W9-AQA-989

Introduction to Algorithms

Third Edition

Thomas H. Cormen
Charles E. Leiserson
Ronald L. Rivest
Clifford Stein

Introduction to Algorithms

Third Edition

The MIT Press
Cambridge, Massachusetts   London, England

© 2009 Massachusetts Institute of Technology

For information about special quantity discounts, please email special_sales@mitpress.mit.edu.

This book was set in Times Roman and Mathtime Pro 2 by the authors.

Printed and bound in the United States of America.

Library of Congress Cataloging-in-Publication Data

Introduction to algorithms / Thomas H. Cormen . . . [et al.].—3rd ed.
   p. cm.
 Includes bibliographical references and index.
 ISBN 978-0-262-03384-8 (hardcover : alk. paper)—ISBN 978-0-262-53305-8 (pbk. : alk. paper)
 1. Computer programming. 2. Computer algorithms. I. Cormen, Thomas H.

QA76.6.I5858 2009
005.1—dc22

2009008593

HARDCOVER: 20 19 18 17 16 15 14 13 12
PAPERBACK: 10 9 8 7 6 5

Contents

Preface   *xiii*

I   *Foundations*

Introduction   *3*

1   The Role of Algorithms in Computing   *5*
1.1   Algorithms   *5*
1.2   Algorithms as a technology   *11*

2   Getting Started   *16*
2.1   Insertion sort   *16*
2.2   Analyzing algorithms   *23*
2.3   Designing algorithms   *29*

3   Growth of Functions   *43*
3.1   Asymptotic notation   *43*
3.2   Standard notations and common functions   *53*

4   Divide-and-Conquer   *65*
4.1   The maximum-subarray problem   *68*
4.2   Strassen's algorithm for matrix multiplication   *75*
4.3   The substitution method for solving recurrences   *83*
4.4   The recursion-tree method for solving recurrences   *88*
4.5   The master method for solving recurrences   *93*
★   4.6   Proof of the master theorem   *97*

5   Probabilistic Analysis and Randomized Algorithms   *114*
5.1   The hiring problem   *114*
5.2   Indicator random variables   *118*
5.3   Randomized algorithms   *122*
★   5.4   Probabilistic analysis and further uses of indicator random variables   *130*

II   Sorting and Order Statistics

Introduction   *147*

6   Heapsort   *151*
6.1   Heaps   *151*
6.2   Maintaining the heap property   *154*
6.3   Building a heap   *156*
6.4   The heapsort algorithm   *159*
6.5   Priority queues   *162*

7   Quicksort   *170*
7.1   Description of quicksort   *170*
7.2   Performance of quicksort   *174*
7.3   A randomized version of quicksort   *179*
7.4   Analysis of quicksort   *180*

8   Sorting in Linear Time   *191*
8.1   Lower bounds for sorting   *191*
8.2   Counting sort   *194*
8.3   Radix sort   *197*
8.4   Bucket sort   *200*

9   Medians and Order Statistics   *213*
9.1   Minimum and maximum   *214*
9.2   Selection in expected linear time   *215*
9.3   Selection in worst-case linear time   *220*

III   Data Structures

Introduction   *229*

10   Elementary Data Structures   *232*
10.1   Stacks and queues   *232*
10.2   Linked lists   *236*
10.3   Implementing pointers and objects   *241*
10.4   Representing rooted trees   *246*

11   Hash Tables   *253*
11.1   Direct-address tables   *254*
11.2   Hash tables   *256*
11.3   Hash functions   *262*
11.4   Open addressing   *269*
★   11.5   Perfect hashing   *277*

12   Binary Search Trees   *286*
   12.1   What is a binary search tree?   *286*
   12.2   Querying a binary search tree   *289*
   12.3   Insertion and deletion   *294*
★ 12.4   Randomly built binary search trees   *299*

13   Red-Black Trees   *308*
   13.1   Properties of red-black trees   *308*
   13.2   Rotations   *312*
   13.3   Insertion   *315*
   13.4   Deletion   *323*

14   Augmenting Data Structures   *339*
   14.1   Dynamic order statistics   *339*
   14.2   How to augment a data structure   *345*
   14.3   Interval trees   *348*

IV   *Advanced Design and Analysis Techniques*

Introduction   *357*

15   Dynamic Programming   *359*
   15.1   Rod cutting   *360*
   15.2   Matrix-chain multiplication   *370*
   15.3   Elements of dynamic programming   *378*
   15.4   Longest common subsequence   *390*
   15.5   Optimal binary search trees   *397*

16   Greedy Algorithms   *414*
   16.1   An activity-selection problem   *415*
   16.2   Elements of the greedy strategy   *423*
   16.3   Huffman codes   *428*
★ 16.4   Matroids and greedy methods   *437*
★ 16.5   A task-scheduling problem as a matroid   *443*

17   Amortized Analysis   *451*
   17.1   Aggregate analysis   *452*
   17.2   The accounting method   *456*
   17.3   The potential method   *459*
   17.4   Dynamic tables   *463*

V Advanced Data Structures

Introduction   *481*

18   B-Trees   *484*
18.1 Definition of B-trees   *488*
18.2 Basic operations on B-trees   *491*
18.3 Deleting a key from a B-tree   *499*

19   Fibonacci Heaps   *505*
19.1 Structure of Fibonacci heaps   *507*
19.2 Mergeable-heap operations   *510*
19.3 Decreasing a key and deleting a node   *518*
19.4 Bounding the maximum degree   *523*

20   van Emde Boas Trees   *531*
20.1 Preliminary approaches   *532*
20.2 A recursive structure   *536*
20.3 The van Emde Boas tree   *545*

21   Data Structures for Disjoint Sets   *561*
21.1 Disjoint-set operations   *561*
21.2 Linked-list representation of disjoint sets   *564*
21.3 Disjoint-set forests   *568*
★ 21.4 Analysis of union by rank with path compression   *573*

VI Graph Algorithms

Introduction   *587*

22   Elementary Graph Algorithms   *589*
22.1 Representations of graphs   *589*
22.2 Breadth-first search   *594*
22.3 Depth-first search   *603*
22.4 Topological sort   *612*
22.5 Strongly connected components   *615*

23   Minimum Spanning Trees   *624*
23.1 Growing a minimum spanning tree   *625*
23.2 The algorithms of Kruskal and Prim   *631*

24 Single-Source Shortest Paths *643*

24.1 The Bellman-Ford algorithm *651*

24.2 Single-source shortest paths in directed acyclic graphs *655*

24.3 Dijkstra's algorithm *658*

24.4 Difference constraints and shortest paths *664*

24.5 Proofs of shortest-paths properties *671*

25 All-Pairs Shortest Paths *684*

25.1 Shortest paths and matrix multiplication *686*

25.2 The Floyd-Warshall algorithm *693*

25.3 Johnson's algorithm for sparse graphs *700*

26 Maximum Flow *708*

26.1 Flow networks *709*

26.2 The Ford-Fulkerson method *714*

26.3 Maximum bipartite matching *732*

★   26.4 Push-relabel algorithms *736*

★   26.5 The relabel-to-front algorithm *748*

VII Selected Topics

Introduction *769*

27 Multithreaded Algorithms *772*

27.1 The basics of dynamic multithreading *774*

27.2 Multithreaded matrix multiplication *792*

27.3 Multithreaded merge sort *797*

28 Matrix Operations *813*

28.1 Solving systems of linear equations *813*

28.2 Inverting matrices *827*

28.3 Symmetric positive-definite matrices and least-squares approximation *832*

29 Linear Programming *843*

29.1 Standard and slack forms *850*

29.2 Formulating problems as linear programs *859*

29.3 The simplex algorithm *864*

29.4 Duality *879*

29.5 The initial basic feasible solution *886*

30   Polynomials and the FFT   898
30.1 Representing polynomials   *900*
30.2 The DFT and FFT   *906*
30.3 Efficient FFT implementations   *915*

31   Number-Theoretic Algorithms   926
31.1 Elementary number-theoretic notions   *927*
31.2 Greatest common divisor   *933*
31.3 Modular arithmetic   *939*
31.4 Solving modular linear equations   *946*
31.5 The Chinese remainder theorem   *950*
31.6 Powers of an element   *954*
31.7 The RSA public-key cryptosystem   *958*
★ 31.8 Primality testing   *965*
★ 31.9 Integer factorization   *975*

32   String Matching   985
32.1 The naive string-matching algorithm   *988*
32.2 The Rabin-Karp algorithm   *990*
32.3 String matching with finite automata   *995*
★ 32.4 The Knuth-Morris-Pratt algorithm   *1002*

33   Computational Geometry   1014
33.1 Line-segment properties   *1015*
33.2 Determining whether any pair of segments intersects   *1021*
33.3 Finding the convex hull   *1029*
33.4 Finding the closest pair of points   *1039*

34   NP-Completeness   1048
34.1 Polynomial time   *1053*
34.2 Polynomial-time verification   *1061*
34.3 NP-completeness and reducibility   *1067*
34.4 NP-completeness proofs   *1078*
34.5 NP-complete problems   *1086*

35   Approximation Algorithms   1106
35.1 The vertex-cover problem   *1108*
35.2 The traveling-salesman problem   *1111*
35.3 The set-covering problem   *1117*
35.4 Randomization and linear programming   *1123*
35.5 The subset-sum problem   *1128*

VIII   Appendix: Mathematical Background

Introduction   *1143*

A   **Summations**   *1145*
A.1   Summation formulas and properties   *1145*
A.2   Bounding summations   *1149*

B   **Sets, Etc.**   *1158*
B.1   Sets   *1158*
B.2   Relations   *1163*
B.3   Functions   *1166*
B.4   Graphs   *1168*
B.5   Trees   *1173*

C   **Counting and Probability**   *1183*
C.1   Counting   *1183*
C.2   Probability   *1189*
C.3   Discrete random variables   *1196*
C.4   The geometric and binomial distributions   *1201*
★   C.5   The tails of the binomial distribution   *1208*

D   **Matrices**   *1217*
D.1   Matrices and matrix operations   *1217*
D.2   Basic matrix properties   *1222*

Bibliography   *1231*
Index   *1251*

Preface

Before there were computers, there were algorithms. But now that there are computers, there are even more algorithms, and algorithms lie at the heart of computing.

This book provides a comprehensive introduction to the modern study of computer algorithms. It presents many algorithms and covers them in considerable depth, yet makes their design and analysis accessible to all levels of readers. We have tried to keep explanations elementary without sacrificing depth of coverage or mathematical rigor.

Each chapter presents an algorithm, a design technique, an application area, or a related topic. Algorithms are described in English and in a pseudocode designed to be readable by anyone who has done a little programming. The book contains 244 figures—many with multiple parts—illustrating how the algorithms work. Since we emphasize *efficiency* as a design criterion, we include careful analyses of the running times of all our algorithms.

The text is intended primarily for use in undergraduate or graduate courses in algorithms or data structures. Because it discusses engineering issues in algorithm design, as well as mathematical aspects, it is equally well suited for self-study by technical professionals.

In this, the third edition, we have once again updated the entire book. The changes cover a broad spectrum, including new chapters, revised pseudocode, and a more active writing style.

To the teacher

We have designed this book to be both versatile and complete. You should find it useful for a variety of courses, from an undergraduate course in data structures up through a graduate course in algorithms. Because we have provided considerably more material than can fit in a typical one-term course, you can consider this book to be a "buffet" or "smorgasbord" from which you can pick and choose the material that best supports the course you wish to teach.

You should find it easy to organize your course around just the chapters you need. We have made chapters relatively self-contained, so that you need not worry about an unexpected and unnecessary dependence of one chapter on another. Each chapter presents the easier material first and the more difficult material later, with section boundaries marking natural stopping points. In an undergraduate course, you might use only the earlier sections from a chapter; in a graduate course, you might cover the entire chapter.

We have included 957 exercises and 158 problems. Each section ends with exercises, and each chapter ends with problems. The exercises are generally short questions that test basic mastery of the material. Some are simple self-check thought exercises, whereas others are more substantial and are suitable as assigned homework. The problems are more elaborate case studies that often introduce new material; they often consist of several questions that lead the student through the steps required to arrive at a solution.

Departing from our practice in previous editions of this book, we have made publicly available solutions to some, but by no means all, of the problems and exercises. Our Web site, http://mitpress.mit.edu/algorithms/, links to these solutions. You will want to check this site to make sure that it does not contain the solution to an exercise or problem that you plan to assign. We expect the set of solutions that we post to grow slowly over time, so you will need to check it each time you teach the course.

We have starred ($\star$) the sections and exercises that are more suitable for graduate students than for undergraduates. A starred section is not necessarily more difficult than an unstarred one, but it may require an understanding of more advanced mathematics. Likewise, starred exercises may require an advanced background or more than average creativity.

To the student

We hope that this textbook provides you with an enjoyable introduction to the field of algorithms. We have attempted to make every algorithm accessible and interesting. To help you when you encounter unfamiliar or difficult algorithms, we describe each one in a step-by-step manner. We also provide careful explanations of the mathematics needed to understand the analysis of the algorithms. If you already have some familiarity with a topic, you will find the chapters organized so that you can skim introductory sections and proceed quickly to the more advanced material.

This is a large book, and your class will probably cover only a portion of its material. We have tried, however, to make this a book that will be useful to you now as a course textbook and also later in your career as a mathematical desk reference or an engineering handbook.

What are the prerequisites for reading this book?

- You should have some programming experience. In particular, you should understand recursive procedures and simple data structures such as arrays and linked lists.

- You should have some facility with mathematical proofs, and especially proofs by mathematical induction. A few portions of the book rely on some knowledge of elementary calculus. Beyond that, Parts I and VIII of this book teach you all the mathematical techniques you will need.

We have heard, loud and clear, the call to supply solutions to problems and exercises. Our Web site, http://mitpress.mit.edu/algorithms/, links to solutions for a few of the problems and exercises. Feel free to check your solutions against ours. We ask, however, that you do not send your solutions to us.

To the professional

The wide range of topics in this book makes it an excellent handbook on algorithms. Because each chapter is relatively self-contained, you can focus on the topics that most interest you.

Most of the algorithms we discuss have great practical utility. We therefore address implementation concerns and other engineering issues. We often provide practical alternatives to the few algorithms that are primarily of theoretical interest.

If you wish to implement any of the algorithms, you should find the translation of our pseudocode into your favorite programming language to be a fairly straightforward task. We have designed the pseudocode to present each algorithm clearly and succinctly. Consequently, we do not address error-handling and other software-engineering issues that require specific assumptions about your programming environment. We attempt to present each algorithm simply and directly without allowing the idiosyncrasies of a particular programming language to obscure its essence.

We understand that if you are using this book outside of a course, then you might be unable to check your solutions to problems and exercises against solutions provided by an instructor. Our Web site, http://mitpress.mit.edu/algorithms/, links to solutions for some of the problems and exercises so that you can check your work. Please do not send your solutions to us.

To our colleagues

We have supplied an extensive bibliography and pointers to the current literature. Each chapter ends with a set of chapter notes that give historical details and references. The chapter notes do not provide a complete reference to the whole field

of algorithms, however. Though it may be hard to believe for a book of this size, space constraints prevented us from including many interesting algorithms.

Despite myriad requests from students for solutions to problems and exercises, we have chosen as a matter of policy not to supply references for problems and exercises, to remove the temptation for students to look up a solution rather than to find it themselves.

Changes for the third edition

What has changed between the second and third editions of this book? The magnitude of the changes is on a par with the changes between the first and second editions. As we said about the second-edition changes, depending on how you look at it, the book changed either not much or quite a bit.

A quick look at the table of contents shows that most of the second-edition chapters and sections appear in the third edition. We removed two chapters and one section, but we have added three new chapters and two new sections apart from these new chapters.

We kept the hybrid organization from the first two editions. Rather than organizing chapters by only problem domains or according only to techniques, this book has elements of both. It contains technique-based chapters on divide-and-conquer, dynamic programming, greedy algorithms, amortized analysis, NP-Completeness, and approximation algorithms. But it also has entire parts on sorting, on data structures for dynamic sets, and on algorithms for graph problems. We find that although you need to know how to apply techniques for designing and analyzing algorithms, problems seldom announce to you which techniques are most amenable to solving them.

Here is a summary of the most significant changes for the third edition:

- We added new chapters on van Emde Boas trees and multithreaded algorithms, and we have broken out material on matrix basics into its own appendix chapter.

- We revised the chapter on recurrences to more broadly cover the divide-and-conquer technique, and its first two sections apply divide-and-conquer to solve two problems. The second section of this chapter presents Strassen's algorithm for matrix multiplication, which we have moved from the chapter on matrix operations.

- We removed two chapters that were rarely taught: binomial heaps and sorting networks. One key idea in the sorting networks chapter, the 0-1 principle, appears in this edition within Problem 8-7 as the 0-1 sorting lemma for compare-exchange algorithms. The treatment of Fibonacci heaps no longer relies on binomial heaps as a precursor.

- We revised our treatment of dynamic programming and greedy algorithms. Dynamic programming now leads off with a more interesting problem, rod cutting, than the assembly-line scheduling problem from the second edition. Furthermore, we emphasize memoization a bit more than we did in the second edition, and we introduce the notion of the subproblem graph as a way to understand the running time of a dynamic-programming algorithm. In our opening example of greedy algorithms, the activity-selection problem, we get to the greedy algorithm more directly than we did in the second edition.

- The way we delete a node from binary search trees (which includes red-black trees) now guarantees that the node requested for deletion is the node that is actually deleted. In the first two editions, in certain cases, some other node would be deleted, with its contents moving into the node passed to the deletion procedure. With our new way to delete nodes, if other components of a program maintain pointers to nodes in the tree, they will not mistakenly end up with stale pointers to nodes that have been deleted.

- The material on flow networks now bases flows entirely on edges. This approach is more intuitive than the net flow used in the first two editions.

- With the material on matrix basics and Strassen's algorithm moved to other chapters, the chapter on matrix operations is smaller than in the second edition.

- We have modified our treatment of the Knuth-Morris-Pratt string-matching algorithm.

- We corrected several errors. Most of these errors were posted on our Web site of second-edition errata, but a few were not.

- Based on many requests, we changed the syntax (as it were) of our pseudocode. We now use "$=$" to indicate assignment and "$==$" to test for equality, just as C, C++, Java, and Python do. Likewise, we have eliminated the keywords **do** and **then** and adopted "**//**" as our comment-to-end-of-line symbol. We also now use dot-notation to indicate object attributes. Our pseudocode remains procedural, rather than object-oriented. In other words, rather than running methods on objects, we simply call procedures, passing objects as parameters.

- We added 100 new exercises and 28 new problems. We also updated many bibliography entries and added several new ones.

- Finally, we went through the entire book and rewrote sentences, paragraphs, and sections to make the writing clearer and more active.

Web site

You can use our Web site, http://mitpress.mit.edu/algorithms/, to obtain supplementary information and to communicate with us. The Web site links to a list of known errors, solutions to selected exercises and problems, and (of course) a list explaining the corny professor jokes, as well as other content that we might add. The Web site also tells you how to report errors or make suggestions.

How we produced this book

Like the second edition, the third edition was produced in LaTeX 2_ε. We used the Times font with mathematics typeset using the MathTime Pro 2 fonts. We thank Michael Spivak from Publish or Perish, Inc., Lance Carnes from Personal TeX, Inc., and Tim Tregubov from Dartmouth College for technical support. As in the previous two editions, we compiled the index using Windex, a C program that we wrote, and the bibliography was produced with BIBTeX. The PDF files for this book were created on a MacBook running OS 10.5.

We drew the illustrations for the third edition using MacDraw Pro, with some of the mathematical expressions in illustrations laid in with the psfrag package for LaTeX 2_ε. Unfortunately, MacDraw Pro is legacy software, having not been marketed for over a decade now. Happily, we still have a couple of Macintoshes that can run the Classic environment under OS 10.4, and hence they can run Mac-Draw Pro—mostly. Even under the Classic environment, we find MacDraw Pro to be far easier to use than any other drawing software for the types of illustrations that accompany computer-science text, and it produces beautiful output.[1] Who knows how long our pre-Intel Macs will continue to run, so if anyone from Apple is listening: *Please create an OS X-compatible version of MacDraw Pro!*

Acknowledgments for the third edition

We have been working with the MIT Press for over two decades now, and what a terrific relationship it has been! We thank Ellen Faran, Bob Prior, Ada Brunstein, and Mary Reilly for their help and support.

We were geographically distributed while producing the third edition, working in the Dartmouth College Department of Computer Science, the MIT Computer

---

[1] We investigated several drawing programs that run under Mac OS X, but all had significant shortcomings compared with MacDraw Pro. We briefly attempted to produce the illustrations for this book with a different, well known drawing program. We found that it took at least five times as long to produce each illustration as it took with MacDraw Pro, and the resulting illustrations did not look as good. Hence the decision to revert to MacDraw Pro running on older Macintoshes.

Science and Artificial Intelligence Laboratory, and the Columbia University Department of Industrial Engineering and Operations Research. We thank our respective universities and colleagues for providing such supportive and stimulating environments.

Julie Sussman, P.P.A., once again bailed us out as the technical copyeditor. Time and again, we were amazed at the errors that eluded us, but that Julie caught. She also helped us improve our presentation in several places. If there is a Hall of Fame for technical copyeditors, Julie is a sure-fire, first-ballot inductee. She is nothing short of phenomenal. Thank you, thank you, thank you, Julie! Priya Natarajan also found some errors that we were able to correct before this book went to press. Any errors that remain (and undoubtedly, some do) are the responsibility of the authors (and probably were inserted after Julie read the material).

The treatment for van Emde Boas trees derives from Erik Demaine's notes, which were in turn influenced by Michael Bender. We also incorporated ideas from Javed Aslam, Bradley Kuszmaul, and Hui Zha into this edition.

The chapter on multithreading was based on notes originally written jointly with Harald Prokop. The material was influenced by several others working on the Cilk project at MIT, including Bradley Kuszmaul and Matteo Frigo. The design of the multithreaded pseudocode took its inspiration from the MIT Cilk extensions to C and by Cilk Arts's Cilk++ extensions to C++.

We also thank the many readers of the first and second editions who reported errors or submitted suggestions for how to improve this book. We corrected all the bona fide errors that were reported, and we incorporated as many suggestions as we could. We rejoice that the number of such contributors has grown so great that we must regret that it has become impractical to list them all.

Finally, we thank our wives—Nicole Cormen, Wendy Leiserson, Gail Rivest, and Rebecca Ivry—and our children—Ricky, Will, Debby, and Katie Leiserson; Alex and Christopher Rivest; and Molly, Noah, and Benjamin Stein—for their love and support while we prepared this book. The patience and encouragement of our families made this project possible. We affectionately dedicate this book to them.

THOMAS H. CORMEN   *Lebanon, New Hampshire*
CHARLES E. LEISERSON   *Cambridge, Massachusetts*
RONALD L. RIVEST   *Cambridge, Massachusetts*
CLIFFORD STEIN   *New York, New York*

February 2009

Introduction to Algorithms

Third Edition

I   Foundations

Introduction

This part will start you thinking about designing and analyzing algorithms. It is intended to be a gentle introduction to how we specify algorithms, some of the design strategies we will use throughout this book, and many of the fundamental ideas used in algorithm analysis. Later parts of this book will build upon this base.

Chapter 1 provides an overview of algorithms and their place in modern computing systems. This chapter defines what an algorithm is and lists some examples. It also makes a case that we should consider algorithms as a technology, alongside technologies such as fast hardware, graphical user interfaces, object-oriented systems, and networks.

In Chapter 2, we see our first algorithms, which solve the problem of sorting a sequence of n numbers. They are written in a pseudocode which, although not directly translatable to any conventional programming language, conveys the structure of the algorithm clearly enough that you should be able to implement it in the language of your choice. The sorting algorithms we examine are insertion sort, which uses an incremental approach, and merge sort, which uses a recursive technique known as "divide-and-conquer." Although the time each requires increases with the value of n, the rate of increase differs between the two algorithms. We determine these running times in Chapter 2, and we develop a useful notation to express them.

Chapter 3 precisely defines this notation, which we call asymptotic notation. It starts by defining several asymptotic notations, which we use for bounding algorithm running times from above and/or below. The rest of Chapter 3 is primarily a presentation of mathematical notation, more to ensure that your use of notation matches that in this book than to teach you new mathematical concepts.

Chapter 4 delves further into the divide-and-conquer method introduced in Chapter 2. It provides additional examples of divide-and-conquer algorithms, including Strassen's surprising method for multiplying two square matrices. Chapter 4 contains methods for solving recurrences, which are useful for describing the running times of recursive algorithms. One powerful technique is the "master method," which we often use to solve recurrences that arise from divide-and-conquer algorithms. Although much of Chapter 4 is devoted to proving the correctness of the master method, you may skip this proof yet still employ the master method.

Chapter 5 introduces probabilistic analysis and randomized algorithms. We typically use probabilistic analysis to determine the running time of an algorithm in cases in which, due to the presence of an inherent probability distribution, the running time may differ on different inputs of the same size. In some cases, we assume that the inputs conform to a known probability distribution, so that we are averaging the running time over all possible inputs. In other cases, the probability distribution comes not from the inputs but from random choices made during the course of the algorithm. An algorithm whose behavior is determined not only by its input but by the values produced by a random-number generator is a randomized algorithm. We can use randomized algorithms to enforce a probability distribution on the inputs—thereby ensuring that no particular input always causes poor performance—or even to bound the error rate of algorithms that are allowed to produce incorrect results on a limited basis.

Appendices A–D contain other mathematical material that you will find helpful as you read this book. You are likely to have seen much of the material in the appendix chapters before having read this book (although the specific definitions and notational conventions we use may differ in some cases from what you have seen in the past), and so you should think of the Appendices as reference material. On the other hand, you probably have not already seen most of the material in Part I. All the chapters in Part I and the Appendices are written with a tutorial flavor.

1   The Role of Algorithms in Computing

What are algorithms? Why is the study of algorithms worthwhile? What is the role of algorithms relative to other technologies used in computers? In this chapter, we will answer these questions.

1.1   Algorithms

Informally, an *algorithm* is any well-defined computational procedure that takes some value, or set of values, as *input* and produces some value, or set of values, as *output*. An algorithm is thus a sequence of computational steps that transform the input into the output.

We can also view an algorithm as a tool for solving a well-specified *computational problem*. The statement of the problem specifies in general terms the desired input/output relationship. The algorithm describes a specific computational procedure for achieving that input/output relationship.

For example, we might need to sort a sequence of numbers into nondecreasing order. This problem arises frequently in practice and provides fertile ground for introducing many standard design techniques and analysis tools. Here is how we formally define the *sorting problem*:

Input: A sequence of n numbers $\langle a_1, a_2, \ldots, a_n \rangle$.

Output: A permutation (reordering) $\langle a_1', a_2', \ldots, a_n' \rangle$ of the input sequence such that $a_1' \leq a_2' \leq \cdots \leq a_n'$.

For example, given the input sequence $\langle 31, 41, 59, 26, 41, 58 \rangle$, a sorting algorithm returns as output the sequence $\langle 26, 31, 41, 41, 58, 59 \rangle$. Such an input sequence is called an *instance* of the sorting problem. In general, an *instance of a problem* consists of the input (satisfying whatever constraints are imposed in the problem statement) needed to compute a solution to the problem.

Because many programs use it as an intermediate step, sorting is a fundamental operation in computer science. As a result, we have a large number of good sorting algorithms at our disposal. Which algorithm is best for a given application depends on—among other factors—the number of items to be sorted, the extent to which the items are already somewhat sorted, possible restrictions on the item values, the architecture of the computer, and the kind of storage devices to be used: main memory, disks, or even tapes.

An algorithm is said to be ***correct*** if, for every input instance, it halts with the correct output. We say that a correct algorithm ***solves*** the given computational problem. An incorrect algorithm might not halt at all on some input instances, or it might halt with an incorrect answer. Contrary to what you might expect, incorrect algorithms can sometimes be useful, if we can control their error rate. We shall see an example of an algorithm with a controllable error rate in Chapter 31 when we study algorithms for finding large prime numbers. Ordinarily, however, we shall be concerned only with correct algorithms.

An algorithm can be specified in English, as a computer program, or even as a hardware design. The only requirement is that the specification must provide a precise description of the computational procedure to be followed.

What kinds of problems are solved by algorithms?

Sorting is by no means the only computational problem for which algorithms have been developed. (You probably suspected as much when you saw the size of this book.) Practical applications of algorithms are ubiquitous and include the following examples:

- The Human Genome Project has made great progress toward the goals of identifying all the 100,000 genes in human DNA, determining the sequences of the 3 billion chemical base pairs that make up human DNA, storing this information in databases, and developing tools for data analysis. Each of these steps requires sophisticated algorithms. Although the solutions to the various problems involved are beyond the scope of this book, many methods to solve these biological problems use ideas from several of the chapters in this book, thereby enabling scientists to accomplish tasks while using resources efficiently. The savings are in time, both human and machine, and in money, as more information can be extracted from laboratory techniques.

- The Internet enables people all around the world to quickly access and retrieve large amounts of information. With the aid of clever algorithms, sites on the Internet are able to manage and manipulate this large volume of data. Examples of problems that make essential use of algorithms include finding good routes on which the data will travel (techniques for solving such problems appear in

Chapter 24), and using a search engine to quickly find pages on which particular information resides (related techniques are in Chapters 11 and 32).

- Electronic commerce enables goods and services to be negotiated and exchanged electronically, and it depends on the privacy of personal information such as credit card numbers, passwords, and bank statements. The core technologies used in electronic commerce include public-key cryptography and digital signatures (covered in Chapter 31), which are based on numerical algorithms and number theory.

- Manufacturing and other commercial enterprises often need to allocate scarce resources in the most beneficial way. An oil company may wish to know where to place its wells in order to maximize its expected profit. A political candidate may want to determine where to spend money buying campaign advertising in order to maximize the chances of winning an election. An airline may wish to assign crews to flights in the least expensive way possible, making sure that each flight is covered and that government regulations regarding crew scheduling are met. An Internet service provider may wish to determine where to place additional resources in order to serve its customers more effectively. All of these are examples of problems that can be solved using linear programming, which we shall study in Chapter 29.

Although some of the details of these examples are beyond the scope of this book, we do give underlying techniques that apply to these problems and problem areas. We also show how to solve many specific problems, including the following:

- We are given a road map on which the distance between each pair of adjacent intersections is marked, and we wish to determine the shortest route from one intersection to another. The number of possible routes can be huge, even if we disallow routes that cross over themselves. How do we choose which of all possible routes is the shortest? Here, we model the road map (which is itself a model of the actual roads) as a graph (which we will meet in Part VI and Appendix B), and we wish to find the shortest path from one vertex to another in the graph. We shall see how to solve this problem efficiently in Chapter 24.

- We are given two ordered sequences of symbols, $X = \langle x_1, x_2, \ldots, x_m \rangle$ and $Y = \langle y_1, y_2, \ldots, y_n \rangle$, and we wish to find a longest common subsequence of X and Y. A subsequence of X is just X with some (or possibly all or none) of its elements removed. For example, one subsequence of $\langle A, B, C, D, E, F, G \rangle$ would be $\langle B, C, E, G \rangle$. The length of a longest common subsequence of X and Y gives one measure of how similar these two sequences are. For example, if the two sequences are base pairs in DNA strands, then we might consider them similar if they have a long common subsequence. If X has m symbols and Y has n symbols, then X and Y have 2^m and 2^n possible subsequences,

respectively. Selecting all possible subsequences of X and Y and matching them up could take a prohibitively long time unless m and n are very small. We shall see in Chapter 15 how to use a general technique known as dynamic programming to solve this problem much more efficiently.

- We are given a mechanical design in terms of a library of parts, where each part may include instances of other parts, and we need to list the parts in order so that each part appears before any part that uses it. If the design comprises n parts, then there are $n!$ possible orders, where $n!$ denotes the factorial function. Because the factorial function grows faster than even an exponential function, we cannot feasibly generate each possible order and then verify that, within that order, each part appears before the parts using it (unless we have only a few parts). This problem is an instance of topological sorting, and we shall see in Chapter 22 how to solve this problem efficiently.

- We are given n points in the plane, and we wish to find the convex hull of these points. The convex hull is the smallest convex polygon containing the points. Intuitively, we can think of each point as being represented by a nail sticking out from a board. The convex hull would be represented by a tight rubber band that surrounds all the nails. Each nail around which the rubber band makes a turn is a vertex of the convex hull. (See Figure 33.6 on page 1029 for an example.) Any of the 2^n subsets of the points might be the vertices of the convex hull. Knowing which points are vertices of the convex hull is not quite enough, either, since we also need to know the order in which they appear. There are many choices, therefore, for the vertices of the convex hull. Chapter 33 gives two good methods for finding the convex hull.

These lists are far from exhaustive (as you again have probably surmised from this book's heft), but exhibit two characteristics that are common to many interesting algorithmic problems:

1. They have many candidate solutions, the overwhelming majority of which do not solve the problem at hand. Finding one that does, or one that is "best," can present quite a challenge.

2. They have practical applications. Of the problems in the above list, finding the shortest path provides the easiest examples. A transportation firm, such as a trucking or railroad company, has a financial interest in finding shortest paths through a road or rail network because taking shorter paths results in lower labor and fuel costs. Or a routing node on the Internet may need to find the shortest path through the network in order to route a message quickly. Or a person wishing to drive from New York to Boston may want to find driving directions from an appropriate Web site, or she may use her GPS while driving.

Not every problem solved by algorithms has an easily identified set of candidate solutions. For example, suppose we are given a set of numerical values representing samples of a signal, and we want to compute the discrete Fourier transform of these samples. The discrete Fourier transform converts the time domain to the frequency domain, producing a set of numerical coefficients, so that we can determine the strength of various frequencies in the sampled signal. In addition to lying at the heart of signal processing, discrete Fourier transforms have applications in data compression and multiplying large polynomials and integers. Chapter 30 gives an efficient algorithm, the fast Fourier transform (commonly called the FFT), for this problem, and the chapter also sketches out the design of a hardware circuit to compute the FFT.

Data structures

This book also contains several data structures. A ***data structure*** is a way to store and organize data in order to facilitate access and modifications. No single data structure works well for all purposes, and so it is important to know the strengths and limitations of several of them.

Technique

Although you can use this book as a "cookbook" for algorithms, you may someday encounter a problem for which you cannot readily find a published algorithm (many of the exercises and problems in this book, for example). This book will teach you techniques of algorithm design and analysis so that you can develop algorithms on your own, show that they give the correct answer, and understand their efficiency. Different chapters address different aspects of algorithmic problem solving. Some chapters address specific problems, such as finding medians and order statistics in Chapter 9, computing minimum spanning trees in Chapter 23, and determining a maximum flow in a network in Chapter 26. Other chapters address techniques, such as divide-and-conquer in Chapter 4, dynamic programming in Chapter 15, and amortized analysis in Chapter 17.

Hard problems

Most of this book is about efficient algorithms. Our usual measure of efficiency is speed, i.e., how long an algorithm takes to produce its result. There are some problems, however, for which no efficient solution is known. Chapter 34 studies an interesting subset of these problems, which are known as NP-complete.

Why are NP-complete problems interesting? First, although no efficient algorithm for an NP-complete problem has ever been found, nobody has ever proven

that an efficient algorithm for one cannot exist. In other words, no one knows whether or not efficient algorithms exist for NP-complete problems. Second, the set of NP-complete problems has the remarkable property that if an efficient algorithm exists for any one of them, then efficient algorithms exist for all of them. This relationship among the NP-complete problems makes the lack of efficient solutions all the more tantalizing. Third, several NP-complete problems are similar, but not identical, to problems for which we do know of efficient algorithms. Computer scientists are intrigued by how a small change to the problem statement can cause a big change to the efficiency of the best known algorithm.

You should know about NP-complete problems because some of them arise surprisingly often in real applications. If you are called upon to produce an efficient algorithm for an NP-complete problem, you are likely to spend a lot of time in a fruitless search. If you can show that the problem is NP-complete, you can instead spend your time developing an efficient algorithm that gives a good, but not the best possible, solution.

As a concrete example, consider a delivery company with a central depot. Each day, it loads up each delivery truck at the depot and sends it around to deliver goods to several addresses. At the end of the day, each truck must end up back at the depot so that it is ready to be loaded for the next day. To reduce costs, the company wants to select an order of delivery stops that yields the lowest overall distance traveled by each truck. This problem is the well-known "traveling-salesman problem," and it is NP-complete. It has no known efficient algorithm. Under certain assumptions, however, we know of efficient algorithms that give an overall distance which is not too far above the smallest possible. Chapter 35 discusses such "approximation algorithms."

Parallelism

For many years, we could count on processor clock speeds increasing at a steady rate. Physical limitations present a fundamental roadblock to ever-increasing clock speeds, however: because power density increases superlinearly with clock speed, chips run the risk of melting once their clock speeds become high enough. In order to perform more computations per second, therefore, chips are being designed to contain not just one but several processing "cores." We can liken these multicore computers to several sequential computers on a single chip; in other words, they are a type of "parallel computer." In order to elicit the best performance from multicore computers, we need to design algorithms with parallelism in mind. Chapter 27 presents a model for "multithreaded" algorithms, which take advantage of multiple cores. This model has advantages from a theoretical standpoint, and it forms the basis of several successful computer programs, including a championship chess program.

Exercises

1.1-1

Give a real-world example that requires sorting or a real-world example that requires computing a convex hull.

1.1-2

Other than speed, what other measures of efficiency might one use in a real-world setting?

1.1-3

Select a data structure that you have seen previously, and discuss its strengths and limitations.

1.1-4

How are the shortest-path and traveling-salesman problems given above similar? How are they different?

1.1-5

Come up with a real-world problem in which only the best solution will do. Then come up with one in which a solution that is "approximately" the best is good enough.

1.2 Algorithms as a technology

Suppose computers were infinitely fast and computer memory was free. Would you have any reason to study algorithms? The answer is yes, if for no other reason than that you would still like to demonstrate that your solution method terminates and does so with the correct answer.

If computers were infinitely fast, any correct method for solving a problem would do. You would probably want your implementation to be within the bounds of good software engineering practice (for example, your implementation should be well designed and documented), but you would most often use whichever method was the easiest to implement.

Of course, computers may be fast, but they are not infinitely fast. And memory may be inexpensive, but it is not free. Computing time is therefore a bounded resource, and so is space in memory. You should use these resources wisely, and algorithms that are efficient in terms of time or space will help you do so.

Efficiency

Different algorithms devised to solve the same problem often differ dramatically in their efficiency. These differences can be much more significant than differences due to hardware and software.

As an example, in Chapter 2, we will see two algorithms for sorting. The first, known as ***insertion sort***, takes time roughly equal to $c_1 n^2$ to sort n items, where c_1 is a constant that does not depend on n. That is, it takes time roughly proportional to n^2. The second, ***merge sort***, takes time roughly equal to $c_2 n \lg n$, where $\lg n$ stands for $\log_2 n$ and c_2 is another constant that also does not depend on n. Insertion sort typically has a smaller constant factor than merge sort, so that $c_1 < c_2$. We shall see that the constant factors can have far less of an impact on the running time than the dependence on the input size n. Let's write insertion sort's running time as $c_1 n \cdot n$ and merge sort's running time as $c_2 n \cdot \lg n$. Then we see that where insertion sort has a factor of n in its running time, merge sort has a factor of $\lg n$, which is much smaller. (For example, when $n = 1000$, $\lg n$ is approximately 10, and when n equals one million, $\lg n$ is approximately only 20.) Although insertion sort usually runs faster than merge sort for small input sizes, once the input size n becomes large enough, merge sort's advantage of $\lg n$ vs. n will more than compensate for the difference in constant factors. No matter how much smaller c_1 is than c_2, there will always be a crossover point beyond which merge sort is faster.

For a concrete example, let us pit a faster computer (computer A) running insertion sort against a slower computer (computer B) running merge sort. They each must sort an array of 10 million numbers. (Although 10 million numbers might seem like a lot, if the numbers are eight-byte integers, then the input occupies about 80 megabytes, which fits in the memory of even an inexpensive laptop computer many times over.) Suppose that computer A executes 10 billion instructions per second (faster than any single sequential computer at the time of this writing) and computer B executes only 10 million instructions per second, so that computer A is 1000 times faster than computer B in raw computing power. To make the difference even more dramatic, suppose that the world's craftiest programmer codes insertion sort in machine language for computer A, and the resulting code requires $2n^2$ instructions to sort n numbers. Suppose further that just an average programmer implements merge sort, using a high-level language with an inefficient compiler, with the resulting code taking $50n \lg n$ instructions. To sort 10 million numbers, computer A takes

$$\frac{2 \cdot (10^7)^2 \text{ instructions}}{10^{10} \text{ instructions/second}} = 20{,}000 \text{ seconds (more than 5.5 hours)},$$

while computer B takes

$$\frac{50 \cdot 10^7 \lg 10^7 \text{ instructions}}{10^7 \text{ instructions/second}} \approx 1163 \text{ seconds (less than 20 minutes)}.$$

By using an algorithm whose running time grows more slowly, even with a poor compiler, computer B runs more than 17 times faster than computer A! The advantage of merge sort is even more pronounced when we sort 100 million numbers: where insertion sort takes more than 23 days, merge sort takes under four hours. In general, as the problem size increases, so does the relative advantage of merge sort.

Algorithms and other technologies

The example above shows that we should consider algorithms, like computer hardware, as a ***technology***. Total system performance depends on choosing efficient algorithms as much as on choosing fast hardware. Just as rapid advances are being made in other computer technologies, they are being made in algorithms as well.

You might wonder whether algorithms are truly that important on contemporary computers in light of other advanced technologies, such as

- advanced computer architectures and fabrication technologies,

- easy-to-use, intuitive, graphical user interfaces (GUIs),

- object-oriented systems,

- integrated Web technologies, and

- fast networking, both wired and wireless.

The answer is yes. Although some applications do not explicitly require algorithmic content at the application level (such as some simple, Web-based applications), many do. For example, consider a Web-based service that determines how to travel from one location to another. Its implementation would rely on fast hardware, a graphical user interface, wide-area networking, and also possibly on object orientation. However, it would also require algorithms for certain operations, such as finding routes (probably using a shortest-path algorithm), rendering maps, and interpolating addresses.

Moreover, even an application that does not require algorithmic content at the application level relies heavily upon algorithms. Does the application rely on fast hardware? The hardware design used algorithms. Does the application rely on graphical user interfaces? The design of any GUI relies on algorithms. Does the application rely on networking? Routing in networks relies heavily on algorithms. Was the application written in a language other than machine code? Then it was processed by a compiler, interpreter, or assembler, all of which make extensive use

of algorithms. Algorithms are at the core of most technologies used in contemporary computers.

Furthermore, with the ever-increasing capacities of computers, we use them to solve larger problems than ever before. As we saw in the above comparison between insertion sort and merge sort, it is at larger problem sizes that the differences in efficiency between algorithms become particularly prominent.

Having a solid base of algorithmic knowledge and technique is one characteristic that separates the truly skilled programmers from the novices. With modern computing technology, you can accomplish some tasks without knowing much about algorithms, but with a good background in algorithms, you can do much, much more.

Exercises

1.2-1
Give an example of an application that requires algorithmic content at the application level, and discuss the function of the algorithms involved.

1.2-2
Suppose we are comparing implementations of insertion sort and merge sort on the same machine. For inputs of size n, insertion sort runs in $8n^2$ steps, while merge sort runs in $64n \lg n$ steps. For which values of n does insertion sort beat merge sort?

1.2-3
What is the smallest value of n such that an algorithm whose running time is $100n^2$ runs faster than an algorithm whose running time is 2^n on the same machine?

Problems

1-1   Comparison of running times
For each function $f(n)$ and time t in the following table, determine the largest size n of a problem that can be solved in time t, assuming that the algorithm to solve the problem takes $f(n)$ microseconds.

	1 second	1 minute	1 hour	1 day	1 month	1 year	1 century
$\lg n$							
$\sqrt{n}$							
n							
$n \lg n$							
n^2							
n^3							
2^n							
$n!$							

Chapter notes

There are many excellent texts on the general topic of algorithms, including those by Aho, Hopcroft, and Ullman [5, 6]; Baase and Van Gelder [28]; Brassard and Bratley [54]; Dasgupta, Papadimitriou, and Vazirani [82]; Goodrich and Tamassia [148]; Hofri [175]; Horowitz, Sahni, and Rajasekaran [181]; Johnsonbaugh and Schaefer [193]; Kingston [205]; Kleinberg and Tardos [208]; Knuth [209, 210, 211]; Kozen [220]; Levitin [235]; Manber [242]; Mehlhorn [249, 250, 251]; Purdom and Brown [287]; Reingold, Nievergelt, and Deo [293]; Sedgewick [306]; Sedgewick and Flajolet [307]; Skiena [318]; and Wilf [356]. Some of the more practical aspects of algorithm design are discussed by Bentley [42, 43] and Gonnet [145]. Surveys of the field of algorithms can also be found in the *Handbook of Theoretical Computer Science, Volume A* [342] and the CRC *Algorithms and Theory of Computation Handbook* [25]. Overviews of the algorithms used in computational biology can be found in textbooks by Gusfield [156], Pevzner [275], Setubal and Meidanis [310], and Waterman [350].

2   Getting Started

This chapter will familiarize you with the framework we shall use throughout the book to think about the design and analysis of algorithms. It is self-contained, but it does include several references to material that we introduce in Chapters 3 and 4. (It also contains several summations, which Appendix A shows how to solve.)

We begin by examining the insertion sort algorithm to solve the sorting problem introduced in Chapter 1. We define a "pseudocode" that should be familiar to you if you have done computer programming, and we use it to show how we shall specify our algorithms. Having specified the insertion sort algorithm, we then argue that it correctly sorts, and we analyze its running time. The analysis introduces a notation that focuses on how that time increases with the number of items to be sorted. Following our discussion of insertion sort, we introduce the divide-and-conquer approach to the design of algorithms and use it to develop an algorithm called merge sort. We end with an analysis of merge sort's running time.

2.1   Insertion sort

Our first algorithm, insertion sort, solves the **sorting problem** introduced in Chapter 1:

Input: A sequence of n numbers $\langle a_1, a_2, \ldots, a_n \rangle$.

Output: A permutation (reordering) $\langle a'_1, a'_2, \ldots, a'_n \rangle$ of the input sequence such that $a'_1 \leq a'_2 \leq \cdots \leq a'_n$.

The numbers that we wish to sort are also known as the **keys**. Although conceptually we are sorting a sequence, the input comes to us in the form of an array with n elements.

In this book, we shall typically describe algorithms as programs written in a **pseudocode** that is similar in many respects to C, C++, Java, Python, or Pascal. If you have been introduced to any of these languages, you should have little trouble

Figure 2.1 Sorting a hand of cards using insertion sort.

reading our algorithms. What separates pseudocode from "real" code is that in pseudocode, we employ whatever expressive method is most clear and concise to specify a given algorithm. Sometimes, the clearest method is English, so do not be surprised if you come across an English phrase or sentence embedded within a section of "real" code. Another difference between pseudocode and real code is that pseudocode is not typically concerned with issues of software engineering. Issues of data abstraction, modularity, and error handling are often ignored in order to convey the essence of the algorithm more concisely.

We start with *insertion sort*, which is an efficient algorithm for sorting a small number of elements. Insertion sort works the way many people sort a hand of playing cards. We start with an empty left hand and the cards face down on the table. We then remove one card at a time from the table and insert it into the correct position in the left hand. To find the correct position for a card, we compare it with each of the cards already in the hand, from right to left, as illustrated in Figure 2.1. At all times, the cards held in the left hand are sorted, and these cards were originally the top cards of the pile on the table.

We present our pseudocode for insertion sort as a procedure called INSERTION-SORT, which takes as a parameter an array $A[1 .. n]$ containing a sequence of length n that is to be sorted. (In the code, the number n of elements in A is denoted by $A.length$.) The algorithm sorts the input numbers *in place*: it rearranges the numbers within the array A, with at most a constant number of them stored outside the array at any time. The input array A contains the sorted output sequence when the INSERTION-SORT procedure is finished.

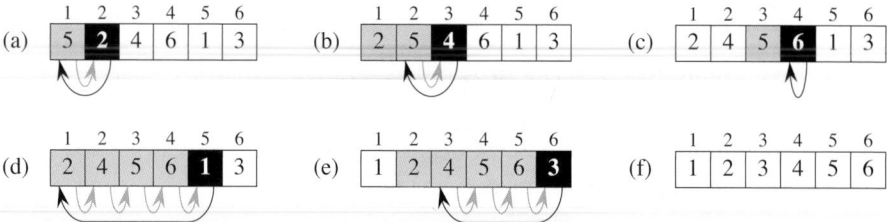

Figure 2.2 The operation of INSERTION-SORT on the array $A = \langle 5, 2, 4, 6, 1, 3 \rangle$. Array indices appear above the rectangles, and values stored in the array positions appear within the rectangles. **(a)–(e)** The iterations of the **for** loop of lines 1–8. In each iteration, the black rectangle holds the key taken from $A[j]$, which is compared with the values in shaded rectangles to its left in the test of line 5. Shaded arrows show array values moved one position to the right in line 6, and black arrows indicate where the key moves to in line 8. **(f)** The final sorted array.

INSERTION-SORT(A)

```
1  for j = 2 to A.length
2      key = A[j]
3      // Insert A[j] into the sorted sequence A[1 .. j − 1].
4      i = j − 1
5      while i > 0 and A[i] > key
6          A[i + 1] = A[i]
7          i = i − 1
8      A[i + 1] = key
```

Loop invariants and the correctness of insertion sort

Figure 2.2 shows how this algorithm works for $A = \langle 5, 2, 4, 6, 1, 3 \rangle$. The index j indicates the "current card" being inserted into the hand. At the beginning of each iteration of the **for** loop, which is indexed by j, the subarray consisting of elements $A[1 .. j − 1]$ constitutes the currently sorted hand, and the remaining subarray $A[j + 1 .. n]$ corresponds to the pile of cards still on the table. In fact, elements $A[1 .. j − 1]$ are the elements *originally* in positions 1 through $j − 1$, but now in sorted order. We state these properties of $A[1 .. j − 1]$ formally as a ***loop invariant***:

> At the start of each iteration of the **for** loop of lines 1–8, the subarray $A[1 .. j − 1]$ consists of the elements originally in $A[1 .. j − 1]$, but in sorted order.

We use loop invariants to help us understand why an algorithm is correct. We must show three things about a loop invariant:

Initialization: It is true prior to the first iteration of the loop.

Maintenance: If it is true before an iteration of the loop, it remains true before the next iteration.

Termination: When the loop terminates, the invariant gives us a useful property that helps show that the algorithm is correct.

When the first two properties hold, the loop invariant is true prior to every iteration of the loop. (Of course, we are free to use established facts other than the loop invariant itself to prove that the loop invariant remains true before each iteration.) Note the similarity to mathematical induction, where to prove that a property holds, you prove a base case and an inductive step. Here, showing that the invariant holds before the first iteration corresponds to the base case, and showing that the invariant holds from iteration to iteration corresponds to the inductive step.

The third property is perhaps the most important one, since we are using the loop invariant to show correctness. Typically, we use the loop invariant along with the condition that caused the loop to terminate. The termination property differs from how we usually use mathematical induction, in which we apply the inductive step infinitely; here, we stop the "induction" when the loop terminates.

Let us see how these properties hold for insertion sort.

Initialization: We start by showing that the loop invariant holds before the first loop iteration, when $j = 2$.[1] The subarray $A[1 . . j - 1]$, therefore, consists of just the single element $A[1]$, which is in fact the original element in $A[1]$. Moreover, this subarray is sorted (trivially, of course), which shows that the loop invariant holds prior to the first iteration of the loop.

Maintenance: Next, we tackle the second property: showing that each iteration maintains the loop invariant. Informally, the body of the **for** loop works by moving $A[j - 1]$, $A[j - 2]$, $A[j - 3]$, and so on by one position to the right until it finds the proper position for $A[j]$ (lines 4–7), at which point it inserts the value of $A[j]$ (line 8). The subarray $A[1 . . j]$ then consists of the elements originally in $A[1 . . j]$, but in sorted order. Incrementing j for the next iteration of the **for** loop then preserves the loop invariant.

A more formal treatment of the second property would require us to state and show a loop invariant for the **while** loop of lines 5–7. At this point, however,

---

[1] When the loop is a **for** loop, the moment at which we check the loop invariant just prior to the first iteration is immediately after the initial assignment to the loop-counter variable and just before the first test in the loop header. In the case of INSERTION-SORT, this time is after assigning 2 to the variable j but before the first test of whether $j \leq A.length$.

we prefer not to get bogged down in such formalism, and so we rely on our informal analysis to show that the second property holds for the outer loop.

Termination: Finally, we examine what happens when the loop terminates. The condition causing the **for** loop to terminate is that $j > A.length = n$. Because each loop iteration increases j by 1, we must have $j = n + 1$ at that time. Substituting $n + 1$ for j in the wording of loop invariant, we have that the subarray $A[1 .. n]$ consists of the elements originally in $A[1 .. n]$, but in sorted order. Observing that the subarray $A[1 .. n]$ is the entire array, we conclude that the entire array is sorted. Hence, the algorithm is correct.

We shall use this method of loop invariants to show correctness later in this chapter and in other chapters as well.

Pseudocode conventions

We use the following conventions in our pseudocode.

- Indentation indicates block structure. For example, the body of the **for** loop that begins on line 1 consists of lines 2–8, and the body of the **while** loop that begins on line 5 contains lines 6–7 but not line 8. Our indentation style applies to **if-else** statements[2] as well. Using indentation instead of conventional indicators of block structure, such as **begin** and **end** statements, greatly reduces clutter while preserving, or even enhancing, clarity.[3]

- The looping constructs **while**, **for**, and **repeat-until** and the **if-else** conditional construct have interpretations similar to those in C, C++, Java, Python, and Pascal.[4] In this book, the loop counter retains its value after exiting the loop, unlike some situations that arise in C++, Java, and Pascal. Thus, immediately after a **for** loop, the loop counter's value is the value that first exceeded the **for** loop bound. We used this property in our correctness argument for insertion sort. The **for** loop header in line 1 is **for** $j = 2$ **to** $A.length$, and so when this loop terminates, $j = A.length + 1$ (or, equivalently, $j = n + 1$, since $n = A.length$). We use the keyword **to** when a **for** loop increments its loop

---

[2]In an **if-else** statement, we indent **else** at the same level as its matching **if**. Although we omit the keyword **then**, we occasionally refer to the portion executed when the test following **if** is true as a *then clause*. For multiway tests, we use **elseif** for tests after the first one.

[3]Each pseudocode procedure in this book appears on one page so that you will not have to discern levels of indentation in code that is split across pages.

[4]Most block-structured languages have equivalent constructs, though the exact syntax may differ. Python lacks **repeat-until** loops, and its **for** loops operate a little differently from the **for** loops in this book.

counter in each iteration, and we use the keyword **downto** when a **for** loop decrements its loop counter. When the loop counter changes by an amount greater than 1, the amount of change follows the optional keyword **by**.

- The symbol "*//*" indicates that the remainder of the line is a comment.

- A multiple assignment of the form $i = j = e$ assigns to both variables i and j the value of expression e; it should be treated as equivalent to the assignment $j = e$ followed by the assignment $i = j$.

- Variables (such as i, j, and *key*) are local to the given procedure. We shall not use global variables without explicit indication.

- We access array elements by specifying the array name followed by the index in square brackets. For example, $A[i]$ indicates the ith element of the array A. The notation ".." is used to indicate a range of values within an array. Thus, $A[1 .. j]$ indicates the subarray of A consisting of the j elements $A[1], A[2], \ldots, A[j]$.

- We typically organize compound data into *objects*, which are composed of *attributes*. We access a particular attribute using the syntax found in many object-oriented programming languages: the object name, followed by a dot, followed by the attribute name. For example, we treat an array as an object with the attribute *length* indicating how many elements it contains. To specify the number of elements in an array A, we write $A.length$.

  We treat a variable representing an array or object as a pointer to the data representing the array or object. For all attributes f of an object x, setting $y = x$ causes $y.f$ to equal $x.f$. Moreover, if we now set $x.f = 3$, then afterward not only does $x.f$ equal 3, but $y.f$ equals 3 as well. In other words, x and y point to the same object after the assignment $y = x$.

  Our attribute notation can "cascade." For example, suppose that the attribute f is itself a pointer to some type of object that has an attribute g. Then the notation $x.f.g$ is implicitly parenthesized as $(x.f).g$. In other words, if we had assigned $y = x.f$, then $x.f.g$ is the same as $y.g$.

  Sometimes, a pointer will refer to no object at all. In this case, we give it the special value NIL.

- We pass parameters to a procedure *by value*: the called procedure receives its own copy of the parameters, and if it assigns a value to a parameter, the change is *not* seen by the calling procedure. When objects are passed, the pointer to the data representing the object is copied, but the object's attributes are not. For example, if x is a parameter of a called procedure, the assignment $x = y$ within the called procedure is not visible to the calling procedure. The assignment $x.f = 3$, however, is visible. Similarly, arrays are passed by pointer, so that

a pointer to the array is passed, rather than the entire array, and changes to individual array elements are visible to the calling procedure.

- A **return** statement immediately transfers control back to the point of call in the calling procedure. Most **return** statements also take a value to pass back to the caller. Our pseudocode differs from many programming languages in that we allow multiple values to be returned in a single **return** statement.

- The boolean operators "and" and "or" are ***short circuiting***. That is, when we evaluate the expression "x and y" we first evaluate x. If x evaluates to FALSE, then the entire expression cannot evaluate to TRUE, and so we do not evaluate y. If, on the other hand, x evaluates to TRUE, we must evaluate y to determine the value of the entire expression. Similarly, in the expression "x or y" we evaluate the expression y only if x evaluates to FALSE. Short-circuiting operators allow us to write boolean expressions such as "$x \neq$ NIL and $x.f = y$" without worrying about what happens when we try to evaluate $x.f$ when x is NIL.

- The keyword **error** indicates that an error occurred because conditions were wrong for the procedure to have been called. The calling procedure is responsible for handling the error, and so we do not specify what action to take.

Exercises

2.1-1
Using Figure 2.2 as a model, illustrate the operation of INSERTION-SORT on the array $A = \langle 31, 41, 59, 26, 41, 58 \rangle$.

2.1-2
Rewrite the INSERTION-SORT procedure to sort into nonincreasing instead of nondecreasing order.

2.1-3
Consider the ***searching problem***:

Input: A sequence of n numbers $A = \langle a_1, a_2, \ldots, a_n \rangle$ and a value v.

Output: An index i such that $v = A[i]$ or the special value NIL if v does not appear in A.

Write pseudocode for ***linear search***, which scans through the sequence, looking for v. Using a loop invariant, prove that your algorithm is correct. Make sure that your loop invariant fulfills the three necessary properties.

2.1-4
Consider the problem of adding two n-bit binary integers, stored in two n-element arrays A and B. The sum of the two integers should be stored in binary form in

an $(n + 1)$-element array C. State the problem formally and write pseudocode for adding the two integers.

2.2 Analyzing algorithms

Analyzing an algorithm has come to mean predicting the resources that the algorithm requires. Occasionally, resources such as memory, communication bandwidth, or computer hardware are of primary concern, but most often it is computational time that we want to measure. Generally, by analyzing several candidate algorithms for a problem, we can identify a most efficient one. Such analysis may indicate more than one viable candidate, but we can often discard several inferior algorithms in the process.

Before we can analyze an algorithm, we must have a model of the implementation technology that we will use, including a model for the resources of that technology and their costs. For most of this book, we shall assume a generic one-processor, ***random-access machine (RAM)*** model of computation as our implementation technology and understand that our algorithms will be implemented as computer programs. In the RAM model, instructions are executed one after another, with no concurrent operations.

Strictly speaking, we should precisely define the instructions of the RAM model and their costs. To do so, however, would be tedious and would yield little insight into algorithm design and analysis. Yet we must be careful not to abuse the RAM model. For example, what if a RAM had an instruction that sorts? Then we could sort in just one instruction. Such a RAM would be unrealistic, since real computers do not have such instructions. Our guide, therefore, is how real computers are designed. The RAM model contains instructions commonly found in real computers: arithmetic (such as add, subtract, multiply, divide, remainder, floor, ceiling), data movement (load, store, copy), and control (conditional and unconditional branch, subroutine call and return). Each such instruction takes a constant amount of time.

The data types in the RAM model are integer and floating point (for storing real numbers). Although we typically do not concern ourselves with precision in this book, in some applications precision is crucial. We also assume a limit on the size of each word of data. For example, when working with inputs of size n, we typically assume that integers are represented by $c \lg n$ bits for some constant $c \geq 1$. We require $c \geq 1$ so that each word can hold the value of n, enabling us to index the individual input elements, and we restrict c to be a constant so that the word size does not grow arbitrarily. (If the word size could grow arbitrarily, we could store huge amounts of data in one word and operate on it all in constant time—clearly an unrealistic scenario.)

Real computers contain instructions not listed above, and such instructions represent a gray area in the RAM model. For example, is exponentiation a constant-time instruction? In the general case, no; it takes several instructions to compute x^y when x and y are real numbers. In restricted situations, however, exponentiation is a constant-time operation. Many computers have a "shift left" instruction, which in constant time shifts the bits of an integer by k positions to the left. In most computers, shifting the bits of an integer by one position to the left is equivalent to multiplication by 2, so that shifting the bits by k positions to the left is equivalent to multiplication by 2^k. Therefore, such computers can compute 2^k in one constant-time instruction by shifting the integer 1 by k positions to the left, as long as k is no more than the number of bits in a computer word. We will endeavor to avoid such gray areas in the RAM model, but we will treat computation of 2^k as a constant-time operation when k is a small enough positive integer.

In the RAM model, we do not attempt to model the memory hierarchy that is common in contemporary computers. That is, we do not model caches or virtual memory. Several computational models attempt to account for memory-hierarchy effects, which are sometimes significant in real programs on real machines. A handful of problems in this book examine memory-hierarchy effects, but for the most part, the analyses in this book will not consider them. Models that include the memory hierarchy are quite a bit more complex than the RAM model, and so they can be difficult to work with. Moreover, RAM-model analyses are usually excellent predictors of performance on actual machines.

Analyzing even a simple algorithm in the RAM model can be a challenge. The mathematical tools required may include combinatorics, probability theory, algebraic dexterity, and the ability to identify the most significant terms in a formula. Because the behavior of an algorithm may be different for each possible input, we need a means for summarizing that behavior in simple, easily understood formulas.

Even though we typically select only one machine model to analyze a given algorithm, we still face many choices in deciding how to express our analysis. We would like a way that is simple to write and manipulate, shows the important characteristics of an algorithm's resource requirements, and suppresses tedious details.

Analysis of insertion sort

The time taken by the INSERTION-SORT procedure depends on the input: sorting a thousand numbers takes longer than sorting three numbers. Moreover, INSERTION-SORT can take different amounts of time to sort two input sequences of the same size depending on how nearly sorted they already are. In general, the time taken by an algorithm grows with the size of the input, so it is traditional to describe the running time of a program as a function of the size of its input. To do so, we need to define the terms "running time" and "size of input" more carefully.

The best notion for **input size** depends on the problem being studied. For many problems, such as sorting or computing discrete Fourier transforms, the most natural measure is the *number of items in the input*—for example, the array size n for sorting. For many other problems, such as multiplying two integers, the best measure of input size is the *total number of bits* needed to represent the input in ordinary binary notation. Sometimes, it is more appropriate to describe the size of the input with two numbers rather than one. For instance, if the input to an algorithm is a graph, the input size can be described by the numbers of vertices and edges in the graph. We shall indicate which input size measure is being used with each problem we study.

The **running time** of an algorithm on a particular input is the number of primitive operations or "steps" executed. It is convenient to define the notion of step so that it is as machine-independent as possible. For the moment, let us adopt the following view. A constant amount of time is required to execute each line of our pseudocode. One line may take a different amount of time than another line, but we shall assume that each execution of the ith line takes time c_i, where c_i is a constant. This viewpoint is in keeping with the RAM model, and it also reflects how the pseudocode would be implemented on most actual computers.[5]

In the following discussion, our expression for the running time of INSERTION-SORT will evolve from a messy formula that uses all the statement costs c_i to a much simpler notation that is more concise and more easily manipulated. This simpler notation will also make it easy to determine whether one algorithm is more efficient than another.

We start by presenting the INSERTION-SORT procedure with the time "cost" of each statement and the number of times each statement is executed. For each $j = 2, 3, \ldots, n$, where $n = A.length$, we let t_j denote the number of times the **while** loop test in line 5 is executed for that value of j. When a **for** or **while** loop exits in the usual way (i.e., due to the test in the loop header), the test is executed one time more than the loop body. We assume that comments are not executable statements, and so they take no time.

---

[5]There are some subtleties here. Computational steps that we specify in English are often variants of a procedure that requires more than just a constant amount of time. For example, later in this book we might say "sort the points by x-coordinate," which, as we shall see, takes more than a constant amount of time. Also, note that a statement that calls a subroutine takes constant time, though the subroutine, once invoked, may take more. That is, we separate the process of **calling** the subroutine—passing parameters to it, etc.—from the process of **executing** the subroutine.

INSERTION-SORT(A)	cost	times
1 **for** $j = 2$ **to** $A.length$	c_1	n
2 $key = A[j]$	c_2	$n - 1$
3 // Insert $A[j]$ into the sorted		
sequence $A[1 .. j - 1]$.	0	$n - 1$
4 $i = j - 1$	c_4	$n - 1$
5 **while** $i > 0$ and $A[i] > key$	c_5	$\sum_{j=2}^{n} t_j$
6 $A[i + 1] = A[i]$	c_6	$\sum_{j=2}^{n}(t_j - 1)$
7 $i = i - 1$	c_7	$\sum_{j=2}^{n}(t_j - 1)$
8 $A[i + 1] = key$	c_8	$n - 1$

The running time of the algorithm is the sum of running times for each state-ment executed; a statement that takes c_i steps to execute and executes n times will contribute $c_i n$ to the total running time.[6] To compute $T(n)$, the running time of INSERTION-SORT on an input of n values, we sum the products of the *cost* and *times* columns, obtaining

$$T(n) \;=\; c_1 n + c_2(n - 1) + c_4(n - 1) + c_5 \sum_{j=2}^{n} t_j + c_6 \sum_{j=2}^{n}(t_j - 1)$$

$$+ c_7 \sum_{j=2}^{n}(t_j - 1) + c_8(n - 1) \,.$$

Even for inputs of a given size, an algorithm's running time may depend on *which* input of that size is given. For example, in INSERTION-SORT, the best case occurs if the array is already sorted. For each $j = 2, 3, \ldots, n$, we then find that $A[i] \le key$ in line 5 when i has its initial value of $j - 1$. Thus $t_j = 1$ for $j = 2, 3, \ldots, n$, and the best-case running time is

$$T(n) \;=\; c_1 n + c_2(n - 1) + c_4(n - 1) + c_5(n - 1) + c_8(n - 1)$$
$$=\; (c_1 + c_2 + c_4 + c_5 + c_8)n - (c_2 + c_4 + c_5 + c_8) \,.$$

We can express this running time as $an + b$ for *constants* a and b that depend on the statement costs c_i; it is thus a ***linear function*** of n.

If the array is in reverse sorted order—that is, in decreasing order—the worst case results. We must compare each element $A[j]$ with each element in the entire sorted subarray $A[1 .. j - 1]$, and so $t_j = j$ for $j = 2, 3, \ldots, n$. Noting that

---

[6]This characteristic does not necessarily hold for a resource such as memory. A statement that references m words of memory and is executed n times does not necessarily reference mn distinct words of memory.

$$\sum_{j=2}^{n} j = \frac{n(n+1)}{2} - 1$$

and

$$\sum_{j=2}^{n}(j-1) = \frac{n(n-1)}{2}$$

(see Appendix A for a review of how to solve these summations), we find that in the worst case, the running time of INSERTION-SORT is

$$
\begin{aligned}
T(n) \;=\; & c_1 n + c_2(n-1) + c_4(n-1) + c_5\left(\frac{n(n+1)}{2} - 1\right) \\
& + c_6\left(\frac{n(n-1)}{2}\right) + c_7\left(\frac{n(n-1)}{2}\right) + c_8(n-1) \\
=\; & \left(\frac{c_5}{2} + \frac{c_6}{2} + \frac{c_7}{2}\right)n^2 + \left(c_1 + c_2 + c_4 + \frac{c_5}{2} - \frac{c_6}{2} - \frac{c_7}{2} + c_8\right)n \\
& - (c_2 + c_4 + c_5 + c_8) \, .
\end{aligned}
$$

We can express this worst-case running time as $an^2 + bn + c$ for constants a, b, and c that again depend on the statement costs c_i; it is thus a ***quadratic function*** of n.

Typically, as in insertion sort, the running time of an algorithm is fixed for a given input, although in later chapters we shall see some interesting "randomized" algorithms whose behavior can vary even for a fixed input.

Worst-case and average-case analysis

In our analysis of insertion sort, we looked at both the best case, in which the input array was already sorted, and the worst case, in which the input array was reverse sorted. For the remainder of this book, though, we shall usually concentrate on finding only the ***worst-case running time***, that is, the longest running time for *any* input of size n. We give three reasons for this orientation.

- The worst-case running time of an algorithm gives us an upper bound on the running time for any input. Knowing it provides a guarantee that the algorithm will never take any longer. We need not make some educated guess about the running time and hope that it never gets much worse.

- For some algorithms, the worst case occurs fairly often. For example, in searching a database for a particular piece of information, the searching algorithm's worst case will often occur when the information is not present in the database. In some applications, searches for absent information may be frequent.

- The "average case" is often roughly as bad as the worst case. Suppose that we randomly choose n numbers and apply insertion sort. How long does it take to determine where in subarray $A[1 .. j - 1]$ to insert element $A[j]$? On average, half the elements in $A[1 .. j - 1]$ are less than $A[j]$, and half the elements are greater. On average, therefore, we check half of the subarray $A[1 .. j - 1]$, and so t_j is about $j/2$. The resulting average-case running time turns out to be a quadratic function of the input size, just like the worst-case running time.

In some particular cases, we shall be interested in the ***average-case*** running time of an algorithm; we shall see the technique of ***probabilistic analysis*** applied to various algorithms throughout this book. The scope of average-case analysis is limited, because it may not be apparent what constitutes an "average" input for a particular problem. Often, we shall assume that all inputs of a given size are equally likely. In practice, this assumption may be violated, but we can sometimes use a ***randomized algorithm***, which makes random choices, to allow a probabilistic analysis and yield an ***expected*** running time. We explore randomized algorithms more in Chapter 5 and in several other subsequent chapters.

Order of growth

We used some simplifying abstractions to ease our analysis of the INSERTION-SORT procedure. First, we ignored the actual cost of each statement, using the constants c_i to represent these costs. Then, we observed that even these constants give us more detail than we really need: we expressed the worst-case running time as $an^2 + bn + c$ for some constants a, b, and c that depend on the statement costs c_i. We thus ignored not only the actual statement costs, but also the abstract costs c_i.

We shall now make one more simplifying abstraction: it is the ***rate of growth***, or ***order of growth***, of the running time that really interests us. We therefore consider only the leading term of a formula (e.g., an^2), since the lower-order terms are relatively insignificant for large values of n. We also ignore the leading term's constant coefficient, since constant factors are less significant than the rate of growth in determining computational efficiency for large inputs. For insertion sort, when we ignore the lower-order terms and the leading term's constant coefficient, we are left with the factor of n^2 from the leading term. We write that insertion sort has a worst-case running time of $\Theta(n^2)$ (pronounced "theta of n-squared"). We shall use Θ-notation informally in this chapter, and we will define it precisely in Chapter 3.

We usually consider one algorithm to be more efficient than another if its worst-case running time has a lower order of growth. Due to constant factors and lower-order terms, an algorithm whose running time has a higher order of growth might take less time for small inputs than an algorithm whose running time has a lower

order of growth. But for large enough inputs, a $\Theta(n^2)$ algorithm, for example, will run more quickly in the worst case than a $\Theta(n^3)$ algorithm.

Exercises

2.2-1
Express the function $n^3/1000 - 100n^2 - 100n + 3$ in terms of Θ-notation.

2.2-2
Consider sorting n numbers stored in array A by first finding the smallest element of A and exchanging it with the element in $A[1]$. Then find the second smallest element of A, and exchange it with $A[2]$. Continue in this manner for the first $n - 1$ elements of A. Write pseudocode for this algorithm, which is known as ***selection sort***. What loop invariant does this algorithm maintain? Why does it need to run for only the first $n - 1$ elements, rather than for all n elements? Give the best-case and worst-case running times of selection sort in Θ-notation.

2.2-3
Consider linear search again (see Exercise 2.1-3). How many elements of the input sequence need to be checked on the average, assuming that the element being searched for is equally likely to be any element in the array? How about in the worst case? What are the average-case and worst-case running times of linear search in Θ-notation? Justify your answers.

2.2-4
How can we modify almost any algorithm to have a good best-case running time?

2.3 Designing algorithms

We can choose from a wide range of algorithm design techniques. For insertion sort, we used an ***incremental*** approach: having sorted the subarray $A[1 \mathinner{.\,.} j - 1]$, we inserted the single element $A[j]$ into its proper place, yielding the sorted subarray $A[1 \mathinner{.\,.} j]$.

In this section, we examine an alternative design approach, known as "divide-and-conquer," which we shall explore in more detail in Chapter 4. We'll use divide-and-conquer to design a sorting algorithm whose worst-case running time is much less than that of insertion sort. One advantage of divide-and-conquer algorithms is that their running times are often easily determined using techniques that we will see in Chapter 4.

2.3.1   The divide-and-conquer approach

Many useful algorithms are *recursive* in structure: to solve a given problem, they call themselves recursively one or more times to deal with closely related subproblems. These algorithms typically follow a *divide-and-conquer* approach: they break the problem into several subproblems that are similar to the original problem but smaller in size, solve the subproblems recursively, and then combine these solutions to create a solution to the original problem.

The divide-and-conquer paradigm involves three steps at each level of the recursion:

Divide the problem into a number of subproblems that are smaller instances of the same problem.

Conquer the subproblems by solving them recursively. If the subproblem sizes are small enough, however, just solve the subproblems in a straightforward manner.

Combine the solutions to the subproblems into the solution for the original problem.

The *merge sort* algorithm closely follows the divide-and-conquer paradigm. Intuitively, it operates as follows.

Divide: Divide the n-element sequence to be sorted into two subsequences of $n/2$ elements each.

Conquer: Sort the two subsequences recursively using merge sort.

Combine: Merge the two sorted subsequences to produce the sorted answer.

The recursion "bottoms out" when the sequence to be sorted has length 1, in which case there is no work to be done, since every sequence of length 1 is already in sorted order.

The key operation of the merge sort algorithm is the merging of two sorted sequences in the "combine" step. We merge by calling an auxiliary procedure MERGE(A, p, q, r), where A is an array and p, q, and r are indices into the array such that $p \leq q < r$. The procedure assumes that the subarrays $A[p \mathinner{\ldotp\ldotp} q]$ and $A[q + 1 \mathinner{\ldotp\ldotp} r]$ are in sorted order. It *merges* them to form a single sorted subarray that replaces the current subarray $A[p \mathinner{\ldotp\ldotp} r]$.

Our MERGE procedure takes time $\Theta(n)$, where $n = r - p + 1$ is the total number of elements being merged, and it works as follows. Returning to our card-playing motif, suppose we have two piles of cards face up on a table. Each pile is sorted, with the smallest cards on top. We wish to merge the two piles into a single sorted output pile, which is to be face down on the table. Our basic step consists of choosing the smaller of the two cards on top of the face-up piles, removing it from its pile (which exposes a new top card), and placing this card face down onto

the output pile. We repeat this step until one input pile is empty, at which time we just take the remaining input pile and place it face down onto the output pile. Computationally, each basic step takes constant time, since we are comparing just the two top cards. Since we perform at most n basic steps, merging takes $\Theta(n)$ time.

The following pseudocode implements the above idea, but with an additional twist that avoids having to check whether either pile is empty in each basic step. We place on the bottom of each pile a ***sentinel*** card, which contains a special value that we use to simplify our code. Here, we use ∞ as the sentinel value, so that whenever a card with ∞ is exposed, it cannot be the smaller card unless both piles have their sentinel cards exposed. But once that happens, all the nonsentinel cards have already been placed onto the output pile. Since we know in advance that exactly $r - p + 1$ cards will be placed onto the output pile, we can stop once we have performed that many basic steps.

MERGE(A, p, q, r)

```
 1   n₁ = q − p + 1
 2   n₂ = r − q
 3   let L[1 .. n₁ + 1] and R[1 .. n₂ + 1] be new arrays
 4   for i = 1 to n₁
 5       L[i] = A[p + i − 1]
 6   for j = 1 to n₂
 7       R[j] = A[q + j]
 8   L[n₁ + 1] = ∞
 9   R[n₂ + 1] = ∞
10   i = 1
11   j = 1
12   for k = p to r
13       if L[i] ≤ R[j]
14           A[k] = L[i]
15           i = i + 1
16       else A[k] = R[j]
17           j = j + 1
```

In detail, the MERGE procedure works as follows. Line 1 computes the length n_1 of the subarray $A[p \, .. \, q]$, and line 2 computes the length n_2 of the subarray $A[q + 1 \, .. \, r]$. We create arrays L and R ("left" and "right"), of lengths $n_1 + 1$ and $n_2 + 1$, respectively, in line 3; the extra position in each array will hold the sentinel. The **for** loop of lines 4–5 copies the subarray $A[p \, .. \, q]$ into $L[1 \, .. \, n_1]$, and the **for** loop of lines 6–7 copies the subarray $A[q + 1 \, .. \, r]$ into $R[1 \, .. \, n_2]$. Lines 8–9 put the sentinels at the ends of the arrays L and R. Lines 10–17, illus-

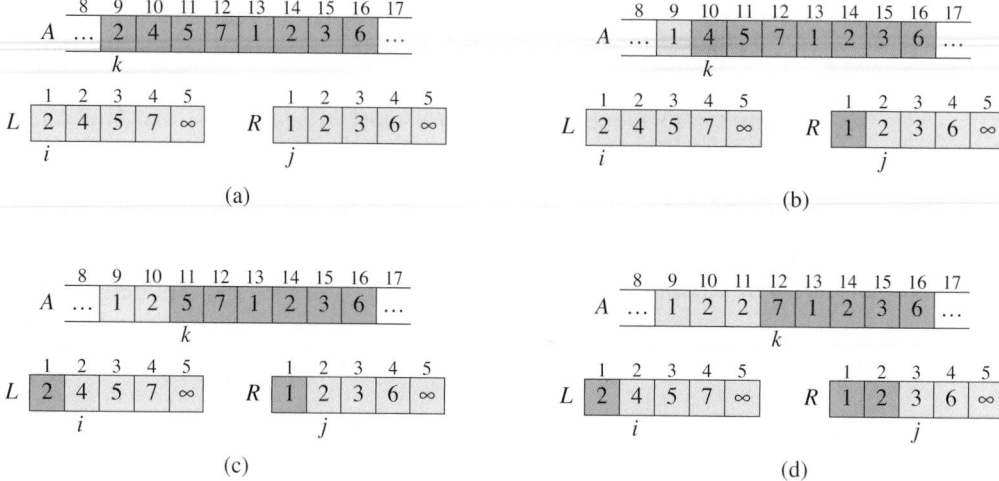

Figure 2.3 The operation of lines 10–17 in the call MERGE($A, 9, 12, 16$), when the subarray $A[9 .. 16]$ contains the sequence $\langle 2, 4, 5, 7, 1, 2, 3, 6 \rangle$. After copying and inserting sentinels, the array L contains $\langle 2, 4, 5, 7, \infty \rangle$, and the array R contains $\langle 1, 2, 3, 6, \infty \rangle$. Lightly shaded positions in A contain their final values, and lightly shaded positions in L and R contain values that have yet to be copied back into A. Taken together, the lightly shaded positions always comprise the values originally in $A[9 .. 16]$, along with the two sentinels. Heavily shaded positions in A contain values that will be copied over, and heavily shaded positions in L and R contain values that have already been copied back into A. **(a)–(h)** The arrays A, L, and R, and their respective indices k, i, and j prior to each iteration of the loop of lines 12–17.

trated in Figure 2.3, perform the $r - p + 1$ basic steps by maintaining the following loop invariant:

> At the start of each iteration of the **for** loop of lines 12–17, the subarray $A[p .. k - 1]$ contains the $k - p$ smallest elements of $L[1 .. n_1 + 1]$ and $R[1 .. n_2 + 1]$, in sorted order. Moreover, $L[i]$ and $R[j]$ are the smallest elements of their arrays that have not been copied back into A.

We must show that this loop invariant holds prior to the first iteration of the **for** loop of lines 12–17, that each iteration of the loop maintains the invariant, and that the invariant provides a useful property to show correctness when the loop terminates.

Initialization: Prior to the first iteration of the loop, we have $k = p$, so that the subarray $A[p .. k - 1]$ is empty. This empty subarray contains the $k - p = 0$ smallest elements of L and R, and since $i = j = 1$, both $L[i]$ and $R[j]$ are the smallest elements of their arrays that have not been copied back into A.

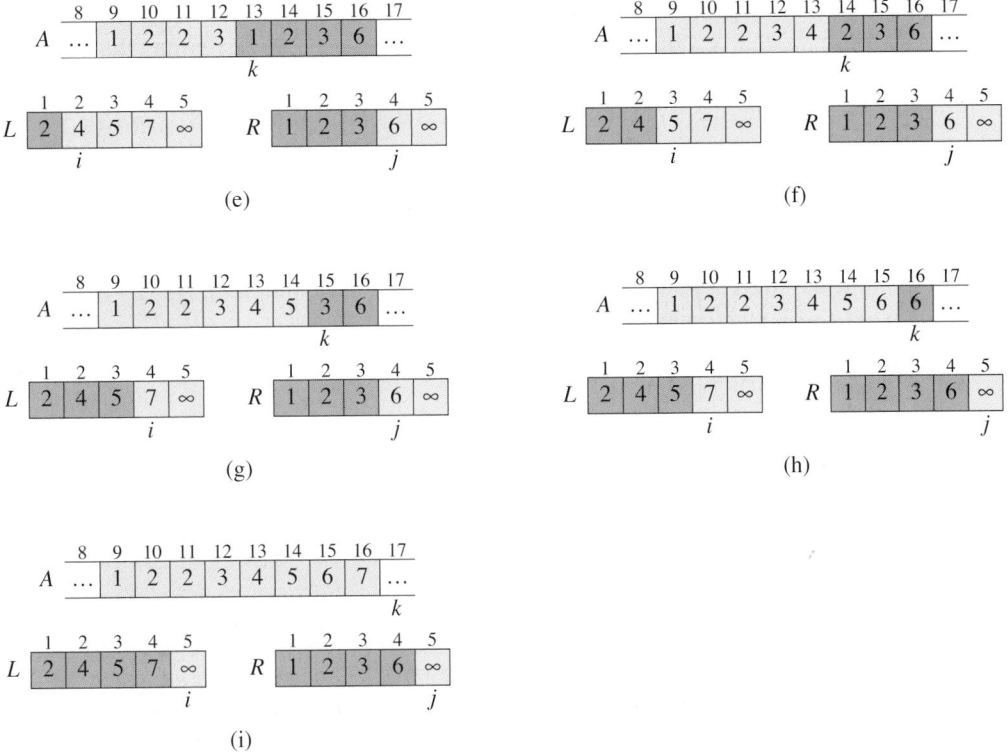

Figure 2.3, continued **(i)** The arrays and indices at termination. At this point, the subarray in $A[9..16]$ is sorted, and the two sentinels in L and R are the only two elements in these arrays that have not been copied into A.

Maintenance: To see that each iteration maintains the loop invariant, let us first suppose that $L[i] \leq R[j]$. Then $L[i]$ is the smallest element not yet copied back into A. Because $A[p..k-1]$ contains the $k-p$ smallest elements, after line 14 copies $L[i]$ into $A[k]$, the subarray $A[p..k]$ will contain the $k-p+1$ smallest elements. Incrementing k (in the **for** loop update) and i (in line 15) reestablishes the loop invariant for the next iteration. If instead $L[i] > R[j]$, then lines 16–17 perform the appropriate action to maintain the loop invariant.

Termination: At termination, $k = r + 1$. By the loop invariant, the subarray $A[p..k-1]$, which is $A[p..r]$, contains the $k - p = r - p + 1$ smallest elements of $L[1..n_1 + 1]$ and $R[1..n_2 + 1]$, in sorted order. The arrays L and R together contain $n_1 + n_2 + 2 = r - p + 3$ elements. All but the two largest have been copied back into A, and these two largest elements are the sentinels.

To see that the MERGE procedure runs in $\Theta(n)$ time, where $n = r - p + 1$, observe that each of lines 1–3 and 8–11 takes constant time, the **for** loops of lines 4–7 take $\Theta(n_1 + n_2) = \Theta(n)$ time,[7] and there are n iterations of the **for** loop of lines 12–17, each of which takes constant time.

We can now use the MERGE procedure as a subroutine in the merge sort algorithm. The procedure MERGE-SORT(A, p, r) sorts the elements in the subarray $A[p \mathinner{.\,.} r]$. If $p \geq r$, the subarray has at most one element and is therefore already sorted. Otherwise, the divide step simply computes an index q that partitions $A[p \mathinner{.\,.} r]$ into two subarrays: $A[p \mathinner{.\,.} q]$, containing $\lceil n/2 \rceil$ elements, and $A[q + 1 \mathinner{.\,.} r]$, containing $\lfloor n/2 \rfloor$ elements.[8]

MERGE-SORT(A, p, r)

1   **if** $p < r$
2       $q = \lfloor (p + r)/2 \rfloor$
3   MERGE-SORT(A, p, q)
4   MERGE-SORT$(A, q + 1, r)$
5   MERGE(A, p, q, r)

To sort the entire sequence $A = \langle A[1], A[2], \ldots, A[n] \rangle$, we make the initial call MERGE-SORT$(A, 1, A.length)$, where once again $A.length = n$. Figure 2.4 illustrates the operation of the procedure bottom-up when n is a power of 2. The algorithm consists of merging pairs of 1-item sequences to form sorted sequences of length 2, merging pairs of sequences of length 2 to form sorted sequences of length 4, and so on, until two sequences of length $n/2$ are merged to form the final sorted sequence of length n.

2.3.2   Analyzing divide-and-conquer algorithms

When an algorithm contains a recursive call to itself, we can often describe its running time by a ***recurrence equation*** or ***recurrence***, which describes the overall running time on a problem of size n in terms of the running time on smaller inputs. We can then use mathematical tools to solve the recurrence and provide bounds on the performance of the algorithm.

---

[7]We shall see in Chapter 3 how to formally interpret equations containing Θ-notation.

[8]The expression $\lceil x \rceil$ denotes the least integer greater than or equal to x, and $\lfloor x \rfloor$ denotes the greatest integer less than or equal to x. These notations are defined in Chapter 3. The easiest way to verify that setting q to $\lfloor (p + r)/2 \rfloor$ yields subarrays $A[p \mathinner{.\,.} q]$ and $A[q + 1 \mathinner{.\,.} r]$ of sizes $\lceil n/2 \rceil$ and $\lfloor n/2 \rfloor$, respectively, is to examine the four cases that arise depending on whether each of p and r is odd or even.

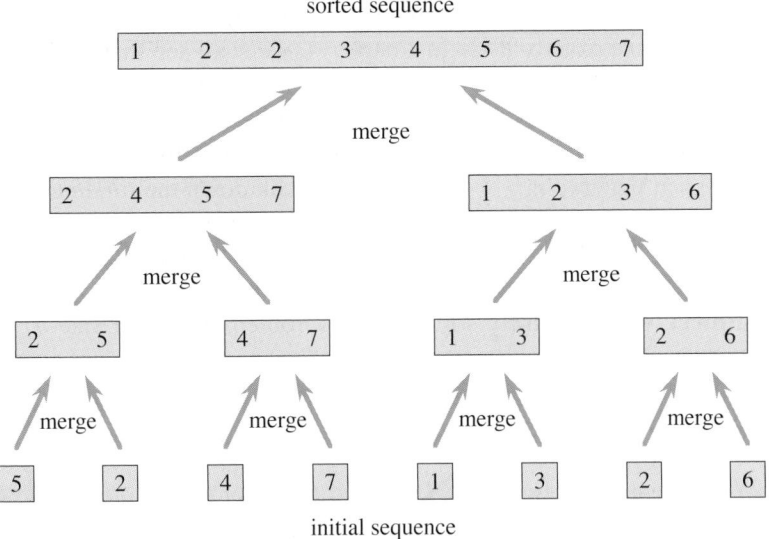

Figure 2.4   The operation of merge sort on the array $A = \langle 5, 2, 4, 7, 1, 3, 2, 6 \rangle$. The lengths of the sorted sequences being merged increase as the algorithm progresses from bottom to top.

A recurrence for the running time of a divide-and-conquer algorithm falls out from the three steps of the basic paradigm. As before, we let $T(n)$ be the running time on a problem of size n. If the problem size is small enough, say $n \le c$ for some constant c, the straightforward solution takes constant time, which we write as $\Theta(1)$. Suppose that our division of the problem yields a subproblems, each of which is $1/b$ the size of the original. (For merge sort, both a and b are 2, but we shall see many divide-and-conquer algorithms in which $a \ne b$.) It takes time $T(n/b)$ to solve one subproblem of size n/b, and so it takes time $aT(n/b)$ to solve a of them. If we take $D(n)$ time to divide the problem into subproblems and $C(n)$ time to combine the solutions to the subproblems into the solution to the original problem, we get the recurrence

$$T(n) = \begin{cases} \Theta(1) & \text{if } n \le c \,, \\ aT(n/b) + D(n) + C(n) & \text{otherwise} \,. \end{cases}$$

In Chapter 4, we shall see how to solve common recurrences of this form.

Analysis of merge sort

Although the pseudocode for MERGE-SORT works correctly when the number of elements is not even, our recurrence-based analysis is simplified if we assume that

the original problem size is a power of 2. Each divide step then yields two subsequences of size exactly $n/2$. In Chapter 4, we shall see that this assumption does not affect the order of growth of the solution to the recurrence.

We reason as follows to set up the recurrence for $T(n)$, the worst-case running time of merge sort on n numbers. Merge sort on just one element takes constant time. When we have $n > 1$ elements, we break down the running time as follows.

Divide: The divide step just computes the middle of the subarray, which takes constant time. Thus, $D(n) = \Theta(1)$.

Conquer: We recursively solve two subproblems, each of size $n/2$, which contributes $2T(n/2)$ to the running time.

Combine: We have already noted that the MERGE procedure on an n-element subarray takes time $\Theta(n)$, and so $C(n) = \Theta(n)$.

When we add the functions $D(n)$ and $C(n)$ for the merge sort analysis, we are adding a function that is $\Theta(n)$ and a function that is $\Theta(1)$. This sum is a linear function of n, that is, $\Theta(n)$. Adding it to the $2T(n/2)$ term from the "conquer" step gives the recurrence for the worst-case running time $T(n)$ of merge sort:

$$T(n) = \begin{cases} \Theta(1) & \text{if } n = 1, \\ 2T(n/2) + \Theta(n) & \text{if } n > 1. \end{cases} \tag{2.1}$$

In Chapter 4, we shall see the "master theorem," which we can use to show that $T(n)$ is $\Theta(n \lg n)$, where $\lg n$ stands for $\log_2 n$. Because the logarithm function grows more slowly than any linear function, for large enough inputs, merge sort, with its $\Theta(n \lg n)$ running time, outperforms insertion sort, whose running time is $\Theta(n^2)$, in the worst case.

We do not need the master theorem to intuitively understand why the solution to the recurrence (2.1) is $T(n) = \Theta(n \lg n)$. Let us rewrite recurrence (2.1) as

$$T(n) = \begin{cases} c & \text{if } n = 1, \\ 2T(n/2) + cn & \text{if } n > 1, \end{cases} \tag{2.2}$$

where the constant c represents the time required to solve problems of size 1 as well as the time per array element of the divide and combine steps.[9]

---

[9]It is unlikely that the same constant exactly represents both the time to solve problems of size 1 and the time per array element of the divide and combine steps. We can get around this problem by letting c be the larger of these times and understanding that our recurrence gives an upper bound on the running time, or by letting c be the lesser of these times and understanding that our recurrence gives a lower bound on the running time. Both bounds are on the order of $n \lg n$ and, taken together, give a $\Theta(n \lg n)$ running time.

Figure 2.5 shows how we can solve recurrence (2.2). For convenience, we assume that n is an exact power of 2. Part (a) of the figure shows $T(n)$, which we expand in part (b) into an equivalent tree representing the recurrence. The cn term is the root (the cost incurred at the top level of recursion), and the two subtrees of the root are the two smaller recurrences $T(n/2)$. Part (c) shows this process carried one step further by expanding $T(n/2)$. The cost incurred at each of the two subnodes at the second level of recursion is $cn/2$. We continue expanding each node in the tree by breaking it into its constituent parts as determined by the recurrence, until the problem sizes get down to 1, each with a cost of c. Part (d) shows the resulting *recursion tree*.

Next, we add the costs across each level of the tree. The top level has total cost cn, the next level down has total cost $c(n/2) + c(n/2) = cn$, the level after that has total cost $c(n/4)+c(n/4)+c(n/4)+c(n/4) = cn$, and so on. In general, the level i below the top has 2^i nodes, each contributing a cost of $c(n/2^i)$, so that the ith level below the top has total cost $2^i c(n/2^i) = cn$. The bottom level has n nodes, each contributing a cost of c, for a total cost of cn.

The total number of levels of the recursion tree in Figure 2.5 is $\lg n + 1$, where n is the number of leaves, corresponding to the input size. An informal inductive argument justifies this claim. The base case occurs when $n = 1$, in which case the tree has only one level. Since $\lg 1 = 0$, we have that $\lg n + 1$ gives the correct number of levels. Now assume as an inductive hypothesis that the number of levels of a recursion tree with 2^i leaves is $\lg 2^i + 1 = i + 1$ (since for any value of i, we have that $\lg 2^i = i$). Because we are assuming that the input size is a power of 2, the next input size to consider is 2^{i+1}. A tree with $n = 2^{i+1}$ leaves has one more level than a tree with 2^i leaves, and so the total number of levels is $(i + 1) + 1 = \lg 2^{i+1} + 1$.

To compute the total cost represented by the recurrence (2.2), we simply add up the costs of all the levels. The recursion tree has $\lg n + 1$ levels, each costing cn, for a total cost of $cn(\lg n + 1) = cn \lg n + cn$. Ignoring the low-order term and the constant c gives the desired result of $\Theta(n \lg n)$.

Exercises

2.3-1
Using Figure 2.4 as a model, illustrate the operation of merge sort on the array $A = \langle 3, 41, 52, 26, 38, 57, 9, 49 \rangle$.

2.3-2
Rewrite the MERGE procedure so that it does not use sentinels, instead stopping once either array L or R has had all its elements copied back to A and then copying the remainder of the other array back into A.

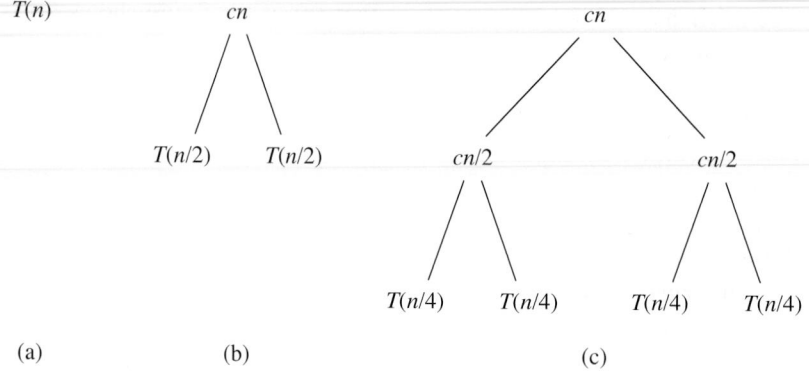

(a)   (b)   (c)

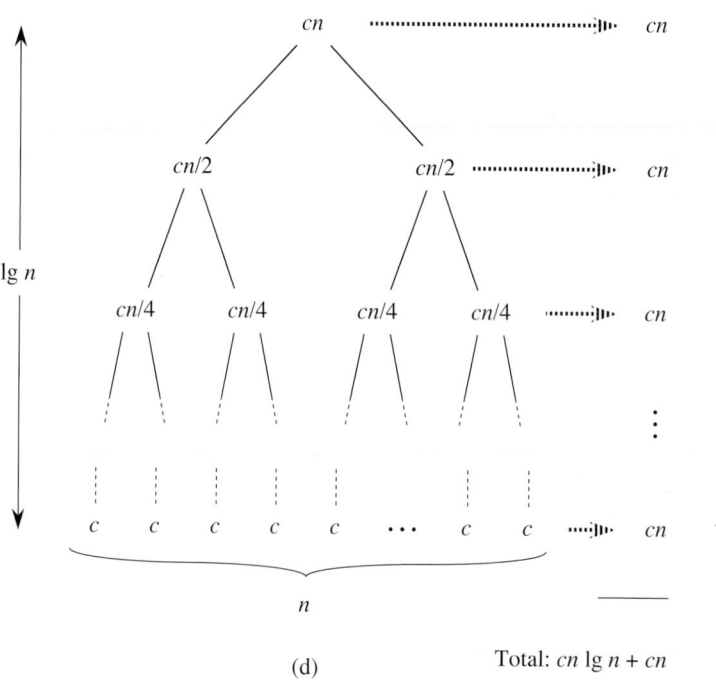

(d)   Total: $cn \lg n + cn$

Figure 2.5 How to construct a recursion tree for the recurrence $T(n) = 2T(n/2) + cn$. Part **(a)** shows $T(n)$, which progressively expands in **(b)**–**(d)** to form the recursion tree. The fully expanded tree in part (d) has $\lg n + 1$ levels (i.e., it has height $\lg n$, as indicated), and each level contributes a total cost of cn. The total cost, therefore, is $cn \lg n + cn$, which is $\Theta(n \lg n)$.

2.3-3
Use mathematical induction to show that when n is an exact power of 2, the solution of the recurrence

$$T(n) = \begin{cases} 2 & \text{if } n = 2, \\ 2T(n/2) + n & \text{if } n = 2^k, \text{ for } k > 1 \end{cases}$$

is $T(n) = n \lg n$.

2.3-4
We can express insertion sort as a recursive procedure as follows. In order to sort $A[1 \mathrel{..} n]$, we recursively sort $A[1 \mathrel{..} n-1]$ and then insert $A[n]$ into the sorted array $A[1 \mathrel{..} n-1]$. Write a recurrence for the worst-case running time of this recursive version of insertion sort.

2.3-5
Referring back to the searching problem (see Exercise 2.1-3), observe that if the sequence A is sorted, we can check the midpoint of the sequence against v and eliminate half of the sequence from further consideration. The ***binary search*** algorithm repeats this procedure, halving the size of the remaining portion of the sequence each time. Write pseudocode, either iterative or recursive, for binary search. Argue that the worst-case running time of binary search is $\Theta(\lg n)$.

2.3-6
Observe that the **while** loop of lines 5–7 of the INSERTION-SORT procedure in Section 2.1 uses a linear search to scan (backward) through the sorted subarray $A[1 \mathrel{..} j-1]$. Can we use a binary search (see Exercise 2.3-5) instead to improve the overall worst-case running time of insertion sort to $\Theta(n \lg n)$?

2.3-7 ⋆
Describe a $\Theta(n \lg n)$-time algorithm that, given a set S of n integers and another integer x, determines whether or not there exist two elements in S whose sum is exactly x.

Problems

2-1 *Insertion sort on small arrays in merge sort*
Although merge sort runs in $\Theta(n \lg n)$ worst-case time and insertion sort runs in $\Theta(n^2)$ worst-case time, the constant factors in insertion sort can make it faster in practice for small problem sizes on many machines. Thus, it makes sense to ***coarsen*** the leaves of the recursion by using insertion sort within merge sort when

subproblems become sufficiently small. Consider a modification to merge sort in which n/k sublists of length k are sorted using insertion sort and then merged using the standard merging mechanism, where k is a value to be determined.

a. Show that insertion sort can sort the n/k sublists, each of length k, in $\Theta(nk)$ worst-case time.

b. Show how to merge the sublists in $\Theta(n \lg(n/k))$ worst-case time.

c. Given that the modified algorithm runs in $\Theta(nk + n \lg(n/k))$ worst-case time, what is the largest value of k as a function of n for which the modified algorithm has the same running time as standard merge sort, in terms of Θ-notation?

d. How should we choose k in practice?

2-2   *Correctness of bubblesort*

Bubblesort is a popular, but inefficient, sorting algorithm. It works by repeatedly swapping adjacent elements that are out of order.

BUBBLESORT(A)

```
1  for i = 1 to A.length − 1
2      for j = A.length downto i + 1
3          if A[j] < A[j − 1]
4              exchange A[j] with A[j − 1]
```

a. Let A' denote the output of BUBBLESORT(A). To prove that BUBBLESORT is correct, we need to prove that it terminates and that

$$A'[1] \le A'[2] \le \cdots \le A'[n] , \tag{2.3}$$

where $n = A.length$. In order to show that BUBBLESORT actually sorts, what else do we need to prove?

The next two parts will prove inequality (2.3).

b. State precisely a loop invariant for the **for** loop in lines 2–4, and prove that this loop invariant holds. Your proof should use the structure of the loop invariant proof presented in this chapter.

c. Using the termination condition of the loop invariant proved in part (b), state a loop invariant for the **for** loop in lines 1–4 that will allow you to prove inequality (2.3). Your proof should use the structure of the loop invariant proof presented in this chapter.

d. What is the worst-case running time of bubblesort? How does it compare to the running time of insertion sort?

2-3 Correctness of Horner's rule

The following code fragment implements Horner's rule for evaluating a polynomial

$$P(x) = \sum_{k=0}^{n} a_k x^k$$

$$= a_0 + x(a_1 + x(a_2 + \cdots + x(a_{n-1} + x a_n) \cdots)),$$

given the coefficients $a_0, a_1, \ldots, a_n$ and a value for x:

```
1  y = 0
2  for i = n downto 0
3      y = a_i + x · y
```

a. In terms of Θ-notation, what is the running time of this code fragment for Horner's rule?

b. Write pseudocode to implement the naive polynomial-evaluation algorithm that computes each term of the polynomial from scratch. What is the running time of this algorithm? How does it compare to Horner's rule?

c. Consider the following loop invariant:

At the start of each iteration of the **for** loop of lines 2–3,

$$y = \sum_{k=0}^{n-(i+1)} a_{k+i+1} x^k .$$

Interpret a summation with no terms as equaling 0. Following the structure of the loop invariant proof presented in this chapter, use this loop invariant to show that, at termination, $y = \sum_{k=0}^{n} a_k x^k$.

d. Conclude by arguing that the given code fragment correctly evaluates a polynomial characterized by the coefficients $a_0, a_1, \ldots, a_n$.

2-4 Inversions

Let $A[1 \mathbin{..} n]$ be an array of n distinct numbers. If $i < j$ and $A[i] > A[j]$, then the pair (i, j) is called an ***inversion*** of A.

a. List the five inversions of the array $\langle 2, 3, 8, 6, 1 \rangle$.

b. What array with elements from the set $\{1, 2, \ldots, n\}$ has the most inversions? How many does it have?

c. What is the relationship between the running time of insertion sort and the number of inversions in the input array? Justify your answer.

d. Give an algorithm that determines the number of inversions in any permutation on n elements in $\Theta(n \lg n)$ worst-case time. (*Hint:* Modify merge sort.)

Chapter notes

In 1968, Knuth published the first of three volumes with the general title *The Art of Computer Programming* [209, 210, 211]. The first volume ushered in the modern study of computer algorithms with a focus on the analysis of running time, and the full series remains an engaging and worthwhile reference for many of the topics presented here. According to Knuth, the word "algorithm" is derived from the name "al-Khowârizmî," a ninth-century Persian mathematician.

Aho, Hopcroft, and Ullman [5] advocated the asymptotic analysis of algorithms—using notations that Chapter 3 introduces, including Θ-notation—as a means of comparing relative performance. They also popularized the use of recurrence relations to describe the running times of recursive algorithms.

Knuth [211] provides an encyclopedic treatment of many sorting algorithms. His comparison of sorting algorithms (page 381) includes exact step-counting analyses, like the one we performed here for insertion sort. Knuth's discussion of insertion sort encompasses several variations of the algorithm. The most important of these is Shell's sort, introduced by D. L. Shell, which uses insertion sort on periodic subsequences of the input to produce a faster sorting algorithm.

Merge sort is also described by Knuth. He mentions that a mechanical collator capable of merging two decks of punched cards in a single pass was invented in 1938. J. von Neumann, one of the pioneers of computer science, apparently wrote a program for merge sort on the EDVAC computer in 1945.

The early history of proving programs correct is described by Gries [153], who credits P. Naur with the first article in this field. Gries attributes loop invariants to R. W. Floyd. The textbook by Mitchell [256] describes more recent progress in proving programs correct.

3   Growth of Functions

The order of growth of the running time of an algorithm, defined in Chapter 2, gives a simple characterization of the algorithm's efficiency and also allows us to compare the relative performance of alternative algorithms. Once the input size n becomes large enough, merge sort, with its $\Theta(n \lg n)$ worst-case running time, beats insertion sort, whose worst-case running time is $\Theta(n^2)$. Although we can sometimes determine the exact running time of an algorithm, as we did for insertion sort in Chapter 2, the extra precision is not usually worth the effort of computing it. For large enough inputs, the multiplicative constants and lower-order terms of an exact running time are dominated by the effects of the input size itself.

When we look at input sizes large enough to make only the order of growth of the running time relevant, we are studying the *asymptotic* efficiency of algorithms. That is, we are concerned with how the running time of an algorithm increases with the size of the input *in the limit*, as the size of the input increases without bound. Usually, an algorithm that is asymptotically more efficient will be the best choice for all but very small inputs.

This chapter gives several standard methods for simplifying the asymptotic analysis of algorithms. The next section begins by defining several types of "asymptotic notation," of which we have already seen an example in Θ-notation. We then present several notational conventions used throughout this book, and finally we review the behavior of functions that commonly arise in the analysis of algorithms.

3.1   Asymptotic notation

The notations we use to describe the asymptotic running time of an algorithm are defined in terms of functions whose domains are the set of natural numbers $\mathbb{N} = \{0, 1, 2, \ldots\}$. Such notations are convenient for describing the worst-case running-time function $T(n)$, which usually is defined only on integer input sizes. We sometimes find it convenient, however, to *abuse* asymptotic notation in a va-

riety of ways. For example, we might extend the notation to the domain of real numbers or, alternatively, restrict it to a subset of the natural numbers. We should make sure, however, to understand the precise meaning of the notation so that when we abuse, we do not *misuse* it. This section defines the basic asymptotic notations and also introduces some common abuses.

Asymptotic notation, functions, and running times

We will use asymptotic notation primarily to describe the running times of algorithms, as when we wrote that insertion sort's worst-case running time is $\Theta(n^2)$. Asymptotic notation actually applies to functions, however. Recall that we characterized insertion sort's worst-case running time as $an^2 + bn + c$, for some constants a, b, and c. By writing that insertion sort's running time is $\Theta(n^2)$, we abstracted away some details of this function. Because asymptotic notation applies to functions, what we were writing as $\Theta(n^2)$ was the function $an^2 + bn + c$, which in that case happened to characterize the worst-case running time of insertion sort.

In this book, the functions to which we apply asymptotic notation will usually characterize the running times of algorithms. But asymptotic notation can apply to functions that characterize some other aspect of algorithms (the amount of space they use, for example), or even to functions that have nothing whatsoever to do with algorithms.

Even when we use asymptotic notation to apply to the running time of an algorithm, we need to understand *which* running time we mean. Sometimes we are interested in the worst-case running time. Often, however, we wish to characterize the running time no matter what the input. In other words, we often wish to make a blanket statement that covers all inputs, not just the worst case. We shall see asymptotic notations that are well suited to characterizing running times no matter what the input.

Θ-notation

In Chapter 2, we found that the worst-case running time of insertion sort is $T(n) = \Theta(n^2)$. Let us define what this notation means. For a given function $g(n)$, we denote by $\Theta(g(n))$ the *set of functions*

$$\Theta(g(n)) = \{f(n) : \text{there exist positive constants } c_1, c_2, \text{ and } n_0 \text{ such that}$$
$$0 \leq c_1 g(n) \leq f(n) \leq c_2 g(n) \text{ for all } n \geq n_0\}\,.[1]$$

---

[1] Within set notation, a colon means "such that."

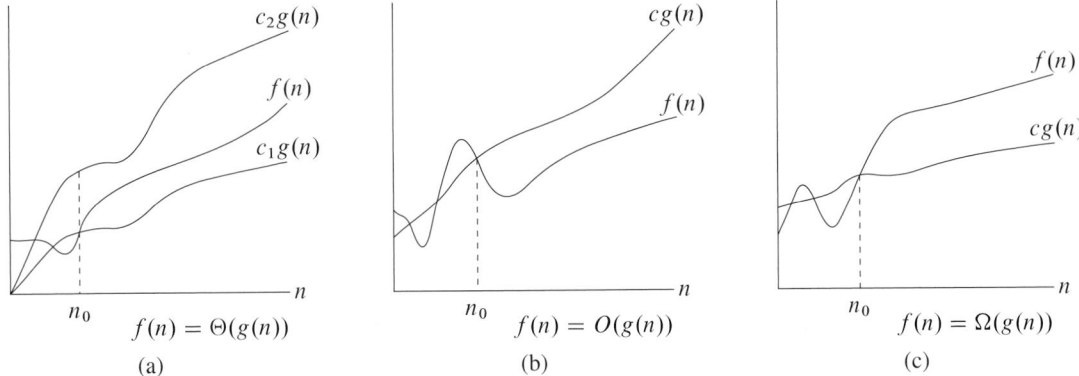

Figure 3.1 Graphic examples of the Θ, O, and Ω notations. In each part, the value of n_0 shown is the minimum possible value; any greater value would also work. **(a)** Θ-notation bounds a function to within constant factors. We write $f(n) = \Theta(g(n))$ if there exist positive constants n_0, c_1, and c_2 such that at and to the right of n_0, the value of $f(n)$ always lies between $c_1 g(n)$ and $c_2 g(n)$ inclusive. **(b)** O-notation gives an upper bound for a function to within a constant factor. We write $f(n) = O(g(n))$ if there are positive constants n_0 and c such that at and to the right of n_0, the value of $f(n)$ always lies on or below $cg(n)$. **(c)** Ω-notation gives a lower bound for a function to within a constant factor. We write $f(n) = \Omega(g(n))$ if there are positive constants n_0 and c such that at and to the right of n_0, the value of $f(n)$ always lies on or above $cg(n)$.

A function $f(n)$ belongs to the set $\Theta(g(n))$ if there exist positive constants c_1 and c_2 such that it can be "sandwiched" between $c_1 g(n)$ and $c_2 g(n)$, for sufficiently large n. Because $\Theta(g(n))$ is a set, we could write "$f(n) \in \Theta(g(n))$" to indicate that $f(n)$ is a member of $\Theta(g(n))$. Instead, we will usually write "$f(n) = \Theta(g(n))$" to express the same notion. You might be confused because we abuse equality in this way, but we shall see later in this section that doing so has its advantages.

Figure 3.1(a) gives an intuitive picture of functions $f(n)$ and $g(n)$, where $f(n) = \Theta(g(n))$. For all values of n at and to the right of n_0, the value of $f(n)$ lies at or above $c_1 g(n)$ and at or below $c_2 g(n)$. In other words, for all $n \geq n_0$, the function $f(n)$ is equal to $g(n)$ to within a constant factor. We say that $g(n)$ is an *asymptotically tight bound* for $f(n)$.

The definition of $\Theta(g(n))$ requires that every member $f(n) \in \Theta(g(n))$ be *asymptotically nonnegative*, that is, that $f(n)$ be nonnegative whenever n is sufficiently large. (An *asymptotically positive* function is one that is positive for all sufficiently large n.) Consequently, the function $g(n)$ itself must be asymptotically nonnegative, or else the set $\Theta(g(n))$ is empty. We shall therefore assume that every function used within Θ-notation is asymptotically nonnegative. This assumption holds for the other asymptotic notations defined in this chapter as well.

In Chapter 2, we introduced an informal notion of Θ-notation that amounted to throwing away lower-order terms and ignoring the leading coefficient of the highest-order term. Let us briefly justify this intuition by using the formal definition to show that $\frac{1}{2}n^2 - 3n = \Theta(n^2)$. To do so, we must determine positive constants c_1, c_2, and n_0 such that

$$c_1 n^2 \leq \frac{1}{2}n^2 - 3n \leq c_2 n^2$$

for all $n \geq n_0$. Dividing by n^2 yields

$$c_1 \leq \frac{1}{2} - \frac{3}{n} \leq c_2 .$$

We can make the right-hand inequality hold for any value of $n \geq 1$ by choosing any constant $c_2 \geq 1/2$. Likewise, we can make the left-hand inequality hold for any value of $n \geq 7$ by choosing any constant $c_1 \leq 1/14$. Thus, by choosing $c_1 = 1/14$, $c_2 = 1/2$, and $n_0 = 7$, we can verify that $\frac{1}{2}n^2 - 3n = \Theta(n^2)$. Certainly, other choices for the constants exist, but the important thing is that *some* choice exists. Note that these constants depend on the function $\frac{1}{2}n^2 - 3n$; a different function belonging to $\Theta(n^2)$ would usually require different constants.

We can also use the formal definition to verify that $6n^3 \neq \Theta(n^2)$. Suppose for the purpose of contradiction that c_2 and n_0 exist such that $6n^3 \leq c_2 n^2$ for all $n \geq n_0$. But then dividing by n^2 yields $n \leq c_2/6$, which cannot possibly hold for arbitrarily large n, since c_2 is constant.

Intuitively, the lower-order terms of an asymptotically positive function can be ignored in determining asymptotically tight bounds because they are insignificant for large n. When n is large, even a tiny fraction of the highest-order term suffices to dominate the lower-order terms. Thus, setting c_1 to a value that is slightly smaller than the coefficient of the highest-order term and setting c_2 to a value that is slightly larger permits the inequalities in the definition of Θ-notation to be satisfied. The coefficient of the highest-order term can likewise be ignored, since it only changes c_1 and c_2 by a constant factor equal to the coefficient.

As an example, consider any quadratic function $f(n) = an^2 + bn + c$, where a, b, and c are constants and $a > 0$. Throwing away the lower-order terms and ignoring the constant yields $f(n) = \Theta(n^2)$. Formally, to show the same thing, we take the constants $c_1 = a/4, c_2 = 7a/4$, and $n_0 = 2 \cdot \max(|b|/a, \sqrt{|c|/a})$. You may verify that $0 \leq c_1 n^2 \leq an^2 + bn + c \leq c_2 n^2$ for all $n \geq n_0$. In general, for any polynomial $p(n) = \sum_{i=0}^{d} a_i n^i$, where the a_i are constants and $a_d > 0$, we have $p(n) = \Theta(n^d)$ (see Problem 3-1).

Since any constant is a degree-0 polynomial, we can express any constant function as $\Theta(n^0)$, or $\Theta(1)$. This latter notation is a minor abuse, however, because the

expression does not indicate what variable is tending to infinity.[2] We shall often use the notation $\Theta(1)$ to mean either a constant or a constant function with respect to some variable.

O-notation

The Θ-notation asymptotically bounds a function from above and below. When we have only an ***asymptotic upper bound***, we use O-notation. For a given function $g(n)$, we denote by $O(g(n))$ (pronounced "big-oh of g of n" or sometimes just "oh of g of n") the set of functions

$O(g(n)) = \{ f(n) :$ there exist positive constants c and n_0 such that
$$0 \le f(n) \le cg(n) \text{ for all } n \ge n_0 \} \,.$$

We use O-notation to give an upper bound on a function, to within a constant factor. Figure 3.1(b) shows the intuition behind O-notation. For all values n at and to the right of n_0, the value of the function $f(n)$ is on or below $cg(n)$.

We write $f(n) = O(g(n))$ to indicate that a function $f(n)$ is a member of the set $O(g(n))$. Note that $f(n) = \Theta(g(n))$ implies $f(n) = O(g(n))$, since Θ-notation is a stronger notion than O-notation. Written set-theoretically, we have $\Theta(g(n)) \subseteq O(g(n))$. Thus, our proof that any quadratic function $an^2 + bn + c$, where $a > 0$, is in $\Theta(n^2)$ also shows that any such quadratic function is in $O(n^2)$. What may be more surprising is that when $a > 0$, any *linear* function $an + b$ is in $O(n^2)$, which is easily verified by taking $c = a + |b|$ and $n_0 = \max(1, -b/a)$.

If you have seen O-notation before, you might find it strange that we should write, for example, $n = O(n^2)$. In the literature, we sometimes find O-notation informally describing asymptotically tight bounds, that is, what we have defined using Θ-notation. In this book, however, when we write $f(n) = O(g(n))$, we are merely claiming that some constant multiple of $g(n)$ is an asymptotic upper bound on $f(n)$, with no claim about how tight an upper bound it is. Distinguishing asymptotic upper bounds from asymptotically tight bounds is standard in the algorithms literature.

Using O-notation, we can often describe the running time of an algorithm merely by inspecting the algorithm's overall structure. For example, the doubly nested loop structure of the insertion sort algorithm from Chapter 2 immediately yields an $O(n^2)$ upper bound on the worst-case running time: the cost of each iteration of the inner loop is bounded from above by $O(1)$ (constant), the indices i

---

[2]The real problem is that our ordinary notation for functions does not distinguish functions from values. In λ-calculus, the parameters to a function are clearly specified: the function n^2 could be written as $\lambda n.n^2$, or even $\lambda r.r^2$. Adopting a more rigorous notation, however, would complicate algebraic manipulations, and so we choose to tolerate the abuse.

and j are both at most n, and the inner loop is executed at most once for each of the n^2 pairs of values for i and j.

Since O-notation describes an upper bound, when we use it to bound the worst-case running time of an algorithm, we have a bound on the running time of the algorithm on every input—the blanket statement we discussed earlier. Thus, the $O(n^2)$ bound on worst-case running time of insertion sort also applies to its running time on every input. The $\Theta(n^2)$ bound on the worst-case running time of insertion sort, however, does not imply a $\Theta(n^2)$ bound on the running time of insertion sort on *every* input. For example, we saw in Chapter 2 that when the input is already sorted, insertion sort runs in $\Theta(n)$ time.

Technically, it is an abuse to say that the running time of insertion sort is $O(n^2)$, since for a given n, the actual running time varies, depending on the particular input of size n. When we say "the running time is $O(n^2)$," we mean that there is a function $f(n)$ that is $O(n^2)$ such that for any value of n, no matter what particular input of size n is chosen, the running time on that input is bounded from above by the value $f(n)$. Equivalently, we mean that the worst-case running time is $O(n^2)$.

Ω-notation

Just as O-notation provides an asymptotic *upper* bound on a function, Ω-notation provides an **asymptotic lower bound**. For a given function $g(n)$, we denote by $\Omega(g(n))$ (pronounced "big-omega of g of n" or sometimes just "omega of g of n") the set of functions

$$\Omega(g(n)) = \{f(n) : \text{there exist positive constants } c \text{ and } n_0 \text{ such that}$$
$$0 \le cg(n) \le f(n) \text{ for all } n \ge n_0\} \ .$$

Figure 3.1(c) shows the intuition behind Ω-notation. For all values n at or to the right of n_0, the value of $f(n)$ is on or above $cg(n)$.

From the definitions of the asymptotic notations we have seen thus far, it is easy to prove the following important theorem (see Exercise 3.1-5).

Theorem 3.1
For any two functions $f(n)$ and $g(n)$, we have $f(n) = \Theta(g(n))$ if and only if $f(n) = O(g(n))$ and $f(n) = \Omega(g(n))$. ■

As an example of the application of this theorem, our proof that $an^2 + bn + c = \Theta(n^2)$ for any constants a, b, and c, where $a > 0$, immediately implies that $an^2 + bn + c = \Omega(n^2)$ and $an^2 + bn + c = O(n^2)$. In practice, rather than using Theorem 3.1 to obtain asymptotic upper and lower bounds from asymptotically tight bounds, as we did for this example, we usually use it to prove asymptotically tight bounds from asymptotic upper and lower bounds.

When we say that the *running time* (no modifier) of an algorithm is $\Omega(g(n))$, we mean that *no matter what particular input of size n is chosen for each value of n*, the running time on that input is at least a constant times $g(n)$, for sufficiently large n. Equivalently, we are giving a lower bound on the best-case running time of an algorithm. For example, the best-case running time of insertion sort is $\Omega(n)$, which implies that the running time of insertion sort is $\Omega(n)$.

The running time of insertion sort therefore belongs to both $\Omega(n)$ and $O(n^2)$, since it falls anywhere between a linear function of n and a quadratic function of n. Moreover, these bounds are asymptotically as tight as possible: for instance, the running time of insertion sort is not $\Omega(n^2)$, since there exists an input for which insertion sort runs in $\Theta(n)$ time (e.g., when the input is already sorted). It is not contradictory, however, to say that the *worst-case* running time of insertion sort is $\Omega(n^2)$, since there exists an input that causes the algorithm to take $\Omega(n^2)$ time.

Asymptotic notation in equations and inequalities

We have already seen how asymptotic notation can be used within mathematical formulas. For example, in introducing O-notation, we wrote "$n = O(n^2)$." We might also write $2n^2 + 3n + 1 = 2n^2 + \Theta(n)$. How do we interpret such formulas?

When the asymptotic notation stands alone (that is, not within a larger formula) on the right-hand side of an equation (or inequality), as in $n = O(n^2)$, we have already defined the equal sign to mean set membership: $n \in O(n^2)$. In general, however, when asymptotic notation appears in a formula, we interpret it as standing for some anonymous function that we do not care to name. For example, the formula $2n^2 + 3n + 1 = 2n^2 + \Theta(n)$ means that $2n^2 + 3n + 1 = 2n^2 + f(n)$, where $f(n)$ is some function in the set $\Theta(n)$. In this case, we let $f(n) = 3n + 1$, which indeed is in $\Theta(n)$.

Using asymptotic notation in this manner can help eliminate inessential detail and clutter in an equation. For example, in Chapter 2 we expressed the worst-case running time of merge sort as the recurrence

$$T(n) = 2T(n/2) + \Theta(n) .$$

If we are interested only in the asymptotic behavior of $T(n)$, there is no point in specifying all the lower-order terms exactly; they are all understood to be included in the anonymous function denoted by the term $\Theta(n)$.

The number of anonymous functions in an expression is understood to be equal to the number of times the asymptotic notation appears. For example, in the expression

$$\sum_{i=1}^{n} O(i) ,$$

there is only a single anonymous function (a function of i). This expression is thus *not* the same as $O(1) + O(2) + \cdots + O(n)$, which doesn't really have a clean interpretation.

In some cases, asymptotic notation appears on the left-hand side of an equation, as in

$$2n^2 + \Theta(n) = \Theta(n^2) \, .$$

We interpret such equations using the following rule: *No matter how the anonymous functions are chosen on the left of the equal sign, there is a way to choose the anonymous functions on the right of the equal sign to make the equation valid.* Thus, our example means that for *any* function $f(n) \in \Theta(n)$, there is *some* function $g(n) \in \Theta(n^2)$ such that $2n^2 + f(n) = g(n)$ for all n. In other words, the right-hand side of an equation provides a coarser level of detail than the left-hand side.

We can chain together a number of such relationships, as in

$$
\begin{aligned}
2n^2 + 3n + 1 &= 2n^2 + \Theta(n) \\
&= \Theta(n^2) \, .
\end{aligned}
$$

We can interpret each equation separately by the rules above. The first equation says that there is *some* function $f(n) \in \Theta(n)$ such that $2n^2 + 3n + 1 = 2n^2 + f(n)$ for all n. The second equation says that for *any* function $g(n) \in \Theta(n)$ (such as the $f(n)$ just mentioned), there is *some* function $h(n) \in \Theta(n^2)$ such that $2n^2 + g(n) = h(n)$ for all n. Note that this interpretation implies that $2n^2 + 3n + 1 = \Theta(n^2)$, which is what the chaining of equations intuitively gives us.

o-notation

The asymptotic upper bound provided by O-notation may or may not be asymptotically tight. The bound $2n^2 = O(n^2)$ is asymptotically tight, but the bound $2n = O(n^2)$ is not. We use o-notation to denote an upper bound that is not asymptotically tight. We formally define $o(g(n))$ ("little-oh of g of n") as the set

$$o(g(n)) = \{ f(n) : \text{for any positive constant } c > 0, \text{there exists a constant} \\ n_0 > 0 \text{ such that } 0 \leq f(n) < cg(n) \text{ for all } n \geq n_0 \} \, .$$

For example, $2n = o(n^2)$, but $2n^2 \neq o(n^2)$.

The definitions of O-notation and o-notation are similar. The main difference is that in $f(n) = O(g(n))$, the bound $0 \leq f(n) \leq cg(n)$ holds for *some* constant $c > 0$, but in $f(n) = o(g(n))$, the bound $0 \leq f(n) < cg(n)$ holds for *all* constants $c > 0$. Intuitively, in o-notation, the function $f(n)$ becomes insignificant relative to $g(n)$ as n approaches infinity; that is,

$$\lim_{n \to \infty} \frac{f(n)}{g(n)} = 0 \, . \tag{3.1}$$

Some authors use this limit as a definition of the o-notation; the definition in this book also restricts the anonymous functions to be asymptotically nonnegative.

ω-notation

By analogy, ω-notation is to Ω-notation as o-notation is to O-notation. We use ω-notation to denote a lower bound that is not asymptotically tight. One way to define it is by

$f(n) \in \omega(g(n))$ if and only if $g(n) \in o(f(n))$.

Formally, however, we define $\omega(g(n))$ ("little-omega of g of n") as the set

$\omega(g(n)) = \{ f(n) :$ for any positive constant $c > 0$, there exists a constant $n_0 > 0$ such that $0 \leq cg(n) < f(n)$ for all $n \geq n_0 \}$.

For example, $n^2/2 = \omega(n)$, but $n^2/2 \neq \omega(n^2)$. The relation $f(n) = \omega(g(n))$ implies that

$$\lim_{n \to \infty} \frac{f(n)}{g(n)} = \infty \, ,$$

if the limit exists. That is, $f(n)$ becomes arbitrarily large relative to $g(n)$ as n approaches infinity.

Comparing functions

Many of the relational properties of real numbers apply to asymptotic comparisons as well. For the following, assume that $f(n)$ and $g(n)$ are asymptotically positive.

Transitivity:

$$f(n) = \Theta(g(n)) \text{ and } g(n) = \Theta(h(n)) \quad \text{imply} \quad f(n) = \Theta(h(n)) \, ,$$
$$f(n) = O(g(n)) \text{ and } g(n) = O(h(n)) \quad \text{imply} \quad f(n) = O(h(n)) \, ,$$
$$f(n) = \Omega(g(n)) \text{ and } g(n) = \Omega(h(n)) \quad \text{imply} \quad f(n) = \Omega(h(n)) \, ,$$
$$f(n) = o(g(n)) \text{ and } g(n) = o(h(n)) \quad \text{imply} \quad f(n) = o(h(n)) \, ,$$
$$f(n) = \omega(g(n)) \text{ and } g(n) = \omega(h(n)) \quad \text{imply} \quad f(n) = \omega(h(n)) \, .$$

Reflexivity:

$$f(n) = \Theta(f(n)) \, ,$$
$$f(n) = O(f(n)) \, ,$$
$$f(n) = \Omega(f(n)) \, .$$

Symmetry:

$$f(n) = \Theta(g(n)) \text{ if and only if } g(n) = \Theta(f(n)).$$

Transpose symmetry:

$$f(n) = O(g(n)) \text{ if and only if } g(n) = \Omega(f(n)),$$
$$f(n) = o(g(n)) \text{ if and only if } g(n) = \omega(f(n)).$$

Because these properties hold for asymptotic notations, we can draw an analogy between the asymptotic comparison of two functions f and g and the comparison of two real numbers a and b:

$$f(n) = O(g(n)) \quad \text{is like} \quad a \leq b,$$
$$f(n) = \Omega(g(n)) \quad \text{is like} \quad a \geq b,$$
$$f(n) = \Theta(g(n)) \quad \text{is like} \quad a = b,$$
$$f(n) = o(g(n)) \quad \text{is like} \quad a < b,$$
$$f(n) = \omega(g(n)) \quad \text{is like} \quad a > b.$$

We say that $f(n)$ is ***asymptotically smaller*** than $g(n)$ if $f(n) = o(g(n))$, and $f(n)$ is ***asymptotically larger*** than $g(n)$ if $f(n) = \omega(g(n))$.

One property of real numbers, however, does not carry over to asymptotic notation:

Trichotomy: For any two real numbers a and b, exactly one of the following must hold: $a < b, a = b$, or $a > b$.

Although any two real numbers can be compared, not all functions are asymptotically comparable. That is, for two functions $f(n)$ and $g(n)$, it may be the case that neither $f(n) = O(g(n))$ nor $f(n) = \Omega(g(n))$ holds. For example, we cannot compare the functions n and $n^{1+\sin n}$ using asymptotic notation, since the value of the exponent in $n^{1+\sin n}$ oscillates between 0 and 2, taking on all values in between.

Exercises

3.1-1
Let $f(n)$ and $g(n)$ be asymptotically nonnegative functions. Using the basic definition of Θ-notation, prove that $\max(f(n), g(n)) = \Theta(f(n) + g(n))$.

3.1-2
Show that for any real constants a and b, where $b > 0$,

$$(n + a)^b = \Theta(n^b). \tag{3.2}$$

3.1-3

Explain why the statement, "The running time of algorithm A is at least $O(n^2)$," is meaningless.

3.1-4

Is $2^{n+1} = O(2^n)$? Is $2^{2n} = O(2^n)$?

3.1-5

Prove Theorem 3.1.

3.1-6

Prove that the running time of an algorithm is $\Theta(g(n))$ if and only if its worst-case running time is $O(g(n))$ and its best-case running time is $\Omega(g(n))$.

3.1-7

Prove that $o(g(n)) \cap \omega(g(n))$ is the empty set.

3.1-8

We can extend our notation to the case of two parameters n and m that can go to infinity independently at different rates. For a given function $g(n, m)$, we denote by $O(g(n, m))$ the set of functions

$$O(g(n,m)) = \{f(n,m) : \text{ there exist positive constants } c, n_0, \text{ and } m_0$$
$$\text{such that } 0 \leq f(n,m) \leq cg(n,m)$$
$$\text{for all } n \geq n_0 \text{ or } m \geq m_0\}\,.$$

Give corresponding definitions for $\Omega(g(n, m))$ and $\Theta(g(n, m))$.

3.2   Standard notations and common functions

This section reviews some standard mathematical functions and notations and explores the relationships among them. It also illustrates the use of the asymptotic notations.

Monotonicity

A function $f(n)$ is **monotonically increasing** if $m \leq n$ implies $f(m) \leq f(n)$. Similarly, it is **monotonically decreasing** if $m \leq n$ implies $f(m) \geq f(n)$. A function $f(n)$ is **strictly increasing** if $m < n$ implies $f(m) < f(n)$ and **strictly decreasing** if $m < n$ implies $f(m) > f(n)$.

Floors and ceilings

For any real number x, we denote the greatest integer less than or equal to x by $\lfloor x \rfloor$ (read "the floor of x") and the least integer greater than or equal to x by $\lceil x \rceil$ (read "the ceiling of x"). For all real x,

$$x - 1 < \lfloor x \rfloor \le x \le \lceil x \rceil < x + 1 . \tag{3.3}$$

For any integer n,

$$\lceil n/2 \rceil + \lfloor n/2 \rfloor = n ,$$

and for any real number $x \ge 0$ and integers $a, b > 0$,

$$\left\lceil \frac{\lceil x/a \rceil}{b} \right\rceil = \left\lceil \frac{x}{ab} \right\rceil , \tag{3.4}$$

$$\left\lfloor \frac{\lfloor x/a \rfloor}{b} \right\rfloor = \left\lfloor \frac{x}{ab} \right\rfloor , \tag{3.5}$$

$$\left\lceil \frac{a}{b} \right\rceil \le \frac{a + (b-1)}{b} , \tag{3.6}$$

$$\left\lfloor \frac{a}{b} \right\rfloor \ge \frac{a - (b-1)}{b} . \tag{3.7}$$

The floor function $f(x) = \lfloor x \rfloor$ is monotonically increasing, as is the ceiling function $f(x) = \lceil x \rceil$.

Modular arithmetic

For any integer a and any positive integer n, the value $a \bmod n$ is the **remainder** (or **residue**) of the quotient a/n:

$$a \bmod n = a - n \lfloor a/n \rfloor . \tag{3.8}$$

It follows that

$$0 \le a \bmod n < n . \tag{3.9}$$

Given a well-defined notion of the remainder of one integer when divided by another, it is convenient to provide special notation to indicate equality of remainders. If $(a \bmod n) = (b \bmod n)$, we write $a \equiv b \pmod{n}$ and say that a is **equivalent** to b, modulo n. In other words, $a \equiv b \pmod{n}$ if a and b have the same remainder when divided by n. Equivalently, $a \equiv b \pmod{n}$ if and only if n is a divisor of $b - a$. We write $a \not\equiv b \pmod{n}$ if a is not equivalent to b, modulo n.

Polynomials

Given a nonnegative integer d, a *polynomial in n of degree d* is a function $p(n)$ of the form

$$p(n) = \sum_{i=0}^{d} a_i n^i,$$

where the constants $a_0, a_1, \ldots, a_d$ are the *coefficients* of the polynomial and $a_d \neq 0$. A polynomial is asymptotically positive if and only if $a_d > 0$. For an asymptotically positive polynomial $p(n)$ of degree d, we have $p(n) = \Theta(n^d)$. For any real constant $a \geq 0$, the function n^a is monotonically increasing, and for any real constant $a \leq 0$, the function n^a is monotonically decreasing. We say that a function $f(n)$ is *polynomially bounded* if $f(n) = O(n^k)$ for some constant k.

Exponentials

For all real $a > 0, m$, and n, we have the following identities:

$$
\begin{aligned}
a^0 &= 1, \\
a^1 &= a, \\
a^{-1} &= 1/a, \\
(a^m)^n &= a^{mn}, \\
(a^m)^n &= (a^n)^m, \\
a^m a^n &= a^{m+n}.
\end{aligned}
$$

For all n and $a \geq 1$, the function a^n is monotonically increasing in n. When convenient, we shall assume $0^0 = 1$.

We can relate the rates of growth of polynomials and exponentials by the following fact. For all real constants a and b such that $a > 1$,

$$\lim_{n \to \infty} \frac{n^b}{a^n} = 0, \tag{3.10}$$

from which we can conclude that

$$n^b = o(a^n).$$

Thus, any exponential function with a base strictly greater than 1 grows faster than any polynomial function.

Using e to denote $2.71828\ldots$, the base of the natural logarithm function, we have for all real x,

$$e^x = 1 + x + \frac{x^2}{2!} + \frac{x^3}{3!} + \cdots = \sum_{i=0}^{\infty} \frac{x^i}{i!}, \tag{3.11}$$

where "!" denotes the factorial function defined later in this section. For all real x, we have the inequality

$$e^x \geq 1 + x \,, \tag{3.12}$$

where equality holds only when $x = 0$. When $|x| \leq 1$, we have the approximation

$$1 + x \leq e^x \leq 1 + x + x^2 \,. \tag{3.13}$$

When $x \to 0$, the approximation of e^x by $1 + x$ is quite good:

$$e^x = 1 + x + \Theta(x^2) \,.$$

(In this equation, the asymptotic notation is used to describe the limiting behavior as $x \to 0$ rather than as $x \to \infty$.) We have for all x,

$$\lim_{n \to \infty} \left(1 + \frac{x}{n}\right)^n = e^x \,. \tag{3.14}$$

Logarithms

We shall use the following notations:

$$
\begin{aligned}
\lg n &= \log_2 n & \text{(binary logarithm)} \,, \\
\ln n &= \log_e n & \text{(natural logarithm)} \,, \\
\lg^k n &= (\lg n)^k & \text{(exponentiation)} \,, \\
\lg \lg n &= \lg(\lg n) & \text{(composition)} \,.
\end{aligned}
$$

An important notational convention we shall adopt is that *logarithm functions will apply only to the next term in the formula*, so that $\lg n + k$ will mean $(\lg n) + k$ and not $\lg(n + k)$. If we hold $b > 1$ constant, then for $n > 0$, the function $\log_b n$ is strictly increasing.

For all real $a > 0, b > 0, c > 0$, and n,

$$
\begin{aligned}
a &= b^{\log_b a} \,, \\
\log_c(ab) &= \log_c a + \log_c b \,, \\
\log_b a^n &= n \log_b a \,, \\
\log_b a &= \frac{\log_c a}{\log_c b} \,, \\
\log_b(1/a) &= -\log_b a \,, \\
\log_b a &= \frac{1}{\log_a b} \,, \\
a^{\log_b c} &= c^{\log_b a} \,,
\end{aligned}
\tag{3.15}
$$

$$\tag{3.16}$$

where, in each equation above, logarithm bases are not 1.

By equation (3.15), changing the base of a logarithm from one constant to another changes the value of the logarithm by only a constant factor, and so we shall often use the notation "$\lg n$" when we don't care about constant factors, such as in O-notation. Computer scientists find 2 to be the most natural base for logarithms because so many algorithms and data structures involve splitting a problem into two parts.

There is a simple series expansion for $\ln(1 + x)$ when $|x| < 1$:

$$\ln(1 + x) = x - \frac{x^2}{2} + \frac{x^3}{3} - \frac{x^4}{4} + \frac{x^5}{5} - \cdots .$$

We also have the following inequalities for $x > -1$:

$$\frac{x}{1 + x} \leq \ln(1 + x) \leq x , \tag{3.17}$$

where equality holds only for $x = 0$.

We say that a function $f(n)$ is **polylogarithmically bounded** if $f(n) = O(\lg^k n)$ for some constant k. We can relate the growth of polynomials and polylogarithms by substituting $\lg n$ for n and 2^a for a in equation (3.10), yielding

$$\lim_{n \to \infty} \frac{\lg^b n}{(2^a)^{\lg n}} = \lim_{n \to \infty} \frac{\lg^b n}{n^a} = 0 .$$

From this limit, we can conclude that

$$\lg^b n = o(n^a)$$

for any constant $a > 0$. Thus, any positive polynomial function grows faster than any polylogarithmic function.

Factorials

The notation $n!$ (read "n factorial") is defined for integers $n \geq 0$ as

$$n! = \begin{cases} 1 & \text{if } n = 0 , \\ n \cdot (n - 1)! & \text{if } n > 0 . \end{cases}$$

Thus, $n! = 1 \cdot 2 \cdot 3 \cdots n$.

A weak upper bound on the factorial function is $n! \leq n^n$, since each of the n terms in the factorial product is at most n. **Stirling's approximation**,

$$n! = \sqrt{2\pi n} \left(\frac{n}{e}\right)^n \left(1 + \Theta\left(\frac{1}{n}\right)\right) , \tag{3.18}$$

where e is the base of the natural logarithm, gives us a tighter upper bound, and a lower bound as well. As Exercise 3.2-3 asks you to prove,

$$n! = o(n^n),$$
$$n! = \omega(2^n),$$
$$\lg(n!) = \Theta(n \lg n), \tag{3.19}$$

where Stirling's approximation is helpful in proving equation (3.19). The following equation also holds for all $n \geq 1$:

$$n! = \sqrt{2\pi n} \left(\frac{n}{e}\right)^n e^{\alpha_n} \tag{3.20}$$

where

$$\frac{1}{12n + 1} < \alpha_n < \frac{1}{12n}. \tag{3.21}$$

Functional iteration

We use the notation $f^{(i)}(n)$ to denote the function $f(n)$ iteratively applied i times to an initial value of n. Formally, let $f(n)$ be a function over the reals. For non-negative integers i, we recursively define

$$f^{(i)}(n) = \begin{cases} n & \text{if } i = 0, \\ f(f^{(i-1)}(n)) & \text{if } i > 0. \end{cases}$$

For example, if $f(n) = 2n$, then $f^{(i)}(n) = 2^i n$.

The iterated logarithm function

We use the notation $\lg^* n$ (read "log star of n") to denote the iterated logarithm, defined as follows. Let $\lg^{(i)} n$ be as defined above, with $f(n) = \lg n$. Because the logarithm of a nonpositive number is undefined, $\lg^{(i)} n$ is defined only if $\lg^{(i-1)} n > 0$. Be sure to distinguish $\lg^{(i)} n$ (the logarithm function applied i times in succession, starting with argument n) from $\lg^i n$ (the logarithm of n raised to the ith power). Then we define the iterated logarithm function as

$$\lg^* n = \min \left\{ i \geq 0 : \lg^{(i)} n \leq 1 \right\}.$$

The iterated logarithm is a *very* slowly growing function:

$$\lg^* 2 = 1,$$
$$\lg^* 4 = 2,$$
$$\lg^* 16 = 3,$$
$$\lg^* 65536 = 4,$$
$$\lg^* (2^{65536}) = 5.$$

Since the number of atoms in the observable universe is estimated to be about 10^{80}, which is much less than 2^{65536}, we rarely encounter an input size n such that $\lg^* n > 5$.

Fibonacci numbers

We define the *Fibonacci numbers* by the following recurrence:

$$
\begin{aligned}
F_0 &= 0, \\
F_1 &= 1, \\
F_i &= F_{i-1} + F_{i-2} \qquad \text{for } i \geq 2.
\end{aligned}
\tag{3.22}
$$

Thus, each Fibonacci number is the sum of the two previous ones, yielding the sequence

$$0, \ 1, \ 1, \ 2, \ 3, \ 5, \ 8, \ 13, \ 21, \ 34, \ 55, \ \ldots .$$

Fibonacci numbers are related to the *golden ratio* ϕ and to its conjugate $\widehat{\phi}$, which are the two roots of the equation

$$x^2 = x + 1 \tag{3.23}$$

and are given by the following formulas (see Exercise 3.2-6):

$$
\begin{aligned}
\phi &= \frac{1 + \sqrt{5}}{2} \\
&= 1.61803\ldots, \\
\widehat{\phi} &= \frac{1 - \sqrt{5}}{2} \\
&= -.61803\ldots .
\end{aligned}
\tag{3.24}
$$

Specifically, we have

$$F_i = \frac{\phi^i - \widehat{\phi}^i}{\sqrt{5}},$$

which we can prove by induction (Exercise 3.2-7). Since $\left|\widehat{\phi}\right| < 1$, we have

$$
\begin{aligned}
\frac{\left|\widehat{\phi}^i\right|}{\sqrt{5}} &< \frac{1}{\sqrt{5}} \\
&< \frac{1}{2},
\end{aligned}
$$

which implies that

$$F_i = \left\lfloor \frac{\phi^i}{\sqrt{5}} + \frac{1}{2} \right\rfloor ,$$ (3.25)

which is to say that the ith Fibonacci number F_i is equal to $\phi^i / \sqrt{5}$ rounded to the nearest integer. Thus, Fibonacci numbers grow exponentially.

Exercises

3.2-1
Show that if $f(n)$ and $g(n)$ are monotonically increasing functions, then so are the functions $f(n) + g(n)$ and $f(g(n))$, and if $f(n)$ and $g(n)$ are in addition nonnegative, then $f(n) \cdot g(n)$ is monotonically increasing.

3.2-2
Prove equation (3.16).

3.2-3
Prove equation (3.19). Also prove that $n! = \omega(2^n)$ and $n! = o(n^n)$.

3.2-4 ★
Is the function $\lceil \lg n \rceil !$ polynomially bounded? Is the function $\lceil \lg \lg n \rceil !$ polynomially bounded?

3.2-5 ★
Which is asymptotically larger: $\lg(\lg^* n)$ or $\lg^*(\lg n)$?

3.2-6
Show that the golden ratio ϕ and its conjugate $\hat{\phi}$ both satisfy the equation $x^2 = x + 1$.

3.2-7
Prove by induction that the ith Fibonacci number satisfies the equality

$$F_i = \frac{\phi^i - \hat{\phi}^i}{\sqrt{5}} ,$$

where ϕ is the golden ratio and $\hat{\phi}$ is its conjugate.

3.2-8
Show that $k \ln k = \Theta(n)$ implies $k = \Theta(n / \ln n)$.

Problems

3-1 Asymptotic behavior of polynomials

Let

$$p(n) = \sum_{i=0}^{d} a_i n^i \, ,$$

where $a_d > 0$, be a degree-d polynomial in n, and let k be a constant. Use the definitions of the asymptotic notations to prove the following properties.

a. If $k \geq d$, then $p(n) = O(n^k)$.

b. If $k \leq d$, then $p(n) = \Omega(n^k)$.

c. If $k = d$, then $p(n) = \Theta(n^k)$.

d. If $k > d$, then $p(n) = o(n^k)$.

e. If $k < d$, then $p(n) = \omega(n^k)$.

3-2 Relative asymptotic growths

Indicate, for each pair of expressions (A, B) in the table below, whether A is O, o, Ω, ω, or Θ of B. Assume that $k \geq 1, \epsilon > 0$, and $c > 1$ are constants. Your answer should be in the form of the table with "yes" or "no" written in each box.

	A	B	O	o	Ω	ω	Θ
a.	$\lg^k n$	n^ϵ					
b.	n^k	c^n					
c.	$\sqrt{n}$	$n^{\sin n}$					
d.	2^n	$2^{n/2}$					
e.	$n^{\lg c}$	$c^{\lg n}$					
f.	$\lg(n!)$	$\lg(n^n)$					

3-3 Ordering by asymptotic growth rates

a. Rank the following functions by order of growth; that is, find an arrangement $g_1, g_2, \ldots, g_{30}$ of the functions satisfying $g_1 = \Omega(g_2)$, $g_2 = \Omega(g_3)$, ..., $g_{29} = \Omega(g_{30})$. Partition your list into equivalence classes such that functions $f(n)$ and $g(n)$ are in the same class if and only if $f(n) = \Theta(g(n))$.

$$\lg(\lg^* n) \qquad 2^{\lg^* n} \qquad (\sqrt{2})^{\lg n} \qquad n^2 \qquad n! \qquad (\lg n)!$$

$$\left(\tfrac{3}{2}\right)^n \qquad n^3 \qquad \lg^2 n \qquad \lg(n!) \qquad 2^{2^n} \qquad n^{1/\lg n}$$

$$\ln\ln n \qquad \lg^* n \qquad n \cdot 2^n \qquad n^{\lg\lg n} \qquad \ln n \qquad 1$$

$$2^{\lg n} \qquad (\lg n)^{\lg n} \qquad e^n \qquad 4^{\lg n} \qquad (n+1)! \qquad \sqrt{\lg n}$$

$$\lg^*(\lg n) \qquad 2^{\sqrt{2\lg n}} \qquad n \qquad 2^n \qquad n\lg n \qquad 2^{2^{n+1}}$$

b. Give an example of a single nonnegative function $f(n)$ such that for all functions $g_i(n)$ in part (a), $f(n)$ is neither $O(g_i(n))$ nor $\Omega(g_i(n))$.

3-4 *Asymptotic notation properties*

Let $f(n)$ and $g(n)$ be asymptotically positive functions. Prove or disprove each of the following conjectures.

a. $f(n) = O(g(n))$ implies $g(n) = O(f(n))$.

b. $f(n) + g(n) = \Theta(\min(f(n), g(n)))$.

c. $f(n) = O(g(n))$ implies $\lg(f(n)) = O(\lg(g(n)))$, where $\lg(g(n)) \geq 1$ and $f(n) \geq 1$ for all sufficiently large n.

d. $f(n) = O(g(n))$ implies $2^{f(n)} = O\left(2^{g(n)}\right)$.

e. $f(n) = O\left((f(n))^2\right)$.

f. $f(n) = O(g(n))$ implies $g(n) = \Omega(f(n))$.

g. $f(n) = \Theta(f(n/2))$.

h. $f(n) + o(f(n)) = \Theta(f(n))$.

3-5 *Variations on O and Ω*

Some authors define Ω in a slightly different way than we do; let's use $\overset{\infty}{\Omega}$ (read "omega infinity") for this alternative definition. We say that $f(n) = \overset{\infty}{\Omega}(g(n))$ if there exists a positive constant c such that $f(n) \geq cg(n) \geq 0$ for infinitely many integers n.

a. Show that for any two functions $f(n)$ and $g(n)$ that are asymptotically nonnegative, either $f(n) = O(g(n))$ or $f(n) = \overset{\infty}{\Omega}(g(n))$ or both, whereas this is not true if we use Ω in place of $\overset{\infty}{\Omega}$.

b. Describe the potential advantages and disadvantages of using $\overset{\infty}{\Omega}$ instead of Ω to characterize the running times of programs.

Some authors also define O in a slightly different manner; let's use O' for the alternative definition. We say that $f(n) = O'(g(n))$ if and only if $|f(n)| = O(g(n))$.

c. What happens to each direction of the "if and only if" in Theorem 3.1 if we substitute O' for O but still use Ω?

Some authors define $\widetilde{O}$ (read "soft-oh") to mean O with logarithmic factors ignored:

$$\widetilde{O}(g(n)) = \{f(n) : \text{there exist positive constants } c, k, \text{ and } n_0 \text{ such that} \\ 0 \le f(n) \le cg(n) \lg^k(n) \text{ for all } n \ge n_0\} .$$

d. Define $\widetilde{\Omega}$ and $\widetilde{\Theta}$ in a similar manner. Prove the corresponding analog to Theorem 3.1.

3-6 *Iterated functions*

We can apply the iteration operator * used in the $\lg^*$ function to any monotonically increasing function $f(n)$ over the reals. For a given constant $c \in \mathbb{R}$, we define the iterated function f_c^* by

$$f_c^*(n) = \min \{i \ge 0 : f^{(i)}(n) \le c\} ,$$

which need not be well defined in all cases. In other words, the quantity $f_c^*(n)$ is the number of iterated applications of the function f required to reduce its argument down to c or less.

For each of the following functions $f(n)$ and constants c, give as tight a bound as possible on $f_c^*(n)$.

	$f(n)$	c	$f_c^*(n)$
a.	$n - 1$	0	
b.	$\lg n$	1	
c.	$n/2$	1	
d.	$n/2$	2	
e.	$\sqrt{n}$	2	
f.	$\sqrt{n}$	1	
g.	$n^{1/3}$	2	
h.	$n/\lg n$	2	

Chapter notes

Knuth [209] traces the origin of the O-notation to a number-theory text by P. Bachmann in 1892. The o-notation was invented by E. Landau in 1909 for his discussion of the distribution of prime numbers. The Ω and Θ notations were advocated by Knuth [213] to correct the popular, but technically sloppy, practice in the literature of using O-notation for both upper and lower bounds. Many people continue to use the O-notation where the Θ-notation is more technically precise. Further discussion of the history and development of asymptotic notations appears in works by Knuth [209, 213] and Brassard and Bratley [54].

Not all authors define the asymptotic notations in the same way, although the various definitions agree in most common situations. Some of the alternative definitions encompass functions that are not asymptotically nonnegative, as long as their absolute values are appropriately bounded.

Equation (3.20) is due to Robbins [297]. Other properties of elementary mathematical functions can be found in any good mathematical reference, such as Abramowitz and Stegun [1] or Zwillinger [362], or in a calculus book, such as Apostol [18] or Thomas et al. [334]. Knuth [209] and Graham, Knuth, and Patashnik [152] contain a wealth of material on discrete mathematics as used in computer science.

4 Divide-and-Conquer

In Section 2.3.1, we saw how merge sort serves as an example of the divide-and-conquer paradigm. Recall that in divide-and-conquer, we solve a problem recursively, applying three steps at each level of the recursion:

Divide the problem into a number of subproblems that are smaller instances of the same problem.

Conquer the subproblems by solving them recursively. If the subproblem sizes are small enough, however, just solve the subproblems in a straightforward manner.

Combine the solutions to the subproblems into the solution for the original problem.

When the subproblems are large enough to solve recursively, we call that the ***recursive case***. Once the subproblems become small enough that we no longer recurse, we say that the recursion "bottoms out" and that we have gotten down to the ***base case***. Sometimes, in addition to subproblems that are smaller instances of the same problem, we have to solve subproblems that are not quite the same as the original problem. We consider solving such subproblems as part of the combine step.

In this chapter, we shall see more algorithms based on divide-and-conquer. The first one solves the maximum-subarray problem: it takes as input an array of numbers, and it determines the contiguous subarray whose values have the greatest sum. Then we shall see two divide-and-conquer algorithms for multiplying $n \times n$ matrices. One runs in $\Theta(n^3)$ time, which is no better than the straightforward method of multiplying square matrices. But the other, Strassen's algorithm, runs in $O(n^{2.81})$ time, which beats the straightforward method asymptotically.

Recurrences

Recurrences go hand in hand with the divide-and-conquer paradigm, because they give us a natural way to characterize the running times of divide-and-conquer algorithms. A ***recurrence*** is an equation or inequality that describes a function in terms

of its value on smaller inputs. For example, in Section 2.3.2 we described the worst-case running time $T(n)$ of the MERGE-SORT procedure by the recurrence

$$T(n) = \begin{cases} \Theta(1) & \text{if } n = 1, \\ 2T(n/2) + \Theta(n) & \text{if } n > 1, \end{cases} \tag{4.1}$$

whose solution we claimed to be $T(n) = \Theta(n \lg n)$.

Recurrences can take many forms. For example, a recursive algorithm might divide subproblems into unequal sizes, such as a 2/3-to-1/3 split. If the divide and combine steps take linear time, such an algorithm would give rise to the recurrence $T(n) = T(2n/3) + T(n/3) + \Theta(n)$.

Subproblems are not necessarily constrained to being a constant fraction of the original problem size. For example, a recursive version of linear search (see Exercise 2.1-3) would create just one subproblem containing only one element fewer than the original problem. Each recursive call would take constant time plus the time for the recursive calls it makes, yielding the recurrence $T(n) = T(n - 1) + \Theta(1)$.

This chapter offers three methods for solving recurrences—that is, for obtaining asymptotic "Θ" or "O" bounds on the solution:

- In the ***substitution method***, we guess a bound and then use mathematical induction to prove our guess correct.

- The ***recursion-tree method*** converts the recurrence into a tree whose nodes represent the costs incurred at various levels of the recursion. We use techniques for bounding summations to solve the recurrence.

- The ***master method*** provides bounds for recurrences of the form

$$T(n) = aT(n/b) + f(n), \tag{4.2}$$

  where $a \geq 1$, $b > 1$, and $f(n)$ is a given function. Such recurrences arise frequently. A recurrence of the form in equation (4.2) characterizes a divide-and-conquer algorithm that creates a subproblems, each of which is $1/b$ the size of the original problem, and in which the divide and combine steps together take $f(n)$ time.

To use the master method, you will need to memorize three cases, but once you do that, you will easily be able to determine asymptotic bounds for many simple recurrences. We will use the master method to determine the running times of the divide-and-conquer algorithms for the maximum-subarray problem and for matrix multiplication, as well as for other algorithms based on divide-and-conquer elsewhere in this book.

Occasionally, we shall see recurrences that are not equalities but rather inequalities, such as $T(n) \leq 2T(n/2) + \Theta(n)$. Because such a recurrence states only an upper bound on $T(n)$, we will couch its solution using O-notation rather than Θ-notation. Similarly, if the inequality were reversed to $T(n) \geq 2T(n/2) + \Theta(n)$, then because the recurrence gives only a lower bound on $T(n)$, we would use Ω-notation in its solution.

Technicalities in recurrences

In practice, we neglect certain technical details when we state and solve recurrences. For example, if we call MERGE-SORT on n elements when n is odd, we end up with subproblems of size $\lfloor n/2 \rfloor$ and $\lceil n/2 \rceil$. Neither size is actually $n/2$, because $n/2$ is not an integer when n is odd. Technically, the recurrence describing the worst-case running time of MERGE-SORT is really

$$T(n) = \begin{cases} \Theta(1) & \text{if } n = 1 \text{,} \\ T(\lceil n/2 \rceil) + T(\lfloor n/2 \rfloor) + \Theta(n) & \text{if } n > 1 \text{.} \end{cases} \tag{4.3}$$

Boundary conditions represent another class of details that we typically ignore. Since the running time of an algorithm on a constant-sized input is a constant, the recurrences that arise from the running times of algorithms generally have $T(n) = \Theta(1)$ for sufficiently small n. Consequently, for convenience, we shall generally omit statements of the boundary conditions of recurrences and assume that $T(n)$ is constant for small n. For example, we normally state recurrence (4.1) as

$$T(n) = 2T(n/2) + \Theta(n) \text{,} \tag{4.4}$$

without explicitly giving values for small n. The reason is that although changing the value of $T(1)$ changes the exact solution to the recurrence, the solution typically doesn't change by more than a constant factor, and so the order of growth is unchanged.

When we state and solve recurrences, we often omit floors, ceilings, and boundary conditions. We forge ahead without these details and later determine whether or not they matter. They usually do not, but you should know when they do. Experience helps, and so do some theorems stating that these details do not affect the asymptotic bounds of many recurrences characterizing divide-and-conquer algorithms (see Theorem 4.1). In this chapter, however, we shall address some of these details and illustrate the fine points of recurrence solution methods.

4.1   The maximum-subarray problem

Suppose that you have been offered the opportunity to invest in the Volatile Chemical Corporation. Like the chemicals the company produces, the stock price of the Volatile Chemical Corporation is rather volatile. You are allowed to buy one unit of stock only one time and then sell it at a later date, buying and selling after the close of trading for the day. To compensate for this restriction, you are allowed to learn what the price of the stock will be in the future. Your goal is to maximize your profit. Figure 4.1 shows the price of the stock over a 17-day period. You may buy the stock at any one time, starting after day 0, when the price is $100 per share. Of course, you would want to "buy low, sell high"—buy at the lowest possible price and later on sell at the highest possible price—to maximize your profit. Unfortunately, you might not be able to buy at the lowest price and then sell at the highest price within a given period. In Figure 4.1, the lowest price occurs after day 7, which occurs after the highest price, after day 1.

You might think that you can always maximize profit by either buying at the lowest price or selling at the highest price. For example, in Figure 4.1, we would maximize profit by buying at the lowest price, after day 7. If this strategy always worked, then it would be easy to determine how to maximize profit: find the highest and lowest prices, and then work left from the highest price to find the lowest prior price, work right from the lowest price to find the highest later price, and take the pair with the greater difference. Figure 4.2 shows a simple counterexample,

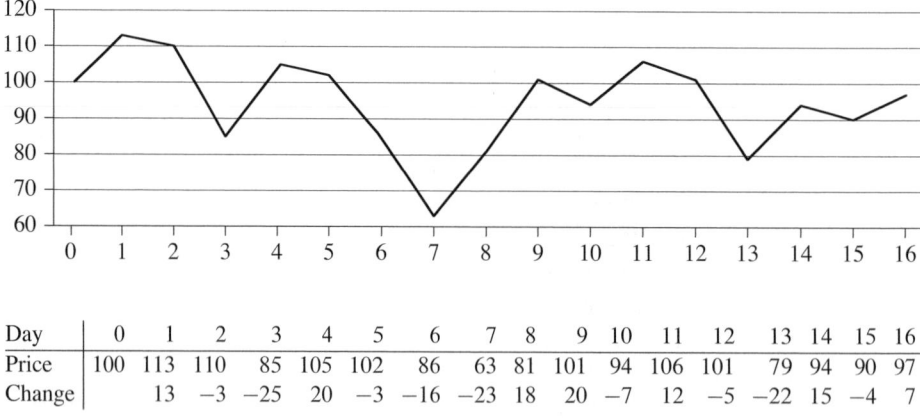

Day	0	1	2	3	4	5	6	7	8	9	10	11	12	13	14	15	16
Price	100	113	110	85	105	102	86	63	81	101	94	106	101	79	94	90	97
Change		13	−3	−25	20	−3	−16	−23	18	20	−7	12	−5	−22	15	−4	7

Figure 4.1   Information about the price of stock in the Volatile Chemical Corporation after the close of trading over a period of 17 days. The horizontal axis of the chart indicates the day, and the vertical axis shows the price. The bottom row of the table gives the change in price from the previous day.

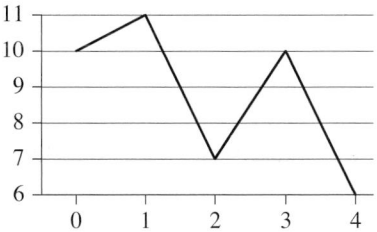

Day	0	1	2	3	4
Price	10	11	7	10	6
Change		1	−4	3	−4

Figure 4.2 An example showing that the maximum profit does not always start at the lowest price or end at the highest price. Again, the horizontal axis indicates the day, and the vertical axis shows the price. Here, the maximum profit of $3 per share would be earned by buying after day 2 and selling after day 3. The price of $7 after day 2 is not the lowest price overall, and the price of $10 after day 3 is not the highest price overall.

demonstrating that the maximum profit sometimes comes neither by buying at the lowest price nor by selling at the highest price.

A brute-force solution

We can easily devise a brute-force solution to this problem: just try every possible pair of buy and sell dates in which the buy date precedes the sell date. A period of n days has $\binom{n}{2}$ such pairs of dates. Since $\binom{n}{2}$ is $\Theta(n^2)$, and the best we can hope for is to evaluate each pair of dates in constant time, this approach would take $\Omega(n^2)$ time. Can we do better?

A transformation

In order to design an algorithm with an $o(n^2)$ running time, we will look at the input in a slightly different way. We want to find a sequence of days over which the net change from the first day to the last is maximum. Instead of looking at the daily prices, let us instead consider the daily change in price, where the change on day i is the difference between the prices after day $i - 1$ and after day i. The table in Figure 4.1 shows these daily changes in the bottom row. If we treat this row as an array A, shown in Figure 4.3, we now want to find the nonempty, contiguous subarray of A whose values have the largest sum. We call this contiguous subarray the ***maximum subarray***. For example, in the array of Figure 4.3, the maximum subarray of $A[1 .. 16]$ is $A[8 .. 11]$, with the sum 43. Thus, you would want to buy the stock just before day 8 (that is, after day 7) and sell it after day 11, earning a profit of $43 per share.

At first glance, this transformation does not help. We still need to check $\binom{n-1}{2} = \Theta(n^2)$ subarrays for a period of n days. Exercise 4.1-2 asks you to show

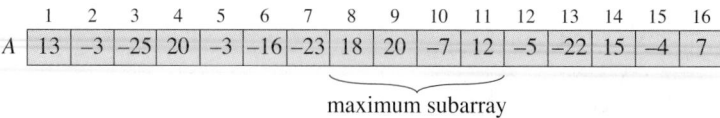

Figure 4.3 The change in stock prices as a maximum-subarray problem. Here, the subarray $A[8 . . 11]$, with sum 43, has the greatest sum of any contiguous subarray of array A.

that although computing the cost of one subarray might take time proportional to the length of the subarray, when computing all $\Theta(n^2)$ subarray sums, we can organize the computation so that each subarray sum takes $O(1)$ time, given the values of previously computed subarray sums, so that the brute-force solution takes $\Theta(n^2)$ time.

So let us seek a more efficient solution to the maximum-subarray problem. When doing so, we will usually speak of "a" maximum subarray rather than "the" maximum subarray, since there could be more than one subarray that achieves the maximum sum.

The maximum-subarray problem is interesting only when the array contains some negative numbers. If all the array entries were nonnegative, then the maximum-subarray problem would present no challenge, since the entire array would give the greatest sum.

A solution using divide-and-conquer

Let's think about how we might solve the maximum-subarray problem using the divide-and-conquer technique. Suppose we want to find a maximum subarray of the subarray $A[low . . high]$. Divide-and-conquer suggests that we divide the subarray into two subarrays of as equal size as possible. That is, we find the midpoint, say mid, of the subarray, and consider the subarrays $A[low . . mid]$ and $A[mid + 1 . . high]$. As Figure 4.4(a) shows, any contiguous subarray $A[i . . j]$ of $A[low . . high]$ must lie in exactly one of the following places:

- entirely in the subarray $A[low . . mid]$, so that $low \leq i \leq j \leq mid$,
- entirely in the subarray $A[mid + 1 . . high]$, so that $mid < i \leq j \leq high$, or
- crossing the midpoint, so that $low \leq i \leq mid < j \leq high$.

Therefore, a maximum subarray of $A[low . . high]$ must lie in exactly one of these places. In fact, a maximum subarray of $A[low . . high]$ must have the greatest sum over all subarrays entirely in $A[low . . mid]$, entirely in $A[mid + 1 . . high]$, or crossing the midpoint. We can find maximum subarrays of $A[low . . mid]$ and $A[mid+1 . . high]$ recursively, because these two subproblems are smaller instances of the problem of finding a maximum subarray. Thus, all that is left to do is find a

The initial call FIND-MAXIMUM-SUBARRAY($A, 1, A.length$) will find a maximum subarray of $A[1 . . n]$.

Similar to FIND-MAX-CROSSING-SUBARRAY, the recursive procedure FIND-MAXIMUM-SUBARRAY returns a tuple containing the indices that demarcate a maximum subarray, along with the sum of the values in a maximum subarray. Line 1 tests for the base case, where the subarray has just one element. A subarray with just one element has only one subarray—itself—and so line 2 returns a tuple with the starting and ending indices of just the one element, along with its value. Lines 3–11 handle the recursive case. Line 3 does the divide part, computing the index *mid* of the midpoint. Let's refer to the subarray $A[low . . mid]$ as the ***left subarray*** and to $A[mid + 1 . . high]$ as the ***right subarray***. Because we know that the subarray $A[low . . high]$ contains at least two elements, each of the left and right subarrays must have at least one element. Lines 4 and 5 conquer by recursively finding maximum subarrays within the left and right subarrays, respectively. Lines 6–11 form the combine part. Line 6 finds a maximum subarray that crosses the midpoint. (Recall that because line 6 solves a subproblem that is not a smaller instance of the original problem, we consider it to be in the combine part.) Line 7 tests whether the left subarray contains a subarray with the maximum sum, and line 8 returns that maximum subarray. Otherwise, line 9 tests whether the right subarray contains a subarray with the maximum sum, and line 10 returns that maximum subarray. If neither the left nor right subarrays contain a subarray achieving the maximum sum, then a maximum subarray must cross the midpoint, and line 11 returns it.

Analyzing the divide-and-conquer algorithm

Next we set up a recurrence that describes the running time of the recursive FIND-MAXIMUM-SUBARRAY procedure. As we did when we analyzed merge sort in Section 2.3.2, we make the simplifying assumption that the original problem size is a power of 2, so that all subproblem sizes are integers. We denote by $T(n)$ the running time of FIND-MAXIMUM-SUBARRAY on a subarray of n elements. For starters, line 1 takes constant time. The base case, when $n = 1$, is easy: line 2 takes constant time, and so

$$T(1) = \Theta(1) .$$ (4.5)

The recursive case occurs when $n > 1$. Lines 1 and 3 take constant time. Each of the subproblems solved in lines 4 and 5 is on a subarray of $n/2$ elements (our assumption that the original problem size is a power of 2 ensures that $n/2$ is an integer), and so we spend $T(n/2)$ time solving each of them. Because we have to solve two subproblems—for the left subarray and for the right subarray—the contribution to the running time from lines 4 and 5 comes to $2T(n/2)$. As we have

already seen, the call to FIND-MAX-CROSSING-SUBARRAY in line 6 takes $\Theta(n)$
time. Lines 7–11 take only $\Theta(1)$ time. For the recursive case, therefore, we have

$$
\begin{aligned}
T(n) &= \Theta(1) + 2T(n/2) + \Theta(n) + \Theta(1) \\
&= 2T(n/2) + \Theta(n) \, .
\end{aligned} \tag{4.6}
$$

Combining equations (4.5) and (4.6) gives us a recurrence for the running
time $T(n)$ of FIND-MAXIMUM-SUBARRAY:

$$
T(n) = \begin{cases} \Theta(1) & \text{if } n = 1 \, , \\ 2T(n/2) + \Theta(n) & \text{if } n > 1 \, . \end{cases} \tag{4.7}
$$

This recurrence is the same as recurrence (4.1) for merge sort. As we shall
see from the master method in Section 4.5, this recurrence has the solution
$T(n) = \Theta(n \lg n)$. You might also revisit the recursion tree in Figure 2.5 to understand why the solution should be $T(n) = \Theta(n \lg n)$.

Thus, we see that the divide-and-conquer method yields an algorithm that is
asymptotically faster than the brute-force method. With merge sort and now the
maximum-subarray problem, we begin to get an idea of how powerful the divide-
and-conquer method can be. Sometimes it will yield the asymptotically fastest
algorithm for a problem, and other times we can do even better. As Exercise 4.1-5
shows, there is in fact a linear-time algorithm for the maximum-subarray problem,
and it does not use divide-and-conquer.

Exercises

4.1-1
What does FIND-MAXIMUM-SUBARRAY return when all elements of A are negative?

4.1-2
Write pseudocode for the brute-force method of solving the maximum-subarray
problem. Your procedure should run in $\Theta(n^2)$ time.

4.1-3
Implement both the brute-force and recursive algorithms for the maximum-
subarray problem on your own computer. What problem size n_0 gives the crossover
point at which the recursive algorithm beats the brute-force algorithm? Then,
change the base case of the recursive algorithm to use the brute-force algorithm
whenever the problem size is less than n_0. Does that change the crossover point?

4.1-4
Suppose we change the definition of the maximum-subarray problem to allow the
result to be an empty subarray, where the sum of the values of an empty subar-

ray is 0. How would you change any of the algorithms that do not allow empty subarrays to permit an empty subarray to be the result?

4.1-5
Use the following ideas to develop a nonrecursive, linear-time algorithm for the maximum-subarray problem. Start at the left end of the array, and progress toward the right, keeping track of the maximum subarray seen so far. Knowing a maximum subarray of $A[1 .. j]$, extend the answer to find a maximum subarray ending at index $j + 1$ by using the following observation: a maximum subarray of $A[1 .. j + 1]$ is either a maximum subarray of $A[1 .. j]$ or a subarray $A[i .. j + 1]$, for some $1 \leq i \leq j + 1$. Determine a maximum subarray of the form $A[i .. j + 1]$ in constant time based on knowing a maximum subarray ending at index j.

4.2   Strassen's algorithm for matrix multiplication

If you have seen matrices before, then you probably know how to multiply them. (Otherwise, you should read Section D.1 in Appendix D.) If $A = (a_{ij})$ and $B = (b_{ij})$ are square $n \times n$ matrices, then in the product $C = A \cdot B$, we define the entry c_{ij}, for $i, j = 1, 2, \ldots, n$, by

$$c_{ij} = \sum_{k=1}^{n} a_{ik} \cdot b_{kj} \ . \tag{4.8}$$

We must compute n^2 matrix entries, and each is the sum of n values. The following procedure takes $n \times n$ matrices A and B and multiplies them, returning their $n \times n$ product C. We assume that each matrix has an attribute *rows*, giving the number of rows in the matrix.

SQUARE-MATRIX-MULTIPLY (A, B)

```
1   n = A.rows
2   let C be a new n × n matrix
3   for i = 1 to n
4       for j = 1 to n
5           c_ij = 0
6           for k = 1 to n
7               c_ij = c_ij + a_ik · b_kj
8   return C
```

The SQUARE-MATRIX-MULTIPLY procedure works as follows. The **for** loop of lines 3–7 computes the entries of each row i, and within a given row i, the

for loop of lines 4–7 computes each of the entries c_{ij}, for each column j. Line 5 initializes c_{ij} to 0 as we start computing the sum given in equation (4.8), and each iteration of the **for** loop of lines 6–7 adds in one more term of equation (4.8).

Because each of the triply-nested **for** loops runs exactly n iterations, and each execution of line 7 takes constant time, the SQUARE-MATRIX-MULTIPLY procedure takes $\Theta(n^3)$ time.

You might at first think that any matrix multiplication algorithm must take $\Omega(n^3)$ time, since the natural definition of matrix multiplication requires that many multiplications. You would be incorrect, however: we have a way to multiply matrices in $o(n^3)$ time. In this section, we shall see Strassen's remarkable recursive algorithm for multiplying $n \times n$ matrices. It runs in $\Theta(n^{\lg 7})$ time, which we shall show in Section 4.5. Since $\lg 7$ lies between 2.80 and 2.81, Strassen's algorithm runs in $O(n^{2.81})$ time, which is asymptotically better than the simple SQUARE-MATRIX-MULTIPLY procedure.

A simple divide-and-conquer algorithm

To keep things simple, when we use a divide-and-conquer algorithm to compute the matrix product $C = A \cdot B$, we assume that n is an exact power of 2 in each of the $n \times n$ matrices. We make this assumption because in each divide step, we will divide $n \times n$ matrices into four $n/2 \times n/2$ matrices, and by assuming that n is an exact power of 2, we are guaranteed that as long as $n \geq 2$, the dimension $n/2$ is an integer.

Suppose that we partition each of A, B, and C into four $n/2 \times n/2$ matrices

$$A = \begin{pmatrix} A_{11} & A_{12} \\ A_{21} & A_{22} \end{pmatrix}, \quad B = \begin{pmatrix} B_{11} & B_{12} \\ B_{21} & B_{22} \end{pmatrix}, \quad C = \begin{pmatrix} C_{11} & C_{12} \\ C_{21} & C_{22} \end{pmatrix}, \tag{4.9}$$

so that we rewrite the equation $C = A \cdot B$ as

$$\begin{pmatrix} C_{11} & C_{12} \\ C_{21} & C_{22} \end{pmatrix} = \begin{pmatrix} A_{11} & A_{12} \\ A_{21} & A_{22} \end{pmatrix} \cdot \begin{pmatrix} B_{11} & B_{12} \\ B_{21} & B_{22} \end{pmatrix}. \tag{4.10}$$

Equation (4.10) corresponds to the four equations

$$C_{11} = A_{11} \cdot B_{11} + A_{12} \cdot B_{21}, \tag{4.11}$$
$$C_{12} = A_{11} \cdot B_{12} + A_{12} \cdot B_{22}, \tag{4.12}$$
$$C_{21} = A_{21} \cdot B_{11} + A_{22} \cdot B_{21}, \tag{4.13}$$
$$C_{22} = A_{21} \cdot B_{12} + A_{22} \cdot B_{22}. \tag{4.14}$$

Each of these four equations specifies two multiplications of $n/2 \times n/2$ matrices and the addition of their $n/2 \times n/2$ products. We can use these equations to create a straightforward, recursive, divide-and-conquer algorithm:

SQUARE-MATRIX-MULTIPLY-RECURSIVE(A, B)

1 $n = A.rows$
2 let C be a new $n \times n$ matrix
3 **if** $n == 1$
4      $c_{11} = a_{11} \cdot b_{11}$
5 **else** partition A, B, and C as in equations (4.9)
6      $C_{11} =$ SQUARE-MATRIX-MULTIPLY-RECURSIVE(A_{11}, B_{11})
            $+$ SQUARE-MATRIX-MULTIPLY-RECURSIVE(A_{12}, B_{21})
7      $C_{12} =$ SQUARE-MATRIX-MULTIPLY-RECURSIVE(A_{11}, B_{12})
            $+$ SQUARE-MATRIX-MULTIPLY-RECURSIVE(A_{12}, B_{22})
8      $C_{21} =$ SQUARE-MATRIX-MULTIPLY-RECURSIVE(A_{21}, B_{11})
            $+$ SQUARE-MATRIX-MULTIPLY-RECURSIVE(A_{22}, B_{21})
9      $C_{22} =$ SQUARE-MATRIX-MULTIPLY-RECURSIVE(A_{21}, B_{12})
            $+$ SQUARE-MATRIX-MULTIPLY-RECURSIVE(A_{22}, B_{22})
10 **return** C

This pseudocode glosses over one subtle but important implementation detail. How do we partition the matrices in line 5? If we were to create 12 new $n/2 \times n/2$ matrices, we would spend $\Theta(n^2)$ time copying entries. In fact, we can partition the matrices without copying entries. The trick is to use index calculations. We identify a submatrix by a range of row indices and a range of column indices of the original matrix. We end up representing a submatrix a little differently from how we represent the original matrix, which is the subtlety we are glossing over. The advantage is that, since we can specify submatrices by index calculations, executing line 5 takes only $\Theta(1)$ time (although we shall see that it makes no difference asymptotically to the overall running time whether we copy or partition in place).

Now, we derive a recurrence to characterize the running time of SQUARE-MATRIX-MULTIPLY-RECURSIVE. Let $T(n)$ be the time to multiply two $n \times n$ matrices using this procedure. In the base case, when $n = 1$, we perform just the one scalar multiplication in line 4, and so

$$T(1) = \Theta(1) . \tag{4.15}$$

The recursive case occurs when $n > 1$. As discussed, partitioning the matrices in line 5 takes $\Theta(1)$ time, using index calculations. In lines 6–9, we recursively call SQUARE-MATRIX-MULTIPLY-RECURSIVE a total of eight times. Because each recursive call multiplies two $n/2 \times n/2$ matrices, thereby contributing $T(n/2)$ to the overall running time, the time taken by all eight recursive calls is $8T(n/2)$. We also must account for the four matrix additions in lines 6–9. Each of these matrices contains $n^2/4$ entries, and so each of the four matrix additions takes $\Theta(n^2)$ time. Since the number of matrix additions is a constant, the total time spent adding ma-

trices in lines 6–9 is $\Theta(n^2)$. (Again, we use index calculations to place the results of the matrix additions into the correct positions of matrix C, with an overhead of $\Theta(1)$ time per entry.) The total time for the recursive case, therefore, is the sum of the partitioning time, the time for all the recursive calls, and the time to add the matrices resulting from the recursive calls:

$$
\begin{aligned}
T(n) &= \Theta(1) + 8T(n/2) + \Theta(n^2) \\
&= 8T(n/2) + \Theta(n^2) \, .
\end{aligned}
\tag{4.16}
$$

Notice that if we implemented partitioning by copying matrices, which would cost $\Theta(n^2)$ time, the recurrence would not change, and hence the overall running time would increase by only a constant factor.

Combining equations (4.15) and (4.16) gives us the recurrence for the running time of SQUARE-MATRIX-MULTIPLY-RECURSIVE:

$$
T(n) = \begin{cases} \Theta(1) & \text{if } n = 1 \, , \\ 8T(n/2) + \Theta(n^2) & \text{if } n > 1 \, . \end{cases}
\tag{4.17}
$$

As we shall see from the master method in Section 4.5, recurrence (4.17) has the solution $T(n) = \Theta(n^3)$. Thus, this simple divide-and-conquer approach is no faster than the straightforward SQUARE-MATRIX-MULTIPLY procedure.

Before we continue on to examining Strassen's algorithm, let us review where the components of equation (4.16) came from. Partitioning each $n \times n$ matrix by index calculation takes $\Theta(1)$ time, but we have two matrices to partition. Although you could say that partitioning the two matrices takes $\Theta(2)$ time, the constant of 2 is subsumed by the Θ-notation. Adding two matrices, each with, say, k entries, takes $\Theta(k)$ time. Since the matrices we add each have $n^2/4$ entries, you could say that adding each pair takes $\Theta(n^2/4)$ time. Again, however, the Θ-notation subsumes the constant factor of $1/4$, and we say that adding two $n/2 \times n/2$ matrices takes $\Theta(n^2)$ time. We have four such matrix additions, and once again, instead of saying that they take $\Theta(4n^2)$ time, we say that they take $\Theta(n^2)$ time. (Of course, you might observe that we could say that the four matrix additions take $\Theta(4n^2/4)$ time, and that $4n^2/4 = n^2$, but the point here is that Θ-notation subsumes constant factors, whatever they are.) Thus, we end up with two terms of $\Theta(n^2)$, which we can combine into one.

When we account for the eight recursive calls, however, we cannot just subsume the constant factor of 8. In other words, we must say that together they take $8T(n/2)$ time, rather than just $T(n/2)$ time. You can get a feel for why by looking back at the recursion tree in Figure 2.5, for recurrence (2.1) (which is identical to recurrence (4.7)), with the recursive case $T(n) = 2T(n/2) + \Theta(n)$. The factor of 2 determined how many children each tree node had, which in turn determined how many terms contributed to the sum at each level of the tree. If we were to ignore

the factor of 8 in equation (4.16) or the factor of 2 in recurrence (4.1), the recursion tree would just be linear, rather than "bushy," and each level would contribute only one term to the sum.

Bear in mind, therefore, that although asymptotic notation subsumes constant multiplicative factors, recursive notation such as $T(n/2)$ does not.

Strassen's method

The key to Strassen's method is to make the recursion tree slightly less bushy. That is, instead of performing eight recursive multiplications of $n/2 \times n/2$ matrices, it performs only seven. The cost of eliminating one matrix multiplication will be several new additions of $n/2 \times n/2$ matrices, but still only a constant number of additions. As before, the constant number of matrix additions will be subsumed by Θ-notation when we set up the recurrence equation to characterize the running time.

Strassen's method is not at all obvious. (This might be the biggest understatement in this book.) It has four steps:

1. Divide the input matrices A and B and output matrix C into $n/2 \times n/2$ submatrices, as in equation (4.9). This step takes $\Theta(1)$ time by index calculation, just as in SQUARE-MATRIX-MULTIPLY-RECURSIVE.

2. Create 10 matrices $S_1, S_2, \ldots, S_{10}$, each of which is $n/2 \times n/2$ and is the sum or difference of two matrices created in step 1. We can create all 10 matrices in $\Theta(n^2)$ time.

3. Using the submatrices created in step 1 and the 10 matrices created in step 2, recursively compute seven matrix products $P_1, P_2, \ldots, P_7$. Each matrix P_i is $n/2 \times n/2$.

4. Compute the desired submatrices $C_{11}, C_{12}, C_{21}, C_{22}$ of the result matrix C by adding and subtracting various combinations of the P_i matrices. We can compute all four submatrices in $\Theta(n^2)$ time.

We shall see the details of steps 2–4 in a moment, but we already have enough information to set up a recurrence for the running time of Strassen's method. Let us assume that once the matrix size n gets down to 1, we perform a simple scalar multiplication, just as in line 4 of SQUARE-MATRIX-MULTIPLY-RECURSIVE. When $n > 1$, steps 1, 2, and 4 take a total of $\Theta(n^2)$ time, and step 3 requires us to perform seven multiplications of $n/2 \times n/2$ matrices. Hence, we obtain the following recurrence for the running time $T(n)$ of Strassen's algorithm:

$$T(n) = \begin{cases} \Theta(1) & \text{if } n = 1, \\ 7T(n/2) + \Theta(n^2) & \text{if } n > 1. \end{cases} \tag{4.18}$$

We have traded off one matrix multiplication for a constant number of matrix additions. Once we understand recurrences and their solutions, we shall see that this tradeoff actually leads to a lower asymptotic running time. By the master method in Section 4.5, recurrence (4.18) has the solution $T(n) = \Theta(n^{\lg 7})$.

We now proceed to describe the details. In step 2, we create the following 10 matrices:

$$
\begin{aligned}
S_1 &= B_{12} - B_{22} , \\
S_2 &= A_{11} + A_{12} , \\
S_3 &= A_{21} + A_{22} , \\
S_4 &= B_{21} - B_{11} , \\
S_5 &= A_{11} + A_{22} , \\
S_6 &= B_{11} + B_{22} , \\
S_7 &= A_{12} - A_{22} , \\
S_8 &= B_{21} + B_{22} , \\
S_9 &= A_{11} - A_{21} , \\
S_{10} &= B_{11} + B_{12} .
\end{aligned}
$$

Since we must add or subtract $n/2 \times n/2$ matrices 10 times, this step does indeed take $\Theta(n^2)$ time.

In step 3, we recursively multiply $n/2 \times n/2$ matrices seven times to compute the following $n/2 \times n/2$ matrices, each of which is the sum or difference of products of A and B submatrices:

$$
\begin{aligned}
P_1 &= A_{11} \cdot S_1 &&= A_{11} \cdot B_{12} - A_{11} \cdot B_{22} , \\
P_2 &= S_2 \cdot B_{22} &&= A_{11} \cdot B_{22} + A_{12} \cdot B_{22} , \\
P_3 &= S_3 \cdot B_{11} &&= A_{21} \cdot B_{11} + A_{22} \cdot B_{11} , \\
P_4 &= A_{22} \cdot S_4 &&= A_{22} \cdot B_{21} - A_{22} \cdot B_{11} , \\
P_5 &= S_5 \cdot S_6 &&= A_{11} \cdot B_{11} + A_{11} \cdot B_{22} + A_{22} \cdot B_{11} + A_{22} \cdot B_{22} , \\
P_6 &= S_7 \cdot S_8 &&= A_{12} \cdot B_{21} + A_{12} \cdot B_{22} - A_{22} \cdot B_{21} - A_{22} \cdot B_{22} , \\
P_7 &= S_9 \cdot S_{10} &&= A_{11} \cdot B_{11} + A_{11} \cdot B_{12} - A_{21} \cdot B_{11} - A_{21} \cdot B_{12} .
\end{aligned}
$$

Note that the only multiplications we need to perform are those in the middle column of the above equations. The right-hand column just shows what these products equal in terms of the original submatrices created in step 1.

Step 4 adds and subtracts the P_i matrices created in step 3 to construct the four $n/2 \times n/2$ submatrices of the product C. We start with

$$C_{11} = P_5 + P_4 - P_2 + P_6 .$$

Expanding out the right-hand side, with the expansion of each P_i on its own line and vertically aligning terms that cancel out, we see that C_{11} equals

$$
\begin{aligned}
A_{11} \cdot B_{11} + A_{11} \cdot B_{22} + A_{22} \cdot B_{11} + A_{22} \cdot B_{22} & \\
- A_{22} \cdot B_{11} \qquad\qquad\quad + A_{22} \cdot B_{21} & \\
- A_{11} \cdot B_{22} \qquad\qquad\qquad\qquad\qquad\quad - A_{12} \cdot B_{22} & \\
- A_{22} \cdot B_{22} - A_{22} \cdot B_{21} + A_{12} \cdot B_{22} + A_{12} \cdot B_{21} &
\end{aligned}
$$

$$
\overline{A_{11} \cdot B_{11} \qquad\qquad\qquad\qquad\qquad\qquad\qquad\qquad + A_{12} \cdot B_{21}} \,,
$$

which corresponds to equation (4.11).

Similarly, we set

$$
C_{12} = P_1 + P_2 \,,
$$

and so C_{12} equals

$$
\begin{aligned}
A_{11} \cdot B_{12} - A_{11} \cdot B_{22} & \\
+ A_{11} \cdot B_{22} + A_{12} \cdot B_{22} &
\end{aligned}
$$

$$
\overline{A_{11} \cdot B_{12} \qquad\qquad + A_{12} \cdot B_{22}} \,,
$$

corresponding to equation (4.12).

Setting

$$
C_{21} = P_3 + P_4
$$

makes C_{21} equal

$$
\begin{aligned}
A_{21} \cdot B_{11} + A_{22} \cdot B_{11} & \\
- A_{22} \cdot B_{11} + A_{22} \cdot B_{21} &
\end{aligned}
$$

$$
\overline{A_{21} \cdot B_{11} \qquad\qquad + A_{22} \cdot B_{21}} \,,
$$

corresponding to equation (4.13).

Finally, we set

$$
C_{22} = P_5 + P_1 - P_3 - P_7 \,,
$$

so that C_{22} equals

$$
\begin{aligned}
A_{11} \cdot B_{11} + A_{11} \cdot B_{22} + A_{22} \cdot B_{11} + A_{22} \cdot B_{22} & \\
- A_{11} \cdot B_{22} \qquad\qquad\qquad\qquad + A_{11} \cdot B_{12} & \\
- A_{22} \cdot B_{11} \qquad\qquad\qquad\qquad - A_{21} \cdot B_{11} & \\
- A_{11} \cdot B_{11} \qquad\qquad\qquad\qquad - A_{11} \cdot B_{12} + A_{21} \cdot B_{11} + A_{21} \cdot B_{12} &
\end{aligned}
$$

$$
\overline{A_{22} \cdot B_{22} \qquad\qquad\qquad\qquad\qquad + A_{21} \cdot B_{12}} \,,
$$

which corresponds to equation (4.14). Altogether, we add or subtract $n/2 \times n/2$ matrices eight times in step 4, and so this step indeed takes $\Theta(n^2)$ time.

Thus, we see that Strassen's algorithm, comprising steps 1–4, produces the correct matrix product and that recurrence (4.18) characterizes its running time. Since we shall see in Section 4.5 that this recurrence has the solution $T(n) = \Theta(n^{\lg 7})$, Strassen's method is asymptotically faster than the straightforward SQUARE-MATRIX-MULTIPLY procedure. The notes at the end of this chapter discuss some of the practical aspects of Strassen's algorithm.

Exercises

Note: Although Exercises 4.2-3, 4.2-4, and 4.2-5 are about variants on Strassen's algorithm, you should read Section 4.5 before trying to solve them.

4.2-1
Use Strassen's algorithm to compute the matrix product

$$\begin{pmatrix} 1 & 3 \\ 7 & 5 \end{pmatrix} \begin{pmatrix} 6 & 8 \\ 4 & 2 \end{pmatrix}.$$

Show your work.

4.2-2
Write pseudocode for Strassen's algorithm.

4.2-3
How would you modify Strassen's algorithm to multiply $n \times n$ matrices in which n is not an exact power of 2? Show that the resulting algorithm runs in time $\Theta(n^{\lg 7})$.

4.2-4
What is the largest k such that if you can multiply 3×3 matrices using k multiplications (not assuming commutativity of multiplication), then you can multiply $n \times n$ matrices in time $o(n^{\lg 7})$? What would the running time of this algorithm be?

4.2-5
V. Pan has discovered a way of multiplying 68×68 matrices using 132,464 multiplications, a way of multiplying 70×70 matrices using 143,640 multiplications, and a way of multiplying 72×72 matrices using 155,424 multiplications. Which method yields the best asymptotic running time when used in a divide-and-conquer matrix-multiplication algorithm? How does it compare to Strassen's algorithm?

4.2-6

How quickly can you multiply a $kn \times n$ matrix by an $n \times kn$ matrix, using Strassen's algorithm as a subroutine? Answer the same question with the order of the input matrices reversed.

4.2-7

Show how to multiply the complex numbers $a + bi$ and $c + di$ using only three multiplications of real numbers. The algorithm should take a, b, c, and d as input and produce the real component $ac - bd$ and the imaginary component $ad + bc$ separately.

4.3 The substitution method for solving recurrences

Now that we have seen how recurrences characterize the running times of divide-and-conquer algorithms, we will learn how to solve recurrences. We start in this section with the "substitution" method.

The *substitution method* for solving recurrences comprises two steps:

1. Guess the form of the solution.

2. Use mathematical induction to find the constants and show that the solution works.

We substitute the guessed solution for the function when applying the inductive hypothesis to smaller values; hence the name "substitution method." This method is powerful, but we must be able to guess the form of the answer in order to apply it.

We can use the substitution method to establish either upper or lower bounds on a recurrence. As an example, let us determine an upper bound on the recurrence

$$T(n) = 2T(\lfloor n/2 \rfloor) + n , \tag{4.19}$$

which is similar to recurrences (4.3) and (4.4). We guess that the solution is $T(n) = O(n \lg n)$. The substitution method requires us to prove that $T(n) \leq cn \lg n$ for an appropriate choice of the constant $c > 0$. We start by assuming that this bound holds for all positive $m < n$, in particular for $m = \lfloor n/2 \rfloor$, yielding $T(\lfloor n/2 \rfloor) \leq c \lfloor n/2 \rfloor \lg(\lfloor n/2 \rfloor)$. Substituting into the recurrence yields

$$
\begin{aligned}
T(n) &\leq 2(c \lfloor n/2 \rfloor \lg(\lfloor n/2 \rfloor)) + n \\
&\leq cn \lg(n/2) + n \\
&= cn \lg n - cn \lg 2 + n \\
&= cn \lg n - cn + n \\
&\leq cn \lg n ,
\end{aligned}
$$

where the last step holds as long as $c \geq 1$.

Mathematical induction now requires us to show that our solution holds for the boundary conditions. Typically, we do so by showing that the boundary conditions are suitable as base cases for the inductive proof. For the recurrence (4.19), we must show that we can choose the constant c large enough so that the bound $T(n) \leq cn \lg n$ works for the boundary conditions as well. This requirement can sometimes lead to problems. Let us assume, for the sake of argument, that $T(1) = 1$ is the sole boundary condition of the recurrence. Then for $n = 1$, the bound $T(n) \leq cn \lg n$ yields $T(1) \leq c1 \lg 1 = 0$, which is at odds with $T(1) = 1$. Consequently, the base case of our inductive proof fails to hold.

We can overcome this obstacle in proving an inductive hypothesis for a specific boundary condition with only a little more effort. In the recurrence (4.19), for example, we take advantage of asymptotic notation requiring us only to prove $T(n) \leq cn \lg n$ for $n \geq n_0$, where n_0 is a constant *that we get to choose*. We keep the troublesome boundary condition $T(1) = 1$, but remove it from consideration in the inductive proof. We do so by first observing that for $n > 3$, the recurrence does not depend directly on $T(1)$. Thus, we can replace $T(1)$ by $T(2)$ and $T(3)$ as the base cases in the inductive proof, letting $n_0 = 2$. Note that we make a distinction between the base case of the recurrence ($n = 1$) and the base cases of the inductive proof ($n = 2$ and $n = 3$). With $T(1) = 1$, we derive from the recurrence that $T(2) = 4$ and $T(3) = 5$. Now we can complete the inductive proof that $T(n) \leq cn \lg n$ for some constant $c \geq 1$ by choosing c large enough so that $T(2) \leq c2 \lg 2$ and $T(3) \leq c3 \lg 3$. As it turns out, any choice of $c \geq 2$ suffices for the base cases of $n = 2$ and $n = 3$ to hold. For most of the recurrences we shall examine, it is straightforward to extend boundary conditions to make the inductive assumption work for small n, and we shall not always explicitly work out the details.

Making a good guess

Unfortunately, there is no general way to guess the correct solutions to recurrences. Guessing a solution takes experience and, occasionally, creativity. Fortunately, though, you can use some heuristics to help you become a good guesser. You can also use recursion trees, which we shall see in Section 4.4, to generate good guesses.

If a recurrence is similar to one you have seen before, then guessing a similar solution is reasonable. As an example, consider the recurrence

$$T(n) = 2T(\lfloor n/2 \rfloor + 17) + n ,$$

which looks difficult because of the added "17" in the argument to T on the right-hand side. Intuitively, however, this additional term cannot substantially affect the

solution to the recurrence. When n is large, the difference between $\lfloor n/2 \rfloor$ and $\lfloor n/2 \rfloor + 17$ is not that large: both cut n nearly evenly in half. Consequently, we make the guess that $T(n) = O(n \lg n)$, which you can verify as correct by using the substitution method (see Exercise 4.3-6).

Another way to make a good guess is to prove loose upper and lower bounds on the recurrence and then reduce the range of uncertainty. For example, we might start with a lower bound of $T(n) = \Omega(n)$ for the recurrence (4.19), since we have the term n in the recurrence, and we can prove an initial upper bound of $T(n) = O(n^2)$. Then, we can gradually lower the upper bound and raise the lower bound until we converge on the correct, asymptotically tight solution of $T(n) = \Theta(n \lg n)$.

Subtleties

Sometimes you might correctly guess an asymptotic bound on the solution of a recurrence, but somehow the math fails to work out in the induction. The problem frequently turns out to be that the inductive assumption is not strong enough to prove the detailed bound. If you revise the guess by subtracting a lower-order term when you hit such a snag, the math often goes through.

Consider the recurrence

$$T(n) = T(\lfloor n/2 \rfloor) + T(\lceil n/2 \rceil) + 1 .$$

We guess that the solution is $T(n) = O(n)$, and we try to show that $T(n) \leq cn$ for an appropriate choice of the constant c. Substituting our guess in the recurrence, we obtain

$$
\begin{aligned}
T(n) &\leq c \lfloor n/2 \rfloor + c \lceil n/2 \rceil + 1 \\
&= cn + 1 ,
\end{aligned}
$$

which does not imply $T(n) \leq cn$ for any choice of c. We might be tempted to try a larger guess, say $T(n) = O(n^2)$. Although we can make this larger guess work, our original guess of $T(n) = O(n)$ is correct. In order to show that it is correct, however, we must make a stronger inductive hypothesis.

Intuitively, our guess is nearly right: we are off only by the constant 1, a lower-order term. Nevertheless, mathematical induction does not work unless we prove the exact form of the inductive hypothesis. We overcome our difficulty by *subtracting* a lower-order term from our previous guess. Our new guess is $T(n) \leq cn - d$, where $d \geq 0$ is a constant. We now have

$$
\begin{aligned}
T(n) &\leq (c \lfloor n/2 \rfloor - d) + (c \lceil n/2 \rceil - d) + 1 \\
&= cn - 2d + 1 \\
&\leq cn - d ,
\end{aligned}
$$

as long as $d \geq 1$. As before, we must choose the constant c large enough to handle the boundary conditions.

You might find the idea of subtracting a lower-order term counterintuitive. After all, if the math does not work out, we should increase our guess, right? Not necessarily! When proving an upper bound by induction, it may actually be more difficult to prove that a weaker upper bound holds, because in order to prove the weaker bound, we must use the same weaker bound inductively in the proof. In our current example, when the recurrence has more than one recursive term, we get to subtract out the lower-order term of the proposed bound once per recursive term. In the above example, we subtracted out the constant d twice, once for the $T(\lfloor n/2 \rfloor)$ term and once for the $T(\lceil n/2 \rceil)$ term. We ended up with the inequality $T(n) \leq cn - 2d + 1$, and it was easy to find values of d to make $cn - 2d + 1$ be less than or equal to $cn - d$.

Avoiding pitfalls

It is easy to err in the use of asymptotic notation. For example, in the recurrence (4.19) we can falsely "prove" $T(n) = O(n)$ by guessing $T(n) \leq cn$ and then arguing

$$
\begin{aligned}
T(n) &\leq 2(c \lfloor n/2 \rfloor) + n \\
&\leq cn + n \\
&= O(n), \qquad \Longleftarrow wrong!!
\end{aligned}
$$

since c is a constant. The error is that we have not proved the *exact form* of the inductive hypothesis, that is, that $T(n) \leq cn$. We therefore will explicitly prove that $T(n) \leq cn$ when we want to show that $T(n) = O(n)$.

Changing variables

Sometimes, a little algebraic manipulation can make an unknown recurrence similar to one you have seen before. As an example, consider the recurrence

$$T(n) = 2T\left(\lfloor \sqrt{n} \rfloor\right) + \lg n,$$

which looks difficult. We can simplify this recurrence, though, with a change of variables. For convenience, we shall not worry about rounding off values, such as $\sqrt{n}$, to be integers. Renaming $m = \lg n$ yields

$$T(2^m) = 2T(2^{m/2}) + m.$$

We can now rename $S(m) = T(2^m)$ to produce the new recurrence

$$S(m) = 2S(m/2) + m,$$

which is very much like recurrence (4.19). Indeed, this new recurrence has the same solution: $S(m) = O(m \lg m)$. Changing back from $S(m)$ to $T(n)$, we obtain

$$T(n) = T(2^m) = S(m) = O(m \lg m) = O(\lg n \lg \lg n) \,.$$

Exercises

4.3-1
Show that the solution of $T(n) = T(n - 1) + n$ is $O(n^2)$.

4.3-2
Show that the solution of $T(n) = T(\lceil n/2 \rceil) + 1$ is $O(\lg n)$.

4.3-3
We saw that the solution of $T(n) = 2T(\lfloor n/2 \rfloor) + n$ is $O(n \lg n)$. Show that the solution of this recurrence is also $\Omega(n \lg n)$. Conclude that the solution is $\Theta(n \lg n)$.

4.3-4
Show that by making a different inductive hypothesis, we can overcome the difficulty with the boundary condition $T(1) = 1$ for recurrence (4.19) without adjusting the boundary conditions for the inductive proof.

4.3-5
Show that $\Theta(n \lg n)$ is the solution to the "exact" recurrence (4.3) for merge sort.

4.3-6
Show that the solution to $T(n) = 2T(\lfloor n/2 \rfloor + 17) + n$ is $O(n \lg n)$.

4.3-7
Using the master method in Section 4.5, you can show that the solution to the recurrence $T(n) = 4T(n/3) + n$ is $T(n) = \Theta(n^{\log_3 4})$. Show that a substitution proof with the assumption $T(n) \le cn^{\log_3 4}$ fails. Then show how to subtract off a lower-order term to make a substitution proof work.

4.3-8
Using the master method in Section 4.5, you can show that the solution to the recurrence $T(n) = 4T(n/2) + n$ is $T(n) = \Theta(n^2)$. Show that a substitution proof with the assumption $T(n) \le cn^2$ fails. Then show how to subtract off a lower-order term to make a substitution proof work.

4.3-9

Solve the recurrence $T(n) = 3T(\sqrt{n}) + \log n$ by making a change of variables. Your solution should be asymptotically tight. Do not worry about whether values are integral.

4.4   The recursion-tree method for solving recurrences

Although you can use the substitution method to provide a succinct proof that a solution to a recurrence is correct, you might have trouble coming up with a good guess. Drawing out a recursion tree, as we did in our analysis of the merge sort recurrence in Section 2.3.2, serves as a straightforward way to devise a good guess. In a ***recursion tree***, each node represents the cost of a single subproblem somewhere in the set of recursive function invocations. We sum the costs within each level of the tree to obtain a set of per-level costs, and then we sum all the per-level costs to determine the total cost of all levels of the recursion.

A recursion tree is best used to generate a good guess, which you can then verify by the substitution method. When using a recursion tree to generate a good guess, you can often tolerate a small amount of "sloppiness," since you will be verifying your guess later on. If you are very careful when drawing out a recursion tree and summing the costs, however, you can use a recursion tree as a direct proof of a solution to a recurrence. In this section, we will use recursion trees to generate good guesses, and in Section 4.6, we will use recursion trees directly to prove the theorem that forms the basis of the master method.

For example, let us see how a recursion tree would provide a good guess for the recurrence $T(n) = 3T(\lfloor n/4 \rfloor) + \Theta(n^2)$. We start by focusing on finding an upper bound for the solution. Because we know that floors and ceilings usually do not matter when solving recurrences (here's an example of sloppiness that we can tolerate), we create a recursion tree for the recurrence $T(n) = 3T(n/4) + cn^2$, having written out the implied constant coefficient $c > 0$.

Figure 4.5 shows how we derive the recursion tree for $T(n) = 3T(n/4) + cn^2$. For convenience, we assume that n is an exact power of 4 (another example of tolerable sloppiness) so that all subproblem sizes are integers. Part (a) of the figure shows $T(n)$, which we expand in part (b) into an equivalent tree representing the recurrence. The cn^2 term at the root represents the cost at the top level of recursion, and the three subtrees of the root represent the costs incurred by the subproblems of size $n/4$. Part (c) shows this process carried one step further by expanding each node with cost $T(n/4)$ from part (b). The cost for each of the three children of the root is $c(n/4)^2$. We continue expanding each node in the tree by breaking it into its constituent parts as determined by the recurrence.

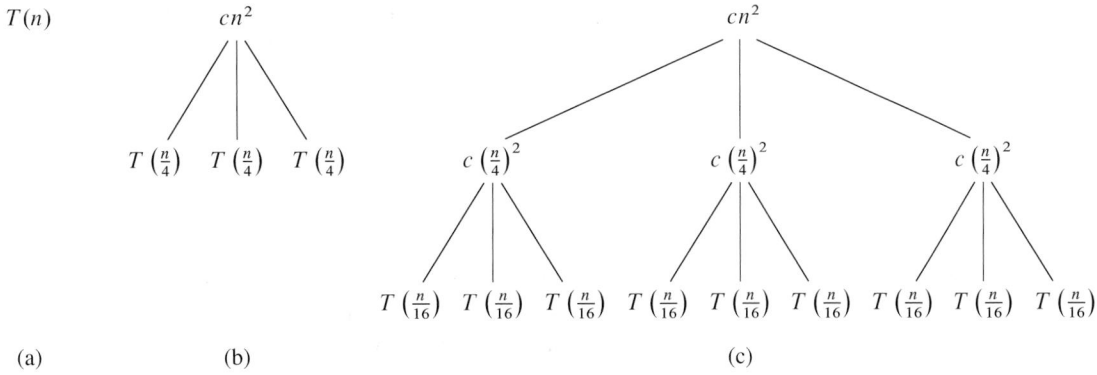

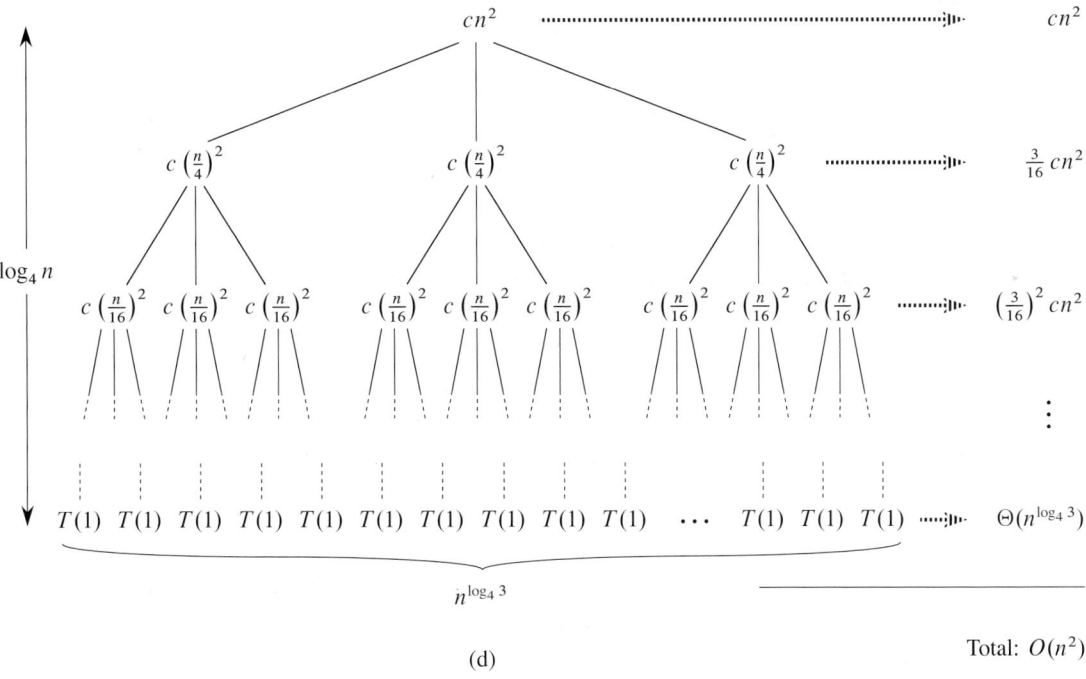

Figure 4.5 Constructing a recursion tree for the recurrence $T(n) = 3T(n/4) + cn^2$. Part **(a)** shows $T(n)$, which progressively expands in **(b)–(d)** to form the recursion tree. The fully expanded tree in part (d) has height $\log_4 n$ (it has $\log_4 n + 1$ levels).

Because subproblem sizes decrease by a factor of 4 each time we go down one level, we eventually must reach a boundary condition. How far from the root do we reach one? The subproblem size for a node at depth i is $n/4^i$. Thus, the subproblem size hits $n = 1$ when $n/4^i = 1$ or, equivalently, when $i = \log_4 n$. Thus, the tree has $\log_4 n + 1$ levels (at depths $0, 1, 2, \ldots, \log_4 n$).

Next we determine the cost at each level of the tree. Each level has three times more nodes than the level above, and so the number of nodes at depth i is 3^i. Because subproblem sizes reduce by a factor of 4 for each level we go down from the root, each node at depth i, for $i = 0, 1, 2, \ldots, \log_4 n - 1$, has a cost of $c(n/4^i)^2$. Multiplying, we see that the total cost over all nodes at depth i, for $i = 0, 1, 2, \ldots, \log_4 n - 1$, is $3^i c(n/4^i)^2 = (3/16)^i cn^2$. The bottom level, at depth $\log_4 n$, has $3^{\log_4 n} = n^{\log_4 3}$ nodes, each contributing cost $T(1)$, for a total cost of $n^{\log_4 3} T(1)$, which is $\Theta(n^{\log_4 3})$, since we assume that $T(1)$ is a constant.

Now we add up the costs over all levels to determine the cost for the entire tree:

$$
\begin{aligned}
T(n) &= cn^2 + \frac{3}{16}cn^2 + \left(\frac{3}{16}\right)^2 cn^2 + \cdots + \left(\frac{3}{16}\right)^{\log_4 n - 1} cn^2 + \Theta(n^{\log_4 3}) \\
&= \sum_{i=0}^{\log_4 n - 1} \left(\frac{3}{16}\right)^i cn^2 + \Theta(n^{\log_4 3}) \\
&= \frac{(3/16)^{\log_4 n} - 1}{(3/16) - 1} cn^2 + \Theta(n^{\log_4 3}) \qquad \text{(by equation (A.5))} .
\end{aligned}
$$

This last formula looks somewhat messy until we realize that we can again take advantage of small amounts of sloppiness and use an infinite decreasing geometric series as an upper bound. Backing up one step and applying equation (A.6), we have

$$
\begin{aligned}
T(n) &= \sum_{i=0}^{\log_4 n - 1} \left(\frac{3}{16}\right)^i cn^2 + \Theta(n^{\log_4 3}) \\
&< \sum_{i=0}^{\infty} \left(\frac{3}{16}\right)^i cn^2 + \Theta(n^{\log_4 3}) \\
&= \frac{1}{1 - (3/16)} cn^2 + \Theta(n^{\log_4 3}) \\
&= \frac{16}{13} cn^2 + \Theta(n^{\log_4 3}) \\
&= O(n^2) .
\end{aligned}
$$

Thus, we have derived a guess of $T(n) = O(n^2)$ for our original recurrence $T(n) = 3T(\lfloor n/4 \rfloor) + \Theta(n^2)$. In this example, the coefficients of cn^2 form a decreasing geometric series and, by equation (A.6), the sum of these coefficients

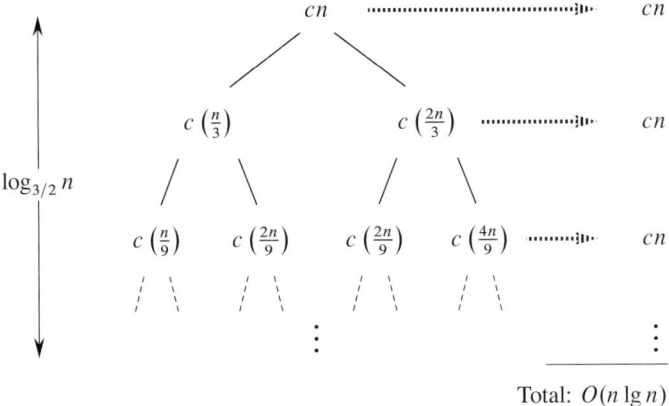

Total: $O(n \lg n)$

Figure 4.6 A recursion tree for the recurrence $T(n) = T(n/3) + T(2n/3) + cn$.

is bounded from above by the constant $16/13$. Since the root's contribution to the total cost is cn^2, the root contributes a constant fraction of the total cost. In other words, the cost of the root dominates the total cost of the tree.

In fact, if $O(n^2)$ is indeed an upper bound for the recurrence (as we shall verify in a moment), then it must be a tight bound. Why? The first recursive call contributes a cost of $\Theta(n^2)$, and so $\Omega(n^2)$ must be a lower bound for the recurrence.

Now we can use the substitution method to verify that our guess was correct, that is, $T(n) = O(n^2)$ is an upper bound for the recurrence $T(n) = 3T(\lfloor n/4 \rfloor) + \Theta(n^2)$. We want to show that $T(n) \le dn^2$ for some constant $d > 0$. Using the same constant $c > 0$ as before, we have

$$
\begin{aligned}
T(n) &\le 3T(\lfloor n/4 \rfloor) + cn^2 \\
&\le 3d\lfloor n/4 \rfloor^2 + cn^2 \\
&\le 3d(n/4)^2 + cn^2 \\
&= \frac{3}{16}dn^2 + cn^2 \\
&\le dn^2 ,
\end{aligned}
$$

where the last step holds as long as $d \ge (16/13)c$.

In another, more intricate, example, Figure 4.6 shows the recursion tree for

$$T(n) = T(n/3) + T(2n/3) + O(n) .$$

(Again, we omit floor and ceiling functions for simplicity.) As before, we let c represent the constant factor in the $O(n)$ term. When we add the values across the levels of the recursion tree shown in the figure, we get a value of cn for every level.

The longest simple path from the root to a leaf is $n \rightarrow (2/3)n \rightarrow (2/3)^2 n \rightarrow \cdots \rightarrow 1$. Since $(2/3)^k n = 1$ when $k = \log_{3/2} n$, the height of the tree is $\log_{3/2} n$.

Intuitively, we expect the solution to the recurrence to be at most the number of levels times the cost of each level, or $O(cn \log_{3/2} n) = O(n \lg n)$. Figure 4.6 shows only the top levels of the recursion tree, however, and not every level in the tree contributes a cost of cn. Consider the cost of the leaves. If this recursion tree were a complete binary tree of height $\log_{3/2} n$, there would be $2^{\log_{3/2} n} = n^{\log_{3/2} 2}$ leaves. Since the cost of each leaf is a constant, the total cost of all leaves would then be $\Theta(n^{\log_{3/2} 2})$ which, since $\log_{3/2} 2$ is a constant strictly greater than 1, is $\omega(n \lg n)$. This recursion tree is not a complete binary tree, however, and so it has fewer than $n^{\log_{3/2} 2}$ leaves. Moreover, as we go down from the root, more and more internal nodes are absent. Consequently, levels toward the bottom of the recursion tree contribute less than cn to the total cost. We could work out an accurate accounting of all costs, but remember that we are just trying to come up with a guess to use in the substitution method. Let us tolerate the sloppiness and attempt to show that a guess of $O(n \lg n)$ for the upper bound is correct.

Indeed, we can use the substitution method to verify that $O(n \lg n)$ is an upper bound for the solution to the recurrence. We show that $T(n) \leq dn \lg n$, where d is a suitable positive constant. We have

$$
\begin{aligned}
T(n) &\leq T(n/3) + T(2n/3) + cn \\
&\leq d(n/3)\lg(n/3) + d(2n/3)\lg(2n/3) + cn \\
&= (d(n/3)\lg n - d(n/3)\lg 3) \\
&\qquad + (d(2n/3)\lg n - d(2n/3)\lg(3/2)) + cn \\
&= dn\lg n - d((n/3)\lg 3 + (2n/3)\lg(3/2)) + cn \\
&= dn\lg n - d((n/3)\lg 3 + (2n/3)\lg 3 - (2n/3)\lg 2) + cn \\
&= dn\lg n - dn(\lg 3 - 2/3) + cn \\
&\leq dn\lg n ,
\end{aligned}
$$

as long as $d \geq c/(\lg 3 - (2/3))$. Thus, we did not need to perform a more accurate accounting of costs in the recursion tree.

Exercises

4.4-1
Use a recursion tree to determine a good asymptotic upper bound on the recurrence $T(n) = 3T(\lfloor n/2 \rfloor) + n$. Use the substitution method to verify your answer.

4.4-2
Use a recursion tree to determine a good asymptotic upper bound on the recurrence $T(n) = T(n/2) + n^2$. Use the substitution method to verify your answer.

4.4-3

Use a recursion tree to determine a good asymptotic upper bound on the recurrence $T(n) = 4T(n/2 + 2) + n$. Use the substitution method to verify your answer.

4.4-4

Use a recursion tree to determine a good asymptotic upper bound on the recurrence $T(n) = 2T(n - 1) + 1$. Use the substitution method to verify your answer.

4.4-5

Use a recursion tree to determine a good asymptotic upper bound on the recurrence $T(n) = T(n-1) + T(n/2) + n$. Use the substitution method to verify your answer.

4.4-6

Argue that the solution to the recurrence $T(n) = T(n/3) + T(2n/3) + cn$, where c is a constant, is $\Omega(n \lg n)$ by appealing to a recursion tree.

4.4-7

Draw the recursion tree for $T(n) = 4T(\lfloor n/2 \rfloor) + cn$, where c is a constant, and provide a tight asymptotic bound on its solution. Verify your bound by the substitution method.

4.4-8

Use a recursion tree to give an asymptotically tight solution to the recurrence $T(n) = T(n - a) + T(a) + cn$, where $a \geq 1$ and $c > 0$ are constants.

4.4-9

Use a recursion tree to give an asymptotically tight solution to the recurrence $T(n) = T(\alpha n) + T((1 - \alpha)n) + cn$, where α is a constant in the range $0 < \alpha < 1$ and $c > 0$ is also a constant.

4.5 The master method for solving recurrences

The master method provides a "cookbook" method for solving recurrences of the form

$$T(n) = aT(n/b) + f(n) \,, \tag{4.20}$$

where $a \geq 1$ and $b > 1$ are constants and $f(n)$ is an asymptotically positive function. To use the master method, you will need to memorize three cases, but then you will be able to solve many recurrences quite easily, often without pencil and paper.

The recurrence (4.20) describes the running time of an algorithm that divides a problem of size n into a subproblems, each of size n/b, where a and b are positive constants. The a subproblems are solved recursively, each in time $T(n/b)$. The function $f(n)$ encompasses the cost of dividing the problem and combining the results of the subproblems. For example, the recurrence arising from Strassen's algorithm has $a = 7$, $b = 2$, and $f(n) = \Theta(n^2)$.

As a matter of technical correctness, the recurrence is not actually well defined, because n/b might not be an integer. Replacing each of the a terms $T(n/b)$ with either $T(\lfloor n/b \rfloor)$ or $T(\lceil n/b \rceil)$ will not affect the asymptotic behavior of the recurrence, however. (We will prove this assertion in the next section.) We normally find it convenient, therefore, to omit the floor and ceiling functions when writing divide-and-conquer recurrences of this form.

The master theorem

The master method depends on the following theorem.

Theorem 4.1 (Master theorem)
Let $a \geq 1$ and $b > 1$ be constants, let $f(n)$ be an asymptotically positive function, and let $T(n)$ be defined on the nonnegative integers by the recurrence

$$T(n) = aT(n/b) + f(n) ,$$

where we interpret n/b to mean either $\lfloor n/b \rfloor$ or $\lceil n/b \rceil$. Then $T(n)$ has the following asymptotic bounds:

1. If $f(n) = O(n^{\log_b a - \epsilon})$ for some constant $\epsilon > 0$, then $T(n) = \Theta(n^{\log_b a})$.

2. If $f(n) = \Theta(n^{\log_b a})$, then $T(n) = \Theta(n^{\log_b a} \lg n)$.

3. If $f(n) = \Omega(n^{\log_b a + \epsilon})$ for some constant $\epsilon > 0$, and if $af(n/b) \leq cf(n)$ for some constant $c < 1$ and all sufficiently large n, then $T(n) = \Theta(f(n))$.   ■

Before applying the master theorem to some examples, let's spend a moment trying to understand what it says. In each of the three cases, we compare the function $f(n)$ with the function $n^{\log_b a}$. Intuitively, the larger of the two functions determines the solution to the recurrence. If, as in case 1, the function $n^{\log_b a}$ is the larger, then the solution is $T(n) = \Theta(n^{\log_b a})$. If, as in case 3, the function $f(n)$ is the larger, then the solution is $T(n) = \Theta(f(n))$. If, as in case 2, the two functions are the same size, we multiply by a logarithmic factor, and the solution is $T(n) = \Theta(n^{\log_b a} \lg n) = \Theta(f(n) \lg n)$.

Beyond this intuition, you need to be aware of some technicalities. In the first case, not only must $f(n)$ be smaller than $n^{\log_b a}$, it must be *polynomially* smaller.

That is, $f(n)$ must be asymptotically smaller than $n^{\log_b a}$ by a factor of n^ϵ for some constant $\epsilon > 0$. In the third case, not only must $f(n)$ be larger than $n^{\log_b a}$, it also must be polynomially larger and in addition satisfy the "regularity" condition that $af(n/b) \leq cf(n)$. This condition is satisfied by most of the polynomially bounded functions that we shall encounter.

Note that the three cases do not cover all the possibilities for $f(n)$. There is a gap between cases 1 and 2 when $f(n)$ is smaller than $n^{\log_b a}$ but not polynomially smaller. Similarly, there is a gap between cases 2 and 3 when $f(n)$ is larger than $n^{\log_b a}$ but not polynomially larger. If the function $f(n)$ falls into one of these gaps, or if the regularity condition in case 3 fails to hold, you cannot use the master method to solve the recurrence.

Using the master method

To use the master method, we simply determine which case (if any) of the master theorem applies and write down the answer.

As a first example, consider

$$T(n) = 9T(n/3) + n .$$

For this recurrence, we have $a = 9$, $b = 3$, $f(n) = n$, and thus we have that $n^{\log_b a} = n^{\log_3 9} = \Theta(n^2)$. Since $f(n) = O(n^{\log_3 9 - \epsilon})$, where $\epsilon = 1$, we can apply case 1 of the master theorem and conclude that the solution is $T(n) = \Theta(n^2)$.

Now consider

$$T(n) = T(2n/3) + 1,$$

in which $a = 1$, $b = 3/2$, $f(n) = 1$, and $n^{\log_b a} = n^{\log_{3/2} 1} = n^0 = 1$. Case 2 applies, since $f(n) = \Theta(n^{\log_b a}) = \Theta(1)$, and thus the solution to the recurrence is $T(n) = \Theta(\lg n)$.

For the recurrence

$$T(n) = 3T(n/4) + n \lg n ,$$

we have $a = 3$, $b = 4$, $f(n) = n \lg n$, and $n^{\log_b a} = n^{\log_4 3} = O(n^{0.793})$. Since $f(n) = \Omega(n^{\log_4 3 + \epsilon})$, where $\epsilon \approx 0.2$, case 3 applies if we can show that the regularity condition holds for $f(n)$. For sufficiently large n, we have that $af(n/b) = 3(n/4) \lg(n/4) \leq (3/4)n \lg n = cf(n)$ for $c = 3/4$. Consequently, by case 3, the solution to the recurrence is $T(n) = \Theta(n \lg n)$.

The master method does not apply to the recurrence

$$T(n) = 2T(n/2) + n \lg n ,$$

even though it appears to have the proper form: $a = 2$, $b = 2$, $f(n) = n \lg n$, and $n^{\log_b a} = n$. You might mistakenly think that case 3 should apply, since

$f(n) = n \lg n$ is asymptotically larger than $n^{\log_b a} = n$. The problem is that it is not *polynomially* larger. The ratio $f(n)/n^{\log_b a} = (n \lg n)/n = \lg n$ is asymptotically less than n^ϵ for any positive constant ϵ. Consequently, the recurrence falls into the gap between case 2 and case 3. (See Exercise 4.6-2 for a solution.)

Let's use the master method to solve the recurrences we saw in Sections 4.1 and 4.2. Recurrence (4.7),

$$T(n) = 2T(n/2) + \Theta(n) ,$$

characterizes the running times of the divide-and-conquer algorithm for both the maximum-subarray problem and merge sort. (As is our practice, we omit stating the base case in the recurrence.) Here, we have $a = 2, b = 2, f(n) = \Theta(n)$, and thus we have that $n^{\log_b a} = n^{\log_2 2} = n$. Case 2 applies, since $f(n) = \Theta(n)$, and so we have the solution $T(n) = \Theta(n \lg n)$.

Recurrence (4.17),

$$T(n) = 8T(n/2) + \Theta(n^2) ,$$

describes the running time of the first divide-and-conquer algorithm that we saw for matrix multiplication. Now we have $a = 8, b = 2$, and $f(n) = \Theta(n^2)$, and so $n^{\log_b a} = n^{\log_2 8} = n^3$. Since n^3 is polynomially larger than $f(n)$ (that is, $f(n) = O(n^{3-\epsilon})$ for $\epsilon = 1$), case 1 applies, and $T(n) = \Theta(n^3)$.

Finally, consider recurrence (4.18),

$$T(n) = 7T(n/2) + \Theta(n^2) ,$$

which describes the running time of Strassen's algorithm. Here, we have $a = 7$, $b = 2$, $f(n) = \Theta(n^2)$, and thus $n^{\log_b a} = n^{\log_2 7}$. Rewriting $\log_2 7$ as $\lg 7$ and recalling that $2.80 < \lg 7 < 2.81$, we see that $f(n) = O(n^{\lg 7 - \epsilon})$ for $\epsilon = 0.8$. Again, case 1 applies, and we have the solution $T(n) = \Theta(n^{\lg 7})$.

Exercises

4.5-1

Use the master method to give tight asymptotic bounds for the following recurrences.

a. $T(n) = 2T(n/4) + 1$.

b. $T(n) = 2T(n/4) + \sqrt{n}$.

c. $T(n) = 2T(n/4) + n$.

d. $T(n) = 2T(n/4) + n^2$.

4.5-2

Professor Caesar wishes to develop a matrix-multiplication algorithm that is asymptotically faster than Strassen's algorithm. His algorithm will use the divide-and-conquer method, dividing each matrix into pieces of size $n/4 \times n/4$, and the divide and combine steps together will take $\Theta(n^2)$ time. He needs to determine how many subproblems his algorithm has to create in order to beat Strassen's algorithm. If his algorithm creates a subproblems, then the recurrence for the running time $T(n)$ becomes $T(n) = aT(n/4) + \Theta(n^2)$. What is the largest integer value of a for which Professor Caesar's algorithm would be asymptotically faster than Strassen's algorithm?

4.5-3

Use the master method to show that the solution to the binary-search recurrence $T(n) = T(n/2) + \Theta(1)$ is $T(n) = \Theta(\lg n)$. (See Exercise 2.3-5 for a description of binary search.)

4.5-4

Can the master method be applied to the recurrence $T(n) = 4T(n/2) + n^2 \lg n$? Why or why not? Give an asymptotic upper bound for this recurrence.

4.5-5   ★

Consider the regularity condition $af(n/b) \leq cf(n)$ for some constant $c < 1$, which is part of case 3 of the master theorem. Give an example of constants $a \geq 1$ and $b > 1$ and a function $f(n)$ that satisfies all the conditions in case 3 of the master theorem except the regularity condition.

★   4.6   Proof of the master theorem

This section contains a proof of the master theorem (Theorem 4.1). You do not need to understand the proof in order to apply the master theorem.

The proof appears in two parts. The first part analyzes the master recurrence (4.20), under the simplifying assumption that $T(n)$ is defined only on exact powers of $b > 1$, that is, for $n = 1, b, b^2, \ldots$. This part gives all the intuition needed to understand why the master theorem is true. The second part shows how to extend the analysis to all positive integers n; it applies mathematical technique to the problem of handling floors and ceilings.

In this section, we shall sometimes abuse our asymptotic notation slightly by using it to describe the behavior of functions that are defined only over exact powers of b. Recall that the definitions of asymptotic notations require that

bounds be proved for all sufficiently large numbers, not just those that are powers of b. Since we could make new asymptotic notations that apply only to the set $\{b^i : i = 0, 1, 2, \ldots\}$, instead of to the nonnegative numbers, this abuse is minor.

Nevertheless, we must always be on guard when we use asymptotic notation over a limited domain lest we draw improper conclusions. For example, proving that $T(n) = O(n)$ when n is an exact power of 2 does not guarantee that $T(n) = O(n)$. The function $T(n)$ could be defined as

$$T(n) = \begin{cases} n & \text{if } n = 1, 2, 4, 8, \ldots, \\ n^2 & \text{otherwise}, \end{cases}$$

in which case the best upper bound that applies to all values of n is $T(n) = O(n^2)$. Because of this sort of drastic consequence, we shall never use asymptotic notation over a limited domain without making it absolutely clear from the context that we are doing so.

4.6.1   The proof for exact powers

The first part of the proof of the master theorem analyzes the recurrence (4.20)

$$T(n) = aT(n/b) + f(n),$$

for the master method, under the assumption that n is an exact power of $b > 1$, where b need not be an integer. We break the analysis into three lemmas. The first reduces the problem of solving the master recurrence to the problem of evaluating an expression that contains a summation. The second determines bounds on this summation. The third lemma puts the first two together to prove a version of the master theorem for the case in which n is an exact power of b.

Lemma 4.2
Let $a \geq 1$ and $b > 1$ be constants, and let $f(n)$ be a nonnegative function defined on exact powers of b. Define $T(n)$ on exact powers of b by the recurrence

$$T(n) = \begin{cases} \Theta(1) & \text{if } n = 1, \\ aT(n/b) + f(n) & \text{if } n = b^i, \end{cases}$$

where i is a positive integer. Then

$$T(n) = \Theta(n^{\log_b a}) + \sum_{j=0}^{\log_b n - 1} a^j f(n/b^j). \tag{4.21}$$

Proof   We use the recursion tree in Figure 4.7. The root of the tree has cost $f(n)$, and it has a children, each with cost $f(n/b)$. (It is convenient to think of a as being

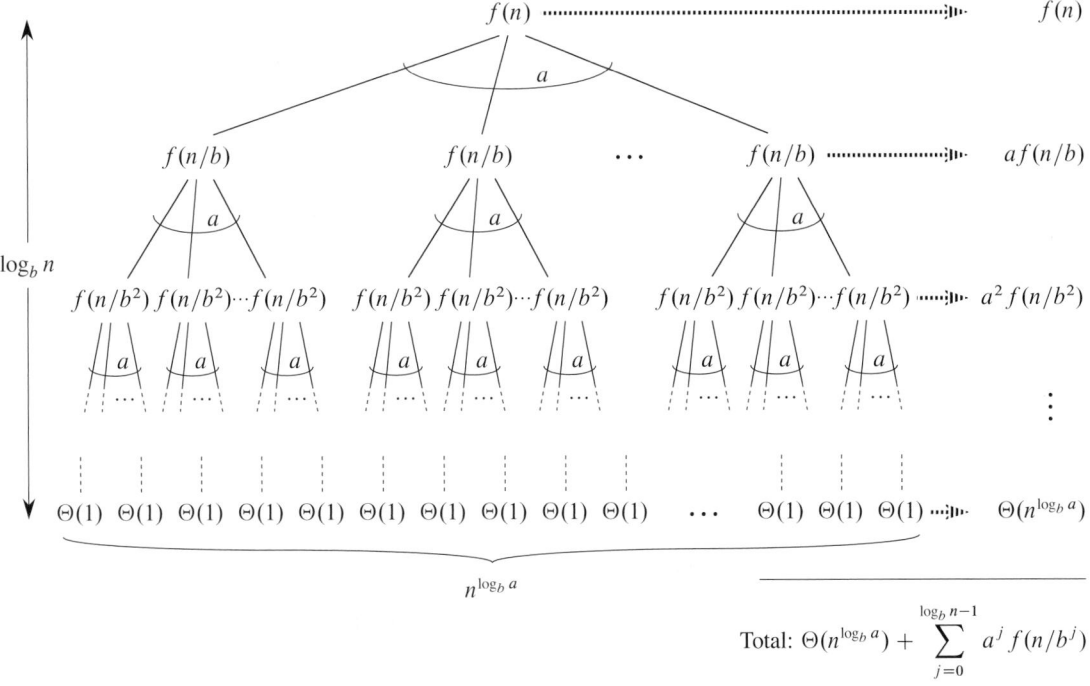

Figure 4.7   The recursion tree generated by $T(n) = aT(n/b) + f(n)$. The tree is a complete a-ary tree with $n^{\log_b a}$ leaves and height $\log_b n$. The cost of the nodes at each depth is shown at the right, and their sum is given in equation (4.21).

an integer, especially when visualizing the recursion tree, but the mathematics does not require it.) Each of these children has a children, making a^2 nodes at depth 2, and each of the a children has cost $f(n/b^2)$. In general, there are a^j nodes at depth j, and each has cost $f(n/b^j)$. The cost of each leaf is $T(1) = \Theta(1)$, and each leaf is at depth $\log_b n$, since $n/b^{\log_b n} = 1$. There are $a^{\log_b n} = n^{\log_b a}$ leaves in the tree.

We can obtain equation (4.21) by summing the costs of the nodes at each depth in the tree, as shown in the figure. The cost for all internal nodes at depth j is $a^j f(n/b^j)$, and so the total cost of all internal nodes is

$$\sum_{j=0}^{\log_b n - 1} a^j f(n/b^j) \, .$$

In the underlying divide-and-conquer algorithm, this sum represents the costs of dividing problems into subproblems and then recombining the subproblems. The

cost of all the leaves, which is the cost of doing all $n^{\log_b a}$ subproblems of size 1, is $\Theta(n^{\log_b a})$. ∎

In terms of the recursion tree, the three cases of the master theorem correspond to cases in which the total cost of the tree is (1) dominated by the costs in the leaves, (2) evenly distributed among the levels of the tree, or (3) dominated by the cost of the root.

The summation in equation (4.21) describes the cost of the dividing and combining steps in the underlying divide-and-conquer algorithm. The next lemma provides asymptotic bounds on the summation's growth.

Lemma 4.3

Let $a \geq 1$ and $b > 1$ be constants, and let $f(n)$ be a nonnegative function defined on exact powers of b. A function $g(n)$ defined over exact powers of b by

$$g(n) = \sum_{j=0}^{\log_b n - 1} a^j f(n/b^j) \tag{4.22}$$

has the following asymptotic bounds for exact powers of b:

1. If $f(n) = O(n^{\log_b a - \epsilon})$ for some constant $\epsilon > 0$, then $g(n) = O(n^{\log_b a})$.

2. If $f(n) = \Theta(n^{\log_b a})$, then $g(n) = \Theta(n^{\log_b a} \lg n)$.

3. If $af(n/b) \leq cf(n)$ for some constant $c < 1$ and for all sufficiently large n, then $g(n) = \Theta(f(n))$.

Proof For case 1, we have $f(n) = O(n^{\log_b a - \epsilon})$, which implies that $f(n/b^j) = O((n/b^j)^{\log_b a - \epsilon})$. Substituting into equation (4.22) yields

$$g(n) = O\left(\sum_{j=0}^{\log_b n - 1} a^j \left(\frac{n}{b^j}\right)^{\log_b a - \epsilon} \right). \tag{4.23}$$

We bound the summation within the O-notation by factoring out terms and simplifying, which leaves an increasing geometric series:

$$\sum_{j=0}^{\log_b n - 1} a^j \left(\frac{n}{b^j}\right)^{\log_b a - \epsilon} = n^{\log_b a - \epsilon} \sum_{j=0}^{\log_b n - 1} \left(\frac{ab^\epsilon}{b^{\log_b a}}\right)^j$$

$$= n^{\log_b a - \epsilon} \sum_{j=0}^{\log_b n - 1} (b^\epsilon)^j$$

$$= n^{\log_b a - \epsilon} \left(\frac{b^{\epsilon \log_b n} - 1}{b^\epsilon - 1}\right)$$

$$= n^{\log_b a - \epsilon} \left(\frac{n^\epsilon - 1}{b^\epsilon - 1} \right) .$$

Since b and ϵ are constants, we can rewrite the last expression as $n^{\log_b a - \epsilon} O(n^\epsilon) = O(n^{\log_b a})$. Substituting this expression for the summation in equation (4.23) yields

$$g(n) = O(n^{\log_b a}) ,$$

thereby proving case 1.

Because case 2 assumes that $f(n) = \Theta(n^{\log_b a})$, we have that $f(n/b^j) = \Theta((n/b^j)^{\log_b a})$. Substituting into equation (4.22) yields

$$g(n) = \Theta \left(\sum_{j=0}^{\log_b n - 1} a^j \left(\frac{n}{b^j} \right)^{\log_b a} \right) . \tag{4.24}$$

We bound the summation within the Θ-notation as in case 1, but this time we do not obtain a geometric series. Instead, we discover that every term of the summation is the same:

$$\sum_{j=0}^{\log_b n - 1} a^j \left(\frac{n}{b^j} \right)^{\log_b a} = n^{\log_b a} \sum_{j=0}^{\log_b n - 1} \left(\frac{a}{b^{\log_b a}} \right)^j$$

$$= n^{\log_b a} \sum_{j=0}^{\log_b n - 1} 1$$

$$= n^{\log_b a} \log_b n .$$

Substituting this expression for the summation in equation (4.24) yields

$$g(n) = \Theta(n^{\log_b a} \log_b n)$$
$$= \Theta(n^{\log_b a} \lg n) ,$$

proving case 2.

We prove case 3 similarly. Since $f(n)$ appears in the definition (4.22) of $g(n)$ and all terms of $g(n)$ are nonnegative, we can conclude that $g(n) = \Omega(f(n))$ for exact powers of b. We assume in the statement of the lemma that $af(n/b) \le cf(n)$ for some constant $c < 1$ and all sufficiently large n. We rewrite this assumption as $f(n/b) \le (c/a)f(n)$ and iterate j times, yielding $f(n/b^j) \le (c/a)^j f(n)$ or, equivalently, $a^j f(n/b^j) \le c^j f(n)$, where we assume that the values we iterate on are sufficiently large. This inequality holds for all but at most a constant number of terms with the smallest such values n/b^j, for which $a^j f(n/b^j) = O(1)$.

Substituting into equation (4.22) and simplifying yields a geometric series, but unlike the series in case 1, this one has decreasing terms. We use an $O(1)$ term to

capture the terms that are not covered by our assumption that n is sufficiently large:

$$
\begin{aligned}
g(n) \;&=\; \sum_{j=0}^{\log_b n - 1} a^j f(n/b^j) \\[2mm]
&\le\; \sum_{j=0}^{\log_b n - 1} c^j f(n) + O(1) \\[2mm]
&\le\; f(n) \sum_{j=0}^{\infty} c^j + O(1) \\[2mm]
&=\; f(n) \left(\frac{1}{1-c} \right) + O(1) \\[2mm]
&=\; O(f(n)),
\end{aligned}
$$

since c is a constant. Thus, we can conclude that $g(n) = \Theta(f(n))$ for exact powers of b. With case 3 proved, the proof of the lemma is complete.   ∎

We can now prove a version of the master theorem for the case in which n is an exact power of b.

Lemma 4.4

Let $a \ge 1$ and $b > 1$ be constants, and let $f(n)$ be a nonnegative function defined on exact powers of b. Define $T(n)$ on exact powers of b by the recurrence

$$
T(n) = \begin{cases} \Theta(1) & \text{if } n = 1, \\ aT(n/b) + f(n) & \text{if } n = b^i, \end{cases}
$$

where i is a positive integer. Then $T(n)$ has the following asymptotic bounds for exact powers of b:

1. If $f(n) = O(n^{\log_b a - \epsilon})$ for some constant $\epsilon > 0$, then $T(n) = \Theta(n^{\log_b a})$.

2. If $f(n) = \Theta(n^{\log_b a})$, then $T(n) = \Theta(n^{\log_b a} \lg n)$.

3. If $f(n) = \Omega(n^{\log_b a + \epsilon})$ for some constant $\epsilon > 0$, and if $af(n/b) \le cf(n)$ for some constant $c < 1$ and all sufficiently large n, then $T(n) = \Theta(f(n))$.

Proof We use the bounds in Lemma 4.3 to evaluate the summation (4.21) from Lemma 4.2. For case 1, we have

$$
\begin{aligned}
T(n) \;&=\; \Theta(n^{\log_b a}) + O(n^{\log_b a}) \\
&=\; \Theta(n^{\log_b a}),
\end{aligned}
$$

and for case 2,

$$
\begin{aligned}
T(n) &= \Theta(n^{\log_b a}) + \Theta(n^{\log_b a} \lg n) \\
&= \Theta(n^{\log_b a} \lg n) \, .
\end{aligned}
$$

For case 3,

$$
\begin{aligned}
T(n) &= \Theta(n^{\log_b a}) + \Theta(f(n)) \\
&= \Theta(f(n)) \, ,
\end{aligned}
$$

because $f(n) = \Omega(n^{\log_b a + \epsilon})$.   ∎

4.6.2   Floors and ceilings

To complete the proof of the master theorem, we must now extend our analysis to the situation in which floors and ceilings appear in the master recurrence, so that the recurrence is defined for all integers, not for just exact powers of b. Obtaining a lower bound on

$$
T(n) = aT(\lceil n/b \rceil) + f(n) \tag{4.25}
$$

and an upper bound on

$$
T(n) = aT(\lfloor n/b \rfloor) + f(n) \tag{4.26}
$$

is routine, since we can push through the bound $\lceil n/b \rceil \geq n/b$ in the first case to yield the desired result, and we can push through the bound $\lfloor n/b \rfloor \leq n/b$ in the second case. We use much the same technique to lower-bound the recurrence (4.26) as to upper-bound the recurrence (4.25), and so we shall present only this latter bound.

We modify the recursion tree of Figure 4.7 to produce the recursion tree in Figure 4.8. As we go down in the recursion tree, we obtain a sequence of recursive invocations on the arguments

n ,

$\lceil n/b \rceil$,

$\lceil \lceil n/b \rceil / b \rceil$,

$\lceil \lceil \lceil n/b \rceil / b \rceil / b \rceil$,

$\vdots$

Let us denote the jth element in the sequence by n_j, where

$$
n_j = \begin{cases} n & \text{if } j = 0 \, , \\ \lceil n_{j-1}/b \rceil & \text{if } j > 0 \, . \end{cases} \tag{4.27}
$$

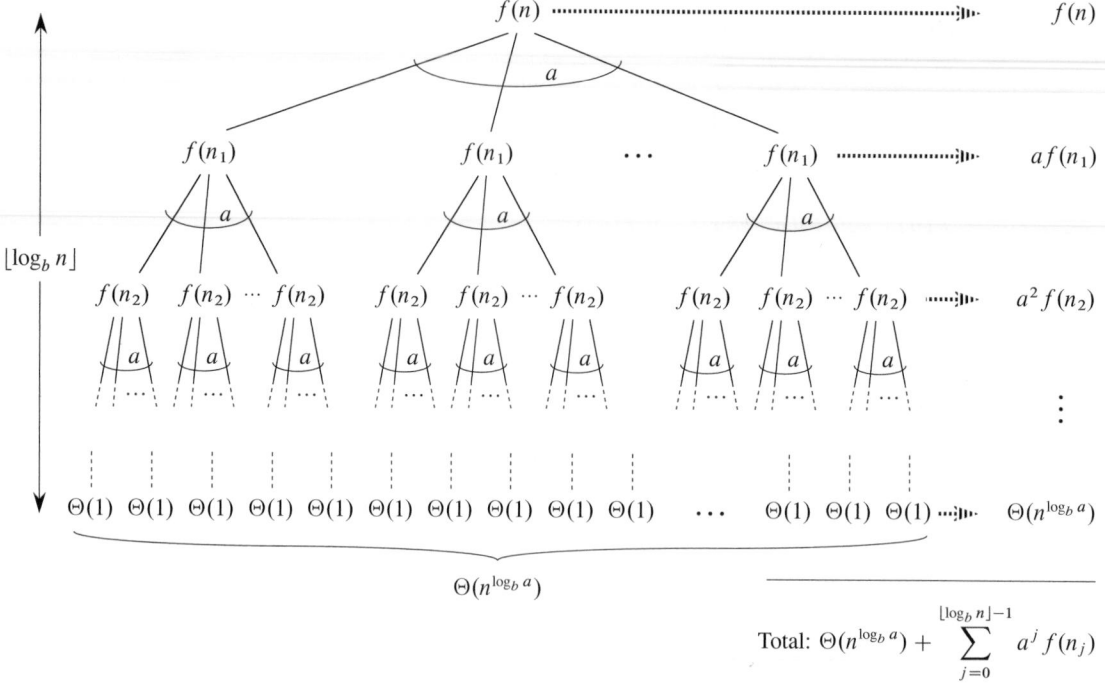

Figure 4.8   The recursion tree generated by $T(n) = aT(\lceil n/b \rceil) + f(n)$. The recursive argument n_j is given by equation (4.27).

Our first goal is to determine the depth k such that n_k is a constant. Using the inequality $\lceil x \rceil \leq x + 1$, we obtain

$$n_0 \leq n \,,$$
$$n_1 \leq \frac{n}{b} + 1 \,,$$
$$n_2 \leq \frac{n}{b^2} + \frac{1}{b} + 1 \,,$$
$$n_3 \leq \frac{n}{b^3} + \frac{1}{b^2} + \frac{1}{b} + 1 \,,$$
$$\vdots$$

In general, we have

$$n_j \leq \frac{n}{b^j} + \sum_{i=0}^{j-1} \frac{1}{b^i}$$

$$< \frac{n}{b^j} + \sum_{i=0}^{\infty} \frac{1}{b^i}$$

$$= \frac{n}{b^j} + \frac{b}{b-1} \; .$$

Letting $j = \lfloor \log_b n \rfloor$, we obtain

$$n_{\lfloor \log_b n \rfloor} < \frac{n}{b^{\lfloor \log_b n \rfloor}} + \frac{b}{b-1}$$

$$< \frac{n}{b^{\log_b n - 1}} + \frac{b}{b-1}$$

$$= \frac{n}{n/b} + \frac{b}{b-1}$$

$$= b + \frac{b}{b-1}$$

$$= O(1) \; ,$$

and thus we see that at depth $\lfloor \log_b n \rfloor$, the problem size is at most a constant.

From Figure 4.8, we see that

$$T(n) = \Theta(n^{\log_b a}) + \sum_{j=0}^{\lfloor \log_b n \rfloor - 1} a^j f(n_j) \; , \tag{4.28}$$

which is much the same as equation (4.21), except that n is an arbitrary integer and not restricted to be an exact power of b.

We can now evaluate the summation

$$g(n) = \sum_{j=0}^{\lfloor \log_b n \rfloor - 1} a^j f(n_j) \tag{4.29}$$

from equation (4.28) in a manner analogous to the proof of Lemma 4.3. Beginning with case 3, if $af(\lceil n/b \rceil) \leq cf(n)$ for $n > b + b/(b-1)$, where $c < 1$ is a constant, then it follows that $a^j f(n_j) \leq c^j f(n)$. Therefore, we can evaluate the sum in equation (4.29) just as in Lemma 4.3. For case 2, we have $f(n) = \Theta(n^{\log_b a})$. If we can show that $f(n_j) = O(n^{\log_b a}/a^j) = O((n/b^j)^{\log_b a})$, then the proof for case 2 of Lemma 4.3 will go through. Observe that $j \leq \lfloor \log_b n \rfloor$ implies $b^j/n \leq 1$. The bound $f(n) = O(n^{\log_b a})$ implies that there exists a constant $c > 0$ such that for all sufficiently large n_j,

$$
\begin{aligned}
f(n_j) \; &\leq \; c\left(\frac{n}{b^j} + \frac{b}{b-1}\right)^{\log_b a} \\
&= \; c\left(\frac{n}{b^j}\left(1 + \frac{b^j}{n}\cdot\frac{b}{b-1}\right)\right)^{\log_b a} \\
&= \; c\left(\frac{n^{\log_b a}}{a^j}\right)\left(1 + \left(\frac{b^j}{n}\cdot\frac{b}{b-1}\right)\right)^{\log_b a} \\
&\leq \; c\left(\frac{n^{\log_b a}}{a^j}\right)\left(1 + \frac{b}{b-1}\right)^{\log_b a} \\
&= \; O\left(\frac{n^{\log_b a}}{a^j}\right) ,
\end{aligned}
$$

since $c(1 + b/(b-1))^{\log_b a}$ is a constant. Thus, we have proved case 2. The proof of case 1 is almost identical. The key is to prove the bound $f(n_j) = O((n/b^j)^{\log_b a - \epsilon})$, which is similar to the corresponding proof of case 2, though the algebra is more intricate.

We have now proved the upper bounds in the master theorem for all integers n. The proof of the lower bounds is similar.

Exercises

4.6-1 ★
Give a simple and exact expression for n_j in equation (4.27) for the case in which b is a positive integer instead of an arbitrary real number.

4.6-2 ★
Show that if $f(n) = \Theta(n^{\log_b a} \lg^k n)$, where $k \geq 0$, then the master recurrence has solution $T(n) = \Theta(n^{\log_b a} \lg^{k+1} n)$. For simplicity, confine your analysis to exact powers of b.

4.6-3 ★
Show that case 3 of the master theorem is overstated, in the sense that the regularity condition $af(n/b) \leq cf(n)$ for some constant $c < 1$ implies that there exists a constant $\epsilon > 0$ such that $f(n) = \Omega(n^{\log_b a + \epsilon})$.

Problems

4-1 Recurrence examples

Give asymptotic upper and lower bounds for $T(n)$ in each of the following recurrences. Assume that $T(n)$ is constant for $n \leq 2$. Make your bounds as tight as possible, and justify your answers.

a. $T(n) = 2T(n/2) + n^4$.

b. $T(n) = T(7n/10) + n$.

c. $T(n) = 16T(n/4) + n^2$.

d. $T(n) = 7T(n/3) + n^2$.

e. $T(n) = 7T(n/2) + n^2$.

f. $T(n) = 2T(n/4) + \sqrt{n}$.

g. $T(n) = T(n - 2) + n^2$.

4-2 Parameter-passing costs

Throughout this book, we assume that parameter passing during procedure calls takes constant time, even if an N-element array is being passed. This assumption is valid in most systems because a pointer to the array is passed, not the array itself. This problem examines the implications of three parameter-passing strategies:

1. An array is passed by pointer. Time $= \Theta(1)$.

2. An array is passed by copying. Time $= \Theta(N)$, where N is the size of the array.

3. An array is passed by copying only the subrange that might be accessed by the called procedure. Time $= \Theta(q - p + 1)$ if the subarray $A[p \mathinner{.\,.} q]$ is passed.

a. Consider the recursive binary search algorithm for finding a number in a sorted array (see Exercise 2.3-5). Give recurrences for the worst-case running times of binary search when arrays are passed using each of the three methods above, and give good upper bounds on the solutions of the recurrences. Let N be the size of the original problem and n be the size of a subproblem.

b. Redo part (a) for the MERGE-SORT algorithm from Section 2.3.1.

4-3   *More recurrence examples*

Give asymptotic upper and lower bounds for $T(n)$ in each of the following recurrences. Assume that $T(n)$ is constant for sufficiently small n. Make your bounds as tight as possible, and justify your answers.

a. $T(n) = 4T(n/3) + n \lg n$.

b. $T(n) = 3T(n/3) + n/\lg n$.

c. $T(n) = 4T(n/2) + n^2 \sqrt{n}$.

d. $T(n) = 3T(n/3 - 2) + n/2$.

e. $T(n) = 2T(n/2) + n/\lg n$.

f. $T(n) = T(n/2) + T(n/4) + T(n/8) + n$.

g. $T(n) = T(n-1) + 1/n$.

h. $T(n) = T(n-1) + \lg n$.

i. $T(n) = T(n-2) + 1/\lg n$.

j. $T(n) = \sqrt{n}\, T(\sqrt{n}) + n$.

4-4   *Fibonacci numbers*

This problem develops properties of the Fibonacci numbers, which are defined by recurrence (3.22). We shall use the technique of generating functions to solve the Fibonacci recurrence. Define the **generating function** (or **formal power series**) $\mathcal{F}$ as

$$
\begin{aligned}
\mathcal{F}(z) &= \sum_{i=0}^{\infty} F_i z^i \\
&= 0 + z + z^2 + 2z^3 + 3z^4 + 5z^5 + 8z^6 + 13z^7 + 21z^8 + \cdots,
\end{aligned}
$$

where F_i is the ith Fibonacci number.

a. Show that $\mathcal{F}(z) = z + z\mathcal{F}(z) + z^2 \mathcal{F}(z)$.

b. Show that

$$
\mathcal{F}(z) = \frac{z}{1 - z - z^2}
$$

$$
= \frac{z}{(1 - \phi z)(1 - \widehat{\phi} z)}
$$

$$
= \frac{1}{\sqrt{5}} \left(\frac{1}{1 - \phi z} - \frac{1}{1 - \widehat{\phi} z} \right),
$$

where

$$
\phi = \frac{1 + \sqrt{5}}{2} = 1.61803\ldots
$$

and

$$
\widehat{\phi} = \frac{1 - \sqrt{5}}{2} = -0.61803\ldots .
$$

c. Show that

$$
\mathcal{F}(z) = \sum_{i=0}^{\infty} \frac{1}{\sqrt{5}} (\phi^i - \widehat{\phi}^i) z^i .
$$

d. Use part (c) to prove that $F_i = \phi^i / \sqrt{5}$ for $i > 0$, rounded to the nearest integer. (*Hint:* Observe that $\left| \widehat{\phi} \right| < 1$.)

4-5 *Chip testing*

Professor Diogenes has n supposedly identical integrated-circuit chips that in principle are capable of testing each other. The professor's test jig accommodates two chips at a time. When the jig is loaded, each chip tests the other and reports whether it is good or bad. A good chip always reports accurately whether the other chip is good or bad, but the professor cannot trust the answer of a bad chip. Thus, the four possible outcomes of a test are as follows:

Chip A says	Chip B says	Conclusion
B is good	A is good	both are good, or both are bad
B is good	A is bad	at least one is bad
B is bad	A is good	at least one is bad
B is bad	A is bad	at least one is bad

a. Show that if at least $n/2$ chips are bad, the professor cannot necessarily determine which chips are good using any strategy based on this kind of pairwise test. Assume that the bad chips can conspire to fool the professor.

b. Consider the problem of finding a single good chip from among n chips, assuming that more than $n/2$ of the chips are good. Show that $\lfloor n/2 \rfloor$ pairwise tests are sufficient to reduce the problem to one of nearly half the size.

c. Show that the good chips can be identified with $\Theta(n)$ pairwise tests, assuming that more than $n/2$ of the chips are good. Give and solve the recurrence that describes the number of tests.

4-6 *Monge arrays*

An $m \times n$ array A of real numbers is a ***Monge array*** if for all i, j, k, and l such that $1 \le i < k \le m$ and $1 \le j < l \le n$, we have

$$A[i, j] + A[k, l] \le A[i, l] + A[k, j].$$

In other words, whenever we pick two rows and two columns of a Monge array and consider the four elements at the intersections of the rows and the columns, the sum of the upper-left and lower-right elements is less than or equal to the sum of the lower-left and upper-right elements. For example, the following array is Monge:

```
10  17  13  28  23
17  22  16  29  23
24  28  22  34  24
11  13   6  17   7
45  44  32  37  23
36  33  19  21   6
75  66  51  53  34
```

a. Prove that an array is Monge if and only if for all $i = 1, 2, ..., m - 1$ and $j = 1, 2, ..., n - 1$, we have

$$A[i, j] + A[i + 1, j + 1] \le A[i, j + 1] + A[i + 1, j].$$

(*Hint:* For the "if" part, use induction separately on rows and columns.)

b. The following array is not Monge. Change one element in order to make it Monge. (*Hint:* Use part (a).)

```
37  23  22  32
21   6   7  10
53  34  30  31
32  13   9   6
43  21  15   8
```

c. Let $f(i)$ be the index of the column containing the leftmost minimum element of row i. Prove that $f(1) \leq f(2) \leq \cdots \leq f(m)$ for any $m \times n$ Monge array.

d. Here is a description of a divide-and-conquer algorithm that computes the leftmost minimum element in each row of an $m \times n$ Monge array A:

> Construct a submatrix A' of A consisting of the even-numbered rows of A. Recursively determine the leftmost minimum for each row of A'. Then compute the leftmost minimum in the odd-numbered rows of A.

Explain how to compute the leftmost minimum in the odd-numbered rows of A (given that the leftmost minimum of the even-numbered rows is known) in $O(m + n)$ time.

e. Write the recurrence describing the running time of the algorithm described in part (d). Show that its solution is $O(m + n \log m)$.

Chapter notes

Divide-and-conquer as a technique for designing algorithms dates back to at least 1962 in an article by Karatsuba and Ofman [194]. It might have been used well before then, however; according to Heideman, Johnson, and Burrus [163], C. F. Gauss devised the first fast Fourier transform algorithm in 1805, and Gauss's formulation breaks the problem into smaller subproblems whose solutions are combined.

The maximum-subarray problem in Section 4.1 is a minor variation on a problem studied by Bentley [43, Chapter 7].

Strassen's algorithm [325] caused much excitement when it was published in 1969. Before then, few imagined the possibility of an algorithm asymptotically faster than the basic SQUARE-MATRIX-MULTIPLY procedure. The asymptotic upper bound for matrix multiplication has been improved since then. The most asymptotically efficient algorithm for multiplying $n \times n$ matrices to date, due to Coppersmith and Winograd [78], has a running time of $O(n^{2.376})$. The best lower bound known is just the obvious $\Omega(n^2)$ bound (obvious because we must fill in n^2 elements of the product matrix).

From a practical point of view, Strassen's algorithm is often not the method of choice for matrix multiplication, for four reasons:

1. The constant factor hidden in the $\Theta(n^{\lg 7})$ running time of Strassen's algorithm is larger than the constant factor in the $\Theta(n^3)$-time SQUARE-MATRIX-MULTIPLY procedure.

2. When the matrices are sparse, methods tailored for sparse matrices are faster.

3. Strassen's algorithm is not quite as numerically stable as SQUARE-MATRIX-MULTIPLY. In other words, because of the limited precision of computer arithmetic on noninteger values, larger errors accumulate in Strassen's algorithm than in SQUARE-MATRIX-MULTIPLY.

4. The submatrices formed at the levels of recursion consume space.

The latter two reasons were mitigated around 1990. Higham [167] demonstrated that the difference in numerical stability had been overemphasized; although Strassen's algorithm is too numerically unstable for some applications, it is within acceptable limits for others. Bailey, Lee, and Simon [32] discuss techniques for reducing the memory requirements for Strassen's algorithm.

In practice, fast matrix-multiplication implementations for dense matrices use Strassen's algorithm for matrix sizes above a "crossover point," and they switch to a simpler method once the subproblem size reduces to below the crossover point. The exact value of the crossover point is highly system dependent. Analyses that count operations but ignore effects from caches and pipelining have produced crossover points as low as $n = 8$ (by Higham [167]) or $n = 12$ (by Huss-Lederman et al. [186]). D'Alberto and Nicolau [81] developed an adaptive scheme, which determines the crossover point by benchmarking when their software package is installed. They found crossover points on various systems ranging from $n = 400$ to $n = 2150$, and they could not find a crossover point on a couple of systems.

Recurrences were studied as early as 1202 by L. Fibonacci, for whom the Fibonacci numbers are named. A. De Moivre introduced the method of generating functions (see Problem 4-4) for solving recurrences. The master method is adapted from Bentley, Haken, and Saxe [44], which provides the extended method justified by Exercise 4.6-2. Knuth [209] and Liu [237] show how to solve linear recurrences using the method of generating functions. Purdom and Brown [287] and Graham, Knuth, and Patashnik [152] contain extended discussions of recurrence solving.

Several researchers, including Akra and Bazzi [13], Roura [299], Verma [346], and Yap [360], have given methods for solving more general divide-and-conquer recurrences than are solved by the master method. We describe the result of Akra and Bazzi here, as modified by Leighton [228]. The Akra-Bazzi method works for recurrences of the form

$$T(x) = \begin{cases} \Theta(1) & \text{if } 1 \leq x \leq x_0 , \\ \sum_{i=1}^{k} a_i T(b_i x) + f(x) & \text{if } x > x_0 , \end{cases} \tag{4.30}$$

where

- $x \geq 1$ is a real number,
- x_0 is a constant such that $x_0 \geq 1/b_i$ and $x_0 \geq 1/(1 - b_i)$ for $i = 1, 2, \ldots, k$,
- a_i is a positive constant for $i = 1, 2, \ldots, k$ and $\sum_{i=1}^{k} a_i \geq 1$,

- b_i is a constant in the range $0 < b_i < 1$ for $i = 1, 2, \ldots, k$,

- $k \geq 1$ is an integer constant, and

- $f(x)$ is a nonnegative function that satisfies the **polynomial-growth condition**: there exist positive constants c_1 and c_2 such that for all $x \geq 1$, for $i = 1, 2, \ldots, k$, and for all u such that $b_i x \leq u \leq x$, we have $c_1 f(x) \leq f(u) \leq c_2 f(x)$. (If $|f'(x)|$ is upper-bounded by some polynomial in x, then $f(x)$ satisfies the polynomial-growth condition. For example, $f(x) = x^\alpha \lg^\beta x$ satisfies this condition for any real constants α and β.)

Although the master method does not apply to a recurrence such as $T(n) = T(\lfloor n/3 \rfloor) + T(\lfloor 2n/3 \rfloor) + O(n)$, the Akra-Bazzi method does. To solve the recurrence (4.30), we first find the unique real number p such that $\sum_{i=1}^{k} a_i b_i^p = 1$. (Such a p always exists.) The solution to the recurrence is then

$$T(x) = \Theta \left(x^p \left(1 + \int_1^x \frac{f(u)}{u^{p+1}} \, du \right) \right) .$$

The Akra-Bazzi method can be somewhat difficult to use, but it serves in solving recurrences that model division of the problem into substantially unequally sized subproblems. The master method is simpler to use, but it applies only when subproblem sizes are equal.

5 Probabilistic Analysis and Randomized Algorithms

This chapter introduces probabilistic analysis and randomized algorithms. If you are unfamiliar with the basics of probability theory, you should read Appendix C, which reviews this material. We shall revisit probabilistic analysis and randomized algorithms several times throughout this book.

5.1 The hiring problem

Suppose that you need to hire a new office assistant. Your previous attempts at hiring have been unsuccessful, and you decide to use an employment agency. The employment agency sends you one candidate each day. You interview that person and then decide either to hire that person or not. You must pay the employment agency a small fee to interview an applicant. To actually hire an applicant is more costly, however, since you must fire your current office assistant and pay a substantial hiring fee to the employment agency. You are committed to having, at all times, the best possible person for the job. Therefore, you decide that, after interviewing each applicant, if that applicant is better qualified than the current office assistant, you will fire the current office assistant and hire the new applicant. You are willing to pay the resulting price of this strategy, but you wish to estimate what that price will be.

The procedure HIRE-ASSISTANT, given below, expresses this strategy for hiring in pseudocode. It assumes that the candidates for the office assistant job are numbered 1 through n. The procedure assumes that you are able to, after interviewing candidate i, determine whether candidate i is the best candidate you have seen so far. To initialize, the procedure creates a dummy candidate, numbered 0, who is less qualified than each of the other candidates.

HIRE-ASSISTANT(n)

```
1   best = 0          // candidate 0 is a least-qualified dummy candidate
2   for i = 1 to n
3       interview candidate i
4       if candidate i is better than candidate best
5           best = i
6           hire candidate i
```

The cost model for this problem differs from the model described in Chapter 2. We focus not on the running time of HIRE-ASSISTANT, but instead on the costs incurred by interviewing and hiring. On the surface, analyzing the cost of this algorithm may seem very different from analyzing the running time of, say, merge sort. The analytical techniques used, however, are identical whether we are analyzing cost or running time. In either case, we are counting the number of times certain basic operations are executed.

Interviewing has a low cost, say c_i, whereas hiring is expensive, costing c_h. Letting m be the number of people hired, the total cost associated with this algorithm is $O(c_i n + c_h m)$. No matter how many people we hire, we always interview n candidates and thus always incur the cost $c_i n$ associated with interviewing. We therefore concentrate on analyzing $c_h m$, the hiring cost. This quantity varies with each run of the algorithm.

This scenario serves as a model for a common computational paradigm. We often need to find the maximum or minimum value in a sequence by examining each element of the sequence and maintaining a current "winner." The hiring problem models how often we update our notion of which element is currently winning.

Worst-case analysis

In the worst case, we actually hire every candidate that we interview. This situation occurs if the candidates come in strictly increasing order of quality, in which case we hire n times, for a total hiring cost of $O(c_h n)$.

Of course, the candidates do not always come in increasing order of quality. In fact, we have no idea about the order in which they arrive, nor do we have any control over this order. Therefore, it is natural to ask what we expect to happen in a typical or average case.

Probabilistic analysis

Probabilistic analysis is the use of probability in the analysis of problems. Most commonly, we use probabilistic analysis to analyze the running time of an algorithm. Sometimes we use it to analyze other quantities, such as the hiring cost

in procedure HIRE-ASSISTANT. In order to perform a probabilistic analysis, we must use knowledge of, or make assumptions about, the distribution of the inputs. Then we analyze our algorithm, computing an average-case running time, where we take the average over the distribution of the possible inputs. Thus we are, in effect, averaging the running time over all possible inputs. When reporting such a running time, we will refer to it as the ***average-case running time***.

We must be very careful in deciding on the distribution of inputs. For some problems, we may reasonably assume something about the set of all possible inputs, and then we can use probabilistic analysis as a technique for designing an efficient algorithm and as a means for gaining insight into a problem. For other problems, we cannot describe a reasonable input distribution, and in these cases we cannot use probabilistic analysis.

For the hiring problem, we can assume that the applicants come in a random order. What does that mean for this problem? We assume that we can compare any two candidates and decide which one is better qualified; that is, there is a total order on the candidates. (See Appendix B for the definition of a total order.) Thus, we can rank each candidate with a unique number from 1 through n, using $rank(i)$ to denote the rank of applicant i, and adopt the convention that a higher rank corresponds to a better qualified applicant. The ordered list $\langle rank(1), rank(2), \ldots, rank(n) \rangle$ is a permutation of the list $\langle 1, 2, \ldots, n \rangle$. Saying that the applicants come in a random order is equivalent to saying that this list of ranks is equally likely to be any one of the $n!$ permutations of the numbers 1 through n. Alternatively, we say that the ranks form a ***uniform random permutation***; that is, each of the possible $n!$ permutations appears with equal probability.

Section 5.2 contains a probabilistic analysis of the hiring problem.

Randomized algorithms

In order to use probabilistic analysis, we need to know something about the distribution of the inputs. In many cases, we know very little about the input distribution. Even if we do know something about the distribution, we may not be able to model this knowledge computationally. Yet we often can use probability and randomness as a tool for algorithm design and analysis, by making the behavior of part of the algorithm random.

In the hiring problem, it may seem as if the candidates are being presented to us in a random order, but we have no way of knowing whether or not they really are. Thus, in order to develop a randomized algorithm for the hiring problem, we must have greater control over the order in which we interview the candidates. We will, therefore, change the model slightly. We say that the employment agency has n candidates, and they send us a list of the candidates in advance. On each day, we choose, randomly, which candidate to interview. Although we know nothing about

the candidates (besides their names), we have made a significant change. Instead of relying on a guess that the candidates come to us in a random order, we have instead gained control of the process and enforced a random order.

More generally, we call an algorithm ***randomized*** if its behavior is determined not only by its input but also by values produced by a ***random-number generator***. We shall assume that we have at our disposal a random-number generator RANDOM. A call to RANDOM(a, b) returns an integer between a and b, inclusive, with each such integer being equally likely. For example, RANDOM($0, 1$) produces 0 with probability $1/2$, and it produces 1 with probability $1/2$. A call to RANDOM($3, 7$) returns either $3, 4, 5, 6$, or 7, each with probability $1/5$. Each integer returned by RANDOM is independent of the integers returned on previous calls. You may imagine RANDOM as rolling a $(b - a + 1)$-sided die to obtain its output. (In practice, most programming environments offer a ***pseudorandom-number generator***: a deterministic algorithm returning numbers that "look" statistically random.)

When analyzing the running time of a randomized algorithm, we take the expectation of the running time over the distribution of values returned by the random number generator. We distinguish these algorithms from those in which the input is random by referring to the running time of a randomized algorithm as an ***expected running time***. In general, we discuss the average-case running time when the probability distribution is over the inputs to the algorithm, and we discuss the expected running time when the algorithm itself makes random choices.

Exercises

5.1-1
Show that the assumption that we are always able to determine which candidate is best, in line 4 of procedure HIRE-ASSISTANT, implies that we know a total order on the ranks of the candidates.

5.1-2 ⋆
Describe an implementation of the procedure RANDOM(a, b) that only makes calls to RANDOM($0, 1$). What is the expected running time of your procedure, as a function of a and b?

5.1-3 ⋆
Suppose that you want to output 0 with probability $1/2$ and 1 with probability $1/2$. At your disposal is a procedure BIASED-RANDOM, that outputs either 0 or 1. It outputs 1 with some probability p and 0 with probability $1 - p$, where $0 < p < 1$, but you do not know what p is. Give an algorithm that uses BIASED-RANDOM as a subroutine, and returns an unbiased answer, returning 0 with probability $1/2$

and 1 with probability $1/2$. What is the expected running time of your algorithm as a function of p?

5.2   Indicator random variables

In order to analyze many algorithms, including the hiring problem, we use indicator random variables. Indicator random variables provide a convenient method for converting between probabilities and expectations. Suppose we are given a sample space S and an event A. Then the *indicator random variable* $I\{A\}$ associated with event A is defined as

$$
I\{A\} = \begin{cases} 1 & \text{if } A \text{ occurs}, \\ 0 & \text{if } A \text{ does not occur} . \end{cases} \tag{5.1}
$$

As a simple example, let us determine the expected number of heads that we obtain when flipping a fair coin. Our sample space is $S = \{H, T\}$, with $\Pr\{H\} = \Pr\{T\} = 1/2$. We can then define an indicator random variable X_H, associated with the coin coming up heads, which is the event H. This variable counts the number of heads obtained in this flip, and it is 1 if the coin comes up heads and 0 otherwise. We write

$$
\begin{aligned}
X_H &= I\{H\} \\
&= \begin{cases} 1 & \text{if } H \text{ occurs}, \\ 0 & \text{if } T \text{ occurs} . \end{cases}
\end{aligned}
$$

The expected number of heads obtained in one flip of the coin is simply the expected value of our indicator variable X_H:

$$
\begin{aligned}
E[X_H] &= E[I\{H\}] \\
&= 1 \cdot \Pr\{H\} + 0 \cdot \Pr\{T\} \\
&= 1 \cdot (1/2) + 0 \cdot (1/2) \\
&= 1/2 .
\end{aligned}
$$

Thus the expected number of heads obtained by one flip of a fair coin is $1/2$. As the following lemma shows, the expected value of an indicator random variable associated with an event A is equal to the probability that A occurs.

Lemma 5.1

Given a sample space S and an event A in the sample space S, let $X_A = I\{A\}$. Then $E[X_A] = \Pr\{A\}$.

Proof   By the definition of an indicator random variable from equation (5.1) and the definition of expected value, we have

$$
\begin{aligned}
\mathrm{E}\left[X_A\right] &= \mathrm{E}\left[\mathrm{I}\{A\}\right] \\
&= 1 \cdot \Pr\{A\} + 0 \cdot \Pr\{\overline{A}\} \\
&= \Pr\{A\} ,
\end{aligned}
$$

where $\overline{A}$ denotes $S - A$, the complement of A.   ∎

Although indicator random variables may seem cumbersome for an application such as counting the expected number of heads on a flip of a single coin, they are useful for analyzing situations in which we perform repeated random trials. For example, indicator random variables give us a simple way to arrive at the result of equation (C.37). In this equation, we compute the number of heads in n coin flips by considering separately the probability of obtaining 0 heads, 1 head, 2 heads, etc. The simpler method proposed in equation (C.38) instead uses indicator random variables implicitly. Making this argument more explicit, we let X_i be the indicator random variable associated with the event in which the ith flip comes up heads: $X_i = \mathrm{I}\{\text{the } i\text{th flip results in the event } H\}$. Let X be the random variable denoting the total number of heads in the n coin flips, so that

$$
X = \sum_{i=1}^{n} X_i .
$$

We wish to compute the expected number of heads, and so we take the expectation of both sides of the above equation to obtain

$$
\mathrm{E}[X] = \mathrm{E}\left[\sum_{i=1}^{n} X_i\right] .
$$

The above equation gives the expectation of the sum of n indicator random variables. By Lemma 5.1, we can easily compute the expectation of each of the random variables. By equation (C.21)—linearity of expectation—it is easy to compute the expectation of the sum: it equals the sum of the expectations of the n random variables. Linearity of expectation makes the use of indicator random variables a powerful analytical technique; it applies even when there is dependence among the random variables. We now can easily compute the expected number of heads:

$$E[X] = E\left[\sum_{i=1}^{n} X_i\right]$$

$$= \sum_{i=1}^{n} E[X_i]$$

$$= \sum_{i=1}^{n} 1/2$$

$$= n/2 .$$

Thus, compared to the method used in equation (C.37), indicator random variables greatly simplify the calculation. We shall use indicator random variables throughout this book.

Analysis of the hiring problem using indicator random variables

Returning to the hiring problem, we now wish to compute the expected number of times that we hire a new office assistant. In order to use a probabilistic analysis, we assume that the candidates arrive in a random order, as discussed in the previous section. (We shall see in Section 5.3 how to remove this assumption.) Let X be the random variable whose value equals the number of times we hire a new office assistant. We could then apply the definition of expected value from equation (C.20) to obtain

$$E[X] = \sum_{x=1}^{n} x \Pr\{X = x\} ,$$

but this calculation would be cumbersome. We shall instead use indicator random variables to greatly simplify the calculation.

To use indicator random variables, instead of computing $E[X]$ by defining one variable associated with the number of times we hire a new office assistant, we define n variables related to whether or not each particular candidate is hired. In particular, we let X_i be the indicator random variable associated with the event in which the ith candidate is hired. Thus,

$$X_i = I\{\text{candidate } i \text{ is hired}\}$$

$$= \begin{cases} 1 & \text{if candidate } i \text{ is hired} , \\ 0 & \text{if candidate } i \text{ is not hired} , \end{cases}$$

and

$$X = X_1 + X_2 + \cdots + X_n . \tag{5.2}$$

By Lemma 5.1, we have that

$$E[X_i] = \Pr\{\text{candidate } i \text{ is hired}\} ,$$

and we must therefore compute the probability that lines 5–6 of HIRE-ASSISTANT are executed.

Candidate i is hired, in line 6, exactly when candidate i is better than each of candidates 1 through $i - 1$. Because we have assumed that the candidates arrive in a random order, the first i candidates have appeared in a random order. Any one of these first i candidates is equally likely to be the best-qualified so far. Candidate i has a probability of $1/i$ of being better qualified than candidates 1 through $i - 1$ and thus a probability of $1/i$ of being hired. By Lemma 5.1, we conclude that

$$E[X_i] = 1/i . \tag{5.3}$$

Now we can compute $E[X]$:

$$
\begin{aligned}
E[X] &= E\left[\sum_{i=1}^{n} X_i\right] && \text{(by equation (5.2))} && \text{(5.4)} \\
&= \sum_{i=1}^{n} E[X_i] && \text{(by linearity of expectation)} \\
&= \sum_{i=1}^{n} 1/i && \text{(by equation (5.3))} \\
&= \ln n + O(1) && \text{(by equation (A.7)) .} && \text{(5.5)}
\end{aligned}
$$

Even though we interview n people, we actually hire only approximately $\ln n$ of them, on average. We summarize this result in the following lemma.

Lemma 5.2

Assuming that the candidates are presented in a random order, algorithm HIRE-ASSISTANT has an average-case total hiring cost of $O(c_h \ln n)$.

Proof The bound follows immediately from our definition of the hiring cost and equation (5.5), which shows that the expected number of hires is approximately $\ln n$. ∎

The average-case hiring cost is a significant improvement over the worst-case hiring cost of $O(c_h n)$.

Exercises

5.2-1

In HIRE-ASSISTANT, assuming that the candidates are presented in a random order, what is the probability that you hire exactly one time? What is the probability that you hire exactly n times?

5.2-2

In HIRE-ASSISTANT, assuming that the candidates are presented in a random order, what is the probability that you hire exactly twice?

5.2-3

Use indicator random variables to compute the expected value of the sum of n dice.

5.2-4

Use indicator random variables to solve the following problem, which is known as the ***hat-check problem***. Each of n customers gives a hat to a hat-check person at a restaurant. The hat-check person gives the hats back to the customers in a random order. What is the expected number of customers who get back their own hat?

5.2-5

Let $A[1..n]$ be an array of n distinct numbers. If $i < j$ and $A[i] > A[j]$, then the pair (i, j) is called an ***inversion*** of A. (See Problem 2-4 for more on inversions.) Suppose that the elements of A form a uniform random permutation of $\langle 1, 2, \ldots, n \rangle$. Use indicator random variables to compute the expected number of inversions.

5.3   Randomized algorithms

In the previous section, we showed how knowing a distribution on the inputs can help us to analyze the average-case behavior of an algorithm. Many times, we do not have such knowledge, thus precluding an average-case analysis. As mentioned in Section 5.1, we may be able to use a randomized algorithm.

For a problem such as the hiring problem, in which it is helpful to assume that all permutations of the input are equally likely, a probabilistic analysis can guide the development of a randomized algorithm. Instead of assuming a distribution of inputs, we impose a distribution. In particular, before running the algorithm, we randomly permute the candidates in order to enforce the property that every permutation is equally likely. Although we have modified the algorithm, we still expect to hire a new office assistant approximately $\ln n$ times. But now we expect

this to be the case for *any* input, rather than for inputs drawn from a particular distribution.

Let us further explore the distinction between probabilistic analysis and randomized algorithms. In Section 5.2, we claimed that, assuming that the candidates arrive in a random order, the expected number of times we hire a new office assistant is about $\ln n$. Note that the algorithm here is deterministic; for any particular input, the number of times a new office assistant is hired is always the same. Furthermore, the number of times we hire a new office assistant differs for different inputs, and it depends on the ranks of the various candidates. Since this number depends only on the ranks of the candidates, we can represent a particular input by listing, in order, the ranks of the candidates, i.e., $\langle rank(1), rank(2), \ldots, rank(n)\rangle$. Given the rank list $A_1 = \langle 1, 2, 3, 4, 5, 6, 7, 8, 9, 10\rangle$, a new office assistant is always hired 10 times, since each successive candidate is better than the previous one, and lines 5–6 are executed in each iteration. Given the list of ranks $A_2 = \langle 10, 9, 8, 7, 6, 5, 4, 3, 2, 1\rangle$, a new office assistant is hired only once, in the first iteration. Given a list of ranks $A_3 = \langle 5, 2, 1, 8, 4, 7, 10, 9, 3, 6\rangle$, a new office assistant is hired three times, upon interviewing the candidates with ranks 5, 8, and 10. Recalling that the cost of our algorithm depends on how many times we hire a new office assistant, we see that there are expensive inputs such as A_1, inexpensive inputs such as A_2, and moderately expensive inputs such as A_3.

Consider, on the other hand, the randomized algorithm that first permutes the candidates and then determines the best candidate. In this case, we randomize in the algorithm, not in the input distribution. Given a particular input, say A_3 above, we cannot say how many times the maximum is updated, because this quantity differs with each run of the algorithm. The first time we run the algorithm on A_3, it may produce the permutation A_1 and perform 10 updates; but the second time we run the algorithm, we may produce the permutation A_2 and perform only one update. The third time we run it, we may perform some other number of updates. Each time we run the algorithm, the execution depends on the random choices made and is likely to differ from the previous execution of the algorithm. For this algorithm and many other randomized algorithms, *no particular input elicits its worst-case behavior*. Even your worst enemy cannot produce a bad input array, since the random permutation makes the input order irrelevant. The randomized algorithm performs badly only if the random-number generator produces an "unlucky" permutation.

For the hiring problem, the only change needed in the code is to randomly permute the array.

RANDOMIZED-HIRE-ASSISTANT(n)

```
1  randomly permute the list of candidates
2  best = 0          // candidate 0 is a least-qualified dummy candidate
3  for i = 1 to n
4      interview candidate i
5      if candidate i is better than candidate best
6          best = i
7          hire candidate i
```

With this simple change, we have created a randomized algorithm whose performance matches that obtained by assuming that the candidates were presented in a random order.

Lemma 5.3

The expected hiring cost of the procedure RANDOMIZED-HIRE-ASSISTANT is $O(c_h \ln n)$.

Proof   After permuting the input array, we have achieved a situation identical to that of the probabilistic analysis of HIRE-ASSISTANT.   ∎

Comparing Lemmas 5.2 and 5.3 highlights the difference between probabilistic analysis and randomized algorithms. In Lemma 5.2, we make an assumption about the input. In Lemma 5.3, we make no such assumption, although randomizing the input takes some additional time. To remain consistent with our terminology, we couched Lemma 5.2 in terms of the average-case hiring cost and Lemma 5.3 in terms of the expected hiring cost. In the remainder of this section, we discuss some issues involved in randomly permuting inputs.

Randomly permuting arrays

Many randomized algorithms randomize the input by permuting the given input array. (There are other ways to use randomization.) Here, we shall discuss two methods for doing so. We assume that we are given an array A which, without loss of generality, contains the elements 1 through n. Our goal is to produce a random permutation of the array.

One common method is to assign each element $A[i]$ of the array a random priority $P[i]$, and then sort the elements of A according to these priorities. For example, if our initial array is $A = \langle 1, 2, 3, 4 \rangle$ and we choose random priorities $P = \langle 36, 3, 62, 19 \rangle$, we would produce an array $B = \langle 2, 4, 1, 3 \rangle$, since the second priority is the smallest, followed by the fourth, then the first, and finally the third. We call this procedure PERMUTE-BY-SORTING:

PERMUTE-BY-SORTING(A)

```
1   n = A.length
2   let P[1 . . n] be a new array
3   for i = 1 to n
4        P[i] = RANDOM(1, n³)
5   sort A, using P as sort keys
```

Line 4 chooses a random number between 1 and n^3. We use a range of 1 to n^3 to make it likely that all the priorities in P are unique. (Exercise 5.3-5 asks you to prove that the probability that all entries are unique is at least $1 - 1/n$, and Exercise 5.3-6 asks how to implement the algorithm even if two or more priorities are identical.) Let us assume that all the priorities are unique.

The time-consuming step in this procedure is the sorting in line 5. As we shall see in Chapter 8, if we use a comparison sort, sorting takes $\Omega(n \lg n)$ time. We can achieve this lower bound, since we have seen that merge sort takes $\Theta(n \lg n)$ time. (We shall see other comparison sorts that take $\Theta(n \lg n)$ time in Part II. Exercise 8.3-4 asks you to solve the very similar problem of sorting numbers in the range 0 to $n^3 - 1$ in $O(n)$ time.) After sorting, if $P[i]$ is the jth smallest priority, then $A[i]$ lies in position j of the output. In this manner we obtain a permutation. It remains to prove that the procedure produces a ***uniform random permutation***, that is, that the procedure is equally likely to produce every permutation of the numbers 1 through n.

Lemma 5.4
Procedure PERMUTE-BY-SORTING produces a uniform random permutation of the input, assuming that all priorities are distinct.

Proof   We start by considering the particular permutation in which each element $A[i]$ receives the ith smallest priority. We shall show that this permutation occurs with probability exactly $1/n!$. For $i = 1, 2, \ldots, n$, let E_i be the event that element $A[i]$ receives the ith smallest priority. Then we wish to compute the probability that for all i, event E_i occurs, which is

$$\Pr\{E_1 \cap E_2 \cap E_3 \cap \cdots \cap E_{n-1} \cap E_n\} \ .$$

Using Exercise C.2-5, this probability is equal to

$$\Pr\{E_1\} \cdot \Pr\{E_2 \mid E_1\} \cdot \Pr\{E_3 \mid E_2 \cap E_1\} \cdot \Pr\{E_4 \mid E_3 \cap E_2 \cap E_1\}$$
$$\cdots \Pr\{E_i \mid E_{i-1} \cap E_{i-2} \cap \cdots \cap E_1\} \cdots \Pr\{E_n \mid E_{n-1} \cap \cdots \cap E_1\} \ .$$

We have that $\Pr\{E_1\} = 1/n$ because it is the probability that one priority chosen randomly out of a set of n is the smallest priority. Next, we observe

that $\Pr\{E_2 \mid E_1\} = 1/(n-1)$ because given that element $A[1]$ has the smallest priority, each of the remaining $n-1$ elements has an equal chance of having the second smallest priority. In general, for $i = 2, 3, \ldots, n$, we have that $\Pr\{E_i \mid E_{i-1} \cap E_{i-2} \cap \cdots \cap E_1\} = 1/(n-i+1)$, since, given that elements $A[1]$ through $A[i-1]$ have the $i-1$ smallest priorities (in order), each of the remaining $n-(i-1)$ elements has an equal chance of having the ith smallest priority. Thus, we have

$$\Pr\{E_1 \cap E_2 \cap E_3 \cap \cdots \cap E_{n-1} \cap E_n\} = \left(\frac{1}{n}\right)\left(\frac{1}{n-1}\right)\cdots\left(\frac{1}{2}\right)\left(\frac{1}{1}\right)$$
$$= \frac{1}{n!},$$

and we have shown that the probability of obtaining the identity permutation is $1/n!$.

We can extend this proof to work for any permutation of priorities. Consider any fixed permutation $\sigma = \langle \sigma(1), \sigma(2), \ldots, \sigma(n) \rangle$ of the set $\{1, 2, \ldots, n\}$. Let us denote by r_i the rank of the priority assigned to element $A[i]$, where the element with the jth smallest priority has rank j. If we define E_i as the event in which element $A[i]$ receives the $\sigma(i)$th smallest priority, or $r_i = \sigma(i)$, the same proof still applies. Therefore, if we calculate the probability of obtaining any particular permutation, the calculation is identical to the one above, so that the probability of obtaining this permutation is also $1/n!$.   ■

You might think that to prove that a permutation is a uniform random permutation, it suffices to show that, for each element $A[i]$, the probability that the element winds up in position j is $1/n$. Exercise 5.3-4 shows that this weaker condition is, in fact, insufficient.

A better method for generating a random permutation is to permute the given array in place. The procedure RANDOMIZE-IN-PLACE does so in $O(n)$ time. In its ith iteration, it chooses the element $A[i]$ randomly from among elements $A[i]$ through $A[n]$. Subsequent to the ith iteration, $A[i]$ is never altered.

RANDOMIZE-IN-PLACE(A)

```
1  n = A.length
2  for i = 1 to n
3      swap A[i] with A[RANDOM(i, n)]
```

We shall use a loop invariant to show that procedure RANDOMIZE-IN-PLACE produces a uniform random permutation. A **k-permutation** on a set of n elements is a sequence containing k of the n elements, with no repetitions. (See Appendix C.) There are $n!/(n-k)!$ such possible k-permutations.

Lemma 5.5
Procedure RANDOMIZE-IN-PLACE computes a uniform random permutation.

Proof We use the following loop invariant:

> Just prior to the ith iteration of the **for** loop of lines 2–3, for each possible $(i - 1)$-permutation of the n elements, the subarray $A[1 . . i - 1]$ contains this $(i - 1)$-permutation with probability $(n - i + 1)!/n!$.

We need to show that this invariant is true prior to the first loop iteration, that each iteration of the loop maintains the invariant, and that the invariant provides a useful property to show correctness when the loop terminates.

Initialization: Consider the situation just before the first loop iteration, so that $i = 1$. The loop invariant says that for each possible 0-permutation, the subarray $A[1 . . 0]$ contains this 0-permutation with probability $(n - i + 1)!/n! = n!/n! = 1$. The subarray $A[1 . . 0]$ is an empty subarray, and a 0-permutation has no elements. Thus, $A[1 . . 0]$ contains any 0-permutation with probability 1, and the loop invariant holds prior to the first iteration.

Maintenance: We assume that just before the ith iteration, each possible $(i - 1)$-permutation appears in the subarray $A[1 . . i - 1]$ with probability $(n - i + 1)!/n!$, and we shall show that after the ith iteration, each possible i-permutation appears in the subarray $A[1 . . i]$ with probability $(n - i)!/n!$. Incrementing i for the next iteration then maintains the loop invariant.

Let us examine the ith iteration. Consider a particular i-permutation, and denote the elements in it by $\langle x_1, x_2, \ldots, x_i \rangle$. This permutation consists of an $(i - 1)$-permutation $\langle x_1, \ldots, x_{i-1} \rangle$ followed by the value x_i that the algorithm places in $A[i]$. Let E_1 denote the event in which the first $i - 1$ iterations have created the particular $(i - 1)$-permutation $\langle x_1, \ldots, x_{i-1} \rangle$ in $A[1 . . i - 1]$. By the loop invariant, $\Pr\{E_1\} = (n - i + 1)!/n!$. Let E_2 be the event that ith iteration puts x_i in position $A[i]$. The i-permutation $\langle x_1, \ldots, x_i \rangle$ appears in $A[1 . . i]$ precisely when both E_1 and E_2 occur, and so we wish to compute $\Pr\{E_2 \cap E_1\}$. Using equation (C.14), we have

$$\Pr\{E_2 \cap E_1\} = \Pr\{E_2 \mid E_1\} \Pr\{E_1\} \ .$$

The probability $\Pr\{E_2 \mid E_1\}$ equals $1/(n - i + 1)$ because in line 3 the algorithm chooses x_i randomly from the $n - i + 1$ values in positions $A[i . . n]$. Thus, we have

$$\begin{aligned}
\Pr\{E_2 \cap E_1\} &= \Pr\{E_2 \mid E_1\}\Pr\{E_1\} \\
&= \frac{1}{n-i+1} \cdot \frac{(n-i+1)!}{n!} \\
&= \frac{(n-i)!}{n!}.
\end{aligned}$$

Termination: At termination, $i = n+1$, and we have that the subarray $A[1 \mathbin{..} n]$ is a given n-permutation with probability $(n-(n+1)+1)!/n! = 0!/n! = 1/n!$.

Thus, RANDOMIZE-IN-PLACE produces a uniform random permutation.   ∎

A randomized algorithm is often the simplest and most efficient way to solve a problem. We shall use randomized algorithms occasionally throughout this book.

Exercises

5.3-1
Professor Marceau objects to the loop invariant used in the proof of Lemma 5.5. He questions whether it is true prior to the first iteration. He reasons that we could just as easily declare that an empty subarray contains no 0-permutations. Therefore, the probability that an empty subarray contains a 0-permutation should be 0, thus invalidating the loop invariant prior to the first iteration. Rewrite the procedure RANDOMIZE-IN-PLACE so that its associated loop invariant applies to a nonempty subarray prior to the first iteration, and modify the proof of Lemma 5.5 for your procedure.

5.3-2
Professor Kelp decides to write a procedure that produces at random any permutation besides the identity permutation. He proposes the following procedure:

PERMUTE-WITHOUT-IDENTITY(A)

```
1   n = A.length
2   for i = 1 to n - 1
3       swap A[i] with A[RANDOM(i + 1, n)]
```

Does this code do what Professor Kelp intends?

5.3-3
Suppose that instead of swapping element $A[i]$ with a random element from the subarray $A[i \mathbin{..} n]$, we swapped it with a random element from anywhere in the array:

PERMUTE-WITH-ALL(A)

1   n = A.length
2   **for** i = 1 **to** n
3   swap A[i] with A[RANDOM(1, n)]

Does this code produce a uniform random permutation? Why or why not?

5.3-4
Professor Armstrong suggests the following procedure for generating a uniform random permutation:

PERMUTE-BY-CYCLIC(A)

1   n = A.length
2   let B[1 .. n] be a new array
3   offset = RANDOM(1, n)
4   **for** i = 1 **to** n
5   dest = i + offset
6   **if** dest > n
7   dest = dest − n
8   B[dest] = A[i]
9   **return** B

Show that each element A[i] has a 1/n probability of winding up in any particular position in B. Then show that Professor Armstrong is mistaken by showing that the resulting permutation is not uniformly random.

5.3-5 ★
Prove that in the array P in procedure PERMUTE-BY-SORTING, the probability that all elements are unique is at least $1 - 1/n$.

5.3-6
Explain how to implement the algorithm PERMUTE-BY-SORTING to handle the case in which two or more priorities are identical. That is, your algorithm should produce a uniform random permutation, even if two or more priorities are identical.

5.3-7
Suppose we want to create a ***random sample*** of the set $\{1, 2, 3, \ldots, n\}$, that is, an m-element subset S, where $0 \le m \le n$, such that each m-subset is equally likely to be created. One way would be to set A[i] = i for i = 1, 2, 3, \ldots, n, call RANDOMIZE-IN-PLACE(A), and then take just the first m array elements. This method would make n calls to the RANDOM procedure. If n is much larger than m, we can create a random sample with fewer calls to RANDOM. Show that

the following recursive procedure returns a random m-subset S of $\{1, 2, 3, \ldots, n\}$, in which each m-subset is equally likely, while making only m calls to RANDOM:

RANDOM-SAMPLE(m, n)

```
1  if m == 0
2      return ∅
3  else S = RANDOM-SAMPLE(m − 1, n − 1)
4      i = RANDOM(1, n)
5      if i ∈ S
6          S = S ∪ {n}
7      else S = S ∪ {i}
8      return S
```

⋆ 5.4   Probabilistic analysis and further uses of indicator random variables

This advanced section further illustrates probabilistic analysis by way of four examples. The first determines the probability that in a room of k people, two of them share the same birthday. The second example examines what happens when we randomly toss balls into bins. The third investigates "streaks" of consecutive heads when we flip coins. The final example analyzes a variant of the hiring problem in which you have to make decisions without actually interviewing all the candidates.

5.4.1   The birthday paradox

Our first example is the **birthday paradox**. How many people must there be in a room before there is a 50% chance that two of them were born on the same day of the year? The answer is surprisingly few. The paradox is that it is in fact far fewer than the number of days in a year, or even half the number of days in a year, as we shall see.

To answer this question, we index the people in the room with the integers $1, 2, \ldots, k$, where k is the number of people in the room. We ignore the issue of leap years and assume that all years have $n = 365$ days. For $i = 1, 2, \ldots, k$, let b_i be the day of the year on which person i's birthday falls, where $1 \leq b_i \leq n$. We also assume that birthdays are uniformly distributed across the n days of the year, so that $\Pr\{b_i = r\} = 1/n$ for $i = 1, 2, \ldots, k$ and $r = 1, 2, \ldots, n$.

The probability that two given people, say i and j, have matching birthdays depends on whether the random selection of birthdays is independent. We assume from now on that birthdays are independent, so that the probability that i's birthday

and j's birthday both fall on day r is

$$
\begin{aligned}
\Pr\{b_i = r \text{ and } b_j = r\} &= \Pr\{b_i = r\}\Pr\{b_j = r\} \\
&= 1/n^2 .
\end{aligned}
$$

Thus, the probability that they both fall on the same day is

$$
\begin{aligned}
\Pr\{b_i = b_j\} &= \sum_{r=1}^{n} \Pr\{b_i = r \text{ and } b_j = r\} \\
&= \sum_{r=1}^{n} (1/n^2) \\
&= 1/n .
\end{aligned}
\tag{5.6}
$$

More intuitively, once b_i is chosen, the probability that b_j is chosen to be the same day is $1/n$. Thus, the probability that i and j have the same birthday is the same as the probability that the birthday of one of them falls on a given day. Notice, however, that this coincidence depends on the assumption that the birthdays are independent.

We can analyze the probability of at least 2 out of k people having matching birthdays by looking at the complementary event. The probability that at least two of the birthdays match is 1 minus the probability that all the birthdays are different. The event that k people have distinct birthdays is

$$
B_k = \bigcap_{i=1}^{k} A_i ,
$$

where A_i is the event that person i's birthday is different from person j's for all $j < i$. Since we can write $B_k = A_k \cap B_{k-1}$, we obtain from equation (C.16) the recurrence

$$
\Pr\{B_k\} = \Pr\{B_{k-1}\}\Pr\{A_k \mid B_{k-1}\} ,
\tag{5.7}
$$

where we take $\Pr\{B_1\} = \Pr\{A_1\} = 1$ as an initial condition. In other words, the probability that $b_1, b_2, \ldots, b_k$ are distinct birthdays is the probability that $b_1, b_2, \ldots, b_{k-1}$ are distinct birthdays times the probability that $b_k \neq b_i$ for $i = 1, 2, \ldots, k - 1$, given that $b_1, b_2, \ldots, b_{k-1}$ are distinct.

If $b_1, b_2, \ldots, b_{k-1}$ are distinct, the conditional probability that $b_k \neq b_i$ for $i = 1, 2, \ldots, k - 1$ is $\Pr\{A_k \mid B_{k-1}\} = (n - k + 1)/n$, since out of the n days, $n - (k - 1)$ days are not taken. We iteratively apply the recurrence (5.7) to obtain

$$
\begin{aligned}
\Pr\{B_k\} &= \Pr\{B_{k-1}\}\Pr\{A_k \mid B_{k-1}\} \\
&= \Pr\{B_{k-2}\}\Pr\{A_{k-1} \mid B_{k-2}\}\Pr\{A_k \mid B_{k-1}\} \\
&\vdots \\
&= \Pr\{B_1\}\Pr\{A_2 \mid B_1\}\Pr\{A_3 \mid B_2\}\cdots\Pr\{A_k \mid B_{k-1}\} \\
&= 1 \cdot \left(\frac{n-1}{n}\right)\left(\frac{n-2}{n}\right)\cdots\left(\frac{n-k+1}{n}\right) \\
&= 1 \cdot \left(1 - \frac{1}{n}\right)\left(1 - \frac{2}{n}\right)\cdots\left(1 - \frac{k-1}{n}\right) .
\end{aligned}
$$

Inequality (3.12), $1 + x \le e^x$, gives us

$$
\begin{aligned}
\Pr\{B_k\} &\le e^{-1/n}e^{-2/n}\cdots e^{-(k-1)/n} \\
&= e^{-\sum_{i=1}^{k-1} i/n} \\
&= e^{-k(k-1)/2n} \\
&\le 1/2
\end{aligned}
$$

when $-k(k-1)/2n \le \ln(1/2)$. The probability that all k birthdays are distinct is at most $1/2$ when $k(k-1) \ge 2n\ln 2$ or, solving the quadratic equation, when $k \ge (1 + \sqrt{1 + (8\ln 2)n})/2$. For $n = 365$, we must have $k \ge 23$. Thus, if at least 23 people are in a room, the probability is at least $1/2$ that at least two people have the same birthday. On Mars, a year is 669 Martian days long; it therefore takes 31 Martians to get the same effect.

An analysis using indicator random variables

We can use indicator random variables to provide a simpler but approximate analysis of the birthday paradox. For each pair (i, j) of the k people in the room, we define the indicator random variable X_{ij}, for $1 \le i < j \le k$, by

$$
\begin{aligned}
X_{ij} &= \mathrm{I}\{\text{person } i \text{ and person } j \text{ have the same birthday}\} \\
&= \begin{cases} 1 & \text{if person } i \text{ and person } j \text{ have the same birthday},\\ 0 & \text{otherwise}. \end{cases}
\end{aligned}
$$

By equation (5.6), the probability that two people have matching birthdays is $1/n$, and thus by Lemma 5.1, we have

$$
\begin{aligned}
\mathrm{E}[X_{ij}] &= \Pr\{\text{person } i \text{ and person } j \text{ have the same birthday}\} \\
&= 1/n .
\end{aligned}
$$

Letting X be the random variable that counts the number of pairs of individuals having the same birthday, we have

$$X = \sum_{i=1}^{k-1} \sum_{j=i+1}^{k} X_{ij} \, .$$

Taking expectations of both sides and applying linearity of expectation, we obtain

$$
\begin{aligned}
\mathrm{E}\,[X] &= \mathrm{E}\left[\sum_{i=1}^{k-1} \sum_{j=i+1}^{k} X_{ij}\right] \\
&= \sum_{i=1}^{k-1} \sum_{j=i+1}^{k} \mathrm{E}\,[X_{ij}] \\
&= \binom{k}{2}\frac{1}{n} \\
&= \frac{k(k-1)}{2n}\, .
\end{aligned}
$$

When $k(k-1) \geq 2n$, therefore, the expected number of pairs of people with the same birthday is at least 1. Thus, if we have at least $\sqrt{2n}+1$ individuals in a room, we can expect at least two to have the same birthday. For $n = 365$, if $k = 28$, the expected number of pairs with the same birthday is $(28 \cdot 27)/(2 \cdot 365) \approx 1.0356$. Thus, with at least 28 people, we expect to find at least one matching pair of birthdays. On Mars, where a year is 669 Martian days long, we need at least 38 Martians.

The first analysis, which used only probabilities, determined the number of people required for the probability to exceed $1/2$ that a matching pair of birthdays exists, and the second analysis, which used indicator random variables, determined the number such that the expected number of matching birthdays is 1. Although the exact numbers of people differ for the two situations, they are the same asymptotically: $\Theta(\sqrt{n})$.

5.4.2   Balls and bins

Consider a process in which we randomly toss identical balls into b bins, numbered $1, 2, \ldots, b$. The tosses are independent, and on each toss the ball is equally likely to end up in any bin. The probability that a tossed ball lands in any given bin is $1/b$. Thus, the ball-tossing process is a sequence of Bernoulli trials (see Appendix C.4) with a probability $1/b$ of success, where success means that the ball falls in the given bin. This model is particularly useful for analyzing hashing (see Chapter 11), and we can answer a variety of interesting questions about the ball-tossing process. (Problem C-1 asks additional questions about balls and bins.)

How many balls fall in a given bin? The number of balls that fall in a given bin follows the binomial distribution $b(k; n, 1/b)$. If we toss n balls, equation (C.37) tells us that the expected number of balls that fall in the given bin is n/b.

How many balls must we toss, on the average, until a given bin contains a ball? The number of tosses until the given bin receives a ball follows the geometric distribution with probability $1/b$ and, by equation (C.32), the expected number of tosses until success is $1/(1/b) = b$.

How many balls must we toss until every bin contains at least one ball? Let us call a toss in which a ball falls into an empty bin a "hit." We want to know the expected number n of tosses required to get b hits.

Using the hits, we can partition the n tosses into stages. The ith stage consists of the tosses after the $(i-1)$st hit until the ith hit. The first stage consists of the first toss, since we are guaranteed to have a hit when all bins are empty. For each toss during the ith stage, $i - 1$ bins contain balls and $b - i + 1$ bins are empty. Thus, for each toss in the ith stage, the probability of obtaining a hit is $(b - i + 1)/b$.

Let n_i denote the number of tosses in the ith stage. Thus, the number of tosses required to get b hits is $n = \sum_{i=1}^{b} n_i$. Each random variable n_i has a geometric distribution with probability of success $(b - i + 1)/b$ and thus, by equation (C.32), we have

$$E[n_i] = \frac{b}{b - i + 1} \, .$$

By linearity of expectation, we have

$$
\begin{aligned}
E[n] &= E\left[\sum_{i=1}^{b} n_i\right] \\
&= \sum_{i=1}^{b} E[n_i] \\
&= \sum_{i=1}^{b} \frac{b}{b - i + 1} \\
&= b \sum_{i=1}^{b} \frac{1}{i} \\
&= b(\ln b + O(1)) \quad \text{(by equation (A.7))} \, .
\end{aligned}
$$

It therefore takes approximately $b \ln b$ tosses before we can expect that every bin has a ball. This problem is also known as the ***coupon collector's problem***, which says that a person trying to collect each of b different coupons expects to acquire approximately $b \ln b$ randomly obtained coupons in order to succeed.

5.4.3   Streaks

Suppose you flip a fair coin n times. What is the longest streak of consecutive heads that you expect to see? The answer is $\Theta(\lg n)$, as the following analysis shows.

We first prove that the expected length of the longest streak of heads is $O(\lg n)$. The probability that each coin flip is a head is $1/2$. Let A_{ik} be the event that a streak of heads of length at least k begins with the ith coin flip or, more precisely, the event that the k consecutive coin flips $i, i + 1, \ldots, i + k - 1$ yield only heads, where $1 \le k \le n$ and $1 \le i \le n-k+1$. Since coin flips are mutually independent, for any given event A_{ik}, the probability that all k flips are heads is

$$\Pr\{A_{ik}\} = 1/2^k \,. \tag{5.8}$$

For $k = 2 \lceil \lg n \rceil$,

$$
\begin{aligned}
\Pr\{A_{i,2\lceil \lg n \rceil}\} &= 1/2^{2\lceil \lg n \rceil} \\
&\le 1/2^{2\lg n} \\
&= 1/n^2 \,,
\end{aligned}
$$

and thus the probability that a streak of heads of length at least $2\lceil \lg n \rceil$ begins in position i is quite small. There are at most $n - 2\lceil \lg n \rceil + 1$ positions where such a streak can begin. The probability that a streak of heads of length at least $2\lceil \lg n \rceil$ begins anywhere is therefore

$$
\begin{aligned}
\Pr\left\{ \bigcup_{i=1}^{n-2\lceil \lg n \rceil+1} A_{i,2\lceil \lg n \rceil} \right\} &\le \sum_{i=1}^{n-2\lceil \lg n \rceil+1} 1/n^2 \\
&< \sum_{i=1}^{n} 1/n^2 \\
&= 1/n \,, \tag{5.9}
\end{aligned}
$$

since by Boole's inequality (C.19), the probability of a union of events is at most the sum of the probabilities of the individual events. (Note that Boole's inequality holds even for events such as these that are not independent.)

We now use inequality (5.9) to bound the length of the longest streak. For $j = 0, 1, 2, \ldots, n$, let L_j be the event that the longest streak of heads has length exactly j, and let L be the length of the longest streak. By the definition of expected value, we have

$$\mathrm{E}[L] = \sum_{j=0}^{n} j \Pr\{L_j\} \,. \tag{5.10}$$

We could try to evaluate this sum using upper bounds on each $\Pr\{L_j\}$ similar to those computed in inequality (5.9). Unfortunately, this method would yield weak bounds. We can use some intuition gained by the above analysis to obtain a good bound, however. Informally, we observe that for no individual term in the summation in equation (5.10) are both the factors j and $\Pr\{L_j\}$ large. Why? When $j \geq 2\lceil \lg n \rceil$, then $\Pr\{L_j\}$ is very small, and when $j < 2\lceil \lg n \rceil$, then j is fairly small. More formally, we note that the events L_j for $j = 0, 1, \ldots, n$ are disjoint, and so the probability that a streak of heads of length at least $2\lceil \lg n \rceil$ begins anywhere is $\sum_{j=2\lceil \lg n \rceil}^{n} \Pr\{L_j\}$. By inequality (5.9), we have $\sum_{j=2\lceil \lg n \rceil}^{n} \Pr\{L_j\} < 1/n$. Also, noting that $\sum_{j=0}^{n} \Pr\{L_j\} = 1$, we have that $\sum_{j=0}^{2\lceil \lg n \rceil - 1} \Pr\{L_j\} \leq 1$. Thus, we obtain

$$
\begin{aligned}
\mathrm{E}[L] &= \sum_{j=0}^{n} j \Pr\{L_j\} \\
&= \sum_{j=0}^{2\lceil \lg n \rceil - 1} j \Pr\{L_j\} + \sum_{j=2\lceil \lg n \rceil}^{n} j \Pr\{L_j\} \\
&< \sum_{j=0}^{2\lceil \lg n \rceil - 1} (2\lceil \lg n \rceil) \Pr\{L_j\} + \sum_{j=2\lceil \lg n \rceil}^{n} n \Pr\{L_j\} \\
&= 2\lceil \lg n \rceil \sum_{j=0}^{2\lceil \lg n \rceil - 1} \Pr\{L_j\} + n \sum_{j=2\lceil \lg n \rceil}^{n} \Pr\{L_j\} \\
&< 2\lceil \lg n \rceil \cdot 1 + n \cdot (1/n) \\
&= O(\lg n) .
\end{aligned}
$$

The probability that a streak of heads exceeds $r\lceil \lg n \rceil$ flips diminishes quickly with r. For $r \geq 1$, the probability that a streak of at least $r\lceil \lg n \rceil$ heads starts in position i is

$$
\begin{aligned}
\Pr\{A_{i, r\lceil \lg n \rceil}\} &= 1/2^{r\lceil \lg n \rceil} \\
&\leq 1/n^r .
\end{aligned}
$$

Thus, the probability is at most $n/n^r = 1/n^{r-1}$ that the longest streak is at least $r\lceil \lg n \rceil$, or equivalently, the probability is at least $1 - 1/n^{r-1}$ that the longest streak has length less than $r\lceil \lg n \rceil$.

As an example, for $n = 1000$ coin flips, the probability of having a streak of at least $2\lceil \lg n \rceil = 20$ heads is at most $1/n = 1/1000$. The chance of having a streak longer than $3\lceil \lg n \rceil = 30$ heads is at most $1/n^2 = 1/1{,}000{,}000$.

We now prove a complementary lower bound: the expected length of the longest streak of heads in n coin flips is $\Omega(\lg n)$. To prove this bound, we look for streaks

of length s by partitioning the n flips into approximately n/s groups of s flips each. If we choose $s = \lfloor (\lg n)/2 \rfloor$, we can show that it is likely that at least one of these groups comes up all heads, and hence it is likely that the longest streak has length at least $s = \Omega(\lg n)$. We then show that the longest streak has expected length $\Omega(\lg n)$.

We partition the n coin flips into at least $\lfloor n/ \lfloor (\lg n)/2 \rfloor \rfloor$ groups of $\lfloor (\lg n)/2 \rfloor$ consecutive flips, and we bound the probability that no group comes up all heads. By equation (5.8), the probability that the group starting in position i comes up all heads is

$$
\begin{aligned}
\Pr\{A_{i,\lfloor (\lg n)/2 \rfloor}\} &= 1/2^{\lfloor (\lg n)/2 \rfloor} \\
&\geq 1/\sqrt{n} .
\end{aligned}
$$

The probability that a streak of heads of length at least $\lfloor (\lg n)/2 \rfloor$ does not begin in position i is therefore at most $1 - 1/\sqrt{n}$. Since the $\lfloor n/ \lfloor (\lg n)/2 \rfloor \rfloor$ groups are formed from mutually exclusive, independent coin flips, the probability that every one of these groups *fails* to be a streak of length $\lfloor (\lg n)/2 \rfloor$ is at most

$$
\begin{aligned}
\left(1 - 1/\sqrt{n}\right)^{\lfloor n/\lfloor (\lg n)/2 \rfloor \rfloor} &\leq \left(1 - 1/\sqrt{n}\right)^{n/\lfloor (\lg n)/2 \rfloor - 1} \\
&\leq \left(1 - 1/\sqrt{n}\right)^{2n/\lg n - 1} \\
&\leq e^{-(2n/\lg n - 1)/\sqrt{n}} \\
&= O(e^{-\lg n}) \\
&= O(1/n) .
\end{aligned}
$$

For this argument, we used inequality (3.12), $1 + x \leq e^x$, and the fact, which you might want to verify, that $(2n/\lg n - 1)/\sqrt{n} \geq \lg n$ for sufficiently large n.

Thus, the probability that the longest streak equals or exceeds $\lfloor (\lg n)/2 \rfloor$ is

$$
\sum_{j=\lfloor (\lg n)/2 \rfloor}^{n} \Pr\{L_j\} \geq 1 - O(1/n) . \tag{5.11}
$$

We can now calculate a lower bound on the expected length of the longest streak, beginning with equation (5.10) and proceeding in a manner similar to our analysis of the upper bound:

$$
\begin{aligned}
\mathrm{E}\,[L] \;&=\; \sum_{j=0}^{n} j\,\Pr\{L_j\} \\[2mm]
&=\; \sum_{j=0}^{\lfloor (\lg n)/2 \rfloor - 1} j\,\Pr\{L_j\} + \sum_{j=\lfloor (\lg n)/2 \rfloor}^{n} j\,\Pr\{L_j\} \\[2mm]
&\geq\; \sum_{j=0}^{\lfloor (\lg n)/2 \rfloor - 1} 0\cdot\Pr\{L_j\} + \sum_{j=\lfloor (\lg n)/2 \rfloor}^{n} \lfloor (\lg n)/2 \rfloor\,\Pr\{L_j\} \\[2mm]
&=\; 0\cdot \sum_{j=0}^{\lfloor (\lg n)/2 \rfloor - 1} \Pr\{L_j\} + \lfloor (\lg n)/2 \rfloor \sum_{j=\lfloor (\lg n)/2 \rfloor}^{n} \Pr\{L_j\} \\[2mm]
&\geq\; 0 + \lfloor (\lg n)/2 \rfloor\,(1 - O(1/n)) \qquad \text{(by inequality (5.11))} \\[2mm]
&=\; \Omega(\lg n)\,.
\end{aligned}
$$

As with the birthday paradox, we can obtain a simpler but approximate analysis using indicator random variables. We let $X_{ik} = \mathrm{I}\{A_{ik}\}$ be the indicator random variable associated with a streak of heads of length at least k beginning with the ith coin flip. To count the total number of such streaks, we define

$$
X = \sum_{i=1}^{n-k+1} X_{ik}\,.
$$

Taking expectations and using linearity of expectation, we have

$$
\begin{aligned}
\mathrm{E}\,[X] \;&=\; \mathrm{E}\left[\sum_{i=1}^{n-k+1} X_{ik}\right] \\[2mm]
&=\; \sum_{i=1}^{n-k+1} \mathrm{E}\,[X_{ik}] \\[2mm]
&=\; \sum_{i=1}^{n-k+1} \Pr\{A_{ik}\} \\[2mm]
&=\; \sum_{i=1}^{n-k+1} 1/2^k \\[2mm]
&=\; \frac{n-k+1}{2^k}\,.
\end{aligned}
$$

By plugging in various values for k, we can calculate the expected number of streaks of length k. If this number is large (much greater than 1), then we expect many streaks of length k to occur and the probability that one occurs is high. If

this number is small (much less than 1), then we expect few streaks of length k to occur and the probability that one occurs is low. If $k = c \lg n$, for some positive constant c, we obtain

$$
\begin{aligned}
E[X] & = \frac{n - c \lg n + 1}{2^{c \lg n}} \\
& = \frac{n - c \lg n + 1}{n^c} \\
& = \frac{1}{n^{c-1}} - \frac{(c \lg n - 1)/n}{n^{c-1}} \\
& = \Theta(1/n^{c-1}) \, .
\end{aligned}
$$

If c is large, the expected number of streaks of length $c \lg n$ is small, and we conclude that they are unlikely to occur. On the other hand, if $c = 1/2$, then we obtain $E[X] = \Theta(1/n^{1/2-1}) = \Theta(n^{1/2})$, and we expect that there are a large number of streaks of length $(1/2) \lg n$. Therefore, one streak of such a length is likely to occur. From these rough estimates alone, we can conclude that the expected length of the longest streak is $\Theta(\lg n)$.

5.4.4 The on-line hiring problem

As a final example, we consider a variant of the hiring problem. Suppose now that we do not wish to interview all the candidates in order to find the best one. We also do not wish to hire and fire as we find better and better applicants. Instead, we are willing to settle for a candidate who is close to the best, in exchange for hiring exactly once. We must obey one company requirement: after each interview we must either immediately offer the position to the applicant or immediately reject the applicant. What is the trade-off between minimizing the amount of interviewing and maximizing the quality of the candidate hired?

We can model this problem in the following way. After meeting an applicant, we are able to give each one a score; let *score*(i) denote the score we give to the ith applicant, and assume that no two applicants receive the same score. After we have seen j applicants, we know which of the j has the highest score, but we do not know whether any of the remaining $n - j$ applicants will receive a higher score. We decide to adopt the strategy of selecting a positive integer $k < n$, interviewing and then rejecting the first k applicants, and hiring the first applicant thereafter who has a higher score than all preceding applicants. If it turns out that the best-qualified applicant was among the first k interviewed, then we hire the nth applicant. We formalize this strategy in the procedure ON-LINE-MAXIMUM(k, n), which returns the index of the candidate we wish to hire.

ON-LINE-MAXIMUM(k, n)

```
1   bestscore = -∞
2   for i = 1 to k
3       if score(i) > bestscore
4           bestscore = score(i)
5   for i = k + 1 to n
6       if score(i) > bestscore
7           return i
8   return n
```

We wish to determine, for each possible value of k, the probability that we hire the most qualified applicant. We then choose the best possible k, and implement the strategy with that value. For the moment, assume that k is fixed. Let $M(j) = \max_{1 \le i \le j} \{score(i)\}$ denote the maximum score among applicants 1 through j. Let S be the event that we succeed in choosing the best-qualified applicant, and let S_i be the event that we succeed when the best-qualified applicant is the ith one interviewed. Since the various S_i are disjoint, we have that $\Pr\{S\} = \sum_{i=1}^{n} \Pr\{S_i\}$. Noting that we never succeed when the best-qualified applicant is one of the first k, we have that $\Pr\{S_i\} = 0$ for $i = 1, 2, \ldots, k$. Thus, we obtain

$$\Pr\{S\} = \sum_{i=k+1}^{n} \Pr\{S_i\} \ . \tag{5.12}$$

We now compute $\Pr\{S_i\}$. In order to succeed when the best-qualified applicant is the ith one, two things must happen. First, the best-qualified applicant must be in position i, an event which we denote by B_i. Second, the algorithm must not select any of the applicants in positions $k + 1$ through $i - 1$, which happens only if, for each j such that $k + 1 \le j \le i - 1$, we find that $score(j) < bestscore$ in line 6. (Because scores are unique, we can ignore the possibility of $score(j) = bestscore$.) In other words, all of the values $score(k + 1)$ through $score(i - 1)$ must be less than $M(k)$; if any are greater than $M(k)$, we instead return the index of the first one that is greater. We use O_i to denote the event that none of the applicants in position $k + 1$ through $i - 1$ are chosen. Fortunately, the two events B_i and O_i are independent. The event O_i depends only on the relative ordering of the values in positions 1 through $i - 1$, whereas B_i depends only on whether the value in position i is greater than the values in all other positions. The ordering of the values in positions 1 through $i - 1$ does not affect whether the value in position i is greater than all of them, and the value in position i does not affect the ordering of the values in positions 1 through $i - 1$. Thus we can apply equation (C.15) to obtain

$$\Pr\{S_i\} = \Pr\{B_i \cap O_i\} = \Pr\{B_i\}\Pr\{O_i\} \ .$$

The probability $\Pr\{B_i\}$ is clearly $1/n$, since the maximum is equally likely to be in any one of the n positions. For event O_i to occur, the maximum value in positions 1 through $i-1$, which is equally likely to be in any of these $i-1$ positions, must be in one of the first k positions. Consequently, $\Pr\{O_i\} = k/(i-1)$ and $\Pr\{S_i\} = k/(n(i-1))$. Using equation (5.12), we have

$$
\begin{aligned}
\Pr\{S\} &= \sum_{i=k+1}^{n} \Pr\{S_i\} \\
&= \sum_{i=k+1}^{n} \frac{k}{n(i-1)} \\
&= \frac{k}{n} \sum_{i=k+1}^{n} \frac{1}{i-1} \\
&= \frac{k}{n} \sum_{i=k}^{n-1} \frac{1}{i} \ .
\end{aligned}
$$

We approximate by integrals to bound this summation from above and below. By the inequalities (A.12), we have

$$\int_{k}^{n} \frac{1}{x}\,dx \le \sum_{i=k}^{n-1} \frac{1}{i} \le \int_{k-1}^{n-1} \frac{1}{x}\,dx \ .$$

Evaluating these definite integrals gives us the bounds

$$\frac{k}{n}(\ln n - \ln k) \le \Pr\{S\} \le \frac{k}{n}(\ln(n-1) - \ln(k-1)) \ ,$$

which provide a rather tight bound for $\Pr\{S\}$. Because we wish to maximize our probability of success, let us focus on choosing the value of k that maximizes the lower bound on $\Pr\{S\}$. (Besides, the lower-bound expression is easier to maximize than the upper-bound expression.) Differentiating the expression $(k/n)(\ln n - \ln k)$ with respect to k, we obtain

$$\frac{1}{n}(\ln n - \ln k - 1) \ .$$

Setting this derivative equal to 0, we see that we maximize the lower bound on the probability when $\ln k = \ln n - 1 = \ln(n/e)$ or, equivalently, when $k = n/e$. Thus, if we implement our strategy with $k = n/e$, we succeed in hiring our best-qualified applicant with probability at least $1/e$.

Exercises

5.4-1

How many people must there be in a room before the probability that someone has the same birthday as you do is at least $1/2$? How many people must there be before the probability that at least two people have a birthday on July 4 is greater than $1/2$?

5.4-2

Suppose that we toss balls into b bins until some bin contains two balls. Each toss is independent, and each ball is equally likely to end up in any bin. What is the expected number of ball tosses?

5.4-3 ★

For the analysis of the birthday paradox, is it important that the birthdays be mutually independent, or is pairwise independence sufficient? Justify your answer.

5.4-4 ★

How many people should be invited to a party in order to make it likely that there are *three* people with the same birthday?

5.4-5 ★

What is the probability that a k-string over a set of size n forms a k-permutation? How does this question relate to the birthday paradox?

5.4-6 ★

Suppose that n balls are tossed into n bins, where each toss is independent and the ball is equally likely to end up in any bin. What is the expected number of empty bins? What is the expected number of bins with exactly one ball?

5.4-7 ★

Sharpen the lower bound on streak length by showing that in n flips of a fair coin, the probability is less than $1/n$ that no streak longer than $\lg n - 2\lg\lg n$ consecutive heads occurs.

Problems

5-1 *Probabilistic counting*

With a b-bit counter, we can ordinarily only count up to $2^b - 1$. With R. Morris's *probabilistic counting*, we can count up to a much larger value at the expense of some loss of precision.

We let a counter value of i represent a count of n_i for $i = 0, 1, \ldots, 2^b - 1$, where the n_i form an increasing sequence of nonnegative values. We assume that the initial value of the counter is 0, representing a count of $n_0 = 0$. The INCREMENT operation works on a counter containing the value i in a probabilistic manner. If $i = 2^b - 1$, then the operation reports an overflow error. Otherwise, the INCREMENT operation increases the counter by 1 with probability $1/(n_{i+1} - n_i)$, and it leaves the counter unchanged with probability $1 - 1/(n_{i+1} - n_i)$.

If we select $n_i = i$ for all $i \geq 0$, then the counter is an ordinary one. More interesting situations arise if we select, say, $n_i = 2^{i-1}$ for $i > 0$ or $n_i = F_i$ (the ith Fibonacci number—see Section 3.2).

For this problem, assume that n_{2^b-1} is large enough that the probability of an overflow error is negligible.

a. Show that the expected value represented by the counter after n INCREMENT operations have been performed is exactly n.

b. The analysis of the variance of the count represented by the counter depends on the sequence of the n_i. Let us consider a simple case: $n_i = 100i$ for all $i \geq 0$. Estimate the variance in the value represented by the register after n INCREMENT operations have been performed.

5-2 *Searching an unsorted array*

This problem examines three algorithms for searching for a value x in an unsorted array A consisting of n elements.

Consider the following randomized strategy: pick a random index i into A. If $A[i] = x$, then we terminate; otherwise, we continue the search by picking a new random index into A. We continue picking random indices into A until we find an index j such that $A[j] = x$ or until we have checked every element of A. Note that we pick from the whole set of indices each time, so that we may examine a given element more than once.

a. Write pseudocode for a procedure RANDOM-SEARCH to implement the strategy above. Be sure that your algorithm terminates when all indices into A have been picked.

b. Suppose that there is exactly one index i such that $A[i] = x$. What is the expected number of indices into A that we must pick before we find x and RANDOM-SEARCH terminates?

c. Generalizing your solution to part (b), suppose that there are $k \geq 1$ indices i such that $A[i] = x$. What is the expected number of indices into A that we must pick before we find x and RANDOM-SEARCH terminates? Your answer should be a function of n and k.

d. Suppose that there are no indices i such that $A[i] = x$. What is the expected number of indices into A that we must pick before we have checked all elements of A and RANDOM-SEARCH terminates?

Now consider a deterministic linear search algorithm, which we refer to as DETERMINISTIC-SEARCH. Specifically, the algorithm searches A for x in order, considering $A[1], A[2], A[3], \ldots, A[n]$ until either it finds $A[i] = x$ or it reaches the end of the array. Assume that all possible permutations of the input array are equally likely.

e. Suppose that there is exactly one index i such that $A[i] = x$. What is the average-case running time of DETERMINISTIC-SEARCH? What is the worst-case running time of DETERMINISTIC-SEARCH?

f. Generalizing your solution to part (e), suppose that there are $k \geq 1$ indices i such that $A[i] = x$. What is the average-case running time of DETERMINISTIC-SEARCH? What is the worst-case running time of DETERMINISTIC-SEARCH? Your answer should be a function of n and k.

g. Suppose that there are no indices i such that $A[i] = x$. What is the average-case running time of DETERMINISTIC-SEARCH? What is the worst-case running time of DETERMINISTIC-SEARCH?

Finally, consider a randomized algorithm SCRAMBLE-SEARCH that works by first randomly permuting the input array and then running the deterministic linear search given above on the resulting permuted array.

h. Letting k be the number of indices i such that $A[i] = x$, give the worst-case and expected running times of SCRAMBLE-SEARCH for the cases in which $k = 0$ and $k = 1$. Generalize your solution to handle the case in which $k \geq 1$.

i. Which of the three searching algorithms would you use? Explain your answer.

Chapter notes

Bollobás [53], Hofri [174], and Spencer [321] contain a wealth of advanced probabilistic techniques. The advantages of randomized algorithms are discussed and surveyed by Karp [200] and Rabin [288]. The textbook by Motwani and Raghavan [262] gives an extensive treatment of randomized algorithms.

Several variants of the hiring problem have been widely studied. These problems are more commonly referred to as "secretary problems." An example of work in this area is the paper by Ajtai, Meggido, and Waarts [11].

II Sorting and Order Statistics

Introduction

This part presents several algorithms that solve the following *sorting problem*:

Input: A sequence of n numbers $\langle a_1, a_2, \ldots, a_n \rangle$.

Output: A permutation (reordering) $\langle a'_1, a'_2, \ldots, a'_n \rangle$ of the input sequence such that $a'_1 \leq a'_2 \leq \cdots \leq a'_n$.

The input sequence is usually an n-element array, although it may be represented in some other fashion, such as a linked list.

The structure of the data

In practice, the numbers to be sorted are rarely isolated values. Each is usually part of a collection of data called a *record*. Each record contains a *key*, which is the value to be sorted. The remainder of the record consists of *satellite data*, which are usually carried around with the key. In practice, when a sorting algorithm permutes the keys, it must permute the satellite data as well. If each record includes a large amount of satellite data, we often permute an array of pointers to the records rather than the records themselves in order to minimize data movement.

In a sense, it is these implementation details that distinguish an algorithm from a full-blown program. A sorting algorithm describes the *method* by which we determine the sorted order, regardless of whether we are sorting individual numbers or large records containing many bytes of satellite data. Thus, when focusing on the problem of sorting, we typically assume that the input consists only of numbers. Translating an algorithm for sorting numbers into a program for sorting records

is conceptually straightforward, although in a given engineering situation other subtleties may make the actual programming task a challenge.

Why sorting?

Many computer scientists consider sorting to be the most fundamental problem in the study of algorithms. There are several reasons:

- Sometimes an application inherently needs to sort information. For example, in order to prepare customer statements, banks need to sort checks by check number.

- Algorithms often use sorting as a key subroutine. For example, a program that renders graphical objects which are layered on top of each other might have to sort the objects according to an "above" relation so that it can draw these objects from bottom to top. We shall see numerous algorithms in this text that use sorting as a subroutine.

- We can draw from among a wide variety of sorting algorithms, and they employ a rich set of techniques. In fact, many important techniques used throughout algorithm design appear in the body of sorting algorithms that have been developed over the years. In this way, sorting is also a problem of historical interest.

- We can prove a nontrivial lower bound for sorting (as we shall do in Chapter 8). Our best upper bounds match the lower bound asymptotically, and so we know that our sorting algorithms are asymptotically optimal. Moreover, we can use the lower bound for sorting to prove lower bounds for certain other problems.

- Many engineering issues come to the fore when implementing sorting algorithms. The fastest sorting program for a particular situation may depend on many factors, such as prior knowledge about the keys and satellite data, the memory hierarchy (caches and virtual memory) of the host computer, and the software environment. Many of these issues are best dealt with at the algorithmic level, rather than by "tweaking" the code.

Sorting algorithms

We introduced two algorithms that sort n real numbers in Chapter 2. Insertion sort takes $\Theta(n^2)$ time in the worst case. Because its inner loops are tight, however, it is a fast in-place sorting algorithm for small input sizes. (Recall that a sorting algorithm sorts **_in place_** if only a constant number of elements of the input array are ever stored outside the array.) Merge sort has a better asymptotic running time, $\Theta(n \lg n)$, but the MERGE procedure it uses does not operate in place.

In this part, we shall introduce two more algorithms that sort arbitrary real numbers. Heapsort, presented in Chapter 6, sorts n numbers in place in $O(n \lg n)$ time. It uses an important data structure, called a heap, with which we can also implement a priority queue.

Quicksort, in Chapter 7, also sorts n numbers in place, but its worst-case running time is $\Theta(n^2)$. Its expected running time is $\Theta(n \lg n)$, however, and it generally outperforms heapsort in practice. Like insertion sort, quicksort has tight code, and so the hidden constant factor in its running time is small. It is a popular algorithm for sorting large input arrays.

Insertion sort, merge sort, heapsort, and quicksort are all comparison sorts: they determine the sorted order of an input array by comparing elements. Chapter 8 begins by introducing the decision-tree model in order to study the performance limitations of comparison sorts. Using this model, we prove a lower bound of $\Omega(n \lg n)$ on the worst-case running time of any comparison sort on n inputs, thus showing that heapsort and merge sort are asymptotically optimal comparison sorts.

Chapter 8 then goes on to show that we can beat this lower bound of $\Omega(n \lg n)$ if we can gather information about the sorted order of the input by means other than comparing elements. The counting sort algorithm, for example, assumes that the input numbers are in the set $\{0, 1, \ldots, k\}$. By using array indexing as a tool for determining relative order, counting sort can sort n numbers in $\Theta(k + n)$ time. Thus, when $k = O(n)$, counting sort runs in time that is linear in the size of the input array. A related algorithm, radix sort, can be used to extend the range of counting sort. If there are n integers to sort, each integer has d digits, and each digit can take on up to k possible values, then radix sort can sort the numbers in $\Theta(d(n + k))$ time. When d is a constant and k is $O(n)$, radix sort runs in linear time. A third algorithm, bucket sort, requires knowledge of the probabilistic distribution of numbers in the input array. It can sort n real numbers uniformly distributed in the half-open interval $[0, 1)$ in average-case $O(n)$ time.

The following table summarizes the running times of the sorting algorithms from Chapters 2 and 6–8. As usual, n denotes the number of items to sort. For counting sort, the items to sort are integers in the set $\{0, 1, \ldots, k\}$. For radix sort, each item is a d-digit number, where each digit takes on k possible values. For bucket sort, we assume that the keys are real numbers uniformly distributed in the half-open interval $[0, 1)$. The rightmost column gives the average-case or expected running time, indicating which it gives when it differs from the worst-case running time. We omit the average-case running time of heapsort because we do not analyze it in this book.

Algorithm	Worst-case running time	Average-case/expected running time
Insertion sort	$\Theta(n^2)$	$\Theta(n^2)$
Merge sort	$\Theta(n \lg n)$	$\Theta(n \lg n)$
Heapsort	$O(n \lg n)$	—
Quicksort	$\Theta(n^2)$	$\Theta(n \lg n)$ (expected)
Counting sort	$\Theta(k + n)$	$\Theta(k + n)$
Radix sort	$\Theta(d(n + k))$	$\Theta(d(n + k))$
Bucket sort	$\Theta(n^2)$	$\Theta(n)$ (average-case)

Order statistics

The ith order statistic of a set of n numbers is the ith smallest number in the set. We can, of course, select the ith order statistic by sorting the input and indexing the ith element of the output. With no assumptions about the input distribution, this method runs in $\Omega(n \lg n)$ time, as the lower bound proved in Chapter 8 shows.

In Chapter 9, we show that we can find the ith smallest element in $O(n)$ time, even when the elements are arbitrary real numbers. We present a randomized algorithm with tight pseudocode that runs in $\Theta(n^2)$ time in the worst case, but whose expected running time is $O(n)$. We also give a more complicated algorithm that runs in $O(n)$ worst-case time.

Background

Although most of this part does not rely on difficult mathematics, some sections do require mathematical sophistication. In particular, analyses of quicksort, bucket sort, and the order-statistic algorithm use probability, which is reviewed in Appendix C, and the material on probabilistic analysis and randomized algorithms in Chapter 5. The analysis of the worst-case linear-time algorithm for order statistics involves somewhat more sophisticated mathematics than the other worst-case analyses in this part.

6   Heapsort

In this chapter, we introduce another sorting algorithm: heapsort. Like merge sort, but unlike insertion sort, heapsort's running time is $O(n \lg n)$. Like insertion sort, but unlike merge sort, heapsort sorts in place: only a constant number of array elements are stored outside the input array at any time. Thus, heapsort combines the better attributes of the two sorting algorithms we have already discussed.

Heapsort also introduces another algorithm design technique: using a data structure, in this case one we call a "heap," to manage information. Not only is the heap data structure useful for heapsort, but it also makes an efficient priority queue. The heap data structure will reappear in algorithms in later chapters.

The term "heap" was originally coined in the context of heapsort, but it has since come to refer to "garbage-collected storage," such as the programming languages Java and Lisp provide. Our heap data structure is *not* garbage-collected storage, and whenever we refer to heaps in this book, we shall mean a data structure rather than an aspect of garbage collection.

6.1   Heaps

The *(binary) heap* data structure is an array object that we can view as a nearly complete binary tree (see Section B.5.3), as shown in Figure 6.1. Each node of the tree corresponds to an element of the array. The tree is completely filled on all levels except possibly the lowest, which is filled from the left up to a point. An array A that represents a heap is an object with two attributes: $A.length$, which (as usual) gives the number of elements in the array, and $A.heap\text{-}size$, which represents how many elements in the heap are stored within array A. That is, although $A[1 .. A.length]$ may contain numbers, only the elements in $A[1 .. A.heap\text{-}size]$, where $0 \leq A.heap\text{-}size \leq A.length$, are valid elements of the heap. The root of the tree is $A[1]$, and given the index i of a node, we can easily compute the indices of its parent, left child, and right child:

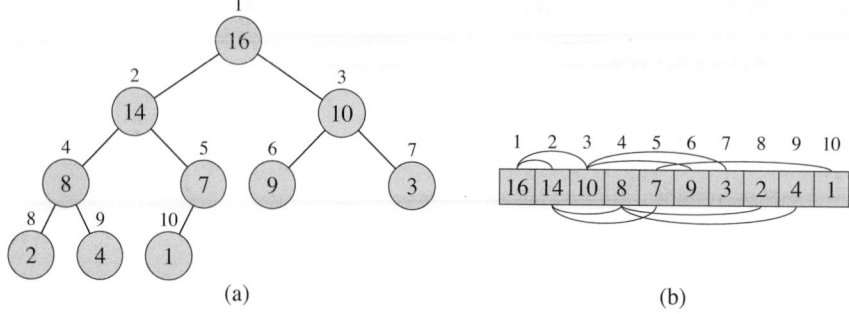

Figure 6.1 A max-heap viewed as **(a)** a binary tree and **(b)** an array. The number within the circle at each node in the tree is the value stored at that node. The number above a node is the corresponding index in the array. Above and below the array are lines showing parent-child relationships; parents are always to the left of their children. The tree has height three; the node at index 4 (with value 8) has height one.

PARENT(i)

1   **return** $\lfloor i/2 \rfloor$

LEFT(i)

1   **return** $2i$

RIGHT(i)

1   **return** $2i + 1$

On most computers, the LEFT procedure can compute $2i$ in one instruction by simply shifting the binary representation of i left by one bit position. Similarly, the RIGHT procedure can quickly compute $2i + 1$ by shifting the binary representation of i left by one bit position and then adding in a 1 as the low-order bit. The PARENT procedure can compute $\lfloor i/2 \rfloor$ by shifting i right one bit position. Good implementations of heapsort often implement these procedures as "macros" or "in-line" procedures.

There are two kinds of binary heaps: max-heaps and min-heaps. In both kinds, the values in the nodes satisfy a **heap property**, the specifics of which depend on the kind of heap. In a **max-heap**, the **max-heap property** is that for every node i other than the root,

$$A[\text{PARENT}(i)] \geq A[i] \,,$$

that is, the value of a node is at most the value of its parent. Thus, the largest element in a max-heap is stored at the root, and the subtree rooted at a node contains

values no larger than that contained at the node itself. A **_min-heap_** is organized in the opposite way; the **_min-heap property_** is that for every node i other than the root,

$$A[\text{PARENT}(i)] \leq A[i] \, .$$

The smallest element in a min-heap is at the root.

For the heapsort algorithm, we use max-heaps. Min-heaps commonly implement priority queues, which we discuss in Section 6.5. We shall be precise in specifying whether we need a max-heap or a min-heap for any particular application, and when properties apply to either max-heaps or min-heaps, we just use the term "heap."

Viewing a heap as a tree, we define the **_height_** of a node in a heap to be the number of edges on the longest simple downward path from the node to a leaf, and we define the height of the heap to be the height of its root. Since a heap of n elements is based on a complete binary tree, its height is $\Theta(\lg n)$ (see Exercise 6.1-2). We shall see that the basic operations on heaps run in time at most proportional to the height of the tree and thus take $O(\lg n)$ time. The remainder of this chapter presents some basic procedures and shows how they are used in a sorting algorithm and a priority-queue data structure.

- The MAX-HEAPIFY procedure, which runs in $O(\lg n)$ time, is the key to maintaining the max-heap property.

- The BUILD-MAX-HEAP procedure, which runs in linear time, produces a max-heap from an unordered input array.

- The HEAPSORT procedure, which runs in $O(n \lg n)$ time, sorts an array in place.

- The MAX-HEAP-INSERT, HEAP-EXTRACT-MAX, HEAP-INCREASE-KEY, and HEAP-MAXIMUM procedures, which run in $O(\lg n)$ time, allow the heap data structure to implement a priority queue.

Exercises

6.1-1
What are the minimum and maximum numbers of elements in a heap of height h?

6.1-2
Show that an n-element heap has height $\lfloor \lg n \rfloor$.

6.1-3
Show that in any subtree of a max-heap, the root of the subtree contains the largest value occurring anywhere in that subtree.

6.1-4

Where in a max-heap might the smallest element reside, assuming that all elements are distinct?

6.1-5

Is an array that is in sorted order a min-heap?

6.1-6

Is the array with values $\langle 23, 17, 14, 6, 13, 10, 1, 5, 7, 12 \rangle$ a max-heap?

6.1-7

Show that, with the array representation for storing an n-element heap, the leaves are the nodes indexed by $\lfloor n/2 \rfloor + 1, \lfloor n/2 \rfloor + 2, \ldots, n$.

6.2   Maintaining the heap property

In order to maintain the max-heap property, we call the procedure MAX-HEAPIFY. Its inputs are an array A and an index i into the array. When it is called, MAX-HEAPIFY assumes that the binary trees rooted at LEFT(i) and RIGHT(i) are max-heaps, but that $A[i]$ might be smaller than its children, thus violating the max-heap property. MAX-HEAPIFY lets the value at $A[i]$ "float down" in the max-heap so that the subtree rooted at index i obeys the max-heap property.

MAX-HEAPIFY(A, i)

```
1   l = LEFT(i)
2   r = RIGHT(i)
3   if l ≤ A.heap-size and A[l] > A[i]
4       largest = l
5   else largest = i
6   if r ≤ A.heap-size and A[r] > A[largest]
7       largest = r
8   if largest ≠ i
9       exchange A[i] with A[largest]
10      MAX-HEAPIFY(A, largest)
```

Figure 6.2 illustrates the action of MAX-HEAPIFY. At each step, the largest of the elements $A[i]$, $A[\text{LEFT}(i)]$, and $A[\text{RIGHT}(i)]$ is determined, and its index is stored in *largest*. If $A[i]$ is largest, then the subtree rooted at node i is already a max-heap and the procedure terminates. Otherwise, one of the two children has the largest element, and $A[i]$ is swapped with $A[largest]$, which causes node i and its

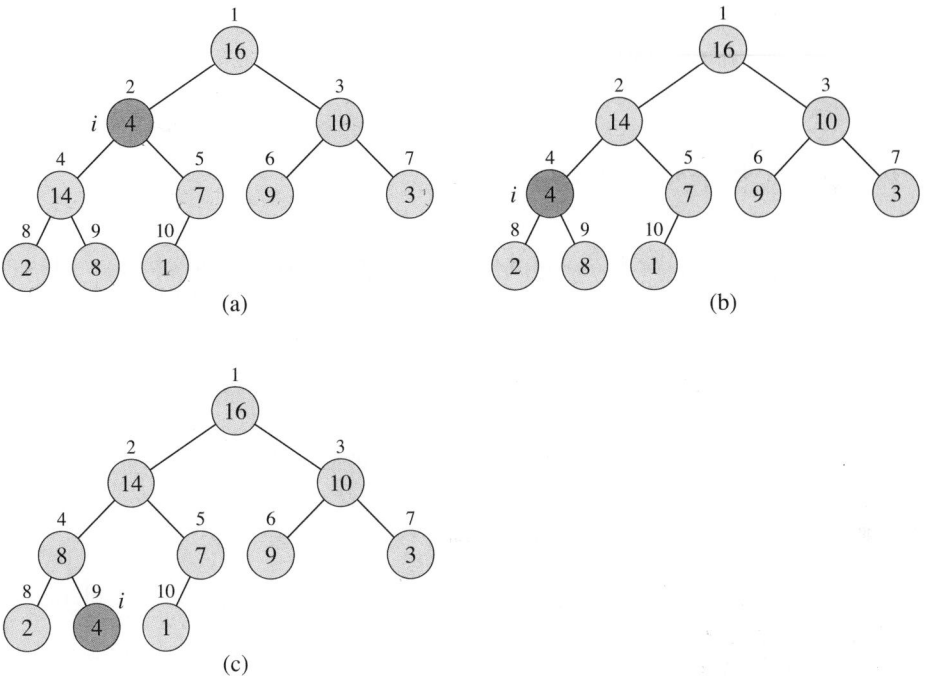

Figure 6.2 The action of MAX-HEAPIFY($A, 2$), where $A.heap\text{-}size = 10$. **(a)** The initial configuration, with $A[2]$ at node $i = 2$ violating the max-heap property since it is not larger than both children. The max-heap property is restored for node 2 in **(b)** by exchanging $A[2]$ with $A[4]$, which destroys the max-heap property for node 4. The recursive call MAX-HEAPIFY($A, 4$) now has $i = 4$. After swapping $A[4]$ with $A[9]$, as shown in **(c)**, node 4 is fixed up, and the recursive call MAX-HEAPIFY($A, 9$) yields no further change to the data structure.

children to satisfy the max-heap property. The node indexed by *largest*, however, now has the original value $A[i]$, and thus the subtree rooted at *largest* might violate the max-heap property. Consequently, we call MAX-HEAPIFY recursively on that subtree.

The running time of MAX-HEAPIFY on a subtree of size n rooted at a given node i is the $\Theta(1)$ time to fix up the relationships among the elements $A[i]$, $A[\text{LEFT}(i)]$, and $A[\text{RIGHT}(i)]$, plus the time to run MAX-HEAPIFY on a subtree rooted at one of the children of node i (assuming that the recursive call occurs). The children's subtrees each have size at most $2n/3$—the worst case occurs when the bottom level of the tree is exactly half full—and therefore we can describe the running time of MAX-HEAPIFY by the recurrence

$$T(n) \leq T(2n/3) + \Theta(1) .$$

The solution to this recurrence, by case 2 of the master theorem (Theorem 4.1), is $T(n) = O(\lg n)$. Alternatively, we can characterize the running time of MAX-HEAPIFY on a node of height h as $O(h)$.

Exercises

6.2-1
Using Figure 6.2 as a model, illustrate the operation of MAX-HEAPIFY$(A, 3)$ on the array $A = \langle 27, 17, 3, 16, 13, 10, 1, 5, 7, 12, 4, 8, 9, 0 \rangle$.

6.2-2
Starting with the procedure MAX-HEAPIFY, write pseudocode for the procedure MIN-HEAPIFY(A, i), which performs the corresponding manipulation on a min-heap. How does the running time of MIN-HEAPIFY compare to that of MAX-HEAPIFY?

6.2-3
What is the effect of calling MAX-HEAPIFY(A, i) when the element $A[i]$ is larger than its children?

6.2-4
What is the effect of calling MAX-HEAPIFY(A, i) for $i > A.heap\text{-}size/2$?

6.2-5
The code for MAX-HEAPIFY is quite efficient in terms of constant factors, except possibly for the recursive call in line 10, which might cause some compilers to produce inefficient code. Write an efficient MAX-HEAPIFY that uses an iterative control construct (a loop) instead of recursion.

6.2-6
Show that the worst-case running time of MAX-HEAPIFY on a heap of size n is $\Omega(\lg n)$. (*Hint:* For a heap with n nodes, give node values that cause MAX-HEAPIFY to be called recursively at every node on a simple path from the root down to a leaf.)

6.3   Building a heap

We can use the procedure MAX-HEAPIFY in a bottom-up manner to convert an array $A[1..n]$, where $n = A.length$, into a max-heap. By Exercise 6.1-7, the elements in the subarray $A[(\lfloor n/2 \rfloor + 1)..n]$ are all leaves of the tree, and so each is

a 1-element heap to begin with. The procedure BUILD-MAX-HEAP goes through the remaining nodes of the tree and runs MAX-HEAPIFY on each one.

BUILD-MAX-HEAP(A)

1   $A.heap\text{-}size = A.length$
2   **for** $i = \lfloor A.length/2 \rfloor$ **downto** 1
3   MAX-HEAPIFY(A, i)

Figure 6.3 shows an example of the action of BUILD-MAX-HEAP.

To show why BUILD-MAX-HEAP works correctly, we use the following loop invariant:

At the start of each iteration of the **for** loop of lines 2–3, each node $i + 1$, $i + 2, \ldots, n$ is the root of a max-heap.

We need to show that this invariant is true prior to the first loop iteration, that each iteration of the loop maintains the invariant, and that the invariant provides a useful property to show correctness when the loop terminates.

Initialization: Prior to the first iteration of the loop, $i = \lfloor n/2 \rfloor$. Each node $\lfloor n/2 \rfloor + 1, \lfloor n/2 \rfloor + 2, \ldots, n$ is a leaf and is thus the root of a trivial max-heap.

Maintenance: To see that each iteration maintains the loop invariant, observe that the children of node i are numbered higher than i. By the loop invariant, therefore, they are both roots of max-heaps. This is precisely the condition required for the call MAX-HEAPIFY(A, i) to make node i a max-heap root. Moreover, the MAX-HEAPIFY call preserves the property that nodes $i + 1, i + 2, \ldots, n$ are all roots of max-heaps. Decrementing i in the **for** loop update reestablishes the loop invariant for the next iteration.

Termination: At termination, $i = 0$. By the loop invariant, each node $1, 2, \ldots, n$ is the root of a max-heap. In particular, node 1 is.

We can compute a simple upper bound on the running time of BUILD-MAX-HEAP as follows. Each call to MAX-HEAPIFY costs $O(\lg n)$ time, and BUILD-MAX-HEAP makes $O(n)$ such calls. Thus, the running time is $O(n \lg n)$. This upper bound, though correct, is not asymptotically tight.

We can derive a tighter bound by observing that the time for MAX-HEAPIFY to run at a node varies with the height of the node in the tree, and the heights of most nodes are small. Our tighter analysis relies on the properties that an n-element heap has height $\lfloor \lg n \rfloor$ (see Exercise 6.1-2) and at most $\lceil n/2^{h+1} \rceil$ nodes of any height h (see Exercise 6.3-3).

The time required by MAX-HEAPIFY when called on a node of height h is $O(h)$, and so we can express the total cost of BUILD-MAX-HEAP as being bounded from above by

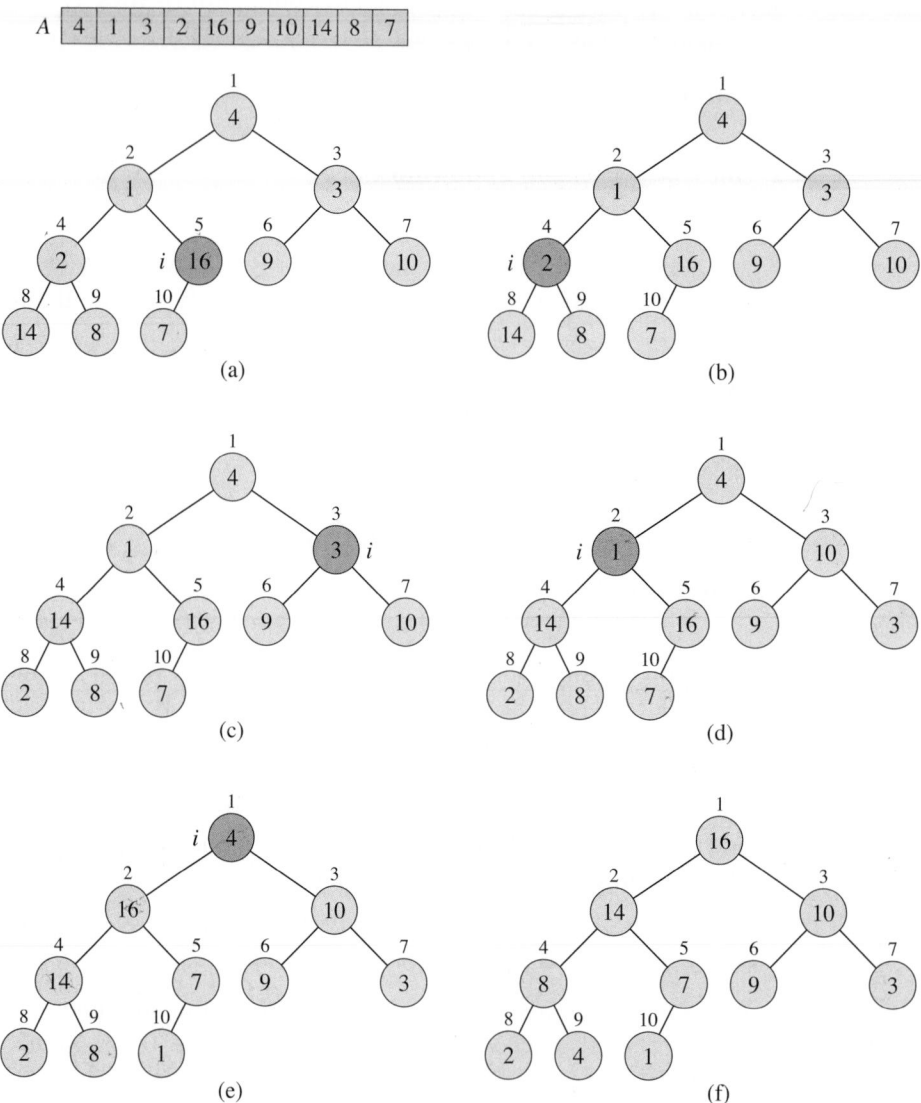

Figure 6.3 The operation of Build-Max-Heap, showing the data structure before the call to Max-Heapify in line 3 of Build-Max-Heap. **(a)** A 10-element input array A and the binary tree it represents. The figure shows that the loop index i refers to node 5 before the call Max-Heapify(A, i). **(b)** The data structure that results. The loop index i for the next iteration refers to node 4. **(c)–(e)** Subsequent iterations of the **for** loop in Build-Max-Heap. Observe that whenever Max-Heapify is called on a node, the two subtrees of that node are both max-heaps. **(f)** The max-heap after Build-Max-Heap finishes.

$$\sum_{h=0}^{\lfloor \lg n \rfloor} \left\lceil \frac{n}{2^{h+1}} \right\rceil O(h) = O \left(n \sum_{h=0}^{\lfloor \lg n \rfloor} \frac{h}{2^h} \right) .$$

We evaluate the last summation by substituting $x = 1/2$ in the formula (A.8), yielding

$$\sum_{h=0}^{\infty} \frac{h}{2^h} = \frac{1/2}{(1 - 1/2)^2}$$
$$= 2 .$$

Thus, we can bound the running time of BUILD-MAX-HEAP as

$$O \left(n \sum_{h=0}^{\lfloor \lg n \rfloor} \frac{h}{2^h} \right) = O \left(n \sum_{h=0}^{\infty} \frac{h}{2^h} \right)$$
$$= O(n) .$$

Hence, we can build a max-heap from an unordered array in linear time.

We can build a min-heap by the procedure BUILD-MIN-HEAP, which is the same as BUILD-MAX-HEAP but with the call to MAX-HEAPIFY in line 3 replaced by a call to MIN-HEAPIFY (see Exercise 6.2-2). BUILD-MIN-HEAP produces a min-heap from an unordered linear array in linear time.

Exercises

6.3-1
Using Figure 6.3 as a model, illustrate the operation of BUILD-MAX-HEAP on the array $A = \langle 5, 3, 17, 10, 84, 19, 6, 22, 9 \rangle$.

6.3-2
Why do we want the loop index i in line 2 of BUILD-MAX-HEAP to decrease from $\lfloor A.length/2 \rfloor$ to 1 rather than increase from 1 to $\lfloor A.length/2 \rfloor$?

6.3-3
Show that there are at most $\lceil n/2^{h+1} \rceil$ nodes of height h in any n-element heap.

6.4   The heapsort algorithm

The heapsort algorithm starts by using BUILD-MAX-HEAP to build a max-heap on the input array $A[1 .. n]$, where $n = A.length$. Since the maximum element of the array is stored at the root $A[1]$, we can put it into its correct final position

by exchanging it with $A[n]$. If we now discard node n from the heap—and we can do so by simply decrementing $A.heap\text{-}size$—we observe that the children of the root remain max-heaps, but the new root element might violate the max-heap property. All we need to do to restore the max-heap property, however, is call MAX-HEAPIFY$(A, 1)$, which leaves a max-heap in $A[1 .. n - 1]$. The heapsort algorithm then repeats this process for the max-heap of size $n - 1$ down to a heap of size 2. (See Exercise 6.4-2 for a precise loop invariant.)

HEAPSORT(A)

1   BUILD-MAX-HEAP(A)
2   **for** $i = A.length$ **downto** 2
3   exchange $A[1]$ with $A[i]$
4       $A.heap\text{-}size = A.heap\text{-}size - 1$
5   MAX-HEAPIFY$(A, 1)$

Figure 6.4 shows an example of the operation of HEAPSORT after line 1 has built the initial max-heap. The figure shows the max-heap before the first iteration of the **for** loop of lines 2–5 and after each iteration.

The HEAPSORT procedure takes time $O(n \lg n)$, since the call to BUILD-MAX-HEAP takes time $O(n)$ and each of the $n - 1$ calls to MAX-HEAPIFY takes time $O(\lg n)$.

Exercises

6.4-1
Using Figure 6.4 as a model, illustrate the operation of HEAPSORT on the array $A = \langle 5, 13, 2, 25, 7, 17, 20, 8, 4 \rangle$.

6.4-2
Argue the correctness of HEAPSORT using the following loop invariant:

> At the start of each iteration of the **for** loop of lines 2–5, the subarray $A[1 .. i]$ is a max-heap containing the i smallest elements of $A[1 .. n]$, and the subarray $A[i + 1 .. n]$ contains the $n - i$ largest elements of $A[1 .. n]$, sorted.

6.4-3
What is the running time of HEAPSORT on an array A of length n that is already sorted in increasing order? What about decreasing order?

6.4-4
Show that the worst-case running time of HEAPSORT is $\Omega(n \lg n)$.

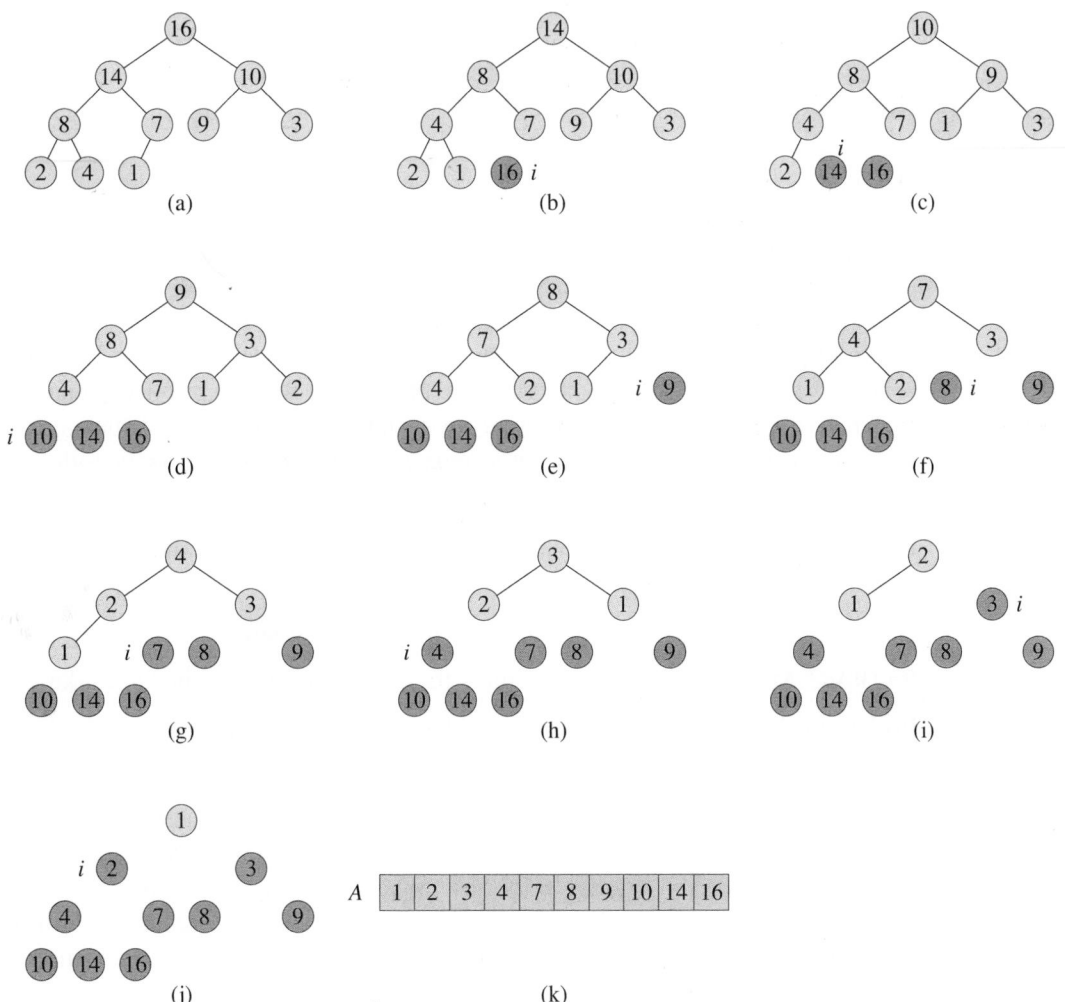

Figure 6.4 The operation of HEAPSORT. **(a)** The max-heap data structure just after BUILD-MAX-HEAP has built it in line 1. **(b)–(j)** The max-heap just after each call of MAX-HEAPIFY in line 5, showing the value of i at that time. Only lightly shaded nodes remain in the heap. **(k)** The resulting sorted array A.

6.4-5 ★

Show that when all elements are distinct, the best-case running time of HEAPSORT is $\Omega(n \lg n)$.

6.5   Priority queues

Heapsort is an excellent algorithm, but a good implementation of quicksort, presented in Chapter 7, usually beats it in practice. Nevertheless, the heap data structure itself has many uses. In this section, we present one of the most popular applications of a heap: as an efficient priority queue. As with heaps, priority queues come in two forms: max-priority queues and min-priority queues. We will focus here on how to implement max-priority queues, which are in turn based on max-heaps; Exercise 6.5-3 asks you to write the procedures for min-priority queues.

A *priority queue* is a data structure for maintaining a set S of elements, each with an associated value called a *key*. A *max-priority queue* supports the following operations:

INSERT(S, x) inserts the element x into the set S, which is equivalent to the operation $S = S \cup \{x\}$.

MAXIMUM(S) returns the element of S with the largest key.

EXTRACT-MAX(S) removes and returns the element of S with the largest key.

INCREASE-KEY(S, x, k) increases the value of element x's key to the new value k, which is assumed to be at least as large as x's current key value.

Among their other applications, we can use max-priority queues to schedule jobs on a shared computer. The max-priority queue keeps track of the jobs to be performed and their relative priorities. When a job is finished or interrupted, the scheduler selects the highest-priority job from among those pending by calling EXTRACT-MAX. The scheduler can add a new job to the queue at any time by calling INSERT.

Alternatively, a *min-priority queue* supports the operations INSERT, MINIMUM, EXTRACT-MIN, and DECREASE-KEY. A min-priority queue can be used in an event-driven simulator. The items in the queue are events to be simulated, each with an associated time of occurrence that serves as its key. The events must be simulated in order of their time of occurrence, because the simulation of an event can cause other events to be simulated in the future. The simulation program calls EXTRACT-MIN at each step to choose the next event to simulate. As new events are produced, the simulator inserts them into the min-priority queue by calling INSERT.

We shall see other uses for min-priority queues, highlighting the DECREASE-KEY operation, in Chapters 23 and 24.

Not surprisingly, we can use a heap to implement a priority queue. In a given application, such as job scheduling or event-driven simulation, elements of a priority queue correspond to objects in the application. We often need to determine which application object corresponds to a given priority-queue element, and vice versa. When we use a heap to implement a priority queue, therefore, we often need to store a *handle* to the corresponding application object in each heap element. The exact makeup of the handle (such as a pointer or an integer) depends on the application. Similarly, we need to store a handle to the corresponding heap element in each application object. Here, the handle would typically be an array index. Because heap elements change locations within the array during heap operations, an actual implementation, upon relocating a heap element, would also have to update the array index in the corresponding application object. Because the details of accessing application objects depend heavily on the application and its implementation, we shall not pursue them here, other than noting that in practice, these handles do need to be correctly maintained.

Now we discuss how to implement the operations of a max-priority queue. The procedure HEAP-MAXIMUM implements the MAXIMUM operation in $\Theta(1)$ time.

HEAP-MAXIMUM(A)

1   **return** $A[1]$

The procedure HEAP-EXTRACT-MAX implements the EXTRACT-MAX operation. It is similar to the **for** loop body (lines 3–5) of the HEAPSORT procedure.

HEAP-EXTRACT-MAX(A)

1   **if** $A.heap\text{-}size < 1$
2   **error** "heap underflow"
3   $max = A[1]$
4   $A[1] = A[A.heap\text{-}size]$
5   $A.heap\text{-}size = A.heap\text{-}size - 1$
6   MAX-HEAPIFY($A, 1$)
7   **return** max

The running time of HEAP-EXTRACT-MAX is $O(\lg n)$, since it performs only a constant amount of work on top of the $O(\lg n)$ time for MAX-HEAPIFY.

The procedure HEAP-INCREASE-KEY implements the INCREASE-KEY operation. An index i into the array identifies the priority-queue element whose key we wish to increase. The procedure first updates the key of element $A[i]$ to its new value. Because increasing the key of $A[i]$ might violate the max-heap property,

the procedure then, in a manner reminiscent of the insertion loop (lines 5–7) of
INSERTION-SORT from Section 2.1, traverses a simple path from this node toward
the root to find a proper place for the newly increased key. As HEAP-INCREASE-
KEY traverses this path, it repeatedly compares an element to its parent, exchanging their keys and continuing if the element's key is larger, and terminating if the element's key is smaller, since the max-heap property now holds. (See Exercise 6.5-5
for a precise loop invariant.)

HEAP-INCREASE-KEY(A, i, key)

```
1   if key < A[i]
2       error "new key is smaller than current key"
3   A[i] = key
4   while i > 1 and A[PARENT(i)] < A[i]
5       exchange A[i] with A[PARENT(i)]
6       i = PARENT(i)
```

Figure 6.5 shows an example of a HEAP-INCREASE-KEY operation. The running
time of HEAP-INCREASE-KEY on an n-element heap is $O(\lg n)$, since the path
traced from the node updated in line 3 to the root has length $O(\lg n)$.

The procedure MAX-HEAP-INSERT implements the INSERT operation. It takes
as an input the key of the new element to be inserted into max-heap A. The procedure first expands the max-heap by adding to the tree a new leaf whose key is $-\infty$.
Then it calls HEAP-INCREASE-KEY to set the key of this new node to its correct
value and maintain the max-heap property.

MAX-HEAP-INSERT(A, key)

```
1   A.heap-size = A.heap-size + 1
2   A[A.heap-size] = -∞
3   HEAP-INCREASE-KEY(A, A.heap-size, key)
```

The running time of MAX-HEAP-INSERT on an n-element heap is $O(\lg n)$.

In summary, a heap can support any priority-queue operation on a set of size n
in $O(\lg n)$ time.

Exercises

6.5-1
Illustrate the operation of HEAP-EXTRACT-MAX on the heap $A = \langle 15, 13, 9, 5,$
$12, 8, 7, 4, 0, 6, 2, 1 \rangle$.

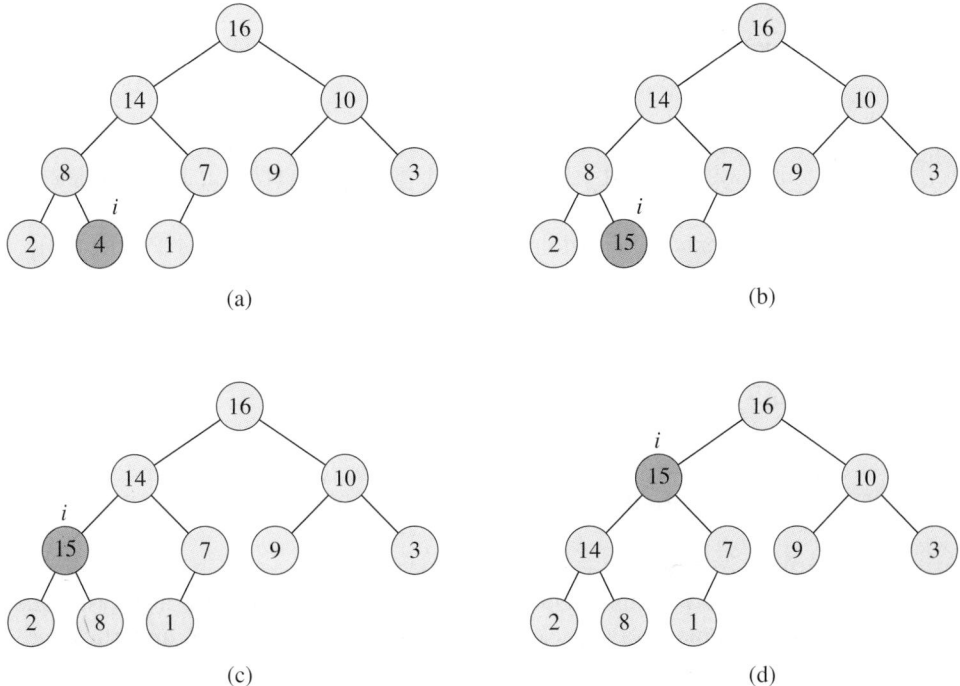

Figure 6.5 The operation of HEAP-INCREASE-KEY. **(a)** The max-heap of Figure 6.4(a) with a node whose index is i heavily shaded. **(b)** This node has its key increased to 15. **(c)** After one iteration of the **while** loop of lines 4–6, the node and its parent have exchanged keys, and the index i moves up to the parent. **(d)** The max-heap after one more iteration of the **while** loop. At this point, $A[\text{PARENT}(i)] \geq A[i]$. The max-heap property now holds and the procedure terminates.

6.5-2
Illustrate the operation of MAX-HEAP-INSERT$(A, 10)$ on the heap $A = \langle 15, 13, 9, 5, 12, 8, 7, 4, 0, 6, 2, 1 \rangle$.

6.5-3
Write pseudocode for the procedures HEAP-MINIMUM, HEAP-EXTRACT-MIN, HEAP-DECREASE-KEY, and MIN-HEAP-INSERT that implement a min-priority queue with a min-heap.

6.5-4
Why do we bother setting the key of the inserted node to $-\infty$ in line 2 of MAX-HEAP-INSERT when the next thing we do is increase its key to the desired value?

6.5-5

Argue the correctness of HEAP-INCREASE-KEY using the following loop invariant:

At the start of each iteration of the **while** loop of lines 4–6, $A[\text{PARENT}(i)] \geq A[\text{LEFT}(i)]$ and $A[\text{PARENT}(i)] \geq A[\text{RIGHT}(i)]$, if these nodes exist, and the subarray $A[1 .. A.heap\text{-}size]$ satisfies the max-heap property, except that there may be one violation: $A[i]$ may be larger than $A[\text{PARENT}(i)]$.

You may assume that the subarray $A[1 .. A.heap\text{-}size]$ satisfies the max-heap property at the time HEAP-INCREASE-KEY is called.

6.5-6

Each exchange operation on line 5 of HEAP-INCREASE-KEY typically requires three assignments. Show how to use the idea of the inner loop of INSERTION-SORT to reduce the three assignments down to just one assignment.

6.5-7

Show how to implement a first-in, first-out queue with a priority queue. Show how to implement a stack with a priority queue. (Queues and stacks are defined in Section 10.1.)

6.5-8

The operation HEAP-DELETE(A, i) deletes the item in node i from heap A. Give an implementation of HEAP-DELETE that runs in $O(\lg n)$ time for an n-element max-heap.

6.5-9

Give an $O(n \lg k)$-time algorithm to merge k sorted lists into one sorted list, where n is the total number of elements in all the input lists. (*Hint:* Use a min-heap for k-way merging.)

Problems

6-1 *Building a heap using insertion*

We can build a heap by repeatedly calling MAX-HEAP-INSERT to insert the elements into the heap. Consider the following variation on the BUILD-MAX-HEAP procedure:

BUILD-MAX-HEAP'(A)

1   $A.heap\text{-}size = 1$
2   **for** $i = 2$ **to** $A.length$
3   MAX-HEAP-INSERT($A, A[i]$)

a. Do the procedures BUILD-MAX-HEAP and BUILD-MAX-HEAP' always create the same heap when run on the same input array? Prove that they do, or provide a counterexample.

b. Show that in the worst case, BUILD-MAX-HEAP' requires $\Theta(n \lg n)$ time to build an n-element heap.

6-2   *Analysis of d-ary heaps*

A ***d-ary heap*** is like a binary heap, but (with one possible exception) non-leaf nodes have d children instead of 2 children.

a. How would you represent a d-ary heap in an array?

b. What is the height of a d-ary heap of n elements in terms of n and d?

c. Give an efficient implementation of EXTRACT-MAX in a d-ary max-heap. Analyze its running time in terms of d and n.

d. Give an efficient implementation of INSERT in a d-ary max-heap. Analyze its running time in terms of d and n.

e. Give an efficient implementation of INCREASE-KEY(A, i, k), which flags an error if $k < A[i]$, but otherwise sets $A[i] = k$ and then updates the d-ary max-heap structure appropriately. Analyze its running time in terms of d and n.

6-3   *Young tableaus*

An $m \times n$ ***Young tableau*** is an $m \times n$ matrix such that the entries of each row are in sorted order from left to right and the entries of each column are in sorted order from top to bottom. Some of the entries of a Young tableau may be ∞, which we treat as nonexistent elements. Thus, a Young tableau can be used to hold $r \leq mn$ finite numbers.

a. Draw a 4×4 Young tableau containing the elements $\{9, 16, 3, 2, 4, 8, 5, 14, 12\}$.

b. Argue that an $m \times n$ Young tableau Y is empty if $Y[1, 1] = \infty$. Argue that Y is full (contains mn elements) if $Y[m, n] < \infty$.

c. Give an algorithm to implement EXTRACT-MIN on a nonempty $m \times n$ Young tableau that runs in $O(m + n)$ time. Your algorithm should use a recursive subroutine that solves an $m \times n$ problem by recursively solving either an $(m - 1) \times n$ or an $m \times (n - 1)$ subproblem. (*Hint:* Think about MAX-HEAPIFY.) Define $T(p)$, where $p = m + n$, to be the maximum running time of EXTRACT-MIN on any $m \times n$ Young tableau. Give and solve a recurrence for $T(p)$ that yields the $O(m + n)$ time bound.

d. Show how to insert a new element into a nonfull $m \times n$ Young tableau in $O(m + n)$ time.

e. Using no other sorting method as a subroutine, show how to use an $n \times n$ Young tableau to sort n^2 numbers in $O(n^3)$ time.

f. Give an $O(m + n)$-time algorithm to determine whether a given number is stored in a given $m \times n$ Young tableau.

Chapter notes

The heapsort algorithm was invented by Williams [357], who also described how to implement a priority queue with a heap. The BUILD-MAX-HEAP procedure was suggested by Floyd [106].

We use min-heaps to implement min-priority queues in Chapters 16, 23, and 24. We also give an implementation with improved time bounds for certain operations in Chapter 19 and, assuming that the keys are drawn from a bounded set of non-negative integers, Chapter 20.

If the data are b-bit integers, and the computer memory consists of addressable b-bit words, Fredman and Willard [115] showed how to implement MINIMUM in $O(1)$ time and INSERT and EXTRACT-MIN in $O(\sqrt{\lg n})$ time. Thorup [337] has improved the $O(\sqrt{\lg n})$ bound to $O(\lg \lg n)$ time. This bound uses an amount of space unbounded in n, but it can be implemented in linear space by using randomized hashing.

An important special case of priority queues occurs when the sequence of EXTRACT-MIN operations is *monotone*, that is, the values returned by successive EXTRACT-MIN operations are monotonically increasing over time. This case arises in several important applications, such as Dijkstra's single-source shortest-paths algorithm, which we discuss in Chapter 24, and in discrete-event simulation. For Dijkstra's algorithm it is particularly important that the DECREASE-KEY operation be implemented efficiently. For the monotone case, if the data are integers in the range $1, 2, \ldots, C$, Ahuja, Mehlhorn, Orlin, and Tarjan [8] describe

how to implement EXTRACT-MIN and INSERT in $O(\lg C)$ amortized time (see Chapter 17 for more on amortized analysis) and DECREASE-KEY in $O(1)$ time, using a data structure called a radix heap. The $O(\lg C)$ bound can be improved to $O(\sqrt{\lg C})$ using Fibonacci heaps (see Chapter 19) in conjunction with radix heaps. Cherkassky, Goldberg, and Silverstein [65] further improved the bound to $O(\lg^{1/3+\epsilon} C)$ expected time by combining the multilevel bucketing structure of Denardo and Fox [85] with the heap of Thorup mentioned earlier. Raman [291] further improved these results to obtain a bound of $O(\min(\lg^{1/4+\epsilon} C, \lg^{1/3+\epsilon} n))$, for any fixed $\epsilon > 0$.

7 Quicksort

The quicksort algorithm has a worst-case running time of $\Theta(n^2)$ on an input array of n numbers. Despite this slow worst-case running time, quicksort is often the best practical choice for sorting because it is remarkably efficient on the average: its expected running time is $\Theta(n \lg n)$, and the constant factors hidden in the $\Theta(n \lg n)$ notation are quite small. It also has the advantage of sorting in place (see page 17), and it works well even in virtual-memory environments.

Section 7.1 describes the algorithm and an important subroutine used by quicksort for partitioning. Because the behavior of quicksort is complex, we start with an intuitive discussion of its performance in Section 7.2 and postpone its precise analysis to the end of the chapter. Section 7.3 presents a version of quicksort that uses random sampling. This algorithm has a good expected running time and, when all elements are distinct, no particular input elicits its worst-case behavior. (See Problem 7-2 for the case in which elements may be equal.) Section 7.4 analyzes the randomized algorithm, showing that it runs in $\Theta(n^2)$ time in the worst case and, assuming distinct elements, in expected $O(n \lg n)$ time.

7.1 Description of quicksort

Quicksort, like merge sort, applies the divide-and-conquer paradigm introduced in Section 2.3.1. Here is the three-step divide-and-conquer process for sorting a typical subarray $A[p \mathinner{.\,.} r]$:

Divide: Partition (rearrange) the array $A[p \mathinner{.\,.} r]$ into two (possibly empty) subarrays $A[p \mathinner{.\,.} q - 1]$ and $A[q + 1 \mathinner{.\,.} r]$ such that each element of $A[p \mathinner{.\,.} q - 1]$ is less than or equal to $A[q]$, which is, in turn, less than or equal to each element of $A[q + 1 \mathinner{.\,.} r]$. Compute the index q as part of this partitioning procedure.

Conquer: Sort the two subarrays $A[p \mathinner{.\,.} q - 1]$ and $A[q + 1 \mathinner{.\,.} r]$ by recursive calls to quicksort.

Combine: Because the subarrays are already sorted, no work is needed to combine them: the entire array $A[p \mathinner{\ldotp\ldotp} r]$ is now sorted.

The following procedure implements quicksort:

QUICKSORT(A, p, r)

1   **if** $p < r$
2       $q =$ PARTITION(A, p, r)
3   QUICKSORT$(A, p, q - 1)$
4   QUICKSORT$(A, q + 1, r)$

To sort an entire array A, the initial call is QUICKSORT$(A, 1, A.length)$.

Partitioning the array

The key to the algorithm is the PARTITION procedure, which rearranges the subarray $A[p \mathinner{\ldotp\ldotp} r]$ in place.

PARTITION(A, p, r)

1   $x = A[r]$
2   $i = p - 1$
3   **for** $j = p$ **to** $r - 1$
4   **if** $A[j] \leq x$
5           $i = i + 1$
6   exchange $A[i]$ with $A[j]$
7   exchange $A[i + 1]$ with $A[r]$
8   **return** $i + 1$

Figure 7.1 shows how PARTITION works on an 8-element array. PARTITION always selects an element $x = A[r]$ as a ***pivot*** element around which to partition the subarray $A[p \mathinner{\ldotp\ldotp} r]$. As the procedure runs, it partitions the array into four (possibly empty) regions. At the start of each iteration of the **for** loop in lines 3–6, the regions satisfy certain properties, shown in Figure 7.2. We state these properties as a loop invariant:

At the beginning of each iteration of the loop of lines 3–6, for any array index k,

1. If $p \leq k \leq i$, then $A[k] \leq x$.
2. If $i + 1 \leq k \leq j - 1$, then $A[k] > x$.
3. If $k = r$, then $A[k] = x$.

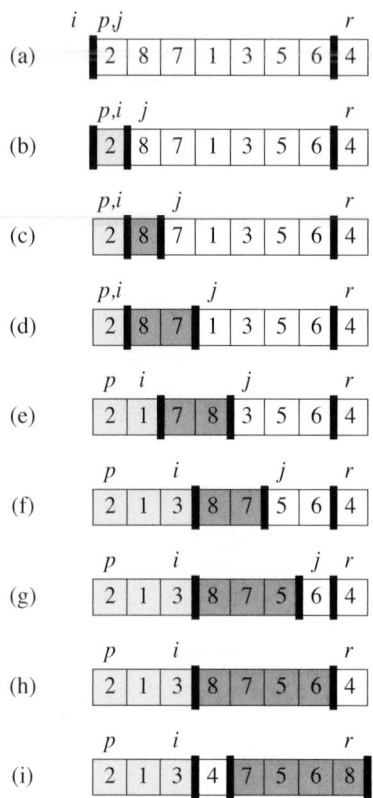

Figure 7.1 The operation of PARTITION on a sample array. Array entry $A[r]$ becomes the pivot element x. Lightly shaded array elements are all in the first partition with values no greater than x. Heavily shaded elements are in the second partition with values greater than x. The unshaded elements have not yet been put in one of the first two partitions, and the final white element is the pivot x. **(a)** The initial array and variable settings. None of the elements have been placed in either of the first two partitions. **(b)** The value 2 is "swapped with itself" and put in the partition of smaller values. **(c)–(d)** The values 8 and 7 are added to the partition of larger values. **(e)** The values 1 and 8 are swapped, and the smaller partition grows. **(f)** The values 3 and 7 are swapped, and the smaller partition grows. **(g)–(h)** The larger partition grows to include 5 and 6, and the loop terminates. **(i)** In lines 7–8, the pivot element is swapped so that it lies between the two partitions.

The indices between j and $r - 1$ are not covered by any of the three cases, and the values in these entries have no particular relationship to the pivot x.

We need to show that this loop invariant is true prior to the first iteration, that each iteration of the loop maintains the invariant, and that the invariant provides a useful property to show correctness when the loop terminates.

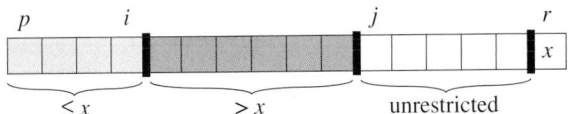

Figure 7.2 The four regions maintained by the procedure PARTITION on a subarray $A[p..r]$. The values in $A[p..i]$ are all less than or equal to x, the values in $A[i+1..j-1]$ are all greater than x, and $A[r] = x$. The subarray $A[j..r-1]$ can take on any values.

Initialization: Prior to the first iteration of the loop, $i = p-1$ and $j = p$. Because no values lie between p and i and no values lie between $i+1$ and $j-1$, the first two conditions of the loop invariant are trivially satisfied. The assignment in line 1 satisfies the third condition.

Maintenance: As Figure 7.3 shows, we consider two cases, depending on the outcome of the test in line 4. Figure 7.3(a) shows what happens when $A[j] > x$; the only action in the loop is to increment j. After j is incremented, condition 2 holds for $A[j-1]$ and all other entries remain unchanged. Figure 7.3(b) shows what happens when $A[j] \leq x$; the loop increments i, swaps $A[i]$ and $A[j]$, and then increments j. Because of the swap, we now have that $A[i] \leq x$, and condition 1 is satisfied. Similarly, we also have that $A[j-1] > x$, since the item that was swapped into $A[j-1]$ is, by the loop invariant, greater than x.

Termination: At termination, $j = r$. Therefore, every entry in the array is in one of the three sets described by the invariant, and we have partitioned the values in the array into three sets: those less than or equal to x, those greater than x, and a singleton set containing x.

The final two lines of PARTITION finish up by swapping the pivot element with the leftmost element greater than x, thereby moving the pivot into its correct place in the partitioned array, and then returning the pivot's new index. The output of PARTITION now satisfies the specifications given for the divide step. In fact, it satisfies a slightly stronger condition: after line 2 of QUICKSORT, $A[q]$ is strictly less than every element of $A[q+1..r]$.

The running time of PARTITION on the subarray $A[p..r]$ is $\Theta(n)$, where $n = r - p + 1$ (see Exercise 7.1-3).

Exercises

7.1-1
Using Figure 7.1 as a model, illustrate the operation of PARTITION on the array $A = \langle 13, 19, 9, 5, 12, 8, 7, 4, 21, 2, 6, 11 \rangle$.

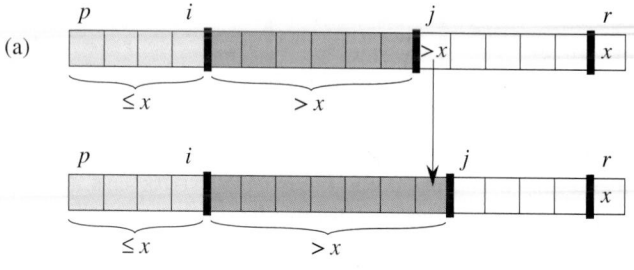

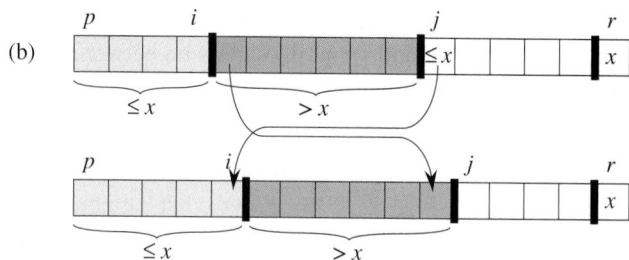

Figure 7.3   The two cases for one iteration of procedure PARTITION. **(a)** If $A[j] > x$, the only action is to increment j, which maintains the loop invariant. **(b)** If $A[j] \leq x$, index i is incremented, $A[i]$ and $A[j]$ are swapped, and then j is incremented. Again, the loop invariant is maintained.

7.1-2

What value of q does PARTITION return when all elements in the array $A[p \mathbin{..} r]$ have the same value? Modify PARTITION so that $q = \lfloor (p + r)/2 \rfloor$ when all elements in the array $A[p \mathbin{..} r]$ have the same value.

7.1-3

Give a brief argument that the running time of PARTITION on a subarray of size n is $\Theta(n)$.

7.1-4

How would you modify QUICKSORT to sort into nonincreasing order?

7.2   Performance of quicksort

The running time of quicksort depends on whether the partitioning is balanced or unbalanced, which in turn depends on which elements are used for partitioning. If the partitioning is balanced, the algorithm runs asymptotically as fast as merge

sort. If the partitioning is unbalanced, however, it can run asymptotically as slowly as insertion sort. In this section, we shall informally investigate how quicksort performs under the assumptions of balanced versus unbalanced partitioning.

Worst-case partitioning

The worst-case behavior for quicksort occurs when the partitioning routine produces one subproblem with $n - 1$ elements and one with 0 elements. (We prove this claim in Section 7.4.1.) Let us assume that this unbalanced partitioning arises in each recursive call. The partitioning costs $\Theta(n)$ time. Since the recursive call on an array of size 0 just returns, $T(0) = \Theta(1)$, and the recurrence for the running time is

$$
\begin{aligned}
T(n) &= T(n-1) + T(0) + \Theta(n) \\
     &= T(n-1) + \Theta(n) .
\end{aligned}
$$

Intuitively, if we sum the costs incurred at each level of the recursion, we get an arithmetic series (equation (A.2)), which evaluates to $\Theta(n^2)$. Indeed, it is straightforward to use the substitution method to prove that the recurrence $T(n) = T(n-1) + \Theta(n)$ has the solution $T(n) = \Theta(n^2)$. (See Exercise 7.2-1.)

Thus, if the partitioning is maximally unbalanced at every recursive level of the algorithm, the running time is $\Theta(n^2)$. Therefore the worst-case running time of quicksort is no better than that of insertion sort. Moreover, the $\Theta(n^2)$ running time occurs when the input array is already completely sorted—a common situation in which insertion sort runs in $O(n)$ time.

Best-case partitioning

In the most even possible split, PARTITION produces two subproblems, each of size no more than $n/2$, since one is of size $\lfloor n/2 \rfloor$ and one of size $\lceil n/2 \rceil - 1$. In this case, quicksort runs much faster. The recurrence for the running time is then

$$
T(n) = 2T(n/2) + \Theta(n) ,
$$

where we tolerate the sloppiness from ignoring the floor and ceiling and from subtracting 1. By case 2 of the master theorem (Theorem 4.1), this recurrence has the solution $T(n) = \Theta(n \lg n)$. By equally balancing the two sides of the partition at every level of the recursion, we get an asymptotically faster algorithm.

Balanced partitioning

The average-case running time of quicksort is much closer to the best case than to the worst case, as the analyses in Section 7.4 will show. The key to understand-

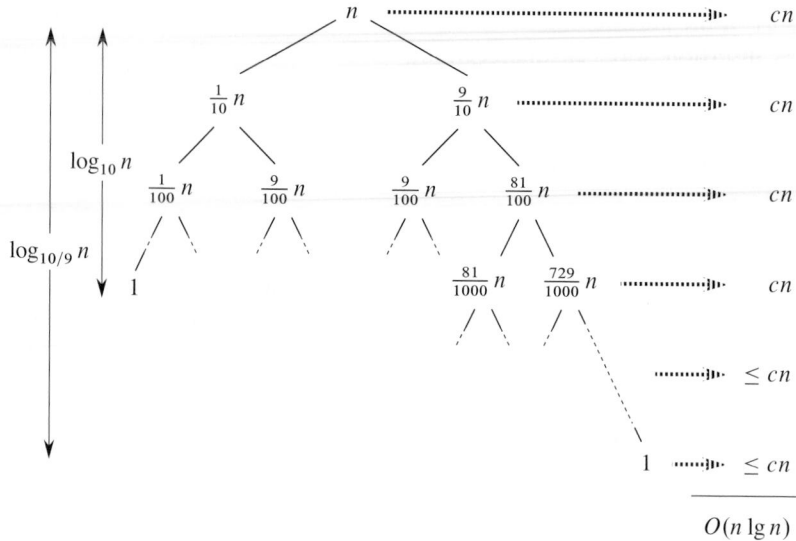

Figure 7.4 A recursion tree for QUICKSORT in which PARTITION always produces a 9-to-1 split, yielding a running time of $O(n \lg n)$. Nodes show subproblem sizes, with per-level costs on the right. The per-level costs include the constant c implicit in the $\Theta(n)$ term.

ing why is to understand how the balance of the partitioning is reflected in the recurrence that describes the running time.

Suppose, for example, that the partitioning algorithm always produces a 9-to-1 proportional split, which at first blush seems quite unbalanced. We then obtain the recurrence

$$T(n) = T(9n/10) + T(n/10) + cn ,$$

on the running time of quicksort, where we have explicitly included the constant c hidden in the $\Theta(n)$ term. Figure 7.4 shows the recursion tree for this recurrence. Notice that every level of the tree has cost cn, until the recursion reaches a boundary condition at depth $\log_{10} n = \Theta(\lg n)$, and then the levels have cost at most cn. The recursion terminates at depth $\log_{10/9} n = \Theta(\lg n)$. The total cost of quicksort is therefore $O(n \lg n)$. Thus, with a 9-to-1 proportional split at every level of recursion, which intuitively seems quite unbalanced, quicksort runs in $O(n \lg n)$ time—asymptotically the same as if the split were right down the middle. Indeed, even a 99-to-1 split yields an $O(n \lg n)$ running time. In fact, any split of *constant* proportionality yields a recursion tree of depth $\Theta(\lg n)$, where the cost at each level is $O(n)$. The running time is therefore $O(n \lg n)$ whenever the split has constant proportionality.

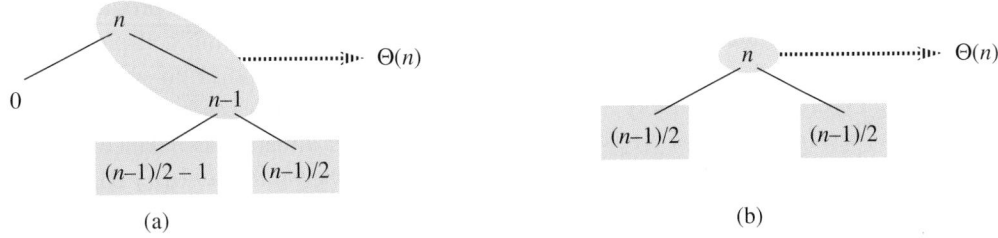

(a)   (b)

Figure 7.5   **(a)** Two levels of a recursion tree for quicksort. The partitioning at the root costs n and produces a "bad" split: two subarrays of sizes 0 and $n - 1$. The partitioning of the subarray of size $n - 1$ costs $n - 1$ and produces a "good" split: subarrays of size $(n - 1)/2 - 1$ and $(n - 1)/2$. **(b)** A single level of a recursion tree that is very well balanced. In both parts, the partitioning cost for the subproblems shown with elliptical shading is $\Theta(n)$. Yet the subproblems remaining to be solved in (a), shown with square shading, are no larger than the corresponding subproblems remaining to be solved in (b).

Intuition for the average case

To develop a clear notion of the randomized behavior of quicksort, we must make an assumption about how frequently we expect to encounter the various inputs. The behavior of quicksort depends on the relative ordering of the values in the array elements given as the input, and not by the particular values in the array. As in our probabilistic analysis of the hiring problem in Section 5.2, we will assume for now that all permutations of the input numbers are equally likely.

When we run quicksort on a random input array, the partitioning is highly unlikely to happen in the same way at every level, as our informal analysis has assumed. We expect that some of the splits will be reasonably well balanced and that some will be fairly unbalanced. For example, Exercise 7.2-6 asks you to show that about 80 percent of the time PARTITION produces a split that is more balanced than 9 to 1, and about 20 percent of the time it produces a split that is less balanced than 9 to 1.

In the average case, PARTITION produces a mix of "good" and "bad" splits. In a recursion tree for an average-case execution of PARTITION, the good and bad splits are distributed randomly throughout the tree. Suppose, for the sake of intuition, that the good and bad splits alternate levels in the tree, and that the good splits are best-case splits and the bad splits are worst-case splits. Figure 7.5(a) shows the splits at two consecutive levels in the recursion tree. At the root of the tree, the cost is n for partitioning, and the subarrays produced have sizes $n - 1$ and 0: the worst case. At the next level, the subarray of size $n - 1$ undergoes best-case partitioning into subarrays of size $(n - 1)/2 - 1$ and $(n - 1)/2$. Let's assume that the boundary-condition cost is 1 for the subarray of size 0.

The combination of the bad split followed by the good split produces three subarrays of sizes 0, $(n - 1)/2 - 1$, and $(n - 1)/2$ at a combined partitioning cost of $\Theta(n) + \Theta(n - 1) = \Theta(n)$. Certainly, this situation is no worse than that in Figure 7.5(b), namely a single level of partitioning that produces two subarrays of size $(n - 1)/2$, at a cost of $\Theta(n)$. Yet this latter situation is balanced! Intuitively, the $\Theta(n - 1)$ cost of the bad split can be absorbed into the $\Theta(n)$ cost of the good split, and the resulting split is good. Thus, the running time of quicksort, when levels alternate between good and bad splits, is like the running time for good splits alone: still $O(n \lg n)$, but with a slightly larger constant hidden by the O-notation. We shall give a rigorous analysis of the expected running time of a randomized version of quicksort in Section 7.4.2.

Exercises

7.2-1
Use the substitution method to prove that the recurrence $T(n) = T(n-1) + \Theta(n)$ has the solution $T(n) = \Theta(n^2)$, as claimed at the beginning of Section 7.2.

7.2-2
What is the running time of QUICKSORT when all elements of array A have the same value?

7.2-3
Show that the running time of QUICKSORT is $\Theta(n^2)$ when the array A contains distinct elements and is sorted in decreasing order.

7.2-4
Banks often record transactions on an account in order of the times of the transactions, but many people like to receive their bank statements with checks listed in order by check number. People usually write checks in order by check number, and merchants usually cash them with reasonable dispatch. The problem of converting time-of-transaction ordering to check-number ordering is therefore the problem of sorting almost-sorted input. Argue that the procedure INSERTION-SORT would tend to beat the procedure QUICKSORT on this problem.

7.2-5
Suppose that the splits at every level of quicksort are in the proportion $1 - \alpha$ to α, where $0 < \alpha \le 1/2$ is a constant. Show that the minimum depth of a leaf in the recursion tree is approximately $-\lg n / \lg \alpha$ and the maximum depth is approximately $-\lg n / \lg(1 - \alpha)$. (Don't worry about integer round-off.)

7.2-6   ★

Argue that for any constant $0 < \alpha \leq 1/2$, the probability is approximately $1 - 2\alpha$ that on a random input array, PARTITION produces a split more balanced than $1 - \alpha$ to α.

7.3   A randomized version of quicksort

In exploring the average-case behavior of quicksort, we have made an assumption that all permutations of the input numbers are equally likely. In an engineering situation, however, we cannot always expect this assumption to hold. (See Exercise 7.2-4.) As we saw in Section 5.3, we can sometimes add randomization to an algorithm in order to obtain good expected performance over all inputs. Many people regard the resulting randomized version of quicksort as the sorting algorithm of choice for large enough inputs.

In Section 5.3, we randomized our algorithm by explicitly permuting the input. We could do so for quicksort also, but a different randomization technique, called **random sampling**, yields a simpler analysis. Instead of always using $A[r]$ as the pivot, we will select a randomly chosen element from the subarray $A[p \mathinner{.\,.} r]$. We do so by first exchanging element $A[r]$ with an element chosen at random from $A[p \mathinner{.\,.} r]$. By randomly sampling the range $p, \ldots, r$, we ensure that the pivot element $x = A[r]$ is equally likely to be any of the $r - p + 1$ elements in the subarray. Because we randomly choose the pivot element, we expect the split of the input array to be reasonably well balanced on average.

The changes to PARTITION and QUICKSORT are small. In the new partition procedure, we simply implement the swap before actually partitioning:

RANDOMIZED-PARTITION(A, p, r)

1 $i = $ RANDOM(p, r)
2 exchange $A[r]$ with $A[i]$
3 **return** PARTITION(A, p, r)

The new quicksort calls RANDOMIZED-PARTITION in place of PARTITION:

RANDOMIZED-QUICKSORT(A, p, r)

1 **if** $p < r$
2      $q = $ RANDOMIZED-PARTITION(A, p, r)
3   RANDOMIZED-QUICKSORT$(A, p, q - 1)$
4   RANDOMIZED-QUICKSORT$(A, q + 1, r)$

We analyze this algorithm in the next section.

Exercises

7.3-1
Why do we analyze the expected running time of a randomized algorithm and not its worst-case running time?

7.3-2
When RANDOMIZED-QUICKSORT runs, how many calls are made to the random-number generator RANDOM in the worst case? How about in the best case? Give your answer in terms of Θ-notation.

7.4   Analysis of quicksort

Section 7.2 gave some intuition for the worst-case behavior of quicksort and for why we expect it to run quickly. In this section, we analyze the behavior of quicksort more rigorously. We begin with a worst-case analysis, which applies to either QUICKSORT or RANDOMIZED-QUICKSORT, and conclude with an analysis of the expected running time of RANDOMIZED-QUICKSORT.

7.4.1   Worst-case analysis

We saw in Section 7.2 that a worst-case split at every level of recursion in quicksort produces a $\Theta(n^2)$ running time, which, intuitively, is the worst-case running time of the algorithm. We now prove this assertion.

Using the substitution method (see Section 4.3), we can show that the running time of quicksort is $O(n^2)$. Let $T(n)$ be the worst-case time for the procedure QUICKSORT on an input of size n. We have the recurrence

$$T(n) = \max_{0 \le q \le n-1} (T(q) + T(n - q - 1)) + \Theta(n) , \tag{7.1}$$

where the parameter q ranges from 0 to $n - 1$ because the procedure PARTITION produces two subproblems with total size $n - 1$. We guess that $T(n) \le cn^2$ for some constant c. Substituting this guess into recurrence (7.1), we obtain

$$
\begin{aligned}
T(n) &\le \max_{0 \le q \le n-1} (cq^2 + c(n - q - 1)^2) + \Theta(n) \\
&= c \cdot \max_{0 \le q \le n-1} (q^2 + (n - q - 1)^2) + \Theta(n) .
\end{aligned}
$$

The expression $q^2 + (n - q - 1)^2$ achieves a maximum over the parameter's range $0 \le q \le n - 1$ at either endpoint. To verify this claim, note that the second derivative of the expression with respect to q is positive (see Exercise 7.4-3). This

observation gives us the bound $\max_{0 \le q \le n-1}(q^2 + (n-q-1)^2) \le (n-1)^2 = n^2 - 2n + 1$. Continuing with our bounding of $T(n)$, we obtain

$$
\begin{aligned}
T(n) &\le cn^2 - c(2n-1) + \Theta(n) \\
&\le cn^2 \,,
\end{aligned}
$$

since we can pick the constant c large enough so that the $c(2n-1)$ term dominates the $\Theta(n)$ term. Thus, $T(n) = O(n^2)$. We saw in Section 7.2 a specific case in which quicksort takes $\Omega(n^2)$ time: when partitioning is unbalanced. Alternatively, Exercise 7.4-1 asks you to show that recurrence (7.1) has a solution of $T(n) = \Omega(n^2)$. Thus, the (worst-case) running time of quicksort is $\Theta(n^2)$.

7.4.2 Expected running time

We have already seen the intuition behind why the expected running time of RANDOMIZED-QUICKSORT is $O(n \lg n)$: if, in each level of recursion, the split induced by RANDOMIZED-PARTITION puts any constant fraction of the elements on one side of the partition, then the recursion tree has depth $\Theta(\lg n)$, and $O(n)$ work is performed at each level. Even if we add a few new levels with the most unbalanced split possible between these levels, the total time remains $O(n \lg n)$. We can analyze the expected running time of RANDOMIZED-QUICKSORT precisely by first understanding how the partitioning procedure operates and then using this understanding to derive an $O(n \lg n)$ bound on the expected running time. This upper bound on the expected running time, combined with the $\Theta(n \lg n)$ best-case bound we saw in Section 7.2, yields a $\Theta(n \lg n)$ expected running time. We assume throughout that the values of the elements being sorted are distinct.

Running time and comparisons

The QUICKSORT and RANDOMIZED-QUICKSORT procedures differ only in how they select pivot elements; they are the same in all other respects. We can therefore couch our analysis of RANDOMIZED-QUICKSORT by discussing the QUICKSORT and PARTITION procedures, but with the assumption that pivot elements are selected randomly from the subarray passed to RANDOMIZED-PARTITION.

The running time of QUICKSORT is dominated by the time spent in the PARTITION procedure. Each time the PARTITION procedure is called, it selects a pivot element, and this element is never included in any future recursive calls to QUICKSORT and PARTITION. Thus, there can be at most n calls to PARTITION over the entire execution of the quicksort algorithm. One call to PARTITION takes $O(1)$ time plus an amount of time that is proportional to the number of iterations of the **for** loop in lines 3–6. Each iteration of this **for** loop performs a comparison in line 4, comparing the pivot element to another element of the array A. Therefore,

if we can count the total number of times that line 4 is executed, we can bound the total time spent in the **for** loop during the entire execution of QUICKSORT.

Lemma 7.1

Let X be the number of comparisons performed in line 4 of PARTITION over the entire execution of QUICKSORT on an n-element array. Then the running time of QUICKSORT is $O(n + X)$.

Proof   By the discussion above, the algorithm makes at most n calls to PARTITION, each of which does a constant amount of work and then executes the **for** loop some number of times. Each iteration of the **for** loop executes line 4.   ∎

Our goal, therefore, is to compute X, the total number of comparisons performed in all calls to PARTITION. We will not attempt to analyze how many comparisons are made in *each* call to PARTITION. Rather, we will derive an overall bound on the total number of comparisons. To do so, we must understand when the algorithm compares two elements of the array and when it does not. For ease of analysis, we rename the elements of the array A as $z_1, z_2, \ldots, z_n$, with z_i being the ith smallest element. We also define the set $Z_{ij} = \{z_i, z_{i+1}, \ldots, z_j\}$ to be the set of elements between z_i and z_j, inclusive.

When does the algorithm compare z_i and z_j? To answer this question, we first observe that each pair of elements is compared at most once. Why? Elements are compared only to the pivot element and, after a particular call of PARTITION finishes, the pivot element used in that call is never again compared to any other elements.

Our analysis uses indicator random variables (see Section 5.2). We define

$$X_{ij} = \mathrm{I}\{z_i \text{ is compared to } z_j\} \ ,$$

where we are considering whether the comparison takes place at any time during the execution of the algorithm, not just during one iteration or one call of PARTITION. Since each pair is compared at most once, we can easily characterize the total number of comparisons performed by the algorithm:

$$X = \sum_{i=1}^{n-1} \sum_{j=i+1}^{n} X_{ij} \ .$$

Taking expectations of both sides, and then using linearity of expectation and Lemma 5.1, we obtain

$$\mathrm{E}[X] \;=\; \mathrm{E}\left[\sum_{i=1}^{n-1} \sum_{j=i+1}^{n} X_{ij}\right]$$

$$= \sum_{i=1}^{n-1} \sum_{j=i+1}^{n} \mathrm{E}[X_{ij}]$$

$$= \sum_{i=1}^{n-1} \sum_{j=i+1}^{n} \Pr\{z_i \text{ is compared to } z_j\} \ . \tag{7.2}$$

It remains to compute $\Pr\{z_i \text{ is compared to } z_j\}$. Our analysis assumes that the RANDOMIZED-PARTITION procedure chooses each pivot randomly and independently.

Let us think about when two items are *not* compared. Consider an input to quicksort of the numbers 1 through 10 (in any order), and suppose that the first pivot element is 7. Then the first call to PARTITION separates the numbers into two sets: $\{1, 2, 3, 4, 5, 6\}$ and $\{8, 9, 10\}$. In doing so, the pivot element 7 is compared to all other elements, but no number from the first set (e.g., 2) is or ever will be compared to any number from the second set (e.g., 9).

In general, because we assume that element values are distinct, once a pivot x is chosen with $z_i < x < z_j$, we know that z_i and z_j cannot be compared at any subsequent time. If, on the other hand, z_i is chosen as a pivot before any other item in Z_{ij}, then z_i will be compared to each item in Z_{ij}, except for itself. Similarly, if z_j is chosen as a pivot before any other item in Z_{ij}, then z_j will be compared to each item in Z_{ij}, except for itself. In our example, the values 7 and 9 are compared because 7 is the first item from $Z_{7,9}$ to be chosen as a pivot. In contrast, 2 and 9 will never be compared because the first pivot element chosen from $Z_{2,9}$ is 7. Thus, z_i and z_j are compared if and only if the first element to be chosen as a pivot from Z_{ij} is either z_i or z_j.

We now compute the probability that this event occurs. Prior to the point at which an element from Z_{ij} has been chosen as a pivot, the whole set Z_{ij} is together in the same partition. Therefore, any element of Z_{ij} is equally likely to be the first one chosen as a pivot. Because the set Z_{ij} has $j - i + 1$ elements, and because pivots are chosen randomly and independently, the probability that any given element is the first one chosen as a pivot is $1/(j - i + 1)$. Thus, we have

$$
\begin{aligned}
\Pr\{z_i \text{ is compared to } z_j\} &= \Pr\{z_i \text{ or } z_j \text{ is first pivot chosen from } Z_{ij}\} \\
&= \Pr\{z_i \text{ is first pivot chosen from } Z_{ij}\} \\
&\quad + \Pr\{z_j \text{ is first pivot chosen from } Z_{ij}\} \\
&= \frac{1}{j - i + 1} + \frac{1}{j - i + 1} \\
&= \frac{2}{j - i + 1} \ .
\end{aligned} \tag{7.3}
$$

The second line follows because the two events are mutually exclusive. Combining equations (7.2) and (7.3), we get that

$$E[X] = \sum_{i=1}^{n-1} \sum_{j=i+1}^{n} \frac{2}{j-i+1} \,.$$

We can evaluate this sum using a change of variables ($k = j - i$) and the bound on the harmonic series in equation (A.7):

$$\begin{aligned}
E[X] &= \sum_{i=1}^{n-1} \sum_{j=i+1}^{n} \frac{2}{j-i+1} \\
&= \sum_{i=1}^{n-1} \sum_{k=1}^{n-i} \frac{2}{k+1} \\
&< \sum_{i=1}^{n-1} \sum_{k=1}^{n} \frac{2}{k} \\
&= \sum_{i=1}^{n-1} O(\lg n) \\
&= O(n \lg n) \,.
\end{aligned} \tag{7.4}$$

Thus we conclude that, using RANDOMIZED-PARTITION, the expected running time of quicksort is $O(n \lg n)$ when element values are distinct.

Exercises

7.4-1
Show that in the recurrence

$$T(n) = \max_{0 \le q \le n-1} (T(q) + T(n-q-1)) + \Theta(n) \,,$$

$$T(n) = \Omega(n^2).$$

7.4-2
Show that quicksort's best-case running time is $\Omega(n \lg n)$.

7.4-3
Show that the expression $q^2 + (n - q - 1)^2$ achieves a maximum over $q = 0, 1, \ldots, n - 1$ when $q = 0$ or $q = n - 1$.

7.4-4
Show that RANDOMIZED-QUICKSORT's expected running time is $\Omega(n \lg n)$.

7.4-5
We can improve the running time of quicksort in practice by taking advantage of the fast running time of insertion sort when its input is "nearly" sorted. Upon calling quicksort on a subarray with fewer than k elements, let it simply return without sorting the subarray. After the top-level call to quicksort returns, run insertion sort on the entire array to finish the sorting process. Argue that this sorting algorithm runs in $O(nk + n\lg(n/k))$ expected time. How should we pick k, both in theory and in practice?

7.4-6 ★
Consider modifying the PARTITION procedure by randomly picking three elements from array A and partitioning about their median (the middle value of the three elements). Approximate the probability of getting at worst an α-to-$(1-\alpha)$ split, as a function of α in the range $0 < \alpha < 1$.

Problems

7-1   *Hoare partition correctness*
The version of PARTITION given in this chapter is not the original partitioning algorithm. Here is the original partition algorithm, which is due to C. A. R. Hoare:

HOARE-PARTITION(A, p, r)

```
1   x = A[p]
2   i = p - 1
3   j = r + 1
4   while TRUE
5       repeat
6           j = j - 1
7       until A[j] ≤ x
8       repeat
9           i = i + 1
10      until A[i] ≥ x
11      if i < j
12          exchange A[i] with A[j]
13      else return j
```

a. Demonstrate the operation of HOARE-PARTITION on the array $A = \langle 13, 19, 9, 5, 12, 8, 7, 4, 11, 2, 6, 21\rangle$, showing the values of the array and auxiliary values after each iteration of the **while** loop in lines 4–13.

The next three questions ask you to give a careful argument that the procedure HOARE-PARTITION is correct. Assuming that the subarray $A[p \mathinner{..} r]$ contains at least two elements, prove the following:

b. The indices i and j are such that we never access an element of A outside the subarray $A[p \mathinner{..} r]$.

c. When HOARE-PARTITION terminates, it returns a value j such that $p \le j < r$.

d. Every element of $A[p \mathinner{..} j]$ is less than or equal to every element of $A[j+1 \mathinner{..} r]$ when HOARE-PARTITION terminates.

The PARTITION procedure in Section 7.1 separates the pivot value (originally in $A[r]$) from the two partitions it forms. The HOARE-PARTITION procedure, on the other hand, always places the pivot value (originally in $A[p]$) into one of the two partitions $A[p \mathinner{..} j]$ and $A[j+1 \mathinner{..} r]$. Since $p \le j < r$, this split is always nontrivial.

e. Rewrite the QUICKSORT procedure to use HOARE-PARTITION.

7-2   *Quicksort with equal element values*

The analysis of the expected running time of randomized quicksort in Section 7.4.2 assumes that all element values are distinct. In this problem, we examine what happens when they are not.

a. Suppose that all element values are equal. What would be randomized quicksort's running time in this case?

b. The PARTITION procedure returns an index q such that each element of $A[p \mathinner{..} q - 1]$ is less than or equal to $A[q]$ and each element of $A[q + 1 \mathinner{..} r]$ is greater than $A[q]$. Modify the PARTITION procedure to produce a procedure PARTITION$'(A, p, r)$, which permutes the elements of $A[p \mathinner{..} r]$ and returns two indices q and t, where $p \le q \le t \le r$, such that

- all elements of $A[q \mathinner{..} t]$ are equal,
- each element of $A[p \mathinner{..} q - 1]$ is less than $A[q]$, and
- each element of $A[t + 1 \mathinner{..} r]$ is greater than $A[q]$.

Like PARTITION, your PARTITION$'$ procedure should take $\Theta(r - p)$ time.

c. Modify the RANDOMIZED-PARTITION procedure to call PARTITION$'$, and name the new procedure RANDOMIZED-PARTITION$'$. Then modify the QUICKSORT procedure to produce a procedure QUICKSORT$'(A, p, r)$ that calls

RANDOMIZED-PARTITION' and recurses only on partitions of elements not known to be equal to each other.

d. Using QUICKSORT', how would you adjust the analysis in Section 7.4.2 to avoid the assumption that all elements are distinct?

7-3 Alternative quicksort analysis

An alternative analysis of the running time of randomized quicksort focuses on the expected running time of each individual recursive call to RANDOMIZED-QUICKSORT, rather than on the number of comparisons performed.

a. Argue that, given an array of size n, the probability that any particular element is chosen as the pivot is $1/n$. Use this to define indicator random variables $X_i = I\{i\text{th smallest element is chosen as the pivot}\}$. What is $E[X_i]$?

b. Let $T(n)$ be a random variable denoting the running time of quicksort on an array of size n. Argue that

$$E[T(n)] = E\left[\sum_{q=1}^{n} X_q\left(T(q-1) + T(n-q) + \Theta(n)\right)\right]. \tag{7.5}$$

c. Show that we can rewrite equation (7.5) as

$$E[T(n)] = \frac{2}{n}\sum_{q=2}^{n-1} E[T(q)] + \Theta(n). \tag{7.6}$$

d. Show that

$$\sum_{k=2}^{n-1} k\lg k \le \frac{1}{2}n^2\lg n - \frac{1}{8}n^2. \tag{7.7}$$

(*Hint:* Split the summation into two parts, one for $k = 2, 3, \ldots, \lceil n/2 \rceil - 1$ and one for $k = \lceil n/2 \rceil, \ldots, n - 1$.)

e. Using the bound from equation (7.7), show that the recurrence in equation (7.6) has the solution $E[T(n)] = \Theta(n\lg n)$. (*Hint:* Show, by substitution, that $E[T(n)] \le an\lg n$ for sufficiently large n and for some positive constant a.)

7-4 *Stack depth for quicksort*

The QUICKSORT algorithm of Section 7.1 contains two recursive calls to itself. After QUICKSORT calls PARTITION, it recursively sorts the left subarray and then it recursively sorts the right subarray. The second recursive call in QUICKSORT is not really necessary; we can avoid it by using an iterative control structure. This technique, called **tail recursion**, is provided automatically by good compilers. Consider the following version of quicksort, which simulates tail recursion:

TAIL-RECURSIVE-QUICKSORT(A, p, r)

```
1  while p < r
2      // Partition and sort left subarray.
3      q = PARTITION(A, p, r)
4      TAIL-RECURSIVE-QUICKSORT(A, p, q − 1)
5      p = q + 1
```

a. Argue that TAIL-RECURSIVE-QUICKSORT$(A, 1, A.length)$ correctly sorts the array A.

Compilers usually execute recursive procedures by using a **stack** that contains pertinent information, including the parameter values, for each recursive call. The information for the most recent call is at the top of the stack, and the information for the initial call is at the bottom. Upon calling a procedure, its information is **pushed** onto the stack; when it terminates, its information is **popped**. Since we assume that array parameters are represented by pointers, the information for each procedure call on the stack requires $O(1)$ stack space. The **stack depth** is the maximum amount of stack space used at any time during a computation.

b. Describe a scenario in which TAIL-RECURSIVE-QUICKSORT's stack depth is $\Theta(n)$ on an n-element input array.

c. Modify the code for TAIL-RECURSIVE-QUICKSORT so that the worst-case stack depth is $\Theta(\lg n)$. Maintain the $O(n \lg n)$ expected running time of the algorithm.

7-5 *Median-of-3 partition*

One way to improve the RANDOMIZED-QUICKSORT procedure is to partition around a pivot that is chosen more carefully than by picking a random element from the subarray. One common approach is the **median-of-3** method: choose the pivot as the median (middle element) of a set of 3 elements randomly selected from the subarray. (See Exercise 7.4-6.) For this problem, let us assume that the elements in the input array $A[1 .. n]$ are distinct and that $n \geq 3$. We denote the

sorted output array by $A'[1 . . n]$. Using the median-of-3 method to choose the pivot element x, define $p_i = \Pr\{x = A'[i]\}$.

a. Give an exact formula for p_i as a function of n and i for $i = 2, 3, \ldots, n - 1$. (Note that $p_1 = p_n = 0$.)

b. By what amount have we increased the likelihood of choosing the pivot as $x = A'[\lfloor (n + 1)/2 \rfloor]$, the median of $A[1 . . n]$, compared with the ordinary implementation? Assume that $n \to \infty$, and give the limiting ratio of these probabilities.

c. If we define a "good" split to mean choosing the pivot as $x = A'[i]$, where $n/3 \le i \le 2n/3$, by what amount have we increased the likelihood of getting a good split compared with the ordinary implementation? (*Hint:* Approximate the sum by an integral.)

d. Argue that in the $\Omega(n \lg n)$ running time of quicksort, the median-of-3 method affects only the constant factor.

7-6 *Fuzzy sorting of intervals*

Consider a sorting problem in which we do not know the numbers exactly. Instead, for each number, we know an interval on the real line to which it belongs. That is, we are given n closed intervals of the form $[a_i, b_i]$, where $a_i \le b_i$. We wish to *fuzzy-sort* these intervals, i.e., to produce a permutation $\langle i_1, i_2, \ldots, i_n \rangle$ of the intervals such that for $j = 1, 2, \ldots, n$, there exist $c_j \in [a_{i_j}, b_{i_j}]$ satisfying $c_1 \le c_2 \le \cdots \le c_n$.

a. Design a randomized algorithm for fuzzy-sorting n intervals. Your algorithm should have the general structure of an algorithm that quicksorts the left endpoints (the a_i values), but it should take advantage of overlapping intervals to improve the running time. (As the intervals overlap more and more, the problem of fuzzy-sorting the intervals becomes progressively easier. Your algorithm should take advantage of such overlapping, to the extent that it exists.)

b. Argue that your algorithm runs in expected time $\Theta(n \lg n)$ in general, but runs in expected time $\Theta(n)$ when all of the intervals overlap (i.e., when there exists a value x such that $x \in [a_i, b_i]$ for all i). Your algorithm should not be checking for this case explicitly; rather, its performance should naturally improve as the amount of overlap increases.

Chapter notes

The quicksort procedure was invented by Hoare [170]; Hoare's version appears in Problem 7-1. The PARTITION procedure given in Section 7.1 is due to N. Lomuto. The analysis in Section 7.4 is due to Avrim Blum. Sedgewick [305] and Bentley [43] provide a good reference on the details of implementation and how they matter.

McIlroy [248] showed how to engineer a "killer adversary" that produces an array on which virtually any implementation of quicksort takes $\Theta(n^2)$ time. If the implementation is randomized, the adversary produces the array after seeing the random choices of the quicksort algorithm.

8   Sorting in Linear Time

We have now introduced several algorithms that can sort n numbers in $O(n \lg n)$ time. Merge sort and heapsort achieve this upper bound in the worst case; quicksort achieves it on average. Moreover, for each of these algorithms, we can produce a sequence of n input numbers that causes the algorithm to run in $\Omega(n \lg n)$ time.

These algorithms share an interesting property: *the sorted order they determine is based only on comparisons between the input elements.* We call such sorting algorithms **comparison sorts**. All the sorting algorithms introduced thus far are comparison sorts.

In Section 8.1, we shall prove that any comparison sort must make $\Omega(n \lg n)$ comparisons in the worst case to sort n elements. Thus, merge sort and heapsort are asymptotically optimal, and no comparison sort exists that is faster by more than a constant factor.

Sections 8.2, 8.3, and 8.4 examine three sorting algorithms—counting sort, radix sort, and bucket sort—that run in linear time. Of course, these algorithms use operations other than comparisons to determine the sorted order. Consequently, the $\Omega(n \lg n)$ lower bound does not apply to them.

8.1   Lower bounds for sorting

In a comparison sort, we use only comparisons between elements to gain order information about an input sequence $\langle a_1, a_2, \ldots, a_n \rangle$. That is, given two elements a_i and a_j, we perform one of the tests $a_i < a_j$, $a_i \leq a_j$, $a_i = a_j$, $a_i \geq a_j$, or $a_i > a_j$ to determine their relative order. We may not inspect the values of the elements or gain order information about them in any other way.

In this section, we assume without loss of generality that all the input elements are distinct. Given this assumption, comparisons of the form $a_i = a_j$ are useless, so we can assume that no comparisons of this form are made. We also note that the comparisons $a_i \leq a_j$, $a_i \geq a_j$, $a_i > a_j$, and $a_i < a_j$ are all equivalent in that

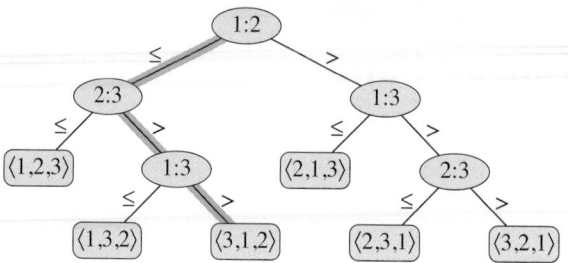

Figure 8.1 The decision tree for insertion sort operating on three elements. An internal node annotated by $i:j$ indicates a comparison between a_i and a_j. A leaf annotated by the permutation $\langle \pi(1), \pi(2), \ldots, \pi(n) \rangle$ indicates the ordering $a_{\pi(1)} \leq a_{\pi(2)} \leq \cdots \leq a_{\pi(n)}$. The shaded path indicates the decisions made when sorting the input sequence $\langle a_1 = 6, a_2 = 8, a_3 = 5 \rangle$; the permutation $\langle 3, 1, 2 \rangle$ at the leaf indicates that the sorted ordering is $a_3 = 5 \leq a_1 = 6 \leq a_2 = 8$. There are $3! = 6$ possible permutations of the input elements, and so the decision tree must have at least 6 leaves.

they yield identical information about the relative order of a_i and a_j. We therefore assume that all comparisons have the form $a_i \leq a_j$.

The decision-tree model

We can view comparison sorts abstractly in terms of decision trees. A ***decision tree*** is a full binary tree that represents the comparisons between elements that are performed by a particular sorting algorithm operating on an input of a given size. Control, data movement, and all other aspects of the algorithm are ignored. Figure 8.1 shows the decision tree corresponding to the insertion sort algorithm from Section 2.1 operating on an input sequence of three elements.

In a decision tree, we annotate each internal node by $i:j$ for some i and j in the range $1 \leq i, j \leq n$, where n is the number of elements in the input sequence. We also annotate each leaf by a permutation $\langle \pi(1), \pi(2), \ldots, \pi(n) \rangle$. (See Section C.1 for background on permutations.) The execution of the sorting algorithm corresponds to tracing a simple path from the root of the decision tree down to a leaf. Each internal node indicates a comparison $a_i \leq a_j$. The left subtree then dictates subsequent comparisons once we know that $a_i \leq a_j$, and the right subtree dictates subsequent comparisons knowing that $a_i > a_j$. When we come to a leaf, the sorting algorithm has established the ordering $a_{\pi(1)} \leq a_{\pi(2)} \leq \cdots \leq a_{\pi(n)}$. Because any correct sorting algorithm must be able to produce each permutation of its input, each of the $n!$ permutations on n elements must appear as one of the leaves of the decision tree for a comparison sort to be correct. Furthermore, each of these leaves must be reachable from the root by a downward path corresponding to an actual

execution of the comparison sort. (We shall refer to such leaves as "reachable.") Thus, we shall consider only decision trees in which each permutation appears as a reachable leaf.

A lower bound for the worst case

The length of the longest simple path from the root of a decision tree to any of its reachable leaves represents the worst-case number of comparisons that the corresponding sorting algorithm performs. Consequently, the worst-case number of comparisons for a given comparison sort algorithm equals the height of its decision tree. A lower bound on the heights of all decision trees in which each permutation appears as a reachable leaf is therefore a lower bound on the running time of any comparison sort algorithm. The following theorem establishes such a lower bound.

Theorem 8.1
Any comparison sort algorithm requires $\Omega(n \lg n)$ comparisons in the worst case.

Proof   From the preceding discussion, it suffices to determine the height of a decision tree in which each permutation appears as a reachable leaf. Consider a decision tree of height h with l reachable leaves corresponding to a comparison sort on n elements. Because each of the $n!$ permutations of the input appears as some leaf, we have $n! \le l$. Since a binary tree of height h has no more than 2^h leaves, we have

$$n! \le l \le 2^h \ ,$$

which, by taking logarithms, implies

$$
\begin{aligned}
h &\ge \lg(n!) \quad \text{(since the lg function is monotonically increasing)} \\
  &= \Omega(n \lg n) \quad \text{(by equation (3.19))} \ .
\end{aligned}
$$
∎

Corollary 8.2
Heapsort and merge sort are asymptotically optimal comparison sorts.

Proof   The $O(n \lg n)$ upper bounds on the running times for heapsort and merge sort match the $\Omega(n \lg n)$ worst-case lower bound from Theorem 8.1.   ∎

Exercises

8.1-1
What is the smallest possible depth of a leaf in a decision tree for a comparison sort?

8.1-2

Obtain asymptotically tight bounds on $\lg(n!)$ without using Stirling's approximation. Instead, evaluate the summation $\sum_{k=1}^{n} \lg k$ using techniques from Section A.2.

8.1-3

Show that there is no comparison sort whose running time is linear for at least half of the $n!$ inputs of length n. What about a fraction of $1/n$ of the inputs of length n? What about a fraction $1/2^n$?

8.1-4

Suppose that you are given a sequence of n elements to sort. The input sequence consists of n/k subsequences, each containing k elements. The elements in a given subsequence are all smaller than the elements in the succeeding subsequence and larger than the elements in the preceding subsequence. Thus, all that is needed to sort the whole sequence of length n is to sort the k elements in each of the n/k subsequences. Show an $\Omega(n \lg k)$ lower bound on the number of comparisons needed to solve this variant of the sorting problem. (*Hint:* It is not rigorous to simply combine the lower bounds for the individual subsequences.)

8.2   Counting sort

Counting sort assumes that each of the n input elements is an integer in the range 0 to k, for some integer k. When $k = O(n)$, the sort runs in $\Theta(n)$ time.

Counting sort determines, for each input element x, the number of elements less than x. It uses this information to place element x directly into its position in the output array. For example, if 17 elements are less than x, then x belongs in output position 18. We must modify this scheme slightly to handle the situation in which several elements have the same value, since we do not want to put them all in the same position.

In the code for counting sort, we assume that the input is an array $A[1 \mathinner{.\,.} n]$, and thus $A.length = n$. We require two other arrays: the array $B[1 \mathinner{.\,.} n]$ holds the sorted output, and the array $C[0 \mathinner{.\,.} k]$ provides temporary working storage.

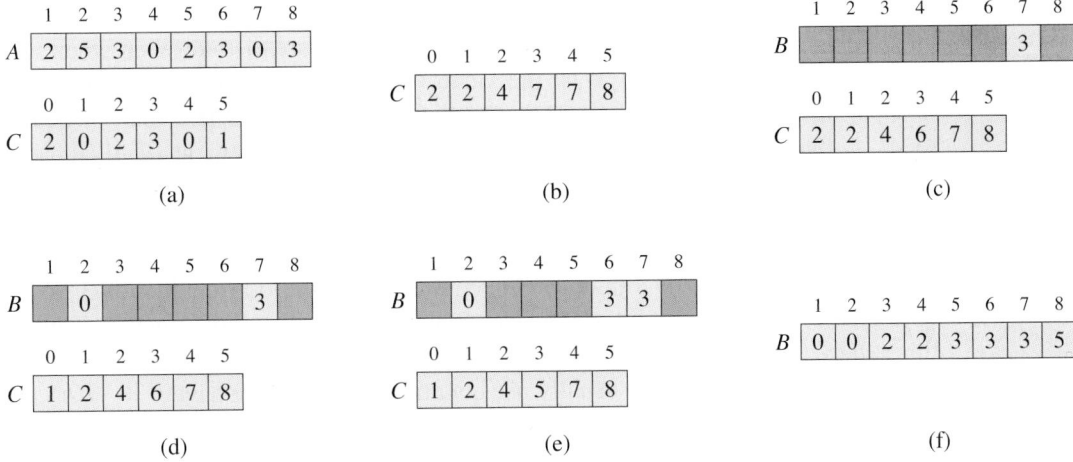

Figure 8.2 The operation of COUNTING-SORT on an input array $A[1 .. 8]$, where each element of A is a nonnegative integer no larger than $k = 5$. **(a)** The array A and the auxiliary array C after line 5. **(b)** The array C after line 8. **(c)–(e)** The output array B and the auxiliary array C after one, two, and three iterations of the loop in lines 10–12, respectively. Only the lightly shaded elements of array B have been filled in. **(f)** The final sorted output array B.

COUNTING-SORT(A, B, k)

```
1   let C[0 .. k] be a new array
2   for i = 0 to k
3       C[i] = 0
4   for j = 1 to A.length
5       C[A[j]] = C[A[j]] + 1
6   // C[i] now contains the number of elements equal to i.
7   for i = 1 to k
8       C[i] = C[i] + C[i − 1]
9   // C[i] now contains the number of elements less than or equal to i.
10  for j = A.length downto 1
11      B[C[A[j]]] = A[j]
12      C[A[j]] = C[A[j]] − 1
```

Figure 8.2 illustrates counting sort. After the **for** loop of lines 2–3 initializes the array C to all zeros, the **for** loop of lines 4–5 inspects each input element. If the value of an input element is i, we increment $C[i]$. Thus, after line 5, $C[i]$ holds the number of input elements equal to i for each integer $i = 0, 1, \ldots, k$. Lines 7–8 determine for each $i = 0, 1, \ldots, k$ how many input elements are less than or equal to i by keeping a running sum of the array C.

Finally, the **for** loop of lines 10–12 places each element $A[j]$ into its correct sorted position in the output array B. If all n elements are distinct, then when we first enter line 10, for each $A[j]$, the value $C[A[j]]$ is the correct final position of $A[j]$ in the output array, since there are $C[A[j]]$ elements less than or equal to $A[j]$. Because the elements might not be distinct, we decrement $C[A[j]]$ each time we place a value $A[j]$ into the B array. Decrementing $C[A[j]]$ causes the next input element with a value equal to $A[j]$, if one exists, to go to the position immediately before $A[j]$ in the output array.

How much time does counting sort require? The **for** loop of lines 2–3 takes time $\Theta(k)$, the **for** loop of lines 4–5 takes time $\Theta(n)$, the **for** loop of lines 7–8 takes time $\Theta(k)$, and the **for** loop of lines 10–12 takes time $\Theta(n)$. Thus, the overall time is $\Theta(k + n)$. In practice, we usually use counting sort when we have $k = O(n)$, in which case the running time is $\Theta(n)$.

Counting sort beats the lower bound of $\Omega(n \lg n)$ proved in Section 8.1 because it is not a comparison sort. In fact, no comparisons between input elements occur anywhere in the code. Instead, counting sort uses the actual values of the elements to index into an array. The $\Omega(n \lg n)$ lower bound for sorting does not apply when we depart from the comparison sort model.

An important property of counting sort is that it is ***stable***: numbers with the same value appear in the output array in the same order as they do in the input array. That is, it breaks ties between two numbers by the rule that whichever number appears first in the input array appears first in the output array. Normally, the property of stability is important only when satellite data are carried around with the element being sorted. Counting sort's stability is important for another reason: counting sort is often used as a subroutine in radix sort. As we shall see in the next section, in order for radix sort to work correctly, counting sort must be stable.

Exercises

8.2-1
Using Figure 8.2 as a model, illustrate the operation of COUNTING-SORT on the array $A = \langle 6, 0, 2, 0, 1, 3, 4, 6, 1, 3, 2 \rangle$.

8.2-2
Prove that COUNTING-SORT is stable.

8.2-3
Suppose that we were to rewrite the **for** loop header in line 10 of the COUNTING-SORT as

10   **for** $j = 1$ **to** $A.length$

Show that the algorithm still works properly. Is the modified algorithm stable?

8.2-4

Describe an algorithm that, given n integers in the range 0 to k, preprocesses its input and then answers any query about how many of the n integers fall into a range $[a .. b]$ in $O(1)$ time. Your algorithm should use $\Theta(n + k)$ preprocessing time.

8.3 Radix sort

Radix sort is the algorithm used by the card-sorting machines you now find only in computer museums. The cards have 80 columns, and in each column a machine can punch a hole in one of 12 places. The sorter can be mechanically "programmed" to examine a given column of each card in a deck and distribute the card into one of 12 bins depending on which place has been punched. An operator can then gather the cards bin by bin, so that cards with the first place punched are on top of cards with the second place punched, and so on.

For decimal digits, each column uses only 10 places. (The other two places are reserved for encoding nonnumeric characters.) A d-digit number would then occupy a field of d columns. Since the card sorter can look at only one column at a time, the problem of sorting n cards on a d-digit number requires a sorting algorithm.

Intuitively, you might sort numbers on their *most significant* digit, sort each of the resulting bins recursively, and then combine the decks in order. Unfortunately, since the cards in 9 of the 10 bins must be put aside to sort each of the bins, this procedure generates many intermediate piles of cards that you would have to keep track of. (See Exercise 8.3-5.)

Radix sort solves the problem of card sorting—counterintuitively—by sorting on the *least significant* digit first. The algorithm then combines the cards into a single deck, with the cards in the 0 bin preceding the cards in the 1 bin preceding the cards in the 2 bin, and so on. Then it sorts the entire deck again on the second-least significant digit and recombines the deck in a like manner. The process continues until the cards have been sorted on all d digits. Remarkably, at that point the cards are fully sorted on the d-digit number. Thus, only d passes through the deck are required to sort. Figure 8.3 shows how radix sort operates on a "deck" of seven 3-digit numbers.

In order for radix sort to work correctly, the digit sorts must be stable. The sort performed by a card sorter is stable, but the operator has to be wary about not changing the order of the cards as they come out of a bin, even though all the cards in a bin have the same digit in the chosen column.

```
329        720        720        329
457        355        329        355
657        436        436        436
839 ····⫶⪼ 457 ····⫶⪼ 839 ····⫶⪼ 457
436        657        355        657
720        329        457        720
355        839        657        839
```

Figure 8.3 The operation of radix sort on a list of seven 3-digit numbers. The leftmost column is the input. The remaining columns show the list after successive sorts on increasingly significant digit positions. Shading indicates the digit position sorted on to produce each list from the previous one.

In a typical computer, which is a sequential random-access machine, we sometimes use radix sort to sort records of information that are keyed by multiple fields. For example, we might wish to sort dates by three keys: year, month, and day. We could run a sorting algorithm with a comparison function that, given two dates, compares years, and if there is a tie, compares months, and if another tie occurs, compares days. Alternatively, we could sort the information three times with a stable sort: first on day, next on month, and finally on year.

The code for radix sort is straightforward. The following procedure assumes that each element in the n-element array A has d digits, where digit 1 is the lowest-order digit and digit d is the highest-order digit.

RADIX-SORT(A, d)

1 **for** $i = 1$ **to** d
2   use a stable sort to sort array A on digit i

Lemma 8.3
Given n d-digit numbers in which each digit can take on up to k possible values, RADIX-SORT correctly sorts these numbers in $\Theta(d(n + k))$ time if the stable sort it uses takes $\Theta(n + k)$ time.

Proof The correctness of radix sort follows by induction on the column being sorted (see Exercise 8.3-3). The analysis of the running time depends on the stable sort used as the intermediate sorting algorithm. When each digit is in the range 0 to $k-1$ (so that it can take on k possible values), and k is not too large, counting sort is the obvious choice. Each pass over n d-digit numbers then takes time $\Theta(n + k)$. There are d passes, and so the total time for radix sort is $\Theta(d(n + k))$. ∎

When d is constant and $k = O(n)$, we can make radix sort run in linear time. More generally, we have some flexibility in how to break each key into digits.

Lemma 8.4

Given n b-bit numbers and any positive integer $r \le b$, RADIX-SORT correctly sorts these numbers in $\Theta((b/r)(n + 2^r))$ time if the stable sort it uses takes $\Theta(n + k)$ time for inputs in the range 0 to k.

Proof For a value $r \le b$, we view each key as having $d = \lceil b/r \rceil$ digits of r bits each. Each digit is an integer in the range 0 to $2^r - 1$, so that we can use counting sort with $k = 2^r$. (For example, we can view a 32-bit word as having four 8-bit digits, so that $b = 32, r = 8, k = 2^r = 256$, and $d = b/r = 4$.) Each pass of counting sort takes time $\Theta(n + k) = \Theta(n + 2^r)$ and there are d passes, for a total running time of $\Theta(d(n + 2^r)) = \Theta((b/r)(n + 2^r))$. ∎

For given values of n and b, we wish to choose the value of r, with $r \le b$, that minimizes the expression $(b/r)(n + 2^r)$. If $b < \lfloor \lg n \rfloor$, then for any value of $r \le b$, we have that $(n + 2^r) = \Theta(n)$. Thus, choosing $r = b$ yields a running time of $(b/b)(n + 2^b) = \Theta(n)$, which is asymptotically optimal. If $b \ge \lfloor \lg n \rfloor$, then choosing $r = \lfloor \lg n \rfloor$ gives the best time to within a constant factor, which we can see as follows. Choosing $r = \lfloor \lg n \rfloor$ yields a running time of $\Theta(bn/ \lg n)$. As we increase r above $\lfloor \lg n \rfloor$, the 2^r term in the numerator increases faster than the r term in the denominator, and so increasing r above $\lfloor \lg n \rfloor$ yields a running time of $\Omega(bn/ \lg n)$. If instead we were to decrease r below $\lfloor \lg n \rfloor$, then the b/r term increases and the $n + 2^r$ term remains at $\Theta(n)$.

Is radix sort preferable to a comparison-based sorting algorithm, such as quicksort? If $b = O(\lg n)$, as is often the case, and we choose $r \approx \lg n$, then radix sort's running time is $\Theta(n)$, which appears to be better than quicksort's expected running time of $\Theta(n \lg n)$. The constant factors hidden in the Θ-notation differ, however. Although radix sort may make fewer passes than quicksort over the n keys, each pass of radix sort may take significantly longer. Which sorting algorithm we prefer depends on the characteristics of the implementations, of the underlying machine (e.g., quicksort often uses hardware caches more effectively than radix sort), and of the input data. Moreover, the version of radix sort that uses counting sort as the intermediate stable sort does not sort in place, which many of the $\Theta(n \lg n)$-time comparison sorts do. Thus, when primary memory storage is at a premium, we might prefer an in-place algorithm such as quicksort.

Exercises

8.3-1

Using Figure 8.3 as a model, illustrate the operation of RADIX-SORT on the following list of English words: COW, DOG, SEA, RUG, ROW, MOB, BOX, TAB, BAR, EAR, TAR, DIG, BIG, TEA, NOW, FOX.

8.3-2

Which of the following sorting algorithms are stable: insertion sort, merge sort, heapsort, and quicksort? Give a simple scheme that makes any comparison sort stable. How much additional time and space does your scheme entail?

8.3-3

Use induction to prove that radix sort works. Where does your proof need the assumption that the intermediate sort is stable?

8.3-4

Show how to sort n integers in the range 0 to $n^3 - 1$ in $O(n)$ time.

8.3-5 ★

In the first card-sorting algorithm in this section, exactly how many sorting passes are needed to sort d-digit decimal numbers in the worst case? How many piles of cards would an operator need to keep track of in the worst case?

8.4 Bucket sort

Bucket sort assumes that the input is drawn from a uniform distribution and has an average-case running time of $O(n)$. Like counting sort, bucket sort is fast because it assumes something about the input. Whereas counting sort assumes that the input consists of integers in a small range, bucket sort assumes that the input is generated by a random process that distributes elements uniformly and independently over the interval $[0, 1)$. (See Section C.2 for a definition of uniform distribution.)

Bucket sort divides the interval $[0, 1)$ into n equal-sized subintervals, or *buckets*, and then distributes the n input numbers into the buckets. Since the inputs are uniformly and independently distributed over $[0, 1)$, we do not expect many numbers to fall into each bucket. To produce the output, we simply sort the numbers in each bucket and then go through the buckets in order, listing the elements in each.

Our code for bucket sort assumes that the input is an n-element array A and that each element $A[i]$ in the array satisfies $0 \leq A[i] < 1$. The code requires an auxiliary array $B[0 \mathinner{.\,.} n - 1]$ of linked lists (buckets) and assumes that there is a mechanism for maintaining such lists. (Section 10.2 describes how to implement basic operations on linked lists.)

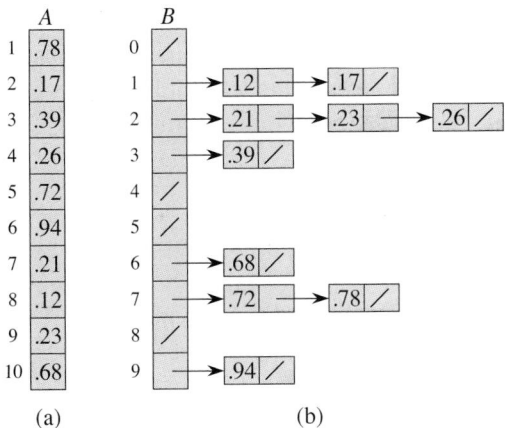

Figure 8.4   The operation of BUCKET-SORT for $n = 10$. **(a)** The input array $A[1 . . 10]$. **(b)** The array $B[0 . . 9]$ of sorted lists (buckets) after line 8 of the algorithm. Bucket i holds values in the half-open interval $[i/10, (i + 1)/10)$. The sorted output consists of a concatenation in order of the lists $B[0], B[1], \ldots, B[9]$.

BUCKET-SORT(A)

```
1   n = A.length
2   let B[0 .. n − 1] be a new array
3   for i = 0 to n − 1
4       make B[i] an empty list
5   for i = 1 to n
6       insert A[i] into list B[⌊nA[i]⌋]
7   for i = 0 to n − 1
8       sort list B[i] with insertion sort
9   concatenate the lists B[0], B[1], . . . , B[n − 1] together in order
```

Figure 8.4 shows the operation of bucket sort on an input array of 10 numbers.

To see that this algorithm works, consider two elements $A[i]$ and $A[j]$. Assume without loss of generality that $A[i] \leq A[j]$. Since $\lfloor nA[i] \rfloor \leq \lfloor nA[j] \rfloor$, either element $A[i]$ goes into the same bucket as $A[j]$ or it goes into a bucket with a lower index. If $A[i]$ and $A[j]$ go into the same bucket, then the **for** loop of lines 7–8 puts them into the proper order. If $A[i]$ and $A[j]$ go into different buckets, then line 9 puts them into the proper order. Therefore, bucket sort works correctly.

To analyze the running time, observe that all lines except line 8 take $O(n)$ time in the worst case. We need to analyze the total time taken by the n calls to insertion sort in line 8.

To analyze the cost of the calls to insertion sort, let n_i be the random variable denoting the number of elements placed in bucket $B[i]$. Since insertion sort runs in quadratic time (see Section 2.2), the running time of bucket sort is

$$T(n) = \Theta(n) + \sum_{i=0}^{n-1} O(n_i^2) \, .$$

We now analyze the average-case running time of bucket sort, by computing the expected value of the running time, where we take the expectation over the input distribution. Taking expectations of both sides and using linearity of expectation, we have

$$
\begin{aligned}
\mathrm{E}\left[T(n)\right] &= \mathrm{E}\left[\Theta(n) + \sum_{i=0}^{n-1} O(n_i^2)\right] \\
&= \Theta(n) + \sum_{i=0}^{n-1} \mathrm{E}\left[O(n_i^2)\right] \quad \text{(by linearity of expectation)} \\
&= \Theta(n) + \sum_{i=0}^{n-1} O\left(\mathrm{E}\left[n_i^2\right]\right) \quad \text{(by equation (C.22))} \, .
\end{aligned}
\tag{8.1}
$$

We claim that

$$\mathrm{E}\left[n_i^2\right] = 2 - 1/n \tag{8.2}$$

for $i = 0, 1, \ldots, n - 1$. It is no surprise that each bucket i has the same value of $\mathrm{E}\left[n_i^2\right]$, since each value in the input array A is equally likely to fall in any bucket. To prove equation (8.2), we define indicator random variables

$$X_{ij} = \mathrm{I}\{A[j] \text{ falls in bucket } i\}$$

for $i = 0, 1, \ldots, n - 1$ and $j = 1, 2, \ldots, n$. Thus,

$$n_i = \sum_{j=1}^{n} X_{ij} \, .$$

To compute $\mathrm{E}\left[n_i^2\right]$, we expand the square and regroup terms:

$$
\begin{aligned}
\mathrm{E}\left[n_i^2\right] &= \mathrm{E}\left[\left(\sum_{j=1}^{n} X_{ij}\right)^2\right] \\
&= \mathrm{E}\left[\sum_{j=1}^{n}\sum_{k=1}^{n} X_{ij} X_{ik}\right] \\
&= \mathrm{E}\left[\sum_{j=1}^{n} X_{ij}^2 + \sum_{1\le j\le n}\sum_{\substack{1\le k\le n \\ k\ne j}} X_{ij} X_{ik}\right] \\
&= \sum_{j=1}^{n}\mathrm{E}\left[X_{ij}^2\right] + \sum_{1\le j\le n}\sum_{\substack{1\le k\le n \\ k\ne j}} \mathrm{E}\left[X_{ij} X_{ik}\right] \,, \quad\quad\quad (8.3)
\end{aligned}
$$

where the last line follows by linearity of expectation. We evaluate the two summations separately. Indicator random variable X_{ij} is 1 with probability $1/n$ and 0 otherwise, and therefore

$$
\begin{aligned}
\mathrm{E}\left[X_{ij}^2\right] &= 1^2 \cdot \frac{1}{n} + 0^2 \cdot \left(1 - \frac{1}{n}\right) \\
&= \frac{1}{n} \,.
\end{aligned}
$$

When $k \ne j$, the variables X_{ij} and X_{ik} are independent, and hence

$$
\begin{aligned}
\mathrm{E}\left[X_{ij} X_{ik}\right] &= \mathrm{E}\left[X_{ij}\right]\mathrm{E}\left[X_{ik}\right] \\
&= \frac{1}{n}\cdot\frac{1}{n} \\
&= \frac{1}{n^2} \,.
\end{aligned}
$$

Substituting these two expected values in equation (8.3), we obtain

$$
\begin{aligned}
\mathrm{E}\left[n_i^2\right] &= \sum_{j=1}^{n}\frac{1}{n} + \sum_{1\le j\le n}\sum_{\substack{1\le k\le n \\ k\ne j}}\frac{1}{n^2} \\
&= n\cdot\frac{1}{n} + n(n-1)\cdot\frac{1}{n^2} \\
&= 1 + \frac{n-1}{n} \\
&= 2 - \frac{1}{n} \,,
\end{aligned}
$$

which proves equation (8.2).

Using this expected value in equation (8.1), we conclude that the average-case running time for bucket sort is $\Theta(n) + n \cdot O(2 - 1/n) = \Theta(n)$.

Even if the input is not drawn from a uniform distribution, bucket sort may still run in linear time. As long as the input has the property that the sum of the squares of the bucket sizes is linear in the total number of elements, equation (8.1) tells us that bucket sort will run in linear time.

Exercises

8.4-1
Using Figure 8.4 as a model, illustrate the operation of BUCKET-SORT on the array $A = \langle .79, .13, .16, .64, .39, .20, .89, .53, .71, .42 \rangle$.

8.4-2
Explain why the worst-case running time for bucket sort is $\Theta(n^2)$. What simple change to the algorithm preserves its linear average-case running time and makes its worst-case running time $O(n \lg n)$?

8.4-3
Let X be a random variable that is equal to the number of heads in two flips of a fair coin. What is $E[X^2]$? What is $E^2[X]$?

8.4-4 ★
We are given n points in the unit circle, $p_i = (x_i, y_i)$, such that $0 < x_i^2 + y_i^2 \le 1$ for $i = 1, 2, \ldots, n$. Suppose that the points are uniformly distributed; that is, the probability of finding a point in any region of the circle is proportional to the area of that region. Design an algorithm with an average-case running time of $\Theta(n)$ to sort the n points by their distances $d_i = \sqrt{x_i^2 + y_i^2}$ from the origin. (*Hint:* Design the bucket sizes in BUCKET-SORT to reflect the uniform distribution of the points in the unit circle.)

8.4-5 ★
A ***probability distribution function*** $P(x)$ for a random variable X is defined by $P(x) = \Pr\{X \le x\}$. Suppose that we draw a list of n random variables $X_1, X_2, \ldots, X_n$ from a continuous probability distribution function P that is computable in $O(1)$ time. Give an algorithm that sorts these numbers in linear average-case time.

Problems

8-1 *Probabilistic lower bounds on comparison sorting*

In this problem, we prove a probabilistic $\Omega(n \lg n)$ lower bound on the running time of any deterministic or randomized comparison sort on n distinct input elements. We begin by examining a deterministic comparison sort A with decision tree T_A. We assume that every permutation of A's inputs is equally likely.

a. Suppose that each leaf of T_A is labeled with the probability that it is reached given a random input. Prove that exactly $n!$ leaves are labeled $1/n!$ and that the rest are labeled 0.

b. Let $D(T)$ denote the external path length of a decision tree T; that is, $D(T)$ is the sum of the depths of all the leaves of T. Let T be a decision tree with $k > 1$ leaves, and let LT and RT be the left and right subtrees of T. Show that $D(T) = D(LT) + D(RT) + k$.

c. Let $d(k)$ be the minimum value of $D(T)$ over all decision trees T with $k > 1$ leaves. Show that $d(k) = \min_{1 \le i \le k-1} \{d(i) + d(k-i) + k\}$. (*Hint:* Consider a decision tree T with k leaves that achieves the minimum. Let i_0 be the number of leaves in LT and $k - i_0$ the number of leaves in RT.)

d. Prove that for a given value of $k > 1$ and i in the range $1 \le i \le k - 1$, the function $i \lg i + (k - i) \lg(k - i)$ is minimized at $i = k/2$. Conclude that $d(k) = \Omega(k \lg k)$.

e. Prove that $D(T_A) = \Omega(n! \lg(n!))$, and conclude that the average-case time to sort n elements is $\Omega(n \lg n)$.

Now, consider a *randomized* comparison sort B. We can extend the decision-tree model to handle randomization by incorporating two kinds of nodes: ordinary comparison nodes and "randomization" nodes. A randomization node models a random choice of the form RANDOM$(1, r)$ made by algorithm B; the node has r children, each of which is equally likely to be chosen during an execution of the algorithm.

f. Show that for any randomized comparison sort B, there exists a deterministic comparison sort A whose expected number of comparisons is no more than those made by B.

8-2 *Sorting in place in linear time*

Suppose that we have an array of n data records to sort and that the key of each record has the value 0 or 1. An algorithm for sorting such a set of records might possess some subset of the following three desirable characteristics:

1. The algorithm runs in $O(n)$ time.

2. The algorithm is stable.

3. The algorithm sorts in place, using no more than a constant amount of storage space in addition to the original array.

   a. Give an algorithm that satisfies criteria 1 and 2 above.

   b. Give an algorithm that satisfies criteria 1 and 3 above.

   c. Give an algorithm that satisfies criteria 2 and 3 above.

   d. Can you use any of your sorting algorithms from parts (a)–(c) as the sorting method used in line 2 of RADIX-SORT, so that RADIX-SORT sorts n records with b-bit keys in $O(bn)$ time? Explain how or why not.

   e. Suppose that the n records have keys in the range from 1 to k. Show how to modify counting sort so that it sorts the records in place in $O(n + k)$ time. You may use $O(k)$ storage outside the input array. Is your algorithm stable? (*Hint:* How would you do it for $k = 3$?)

8-3 *Sorting variable-length items*

   a. You are given an array of integers, where different integers may have different numbers of digits, but the total number of digits over *all* the integers in the array is n. Show how to sort the array in $O(n)$ time.

   b. You are given an array of strings, where different strings may have different numbers of characters, but the total number of characters over all the strings is n. Show how to sort the strings in $O(n)$ time.

   (Note that the desired order here is the standard alphabetical order; for example, a < ab < b.)

8-4 *Water jugs*

Suppose that you are given n red and n blue water jugs, all of different shapes and sizes. All red jugs hold different amounts of water, as do the blue ones. Moreover, for every red jug, there is a blue jug that holds the same amount of water, and vice versa.

Your task is to find a grouping of the jugs into pairs of red and blue jugs that hold the same amount of water. To do so, you may perform the following operation: pick a pair of jugs in which one is red and one is blue, fill the red jug with water, and then pour the water into the blue jug. This operation will tell you whether the red or the blue jug can hold more water, or that they have the same volume. Assume that such a comparison takes one time unit. Your goal is to find an algorithm that makes a minimum number of comparisons to determine the grouping. Remember that you may not directly compare two red jugs or two blue jugs.

a. Describe a deterministic algorithm that uses $\Theta(n^2)$ comparisons to group the jugs into pairs.

b. Prove a lower bound of $\Omega(n \lg n)$ for the number of comparisons that an algorithm solving this problem must make.

c. Give a randomized algorithm whose expected number of comparisons is $O(n \lg n)$, and prove that this bound is correct. What is the worst-case number of comparisons for your algorithm?

8-5 *Average sorting*

Suppose that, instead of sorting an array, we just require that the elements increase on average. More precisely, we call an n-element array A *k-sorted* if, for all $i = 1, 2, \ldots, n - k$, the following holds:

$$\frac{\sum_{j=i}^{i+k-1} A[j]}{k} \leq \frac{\sum_{j=i+1}^{i+k} A[j]}{k} .$$

a. What does it mean for an array to be 1-sorted?

b. Give a permutation of the numbers $1, 2, \ldots, 10$ that is 2-sorted, but not sorted.

c. Prove that an n-element array is k-sorted if and only if $A[i] \leq A[i + k]$ for all $i = 1, 2, \ldots, n - k$.

d. Give an algorithm that k-sorts an n-element array in $O(n \lg(n/k))$ time.

We can also show a lower bound on the time to produce a k-sorted array, when k is a constant.

e. Show that we can sort a k-sorted array of length n in $O(n \lg k)$ time. (*Hint:* Use the solution to Exercise 6.5-9.)

f. Show that when k is a constant, k-sorting an n-element array requires $\Omega(n \lg n)$ time. (*Hint:* Use the solution to the previous part along with the lower bound on comparison sorts.)

8-6   *Lower bound on merging sorted lists*

The problem of merging two sorted lists arises frequently. We have seen a procedure for it as the subroutine MERGE in Section 2.3.1. In this problem, we will prove a lower bound of $2n - 1$ on the worst-case number of comparisons required to merge two sorted lists, each containing n items.

First we will show a lower bound of $2n - o(n)$ comparisons by using a decision tree.

a. Given $2n$ numbers, compute the number of possible ways to divide them into two sorted lists, each with n numbers.

b. Using a decision tree and your answer to part (a), show that any algorithm that correctly merges two sorted lists must perform at least $2n - o(n)$ comparisons.

Now we will show a slightly tighter $2n - 1$ bound.

c. Show that if two elements are consecutive in the sorted order and from different lists, then they must be compared.

d. Use your answer to the previous part to show a lower bound of $2n - 1$ comparisons for merging two sorted lists.

8-7   *The 0-1 sorting lemma and columnsort*

A ***compare-exchange*** operation on two array elements $A[i]$ and $A[j]$, where $i < j$, has the form

COMPARE-EXCHANGE(A, i, j)

```
1   if A[i] > A[j]
2       exchange A[i] with A[j]
```

After the compare-exchange operation, we know that $A[i] \leq A[j]$.

An ***oblivious compare-exchange algorithm*** operates solely by a sequence of prespecified compare-exchange operations. The indices of the positions compared in the sequence must be determined in advance, and although they can depend on the number of elements being sorted, they cannot depend on the values being sorted, nor can they depend on the result of any prior compare-exchange operation. For example, here is insertion sort expressed as an oblivious compare-exchange algorithm:

INSERTION-SORT(A)

```
1   for j = 2 to A.length
2       for i = j − 1 downto 1
3           COMPARE-EXCHANGE(A, i, i + 1)
```

The **0-1 sorting lemma** provides a powerful way to prove that an oblivious compare-exchange algorithm produces a sorted result. It states that if an oblivious compare-exchange algorithm correctly sorts all input sequences consisting of only 0s and 1s, then it correctly sorts all inputs containing arbitrary values.

You will prove the 0-1 sorting lemma by proving its contrapositive: if an oblivious compare-exchange algorithm fails to sort an input containing arbitrary values, then it fails to sort some 0-1 input. Assume that an oblivious compare-exchange algorithm X fails to correctly sort the array $A[1 .. n]$. Let $A[p]$ be the smallest value in A that algorithm X puts into the wrong location, and let $A[q]$ be the value that algorithm X moves to the location into which $A[p]$ should have gone. Define an array $B[1 .. n]$ of 0s and 1s as follows:

$$B[i] = \begin{cases} 0 & \text{if } A[i] \leq A[p], \\ 1 & \text{if } A[i] > A[p]. \end{cases}$$

a. Argue that $A[q] > A[p]$, so that $B[p] = 0$ and $B[q] = 1$.

b. To complete the proof of the 0-1 sorting lemma, prove that algorithm X fails to sort array B correctly.

Now you will use the 0-1 sorting lemma to prove that a particular sorting algorithm works correctly. The algorithm, **columnsort**, works on a rectangular array of n elements. The array has r rows and s columns (so that $n = rs$), subject to three restrictions:

- r must be even,
- s must be a divisor of r, and
- $r \geq 2s^2$.

When columnsort completes, the array is sorted in **column-major order**: reading down the columns, from left to right, the elements monotonically increase.

Columnsort operates in eight steps, regardless of the value of n. The odd steps are all the same: sort each column individually. Each even step is a fixed permutation. Here are the steps:

1. Sort each column.

2. Transpose the array, but reshape it back to r rows and s columns. In other words, turn the leftmost column into the top r/s rows, in order; turn the next column into the next r/s rows, in order; and so on.

3. Sort each column.

4. Perform the inverse of the permutation performed in step 2.

10	14	5
8	7	17
12	1	6
16	9	11
4	15	2
18	3	13

(a)

4	1	2
8	3	5
10	7	6
12	9	11
16	14	13
18	15	17

(b)

4	8	10
12	16	18
1	3	7
9	14	15
2	5	6
11	13	17

(c)

1	3	6
2	5	7
4	8	10
9	13	15
11	14	17
12	16	18

(d)

1	4	11
3	8	14
6	10	17
2	9	12
5	13	16
7	15	18

(e)

1	4	11
2	8	12
3	9	14
5	10	16
6	13	17
7	15	18

(f)

	5	10	16
	6	13	17
	7	15	18
1	4	11
2	8	12
3	9	14

(g)

	4	10	16
	5	11	17
	6	12	18
1	7	13
2	8	14
3	9	15

(h)

1	7	13
2	8	14
3	9	15
4	10	16
5	11	17
6	12	18

(i)

Figure 8.5 The steps of columnsort. **(a)** The input array with 6 rows and 3 columns. **(b)** After sorting each column in step 1. **(c)** After transposing and reshaping in step 2. **(d)** After sorting each column in step 3. **(e)** After performing step 4, which inverts the permutation from step 2. **(f)** After sorting each column in step 5. **(g)** After shifting by half a column in step 6. **(h)** After sorting each column in step 7. **(i)** After performing step 8, which inverts the permutation from step 6. The array is now sorted in column-major order.

5. Sort each column.

6. Shift the top half of each column into the bottom half of the same column, and shift the bottom half of each column into the top half of the next column to the right. Leave the top half of the leftmost column empty. Shift the bottom half of the last column into the top half of a new rightmost column, and leave the bottom half of this new column empty.

7. Sort each column.

8. Perform the inverse of the permutation performed in step 6.

Figure 8.5 shows an example of the steps of columnsort with $r = 6$ and $s = 3$. (Even though this example violates the requirement that $r \geq 2s^2$, it happens to work.)

c. Argue that we can treat columnsort as an oblivious compare-exchange algorithm, even if we do not know what sorting method the odd steps use.

Although it might seem hard to believe that columnsort actually sorts, you will use the 0-1 sorting lemma to prove that it does. The 0-1 sorting lemma applies because we can treat columnsort as an oblivious compare-exchange algorithm. A

couple of definitions will help you apply the 0-1 sorting lemma. We say that an area of an array is **clean** if we know that it contains either all 0s or all 1s. Otherwise, the area might contain mixed 0s and 1s, and it is **dirty**. From here on, assume that the input array contains only 0s and 1s, and that we can treat it as an array with r rows and s columns.

d. Prove that after steps 1–3, the array consists of some clean rows of 0s at the top, some clean rows of 1s at the bottom, and at most s dirty rows between them.

e. Prove that after step 4, the array, read in column-major order, starts with a clean area of 0s, ends with a clean area of 1s, and has a dirty area of at most s^2 elements in the middle.

f. Prove that steps 5–8 produce a fully sorted 0-1 output. Conclude that column-sort correctly sorts all inputs containing arbitrary values.

g. Now suppose that s does not divide r. Prove that after steps 1–3, the array consists of some clean rows of 0s at the top, some clean rows of 1s at the bottom, and at most $2s - 1$ dirty rows between them. How large must r be, compared with s, for columnsort to correctly sort when s does not divide r?

h. Suggest a simple change to step 1 that allows us to maintain the requirement that $r \geq 2s^2$ even when s does not divide r, and prove that with your change, columnsort correctly sorts.

Chapter notes

The decision-tree model for studying comparison sorts was introduced by Ford and Johnson [110]. Knuth's comprehensive treatise on sorting [211] covers many variations on the sorting problem, including the information-theoretic lower bound on the complexity of sorting given here. Ben-Or [39] studied lower bounds for sorting using generalizations of the decision-tree model.

Knuth credits H. H. Seward with inventing counting sort in 1954, as well as with the idea of combining counting sort with radix sort. Radix sorting starting with the least significant digit appears to be a folk algorithm widely used by operators of mechanical card-sorting machines. According to Knuth, the first published reference to the method is a 1929 document by L. J. Comrie describing punched-card equipment. Bucket sorting has been in use since 1956, when the basic idea was proposed by E. J. Isaac and R. C. Singleton [188].

Munro and Raman [263] give a stable sorting algorithm that performs $O(n^{1+\epsilon})$ comparisons in the worst case, where $0 < \epsilon \leq 1$ is any fixed constant. Although

any of the $O(n \lg n)$-time algorithms make fewer comparisons, the algorithm by Munro and Raman moves data only $O(n)$ times and operates in place.

The case of sorting n b-bit integers in $o(n \lg n)$ time has been considered by many researchers. Several positive results have been obtained, each under slightly different assumptions about the model of computation and the restrictions placed on the algorithm. All the results assume that the computer memory is divided into addressable b-bit words. Fredman and Willard [115] introduced the fusion tree data structure and used it to sort n integers in $O(n \lg n / \lg \lg n)$ time. This bound was later improved to $O(n \sqrt{\lg n})$ time by Andersson [16]. These algorithms require the use of multiplication and several precomputed constants. Andersson, Hagerup, Nilsson, and Raman [17] have shown how to sort n integers in $O(n \lg \lg n)$ time without using multiplication, but their method requires storage that can be unbounded in terms of n. Using multiplicative hashing, we can reduce the storage needed to $O(n)$, but then the $O(n \lg \lg n)$ worst-case bound on the running time becomes an expected-time bound. Generalizing the exponential search trees of Andersson [16], Thorup [335] gave an $O(n(\lg \lg n)^2)$-time sorting algorithm that does not use multiplication or randomization, and it uses linear space. Combining these techniques with some new ideas, Han [158] improved the bound for sorting to $O(n \lg \lg n \lg \lg \lg n)$ time. Although these algorithms are important theoretical breakthroughs, they are all fairly complicated and at the present time seem unlikely to compete with existing sorting algorithms in practice.

The columnsort algorithm in Problem 8-7 is by Leighton [227].

9   Medians and Order Statistics

The ith *order statistic* of a set of n elements is the ith smallest element. For example, the *minimum* of a set of elements is the first order statistic ($i = 1$), and the *maximum* is the nth order statistic ($i = n$). A *median*, informally, is the "halfway point" of the set. When n is odd, the median is unique, occurring at $i = (n + 1)/2$. When n is even, there are two medians, occurring at $i = n/2$ and $i = n/2 + 1$. Thus, regardless of the parity of n, medians occur at $i = \lfloor (n + 1)/2 \rfloor$ (the *lower median*) and $i = \lceil (n + 1)/2 \rceil$ (the *upper median*). For simplicity in this text, however, we consistently use the phrase "the median" to refer to the lower median.

This chapter addresses the problem of selecting the ith order statistic from a set of n distinct numbers. We assume for convenience that the set contains distinct numbers, although virtually everything that we do extends to the situation in which a set contains repeated values. We formally specify the *selection problem* as follows:

Input: A set A of n (distinct) numbers and an integer i, with $1 \leq i \leq n$.

Output: The element $x \in A$ that is larger than exactly $i - 1$ other elements of A.

We can solve the selection problem in $O(n \lg n)$ time, since we can sort the numbers using heapsort or merge sort and then simply index the ith element in the output array. This chapter presents faster algorithms.

In Section 9.1, we examine the problem of selecting the minimum and maximum of a set of elements. More interesting is the general selection problem, which we investigate in the subsequent two sections. Section 9.2 analyzes a practical randomized algorithm that achieves an $O(n)$ expected running time, assuming distinct elements. Section 9.3 contains an algorithm of more theoretical interest that achieves the $O(n)$ running time in the worst case.

9.1   Minimum and maximum

How many comparisons are necessary to determine the minimum of a set of n elements? We can easily obtain an upper bound of $n - 1$ comparisons: examine each element of the set in turn and keep track of the smallest element seen so far. In the following procedure, we assume that the set resides in array A, where $A.length = n$.

MINIMUM(A)

```
1   min = A[1]
2   for i = 2 to A.length
3       if min > A[i]
4           min = A[i]
5   return min
```

We can, of course, find the maximum with $n - 1$ comparisons as well.

Is this the best we can do? Yes, since we can obtain a lower bound of $n - 1$ comparisons for the problem of determining the minimum. Think of any algorithm that determines the minimum as a tournament among the elements. Each comparison is a match in the tournament in which the smaller of the two elements wins. Observing that every element except the winner must lose at least one match, we conclude that $n - 1$ comparisons are necessary to determine the minimum. Hence, the algorithm MINIMUM is optimal with respect to the number of comparisons performed.

Simultaneous minimum and maximum

In some applications, we must find both the minimum and the maximum of a set of n elements. For example, a graphics program may need to scale a set of (x, y) data to fit onto a rectangular display screen or other graphical output device. To do so, the program must first determine the minimum and maximum value of each coordinate.

At this point, it should be obvious how to determine both the minimum and the maximum of n elements using $\Theta(n)$ comparisons, which is asymptotically optimal: simply find the minimum and maximum independently, using $n - 1$ comparisons for each, for a total of $2n - 2$ comparisons.

In fact, we can find both the minimum and the maximum using at most $3 \lfloor n/2 \rfloor$ comparisons. We do so by maintaining both the minimum and maximum elements seen thus far. Rather than processing each element of the input by comparing it against the current minimum and maximum, at a cost of 2 comparisons per element,

we process elements in pairs. We compare pairs of elements from the input first *with each other*, and then we compare the smaller with the current minimum and the larger to the current maximum, at a cost of 3 comparisons for every 2 elements.

How we set up initial values for the current minimum and maximum depends on whether n is odd or even. If n is odd, we set both the minimum and maximum to the value of the first element, and then we process the rest of the elements in pairs. If n is even, we perform 1 comparison on the first 2 elements to determine the initial values of the minimum and maximum, and then process the rest of the elements in pairs as in the case for odd n.

Let us analyze the total number of comparisons. If n is odd, then we perform $3 \lfloor n/2 \rfloor$ comparisons. If n is even, we perform 1 initial comparison followed by $3(n - 2)/2$ comparisons, for a total of $3n/2 - 2$. Thus, in either case, the total number of comparisons is at most $3 \lfloor n/2 \rfloor$.

Exercises

9.1-1
Show that the second smallest of n elements can be found with $n + \lceil \lg n \rceil - 2$ comparisons in the worst case. (*Hint:* Also find the smallest element.)

9.1-2   ★
Prove the lower bound of $\lceil 3n/2 \rceil - 2$ comparisons in the worst case to find both the maximum and minimum of n numbers. (*Hint:* Consider how many numbers are potentially either the maximum or minimum, and investigate how a comparison affects these counts.)

9.2   Selection in expected linear time

The general selection problem appears more difficult than the simple problem of finding a minimum. Yet, surprisingly, the asymptotic running time for both problems is the same: $\Theta(n)$. In this section, we present a divide-and-conquer algorithm for the selection problem. The algorithm RANDOMIZED-SELECT is modeled after the quicksort algorithm of Chapter 7. As in quicksort, we partition the input array recursively. But unlike quicksort, which recursively processes both sides of the partition, RANDOMIZED-SELECT works on only one side of the partition. This difference shows up in the analysis: whereas quicksort has an expected running time of $\Theta(n \lg n)$, the expected running time of RANDOMIZED-SELECT is $\Theta(n)$, assuming that the elements are distinct.

RANDOMIZED-SELECT uses the procedure RANDOMIZED-PARTITION introduced in Section 7.3. Thus, like RANDOMIZED-QUICKSORT, it is a randomized algorithm, since its behavior is determined in part by the output of a random-number
generator. The following code for RANDOMIZED-SELECT returns the ith smallest
element of the array $A[p..r]$.

RANDOMIZED-SELECT(A, p, r, i)

```
1   if p == r
2       return A[p]
3   q = RANDOMIZED-PARTITION(A, p, r)
4   k = q − p + 1
5   if i == k              // the pivot value is the answer
6       return A[q]
7   elseif i < k
8       return RANDOMIZED-SELECT(A, p, q − 1, i)
9   else return RANDOMIZED-SELECT(A, q + 1, r, i − k)
```

The RANDOMIZED-SELECT procedure works as follows. Line 1 checks for the
base case of the recursion, in which the subarray $A[p..r]$ consists of just one
element. In this case, i must equal 1, and we simply return $A[p]$ in line 2 as the
ith smallest element. Otherwise, the call to RANDOMIZED-PARTITION in line 3
partitions the array $A[p..r]$ into two (possibly empty) subarrays $A[p..q − 1]$
and $A[q + 1..r]$ such that each element of $A[p..q − 1]$ is less than or equal
to $A[q]$, which in turn is less than each element of $A[q + 1..r]$. As in quicksort,
we will refer to $A[q]$ as the ***pivot*** element. Line 4 computes the number k of
elements in the subarray $A[p..q]$, that is, the number of elements in the low side
of the partition, plus one for the pivot element. Line 5 then checks whether $A[q]$ is
the ith smallest element. If it is, then line 6 returns $A[q]$. Otherwise, the algorithm
determines in which of the two subarrays $A[p..q − 1]$ and $A[q + 1..r]$ the ith
smallest element lies. If $i < k$, then the desired element lies on the low side of
the partition, and line 8 recursively selects it from the subarray. If $i > k$, however,
then the desired element lies on the high side of the partition. Since we already
know k values that are smaller than the ith smallest element of $A[p..r]$—namely,
the elements of $A[p..q]$—the desired element is the $(i − k)$th smallest element
of $A[q + 1..r]$, which line 9 finds recursively. The code appears to allow recursive
calls to subarrays with 0 elements, but Exercise 9.2-1 asks you to show that this
situation cannot happen.

The worst-case running time for RANDOMIZED-SELECT is $\Theta(n^2)$, even to find
the minimum, because we could be extremely unlucky and always partition around
the largest remaining element, and partitioning takes $\Theta(n)$ time. We will see that

the algorithm has a linear expected running time, though, and because it is random-ized, no particular input elicits the worst-case behavior.

To analyze the expected running time of RANDOMIZED-SELECT, we let the run-ning time on an input array $A[p \mathrel{..} r]$ of n elements be a random variable that we denote by $T(n)$, and we obtain an upper bound on $\mathrm{E}\left[T(n)\right]$ as follows. The pro-cedure RANDOMIZED-PARTITION is equally likely to return any element as the pivot. Therefore, for each k such that $1 \leq k \leq n$, the subarray $A[p \mathrel{..} q]$ has k ele-ments (all less than or equal to the pivot) with probability $1/n$. For $k = 1, 2, \ldots, n$, we define indicator random variables X_k where

$$X_k = \mathrm{I}\{\text{the subarray } A[p \mathrel{..} q] \text{ has exactly } k \text{ elements}\} \;,$$

and so, assuming that the elements are distinct, we have

$$\mathrm{E}\left[X_k\right] = 1/n \;. \tag{9.1}$$

When we call RANDOMIZED-SELECT and choose $A[q]$ as the pivot element, we do not know, a priori, if we will terminate immediately with the correct answer, recurse on the subarray $A[p \mathrel{..} q - 1]$, or recurse on the subarray $A[q + 1 \mathrel{..} r]$. This decision depends on where the ith smallest element falls relative to $A[q]$. Assuming that $T(n)$ is monotonically increasing, we can upper-bound the time needed for the recursive call by the time needed for the recursive call on the largest possible input. In other words, to obtain an upper bound, we assume that the ith element is always on the side of the partition with the greater number of elements. For a given call of RANDOMIZED-SELECT, the indicator random variable X_k has the value 1 for exactly one value of k, and it is 0 for all other k. When $X_k = 1$, the two subarrays on which we might recurse have sizes $k - 1$ and $n - k$. Hence, we have the recurrence

$$
\begin{aligned}
T(n) \;\leq\; & \sum_{k=1}^{n} X_k \cdot \left(T(\max(k - 1, n - k)) + O(n)\right) \\
=\; & \sum_{k=1}^{n} X_k \cdot T(\max(k - 1, n - k)) + O(n) \;.
\end{aligned}
$$

Taking expected values, we have

$$E[T(n)]$$

$$\leq \; E\left[\sum_{k=1}^{n} X_k \cdot T(\max(k-1, n-k)) + O(n)\right]$$

$$= \; \sum_{k=1}^{n} E[X_k \cdot T(\max(k-1, n-k))] + O(n) \qquad \text{(by linearity of expectation)}$$

$$= \; \sum_{k=1}^{n} E[X_k] \cdot E[T(\max(k-1, n-k))] + O(n) \quad \text{(by equation (C.24))}$$

$$= \; \sum_{k=1}^{n} \frac{1}{n} \cdot E[T(\max(k-1, n-k))] + O(n) \qquad \text{(by equation (9.1))}\;.$$

In order to apply equation (C.24), we rely on X_k and $T(\max(k-1, n-k))$ being independent random variables. Exercise 9.2-2 asks you to justify this assertion.

Let us consider the expression $\max(k-1, n-k)$. We have

$$\max(k-1, n-k) = \begin{cases} k-1 & \text{if } k > \lceil n/2 \rceil\,, \\ n-k & \text{if } k \leq \lceil n/2 \rceil\,. \end{cases}$$

If n is even, each term from $T(\lceil n/2 \rceil)$ up to $T(n-1)$ appears exactly twice in the summation, and if n is odd, all these terms appear twice and $T(\lfloor n/2 \rfloor)$ appears once. Thus, we have

$$E[T(n)] \leq \frac{2}{n} \sum_{k=\lfloor n/2 \rfloor}^{n-1} E[T(k)] + O(n)\;.$$

We show that $E[T(n)] = O(n)$ by substitution. Assume that $E[T(n)] \leq cn$ for some constant c that satisfies the initial conditions of the recurrence. We assume that $T(n) = O(1)$ for n less than some constant; we shall pick this constant later. We also pick a constant a such that the function described by the $O(n)$ term above (which describes the non-recursive component of the running time of the algorithm) is bounded from above by an for all $n > 0$. Using this inductive hypothesis, we have

$$E[T(n)] \; \leq \; \frac{2}{n} \sum_{k=\lfloor n/2 \rfloor}^{n-1} ck + an$$

$$= \; \frac{2c}{n} \left(\sum_{k=1}^{n-1} k - \sum_{k=1}^{\lfloor n/2 \rfloor - 1} k\right) + an$$

$$= \frac{2c}{n} \left(\frac{(n-1)n}{2} - \frac{(\lfloor n/2 \rfloor - 1) \lfloor n/2 \rfloor}{2} \right) + an$$

$$\leq \frac{2c}{n} \left(\frac{(n-1)n}{2} - \frac{(n/2 - 2)(n/2 - 1)}{2} \right) + an$$

$$= \frac{2c}{n} \left(\frac{n^2 - n}{2} - \frac{n^2/4 - 3n/2 + 2}{2} \right) + an$$

$$= \frac{c}{n} \left(\frac{3n^2}{4} + \frac{n}{2} - 2 \right) + an$$

$$= c \left(\frac{3n}{4} + \frac{1}{2} - \frac{2}{n} \right) + an$$

$$\leq \frac{3cn}{4} + \frac{c}{2} + an$$

$$= cn - \left(\frac{cn}{4} - \frac{c}{2} - an \right) .$$

In order to complete the proof, we need to show that for sufficiently large n, this last expression is at most cn or, equivalently, that $cn/4 - c/2 - an \geq 0$. If we add $c/2$ to both sides and factor out n, we get $n(c/4 - a) \geq c/2$. As long as we choose the constant c so that $c/4 - a > 0$, i.e., $c > 4a$, we can divide both sides by $c/4 - a$, giving

$$n \geq \frac{c/2}{c/4 - a} = \frac{2c}{c - 4a} .$$

Thus, if we assume that $T(n) = O(1)$ for $n < 2c/(c-4a)$, then $\mathrm{E}\left[T(n)\right] = O(n)$. We conclude that we can find any order statistic, and in particular the median, in expected linear time, assuming that the elements are distinct.

Exercises

9.2-1
Show that RANDOMIZED-SELECT never makes a recursive call to a 0-length array.

9.2-2
Argue that the indicator random variable X_k and the value $T(\max(k - 1, n - k))$ are independent.

9.2-3
Write an iterative version of RANDOMIZED-SELECT.

9.2-4

Suppose we use RANDOMIZED-SELECT to select the minimum element of the array $A = \langle 3, 2, 9, 0, 7, 5, 4, 8, 6, 1 \rangle$. Describe a sequence of partitions that results in a worst-case performance of RANDOMIZED-SELECT.

9.3   Selection in worst-case linear time

We now examine a selection algorithm whose running time is $O(n)$ in the worst case. Like RANDOMIZED-SELECT, the algorithm SELECT finds the desired element by recursively partitioning the input array. Here, however, we *guarantee* a good split upon partitioning the array. SELECT uses the deterministic partitioning algorithm PARTITION from quicksort (see Section 7.1), but modified to take the element to partition around as an input parameter.

The SELECT algorithm determines the ith smallest of an input array of $n > 1$ distinct elements by executing the following steps. (If $n = 1$, then SELECT merely returns its only input value as the ith smallest.)

1. Divide the n elements of the input array into $\lfloor n/5 \rfloor$ groups of 5 elements each and at most one group made up of the remaining $n \bmod 5$ elements.

2. Find the median of each of the $\lceil n/5 \rceil$ groups by first insertion-sorting the elements of each group (of which there are at most 5) and then picking the median from the sorted list of group elements.

3. Use SELECT recursively to find the median x of the $\lceil n/5 \rceil$ medians found in step 2. (If there are an even number of medians, then by our convention, x is the lower median.)

4. Partition the input array around the median-of-medians x using the modified version of PARTITION. Let k be one more than the number of elements on the low side of the partition, so that x is the kth smallest element and there are $n - k$ elements on the high side of the partition.

5. If $i = k$, then return x. Otherwise, use SELECT recursively to find the ith smallest element on the low side if $i < k$, or the $(i - k)$th smallest element on the high side if $i > k$.

To analyze the running time of SELECT, we first determine a lower bound on the number of elements that are greater than the partitioning element x. Figure 9.1 helps us to visualize this bookkeeping. At least half of the medians found in

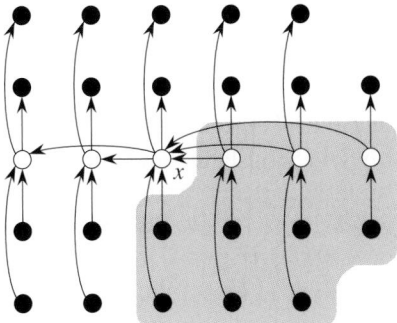

Figure 9.1 Analysis of the algorithm SELECT. The n elements are represented by small circles, and each group of 5 elements occupies a column. The medians of the groups are whitened, and the median-of-medians x is labeled. (When finding the median of an even number of elements, we use the lower median.) Arrows go from larger elements to smaller, from which we can see that 3 out of every full group of 5 elements to the right of x are greater than x, and 3 out of every group of 5 elements to the left of x are less than x. The elements known to be greater than x appear on a shaded background.

step 2 are greater than or equal to the median-of-medians x.[1] Thus, at least half of the $\lceil n/5 \rceil$ groups contribute at least 3 elements that are greater than x, except for the one group that has fewer than 5 elements if 5 does not divide n exactly, and the one group containing x itself. Discounting these two groups, it follows that the number of elements greater than x is at least

$$3\left(\left\lceil \frac{1}{2}\left\lceil \frac{n}{5}\right\rceil\right\rceil - 2\right) \geq \frac{3n}{10} - 6 .$$

Similarly, at least $3n/10 - 6$ elements are less than x. Thus, in the worst case, step 5 calls SELECT recursively on at most $7n/10 + 6$ elements.

We can now develop a recurrence for the worst-case running time $T(n)$ of the algorithm SELECT. Steps 1, 2, and 4 take $O(n)$ time. (Step 2 consists of $O(n)$ calls of insertion sort on sets of size $O(1)$.) Step 3 takes time $T(\lceil n/5 \rceil)$, and step 5 takes time at most $T(7n/10 + 6)$, assuming that T is monotonically increasing. We make the assumption, which seems unmotivated at first, that any input of fewer than 140 elements requires $O(1)$ time; the origin of the magic constant 140 will be clear shortly. We can therefore obtain the recurrence

---

[1]Because of our assumption that the numbers are distinct, all medians except x are either greater than or less than x.

$$T(n) \leq \begin{cases} O(1) & \text{if } n < 140\,, \\ T(\lceil n/5 \rceil) + T(7n/10 + 6) + O(n) & \text{if } n \geq 140\,. \end{cases}$$

We show that the running time is linear by substitution. More specifically, we will show that $T(n) \leq cn$ for some suitably large constant c and all $n > 0$. We begin by assuming that $T(n) \leq cn$ for some suitably large constant c and all $n < 140$; this assumption holds if c is large enough. We also pick a constant a such that the function described by the $O(n)$ term above (which describes the non-recursive component of the running time of the algorithm) is bounded above by an for all $n > 0$. Substituting this inductive hypothesis into the right-hand side of the recurrence yields

$$\begin{aligned} T(n) &\leq& c \lceil n/5 \rceil + c(7n/10 + 6) + an \\ &\leq& cn/5 + c + 7cn/10 + 6c + an \\ &=& 9cn/10 + 7c + an \\ &=& cn + (-cn/10 + 7c + an)\,, \end{aligned}$$

which is at most cn if

$$-cn/10 + 7c + an \leq 0\,. \tag{9.2}$$

Inequality (9.2) is equivalent to the inequality $c \geq 10a(n/(n - 70))$ when $n > 70$. Because we assume that $n \geq 140$, we have $n/(n - 70) \leq 2$, and so choosing $c \geq 20a$ will satisfy inequality (9.2). (Note that there is nothing special about the constant 140; we could replace it by any integer strictly greater than 70 and then choose c accordingly.) The worst-case running time of SELECT is therefore linear.

As in a comparison sort (see Section 8.1), SELECT and RANDOMIZED-SELECT determine information about the relative order of elements only by comparing elements. Recall from Chapter 8 that sorting requires $\Omega(n \lg n)$ time in the comparison model, even on average (see Problem 8-1). The linear-time sorting algorithms in Chapter 8 make assumptions about the input. In contrast, the linear-time selection algorithms in this chapter do not require any assumptions about the input. They are not subject to the $\Omega(n \lg n)$ lower bound because they manage to solve the selection problem without sorting. Thus, solving the selection problem by sorting and indexing, as presented in the introduction to this chapter, is asymptotically inefficient.

Exercises

9.3-1

In the algorithm SELECT, the input elements are divided into groups of 5. Will the algorithm work in linear time if they are divided into groups of 7? Argue that SELECT does not run in linear time if groups of 3 are used.

9.3-2

Analyze SELECT to show that if $n \geq 140$, then at least $\lceil n/4 \rceil$ elements are greater than the median-of-medians x and at least $\lceil n/4 \rceil$ elements are less than x.

9.3-3

Show how quicksort can be made to run in $O(n \lg n)$ time in the worst case, assuming that all elements are distinct.

9.3-4 ★

Suppose that an algorithm uses only comparisons to find the ith smallest element in a set of n elements. Show that it can also find the $i - 1$ smaller elements and the $n - i$ larger elements without performing any additional comparisons.

9.3-5

Suppose that you have a "black-box" worst-case linear-time median subroutine. Give a simple, linear-time algorithm that solves the selection problem for an arbitrary order statistic.

9.3-6

The kth *quantiles* of an n-element set are the $k - 1$ order statistics that divide the sorted set into k equal-sized sets (to within 1). Give an $O(n \lg k)$-time algorithm to list the kth quantiles of a set.

9.3-7

Describe an $O(n)$-time algorithm that, given a set S of n distinct numbers and a positive integer $k \leq n$, determines the k numbers in S that are closest to the median of S.

9.3-8

Let $X[1 .. n]$ and $Y[1 .. n]$ be two arrays, each containing n numbers already in sorted order. Give an $O(\lg n)$-time algorithm to find the median of all $2n$ elements in arrays X and Y.

9.3-9

Professor Olay is consulting for an oil company, which is planning a large pipeline running east to west through an oil field of n wells. The company wants to connect

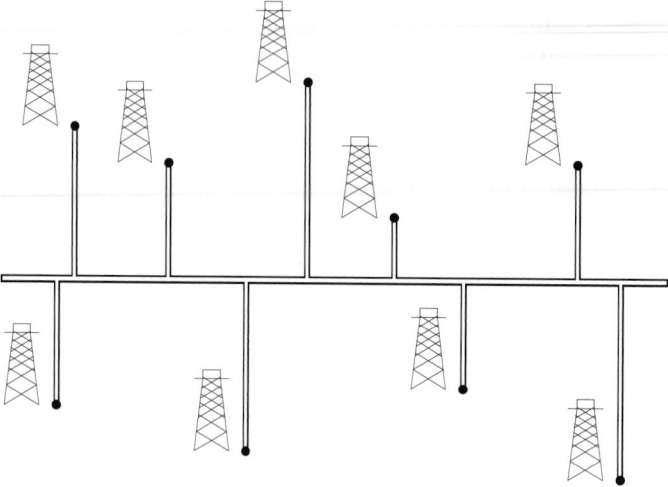

Figure 9.2 Professor Olay needs to determine the position of the east-west oil pipeline that minimizes the total length of the north-south spurs.

a spur pipeline from each well directly to the main pipeline along a shortest route (either north or south), as shown in Figure 9.2. Given the x- and y-coordinates of the wells, how should the professor pick the optimal location of the main pipeline, which would be the one that minimizes the total length of the spurs? Show how to determine the optimal location in linear time.

Problems

9-1 *Largest i numbers in sorted order*

Given a set of n numbers, we wish to find the i largest in sorted order using a comparison-based algorithm. Find the algorithm that implements each of the following methods with the best asymptotic worst-case running time, and analyze the running times of the algorithms in terms of n and i.

a. Sort the numbers, and list the i largest.

b. Build a max-priority queue from the numbers, and call EXTRACT-MAX i times.

c. Use an order-statistic algorithm to find the ith largest number, partition around that number, and sort the i largest numbers.

9-2 Weighted median

For n distinct elements $x_1, x_2, \ldots, x_n$ with positive weights $w_1, w_2, \ldots, w_n$ such that $\sum_{i=1}^{n} w_i = 1$, the **weighted (lower) median** is the element x_k satisfying

$$\sum_{x_i < x_k} w_i < \frac{1}{2}$$

and

$$\sum_{x_i > x_k} w_i \leq \frac{1}{2} \, .$$

For example, if the elements are $0.1, 0.35, 0.05, 0.1, 0.15, 0.05, 0.2$ and each element equals its weight (that is, $w_i = x_i$ for $i = 1, 2, \ldots, 7$), then the median is 0.1, but the weighted median is 0.2.

a. Argue that the median of $x_1, x_2, \ldots, x_n$ is the weighted median of the x_i with weights $w_i = 1/n$ for $i = 1, 2, \ldots, n$.

b. Show how to compute the weighted median of n elements in $O(n \lg n)$ worst-case time using sorting.

c. Show how to compute the weighted median in $\Theta(n)$ worst-case time using a linear-time median algorithm such as SELECT from Section 9.3.

The **post-office location problem** is defined as follows. We are given n points $p_1, p_2, \ldots, p_n$ with associated weights $w_1, w_2, \ldots, w_n$. We wish to find a point p (not necessarily one of the input points) that minimizes the sum $\sum_{i=1}^{n} w_i \, d(p, p_i)$, where $d(a, b)$ is the distance between points a and b.

d. Argue that the weighted median is a best solution for the 1-dimensional post-office location problem, in which points are simply real numbers and the distance between points a and b is $d(a, b) = |a - b|$.

e. Find the best solution for the 2-dimensional post-office location problem, in which the points are (x, y) coordinate pairs and the distance between points $a = (x_1, y_1)$ and $b = (x_2, y_2)$ is the **Manhattan distance** given by $d(a, b) = |x_1 - x_2| + |y_1 - y_2|$.

9-3 Small order statistics

We showed that the worst-case number $T(n)$ of comparisons used by SELECT to select the ith order statistic from n numbers satisfies $T(n) = \Theta(n)$, but the constant hidden by the Θ-notation is rather large. When i is small relative to n, we can implement a different procedure that uses SELECT as a subroutine but makes fewer comparisons in the worst case.

a. Describe an algorithm that uses $U_i(n)$ comparisons to find the ith smallest of n elements, where

$$U_i(n) = \begin{cases} T(n) & \text{if } i \geq n/2, \\ \lfloor n/2 \rfloor + U_i(\lceil n/2 \rceil) + T(2i) & \text{otherwise .} \end{cases}$$

(*Hint:* Begin with $\lfloor n/2 \rfloor$ disjoint pairwise comparisons, and recurse on the set containing the smaller element from each pair.)

b. Show that, if $i < n/2$, then $U_i(n) = n + O(T(2i) \lg(n/i))$.

c. Show that if i is a constant less than $n/2$, then $U_i(n) = n + O(\lg n)$.

d. Show that if $i = n/k$ for $k \geq 2$, then $U_i(n) = n + O(T(2n/k) \lg k)$.

9-4   *Alternative analysis of randomized selection*

In this problem, we use indicator random variables to analyze the RANDOMIZED-SELECT procedure in a manner akin to our analysis of RANDOMIZED-QUICKSORT in Section 7.4.2.

As in the quicksort analysis, we assume that all elements are distinct, and we rename the elements of the input array A as $z_1, z_2, \ldots, z_n$, where z_i is the ith smallest element. Thus, the call RANDOMIZED-SELECT$(A, 1, n, k)$ returns z_k.

For $1 \leq i < j \leq n$, let

$$X_{ijk} = I\{z_i \text{ is compared with } z_j \text{ sometime during the execution of the algorithm to find } z_k\} .$$

a. Give an exact expression for $E[X_{ijk}]$. (*Hint:* Your expression may have different values, depending on the values of i, j, and k.)

b. Let X_k denote the total number of comparisons between elements of array A when finding z_k. Show that

$$E[X_k] \leq 2 \left(\sum_{i=1}^{k} \sum_{j=k}^{n} \frac{1}{j-i+1} + \sum_{j=k+1}^{n} \frac{j-k-1}{j-k+1} + \sum_{i=1}^{k-2} \frac{k-i-1}{k-i+1} \right) .$$

c. Show that $E[X_k] \leq 4n$.

d. Conclude that, assuming all elements of array A are distinct, RANDOMIZED-SELECT runs in expected time $O(n)$.

Chapter notes

The worst-case linear-time median-finding algorithm was devised by Blum, Floyd, Pratt, Rivest, and Tarjan [50]. The fast randomized version is due to Hoare [169]. Floyd and Rivest [108] have developed an improved randomized version that partitions around an element recursively selected from a small sample of the elements.

It is still unknown exactly how many comparisons are needed to determine the median. Bent and John [41] gave a lower bound of $2n$ comparisons for median finding, and Schönhage, Paterson, and Pippenger [302] gave an upper bound of $3n$. Dor and Zwick have improved on both of these bounds. Their upper bound [93] is slightly less than $2.95n$, and their lower bound [94] is $(2 + \epsilon)n$, for a small positive constant ϵ, thereby improving slightly on related work by Dor et al. [92]. Paterson [272] describes some of these results along with other related work.

III   Data Structures

Introduction

Sets are as fundamental to computer science as they are to mathematics. Whereas mathematical sets are unchanging, the sets manipulated by algorithms can grow, shrink, or otherwise change over time. We call such sets *dynamic*. The next five chapters present some basic techniques for representing finite dynamic sets and manipulating them on a computer.

Algorithms may require several different types of operations to be performed on sets. For example, many algorithms need only the ability to insert elements into, delete elements from, and test membership in a set. We call a dynamic set that supports these operations a *dictionary*. Other algorithms require more complicated operations. For example, min-priority queues, which Chapter 6 introduced in the context of the heap data structure, support the operations of inserting an element into and extracting the smallest element from a set. The best way to implement a dynamic set depends upon the operations that must be supported.

Elements of a dynamic set

In a typical implementation of a dynamic set, each element is represented by an object whose attributes can be examined and manipulated if we have a pointer to the object. (Section 10.3 discusses the implementation of objects and pointers in programming environments that do not contain them as basic data types.) Some kinds of dynamic sets assume that one of the object's attributes is an identifying *key*. If the keys are all different, we can think of the dynamic set as being a set of key values. The object may contain *satellite data*, which are carried around in other object attributes but are otherwise unused by the set implementation. It may

also have attributes that are manipulated by the set operations; these attributes may contain data or pointers to other objects in the set.

Some dynamic sets presuppose that the keys are drawn from a totally ordered set, such as the real numbers, or the set of all words under the usual alphabetic ordering. A total ordering allows us to define the minimum element of the set, for example, or to speak of the next element larger than a given element in a set.

Operations on dynamic sets

Operations on a dynamic set can be grouped into two categories: *queries*, which simply return information about the set, and *modifying operations*, which change the set. Here is a list of typical operations. Any specific application will usually require only a few of these to be implemented.

SEARCH(S, k)

> A query that, given a set S and a key value k, returns a pointer x to an element in S such that $x.key = k$, or NIL if no such element belongs to S.

INSERT(S, x)

> A modifying operation that augments the set S with the element pointed to by x. We usually assume that any attributes in element x needed by the set implementation have already been initialized.

DELETE(S, x)

> A modifying operation that, given a pointer x to an element in the set S, removes x from S. (Note that this operation takes a pointer to an element x, not a key value.)

MINIMUM(S)

> A query on a totally ordered set S that returns a pointer to the element of S with the smallest key.

MAXIMUM(S)

> A query on a totally ordered set S that returns a pointer to the element of S with the largest key.

SUCCESSOR(S, x)

> A query that, given an element x whose key is from a totally ordered set S, returns a pointer to the next larger element in S, or NIL if x is the maximum element.

PREDECESSOR(S, x)

> A query that, given an element x whose key is from a totally ordered set S, returns a pointer to the next smaller element in S, or NIL if x is the minimum element.

In some situations, we can extend the queries SUCCESSOR and PREDECESSOR so that they apply to sets with nondistinct keys. For a set on n keys, the normal presumption is that a call to MINIMUM followed by $n - 1$ calls to SUCCESSOR enumerates the elements in the set in sorted order.

We usually measure the time taken to execute a set operation in terms of the size of the set. For example, Chapter 13 describes a data structure that can support any of the operations listed above on a set of size n in time $O(\lg n)$.

Overview of Part III

Chapters 10–14 describe several data structures that we can use to implement dynamic sets; we shall use many of these later to construct efficient algorithms for a variety of problems. We already saw another important data structure—the heap—in Chapter 6.

Chapter 10 presents the essentials of working with simple data structures such as stacks, queues, linked lists, and rooted trees. It also shows how to implement objects and pointers in programming environments that do not support them as primitives. If you have taken an introductory programming course, then much of this material should be familiar to you.

Chapter 11 introduces hash tables, which support the dictionary operations IN-SERT, DELETE, and SEARCH. In the worst case, hashing requires $\Theta(n)$ time to perform a SEARCH operation, but the expected time for hash-table operations is $O(1)$. The analysis of hashing relies on probability, but most of the chapter requires no background in the subject.

Binary search trees, which are covered in Chapter 12, support all the dynamic-set operations listed above. In the worst case, each operation takes $\Theta(n)$ time on a tree with n elements, but on a randomly built binary search tree, the expected time for each operation is $O(\lg n)$. Binary search trees serve as the basis for many other data structures.

Chapter 13 introduces red-black trees, which are a variant of binary search trees. Unlike ordinary binary search trees, red-black trees are guaranteed to perform well: operations take $O(\lg n)$ time in the worst case. A red-black tree is a balanced search tree; Chapter 18 in Part V presents another kind of balanced search tree, called a B-tree. Although the mechanics of red-black trees are somewhat intricate, you can glean most of their properties from the chapter without studying the mechanics in detail. Nevertheless, you probably will find walking through the code to be quite instructive.

In Chapter 14, we show how to augment red-black trees to support operations other than the basic ones listed above. First, we augment them so that we can dynamically maintain order statistics for a set of keys. Then, we augment them in a different way to maintain intervals of real numbers.

10 Elementary Data Structures

In this chapter, we examine the representation of dynamic sets by simple data structures that use pointers. Although we can construct many complex data structures using pointers, we present only the rudimentary ones: stacks, queues, linked lists, and rooted trees. We also show ways to synthesize objects and pointers from arrays.

10.1 Stacks and queues

Stacks and queues are dynamic sets in which the element removed from the set by the DELETE operation is prespecified. In a *stack*, the element deleted from the set is the one most recently inserted: the stack implements a *last-in, first-out*, or *LIFO*, policy. Similarly, in a *queue*, the element deleted is always the one that has been in the set for the longest time: the queue implements a *first-in, first-out*, or *FIFO*, policy. There are several efficient ways to implement stacks and queues on a computer. In this section we show how to use a simple array to implement each.

Stacks

The INSERT operation on a stack is often called PUSH, and the DELETE operation, which does not take an element argument, is often called POP. These names are allusions to physical stacks, such as the spring-loaded stacks of plates used in cafeterias. The order in which plates are popped from the stack is the reverse of the order in which they were pushed onto the stack, since only the top plate is accessible.

As Figure 10.1 shows, we can implement a stack of at most n elements with an array $S[1 \, .. \, n]$. The array has an attribute $S.top$ that indexes the most recently

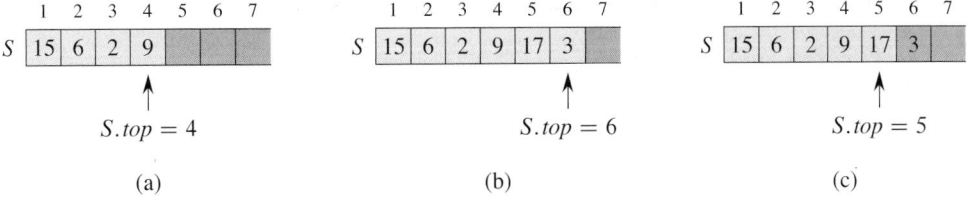

Figure 10.1 An array implementation of a stack S. Stack elements appear only in the lightly shaded positions. **(a)** Stack S has 4 elements. The top element is 9. **(b)** Stack S after the calls PUSH$(S, 17)$ and PUSH$(S, 3)$. **(c)** Stack S after the call POP(S) has returned the element 3, which is the one most recently pushed. Although element 3 still appears in the array, it is no longer in the stack; the top is element 17.

inserted element. The stack consists of elements $S[1 .. S.top]$, where $S[1]$ is the element at the bottom of the stack and $S[S.top]$ is the element at the top.

When $S.top = 0$, the stack contains no elements and is ***empty***. We can test to see whether the stack is empty by query operation STACK-EMPTY. If we attempt to pop an empty stack, we say the stack ***underflows***, which is normally an error. If $S.top$ exceeds n, the stack ***overflows***. (In our pseudocode implementation, we don't worry about stack overflow.)

We can implement each of the stack operations with just a few lines of code:

STACK-EMPTY(S)

```
1   if S.top == 0
2        return TRUE
3   else return FALSE
```

PUSH(S, x)

```
1   S.top = S.top + 1
2   S[S.top] = x
```

POP(S)

```
1   if STACK-EMPTY(S)
2        error "underflow"
3   else S.top = S.top - 1
4        return S[S.top + 1]
```

Figure 10.1 shows the effects of the modifying operations PUSH and POP. Each of the three stack operations takes $O(1)$ time.

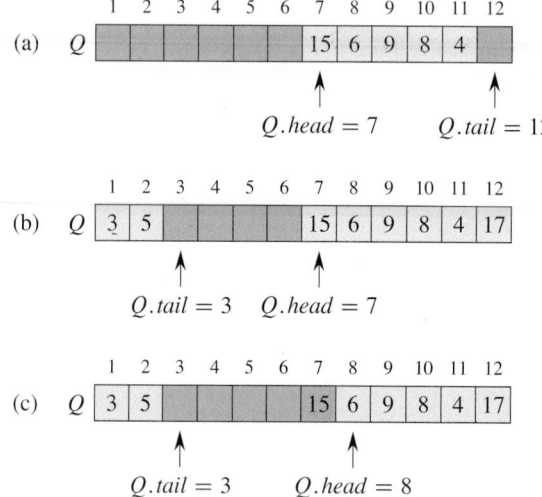

Figure 10.2 A queue implemented using an array $Q[1 . . 12]$. Queue elements appear only in the lightly shaded positions. **(a)** The queue has 5 elements, in locations $Q[7 . . 11]$. **(b)** The configuration of the queue after the calls ENQUEUE(Q, 17), ENQUEUE(Q, 3), and ENQUEUE(Q, 5). **(c)** The configuration of the queue after the call DEQUEUE(Q) returns the key value 15 formerly at the head of the queue. The new head has key 6.

Queues

We call the INSERT operation on a queue ENQUEUE, and we call the DELETE operation DEQUEUE; like the stack operation POP, DEQUEUE takes no element argument. The FIFO property of a queue causes it to operate like a line of customers waiting to pay a cashier. The queue has a ***head*** and a ***tail***. When an element is enqueued, it takes its place at the tail of the queue, just as a newly arriving customer takes a place at the end of the line. The element dequeued is always the one at the head of the queue, like the customer at the head of the line who has waited the longest.

Figure 10.2 shows one way to implement a queue of at most $n - 1$ elements using an array $Q[1 . . n]$. The queue has an attribute $Q.head$ that indexes, or points to, its head. The attribute $Q.tail$ indexes the next location at which a newly arriving element will be inserted into the queue. The elements in the queue reside in locations $Q.head, Q.head + 1, . . . , Q.tail - 1$, where we "wrap around" in the sense that location 1 immediately follows location n in a circular order. When $Q.head = Q.tail$, the queue is empty. Initially, we have $Q.head = Q.tail = 1$. If we attempt to dequeue an element from an empty queue, the queue underflows.

When $Q.head = Q.tail + 1$ or both $Q.head = 1$ and $Q.tail = Q.length$, the queue is full, and if we attempt to enqueue an element, then the queue overflows.

In our procedures ENQUEUE and DEQUEUE, we have omitted the error checking for underflow and overflow. (Exercise 10.1-4 asks you to supply code that checks for these two error conditions.) The pseudocode assumes that $n = Q.length$.

ENQUEUE(Q, x)

```
1   Q[Q.tail] = x
2   if Q.tail == Q.length
3       Q.tail = 1
4   else Q.tail = Q.tail + 1
```

DEQUEUE(Q)

```
1   x = Q[Q.head]
2   if Q.head == Q.length
3       Q.head = 1
4   else Q.head = Q.head + 1
5   return x
```

Figure 10.2 shows the effects of the ENQUEUE and DEQUEUE operations. Each operation takes $O(1)$ time.

Exercises

10.1-1
Using Figure 10.1 as a model, illustrate the result of each operation in the sequence PUSH($S, 4$), PUSH($S, 1$), PUSH($S, 3$), POP(S), PUSH($S, 8$), and POP(S) on an initially empty stack S stored in array $S[1 .. 6]$.

10.1-2
Explain how to implement two stacks in one array $A[1 .. n]$ in such a way that neither stack overflows unless the total number of elements in both stacks together is n. The PUSH and POP operations should run in $O(1)$ time.

10.1-3
Using Figure 10.2 as a model, illustrate the result of each operation in the sequence ENQUEUE($Q, 4$), ENQUEUE($Q, 1$), ENQUEUE($Q, 3$), DEQUEUE(Q), ENQUEUE($Q, 8$), and DEQUEUE(Q) on an initially empty queue Q stored in array $Q[1 .. 6]$.

10.1-4
Rewrite ENQUEUE and DEQUEUE to detect underflow and overflow of a queue.

10.1-5

Whereas a stack allows insertion and deletion of elements at only one end, and a queue allows insertion at one end and deletion at the other end, a ***deque*** (double-ended queue) allows insertion and deletion at both ends. Write four $O(1)$-time procedures to insert elements into and delete elements from both ends of a deque implemented by an array.

10.1-6

Show how to implement a queue using two stacks. Analyze the running time of the queue operations.

10.1-7

Show how to implement a stack using two queues. Analyze the running time of the stack operations.

10.2   Linked lists

A ***linked list*** is a data structure in which the objects are arranged in a linear order. Unlike an array, however, in which the linear order is determined by the array indices, the order in a linked list is determined by a pointer in each object. Linked lists provide a simple, flexible representation for dynamic sets, supporting (though not necessarily efficiently) all the operations listed on page 230.

As shown in Figure 10.3, each element of a ***doubly linked list*** L is an object with an attribute *key* and two other pointer attributes: *next* and *prev*. The object may also contain other satellite data. Given an element x in the list, $x.next$ points to its successor in the linked list, and $x.prev$ points to its predecessor. If $x.prev = \text{NIL}$, the element x has no predecessor and is therefore the first element, or ***head***, of the list. If $x.next = \text{NIL}$, the element x has no successor and is therefore the last element, or ***tail***, of the list. An attribute $L.head$ points to the first element of the list. If $L.head = \text{NIL}$, the list is empty.

A list may have one of several forms. It may be either singly linked or doubly linked, it may be sorted or not, and it may be circular or not. If a list is ***singly linked***, we omit the *prev* pointer in each element. If a list is ***sorted***, the linear order of the list corresponds to the linear order of keys stored in elements of the list; the minimum element is then the head of the list, and the maximum element is the tail. If the list is ***unsorted***, the elements can appear in any order. In a ***circular list***, the *prev* pointer of the head of the list points to the tail, and the *next* pointer of the tail of the list points to the head. We can think of a circular list as a ring of

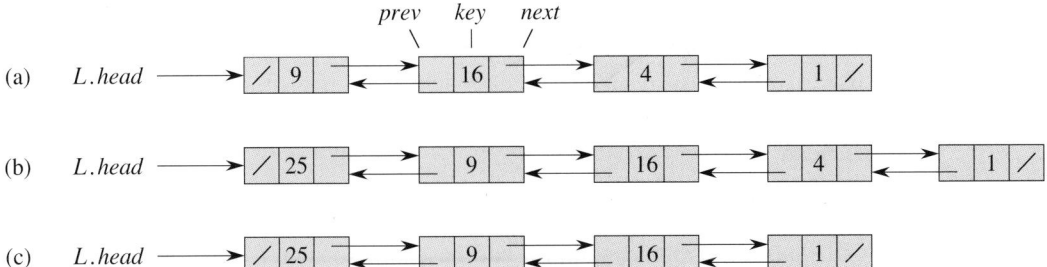

Figure 10.3   **(a)** A doubly linked list L representing the dynamic set $\{1, 4, 9, 16\}$. Each element in the list is an object with attributes for the key and pointers (shown by arrows) to the next and previous objects. The *next* attribute of the tail and the *prev* attribute of the head are NIL, indicated by a diagonal slash. The attribute $L.head$ points to the head. **(b)** Following the execution of LIST-INSERT(L, x), where $x.key = 25$, the linked list has a new object with key 25 as the new head. This new object points to the old head with key 9. **(c)** The result of the subsequent call LIST-DELETE(L, x), where x points to the object with key 4.

elements. In the remainder of this section, we assume that the lists with which we are working are unsorted and doubly linked.

Searching a linked list

The procedure LIST-SEARCH(L, k) finds the first element with key k in list L by a simple linear search, returning a pointer to this element. If no object with key k appears in the list, then the procedure returns NIL. For the linked list in Figure 10.3(a), the call LIST-SEARCH$(L, 4)$ returns a pointer to the third element, and the call LIST-SEARCH$(L, 7)$ returns NIL.

LIST-SEARCH(L, k)

1 $x = L.head$
2 **while** $x \neq$ NIL and $x.key \neq k$
3      $x = x.next$
4 **return** x

To search a list of n objects, the LIST-SEARCH procedure takes $\Theta(n)$ time in the worst case, since it may have to search the entire list.

Inserting into a linked list

Given an element x whose *key* attribute has already been set, the LIST-INSERT procedure "splices" x onto the front of the linked list, as shown in Figure 10.3(b).

LIST-INSERT(L, x)

1 $x.next = L.head$
2 **if** $L.head \neq$ NIL
3      $L.head.prev = x$
4 $L.head = x$
5 $x.prev =$ NIL

(Recall that our attribute notation can cascade, so that $L.head.prev$ denotes the *prev* attribute of the object that $L.head$ points to.) The running time for LIST-INSERT on a list of n elements is $O(1)$.

Deleting from a linked list

The procedure LIST-DELETE removes an element x from a linked list L. It must be given a pointer to x, and it then "splices" x out of the list by updating pointers. If we wish to delete an element with a given key, we must first call LIST-SEARCH to retrieve a pointer to the element.

LIST-DELETE(L, x)

1 **if** $x.prev \neq$ NIL
2      $x.prev.next = x.next$
3 **else** $L.head = x.next$
4 **if** $x.next \neq$ NIL
5      $x.next.prev = x.prev$

Figure 10.3(c) shows how an element is deleted from a linked list. LIST-DELETE runs in $O(1)$ time, but if we wish to delete an element with a given key, $\Theta(n)$ time is required in the worst case because we must first call LIST-SEARCH to find the element.

Sentinels

The code for LIST-DELETE would be simpler if we could ignore the boundary conditions at the head and tail of the list:

LIST-DELETE$'(L, x)$

1 $x.prev.next = x.next$
2 $x.next.prev = x.prev$

A **sentinel** is a dummy object that allows us to simplify boundary conditions. For example, suppose that we provide with list L an object $L.nil$ that represents NIL

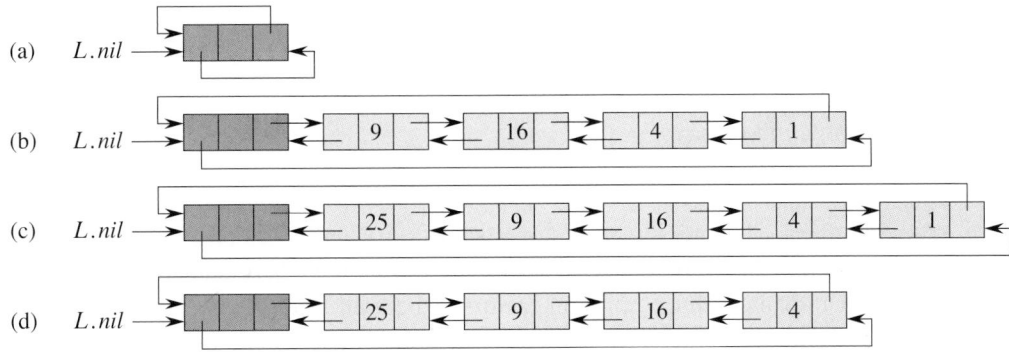

Figure 10.4   A circular, doubly linked list with a sentinel. The sentinel *L.nil* appears between the head and tail. The attribute *L.head* is no longer needed, since we can access the head of the list by *L.nil.next*. **(a)** An empty list. **(b)** The linked list from Figure 10.3(a), with key 9 at the head and key 1 at the tail. **(c)** The list after executing LIST-INSERT$'(L, x)$, where $x.key = 25$. The new object becomes the head of the list. **(d)** The list after deleting the object with key 1. The new tail is the object with key 4.

but has all the attributes of the other objects in the list. Wherever we have a reference to NIL in list code, we replace it by a reference to the sentinel *L.nil*. As shown in Figure 10.4, this change turns a regular doubly linked list into a ***circular, doubly linked list with a sentinel***, in which the sentinel *L.nil* lies between the head and tail. The attribute *L.nil.next* points to the head of the list, and *L.nil.prev* points to the tail. Similarly, both the *next* attribute of the tail and the *prev* attribute of the head point to *L.nil*. Since *L.nil.next* points to the head, we can eliminate the attribute *L.head* altogether, replacing references to it by references to *L.nil.next*. Figure 10.4(a) shows that an empty list consists of just the sentinel, and both *L.nil.next* and *L.nil.prev* point to *L.nil*.

The code for LIST-SEARCH remains the same as before, but with the references to NIL and *L.head* changed as specified above:

LIST-SEARCH$'(L, k)$

```
1   x = L.nil.next
2   while x ≠ L.nil and x.key ≠ k
3       x = x.next
4   return x
```

We use the two-line procedure LIST-DELETE$'$ from before to delete an element from the list. The following procedure inserts an element into the list:

LIST-INSERT$'(L, x)$

1   $x.next = L.nil.next$
2   $L.nil.next.prev = x$
3   $L.nil.next = x$
4   $x.prev = L.nil$

Figure 10.4 shows the effects of LIST-INSERT$'$ and LIST-DELETE$'$ on a sample list.

Sentinels rarely reduce the asymptotic time bounds of data structure operations, but they can reduce constant factors. The gain from using sentinels within loops is usually a matter of clarity of code rather than speed; the linked list code, for example, becomes simpler when we use sentinels, but we save only $O(1)$ time in the LIST-INSERT$'$ and LIST-DELETE$'$ procedures. In other situations, however, the use of sentinels helps to tighten the code in a loop, thus reducing the coefficient of, say, n or n^2 in the running time.

We should use sentinels judiciously. When there are many small lists, the extra storage used by their sentinels can represent significant wasted memory. In this book, we use sentinels only when they truly simplify the code.

Exercises

10.2-1
Can you implement the dynamic-set operation INSERT on a singly linked list in $O(1)$ time? How about DELETE?

10.2-2
Implement a stack using a singly linked list L. The operations PUSH and POP should still take $O(1)$ time.

10.2-3
Implement a queue by a singly linked list L. The operations ENQUEUE and DE-QUEUE should still take $O(1)$ time.

10.2-4
As written, each loop iteration in the LIST-SEARCH$'$ procedure requires two tests: one for $x \neq L.nil$ and one for $x.key \neq k$. Show how to eliminate the test for $x \neq L.nil$ in each iteration.

10.2-5
Implement the dictionary operations INSERT, DELETE, and SEARCH using singly linked, circular lists. What are the running times of your procedures?

10.2-6

The dynamic-set operation UNION takes two disjoint sets S_1 and S_2 as input, and it returns a set $S = S_1 \cup S_2$ consisting of all the elements of S_1 and S_2. The sets S_1 and S_2 are usually destroyed by the operation. Show how to support UNION in $O(1)$ time using a suitable list data structure.

10.2-7

Give a $\Theta(n)$-time nonrecursive procedure that reverses a singly linked list of n elements. The procedure should use no more than constant storage beyond that needed for the list itself.

10.2-8 ★

Explain how to implement doubly linked lists using only one pointer value $x.np$ per item instead of the usual two (*next* and *prev*). Assume that all pointer values can be interpreted as k-bit integers, and define $x.np$ to be $x.np = x.next$ XOR $x.prev$, the k-bit "exclusive-or" of $x.next$ and $x.prev$. (The value NIL is represented by 0.) Be sure to describe what information you need to access the head of the list. Show how to implement the SEARCH, INSERT, and DELETE operations on such a list. Also show how to reverse such a list in $O(1)$ time.

10.3   Implementing pointers and objects

How do we implement pointers and objects in languages that do not provide them? In this section, we shall see two ways of implementing linked data structures without an explicit pointer data type. We shall synthesize objects and pointers from arrays and array indices.

A multiple-array representation of objects

We can represent a collection of objects that have the same attributes by using an array for each attribute. As an example, Figure 10.5 shows how we can implement the linked list of Figure 10.3(a) with three arrays. The array *key* holds the values of the keys currently in the dynamic set, and the pointers reside in the arrays *next* and *prev*. For a given array index x, the array entries $key[x]$, $next[x]$, and $prev[x]$ represent an object in the linked list. Under this interpretation, a pointer x is simply a common index into the *key*, *next*, and *prev* arrays.

In Figure 10.3(a), the object with key 4 follows the object with key 16 in the linked list. In Figure 10.5, key 4 appears in $key[2]$, and key 16 appears in $key[5]$, and so $next[5] = 2$ and $prev[2] = 5$. Although the constant NIL appears in the *next*

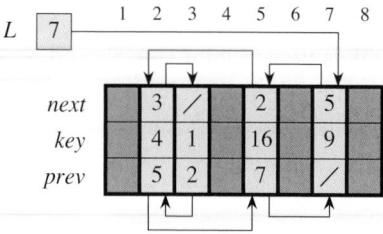

Figure 10.5   The linked list of Figure 10.3(a) represented by the arrays *key*, *next*, and *prev*. Each vertical slice of the arrays represents a single object. Stored pointers correspond to the array indices shown at the top; the arrows show how to interpret them. Lightly shaded object positions contain list elements. The variable *L* keeps the index of the head.

attribute of the tail and the *prev* attribute of the head, we usually use an integer (such as 0 or -1) that cannot possibly represent an actual index into the arrays. A variable *L* holds the index of the head of the list.

A single-array representation of objects

The words in a computer memory are typically addressed by integers from 0 to $M - 1$, where M is a suitably large integer. In many programming languages, an object occupies a contiguous set of locations in the computer memory. A pointer is simply the address of the first memory location of the object, and we can address other memory locations within the object by adding an offset to the pointer.

We can use the same strategy for implementing objects in programming environments that do not provide explicit pointer data types. For example, Figure 10.6 shows how to use a single array A to store the linked list from Figures 10.3(a) and 10.5. An object occupies a contiguous subarray $A[j \mathinner{.\,.} k]$. Each attribute of the object corresponds to an offset in the range from 0 to $k - j$, and a pointer to the object is the index j. In Figure 10.6, the offsets corresponding to *key*, *next*, and *prev* are 0, 1, and 2, respectively. To read the value of $i.prev$, given a pointer i, we add the value i of the pointer to the offset 2, thus reading $A[i + 2]$.

The single-array representation is flexible in that it permits objects of different lengths to be stored in the same array. The problem of managing such a heterogeneous collection of objects is more difficult than the problem of managing a homogeneous collection, where all objects have the same attributes. Since most of the data structures we shall consider are composed of homogeneous elements, it will be sufficient for our purposes to use the multiple-array representation of objects.

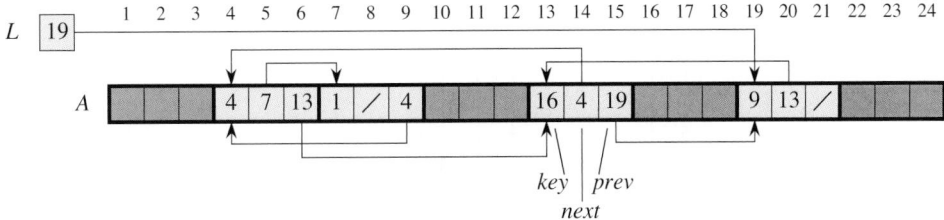

Figure 10.6 The linked list of Figures 10.3(a) and 10.5 represented in a single array A. Each list element is an object that occupies a contiguous subarray of length 3 within the array. The three attributes *key*, *next*, and *prev* correspond to the offsets 0, 1, and 2, respectively, within each object. A pointer to an object is the index of the first element of the object. Objects containing list elements are lightly shaded, and arrows show the list ordering.

Allocating and freeing objects

To insert a key into a dynamic set represented by a doubly linked list, we must allocate a pointer to a currently unused object in the linked-list representation. Thus, it is useful to manage the storage of objects not currently used in the linked-list representation so that one can be allocated. In some systems, a ***garbage collector*** is responsible for determining which objects are unused. Many applications, however, are simple enough that they can bear responsibility for returning an unused object to a storage manager. We shall now explore the problem of allocating and freeing (or deallocating) homogeneous objects using the example of a doubly linked list represented by multiple arrays.

Suppose that the arrays in the multiple-array representation have length m and that at some moment the dynamic set contains $n \leq m$ elements. Then n objects represent elements currently in the dynamic set, and the remaining $m-n$ objects are *free*; the free objects are available to represent elements inserted into the dynamic set in the future.

We keep the free objects in a singly linked list, which we call the *free list*. The free list uses only the *next* array, which stores the *next* pointers within the list. The head of the free list is held in the global variable *free*. When the dynamic set represented by linked list L is nonempty, the free list may be intertwined with list L, as shown in Figure 10.7. Note that each object in the representation is either in list L or in the free list, but not in both.

The free list acts like a stack: the next object allocated is the last one freed. We can use a list implementation of the stack operations PUSH and POP to implement the procedures for freeing and allocating objects, respectively. We assume that the global variable *free* used in the following procedures points to the first element of the free list.

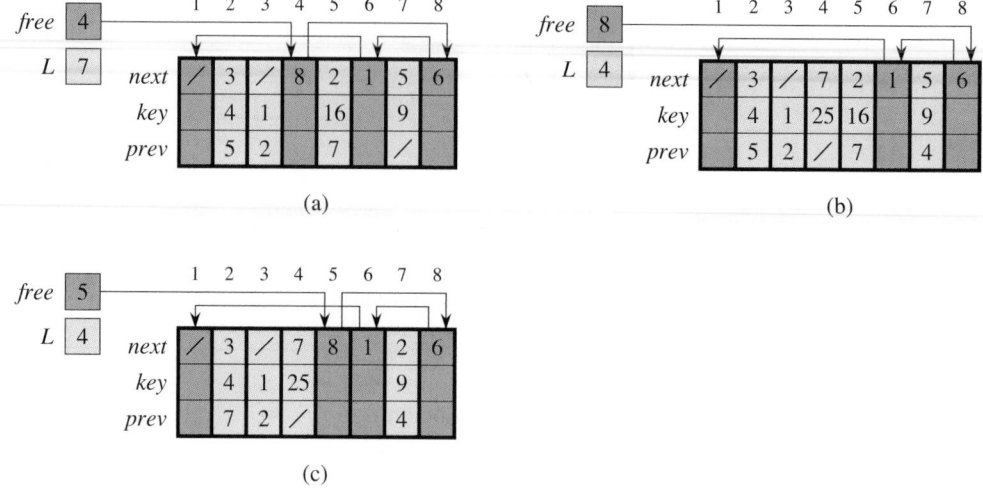

Figure 10.7 The effect of the ALLOCATE-OBJECT and FREE-OBJECT procedures. **(a)** The list of Figure 10.5 (lightly shaded) and a free list (heavily shaded). Arrows show the free-list structure. **(b)** The result of calling ALLOCATE-OBJECT() (which returns index 4), setting $key[4]$ to 25, and calling LIST-INSERT(L, 4). The new free-list head is object 8, which had been $next[4]$ on the free list. **(c)** After executing LIST-DELETE(L, 5), we call FREE-OBJECT(5). Object 5 becomes the new free-list head, with object 8 following it on the free list.

ALLOCATE-OBJECT()

```
1   if free == NIL
2       error "out of space"
3   else x = free
4       free = x.next
5       return x
```

FREE-OBJECT(x)

```
1   x.next = free
2   free = x
```

The free list initially contains all n unallocated objects. Once the free list has been exhausted, running the ALLOCATE-OBJECT procedure signals an error. We can even service several linked lists with just a single free list. Figure 10.8 shows two linked lists and a free list intertwined through key, $next$, and $prev$ arrays.

The two procedures run in $O(1)$ time, which makes them quite practical. We can modify them to work for any homogeneous collection of objects by letting any one of the attributes in the object act like a $next$ attribute in the free list.

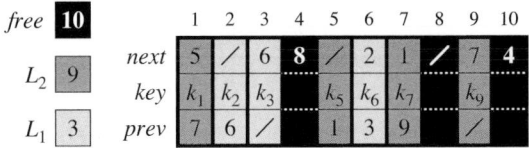

Figure 10.8 Two linked lists, L_1 (lightly shaded) and L_2 (heavily shaded), and a free list (darkened) intertwined.

Exercises

10.3-1
Draw a picture of the sequence $\langle 13, 4, 8, 19, 5, 11 \rangle$ stored as a doubly linked list using the multiple-array representation. Do the same for the single-array representation.

10.3-2
Write the procedures ALLOCATE-OBJECT and FREE-OBJECT for a homogeneous collection of objects implemented by the single-array representation.

10.3-3
Why don't we need to set or reset the *prev* attributes of objects in the implementation of the ALLOCATE-OBJECT and FREE-OBJECT procedures?

10.3-4
It is often desirable to keep all elements of a doubly linked list compact in storage, using, for example, the first m index locations in the multiple-array representation. (This is the case in a paged, virtual-memory computing environment.) Explain how to implement the procedures ALLOCATE-OBJECT and FREE-OBJECT so that the representation is compact. Assume that there are no pointers to elements of the linked list outside the list itself. (*Hint:* Use the array implementation of a stack.)

10.3-5
Let L be a doubly linked list of length n stored in arrays *key*, *prev*, and *next* of length m. Suppose that these arrays are managed by ALLOCATE-OBJECT and FREE-OBJECT procedures that keep a doubly linked free list F. Suppose further that of the m items, exactly n are on list L and $m - n$ are on the free list. Write a procedure COMPACTIFY-LIST(L, F) that, given the list L and the free list F, moves the items in L so that they occupy array positions $1, 2, \ldots, n$ and adjusts the free list F so that it remains correct, occupying array positions $n + 1, n + 2, \ldots, m$. The running time of your procedure should be $\Theta(n)$, and it should use only a constant amount of extra space. Argue that your procedure is correct.

10.4   Representing rooted trees

The methods for representing lists given in the previous section extend to any homogeneous data structure. In this section, we look specifically at the problem of representing rooted trees by linked data structures. We first look at binary trees, and then we present a method for rooted trees in which nodes can have an arbitrary number of children.

We represent each node of a tree by an object. As with linked lists, we assume that each node contains a *key* attribute. The remaining attributes of interest are pointers to other nodes, and they vary according to the type of tree.

Binary trees

Figure 10.9 shows how we use the attributes p, *left*, and *right* to store pointers to the parent, left child, and right child of each node in a binary tree T. If $x.p = \text{NIL}$, then x is the root. If node x has no left child, then $x.left = \text{NIL}$, and similarly for the right child. The root of the entire tree T is pointed to by the attribute $T.root$. If $T.root = \text{NIL}$, then the tree is empty.

Rooted trees with unbounded branching

We can extend the scheme for representing a binary tree to any class of trees in which the number of children of each node is at most some constant k: we replace the *left* and *right* attributes by $child_1, child_2, \ldots, child_k$. This scheme no longer works when the number of children of a node is unbounded, since we do not know how many attributes (arrays in the multiple-array representation) to allocate in advance. Moreover, even if the number of children k is bounded by a large constant but most nodes have a small number of children, we may waste a lot of memory.

Fortunately, there is a clever scheme to represent trees with arbitrary numbers of children. It has the advantage of using only $O(n)$ space for any n-node rooted tree. The ***left-child, right-sibling representation*** appears in Figure 10.10. As before, each node contains a parent pointer p, and $T.root$ points to the root of tree T. Instead of having a pointer to each of its children, however, each node x has only two pointers:

1. $x.left$-$child$ points to the leftmost child of node x, and

2. $x.right$-$sibling$ points to the sibling of x immediately to its right.

If node x has no children, then $x.left$-$child = \text{NIL}$, and if node x is the rightmost child of its parent, then $x.right$-$sibling = \text{NIL}$.

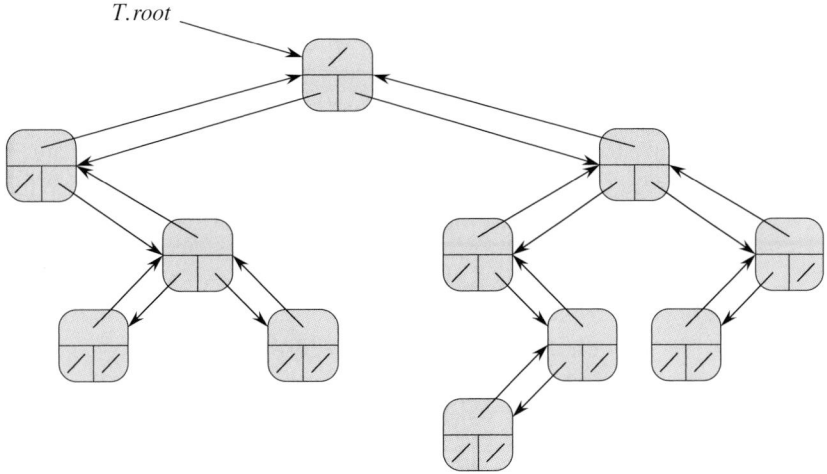

Figure 10.9   The representation of a binary tree T. Each node x has the attributes $x.p$ (top), $x.left$ (lower left), and $x.right$ (lower right). The *key* attributes are not shown.

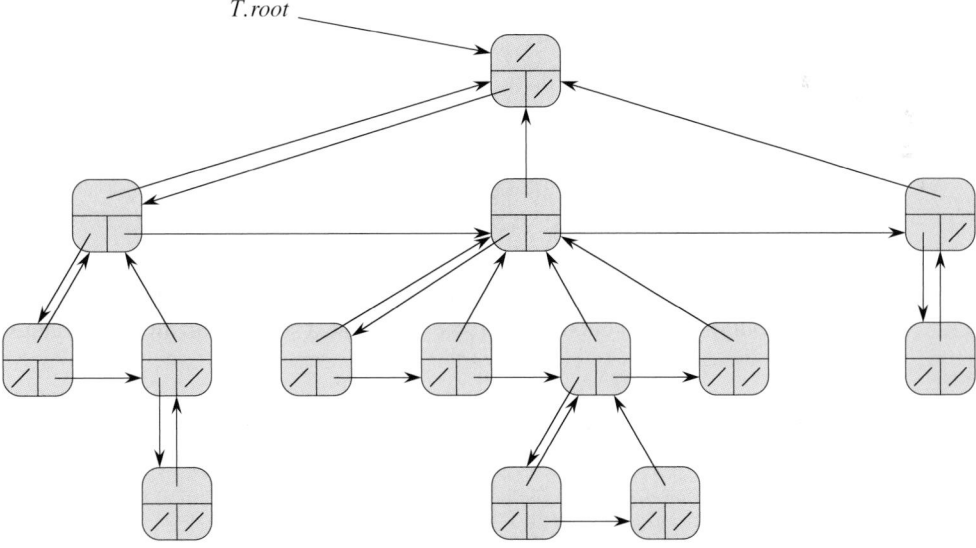

Figure 10.10   The left-child, right-sibling representation of a tree T. Each node x has attributes $x.p$ (top), $x.left$-$child$ (lower left), and $x.right$-$sibling$ (lower right). The *key* attributes are not shown.

Other tree representations

We sometimes represent rooted trees in other ways. In Chapter 6, for example, we represented a heap, which is based on a complete binary tree, by a single array plus the index of the last node in the heap. The trees that appear in Chapter 21 are traversed only toward the root, and so only the parent pointers are present; there are no pointers to children. Many other schemes are possible. Which scheme is best depends on the application.

Exercises

10.4-1
Draw the binary tree rooted at index 6 that is represented by the following attributes:

index	key	left	right
1	12	7	3
2	15	8	NIL
3	4	10	NIL
4	10	5	9
5	2	NIL	NIL
6	18	1	4
7	7	NIL	NIL
8	14	6	2
9	21	NIL	NIL
10	5	NIL	NIL

10.4-2
Write an $O(n)$-time recursive procedure that, given an n-node binary tree, prints out the key of each node in the tree.

10.4-3
Write an $O(n)$-time nonrecursive procedure that, given an n-node binary tree, prints out the key of each node in the tree. Use a stack as an auxiliary data structure.

10.4-4
Write an $O(n)$-time procedure that prints all the keys of an arbitrary rooted tree with n nodes, where the tree is stored using the left-child, right-sibling representation.

10.4-5 ★
Write an $O(n)$-time nonrecursive procedure that, given an n-node binary tree, prints out the key of each node. Use no more than constant extra space outside

of the tree itself and do not modify the tree, even temporarily, during the procedure.

10.4-6 ★

The left-child, right-sibling representation of an arbitrary rooted tree uses three pointers in each node: *left-child*, *right-sibling*, and *parent*. From any node, its parent can be reached and identified in constant time and all its children can be reached and identified in time linear in the number of children. Show how to use only two pointers and one boolean value in each node so that the parent of a node or all of its children can be reached and identified in time linear in the number of children.

Problems

10-1 *Comparisons among lists*

For each of the four types of lists in the following table, what is the asymptotic worst-case running time for each dynamic-set operation listed?

	unsorted, singly linked	sorted, singly linked	unsorted, doubly linked	sorted, doubly linked
SEARCH(L,k)				
INSERT(L,x)				
DELETE(L,x)				
SUCCESSOR(L,x)				
PREDECESSOR(L,x)				
MINIMUM(L)				
MAXIMUM(L)				

10-2   Mergeable heaps using linked lists

A *mergeable heap* supports the following operations: MAKE-HEAP (which creates an empty mergeable heap), INSERT, MINIMUM, EXTRACT-MIN, and UNION.[1] Show how to implement mergeable heaps using linked lists in each of the following cases. Try to make each operation as efficient as possible. Analyze the running time of each operation in terms of the size of the dynamic set(s) being operated on.

a. Lists are sorted.

b. Lists are unsorted.

c. Lists are unsorted, and dynamic sets to be merged are disjoint.

10-3   Searching a sorted compact list

Exercise 10.3-4 asked how we might maintain an n-element list compactly in the first n positions of an array. We shall assume that all keys are distinct and that the compact list is also sorted, that is, $key[i] < key[next[i]]$ for all $i = 1, 2, \ldots, n$ such that $next[i] \neq$ NIL. We will also assume that we have a variable L that contains the index of the first element on the list. Under these assumptions, you will show that we can use the following randomized algorithm to search the list in $O(\sqrt{n})$ expected time.

COMPACT-LIST-SEARCH(L, n, k)

```
 1   i = L
 2   while i ≠ NIL and key[i] < k
 3        j = RANDOM(1, n)
 4        if key[i] < key[j] and key[j] ≤ k
 5            i = j
 6            if key[i] == k
 7                return i
 8        i = next[i]
 9   if i == NIL or key[i] > k
10        return NIL
11   else return i
```

If we ignore lines 3–7 of the procedure, we have an ordinary algorithm for searching a sorted linked list, in which index i points to each position of the list in

---

[1]Because we have defined a mergeable heap to support MINIMUM and EXTRACT-MIN, we can also refer to it as a *mergeable min-heap*. Alternatively, if it supported MAXIMUM and EXTRACT-MAX, it would be a *mergeable max-heap*.

turn. The search terminates once the index i "falls off" the end of the list or once $key[i] \geq k$. In the latter case, if $key[i] = k$, clearly we have found a key with the value k. If, however, $key[i] > k$, then we will never find a key with the value k, and so terminating the search was the right thing to do.

Lines 3–7 attempt to skip ahead to a randomly chosen position j. Such a skip benefits us if $key[j]$ is larger than $key[i]$ and no larger than k; in such a case, j marks a position in the list that i would have to reach during an ordinary list search. Because the list is compact, we know that any choice of j between 1 and n indexes some object in the list rather than a slot on the free list.

Instead of analyzing the performance of COMPACT-LIST-SEARCH directly, we shall analyze a related algorithm, COMPACT-LIST-SEARCH$'$, which executes two separate loops. This algorithm takes an additional parameter t which determines an upper bound on the number of iterations of the first loop.

COMPACT-LIST-SEARCH$'(L, n, k, t)$

```
 1  i = L
 2  for q = 1 to t
 3      j = RANDOM(1, n)
 4      if key[i] < key[j] and key[j] ≤ k
 5          i = j
 6          if key[i] == k
 7              return i
 8  while i ≠ NIL and key[i] < k
 9      i = next[i]
10  if i == NIL or key[i] > k
11      return NIL
12  else return i
```

To compare the execution of the algorithms COMPACT-LIST-SEARCH(L, n, k) and COMPACT-LIST-SEARCH$'(L, n, k, t)$, assume that the sequence of integers returned by the calls of RANDOM$(1, n)$ is the same for both algorithms.

a. Suppose that COMPACT-LIST-SEARCH(L, n, k) takes t iterations of the **while** loop of lines 2–8. Argue that COMPACT-LIST-SEARCH$'(L, n, k, t)$ returns the same answer and that the total number of iterations of both the **for** and **while** loops within COMPACT-LIST-SEARCH$'$ is at least t.

In the call COMPACT-LIST-SEARCH$'(L, n, k, t)$, let X_t be the random variable that describes the distance in the linked list (that is, through the chain of *next* pointers) from position i to the desired key k after t iterations of the **for** loop of lines 2–7 have occurred.

b. Argue that the expected running time of COMPACT-LIST-SEARCH$'(L, n, k, t)$ is $O(t + E[X_t])$.

c. Show that $E[X_t] \leq \sum_{r=1}^{n}(1 - r/n)^t$. (*Hint:* Use equation (C.25).)

d. Show that $\sum_{r=0}^{n-1} r^t \leq n^{t+1}/(t + 1)$.

e. Prove that $E[X_t] \leq n/(t + 1)$.

f. Show that COMPACT-LIST-SEARCH$'(L, n, k, t)$ runs in $O(t + n/t)$ expected time.

g. Conclude that COMPACT-LIST-SEARCH runs in $O(\sqrt{n})$ expected time.

h. Why do we assume that all keys are distinct in COMPACT-LIST-SEARCH? Argue that random skips do not necessarily help asymptotically when the list contains repeated key values.

Chapter notes

Aho, Hopcroft, and Ullman [6] and Knuth [209] are excellent references for elementary data structures. Many other texts cover both basic data structures and their implementation in a particular programming language. Examples of these types of textbooks include Goodrich and Tamassia [147], Main [241], Shaffer [311], and Weiss [352, 353, 354]. Gonnet [145] provides experimental data on the performance of many data-structure operations.

The origin of stacks and queues as data structures in computer science is unclear, since corresponding notions already existed in mathematics and paper-based business practices before the introduction of digital computers. Knuth [209] cites A. M. Turing for the development of stacks for subroutine linkage in 1947.

Pointer-based data structures also seem to be a folk invention. According to Knuth, pointers were apparently used in early computers with drum memories. The A-1 language developed by G. M. Hopper in 1951 represented algebraic formulas as binary trees. Knuth credits the IPL-II language, developed in 1956 by A. Newell, J. C. Shaw, and H. A. Simon, for recognizing the importance and promoting the use of pointers. Their IPL-III language, developed in 1957, included explicit stack operations.

11 Hash Tables

Many applications require a dynamic set that supports only the dictionary operations INSERT, SEARCH, and DELETE. For example, a compiler that translates a programming language maintains a symbol table, in which the keys of elements are arbitrary character strings corresponding to identifiers in the language. A hash table is an effective data structure for implementing dictionaries. Although searching for an element in a hash table can take as long as searching for an element in a linked list — $\Theta(n)$ time in the worst case — in practice, hashing performs extremely well. Under reasonable assumptions, the average time to search for an element in a hash table is $O(1)$.

A hash table generalizes the simpler notion of an ordinary array. Directly addressing into an ordinary array makes effective use of our ability to examine an arbitrary position in an array in $O(1)$ time. Section 11.1 discusses direct addressing in more detail. We can take advantage of direct addressing when we can afford to allocate an array that has one position for every possible key.

When the number of keys actually stored is small relative to the total number of possible keys, hash tables become an effective alternative to directly addressing an array, since a hash table typically uses an array of size proportional to the number of keys actually stored. Instead of using the key as an array index directly, the array index is *computed* from the key. Section 11.2 presents the main ideas, focusing on "chaining" as a way to handle "collisions," in which more than one key maps to the same array index. Section 11.3 describes how we can compute array indices from keys using hash functions. We present and analyze several variations on the basic theme. Section 11.4 looks at "open addressing," which is another way to deal with collisions. The bottom line is that hashing is an extremely effective and practical technique: the basic dictionary operations require only $O(1)$ time on the average. Section 11.5 explains how "perfect hashing" can support searches in $O(1)$ *worst-case* time, when the set of keys being stored is static (that is, when the set of keys never changes once stored).

11.1   Direct-address tables

Direct addressing is a simple technique that works well when the universe U of keys is reasonably small. Suppose that an application needs a dynamic set in which each element has a key drawn from the universe $U = \{0, 1, \ldots, m - 1\}$, where m is not too large. We shall assume that no two elements have the same key.

To represent the dynamic set, we use an array, or ***direct-address table***, denoted by $T[0 \mathinner{.\,.} m - 1]$, in which each position, or ***slot***, corresponds to a key in the universe U. Figure 11.1 illustrates the approach; slot k points to an element in the set with key k. If the set contains no element with key k, then $T[k] = \text{NIL}$.

The dictionary operations are trivial to implement:

DIRECT-ADDRESS-SEARCH(T, k)

1   **return** $T[k]$

DIRECT-ADDRESS-INSERT(T, x)

1   $T[x.key] = x$

DIRECT-ADDRESS-DELETE(T, x)

1   $T[x.key] = \text{NIL}$

Each of these operations takes only $O(1)$ time.

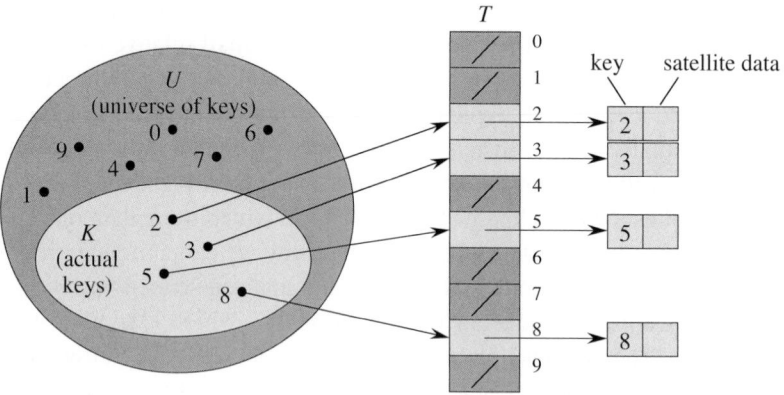

Figure 11.1   How to implement a dynamic set by a direct-address table T. Each key in the universe $U = \{0, 1, \ldots, 9\}$ corresponds to an index in the table. The set $K = \{2, 3, 5, 8\}$ of actual keys determines the slots in the table that contain pointers to elements. The other slots, heavily shaded, contain NIL.

For some applications, the direct-address table itself can hold the elements in the dynamic set. That is, rather than storing an element's key and satellite data in an object external to the direct-address table, with a pointer from a slot in the table to the object, we can store the object in the slot itself, thus saving space. We would use a special key within an object to indicate an empty slot. Moreover, it is often unnecessary to store the key of the object, since if we have the index of an object in the table, we have its key. If keys are not stored, however, we must have some way to tell whether the slot is empty.

Exercises

11.1-1
Suppose that a dynamic set S is represented by a direct-address table T of length m. Describe a procedure that finds the maximum element of S. What is the worst-case performance of your procedure?

11.1-2
A ***bit vector*** is simply an array of bits (0s and 1s). A bit vector of length m takes much less space than an array of m pointers. Describe how to use a bit vector to represent a dynamic set of distinct elements with no satellite data. Dictionary operations should run in $O(1)$ time.

11.1-3
Suggest how to implement a direct-address table in which the keys of stored elements do not need to be distinct and the elements can have satellite data. All three dictionary operations (INSERT, DELETE, and SEARCH) should run in $O(1)$ time. (Don't forget that DELETE takes as an argument a pointer to an object to be deleted, not a key.)

11.1-4   ★
We wish to implement a dictionary by using direct addressing on a *huge* array. At the start, the array entries may contain garbage, and initializing the entire array is impractical because of its size. Describe a scheme for implementing a direct-address dictionary on a huge array. Each stored object should use $O(1)$ space; the operations SEARCH, INSERT, and DELETE should take $O(1)$ time each; and initializing the data structure should take $O(1)$ time. (*Hint:* Use an additional array, treated somewhat like a stack whose size is the number of keys actually stored in the dictionary, to help determine whether a given entry in the huge array is valid or not.)

11.2   Hash tables

The downside of direct addressing is obvious: if the universe U is large, storing a table T of size $|U|$ may be impractical, or even impossible, given the memory available on a typical computer. Furthermore, the set K of keys *actually stored* may be so small relative to U that most of the space allocated for T would be wasted.

When the set K of keys stored in a dictionary is much smaller than the universe U of all possible keys, a hash table requires much less storage than a direct-address table. Specifically, we can reduce the storage requirement to $\Theta(|K|)$ while we maintain the benefit that searching for an element in the hash table still requires only $O(1)$ time. The catch is that this bound is for the *average-case time*, whereas for direct addressing it holds for the *worst-case time*.

With direct addressing, an element with key k is stored in slot k. With hashing, this element is stored in slot $h(k)$; that is, we use a **hash function** h to compute the slot from the key k. Here, h maps the universe U of keys into the slots of a **hash table** $T[0..m-1]$:

$$h : U \rightarrow \{0, 1, \ldots, m-1\} \ ,$$

where the size m of the hash table is typically much less than $|U|$. We say that an element with key k **hashes** to slot $h(k)$; we also say that $h(k)$ is the **hash value** of key k. Figure 11.2 illustrates the basic idea. The hash function reduces the range of array indices and hence the size of the array. Instead of a size of $|U|$, the array can have size m.

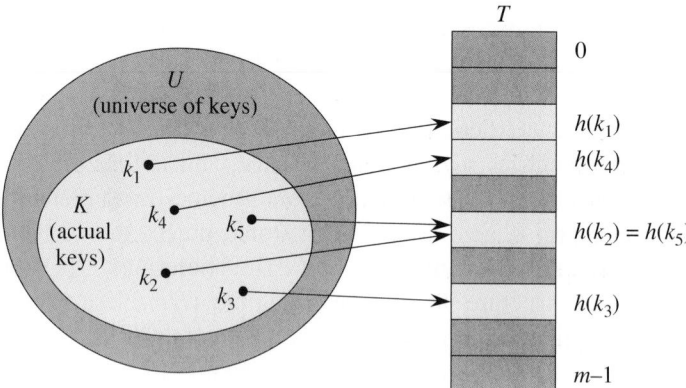

Figure 11.2   Using a hash function h to map keys to hash-table slots. Because keys k_2 and k_5 map to the same slot, they collide.

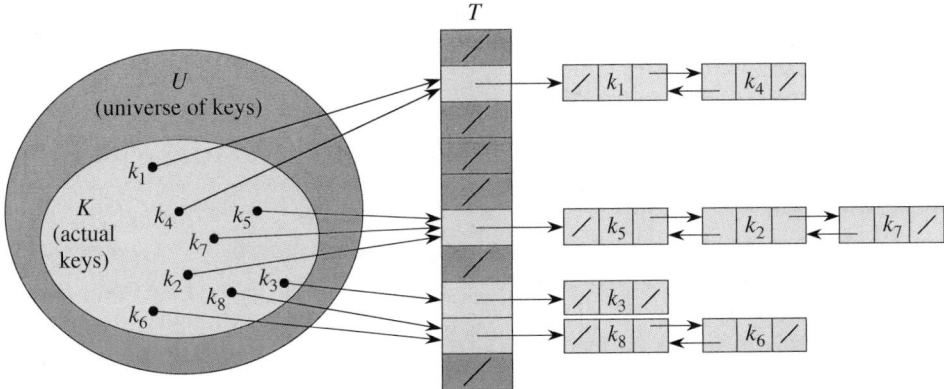

Figure 11.3 Collision resolution by chaining. Each hash-table slot $T[j]$ contains a linked list of all the keys whose hash value is j. For example, $h(k_1) = h(k_4)$ and $h(k_5) = h(k_7) = h(k_2)$. The linked list can be either singly or doubly linked; we show it as doubly linked because deletion is faster that way.

There is one hitch: two keys may hash to the same slot. We call this situation a ***collision***. Fortunately, we have effective techniques for resolving the conflict created by collisions.

Of course, the ideal solution would be to avoid collisions altogether. We might try to achieve this goal by choosing a suitable hash function h. One idea is to make h appear to be "random," thus avoiding collisions or at least minimizing their number. The very term "to hash," evoking images of random mixing and chopping, captures the spirit of this approach. (Of course, a hash function h must be deterministic in that a given input k should always produce the same output $h(k)$.) Because $|U| > m$, however, there must be at least two keys that have the same hash value; avoiding collisions altogether is therefore impossible. Thus, while a well-designed, "random"-looking hash function can minimize the number of collisions, we still need a method for resolving the collisions that do occur.

The remainder of this section presents the simplest collision resolution technique, called chaining. Section 11.4 introduces an alternative method for resolving collisions, called open addressing.

Collision resolution by chaining

In ***chaining***, we place all the elements that hash to the same slot into the same linked list, as Figure 11.3 shows. Slot j contains a pointer to the head of the list of all stored elements that hash to j; if there are no such elements, slot j contains NIL.

The dictionary operations on a hash table T are easy to implement when collisions are resolved by chaining:

CHAINED-HASH-INSERT(T, x)

1   insert x at the head of list $T[h(x.key)]$

CHAINED-HASH-SEARCH(T, k)

1   search for an element with key k in list $T[h(k)]$

CHAINED-HASH-DELETE(T, x)

1   delete x from the list $T[h(x.key)]$

The worst-case running time for insertion is $O(1)$. The insertion procedure is fast in part because it assumes that the element x being inserted is not already present in the table; if necessary, we can check this assumption (at additional cost) by searching for an element whose key is $x.key$ before we insert. For searching, the worst-case running time is proportional to the length of the list; we shall analyze this operation more closely below. We can delete an element in $O(1)$ time if the lists are doubly linked, as Figure 11.3 depicts. (Note that CHAINED-HASH-DELETE takes as input an element x and not its key k, so that we don't have to search for x first. If the hash table supports deletion, then its linked lists should be doubly linked so that we can delete an item quickly. If the lists were only singly linked, then to delete element x, we would first have to find x in the list $T[h(x.key)]$ so that we could update the *next* attribute of x's predecessor. With singly linked lists, both deletion and searching would have the same asymptotic running times.)

Analysis of hashing with chaining

How well does hashing with chaining perform? In particular, how long does it take to search for an element with a given key?

Given a hash table T with m slots that stores n elements, we define the **load factor** α for T as n/m, that is, the average number of elements stored in a chain. Our analysis will be in terms of α, which can be less than, equal to, or greater than 1.

The worst-case behavior of hashing with chaining is terrible: all n keys hash to the same slot, creating a list of length n. The worst-case time for searching is thus $\Theta(n)$ plus the time to compute the hash function—no better than if we used one linked list for all the elements. Clearly, we do not use hash tables for their worst-case performance. (Perfect hashing, described in Section 11.5, does provide good worst-case performance when the set of keys is static, however.)

The average-case performance of hashing depends on how well the hash function h distributes the set of keys to be stored among the m slots, on the average.

Section 11.3 discusses these issues, but for now we shall assume that any given element is equally likely to hash into any of the m slots, independently of where any other element has hashed to. We call this the assumption of **simple uniform hashing**.

For $j = 0, 1, \ldots, m - 1$, let us denote the length of the list $T[j]$ by n_j, so that

$$n = n_0 + n_1 + \cdots + n_{m-1} \, , \tag{11.1}$$

and the expected value of n_j is $\mathrm{E}[n_j] = \alpha = n/m$.

We assume that $O(1)$ time suffices to compute the hash value $h(k)$, so that the time required to search for an element with key k depends linearly on the length $n_{h(k)}$ of the list $T[h(k)]$. Setting aside the $O(1)$ time required to compute the hash function and to access slot $h(k)$, let us consider the expected number of elements examined by the search algorithm, that is, the number of elements in the list $T[h(k)]$ that the algorithm checks to see whether any have a key equal to k. We shall consider two cases. In the first, the search is unsuccessful: no element in the table has key k. In the second, the search successfully finds an element with key k.

Theorem 11.1
In a hash table in which collisions are resolved by chaining, an unsuccessful search takes average-case time $\Theta(1+\alpha)$, under the assumption of simple uniform hashing.

Proof Under the assumption of simple uniform hashing, any key k not already stored in the table is equally likely to hash to any of the m slots. The expected time to search unsuccessfully for a key k is the expected time to search to the end of list $T[h(k)]$, which has expected length $\mathrm{E}[n_{h(k)}] = \alpha$. Thus, the expected number of elements examined in an unsuccessful search is α, and the total time required (including the time for computing $h(k)$) is $\Theta(1 + \alpha)$. ∎

The situation for a successful search is slightly different, since each list is not equally likely to be searched. Instead, the probability that a list is searched is proportional to the number of elements it contains. Nonetheless, the expected search time still turns out to be $\Theta(1 + \alpha)$.

Theorem 11.2
In a hash table in which collisions are resolved by chaining, a successful search takes average-case time $\Theta(1+\alpha)$, under the assumption of simple uniform hashing.

Proof We assume that the element being searched for is equally likely to be any of the n elements stored in the table. The number of elements examined during a successful search for an element x is one more than the number of elements that

appear before x in x's list. Because new elements are placed at the front of the list, elements before x in the list were all inserted after x was inserted. To find the expected number of elements examined, we take the average, over the n elements x in the table, of 1 plus the expected number of elements added to x's list after x was added to the list. Let x_i denote the ith element inserted into the table, for $i = 1, 2, \ldots, n$, and let $k_i = x_i.key$. For keys k_i and k_j, we define the indicator random variable $X_{ij} = \text{I}\{h(k_i) = h(k_j)\}$. Under the assumption of simple uniform hashing, we have $\Pr\{h(k_i) = h(k_j)\} = 1/m$, and so by Lemma 5.1, $\text{E}[X_{ij}] = 1/m$. Thus, the expected number of elements examined in a successful search is

$$
\begin{aligned}
\frac{1}{n} \sum_{i=1}^{n} \left(1 + \text{E}\left[\sum_{j=i+1}^{n} X_{ij}\right]\right) \\
= \ \frac{1}{n} \sum_{i=1}^{n} \left(1 + \sum_{j=i+1}^{n} \text{E}[X_{ij}]\right) \quad &\text{(by linearity of expectation)} \\
= \ \frac{1}{n} \sum_{i=1}^{n} \left(1 + \sum_{j=i+1}^{n} \frac{1}{m}\right) \\
= \ 1 + \frac{1}{nm} \sum_{i=1}^{n} (n - i) \\
= \ 1 + \frac{1}{nm} \left(\sum_{i=1}^{n} n - \sum_{i=1}^{n} i\right) \\
= \ 1 + \frac{1}{nm} \left(n^2 - \frac{n(n+1)}{2}\right) \quad &\text{(by equation (A.1))} \\
= \ 1 + \frac{n-1}{2m} \\
= \ 1 + \frac{\alpha}{2} - \frac{\alpha}{2n} \ .
\end{aligned}
$$

Thus, the total time required for a successful search (including the time for computing the hash function) is $\Theta(2 + \alpha/2 - \alpha/2n) = \Theta(1 + \alpha)$. ∎

What does this analysis mean? If the number of hash-table slots is at least proportional to the number of elements in the table, we have $n = O(m)$ and, consequently, $\alpha = n/m = O(m)/m = O(1)$. Thus, searching takes constant time on average. Since insertion takes $O(1)$ worst-case time and deletion takes $O(1)$ worst-case time when the lists are doubly linked, we can support all dictionary operations in $O(1)$ time on average.

Exercises

11.2-1
Suppose we use a hash function h to hash n distinct keys into an array T of length m. Assuming simple uniform hashing, what is the expected number of collisions? More precisely, what is the expected cardinality of $\{\{k, l\} : k \neq l$ and $h(k) = h(l)\}$?

11.2-2
Demonstrate what happens when we insert the keys $5, 28, 19, 15, 20, 33, 12, 17, 10$ into a hash table with collisions resolved by chaining. Let the table have 9 slots, and let the hash function be $h(k) = k \bmod 9$.

11.2-3
Professor Marley hypothesizes that he can obtain substantial performance gains by modifying the chaining scheme to keep each list in sorted order. How does the professor's modification affect the running time for successful searches, unsuccessful searches, insertions, and deletions?

11.2-4
Suggest how to allocate and deallocate storage for elements within the hash table itself by linking all unused slots into a free list. Assume that one slot can store a flag and either one element plus a pointer or two pointers. All dictionary and free-list operations should run in $O(1)$ expected time. Does the free list need to be doubly linked, or does a singly linked free list suffice?

11.2-5
Suppose that we are storing a set of n keys into a hash table of size m. Show that if the keys are drawn from a universe U with $|U| > nm$, then U has a subset of size n consisting of keys that all hash to the same slot, so that the worst-case searching time for hashing with chaining is $\Theta(n)$.

11.2-6
Suppose we have stored n keys in a hash table of size m, with collisions resolved by chaining, and that we know the length of each chain, including the length L of the longest chain. Describe a procedure that selects a key uniformly at random from among the keys in the hash table and returns it in expected time $O(L \cdot (1 + 1/\alpha))$.

11.3   Hash functions

In this section, we discuss some issues regarding the design of good hash functions and then present three schemes for their creation. Two of the schemes, hashing by division and hashing by multiplication, are heuristic in nature, whereas the third scheme, universal hashing, uses randomization to provide provably good performance.

What makes a good hash function?

A good hash function satisfies (approximately) the assumption of simple uniform hashing: each key is equally likely to hash to any of the m slots, independently of where any other key has hashed to. Unfortunately, we typically have no way to check this condition, since we rarely know the probability distribution from which the keys are drawn. Moreover, the keys might not be drawn independently.

Occasionally we do know the distribution. For example, if we know that the keys are random real numbers k independently and uniformly distributed in the range $0 \leq k < 1$, then the hash function

$$h(k) = \lfloor km \rfloor$$

satisfies the condition of simple uniform hashing.

In practice, we can often employ heuristic techniques to create a hash function that performs well. Qualitative information about the distribution of keys may be useful in this design process. For example, consider a compiler's symbol table, in which the keys are character strings representing identifiers in a program. Closely related symbols, such as `pt` and `pts`, often occur in the same program. A good hash function would minimize the chance that such variants hash to the same slot.

A good approach derives the hash value in a way that we expect to be independent of any patterns that might exist in the data. For example, the "division method" (discussed in Section 11.3.1) computes the hash value as the remainder when the key is divided by a specified prime number. This method frequently gives good results, assuming that we choose a prime number that is unrelated to any patterns in the distribution of keys.

Finally, we note that some applications of hash functions might require stronger properties than are provided by simple uniform hashing. For example, we might want keys that are "close" in some sense to yield hash values that are far apart. (This property is especially desirable when we are using linear probing, defined in Section 11.4.) Universal hashing, described in Section 11.3.3, often provides the desired properties.

Interpreting keys as natural numbers

Most hash functions assume that the universe of keys is the set $\mathbb{N} = \{0, 1, 2, \ldots\}$ of natural numbers. Thus, if the keys are not natural numbers, we find a way to interpret them as natural numbers. For example, we can interpret a character string as an integer expressed in suitable radix notation. Thus, we might interpret the identifier pt as the pair of decimal integers $(112, 116)$, since p = 112 and t = 116 in the ASCII character set; then, expressed as a radix-128 integer, pt becomes $(112 \cdot 128) + 116 = 14452$. In the context of a given application, we can usually devise some such method for interpreting each key as a (possibly large) natural number. In what follows, we assume that the keys are natural numbers.

11.3.1 The division method

In the ***division method*** for creating hash functions, we map a key k into one of m slots by taking the remainder of k divided by m. That is, the hash function is

$$h(k) = k \bmod m \, .$$

For example, if the hash table has size $m = 12$ and the key is $k = 100$, then $h(k) = 4$. Since it requires only a single division operation, hashing by division is quite fast.

When using the division method, we usually avoid certain values of m. For example, m should not be a power of 2, since if $m = 2^p$, then $h(k)$ is just the p lowest-order bits of k. Unless we know that all low-order p-bit patterns are equally likely, we are better off designing the hash function to depend on all the bits of the key. As Exercise 11.3-3 asks you to show, choosing $m = 2^p - 1$ when k is a character string interpreted in radix 2^p may be a poor choice, because permuting the characters of k does not change its hash value.

A prime not too close to an exact power of 2 is often a good choice for m. For example, suppose we wish to allocate a hash table, with collisions resolved by chaining, to hold roughly $n = 2000$ character strings, where a character has 8 bits. We don't mind examining an average of 3 elements in an unsuccessful search, and so we allocate a hash table of size $m = 701$. We could choose $m = 701$ because it is a prime near $2000/3$ but not near any power of 2. Treating each key k as an integer, our hash function would be

$$h(k) = k \bmod 701 \, .$$

11.3.2 The multiplication method

The ***multiplication method*** for creating hash functions operates in two steps. First, we multiply the key k by a constant A in the range $0 < A < 1$ and extract the

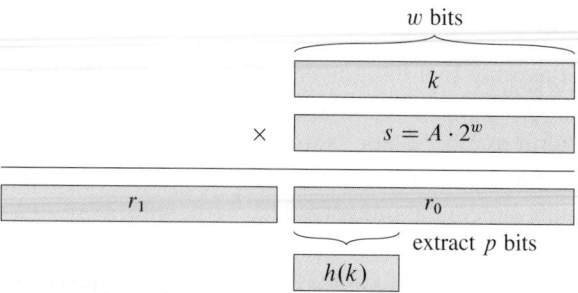

Figure 11.4 The multiplication method of hashing. The w-bit representation of the key k is multiplied by the w-bit value $s = A \cdot 2^w$. The p highest-order bits of the lower w-bit half of the product form the desired hash value $h(k)$.

fractional part of kA. Then, we multiply this value by m and take the floor of the result. In short, the hash function is

$$h(k) = \lfloor m\,(kA \bmod 1) \rfloor \,,$$

where "$kA \bmod 1$" means the fractional part of kA, that is, $kA - \lfloor kA \rfloor$.

An advantage of the multiplication method is that the value of m is not critical. We typically choose it to be a power of 2 ($m = 2^p$ for some integer p), since we can then easily implement the function on most computers as follows. Suppose that the word size of the machine is w bits and that k fits into a single word. We restrict A to be a fraction of the form $s/2^w$, where s is an integer in the range $0 < s < 2^w$. Referring to Figure 11.4, we first multiply k by the w-bit integer $s = A \cdot 2^w$. The result is a $2w$-bit value $r_1 2^w + r_0$, where r_1 is the high-order word of the product and r_0 is the low-order word of the product. The desired p-bit hash value consists of the p most significant bits of r_0.

Although this method works with any value of the constant A, it works better with some values than with others. The optimal choice depends on the characteristics of the data being hashed. Knuth [211] suggests that

$$A \approx (\sqrt{5} - 1)/2 = 0.6180339887\ldots \tag{11.2}$$

is likely to work reasonably well.

As an example, suppose we have $k = 123456$, $p = 14$, $m = 2^{14} = 16384$, and $w = 32$. Adapting Knuth's suggestion, we choose A to be the fraction of the form $s/2^{32}$ that is closest to $(\sqrt{5} - 1)/2$, so that $A = 2654435769/2^{32}$. Then $k \cdot s = 327706022297664 = (76300 \cdot 2^{32}) + 17612864$, and so $r_1 = 76300$ and $r_0 = 17612864$. The 14 most significant bits of r_0 yield the value $h(k) = 67$.

★ **11.3.3 Universal hashing**

If a malicious adversary chooses the keys to be hashed by some fixed hash function, then the adversary can choose n keys that all hash to the same slot, yielding an average retrieval time of $\Theta(n)$. Any fixed hash function is vulnerable to such terrible worst-case behavior; the only effective way to improve the situation is to choose the hash function *randomly* in a way that is *independent* of the keys that are actually going to be stored. This approach, called **universal hashing**, can yield provably good performance on average, no matter which keys the adversary chooses.

In universal hashing, at the beginning of execution we select the hash function at random from a carefully designed class of functions. As in the case of quicksort, randomization guarantees that no single input will always evoke worst-case behavior. Because we randomly select the hash function, the algorithm can behave differently on each execution, even for the same input, guaranteeing good average-case performance for any input. Returning to the example of a compiler's symbol table, we find that the programmer's choice of identifiers cannot now cause consistently poor hashing performance. Poor performance occurs only when the compiler chooses a random hash function that causes the set of identifiers to hash poorly, but the probability of this situation occurring is small and is the same for any set of identifiers of the same size.

Let $\mathcal{H}$ be a finite collection of hash functions that map a given universe U of keys into the range $\{0, 1, \ldots, m-1\}$. Such a collection is said to be **universal** if for each pair of distinct keys $k, l \in U$, the number of hash functions $h \in \mathcal{H}$ for which $h(k) = h(l)$ is at most $|\mathcal{H}|/m$. In other words, with a hash function randomly chosen from $\mathcal{H}$, the chance of a collision between distinct keys k and l is no more than the chance $1/m$ of a collision if $h(k)$ and $h(l)$ were randomly and independently chosen from the set $\{0, 1, \ldots, m-1\}$.

The following theorem shows that a universal class of hash functions gives good average-case behavior. Recall that n_i denotes the length of list $T[i]$.

Theorem 11.3
Suppose that a hash function h is chosen randomly from a universal collection of hash functions and has been used to hash n keys into a table T of size m, using chaining to resolve collisions. If key k is not in the table, then the expected length $\mathrm{E}[n_{h(k)}]$ of the list that key k hashes to is at most the load factor $\alpha = n/m$. If key k is in the table, then the expected length $\mathrm{E}[n_{h(k)}]$ of the list containing key k is at most $1 + \alpha$.

Proof We note that the expectations here are over the choice of the hash function and do not depend on any assumptions about the distribution of the keys. For each pair k and l of distinct keys, define the indicator random variable

$X_{kl} = I\{h(k) = h(l)\}$. Since by the definition of a universal collection of hash functions, a single pair of keys collides with probability at most $1/m$, we have $\Pr\{h(k) = h(l)\} \leq 1/m$. By Lemma 5.1, therefore, we have $E[X_{kl}] \leq 1/m$.

Next we define, for each key k, the random variable Y_k that equals the number of keys other than k that hash to the same slot as k, so that

$$Y_k = \sum_{\substack{l \in T \\ l \neq k}} X_{kl} .$$

Thus we have

$$
\begin{aligned}
E[Y_k] &= E\left[\sum_{\substack{l \in T \\ l \neq k}} X_{kl}\right] \\
&= \sum_{\substack{l \in T \\ l \neq k}} E[X_{kl}] \qquad \text{(by linearity of expectation)} \\
&\leq \sum_{\substack{l \in T \\ l \neq k}} \frac{1}{m} .
\end{aligned}
$$

The remainder of the proof depends on whether key k is in table T.

- If $k \notin T$, then $n_{h(k)} = Y_k$ and $|\{l : l \in T \text{ and } l \neq k\}| = n$. Thus $E[n_{h(k)}] = E[Y_k] \leq n/m = \alpha$.

- If $k \in T$, then because key k appears in list $T[h(k)]$ and the count Y_k does not include key k, we have $n_{h(k)} = Y_k + 1$ and $|\{l : l \in T \text{ and } l \neq k\}| = n - 1$. Thus $E[n_{h(k)}] = E[Y_k] + 1 \leq (n-1)/m + 1 = 1 + \alpha - 1/m < 1 + \alpha$.   ∎

The following corollary says universal hashing provides the desired payoff: it has now become impossible for an adversary to pick a sequence of operations that forces the worst-case running time. By cleverly randomizing the choice of hash function at run time, we guarantee that we can process every sequence of operations with a good average-case running time.

Corollary 11.4
Using universal hashing and collision resolution by chaining in an initially empty table with m slots, it takes expected time $\Theta(s)$ to handle any sequence of s INSERT, SEARCH, and DELETE operations containing $n = O(m)$ INSERT operations.

Proof   Since the number n of insertions is $O(m)$, we have that $\alpha = O(1)$. The INSERT and DELETE operations take constant time and, by Theorem 11.3, the expected time for each SEARCH operation is $O(1)$. By linearity of expectation,

therefore, the expected time for the entire sequence of s operations is $O(s)$. Since each operation takes $\Omega(1)$ time, the $\Theta(s)$ bound follows. ∎

Designing a universal class of hash functions

It is quite easy to design a universal class of hash functions, as a little number theory will help us prove. You may wish to consult Chapter 31 first if you are unfamiliar with number theory.

We begin by choosing a prime number p large enough so that every possible key k is in the range 0 to $p - 1$, inclusive. Let $\mathbb{Z}_p$ denote the set $\{0, 1, \ldots, p - 1\}$, and let $\mathbb{Z}_p^*$ denote the set $\{1, 2, \ldots, p - 1\}$. Since p is prime, we can solve equations modulo p with the methods given in Chapter 31. Because we assume that the size of the universe of keys is greater than the number of slots in the hash table, we have $p > m$.

We now define the hash function h_{ab} for any $a \in \mathbb{Z}_p^*$ and any $b \in \mathbb{Z}_p$ using a linear transformation followed by reductions modulo p and then modulo m:

$$h_{ab}(k) = ((ak + b) \bmod p) \bmod m \, . \tag{11.3}$$

For example, with $p = 17$ and $m = 6$, we have $h_{3,4}(8) = 5$. The family of all such hash functions is

$$\mathcal{H}_{pm} = \{h_{ab} : a \in \mathbb{Z}_p^* \text{ and } b \in \mathbb{Z}_p\} \, . \tag{11.4}$$

Each hash function h_{ab} maps $\mathbb{Z}_p$ to $\mathbb{Z}_m$. This class of hash functions has the nice property that the size m of the output range is arbitrary—not necessarily prime—a feature which we shall use in Section 11.5. Since we have $p - 1$ choices for a and p choices for b, the collection $\mathcal{H}_{pm}$ contains $p(p - 1)$ hash functions.

Theorem 11.5
The class $\mathcal{H}_{pm}$ of hash functions defined by equations (11.3) and (11.4) is universal.

Proof   Consider two distinct keys k and l from $\mathbb{Z}_p$, so that $k \neq l$. For a given hash function h_{ab} we let

$$r = (ak + b) \bmod p \, ,$$
$$s = (al + b) \bmod p \, .$$

We first note that $r \neq s$. Why? Observe that

$$r - s \equiv a(k - l) \pmod{p} \, .$$

It follows that $r \neq s$ because p is prime and both a and $(k - l)$ are nonzero modulo p, and so their product must also be nonzero modulo p by Theorem 31.6. Therefore, when computing any $h_{ab} \in \mathcal{H}_{pm}$, distinct inputs k and l map to distinct

values r and s modulo p; there are no collisions yet at the "mod p level." Moreover, each of the possible $p(p-1)$ choices for the pair (a, b) with $a \neq 0$ yields a *different* resulting pair (r, s) with $r \neq s$, since we can solve for a and b given r and s:

$$a = \left((r - s)((k - l)^{-1} \bmod p)\right) \bmod p ,$$
$$b = (r - ak) \bmod p ,$$

where $((k - l)^{-1} \bmod p)$ denotes the unique multiplicative inverse, modulo p, of $k - l$. Since there are only $p(p - 1)$ possible pairs (r, s) with $r \neq s$, there is a one-to-one correspondence between pairs (a, b) with $a \neq 0$ and pairs (r, s) with $r \neq s$. Thus, for any given pair of inputs k and l, if we pick (a, b) uniformly at random from $\mathbb{Z}_p^* \times \mathbb{Z}_p$, the resulting pair (r, s) is equally likely to be any pair of distinct values modulo p.

Therefore, the probability that distinct keys k and l collide is equal to the probability that $r \equiv s \pmod{m}$ when r and s are randomly chosen as distinct values modulo p. For a given value of r, of the $p - 1$ possible remaining values for s, the number of values s such that $s \neq r$ and $s \equiv r \pmod{m}$ is at most

$$\lceil p/m \rceil - 1 \leq ((p + m - 1)/m) - 1 \quad \text{(by inequality (3.6))}$$
$$= (p - 1)/m .$$

The probability that s collides with r when reduced modulo m is at most $((p - 1)/m)/(p - 1) = 1/m$.

Therefore, for any pair of distinct values $k, l \in \mathbb{Z}_p$,

$$\Pr\{h_{ab}(k) = h_{ab}(l)\} \leq 1/m ,$$

so that $\mathcal{H}_{pm}$ is indeed universal.   ∎

Exercises

11.3-1
Suppose we wish to search a linked list of length n, where each element contains a key k along with a hash value $h(k)$. Each key is a long character string. How might we take advantage of the hash values when searching the list for an element with a given key?

11.3-2
Suppose that we hash a string of r characters into m slots by treating it as a radix-128 number and then using the division method. We can easily represent the number m as a 32-bit computer word, but the string of r characters, treated as a radix-128 number, takes many words. How can we apply the division method to compute the hash value of the character string without using more than a constant number of words of storage outside the string itself?

11.3-3
Consider a version of the division method in which $h(k) = k \bmod m$, where $m = 2^p - 1$ and k is a character string interpreted in radix 2^p. Show that if we can derive string x from string y by permuting its characters, then x and y hash to the same value. Give an example of an application in which this property would be undesirable in a hash function.

11.3-4
Consider a hash table of size $m = 1000$ and a corresponding hash function $h(k) = \lfloor m(kA \bmod 1) \rfloor$ for $A = (\sqrt{5} - 1)/2$. Compute the locations to which the keys $61, 62, 63, 64$, and 65 are mapped.

11.3-5 ⋆
Define a family $\mathcal{H}$ of hash functions from a finite set U to a finite set B to be **ϵ-universal** if for all pairs of distinct elements k and l in U,

$$\Pr\{h(k) = h(l)\} \le \epsilon ,$$

where the probability is over the choice of the hash function h drawn at random from the family $\mathcal{H}$. Show that an ϵ-universal family of hash functions must have

$$\epsilon \ge \frac{1}{|B|} - \frac{1}{|U|} .$$

11.3-6 ⋆
Let U be the set of n-tuples of values drawn from $\mathbb{Z}_p$, and let $B = \mathbb{Z}_p$, where p is prime. Define the hash function $h_b : U \to B$ for $b \in \mathbb{Z}_p$ on an input n-tuple $\langle a_0, a_1, \ldots, a_{n-1} \rangle$ from U as

$$h_b(\langle a_0, a_1, \ldots, a_{n-1} \rangle) = \left(\sum_{j=0}^{n-1} a_j b^j \right) \bmod p ,$$

and let $\mathcal{H} = \{h_b : b \in \mathbb{Z}_p\}$. Argue that $\mathcal{H}$ is $((n-1)/p)$-universal according to the definition of ϵ-universal in Exercise 11.3-5. (*Hint:* See Exercise 31.4-4.)

11.4 Open addressing

In **open addressing**, all elements occupy the hash table itself. That is, each table entry contains either an element of the dynamic set or NIL. When searching for an element, we systematically examine table slots until either we find the desired element or we have ascertained that the element is not in the table. No lists and

no elements are stored outside the table, unlike in chaining. Thus, in open addressing, the hash table can "fill up" so that no further insertions can be made; one consequence is that the load factor α can never exceed 1.

Of course, we could store the linked lists for chaining inside the hash table, in the otherwise unused hash-table slots (see Exercise 11.2-4), but the advantage of open addressing is that it avoids pointers altogether. Instead of following pointers, we *compute* the sequence of slots to be examined. The extra memory freed by not storing pointers provides the hash table with a larger number of slots for the same amount of memory, potentially yielding fewer collisions and faster retrieval.

To perform insertion using open addressing, we successively examine, or *probe*, the hash table until we find an empty slot in which to put the key. Instead of being fixed in the order $0, 1, \ldots, m - 1$ (which requires $\Theta(n)$ search time), the sequence of positions probed *depends upon the key being inserted*. To determine which slots to probe, we extend the hash function to include the probe number (starting from 0) as a second input. Thus, the hash function becomes

$$h : U \times \{0, 1, \ldots, m - 1\} \rightarrow \{0, 1, \ldots, m - 1\} \ .$$

With open addressing, we require that for every key k, the *probe sequence*

$$\langle h(k, 0), h(k, 1), \ldots, h(k, m - 1) \rangle$$

be a permutation of $\langle 0, 1, \ldots, m - 1 \rangle$, so that every hash-table position is eventually considered as a slot for a new key as the table fills up. In the following pseudocode, we assume that the elements in the hash table T are keys with no satellite information; the key k is identical to the element containing key k. Each slot contains either a key or NIL (if the slot is empty). The HASH-INSERT procedure takes as input a hash table T and a key k. It either returns the slot number where it stores key k or flags an error because the hash table is already full.

HASH-INSERT(T, k)

```
1   i = 0
2   repeat
3       j = h(k, i)
4       if T[j] == NIL
5           T[j] = k
6           return j
7       else i = i + 1
8   until i == m
9   error "hash table overflow"
```

The algorithm for searching for key k probes the same sequence of slots that the insertion algorithm examined when key k was inserted. Therefore, the search can

terminate (unsuccessfully) when it finds an empty slot, since k would have been inserted there and not later in its probe sequence. (This argument assumes that keys are not deleted from the hash table.) The procedure HASH-SEARCH takes as input a hash table T and a key k, returning j if it finds that slot j contains key k, or NIL if key k is not present in table T.

HASH-SEARCH(T, k)

1   $i = 0$
2   **repeat**
3         $j = h(k, i)$
4   **if** $T[j] == k$
5   **return** j
6         $i = i + 1$
7   **until** $T[j] ==$ NIL or $i == m$
8   **return** NIL

Deletion from an open-address hash table is difficult. When we delete a key from slot i, we cannot simply mark that slot as empty by storing NIL in it. If we did, we might be unable to retrieve any key k during whose insertion we had probed slot i and found it occupied. We can solve this problem by marking the slot, storing in it the special value DELETED instead of NIL. We would then modify the procedure HASH-INSERT to treat such a slot as if it were empty so that we can insert a new key there. We do not need to modify HASH-SEARCH, since it will pass over DELETED values while searching. When we use the special value DELETED, however, search times no longer depend on the load factor α, and for this reason chaining is more commonly selected as a collision resolution technique when keys must be deleted.

In our analysis, we assume *__uniform hashing__*: the probe sequence of each key is equally likely to be any of the $m!$ permutations of $\langle 0, 1, \ldots, m - 1 \rangle$. Uniform hashing generalizes the notion of simple uniform hashing defined earlier to a hash function that produces not just a single number, but a whole probe sequence. True uniform hashing is difficult to implement, however, and in practice suitable approximations (such as double hashing, defined below) are used.

We will examine three commonly used techniques to compute the probe sequences required for open addressing: linear probing, quadratic probing, and double hashing. These techniques all guarantee that $\langle h(k, 0), h(k, 1), \ldots, h(k, m - 1) \rangle$ is a permutation of $\langle 0, 1, \ldots, m - 1 \rangle$ for each key k. None of these techniques fulfills the assumption of uniform hashing, however, since none of them is capable of generating more than m^2 different probe sequences (instead of the $m!$ that uniform hashing requires). Double hashing has the greatest number of probe sequences and, as one might expect, seems to give the best results.

Linear probing

Given an ordinary hash function $h' : U \to \{0, 1, \ldots, m - 1\}$, which we refer to as an ***auxiliary hash function***, the method of ***linear probing*** uses the hash function

$$h(k, i) = (h'(k) + i) \bmod m$$

for $i = 0, 1, \ldots, m - 1$. Given key k, we first probe $T[h'(k)]$, i.e., the slot given by the auxiliary hash function. We next probe slot $T[h'(k) + 1]$, and so on up to slot $T[m - 1]$. Then we wrap around to slots $T[0], T[1], \ldots$ until we finally probe slot $T[h'(k) - 1]$. Because the initial probe determines the entire probe sequence, there are only m distinct probe sequences.

Linear probing is easy to implement, but it suffers from a problem known as ***primary clustering***. Long runs of occupied slots build up, increasing the average search time. Clusters arise because an empty slot preceded by i full slots gets filled next with probability $(i + 1)/m$. Long runs of occupied slots tend to get longer, and the average search time increases.

Quadratic probing

Quadratic probing uses a hash function of the form

$$h(k, i) = (h'(k) + c_1 i + c_2 i^2) \bmod m \ , \tag{11.5}$$

where h' is an auxiliary hash function, c_1 and c_2 are positive auxiliary constants, and $i = 0, 1, \ldots, m - 1$. The initial position probed is $T[h'(k)]$; later positions probed are offset by amounts that depend in a quadratic manner on the probe number i. This method works much better than linear probing, but to make full use of the hash table, the values of c_1, c_2, and m are constrained. Problem 11-3 shows one way to select these parameters. Also, if two keys have the same initial probe position, then their probe sequences are the same, since $h(k_1, 0) = h(k_2, 0)$ implies $h(k_1, i) = h(k_2, i)$. This property leads to a milder form of clustering, called ***secondary clustering***. As in linear probing, the initial probe determines the entire sequence, and so only m distinct probe sequences are used.

Double hashing

Double hashing offers one of the best methods available for open addressing because the permutations produced have many of the characteristics of randomly chosen permutations. ***Double hashing*** uses a hash function of the form

$$h(k, i) = (h_1(k) + i h_2(k)) \bmod m \ ,$$

where both h_1 and h_2 are auxiliary hash functions. The initial probe goes to position $T[h_1(k)]$; successive probe positions are offset from previous positions by the

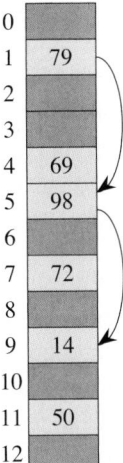

Figure 11.5   Insertion by double hashing. Here we have a hash table of size 13 with $h_1(k) = k \bmod 13$ and $h_2(k) = 1 + (k \bmod 11)$. Since $14 \equiv 1 \pmod{13}$ and $14 \equiv 3 \pmod{11}$, we insert the key 14 into empty slot 9, after examining slots 1 and 5 and finding them to be occupied.

amount $h_2(k)$, modulo m. Thus, unlike the case of linear or quadratic probing, the probe sequence here depends in two ways upon the key k, since the initial probe position, the offset, or both, may vary. Figure 11.5 gives an example of insertion by double hashing.

The value $h_2(k)$ must be relatively prime to the hash-table size m for the entire hash table to be searched. (See Exercise 11.4-4.) A convenient way to ensure this condition is to let m be a power of 2 and to design h_2 so that it always produces an odd number. Another way is to let m be prime and to design h_2 so that it always returns a positive integer less than m. For example, we could choose m prime and let

$$h_1(k) = k \bmod m ,$$
$$h_2(k) = 1 + (k \bmod m') ,$$

where m' is chosen to be slightly less than m (say, $m - 1$). For example, if $k = 123456, m = 701$, and $m' = 700$, we have $h_1(k) = 80$ and $h_2(k) = 257$, so that we first probe position 80, and then we examine every 257th slot (modulo m) until we find the key or have examined every slot.

When m is prime or a power of 2, double hashing improves over linear or quadratic probing in that $\Theta(m^2)$ probe sequences are used, rather than $\Theta(m)$, since each possible $(h_1(k), h_2(k))$ pair yields a distinct probe sequence. As a result, for

such values of m, the performance of double hashing appears to be very close to the performance of the "ideal" scheme of uniform hashing.

Although values of m other than primes or powers of 2 could in principle be used with double hashing, in practice it becomes more difficult to efficiently generate $h_2(k)$ in a way that ensures that it is relatively prime to m, in part because the relative density $\phi(m)/m$ of such numbers may be small (see equation (31.24)).

Analysis of open-address hashing

As in our analysis of chaining, we express our analysis of open addressing in terms of the load factor $\alpha = n/m$ of the hash table. Of course, with open addressing, at most one element occupies each slot, and thus $n \le m$, which implies $\alpha \le 1$.

We assume that we are using uniform hashing. In this idealized scheme, the probe sequence $\langle h(k, 0), h(k, 1), \ldots, h(k, m-1) \rangle$ used to insert or search for each key k is equally likely to be any permutation of $\langle 0, 1, \ldots, m-1 \rangle$. Of course, a given key has a unique fixed probe sequence associated with it; what we mean here is that, considering the probability distribution on the space of keys and the operation of the hash function on the keys, each possible probe sequence is equally likely.

We now analyze the expected number of probes for hashing with open addressing under the assumption of uniform hashing, beginning with an analysis of the number of probes made in an unsuccessful search.

Theorem 11.6
Given an open-address hash table with load factor $\alpha = n/m < 1$, the expected number of probes in an unsuccessful search is at most $1/(1-\alpha)$, assuming uniform hashing.

Proof   In an unsuccessful search, every probe but the last accesses an occupied slot that does not contain the desired key, and the last slot probed is empty. Let us define the random variable X to be the number of probes made in an unsuccessful search, and let us also define the event A_i, for $i = 1, 2, \ldots$, to be the event that an ith probe occurs and it is to an occupied slot. Then the event $\{X \ge i\}$ is the intersection of events $A_1 \cap A_2 \cap \cdots \cap A_{i-1}$. We will bound $\Pr\{X \ge i\}$ by bounding $\Pr\{A_1 \cap A_2 \cap \cdots \cap A_{i-1}\}$. By Exercise C.2-5,

$$\Pr\{A_1 \cap A_2 \cap \cdots \cap A_{i-1}\} = \Pr\{A_1\} \cdot \Pr\{A_2 \mid A_1\} \cdot \Pr\{A_3 \mid A_1 \cap A_2\} \cdots$$
$$\Pr\{A_{i-1} \mid A_1 \cap A_2 \cap \cdots \cap A_{i-2}\} \;.$$

Since there are n elements and m slots, $\Pr\{A_1\} = n/m$. For $j > 1$, the probability that there is a jth probe and it is to an occupied slot, given that the first $j - 1$ probes were to occupied slots, is $(n - j + 1)/(m - j + 1)$. This probability follows

because we would be finding one of the remaining $(n - (j - 1))$ elements in one of the $(m - (j - 1))$ unexamined slots, and by the assumption of uniform hashing, the probability is the ratio of these quantities. Observing that $n < m$ implies that $(n - j)/(m - j) \leq n/m$ for all j such that $0 \leq j < m$, we have for all i such that $1 \leq i \leq m$,

$$\Pr\{X \geq i\} = \frac{n}{m} \cdot \frac{n-1}{m-1} \cdot \frac{n-2}{m-2} \cdots \frac{n-i+2}{m-i+2}$$

$$\leq \left(\frac{n}{m}\right)^{i-1}$$

$$= \alpha^{i-1}.$$

Of course, $\Pr\{X \geq i\} = 0$ for $i > m$. Now, we use equation (C.25) to bound the expected number of probes:

$$\mathrm{E}[X] = \sum_{i=1}^{\infty} \Pr\{X \geq i\}$$

$$= \sum_{i=1}^{m} \Pr\{X \geq i\} + \sum_{i>m} \Pr\{X \geq i\}$$

$$\leq \sum_{i=1}^{\infty} \alpha^{i-1} + 0$$

$$= \sum_{i=0}^{\infty} \alpha^{i}$$

$$= \frac{1}{1-\alpha}. \qquad \blacksquare$$

This bound of $1/(1-\alpha) = 1 + \alpha + \alpha^2 + \alpha^3 + \cdots$ has an intuitive interpretation. We always make the first probe. With probability approximately α, the first probe finds an occupied slot, so that we need to probe a second time. With probability approximately α^2, the first two slots are occupied so that we make a third probe, and so on.

If α is a constant, Theorem 11.6 predicts that an unsuccessful search runs in $O(1)$ time. For example, if the hash table is half full, the average number of probes in an unsuccessful search is at most $1/(1 - .5) = 2$. If it is 90 percent full, the average number of probes is at most $1/(1 - .9) = 10$.

Theorem 11.6 gives us the performance of the HASH-INSERT procedure almost immediately.

Corollary 11.7

Inserting an element into an open-address hash table with load factor α requires at most $1/(1-\alpha)$ probes on average, assuming uniform hashing.

Proof   An element is inserted only if there is room in the table, and thus $\alpha < 1$. Inserting a key requires an unsuccessful search followed by placing the key into the first empty slot found. Thus, the expected number of probes is at most $1/(1-\alpha)$. ■

We have to do a little more work to compute the expected number of probes for a successful search.

Theorem 11.8

Given an open-address hash table with load factor $\alpha < 1$, the expected number of probes in a successful search is at most

$$\frac{1}{\alpha} \ln \frac{1}{1-\alpha} \, ,$$

assuming uniform hashing and assuming that each key in the table is equally likely to be searched for.

Proof   A search for a key k reproduces the same probe sequence as when the element with key k was inserted. By Corollary 11.7, if k was the $(i + 1)$st key inserted into the hash table, the expected number of probes made in a search for k is at most $1/(1 - i/m) = m/(m - i)$. Averaging over all n keys in the hash table gives us the expected number of probes in a successful search:

$$
\begin{aligned}
\frac{1}{n} \sum_{i=0}^{n-1} \frac{m}{m-i} &= \frac{m}{n} \sum_{i=0}^{n-1} \frac{1}{m-i} \\
&= \frac{1}{\alpha} \sum_{k=m-n+1}^{m} \frac{1}{k} \\
&\leq \frac{1}{\alpha} \int_{m-n}^{m} (1/x)\,dx \quad \text{(by inequality (A.12))} \\
&= \frac{1}{\alpha} \ln \frac{m}{m-n} \\
&= \frac{1}{\alpha} \ln \frac{1}{1-\alpha} \, .
\end{aligned}
$$

■

If the hash table is half full, the expected number of probes in a successful search is less than 1.387. If the hash table is 90 percent full, the expected number of probes is less than 2.559.

Exercises

11.4-1
Consider inserting the keys $10, 22, 31, 4, 15, 28, 17, 88, 59$ into a hash table of
length $m = 11$ using open addressing with the auxiliary hash function $h'(k) = k$.
Illustrate the result of inserting these keys using linear probing, using quadratic
probing with $c_1 = 1$ and $c_2 = 3$, and using double hashing with $h_1(k) = k$ and
$h_2(k) = 1 + (k \bmod (m - 1))$.

11.4-2
Write pseudocode for HASH-DELETE as outlined in the text, and modify HASH-
INSERT to handle the special value DELETED.

11.4-3
Consider an open-address hash table with uniform hashing. Give upper bounds
on the expected number of probes in an unsuccessful search and on the expected
number of probes in a successful search when the load factor is $3/4$ and when it
is $7/8$.

11.4-4   ★
Suppose that we use double hashing to resolve collisions—that is, we use the hash
function $h(k, i) = (h_1(k) + i h_2(k)) \bmod m$. Show that if m and $h_2(k)$ have
greatest common divisor $d \geq 1$ for some key k, then an unsuccessful search for
key k examines $(1/d)$th of the hash table before returning to slot $h_1(k)$. Thus,
when $d = 1$, so that m and $h_2(k)$ are relatively prime, the search may examine the
entire hash table. (*Hint:* See Chapter 31.)

11.4-5   ★
Consider an open-address hash table with a load factor α. Find the nonzero value α
for which the expected number of probes in an unsuccessful search equals twice
the expected number of probes in a successful search. Use the upper bounds given
by Theorems 11.6 and 11.8 for these expected numbers of probes.

★   **11.5   Perfect hashing**

Although hashing is often a good choice for its excellent average-case performance, hashing can also provide excellent *worst-case* performance when the set of
keys is *static*: once the keys are stored in the table, the set of keys never changes.
Some applications naturally have static sets of keys: consider the set of reserved
words in a programming language, or the set of file names on a CD-ROM. We

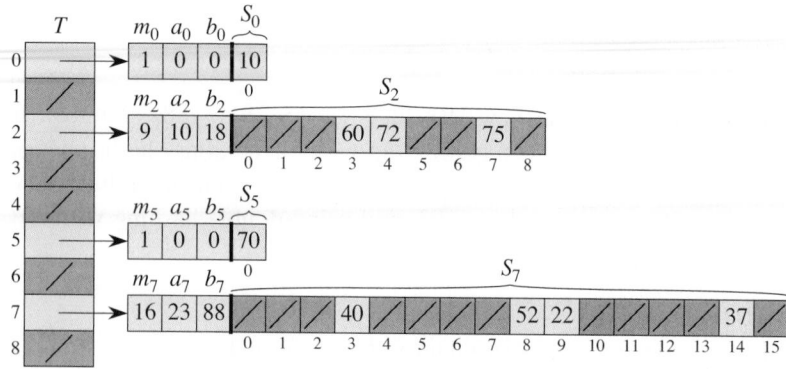

Figure 11.6 Using perfect hashing to store the set $K = \{10, 22, 37, 40, 52, 60, 70, 72, 75\}$. The outer hash function is $h(k) = ((ak + b) \bmod p) \bmod m$, where $a = 3$, $b = 42$, $p = 101$, and $m = 9$. For example, $h(75) = 2$, and so key 75 hashes to slot 2 of table T. A secondary hash table S_j stores all keys hashing to slot j. The size of hash table S_j is $m_j = n_j^2$, and the associated hash function is $h_j(k) = ((a_j k + b_j) \bmod p) \bmod m_j$. Since $h_2(75) = 7$, key 75 is stored in slot 7 of secondary hash table S_2. No collisions occur in any of the secondary hash tables, and so searching takes constant time in the worst case.

call a hashing technique ***perfect hashing*** if $O(1)$ memory accesses are required to perform a search in the worst case.

To create a perfect hashing scheme, we use two levels of hashing, with universal hashing at each level. Figure 11.6 illustrates the approach.

The first level is essentially the same as for hashing with chaining: we hash the n keys into m slots using a hash function h carefully selected from a family of universal hash functions.

Instead of making a linked list of the keys hashing to slot j, however, we use a small ***secondary hash table*** S_j with an associated hash function h_j. By choosing the hash functions h_j carefully, we can guarantee that there are no collisions at the secondary level.

In order to guarantee that there are no collisions at the secondary level, however, we will need to let the size m_j of hash table S_j be the square of the number n_j of keys hashing to slot j. Although you might think that the quadratic dependence of m_j on n_j may seem likely to cause the overall storage requirement to be excessive, we shall show that by choosing the first-level hash function well, we can limit the expected total amount of space used to $O(n)$.

We use hash functions chosen from the universal classes of hash functions of Section 11.3.3. The first-level hash function comes from the class $\mathcal{H}_{pm}$, where as in Section 11.3.3, p is a prime number greater than any key value. Those keys

hashing to slot j are re-hashed into a secondary hash table S_j of size m_j using a hash function h_j chosen from the class $\mathcal{H}_{p,m_j}$.[1]

We shall proceed in two steps. First, we shall determine how to ensure that the secondary tables have no collisions. Second, we shall show that the expected amount of memory used overall—for the primary hash table and all the secondary hash tables—is $O(n)$.

Theorem 11.9
Suppose that we store n keys in a hash table of size $m = n^2$ using a hash function h randomly chosen from a universal class of hash functions. Then, the probability is less than $1/2$ that there are any collisions.

Proof   There are $\binom{n}{2}$ pairs of keys that may collide; each pair collides with probability $1/m$ if h is chosen at random from a universal family $\mathcal{H}$ of hash functions. Let X be a random variable that counts the number of collisions. When $m = n^2$, the expected number of collisions is

$$
\begin{aligned}
\mathrm{E}\left[X\right] &= \binom{n}{2} \cdot \frac{1}{n^2} \\
&= \frac{n^2 - n}{2} \cdot \frac{1}{n^2} \\
&< 1/2 \, .
\end{aligned}
$$

(This analysis is similar to the analysis of the birthday paradox in Section 5.4.1.) Applying Markov's inequality (C.30), $\Pr\{X \geq t\} \leq \mathrm{E}\left[X\right]/t$, with $t = 1$, completes the proof.   ∎

In the situation described in Theorem 11.9, where $m = n^2$, it follows that a hash function h chosen at random from $\mathcal{H}$ is more likely than not to have *no* collisions. Given the set K of n keys to be hashed (remember that K is static), it is thus easy to find a collision-free hash function h with a few random trials.

When n is large, however, a hash table of size $m = n^2$ is excessive. Therefore, we adopt the two-level hashing approach, and we use the approach of Theorem 11.9 only to hash the entries within each slot. We use an outer, or first-level, hash function h to hash the keys into $m = n$ slots. Then, if n_j keys hash to slot j, we use a secondary hash table S_j of size $m_j = n_j^2$ to provide collision-free constant-time lookup.

---

[1] When $n_j = m_j = 1$, we don't really need a hash function for slot j; when we choose a hash function $h_{ab}(k) = ((ak + b) \bmod p) \bmod m_j$ for such a slot, we just use $a = b = 0$.

We now turn to the issue of ensuring that the overall memory used is $O(n)$. Since the size m_j of the jth secondary hash table grows quadratically with the number n_j of keys stored, we run the risk that the overall amount of storage could be excessive.

If the first-level table size is $m = n$, then the amount of memory used is $O(n)$ for the primary hash table, for the storage of the sizes m_j of the secondary hash tables, and for the storage of the parameters a_j and b_j defining the secondary hash functions h_j drawn from the class $\mathcal{H}_{p,m_j}$ of Section 11.3.3 (except when $n_j = 1$ and we use $a = b = 0$). The following theorem and a corollary provide a bound on the expected combined sizes of all the secondary hash tables. A second corollary bounds the probability that the combined size of all the secondary hash tables is superlinear (actually, that it equals or exceeds $4n$).

Theorem 11.10
Suppose that we store n keys in a hash table of size $m = n$ using a hash function h randomly chosen from a universal class of hash functions. Then, we have

$$
\mathrm{E}\left[\sum_{j=0}^{m-1} n_j^2\right] < 2n \, ,
$$

where n_j is the number of keys hashing to slot j.

Proof   We start with the following identity, which holds for any nonnegative integer a:

$$
a^2 = a + 2\binom{a}{2} \, . \tag{11.6}
$$

We have

$$
\mathrm{E}\left[\sum_{j=0}^{m-1} n_j^2\right]
$$

$$
= \mathrm{E}\left[\sum_{j=0}^{m-1}\left(n_j + 2\binom{n_j}{2}\right)\right] \qquad \text{(by equation (11.6))}
$$

$$
= \mathrm{E}\left[\sum_{j=0}^{m-1} n_j\right] + 2\,\mathrm{E}\left[\sum_{j=0}^{m-1}\binom{n_j}{2}\right] \qquad \text{(by linearity of expectation)}
$$

$$
= \mathrm{E}\left[n\right] + 2\,\mathrm{E}\left[\sum_{j=0}^{m-1}\binom{n_j}{2}\right] \qquad \text{(by equation (11.1))}
$$

$$= \quad n + 2\,\mathrm{E}\left[\sum_{j=0}^{m-1}\binom{n_j}{2}\right] \qquad\qquad \text{(since } n \text{ is not a random variable)} \;.$$

To evaluate the summation $\sum_{j=0}^{m-1}\binom{n_j}{2}$, we observe that it is just the total number of pairs of keys in the hash table that collide. By the properties of universal hashing, the expected value of this summation is at most

$$\binom{n}{2}\frac{1}{m} \quad=\quad \frac{n(n-1)}{2m}$$

$$=\quad \frac{n-1}{2}\,,$$

since $m = n$. Thus,

$$\mathrm{E}\left[\sum_{j=0}^{m-1}n_j^2\right] \quad\leq\quad n + 2\,\frac{n-1}{2}$$

$$=\quad 2n-1$$

$$<\quad 2n\;. \qquad\qquad\qquad\blacksquare$$

Corollary 11.11

Suppose that we store n keys in a hash table of size $m = n$ using a hash function h randomly chosen from a universal class of hash functions, and we set the size of each secondary hash table to $m_j = n_j^2$ for $j = 0, 1, \ldots, m - 1$. Then, the expected amount of storage required for all secondary hash tables in a perfect hashing scheme is less than $2n$.

Proof Since $m_j = n_j^2$ for $j = 0, 1, \ldots, m - 1$, Theorem 11.10 gives

$$\mathrm{E}\left[\sum_{j=0}^{m-1}m_j\right] \quad=\quad \mathrm{E}\left[\sum_{j=0}^{m-1}n_j^2\right]$$

$$<\quad 2n\,, \qquad\qquad\qquad\qquad (11.7)$$

which completes the proof. $\blacksquare$

Corollary 11.12

Suppose that we store n keys in a hash table of size $m = n$ using a hash function h randomly chosen from a universal class of hash functions, and we set the size of each secondary hash table to $m_j = n_j^2$ for $j = 0, 1, \ldots, m - 1$. Then, the probability is less than $1/2$ that the total storage used for secondary hash tables equals or exceeds $4n$.

Proof   Again we apply Markov's inequality (C.30), $\Pr\{X \geq t\} \leq \mathrm{E}[X]/t$, this time to inequality (11.7), with $X = \sum_{j=0}^{m-1} m_j$ and $t = 4n$:

$$
\Pr\left\{\sum_{j=0}^{m-1} m_j \geq 4n\right\} \leq \frac{\mathrm{E}\left[\sum_{j=0}^{m-1} m_j\right]}{4n}
$$

$$
< \frac{2n}{4n}
$$

$$
= 1/2 \;. \qquad \blacksquare
$$

From Corollary 11.12, we see that if we test a few randomly chosen hash functions from the universal family, we will quickly find one that uses a reasonable amount of storage.

Exercises

11.5-1   ★
Suppose that we insert n keys into a hash table of size m using open addressing and uniform hashing. Let $p(n, m)$ be the probability that no collisions occur. Show that $p(n, m) \leq e^{-n(n-1)/2m}$. (*Hint:* See equation (3.12).) Argue that when n exceeds $\sqrt{m}$, the probability of avoiding collisions goes rapidly to zero.

Problems

11-1   *Longest-probe bound for hashing*
Suppose that we use an open-addressed hash table of size m to store $n \leq m/2$ items.

a. Assuming uniform hashing, show that for $i = 1, 2, \ldots, n$, the probability is at most 2^{-k} that the ith insertion requires strictly more than k probes.

b. Show that for $i = 1, 2, \ldots, n$, the probability is $O(1/n^2)$ that the ith insertion requires more than $2 \lg n$ probes.

Let the random variable X_i denote the number of probes required by the ith insertion. You have shown in part (b) that $\Pr\{X_i > 2 \lg n\} = O(1/n^2)$. Let the random variable $X = \max_{1 \leq i \leq n} X_i$ denote the maximum number of probes required by any of the n insertions.

c. Show that $\Pr\{X > 2 \lg n\} = O(1/n)$.

d. Show that the expected length $\mathrm{E}[X]$ of the longest probe sequence is $O(\lg n)$.

11-2 Slot-size bound for chaining

Suppose that we have a hash table with n slots, with collisions resolved by chaining, and suppose that n keys are inserted into the table. Each key is equally likely to be hashed to each slot. Let M be the maximum number of keys in any slot after all the keys have been inserted. Your mission is to prove an $O(\lg n / \lg \lg n)$ upper bound on $\mathrm{E}[M]$, the expected value of M.

a. Argue that the probability Q_k that exactly k keys hash to a particular slot is given by

$$Q_k = \left(\frac{1}{n}\right)^k \left(1 - \frac{1}{n}\right)^{n-k} \binom{n}{k}.$$

b. Let P_k be the probability that $M = k$, that is, the probability that the slot containing the most keys contains k keys. Show that $P_k \le n Q_k$.

c. Use Stirling's approximation, equation (3.18), to show that $Q_k < e^k / k^k$.

d. Show that there exists a constant $c > 1$ such that $Q_{k_0} < 1/n^3$ for $k_0 = c \lg n / \lg \lg n$. Conclude that $P_k < 1/n^2$ for $k \ge k_0 = c \lg n / \lg \lg n$.

e. Argue that

$$\mathrm{E}[M] \le \Pr\left\{M > \frac{c \lg n}{\lg \lg n}\right\} \cdot n + \Pr\left\{M \le \frac{c \lg n}{\lg \lg n}\right\} \cdot \frac{c \lg n}{\lg \lg n}.$$

Conclude that $\mathrm{E}[M] = O(\lg n / \lg \lg n)$.

11-3 Quadratic probing

Suppose that we are given a key k to search for in a hash table with positions $0, 1, \ldots, m - 1$, and suppose that we have a hash function h mapping the key space into the set $\{0, 1, \ldots, m - 1\}$. The search scheme is as follows:

1. Compute the value $j = h(k)$, and set $i = 0$.

2. Probe in position j for the desired key k. If you find it, or if this position is empty, terminate the search.

3. Set $i = i + 1$. If i now equals m, the table is full, so terminate the search. Otherwise, set $j = (i + j) \bmod m$, and return to step 2.

Assume that m is a power of 2.

a. Show that this scheme is an instance of the general "quadratic probing" scheme by exhibiting the appropriate constants c_1 and c_2 for equation (11.5).

b. Prove that this algorithm examines every table position in the worst case.

11-4   *Hashing and authentication*

Let $\mathcal{H}$ be a class of hash functions in which each hash function $h \in \mathcal{H}$ maps the universe U of keys to $\{0, 1, \ldots, m - 1\}$. We say that $\mathcal{H}$ is **k-universal** if, for every fixed sequence of k distinct keys $\langle x^{(1)}, x^{(2)}, \ldots, x^{(k)} \rangle$ and for any h chosen at random from $\mathcal{H}$, the sequence $\langle h(x^{(1)}), h(x^{(2)}), \ldots, h(x^{(k)}) \rangle$ is equally likely to be any of the m^k sequences of length k with elements drawn from $\{0, 1, \ldots, m - 1\}$.

a. Show that if the family $\mathcal{H}$ of hash functions is 2-universal, then it is universal.

b. Suppose that the universe U is the set of n-tuples of values drawn from $\mathbb{Z}_p = \{0, 1, \ldots, p - 1\}$, where p is prime. Consider an element $x = \langle x_0, x_1, \ldots, x_{n-1} \rangle \in U$. For any n-tuple $a = \langle a_0, a_1, \ldots, a_{n-1} \rangle \in U$, define the hash function h_a by

$$h_a(x) = \left(\sum_{j=0}^{n-1} a_j x_j \right) \bmod p .$$

Let $\mathcal{H} = \{h_a\}$. Show that $\mathcal{H}$ is universal, but not 2-universal. (*Hint:* Find a key for which all hash functions in $\mathcal{H}$ produce the same value.)

c. Suppose that we modify $\mathcal{H}$ slightly from part (b): for any $a \in U$ and for any $b \in \mathbb{Z}_p$, define

$$h'_{ab}(x) = \left(\sum_{j=0}^{n-1} a_j x_j + b \right) \bmod p$$

and $\mathcal{H}' = \{h'_{ab}\}$. Argue that $\mathcal{H}'$ is 2-universal. (*Hint:* Consider fixed n-tuples $x \in U$ and $y \in U$, with $x_i \neq y_i$ for some i. What happens to $h'_{ab}(x)$ and $h'_{ab}(y)$ as a_i and b range over $\mathbb{Z}_p$?)

d. Suppose that Alice and Bob secretly agree on a hash function h from a 2-universal family $\mathcal{H}$ of hash functions. Each $h \in \mathcal{H}$ maps from a universe of keys U to $\mathbb{Z}_p$, where p is prime. Later, Alice sends a message m to Bob over the Internet, where $m \in U$. She authenticates this message to Bob by also sending an authentication tag $t = h(m)$, and Bob checks that the pair (m, t) he receives indeed satisfies $t = h(m)$. Suppose that an adversary intercepts (m, t) en route and tries to fool Bob by replacing the pair (m, t) with a different pair (m', t'). Argue that the probability that the adversary succeeds in fooling Bob into accepting (m', t') is at most $1/p$, no matter how much computing power the adversary has, and even if the adversary knows the family $\mathcal{H}$ of hash functions used.

Chapter notes

Knuth [211] and Gonnet [145] are excellent references for the analysis of hashing algorithms. Knuth credits H. P. Luhn (1953) for inventing hash tables, along with the chaining method for resolving collisions. At about the same time, G. M. Amdahl originated the idea of open addressing.

Carter and Wegman introduced the notion of universal classes of hash functions in 1979 [58].

Fredman, Komlós, and Szemerédi [112] developed the perfect hashing scheme for static sets presented in Section 11.5. An extension of their method to dynamic sets, handling insertions and deletions in amortized expected time $O(1)$, has been given by Dietzfelbinger et al. [86].

12 Binary Search Trees

The search tree data structure supports many dynamic-set operations, including SEARCH, MINIMUM, MAXIMUM, PREDECESSOR, SUCCESSOR, INSERT, and DELETE. Thus, we can use a search tree both as a dictionary and as a priority queue.

Basic operations on a binary search tree take time proportional to the height of the tree. For a complete binary tree with n nodes, such operations run in $\Theta(\lg n)$ worst-case time. If the tree is a linear chain of n nodes, however, the same operations take $\Theta(n)$ worst-case time. We shall see in Section 12.4 that the expected height of a randomly built binary search tree is $O(\lg n)$, so that basic dynamic-set operations on such a tree take $\Theta(\lg n)$ time on average.

In practice, we can't always guarantee that binary search trees are built randomly, but we can design variations of binary search trees with good guaranteed worst-case performance on basic operations. Chapter 13 presents one such variation, red-black trees, which have height $O(\lg n)$. Chapter 18 introduces B-trees, which are particularly good for maintaining databases on secondary (disk) storage.

After presenting the basic properties of binary search trees, the following sections show how to walk a binary search tree to print its values in sorted order, how to search for a value in a binary search tree, how to find the minimum or maximum element, how to find the predecessor or successor of an element, and how to insert into or delete from a binary search tree. The basic mathematical properties of trees appear in Appendix B.

12.1 What is a binary search tree?

A binary search tree is organized, as the name suggests, in a binary tree, as shown in Figure 12.1. We can represent such a tree by a linked data structure in which each node is an object. In addition to a *key* and satellite data, each node contains attributes *left*, *right*, and p that point to the nodes corresponding to its left child,

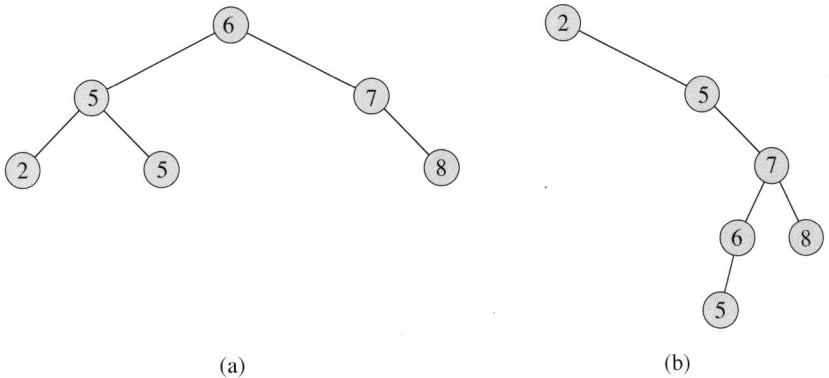

(a)   (b)

Figure 12.1   Binary search trees. For any node x, the keys in the left subtree of x are at most $x.key$, and the keys in the right subtree of x are at least $x.key$. Different binary search trees can represent the same set of values. The worst-case running time for most search-tree operations is proportional to the height of the tree. **(a)** A binary search tree on 6 nodes with height 2. **(b)** A less efficient binary search tree with height 4 that contains the same keys.

its right child, and its parent, respectively. If a child or the parent is missing, the appropriate attribute contains the value NIL. The root node is the only node in the tree whose parent is NIL.

The keys in a binary search tree are always stored in such a way as to satisfy the ***binary-search-tree property***:

> Let x be a node in a binary search tree. If y is a node in the left subtree of x, then $y.key \leq x.key$. If y is a node in the right subtree of x, then $y.key \geq x.key$.

Thus, in Figure 12.1(a), the key of the root is 6, the keys 2, 5, and 5 in its left subtree are no larger than 6, and the keys 7 and 8 in its right subtree are no smaller than 6. The same property holds for every node in the tree. For example, the key 5 in the root's left child is no smaller than the key 2 in that node's left subtree and no larger than the key 5 in the right subtree.

The binary-search-tree property allows us to print out all the keys in a binary search tree in sorted order by a simple recursive algorithm, called an ***inorder tree walk***. This algorithm is so named because it prints the key of the root of a subtree between printing the values in its left subtree and printing those in its right subtree. (Similarly, a ***preorder tree walk*** prints the root before the values in either subtree, and a ***postorder tree walk*** prints the root after the values in its subtrees.) To use the following procedure to print all the elements in a binary search tree T, we call INORDER-TREE-WALK($T.root$).

INORDER-TREE-WALK(x)

1 **if** $x \neq$ NIL
2   INORDER-TREE-WALK($x.left$)
3   print $x.key$
4   INORDER-TREE-WALK($x.right$)

As an example, the inorder tree walk prints the keys in each of the two binary search trees from Figure 12.1 in the order $2, 5, 5, 6, 7, 8$. The correctness of the algorithm follows by induction directly from the binary-search-tree property.

It takes $\Theta(n)$ time to walk an n-node binary search tree, since after the initial call, the procedure calls itself recursively exactly twice for each node in the tree—once for its left child and once for its right child. The following theorem gives a formal proof that it takes linear time to perform an inorder tree walk.

Theorem 12.1
If x is the root of an n-node subtree, then the call INORDER-TREE-WALK(x) takes $\Theta(n)$ time.

Proof Let $T(n)$ denote the time taken by INORDER-TREE-WALK when it is called on the root of an n-node subtree. Since INORDER-TREE-WALK visits all n nodes of the subtree, we have $T(n) = \Omega(n)$. It remains to show that $T(n) = O(n)$.

Since INORDER-TREE-WALK takes a small, constant amount of time on an empty subtree (for the test $x \neq$ NIL), we have $T(0) = c$ for some constant $c > 0$.

For $n > 0$, suppose that INORDER-TREE-WALK is called on a node x whose left subtree has k nodes and whose right subtree has $n - k - 1$ nodes. The time to perform INORDER-TREE-WALK(x) is bounded by $T(n) \leq T(k) + T(n-k-1) + d$ for some constant $d > 0$ that reflects an upper bound on the time to execute the body of INORDER-TREE-WALK(x), exclusive of the time spent in recursive calls.

We use the substitution method to show that $T(n) = O(n)$ by proving that $T(n) \leq (c+d)n + c$. For $n = 0$, we have $(c+d) \cdot 0 + c = c = T(0)$. For $n > 0$, we have

$$
\begin{aligned}
T(n) &\leq T(k) + T(n - k - 1) + d \\
&\leq ((c+d)k + c) + ((c+d)(n-k-1) + c) + d \\
&= (c+d)n + c - (c+d) + c + d \\
&= (c+d)n + c \,,
\end{aligned}
$$

which completes the proof.   ∎

Exercises

12.1-1
For the set of {1, 4, 5, 10, 16, 17, 21} of keys, draw binary search trees of heights 2, 3, 4, 5, and 6.

12.1-2
What is the difference between the binary-search-tree property and the min-heap property (see page 153)? Can the min-heap property be used to print out the keys of an n-node tree in sorted order in $O(n)$ time? Show how, or explain why not.

12.1-3
Give a nonrecursive algorithm that performs an inorder tree walk. (*Hint:* An easy solution uses a stack as an auxiliary data structure. A more complicated, but elegant, solution uses no stack but assumes that we can test two pointers for equality.)

12.1-4
Give recursive algorithms that perform preorder and postorder tree walks in $\Theta(n)$ time on a tree of n nodes.

12.1-5
Argue that since sorting n elements takes $\Omega(n \lg n)$ time in the worst case in the comparison model, any comparison-based algorithm for constructing a binary search tree from an arbitrary list of n elements takes $\Omega(n \lg n)$ time in the worst case.

12.2   Querying a binary search tree

We often need to search for a key stored in a binary search tree. Besides the SEARCH operation, binary search trees can support such queries as MINIMUM, MAXIMUM, SUCCESSOR, and PREDECESSOR. In this section, we shall examine these operations and show how to support each one in time $O(h)$ on any binary search tree of height h.

Searching

We use the following procedure to search for a node with a given key in a binary search tree. Given a pointer to the root of the tree and a key k, TREE-SEARCH returns a pointer to a node with key k if one exists; otherwise, it returns NIL.

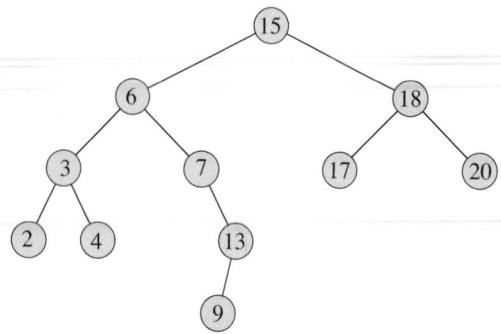

Figure 12.2 Queries on a binary search tree. To search for the key 13 in the tree, we follow the path $15 \rightarrow 6 \rightarrow 7 \rightarrow 13$ from the root. The minimum key in the tree is 2, which is found by following *left* pointers from the root. The maximum key 20 is found by following *right* pointers from the root. The successor of the node with key 15 is the node with key 17, since it is the minimum key in the right subtree of 15. The node with key 13 has no right subtree, and thus its successor is its lowest ancestor whose left child is also an ancestor. In this case, the node with key 15 is its successor.

TREE-SEARCH(x, k)

1   **if** $x ==$ NIL or $k == x.key$
2   **return** x
3   **if** $k < x.key$
4   **return** TREE-SEARCH$(x.left, k)$
5   **else return** TREE-SEARCH$(x.right, k)$

The procedure begins its search at the root and traces a simple path downward in the tree, as shown in Figure 12.2. For each node x it encounters, it compares the key k with $x.key$. If the two keys are equal, the search terminates. If k is smaller than $x.key$, the search continues in the left subtree of x, since the binary-search-tree property implies that k could not be stored in the right subtree. Symmetrically, if k is larger than $x.key$, the search continues in the right subtree. The nodes encountered during the recursion form a simple path downward from the root of the tree, and thus the running time of TREE-SEARCH is $O(h)$, where h is the height of the tree.

We can rewrite this procedure in an iterative fashion by "unrolling" the recursion into a **while** loop. On most computers, the iterative version is more efficient.

ITERATIVE-TREE-SEARCH(x, k)

```
1  while x ≠ NIL and k ≠ x.key
2      if k < x.key
3          x = x.left
4      else x = x.right
5  return x
```

Minimum and maximum

We can always find an element in a binary search tree whose key is a minimum by following *left* child pointers from the root until we encounter a NIL, as shown in Figure 12.2. The following procedure returns a pointer to the minimum element in the subtree rooted at a given node x, which we assume to be non-NIL:

TREE-MINIMUM(x)

```
1  while x.left ≠ NIL
2      x = x.left
3  return x
```

The binary-search-tree property guarantees that TREE-MINIMUM is correct. If a node x has no left subtree, then since every key in the right subtree of x is at least as large as $x.key$, the minimum key in the subtree rooted at x is $x.key$. If node x has a left subtree, then since no key in the right subtree is smaller than $x.key$ and every key in the left subtree is not larger than $x.key$, the minimum key in the subtree rooted at x resides in the subtree rooted at $x.left$.

The pseudocode for TREE-MAXIMUM is symmetric:

TREE-MAXIMUM(x)

```
1  while x.right ≠ NIL
2      x = x.right
3  return x
```

Both of these procedures run in $O(h)$ time on a tree of height h since, as in TREE-SEARCH, the sequence of nodes encountered forms a simple path downward from the root.

Successor and predecessor

Given a node in a binary search tree, sometimes we need to find its successor in the sorted order determined by an inorder tree walk. If all keys are distinct, the

successor of a node x is the node with the smallest key greater than $x.key$. The structure of a binary search tree allows us to determine the successor of a node without ever comparing keys. The following procedure returns the successor of a node x in a binary search tree if it exists, and NIL if x has the largest key in the tree:

TREE-SUCCESSOR(x)

```
1  if x.right ≠ NIL
2      return TREE-MINIMUM(x.right)
3  y = x.p
4  while y ≠ NIL and x == y.right
5      x = y
6      y = y.p
7  return y
```

We break the code for TREE-SUCCESSOR into two cases. If the right subtree of node x is nonempty, then the successor of x is just the leftmost node in x's right subtree, which we find in line 2 by calling TREE-MINIMUM($x.right$). For example, the successor of the node with key 15 in Figure 12.2 is the node with key 17.

On the other hand, as Exercise 12.2-6 asks you to show, if the right subtree of node x is empty and x has a successor y, then y is the lowest ancestor of x whose left child is also an ancestor of x. In Figure 12.2, the successor of the node with key 13 is the node with key 15. To find y, we simply go up the tree from x until we encounter a node that is the left child of its parent; lines 3–7 of TREE-SUCCESSOR handle this case.

The running time of TREE-SUCCESSOR on a tree of height h is $O(h)$, since we either follow a simple path up the tree or follow a simple path down the tree. The procedure TREE-PREDECESSOR, which is symmetric to TREE-SUCCESSOR, also runs in time $O(h)$.

Even if keys are not distinct, we define the successor and predecessor of any node x as the node returned by calls made to TREE-SUCCESSOR(x) and TREE-PREDECESSOR(x), respectively.

In summary, we have proved the following theorem.

Theorem 12.2

We can implement the dynamic-set operations SEARCH, MINIMUM, MAXIMUM, SUCCESSOR, and PREDECESSOR so that each one runs in $O(h)$ time on a binary search tree of height h.   ∎

Exercises

12.2-1
Suppose that we have numbers between 1 and 1000 in a binary search tree, and we want to search for the number 363. Which of the following sequences could *not* be the sequence of nodes examined?

a. 2, 252, 401, 398, 330, 344, 397, 363.

b. 924, 220, 911, 244, 898, 258, 362, 363.

c. 925, 202, 911, 240, 912, 245, 363.

d. 2, 399, 387, 219, 266, 382, 381, 278, 363.

e. 935, 278, 347, 621, 299, 392, 358, 363.

12.2-2
Write recursive versions of TREE-MINIMUM and TREE-MAXIMUM.

12.2-3
Write the TREE-PREDECESSOR procedure.

12.2-4
Professor Bunyan thinks he has discovered a remarkable property of binary search trees. Suppose that the search for key k in a binary search tree ends up in a leaf. Consider three sets: A, the keys to the left of the search path; B, the keys on the search path; and C, the keys to the right of the search path. Professor Bunyan claims that any three keys $a \in A$, $b \in B$, and $c \in C$ must satisfy $a \leq b \leq c$. Give a smallest possible counterexample to the professor's claim.

12.2-5
Show that if a node in a binary search tree has two children, then its successor has no left child and its predecessor has no right child.

12.2-6
Consider a binary search tree T whose keys are distinct. Show that if the right subtree of a node x in T is empty and x has a successor y, then y is the lowest ancestor of x whose left child is also an ancestor of x. (Recall that every node is its own ancestor.)

12.2-7
An alternative method of performing an inorder tree walk of an n-node binary search tree finds the minimum element in the tree by calling TREE-MINIMUM and then making $n - 1$ calls to TREE-SUCCESSOR. Prove that this algorithm runs in $\Theta(n)$ time.

12.2-8

Prove that no matter what node we start at in a height-h binary search tree, k successive calls to TREE-SUCCESSOR take $O(k + h)$ time.

12.2-9

Let T be a binary search tree whose keys are distinct, let x be a leaf node, and let y be its parent. Show that $y.key$ is either the smallest key in T larger than $x.key$ or the largest key in T smaller than $x.key$.

12.3   Insertion and deletion

The operations of insertion and deletion cause the dynamic set represented by a binary search tree to change. The data structure must be modified to reflect this change, but in such a way that the binary-search-tree property continues to hold. As we shall see, modifying the tree to insert a new element is relatively straightforward, but handling deletion is somewhat more intricate.

Insertion

To insert a new value v into a binary search tree T, we use the procedure TREE-INSERT. The procedure takes a node z for which $z.key = v$, $z.left = $ NIL, and $z.right = $ NIL. It modifies T and some of the attributes of z in such a way that it inserts z into an appropriate position in the tree.

TREE-INSERT(T, z)

```
 1   y = NIL
 2   x = T.root
 3   while x ≠ NIL
 4       y = x
 5       if z.key < x.key
 6           x = x.left
 7       else x = x.right
 8   z.p = y
 9   if y == NIL
10       T.root = z        // tree T was empty
11   elseif z.key < y.key
12       y.left = z
13   else y.right = z
```

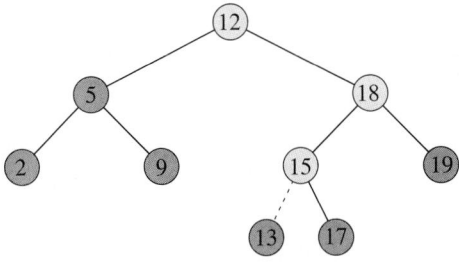

Figure 12.3 Inserting an item with key 13 into a binary search tree. Lightly shaded nodes indicate the simple path from the root down to the position where the item is inserted. The dashed line indicates the link in the tree that is added to insert the item.

Figure 12.3 shows how TREE-INSERT works. Just like the procedures TREE-SEARCH and ITERATIVE-TREE-SEARCH, TREE-INSERT begins at the root of the tree and the pointer x traces a simple path downward looking for a NIL to replace with the input item z. The procedure maintains the *trailing pointer* y as the parent of x. After initialization, the **while** loop in lines 3–7 causes these two pointers to move down the tree, going left or right depending on the comparison of $z.key$ with $x.key$, until x becomes NIL. This NIL occupies the position where we wish to place the input item z. We need the trailing pointer y, because by the time we find the NIL where z belongs, the search has proceeded one step beyond the node that needs to be changed. Lines 8–13 set the pointers that cause z to be inserted.

Like the other primitive operations on search trees, the procedure TREE-INSERT runs in $O(h)$ time on a tree of height h.

Deletion

The overall strategy for deleting a node z from a binary search tree T has three basic cases but, as we shall see, one of the cases is a bit tricky.

- If z has no children, then we simply remove it by modifying its parent to replace z with NIL as its child.

- If z has just one child, then we elevate that child to take z's position in the tree by modifying z's parent to replace z by z's child.

- If z has two children, then we find z's successor y—which must be in z's right subtree—and have y take z's position in the tree. The rest of z's original right subtree becomes y's new right subtree, and z's left subtree becomes y's new left subtree. This case is the tricky one because, as we shall see, it matters whether y is z's right child.

The procedure for deleting a given node z from a binary search tree T takes as arguments pointers to T and z. It organizes its cases a bit differently from the three cases outlined previously by considering the four cases shown in Figure 12.4.

- If z has no left child (part (a) of the figure), then we replace z by its right child, which may or may not be NIL. When z's right child is NIL, this case deals with the situation in which z has no children. When z's right child is non-NIL, this case handles the situation in which z has just one child, which is its right child.

- If z has just one child, which is its left child (part (b) of the figure), then we replace z by its left child.

- Otherwise, z has both a left and a right child. We find z's successor y, which lies in z's right subtree and has no left child (see Exercise 12.2-5). We want to splice y out of its current location and have it replace z in the tree.

    - If y is z's right child (part (c)), then we replace z by y, leaving y's right child alone.

    - Otherwise, y lies within z's right subtree but is not z's right child (part (d)). In this case, we first replace y by its own right child, and then we replace z by y.

In order to move subtrees around within the binary search tree, we define a subroutine TRANSPLANT, which replaces one subtree as a child of its parent with another subtree. When TRANSPLANT replaces the subtree rooted at node u with the subtree rooted at node v, node u's parent becomes node v's parent, and u's parent ends up having v as its appropriate child.

TRANSPLANT(T, u, v)

```
1  if u.p == NIL
2      T.root = v
3  elseif u == u.p.left
4      u.p.left = v
5  else u.p.right = v
6  if v ≠ NIL
7      v.p = u.p
```

Lines 1–2 handle the case in which u is the root of T. Otherwise, u is either a left child or a right child of its parent. Lines 3–4 take care of updating $u.p.left$ if u is a left child, and line 5 updates $u.p.right$ if u is a right child. We allow v to be NIL, and lines 6–7 update $v.p$ if v is non-NIL. Note that TRANSPLANT does not attempt to update $v.left$ and $v.right$; doing so, or not doing so, is the responsibility of TRANSPLANT's caller.

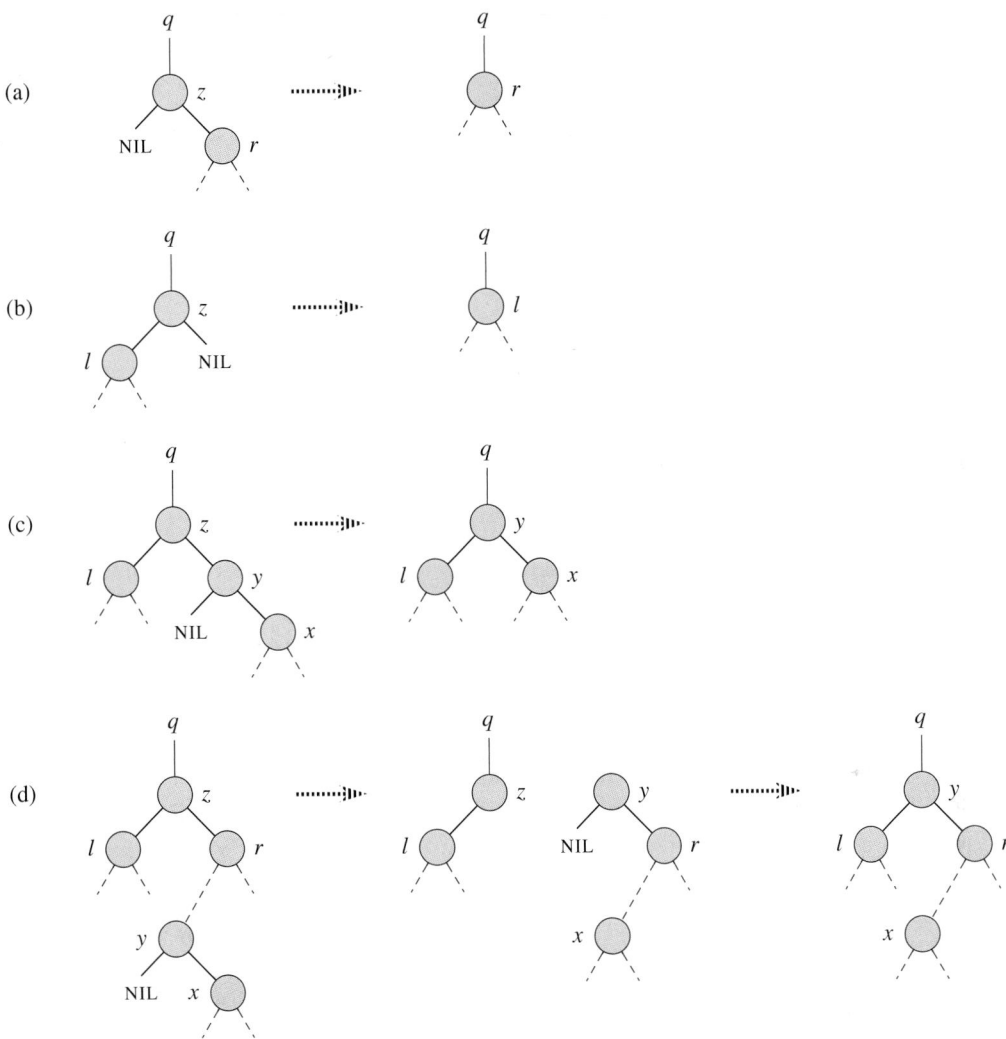

Figure 12.4 Deleting a node z from a binary search tree. Node z may be the root, a left child of node q, or a right child of q. **(a)** Node z has no left child. We replace z by its right child r, which may or may not be NIL. **(b)** Node z has a left child l but no right child. We replace z by l. **(c)** Node z has two children; its left child is node l, its right child is its successor y, and y's right child is node x. We replace z by y, updating y's left child to become l, but leaving x as y's right child. **(d)** Node z has two children (left child l and right child r), and its successor $y \neq r$ lies within the subtree rooted at r. We replace y by its own right child x, and we set y to be r's parent. Then, we set y to be q's child and the parent of l.

With the TRANSPLANT procedure in hand, here is the procedure that deletes node z from binary search tree T:

TREE-DELETE(T, z)

```
 1   if z.left == NIL
 2       TRANSPLANT(T, z, z.right)
 3   elseif z.right == NIL
 4       TRANSPLANT(T, z, z.left)
 5   else y = TREE-MINIMUM(z.right)
 6       if y.p ≠ z
 7           TRANSPLANT(T, y, y.right)
 8           y.right = z.right
 9           y.right.p = y
10       TRANSPLANT(T, z, y)
11       y.left = z.left
12       y.left.p = y
```

The TREE-DELETE procedure executes the four cases as follows. Lines 1–2 handle the case in which node z has no left child, and lines 3–4 handle the case in which z has a left child but no right child. Lines 5–12 deal with the remaining two cases, in which z has two children. Line 5 finds node y, which is the successor of z. Because z has a nonempty right subtree, its successor must be the node in that subtree with the smallest key; hence the call to TREE-MINIMUM$(z.right)$. As we noted before, y has no left child. We want to splice y out of its current location, and it should replace z in the tree. If y is z's right child, then lines 10–12 replace z as a child of its parent by y and replace y's left child by z's left child. If y is not z's right child, lines 7–9 replace y as a child of its parent by y's right child and turn z's right child into y's right child, and then lines 10–12 replace z as a child of its parent by y and replace y's left child by z's left child.

Each line of TREE-DELETE, including the calls to TRANSPLANT, takes constant time, except for the call to TREE-MINIMUM in line 5. Thus, TREE-DELETE runs in $O(h)$ time on a tree of height h.

In summary, we have proved the following theorem.

Theorem 12.3
We can implement the dynamic-set operations INSERT and DELETE so that each one runs in $O(h)$ time on a binary search tree of height h.   ∎

Exercises

12.3-1
Give a recursive version of the TREE-INSERT procedure.

12.3-2
Suppose that we construct a binary search tree by repeatedly inserting distinct values into the tree. Argue that the number of nodes examined in searching for a value in the tree is one plus the number of nodes examined when the value was first inserted into the tree.

12.3-3
We can sort a given set of n numbers by first building a binary search tree containing these numbers (using TREE-INSERT repeatedly to insert the numbers one by one) and then printing the numbers by an inorder tree walk. What are the worst-case and best-case running times for this sorting algorithm?

12.3-4
Is the operation of deletion "commutative" in the sense that deleting x and then y from a binary search tree leaves the same tree as deleting y and then x? Argue why it is or give a counterexample.

12.3-5
Suppose that instead of each node x keeping the attribute $x.p$, pointing to x's parent, it keeps $x.succ$, pointing to x's successor. Give pseudocode for SEARCH, INSERT, and DELETE on a binary search tree T using this representation. These procedures should operate in time $O(h)$, where h is the height of the tree T. (*Hint:* You may wish to implement a subroutine that returns the parent of a node.)

12.3-6
When node z in TREE-DELETE has two children, we could choose node y as its predecessor rather than its successor. What other changes to TREE-DELETE would be necessary if we did so? Some have argued that a fair strategy, giving equal priority to predecessor and successor, yields better empirical performance. How might TREE-DELETE be changed to implement such a fair strategy?

★ **12.4 Randomly built binary search trees**

We have shown that each of the basic operations on a binary search tree runs in $O(h)$ time, where h is the height of the tree. The height of a binary search

tree varies, however, as items are inserted and deleted. If, for example, the n items are inserted in strictly increasing order, the tree will be a chain with height $n - 1$. On the other hand, Exercise B.5-4 shows that $h \geq \lfloor \lg n \rfloor$. As with quicksort, we can show that the behavior of the average case is much closer to the best case than to the worst case.

Unfortunately, little is known about the average height of a binary search tree when both insertion and deletion are used to create it. When the tree is created by insertion alone, the analysis becomes more tractable. Let us therefore define a ***randomly built binary search tree*** on n keys as one that arises from inserting the keys in random order into an initially empty tree, where each of the $n!$ permutations of the input keys is equally likely. (Exercise 12.4-3 asks you to show that this notion is different from assuming that every binary search tree on n keys is equally likely.) In this section, we shall prove the following theorem.

Theorem 12.4
The expected height of a randomly built binary search tree on n distinct keys is $O(\lg n)$.

Proof   We start by defining three random variables that help measure the height of a randomly built binary search tree. We denote the height of a randomly built binary search tree on n keys by X_n, and we define the ***exponential height*** $Y_n = 2^{X_n}$. When we build a binary search tree on n keys, we choose one key as that of the root, and we let R_n denote the random variable that holds this key's ***rank*** within the set of n keys; that is, R_n holds the position that this key would occupy if the set of keys were sorted. The value of R_n is equally likely to be any element of the set $\{1, 2, \ldots, n\}$. If $R_n = i$, then the left subtree of the root is a randomly built binary search tree on $i - 1$ keys, and the right subtree is a randomly built binary search tree on $n - i$ keys. Because the height of a binary tree is 1 more than the larger of the heights of the two subtrees of the root, the exponential height of a binary tree is twice the larger of the exponential heights of the two subtrees of the root. If we know that $R_n = i$, it follows that

$$Y_n = 2 \cdot \max(Y_{i-1}, Y_{n-i}) .$$

As base cases, we have that $Y_1 = 1$, because the exponential height of a tree with 1 node is $2^0 = 1$ and, for convenience, we define $Y_0 = 0$.

Next, define indicator random variables $Z_{n,1}, Z_{n,2}, \ldots, Z_{n,n}$, where

$$Z_{n,i} = \mathrm{I}\{R_n = i\} .$$

Because R_n is equally likely to be any element of $\{1, 2, \ldots, n\}$, it follows that $\Pr\{R_n = i\} = 1/n$ for $i = 1, 2, \ldots, n$, and hence, by Lemma 5.1, we have

$$\mathrm{E}[Z_{n,i}] = 1/n , \tag{12.1}$$

for $i = 1, 2, \ldots, n$. Because exactly one value of $Z_{n,i}$ is 1 and all others are 0, we also have

$$Y_n = \sum_{i=1}^{n} Z_{n,i} \left(2 \cdot \max(Y_{i-1}, Y_{n-i}) \right) .$$

We shall show that $\mathrm{E}\,[Y_n]$ is polynomial in n, which will ultimately imply that $\mathrm{E}\,[X_n] = O(\lg n)$.

We claim that the indicator random variable $Z_{n,i} = \mathrm{I}\,\{R_n = i\}$ is independent of the values of Y_{i-1} and Y_{n-i}. Having chosen $R_n = i$, the left subtree (whose exponential height is Y_{i-1}) is randomly built on the $i - 1$ keys whose ranks are less than i. This subtree is just like any other randomly built binary search tree on $i - 1$ keys. Other than the number of keys it contains, this subtree's structure is not affected at all by the choice of $R_n = i$, and hence the random variables Y_{i-1} and $Z_{n,i}$ are independent. Likewise, the right subtree, whose exponential height is Y_{n-i}, is randomly built on the $n - i$ keys whose ranks are greater than i. Its structure is independent of the value of R_n, and so the random variables Y_{n-i} and $Z_{n,i}$ are independent. Hence, we have

$$
\begin{aligned}
\mathrm{E}\,[Y_n] &= \mathrm{E}\left[\sum_{i=1}^{n} Z_{n,i} \left(2 \cdot \max(Y_{i-1}, Y_{n-i}) \right) \right] \\
&= \sum_{i=1}^{n} \mathrm{E}\,[Z_{n,i} \left(2 \cdot \max(Y_{i-1}, Y_{n-i}) \right)] \quad \text{(by linearity of expectation)} \\
&= \sum_{i=1}^{n} \mathrm{E}\,[Z_{n,i}]\, \mathrm{E}\,[2 \cdot \max(Y_{i-1}, Y_{n-i})] \quad \text{(by independence)} \\
&= \sum_{i=1}^{n} \frac{1}{n} \cdot \mathrm{E}\,[2 \cdot \max(Y_{i-1}, Y_{n-i})] \quad \text{(by equation (12.1))} \\
&= \frac{2}{n} \sum_{i=1}^{n} \mathrm{E}\,[\max(Y_{i-1}, Y_{n-i})] \quad \text{(by equation (C.22))} \\
&\leq \frac{2}{n} \sum_{i=1}^{n} (\mathrm{E}\,[Y_{i-1}] + \mathrm{E}\,[Y_{n-i}]) \quad \text{(by Exercise C.3-4) .}
\end{aligned}
$$

Since each term $\mathrm{E}\,[Y_0], \mathrm{E}\,[Y_1], \ldots, \mathrm{E}\,[Y_{n-1}]$ appears twice in the last summation, once as $\mathrm{E}\,[Y_{i-1}]$ and once as $\mathrm{E}\,[Y_{n-i}]$, we have the recurrence

$$\mathrm{E}\,[Y_n] \leq \frac{4}{n} \sum_{i=0}^{n-1} \mathrm{E}\,[Y_i] . \tag{12.2}$$

Using the substitution method, we shall show that for all positive integers n, the recurrence (12.2) has the solution

$$E[Y_n] \leq \frac{1}{4}\binom{n+3}{3}.$$

In doing so, we shall use the identity

$$\sum_{i=0}^{n-1}\binom{i+3}{3} = \binom{n+3}{4}. \tag{12.3}$$

(Exercise 12.4-1 asks you to prove this identity.)

For the base cases, we note that the bounds $0 = Y_0 = E[Y_0] \leq (1/4)\binom{3}{3} = 1/4$ and $1 = Y_1 = E[Y_1] \leq (1/4)\binom{1+3}{3} = 1$ hold. For the inductive case, we have that

$$
\begin{aligned}
E[Y_n] &\leq \frac{4}{n}\sum_{i=0}^{n-1}E[Y_i] \\
&\leq \frac{4}{n}\sum_{i=0}^{n-1}\frac{1}{4}\binom{i+3}{3} && \text{(by the inductive hypothesis)} \\
&= \frac{1}{n}\sum_{i=0}^{n-1}\binom{i+3}{3} \\
&= \frac{1}{n}\binom{n+3}{4} && \text{(by equation (12.3))} \\
&= \frac{1}{n}\cdot\frac{(n+3)!}{4!\,(n-1)!} \\
&= \frac{1}{4}\cdot\frac{(n+3)!}{3!\,n!} \\
&= \frac{1}{4}\binom{n+3}{3}.
\end{aligned}
$$

We have bounded $E[Y_n]$, but our ultimate goal is to bound $E[X_n]$. As Exercise 12.4-4 asks you to show, the function $f(x) = 2^x$ is convex (see page 1199). Therefore, we can employ Jensen's inequality (C.26), which says that

$$
\begin{aligned}
2^{E[X_n]} &\leq E[2^{X_n}] \\
&= E[Y_n],
\end{aligned}
$$

as follows:

$$2^{E[X_n]} \leq \frac{1}{4}\binom{n+3}{3}$$

$$= \frac{1}{4} \cdot \frac{(n+3)(n+2)(n+1)}{6}$$
$$= \frac{n^3 + 6n^2 + 11n + 6}{24} .$$

Taking logarithms of both sides gives $E[X_n] = O(\lg n)$.   ∎

Exercises

12.4-1
Prove equation (12.3).

12.4-2
Describe a binary search tree on n nodes such that the average depth of a node in the tree is $\Theta(\lg n)$ but the height of the tree is $\omega(\lg n)$. Give an asymptotic upper bound on the height of an n-node binary search tree in which the average depth of a node is $\Theta(\lg n)$.

12.4-3
Show that the notion of a randomly chosen binary search tree on n keys, where each binary search tree of n keys is equally likely to be chosen, is different from the notion of a randomly built binary search tree given in this section. (*Hint:* List the possibilities when $n = 3$.)

12.4-4
Show that the function $f(x) = 2^x$ is convex.

12.4-5 ★
Consider RANDOMIZED-QUICKSORT operating on a sequence of n distinct input numbers. Prove that for any constant $k > 0$, all but $O(1/n^k)$ of the $n!$ input permutations yield an $O(n \lg n)$ running time.

Problems

12-1 Binary search trees with equal keys
Equal keys pose a problem for the implementation of binary search trees.

    a. What is the asymptotic performance of TREE-INSERT when used to insert n items with identical keys into an initially empty binary search tree?

We propose to improve TREE-INSERT by testing before line 5 to determine whether $z.key = x.key$ and by testing before line 11 to determine whether $z.key = y.key$.

If equality holds, we implement one of the following strategies. For each strategy, find the asymptotic performance of inserting n items with identical keys into an initially empty binary search tree. (The strategies are described for line 5, in which we compare the keys of z and x. Substitute y for x to arrive at the strategies for line 11.)

b. Keep a boolean flag $x.b$ at node x, and set x to either $x.left$ or $x.right$ based on the value of $x.b$, which alternates between FALSE and TRUE each time we visit x while inserting a node with the same key as x.

c. Keep a list of nodes with equal keys at x, and insert z into the list.

d. Randomly set x to either $x.left$ or $x.right$. (Give the worst-case performance and informally derive the expected running time.)

12-2   Radix trees

Given two strings $a = a_0 a_1 \ldots a_p$ and $b = b_0 b_1 \ldots b_q$, where each a_i and each b_j is in some ordered set of characters, we say that string a is **lexicographically less than** string b if either

1. there exists an integer j, where $0 \le j \le \min(p, q)$, such that $a_i = b_i$ for all $i = 0, 1, \ldots, j - 1$ and $a_j < b_j$, or

2. $p < q$ and $a_i = b_i$ for all $i = 0, 1, \ldots, p$.

For example, if a and b are bit strings, then $10100 < 10110$ by rule 1 (letting $j = 3$) and $10100 < 101000$ by rule 2. This ordering is similar to that used in English-language dictionaries.

The **radix tree** data structure shown in Figure 12.5 stores the bit strings 1011, 10, 011, 100, and 0. When searching for a key $a = a_0 a_1 \ldots a_p$, we go left at a node of depth i if $a_i = 0$ and right if $a_i = 1$. Let S be a set of distinct bit strings whose lengths sum to n. Show how to use a radix tree to sort S lexicographically in $\Theta(n)$ time. For the example in Figure 12.5, the output of the sort should be the sequence 0, 011, 10, 100, 1011.

12-3   Average node depth in a randomly built binary search tree

In this problem, we prove that the average depth of a node in a randomly built binary search tree with n nodes is $O(\lg n)$. Although this result is weaker than that of Theorem 12.4, the technique we shall use reveals a surprising similarity between the building of a binary search tree and the execution of RANDOMIZED-QUICKSORT from Section 7.3.

We define the **total path length** $P(T)$ of a binary tree T as the sum, over all nodes x in T, of the depth of node x, which we denote by $d(x, T)$.

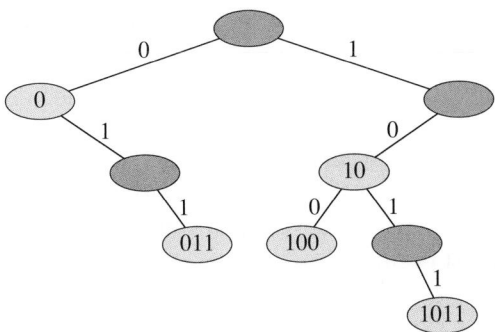

Figure 12.5 A radix tree storing the bit strings 1011, 10, 011, 100, and 0. We can determine each node's key by traversing the simple path from the root to that node. There is no need, therefore, to store the keys in the nodes; the keys appear here for illustrative purposes only. Nodes are heavily shaded if the keys corresponding to them are not in the tree; such nodes are present only to establish a path to other nodes.

a. Argue that the average depth of a node in T is

$$\frac{1}{n} \sum_{x \in T} d(x, T) = \frac{1}{n} P(T) .$$

Thus, we wish to show that the expected value of $P(T)$ is $O(n \lg n)$.

b. Let T_L and T_R denote the left and right subtrees of tree T, respectively. Argue that if T has n nodes, then

$$P(T) = P(T_L) + P(T_R) + n - 1 .$$

c. Let $P(n)$ denote the average total path length of a randomly built binary search tree with n nodes. Show that

$$P(n) = \frac{1}{n} \sum_{i=0}^{n-1} (P(i) + P(n - i - 1) + n - 1) .$$

d. Show how to rewrite $P(n)$ as

$$P(n) = \frac{2}{n} \sum_{k=1}^{n-1} P(k) + \Theta(n) .$$

e. Recalling the alternative analysis of the randomized version of quicksort given in Problem 7-3, conclude that $P(n) = O(n \lg n)$.

At each recursive invocation of quicksort, we choose a random pivot element to partition the set of elements being sorted. Each node of a binary search tree partitions the set of elements that fall into the subtree rooted at that node.

f. Describe an implementation of quicksort in which the comparisons to sort a set of elements are exactly the same as the comparisons to insert the elements into a binary search tree. (The order in which comparisons are made may differ, but the same comparisons must occur.)

12-4   *Number of different binary trees*

Let b_n denote the number of different binary trees with n nodes. In this problem, you will find a formula for b_n, as well as an asymptotic estimate.

a. Show that $b_0 = 1$ and that, for $n \geq 1$,

$$b_n = \sum_{k=0}^{n-1} b_k b_{n-1-k} \; .$$

b. Referring to Problem 4-4 for the definition of a generating function, let $B(x)$ be the generating function

$$B(x) = \sum_{n=0}^{\infty} b_n x^n \; .$$

Show that $B(x) = xB(x)^2 + 1$, and hence one way to express $B(x)$ in closed form is

$$B(x) = \frac{1}{2x} \left(1 - \sqrt{1 - 4x} \right) \; .$$

The ***Taylor expansion*** of $f(x)$ around the point $x = a$ is given by

$$f(x) = \sum_{k=0}^{\infty} \frac{f^{(k)}(a)}{k!} (x - a)^k \; ,$$

where $f^{(k)}(x)$ is the kth derivative of f evaluated at x.

c. Show that

$$b_n = \frac{1}{n+1} \binom{2n}{n}$$

(the nth **Catalan number**) by using the Taylor expansion of $\sqrt{1-4x}$ around $x = 0$. (If you wish, instead of using the Taylor expansion, you may use the generalization of the binomial expansion (C.4) to nonintegral exponents n, where for any real number n and for any integer k, we interpret $\binom{n}{k}$ to be $n(n-1)\cdots(n-k+1)/k!$ if $k \geq 0$, and 0 otherwise.)

d. Show that

$$b_n = \frac{4^n}{\sqrt{\pi}n^{3/2}}\left(1 + O(1/n)\right) .$$

Chapter notes

Knuth [211] contains a good discussion of simple binary search trees as well as many variations. Binary search trees seem to have been independently discovered by a number of people in the late 1950s. Radix trees are often called "tries," which comes from the middle letters in the word *retrieval*. Knuth [211] also discusses them.

Many texts, including the first two editions of this book, have a somewhat simpler method of deleting a node from a binary search tree when both of its children are present. Instead of replacing node z by its successor y, we delete node y but copy its key and satellite data into node z. The downside of this approach is that the node actually deleted might not be the node passed to the delete procedure. If other components of a program maintain pointers to nodes in the tree, they could mistakenly end up with "stale" pointers to nodes that have been deleted. Although the deletion method presented in this edition of this book is a bit more complicated, it guarantees that a call to delete node z deletes node z and only node z.

Section 15.5 will show how to construct an optimal binary search tree when we know the search frequencies before constructing the tree. That is, given the frequencies of searching for each key and the frequencies of searching for values that fall between keys in the tree, we construct a binary search tree for which a set of searches that follows these frequencies examines the minimum number of nodes.

The proof in Section 12.4 that bounds the expected height of a randomly built binary search tree is due to Aslam [24]. Martínez and Roura [243] give randomized algorithms for insertion into and deletion from binary search trees in which the result of either operation is a random binary search tree. Their definition of a random binary search tree differs—only slightly—from that of a randomly built binary search tree in this chapter, however.

13   **Red-Black Trees**

Chapter 12 showed that a binary search tree of height h can support any of the basic dynamic-set operations—such as SEARCH, PREDECESSOR, SUCCESSOR, MINIMUM, MAXIMUM, INSERT, and DELETE—in $O(h)$ time. Thus, the set operations are fast if the height of the search tree is small. If its height is large, however, the set operations may run no faster than with a linked list. Red-black trees are one of many search-tree schemes that are "balanced" in order to guarantee that basic dynamic-set operations take $O(\lg n)$ time in the worst case.

13.1   Properties of red-black trees

A ***red-black tree*** is a binary search tree with one extra bit of storage per node: its ***color***, which can be either RED or BLACK. By constraining the node colors on any simple path from the root to a leaf, red-black trees ensure that no such path is more than twice as long as any other, so that the tree is approximately ***balanced***.

Each node of the tree now contains the attributes *color*, *key*, *left*, *right*, and *p*. If a child or the parent of a node does not exist, the corresponding pointer attribute of the node contains the value NIL. We shall regard these NILs as being pointers to leaves (external nodes) of the binary search tree and the normal, key-bearing nodes as being internal nodes of the tree.

A red-black tree is a binary tree that satisfies the following ***red-black properties***:

1. Every node is either red or black.

2. The root is black.

3. Every leaf (NIL) is black.

4. If a node is red, then both its children are black.

5. For each node, all simple paths from the node to descendant leaves contain the same number of black nodes.

Figure 13.1(a) shows an example of a red-black tree.

As a matter of convenience in dealing with boundary conditions in red-black tree code, we use a single sentinel to represent NIL (see page 238). For a red-black tree T, the sentinel $T.nil$ is an object with the same attributes as an ordinary node in the tree. Its *color* attribute is BLACK, and its other attributes—p, *left*, *right*, and *key*—can take on arbitrary values. As Figure 13.1(b) shows, all pointers to NIL are replaced by pointers to the sentinel $T.nil$.

We use the sentinel so that we can treat a NIL child of a node x as an ordinary node whose parent is x. Although we instead could add a distinct sentinel node for each NIL in the tree, so that the parent of each NIL is well defined, that approach would waste space. Instead, we use the one sentinel $T.nil$ to represent all the NILs—all leaves and the root's parent. The values of the attributes p, *left*, *right*, and *key* of the sentinel are immaterial, although we may set them during the course of a procedure for our convenience.

We generally confine our interest to the internal nodes of a red-black tree, since they hold the key values. In the remainder of this chapter, we omit the leaves when we draw red-black trees, as shown in Figure 13.1(c).

We call the number of black nodes on any simple path from, but not including, a node x down to a leaf the ***black-height*** of the node, denoted bh(x). By property 5, the notion of black-height is well defined, since all descending simple paths from the node have the same number of black nodes. We define the black-height of a red-black tree to be the black-height of its root.

The following lemma shows why red-black trees make good search trees.

Lemma 13.1
A red-black tree with n internal nodes has height at most $2 \lg(n + 1)$.

Proof We start by showing that the subtree rooted at any node x contains at least $2^{\text{bh}(x)} - 1$ internal nodes. We prove this claim by induction on the height of x. If the height of x is 0, then x must be a leaf ($T.nil$), and the subtree rooted at x indeed contains at least $2^{\text{bh}(x)} - 1 = 2^0 - 1 = 0$ internal nodes. For the inductive step, consider a node x that has positive height and is an internal node with two children. Each child has a black-height of either bh(x) or bh(x) − 1, depending on whether its color is red or black, respectively. Since the height of a child of x is less than the height of x itself, we can apply the inductive hypothesis to conclude that each child has at least $2^{\text{bh}(x)-1} - 1$ internal nodes. Thus, the subtree rooted at x contains at least $(2^{\text{bh}(x)-1} - 1) + (2^{\text{bh}(x)-1} - 1) + 1 = 2^{\text{bh}(x)} - 1$ internal nodes, which proves the claim.

To complete the proof of the lemma, let h be the height of the tree. According to property 4, at least half the nodes on any simple path from the root to a leaf, not

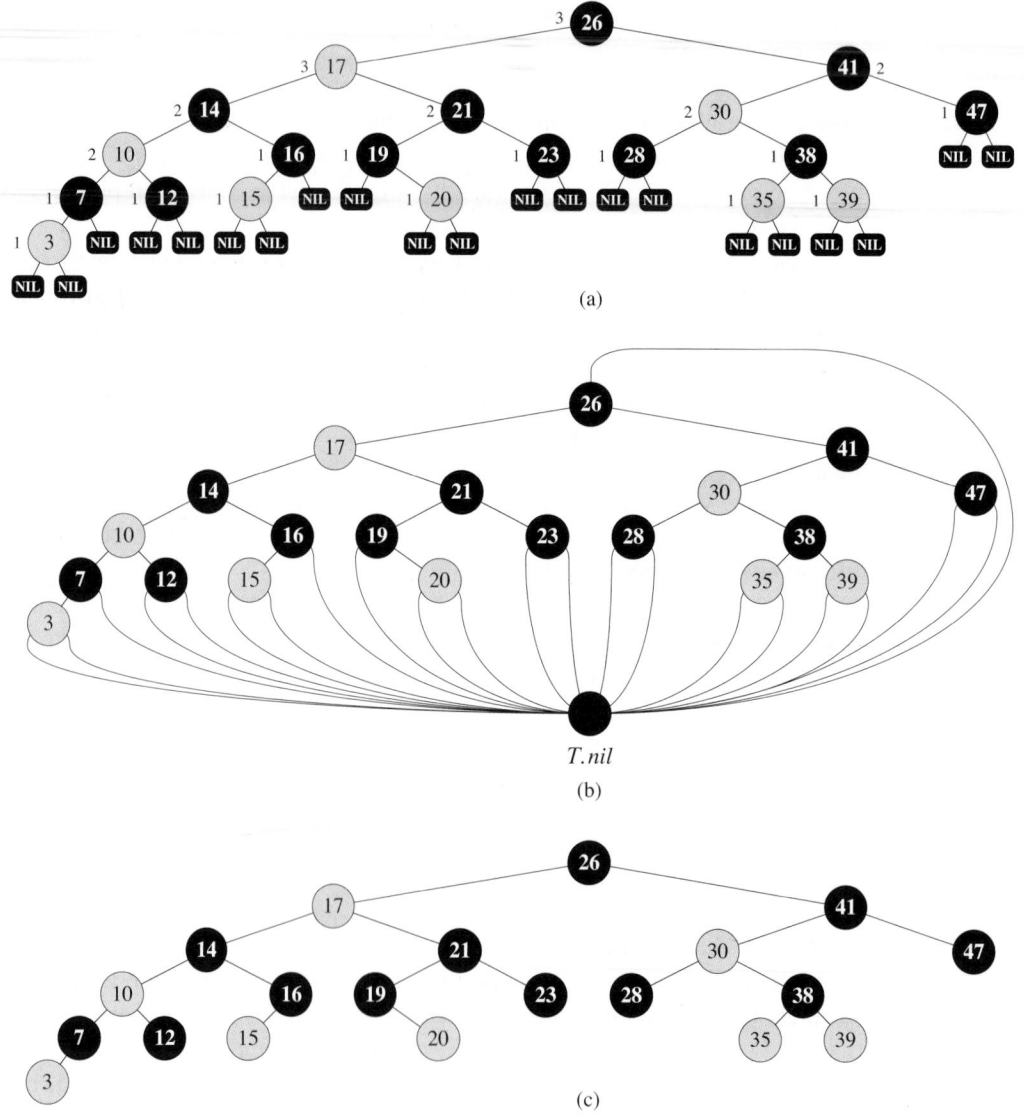

Figure 13.1 A red-black tree with black nodes darkened and red nodes shaded. Every node in a red-black tree is either red or black, the children of a red node are both black, and every simple path from a node to a descendant leaf contains the same number of black nodes. **(a)** Every leaf, shown as a NIL, is black. Each non-NIL node is marked with its black-height; NILs have black-height 0. **(b)** The same red-black tree but with each NIL replaced by the single sentinel $T.nil$, which is always black, and with black-heights omitted. The root's parent is also the sentinel. **(c)** The same red-black tree but with leaves and the root's parent omitted entirely. We shall use this drawing style in the remainder of this chapter.

including the root, must be black. Consequently, the black-height of the root must be at least $h/2$; thus,

$$n \geq 2^{h/2} - 1 .$$

Moving the 1 to the left-hand side and taking logarithms on both sides yields $\lg(n + 1) \geq h/2$, or $h \leq 2\lg(n + 1)$.   ■

As an immediate consequence of this lemma, we can implement the dynamic-set operations SEARCH, MINIMUM, MAXIMUM, SUCCESSOR, and PREDECESSOR in $O(\lg n)$ time on red-black trees, since each can run in $O(h)$ time on a binary search tree of height h (as shown in Chapter 12) and any red-black tree on n nodes is a binary search tree with height $O(\lg n)$. (Of course, references to NIL in the algorithms of Chapter 12 would have to be replaced by $T.nil$.) Although the algorithms TREE-INSERT and TREE-DELETE from Chapter 12 run in $O(\lg n)$ time when given a red-black tree as input, they do not directly support the dynamic-set operations INSERT and DELETE, since they do not guarantee that the modified binary search tree will be a red-black tree. We shall see in Sections 13.3 and 13.4, however, how to support these two operations in $O(\lg n)$ time.

Exercises

13.1-1
In the style of Figure 13.1(a), draw the complete binary search tree of height 3 on the keys $\{1, 2, \ldots, 15\}$. Add the NIL leaves and color the nodes in three different ways such that the black-heights of the resulting red-black trees are 2, 3, and 4.

13.1-2
Draw the red-black tree that results after TREE-INSERT is called on the tree in Figure 13.1 with key 36. If the inserted node is colored red, is the resulting tree a red-black tree? What if it is colored black?

13.1-3
Let us define a ***relaxed red-black tree*** as a binary search tree that satisfies red-black properties 1, 3, 4, and 5. In other words, the root may be either red or black. Consider a relaxed red-black tree T whose root is red. If we color the root of T black but make no other changes to T, is the resulting tree a red-black tree?

13.1-4
Suppose that we "absorb" every red node in a red-black tree into its black parent, so that the children of the red node become children of the black parent. (Ignore what happens to the keys.) What are the possible degrees of a black node after all

its red children are absorbed? What can you say about the depths of the leaves of the resulting tree?

13.1-5

Show that the longest simple path from a node x in a red-black tree to a descendant leaf has length at most twice that of the shortest simple path from node x to a descendant leaf.

13.1-6

What is the largest possible number of internal nodes in a red-black tree with black-height k? What is the smallest possible number?

13.1-7

Describe a red-black tree on n keys that realizes the largest possible ratio of red internal nodes to black internal nodes. What is this ratio? What tree has the smallest possible ratio, and what is the ratio?

13.2   Rotations

The search-tree operations TREE-INSERT and TREE-DELETE, when run on a red-black tree with n keys, take $O(\lg n)$ time. Because they modify the tree, the result may violate the red-black properties enumerated in Section 13.1. To restore these properties, we must change the colors of some of the nodes in the tree and also change the pointer structure.

We change the pointer structure through **rotation**, which is a local operation in a search tree that preserves the binary-search-tree property. Figure 13.2 shows the two kinds of rotations: left rotations and right rotations. When we do a left rotation on a node x, we assume that its right child y is not $T.nil$; x may be any node in the tree whose right child is not $T.nil$. The left rotation "pivots" around the link from x to y. It makes y the new root of the subtree, with x as y's left child and y's left child as x's right child.

The pseudocode for LEFT-ROTATE assumes that $x.right \neq T.nil$ and that the root's parent is $T.nil$.

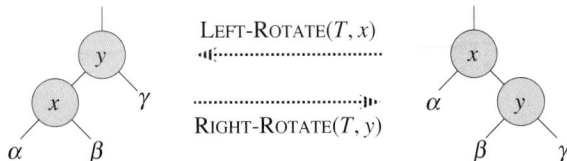

Figure 13.2   The rotation operations on a binary search tree. The operation LEFT-ROTATE(T, x) transforms the configuration of the two nodes on the right into the configuration on the left by changing a constant number of pointers. The inverse operation RIGHT-ROTATE(T, y) transforms the configuration on the left into the configuration on the right. The letters α, β, and γ represent arbitrary subtrees. A rotation operation preserves the binary-search-tree property: the keys in α precede $x.key$, which precedes the keys in β, which precede $y.key$, which precedes the keys in γ.

LEFT-ROTATE(T, x)

```
 1   y = x.right                 // set y
 2   x.right = y.left            // turn y's left subtree into x's right subtree
 3   if y.left ≠ T.nil
 4       y.left.p = x
 5   y.p = x.p                   // link x's parent to y
 6   if x.p == T.nil
 7       T.root = y
 8   elseif x == x.p.left
 9       x.p.left = y
10   else x.p.right = y
11   y.left = x                  // put x on y's left
12   x.p = y
```

Figure 13.3 shows an example of how LEFT-ROTATE modifies a binary search tree. The code for RIGHT-ROTATE is symmetric. Both LEFT-ROTATE and RIGHT-ROTATE run in $O(1)$ time. Only pointers are changed by a rotation; all other attributes in a node remain the same.

Exercises

13.2-1
Write pseudocode for RIGHT-ROTATE.

13.2-2
Argue that in every n-node binary search tree, there are exactly $n - 1$ possible rotations.

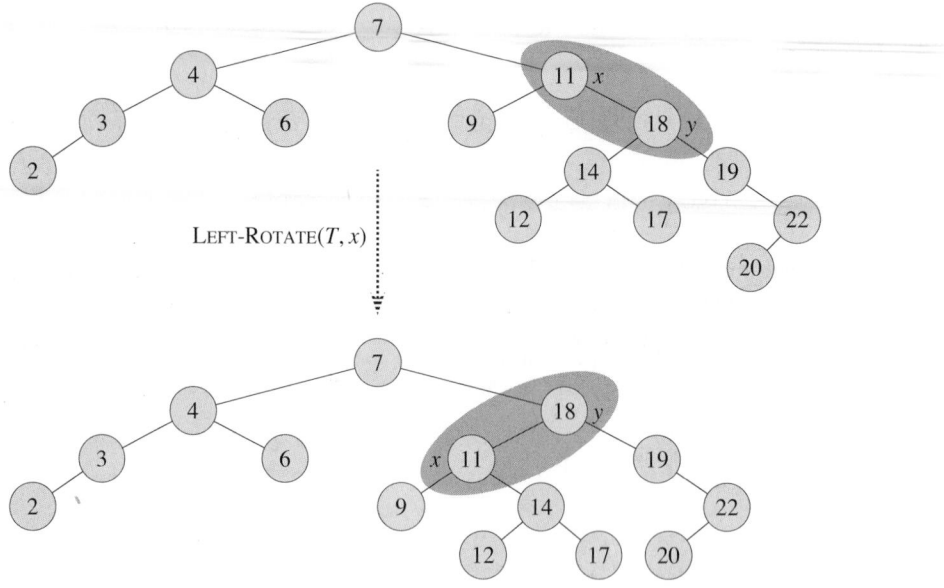

Figure 13.3 An example of how the procedure LEFT-ROTATE(T, x) modifies a binary search tree. Inorder tree walks of the input tree and the modified tree produce the same listing of key values.

13.2-3

Let $a, b,$ and c be arbitrary nodes in subtrees $\alpha, \beta,$ and $\gamma,$ respectively, in the right tree of Figure 13.2. How do the depths of $a, b,$ and c change when a left rotation is performed on node x in the figure?

13.2-4

Show that any arbitrary n-node binary search tree can be transformed into any other arbitrary n-node binary search tree using $O(n)$ rotations. (*Hint:* First show that at most $n - 1$ right rotations suffice to transform the tree into a right-going chain.)

13.2-5 ★

We say that a binary search tree T_1 can be ***right-converted*** to binary search tree T_2 if it is possible to obtain T_2 from T_1 via a series of calls to RIGHT-ROTATE. Give an example of two trees T_1 and T_2 such that T_1 cannot be right-converted to T_2. Then, show that if a tree T_1 can be right-converted to T_2, it can be right-converted using $O(n^2)$ calls to RIGHT-ROTATE.

13.3 Insertion

We can insert a node into an n-node red-black tree in $O(\lg n)$ time. To do so, we use a slightly modified version of the TREE-INSERT procedure (Section 12.3) to insert node z into the tree T as if it were an ordinary binary search tree, and then we color z red. (Exercise 13.3-1 asks you to explain why we choose to make node z red rather than black.) To guarantee that the red-black properties are preserved, we then call an auxiliary procedure RB-INSERT-FIXUP to recolor nodes and perform rotations. The call RB-INSERT(T, z) inserts node z, whose *key* is assumed to have already been filled in, into the red-black tree T.

RB-INSERT(T, z)

```
 1   y = T.nil
 2   x = T.root
 3   while x ≠ T.nil
 4       y = x
 5       if z.key < x.key
 6           x = x.left
 7       else x = x.right
 8   z.p = y
 9   if y == T.nil
10       T.root = z
11   elseif z.key < y.key
12       y.left = z
13   else y.right = z
14   z.left = T.nil
15   z.right = T.nil
16   z.color = RED
17   RB-INSERT-FIXUP(T, z)
```

The procedures TREE-INSERT and RB-INSERT differ in four ways. First, all instances of NIL in TREE-INSERT are replaced by $T.nil$. Second, we set $z.left$ and $z.right$ to $T.nil$ in lines 14–15 of RB-INSERT, in order to maintain the proper tree structure. Third, we color z red in line 16. Fourth, because coloring z red may cause a violation of one of the red-black properties, we call RB-INSERT-FIXUP(T, z) in line 17 of RB-INSERT to restore the red-black properties.

RB-INSERT-FIXUP(T, z)

```
 1   while z.p.color == RED
 2       if z.p == z.p.p.left
 3           y = z.p.p.right
 4           if y.color == RED
 5               z.p.color = BLACK              // case 1
 6               y.color = BLACK                // case 1
 7               z.p.p.color = RED              // case 1
 8               z = z.p.p                      // case 1
 9           else if z == z.p.right
10               z = z.p                        // case 2
11               LEFT-ROTATE(T, z)              // case 2
12               z.p.color = BLACK              // case 3
13               z.p.p.color = RED              // case 3
14               RIGHT-ROTATE(T, z.p.p)         // case 3
15       else (same as then clause
                 with "right" and "left" exchanged)
16   T.root.color = BLACK
```

To understand how RB-INSERT-FIXUP works, we shall break our examination of the code into three major steps. First, we shall determine what violations of the red-black properties are introduced in RB-INSERT when node z is inserted and colored red. Second, we shall examine the overall goal of the **while** loop in lines 1–15. Finally, we shall explore each of the three cases[1] within the **while** loop's body and see how they accomplish the goal. Figure 13.4 shows how RB-INSERT-FIXUP operates on a sample red-black tree.

Which of the red-black properties might be violated upon the call to RB-INSERT-FIXUP? Property 1 certainly continues to hold, as does property 3, since both children of the newly inserted red node are the sentinel $T.nil$. Property 5, which says that the number of black nodes is the same on every simple path from a given node, is satisfied as well, because node z replaces the (black) sentinel, and node z is red with sentinel children. Thus, the only properties that might be violated are property 2, which requires the root to be black, and property 4, which says that a red node cannot have a red child. Both possible violations are due to z being colored red. Property 2 is violated if z is the root, and property 4 is violated if z's parent is red. Figure 13.4(a) shows a violation of property 4 after the node z has been inserted.

---

[1]Case 2 falls through into case 3, and so these two cases are not mutually exclusive.

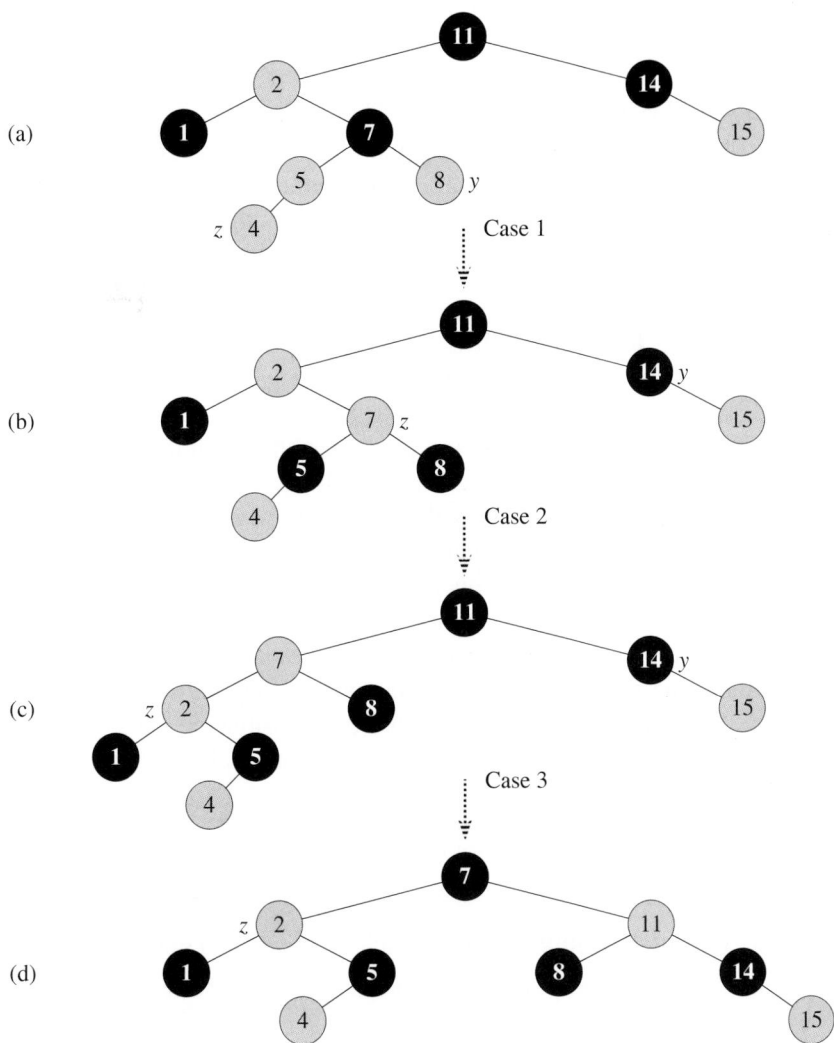

Figure 13.4 The operation of RB-INSERT-FIXUP. **(a)** A node z after insertion. Because both z and its parent $z.p$ are red, a violation of property 4 occurs. Since z's uncle y is red, case 1 in the code applies. We recolor nodes and move the pointer z up the tree, resulting in the tree shown in **(b)**. Once again, z and its parent are both red, but z's uncle y is black. Since z is the right child of $z.p$, case 2 applies. We perform a left rotation, and the tree that results is shown in **(c)**. Now, z is the left child of its parent, and case 3 applies. Recoloring and right rotation yield the tree in **(d)**, which is a legal red-black tree.

The **while** loop in lines 1–15 maintains the following three-part invariant at the start of each iteration of the loop:

a. Node z is red.

b. If $z.p$ is the root, then $z.p$ is black.

c. If the tree violates any of the red-black properties, then it violates at most one of them, and the violation is of either property 2 or property 4. If the tree violates property 2, it is because z is the root and is red. If the tree violates property 4, it is because both z and $z.p$ are red.

Part (c), which deals with violations of red-black properties, is more central to showing that RB-INSERT-FIXUP restores the red-black properties than parts (a) and (b), which we use along the way to understand situations in the code. Because we'll be focusing on node z and nodes near it in the tree, it helps to know from part (a) that z is red. We shall use part (b) to show that the node $z.p.p$ exists when we reference it in lines 2, 3, 7, 8, 13, and 14.

Recall that we need to show that a loop invariant is true prior to the first iteration of the loop, that each iteration maintains the loop invariant, and that the loop invariant gives us a useful property at loop termination.

We start with the initialization and termination arguments. Then, as we examine how the body of the loop works in more detail, we shall argue that the loop maintains the invariant upon each iteration. Along the way, we shall also demonstrate that each iteration of the loop has two possible outcomes: either the pointer z moves up the tree, or we perform some rotations and then the loop terminates.

Initialization: Prior to the first iteration of the loop, we started with a red-black tree with no violations, and we added a red node z. We show that each part of the invariant holds at the time RB-INSERT-FIXUP is called:

a. When RB-INSERT-FIXUP is called, z is the red node that was added.

b. If $z.p$ is the root, then $z.p$ started out black and did not change prior to the call of RB-INSERT-FIXUP.

c. We have already seen that properties 1, 3, and 5 hold when RB-INSERT-FIXUP is called.

If the tree violates property 2, then the red root must be the newly added node z, which is the only internal node in the tree. Because the parent and both children of z are the sentinel, which is black, the tree does not also violate property 4. Thus, this violation of property 2 is the only violation of red-black properties in the entire tree.

If the tree violates property 4, then, because the children of node z are black sentinels and the tree had no other violations prior to z being added, the

violation must be because both z and $z.p$ are red. Moreover, the tree violates no other red-black properties.

Termination: When the loop terminates, it does so because $z.p$ is black. (If z is the root, then $z.p$ is the sentinel $T.nil$, which is black.) Thus, the tree does not violate property 4 at loop termination. By the loop invariant, the only property that might fail to hold is property 2. Line 16 restores this property, too, so that when RB-INSERT-FIXUP terminates, all the red-black properties hold.

Maintenance: We actually need to consider six cases in the **while** loop, but three of them are symmetric to the other three, depending on whether line 2 determines z's parent $z.p$ to be a left child or a right child of z's grandparent $z.p.p$. We have given the code only for the situation in which $z.p$ is a left child. The node $z.p.p$ exists, since by part (b) of the loop invariant, if $z.p$ is the root, then $z.p$ is black. Since we enter a loop iteration only if $z.p$ is red, we know that $z.p$ cannot be the root. Hence, $z.p.p$ exists.

We distinguish case 1 from cases 2 and 3 by the color of z's parent's sibling, or "uncle." Line 3 makes y point to z's uncle $z.p.p.right$, and line 4 tests y's color. If y is red, then we execute case 1. Otherwise, control passes to cases 2 and 3. In all three cases, z's grandparent $z.p.p$ is black, since its parent $z.p$ is red, and property 4 is violated only between z and $z.p$.

Case 1: z's uncle y is red

Figure 13.5 shows the situation for case 1 (lines 5–8), which occurs when both $z.p$ and y are red. Because $z.p.p$ is black, we can color both $z.p$ and y black, thereby fixing the problem of z and $z.p$ both being red, and we can color $z.p.p$ red, thereby maintaining property 5. We then repeat the **while** loop with $z.p.p$ as the new node z. The pointer z moves up two levels in the tree.

Now, we show that case 1 maintains the loop invariant at the start of the next iteration. We use z to denote node z in the current iteration, and $z' = z.p.p$ to denote the node that will be called node z at the test in line 1 upon the next iteration.

a. Because this iteration colors $z.p.p$ red, node z' is red at the start of the next iteration.

b. The node $z'.p$ is $z.p.p.p$ in this iteration, and the color of this node does not change. If this node is the root, it was black prior to this iteration, and it remains black at the start of the next iteration.

c. We have already argued that case 1 maintains property 5, and it does not introduce a violation of properties 1 or 3.

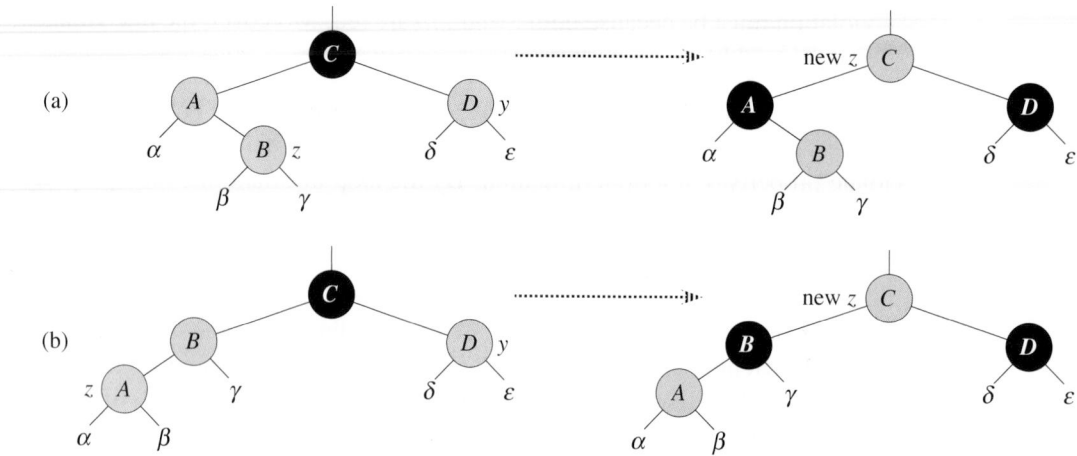

Figure 13.5 Case 1 of the procedure RB-INSERT-FIXUP. Property 4 is violated, since z and its parent $z.p$ are both red. We take the same action whether **(a)** z is a right child or **(b)** z is a left child. Each of the subtrees α, β, γ, δ, and ε has a black root, and each has the same black-height. The code for case 1 changes the colors of some nodes, preserving property 5: all downward simple paths from a node to a leaf have the same number of blacks. The **while** loop continues with node z's grandparent $z.p.p$ as the new z. Any violation of property 4 can now occur only between the new z, which is red, and its parent, if it is red as well.

If node z' is the root at the start of the next iteration, then case 1 corrected the lone violation of property 4 in this iteration. Since z' is red and it is the root, property 2 becomes the only one that is violated, and this violation is due to z'.

If node z' is not the root at the start of the next iteration, then case 1 has not created a violation of property 2. Case 1 corrected the lone violation of property 4 that existed at the start of this iteration. It then made z' red and left $z'.p$ alone. If $z'.p$ was black, there is no violation of property 4. If $z'.p$ was red, coloring z' red created one violation of property 4 between z' and $z'.p$.

Case 2: z's uncle y is black and z is a right child
Case 3: z's uncle y is black and z is a left child

In cases 2 and 3, the color of z's uncle y is black. We distinguish the two cases according to whether z is a right or left child of $z.p$. Lines 10–11 constitute case 2, which is shown in Figure 13.6 together with case 3. In case 2, node z is a right child of its parent. We immediately use a left rotation to transform the situation into case 3 (lines 12–14), in which node z is a left child. Because

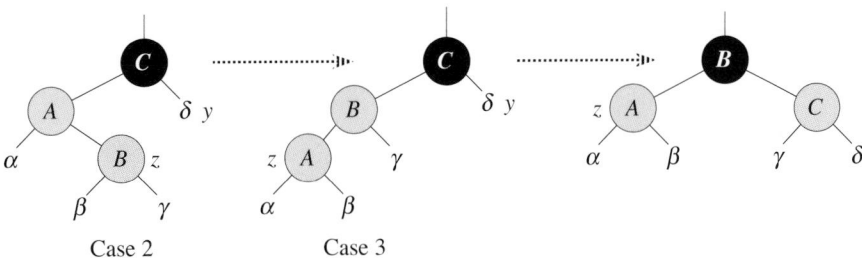

Figure 13.6 Cases 2 and 3 of the procedure RB-INSERT-FIXUP. As in case 1, property 4 is violated in either case 2 or case 3 because z and its parent $z.p$ are both red. Each of the subtrees α, β, γ, and δ has a black root (α, β, and γ from property 4, and δ because otherwise we would be in case 1), and each has the same black-height. We transform case 2 into case 3 by a left rotation, which preserves property 5: all downward simple paths from a node to a leaf have the same number of blacks. Case 3 causes some color changes and a right rotation, which also preserve property 5. The **while** loop then terminates, because property 4 is satisfied: there are no longer two red nodes in a row.

both z and $z.p$ are red, the rotation affects neither the black-height of nodes nor property 5. Whether we enter case 3 directly or through case 2, z's uncle y is black, since otherwise we would have executed case 1. Additionally, the node $z.p.p$ exists, since we have argued that this node existed at the time that lines 2 and 3 were executed, and after moving z up one level in line 10 and then down one level in line 11, the identity of $z.p.p$ remains unchanged. In case 3, we execute some color changes and a right rotation, which preserve property 5, and then, since we no longer have two red nodes in a row, we are done. The **while** loop does not iterate another time, since $z.p$ is now black.

We now show that cases 2 and 3 maintain the loop invariant. (As we have just argued, $z.p$ will be black upon the next test in line 1, and the loop body will not execute again.)

a. Case 2 makes z point to $z.p$, which is red. No further change to z or its color occurs in cases 2 and 3.

b. Case 3 makes $z.p$ black, so that if $z.p$ is the root at the start of the next iteration, it is black.

c. As in case 1, properties 1, 3, and 5 are maintained in cases 2 and 3.

   Since node z is not the root in cases 2 and 3, we know that there is no violation of property 2. Cases 2 and 3 do not introduce a violation of property 2, since the only node that is made red becomes a child of a black node by the rotation in case 3.

   Cases 2 and 3 correct the lone violation of property 4, and they do not introduce another violation.

Having shown that each iteration of the loop maintains the invariant, we have shown that RB-INSERT-FIXUP correctly restores the red-black properties.

Analysis

What is the running time of RB-INSERT? Since the height of a red-black tree on n nodes is $O(\lg n)$, lines 1–16 of RB-INSERT take $O(\lg n)$ time. In RB-INSERT-FIXUP, the **while** loop repeats only if case 1 occurs, and then the pointer z moves two levels up the tree. The total number of times the **while** loop can be executed is therefore $O(\lg n)$. Thus, RB-INSERT takes a total of $O(\lg n)$ time. Moreover, it never performs more than two rotations, since the **while** loop terminates if case 2 or case 3 is executed.

Exercises

13.3-1
In line 16 of RB-INSERT, we set the color of the newly inserted node z to red. Observe that if we had chosen to set z's color to black, then property 4 of a red-black tree would not be violated. Why didn't we choose to set z's color to black?

13.3-2
Show the red-black trees that result after successively inserting the keys $41, 38, 31, 12, 19, 8$ into an initially empty red-black tree.

13.3-3
Suppose that the black-height of each of the subtrees $\alpha, \beta, \gamma, \delta, \varepsilon$ in Figures 13.5 and 13.6 is k. Label each node in each figure with its black-height to verify that the indicated transformation preserves property 5.

13.3-4
Professor Teach is concerned that RB-INSERT-FIXUP might set $T.nil.color$ to RED, in which case the test in line 1 would not cause the loop to terminate when z is the root. Show that the professor's concern is unfounded by arguing that RB-INSERT-FIXUP never sets $T.nil.color$ to RED.

13.3-5
Consider a red-black tree formed by inserting n nodes with RB-INSERT. Argue that if $n > 1$, the tree has at least one red node.

13.3-6
Suggest how to implement RB-INSERT efficiently if the representation for red-black trees includes no storage for parent pointers.

13.4 Deletion

Like the other basic operations on an n-node red-black tree, deletion of a node takes time $O(\lg n)$. Deleting a node from a red-black tree is a bit more complicated than inserting a node.

The procedure for deleting a node from a red-black tree is based on the TREE-DELETE procedure (Section 12.3). First, we need to customize the TRANSPLANT subroutine that TREE-DELETE calls so that it applies to a red-black tree:

RB-TRANSPLANT(T, u, v)

```
1  if u.p == T.nil
2      T.root = v
3  elseif u == u.p.left
4      u.p.left = v
5  else u.p.right = v
6  v.p = u.p
```

The procedure RB-TRANSPLANT differs from TRANSPLANT in two ways. First, line 1 references the sentinel $T.nil$ instead of NIL. Second, the assignment to $v.p$ in line 6 occurs unconditionally: we can assign to $v.p$ even if v points to the sentinel. In fact, we shall exploit the ability to assign to $v.p$ when $v = T.nil$.

The procedure RB-DELETE is like the TREE-DELETE procedure, but with additional lines of pseudocode. Some of the additional lines keep track of a node y that might cause violations of the red-black properties. When we want to delete node z and z has fewer than two children, then z is removed from the tree, and we want y to be z. When z has two children, then y should be z's successor, and y moves into z's position in the tree. We also remember y's color before it is removed from or moved within the tree, and we keep track of the node x that moves into y's original position in the tree, because node x might also cause violations of the red-black properties. After deleting node z, RB-DELETE calls an auxiliary procedure RB-DELETE-FIXUP, which changes colors and performs rotations to restore the red-black properties.

RB-DELETE(T, z)

```
 1  y = z
 2  y-original-color = y.color
 3  if z.left == T.nil
 4      x = z.right
 5      RB-TRANSPLANT(T, z, z.right)
 6  elseif z.right == T.nil
 7      x = z.left
 8      RB-TRANSPLANT(T, z, z.left)
 9  else y = TREE-MINIMUM(z.right)
10      y-original-color = y.color
11      x = y.right
12      if y.p == z
13          x.p = y
14      else RB-TRANSPLANT(T, y, y.right)
15          y.right = z.right
16          y.right.p = y
17      RB-TRANSPLANT(T, z, y)
18      y.left = z.left
19      y.left.p = y
20      y.color = z.color
21  if y-original-color == BLACK
22      RB-DELETE-FIXUP(T, x)
```

Although RB-DELETE contains almost twice as many lines of pseudocode as TREE-DELETE, the two procedures have the same basic structure. You can find each line of TREE-DELETE within RB-DELETE (with the changes of replacing NIL by *T.nil* and replacing calls to TRANSPLANT by calls to RB-TRANSPLANT), executed under the same conditions.

Here are the other differences between the two procedures:

- We maintain node y as the node either removed from the tree or moved within the tree. Line 1 sets y to point to node z when z has fewer than two children and is therefore removed. When z has two children, line 9 sets y to point to z's successor, just as in TREE-DELETE, and y will move into z's position in the tree.

- Because node y's color might change, the variable *y-original-color* stores y's color before any changes occur. Lines 2 and 10 set this variable immediately after assignments to y. When z has two children, then $y \neq z$ and node y moves into node z's original position in the red-black tree; line 20 gives y the same color as z. We need to save y's original color in order to test it at the

end of RB-DELETE; if it was black, then removing or moving y could cause violations of the red-black properties.

• As discussed, we keep track of the node x that moves into node y's original position. The assignments in lines 4, 7, and 11 set x to point to either y's only child or, if y has no children, the sentinel $T.nil$. (Recall from Section 12.3 that y has no left child.)

• Since node x moves into node y's original position, the attribute $x.p$ is always set to point to the original position in the tree of y's parent, even if x is, in fact, the sentinel $T.nil$. Unless z is y's original parent (which occurs only when z has two children and its successor y is z's right child), the assignment to $x.p$ takes place in line 6 of RB-TRANSPLANT. (Observe that when RB-TRANSPLANT is called in lines 5, 8, or 14, the third parameter passed is the same as x.)

When y's original parent is z, however, we do not want $x.p$ to point to y's original parent, since we are removing that node from the tree. Because node y will move up to take z's position in the tree, setting $x.p$ to y in line 13 causes $x.p$ to point to the original position of y's parent, even if $x = T.nil$.

• Finally, if node y was black, we might have introduced one or more violations of the red-black properties, and so we call RB-DELETE-FIXUP in line 22 to restore the red-black properties. If y was red, the red-black properties still hold when y is removed or moved, for the following reasons:

1. No black-heights in the tree have changed.
2. No red nodes have been made adjacent. Because y takes z's place in the tree, along with z's color, we cannot have two adjacent red nodes at y's new position in the tree. In addition, if y was not z's right child, then y's original right child x replaces y in the tree. If y is red, then x must be black, and so replacing y by x cannot cause two red nodes to become adjacent.
3. Since y could not have been the root if it was red, the root remains black.

If node y was black, three problems may arise, which the call of RB-DELETE-FIXUP will remedy. First, if y had been the root and a red child of y becomes the new root, we have violated property 2. Second, if both x and $x.p$ are red, then we have violated property 4. Third, moving y within the tree causes any simple path that previously contained y to have one fewer black node. Thus, property 5 is now violated by any ancestor of y in the tree. We can correct the violation of property 5 by saying that node x, now occupying y's original position, has an "extra" black. That is, if we add 1 to the count of black nodes on any simple path that contains x, then under this interpretation, property 5 holds. When we remove or move the black node y, we "push" its blackness onto node x. The problem is that now node x is neither red nor black, thereby violating property 1. Instead,

node x is either "doubly black" or "red-and-black," and it contributes either 2 or 1, respectively, to the count of black nodes on simple paths containing x. The *color* attribute of x will still be either RED (if x is red-and-black) or BLACK (if x is doubly black). In other words, the extra black on a node is reflected in x's pointing to the node rather than in the *color* attribute.

We can now see the procedure RB-DELETE-FIXUP and examine how it restores the red-black properties to the search tree.

RB-DELETE-FIXUP(T, x)

```
 1  while x ≠ T.root and x.color == BLACK
 2      if x == x.p.left
 3          w = x.p.right
 4          if w.color == RED
 5              w.color = BLACK                                    // case 1
 6              x.p.color = RED                                    // case 1
 7              LEFT-ROTATE(T, x.p)                                // case 1
 8              w = x.p.right                                      // case 1
 9          if w.left.color == BLACK and w.right.color == BLACK
10              w.color = RED                                      // case 2
11              x = x.p                                            // case 2
12          else if w.right.color == BLACK
13                  w.left.color = BLACK                           // case 3
14                  w.color = RED                                  // case 3
15                  RIGHT-ROTATE(T, w)                             // case 3
16                  w = x.p.right                                  // case 3
17              w.color = x.p.color                                // case 4
18              x.p.color = BLACK                                  // case 4
19              w.right.color = BLACK                              // case 4
20              LEFT-ROTATE(T, x.p)                                // case 4
21              x = T.root                                         // case 4
22      else (same as then clause with "right" and "left" exchanged)
23  x.color = BLACK
```

The procedure RB-DELETE-FIXUP restores properties 1, 2, and 4. Exercises 13.4-1 and 13.4-2 ask you to show that the procedure restores properties 2 and 4, and so in the remainder of this section, we shall focus on property 1. The goal of the **while** loop in lines 1–22 is to move the extra black up the tree until

1. x points to a red-and-black node, in which case we color x (singly) black in line 23;

2. x points to the root, in which case we simply "remove" the extra black; or

3. having performed suitable rotations and recolorings, we exit the loop.

Within the **while** loop, x always points to a nonroot doubly black node. We determine in line 2 whether x is a left child or a right child of its parent $x.p$. (We have given the code for the situation in which x is a left child; the situation in which x is a right child—line 22—is symmetric.) We maintain a pointer w to the sibling of x. Since node x is doubly black, node w cannot be $T.nil$, because otherwise, the number of blacks on the simple path from $x.p$ to the (singly black) leaf w would be smaller than the number on the simple path from $x.p$ to x.

The four cases[2] in the code appear in Figure 13.7. Before examining each case in detail, let's look more generally at how we can verify that the transformation in each of the cases preserves property 5. The key idea is that in each case, the transformation applied preserves the number of black nodes (including x's extra black) from (and including) the root of the subtree shown to each of the subtrees $\alpha, \beta, \ldots, \zeta$. Thus, if property 5 holds prior to the transformation, it continues to hold afterward. For example, in Figure 13.7(a), which illustrates case 1, the number of black nodes from the root to either subtree α or β is 3, both before and after the transformation. (Again, remember that node x adds an extra black.) Similarly, the number of black nodes from the root to any of γ, δ, ε, and ζ is 2, both before and after the transformation. In Figure 13.7(b), the counting must involve the value c of the *color* attribute of the root of the subtree shown, which can be either RED or BLACK. If we define count(RED) $= 0$ and count(BLACK) $= 1$, then the number of black nodes from the root to α is $2 + \text{count}(c)$, both before and after the transformation. In this case, after the transformation, the new node x has *color* attribute c, but this node is really either red-and-black (if $c = $ RED) or doubly black (if $c = $ BLACK). You can verify the other cases similarly (see Exercise 13.4-5).

Case 1: x's sibling w is red

Case 1 (lines 5–8 of RB-DELETE-FIXUP and Figure 13.7(a)) occurs when node w, the sibling of node x, is red. Since w must have black children, we can switch the colors of w and $x.p$ and then perform a left-rotation on $x.p$ without violating any of the red-black properties. The new sibling of x, which is one of w's children prior to the rotation, is now black, and thus we have converted case 1 into case 2, 3, or 4.

Cases 2, 3, and 4 occur when node w is black; they are distinguished by the colors of w's children.

---

[2]As in RB-INSERT-FIXUP, the cases in RB-DELETE-FIXUP are not mutually exclusive.

Case 2: x's sibling w is black, and both of w's children are black

In case 2 (lines 10–11 of RB-DELETE-FIXUP and Figure 13.7(b)), both of w's children are black. Since w is also black, we take one black off both x and w, leaving x with only one black and leaving w red. To compensate for removing one black from x and w, we would like to add an extra black to $x.p$, which was originally either red or black. We do so by repeating the **while** loop with $x.p$ as the new node x. Observe that if we enter case 2 through case 1, the new node x is red-and-black, since the original $x.p$ was red. Hence, the value c of the *color* attribute of the new node x is RED, and the loop terminates when it tests the loop condition. We then color the new node x (singly) black in line 23.

Case 3: x's sibling w is black, w's left child is red, and w's right child is black

Case 3 (lines 13–16 and Figure 13.7(c)) occurs when w is black, its left child is red, and its right child is black. We can switch the colors of w and its left child $w.left$ and then perform a right rotation on w without violating any of the red-black properties. The new sibling w of x is now a black node with a red right child, and thus we have transformed case 3 into case 4.

Case 4: x's sibling w is black, and w's right child is red

Case 4 (lines 17–21 and Figure 13.7(d)) occurs when node x's sibling w is black and w's right child is red. By making some color changes and performing a left rotation on $x.p$, we can remove the extra black on x, making it singly black, without violating any of the red-black properties. Setting x to be the root causes the **while** loop to terminate when it tests the loop condition.

Analysis

What is the running time of RB-DELETE? Since the height of a red-black tree of n nodes is $O(\lg n)$, the total cost of the procedure without the call to RB-DELETE-FIXUP takes $O(\lg n)$ time. Within RB-DELETE-FIXUP, each of cases 1, 3, and 4 lead to termination after performing a constant number of color changes and at most three rotations. Case 2 is the only case in which the **while** loop can be repeated, and then the pointer x moves up the tree at most $O(\lg n)$ times, performing no rotations. Thus, the procedure RB-DELETE-FIXUP takes $O(\lg n)$ time and performs at most three rotations, and the overall time for RB-DELETE is therefore also $O(\lg n)$.

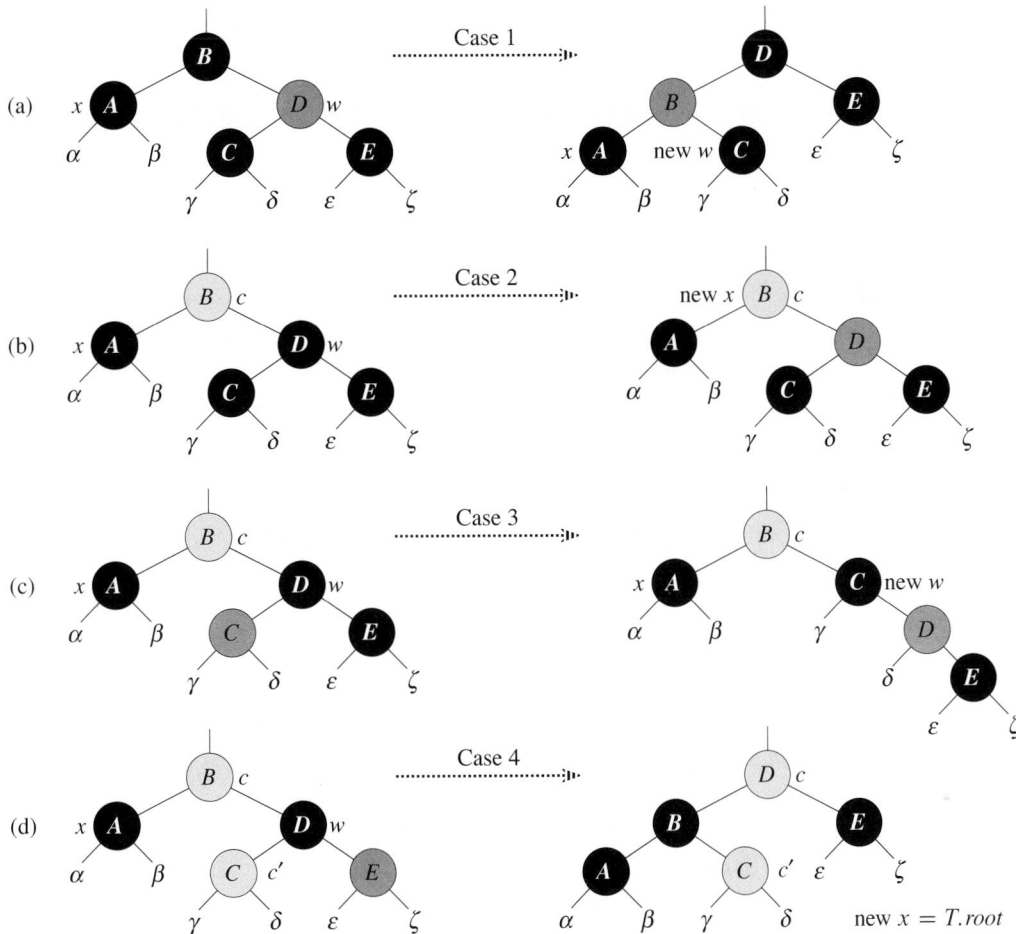

Figure 13.7   The cases in the **while** loop of the procedure RB-DELETE-FIXUP. Darkened nodes have *color* attributes BLACK, heavily shaded nodes have *color* attributes RED, and lightly shaded nodes have *color* attributes represented by c and c′, which may be either RED or BLACK. The letters α, β, . . . , ζ represent arbitrary subtrees. Each case transforms the configuration on the left into the configuration on the right by changing some colors and/or performing a rotation. Any node pointed to by x has an extra black and is either doubly black or red-and-black. Only case 2 causes the loop to repeat. **(a)** Case 1 is transformed to case 2, 3, or 4 by exchanging the colors of nodes B and D and performing a left rotation. **(b)** In case 2, the extra black represented by the pointer x moves up the tree by coloring node D red and setting x to point to node B. If we enter case 2 through case 1, the **while** loop terminates because the new node x is red-and-black, and therefore the value c of its *color* attribute is RED. **(c)** Case 3 is transformed to case 4 by exchanging the colors of nodes C and D and performing a right rotation. **(d)** Case 4 removes the extra black represented by x by changing some colors and performing a left rotation (without violating the red-black properties), and then the loop terminates.

Exercises

13.4-1
Argue that after executing RB-DELETE-FIXUP, the root of the tree must be black.

13.4-2
Argue that if in RB-DELETE both x and $x.p$ are red, then property 4 is restored by the call to RB-DELETE-FIXUP(T, x).

13.4-3
In Exercise 13.3-2, you found the red-black tree that results from successively inserting the keys $41, 38, 31, 12, 19, 8$ into an initially empty tree. Now show the red-black trees that result from the successive deletion of the keys in the order $8, 12, 19, 31, 38, 41$.

13.4-4
In which lines of the code for RB-DELETE-FIXUP might we examine or modify the sentinel $T.nil$?

13.4-5
In each of the cases of Figure 13.7, give the count of black nodes from the root of the subtree shown to each of the subtrees $\alpha, \beta, \ldots, \zeta$, and verify that each count remains the same after the transformation. When a node has a *color* attribute c or c', use the notation count(c) or count(c') symbolically in your count.

13.4-6
Professors Skelton and Baron are concerned that at the start of case 1 of RB-DELETE-FIXUP, the node $x.p$ might not be black. If the professors are correct, then lines 5–6 are wrong. Show that $x.p$ must be black at the start of case 1, so that the professors have nothing to worry about.

13.4-7
Suppose that a node x is inserted into a red-black tree with RB-INSERT and then is immediately deleted with RB-DELETE. Is the resulting red-black tree the same as the initial red-black tree? Justify your answer.

Problems

13-1 *Persistent dynamic sets*

During the course of an algorithm, we sometimes find that we need to maintain past versions of a dynamic set as it is updated. We call such a set ***persistent***. One way to implement a persistent set is to copy the entire set whenever it is modified, but this approach can slow down a program and also consume much space. Sometimes, we can do much better.

Consider a persistent set S with the operations INSERT, DELETE, and SEARCH, which we implement using binary search trees as shown in Figure 13.8(a). We maintain a separate root for every version of the set. In order to insert the key 5 into the set, we create a new node with key 5. This node becomes the left child of a new node with key 7, since we cannot modify the existing node with key 7. Similarly, the new node with key 7 becomes the left child of a new node with key 8 whose right child is the existing node with key 10. The new node with key 8 becomes, in turn, the right child of a new root r' with key 4 whose left child is the existing node with key 3. We thus copy only part of the tree and share some of the nodes with the original tree, as shown in Figure 13.8(b).

Assume that each tree node has the attributes *key*, *left*, and *right* but no parent. (See also Exercise 13.3-6.)

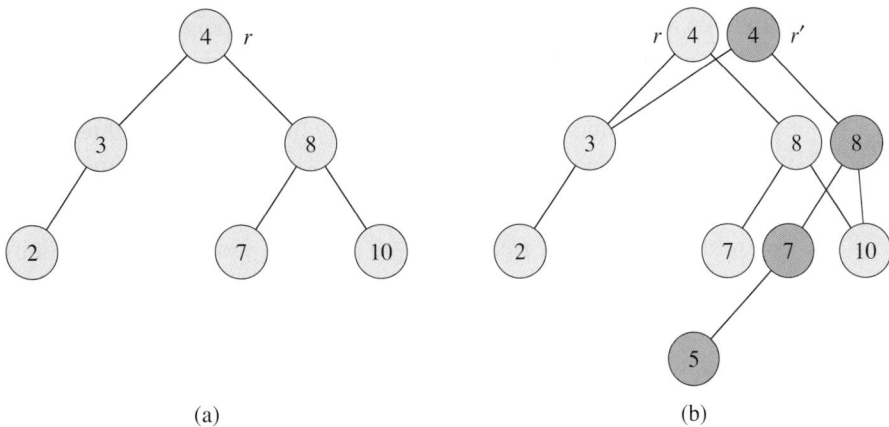

(a)   (b)

Figure 13.8 (a) A binary search tree with keys $2, 3, 4, 7, 8, 10$. (b) The persistent binary search tree that results from the insertion of key 5. The most recent version of the set consists of the nodes reachable from the root r', and the previous version consists of the nodes reachable from r. Heavily shaded nodes are added when key 5 is inserted.

a. For a general persistent binary search tree, identify the nodes that we need to change to insert a key k or delete a node y.

b. Write a procedure PERSISTENT-TREE-INSERT that, given a persistent tree T and a key k to insert, returns a new persistent tree T' that is the result of inserting k into T.

c. If the height of the persistent binary search tree T is h, what are the time and space requirements of your implementation of PERSISTENT-TREE-INSERT? (The space requirement is proportional to the number of new nodes allocated.)

d. Suppose that we had included the parent attribute in each node. In this case, PERSISTENT-TREE-INSERT would need to perform additional copying. Prove that PERSISTENT-TREE-INSERT would then require $\Omega(n)$ time and space, where n is the number of nodes in the tree.

e. Show how to use red-black trees to guarantee that the worst-case running time and space are $O(\lg n)$ per insertion or deletion.

13-2 *Join operation on red-black trees*

The *join* operation takes two dynamic sets S_1 and S_2 and an element x such that for any $x_1 \in S_1$ and $x_2 \in S_2$, we have $x_1.key \leq x.key \leq x_2.key$. It returns a set $S = S_1 \cup \{x\} \cup S_2$. In this problem, we investigate how to implement the join operation on red-black trees.

a. Given a red-black tree T, let us store its black-height as the new attribute $T.bh$. Argue that RB-INSERT and RB-DELETE can maintain the bh attribute without requiring extra storage in the nodes of the tree and without increasing the asymptotic running times. Show that while descending through T, we can determine the black-height of each node we visit in $O(1)$ time per node visited.

We wish to implement the operation RB-JOIN(T_1, x, T_2), which destroys T_1 and T_2 and returns a red-black tree $T = T_1 \cup \{x\} \cup T_2$. Let n be the total number of nodes in T_1 and T_2.

b. Assume that $T_1.bh \geq T_2.bh$. Describe an $O(\lg n)$-time algorithm that finds a black node y in T_1 with the largest key from among those nodes whose black-height is $T_2.bh$.

c. Let T_y be the subtree rooted at y. Describe how $T_y \cup \{x\} \cup T_2$ can replace T_y in $O(1)$ time without destroying the binary-search-tree property.

d. What color should we make x so that red-black properties 1, 3, and 5 are maintained? Describe how to enforce properties 2 and 4 in $O(\lg n)$ time.

e. Argue that no generality is lost by making the assumption in part (b). Describe the symmetric situation that arises when $T_1.bh \leq T_2.bh$.

f. Argue that the running time of RB-JOIN is $O(\lg n)$.

13-3 AVL trees

An **AVL tree** is a binary search tree that is **height balanced**: for each node x, the heights of the left and right subtrees of x differ by at most 1. To implement an AVL tree, we maintain an extra attribute in each node: $x.h$ is the height of node x. As for any other binary search tree T, we assume that $T.root$ points to the root node.

a. Prove that an AVL tree with n nodes has height $O(\lg n)$. (*Hint:* Prove that an AVL tree of height h has at least F_h nodes, where F_h is the hth Fibonacci number.)

b. To insert into an AVL tree, we first place a node into the appropriate place in binary search tree order. Afterward, the tree might no longer be height balanced. Specifically, the heights of the left and right children of some node might differ by 2. Describe a procedure BALANCE(x), which takes a subtree rooted at x whose left and right children are height balanced and have heights that differ by at most 2, i.e., $|x.right.h - x.left.h| \leq 2$, and alters the subtree rooted at x to be height balanced. (*Hint:* Use rotations.)

c. Using part (b), describe a recursive procedure AVL-INSERT(x, z) that takes a node x within an AVL tree and a newly created node z (whose key has already been filled in), and adds z to the subtree rooted at x, maintaining the property that x is the root of an AVL tree. As in TREE-INSERT from Section 12.3, assume that $z.key$ has already been filled in and that $z.left = $ NIL and $z.right = $ NIL; also assume that $z.h = 0$. Thus, to insert the node z into the AVL tree T, we call AVL-INSERT($T.root, z$).

d. Show that AVL-INSERT, run on an n-node AVL tree, takes $O(\lg n)$ time and performs $O(1)$ rotations.

13-4 Treaps

If we insert a set of n items into a binary search tree, the resulting tree may be horribly unbalanced, leading to long search times. As we saw in Section 12.4, however, randomly built binary search trees tend to be balanced. Therefore, one strategy that, on average, builds a balanced tree for a fixed set of items would be to randomly permute the items and then insert them in that order into the tree.

What if we do not have all the items at once? If we receive the items one at a time, can we still randomly build a binary search tree out of them?

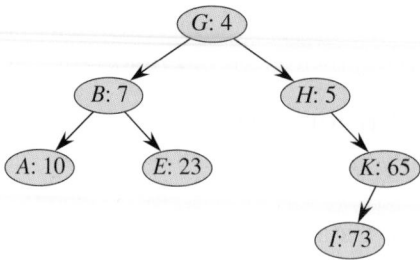

Figure 13.9   A treap. Each node x is labeled with $x.key: x.priority$. For example, the root has key G and priority 4.

We will examine a data structure that answers this question in the affirmative. A **treap** is a binary search tree with a modified way of ordering the nodes. Figure 13.9 shows an example. As usual, each node x in the tree has a key value $x.key$. In addition, we assign $x.priority$, which is a random number chosen independently for each node. We assume that all priorities are distinct and also that all keys are distinct. The nodes of the treap are ordered so that the keys obey the binary-search-tree property and the priorities obey the min-heap order property:

- If v is a left child of u, then $v.key < u.key$.

- If v is a right child of u, then $v.key > u.key$.

- If v is a child of u, then $v.priority > u.priority$.

(This combination of properties is why the tree is called a "treap": it has features of both a binary search tree and a heap.)

It helps to think of treaps in the following way. Suppose that we insert nodes $x_1, x_2, \ldots, x_n$, with associated keys, into a treap. Then the resulting treap is the tree that would have been formed if the nodes had been inserted into a normal binary search tree in the order given by their (randomly chosen) priorities, i.e., $x_i.priority < x_j.priority$ means that we had inserted x_i before x_j.

a. Show that given a set of nodes $x_1, x_2, \ldots, x_n$, with associated keys and priorities, all distinct, the treap associated with these nodes is unique.

b. Show that the expected height of a treap is $\Theta(\lg n)$, and hence the expected time to search for a value in the treap is $\Theta(\lg n)$.

Let us see how to insert a new node into an existing treap. The first thing we do is assign to the new node a random priority. Then we call the insertion algorithm, which we call TREAP-INSERT, whose operation is illustrated in Figure 13.10.

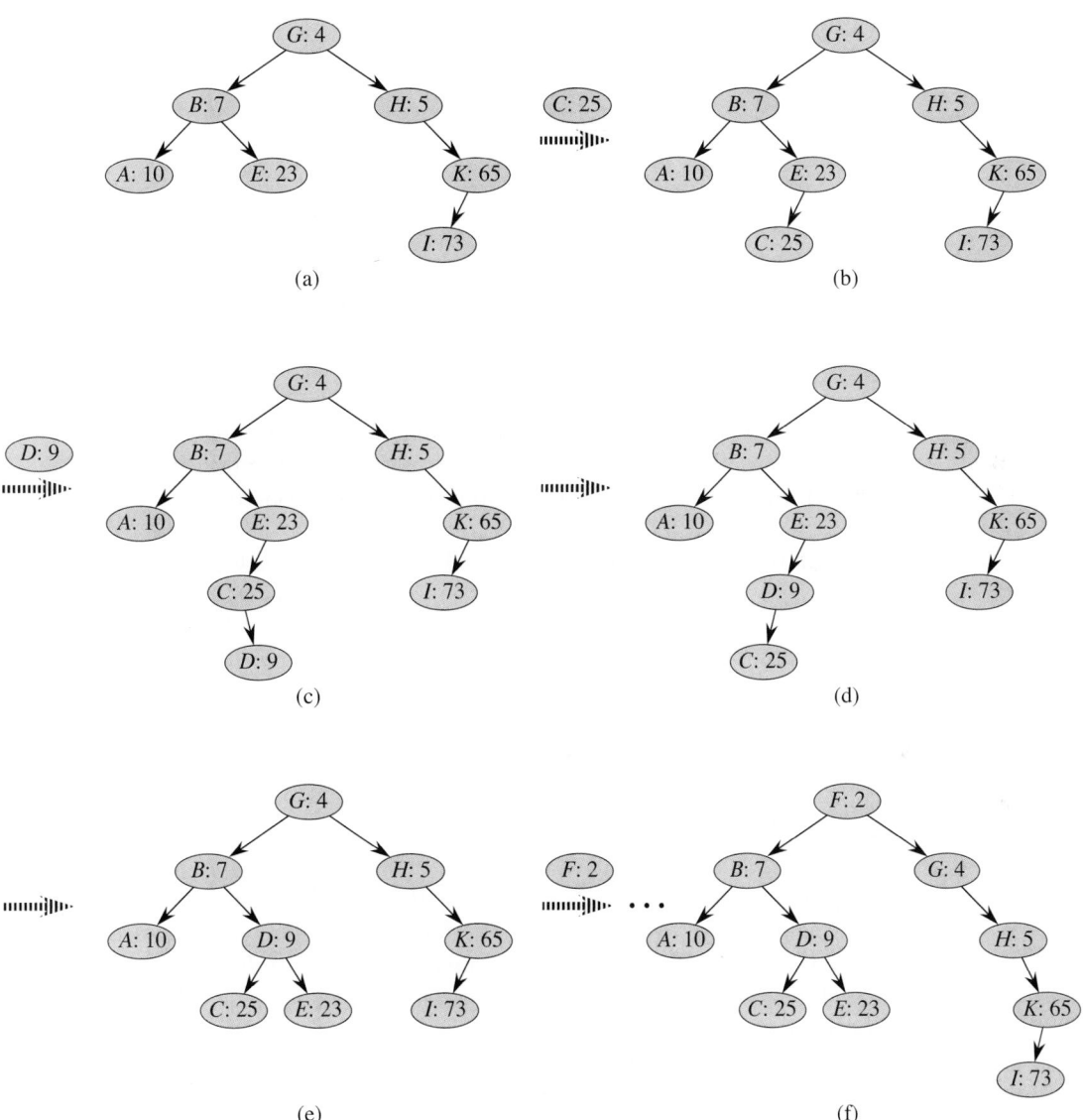

Figure 13.10 The operation of TREAP-INSERT. **(a)** The original treap, prior to insertion. **(b)** The treap after inserting a node with key C and priority 25. **(c)–(d)** Intermediate stages when inserting a node with key D and priority 9. **(e)** The treap after the insertion of parts (c) and (d) is done. **(f)** The treap after inserting a node with key F and priority 2.

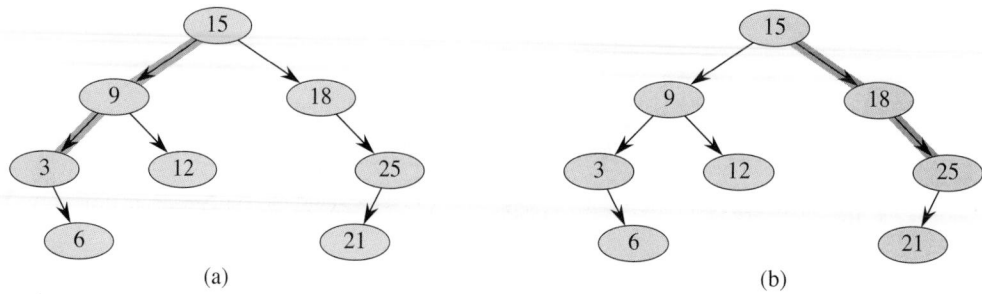

Figure 13.11   Spines of a binary search tree. The left spine is shaded in **(a)**, and the right spine is shaded in **(b)**.

   c. Explain how TREAP-INSERT works. Explain the idea in English and give pseudocode. (*Hint:* Execute the usual binary-search-tree insertion procedure and then perform rotations to restore the min-heap order property.)

   d. Show that the expected running time of TREAP-INSERT is $\Theta(\lg n)$.

TREAP-INSERT performs a search and then a sequence of rotations. Although these two operations have the same expected running time, they have different costs in practice. A search reads information from the treap without modifying it. In contrast, a rotation changes parent and child pointers within the treap. On most computers, read operations are much faster than write operations. Thus we would like TREAP-INSERT to perform few rotations. We will show that the expected number of rotations performed is bounded by a constant.

   In order to do so, we will need some definitions, which Figure 13.11 depicts. The *left spine* of a binary search tree T is the simple path from the root to the node with the smallest key. In other words, the left spine is the simple path from the root that consists of only left edges. Symmetrically, the *right spine* of T is the simple path from the root consisting of only right edges. The *length* of a spine is the number of nodes it contains.

   e. Consider the treap T immediately after TREAP-INSERT has inserted node x. Let C be the length of the right spine of the left subtree of x. Let D be the length of the left spine of the right subtree of x. Prove that the total number of rotations that were performed during the insertion of x is equal to $C + D$.

We will now calculate the expected values of C and D. Without loss of generality, we assume that the keys are $1, 2, \ldots, n$, since we are comparing them only to one another.

For nodes x and y in treap T, where $y \neq x$, let $k = x.key$ and $i = y.key$. We define indicator random variables

$$X_{ik} = \text{I}\{y \text{ is in the right spine of the left subtree of } x\} \ .$$

f. Show that $X_{ik} = 1$ if and only if $y.priority > x.priority$, $y.key < x.key$, and, for every z such that $y.key < z.key < x.key$, we have $y.priority < z.priority$.

g. Show that

$$\Pr\{X_{ik} = 1\} = \frac{(k-i-1)!}{(k-i+1)!}$$

$$= \frac{1}{(k-i+1)(k-i)} \ .$$

h. Show that

$$\text{E}[C] = \sum_{j=1}^{k-1} \frac{1}{j(j+1)}$$

$$= 1 - \frac{1}{k} \ .$$

i. Use a symmetry argument to show that

$$\text{E}[D] = 1 - \frac{1}{n-k+1} \ .$$

j. Conclude that the expected number of rotations performed when inserting a node into a treap is less than 2.

Chapter notes

The idea of balancing a search tree is due to Adel'son-Vel'skiĭ and Landis [2], who introduced a class of balanced search trees called "AVL trees" in 1962, described in Problem 13-3. Another class of search trees, called "2-3 trees," was introduced by J. E. Hopcroft (unpublished) in 1970. A 2-3 tree maintains balance by manipulating the degrees of nodes in the tree. Chapter 18 covers a generalization of 2-3 trees introduced by Bayer and McCreight [35], called "B-trees."

Red-black trees were invented by Bayer [34] under the name "symmetric binary B-trees." Guibas and Sedgewick [155] studied their properties at length and introduced the red/black color convention. Andersson [15] gives a simpler-to-code

variant of red-black trees. Weiss [351] calls this variant AA-trees. An AA-tree is similar to a red-black tree except that left children may never be red.

Treaps, the subject of Problem 13-4, were proposed by Seidel and Aragon [309]. They are the default implementation of a dictionary in LEDA [253], which is a well-implemented collection of data structures and algorithms.

There are many other variations on balanced binary trees, including weight-balanced trees [264], k-neighbor trees [245], and scapegoat trees [127]. Perhaps the most intriguing are the "splay trees" introduced by Sleator and Tarjan [320], which are "self-adjusting." (See Tarjan [330] for a good description of splay trees.) Splay trees maintain balance without any explicit balance condition such as color. Instead, "splay operations" (which involve rotations) are performed within the tree every time an access is made. The amortized cost (see Chapter 17) of each operation on an n-node tree is $O(\lg n)$.

Skip lists [286] provide an alternative to balanced binary trees. A skip list is a linked list that is augmented with a number of additional pointers. Each dictionary operation runs in expected time $O(\lg n)$ on a skip list of n items.

14   Augmenting Data Structures

Some engineering situations require no more than a "textbook" data structure—such as a doubly linked list, a hash table, or a binary search tree—but many others require a dash of creativity. Only in rare situations will you need to create an entirely new type of data structure, though. More often, it will suffice to augment a textbook data structure by storing additional information in it. You can then program new operations for the data structure to support the desired application. Augmenting a data structure is not always straightforward, however, since the added information must be updated and maintained by the ordinary operations on the data structure.

This chapter discusses two data structures that we construct by augmenting red-black trees. Section 14.1 describes a data structure that supports general order-statistic operations on a dynamic set. We can then quickly find the ith smallest number in a set or the rank of a given element in the total ordering of the set. Section 14.2 abstracts the process of augmenting a data structure and provides a theorem that can simplify the process of augmenting red-black trees. Section 14.3 uses this theorem to help design a data structure for maintaining a dynamic set of intervals, such as time intervals. Given a query interval, we can then quickly find an interval in the set that overlaps it.

14.1   Dynamic order statistics

Chapter 9 introduced the notion of an order statistic. Specifically, the ith order statistic of a set of n elements, where $i \in \{1, 2, \ldots, n\}$, is simply the element in the set with the ith smallest key. We saw how to determine any order statistic in $O(n)$ time from an unordered set. In this section, we shall see how to modify red-black trees so that we can determine any order statistic for a dynamic set in $O(\lg n)$ time. We shall also see how to compute the *rank* of an element—its position in the linear order of the set—in $O(\lg n)$ time.

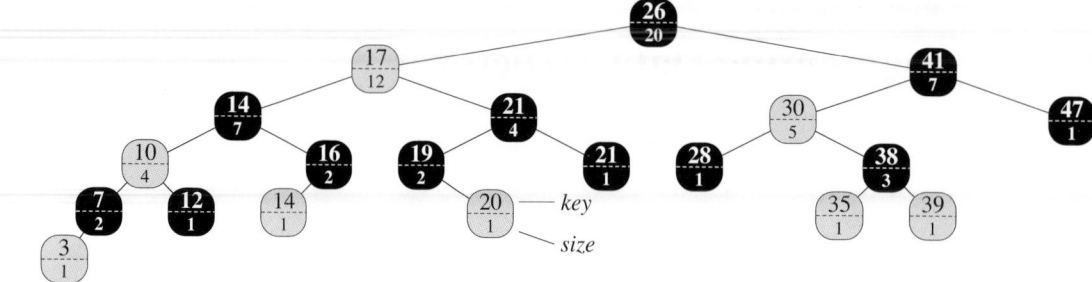

Figure 14.1 An order-statistic tree, which is an augmented red-black tree. Shaded nodes are red, and darkened nodes are black. In addition to its usual attributes, each node x has an attribute $x.size$, which is the number of nodes, other than the sentinel, in the subtree rooted at x.

Figure 14.1 shows a data structure that can support fast order-statistic operations. An ***order-statistic tree*** T is simply a red-black tree with additional information stored in each node. Besides the usual red-black tree attributes $x.key$, $x.color$, $x.p$, $x.left$, and $x.right$ in a node x, we have another attribute, $x.size$. This attribute contains the number of (internal) nodes in the subtree rooted at x (including x itself), that is, the size of the subtree. If we define the sentinel's size to be 0—that is, we set $T.nil.size$ to be 0—then we have the identity

$$x.size = x.left.size + x.right.size + 1 \ .$$

We do not require keys to be distinct in an order-statistic tree. (For example, the tree in Figure 14.1 has two keys with value 14 and two keys with value 21.) In the presence of equal keys, the above notion of rank is not well defined. We remove this ambiguity for an order-statistic tree by defining the rank of an element as the position at which it would be printed in an inorder walk of the tree. In Figure 14.1, for example, the key 14 stored in a black node has rank 5, and the key 14 stored in a red node has rank 6.

Retrieving an element with a given rank

Before we show how to maintain this size information during insertion and deletion, let us examine the implementation of two order-statistic queries that use this additional information. We begin with an operation that retrieves an element with a given rank. The procedure OS-SELECT(x, i) returns a pointer to the node containing the ith smallest key in the subtree rooted at x. To find the node with the ith smallest key in an order-statistic tree T, we call OS-SELECT$(T.root, i)$.

OS-SELECT(x, i)

```
1   r = x.left.size + 1
2   if i == r
3       return x
4   elseif i < r
5       return OS-SELECT(x.left, i)
6   else return OS-SELECT(x.right, i − r)
```

In line 1 of OS-SELECT, we compute r, the rank of node x within the subtree rooted at x. The value of $x.left.size$ is the number of nodes that come before x in an inorder tree walk of the subtree rooted at x. Thus, $x.left.size + 1$ is the rank of x within the subtree rooted at x. If $i = r$, then node x is the ith smallest element, and so we return x in line 3. If $i < r$, then the ith smallest element resides in x's left subtree, and so we recurse on $x.left$ in line 5. If $i > r$, then the ith smallest element resides in x's right subtree. Since the subtree rooted at x contains r elements that come before x's right subtree in an inorder tree walk, the ith smallest element in the subtree rooted at x is the $(i − r)$th smallest element in the subtree rooted at $x.right$. Line 6 determines this element recursively.

To see how OS-SELECT operates, consider a search for the 17th smallest element in the order-statistic tree of Figure 14.1. We begin with x as the root, whose key is 26, and with $i = 17$. Since the size of 26's left subtree is 12, its rank is 13. Thus, we know that the node with rank 17 is the $17 − 13 = 4$th smallest element in 26's right subtree. After the recursive call, x is the node with key 41, and $i = 4$. Since the size of 41's left subtree is 5, its rank within its subtree is 6. Thus, we know that the node with rank 4 is the 4th smallest element in 41's left subtree. After the recursive call, x is the node with key 30, and its rank within its subtree is 2. Thus, we recurse once again to find the $4 − 2 = 2$nd smallest element in the subtree rooted at the node with key 38. We now find that its left subtree has size 1, which means it is the second smallest element. Thus, the procedure returns a pointer to the node with key 38.

Because each recursive call goes down one level in the order-statistic tree, the total time for OS-SELECT is at worst proportional to the height of the tree. Since the tree is a red-black tree, its height is $O(\lg n)$, where n is the number of nodes. Thus, the running time of OS-SELECT is $O(\lg n)$ for a dynamic set of n elements.

Determining the rank of an element

Given a pointer to a node x in an order-statistic tree T, the procedure OS-RANK returns the position of x in the linear order determined by an inorder tree walk of T.

OS-RANK(T, x)

```
1   r = x.left.size + 1
2   y = x
3   while y ≠ T.root
4       if y == y.p.right
5           r = r + y.p.left.size + 1
6       y = y.p
7   return r
```

The procedure works as follows. We can think of node x's rank as the number of nodes preceding x in an inorder tree walk, plus 1 for x itself. OS-RANK maintains the following loop invariant:

> At the start of each iteration of the **while** loop of lines 3–6, r is the rank of $x.key$ in the subtree rooted at node y.

We use this loop invariant to show that OS-RANK works correctly as follows:

Initialization: Prior to the first iteration, line 1 sets r to be the rank of $x.key$ within the subtree rooted at x. Setting $y = x$ in line 2 makes the invariant true the first time the test in line 3 executes.

Maintenance: At the end of each iteration of the **while** loop, we set $y = y.p$. Thus we must show that if r is the rank of $x.key$ in the subtree rooted at y at the start of the loop body, then r is the rank of $x.key$ in the subtree rooted at $y.p$ at the end of the loop body. In each iteration of the **while** loop, we consider the subtree rooted at $y.p$. We have already counted the number of nodes in the subtree rooted at node y that precede x in an inorder walk, and so we must add the nodes in the subtree rooted at y's sibling that precede x in an inorder walk, plus 1 for $y.p$ if it, too, precedes x. If y is a left child, then neither $y.p$ nor any node in $y.p$'s right subtree precedes x, and so we leave r alone. Otherwise, y is a right child and all the nodes in $y.p$'s left subtree precede x, as does $y.p$ itself. Thus, in line 5, we add $y.p.left.size + 1$ to the current value of r.

Termination: The loop terminates when $y = T.root$, so that the subtree rooted at y is the entire tree. Thus, the value of r is the rank of $x.key$ in the entire tree.

As an example, when we run OS-RANK on the order-statistic tree of Figure 14.1 to find the rank of the node with key 38, we get the following sequence of values of $y.key$ and r at the top of the **while** loop:

iteration	$y.key$	r
1	38	2
2	30	4
3	41	4
4	26	17

The procedure returns the rank 17.

Since each iteration of the **while** loop takes $O(1)$ time, and y goes up one level in the tree with each iteration, the running time of OS-RANK is at worst proportional to the height of the tree: $O(\lg n)$ on an n-node order-statistic tree.

Maintaining subtree sizes

Given the *size* attribute in each node, OS-SELECT and OS-RANK can quickly compute order-statistic information. But unless we can efficiently maintain these attributes within the basic modifying operations on red-black trees, our work will have been for naught. We shall now show how to maintain subtree sizes for both insertion and deletion without affecting the asymptotic running time of either operation.

We noted in Section 13.3 that insertion into a red-black tree consists of two phases. The first phase goes down the tree from the root, inserting the new node as a child of an existing node. The second phase goes up the tree, changing colors and performing rotations to maintain the red-black properties.

To maintain the subtree sizes in the first phase, we simply increment $x.size$ for each node x on the simple path traversed from the root down toward the leaves. The new node added gets a *size* of 1. Since there are $O(\lg n)$ nodes on the traversed path, the additional cost of maintaining the *size* attributes is $O(\lg n)$.

In the second phase, the only structural changes to the underlying red-black tree are caused by rotations, of which there are at most two. Moreover, a rotation is a local operation: only two nodes have their *size* attributes invalidated. The link around which the rotation is performed is incident on these two nodes. Referring to the code for LEFT-ROTATE(T, x) in Section 13.2, we add the following lines:

13   $y.size = x.size$
14   $x.size = x.left.size + x.right.size + 1$

Figure 14.2 illustrates how the attributes are updated. The change to RIGHT-ROTATE is symmetric.

Since at most two rotations are performed during insertion into a red-black tree, we spend only $O(1)$ additional time updating *size* attributes in the second phase. Thus, the total time for insertion into an n-node order-statistic tree is $O(\lg n)$, which is asymptotically the same as for an ordinary red-black tree.

Deletion from a red-black tree also consists of two phases: the first operates on the underlying search tree, and the second causes at most three rotations and otherwise performs no structural changes. (See Section 13.4.) The first phase removes one node z from the tree and could move up to two other nodes within the tree (nodes y and x in Figure 12.4). To update the subtree sizes, we simply traverse a simple path from the lowest node that moves (starting from its original

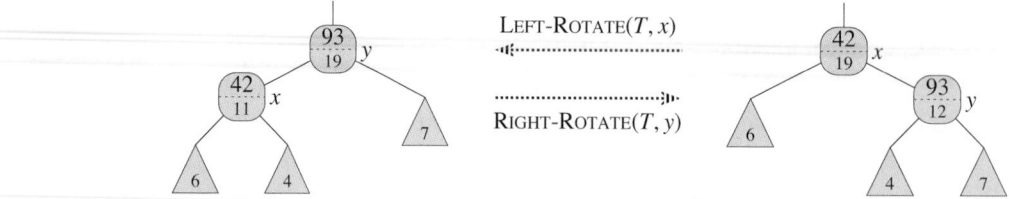

Figure 14.2 Updating subtree sizes during rotations. The link around which we rotate is incident on the two nodes whose *size* attributes need to be updated. The updates are local, requiring only the *size* information stored in x, y, and the roots of the subtrees shown as triangles.

position within the tree) up to the root, decrementing the *size* attribute of each node on the path. Since this path has length $O(\lg n)$ in an n-node red-black tree, the additional time spent maintaining *size* attributes in the first phase is $O(\lg n)$. We handle the $O(1)$ rotations in the second phase of deletion in the same manner as for insertion. Thus, both insertion and deletion, including maintaining the *size* attributes, take $O(\lg n)$ time for an n-node order-statistic tree.

Exercises

14.1-1
Show how OS-SELECT($T.root$, 10) operates on the red-black tree T of Figure 14.1.

14.1-2
Show how OS-RANK(T, x) operates on the red-black tree T of Figure 14.1 and the node x with $x.key = 35$.

14.1-3
Write a nonrecursive version of OS-SELECT.

14.1-4
Write a recursive procedure OS-KEY-RANK(T, k) that takes as input an order-statistic tree T and a key k and returns the rank of k in the dynamic set represented by T. Assume that the keys of T are distinct.

14.1-5
Given an element x in an n-node order-statistic tree and a natural number i, how can we determine the ith successor of x in the linear order of the tree in $O(\lg n)$ time?

14.1-6
Observe that whenever we reference the *size* attribute of a node in either OS-SELECT or OS-RANK, we use it only to compute a rank. Accordingly, suppose we store in each node its rank in the subtree of which it is the root. Show how to maintain this information during insertion and deletion. (Remember that these two operations can cause rotations.)

14.1-7
Show how to use an order-statistic tree to count the number of inversions (see Problem 2-4) in an array of size n in time $O(n \lg n)$.

14.1-8 ★
Consider n chords on a circle, each defined by its endpoints. Describe an $O(n \lg n)$-time algorithm to determine the number of pairs of chords that intersect inside the circle. (For example, if the n chords are all diameters that meet at the center, then the correct answer is $\binom{n}{2}$.) Assume that no two chords share an endpoint.

14.2 How to augment a data structure

The process of augmenting a basic data structure to support additional functionality occurs quite frequently in algorithm design. We shall use it again in the next section to design a data structure that supports operations on intervals. In this section, we examine the steps involved in such augmentation. We shall also prove a theorem that allows us to augment red-black trees easily in many cases.

We can break the process of augmenting a data structure into four steps:

1. Choose an underlying data structure.

2. Determine additional information to maintain in the underlying data structure.

3. Verify that we can maintain the additional information for the basic modifying operations on the underlying data structure.

4. Develop new operations.

As with any prescriptive design method, you should not blindly follow the steps in the order given. Most design work contains an element of trial and error, and progress on all steps usually proceeds in parallel. There is no point, for example, in determining additional information and developing new operations (steps 2 and 4) if we will not be able to maintain the additional information efficiently. Nevertheless, this four-step method provides a good focus for your efforts in augmenting a data structure, and it is also a good way to organize the documentation of an augmented data structure.

We followed these steps in Section 14.1 to design our order-statistic trees. For step 1, we chose red-black trees as the underlying data structure. A clue to the suitability of red-black trees comes from their efficient support of other dynamic-set operations on a total order, such as MINIMUM, MAXIMUM, SUCCESSOR, and PREDECESSOR.

For step 2, we added the *size* attribute, in which each node x stores the size of the subtree rooted at x. Generally, the additional information makes operations more efficient. For example, we could have implemented OS-SELECT and OS-RANK using just the keys stored in the tree, but they would not have run in $O(\lg n)$ time. Sometimes, the additional information is pointer information rather than data, as in Exercise 14.2-1.

For step 3, we ensured that insertion and deletion could maintain the *size* attributes while still running in $O(\lg n)$ time. Ideally, we should need to update only a few elements of the data structure in order to maintain the additional information. For example, if we simply stored in each node its rank in the tree, the OS-SELECT and OS-RANK procedures would run quickly, but inserting a new minimum element would cause a change to this information in every node of the tree. When we store subtree sizes instead, inserting a new element causes information to change in only $O(\lg n)$ nodes.

For step 4, we developed the operations OS-SELECT and OS-RANK. After all, the need for new operations is why we bother to augment a data structure in the first place. Occasionally, rather than developing new operations, we use the additional information to expedite existing ones, as in Exercise 14.2-1.

Augmenting red-black trees

When red-black trees underlie an augmented data structure, we can prove that insertion and deletion can always efficiently maintain certain kinds of additional information, thereby making step 3 very easy. The proof of the following theorem is similar to the argument from Section 14.1 that we can maintain the *size* attribute for order-statistic trees.

Theorem 14.1 (Augmenting a red-black tree)
Let f be an attribute that augments a red-black tree T of n nodes, and suppose that the value of f for each node x depends on only the information in nodes x, $x.left$, and $x.right$, possibly including $x.left.f$ and $x.right.f$. Then, we can maintain the values of f in all nodes of T during insertion and deletion without asymptotically affecting the $O(\lg n)$ performance of these operations.

Proof The main idea of the proof is that a change to an f attribute in a node x propagates only to ancestors of x in the tree. That is, changing $x.f$ may re-

quire $x.p.f$ to be updated, but nothing else; updating $x.p.f$ may require $x.p.p.f$ to be updated, but nothing else; and so on up the tree. Once we have updated $T.root.f$, no other node will depend on the new value, and so the process terminates. Since the height of a red-black tree is $O(\lg n)$, changing an f attribute in a node costs $O(\lg n)$ time in updating all nodes that depend on the change.

Insertion of a node x into T consists of two phases. (See Section 13.3.) The first phase inserts x as a child of an existing node $x.p$. We can compute the value of $x.f$ in $O(1)$ time since, by supposition, it depends only on information in the other attributes of x itself and the information in x's children, but x's children are both the sentinel $T.nil$. Once we have computed $x.f$, the change propagates up the tree. Thus, the total time for the first phase of insertion is $O(\lg n)$. During the second phase, the only structural changes to the tree come from rotations. Since only two nodes change in a rotation, the total time for updating the f attributes is $O(\lg n)$ per rotation. Since the number of rotations during insertion is at most two, the total time for insertion is $O(\lg n)$.

Like insertion, deletion has two phases. (See Section 13.4.) In the first phase, changes to the tree occur when a node is deleted, and at most two other nodes could move within the tree. Propagating the updates to f caused by these changes costs at most $O(\lg n)$, since the changes modify the tree locally along a simple path from the lowest changed node to the root. Fixing up the red-black tree during the second phase requires at most three rotations, and each rotation requires at most $O(\lg n)$ time to propagate the updates to f. Thus, like insertion, the total time for deletion is $O(\lg n)$.   ∎

In many cases, such as maintaining the *size* attributes in order-statistic trees, the cost of updating after a rotation is $O(1)$, rather than the $O(\lg n)$ derived in the proof of Theorem 14.1. Exercise 14.2-3 gives an example.

Exercises

14.2-1
Show, by adding pointers to the nodes, how to support each of the dynamic-set queries MINIMUM, MAXIMUM, SUCCESSOR, and PREDECESSOR in $O(1)$ worst-case time on an augmented order-statistic tree. The asymptotic performance of other operations on order-statistic trees should not be affected.

14.2-2
Can we maintain the black-heights of nodes in a red-black tree as attributes in the nodes of the tree without affecting the asymptotic performance of any of the red-black tree operations? Show how, or argue why not. How about maintaining the depths of nodes?

14.2-3 ★

Let $\otimes$ be an associative binary operator, and let a be an attribute maintained in each node of a red-black tree. Suppose that we want to include in each node x an additional attribute f such that $x.f = x_1.a \otimes x_2.a \otimes \cdots \otimes x_m.a$, where $x_1, x_2, \ldots, x_m$ is the inorder listing of nodes in the subtree rooted at x. Show how to update the f attributes in $O(1)$ time after a rotation. Modify your argument slightly to apply it to the *size* attributes in order-statistic trees.

14.2-4 ★

We wish to augment red-black trees with an operation RB-ENUMERATE(x, a, b) that outputs all the keys k such that $a \leq k \leq b$ in a red-black tree rooted at x. Describe how to implement RB-ENUMERATE in $\Theta(m + \lg n)$ time, where m is the number of keys that are output and n is the number of internal nodes in the tree. (*Hint:* You do not need to add new attributes to the red-black tree.)

14.3   Interval trees

In this section, we shall augment red-black trees to support operations on dynamic sets of intervals. A ***closed interval*** is an ordered pair of real numbers $[t_1, t_2]$, with $t_1 \leq t_2$. The interval $[t_1, t_2]$ represents the set $\{t \in \mathbb{R} : t_1 \leq t \leq t_2\}$. ***Open*** and ***half-open*** intervals omit both or one of the endpoints from the set, respectively. In this section, we shall assume that intervals are closed; extending the results to open and half-open intervals is conceptually straightforward.

Intervals are convenient for representing events that each occupy a continuous period of time. We might, for example, wish to query a database of time intervals to find out what events occurred during a given interval. The data structure in this section provides an efficient means for maintaining such an interval database.

We can represent an interval $[t_1, t_2]$ as an object i, with attributes $i.low = t_1$ (the ***low endpoint***) and $i.high = t_2$ (the ***high endpoint***). We say that intervals i and i' ***overlap*** if $i \cap i' \neq \emptyset$, that is, if $i.low \leq i'.high$ and $i'.low \leq i.high$. As Figure 14.3 shows, any two intervals i and i' satisfy the ***interval trichotomy***; that is, exactly one of the following three properties holds:

a. i and i' overlap,

b. i is to the left of i' (i.e., $i.high < i'.low$),

c. i is to the right of i' (i.e., $i'.high < i.low$).

An ***interval tree*** is a red-black tree that maintains a dynamic set of elements, with each element x containing an interval $x.int$. Interval trees support the following operations:

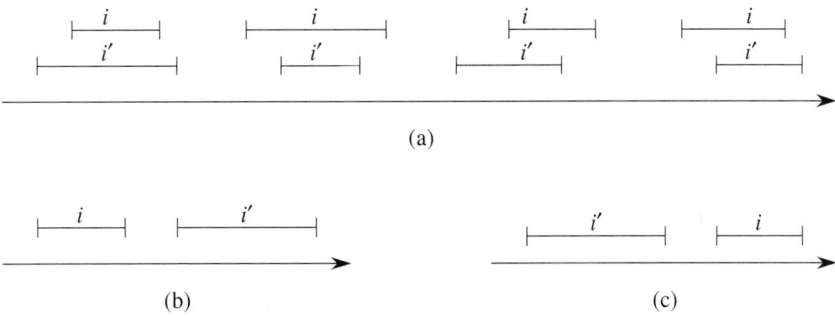

Figure 14.3   The interval trichotomy for two closed intervals i and i'. **(a)** If i and i' overlap, there are four situations; in each, $i.low \leq i'.high$ and $i'.low \leq i.high$. **(b)** The intervals do not overlap, and $i.high < i'.low$. **(c)** The intervals do not overlap, and $i'.high < i.low$.

INTERVAL-INSERT(T, x) adds the element x, whose *int* attribute is assumed to contain an interval, to the interval tree T.

INTERVAL-DELETE(T, x) removes the element x from the interval tree T.

INTERVAL-SEARCH(T, i) returns a pointer to an element x in the interval tree T such that $x.int$ overlaps interval i, or a pointer to the sentinel $T.nil$ if no such element is in the set.

Figure 14.4 shows how an interval tree represents a set of intervals. We shall track the four-step method from Section 14.2 as we review the design of an interval tree and the operations that run on it.

Step 1: Underlying data structure

We choose a red-black tree in which each node x contains an interval $x.int$ and the key of x is the low endpoint, $x.int.low$, of the interval. Thus, an inorder tree walk of the data structure lists the intervals in sorted order by low endpoint.

Step 2: Additional information

In addition to the intervals themselves, each node x contains a value $x.max$, which is the maximum value of any interval endpoint stored in the subtree rooted at x.

Step 3: Maintaining the information

We must verify that insertion and deletion take $O(\lg n)$ time on an interval tree of n nodes. We can determine $x.max$ given interval $x.int$ and the *max* values of node x's children:

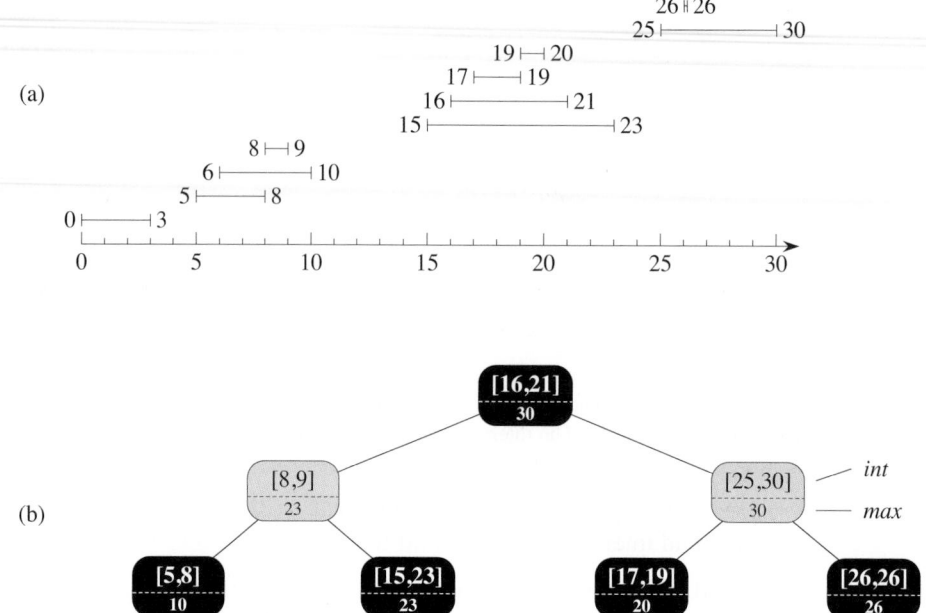

Figure 14.4 An interval tree. **(a)** A set of 10 intervals, shown sorted bottom to top by left endpoint. **(b)** The interval tree that represents them. Each node x contains an interval, shown above the dashed line, and the maximum value of any interval endpoint in the subtree rooted at x, shown below the dashed line. An inorder tree walk of the tree lists the nodes in sorted order by left endpoint.

$$x.max = \max(x.int.high, x.left.max, x.right.max) \ .$$

Thus, by Theorem 14.1, insertion and deletion run in $O(\lg n)$ time. In fact, we can update the *max* attributes after a rotation in $O(1)$ time, as Exercises 14.2-3 and 14.3-1 show.

Step 4: Developing new operations

The only new operation we need is INTERVAL-SEARCH(T, i), which finds a node in tree T whose interval overlaps interval i. If there is no interval that overlaps i in the tree, the procedure returns a pointer to the sentinel $T.nil$.

INTERVAL-SEARCH(T, i)

```
1   x = T.root
2   while x ≠ T.nil and i does not overlap x.int
3       if x.left ≠ T.nil and x.left.max ≥ i.low
4           x = x.left
5       else x = x.right
6   return x
```

The search for an interval that overlaps i starts with x at the root of the tree and proceeds downward. It terminates when either it finds an overlapping interval or x points to the sentinel $T.nil$. Since each iteration of the basic loop takes $O(1)$ time, and since the height of an n-node red-black tree is $O(\lg n)$, the INTERVAL-SEARCH procedure takes $O(\lg n)$ time.

Before we see why INTERVAL-SEARCH is correct, let's examine how it works on the interval tree in Figure 14.4. Suppose we wish to find an interval that overlaps the interval $i = [22, 25]$. We begin with x as the root, which contains $[16, 21]$ and does not overlap i. Since $x.left.max = 23$ is greater than $i.low = 22$, the loop continues with x as the left child of the root—the node containing $[8, 9]$, which also does not overlap i. This time, $x.left.max = 10$ is less than $i.low = 22$, and so the loop continues with the right child of x as the new x. Because the interval $[15, 23]$ stored in this node overlaps i, the procedure returns this node.

As an example of an unsuccessful search, suppose we wish to find an interval that overlaps $i = [11, 14]$ in the interval tree of Figure 14.4. We once again begin with x as the root. Since the root's interval $[16, 21]$ does not overlap i, and since $x.left.max = 23$ is greater than $i.low = 11$, we go left to the node containing $[8, 9]$. Interval $[8, 9]$ does not overlap i, and $x.left.max = 10$ is less than $i.low = 11$, and so we go right. (Note that no interval in the left subtree overlaps i.) Interval $[15, 23]$ does not overlap i, and its left child is $T.nil$, so again we go right, the loop terminates, and we return the sentinel $T.nil$.

To see why INTERVAL-SEARCH is correct, we must understand why it suffices to examine a single path from the root. The basic idea is that at any node x, if $x.int$ does not overlap i, the search always proceeds in a safe direction: the search will definitely find an overlapping interval if the tree contains one. The following theorem states this property more precisely.

Theorem 14.2
Any execution of INTERVAL-SEARCH(T, i) either returns a node whose interval overlaps i, or it returns $T.nil$ and the tree T contains no node whose interval overlaps i.

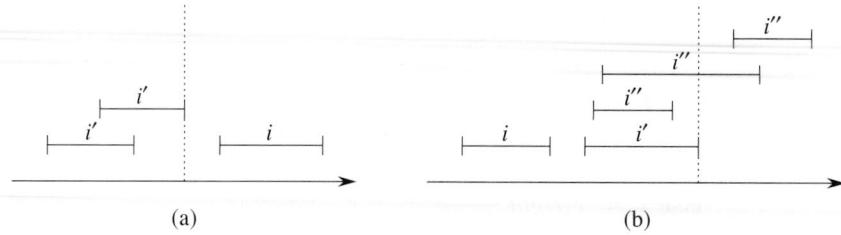

(a)   (b)

Figure 14.5   Intervals in the proof of Theorem 14.2. The value of $x.left.max$ is shown in each case as a dashed line. **(a)** The search goes right. No interval i' in x's left subtree can overlap i. **(b)** The search goes left. The left subtree of x contains an interval that overlaps i (situation not shown), or x's left subtree contains an interval i' such that $i'.high = x.left.max$. Since i does not overlap i', neither does it overlap any interval i'' in x's right subtree, since $i'.low \leq i''.low$.

Proof   The **while** loop of lines 2–5 terminates either when $x = T.nil$ or i overlaps $x.int$. In the latter case, it is certainly correct to return x. Therefore, we focus on the former case, in which the **while** loop terminates because $x = T.nil$.

We use the following invariant for the **while** loop of lines 2–5:

> If tree T contains an interval that overlaps i, then the subtree rooted at x contains such an interval.

We use this loop invariant as follows:

Initialization: Prior to the first iteration, line 1 sets x to be the root of T, so that the invariant holds.

Maintenance: Each iteration of the **while** loop executes either line 4 or line 5. We shall show that both cases maintain the loop invariant.

If line 5 is executed, then because of the branch condition in line 3, we have $x.left = T.nil$, or $x.left.max < i.low$. If $x.left = T.nil$, the subtree rooted at $x.left$ clearly contains no interval that overlaps i, and so setting x to $x.right$ maintains the invariant. Suppose, therefore, that $x.left \neq T.nil$ and $x.left.max < i.low$. As Figure 14.5(a) shows, for each interval i' in x's left subtree, we have

$$
\begin{aligned}
i'.high \ &\leq \ x.left.max \\
&< \ i.low \,.
\end{aligned}
$$

By the interval trichotomy, therefore, i' and i do not overlap. Thus, the left subtree of x contains no intervals that overlap i, so that setting x to $x.right$ maintains the invariant.

If, on the other hand, line 4 is executed, then we will show that the contrapositive of the loop invariant holds. That is, if the subtree rooted at $x.left$ contains no interval overlapping i, then no interval anywhere in the tree overlaps i. Since line 4 is executed, then because of the branch condition in line 3, we have $x.left.max \geq i.low$. Moreover, by definition of the max attribute, x's left subtree must contain some interval i' such that

$$
\begin{aligned}
i'.high \ &= \ x.left.max \\
&\geq \ i.low \, .
\end{aligned}
$$

(Figure 14.5(b) illustrates the situation.) Since i and i' do not overlap, and since it is not true that $i'.high < i.low$, it follows by the interval trichotomy that $i.high < i'.low$. Interval trees are keyed on the low endpoints of intervals, and thus the search-tree property implies that for any interval i'' in x's right subtree,

$$
\begin{aligned}
i.high \ &< \ i'.low \\
&\leq \ i''.low \, .
\end{aligned}
$$

By the interval trichotomy, i and i'' do not overlap. We conclude that whether or not any interval in x's left subtree overlaps i, setting x to $x.left$ maintains the invariant.

Termination: If the loop terminates when $x = T.nil$, then the subtree rooted at x contains no interval overlapping i. The contrapositive of the loop invariant implies that T contains no interval that overlaps i. Hence it is correct to return $x = T.nil$.   ∎

Thus, the INTERVAL-SEARCH procedure works correctly.

Exercises

14.3-1
Write pseudocode for LEFT-ROTATE that operates on nodes in an interval tree and updates the max attributes in $O(1)$ time.

14.3-2
Rewrite the code for INTERVAL-SEARCH so that it works properly when all intervals are open.

14.3-3
Describe an efficient algorithm that, given an interval i, returns an interval overlapping i that has the minimum low endpoint, or $T.nil$ if no such interval exists.

14.3-4

Given an interval tree T and an interval i, describe how to list all intervals in T that overlap i in $O(\min(n, k \lg n))$ time, where k is the number of intervals in the output list. (*Hint:* One simple method makes several queries, modifying the tree between queries. A slightly more complicated method does not modify the tree.)

14.3-5

Suggest modifications to the interval-tree procedures to support the new operation INTERVAL-SEARCH-EXACTLY(T, i), where T is an interval tree and i is an interval. The operation should return a pointer to a node x in T such that $x.int.low = i.low$ and $x.int.high = i.high$, or $T.nil$ if T contains no such node. All operations, including INTERVAL-SEARCH-EXACTLY, should run in $O(\lg n)$ time on an n-node interval tree.

14.3-6

Show how to maintain a dynamic set Q of numbers that supports the operation MIN-GAP, which gives the magnitude of the difference of the two closest numbers in Q. For example, if $Q = \{1, 5, 9, 15, 18, 22\}$, then MIN-GAP$(Q)$ returns $18 - 15 = 3$, since 15 and 18 are the two closest numbers in Q. Make the operations INSERT, DELETE, SEARCH, and MIN-GAP as efficient as possible, and analyze their running times.

14.3-7 ★

VLSI databases commonly represent an integrated circuit as a list of rectangles. Assume that each rectangle is rectilinearly oriented (sides parallel to the x- and y-axes), so that we represent a rectangle by its minimum and maximum x- and y-coordinates. Give an $O(n \lg n)$-time algorithm to decide whether or not a set of n rectangles so represented contains two rectangles that overlap. Your algorithm need not report all intersecting pairs, but it must report that an overlap exists if one rectangle entirely covers another, even if the boundary lines do not intersect. (*Hint:* Move a "sweep" line across the set of rectangles.)

Problems

14-1   *Point of maximum overlap*

Suppose that we wish to keep track of a ***point of maximum overlap*** in a set of intervals—a point with the largest number of intervals in the set that overlap it.

    a. Show that there will always be a point of maximum overlap that is an endpoint of one of the segments.

b. Design a data structure that efficiently supports the operations INTERVAL-INSERT, INTERVAL-DELETE, and FIND-POM, which returns a point of maximum overlap. (*Hint:* Keep a red-black tree of all the endpoints. Associate a value of $+1$ with each left endpoint, and associate a value of -1 with each right endpoint. Augment each node of the tree with some extra information to maintain the point of maximum overlap.)

14-2 *Josephus permutation*

We define the ***Josephus problem*** as follows. Suppose that n people form a circle and that we are given a positive integer $m \leq n$. Beginning with a designated first person, we proceed around the circle, removing every mth person. After each person is removed, counting continues around the circle that remains. This process continues until we have removed all n people. The order in which the people are removed from the circle defines the ***(n, m)-Josephus permutation*** of the integers $1, 2, \ldots, n$. For example, the $(7, 3)$-Josephus permutation is $\langle 3, 6, 2, 7, 5, 1, 4 \rangle$.

a. Suppose that m is a constant. Describe an $O(n)$-time algorithm that, given an integer n, outputs the (n, m)-Josephus permutation.

b. Suppose that m is not a constant. Describe an $O(n \lg n)$-time algorithm that, given integers n and m, outputs the (n, m)-Josephus permutation.

Chapter notes

In their book, Preparata and Shamos [282] describe several of the interval trees that appear in the literature, citing work by H. Edelsbrunner (1980) and E. M. McCreight (1981). The book details an interval tree that, given a static database of n intervals, allows us to enumerate all k intervals that overlap a given query interval in $O(k + \lg n)$ time.

IV Advanced Design and Analysis Techniques

Introduction

This part covers three important techniques used in designing and analyzing efficient algorithms: dynamic programming (Chapter 15), greedy algorithms (Chapter 16), and amortized analysis (Chapter 17). Earlier parts have presented other widely applicable techniques, such as divide-and-conquer, randomization, and how to solve recurrences. The techniques in this part are somewhat more sophisticated, but they help us to attack many computational problems. The themes introduced in this part will recur later in this book.

Dynamic programming typically applies to optimization problems in which we make a set of choices in order to arrive at an optimal solution. As we make each choice, subproblems of the same form often arise. Dynamic programming is effective when a given subproblem may arise from more than one partial set of choices; the key technique is to store the solution to each such subproblem in case it should reappear. Chapter 15 shows how this simple idea can sometimes transform exponential-time algorithms into polynomial-time algorithms.

Like dynamic-programming algorithms, greedy algorithms typically apply to optimization problems in which we make a set of choices in order to arrive at an optimal solution. The idea of a greedy algorithm is to make each choice in a locally optimal manner. A simple example is coin-changing: to minimize the number of U.S. coins needed to make change for a given amount, we can repeatedly select the largest-denomination coin that is not larger than the amount that remains. A greedy approach provides an optimal solution for many such problems much more quickly than would a dynamic-programming approach. We cannot always easily tell whether a greedy approach will be effective, however. Chapter 16 introduces

matroid theory, which provides a mathematical basis that can help us to show that a greedy algorithm yields an optimal solution.

We use amortized analysis to analyze certain algorithms that perform a sequence of similar operations. Instead of bounding the cost of the sequence of operations by bounding the actual cost of each operation separately, an amortized analysis provides a bound on the actual cost of the entire sequence. One advantage of this approach is that although some operations might be expensive, many others might be cheap. In other words, many of the operations might run in well under the worst-case time. Amortized analysis is not just an analysis tool, however; it is also a way of thinking about the design of algorithms, since the design of an algorithm and the analysis of its running time are often closely intertwined. Chapter 17 introduces three ways to perform an amortized analysis of an algorithm.

15   Dynamic Programming

Dynamic programming, like the divide-and-conquer method, solves problems by combining the solutions to subproblems. ("Programming" in this context refers to a tabular method, not to writing computer code.) As we saw in Chapters 2 and 4, divide-and-conquer algorithms partition the problem into disjoint subproblems, solve the subproblems recursively, and then combine their solutions to solve the original problem. In contrast, dynamic programming applies when the subproblems overlap—that is, when subproblems share subsubproblems. In this context, a divide-and-conquer algorithm does more work than necessary, repeatedly solving the common subsubproblems. A dynamic-programming algorithm solves each subsubproblem just once and then saves its answer in a table, thereby avoiding the work of recomputing the answer every time it solves each subsubproblem.

We typically apply dynamic programming to *optimization problems*. Such problems can have many possible solutions. Each solution has a value, and we wish to find a solution with the optimal (minimum or maximum) value. We call such a solution *an* optimal solution to the problem, as opposed to *the* optimal solution, since there may be several solutions that achieve the optimal value.

When developing a dynamic-programming algorithm, we follow a sequence of four steps:

1. Characterize the structure of an optimal solution.

2. Recursively define the value of an optimal solution.

3. Compute the value of an optimal solution, typically in a bottom-up fashion.

4. Construct an optimal solution from computed information.

Steps 1–3 form the basis of a dynamic-programming solution to a problem. If we need only the value of an optimal solution, and not the solution itself, then we can omit step 4. When we do perform step 4, we sometimes maintain additional information during step 3 so that we can easily construct an optimal solution.

The sections that follow use the dynamic-programming method to solve some optimization problems. Section 15.1 examines the problem of cutting a rod into

rods of smaller length in a way that maximizes their total value. Section 15.2 asks how we can multiply a chain of matrices while performing the fewest total scalar multiplications. Given these examples of dynamic programming, Section 15.3 discusses two key characteristics that a problem must have for dynamic programming to be a viable solution technique. Section 15.4 then shows how to find the longest common subsequence of two sequences via dynamic programming. Finally, Section 15.5 uses dynamic programming to construct binary search trees that are optimal, given a known distribution of keys to be looked up.

15.1   Rod cutting

Our first example uses dynamic programming to solve a simple problem in deciding where to cut steel rods. Serling Enterprises buys long steel rods and cuts them into shorter rods, which it then sells. Each cut is free. The management of Serling Enterprises wants to know the best way to cut up the rods.

We assume that we know, for $i = 1, 2, \ldots$, the price p_i in dollars that Serling Enterprises charges for a rod of length i inches. Rod lengths are always an integral number of inches. Figure 15.1 gives a sample price table.

The *rod-cutting problem* is the following. Given a rod of length n inches and a table of prices p_i for $i = 1, 2, \ldots, n$, determine the maximum revenue r_n obtainable by cutting up the rod and selling the pieces. Note that if the price p_n for a rod of length n is large enough, an optimal solution may require no cutting at all.

Consider the case when $n = 4$. Figure 15.2 shows all the ways to cut up a rod of 4 inches in length, including the way with no cuts at all. We see that cutting a 4-inch rod into two 2-inch pieces produces revenue $p_2 + p_2 = 5 + 5 = 10$, which is optimal.

We can cut up a rod of length n in 2^{n-1} different ways, since we have an independent option of cutting, or not cutting, at distance i inches from the left end,

length i	1	2	3	4	5	6	7	8	9	10
price p_i	1	5	8	9	10	17	17	20	24	30

Figure 15.1   A sample price table for rods. Each rod of length i inches earns the company p_i dollars of revenue.

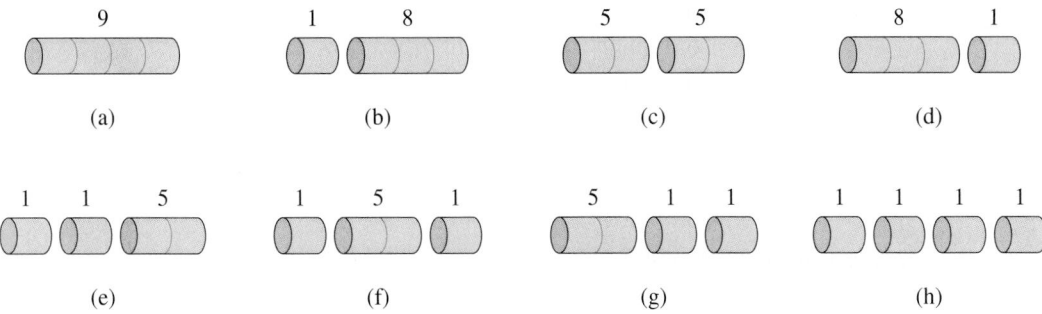

Figure 15.2 The 8 possible ways of cutting up a rod of length 4. Above each piece is the value of that piece, according to the sample price chart of Figure 15.1. The optimal strategy is part (c)—cutting the rod into two pieces of length 2—which has total value 10.

for $i = 1, 2, \ldots, n - 1$.[1] We denote a decomposition into pieces using ordinary additive notation, so that $7 = 2 + 2 + 3$ indicates that a rod of length 7 is cut into three pieces—two of length 2 and one of length 3. If an optimal solution cuts the rod into k pieces, for some $1 \le k \le n$, then an optimal decomposition

$$n = i_1 + i_2 + \cdots + i_k$$

of the rod into pieces of lengths $i_1, i_2, \ldots, i_k$ provides maximum corresponding revenue

$$r_n = p_{i_1} + p_{i_2} + \cdots + p_{i_k} \, .$$

For our sample problem, we can determine the optimal revenue figures r_i, for $i = 1, 2, \ldots, 10$, by inspection, with the corresponding optimal decompositions

---

[1]If we required the pieces to be cut in order of nondecreasing size, there would be fewer ways to consider. For $n = 4$, we would consider only 5 such ways: parts (a), (b), (c), (e), and (h) in Figure 15.2. The number of ways is called the **partition function**; it is approximately equal to $e^{\pi \sqrt{2n/3}}/4n\sqrt{3}$. This quantity is less than 2^{n-1}, but still much greater than any polynomial in n. We shall not pursue this line of inquiry further, however.

$$
\begin{aligned}
r_1 &= 1 && \text{from solution } 1 = 1 \quad \text{(no cuts)}, \\
r_2 &= 5 && \text{from solution } 2 = 2 \quad \text{(no cuts)}, \\
r_3 &= 8 && \text{from solution } 3 = 3 \quad \text{(no cuts)}, \\
r_4 &= 10 && \text{from solution } 4 = 2 + 2, \\
r_5 &= 13 && \text{from solution } 5 = 2 + 3, \\
r_6 &= 17 && \text{from solution } 6 = 6 \quad \text{(no cuts)}, \\
r_7 &= 18 && \text{from solution } 7 = 1 + 6 \ \text{ or } \ 7 = 2 + 2 + 3, \\
r_8 &= 22 && \text{from solution } 8 = 2 + 6, \\
r_9 &= 25 && \text{from solution } 9 = 3 + 6, \\
r_{10} &= 30 && \text{from solution } 10 = 10 \quad \text{(no cuts)}.
\end{aligned}
$$

More generally, we can frame the values r_n for $n \geq 1$ in terms of optimal revenues from shorter rods:

$$
r_n = \max\left(p_n, r_1 + r_{n-1}, r_2 + r_{n-2}, \ldots, r_{n-1} + r_1\right). \tag{15.1}
$$

The first argument, p_n, corresponds to making no cuts at all and selling the rod of length n as is. The other $n - 1$ arguments to max correspond to the maximum revenue obtained by making an initial cut of the rod into two pieces of size i and $n - i$, for each $i = 1, 2, \ldots, n - 1$, and then optimally cutting up those pieces further, obtaining revenues r_i and r_{n-i} from those two pieces. Since we don't know ahead of time which value of i optimizes revenue, we have to consider all possible values for i and pick the one that maximizes revenue. We also have the option of picking no i at all if we can obtain more revenue by selling the rod uncut.

Note that to solve the original problem of size n, we solve smaller problems of the same type, but of smaller sizes. Once we make the first cut, we may consider the two pieces as independent instances of the rod-cutting problem. The overall optimal solution incorporates optimal solutions to the two related subproblems, maximizing revenue from each of those two pieces. We say that the rod-cutting problem exhibits **optimal substructure**: optimal solutions to a problem incorporate optimal solutions to related subproblems, which we may solve independently.

In a related, but slightly simpler, way to arrange a recursive structure for the rod-cutting problem, we view a decomposition as consisting of a first piece of length i cut off the left-hand end, and then a right-hand remainder of length $n - i$. Only the remainder, and not the first piece, may be further divided. We may view every decomposition of a length-n rod in this way: as a first piece followed by some decomposition of the remainder. When doing so, we can couch the solution with no cuts at all as saying that the first piece has size $i = n$ and revenue p_n and that the remainder has size 0 with corresponding revenue $r_0 = 0$. We thus obtain the following simpler version of equation (15.1):

$$
r_n = \max_{1 \leq i \leq n}\left(p_i + r_{n-i}\right). \tag{15.2}
$$

In this formulation, an optimal solution embodies the solution to only *one* related subproblem—the remainder—rather than two.

Recursive top-down implementation

The following procedure implements the computation implicit in equation (15.2) in a straightforward, top-down, recursive manner.

CUT-ROD(p, n)

```
1  if n == 0
2      return 0
3  q = −∞
4  for i = 1 to n
5      q = max(q, p[i] + CUT-ROD(p, n − i))
6  return q
```

Procedure CUT-ROD takes as input an array $p[1 . . n]$ of prices and an integer n, and it returns the maximum revenue possible for a rod of length n. If $n = 0$, no revenue is possible, and so CUT-ROD returns 0 in line 2. Line 3 initializes the maximum revenue q to $-\infty$, so that the **for** loop in lines 4–5 correctly computes $q = \max_{1 \le i \le n}(p_i + \text{CUT-ROD}(p, n - i))$; line 6 then returns this value. A simple induction on n proves that this answer is equal to the desired answer r_n, using equation (15.2).

If you were to code up CUT-ROD in your favorite programming language and run it on your computer, you would find that once the input size becomes moderately large, your program would take a long time to run. For $n = 40$, you would find that your program takes at least several minutes, and most likely more than an hour. In fact, you would find that each time you increase n by 1, your program's running time would approximately double.

Why is CUT-ROD so inefficient? The problem is that CUT-ROD calls itself recursively over and over again with the same parameter values; it solves the same subproblems repeatedly. Figure 15.3 illustrates what happens for $n = 4$: CUT-ROD(p, n) calls CUT-ROD($p, n - i$) for $i = 1, 2, \ldots, n$. Equivalently, CUT-ROD(p, n) calls CUT-ROD(p, j) for each $j = 0, 1, \ldots, n - 1$. When this process unfolds recursively, the amount of work done, as a function of n, grows explosively.

To analyze the running time of CUT-ROD, let $T(n)$ denote the total number of calls made to CUT-ROD when called with its second parameter equal to n. This expression equals the number of nodes in a subtree whose root is labeled n in the recursion tree. The count includes the initial call at its root. Thus, $T(0) = 1$ and

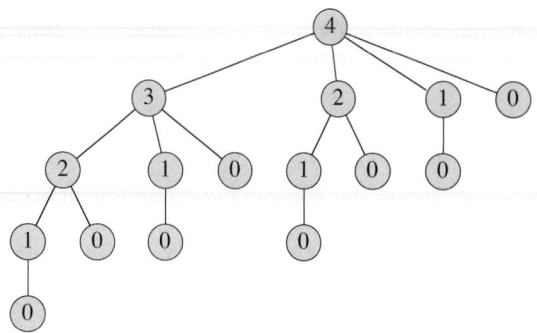

Figure 15.3 The recursion tree showing recursive calls resulting from a call CUT-ROD(p, n) for $n = 4$. Each node label gives the size n of the corresponding subproblem, so that an edge from a parent with label s to a child with label t corresponds to cutting off an initial piece of size $s - t$ and leaving a remaining subproblem of size t. A path from the root to a leaf corresponds to one of the 2^{n-1} ways of cutting up a rod of length n. In general, this recursion tree has 2^n nodes and 2^{n-1} leaves.

$$T(n) = 1 + \sum_{j=0}^{n-1} T(j) \, . \tag{15.3}$$

The initial 1 is for the call at the root, and the term $T(j)$ counts the number of calls (including recursive calls) due to the call CUT-ROD($p, n - i$), where $j = n - i$. As Exercise 15.1-1 asks you to show,

$$T(n) = 2^n \, , \tag{15.4}$$

and so the running time of CUT-ROD is exponential in n.

In retrospect, this exponential running time is not so surprising. CUT-ROD explicitly considers all the 2^{n-1} possible ways of cutting up a rod of length n. The tree of recursive calls has 2^{n-1} leaves, one for each possible way of cutting up the rod. The labels on the simple path from the root to a leaf give the sizes of each remaining right-hand piece before making each cut. That is, the labels give the corresponding cut points, measured from the right-hand end of the rod.

Using dynamic programming for optimal rod cutting

We now show how to convert CUT-ROD into an efficient algorithm, using dynamic programming.

The dynamic-programming method works as follows. Having observed that a naive recursive solution is inefficient because it solves the same subproblems repeatedly, we arrange for each subproblem to be solved only *once*, saving its solution. If we need to refer to this subproblem's solution again later, we can just look it

up, rather than recompute it. Dynamic programming thus uses additional memory to save computation time; it serves an example of a ***time-memory trade-off***. The savings may be dramatic: an exponential-time solution may be transformed into a polynomial-time solution. A dynamic-programming approach runs in polynomial time when the number of *distinct* subproblems involved is polynomial in the input size and we can solve each such subproblem in polynomial time.

There are usually two equivalent ways to implement a dynamic-programming approach. We shall illustrate both of them with our rod-cutting example.

The first approach is ***top-down with memoization***.[2] In this approach, we write the procedure recursively in a natural manner, but modified to save the result of each subproblem (usually in an array or hash table). The procedure now first checks to see whether it has previously solved this subproblem. If so, it returns the saved value, saving further computation at this level; if not, the procedure computes the value in the usual manner. We say that the recursive procedure has been ***memoized***; it "remembers" what results it has computed previously.

The second approach is the ***bottom-up method***. This approach typically depends on some natural notion of the "size" of a subproblem, such that solving any particular subproblem depends only on solving "smaller" subproblems. We sort the subproblems by size and solve them in size order, smallest first. When solving a particular subproblem, we have already solved all of the smaller subproblems its solution depends upon, and we have saved their solutions. We solve each subproblem only once, and when we first see it, we have already solved all of its prerequisite subproblems.

These two approaches yield algorithms with the same asymptotic running time, except in unusual circumstances where the top-down approach does not actually recurse to examine all possible subproblems. The bottom-up approach often has much better constant factors, since it has less overhead for procedure calls.

Here is the pseudocode for the top-down CUT-ROD procedure, with memoization added:

MEMOIZED-CUT-ROD(p, n)

```
1  let r[0 . . n] be a new array
2  for i = 0 to n
3      r[i] = −∞
4  return MEMOIZED-CUT-ROD-AUX(p, n, r)
```

---

[2]This is not a misspelling. The word really is *memoization*, not *memorization*. *Memoization* comes from *memo*, since the technique consists of recording a value so that we can look it up later.

MEMOIZED-CUT-ROD-AUX(p, n, r)

```
1   if r[n] ≥ 0
2       return r[n]
3   if n == 0
4       q = 0
5   else q = -∞
6       for i = 1 to n
7           q = max(q, p[i] + MEMOIZED-CUT-ROD-AUX(p, n - i, r))
8   r[n] = q
9   return q
```

Here, the main procedure MEMOIZED-CUT-ROD initializes a new auxiliary array $r[0 \mathinner{\ldotp\ldotp} n]$ with the value $-\infty$, a convenient choice with which to denote "unknown." (Known revenue values are always nonnegative.) It then calls its helper routine, MEMOIZED-CUT-ROD-AUX.

The procedure MEMOIZED-CUT-ROD-AUX is just the memoized version of our previous procedure, CUT-ROD. It first checks in line 1 to see whether the desired value is already known and, if it is, then line 2 returns it. Otherwise, lines 3–7 compute the desired value q in the usual manner, line 8 saves it in $r[n]$, and line 9 returns it.

The bottom-up version is even simpler:

BOTTOM-UP-CUT-ROD(p, n)

```
1   let r[0..n] be a new array
2   r[0] = 0
3   for j = 1 to n
4       q = -∞
5       for i = 1 to j
6           q = max(q, p[i] + r[j - i])
7       r[j] = q
8   return r[n]
```

For the bottom-up dynamic-programming approach, BOTTOM-UP-CUT-ROD uses the natural ordering of the subproblems: a subproblem of size i is "smaller" than a subproblem of size j if $i < j$. Thus, the procedure solves subproblems of sizes $j = 0, 1, \ldots, n$, in that order.

Line 1 of procedure BOTTOM-UP-CUT-ROD creates a new array $r[0 \mathinner{\ldotp\ldotp} n]$ in which to save the results of the subproblems, and line 2 initializes $r[0]$ to 0, since a rod of length 0 earns no revenue. Lines 3–6 solve each subproblem of size j, for $j = 1, 2, \ldots, n$, in order of increasing size. The approach used to solve a problem of a particular size j is the same as that used by CUT-ROD, except that line 6 now

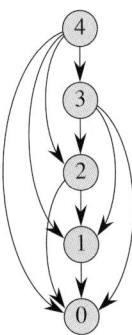

Figure 15.4   The subproblem graph for the rod-cutting problem with $n = 4$. The vertex labels give the sizes of the corresponding subproblems. A directed edge (x, y) indicates that we need a solution to subproblem y when solving subproblem x. This graph is a reduced version of the tree of Figure 15.3, in which all nodes with the same label are collapsed into a single vertex and all edges go from parent to child.

directly references array entry $r[j - i]$ instead of making a recursive call to solve the subproblem of size $j - i$. Line 7 saves in $r[j]$ the solution to the subproblem of size j. Finally, line 8 returns $r[n]$, which equals the optimal value r_n.

The bottom-up and top-down versions have the same asymptotic running time. The running time of procedure BOTTOM-UP-CUT-ROD is $\Theta(n^2)$, due to its doubly-nested loop structure. The number of iterations of its inner **for** loop, in lines 5–6, forms an arithmetic series. The running time of its top-down counterpart, MEMOIZED-CUT-ROD, is also $\Theta(n^2)$, although this running time may be a little harder to see. Because a recursive call to solve a previously solved subproblem returns immediately, MEMOIZED-CUT-ROD solves each subproblem just once. It solves subproblems for sizes $0, 1, \ldots, n$. To solve a subproblem of size n, the **for** loop of lines 6–7 iterates n times. Thus, the total number of iterations of this **for** loop, over all recursive calls of MEMOIZED-CUT-ROD, forms an arithmetic series, giving a total of $\Theta(n^2)$ iterations, just like the inner **for** loop of BOTTOM-UP-CUT-ROD. (We actually are using a form of aggregate analysis here. We shall see aggregate analysis in detail in Section 17.1.)

Subproblem graphs

When we think about a dynamic-programming problem, we should understand the set of subproblems involved and how subproblems depend on one another.

The *subproblem graph* for the problem embodies exactly this information. Figure 15.4 shows the subproblem graph for the rod-cutting problem with $n = 4$. It is a directed graph, containing one vertex for each distinct subproblem. The sub-

problem graph has a directed edge from the vertex for subproblem x to the vertex for subproblem y if determining an optimal solution for subproblem x involves directly considering an optimal solution for subproblem y. For example, the subproblem graph contains an edge from x to y if a top-down recursive procedure for solving x directly calls itself to solve y. We can think of the subproblem graph as a "reduced" or "collapsed" version of the recursion tree for the top-down recursive method, in which we coalesce all nodes for the same subproblem into a single vertex and direct all edges from parent to child.

The bottom-up method for dynamic programming considers the vertices of the subproblem graph in such an order that we solve the subproblems y adjacent to a given subproblem x before we solve subproblem x. (Recall from Section B.4 that the adjacency relation is not necessarily symmetric.) Using the terminology from Chapter 22, in a bottom-up dynamic-programming algorithm, we consider the vertices of the subproblem graph in an order that is a "reverse topological sort," or a "topological sort of the transpose" (see Section 22.4) of the subproblem graph. In other words, no subproblem is considered until all of the subproblems it depends upon have been solved. Similarly, using notions from the same chapter, we can view the top-down method (with memoization) for dynamic programming as a "depth-first search" of the subproblem graph (see Section 22.3).

The size of the subproblem graph $G = (V, E)$ can help us determine the running time of the dynamic programming algorithm. Since we solve each subproblem just once, the running time is the sum of the times needed to solve each subproblem. Typically, the time to compute the solution to a subproblem is proportional to the out-degree (number of outgoing edges) of the corresponding vertex in the subproblem graph, and the number of subproblems is equal to the number of vertices in the subproblem graph. In this common case, the running time of dynamic programming is linear in the number of vertices and edges.

Reconstructing a solution

Our dynamic-programming solutions to the rod-cutting problem return the value of an optimal solution, but they do not return an actual solution: a list of piece sizes. We can extend the dynamic-programming approach to record not only the optimal *value* computed for each subproblem, but also a *choice* that led to the optimal value. With this information, we can readily print an optimal solution.

Here is an extended version of BOTTOM-UP-CUT-ROD that computes, for each rod size j, not only the maximum revenue r_j, but also s_j, the optimal size of the first piece to cut off:

EXTENDED-BOTTOM-UP-CUT-ROD(p, n)

```
1   let r[0 .. n] and s[1 .. n] be new arrays
2   r[0] = 0
3   for j = 1 to n
4       q = -∞
5       for i = 1 to j
6           if q < p[i] + r[j - i]
7               q = p[i] + r[j - i]
8               s[j] = i
9       r[j] = q
10  return r and s
```

This procedure is similar to BOTTOM-UP-CUT-ROD, except that it creates the array s in line 1, and it updates $s[j]$ in line 8 to hold the optimal size i of the first piece to cut off when solving a subproblem of size j.

The following procedure takes a price table p and a rod size n, and it calls EXTENDED-BOTTOM-UP-CUT-ROD to compute the array $s[1 .. n]$ of optimal first-piece sizes and then prints out the complete list of piece sizes in an optimal decomposition of a rod of length n:

PRINT-CUT-ROD-SOLUTION(p, n)

```
1   (r, s) = EXTENDED-BOTTOM-UP-CUT-ROD(p, n)
2   while n > 0
3       print s[n]
4       n = n - s[n]
```

In our rod-cutting example, the call EXTENDED-BOTTOM-UP-CUT-ROD($p, 10$) would return the following arrays:

i	0	1	2	3	4	5	6	7	8	9	10
$r[i]$	0	1	5	8	10	13	17	18	22	25	30
$s[i]$		1	2	3	2	2	6	1	2	3	10

A call to PRINT-CUT-ROD-SOLUTION($p, 10$) would print just 10, but a call with $n = 7$ would print the cuts 1 and 6, corresponding to the first optimal decomposition for r_7 given earlier.

Exercises

15.1-1
Show that equation (15.4) follows from equation (15.3) and the initial condition $T(0) = 1$.

15.1-2

Show, by means of a counterexample, that the following "greedy" strategy does not always determine an optimal way to cut rods. Define the ***density*** of a rod of length i to be p_i / i, that is, its value per inch. The greedy strategy for a rod of length n cuts off a first piece of length i, where $1 \leq i \leq n$, having maximum density. It then continues by applying the greedy strategy to the remaining piece of length $n - i$.

15.1-3

Consider a modification of the rod-cutting problem in which, in addition to a price p_i for each rod, each cut incurs a fixed cost of c. The revenue associated with a solution is now the sum of the prices of the pieces minus the costs of making the cuts. Give a dynamic-programming algorithm to solve this modified problem.

15.1-4

Modify MEMOIZED-CUT-ROD to return not only the value but the actual solution, too.

15.1-5

The Fibonacci numbers are defined by recurrence (3.22). Give an $O(n)$-time dynamic-programming algorithm to compute the nth Fibonacci number. Draw the subproblem graph. How many vertices and edges are in the graph?

15.2   Matrix-chain multiplication

Our next example of dynamic programming is an algorithm that solves the problem of matrix-chain multiplication. We are given a sequence (chain) $\langle A_1, A_2, \ldots, A_n \rangle$ of n matrices to be multiplied, and we wish to compute the product

$$A_1 A_2 \cdots A_n . \tag{15.5}$$

We can evaluate the expression (15.5) using the standard algorithm for multiplying pairs of matrices as a subroutine once we have parenthesized it to resolve all ambiguities in how the matrices are multiplied together. Matrix multiplication is associative, and so all parenthesizations yield the same product. A product of matrices is ***fully parenthesized*** if it is either a single matrix or the product of two fully parenthesized matrix products, surrounded by parentheses. For example, if the chain of matrices is $\langle A_1, A_2, A_3, A_4 \rangle$, then we can fully parenthesize the product $A_1 A_2 A_3 A_4$ in five distinct ways:

$$(A_1(A_2(A_3 A_4)))\,,$$
$$(A_1((A_2 A_3)A_4))\,,$$
$$((A_1 A_2)(A_3 A_4))\,,$$
$$((A_1(A_2 A_3))A_4)\,,$$
$$(((A_1 A_2)A_3)A_4)\,.$$

How we parenthesize a chain of matrices can have a dramatic impact on the cost of evaluating the product. Consider first the cost of multiplying two matrices. The standard algorithm is given by the following pseudocode, which generalizes the SQUARE-MATRIX-MULTIPLY procedure from Section 4.2. The attributes *rows* and *columns* are the numbers of rows and columns in a matrix.

MATRIX-MULTIPLY(A, B)

```
1  if A.columns ≠ B.rows
2      error "incompatible dimensions"
3  else let C be a new A.rows × B.columns matrix
4      for i = 1 to A.rows
5          for j = 1 to B.columns
6              c_ij = 0
7              for k = 1 to A.columns
8                  c_ij = c_ij + a_ik · b_kj
9      return C
```

We can multiply two matrices A and B only if they are ***compatible***: the number of columns of A must equal the number of rows of B. If A is a $p \times q$ matrix and B is a $q \times r$ matrix, the resulting matrix C is a $p \times r$ matrix. The time to compute C is dominated by the number of scalar multiplications in line 8, which is pqr. In what follows, we shall express costs in terms of the number of scalar multiplications.

To illustrate the different costs incurred by different parenthesizations of a matrix product, consider the problem of a chain $\langle A_1, A_2, A_3 \rangle$ of three matrices. Suppose that the dimensions of the matrices are 10×100, 100×5, and 5×50, respectively. If we multiply according to the parenthesization $((A_1 A_2)A_3)$, we perform $10 \cdot 100 \cdot 5 = 5000$ scalar multiplications to compute the 10×5 matrix product $A_1 A_2$, plus another $10 \cdot 5 \cdot 50 = 2500$ scalar multiplications to multiply this matrix by A_3, for a total of 7500 scalar multiplications. If instead we multiply according to the parenthesization $(A_1(A_2 A_3))$, we perform $100 \cdot 5 \cdot 50 = 25{,}000$ scalar multiplications to compute the 100×50 matrix product $A_2 A_3$, plus another $10 \cdot 100 \cdot 50 = 50{,}000$ scalar multiplications to multiply A_1 by this matrix, for a total of 75,000 scalar multiplications. Thus, computing the product according to the first parenthesization is 10 times faster.

We state the ***matrix-chain multiplication problem*** as follows: given a chain $\langle A_1, A_2, \ldots, A_n \rangle$ of n matrices, where for $i = 1, 2, \ldots, n$, matrix A_i has dimension

$p_{i-1} \times p_i$, fully parenthesize the product $A_1 A_2 \cdots A_n$ in a way that minimizes the number of scalar multiplications.

Note that in the matrix-chain multiplication problem, we are not actually multiplying matrices. Our goal is only to determine an order for multiplying matrices that has the lowest cost. Typically, the time invested in determining this optimal order is more than paid for by the time saved later on when actually performing the matrix multiplications (such as performing only 7500 scalar multiplications instead of 75,000).

Counting the number of parenthesizations

Before solving the matrix-chain multiplication problem by dynamic programming, let us convince ourselves that exhaustively checking all possible parenthesizations does not yield an efficient algorithm. Denote the number of alternative parenthesizations of a sequence of n matrices by $P(n)$. When $n = 1$, we have just one matrix and therefore only one way to fully parenthesize the matrix product. When $n \geq 2$, a fully parenthesized matrix product is the product of two fully parenthesized matrix subproducts, and the split between the two subproducts may occur between the kth and $(k + 1)$st matrices for any $k = 1, 2, \ldots, n - 1$. Thus, we obtain the recurrence

$$P(n) = \begin{cases} 1 & \text{if } n = 1, \\ \displaystyle\sum_{k=1}^{n-1} P(k)P(n - k) & \text{if } n \geq 2. \end{cases} \tag{15.6}$$

Problem 12-4 asked you to show that the solution to a similar recurrence is the sequence of *Catalan numbers*, which grows as $\Omega(4^n / n^{3/2})$. A simpler exercise (see Exercise 15.2-3) is to show that the solution to the recurrence (15.6) is $\Omega(2^n)$. The number of solutions is thus exponential in n, and the brute-force method of exhaustive search makes for a poor strategy when determining how to optimally parenthesize a matrix chain.

Applying dynamic programming

We shall use the dynamic-programming method to determine how to optimally parenthesize a matrix chain. In so doing, we shall follow the four-step sequence that we stated at the beginning of this chapter:

1. Characterize the structure of an optimal solution.

2. Recursively define the value of an optimal solution.

3. Compute the value of an optimal solution.

4. Construct an optimal solution from computed information.

We shall go through these steps in order, demonstrating clearly how we apply each step to the problem.

Step 1: The structure of an optimal parenthesization

For our first step in the dynamic-programming paradigm, we find the optimal substructure and then use it to construct an optimal solution to the problem from optimal solutions to subproblems. In the matrix-chain multiplication problem, we can perform this step as follows. For convenience, let us adopt the notation $A_{i..j}$, where $i \leq j$, for the matrix that results from evaluating the product $A_i A_{i+1} \cdots A_j$. Observe that if the problem is nontrivial, i.e., $i < j$, then to parenthesize the product $A_i A_{i+1} \cdots A_j$, we must split the product between A_k and A_{k+1} for some integer k in the range $i \leq k < j$. That is, for some value of k, we first compute the matrices $A_{i..k}$ and $A_{k+1..j}$ and then multiply them together to produce the final product $A_{i..j}$. The cost of parenthesizing this way is the cost of computing the matrix $A_{i..k}$, plus the cost of computing $A_{k+1..j}$, plus the cost of multiplying them together.

The optimal substructure of this problem is as follows. Suppose that to optimally parenthesize $A_i A_{i+1} \cdots A_j$, we split the product between A_k and A_{k+1}. Then the way we parenthesize the "prefix" subchain $A_i A_{i+1} \cdots A_k$ within this optimal parenthesization of $A_i A_{i+1} \cdots A_j$ must be an optimal parenthesization of $A_i A_{i+1} \cdots A_k$. Why? If there were a less costly way to parenthesize $A_i A_{i+1} \cdots A_k$, then we could substitute that parenthesization in the optimal parenthesization of $A_i A_{i+1} \cdots A_j$ to produce another way to parenthesize $A_i A_{i+1} \cdots A_j$ whose cost was lower than the optimum: a contradiction. A similar observation holds for how we parenthesize the subchain $A_{k+1} A_{k+2} \cdots A_j$ in the optimal parenthesization of $A_i A_{i+1} \cdots A_j$: it must be an optimal parenthesization of $A_{k+1} A_{k+2} \cdots A_j$.

Now we use our optimal substructure to show that we can construct an optimal solution to the problem from optimal solutions to subproblems. We have seen that any solution to a nontrivial instance of the matrix-chain multiplication problem requires us to split the product, and that any optimal solution contains within it optimal solutions to subproblem instances. Thus, we can build an optimal solution to an instance of the matrix-chain multiplication problem by splitting the problem into two subproblems (optimally parenthesizing $A_i A_{i+1} \cdots A_k$ and $A_{k+1} A_{k+2} \cdots A_j$), finding optimal solutions to subproblem instances, and then combining these optimal subproblem solutions. We must ensure that when we search for the correct place to split the product, we have considered all possible places, so that we are sure of having examined the optimal one.

Step 2: A recursive solution

Next, we define the cost of an optimal solution recursively in terms of the optimal solutions to subproblems. For the matrix-chain multiplication problem, we pick as our subproblems the problems of determining the minimum cost of parenthesizing $A_i A_{i+1} \cdots A_j$ for $1 \leq i \leq j \leq n$. Let $m[i, j]$ be the minimum number of scalar multiplications needed to compute the matrix $A_{i..j}$; for the full problem, the lowest-cost way to compute $A_{1..n}$ would thus be $m[1, n]$.

We can define $m[i, j]$ recursively as follows. If $i = j$, the problem is trivial; the chain consists of just one matrix $A_{i..i} = A_i$, so that no scalar multiplications are necessary to compute the product. Thus, $m[i, i] = 0$ for $i = 1, 2, \ldots, n$. To compute $m[i, j]$ when $i < j$, we take advantage of the structure of an optimal solution from step 1. Let us assume that to optimally parenthesize, we split the product $A_i A_{i+1} \cdots A_j$ between A_k and A_{k+1}, where $i \leq k < j$. Then, $m[i, j]$ equals the minimum cost for computing the subproducts $A_{i..k}$ and $A_{k+1..j}$, plus the cost of multiplying these two matrices together. Recalling that each matrix A_i is $p_{i-1} \times p_i$, we see that computing the matrix product $A_{i..k} A_{k+1..j}$ takes $p_{i-1} p_k p_j$ scalar multiplications. Thus, we obtain

$$m[i, j] = m[i, k] + m[k + 1, j] + p_{i-1} p_k p_j .$$

This recursive equation assumes that we know the value of k, which we do not. There are only $j - i$ possible values for k, however, namely $k = i, i+1, \ldots, j-1$. Since the optimal parenthesization must use one of these values for k, we need only check them all to find the best. Thus, our recursive definition for the minimum cost of parenthesizing the product $A_i A_{i+1} \cdots A_j$ becomes

$$m[i, j] = \begin{cases} 0 & \text{if } i = j , \\ \min_{i \leq k < j} \{m[i, k] + m[k + 1, j] + p_{i-1} p_k p_j\} & \text{if } i < j . \end{cases} \quad (15.7)$$

The $m[i, j]$ values give the costs of optimal solutions to subproblems, but they do not provide all the information we need to construct an optimal solution. To help us do so, we define $s[i, j]$ to be a value of k at which we split the product $A_i A_{i+1} \cdots A_j$ in an optimal parenthesization. That is, $s[i, j]$ equals a value k such that $m[i, j] = m[i, k] + m[k + 1, j] + p_{i-1} p_k p_j$.

Step 3: Computing the optimal costs

At this point, we could easily write a recursive algorithm based on recurrence (15.7) to compute the minimum cost $m[1, n]$ for multiplying $A_1 A_2 \cdots A_n$. As we saw for the rod-cutting problem, and as we shall see in Section 15.3, this recursive algorithm takes exponential time, which is no better than the brute-force method of checking each way of parenthesizing the product.

Observe that we have relatively few distinct subproblems: one subproblem for each choice of i and j satisfying $1 \leq i \leq j \leq n$, or $\binom{n}{2} + n = \Theta(n^2)$ in all. A recursive algorithm may encounter each subproblem many times in different branches of its recursion tree. This property of overlapping subproblems is the second hallmark of when dynamic programming applies (the first hallmark being optimal substructure).

Instead of computing the solution to recurrence (15.7) recursively, we compute the optimal cost by using a tabular, bottom-up approach. (We present the corresponding top-down approach using memoization in Section 15.3.)

We shall implement the tabular, bottom-up method in the procedure MATRIX-CHAIN-ORDER, which appears below. This procedure assumes that matrix A_i has dimensions $p_{i-1} \times p_i$ for $i = 1, 2, \ldots, n$. Its input is a sequence $p = \langle p_0, p_1, \ldots, p_n \rangle$, where $p.length = n + 1$. The procedure uses an auxiliary table $m[1 .. n, 1 .. n]$ for storing the $m[i, j]$ costs and another auxiliary table $s[1 .. n-1, 2 .. n]$ that records which index of k achieved the optimal cost in computing $m[i, j]$. We shall use the table s to construct an optimal solution.

In order to implement the bottom-up approach, we must determine which entries of the table we refer to when computing $m[i, j]$. Equation (15.7) shows that the cost $m[i, j]$ of computing a matrix-chain product of $j - i + 1$ matrices depends only on the costs of computing matrix-chain products of fewer than $j - i + 1$ matrices. That is, for $k = i, i + 1, \ldots, j - 1$, the matrix $A_{i..k}$ is a product of $k - i + 1 < j - i + 1$ matrices and the matrix $A_{k+1..j}$ is a product of $j - k < j - i + 1$ matrices. Thus, the algorithm should fill in the table m in a manner that corresponds to solving the parenthesization problem on matrix chains of increasing length. For the subproblem of optimally parenthesizing the chain $A_i A_{i+1} \cdots A_j$, we consider the subproblem size to be the length $j - i + 1$ of the chain.

MATRIX-CHAIN-ORDER(p)

```
 1   n = p.length − 1
 2   let m[1 .. n, 1 .. n] and s[1 .. n − 1, 2 .. n] be new tables
 3   for i = 1 to n
 4       m[i, i] = 0
 5   for l = 2 to n                  // l is the chain length
 6       for i = 1 to n − l + 1
 7           j = i + l − 1
 8           m[i, j] = ∞
 9           for k = i to j − 1
10               q = m[i, k] + m[k + 1, j] + p_{i−1} p_k p_j
11               if q < m[i, j]
12                   m[i, j] = q
13                   s[i, j] = k
14   return m and s
```

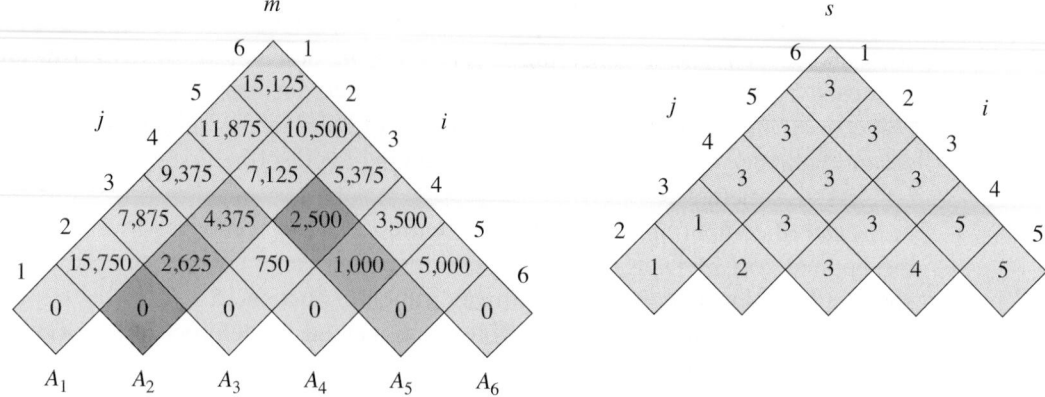

Figure 15.5 The m and s tables computed by MATRIX-CHAIN-ORDER for $n = 6$ and the following matrix dimensions:

matrix	A_1	A_2	A_3	A_4	A_5	A_6
dimension	30×35	35×15	15×5	5×10	10×20	20×25

The tables are rotated so that the main diagonal runs horizontally. The m table uses only the main diagonal and upper triangle, and the s table uses only the upper triangle. The minimum number of scalar multiplications to multiply the 6 matrices is $m[1, 6] = 15{,}125$. Of the darker entries, the pairs that have the same shading are taken together in line 10 when computing

$$m[2, 5] = \min \begin{cases} m[2, 2] + m[3, 5] + p_1 p_2 p_5 = 0 + 2500 + 35 \cdot 15 \cdot 20 = 13{,}000 , \\ m[2, 3] + m[4, 5] + p_1 p_3 p_5 = 2625 + 1000 + 35 \cdot 5 \cdot 20 = 7125 , \\ m[2, 4] + m[5, 5] + p_1 p_4 p_5 = 4375 + 0 + 35 \cdot 10 \cdot 20 = 11{,}375 \end{cases}$$
$$= 7125 .$$

The algorithm first computes $m[i, i] = 0$ for $i = 1, 2, \ldots, n$ (the minimum costs for chains of length 1) in lines 3–4. It then uses recurrence (15.7) to compute $m[i, i + 1]$ for $i = 1, 2, \ldots, n - 1$ (the minimum costs for chains of length $l = 2$) during the first execution of the **for** loop in lines 5–13. The second time through the loop, it computes $m[i, i+2]$ for $i = 1, 2, \ldots, n-2$ (the minimum costs for chains of length $l = 3$), and so forth. At each step, the $m[i, j]$ cost computed in lines 10–13 depends only on table entries $m[i, k]$ and $m[k + 1, j]$ already computed.

Figure 15.5 illustrates this procedure on a chain of $n = 6$ matrices. Since we have defined $m[i, j]$ only for $i \leq j$, only the portion of the table m on or above the main diagonal is used. The figure shows the table rotated to make the main diagonal run horizontally. The matrix chain is listed along the bottom. Using this layout, we can find the minimum cost $m[i, j]$ for multiplying a subchain $A_i A_{i+1} \cdots A_j$ of matrices at the intersection of lines running northeast from A_i and northwest

from A_j. Each horizontal row in the table contains the entries for matrix chains of the same length. MATRIX-CHAIN-ORDER computes the rows from bottom to top and from left to right within each row. It computes each entry $m[i, j]$ using the products $p_{i-1} p_k p_j$ for $k = i, i + 1, \ldots, j - 1$ and all entries southwest and southeast from $m[i, j]$.

A simple inspection of the nested loop structure of MATRIX-CHAIN-ORDER yields a running time of $O(n^3)$ for the algorithm. The loops are nested three deep, and each loop index (l, i, and k) takes on at most $n - 1$ values. Exercise 15.2-5 asks you to show that the running time of this algorithm is in fact also $\Omega(n^3)$. The algorithm requires $\Theta(n^2)$ space to store the m and s tables. Thus, MATRIX-CHAIN-ORDER is much more efficient than the exponential-time method of enumerating all possible parenthesizations and checking each one.

Step 4: Constructing an optimal solution

Although MATRIX-CHAIN-ORDER determines the optimal number of scalar multiplications needed to compute a matrix-chain product, it does not directly show how to multiply the matrices. The table $s[1 .. n - 1, 2 .. n]$ gives us the information we need to do so. Each entry $s[i, j]$ records a value of k such that an optimal parenthesization of $A_i A_{i+1} \cdots A_j$ splits the product between A_k and A_{k+1}. Thus, we know that the final matrix multiplication in computing $A_{1..n}$ optimally is $A_{1..s[1,n]} A_{s[1,n]+1..n}$. We can determine the earlier matrix multiplications recursively, since $s[1, s[1, n]]$ determines the last matrix multiplication when computing $A_{1..s[1,n]}$ and $s[s[1, n] + 1, n]$ determines the last matrix multiplication when computing $A_{s[1,n]+1..n}$. The following recursive procedure prints an optimal parenthesization of $\langle A_i, A_{i+1}, \ldots, A_j \rangle$, given the s table computed by MATRIX-CHAIN-ORDER and the indices i and j. The initial call PRINT-OPTIMAL-PARENS$(s, 1, n)$ prints an optimal parenthesization of $\langle A_1, A_2, \ldots, A_n \rangle$.

PRINT-OPTIMAL-PARENS(s, i, j)

```
1  if i == j
2      print "A"_i
3  else print "("
4      PRINT-OPTIMAL-PARENS(s, i, s[i, j])
5      PRINT-OPTIMAL-PARENS(s, s[i, j] + 1, j)
6      print ")"
```

In the example of Figure 15.5, the call PRINT-OPTIMAL-PARENS$(s, 1, 6)$ prints the parenthesization $((A_1(A_2 A_3))((A_4 A_5) A_6))$.

Exercises

15.2-1
Find an optimal parenthesization of a matrix-chain product whose sequence of dimensions is $\langle 5, 10, 3, 12, 5, 50, 6 \rangle$.

15.2-2
Give a recursive algorithm MATRIX-CHAIN-MULTIPLY(A, s, i, j) that actually performs the optimal matrix-chain multiplication, given the sequence of matrices $\langle A_1, A_2, \ldots, A_n \rangle$, the s table computed by MATRIX-CHAIN-ORDER, and the indices i and j. (The initial call would be MATRIX-CHAIN-MULTIPLY$(A, s, 1, n)$.)

15.2-3
Use the substitution method to show that the solution to the recurrence (15.6) is $\Omega(2^n)$.

15.2-4
Describe the subproblem graph for matrix-chain multiplication with an input chain of length n. How many vertices does it have? How many edges does it have, and which edges are they?

15.2-5
Let $R(i, j)$ be the number of times that table entry $m[i, j]$ is referenced while computing other table entries in a call of MATRIX-CHAIN-ORDER. Show that the total number of references for the entire table is

$$\sum_{i=1}^{n} \sum_{j=i}^{n} R(i, j) = \frac{n^3 - n}{3}.$$

(*Hint:* You may find equation (A.3) useful.)

15.2-6
Show that a full parenthesization of an n-element expression has exactly $n - 1$ pairs of parentheses.

15.3   Elements of dynamic programming

Although we have just worked through two examples of the dynamic-programming method, you might still be wondering just when the method applies. From an engineering perspective, when should we look for a dynamic-programming solution to a problem? In this section, we examine the two key ingredients that an opti-

mization problem must have in order for dynamic programming to apply: optimal substructure and overlapping subproblems. We also revisit and discuss more fully how memoization might help us take advantage of the overlapping-subproblems property in a top-down recursive approach.

Optimal substructure

The first step in solving an optimization problem by dynamic programming is to characterize the structure of an optimal solution. Recall that a problem exhibits *optimal substructure* if an optimal solution to the problem contains within it optimal solutions to subproblems. Whenever a problem exhibits optimal substructure, we have a good clue that dynamic programming might apply. (As Chapter 16 discusses, it also might mean that a greedy strategy applies, however.) In dynamic programming, we build an optimal solution to the problem from optimal solutions to subproblems. Consequently, we must take care to ensure that the range of subproblems we consider includes those used in an optimal solution.

We discovered optimal substructure in both of the problems we have examined in this chapter so far. In Section 15.1, we observed that the optimal way of cutting up a rod of length n (if we make any cuts at all) involves optimally cutting up the two pieces resulting from the first cut. In Section 15.2, we observed that an optimal parenthesization of $A_i A_{i+1} \cdots A_j$ that splits the product between A_k and A_{k+1} contains within it optimal solutions to the problems of parenthesizing $A_i A_{i+1} \cdots A_k$ and $A_{k+1} A_{k+2} \cdots A_j$.

You will find yourself following a common pattern in discovering optimal substructure:

1. You show that a solution to the problem consists of making a choice, such as choosing an initial cut in a rod or choosing an index at which to split the matrix chain. Making this choice leaves one or more subproblems to be solved.

2. You suppose that for a given problem, you are given the choice that leads to an optimal solution. You do not concern yourself yet with how to determine this choice. You just assume that it has been given to you.

3. Given this choice, you determine which subproblems ensue and how to best characterize the resulting space of subproblems.

4. You show that the solutions to the subproblems used within an optimal solution to the problem must themselves be optimal by using a "cut-and-paste" technique. You do so by supposing that each of the subproblem solutions is not optimal and then deriving a contradiction. In particular, by "cutting out" the nonoptimal solution to each subproblem and "pasting in" the optimal one, you show that you can get a better solution to the original problem, thus contradicting your supposition that you already had an optimal solution. If an optimal

solution gives rise to more than one subproblem, they are typically so similar that you can modify the cut-and-paste argument for one to apply to the others with little effort.

To characterize the space of subproblems, a good rule of thumb says to try to keep the space as simple as possible and then expand it as necessary. For example, the space of subproblems that we considered for the rod-cutting problem contained the problems of optimally cutting up a rod of length i for each size i. This subproblem space worked well, and we had no need to try a more general space of subproblems.

Conversely, suppose that we had tried to constrain our subproblem space for matrix-chain multiplication to matrix products of the form $A_1 A_2 \cdots A_j$. As before, an optimal parenthesization must split this product between A_k and A_{k+1} for some $1 \leq k < j$. Unless we could guarantee that k always equals $j - 1$, we would find that we had subproblems of the form $A_1 A_2 \cdots A_k$ and $A_{k+1} A_{k+2} \cdots A_j$, and that the latter subproblem is not of the form $A_1 A_2 \cdots A_j$. For this problem, we needed to allow our subproblems to vary at "both ends," that is, to allow both i and j to vary in the subproblem $A_i A_{i+1} \cdots A_j$.

Optimal substructure varies across problem domains in two ways:

1. how many subproblems an optimal solution to the original problem uses, and

2. how many choices we have in determining which subproblem(s) to use in an optimal solution.

In the rod-cutting problem, an optimal solution for cutting up a rod of size n uses just one subproblem (of size $n - i$), but we must consider n choices for i in order to determine which one yields an optimal solution. Matrix-chain multiplication for the subchain $A_i A_{i+1} \cdots A_j$ serves as an example with two subproblems and $j - i$ choices. For a given matrix A_k at which we split the product, we have two subproblems—parenthesizing $A_i A_{i+1} \cdots A_k$ and parenthesizing $A_{k+1} A_{k+2} \cdots A_j$—and we must solve *both* of them optimally. Once we determine the optimal solutions to subproblems, we choose from among $j - i$ candidates for the index k.

Informally, the running time of a dynamic-programming algorithm depends on the product of two factors: the number of subproblems overall and how many choices we look at for each subproblem. In rod cutting, we had $\Theta(n)$ subproblems overall, and at most n choices to examine for each, yielding an $O(n^2)$ running time. Matrix-chain multiplication had $\Theta(n^2)$ subproblems overall, and in each we had at most $n - 1$ choices, giving an $O(n^3)$ running time (actually, a $\Theta(n^3)$ running time, by Exercise 15.2-5).

Usually, the subproblem graph gives an alternative way to perform the same analysis. Each vertex corresponds to a subproblem, and the choices for a sub-

problem are the edges incident from that subproblem. Recall that in rod cutting, the subproblem graph had n vertices and at most n edges per vertex, yielding an $O(n^2)$ running time. For matrix-chain multiplication, if we were to draw the subproblem graph, it would have $\Theta(n^2)$ vertices and each vertex would have degree at most $n - 1$, giving a total of $O(n^3)$ vertices and edges.

Dynamic programming often uses optimal substructure in a bottom-up fashion. That is, we first find optimal solutions to subproblems and, having solved the subproblems, we find an optimal solution to the problem. Finding an optimal solution to the problem entails making a choice among subproblems as to which we will use in solving the problem. The cost of the problem solution is usually the subproblem costs plus a cost that is directly attributable to the choice itself. In rod cutting, for example, first we solved the subproblems of determining optimal ways to cut up rods of length i for $i = 0, 1, \ldots, n - 1$, and then we determined which such subproblem yielded an optimal solution for a rod of length n, using equation (15.2). The cost attributable to the choice itself is the term p_i in equation (15.2). In matrix-chain multiplication, we determined optimal parenthesizations of subchains of $A_i A_{i+1} \cdots A_j$, and then we chose the matrix A_k at which to split the product. The cost attributable to the choice itself is the term $p_{i-1} p_k p_j$.

In Chapter 16, we shall examine "greedy algorithms," which have many similarities to dynamic programming. In particular, problems to which greedy algorithms apply have optimal substructure. One major difference between greedy algorithms and dynamic programming is that instead of first finding optimal solutions to subproblems and then making an informed choice, greedy algorithms first make a "greedy" choice—the choice that looks best at the time—and then solve a resulting subproblem, without bothering to solve all possible related smaller subproblems. Surprisingly, in some cases this strategy works!

Subtleties

You should be careful not to assume that optimal substructure applies when it does not. Consider the following two problems in which we are given a directed graph $G = (V, E)$ and vertices $u, v \in V$.

Unweighted shortest path:[3] Find a path from u to v consisting of the fewest edges. Such a path must be simple, since removing a cycle from a path produces a path with fewer edges.

---

[3] We use the term "unweighted" to distinguish this problem from that of finding shortest paths with weighted edges, which we shall see in Chapters 24 and 25. We can use the breadth-first search technique of Chapter 22 to solve the unweighted problem.

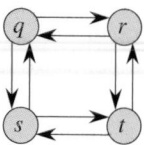

Figure 15.6 A directed graph showing that the problem of finding a longest simple path in an unweighted directed graph does not have optimal substructure. The path $q \to r \to t$ is a longest simple path from q to t, but the subpath $q \to r$ is not a longest simple path from q to r, nor is the subpath $r \to t$ a longest simple path from r to t.

Unweighted longest simple path: Find a simple path from u to v consisting of the most edges. We need to include the requirement of simplicity because otherwise we can traverse a cycle as many times as we like to create paths with an arbitrarily large number of edges.

The unweighted shortest-path problem exhibits optimal substructure, as follows. Suppose that $u \neq v$, so that the problem is nontrivial. Then, any path p from u to v must contain an intermediate vertex, say w. (Note that w may be u or v.) Thus, we can decompose the path $u \stackrel{p}{\rightsquigarrow} v$ into subpaths $u \stackrel{p_1}{\rightsquigarrow} w \stackrel{p_2}{\rightsquigarrow} v$. Clearly, the number of edges in p equals the number of edges in p_1 plus the number of edges in p_2. We claim that if p is an optimal (i.e., shortest) path from u to v, then p_1 must be a shortest path from u to w. Why? We use a "cut-and-paste" argument: if there were another path, say p_1', from u to w with fewer edges than p_1, then we could cut out p_1 and paste in p_1' to produce a path $u \stackrel{p_1'}{\rightsquigarrow} w \stackrel{p_2}{\rightsquigarrow} v$ with fewer edges than p, thus contradicting p's optimality. Symmetrically, p_2 must be a shortest path from w to v. Thus, we can find a shortest path from u to v by considering all intermediate vertices w, finding a shortest path from u to w and a shortest path from w to v, and choosing an intermediate vertex w that yields the overall shortest path. In Section 25.2, we use a variant of this observation of optimal substructure to find a shortest path between every pair of vertices on a weighted, directed graph.

You might be tempted to assume that the problem of finding an unweighted longest simple path exhibits optimal substructure as well. After all, if we decompose a longest simple path $u \stackrel{p}{\rightsquigarrow} v$ into subpaths $u \stackrel{p_1}{\rightsquigarrow} w \stackrel{p_2}{\rightsquigarrow} v$, then mustn't p_1 be a longest simple path from u to w, and mustn't p_2 be a longest simple path from w to v? The answer is no! Figure 15.6 supplies an example. Consider the path $q \to r \to t$, which is a longest simple path from q to t. Is $q \to r$ a longest simple path from q to r? No, for the path $q \to s \to t \to r$ is a simple path that is longer. Is $r \to t$ a longest simple path from r to t? No again, for the path $r \to q \to s \to t$ is a simple path that is longer.

This example shows that for longest simple paths, not only does the problem lack optimal substructure, but we cannot necessarily assemble a "legal" solution to the problem from solutions to subproblems. If we combine the longest simple paths $q \rightarrow s \rightarrow t \rightarrow r$ and $r \rightarrow q \rightarrow s \rightarrow t$, we get the path $q \rightarrow s \rightarrow t \rightarrow r \rightarrow q \rightarrow s \rightarrow t$, which is not simple. Indeed, the problem of finding an unweighted longest simple path does not appear to have any sort of optimal substructure. No efficient dynamic-programming algorithm for this problem has ever been found. In fact, this problem is NP-complete, which—as we shall see in Chapter 34—means that we are unlikely to find a way to solve it in polynomial time.

Why is the substructure of a longest simple path so different from that of a short-est path? Although a solution to a problem for both longest and shortest paths uses two subproblems, the subproblems in finding the longest simple path are not ***independent***, whereas for shortest paths they are. What do we mean by subproblems being independent? We mean that the solution to one subproblem does not affect the solution to another subproblem of the same problem. For the example of Fig-ure 15.6, we have the problem of finding a longest simple path from q to t with two subproblems: finding longest simple paths from q to r and from r to t. For the first of these subproblems, we choose the path $q \rightarrow s \rightarrow t \rightarrow r$, and so we have also used the vertices s and t. We can no longer use these vertices in the second sub-problem, since the combination of the two solutions to subproblems would yield a path that is not simple. If we cannot use vertex t in the second problem, then we cannot solve it at all, since t is required to be on the path that we find, and it is not the vertex at which we are "splicing" together the subproblem solutions (that vertex being r). Because we use vertices s and t in one subproblem solution, we cannot use them in the other subproblem solution. We must use at least one of them to solve the other subproblem, however, and we must use both of them to solve it optimally. Thus, we say that these subproblems are not independent. Looked at another way, using resources in solving one subproblem (those resources being vertices) renders them unavailable for the other subproblem.

Why, then, are the subproblems independent for finding a shortest path? The answer is that by nature, the subproblems do not share resources. We claim that if a vertex w is on a shortest path p from u to v, then we can splice together *any* shortest path $u \overset{p_1}{\rightsquigarrow} w$ and *any* shortest path $w \overset{p_2}{\rightsquigarrow} v$ to produce a shortest path from u to v. We are assured that, other than w, no vertex can appear in both paths p_1 and p_2. Why? Suppose that some vertex $x \neq w$ appears in both p_1 and p_2, so that we can decompose p_1 as $u \overset{p_{ux}}{\rightsquigarrow} x \rightsquigarrow w$ and p_2 as $w \rightsquigarrow x \overset{p_{xv}}{\rightsquigarrow} v$. By the optimal substructure of this problem, path p has as many edges as p_1 and p_2 together; let's say that p has e edges. Now let us construct a path $p' = u \overset{p_{ux}}{\rightsquigarrow} x \overset{p_{xv}}{\rightsquigarrow} v$ from u to v. Because we have excised the paths from x to w and from w to x, each of which contains at least one edge, path p' contains at most $e - 2$ edges, which contradicts

the assumption that p is a shortest path. Thus, we are assured that the subproblems for the shortest-path problem are independent.

Both problems examined in Sections 15.1 and 15.2 have independent subproblems. In matrix-chain multiplication, the subproblems are multiplying subchains $A_i A_{i+1} \cdots A_k$ and $A_{k+1} A_{k+2} \cdots A_j$. These subchains are disjoint, so that no matrix could possibly be included in both of them. In rod cutting, to determine the best way to cut up a rod of length n, we look at the best ways of cutting up rods of length i for $i = 0, 1, \ldots, n - 1$. Because an optimal solution to the length-n problem includes just one of these subproblem solutions (after we have cut off the first piece), independence of subproblems is not an issue.

Overlapping subproblems

The second ingredient that an optimization problem must have for dynamic programming to apply is that the space of subproblems must be "small" in the sense that a recursive algorithm for the problem solves the same subproblems over and over, rather than always generating new subproblems. Typically, the total number of distinct subproblems is a polynomial in the input size. When a recursive algorithm revisits the same problem repeatedly, we say that the optimization problem has ***overlapping subproblems***.[4] In contrast, a problem for which a divide-and-conquer approach is suitable usually generates brand-new problems at each step of the recursion. Dynamic-programming algorithms typically take advantage of overlapping subproblems by solving each subproblem once and then storing the solution in a table where it can be looked up when needed, using constant time per lookup.

In Section 15.1, we briefly examined how a recursive solution to rod cutting makes exponentially many calls to find solutions of smaller subproblems. Our dynamic-programming solution takes an exponential-time recursive algorithm down to quadratic time.

To illustrate the overlapping-subproblems property in greater detail, let us re-examine the matrix-chain multiplication problem. Referring back to Figure 15.5, observe that MATRIX-CHAIN-ORDER repeatedly looks up the solution to subproblems in lower rows when solving subproblems in higher rows. For example, it references entry $m[3, 4]$ four times: during the computations of $m[2, 4]$, $m[1, 4]$,

---

[4]It may seem strange that dynamic programming relies on subproblems being both independent and overlapping. Although these requirements may sound contradictory, they describe two different notions, rather than two points on the same axis. Two subproblems of the same problem are independent if they do not share resources. Two subproblems are overlapping if they are really the same subproblem that occurs as a subproblem of different problems.

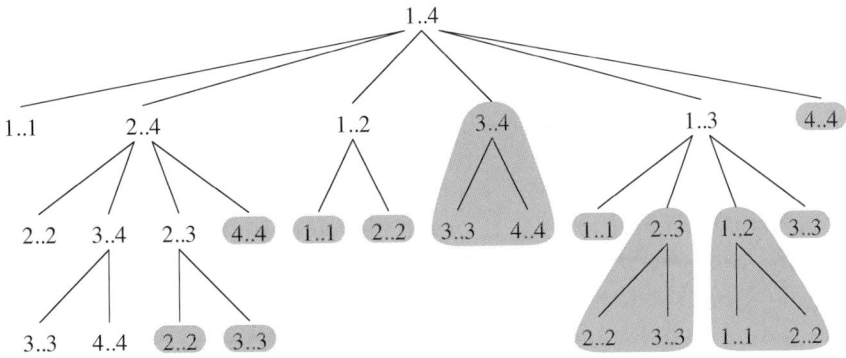

Figure 15.7 The recursion tree for the computation of RECURSIVE-MATRIX-CHAIN($p, 1, 4$). Each node contains the parameters i and j. The computations performed in a shaded subtree are replaced by a single table lookup in MEMOIZED-MATRIX-CHAIN.

$m[3, 5]$, and $m[3, 6]$. If we were to recompute $m[3, 4]$ each time, rather than just looking it up, the running time would increase dramatically. To see how, consider the following (inefficient) recursive procedure that determines $m[i, j]$, the minimum number of scalar multiplications needed to compute the matrix-chain product $A_{i..j} = A_i A_{i+1} \cdots A_j$. The procedure is based directly on the recurrence (15.7).

RECURSIVE-MATRIX-CHAIN(p, i, j)

```
1   if i == j
2        return 0
3   m[i, j] = ∞
4   for k = i to j − 1
5        q = RECURSIVE-MATRIX-CHAIN(p, i, k)
                + RECURSIVE-MATRIX-CHAIN(p, k + 1, j)
                + p_{i−1} p_k p_j
6        if q < m[i, j]
7             m[i, j] = q
8   return m[i, j]
```

Figure 15.7 shows the recursion tree produced by the call RECURSIVE-MATRIX-CHAIN($p, 1, 4$). Each node is labeled by the values of the parameters i and j. Observe that some pairs of values occur many times.

In fact, we can show that the time to compute $m[1, n]$ by this recursive procedure is at least exponential in n. Let $T(n)$ denote the time taken by RECURSIVE-MATRIX-CHAIN to compute an optimal parenthesization of a chain of n matrices. Because the execution of lines 1–2 and of lines 6–7 each take at least unit time, as

does the multiplication in line 5, inspection of the procedure yields the recurrence

$$T(1) \geq 1 ,$$

$$T(n) \geq 1 + \sum_{k=1}^{n-1} (T(k) + T(n-k) + 1) \qquad \text{for } n > 1 .$$

Noting that for $i = 1, 2, \ldots, n-1$, each term $T(i)$ appears once as $T(k)$ and once as $T(n-k)$, and collecting the $n-1$ 1s in the summation together with the 1 out front, we can rewrite the recurrence as

$$T(n) \geq 2 \sum_{i=1}^{n-1} T(i) + n . \tag{15.8}$$

We shall prove that $T(n) = \Omega(2^n)$ using the substitution method. Specifically, we shall show that $T(n) \geq 2^{n-1}$ for all $n \geq 1$. The basis is easy, since $T(1) \geq 1 = 2^0$. Inductively, for $n \geq 2$ we have

$$
\begin{aligned}
T(n) &\geq 2 \sum_{i=1}^{n-1} 2^{i-1} + n \\
&= 2 \sum_{i=0}^{n-2} 2^i + n \\
&= 2(2^{n-1} - 1) + n \quad \text{(by equation (A.5))} \\
&= 2^n - 2 + n \\
&\geq 2^{n-1} ,
\end{aligned}
$$

which completes the proof. Thus, the total amount of work performed by the call RECURSIVE-MATRIX-CHAIN($p, 1, n$) is at least exponential in n.

Compare this top-down, recursive algorithm (without memoization) with the bottom-up dynamic-programming algorithm. The latter is more efficient because it takes advantage of the overlapping-subproblems property. Matrix-chain multiplication has only $\Theta(n^2)$ distinct subproblems, and the dynamic-programming algorithm solves each exactly once. The recursive algorithm, on the other hand, must again solve each subproblem every time it reappears in the recursion tree. Whenever a recursion tree for the natural recursive solution to a problem contains the same subproblem repeatedly, and the total number of distinct subproblems is small, dynamic programming can improve efficiency, sometimes dramatically.

Reconstructing an optimal solution

As a practical matter, we often store which choice we made in each subproblem in a table so that we do not have to reconstruct this information from the costs that we stored.

For matrix-chain multiplication, the table $s[i, j]$ saves us a significant amount of work when reconstructing an optimal solution. Suppose that we did not maintain the $s[i, j]$ table, having filled in only the table $m[i, j]$ containing optimal subproblem costs. We choose from among $j - i$ possibilities when we determine which subproblems to use in an optimal solution to parenthesizing $A_i A_{i+1} \cdots A_j$, and $j - i$ is not a constant. Therefore, it would take $\Theta(j - i) = \omega(1)$ time to reconstruct which subproblems we chose for a solution to a given problem. By storing in $s[i, j]$ the index of the matrix at which we split the product $A_i A_{i+1} \cdots A_j$, we can reconstruct each choice in $O(1)$ time.

Memoization

As we saw for the rod-cutting problem, there is an alternative approach to dynamic programming that often offers the efficiency of the bottom-up dynamic-programming approach while maintaining a top-down strategy. The idea is to *memoize* the natural, but inefficient, recursive algorithm. As in the bottom-up approach, we maintain a table with subproblem solutions, but the control structure for filling in the table is more like the recursive algorithm.

A memoized recursive algorithm maintains an entry in a table for the solution to each subproblem. Each table entry initially contains a special value to indicate that the entry has yet to be filled in. When the subproblem is first encountered as the recursive algorithm unfolds, its solution is computed and then stored in the table. Each subsequent time that we encounter this subproblem, we simply look up the value stored in the table and return it.[5]

Here is a memoized version of RECURSIVE-MATRIX-CHAIN. Note where it resembles the memoized top-down method for the rod-cutting problem.

---

[5]This approach presupposes that we know the set of all possible subproblem parameters and that we have established the relationship between table positions and subproblems. Another, more general, approach is to memoize by using hashing with the subproblem parameters as keys.

MEMOIZED-MATRIX-CHAIN(p)

```
1   n = p.length - 1
2   let m[1..n, 1..n] be a new table
3   for i = 1 to n
4       for j = i to n
5           m[i, j] = ∞
6   return LOOKUP-CHAIN(m, p, 1, n)
```

LOOKUP-CHAIN(m, p, i, j)

```
1   if m[i, j] < ∞
2       return m[i, j]
3   if i == j
4       m[i, j] = 0
5   else for k = i to j - 1
6           q = LOOKUP-CHAIN(m, p, i, k)
                + LOOKUP-CHAIN(m, p, k + 1, j) + p_{i-1} p_k p_j
7           if q < m[i, j]
8               m[i, j] = q
9   return m[i, j]
```

The MEMOIZED-MATRIX-CHAIN procedure, like MATRIX-CHAIN-ORDER, maintains a table $m[1..n, 1..n]$ of computed values of $m[i, j]$, the minimum number of scalar multiplications needed to compute the matrix $A_{i..j}$. Each table entry initially contains the value ∞ to indicate that the entry has yet to be filled in. Upon calling LOOKUP-CHAIN(m, p, i, j), if line 1 finds that $m[i, j] < \infty$, then the procedure simply returns the previously computed cost $m[i, j]$ in line 2. Otherwise, the cost is computed as in RECURSIVE-MATRIX-CHAIN, stored in $m[i, j]$, and returned. Thus, LOOKUP-CHAIN(m, p, i, j) always returns the value of $m[i, j]$, but it computes it only upon the first call of LOOKUP-CHAIN with these specific values of i and j.

Figure 15.7 illustrates how MEMOIZED-MATRIX-CHAIN saves time compared with RECURSIVE-MATRIX-CHAIN. Shaded subtrees represent values that it looks up rather than recomputes.

Like the bottom-up dynamic-programming algorithm MATRIX-CHAIN-ORDER, the procedure MEMOIZED-MATRIX-CHAIN runs in $O(n^3)$ time. Line 5 of MEMOIZED-MATRIX-CHAIN executes $\Theta(n^2)$ times. We can categorize the calls of LOOKUP-CHAIN into two types:

1. calls in which $m[i, j] = \infty$, so that lines 3–9 execute, and

2. calls in which $m[i, j] < \infty$, so that LOOKUP-CHAIN simply returns in line 2.

There are $\Theta(n^2)$ calls of the first type, one per table entry. All calls of the second type are made as recursive calls by calls of the first type. Whenever a given call of LOOKUP-CHAIN makes recursive calls, it makes $O(n)$ of them. Therefore, there are $O(n^3)$ calls of the second type in all. Each call of the second type takes $O(1)$ time, and each call of the first type takes $O(n)$ time plus the time spent in its recursive calls. The total time, therefore, is $O(n^3)$. Memoization thus turns an $\Omega(2^n)$-time algorithm into an $O(n^3)$-time algorithm.

In summary, we can solve the matrix-chain multiplication problem by either a top-down, memoized dynamic-programming algorithm or a bottom-up dynamic-programming algorithm in $O(n^3)$ time. Both methods take advantage of the overlapping-subproblems property. There are only $\Theta(n^2)$ distinct subproblems in total, and either of these methods computes the solution to each subproblem only once. Without memoization, the natural recursive algorithm runs in exponential time, since solved subproblems are repeatedly solved.

In general practice, if all subproblems must be solved at least once, a bottom-up dynamic-programming algorithm usually outperforms the corresponding top-down memoized algorithm by a constant factor, because the bottom-up algorithm has no overhead for recursion and less overhead for maintaining the table. Moreover, for some problems we can exploit the regular pattern of table accesses in the dynamic-programming algorithm to reduce time or space requirements even further. Alternatively, if some subproblems in the subproblem space need not be solved at all, the memoized solution has the advantage of solving only those subproblems that are definitely required.

Exercises

15.3-1
Which is a more efficient way to determine the optimal number of multiplications in a matrix-chain multiplication problem: enumerating all the ways of parenthesizing the product and computing the number of multiplications for each, or running RECURSIVE-MATRIX-CHAIN? Justify your answer.

15.3-2
Draw the recursion tree for the MERGE-SORT procedure from Section 2.3.1 on an array of 16 elements. Explain why memoization fails to speed up a good divide-and-conquer algorithm such as MERGE-SORT.

15.3-3
Consider a variant of the matrix-chain multiplication problem in which the goal is to parenthesize the sequence of matrices so as to maximize, rather than minimize,

the number of scalar multiplications. Does this problem exhibit optimal substructure?

15.3-4

As stated, in dynamic programming we first solve the subproblems and then choose which of them to use in an optimal solution to the problem. Professor Capulet claims that we do not always need to solve all the subproblems in order to find an optimal solution. She suggests that we can find an optimal solution to the matrix-chain multiplication problem by always choosing the matrix A_k at which to split the subproduct $A_i A_{i+1} \cdots A_j$ (by selecting k to minimize the quantity $p_{i-1} p_k p_j$) *before* solving the subproblems. Find an instance of the matrix-chain multiplication problem for which this greedy approach yields a suboptimal solution.

15.3-5

Suppose that in the rod-cutting problem of Section 15.1, we also had limit l_i on the number of pieces of length i that we are allowed to produce, for $i = 1, 2, \ldots, n$. Show that the optimal-substructure property described in Section 15.1 no longer holds.

15.3-6

Imagine that you wish to exchange one currency for another. You realize that instead of directly exchanging one currency for another, you might be better off making a series of trades through other currencies, winding up with the currency you want. Suppose that you can trade n different currencies, numbered $1, 2, \ldots, n$, where you start with currency 1 and wish to wind up with currency n. You are given, for each pair of currencies i and j, an exchange rate r_{ij}, meaning that if you start with d units of currency i, you can trade for dr_{ij} units of currency j. A sequence of trades may entail a commission, which depends on the number of trades you make. Let c_k be the commission that you are charged when you make k trades. Show that, if $c_k = 0$ for all $k = 1, 2, \ldots, n$, then the problem of finding the best sequence of exchanges from currency 1 to currency n exhibits optimal substructure. Then show that if commissions c_k are arbitrary values, then the problem of finding the best sequence of exchanges from currency 1 to currency n does not necessarily exhibit optimal substructure.

15.4   Longest common subsequence

Biological applications often need to compare the DNA of two (or more) different organisms. A strand of DNA consists of a string of molecules called

bases, where the possible bases are adenine, guanine, cytosine, and thymine. Representing each of these bases by its initial letter, we can express a strand of DNA as a string over the finite set $\{A, C, G, T\}$. (See Appendix C for the definition of a string.)   For example, the DNA of one organism may be $S_1 = \text{ACCGGTCGAGTGCGCGGAAGCCGGCCGAA}$, and the DNA of another organism may be $S_2 = \text{GTCGTTCGGAATGCCGTTGCTCTGTAAA}$. One reason to compare two strands of DNA is to determine how "similar" the two strands are, as some measure of how closely related the two organisms are. We can, and do, define similarity in many different ways. For example, we can say that two DNA strands are similar if one is a substring of the other. (Chapter 32 explores algorithms to solve this problem.) In our example, neither S_1 nor S_2 is a substring of the other. Alternatively, we could say that two strands are similar if the number of changes needed to turn one into the other is small. (Problem 15-5 looks at this notion.) Yet another way to measure the similarity of strands S_1 and S_2 is by finding a third strand S_3 in which the bases in S_3 appear in each of S_1 and S_2; these bases must appear in the same order, but not necessarily consecutively. The longer the strand S_3 we can find, the more similar S_1 and S_2 are. In our example, the longest strand S_3 is $\text{GTCGTCGGAAGCCGGCCGAA}$.

We formalize this last notion of similarity as the longest-common-subsequence problem. A subsequence of a given sequence is just the given sequence with zero or more elements left out. Formally, given a sequence $X = \langle x_1, x_2, \ldots, x_m \rangle$, another sequence $Z = \langle z_1, z_2, \ldots, z_k \rangle$ is a ***subsequence*** of X if there exists a strictly increasing sequence $\langle i_1, i_2, \ldots, i_k \rangle$ of indices of X such that for all $j = 1, 2, \ldots, k$, we have $x_{i_j} = z_j$. For example, $Z = \langle B, C, D, B \rangle$ is a subsequence of $X = \langle A, B, C, B, D, A, B \rangle$ with corresponding index sequence $\langle 2, 3, 5, 7 \rangle$.

Given two sequences X and Y, we say that a sequence Z is a ***common subsequence*** of X and Y if Z is a subsequence of both X and Y. For example, if $X = \langle A, B, C, B, D, A, B \rangle$ and $Y = \langle B, D, C, A, B, A \rangle$, the sequence $\langle B, C, A \rangle$ is a common subsequence of both X and Y. The sequence $\langle B, C, A \rangle$ is not a *longest* common subsequence (LCS) of X and Y, however, since it has length 3 and the sequence $\langle B, C, B, A \rangle$, which is also common to both X and Y, has length 4. The sequence $\langle B, C, B, A \rangle$ is an LCS of X and Y, as is the sequence $\langle B, D, A, B \rangle$, since X and Y have no common subsequence of length 5 or greater.

In the ***longest-common-subsequence problem***, we are given two sequences $X = \langle x_1, x_2, \ldots, x_m \rangle$ and $Y = \langle y_1, y_2, \ldots, y_n \rangle$ and wish to find a maximum-length common subsequence of X and Y. This section shows how to efficiently solve the LCS problem using dynamic programming.

Step 1: Characterizing a longest common subsequence

In a brute-force approach to solving the LCS problem, we would enumerate all subsequences of X and check each subsequence to see whether it is also a subsequence of Y, keeping track of the longest subsequence we find. Each subsequence of X corresponds to a subset of the indices $\{1, 2, \dots, m\}$ of X. Because X has 2^m subsequences, this approach requires exponential time, making it impractical for long sequences.

The LCS problem has an optimal-substructure property, however, as the following theorem shows. As we shall see, the natural classes of subproblems correspond to pairs of "prefixes" of the two input sequences. To be precise, given a sequence $X = \langle x_1, x_2, \dots, x_m \rangle$, we define the ith **prefix** of X, for $i = 0, 1, \dots, m$, as $X_i = \langle x_1, x_2, \dots, x_i \rangle$. For example, if $X = \langle A, B, C, B, D, A, B \rangle$, then $X_4 = \langle A, B, C, B \rangle$ and X_0 is the empty sequence.

Theorem 15.1 (Optimal substructure of an LCS)
Let $X = \langle x_1, x_2, \dots, x_m \rangle$ and $Y = \langle y_1, y_2, \dots, y_n \rangle$ be sequences, and let $Z = \langle z_1, z_2, \dots, z_k \rangle$ be any LCS of X and Y.

1. If $x_m = y_n$, then $z_k = x_m = y_n$ and Z_{k-1} is an LCS of X_{m-1} and Y_{n-1}.

2. If $x_m \neq y_n$, then $z_k \neq x_m$ implies that Z is an LCS of X_{m-1} and Y.

3. If $x_m \neq y_n$, then $z_k \neq y_n$ implies that Z is an LCS of X and Y_{n-1}.

Proof   (1) If $z_k \neq x_m$, then we could append $x_m = y_n$ to Z to obtain a common subsequence of X and Y of length $k + 1$, contradicting the supposition that Z is a *longest* common subsequence of X and Y. Thus, we must have $z_k = x_m = y_n$. Now, the prefix Z_{k-1} is a length-$(k - 1)$ common subsequence of X_{m-1} and Y_{n-1}. We wish to show that it is an LCS. Suppose for the purpose of contradiction that there exists a common subsequence W of X_{m-1} and Y_{n-1} with length greater than $k - 1$. Then, appending $x_m = y_n$ to W produces a common subsequence of X and Y whose length is greater than k, which is a contradiction.

(2) If $z_k \neq x_m$, then Z is a common subsequence of X_{m-1} and Y. If there were a common subsequence W of X_{m-1} and Y with length greater than k, then W would also be a common subsequence of X_m and Y, contradicting the assumption that Z is an LCS of X and Y.

(3) The proof is symmetric to (2).   ∎

The way that Theorem 15.1 characterizes longest common subsequences tells us that an LCS of two sequences contains within it an LCS of prefixes of the two sequences. Thus, the LCS problem has an optimal-substructure property. A recur-

sive solution also has the overlapping-subproblems property, as we shall see in a moment.

Step 2: A recursive solution

Theorem 15.1 implies that we should examine either one or two subproblems when finding an LCS of $X = \langle x_1, x_2, \ldots, x_m \rangle$ and $Y = \langle y_1, y_2, \ldots, y_n \rangle$. If $x_m = y_n$, we must find an LCS of X_{m-1} and Y_{n-1}. Appending $x_m = y_n$ to this LCS yields an LCS of X and Y. If $x_m \neq y_n$, then we must solve two subproblems: finding an LCS of X_{m-1} and Y and finding an LCS of X and Y_{n-1}. Whichever of these two LCSs is longer is an LCS of X and Y. Because these cases exhaust all possibilities, we know that one of the optimal subproblem solutions must appear within an LCS of X and Y.

We can readily see the overlapping-subproblems property in the LCS problem. To find an LCS of X and Y, we may need to find the LCSs of X and Y_{n-1} and of X_{m-1} and Y. But each of these subproblems has the subsubproblem of finding an LCS of X_{m-1} and Y_{n-1}. Many other subproblems share subsubproblems.

As in the matrix-chain multiplication problem, our recursive solution to the LCS problem involves establishing a recurrence for the value of an optimal solution. Let us define $c[i, j]$ to be the length of an LCS of the sequences X_i and Y_j. If either $i = 0$ or $j = 0$, one of the sequences has length 0, and so the LCS has length 0. The optimal substructure of the LCS problem gives the recursive formula

$$c[i, j] = \begin{cases} 0 & \text{if } i = 0 \text{ or } j = 0, \\ c[i-1, j-1] + 1 & \text{if } i, j > 0 \text{ and } x_i = y_j, \\ \max(c[i, j-1], c[i-1, j]) & \text{if } i, j > 0 \text{ and } x_i \neq y_j. \end{cases} \quad (15.9)$$

Observe that in this recursive formulation, a condition in the problem restricts which subproblems we may consider. When $x_i = y_j$, we can and should consider the subproblem of finding an LCS of X_{i-1} and Y_{j-1}. Otherwise, we instead consider the two subproblems of finding an LCS of X_i and Y_{j-1} and of X_{i-1} and Y_j. In the previous dynamic-programming algorithms we have examined—for rod cutting and matrix-chain multiplication—we ruled out no subproblems due to conditions in the problem. Finding an LCS is not the only dynamic-programming algorithm that rules out subproblems based on conditions in the problem. For example, the edit-distance problem (see Problem 15-5) has this characteristic.

Step 3: Computing the length of an LCS

Based on equation (15.9), we could easily write an exponential-time recursive algorithm to compute the length of an LCS of two sequences. Since the LCS problem

has only $\Theta(mn)$ distinct subproblems, however, we can use dynamic programming to compute the solutions bottom up.

Procedure LCS-LENGTH takes two sequences $X = \langle x_1, x_2, \ldots, x_m \rangle$ and $Y = \langle y_1, y_2, \ldots, y_n \rangle$ as inputs. It stores the $c[i, j]$ values in a table $c[0 \ldotp\ldotp m, 0 \ldotp\ldotp n]$, and it computes the entries in ***row-major*** order. (That is, the procedure fills in the first row of c from left to right, then the second row, and so on.) The procedure also maintains the table $b[1 \ldotp\ldotp m, 1 \ldotp\ldotp n]$ to help us construct an optimal solution. Intuitively, $b[i, j]$ points to the table entry corresponding to the optimal subproblem solution chosen when computing $c[i, j]$. The procedure returns the b and c tables; $c[m, n]$ contains the length of an LCS of X and Y.

LCS-LENGTH(X, Y)

```
 1   m = X.length
 2   n = Y.length
 3   let b[1..m, 1..n] and c[0..m, 0..n] be new tables
 4   for i = 1 to m
 5       c[i, 0] = 0
 6   for j = 0 to n
 7       c[0, j] = 0
 8   for i = 1 to m
 9       for j = 1 to n
10           if x_i == y_j
11               c[i, j] = c[i − 1, j − 1] + 1
12               b[i, j] = "↖"
13           elseif c[i − 1, j] ≥ c[i, j − 1]
14               c[i, j] = c[i − 1, j]
15               b[i, j] = "↑"
16           else c[i, j] = c[i, j − 1]
17               b[i, j] = "←"
18   return c and b
```

Figure 15.8 shows the tables produced by LCS-LENGTH on the sequences $X = \langle A, B, C, B, D, A, B \rangle$ and $Y = \langle B, D, C, A, B, A \rangle$. The running time of the procedure is $\Theta(mn)$, since each table entry takes $\Theta(1)$ time to compute.

Step 4: Constructing an LCS

The b table returned by LCS-LENGTH enables us to quickly construct an LCS of $X = \langle x_1, x_2, \ldots, x_m \rangle$ and $Y = \langle y_1, y_2, \ldots, y_n \rangle$. We simply begin at $b[m, n]$ and trace through the table by following the arrows. Whenever we encounter a "↖" in entry $b[i, j]$, it implies that $x_i = y_j$ is an element of the LCS that LCS-LENGTH

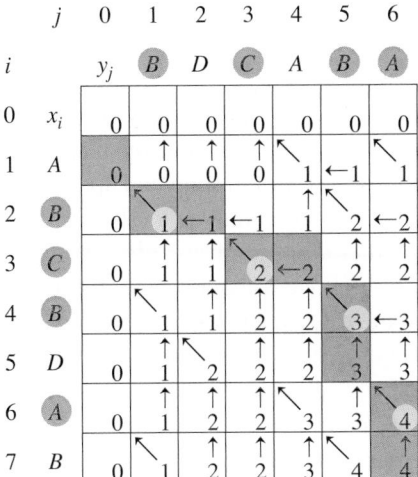

Figure 15.8 The c and b tables computed by LCS-LENGTH on the sequences $X = \langle A, B, C, B, D, A, B\rangle$ and $Y = \langle B, D, C, A, B, A\rangle$. The square in row i and column j contains the value of $c[i, j]$ and the appropriate arrow for the value of $b[i, j]$. The entry 4 in $c[7, 6]$ — the lower right-hand corner of the table — is the length of an LCS $\langle B, C, B, A\rangle$ of X and Y. For $i, j > 0$, entry $c[i, j]$ depends only on whether $x_i = y_j$ and the values in entries $c[i - 1, j]$, $c[i, j - 1]$, and $c[i - 1, j - 1]$, which are computed before $c[i, j]$. To reconstruct the elements of an LCS, follow the $b[i, j]$ arrows from the lower right-hand corner; the sequence is shaded. Each "$\nwarrow$" on the shaded sequence corresponds to an entry (highlighted) for which $x_i = y_j$ is a member of an LCS.

found. With this method, we encounter the elements of this LCS in reverse order. The following recursive procedure prints out an LCS of X and Y in the proper, forward order. The initial call is PRINT-LCS$(b, X, X.length, Y.length)$.

PRINT-LCS(b, X, i, j)

1 **if** $i == 0$ or $j == 0$
2   **return**
3 **if** $b[i, j] ==$ "$\nwarrow$"
4   PRINT-LCS$(b, X, i - 1, j - 1)$
5   print x_i
6 **elseif** $b[i, j] ==$ "$\uparrow$"
7   PRINT-LCS$(b, X, i - 1, j)$
8 **else** PRINT-LCS$(b, X, i, j - 1)$

For the b table in Figure 15.8, this procedure prints $BCBA$. The procedure takes time $O(m + n)$, since it decrements at least one of i and j in each recursive call.

Improving the code

Once you have developed an algorithm, you will often find that you can improve on the time or space it uses. Some changes can simplify the code and improve constant factors but otherwise yield no asymptotic improvement in performance. Others can yield substantial asymptotic savings in time and space.

In the LCS algorithm, for example, we can eliminate the b table altogether. Each $c[i, j]$ entry depends on only three other c table entries: $c[i-1, j-1], c[i-1, j]$, and $c[i, j-1]$. Given the value of $c[i, j]$, we can determine in $O(1)$ time which of these three values was used to compute $c[i, j]$, without inspecting table b. Thus, we can reconstruct an LCS in $O(m+n)$ time using a procedure similar to PRINT-LCS. (Exercise 15.4-2 asks you to give the pseudocode.) Although we save $\Theta(mn)$ space by this method, the auxiliary space requirement for computing an LCS does not asymptotically decrease, since we need $\Theta(mn)$ space for the c table anyway.

We can, however, reduce the asymptotic space requirements for LCS-LENGTH, since it needs only two rows of table c at a time: the row being computed and the previous row. (In fact, as Exercise 15.4-4 asks you to show, we can use only slightly more than the space for one row of c to compute the length of an LCS.) This improvement works if we need only the length of an LCS; if we need to reconstruct the elements of an LCS, the smaller table does not keep enough information to retrace our steps in $O(m + n)$ time.

Exercises

15.4-1
Determine an LCS of $\langle 1, 0, 0, 1, 0, 1, 0, 1 \rangle$ and $\langle 0, 1, 0, 1, 1, 0, 1, 1, 0 \rangle$.

15.4-2
Give pseudocode to reconstruct an LCS from the completed c table and the original sequences $X = \langle x_1, x_2, \ldots, x_m \rangle$ and $Y = \langle y_1, y_2, \ldots, y_n \rangle$ in $O(m + n)$ time, without using the b table.

15.4-3
Give a memoized version of LCS-LENGTH that runs in $O(mn)$ time.

15.4-4
Show how to compute the length of an LCS using only $2 \cdot \min(m, n)$ entries in the c table plus $O(1)$ additional space. Then show how to do the same thing, but using $\min(m, n)$ entries plus $O(1)$ additional space.

15.4-5

Give an $O(n^2)$-time algorithm to find the longest monotonically increasing subsequence of a sequence of n numbers.

15.4-6 ★

Give an $O(n \lg n)$-time algorithm to find the longest monotonically increasing subsequence of a sequence of n numbers. (*Hint:* Observe that the last element of a candidate subsequence of length i is at least as large as the last element of a candidate subsequence of length $i - 1$. Maintain candidate subsequences by linking them through the input sequence.)

15.5 Optimal binary search trees

Suppose that we are designing a program to translate text from English to French. For each occurrence of each English word in the text, we need to look up its French equivalent. We could perform these lookup operations by building a binary search tree with n English words as keys and their French equivalents as satellite data. Because we will search the tree for each individual word in the text, we want the total time spent searching to be as low as possible. We could ensure an $O(\lg n)$ search time per occurrence by using a red-black tree or any other balanced binary search tree. Words appear with different frequencies, however, and a frequently used word such as *the* may appear far from the root while a rarely used word such as *machicolation* appears near the root. Such an organization would slow down the translation, since the number of nodes visited when searching for a key in a binary search tree equals one plus the depth of the node containing the key. We want words that occur frequently in the text to be placed nearer the root.[6] Moreover, some words in the text might have no French translation,[7] and such words would not appear in the binary search tree at all. How do we organize a binary search tree so as to minimize the number of nodes visited in all searches, given that we know how often each word occurs?

What we need is known as an ***optimal binary search tree***. Formally, we are given a sequence $K = \langle k_1, k_2, \ldots, k_n \rangle$ of n distinct keys in sorted order (so that $k_1 < k_2 < \cdots < k_n$), and we wish to build a binary search tree from these keys. For each key k_i, we have a probability p_i that a search will be for k_i. Some searches may be for values not in K, and so we also have $n + 1$ "dummy keys"

---

[6]If the subject of the text is castle architecture, we might want *machicolation* to appear near the root.

[7]Yes, *machicolation* has a French counterpart: *mâchicoulis*.

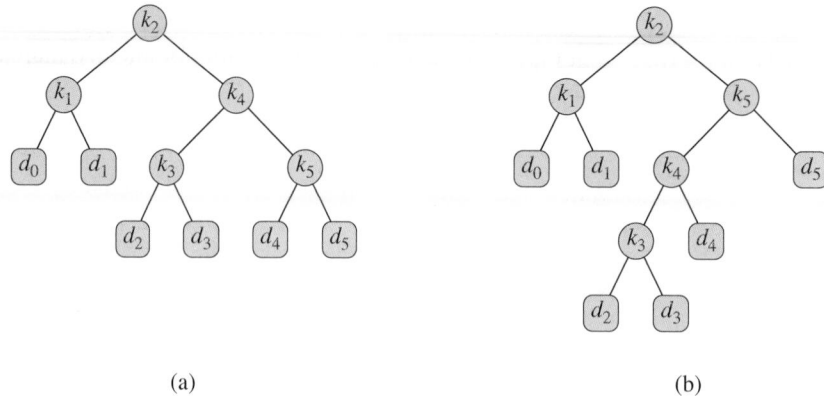

(a)   (b)

Figure 15.9   Two binary search trees for a set of $n = 5$ keys with the following probabilities:

i	0	1	2	3	4	5
p_i		0.15	0.10	0.05	0.10	0.20
q_i	0.05	0.10	0.05	0.05	0.05	0.10

(a) A binary search tree with expected search cost 2.80. **(b)** A binary search tree with expected search cost 2.75. This tree is optimal.

$d_0, d_1, d_2, \ldots, d_n$ representing values not in K. In particular, d_0 represents all values less than k_1, d_n represents all values greater than k_n, and for $i = 1, 2, \ldots, n-1$, the dummy key d_i represents all values between k_i and k_{i+1}. For each dummy key d_i, we have a probability q_i that a search will correspond to d_i. Figure 15.9 shows two binary search trees for a set of $n = 5$ keys. Each key k_i is an internal node, and each dummy key d_i is a leaf. Every search is either successful (finding some key k_i) or unsuccessful (finding some dummy key d_i), and so we have

$$\sum_{i=1}^{n} p_i + \sum_{i=0}^{n} q_i = 1 . \tag{15.10}$$

Because we have probabilities of searches for each key and each dummy key, we can determine the expected cost of a search in a given binary search tree T. Let us assume that the actual cost of a search equals the number of nodes examined, i.e., the depth of the node found by the search in T, plus 1. Then the expected cost of a search in T is

$$\text{E}\left[\text{search cost in } T\right] = \sum_{i=1}^{n} (\text{depth}_T(k_i) + 1) \cdot p_i + \sum_{i=0}^{n} (\text{depth}_T(d_i) + 1) \cdot q_i$$

$$= 1 + \sum_{i=1}^{n} \text{depth}_T(k_i) \cdot p_i + \sum_{i=0}^{n} \text{depth}_T(d_i) \cdot q_i , \tag{15.11}$$

where depth$_T$ denotes a node's depth in the tree T. The last equality follows from equation (15.10). In Figure 15.9(a), we can calculate the expected search cost node by node:

node	depth	probability	contribution
k_1	1	0.15	0.30
k_2	0	0.10	0.10
k_3	2	0.05	0.15
k_4	1	0.10	0.20
k_5	2	0.20	0.60
d_0	2	0.05	0.15
d_1	2	0.10	0.30
d_2	3	0.05	0.20
d_3	3	0.05	0.20
d_4	3	0.05	0.20
d_5	3	0.10	0.40
Total			2.80

For a given set of probabilities, we wish to construct a binary search tree whose expected search cost is smallest. We call such a tree an ***optimal binary search tree***. Figure 15.9(b) shows an optimal binary search tree for the probabilities given in the figure caption; its expected cost is 2.75. This example shows that an optimal binary search tree is not necessarily a tree whose overall height is smallest. Nor can we necessarily construct an optimal binary search tree by always putting the key with the greatest probability at the root. Here, key k_5 has the greatest search probability of any key, yet the root of the optimal binary search tree shown is k_2. (The lowest expected cost of any binary search tree with k_5 at the root is 2.85.)

As with matrix-chain multiplication, exhaustive checking of all possibilities fails to yield an efficient algorithm. We can label the nodes of any n-node binary tree with the keys $k_1, k_2, \ldots, k_n$ to construct a binary search tree, and then add in the dummy keys as leaves. In Problem 12-4, we saw that the number of binary trees with n nodes is $\Omega(4^n / n^{3/2})$, and so we would have to examine an exponential number of binary search trees in an exhaustive search. Not surprisingly, we shall solve this problem with dynamic programming.

Step 1: The structure of an optimal binary search tree

To characterize the optimal substructure of optimal binary search trees, we start with an observation about subtrees. Consider any subtree of a binary search tree. It must contain keys in a contiguous range $k_i, \ldots, k_j$, for some $1 \le i \le j \le n$. In addition, a subtree that contains keys $k_i, \ldots, k_j$ must also have as its leaves the dummy keys $d_{i-1}, \ldots, d_j$.

Now we can state the optimal substructure: if an optimal binary search tree T has a subtree T' containing keys $k_i, \ldots, k_j$, then this subtree T' must be optimal as

well for the subproblem with keys $k_i, \ldots, k_j$ and dummy keys $d_{i-1}, \ldots, d_j$. The usual cut-and-paste argument applies. If there were a subtree T'' whose expected cost is lower than that of T', then we could cut T' out of T and paste in T'', resulting in a binary search tree of lower expected cost than T, thus contradicting the optimality of T.

We need to use the optimal substructure to show that we can construct an optimal solution to the problem from optimal solutions to subproblems. Given keys $k_i, \ldots, k_j$, one of these keys, say k_r ($i \le r \le j$), is the root of an optimal subtree containing these keys. The left subtree of the root k_r contains the keys $k_i, \ldots, k_{r-1}$ (and dummy keys $d_{i-1}, \ldots, d_{r-1}$), and the right subtree contains the keys $k_{r+1}, \ldots, k_j$ (and dummy keys $d_r, \ldots, d_j$). As long as we examine all candidate roots k_r, where $i \le r \le j$, and we determine all optimal binary search trees containing $k_i, \ldots, k_{r-1}$ and those containing $k_{r+1}, \ldots, k_j$, we are guaranteed that we will find an optimal binary search tree.

There is one detail worth noting about "empty" subtrees. Suppose that in a subtree with keys $k_i, \ldots, k_j$, we select k_i as the root. By the above argument, k_i's left subtree contains the keys $k_i, \ldots, k_{i-1}$. We interpret this sequence as containing no keys. Bear in mind, however, that subtrees also contain dummy keys. We adopt the convention that a subtree containing keys $k_i, \ldots, k_{i-1}$ has no actual keys but does contain the single dummy key d_{i-1}. Symmetrically, if we select k_j as the root, then k_j's right subtree contains the keys $k_{j+1}, \ldots, k_j$; this right subtree contains no actual keys, but it does contain the dummy key d_j.

Step 2: A recursive solution

We are ready to define the value of an optimal solution recursively. We pick our subproblem domain as finding an optimal binary search tree containing the keys $k_i, \ldots, k_j$, where $i \ge 1$, $j \le n$, and $j \ge i - 1$. (When $j = i - 1$, there are no actual keys; we have just the dummy key d_{i-1}.) Let us define $e[i, j]$ as the expected cost of searching an optimal binary search tree containing the keys $k_i, \ldots, k_j$. Ultimately, we wish to compute $e[1, n]$.

The easy case occurs when $j = i - 1$. Then we have just the dummy key d_{i-1}. The expected search cost is $e[i, i - 1] = q_{i-1}$.

When $j \ge i$, we need to select a root k_r from among $k_i, \ldots, k_j$ and then make an optimal binary search tree with keys $k_i, \ldots, k_{r-1}$ as its left subtree and an optimal binary search tree with keys $k_{r+1}, \ldots, k_j$ as its right subtree. What happens to the expected search cost of a subtree when it becomes a subtree of a node? The depth of each node in the subtree increases by 1. By equation (15.11), the expected search cost of this subtree increases by the sum of all the probabilities in the subtree. For a subtree with keys $k_i, \ldots, k_j$, let us denote this sum of probabilities as

$$w(i, j) = \sum_{l=i}^{j} p_l + \sum_{l=i-1}^{j} q_l \, . \tag{15.12}$$

Thus, if k_r is the root of an optimal subtree containing keys $k_i, \ldots, k_j$, we have

$$e[i, j] = p_r + (e[i, r-1] + w(i, r-1)) + (e[r+1, j] + w(r+1, j)) \, .$$

Noting that

$$w(i, j) = w(i, r-1) + p_r + w(r+1, j) \, ,$$

we rewrite $e[i, j]$ as

$$e[i, j] = e[i, r-1] + e[r+1, j] + w(i, j) \, . \tag{15.13}$$

The recursive equation (15.13) assumes that we know which node k_r to use as the root. We choose the root that gives the lowest expected search cost, giving us our final recursive formulation:

$$e[i, j] = \begin{cases} q_{i-1} & \text{if } j = i - 1 \, , \\ \min_{i \le r \le j} \{e[i, r-1] + e[r+1, j] + w(i, j)\} & \text{if } i \le j \, . \end{cases} \tag{15.14}$$

The $e[i, j]$ values give the expected search costs in optimal binary search trees. To help us keep track of the structure of optimal binary search trees, we define $root[i, j]$, for $1 \le i \le j \le n$, to be the index r for which k_r is the root of an optimal binary search tree containing keys $k_i, \ldots, k_j$. Although we will see how to compute the values of $root[i, j]$, we leave the construction of an optimal binary search tree from these values as Exercise 15.5-1.

Step 3: Computing the expected search cost of an optimal binary search tree

At this point, you may have noticed some similarities between our characterizations of optimal binary search trees and matrix-chain multiplication. For both problem domains, our subproblems consist of contiguous index subranges. A direct, recursive implementation of equation (15.14) would be as inefficient as a direct, recursive matrix-chain multiplication algorithm. Instead, we store the $e[i, j]$ values in a table $e[1 \mathbin{..} n+1, 0 \mathbin{..} n]$. The first index needs to run to $n+1$ rather than n because in order to have a subtree containing only the dummy key d_n, we need to compute and store $e[n+1, n]$. The second index needs to start from 0 because in order to have a subtree containing only the dummy key d_0, we need to compute and store $e[1, 0]$. We use only the entries $e[i, j]$ for which $j \ge i - 1$. We also use a table $root[i, j]$, for recording the root of the subtree containing keys $k_i, \ldots, k_j$. This table uses only the entries for which $1 \le i \le j \le n$.

We will need one other table for efficiency. Rather than compute the value of $w(i, j)$ from scratch every time we are computing $e[i, j]$—which would take

$\Theta(j - i)$ additions—we store these values in a table $w[1 \mathbin{..} n + 1, 0 \mathbin{..} n]$. For the base case, we compute $w[i, i - 1] = q_{i-1}$ for $1 \leq i \leq n + 1$. For $j \geq i$, we compute

$$w[i, j] = w[i, j - 1] + p_j + q_j \,. \tag{15.15}$$

Thus, we can compute the $\Theta(n^2)$ values of $w[i, j]$ in $\Theta(1)$ time each.

The pseudocode that follows takes as inputs the probabilities $p_1, \ldots, p_n$ and $q_0, \ldots, q_n$ and the size n, and it returns the tables e and $root$.

OPTIMAL-BST(p, q, n)

```
 1   let e[1..n + 1, 0..n], w[1..n + 1, 0..n],
            and root[1..n, 1..n] be new tables
 2   for i = 1 to n + 1
 3       e[i, i − 1] = q_{i−1}
 4       w[i, i − 1] = q_{i−1}
 5   for l = 1 to n
 6       for i = 1 to n − l + 1
 7           j = i + l − 1
 8           e[i, j] = ∞
 9           w[i, j] = w[i, j − 1] + p_j + q_j
10           for r = i to j
11               t = e[i, r − 1] + e[r + 1, j] + w[i, j]
12               if t < e[i, j]
13                   e[i, j] = t
14                   root[i, j] = r
15   return e and root
```

From the description above and the similarity to the MATRIX-CHAIN-ORDER procedure in Section 15.2, you should find the operation of this procedure to be fairly straightforward. The **for** loop of lines 2–4 initializes the values of $e[i, i - 1]$ and $w[i, i - 1]$. The **for** loop of lines 5–14 then uses the recurrences (15.14) and (15.15) to compute $e[i, j]$ and $w[i, j]$ for all $1 \leq i \leq j \leq n$. In the first iteration, when $l = 1$, the loop computes $e[i, i]$ and $w[i, i]$ for $i = 1, 2, \ldots, n$. The second iteration, with $l = 2$, computes $e[i, i+1]$ and $w[i, i+1]$ for $i = 1, 2, \ldots, n-1$, and so forth. The innermost **for** loop, in lines 10–14, tries each candidate index r to determine which key k_r to use as the root of an optimal binary search tree containing keys $k_i, \ldots, k_j$. This **for** loop saves the current value of the index r in $root[i, j]$ whenever it finds a better key to use as the root.

Figure 15.10 shows the tables $e[i, j]$, $w[i, j]$, and $root[i, j]$ computed by the procedure OPTIMAL-BST on the key distribution shown in Figure 15.9. As in the matrix-chain multiplication example of Figure 15.5, the tables are rotated to make

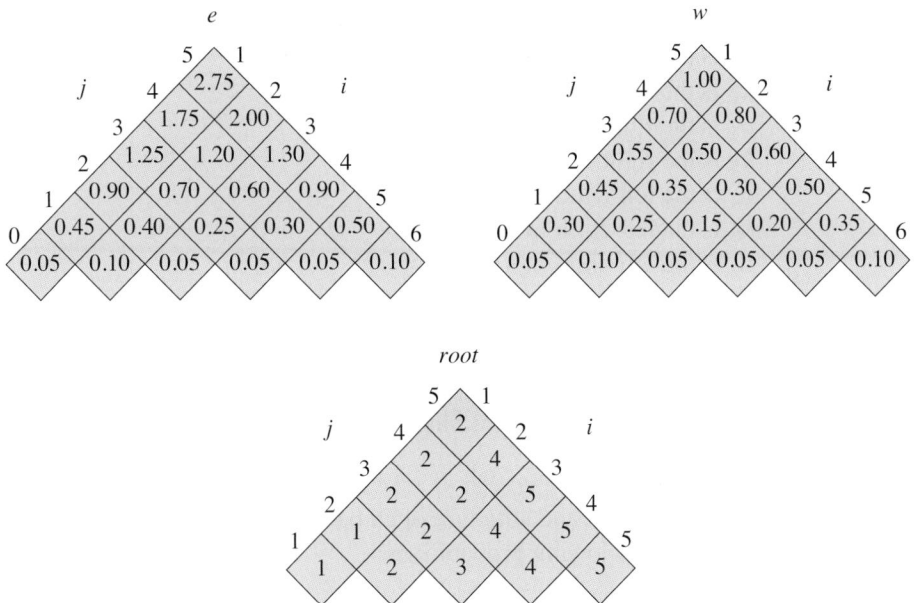

Figure 15.10   The tables $e[i, j]$, $w[i, j]$, and *root*$[i, j]$ computed by OPTIMAL-BST on the key distribution shown in Figure 15.9. The tables are rotated so that the diagonals run horizontally.

the diagonals run horizontally. OPTIMAL-BST computes the rows from bottom to top and from left to right within each row.

The OPTIMAL-BST procedure takes $\Theta(n^3)$ time, just like MATRIX-CHAIN-ORDER. We can easily see that its running time is $O(n^3)$, since its **for** loops are nested three deep and each loop index takes on at most n values. The loop indices in OPTIMAL-BST do not have exactly the same bounds as those in MATRIX-CHAIN-ORDER, but they are within at most 1 in all directions. Thus, like MATRIX-CHAIN-ORDER, the OPTIMAL-BST procedure takes $\Omega(n^3)$ time.

Exercises

15.5-1
Write pseudocode for the procedure CONSTRUCT-OPTIMAL-BST(*root*) which, given the table *root*, outputs the structure of an optimal binary search tree. For the example in Figure 15.10, your procedure should print out the structure

k_2 is the root
k_1 is the left child of k_2
d_0 is the left child of k_1
d_1 is the right child of k_1
k_5 is the right child of k_2
k_4 is the left child of k_5
k_3 is the left child of k_4
d_2 is the left child of k_3
d_3 is the right child of k_3
d_4 is the right child of k_4
d_5 is the right child of k_5

corresponding to the optimal binary search tree shown in Figure 15.9(b).

15.5-2

Determine the cost and structure of an optimal binary search tree for a set of $n = 7$ keys with the following probabilities:

i	0	1	2	3	4	5	6	7
p_i		0.04	0.06	0.08	0.02	0.10	0.12	0.14
q_i	0.06	0.06	0.06	0.06	0.05	0.05	0.05	0.05

15.5-3

Suppose that instead of maintaining the table $w[i, j]$, we computed the value of $w(i, j)$ directly from equation (15.12) in line 9 of OPTIMAL-BST and used this computed value in line 11. How would this change affect the asymptotic running time of OPTIMAL-BST?

15.5-4 ★

Knuth [212] has shown that there are always roots of optimal subtrees such that $root[i, j - 1] \le root[i, j] \le root[i + 1, j]$ for all $1 \le i < j \le n$. Use this fact to modify the OPTIMAL-BST procedure to run in $\Theta(n^2)$ time.

Problems

15-1   *Longest simple path in a directed acyclic graph*

Suppose that we are given a directed acyclic graph $G = (V, E)$ with real-valued edge weights and two distinguished vertices s and t. Describe a dynamic-programming approach for finding a longest weighted simple path from s to t. What does the subproblem graph look like? What is the efficiency of your algorithm?

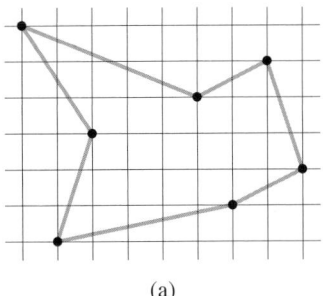 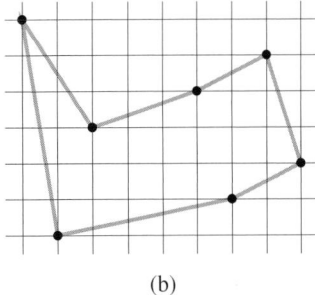

(a) (b)

Figure 15.11 Seven points in the plane, shown on a unit grid. **(a)** The shortest closed tour, with length approximately 24.89. This tour is not bitonic. **(b)** The shortest bitonic tour for the same set of points. Its length is approximately 25.58.

15-2 *Longest palindrome subsequence*

A *palindrome* is a nonempty string over some alphabet that reads the same forward and backward. Examples of palindromes are all strings of length 1, `civic`, `racecar`, and `aibohphobia` (fear of palindromes).

Give an efficient algorithm to find the longest palindrome that is a subsequence of a given input string. For example, given the input `character`, your algorithm should return `carac`. What is the running time of your algorithm?

15-3 *Bitonic euclidean traveling-salesman problem*

In the *euclidean traveling-salesman problem*, we are given a set of n points in the plane, and we wish to find the shortest closed tour that connects all n points. Figure 15.11(a) shows the solution to a 7-point problem. The general problem is NP-hard, and its solution is therefore believed to require more than polynomial time (see Chapter 34).

J. L. Bentley has suggested that we simplify the problem by restricting our attention to *bitonic tours*, that is, tours that start at the leftmost point, go strictly rightward to the rightmost point, and then go strictly leftward back to the starting point. Figure 15.11(b) shows the shortest bitonic tour of the same 7 points. In this case, a polynomial-time algorithm is possible.

Describe an $O(n^2)$-time algorithm for determining an optimal bitonic tour. You may assume that no two points have the same x-coordinate and that all operations on real numbers take unit time. (*Hint:* Scan left to right, maintaining optimal possibilities for the two parts of the tour.)

15-4 *Printing neatly*

Consider the problem of neatly printing a paragraph with a monospaced font (all characters having the same width) on a printer. The input text is a sequence of n

words of lengths $l_1, l_2, \ldots, l_n$, measured in characters. We want to print this paragraph neatly on a number of lines that hold a maximum of M characters each. Our criterion of "neatness" is as follows. If a given line contains words i through j, where $i \leq j$, and we leave exactly one space between words, the number of extra space characters at the end of the line is $M - j + i - \sum_{k=i}^{j} l_k$, which must be nonnegative so that the words fit on the line. We wish to minimize the sum, over all lines except the last, of the cubes of the numbers of extra space characters at the ends of lines. Give a dynamic-programming algorithm to print a paragraph of n words neatly on a printer. Analyze the running time and space requirements of your algorithm.

15-5   *Edit distance*

In order to transform one source string of text $x[1 .. m]$ to a target string $y[1 .. n]$, we can perform various transformation operations. Our goal is, given x and y, to produce a series of transformations that change x to y. We use an array z—assumed to be large enough to hold all the characters it will need—to hold the intermediate results. Initially, z is empty, and at termination, we should have $z[j] = y[j]$ for $j = 1, 2, \ldots, n$. We maintain current indices i into x and j into z, and the operations are allowed to alter z and these indices. Initially, $i = j = 1$. We are required to examine every character in x during the transformation, which means that at the end of the sequence of transformation operations, we must have $i = m + 1$.

We may choose from among six transformation operations:

Copy a character from x to z by setting $z[j] = x[i]$ and then incrementing both i and j. This operation examines $x[i]$.

Replace a character from x by another character c, by setting $z[j] = c$, and then incrementing both i and j. This operation examines $x[i]$.

Delete a character from x by incrementing i but leaving j alone. This operation examines $x[i]$.

Insert the character c into z by setting $z[j] = c$ and then incrementing j, but leaving i alone. This operation examines no characters of x.

Twiddle (i.e., exchange) the next two characters by copying them from x to z but in the opposite order; we do so by setting $z[j] = x[i + 1]$ and $z[j + 1] = x[i]$ and then setting $i = i + 2$ and $j = j + 2$. This operation examines $x[i]$ and $x[i + 1]$.

Kill the remainder of x by setting $i = m + 1$. This operation examines all characters in x that have not yet been examined. This operation, if performed, must be the final operation.

As an example, one way to transform the source string `algorithm` to the target string `altruistic` is to use the following sequence of operations, where the underlined characters are $x[i]$ and $z[j]$ after the operation:

Operation	x	z
initial strings	<u>a</u>lgorithm	_
copy	a<u>l</u>gorithm	a_
copy	al<u>g</u>orithm	al_
replace by t	alg<u>o</u>rithm	alt_
delete	algo<u>r</u>ithm	alt_
copy	algor<u>i</u>thm	altr_
insert u	algor<u>i</u>thm	altru_
insert i	algor<u>i</u>thm	altrui_
insert s	algor<u>i</u>thm	altruis_
twiddle	algorit<u>hm</u>	altruisti_
insert c	algorit<u>hm</u>	altruistic_
kill	algorithm<u> </u>	altruistic_

Note that there are several other sequences of transformation operations that transform `algorithm` to `altruistic`.

Each of the transformation operations has an associated cost. The cost of an operation depends on the specific application, but we assume that each operation's cost is a constant that is known to us. We also assume that the individual costs of the copy and replace operations are less than the combined costs of the delete and insert operations; otherwise, the copy and replace operations would not be used. The cost of a given sequence of transformation operations is the sum of the costs of the individual operations in the sequence. For the sequence above, the cost of transforming `algorithm` to `altruistic` is

$$(3 \cdot \text{cost(copy)}) + \text{cost(replace)} + \text{cost(delete)} + (4 \cdot \text{cost(insert)})$$
$$+ \text{cost(twiddle)} + \text{cost(kill)} \ .$$

a. Given two sequences $x[1 .. m]$ and $y[1 .. n]$ and set of transformation-operation costs, the ***edit distance*** from x to y is the cost of the least expensive operation sequence that transforms x to y. Describe a dynamic-programming algorithm that finds the edit distance from $x[1 .. m]$ to $y[1 .. n]$ and prints an optimal operation sequence. Analyze the running time and space requirements of your algorithm.

The edit-distance problem generalizes the problem of aligning two DNA sequences (see, for example, Setubal and Meidanis [310, Section 3.2]). There are several methods for measuring the similarity of two DNA sequences by aligning them. One such method to align two sequences x and y consists of inserting spaces at

arbitrary locations in the two sequences (including at either end) so that the resulting sequences x' and y' have the same length but do not have a space in the same position (i.e., for no position j are both $x'[j]$ and $y'[j]$ a space). Then we assign a "score" to each position. Position j receives a score as follows:

- $+1$ if $x'[j] = y'[j]$ and neither is a space,
- -1 if $x'[j] \neq y'[j]$ and neither is a space,
- -2 if either $x'[j]$ or $y'[j]$ is a space.

The score for the alignment is the sum of the scores of the individual positions. For example, given the sequences $x = $ GATCGGCAT and $y = $ CAATGTGAATC, one alignment is

```
G ATCG GCAT
CAAT GTGAATC
-*++*+*+-++*
```

A + under a position indicates a score of $+1$ for that position, a – indicates a score of -1, and a $*$ indicates a score of -2, so that this alignment has a total score of $6 \cdot 1 - 2 \cdot 1 - 4 \cdot 2 = -4$.

b. Explain how to cast the problem of finding an optimal alignment as an edit distance problem using a subset of the transformation operations copy, replace, delete, insert, twiddle, and kill.

15-6 *Planning a company party*

Professor Stewart is consulting for the president of a corporation that is planning a company party. The company has a hierarchical structure; that is, the supervisor relation forms a tree rooted at the president. The personnel office has ranked each employee with a conviviality rating, which is a real number. In order to make the party fun for all attendees, the president does not want both an employee and his or her immediate supervisor to attend.

Professor Stewart is given the tree that describes the structure of the corporation, using the left-child, right-sibling representation described in Section 10.4. Each node of the tree holds, in addition to the pointers, the name of an employee and that employee's conviviality ranking. Describe an algorithm to make up a guest list that maximizes the sum of the conviviality ratings of the guests. Analyze the running time of your algorithm.

15-7 *Viterbi algorithm*

We can use dynamic programming on a directed graph $G = (V, E)$ for speech recognition. Each edge $(u, v) \in E$ is labeled with a sound $\sigma(u, v)$ from a finite set Σ of sounds. The labeled graph is a formal model of a person speaking

a restricted language. Each path in the graph starting from a distinguished vertex $v_0 \in V$ corresponds to a possible sequence of sounds produced by the model. We define the label of a directed path to be the concatenation of the labels of the edges on that path.

a. Describe an efficient algorithm that, given an edge-labeled graph G with distinguished vertex v_0 and a sequence $s = \langle \sigma_1, \sigma_2, \ldots, \sigma_k \rangle$ of sounds from Σ, returns a path in G that begins at v_0 and has s as its label, if any such path exists. Otherwise, the algorithm should return NO-SUCH-PATH. Analyze the running time of your algorithm. (*Hint:* You may find concepts from Chapter 22 useful.)

Now, suppose that every edge $(u, v) \in E$ has an associated nonnegative probability $p(u, v)$ of traversing the edge (u, v) from vertex u and thus producing the corresponding sound. The sum of the probabilities of the edges leaving any vertex equals 1. The probability of a path is defined to be the product of the probabilities of its edges. We can view the probability of a path beginning at v_0 as the probability that a "random walk" beginning at v_0 will follow the specified path, where we randomly choose which edge to take leaving a vertex u according to the probabilities of the available edges leaving u.

b. Extend your answer to part (a) so that if a path is returned, it is a *most probable path* starting at v_0 and having label s. Analyze the running time of your algorithm.

15-8 *Image compression by seam carving*

We are given a color picture consisting of an $m \times n$ array $A[1 .. m, 1 .. n]$ of pixels, where each pixel specifies a triple of red, green, and blue (RGB) intensities. Suppose that we wish to compress this picture slightly. Specifically, we wish to remove one pixel from each of the m rows, so that the whole picture becomes one pixel narrower. To avoid disturbing visual effects, however, we require that the pixels removed in two adjacent rows be in the same or adjacent columns; the pixels removed form a "seam" from the top row to the bottom row where successive pixels in the seam are adjacent vertically or diagonally.

a. Show that the number of such possible seams grows at least exponentially in m, assuming that $n > 1$.

b. Suppose now that along with each pixel $A[i, j]$, we have calculated a real-valued disruption measure $d[i, j]$, indicating how disruptive it would be to remove pixel $A[i, j]$. Intuitively, the lower a pixel's disruption measure, the more similar the pixel is to its neighbors. Suppose further that we define the disruption measure of a seam to be the sum of the disruption measures of its pixels.

Give an algorithm to find a seam with the lowest disruption measure. How efficient is your algorithm?

15-9   *Breaking a string*

A certain string-processing language allows a programmer to break a string into two pieces. Because this operation copies the string, it costs n time units to break a string of n characters into two pieces. Suppose a programmer wants to break a string into many pieces. The order in which the breaks occur can affect the total amount of time used. For example, suppose that the programmer wants to break a 20-character string after characters 2, 8, and 10 (numbering the characters in ascending order from the left-hand end, starting from 1). If she programs the breaks to occur in left-to-right order, then the first break costs 20 time units, the second break costs 18 time units (breaking the string from characters 3 to 20 at character 8), and the third break costs 12 time units, totaling 50 time units. If she programs the breaks to occur in right-to-left order, however, then the first break costs 20 time units, the second break costs 10 time units, and the third break costs 8 time units, totaling 38 time units. In yet another order, she could break first at 8 (costing 20), then break the left piece at 2 (costing 8), and finally the right piece at 10 (costing 12), for a total cost of 40.

Design an algorithm that, given the numbers of characters after which to break, determines a least-cost way to sequence those breaks. More formally, given a string S with n characters and an array $L[1 \mathinner{.\,.} m]$ containing the break points, compute the lowest cost for a sequence of breaks, along with a sequence of breaks that achieves this cost.

15-10   *Planning an investment strategy*

Your knowledge of algorithms helps you obtain an exciting job with the Acme Computer Company, along with a \$10,000 signing bonus. You decide to invest this money with the goal of maximizing your return at the end of 10 years. You decide to use the Amalgamated Investment Company to manage your investments. Amalgamated Investments requires you to observe the following rules. It offers n different investments, numbered 1 through n. In each year j, investment i provides a return rate of r_{ij}. In other words, if you invest d dollars in investment i in year j, then at the end of year j, you have dr_{ij} dollars. The return rates are guaranteed, that is, you are given all the return rates for the next 10 years for each investment. You make investment decisions only once per year. At the end of each year, you can leave the money made in the previous year in the same investments, or you can shift money to other investments, by either shifting money between existing investments or moving money to a new investment. If you do not move your money between two consecutive years, you pay a fee of f_1 dollars, whereas if you switch your money, you pay a fee of f_2 dollars, where $f_2 > f_1$.

a. The problem, as stated, allows you to invest your money in multiple investments in each year. Prove that there exists an optimal investment strategy that, in each year, puts all the money into a single investment. (Recall that an optimal investment strategy maximizes the amount of money after 10 years and is not concerned with any other objectives, such as minimizing risk.)

b. Prove that the problem of planning your optimal investment strategy exhibits optimal substructure.

c. Design an algorithm that plans your optimal investment strategy. What is the running time of your algorithm?

d. Suppose that Amalgamated Investments imposed the additional restriction that, at any point, you can have no more than $15,000 in any one investment. Show that the problem of maximizing your income at the end of 10 years no longer exhibits optimal substructure.

15-11 *Inventory planning*

The Rinky Dink Company makes machines that resurface ice rinks. The demand for such products varies from month to month, and so the company needs to develop a strategy to plan its manufacturing given the fluctuating, but predictable, demand. The company wishes to design a plan for the next n months. For each month i, the company knows the demand d_i, that is, the number of machines that it will sell. Let $D = \sum_{i=1}^{n} d_i$ be the total demand over the next n months. The company keeps a full-time staff who provide labor to manufacture up to m machines per month. If the company needs to make more than m machines in a given month, it can hire additional, part-time labor, at a cost that works out to c dollars per machine. Furthermore, if, at the end of a month, the company is holding any unsold machines, it must pay inventory costs. The cost for holding j machines is given as a function $h(j)$ for $j = 1, 2, \ldots, D$, where $h(j) \geq 0$ for $1 \leq j \leq D$ and $h(j) \leq h(j + 1)$ for $1 \leq j \leq D - 1$.

Give an algorithm that calculates a plan for the company that minimizes its costs while fulfilling all the demand. The running time should be polynomial in n and D.

15-12 *Signing free-agent baseball players*

Suppose that you are the general manager for a major-league baseball team. During the off-season, you need to sign some free-agent players for your team. The team owner has given you a budget of $\$X$ to spend on free agents. You are allowed to spend less than $\$X$ altogether, but the owner will fire you if you spend any more than $\$X$.

You are considering N different positions, and for each position, P free-agent players who play that position are available.[8] Because you do not want to overload your roster with too many players at any position, for each position you may sign at most one free agent who plays that position. (If you do not sign any players at a particular position, then you plan to stick with the players you already have at that position.)

To determine how valuable a player is going to be, you decide to use a sabermetric statistic[9] known as "VORP," or "value over replacement player." A player with a higher VORP is more valuable than a player with a lower VORP. A player with a higher VORP is not necessarily more expensive to sign than a player with a lower VORP, because factors other than a player's value determine how much it costs to sign him.

For each available free-agent player, you have three pieces of information:

- the player's position,

- the amount of money it will cost to sign the player, and

- the player's VORP.

Devise an algorithm that maximizes the total VORP of the players you sign while spending no more than $\$X$ altogether. You may assume that each player signs for a multiple of $\$100,000$. Your algorithm should output the total VORP of the players you sign, the total amount of money you spend, and a list of which players you sign. Analyze the running time and space requirement of your algorithm.

Chapter notes

R. Bellman began the systematic study of dynamic programming in 1955. The word "programming," both here and in linear programming, refers to using a tabular solution method. Although optimization techniques incorporating elements of dynamic programming were known earlier, Bellman provided the area with a solid mathematical basis [37].

---

[8] Although there are nine positions on a baseball team, N is not necessarily equal to 9 because some general managers have particular ways of thinking about positions. For example, a general manager might consider right-handed pitchers and left-handed pitchers to be separate "positions," as well as starting pitchers, long relief pitchers (relief pitchers who can pitch several innings), and short relief pitchers (relief pitchers who normally pitch at most only one inning).

[9] *Sabermetrics* is the application of statistical analysis to baseball records. It provides several ways to compare the relative values of individual players.

Galil and Park [125] classify dynamic-programming algorithms according to the size of the table and the number of other table entries each entry depends on. They call a dynamic-programming algorithm tD/eD if its table size is $O(n^t)$ and each entry depends on $O(n^e)$ other entries. For example, the matrix-chain multiplication algorithm in Section 15.2 would be $2D/1D$, and the longest-common-subsequence algorithm in Section 15.4 would be $2D/0D$.

Hu and Shing [182, 183] give an $O(n \lg n)$-time algorithm for the matrix-chain multiplication problem.

The $O(mn)$-time algorithm for the longest-common-subsequence problem appears to be a folk algorithm. Knuth [70] posed the question of whether subquadratic algorithms for the LCS problem exist. Masek and Paterson [244] answered this question in the affirmative by giving an algorithm that runs in $O(mn/\lg n)$ time, where $n \leq m$ and the sequences are drawn from a set of bounded size. For the special case in which no element appears more than once in an input sequence, Szymanski [326] shows how to solve the problem in $O((n + m) \lg(n + m))$ time. Many of these results extend to the problem of computing string edit distances (Problem 15-5).

An early paper on variable-length binary encodings by Gilbert and Moore [133] had applications to constructing optimal binary search trees for the case in which all probabilities p_i are 0; this paper contains an $O(n^3)$-time algorithm. Aho, Hopcroft, and Ullman [5] present the algorithm from Section 15.5. Exercise 15.5-4 is due to Knuth [212]. Hu and Tucker [184] devised an algorithm for the case in which all probabilities p_i are 0 that uses $O(n^2)$ time and $O(n)$ space; subsequently, Knuth [211] reduced the time to $O(n \lg n)$.

Problem 15-8 is due to Avidan and Shamir [27], who have posted on the Web a wonderful video illustrating this image-compression technique.

16 Greedy Algorithms

Algorithms for optimization problems typically go through a sequence of steps, with a set of choices at each step. For many optimization problems, using dynamic programming to determine the best choices is overkill; simpler, more efficient algorithms will do. A *greedy algorithm* always makes the choice that looks best at the moment. That is, it makes a locally optimal choice in the hope that this choice will lead to a globally optimal solution. This chapter explores optimization problems for which greedy algorithms provide optimal solutions. Before reading this chapter, you should read about dynamic programming in Chapter 15, particularly Section 15.3.

Greedy algorithms do not always yield optimal solutions, but for many problems they do. We shall first examine, in Section 16.1, a simple but nontrivial problem, the activity-selection problem, for which a greedy algorithm efficiently computes an optimal solution. We shall arrive at the greedy algorithm by first considering a dynamic-programming approach and then showing that we can always make greedy choices to arrive at an optimal solution. Section 16.2 reviews the basic elements of the greedy approach, giving a direct approach for proving greedy algorithms correct. Section 16.3 presents an important application of greedy techniques: designing data-compression (Huffman) codes. In Section 16.4, we investigate some of the theory underlying combinatorial structures called "matroids," for which a greedy algorithm always produces an optimal solution. Finally, Section 16.5 applies matroids to solve a problem of scheduling unit-time tasks with deadlines and penalties.

The greedy method is quite powerful and works well for a wide range of problems. Later chapters will present many algorithms that we can view as applications of the greedy method, including minimum-spanning-tree algorithms (Chapter 23), Dijkstra's algorithm for shortest paths from a single source (Chapter 24), and Chvátal's greedy set-covering heuristic (Chapter 35). Minimum-spanning-tree algorithms furnish a classic example of the greedy method. Although you can read

this chapter and Chapter 23 independently of each other, you might find it useful to read them together.

16.1 An activity-selection problem

Our first example is the problem of scheduling several competing activities that require exclusive use of a common resource, with a goal of selecting a maximum-size set of mutually compatible activities. Suppose we have a set $S = \{a_1, a_2, \ldots, a_n\}$ of n proposed *activities* that wish to use a resource, such as a lecture hall, which can serve only one activity at a time. Each activity a_i has a *start time* s_i and a *finish time* f_i, where $0 \leq s_i < f_i < \infty$. If selected, activity a_i takes place during the half-open time interval $[s_i, f_i)$. Activities a_i and a_j are *compatible* if the intervals $[s_i, f_i)$ and $[s_j, f_j)$ do not overlap. That is, a_i and a_j are compatible if $s_i \geq f_j$ or $s_j \geq f_i$. In the *activity-selection problem*, we wish to select a maximum-size subset of mutually compatible activities. We assume that the activities are sorted in monotonically increasing order of finish time:

$$f_1 \leq f_2 \leq f_3 \leq \cdots \leq f_{n-1} \leq f_n . \tag{16.1}$$

(We shall see later the advantage that this assumption provides.) For example, consider the following set S of activities:

i	1	2	3	4	5	6	7	8	9	10	11
s_i	1	3	0	5	3	5	6	8	8	2	12
f_i	4	5	6	7	9	9	10	11	12	14	16

For this example, the subset $\{a_3, a_9, a_{11}\}$ consists of mutually compatible activities. It is not a maximum subset, however, since the subset $\{a_1, a_4, a_8, a_{11}\}$ is larger. In fact, $\{a_1, a_4, a_8, a_{11}\}$ is a largest subset of mutually compatible activities; another largest subset is $\{a_2, a_4, a_9, a_{11}\}$.

We shall solve this problem in several steps. We start by thinking about a dynamic-programming solution, in which we consider several choices when determining which subproblems to use in an optimal solution. We shall then observe that we need to consider only one choice—the greedy choice—and that when we make the greedy choice, only one subproblem remains. Based on these observations, we shall develop a recursive greedy algorithm to solve the activity-scheduling problem. We shall complete the process of developing a greedy solution by converting the recursive algorithm to an iterative one. Although the steps we shall go through in this section are slightly more involved than is typical when developing a greedy algorithm, they illustrate the relationship between greedy algorithms and dynamic programming.

The optimal substructure of the activity-selection problem

We can easily verify that the activity-selection problem exhibits optimal substructure. Let us denote by S_{ij} the set of activities that start after activity a_i finishes and that finish before activity a_j starts. Suppose that we wish to find a maximum set of mutually compatible activities in S_{ij}, and suppose further that such a maximum set is A_{ij}, which includes some activity a_k. By including a_k in an optimal solution, we are left with two subproblems: finding mutually compatible activities in the set S_{ik} (activities that start after activity a_i finishes and that finish before activity a_k starts) and finding mutually compatible activities in the set S_{kj} (activities that start after activity a_k finishes and that finish before activity a_j starts). Let $A_{ik} = A_{ij} \cap S_{ik}$ and $A_{kj} = A_{ij} \cap S_{kj}$, so that A_{ik} contains the activities in A_{ij} that finish before a_k starts and A_{kj} contains the activities in A_{ij} that start after a_k finishes. Thus, we have $A_{ij} = A_{ik} \cup \{a_k\} \cup A_{kj}$, and so the maximum-size set A_{ij} of mutually compatible activities in S_{ij} consists of $|A_{ij}| = |A_{ik}| + |A_{kj}| + 1$ activities.

The usual cut-and-paste argument shows that the optimal solution A_{ij} must also include optimal solutions to the two subproblems for S_{ik} and S_{kj}. If we could find a set A'_{kj} of mutually compatible activities in S_{kj} where $|A'_{kj}| > |A_{kj}|$, then we could use A'_{kj}, rather than A_{kj}, in a solution to the subproblem for S_{ij}. We would have constructed a set of $|A_{ik}| + |A'_{kj}| + 1 > |A_{ik}| + |A_{kj}| + 1 = |A_{ij}|$ mutually compatible activities, which contradicts the assumption that A_{ij} is an optimal solution. A symmetric argument applies to the activities in S_{ik}.

This way of characterizing optimal substructure suggests that we might solve the activity-selection problem by dynamic programming. If we denote the size of an optimal solution for the set S_{ij} by $c[i, j]$, then we would have the recurrence

$$c[i, j] = c[i, k] + c[k, j] + 1 .$$

Of course, if we did not know that an optimal solution for the set S_{ij} includes activity a_k, we would have to examine all activities in S_{ij} to find which one to choose, so that

$$c[i, j] = \begin{cases} 0 & \text{if } S_{ij} = \emptyset , \\ \max_{a_k \in S_{ij}} \{c[i, k] + c[k, j] + 1\} & \text{if } S_{ij} \neq \emptyset . \end{cases} \quad (16.2)$$

We could then develop a recursive algorithm and memoize it, or we could work bottom-up and fill in table entries as we go along. But we would be overlooking another important characteristic of the activity-selection problem that we can use to great advantage.

Making the greedy choice

What if we could choose an activity to add to our optimal solution without having to first solve all the subproblems? That could save us from having to consider all the choices inherent in recurrence (16.2). In fact, for the activity-selection problem, we need consider only one choice: the greedy choice.

What do we mean by the greedy choice for the activity-selection problem? Intuition suggests that we should choose an activity that leaves the resource available for as many other activities as possible. Now, of the activities we end up choosing, one of them must be the first one to finish. Our intuition tells us, therefore, to choose the activity in S with the earliest finish time, since that would leave the resource available for as many of the activities that follow it as possible. (If more than one activity in S has the earliest finish time, then we can choose any such activity.) In other words, since the activities are sorted in monotonically increasing order by finish time, the greedy choice is activity a_1. Choosing the first activity to finish is not the only way to think of making a greedy choice for this problem; Exercise 16.1-3 asks you to explore other possibilities.

If we make the greedy choice, we have only one remaining subproblem to solve: finding activities that start after a_1 finishes. Why don't we have to consider activities that finish before a_1 starts? We have that $s_1 < f_1$, and f_1 is the earliest finish time of any activity, and therefore no activity can have a finish time less than or equal to s_1. Thus, all activities that are compatible with activity a_1 must start after a_1 finishes.

Furthermore, we have already established that the activity-selection problem exhibits optimal substructure. Let $S_k = \{a_i \in S : s_i \geq f_k\}$ be the set of activities that start after activity a_k finishes. If we make the greedy choice of activity a_1, then S_1 remains as the only subproblem to solve.[1] Optimal substructure tells us that if a_1 is in the optimal solution, then an optimal solution to the original problem consists of activity a_1 and all the activities in an optimal solution to the subproblem S_1.

One big question remains: is our intuition correct? Is the greedy choice—in which we choose the first activity to finish—always part of some optimal solution? The following theorem shows that it is.

---

[1] We sometimes refer to the sets S_k as subproblems rather than as just sets of activities. It will always be clear from the context whether we are referring to S_k as a set of activities or as a subproblem whose input is that set.

Theorem 16.1

Consider any nonempty subproblem S_k, and let a_m be an activity in S_k with the earliest finish time. Then a_m is included in some maximum-size subset of mutually compatible activities of S_k.

Proof   Let A_k be a maximum-size subset of mutually compatible activities in S_k, and let a_j be the activity in A_k with the earliest finish time. If $a_j = a_m$, we are done, since we have shown that a_m is in some maximum-size subset of mutually compatible activities of S_k. If $a_j \neq a_m$, let the set $A'_k = A_k - \{a_j\} \cup \{a_m\}$ be A_k but substituting a_m for a_j. The activities in A'_k are disjoint, which follows because the activities in A_k are disjoint, a_j is the first activity in A_k to finish, and $f_m \leq f_j$. Since $|A'_k| = |A_k|$, we conclude that A'_k is a maximum-size subset of mutually compatible activities of S_k, and it includes a_m.   ∎

Thus, we see that although we might be able to solve the activity-selection problem with dynamic programming, we don't need to. (Besides, we have not yet examined whether the activity-selection problem even has overlapping subproblems.) Instead, we can repeatedly choose the activity that finishes first, keep only the activities compatible with this activity, and repeat until no activities remain. Moreover, because we always choose the activity with the earliest finish time, the finish times of the activities we choose must strictly increase. We can consider each activity just once overall, in monotonically increasing order of finish times.

An algorithm to solve the activity-selection problem does not need to work bottom-up, like a table-based dynamic-programming algorithm. Instead, it can work top-down, choosing an activity to put into the optimal solution and then solving the subproblem of choosing activities from those that are compatible with those already chosen. Greedy algorithms typically have this top-down design: make a choice and then solve a subproblem, rather than the bottom-up technique of solving subproblems before making a choice.

A recursive greedy algorithm

Now that we have seen how to bypass the dynamic-programming approach and instead use a top-down, greedy algorithm, we can write a straightforward, recursive procedure to solve the activity-selection problem. The procedure RECURSIVE-ACTIVITY-SELECTOR takes the start and finish times of the activities, represented as arrays s and f,[2] the index k that defines the subproblem S_k it is to solve, and

---

[2]Because the pseudocode takes s and f as arrays, it indexes into them with square brackets rather than subscripts.

the size n of the original problem. It returns a maximum-size set of mutually compatible activities in S_k. We assume that the n input activities are already ordered by monotonically increasing finish time, according to equation (16.1). If not, we can sort them into this order in $O(n \lg n)$ time, breaking ties arbitrarily. In order to start, we add the fictitious activity a_0 with $f_0 = 0$, so that subproblem S_0 is the entire set of activities S. The initial call, which solves the entire problem, is RECURSIVE-ACTIVITY-SELECTOR$(s, f, 0, n)$.

RECURSIVE-ACTIVITY-SELECTOR(s, f, k, n)

```
1   m = k + 1
2   while m ≤ n and s[m] < f[k]        // find the first activity in S_k to finish
3       m = m + 1
4   if m ≤ n
5       return {a_m} ∪ RECURSIVE-ACTIVITY-SELECTOR(s, f, m, n)
6   else return ∅
```

Figure 16.1 shows the operation of the algorithm. In a given recursive call RECURSIVE-ACTIVITY-SELECTOR(s, f, k, n), the **while** loop of lines 2–3 looks for the first activity in S_k to finish. The loop examines $a_{k+1}, a_{k+2}, \ldots, a_n$, until it finds the first activity a_m that is compatible with a_k; such an activity has $s_m \geq f_k$. If the loop terminates because it finds such an activity, line 5 returns the union of $\{a_m\}$ and the maximum-size subset of S_m returned by the recursive call RECURSIVE-ACTIVITY-SELECTOR(s, f, m, n). Alternatively, the loop may terminate because $m > n$, in which case we have examined all activities in S_k without finding one that is compatible with a_k. In this case, $S_k = \emptyset$, and so the procedure returns $\emptyset$ in line 6.

Assuming that the activities have already been sorted by finish times, the running time of the call RECURSIVE-ACTIVITY-SELECTOR$(s, f, 0, n)$ is $\Theta(n)$, which we can see as follows. Over all recursive calls, each activity is examined exactly once in the **while** loop test of line 2. In particular, activity a_i is examined in the last call made in which $k < i$.

An iterative greedy algorithm

We easily can convert our recursive procedure to an iterative one. The procedure RECURSIVE-ACTIVITY-SELECTOR is almost "tail recursive" (see Problem 7-4): it ends with a recursive call to itself followed by a union operation. It is usually a straightforward task to transform a tail-recursive procedure to an iterative form; in fact, some compilers for certain programming languages perform this task automatically. As written, RECURSIVE-ACTIVITY-SELECTOR works for subproblems S_k, i.e., subproblems that consist of the last activities to finish.

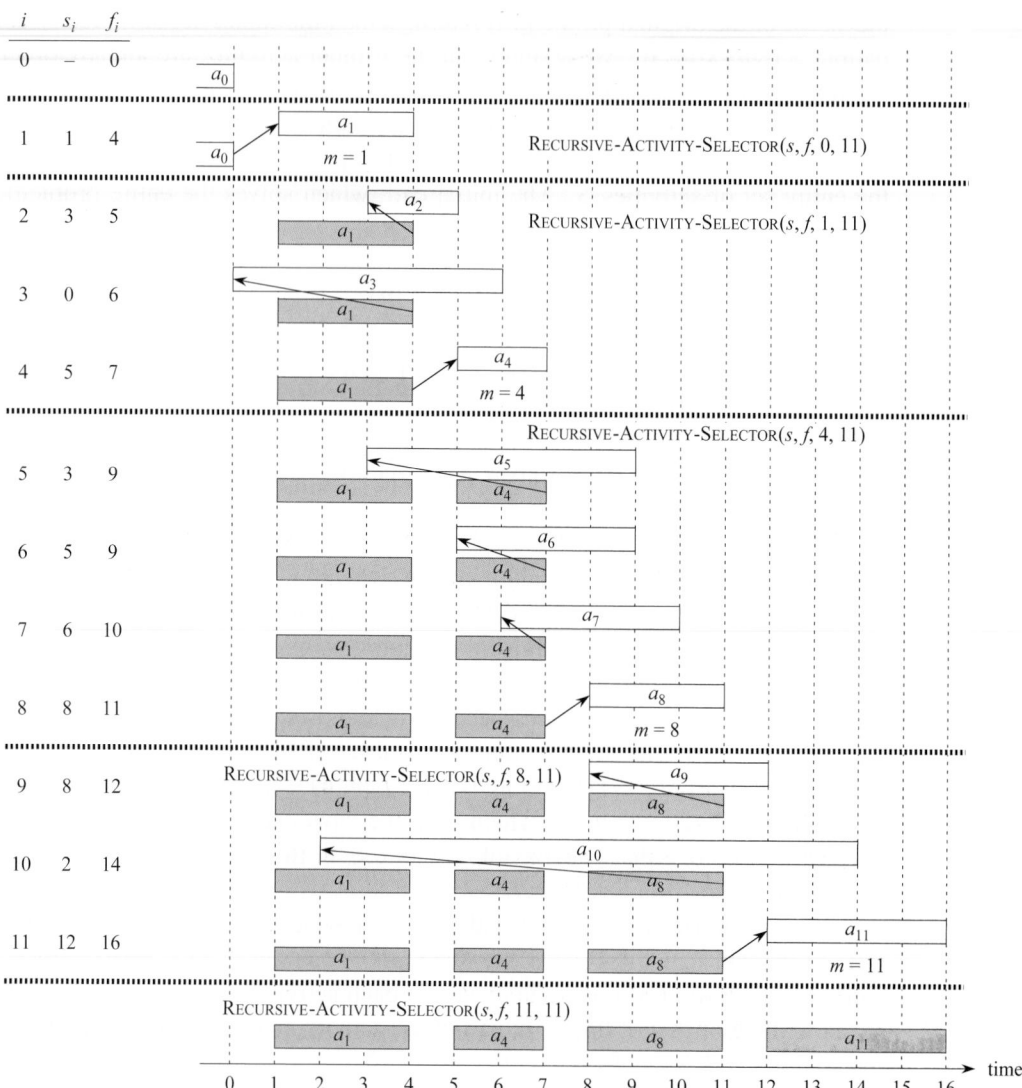

Figure 16.1   The operation of RECURSIVE-ACTIVITY-SELECTOR on the 11 activities given earlier. Activities considered in each recursive call appear between horizontal lines. The fictitious activity a_0 finishes at time 0, and the initial call RECURSIVE-ACTIVITY-SELECTOR$(s, f, 0, 11)$, selects activity a_1. In each recursive call, the activities that have already been selected are shaded, and the activity shown in white is being considered. If the starting time of an activity occurs before the finish time of the most recently added activity (the arrow between them points left), it is rejected. Otherwise (the arrow points directly up or to the right), it is selected. The last recursive call, RECURSIVE-ACTIVITY-SELECTOR$(s, f, 11, 11)$, returns $\emptyset$. The resulting set of selected activities is $\{a_1, a_4, a_8, a_{11}\}$.

The procedure GREEDY-ACTIVITY-SELECTOR is an iterative version of the procedure RECURSIVE-ACTIVITY-SELECTOR. It also assumes that the input activities are ordered by monotonically increasing finish time. It collects selected activities into a set A and returns this set when it is done.

GREEDY-ACTIVITY-SELECTOR(s, f)

```
1   n = s.length
2   A = {a₁}
3   k = 1
4   for m = 2 to n
5       if s[m] ≥ f[k]
6           A = A ∪ {aₘ}
7           k = m
8   return A
```

The procedure works as follows. The variable k indexes the most recent addition to A, corresponding to the activity a_k in the recursive version. Since we consider the activities in order of monotonically increasing finish time, f_k is always the maximum finish time of any activity in A. That is,

$$f_k = \max \{ f_i : a_i \in A \} \; . \tag{16.3}$$

Lines 2–3 select activity a_1, initialize A to contain just this activity, and initialize k to index this activity. The **for** loop of lines 4–7 finds the earliest activity in S_k to finish. The loop considers each activity a_m in turn and adds a_m to A if it is compatible with all previously selected activities; such an activity is the earliest in S_k to finish. To see whether activity a_m is compatible with every activity currently in A, it suffices by equation (16.3) to check (in line 5) that its start time s_m is not earlier than the finish time f_k of the activity most recently added to A. If activity a_m is compatible, then lines 6–7 add activity a_m to A and set k to m. The set A returned by the call GREEDY-ACTIVITY-SELECTOR(s, f) is precisely the set returned by the call RECURSIVE-ACTIVITY-SELECTOR$(s, f, 0, n)$.

Like the recursive version, GREEDY-ACTIVITY-SELECTOR schedules a set of n activities in $\Theta(n)$ time, assuming that the activities were already sorted initially by their finish times.

Exercises

16.1-1

Give a dynamic-programming algorithm for the activity-selection problem, based on recurrence (16.2). Have your algorithm compute the sizes $c[i, j]$ as defined above and also produce the maximum-size subset of mutually compatible activities.

Assume that the inputs have been sorted as in equation (16.1). Compare the running time of your solution to the running time of GREEDY-ACTIVITY-SELECTOR.

16.1-2

Suppose that instead of always selecting the first activity to finish, we instead select the last activity to start that is compatible with all previously selected activities. Describe how this approach is a greedy algorithm, and prove that it yields an optimal solution.

16.1-3

Not just any greedy approach to the activity-selection problem produces a maximum-size set of mutually compatible activities. Give an example to show that the approach of selecting the activity of least duration from among those that are compatible with previously selected activities does not work. Do the same for the approaches of always selecting the compatible activity that overlaps the fewest other remaining activities and always selecting the compatible remaining activity with the earliest start time.

16.1-4

Suppose that we have a set of activities to schedule among a large number of lecture halls, where any activity can take place in any lecture hall. We wish to schedule all the activities using as few lecture halls as possible. Give an efficient greedy algorithm to determine which activity should use which lecture hall.

(This problem is also known as the ***interval-graph coloring problem***. We can create an interval graph whose vertices are the given activities and whose edges connect incompatible activities. The smallest number of colors required to color every vertex so that no two adjacent vertices have the same color corresponds to finding the fewest lecture halls needed to schedule all of the given activities.)

16.1-5

Consider a modification to the activity-selection problem in which each activity a_i has, in addition to a start and finish time, a value v_i. The objective is no longer to maximize the number of activities scheduled, but instead to maximize the total value of the activities scheduled. That is, we wish to choose a set A of compatible activities such that $\sum_{a_k \in A} v_k$ is maximized. Give a polynomial-time algorithm for this problem.

16.2 Elements of the greedy strategy

A greedy algorithm obtains an optimal solution to a problem by making a sequence of choices. At each decision point, the algorithm makes the choice that seems best at the moment. This heuristic strategy does not always produce an optimal solution, but as we saw in the activity-selection problem, sometimes it does. This section discusses some of the general properties of greedy methods.

The process that we followed in Section 16.1 to develop a greedy algorithm was a bit more involved than is typical. We went through the following steps:

1. Determine the optimal substructure of the problem.

2. Develop a recursive solution. (For the activity-selection problem, we formulated recurrence (16.2), but we bypassed developing a recursive algorithm based on this recurrence.)

3. Show that if we make the greedy choice, then only one subproblem remains.

4. Prove that it is always safe to make the greedy choice. (Steps 3 and 4 can occur in either order.)

5. Develop a recursive algorithm that implements the greedy strategy.

6. Convert the recursive algorithm to an iterative algorithm.

In going through these steps, we saw in great detail the dynamic-programming underpinnings of a greedy algorithm. For example, in the activity-selection problem, we first defined the subproblems S_{ij}, where both i and j varied. We then found that if we always made the greedy choice, we could restrict the subproblems to be of the form S_k.

Alternatively, we could have fashioned our optimal substructure with a greedy choice in mind, so that the choice leaves just one subproblem to solve. In the activity-selection problem, we could have started by dropping the second subscript and defining subproblems of the form S_k. Then, we could have proven that a greedy choice (the first activity a_m to finish in S_k), combined with an optimal solution to the remaining set S_m of compatible activities, yields an optimal solution to S_k. More generally, we design greedy algorithms according to the following sequence of steps:

1. Cast the optimization problem as one in which we make a choice and are left with one subproblem to solve.

2. Prove that there is always an optimal solution to the original problem that makes the greedy choice, so that the greedy choice is always safe.

3. Demonstrate optimal substructure by showing that, having made the greedy choice, what remains is a subproblem with the property that if we combine an optimal solution to the subproblem with the greedy choice we have made, we arrive at an optimal solution to the original problem.

We shall use this more direct process in later sections of this chapter. Nevertheless, beneath every greedy algorithm, there is almost always a more cumbersome dynamic-programming solution.

How can we tell whether a greedy algorithm will solve a particular optimization problem? No way works all the time, but the greedy-choice property and optimal substructure are the two key ingredients. If we can demonstrate that the problem has these properties, then we are well on the way to developing a greedy algorithm for it.

Greedy-choice property

The first key ingredient is the *greedy-choice property*: we can assemble a globally optimal solution by making locally optimal (greedy) choices. In other words, when we are considering which choice to make, we make the choice that looks best in the current problem, without considering results from subproblems.

Here is where greedy algorithms differ from dynamic programming. In dynamic programming, we make a choice at each step, but the choice usually depends on the solutions to subproblems. Consequently, we typically solve dynamic-programming problems in a bottom-up manner, progressing from smaller subproblems to larger subproblems. (Alternatively, we can solve them top down, but memoizing. Of course, even though the code works top down, we still must solve the subproblems before making a choice.) In a greedy algorithm, we make whatever choice seems best at the moment and then solve the subproblem that remains. The choice made by a greedy algorithm may depend on choices so far, but it cannot depend on any future choices or on the solutions to subproblems. Thus, unlike dynamic programming, which solves the subproblems before making the first choice, a greedy algorithm makes its first choice before solving any subproblems. A dynamic-programming algorithm proceeds bottom up, whereas a greedy strategy usually progresses in a top-down fashion, making one greedy choice after another, reducing each given problem instance to a smaller one.

Of course, we must prove that a greedy choice at each step yields a globally optimal solution. Typically, as in the case of Theorem 16.1, the proof examines a globally optimal solution to some subproblem. It then shows how to modify the solution to substitute the greedy choice for some other choice, resulting in one similar, but smaller, subproblem.

We can usually make the greedy choice more efficiently than when we have to consider a wider set of choices. For example, in the activity-selection problem, as-

suming that we had already sorted the activities in monotonically increasing order of finish times, we needed to examine each activity just once. By preprocessing the input or by using an appropriate data structure (often a priority queue), we often can make greedy choices quickly, thus yielding an efficient algorithm.

Optimal substructure

A problem exhibits *optimal substructure* if an optimal solution to the problem contains within it optimal solutions to subproblems. This property is a key ingredient of assessing the applicability of dynamic programming as well as greedy algorithms. As an example of optimal substructure, recall how we demonstrated in Section 16.1 that if an optimal solution to subproblem S_{ij} includes an activity a_k, then it must also contain optimal solutions to the subproblems S_{ik} and S_{kj}. Given this optimal substructure, we argued that if we knew which activity to use as a_k, we could construct an optimal solution to S_{ij} by selecting a_k along with all activities in optimal solutions to the subproblems S_{ik} and S_{kj}. Based on this observation of optimal substructure, we were able to devise the recurrence (16.2) that described the value of an optimal solution.

We usually use a more direct approach regarding optimal substructure when applying it to greedy algorithms. As mentioned above, we have the luxury of assuming that we arrived at a subproblem by having made the greedy choice in the original problem. All we really need to do is argue that an optimal solution to the subproblem, combined with the greedy choice already made, yields an optimal solution to the original problem. This scheme implicitly uses induction on the subproblems to prove that making the greedy choice at every step produces an optimal solution.

Greedy versus dynamic programming

Because both the greedy and dynamic-programming strategies exploit optimal substructure, you might be tempted to generate a dynamic-programming solution to a problem when a greedy solution suffices or, conversely, you might mistakenly think that a greedy solution works when in fact a dynamic-programming solution is required. To illustrate the subtleties between the two techniques, let us investigate two variants of a classical optimization problem.

The *0-1 knapsack problem* is the following. A thief robbing a store finds n items. The ith item is worth v_i dollars and weighs w_i pounds, where v_i and w_i are integers. The thief wants to take as valuable a load as possible, but he can carry at most W pounds in his knapsack, for some integer W. Which items should he take? (We call this the 0-1 knapsack problem because for each item, the thief must either

take it or leave it behind; he cannot take a fractional amount of an item or take an item more than once.)

In the *fractional knapsack problem*, the setup is the same, but the thief can take fractions of items, rather than having to make a binary (0-1) choice for each item. You can think of an item in the 0-1 knapsack problem as being like a gold ingot and an item in the fractional knapsack problem as more like gold dust.

Both knapsack problems exhibit the optimal-substructure property. For the 0-1 problem, consider the most valuable load that weighs at most W pounds. If we remove item j from this load, the remaining load must be the most valuable load weighing at most $W - w_j$ that the thief can take from the $n - 1$ original items excluding j. For the comparable fractional problem, consider that if we remove a weight w of one item j from the optimal load, the remaining load must be the most valuable load weighing at most $W - w$ that the thief can take from the $n - 1$ original items plus $w_j - w$ pounds of item j.

Although the problems are similar, we can solve the fractional knapsack problem by a greedy strategy, but we cannot solve the 0-1 problem by such a strategy. To solve the fractional problem, we first compute the value per pound v_i/w_i for each item. Obeying a greedy strategy, the thief begins by taking as much as possible of the item with the greatest value per pound. If the supply of that item is exhausted and he can still carry more, he takes as much as possible of the item with the next greatest value per pound, and so forth, until he reaches his weight limit W. Thus, by sorting the items by value per pound, the greedy algorithm runs in $O(n \lg n)$ time. We leave the proof that the fractional knapsack problem has the greedy-choice property as Exercise 16.2-1.

To see that this greedy strategy does not work for the 0-1 knapsack problem, consider the problem instance illustrated in Figure 16.2(a). This example has 3 items and a knapsack that can hold 50 pounds. Item 1 weighs 10 pounds and is worth 60 dollars. Item 2 weighs 20 pounds and is worth 100 dollars. Item 3 weighs 30 pounds and is worth 120 dollars. Thus, the value per pound of item 1 is 6 dollars per pound, which is greater than the value per pound of either item 2 (5 dollars per pound) or item 3 (4 dollars per pound). The greedy strategy, therefore, would take item 1 first. As you can see from the case analysis in Figure 16.2(b), however, the optimal solution takes items 2 and 3, leaving item 1 behind. The two possible solutions that take item 1 are both suboptimal.

For the comparable fractional problem, however, the greedy strategy, which takes item 1 first, does yield an optimal solution, as shown in Figure 16.2(c). Taking item 1 doesn't work in the 0-1 problem because the thief is unable to fill his knapsack to capacity, and the empty space lowers the effective value per pound of his load. In the 0-1 problem, when we consider whether to include an item in the knapsack, we must compare the solution to the subproblem that includes the item with the solution to the subproblem that excludes the item before we can make the

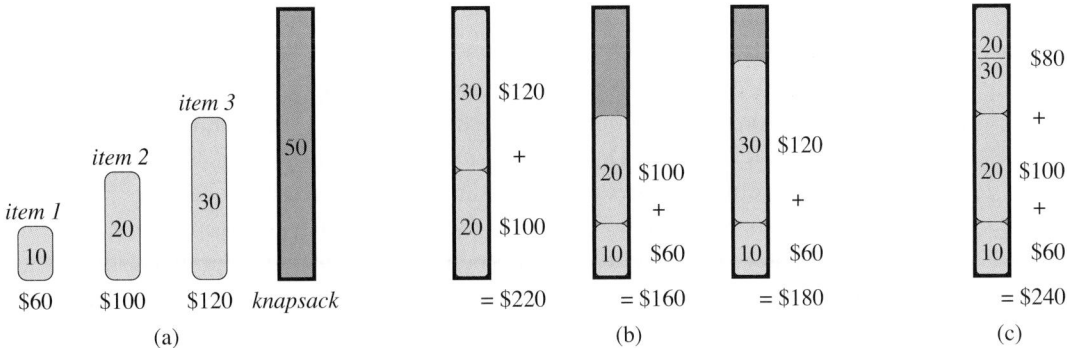

Figure 16.2   An example showing that the greedy strategy does not work for the 0-1 knapsack problem. **(a)** The thief must select a subset of the three items shown whose weight must not exceed 50 pounds. **(b)** The optimal subset includes items 2 and 3. Any solution with item 1 is suboptimal, even though item 1 has the greatest value per pound. **(c)** For the fractional knapsack problem, taking the items in order of greatest value per pound yields an optimal solution.

choice. The problem formulated in this way gives rise to many overlapping sub-problems—a hallmark of dynamic programming, and indeed, as Exercise 16.2-2 asks you to show, we can use dynamic programming to solve the 0-1 problem.

Exercises

16.2-1
Prove that the fractional knapsack problem has the greedy-choice property.

16.2-2
Give a dynamic-programming solution to the 0-1 knapsack problem that runs in $O(n\,W)$ time, where n is the number of items and W is the maximum weight of items that the thief can put in his knapsack.

16.2-3
Suppose that in a 0-1 knapsack problem, the order of the items when sorted by increasing weight is the same as their order when sorted by decreasing value. Give an efficient algorithm to find an optimal solution to this variant of the knapsack problem, and argue that your algorithm is correct.

16.2-4
Professor Gekko has always dreamed of inline skating across North Dakota. He plans to cross the state on highway U.S. 2, which runs from Grand Forks, on the eastern border with Minnesota, to Williston, near the western border with Montana.

The professor can carry two liters of water, and he can skate m miles before running out of water. (Because North Dakota is relatively flat, the professor does not have to worry about drinking water at a greater rate on uphill sections than on flat or downhill sections.) The professor will start in Grand Forks with two full liters of water. His official North Dakota state map shows all the places along U.S. 2 at which he can refill his water and the distances between these locations.

The professor's goal is to minimize the number of water stops along his route across the state. Give an efficient method by which he can determine which water stops he should make. Prove that your strategy yields an optimal solution, and give its running time.

16.2-5
Describe an efficient algorithm that, given a set $\{x_1, x_2, \ldots, x_n\}$ of points on the real line, determines the smallest set of unit-length closed intervals that contains all of the given points. Argue that your algorithm is correct.

16.2-6 ⋆
Show how to solve the fractional knapsack problem in $O(n)$ time.

16.2-7
Suppose you are given two sets A and B, each containing n positive integers. You can choose to reorder each set however you like. After reordering, let a_i be the ith element of set A, and let b_i be the ith element of set B. You then receive a payoff of $\prod_{i=1}^{n} a_i^{b_i}$. Give an algorithm that will maximize your payoff. Prove that your algorithm maximizes the payoff, and state its running time.

16.3   Huffman codes

Huffman codes compress data very effectively: savings of 20% to 90% are typical, depending on the characteristics of the data being compressed. We consider the data to be a sequence of characters. Huffman's greedy algorithm uses a table giving how often each character occurs (i.e., its frequency) to build up an optimal way of representing each character as a binary string.

Suppose we have a 100,000-character data file that we wish to store compactly. We observe that the characters in the file occur with the frequencies given by Figure 16.3. That is, only 6 different characters appear, and the character a occurs 45,000 times.

We have many options for how to represent such a file of information. Here, we consider the problem of designing a **binary character code** (or **code** for short)

	a	b	c	d	e	f
Frequency (in thousands)	45	13	12	16	9	5
Fixed-length codeword	000	001	010	011	100	101
Variable-length codeword	0	101	100	111	1101	1100

Figure 16.3   A character-coding problem. A data file of 100,000 characters contains only the characters a–f, with the frequencies indicated. If we assign each character a 3-bit codeword, we can encode the file in 300,000 bits. Using the variable-length code shown, we can encode the file in only 224,000 bits.

in which each character is represented by a unique binary string, which we call a *codeword*. If we use a *fixed-length code*, we need 3 bits to represent 6 characters: a = 000, b = 001, ..., f = 101. This method requires 300,000 bits to code the entire file. Can we do better?

A *variable-length code* can do considerably better than a fixed-length code, by giving frequent characters short codewords and infrequent characters long codewords. Figure 16.3 shows such a code; here the 1-bit string 0 represents a, and the 4-bit string 1100 represents f. This code requires

$$(45 \cdot 1 + 13 \cdot 3 + 12 \cdot 3 + 16 \cdot 3 + 9 \cdot 4 + 5 \cdot 4) \cdot 1{,}000 = 224{,}000 \text{ bits}$$

to represent the file, a savings of approximately 25%. In fact, this is an optimal character code for this file, as we shall see.

Prefix codes

We consider here only codes in which no codeword is also a prefix of some other codeword. Such codes are called *prefix codes*.[3] Although we won't prove it here, a prefix code can always achieve the optimal data compression among any character code, and so we suffer no loss of generality by restricting our attention to prefix codes.

Encoding is always simple for any binary character code; we just concatenate the codewords representing each character of the file. For example, with the variable-length prefix code of Figure 16.3, we code the 3-character file abc as $0 \cdot 101 \cdot 100 = 0101100$, where "·" denotes concatenation.

Prefix codes are desirable because they simplify decoding. Since no codeword is a prefix of any other, the codeword that begins an encoded file is unambiguous. We can simply identify the initial codeword, translate it back to the original char-

---

[3]Perhaps "prefix-free codes" would be a better name, but the term "prefix codes" is standard in the literature.

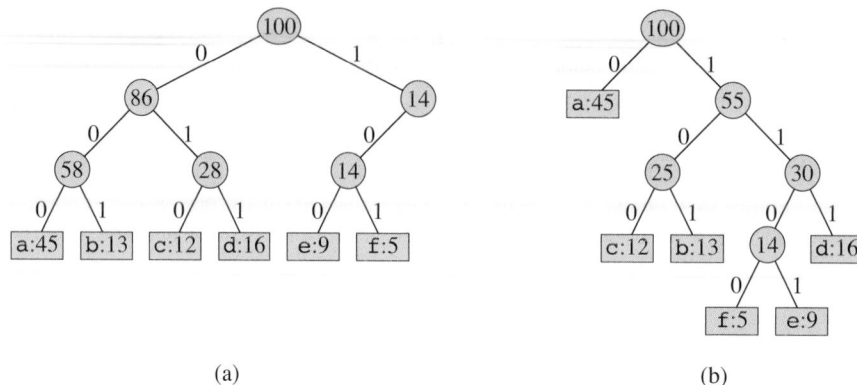

Figure 16.4 Trees corresponding to the coding schemes in Figure 16.3. Each leaf is labeled with a character and its frequency of occurrence. Each internal node is labeled with the sum of the frequencies of the leaves in its subtree. **(a)** The tree corresponding to the fixed-length code $a = 000, \ldots$, $f = 101$. **(b)** The tree corresponding to the optimal prefix code $a = 0, b = 101, \ldots, f = 1100$.

acter, and repeat the decoding process on the remainder of the encoded file. In our example, the string 001011101 parses uniquely as $0 \cdot 0 \cdot 101 \cdot 1101$, which decodes to aabe.

The decoding process needs a convenient representation for the prefix code so that we can easily pick off the initial codeword. A binary tree whose leaves are the given characters provides one such representation. We interpret the binary codeword for a character as the simple path from the root to that character, where 0 means "go to the left child" and 1 means "go to the right child." Figure 16.4 shows the trees for the two codes of our example. Note that these are not binary search trees, since the leaves need not appear in sorted order and internal nodes do not contain character keys.

An optimal code for a file is always represented by a *full* binary tree, in which every nonleaf node has two children (see Exercise 16.3-2). The fixed-length code in our example is not optimal since its tree, shown in Figure 16.4(a), is not a full binary tree: it contains codewords beginning $10\ldots$, but none beginning $11\ldots$. Since we can now restrict our attention to full binary trees, we can say that if C is the alphabet from which the characters are drawn and all character frequencies are positive, then the tree for an optimal prefix code has exactly $|C|$ leaves, one for each letter of the alphabet, and exactly $|C| - 1$ internal nodes (see Exercise B.5-3).

Given a tree T corresponding to a prefix code, we can easily compute the number of bits required to encode a file. For each character c in the alphabet C, let the attribute $c.freq$ denote the frequency of c in the file and let $d_T(c)$ denote the depth

of c's leaf in the tree. Note that $d_T(c)$ is also the length of the codeword for character c. The number of bits required to encode a file is thus

$$B(T) = \sum_{c \in C} c.\mathit{freq} \cdot d_T(c) , \tag{16.4}$$

which we define as the **cost** of the tree T.

Constructing a Huffman code

Huffman invented a greedy algorithm that constructs an optimal prefix code called a **Huffman code**. In line with our observations in Section 16.2, its proof of correctness relies on the greedy-choice property and optimal substructure. Rather than demonstrating that these properties hold and then developing pseudocode, we present the pseudocode first. Doing so will help clarify how the algorithm makes greedy choices.

In the pseudocode that follows, we assume that C is a set of n characters and that each character $c \in C$ is an object with an attribute $c.\mathit{freq}$ giving its frequency. The algorithm builds the tree T corresponding to the optimal code in a bottom-up manner. It begins with a set of $|C|$ leaves and performs a sequence of $|C| - 1$ "merging" operations to create the final tree. The algorithm uses a min-priority queue Q, keyed on the *freq* attribute, to identify the two least-frequent objects to merge together. When we merge two objects, the result is a new object whose frequency is the sum of the frequencies of the two objects that were merged.

HUFFMAN(C)

```
1   n = |C|
2   Q = C
3   for i = 1 to n − 1
4       allocate a new node z
5       z.left = x = EXTRACT-MIN(Q)
6       z.right = y = EXTRACT-MIN(Q)
7       z.freq = x.freq + y.freq
8       INSERT(Q, z)
9   return EXTRACT-MIN(Q)      // return the root of the tree
```

For our example, Huffman's algorithm proceeds as shown in Figure 16.5. Since the alphabet contains 6 letters, the initial queue size is $n = 6$, and 5 merge steps build the tree. The final tree represents the optimal prefix code. The codeword for a letter is the sequence of edge labels on the simple path from the root to the letter.

Line 2 initializes the min-priority queue Q with the characters in C. The **for** loop in lines 3–8 repeatedly extracts the two nodes x and y of lowest frequency

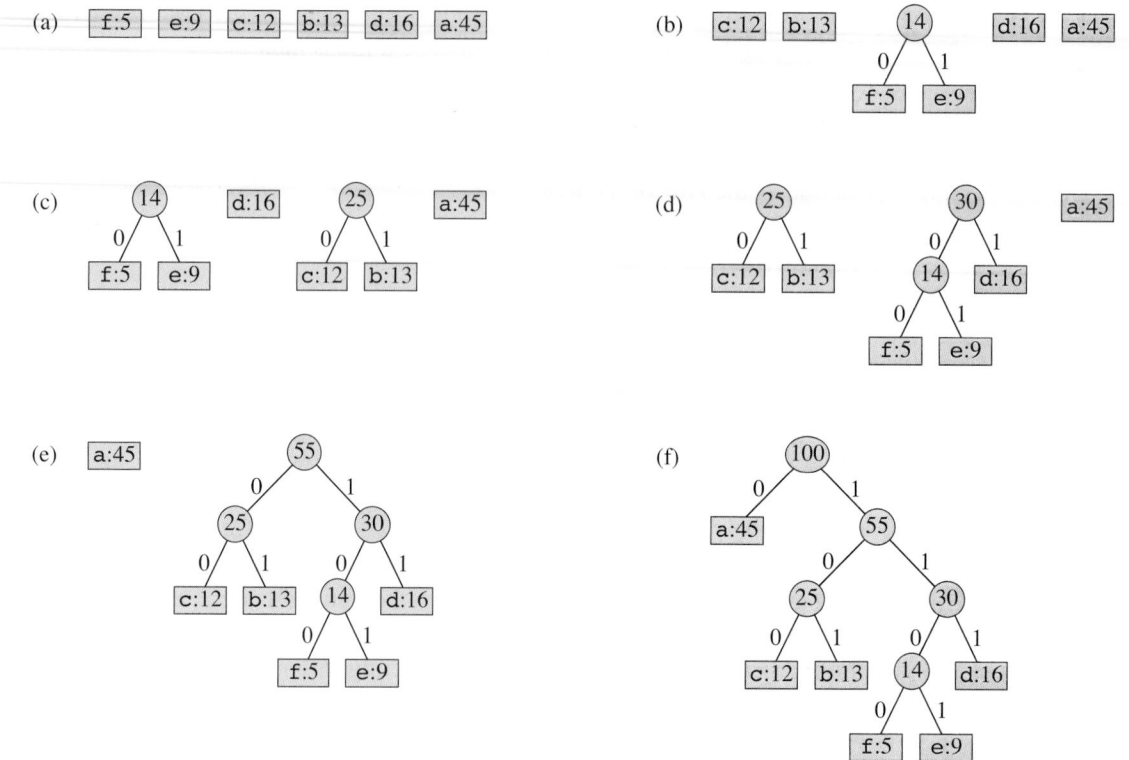

Figure 16.5 The steps of Huffman's algorithm for the frequencies given in Figure 16.3. Each part shows the contents of the queue sorted into increasing order by frequency. At each step, the two trees with lowest frequencies are merged. Leaves are shown as rectangles containing a character and its frequency. Internal nodes are shown as circles containing the sum of the frequencies of their children. An edge connecting an internal node with its children is labeled 0 if it is an edge to a left child and 1 if it is an edge to a right child. The codeword for a letter is the sequence of labels on the edges connecting the root to the leaf for that letter. **(a)** The initial set of $n = 6$ nodes, one for each letter. **(b)–(e)** Intermediate stages. **(f)** The final tree.

from the queue, replacing them in the queue with a new node z representing their merger. The frequency of z is computed as the sum of the frequencies of x and y in line 7. The node z has x as its left child and y as its right child. (This order is arbitrary; switching the left and right child of any node yields a different code of the same cost.) After $n - 1$ mergers, line 9 returns the one node left in the queue, which is the root of the code tree.

Although the algorithm would produce the same result if we were to excise the variables x and y—assigning directly to $z.left$ and $z.right$ in lines 5 and 6, and changing line 7 to $z.freq = z.left.freq + z.right.freq$—we shall use the node

names x and y in the proof of correctness. Therefore, we find it convenient to leave them in.

To analyze the running time of Huffman's algorithm, we assume that Q is implemented as a binary min-heap (see Chapter 6). For a set C of n characters, we can initialize Q in line 2 in $O(n)$ time using the BUILD-MIN-HEAP procedure discussed in Section 6.3. The **for** loop in lines 3–8 executes exactly $n - 1$ times, and since each heap operation requires time $O(\lg n)$, the loop contributes $O(n \lg n)$ to the running time. Thus, the total running time of HUFFMAN on a set of n characters is $O(n \lg n)$. We can reduce the running time to $O(n \lg \lg n)$ by replacing the binary min-heap with a van Emde Boas tree (see Chapter 20).

Correctness of Huffman's algorithm

To prove that the greedy algorithm HUFFMAN is correct, we show that the problem of determining an optimal prefix code exhibits the greedy-choice and optimal-substructure properties. The next lemma shows that the greedy-choice property holds.

Lemma 16.2
Let C be an alphabet in which each character $c \in C$ has frequency $c.freq$. Let x and y be two characters in C having the lowest frequencies. Then there exists an optimal prefix code for C in which the codewords for x and y have the same length and differ only in the last bit.

Proof   The idea of the proof is to take the tree T representing an arbitrary optimal prefix code and modify it to make a tree representing another optimal prefix code such that the characters x and y appear as sibling leaves of maximum depth in the new tree. If we can construct such a tree, then the codewords for x and y will have the same length and differ only in the last bit.

Let a and b be two characters that are sibling leaves of maximum depth in T. Without loss of generality, we assume that $a.freq \le b.freq$ and $x.freq \le y.freq$. Since $x.freq$ and $y.freq$ are the two lowest leaf frequencies, in order, and $a.freq$ and $b.freq$ are two arbitrary frequencies, in order, we have $x.freq \le a.freq$ and $y.freq \le b.freq$.

In the remainder of the proof, it is possible that we could have $x.freq = a.freq$ or $y.freq = b.freq$. However, if we had $x.freq = b.freq$, then we would also have $a.freq = b.freq = x.freq = y.freq$ (see Exercise 16.3-1), and the lemma would be trivially true. Thus, we will assume that $x.freq \ne b.freq$, which means that $x \ne b$.

As Figure 16.6 shows, we exchange the positions in T of a and x to produce a tree T', and then we exchange the positions in T' of b and y to produce a tree T''

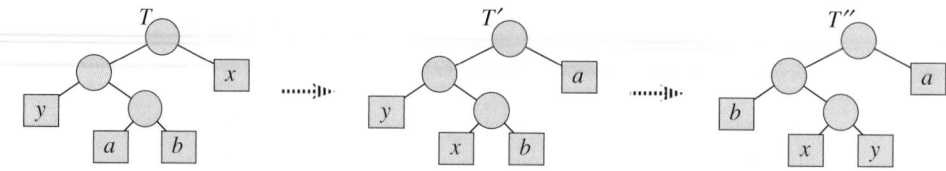

Figure 16.6   An illustration of the key step in the proof of Lemma 16.2. In the optimal tree T, leaves a and b are two siblings of maximum depth. Leaves x and y are the two characters with the lowest frequencies; they appear in arbitrary positions in T. Assuming that $x \neq b$, swapping leaves a and x produces tree T', and then swapping leaves b and y produces tree T''. Since each swap does not increase the cost, the resulting tree T'' is also an optimal tree.

in which x and y are sibling leaves of maximum depth. (Note that if $x = b$ but $y \neq a$, then tree T'' does not have x and y as sibling leaves of maximum depth. Because we assume that $x \neq b$, this situation cannot occur.) By equation (16.4), the difference in cost between T and T' is

$$
\begin{aligned}
B(T) - B(T') \\
= \sum_{c \in C} c.\mathit{freq} \cdot d_T(c) - \sum_{c \in C} c.\mathit{freq} \cdot d_{T'}(c) \\
= x.\mathit{freq} \cdot d_T(x) + a.\mathit{freq} \cdot d_T(a) - x.\mathit{freq} \cdot d_{T'}(x) - a.\mathit{freq} \cdot d_{T'}(a) \\
= x.\mathit{freq} \cdot d_T(x) + a.\mathit{freq} \cdot d_T(a) - x.\mathit{freq} \cdot d_T(a) - a.\mathit{freq} \cdot d_T(x) \\
= (a.\mathit{freq} - x.\mathit{freq})(d_T(a) - d_T(x)) \\
\geq 0 \,,
\end{aligned}
$$

because both $a.\mathit{freq} - x.\mathit{freq}$ and $d_T(a) - d_T(x)$ are nonnegative. More specifically, $a.\mathit{freq} - x.\mathit{freq}$ is nonnegative because x is a minimum-frequency leaf, and $d_T(a) - d_T(x)$ is nonnegative because a is a leaf of maximum depth in T. Similarly, exchanging y and b does not increase the cost, and so $B(T') - B(T'')$ is nonnegative. Therefore, $B(T'') \leq B(T)$, and since T is optimal, we have $B(T) \leq B(T'')$, which implies $B(T'') = B(T)$. Thus, T'' is an optimal tree in which x and y appear as sibling leaves of maximum depth, from which the lemma follows. ■

Lemma 16.2 implies that the process of building up an optimal tree by mergers can, without loss of generality, begin with the greedy choice of merging together those two characters of lowest frequency. Why is this a greedy choice? We can view the cost of a single merger as being the sum of the frequencies of the two items being merged. Exercise 16.3-4 shows that the total cost of the tree constructed equals the sum of the costs of its mergers. Of all possible mergers at each step, HUFFMAN chooses the one that incurs the least cost.

The next lemma shows that the problem of constructing optimal prefix codes has the optimal-substructure property.

Lemma 16.3
Let C be a given alphabet with frequency $c.freq$ defined for each character $c \in C$. Let x and y be two characters in C with minimum frequency. Let C' be the alphabet C with the characters x and y removed and a new character z added, so that $C' = C - \{x, y\} \cup \{z\}$. Define $freq$ for C' as for C, except that $z.freq = x.freq + y.freq$. Let T' be any tree representing an optimal prefix code for the alphabet C'. Then the tree T, obtained from T' by replacing the leaf node for z with an internal node having x and y as children, represents an optimal prefix code for the alphabet C.

Proof   We first show how to express the cost $B(T)$ of tree T in terms of the cost $B(T')$ of tree T', by considering the component costs in equation (16.4). For each character $c \in C - \{x, y\}$, we have that $d_T(c) = d_{T'}(c)$, and hence $c.freq \cdot d_T(c) = c.freq \cdot d_{T'}(c)$. Since $d_T(x) = d_T(y) = d_{T'}(z) + 1$, we have

$$
\begin{aligned}
x.freq \cdot d_T(x) + y.freq \cdot d_T(y) &= (x.freq + y.freq)(d_{T'}(z) + 1) \\
&= z.freq \cdot d_{T'}(z) + (x.freq + y.freq) \,,
\end{aligned}
$$

from which we conclude that

$$
B(T) = B(T') + x.freq + y.freq
$$

or, equivalently,

$$
B(T') = B(T) - x.freq - y.freq \,.
$$

We now prove the lemma by contradiction. Suppose that T does not represent an optimal prefix code for C. Then there exists an optimal tree T'' such that $B(T'') < B(T)$. Without loss of generality (by Lemma 16.2), T'' has x and y as siblings. Let T''' be the tree T'' with the common parent of x and y replaced by a leaf z with frequency $z.freq = x.freq + y.freq$. Then

$$
\begin{aligned}
B(T''') &= B(T'') - x.freq - y.freq \\
&< B(T) - x.freq - y.freq \\
&= B(T') \,,
\end{aligned}
$$

yielding a contradiction to the assumption that T' represents an optimal prefix code for C'. Thus, T must represent an optimal prefix code for the alphabet C.   ∎

Theorem 16.4
Procedure HUFFMAN produces an optimal prefix code.

Proof   Immediate from Lemmas 16.2 and 16.3.   ∎

Exercises

16.3-1
Explain why, in the proof of Lemma 16.2, if $x.freq = b.freq$, then we must have $a.freq = b.freq = x.freq = y.freq$.

16.3-2
Prove that a binary tree that is not full cannot correspond to an optimal prefix code.

16.3-3
What is an optimal Huffman code for the following set of frequencies, based on the first 8 Fibonacci numbers?

a:1 b:1 c:2 d:3 e:5 f:8 g:13 h:21

Can you generalize your answer to find the optimal code when the frequencies are the first n Fibonacci numbers?

16.3-4
Prove that we can also express the total cost of a tree for a code as the sum, over all internal nodes, of the combined frequencies of the two children of the node.

16.3-5
Prove that if we order the characters in an alphabet so that their frequencies are monotonically decreasing, then there exists an optimal code whose codeword lengths are monotonically increasing.

16.3-6
Suppose we have an optimal prefix code on a set $C = \{0, 1, \ldots, n-1\}$ of characters and we wish to transmit this code using as few bits as possible. Show how to represent any optimal prefix code on C using only $2n - 1 + n \lceil \lg n \rceil$ bits. (*Hint:* Use $2n - 1$ bits to specify the structure of the tree, as discovered by a walk of the tree.)

16.3-7
Generalize Huffman's algorithm to ternary codewords (i.e., codewords using the symbols 0, 1, and 2), and prove that it yields optimal ternary codes.

16.3-8
Suppose that a data file contains a sequence of 8-bit characters such that all 256 characters are about equally common: the maximum character frequency is less than twice the minimum character frequency. Prove that Huffman coding in this case is no more efficient than using an ordinary 8-bit fixed-length code.

16.3-9

Show that no compression scheme can expect to compress a file of randomly chosen 8-bit characters by even a single bit. (*Hint:* Compare the number of possible files with the number of possible encoded files.)

★ 16.4 Matroids and greedy methods

In this section, we sketch a beautiful theory about greedy algorithms. This theory describes many situations in which the greedy method yields optimal solutions. It involves combinatorial structures known as "matroids." Although this theory does not cover all cases for which a greedy method applies (for example, it does not cover the activity-selection problem of Section 16.1 or the Huffman-coding problem of Section 16.3), it does cover many cases of practical interest. Furthermore, this theory has been extended to cover many applications; see the notes at the end of this chapter for references.

Matroids

A **matroid** is an ordered pair $M = (S, \mathcal{I})$ satisfying the following conditions.

1. S is a finite set.

2. $\mathcal{I}$ is a nonempty family of subsets of S, called the **independent** subsets of S, such that if $B \in \mathcal{I}$ and $A \subseteq B$, then $A \in \mathcal{I}$. We say that $\mathcal{I}$ is **hereditary** if it satisfies this property. Note that the empty set $\emptyset$ is necessarily a member of $\mathcal{I}$.

3. If $A \in \mathcal{I}$, $B \in \mathcal{I}$, and $|A| < |B|$, then there exists some element $x \in B - A$ such that $A \cup \{x\} \in \mathcal{I}$. We say that M satisfies the **exchange property**.

The word "matroid" is due to Hassler Whitney. He was studying **matric matroids**, in which the elements of S are the rows of a given matrix and a set of rows is independent if they are linearly independent in the usual sense. As Exercise 16.4-2 asks you to show, this structure defines a matroid.

As another example of matroids, consider the **graphic matroid** $M_G = (S_G, \mathcal{I}_G)$ defined in terms of a given undirected graph $G = (V, E)$ as follows:

- The set S_G is defined to be E, the set of edges of G.

- If A is a subset of E, then $A \in \mathcal{I}_G$ if and only if A is acyclic. That is, a set of edges A is independent if and only if the subgraph $G_A = (V, A)$ forms a forest.

The graphic matroid M_G is closely related to the minimum-spanning-tree problem, which Chapter 23 covers in detail.

Theorem 16.5

If $G = (V, E)$ is an undirected graph, then $M_G = (S_G, \mathcal{I}_G)$ is a matroid.

Proof   Clearly, $S_G = E$ is a finite set. Furthermore, $\mathcal{I}_G$ is hereditary, since a subset of a forest is a forest. Putting it another way, removing edges from an acyclic set of edges cannot create cycles.

Thus, it remains to show that M_G satisfies the exchange property. Suppose that $G_A = (V, A)$ and $G_B = (V, B)$ are forests of G and that $|B| > |A|$. That is, A and B are acyclic sets of edges, and B contains more edges than A does.

We claim that a forest $F = (V_F, E_F)$ contains exactly $|V_F| - |E_F|$ trees. To see why, suppose that F consists of t trees, where the ith tree contains v_i vertices and e_i edges. Then, we have

$$
\begin{aligned}
|E_F| &= \sum_{i=1}^{t} e_i \\
&= \sum_{i=1}^{t} (v_i - 1) \quad \text{(by Theorem B.2)} \\
&= \sum_{i=1}^{t} v_i - t \\
&= |V_F| - t ,
\end{aligned}
$$

which implies that $t = |V_F| - |E_F|$. Thus, forest G_A contains $|V| - |A|$ trees, and forest G_B contains $|V| - |B|$ trees.

Since forest G_B has fewer trees than forest G_A does, forest G_B must contain some tree T whose vertices are in two different trees in forest G_A. Moreover, since T is connected, it must contain an edge (u, v) such that vertices u and v are in different trees in forest G_A. Since the edge (u, v) connects vertices in two different trees in forest G_A, we can add the edge (u, v) to forest G_A without creating a cycle. Therefore, M_G satisfies the exchange property, completing the proof that M_G is a matroid.   ∎

Given a matroid $M = (S, \mathcal{I})$, we call an element $x \notin A$ an **extension** of $A \in \mathcal{I}$ if we can add x to A while preserving independence; that is, x is an extension of A if $A \cup \{x\} \in \mathcal{I}$. As an example, consider a graphic matroid M_G. If A is an independent set of edges, then edge e is an extension of A if and only if e is not in A and the addition of e to A does not create a cycle.

If A is an independent subset in a matroid M, we say that A is **maximal** if it has no extensions. That is, A is maximal if it is not contained in any larger independent subset of M. The following property is often useful.

Theorem 16.6
All maximal independent subsets in a matroid have the same size.

Proof   Suppose to the contrary that A is a maximal independent subset of M and there exists another larger maximal independent subset B of M. Then, the exchange property implies that for some $x \in B - A$, we can extend A to a larger independent set $A \cup \{x\}$, contradicting the assumption that A is maximal.   ■

As an illustration of this theorem, consider a graphic matroid M_G for a connected, undirected graph G. Every maximal independent subset of M_G must be a free tree with exactly $|V| - 1$ edges that connects all the vertices of G. Such a tree is called a ***spanning tree*** of G.

We say that a matroid $M = (S, \mathcal{I})$ is ***weighted*** if it is associated with a weight function w that assigns a strictly positive weight $w(x)$ to each element $x \in S$. The weight function w extends to subsets of S by summation:

$$w(A) = \sum_{x \in A} w(x)$$

for any $A \subseteq S$. For example, if we let $w(e)$ denote the weight of an edge e in a graphic matroid M_G, then $w(A)$ is the total weight of the edges in edge set A.

Greedy algorithms on a weighted matroid

Many problems for which a greedy approach provides optimal solutions can be formulated in terms of finding a maximum-weight independent subset in a weighted matroid. That is, we are given a weighted matroid $M = (S, \mathcal{I})$, and we wish to find an independent set $A \in \mathcal{I}$ such that $w(A)$ is maximized. We call such a subset that is independent and has maximum possible weight an ***optimal*** subset of the matroid. Because the weight $w(x)$ of any element $x \in S$ is positive, an optimal subset is always a maximal independent subset—it always helps to make A as large as possible.

For example, in the ***minimum-spanning-tree problem***, we are given a connected undirected graph $G = (V, E)$ and a length function w such that $w(e)$ is the (positive) length of edge e. (We use the term "length" here to refer to the original edge weights for the graph, reserving the term "weight" to refer to the weights in the associated matroid.) We wish to find a subset of the edges that connects all of the vertices together and has minimum total length. To view this as a problem of finding an optimal subset of a matroid, consider the weighted matroid M_G with weight function w', where $w'(e) = w_0 - w(e)$ and w_0 is larger than the maximum length of any edge. In this weighted matroid, all weights are positive and an optimal subset is a spanning tree of minimum total length in the original graph. More specifically, each maximal independent subset A corresponds to a spanning tree

with $|V| - 1$ edges, and since

$$
\begin{aligned}
w'(A) &= \sum_{e \in A} w'(e) \\
&= \sum_{e \in A} (w_0 - w(e)) \\
&= (|V| - 1)w_0 - \sum_{e \in A} w(e) \\
&= (|V| - 1)w_0 - w(A)
\end{aligned}
$$

for any maximal independent subset A, an independent subset that maximizes the quantity $w'(A)$ must minimize $w(A)$. Thus, any algorithm that can find an optimal subset A in an arbitrary matroid can solve the minimum-spanning-tree problem.

Chapter 23 gives algorithms for the minimum-spanning-tree problem, but here we give a greedy algorithm that works for any weighted matroid. The algorithm takes as input a weighted matroid $M = (S, \mathcal{I})$ with an associated positive weight function w, and it returns an optimal subset A. In our pseudocode, we denote the components of M by $M.S$ and $M.\mathcal{I}$ and the weight function by w. The algorithm is greedy because it considers in turn each element $x \in S$, in order of monotonically decreasing weight, and immediately adds it to the set A being accumulated if $A \cup \{x\}$ is independent.

GREEDY(M, w)

```
1  A = ∅
2  sort M.S into monotonically decreasing order by weight w
3  for each x ∈ M.S, taken in monotonically decreasing order by weight w(x)
4      if A ∪ {x} ∈ M.I
5          A = A ∪ {x}
6  return A
```

Line 4 checks whether adding each element x to A would maintain A as an independent set. If A would remain independent, then line 5 adds x to A. Otherwise, x is discarded. Since the empty set is independent, and since each iteration of the **for** loop maintains A's independence, the subset A is always independent, by induction. Therefore, GREEDY always returns an independent subset A. We shall see in a moment that A is a subset of maximum possible weight, so that A is an optimal subset.

The running time of GREEDY is easy to analyze. Let n denote $|S|$. The sorting phase of GREEDY takes time $O(n \lg n)$. Line 4 executes exactly n times, once for each element of S. Each execution of line 4 requires a check on whether or not the set $A \cup \{x\}$ is independent. If each such check takes time $O(f(n))$, the entire algorithm runs in time $O(n \lg n + n f(n))$.

We now prove that GREEDY returns an optimal subset.

Lemma 16.7 (Matroids exhibit the greedy-choice property)

Suppose that $M = (S, \mathcal{I})$ is a weighted matroid with weight function w and that S is sorted into monotonically decreasing order by weight. Let x be the first element of S such that $\{x\}$ is independent, if any such x exists. If x exists, then there exists an optimal subset A of S that contains x.

Proof If no such x exists, then the only independent subset is the empty set and the lemma is vacuously true. Otherwise, let B be any nonempty optimal subset. Assume that $x \notin B$; otherwise, letting $A = B$ gives an optimal subset of S that contains x.

No element of B has weight greater than $w(x)$. To see why, observe that $y \in B$ implies that $\{y\}$ is independent, since $B \in \mathcal{I}$ and $\mathcal{I}$ is hereditary. Our choice of x therefore ensures that $w(x) \geq w(y)$ for any $y \in B$.

Construct the set A as follows. Begin with $A = \{x\}$. By the choice of x, set A is independent. Using the exchange property, repeatedly find a new element of B that we can add to A until $|A| = |B|$, while preserving the independence of A. At that point, A and B are the same except that A has x and B has some other element y. That is, $A = B - \{y\} \cup \{x\}$ for some $y \in B$, and so

$$
\begin{aligned}
w(A) &= w(B) - w(y) + w(x) \\
&\geq w(B) \, .
\end{aligned}
$$

Because set B is optimal, set A, which contains x, must also be optimal. ■

We next show that if an element is not an option initially, then it cannot be an option later.

Lemma 16.8

Let $M = (S, \mathcal{I})$ be any matroid. If x is an element of S that is an extension of some independent subset A of S, then x is also an extension of $\emptyset$.

Proof Since x is an extension of A, we have that $A \cup \{x\}$ is independent. Since $\mathcal{I}$ is hereditary, $\{x\}$ must be independent. Thus, x is an extension of $\emptyset$. ■

Corollary 16.9

Let $M = (S, \mathcal{I})$ be any matroid. If x is an element of S such that x is not an extension of $\emptyset$, then x is not an extension of any independent subset A of S.

Proof This corollary is simply the contrapositive of Lemma 16.8. ■

Corollary 16.9 says that any element that cannot be used immediately can never be used. Therefore, GREEDY cannot make an error by passing over any initial elements in S that are not an extension of $\emptyset$, since they can never be used.

Lemma 16.10 (Matroids exhibit the optimal-substructure property)

Let x be the first element of S chosen by GREEDY for the weighted matroid $M = (S, I)$. The remaining problem of finding a maximum-weight independent subset containing x reduces to finding a maximum-weight independent subset of the weighted matroid $M' = (S', I')$, where

$$S' = \{y \in S : \{x, y\} \in I\} \, ,$$
$$I' = \{B \subseteq S - \{x\} : B \cup \{x\} \in I\} \, ,$$

and the weight function for M' is the weight function for M, restricted to S'. (We call M' the **contraction** of M by the element x.)

Proof If A is any maximum-weight independent subset of M containing x, then $A' = A - \{x\}$ is an independent subset of M'. Conversely, any independent subset A' of M' yields an independent subset $A = A' \cup \{x\}$ of M. Since we have in both cases that $w(A) = w(A') + w(x)$, a maximum-weight solution in M containing x yields a maximum-weight solution in M', and vice versa. ∎

Theorem 16.11 (Correctness of the greedy algorithm on matroids)

If $M = (S, I)$ is a weighted matroid with weight function w, then GREEDY(M, w) returns an optimal subset.

Proof By Corollary 16.9, any elements that GREEDY passes over initially because they are not extensions of $\emptyset$ can be forgotten about, since they can never be useful. Once GREEDY selects the first element x, Lemma 16.7 implies that the algorithm does not err by adding x to A, since there exists an optimal subset containing x. Finally, Lemma 16.10 implies that the remaining problem is one of finding an optimal subset in the matroid M' that is the contraction of M by x. After the procedure GREEDY sets A to $\{x\}$, we can interpret all of its remaining steps as acting in the matroid $M' = (S', I')$, because B is independent in M' if and only if $B \cup \{x\}$ is independent in M, for all sets $B \in I'$. Thus, the subsequent operation of GREEDY will find a maximum-weight independent subset for M', and the overall operation of GREEDY will find a maximum-weight independent subset for M. ∎

Exercises

16.4-1
Show that $(S, \mathcal{I}_k)$ is a matroid, where S is any finite set and $\mathcal{I}_k$ is the set of all subsets of S of size at most k, where $k \leq |S|$.

16.4-2   ★
Given an $m \times n$ matrix T over some field (such as the reals), show that $(S, \mathcal{I})$ is a matroid, where S is the set of columns of T and $A \in \mathcal{I}$ if and only if the columns in A are linearly independent.

16.4-3   ★
Show that if $(S, \mathcal{I})$ is a matroid, then $(S, \mathcal{I}')$ is a matroid, where

$$\mathcal{I}' = \{A' : S - A' \text{ contains some maximal } A \in \mathcal{I}\} \ .$$

That is, the maximal independent sets of $(S, \mathcal{I}')$ are just the complements of the maximal independent sets of $(S, \mathcal{I})$.

16.4-4   ★
Let S be a finite set and let $S_1, S_2, \ldots, S_k$ be a partition of S into nonempty disjoint subsets. Define the structure $(S, \mathcal{I})$ by the condition that $\mathcal{I} = \{A : |A \cap S_i| \leq 1$ for $i = 1, 2, \ldots, k\}$. Show that $(S, \mathcal{I})$ is a matroid. That is, the set of all sets A that contain at most one member of each subset in the partition determines the independent sets of a matroid.

16.4-5
Show how to transform the weight function of a weighted matroid problem, where the desired optimal solution is a *minimum-weight* maximal independent subset, to make it a standard weighted-matroid problem. Argue carefully that your transformation is correct.

★   **16.5   A task-scheduling problem as a matroid**

An interesting problem that we can solve using matroids is the problem of optimally scheduling unit-time tasks on a single processor, where each task has a deadline, along with a penalty paid if the task misses its deadline. The problem looks complicated, but we can solve it in a surprisingly simple manner by casting it as a matroid and using a greedy algorithm.

A ***unit-time task*** is a job, such as a program to be run on a computer, that requires exactly one unit of time to complete. Given a finite set S of unit-time tasks, a

schedule for S is a permutation of S specifying the order in which to perform these tasks. The first task in the schedule begins at time 0 and finishes at time 1, the second task begins at time 1 and finishes at time 2, and so on.

The problem of *scheduling unit-time tasks with deadlines and penalties for a single processor* has the following inputs:

- a set $S = \{a_1, a_2, \ldots, a_n\}$ of n unit-time tasks;

- a set of n integer *deadlines* $d_1, d_2, \ldots, d_n$, such that each d_i satisfies $1 \leq d_i \leq n$ and task a_i is supposed to finish by time d_i; and

- a set of n nonnegative weights or *penalties* $w_1, w_2, \ldots, w_n$, such that we incur a penalty of w_i if task a_i is not finished by time d_i, and we incur no penalty if a task finishes by its deadline.

We wish to find a schedule for S that minimizes the total penalty incurred for missed deadlines.

Consider a given schedule. We say that a task is *late* in this schedule if it finishes after its deadline. Otherwise, the task is *early* in the schedule. We can always transform an arbitrary schedule into *early-first form*, in which the early tasks precede the late tasks. To see why, note that if some early task a_i follows some late task a_j, then we can switch the positions of a_i and a_j, and a_i will still be early and a_j will still be late.

Furthermore, we claim that we can always transform an arbitrary schedule into *canonical form*, in which the early tasks precede the late tasks and we schedule the early tasks in order of monotonically increasing deadlines. To do so, we put the schedule into early-first form. Then, as long as there exist two early tasks a_i and a_j finishing at respective times k and $k + 1$ in the schedule such that $d_j < d_i$, we swap the positions of a_i and a_j. Since a_j is early before the swap, $k + 1 \leq d_j$. Therefore, $k + 1 < d_i$, and so a_i is still early after the swap. Because task a_j is moved earlier in the schedule, it remains early after the swap.

The search for an optimal schedule thus reduces to finding a set A of tasks that we assign to be early in the optimal schedule. Having determined A, we can create the actual schedule by listing the elements of A in order of monotonically increasing deadlines, then listing the late tasks (i.e., $S - A$) in any order, producing a canonical ordering of the optimal schedule.

We say that a set A of tasks is *independent* if there exists a schedule for these tasks such that no tasks are late. Clearly, the set of early tasks for a schedule forms an independent set of tasks. Let $\mathcal{I}$ denote the set of all independent sets of tasks.

Consider the problem of determining whether a given set A of tasks is independent. For $t = 0, 1, 2, \ldots, n$, let $N_t(A)$ denote the number of tasks in A whose deadline is t or earlier. Note that $N_0(A) = 0$ for any set A.

Lemma 16.12
For any set of tasks A, the following statements are equivalent.

1. The set A is independent.

2. For $t = 0, 1, 2, \ldots, n$, we have $N_t(A) \leq t$.

3. If the tasks in A are scheduled in order of monotonically increasing deadlines, then no task is late.

Proof   To show that (1) implies (2), we prove the contrapositive: if $N_t(A) > t$ for some t, then there is no way to make a schedule with no late tasks for set A, because more than t tasks must finish before time t. Therefore, (1) implies (2). If (2) holds, then (3) must follow: there is no way to "get stuck" when scheduling the tasks in order of monotonically increasing deadlines, since (2) implies that the ith largest deadline is at least i. Finally, (3) trivially implies (1).   ■

Using property 2 of Lemma 16.12, we can easily compute whether or not a given set of tasks is independent (see Exercise 16.5-2).

The problem of minimizing the sum of the penalties of the late tasks is the same as the problem of maximizing the sum of the penalties of the early tasks. The following theorem thus ensures that we can use the greedy algorithm to find an independent set A of tasks with the maximum total penalty.

Theorem 16.13
If S is a set of unit-time tasks with deadlines, and $\mathcal{I}$ is the set of all independent sets of tasks, then the corresponding system $(S, \mathcal{I})$ is a matroid.

Proof   Every subset of an independent set of tasks is certainly independent. To prove the exchange property, suppose that B and A are independent sets of tasks and that $|B| > |A|$. Let k be the largest t such that $N_t(B) \leq N_t(A)$. (Such a value of t exists, since $N_0(A) = N_0(B) = 0$.) Since $N_n(B) = |B|$ and $N_n(A) = |A|$, but $|B| > |A|$, we must have that $k < n$ and that $N_j(B) > N_j(A)$ for all j in the range $k + 1 \leq j \leq n$. Therefore, B contains more tasks with deadline $k + 1$ than A does. Let a_i be a task in $B - A$ with deadline $k + 1$. Let $A' = A \cup \{a_i\}$.

We now show that A' must be independent by using property 2 of Lemma 16.12. For $0 \leq t \leq k$, we have $N_t(A') = N_t(A) \leq t$, since A is independent. For $k < t \leq n$, we have $N_t(A') \leq N_t(B) \leq t$, since B is independent. Therefore, A' is independent, completing our proof that $(S, \mathcal{I})$ is a matroid.   ■

By Theorem 16.11, we can use a greedy algorithm to find a maximum-weight independent set of tasks A. We can then create an optimal schedule having the tasks in A as its early tasks. This method is an efficient algorithm for scheduling

		Task					
a_i	1	2	3	4	5	6	7
d_i	4	2	4	3	1	4	6
w_i	70	60	50	40	30	20	10

Figure 16.7   An instance of the problem of scheduling unit-time tasks with deadlines and penalties for a single processor.

unit-time tasks with deadlines and penalties for a single processor. The running time is $O(n^2)$ using GREEDY, since each of the $O(n)$ independence checks made by that algorithm takes time $O(n)$ (see Exercise 16.5-2). Problem 16-4 gives a faster implementation.

Figure 16.7 demonstrates an example of the problem of scheduling unit-time tasks with deadlines and penalties for a single processor. In this example, the greedy algorithm selects, in order, tasks a_1, a_2, a_3, and a_4, then rejects a_5 (because $N_4(\{a_1, a_2, a_3, a_4, a_5\}) = 5$) and a_6 (because $N_4(\{a_1, a_2, a_3, a_4, a_6\}) = 5$), and finally accepts a_7. The final optimal schedule is

$$\langle a_2, a_4, a_1, a_3, a_7, a_5, a_6 \rangle ,$$

which has a total penalty incurred of $w_5 + w_6 = 50$.

Exercises

16.5-1
Solve the instance of the scheduling problem given in Figure 16.7, but with each penalty w_i replaced by $80 - w_i$.

16.5-2
Show how to use property 2 of Lemma 16.12 to determine in time $O(|A|)$ whether or not a given set A of tasks is independent.

Problems

16-1   Coin changing
Consider the problem of making change for n cents using the fewest number of coins. Assume that each coin's value is an integer.

a. Describe a greedy algorithm to make change consisting of quarters, dimes, nickels, and pennies. Prove that your algorithm yields an optimal solution.

b. Suppose that the available coins are in the denominations that are powers of c, i.e., the denominations are $c^0, c^1, \ldots, c^k$ for some integers $c > 1$ and $k \geq 1$. Show that the greedy algorithm always yields an optimal solution.

c. Give a set of coin denominations for which the greedy algorithm does not yield an optimal solution. Your set should include a penny so that there is a solution for every value of n.

d. Give an $O(nk)$-time algorithm that makes change for any set of k different coin denominations, assuming that one of the coins is a penny.

16-2 *Scheduling to minimize average completion time*

Suppose you are given a set $S = \{a_1, a_2, \ldots, a_n\}$ of tasks, where task a_i requires p_i units of processing time to complete, once it has started. You have one computer on which to run these tasks, and the computer can run only one task at a time. Let c_i be the *completion time* of task a_i, that is, the time at which task a_i completes processing. Your goal is to minimize the average completion time, that is, to minimize $(1/n) \sum_{i=1}^{n} c_i$. For example, suppose there are two tasks, a_1 and a_2, with $p_1 = 3$ and $p_2 = 5$, and consider the schedule in which a_2 runs first, followed by a_1. Then $c_2 = 5$, $c_1 = 8$, and the average completion time is $(5 + 8)/2 = 6.5$. If task a_1 runs first, however, then $c_1 = 3$, $c_2 = 8$, and the average completion time is $(3 + 8)/2 = 5.5$.

a. Give an algorithm that schedules the tasks so as to minimize the average completion time. Each task must run non-preemptively, that is, once task a_i starts, it must run continuously for p_i units of time. Prove that your algorithm minimizes the average completion time, and state the running time of your algorithm.

b. Suppose now that the tasks are not all available at once. That is, each task cannot start until its *release time* r_i. Suppose also that we allow *preemption*, so that a task can be suspended and restarted at a later time. For example, a task a_i with processing time $p_i = 6$ and release time $r_i = 1$ might start running at time 1 and be preempted at time 4. It might then resume at time 10 but be preempted at time 11, and it might finally resume at time 13 and complete at time 15. Task a_i has run for a total of 6 time units, but its running time has been divided into three pieces. In this scenario, a_i's completion time is 15. Give an algorithm that schedules the tasks so as to minimize the average completion time in this new scenario. Prove that your algorithm minimizes the average completion time, and state the running time of your algorithm.

16-3   Acyclic subgraphs

a. The ***incidence matrix*** for an undirected graph $G = (V, E)$ is a $|V| \times |E|$ matrix M such that $M_{ve} = 1$ if edge e is incident on vertex v, and $M_{ve} = 0$ otherwise. Argue that a set of columns of M is linearly independent over the field of integers modulo 2 if and only if the corresponding set of edges is acyclic.

b. Suppose that we associate a nonnegative weight $w(e)$ with each edge in an undirected graph $G = (V, E)$. Give an efficient algorithm to find an acyclic subset of E of maximum total weight.

c. Let $G(V, E)$ be an arbitrary directed graph, and let $(E, \mathcal{I})$ be defined so that $A \in \mathcal{I}$ if and only if A does not contain any directed cycles. Give an example of a directed graph G such that the associated system $(E, \mathcal{I})$ is not a matroid. Specify which defining condition for a matroid fails to hold.

d. The ***incidence matrix*** for a directed graph $G = (V, E)$ with no self-loops is a $|V| \times |E|$ matrix M such that $M_{ve} = -1$ if edge e leaves vertex v, $M_{ve} = 1$ if edge e enters vertex v, and $M_{ve} = 0$ otherwise. Argue that if a set of columns of M is linearly independent, then the corresponding set of edges does not contain a directed cycle.

e. Exercise 16.4-2 tells us that the set of linearly independent sets of columns of any matrix M forms a matroid. Explain carefully why the results of parts (c) and (d) are not contradictory. How can there fail to be a perfect correspondence between the notion of a set of edges being acyclic and the notion of the associated set of columns of the incidence matrix being linearly independent?

16-4   Scheduling variations

Consider the following algorithm for the problem from Section 16.5 of scheduling unit-time tasks with deadlines and penalties. Let all n time slots be initially empty, where time slot i is the unit-length slot of time that finishes at time i. We consider the tasks in order of monotonically decreasing penalty. When considering task a_j, if there exists a time slot at or before a_j's deadline d_j that is still empty, assign a_j to the latest such slot, filling it. If there is no such slot, assign task a_j to the latest of the as yet unfilled slots.

a. Argue that this algorithm always gives an optimal answer.

b. Use the fast disjoint-set forest presented in Section 21.3 to implement the algorithm efficiently. Assume that the set of input tasks has already been sorted into monotonically decreasing order by penalty. Analyze the running time of your implementation.

16-5   Off-line caching

Modern computers use a cache to store a small amount of data in a fast memory. Even though a program may access large amounts of data, by storing a small subset of the main memory in the ***cache***—a small but faster memory—overall access time can greatly decrease. When a computer program executes, it makes a sequence $\langle r_1, r_2, \ldots, r_n \rangle$ of n memory requests, where each request is for a particular data element. For example, a program that accesses 4 distinct elements $\{a, b, c, d\}$ might make the sequence of requests $\langle d, b, d, b, d, a, c, d, b, a, c, b \rangle$. Let k be the size of the cache. When the cache contains k elements and the program requests the $(k + 1)$st element, the system must decide, for this and each subsequent request, which k elements to keep in the cache. More precisely, for each request r_i, the cache-management algorithm checks whether element r_i is already in the cache. If it is, then we have a ***cache hit***; otherwise, we have a ***cache miss***. Upon a cache miss, the system retrieves r_i from the main memory, and the cache-management algorithm must decide whether to keep r_i in the cache. If it decides to keep r_i and the cache already holds k elements, then it must evict one element to make room for r_i. The cache-management algorithm evicts data with the goal of minimizing the number of cache misses over the entire sequence of requests.

Typically, caching is an on-line problem. That is, we have to make decisions about which data to keep in the cache without knowing the future requests. Here, however, we consider the off-line version of this problem, in which we are given in advance the entire sequence of n requests and the cache size k, and we wish to minimize the total number of cache misses.

We can solve this off-line problem by a greedy strategy called ***furthest-in-future***, which chooses to evict the item in the cache whose next access in the request sequence comes furthest in the future.

a. Write pseudocode for a cache manager that uses the furthest-in-future strategy. The input should be a sequence $\langle r_1, r_2, \ldots, r_n \rangle$ of requests and a cache size k, and the output should be a sequence of decisions about which data element (if any) to evict upon each request. What is the running time of your algorithm?

b. Show that the off-line caching problem exhibits optimal substructure.

c. Prove that furthest-in-future produces the minimum possible number of cache misses.

Chapter notes

Much more material on greedy algorithms and matroids can be found in Lawler [224] and Papadimitriou and Steiglitz [271].

The greedy algorithm first appeared in the combinatorial optimization literature in a 1971 article by Edmonds [101], though the theory of matroids dates back to a 1935 article by Whitney [355].

Our proof of the correctness of the greedy algorithm for the activity-selection problem is based on that of Gavril [131]. The task-scheduling problem is studied in Lawler [224]; Horowitz, Sahni, and Rajasekaran [181]; and Brassard and Bratley [54].

Huffman codes were invented in 1952 [185]; Lelewer and Hirschberg [231] surveys data-compression techniques known as of 1987.

An extension of matroid theory to greedoid theory was pioneered by Korte and Lovász [216, 217, 218, 219], who greatly generalize the theory presented here.

17 Amortized Analysis

In an ***amortized analysis***, we average the time required to perform a sequence of data-structure operations over all the operations performed. With amortized analysis, we can show that the average cost of an operation is small, if we average over a sequence of operations, even though a single operation within the sequence might be expensive. Amortized analysis differs from average-case analysis in that probability is not involved; an amortized analysis guarantees the *average performance of each operation in the worst case*.

The first three sections of this chapter cover the three most common techniques used in amortized analysis. Section 17.1 starts with aggregate analysis, in which we determine an upper bound $T(n)$ on the total cost of a sequence of n operations. The average cost per operation is then $T(n)/n$. We take the average cost as the amortized cost of each operation, so that all operations have the same amortized cost.

Section 17.2 covers the accounting method, in which we determine an amortized cost of each operation. When there is more than one type of operation, each type of operation may have a different amortized cost. The accounting method overcharges some operations early in the sequence, storing the overcharge as "prepaid credit" on specific objects in the data structure. Later in the sequence, the credit pays for operations that are charged less than they actually cost.

Section 17.3 discusses the potential method, which is like the accounting method in that we determine the amortized cost of each operation and may overcharge operations early on to compensate for undercharges later. The potential method maintains the credit as the "potential energy" of the data structure as a whole instead of associating the credit with individual objects within the data structure.

We shall use two examples to examine these three methods. One is a stack with the additional operation MULTIPOP, which pops several objects at once. The other is a binary counter that counts up from 0 by means of the single operation INCREMENT.

While reading this chapter, bear in mind that the charges assigned during an amortized analysis are for analysis purposes only. They need not—and should not—appear in the code. If, for example, we assign a credit to an object x when using the accounting method, we have no need to assign an appropriate amount to some attribute, such as $x.credit$, in the code.

When we perform an amortized analysis, we often gain insight into a particular data structure, and this insight can help us optimize the design. In Section 17.4, for example, we shall use the potential method to analyze a dynamically expanding and contracting table.

17.1   Aggregate analysis

In **aggregate analysis**, we show that for all n, a sequence of n operations takes *worst-case* time $T(n)$ in total. In the worst case, the average cost, or **amortized cost**, per operation is therefore $T(n)/n$. Note that this amortized cost applies to each operation, even when there are several types of operations in the sequence. The other two methods we shall study in this chapter, the accounting method and the potential method, may assign different amortized costs to different types of operations.

Stack operations

In our first example of aggregate analysis, we analyze stacks that have been augmented with a new operation. Section 10.1 presented the two fundamental stack operations, each of which takes $O(1)$ time:

PUSH(S, x) pushes object x onto stack S.

POP(S) pops the top of stack S and returns the popped object. Calling POP on an empty stack generates an error.

Since each of these operations runs in $O(1)$ time, let us consider the cost of each to be 1. The total cost of a sequence of n PUSH and POP operations is therefore n, and the actual running time for n operations is therefore $\Theta(n)$.

Now we add the stack operation MULTIPOP(S, k), which removes the k top objects of stack S, popping the entire stack if the stack contains fewer than k objects. Of course, we assume that k is positive; otherwise the MULTIPOP operation leaves the stack unchanged. In the following pseudocode, the operation STACK-EMPTY returns TRUE if there are no objects currently on the stack, and FALSE otherwise.

$\sum_{i=1}^{n} \hat{c}_i - \sum_{i=1}^{n} c_i$. By inequality (17.1), the total credit associated with the data structure must be nonnegative at all times. If we ever were to allow the total credit to become negative (the result of undercharging early operations with the promise of repaying the account later on), then the total amortized costs incurred at that time would be below the total actual costs incurred; for the sequence of operations up to that time, the total amortized cost would not be an upper bound on the total actual cost. Thus, we must take care that the total credit in the data structure never becomes negative.

Stack operations

To illustrate the accounting method of amortized analysis, let us return to the stack example. Recall that the actual costs of the operations were

PUSH   1 ,
POP   1 ,
MULTIPOP $\min(k, s)$,

where k is the argument supplied to MULTIPOP and s is the stack size when it is called. Let us assign the following amortized costs:

PUSH   2 ,
POP   0 ,
MULTIPOP   0 .

Note that the amortized cost of MULTIPOP is a constant (0), whereas the actual cost is variable. Here, all three amortized costs are constant. In general, the amortized costs of the operations under consideration may differ from each other, and they may even differ asymptotically.

We shall now show that we can pay for any sequence of stack operations by charging the amortized costs. Suppose we use a dollar bill to represent each unit of cost. We start with an empty stack. Recall the analogy of Section 10.1 between the stack data structure and a stack of plates in a cafeteria. When we push a plate on the stack, we use 1 dollar to pay the actual cost of the push and are left with a credit of 1 dollar (out of the 2 dollars charged), which we leave on top of the plate. At any point in time, every plate on the stack has a dollar of credit on it.

The dollar stored on the plate serves as prepayment for the cost of popping it from the stack. When we execute a POP operation, we charge the operation nothing and pay its actual cost using the credit stored in the stack. To pop a plate, we take the dollar of credit off the plate and use it to pay the actual cost of the operation. Thus, by charging the PUSH operation a little bit more, we can charge the POP operation nothing.

Moreover, we can also charge MULTIPOP operations nothing. To pop the first plate, we take the dollar of credit off the plate and use it to pay the actual cost of a POP operation. To pop a second plate, we again have a dollar of credit on the plate to pay for the POP operation, and so on. Thus, we have always charged enough up front to pay for MULTIPOP operations. In other words, since each plate on the stack has 1 dollar of credit on it, and the stack always has a nonnegative number of plates, we have ensured that the amount of credit is always nonnegative. Thus, for *any* sequence of n PUSH, POP, and MULTIPOP operations, the total amortized cost is an upper bound on the total actual cost. Since the total amortized cost is $O(n)$, so is the total actual cost.

Incrementing a binary counter

As another illustration of the accounting method, we analyze the INCREMENT operation on a binary counter that starts at zero. As we observed earlier, the running time of this operation is proportional to the number of bits flipped, which we shall use as our cost for this example. Let us once again use a dollar bill to represent each unit of cost (the flipping of a bit in this example).

For the amortized analysis, let us charge an amortized cost of 2 dollars to set a bit to 1. When a bit is set, we use 1 dollar (out of the 2 dollars charged) to pay for the actual setting of the bit, and we place the other dollar on the bit as credit to be used later when we flip the bit back to 0. At any point in time, every 1 in the counter has a dollar of credit on it, and thus we can charge nothing to reset a bit to 0; we just pay for the reset with the dollar bill on the bit.

Now we can determine the amortized cost of INCREMENT. The cost of resetting the bits within the **while** loop is paid for by the dollars on the bits that are reset. The INCREMENT procedure sets at most one bit, in line 6, and therefore the amortized cost of an INCREMENT operation is at most 2 dollars. The number of 1s in the counter never becomes negative, and thus the amount of credit stays nonnegative at all times. Thus, for n INCREMENT operations, the total amortized cost is $O(n)$, which bounds the total actual cost.

Exercises

17.2-1

Suppose we perform a sequence of stack operations on a stack whose size never exceeds k. After every k operations, we make a copy of the entire stack for backup purposes. Show that the cost of n stack operations, including copying the stack, is $O(n)$ by assigning suitable amortized costs to the various stack operations.

17.2-2
Redo Exercise 17.1-3 using an accounting method of analysis.

17.2-3
Suppose we wish not only to increment a counter but also to reset it to zero (i.e., make all bits in it 0). Counting the time to examine or modify a bit as $\Theta(1)$, show how to implement a counter as an array of bits so that any sequence of n INCREMENT and RESET operations takes time $O(n)$ on an initially zero counter. (*Hint:* Keep a pointer to the high-order 1.)

17.3   The potential method

Instead of representing prepaid work as credit stored with specific objects in the data structure, the **potential method** of amortized analysis represents the prepaid work as "potential energy," or just "potential," which can be released to pay for future operations. We associate the potential with the data structure as a whole rather than with specific objects within the data structure.

The potential method works as follows. We will perform n operations, starting with an initial data structure D_0. For each $i = 1, 2, \ldots, n$, we let c_i be the actual cost of the ith operation and D_i be the data structure that results after applying the ith operation to data structure D_{i-1}. A **potential function** Φ maps each data structure D_i to a real number $\Phi(D_i)$, which is the **potential** associated with data structure D_i. The **amortized cost** $\widehat{c}_i$ of the ith operation with respect to potential function Φ is defined by

$$\widehat{c}_i = c_i + \Phi(D_i) - \Phi(D_{i-1}) \,. \tag{17.2}$$

The amortized cost of each operation is therefore its actual cost plus the change in potential due to the operation. By equation (17.2), the total amortized cost of the n operations is

$$
\begin{aligned}
\sum_{i=1}^{n} \widehat{c}_i &= \sum_{i=1}^{n} (c_i + \Phi(D_i) - \Phi(D_{i-1})) \\
&= \sum_{i=1}^{n} c_i + \Phi(D_n) - \Phi(D_0) \,. \tag{17.3}
\end{aligned}
$$

The second equality follows from equation (A.9) because the $\Phi(D_i)$ terms telescope.

If we can define a potential function Φ so that $\Phi(D_n) \geq \Phi(D_0)$, then the total amortized cost $\sum_{i=1}^{n} \widehat{c}_i$ gives an upper bound on the total actual cost $\sum_{i=1}^{n} c_i$.

In practice, we do not always know how many operations might be performed. Therefore, if we require that $\Phi(D_i) \geq \Phi(D_0)$ for all i, then we guarantee, as in the accounting method, that we pay in advance. We usually just define $\Phi(D_0)$ to be 0 and then show that $\Phi(D_i) \geq 0$ for all i. (See Exercise 17.3-1 for an easy way to handle cases in which $\Phi(D_0) \neq 0$.)

Intuitively, if the potential difference $\Phi(D_i) - \Phi(D_{i-1})$ of the ith operation is positive, then the amortized cost $\hat{c}_i$ represents an overcharge to the ith operation, and the potential of the data structure increases. If the potential difference is negative, then the amortized cost represents an undercharge to the ith operation, and the decrease in the potential pays for the actual cost of the operation.

The amortized costs defined by equations (17.2) and (17.3) depend on the choice of the potential function Φ. Different potential functions may yield different amortized costs yet still be upper bounds on the actual costs. We often find trade-offs that we can make in choosing a potential function; the best potential function to use depends on the desired time bounds.

Stack operations

To illustrate the potential method, we return once again to the example of the stack operations PUSH, POP, and MULTIPOP. We define the potential function Φ on a stack to be the number of objects in the stack. For the empty stack D_0 with which we start, we have $\Phi(D_0) = 0$. Since the number of objects in the stack is never negative, the stack D_i that results after the ith operation has nonnegative potential, and thus

$$
\begin{aligned}
\Phi(D_i) &\geq 0 \\
&= \Phi(D_0) \, .
\end{aligned}
$$

The total amortized cost of n operations with respect to Φ therefore represents an upper bound on the actual cost.

Let us now compute the amortized costs of the various stack operations. If the ith operation on a stack containing s objects is a PUSH operation, then the potential difference is

$$
\begin{aligned}
\Phi(D_i) - \Phi(D_{i-1}) &= (s+1) - s \\
&= 1 \, .
\end{aligned}
$$

By equation (17.2), the amortized cost of this PUSH operation is

$$
\begin{aligned}
\hat{c}_i &= c_i + \Phi(D_i) - \Phi(D_{i-1}) \\
&= 1 + 1 \\
&= 2 \, .
\end{aligned}
$$

Suppose that the ith operation on the stack is MULTIPOP(S, k), which causes $k' = \min(k, s)$ objects to be popped off the stack. The actual cost of the operation is k', and the potential difference is

$$\Phi(D_i) - \Phi(D_{i-1}) = -k' \, .$$

Thus, the amortized cost of the MULTIPOP operation is

$$
\begin{aligned}
\hat{c}_i &= c_i + \Phi(D_i) - \Phi(D_{i-1}) \\
&= k' - k' \\
&= 0 \, .
\end{aligned}
$$

Similarly, the amortized cost of an ordinary POP operation is 0.

The amortized cost of each of the three operations is $O(1)$, and thus the total amortized cost of a sequence of n operations is $O(n)$. Since we have already argued that $\Phi(D_i) \geq \Phi(D_0)$, the total amortized cost of n operations is an upper bound on the total actual cost. The worst-case cost of n operations is therefore $O(n)$.

Incrementing a binary counter

As another example of the potential method, we again look at incrementing a binary counter. This time, we define the potential of the counter after the ith INCREMENT operation to be b_i, the number of 1s in the counter after the ith operation.

Let us compute the amortized cost of an INCREMENT operation. Suppose that the ith INCREMENT operation resets t_i bits. The actual cost of the operation is therefore at most $t_i + 1$, since in addition to resetting t_i bits, it sets at most one bit to 1. If $b_i = 0$, then the ith operation resets all k bits, and so $b_{i-1} = t_i = k$. If $b_i > 0$, then $b_i = b_{i-1} - t_i + 1$. In either case, $b_i \leq b_{i-1} - t_i + 1$, and the potential difference is

$$
\begin{aligned}
\Phi(D_i) - \Phi(D_{i-1}) &\leq (b_{i-1} - t_i + 1) - b_{i-1} \\
&= 1 - t_i \, .
\end{aligned}
$$

The amortized cost is therefore

$$
\begin{aligned}
\hat{c}_i &= c_i + \Phi(D_i) - \Phi(D_{i-1}) \\
&\leq (t_i + 1) + (1 - t_i) \\
&= 2 \, .
\end{aligned}
$$

If the counter starts at zero, then $\Phi(D_0) = 0$. Since $\Phi(D_i) \geq 0$ for all i, the total amortized cost of a sequence of n INCREMENT operations is an upper bound on the total actual cost, and so the worst-case cost of n INCREMENT operations is $O(n)$.

The potential method gives us an easy way to analyze the counter even when it does not start at zero. The counter starts with b_0 1s, and after n INCREMENT

operations it has b_n 1s, where $0 \le b_0, b_n \le k$. (Recall that k is the number of bits in the counter.) We can rewrite equation (17.3) as

$$\sum_{i=1}^{n} c_i = \sum_{i=1}^{n} \widehat{c}_i - \Phi(D_n) + \Phi(D_0) \,. \tag{17.4}$$

We have $\widehat{c}_i \le 2$ for all $1 \le i \le n$. Since $\Phi(D_0) = b_0$ and $\Phi(D_n) = b_n$, the total actual cost of n INCREMENT operations is

$$\begin{aligned} \sum_{i=1}^{n} c_i &\le \sum_{i=1}^{n} 2 - b_n + b_0 \\ &= 2n - b_n + b_0 \,. \end{aligned}$$

Note in particular that since $b_0 \le k$, as long as $k = O(n)$, the total actual cost is $O(n)$. In other words, if we execute at least $n = \Omega(k)$ INCREMENT operations, the total actual cost is $O(n)$, no matter what initial value the counter contains.

Exercises

17.3-1
Suppose we have a potential function Φ such that $\Phi(D_i) \ge \Phi(D_0)$ for all i, but $\Phi(D_0) \ne 0$. Show that there exists a potential function Φ' such that $\Phi'(D_0) = 0$, $\Phi'(D_i) \ge 0$ for all $i \ge 1$, and the amortized costs using Φ' are the same as the amortized costs using Φ.

17.3-2
Redo Exercise 17.1-3 using a potential method of analysis.

17.3-3
Consider an ordinary binary min-heap data structure with n elements supporting the instructions INSERT and EXTRACT-MIN in $O(\lg n)$ worst-case time. Give a potential function Φ such that the amortized cost of INSERT is $O(\lg n)$ and the amortized cost of EXTRACT-MIN is $O(1)$, and show that it works.

17.3-4
What is the total cost of executing n of the stack operations PUSH, POP, and MULTIPOP, assuming that the stack begins with s_0 objects and finishes with s_n objects?

17.3-5
Suppose that a counter begins at a number with b 1s in its binary representation, rather than at 0. Show that the cost of performing n INCREMENT operations is $O(n)$ if $n = \Omega(b)$. (Do not assume that b is constant.)

17.3-6
Show how to implement a queue with two ordinary stacks (Exercise 10.1-6) so that the amortized cost of each ENQUEUE and each DEQUEUE operation is $O(1)$.

17.3-7
Design a data structure to support the following two operations for a dynamic multiset S of integers, which allows duplicate values:

INSERT(S, x) inserts x into S.

DELETE-LARGER-HALF(S) deletes the largest $\lceil |S| / 2 \rceil$ elements from S.

Explain how to implement this data structure so that any sequence of m INSERT and DELETE-LARGER-HALF operations runs in $O(m)$ time. Your implementation should also include a way to output the elements of S in $O(|S|)$ time.

17.4 Dynamic tables

We do not always know in advance how many objects some applications will store in a table. We might allocate space for a table, only to find out later that it is not enough. We must then reallocate the table with a larger size and copy all objects stored in the original table over into the new, larger table. Similarly, if many objects have been deleted from the table, it may be worthwhile to reallocate the table with a smaller size. In this section, we study this problem of dynamically expanding and contracting a table. Using amortized analysis, we shall show that the amortized cost of insertion and deletion is only $O(1)$, even though the actual cost of an operation is large when it triggers an expansion or a contraction. Moreover, we shall see how to guarantee that the unused space in a dynamic table never exceeds a constant fraction of the total space.

We assume that the dynamic table supports the operations TABLE-INSERT and TABLE-DELETE. TABLE-INSERT inserts into the table an item that occupies a single *slot*, that is, a space for one item. Likewise, TABLE-DELETE removes an item from the table, thereby freeing a slot. The details of the data-structuring method used to organize the table are unimportant; we might use a stack (Section 10.1), a heap (Chapter 6), or a hash table (Chapter 11). We might also use an array or collection of arrays to implement object storage, as we did in Section 10.3.

We shall find it convenient to use a concept introduced in our analysis of hashing (Chapter 11). We define the *load factor* $\alpha(T)$ of a nonempty table T to be the number of items stored in the table divided by the size (number of slots) of the table. We assign an empty table (one with no slots) size 0, and we define its load factor to be 1. If the load factor of a dynamic table is bounded below by a constant,

the unused space in the table is never more than a constant fraction of the total amount of space.

We start by analyzing a dynamic table in which we only insert items. We then consider the more general case in which we both insert and delete items.

17.4.1   Table expansion

Let us assume that storage for a table is allocated as an array of slots. A table fills up when all slots have been used or, equivalently, when its load factor is 1.[1] In some software environments, upon attempting to insert an item into a full table, the only alternative is to abort with an error. We shall assume, however, that our software environment, like many modern ones, provides a memory-management system that can allocate and free blocks of storage on request. Thus, upon inserting an item into a full table, we can **expand** the table by allocating a new table with more slots than the old table had. Because we always need the table to reside in contiguous memory, we must allocate a new array for the larger table and then copy items from the old table into the new table.

A common heuristic allocates a new table with twice as many slots as the old one. If the only table operations are insertions, then the load factor of the table is always at least $1/2$, and thus the amount of wasted space never exceeds half the total space in the table.

In the following pseudocode, we assume that T is an object representing the table. The attribute $T.table$ contains a pointer to the block of storage representing the table, $T.num$ contains the number of items in the table, and $T.size$ gives the total number of slots in the table. Initially, the table is empty: $T.num = T.size = 0$.

TABLE-INSERT(T, x)

```
 1   if T.size == 0
 2        allocate T.table with 1 slot
 3        T.size = 1
 4   if T.num == T.size
 5        allocate new-table with 2 · T.size slots
 6        insert all items in T.table into new-table
 7        free T.table
 8        T.table = new-table
 9        T.size = 2 · T.size
10   insert x into T.table
11   T.num = T.num + 1
```

---

[1]In some situations, such as an open-address hash table, we may wish to consider a table to be full if its load factor equals some constant strictly less than 1. (See Exercise 17.4-1.)

Notice that we have two "insertion" procedures here: the TABLE-INSERT procedure itself and the ***elementary insertion*** into a table in lines 6 and 10. We can analyze the running time of TABLE-INSERT in terms of the number of elementary insertions by assigning a cost of 1 to each elementary insertion. We assume that the actual running time of TABLE-INSERT is linear in the time to insert individual items, so that the overhead for allocating an initial table in line 2 is constant and the overhead for allocating and freeing storage in lines 5 and 7 is dominated by the cost of transferring items in line 6. We call the event in which lines 5–9 are executed an ***expansion***.

Let us analyze a sequence of n TABLE-INSERT operations on an initially empty table. What is the cost c_i of the ith operation? If the current table has room for the new item (or if this is the first operation), then $c_i = 1$, since we need only perform the one elementary insertion in line 10. If the current table is full, however, and an expansion occurs, then $c_i = i$: the cost is 1 for the elementary insertion in line 10 plus $i - 1$ for the items that we must copy from the old table to the new table in line 6. If we perform n operations, the worst-case cost of an operation is $O(n)$, which leads to an upper bound of $O(n^2)$ on the total running time for n operations.

This bound is not tight, because we rarely expand the table in the course of n TABLE-INSERT operations. Specifically, the ith operation causes an expansion only when $i - 1$ is an exact power of 2. The amortized cost of an operation is in fact $O(1)$, as we can show using aggregate analysis. The cost of the ith operation is

$$c_i = \begin{cases} i & \text{if } i - 1 \text{ is an exact power of 2,} \\ 1 & \text{otherwise.} \end{cases}$$

The total cost of n TABLE-INSERT operations is therefore

$$\begin{aligned} \sum_{i=1}^{n} c_i & \le n + \sum_{j=0}^{\lfloor \lg n \rfloor} 2^j \\ & < n + 2n \\ & = 3n, \end{aligned}$$

because at most n operations cost 1 and the costs of the remaining operations form a geometric series. Since the total cost of n TABLE-INSERT operations is bounded by $3n$, the amortized cost of a single operation is at most 3.

By using the accounting method, we can gain some feeling for why the amortized cost of a TABLE-INSERT operation should be 3. Intuitively, each item pays for 3 elementary insertions: inserting itself into the current table, moving itself when the table expands, and moving another item that has already been moved once when the table expands. For example, suppose that the size of the table is m immediately after an expansion. Then the table holds $m/2$ items, and it contains

no credit. We charge 3 dollars for each insertion. The elementary insertion that occurs immediately costs 1 dollar. We place another dollar as credit on the item inserted. We place the third dollar as credit on one of the $m/2$ items already in the table. The table will not fill again until we have inserted another $m/2 - 1$ items, and thus, by the time the table contains m items and is full, we will have placed a dollar on each item to pay to reinsert it during the expansion.

We can use the potential method to analyze a sequence of n TABLE-INSERT operations, and we shall use it in Section 17.4.2 to design a TABLE-DELETE operation that has an $O(1)$ amortized cost as well. We start by defining a potential function Φ that is 0 immediately after an expansion but builds to the table size by the time the table is full, so that we can pay for the next expansion by the potential. The function

$$\Phi(T) = 2 \cdot T.num - T.size \tag{17.5}$$

is one possibility. Immediately after an expansion, we have $T.num = T.size/2$, and thus $\Phi(T) = 0$, as desired. Immediately before an expansion, we have $T.num = T.size$, and thus $\Phi(T) = T.num$, as desired. The initial value of the potential is 0, and since the table is always at least half full, $T.num \geq T.size/2$, which implies that $\Phi(T)$ is always nonnegative. Thus, the sum of the amortized costs of n TABLE-INSERT operations gives an upper bound on the sum of the actual costs.

To analyze the amortized cost of the ith TABLE-INSERT operation, we let num_i denote the number of items stored in the table after the ith operation, $size_i$ denote the total size of the table after the ith operation, and Φ_i denote the potential after the ith operation. Initially, we have $num_0 = 0$, $size_0 = 0$, and $\Phi_0 = 0$.

If the ith TABLE-INSERT operation does not trigger an expansion, then we have $size_i = size_{i-1}$ and the amortized cost of the operation is

$$
\begin{aligned}
\hat{c}_i &= c_i + \Phi_i - \Phi_{i-1} \\
&= 1 + (2 \cdot num_i - size_i) - (2 \cdot num_{i-1} - size_{i-1}) \\
&= 1 + (2 \cdot num_i - size_i) - (2(num_i - 1) - size_i) \\
&= 3 .
\end{aligned}
$$

If the ith operation does trigger an expansion, then we have $size_i = 2 \cdot size_{i-1}$ and $size_{i-1} = num_{i-1} = num_i - 1$, which implies that $size_i = 2 \cdot (num_i - 1)$. Thus, the amortized cost of the operation is

$$
\begin{aligned}
\hat{c}_i &= c_i + \Phi_i - \Phi_{i-1} \\
&= num_i + (2 \cdot num_i - size_i) - (2 \cdot num_{i-1} - size_{i-1}) \\
&= num_i + (2 \cdot num_i - 2 \cdot (num_i - 1)) - (2(num_i - 1) - (num_i - 1)) \\
&= num_i + 2 - (num_i - 1) \\
&= 3 .
\end{aligned}
$$

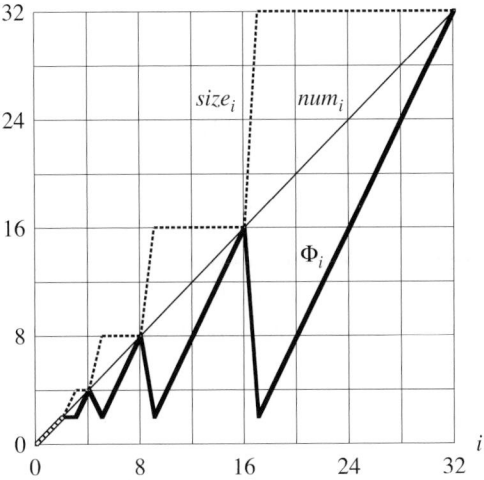

Figure 17.3   The effect of a sequence of n TABLE-INSERT operations on the number num_i of items in the table, the number $size_i$ of slots in the table, and the potential $\Phi_i = 2 \cdot num_i - size_i$, each being measured after the ith operation. The thin line shows num_i, the dashed line shows $size_i$, and the thick line shows Φ_i. Notice that immediately before an expansion, the potential has built up to the number of items in the table, and therefore it can pay for moving all the items to the new table. Afterwards, the potential drops to 0, but it is immediately increased by 2 upon inserting the item that caused the expansion.

Figure 17.3 plots the values of num_i, $size_i$, and Φ_i against i. Notice how the potential builds to pay for expanding the table.

17.4.2   Table expansion and contraction

To implement a TABLE-DELETE operation, it is simple enough to remove the specified item from the table. In order to limit the amount of wasted space, however, we might wish to *contract* the table when the load factor becomes too small. Table contraction is analogous to table expansion: when the number of items in the table drops too low, we allocate a new, smaller table and then copy the items from the old table into the new one. We can then free the storage for the old table by returning it to the memory-management system. Ideally, we would like to preserve two properties:

- the load factor of the dynamic table is bounded below by a positive constant, and

- the amortized cost of a table operation is bounded above by a constant.

We assume that we measure the cost in terms of elementary insertions and deletions.

You might think that we should double the table size upon inserting an item into a full table and halve the size when a deleting an item would cause the table to become less than half full. This strategy would guarantee that the load factor of the table never drops below $1/2$, but unfortunately, it can cause the amortized cost of an operation to be quite large. Consider the following scenario. We perform n operations on a table T, where n is an exact power of 2. The first $n/2$ operations are insertions, which by our previous analysis cost a total of $\Theta(n)$. At the end of this sequence of insertions, $T.num = T.size = n/2$. For the second $n/2$ operations, we perform the following sequence:

insert, delete, delete, insert, insert, delete, delete, insert, insert, ...

The first insertion causes the table to expand to size n. The two following deletions cause the table to contract back to size $n/2$. Two further insertions cause another expansion, and so forth. The cost of each expansion and contraction is $\Theta(n)$, and there are $\Theta(n)$ of them. Thus, the total cost of the n operations is $\Theta(n^2)$, making the amortized cost of an operation $\Theta(n)$.

The downside of this strategy is obvious: after expanding the table, we do not delete enough items to pay for a contraction. Likewise, after contracting the table, we do not insert enough items to pay for an expansion.

We can improve upon this strategy by allowing the load factor of the table to drop below $1/2$. Specifically, we continue to double the table size upon inserting an item into a full table, but we halve the table size when deleting an item causes the table to become less than $1/4$ full, rather than $1/2$ full as before. The load factor of the table is therefore bounded below by the constant $1/4$.

Intuitively, we would consider a load factor of $1/2$ to be ideal, and the table's potential would then be 0. As the load factor deviates from $1/2$, the potential increases so that by the time we expand or contract the table, the table has garnered sufficient potential to pay for copying all the items into the newly allocated table. Thus, we will need a potential function that has grown to $T.num$ by the time that the load factor has either increased to 1 or decreased to $1/4$. After either expanding or contracting the table, the load factor goes back to $1/2$ and the table's potential reduces back to 0.

We omit the code for TABLE-DELETE, since it is analogous to TABLE-INSERT. For our analysis, we shall assume that whenever the number of items in the table drops to 0, we free the storage for the table. That is, if $T.num = 0$, then $T.size = 0$.

We can now use the potential method to analyze the cost of a sequence of n TABLE-INSERT and TABLE-DELETE operations. We start by defining a potential function Φ that is 0 immediately after an expansion or contraction and builds as the load factor increases to 1 or decreases to $1/4$. Let us denote the load fac-

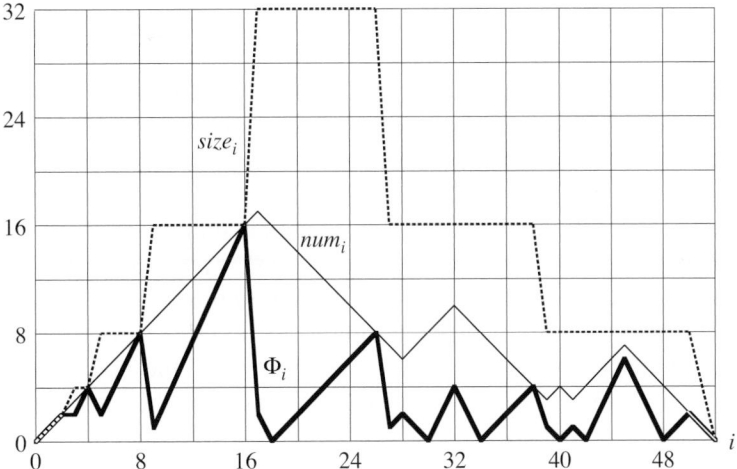

Figure 17.4 The effect of a sequence of n TABLE-INSERT and TABLE-DELETE operations on the number num_i of items in the table, the number $size_i$ of slots in the table, and the potential

$$\Phi_i = \begin{cases} 2 \cdot num_i - size_i & \text{if } \alpha_i \geq 1/2 \,, \\ size_i/2 - num_i & \text{if } \alpha_i < 1/2 \,, \end{cases}$$

each measured after the ith operation. The thin line shows num_i, the dashed line shows $size_i$, and the thick line shows Φ_i. Notice that immediately before an expansion, the potential has built up to the number of items in the table, and therefore it can pay for moving all the items to the new table. Likewise, immediately before a contraction, the potential has built up to the number of items in the table.

tor of a nonempty table T by $\alpha(T) = T.num/T.size$. Since for an empty table, $T.num = T.size = 0$ and $\alpha(T) = 1$, we always have $T.num = \alpha(T) \cdot T.size$, whether the table is empty or not. We shall use as our potential function

$$\Phi(T) = \begin{cases} 2 \cdot T.num - T.size & \text{if } \alpha(T) \geq 1/2 \,, \\ T.size/2 - T.num & \text{if } \alpha(T) < 1/2 \,. \end{cases} \tag{17.6}$$

Observe that the potential of an empty table is 0 and that the potential is never negative. Thus, the total amortized cost of a sequence of operations with respect to Φ provides an upper bound on the actual cost of the sequence.

Before proceeding with a precise analysis, we pause to observe some properties of the potential function, as illustrated in Figure 17.4. Notice that when the load factor is $1/2$, the potential is 0. When the load factor is 1, we have $T.size = T.num$, which implies $\Phi(T) = T.num$, and thus the potential can pay for an expansion if an item is inserted. When the load factor is $1/4$, we have $T.size = 4 \cdot T.num$, which

implies $\Phi(T) = T.num$, and thus the potential can pay for a contraction if an item is deleted.

To analyze a sequence of n TABLE-INSERT and TABLE-DELETE operations, we let c_i denote the actual cost of the ith operation, $\hat{c}_i$ denote its amortized cost with respect to Φ, num_i denote the number of items stored in the table after the ith operation, $size_i$ denote the total size of the table after the ith operation, α_i denote the load factor of the table after the ith operation, and Φ_i denote the potential after the ith operation. Initially, $num_0 = 0$, $size_0 = 0$, $\alpha_0 = 1$, and $\Phi_0 = 0$.

We start with the case in which the ith operation is TABLE-INSERT. The analysis is identical to that for table expansion in Section 17.4.1 if $\alpha_{i-1} \geq 1/2$. Whether the table expands or not, the amortized cost $\hat{c}_i$ of the operation is at most 3. If $\alpha_{i-1} < 1/2$, the table cannot expand as a result of the operation, since the table expands only when $\alpha_{i-1} = 1$. If $\alpha_i < 1/2$ as well, then the amortized cost of the ith operation is

$$
\begin{aligned}
\hat{c}_i &= c_i + \Phi_i - \Phi_{i-1} \\
&= 1 + (size_i/2 - num_i) - (size_{i-1}/2 - num_{i-1}) \\
&= 1 + (size_i/2 - num_i) - (size_i/2 - (num_i - 1)) \\
&= 0 .
\end{aligned}
$$

If $\alpha_{i-1} < 1/2$ but $\alpha_i \geq 1/2$, then

$$
\begin{aligned}
\hat{c}_i &= c_i + \Phi_i - \Phi_{i-1} \\
&= 1 + (2 \cdot num_i - size_i) - (size_{i-1}/2 - num_{i-1}) \\
&= 1 + (2(num_{i-1} + 1) - size_{i-1}) - (size_{i-1}/2 - num_{i-1}) \\
&= 3 \cdot num_{i-1} - \frac{3}{2} size_{i-1} + 3 \\
&= 3\alpha_{i-1} size_{i-1} - \frac{3}{2} size_{i-1} + 3 \\
&< \frac{3}{2} size_{i-1} - \frac{3}{2} size_{i-1} + 3 \\
&= 3 .
\end{aligned}
$$

Thus, the amortized cost of a TABLE-INSERT operation is at most 3.

We now turn to the case in which the ith operation is TABLE-DELETE. In this case, $num_i = num_{i-1} - 1$. If $\alpha_{i-1} < 1/2$, then we must consider whether the operation causes the table to contract. If it does not, then $size_i = size_{i-1}$ and the amortized cost of the operation is

$$
\begin{aligned}
\hat{c}_i &= c_i + \Phi_i - \Phi_{i-1} \\
&= 1 + (size_i/2 - num_i) - (size_{i-1}/2 - num_{i-1}) \\
&= 1 + (size_i/2 - num_i) - (size_i/2 - (num_i + 1)) \\
&= 2 .
\end{aligned}
$$

If $\alpha_{i-1} < 1/2$ and the ith operation does trigger a contraction, then the actual cost of the operation is $c_i = num_i + 1$, since we delete one item and move num_i items. We have $size_i/2 = size_{i-1}/4 = num_{i-1} = num_i + 1$, and the amortized cost of the operation is

$$
\begin{aligned}
\widehat{c}_i &= c_i + \Phi_i - \Phi_{i-1} \\
&= (num_i + 1) + (size_i/2 - num_i) - (size_{i-1}/2 - num_{i-1}) \\
&= (num_i + 1) + ((num_i + 1) - num_i) - ((2 \cdot num_i + 2) - (num_i + 1)) \\
&= 1 .
\end{aligned}
$$

When the ith operation is a TABLE-DELETE and $\alpha_{i-1} \geq 1/2$, the amortized cost is also bounded above by a constant. We leave the analysis as Exercise 17.4-2.

In summary, since the amortized cost of each operation is bounded above by a constant, the actual time for any sequence of n operations on a dynamic table is $O(n)$.

Exercises

17.4-1
Suppose that we wish to implement a dynamic, open-address hash table. Why might we consider the table to be full when its load factor reaches some value α that is strictly less than 1? Describe briefly how to make insertion into a dynamic, open-address hash table run in such a way that the expected value of the amortized cost per insertion is $O(1)$. Why is the expected value of the actual cost per insertion not necessarily $O(1)$ for all insertions?

17.4-2
Show that if $\alpha_{i-1} \geq 1/2$ and the ith operation on a dynamic table is TABLE-DELETE, then the amortized cost of the operation with respect to the potential function (17.6) is bounded above by a constant.

17.4-3
Suppose that instead of contracting a table by halving its size when its load factor drops below $1/4$, we contract it by multiplying its size by $2/3$ when its load factor drops below $1/3$. Using the potential function

$$\Phi(T) = |2 \cdot T.num - T.size| ,$$

show that the amortized cost of a TABLE-DELETE that uses this strategy is bounded above by a constant.

Problems

17-1   Bit-reversed binary counter

Chapter 30 examines an important algorithm called the fast Fourier transform, or FFT. The first step of the FFT algorithm performs a *bit-reversal permutation* on an input array $A[0 \ldots n-1]$ whose length is $n = 2^k$ for some nonnegative integer k. This permutation swaps elements whose indices have binary representations that are the reverse of each other.

We can express each index a as a k-bit sequence $\langle a_{k-1}, a_{k-2}, \ldots, a_0 \rangle$, where $a = \sum_{i=0}^{k-1} a_i \, 2^i$. We define

$$\text{rev}_k(\langle a_{k-1}, a_{k-2}, \ldots, a_0 \rangle) = \langle a_0, a_1, \ldots, a_{k-1} \rangle \, ;$$

thus,

$$\text{rev}_k(a) = \sum_{i=0}^{k-1} a_{k-i-1} 2^i \, .$$

For example, if $n = 16$ (or, equivalently, $k = 4$), then $\text{rev}_k(3) = 12$, since the 4-bit representation of 3 is 0011, which when reversed gives 1100, the 4-bit representation of 12.

a. Given a function rev_k that runs in $\Theta(k)$ time, write an algorithm to perform the bit-reversal permutation on an array of length $n = 2^k$ in $O(nk)$ time.

We can use an algorithm based on an amortized analysis to improve the running time of the bit-reversal permutation. We maintain a "bit-reversed counter" and a procedure BIT-REVERSED-INCREMENT that, when given a bit-reversed-counter value a, produces $\text{rev}_k(\text{rev}_k(a) + 1)$. If $k = 4$, for example, and the bit-reversed counter starts at 0, then successive calls to BIT-REVERSED-INCREMENT produce the sequence

$$0000, 1000, 0100, 1100, 0010, 1010, \ldots = 0, 8, 4, 12, 2, 10, \ldots \, .$$

b. Assume that the words in your computer store k-bit values and that in unit time, your computer can manipulate the binary values with operations such as shifting left or right by arbitrary amounts, bitwise-AND, bitwise-OR, etc. Describe an implementation of the BIT-REVERSED-INCREMENT procedure that allows the bit-reversal permutation on an n-element array to be performed in a total of $O(n)$ time.

c. Suppose that you can shift a word left or right by only one bit in unit time. Is it still possible to implement an $O(n)$-time bit-reversal permutation?

17-2 Making binary search dynamic

Binary search of a sorted array takes logarithmic search time, but the time to insert a new element is linear in the size of the array. We can improve the time for insertion by keeping several sorted arrays.

Specifically, suppose that we wish to support SEARCH and INSERT on a set of n elements. Let $k = \lceil \lg(n + 1) \rceil$, and let the binary representation of n be $\langle n_{k-1}, n_{k-2}, \ldots, n_0 \rangle$. We have k sorted arrays $A_0, A_1, \ldots, A_{k-1}$, where for $i = 0, 1, \ldots, k - 1$, the length of array A_i is 2^i. Each array is either full or empty, depending on whether $n_i = 1$ or $n_i = 0$, respectively. The total number of elements held in all k arrays is therefore $\sum_{i=0}^{k-1} n_i \, 2^i = n$. Although each individual array is sorted, elements in different arrays bear no particular relationship to each other.

a. Describe how to perform the SEARCH operation for this data structure. Analyze its worst-case running time.

b. Describe how to perform the INSERT operation. Analyze its worst-case and amortized running times.

c. Discuss how to implement DELETE.

17-3 Amortized weight-balanced trees

Consider an ordinary binary search tree augmented by adding to each node x the attribute $x.size$ giving the number of keys stored in the subtree rooted at x. Let α be a constant in the range $1/2 \leq \alpha < 1$. We say that a given node x is *α-balanced* if $x.left.size \leq \alpha \cdot x.size$ and $x.right.size \leq \alpha \cdot x.size$. The tree as a whole is *α-balanced* if every node in the tree is α-balanced. The following amortized approach to maintaining weight-balanced trees was suggested by G. Varghese.

a. A $1/2$-balanced tree is, in a sense, as balanced as it can be. Given a node x in an arbitrary binary search tree, show how to rebuild the subtree rooted at x so that it becomes $1/2$-balanced. Your algorithm should run in time $\Theta(x.size)$, and it can use $O(x.size)$ auxiliary storage.

b. Show that performing a search in an n-node α-balanced binary search tree takes $O(\lg n)$ worst-case time.

For the remainder of this problem, assume that the constant α is strictly greater than $1/2$. Suppose that we implement INSERT and DELETE as usual for an n-node binary search tree, except that after every such operation, if any node in the tree is no longer α-balanced, then we "rebuild" the subtree rooted at the highest such node in the tree so that it becomes $1/2$-balanced.

We shall analyze this rebuilding scheme using the potential method. For a node x in a binary search tree T, we define

$$\Delta(x) = |x.left.size - x.right.size| \ ,$$

and we define the potential of T as

$$\Phi(T) = c \sum_{x \in T : \Delta(x) \geq 2} \Delta(x) \ ,$$

where c is a sufficiently large constant that depends on α.

c. Argue that any binary search tree has nonnegative potential and that a $1/2$-balanced tree has potential 0.

d. Suppose that m units of potential can pay for rebuilding an m-node subtree. How large must c be in terms of α in order for it to take $O(1)$ amortized time to rebuild a subtree that is not α-balanced?

e. Show that inserting a node into or deleting a node from an n-node α-balanced tree costs $O(\lg n)$ amortized time.

17-4 *The cost of restructuring red-black trees*

There are four basic operations on red-black trees that perform ***structural modifications***: node insertions, node deletions, rotations, and color changes. We have seen that RB-INSERT and RB-DELETE use only $O(1)$ rotations, node insertions, and node deletions to maintain the red-black properties, but they may make many more color changes.

a. Describe a legal red-black tree with n nodes such that calling RB-INSERT to add the $(n + 1)$st node causes $\Omega(\lg n)$ color changes. Then describe a legal red-black tree with n nodes for which calling RB-DELETE on a particular node causes $\Omega(\lg n)$ color changes.

Although the worst-case number of color changes per operation can be logarithmic, we shall prove that any sequence of m RB-INSERT and RB-DELETE operations on an initially empty red-black tree causes $O(m)$ structural modifications in the worst case. Note that we count each color change as a structural modification.

b. Some of the cases handled by the main loop of the code of both RB-INSERT-FIXUP and RB-DELETE-FIXUP are ***terminating***: once encountered, they cause the loop to terminate after a constant number of additional operations. For each of the cases of RB-INSERT-FIXUP and RB-DELETE-FIXUP, specify which are terminating and which are not. (*Hint:* Look at Figures 13.5, 13.6, and 13.7.)

We shall first analyze the structural modifications when only insertions are performed. Let T be a red-black tree, and define $\Phi(T)$ to be the number of red nodes in T. Assume that 1 unit of potential can pay for the structural modifications performed by any of the three cases of RB-INSERT-FIXUP.

c. Let T' be the result of applying Case 1 of RB-INSERT-FIXUP to T. Argue that $\Phi(T') = \Phi(T) - 1$.

d. When we insert a node into a red-black tree using RB-INSERT, we can break the operation into three parts. List the structural modifications and potential changes resulting from lines 1–16 of RB-INSERT, from nonterminating cases of RB-INSERT-FIXUP, and from terminating cases of RB-INSERT-FIXUP.

e. Using part (d), argue that the amortized number of structural modifications performed by any call of RB-INSERT is $O(1)$.

We now wish to prove that there are $O(m)$ structural modifications when there are both insertions and deletions. Let us define, for each node x,

$$w(x) = \begin{cases} 0 & \text{if } x \text{ is red }, \\ 1 & \text{if } x \text{ is black and has no red children }, \\ 0 & \text{if } x \text{ is black and has one red child }, \\ 2 & \text{if } x \text{ is black and has two red children }. \end{cases}$$

Now we redefine the potential of a red-black tree T as

$$\Phi(T) = \sum_{x \in T} w(x) ,$$

and let T' be the tree that results from applying any nonterminating case of RB-INSERT-FIXUP or RB-DELETE-FIXUP to T.

f. Show that $\Phi(T') \leq \Phi(T) - 1$ for all nonterminating cases of RB-INSERT-FIXUP. Argue that the amortized number of structural modifications performed by any call of RB-INSERT-FIXUP is $O(1)$.

g. Show that $\Phi(T') \leq \Phi(T) - 1$ for all nonterminating cases of RB-DELETE-FIXUP. Argue that the amortized number of structural modifications performed by any call of RB-DELETE-FIXUP is $O(1)$.

h. Complete the proof that in the worst case, any sequence of m RB-INSERT and RB-DELETE operations performs $O(m)$ structural modifications.

17-5   Competitive analysis of self-organizing lists with move-to-front

A *self-organizing list* is a linked list of n elements, in which each element has a unique key. When we search for an element in the list, we are given a key, and we want to find an element with that key.

A self-organizing list has two important properties:

1. To find an element in the list, given its key, we must traverse the list from the beginning until we encounter the element with the given key. If that element is the kth element from the start of the list, then the cost to find the element is k.

2. We may reorder the list elements after any operation, according to a given rule with a given cost. We may choose any heuristic we like to decide how to reorder the list.

Assume that we start with a given list of n elements, and we are given an access sequence $\sigma = \langle \sigma_1, \sigma_2, \ldots, \sigma_m \rangle$ of keys to find, in order. The cost of the sequence is the sum of the costs of the individual accesses in the sequence.

Out of the various possible ways to reorder the list after an operation, this problem focuses on transposing adjacent list elements—switching their positions in the list—with a unit cost for each transpose operation. You will show, by means of a potential function, that a particular heuristic for reordering the list, move-to-front, entails a total cost no worse than 4 times that of any other heuristic for maintaining the list order—even if the other heuristic knows the access sequence in advance! We call this type of analysis a *competitive analysis*.

For a heuristic H and a given initial ordering of the list, denote the access cost of sequence σ by $C_H(\sigma)$. Let m be the number of accesses in σ.

a. Argue that if heuristic H does not know the access sequence in advance, then the worst-case cost for H on an access sequence σ is $C_H(\sigma) = \Omega(mn)$.

With the *move-to-front* heuristic, immediately after searching for an element x, we move x to the first position on the list (i.e., the front of the list).

Let $\mathrm{rank}_L(x)$ denote the rank of element x in list L, that is, the position of x in list L. For example, if x is the fourth element in L, then $\mathrm{rank}_L(x) = 4$. Let c_i denote the cost of access σ_i using the move-to-front heuristic, which includes the cost of finding the element in the list and the cost of moving it to the front of the list by a series of transpositions of adjacent list elements.

b. Show that if σ_i accesses element x in list L using the move-to-front heuristic, then $c_i = 2 \cdot \mathrm{rank}_L(x) - 1$.

Now we compare move-to-front with any other heuristic H that processes an access sequence according to the two properties above. Heuristic H may transpose

elements in the list in any way it wants, and it might even know the entire access sequence in advance.

Let L_i be the list after access σ_i using move-to-front, and let L_i^* be the list after access σ_i using heuristic H. We denote the cost of access σ_i by c_i for move-to-front and by c_i^* for heuristic H. Suppose that heuristic H performs t_i^* transpositions during access σ_i.

c. In part (b), you showed that $c_i = 2 \cdot \mathrm{rank}_{L_{i-1}}(x) - 1$. Now show that $c_i^* = \mathrm{rank}_{L_{i-1}^*}(x) + t_i^*$.

We define an ***inversion*** in list L_i as a pair of elements y and z such that y precedes z in L_i and z precedes y in list L_i^*. Suppose that list L_i has q_i inversions after processing the access sequence $\langle \sigma_1, \sigma_2, \ldots, \sigma_i \rangle$. Then, we define a potential function Φ that maps L_i to a real number by $\Phi(L_i) = 2q_i$. For example, if L_i has the elements $\langle e, c, a, d, b \rangle$ and L_i^* has the elements $\langle c, a, b, d, e \rangle$, then L_i has 5 inversions $((e,c), (e,a), (e,d), (e,b), (d,b))$, and so $\Phi(L_i) = 10$. Observe that $\Phi(L_i) \geq 0$ for all i and that, if move-to-front and heuristic H start with the same list L_0, then $\Phi(L_0) = 0$.

d. Argue that a transposition either increases the potential by 2 or decreases the potential by 2.

Suppose that access σ_i finds the element x. To understand how the potential changes due to σ_i, let us partition the elements other than x into four sets, depending on where they are in the lists just before the ith access:

- Set A consists of elements that precede x in both L_{i-1} and L_{i-1}^*.

- Set B consists of elements that precede x in L_{i-1} and follow x in L_{i-1}^*.

- Set C consists of elements that follow x in L_{i-1} and precede x in L_{i-1}^*.

- Set D consists of elements that follow x in both L_{i-1} and L_{i-1}^*.

e. Argue that $\mathrm{rank}_{L_{i-1}}(x) = |A| + |B| + 1$ and $\mathrm{rank}_{L_{i-1}^*}(x) = |A| + |C| + 1$.

f. Show that access σ_i causes a change in potential of

$$\Phi(L_i) - \Phi(L_{i-1}) \leq 2(|A| - |B| + t_i^*) ,$$

where, as before, heuristic H performs t_i^* transpositions during access σ_i.

Define the amortized cost $\hat{c}_i$ of access σ_i by $\hat{c}_i = c_i + \Phi(L_i) - \Phi(L_{i-1})$.

g. Show that the amortized cost $\hat{c}_i$ of access σ_i is bounded from above by $4c_i^*$.

h. Conclude that the cost $C_{\mathrm{MTF}}(\sigma)$ of access sequence σ with move-to-front is at most 4 times the cost $C_H(\sigma)$ of σ with any other heuristic H, assuming that both heuristics start with the same list.

Chapter notes

Aho, Hopcroft, and Ullman [5] used aggregate analysis to determine the running time of operations on a disjoint-set forest; we shall analyze this data structure using the potential method in Chapter 21. Tarjan [331] surveys the accounting and potential methods of amortized analysis and presents several applications. He attributes the accounting method to several authors, including M. R. Brown, R. E. Tarjan, S. Huddleston, and K. Mehlhorn. He attributes the potential method to D. D. Sleator. The term "amortized" is due to D. D. Sleator and R. E. Tarjan.

Potential functions are also useful for proving lower bounds for certain types of problems. For each configuration of the problem, we define a potential function that maps the configuration to a real number. Then we determine the potential Φ_{init} of the initial configuration, the potential Φ_{final} of the final configuration, and the maximum change in potential $\Delta\Phi_{\max}$ due to any step. The number of steps must therefore be at least $|\Phi_{\text{final}} - \Phi_{\text{init}}| / |\Delta\Phi_{\max}|$. Examples of potential functions to prove lower bounds in I/O complexity appear in works by Cormen, Sundquist, and Wisniewski [79]; Floyd [107]; and Aggarwal and Vitter [3]. Krumme, Cybenko, and Venkataraman [221] applied potential functions to prove lower bounds on *gossiping*: communicating a unique item from each vertex in a graph to every other vertex.

The move-to-front heuristic from Problem 17-5 works quite well in practice. Moreover, if we recognize that when we find an element, we can splice it out of its position in the list and relocate it to the front of the list in constant time, we can show that the cost of move-to-front is at most twice the cost of any other heuristic including, again, one that knows the entire access sequence in advance.

V *Advanced Data Structures*

Introduction

This part returns to studying data structures that support operations on dynamic sets, but at a more advanced level than Part III. Two of the chapters, for example, make extensive use of the amortized analysis techniques we saw in Chapter 17.

Chapter 18 presents B-trees, which are balanced search trees specifically designed to be stored on disks. Because disks operate much more slowly than random-access memory, we measure the performance of B-trees not only by how much computing time the dynamic-set operations consume but also by how many disk accesses they perform. For each B-tree operation, the number of disk accesses increases with the height of the B-tree, but B-tree operations keep the height low.

Chapter 19 gives an implementation of a mergeable heap, which supports the operations INSERT, MINIMUM, EXTRACT-MIN, and UNION.[1] The UNION operation unites, or merges, two heaps. Fibonacci heaps—the data structure in Chapter 19—also support the operations DELETE and DECREASE-KEY. We use amortized time bounds to measure the performance of Fibonacci heaps. The operations INSERT, MINIMUM, and UNION take only $O(1)$ actual and amortized time on Fibonacci heaps, and the operations EXTRACT-MIN and DELETE take $O(\lg n)$ amortized time. The most significant advantage of Fibonacci heaps, however, is that DECREASE-KEY takes only $O(1)$ amortized time. Because the DECREASE-

---

[1] As in Problem 10-2, we have defined a mergeable heap to support MINIMUM and EXTRACT-MIN, and so we can also refer to it as a *mergeable min-heap*. Alternatively, if it supported MAXIMUM and EXTRACT-MAX, it would be a *mergeable max-heap*. Unless we specify otherwise, mergeable heaps will be by default mergeable min-heaps.

KEY operation takes constant amortized time, Fibonacci heaps are key components of some of the asymptotically fastest algorithms to date for graph problems.

Noting that we can beat the $\Omega(n \lg n)$ lower bound for sorting when the keys are integers in a restricted range, Chapter 20 asks whether we can design a data structure that supports the dynamic-set operations SEARCH, INSERT, DELETE, MINIMUM, MAXIMUM, SUCCESSOR, and PREDECESSOR in $o(\lg n)$ time when the keys are integers in a restricted range. The answer turns out to be that we can, by using a recursive data structure known as a van Emde Boas tree. If the keys are unique integers drawn from the set $\{0, 1, 2, \ldots, u - 1\}$, where u is an exact power of 2, then van Emde Boas trees support each of the above operations in $O(\lg \lg u)$ time.

Finally, Chapter 21 presents data structures for disjoint sets. We have a universe of n elements that are partitioned into dynamic sets. Initially, each element belongs to its own singleton set. The operation UNION unites two sets, and the query FIND-SET identifies the unique set that contains a given element at the moment. By representing each set as a simple rooted tree, we obtain surprisingly fast operations: a sequence of m operations runs in $O(m \, \alpha(n))$ time, where $\alpha(n)$ is an incredibly slowly growing function—$\alpha(n)$ is at most 4 in any conceivable application. The amortized analysis that proves this time bound is as complex as the data structure is simple.

The topics covered in this part are by no means the only examples of "advanced" data structures. Other advanced data structures include the following:

- *Dynamic trees*, introduced by Sleator and Tarjan [319] and discussed by Tarjan [330], maintain a forest of disjoint rooted trees. Each edge in each tree has a real-valued cost. Dynamic trees support queries to find parents, roots, edge costs, and the minimum edge cost on a simple path from a node up to a root. Trees may be manipulated by cutting edges, updating all edge costs on a simple path from a node up to a root, linking a root into another tree, and making a node the root of the tree it appears in. One implementation of dynamic trees gives an $O(\lg n)$ amortized time bound for each operation; a more complicated implementation yields $O(\lg n)$ worst-case time bounds. Dynamic trees are used in some of the asymptotically fastest network-flow algorithms.

- *Splay trees*, developed by Sleator and Tarjan [320] and, again, discussed by Tarjan [330], are a form of binary search tree on which the standard search-tree operations run in $O(\lg n)$ amortized time. One application of splay trees simplifies dynamic trees.

- *Persistent* data structures allow queries, and sometimes updates as well, on past versions of a data structure. Driscoll, Sarnak, Sleator, and Tarjan [97] present techniques for making linked data structures persistent with only a small time

and space cost. Problem 13-1 gives a simple example of a persistent dynamic set.

- As in Chapter 20, several data structures allow a faster implementation of dictionary operations (INSERT, DELETE, and SEARCH) for a restricted universe of keys. By taking advantage of these restrictions, they are able to achieve better worst-case asymptotic running times than comparison-based data structures. Fredman and Willard introduced *fusion trees* [115], which were the first data structure to allow faster dictionary operations when the universe is restricted to integers. They showed how to implement these operations in $O(\lg n / \lg \lg n)$ time. Several subsequent data structures, including **exponential search trees** [16], have also given improved bounds on some or all of the dictionary operations and are mentioned in the chapter notes throughout this book.

- *Dynamic graph data structures* support various queries while allowing the structure of a graph to change through operations that insert or delete vertices or edges. Examples of the queries that they support include vertex connectivity [166], edge connectivity, minimum spanning trees [165], biconnectivity, and transitive closure [164].

Chapter notes throughout this book mention additional data structures.

18   B-Trees

B-trees are balanced search trees designed to work well on disks or other direct-access secondary storage devices. B-trees are similar to red-black trees (Chapter 13), but they are better at minimizing disk I/O operations. Many database systems use B-trees, or variants of B-trees, to store information.

B-trees differ from red-black trees in that B-tree nodes may have many children, from a few to thousands. That is, the "branching factor" of a B-tree can be quite large, although it usually depends on characteristics of the disk unit used. B-trees are similar to red-black trees in that every n-node B-tree has height $O(\lg n)$. The exact height of a B-tree can be considerably less than that of a red-black tree, however, because its branching factor, and hence the base of the logarithm that expresses its height, can be much larger. Therefore, we can also use B-trees to implement many dynamic-set operations in time $O(\lg n)$.

B-trees generalize binary search trees in a natural manner. Figure 18.1 shows a simple B-tree. If an internal B-tree node x contains $x.n$ keys, then x has $x.n + 1$ children. The keys in node x serve as dividing points separating the range of keys handled by x into $x.n + 1$ subranges, each handled by one child of x. When searching for a key in a B-tree, we make an $(x.n + 1)$-way decision based on comparisons with the $x.n$ keys stored at node x. The structure of leaf nodes differs from that of internal nodes; we will examine these differences in Section 18.1.

Section 18.1 gives a precise definition of B-trees and proves that the height of a B-tree grows only logarithmically with the number of nodes it contains. Section 18.2 describes how to search for a key and insert a key into a B-tree, and Section 18.3 discusses deletion. Before proceeding, however, we need to ask why we evaluate data structures designed to work on a disk differently from data structures designed to work in main random-access memory.

Data structures on secondary storage

Computer systems take advantage of various technologies that provide memory capacity. The ***primary memory*** (or ***main memory***) of a computer system normally

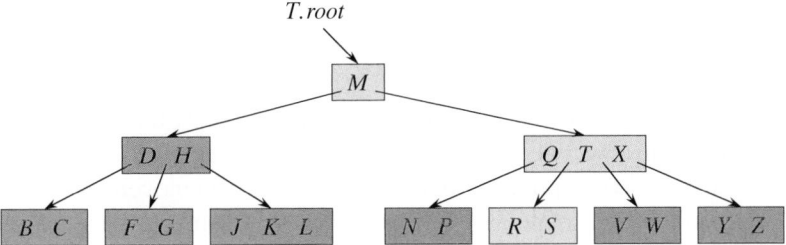

T.root

Figure 18.1   A B-tree whose keys are the consonants of English. An internal node x containing $x.n$ keys has $x.n + 1$ children. All leaves are at the same depth in the tree. The lightly shaded nodes are examined in a search for the letter R.

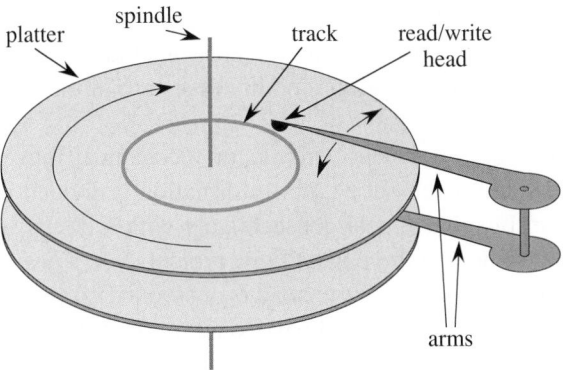

Figure 18.2   A typical disk drive. It comprises one or more platters (two platters are shown here) that rotate around a spindle. Each platter is read and written with a head at the end of an arm. Arms rotate around a common pivot axis. A track is the surface that passes beneath the read/write head when the head is stationary.

consists of silicon memory chips. This technology is typically more than an order of magnitude more expensive per bit stored than magnetic storage technology, such as tapes or disks. Most computer systems also have ***secondary storage*** based on magnetic disks; the amount of such secondary storage often exceeds the amount of primary memory by at least two orders of magnitude.

Figure 18.2 shows a typical disk drive. The drive consists of one or more ***platters***, which rotate at a constant speed around a common ***spindle***. A magnetizable material covers the surface of each platter. The drive reads and writes each platter by a ***head*** at the end of an ***arm***. The arms can move their heads toward or away

from the spindle. When a given head is stationary, the surface that passes underneath it is called a **track**. Multiple platters increase only the disk drive's capacity and not its performance.

Although disks are cheaper and have higher capacity than main memory, they are much, much slower because they have moving mechanical parts.[1] The mechanical motion has two components: platter rotation and arm movement. As of this writing, commodity disks rotate at speeds of 5400–15,000 revolutions per minute (RPM). We typically see 15,000 RPM speeds in server-grade drives, 7200 RPM speeds in drives for desktops, and 5400 RPM speeds in drives for laptops. Although 7200 RPM may seem fast, one rotation takes 8.33 milliseconds, which is over 5 orders of magnitude longer than the 50 nanosecond access times (more or less) commonly found for silicon memory. In other words, if we have to wait a full rotation for a particular item to come under the read/write head, we could access main memory more than 100,000 times during that span. On average we have to wait for only half a rotation, but still, the difference in access times for silicon memory compared with disks is enormous. Moving the arms also takes some time. As of this writing, average access times for commodity disks are in the range of 8 to 11 milliseconds.

In order to amortize the time spent waiting for mechanical movements, disks access not just one item but several at a time. Information is divided into a number of equal-sized **pages** of bits that appear consecutively within tracks, and each disk read or write is of one or more entire pages. For a typical disk, a page might be 2^{11} to 2^{14} bytes in length. Once the read/write head is positioned correctly and the disk has rotated to the beginning of the desired page, reading or writing a magnetic disk is entirely electronic (aside from the rotation of the disk), and the disk can quickly read or write large amounts of data.

Often, accessing a page of information and reading it from a disk takes longer than examining all the information read. For this reason, in this chapter we shall look separately at the two principal components of the running time:

- the number of disk accesses, and

- the CPU (computing) time.

We measure the number of disk accesses in terms of the number of pages of information that need to be read from or written to the disk. We note that disk-access time is not constant—it depends on the distance between the current track and the desired track and also on the initial rotational position of the disk. We shall

---

[1] As of this writing, solid-state drives have recently come onto the consumer market. Although they are faster than mechanical disk drives, they cost more per gigabyte and have lower capacities than mechanical disk drives.

nonetheless use the number of pages read or written as a first-order approximation of the total time spent accessing the disk.

In a typical B-tree application, the amount of data handled is so large that all the data do not fit into main memory at once. The B-tree algorithms copy selected pages from disk into main memory as needed and write back onto disk the pages that have changed. B-tree algorithms keep only a constant number of pages in main memory at any time; thus, the size of main memory does not limit the size of B-trees that can be handled.

We model disk operations in our pseudocode as follows. Let x be a pointer to an object. If the object is currently in the computer's main memory, then we can refer to the attributes of the object as usual: $x.key$, for example. If the object referred to by x resides on disk, however, then we must perform the operation DISK-READ(x) to read object x into main memory before we can refer to its attributes. (We assume that if x is already in main memory, then DISK-READ(x) requires no disk accesses; it is a "no-op.") Similarly, the operation DISK-WRITE(x) is used to save any changes that have been made to the attributes of object x. That is, the typical pattern for working with an object is as follows:

> $x =$ a pointer to some object
> DISK-READ(x)
> operations that access and/or modify the attributes of x
> DISK-WRITE(x)   **//** omitted if no attributes of x were changed
> other operations that access but do not modify attributes of x

The system can keep only a limited number of pages in main memory at any one time. We shall assume that the system flushes from main memory pages no longer in use; our B-tree algorithms will ignore this issue.

Since in most systems the running time of a B-tree algorithm depends primarily on the number of DISK-READ and DISK-WRITE operations it performs, we typically want each of these operations to read or write as much information as possible. Thus, a B-tree node is usually as large as a whole disk page, and this size limits the number of children a B-tree node can have.

For a large B-tree stored on a disk, we often see branching factors between 50 and 2000, depending on the size of a key relative to the size of a page. A large branching factor dramatically reduces both the height of the tree and the number of disk accesses required to find any key. Figure 18.3 shows a B-tree with a branching factor of 1001 and height 2 that can store over one billion keys; nevertheless, since we can keep the root node permanently in main memory, we can find any key in this tree by making at most only two disk accesses.

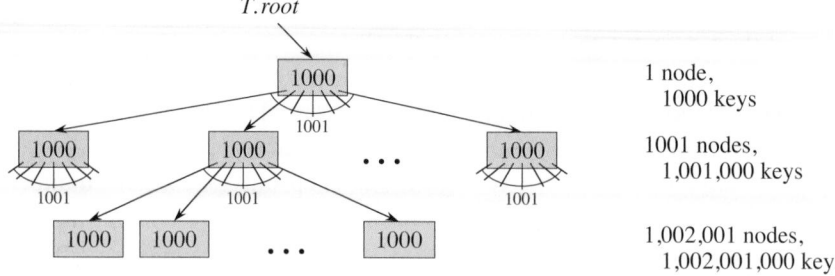

Figure 18.3 A B-tree of height 2 containing over one billion keys. Shown inside each node x is $x.n$, the number of keys in x. Each internal node and leaf contains 1000 keys. This B-tree has 1001 nodes at depth 1 and over one million leaves at depth 2.

18.1   Definition of B-trees

To keep things simple, we assume, as we have for binary search trees and red-black trees, that any "satellite information" associated with a key resides in the same node as the key. In practice, one might actually store with each key just a pointer to another disk page containing the satellite information for that key. The pseudocode in this chapter implicitly assumes that the satellite information associated with a key, or the pointer to such satellite information, travels with the key whenever the key is moved from node to node. A common variant on a B-tree, known as a **B$^+$-tree**, stores all the satellite information in the leaves and stores only keys and child pointers in the internal nodes, thus maximizing the branching factor of the internal nodes.

A **B-tree** T is a rooted tree (whose root is $T.root$) having the following properties:

1. Every node x has the following attributes:

   a. $x.n$, the number of keys currently stored in node x,

   b. the $x.n$ keys themselves, $x.key_1, x.key_2, \ldots, x.key_{x.n}$, stored in nondecreasing order, so that $x.key_1 \le x.key_2 \le \cdots \le x.key_{x.n}$,

   c. $x.leaf$, a boolean value that is TRUE if x is a leaf and FALSE if x is an internal node.

2. Each internal node x also contains $x.n + 1$ pointers $x.c_1, x.c_2, \ldots, x.c_{x.n+1}$ to its children. Leaf nodes have no children, and so their c_i attributes are undefined.

3. The keys $x.key_i$ separate the ranges of keys stored in each subtree: if k_i is any key stored in the subtree with root $x.c_i$, then

$$k_1 \leq x.key_1 \leq k_2 \leq x.key_2 \leq \cdots \leq x.key_{x.n} \leq k_{x.n+1} .$$

4. All leaves have the same depth, which is the tree's height h.

5. Nodes have lower and upper bounds on the number of keys they can contain. We express these bounds in terms of a fixed integer $t \geq 2$ called the ***minimum degree*** of the B-tree:

   a. Every node other than the root must have at least $t - 1$ keys. Every internal node other than the root thus has at least t children. If the tree is nonempty, the root must have at least one key.

   b. Every node may contain at most $2t - 1$ keys. Therefore, an internal node may have at most $2t$ children. We say that a node is ***full*** if it contains exactly $2t - 1$ keys.[2]

The simplest B-tree occurs when $t = 2$. Every internal node then has either 2, 3, or 4 children, and we have a ***2-3-4 tree***. In practice, however, much larger values of t yield B-trees with smaller height.

The height of a B-tree

The number of disk accesses required for most operations on a B-tree is proportional to the height of the B-tree. We now analyze the worst-case height of a B-tree.

Theorem 18.1
If $n \geq 1$, then for any n-key B-tree T of height h and minimum degree $t \geq 2$,

$$h \leq \log_t \frac{n + 1}{2} .$$

Proof The root of a B-tree T contains at least one key, and all other nodes contain at least $t - 1$ keys. Thus, T, whose height is h, has at least 2 nodes at depth 1, at least $2t$ nodes at depth 2, at least $2t^2$ nodes at depth 3, and so on, until at depth h it has at least $2t^{h-1}$ nodes. Figure 18.4 illustrates such a tree for $h = 3$. Thus, the

---

[2]Another common variant on a B-tree, known as a ***B*-tree***, requires each internal node to be at least 2/3 full, rather than at least half full, as a B-tree requires.

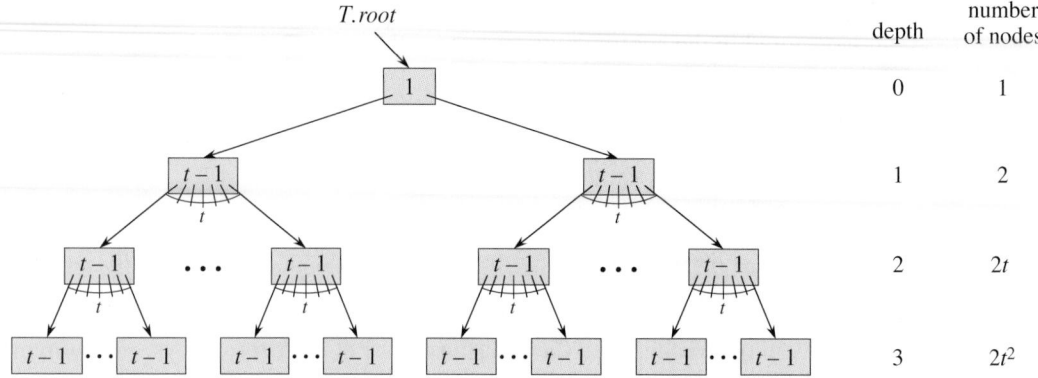

Figure 18.4 A B-tree of height 3 containing a minimum possible number of keys. Shown inside each node x is $x.n$.

number n of keys satisfies the inequality

$$
\begin{aligned}
n &\geq 1 + (t-1)\sum_{i=1}^{h} 2t^{i-1} \\
&= 1 + 2(t-1)\left(\frac{t^h - 1}{t - 1}\right) \\
&= 2t^h - 1 .
\end{aligned}
$$

By simple algebra, we get $t^h \leq (n+1)/2$. Taking base-t logarithms of both sides proves the theorem. ■

Here we see the power of B-trees, as compared with red-black trees. Although the height of the tree grows as $O(\lg n)$ in both cases (recall that t is a constant), for B-trees the base of the logarithm can be many times larger. Thus, B-trees save a factor of about $\lg t$ over red-black trees in the number of nodes examined for most tree operations. Because we usually have to access the disk to examine an arbitrary node in a tree, B-trees avoid a substantial number of disk accesses.

Exercises

18.1-1
Why don't we allow a minimum degree of $t = 1$?

18.1-2
For what values of t is the tree of Figure 18.1 a legal B-tree?

18.1-3
Show all legal B-trees of minimum degree 2 that represent $\{1, 2, 3, 4, 5\}$.

18.1-4
As a function of the minimum degree t, what is the maximum number of keys that can be stored in a B-tree of height h?

18.1-5
Describe the data structure that would result if each black node in a red-black tree were to absorb its red children, incorporating their children with its own.

18.2   Basic operations on B-trees

In this section, we present the details of the operations B-TREE-SEARCH, B-TREE-CREATE, and B-TREE-INSERT. In these procedures, we adopt two conventions:

- The root of the B-tree is always in main memory, so that we never need to perform a DISK-READ on the root; we do have to perform a DISK-WRITE of the root, however, whenever the root node is changed.

- Any nodes that are passed as parameters must already have had a DISK-READ operation performed on them.

The procedures we present are all "one-pass" algorithms that proceed downward from the root of the tree, without having to back up.

Searching a B-tree

Searching a B-tree is much like searching a binary search tree, except that instead of making a binary, or "two-way," branching decision at each node, we make a multiway branching decision according to the number of the node's children. More precisely, at each internal node x, we make an $(x.n + 1)$-way branching decision.

B-TREE-SEARCH is a straightforward generalization of the TREE-SEARCH procedure defined for binary search trees. B-TREE-SEARCH takes as input a pointer to the root node x of a subtree and a key k to be searched for in that subtree. The top-level call is thus of the form B-TREE-SEARCH$(T.root, k)$. If k is in the B-tree, B-TREE-SEARCH returns the ordered pair (y, i) consisting of a node y and an index i such that $y.key_i = k$. Otherwise, the procedure returns NIL.

B-Tree-Search(x, k)

```
1  i = 1
2  while i ≤ x.n and k > x.key_i
3      i = i + 1
4  if i ≤ x.n and k == x.key_i
5      return (x, i)
6  elseif x.leaf
7      return NIL
8  else DISK-READ(x.c_i)
9      return B-TREE-SEARCH(x.c_i, k)
```

Using a linear-search procedure, lines 1–3 find the smallest index i such that $k \leq x.key_i$, or else they set i to $x.n + 1$. Lines 4–5 check to see whether we have now discovered the key, returning if we have. Otherwise, lines 6–9 either terminate the search unsuccessfully (if x is a leaf) or recurse to search the appropriate subtree of x, after performing the necessary DISK-READ on that child.

Figure 18.1 illustrates the operation of B-TREE-SEARCH. The procedure examines the lightly shaded nodes during a search for the key R.

As in the TREE-SEARCH procedure for binary search trees, the nodes encountered during the recursion form a simple path downward from the root of the tree. The B-TREE-SEARCH procedure therefore accesses $O(h) = O(\log_t n)$ disk pages, where h is the height of the B-tree and n is the number of keys in the B-tree. Since $x.n < 2t$, the **while** loop of lines 2–3 takes $O(t)$ time within each node, and the total CPU time is $O(th) = O(t \log_t n)$.

Creating an empty B-tree

To build a B-tree T, we first use B-TREE-CREATE to create an empty root node and then call B-TREE-INSERT to add new keys. Both of these procedures use an auxiliary procedure ALLOCATE-NODE, which allocates one disk page to be used as a new node in $O(1)$ time. We can assume that a node created by ALLOCATE-NODE requires no DISK-READ, since there is as yet no useful information stored on the disk for that node.

B-Tree-Create(T)

```
1  x = ALLOCATE-NODE()
2  x.leaf = TRUE
3  x.n = 0
4  DISK-WRITE(x)
5  T.root = x
```

B-TREE-CREATE requires $O(1)$ disk operations and $O(1)$ CPU time.

Inserting a key into a B-tree

Inserting a key into a B-tree is significantly more complicated than inserting a key into a binary search tree. As with binary search trees, we search for the leaf position at which to insert the new key. With a B-tree, however, we cannot simply create a new leaf node and insert it, as the resulting tree would fail to be a valid B-tree. Instead, we insert the new key into an existing leaf node. Since we cannot insert a key into a leaf node that is full, we introduce an operation that *splits* a full node y (having $2t - 1$ keys) around its *median key* $y.key_t$ into two nodes having only $t - 1$ keys each. The median key moves up into y's parent to identify the dividing point between the two new trees. But if y's parent is also full, we must split it before we can insert the new key, and thus we could end up splitting full nodes all the way up the tree.

As with a binary search tree, we can insert a key into a B-tree in a single pass down the tree from the root to a leaf. To do so, we do not wait to find out whether we will actually need to split a full node in order to do the insertion. Instead, as we travel down the tree searching for the position where the new key belongs, we split each full node we come to along the way (including the leaf itself). Thus whenever we want to split a full node y, we are assured that its parent is not full.

Splitting a node in a B-tree

The procedure B-TREE-SPLIT-CHILD takes as input a *nonfull* internal node x (assumed to be in main memory) and an index i such that $x.c_i$ (also assumed to be in main memory) is a *full* child of x. The procedure then splits this child in two and adjusts x so that it has an additional child. To split a full root, we will first make the root a child of a new empty root node, so that we can use B-TREE-SPLIT-CHILD. The tree thus grows in height by one; splitting is the only means by which the tree grows.

Figure 18.5 illustrates this process. We split the full node $y = x.c_i$ about its median key S, which moves up into y's parent node x. Those keys in y that are greater than the median key move into a new node z, which becomes a new child of x.

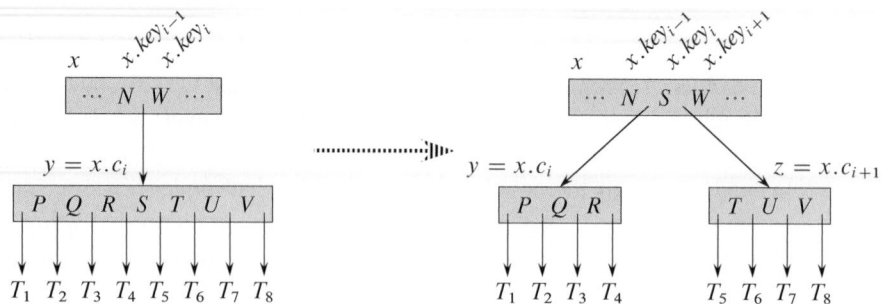

Figure 18.5 Splitting a node with $t = 4$. Node $y = x.c_i$ splits into two nodes, y and z, and the median key S of y moves up into y's parent.

B-TREE-SPLIT-CHILD(x, i)

```
 1   z = ALLOCATE-NODE()
 2   y = x.c_i
 3   z.leaf = y.leaf
 4   z.n = t − 1
 5   for j = 1 to t − 1
 6       z.key_j = y.key_{j+t}
 7   if not y.leaf
 8       for j = 1 to t
 9           z.c_j = y.c_{j+t}
10   y.n = t − 1
11   for j = x.n + 1 downto i + 1
12       x.c_{j+1} = x.c_j
13   x.c_{i+1} = z
14   for j = x.n downto i
15       x.key_{j+1} = x.key_j
16   x.key_i = y.key_t
17   x.n = x.n + 1
18   DISK-WRITE(y)
19   DISK-WRITE(z)
20   DISK-WRITE(x)
```

B-TREE-SPLIT-CHILD works by straightforward "cutting and pasting." Here, x is the parent of the node being split, and y is x's ith child (set in line 2). Node y originally has $2t$ children ($2t - 1$ keys) but is reduced to t children ($t - 1$ keys) by this operation. Node z takes the t largest children ($t - 1$ keys) from y, and

z becomes a new child of x, positioned just after y in x's table of children. The median key of y moves up to become the key in x that separates y and z.

Lines 1–9 create node z and give it the largest $t - 1$ keys and corresponding t children of y. Line 10 adjusts the key count for y. Finally, lines 11–17 insert z as a child of x, move the median key from y up to x in order to separate y from z, and adjust x's key count. Lines 18–20 write out all modified disk pages. The CPU time used by B-TREE-SPLIT-CHILD is $\Theta(t)$, due to the loops on lines 5–6 and 8–9. (The other loops run for $O(t)$ iterations.) The procedure performs $O(1)$ disk operations.

Inserting a key into a B-tree in a single pass down the tree

We insert a key k into a B-tree T of height h in a single pass down the tree, requiring $O(h)$ disk accesses. The CPU time required is $O(th) = O(t \log_t n)$. The B-TREE-INSERT procedure uses B-TREE-SPLIT-CHILD to guarantee that the recursion never descends to a full node.

B-TREE-INSERT(T, k)

```
 1   r = T.root
 2   if r.n == 2t − 1
 3       s = ALLOCATE-NODE()
 4       T.root = s
 5       s.leaf = FALSE
 6       s.n = 0
 7       s.c₁ = r
 8       B-TREE-SPLIT-CHILD(s, 1)
 9       B-TREE-INSERT-NONFULL(s, k)
10   else B-TREE-INSERT-NONFULL(r, k)
```

Lines 3–9 handle the case in which the root node r is full: the root splits and a new node s (having two children) becomes the root. Splitting the root is the only way to increase the height of a B-tree. Figure 18.6 illustrates this case. Unlike a binary search tree, a B-tree increases in height at the top instead of at the bottom. The procedure finishes by calling B-TREE-INSERT-NONFULL to insert key k into the tree rooted at the nonfull root node. B-TREE-INSERT-NONFULL recurses as necessary down the tree, at all times guaranteeing that the node to which it recurses is not full by calling B-TREE-SPLIT-CHILD as necessary.

The auxiliary recursive procedure B-TREE-INSERT-NONFULL inserts key k into node x, which is assumed to be nonfull when the procedure is called. The operation of B-TREE-INSERT and the recursive operation of B-TREE-INSERT-NONFULL guarantee that this assumption is true.

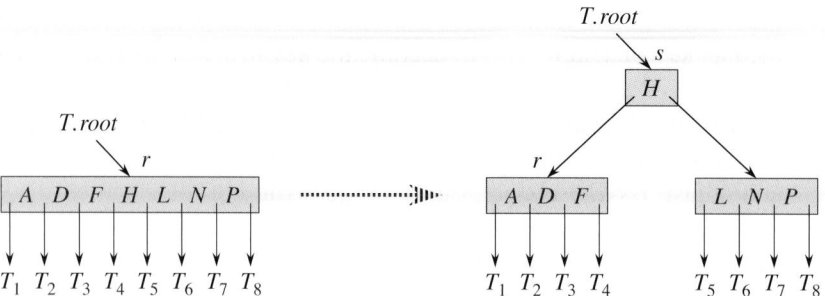

Figure 18.6 Splitting the root with $t = 4$. Root node r splits in two, and a new root node s is created. The new root contains the median key of r and has the two halves of r as children. The B-tree grows in height by one when the root is split.

B-TREE-INSERT-NONFULL(x, k)

```
 1   i = x.n
 2   if x.leaf
 3       while i ≥ 1 and k < x.key_i
 4           x.key_{i+1} = x.key_i
 5           i = i − 1
 6       x.key_{i+1} = k
 7       x.n = x.n + 1
 8       DISK-WRITE(x)
 9   else while i ≥ 1 and k < x.key_i
10           i = i − 1
11       i = i + 1
12       DISK-READ(x.c_i)
13       if x.c_i.n == 2t − 1
14           B-TREE-SPLIT-CHILD(x, i)
15           if k > x.key_i
16               i = i + 1
17       B-TREE-INSERT-NONFULL(x.c_i, k)
```

The B-TREE-INSERT-NONFULL procedure works as follows. Lines 3–8 handle the case in which x is a leaf node by inserting key k into x. If x is not a leaf node, then we must insert k into the appropriate leaf node in the subtree rooted at internal node x. In this case, lines 9–11 determine the child of x to which the recursion descends. Line 13 detects whether the recursion would descend to a full child, in which case line 14 uses B-TREE-SPLIT-CHILD to split that child into two nonfull children, and lines 15–16 determine which of the two children is now the

correct one to descend to. (Note that there is no need for a DISK-READ($x.c_i$) after line 16 increments i, since the recursion will descend in this case to a child that was just created by B-TREE-SPLIT-CHILD.) The net effect of lines 13–16 is thus to guarantee that the procedure never recurses to a full node. Line 17 then recurses to insert k into the appropriate subtree. Figure 18.7 illustrates the various cases of inserting into a B-tree.

For a B-tree of height h, B-TREE-INSERT performs $O(h)$ disk accesses, since only $O(1)$ DISK-READ and DISK-WRITE operations occur between calls to B-TREE-INSERT-NONFULL. The total CPU time used is $O(th) = O(t \log_t n)$. Since B-TREE-INSERT-NONFULL is tail-recursive, we can alternatively implement it as a **while** loop, thereby demonstrating that the number of pages that need to be in main memory at any time is $O(1)$.

Exercises

18.2-1
Show the results of inserting the keys

$$F, S, Q, K, C, L, H, T, V, W, M, R, N, P, A, B, X, Y, D, Z, E$$

in order into an empty B-tree with minimum degree 2. Draw only the configurations of the tree just before some node must split, and also draw the final configuration.

18.2-2
Explain under what circumstances, if any, redundant DISK-READ or DISK-WRITE operations occur during the course of executing a call to B-TREE-INSERT. (A redundant DISK-READ is a DISK-READ for a page that is already in memory. A redundant DISK-WRITE writes to disk a page of information that is identical to what is already stored there.)

18.2-3
Explain how to find the minimum key stored in a B-tree and how to find the predecessor of a given key stored in a B-tree.

18.2-4 ★
Suppose that we insert the keys $\{1, 2, \ldots, n\}$ into an empty B-tree with minimum degree 2. How many nodes does the final B-tree have?

18.2-5
Since leaf nodes require no pointers to children, they could conceivably use a different (larger) t value than internal nodes for the same disk page size. Show how to modify the procedures for creating and inserting into a B-tree to handle this variation.

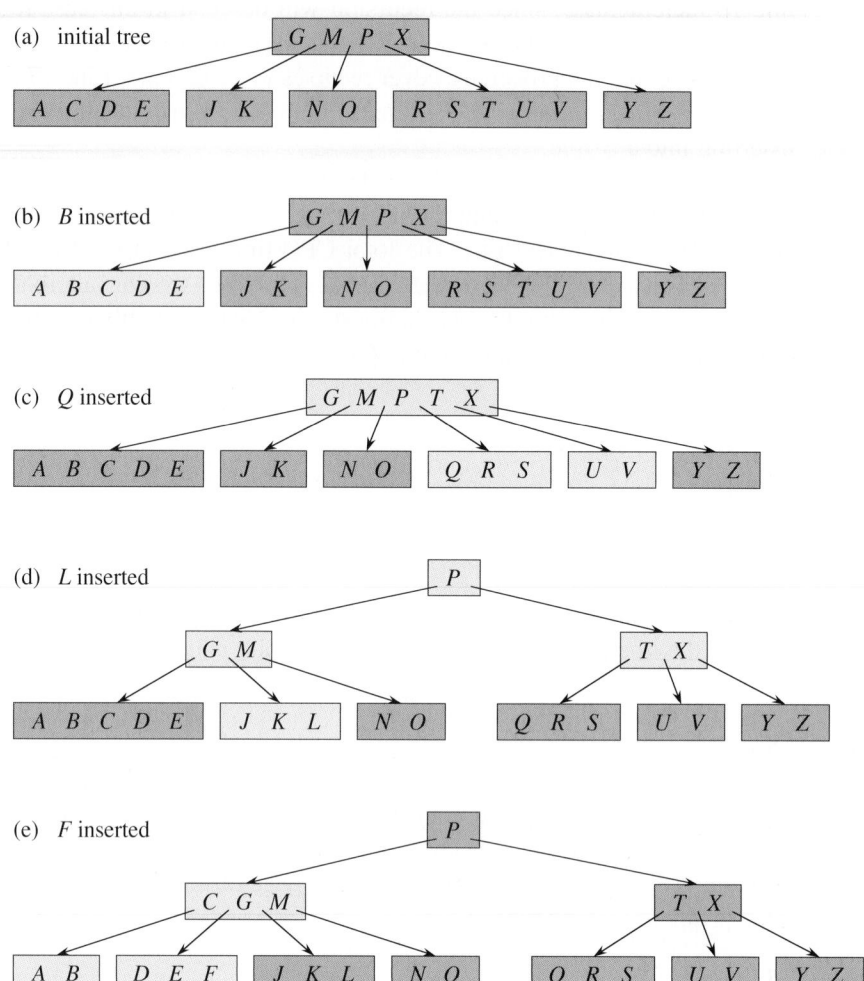

Figure 18.7 Inserting keys into a B-tree. The minimum degree t for this B-tree is 3, so a node can hold at most 5 keys. Nodes that are modified by the insertion process are lightly shaded. **(a)** The initial tree for this example. **(b)** The result of inserting B into the initial tree; this is a simple insertion into a leaf node. **(c)** The result of inserting Q into the previous tree. The node $RSTUV$ splits into two nodes containing RS and UV, the key T moves up to the root, and Q is inserted in the leftmost of the two halves (the RS node). **(d)** The result of inserting L into the previous tree. The root splits right away, since it is full, and the B-tree grows in height by one. Then L is inserted into the leaf containing JK. **(e)** The result of inserting F into the previous tree. The node $ABCDE$ splits before F is inserted into the rightmost of the two halves (the DE node).

18.2-6

Suppose that we were to implement B-TREE-SEARCH to use binary search rather than linear search within each node. Show that this change makes the CPU time required $O(\lg n)$, independently of how t might be chosen as a function of n.

18.2-7

Suppose that disk hardware allows us to choose the size of a disk page arbitrarily, but that the time it takes to read the disk page is $a + bt$, where a and b are specified constants and t is the minimum degree for a B-tree using pages of the selected size. Describe how to choose t so as to minimize (approximately) the B-tree search time. Suggest an optimal value of t for the case in which $a = 5$ milliseconds and $b = 10$ microseconds.

18.3   Deleting a key from a B-tree

Deletion from a B-tree is analogous to insertion but a little more complicated, because we can delete a key from any node—not just a leaf—and when we delete a key from an internal node, we will have to rearrange the node's children. As in insertion, we must guard against deletion producing a tree whose structure violates the B-tree properties. Just as we had to ensure that a node didn't get too big due to insertion, we must ensure that a node doesn't get too small during deletion (except that the root is allowed to have fewer than the minimum number $t - 1$ of keys). Just as a simple insertion algorithm might have to back up if a node on the path to where the key was to be inserted was full, a simple approach to deletion might have to back up if a node (other than the root) along the path to where the key is to be deleted has the minimum number of keys.

The procedure B-TREE-DELETE deletes the key k from the subtree rooted at x. We design this procedure to guarantee that whenever it calls itself recursively on a node x, the number of keys in x is at least the minimum degree t. Note that this condition requires one more key than the minimum required by the usual B-tree conditions, so that sometimes a key may have to be moved into a child node before recursion descends to that child. This strengthened condition allows us to delete a key from the tree in one downward pass without having to "back up" (with one exception, which we'll explain). You should interpret the following specification for deletion from a B-tree with the understanding that if the root node x ever becomes an internal node having no keys (this situation can occur in cases 2c and 3b on pages 501–502), then we delete x, and x's only child $x.c_1$ becomes the new root of the tree, decreasing the height of the tree by one and preserving the property that the root of the tree contains at least one key (unless the tree is empty).

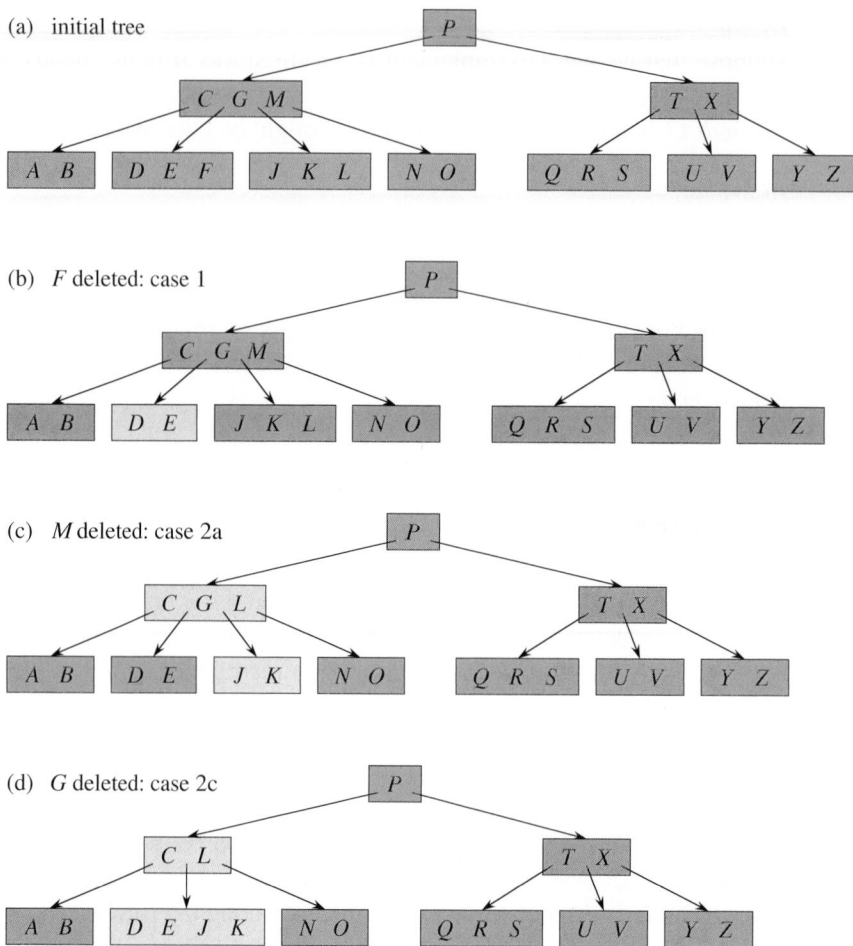

Figure 18.8   Deleting keys from a B-tree. The minimum degree for this B-tree is $t = 3$, so a node (other than the root) cannot have fewer than 2 keys. Nodes that are modified are lightly shaded. **(a)** The B-tree of Figure 18.7(e). **(b)** Deletion of F. This is case 1: simple deletion from a leaf. **(c)** Deletion of M. This is case 2a: the predecessor L of M moves up to take M's position. **(d)** Deletion of G. This is case 2c: we push G down to make node $DEGJK$ and then delete G from this leaf (case 1).

   We sketch how deletion works instead of presenting the pseudocode. Figure 18.8 illustrates the various cases of deleting keys from a B-tree.

1. If the key k is in node x and x is a leaf, delete the key k from x.

2. If the key k is in node x and x is an internal node, do the following:

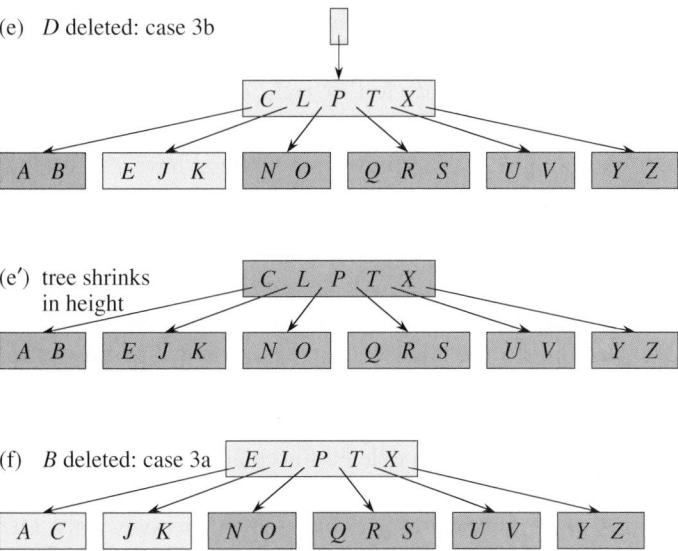

(e) *D* deleted: case 3b

(e') tree shrinks in height

(f) *B* deleted: case 3a

Figure 18.8, continued **(e)** Deletion of *D*. This is case 3b: the recursion cannot descend to node *CL* because it has only 2 keys, so we push *P* down and merge it with *CL* and *TX* to form *CLPTX*; then we delete *D* from a leaf (case 1). **(e')** After (e), we delete the root and the tree shrinks in height by one. **(f)** Deletion of *B*. This is case 3a: *C* moves to fill *B*'s position and *E* moves to fill *C*'s position.

   a. If the child *y* that precedes *k* in node *x* has at least *t* keys, then find the predecessor *k'* of *k* in the subtree rooted at *y*. Recursively delete *k'*, and replace *k* by *k'* in *x*. (We can find *k'* and delete it in a single downward pass.)

   b. If *y* has fewer than *t* keys, then, symmetrically, examine the child *z* that follows *k* in node *x*. If *z* has at least *t* keys, then find the successor *k'* of *k* in the subtree rooted at *z*. Recursively delete *k'*, and replace *k* by *k'* in *x*. (We can find *k'* and delete it in a single downward pass.)

   c. Otherwise, if both *y* and *z* have only $t - 1$ keys, merge *k* and all of *z* into *y*, so that *x* loses both *k* and the pointer to *z*, and *y* now contains $2t - 1$ keys. Then free *z* and recursively delete *k* from *y*.

3. If the key *k* is not present in internal node *x*, determine the root $x.c_i$ of the appropriate subtree that must contain *k*, if *k* is in the tree at all. If $x.c_i$ has only $t - 1$ keys, execute step 3a or 3b as necessary to guarantee that we descend to a node containing at least *t* keys. Then finish by recursing on the appropriate child of *x*.

a. If $x.c_i$ has only $t - 1$ keys but has an immediate sibling with at least t keys, give $x.c_i$ an extra key by moving a key from x down into $x.c_i$, moving a key from $x.c_i$'s immediate left or right sibling up into x, and moving the appropriate child pointer from the sibling into $x.c_i$.

b. If $x.c_i$ and both of $x.c_i$'s immediate siblings have $t - 1$ keys, merge $x.c_i$ with one sibling, which involves moving a key from x down into the new merged node to become the median key for that node.

Since most of the keys in a B-tree are in the leaves, we may expect that in practice, deletion operations are most often used to delete keys from leaves. The B-TREE-DELETE procedure then acts in one downward pass through the tree, without having to back up. When deleting a key in an internal node, however, the procedure makes a downward pass through the tree but may have to return to the node from which the key was deleted to replace the key with its predecessor or successor (cases 2a and 2b).

Although this procedure seems complicated, it involves only $O(h)$ disk operations for a B-tree of height h, since only $O(1)$ calls to DISK-READ and DISK-WRITE are made between recursive invocations of the procedure. The CPU time required is $O(th) = O(t \log_t n)$.

Exercises

18.3-1
Show the results of deleting C, P, and V, in order, from the tree of Figure 18.8(f).

18.3-2
Write pseudocode for B-TREE-DELETE.

Problems

18-1   Stacks on secondary storage
Consider implementing a stack in a computer that has a relatively small amount of fast primary memory and a relatively large amount of slower disk storage. The operations PUSH and POP work on single-word values. The stack we wish to support can grow to be much larger than can fit in memory, and thus most of it must be stored on disk.

A simple, but inefficient, stack implementation keeps the entire stack on disk. We maintain in memory a stack pointer, which is the disk address of the top element on the stack. If the pointer has value p, the top element is the $(p \bmod m)$th word on page $\lfloor p/m \rfloor$ of the disk, where m is the number of words per page.

To implement the PUSH operation, we increment the stack pointer, read the appropriate page into memory from disk, copy the element to be pushed to the appropriate word on the page, and write the page back to disk. A POP operation is similar. We save the top of the stack, decrement the stack pointer, read in the appropriate page from disk, and return the saved value. We need not write back the page, since it was not modified.

Because disk operations are relatively expensive, we count two costs for any implementation: the total number of disk accesses and the total CPU time. Any disk access to a page of m words incurs charges of one disk access and $\Theta(m)$ CPU time.

a. Asymptotically, what is the worst-case number of disk accesses for n stack operations using this simple implementation? What is the CPU time for n stack operations? (Express your answer in terms of m and n for this and subsequent parts.)

Now consider a stack implementation in which we keep one page of the stack in memory. (We also maintain a small amount of memory to keep track of which page is currently in memory.) We can perform a stack operation only if the relevant disk page resides in memory. If necessary, we can write the page currently in memory to the disk and read in the new page from the disk to memory. If the relevant disk page is already in memory, then no disk accesses are required.

b. What is the worst-case number of disk accesses required for n PUSH operations? What is the CPU time?

c. What is the worst-case number of disk accesses required for n stack operations? What is the CPU time?

Suppose that we now implement the stack by keeping two pages in memory (in addition to a small number of words for bookkeeping).

d. Describe how to manage the stack pages so that the amortized number of disk accesses for any stack operation is $O(1/m)$ and the amortized CPU time for any stack operation is $O(1)$.

18-2 *Joining and splitting 2-3-4 trees*

The *join* operation takes two dynamic sets S' and S'' and an element x such that for any $x' \in S'$ and $x'' \in S''$, we have $x'.key < x.key < x''.key$. It returns a set $S = S' \cup \{x\} \cup S''$. The *split* operation is like an "inverse" join: given a dynamic set S and an element $x \in S$, it creates a set S' that consists of all elements in $S - \{x\}$ whose keys are less than $x.key$ and a set S'' that consists of all elements in $S - \{x\}$ whose keys are greater than $x.key$. In this problem, we investigate

how to implement these operations on 2-3-4 trees. We assume for convenience that elements consist only of keys and that all key values are distinct.

a. Show how to maintain, for every node x of a 2-3-4 tree, the height of the subtree rooted at x as an attribute $x.height$. Make sure that your implementation does not affect the asymptotic running times of searching, insertion, and deletion.

b. Show how to implement the join operation. Given two 2-3-4 trees T' and T'' and a key k, the join operation should run in $O(1 + |h' - h''|)$ time, where h' and h'' are the heights of T' and T'', respectively.

c. Consider the simple path p from the root of a 2-3-4 tree T to a given key k, the set S' of keys in T that are less than k, and the set S'' of keys in T that are greater than k. Show that p breaks S' into a set of trees $\{T'_0, T'_1, \ldots, T'_m\}$ and a set of keys $\{k'_1, k'_2, \ldots, k'_m\}$, where, for $i = 1, 2, \ldots, m$, we have $y < k'_i < z$ for any keys $y \in T'_{i-1}$ and $z \in T'_i$. What is the relationship between the heights of T'_{i-1} and T'_i? Describe how p breaks S'' into sets of trees and keys.

d. Show how to implement the split operation on T. Use the join operation to assemble the keys in S' into a single 2-3-4 tree T' and the keys in S'' into a single 2-3-4 tree T''. The running time of the split operation should be $O(\lg n)$, where n is the number of keys in T. (*Hint:* The costs for joining should telescope.)

Chapter notes

Knuth [211], Aho, Hopcroft, and Ullman [5], and Sedgewick [306] give further discussions of balanced-tree schemes and B-trees. Comer [74] provides a comprehensive survey of B-trees. Guibas and Sedgewick [155] discuss the relationships among various kinds of balanced-tree schemes, including red-black trees and 2-3-4 trees.

In 1970, J. E. Hopcroft invented 2-3 trees, a precursor to B-trees and 2-3-4 trees, in which every internal node has either two or three children. Bayer and McCreight [35] introduced B-trees in 1972; they did not explain their choice of name.

Bender, Demaine, and Farach-Colton [40] studied how to make B-trees perform well in the presence of memory-hierarchy effects. Their ***cache-oblivious*** algorithms work efficiently without explicitly knowing the data transfer sizes within the memory hierarchy.

19   Fibonacci Heaps

The Fibonacci heap data structure serves a dual purpose. First, it supports a set of operations that constitutes what is known as a "mergeable heap." Second, several Fibonacci-heap operations run in constant amortized time, which makes this data structure well suited for applications that invoke these operations frequently.

Mergeable heaps

A *mergeable heap* is any data structure that supports the following five operations, in which each element has a *key*:

MAKE-HEAP() creates and returns a new heap containing no elements.

INSERT(H, x) inserts element x, whose *key* has already been filled in, into heap H.

MINIMUM(H) returns a pointer to the element in heap H whose key is minimum.

EXTRACT-MIN(H) deletes the element from heap H whose key is minimum, returning a pointer to the element.

UNION(H_1, H_2) creates and returns a new heap that contains all the elements of heaps H_1 and H_2. Heaps H_1 and H_2 are "destroyed" by this operation.

In addition to the mergeable-heap operations above, Fibonacci heaps also support the following two operations:

DECREASE-KEY(H, x, k) assigns to element x within heap H the new key value k, which we assume to be no greater than its current key value.[1]

DELETE(H, x) deletes element x from heap H.

---

[1] As mentioned in the introduction to Part V, our default mergeable heaps are mergeable min-heaps, and so the operations MINIMUM, EXTRACT-MIN, and DECREASE-KEY apply. Alternatively, we could define a *mergeable max-heap* with the operations MAXIMUM, EXTRACT-MAX, and INCREASE-KEY.

Procedure	Binary heap (worst-case)	Fibonacci heap (amortized)
MAKE-HEAP	$\Theta(1)$	$\Theta(1)$
INSERT	$\Theta(\lg n)$	$\Theta(1)$
MINIMUM	$\Theta(1)$	$\Theta(1)$
EXTRACT-MIN	$\Theta(\lg n)$	$O(\lg n)$
UNION	$\Theta(n)$	$\Theta(1)$
DECREASE-KEY	$\Theta(\lg n)$	$\Theta(1)$
DELETE	$\Theta(\lg n)$	$O(\lg n)$

Figure 19.1 Running times for operations on two implementations of mergeable heaps. The number of items in the heap(s) at the time of an operation is denoted by n.

As the table in Figure 19.1 shows, if we don't need the UNION operation, ordinary binary heaps, as used in heapsort (Chapter 6), work fairly well. Operations other than UNION run in worst-case time $O(\lg n)$ on a binary heap. If we need to support the UNION operation, however, binary heaps perform poorly. By concatenating the two arrays that hold the binary heaps to be merged and then running BUILD-MIN-HEAP (see Section 6.3), the UNION operation takes $\Theta(n)$ time in the worst case.

Fibonacci heaps, on the other hand, have better asymptotic time bounds than binary heaps for the INSERT, UNION, and DECREASE-KEY operations, and they have the same asymptotic running times for the remaining operations. Note, however, that the running times for Fibonacci heaps in Figure 19.1 are amortized time bounds, not worst-case per-operation time bounds. The UNION operation takes only constant amortized time in a Fibonacci heap, which is significantly better than the linear worst-case time required in a binary heap (assuming, of course, that an amortized time bound suffices).

Fibonacci heaps in theory and practice

From a theoretical standpoint, Fibonacci heaps are especially desirable when the number of EXTRACT-MIN and DELETE operations is small relative to the number of other operations performed. This situation arises in many applications. For example, some algorithms for graph problems may call DECREASE-KEY once per edge. For dense graphs, which have many edges, the $\Theta(1)$ amortized time of each call of DECREASE-KEY adds up to a big improvement over the $\Theta(\lg n)$ worst-case time of binary heaps. Fast algorithms for problems such as computing minimum spanning trees (Chapter 23) and finding single-source shortest paths (Chapter 24) make essential use of Fibonacci heaps.

From a practical point of view, however, the constant factors and programming complexity of Fibonacci heaps make them less desirable than ordinary binary (or k-ary) heaps for most applications, except for certain applications that manage large amounts of data. Thus, Fibonacci heaps are predominantly of theoretical interest. If a much simpler data structure with the same amortized time bounds as Fibonacci heaps were developed, it would be of practical use as well.

Both binary heaps and Fibonacci heaps are inefficient in how they support the operation SEARCH; it can take a while to find an element with a given key. For this reason, operations such as DECREASE-KEY and DELETE that refer to a given element require a pointer to that element as part of their input. As in our discussion of priority queues in Section 6.5, when we use a mergeable heap in an application, we often store a handle to the corresponding application object in each mergeable-heap element, as well as a handle to the corresponding mergeable-heap element in each application object. The exact nature of these handles depends on the application and its implementation.

Like several other data structures that we have seen, Fibonacci heaps are based on rooted trees. We represent each element by a node within a tree, and each node has a *key* attribute. For the remainder of this chapter, we shall use the term "node" instead of "element." We shall also ignore issues of allocating nodes prior to insertion and freeing nodes following deletion, assuming instead that the code calling the heap procedures deals with these details.

Section 19.1 defines Fibonacci heaps, discusses how we represent them, and presents the potential function used for their amortized analysis. Section 19.2 shows how to implement the mergeable-heap operations and achieve the amortized time bounds shown in Figure 19.1. The remaining two operations, DECREASE-KEY and DELETE, form the focus of Section 19.3. Finally, Section 19.4 finishes a key part of the analysis and also explains the curious name of the data structure.

19.1 Structure of Fibonacci heaps

A *Fibonacci heap* is a collection of rooted trees that are *min-heap ordered*. That is, each tree obeys the *min-heap property*: the key of a node is greater than or equal to the key of its parent. Figure 19.2(a) shows an example of a Fibonacci heap.

As Figure 19.2(b) shows, each node x contains a pointer $x.p$ to its parent and a pointer $x.child$ to any one of its children. The children of x are linked together in a circular, doubly linked list, which we call the *child list* of x. Each child y in a child list has pointers $y.left$ and $y.right$ that point to y's left and right siblings, respectively. If node y is an only child, then $y.left = y.right = y$. Siblings may appear in a child list in any order.

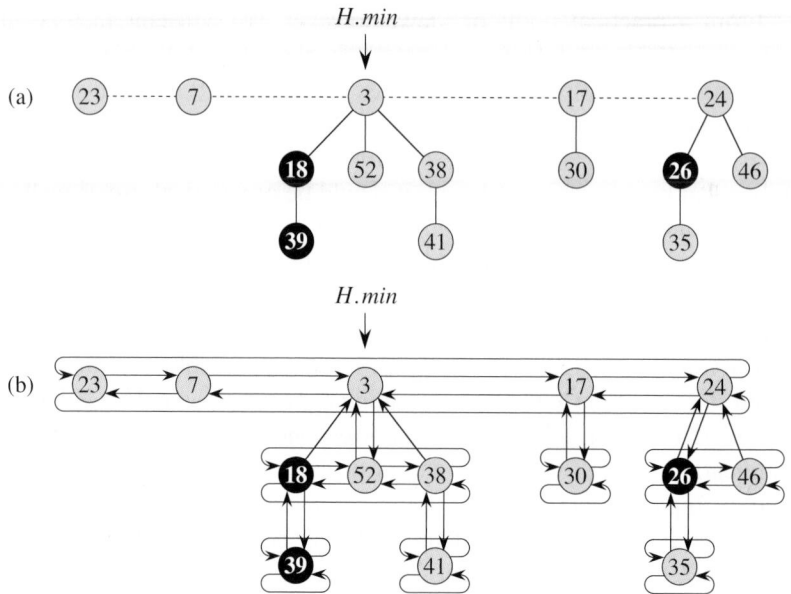

Figure 19.2   **(a)** A Fibonacci heap consisting of five min-heap-ordered trees and 14 nodes. The dashed line indicates the root list. The minimum node of the heap is the node containing the key 3. Black nodes are marked. The potential of this particular Fibonacci heap is $5 + 2 \cdot 3 = 11$. **(b)** A more complete representation showing pointers p (up arrows), *child* (down arrows), and *left* and *right* (sideways arrows). The remaining figures in this chapter omit these details, since all the information shown here can be determined from what appears in part (a).

Circular, doubly linked lists (see Section 10.2) have two advantages for use in Fibonacci heaps. First, we can insert a node into any location or remove a node from anywhere in a circular, doubly linked list in $O(1)$ time. Second, given two such lists, we can concatenate them (or "splice" them together) into one circular, doubly linked list in $O(1)$ time. In the descriptions of Fibonacci heap operations, we shall refer to these operations informally, letting you fill in the details of their implementations if you wish.

Each node has two other attributes. We store the number of children in the child list of node x in $x.degree$. The boolean-valued attribute $x.mark$ indicates whether node x has lost a child since the last time x was made the child of another node. Newly created nodes are unmarked, and a node x becomes unmarked whenever it is made the child of another node. Until we look at the DECREASE-KEY operation in Section 19.3, we will just set all *mark* attributes to FALSE.

We access a given Fibonacci heap H by a pointer $H.min$ to the root of a tree containing the minimum key; we call this node the ***minimum node*** of the Fibonacci

heap. If more than one root has a key with the minimum value, then any such root may serve as the minimum node. When a Fibonacci heap H is empty, $H.min$ is NIL.

The roots of all the trees in a Fibonacci heap are linked together using their *left* and *right* pointers into a circular, doubly linked list called the **root list** of the Fibonacci heap. The pointer $H.min$ thus points to the node in the root list whose key is minimum. Trees may appear in any order within a root list.

We rely on one other attribute for a Fibonacci heap H: $H.n$, the number of nodes currently in H.

Potential function

As mentioned, we shall use the potential method of Section 17.3 to analyze the performance of Fibonacci heap operations. For a given Fibonacci heap H, we indicate by $t(H)$ the number of trees in the root list of H and by $m(H)$ the number of marked nodes in H. We then define the potential $\Phi(H)$ of Fibonacci heap H by

$$\Phi(H) = t(H) + 2m(H) . \tag{19.1}$$

(We will gain some intuition for this potential function in Section 19.3.) For example, the potential of the Fibonacci heap shown in Figure 19.2 is $5 + 2 \cdot 3 = 11$. The potential of a set of Fibonacci heaps is the sum of the potentials of its constituent Fibonacci heaps. We shall assume that a unit of potential can pay for a constant amount of work, where the constant is sufficiently large to cover the cost of any of the specific constant-time pieces of work that we might encounter.

We assume that a Fibonacci heap application begins with no heaps. The initial potential, therefore, is 0, and by equation (19.1), the potential is nonnegative at all subsequent times. From equation (17.3), an upper bound on the total amortized cost provides an upper bound on the total actual cost for the sequence of operations.

Maximum degree

The amortized analyses we shall perform in the remaining sections of this chapter assume that we know an upper bound $D(n)$ on the maximum degree of any node in an n-node Fibonacci heap. We won't prove it, but when only the mergeable-heap operations are supported, $D(n) \leq \lfloor \lg n \rfloor$. (Problem 19-2(d) asks you to prove this property.) In Sections 19.3 and 19.4, we shall show that when we support DECREASE-KEY and DELETE as well, $D(n) = O(\lg n)$.

19.2   Mergeable-heap operations

The mergeable-heap operations on Fibonacci heaps delay work as long as possible. The various operations have performance trade-offs. For example, we insert a node by adding it to the root list, which takes just constant time. If we were to start with an empty Fibonacci heap and then insert k nodes, the Fibonacci heap would consist of just a root list of k nodes. The trade-off is that if we then perform an EXTRACT-MIN operation on Fibonacci heap H, after removing the node that $H.min$ points to, we would have to look through each of the remaining $k - 1$ nodes in the root list to find the new minimum node. As long as we have to go through the entire root list during the EXTRACT-MIN operation, we also consolidate nodes into min-heap-ordered trees to reduce the size of the root list. We shall see that, no matter what the root list looks like before an EXTRACT-MIN operation, afterward each node in the root list has a degree that is unique within the root list, which leads to a root list of size at most $D(n) + 1$.

Creating a new Fibonacci heap

To make an empty Fibonacci heap, the MAKE-FIB-HEAP procedure allocates and returns the Fibonacci heap object H, where $H.n = 0$ and $H.min =$ NIL; there are no trees in H. Because $t(H) = 0$ and $m(H) = 0$, the potential of the empty Fibonacci heap is $\Phi(H) = 0$. The amortized cost of MAKE-FIB-HEAP is thus equal to its $O(1)$ actual cost.

Inserting a node

The following procedure inserts node x into Fibonacci heap H, assuming that the node has already been allocated and that $x.key$ has already been filled in.

FIB-HEAP-INSERT(H, x)

```
 1   x.degree = 0
 2   x.p = NIL
 3   x.child = NIL
 4   x.mark = FALSE
 5   if H.min == NIL
 6       create a root list for H containing just x
 7       H.min = x
 8   else insert x into H's root list
 9       if x.key < H.min.key
10           H.min = x
11   H.n = H.n + 1
```

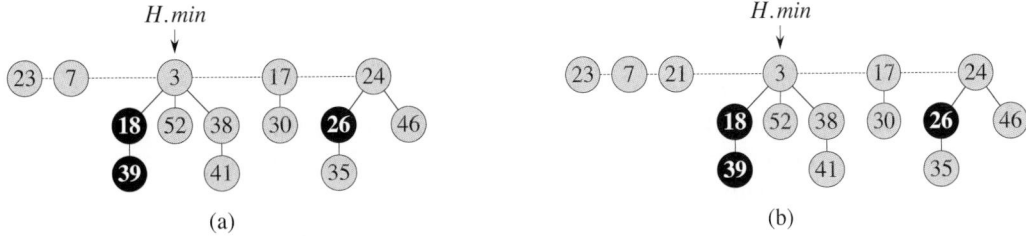

Figure 19.3   Inserting a node into a Fibonacci heap. **(a)** A Fibonacci heap H. **(b)** Fibonacci heap H after inserting the node with key 21. The node becomes its own min-heap-ordered tree and is then added to the root list, becoming the left sibling of the root.

Lines 1–4 initialize some of the structural attributes of node x. Line 5 tests to see whether Fibonacci heap H is empty. If it is, then lines 6–7 make x be the only node in H's root list and set $H.min$ to point to x. Otherwise, lines 8–10 insert x into H's root list and update $H.min$ if necessary. Finally, line 11 increments $H.n$ to reflect the addition of the new node. Figure 19.3 shows a node with key 21 inserted into the Fibonacci heap of Figure 19.2.

To determine the amortized cost of FIB-HEAP-INSERT, let H be the input Fibonacci heap and H' be the resulting Fibonacci heap. Then, $t(H') = t(H) + 1$ and $m(H') = m(H)$, and the increase in potential is

$$((t(H) + 1) + 2m(H)) - (t(H) + 2m(H)) = 1.$$

Since the actual cost is $O(1)$, the amortized cost is $O(1) + 1 = O(1)$.

Finding the minimum node

The minimum node of a Fibonacci heap H is given by the pointer $H.min$, so we can find the minimum node in $O(1)$ actual time. Because the potential of H does not change, the amortized cost of this operation is equal to its $O(1)$ actual cost.

Uniting two Fibonacci heaps

The following procedure unites Fibonacci heaps H_1 and H_2, destroying H_1 and H_2 in the process. It simply concatenates the root lists of H_1 and H_2 and then determines the new minimum node. Afterward, the objects representing H_1 and H_2 will never be used again.

FIB-HEAP-UNION(H_1, H_2)

1   $H =$ MAKE-FIB-HEAP()
2   $H.min = H_1.min$
3   concatenate the root list of H_2 with the root list of H
4   **if** ($H_1.min ==$ NIL) or ($H_2.min \neq$ NIL and $H_2.min.key < H_1.min.key$)
5       $H.min = H_2.min$
6   $H.n = H_1.n + H_2.n$
7   **return** H

Lines 1–3 concatenate the root lists of H_1 and H_2 into a new root list H. Lines 2, 4, and 5 set the minimum node of H, and line 6 sets $H.n$ to the total number of nodes. Line 7 returns the resulting Fibonacci heap H. As in the FIB-HEAP-INSERT procedure, all roots remain roots.

The change in potential is

$$
\begin{aligned}
\Phi(H) &- (\Phi(H_1) + \Phi(H_2)) \\
&= (t(H) + 2m(H)) - ((t(H_1) + 2m(H_1)) + (t(H_2) + 2m(H_2))) \\
&= 0,
\end{aligned}
$$

because $t(H) = t(H_1) + t(H_2)$ and $m(H) = m(H_1) + m(H_2)$. The amortized cost of FIB-HEAP-UNION is therefore equal to its $O(1)$ actual cost.

Extracting the minimum node

The process of extracting the minimum node is the most complicated of the operations presented in this section. It is also where the delayed work of consolidating trees in the root list finally occurs. The following pseudocode extracts the minimum node. The code assumes for convenience that when a node is removed from a linked list, pointers remaining in the list are updated, but pointers in the extracted node are left unchanged. It also calls the auxiliary procedure CONSOLIDATE, which we shall see shortly.

FIB-HEAP-EXTRACT-MIN(H)

```
 1  z = H.min
 2  if z ≠ NIL
 3      for each child x of z
 4          add x to the root list of H
 5          x.p = NIL
 6      remove z from the root list of H
 7      if z == z.right
 8          H.min = NIL
 9      else H.min = z.right
10          CONSOLIDATE(H)
11      H.n = H.n − 1
12  return z
```

As Figure 19.4 illustrates, FIB-HEAP-EXTRACT-MIN works by first making a root out of each of the minimum node's children and removing the minimum node from the root list. It then consolidates the root list by linking roots of equal degree until at most one root remains of each degree.

We start in line 1 by saving a pointer z to the minimum node; the procedure returns this pointer at the end. If z is NIL, then Fibonacci heap H is already empty and we are done. Otherwise, we delete node z from H by making all of z's children roots of H in lines 3–5 (putting them into the root list) and removing z from the root list in line 6. If z is its own right sibling after line 6, then z was the only node on the root list and it had no children, so all that remains is to make the Fibonacci heap empty in line 8 before returning z. Otherwise, we set the pointer $H.min$ into the root list to point to a root other than z (in this case, z's right sibling), which is not necessarily going to be the new minimum node when FIB-HEAP-EXTRACT-MIN is done. Figure 19.4(b) shows the Fibonacci heap of Figure 19.4(a) after executing line 9.

The next step, in which we reduce the number of trees in the Fibonacci heap, is *consolidating* the root list of H, which the call CONSOLIDATE(H) accomplishes. Consolidating the root list consists of repeatedly executing the following steps until every root in the root list has a distinct *degree* value:

1. Find two roots x and y in the root list with the same degree. Without loss of generality, let $x.key \leq y.key$.

2. **Link** y to x: remove y from the root list, and make y a child of x by calling the FIB-HEAP-LINK procedure. This procedure increments the attribute $x.degree$ and clears the mark on y.

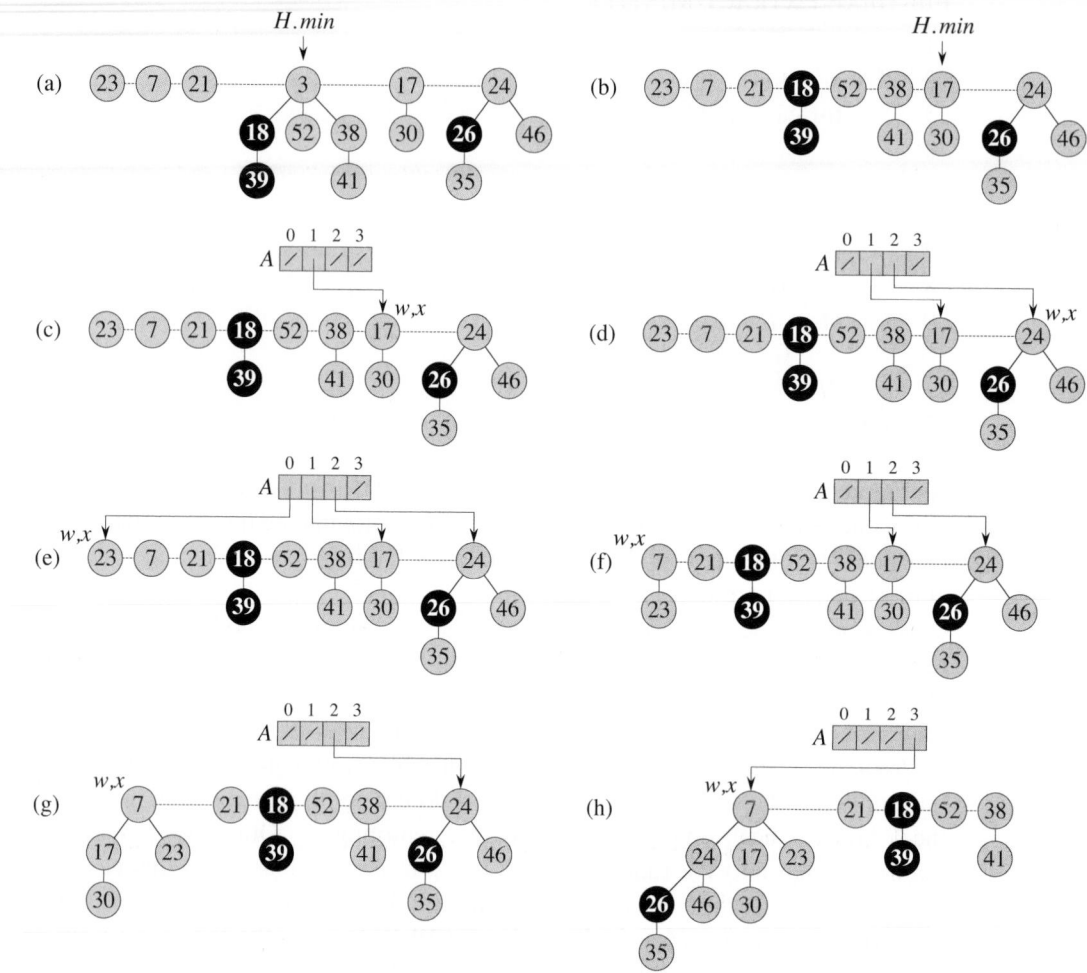

Figure 19.4 The action of FIB-HEAP-EXTRACT-MIN. **(a)** A Fibonacci heap H. **(b)** The situation after removing the minimum node z from the root list and adding its children to the root list. **(c)–(e)** The array A and the trees after each of the first three iterations of the **for** loop of lines 4–14 of the procedure CONSOLIDATE. The procedure processes the root list by starting at the node pointed to by $H.min$ and following *right* pointers. Each part shows the values of w and x at the end of an iteration. **(f)–(h)** The next iteration of the **for** loop, with the values of w and x shown at the end of each iteration of the **while** loop of lines 7–13. Part (f) shows the situation after the first time through the **while** loop. The node with key 23 has been linked to the node with key 7, which x now points to. In part (g), the node with key 17 has been linked to the node with key 7, which x still points to. In part (h), the node with key 24 has been linked to the node with key 7. Since no node was previously pointed to by $A[3]$, at the end of the **for** loop iteration, $A[3]$ is set to point to the root of the resulting tree.

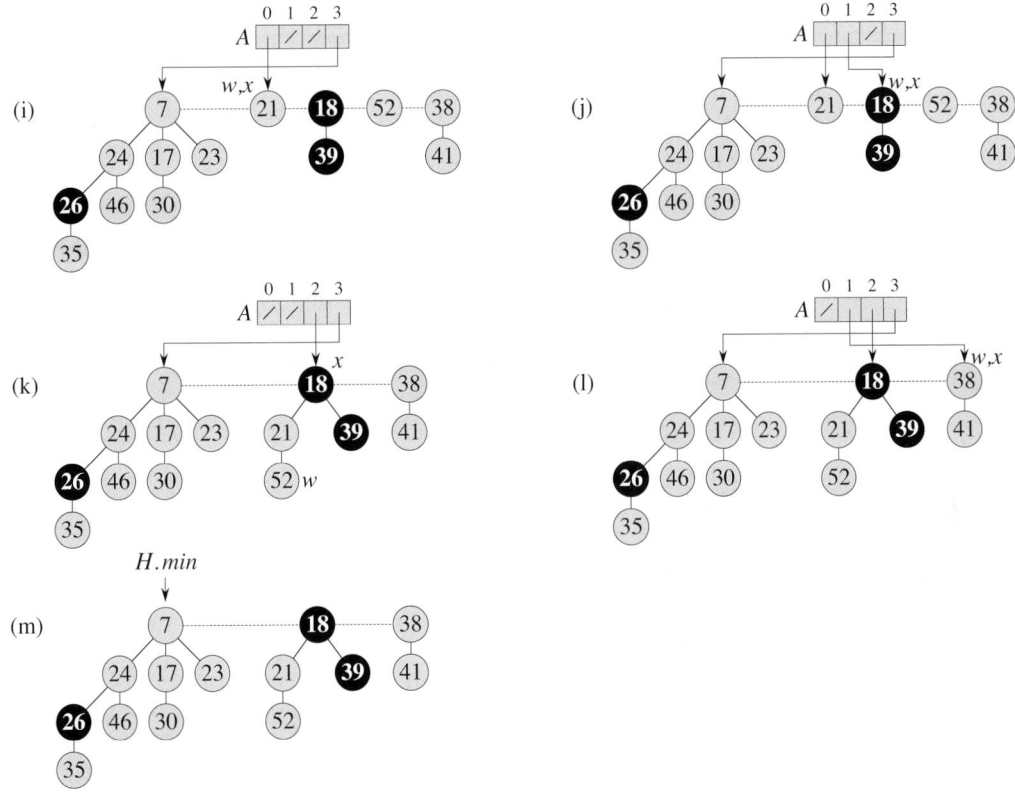

Figure 19.4, continued   **(i)–(l)** The situation after each of the next four iterations of the **for** loop. **(m)** Fibonacci heap H after reconstructing the root list from the array A and determining the new $H.min$ pointer.

The procedure CONSOLIDATE uses an auxiliary array $A[0 .. D(H.n)]$ to keep track of roots according to their degrees. If $A[i] = y$, then y is currently a root with $y.degree = i$. Of course, in order to allocate the array we have to know how to calculate the upper bound $D(H.n)$ on the maximum degree, but we will see how to do so in Section 19.4.

CONSOLIDATE(H)

```
 1   let A[0 .. D(H.n)] be a new array
 2   for i = 0 to D(H.n)
 3       A[i] = NIL
 4   for each node w in the root list of H
 5       x = w
 6       d = x.degree
 7       while A[d] ≠ NIL
 8           y = A[d]          // another node with the same degree as x
 9           if x.key > y.key
10               exchange x with y
11           FIB-HEAP-LINK(H, y, x)
12           A[d] = NIL
13           d = d + 1
14       A[d] = x
15   H.min = NIL
16   for i = 0 to D(H.n)
17       if A[i] ≠ NIL
18           if H.min == NIL
19               create a root list for H containing just A[i]
20               H.min = A[i]
21           else insert A[i] into H's root list
22               if A[i].key < H.min.key
23                   H.min = A[i]
```

FIB-HEAP-LINK(H, y, x)

```
1   remove y from the root list of H
2   make y a child of x, incrementing x.degree
3   y.mark = FALSE
```

In detail, the CONSOLIDATE procedure works as follows. Lines 1–3 allocate and initialize the array A by making each entry NIL. The **for** loop of lines 4–14 processes each root w in the root list. As we link roots together, w may be linked to some other node and no longer be a root. Nevertheless, w is always in a tree rooted at some node x, which may or may not be w itself. Because we want at most one root with each degree, we look in the array A to see whether it contains a root y with the same degree as x. If it does, then we link the roots x and y but guaranteeing that x remains a root after linking. That is, we link y to x after first exchanging the pointers to the two roots if y's key is smaller than x's key. After we link y to x, the degree of x has increased by 1, and so we continue this process, linking x and another root whose degree equals x's new degree, until no other root

that we have processed has the same degree as x. We then set the appropriate entry of A to point to x, so that as we process roots later on, we have recorded that x is the unique root of its degree that we have already processed. When this **for** loop terminates, at most one root of each degree will remain, and the array A will point to each remaining root.

The **while** loop of lines 7–13 repeatedly links the root x of the tree containing node w to another tree whose root has the same degree as x, until no other root has the same degree. This **while** loop maintains the following invariant:

At the start of each iteration of the **while** loop, $d = x.degree$.

We use this loop invariant as follows:

Initialization: Line 6 ensures that the loop invariant holds the first time we enter the loop.

Maintenance: In each iteration of the **while** loop, $A[d]$ points to some root y. Because $d = x.degree = y.degree$, we want to link x and y. Whichever of x and y has the smaller key becomes the parent of the other as a result of the link operation, and so lines 9–10 exchange the pointers to x and y if necessary. Next, we link y to x by the call FIB-HEAP-LINK(H, y, x) in line 11. This call increments $x.degree$ but leaves $y.degree$ as d. Node y is no longer a root, and so line 12 removes the pointer to it in array A. Because the call of FIB-HEAP-LINK increments the value of $x.degree$, line 13 restores the invariant that $d = x.degree$.

Termination: We repeat the **while** loop until $A[d] = \text{NIL}$, in which case there is no other root with the same degree as x.

After the **while** loop terminates, we set $A[d]$ to x in line 14 and perform the next iteration of the **for** loop.

Figures 19.4(c)–(e) show the array A and the resulting trees after the first three iterations of the **for** loop of lines 4–14. In the next iteration of the **for** loop, three links occur; their results are shown in Figures 19.4(f)–(h). Figures 19.4(i)–(l) show the result of the next four iterations of the **for** loop.

All that remains is to clean up. Once the **for** loop of lines 4–14 completes, line 15 empties the root list, and lines 16–23 reconstruct it from the array A. The resulting Fibonacci heap appears in Figure 19.4(m). After consolidating the root list, FIB-HEAP-EXTRACT-MIN finishes up by decrementing $H.n$ in line 11 and returning a pointer to the deleted node z in line 12.

We are now ready to show that the amortized cost of extracting the minimum node of an n-node Fibonacci heap is $O(D(n))$. Let H denote the Fibonacci heap just prior to the FIB-HEAP-EXTRACT-MIN operation.

We start by accounting for the actual cost of extracting the minimum node. An $O(D(n))$ contribution comes from FIB-HEAP-EXTRACT-MIN processing at

most $D(n)$ children of the minimum node and from the work in lines 2–3 and 16–23 of CONSOLIDATE. It remains to analyze the contribution from the **for** loop of lines 4–14 in CONSOLIDATE, for which we use an aggregate analysis. The size of the root list upon calling CONSOLIDATE is at most $D(n) + t(H) - 1$, since it consists of the original $t(H)$ root-list nodes, minus the extracted root node, plus the children of the extracted node, which number at most $D(n)$. Within a given iteration of the **for** loop of lines 4–14, the number of iterations of the **while** loop of lines 7–13 depends on the root list. But we know that every time through the **while** loop, one of the roots is linked to another, and thus the total number of iterations of the **while** loop over all iterations of the **for** loop is at most the number of roots in the root list. Hence, the total amount of work performed in the **for** loop is at most proportional to $D(n) + t(H)$. Thus, the total actual work in extracting the minimum node is $O(D(n) + t(H))$.

The potential before extracting the minimum node is $t(H) + 2m(H)$, and the potential afterward is at most $(D(n) + 1) + 2m(H)$, since at most $D(n) + 1$ roots remain and no nodes become marked during the operation. The amortized cost is thus at most

$$
\begin{aligned}
O(D(n) + t(H)) &+ ((D(n) + 1) + 2m(H)) - (t(H) + 2m(H)) \\
&= O(D(n)) + O(t(H)) - t(H) \\
&= O(D(n)) \,,
\end{aligned}
$$

since we can scale up the units of potential to dominate the constant hidden in $O(t(H))$. Intuitively, the cost of performing each link is paid for by the reduction in potential due to the link's reducing the number of roots by one. We shall see in Section 19.4 that $D(n) = O(\lg n)$, so that the amortized cost of extracting the minimum node is $O(\lg n)$.

Exercises

19.2-1
Show the Fibonacci heap that results from calling FIB-HEAP-EXTRACT-MIN on the Fibonacci heap shown in Figure 19.4(m).

19.3   Decreasing a key and deleting a node

In this section, we show how to decrease the key of a node in a Fibonacci heap in $O(1)$ amortized time and how to delete any node from an n-node Fibonacci heap in $O(D(n))$ amortized time. In Section 19.4, we will show that the maxi-

mum degree $D(n)$ is $O(\lg n)$, which will imply that Fib-Heap-Extract-Min and Fib-Heap-Delete run in $O(\lg n)$ amortized time.

Decreasing a key

In the following pseudocode for the operation Fib-Heap-Decrease-Key, we assume as before that removing a node from a linked list does not change any of the structural attributes in the removed node.

Fib-Heap-Decrease-Key(H, x, k)

```
1  if k > x.key
2      error "new key is greater than current key"
3  x.key = k
4  y = x.p
5  if y ≠ NIL and x.key < y.key
6      Cut(H, x, y)
7      Cascading-Cut(H, y)
8  if x.key < H.min.key
9      H.min = x
```

Cut(H, x, y)

```
1  remove x from the child list of y, decrementing y.degree
2  add x to the root list of H
3  x.p = NIL
4  x.mark = FALSE
```

Cascading-Cut(H, y)

```
1  z = y.p
2  if z ≠ NIL
3      if y.mark == FALSE
4          y.mark = TRUE
5      else Cut(H, y, z)
6          Cascading-Cut(H, z)
```

The Fib-Heap-Decrease-Key procedure works as follows. Lines 1–3 ensure that the new key is no greater than the current key of x and then assign the new key to x. If x is a root or if $x.key \geq y.key$, where y is x's parent, then no structural changes need occur, since min-heap order has not been violated. Lines 4–5 test for this condition.

If min-heap order has been violated, many changes may occur. We start by *cutting* x in line 6. The Cut procedure "cuts" the link between x and its parent y, making x a root.

We use the *mark* attributes to obtain the desired time bounds. They record a little piece of the history of each node. Suppose that the following events have happened to node x:

1. at some time, x was a root,

2. then x was linked to (made the child of) another node,

3. then two children of x were removed by cuts.

As soon as the second child has been lost, we cut x from its parent, making it a new root. The attribute $x.mark$ is TRUE if steps 1 and 2 have occurred and one child of x has been cut. The CUT procedure, therefore, clears $x.mark$ in line 4, since it performs step 1. (We can now see why line 3 of FIB-HEAP-LINK clears $y.mark$: node y is being linked to another node, and so step 2 is being performed. The next time a child of y is cut, $y.mark$ will be set to TRUE.)

We are not yet done, because x might be the second child cut from its parent y since the time that y was linked to another node. Therefore, line 7 of FIB-HEAP-DECREASE-KEY attempts to perform a ***cascading-cut*** operation on y. If y is a root, then the test in line 2 of CASCADING-CUT causes the procedure to just return. If y is unmarked, the procedure marks it in line 4, since its first child has just been cut, and returns. If y is marked, however, it has just lost its second child; y is cut in line 5, and CASCADING-CUT calls itself recursively in line 6 on y's parent z. The CASCADING-CUT procedure recurses its way up the tree until it finds either a root or an unmarked node.

Once all the cascading cuts have occurred, lines 8–9 of FIB-HEAP-DECREASE-KEY finish up by updating $H.min$ if necessary. The only node whose key changed was the node x whose key decreased. Thus, the new minimum node is either the original minimum node or node x.

Figure 19.5 shows the execution of two calls of FIB-HEAP-DECREASE-KEY, starting with the Fibonacci heap shown in Figure 19.5(a). The first call, shown in Figure 19.5(b), involves no cascading cuts. The second call, shown in Figures 19.5(c)–(e), invokes two cascading cuts.

We shall now show that the amortized cost of FIB-HEAP-DECREASE-KEY is only $O(1)$. We start by determining its actual cost. The FIB-HEAP-DECREASE-KEY procedure takes $O(1)$ time, plus the time to perform the cascading cuts. Suppose that a given invocation of FIB-HEAP-DECREASE-KEY results in c calls of CASCADING-CUT (the call made from line 7 of FIB-HEAP-DECREASE-KEY followed by $c - 1$ recursive calls of CASCADING-CUT). Each call of CASCADING-CUT takes $O(1)$ time exclusive of recursive calls. Thus, the actual cost of FIB-HEAP-DECREASE-KEY, including all recursive calls, is $O(c)$.

We next compute the change in potential. Let H denote the Fibonacci heap just prior to the FIB-HEAP-DECREASE-KEY operation. The call to CUT in line 6 of

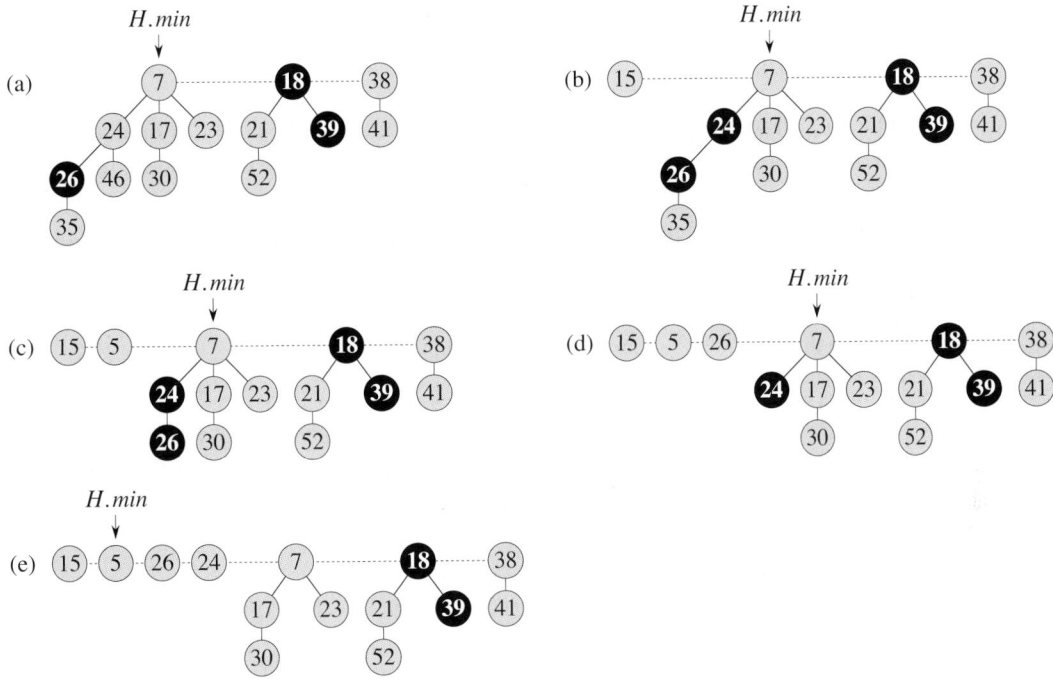

Figure 19.5 Two calls of FIB-HEAP-DECREASE-KEY. **(a)** The initial Fibonacci heap. **(b)** The node with key 46 has its key decreased to 15. The node becomes a root, and its parent (with key 24), which had previously been unmarked, becomes marked. **(c)–(e)** The node with key 35 has its key decreased to 5. In part (c), the node, now with key 5, becomes a root. Its parent, with key 26, is marked, so a cascading cut occurs. The node with key 26 is cut from its parent and made an unmarked root in (d). Another cascading cut occurs, since the node with key 24 is marked as well. This node is cut from its parent and made an unmarked root in part (e). The cascading cuts stop at this point, since the node with key 7 is a root. (Even if this node were not a root, the cascading cuts would stop, since it is unmarked.) Part (e) shows the result of the FIB-HEAP-DECREASE-KEY operation, with *H.min* pointing to the new minimum node.

FIB-HEAP-DECREASE-KEY creates a new tree rooted at node x and clears x's mark bit (which may have already been FALSE). Each call of CASCADING-CUT, except for the last one, cuts a marked node and clears the mark bit. Afterward, the Fibonacci heap contains $t(H) + c$ trees (the original $t(H)$ trees, $c - 1$ trees produced by cascading cuts, and the tree rooted at x) and at most $m(H) - c + 2$ marked nodes ($c - 1$ were unmarked by cascading cuts and the last call of CASCADING-CUT may have marked a node). The change in potential is therefore at most

$$((t(H) + c) + 2(m(H) - c + 2)) - (t(H) + 2m(H)) = 4 - c .$$

Thus, the amortized cost of FIB-HEAP-DECREASE-KEY is at most

$$O(c) + 4 - c = O(1) \,,$$

since we can scale up the units of potential to dominate the constant hidden in $O(c)$.

You can now see why we defined the potential function to include a term that is twice the number of marked nodes. When a marked node y is cut by a cascading cut, its mark bit is cleared, which reduces the potential by 2. One unit of potential pays for the cut and the clearing of the mark bit, and the other unit compensates for the unit increase in potential due to node y becoming a root.

Deleting a node

The following pseudocode deletes a node from an n-node Fibonacci heap in $O(D(n))$ amortized time. We assume that there is no key value of $-\infty$ currently in the Fibonacci heap.

FIB-HEAP-DELETE(H, x)

1   FIB-HEAP-DECREASE-KEY($H, x, -\infty$)
2   FIB-HEAP-EXTRACT-MIN(H)

FIB-HEAP-DELETE makes x become the minimum node in the Fibonacci heap by giving it a uniquely small key of $-\infty$. The FIB-HEAP-EXTRACT-MIN procedure then removes node x from the Fibonacci heap. The amortized time of FIB-HEAP-DELETE is the sum of the $O(1)$ amortized time of FIB-HEAP-DECREASE-KEY and the $O(D(n))$ amortized time of FIB-HEAP-EXTRACT-MIN. Since we shall see in Section 19.4 that $D(n) = O(\lg n)$, the amortized time of FIB-HEAP-DELETE is $O(\lg n)$.

Exercises

19.3-1
Suppose that a root x in a Fibonacci heap is marked. Explain how x came to be a marked root. Argue that it doesn't matter to the analysis that x is marked, even though it is not a root that was first linked to another node and then lost one child.

19.3-2
Justify the $O(1)$ amortized time of FIB-HEAP-DECREASE-KEY as an average cost per operation by using aggregate analysis.

19.4 Bounding the maximum degree

To prove that the amortized time of FIB-HEAP-EXTRACT-MIN and FIB-HEAP-DELETE is $O(\lg n)$, we must show that the upper bound $D(n)$ on the degree of any node of an n-node Fibonacci heap is $O(\lg n)$. In particular, we shall show that $D(n) \leq \lfloor \log_\phi n \rfloor$, where ϕ is the golden ratio, defined in equation (3.24) as

$$\phi = (1 + \sqrt{5})/2 = 1.61803\ldots .$$

The key to the analysis is as follows. For each node x within a Fibonacci heap, define $size(x)$ to be the number of nodes, including x itself, in the subtree rooted at x. (Note that x need not be in the root list—it can be any node at all.) We shall show that $size(x)$ is exponential in $x.degree$. Bear in mind that $x.degree$ is always maintained as an accurate count of the degree of x.

Lemma 19.1
Let x be any node in a Fibonacci heap, and suppose that $x.degree = k$. Let $y_1, y_2, \ldots, y_k$ denote the children of x in the order in which they were linked to x, from the earliest to the latest. Then, $y_1.degree \geq 0$ and $y_i.degree \geq i - 2$ for $i = 2, 3, \ldots, k$.

Proof Obviously, $y_1.degree \geq 0$.

For $i \geq 2$, we note that when y_i was linked to x, all of $y_1, y_2, \ldots, y_{i-1}$ were children of x, and so we must have had $x.degree \geq i - 1$. Because node y_i is linked to x (by CONSOLIDATE) only if $x.degree = y_i.degree$, we must have also had $y_i.degree \geq i - 1$ at that time. Since then, node y_i has lost at most one child, since it would have been cut from x (by CASCADING-CUT) if it had lost two children. We conclude that $y_i.degree \geq i - 2$. ∎

We finally come to the part of the analysis that explains the name "Fibonacci heaps." Recall from Section 3.2 that for $k = 0, 1, 2, \ldots$, the kth Fibonacci number is defined by the recurrence

$$F_k = \begin{cases} 0 & \text{if } k = 0, \\ 1 & \text{if } k = 1, \\ F_{k-1} + F_{k-2} & \text{if } k \geq 2. \end{cases}$$

The following lemma gives another way to express F_k.

Lemma 19.2
For all integers $k \geq 0$,

$$F_{k+2} = 1 + \sum_{i=0}^{k} F_i \; .$$

Proof   The proof is by induction on k. When $k = 0$,

$$
\begin{aligned}
1 + \sum_{i=0}^{0} F_i &= 1 + F_0 \\
&= 1 + 0 \\
&= F_2 \; .
\end{aligned}
$$

We now assume the inductive hypothesis that $F_{k+1} = 1 + \sum_{i=0}^{k-1} F_i$, and we have

$$
\begin{aligned}
F_{k+2} &= F_k + F_{k+1} \\
&= F_k + \left(1 + \sum_{i=0}^{k-1} F_i \right) \\
&= 1 + \sum_{i=0}^{k} F_i \; .
\end{aligned}
$$
■

Lemma 19.3
For all integers $k \geq 0$, the $(k + 2)$nd Fibonacci number satisfies $F_{k+2} \geq \phi^k$.

Proof   The proof is by induction on k. The base cases are for $k = 0$ and $k = 1$. When $k = 0$ we have $F_2 = 1 = \phi^0$, and when $k = 1$ we have $F_3 = 2 > 1.619 > \phi^1$. The inductive step is for $k \geq 2$, and we assume that $F_{i+2} > \phi^i$ for $i = 0, 1, \ldots, k-1$. Recall that ϕ is the positive root of equation (3.23), $x^2 = x+1$. Thus, we have

$$
\begin{aligned}
F_{k+2} &= F_{k+1} + F_k \\
&\geq \phi^{k-1} + \phi^{k-2} \quad \text{(by the inductive hypothesis)} \\
&= \phi^{k-2}(\phi + 1) \\
&= \phi^{k-2} \cdot \phi^2 \quad \text{(by equation (3.23))} \\
&= \phi^k \; .
\end{aligned}
$$
■

The following lemma and its corollary complete the analysis.

Lemma 19.4
Let x be any node in a Fibonacci heap, and let $k = x.degree$. Then size$(x) \geq F_{k+2} \geq \phi^k$, where $\phi = (1 + \sqrt{5})/2$.

Proof   Let s_k denote the minimum possible size of any node of degree k in any Fibonacci heap. Trivially, $s_0 = 1$ and $s_1 = 2$. The number s_k is at most size(x) and, because adding children to a node cannot decrease the node's size, the value of s_k increases monotonically with k. Consider some node z, in any Fibonacci heap, such that $z.degree = k$ and size$(z) = s_k$. Because $s_k \leq$ size(x), we compute a lower bound on size(x) by computing a lower bound on s_k. As in Lemma 19.1, let $y_1, y_2, \ldots, y_k$ denote the children of z in the order in which they were linked to z. To bound s_k, we count one for z itself and one for the first child y_1 (for which size$(y_1) \geq 1$), giving

$$
\begin{aligned}
\text{size}(x) \;\geq\; & s_k \\
\geq\; & 2 + \sum_{i=2}^{k} s_{y_i.degree} \\
\geq\; & 2 + \sum_{i=2}^{k} s_{i-2} \,,
\end{aligned}
$$

where the last line follows from Lemma 19.1 (so that $y_i.degree \geq i - 2$) and the monotonicity of s_k (so that $s_{y_i.degree} \geq s_{i-2}$).

We now show by induction on k that $s_k \geq F_{k+2}$ for all nonnegative integers k. The bases, for $k = 0$ and $k = 1$, are trivial. For the inductive step, we assume that $k \geq 2$ and that $s_i \geq F_{i+2}$ for $i = 0, 1, \ldots, k - 1$. We have

$$
\begin{aligned}
s_k \;\geq\; & 2 + \sum_{i=2}^{k} s_{i-2} \\
\geq\; & 2 + \sum_{i=2}^{k} F_i \\
=\; & 1 + \sum_{i=0}^{k} F_i \\
=\; & F_{k+2} \qquad \text{(by Lemma 19.2)} \\
\geq\; & \phi^k \qquad \text{(by Lemma 19.3) .}
\end{aligned}
$$

Thus, we have shown that size$(x) \geq s_k \geq F_{k+2} \geq \phi^k$.   ∎

Corollary 19.5

The maximum degree $D(n)$ of any node in an n-node Fibonacci heap is $O(\lg n)$.

Proof Let x be any node in an n-node Fibonacci heap, and let $k = x.degree$. By Lemma 19.4, we have $n \geq \text{size}(x) \geq \phi^k$. Taking base-$\phi$ logarithms gives us $k \leq \log_\phi n$. (In fact, because k is an integer, $k \leq \lfloor \log_\phi n \rfloor$.) The maximum degree $D(n)$ of any node is thus $O(\lg n)$.   ∎

Exercises

19.4-1

Professor Pinocchio claims that the height of an n-node Fibonacci heap is $O(\lg n)$. Show that the professor is mistaken by exhibiting, for any positive integer n, a sequence of Fibonacci-heap operations that creates a Fibonacci heap consisting of just one tree that is a linear chain of n nodes.

19.4-2

Suppose we generalize the cascading-cut rule to cut a node x from its parent as soon as it loses its kth child, for some integer constant k. (The rule in Section 19.3 uses $k = 2$.) For what values of k is $D(n) = O(\lg n)$ and the asymptotic amortized operation costs remain unchanged?

Problems

19-1   *Alternative implementation of deletion*

Professor Pisano has proposed the following variant of the FIB-HEAP-DELETE procedure, claiming that it runs faster when the node being deleted is not the node pointed to by $H.min$.

PISANO-DELETE(H, x)

```
1  if x == H.min
2       FIB-HEAP-EXTRACT-MIN(H)
3  else y = x.p
4       if y ≠ NIL
5            CUT(H, x, y)
6            CASCADING-CUT(H, y)
7       add x's child list to the root list of H
8       remove x from the root list of H
```

a. The professor's claim that this procedure runs faster is based partly on the assumption that line 7 can be performed in $O(1)$ actual time. What is wrong with this assumption?

b. Give a good upper bound on the actual time of PISANO-DELETE when x is not $H.min$. Your bound should be in terms of $x.degree$ and the number c of calls to the CASCADING-CUT procedure.

c. Suppose that we call PISANO-DELETE(H, x), and let H' be the Fibonacci heap that results. Assuming that node x is not a root, bound the potential of H' in terms of $x.degree, c, t(H)$, and $m(H)$.

d. Conclude that the amortized time for PISANO-DELETE is asymptotically no better than for FIB-HEAP-DELETE, even when $x \neq H.min$.

19-2 *Binomial trees and binomial heaps*

The ***binomial tree*** B_k is an ordered tree (see Section B.5.2) defined recursively. As shown in Figure 19.6(a), the binomial tree B_0 consists of a single node. The binomial tree B_k consists of two binomial trees B_{k-1} that are linked together so that the root of one is the leftmost child of the root of the other. Figure 19.6(b) shows the binomial trees B_0 through B_4.

a. Show that for the binomial tree B_k,

1. there are 2^k nodes,
2. the height of the tree is k,
3. there are exactly $\binom{k}{i}$ nodes at depth i for $i = 0, 1, \ldots, k$, and
4. the root has degree k, which is greater than that of any other node; moreover, as Figure 19.6(c) shows, if we number the children of the root from left to right by $k - 1, k - 2, \ldots, 0$, then child i is the root of a subtree B_i.

A ***binomial heap*** H is a set of binomial trees that satisfies the following properties:

1. Each node has a *key* (like a Fibonacci heap).
2. Each binomial tree in H obeys the min-heap property.
3. For any nonnegative integer k, there is at most one binomial tree in H whose root has degree k.

b. Suppose that a binomial heap H has a total of n nodes. Discuss the relationship between the binomial trees that H contains and the binary representation of n. Conclude that H consists of at most $\lfloor \lg n \rfloor + 1$ binomial trees.

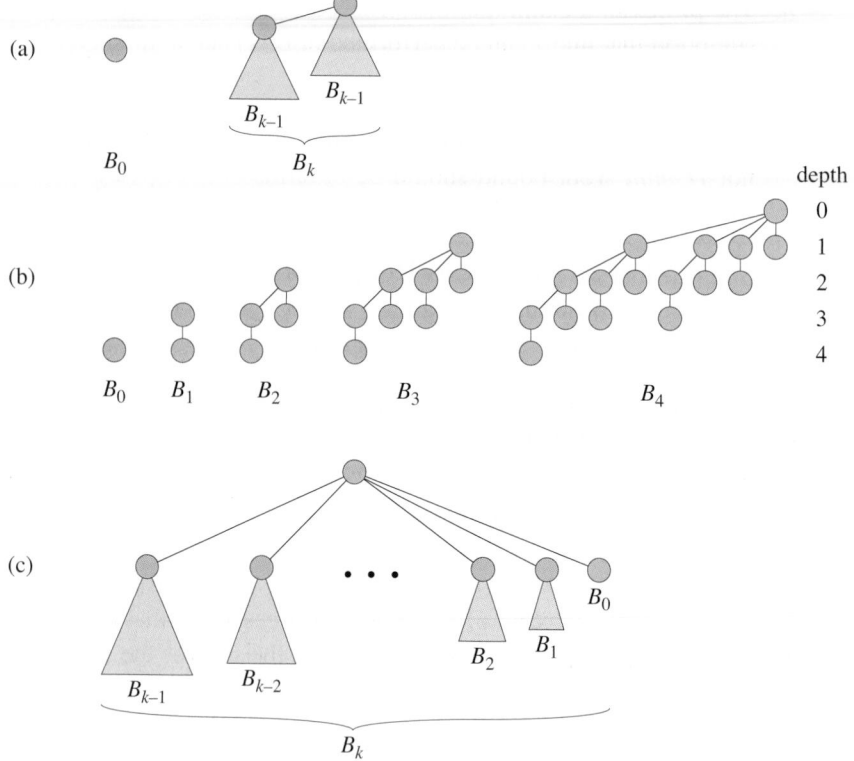

Figure 19.6 **(a)** The recursive definition of the binomial tree B_k. Triangles represent rooted sub-trees. **(b)** The binomial trees B_0 through B_4. Node depths in B_4 are shown. **(c)** Another way of looking at the binomial tree B_k.

Suppose that we represent a binomial heap as follows. The left-child, right-sibling scheme of Section 10.4 represents each binomial tree within a binomial heap. Each node contains its key; pointers to its parent, to its leftmost child, and to the sibling immediately to its right (these pointers are NIL when appropriate); and its degree (as in Fibonacci heaps, how many children it has). The roots form a singly linked root list, ordered by the degrees of the roots (from low to high), and we access the binomial heap by a pointer to the first node on the root list.

c. Complete the description of how to represent a binomial heap (i.e., name the attributes, describe when attributes have the value NIL, and define how the root list is organized), and show how to implement the same seven operations on binomial heaps as this chapter implemented on Fibonacci heaps. Each operation should run in $O(\lg n)$ worst-case time, where n is the number of nodes in

the binomial heap (or in the case of the UNION operation, in the two binomial heaps that are being united). The MAKE-HEAP operation should take constant time.

d. Suppose that we were to implement only the mergeable-heap operations on a Fibonacci heap (i.e., we do not implement the DECREASE-KEY or DELETE operations). How would the trees in a Fibonacci heap resemble those in a binomial heap? How would they differ? Show that the maximum degree in an n-node Fibonacci heap would be at most $\lfloor \lg n \rfloor$.

e. Professor McGee has devised a new data structure based on Fibonacci heaps. A McGee heap has the same structure as a Fibonacci heap and supports just the mergeable-heap operations. The implementations of the operations are the same as for Fibonacci heaps, except that insertion and union consolidate the root list as their last step. What are the worst-case running times of operations on McGee heaps?

19-3 *More Fibonacci-heap operations*

We wish to augment a Fibonacci heap H to support two new operations without changing the amortized running time of any other Fibonacci-heap operations.

a. The operation FIB-HEAP-CHANGE-KEY(H, x, k) changes the key of node x to the value k. Give an efficient implementation of FIB-HEAP-CHANGE-KEY, and analyze the amortized running time of your implementation for the cases in which k is greater than, less than, or equal to $x.key$.

b. Give an efficient implementation of FIB-HEAP-PRUNE(H, r), which deletes $q = \min(r, H.n)$ nodes from H. You may choose any q nodes to delete. Analyze the amortized running time of your implementation. (*Hint:* You may need to modify the data structure and potential function.)

19-4 *2-3-4 heaps*

Chapter 18 introduced the 2-3-4 tree, in which every internal node (other than possibly the root) has two, three, or four children and all leaves have the same depth. In this problem, we shall implement *2-3-4 heaps*, which support the mergeable-heap operations.

The 2-3-4 heaps differ from 2-3-4 trees in the following ways. In 2-3-4 heaps, only leaves store keys, and each leaf x stores exactly one key in the attribute $x.key$. The keys in the leaves may appear in any order. Each internal node x contains a value $x.small$ that is equal to the smallest key stored in any leaf in the subtree rooted at x. The root r contains an attribute $r.height$ that gives the height of the

tree. Finally, 2-3-4 heaps are designed to be kept in main memory, so that disk reads and writes are not needed.

Implement the following 2-3-4 heap operations. In parts (a)–(e), each operation should run in $O(\lg n)$ time on a 2-3-4 heap with n elements. The UNION operation in part (f) should run in $O(\lg n)$ time, where n is the number of elements in the two input heaps.

a. MINIMUM, which returns a pointer to the leaf with the smallest key.

b. DECREASE-KEY, which decreases the key of a given leaf x to a given value $k \leq x.key$.

c. INSERT, which inserts leaf x with key k.

d. DELETE, which deletes a given leaf x.

e. EXTRACT-MIN, which extracts the leaf with the smallest key.

f. UNION, which unites two 2-3-4 heaps, returning a single 2-3-4 heap and destroying the input heaps.

Chapter notes

Fredman and Tarjan [114] introduced Fibonacci heaps. Their paper also describes the application of Fibonacci heaps to the problems of single-source shortest paths, all-pairs shortest paths, weighted bipartite matching, and the minimum-spanning-tree problem.

Subsequently, Driscoll, Gabow, Shrairman, and Tarjan [96] developed "relaxed heaps" as an alternative to Fibonacci heaps. They devised two varieties of relaxed heaps. One gives the same amortized time bounds as Fibonacci heaps. The other allows DECREASE-KEY to run in $O(1)$ worst-case (not amortized) time and EXTRACT-MIN and DELETE to run in $O(\lg n)$ worst-case time. Relaxed heaps also have some advantages over Fibonacci heaps in parallel algorithms.

See also the chapter notes for Chapter 6 for other data structures that support fast DECREASE-KEY operations when the sequence of values returned by EXTRACT-MIN calls are monotonically increasing over time and the data are integers in a specific range.

20   van Emde Boas Trees

In previous chapters, we saw data structures that support the operations of a priority queue—binary heaps in Chapter 6, red-black trees in Chapter 13,[1] and Fibonacci heaps in Chapter 19. In each of these data structures, at least one important operation took $O(\lg n)$ time, either worst case or amortized. In fact, because each of these data structures bases its decisions on comparing keys, the $\Omega(n \lg n)$ lower bound for sorting in Section 8.1 tells us that at least one operation will have to take $\Omega(\lg n)$ time. Why? If we could perform both the INSERT and EXTRACT-MIN operations in $o(\lg n)$ time, then we could sort n keys in $o(n \lg n)$ time by first performing n INSERT operations, followed by n EXTRACT-MIN operations.

We saw in Chapter 8, however, that sometimes we can exploit additional information about the keys to sort in $o(n \lg n)$ time. In particular, with counting sort we can sort n keys, each an integer in the range 0 to k, in time $\Theta(n + k)$, which is $\Theta(n)$ when $k = O(n)$.

Since we can circumvent the $\Omega(n \lg n)$ lower bound for sorting when the keys are integers in a bounded range, you might wonder whether we can perform each of the priority-queue operations in $o(\lg n)$ time in a similar scenario. In this chapter, we shall see that we can: van Emde Boas trees support the priority-queue operations, and a few others, each in $O(\lg \lg n)$ worst-case time. The hitch is that the keys must be integers in the range 0 to $n - 1$, with no duplicates allowed.

Specifically, van Emde Boas trees support each of the dynamic set operations listed on page 230—SEARCH, INSERT, DELETE, MINIMUM, MAXIMUM, SUCCESSOR, and PREDECESSOR—in $O(\lg \lg n)$ time. In this chapter, we will omit discussion of satellite data and focus only on storing keys. Because we concentrate on keys and disallow duplicate keys to be stored, instead of describing the SEARCH

---

[1] Chapter 13 does not explicitly discuss how to implement EXTRACT-MIN and DECREASE-KEY, but we can easily build these operations for any data structure that supports MINIMUM, DELETE, and INSERT.

operation, we will implement the simpler operation MEMBER(S, x), which returns a boolean indicating whether the value x is currently in dynamic set S.

So far, we have used the parameter n for two distinct purposes: the number of elements in the dynamic set, and the range of the possible values. To avoid any further confusion, from here on we will use n to denote the number of elements currently in the set and u as the range of possible values, so that each van Emde Boas tree operation runs in $O(\lg \lg u)$ time. We call the set $\{0, 1, 2, \ldots, u-1\}$ the **universe** of values that can be stored and u the **universe size**. We assume throughout this chapter that u is an exact power of 2, i.e., $u = 2^k$ for some integer $k \geq 1$.

Section 20.1 starts us out by examining some simple approaches that will get us going in the right direction. We enhance these approaches in Section 20.2, introducing proto van Emde Boas structures, which are recursive but do not achieve our goal of $O(\lg \lg u)$-time operations. Section 20.3 modifies proto van Emde Boas structures to develop van Emde Boas trees, and it shows how to implement each operation in $O(\lg \lg u)$ time.

20.1   Preliminary approaches

In this section, we shall examine various approaches for storing a dynamic set. Although none will achieve the $O(\lg \lg u)$ time bounds that we desire, we will gain insights that will help us understand van Emde Boas trees when we see them later in this chapter.

Direct addressing

Direct addressing, as we saw in Section 11.1, provides the simplest approach to storing a dynamic set. Since in this chapter we are concerned only with storing keys, we can simplify the direct-addressing approach to store the dynamic set as a bit vector, as discussed in Exercise 11.1-2. To store a dynamic set of values from the universe $\{0, 1, 2, \ldots, u-1\}$, we maintain an array $A[0 \mathbin{..} u-1]$ of u bits. The entry $A[x]$ holds a 1 if the value x is in the dynamic set, and it holds a 0 otherwise. Although we can perform each of the INSERT, DELETE, and MEMBER operations in $O(1)$ time with a bit vector, the remaining operations—MINIMUM, MAXIMUM, SUCCESSOR, and PREDECESSOR—each take $\Theta(u)$ time in the worst case because

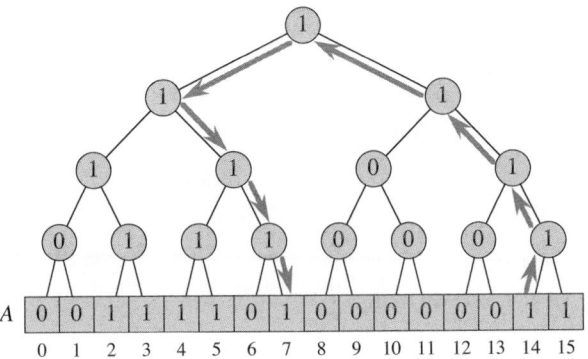

Figure 20.1 A binary tree of bits superimposed on top of a bit vector representing the set $\{2, 3, 4, 5, 7, 14, 15\}$ when $u = 16$. Each internal node contains a 1 if and only if some leaf in its subtree contains a 1. The arrows show the path followed to determine the predecessor of 14 in the set.

we might have to scan through $\Theta(u)$ elements.[2] For example, if a set contains only the values 0 and $u - 1$, then to find the successor of 0, we would have to scan entries 1 through $u - 2$ before finding a 1 in $A[u - 1]$.

Superimposing a binary tree structure

We can short-cut long scans in the bit vector by superimposing a binary tree of bits on top of it. Figure 20.1 shows an example. The entries of the bit vector form the leaves of the binary tree, and each internal node contains a 1 if and only if any leaf in its subtree contains a 1. In other words, the bit stored in an internal node is the logical-or of its two children.

The operations that took $\Theta(u)$ worst-case time with an unadorned bit vector now use the tree structure:

- To find the minimum value in the set, start at the root and head down toward the leaves, always taking the leftmost node containing a 1.

- To find the maximum value in the set, start at the root and head down toward the leaves, always taking the rightmost node containing a 1.

---

[2]We assume throughout this chapter that MINIMUM and MAXIMUM return NIL if the dynamic set is empty and that SUCCESSOR and PREDECESSOR return NIL if the element they are given has no successor or predecessor, respectively.

- To find the successor of x, start at the leaf indexed by x, and head up toward the root until we enter a node from the left and this node has a 1 in its right child z. Then head down through node z, always taking the leftmost node containing a 1 (i.e., find the minimum value in the subtree rooted at the right child z).

- To find the predecessor of x, start at the leaf indexed by x, and head up toward the root until we enter a node from the right and this node has a 1 in its left child z. Then head down through node z, always taking the rightmost node containing a 1 (i.e., find the maximum value in the subtree rooted at the left child z).

Figure 20.1 shows the path taken to find the predecessor, 7, of the value 14.

We also augment the INSERT and DELETE operations appropriately. When inserting a value, we store a 1 in each node on the simple path from the appropriate leaf up to the root. When deleting a value, we go from the appropriate leaf up to the root, recomputing the bit in each internal node on the path as the logical-or of its two children.

Since the height of the tree is $\lg u$ and each of the above operations makes at most one pass up the tree and at most one pass down, each operation takes $O(\lg u)$ time in the worst case.

This approach is only marginally better than just using a red-black tree. We can still perform the MEMBER operation in $O(1)$ time, whereas searching a red-black tree takes $O(\lg n)$ time. Then again, if the number n of elements stored is much smaller than the size u of the universe, a red-black tree would be faster for all the other operations.

Superimposing a tree of constant height

What happens if we superimpose a tree with greater degree? Let us assume that the size of the universe is $u = 2^{2k}$ for some integer k, so that $\sqrt{u}$ is an integer. Instead of superimposing a binary tree on top of the bit vector, we superimpose a tree of degree $\sqrt{u}$. Figure 20.2(a) shows such a tree for the same bit vector as in Figure 20.1. The height of the resulting tree is always 2.

As before, each internal node stores the logical-or of the bits within its subtree, so that the $\sqrt{u}$ internal nodes at depth 1 summarize each group of $\sqrt{u}$ values. As Figure 20.2(b) demonstrates, we can think of these nodes as an array $summary[0 .. \sqrt{u} - 1]$, where $summary[i]$ contains a 1 if and only if the subarray $A[i\sqrt{u} .. (i + 1)\sqrt{u} - 1]$ contains a 1. We call this $\sqrt{u}$-bit subarray of A the ith **cluster**. For a given value of x, the bit $A[x]$ appears in cluster number $\lfloor x/\sqrt{u} \rfloor$. Now INSERT becomes an $O(1)$-time operation: to insert x, set both $A[x]$ and $summary[\lfloor x/\sqrt{u} \rfloor]$ to 1. We can use the $summary$ array to perform

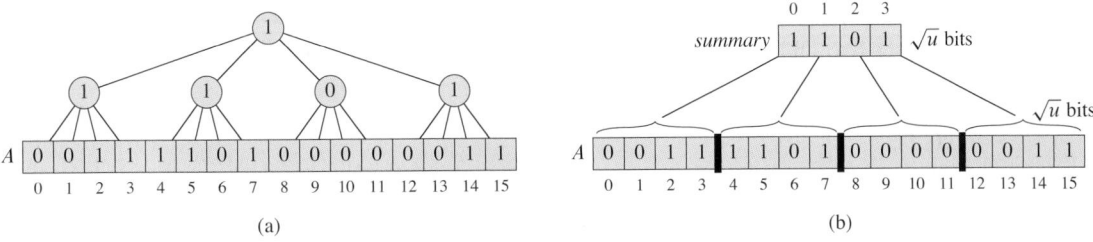

(a)   (b)

Figure 20.2   **(a)** A tree of degree $\sqrt{u}$ superimposed on top of the same bit vector as in Figure 20.1. Each internal node stores the logical-or of the bits in its subtree. **(b)** A view of the same structure, but with the internal nodes at depth 1 treated as an array $summary[0 \mathinner{.\,.} \sqrt{u} - 1]$, where $summary[i]$ is the logical-or of the subarray $A[i \sqrt{u} \mathinner{.\,.} (i + 1) \sqrt{u} - 1]$.

each of the operations MINIMUM, MAXIMUM, SUCCESSOR, PREDECESSOR, and DELETE in $O(\sqrt{u})$ time:

- To find the minimum (maximum) value, find the leftmost (rightmost) entry in *summary* that contains a 1, say $summary[i]$, and then do a linear search within the ith cluster for the leftmost (rightmost) 1.

- To find the successor (predecessor) of x, first search to the right (left) within its cluster. If we find a 1, that position gives the result. Otherwise, let $i = \lfloor x/\sqrt{u} \rfloor$ and search to the right (left) within the *summary* array from index i. The first position that holds a 1 gives the index of a cluster. Search within that cluster for the leftmost (rightmost) 1. That position holds the successor (predecessor).

- To delete the value x, let $i = \lfloor x/\sqrt{u} \rfloor$. Set $A[x]$ to 0 and then set $summary[i]$ to the logical-or of the bits in the ith cluster.

In each of the above operations, we search through at most two clusters of $\sqrt{u}$ bits plus the *summary* array, and so each operation takes $O(\sqrt{u})$ time.

At first glance, it seems as though we have made negative progress. Superimposing a binary tree gave us $O(\lg u)$-time operations, which are asymptotically faster than $O(\sqrt{u})$ time. Using a tree of degree $\sqrt{u}$ will turn out to be a key idea of van Emde Boas trees, however. We continue down this path in the next section.

Exercises

20.1-1
Modify the data structures in this section to support duplicate keys.

20.1-2

Modify the data structures in this section to support keys that have associated satellite data.

20.1-3

Observe that, using the structures in this section, the way we find the successor and predecessor of a value x does not depend on whether x is in the set at the time. Show how to find the successor of x in a binary search tree when x is not stored in the tree.

20.1-4

Suppose that instead of superimposing a tree of degree $\sqrt{u}$, we were to superimpose a tree of degree $u^{1/k}$, where $k > 1$ is a constant. What would be the height of such a tree, and how long would each of the operations take?

20.2   A recursive structure

In this section, we modify the idea of superimposing a tree of degree $\sqrt{u}$ on top of a bit vector. In the previous section, we used a summary structure of size $\sqrt{u}$, with each entry pointing to another structure of size $\sqrt{u}$. Now, we make the structure recursive, shrinking the universe size by the square root at each level of recursion. Starting with a universe of size u, we make structures holding $\sqrt{u} = u^{1/2}$ items, which themselves hold structures of $u^{1/4}$ items, which hold structures of $u^{1/8}$ items, and so on, down to a base size of 2.

For simplicity, in this section, we assume that $u = 2^{2^k}$ for some integer k, so that $u, u^{1/2}, u^{1/4}, \ldots$ are integers. This restriction would be quite severe in practice, allowing only values of u in the sequence $2, 4, 16, 256, 65536, \ldots$ We shall see in the next section how to relax this assumption and assume only that $u = 2^k$ for some integer k. Since the structure we examine in this section is only a precursor to the true van Emde Boas tree structure, we tolerate this restriction in favor of aiding our understanding.

Recalling that our goal is to achieve running times of $O(\lg \lg u)$ for the operations, let's think about how we might obtain such running times. At the end of Section 4.3, we saw that by changing variables, we could show that the recurrence

$$T(n) = 2T\left(\lfloor \sqrt{n} \rfloor\right) + \lg n \tag{20.1}$$

has the solution $T(n) = O(\lg n \lg \lg n)$. Let's consider a similar, but simpler, recurrence:

$$T(u) = T(\sqrt{u}) + O(1) . \tag{20.2}$$

If we use the same technique, changing variables, we can show that recurrence (20.2) has the solution $T(u) = O(\lg \lg u)$. Let $m = \lg u$, so that $u = 2^m$ and we have

$$T(2^m) = T(2^{m/2}) + O(1) .$$

Now we rename $S(m) = T(2^m)$, giving the new recurrence

$$S(m) = S(m/2) + O(1) .$$

By case 2 of the master method, this recurrence has the solution $S(m) = O(\lg m)$. We change back from $S(m)$ to $T(u)$, giving $T(u) = T(2^m) = S(m) = O(\lg m) = O(\lg \lg u)$.

Recurrence (20.2) will guide our search for a data structure. We will design a recursive data structure that shrinks by a factor of $\sqrt{u}$ in each level of its recursion. When an operation traverses this data structure, it will spend a constant amount of time at each level before recursing to the level below. Recurrence (20.2) will then characterize the running time of the operation.

Here is another way to think of how the term $\lg \lg u$ ends up in the solution to recurrence (20.2). As we look at the universe size in each level of the recursive data structure, we see the sequence $u, u^{1/2}, u^{1/4}, u^{1/8}, \ldots$. If we consider how many bits we need to store the universe size at each level, we need $\lg u$ at the top level, and each level needs half the bits of the previous level. In general, if we start with b bits and halve the number of bits at each level, then after $\lg b$ levels, we get down to just one bit. Since $b = \lg u$, we see that after $\lg \lg u$ levels, we have a universe size of 2.

Looking back at the data structure in Figure 20.2, a given value x resides in cluster number $\lfloor x/\sqrt{u} \rfloor$. If we view x as a $\lg u$-bit binary integer, that cluster number, $\lfloor x/\sqrt{u} \rfloor$, is given by the most significant $(\lg u)/2$ bits of x. Within its cluster, x appears in position $x \bmod \sqrt{u}$, which is given by the least significant $(\lg u)/2$ bits of x. We will need to index in this way, and so let us define some functions that will help us do so:

$$\begin{aligned}
\text{high}(x) &= \lfloor x/\sqrt{u} \rfloor , \\
\text{low}(x) &= x \bmod \sqrt{u} , \\
\text{index}(x, y) &= x\sqrt{u} + y .
\end{aligned}$$

The function $\text{high}(x)$ gives the most significant $(\lg u)/2$ bits of x, producing the number of x's cluster. The function $\text{low}(x)$ gives the least significant $(\lg u)/2$ bits of x and provides x's position within its cluster. The function $\text{index}(x, y)$ builds an element number from x and y, treating x as the most significant $(\lg u)/2$ bits of the element number and y as the least significant $(\lg u)/2$ bits. We have the identity $x = \text{index}(\text{high}(x), \text{low}(x))$. The value of u used by each of these functions will

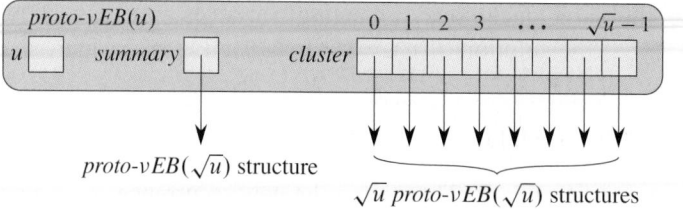

Figure 20.3   The information in a *proto-vEB(u)* structure when $u \geq 4$. The structure contains the universe size u, a pointer *summary* to a *proto-vEB($\sqrt{u}$)* structure, and an array *cluster*$[0 . . \sqrt{u} - 1]$ of $\sqrt{u}$ pointers to *proto-vEB($\sqrt{u}$)* structures.

always be the universe size of the data structure in which we call the function, which changes as we descend into the recursive structure.

20.2.1   Proto van Emde Boas structures

Taking our cue from recurrence (20.2), let us design a recursive data structure to support the operations. Although this data structure will fail to achieve our goal of $O(\lg \lg u)$ time for some operations, it serves as a basis for the van Emde Boas tree structure that we will see in Section 20.3.

For the universe $\{0, 1, 2, \ldots, u - 1\}$, we define a ***proto van Emde Boas structure***, or ***proto-vEB structure***, which we denote as *proto-vEB(u)*, recursively as follows. Each *proto-vEB(u)* structure contains an attribute u giving its universe size. In addition, it contains the following:

- If $u = 2$, then it is the base size, and it contains an array $A[0 . . 1]$ of two bits.

- Otherwise, $u = 2^{2^k}$ for some integer $k \geq 1$, so that $u \geq 4$. In addition to the universe size u, the data structure *proto-vEB(u)* contains the following attributes, illustrated in Figure 20.3:

  - a pointer named *summary* to a *proto-vEB($\sqrt{u}$)* structure and
  - an array *cluster*$[0 . . \sqrt{u} - 1]$ of $\sqrt{u}$ pointers, each to a *proto-vEB($\sqrt{u}$)* structure.

The element x, where $0 \leq x < u$, is recursively stored in the cluster numbered high(x) as element low(x) within that cluster.

In the two-level structure of the previous section, the root stores a summary array of size $\sqrt{u}$, in which each entry contains a bit. From the index of each entry, we can compute the starting index of the subarray of size $\sqrt{u}$ that the bit summarizes. In the proto-vEB structure, we use explicit pointers rather than index calculations.

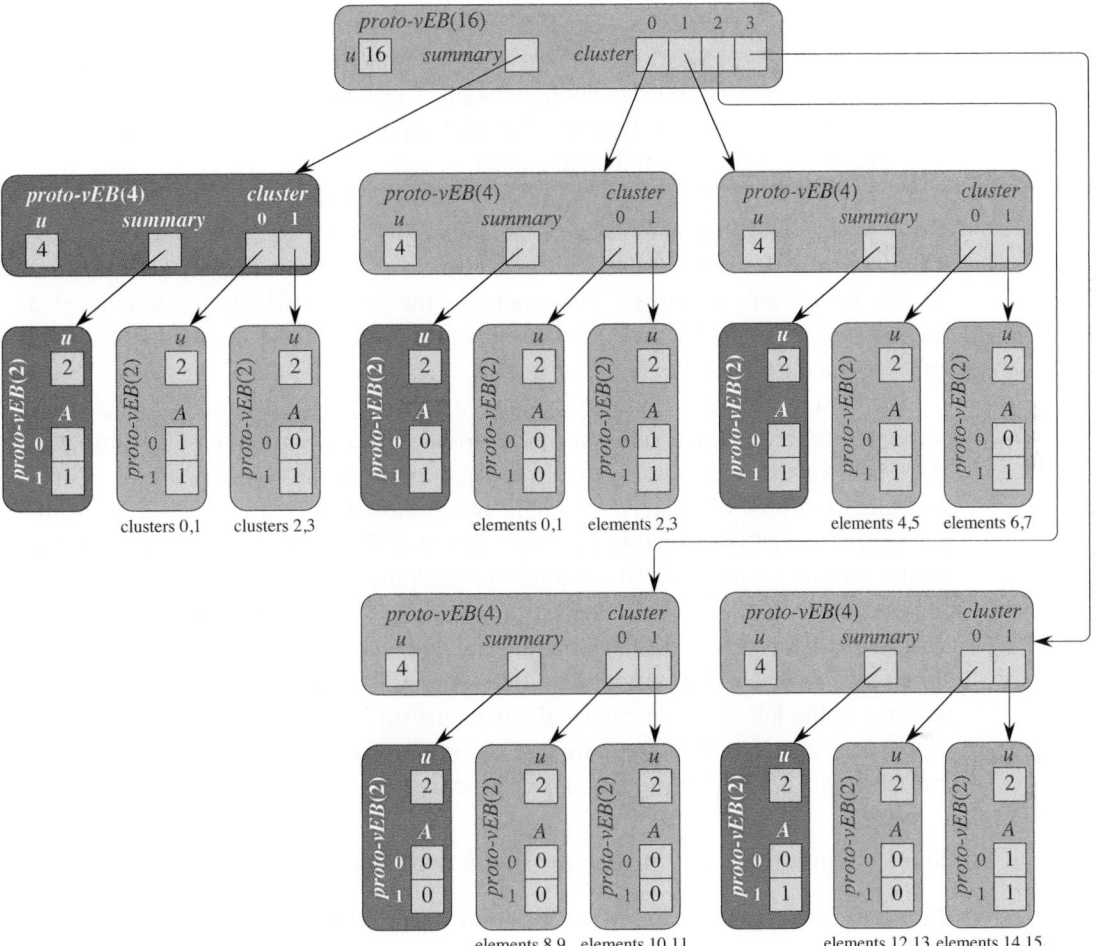

Figure 20.4 A *proto-vEB*(16) structure representing the set {2, 3, 4, 5, 7, 14, 15}. It points to four *proto-vEB*(4) structures in *cluster*[0 . . 3], and to a summary structure, which is also a *proto-vEB*(4). Each *proto-vEB*(4) structure points to two *proto-vEB*(2) structures in *cluster*[0 . . 1], and to a *proto-vEB*(2) summary. Each *proto-vEB*(2) structure contains just an array A[0 . . 1] of two bits. The *proto-vEB*(2) structures above "elements *i,j*" store bits *i* and *j* of the actual dynamic set, and the *proto-vEB*(2) structures above "clusters *i,j*" store the summary bits for clusters *i* and *j* in the top-level *proto-vEB*(16) structure. For clarity, heavy shading indicates the top level of a proto-vEB structure that stores summary information for its parent structure; such a proto-vEB structure is otherwise identical to any other proto-vEB structure with the same universe size.

The array *summary* contains the summary bits stored recursively in a proto-vEB structure, and the array *cluster* contains $\sqrt{u}$ pointers.

Figure 20.4 shows a fully expanded *proto-vEB*(16) structure representing the set $\{2, 3, 4, 5, 7, 14, 15\}$. If the value i is in the proto-vEB structure pointed to by *summary*, then the ith cluster contains some value in the set being represented. As in the tree of constant height, *cluster*[i] represents the values $i\sqrt{u}$ through $(i + 1)\sqrt{u} - 1$, which form the ith cluster.

At the base level, the elements of the actual dynamic sets are stored in some of the *proto-vEB*(2) structures, and the remaining *proto-vEB*(2) structures store summary bits. Beneath each of the non-summary base structures, the figure indicates which bits it stores. For example, the *proto-vEB*(2) structure labeled "elements 6,7" stores bit 6 (0, since element 6 is not in the set) in its $A[0]$ and bit 7 (1, since element 7 is in the set) in its $A[1]$.

Like the clusters, each summary is just a dynamic set with universe size $\sqrt{u}$, and so we represent each summary as a *proto-vEB*($\sqrt{u}$) structure. The four summary bits for the main *proto-vEB*(16) structure are in the leftmost *proto-vEB*(4) structure, and they ultimately appear in two *proto-vEB*(2) structures. For example, the *proto-vEB*(2) structure labeled "clusters 2,3" has $A[0] = 0$, indicating that cluster 2 of the *proto-vEB*(16) structure (containing elements $8, 9, 10, 11$) is all 0, and $A[1] = 1$, telling us that cluster 3 (containing elements $12, 13, 14, 15$) has at least one 1. Each *proto-vEB*(4) structure points to its own summary, which is itself stored as a *proto-vEB*(2) structure. For example, look at the *proto-vEB*(2) structure just to the left of the one labeled "elements 0,1." Because its $A[0]$ is 0, it tells us that the "elements 0,1" structure is all 0, and because its $A[1]$ is 1, we know that the "elements 2,3" structure contains at least one 1.

20.2.2   Operations on a proto van Emde Boas structure

We shall now describe how to perform operations on a proto-vEB structure. We first examine the query operations—MEMBER, MINIMUM, and SUCCESSOR—which do not change the proto-vEB structure. We then discuss INSERT and DELETE. We leave MAXIMUM and PREDECESSOR, which are symmetric to MINIMUM and SUCCESSOR, respectively, as Exercise 20.2-1.

Each of the MEMBER, SUCCESSOR, PREDECESSOR, INSERT, and DELETE operations takes a parameter x, along with a proto-vEB structure V. Each of these operations assumes that $0 \leq x < V.u$.

Determining whether a value is in the set

To perform MEMBER(x), we need to find the bit corresponding to x within the appropriate *proto-vEB*(2) structure. We can do so in $O(\lg \lg u)$ time, bypassing

the *summary* structures altogether. The following procedure takes a *proto-vEB* structure V and a value x, and it returns a bit indicating whether x is in the dynamic set held by V.

PROTO-VEB-MEMBER(V, x)

1   **if** $V.u == 2$
2   **return** $V.A[x]$
3   **else return** PROTO-VEB-MEMBER$(V.cluster[\text{high}(x)], \text{low}(x))$

The PROTO-VEB-MEMBER procedure works as follows. Line 1 tests whether we are in a base case, where V is a *proto-vEB*(2) structure. Line 2 handles the base case, simply returning the appropriate bit of array A. Line 3 deals with the recursive case, "drilling down" into the appropriate smaller proto-vEB structure. The value high(x) says which *proto-vEB*$(\sqrt{u})$ structure we visit, and low(x) determines which element within that *proto-vEB*$(\sqrt{u})$ structure we are querying.

Let's see what happens when we call PROTO-VEB-MEMBER$(V, 6)$ on the *proto-vEB*(16) structure in Figure 20.4. Since high$(6) = 1$ when $u = 16$, we recurse into the *proto-vEB*(4) structure in the upper right, and we ask about element low$(6) = 2$ of that structure. In this recursive call, $u = 4$, and so we recurse again. With $u = 4$, we have high$(2) = 1$ and low$(2) = 0$, and so we ask about element 0 of the *proto-vEB*(2) structure in the upper right. This recursive call turns out to be a base case, and so it returns $A[0] = 0$ back up through the chain of recursive calls. Thus, we get the result that PROTO-VEB-MEMBER$(V, 6)$ returns 0, indicating that 6 is not in the set.

To determine the running time of PROTO-VEB-MEMBER, let $T(u)$ denote its running time on a *proto-vEB*(u) structure. Each recursive call takes constant time, not including the time taken by the recursive calls that it makes. When PROTO-VEB-MEMBER makes a recursive call, it makes a call on a *proto-vEB*$(\sqrt{u})$ structure. Thus, we can characterize the running time by the recurrence $T(u) = T(\sqrt{u}) + O(1)$, which we have already seen as recurrence (20.2). Its solution is $T(u) = O(\lg \lg u)$, and so we conclude that PROTO-VEB-MEMBER runs in time $O(\lg \lg u)$.

Finding the minimum element

Now we examine how to perform the MINIMUM operation. The procedure PROTO-VEB-MINIMUM(V) returns the minimum element in the proto-vEB structure V, or NIL if V represents an empty set.

PROTO-VEB-MINIMUM(V)

```
 1  if V.u == 2
 2      if V.A[0] == 1
 3          return 0
 4      elseif V.A[1] == 1
 5          return 1
 6      else return NIL
 7  else min-cluster = PROTO-VEB-MINIMUM(V.summary)
 8      if min-cluster == NIL
 9          return NIL
10      else offset = PROTO-VEB-MINIMUM(V.cluster[min-cluster])
11          return index(min-cluster, offset)
```

This procedure works as follows. Line 1 tests for the base case, which lines 2–6 handle by brute force. Lines 7–11 handle the recursive case. First, line 7 finds the number of the first cluster that contains an element of the set. It does so by recursively calling PROTO-VEB-MINIMUM on $V.summary$, which is a $proto\text{-}vEB(\sqrt{u})$ structure. Line 7 assigns this cluster number to the variable $min\text{-}cluster$. If the set is empty, then the recursive call returned NIL, and line 9 returns NIL. Otherwise, the minimum element of the set is somewhere in cluster number $min\text{-}cluster$. The recursive call in line 10 finds the offset within the cluster of the minimum element in this cluster. Finally, line 11 constructs the value of the minimum element from the cluster number and offset, and it returns this value.

Although querying the summary information allows us to quickly find the cluster containing the minimum element, because this procedure makes two recursive calls on $proto\text{-}vEB(\sqrt{u})$ structures, it does not run in $O(\lg\lg u)$ time in the worst case. Letting $T(u)$ denote the worst-case time for PROTO-VEB-MINIMUM on a $proto\text{-}vEB(u)$ structure, we have the recurrence

$$T(u) = 2T(\sqrt{u}) + O(1) \ . \tag{20.3}$$

Again, we use a change of variables to solve this recurrence, letting $m = \lg u$, which gives

$$T(2^m) = 2T(2^{m/2}) + O(1) \ .$$

Renaming $S(m) = T(2^m)$ gives

$$S(m) = 2S(m/2) + O(1) \ ,$$

which, by case 1 of the master method, has the solution $S(m) = \Theta(m)$. By changing back from $S(m)$ to $T(u)$, we have that $T(u) = T(2^m) = S(m) = \Theta(m) = \Theta(\lg u)$. Thus, we see that because of the second recursive call, PROTO-VEB-MINIMUM runs in $\Theta(\lg u)$ time rather than the desired $O(\lg\lg u)$ time.

Finding the successor

The SUCCESSOR operation is even worse. In the worst case, it makes two recursive calls, along with a call to PROTO-VEB-MINIMUM. The procedure PROTO-VEB-SUCCESSOR(V, x) returns the smallest element in the proto-vEB structure V that is greater than x, or NIL if no element in V is greater than x. It does not require x to be a member of the set, but it does assume that $0 \leq x < V.u$.

PROTO-VEB-SUCCESSOR(V, x)

```
 1  if V.u == 2
 2      if x == 0 and V.A[1] == 1
 3          return 1
 4      else return NIL
 5  else offset = PROTO-VEB-SUCCESSOR(V.cluster[high(x)], low(x))
 6      if offset ≠ NIL
 7          return index(high(x), offset)
 8      else succ-cluster = PROTO-VEB-SUCCESSOR(V.summary, high(x))
 9          if succ-cluster == NIL
10              return NIL
11          else offset = PROTO-VEB-MINIMUM(V.cluster[succ-cluster])
12              return index(succ-cluster, offset)
```

The PROTO-VEB-SUCCESSOR procedure works as follows. As usual, line 1 tests for the base case, which lines 2–4 handle by brute force: the only way that x can have a successor within a *proto-vEB(2)* structure is when $x = 0$ and $A[1]$ is 1. Lines 5–12 handle the recursive case. Line 5 searches for a successor to x within x's cluster, assigning the result to *offset*. Line 6 determines whether x has a successor within its cluster; if it does, then line 7 computes and returns the value of this successor. Otherwise, we have to search in other clusters. Line 8 assigns to *succ-cluster* the number of the next nonempty cluster, using the summary information to find it. Line 9 tests whether *succ-cluster* is NIL, with line 10 returning NIL if all succeeding clusters are empty. If *succ-cluster* is non-NIL, line 11 assigns the first element within that cluster to *offset*, and line 12 computes and returns the minimum element in that cluster.

In the worst case, PROTO-VEB-SUCCESSOR calls itself recursively twice on *proto-vEB($\sqrt{u}$)* structures, and it makes one call to PROTO-VEB-MINIMUM on a *proto-vEB($\sqrt{u}$)* structure. Thus, the recurrence for the worst-case running time $T(u)$ of PROTO-VEB-SUCCESSOR is

$$
\begin{aligned}
T(u) &= 2T(\sqrt{u}) + \Theta(\lg \sqrt{u}) \\
     &= 2T(\sqrt{u}) + \Theta(\lg u) \, .
\end{aligned}
$$

We can employ the same technique that we used for recurrence (20.1) to show that this recurrence has the solution $T(u) = \Theta(\lg u \lg \lg u)$. Thus, PROTO-VEB-SUCCESSOR is asymptotically slower than PROTO-VEB-MINIMUM.

Inserting an element

To insert an element, we need to insert it into the appropriate cluster and also set the summary bit for that cluster to 1. The procedure PROTO-VEB-INSERT(V, x) inserts the value x into the proto-vEB structure V.

PROTO-VEB-INSERT(V, x)

```
1   if V.u == 2
2       V.A[x] = 1
3   else PROTO-VEB-INSERT(V.cluster[high(x)], low(x))
4        PROTO-VEB-INSERT(V.summary, high(x))
```

In the base case, line 2 sets the appropriate bit in the array A to 1. In the recursive case, the recursive call in line 3 inserts x into the appropriate cluster, and line 4 sets the summary bit for that cluster to 1.

Because PROTO-VEB-INSERT makes two recursive calls in the worst case, recurrence (20.3) characterizes its running time. Hence, PROTO-VEB-INSERT runs in $\Theta(\lg u)$ time.

Deleting an element

The DELETE operation is more complicated than insertion. Whereas we can always set a summary bit to 1 when inserting, we cannot always reset the same summary bit to 0 when deleting. We need to determine whether any bit in the appropriate cluster is 1. As we have defined proto-vEB structures, we would have to examine all $\sqrt{u}$ bits within a cluster to determine whether any of them are 1. Alternatively, we could add an attribute n to the proto-vEB structure, counting how many elements it has. We leave implementation of PROTO-VEB-DELETE as Exercises 20.2-2 and 20.2-3.

Clearly, we need to modify the proto-vEB structure to get each operation down to making at most one recursive call. We will see in the next section how to do so.

Exercises

20.2-1
Write pseudocode for the procedures PROTO-VEB-MAXIMUM and PROTO-VEB-PREDECESSOR.

20.2-2

Write pseudocode for PROTO-VEB-DELETE. It should update the appropriate summary bit by scanning the related bits within the cluster. What is the worst-case running time of your procedure?

20.2-3

Add the attribute n to each proto-vEB structure, giving the number of elements currently in the set it represents, and write pseudocode for PROTO-VEB-DELETE that uses the attribute n to decide when to reset summary bits to 0. What is the worst-case running time of your procedure? What other procedures need to change because of the new attribute? Do these changes affect their running times?

20.2-4

Modify the proto-vEB structure to support duplicate keys.

20.2-5

Modify the proto-vEB structure to support keys that have associated satellite data.

20.2-6

Write pseudocode for a procedure that creates a *proto-vEB(u)* structure.

20.2-7

Argue that if line 9 of PROTO-VEB-MINIMUM is executed, then the proto-vEB structure is empty.

20.2-8

Suppose that we designed a proto-vEB structure in which each *cluster* array had only $u^{1/4}$ elements. What would the running times of each operation be?

20.3   The van Emde Boas tree

The proto-vEB structure of the previous section is close to what we need to achieve $O(\lg \lg u)$ running times. It falls short because we have to recurse too many times in most of the operations. In this section, we shall design a data structure that is similar to the proto-vEB structure but stores a little more information, thereby removing the need for some of the recursion.

In Section 20.2, we observed that the assumption that we made about the universe size—that $u = 2^{2^k}$ for some integer k—is unduly restrictive, confining the possible values of u to an overly sparse set. From this point on, therefore, we will allow the universe size u to be any exact power of 2, and when $\sqrt{u}$ is not an inte-

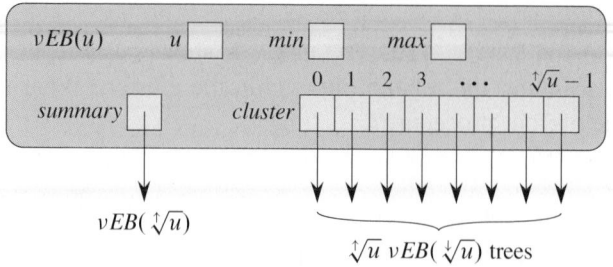

Figure 20.5 The information in a $vEB(u)$ tree when $u > 2$. The structure contains the universe size u, elements *min* and *max*, a pointer *summary* to a $vEB(\sqrt[\uparrow]{u})$ tree, and an array *cluster*[$0 .. \sqrt[\uparrow]{u} - 1$] of $\sqrt[\uparrow]{u}$ pointers to $vEB(\sqrt[\downarrow]{u})$ trees.

ger—that is, if u is an odd power of 2 ($u = 2^{2k+1}$ for some integer $k \geq 0$)—then we will divide the $\lg u$ bits of a number into the most significant $\lceil (\lg u)/2 \rceil$ bits and the least significant $\lfloor (\lg u)/2 \rfloor$ bits. For convenience, we denote $2^{\lceil (\lg u)/2 \rceil}$ (the "upper square root" of u) by $\sqrt[\uparrow]{u}$ and $2^{\lfloor (\lg u)/2 \rfloor}$ (the "lower square root" of u) by $\sqrt[\downarrow]{u}$, so that $u = \sqrt[\uparrow]{u} \cdot \sqrt[\downarrow]{u}$ and, when u is an even power of 2 ($u = 2^{2k}$ for some integer k), $\sqrt[\uparrow]{u} = \sqrt[\downarrow]{u} = \sqrt{u}$. Because we now allow u to be an odd power of 2, we must redefine our helpful functions from Section 20.2:

$$\begin{aligned} \text{high}(x) &= \left\lfloor x/\sqrt[\downarrow]{u} \right\rfloor , \\ \text{low}(x) &= x \bmod \sqrt[\downarrow]{u} , \\ \text{index}(x, y) &= x \sqrt[\downarrow]{u} + y . \end{aligned}$$

20.3.1   van Emde Boas trees

The **van Emde Boas tree**, or **vEB tree**, modifies the proto-vEB structure. We denote a vEB tree with a universe size of u as $vEB(u)$ and, unless u equals the base size of 2, the attribute *summary* points to a $vEB(\sqrt[\uparrow]{u})$ tree and the array *cluster*[$0 .. \sqrt[\uparrow]{u} - 1$] points to $\sqrt[\uparrow]{u}$ $vEB(\sqrt[\downarrow]{u})$ trees. As Figure 20.5 illustrates, a vEB tree contains two attributes not found in a proto-vEB structure:

- *min* stores the minimum element in the vEB tree, and

- *max* stores the maximum element in the vEB tree.

Furthermore, the element stored in *min* does not appear in any of the recursive $vEB(\sqrt[\downarrow]{u})$ trees that the *cluster* array points to. The elements stored in a $vEB(u)$ tree V, therefore, are $V.min$ plus all the elements recursively stored in the $vEB(\sqrt[\downarrow]{u})$ trees pointed to by $V.cluster[0 .. \sqrt[\uparrow]{u} - 1]$. Note that when a vEB tree contains two or more elements, we treat *min* and *max* differently: the element

stored in *min* does not appear in any of the clusters, but unless the vEB tree contains just one element (so that the minimum and maximum elements are the same), the element stored in *max* does.

Since the base size is 2, a $vEB(2)$ tree does not need the array A that the corresponding $proto\text{-}vEB(2)$ structure has. Instead, we can determine its elements from its *min* and *max* attributes. In a vEB tree with no elements, regardless of its universe size u, both *min* and *max* are NIL.

Figure 20.6 shows a $vEB(16)$ tree V holding the set $\{2, 3, 4, 5, 7, 14, 15\}$. Because the smallest element is 2, $V.min$ equals 2, and even though high(2) = 0, the element 2 does not appear in the $vEB(4)$ tree pointed to by $V.cluster[0]$: notice that $V.cluster[0].min$ equals 3, and so 2 is not in this vEB tree. Similarly, since $V.cluster[0].min$ equals 3, and 2 and 3 are the only elements in $V.cluster[0]$, the $vEB(2)$ clusters within $V.cluster[0]$ are empty.

The *min* and *max* attributes will turn out to be key to reducing the number of recursive calls within the operations on vEB trees. These attributes will help us in four ways:

1. The MINIMUM and MAXIMUM operations do not even need to recurse, for they can just return the values of *min* or *max*.

2. The SUCCESSOR operation can avoid making a recursive call to determine whether the successor of a value x lies within high(x). That is because x's successor lies within its cluster if and only if x is strictly less than the *max* attribute of its cluster. A symmetric argument holds for PREDECESSOR and *min*.

3. We can tell whether a vEB tree has no elements, exactly one element, or at least two elements in constant time from its *min* and *max* values. This ability will help in the INSERT and DELETE operations. If *min* and *max* are both NIL, then the vEB tree has no elements. If *min* and *max* are non-NIL but are equal to each other, then the vEB tree has exactly one element. Otherwise, both *min* and *max* are non-NIL but are unequal, and the vEB tree has two or more elements.

4. If we know that a vEB tree is empty, we can insert an element into it by updating only its *min* and *max* attributes. Hence, we can insert into an empty vEB tree in constant time. Similarly, if we know that a vEB tree has only one element, we can delete that element in constant time by updating only *min* and *max*. These properties will allow us to cut short the chain of recursive calls.

Even if the universe size u is an odd power of 2, the difference in the sizes of the summary vEB tree and the clusters will not turn out to affect the asymptotic running times of the vEB-tree operations. The recursive procedures that implement the vEB-tree operations will all have running times characterized by the recurrence

$$T(u) \leq T(\sqrt[\uparrow]{u}) + O(1) . \tag{20.4}$$

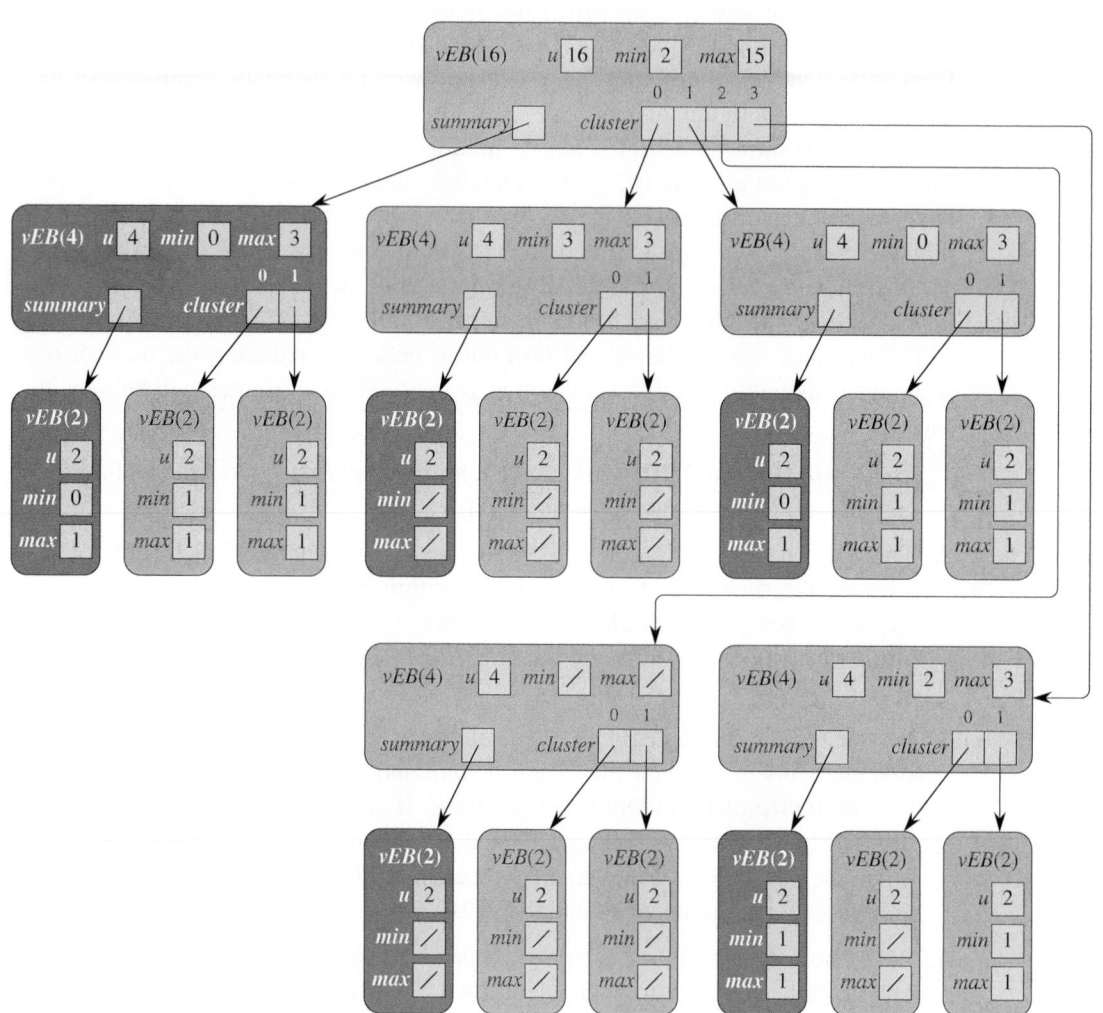

Figure 20.6 A $vEB(16)$ tree corresponding to the proto-vEB tree in Figure 20.4. It stores the set $\{2, 3, 4, 5, 7, 14, 15\}$. Slashes indicate NIL values. The value stored in the *min* attribute of a vEB tree does not appear in any of its clusters. Heavy shading serves the same purpose here as in Figure 20.4.

This recurrence looks similar to recurrence (20.2), and we will solve it in a similar fashion. Letting $m = \lg u$, we rewrite it as

$$T(2^m) \leq T(2^{\lceil m/2 \rceil}) + O(1) \ .$$

Noting that $\lceil m/2 \rceil \leq 2m/3$ for all $m \geq 2$, we have

$$T(2^m) \leq T(2^{2m/3}) + O(1) \ .$$

Letting $S(m) = T(2^m)$, we rewrite this last recurrence as

$$S(m) \leq S(2m/3) + O(1) \ ,$$

which, by case 2 of the master method, has the solution $S(m) = O(\lg m)$. (In terms of the asymptotic solution, the fraction $2/3$ does not make any difference compared with the fraction $1/2$, because when we apply the master method, we find that $\log_{3/2} 1 = \log_2 1 = 0$.) Thus, we have $T(u) = T(2^m) = S(m) = O(\lg m) = O(\lg \lg u)$.

Before using a van Emde Boas tree, we must know the universe size u, so that we can create a van Emde Boas tree of the appropriate size that initially represents an empty set. As Problem 20-1 asks you to show, the total space requirement of a van Emde Boas tree is $O(u)$, and it is straightforward to create an empty tree in $\Theta(u)$ time. In contrast, we can create an empty red-black tree in constant time. Therefore, we might not want to use a van Emde Boas tree when we perform only a small number of operations, since the time to create the data structure would exceed the time saved in the individual operations. This drawback is usually not significant, since we typically use a simple data structure, such as an array or linked list, to represent a set with only a few elements.

20.3.2   Operations on a van Emde Boas tree

We are now ready to see how to perform operations on a van Emde Boas tree. As we did for the proto van Emde Boas structure, we will consider the querying operations first, and then INSERT and DELETE. Due to the slight asymmetry between the minimum and maximum elements in a vEB tree—when a vEB tree contains at least two elements, the minimum element does not appear within a cluster but the maximum element does—we will provide pseudocode for all five querying operations. As in the operations on proto van Emde Boas structures, the operations here that take parameters V and x, where V is a van Emde Boas tree and x is an element, assume that $0 \leq x < V.u$.

Finding the minimum and maximum elements

Because we store the minimum and maximum in the attributes *min* and *max*, two of the operations are one-liners, taking constant time:

VEB-TREE-MINIMUM(V)

1   **return** $V.min$

VEB-TREE-MAXIMUM(V)

1   **return** $V.max$

Determining whether a value is in the set

The procedure VEB-TREE-MEMBER(V, x) has a recursive case like that of PROTO-VEB-MEMBER, but the base case is a little different. We also check directly whether x equals the minimum or maximum element. Since a vEB tree doesn't store bits as a proto-vEB structure does, we design VEB-TREE-MEMBER to return TRUE or FALSE rather than 1 or 0.

VEB-TREE-MEMBER(V, x)

1   **if** $x == V.min$ or $x == V.max$
2   **return** TRUE
3   **elseif** $V.u == 2$
4   **return** FALSE
5   **else return** VEB-TREE-MEMBER($V.cluster[high(x)], low(x)$)

Line 1 checks to see whether x equals either the minimum or maximum element. If it does, line 2 returns TRUE. Otherwise, line 3 tests for the base case. Since a $vEB(2)$ tree has no elements other than those in *min* and *max*, if it is the base case, line 4 returns FALSE. The other possibility—it is not a base case and x equals neither *min* nor *max*—is handled by the recursive call in line 5.

Recurrence (20.4) characterizes the running time of the VEB-TREE-MEMBER procedure, and so this procedure takes $O(\lg \lg u)$ time.

Finding the successor and predecessor

Next we see how to implement the SUCCESSOR operation. Recall that the procedure PROTO-VEB-SUCCESSOR(V, x) could make two recursive calls: one to determine whether x's successor resides in the same cluster as x and, if it does not, one to find the cluster containing x's successor. Because we can access the maximum value in a vEB tree quickly, we can avoid making two recursive calls, and instead make one recursive call on either a cluster or on the summary, but not on both.

VEB-TREE-SUCCESSOR(V, x)

```
 1  if V.u == 2
 2      if x == 0 and V.max == 1
 3          return 1
 4      else return NIL
 5  elseif V.min ≠ NIL and x < V.min
 6      return V.min
 7  else max-low = VEB-TREE-MAXIMUM(V.cluster[high(x)])
 8      if max-low ≠ NIL and low(x) < max-low
 9          offset = VEB-TREE-SUCCESSOR(V.cluster[high(x)], low(x))
10          return index(high(x), offset)
11      else succ-cluster = VEB-TREE-SUCCESSOR(V.summary, high(x))
12          if succ-cluster == NIL
13              return NIL
14          else offset = VEB-TREE-MINIMUM(V.cluster[succ-cluster])
15              return index(succ-cluster, offset)
```

This procedure has six **return** statements and several cases. We start with the base case in lines 2–4, which returns 1 in line 3 if we are trying to find the successor of 0 and 1 is in the 2-element set; otherwise, the base case returns NIL in line 4.

If we are not in the base case, we next check in line 5 whether x is strictly less than the minimum element. If so, then we simply return the minimum element in line 6.

If we get to line 7, then we know that we are not in a base case and that x is greater than or equal to the minimum value in the vEB tree V. Line 7 assigns to *max-low* the maximum element in x's cluster. If x's cluster contains some element that is greater than x, then we know that x's successor lies somewhere within x's cluster. Line 8 tests for this condition. If x's successor is within x's cluster, then line 9 determines where in the cluster it is, and line 10 returns the successor in the same way as line 7 of PROTO-VEB-SUCCESSOR.

We get to line 11 if x is greater than or equal to the greatest element in its cluster. In this case, lines 11–15 find x's successor in the same way as lines 8–12 of PROTO-VEB-SUCCESSOR.

It is easy to see how recurrence (20.4) characterizes the running time of VEB-TREE-SUCCESSOR. Depending on the result of the test in line 8, the procedure calls itself recursively in either line 9 (on a vEB tree with universe size $\sqrt[\downarrow]{u}$) or line 11 (on a vEB tree with universe size $\sqrt[\uparrow]{u}$). In either case, the one recursive call is on a vEB tree with universe size at most $\sqrt[\uparrow]{u}$. The remainder of the procedure, including the calls to VEB-TREE-MINIMUM and VEB-TREE-MAXIMUM, takes $O(1)$ time. Hence, VEB-TREE-SUCCESSOR runs in $O(\lg \lg u)$ worst-case time.

The VEB-TREE-PREDECESSOR procedure is symmetric to the VEB-TREE-SUCCESSOR procedure, but with one additional case:

VEB-TREE-PREDECESSOR(V, x)

```
 1   if V.u == 2
 2       if x == 1 and V.min == 0
 3           return 0
 4       else return NIL
 5   elseif V.max ≠ NIL and x > V.max
 6       return V.max
 7   else min-low = VEB-TREE-MINIMUM(V.cluster[high(x)])
 8       if min-low ≠ NIL and low(x) > min-low
 9           offset = VEB-TREE-PREDECESSOR(V.cluster[high(x)], low(x))
10           return index(high(x), offset)
11       else pred-cluster = VEB-TREE-PREDECESSOR(V.summary, high(x))
12           if pred-cluster == NIL
13               if V.min ≠ NIL and x > V.min
14                   return V.min
15               else return NIL
16           else offset = VEB-TREE-MAXIMUM(V.cluster[pred-cluster])
17               return index(pred-cluster, offset)
```

Lines 13–14 form the additional case. This case occurs when x's predecessor, if it exists, does not reside in x's cluster. In VEB-TREE-SUCCESSOR, we were assured that if x's successor resides outside of x's cluster, then it must reside in a higher-numbered cluster. But if x's predecessor is the minimum value in vEB tree V, then the predecessor resides in no cluster at all. Line 13 checks for this condition, and line 14 returns the minimum value as appropriate.

This extra case does not affect the asymptotic running time of VEB-TREE-PREDECESSOR when compared with VEB-TREE-SUCCESSOR, and so VEB-TREE-PREDECESSOR runs in $O(\lg \lg u)$ worst-case time.

Inserting an element

Now we examine how to insert an element into a vEB tree. Recall that PROTO-VEB-INSERT made two recursive calls: one to insert the element and one to insert the element's cluster number into the summary. The VEB-TREE-INSERT procedure will make only one recursive call. How can we get away with just one? When we insert an element, either the cluster that it goes into already has another element or it does not. If the cluster already has another element, then the cluster number is already in the summary, and so we do not need to make that recursive call. If

the cluster does not already have another element, then the element being inserted becomes the only element in the cluster, and we do not need to recurse to insert an element into an empty vEB tree:

VEB-EMPTY-TREE-INSERT(V, x)

1   $V.min = x$
2   $V.max = x$

With this procedure in hand, here is the pseudocode for VEB-TREE-INSERT(V, x), which assumes that x is not already an element in the set represented by vEB tree V:

VEB-TREE-INSERT(V, x)

 1   **if** $V.min$ == NIL
 2   VEB-EMPTY-TREE-INSERT(V, x)
 3   **else if** $x < V.min$
 4   exchange x with $V.min$
 5   **if** $V.u > 2$
 6   **if** VEB-TREE-MINIMUM$(V.cluster[\text{high}(x)])$ == NIL
 7   VEB-TREE-INSERT$(V.summary, \text{high}(x))$
 8   VEB-EMPTY-TREE-INSERT$(V.cluster[\text{high}(x)], \text{low}(x))$
 9   **else** VEB-TREE-INSERT$(V.cluster[\text{high}(x)], \text{low}(x))$
10   **if** $x > V.max$
11      $V.max = x$

This procedure works as follows. Line 1 tests whether V is an empty vEB tree and, if it is, then line 2 handles this easy case. Lines 3–11 assume that V is not empty, and therefore some element will be inserted into one of V's clusters. But that element might not necessarily be the element x passed to VEB-TREE-INSERT. If $x < min$, as tested in line 3, then x needs to become the new min. We don't want to lose the original min, however, and so we need to insert it into one of V's clusters. In this case, line 4 exchanges x with min, so that we insert the original min into one of V's clusters.

We execute lines 6–9 only if V is not a base-case vEB tree. Line 6 determines whether the cluster that x will go into is currently empty. If so, then line 7 inserts x's cluster number into the summary and line 8 handles the easy case of inserting x into an empty cluster. If x's cluster is not currently empty, then line 9 inserts x into its cluster. In this case, we do not need to update the summary, since x's cluster number is already a member of the summary.

Finally, lines 10–11 take care of updating max if $x > max$. Note that if V is a base-case vEB tree that is not empty, then lines 3–4 and 10–11 update min and max properly.

Once again, we can easily see how recurrence (20.4) characterizes the running time. Depending on the result of the test in line 6, either the recursive call in line 7 (run on a vEB tree with universe size $\sqrt[\uparrow]{u}$) or the recursive call in line 9 (run on a vEB with universe size $\sqrt[\downarrow]{u}$) executes. In either case, the one recursive call is on a vEB tree with universe size at most $\sqrt[\uparrow]{u}$. Because the remainder of VEB-TREE-INSERT takes $O(1)$ time, recurrence (20.4) applies, and so the running time is $O(\lg \lg u)$.

Deleting an element

Finally, we look at how to delete an element from a vEB tree. The procedure VEB-TREE-DELETE(V, x) assumes that x is currently an element in the set represented by the vEB tree V.

VEB-TREE-DELETE(V, x)

```
 1  if V.min == V.max
 2      V.min = NIL
 3      V.max = NIL
 4  elseif V.u == 2
 5      if x == 0
 6          V.min = 1
 7      else V.min = 0
 8      V.max = V.min
 9  else if x == V.min
10          first-cluster = VEB-TREE-MINIMUM(V.summary)
11          x = index(first-cluster,
                    VEB-TREE-MINIMUM(V.cluster[first-cluster]))
12          V.min = x
13      VEB-TREE-DELETE(V.cluster[high(x)], low(x))
14      if VEB-TREE-MINIMUM(V.cluster[high(x)]) == NIL
15          VEB-TREE-DELETE(V.summary, high(x))
16          if x == V.max
17              summary-max = VEB-TREE-MAXIMUM(V.summary)
18              if summary-max == NIL
19                  V.max = V.min
20              else V.max = index(summary-max,
                        VEB-TREE-MAXIMUM(V.cluster[summary-max]))
21      elseif x == V.max
22          V.max = index(high(x),
                    VEB-TREE-MAXIMUM(V.cluster[high(x)]))
```

The VEB-TREE-DELETE procedure works as follows. If the vEB tree V contains only one element, then it's just as easy to delete it as it was to insert an element into an empty vEB tree: just set min and max to NIL. Lines 1–3 handle this case. Otherwise, V has at least two elements. Line 4 tests whether V is a base-case vEB tree and, if so, lines 5–8 set min and max to the one remaining element.

Lines 9–22 assume that V has two or more elements and that $u \geq 4$. In this case, we will have to delete an element from a cluster. The element we delete from a cluster might not be x, however, because if x equals min, then once we have deleted x, some other element within one of V's clusters becomes the new min, and we have to delete that other element from its cluster. If the test in line 9 reveals that we are in this case, then line 10 sets $first\text{-}cluster$ to the number of the cluster that contains the lowest element other than min, and line 11 sets x to the value of the lowest element in that cluster. This element becomes the new min in line 12 and, because we set x to its value, it is the element that will be deleted from its cluster.

When we reach line 13, we know that we need to delete element x from its cluster, whether x was the value originally passed to VEB-TREE-DELETE or x is the element becoming the new minimum. Line 13 deletes x from its cluster. That cluster might now become empty, which line 14 tests, and if it does, then we need to remove x's cluster number from the summary, which line 15 handles. After updating the summary, we might need to update max. Line 16 checks to see whether we are deleting the maximum element in V and, if we are, then line 17 sets $summary\text{-}max$ to the number of the highest-numbered nonempty cluster. (The call VEB-TREE-MAXIMUM($V.summary$) works because we have already recursively called VEB-TREE-DELETE on $V.summary$, and therefore $V.summary.max$ has already been updated as necessary.) If all of V's clusters are empty, then the only remaining element in V is min; line 18 checks for this case, and line 19 updates max appropriately. Otherwise, line 20 sets max to the maximum element in the highest-numbered nonempty cluster. (If this cluster is where the element has been deleted, we again rely on the recursive call in line 13 having already corrected that cluster's max attribute.)

Finally, we have to handle the case in which x's cluster did not become empty due to x being deleted. Although we do not have to update the summary in this case, we might have to update max. Line 21 tests for this case, and if we have to update max, line 22 does so (again relying on the recursive call to have corrected max in the cluster).

Now we show that VEB-TREE-DELETE runs in $O(\lg \lg u)$ time in the worst case. At first glance, you might think that recurrence (20.4) does not always apply, because a single call of VEB-TREE-DELETE can make two recursive calls: one on line 13 and one on line 15. Although the procedure can make both recursive calls, let's think about what happens when it does. In order for the recursive call on

line 15 to occur, the test on line 14 must show that x's cluster is empty. The only way that x's cluster can be empty is if x was the only element in its cluster when we made the recursive call on line 13. But if x was the only element in its cluster, then that recursive call took $O(1)$ time, because it executed only lines 1–3. Thus, we have two mutually exclusive possibilities:

- The recursive call on line 13 took constant time.

- The recursive call on line 15 did not occur.

In either case, recurrence (20.4) characterizes the running time of VEB-TREE-DELETE, and hence its worst-case running time is $O(\lg \lg u)$.

Exercises

20.3-1
Modify vEB trees to support duplicate keys.

20.3-2
Modify vEB trees to support keys that have associated satellite data.

20.3-3
Write pseudocode for a procedure that creates an empty van Emde Boas tree.

20.3-4
What happens if you call VEB-TREE-INSERT with an element that is already in the vEB tree? What happens if you call VEB-TREE-DELETE with an element that is not in the vEB tree? Explain why the procedures exhibit the behavior that they do. Show how to modify vEB trees and their operations so that we can check in constant time whether an element is present.

20.3-5
Suppose that instead of $\sqrt[+]{u}$ clusters, each with universe size $\sqrt[+]{u}$, we constructed vEB trees to have $u^{1/k}$ clusters, each with universe size $u^{1-1/k}$, where $k > 1$ is a constant. If we were to modify the operations appropriately, what would be their running times? For the purpose of analysis, assume that $u^{1/k}$ and $u^{1-1/k}$ are always integers.

20.3-6
Creating a vEB tree with universe size u requires $\Theta(u)$ time. Suppose we wish to explicitly account for that time. What is the smallest number of operations n for which the amortized time of each operation in a vEB tree is $O(\lg \lg u)$?

Problems

20-1   *Space requirements for van Emde Boas trees*

This problem explores the space requirements for van Emde Boas trees and suggests a way to modify the data structure to make its space requirement depend on the number n of elements actually stored in the tree, rather than on the universe size u. For simplicity, assume that $\sqrt{u}$ is always an integer.

a. Explain why the following recurrence characterizes the space requirement $P(u)$ of a van Emde Boas tree with universe size u:

$$P(u) = (\sqrt{u} + 1)P(\sqrt{u}) + \Theta(\sqrt{u}) . \tag{20.5}$$

b. Prove that recurrence (20.5) has the solution $P(u) = O(u)$.

In order to reduce the space requirements, let us define a ***reduced-space van Emde Boas tree***, or ***RS-vEB tree***, as a vEB tree V but with the following changes:

- The attribute $V.cluster$, rather than being stored as a simple array of pointers to vEB trees with universe size $\sqrt{u}$, is a hash table (see Chapter 11) stored as a dynamic table (see Section 17.4). Corresponding to the array version of $V.cluster$, the hash table stores pointers to RS-vEB trees with universe size $\sqrt{u}$. To find the ith cluster, we look up the key i in the hash table, so that we can find the ith cluster by a single search in the hash table.

- The hash table stores only pointers to nonempty clusters. A search in the hash table for an empty cluster returns NIL, indicating that the cluster is empty.

- The attribute $V.summary$ is NIL if all clusters are empty. Otherwise, $V.summary$ points to an RS-vEB tree with universe size $\sqrt{u}$.

Because the hash table is implemented with a dynamic table, the space it requires is proportional to the number of nonempty clusters.

When we need to insert an element into an empty RS-vEB tree, we create the RS-vEB tree by calling the following procedure, where the parameter u is the universe size of the RS-vEB tree:

CREATE-NEW-RS-VEB-TREE(u)

```
1   allocate a new vEB tree V
2   V.u = u
3   V.min = NIL
4   V.max = NIL
5   V.summary = NIL
6   create V.cluster as an empty dynamic hash table
7   return V
```

c. Modify the VEB-TREE-INSERT procedure to produce pseudocode for the procedure RS-VEB-TREE-INSERT(V, x), which inserts x into the RS-vEB tree V, calling CREATE-NEW-RS-VEB-TREE as appropriate.

d. Modify the VEB-TREE-SUCCESSOR procedure to produce pseudocode for the procedure RS-VEB-TREE-SUCCESSOR(V, x), which returns the successor of x in RS-vEB tree V, or NIL if x has no successor in V.

e. Prove that, under the assumption of simple uniform hashing, your RS-VEB-TREE-INSERT and RS-VEB-TREE-SUCCESSOR procedures run in $O(\lg \lg u)$ expected amortized time.

f. Assuming that elements are never deleted from a vEB tree, prove that the space requirement for the RS-vEB tree structure is $O(n)$, where n is the number of elements actually stored in the RS-vEB tree.

g. RS-vEB trees have another advantage over vEB trees: they require less time to create. How long does it take to create an empty RS-vEB tree?

20-2   *y-fast tries*

This problem investigates D. Willard's "y-fast tries" which, like van Emde Boas trees, perform each of the operations MEMBER, MINIMUM, MAXIMUM, PRE-DECESSOR, and SUCCESSOR on elements drawn from a universe with size u in $O(\lg \lg u)$ worst-case time. The INSERT and DELETE operations take $O(\lg \lg u)$ amortized time. Like reduced-space van Emde Boas trees (see Problem 20-1), y-fast tries use only $O(n)$ space to store n elements. The design of y-fast tries relies on perfect hashing (see Section 11.5).

As a preliminary structure, suppose that we create a perfect hash table containing not only every element in the dynamic set, but every prefix of the binary representation of every element in the set. For example, if $u = 16$, so that $\lg u = 4$, and $x = 13$ is in the set, then because the binary representation of 13 is 1101, the perfect hash table would contain the strings 1, 11, 110, and 1101. In addition to the hash table, we create a doubly linked list of the elements currently in the set, in increasing order.

a. How much space does this structure require?

b. Show how to perform the MINIMUM and MAXIMUM operations in $O(1)$ time; the MEMBER, PREDECESSOR, and SUCCESSOR operations in $O(\lg \lg u)$ time; and the INSERT and DELETE operations in $O(\lg u)$ time.

To reduce the space requirement to $O(n)$, we make the following changes to the data structure:

- We cluster the n elements into $n / \lg u$ groups of size $\lg u$. (Assume for now that $\lg u$ divides n.) The first group consists of the $\lg u$ smallest elements in the set, the second group consists of the next $\lg u$ smallest elements, and so on.

- We designate a "representative" value for each group. The representative of the ith group is at least as large as the largest element in the ith group, and it is smaller than every element of the $(i + 1)$st group. (The representative of the last group can be the maximum possible element $u - 1$.) Note that a representative might be a value not currently in the set.

- We store the $\lg u$ elements of each group in a balanced binary search tree, such as a red-black tree. Each representative points to the balanced binary search tree for its group, and each balanced binary search tree points to its group's representative.

- The perfect hash table stores only the representatives, which are also stored in a doubly linked list in increasing order.

We call this structure a *y-fast trie*.

c. Show that a y-fast trie requires only $O(n)$ space to store n elements.

d. Show how to perform the MINIMUM and MAXIMUM operations in $O(\lg \lg u)$ time with a y-fast trie.

e. Show how to perform the MEMBER operation in $O(\lg \lg u)$ time.

f. Show how to perform the PREDECESSOR and SUCCESSOR operations in $O(\lg \lg u)$ time.

g. Explain why the INSERT and DELETE operations take $\Omega(\lg \lg u)$ time.

h. Show how to relax the requirement that each group in a y-fast trie has exactly $\lg u$ elements to allow INSERT and DELETE to run in $O(\lg \lg u)$ amortized time without affecting the asymptotic running times of the other operations.

Chapter notes

The data structure in this chapter is named after P. van Emde Boas, who described an early form of the idea in 1975 [339]. Later papers by van Emde Boas [340] and van Emde Boas, Kaas, and Zijlstra [341] refined the idea and the exposition. Mehlhorn and Näher [252] subsequently extended the ideas to apply to universe

sizes that are prime. Mehlhorn's book [249] contains a slightly different treatment of van Emde Boas trees than the one in this chapter.

Using the ideas behind van Emde Boas trees, Dementiev et al. [83] developed a nonrecursive, three-level search tree that ran faster than van Emde Boas trees in their own experiments.

Wang and Lin [347] designed a hardware-pipelined version of van Emde Boas trees, which achieves constant amortized time per operation and uses $O(\lg \lg u)$ stages in the pipeline.

A lower bound by Pătraşcu and Thorup [273, 274] for finding the predecessor shows that van Emde Boas trees are optimal for this operation, even if randomization is allowed.

21   Data Structures for Disjoint Sets

Some applications involve grouping n distinct elements into a collection of disjoint sets. These applications often need to perform two operations in particular: finding the unique set that contains a given element and uniting two sets. This chapter explores methods for maintaining a data structure that supports these operations.

Section 21.1 describes the operations supported by a disjoint-set data structure and presents a simple application. In Section 21.2, we look at a simple linked-list implementation for disjoint sets. Section 21.3 presents a more efficient representation using rooted trees. The running time using the tree representation is theoretically superlinear, but for all practical purposes it is linear. Section 21.4 defines and discusses a very quickly growing function and its very slowly growing inverse, which appears in the running time of operations on the tree-based implementation, and then, by a complex amortized analysis, proves an upper bound on the running time that is just barely superlinear.

21.1   Disjoint-set operations

A *disjoint-set data structure* maintains a collection $\mathcal{S} = \{S_1, S_2, \ldots, S_k\}$ of disjoint dynamic sets. We identify each set by a *representative*, which is some member of the set. In some applications, it doesn't matter which member is used as the representative; we care only that if we ask for the representative of a dynamic set twice without modifying the set between the requests, we get the same answer both times. Other applications may require a prespecified rule for choosing the representative, such as choosing the smallest member in the set (assuming, of course, that the elements can be ordered).

As in the other dynamic-set implementations we have studied, we represent each element of a set by an object. Letting x denote an object, we wish to support the following operations:

MAKE-SET(x) creates a new set whose only member (and thus representative) is x. Since the sets are disjoint, we require that x not already be in some other set.

UNION(x, y) unites the dynamic sets that contain x and y, say S_x and S_y, into a new set that is the union of these two sets. We assume that the two sets are disjoint prior to the operation. The representative of the resulting set is any member of $S_x \cup S_y$, although many implementations of UNION specifically choose the representative of either S_x or S_y as the new representative. Since we require the sets in the collection to be disjoint, conceptually we destroy sets S_x and S_y, removing them from the collection $\mathcal{S}$. In practice, we often absorb the elements of one of the sets into the other set.

FIND-SET(x) returns a pointer to the representative of the (unique) set containing x.

Throughout this chapter, we shall analyze the running times of disjoint-set data structures in terms of two parameters: n, the number of MAKE-SET operations, and m, the total number of MAKE-SET, UNION, and FIND-SET operations. Since the sets are disjoint, each UNION operation reduces the number of sets by one. After $n - 1$ UNION operations, therefore, only one set remains. The number of UNION operations is thus at most $n - 1$. Note also that since the MAKE-SET operations are included in the total number of operations m, we have $m \geq n$. We assume that the n MAKE-SET operations are the first n operations performed.

An application of disjoint-set data structures

One of the many applications of disjoint-set data structures arises in determining the connected components of an undirected graph (see Section B.4). Figure 21.1(a), for example, shows a graph with four connected components.

The procedure CONNECTED-COMPONENTS that follows uses the disjoint-set operations to compute the connected components of a graph. Once CONNECTED-COMPONENTS has preprocessed the graph, the procedure SAME-COMPONENT answers queries about whether two vertices are in the same connected component.[1] (In pseudocode, we denote the set of vertices of a graph G by $G.V$ and the set of edges by $G.E$.)

---

[1]When the edges of the graph are static—not changing over time—we can compute the connected components faster by using depth-first search (Exercise 22.3-12). Sometimes, however, the edges are added dynamically and we need to maintain the connected components as each edge is added. In this case, the implementation given here can be more efficient than running a new depth-first search for each new edge.

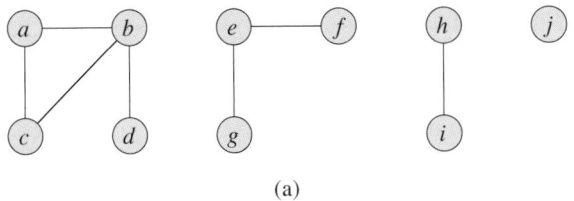

(a)

Edge processed	Collection of disjoint sets									
initial sets	{a}	{b}	{c}	{d}	{e}	{f}	{g}	{h}	{i}	{j}
(b,d)	{a}	{b,d}	{c}		{e}	{f}	{g}	{h}	{i}	{j}
(e,g)	{a}	{b,d}	{c}		{e,g}	{f}		{h}	{i}	{j}
(a,c)	{a,c}	{b,d}			{e,g}	{f}		{h}	{i}	{j}
(h,i)	{a,c}	{b,d}			{e,g}	{f}		{h,i}		{j}
(a,b)	{a,b,c,d}				{e,g}	{f}		{h,i}		{j}
(e,f)	{a,b,c,d}				{e,f,g}			{h,i}		{j}
(b,c)	{a,b,c,d}				{e,f,g}			{h,i}		{j}

(b)

Figure 21.1 (a) A graph with four connected components: $\{a,b,c,d\}$, $\{e,f,g\}$, $\{h,i\}$, and $\{j\}$. (b) The collection of disjoint sets after processing each edge.

CONNECTED-COMPONENTS(G)

1   **for** each vertex $v \in G.V$
2   MAKE-SET(v)
3   **for** each edge $(u, v) \in G.E$
4   **if** FIND-SET(u) $\neq$ FIND-SET(v)
5   UNION(u, v)

SAME-COMPONENT(u, v)

1   **if** FIND-SET(u) == FIND-SET(v)
2   **return** TRUE
3   **else return** FALSE

The procedure CONNECTED-COMPONENTS initially places each vertex v in its own set. Then, for each edge (u, v), it unites the sets containing u and v. By Exercise 21.1-2, after processing all the edges, two vertices are in the same connected component if and only if the corresponding objects are in the same set. Thus, CONNECTED-COMPONENTS computes sets in such a way that the procedure SAME-COMPONENT can determine whether two vertices are in the same con-

nected component. Figure 21.1(b) illustrates how CONNECTED-COMPONENTS computes the disjoint sets.

In an actual implementation of this connected-components algorithm, the representations of the graph and the disjoint-set data structure would need to reference each other. That is, an object representing a vertex would contain a pointer to the corresponding disjoint-set object, and vice versa. These programming details depend on the implementation language, and we do not address them further here.

Exercises

21.1-1
Suppose that CONNECTED-COMPONENTS is run on the undirected graph $G = (V, E)$, where $V = \{a, b, c, d, e, f, g, h, i, j, k\}$ and the edges of E are processed in the order $(d, i), (f, k), (g, i), (b, g), (a, h), (i, j), (d, k), (b, j), (d, f), (g, j), (a, e)$. List the vertices in each connected component after each iteration of lines 3–5.

21.1-2
Show that after all edges are processed by CONNECTED-COMPONENTS, two vertices are in the same connected component if and only if they are in the same set.

21.1-3
During the execution of CONNECTED-COMPONENTS on an undirected graph $G = (V, E)$ with k connected components, how many times is FIND-SET called? How many times is UNION called? Express your answers in terms of $|V|, |E|$, and k.

21.2   Linked-list representation of disjoint sets

Figure 21.2(a) shows a simple way to implement a disjoint-set data structure: each set is represented by its own linked list. The object for each set has attributes *head*, pointing to the first object in the list, and *tail*, pointing to the last object. Each object in the list contains a set member, a pointer to the next object in the list, and a pointer back to the set object. Within each linked list, the objects may appear in any order. The representative is the set member in the first object in the list.

With this linked-list representation, both MAKE-SET and FIND-SET are easy, requiring $O(1)$ time. To carry out MAKE-SET(x), we create a new linked list whose only object is x. For FIND-SET(x), we just follow the pointer from x back to its set object and then return the member in the object that *head* points to. For example, in Figure 21.2(a), the call FIND-SET(g) would return f.

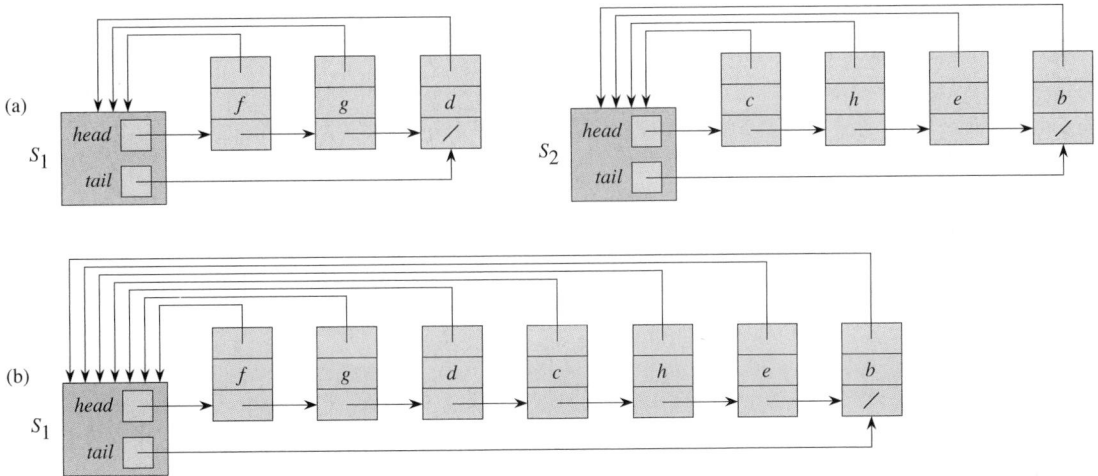

Figure 21.2   **(a)** Linked-list representations of two sets. Set S_1 contains members d, f, and g, with representative f, and set S_2 contains members b, c, e, and h, with representative c. Each object in the list contains a set member, a pointer to the next object in the list, and a pointer back to the set object. Each set object has pointers *head* and *tail* to the first and last objects, respectively. **(b)** The result of UNION(g, e), which appends the linked list containing e to the linked list containing g. The representative of the resulting set is f. The set object for e's list, S_2, is destroyed.

A simple implementation of union

The simplest implementation of the UNION operation using the linked-list set representation takes significantly more time than MAKE-SET or FIND-SET. As Figure 21.2(b) shows, we perform UNION(x, y) by appending y's list onto the end of x's list. The representative of x's list becomes the representative of the resulting set. We use the *tail* pointer for x's list to quickly find where to append y's list. Because all members of y's list join x's list, we can destroy the set object for y's list. Unfortunately, we must update the pointer to the set object for each object originally on y's list, which takes time linear in the length of y's list. In Figure 21.2, for example, the operation UNION(g, e) causes pointers to be updated in the objects for b, c, e, and h.

In fact, we can easily construct a sequence of m operations on n objects that requires $\Theta(n^2)$ time. Suppose that we have objects $x_1, x_2, \ldots, x_n$. We execute the sequence of n MAKE-SET operations followed by $n - 1$ UNION operations shown in Figure 21.3, so that $m = 2n - 1$. We spend $\Theta(n)$ time performing the n MAKE-SET operations. Because the ith UNION operation updates i objects, the total number of objects updated by all $n - 1$ UNION operations is

Operation	Number of objects updated
MAKE-SET(x_1)	1
MAKE-SET(x_2)	1
$\vdots$	$\vdots$
MAKE-SET(x_n)	1
UNION(x_2, x_1)	1
UNION(x_3, x_2)	2
UNION(x_4, x_3)	3
$\vdots$	$\vdots$
UNION(x_n, x_{n-1})	$n-1$

Figure 21.3 A sequence of $2n - 1$ operations on n objects that takes $\Theta(n^2)$ time, or $\Theta(n)$ time per operation on average, using the linked-list set representation and the simple implementation of UNION.

$$\sum_{i=1}^{n-1} i = \Theta(n^2) \, .$$

The total number of operations is $2n - 1$, and so each operation on average requires $\Theta(n)$ time. That is, the amortized time of an operation is $\Theta(n)$.

A weighted-union heuristic

In the worst case, the above implementation of the UNION procedure requires an average of $\Theta(n)$ time per call because we may be appending a longer list onto a shorter list; we must update the pointer to the set object for each member of the longer list. Suppose instead that each list also includes the length of the list (which we can easily maintain) and that we always append the shorter list onto the longer, breaking ties arbitrarily. With this simple *weighted-union heuristic*, a single UNION operation can still take $\Omega(n)$ time if both sets have $\Omega(n)$ members. As the following theorem shows, however, a sequence of m MAKE-SET, UNION, and FIND-SET operations, n of which are MAKE-SET operations, takes $O(m + n \lg n)$ time.

Theorem 21.1
Using the linked-list representation of disjoint sets and the weighted-union heuristic, a sequence of m MAKE-SET, UNION, and FIND-SET operations, n of which are MAKE-SET operations, takes $O(m + n \lg n)$ time.

Proof   Because each UNION operation unites two disjoint sets, we perform at most $n - 1$ UNION operations over all. We now bound the total time taken by these UNION operations. We start by determining, for each object, an upper bound on the number of times the object's pointer back to its set object is updated. Consider a particular object x. We know that each time x's pointer was updated, x must have started in the smaller set. The first time x's pointer was updated, therefore, the resulting set must have had at least 2 members. Similarly, the next time x's pointer was updated, the resulting set must have had at least 4 members. Continuing on, we observe that for any $k \leq n$, after x's pointer has been updated $\lceil \lg k \rceil$ times, the resulting set must have at least k members. Since the largest set has at most n members, each object's pointer is updated at most $\lceil \lg n \rceil$ times over all the UNION operations. Thus the total time spent updating object pointers over all UNION operations is $O(n \lg n)$. We must also account for updating the *tail* pointers and the list lengths, which take only $\Theta(1)$ time per UNION operation. The total time spent in all UNION operations is thus $O(n \lg n)$.

The time for the entire sequence of m operations follows easily. Each MAKE-SET and FIND-SET operation takes $O(1)$ time, and there are $O(m)$ of them. The total time for the entire sequence is thus $O(m + n \lg n)$.   ■

Exercises

21.2-1
Write pseudocode for MAKE-SET, FIND-SET, and UNION using the linked-list representation and the weighted-union heuristic. Make sure to specify the attributes that you assume for set objects and list objects.

21.2-2
Show the data structure that results and the answers returned by the FIND-SET operations in the following program. Use the linked-list representation with the weighted-union heuristic.

```
 1   for i = 1 to 16
 2        MAKE-SET(x_i)
 3   for i = 1 to 15 by 2
 4        UNION(x_i, x_{i+1})
 5   for i = 1 to 13 by 4
 6        UNION(x_i, x_{i+2})
 7   UNION(x_1, x_5)
 8   UNION(x_{11}, x_{13})
 9   UNION(x_1, x_{10})
10   FIND-SET(x_2)
11   FIND-SET(x_9)
```

Assume that if the sets containing x_i and x_j have the same size, then the operation UNION(x_i, x_j) appends x_j's list onto x_i's list.

21.2-3

Adapt the aggregate proof of Theorem 21.1 to obtain amortized time bounds of $O(1)$ for MAKE-SET and FIND-SET and $O(\lg n)$ for UNION using the linked-list representation and the weighted-union heuristic.

21.2-4

Give a tight asymptotic bound on the running time of the sequence of operations in Figure 21.3 assuming the linked-list representation and the weighted-union heuristic.

21.2-5

Professor Gompers suspects that it might be possible to keep just one pointer in each set object, rather than two (*head* and *tail*), while keeping the number of pointers in each list element at two. Show that the professor's suspicion is well founded by describing how to represent each set by a linked list such that each operation has the same running time as the operations described in this section. Describe also how the operations work. Your scheme should allow for the weighted-union heuristic, with the same effect as described in this section. (*Hint:* Use the tail of a linked list as its set's representative.)

21.2-6

Suggest a simple change to the UNION procedure for the linked-list representation that removes the need to keep the *tail* pointer to the last object in each list. Whether or not the weighted-union heuristic is used, your change should not change the asymptotic running time of the UNION procedure. (*Hint:* Rather than appending one list to another, splice them together.)

21.3   Disjoint-set forests

In a faster implementation of disjoint sets, we represent sets by rooted trees, with each node containing one member and each tree representing one set. In a ***disjoint-set forest***, illustrated in Figure 21.4(a), each member points only to its parent. The root of each tree contains the representative and is its own parent. As we shall see, although the straightforward algorithms that use this representation are no faster than ones that use the linked-list representation, by introducing two heuristics—"union by rank" and "path compression"—we can achieve an asymptotically optimal disjoint-set data structure.

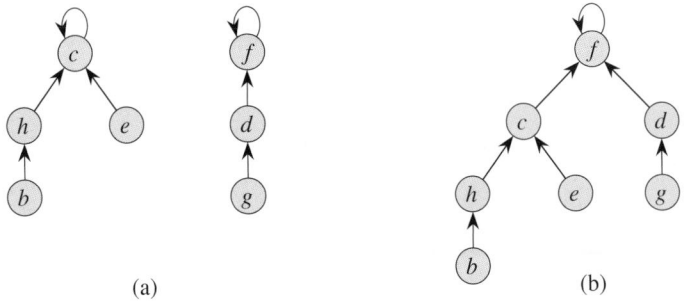

Figure 21.4   A disjoint-set forest. **(a)** Two trees representing the two sets of Figure 21.2. The tree on the left represents the set $\{b, c, e, h\}$, with c as the representative, and the tree on the right represents the set $\{d, f, g\}$, with f as the representative. **(b)** The result of UNION(e, g).

We perform the three disjoint-set operations as follows. A MAKE-SET operation simply creates a tree with just one node. We perform a FIND-SET operation by following parent pointers until we find the root of the tree. The nodes visited on this simple path toward the root constitute the *find path*. A UNION operation, shown in Figure 21.4(b), causes the root of one tree to point to the root of the other.

Heuristics to improve the running time

So far, we have not improved on the linked-list implementation. A sequence of $n - 1$ UNION operations may create a tree that is just a linear chain of n nodes. By using two heuristics, however, we can achieve a running time that is almost linear in the total number of operations m.

The first heuristic, ***union by rank***, is similar to the weighted-union heuristic we used with the linked-list representation. The obvious approach would be to make the root of the tree with fewer nodes point to the root of the tree with more nodes. Rather than explicitly keeping track of the size of the subtree rooted at each node, we shall use an approach that eases the analysis. For each node, we maintain a ***rank***, which is an upper bound on the height of the node. In union by rank, we make the root with smaller rank point to the root with larger rank during a UNION operation.

The second heuristic, ***path compression***, is also quite simple and highly effective. As shown in Figure 21.5, we use it during FIND-SET operations to make each node on the find path point directly to the root. Path compression does not change any ranks.

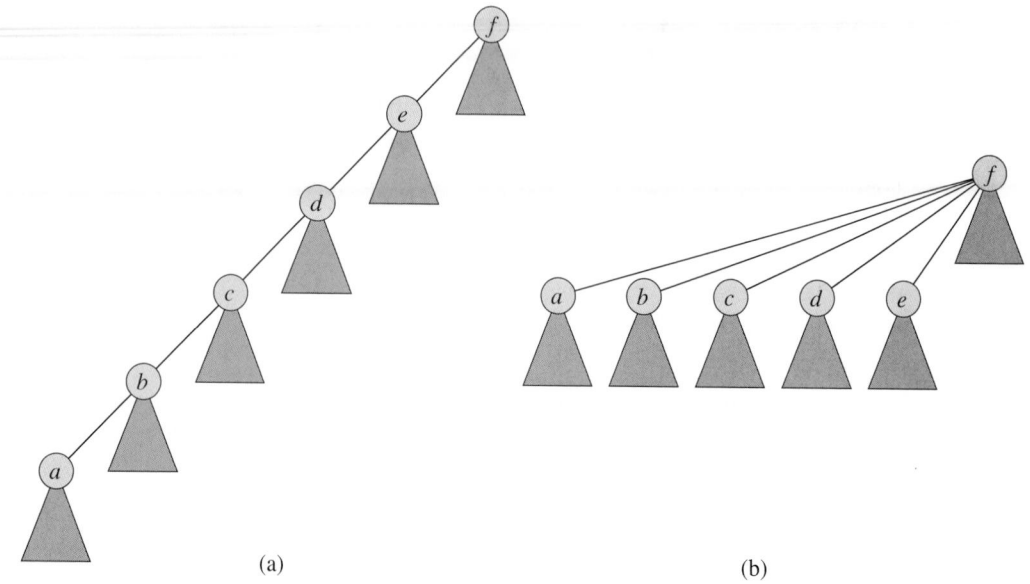

(a)   (b)

Figure 21.5 Path compression during the operation FIND-SET. Arrows and self-loops at roots are omitted. **(a)** A tree representing a set prior to executing FIND-SET(a). Triangles represent subtrees whose roots are the nodes shown. Each node has a pointer to its parent. **(b)** The same set after executing FIND-SET(a). Each node on the find path now points directly to the root.

Pseudocode for disjoint-set forests

To implement a disjoint-set forest with the union-by-rank heuristic, we must keep track of ranks. With each node x, we maintain the integer value $x.rank$, which is an upper bound on the height of x (the number of edges in the longest simple path from a descendant leaf to x). When MAKE-SET creates a singleton set, the single node in the corresponding tree has an initial rank of 0. Each FIND-SET operation leaves all ranks unchanged. The UNION operation has two cases, depending on whether the roots of the trees have equal rank. If the roots have unequal rank, we make the root with higher rank the parent of the root with lower rank, but the ranks themselves remain unchanged. If, instead, the roots have equal ranks, we arbitrarily choose one of the roots as the parent and increment its rank.

Let us put this method into pseudocode. We designate the parent of node x by $x.p$. The LINK procedure, a subroutine called by UNION, takes pointers to two roots as inputs.

MAKE-SET(x)

1   $x.p = x$
2   $x.rank = 0$

UNION(x, y)

1   LINK(FIND-SET(x), FIND-SET(y))

LINK(x, y)

1   **if** $x.rank > y.rank$
2       $y.p = x$
3   **else** $x.p = y$
4   **if** $x.rank == y.rank$
5           $y.rank = y.rank + 1$

The FIND-SET procedure with path compression is quite simple:

FIND-SET(x)

1   **if** $x \neq x.p$
2       $x.p =$ FIND-SET($x.p$)
3   **return** $x.p$

The FIND-SET procedure is a ***two-pass method***: as it recurses, it makes one pass up the find path to find the root, and as the recursion unwinds, it makes a second pass back down the find path to update each node to point directly to the root. Each call of FIND-SET(x) returns $x.p$ in line 3. If x is the root, then FIND-SET skips line 2 and instead returns $x.p$, which is x; this is the case in which the recursion bottoms out. Otherwise, line 2 executes, and the recursive call with parameter $x.p$ returns a pointer to the root. Line 2 updates node x to point directly to the root, and line 3 returns this pointer.

Effect of the heuristics on the running time

Separately, either union by rank or path compression improves the running time of the operations on disjoint-set forests, and the improvement is even greater when we use the two heuristics together. Alone, union by rank yields a running time of $O(m \lg n)$ (see Exercise 21.4-4), and this bound is tight (see Exercise 21.3-3). Although we shall not prove it here, for a sequence of n MAKE-SET operations (and hence at most $n - 1$ UNION operations) and f FIND-SET operations, the path-compression heuristic alone gives a worst-case running time of $\Theta(n + f \cdot (1 + \log_{2+f/n} n))$.

When we use both union by rank and path compression, the worst-case running time is $O(m\,\alpha(n))$, where $\alpha(n)$ is a *very* slowly growing function, which we define in Section 21.4. In any conceivable application of a disjoint-set data structure, $\alpha(n) \leq 4$; thus, we can view the running time as linear in m in all practical situations. Strictly speaking, however, it is superlinear. In Section 21.4, we prove this upper bound.

Exercises

21.3-1
Redo Exercise 21.2-2 using a disjoint-set forest with union by rank and path compression.

21.3-2
Write a nonrecursive version of FIND-SET with path compression.

21.3-3
Give a sequence of m MAKE-SET, UNION, and FIND-SET operations, n of which are MAKE-SET operations, that takes $\Omega(m \lg n)$ time when we use union by rank only.

21.3-4
Suppose that we wish to add the operation PRINT-SET(x), which is given a node x and prints all the members of x's set, in any order. Show how we can add just a single attribute to each node in a disjoint-set forest so that PRINT-SET(x) takes time linear in the number of members of x's set and the asymptotic running times of the other operations are unchanged. Assume that we can print each member of the set in $O(1)$ time.

21.3-5 ★
Show that any sequence of m MAKE-SET, FIND-SET, and LINK operations, where all the LINK operations appear before any of the FIND-SET operations, takes only $O(m)$ time if we use both path compression and union by rank. What happens in the same situation if we use only the path-compression heuristic?

★ 21.4   Analysis of union by rank with path compression

As noted in Section 21.3, the combined union-by-rank and path-compression heuristic runs in time $O(m \, \alpha(n))$ for m disjoint-set operations on n elements. In this section, we shall examine the function α to see just how slowly it grows. Then we prove this running time using the potential method of amortized analysis.

A very quickly growing function and its very slowly growing inverse

For integers $k \geq 0$ and $j \geq 1$, we define the function $A_k(j)$ as

$$A_k(j) = \begin{cases} j + 1 & \text{if } k = 0 , \\ A_{k-1}^{(j+1)}(j) & \text{if } k \geq 1 , \end{cases}$$

where the expression $A_{k-1}^{(j+1)}(j)$ uses the functional-iteration notation given in Section 3.2. Specifically, $A_{k-1}^{(0)}(j) = j$ and $A_{k-1}^{(i)}(j) = A_{k-1}(A_{k-1}^{(i-1)}(j))$ for $i \geq 1$. We will refer to the parameter k as the *level* of the function A.

The function $A_k(j)$ strictly increases with both j and k. To see just how quickly this function grows, we first obtain closed-form expressions for $A_1(j)$ and $A_2(j)$.

Lemma 21.2
For any integer $j \geq 1$, we have $A_1(j) = 2j + 1$.

Proof   We first use induction on i to show that $A_0^{(i)}(j) = j + i$. For the base case, we have $A_0^{(0)}(j) = j = j + 0$. For the inductive step, assume that $A_0^{(i-1)}(j) = j + (i - 1)$. Then $A_0^{(i)}(j) = A_0(A_0^{(i-1)}(j)) = (j + (i - 1)) + 1 = j + i$. Finally, we note that $A_1(j) = A_0^{(j+1)}(j) = j + (j + 1) = 2j + 1$.   ∎

Lemma 21.3
For any integer $j \geq 1$, we have $A_2(j) = 2^{j+1}(j + 1) - 1$.

Proof   We first use induction on i to show that $A_1^{(i)}(j) = 2^i(j + 1) - 1$. For the base case, we have $A_1^{(0)}(j) = j = 2^0(j + 1) - 1$. For the inductive step, assume that $A_1^{(i-1)}(j) = 2^{i-1}(j + 1) - 1$. Then $A_1^{(i)}(j) = A_1(A_1^{(i-1)}(j)) = A_1(2^{i-1}(j + 1) - 1) = 2 \cdot (2^{i-1}(j+1)-1)+1 = 2^i(j+1)-2+1 = 2^i(j+1)-1$. Finally, we note that $A_2(j) = A_1^{(j+1)}(j) = 2^{j+1}(j + 1) - 1$.   ∎

Now we can see how quickly $A_k(j)$ grows by simply examining $A_k(1)$ for levels $k = 0, 1, 2, 3, 4$. From the definition of $A_0(j)$ and the above lemmas, we have $A_0(1) = 1 + 1 = 2$, $A_1(1) = 2 \cdot 1 + 1 = 3$, and $A_2(1) = 2^{1+1} \cdot (1 + 1) - 1 = 7$.

We also have

$$
\begin{aligned}
A_3(1) &= A_2^{(2)}(1) \\
&= A_2(A_2(1)) \\
&= A_2(7) \\
&= 2^8 \cdot 8 - 1 \\
&= 2^{11} - 1 \\
&= 2047
\end{aligned}
$$

and

$$
\begin{aligned}
A_4(1) &= A_3^{(2)}(1) \\
&= A_3(A_3(1)) \\
&= A_3(2047) \\
&= A_2^{(2048)}(2047) \\
&\gg A_2(2047) \\
&= 2^{2048} \cdot 2048 - 1 \\
&> 2^{2048} \\
&= (2^4)^{512} \\
&= 16^{512} \\
&\gg 10^{80} ,
\end{aligned}
$$

which is the estimated number of atoms in the observable universe. (The symbol "$\gg$" denotes the "much-greater-than" relation.)

We define the inverse of the function $A_k(n)$, for integer $n \geq 0$, by

$$\alpha(n) = \min\{k : A_k(1) \geq n\} \ .$$

In words, $\alpha(n)$ is the lowest level k for which $A_k(1)$ is at least n. From the above values of $A_k(1)$, we see that

$$
\alpha(n) = \begin{cases}
0 & \text{for } 0 \leq n \leq 2 , \\
1 & \text{for } n = 3 , \\
2 & \text{for } 4 \leq n \leq 7 , \\
3 & \text{for } 8 \leq n \leq 2047 , \\
4 & \text{for } 2048 \leq n \leq A_4(1) .
\end{cases}
$$

It is only for values of n so large that the term "astronomical" understates them (greater than $A_4(1)$, a huge number) that $\alpha(n) > 4$, and so $\alpha(n) \leq 4$ for all practical purposes.

Properties of ranks

In the remainder of this section, we prove an $O(m\,\alpha(n))$ bound on the running time of the disjoint-set operations with union by rank and path compression. In order to prove this bound, we first prove some simple properties of ranks.

Lemma 21.4
For all nodes x, we have $x.rank \le x.p.rank$, with strict inequality if $x \ne x.p$. The value of $x.rank$ is initially 0 and increases through time until $x \ne x.p$; from then on, $x.rank$ does not change. The value of $x.p.rank$ monotonically increases over time.

Proof The proof is a straightforward induction on the number of operations, using the implementations of MAKE-SET, UNION, and FIND-SET that appear in Section 21.3. We leave it as Exercise 21.4-1. ∎

Corollary 21.5
As we follow the simple path from any node toward a root, the node ranks strictly increase. ∎

Lemma 21.6
Every node has rank at most $n - 1$.

Proof Each node's rank starts at 0, and it increases only upon LINK operations. Because there are at most $n - 1$ UNION operations, there are also at most $n - 1$ LINK operations. Because each LINK operation either leaves all ranks alone or increases some node's rank by 1, all ranks are at most $n - 1$. ∎

Lemma 21.6 provides a weak bound on ranks. In fact, every node has rank at most $\lfloor \lg n \rfloor$ (see Exercise 21.4-2). The looser bound of Lemma 21.6 will suffice for our purposes, however.

Proving the time bound

We shall use the potential method of amortized analysis (see Section 17.3) to prove the $O(m\,\alpha(n))$ time bound. In performing the amortized analysis, we will find it convenient to assume that we invoke the LINK operation rather than the UNION operation. That is, since the parameters of the LINK procedure are pointers to two roots, we act as though we perform the appropriate FIND-SET operations separately. The following lemma shows that even if we count the extra FIND-SET operations induced by UNION calls, the asymptotic running time remains unchanged.

Lemma 21.7

Suppose we convert a sequence S' of m' MAKE-SET, UNION, and FIND-SET operations into a sequence S of m MAKE-SET, LINK, and FIND-SET operations by turning each UNION into two FIND-SET operations followed by a LINK. Then, if sequence S runs in $O(m\,\alpha(n))$ time, sequence S' runs in $O(m'\,\alpha(n))$ time.

Proof   Since each UNION operation in sequence S' is converted into three operations in S, we have $m' \leq m \leq 3m'$. Since $m = O(m')$, an $O(m\,\alpha(n))$ time bound for the converted sequence S implies an $O(m'\,\alpha(n))$ time bound for the original sequence S'.   ∎

In the remainder of this section, we shall assume that the initial sequence of m' MAKE-SET, UNION, and FIND-SET operations has been converted to a sequence of m MAKE-SET, LINK, and FIND-SET operations. We now prove an $O(m\,\alpha(n))$ time bound for the converted sequence and appeal to Lemma 21.7 to prove the $O(m'\,\alpha(n))$ running time of the original sequence of m' operations.

Potential function

The potential function we use assigns a potential $\phi_q(x)$ to each node x in the disjoint-set forest after q operations. We sum the node potentials for the potential of the entire forest: $\Phi_q = \sum_x \phi_q(x)$, where Φ_q denotes the potential of the forest after q operations. The forest is empty prior to the first operation, and we arbitrarily set $\Phi_0 = 0$. No potential Φ_q will ever be negative.

The value of $\phi_q(x)$ depends on whether x is a tree root after the qth operation. If it is, or if $x.rank = 0$, then $\phi_q(x) = \alpha(n) \cdot x.rank$.

Now suppose that after the qth operation, x is not a root and that $x.rank \geq 1$. We need to define two auxiliary functions on x before we can define $\phi_q(x)$. First we define

$$\text{level}(x) = \max\{k : x.p.rank \geq A_k(x.rank)\}\,.$$

That is, $\text{level}(x)$ is the greatest level k for which A_k, applied to x's rank, is no greater than x's parent's rank.

We claim that

$$0 \leq \text{level}(x) < \alpha(n)\,, \tag{21.1}$$

which we see as follows. We have

$$
\begin{aligned}
x.p.rank &\geq x.rank + 1 &&\text{(by Lemma 21.4)}\\
&= A_0(x.rank) &&\text{(by definition of } A_0(j))\,,
\end{aligned}
$$

which implies that $\text{level}(x) \geq 0$, and we have

$$
\begin{aligned}
A_{\alpha(n)}(x.rank) \;&\geq\; A_{\alpha(n)}(1) \quad \text{(because } A_k(j) \text{ is strictly increasing)} \\
&\geq\; n \qquad\qquad \text{(by the definition of } \alpha(n)) \\
&>\; x.p.rank \quad \text{(by Lemma 21.6)} ,
\end{aligned}
$$

which implies that $\mathrm{level}(x) < \alpha(n)$. Note that because $x.p.rank$ monotonically increases over time, so does $\mathrm{level}(x)$.

The second auxiliary function applies when $x.rank \geq 1$:

$$
\mathrm{iter}(x) = \max\left\{ i : x.p.rank \geq A_{\mathrm{level}(x)}^{(i)}(x.rank)\right\} .
$$

That is, $\mathrm{iter}(x)$ is the largest number of times we can iteratively apply $A_{\mathrm{level}(x)}$, applied initially to x's rank, before we get a value greater than x's parent's rank.

We claim that when $x.rank \geq 1$, we have

$$
1 \leq \mathrm{iter}(x) \leq x.rank , \tag{21.2}
$$

which we see as follows. We have

$$
\begin{aligned}
x.p.rank \;&\geq\; A_{\mathrm{level}(x)}(x.rank) \quad \text{(by definition of } \mathrm{level}(x)) \\
&=\; A_{\mathrm{level}(x)}^{(1)}(x.rank) \quad \text{(by definition of functional iteration)} ,
\end{aligned}
$$

which implies that $\mathrm{iter}(x) \geq 1$, and we have

$$
\begin{aligned}
A_{\mathrm{level}(x)}^{(x.rank+1)}(x.rank) \;&=\; A_{\mathrm{level}(x)+1}(x.rank) \quad \text{(by definition of } A_k(j)) \\
&>\; x.p.rank \qquad\qquad \text{(by definition of } \mathrm{level}(x)) ,
\end{aligned}
$$

which implies that $\mathrm{iter}(x) \leq x.rank$. Note that because $x.p.rank$ monotonically increases over time, in order for $\mathrm{iter}(x)$ to decrease, $\mathrm{level}(x)$ must increase. As long as $\mathrm{level}(x)$ remains unchanged, $\mathrm{iter}(x)$ must either increase or remain unchanged.

With these auxiliary functions in place, we are ready to define the potential of node x after q operations:

$$
\phi_q(x) = \begin{cases} \alpha(n) \cdot x.rank & \text{if } x \text{ is a root or } x.rank = 0 , \\ (\alpha(n) - \mathrm{level}(x)) \cdot x.rank - \mathrm{iter}(x) & \text{if } x \text{ is not a root and } x.rank \geq 1 . \end{cases}
$$

We next investigate some useful properties of node potentials.

Lemma 21.8
For every node x, and for all operation counts q, we have

$$
0 \leq \phi_q(x) \leq \alpha(n) \cdot x.rank .
$$

Proof   If x is a root or $x.rank = 0$, then $\phi_q(x) = \alpha(n){\cdot}x.rank$ by definition. Now suppose that x is not a root and that $x.rank \geq 1$. We obtain a lower bound on $\phi_q(x)$ by maximizing level(x) and iter(x). By the bound (21.1), level$(x) \leq \alpha(n) - 1$, and by the bound (21.2), iter$(x) \leq x.rank$. Thus,

$$
\begin{aligned}
\phi_q(x) &= (\alpha(n) - \text{level}(x)) \cdot x.rank - \text{iter}(x) \\
&\geq (\alpha(n) - (\alpha(n) - 1)) \cdot x.rank - x.rank \\
&= x.rank - x.rank \\
&= 0 .
\end{aligned}
$$

Similarly, we obtain an upper bound on $\phi_q(x)$ by minimizing level(x) and iter(x). By the bound (21.1), level$(x) \geq 0$, and by the bound (21.2), iter$(x) \geq 1$. Thus,

$$
\begin{aligned}
\phi_q(x) &\leq (\alpha(n) - 0) \cdot x.rank - 1 \\
&= \alpha(n) \cdot x.rank - 1 \\
&< \alpha(n) \cdot x.rank .
\end{aligned}
$$

∎

Corollary 21.9
If node x is not a root and $x.rank > 0$, then $\phi_q(x) < \alpha(n) \cdot x.rank$.   ∎

Potential changes and amortized costs of operations

We are now ready to examine how the disjoint-set operations affect node potentials. With an understanding of the change in potential due to each operation, we can determine each operation's amortized cost.

Lemma 21.10
Let x be a node that is not a root, and suppose that the qth operation is either a LINK or FIND-SET. Then after the qth operation, $\phi_q(x) \leq \phi_{q-1}(x)$. Moreover, if $x.rank \geq 1$ and either level(x) or iter(x) changes due to the qth operation, then $\phi_q(x) \leq \phi_{q-1}(x) - 1$. That is, x's potential cannot increase, and if it has positive rank and either level(x) or iter(x) changes, then x's potential drops by at least 1.

Proof   Because x is not a root, the qth operation does not change $x.rank$, and because n does not change after the initial n MAKE-SET operations, $\alpha(n)$ remains unchanged as well. Hence, these components of the formula for x's potential remain the same after the qth operation. If $x.rank = 0$, then $\phi_q(x) = \phi_{q-1}(x) = 0$. Now assume that $x.rank \geq 1$.

Recall that level(x) monotonically increases over time. If the qth operation leaves level(x) unchanged, then iter(x) either increases or remains unchanged. If both level(x) and iter(x) are unchanged, then $\phi_q(x) = \phi_{q-1}(x)$. If level$(x)$

is unchanged and iter(x) increases, then it increases by at least 1, and so $\phi_q(x) \leq \phi_{q-1}(x) - 1$.

Finally, if the qth operation increases level(x), it increases by at least 1, so that the value of the term $(\alpha(n) - \text{level}(x)) \cdot x.rank$ drops by at least $x.rank$. Because level(x) increased, the value of iter(x) might drop, but according to the bound (21.2), the drop is by at most $x.rank - 1$. Thus, the increase in potential due to the change in iter(x) is less than the decrease in potential due to the change in level(x), and we conclude that $\phi_q(x) \leq \phi_{q-1}(x) - 1$. ∎

Our final three lemmas show that the amortized cost of each MAKE-SET, LINK, and FIND-SET operation is $O(\alpha(n))$. Recall from equation (17.2) that the amortized cost of each operation is its actual cost plus the change in potential due to the operation.

Lemma 21.11
The amortized cost of each MAKE-SET operation is $O(1)$.

Proof Suppose that the qth operation is MAKE-SET(x). This operation creates node x with rank 0, so that $\phi_q(x) = 0$. No other ranks or potentials change, and so $\Phi_q = \Phi_{q-1}$. Noting that the actual cost of the MAKE-SET operation is $O(1)$ completes the proof. ∎

Lemma 21.12
The amortized cost of each LINK operation is $O(\alpha(n))$.

Proof Suppose that the qth operation is LINK(x, y). The actual cost of the LINK operation is $O(1)$. Without loss of generality, suppose that the LINK makes y the parent of x.

To determine the change in potential due to the LINK, we note that the only nodes whose potentials may change are x, y, and the children of y just prior to the operation. We shall show that the only node whose potential can increase due to the LINK is y, and that its increase is at most $\alpha(n)$:

- By Lemma 21.10, any node that is y's child just before the LINK cannot have its potential increase due to the LINK.

- From the definition of $\phi_q(x)$, we see that, since x was a root just before the qth operation, $\phi_{q-1}(x) = \alpha(n) \cdot x.rank$. If $x.rank = 0$, then $\phi_q(x) = \phi_{q-1}(x) = 0$. Otherwise,

$$\phi_q(x) \; < \; \alpha(n) \cdot x.rank \quad \text{(by Corollary 21.9)}$$
$$= \; \phi_{q-1}(x) ,$$

and so x's potential decreases.

- Because y is a root prior to the LINK, $\phi_{q-1}(y) = \alpha(n) \cdot y.rank$. The LINK operation leaves y as a root, and it either leaves y's rank alone or it increases y's rank by 1. Therefore, either $\phi_q(y) = \phi_{q-1}(y)$ or $\phi_q(y) = \phi_{q-1}(y) + \alpha(n)$.

The increase in potential due to the LINK operation, therefore, is at most $\alpha(n)$. The amortized cost of the LINK operation is $O(1) + \alpha(n) = O(\alpha(n))$. ∎

Lemma 21.13
The amortized cost of each FIND-SET operation is $O(\alpha(n))$.

Proof Suppose that the qth operation is a FIND-SET and that the find path contains s nodes. The actual cost of the FIND-SET operation is $O(s)$. We shall show that no node's potential increases due to the FIND-SET and that at least $\max(0, s - (\alpha(n) + 2))$ nodes on the find path have their potential decrease by at least 1.

To see that no node's potential increases, we first appeal to Lemma 21.10 for all nodes other than the root. If x is the root, then its potential is $\alpha(n) \cdot x.rank$, which does not change.

Now we show that at least $\max(0, s - (\alpha(n) + 2))$ nodes have their potential decrease by at least 1. Let x be a node on the find path such that $x.rank > 0$ and x is followed somewhere on the find path by another node y that is not a root, where $\mathrm{level}(y) = \mathrm{level}(x)$ just before the FIND-SET operation. (Node y need not *immediately* follow x on the find path.) All but at most $\alpha(n) + 2$ nodes on the find path satisfy these constraints on x. Those that do not satisfy them are the first node on the find path (if it has rank 0), the last node on the path (i.e., the root), and the last node w on the path for which $\mathrm{level}(w) = k$, for each $k = 0, 1, 2, \ldots, \alpha(n) - 1$.

Let us fix such a node x, and we shall show that x's potential decreases by at least 1. Let $k = \mathrm{level}(x) = \mathrm{level}(y)$. Just prior to the path compression caused by the FIND-SET, we have

$$
\begin{aligned}
x.p.rank &\geq A_k^{(\mathrm{iter}(x))}(x.rank) &&\text{(by definition of } \mathrm{iter}(x)) \ , \\
y.p.rank &\geq A_k(y.rank) &&\text{(by definition of } \mathrm{level}(y)) \ , \\
y.rank &\geq x.p.rank &&\text{(by Corollary 21.5 and because} \\
& && \quad y \text{ follows } x \text{ on the find path)} \ .
\end{aligned}
$$

Putting these inequalities together and letting i be the value of $\mathrm{iter}(x)$ before path compression, we have

$$
\begin{aligned}
y.p.rank &\geq A_k(y.rank) \\
&\geq A_k(x.p.rank) &&\text{(because } A_k(j) \text{ is strictly increasing)} \\
&\geq A_k(A_k^{(\mathrm{iter}(x))}(x.rank)) \\
&= A_k^{(i+1)}(x.rank) \ .
\end{aligned}
$$

Because path compression will make x and y have the same parent, we know that after path compression, $x.p.rank = y.p.rank$ and that the path compression does not decrease $y.p.rank$. Since $x.rank$ does not change, after path compression we have that $x.p.rank \geq A_k^{(i+1)}(x.rank)$. Thus, path compression will cause either iter(x) to increase (to at least $i + 1$) or level(x) to increase (which occurs if iter(x) increases to at least $x.rank + 1$). In either case, by Lemma 21.10, we have $\phi_q(x) \leq \phi_{q-1}(x) - 1$. Hence, x's potential decreases by at least 1.

The amortized cost of the FIND-SET operation is the actual cost plus the change in potential. The actual cost is $O(s)$, and we have shown that the total potential decreases by at least $\max(0, s - (\alpha(n) + 2))$. The amortized cost, therefore, is at most $O(s) - (s - (\alpha(n) + 2)) = O(s) - s + O(\alpha(n)) = O(\alpha(n))$, since we can scale up the units of potential to dominate the constant hidden in $O(s)$.   ■

Putting the preceding lemmas together yields the following theorem.

Theorem 21.14
A sequence of m MAKE-SET, UNION, and FIND-SET operations, n of which are MAKE-SET operations, can be performed on a disjoint-set forest with union by rank and path compression in worst-case time $O(m\, \alpha(n))$.

Proof   Immediate from Lemmas 21.7, 21.11, 21.12, and 21.13.   ■

Exercises

21.4-1
Prove Lemma 21.4.

21.4-2
Prove that every node has rank at most $\lfloor \lg n \rfloor$.

21.4-3
In light of Exercise 21.4-2, how many bits are necessary to store $x.rank$ for each node x?

21.4-4
Using Exercise 21.4-2, give a simple proof that operations on a disjoint-set forest with union by rank but without path compression run in $O(m \lg n)$ time.

21.4-5
Professor Dante reasons that because node ranks increase strictly along a simple path to the root, node levels must monotonically increase along the path. In other

words, if $x.rank > 0$ and $x.p$ is not a root, then $\text{level}(x) \leq \text{level}(x.p)$. Is the professor correct?

21.4-6 ★

Consider the function $\alpha'(n) = \min\{k : A_k(1) \geq \lg(n+1)\}$. Show that $\alpha'(n) \leq 3$ for all practical values of n and, using Exercise 21.4-2, show how to modify the potential-function argument to prove that we can perform a sequence of m MAKE-SET, UNION, and FIND-SET operations, n of which are MAKE-SET operations, on a disjoint-set forest with union by rank and path compression in worst-case time $O(m \, \alpha'(n))$.

Problems

21-1   *Off-line minimum*

The ***off-line minimum problem*** asks us to maintain a dynamic set T of elements from the domain $\{1, 2, \ldots, n\}$ under the operations INSERT and EXTRACT-MIN. We are given a sequence S of n INSERT and m EXTRACT-MIN calls, where each key in $\{1, 2, \ldots, n\}$ is inserted exactly once. We wish to determine which key is returned by each EXTRACT-MIN call. Specifically, we wish to fill in an array *extracted*$[1 .. m]$, where for $i = 1, 2, \ldots, m$, *extracted*$[i]$ is the key returned by the ith EXTRACT-MIN call. The problem is "off-line" in the sense that we are allowed to process the entire sequence S before determining any of the returned keys.

a. In the following instance of the off-line minimum problem, each operation INSERT(i) is represented by the value of i and each EXTRACT-MIN is represented by the letter E:

$$4, 8, \text{E}, 3, \text{E}, 9, 2, 6, \text{E}, \text{E}, \text{E}, 1, 7, \text{E}, 5 \; .$$

Fill in the correct values in the *extracted* array.

To develop an algorithm for this problem, we break the sequence S into homogeneous subsequences. That is, we represent S by

$$\text{I}_1, \text{E}, \text{I}_2, \text{E}, \text{I}_3, \ldots, \text{I}_m, \text{E}, \text{I}_{m+1} \; ,$$

where each E represents a single EXTRACT-MIN call and each I_j represents a (possibly empty) sequence of INSERT calls. For each subsequence I_j, we initially place the keys inserted by these operations into a set K_j, which is empty if I_j is empty. We then do the following:

OFF-LINE-MINIMUM(m, n)

```
1  for i = 1 to n
2      determine j such that i ∈ K_j
3      if j ≠ m + 1
4          extracted[j] = i
5          let l be the smallest value greater than j
                 for which set K_l exists
6          K_l = K_j ∪ K_l, destroying K_j
7  return extracted
```

b. Argue that the array *extracted* returned by OFF-LINE-MINIMUM is correct.

c. Describe how to implement OFF-LINE-MINIMUM efficiently with a disjoint-set data structure. Give a tight bound on the worst-case running time of your implementation.

21-2 *Depth determination*

In the ***depth-determination problem***, we maintain a forest $\mathscr{F} = \{T_i\}$ of rooted trees under three operations:

MAKE-TREE(v) creates a tree whose only node is v.

FIND-DEPTH(v) returns the depth of node v within its tree.

GRAFT(r, v) makes node r, which is assumed to be the root of a tree, become the child of node v, which is assumed to be in a different tree than r but may or may not itself be a root.

a. Suppose that we use a tree representation similar to a disjoint-set forest: $v.p$ is the parent of node v, except that $v.p = v$ if v is a root. Suppose further that we implement GRAFT(r, v) by setting $r.p = v$ and FIND-DEPTH(v) by following the find path up to the root, returning a count of all nodes other than v encountered. Show that the worst-case running time of a sequence of m MAKE-TREE, FIND-DEPTH, and GRAFT operations is $\Theta(m^2)$.

By using the union-by-rank and path-compression heuristics, we can reduce the worst-case running time. We use the disjoint-set forest $\mathscr{S} = \{S_i\}$, where each set S_i (which is itself a tree) corresponds to a tree T_i in the forest $\mathscr{F}$. The tree structure within a set S_i, however, does not necessarily correspond to that of T_i. In fact, the implementation of S_i does not record the exact parent-child relationships but nevertheless allows us to determine any node's depth in T_i.

The key idea is to maintain in each node v a "pseudodistance" $v.d$, which is defined so that the sum of the pseudodistances along the simple path from v to the

root of its set S_i equals the depth of v in T_i. That is, if the simple path from v to its root in S_i is $v_0, v_1, \ldots, v_k$, where $v_0 = v$ and v_k is S_i's root, then the depth of v in T_i is $\sum_{j=0}^{k} v_j.d$.

b. Give an implementation of MAKE-TREE.

c. Show how to modify FIND-SET to implement FIND-DEPTH. Your implementation should perform path compression, and its running time should be linear in the length of the find path. Make sure that your implementation updates pseudodistances correctly.

d. Show how to implement GRAFT(r, v), which combines the sets containing r and v, by modifying the UNION and LINK procedures. Make sure that your implementation updates pseudodistances correctly. Note that the root of a set S_i is not necessarily the root of the corresponding tree T_i.

e. Give a tight bound on the worst-case running time of a sequence of m MAKE-TREE, FIND-DEPTH, and GRAFT operations, n of which are MAKE-TREE operations.

21-3   *Tarjan's off-line least-common-ancestors algorithm*

The ***least common ancestor*** of two nodes u and v in a rooted tree T is the node w that is an ancestor of both u and v and that has the greatest depth in T. In the ***off-line least-common-ancestors problem***, we are given a rooted tree T and an arbitrary set $P = \{\{u, v\}\}$ of unordered pairs of nodes in T, and we wish to determine the least common ancestor of each pair in P.

To solve the off-line least-common-ancestors problem, the following procedure performs a tree walk of T with the initial call LCA($T.root$). We assume that each node is colored WHITE prior to the walk.

LCA(u)

```
 1   MAKE-SET(u)
 2   FIND-SET(u).ancestor = u
 3   for each child v of u in T
 4       LCA(v)
 5       UNION(u, v)
 6       FIND-SET(u).ancestor = u
 7   u.color = BLACK
 8   for each node v such that {u, v} ∈ P
 9       if v.color == BLACK
10           print "The least common ancestor of"
                 u "and" v "is" FIND-SET(v).ancestor
```

a. Argue that line 10 executes exactly once for each pair $\{u, v\} \in P$.

b. Argue that at the time of the call LCA(u), the number of sets in the disjoint-set data structure equals the depth of u in T.

c. Prove that LCA correctly prints the least common ancestor of u and v for each pair $\{u, v\} \in P$.

d. Analyze the running time of LCA, assuming that we use the implementation of the disjoint-set data structure in Section 21.3.

Chapter notes

Many of the important results for disjoint-set data structures are due at least in part to R. E. Tarjan. Using aggregate analysis, Tarjan [328, 330] gave the first tight upper bound in terms of the very slowly growing inverse $\hat{\alpha}(m, n)$ of Ackermann's function. (The function $A_k(j)$ given in Section 21.4 is similar to Ackermann's function, and the function $\alpha(n)$ is similar to the inverse. Both $\alpha(n)$ and $\hat{\alpha}(m, n)$ are at most 4 for all conceivable values of m and n.) An $O(m \lg^* n)$ upper bound was proven earlier by Hopcroft and Ullman [5, 179]. The treatment in Section 21.4 is adapted from a later analysis by Tarjan [332], which is in turn based on an analysis by Kozen [220]. Harfst and Reingold [161] give a potential-based version of Tarjan's earlier bound.

Tarjan and van Leeuwen [333] discuss variants on the path-compression heuristic, including "one-pass methods," which sometimes offer better constant factors in their performance than do two-pass methods. As with Tarjan's earlier analyses of the basic path-compression heuristic, the analyses by Tarjan and van Leeuwen are aggregate. Harfst and Reingold [161] later showed how to make a small change to the potential function to adapt their path-compression analysis to these one-pass variants. Gabow and Tarjan [121] show that in certain applications, the disjoint-set operations can be made to run in $O(m)$ time.

Tarjan [329] showed that a lower bound of $\Omega(m \,\hat{\alpha}(m, n))$ time is required for operations on any disjoint-set data structure satisfying certain technical conditions. This lower bound was later generalized by Fredman and Saks [113], who showed that in the worst case, $\Omega(m \,\hat{\alpha}(m, n))$ ($\lg n$)-bit words of memory must be accessed.

VI Graph Algorithms

Introduction

Graph problems pervade computer science, and algorithms for working with them
are fundamental to the field. Hundreds of interesting computational problems are
couched in terms of graphs. In this part, we touch on a few of the more significant
ones.

Chapter 22 shows how we can represent a graph in a computer and then discusses
algorithms based on searching a graph using either breadth-first search or depth-
first search. The chapter gives two applications of depth-first search: topologically
sorting a directed acyclic graph and decomposing a directed graph into its strongly
connected components.

Chapter 23 describes how to compute a minimum-weight spanning tree of a
graph: the least-weight way of connecting all of the vertices together when each
edge has an associated weight. The algorithms for computing minimum spanning
trees serve as good examples of greedy algorithms (see Chapter 16).

Chapters 24 and 25 consider how to compute shortest paths between vertices
when each edge has an associated length or "weight." Chapter 24 shows how to
find shortest paths from a given source vertex to all other vertices, and Chapter 25
examines methods to compute shortest paths between every pair of vertices.

Finally, Chapter 26 shows how to compute a maximum flow of material in a flow
network, which is a directed graph having a specified source vertex of material, a
specified sink vertex, and specified capacities for the amount of material that can
traverse each directed edge. This general problem arises in many forms, and a
good algorithm for computing maximum flows can help solve a variety of related
problems efficiently.

When we characterize the running time of a graph algorithm on a given graph $G = (V, E)$, we usually measure the size of the input in terms of the number of vertices $|V|$ and the number of edges $|E|$ of the graph. That is, we describe the size of the input with two parameters, not just one. We adopt a common notational convention for these parameters. Inside asymptotic notation (such as O-notation or Θ-notation), and *only* inside such notation, the symbol V denotes $|V|$ and the symbol E denotes $|E|$. For example, we might say, "the algorithm runs in time $O(VE)$," meaning that the algorithm runs in time $O(|V||E|)$. This convention makes the running-time formulas easier to read, without risk of ambiguity.

Another convention we adopt appears in pseudocode. We denote the vertex set of a graph G by $G.V$ and its edge set by $G.E$. That is, the pseudocode views vertex and edge sets as attributes of a graph.

22   Elementary Graph Algorithms

This chapter presents methods for representing a graph and for searching a graph. Searching a graph means systematically following the edges of the graph so as to visit the vertices of the graph. A graph-searching algorithm can discover much about the structure of a graph. Many algorithms begin by searching their input graph to obtain this structural information. Several other graph algorithms elaborate on basic graph searching. Techniques for searching a graph lie at the heart of the field of graph algorithms.

Section 22.1 discusses the two most common computational representations of graphs: as adjacency lists and as adjacency matrices. Section 22.2 presents a simple graph-searching algorithm called breadth-first search and shows how to create a breadth-first tree. Section 22.3 presents depth-first search and proves some standard results about the order in which depth-first search visits vertices. Section 22.4 provides our first real application of depth-first search: topologically sorting a directed acyclic graph. A second application of depth-first search, finding the strongly connected components of a directed graph, is the topic of Section 22.5.

22.1   Representations of graphs

We can choose between two standard ways to represent a graph $G = (V, E)$: as a collection of adjacency lists or as an adjacency matrix. Either way applies to both directed and undirected graphs. Because the adjacency-list representation provides a compact way to represent *sparse* graphs—those for which $|E|$ is much less than $|V|^2$—it is usually the method of choice. Most of the graph algorithms presented in this book assume that an input graph is represented in adjacency-list form. We may prefer an adjacency-matrix representation, however, when the graph is *dense*—$|E|$ is close to $|V|^2$—or when we need to be able to tell quickly if there is an edge connecting two given vertices. For example, two of the all-pairs

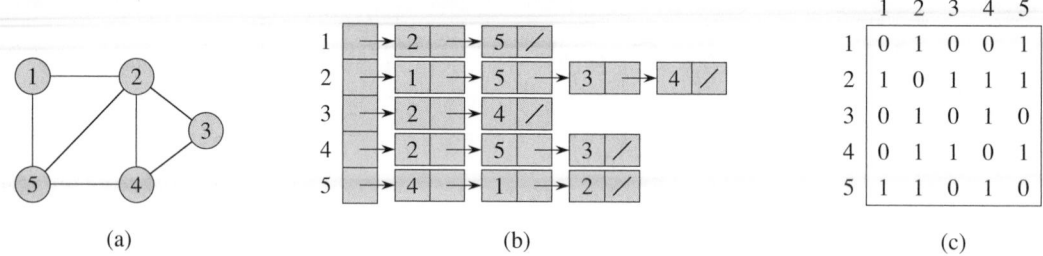

Figure 22.1 Two representations of an undirected graph. **(a)** An undirected graph G with 5 vertices and 7 edges. **(b)** An adjacency-list representation of G. **(c)** The adjacency-matrix representation of G.

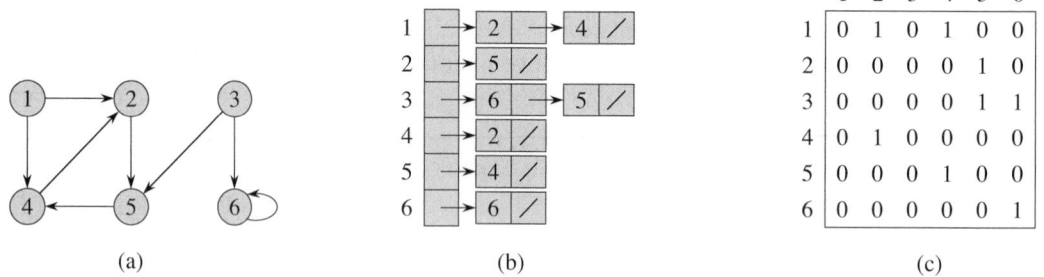

Figure 22.2 Two representations of a directed graph. **(a)** A directed graph G with 6 vertices and 8 edges. **(b)** An adjacency-list representation of G. **(c)** The adjacency-matrix representation of G.

shortest-paths algorithms presented in Chapter 25 assume that their input graphs are represented by adjacency matrices.

The ***adjacency-list representation*** of a graph $G = (V, E)$ consists of an array *Adj* of $|V|$ lists, one for each vertex in V. For each $u \in V$, the adjacency list *Adj*[u] contains all the vertices v such that there is an edge $(u, v) \in E$. That is, *Adj*[u] consists of all the vertices adjacent to u in G. (Alternatively, it may contain pointers to these vertices.) Since the adjacency lists represent the edges of a graph, in pseudocode we treat the array *Adj* as an attribute of the graph, just as we treat the edge set E. In pseudocode, therefore, we will see notation such as $G.Adj[u]$. Figure 22.1(b) is an adjacency-list representation of the undirected graph in Figure 22.1(a). Similarly, Figure 22.2(b) is an adjacency-list representation of the directed graph in Figure 22.2(a).

If G is a directed graph, the sum of the lengths of all the adjacency lists is $|E|$, since an edge of the form (u, v) is represented by having v appear in *Adj*[u]. If G is

an undirected graph, the sum of the lengths of all the adjacency lists is $2|E|$, since if (u, v) is an undirected edge, then u appears in v's adjacency list and vice versa. For both directed and undirected graphs, the adjacency-list representation has the desirable property that the amount of memory it requires is $\Theta(V + E)$.

We can readily adapt adjacency lists to represent *weighted graphs*, that is, graphs for which each edge has an associated *weight*, typically given by a *weight function* $w : E \rightarrow \mathbb{R}$. For example, let $G = (V, E)$ be a weighted graph with weight function w. We simply store the weight $w(u, v)$ of the edge $(u, v) \in E$ with vertex v in u's adjacency list. The adjacency-list representation is quite robust in that we can modify it to support many other graph variants.

A potential disadvantage of the adjacency-list representation is that it provides no quicker way to determine whether a given edge (u, v) is present in the graph than to search for v in the adjacency list $Adj[u]$. An adjacency-matrix representation of the graph remedies this disadvantage, but at the cost of using asymptotically more memory. (See Exercise 22.1-8 for suggestions of variations on adjacency lists that permit faster edge lookup.)

For the *adjacency-matrix representation* of a graph $G = (V, E)$, we assume that the vertices are numbered $1, 2, \ldots, |V|$ in some arbitrary manner. Then the adjacency-matrix representation of a graph G consists of a $|V| \times |V|$ matrix $A = (a_{ij})$ such that

$$a_{ij} = \begin{cases} 1 & \text{if } (i, j) \in E \text{ ,} \\ 0 & \text{otherwise .} \end{cases}$$

Figures 22.1(c) and 22.2(c) are the adjacency matrices of the undirected and directed graphs in Figures 22.1(a) and 22.2(a), respectively. The adjacency matrix of a graph requires $\Theta(V^2)$ memory, independent of the number of edges in the graph.

Observe the symmetry along the main diagonal of the adjacency matrix in Figure 22.1(c). Since in an undirected graph, (u, v) and (v, u) represent the same edge, the adjacency matrix A of an undirected graph is its own transpose: $A = A^{\mathrm{T}}$. In some applications, it pays to store only the entries on and above the diagonal of the adjacency matrix, thereby cutting the memory needed to store the graph almost in half.

Like the adjacency-list representation of a graph, an adjacency matrix can represent a weighted graph. For example, if $G = (V, E)$ is a weighted graph with edge-weight function w, we can simply store the weight $w(u, v)$ of the edge $(u, v) \in E$ as the entry in row u and column v of the adjacency matrix. If an edge does not exist, we can store a NIL value as its corresponding matrix entry, though for many problems it is convenient to use a value such as 0 or ∞.

Although the adjacency-list representation is asymptotically at least as space-efficient as the adjacency-matrix representation, adjacency matrices are simpler, and so we may prefer them when graphs are reasonably small. Moreover, adja-

cency matrices carry a further advantage for unweighted graphs: they require only one bit per entry.

Representing attributes

Most algorithms that operate on graphs need to maintain attributes for vertices and/or edges. We indicate these attributes using our usual notation, such as $v.d$ for an attribute d of a vertex v. When we indicate edges as pairs of vertices, we use the same style of notation. For example, if edges have an attribute f, then we denote this attribute for edge (u, v) by $(u, v).f$. For the purpose of presenting and understanding algorithms, our attribute notation suffices.

Implementing vertex and edge attributes in real programs can be another story entirely. There is no one best way to store and access vertex and edge attributes. For a given situation, your decision will likely depend on the programming language you are using, the algorithm you are implementing, and how the rest of your program uses the graph. If you represent a graph using adjacency lists, one design represents vertex attributes in additional arrays, such as an array $d[1 \mathinner{\ldotp\ldotp} |V|]$ that parallels the *Adj* array. If the vertices adjacent to u are in $Adj[u]$, then what we call the attribute $u.d$ would actually be stored in the array entry $d[u]$. Many other ways of implementing attributes are possible. For example, in an object-oriented programming language, vertex attributes might be represented as instance variables within a subclass of a `Vertex` class.

Exercises

22.1-1
Given an adjacency-list representation of a directed graph, how long does it take to compute the out-degree of every vertex? How long does it take to compute the in-degrees?

22.1-2
Give an adjacency-list representation for a complete binary tree on 7 vertices. Give an equivalent adjacency-matrix representation. Assume that vertices are numbered from 1 to 7 as in a binary heap.

22.1-3
The *transpose* of a directed graph $G = (V, E)$ is the graph $G^{\mathrm{T}} = (V, E^{\mathrm{T}})$, where $E^{\mathrm{T}} = \{(v, u) \in V \times V : (u, v) \in E\}$. Thus, G^{T} is G with all its edges reversed. Describe efficient algorithms for computing G^{T} from G, for both the adjacency-list and adjacency-matrix representations of G. Analyze the running times of your algorithms.

22.1-4

Given an adjacency-list representation of a multigraph $G = (V, E)$, describe an $O(V + E)$-time algorithm to compute the adjacency-list representation of the "equivalent" undirected graph $G' = (V, E')$, where E' consists of the edges in E with all multiple edges between two vertices replaced by a single edge and with all self-loops removed.

22.1-5

The *square* of a directed graph $G = (V, E)$ is the graph $G^2 = (V, E^2)$ such that $(u, v) \in E^2$ if and only if G contains a path with at most two edges between u and v. Describe efficient algorithms for computing G^2 from G for both the adjacency-list and adjacency-matrix representations of G. Analyze the running times of your algorithms.

22.1-6

Most graph algorithms that take an adjacency-matrix representation as input require time $\Omega(V^2)$, but there are some exceptions. Show how to determine whether a directed graph G contains a *universal sink*—a vertex with in-degree $|V| - 1$ and out-degree 0—in time $O(V)$, given an adjacency matrix for G.

22.1-7

The *incidence matrix* of a directed graph $G = (V, E)$ with no self-loops is a $|V| \times |E|$ matrix $B = (b_{ij})$ such that

$$
b_{ij} = \begin{cases} -1 & \text{if edge } j \text{ leaves vertex } i \text{ ,} \\ 1 & \text{if edge } j \text{ enters vertex } i \text{ ,} \\ 0 & \text{otherwise .} \end{cases}
$$

Describe what the entries of the matrix product BB^{T} represent, where B^{T} is the transpose of B.

22.1-8

Suppose that instead of a linked list, each array entry $Adj[u]$ is a hash table containing the vertices v for which $(u, v) \in E$. If all edge lookups are equally likely, what is the expected time to determine whether an edge is in the graph? What disadvantages does this scheme have? Suggest an alternate data structure for each edge list that solves these problems. Does your alternative have disadvantages compared to the hash table?

22.2   Breadth-first search

Breadth-first search is one of the simplest algorithms for searching a graph and the archetype for many important graph algorithms. Prim's minimum-spanning-tree algorithm (Section 23.2) and Dijkstra's single-source shortest-paths algorithm (Section 24.3) use ideas similar to those in breadth-first search.

Given a graph $G = (V, E)$ and a distinguished ***source*** vertex s, breadth-first search systematically explores the edges of G to "discover" every vertex that is reachable from s. It computes the distance (smallest number of edges) from s to each reachable vertex. It also produces a "breadth-first tree" with root s that contains all reachable vertices. For any vertex v reachable from s, the simple path in the breadth-first tree from s to v corresponds to a "shortest path" from s to v in G, that is, a path containing the smallest number of edges. The algorithm works on both directed and undirected graphs.

Breadth-first search is so named because it expands the frontier between discovered and undiscovered vertices uniformly across the breadth of the frontier. That is, the algorithm discovers all vertices at distance k from s before discovering any vertices at distance $k + 1$.

To keep track of progress, breadth-first search colors each vertex white, gray, or black. All vertices start out white and may later become gray and then black. A vertex is ***discovered*** the first time it is encountered during the search, at which time it becomes nonwhite. Gray and black vertices, therefore, have been discovered, but breadth-first search distinguishes between them to ensure that the search proceeds in a breadth-first manner.[1] If $(u, v) \in E$ and vertex u is black, then vertex v is either gray or black; that is, all vertices adjacent to black vertices have been discovered. Gray vertices may have some adjacent white vertices; they represent the frontier between discovered and undiscovered vertices.

Breadth-first search constructs a breadth-first tree, initially containing only its root, which is the source vertex s. Whenever the search discovers a white vertex v in the course of scanning the adjacency list of an already discovered vertex u, the vertex v and the edge (u, v) are added to the tree. We say that u is the ***predecessor*** or ***parent*** of v in the breadth-first tree. Since a vertex is discovered at most once, it has at most one parent. Ancestor and descendant relationships in the breadth-first tree are defined relative to the root s as usual: if u is on the simple path in the tree from the root s to vertex v, then u is an ancestor of v and v is a descendant of u.

---

[1] We distinguish between gray and black vertices to help us understand how breadth-first search operates. In fact, as Exercise 22.2-3 shows, we would get the same result even if we did not distinguish between gray and black vertices.

The breadth-first-search procedure BFS below assumes that the input graph $G = (V, E)$ is represented using adjacency lists. It attaches several additional attributes to each vertex in the graph. We store the color of each vertex $u \in V$ in the attribute $u.color$ and the predecessor of u in the attribute $u.\pi$. If u has no predecessor (for example, if $u = s$ or u has not been discovered), then $u.\pi = \text{NIL}$. The attribute $u.d$ holds the distance from the source s to vertex u computed by the algorithm. The algorithm also uses a first-in, first-out queue Q (see Section 10.1) to manage the set of gray vertices.

BFS(G, s)

```
 1   for each vertex u ∈ G.V − {s}
 2        u.color = WHITE
 3        u.d = ∞
 4        u.π = NIL
 5   s.color = GRAY
 6   s.d = 0
 7   s.π = NIL
 8   Q = ∅
 9   ENQUEUE(Q, s)
10   while Q ≠ ∅
11        u = DEQUEUE(Q)
12        for each v ∈ G.Adj[u]
13             if v.color == WHITE
14                  v.color = GRAY
15                  v.d = u.d + 1
16                  v.π = u
17                  ENQUEUE(Q, v)
18        u.color = BLACK
```

Figure 22.3 illustrates the progress of BFS on a sample graph.

The procedure BFS works as follows. With the exception of the source vertex s, lines 1–4 paint every vertex white, set $u.d$ to be infinity for each vertex u, and set the parent of every vertex to be NIL. Line 5 paints s gray, since we consider it to be discovered as the procedure begins. Line 6 initializes $s.d$ to 0, and line 7 sets the predecessor of the source to be NIL. Lines 8–9 initialize Q to the queue containing just the vertex s.

The **while** loop of lines 10–18 iterates as long as there remain gray vertices, which are discovered vertices that have not yet had their adjacency lists fully examined. This **while** loop maintains the following invariant:

At the test in line 10, the queue Q consists of the set of gray vertices.

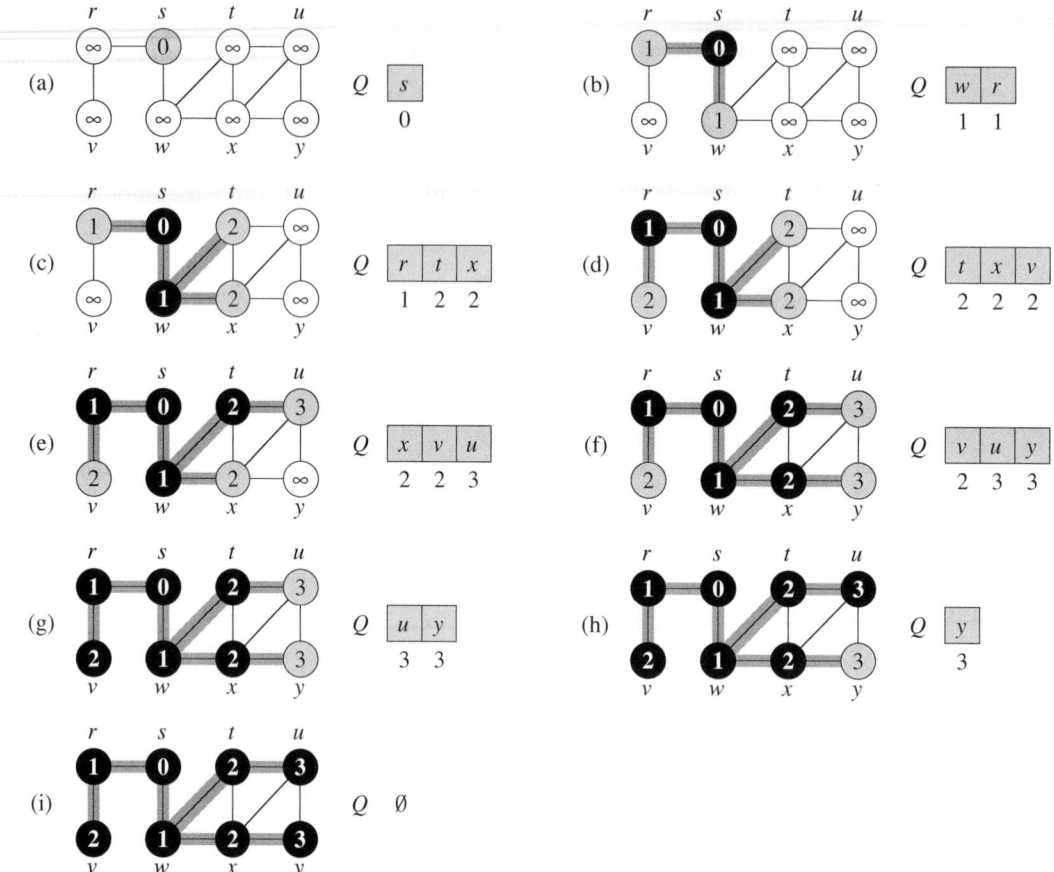

Figure 22.3 The operation of BFS on an undirected graph. Tree edges are shown shaded as they are produced by BFS. The value of $u.d$ appears within each vertex u. The queue Q is shown at the beginning of each iteration of the **while** loop of lines 10–18. Vertex distances appear below vertices in the queue.

Although we won't use this loop invariant to prove correctness, it is easy to see that it holds prior to the first iteration and that each iteration of the loop maintains the invariant. Prior to the first iteration, the only gray vertex, and the only vertex in Q, is the source vertex s. Line 11 determines the gray vertex u at the head of the queue Q and removes it from Q. The **for** loop of lines 12–17 considers each vertex v in the adjacency list of u. If v is white, then it has not yet been discovered, and the procedure discovers it by executing lines 14–17. The procedure paints vertex v gray, sets its distance $v.d$ to $u.d+1$, records u as its parent $v.\pi$, and places it at the tail of the queue Q. Once the procedure has examined all the vertices on u's

adjacency list, it blackens u in line 18. The loop invariant is maintained because whenever a vertex is painted gray (in line 14) it is also enqueued (in line 17), and whenever a vertex is dequeued (in line 11) it is also painted black (in line 18).

The results of breadth-first search may depend upon the order in which the neighbors of a given vertex are visited in line 12: the breadth-first tree may vary, but the distances d computed by the algorithm will not. (See Exercise 22.2-5.)

Analysis

Before proving the various properties of breadth-first search, we take on the somewhat easier job of analyzing its running time on an input graph $G = (V, E)$. We use aggregate analysis, as we saw in Section 17.1. After initialization, breadth-first search never whitens a vertex, and thus the test in line 13 ensures that each vertex is enqueued at most once, and hence dequeued at most once. The operations of enqueuing and dequeuing take $O(1)$ time, and so the total time devoted to queue operations is $O(V)$. Because the procedure scans the adjacency list of each vertex only when the vertex is dequeued, it scans each adjacency list at most once. Since the sum of the lengths of all the adjacency lists is $\Theta(E)$, the total time spent in scanning adjacency lists is $O(E)$. The overhead for initialization is $O(V)$, and thus the total running time of the BFS procedure is $O(V + E)$. Thus, breadth-first search runs in time linear in the size of the adjacency-list representation of G.

Shortest paths

At the beginning of this section, we claimed that breadth-first search finds the distance to each reachable vertex in a graph $G = (V, E)$ from a given source vertex $s \in V$. Define the ***shortest-path distance*** $\delta(s, v)$ from s to v as the minimum number of edges in any path from vertex s to vertex v; if there is no path from s to v, then $\delta(s, v) = \infty$. We call a path of length $\delta(s, v)$ from s to v a ***shortest path***[2] from s to v. Before showing that breadth-first search correctly computes shortest-path distances, we investigate an important property of shortest-path distances.

---

[2]In Chapters 24 and 25, we shall generalize our study of shortest paths to weighted graphs, in which every edge has a real-valued weight and the weight of a path is the sum of the weights of its constituent edges. The graphs considered in the present chapter are unweighted or, equivalently, all edges have unit weight.

Lemma 22.1

Let $G = (V, E)$ be a directed or undirected graph, and let $s \in V$ be an arbitrary vertex. Then, for any edge $(u, v) \in E$,

$$\delta(s, v) \leq \delta(s, u) + 1 .$$

Proof   If u is reachable from s, then so is v. In this case, the shortest path from s to v cannot be longer than the shortest path from s to u followed by the edge (u, v), and thus the inequality holds. If u is not reachable from s, then $\delta(s, u) = \infty$, and the inequality holds.   ∎

We want to show that BFS properly computes $v.d = \delta(s, v)$ for each vertex $v \in V$. We first show that $v.d$ bounds $\delta(s, v)$ from above.

Lemma 22.2

Let $G = (V, E)$ be a directed or undirected graph, and suppose that BFS is run on G from a given source vertex $s \in V$. Then upon termination, for each vertex $v \in V$, the value $v.d$ computed by BFS satisfies $v.d \geq \delta(s, v)$.

Proof   We use induction on the number of ENQUEUE operations. Our inductive hypothesis is that $v.d \geq \delta(s, v)$ for all $v \in V$.

The basis of the induction is the situation immediately after enqueuing s in line 9 of BFS. The inductive hypothesis holds here, because $s.d = 0 = \delta(s, s)$ and $v.d = \infty \geq \delta(s, v)$ for all $v \in V - \{s\}$.

For the inductive step, consider a white vertex v that is discovered during the search from a vertex u. The inductive hypothesis implies that $u.d \geq \delta(s, u)$. From the assignment performed by line 15 and from Lemma 22.1, we obtain

$$
\begin{aligned}
v.d &= u.d + 1 \\
&\geq \delta(s, u) + 1 \\
&\geq \delta(s, v) .
\end{aligned}
$$

Vertex v is then enqueued, and it is never enqueued again because it is also grayed and the **then** clause of lines 14–17 is executed only for white vertices. Thus, the value of $v.d$ never changes again, and the inductive hypothesis is maintained.   ∎

To prove that $v.d = \delta(s, v)$, we must first show more precisely how the queue Q operates during the course of BFS. The next lemma shows that at all times, the queue holds at most two distinct d values.

Lemma 22.3
Suppose that during the execution of BFS on a graph $G = (V, E)$, the queue Q contains the vertices $\langle v_1, v_2, \ldots, v_r \rangle$, where v_1 is the head of Q and v_r is the tail. Then, $v_r.d \le v_1.d + 1$ and $v_i.d \le v_{i+1}.d$ for $i = 1, 2, \ldots, r - 1$.

Proof   The proof is by induction on the number of queue operations. Initially, when the queue contains only s, the lemma certainly holds.

For the inductive step, we must prove that the lemma holds after both dequeuing and enqueuing a vertex. If the head v_1 of the queue is dequeued, v_2 becomes the new head. (If the queue becomes empty, then the lemma holds vacuously.) By the inductive hypothesis, $v_1.d \le v_2.d$. But then we have $v_r.d \le v_1.d + 1 \le v_2.d + 1$, and the remaining inequalities are unaffected. Thus, the lemma follows with v_2 as the head.

In order to understand what happens upon enqueuing a vertex, we need to examine the code more closely. When we enqueue a vertex v in line 17 of BFS, it becomes v_{r+1}. At that time, we have already removed vertex u, whose adjacency list is currently being scanned, from the queue Q, and by the inductive hypothesis, the new head v_1 has $v_1.d \ge u.d$. Thus, $v_{r+1}.d = v.d = u.d + 1 \le v_1.d + 1$. From the inductive hypothesis, we also have $v_r.d \le u.d + 1$, and so $v_r.d \le u.d + 1 = v.d = v_{r+1}.d$, and the remaining inequalities are unaffected. Thus, the lemma follows when v is enqueued.   ∎

The following corollary shows that the d values at the time that vertices are enqueued are monotonically increasing over time.

Corollary 22.4
Suppose that vertices v_i and v_j are enqueued during the execution of BFS, and that v_i is enqueued before v_j. Then $v_i.d \le v_j.d$ at the time that v_j is enqueued.

Proof   Immediate from Lemma 22.3 and the property that each vertex receives a finite d value at most once during the course of BFS.   ∎

We can now prove that breadth-first search correctly finds shortest-path distances.

Theorem 22.5 (Correctness of breadth-first search)
Let $G = (V, E)$ be a directed or undirected graph, and suppose that BFS is run on G from a given source vertex $s \in V$. Then, during its execution, BFS discovers every vertex $v \in V$ that is reachable from the source s, and upon termination, $v.d = \delta(s, v)$ for all $v \in V$. Moreover, for any vertex $v \ne s$ that is reachable

from s, one of the shortest paths from s to v is a shortest path from s to $v.\pi$ followed by the edge $(v.\pi, v)$.

Proof Assume, for the purpose of contradiction, that some vertex receives a d value not equal to its shortest-path distance. Let v be the vertex with minimum $\delta(s, v)$ that receives such an incorrect d value; clearly $v \neq s$. By Lemma 22.2, $v.d \geq \delta(s, v)$, and thus we have that $v.d > \delta(s, v)$. Vertex v must be reachable from s, for if it is not, then $\delta(s, v) = \infty \geq v.d$. Let u be the vertex immediately preceding v on a shortest path from s to v, so that $\delta(s, v) = \delta(s, u) + 1$. Because $\delta(s, u) < \delta(s, v)$, and because of how we chose v, we have $u.d = \delta(s, u)$. Putting these properties together, we have

$$v.d > \delta(s, v) = \delta(s, u) + 1 = u.d + 1 . \tag{22.1}$$

Now consider the time when BFS chooses to dequeue vertex u from Q in line 11. At this time, vertex v is either white, gray, or black. We shall show that in each of these cases, we derive a contradiction to inequality (22.1). If v is white, then line 15 sets $v.d = u.d + 1$, contradicting inequality (22.1). If v is black, then it was already removed from the queue and, by Corollary 22.4, we have $v.d \leq u.d$, again contradicting inequality (22.1). If v is gray, then it was painted gray upon dequeuing some vertex w, which was removed from Q earlier than u and for which $v.d = w.d + 1$. By Corollary 22.4, however, $w.d \leq u.d$, and so we have $v.d = w.d + 1 \leq u.d + 1$, once again contradicting inequality (22.1).

Thus we conclude that $v.d = \delta(s, v)$ for all $v \in V$. All vertices v reachable from s must be discovered, for otherwise they would have $\infty = v.d > \delta(s, v)$. To conclude the proof of the theorem, observe that if $v.\pi = u$, then $v.d = u.d + 1$. Thus, we can obtain a shortest path from s to v by taking a shortest path from s to $v.\pi$ and then traversing the edge $(v.\pi, v)$.   ∎

Breadth-first trees

The procedure BFS builds a breadth-first tree as it searches the graph, as Figure 22.3 illustrates. The tree corresponds to the π attributes. More formally, for a graph $G = (V, E)$ with source s, we define the ***predecessor subgraph*** of G as $G_\pi = (V_\pi, E_\pi)$, where

$$V_\pi = \{v \in V : v.\pi \neq \text{NIL}\} \cup \{s\}$$

and

$$E_\pi = \{(v.\pi, v) : v \in V_\pi - \{s\}\} .$$

The predecessor subgraph G_π is a ***breadth-first tree*** if V_π consists of the vertices reachable from s and, for all $v \in V_\pi$, the subgraph G_π contains a unique simple

path from s to v that is also a shortest path from s to v in G. A breadth-first tree is in fact a tree, since it is connected and $|E_\pi| = |V_\pi| - 1$ (see Theorem B.2). We call the edges in E_π **tree edges**.

The following lemma shows that the predecessor subgraph produced by the BFS procedure is a breadth-first tree.

Lemma 22.6
When applied to a directed or undirected graph $G = (V, E)$, procedure BFS constructs π so that the predecessor subgraph $G_\pi = (V_\pi, E_\pi)$ is a breadth-first tree.

Proof Line 16 of BFS sets $v.\pi = u$ if and only if $(u, v) \in E$ and $\delta(s, v) < \infty$—that is, if v is reachable from s—and thus V_π consists of the vertices in V reachable from s. Since G_π forms a tree, by Theorem B.2, it contains a unique simple path from s to each vertex in V_π. By applying Theorem 22.5 inductively, we conclude that every such path is a shortest path in G. ∎

The following procedure prints out the vertices on a shortest path from s to v, assuming that BFS has already computed a breadth-first tree:

PRINT-PATH(G, s, v)

```
1  if v == s
2      print s
3  elseif v.π == NIL
4      print "no path from" s "to" v "exists"
5  else PRINT-PATH(G, s, v.π)
6      print v
```

This procedure runs in time linear in the number of vertices in the path printed, since each recursive call is for a path one vertex shorter.

Exercises

22.2-1
Show the d and π values that result from running breadth-first search on the directed graph of Figure 22.2(a), using vertex 3 as the source.

22.2-2
Show the d and π values that result from running breadth-first search on the undirected graph of Figure 22.3, using vertex u as the source.

22.2-3

Show that using a single bit to store each vertex color suffices by arguing that the BFS procedure would produce the same result if line 18 were removed.

22.2-4

What is the running time of BFS if we represent its input graph by an adjacency matrix and modify the algorithm to handle this form of input?

22.2-5

Argue that in a breadth-first search, the value $u.d$ assigned to a vertex u is independent of the order in which the vertices appear in each adjacency list. Using Figure 22.3 as an example, show that the breadth-first tree computed by BFS can depend on the ordering within adjacency lists.

22.2-6

Give an example of a directed graph $G = (V, E)$, a source vertex $s \in V$, and a set of tree edges $E_\pi \subseteq E$ such that for each vertex $v \in V$, the unique simple path in the graph (V, E_π) from s to v is a shortest path in G, yet the set of edges E_π cannot be produced by running BFS on G, no matter how the vertices are ordered in each adjacency list.

22.2-7

There are two types of professional wrestlers: "babyfaces" ("good guys") and "heels" ("bad guys"). Between any pair of professional wrestlers, there may or may not be a rivalry. Suppose we have n professional wrestlers and we have a list of r pairs of wrestlers for which there are rivalries. Give an $O(n + r)$-time algorithm that determines whether it is possible to designate some of the wrestlers as babyfaces and the remainder as heels such that each rivalry is between a babyface and a heel. If it is possible to perform such a designation, your algorithm should produce it.

22.2-8 ★

The *diameter* of a tree $T = (V, E)$ is defined as $\max_{u,v \in V} \delta(u, v)$, that is, the largest of all shortest-path distances in the tree. Give an efficient algorithm to compute the diameter of a tree, and analyze the running time of your algorithm.

22.2-9

Let $G = (V, E)$ be a connected, undirected graph. Give an $O(V + E)$-time algorithm to compute a path in G that traverses each edge in E exactly once in each direction. Describe how you can find your way out of a maze if you are given a large supply of pennies.

22.3 Depth-first search

The strategy followed by depth-first search is, as its name implies, to search "deeper" in the graph whenever possible. Depth-first search explores edges out of the most recently discovered vertex v that still has unexplored edges leaving it. Once all of v's edges have been explored, the search "backtracks" to explore edges leaving the vertex from which v was discovered. This process continues until we have discovered all the vertices that are reachable from the original source vertex. If any undiscovered vertices remain, then depth-first search selects one of them as a new source, and it repeats the search from that source. The algorithm repeats this entire process until it has discovered every vertex.[3]

As in breadth-first search, whenever depth-first search discovers a vertex v during a scan of the adjacency list of an already discovered vertex u, it records this event by setting v's predecessor attribute $v.\pi$ to u. Unlike breadth-first search, whose predecessor subgraph forms a tree, the predecessor subgraph produced by a depth-first search may be composed of several trees, because the search may repeat from multiple sources. Therefore, we define the *predecessor subgraph* of a depth-first search slightly differently from that of a breadth-first search: we let $G_\pi = (V, E_\pi)$, where

$$E_\pi = \{(v.\pi, v) : v \in V \text{ and } v.\pi \neq \text{NIL}\} \ .$$

The predecessor subgraph of a depth-first search forms a *depth-first forest* comprising several *depth-first trees*. The edges in E_π are *tree edges*.

As in breadth-first search, depth-first search colors vertices during the search to indicate their state. Each vertex is initially white, is grayed when it is *discovered* in the search, and is blackened when it is *finished*, that is, when its adjacency list has been examined completely. This technique guarantees that each vertex ends up in exactly one depth-first tree, so that these trees are disjoint.

Besides creating a depth-first forest, depth-first search also *timestamps* each vertex. Each vertex v has two timestamps: the first timestamp $v.d$ records when v is first discovered (and grayed), and the second timestamp $v.f$ records when the search finishes examining v's adjacency list (and blackens v). These timestamps

---

[3]It may seem arbitrary that breadth-first search is limited to only one source whereas depth-first search may search from multiple sources. Although conceptually, breadth-first search could proceed from multiple sources and depth-first search could be limited to one source, our approach reflects how the results of these searches are typically used. Breadth-first search usually serves to find shortest-path distances (and the associated predecessor subgraph) from a given source. Depth-first search is often a subroutine in another algorithm, as we shall see later in this chapter.

provide important information about the structure of the graph and are generally helpful in reasoning about the behavior of depth-first search.

The procedure DFS below records when it discovers vertex u in the attribute $u.d$ and when it finishes vertex u in the attribute $u.f$. These timestamps are integers between 1 and $2|V|$, since there is one discovery event and one finishing event for each of the $|V|$ vertices. For every vertex u,

$$u.d < u.f . \tag{22.2}$$

Vertex u is WHITE before time $u.d$, GRAY between time $u.d$ and time $u.f$, and BLACK thereafter.

The following pseudocode is the basic depth-first-search algorithm. The input graph G may be undirected or directed. The variable *time* is a global variable that we use for timestamping.

DFS(G)

```
1   for each vertex u ∈ G.V
2       u.color = WHITE
3       u.π = NIL
4   time = 0
5   for each vertex u ∈ G.V
6       if u.color == WHITE
7           DFS-VISIT(G, u)
```

DFS-VISIT(G, u)

```
 1   time = time + 1          // white vertex u has just been discovered
 2   u.d = time
 3   u.color = GRAY
 4   for each v ∈ G.Adj[u]    // explore edge (u, v)
 5       if v.color == WHITE
 6           v.π = u
 7           DFS-VISIT(G, v)
 8   u.color = BLACK          // blacken u; it is finished
 9   time = time + 1
10   u.f = time
```

Figure 22.4 illustrates the progress of DFS on the graph shown in Figure 22.2.

Procedure DFS works as follows. Lines 1–3 paint all vertices white and initialize their π attributes to NIL. Line 4 resets the global time counter. Lines 5–7 check each vertex in V in turn and, when a white vertex is found, visit it using DFS-VISIT. Every time DFS-VISIT(G, u) is called in line 7, vertex u becomes

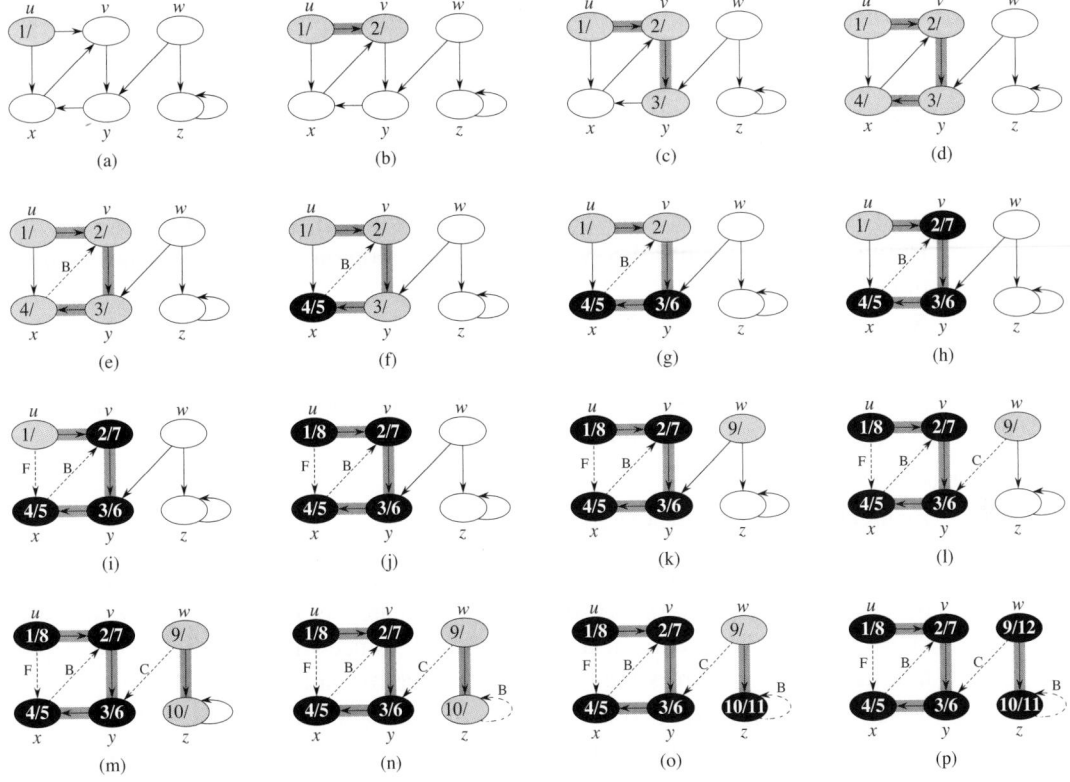

Figure 22.4 The progress of the depth-first-search algorithm DFS on a directed graph. As edges are explored by the algorithm, they are shown as either shaded (if they are tree edges) or dashed (otherwise). Nontree edges are labeled B, C, or F according to whether they are back, cross, or forward edges. Timestamps within vertices indicate discovery time/finishing times.

the root of a new tree in the depth-first forest. When DFS returns, every vertex u has been assigned a *discovery time* $u.d$ and a *finishing time* $u.f$.

In each call DFS-VISIT(G, u), vertex u is initially white. Line 1 increments the global variable *time*, line 2 records the new value of *time* as the discovery time $u.d$, and line 3 paints u gray. Lines 4–7 examine each vertex v adjacent to u and recursively visit v if it is white. As each vertex $v \in Adj[u]$ is considered in line 4, we say that edge (u, v) is *explored* by the depth-first search. Finally, after every edge leaving u has been explored, lines 8–10 paint u black, increment *time*, and record the finishing time in $u.f$.

Note that the results of depth-first search may depend upon the order in which line 5 of DFS examines the vertices and upon the order in which line 4 of DFS-VISIT visits the neighbors of a vertex. These different visitation orders tend not

to cause problems in practice, as we can usually use *any* depth-first search result effectively, with essentially equivalent results.

What is the running time of DFS? The loops on lines 1–3 and lines 5–7 of DFS take time $\Theta(V)$, exclusive of the time to execute the calls to DFS-VISIT. As we did for breadth-first search, we use aggregate analysis. The procedure DFS-VISIT is called exactly once for each vertex $v \in V$, since the vertex u on which DFS-VISIT is invoked must be white and the first thing DFS-VISIT does is paint vertex u gray. During an execution of DFS-VISIT(G, v), the loop on lines 4–7 executes $|Adj[v]|$ times. Since

$$\sum_{v \in V} |Adj[v]| = \Theta(E) \,,$$

the total cost of executing lines 4–7 of DFS-VISIT is $\Theta(E)$. The running time of DFS is therefore $\Theta(V + E)$.

Properties of depth-first search

Depth-first search yields valuable information about the structure of a graph. Perhaps the most basic property of depth-first search is that the predecessor subgraph G_π does indeed form a forest of trees, since the structure of the depth-first trees exactly mirrors the structure of recursive calls of DFS-VISIT. That is, $u = v.\pi$ if and only if DFS-VISIT(G, v) was called during a search of u's adjacency list. Additionally, vertex v is a descendant of vertex u in the depth-first forest if and only if v is discovered during the time in which u is gray.

Another important property of depth-first search is that discovery and finishing times have **parenthesis structure**. If we represent the discovery of vertex u with a left parenthesis "(u" and represent its finishing by a right parenthesis "u)", then the history of discoveries and finishings makes a well-formed expression in the sense that the parentheses are properly nested. For example, the depth-first search of Figure 22.5(a) corresponds to the parenthesization shown in Figure 22.5(b). The following theorem provides another way to characterize the parenthesis structure.

Theorem 22.7 (Parenthesis theorem)
In any depth-first search of a (directed or undirected) graph $G = (V, E)$, for any two vertices u and v, exactly one of the following three conditions holds:

- the intervals $[u.d, u.f]$ and $[v.d, v.f]$ are entirely disjoint, and neither u nor v is a descendant of the other in the depth-first forest,

- the interval $[u.d, u.f]$ is contained entirely within the interval $[v.d, v.f]$, and u is a descendant of v in a depth-first tree, or

- the interval $[v.d, v.f]$ is contained entirely within the interval $[u.d, u.f]$, and v is a descendant of u in a depth-first tree.

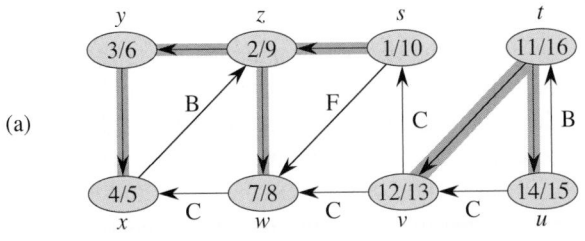

(a)

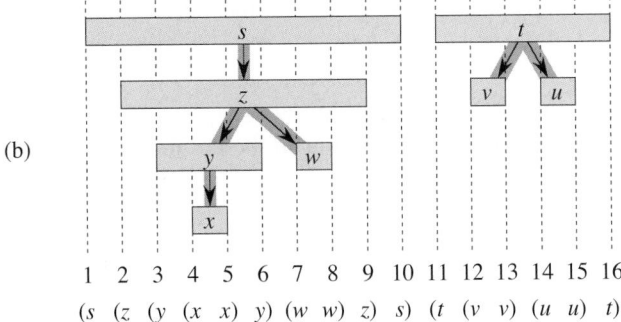

(b)

1   2   3   4   5   6   7   8   9   10 11 12 13 14 15 16

(s   (z   (y   (x   x)   y)   (w   w)   z)   s)   (t   (v   v)   (u   u)   t)

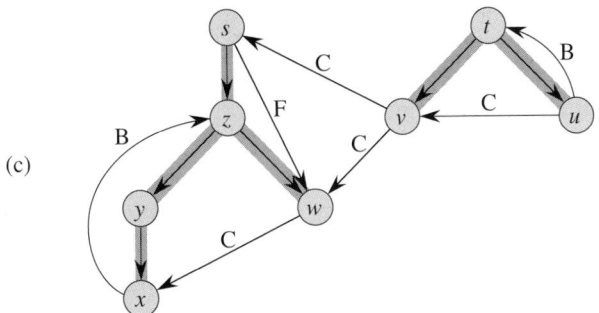

(c)

Figure 22.5   Properties of depth-first search. **(a)** The result of a depth-first search of a directed graph. Vertices are timestamped and edge types are indicated as in Figure 22.4. **(b)** Intervals for the discovery time and finishing time of each vertex correspond to the parenthesization shown. Each rectangle spans the interval given by the discovery and finishing times of the corresponding vertex. Only tree edges are shown. If two intervals overlap, then one is nested within the other, and the vertex corresponding to the smaller interval is a descendant of the vertex corresponding to the larger. **(c)** The graph of part (a) redrawn with all tree and forward edges going down within a depth-first tree and all back edges going up from a descendant to an ancestor.

Proof   We begin with the case in which $u.d < v.d$. We consider two subcases, according to whether $v.d < u.f$ or not. The first subcase occurs when $v.d < u.f$, so v was discovered while u was still gray, which implies that v is a descendant of u. Moreover, since v was discovered more recently than u, all of its outgoing edges are explored, and v is finished, before the search returns to and finishes u. In this case, therefore, the interval $[v.d, v.f]$ is entirely contained within the interval $[u.d, u.f]$. In the other subcase, $u.f < v.d$, and by inequality (22.2), $u.d < u.f < v.d < v.f$; thus the intervals $[u.d, u.f]$ and $[v.d, v.f]$ are disjoint. Because the intervals are disjoint, neither vertex was discovered while the other was gray, and so neither vertex is a descendant of the other.

The case in which $v.d < u.d$ is similar, with the roles of u and v reversed in the above argument.   ∎

Corollary 22.8 (Nesting of descendants' intervals)
Vertex v is a proper descendant of vertex u in the depth-first forest for a (directed or undirected) graph G if and only if $u.d < v.d < v.f < u.f$.

Proof   Immediate from Theorem 22.7.   ∎

The next theorem gives another important characterization of when one vertex is a descendant of another in the depth-first forest.

Theorem 22.9 (White-path theorem)
In a depth-first forest of a (directed or undirected) graph $G = (V, E)$, vertex v is a descendant of vertex u if and only if at the time $u.d$ that the search discovers u, there is a path from u to v consisting entirely of white vertices.

Proof   ⇒: If $v = u$, then the path from u to v contains just vertex u, which is still white when we set the value of $u.d$. Now, suppose that v is a proper descendant of u in the depth-first forest. By Corollary 22.8, $u.d < v.d$, and so v is white at time $u.d$. Since v can be any descendant of u, all vertices on the unique simple path from u to v in the depth-first forest are white at time $u.d$.

⇐: Suppose that there is a path of white vertices from u to v at time $u.d$, but v does not become a descendant of u in the depth-first tree. Without loss of generality, assume that every vertex other than v along the path becomes a descendant of u. (Otherwise, let v be the closest vertex to u along the path that doesn't become a descendant of u.) Let w be the predecessor of v in the path, so that w is a descendant of u (w and u may in fact be the same vertex). By Corollary 22.8, $w.f \le u.f$. Because v must be discovered after u is discovered, but before w is finished, we have $u.d < v.d < w.f \le u.f$. Theorem 22.7 then implies that the interval $[v.d, v.f]$

is contained entirely within the interval $[u.d, u.f]$. By Corollary 22.8, v must after all be a descendant of u.   ∎

Classification of edges

Another interesting property of depth-first search is that the search can be used to classify the edges of the input graph $G = (V, E)$. The type of each edge can provide important information about a graph. For example, in the next section, we shall see that a directed graph is acyclic if and only if a depth-first search yields no "back" edges (Lemma 22.11).

We can define four edge types in terms of the depth-first forest G_π produced by a depth-first search on G:

1. **Tree edges** are edges in the depth-first forest G_π. Edge (u, v) is a tree edge if v was first discovered by exploring edge (u, v).

2. **Back edges** are those edges (u, v) connecting a vertex u to an ancestor v in a depth-first tree. We consider self-loops, which may occur in directed graphs, to be back edges.

3. **Forward edges** are those nontree edges (u, v) connecting a vertex u to a descendant v in a depth-first tree.

4. **Cross edges** are all other edges. They can go between vertices in the same depth-first tree, as long as one vertex is not an ancestor of the other, or they can go between vertices in different depth-first trees.

In Figures 22.4 and 22.5, edge labels indicate edge types. Figure 22.5(c) also shows how to redraw the graph of Figure 22.5(a) so that all tree and forward edges head downward in a depth-first tree and all back edges go up. We can redraw any graph in this fashion.

The DFS algorithm has enough information to classify some edges as it encounters them. The key idea is that when we first explore an edge (u, v), the color of vertex v tells us something about the edge:

1. WHITE indicates a tree edge,

2. GRAY indicates a back edge, and

3. BLACK indicates a forward or cross edge.

The first case is immediate from the specification of the algorithm. For the second case, observe that the gray vertices always form a linear chain of descendants corresponding to the stack of active DFS-VISIT invocations; the number of gray vertices is one more than the depth in the depth-first forest of the vertex most recently discovered. Exploration always proceeds from the deepest gray vertex, so

an edge that reaches another gray vertex has reached an ancestor. The third case handles the remaining possibility; Exercise 22.3-5 asks you to show that such an edge (u, v) is a forward edge if $u.d < v.d$ and a cross edge if $u.d > v.d$.

An undirected graph may entail some ambiguity in how we classify edges, since (u, v) and (v, u) are really the same edge. In such a case, we classify the edge as the *first* type in the classification list that applies. Equivalently (see Exercise 22.3-6), we classify the edge according to whichever of (u, v) or (v, u) the search encounters first.

We now show that forward and cross edges never occur in a depth-first search of an undirected graph.

Theorem 22.10
In a depth-first search of an undirected graph G, every edge of G is either a tree edge or a back edge.

Proof   Let (u, v) be an arbitrary edge of G, and suppose without loss of generality that $u.d < v.d$. Then the search must discover and finish v before it finishes u (while u is gray), since v is on u's adjacency list. If the first time that the search explores edge (u, v), it is in the direction from u to v, then v is undiscovered (white) until that time, for otherwise the search would have explored this edge already in the direction from v to u. Thus, (u, v) becomes a tree edge. If the search explores (u, v) first in the direction from v to u, then (u, v) is a back edge, since u is still gray at the time the edge is first explored.   ■

We shall see several applications of these theorems in the following sections.

Exercises

22.3-1
Make a 3-by-3 chart with row and column labels WHITE, GRAY, and BLACK. In each cell (i, j), indicate whether, at any point during a depth-first search of a directed graph, there can be an edge from a vertex of color i to a vertex of color j. For each possible edge, indicate what edge types it can be. Make a second such chart for depth-first search of an undirected graph.

22.3-2
Show how depth-first search works on the graph of Figure 22.6. Assume that the **for** loop of lines 5–7 of the DFS procedure considers the vertices in alphabetical order, and assume that each adjacency list is ordered alphabetically. Show the discovery and finishing times for each vertex, and show the classification of each edge.

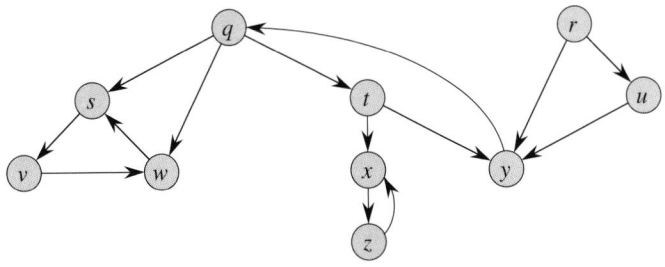

Figure 22.6   A directed graph for use in Exercises 22.3-2 and 22.5-2.

22.3-3
Show the parenthesis structure of the depth-first search of Figure 22.4.

22.3-4
Show that using a single bit to store each vertex color suffices by arguing that the DFS procedure would produce the same result if line 8 of DFS-VISIT was removed.

22.3-5
Show that edge (u, v) is

a. a tree edge or forward edge if and only if $u.d < v.d < v.f < u.f$,

b. a back edge if and only if $v.d \leq u.d < u.f \leq v.f$, and

c. a cross edge if and only if $v.d < v.f < u.d < u.f$.

22.3-6
Show that in an undirected graph, classifying an edge (u, v) as a tree edge or a back edge according to whether (u, v) or (v, u) is encountered first during the depth-first search is equivalent to classifying it according to the ordering of the four types in the classification scheme.

22.3-7
Rewrite the procedure DFS, using a stack to eliminate recursion.

22.3-8
Give a counterexample to the conjecture that if a directed graph G contains a path from u to v, and if $u.d < v.d$ in a depth-first search of G, then v is a descendant of u in the depth-first forest produced.

22.3-9
Give a counterexample to the conjecture that if a directed graph G contains a path from u to v, then any depth-first search must result in $v.d \leq u.f$.

22.3-10
Modify the pseudocode for depth-first search so that it prints out every edge in the directed graph G, together with its type. Show what modifications, if any, you need to make if G is undirected.

22.3-11
Explain how a vertex u of a directed graph can end up in a depth-first tree containing only u, even though u has both incoming and outgoing edges in G.

22.3-12
Show that we can use a depth-first search of an undirected graph G to identify the connected components of G, and that the depth-first forest contains as many trees as G has connected components. More precisely, show how to modify depth-first search so that it assigns to each vertex v an integer label $v.cc$ between 1 and k, where k is the number of connected components of G, such that $u.cc = v.cc$ if and only if u and v are in the same connected component.

22.3-13 ★
A directed graph $G = (V, E)$ is ***singly connected*** if $u \rightsquigarrow v$ implies that G contains at most one simple path from u to v for all vertices $u, v \in V$. Give an efficient algorithm to determine whether or not a directed graph is singly connected.

22.4   Topological sort

This section shows how we can use depth-first search to perform a topological sort of a directed acyclic graph, or a "dag" as it is sometimes called. A ***topological sort*** of a dag $G = (V, E)$ is a linear ordering of all its vertices such that if G contains an edge (u, v), then u appears before v in the ordering. (If the graph contains a cycle, then no linear ordering is possible.) We can view a topological sort of a graph as an ordering of its vertices along a horizontal line so that all directed edges go from left to right. Topological sorting is thus different from the usual kind of "sorting" studied in Part II.

Many applications use directed acyclic graphs to indicate precedences among events. Figure 22.7 gives an example that arises when Professor Bumstead gets dressed in the morning. The professor must don certain garments before others (e.g., socks before shoes). Other items may be put on in any order (e.g., socks and

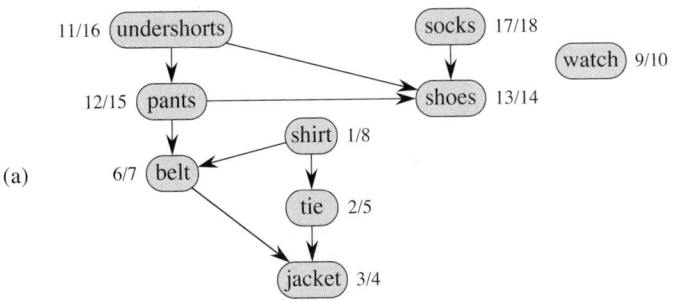

(a)

(b)

Figure 22.7   **(a)** Professor Bumstead topologically sorts his clothing when getting dressed. Each directed edge (u, v) means that garment u must be put on before garment v. The discovery and finishing times from a depth-first search are shown next to each vertex. **(b)** The same graph shown topologically sorted, with its vertices arranged from left to right in order of decreasing finishing time. All directed edges go from left to right.

pants). A directed edge (u, v) in the dag of Figure 22.7(a) indicates that garment u must be donned before garment v. A topological sort of this dag therefore gives an order for getting dressed. Figure 22.7(b) shows the topologically sorted dag as an ordering of vertices along a horizontal line such that all directed edges go from left to right.

The following simple algorithm topologically sorts a dag:

TOPOLOGICAL-SORT(G)

1   call DFS(G) to compute finishing times $v.f$ for each vertex v
2   as each vertex is finished, insert it onto the front of a linked list
3   **return** the linked list of vertices

Figure 22.7(b) shows how the topologically sorted vertices appear in reverse order of their finishing times.

We can perform a topological sort in time $\Theta(V + E)$, since depth-first search takes $\Theta(V + E)$ time and it takes $O(1)$ time to insert each of the $|V|$ vertices onto the front of the linked list.

We prove the correctness of this algorithm using the following key lemma characterizing directed acyclic graphs.

Lemma 22.11

A directed graph G is acyclic if and only if a depth-first search of G yields no back edges.

Proof $\Rightarrow$: Suppose that a depth-first search produces a back edge (u, v). Then vertex v is an ancestor of vertex u in the depth-first forest. Thus, G contains a path from v to u, and the back edge (u, v) completes a cycle.

$\Leftarrow$: Suppose that G contains a cycle c. We show that a depth-first search of G yields a back edge. Let v be the first vertex to be discovered in c, and let (u, v) be the preceding edge in c. At time $v.d$, the vertices of c form a path of white vertices from v to u. By the white-path theorem, vertex u becomes a descendant of v in the depth-first forest. Therefore, (u, v) is a back edge. ∎

Theorem 22.12

TOPOLOGICAL-SORT produces a topological sort of the directed acyclic graph provided as its input.

Proof Suppose that DFS is run on a given dag $G = (V, E)$ to determine finishing times for its vertices. It suffices to show that for any pair of distinct vertices $u, v \in V$, if G contains an edge from u to v, then $v.f < u.f$. Consider any edge (u, v) explored by $\text{DFS}(G)$. When this edge is explored, v cannot be gray, since then v would be an ancestor of u and (u, v) would be a back edge, contradicting Lemma 22.11. Therefore, v must be either white or black. If v is white, it becomes a descendant of u, and so $v.f < u.f$. If v is black, it has already been finished, so that $v.f$ has already been set. Because we are still exploring from u, we have yet to assign a timestamp to $u.f$, and so once we do, we will have $v.f < u.f$ as well. Thus, for any edge (u, v) in the dag, we have $v.f < u.f$, proving the theorem. ∎

Exercises

22.4-1

Show the ordering of vertices produced by TOPOLOGICAL-SORT when it is run on the dag of Figure 22.8, under the assumption of Exercise 22.3-2.

22.4-2

Give a linear-time algorithm that takes as input a directed acyclic graph $G = (V, E)$ and two vertices s and t, and returns the number of simple paths from s to t in G. For example, the directed acyclic graph of Figure 22.8 contains exactly four simple paths from vertex p to vertex v: pov, $poryv$, $posryv$, and $psryv$. (Your algorithm needs only to count the simple paths, not list them.)

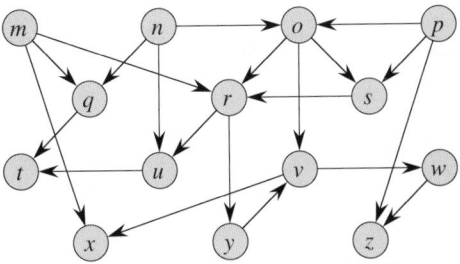

Figure 22.8 A dag for topological sorting.

22.4-3
Give an algorithm that determines whether or not a given undirected graph $G = (V, E)$ contains a simple cycle. Your algorithm should run in $O(V)$ time, independent of $|E|$.

22.4-4
Prove or disprove: If a directed graph G contains cycles, then TOPOLOGICAL-SORT(G) produces a vertex ordering that minimizes the number of "bad" edges that are inconsistent with the ordering produced.

22.4-5
Another way to perform topological sorting on a directed acyclic graph $G = (V, E)$ is to repeatedly find a vertex of in-degree 0, output it, and remove it and all of its outgoing edges from the graph. Explain how to implement this idea so that it runs in time $O(V + E)$. What happens to this algorithm if G has cycles?

22.5 Strongly connected components

We now consider a classic application of depth-first search: decomposing a directed graph into its strongly connected components. This section shows how to do so using two depth-first searches. Many algorithms that work with directed graphs begin with such a decomposition. After decomposing the graph into strongly connected components, such algorithms run separately on each one and then combine the solutions according to the structure of connections among components.

Recall from Appendix B that a strongly connected component of a directed graph $G = (V, E)$ is a maximal set of vertices $C \subseteq V$ such that for every pair of vertices u and v in C, we have both $u \rightsquigarrow v$ and $v \rightsquigarrow u$; that is, vertices u and v are reachable from each other. Figure 22.9 shows an example.

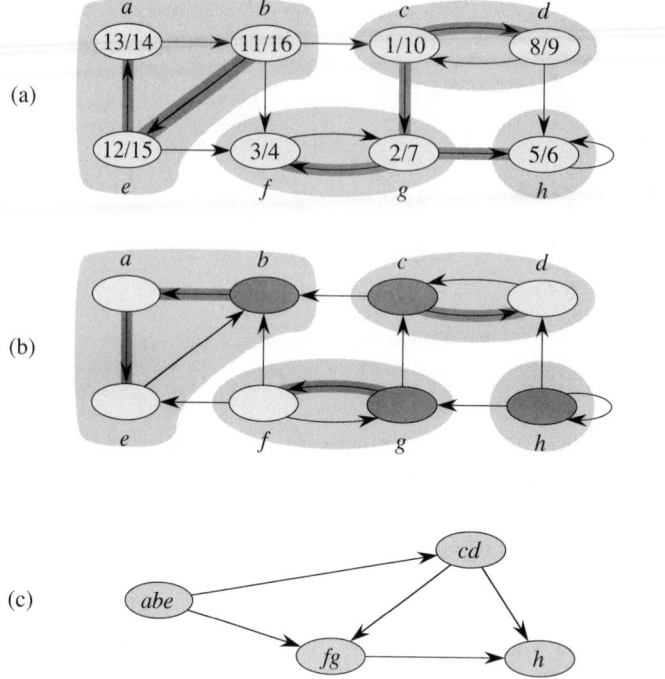

Figure 22.9 **(a)** A directed graph G. Each shaded region is a strongly connected component of G. Each vertex is labeled with its discovery and finishing times in a depth-first search, and tree edges are shaded. **(b)** The graph G^T, the transpose of G, with the depth-first forest computed in line 3 of STRONGLY-CONNECTED-COMPONENTS shown and tree edges shaded. Each strongly connected component corresponds to one depth-first tree. Vertices b, c, g, and h, which are heavily shaded, are the roots of the depth-first trees produced by the depth-first search of G^T. **(c)** The acyclic component graph G^{SCC} obtained by contracting all edges within each strongly connected component of G so that only a single vertex remains in each component.

Our algorithm for finding strongly connected components of a graph $G = (V, E)$ uses the transpose of G, which we defined in Exercise 22.1-3 to be the graph $G^T = (V, E^T)$, where $E^T = \{(u, v) : (v, u) \in E\}$. That is, E^T consists of the edges of G with their directions reversed. Given an adjacency-list representation of G, the time to create G^T is $O(V + E)$. It is interesting to observe that G and G^T have exactly the same strongly connected components: u and v are reachable from each other in G if and only if they are reachable from each other in G^T. Figure 22.9(b) shows the transpose of the graph in Figure 22.9(a), with the strongly connected components shaded.

The following linear-time (i.e., $\Theta(V+E)$-time) algorithm computes the strongly connected components of a directed graph $G = (V, E)$ using two depth-first searches, one on G and one on G^{T}.

STRONGLY-CONNECTED-COMPONENTS(G)

1   call DFS(G) to compute finishing times $u.f$ for each vertex u
2   compute G^{T}
3   call DFS(G^{T}), but in the main loop of DFS, consider the vertices
         in order of decreasing $u.f$ (as computed in line 1)
4   output the vertices of each tree in the depth-first forest formed in line 3 as a
         separate strongly connected component

The idea behind this algorithm comes from a key property of the *component graph* $G^{\mathrm{SCC}} = (V^{\mathrm{SCC}}, E^{\mathrm{SCC}})$, which we define as follows. Suppose that G has strongly connected components $C_1, C_2, \ldots, C_k$. The vertex set V^{SCC} is $\{v_1, v_2, \ldots, v_k\}$, and it contains a vertex v_i for each strongly connected component C_i of G. There is an edge $(v_i, v_j) \in E^{\mathrm{SCC}}$ if G contains a directed edge (x, y) for some $x \in C_i$ and some $y \in C_j$. Looked at another way, by contracting all edges whose incident vertices are within the same strongly connected component of G, the resulting graph is G^{SCC}. Figure 22.9(c) shows the component graph of the graph in Figure 22.9(a).

The key property is that the component graph is a dag, which the following lemma implies.

Lemma 22.13
Let C and C' be distinct strongly connected components in directed graph $G = (V, E)$, let $u, v \in C$, let $u', v' \in C'$, and suppose that G contains a path $u \rightsquigarrow u'$. Then G cannot also contain a path $v' \rightsquigarrow v$.

Proof   If G contains a path $v' \rightsquigarrow v$, then it contains paths $u \rightsquigarrow u' \rightsquigarrow v'$ and $v' \rightsquigarrow v \rightsquigarrow u$. Thus, u and v' are reachable from each other, thereby contradicting the assumption that C and C' are distinct strongly connected components.   ∎

We shall see that by considering vertices in the second depth-first search in decreasing order of the finishing times that were computed in the first depth-first search, we are, in essence, visiting the vertices of the component graph (each of which corresponds to a strongly connected component of G) in topologically sorted order.

Because the STRONGLY-CONNECTED-COMPONENTS procedure performs two depth-first searches, there is the potential for ambiguity when we discuss $u.d$ or $u.f$. In this section, these values always refer to the discovery and finishing times as computed by the first call of DFS, in line 1.

We extend the notation for discovery and finishing times to sets of vertices. If $U \subseteq V$, then we define $d(U) = \min_{u \in U} \{u.d\}$ and $f(U) = \max_{u \in U} \{u.f\}$. That is, $d(U)$ and $f(U)$ are the earliest discovery time and latest finishing time, respectively, of any vertex in U.

The following lemma and its corollary give a key property relating strongly connected components and finishing times in the first depth-first search.

Lemma 22.14
Let C and C' be distinct strongly connected components in directed graph $G = (V, E)$. Suppose that there is an edge $(u, v) \in E$, where $u \in C$ and $v \in C'$. Then $f(C) > f(C')$.

Proof   We consider two cases, depending on which strongly connected component, C or C', had the first discovered vertex during the depth-first search.

If $d(C) < d(C')$, let x be the first vertex discovered in C. At time $x.d$, all vertices in C and C' are white. At that time, G contains a path from x to each vertex in C consisting only of white vertices. Because $(u, v) \in E$, for any vertex $w \in C'$, there is also a path in G at time $x.d$ from x to w consisting only of white vertices: $x \rightsquigarrow u \rightarrow v \rightsquigarrow w$. By the white-path theorem, all vertices in C and C' become descendants of x in the depth-first tree. By Corollary 22.8, x has the latest finishing time of any of its descendants, and so $x.f = f(C) > f(C')$.

If instead we have $d(C) > d(C')$, let y be the first vertex discovered in C'. At time $y.d$, all vertices in C' are white and G contains a path from y to each vertex in C' consisting only of white vertices. By the white-path theorem, all vertices in C' become descendants of y in the depth-first tree, and by Corollary 22.8, $y.f = f(C')$. At time $y.d$, all vertices in C are white. Since there is an edge (u, v) from C to C', Lemma 22.13 implies that there cannot be a path from C' to C. Hence, no vertex in C is reachable from y. At time $y.f$, therefore, all vertices in C are still white. Thus, for any vertex $w \in C$, we have $w.f > y.f$, which implies that $f(C) > f(C')$.   ∎

The following corollary tells us that each edge in G^{T} that goes between different strongly connected components goes from a component with an earlier finishing time (in the first depth-first search) to a component with a later finishing time.

Corollary 22.15
Let C and C' be distinct strongly connected components in directed graph $G = (V, E)$. Suppose that there is an edge $(u, v) \in E^{\mathrm{T}}$, where $u \in C$ and $v \in C'$. Then $f(C) < f(C')$.

Proof   Since $(u, v) \in E^T$, we have $(v, u) \in E$. Because the strongly connected components of G and G^T are the same, Lemma 22.14 implies that
$f(C) < f(C')$.   ■

Corollary 22.15 provides the key to understanding why the strongly connected
components algorithm works. Let us examine what happens when we perform the
second depth-first search, which is on G^T. We start with the strongly connected
component C whose finishing time $f(C)$ is maximum. The search starts from
some vertex $x \in C$, and it visits all vertices in C. By Corollary 22.15, G^T contains
no edges from C to any other strongly connected component, and so the search
from x will not visit vertices in any other component. Thus, the tree rooted at x
contains exactly the vertices of C. Having completed visiting all vertices in C,
the search in line 3 selects as a root a vertex from some other strongly connected
component C' whose finishing time $f(C')$ is maximum over all components other
than C. Again, the search will visit all vertices in C', but by Corollary 22.15,
the only edges in G^T from C' to any other component must be to C, which we
have already visited. In general, when the depth-first search of G^T in line 3 visits
any strongly connected component, any edges out of that component must be to
components that the search already visited. Each depth-first tree, therefore, will be
exactly one strongly connected component. The following theorem formalizes this
argument.

Theorem 22.16
The STRONGLY-CONNECTED-COMPONENTS procedure correctly computes the
strongly connected components of the directed graph G provided as its input.

Proof   We argue by induction on the number of depth-first trees found in the
depth-first search of G^T in line 3 that the vertices of each tree form a strongly
connected component. The inductive hypothesis is that the first k trees produced
in line 3 are strongly connected components. The basis for the induction, when
$k = 0$, is trivial.

In the inductive step, we assume that each of the first k depth-first trees produced
in line 3 is a strongly connected component, and we consider the $(k + 1)$st tree
produced. Let the root of this tree be vertex u, and let u be in strongly connected
component C. Because of how we choose roots in the depth-first search in line 3,
$u.f = f(C) > f(C')$ for any strongly connected component C' other than C
that has yet to be visited. By the inductive hypothesis, at the time that the search
visits u, all other vertices of C are white. By the white-path theorem, therefore, all
other vertices of C are descendants of u in its depth-first tree. Moreover, by the
inductive hypothesis and by Corollary 22.15, any edges in G^T that leave C must be
to strongly connected components that have already been visited. Thus, no vertex

in any strongly connected component other than C will be a descendant of u during the depth-first search of G^{T}. Thus, the vertices of the depth-first tree in G^{T} that is rooted at u form exactly one strongly connected component, which completes the inductive step and the proof.   ∎

Here is another way to look at how the second depth-first search operates. Consider the component graph $(G^{\mathrm{T}})^{\mathrm{SCC}}$ of G^{T}. If we map each strongly connected component visited in the second depth-first search to a vertex of $(G^{\mathrm{T}})^{\mathrm{SCC}}$, the second depth-first search visits vertices of $(G^{\mathrm{T}})^{\mathrm{SCC}}$ in the reverse of a topologically sorted order. If we reverse the edges of $(G^{\mathrm{T}})^{\mathrm{SCC}}$, we get the graph $((G^{\mathrm{T}})^{\mathrm{SCC}})^{\mathrm{T}}$. Because $((G^{\mathrm{T}})^{\mathrm{SCC}})^{\mathrm{T}} = G^{\mathrm{SCC}}$ (see Exercise 22.5-4), the second depth-first search visits the vertices of G^{SCC} in topologically sorted order.

Exercises

22.5-1
How can the number of strongly connected components of a graph change if a new edge is added?

22.5-2
Show how the procedure STRONGLY-CONNECTED-COMPONENTS works on the graph of Figure 22.6. Specifically, show the finishing times computed in line 1 and the forest produced in line 3. Assume that the loop of lines 5–7 of DFS considers vertices in alphabetical order and that the adjacency lists are in alphabetical order.

22.5-3
Professor Bacon claims that the algorithm for strongly connected components would be simpler if it used the original (instead of the transpose) graph in the second depth-first search and scanned the vertices in order of *increasing* finishing times. Does this simpler algorithm always produce correct results?

22.5-4
Prove that for any directed graph G, we have $((G^{\mathrm{T}})^{\mathrm{SCC}})^{\mathrm{T}} = G^{\mathrm{SCC}}$. That is, the transpose of the component graph of G^{T} is the same as the component graph of G.

22.5-5
Give an $O(V + E)$-time algorithm to compute the component graph of a directed graph $G = (V, E)$. Make sure that there is at most one edge between two vertices in the component graph your algorithm produces.

22.5-6
Given a directed graph $G = (V, E)$, explain how to create another graph $G' = (V, E')$ such that (a) G' has the same strongly connected components as G, (b) G' has the same component graph as G, and (c) E' is as small as possible. Describe a fast algorithm to compute G'.

22.5-7
A directed graph $G = (V, E)$ is *semiconnected* if, for all pairs of vertices $u, v \in V$, we have $u \rightsquigarrow v$ or $v \rightsquigarrow u$. Give an efficient algorithm to determine whether or not G is semiconnected. Prove that your algorithm is correct, and analyze its running time.

Problems

22-1 *Classifying edges by breadth-first search*
A depth-first forest classifies the edges of a graph into tree, back, forward, and cross edges. A breadth-first tree can also be used to classify the edges reachable from the source of the search into the same four categories.

a. Prove that in a breadth-first search of an undirected graph, the following properties hold:

1. There are no back edges and no forward edges.
2. For each tree edge (u, v), we have $v.d = u.d + 1$.
3. For each cross edge (u, v), we have $v.d = u.d$ or $v.d = u.d + 1$.

b. Prove that in a breadth-first search of a directed graph, the following properties hold:

1. There are no forward edges.
2. For each tree edge (u, v), we have $v.d = u.d + 1$.
3. For each cross edge (u, v), we have $v.d \le u.d + 1$.
4. For each back edge (u, v), we have $0 \le v.d \le u.d$.

22-2 *Articulation points, bridges, and biconnected components*
Let $G = (V, E)$ be a connected, undirected graph. An *articulation point* of G is a vertex whose removal disconnects G. A *bridge* of G is an edge whose removal disconnects G. A *biconnected component* of G is a maximal set of edges such that any two edges in the set lie on a common simple cycle. Figure 22.10 illustrates

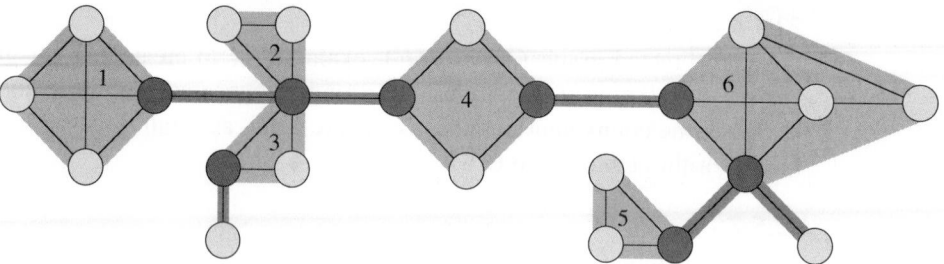

Figure 22.10   The articulation points, bridges, and biconnected components of a connected, undirected graph for use in Problem 22-2. The articulation points are the heavily shaded vertices, the bridges are the heavily shaded edges, and the biconnected components are the edges in the shaded regions, with a *bcc* numbering shown.

these definitions. We can determine articulation points, bridges, and biconnected components using depth-first search. Let $G_\pi = (V, E_\pi)$ be a depth-first tree of G.

a. Prove that the root of G_π is an articulation point of G if and only if it has at least two children in G_π.

b. Let v be a nonroot vertex of G_π. Prove that v is an articulation point of G if and only if v has a child s such that there is no back edge from s or any descendant of s to a proper ancestor of v.

c. Let

$$v.low = \min \begin{cases} v.d \,, \\ w.d : (u, w) \text{ is a back edge for some descendant } u \text{ of } v \,. \end{cases}$$

Show how to compute $v.low$ for all vertices $v \in V$ in $O(E)$ time.

d. Show how to compute all articulation points in $O(E)$ time.

e. Prove that an edge of G is a bridge if and only if it does not lie on any simple cycle of G.

f. Show how to compute all the bridges of G in $O(E)$ time.

g. Prove that the biconnected components of G partition the nonbridge edges of G.

h. Give an $O(E)$-time algorithm to label each edge e of G with a positive integer $e.bcc$ such that $e.bcc = e'.bcc$ if and only if e and e' are in the same biconnected component.

22-3 *Euler tour*

An *Euler tour* of a strongly connected, directed graph $G = (V, E)$ is a cycle that traverses each edge of G exactly once, although it may visit a vertex more than once.

a. Show that G has an Euler tour if and only if in-degree$(v) = $ out-degree(v) for each vertex $v \in V$.

b. Describe an $O(E)$-time algorithm to find an Euler tour of G if one exists. (*Hint:* Merge edge-disjoint cycles.)

22-4 *Reachability*

Let $G = (V, E)$ be a directed graph in which each vertex $u \in V$ is labeled with a unique integer $L(u)$ from the set $\{1, 2, \ldots, |V|\}$. For each vertex $u \in V$, let $R(u) = \{v \in V : u \rightsquigarrow v\}$ be the set of vertices that are reachable from u. Define $\min(u)$ to be the vertex in $R(u)$ whose label is minimum, i.e., $\min(u)$ is the vertex v such that $L(v) = \min\{L(w) : w \in R(u)\}$. Give an $O(V + E)$-time algorithm that computes $\min(u)$ for all vertices $u \in V$.

Chapter notes

Even [103] and Tarjan [330] are excellent references for graph algorithms.

Breadth-first search was discovered by Moore [260] in the context of finding paths through mazes. Lee [226] independently discovered the same algorithm in the context of routing wires on circuit boards.

Hopcroft and Tarjan [178] advocated the use of the adjacency-list representation over the adjacency-matrix representation for sparse graphs and were the first to recognize the algorithmic importance of depth-first search. Depth-first search has been widely used since the late 1950s, especially in artificial intelligence programs.

Tarjan [327] gave a linear-time algorithm for finding strongly connected components. The algorithm for strongly connected components in Section 22.5 is adapted from Aho, Hopcroft, and Ullman [6], who credit it to S. R. Kosaraju (unpublished) and M. Sharir [314]. Gabow [119] also developed an algorithm for strongly connected components that is based on contracting cycles and uses two stacks to make it run in linear time. Knuth [209] was the first to give a linear-time algorithm for topological sorting.

23 Minimum Spanning Trees

Electronic circuit designs often need to make the pins of several components electrically equivalent by wiring them together. To interconnect a set of n pins, we can use an arrangement of $n - 1$ wires, each connecting two pins. Of all such arrangements, the one that uses the least amount of wire is usually the most desirable.

We can model this wiring problem with a connected, undirected graph $G = (V, E)$, where V is the set of pins, E is the set of possible interconnections between pairs of pins, and for each edge $(u, v) \in E$, we have a weight $w(u, v)$ specifying the cost (amount of wire needed) to connect u and v. We then wish to find an acyclic subset $T \subseteq E$ that connects all of the vertices and whose total weight

$$w(T) = \sum_{(u,v) \in T} w(u, v)$$

is minimized. Since T is acyclic and connects all of the vertices, it must form a tree, which we call a *spanning tree* since it "spans" the graph G. We call the problem of determining the tree T the *minimum-spanning-tree problem*.[1] Figure 23.1 shows an example of a connected graph and a minimum spanning tree.

In this chapter, we shall examine two algorithms for solving the minimum-spanning-tree problem: Kruskal's algorithm and Prim's algorithm. We can easily make each of them run in time $O(E \lg V)$ using ordinary binary heaps. By using Fibonacci heaps, Prim's algorithm runs in time $O(E + V \lg V)$, which improves over the binary-heap implementation if $|V|$ is much smaller than $|E|$.

The two algorithms are greedy algorithms, as described in Chapter 16. Each step of a greedy algorithm must make one of several possible choices. The greedy strategy advocates making the choice that is the best at the moment. Such a strategy does not generally guarantee that it will always find globally optimal solutions

---

[1] The phrase "minimum spanning tree" is a shortened form of the phrase "minimum-weight spanning tree." We are not, for example, minimizing the number of edges in T, since all spanning trees have exactly $|V| - 1$ edges by Theorem B.2.

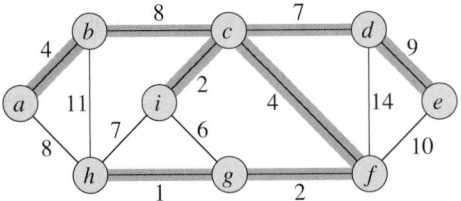

Figure 23.1   A minimum spanning tree for a connected graph. The weights on edges are shown, and the edges in a minimum spanning tree are shaded. The total weight of the tree shown is 37. This minimum spanning tree is not unique: removing the edge (b, c) and replacing it with the edge (a, h) yields another spanning tree with weight 37.

to problems. For the minimum-spanning-tree problem, however, we can prove that certain greedy strategies do yield a spanning tree with minimum weight. Although you can read this chapter independently of Chapter 16, the greedy methods presented here are a classic application of the theoretical notions introduced there.

Section 23.1 introduces a "generic" minimum-spanning-tree method that grows a spanning tree by adding one edge at a time. Section 23.2 gives two algorithms that implement the generic method. The first algorithm, due to Kruskal, is similar to the connected-components algorithm from Section 21.1. The second, due to Prim, resembles Dijkstra's shortest-paths algorithm (Section 24.3).

Because a tree is a type of graph, in order to be precise we must define a tree in terms of not just its edges, but its vertices as well. Although this chapter focuses on trees in terms of their edges, we shall operate with the understanding that the vertices of a tree T are those that some edge of T is incident on.

23.1   Growing a minimum spanning tree

Assume that we have a connected, undirected graph $G = (V, E)$ with a weight function $w : E \rightarrow \mathbb{R}$, and we wish to find a minimum spanning tree for G. The two algorithms we consider in this chapter use a greedy approach to the problem, although they differ in how they apply this approach.

This greedy strategy is captured by the following generic method, which grows the minimum spanning tree one edge at a time. The generic method manages a set of edges A, maintaining the following loop invariant:

Prior to each iteration, A is a subset of some minimum spanning tree.

At each step, we determine an edge (u, v) that we can add to A without violating this invariant, in the sense that $A \cup \{(u, v)\}$ is also a subset of a minimum spanning

tree. We call such an edge a *safe edge* for A, since we can add it safely to A while maintaining the invariant.

GENERIC-MST(G, w)

1   $A = \emptyset$
2   **while** A does not form a spanning tree
3   find an edge (u, v) that is safe for A
4       $A = A \cup \{(u, v)\}$
5   **return** A

We use the loop invariant as follows:

Initialization: After line 1, the set A trivially satisfies the loop invariant.

Maintenance: The loop in lines 2–4 maintains the invariant by adding only safe edges.

Termination: All edges added to A are in a minimum spanning tree, and so the set A returned in line 5 must be a minimum spanning tree.

The tricky part is, of course, finding a safe edge in line 3. One must exist, since when line 3 is executed, the invariant dictates that there is a spanning tree T such that $A \subseteq T$. Within the **while** loop body, A must be a proper subset of T, and therefore there must be an edge $(u, v) \in T$ such that $(u, v) \notin A$ and (u, v) is safe for A.

In the remainder of this section, we provide a rule (Theorem 23.1) for recognizing safe edges. The next section describes two algorithms that use this rule to find safe edges efficiently.

We first need some definitions. A *cut* $(S, V - S)$ of an undirected graph $G = (V, E)$ is a partition of V. Figure 23.2 illustrates this notion. We say that an edge $(u, v) \in E$ *crosses* the cut $(S, V - S)$ if one of its endpoints is in S and the other is in $V - S$. We say that a cut *respects* a set A of edges if no edge in A crosses the cut. An edge is a *light edge* crossing a cut if its weight is the minimum of any edge crossing the cut. Note that there can be more than one light edge crossing a cut in the case of ties. More generally, we say that an edge is a *light edge* satisfying a given property if its weight is the minimum of any edge satisfying the property.

Our rule for recognizing safe edges is given by the following theorem.

Theorem 23.1

Let $G = (V, E)$ be a connected, undirected graph with a real-valued weight function w defined on E. Let A be a subset of E that is included in some minimum spanning tree for G, let $(S, V - S)$ be any cut of G that respects A, and let (u, v) be a light edge crossing $(S, V - S)$. Then, edge (u, v) is safe for A.

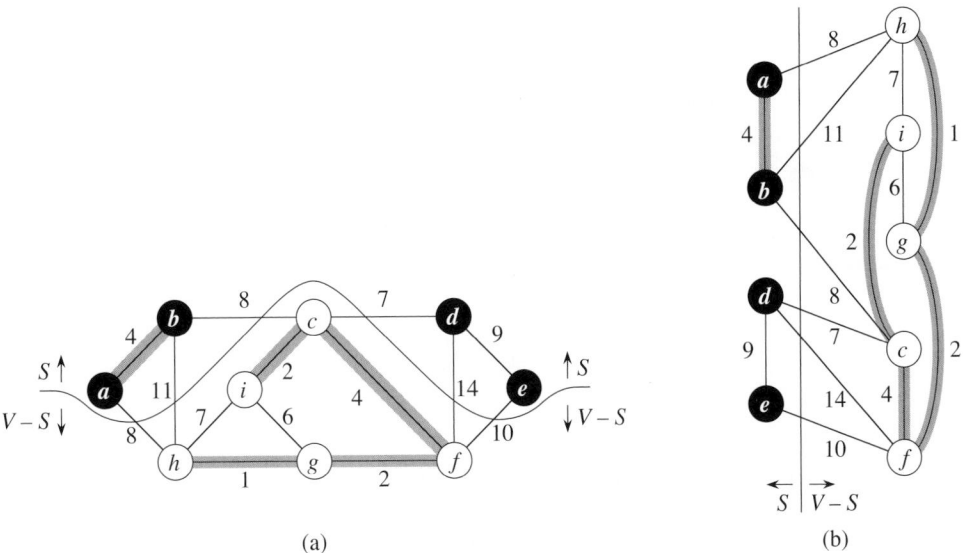

(a)   (b)

Figure 23.2 Two ways of viewing a cut $(S, V - S)$ of the graph from Figure 23.1. **(a)** Black vertices are in the set S, and white vertices are in $V - S$. The edges crossing the cut are those connecting white vertices with black vertices. The edge (d, c) is the unique light edge crossing the cut. A subset A of the edges is shaded; note that the cut $(S, V - S)$ respects A, since no edge of A crosses the cut. **(b)** The same graph with the vertices in the set S on the left and the vertices in the set $V - S$ on the right. An edge crosses the cut if it connects a vertex on the left with a vertex on the right.

Proof Let T be a minimum spanning tree that includes A, and assume that T does not contain the light edge (u, v), since if it does, we are done. We shall construct another minimum spanning tree T' that includes $A \cup \{(u, v)\}$ by using a cut-and-paste technique, thereby showing that (u, v) is a safe edge for A.

The edge (u, v) forms a cycle with the edges on the simple path p from u to v in T, as Figure 23.3 illustrates. Since u and v are on opposite sides of the cut $(S, V - S)$, at least one edge in T lies on the simple path p and also crosses the cut. Let (x, y) be any such edge. The edge (x, y) is not in A, because the cut respects A. Since (x, y) is on the unique simple path from u to v in T, removing (x, y) breaks T into two components. Adding (u, v) reconnects them to form a new spanning tree $T' = T - \{(x, y)\} \cup \{(u, v)\}$.

We next show that T' is a minimum spanning tree. Since (u, v) is a light edge crossing $(S, V - S)$ and (x, y) also crosses this cut, $w(u, v) \leq w(x, y)$. Therefore,

$$
\begin{aligned}
w(T') &= w(T) - w(x, y) + w(u, v) \\
&\leq w(T).
\end{aligned}
$$

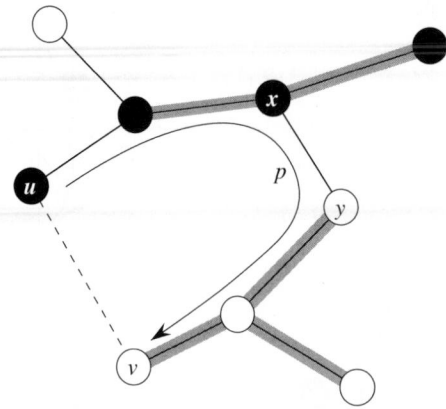

Figure 23.3 The proof of Theorem 23.1. Black vertices are in S, and white vertices are in $V - S$. The edges in the minimum spanning tree T are shown, but the edges in the graph G are not. The edges in A are shaded, and (u, v) is a light edge crossing the cut $(S, V - S)$. The edge (x, y) is an edge on the unique simple path p from u to v in T. To form a minimum spanning tree T' that contains (u, v), remove the edge (x, y) from T and add the edge (u, v).

But T is a minimum spanning tree, so that $w(T) \leq w(T')$; thus, T' must be a minimum spanning tree also.

It remains to show that (u, v) is actually a safe edge for A. We have $A \subseteq T'$, since $A \subseteq T$ and $(x, y) \notin A$; thus, $A \cup \{(u, v)\} \subseteq T'$. Consequently, since T' is a minimum spanning tree, (u, v) is safe for A.   ■

Theorem 23.1 gives us a better understanding of the workings of the GENERIC-MST method on a connected graph $G = (V, E)$. As the method proceeds, the set A is always acyclic; otherwise, a minimum spanning tree including A would contain a cycle, which is a contradiction. At any point in the execution, the graph $G_A = (V, A)$ is a forest, and each of the connected components of G_A is a tree. (Some of the trees may contain just one vertex, as is the case, for example, when the method begins: A is empty and the forest contains $|V|$ trees, one for each vertex.) Moreover, any safe edge (u, v) for A connects distinct components of G_A, since $A \cup \{(u, v)\}$ must be acyclic.

The **while** loop in lines 2–4 of GENERIC-MST executes $|V| - 1$ times because it finds one of the $|V| - 1$ edges of a minimum spanning tree in each iteration. Initially, when $A = \emptyset$, there are $|V|$ trees in G_A, and each iteration reduces that number by 1. When the forest contains only a single tree, the method terminates.

The two algorithms in Section 23.2 use the following corollary to Theorem 23.1.

Corollary 23.2
Let $G = (V, E)$ be a connected, undirected graph with a real-valued weight function w defined on E. Let A be a subset of E that is included in some minimum spanning tree for G, and let $C = (V_C, E_C)$ be a connected component (tree) in the forest $G_A = (V, A)$. If (u, v) is a light edge connecting C to some other component in G_A, then (u, v) is safe for A.

Proof   The cut $(V_C, V - V_C)$ respects A, and (u, v) is a light edge for this cut. Therefore, (u, v) is safe for A.   ∎

Exercises

23.1-1
Let (u, v) be a minimum-weight edge in a connected graph G. Show that (u, v) belongs to some minimum spanning tree of G.

23.1-2
Professor Sabatier conjectures the following converse of Theorem 23.1. Let $G = (V, E)$ be a connected, undirected graph with a real-valued weight function w defined on E. Let A be a subset of E that is included in some minimum spanning tree for G, let $(S, V - S)$ be any cut of G that respects A, and let (u, v) be a safe edge for A crossing $(S, V - S)$. Then, (u, v) is a light edge for the cut. Show that the professor's conjecture is incorrect by giving a counterexample.

23.1-3
Show that if an edge (u, v) is contained in some minimum spanning tree, then it is a light edge crossing some cut of the graph.

23.1-4
Give a simple example of a connected graph such that the set of edges $\{(u, v) :$ there exists a cut $(S, V - S)$ such that (u, v) is a light edge crossing $(S, V - S)\}$ does not form a minimum spanning tree.

23.1-5
Let e be a maximum-weight edge on some cycle of connected graph $G = (V, E)$. Prove that there is a minimum spanning tree of $G' = (V, E - \{e\})$ that is also a minimum spanning tree of G. That is, there is a minimum spanning tree of G that does not include e.

23.1-6

Show that a graph has a unique minimum spanning tree if, for every cut of the graph, there is a unique light edge crossing the cut. Show that the converse is not true by giving a counterexample.

23.1-7

Argue that if all edge weights of a graph are positive, then any subset of edges that connects all vertices and has minimum total weight must be a tree. Give an example to show that the same conclusion does not follow if we allow some weights to be nonpositive.

23.1-8

Let T be a minimum spanning tree of a graph G, and let L be the sorted list of the edge weights of T. Show that for any other minimum spanning tree T' of G, the list L is also the sorted list of edge weights of T'.

23.1-9

Let T be a minimum spanning tree of a graph $G = (V, E)$, and let V' be a subset of V. Let T' be the subgraph of T induced by V', and let G' be the subgraph of G induced by V'. Show that if T' is connected, then T' is a minimum spanning tree of G'.

23.1-10

Given a graph G and a minimum spanning tree T, suppose that we decrease the weight of one of the edges in T. Show that T is still a minimum spanning tree for G. More formally, let T be a minimum spanning tree for G with edge weights given by weight function w. Choose one edge $(x, y) \in T$ and a positive number k, and define the weight function w' by

$$w'(u, v) = \begin{cases} w(u, v) & \text{if } (u, v) \neq (x, y), \\ w(x, y) - k & \text{if } (u, v) = (x, y). \end{cases}$$

Show that T is a minimum spanning tree for G with edge weights given by w'.

23.1-11 ★

Given a graph G and a minimum spanning tree T, suppose that we decrease the weight of one of the edges not in T. Give an algorithm for finding the minimum spanning tree in the modified graph.

23.2   The algorithms of Kruskal and Prim

The two minimum-spanning-tree algorithms described in this section elaborate on the generic method. They each use a specific rule to determine a safe edge in line 3 of GENERIC-MST. In Kruskal's algorithm, the set A is a forest whose vertices are all those of the given graph. The safe edge added to A is always a least-weight edge in the graph that connects two distinct components. In Prim's algorithm, the set A forms a single tree. The safe edge added to A is always a least-weight edge connecting the tree to a vertex not in the tree.

Kruskal's algorithm

Kruskal's algorithm finds a safe edge to add to the growing forest by finding, of all the edges that connect any two trees in the forest, an edge (u, v) of least weight. Let C_1 and C_2 denote the two trees that are connected by (u, v). Since (u, v) must be a light edge connecting C_1 to some other tree, Corollary 23.2 implies that (u, v) is a safe edge for C_1. Kruskal's algorithm qualifies as a greedy algorithm because at each step it adds to the forest an edge of least possible weight.

Our implementation of Kruskal's algorithm is like the algorithm to compute connected components from Section 21.1. It uses a disjoint-set data structure to maintain several disjoint sets of elements. Each set contains the vertices in one tree of the current forest. The operation FIND-SET(u) returns a representative element from the set that contains u. Thus, we can determine whether two vertices u and v belong to the same tree by testing whether FIND-SET(u) equals FIND-SET(v). To combine trees, Kruskal's algorithm calls the UNION procedure.

MST-KRUSKAL(G, w)

```
1   A = ∅
2   for each vertex v ∈ G.V
3       MAKE-SET(v)
4   sort the edges of G.E into nondecreasing order by weight w
5   for each edge (u, v) ∈ G.E, taken in nondecreasing order by weight
6       if FIND-SET(u) ≠ FIND-SET(v)
7           A = A ∪ {(u, v)}
8           UNION(u, v)
9   return A
```

Figure 23.4 shows how Kruskal's algorithm works. Lines 1–3 initialize the set A to the empty set and create $|V|$ trees, one containing each vertex. The **for** loop in lines 5–8 examines edges in order of weight, from lowest to highest. The loop

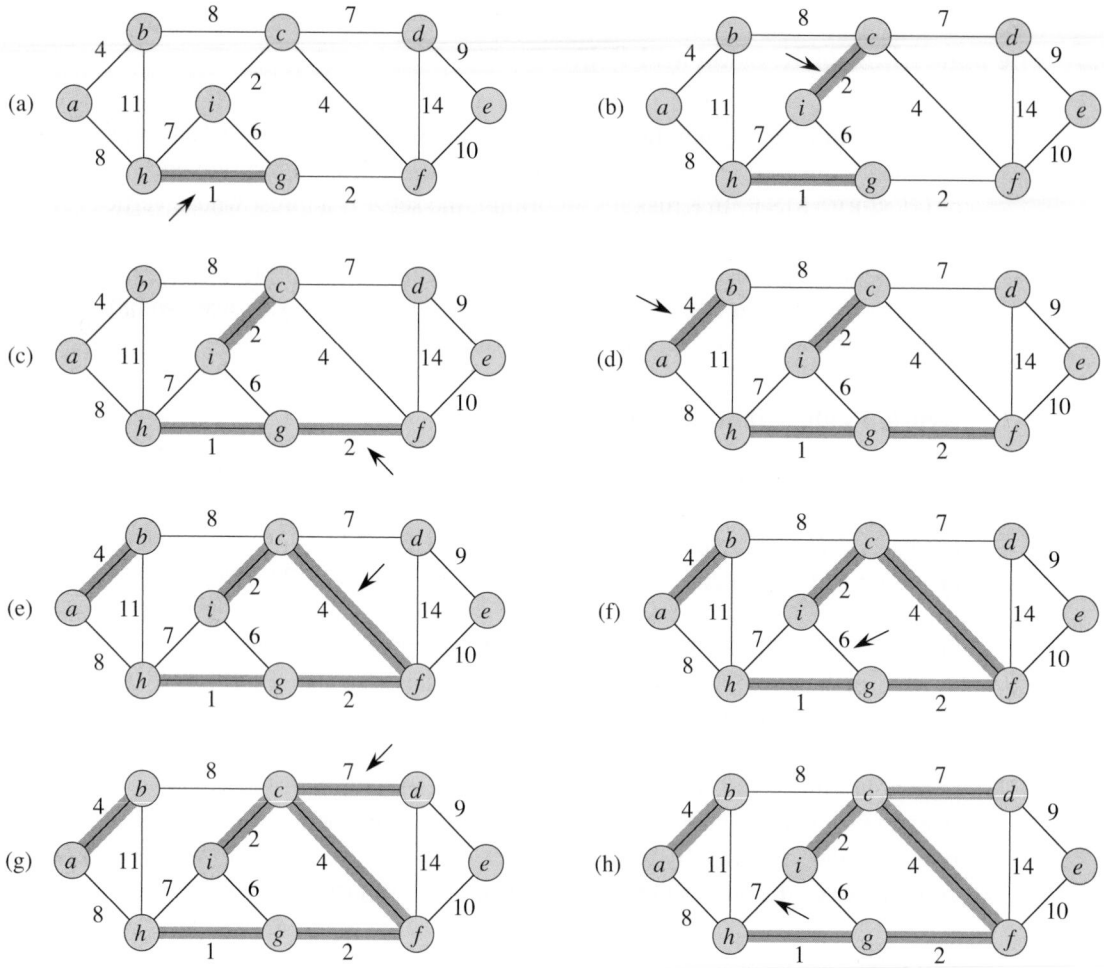

Figure 23.4   The execution of Kruskal's algorithm on the graph from Figure 23.1. Shaded edges belong to the forest A being grown. The algorithm considers each edge in sorted order by weight. An arrow points to the edge under consideration at each step of the algorithm. If the edge joins two distinct trees in the forest, it is added to the forest, thereby merging the two trees.

checks, for each edge (u, v), whether the endpoints u and v belong to the same tree. If they do, then the edge (u, v) cannot be added to the forest without creating a cycle, and the edge is discarded. Otherwise, the two vertices belong to different trees. In this case, line 7 adds the edge (u, v) to A, and line 8 merges the vertices in the two trees.

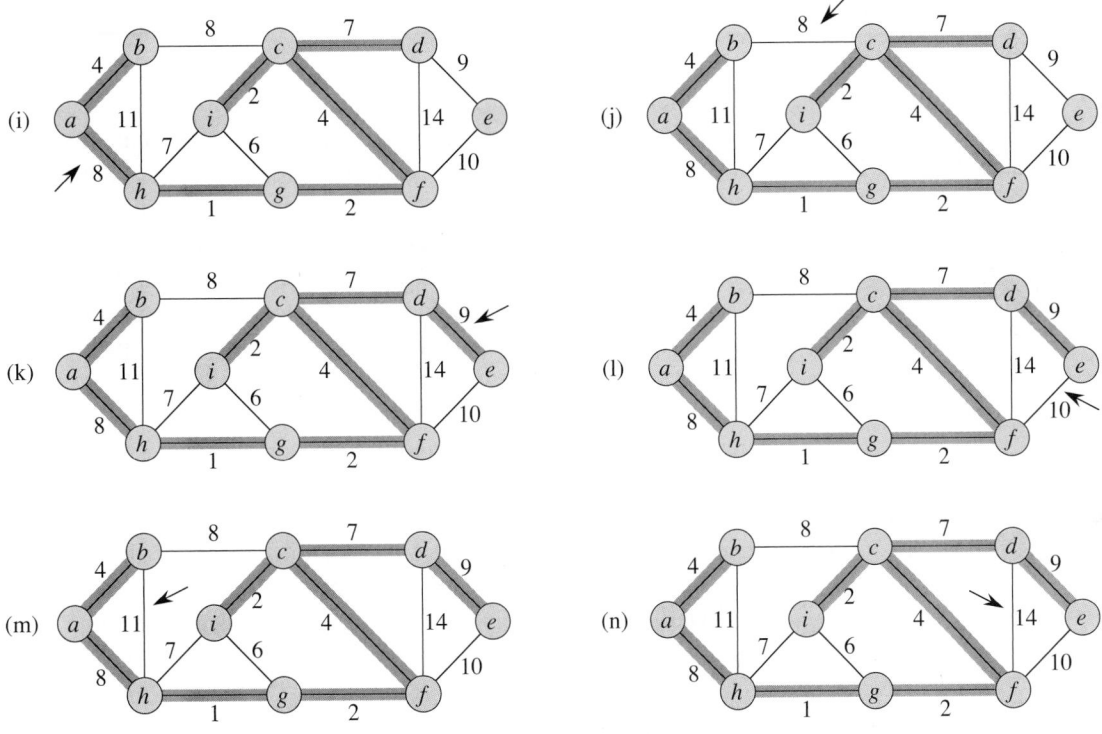

Figure 23.4, continued Further steps in the execution of Kruskal's algorithm.

The running time of Kruskal's algorithm for a graph $G = (V, E)$ depends on how we implement the disjoint-set data structure. We assume that we use the disjoint-set-forest implementation of Section 21.3 with the union-by-rank and path-compression heuristics, since it is the asymptotically fastest implementation known. Initializing the set A in line 1 takes $O(1)$ time, and the time to sort the edges in line 4 is $O(E \lg E)$. (We will account for the cost of the $|V|$ MAKE-SET operations in the **for** loop of lines 2–3 in a moment.) The **for** loop of lines 5–8 performs $O(E)$ FIND-SET and UNION operations on the disjoint-set forest. Along with the $|V|$ MAKE-SET operations, these take a total of $O((V + E)\,\alpha(V))$ time, where α is the very slowly growing function defined in Section 21.4. Because we assume that G is connected, we have $|E| \geq |V| - 1$, and so the disjoint-set operations take $O(E\alpha(V))$ time. Moreover, since $\alpha(|V|) = O(\lg V) = O(\lg E)$, the total running time of Kruskal's algorithm is $O(E \lg E)$. Observing that $|E| < |V|^2$, we have $\lg |E| = O(\lg V)$, and so we can restate the running time of Kruskal's algorithm as $O(E \lg V)$.

Prim's algorithm

Like Kruskal's algorithm, Prim's algorithm is a special case of the generic minimum-spanning-tree method from Section 23.1. Prim's algorithm operates much like Dijkstra's algorithm for finding shortest paths in a graph, which we shall see in Section 24.3. Prim's algorithm has the property that the edges in the set A always form a single tree. As Figure 23.5 shows, the tree starts from an arbitrary root vertex r and grows until the tree spans all the vertices in V. Each step adds to the tree A a light edge that connects A to an isolated vertex—one on which no edge of A is incident. By Corollary 23.2, this rule adds only edges that are safe for A; therefore, when the algorithm terminates, the edges in A form a minimum spanning tree. This strategy qualifies as greedy since at each step it adds to the tree an edge that contributes the minimum amount possible to the tree's weight.

In order to implement Prim's algorithm efficiently, we need a fast way to select a new edge to add to the tree formed by the edges in A. In the pseudocode below, the connected graph G and the root r of the minimum spanning tree to be grown are inputs to the algorithm. During execution of the algorithm, all vertices that are *not* in the tree reside in a min-priority queue Q based on a *key* attribute. For each vertex v, the attribute $v.key$ is the minimum weight of any edge connecting v to a vertex in the tree; by convention, $v.key = \infty$ if there is no such edge. The attribute $v.\pi$ names the parent of v in the tree. The algorithm implicitly maintains the set A from GENERIC-MST as

$$A = \{(v, v.\pi) : v \in V - \{r\} - Q\} \ .$$

When the algorithm terminates, the min-priority queue Q is empty; the minimum spanning tree A for G is thus

$$A = \{(v, v.\pi) : v \in V - \{r\}\} \ .$$

MST-PRIM(G, w, r)

```
 1   for each u ∈ G.V
 2       u.key = ∞
 3       u.π = NIL
 4   r.key = 0
 5   Q = G.V
 6   while Q ≠ ∅
 7       u = EXTRACT-MIN(Q)
 8       for each v ∈ G.Adj[u]
 9           if v ∈ Q and w(u, v) < v.key
10               v.π = u
11               v.key = w(u, v)
```

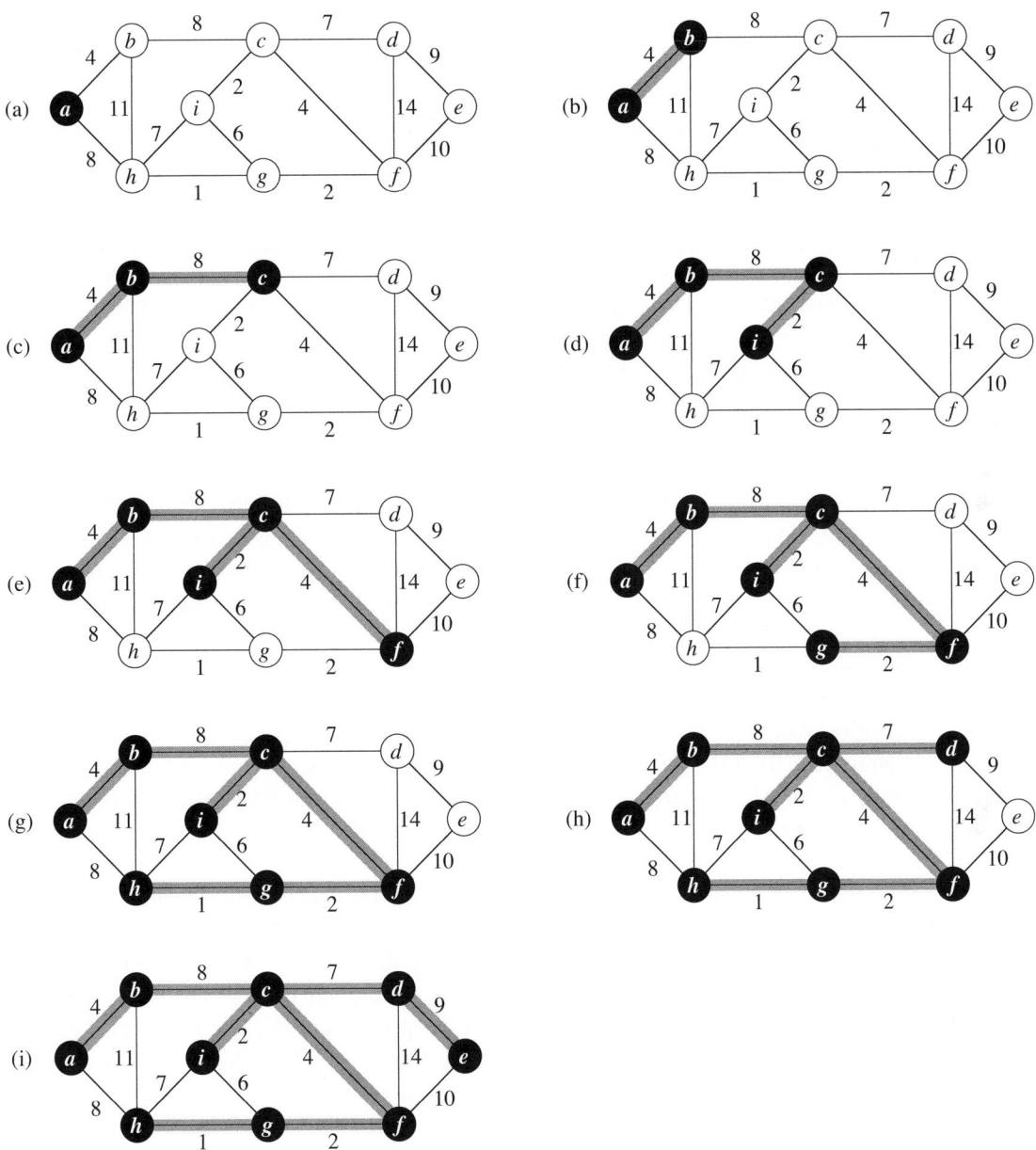

Figure 23.5   The execution of Prim's algorithm on the graph from Figure 23.1. The root vertex is a. Shaded edges are in the tree being grown, and black vertices are in the tree. At each step of the algorithm, the vertices in the tree determine a cut of the graph, and a light edge crossing the cut is added to the tree. In the second step, for example, the algorithm has a choice of adding either edge (b, c) or edge (a, h) to the tree since both are light edges crossing the cut.

Figure 23.5 shows how Prim's algorithm works. Lines 1–5 set the key of each vertex to ∞ (except for the root r, whose key is set to 0 so that it will be the first vertex processed), set the parent of each vertex to NIL, and initialize the min-priority queue Q to contain all the vertices. The algorithm maintains the following three-part loop invariant:

Prior to each iteration of the **while** loop of lines 6–11,

1. $A = \{(v, v.\pi) : v \in V - \{r\} - Q\}$.

2. The vertices already placed into the minimum spanning tree are those in $V - Q$.

3. For all vertices $v \in Q$, if $v.\pi \neq$ NIL, then $v.key < \infty$ and $v.key$ is the weight of a light edge $(v, v.\pi)$ connecting v to some vertex already placed into the minimum spanning tree.

Line 7 identifies a vertex $u \in Q$ incident on a light edge that crosses the cut $(V - Q, Q)$ (with the exception of the first iteration, in which $u = r$ due to line 4). Removing u from the set Q adds it to the set $V - Q$ of vertices in the tree, thus adding $(u, u.\pi)$ to A. The **for** loop of lines 8–11 updates the *key* and π attributes of every vertex v adjacent to u but not in the tree, thereby maintaining the third part of the loop invariant.

The running time of Prim's algorithm depends on how we implement the min-priority queue Q. If we implement Q as a binary min-heap (see Chapter 6), we can use the BUILD-MIN-HEAP procedure to perform lines 1–5 in $O(V)$ time. The body of the **while** loop executes $|V|$ times, and since each EXTRACT-MIN operation takes $O(\lg V)$ time, the total time for all calls to EXTRACT-MIN is $O(V \lg V)$. The **for** loop in lines 8–11 executes $O(E)$ times altogether, since the sum of the lengths of all adjacency lists is $2|E|$. Within the **for** loop, we can implement the test for membership in Q in line 9 in constant time by keeping a bit for each vertex that tells whether or not it is in Q, and updating the bit when the vertex is removed from Q. The assignment in line 11 involves an implicit DECREASE-KEY operation on the min-heap, which a binary min-heap supports in $O(\lg V)$ time. Thus, the total time for Prim's algorithm is $O(V \lg V + E \lg V) = O(E \lg V)$, which is asymptotically the same as for our implementation of Kruskal's algorithm.

We can improve the asymptotic running time of Prim's algorithm by using Fibonacci heaps. Chapter 19 shows that if a Fibonacci heap holds $|V|$ elements, an EXTRACT-MIN operation takes $O(\lg V)$ amortized time and a DECREASE-KEY operation (to implement line 11) takes $O(1)$ amortized time. Therefore, if we use a Fibonacci heap to implement the min-priority queue Q, the running time of Prim's algorithm improves to $O(E + V \lg V)$.

Exercises

23.2-1
Kruskal's algorithm can return different spanning trees for the same input graph G, depending on how it breaks ties when the edges are sorted into order. Show that for each minimum spanning tree T of G, there is a way to sort the edges of G in Kruskal's algorithm so that the algorithm returns T.

23.2-2
Suppose that we represent the graph $G = (V, E)$ as an adjacency matrix. Give a simple implementation of Prim's algorithm for this case that runs in $O(V^2)$ time.

23.2-3
For a sparse graph $G = (V, E)$, where $|E| = \Theta(V)$, is the implementation of Prim's algorithm with a Fibonacci heap asymptotically faster than the binary-heap implementation? What about for a dense graph, where $|E| = \Theta(V^2)$? How must the sizes $|E|$ and $|V|$ be related for the Fibonacci-heap implementation to be asymptotically faster than the binary-heap implementation?

23.2-4
Suppose that all edge weights in a graph are integers in the range from 1 to $|V|$. How fast can you make Kruskal's algorithm run? What if the edge weights are integers in the range from 1 to W for some constant W?

23.2-5
Suppose that all edge weights in a graph are integers in the range from 1 to $|V|$. How fast can you make Prim's algorithm run? What if the edge weights are integers in the range from 1 to W for some constant W?

23.2-6   ★
Suppose that the edge weights in a graph are uniformly distributed over the half-open interval $[0, 1)$. Which algorithm, Kruskal's or Prim's, can you make run faster?

23.2-7   ★
Suppose that a graph G has a minimum spanning tree already computed. How quickly can we update the minimum spanning tree if we add a new vertex and incident edges to G?

23.2-8
Professor Borden proposes a new divide-and-conquer algorithm for computing minimum spanning trees, which goes as follows. Given a graph $G = (V, E)$, partition the set V of vertices into two sets V_1 and V_2 such that $|V_1|$ and $|V_2|$ differ

by at most 1. Let E_1 be the set of edges that are incident only on vertices in V_1, and let E_2 be the set of edges that are incident only on vertices in V_2. Recursively solve a minimum-spanning-tree problem on each of the two subgraphs $G_1 = (V_1, E_1)$ and $G_2 = (V_2, E_2)$. Finally, select the minimum-weight edge in E that crosses the cut (V_1, V_2), and use this edge to unite the resulting two minimum spanning trees into a single spanning tree.

Either argue that the algorithm correctly computes a minimum spanning tree of G, or provide an example for which the algorithm fails.

Problems

23-1   *Second-best minimum spanning tree*
Let $G = (V, E)$ be an undirected, connected graph whose weight function is $w : E \to \mathbb{R}$, and suppose that $|E| \geq |V|$ and all edge weights are distinct.

We define a second-best minimum spanning tree as follows. Let $\mathcal{T}$ be the set of all spanning trees of G, and let T' be a minimum spanning tree of G. Then a ***second-best minimum spanning tree*** is a spanning tree T such that $w(T) = \min_{T'' \in \mathcal{T} - \{T'\}} \{w(T'')\}$.

a. Show that the minimum spanning tree is unique, but that the second-best minimum spanning tree need not be unique.

b. Let T be the minimum spanning tree of G. Prove that G contains edges $(u, v) \in T$ and $(x, y) \notin T$ such that $T - \{(u, v)\} \cup \{(x, y)\}$ is a second-best minimum spanning tree of G.

c. Let T be a spanning tree of G and, for any two vertices $u, v \in V$, let $max[u, v]$ denote an edge of maximum weight on the unique simple path between u and v in T. Describe an $O(V^2)$-time algorithm that, given T, computes $max[u, v]$ for all $u, v \in V$.

d. Give an efficient algorithm to compute the second-best minimum spanning tree of G.

23-2   *Minimum spanning tree in sparse graphs*
For a very sparse connected graph $G = (V, E)$, we can further improve upon the $O(E + V \lg V)$ running time of Prim's algorithm with Fibonacci heaps by preprocessing G to decrease the number of vertices before running Prim's algorithm. In particular, we choose, for each vertex u, the minimum-weight edge (u, v) incident on u, and we put (u, v) into the minimum spanning tree under construction. We

then contract all chosen edges (see Section B.4). Rather than contracting these edges one at a time, we first identify sets of vertices that are united into the same new vertex. Then we create the graph that would have resulted from contracting these edges one at a time, but we do so by "renaming" edges according to the sets into which their endpoints were placed. Several edges from the original graph may be renamed the same as each other. In such a case, only one edge results, and its weight is the minimum of the weights of the corresponding original edges.

Initially, we set the minimum spanning tree T being constructed to be empty, and for each edge $(u, v) \in E$, we initialize the attributes $(u, v).orig = (u, v)$ and $(u, v).c = w(u, v)$. We use the $orig$ attribute to reference the edge from the initial graph that is associated with an edge in the contracted graph. The c attribute holds the weight of an edge, and as edges are contracted, we update it according to the above scheme for choosing edge weights. The procedure MST-REDUCE takes inputs G and T, and it returns a contracted graph G' with updated attributes $orig'$ and c'. The procedure also accumulates edges of G into the minimum spanning tree T.

MST-REDUCE(G, T)

```
 1  for each v ∈ G.V
 2      v.mark = FALSE
 3      MAKE-SET(v)
 4  for each u ∈ G.V
 5      if u.mark == FALSE
 6          choose v ∈ G.Adj[u] such that (u, v).c is minimized
 7          UNION(u, v)
 8          T = T ∪ {(u, v).orig}
 9          u.mark = v.mark = TRUE
10  G'.V = {FIND-SET(v) : v ∈ G.V}
11  G'.E = ∅
12  for each (x, y) ∈ G.E
13      u = FIND-SET(x)
14      v = FIND-SET(y)
15      if u ≠ v
16          if (u, v) ∉ G'.E
17              G'.E = G'.E ∪ {(u, v)}
18              (u, v).orig' = (x, y).orig
19              (u, v).c' = (x, y).c
20          else if (x, y).c < (u, v).c'
21              (u, v).orig' = (x, y).orig
22              (u, v).c' = (x, y).c
23  construct adjacency lists G'.Adj for G'
24  return G' and T
```

a. Let T be the set of edges returned by MST-REDUCE, and let A be the minimum spanning tree of the graph G' formed by the call MST-PRIM(G', c', r), where c' is the weight attribute on the edges of $G'.E$ and r is any vertex in $G'.V$. Prove that $T \cup \{(x, y).orig' : (x, y) \in A\}$ is a minimum spanning tree of G.

b. Argue that $|G'.V| \leq |V|/2$.

c. Show how to implement MST-REDUCE so that it runs in $O(E)$ time. (*Hint:* Use simple data structures.)

d. Suppose that we run k phases of MST-REDUCE, using the output G' produced by one phase as the input G to the next phase and accumulating edges in T. Argue that the overall running time of the k phases is $O(kE)$.

e. Suppose that after running k phases of MST-REDUCE, as in part (d), we run Prim's algorithm by calling MST-PRIM(G', c', r), where G', with weight attribute c', is returned by the last phase and r is any vertex in $G'.V$. Show how to pick k so that the overall running time is $O(E \lg \lg V)$. Argue that your choice of k minimizes the overall asymptotic running time.

f. For what values of $|E|$ (in terms of $|V|$) does Prim's algorithm with preprocessing asymptotically beat Prim's algorithm without preprocessing?

23-3   *Bottleneck spanning tree*

A ***bottleneck spanning tree*** T of an undirected graph G is a spanning tree of G whose largest edge weight is minimum over all spanning trees of G. We say that the value of the bottleneck spanning tree is the weight of the maximum-weight edge in T.

a. Argue that a minimum spanning tree is a bottleneck spanning tree.

Part (a) shows that finding a bottleneck spanning tree is no harder than finding a minimum spanning tree. In the remaining parts, we will show how to find a bottleneck spanning tree in linear time.

b. Give a linear-time algorithm that given a graph G and an integer b, determines whether the value of the bottleneck spanning tree is at most b.

c. Use your algorithm for part (b) as a subroutine in a linear-time algorithm for the bottleneck-spanning-tree problem. (*Hint:* You may want to use a subroutine that contracts sets of edges, as in the MST-REDUCE procedure described in Problem 23-2.)

23-4 *Alternative minimum-spanning-tree algorithms*

In this problem, we give pseudocode for three different algorithms. Each one takes a connected graph and a weight function as input and returns a set of edges T. For each algorithm, either prove that T is a minimum spanning tree or prove that T is not necessarily a minimum spanning tree. Also describe the most efficient implementation of each algorithm, whether or not it computes a minimum spanning tree.

a. MAYBE-MST-A(G, w)

```
1  sort the edges into nonincreasing order of edge weights w
2  T = E
3  for each edge e, taken in nonincreasing order by weight
4      if T − {e} is a connected graph
5          T = T − {e}
6  return T
```

b. MAYBE-MST-B(G, w)

```
1  T = ∅
2  for each edge e, taken in arbitrary order
3      if T ∪ {e} has no cycles
4          T = T ∪ {e}
5  return T
```

c. MAYBE-MST-C(G, w)

```
1  T = ∅
2  for each edge e, taken in arbitrary order
3      T = T ∪ {e}
4      if T has a cycle c
5          let e′ be a maximum-weight edge on c
6          T = T − {e′}
7  return T
```

Chapter notes

Tarjan [330] surveys the minimum-spanning-tree problem and provides excellent advanced material. Graham and Hell [151] compiled a history of the minimum-spanning-tree problem.

Tarjan attributes the first minimum-spanning-tree algorithm to a 1926 paper by O. Borůvka. Borůvka's algorithm consists of running $O(\lg V)$ iterations of the

procedure MST-REDUCE described in Problem 23-2. Kruskal's algorithm was reported by Kruskal [222] in 1956. The algorithm commonly known as Prim's algorithm was indeed invented by Prim [285], but it was also invented earlier by V. Jarník in 1930.

The reason underlying why greedy algorithms are effective at finding minimum spanning trees is that the set of forests of a graph forms a graphic matroid. (See Section 16.4.)

When $|E| = \Omega(V \lg V)$, Prim's algorithm, implemented with Fibonacci heaps, runs in $O(E)$ time. For sparser graphs, using a combination of the ideas from Prim's algorithm, Kruskal's algorithm, and Borůvka's algorithm, together with advanced data structures, Fredman and Tarjan [114] give an algorithm that runs in $O(E \lg^* V)$ time. Gabow, Galil, Spencer, and Tarjan [120] improved this algorithm to run in $O(E \lg \lg^* V)$ time. Chazelle [60] gives an algorithm that runs in $O(E \, \hat{\alpha}(E, V))$ time, where $\hat{\alpha}(E, V)$ is the functional inverse of Ackermann's function. (See the chapter notes for Chapter 21 for a brief discussion of Ackermann's function and its inverse.) Unlike previous minimum-spanning-tree algorithms, Chazelle's algorithm does not follow the greedy method.

A related problem is ***spanning-tree verification***, in which we are given a graph $G = (V, E)$ and a tree $T \subseteq E$, and we wish to determine whether T is a minimum spanning tree of G. King [203] gives a linear-time algorithm to verify a spanning tree, building on earlier work of Komlós [215] and Dixon, Rauch, and Tarjan [90].

The above algorithms are all deterministic and fall into the comparison-based model described in Chapter 8. Karger, Klein, and Tarjan [195] give a randomized minimum-spanning-tree algorithm that runs in $O(V + E)$ expected time. This algorithm uses recursion in a manner similar to the linear-time selection algorithm in Section 9.3: a recursive call on an auxiliary problem identifies a subset of the edges E' that cannot be in any minimum spanning tree. Another recursive call on $E - E'$ then finds the minimum spanning tree. The algorithm also uses ideas from Borůvka's algorithm and King's algorithm for spanning-tree verification.

Fredman and Willard [116] showed how to find a minimum spanning tree in $O(V + E)$ time using a deterministic algorithm that is not comparison based. Their algorithm assumes that the data are b-bit integers and that the computer memory consists of addressable b-bit words.

24 Single-Source Shortest Paths

Professor Patrick wishes to find the shortest possible route from Phoenix to Indianapolis. Given a road map of the United States on which the distance between each pair of adjacent intersections is marked, how can she determine this shortest route?

One possible way would be to enumerate all the routes from Phoenix to Indianapolis, add up the distances on each route, and select the shortest. It is easy to see, however, that even disallowing routes that contain cycles, Professor Patrick would have to examine an enormous number of possibilities, most of which are simply not worth considering. For example, a route from Phoenix to Indianapolis that passes through Seattle is obviously a poor choice, because Seattle is several hundred miles out of the way.

In this chapter and in Chapter 25, we show how to solve such problems efficiently. In a *shortest-paths problem*, we are given a weighted, directed graph $G = (V, E)$, with weight function $w : E \rightarrow \mathbb{R}$ mapping edges to real-valued weights. The *weight* $w(p)$ of path $p = \langle v_0, v_1, \ldots, v_k \rangle$ is the sum of the weights of its constituent edges:

$$w(p) = \sum_{i=1}^{k} w(v_{i-1}, v_i) .$$

We define the *shortest-path weight* $\delta(u, v)$ from u to v by

$$\delta(u, v) = \begin{cases} \min\{w(p) : u \overset{p}{\leadsto} v\} & \text{if there is a path from } u \text{ to } v , \\ \infty & \text{otherwise} . \end{cases}$$

A *shortest path* from vertex u to vertex v is then defined as any path p with weight $w(p) = \delta(u, v)$.

In the Phoenix-to-Indianapolis example, we can model the road map as a graph: vertices represent intersections, edges represent road segments between intersections, and edge weights represent road distances. Our goal is to find a shortest path from a given intersection in Phoenix to a given intersection in Indianapolis.

Edge weights can represent metrics other than distances, such as time, cost, penalties, loss, or any other quantity that accumulates linearly along a path and that we would want to minimize.

The breadth-first-search algorithm from Section 22.2 is a shortest-paths algorithm that works on unweighted graphs, that is, graphs in which each edge has unit weight. Because many of the concepts from breadth-first search arise in the study of shortest paths in weighted graphs, you might want to review Section 22.2 before proceeding.

Variants

In this chapter, we shall focus on the *single-source shortest-paths problem*: given a graph $G = (V, E)$, we want to find a shortest path from a given *source* vertex $s \in V$ to each vertex $v \in V$. The algorithm for the single-source problem can solve many other problems, including the following variants.

Single-destination shortest-paths problem: Find a shortest path to a given *destination* vertex t from each vertex v. By reversing the direction of each edge in the graph, we can reduce this problem to a single-source problem.

Single-pair shortest-path problem: Find a shortest path from u to v for given vertices u and v. If we solve the single-source problem with source vertex u, we solve this problem also. Moreover, all known algorithms for this problem have the same worst-case asymptotic running time as the best single-source algorithms.

All-pairs shortest-paths problem: Find a shortest path from u to v for every pair of vertices u and v. Although we can solve this problem by running a single-source algorithm once from each vertex, we usually can solve it faster. Additionally, its structure is interesting in its own right. Chapter 25 addresses the all-pairs problem in detail.

Optimal substructure of a shortest path

Shortest-paths algorithms typically rely on the property that a shortest path between two vertices contains other shortest paths within it. (The Edmonds-Karp maximum-flow algorithm in Chapter 26 also relies on this property.) Recall that optimal substructure is one of the key indicators that dynamic programming (Chapter 15) and the greedy method (Chapter 16) might apply. Dijkstra's algorithm, which we shall see in Section 24.3, is a greedy algorithm, and the Floyd-Warshall algorithm, which finds shortest paths between all pairs of vertices (see Section 25.2), is a dynamic-programming algorithm. The following lemma states the optimal-substructure property of shortest paths more precisely.

Lemma 24.1 (Subpaths of shortest paths are shortest paths)
Given a weighted, directed graph $G = (V, E)$ with weight function $w : E \to \mathbb{R}$, let $p = \langle v_0, v_1, \ldots, v_k \rangle$ be a shortest path from vertex v_0 to vertex v_k and, for any i and j such that $0 \leq i \leq j \leq k$, let $p_{ij} = \langle v_i, v_{i+1}, \ldots, v_j \rangle$ be the subpath of p from vertex v_i to vertex v_j. Then, p_{ij} is a shortest path from v_i to v_j.

Proof If we decompose path p into $v_0 \overset{p_{0i}}{\leadsto} v_i \overset{p_{ij}}{\leadsto} v_j \overset{p_{jk}}{\leadsto} v_k$, then we have that $w(p) = w(p_{0i}) + w(p_{ij}) + w(p_{jk})$. Now, assume that there is a path p'_{ij} from v_i to v_j with weight $w(p'_{ij}) < w(p_{ij})$. Then, $v_0 \overset{p_{0i}}{\leadsto} v_i \overset{p'_{ij}}{\leadsto} v_j \overset{p_{jk}}{\leadsto} v_k$ is a path from v_0 to v_k whose weight $w(p_{0i}) + w(p'_{ij}) + w(p_{jk})$ is less than $w(p)$, which contradicts the assumption that p is a shortest path from v_0 to v_k. ∎

Negative-weight edges

Some instances of the single-source shortest-paths problem may include edges whose weights are negative. If the graph $G = (V, E)$ contains no negative-weight cycles reachable from the source s, then for all $v \in V$, the shortest-path weight $\delta(s, v)$ remains well defined, even if it has a negative value. If the graph contains a negative-weight cycle reachable from s, however, shortest-path weights are not well defined. No path from s to a vertex on the cycle can be a shortest path—we can always find a path with lower weight by following the proposed "shortest" path and then traversing the negative-weight cycle. If there is a negative-weight cycle on some path from s to v, we define $\delta(s, v) = -\infty$.

Figure 24.1 illustrates the effect of negative weights and negative-weight cycles on shortest-path weights. Because there is only one path from s to a (the path $\langle s, a \rangle$), we have $\delta(s, a) = w(s, a) = 3$. Similarly, there is only one path from s to b, and so $\delta(s, b) = w(s, a) + w(a, b) = 3 + (-4) = -1$. There are infinitely many paths from s to c: $\langle s, c \rangle$, $\langle s, c, d, c \rangle$, $\langle s, c, d, c, d, c \rangle$, and so on. Because the cycle $\langle c, d, c \rangle$ has weight $6 + (-3) = 3 > 0$, the shortest path from s to c is $\langle s, c \rangle$, with weight $\delta(s, c) = w(s, c) = 5$. Similarly, the shortest path from s to d is $\langle s, c, d \rangle$, with weight $\delta(s, d) = w(s, c) + w(c, d) = 11$. Analogously, there are infinitely many paths from s to e: $\langle s, e \rangle$, $\langle s, e, f, e \rangle$, $\langle s, e, f, e, f, e \rangle$, and so on. Because the cycle $\langle e, f, e \rangle$ has weight $3 + (-6) = -3 < 0$, however, there is no shortest path from s to e. By traversing the negative-weight cycle $\langle e, f, e \rangle$ arbitrarily many times, we can find paths from s to e with arbitrarily large negative weights, and so $\delta(s, e) = -\infty$. Similarly, $\delta(s, f) = -\infty$. Because g is reachable from f, we can also find paths with arbitrarily large negative weights from s to g, and so $\delta(s, g) = -\infty$. Vertices h, i, and j also form a negative-weight cycle. They are not reachable from s, however, and so $\delta(s, h) = \delta(s, i) = \delta(s, j) = \infty$.

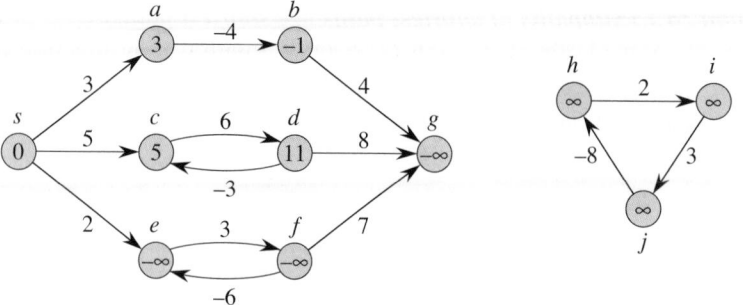

Figure 24.1 Negative edge weights in a directed graph. The shortest-path weight from source s appears within each vertex. Because vertices e and f form a negative-weight cycle reachable from s, they have shortest-path weights of $-\infty$. Because vertex g is reachable from a vertex whose shortest-path weight is $-\infty$, it, too, has a shortest-path weight of $-\infty$. Vertices such as h, i, and j are not reachable from s, and so their shortest-path weights are ∞, even though they lie on a negative-weight cycle.

Some shortest-paths algorithms, such as Dijkstra's algorithm, assume that all edge weights in the input graph are nonnegative, as in the road-map example. Others, such as the Bellman-Ford algorithm, allow negative-weight edges in the input graph and produce a correct answer as long as no negative-weight cycles are reachable from the source. Typically, if there is such a negative-weight cycle, the algorithm can detect and report its existence.

Cycles

Can a shortest path contain a cycle? As we have just seen, it cannot contain a negative-weight cycle. Nor can it contain a positive-weight cycle, since removing the cycle from the path produces a path with the same source and destination vertices and a lower path weight. That is, if $p = \langle v_0, v_1, \ldots, v_k \rangle$ is a path and $c = \langle v_i, v_{i+1}, \ldots, v_j \rangle$ is a positive-weight cycle on this path (so that $v_i = v_j$ and $w(c) > 0$), then the path $p' = \langle v_0, v_1, \ldots, v_i, v_{j+1}, v_{j+2}, \ldots, v_k \rangle$ has weight $w(p') = w(p) - w(c) < w(p)$, and so p cannot be a shortest path from v_0 to v_k.

That leaves only 0-weight cycles. We can remove a 0-weight cycle from any path to produce another path whose weight is the same. Thus, if there is a shortest path from a source vertex s to a destination vertex v that contains a 0-weight cycle, then there is another shortest path from s to v without this cycle. As long as a shortest path has 0-weight cycles, we can repeatedly remove these cycles from the path until we have a shortest path that is cycle-free. Therefore, without loss of generality we can assume that when we are finding shortest paths, they have no cycles, i.e., they are simple paths. Since any acyclic path in a graph $G = (V, E)$

contains at most $|V|$ distinct vertices, it also contains at most $|V| - 1$ edges. Thus, we can restrict our attention to shortest paths of at most $|V| - 1$ edges.

Representing shortest paths

We often wish to compute not only shortest-path weights, but the vertices on shortest paths as well. We represent shortest paths similarly to how we represented breadth-first trees in Section 22.2. Given a graph $G = (V, E)$, we maintain for each vertex $v \in V$ a ***predecessor*** $v.\pi$ that is either another vertex or NIL. The shortest-paths algorithms in this chapter set the π attributes so that the chain of predecessors originating at a vertex v runs backwards along a shortest path from s to v. Thus, given a vertex v for which $v.\pi \neq$ NIL, the procedure PRINT-PATH(G, s, v) from Section 22.2 will print a shortest path from s to v.

In the midst of executing a shortest-paths algorithm, however, the π values might not indicate shortest paths. As in breadth-first search, we shall be interested in the ***predecessor subgraph*** $G_\pi = (V_\pi, E_\pi)$ induced by the π values. Here again, we define the vertex set V_π to be the set of vertices of G with non-NIL predecessors, plus the source s:

$$V_\pi = \{v \in V : v.\pi \neq \text{NIL}\} \cup \{s\} \ .$$

The directed edge set E_π is the set of edges induced by the π values for vertices in V_π:

$$E_\pi = \{(v.\pi, v) \in E : v \in V_\pi - \{s\}\} \ .$$

We shall prove that the π values produced by the algorithms in this chapter have the property that at termination G_π is a "shortest-paths tree"—informally, a rooted tree containing a shortest path from the source s to every vertex that is reachable from s. A shortest-paths tree is like the breadth-first tree from Section 22.2, but it contains shortest paths from the source defined in terms of edge weights instead of numbers of edges. To be precise, let $G = (V, E)$ be a weighted, directed graph with weight function $w : E \to \mathbb{R}$, and assume that G contains no negative-weight cycles reachable from the source vertex $s \in V$, so that shortest paths are well defined. A ***shortest-paths tree*** rooted at s is a directed subgraph $G' = (V', E')$, where $V' \subseteq V$ and $E' \subseteq E$, such that

1. V' is the set of vertices reachable from s in G,

2. G' forms a rooted tree with root s, and

3. for all $v \in V'$, the unique simple path from s to v in G' is a shortest path from s to v in G.

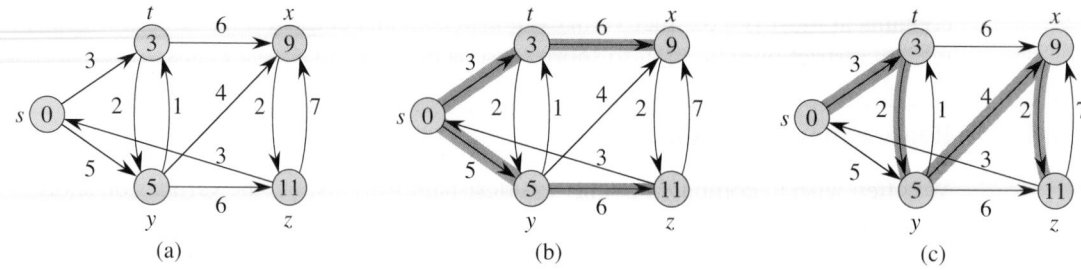

Figure 24.2 **(a)** A weighted, directed graph with shortest-path weights from source s. **(b)** The shaded edges form a shortest-paths tree rooted at the source s. **(c)** Another shortest-paths tree with the same root.

Shortest paths are not necessarily unique, and neither are shortest-paths trees. For example, Figure 24.2 shows a weighted, directed graph and two shortest-paths trees with the same root.

Relaxation

The algorithms in this chapter use the technique of ***relaxation***. For each vertex $v \in V$, we maintain an attribute $v.d$, which is an upper bound on the weight of a shortest path from source s to v. We call $v.d$ a ***shortest-path estimate***. We initialize the shortest-path estimates and predecessors by the following $\Theta(V)$-time procedure:

INITIALIZE-SINGLE-SOURCE(G, s)

1 **for** each vertex $v \in G.V$
2      $v.d = \infty$
3      $v.\pi = $ NIL
4 $s.d = 0$

After initialization, we have $v.\pi = $ NIL for all $v \in V$, $s.d = 0$, and $v.d = \infty$ for $v \in V - \{s\}$.

The process of ***relaxing*** an edge (u, v) consists of testing whether we can improve the shortest path to v found so far by going through u and, if so, updating $v.d$ and $v.\pi$. A relaxation step[1] may decrease the value of the shortest-path

---

[1] It may seem strange that the term "relaxation" is used for an operation that tightens an upper bound. The use of the term is historical. The outcome of a relaxation step can be viewed as a relaxation of the constraint $v.d \leq u.d + w(u, v)$, which, by the triangle inequality (Lemma 24.10), must be satisfied if $u.d = \delta(s, u)$ and $v.d = \delta(s, v)$. That is, if $v.d \leq u.d + w(u, v)$, there is no "pressure" to satisfy this constraint, so the constraint is "relaxed."

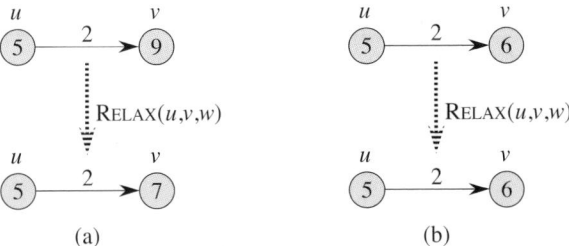

Figure 24.3   Relaxing an edge (u, v) with weight $w(u, v) = 2$. The shortest-path estimate of each vertex appears within the vertex. **(a)** Because $v.d > u.d + w(u, v)$ prior to relaxation, the value of $v.d$ decreases. **(b)** Here, $v.d \leq u.d + w(u, v)$ before relaxing the edge, and so the relaxation step leaves $v.d$ unchanged.

estimate $v.d$ and update v's predecessor attribute $v.\pi$. The following code performs a relaxation step on edge (u, v) in $O(1)$ time:

RELAX(u, v, w)

1   **if** $v.d > u.d + w(u, v)$
2       $v.d = u.d + w(u, v)$
3       $v.\pi = u$

Figure 24.3 shows two examples of relaxing an edge, one in which a shortest-path estimate decreases and one in which no estimate changes.

Each algorithm in this chapter calls INITIALIZE-SINGLE-SOURCE and then repeatedly relaxes edges. Moreover, relaxation is the only means by which shortest-path estimates and predecessors change. The algorithms in this chapter differ in how many times they relax each edge and the order in which they relax edges. Dijkstra's algorithm and the shortest-paths algorithm for directed acyclic graphs relax each edge exactly once. The Bellman-Ford algorithm relaxes each edge $|V| - 1$ times.

Properties of shortest paths and relaxation

To prove the algorithms in this chapter correct, we shall appeal to several properties of shortest paths and relaxation. We state these properties here, and Section 24.5 proves them formally. For your reference, each property stated here includes the appropriate lemma or corollary number from Section 24.5. The latter five of these properties, which refer to shortest-path estimates or the predecessor subgraph, implicitly assume that the graph is initialized with a call to INITIALIZE-SINGLE-SOURCE(G, s) and that the only way that shortest-path estimates and the predecessor subgraph change are by some sequence of relaxation steps.

Triangle inequality (Lemma 24.10)

For any edge $(u, v) \in E$, we have $\delta(s, v) \leq \delta(s, u) + w(u, v)$.

Upper-bound property (Lemma 24.11)

We always have $v.d \geq \delta(s, v)$ for all vertices $v \in V$, and once $v.d$ achieves the value $\delta(s, v)$, it never changes.

No-path property (Corollary 24.12)

If there is no path from s to v, then we always have $v.d = \delta(s, v) = \infty$.

Convergence property (Lemma 24.14)

If $s \rightsquigarrow u \to v$ is a shortest path in G for some $u, v \in V$, and if $u.d = \delta(s, u)$ at any time prior to relaxing edge (u, v), then $v.d = \delta(s, v)$ at all times afterward.

Path-relaxation property (Lemma 24.15)

If $p = \langle v_0, v_1, \ldots, v_k \rangle$ is a shortest path from $s = v_0$ to v_k, and we relax the edges of p in the order $(v_0, v_1), (v_1, v_2), \ldots, (v_{k-1}, v_k)$, then $v_k.d = \delta(s, v_k)$. This property holds regardless of any other relaxation steps that occur, even if they are intermixed with relaxations of the edges of p.

Predecessor-subgraph property (Lemma 24.17)

Once $v.d = \delta(s, v)$ for all $v \in V$, the predecessor subgraph is a shortest-paths tree rooted at s.

Chapter outline

Section 24.1 presents the Bellman-Ford algorithm, which solves the single-source shortest-paths problem in the general case in which edges can have negative weight. The Bellman-Ford algorithm is remarkably simple, and it has the further benefit of detecting whether a negative-weight cycle is reachable from the source. Section 24.2 gives a linear-time algorithm for computing shortest paths from a single source in a directed acyclic graph. Section 24.3 covers Dijkstra's algorithm, which has a lower running time than the Bellman-Ford algorithm but requires the edge weights to be nonnegative. Section 24.4 shows how we can use the Bellman-Ford algorithm to solve a special case of linear programming. Finally, Section 24.5 proves the properties of shortest paths and relaxation stated above.

We require some conventions for doing arithmetic with infinities. We shall assume that for any real number $a \neq -\infty$, we have $a + \infty = \infty + a = \infty$. Also, to make our proofs hold in the presence of negative-weight cycles, we shall assume that for any real number $a \neq \infty$, we have $a + (-\infty) = (-\infty) + a = -\infty$.

All algorithms in this chapter assume that the directed graph G is stored in the adjacency-list representation. Additionally, stored with each edge is its weight, so that as we traverse each adjacency list, we can determine the edge weights in $O(1)$ time per edge.

24.1   The Bellman-Ford algorithm

The ***Bellman-Ford algorithm*** solves the single-source shortest-paths problem in the general case in which edge weights may be negative. Given a weighted, directed graph $G = (V, E)$ with source s and weight function $w : E \to \mathbb{R}$, the Bellman-Ford algorithm returns a boolean value indicating whether or not there is a negative-weight cycle that is reachable from the source. If there is such a cycle, the algorithm indicates that no solution exists. If there is no such cycle, the algorithm produces the shortest paths and their weights.

The algorithm relaxes edges, progressively decreasing an estimate $v.d$ on the weight of a shortest path from the source s to each vertex $v \in V$ until it achieves the actual shortest-path weight $\delta(s, v)$. The algorithm returns TRUE if and only if the graph contains no negative-weight cycles that are reachable from the source.

BELLMAN-FORD(G, w, s)

```
1   INITIALIZE-SINGLE-SOURCE(G, s)
2   for i = 1 to |G.V| − 1
3       for each edge (u, v) ∈ G.E
4           RELAX(u, v, w)
5   for each edge (u, v) ∈ G.E
6       if v.d > u.d + w(u, v)
7           return FALSE
8   return TRUE
```

Figure 24.4 shows the execution of the Bellman-Ford algorithm on a graph with 5 vertices. After initializing the d and π values of all vertices in line 1, the algorithm makes $|V| - 1$ passes over the edges of the graph. Each pass is one iteration of the **for** loop of lines 2–4 and consists of relaxing each edge of the graph once. Figures 24.4(b)–(e) show the state of the algorithm after each of the four passes over the edges. After making $|V| - 1$ passes, lines 5–8 check for a negative-weight cycle and return the appropriate boolean value. (We'll see a little later why this check works.)

The Bellman-Ford algorithm runs in time $O(VE)$, since the initialization in line 1 takes $\Theta(V)$ time, each of the $|V| - 1$ passes over the edges in lines 2–4 takes $\Theta(E)$ time, and the **for** loop of lines 5–7 takes $O(E)$ time.

To prove the correctness of the Bellman-Ford algorithm, we start by showing that if there are no negative-weight cycles, the algorithm computes correct shortest-path weights for all vertices reachable from the source.

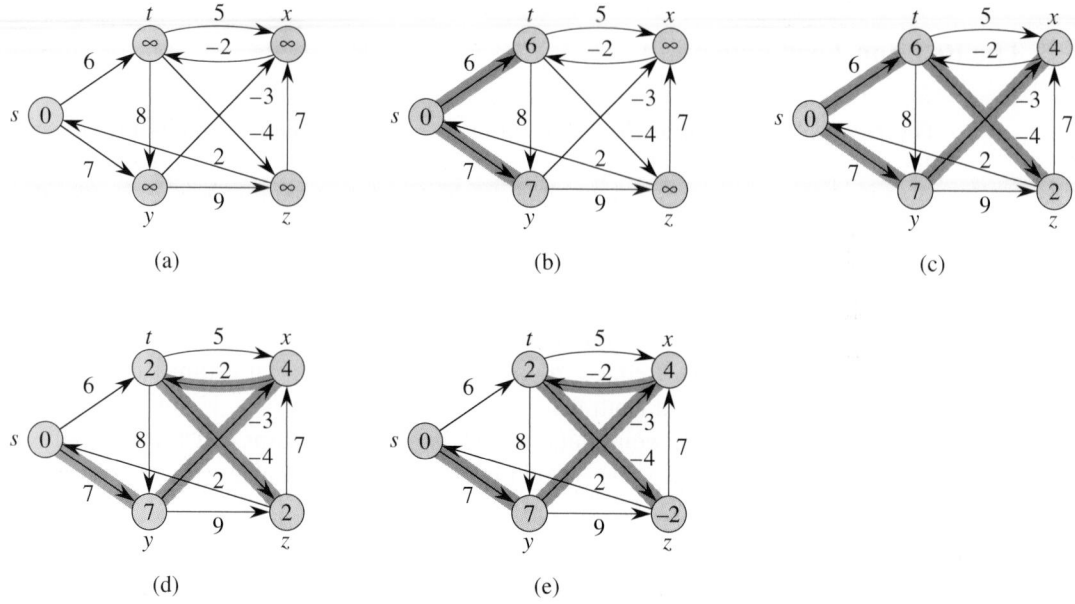

(a)   (b)   (c)

(d)   (e)

Figure 24.4 The execution of the Bellman-Ford algorithm. The source is vertex s. The d values appear within the vertices, and shaded edges indicate predecessor values: if edge (u, v) is shaded, then $v.\pi = u$. In this particular example, each pass relaxes the edges in the order $(t, x), (t, y), (t, z), (x, t), (y, x), (y, z), (z, x), (z, s), (s, t), (s, y)$. **(a)** The situation just before the first pass over the edges. **(b)–(e)** The situation after each successive pass over the edges. The d and π values in part (e) are the final values. The Bellman-Ford algorithm returns TRUE in this example.

Lemma 24.2

Let $G = (V, E)$ be a weighted, directed graph with source s and weight function $w : E \rightarrow \mathbb{R}$, and assume that G contains no negative-weight cycles that are reachable from s. Then, after the $|V| - 1$ iterations of the **for** loop of lines 2–4 of BELLMAN-FORD, we have $v.d = \delta(s, v)$ for all vertices v that are reachable from s.

Proof We prove the lemma by appealing to the path-relaxation property. Consider any vertex v that is reachable from s, and let $p = \langle v_0, v_1, \ldots, v_k \rangle$, where $v_0 = s$ and $v_k = v$, be any shortest path from s to v. Because shortest paths are simple, p has at most $|V| - 1$ edges, and so $k \leq |V| - 1$. Each of the $|V| - 1$ iterations of the **for** loop of lines 2–4 relaxes all $|E|$ edges. Among the edges relaxed in the ith iteration, for $i = 1, 2, \ldots, k$, is (v_{i-1}, v_i). By the path-relaxation property, therefore, $v.d = v_k.d = \delta(s, v_k) = \delta(s, v)$. ∎

Corollary 24.3

Let $G = (V, E)$ be a weighted, directed graph with source vertex s and weight function $w : E \rightarrow \mathbb{R}$. Then, for each vertex $v \in V$, there is a path from s to v if and only if BELLMAN-FORD terminates with $v.d < \infty$ when it is run on G.

Proof   The proof is left as Exercise 24.1-2. Note that this corollary allows G to have negative-weight cycles that are reachable from s, but that Lemma 24.2 does not.   ∎

Theorem 24.4 (Correctness of the Bellman-Ford algorithm)

Let BELLMAN-FORD be run on a weighted, directed graph $G = (V, E)$ with source s and weight function $w : E \rightarrow \mathbb{R}$. If G contains no negative-weight cycles that are reachable from s, then the algorithm returns TRUE, we have $v.d = \delta(s, v)$ for all vertices $v \in V$, and the predecessor subgraph G_π is a shortest-paths tree rooted at s. If G does contain a negative-weight cycle reachable from s, then the algorithm returns FALSE.

Proof   Suppose that graph G contains no negative-weight cycles that are reachable from the source s. We first prove the claim that at termination, $v.d = \delta(s, v)$ for all vertices $v \in V$. If vertex v is reachable from s, then Lemma 24.2 proves this claim. If v is not reachable from s, then the claim follows from the no-path property. Thus, the claim is proven. The predecessor-subgraph property, along with the claim, implies that G_π is a shortest-paths tree. Now we use the claim to show that BELLMAN-FORD returns TRUE. At termination, we have for all edges $(u, v) \in E$,

$$
\begin{aligned}
v.d &= \delta(s, v) \\
&\leq \delta(s, u) + w(u, v) \quad \text{(by the triangle inequality)} \\
&= u.d + w(u, v) \, ,
\end{aligned}
$$

and so none of the tests in line 6 causes BELLMAN-FORD to return FALSE. Therefore, it returns TRUE.

Now, suppose that graph G contains a negative-weight cycle that is reachable from the source s; let this cycle be $c = \langle v_0, v_1, \ldots, v_k \rangle$, where $v_0 = v_k$. Then,

$$
\sum_{i=1}^{k} w(v_{i-1}, v_i) < 0 \, . \tag{24.1}
$$

Assume for the purpose of contradiction that the Bellman-Ford algorithm returns TRUE. Thus, $v_i.d \leq v_{i-1}.d + w(v_{i-1}, v_i)$ for $i = 1, 2, \ldots, k$. Summing the inequalities around cycle c gives us

$$\sum_{i=1}^{k} v_i.d \;\leq\; \sum_{i=1}^{k}(v_{i-1}.d + w(v_{i-1}, v_i))$$

$$= \sum_{i=1}^{k} v_{i-1}.d + \sum_{i=1}^{k} w(v_{i-1}, v_i) \,.$$

Since $v_0 = v_k$, each vertex in c appears exactly once in each of the summations $\sum_{i=1}^{k} v_i.d$ and $\sum_{i=1}^{k} v_{i-1}.d$, and so

$$\sum_{i=1}^{k} v_i.d = \sum_{i=1}^{k} v_{i-1}.d \,.$$

Moreover, by Corollary 24.3, $v_i.d$ is finite for $i = 1, 2, \ldots, k$. Thus,

$$0 \leq \sum_{i=1}^{k} w(v_{i-1}, v_i) \,,$$

which contradicts inequality (24.1). We conclude that the Bellman-Ford algorithm returns TRUE if graph G contains no negative-weight cycles reachable from the source, and FALSE otherwise.   ∎

Exercises

24.1-1
Run the Bellman-Ford algorithm on the directed graph of Figure 24.4, using vertex z as the source. In each pass, relax edges in the same order as in the figure, and show the d and π values after each pass. Now, change the weight of edge (z, x) to 4 and run the algorithm again, using s as the source.

24.1-2
Prove Corollary 24.3.

24.1-3
Given a weighted, directed graph $G = (V, E)$ with no negative-weight cycles, let m be the maximum over all vertices $v \in V$ of the minimum number of edges in a shortest path from the source s to v. (Here, the shortest path is by weight, not the number of edges.) Suggest a simple change to the Bellman-Ford algorithm that allows it to terminate in $m + 1$ passes, even if m is not known in advance.

24.1-4
Modify the Bellman-Ford algorithm so that it sets $v.d$ to $-\infty$ for all vertices v for which there is a negative-weight cycle on some path from the source to v.

24.1-5   ★
Let $G = (V, E)$ be a weighted, directed graph with weight function $w : E \to \mathbb{R}$. Give an $O(VE)$-time algorithm to find, for each vertex $v \in V$, the value $\delta^*(v) = \min_{u \in V} \{\delta(u, v)\}$.

24.1-6   ★
Suppose that a weighted, directed graph $G = (V, E)$ has a negative-weight cycle. Give an efficient algorithm to list the vertices of one such cycle. Prove that your algorithm is correct.

24.2   Single-source shortest paths in directed acyclic graphs

By relaxing the edges of a weighted dag (directed acyclic graph) $G = (V, E)$ according to a topological sort of its vertices, we can compute shortest paths from a single source in $\Theta(V + E)$ time. Shortest paths are always well defined in a dag, since even if there are negative-weight edges, no negative-weight cycles can exist.

The algorithm starts by topologically sorting the dag (see Section 22.4) to impose a linear ordering on the vertices. If the dag contains a path from vertex u to vertex v, then u precedes v in the topological sort. We make just one pass over the vertices in the topologically sorted order. As we process each vertex, we relax each edge that leaves the vertex.

DAG-SHORTEST-PATHS(G, w, s)

1   topologically sort the vertices of G
2   INITIALIZE-SINGLE-SOURCE(G, s)
3   **for** each vertex u, taken in topologically sorted order
4   **for** each vertex $v \in G.Adj[u]$
5   RELAX(u, v, w)

Figure 24.5 shows the execution of this algorithm.

The running time of this algorithm is easy to analyze. As shown in Section 22.4, the topological sort of line 1 takes $\Theta(V + E)$ time. The call of INITIALIZE-SINGLE-SOURCE in line 2 takes $\Theta(V)$ time. The **for** loop of lines 3–5 makes one iteration per vertex. Altogether, the **for** loop of lines 4–5 relaxes each edge exactly once. (We have used an aggregate analysis here.) Because each iteration of the inner **for** loop takes $\Theta(1)$ time, the total running time is $\Theta(V + E)$, which is linear in the size of an adjacency-list representation of the graph.

The following theorem shows that the DAG-SHORTEST-PATHS procedure correctly computes the shortest paths.

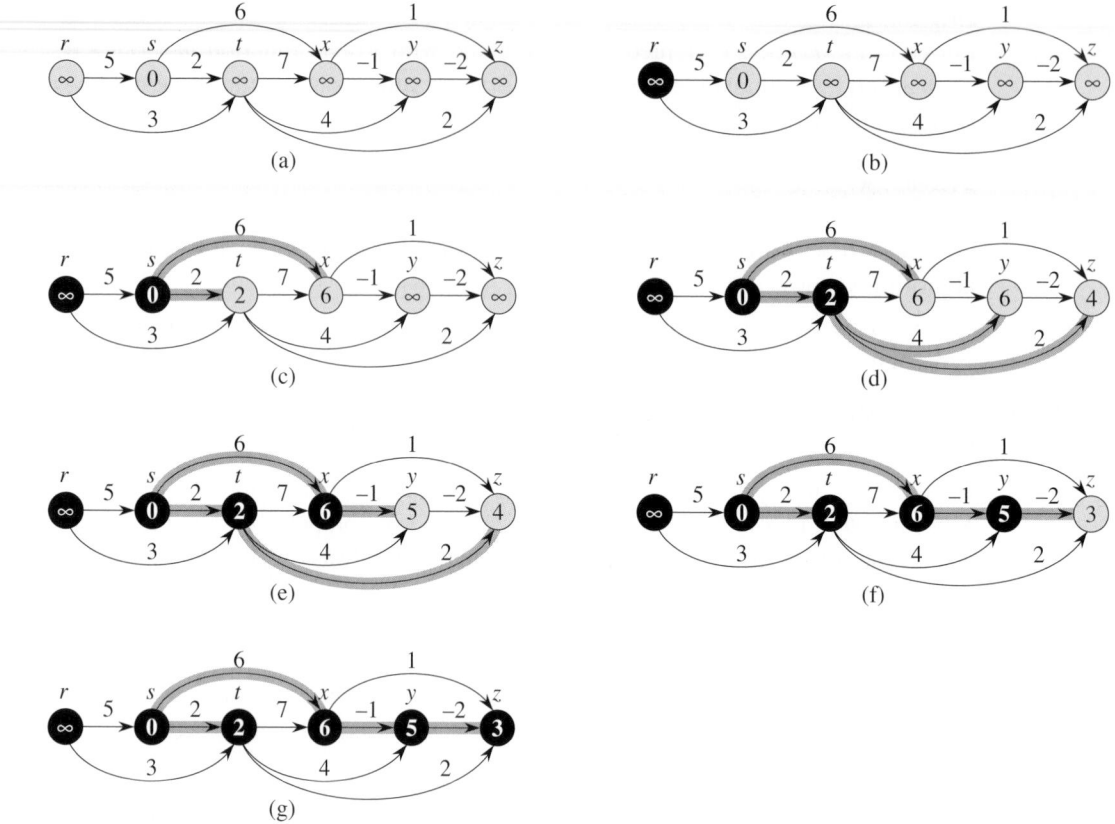

Figure 24.5 The execution of the algorithm for shortest paths in a directed acyclic graph. The vertices are topologically sorted from left to right. The source vertex is s. The d values appear within the vertices, and shaded edges indicate the π values. **(a)** The situation before the first iteration of the **for** loop of lines 3–5. **(b)–(g)** The situation after each iteration of the **for** loop of lines 3–5. The newly blackened vertex in each iteration was used as u in that iteration. The values shown in part (g) are the final values.

Theorem 24.5

If a weighted, directed graph $G = (V, E)$ has source vertex s and no cycles, then at the termination of the DAG-SHORTEST-PATHS procedure, $v.d = \delta(s, v)$ for all vertices $v \in V$, and the predecessor subgraph G_π is a shortest-paths tree.

Proof We first show that $v.d = \delta(s, v)$ for all vertices $v \in V$ at termination. If v is not reachable from s, then $v.d = \delta(s, v) = \infty$ by the no-path property. Now, suppose that v is reachable from s, so that there is a shortest path $p = \langle v_0, v_1, \ldots, v_k \rangle$, where $v_0 = s$ and $v_k = v$. Because we pro-

cess the vertices in topologically sorted order, we relax the edges on p in the order $(v_0, v_1), (v_1, v_2), \ldots, (v_{k-1}, v_k)$. The path-relaxation property implies that $v_i.d = \delta(s, v_i)$ at termination for $i = 0, 1, \ldots, k$. Finally, by the predecessor-subgraph property, G_π is a shortest-paths tree. ∎

An interesting application of this algorithm arises in determining critical paths in *PERT chart*[2] analysis. Edges represent jobs to be performed, and edge weights represent the times required to perform particular jobs. If edge (u, v) enters vertex v and edge (v, x) leaves v, then job (u, v) must be performed before job (v, x). A path through this dag represents a sequence of jobs that must be performed in a particular order. A *critical path* is a *longest* path through the dag, corresponding to the longest time to perform any sequence of jobs. Thus, the weight of a critical path provides a lower bound on the total time to perform all the jobs. We can find a critical path by either

- negating the edge weights and running DAG-SHORTEST-PATHS, or

- running DAG-SHORTEST-PATHS, with the modification that we replace "∞" by "$-\infty$" in line 2 of INITIALIZE-SINGLE-SOURCE and "$>$" by "$<$" in the RELAX procedure.

Exercises

24.2-1
Run DAG-SHORTEST-PATHS on the directed graph of Figure 24.5, using vertex r as the source.

24.2-2
Suppose we change line 3 of DAG-SHORTEST-PATHS to read

3   **for** the first $|V| - 1$ vertices, taken in topologically sorted order

Show that the procedure would remain correct.

24.2-3
The PERT chart formulation given above is somewhat unnatural. In a more natural structure, vertices would represent jobs and edges would represent sequencing constraints; that is, edge (u, v) would indicate that job u must be performed before job v. We would then assign weights to vertices, not edges. Modify the DAG-SHORTEST-PATHS procedure so that it finds a longest path in a directed acyclic graph with weighted vertices in linear time.

---

[2]"PERT" is an acronym for "program evaluation and review technique."

24.2-4

Give an efficient algorithm to count the total number of paths in a directed acyclic graph. Analyze your algorithm.

24.3   Dijkstra's algorithm

Dijkstra's algorithm solves the single-source shortest-paths problem on a weighted, directed graph $G = (V, E)$ for the case in which all edge weights are nonnegative. In this section, therefore, we assume that $w(u, v) \geq 0$ for each edge $(u, v) \in E$. As we shall see, with a good implementation, the running time of Dijkstra's algorithm is lower than that of the Bellman-Ford algorithm.

Dijkstra's algorithm maintains a set S of vertices whose final shortest-path weights from the source s have already been determined. The algorithm repeatedly selects the vertex $u \in V - S$ with the minimum shortest-path estimate, adds u to S, and relaxes all edges leaving u. In the following implementation, we use a min-priority queue Q of vertices, keyed by their d values.

DIJKSTRA(G, w, s)

```
1   INITIALIZE-SINGLE-SOURCE(G, s)
2   S = ∅
3   Q = G.V
4   while Q ≠ ∅
5       u = EXTRACT-MIN(Q)
6       S = S ∪ {u}
7       for each vertex v ∈ G.Adj[u]
8           RELAX(u, v, w)
```

Dijkstra's algorithm relaxes edges as shown in Figure 24.6. Line 1 initializes the d and π values in the usual way, and line 2 initializes the set S to the empty set. The algorithm maintains the invariant that $Q = V - S$ at the start of each iteration of the **while** loop of lines 4–8. Line 3 initializes the min-priority queue Q to contain all the vertices in V; since $S = \emptyset$ at that time, the invariant is true after line 3. Each time through the **while** loop of lines 4–8, line 5 extracts a vertex u from $Q = V - S$ and line 6 adds it to set S, thereby maintaining the invariant. (The first time through this loop, $u = s$.) Vertex u, therefore, has the smallest shortest-path estimate of any vertex in $V - S$. Then, lines 7–8 relax each edge (u, v) leaving u, thus updating the estimate $v.d$ and the predecessor $v.\pi$ if we can improve the shortest path to v found so far by going through u. Observe that the algorithm never inserts vertices into Q after line 3 and that each vertex is extracted from Q

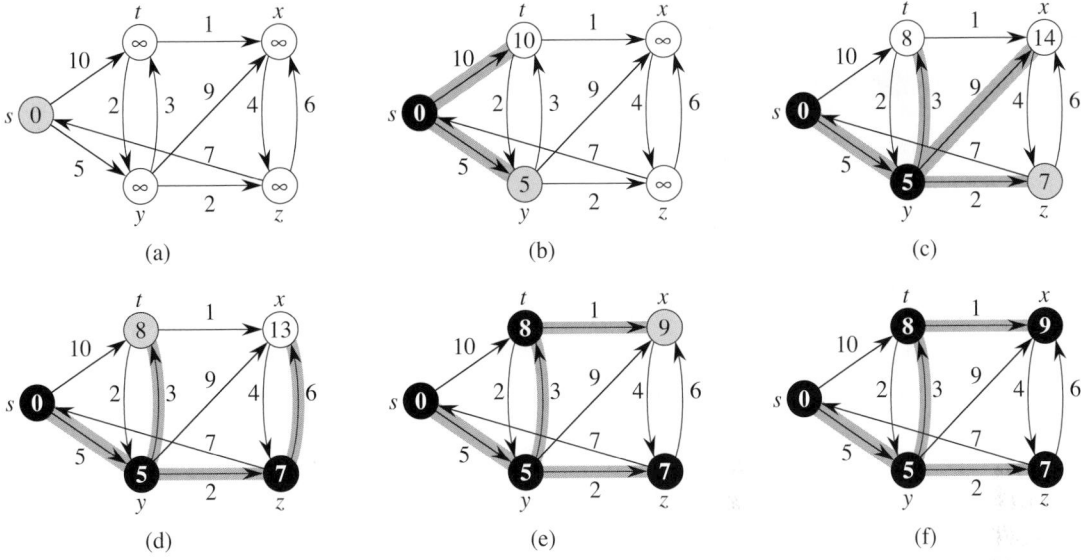

Figure 24.6 The execution of Dijkstra's algorithm. The source s is the leftmost vertex. The shortest-path estimates appear within the vertices, and shaded edges indicate predecessor values. Black vertices are in the set S, and white vertices are in the min-priority queue $Q = V - S$. **(a)** The situation just before the first iteration of the **while** loop of lines 4–8. The shaded vertex has the minimum d value and is chosen as vertex u in line 5. **(b)–(f)** The situation after each successive iteration of the **while** loop. The shaded vertex in each part is chosen as vertex u in line 5 of the next iteration. The d values and predecessors shown in part (f) are the final values.

and added to S exactly once, so that the **while** loop of lines 4–8 iterates exactly $|V|$ times.

Because Dijkstra's algorithm always chooses the "lightest" or "closest" vertex in $V - S$ to add to set S, we say that it uses a greedy strategy. Chapter 16 explains greedy strategies in detail, but you need not have read that chapter to understand Dijkstra's algorithm. Greedy strategies do not always yield optimal results in general, but as the following theorem and its corollary show, Dijkstra's algorithm does indeed compute shortest paths. The key is to show that each time it adds a vertex u to set S, we have $u.d = \delta(s, u)$.

Theorem 24.6 (Correctness of Dijkstra's algorithm)
Dijkstra's algorithm, run on a weighted, directed graph $G = (V, E)$ with non-negative weight function w and source s, terminates with $u.d = \delta(s, u)$ for all vertices $u \in V$.

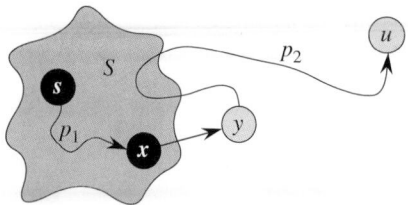

Figure 24.7   The proof of Theorem 24.6. Set S is nonempty just before vertex u is added to it. We decompose a shortest path p from source s to vertex u into $s \overset{p_1}{\leadsto} x \to y \overset{p_2}{\leadsto} u$, where y is the first vertex on the path that is not in S and $x \in S$ immediately precedes y. Vertices x and y are distinct, but we may have $s = x$ or $y = u$. Path p_2 may or may not reenter set S.

Proof   We use the following loop invariant:

> At the start of each iteration of the **while** loop of lines 4–8, $v.d = \delta(s, v)$ for each vertex $v \in S$.

It suffices to show for each vertex $u \in V$, we have $u.d = \delta(s, u)$ at the time when u is added to set S. Once we show that $u.d = \delta(s, u)$, we rely on the upper-bound property to show that the equality holds at all times thereafter.

Initialization: Initially, $S = \emptyset$, and so the invariant is trivially true.

Maintenance: We wish to show that in each iteration, $u.d = \delta(s, u)$ for the vertex added to set S. For the purpose of contradiction, let u be the first vertex for which $u.d \neq \delta(s, u)$ when it is added to set S. We shall focus our attention on the situation at the beginning of the iteration of the **while** loop in which u is added to S and derive the contradiction that $u.d = \delta(s, u)$ at that time by examining a shortest path from s to u. We must have $u \neq s$ because s is the first vertex added to set S and $s.d = \delta(s, s) = 0$ at that time. Because $u \neq s$, we also have that $S \neq \emptyset$ just before u is added to S. There must be some path from s to u, for otherwise $u.d = \delta(s, u) = \infty$ by the no-path property, which would violate our assumption that $u.d \neq \delta(s, u)$. Because there is at least one path, there is a shortest path p from s to u. Prior to adding u to S, path p connects a vertex in S, namely s, to a vertex in $V - S$, namely u. Let us consider the first vertex y along p such that $y \in V - S$, and let $x \in S$ be y's predecessor along p. Thus, as Figure 24.7 illustrates, we can decompose path p into $s \overset{p_1}{\leadsto} x \to y \overset{p_2}{\leadsto} u$. (Either of paths p_1 or p_2 may have no edges.)

We claim that $y.d = \delta(s, y)$ when u is added to S. To prove this claim, observe that $x \in S$. Then, because we chose u as the first vertex for which $u.d \neq \delta(s, u)$ when it is added to S, we had $x.d = \delta(s, x)$ when x was added

to S. Edge (x, y) was relaxed at that time, and the claim follows from the convergence property.

We can now obtain a contradiction to prove that $u.d = \delta(s, u)$. Because y appears before u on a shortest path from s to u and all edge weights are nonnegative (notably those on path p_2), we have $\delta(s, y) \le \delta(s, u)$, and thus

$$
\begin{aligned}
y.d &= \delta(s, y) \\
&\le \delta(s, u) \\
&\le u.d \quad \text{(by the upper-bound property)} .
\end{aligned}
\tag{24.2}
$$

But because both vertices u and y were in $V - S$ when u was chosen in line 5, we have $u.d \le y.d$. Thus, the two inequalities in (24.2) are in fact equalities, giving

$$
y.d = \delta(s, y) = \delta(s, u) = u.d .
$$

Consequently, $u.d = \delta(s, u)$, which contradicts our choice of u. We conclude that $u.d = \delta(s, u)$ when u is added to S, and that this equality is maintained at all times thereafter.

Termination: At termination, $Q = \emptyset$ which, along with our earlier invariant that $Q = V - S$, implies that $S = V$. Thus, $u.d = \delta(s, u)$ for all vertices $u \in V$. ∎

Corollary 24.7
If we run Dijkstra's algorithm on a weighted, directed graph $G = (V, E)$ with nonnegative weight function w and source s, then at termination, the predecessor subgraph G_π is a shortest-paths tree rooted at s.

Proof Immediate from Theorem 24.6 and the predecessor-subgraph property. ∎

Analysis

How fast is Dijkstra's algorithm? It maintains the min-priority queue Q by calling three priority-queue operations: INSERT (implicit in line 3), EXTRACT-MIN (line 5), and DECREASE-KEY (implicit in RELAX, which is called in line 8). The algorithm calls both INSERT and EXTRACT-MIN once per vertex. Because each vertex $u \in V$ is added to set S exactly once, each edge in the adjacency list $Adj[u]$ is examined in the **for** loop of lines 7–8 exactly once during the course of the algorithm. Since the total number of edges in all the adjacency lists is $|E|$, this **for** loop iterates a total of $|E|$ times, and thus the algorithm calls DECREASE-KEY at most $|E|$ times overall. (Observe once again that we are using aggregate analysis.)

The running time of Dijkstra's algorithm depends on how we implement the min-priority queue. Consider first the case in which we maintain the min-priority

queue by taking advantage of the vertices being numbered 1 to $|V|$. We simply store $v.d$ in the vth entry of an array. Each INSERT and DECREASE-KEY operation takes $O(1)$ time, and each EXTRACT-MIN operation takes $O(V)$ time (since we have to search through the entire array), for a total time of $O(V^2 + E) = O(V^2)$.

If the graph is sufficiently sparse—in particular, $E = o(V^2/\lg V)$—we can improve the algorithm by implementing the min-priority queue with a binary min-heap. (As discussed in Section 6.5, the implementation should make sure that vertices and corresponding heap elements maintain handles to each other.) Each EXTRACT-MIN operation then takes time $O(\lg V)$. As before, there are $|V|$ such operations. The time to build the binary min-heap is $O(V)$. Each DECREASE-KEY operation takes time $O(\lg V)$, and there are still at most $|E|$ such operations. The total running time is therefore $O((V + E)\lg V)$, which is $O(E \lg V)$ if all vertices are reachable from the source. This running time improves upon the straightforward $O(V^2)$-time implementation if $E = o(V^2/\lg V)$.

We can in fact achieve a running time of $O(V \lg V + E)$ by implementing the min-priority queue with a Fibonacci heap (see Chapter 19). The amortized cost of each of the $|V|$ EXTRACT-MIN operations is $O(\lg V)$, and each DECREASE-KEY call, of which there are at most $|E|$, takes only $O(1)$ amortized time. Historically, the development of Fibonacci heaps was motivated by the observation that Dijkstra's algorithm typically makes many more DECREASE-KEY calls than EXTRACT-MIN calls, so that any method of reducing the amortized time of each DECREASE-KEY operation to $o(\lg V)$ without increasing the amortized time of EXTRACT-MIN would yield an asymptotically faster implementation than with binary heaps.

Dijkstra's algorithm resembles both breadth-first search (see Section 22.2) and Prim's algorithm for computing minimum spanning trees (see Section 23.2). It is like breadth-first search in that set S corresponds to the set of black vertices in a breadth-first search; just as vertices in S have their final shortest-path weights, so do black vertices in a breadth-first search have their correct breadth-first distances. Dijkstra's algorithm is like Prim's algorithm in that both algorithms use a min-priority queue to find the "lightest" vertex outside a given set (the set S in Dijkstra's algorithm and the tree being grown in Prim's algorithm), add this vertex into the set, and adjust the weights of the remaining vertices outside the set accordingly.

Exercises

24.3-1
Run Dijkstra's algorithm on the directed graph of Figure 24.2, first using vertex s as the source and then using vertex z as the source. In the style of Figure 24.6, show the d and π values and the vertices in set S after each iteration of the **while** loop.

24.3-2
Give a simple example of a directed graph with negative-weight edges for which Dijkstra's algorithm produces incorrect answers. Why doesn't the proof of Theorem 24.6 go through when negative-weight edges are allowed?

24.3-3
Suppose we change line 4 of Dijkstra's algorithm to the following.

4   **while** $|Q| > 1$

This change causes the **while** loop to execute $|V| - 1$ times instead of $|V|$ times. Is this proposed algorithm correct?

24.3-4
Professor Gaedel has written a program that he claims implements Dijkstra's algorithm. The program produces $v.d$ and $v.\pi$ for each vertex $v \in V$. Give an $O(V + E)$-time algorithm to check the output of the professor's program. It should determine whether the d and π attributes match those of some shortest-paths tree. You may assume that all edge weights are nonnegative.

24.3-5
Professor Newman thinks that he has worked out a simpler proof of correctness for Dijkstra's algorithm. He claims that Dijkstra's algorithm relaxes the edges of every shortest path in the graph in the order in which they appear on the path, and therefore the path-relaxation property applies to every vertex reachable from the source. Show that the professor is mistaken by constructing a directed graph for which Dijkstra's algorithm could relax the edges of a shortest path out of order.

24.3-6
We are given a directed graph $G = (V, E)$ on which each edge $(u, v) \in E$ has an associated value $r(u, v)$, which is a real number in the range $0 \le r(u, v) \le 1$ that represents the reliability of a communication channel from vertex u to vertex v. We interpret $r(u, v)$ as the probability that the channel from u to v will not fail, and we assume that these probabilities are independent. Give an efficient algorithm to find the most reliable path between two given vertices.

24.3-7
Let $G = (V, E)$ be a weighted, directed graph with positive weight function $w : E \to \{1, 2, \ldots, W\}$ for some positive integer W, and assume that no two vertices have the same shortest-path weights from source vertex s. Now suppose that we define an unweighted, directed graph $G' = (V \cup V', E')$ by replacing each edge $(u, v) \in E$ with $w(u, v)$ unit-weight edges in series. How many vertices does G' have? Now suppose that we run a breadth-first search on G'. Show that

the order in which the breadth-first search of G' colors vertices in V black is the same as the order in which Dijkstra's algorithm extracts the vertices of V from the priority queue when it runs on G.

24.3-8
Let $G = (V, E)$ be a weighted, directed graph with nonnegative weight function $w : E \rightarrow \{0, 1, \ldots, W\}$ for some nonnegative integer W. Modify Dijkstra's algorithm to compute the shortest paths from a given source vertex s in $O(WV + E)$ time.

24.3-9
Modify your algorithm from Exercise 24.3-8 to run in $O((V + E) \lg W)$ time. (*Hint:* How many distinct shortest-path estimates can there be in $V - S$ at any point in time?)

24.3-10
Suppose that we are given a weighted, directed graph $G = (V, E)$ in which edges that leave the source vertex s may have negative weights, all other edge weights are nonnegative, and there are no negative-weight cycles. Argue that Dijkstra's algorithm correctly finds shortest paths from s in this graph.

24.4   Difference constraints and shortest paths

Chapter 29 studies the general linear-programming problem, in which we wish to optimize a linear function subject to a set of linear inequalities. In this section, we investigate a special case of linear programming that we reduce to finding shortest paths from a single source. We can then solve the single-source shortest-paths problem that results by running the Bellman-Ford algorithm, thereby also solving the linear-programming problem.

Linear programming

In the general *linear-programming problem*, we are given an $m \times n$ matrix A, an m-vector b, and an n-vector c. We wish to find a vector x of n elements that maximizes the *objective function* $\sum_{i=1}^{n} c_i x_i$ subject to the m constraints given by $Ax \leq b$.

Although the simplex algorithm, which is the focus of Chapter 29, does not always run in time polynomial in the size of its input, there are other linear-programming algorithms that do run in polynomial time. We offer here two reasons to understand the setup of linear-programming problems. First, if we know that we

can cast a given problem as a polynomial-sized linear-programming problem, then we immediately have a polynomial-time algorithm to solve the problem. Second, faster algorithms exist for many special cases of linear programming. For example, the single-pair shortest-path problem (Exercise 24.4-4) and the maximum-flow problem (Exercise 26.1-5) are special cases of linear programming.

Sometimes we don't really care about the objective function; we just wish to find any *feasible solution*, that is, any vector x that satisfies $Ax \leq b$, or to determine that no feasible solution exists. We shall focus on one such *feasibility problem*.

Systems of difference constraints

In a *system of difference constraints*, each row of the linear-programming matrix A contains one 1 and one -1, and all other entries of A are 0. Thus, the constraints given by $Ax \leq b$ are a set of m *difference constraints* involving n unknowns, in which each constraint is a simple linear inequality of the form

$$x_j - x_i \leq b_k ,$$

where $1 \leq i, j \leq n, i \neq j$, and $1 \leq k \leq m$.

For example, consider the problem of finding a 5-vector $x = (x_i)$ that satisfies

$$
\begin{pmatrix}
1 & -1 & 0 & 0 & 0 \\
1 & 0 & 0 & 0 & -1 \\
0 & 1 & 0 & 0 & -1 \\
-1 & 0 & 1 & 0 & 0 \\
-1 & 0 & 0 & 1 & 0 \\
0 & 0 & -1 & 1 & 0 \\
0 & 0 & -1 & 0 & 1 \\
0 & 0 & 0 & -1 & 1
\end{pmatrix}
\begin{pmatrix}
x_1 \\
x_2 \\
x_3 \\
x_4 \\
x_5
\end{pmatrix}
\leq
\begin{pmatrix}
0 \\
-1 \\
1 \\
5 \\
4 \\
-1 \\
-3 \\
-3
\end{pmatrix} .
$$

This problem is equivalent to finding values for the unknowns x_1, x_2, x_3, x_4, x_5, satisfying the following 8 difference constraints:

$$x_1 - x_2 \leq 0 , \tag{24.3}$$
$$x_1 - x_5 \leq -1 , \tag{24.4}$$
$$x_2 - x_5 \leq 1 , \tag{24.5}$$
$$x_3 - x_1 \leq 5 , \tag{24.6}$$
$$x_4 - x_1 \leq 4 , \tag{24.7}$$
$$x_4 - x_3 \leq -1 , \tag{24.8}$$
$$x_5 - x_3 \leq -3 , \tag{24.9}$$
$$x_5 - x_4 \leq -3 . \tag{24.10}$$

One solution to this problem is $x = (-5, -3, 0, -1, -4)$, which you can verify directly by checking each inequality. In fact, this problem has more than one solution. Another is $x' = (0, 2, 5, 4, 1)$. These two solutions are related: each component of x' is 5 larger than the corresponding component of x. This fact is not mere coincidence.

Lemma 24.8

Let $x = (x_1, x_2, \ldots, x_n)$ be a solution to a system $Ax \leq b$ of difference constraints, and let d be any constant. Then $x + d = (x_1 + d, x_2 + d, \ldots, x_n + d)$ is a solution to $Ax \leq b$ as well.

Proof   For each x_i and x_j, we have $(x_j + d) - (x_i + d) = x_j - x_i$. Thus, if x satisfies $Ax \leq b$, so does $x + d$.   ∎

Systems of difference constraints occur in many different applications. For example, the unknowns x_i may be times at which events are to occur. Each constraint states that at least a certain amount of time, or at most a certain amount of time, must elapse between two events. Perhaps the events are jobs to be performed during the assembly of a product. If we apply an adhesive that takes 2 hours to set at time x_1 and we have to wait until it sets to install a part at time x_2, then we have the constraint that $x_2 \geq x_1 + 2$ or, equivalently, that $x_1 - x_2 \leq -2$. Alternatively, we might require that the part be installed after the adhesive has been applied but no later than the time that the adhesive has set halfway. In this case, we get the pair of constraints $x_2 \geq x_1$ and $x_2 \leq x_1 + 1$ or, equivalently, $x_1 - x_2 \leq 0$ and $x_2 - x_1 \leq 1$.

Constraint graphs

We can interpret systems of difference constraints from a graph-theoretic point of view. In a system $Ax \leq b$ of difference constraints, we view the $m \times n$ linear-programming matrix A as the transpose of an incidence matrix (see Exercise 22.1-7) for a graph with n vertices and m edges. Each vertex v_i in the graph, for $i = 1, 2, \ldots, n$, corresponds to one of the n unknown variables x_i. Each directed edge in the graph corresponds to one of the m inequalities involving two unknowns.

More formally, given a system $Ax \leq b$ of difference constraints, the corresponding *constraint graph* is a weighted, directed graph $G = (V, E)$, where

$$V = \{v_0, v_1, \ldots, v_n\}$$

and

$$E = \{(v_i, v_j) : x_j - x_i \leq b_k \text{ is a constraint}\}$$
$$\cup \{(v_0, v_1), (v_0, v_2), (v_0, v_3), \ldots, (v_0, v_n)\} \ .$$

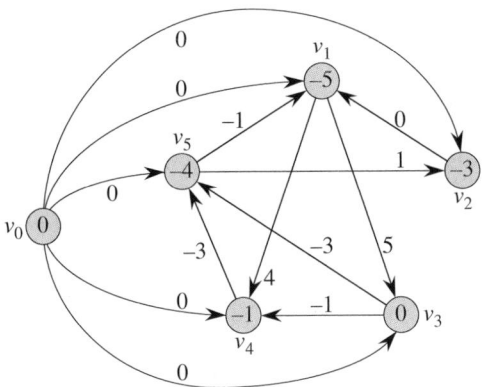

Figure 24.8 The constraint graph corresponding to the system (24.3)–(24.10) of difference constraints. The value of $\delta(v_0, v_i)$ appears in each vertex v_i. One feasible solution to the system is $x = (-5, -3, 0, -1, -4)$.

The constraint graph contains the additional vertex v_0, as we shall see shortly, to guarantee that the graph has some vertex which can reach all other vertices. Thus, the vertex set V consists of a vertex v_i for each unknown x_i, plus an additional vertex v_0. The edge set E contains an edge for each difference constraint, plus an edge (v_0, v_i) for each unknown x_i. If $x_j - x_i \le b_k$ is a difference constraint, then the weight of edge (v_i, v_j) is $w(v_i, v_j) = b_k$. The weight of each edge leaving v_0 is 0. Figure 24.8 shows the constraint graph for the system (24.3)–(24.10) of difference constraints.

The following theorem shows that we can find a solution to a system of difference constraints by finding shortest-path weights in the corresponding constraint graph.

Theorem 24.9
Given a system $Ax \le b$ of difference constraints, let $G = (V, E)$ be the corresponding constraint graph. If G contains no negative-weight cycles, then

$$x = (\delta(v_0, v_1), \delta(v_0, v_2), \delta(v_0, v_3), \ldots, \delta(v_0, v_n)) \qquad (24.11)$$

is a feasible solution for the system. If G contains a negative-weight cycle, then there is no feasible solution for the system.

Proof We first show that if the constraint graph contains no negative-weight cycles, then equation (24.11) gives a feasible solution. Consider any edge $(v_i, v_j) \in E$. By the triangle inequality, $\delta(v_0, v_j) \le \delta(v_0, v_i) + w(v_i, v_j)$ or, equivalently, $\delta(v_0, v_j) - \delta(v_0, v_i) \le w(v_i, v_j)$. Thus, letting $x_i = \delta(v_0, v_i)$ and

$x_j = \delta(v_0, v_j)$ satisfies the difference constraint $x_j - x_i \leq w(v_i, v_j)$ that corresponds to edge (v_i, v_j).

Now we show that if the constraint graph contains a negative-weight cycle, then the system of difference constraints has no feasible solution. Without loss of generality, let the negative-weight cycle be $c = \langle v_1, v_2, \ldots, v_k \rangle$, where $v_1 = v_k$. (The vertex v_0 cannot be on cycle c, because it has no entering edges.) Cycle c corresponds to the following difference constraints:

$$
\begin{aligned}
x_2 - x_1 &\leq w(v_1, v_2), \\
x_3 - x_2 &\leq w(v_2, v_3), \\
&\vdots \\
x_{k-1} - x_{k-2} &\leq w(v_{k-2}, v_{k-1}), \\
x_k - x_{k-1} &\leq w(v_{k-1}, v_k).
\end{aligned}
$$

We will assume that x has a solution satisfying each of these k inequalities and then derive a contradiction. The solution must also satisfy the inequality that results when we sum the k inequalities together. If we sum the left-hand sides, each unknown x_i is added in once and subtracted out once (remember that $v_1 = v_k$ implies $x_1 = x_k$), so that the left-hand side of the sum is 0. The right-hand side sums to $w(c)$, and thus we obtain $0 \leq w(c)$. But since c is a negative-weight cycle, $w(c) < 0$, and we obtain the contradiction that $0 \leq w(c) < 0$. ∎

Solving systems of difference constraints

Theorem 24.9 tells us that we can use the Bellman-Ford algorithm to solve a system of difference constraints. Because the constraint graph contains edges from the source vertex v_0 to all other vertices, any negative-weight cycle in the constraint graph is reachable from v_0. If the Bellman-Ford algorithm returns TRUE, then the shortest-path weights give a feasible solution to the system. In Figure 24.8, for example, the shortest-path weights provide the feasible solution $x = (-5, -3, 0, -1, -4)$, and by Lemma 24.8, $x = (d - 5, d - 3, d, d - 1, d - 4)$ is also a feasible solution for any constant d. If the Bellman-Ford algorithm returns FALSE, there is no feasible solution to the system of difference constraints.

A system of difference constraints with m constraints on n unknowns produces a graph with $n + 1$ vertices and $n + m$ edges. Thus, using the Bellman-Ford algorithm, we can solve the system in $O((n + 1)(n + m)) = O(n^2 + nm)$ time. Exercise 24.4-5 asks you to modify the algorithm to run in $O(nm)$ time, even if m is much less than n.

Exercises

24.4-1

Find a feasible solution or determine that no feasible solution exists for the following system of difference constraints:

$$
\begin{aligned}
x_1 - x_2 &\leq 1, \\
x_1 - x_4 &\leq -4, \\
x_2 - x_3 &\leq 2, \\
x_2 - x_5 &\leq 7, \\
x_2 - x_6 &\leq 5, \\
x_3 - x_6 &\leq 10, \\
x_4 - x_2 &\leq 2, \\
x_5 - x_1 &\leq -1, \\
x_5 - x_4 &\leq 3, \\
x_6 - x_3 &\leq -8.
\end{aligned}
$$

24.4-2

Find a feasible solution or determine that no feasible solution exists for the following system of difference constraints:

$$
\begin{aligned}
x_1 - x_2 &\leq 4, \\
x_1 - x_5 &\leq 5, \\
x_2 - x_4 &\leq -6, \\
x_3 - x_2 &\leq 1, \\
x_4 - x_1 &\leq 3, \\
x_4 - x_3 &\leq 5, \\
x_4 - x_5 &\leq 10, \\
x_5 - x_3 &\leq -4, \\
x_5 - x_4 &\leq -8.
\end{aligned}
$$

24.4-3

Can any shortest-path weight from the new vertex v_0 in a constraint graph be positive? Explain.

24.4-4

Express the single-pair shortest-path problem as a linear program.

24.4-5

Show how to modify the Bellman-Ford algorithm slightly so that when we use it to solve a system of difference constraints with m inequalities on n unknowns, the running time is $O(nm)$.

24.4-6

Suppose that in addition to a system of difference constraints, we want to handle *equality constraints* of the form $x_i = x_j + b_k$. Show how to adapt the Bellman-Ford algorithm to solve this variety of constraint system.

24.4-7

Show how to solve a system of difference constraints by a Bellman-Ford-like algorithm that runs on a constraint graph without the extra vertex v_0.

24.4-8 ★

Let $Ax \leq b$ be a system of m difference constraints in n unknowns. Show that the Bellman-Ford algorithm, when run on the corresponding constraint graph, maximizes $\sum_{i=1}^{n} x_i$ subject to $Ax \leq b$ and $x_i \leq 0$ for all x_i.

24.4-9 ★

Show that the Bellman-Ford algorithm, when run on the constraint graph for a system $Ax \leq b$ of difference constraints, minimizes the quantity $(\max\{x_i\} - \min\{x_i\})$ subject to $Ax \leq b$. Explain how this fact might come in handy if the algorithm is used to schedule construction jobs.

24.4-10

Suppose that every row in the matrix A of a linear program $Ax \leq b$ corresponds to a difference constraint, a single-variable constraint of the form $x_i \leq b_k$, or a single-variable constraint of the form $-x_i \leq b_k$. Show how to adapt the Bellman-Ford algorithm to solve this variety of constraint system.

24.4-11

Give an efficient algorithm to solve a system $Ax \leq b$ of difference constraints when all of the elements of b are real-valued and all of the unknowns x_i must be integers.

24.4-12 ★

Give an efficient algorithm to solve a system $Ax \leq b$ of difference constraints when all of the elements of b are real-valued and a specified subset of some, but not necessarily all, of the unknowns x_i must be integers.

24.5   Proofs of shortest-paths properties

Throughout this chapter, our correctness arguments have relied on the triangle inequality, upper-bound property, no-path property, convergence property, path-relaxation property, and predecessor-subgraph property. We stated these properties without proof at the beginning of this chapter. In this section, we prove them.

The triangle inequality

In studying breadth-first search (Section 22.2), we proved as Lemma 22.1 a simple property of shortest distances in unweighted graphs. The triangle inequality generalizes the property to weighted graphs.

Lemma 24.10 (Triangle inequality)
Let $G = (V, E)$ be a weighted, directed graph with weight function $w : E \to \mathbb{R}$ and source vertex s. Then, for all edges $(u, v) \in E$, we have

$$\delta(s, v) \leq \delta(s, u) + w(u, v) .$$

Proof   Suppose that p is a shortest path from source s to vertex v. Then p has no more weight than any other path from s to v. Specifically, path p has no more weight than the particular path that takes a shortest path from source s to vertex u and then takes edge (u, v).

Exercise 24.5-3 asks you to handle the case in which there is no shortest path from s to v.   ∎

Effects of relaxation on shortest-path estimates

The next group of lemmas describes how shortest-path estimates are affected when we execute a sequence of relaxation steps on the edges of a weighted, directed graph that has been initialized by INITIALIZE-SINGLE-SOURCE.

Lemma 24.11 (Upper-bound property)
Let $G = (V, E)$ be a weighted, directed graph with weight function $w : E \to \mathbb{R}$. Let $s \in V$ be the source vertex, and let the graph be initialized by INITIALIZE-SINGLE-SOURCE(G, s). Then, $v.d \geq \delta(s, v)$ for all $v \in V$, and this invariant is maintained over any sequence of relaxation steps on the edges of G. Moreover, once $v.d$ achieves its lower bound $\delta(s, v)$, it never changes.

Proof   We prove the invariant $v.d \geq \delta(s, v)$ for all vertices $v \in V$ by induction over the number of relaxation steps.

For the basis, $v.d \geq \delta(s, v)$ is certainly true after initialization, since $v.d = \infty$ implies $v.d \geq \delta(s, v)$ for all $v \in V - \{s\}$, and since $s.d = 0 \geq \delta(s, s)$ (note that $\delta(s, s) = -\infty$ if s is on a negative-weight cycle and 0 otherwise).

For the inductive step, consider the relaxation of an edge (u, v). By the inductive hypothesis, $x.d \geq \delta(s, x)$ for all $x \in V$ prior to the relaxation. The only d value that may change is $v.d$. If it changes, we have

$$
\begin{aligned}
v.d &= u.d + w(u, v) \\
&\geq \delta(s, u) + w(u, v) \quad \text{(by the inductive hypothesis)} \\
&\geq \delta(s, v) \quad\quad\quad\quad\;\; \text{(by the triangle inequality)} ,
\end{aligned}
$$

and so the invariant is maintained.

To see that the value of $v.d$ never changes once $v.d = \delta(s, v)$, note that having achieved its lower bound, $v.d$ cannot decrease because we have just shown that $v.d \geq \delta(s, v)$, and it cannot increase because relaxation steps do not increase d values.   ∎

Corollary 24.12 (No-path property)
Suppose that in a weighted, directed graph $G = (V, E)$ with weight function $w : E \to \mathbb{R}$, no path connects a source vertex $s \in V$ to a given vertex $v \in V$. Then, after the graph is initialized by INITIALIZE-SINGLE-SOURCE(G, s), we have $v.d = \delta(s, v) = \infty$, and this equality is maintained as an invariant over any sequence of relaxation steps on the edges of G.

Proof   By the upper-bound property, we always have $\infty = \delta(s, v) \leq v.d$, and thus $v.d = \infty = \delta(s, v)$.   ∎

Lemma 24.13
Let $G = (V, E)$ be a weighted, directed graph with weight function $w : E \to \mathbb{R}$, and let $(u, v) \in E$. Then, immediately after relaxing edge (u, v) by executing RELAX(u, v, w), we have $v.d \leq u.d + w(u, v)$.

Proof   If, just prior to relaxing edge (u, v), we have $v.d > u.d + w(u, v)$, then $v.d = u.d + w(u, v)$ afterward. If, instead, $v.d \leq u.d + w(u, v)$ just before the relaxation, then neither $u.d$ nor $v.d$ changes, and so $v.d \leq u.d + w(u, v)$ afterward.   ∎

Lemma 24.14 (Convergence property)
Let $G = (V, E)$ be a weighted, directed graph with weight function $w : E \to \mathbb{R}$, let $s \in V$ be a source vertex, and let $s \rightsquigarrow u \to v$ be a shortest path in G for

some vertices $u, v \in V$. Suppose that G is initialized by INITIALIZE-SINGLE-SOURCE(G, s) and then a sequence of relaxation steps that includes the call RELAX(u, v, w) is executed on the edges of G. If $u.d = \delta(s, u)$ at any time prior to the call, then $v.d = \delta(s, v)$ at all times after the call.

Proof By the upper-bound property, if $u.d = \delta(s, u)$ at some point prior to relaxing edge (u, v), then this equality holds thereafter. In particular, after relaxing edge (u, v), we have

$$
\begin{aligned}
v.d \;\; &\leq \;\; u.d + w(u, v) &&\text{(by Lemma 24.13)} \\
&= \;\; \delta(s, u) + w(u, v) \\
&= \;\; \delta(s, v) &&\text{(by Lemma 24.1) .}
\end{aligned}
$$

By the upper-bound property, $v.d \geq \delta(s, v)$, from which we conclude that $v.d = \delta(s, v)$, and this equality is maintained thereafter. ∎

Lemma 24.15 (Path-relaxation property)
Let $G = (V, E)$ be a weighted, directed graph with weight function $w : E \to \mathbb{R}$, and let $s \in V$ be a source vertex. Consider any shortest path $p = \langle v_0, v_1, \ldots, v_k \rangle$ from $s = v_0$ to v_k. If G is initialized by INITIALIZE-SINGLE-SOURCE(G, s) and then a sequence of relaxation steps occurs that includes, in order, relaxing the edges $(v_0, v_1), (v_1, v_2), \ldots, (v_{k-1}, v_k)$, then $v_k.d = \delta(s, v_k)$ after these relaxations and at all times afterward. This property holds no matter what other edge relaxations occur, including relaxations that are intermixed with relaxations of the edges of p.

Proof We show by induction that after the ith edge of path p is relaxed, we have $v_i.d = \delta(s, v_i)$. For the basis, $i = 0$, and before any edges of p have been relaxed, we have from the initialization that $v_0.d = s.d = 0 = \delta(s, s)$. By the upper-bound property, the value of $s.d$ never changes after initialization.

For the inductive step, we assume that $v_{i-1}.d = \delta(s, v_{i-1})$, and we examine what happens when we relax edge (v_{i-1}, v_i). By the convergence property, after relaxing this edge, we have $v_i.d = \delta(s, v_i)$, and this equality is maintained at all times thereafter. ∎

Relaxation and shortest-paths trees

We now show that once a sequence of relaxations has caused the shortest-path estimates to converge to shortest-path weights, the predecessor subgraph G_π induced by the resulting π values is a shortest-paths tree for G. We start with the following lemma, which shows that the predecessor subgraph always forms a rooted tree whose root is the source.

Lemma 24.16

Let $G = (V, E)$ be a weighted, directed graph with weight function $w : E \to \mathbb{R}$, let $s \in V$ be a source vertex, and assume that G contains no negative-weight cycles that are reachable from s. Then, after the graph is initialized by INITIALIZE-SINGLE-SOURCE(G, s), the predecessor subgraph G_π forms a rooted tree with root s, and any sequence of relaxation steps on edges of G maintains this property as an invariant.

Proof   Initially, the only vertex in G_π is the source vertex, and the lemma is trivially true. Consider a predecessor subgraph G_π that arises after a sequence of relaxation steps. We shall first prove that G_π is acyclic. Suppose for the sake of contradiction that some relaxation step creates a cycle in the graph G_π. Let the cycle be $c = \langle v_0, v_1, \ldots, v_k \rangle$, where $v_k = v_0$. Then, $v_i.\pi = v_{i-1}$ for $i = 1, 2, \ldots, k$ and, without loss of generality, we can assume that relaxing edge (v_{k-1}, v_k) created the cycle in G_π.

We claim that all vertices on cycle c are reachable from the source s. Why? Each vertex on c has a non-NIL predecessor, and so each vertex on c was assigned a finite shortest-path estimate when it was assigned its non-NIL π value. By the upper-bound property, each vertex on cycle c has a finite shortest-path weight, which implies that it is reachable from s.

We shall examine the shortest-path estimates on c just prior to the call RELAX(v_{k-1}, v_k, w) and show that c is a negative-weight cycle, thereby contradicting the assumption that G contains no negative-weight cycles that are reachable from the source. Just before the call, we have $v_i.\pi = v_{i-1}$ for $i = 1, 2, \ldots, k - 1$. Thus, for $i = 1, 2, \ldots, k - 1$, the last update to $v_i.d$ was by the assignment $v_i.d = v_{i-1}.d + w(v_{i-1}, v_i)$. If $v_{i-1}.d$ changed since then, it decreased. Therefore, just before the call RELAX(v_{k-1}, v_k, w), we have

$$v_i.d \geq v_{i-1}.d + w(v_{i-1}, v_i) \qquad \text{for all } i = 1, 2, \ldots, k - 1 \,. \tag{24.12}$$

Because $v_k.\pi$ is changed by the call, immediately beforehand we also have the strict inequality

$$v_k.d > v_{k-1}.d + w(v_{k-1}, v_k) \,.$$

Summing this strict inequality with the $k - 1$ inequalities (24.12), we obtain the sum of the shortest-path estimates around cycle c:

$$\sum_{i=1}^{k} v_i.d \;>\; \sum_{i=1}^{k} (v_{i-1}.d + w(v_{i-1}, v_i))$$

$$= \sum_{i=1}^{k} v_{i-1}.d + \sum_{i=1}^{k} w(v_{i-1}, v_i) \,.$$

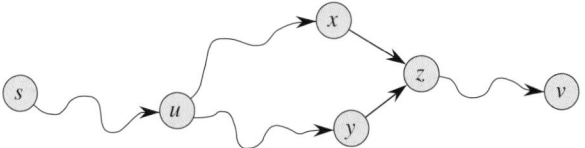

Figure 24.9 Showing that a simple path in G_π from source s to vertex v is unique. If there are two paths p_1 ($s \rightsquigarrow u \rightsquigarrow x \rightarrow z \rightsquigarrow v$) and p_2 ($s \rightsquigarrow u \rightsquigarrow y \rightarrow z \rightsquigarrow v$), where $x \neq y$, then $z.\pi = x$ and $z.\pi = y$, a contradiction.

But

$$\sum_{i=1}^{k} v_i.d = \sum_{i=1}^{k} v_{i-1}.d \,,$$

since each vertex in the cycle c appears exactly once in each summation. This equality implies

$$0 > \sum_{i=1}^{k} w(v_{i-1}, v_i) \,.$$

Thus, the sum of weights around the cycle c is negative, which provides the desired contradiction.

We have now proven that G_π is a directed, acyclic graph. To show that it forms a rooted tree with root s, it suffices (see Exercise B.5-2) to prove that for each vertex $v \in V_\pi$, there is a unique simple path from s to v in G_π.

We first must show that a path from s exists for each vertex in V_π. The vertices in V_π are those with non-NIL π values, plus s. The idea here is to prove by induction that a path exists from s to all vertices in V_π. We leave the details as Exercise 24.5-6.

To complete the proof of the lemma, we must now show that for any vertex $v \in V_\pi$, the graph G_π contains at most one simple path from s to v. Suppose otherwise. That is, suppose that, as Figure 24.9 illustrates, G_π contains two simple paths from s to some vertex v: p_1, which we decompose into $s \rightsquigarrow u \rightsquigarrow x \rightarrow z \rightsquigarrow v$, and p_2, which we decompose into $s \rightsquigarrow u \rightsquigarrow y \rightarrow z \rightsquigarrow v$, where $x \neq y$ (though u could be s and z could be v). But then, $z.\pi = x$ and $z.\pi = y$, which implies the contradiction that $x = y$. We conclude that G_π contains a unique simple path from s to v, and thus G_π forms a rooted tree with root s. ∎

We can now show that if, after we have performed a sequence of relaxation steps, all vertices have been assigned their true shortest-path weights, then the predecessor subgraph G_π is a shortest-paths tree.

Lemma 24.17 (Predecessor-subgraph property)

Let $G = (V, E)$ be a weighted, directed graph with weight function $w : E \to \mathbb{R}$, let $s \in V$ be a source vertex, and assume that G contains no negative-weight cycles that are reachable from s. Let us call INITIALIZE-SINGLE-SOURCE(G, s) and then execute any sequence of relaxation steps on edges of G that produces $v.d = \delta(s, v)$ for all $v \in V$. Then, the predecessor subgraph G_π is a shortest-paths tree rooted at s.

Proof We must prove that the three properties of shortest-paths trees given on page 647 hold for G_π. To show the first property, we must show that V_π is the set of vertices reachable from s. By definition, a shortest-path weight $\delta(s, v)$ is finite if and only if v is reachable from s, and thus the vertices that are reachable from s are exactly those with finite d values. But a vertex $v \in V - \{s\}$ has been assigned a finite value for $v.d$ if and only if $v.\pi \neq$ NIL. Thus, the vertices in V_π are exactly those reachable from s.

The second property follows directly from Lemma 24.16.

It remains, therefore, to prove the last property of shortest-paths trees: for each vertex $v \in V_\pi$, the unique simple path $s \overset{p}{\rightsquigarrow} v$ in G_π is a shortest path from s to v in G. Let $p = \langle v_0, v_1, \ldots, v_k \rangle$, where $v_0 = s$ and $v_k = v$. For $i = 1, 2, \ldots, k$, we have both $v_i.d = \delta(s, v_i)$ and $v_i.d \geq v_{i-1}.d + w(v_{i-1}, v_i)$, from which we conclude $w(v_{i-1}, v_i) \leq \delta(s, v_i) - \delta(s, v_{i-1})$. Summing the weights along path p yields

$$
\begin{aligned}
w(p) &= \sum_{i=1}^{k} w(v_{i-1}, v_i) \\
&\leq \sum_{i=1}^{k} (\delta(s, v_i) - \delta(s, v_{i-1})) \\
&= \delta(s, v_k) - \delta(s, v_0) \qquad \text{(because the sum telescopes)} \\
&= \delta(s, v_k) \qquad \text{(because } \delta(s, v_0) = \delta(s, s) = 0) \ .
\end{aligned}
$$

Thus, $w(p) \leq \delta(s, v_k)$. Since $\delta(s, v_k)$ is a lower bound on the weight of any path from s to v_k, we conclude that $w(p) = \delta(s, v_k)$, and thus p is a shortest path from s to $v = v_k$.   ∎

Exercises

24.5-1
Give two shortest-paths trees for the directed graph of Figure 24.2 (on page 648) other than the two shown.

24.5-2

Give an example of a weighted, directed graph $G = (V, E)$ with weight function $w : E \to \mathbb{R}$ and source vertex s such that G satisfies the following property: For every edge $(u, v) \in E$, there is a shortest-paths tree rooted at s that contains (u, v) and another shortest-paths tree rooted at s that does not contain (u, v).

24.5-3

Embellish the proof of Lemma 24.10 to handle cases in which shortest-path weights are ∞ or $-\infty$.

24.5-4

Let $G = (V, E)$ be a weighted, directed graph with source vertex s, and let G be initialized by INITIALIZE-SINGLE-SOURCE(G, s). Prove that if a sequence of relaxation steps sets $s.\pi$ to a non-NIL value, then G contains a negative-weight cycle.

24.5-5

Let $G = (V, E)$ be a weighted, directed graph with no negative-weight edges. Let $s \in V$ be the source vertex, and suppose that we allow $v.\pi$ to be the predecessor of v on *any* shortest path to v from source s if $v \in V - \{s\}$ is reachable from s, and NIL otherwise. Give an example of such a graph G and an assignment of π values that produces a cycle in G_π. (By Lemma 24.16, such an assignment cannot be produced by a sequence of relaxation steps.)

24.5-6

Let $G = (V, E)$ be a weighted, directed graph with weight function $w : E \to \mathbb{R}$ and no negative-weight cycles. Let $s \in V$ be the source vertex, and let G be initialized by INITIALIZE-SINGLE-SOURCE(G, s). Prove that for every vertex $v \in V_\pi$, there exists a path from s to v in G_π and that this property is maintained as an invariant over any sequence of relaxations.

24.5-7

Let $G = (V, E)$ be a weighted, directed graph that contains no negative-weight cycles. Let $s \in V$ be the source vertex, and let G be initialized by INITIALIZE-SINGLE-SOURCE(G, s). Prove that there exists a sequence of $|V| - 1$ relaxation steps that produces $v.d = \delta(s, v)$ for all $v \in V$.

24.5-8

Let G be an arbitrary weighted, directed graph with a negative-weight cycle reachable from the source vertex s. Show how to construct an infinite sequence of relaxations of the edges of G such that every relaxation causes a shortest-path estimate to change.

Problems

24-1   Yen's improvement to Bellman-Ford

Suppose that we order the edge relaxations in each pass of the Bellman-Ford algorithm as follows. Before the first pass, we assign an arbitrary linear order $v_1, v_2, \ldots, v_{|V|}$ to the vertices of the input graph $G = (V, E)$. Then, we partition the edge set E into $E_f \cup E_b$, where $E_f = \{(v_i, v_j) \in E : i < j\}$ and $E_b = \{(v_i, v_j) \in E : i > j\}$. (Assume that G contains no self-loops, so that every edge is in either E_f or E_b.) Define $G_f = (V, E_f)$ and $G_b = (V, E_b)$.

a. Prove that G_f is acyclic with topological sort $\langle v_1, v_2, \ldots, v_{|V|} \rangle$ and that G_b is acyclic with topological sort $\langle v_{|V|}, v_{|V|-1}, \ldots, v_1 \rangle$.

Suppose that we implement each pass of the Bellman-Ford algorithm in the following way. We visit each vertex in the order $v_1, v_2, \ldots, v_{|V|}$, relaxing edges of E_f that leave the vertex. We then visit each vertex in the order $v_{|V|}, v_{|V|-1}, \ldots, v_1$, relaxing edges of E_b that leave the vertex.

b. Prove that with this scheme, if G contains no negative-weight cycles that are reachable from the source vertex s, then after only $\lceil |V|/2 \rceil$ passes over the edges, $v.d = \delta(s, v)$ for all vertices $v \in V$.

c. Does this scheme improve the asymptotic running time of the Bellman-Ford algorithm?

24-2   Nesting boxes

A d-dimensional box with dimensions $(x_1, x_2, \ldots, x_d)$ ***nests*** within another box with dimensions $(y_1, y_2, \ldots, y_d)$ if there exists a permutation π on $\{1, 2, \ldots, d\}$ such that $x_{\pi(1)} < y_1, x_{\pi(2)} < y_2, \ldots, x_{\pi(d)} < y_d$.

a. Argue that the nesting relation is transitive.

b. Describe an efficient method to determine whether or not one d-dimensional box nests inside another.

c. Suppose that you are given a set of n d-dimensional boxes $\{B_1, B_2, \ldots, B_n\}$. Give an efficient algorithm to find the longest sequence $\langle B_{i_1}, B_{i_2}, \ldots, B_{i_k} \rangle$ of boxes such that B_{i_j} nests within $B_{i_{j+1}}$ for $j = 1, 2, \ldots, k - 1$. Express the running time of your algorithm in terms of n and d.

24-3   *Arbitrage*

Arbitrage is the use of discrepancies in currency exchange rates to transform one unit of a currency into more than one unit of the same currency. For example, suppose that 1 U.S. dollar buys 49 Indian rupees, 1 Indian rupee buys 2 Japanese yen, and 1 Japanese yen buys 0.0107 U.S. dollars. Then, by converting currencies, a trader can start with 1 U.S. dollar and buy $49 \times 2 \times 0.0107 = 1.0486$ U.S. dollars, thus turning a profit of 4.86 percent.

Suppose that we are given n currencies $c_1, c_2, \ldots, c_n$ and an $n \times n$ table R of exchange rates, such that one unit of currency c_i buys $R[i, j]$ units of currency c_j.

a. Give an efficient algorithm to determine whether or not there exists a sequence of currencies $\langle c_{i_1}, c_{i_2}, \ldots, c_{i_k} \rangle$ such that

$$R[i_1, i_2] \cdot R[i_2, i_3] \cdots R[i_{k-1}, i_k] \cdot R[i_k, i_1] > 1 \ .$$

Analyze the running time of your algorithm.

b. Give an efficient algorithm to print out such a sequence if one exists. Analyze the running time of your algorithm.

24-4   *Gabow's scaling algorithm for single-source shortest paths*

A *scaling* algorithm solves a problem by initially considering only the highest-order bit of each relevant input value (such as an edge weight). It then refines the initial solution by looking at the two highest-order bits. It progressively looks at more and more high-order bits, refining the solution each time, until it has examined all bits and computed the correct solution.

In this problem, we examine an algorithm for computing the shortest paths from a single source by scaling edge weights. We are given a directed graph $G = (V, E)$ with nonnegative integer edge weights w. Let $W = \max_{(u,v) \in E} \{w(u, v)\}$. Our goal is to develop an algorithm that runs in $O(E \lg W)$ time. We assume that all vertices are reachable from the source.

The algorithm uncovers the bits in the binary representation of the edge weights one at a time, from the most significant bit to the least significant bit. Specifically, let $k = \lceil \lg(W + 1) \rceil$ be the number of bits in the binary representation of W, and for $i = 1, 2, \ldots, k$, let $w_i(u, v) = \lfloor w(u, v)/2^{k-i} \rfloor$. That is, $w_i(u, v)$ is the "scaled-down" version of $w(u, v)$ given by the i most significant bits of $w(u, v)$. (Thus, $w_k(u, v) = w(u, v)$ for all $(u, v) \in E$.) For example, if $k = 5$ and $w(u, v) = 25$, which has the binary representation $\langle 11001 \rangle$, then $w_3(u, v) = \langle 110 \rangle = 6$. As another example with $k = 5$, if $w(u, v) = \langle 00100 \rangle = 4$, then $w_3(u, v) = \langle 001 \rangle = 1$. Let us define $\delta_i(u, v)$ as the shortest-path weight from vertex u to vertex v using weight function w_i. Thus, $\delta_k(u, v) = \delta(u, v)$ for all $u, v \in V$. For a given source vertex s, the scaling algorithm first computes the

shortest-path weights $\delta_1(s, v)$ for all $v \in V$, then computes $\delta_2(s, v)$ for all $v \in V$, and so on, until it computes $\delta_k(s, v)$ for all $v \in V$. We assume throughout that $|E| \geq |V| - 1$, and we shall see that computing δ_i from δ_{i-1} takes $O(E)$ time, so that the entire algorithm takes $O(kE) = O(E \lg W)$ time.

a. Suppose that for all vertices $v \in V$, we have $\delta(s, v) \leq |E|$. Show that we can compute $\delta(s, v)$ for all $v \in V$ in $O(E)$ time.

b. Show that we can compute $\delta_1(s, v)$ for all $v \in V$ in $O(E)$ time.

Let us now focus on computing δ_i from δ_{i-1}.

c. Prove that for $i = 2, 3, \ldots, k$, we have either $w_i(u, v) = 2w_{i-1}(u, v)$ or $w_i(u, v) = 2w_{i-1}(u, v) + 1$. Then, prove that

$$2\delta_{i-1}(s, v) \leq \delta_i(s, v) \leq 2\delta_{i-1}(s, v) + |V| - 1$$

for all $v \in V$.

d. Define for $i = 2, 3, \ldots, k$ and all $(u, v) \in E$,

$$\hat{w}_i(u, v) = w_i(u, v) + 2\delta_{i-1}(s, u) - 2\delta_{i-1}(s, v) .$$

Prove that for $i = 2, 3, \ldots, k$ and all $u, v \in V$, the "reweighted" value $\hat{w}_i(u, v)$ of edge (u, v) is a nonnegative integer.

e. Now, define $\hat{\delta}_i(s, v)$ as the shortest-path weight from s to v using the weight function $\hat{w}_i$. Prove that for $i = 2, 3, \ldots, k$ and all $v \in V$,

$$\delta_i(s, v) = \hat{\delta}_i(s, v) + 2\delta_{i-1}(s, v)$$

and that $\hat{\delta}_i(s, v) \leq |E|$.

f. Show how to compute $\delta_i(s, v)$ from $\delta_{i-1}(s, v)$ for all $v \in V$ in $O(E)$ time, and conclude that we can compute $\delta(s, v)$ for all $v \in V$ in $O(E \lg W)$ time.

24-5   Karp's minimum mean-weight cycle algorithm

Let $G = (V, E)$ be a directed graph with weight function $w : E \rightarrow \mathbb{R}$, and let $n = |V|$. We define the *mean weight* of a cycle $c = \langle e_1, e_2, \ldots, e_k \rangle$ of edges in E to be

$$\mu(c) = \frac{1}{k} \sum_{i=1}^{k} w(e_i) .$$

Let $\mu^* = \min_c \mu(c)$, where c ranges over all directed cycles in G. We call a cycle c for which $\mu(c) = \mu^*$ a ***minimum mean-weight cycle***. This problem investigates an efficient algorithm for computing μ^*.

Assume without loss of generality that every vertex $v \in V$ is reachable from a source vertex $s \in V$. Let $\delta(s, v)$ be the weight of a shortest path from s to v, and let $\delta_k(s, v)$ be the weight of a shortest path from s to v consisting of *exactly* k edges. If there is no path from s to v with exactly k edges, then $\delta_k(s, v) = \infty$.

a. Show that if $\mu^* = 0$, then G contains no negative-weight cycles and $\delta(s, v) = \min_{0 \le k \le n-1} \delta_k(s, v)$ for all vertices $v \in V$.

b. Show that if $\mu^* = 0$, then

$$\max_{0 \le k \le n-1} \frac{\delta_n(s, v) - \delta_k(s, v)}{n - k} \ge 0$$

for all vertices $v \in V$. (*Hint:* Use both properties from part (a).)

c. Let c be a 0-weight cycle, and let u and v be any two vertices on c. Suppose that $\mu^* = 0$ and that the weight of the simple path from u to v along the cycle is x. Prove that $\delta(s, v) = \delta(s, u) + x$. (*Hint:* The weight of the simple path from v to u along the cycle is $-x$.)

d. Show that if $\mu^* = 0$, then on each minimum mean-weight cycle there exists a vertex v such that

$$\max_{0 \le k \le n-1} \frac{\delta_n(s, v) - \delta_k(s, v)}{n - k} = 0 .$$

(*Hint:* Show how to extend a shortest path to any vertex on a minimum mean-weight cycle along the cycle to make a shortest path to the next vertex on the cycle.)

e. Show that if $\mu^* = 0$, then

$$\min_{v \in V} \max_{0 \le k \le n-1} \frac{\delta_n(s, v) - \delta_k(s, v)}{n - k} = 0 .$$

f. Show that if we add a constant t to the weight of each edge of G, then μ^* increases by t. Use this fact to show that

$$\mu^* = \min_{v \in V} \max_{0 \le k \le n-1} \frac{\delta_n(s, v) - \delta_k(s, v)}{n - k} .$$

g. Give an $O(VE)$-time algorithm to compute μ^*.

24-6   Bitonic shortest paths

A sequence is ***bitonic*** if it monotonically increases and then monotonically decreases, or if by a circular shift it monotonically increases and then monotonically decreases. For example the sequences $\langle 1, 4, 6, 8, 3, -2 \rangle$, $\langle 9, 2, -4, -10, -5 \rangle$, and $\langle 1, 2, 3, 4 \rangle$ are bitonic, but $\langle 1, 3, 12, 4, 2, 10 \rangle$ is not bitonic. (See Problem 15-3 for the bitonic euclidean traveling-salesman problem.)

Suppose that we are given a directed graph $G = (V, E)$ with weight function $w : E \rightarrow \mathbb{R}$, where all edge weights are unique, and we wish to find single-source shortest paths from a source vertex s. We are given one additional piece of information: for each vertex $v \in V$, the weights of the edges along any shortest path from s to v form a bitonic sequence.

Give the most efficient algorithm you can to solve this problem, and analyze its running time.

Chapter notes

Dijkstra's algorithm [88] appeared in 1959, but it contained no mention of a priority queue. The Bellman-Ford algorithm is based on separate algorithms by Bellman [38] and Ford [109]. Bellman describes the relation of shortest paths to difference constraints. Lawler [224] describes the linear-time algorithm for shortest paths in a dag, which he considers part of the folklore.

When edge weights are relatively small nonnegative integers, we have more efficient algorithms to solve the single-source shortest-paths problem. The sequence of values returned by the EXTRACT-MIN calls in Dijkstra's algorithm monotonically increases over time. As discussed in the chapter notes for Chapter 6, in this case several data structures can implement the various priority-queue operations more efficiently than a binary heap or a Fibonacci heap. Ahuja, Mehlhorn, Orlin, and Tarjan [8] give an algorithm that runs in $O(E + V \sqrt{\lg W})$ time on graphs with nonnegative edge weights, where W is the largest weight of any edge in the graph. The best bounds are by Thorup [337], who gives an algorithm that runs in $O(E \lg \lg V)$ time, and by Raman [291], who gives an algorithm that runs in $O\left(E + V \min\left\{(\lg V)^{1/3+\epsilon}, (\lg W)^{1/4+\epsilon}\right\}\right)$ time. These two algorithms use an amount of space that depends on the word size of the underlying machine. Although the amount of space used can be unbounded in the size of the input, it can be reduced to be linear in the size of the input using randomized hashing.

For undirected graphs with integer weights, Thorup [336] gives an $O(V + E)$-time algorithm for single-source shortest paths. In contrast to the algorithms mentioned in the previous paragraph, this algorithm is not an implementation of Dijk-

stra's algorithm, since the sequence of values returned by EXTRACT-MIN calls does not monotonically increase over time.

For graphs with negative edge weights, an algorithm due to Gabow and Tarjan [122] runs in $O(\sqrt{V} E \lg(VW))$ time, and one by Goldberg [137] runs in $O(\sqrt{V} E \lg W)$ time, where $W = \max_{(u,v) \in E} \{|w(u,v)|\}$.

Cherkassky, Goldberg, and Radzik [64] conducted extensive experiments comparing various shortest-path algorithms.

25 All-Pairs Shortest Paths

In this chapter, we consider the problem of finding shortest paths between all pairs of vertices in a graph. This problem might arise in making a table of distances between all pairs of cities for a road atlas. As in Chapter 24, we are given a weighted, directed graph $G = (V, E)$ with a weight function $w : E \rightarrow \mathbb{R}$ that maps edges to real-valued weights. We wish to find, for every pair of vertices $u, v \in V$, a shortest (least-weight) path from u to v, where the weight of a path is the sum of the weights of its constituent edges. We typically want the output in tabular form: the entry in u's row and v's column should be the weight of a shortest path from u to v.

We can solve an all-pairs shortest-paths problem by running a single-source shortest-paths algorithm $|V|$ times, once for each vertex as the source. If all edge weights are nonnegative, we can use Dijkstra's algorithm. If we use the linear-array implementation of the min-priority queue, the running time is $O(V^3 + VE) = O(V^3)$. The binary min-heap implementation of the min-priority queue yields a running time of $O(VE \lg V)$, which is an improvement if the graph is sparse. Alternatively, we can implement the min-priority queue with a Fibonacci heap, yielding a running time of $O(V^2 \lg V + VE)$.

If the graph has negative-weight edges, we cannot use Dijkstra's algorithm. Instead, we must run the slower Bellman-Ford algorithm once from each vertex. The resulting running time is $O(V^2 E)$, which on a dense graph is $O(V^4)$. In this chapter we shall see how to do better. We also investigate the relation of the all-pairs shortest-paths problem to matrix multiplication and study its algebraic structure.

Unlike the single-source algorithms, which assume an adjacency-list representation of the graph, most of the algorithms in this chapter use an adjacency-matrix representation. (Johnson's algorithm for sparse graphs, in Section 25.3, uses adjacency lists.) For convenience, we assume that the vertices are numbered $1, 2, \ldots, |V|$, so that the input is an $n \times n$ matrix W representing the edge weights of an n-vertex directed graph $G = (V, E)$. That is, $W = (w_{ij})$, where

$$w_{ij} = \begin{cases} 0 & \text{if } i = j \text{ ,} \\ \text{the weight of directed edge } (i, j) & \text{if } i \neq j \text{ and } (i, j) \in E \text{ ,} \\ \infty & \text{if } i \neq j \text{ and } (i, j) \notin E \text{ .} \end{cases} \qquad (25.1)$$

We allow negative-weight edges, but we assume for the time being that the input graph contains no negative-weight cycles.

The tabular output of the all-pairs shortest-paths algorithms presented in this chapter is an $n \times n$ matrix $D = (d_{ij})$, where entry d_{ij} contains the weight of a shortest path from vertex i to vertex j. That is, if we let $\delta(i, j)$ denote the shortest-path weight from vertex i to vertex j (as in Chapter 24), then $d_{ij} = \delta(i, j)$ at termination.

To solve the all-pairs shortest-paths problem on an input adjacency matrix, we need to compute not only the shortest-path weights but also a ***predecessor matrix*** $\Pi = (\pi_{ij})$, where π_{ij} is NIL if either $i = j$ or there is no path from i to j, and otherwise π_{ij} is the predecessor of j on some shortest path from i. Just as the predecessor subgraph G_π from Chapter 24 is a shortest-paths tree for a given source vertex, the subgraph induced by the ith row of the Π matrix should be a shortest-paths tree with root i. For each vertex $i \in V$, we define the ***predecessor subgraph*** of G for i as $G_{\pi,i} = (V_{\pi,i}, E_{\pi,i})$, where

$$V_{\pi,i} = \{j \in V : \pi_{ij} \neq \text{NIL}\} \cup \{i\}$$

and

$$E_{\pi,i} = \{(\pi_{ij}, j) : j \in V_{\pi,i} - \{i\}\} \text{ .}$$

If $G_{\pi,i}$ is a shortest-paths tree, then the following procedure, which is a modified version of the PRINT-PATH procedure from Chapter 22, prints a shortest path from vertex i to vertex j.

PRINT-ALL-PAIRS-SHORTEST-PATH(Π, i, j)

1 **if** $i == j$
2   print i
3 **elseif** $\pi_{ij} ==$ NIL
4   print "no path from" i "to" j "exists"
5 **else** PRINT-ALL-PAIRS-SHORTEST-PATH(Π, i, π_{ij})
6   print j

In order to highlight the essential features of the all-pairs algorithms in this chapter, we won't cover the creation and properties of predecessor matrices as extensively as we dealt with predecessor subgraphs in Chapter 24. Some of the exercises cover the basics.

Chapter outline

Section 25.1 presents a dynamic-programming algorithm based on matrix multiplication to solve the all-pairs shortest-paths problem. Using the technique of "repeated squaring," we can achieve a running time of $\Theta(V^3 \lg V)$. Section 25.2 gives another dynamic-programming algorithm, the Floyd-Warshall algorithm, which runs in time $\Theta(V^3)$. Section 25.2 also covers the problem of finding the transitive closure of a directed graph, which is related to the all-pairs shortest-paths problem. Finally, Section 25.3 presents Johnson's algorithm, which solves the all-pairs shortest-paths problem in $O(V^2 \lg V + VE)$ time and is a good choice for large, sparse graphs.

Before proceeding, we need to establish some conventions for adjacency-matrix representations. First, we shall generally assume that the input graph $G = (V, E)$ has n vertices, so that $n = |V|$. Second, we shall use the convention of denoting matrices by uppercase letters, such as W, L, or D, and their individual elements by subscripted lowercase letters, such as w_{ij}, l_{ij}, or d_{ij}. Some matrices will have parenthesized superscripts, as in $L^{(m)} = \left(l_{ij}^{(m)}\right)$ or $D^{(m)} = \left(d_{ij}^{(m)}\right)$, to indicate iterates. Finally, for a given $n \times n$ matrix A, we shall assume that the value of n is stored in the attribute $A.rows$.

25.1   Shortest paths and matrix multiplication

This section presents a dynamic-programming algorithm for the all-pairs shortest-paths problem on a directed graph $G = (V, E)$. Each major loop of the dynamic program will invoke an operation that is very similar to matrix multiplication, so that the algorithm will look like repeated matrix multiplication. We shall start by developing a $\Theta(V^4)$-time algorithm for the all-pairs shortest-paths problem and then improve its running time to $\Theta(V^3 \lg V)$.

Before proceeding, let us briefly recap the steps given in Chapter 15 for developing a dynamic-programming algorithm.

1. Characterize the structure of an optimal solution.

2. Recursively define the value of an optimal solution.

3. Compute the value of an optimal solution in a bottom-up fashion.

We reserve the fourth step—constructing an optimal solution from computed information—for the exercises.

The structure of a shortest path

We start by characterizing the structure of an optimal solution. For the all-pairs shortest-paths problem on a graph $G = (V, E)$, we have proven (Lemma 24.1) that all subpaths of a shortest path are shortest paths. Suppose that we represent the graph by an adjacency matrix $W = (w_{ij})$. Consider a shortest path p from vertex i to vertex j, and suppose that p contains at most m edges. Assuming that there are no negative-weight cycles, m is finite. If $i = j$, then p has weight 0 and no edges. If vertices i and j are distinct, then we decompose path p into $i \overset{p'}{\rightsquigarrow} k \rightarrow j$, where path p' now contains at most $m - 1$ edges. By Lemma 24.1, p' is a shortest path from i to k, and so $\delta(i, j) = \delta(i, k) + w_{kj}$.

A recursive solution to the all-pairs shortest-paths problem

Now, let $l_{ij}^{(m)}$ be the minimum weight of any path from vertex i to vertex j that contains at most m edges. When $m = 0$, there is a shortest path from i to j with no edges if and only if $i = j$. Thus,

$$l_{ij}^{(0)} = \begin{cases} 0 & \text{if } i = j \text{ ,} \\ \infty & \text{if } i \neq j \text{ .} \end{cases}$$

For $m \geq 1$, we compute $l_{ij}^{(m)}$ as the minimum of $l_{ij}^{(m-1)}$ (the weight of a shortest path from i to j consisting of at most $m - 1$ edges) and the minimum weight of any path from i to j consisting of at most m edges, obtained by looking at all possible predecessors k of j. Thus, we recursively define

$$\begin{aligned} l_{ij}^{(m)} &= \min \left(l_{ij}^{(m-1)}, \min_{1 \leq k \leq n} \left\{ l_{ik}^{(m-1)} + w_{kj} \right\} \right) \\ &= \min_{1 \leq k \leq n} \left\{ l_{ik}^{(m-1)} + w_{kj} \right\} \text{ .} \end{aligned} \tag{25.2}$$

The latter equality follows since $w_{jj} = 0$ for all j.

What are the actual shortest-path weights $\delta(i, j)$? If the graph contains no negative-weight cycles, then for every pair of vertices i and j for which $\delta(i, j) < \infty$, there is a shortest path from i to j that is simple and thus contains at most $n - 1$ edges. A path from vertex i to vertex j with more than $n - 1$ edges cannot have lower weight than a shortest path from i to j. The actual shortest-path weights are therefore given by

$$\delta(i, j) = l_{ij}^{(n-1)} = l_{ij}^{(n)} = l_{ij}^{(n+1)} = \cdots \text{ .} \tag{25.3}$$

Computing the shortest-path weights bottom up

Taking as our input the matrix $W = (w_{ij})$, we now compute a series of matrices $L^{(1)}, L^{(2)}, \ldots, L^{(n-1)}$, where for $m = 1, 2, \ldots, n - 1$, we have $L^{(m)} = \left(l_{ij}^{(m)}\right)$. The final matrix $L^{(n-1)}$ contains the actual shortest-path weights. Observe that $l_{ij}^{(1)} = w_{ij}$ for all vertices $i, j \in V$, and so $L^{(1)} = W$.

The heart of the algorithm is the following procedure, which, given matrices $L^{(m-1)}$ and W, returns the matrix $L^{(m)}$. That is, it extends the shortest paths computed so far by one more edge.

EXTEND-SHORTEST-PATHS(L, W)

```
1   n = L.rows
2   let L' = (l'_{ij}) be a new n × n matrix
3   for i = 1 to n
4       for j = 1 to n
5           l'_{ij} = ∞
6           for k = 1 to n
7               l'_{ij} = min(l'_{ij}, l_{ik} + w_{kj})
8   return L'
```

The procedure computes a matrix $L' = (l'_{ij})$, which it returns at the end. It does so by computing equation (25.2) for all i and j, using L for $L^{(m-1)}$ and L' for $L^{(m)}$. (It is written without the superscripts to make its input and output matrices independent of m.) Its running time is $\Theta(n^3)$ due to the three nested **for** loops.

Now we can see the relation to matrix multiplication. Suppose we wish to compute the matrix product $C = A \cdot B$ of two $n \times n$ matrices A and B. Then, for $i, j = 1, 2, \ldots, n$, we compute

$$c_{ij} = \sum_{k=1}^{n} a_{ik} \cdot b_{kj} \,. \tag{25.4}$$

Observe that if we make the substitutions

$$
\begin{aligned}
l^{(m-1)} &\rightarrow a \,, \\
w &\rightarrow b \,, \\
l^{(m)} &\rightarrow c \,, \\
\min &\rightarrow + \,, \\
+ &\rightarrow \cdot
\end{aligned}
$$

in equation (25.2), we obtain equation (25.4). Thus, if we make these changes to EXTEND-SHORTEST-PATHS and also replace ∞ (the identity for min) by 0 (the

identity for $+$), we obtain the same $\Theta(n^3)$-time procedure for multiplying square matrices that we saw in Section 4.2:

SQUARE-MATRIX-MULTIPLY(A, B)

```
1   n = A.rows
2   let C be a new n × n matrix
3   for i = 1 to n
4       for j = 1 to n
5           c_ij = 0
6           for k = 1 to n
7               c_ij = c_ij + a_ik · b_kj
8   return C
```

Returning to the all-pairs shortest-paths problem, we compute the shortest-path weights by extending shortest paths edge by edge. Letting $A \cdot B$ denote the matrix "product" returned by EXTEND-SHORTEST-PATHS(A, B), we compute the sequence of $n - 1$ matrices

$$
\begin{aligned}
L^{(1)} &= L^{(0)} \cdot W &= W\,, \\
L^{(2)} &= L^{(1)} \cdot W &= W^2\,, \\
L^{(3)} &= L^{(2)} \cdot W &= W^3\,, \\
&\;\;\vdots \\
L^{(n-1)} &= L^{(n-2)} \cdot W &= W^{n-1}\,.
\end{aligned}
$$

As we argued above, the matrix $L^{(n-1)} = W^{n-1}$ contains the shortest-path weights. The following procedure computes this sequence in $\Theta(n^4)$ time.

SLOW-ALL-PAIRS-SHORTEST-PATHS(W)

```
1   n = W.rows
2   L^(1) = W
3   for m = 2 to n - 1
4       let L^(m) be a new n × n matrix
5       L^(m) = EXTEND-SHORTEST-PATHS(L^(m-1), W)
6   return L^(n-1)
```

Figure 25.1 shows a graph and the matrices $L^{(m)}$ computed by the procedure SLOW-ALL-PAIRS-SHORTEST-PATHS.

Improving the running time

Our goal, however, is not to compute *all* the $L^{(m)}$ matrices: we are interested only in matrix $L^{(n-1)}$. Recall that in the absence of negative-weight cycles, equa-

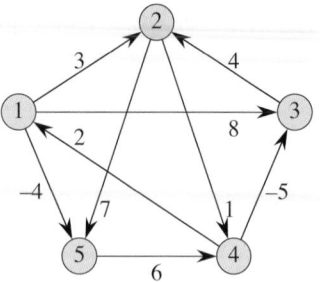

$$L^{(1)} = \begin{pmatrix} 0 & 3 & 8 & \infty & -4 \\ \infty & 0 & \infty & 1 & 7 \\ \infty & 4 & 0 & \infty & \infty \\ 2 & \infty & -5 & 0 & \infty \\ \infty & \infty & \infty & 6 & 0 \end{pmatrix} \quad L^{(2)} = \begin{pmatrix} 0 & 3 & 8 & 2 & -4 \\ 3 & 0 & -4 & 1 & 7 \\ \infty & 4 & 0 & 5 & 11 \\ 2 & -1 & -5 & 0 & -2 \\ 8 & \infty & 1 & 6 & 0 \end{pmatrix}$$

$$L^{(3)} = \begin{pmatrix} 0 & 3 & -3 & 2 & -4 \\ 3 & 0 & -4 & 1 & -1 \\ 7 & 4 & 0 & 5 & 11 \\ 2 & -1 & -5 & 0 & -2 \\ 8 & 5 & 1 & 6 & 0 \end{pmatrix} \quad L^{(4)} = \begin{pmatrix} 0 & 1 & -3 & 2 & -4 \\ 3 & 0 & -4 & 1 & -1 \\ 7 & 4 & 0 & 5 & 3 \\ 2 & -1 & -5 & 0 & -2 \\ 8 & 5 & 1 & 6 & 0 \end{pmatrix}$$

Figure 25.1 A directed graph and the sequence of matrices $L^{(m)}$ computed by SLOW-ALL-PAIRS-SHORTEST-PATHS. You might want to verify that $L^{(5)}$, defined as $L^{(4)} \cdot W$, equals $L^{(4)}$, and thus $L^{(m)} = L^{(4)}$ for all $m \geq 4$.

tion (25.3) implies $L^{(m)} = L^{(n-1)}$ for all integers $m \geq n - 1$. Just as traditional matrix multiplication is associative, so is matrix multiplication defined by the EXTEND-SHORTEST-PATHS procedure (see Exercise 25.1-4). Therefore, we can compute $L^{(n-1)}$ with only $\lceil \lg(n-1) \rceil$ matrix products by computing the sequence

$$\begin{aligned} L^{(1)} &= & W \,, & \\ L^{(2)} &= & W^2 &= W \cdot W \,, \\ L^{(4)} &= & W^4 &= W^2 \cdot W^2 \\ L^{(8)} &= & W^8 &= W^4 \cdot W^4 \,, \\ & & \vdots & \\ L^{(2^{\lceil \lg(n-1) \rceil})} &= & W^{2^{\lceil \lg(n-1) \rceil}} &= W^{2^{\lceil \lg(n-1) \rceil - 1}} \cdot W^{2^{\lceil \lg(n-1) \rceil - 1}} \,. \end{aligned}$$

Since $2^{\lceil \lg(n-1) \rceil} \geq n - 1$, the final product $L^{(2^{\lceil \lg(n-1) \rceil})}$ is equal to $L^{(n-1)}$.

The following procedure computes the above sequence of matrices by using this technique of ***repeated squaring***.

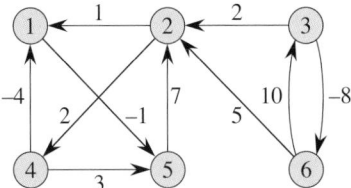

Figure 25.2   A weighted, directed graph for use in Exercises 25.1-1, 25.2-1, and 25.3-1.

FASTER-ALL-PAIRS-SHORTEST-PATHS(W)

```
1   n = W.rows
2   L⁽¹⁾ = W
3   m = 1
4   while m < n − 1
5       let L⁽²ᵐ⁾ be a new n × n matrix
6       L⁽²ᵐ⁾ = EXTEND-SHORTEST-PATHS(L⁽ᵐ⁾, L⁽ᵐ⁾)
7       m = 2m
8   return L⁽ᵐ⁾
```

In each iteration of the **while** loop of lines 4–7, we compute $L^{(2m)} = \left(L^{(m)}\right)^2$, starting with $m = 1$. At the end of each iteration, we double the value of m. The final iteration computes $L^{(n-1)}$ by actually computing $L^{(2m)}$ for some $n - 1 \leq 2m < 2n - 2$. By equation (25.3), $L^{(2m)} = L^{(n-1)}$. The next time the test in line 4 is performed, m has been doubled, so now $m \geq n - 1$, the test fails, and the procedure returns the last matrix it computed.

Because each of the $\lceil \lg(n - 1) \rceil$ matrix products takes $\Theta(n^3)$ time, FASTER-ALL-PAIRS-SHORTEST-PATHS runs in $\Theta(n^3 \lg n)$ time. Observe that the code is tight, containing no elaborate data structures, and the constant hidden in the Θ-notation is therefore small.

Exercises

25.1-1
Run SLOW-ALL-PAIRS-SHORTEST-PATHS on the weighted, directed graph of Figure 25.2, showing the matrices that result for each iteration of the loop. Then do the same for FASTER-ALL-PAIRS-SHORTEST-PATHS.

25.1-2
Why do we require that $w_{ii} = 0$ for all $1 \leq i \leq n$?

25.1-3

What does the matrix

$$L^{(0)} = \begin{pmatrix} 0 & \infty & \infty & \cdots & \infty \\ \infty & 0 & \infty & \cdots & \infty \\ \infty & \infty & 0 & \cdots & \infty \\ \vdots & \vdots & \vdots & \ddots & \vdots \\ \infty & \infty & \infty & \cdots & 0 \end{pmatrix}$$

used in the shortest-paths algorithms correspond to in regular matrix multiplication?

25.1-4

Show that matrix multiplication defined by EXTEND-SHORTEST-PATHS is associative.

25.1-5

Show how to express the single-source shortest-paths problem as a product of matrices and a vector. Describe how evaluating this product corresponds to a Bellman-Ford-like algorithm (see Section 24.1).

25.1-6

Suppose we also wish to compute the vertices on shortest paths in the algorithms of this section. Show how to compute the predecessor matrix Π from the completed matrix L of shortest-path weights in $O(n^3)$ time.

25.1-7

We can also compute the vertices on shortest paths as we compute the shortest-path weights. Define $\pi_{ij}^{(m)}$ as the predecessor of vertex j on any minimum-weight path from i to j that contains at most m edges. Modify the EXTEND-SHORTEST-PATHS and SLOW-ALL-PAIRS-SHORTEST-PATHS procedures to compute the matrices $\Pi^{(1)}, \Pi^{(2)}, \ldots, \Pi^{(n-1)}$ as the matrices $L^{(1)}, L^{(2)}, \ldots, L^{(n-1)}$ are computed.

25.1-8

The FASTER-ALL-PAIRS-SHORTEST-PATHS procedure, as written, requires us to store $\lceil \lg(n-1) \rceil$ matrices, each with n^2 elements, for a total space requirement of $\Theta(n^2 \lg n)$. Modify the procedure to require only $\Theta(n^2)$ space by using only two $n \times n$ matrices.

25.1-9

Modify FASTER-ALL-PAIRS-SHORTEST-PATHS so that it can determine whether the graph contains a negative-weight cycle.

25.1-10
Give an efficient algorithm to find the length (number of edges) of a minimum-length negative-weight cycle in a graph.

25.2   The Floyd-Warshall algorithm

In this section, we shall use a different dynamic-programming formulation to solve the all-pairs shortest-paths problem on a directed graph $G = (V, E)$. The resulting algorithm, known as the ***Floyd-Warshall algorithm***, runs in $\Theta(V^3)$ time. As before, negative-weight edges may be present, but we assume that there are no negative-weight cycles. As in Section 25.1, we follow the dynamic-programming process to develop the algorithm. After studying the resulting algorithm, we present a similar method for finding the transitive closure of a directed graph.

The structure of a shortest path

In the Floyd-Warshall algorithm, we characterize the structure of a shortest path differently from how we characterized it in Section 25.1. The Floyd-Warshall algorithm considers the intermediate vertices of a shortest path, where an ***intermediate*** vertex of a simple path $p = \langle v_1, v_2, \ldots, v_l \rangle$ is any vertex of p other than v_1 or v_l, that is, any vertex in the set $\{v_2, v_3, \ldots, v_{l-1}\}$.

The Floyd-Warshall algorithm relies on the following observation. Under our assumption that the vertices of G are $V = \{1, 2, \ldots, n\}$, let us consider a subset $\{1, 2, \ldots, k\}$ of vertices for some k. For any pair of vertices $i, j \in V$, consider all paths from i to j whose intermediate vertices are all drawn from $\{1, 2, \ldots, k\}$, and let p be a minimum-weight path from among them. (Path p is simple.) The Floyd-Warshall algorithm exploits a relationship between path p and shortest paths from i to j with all intermediate vertices in the set $\{1, 2, \ldots, k-1\}$. The relationship depends on whether or not k is an intermediate vertex of path p.

- If k is not an intermediate vertex of path p, then all intermediate vertices of path p are in the set $\{1, 2, \ldots, k-1\}$. Thus, a shortest path from vertex i to vertex j with all intermediate vertices in the set $\{1, 2, \ldots, k-1\}$ is also a shortest path from i to j with all intermediate vertices in the set $\{1, 2, \ldots, k\}$.

- If k is an intermediate vertex of path p, then we decompose p into $i \overset{p_1}{\rightsquigarrow} k \overset{p_2}{\rightsquigarrow} j$, as Figure 25.3 illustrates. By Lemma 24.1, p_1 is a shortest path from i to k with all intermediate vertices in the set $\{1, 2, \ldots, k\}$. In fact, we can make a slightly stronger statement. Because vertex k is not an intermediate vertex of path p_1, all intermediate vertices of p_1 are in the set $\{1, 2, \ldots, k-1\}$. There-

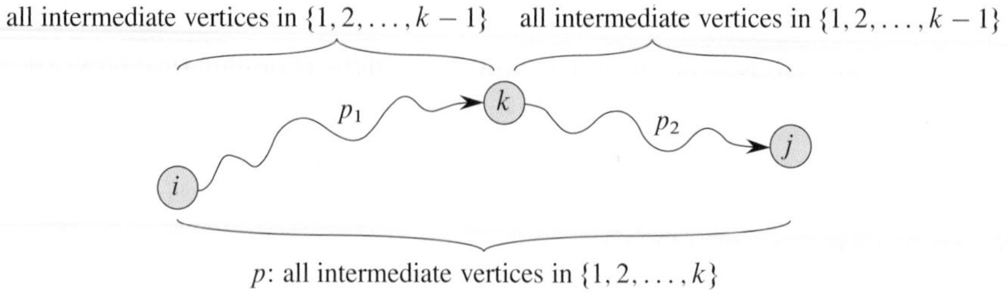

$$p: \text{all intermediate vertices in } \{1, 2, \ldots, k\}$$

Figure 25.3 Path p is a shortest path from vertex i to vertex j, and k is the highest-numbered intermediate vertex of p. Path p_1, the portion of path p from vertex i to vertex k, has all intermediate vertices in the set $\{1, 2, \ldots, k-1\}$. The same holds for path p_2 from vertex k to vertex j.

fore, p_1 is a shortest path from i to k with all intermediate vertices in the set $\{1, 2, \ldots, k-1\}$. Similarly, p_2 is a shortest path from vertex k to vertex j with all intermediate vertices in the set $\{1, 2, \ldots, k-1\}$.

A recursive solution to the all-pairs shortest-paths problem

Based on the above observations, we define a recursive formulation of shortest-path estimates that differs from the one in Section 25.1. Let $d_{ij}^{(k)}$ be the weight of a shortest path from vertex i to vertex j for which all intermediate vertices are in the set $\{1, 2, \ldots, k\}$. When $k = 0$, a path from vertex i to vertex j with no intermediate vertex numbered higher than 0 has no intermediate vertices at all. Such a path has at most one edge, and hence $d_{ij}^{(0)} = w_{ij}$. Following the above discussion, we define $d_{ij}^{(k)}$ recursively by

$$d_{ij}^{(k)} = \begin{cases} w_{ij} & \text{if } k = 0, \\ \min\left(d_{ij}^{(k-1)}, d_{ik}^{(k-1)} + d_{kj}^{(k-1)}\right) & \text{if } k \geq 1. \end{cases} \tag{25.5}$$

Because for any path, all intermediate vertices are in the set $\{1, 2, \ldots, n\}$, the matrix $D^{(n)} = \left(d_{ij}^{(n)}\right)$ gives the final answer: $d_{ij}^{(n)} = \delta(i, j)$ for all $i, j \in V$.

Computing the shortest-path weights bottom up

Based on recurrence (25.5), we can use the following bottom-up procedure to compute the values $d_{ij}^{(k)}$ in order of increasing values of k. Its input is an $n \times n$ matrix W defined as in equation (25.1). The procedure returns the matrix $D^{(n)}$ of shortest-path weights.

Floyd-Warshall(W)

```
1   n = W.rows
2   D^(0) = W
3   for k = 1 to n
4       let D^(k) = (d_{ij}^(k)) be a new n × n matrix
5       for i = 1 to n
6           for j = 1 to n
7               d_{ij}^(k) = min (d_{ij}^(k-1), d_{ik}^(k-1) + d_{kj}^(k-1))
8   return D^(n)
```

Figure 25.4 shows the matrices $D^{(k)}$ computed by the Floyd-Warshall algorithm for the graph in Figure 25.1.

The running time of the Floyd-Warshall algorithm is determined by the triply nested **for** loops of lines 3–7. Because each execution of line 7 takes $O(1)$ time, the algorithm runs in time $\Theta(n^3)$. As in the final algorithm in Section 25.1, the code is tight, with no elaborate data structures, and so the constant hidden in the Θ-notation is small. Thus, the Floyd-Warshall algorithm is quite practical for even moderate-sized input graphs.

Constructing a shortest path

There are a variety of different methods for constructing shortest paths in the Floyd-Warshall algorithm. One way is to compute the matrix D of shortest-path weights and then construct the predecessor matrix Π from the D matrix. Exercise 25.1-6 asks you to implement this method so that it runs in $O(n^3)$ time. Given the predecessor matrix Π, the Print-All-Pairs-Shortest-Path procedure will print the vertices on a given shortest path.

Alternatively, we can compute the predecessor matrix Π while the algorithm computes the matrices $D^{(k)}$. Specifically, we compute a sequence of matrices $\Pi^{(0)}, \Pi^{(1)}, \ldots, \Pi^{(n)}$, where $\Pi = \Pi^{(n)}$ and we define $\pi_{ij}^{(k)}$ as the predecessor of vertex j on a shortest path from vertex i with all intermediate vertices in the set $\{1, 2, \ldots, k\}$.

We can give a recursive formulation of $\pi_{ij}^{(k)}$. When $k = 0$, a shortest path from i to j has no intermediate vertices at all. Thus,

$$\pi_{ij}^{(0)} = \begin{cases} \text{NIL} & \text{if } i = j \text{ or } w_{ij} = \infty, \\ i & \text{if } i \neq j \text{ and } w_{ij} < \infty. \end{cases} \tag{25.6}$$

For $k \geq 1$, if we take the path $i \rightsquigarrow k \rightsquigarrow j$, where $k \neq j$, then the predecessor of j we choose is the same as the predecessor of j we chose on a shortest path from k with all intermediate vertices in the set $\{1, 2, \ldots, k - 1\}$. Otherwise, we

$$D^{(0)} = \begin{pmatrix} 0 & 3 & 8 & \infty & -4 \\ \infty & 0 & \infty & 1 & 7 \\ \infty & 4 & 0 & \infty & \infty \\ 2 & \infty & -5 & 0 & \infty \\ \infty & \infty & \infty & 6 & 0 \end{pmatrix} \quad \Pi^{(0)} = \begin{pmatrix} \text{NIL} & 1 & 1 & \text{NIL} & 1 \\ \text{NIL} & \text{NIL} & \text{NIL} & 2 & 2 \\ \text{NIL} & 3 & \text{NIL} & \text{NIL} & \text{NIL} \\ 4 & \text{NIL} & 4 & \text{NIL} & \text{NIL} \\ \text{NIL} & \text{NIL} & \text{NIL} & 5 & \text{NIL} \end{pmatrix}$$

$$D^{(1)} = \begin{pmatrix} 0 & 3 & 8 & \infty & -4 \\ \infty & 0 & \infty & 1 & 7 \\ \infty & 4 & 0 & \infty & \infty \\ 2 & 5 & -5 & 0 & -2 \\ \infty & \infty & \infty & 6 & 0 \end{pmatrix} \quad \Pi^{(1)} = \begin{pmatrix} \text{NIL} & 1 & 1 & \text{NIL} & 1 \\ \text{NIL} & \text{NIL} & \text{NIL} & 2 & 2 \\ \text{NIL} & 3 & \text{NIL} & \text{NIL} & \text{NIL} \\ 4 & 1 & 4 & \text{NIL} & 1 \\ \text{NIL} & \text{NIL} & \text{NIL} & 5 & \text{NIL} \end{pmatrix}$$

$$D^{(2)} = \begin{pmatrix} 0 & 3 & 8 & 4 & -4 \\ \infty & 0 & \infty & 1 & 7 \\ \infty & 4 & 0 & 5 & 11 \\ 2 & 5 & -5 & 0 & -2 \\ \infty & \infty & \infty & 6 & 0 \end{pmatrix} \quad \Pi^{(2)} = \begin{pmatrix} \text{NIL} & 1 & 1 & 2 & 1 \\ \text{NIL} & \text{NIL} & \text{NIL} & 2 & 2 \\ \text{NIL} & 3 & \text{NIL} & 2 & 2 \\ 4 & 1 & 4 & \text{NIL} & 1 \\ \text{NIL} & \text{NIL} & \text{NIL} & 5 & \text{NIL} \end{pmatrix}$$

$$D^{(3)} = \begin{pmatrix} 0 & 3 & 8 & 4 & -4 \\ \infty & 0 & \infty & 1 & 7 \\ \infty & 4 & 0 & 5 & 11 \\ 2 & -1 & -5 & 0 & -2 \\ \infty & \infty & \infty & 6 & 0 \end{pmatrix} \quad \Pi^{(3)} = \begin{pmatrix} \text{NIL} & 1 & 1 & 2 & 1 \\ \text{NIL} & \text{NIL} & \text{NIL} & 2 & 2 \\ \text{NIL} & 3 & \text{NIL} & 2 & 2 \\ 4 & 3 & 4 & \text{NIL} & 1 \\ \text{NIL} & \text{NIL} & \text{NIL} & 5 & \text{NIL} \end{pmatrix}$$

$$D^{(4)} = \begin{pmatrix} 0 & 3 & -1 & 4 & -4 \\ 3 & 0 & -4 & 1 & -1 \\ 7 & 4 & 0 & 5 & 3 \\ 2 & -1 & -5 & 0 & -2 \\ 8 & 5 & 1 & 6 & 0 \end{pmatrix} \quad \Pi^{(4)} = \begin{pmatrix} \text{NIL} & 1 & 4 & 2 & 1 \\ 4 & \text{NIL} & 4 & 2 & 1 \\ 4 & 3 & \text{NIL} & 2 & 1 \\ 4 & 3 & 4 & \text{NIL} & 1 \\ 4 & 3 & 4 & 5 & \text{NIL} \end{pmatrix}$$

$$D^{(5)} = \begin{pmatrix} 0 & 1 & -3 & 2 & -4 \\ 3 & 0 & -4 & 1 & -1 \\ 7 & 4 & 0 & 5 & 3 \\ 2 & -1 & -5 & 0 & -2 \\ 8 & 5 & 1 & 6 & 0 \end{pmatrix} \quad \Pi^{(5)} = \begin{pmatrix} \text{NIL} & 3 & 4 & 5 & 1 \\ 4 & \text{NIL} & 4 & 2 & 1 \\ 4 & 3 & \text{NIL} & 2 & 1 \\ 4 & 3 & 4 & \text{NIL} & 1 \\ 4 & 3 & 4 & 5 & \text{NIL} \end{pmatrix}$$

Figure 25.4 The sequence of matrices $D^{(k)}$ and $\Pi^{(k)}$ computed by the Floyd-Warshall algorithm for the graph in Figure 25.1.

choose the same predecessor of j that we chose on a shortest path from i with all intermediate vertices in the set $\{1, 2, \ldots, k-1\}$. Formally, for $k \geq 1$,

$$\pi_{ij}^{(k)} = \begin{cases} \pi_{ij}^{(k-1)} & \text{if } d_{ij}^{(k-1)} \leq d_{ik}^{(k-1)} + d_{kj}^{(k-1)} \,, \\ \pi_{kj}^{(k-1)} & \text{if } d_{ij}^{(k-1)} > d_{ik}^{(k-1)} + d_{kj}^{(k-1)} \,. \end{cases} \tag{25.7}$$

We leave the incorporation of the $\Pi^{(k)}$ matrix computations into the FLOYD-WARSHALL procedure as Exercise 25.2-3. Figure 25.4 shows the sequence of $\Pi^{(k)}$ matrices that the resulting algorithm computes for the graph of Figure 25.1. The exercise also asks for the more difficult task of proving that the predecessor subgraph $G_{\pi,i}$ is a shortest-paths tree with root i. Exercise 25.2-7 asks for yet another way to reconstruct shortest paths.

Transitive closure of a directed graph

Given a directed graph $G = (V, E)$ with vertex set $V = \{1, 2, \ldots, n\}$, we might wish to determine whether G contains a path from i to j for all vertex pairs $i, j \in V$. We define the ***transitive closure*** of G as the graph $G^* = (V, E^*)$, where

$$E^* = \{(i, j) : \text{there is a path from vertex } i \text{ to vertex } j \text{ in } G\} \,.$$

One way to compute the transitive closure of a graph in $\Theta(n^3)$ time is to assign a weight of 1 to each edge of E and run the Floyd-Warshall algorithm. If there is a path from vertex i to vertex j, we get $d_{ij} < n$. Otherwise, we get $d_{ij} = \infty$.

There is another, similar way to compute the transitive closure of G in $\Theta(n^3)$ time that can save time and space in practice. This method substitutes the logical operations $\vee$ (logical OR) and $\wedge$ (logical AND) for the arithmetic operations min and $+$ in the Floyd-Warshall algorithm. For $i, j, k = 1, 2, \ldots, n$, we define $t_{ij}^{(k)}$ to be 1 if there exists a path in graph G from vertex i to vertex j with all intermediate vertices in the set $\{1, 2, \ldots, k\}$, and 0 otherwise. We construct the transitive closure $G^* = (V, E^*)$ by putting edge (i, j) into E^* if and only if $t_{ij}^{(n)} = 1$. A recursive definition of $t_{ij}^{(k)}$, analogous to recurrence (25.5), is

$$t_{ij}^{(0)} = \begin{cases} 0 & \text{if } i \neq j \text{ and } (i, j) \notin E \,, \\ 1 & \text{if } i = j \text{ or } (i, j) \in E \,, \end{cases}$$

and for $k \geq 1$,

$$t_{ij}^{(k)} = t_{ij}^{(k-1)} \vee \left(t_{ik}^{(k-1)} \wedge t_{kj}^{(k-1)} \right) \,. \tag{25.8}$$

As in the Floyd-Warshall algorithm, we compute the matrices $T^{(k)} = \left(t_{ij}^{(k)} \right)$ in order of increasing k.

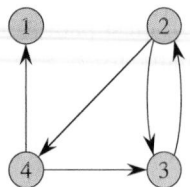

$$T^{(0)} = \begin{pmatrix} 1 & 0 & 0 & 0 \\ 0 & 1 & 1 & 1 \\ 0 & 1 & 1 & 0 \\ 1 & 0 & 1 & 1 \end{pmatrix} \quad T^{(1)} = \begin{pmatrix} 1 & 0 & 0 & 0 \\ 0 & 1 & 1 & 1 \\ 0 & 1 & 1 & 0 \\ 1 & 0 & 1 & 1 \end{pmatrix} \quad T^{(2)} = \begin{pmatrix} 1 & 0 & 0 & 0 \\ 0 & 1 & 1 & 1 \\ 0 & 1 & 1 & 1 \\ 1 & 0 & 1 & 1 \end{pmatrix}$$

$$T^{(3)} = \begin{pmatrix} 1 & 0 & 0 & 0 \\ 0 & 1 & 1 & 1 \\ 0 & 1 & 1 & 1 \\ 1 & 1 & 1 & 1 \end{pmatrix} \quad T^{(4)} = \begin{pmatrix} 1 & 0 & 0 & 0 \\ 1 & 1 & 1 & 1 \\ 1 & 1 & 1 & 1 \\ 1 & 1 & 1 & 1 \end{pmatrix}$$

Figure 25.5   A directed graph and the matrices $T^{(k)}$ computed by the transitive-closure algorithm.

TRANSITIVE-CLOSURE(G)

```
 1  n = |G.V|
 2  let T^(0) = (t_ij^(0)) be a new n × n matrix
 3  for i = 1 to n
 4      for j = 1 to n
 5          if i == j or (i, j) ∈ G.E
 6              t_ij^(0) = 1
 7          else t_ij^(0) = 0
 8  for k = 1 to n
 9      let T^(k) = (t_ij^(k)) be a new n × n matrix
10      for i = 1 to n
11          for j = 1 to n
12              t_ij^(k) = t_ij^(k-1) ∨ (t_ik^(k-1) ∧ t_kj^(k-1))
13  return T^(n)
```

Figure 25.5 shows the matrices $T^{(k)}$ computed by the TRANSITIVE-CLOSURE procedure on a sample graph. The TRANSITIVE-CLOSURE procedure, like the Floyd-Warshall algorithm, runs in $\Theta(n^3)$ time. On some computers, though, logical operations on single-bit values execute faster than arithmetic operations on integer words of data. Moreover, because the direct transitive-closure algorithm uses only boolean values rather than integer values, its space requirement is less

than the Floyd-Warshall algorithm's by a factor corresponding to the size of a word of computer storage.

Exercises

25.2-1
Run the Floyd-Warshall algorithm on the weighted, directed graph of Figure 25.2. Show the matrix $D^{(k)}$ that results for each iteration of the outer loop.

25.2-2
Show how to compute the transitive closure using the technique of Section 25.1.

25.2-3
Modify the FLOYD-WARSHALL procedure to compute the $\Pi^{(k)}$ matrices according to equations (25.6) and (25.7). Prove rigorously that for all $i \in V$, the predecessor subgraph $G_{\pi,i}$ is a shortest-paths tree with root i. (*Hint:* To show that $G_{\pi,i}$ is acyclic, first show that $\pi_{ij}^{(k)} = l$ implies $d_{ij}^{(k)} \geq d_{il}^{(k)} + w_{lj}$, according to the definition of $\pi_{ij}^{(k)}$. Then, adapt the proof of Lemma 24.16.)

25.2-4
As it appears above, the Floyd-Warshall algorithm requires $\Theta(n^3)$ space, since we compute $d_{ij}^{(k)}$ for $i, j, k = 1, 2, \ldots, n$. Show that the following procedure, which simply drops all the superscripts, is correct, and thus only $\Theta(n^2)$ space is required.

FLOYD-WARSHALL$'(W)$

```
1  n = W.rows
2  D = W
3  for k = 1 to n
4      for i = 1 to n
5          for j = 1 to n
6              dij = min (dij, dik + dkj)
7  return D
```

25.2-5
Suppose that we modify the way in which equation (25.7) handles equality:

$$\pi_{ij}^{(k)} = \begin{cases} \pi_{ij}^{(k-1)} & \text{if } d_{ij}^{(k-1)} < d_{ik}^{(k-1)} + d_{kj}^{(k-1)} , \\ \pi_{kj}^{(k-1)} & \text{if } d_{ij}^{(k-1)} \geq d_{ik}^{(k-1)} + d_{kj}^{(k-1)} . \end{cases}$$

Is this alternative definition of the predecessor matrix Π correct?

25.2-6

How can we use the output of the Floyd-Warshall algorithm to detect the presence of a negative-weight cycle?

25.2-7

Another way to reconstruct shortest paths in the Floyd-Warshall algorithm uses values $\phi_{ij}^{(k)}$ for $i, j, k = 1, 2, \ldots, n$, where $\phi_{ij}^{(k)}$ is the highest-numbered intermediate vertex of a shortest path from i to j in which all intermediate vertices are in the set $\{1, 2, \ldots, k\}$. Give a recursive formulation for $\phi_{ij}^{(k)}$, modify the FLOYD-WARSHALL procedure to compute the $\phi_{ij}^{(k)}$ values, and rewrite the PRINT-ALL-PAIRS-SHORTEST-PATH procedure to take the matrix $\Phi = \left(\phi_{ij}^{(n)}\right)$ as an input. How is the matrix Φ like the s table in the matrix-chain multiplication problem of Section 15.2?

25.2-8

Give an $O(VE)$-time algorithm for computing the transitive closure of a directed graph $G = (V, E)$.

25.2-9

Suppose that we can compute the transitive closure of a directed acyclic graph in $f(|V|, |E|)$ time, where f is a monotonically increasing function of $|V|$ and $|E|$. Show that the time to compute the transitive closure $G^* = (V, E^*)$ of a general directed graph $G = (V, E)$ is then $O(f(|V|, |E|) + V + E^*)$.

25.3   Johnson's algorithm for sparse graphs

Johnson's algorithm finds shortest paths between all pairs in $O(V^2 \lg V + VE)$ time. For sparse graphs, it is asymptotically faster than either repeated squaring of matrices or the Floyd-Warshall algorithm. The algorithm either returns a matrix of shortest-path weights for all pairs of vertices or reports that the input graph contains a negative-weight cycle. Johnson's algorithm uses as subroutines both Dijkstra's algorithm and the Bellman-Ford algorithm, which Chapter 24 describes.

Johnson's algorithm uses the technique of ***reweighting***, which works as follows. If all edge weights w in a graph $G = (V, E)$ are nonnegative, we can find shortest paths between all pairs of vertices by running Dijkstra's algorithm once from each vertex; with the Fibonacci-heap min-priority queue, the running time of this all-pairs algorithm is $O(V^2 \lg V + VE)$. If G has negative-weight edges but no negative-weight cycles, we simply compute a new set of nonnegative edge weights

that allows us to use the same method. The new set of edge weights $\hat{w}$ must satisfy two important properties:

1. For all pairs of vertices $u, v \in V$, a path p is a shortest path from u to v using weight function w if and only if p is also a shortest path from u to v using weight function $\hat{w}$.

2. For all edges (u, v), the new weight $\hat{w}(u, v)$ is nonnegative.

As we shall see in a moment, we can preprocess G to determine the new weight function $\hat{w}$ in $O(VE)$ time.

Preserving shortest paths by reweighting

The following lemma shows how easily we can reweight the edges to satisfy the first property above. We use δ to denote shortest-path weights derived from weight function w and $\hat{\delta}$ to denote shortest-path weights derived from weight function $\hat{w}$.

Lemma 25.1 (Reweighting does not change shortest paths)
Given a weighted, directed graph $G = (V, E)$ with weight function $w : E \to \mathbb{R}$, let $h : V \to \mathbb{R}$ be any function mapping vertices to real numbers. For each edge $(u, v) \in E$, define

$$\hat{w}(u, v) = w(u, v) + h(u) - h(v) . \tag{25.9}$$

Let $p = \langle v_0, v_1, \ldots, v_k \rangle$ be any path from vertex v_0 to vertex v_k. Then p is a shortest path from v_0 to v_k with weight function w if and only if it is a shortest path with weight function $\hat{w}$. That is, $w(p) = \delta(v_0, v_k)$ if and only if $\hat{w}(p) = \hat{\delta}(v_0, v_k)$. Furthermore, G has a negative-weight cycle using weight function w if and only if G has a negative-weight cycle using weight function $\hat{w}$.

Proof We start by showing that

$$\hat{w}(p) = w(p) + h(v_0) - h(v_k) . \tag{25.10}$$

We have

$$
\begin{aligned}
\hat{w}(p) &= \sum_{i=1}^{k} \hat{w}(v_{i-1}, v_i) \\
&= \sum_{i=1}^{k} (w(v_{i-1}, v_i) + h(v_{i-1}) - h(v_i)) \\
&= \sum_{i=1}^{k} w(v_{i-1}, v_i) + h(v_0) - h(v_k) \quad \text{(because the sum telescopes)} \\
&= w(p) + h(v_0) - h(v_k) .
\end{aligned}
$$

Therefore, any path p from v_0 to v_k has $\hat{w}(p) = w(p) + h(v_0) - h(v_k)$. Be-cause $h(v_0)$ and $h(v_k)$ do not depend on the path, if one path from v_0 to v_k is shorter than another using weight function w, then it is also shorter using $\hat{w}$. Thus, $w(p) = \delta(v_0, v_k)$ if and only if $\hat{w}(p) = \hat{\delta}(v_0, v_k)$.

Finally, we show that G has a negative-weight cycle using weight function w if and only if G has a negative-weight cycle using weight function $\hat{w}$. Consider any cycle $c = \langle v_0, v_1, \ldots, v_k \rangle$, where $v_0 = v_k$. By equation (25.10),

$$
\begin{aligned}
\hat{w}(c) &= w(c) + h(v_0) - h(v_k) \\
&= w(c),
\end{aligned}
$$

and thus c has negative weight using w if and only if it has negative weight us-ing $\hat{w}$. ∎

Producing nonnegative weights by reweighting

Our next goal is to ensure that the second property holds: we want $\hat{w}(u, v)$ to be nonnegative for all edges $(u, v) \in E$. Given a weighted, directed graph $G = (V, E)$ with weight function $w : E \rightarrow \mathbb{R}$, we make a new graph $G' = (V', E')$, where $V' = V \cup \{s\}$ for some new vertex $s \notin V$ and $E' = E \cup \{(s, v) : v \in V\}$. We extend the weight function w so that $w(s, v) = 0$ for all $v \in V$. Note that because s has no edges that enter it, no shortest paths in G', other than those with source s, contain s. Moreover, G' has no negative-weight cycles if and only if G has no negative-weight cycles. Figure 25.6(a) shows the graph G' corresponding to the graph G of Figure 25.1.

Now suppose that G and G' have no negative-weight cycles. Let us define $h(v) = \delta(s, v)$ for all $v \in V'$. By the triangle inequality (Lemma 24.10), we have $h(v) \leq h(u) + w(u, v)$ for all edges $(u, v) \in E'$. Thus, if we de-fine the new weights $\hat{w}$ by reweighting according to equation (25.9), we have $\hat{w}(u, v) = w(u, v) + h(u) - h(v) \geq 0$, and we have satisfied the second property. Figure 25.6(b) shows the graph G' from Figure 25.6(a) with reweighted edges.

Computing all-pairs shortest paths

Johnson's algorithm to compute all-pairs shortest paths uses the Bellman-Ford al-gorithm (Section 24.1) and Dijkstra's algorithm (Section 24.3) as subroutines. It assumes implicitly that the edges are stored in adjacency lists. The algorithm re-turns the usual $|V| \times |V|$ matrix $D = d_{ij}$, where $d_{ij} = \delta(i, j)$, or it reports that the input graph contains a negative-weight cycle. As is typical for an all-pairs shortest-paths algorithm, we assume that the vertices are numbered from 1 to $|V|$.

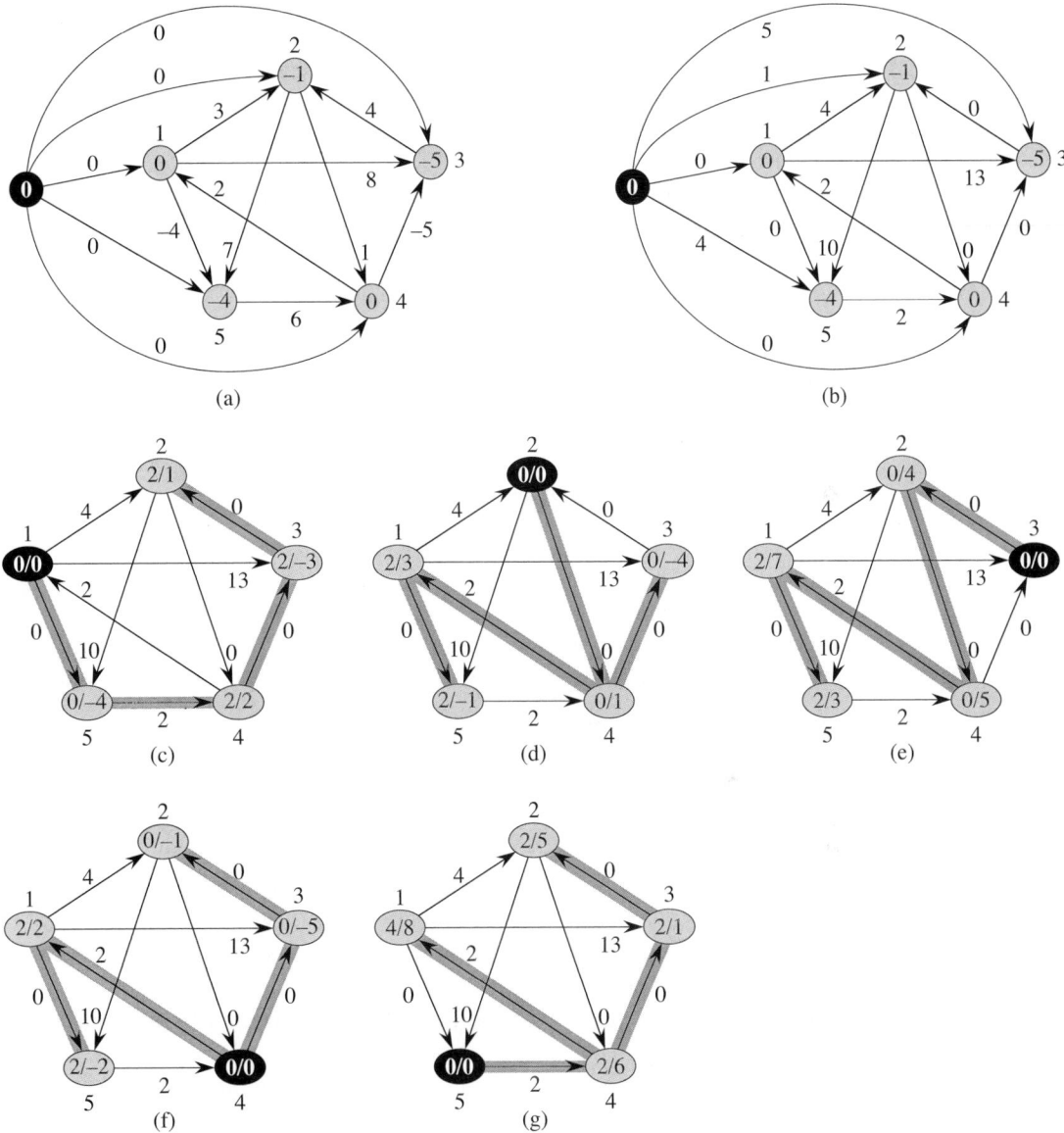

Figure 25.6 Johnson's all-pairs shortest-paths algorithm run on the graph of Figure 25.1. Vertex numbers appear outside the vertices. (**a**) The graph G' with the original weight function w. The new vertex s is black. Within each vertex v is $h(v) = \delta(s, v)$. (**b**) After reweighting each edge (u, v) with weight function $\hat{w}(u, v) = w(u, v) + h(u) - h(v)$. (**c**)–(**g**) The result of running Dijkstra's algorithm on each vertex of G using weight function $\hat{w}$. In each part, the source vertex u is black, and shaded edges are in the shortest-paths tree computed by the algorithm. Within each vertex v are the values $\hat{\delta}(u, v)$ and $\delta(u, v)$, separated by a slash. The value $d_{uv} = \delta(u, v)$ is equal to $\hat{\delta}(u, v) + h(v) - h(u)$.

JOHNSON(G, w)

```
 1   compute G', where G'.V = G.V ∪ {s},
         G'.E = G.E ∪ {(s, v) : v ∈ G.V}, and
         w(s, v) = 0 for all v ∈ G.V
 2   if BELLMAN-FORD(G', w, s) == FALSE
 3       print "the input graph contains a negative-weight cycle"
 4   else for each vertex v ∈ G'.V
 5           set h(v) to the value of δ(s, v)
                 computed by the Bellman-Ford algorithm
 6       for each edge (u, v) ∈ G'.E
 7           ŵ(u, v) = w(u, v) + h(u) − h(v)
 8       let D = (d_uv) be a new n × n matrix
 9       for each vertex u ∈ G.V
10           run DIJKSTRA(G, ŵ, u) to compute δ̂(u, v) for all v ∈ G.V
11           for each vertex v ∈ G.V
12               d_uv = δ̂(u, v) + h(v) − h(u)
13       return D
```

This code simply performs the actions we specified earlier. Line 1 produces G'. Line 2 runs the Bellman-Ford algorithm on G' with weight function w and source vertex s. If G', and hence G, contains a negative-weight cycle, line 3 reports the problem. Lines 4–12 assume that G' contains no negative-weight cycles. Lines 4–5 set $h(v)$ to the shortest-path weight $\delta(s, v)$ computed by the Bellman-Ford algorithm for all $v \in V'$. Lines 6–7 compute the new weights $\hat{w}$. For each pair of vertices $u, v \in V$, the **for** loop of lines 9–12 computes the shortest-path weight $\hat{\delta}(u, v)$ by calling Dijkstra's algorithm once from each vertex in V. Line 12 stores in matrix entry d_{uv} the correct shortest-path weight $\delta(u, v)$, calculated using equation (25.10). Finally, line 13 returns the completed D matrix. Figure 25.6 depicts the execution of Johnson's algorithm.

If we implement the min-priority queue in Dijkstra's algorithm by a Fibonacci heap, Johnson's algorithm runs in $O(V^2 \lg V + VE)$ time. The simpler binary min-heap implementation yields a running time of $O(VE \lg V)$, which is still asymptotically faster than the Floyd-Warshall algorithm if the graph is sparse.

Exercises

25.3-1
Use Johnson's algorithm to find the shortest paths between all pairs of vertices in the graph of Figure 25.2. Show the values of h and $\hat{w}$ computed by the algorithm.

25.3-2
What is the purpose of adding the new vertex s to V, yielding V'?

25.3-3
Suppose that $w(u, v) \geq 0$ for all edges $(u, v) \in E$. What is the relationship between the weight functions w and $\hat{w}$?

25.3-4
Professor Greenstreet claims that there is a simpler way to reweight edges than the method used in Johnson's algorithm. Letting $w^* = \min_{(u,v) \in E} \{w(u, v)\}$, just define $\hat{w}(u, v) = w(u, v) - w^*$ for all edges $(u, v) \in E$. What is wrong with the professor's method of reweighting?

25.3-5
Suppose that we run Johnson's algorithm on a directed graph G with weight function w. Show that if G contains a 0-weight cycle c, then $\hat{w}(u, v) = 0$ for every edge (u, v) in c.

25.3-6
Professor Michener claims that there is no need to create a new source vertex in line 1 of JOHNSON. He claims that instead we can just use $G' = G$ and let s be any vertex. Give an example of a weighted, directed graph G for which incorporating the professor's idea into JOHNSON causes incorrect answers. Then show that if G is strongly connected (every vertex is reachable from every other vertex), the results returned by JOHNSON with the professor's modification are correct.

Problems

25-1 *Transitive closure of a dynamic graph*
Suppose that we wish to maintain the transitive closure of a directed graph $G = (V, E)$ as we insert edges into E. That is, after each edge has been inserted, we want to update the transitive closure of the edges inserted so far. Assume that the graph G has no edges initially and that we represent the transitive closure as a boolean matrix.

a. Show how to update the transitive closure $G^* = (V, E^*)$ of a graph $G = (V, E)$ in $O(V^2)$ time when a new edge is added to G.

b. Give an example of a graph G and an edge e such that $\Omega(V^2)$ time is required to update the transitive closure after the insertion of e into G, no matter what algorithm is used.

c. Describe an efficient algorithm for updating the transitive closure as edges are inserted into the graph. For any sequence of n insertions, your algorithm should run in total time $\sum_{i=1}^{n} t_i = O(V^3)$, where t_i is the time to update the transitive closure upon inserting the ith edge. Prove that your algorithm attains this time bound.

25-2   *Shortest paths in ϵ-dense graphs*

A graph $G = (V, E)$ is ϵ-*dense* if $|E| = \Theta(V^{1+\epsilon})$ for some constant ϵ in the range $0 < \epsilon \le 1$. By using d-ary min-heaps (see Problem 6-2) in shortest-paths algorithms on ϵ-dense graphs, we can match the running times of Fibonacci-heap-based algorithms without using as complicated a data structure.

a. What are the asymptotic running times for INSERT, EXTRACT-MIN, and DECREASE-KEY, as a function of d and the number n of elements in a d-ary min-heap? What are these running times if we choose $d = \Theta(n^\alpha)$ for some constant $0 < \alpha \le 1$? Compare these running times to the amortized costs of these operations for a Fibonacci heap.

b. Show how to compute shortest paths from a single source on an ϵ-dense directed graph $G = (V, E)$ with no negative-weight edges in $O(E)$ time. (*Hint:* Pick d as a function of ϵ.)

c. Show how to solve the all-pairs shortest-paths problem on an ϵ-dense directed graph $G = (V, E)$ with no negative-weight edges in $O(VE)$ time.

d. Show how to solve the all-pairs shortest-paths problem in $O(VE)$ time on an ϵ-dense directed graph $G = (V, E)$ that may have negative-weight edges but has no negative-weight cycles.

Chapter notes

Lawler [224] has a good discussion of the all-pairs shortest-paths problem, although he does not analyze solutions for sparse graphs. He attributes the matrix-multiplication algorithm to the folklore. The Floyd-Warshall algorithm is due to Floyd [105], who based it on a theorem of Warshall [349] that describes how to compute the transitive closure of boolean matrices. Johnson's algorithm is taken from [192].

Several researchers have given improved algorithms for computing shortest paths via matrix multiplication. Fredman [111] shows how to solve the all-pairs shortest paths problem using $O(V^{5/2})$ comparisons between sums of edge

weights and obtains an algorithm that runs in $O(V^3(\lg \lg V / \lg V)^{1/3})$ time, which is slightly better than the running time of the Floyd-Warshall algorithm. Han [159] reduced the running time to $O(V^3(\lg \lg V / \lg V)^{5/4})$. Another line of research demonstrates that we can apply algorithms for fast matrix multiplication (see the chapter notes for Chapter 4) to the all-pairs shortest paths problem. Let $O(n^\omega)$ be the running time of the fastest algorithm for multiplying $n \times n$ matrices; currently $\omega < 2.376$ [78]. Galil and Margalit [123, 124] and Seidel [308] designed algorithms that solve the all-pairs shortest paths problem in undirected, unweighted graphs in $(V^\omega p(V))$ time, where $p(n)$ denotes a particular function that is polylogarithmically bounded in n. In dense graphs, these algorithms are faster than the $O(VE)$ time needed to perform $|V|$ breadth-first searches. Several researchers have extended these results to give algorithms for solving the all-pairs shortest paths problem in undirected graphs in which the edge weights are integers in the range $\{1, 2, \ldots, W\}$. The asymptotically fastest such algorithm, by Shoshan and Zwick [316], runs in time $O(WV^\omega p(VW))$.

Karger, Koller, and Phillips [196] and independently McGeoch [247] have given a time bound that depends on E^*, the set of edges in E that participate in some shortest path. Given a graph with nonnegative edge weights, their algorithms run in $O(VE^* + V^2 \lg V)$ time and improve upon running Dijkstra's algorithm $|V|$ times when $|E^*| = o(E)$.

Baswana, Hariharan, and Sen [33] examined decremental algorithms for maintaining all-pairs shortest paths and transitive-closure information. Decremental algorithms allow a sequence of intermixed edge deletions and queries; by comparison, Problem 25-1, in which edges are inserted, asks for an incremental algorithm. The algorithms by Baswana, Hariharan, and Sen are randomized and, when a path exists, their transitive-closure algorithm can fail to report it with probability $1/n^c$ for an arbitrary $c > 0$. The query times are $O(1)$ with high probability. For transitive closure, the amortized time for each update is $O(V^{4/3} \lg^{1/3} V)$. For all-pairs shortest paths, the update times depend on the queries. For queries just giving the shortest-path weights, the amortized time per update is $O(V^3/E \lg^2 V)$. To report the actual shortest path, the amortized update time is $\min(O(V^{3/2}\sqrt{\lg V}), O(V^3/E \lg^2 V))$. Demetrescu and Italiano [84] showed how to handle update and query operations when edges are both inserted and deleted, as long as each given edge has a bounded range of possible values drawn from the real numbers.

Aho, Hopcroft, and Ullman [5] defined an algebraic structure known as a "closed semiring," which serves as a general framework for solving path problems in directed graphs. Both the Floyd-Warshall algorithm and the transitive-closure algorithm from Section 25.2 are instantiations of an all-pairs algorithm based on closed semirings. Maggs and Plotkin [240] showed how to find minimum spanning trees using a closed semiring.

26 Maximum Flow

Just as we can model a road map as a directed graph in order to find the shortest path from one point to another, we can also interpret a directed graph as a "flow network" and use it to answer questions about material flows. Imagine a material coursing through a system from a source, where the material is produced, to a sink, where it is consumed. The source produces the material at some steady rate, and the sink consumes the material at the same rate. The "flow" of the material at any point in the system is intuitively the rate at which the material moves. Flow networks can model many problems, including liquids flowing through pipes, parts through assembly lines, current through electrical networks, and information through communication networks.

We can think of each directed edge in a flow network as a conduit for the material. Each conduit has a stated capacity, given as a maximum rate at which the material can flow through the conduit, such as 200 gallons of liquid per hour through a pipe or 20 amperes of electrical current through a wire. Vertices are conduit junctions, and other than the source and sink, material flows through the vertices without collecting in them. In other words, the rate at which material enters a vertex must equal the rate at which it leaves the vertex. We call this property "flow conservation," and it is equivalent to Kirchhoff's current law when the material is electrical current.

In the maximum-flow problem, we wish to compute the greatest rate at which we can ship material from the source to the sink without violating any capacity constraints. It is one of the simplest problems concerning flow networks and, as we shall see in this chapter, this problem can be solved by efficient algorithms. Moreover, we can adapt the basic techniques used in maximum-flow algorithms to solve other network-flow problems.

This chapter presents two general methods for solving the maximum-flow problem. Section 26.1 formalizes the notions of flow networks and flows, formally defining the maximum-flow problem. Section 26.2 describes the classical method of Ford and Fulkerson for finding maximum flows. An application of this method,

finding a maximum matching in an undirected bipartite graph, appears in Section 26.3. Section 26.4 presents the push-relabel method, which underlies many of the fastest algorithms for network-flow problems. Section 26.5 covers the "relabel-to-front" algorithm, a particular implementation of the push-relabel method that runs in time $O(V^3)$. Although this algorithm is not the fastest algorithm known, it illustrates some of the techniques used in the asymptotically fastest algorithms, and it is reasonably efficient in practice.

26.1 Flow networks

In this section, we give a graph-theoretic definition of flow networks, discuss their properties, and define the maximum-flow problem precisely. We also introduce some helpful notation.

Flow networks and flows

A *flow network* $G = (V, E)$ is a directed graph in which each edge $(u, v) \in E$ has a nonnegative *capacity* $c(u, v) \geq 0$. We further require that if E contains an edge (u, v), then there is no edge (v, u) in the reverse direction. (We shall see shortly how to work around this restriction.) If $(u, v) \notin E$, then for convenience we define $c(u, v) = 0$, and we disallow self-loops. We distinguish two vertices in a flow network: a *source* s and a *sink* t. For convenience, we assume that each vertex lies on some path from the source to the sink. That is, for each vertex $v \in V$, the flow network contains a path $s \rightsquigarrow v \rightsquigarrow t$. The graph is therefore connected and, since each vertex other than s has at least one entering edge, $|E| \geq |V| - 1$. Figure 26.1 shows an example of a flow network.

We are now ready to define flows more formally. Let $G = (V, E)$ be a flow network with a capacity function c. Let s be the source of the network, and let t be the sink. A *flow* in G is a real-valued function $f : V \times V \rightarrow \mathbb{R}$ that satisfies the following two properties:

Capacity constraint: For all $u, v \in V$, we require $0 \leq f(u, v) \leq c(u, v)$.

Flow conservation: For all $u \in V - \{s, t\}$, we require

$$\sum_{v \in V} f(v, u) = \sum_{v \in V} f(u, v) .$$

When $(u, v) \notin E$, there can be no flow from u to v, and $f(u, v) = 0$.

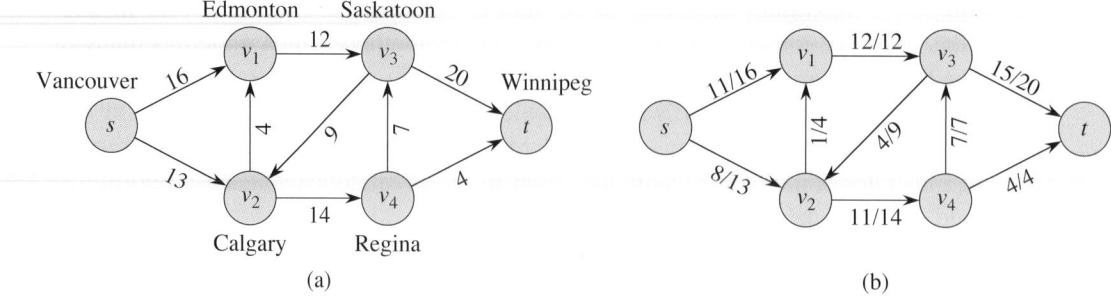

Figure 26.1 (a) A flow network $G = (V, E)$ for the Lucky Puck Company's trucking problem. The Vancouver factory is the source s, and the Winnipeg warehouse is the sink t. The company ships pucks through intermediate cities, but only $c(u, v)$ crates per day can go from city u to city v. Each edge is labeled with its capacity. (b) A flow f in G with value $|f| = 19$. Each edge (u, v) is labeled by $f(u, v)/c(u, v)$. The slash notation merely separates the flow and capacity; it does not indicate division.

We call the nonnegative quantity $f(u, v)$ the flow from vertex u to vertex v. The *value* $|f|$ of a flow f is defined as

$$|f| = \sum_{v \in V} f(s, v) - \sum_{v \in V} f(v, s) \,, \tag{26.1}$$

that is, the total flow out of the source minus the flow into the source. (Here, the $|\cdot|$ notation denotes flow value, not absolute value or cardinality.) Typically, a flow network will not have any edges into the source, and the flow into the source, given by the summation $\sum_{v \in V} f(v, s)$, will be 0. We include it, however, because when we introduce residual networks later in this chapter, the flow into the source will become significant. In the *maximum-flow problem*, we are given a flow network G with source s and sink t, and we wish to find a flow of maximum value.

Before seeing an example of a network-flow problem, let us briefly explore the definition of flow and the two flow properties. The capacity constraint simply says that the flow from one vertex to another must be nonnegative and must not exceed the given capacity. The flow-conservation property says that the total flow into a vertex other than the source or sink must equal the total flow out of that vertex—informally, "flow in equals flow out."

An example of flow

A flow network can model the trucking problem shown in Figure 26.1(a). The Lucky Puck Company has a factory (source s) in Vancouver that manufactures hockey pucks, and it has a warehouse (sink t) in Winnipeg that stocks them. Lucky

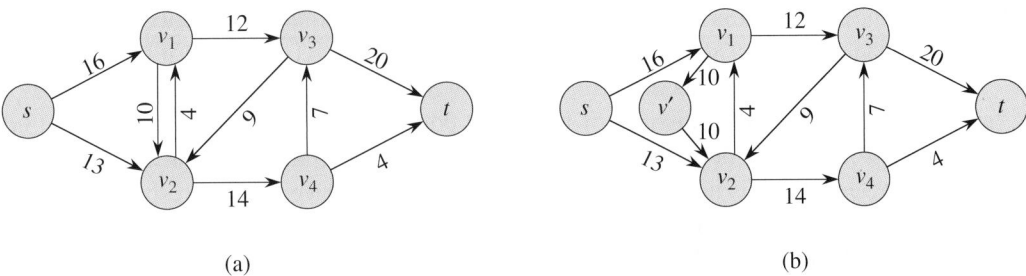

(a) (b)

Figure 26.2 Converting a network with antiparallel edges to an equivalent one with no antiparallel edges. **(a)** A flow network containing both the edges (v_1, v_2) and (v_2, v_1). **(b)** An equivalent network with no antiparallel edges. We add the new vertex v', and we replace edge (v_1, v_2) by the pair of edges (v_1, v') and (v', v_2), both with the same capacity as (v_1, v_2).

Puck leases space on trucks from another firm to ship the pucks from the factory to the warehouse. Because the trucks travel over specified routes (edges) between cities (vertices) and have a limited capacity, Lucky Puck can ship at most $c(u, v)$ crates per day between each pair of cities u and v in Figure 26.1(a). Lucky Puck has no control over these routes and capacities, and so the company cannot alter the flow network shown in Figure 26.1(a). They need to determine the largest number p of crates per day that they can ship and then to produce this amount, since there is no point in producing more pucks than they can ship to their warehouse. Lucky Puck is not concerned with how long it takes for a given puck to get from the factory to the warehouse; they care only that p crates per day leave the factory and p crates per day arrive at the warehouse.

We can model the "flow" of shipments with a flow in this network because the number of crates shipped per day from one city to another is subject to a capacity constraint. Additionally, the model must obey flow conservation, for in a steady state, the rate at which pucks enter an intermediate city must equal the rate at which they leave. Otherwise, crates would accumulate at intermediate cities.

Modeling problems with antiparallel edges

Suppose that the trucking firm offered Lucky Puck the opportunity to lease space for 10 crates in trucks going from Edmonton to Calgary. It would seem natural to add this opportunity to our example and form the network shown in Figure 26.2(a). This network suffers from one problem, however: it violates our original assumption that if an edge $(v_1, v_2) \in E$, then $(v_2, v_1) \notin E$. We call the two edges (v_1, v_2) and (v_2, v_1) *antiparallel*. Thus, if we wish to model a flow problem with antiparallel edges, we must transform the network into an equivalent one containing no

antiparallel edges. Figure 26.2(b) displays this equivalent network. We choose one of the two antiparallel edges, in this case (v_1, v_2), and split it by adding a new vertex v' and replacing edge (v_1, v_2) with the pair of edges (v_1, v') and (v', v_2). We also set the capacity of both new edges to the capacity of the original edge. The resulting network satisfies the property that if an edge is in the network, the reverse edge is not. Exercise 26.1-1 asks you to prove that the resulting network is equivalent to the original one.

Thus, we see that a real-world flow problem might be most naturally modeled by a network with antiparallel edges. It will be convenient to disallow antiparallel edges, however, and so we have a straightforward way to convert a network containing antiparallel edges into an equivalent one with no antiparallel edges.

Networks with multiple sources and sinks

A maximum-flow problem may have several sources and sinks, rather than just one of each. The Lucky Puck Company, for example, might actually have a set of m factories $\{s_1, s_2, \ldots, s_m\}$ and a set of n warehouses $\{t_1, t_2, \ldots, t_n\}$, as shown in Figure 26.3(a). Fortunately, this problem is no harder than ordinary maximum flow.

We can reduce the problem of determining a maximum flow in a network with multiple sources and multiple sinks to an ordinary maximum-flow problem. Figure 26.3(b) shows how to convert the network from (a) to an ordinary flow network with only a single source and a single sink. We add a ***supersource*** s and add a directed edge (s, s_i) with capacity $c(s, s_i) = \infty$ for each $i = 1, 2, \ldots, m$. We also create a new ***supersink*** t and add a directed edge (t_i, t) with capacity $c(t_i, t) = \infty$ for each $i = 1, 2, \ldots, n$. Intuitively, any flow in the network in (a) corresponds to a flow in the network in (b), and vice versa. The single source s simply provides as much flow as desired for the multiple sources s_i, and the single sink t likewise consumes as much flow as desired for the multiple sinks t_i. Exercise 26.1-2 asks you to prove formally that the two problems are equivalent.

Exercises

26.1-1
Show that splitting an edge in a flow network yields an equivalent network. More formally, suppose that flow network G contains edge (u, v), and we create a new flow network G' by creating a new vertex x and replacing (u, v) by new edges (u, x) and (x, v) with $c(u, x) = c(x, v) = c(u, v)$. Show that a maximum flow in G' has the same value as a maximum flow in G.

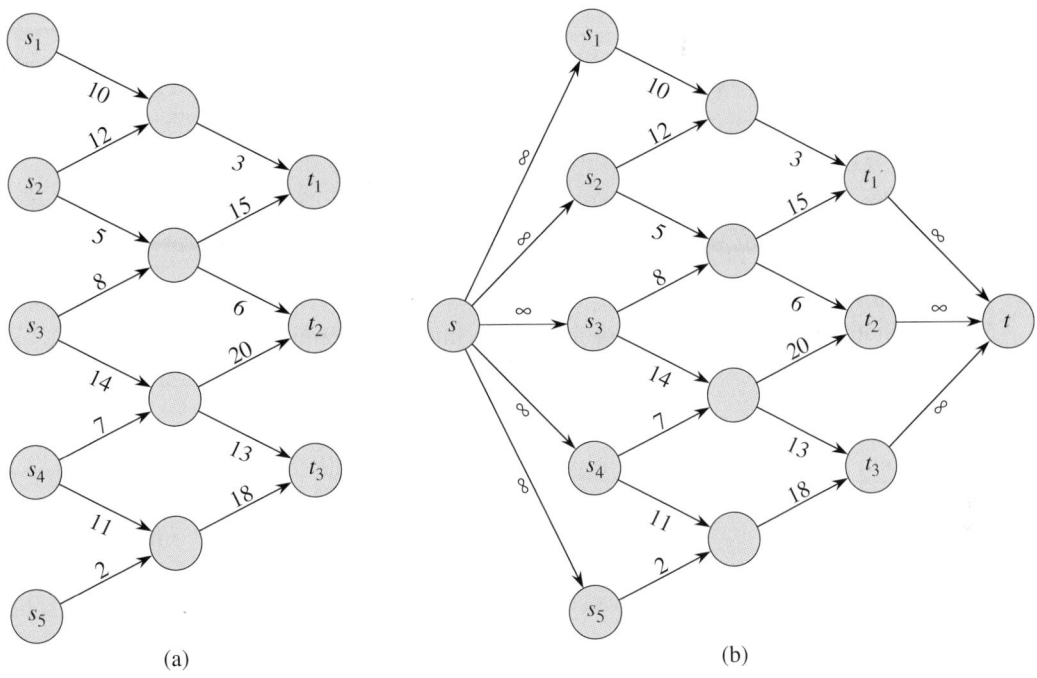

Figure 26.3 Converting a multiple-source, multiple-sink maximum-flow problem into a problem with a single source and a single sink. **(a)** A flow network with five sources $S = \{s_1, s_2, s_3, s_4, s_5\}$ and three sinks $T = \{t_1, t_2, t_3\}$. **(b)** An equivalent single-source, single-sink flow network. We add a supersource s and an edge with infinite capacity from s to each of the multiple sources. We also add a supersink t and an edge with infinite capacity from each of the multiple sinks to t.

26.1-2
Extend the flow properties and definitions to the multiple-source, multiple-sink problem. Show that any flow in a multiple-source, multiple-sink flow network corresponds to a flow of identical value in the single-source, single-sink network obtained by adding a supersource and a supersink, and vice versa.

26.1-3
Suppose that a flow network $G = (V, E)$ violates the assumption that the network contains a path $s \rightsquigarrow v \rightsquigarrow t$ for all vertices $v \in V$. Let u be a vertex for which there is no path $s \rightsquigarrow u \rightsquigarrow t$. Show that there must exist a maximum flow f in G such that $f(u, v) = f(v, u) = 0$ for all vertices $v \in V$.

26.1-4

Let f be a flow in a network, and let α be a real number. The ***scalar flow product***, denoted αf, is a function from $V \times V$ to $\mathbb{R}$ defined by

$$(\alpha f)(u, v) = \alpha \cdot f(u, v) .$$

Prove that the flows in a network form a ***convex set***. That is, show that if f_1 and f_2 are flows, then so is $\alpha f_1 + (1 - \alpha) f_2$ for all α in the range $0 \le \alpha \le 1$.

26.1-5

State the maximum-flow problem as a linear-programming problem.

26.1-6

Professor Adam has two children who, unfortunately, dislike each other. The problem is so severe that not only do they refuse to walk to school together, but in fact each one refuses to walk on any block that the other child has stepped on that day. The children have no problem with their paths crossing at a corner. Fortunately both the professor's house and the school are on corners, but beyond that he is not sure if it is going to be possible to send both of his children to the same school. The professor has a map of his town. Show how to formulate the problem of determining whether both his children can go to the same school as a maximum-flow problem.

26.1-7

Suppose that, in addition to edge capacities, a flow network has ***vertex capacities***. That is each vertex v has a limit $l(v)$ on how much flow can pass through v. Show how to transform a flow network $G = (V, E)$ with vertex capacities into an equivalent flow network $G' = (V', E')$ without vertex capacities, such that a maximum flow in G' has the same value as a maximum flow in G. How many vertices and edges does G' have?

26.2   The Ford-Fulkerson method

This section presents the Ford-Fulkerson method for solving the maximum-flow problem. We call it a "method" rather than an "algorithm" because it encompasses several implementations with differing running times. The Ford-Fulkerson method depends on three important ideas that transcend the method and are relevant to many flow algorithms and problems: residual networks, augmenting paths, and cuts. These ideas are essential to the important max-flow min-cut theorem (Theorem 26.6), which characterizes the value of a maximum flow in terms of cuts of

the flow network. We end this section by presenting one specific implementation of the Ford-Fulkerson method and analyzing its running time.

The Ford-Fulkerson method iteratively increases the value of the flow. We start with $f(u, v) = 0$ for all $u, v \in V$, giving an initial flow of value 0. At each iteration, we increase the flow value in G by finding an "augmenting path" in an associated "residual network" G_f. Once we know the edges of an augmenting path in G_f, we can easily identify specific edges in G for which we can change the flow so that we increase the value of the flow. Although each iteration of the Ford-Fulkerson method increases the value of the flow, we shall see that the flow on any particular edge of G may increase or decrease; decreasing the flow on some edges may be necessary in order to enable an algorithm to send more flow from the source to the sink. We repeatedly augment the flow until the residual network has no more augmenting paths. The max-flow min-cut theorem will show that upon termination, this process yields a maximum flow.

FORD-FULKERSON-METHOD(G, s, t)

1   initialize flow f to 0
2   **while** there exists an augmenting path p in the residual network G_f
3   augment flow f along p
4   **return** f

In order to implement and analyze the Ford-Fulkerson method, we need to introduce several additional concepts.

Residual networks

Intuitively, given a flow network G and a flow f, the residual network G_f consists of edges with capacities that represent how we can change the flow on edges of G. An edge of the flow network can admit an amount of additional flow equal to the edge's capacity minus the flow on that edge. If that value is positive, we place that edge into G_f with a "residual capacity" of $c_f(u, v) = c(u, v) - f(u, v)$. The only edges of G that are in G_f are those that can admit more flow; those edges (u, v) whose flow equals their capacity have $c_f(u, v) = 0$, and they are not in G_f.

The residual network G_f may also contain edges that are not in G, however. As an algorithm manipulates the flow, with the goal of increasing the total flow, it might need to decrease the flow on a particular edge. In order to represent a possible decrease of a positive flow $f(u, v)$ on an edge in G, we place an edge (v, u) into G_f with residual capacity $c_f(v, u) = f(u, v)$—that is, an edge that can admit flow in the opposite direction to (u, v), at most canceling out the flow on (u, v). These reverse edges in the residual network allow an algorithm to send back flow

it has already sent along an edge. Sending flow back along an edge is equivalent to *decreasing* the flow on the edge, which is a necessary operation in many algorithms.

More formally, suppose that we have a flow network $G = (V, E)$ with source s and sink t. Let f be a flow in G, and consider a pair of vertices $u, v \in V$. We define the *residual capacity* $c_f(u, v)$ by

$$c_f(u, v) = \begin{cases} c(u, v) - f(u, v) & \text{if } (u, v) \in E, \\ f(v, u) & \text{if } (v, u) \in E, \\ 0 & \text{otherwise}. \end{cases} \tag{26.2}$$

Because of our assumption that $(u, v) \in E$ implies $(v, u) \notin E$, exactly one case in equation (26.2) applies to each ordered pair of vertices.

As an example of equation (26.2), if $c(u, v) = 16$ and $f(u, v) = 11$, then we can increase $f(u, v)$ by up to $c_f(u, v) = 5$ units before we exceed the capacity constraint on edge (u, v). We also wish to allow an algorithm to return up to 11 units of flow from v to u, and hence $c_f(v, u) = 11$.

Given a flow network $G = (V, E)$ and a flow f, the *residual network* of G induced by f is $G_f = (V, E_f)$, where

$$E_f = \{(u, v) \in V \times V : c_f(u, v) > 0\} . \tag{26.3}$$

That is, as promised above, each edge of the residual network, or *residual edge*, can admit a flow that is greater than 0. Figure 26.4(a) repeats the flow network G and flow f of Figure 26.1(b), and Figure 26.4(b) shows the corresponding residual network G_f. The edges in E_f are either edges in E or their reversals, and thus

$$|E_f| \le 2 |E| .$$

Observe that the residual network G_f is similar to a flow network with capacities given by c_f. It does not satisfy our definition of a flow network because it may contain both an edge (u, v) and its reversal (v, u). Other than this difference, a residual network has the same properties as a flow network, and we can define a flow in the residual network as one that satisfies the definition of a flow, but with respect to capacities c_f in the network G_f.

A flow in a residual network provides a roadmap for adding flow to the original flow network. If f is a flow in G and f' is a flow in the corresponding residual network G_f, we define $f \uparrow f'$, the *augmentation* of flow f by f', to be a function from $V \times V$ to $\mathbb{R}$, defined by

$$(f \uparrow f')(u, v) = \begin{cases} f(u, v) + f'(u, v) - f'(v, u) & \text{if } (u, v) \in E, \\ 0 & \text{otherwise}. \end{cases} \tag{26.4}$$

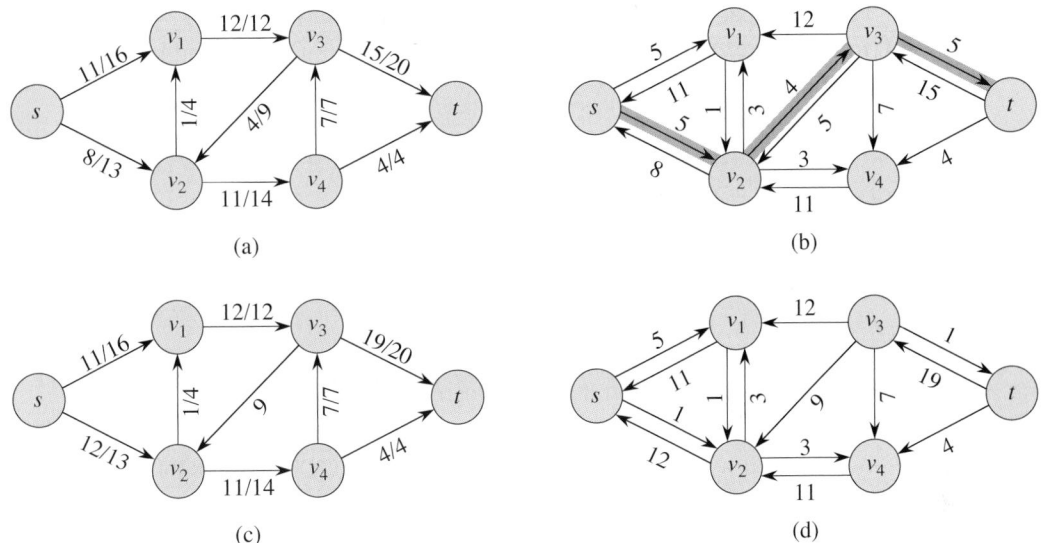

Figure 26.4 **(a)** The flow network G and flow f of Figure 26.1(b). **(b)** The residual network G_f with augmenting path p shaded; its residual capacity is $c_f(p) = c_f(v_2, v_3) = 4$. Edges with residual capacity equal to 0, such as (v_1, v_3), are not shown, a convention we follow in the remainder of this section. **(c)** The flow in G that results from augmenting along path p by its residual capacity 4. Edges carrying no flow, such as (v_3, v_2), are labeled only by their capacity, another convention we follow throughout. **(d)** The residual network induced by the flow in (c).

The intuition behind this definition follows the definition of the residual network. We increase the flow on (u, v) by $f'(u, v)$ but decrease it by $f'(v, u)$ because pushing flow on the reverse edge in the residual network signifies decreasing the flow in the original network. Pushing flow on the reverse edge in the residual network is also known as ***cancellation***. For example, if we send 5 crates of hockey pucks from u to v and send 2 crates from v to u, we could equivalently (from the perspective of the final result) just send 3 crates from u to v and none from v to u. Cancellation of this type is crucial for any maximum-flow algorithm.

Lemma 26.1
Let $G = (V, E)$ be a flow network with source s and sink t, and let f be a flow in G. Let G_f be the residual network of G induced by f, and let f' be a flow in G_f. Then the function $f \uparrow f'$ defined in equation (26.4) is a flow in G with value $|f \uparrow f'| = |f| + |f'|$.

Proof We first verify that $f \uparrow f'$ obeys the capacity constraint for each edge in E and flow conservation at each vertex in $V - \{s, t\}$.

For the capacity constraint, first observe that if $(u, v) \in E$, then $c_f(v, u) = f(u, v)$. Therefore, we have $f'(v, u) \le c_f(v, u) = f(u, v)$, and hence

$$
\begin{aligned}
(f \uparrow f')(u, v) &= f(u, v) + f'(u, v) - f'(v, u) && \text{(by equation (26.4))} \\
&\ge f(u, v) + f'(u, v) - f(u, v) && \text{(because } f'(v, u) \le f(u, v)) \\
&= f'(u, v) \\
&\ge 0 .
\end{aligned}
$$

In addition,

$$
\begin{aligned}
(f \uparrow f')(u, v) \\
= f(u, v) + f'(u, v) - f'(v, u) && \text{(by equation (26.4))} \\
\le f(u, v) + f'(u, v) && \text{(because flows are nonnegative)} \\
\le f(u, v) + c_f(u, v) && \text{(capacity constraint)} \\
= f(u, v) + c(u, v) - f(u, v) && \text{(definition of } c_f) \\
= c(u, v) .
\end{aligned}
$$

To show that flow conservation holds and that $|f \uparrow f'| = |f| + |f'|$, we first prove the claim that for all $u \in V$, we have

$$
\sum_{v \in V} (f \uparrow f')(u, v) - \sum_{v \in V} (f \uparrow f')(v, u)
$$

$$
= \sum_{v \in V} f(u, v) - \sum_{v \in V} f(v, u) + \sum_{v \in V} f'(u, v) - \sum_{v \in V} f'(v, u) . \quad (26.5)
$$

Because we disallow antiparallel edges in G (but not in G_f), we know that for each vertex u, there can be an edge (u, v) or (v, u) in G, but never both. For a fixed vertex u, let's define $V_1(u) = \{v : (u, v) \in E\}$ to be the set of vertices with edges from u, and $V_2(u) = \{v : (v, u) \in E\}$ to be the set of vertices with edges to u. We have $V_1(u) \cup V_2(u) \subseteq V$ and, because we disallow antiparallel edges, $V_1(u) \cap V_2(u) = \emptyset$. By the definition of flow augmentation in equation (26.4), only vertices in $V_1(u)$ can have positive $(f \uparrow f')(u, v)$, and only vertices in $V_2(u)$ can have positive $(f \uparrow f')(v, u)$. Starting from the left-hand side of equation (26.5), we use this fact and then reorder and group terms, giving

$$
\sum_{v \in V} (f \uparrow f')(u, v) - \sum_{v \in V} (f \uparrow f')(v, u)
$$

$$
= \sum_{v \in V_1(u)} (f \uparrow f')(u, v) - \sum_{v \in V_2(u)} (f \uparrow f')(v, u)
$$

$$
= \sum_{v \in V_1(u)} (f(u, v) + f'(u, v) - f'(v, u)) - \sum_{v \in V_2(u)} (f(v, u) + f'(v, u) - f'(u, v))
$$

$$= \sum_{v \in V_1(u)} f(u, v) + \sum_{v \in V_1(u)} f'(u, v) - \sum_{v \in V_1(u)} f'(v, u)$$

$$- \sum_{v \in V_2(u)} f(v, u) - \sum_{v \in V_2(u)} f'(v, u) + \sum_{v \in V_2(u)} f'(u, v)$$

$$= \sum_{v \in V_1(u)} f(u, v) - \sum_{v \in V_2(u)} f(v, u)$$

$$+ \sum_{v \in V_1(u)} f'(u, v) + \sum_{v \in V_2(u)} f'(u, v) - \sum_{v \in V_1(u)} f'(v, u) - \sum_{v \in V_2(u)} f'(v, u)$$

$$= \sum_{v \in V_1(u)} f(u, v) - \sum_{v \in V_2(u)} f(v, u) + \sum_{v \in V_1(u) \cup V_2(u)} f'(u, v) - \sum_{v \in V_1(u) \cup V_2(u)} f'(v, u) \,. \qquad (26.6)$$

In equation (26.6), we can extend all four summations to sum over V, since each additional term has value 0. (Exercise 26.2-1 asks you to prove this formally.) With all four summations over V, instead of just subsets of V, we get equation (26.5).

Now we are ready to prove flow conservation for $f \uparrow f'$ and that $|f \uparrow f'| = |f| + |f'|$. For the latter property, let $u = s$ in equation (26.5). Then, we have

$$|f \uparrow f'| = \sum_{v \in V} (f \uparrow f')(s, v) - \sum_{v \in V} (f \uparrow f')(v, s)$$

$$= \sum_{v \in V} f(s, v) - \sum_{v \in V} f(v, s) + \sum_{v \in V} f'(s, v) - \sum_{v \in V} f'(v, s)$$

$$= |f| + |f'| \,. \qquad (26.7)$$

For flow conservation, observe that for any vertex u that is neither s nor t, flow conservation for f and f' means that the right-hand side of equation (26.5) is 0, and thus $\sum_{v \in V}(f \uparrow f')(u, v) = \sum_{v \in V}(f \uparrow f')(v, u)$.   ■

Augmenting paths

Given a flow network $G = (V, E)$ and a flow f, an ***augmenting path*** p is a simple path from s to t in the residual network G_f. By the definition of the residual network, we may increase the flow on an edge (u, v) of an augmenting path by up to $c_f(u, v)$ without violating the capacity constraint on whichever of (u, v) and (v, u) is in the original flow network G.

The shaded path in Figure 26.4(b) is an augmenting path. Treating the residual network G_f in the figure as a flow network, we can increase the flow through each edge of this path by up to 4 units without violating a capacity constraint, since the smallest residual capacity on this path is $c_f(v_2, v_3) = 4$. We call the maximum amount by which we can increase the flow on each edge in an augmenting path p the ***residual capacity*** of p, given by

$$c_f(p) = \min \{c_f(u, v) : (u, v) \text{ is on } p\} \ .$$

The following lemma, whose proof we leave as Exercise 26.2-7, makes the above argument more precise.

Lemma 26.2
Let $G = (V, E)$ be a flow network, let f be a flow in G, and let p be an augmenting path in G_f. Define a function $f_p : V \times V \to \mathbb{R}$ by

$$f_p(u, v) = \begin{cases} c_f(p) & \text{if } (u, v) \text{ is on } p, \\ 0 & \text{otherwise} . \end{cases} \tag{26.8}$$

Then, f_p is a flow in G_f with value $|f_p| = c_f(p) > 0$.   ∎

The following corollary shows that if we augment f by f_p, we get another flow in G whose value is closer to the maximum. Figure 26.4(c) shows the result of augmenting the flow f from Figure 26.4(a) by the flow f_p in Figure 26.4(b), and Figure 26.4(d) shows the ensuing residual network.

Corollary 26.3
Let $G = (V, E)$ be a flow network, let f be a flow in G, and let p be an augmenting path in G_f. Let f_p be defined as in equation (26.8), and suppose that we augment f by f_p. Then the function $f \uparrow f_p$ is a flow in G with value $|f \uparrow f_p| = |f| + |f_p| > |f|$.

Proof   Immediate from Lemmas 26.1 and 26.2.   ∎

Cuts of flow networks

The Ford-Fulkerson method repeatedly augments the flow along augmenting paths until it has found a maximum flow. How do we know that when the algorithm terminates, we have actually found a maximum flow? The max-flow min-cut theorem, which we shall prove shortly, tells us that a flow is maximum if and only if its residual network contains no augmenting path. To prove this theorem, though, we must first explore the notion of a cut of a flow network.

A **cut** (S, T) of flow network $G = (V, E)$ is a partition of V into S and $T = V - S$ such that $s \in S$ and $t \in T$. (This definition is similar to the definition of "cut" that we used for minimum spanning trees in Chapter 23, except that here we are cutting a directed graph rather than an undirected graph, and we insist that $s \in S$ and $t \in T$.) If f is a flow, then the **net flow** $f(S, T)$ across the cut (S, T) is defined to be

$$f(S, T) = \sum_{u \in S} \sum_{v \in T} f(u, v) - \sum_{u \in S} \sum_{v \in T} f(v, u) \ . \tag{26.9}$$

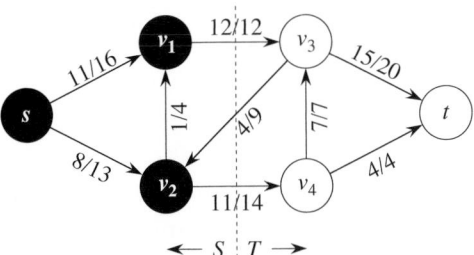

Figure 26.5   A cut (S, T) in the flow network of Figure 26.1(b), where $S = \{s, v_1, v_2\}$ and $T = \{v_3, v_4, t\}$. The vertices in S are black, and the vertices in T are white. The net flow across (S, T) is $f(S, T) = 19$, and the capacity is $c(S, T) = 26$.

The **capacity** of the cut (S, T) is

$$c(S, T) = \sum_{u \in S} \sum_{v \in T} c(u, v) \, . \tag{26.10}$$

A **minimum cut** of a network is a cut whose capacity is minimum over all cuts of the network.

The asymmetry between the definitions of flow and capacity of a cut is intentional and important. For capacity, we count only the capacities of edges going from S to T, ignoring edges in the reverse direction. For flow, we consider the flow going from S to T minus the flow going in the reverse direction from T to S. The reason for this difference will become clear later in this section.

Figure 26.5 shows the cut $(\{s, v_1, v_2\}, \{v_3, v_4, t\})$ in the flow network of Figure 26.1(b). The net flow across this cut is

$$
\begin{aligned}
f(v_1, v_3) + f(v_2, v_4) - f(v_3, v_2) &= 12 + 11 - 4 \\
&= 19 \, ,
\end{aligned}
$$

and the capacity of this cut is

$$
\begin{aligned}
c(v_1, v_3) + c(v_2, v_4) &= 12 + 14 \\
&= 26 \, .
\end{aligned}
$$

The following lemma shows that, for a given flow f, the net flow across any cut is the same, and it equals $|f|$, the value of the flow.

Lemma 26.4
Let f be a flow in a flow network G with source s and sink t, and let (S, T) be any cut of G. Then the net flow across (S, T) is $f(S, T) = |f|$.

Proof   We can rewrite the flow-conservation condition for any node $u \in V - \{s, t\}$ as

$$\sum_{v \in V} f(u, v) - \sum_{v \in V} f(v, u) = 0 . \tag{26.11}$$

Taking the definition of $|f|$ from equation (26.1) and adding the left-hand side of equation (26.11), which equals 0, summed over all vertices in $S - \{s\}$, gives

$$|f| = \sum_{v \in V} f(s, v) - \sum_{v \in V} f(v, s) + \sum_{u \in S - \{s\}} \left(\sum_{v \in V} f(u, v) - \sum_{v \in V} f(v, u) \right) .$$

Expanding the right-hand summation and regrouping terms yields

$$
\begin{aligned}
|f| &= \sum_{v \in V} f(s, v) - \sum_{v \in V} f(v, s) + \sum_{u \in S - \{s\}} \sum_{v \in V} f(u, v) - \sum_{u \in S - \{s\}} \sum_{v \in V} f(v, u) \\
&= \sum_{v \in V} \left(f(s, v) + \sum_{u \in S - \{s\}} f(u, v) \right) - \sum_{v \in V} \left(f(v, s) + \sum_{u \in S - \{s\}} f(v, u) \right) \\
&= \sum_{v \in V} \sum_{u \in S} f(u, v) - \sum_{v \in V} \sum_{u \in S} f(v, u) .
\end{aligned}
$$

Because $V = S \cup T$ and $S \cap T = \emptyset$, we can split each summation over V into summations over S and T to obtain

$$
\begin{aligned}
|f| &= \sum_{v \in S} \sum_{u \in S} f(u, v) + \sum_{v \in T} \sum_{u \in S} f(u, v) - \sum_{v \in S} \sum_{u \in S} f(v, u) - \sum_{v \in T} \sum_{u \in S} f(v, u) \\
&= \sum_{v \in T} \sum_{u \in S} f(u, v) - \sum_{v \in T} \sum_{u \in S} f(v, u) \\
&\quad + \left(\sum_{v \in S} \sum_{u \in S} f(u, v) - \sum_{v \in S} \sum_{u \in S} f(v, u) \right) .
\end{aligned}
$$

The two summations within the parentheses are actually the same, since for all vertices $x, y \in S$, the term $f(x, y)$ appears once in each summation. Hence, these summations cancel, and we have

$$
\begin{aligned}
|f| &= \sum_{u \in S} \sum_{v \in T} f(u, v) - \sum_{u \in S} \sum_{v \in T} f(v, u) \\
&= f(S, T) . \qquad \blacksquare
\end{aligned}
$$

A corollary to Lemma 26.4 shows how we can use cut capacities to bound the value of a flow.

Corollary 26.5
The value of any flow f in a flow network G is bounded from above by the capacity of any cut of G.

Proof   Let (S, T) be any cut of G and let f be any flow. By Lemma 26.4 and the capacity constraint,

$$
\begin{aligned}
|f| &= f(S, T) \\
&= \sum_{u \in S} \sum_{v \in T} f(u, v) - \sum_{u \in S} \sum_{v \in T} f(v, u) \\
&\le \sum_{u \in S} \sum_{v \in T} f(u, v) \\
&\le \sum_{u \in S} \sum_{v \in T} c(u, v) \\
&= c(S, T) .
\end{aligned}
$$
■

Corollary 26.5 yields the immediate consequence that the value of a maximum flow in a network is bounded from above by the capacity of a minimum cut of the network. The important max-flow min-cut theorem, which we now state and prove, says that the value of a maximum flow is in fact equal to the capacity of a minimum cut.

Theorem 26.6 (Max-flow min-cut theorem)
If f is a flow in a flow network $G = (V, E)$ with source s and sink t, then the following conditions are equivalent:

1. f is a maximum flow in G.

2. The residual network G_f contains no augmenting paths.

3. $|f| = c(S, T)$ for some cut (S, T) of G.

Proof   (1) $\Rightarrow$ (2): Suppose for the sake of contradiction that f is a maximum flow in G but that G_f has an augmenting path p. Then, by Corollary 26.3, the flow found by augmenting f by f_p, where f_p is given by equation (26.8), is a flow in G with value strictly greater than $|f|$, contradicting the assumption that f is a maximum flow.

(2) $\Rightarrow$ (3): Suppose that G_f has no augmenting path, that is, that G_f contains no path from s to t. Define

$S = \{v \in V : \text{there exists a path from } s \text{ to } v \text{ in } G_f\}$

and $T = V - S$. The partition (S, T) is a cut: we have $s \in S$ trivially and $t \notin S$ because there is no path from s to t in G_f. Now consider a pair of vertices

$u \in S$ and $v \in T$. If $(u, v) \in E$, we must have $f(u, v) = c(u, v)$, since otherwise $(u, v) \in E_f$, which would place v in set S. If $(v, u) \in E$, we must have $f(v, u) = 0$, because otherwise $c_f(u, v) = f(v, u)$ would be positive and we would have $(u, v) \in E_f$, which would place v in S. Of course, if neither (u, v) nor (v, u) is in E, then $f(u, v) = f(v, u) = 0$. We thus have

$$
\begin{aligned}
f(S, T) &= \sum_{u \in S} \sum_{v \in T} f(u, v) - \sum_{v \in T} \sum_{u \in S} f(v, u) \\
&= \sum_{u \in S} \sum_{v \in T} c(u, v) - \sum_{v \in T} \sum_{u \in S} 0 \\
&= c(S, T) \, .
\end{aligned}
$$

By Lemma 26.4, therefore, $|f| = f(S, T) = c(S, T)$.

(3) $\Rightarrow$ (1): By Corollary 26.5, $|f| \le c(S, T)$ for all cuts (S, T). The condition $|f| = c(S, T)$ thus implies that f is a maximum flow. ∎

The basic Ford-Fulkerson algorithm

In each iteration of the Ford-Fulkerson method, we find *some* augmenting path p and use p to modify the flow f. As Lemma 26.2 and Corollary 26.3 suggest, we replace f by $f \uparrow f_p$, obtaining a new flow whose value is $|f| + |f_p|$. The following implementation of the method computes the maximum flow in a flow network $G = (V, E)$ by updating the flow attribute $(u, v).f$ for each edge $(u, v) \in E$.[1] If $(u, v) \notin E$, we assume implicitly that $(u, v).f = 0$. We also assume that we are given the capacities $c(u, v)$ along with the flow network, and $c(u, v) = 0$ if $(u, v) \notin E$. We compute the residual capacity $c_f(u, v)$ in accordance with the formula (26.2). The expression $c_f(p)$ in the code is just a temporary variable that stores the residual capacity of the path p.

FORD-FULKERSON(G, s, t)

```
1  for each edge (u, v) ∈ G.E
2      (u, v).f = 0
3  while there exists a path p from s to t in the residual network G_f
4      c_f(p) = min {c_f(u, v) : (u, v) is in p}
5      for each edge (u, v) in p
6          if (u, v) ∈ G.E
7              (u, v).f = (u, v).f + c_f(p)
8          else (v, u).f = (v, u).f − c_f(p)
```

---

[1] Recall from Section 22.1 that we represent an attribute f for edge (u, v) with the same style of notation—$(u, v).f$—that we use for an attribute of any other object.

The FORD-FULKERSON algorithm simply expands on the FORD-FULKERSON-
METHOD pseudocode given earlier. Figure 26.6 shows the result of each iteration
in a sample run. Lines 1–2 initialize the flow f to 0. The **while** loop of lines 3–8
repeatedly finds an augmenting path p in G_f and augments flow f along p by
the residual capacity $c_f(p)$. Each residual edge in path p is either an edge in the
original network or the reversal of an edge in the original network. Lines 6–8
update the flow in each case appropriately, adding flow when the residual edge is
an original edge and subtracting it otherwise. When no augmenting paths exist, the
flow f is a maximum flow.

Analysis of Ford-Fulkerson

The running time of FORD-FULKERSON depends on how we find the augmenting
path p in line 3. If we choose it poorly, the algorithm might not even terminate: the
value of the flow will increase with successive augmentations, but it need not even
converge to the maximum flow value.[2] If we find the augmenting path by using a
breadth-first search (which we saw in Section 22.2), however, the algorithm runs in
polynomial time. Before proving this result, we obtain a simple bound for the case
in which we choose the augmenting path arbitrarily and all capacities are integers.

In practice, the maximum-flow problem often arises with integral capacities. If
the capacities are rational numbers, we can apply an appropriate scaling transformation to make them all integral. If f^* denotes a maximum flow in the transformed
network, then a straightforward implementation of FORD-FULKERSON executes
the **while** loop of lines 3–8 at most $|f^*|$ times, since the flow value increases by at
least one unit in each iteration.

We can perform the work done within the **while** loop efficiently if we implement
the flow network $G = (V, E)$ with the right data structure and find an augmenting
path by a linear-time algorithm. Let us assume that we keep a data structure corresponding to a directed graph $G' = (V, E')$, where $E' = \{(u, v) : (u, v) \in E$ or
$(v, u) \in E\}$. Edges in the network G are also edges in G', and therefore we can
easily maintain capacities and flows in this data structure. Given a flow f on G,
the edges in the residual network G_f consist of all edges (u, v) of G' such that
$c_f(u, v) > 0$, where c_f conforms to equation (26.2). The time to find a path in
a residual network is therefore $O(V + E') = O(E)$ if we use either depth-first
search or breadth-first search. Each iteration of the **while** loop thus takes $O(E)$
time, as does the initialization in lines 1–2, making the total running time of the
FORD-FULKERSON algorithm $O(E\,|f^*|)$.

---

[2]The Ford-Fulkerson method might fail to terminate only if edge capacities are irrational numbers.

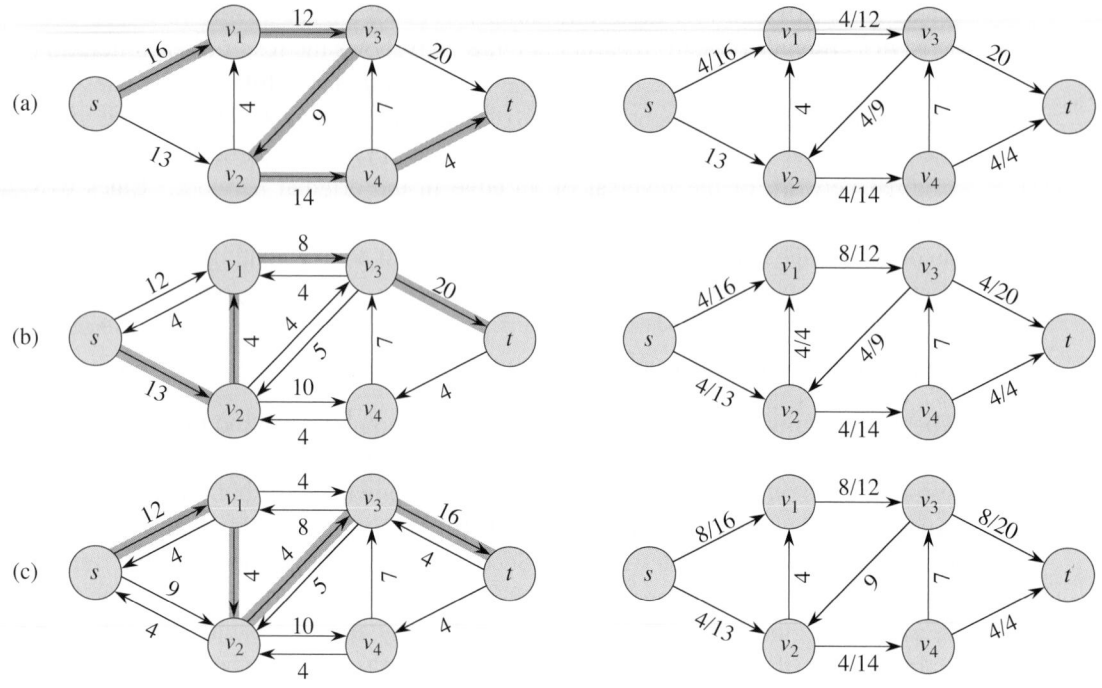

Figure 26.6 The execution of the basic Ford-Fulkerson algorithm. **(a)–(e)** Successive iterations of the **while** loop. The left side of each part shows the residual network G_f from line 3 with a shaded augmenting path p. The right side of each part shows the new flow f that results from augmenting f by f_p. The residual network in (a) is the input network G.

When the capacities are integral and the optimal flow value $|f^*|$ is small, the running time of the Ford-Fulkerson algorithm is good. Figure 26.7(a) shows an example of what can happen on a simple flow network for which $|f^*|$ is large. A maximum flow in this network has value 2,000,000: 1,000,000 units of flow traverse the path $s \rightarrow u \rightarrow t$, and another 1,000,000 units traverse the path $s \rightarrow v \rightarrow t$. If the first augmenting path found by FORD-FULKERSON is $s \rightarrow u \rightarrow v \rightarrow t$, shown in Figure 26.7(a), the flow has value 1 after the first iteration. The resulting residual network appears in Figure 26.7(b). If the second iteration finds the augmenting path $s \rightarrow v \rightarrow u \rightarrow t$, as shown in Figure 26.7(b), the flow then has value 2. Figure 26.7(c) shows the resulting residual network. We can continue, choosing the augmenting path $s \rightarrow u \rightarrow v \rightarrow t$ in the odd-numbered iterations and the augmenting path $s \rightarrow v \rightarrow u \rightarrow t$ in the even-numbered iterations. We would perform a total of 2,000,000 augmentations, increasing the flow value by only 1 unit in each.

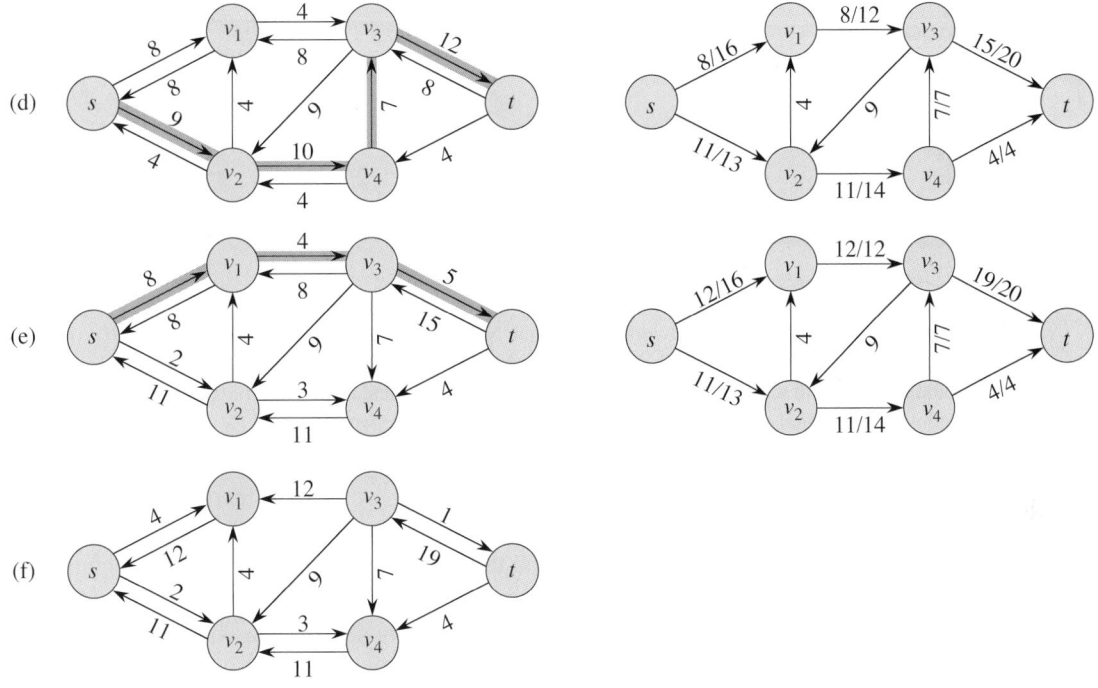

Figure 26.6, continued **(f)** The residual network at the last **while** loop test. It has no augmenting paths, and the flow f shown in (e) is therefore a maximum flow. The value of the maximum flow found is 23.

The Edmonds-Karp algorithm

We can improve the bound on FORD-FULKERSON by finding the augmenting path p in line 3 with a breadth-first search. That is, we choose the augmenting path as a *shortest* path from s to t in the residual network, where each edge has unit distance (weight). We call the Ford-Fulkerson method so implemented the *Edmonds-Karp algorithm*. We now prove that the Edmonds-Karp algorithm runs in $O(VE^2)$ time.

The analysis depends on the distances to vertices in the residual network G_f. The following lemma uses the notation $\delta_f(u, v)$ for the shortest-path distance from u to v in G_f, where each edge has unit distance.

Lemma 26.7

If the Edmonds-Karp algorithm is run on a flow network $G = (V, E)$ with source s and sink t, then for all vertices $v \in V - \{s, t\}$, the shortest-path distance $\delta_f(s, v)$ in the residual network G_f increases monotonically with each flow augmentation.

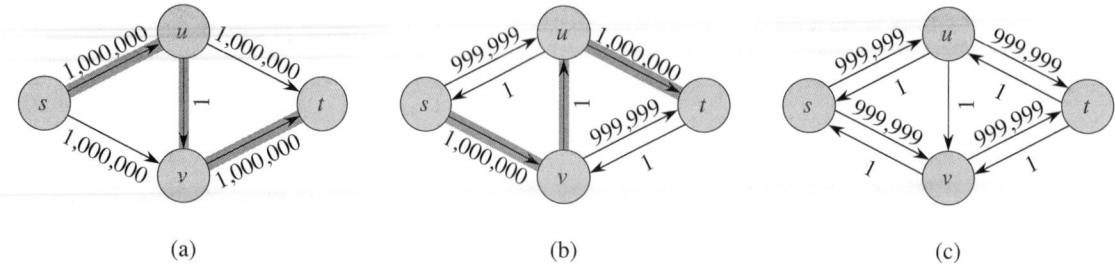

(a)   (b)   (c)

Figure 26.7 (a) A flow network for which FORD-FULKERSON can take $\Theta(E\,|f^*|)$ time, where f^* is a maximum flow, shown here with $|f^*| = 2,000,000$. The shaded path is an augmenting path with residual capacity 1. (b) The resulting residual network, with another augmenting path whose residual capacity is 1. (c) The resulting residual network.

Proof We will suppose that for some vertex $v \in V - \{s,t\}$, there is a flow augmentation that causes the shortest-path distance from s to v to decrease, and then we will derive a contradiction. Let f be the flow just before the first augmentation that decreases some shortest-path distance, and let f' be the flow just afterward. Let v be the vertex with the minimum $\delta_{f'}(s,v)$ whose distance was decreased by the augmentation, so that $\delta_{f'}(s,v) < \delta_f(s,v)$. Let $p = s \rightsquigarrow u \to v$ be a shortest path from s to v in $G_{f'}$, so that $(u,v) \in E_{f'}$ and

$$\delta_{f'}(s,u) = \delta_{f'}(s,v) - 1 \, . \tag{26.12}$$

Because of how we chose v, we know that the distance of vertex u from the source s did not decrease, i.e.,

$$\delta_{f'}(s,u) \geq \delta_f(s,u) \, . \tag{26.13}$$

We claim that $(u,v) \notin E_f$. Why? If we had $(u,v) \in E_f$, then we would also have

$$
\begin{aligned}
\delta_f(s,v) &\leq \delta_f(s,u) + 1 &&\text{(by Lemma 24.10, the triangle inequality)} \\
&\leq \delta_{f'}(s,u) + 1 &&\text{(by inequality (26.13))} \\
&= \delta_{f'}(s,v) &&\text{(by equation (26.12))} \, ,
\end{aligned}
$$

which contradicts our assumption that $\delta_{f'}(s,v) < \delta_f(s,v)$.

How can we have $(u,v) \notin E_f$ and $(u,v) \in E_{f'}$? The augmentation must have increased the flow from v to u. The Edmonds-Karp algorithm always augments flow along shortest paths, and therefore it augmented along a shortest path from s to u in G_f that has (v,u) as its last edge. Therefore,

$$
\begin{aligned}
\delta_f(s,v) &= \delta_f(s,u) - 1 \\
&\leq \delta_{f'}(s,u) - 1 &&\text{(by inequality (26.13))} \\
&= \delta_{f'}(s,v) - 2 &&\text{(by equation (26.12))} \, ,
\end{aligned}
$$

which contradicts our assumption that $\delta_{f'}(s, v) < \delta_f(s, v)$. We conclude that our assumption that such a vertex v exists is incorrect.   ∎

The next theorem bounds the number of iterations of the Edmonds-Karp algorithm.

Theorem 26.8
If the Edmonds-Karp algorithm is run on a flow network $G = (V, E)$ with source s and sink t, then the total number of flow augmentations performed by the algorithm is $O(VE)$.

Proof   We say that an edge (u, v) in a residual network G_f is ***critical*** on an augmenting path p if the residual capacity of p is the residual capacity of (u, v), that is, if $c_f(p) = c_f(u, v)$. After we have augmented flow along an augmenting path, any critical edge on the path disappears from the residual network. Moreover, at least one edge on any augmenting path must be critical. We will show that each of the $|E|$ edges can become critical at most $|V|/2$ times.

Let u and v be vertices in V that are connected by an edge in E. Since augmenting paths are shortest paths, when (u, v) is critical for the first time, we have

$$\delta_f(s, v) = \delta_f(s, u) + 1 .$$

Once the flow is augmented, the edge (u, v) disappears from the residual network. It cannot reappear later on another augmenting path until after the flow from u to v is decreased, which occurs only if (v, u) appears on an augmenting path. If f' is the flow in G when this event occurs, then we have

$$\delta_{f'}(s, u) = \delta_{f'}(s, v) + 1 .$$

Since $\delta_f(s, v) \leq \delta_{f'}(s, v)$ by Lemma 26.7, we have

$$
\begin{aligned}
\delta_{f'}(s, u) &= \delta_{f'}(s, v) + 1 \\
&\geq \delta_f(s, v) + 1 \\
&= \delta_f(s, u) + 2 .
\end{aligned}
$$

Consequently, from the time (u, v) becomes critical to the time when it next becomes critical, the distance of u from the source increases by at least 2. The distance of u from the source is initially at least 0. The intermediate vertices on a shortest path from s to u cannot contain s, u, or t (since (u, v) on an augmenting path implies that $u \neq t$). Therefore, until u becomes unreachable from the source, if ever, its distance is at most $|V| - 2$. Thus, after the first time that (u, v) becomes critical, it can become critical at most $(|V| - 2)/2 = |V|/2 - 1$ times more, for a total of at most $|V|/2$ times. Since there are $O(E)$ pairs of vertices that can have an edge between them in a residual network, the total number of critical edges during

the entire execution of the Edmonds-Karp algorithm is $O(VE)$. Each augmenting path has at least one critical edge, and hence the theorem follows. ∎

Because we can implement each iteration of FORD-FULKERSON in $O(E)$ time when we find the augmenting path by breadth-first search, the total running time of the Edmonds-Karp algorithm is $O(VE^2)$. We shall see that push-relabel algorithms can yield even better bounds. The algorithm of Section 26.4 gives a method for achieving an $O(V^2E)$ running time, which forms the basis for the $O(V^3)$-time algorithm of Section 26.5.

Exercises

26.2-1
Prove that the summations in equation (26.6) equal the summations in equation (26.5).

26.2-2
In Figure 26.1(b), what is the flow across the cut $(\{s, v_2, v_4\}, \{v_1, v_3, t\})$? What is the capacity of this cut?

26.2-3
Show the execution of the Edmonds-Karp algorithm on the flow network of Figure 26.1(a).

26.2-4
In the example of Figure 26.6, what is the minimum cut corresponding to the maximum flow shown? Of the augmenting paths appearing in the example, which one cancels flow?

26.2-5
Recall that the construction in Section 26.1 that converts a flow network with multiple sources and sinks into a single-source, single-sink network adds edges with infinite capacity. Prove that any flow in the resulting network has a finite value if the edges of the original network with multiple sources and sinks have finite capacity.

26.2-6
Suppose that each source s_i in a flow network with multiple sources and sinks produces exactly p_i units of flow, so that $\sum_{v \in V} f(s_i, v) = p_i$. Suppose also that each sink t_j consumes exactly q_j units, so that $\sum_{v \in V} f(v, t_j) = q_j$, where $\sum_i p_i = \sum_j q_j$. Show how to convert the problem of finding a flow f that obeys

these additional constraints into the problem of finding a maximum flow in a single-source, single-sink flow network.

26.2-7
Prove Lemma 26.2.

26.2-8
Suppose that we redefine the residual network to disallow edges into s. Argue that the procedure FORD-FULKERSON still correctly computes a maximum flow.

26.2-9
Suppose that both f and f' are flows in a network G and we compute flow $f \uparrow f'$. Does the augmented flow satisfy the flow conservation property? Does it satisfy the capacity constraint?

26.2-10
Show how to find a maximum flow in a network $G = (V, E)$ by a sequence of at most $|E|$ augmenting paths. (*Hint:* Determine the paths *after* finding the maximum flow.)

26.2-11
The ***edge connectivity*** of an undirected graph is the minimum number k of edges that must be removed to disconnect the graph. For example, the edge connectivity of a tree is 1, and the edge connectivity of a cyclic chain of vertices is 2. Show how to determine the edge connectivity of an undirected graph $G = (V, E)$ by running a maximum-flow algorithm on at most $|V|$ flow networks, each having $O(V)$ vertices and $O(E)$ edges.

26.2-12
Suppose that you are given a flow network G, and G has edges entering the source s. Let f be a flow in G with $|f| \geq 0$ and in which one of the edges (v, s) entering the source has $f(v, s) = 1$. Prove that there must exist another flow f' with $f'(v, s) = 0$ such that $|f| = |f'|$. Give an $O(E)$-time algorithm to compute f', given f, and assuming that all edge capacities are integers.

26.2-13
Suppose that you wish to find, among all minimum cuts in a flow network G with integral capacities, one that contains the smallest number of edges. Show how to modify the capacities of G to create a new flow network G' in which any minimum cut in G' is a minimum cut with the smallest number of edges in G.

26.3   Maximum bipartite matching

Some combinatorial problems can easily be cast as maximum-flow problems. The multiple-source, multiple-sink maximum-flow problem from Section 26.1 gave us one example. Some other combinatorial problems seem on the surface to have little to do with flow networks, but can in fact be reduced to maximum-flow problems. This section presents one such problem: finding a maximum matching in a bipartite graph. In order to solve this problem, we shall take advantage of an integrality property provided by the Ford-Fulkerson method. We shall also see how to use the Ford-Fulkerson method to solve the maximum-bipartite-matching problem on a graph $G = (V, E)$ in $O(VE)$ time.

The maximum-bipartite-matching problem

Given an undirected graph $G = (V, E)$, a **matching** is a subset of edges $M \subseteq E$ such that for all vertices $v \in V$, at most one edge of M is incident on v. We say that a vertex $v \in V$ is **matched** by the matching M if some edge in M is incident on v; otherwise, v is **unmatched**. A **maximum matching** is a matching of maximum cardinality, that is, a matching M such that for any matching M', we have $|M| \geq |M'|$. In this section, we shall restrict our attention to finding maximum matchings in bipartite graphs: graphs in which the vertex set can be partitioned into $V = L \cup R$, where L and R are disjoint and all edges in E go between L and R. We further assume that every vertex in V has at least one incident edge. Figure 26.8 illustrates the notion of a matching in a bipartite graph.

The problem of finding a maximum matching in a bipartite graph has many practical applications. As an example, we might consider matching a set L of machines with a set R of tasks to be performed simultaneously. We take the presence of edge (u, v) in E to mean that a particular machine $u \in L$ is capable of performing a particular task $v \in R$. A maximum matching provides work for as many machines as possible.

Finding a maximum bipartite matching

We can use the Ford-Fulkerson method to find a maximum matching in an undirected bipartite graph $G = (V, E)$ in time polynomial in $|V|$ and $|E|$. The trick is to construct a flow network in which flows correspond to matchings, as shown in Figure 26.8(c). We define the **corresponding flow network** $G' = (V', E')$ for the bipartite graph G as follows. We let the source s and sink t be new vertices not in V, and we let $V' = V \cup \{s, t\}$. If the vertex partition of G is $V = L \cup R$, the

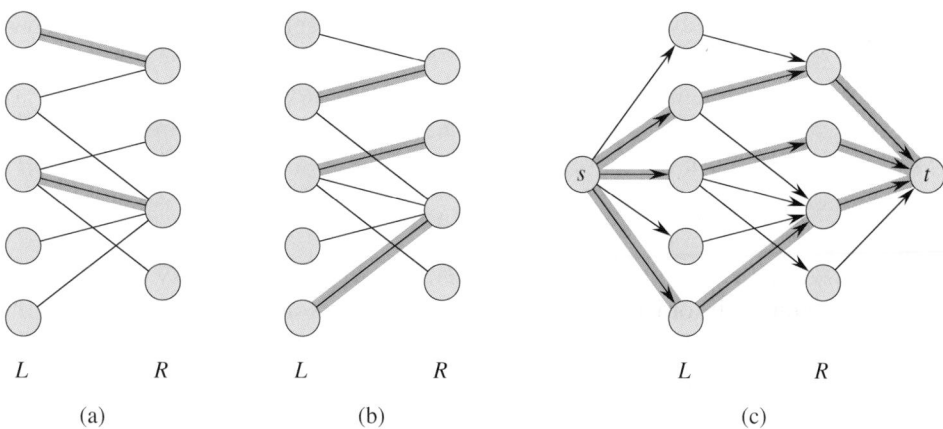

L   R   L   R   L   R

(a)   (b)   (c)

Figure 26.8   A bipartite graph $G = (V, E)$ with vertex partition $V = L \cup R$. **(a)** A matching with cardinality 2, indicated by shaded edges. **(b)** A maximum matching with cardinality 3. **(c)** The corresponding flow network G' with a maximum flow shown. Each edge has unit capacity. Shaded edges have a flow of 1, and all other edges carry no flow. The shaded edges from L to R correspond to those in the maximum matching from (b).

directed edges of G' are the edges of E, directed from L to R, along with $|V|$ new directed edges:

$$E' = \{(s, u) : u \in L\} \cup \{(u, v) : (u, v) \in E\} \cup \{(v, t) : v \in R\} \ .$$

To complete the construction, we assign unit capacity to each edge in E'. Since each vertex in V has at least one incident edge, $|E| \geq |V|/2$. Thus, $|E| \leq |E'| = |E| + |V| \leq 3|E|$, and so $|E'| = \Theta(E)$.

The following lemma shows that a matching in G corresponds directly to a flow in G's corresponding flow network G'. We say that a flow f on a flow network $G = (V, E)$ is *integer-valued* if $f(u, v)$ is an integer for all $(u, v) \in V \times V$.

Lemma 26.9
Let $G = (V, E)$ be a bipartite graph with vertex partition $V = L \cup R$, and let $G' = (V', E')$ be its corresponding flow network. If M is a matching in G, then there is an integer-valued flow f in G' with value $|f| = |M|$. Conversely, if f is an integer-valued flow in G', then there is a matching M in G with cardinality $|M| = |f|$.

Proof   We first show that a matching M in G corresponds to an integer-valued flow f in G'. Define f as follows. If $(u, v) \in M$, then $f(s, u) = f(u, v) = f(v, t) = 1$. For all other edges $(u, v) \in E'$, we define $f(u, v) = 0$. It is simple to verify that f satisfies the capacity constraint and flow conservation.

Intuitively, each edge $(u, v) \in M$ corresponds to one unit of flow in G' that traverses the path $s \rightarrow u \rightarrow v \rightarrow t$. Moreover, the paths induced by edges in M are vertex-disjoint, except for s and t. The net flow across cut $(L \cup \{s\}, R \cup \{t\})$ is equal to $|M|$; thus, by Lemma 26.4, the value of the flow is $|f| = |M|$.

To prove the converse, let f be an integer-valued flow in G', and let

$$M = \{(u, v) : u \in L,\ v \in R,\ \text{and}\ f(u, v) > 0\}\ .$$

Each vertex $u \in L$ has only one entering edge, namely (s, u), and its capacity is 1. Thus, each $u \in L$ has at most one unit of flow entering it, and if one unit of flow does enter, by flow conservation, one unit of flow must leave. Furthermore, since f is integer-valued, for each $u \in L$, the one unit of flow can enter on at most one edge and can leave on at most one edge. Thus, one unit of flow enters u if and only if there is exactly one vertex $v \in R$ such that $f(u, v) = 1$, and at most one edge leaving each $u \in L$ carries positive flow. A symmetric argument applies to each $v \in R$. The set M is therefore a matching.

To see that $|M| = |f|$, observe that for every matched vertex $u \in L$, we have $f(s, u) = 1$, and for every edge $(u, v) \in E - M$, we have $f(u, v) = 0$. Consequently, $f(L \cup \{s\}, R \cup \{t\})$, the net flow across cut $(L \cup \{s\}, R \cup \{t\})$, is equal to $|M|$. Applying Lemma 26.4, we have that $|f| = f(L \cup \{s\}, R \cup \{t\}) = |M|$. ∎

Based on Lemma 26.9, we would like to conclude that a maximum matching in a bipartite graph G corresponds to a maximum flow in its corresponding flow network G', and we can therefore compute a maximum matching in G by running a maximum-flow algorithm on G'. The only hitch in this reasoning is that the maximum-flow algorithm might return a flow in G' for which some $f(u, v)$ is not an integer, even though the flow value $|f|$ must be an integer. The following theorem shows that if we use the Ford-Fulkerson method, this difficulty cannot arise.

Theorem 26.10 (Integrality theorem)
If the capacity function c takes on only integral values, then the maximum flow f produced by the Ford-Fulkerson method has the property that $|f|$ is an integer. Moreover, for all vertices u and v, the value of $f(u, v)$ is an integer.

Proof The proof is by induction on the number of iterations. We leave it as Exercise 26.3-2. ∎

We can now prove the following corollary to Lemma 26.9.

Corollary 26.11
The cardinality of a maximum matching M in a bipartite graph G equals the value of a maximum flow f in its corresponding flow network G'.

Proof We use the nomenclature from Lemma 26.9. Suppose that M is a maximum matching in G and that the corresponding flow f in G' is not maximum. Then there is a maximum flow f' in G' such that $|f'| > |f|$. Since the capacities in G' are integer-valued, by Theorem 26.10, we can assume that f' is integer-valued. Thus, f' corresponds to a matching M' in G with cardinality $|M'| = |f'| > |f| = |M|$, contradicting our assumption that M is a maximum matching. In a similar manner, we can show that if f is a maximum flow in G', its corresponding matching is a maximum matching on G. ∎

Thus, given a bipartite undirected graph G, we can find a maximum matching by creating the flow network G', running the Ford-Fulkerson method, and directly obtaining a maximum matching M from the integer-valued maximum flow f found. Since any matching in a bipartite graph has cardinality at most $\min(L, R) = O(V)$, the value of the maximum flow in G' is $O(V)$. We can therefore find a maximum matching in a bipartite graph in time $O(VE') = O(VE)$, since $|E'| = \Theta(E)$.

Exercises

26.3-1
Run the Ford-Fulkerson algorithm on the flow network in Figure 26.8(c) and show the residual network after each flow augmentation. Number the vertices in L top to bottom from 1 to 5 and in R top to bottom from 6 to 9. For each iteration, pick the augmenting path that is lexicographically smallest.

26.3-2
Prove Theorem 26.10.

26.3-3
Let $G = (V, E)$ be a bipartite graph with vertex partition $V = L \cup R$, and let G' be its corresponding flow network. Give a good upper bound on the length of any augmenting path found in G' during the execution of FORD-FULKERSON.

26.3-4 ★
A ***perfect matching*** is a matching in which every vertex is matched. Let $G = (V, E)$ be an undirected bipartite graph with vertex partition $V = L \cup R$, where $|L| = |R|$. For any $X \subseteq V$, define the ***neighborhood*** of X as

$$N(X) = \{y \in V : (x, y) \in E \text{ for some } x \in X\} \ ,$$

that is, the set of vertices adjacent to some member of X. Prove **Hall's theorem**: there exists a perfect matching in G if and only if $|A| \leq |N(A)|$ for every subset $A \subseteq L$.

26.3-5 ★

We say that a bipartite graph $G = (V, E)$, where $V = L \cup R$, is ***d-regular*** if every vertex $v \in V$ has degree exactly d. Every d-regular bipartite graph has $|L| = |R|$. Prove that every d-regular bipartite graph has a matching of cardinality $|L|$ by arguing that a minimum cut of the corresponding flow network has capacity $|L|$.

★ **26.4   Push-relabel algorithms**

In this section, we present the "push-relabel" approach to computing maximum flows. To date, many of the asymptotically fastest maximum-flow algorithms are push-relabel algorithms, and the fastest actual implementations of maximum-flow algorithms are based on the push-relabel method. Push-relabel methods also efficiently solve other flow problems, such as the minimum-cost flow problem. This section introduces Goldberg's "generic" maximum-flow algorithm, which has a simple implementation that runs in $O(V^2 E)$ time, thereby improving upon the $O(VE^2)$ bound of the Edmonds-Karp algorithm. Section 26.5 refines the generic algorithm to obtain another push-relabel algorithm that runs in $O(V^3)$ time.

Push-relabel algorithms work in a more localized manner than the Ford-Fulkerson method. Rather than examine the entire residual network to find an augmenting path, push-relabel algorithms work on one vertex at a time, looking only at the vertex's neighbors in the residual network. Furthermore, unlike the Ford-Fulkerson method, push-relabel algorithms do not maintain the flow-conservation property throughout their execution. They do, however, maintain a ***preflow***, which is a function $f : V \times V \to \mathbb{R}$ that satisfies the capacity constraint and the following relaxation of flow conservation:

$$\sum_{v \in V} f(v, u) - \sum_{v \in V} f(u, v) \geq 0$$

for all vertices $u \in V - \{s\}$. That is, the flow into a vertex may exceed the flow out. We call the quantity

$$e(u) = \sum_{v \in V} f(v, u) - \sum_{v \in V} f(u, v) \tag{26.14}$$

the ***excess flow*** into vertex u. The excess at a vertex is the amount by which the flow in exceeds the flow out. We say that a vertex $u \in V - \{s, t\}$ is ***overflowing*** if $e(u) > 0$.

We shall begin this section by describing the intuition behind the push-relabel method. We shall then investigate the two operations employed by the method: "pushing" preflow and "relabeling" a vertex. Finally, we shall present a generic push-relabel algorithm and analyze its correctness and running time.

Intuition

You can understand the intuition behind the push-relabel method in terms of fluid flows: we consider a flow network $G = (V, E)$ to be a system of interconnected pipes of given capacities. Applying this analogy to the Ford-Fulkerson method, we might say that each augmenting path in the network gives rise to an additional stream of fluid, with no branch points, flowing from the source to the sink. The Ford-Fulkerson method iteratively adds more streams of flow until no more can be added.

The generic push-relabel algorithm has a rather different intuition. As before, directed edges correspond to pipes. Vertices, which are pipe junctions, have two interesting properties. First, to accommodate excess flow, each vertex has an out-flow pipe leading to an arbitrarily large reservoir that can accumulate fluid. Second, each vertex, its reservoir, and all its pipe connections sit on a platform whose height increases as the algorithm progresses.

Vertex heights determine how flow is pushed: we push flow only downhill, that is, from a higher vertex to a lower vertex. The flow from a lower vertex to a higher vertex may be positive, but operations that push flow push it only downhill. We fix the height of the source at $|V|$ and the height of the sink at 0. All other vertex heights start at 0 and increase with time. The algorithm first sends as much flow as possible downhill from the source toward the sink. The amount it sends is exactly enough to fill each outgoing pipe from the source to capacity; that is, it sends the capacity of the cut $(s, V - \{s\})$. When flow first enters an intermediate vertex, it collects in the vertex's reservoir. From there, we eventually push it downhill.

We may eventually find that the only pipes that leave a vertex u and are not already saturated with flow connect to vertices that are on the same level as u or are uphill from u. In this case, to rid an overflowing vertex u of its excess flow, we must increase its height—an operation called "relabeling" vertex u. We increase its height to one unit more than the height of the lowest of its neighbors to which it has an unsaturated pipe. After a vertex is relabeled, therefore, it has at least one outgoing pipe through which we can push more flow.

Eventually, all the flow that can possibly get through to the sink has arrived there. No more can arrive, because the pipes obey the capacity constraints; the amount of flow across any cut is still limited by the capacity of the cut. To make the preflow a "legal" flow, the algorithm then sends the excess collected in the reservoirs of overflowing vertices back to the source by continuing to relabel vertices to above

the fixed height $|V|$ of the source. As we shall see, once we have emptied all the reservoirs, the preflow is not only a "legal" flow, it is also a maximum flow.

The basic operations

From the preceding discussion, we see that a push-relabel algorithm performs two basic operations: pushing flow excess from a vertex to one of its neighbors and relabeling a vertex. The situations in which these operations apply depend on the heights of vertices, which we now define precisely.

Let $G = (V, E)$ be a flow network with source s and sink t, and let f be a preflow in G. A function $h : V \rightarrow \mathbb{N}$ is a *height function*[3] if $h(s) = |V|$, $h(t) = 0$, and

$$h(u) \leq h(v) + 1$$

for every residual edge $(u, v) \in E_f$. We immediately obtain the following lemma.

Lemma 26.12
Let $G = (V, E)$ be a flow network, let f be a preflow in G, and let h be a height function on V. For any two vertices $u, v \in V$, if $h(u) > h(v) + 1$, then (u, v) is not an edge in the residual network.   ■

The push operation
The basic operation PUSH(u, v) applies if u is an overflowing vertex, $c_f (u, v) > 0$, and $h(u) = h(v) + 1$. The pseudocode below updates the preflow f and the excess flows for u and v. It assumes that we can compute residual capacity $c_f (u, v)$ in constant time given c and f. We maintain the excess flow stored at a vertex u as the attribute $u.e$ and the height of u as the attribute $u.h$. The expression $\Delta_f (u, v)$ is a temporary variable that stores the amount of flow that we can push from u to v.

---

[3] In the literature, a height function is typically called a "distance function," and the height of a vertex is called a "distance label." We use the term "height" because it is more suggestive of the intuition behind the algorithm. We retain the use of the term "relabel" to refer to the operation that increases the height of a vertex. The height of a vertex is related to its distance from the sink t, as would be found in a breadth-first search of the transpose G^T.

Push(u, v)

1 **// Applies when**: u is overflowing, $c_f(u, v) > 0$, and $u.h = v.h + 1$.
2 **// Action:** Push $\Delta_f(u, v) = \min(u.e, c_f(u, v))$ units of flow from u to v.
3 $\Delta_f(u, v) = \min(u.e, c_f(u, v))$
4 **if** $(u, v) \in E$
5      $(u, v).f = (u, v).f + \Delta_f(u, v)$
6 **else** $(v, u).f = (v, u).f - \Delta_f(u, v)$
7 $u.e = u.e - \Delta_f(u, v)$
8 $v.e = v.e + \Delta_f(u, v)$

The code for PUSH operates as follows. Because vertex u has a positive excess $u.e$ and the residual capacity of (u, v) is positive, we can increase the flow from u to v by $\Delta_f(u, v) = \min(u.e, c_f(u, v))$ without causing $u.e$ to become negative or the capacity $c(u, v)$ to be exceeded. Line 3 computes the value $\Delta_f(u, v)$, and lines 4–6 update f. Line 5 increases the flow on edge (u, v), because we are pushing flow over a residual edge that is also an original edge. Line 6 decreases the flow on edge (v, u), because the residual edge is actually the reverse of an edge in the original network. Finally, lines 7–8 update the excess flows into vertices u and v. Thus, if f is a preflow before PUSH is called, it remains a preflow afterward.

Observe that nothing in the code for PUSH depends on the heights of u and v, yet we prohibit it from being invoked unless $u.h = v.h + 1$. Thus, we push excess flow downhill only by a height differential of 1. By Lemma 26.12, no residual edges exist between two vertices whose heights differ by more than 1, and thus, as long as the attribute h is indeed a height function, we would gain nothing by allowing flow to be pushed downhill by a height differential of more than 1.

We call the operation PUSH(u, v) a **push** from u to v. If a push operation applies to some edge (u, v) leaving a vertex u, we also say that the push operation applies to u. It is a **saturating push** if edge (u, v) in the residual network becomes **saturated** ($c_f(u, v) = 0$ afterward); otherwise, it is a **nonsaturating push**. If an edge becomes saturated, it disappears from the residual network. A simple lemma characterizes one result of a nonsaturating push.

Lemma 26.13
After a nonsaturating push from u to v, the vertex u is no longer overflowing.

Proof Since the push was nonsaturating, the amount of flow $\Delta_f(u, v)$ actually pushed must equal $u.e$ prior to the push. Since $u.e$ is reduced by this amount, it becomes 0 after the push. ∎

The relabel operation

The basic operation RELABEL(u) applies if u is overflowing and if $u.h \leq v.h$ for all edges $(u, v) \in E_f$. In other words, we can relabel an overflowing vertex u if for every vertex v for which there is residual capacity from u to v, flow cannot be pushed from u to v because v is not downhill from u. (Recall that by definition, neither the source s nor the sink t can be overflowing, and so s and t are ineligible for relabeling.)

RELABEL(u)

1 **// Applies when:** u is overflowing and for all $v \in V$ such that $(u, v) \in E_f$,
        we have $u.h \leq v.h$.
2 **// Action:** Increase the height of u.
3 $u.h = 1 + \min \{v.h : (u, v) \in E_f\}$

When we call the operation RELABEL(u), we say that vertex u is **relabeled**. Note that when u is relabeled, E_f must contain at least one edge that leaves u, so that the minimization in the code is over a nonempty set. This property follows from the assumption that u is overflowing, which in turn tells us that

$$u.e = \sum_{v \in V} f(v, u) - \sum_{v \in V} f(u, v) > 0 .$$

Since all flows are nonnegative, we must therefore have at least one vertex v such that $(v, u).f > 0$. But then, $c_f(u, v) > 0$, which implies that $(u, v) \in E_f$. The operation RELABEL(u) thus gives u the greatest height allowed by the constraints on height functions.

The generic algorithm

The generic push-relabel algorithm uses the following subroutine to create an initial preflow in the flow network.

INITIALIZE-PREFLOW(G, s)

1 **for** each vertex $v \in G.V$
2       $v.h = 0$
3       $v.e = 0$
4 **for** each edge $(u, v) \in G.E$
5       $(u, v).f = 0$
6 $s.h = |G.V|$
7 **for** each vertex $v \in s.Adj$
8       $(s, v).f = c(s, v)$
9       $v.e = c(s, v)$
10      $s.e = s.e - c(s, v)$

INITIALIZE-PREFLOW creates an initial preflow f defined by

$$(u, v).f = \begin{cases} c(u, v) & \text{if } u = s, \\ 0 & \text{otherwise}. \end{cases} \tag{26.15}$$

That is, we fill to capacity each edge leaving the source s, and all other edges carry no flow. For each vertex v adjacent to the source, we initially have $v.e = c(s, v)$, and we initialize $s.e$ to the negative of the sum of these capacities. The generic algorithm also begins with an initial height function h, given by

$$u.h = \begin{cases} |V| & \text{if } u = s, \\ 0 & \text{otherwise}. \end{cases} \tag{26.16}$$

Equation (26.16) defines a height function because the only edges (u, v) for which $u.h > v.h + 1$ are those for which $u = s$, and those edges are saturated, which means that they are not in the residual network.

Initialization, followed by a sequence of push and relabel operations, executed in no particular order, yields the GENERIC-PUSH-RELABEL algorithm:

GENERIC-PUSH-RELABEL(G)

1   INITIALIZE-PREFLOW(G, s)
2   **while** there exists an applicable push or relabel operation
3   select an applicable push or relabel operation and perform it

The following lemma tells us that as long as an overflowing vertex exists, at least one of the two basic operations applies.

Lemma 26.14 (An overflowing vertex can be either pushed or relabeled)
Let $G = (V, E)$ be a flow network with source s and sink t, let f be a preflow, and let h be any height function for f. If u is any overflowing vertex, then either a push or relabel operation applies to it.

Proof For any residual edge (u, v), we have $h(u) \leq h(v) + 1$ because h is a height function. If a push operation does not apply to an overflowing vertex u, then for all residual edges (u, v), we must have $h(u) < h(v) + 1$, which implies $h(u) \leq h(v)$. Thus, a relabel operation applies to u.   ∎

Correctness of the push-relabel method

To show that the generic push-relabel algorithm solves the maximum-flow problem, we shall first prove that if it terminates, the preflow f is a maximum flow. We shall later prove that it terminates. We start with some observations about the height function h.

Lemma 26.15 (Vertex heights never decrease)
During the execution of the GENERIC-PUSH-RELABEL procedure on a flow network $G = (V, E)$, for each vertex $u \in V$, the height $u.h$ never decreases. Moreover, whenever a relabel operation is applied to a vertex u, its height $u.h$ increases by at least 1.

Proof   Because vertex heights change only during relabel operations, it suffices to prove the second statement of the lemma. If vertex u is about to be relabeled, then for all vertices v such that $(u, v) \in E_f$, we have $u.h \le v.h$. Thus, $u.h < 1 + \min\{v.h : (u, v) \in E_f\}$, and so the operation must increase $u.h$. ∎

Lemma 26.16
Let $G = (V, E)$ be a flow network with source s and sink t. Then the execution of GENERIC-PUSH-RELABEL on G maintains the attribute h as a height function.

Proof   The proof is by induction on the number of basic operations performed. Initially, h is a height function, as we have already observed.

We claim that if h is a height function, then an operation RELABEL(u) leaves h a height function. If we look at a residual edge $(u, v) \in E_f$ that leaves u, then the operation RELABEL(u) ensures that $u.h \le v.h + 1$ afterward. Now consider a residual edge (w, u) that enters u. By Lemma 26.15, $w.h \le u.h + 1$ before the operation RELABEL(u) implies $w.h < u.h + 1$ afterward. Thus, the operation RELABEL(u) leaves h a height function.

Now, consider an operation PUSH(u, v). This operation may add the edge (v, u) to E_f, and it may remove (u, v) from E_f. In the former case, we have $v.h = u.h - 1 < u.h + 1$, and so h remains a height function. In the latter case, removing (u, v) from the residual network removes the corresponding constraint, and h again remains a height function. ∎

The following lemma gives an important property of height functions.

Lemma 26.17
Let $G = (V, E)$ be a flow network with source s and sink t, let f be a preflow in G, and let h be a height function on V. Then there is no path from the source s to the sink t in the residual network G_f.

Proof   Assume for the sake of contradiction that G_f contains a path p from s to t, where $p = \langle v_0, v_1, \ldots, v_k \rangle$, $v_0 = s$, and $v_k = t$. Without loss of generality, p is a simple path, and so $k < |V|$. For $i = 0, 1, \ldots, k - 1$, edge $(v_i, v_{i+1}) \in E_f$. Because h is a height function, $h(v_i) \le h(v_{i+1}) + 1$ for $i = 0, 1, \ldots, k - 1$. Combining these inequalities over path p yields $h(s) \le h(t) + k$. But because $h(t) = 0$,

we have $h(s) \leq k < |V|$, which contradicts the requirement that $h(s) = |V|$ in a height function.   ∎

We are now ready to show that if the generic push-relabel algorithm terminates, the preflow it computes is a maximum flow.

Theorem 26.18 (Correctness of the generic push-relabel algorithm)
If the algorithm GENERIC-PUSH-RELABEL terminates when run on a flow network $G = (V, E)$ with source s and sink t, then the preflow f it computes is a maximum flow for G.

Proof   We use the following loop invariant:

> Each time the **while** loop test in line 2 in GENERIC-PUSH-RELABEL is executed, f is a preflow.

Initialization: INITIALIZE-PREFLOW makes f a preflow.

Maintenance: The only operations within the **while** loop of lines 2–3 are push and relabel. Relabel operations affect only height attributes and not the flow values; hence they do not affect whether f is a preflow. As argued on page 739, if f is a preflow prior to a push operation, it remains a preflow afterward.

Termination: At termination, each vertex in $V - \{s, t\}$ must have an excess of 0, because by Lemma 26.14 and the invariant that f is always a preflow, there are no overflowing vertices. Therefore, f is a flow. Lemma 26.16 shows that h is a height function at termination, and thus Lemma 26.17 tells us that there is no path from s to t in the residual network G_f. By the max-flow min-cut theorem (Theorem 26.6), therefore, f is a maximum flow.   ∎

Analysis of the push-relabel method

To show that the generic push-relabel algorithm indeed terminates, we shall bound the number of operations it performs. We bound separately each of the three types of operations: relabels, saturating pushes, and nonsaturating pushes. With knowledge of these bounds, it is a straightforward problem to construct an algorithm that runs in $O(V^2 E)$ time. Before beginning the analysis, however, we prove an important lemma. Recall that we allow edges into the source in the residual network.

Lemma 26.19
Let $G = (V, E)$ be a flow network with source s and sink t, and let f be a preflow in G. Then, for any overflowing vertex x, there is a simple path from x to s in the residual network G_f.

Proof   For an overflowing vertex x, let $U = \{v : \text{there exists a simple path from } x \text{ to } v \text{ in } G_f\}$, and suppose for the sake of contradiction that $s \notin U$. Let $\overline{U} = V - U$.

We take the definition of excess from equation (26.14), sum over all vertices in U, and note that $V = U \cup \overline{U}$, to obtain

$$\sum_{u \in U} e(u)$$

$$= \sum_{u \in U} \left(\sum_{v \in V} f(v, u) - \sum_{v \in V} f(u, v) \right)$$

$$= \sum_{u \in U} \left(\left(\sum_{v \in U} f(v, u) + \sum_{v \in \overline{U}} f(v, u) \right) - \left(\sum_{v \in U} f(u, v) + \sum_{v \in \overline{U}} f(u, v) \right) \right)$$

$$= \sum_{u \in U} \sum_{v \in U} f(v, u) + \sum_{u \in U} \sum_{v \in \overline{U}} f(v, u) - \sum_{u \in U} \sum_{v \in U} f(u, v) - \sum_{u \in U} \sum_{v \in \overline{U}} f(u, v)$$

$$= \sum_{u \in U} \sum_{v \in \overline{U}} f(v, u) - \sum_{u \in U} \sum_{v \in \overline{U}} f(u, v) .$$

We know that the quantity $\sum_{u \in U} e(u)$ must be positive because $e(x) > 0$, $x \in U$, all vertices other than s have nonnegative excess, and, by assumption, $s \notin U$. Thus, we have

$$\sum_{u \in U} \sum_{v \in \overline{U}} f(v, u) - \sum_{u \in U} \sum_{v \in \overline{U}} f(u, v) > 0 . \tag{26.17}$$

All edge flows are nonnegative, and so for equation (26.17) to hold, we must have $\sum_{u \in U} \sum_{v \in \overline{U}} f(v, u) > 0$. Hence, there must exist at least one pair of vertices $u' \in U$ and $v' \in \overline{U}$ with $f(v', u') > 0$. But, if $f(v', u') > 0$, there must be a residual edge (u', v'), which means that there is a simple path from x to v' (the path $x \rightsquigarrow u' \rightarrow v'$), thus contradicting the definition of U.   ∎

The next lemma bounds the heights of vertices, and its corollary bounds the number of relabel operations that are performed in total.

Lemma 26.20
Let $G = (V, E)$ be a flow network with source s and sink t. At any time during the execution of GENERIC-PUSH-RELABEL on G, we have $u.h \le 2|V| - 1$ for all vertices $u \in V$.

Proof   The heights of the source s and the sink t never change because these vertices are by definition not overflowing. Thus, we always have $s.h = |V|$ and $t.h = 0$, both of which are no greater than $2|V| - 1$.

Now consider any vertex $u \in V - \{s, t\}$. Initially, $u.h = 0 \le 2|V| - 1$. We shall show that after each relabeling operation, we still have $u.h \le 2|V| - 1$. When u is

relabeled, it is overflowing, and Lemma 26.19 tells us that there is a simple path p from u to s in G_f. Let $p = \langle v_0, v_1, \ldots, v_k \rangle$, where $v_0 = u$, $v_k = s$, and $k \leq |V| - 1$ because p is simple. For $i = 0, 1, \ldots, k - 1$, we have $(v_i, v_{i+1}) \in E_f$, and therefore, by Lemma 26.16, $v_i.h \leq v_{i+1}.h + 1$. Expanding these inequalities over path p yields $u.h = v_0.h \leq v_k.h + k \leq s.h + (|V| - 1) = 2|V| - 1$. ∎

Corollary 26.21 (Bound on relabel operations)

Let $G = (V, E)$ be a flow network with source s and sink t. Then, during the execution of GENERIC-PUSH-RELABEL on G, the number of relabel operations is at most $2|V| - 1$ per vertex and at most $(2|V| - 1)(|V| - 2) < 2|V|^2$ overall.

Proof Only the $|V| - 2$ vertices in $V - \{s, t\}$ may be relabeled. Let $u \in V - \{s, t\}$. The operation RELABEL(u) increases $u.h$. The value of $u.h$ is initially 0 and by Lemma 26.20, it grows to at most $2|V| - 1$. Thus, each vertex $u \in V - \{s, t\}$ is relabeled at most $2|V| - 1$ times, and the total number of relabel operations performed is at most $(2|V| - 1)(|V| - 2) < 2|V|^2$. ∎

Lemma 26.20 also helps us to bound the number of saturating pushes.

Lemma 26.22 (Bound on saturating pushes)

During the execution of GENERIC-PUSH-RELABEL on any flow network $G = (V, E)$, the number of saturating pushes is less than $2|V||E|$.

Proof For any pair of vertices $u, v \in V$, we will count the saturating pushes from u to v and from v to u together, calling them the saturating pushes between u and v. If there are any such pushes, at least one of (u, v) and (v, u) is actually an edge in E. Now, suppose that a saturating push from u to v has occurred. At that time, $v.h = u.h - 1$. In order for another saturating push from u to v to occur later, the algorithm must first push flow from v to u, which cannot happen until $v.h = u.h + 1$. Since $u.h$ never decreases, in order for $v.h = u.h + 1$, the value of $v.h$ must increase by at least 2. Likewise, $u.h$ must increase by at least 2 between saturating pushes from v to u. Heights start at 0 and, by Lemma 26.20, never exceed $2|V| - 1$, which implies that the number of times any vertex can have its height increase by 2 is less than $|V|$. Since at least one of $u.h$ and $v.h$ must increase by 2 between any two saturating pushes between u and v, there are fewer than $2|V|$ saturating pushes between u and v. Multiplying by the number of edges gives a bound of less than $2|V||E|$ on the total number of saturating pushes. ∎

The following lemma bounds the number of nonsaturating pushes in the generic push-relabel algorithm.

Lemma 26.23 (Bound on nonsaturating pushes)

During the execution of GENERIC-PUSH-RELABEL on any flow network $G = (V, E)$, the number of nonsaturating pushes is less than $4|V|^2(|V| + |E|)$.

Proof   Define a potential function $\Phi = \sum_{v:e(v)>0} v.h$. Initially, $\Phi = 0$, and the value of Φ may change after each relabeling, saturating push, and nonsaturating push. We will bound the amount that saturating pushes and relabelings can contribute to the increase of Φ. Then we will show that each nonsaturating push must decrease Φ by at least 1, and will use these bounds to derive an upper bound on the number of nonsaturating pushes.

Let us examine the two ways in which Φ might increase. First, relabeling a vertex u increases Φ by less than $2|V|$, since the set over which the sum is taken is the same and the relabeling cannot increase u's height by more than its maximum possible height, which, by Lemma 26.20, is at most $2|V| - 1$. Second, a saturating push from a vertex u to a vertex v increases Φ by less than $2|V|$, since no heights change and only vertex v, whose height is at most $2|V| - 1$, can possibly become overflowing.

Now we show that a nonsaturating push from u to v decreases Φ by at least 1. Why? Before the nonsaturating push, u was overflowing, and v may or may not have been overflowing. By Lemma 26.13, u is no longer overflowing after the push. In addition, unless v is the source, it may or may not be overflowing after the push. Therefore, the potential function Φ has decreased by exactly $u.h$, and it has increased by either 0 or $v.h$. Since $u.h - v.h = 1$, the net effect is that the potential function has decreased by at least 1.

Thus, during the course of the algorithm, the total amount of increase in Φ is due to relabelings and saturated pushes, and Corollary 26.21 and Lemma 26.22 constrain the increase to be less than $(2|V|)(2|V|^2) + (2|V|)(2|V||E|) = 4|V|^2(|V| + |E|)$. Since $\Phi \geq 0$, the total amount of decrease, and therefore the total number of nonsaturating pushes, is less than $4|V|^2(|V| + |E|)$.   ∎

Having bounded the number of relabelings, saturating pushes, and nonsaturating pushes, we have set the stage for the following analysis of the GENERIC-PUSH-RELABEL procedure, and hence of any algorithm based on the push-relabel method.

Theorem 26.24

During the execution of GENERIC-PUSH-RELABEL on any flow network $G = (V, E)$, the number of basic operations is $O(V^2E)$.

Proof   Immediate from Corollary 26.21 and Lemmas 26.22 and 26.23.   ∎

Thus, the algorithm terminates after $O(V^2E)$ operations. All that remains is to give an efficient method for implementing each operation and for choosing an appropriate operation to execute.

Corollary 26.25
There is an implementation of the generic push-relabel algorithm that runs in $O(V^2E)$ time on any flow network $G = (V, E)$.

Proof Exercise 26.4-2 asks you to show how to implement the generic algorithm with an overhead of $O(V)$ per relabel operation and $O(1)$ per push. It also asks you to design a data structure that allows you to pick an applicable operation in $O(1)$ time. The corollary then follows. ∎

Exercises

26.4-1
Prove that, after the procedure INITIALIZE-PREFLOW(G, s) terminates, we have $s.e \le -|f^*|$, where f^* is a maximum flow for G.

26.4-2
Show how to implement the generic push-relabel algorithm using $O(V)$ time per relabel operation, $O(1)$ time per push, and $O(1)$ time to select an applicable operation, for a total time of $O(V^2E)$.

26.4-3
Prove that the generic push-relabel algorithm spends a total of only $O(VE)$ time in performing all the $O(V^2)$ relabel operations.

26.4-4
Suppose that we have found a maximum flow in a flow network $G = (V, E)$ using a push-relabel algorithm. Give a fast algorithm to find a minimum cut in G.

26.4-5
Give an efficient push-relabel algorithm to find a maximum matching in a bipartite graph. Analyze your algorithm.

26.4-6
Suppose that all edge capacities in a flow network $G = (V, E)$ are in the set $\{1, 2, \ldots, k\}$. Analyze the running time of the generic push-relabel algorithm in terms of $|V|$, $|E|$, and k. (*Hint:* How many times can each edge support a nonsaturating push before it becomes saturated?)

26.4-7
Show that we could change line 6 of INITIALIZE-PREFLOW to

6    $s.h = |G.V| - 2$

without affecting the correctness or asymptotic performance of the generic push-relabel algorithm.

26.4-8
Let $\delta_f(u, v)$ be the distance (number of edges) from u to v in the residual network G_f. Show that the GENERIC-PUSH-RELABEL procedure maintains the properties that $u.h < |V|$ implies $u.h \leq \delta_f(u, t)$ and that $u.h \geq |V|$ implies $u.h - |V| \leq \delta_f(u, s)$.

26.4-9 ★
As in the previous exercise, let $\delta_f(u, v)$ be the distance from u to v in the residual network G_f. Show how to modify the generic push-relabel algorithm to maintain the property that $u.h < |V|$ implies $u.h = \delta_f(u, t)$ and that $u.h \geq |V|$ implies $u.h - |V| = \delta_f(u, s)$. The total time that your implementation dedicates to maintaining this property should be $O(VE)$.

26.4-10
Show that the number of nonsaturating pushes executed by the GENERIC-PUSH-RELABEL procedure on a flow network $G = (V, E)$ is at most $4|V|^2|E|$ for $|V| \geq 4$.

★ **26.5   The relabel-to-front algorithm**

The push-relabel method allows us to apply the basic operations in any order at all. By choosing the order carefully and managing the network data structure efficiently, however, we can solve the maximum-flow problem faster than the $O(V^2 E)$ bound given by Corollary 26.25. We shall now examine the relabel-to-front algorithm, a push-relabel algorithm whose running time is $O(V^3)$, which is asymptotically at least as good as $O(V^2 E)$, and even better for dense networks.

The relabel-to-front algorithm maintains a list of the vertices in the network. Beginning at the front, the algorithm scans the list, repeatedly selecting an overflowing vertex u and then "discharging" it, that is, performing push and relabel operations until u no longer has a positive excess. Whenever we relabel a vertex, we move it to the front of the list (hence the name "relabel-to-front") and the algorithm begins its scan anew.

The correctness and analysis of the relabel-to-front algorithm depend on the notion of "admissible" edges: those edges in the residual network through which flow can be pushed. After proving some properties about the network of admissible edges, we shall investigate the discharge operation and then present and analyze the relabel-to-front algorithm itself.

Admissible edges and networks

If $G = (V, E)$ is a flow network with source s and sink t, f is a preflow in G, and h is a height function, then we say that (u, v) is an ***admissible edge*** if $c_f(u, v) > 0$ and $h(u) = h(v) + 1$. Otherwise, (u, v) is ***inadmissible***. The ***admissible network*** is $G_{f,h} = (V, E_{f,h})$, where $E_{f,h}$ is the set of admissible edges.

The admissible network consists of those edges through which we can push flow. The following lemma shows that this network is a directed acyclic graph (dag).

Lemma 26.26 (The admissible network is acyclic)
If $G = (V, E)$ is a flow network, f is a preflow in G, and h is a height function on G, then the admissible network $G_{f,h} = (V, E_{f,h})$ is acyclic.

Proof   The proof is by contradiction. Suppose that $G_{f,h}$ contains a cycle $p = \langle v_0, v_1, \ldots, v_k \rangle$, where $v_0 = v_k$ and $k > 0$. Since each edge in p is admissible, we have $h(v_{i-1}) = h(v_i) + 1$ for $i = 1, 2, \ldots, k$. Summing around the cycle gives

$$\sum_{i=1}^{k} h(v_{i-1}) = \sum_{i=1}^{k} (h(v_i) + 1)$$

$$= \sum_{i=1}^{k} h(v_i) + k .$$

Because each vertex in cycle p appears once in each of the summations, we derive the contradiction that $0 = k$.   ∎

The next two lemmas show how push and relabel operations change the admissible network.

Lemma 26.27
Let $G = (V, E)$ be a flow network, let f be a preflow in G, and suppose that the attribute h is a height function. If a vertex u is overflowing and (u, v) is an admissible edge, then PUSH(u, v) applies. The operation does not create any new admissible edges, but it may cause (u, v) to become inadmissible.

Proof By the definition of an admissible edge, we can push flow from u to v. Since u is overflowing, the operation $\text{PUSH}(u, v)$ applies. The only new residual edge that pushing flow from u to v can create is (v, u). Since $v.h = u.h - 1$, edge (v, u) cannot become admissible. If the operation is a saturating push, then $c_f(u, v) = 0$ afterward and (u, v) becomes inadmissible.   ∎

Lemma 26.28

Let $G = (V, E)$ be a flow network, let f be a preflow in G, and suppose that the attribute h is a height function. If a vertex u is overflowing and there are no admissible edges leaving u, then $\text{RELABEL}(u)$ applies. After the relabel operation, there is at least one admissible edge leaving u, but there are no admissible edges entering u.

Proof If u is overflowing, then by Lemma 26.14, either a push or a relabel operation applies to it. If there are no admissible edges leaving u, then no flow can be pushed from u and so $\text{RELABEL}(u)$ applies. After the relabel operation, $u.h = 1 + \min\{v.h : (u, v) \in E_f\}$. Thus, if v is a vertex that realizes the minimum in this set, the edge (u, v) becomes admissible. Hence, after the relabel, there is at least one admissible edge leaving u.

To show that no admissible edges enter u after a relabel operation, suppose that there is a vertex v such that (v, u) is admissible. Then, $v.h = u.h + 1$ after the relabel, and so $v.h > u.h + 1$ just before the relabel. But by Lemma 26.12, no residual edges exist between vertices whose heights differ by more than 1. Moreover, relabeling a vertex does not change the residual network. Thus, (v, u) is not in the residual network, and hence it cannot be in the admissible network.   ∎

Neighbor lists

Edges in the relabel-to-front algorithm are organized into "neighbor lists." Given a flow network $G = (V, E)$, the ***neighbor list*** $u.N$ for a vertex $u \in V$ is a singly linked list of the neighbors of u in G. Thus, vertex v appears in the list $u.N$ if $(u, v) \in E$ or $(v, u) \in E$. The neighbor list $u.N$ contains exactly those vertices v for which there may be a residual edge (u, v). The attribute $u.N.head$ points to the first vertex in $u.N$, and $v.next\text{-}neighbor$ points to the vertex following v in a neighbor list; this pointer is NIL if v is the last vertex in the neighbor list.

The relabel-to-front algorithm cycles through each neighbor list in an arbitrary order that is fixed throughout the execution of the algorithm. For each vertex u, the attribute $u.current$ points to the vertex currently under consideration in $u.N$. Initially, $u.current$ is set to $u.N.head$.

Discharging an overflowing vertex

An overflowing vertex u is **discharged** by pushing all of its excess flow through admissible edges to neighboring vertices, relabeling u as necessary to cause edges leaving u to become admissible. The pseudocode goes as follows.

DISCHARGE(u)

```
1   while u.e > 0
2       v = u.current
3       if v == NIL
4           RELABEL(u)
5           u.current = u.N.head
6       elseif c_f(u, v) > 0 and u.h == v.h + 1
7           PUSH(u, v)
8       else u.current = v.next-neighbor
```

Figure 26.9 steps through several iterations of the **while** loop of lines 1–8, which executes as long as vertex u has positive excess. Each iteration performs exactly one of three actions, depending on the current vertex v in the neighbor list $u.N$.

1. If v is NIL, then we have run off the end of $u.N$. Line 4 relabels vertex u, and then line 5 resets the current neighbor of u to be the first one in $u.N$. (Lemma 26.29 below states that the relabel operation applies in this situation.)

2. If v is non-NIL and (u, v) is an admissible edge (determined by the test in line 6), then line 7 pushes some (or possibly all) of u's excess to vertex v.

3. If v is non-NIL but (u, v) is inadmissible, then line 8 advances $u.current$ one position further in the neighbor list $u.N$.

Observe that if DISCHARGE is called on an overflowing vertex u, then the last action performed by DISCHARGE must be a push from u. Why? The procedure terminates only when $u.e$ becomes zero, and neither the relabel operation nor advancing the pointer $u.current$ affects the value of $u.e$.

We must be sure that when PUSH or RELABEL is called by DISCHARGE, the operation applies. The next lemma proves this fact.

Lemma 26.29

If DISCHARGE calls PUSH(u, v) in line 7, then a push operation applies to (u, v). If DISCHARGE calls RELABEL(u) in line 4, then a relabel operation applies to u.

Proof   The tests in lines 1 and 6 ensure that a push operation occurs only if the operation applies, which proves the first statement in the lemma.

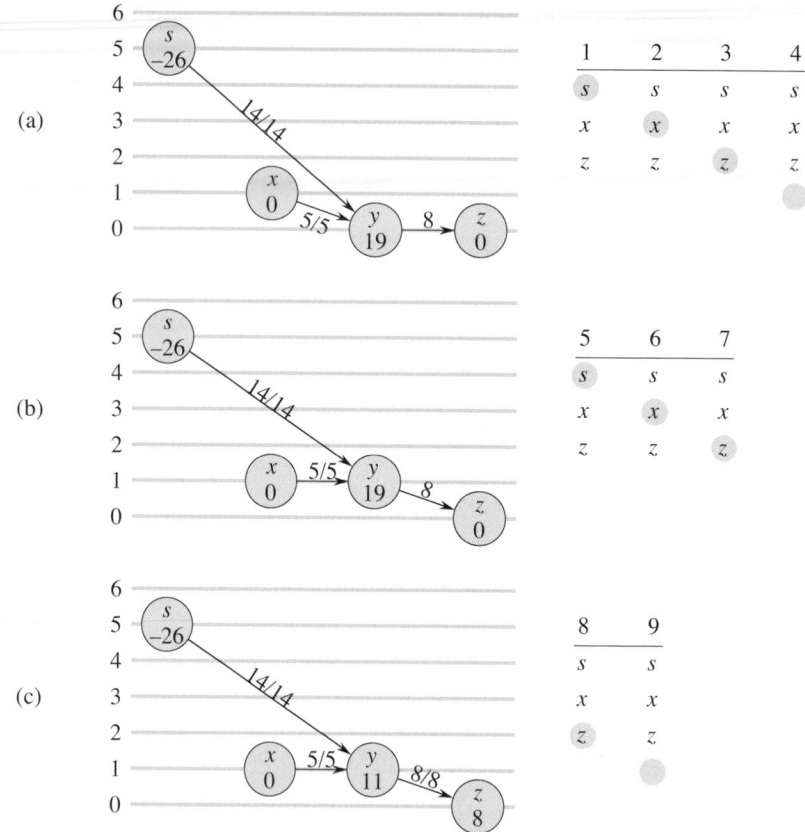

Figure 26.9 Discharging a vertex y. It takes 15 iterations of the **while** loop of DISCHARGE to push all the excess flow from y. Only the neighbors of y and edges of the flow network that enter or leave y are shown. In each part of the figure, the number inside each vertex is its excess at the beginning of the first iteration shown in the part, and each vertex is shown at its height throughout the part. The neighbor list $y.N$ at the beginning of each iteration appears on the right, with the iteration number on top. The shaded neighbor is $y.current$. **(a)** Initially, there are 19 units of excess to push from y, and $y.current = s$. Iterations 1, 2, and 3 just advance $y.current$, since there are no admissible edges leaving y. In iteration 4, $y.current = $ NIL (shown by the shading being below the neighbor list), and so y is relabeled and $y.current$ is reset to the head of the neighbor list. **(b)** After relabeling, vertex y has height 1. In iterations 5 and 6, edges (y, s) and (y, x) are found to be inadmissible, but iteration 7 pushes 8 units of excess flow from y to z. Because of the push, $y.current$ does not advance in this iteration. **(c)** Because the push in iteration 7 saturated edge (y, z), it is found inadmissible in iteration 8. In iteration 9, $y.current = $ NIL, and so vertex y is again relabeled and $y.current$ is reset.

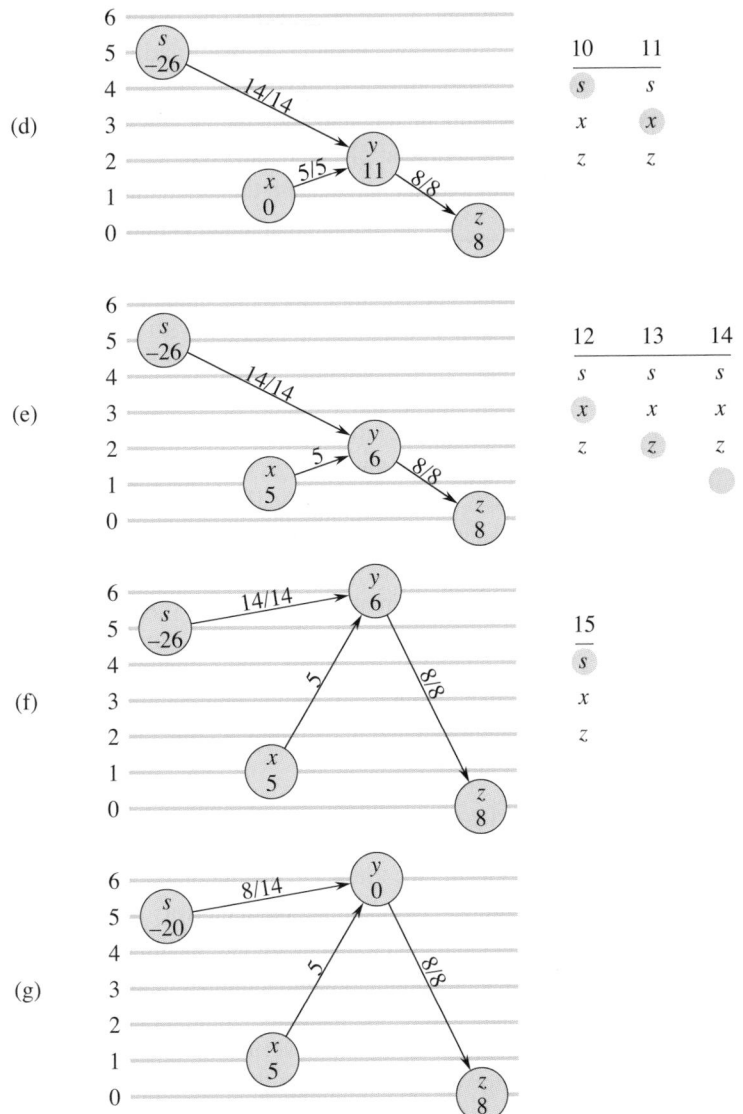

Figure 26.9, continued   **(d)** In iteration 10, (y, s) is inadmissible, but iteration 11 pushes 5 units of excess flow from y to x. **(e)** Because $y.current$ did not advance in iteration 11, iteration 12 finds (y, x) to be inadmissible. Iteration 13 finds (y, z) inadmissible, and iteration 14 relabels vertex y and resets $y.current$. **(f)** Iteration 15 pushes 6 units of excess flow from y to s. **(g)** Vertex y now has no excess flow, and DISCHARGE terminates. In this example, DISCHARGE both starts and finishes with the current pointer at the head of the neighbor list, but in general this need not be the case.

To prove the second statement, according to the test in line 1 and Lemma 26.28, we need only show that all edges leaving u are inadmissible. If a call to DISCHARGE(u) starts with the pointer $u.current$ at the head of u's neighbor list and finishes with it off the end of the list, then all of u's outgoing edges are inadmissible and a relabel operation applies. It is possible, however, that during a call to DISCHARGE(u), the pointer $u.current$ traverses only part of the list before the procedure returns. Calls to DISCHARGE on other vertices may then occur, but $u.current$ will continue moving through the list during the next call to DISCHARGE(u). We now consider what happens during a complete pass through the list, which begins at the head of $u.N$ and finishes with $u.current =$ NIL. Once $u.current$ reaches the end of the list, the procedure relabels u and begins a new pass. For the $u.current$ pointer to advance past a vertex $v \in u.N$ during a pass, the edge (u, v) must be deemed inadmissible by the test in line 6. Thus, by the time the pass completes, every edge leaving u has been determined to be inadmissible at some time during the pass. The key observation is that at the end of the pass, every edge leaving u is still inadmissible. Why? By Lemma 26.27, pushes cannot create any admissible edges, regardless of which vertex the flow is pushed from. Thus, any admissible edge must be created by a relabel operation. But the vertex u is not relabeled during the pass, and by Lemma 26.28, any other vertex v that is relabeled during the pass (resulting from a call of DISCHARGE(v)) has no entering admissible edges after relabeling. Thus, at the end of the pass, all edges leaving u remain inadmissible, which completes the proof.   ∎

The relabel-to-front algorithm

In the relabel-to-front algorithm, we maintain a linked list L consisting of all vertices in $V - \{s, t\}$. A key property is that the vertices in L are topologically sorted according to the admissible network, as we shall see in the loop invariant that follows. (Recall from Lemma 26.26 that the admissible network is a dag.)

The pseudocode for the relabel-to-front algorithm assumes that the neighbor lists $u.N$ have already been created for each vertex u. It also assumes that $u.next$ points to the vertex that follows u in list L and that, as usual, $u.next =$ NIL if u is the last vertex in the list.

RELABEL-TO-FRONT(G, s, t)

```
 1   INITIALIZE-PREFLOW(G, s)
 2   L = G.V − {s, t}, in any order
 3   for each vertex u ∈ G.V − {s, t}
 4       u.current = u.N.head
 5   u = L.head
 6   while u ≠ NIL
 7       old-height = u.h
 8       DISCHARGE(u)
 9       if u.h > old-height
10           move u to the front of list L
11       u = u.next
```

The relabel-to-front algorithm works as follows. Line 1 initializes the preflow and heights to the same values as in the generic push-relabel algorithm. Line 2 initializes the list L to contain all potentially overflowing vertices, in any order. Lines 3–4 initialize the *current* pointer of each vertex u to the first vertex in u's neighbor list.

As Figure 26.10 illustrates, the **while** loop of lines 6–11 runs through the list L, discharging vertices. Line 5 makes it start with the first vertex in the list. Each time through the loop, line 8 discharges a vertex u. If u was relabeled by the DISCHARGE procedure, line 10 moves it to the front of list L. We can determine whether u was relabeled by comparing its height before the discharge operation, saved into the variable *old-height* in line 7, with its height afterward, in line 9. Line 11 makes the next iteration of the **while** loop use the vertex following u in list L. If line 10 moved u to the front of the list, the vertex used in the next iteration is the one following u in its new position in the list.

To show that RELABEL-TO-FRONT computes a maximum flow, we shall show that it is an implementation of the generic push-relabel algorithm. First, observe that it performs push and relabel operations only when they apply, since Lemma 26.29 guarantees that DISCHARGE performs them only when they apply. It remains to show that when RELABEL-TO-FRONT terminates, no basic operations apply. The remainder of the correctness argument relies on the following loop invariant:

> At each test in line 6 of RELABEL-TO-FRONT, list L is a topological sort of the vertices in the admissible network $G_{f,h} = (V, E_{f,h})$, and no vertex before u in the list has excess flow.

Initialization: Immediately after INITIALIZE-PREFLOW has been run, $s.h = |V|$ and $v.h = 0$ for all $v \in V − \{s\}$. Since $|V| \geq 2$ (because V contains at

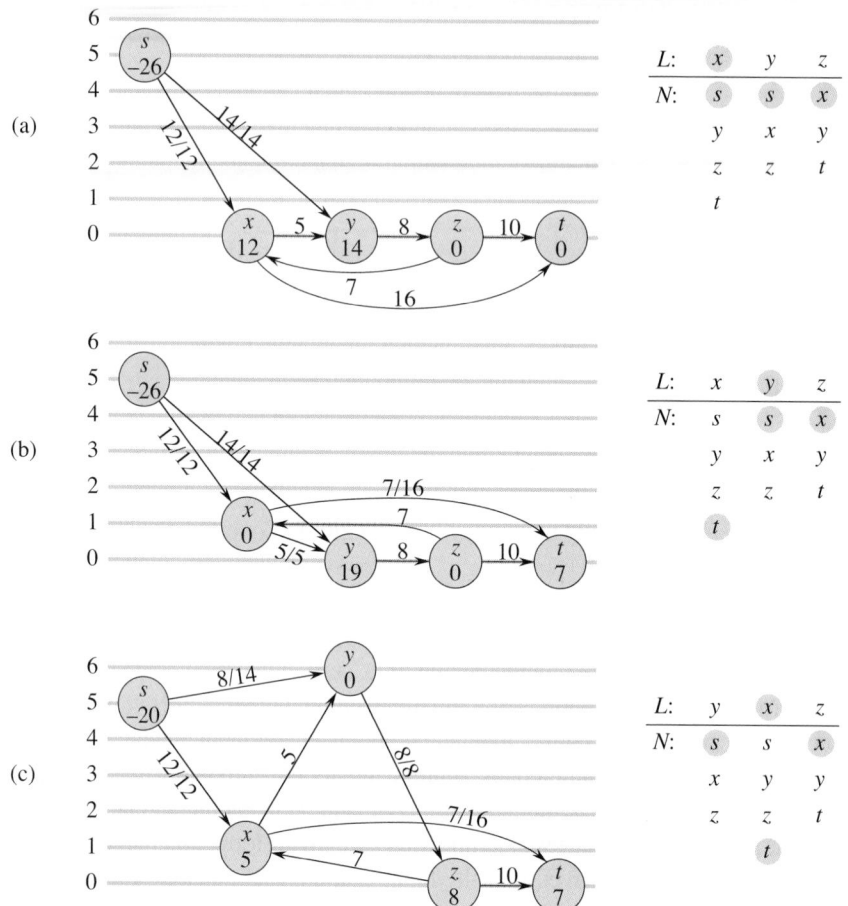

Figure 26.10 The action of RELABEL-TO-FRONT. **(a)** A flow network just before the first iteration of the **while** loop. Initially, 26 units of flow leave source s. On the right is shown the initial list $L = \langle x, y, z \rangle$, where initially $u = x$. Under each vertex in list L is its neighbor list, with the current neighbor shaded. Vertex x is discharged. It is relabeled to height 1, 5 units of excess flow are pushed to y, and the 7 remaining units of excess are pushed to the sink t. Because x is relabeled, it moves to the head of L, which in this case does not change the structure of L. **(b)** After x, the next vertex in L that is discharged is y. Figure 26.9 shows the detailed action of discharging y in this situation. Because y is relabeled, it is moved to the head of L. **(c)** Vertex x now follows y in L, and so it is again discharged, pushing all 5 units of excess flow to t. Because vertex x is not relabeled in this discharge operation, it remains in place in list L.

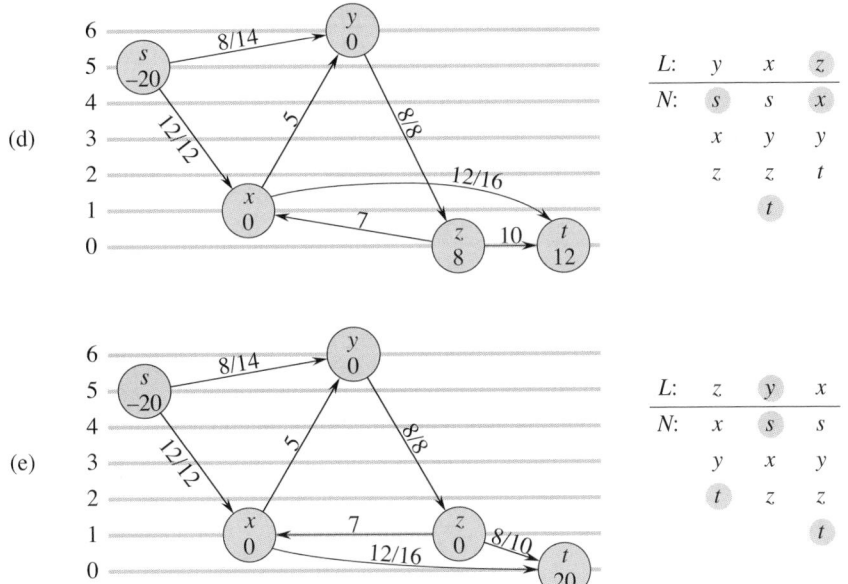

Figure 26.10, continued   **(d)** Since vertex z follows vertex x in L, it is discharged. It is relabeled to height 1 and all 8 units of excess flow are pushed to t. Because z is relabeled, it moves to the front of L. **(e)** Vertex y now follows vertex z in L and is therefore discharged. But because y has no excess, DISCHARGE immediately returns, and y remains in place in L. Vertex x is then discharged. Because it, too, has no excess, DISCHARGE again returns, and x remains in place in L. RELABEL-TO-FRONT has reached the end of list L and terminates. There are no overflowing vertices, and the preflow is a maximum flow.

least s and t), no edge can be admissible. Thus, $E_{f,h} = \emptyset$, and any ordering of $V - \{s, t\}$ is a topological sort of $G_{f,h}$.

Because u is initially the head of the list L, there are no vertices before it and so there are none before it with excess flow.

Maintenance: To see that each iteration of the **while** loop maintains the topological sort, we start by observing that the admissible network is changed only by push and relabel operations. By Lemma 26.27, push operations do not cause edges to become admissible. Thus, only relabel operations can create admissible edges. After a vertex u is relabeled, however, Lemma 26.28 states that there are no admissible edges entering u but there may be admissible edges leaving u. Thus, by moving u to the front of L, the algorithm ensures that any admissible edges leaving u satisfy the topological sort ordering.

To see that no vertex preceding u in L has excess flow, we denote the vertex that will be u in the next iteration by u'. The vertices that will precede u' in the next iteration include the current u (due to line 11) and either no other vertices (if u is relabeled) or the same vertices as before (if u is not relabeled). When u is discharged, it has no excess flow afterward. Thus, if u is relabeled during the discharge, no vertices preceding u' have excess flow. If u is not relabeled during the discharge, no vertices before it on the list acquired excess flow during this discharge, because L remained topologically sorted at all times during the discharge (as just pointed out, admissible edges are created only by relabeling, not pushing), and so each push operation causes excess flow to move only to vertices further down the list (or to s or t). Again, no vertices preceding u' have excess flow.

Termination: When the loop terminates, u is just past the end of L, and so the loop invariant ensures that the excess of every vertex is 0. Thus, no basic operations apply.

Analysis

We shall now show that RELABEL-TO-FRONT runs in $O(V^3)$ time on any flow network $G = (V, E)$. Since the algorithm is an implementation of the generic push-relabel algorithm, we shall take advantage of Corollary 26.21, which provides an $O(V)$ bound on the number of relabel òperations executed per vertex and an $O(V^2)$ bound on the total number of relabel operations overall. In addition, Exercise 26.4-3 provides an $O(VE)$ bound on the total time spent performing relabel operations, and Lemma 26.22 provides an $O(VE)$ bound on the total number of saturating push operations.

Theorem 26.30
The running time of RELABEL-TO-FRONT on any flow network $G = (V, E)$ is $O(V^3)$.

Proof   Let us consider a "phase" of the relabel-to-front algorithm to be the time between two consecutive relabel operations. There are $O(V^2)$ phases, since there are $O(V^2)$ relabel operations. Each phase consists of at most $|V|$ calls to DISCHARGE, which we can see as follows. If DISCHARGE does not perform a relabel operation, then the next call to DISCHARGE is further down the list L, and the length of L is less than $|V|$. If DISCHARGE does perform a relabel, the next call to DISCHARGE belongs to a different phase. Since each phase contains at most $|V|$ calls to DISCHARGE and there are $O(V^2)$ phases, the number of times DISCHARGE is called in line 8 of RELABEL-TO-FRONT is $O(V^3)$. Thus, the total

work performed by the **while** loop in RELABEL-TO-FRONT, excluding the work performed within DISCHARGE, is at most $O(V^3)$.

We must now bound the work performed within DISCHARGE during the execution of the algorithm. Each iteration of the **while** loop within DISCHARGE performs one of three actions. We shall analyze the total amount of work involved in performing each of these actions.

We start with relabel operations (lines 4–5). Exercise 26.4-3 provides an $O(VE)$ time bound on all the $O(V^2)$ relabels that are performed.

Now, suppose that the action updates the $u.current$ pointer in line 8. This action occurs $O(\text{degree}(u))$ times each time a vertex u is relabeled, and $O(V \cdot \text{degree}(u))$ times overall for the vertex. For all vertices, therefore, the total amount of work done in advancing pointers in neighbor lists is $O(VE)$ by the handshaking lemma (Exercise B.4-1).

The third type of action performed by DISCHARGE is a push operation (line 7). We already know that the total number of saturating push operations is $O(VE)$. Observe that if a nonsaturating push is executed, DISCHARGE immediately returns, since the push reduces the excess to 0. Thus, there can be at most one nonsaturating push per call to DISCHARGE. As we have observed, DISCHARGE is called $O(V^3)$ times, and thus the total time spent performing nonsaturating pushes is $O(V^3)$.

The running time of RELABEL-TO-FRONT is therefore $O(V^3 + VE)$, which is $O(V^3)$. ∎

Exercises

26.5-1
Illustrate the execution of RELABEL-TO-FRONT in the manner of Figure 26.10 for the flow network in Figure 26.1(a). Assume that the initial ordering of vertices in L is $\langle v_1, v_2, v_3, v_4 \rangle$ and that the neighbor lists are

$$
\begin{aligned}
v_1.N &= \langle s, v_2, v_3 \rangle, \\
v_2.N &= \langle s, v_1, v_3, v_4 \rangle, \\
v_3.N &= \langle v_1, v_2, v_4, t \rangle, \\
v_4.N &= \langle v_2, v_3, t \rangle.
\end{aligned}
$$

26.5-2 ⋆
We would like to implement a push-relabel algorithm in which we maintain a first-in, first-out queue of overflowing vertices. The algorithm repeatedly discharges the vertex at the head of the queue, and any vertices that were not overflowing before the discharge but are overflowing afterward are placed at the end of the queue. After the vertex at the head of the queue is discharged, it is removed. When the

queue is empty, the algorithm terminates. Show how to implement this algorithm to compute a maximum flow in $O(V^3)$ time.

26.5-3

Show that the generic algorithm still works if RELABEL updates $u.h$ by simply computing $u.h = u.h + 1$. How would this change affect the analysis of RELABEL-TO-FRONT?

26.5-4 ★

Show that if we always discharge a highest overflowing vertex, we can make the push-relabel method run in $O(V^3)$ time.

26.5-5

Suppose that at some point in the execution of a push-relabel algorithm, there exists an integer $0 < k \leq |V| - 1$ for which no vertex has $v.h = k$. Show that all vertices with $v.h > k$ are on the source side of a minimum cut. If such a k exists, the **gap heuristic** updates every vertex $v \in V - \{s\}$ for which $v.h > k$, to set $v.h = \max(v.h, |V| + 1)$. Show that the resulting attribute h is a height function. (The gap heuristic is crucial in making implementations of the push-relabel method perform well in practice.)

Problems

26-1 *Escape problem*

An $n \times n$ **grid** is an undirected graph consisting of n rows and n columns of vertices, as shown in Figure 26.11. We denote the vertex in the ith row and the jth column by (i, j). All vertices in a grid have exactly four neighbors, except for the boundary vertices, which are the points (i, j) for which $i = 1, i = n, j = 1,$ or $j = n$.

Given $m \leq n^2$ starting points $(x_1, y_1), (x_2, y_2), \ldots, (x_m, y_m)$ in the grid, the **escape problem** is to determine whether or not there are m vertex-disjoint paths from the starting points to any m different points on the boundary. For example, the grid in Figure 26.11(a) has an escape, but the grid in Figure 26.11(b) does not.

a. Consider a flow network in which vertices, as well as edges, have capacities. That is, the total positive flow entering any given vertex is subject to a capacity constraint. Show that determining the maximum flow in a network with edge and vertex capacities can be reduced to an ordinary maximum-flow problem on a flow network of comparable size.

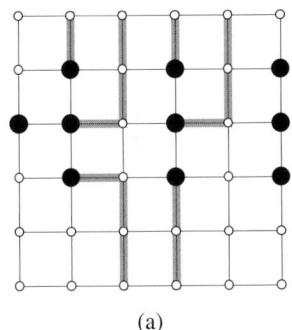 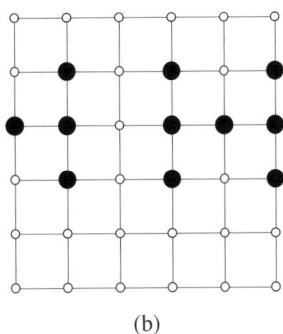

(a)   (b)

Figure 26.11 Grids for the escape problem. Starting points are black, and other grid vertices are white. **(a)** A grid with an escape, shown by shaded paths. **(b)** A grid with no escape.

b. Describe an efficient algorithm to solve the escape problem, and analyze its running time.

26-2 *Minimum path cover*

A *path cover* of a directed graph $G = (V, E)$ is a set P of vertex-disjoint paths such that every vertex in V is included in exactly one path in P. Paths may start and end anywhere, and they may be of any length, including 0. A *minimum path cover* of G is a path cover containing the fewest possible paths.

a. Give an efficient algorithm to find a minimum path cover of a directed acyclic graph $G = (V, E)$. (*Hint:* Assuming that $V = \{1, 2, \ldots, n\}$, construct the graph $G' = (V', E')$, where

$$V' = \{x_0, x_1, \ldots, x_n\} \cup \{y_0, y_1, \ldots, y_n\} \ ,$$
$$E' = \{(x_0, x_i) : i \in V\} \cup \{(y_i, y_0) : i \in V\} \cup \{(x_i, y_j) : (i, j) \in E\} \ ,$$

and run a maximum-flow algorithm.)

b. Does your algorithm work for directed graphs that contain cycles? Explain.

26-3 *Algorithmic consulting*

Professor Gore wants to open up an algorithmic consulting company. He has identified n important subareas of algorithms (roughly corresponding to different portions of this textbook), which he represents by the set $A = \{A_1, A_2, \ldots, A_n\}$. In each subarea A_k, he can hire an expert in that area for c_k dollars. The consulting company has lined up a set $J = \{J_1, J_2, \ldots, J_m\}$ of potential jobs. In order to perform job J_i, the company needs to have hired experts in a subset $R_i \subseteq A$ of

subareas. Each expert can work on multiple jobs simultaneously. If the company chooses to accept job J_i, it must have hired experts in all subareas in R_i, and it will take in revenue of p_i dollars.

Professor Gore's job is to determine which subareas to hire experts in and which jobs to accept in order to maximize the net revenue, which is the total income from jobs accepted minus the total cost of employing the experts.

Consider the following flow network G. It contains a source vertex s, vertices $A_1, A_2, \ldots, A_n$, vertices $J_1, J_2, \ldots, J_m$, and a sink vertex t. For $k = 1, 2 \ldots, n$, the flow network contains an edge (s, A_k) with capacity $c(s, A_k) = c_k$, and for $i = 1, 2, \ldots, m$, the flow network contains an edge (J_i, t) with capacity $c(J_i, t) = p_i$. For $k = 1, 2, \ldots, n$ and $i = 1, 2, \ldots, m$, if $A_k \in R_i$, then G contains an edge (A_k, J_i) with capacity $c(A_k, J_i) = \infty$.

a. Show that if $J_i \in T$ for a finite-capacity cut (S, T) of G, then $A_k \in T$ for each $A_k \in R_i$.

b. Show how to determine the maximum net revenue from the capacity of a minimum cut of G and the given p_i values.

c. Give an efficient algorithm to determine which jobs to accept and which experts to hire. Analyze the running time of your algorithm in terms of m, n, and $r = \sum_{i=1}^{m} |R_i|$.

26-4   *Updating maximum flow*
Let $G = (V, E)$ be a flow network with source s, sink t, and integer capacities. Suppose that we are given a maximum flow in G.

a. Suppose that we increase the capacity of a single edge $(u, v) \in E$ by 1. Give an $O(V + E)$-time algorithm to update the maximum flow.

b. Suppose that we decrease the capacity of a single edge $(u, v) \in E$ by 1. Give an $O(V + E)$-time algorithm to update the maximum flow.

26-5   *Maximum flow by scaling*
Let $G = (V, E)$ be a flow network with source s, sink t, and an integer capacity $c(u, v)$ on each edge $(u, v) \in E$. Let $C = \max_{(u,v) \in E} c(u, v)$.

a. Argue that a minimum cut of G has capacity at most $C |E|$.

b. For a given number K, show how to find an augmenting path of capacity at least K in $O(E)$ time, if such a path exists.

We can use the following modification of FORD-FULKERSON-METHOD to compute a maximum flow in G:

MAX-FLOW-BY-SCALING(G, s, t)

```
1   C = max(u,v)∈E c(u, v)
2   initialize flow f to 0
3   K = 2^⌊lg C⌋
4   while K ≥ 1
5       while there exists an augmenting path p of capacity at least K
6           augment flow f along p
7       K = K/2
8   return f
```

c. Argue that MAX-FLOW-BY-SCALING returns a maximum flow.

d. Show that the capacity of a minimum cut of the residual network G_f is at most $2K |E|$ each time line 4 is executed.

e. Argue that the inner **while** loop of lines 5–6 executes $O(E)$ times for each value of K.

f. Conclude that MAX-FLOW-BY-SCALING can be implemented so that it runs in $O(E^2 \lg C)$ time.

26-6 *The Hopcroft-Karp bipartite matching algorithm*

In this problem, we describe a faster algorithm, due to Hopcroft and Karp, for finding a maximum matching in a bipartite graph. The algorithm runs in $O(\sqrt{V} E)$ time. Given an undirected, bipartite graph $G = (V, E)$, where $V = L \cup R$ and all edges have exactly one endpoint in L, let M be a matching in G. We say that a simple path P in G is an ***augmenting path*** with respect to M if it starts at an unmatched vertex in L, ends at an unmatched vertex in R, and its edges belong alternately to M and $E - M$. (This definition of an augmenting path is related to, but different from, an augmenting path in a flow network.) In this problem, we treat a path as a sequence of edges, rather than as a sequence of vertices. A shortest augmenting path with respect to a matching M is an augmenting path with a minimum number of edges.

Given two sets A and B, the ***symmetric difference*** $A \oplus B$ is defined as $(A - B) \cup (B - A)$, that is, the elements that are in exactly one of the two sets.

a. Show that if M is a matching and P is an augmenting path with respect to M, then the symmetric difference $M \oplus P$ is a matching and $|M \oplus P| = |M| + 1$. Show that if $P_1, P_2, \ldots, P_k$ are vertex-disjoint augmenting paths with respect to M, then the symmetric difference $M \oplus (P_1 \cup P_2 \cup \cdots \cup P_k)$ is a matching with cardinality $|M| + k$.

The general structure of our algorithm is the following:

HOPCROFT-KARP(G)

```
1  M = Ø
2  repeat
3      let 𝒫 = {P₁, P₂, ..., Pₖ} be a maximal set of vertex-disjoint
              shortest augmenting paths with respect to M
4      M = M ⊕ (P₁ ∪ P₂ ∪ ··· ∪ Pₖ)
5  until 𝒫 == Ø
6  return M
```

The remainder of this problem asks you to analyze the number of iterations in the algorithm (that is, the number of iterations in the **repeat** loop) and to describe an implementation of line 3.

b. Given two matchings M and M^* in G, show that every vertex in the graph $G' = (V, M \oplus M^*)$ has degree at most 2. Conclude that G' is a disjoint union of simple paths or cycles. Argue that edges in each such simple path or cycle belong alternately to M or M^*. Prove that if $|M| \leq |M^*|$, then $M \oplus M^*$ contains at least $|M^*| - |M|$ vertex-disjoint augmenting paths with respect to M.

Let l be the length of a shortest augmenting path with respect to a matching M, and let $P_1, P_2, \ldots, P_k$ be a maximal set of vertex-disjoint augmenting paths of length l with respect to M. Let $M' = M \oplus (P_1 \cup \cdots \cup P_k)$, and suppose that P is a shortest augmenting path with respect to M'.

c. Show that if P is vertex-disjoint from $P_1, P_2, \ldots, P_k$, then P has more than l edges.

d. Now suppose that P is not vertex-disjoint from $P_1, P_2, \ldots, P_k$. Let A be the set of edges $(M \oplus M') \oplus P$. Show that $A = (P_1 \cup P_2 \cup \cdots \cup P_k) \oplus P$ and that $|A| \geq (k + 1)l$. Conclude that P has more than l edges.

e. Prove that if a shortest augmenting path with respect to M has l edges, the size of the maximum matching is at most $|M| + |V|/(l + 1)$.

f. Show that the number of **repeat** loop iterations in the algorithm is at most $2\sqrt{|V|}$. (*Hint:* By how much can M grow after iteration number $\sqrt{|V|}$?)

g. Give an algorithm that runs in $O(E)$ time to find a maximal set of vertex-disjoint shortest augmenting paths $P_1, P_2, \ldots, P_k$ for a given matching M. Conclude that the total running time of Hopcroft-Karp is $O(\sqrt{V}E)$.

Chapter notes

Ahuja, Magnanti, and Orlin [7], Even [103], Lawler [224], Papadimitriou and Steiglitz [271], and Tarjan [330] are good references for network flow and related algorithms. Goldberg, Tardos, and Tarjan [139] also provide a nice survey of algorithms for network-flow problems, and Schrijver [304] has written an interesting review of historical developments in the field of network flows.

The Ford-Fulkerson method is due to Ford and Fulkerson [109], who originated the formal study of many of the problems in the area of network flow, including the maximum-flow and bipartite-matching problems. Many early implementations of the Ford-Fulkerson method found augmenting paths using breadth-first search; Edmonds and Karp [102], and independently Dinic [89], proved that this strategy yields a polynomial-time algorithm. A related idea, that of using "blocking flows," was also first developed by Dinic [89]. Karzanov [202] first developed the idea of preflows. The push-relabel method is due to Goldberg [136] and Goldberg and Tarjan [140]. Goldberg and Tarjan gave an $O(V^3)$-time algorithm that uses a queue to maintain the set of overflowing vertices, as well as an algorithm that uses dynamic trees to achieve a running time of $O(VE \lg(V^2/E + 2))$. Several other researchers have developed push-relabel maximum-flow algorithms. Ahuja and Orlin [9] and Ahuja, Orlin, and Tarjan [10] gave algorithms that used scaling. Cheriyan and Maheshwari [62] proposed pushing flow from the overflowing vertex of maximum height. Cheriyan and Hagerup [61] suggested randomly permuting the neighbor lists, and several researchers [14, 204, 276] developed clever derandomizations of this idea, leading to a sequence of faster algorithms. The algorithm of King, Rao, and Tarjan [204] is the fastest such algorithm and runs in $O(VE \log_{E/(V \lg V)} V)$ time.

The asymptotically fastest algorithm to date for the maximum-flow problem, by Goldberg and Rao [138], runs in time $O(\min(V^{2/3}, E^{1/2})E \lg(V^2/E + 2) \lg C)$, where $C = \max_{(u,v) \in E} c(u, v)$. This algorithm does not use the push-relabel method but instead is based on finding blocking flows. All previous maximum-flow algorithms, including the ones in this chapter, use some notion of distance (the push-relabel algorithms use the analogous notion of height), with a length of 1

assigned implicitly to each edge. This new algorithm takes a different approach and assigns a length of 0 to high-capacity edges and a length of 1 to low-capacity edges. Informally, with respect to these lengths, shortest paths from the source to the sink tend to have high capacity, which means that fewer iterations need be performed.

In practice, push-relabel algorithms currently dominate augmenting-path or linear-programming based algorithms for the maximum-flow problem. A study by Cherkassky and Goldberg [63] underscores the importance of using two heuristics when implementing a push-relabel algorithm. The first heuristic is to periodically perform a breadth-first search of the residual network in order to obtain more accurate height values. The second heuristic is the gap heuristic, described in Exercise 26.5-5. Cherkassky and Goldberg conclude that the best choice of push-relabel variants is the one that chooses to discharge the overflowing vertex with the maximum height.

The best algorithm to date for maximum bipartite matching, discovered by Hopcroft and Karp [176], runs in $O(\sqrt{V} E)$ time and is described in Problem 26-6. The book by Lovász and Plummer [239] is an excellent reference on matching problems.

VII   Selected Topics

Introduction

This part contains a selection of algorithmic topics that extend and complement earlier material in this book. Some chapters introduce new models of computation such as circuits or parallel computers. Others cover specialized domains such as computational geometry or number theory. The last two chapters discuss some of the known limitations to the design of efficient algorithms and introduce techniques for coping with those limitations.

Chapter 27 presents an algorithmic model for parallel computing based on dynamic multithreading. The chapter introduces the basics of the model, showing how to quantify parallelism in terms of the measures of work and span. It then investigates several interesting multithreaded algorithms, including algorithms for matrix multiplication and merge sorting.

Chapter 28 studies efficient algorithms for operating on matrices. It presents two general methods—LU decomposition and LUP decomposition—for solving linear equations by Gaussian elimination in $O(n^3)$ time. It also shows that matrix inversion and matrix multiplication can be performed equally fast. The chapter concludes by showing how to compute a least-squares approximate solution when a set of linear equations has no exact solution.

Chapter 29 studies linear programming, in which we wish to maximize or minimize an objective, given limited resources and competing constraints. Linear programming arises in a variety of practical application areas. This chapter covers how to formulate and solve linear programs. The solution method covered is the simplex algorithm, which is the oldest algorithm for linear programming. In contrast to many algorithms in this book, the simplex algorithm does not run in polynomial time in the worst case, but it is fairly efficient and widely used in practice.

Chapter 30 studies operations on polynomials and shows how to use a well-known signal-processing technique—the fast Fourier transform (FFT)—to multiply two degree-n polynomials in $O(n \lg n)$ time. It also investigates efficient implementations of the FFT, including a parallel circuit.

Chapter 31 presents number-theoretic algorithms. After reviewing elementary number theory, it presents Euclid's algorithm for computing greatest common divisors. Next, it studies algorithms for solving modular linear equations and for raising one number to a power modulo another number. Then, it explores an important application of number-theoretic algorithms: the RSA public-key cryptosystem. This cryptosystem can be used not only to encrypt messages so that an adversary cannot read them, but also to provide digital signatures. The chapter then presents the Miller-Rabin randomized primality test, with which we can find large primes efficiently—an essential requirement for the RSA system. Finally, the chapter covers Pollard's "rho" heuristic for factoring integers and discusses the state of the art of integer factorization.

Chapter 32 studies the problem of finding all occurrences of a given pattern string in a given text string, a problem that arises frequently in text-editing programs. After examining the naive approach, the chapter presents an elegant approach due to Rabin and Karp. Then, after showing an efficient solution based on finite automata, the chapter presents the Knuth-Morris-Pratt algorithm, which modifies the automaton-based algorithm to save space by cleverly preprocessing the pattern.

Chapter 33 considers a few problems in computational geometry. After discussing basic primitives of computational geometry, the chapter shows how to use a "sweeping" method to efficiently determine whether a set of line segments contains any intersections. Two clever algorithms for finding the convex hull of a set of points—Graham's scan and Jarvis's march—also illustrate the power of sweeping methods. The chapter closes with an efficient algorithm for finding the closest pair from among a given set of points in the plane.

Chapter 34 concerns NP-complete problems. Many interesting computational problems are NP-complete, but no polynomial-time algorithm is known for solving any of them. This chapter presents techniques for determining when a problem is NP-complete. Several classic problems are proved to be NP-complete: determining whether a graph has a hamiltonian cycle, determining whether a boolean formula is satisfiable, and determining whether a given set of numbers has a subset that adds up to a given target value. The chapter also proves that the famous traveling-salesman problem is NP-complete.

Chapter 35 shows how to find approximate solutions to NP-complete problems efficiently by using approximation algorithms. For some NP-complete problems, approximate solutions that are near optimal are quite easy to produce, but for others even the best approximation algorithms known work progressively more poorly as

the problem size increases. Then, there are some problems for which we can invest increasing amounts of computation time in return for increasingly better approximate solutions. This chapter illustrates these possibilities with the vertex-cover problem (unweighted and weighted versions), an optimization version of 3-CNF satisfiability, the traveling-salesman problem, the set-covering problem, and the subset-sum problem.

27   Multithreaded Algorithms

The vast majority of algorithms in this book are ***serial algorithms*** suitable for running on a uniprocessor computer in which only one instruction executes at a time. In this chapter, we shall extend our algorithmic model to encompass ***parallel algorithms***, which can run on a multiprocessor computer that permits multiple instructions to execute concurrently. In particular, we shall explore the elegant model of dynamic multithreaded algorithms, which are amenable to algorithmic design and analysis, as well as to efficient implementation in practice.

Parallel computers—computers with multiple processing units—have become increasingly common, and they span a wide range of prices and performance. Relatively inexpensive desktop and laptop ***chip multiprocessors*** contain a single ***multicore*** integrated-circuit chip that houses multiple processing "cores," each of which is a full-fledged processor that can access a common memory. At an intermediate price/performance point are clusters built from individual computers—often simple PC-class machines—with a dedicated network interconnecting them. The highest-priced machines are supercomputers, which often use a combination of custom architectures and custom networks to deliver the highest performance in terms of instructions executed per second.

Multiprocessor computers have been around, in one form or another, for decades. Although the computing community settled on the random-access machine model for serial computing early on in the history of computer science, no single model for parallel computing has gained as wide acceptance. A major reason is that vendors have not agreed on a single architectural model for parallel computers. For example, some parallel computers feature ***shared memory***, where each processor can directly access any location of memory. Other parallel computers employ ***distributed memory***, where each processor's memory is private, and an explicit message must be sent between processors in order for one processor to access the memory of another. With the advent of multicore technology, however, every new laptop and desktop machine is now a shared-memory parallel computer,

and the trend appears to be toward shared-memory multiprocessing. Although time will tell, that is the approach we shall take in this chapter.

One common means of programming chip multiprocessors and other shared-memory parallel computers is by using *static threading*, which provides a software abstraction of "virtual processors," or *threads*, sharing a common memory. Each thread maintains an associated program counter and can execute code independently of the other threads. The operating system loads a thread onto a processor for execution and switches it out when another thread needs to run. Although the operating system allows programmers to create and destroy threads, these operations are comparatively slow. Thus, for most applications, threads persist for the duration of a computation, which is why we call them "static."

Unfortunately, programming a shared-memory parallel computer directly using static threads is difficult and error-prone. One reason is that dynamically partitioning the work among the threads so that each thread receives approximately the same load turns out to be a complicated undertaking. For any but the simplest of applications, the programmer must use complex communication protocols to implement a scheduler to load-balance the work. This state of affairs has led toward the creation of *concurrency platforms*, which provide a layer of software that coordinates, schedules, and manages the parallel-computing resources. Some concurrency platforms are built as runtime libraries, but others provide full-fledged parallel languages with compiler and runtime support.

Dynamic multithreaded programming

One important class of concurrency platform is *dynamic multithreading*, which is the model we shall adopt in this chapter. Dynamic multithreading allows programmers to specify parallelism in applications without worrying about communication protocols, load balancing, and other vagaries of static-thread programming. The concurrency platform contains a scheduler, which load-balances the computation automatically, thereby greatly simplifying the programmer's chore. Although the functionality of dynamic-multithreading environments is still evolving, almost all support two features: nested parallelism and parallel loops. Nested parallelism allows a subroutine to be "spawned," allowing the caller to proceed while the spawned subroutine is computing its result. A parallel loop is like an ordinary **for** loop, except that the iterations of the loop can execute concurrently.

These two features form the basis of the model for dynamic multithreading that we shall study in this chapter. A key aspect of this model is that the programmer needs to specify only the logical parallelism within a computation, and the threads within the underlying concurrency platform schedule and load-balance the computation among themselves. We shall investigate multithreaded algorithms written

for this model, as well as how the underlying concurrency platform can schedule computations efficiently.

Our model for dynamic multithreading offers several important advantages:

- It is a simple extension of our serial programming model. We can describe a multithreaded algorithm by adding to our pseudocode just four "concurrency" keywords: **parallel**, **spawn**, **sync**, and **new**. Moreover, if we delete these concurrency keywords from the multithreaded pseudocode, the resulting text is serial pseudocode for the same problem, which we call the "serialization" of the multithreaded algorithm.

- It provides a theoretically clean way to quantify parallelism based on the notions of "work" and "span."

- Many multithreaded algorithms involving nested parallelism follow naturally from the divide-and-conquer paradigm. Moreover, just as serial divide-and-conquer algorithms lend themselves to analysis by solving recurrences, so do multithreaded algorithms.

- The model is faithful to how parallel-computing practice is evolving. A growing number of concurrency platforms support one variant or another of dynamic multithreading, including Cilk [51, 118], Cilk++ [71], OpenMP [59], Task Parallel Library [230], and Threading Building Blocks [292].

Section 27.1 introduces the dynamic multithreading model and presents the metrics of work, span, and parallelism, which we shall use to analyze multithreaded algorithms. Section 27.2 investigates how to multiply matrices with multithreading, and Section 27.3 tackles the tougher problem of multithreading merge sort.

27.1   The basics of dynamic multithreading

We shall begin our exploration of dynamic multithreading using the example of computing Fibonacci numbers recursively. Recall that the Fibonacci numbers are defined by recurrence (3.22):

$$
\begin{aligned}
F_0 &= 0, \\
F_1 &= 1, \\
F_i &= F_{i-1} + F_{i-2} \qquad \text{for } i \geq 2.
\end{aligned}
$$

Here is a simple, recursive, serial algorithm to compute the nth Fibonacci number:

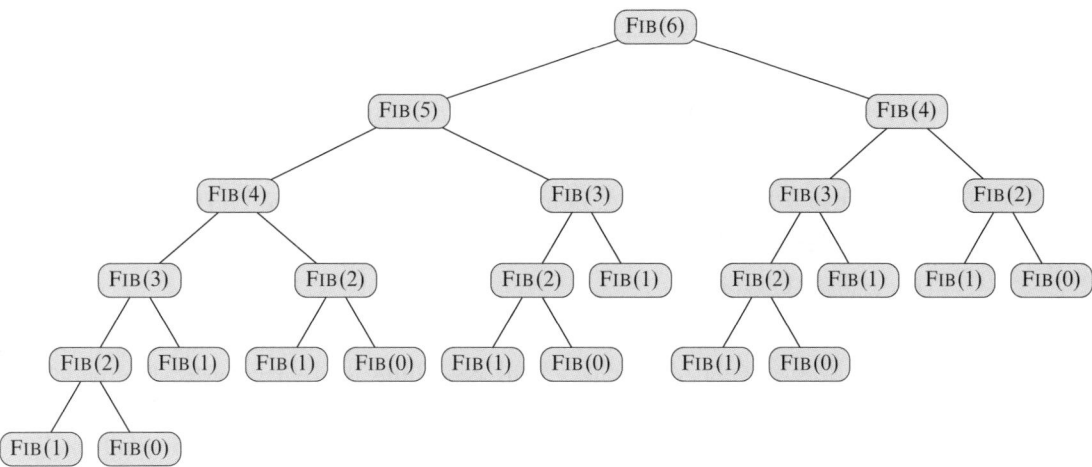

Figure 27.1   The tree of recursive procedure instances when computing FIB(6). Each instance of FIB with the same argument does the same work to produce the same result, providing an inefficient but interesting way to compute Fibonacci numbers.

FIB(n)

1   **if** $n \leq 1$
2   **return** n
3   **else** $x = \text{FIB}(n - 1)$
4       $y = \text{FIB}(n - 2)$
5   **return** $x + y$

You would not really want to compute large Fibonacci numbers this way, because this computation does much repeated work. Figure 27.1 shows the tree of recursive procedure instances that are created when computing F_6. For example, a call to FIB(6) recursively calls FIB(5) and then FIB(4). But, the call to FIB(5) also results in a call to FIB(4). Both instances of FIB(4) return the same result ($F_4 = 3$). Since the FIB procedure does not memoize, the second call to FIB(4) replicates the work that the first call performs.

Let $T(n)$ denote the running time of FIB(n). Since FIB(n) contains two recursive calls plus a constant amount of extra work, we obtain the recurrence

$$T(n) = T(n - 1) + T(n - 2) + \Theta(1) .$$

This recurrence has solution $T(n) = \Theta(F_n)$, which we can show using the substitution method. For an inductive hypothesis, assume that $T(n) \leq a F_n - b$, where $a > 1$ and $b > 0$ are constants. Substituting, we obtain

$$
\begin{aligned}
T(n) &\le (aF_{n-1} - b) + (aF_{n-2} - b) + \Theta(1) \\
&= a(F_{n-1} + F_{n-2}) - 2b + \Theta(1) \\
&= aF_n - b - (b - \Theta(1)) \\
&\le aF_n - b
\end{aligned}
$$

if we choose b large enough to dominate the constant in the $\Theta(1)$. We can then choose a large enough to satisfy the initial condition. The analytical bound

$$
T(n) = \Theta(\phi^n) , \tag{27.1}
$$

where $\phi = (1 + \sqrt{5})/2$ is the golden ratio, now follows from equation (3.25). Since F_n grows exponentially in n, this procedure is a particularly slow way to compute Fibonacci numbers. (See Problem 31-3 for much faster ways.)

Although the FIB procedure is a poor way to compute Fibonacci numbers, it makes a good example for illustrating key concepts in the analysis of multithreaded algorithms. Observe that within FIB(n), the two recursive calls in lines 3 and 4 to FIB$(n-1)$ and FIB$(n-2)$, respectively, are independent of each other: they could be called in either order, and the computation performed by one in no way affects the other. Therefore, the two recursive calls can run in parallel.

We augment our pseudocode to indicate parallelism by adding the ***concurrency keywords*** **spawn** and **sync**. Here is how we can rewrite the FIB procedure to use dynamic multithreading:

P-FIB(n)

```
1  if n ≤ 1
2      return n
3  else x = spawn P-FIB(n − 1)
4      y = P-FIB(n − 2)
5      sync
6      return x + y
```

Notice that if we delete the concurrency keywords **spawn** and **sync** from P-FIB, the resulting pseudocode text is identical to FIB (other than renaming the procedure in the header and in the two recursive calls). We define the ***serialization*** of a multithreaded algorithm to be the serial algorithm that results from deleting the multithreaded keywords: **spawn**, **sync**, and when we examine parallel loops, **parallel** and **new**. Indeed, our multithreaded pseudocode has the nice property that a serialization is always ordinary serial pseudocode to solve the same problem.

Nested parallelism occurs when the keyword **spawn** precedes a procedure call, as in line 3. The semantics of a spawn differs from an ordinary procedure call in that the procedure instance that executes the spawn—the ***parent***—may continue to execute in parallel with the spawned subroutine—its ***child***—instead of waiting

for the child to complete, as would normally happen in a serial execution. In this case, while the spawned child is computing P-FIB$(n - 1)$, the parent may go on to compute P-FIB$(n - 2)$ in line 4 in parallel with the spawned child. Since the P-FIB procedure is recursive, these two subroutine calls themselves create nested parallelism, as do their children, thereby creating a potentially vast tree of subcomputations, all executing in parallel.

The keyword **spawn** does not say, however, that a procedure *must* execute concurrently with its spawned children, only that it *may*. The concurrency keywords express the *logical parallelism* of the computation, indicating which parts of the computation may proceed in parallel. At runtime, it is up to a *scheduler* to determine which subcomputations actually run concurrently by assigning them to available processors as the computation unfolds. We shall discuss the theory behind schedulers shortly.

A procedure cannot safely use the values returned by its spawned children until after it executes a **sync** statement, as in line 5. The keyword **sync** indicates that the procedure must wait as necessary for all its spawned children to complete before proceeding to the statement after the **sync**. In the P-FIB procedure, a **sync** is required before the **return** statement in line 6 to avoid the anomaly that would occur if x and y were summed before x was computed. In addition to explicit synchronization provided by the **sync** statement, every procedure executes a **sync** implicitly before it returns, thus ensuring that all its children terminate before it does.

A model for multithreaded execution

It helps to think of a *multithreaded computation*—the set of runtime instructions executed by a processor on behalf of a multithreaded program—as a directed acyclic graph $G = (V, E)$, called a *computation dag*. As an example, Figure 27.2 shows the computation dag that results from computing P-FIB(4). Conceptually, the vertices in V are instructions, and the edges in E represent dependencies between instructions, where $(u, v) \in E$ means that instruction u must execute before instruction v. For convenience, however, if a chain of instructions contains no parallel control (no **spawn**, **sync**, or **return** from a spawn—via either an explicit **return** statement or the return that happens implicitly upon reaching the end of a procedure), we may group them into a single *strand*, each of which represents one or more instructions. Instructions involving parallel control are not included in strands, but are represented in the structure of the dag. For example, if a strand has two successors, one of them must have been spawned, and a strand with multiple predecessors indicates the predecessors joined because of a **sync** statement. Thus, in the general case, the set V forms the set of strands, and the set E of directed edges represents dependencies between strands induced by parallel control.

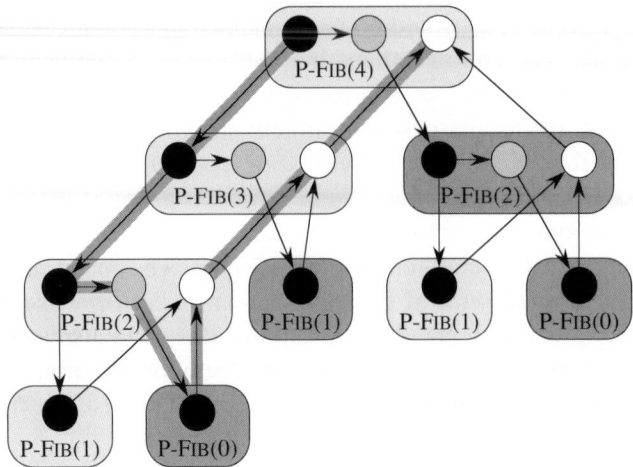

Figure 27.2   A directed acyclic graph representing the computation of P-FIB(4). Each circle represents one strand, with black circles representing either base cases or the part of the procedure (instance) up to the spawn of P-FIB($n-1$) in line 3, shaded circles representing the part of the procedure that calls P-FIB($n-2$) in line 4 up to the **sync** in line 5, where it suspends until the spawn of P-FIB($n-1$) returns, and white circles representing the part of the procedure after the **sync** where it sums x and y up to the point where it returns the result. Each group of strands belonging to the same procedure is surrounded by a rounded rectangle, lightly shaded for spawned procedures and heavily shaded for called procedures. Spawn edges and call edges point downward, continuation edges point horizontally to the right, and return edges point upward. Assuming that each strand takes unit time, the work equals 17 time units, since there are 17 strands, and the span is 8 time units, since the critical path—shown with shaded edges—contains 8 strands.

If G has a directed path from strand u to strand v, we say that the two strands are *(logically) in series*. Otherwise, strands u and v are *(logically) in parallel*.

We can picture a multithreaded computation as a dag of strands embedded in a tree of procedure instances. For example, Figure 27.1 shows the tree of procedure instances for P-FIB(6) without the detailed structure showing strands. Figure 27.2 zooms in on a section of that tree, showing the strands that constitute each procedure. All directed edges connecting strands run either within a procedure or along undirected edges in the procedure tree.

We can classify the edges of a computation dag to indicate the kind of dependencies between the various strands. A *continuation edge* (u, u'), drawn horizontally in Figure 27.2, connects a strand u to its successor u' within the same procedure instance. When a strand u spawns a strand v, the dag contains a *spawn edge* (u, v), which points downward in the figure. *Call edges*, representing normal procedure calls, also point downward. Strand u spawning strand v differs from u calling v in that a spawn induces a horizontal continuation edge from u to the strand u' fol-

lowing u in its procedure, indicating that u' is free to execute at the same time as v, whereas a call induces no such edge. When a strand u returns to its calling procedure and x is the strand immediately following the next **sync** in the calling procedure, the computation dag contains *return edge* (u, x), which points upward. A computation starts with a single *initial strand*—the black vertex in the procedure labeled P-FIB(4) in Figure 27.2—and ends with a single *final strand*—the white vertex in the procedure labeled P-FIB(4).

We shall study the execution of multithreaded algorithms on an *ideal parallel computer*, which consists of a set of processors and a *sequentially consistent* shared memory. Sequential consistency means that the shared memory, which may in reality be performing many loads and stores from the processors at the same time, produces the same results as if at each step, exactly one instruction from one of the processors is executed. That is, the memory behaves as if the instructions were executed sequentially according to some global linear order that preserves the individual orders in which each processor issues its own instructions. For dynamic multithreaded computations, which are scheduled onto processors automatically by the concurrency platform, the shared memory behaves as if the multithreaded computation's instructions were interleaved to produce a linear order that preserves the partial order of the computation dag. Depending on scheduling, the ordering could differ from one run of the program to another, but the behavior of any execution can be understood by assuming that the instructions are executed in some linear order consistent with the computation dag.

In addition to making assumptions about semantics, the ideal-parallel-computer model makes some performance assumptions. Specifically, it assumes that each processor in the machine has equal computing power, and it ignores the cost of scheduling. Although this last assumption may sound optimistic, it turns out that for algorithms with sufficient "parallelism" (a term we shall define precisely in a moment), the overhead of scheduling is generally minimal in practice.

Performance measures

We can gauge the theoretical efficiency of a multithreaded algorithm by using two metrics: "work" and "span." The *work* of a multithreaded computation is the total time to execute the entire computation on one processor. In other words, the work is the sum of the times taken by each of the strands. For a computation dag in which each strand takes unit time, the work is just the number of vertices in the dag. The *span* is the longest time to execute the strands along any path in the dag. Again, for a dag in which each strand takes unit time, the span equals the number of vertices on a longest or *critical path* in the dag. (Recall from Section 24.2 that we can find a critical path in a dag $G = (V, E)$ in $\Theta(V + E)$ time.) For example, the computation dag of Figure 27.2 has 17 vertices in all and 8 vertices on its critical

path, so that if each strand takes unit time, its work is 17 time units and its span is 8 time units.

The actual running time of a multithreaded computation depends not only on its work and its span, but also on how many processors are available and how the scheduler allocates strands to processors. To denote the running time of a multithreaded computation on P processors, we shall subscript by P. For example, we might denote the running time of an algorithm on P processors by T_P. The work is the running time on a single processor, or T_1. The span is the running time if we could run each strand on its own processor—in other words, if we had an unlimited number of processors—and so we denote the span by T_∞.

The work and span provide lower bounds on the running time T_P of a multi-threaded computation on P processors:

- In one step, an ideal parallel computer with P processors can do at most P units of work, and thus in T_P time, it can perform at most $P T_P$ work. Since the total work to do is T_1, we have $P T_P \geq T_1$. Dividing by P yields the **work law**:

$$T_P \geq T_1/P \ . \tag{27.2}$$

- A P-processor ideal parallel computer cannot run any faster than a machine with an unlimited number of processors. Looked at another way, a machine with an unlimited number of processors can emulate a P-processor machine by using just P of its processors. Thus, the **span law** follows:

$$T_P \geq T_\infty \ . \tag{27.3}$$

We define the **speedup** of a computation on P processors by the ratio T_1/T_P, which says how many times faster the computation is on P processors than on 1 processor. By the work law, we have $T_P \geq T_1/P$, which implies that $T_1/T_P \leq P$. Thus, the speedup on P processors can be at most P. When the speedup is linear in the number of processors, that is, when $T_1/T_P = \Theta(P)$, the computation exhibits **linear speedup**, and when $T_1/T_P = P$, we have **perfect linear speedup**.

The ratio T_1/T_∞ of the work to the span gives the **parallelism** of the multi-threaded computation. We can view the parallelism from three perspectives. As a ratio, the parallelism denotes the average amount of work that can be performed in parallel for each step along the critical path. As an upper bound, the parallelism gives the maximum possible speedup that can be achieved on any number of processors. Finally, and perhaps most important, the parallelism provides a limit on the possibility of attaining perfect linear speedup. Specifically, once the number of processors exceeds the parallelism, the computation cannot possibly achieve perfect linear speedup. To see this last point, suppose that $P > T_1/T_\infty$, in which case

the span law implies that the speedup satisfies $T_1/T_P \leq T_1/T_\infty < P$. Moreover, if the number P of processors in the ideal parallel computer greatly exceeds the parallelism—that is, if $P \gg T_1/T_\infty$—then $T_1/T_P \ll P$, so that the speedup is much less than the number of processors. In other words, the more processors we use beyond the parallelism, the less perfect the speedup.

As an example, consider the computation P-FIB(4) in Figure 27.2, and assume that each strand takes unit time. Since the work is $T_1 = 17$ and the span is $T_\infty = 8$, the parallelism is $T_1/T_\infty = 17/8 = 2.125$. Consequently, achieving much more than double the speedup is impossible, no matter how many processors we employ to execute the computation. For larger input sizes, however, we shall see that P-FIB(n) exhibits substantial parallelism.

We define the *(parallel) slackness* of a multithreaded computation executed on an ideal parallel computer with P processors to be the ratio $(T_1/T_\infty)/P = T_1/(PT_\infty)$, which is the factor by which the parallelism of the computation exceeds the number of processors in the machine. Thus, if the slackness is less than 1, we cannot hope to achieve perfect linear speedup, because $T_1/(PT_\infty) < 1$ and the span law imply that the speedup on P processors satisfies $T_1/T_P \leq T_1/T_\infty < P$. Indeed, as the slackness decreases from 1 toward 0, the speedup of the computation diverges further and further from perfect linear speedup. If the slackness is greater than 1, however, the work per processor is the limiting constraint. As we shall see, as the slackness increases from 1, a good scheduler can achieve closer and closer to perfect linear speedup.

Scheduling

Good performance depends on more than just minimizing the work and span. The strands must also be scheduled efficiently onto the processors of the parallel machine. Our multithreaded programming model provides no way to specify which strands to execute on which processors. Instead, we rely on the concurrency platform's scheduler to map the dynamically unfolding computation to individual processors. In practice, the scheduler maps the strands to static threads, and the operating system schedules the threads on the processors themselves, but this extra level of indirection is unnecessary for our understanding of scheduling. We can just imagine that the concurrency platform's scheduler maps strands to processors directly.

A multithreaded scheduler must schedule the computation with no advance knowledge of when strands will be spawned or when they will complete—it must operate *on-line*. Moreover, a good scheduler operates in a distributed fashion, where the threads implementing the scheduler cooperate to load-balance the computation. Provably good on-line, distributed schedulers exist, but analyzing them is complicated.

Instead, to keep our analysis simple, we shall investigate an on-line *centralized* scheduler, which knows the global state of the computation at any given time. In particular, we shall analyze *greedy schedulers*, which assign as many strands to processors as possible in each time step. If at least P strands are ready to execute during a time step, we say that the step is a *complete step*, and a greedy scheduler assigns any P of the ready strands to processors. Otherwise, fewer than P strands are ready to execute, in which case we say that the step is an *incomplete step*, and the scheduler assigns each ready strand to its own processor.

From the work law, the best running time we can hope for on P processors is $T_P = T_1/P$, and from the span law the best we can hope for is $T_P = T_\infty$. The following theorem shows that greedy scheduling is provably good in that it achieves the sum of these two lower bounds as an upper bound.

Theorem 27.1
On an ideal parallel computer with P processors, a greedy scheduler executes a multithreaded computation with work T_1 and span T_∞ in time

$$T_P \leq T_1/P + T_\infty \,. \tag{27.4}$$

Proof   We start by considering the complete steps. In each complete step, the P processors together perform a total of P work. Suppose for the purpose of contradiction that the number of complete steps is strictly greater than $\lfloor T_1/P \rfloor$. Then, the total work of the complete steps is at least

$$
\begin{aligned}
P \cdot (\lfloor T_1/P \rfloor + 1) \;&=\; P \lfloor T_1/P \rfloor + P \\
&=\; T_1 - (T_1 \bmod P) + P \quad \text{(by equation (3.8))} \\
&>\; T_1 \quad\quad\quad\quad\quad\quad\quad \text{(by inequality (3.9))} \,.
\end{aligned}
$$

Thus, we obtain the contradiction that the P processors would perform more work than the computation requires, which allows us to conclude that the number of complete steps is at most $\lfloor T_1/P \rfloor$.

Now, consider an incomplete step. Let G be the dag representing the entire computation, and without loss of generality, assume that each strand takes unit time. (We can replace each longer strand by a chain of unit-time strands.) Let G' be the subgraph of G that has yet to be executed at the start of the incomplete step, and let G'' be the subgraph remaining to be executed after the incomplete step. A longest path in a dag must necessarily start at a vertex with in-degree 0. Since an incomplete step of a greedy scheduler executes all strands with in-degree 0 in G', the length of a longest path in G'' must be 1 less than the length of a longest path in G'. In other words, an incomplete step decreases the span of the unexecuted dag by 1. Hence, the number of incomplete steps is at most T_∞.

Since each step is either complete or incomplete, the theorem follows.   ∎

The following corollary to Theorem 27.1 shows that a greedy scheduler always performs well.

Corollary 27.2
The running time T_P of any multithreaded computation scheduled by a greedy scheduler on an ideal parallel computer with P processors is within a factor of 2 of optimal.

Proof   Let T_P^* be the running time produced by an optimal scheduler on a machine with P processors, and let T_1 and T_∞ be the work and span of the computation, respectively. Since the work and span laws—inequalities (27.2) and (27.3)—give us $T_P^* \geq \max(T_1/P, T_\infty)$, Theorem 27.1 implies that

$$
\begin{aligned}
T_P &\leq & T_1/P + T_\infty \\
&\leq & 2 \cdot \max(T_1/P, T_\infty) \\
&\leq & 2T_P^* .
\end{aligned}
$$

■

The next corollary shows that, in fact, a greedy scheduler achieves near-perfect linear speedup on any multithreaded computation as the slackness grows.

Corollary 27.3
Let T_P be the running time of a multithreaded computation produced by a greedy scheduler on an ideal parallel computer with P processors, and let T_1 and T_∞ be the work and span of the computation, respectively. Then, if $P \ll T_1/T_\infty$, we have $T_P \approx T_1/P$, or equivalently, a speedup of approximately P.

Proof   If we suppose that $P \ll T_1/T_\infty$, then we also have $T_\infty \ll T_1/P$, and hence Theorem 27.1 gives us $T_P \leq T_1/P + T_\infty \approx T_1/P$. Since the work law (27.2) dictates that $T_P \geq T_1/P$, we conclude that $T_P \approx T_1/P$, or equivalently, that the speedup is $T_1/T_P \approx P$.

■

The $\ll$ symbol denotes "much less," but how much is "much less"? As a rule of thumb, a slackness of at least 10—that is, 10 times more parallelism than processors—generally suffices to achieve good speedup. Then, the span term in the greedy bound, inequality (27.4), is less than 10% of the work-per-processor term, which is good enough for most engineering situations. For example, if a computation runs on only 10 or 100 processors, it doesn't make sense to value parallelism of, say 1,000,000 over parallelism of 10,000, even with the factor of 100 difference. As Problem 27-2 shows, sometimes by reducing extreme parallelism, we can obtain algorithms that are better with respect to other concerns and which still scale up well on reasonable numbers of processors.

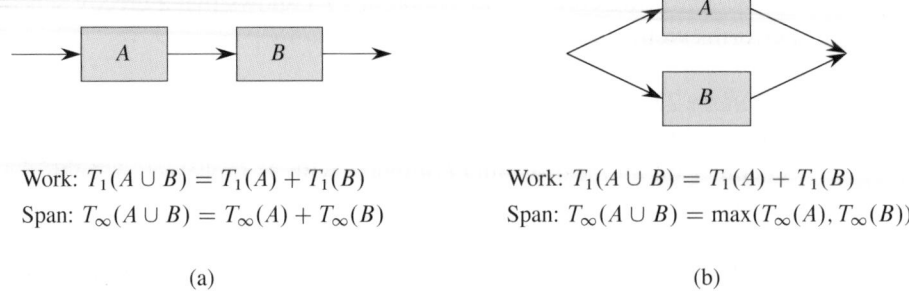

Work: $T_1(A \cup B) = T_1(A) + T_1(B)$

Span: $T_\infty(A \cup B) = T_\infty(A) + T_\infty(B)$

Work: $T_1(A \cup B) = T_1(A) + T_1(B)$

Span: $T_\infty(A \cup B) = \max(T_\infty(A), T_\infty(B))$

(a)   (b)

Figure 27.3 The work and span of composed subcomputations. **(a)** When two subcomputations are joined in series, the work of the composition is the sum of their work, and the span of the composition is the sum of their spans. **(b)** When two subcomputations are joined in parallel, the work of the composition remains the sum of their work, but the span of the composition is only the maximum of their spans.

Analyzing multithreaded algorithms

We now have all the tools we need to analyze multithreaded algorithms and provide good bounds on their running times on various numbers of processors. Analyzing the work is relatively straightforward, since it amounts to nothing more than analyzing the running time of an ordinary serial algorithm—namely, the serialization of the multithreaded algorithm—which you should already be familiar with, since that is what most of this textbook is about! Analyzing the span is more interesting, but generally no harder once you get the hang of it. We shall investigate the basic ideas using the P-FIB program.

Analyzing the work $T_1(n)$ of P-FIB(n) poses no hurdles, because we've already done it. The original FIB procedure is essentially the serialization of P-FIB, and hence $T_1(n) = T(n) = \Theta(\phi^n)$ from equation (27.1).

Figure 27.3 illustrates how to analyze the span. If two subcomputations are joined in series, their spans add to form the span of their composition, whereas if they are joined in parallel, the span of their composition is the maximum of the spans of the two subcomputations. For P-FIB(n), the spawned call to P-FIB$(n-1)$ in line 3 runs in parallel with the call to P-FIB$(n - 2)$ in line 4. Hence, we can express the span of P-FIB(n) as the recurrence

$$
\begin{aligned}
T_\infty(n) &= \max(T_\infty(n-1), T_\infty(n-2)) + \Theta(1) \\
&= T_\infty(n-1) + \Theta(1) ,
\end{aligned}
$$

which has solution $T_\infty(n) = \Theta(n)$.

The parallelism of P-FIB(n) is $T_1(n)/T_\infty(n) = \Theta(\phi^n/n)$, which grows dramatically as n gets large. Thus, on even the largest parallel computers, a modest

value for n suffices to achieve near perfect linear speedup for P-FIB(n), because this procedure exhibits considerable parallel slackness.

Parallel loops

Many algorithms contain loops all of whose iterations can operate in parallel. As we shall see, we can parallelize such loops using the **spawn** and **sync** keywords, but it is much more convenient to specify directly that the iterations of such loops can run concurrently. Our pseudocode provides this functionality via the **parallel** concurrency keyword, which precedes the **for** keyword in a **for** loop statement.

As an example, consider the problem of multiplying an $n \times n$ matrix $A = (a_{ij})$ by an n-vector $x = (x_j)$. The resulting n-vector $y = (y_i)$ is given by the equation

$$y_i = \sum_{j=1}^{n} a_{ij} x_j \; ,$$

for $i = 1, 2, \ldots, n$. We can perform matrix-vector multiplication by computing all the entries of y in parallel as follows:

MAT-VEC(A, x)

```
1   n = A.rows
2   let y be a new vector of length n
3   parallel for i = 1 to n
4       y_i = 0
5   parallel for i = 1 to n
6       for new j = 1 to n
7           y_i = y_i + a_ij x_j
8   return y
```

In this code, the **parallel for** keywords in lines 3 and 5 indicate that the iterations of the respective loops may be run concurrently. The **new** keyword in line 6 indicates that a new variable j should be allocated for each iteration of i, rather than reusing the same variable, precluding different iterations of i from attempting to update the same variable j and causing a "race condition," which we shall examine in more detail starting on page 787.

A compiler can implement each **parallel for** loop as a divide-and-conquer subroutine using nested parallelism. For example, the **parallel for** loop in lines 5–7 can be implemented with the call MAT-VEC-MAIN-LOOP$(A, x, y, n, 1, n)$, where the compiler produces the auxiliary subroutine MAT-VEC-MAIN-LOOP as follows:

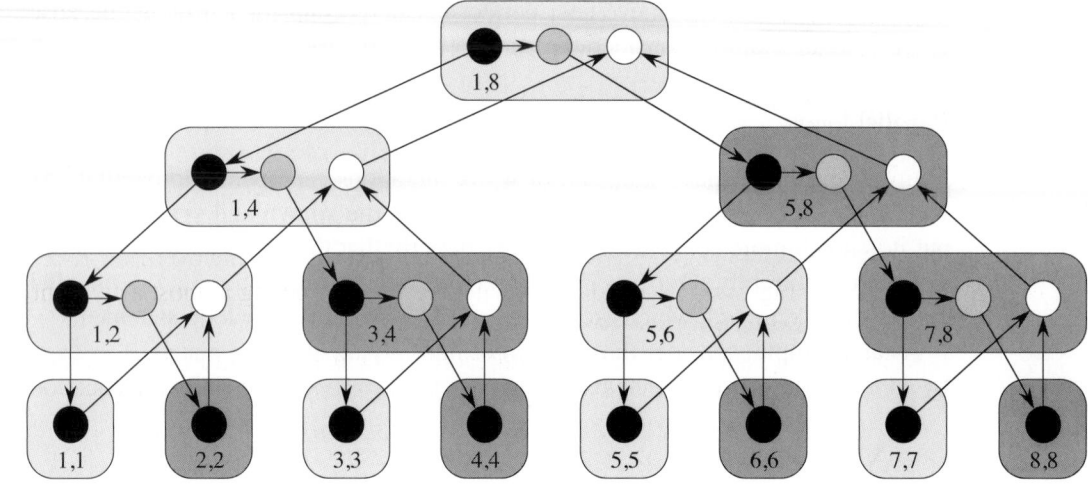

Figure 27.4   A dag representing the computation of MAT-VEC-MAIN-LOOP($A, x, y, 8, 1, 8$). The two numbers within each rounded rectangle give the values of the last two parameters (i and i' in the procedure header) in the invocation (spawn or call) of the procedure. The black circles represent strands corresponding to either the base case or the part of the procedure up to the spawn of MAT-VEC-MAIN-LOOP in line 5; the shaded circles represent strands corresponding to the part of the procedure that calls MAT-VEC-MAIN-LOOP in line 6 up to the **sync** in line 7, where it suspends until the spawned subroutine in line 5 returns; and the white circles represent strands corresponding to the (negligible) part of the procedure after the **sync** up to the point where it returns.

MAT-VEC-MAIN-LOOP(A, x, y, n, i, i')

1   **if** $i == i'$
2   **for** $j = 1$ **to** n
3            $y_i = y_i + a_{ij}x_j$
4   **else** $mid = \lfloor (i + i')/2 \rfloor$
5   **spawn** MAT-VEC-MAIN-LOOP(A, x, y, n, i, mid)
6   MAT-VEC-MAIN-LOOP($A, x, y, n, mid + 1, i'$)
7   **sync**

This code recursively spawns the first half of the iterations of the loop to execute in parallel with the second half of the iterations and then executes a **sync**, thereby creating a binary tree of execution where the leaves are individual loop iterations, as shown in Figure 27.4.

To calculate the work $T_1(n)$ of MAT-VEC on an $n \times n$ matrix, we simply compute the running time of its serialization, which we obtain by replacing the **parallel for** loops with ordinary **for** loops. Thus, we have $T_1(n) = \Theta(n^2)$, because the quadratic running time of the doubly nested loops in lines 5–7 dominates. This analysis

seems to ignore the overhead for recursive spawning in implementing the parallel
loops, however. In fact, the overhead of recursive spawning does increase the work
of a parallel loop compared with that of its serialization, but not asymptotically.
To see why, observe that since the tree of recursive procedure instances is a full
binary tree, the number of internal nodes is 1 fewer than the number of leaves (see
Exercise B.5-3). Each internal node performs constant work to divide the iteration
range, and each leaf corresponds to an iteration of the loop, which takes at least
constant time ($\Theta(n)$ time in this case). Thus, we can amortize the overhead of recursive spawning against the work of the iterations, contributing at most a constant
factor to the overall work.

   As a practical matter, dynamic-multithreading concurrency platforms sometimes
coarsen the leaves of the recursion by executing several iterations in a single leaf,
either automatically or under programmer control, thereby reducing the overhead
of recursive spawning. This reduced overhead comes at the expense of also reducing the parallelism, however, but if the computation has sufficient parallel slackness, near-perfect linear speedup need not be sacrificed.

   We must also account for the overhead of recursive spawning when analyzing the
span of a parallel-loop construct. Since the depth of recursive calling is logarithmic
in the number of iterations, for a parallel loop with n iterations in which the ith
iteration has span $iter_\infty(i)$, the span is

$$T_\infty(n) = \Theta(\lg n) + \max_{1 \le i \le n} iter_\infty(i) .$$

For example, for MAT-VEC on an $n \times n$ matrix, the parallel initialization loop in
lines 3–4 has span $\Theta(\lg n)$, because the recursive spawning dominates the constant-
time work of each iteration. The span of the doubly nested loops in lines 5–7
is $\Theta(n)$, because each iteration of the outer **parallel for** loop contains n iterations
of the inner (serial) **for** loop. The span of the remaining code in the procedure
is constant, and thus the span is dominated by the doubly nested loops, yielding
an overall span of $\Theta(n)$ for the whole procedure. Since the work is $\Theta(n^2)$, the
parallelism is $\Theta(n^2)/\Theta(n) = \Theta(n)$. (Exercise 27.1-6 asks you to provide an
implementation with even more parallelism.)

Race conditions

A multithreaded algorithm is *deterministic* if it always does the same thing on the
same input, no matter how the instructions are scheduled on the multicore computer. It is *nondeterministic* if its behavior might vary from run to run. Often, a
multithreaded algorithm that is intended to be deterministic fails to be, because it
contains a "determinacy race."

   Race conditions are the bane of concurrency. Famous race bugs include the
Therac-25 radiation therapy machine, which killed three people and injured sev-

eral others, and the North American Blackout of 2003, which left over 50 million people without power. These pernicious bugs are notoriously hard to find. You can run tests in the lab for days without a failure only to discover that your software sporadically crashes in the field.

A ***determinacy race*** occurs when two logically parallel instructions access the same memory location and at least one of the instructions performs a write. The following procedure illustrates a race condition:

RACE-EXAMPLE( )

1   $x = 0$
2   **parallel for** $i = 1$ **to** 2
3       $x = x + 1$
4   print x

After initializing x to 0 in line 1, RACE-EXAMPLE creates two parallel strands, each of which increments x in line 3. Although it might seem that RACE-EXAMPLE should always print the value 2 (its serialization certainly does), it could instead print the value 1. Let's see how this anomaly might occur.

When a processor increments x, the operation is not indivisible, but is composed of a sequence of instructions:

1. Read x from memory into one of the processor's registers.

2. Increment the value in the register.

3. Write the value in the register back into x in memory.

Figure 27.5(a) illustrates a computation dag representing the execution of RACE-EXAMPLE, with the strands broken down to individual instructions. Recall that since an ideal parallel computer supports sequential consistency, we can view the parallel execution of a multithreaded algorithm as an interleaving of instructions that respects the dependencies in the dag. Part (b) of the figure shows the values in an execution of the computation that elicits the anomaly. The value x is stored in memory, and r_1 and r_2 are processor registers. In step 1, one of the processors sets x to 0. In steps 2 and 3, processor 1 reads x from memory into its register r_1 and increments it, producing the value 1 in r_1. At that point, processor 2 comes into the picture, executing instructions 4–6. Processor 2 reads x from memory into register r_2; increments it, producing the value 1 in r_2; and then stores this value into x, setting x to 1. Now, processor 1 resumes with step 7, storing the value 1 in r_1 into x, which leaves the value of x unchanged. Therefore, step 8 prints the value 1, rather than 2, as the serialization would print.

We can see what has happened. If the effect of the parallel execution were that processor 1 executed all its instructions before processor 2, the value 2 would be

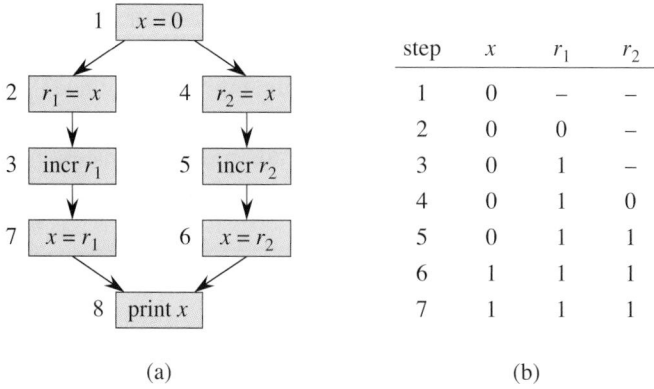

$$\text{(a)} \qquad\qquad\qquad\qquad\qquad \text{(b)}$$

Figure 27.5   Illustration of the determinacy race in RACE-EXAMPLE. **(a)** A computation dag showing the dependencies among individual instructions. The processor registers are r_1 and r_2. Instructions unrelated to the race, such as the implementation of loop control, are omitted. **(b)** An execution
sequence that elicits the bug, showing the values of x in memory and registers r_1 and r_2 for each
step in the execution sequence.

printed. Conversely, if the effect were that processor 2 executed all its instructions
before processor 1, the value 2 would still be printed. When the instructions of the
two processors execute at the same time, however, it is possible, as in this example
execution, that one of the updates to x is lost.

Of course, many executions do not elicit the bug. For example, if the execution
order were $\langle 1, 2, 3, 7, 4, 5, 6, 8 \rangle$ or $\langle 1, 4, 5, 6, 2, 3, 7, 8 \rangle$, we would get the correct result. That's the problem with determinacy races. Generally, most orderings
produce correct results—such as any in which the instructions on the left execute
before the instructions on the right, or vice versa. But some orderings generate
improper results when the instructions interleave. Consequently, races can be extremely hard to test for. You can run tests for days and never see the bug, only to
experience a catastrophic system crash in the field when the outcome is critical.

Although we can cope with races in a variety of ways, including using mutual-
exclusion locks and other methods of synchronization, for our purposes, we shall
simply ensure that strands that operate in parallel are *independent*: they have no
determinacy races among them. Thus, in a **parallel for** construct, all the iterations
should be independent. Sometimes that means using the **new** keyword to ensure
that different iterations do not operate on the same variable, as in MAT-VEC. The
new keyword allows the same variable name to be used in multiple iterations while
referring to different memory locations, which renders accesses to the variable
in the different iterations independent. Between a **spawn** and the corresponding
sync, the code of the spawned child should be independent of the code of the

parent, including code executed by additional spawned or called children. Note that arguments to a spawned child are evaluated in the parent before the actual spawn occurs, and thus the evaluation of arguments to a spawned subroutine is in series with any accesses to those arguments after the spawn.

As an example of how easy it is to generate code with races, here is a faulty implementation of multithreaded matrix-vector multiplication that achieves a span of $\Theta(\lg n)$ by parallelizing the inner **for** loop:

MAT-VEC-WRONG(A, x)

```
1   n = A.rows
2   let y be a new vector of length n
3   parallel for i = 1 to n
4        y_i = 0
5   parallel for i = 1 to n
6        parallel for new j = 1 to n
7             y_i = y_i + a_ij x_j
8   return y
```

This procedure is, unfortunately, incorrect due to races on updating y_i in line 7, which executes concurrently for all n values of j. Exercise 27.1-6 asks you to give a correct implementation with $\Theta(\lg n)$ span.

A multithreaded algorithm with races can sometimes be correct. As an example, two parallel threads might store the same value into a shared variable, and it wouldn't matter which stored the value first. Generally, however, we shall consider code with races to be illegal.

A chess lesson

We close this section with a true story that occurred during the development of the world-class multithreaded chess-playing program ★Socrates [80], although the timings below have been simplified for exposition. The program was prototyped on a 32-processor computer but was ultimately to run on a supercomputer with 512 processors. At one point, the developers incorporated an optimization into the program that reduced its running time on an important benchmark on the 32-processor machine from $T_{32} = 65$ seconds to $T'_{32} = 40$ seconds. Yet, the developers used the work and span performance measures to conclude that the optimized version, which was faster on 32 processors, would actually be slower than the original version on 512 processors. As a result, they abandoned the "optimization."

Here is their analysis. The original version of the program had work $T_1 = 2048$ seconds and span $T_\infty = 1$ second. If we treat inequality (27.4) as an equation, $T_P = T_1/P + T_\infty$, and use it as an approximation to the running time on P processors, we see that indeed $T_{32} = 2048/32 + 1 = 65$. With the optimization, the

work became $T_1' = 1024$ seconds and the span became $T_\infty' = 8$ seconds. Again using our approximation, we get $T_{32}' = 1024/32 + 8 = 40$.

The relative speeds of the two versions switch when we calculate the running times on 512 processors, however. In particular, we have $T_{512} = 2048/512 + 1 = 5$ seconds, and $T_{512}' = 1024/512 + 8 = 10$ seconds. The optimization that sped up the program on 32 processors would have made the program twice as slow on 512 processors! The optimized version's span of 8, which was not the dominant term in the running time on 32 processors, became the dominant term on 512 processors, nullifying the advantage from using more processors.

The moral of the story is that work and span can provide a better means of extrapolating performance than can measured running times.

Exercises

27.1-1
Suppose that we spawn P-FIB$(n - 2)$ in line 4 of P-FIB, rather than calling it as is done in the code. What is the impact on the asymptotic work, span, and parallelism?

27.1-2
Draw the computation dag that results from executing P-FIB(5). Assuming that each strand in the computation takes unit time, what are the work, span, and parallelism of the computation? Show how to schedule the dag on 3 processors using greedy scheduling by labeling each strand with the time step in which it is executed.

27.1-3
Prove that a greedy scheduler achieves the following time bound, which is slightly stronger than the bound proved in Theorem 27.1:

$$T_P \leq \frac{T_1 - T_\infty}{P} + T_\infty . \tag{27.5}$$

27.1-4
Construct a computation dag for which one execution of a greedy scheduler can take nearly twice the time of another execution of a greedy scheduler on the same number of processors. Describe how the two executions would proceed.

27.1-5
Professor Karan measures her deterministic multithreaded algorithm on 4, 10, and 64 processors of an ideal parallel computer using a greedy scheduler. She claims that the three runs yielded $T_4 = 80$ seconds, $T_{10} = 42$ seconds, and $T_{64} = 10$ seconds. Argue that the professor is either lying or incompetent. (*Hint:*

Use the work law (27.2), the span law (27.3), and inequality (27.5) from Exercise 27.1-3.)

27.1-6
Give a multithreaded algorithm to multiply an $n \times n$ matrix by an n-vector that achieves $\Theta(n^2/\lg n)$ parallelism while maintaining $\Theta(n^2)$ work.

27.1-7
Consider the following multithreaded pseudocode for transposing an $n \times n$ matrix A in place:

P-TRANSPOSE(A)

```
1   n = A.rows
2   parallel for j = 2 to n
3       parallel for new i = 1 to j − 1
4           exchange a_ij with a_ji
```

Analyze the work, span, and parallelism of this algorithm.

27.1-8
Suppose that we replace the **parallel for** loop in line 3 of P-TRANSPOSE (see Exercise 27.1-7) with an ordinary **for** loop. Analyze the work, span, and parallelism of the resulting algorithm.

27.1-9
For how many processors do the two versions of the chess program run equally fast, assuming that $T_P = T_1/P + T_\infty$?

27.2 Multithreaded matrix multiplication

In this section, we examine how to multithread matrix multiplication, a problem whose serial running time we studied in Section 4.2. We'll look at multithreaded algorithms based on the standard triply nested loop, as well as divide-and-conquer algorithms.

Multithreaded matrix multiplication

The first algorithm we study is the straightforward algorithm based on parallelizing the loops in the procedure SQUARE-MATRIX-MULTIPLY on page 75:

P-SQUARE-MATRIX-MULTIPLY(A, B)

1   $n = A.rows$
2   let C be a new $n \times n$ matrix
3   **parallel for** $i = 1$ **to** n
4   **parallel for new** $j = 1$ **to** n
5               $c_{ij} = 0$
6   **for new** $k = 1$ **to** n
7                     $c_{ij} = c_{ij} + a_{ik} \cdot b_{kj}$
8   **return** C

To analyze this algorithm, observe that since the serialization of the algorithm is just SQUARE-MATRIX-MULTIPLY, the work is therefore simply $T_1(n) = \Theta(n^3)$, the same as the running time of SQUARE-MATRIX-MULTIPLY. The span is $T_\infty(n) = \Theta(n)$, because it follows a path down the tree of recursion for the **parallel for** loop starting in line 3, then down the tree of recursion for the **parallel for** loop starting in line 4, and then executes all n iterations of the ordinary **for** loop starting in line 6, resulting in a total span of $\Theta(\lg n) + \Theta(\lg n) + \Theta(n) = \Theta(n)$. Thus, the parallelism is $\Theta(n^3)/\Theta(n) = \Theta(n^2)$. Exercise 27.2-3 asks you to parallelize the inner loop to obtain a parallelism of $\Theta(n^3/\lg n)$, which you cannot do straightforwardly using **parallel for**, because you would create races.

A divide-and-conquer multithreaded algorithm for matrix multiplication

As we learned in Section 4.2, we can multiply $n \times n$ matrices serially in time $\Theta(n^{\lg 7}) = O(n^{2.81})$ using Strassen's divide-and-conquer strategy, which motivates us to look at multithreading such an algorithm. We begin, as we did in Section 4.2, with multithreading a simpler divide-and-conquer algorithm.

Recall from page 77 that the SQUARE-MATRIX-MULTIPLY-RECURSIVE procedure, which multiplies two $n \times n$ matrices A and B to produce the $n \times n$ matrix C, relies on partitioning each of the three matrices into four $n/2 \times n/2$ submatrices:

$$A = \begin{pmatrix} A_{11} & A_{12} \\ A_{21} & A_{22} \end{pmatrix}, \quad B = \begin{pmatrix} B_{11} & B_{12} \\ B_{21} & B_{22} \end{pmatrix}, \quad C = \begin{pmatrix} C_{11} & C_{12} \\ C_{21} & C_{22} \end{pmatrix}.$$

Then, we can write the matrix product as

$$\begin{pmatrix} C_{11} & C_{12} \\ C_{21} & C_{22} \end{pmatrix} = \begin{pmatrix} A_{11} & A_{12} \\ A_{21} & A_{22} \end{pmatrix}\begin{pmatrix} B_{11} & B_{12} \\ B_{21} & B_{22} \end{pmatrix}$$

$$= \begin{pmatrix} A_{11}B_{11} & A_{11}B_{12} \\ A_{21}B_{11} & A_{21}B_{12} \end{pmatrix} + \begin{pmatrix} A_{12}B_{21} & A_{12}B_{22} \\ A_{22}B_{21} & A_{22}B_{22} \end{pmatrix}. \tag{27.6}$$

Thus, to multiply two $n \times n$ matrices, we perform eight multiplications of $n/2 \times n/2$ matrices and one addition of $n \times n$ matrices. The following pseudocode implements

this divide-and-conquer strategy using nested parallelism. Unlike the SQUARE-MATRIX-MULTIPLY-RECURSIVE procedure on which it is based, P-MATRIX-MULTIPLY-RECURSIVE takes the output matrix as a parameter to avoid allocating matrices unnecessarily.

P-MATRIX-MULTIPLY-RECURSIVE(C, A, B)

```
 1  n = A.rows
 2  if n == 1
 3      c₁₁ = a₁₁b₁₁
 4  else let T be a new n × n matrix
 5      partition A, B, C, and T into n/2 × n/2 submatrices
            A₁₁, A₁₂, A₂₁, A₂₂; B₁₁, B₁₂, B₂₁, B₂₂; C₁₁, C₁₂, C₂₁, C₂₂;
            and T₁₁, T₁₂, T₂₁, T₂₂; respectively
 6      spawn P-MATRIX-MULTIPLY-RECURSIVE(C₁₁, A₁₁, B₁₁)
 7      spawn P-MATRIX-MULTIPLY-RECURSIVE(C₁₂, A₁₁, B₁₂)
 8      spawn P-MATRIX-MULTIPLY-RECURSIVE(C₂₁, A₂₁, B₁₁)
 9      spawn P-MATRIX-MULTIPLY-RECURSIVE(C₂₂, A₂₁, B₁₂)
10      spawn P-MATRIX-MULTIPLY-RECURSIVE(T₁₁, A₁₂, B₂₁)
11      spawn P-MATRIX-MULTIPLY-RECURSIVE(T₁₂, A₁₂, B₂₂)
12      spawn P-MATRIX-MULTIPLY-RECURSIVE(T₂₁, A₂₂, B₂₁)
13      P-MATRIX-MULTIPLY-RECURSIVE(T₂₂, A₂₂, B₂₂)
14      sync
15      parallel for i = 1 to n
16          parallel for new j = 1 to n
17              cᵢⱼ = cᵢⱼ + tᵢⱼ
```

Line 3 handles the base case, where we are multiplying 1×1 matrices. We handle the recursive case in lines 4–17. We allocate a temporary matrix T in line 4, and line 5 partitions each of the matrices A, B, C, and T into $n/2 \times n/2$ submatrices. (As with SQUARE-MATRIX-MULTIPLY-RECURSIVE on page 77, we gloss over the minor issue of how to use index calculations to represent submatrix sections of a matrix.) The recursive call in line 6 sets the submatrix C_{11} to the submatrix product $A_{11}B_{11}$, so that C_{11} equals the first of the two terms that form its sum in equation (27.6). Similarly, lines 7–9 set C_{12}, C_{21}, and C_{22} to the first of the two terms that equal their sums in equation (27.6). Line 10 sets the submatrix T_{11} to the submatrix product $A_{12}B_{21}$, so that T_{11} equals the second of the two terms that form C_{11}'s sum. Lines 11–13 set T_{12}, T_{21}, and T_{22} to the second of the two terms that form the sums of C_{12}, C_{21}, and C_{22}, respectively. The first seven recursive calls are spawned, and the last one runs in the main strand. The **sync** statement in line 14 ensures that all the submatrix products in lines 6–13 have been computed,

after which we add the products from T into C using the doubly nested **parallel for** loops in lines 15–17.

We first analyze the work $M_1(n)$ of the P-MATRIX-MULTIPLY-RECURSIVE procedure, echoing the serial running-time analysis of its progenitor SQUARE-MATRIX-MULTIPLY-RECURSIVE. In the recursive case, we partition in $\Theta(1)$ time, perform eight recursive multiplications of $n/2 \times n/2$ matrices, and finish up with the $\Theta(n^2)$ work from adding two $n \times n$ matrices. Thus, the recurrence for the work $M_1(n)$ is

$$
\begin{aligned}
M_1(n) &= 8M_1(n/2) + \Theta(n^2) \\
&= \Theta(n^3)
\end{aligned}
$$

by case 1 of the master theorem. In other words, the work of our multithreaded algorithm is asymptotically the same as the running time of the procedure SQUARE-MATRIX-MULTIPLY in Section 4.2, with its triply nested loops.

To determine the span $M_\infty(n)$ of P-MATRIX-MULTIPLY-RECURSIVE, we first observe that the span for partitioning is $\Theta(1)$, which is dominated by the $\Theta(\lg n)$ span of the doubly nested **parallel for** loops in lines 15–17. Because the eight parallel recursive calls all execute on matrices of the same size, the maximum span for any recursive call is just the span of any one. Hence, the recurrence for the span $M_\infty(n)$ of P-MATRIX-MULTIPLY-RECURSIVE is

$$
M_\infty(n) = M_\infty(n/2) + \Theta(\lg n) . \tag{27.7}
$$

This recurrence does not fall under any of the cases of the master theorem, but it does meet the condition of Exercise 4.6-2. By Exercise 4.6-2, therefore, the solution to recurrence (27.7) is $M_\infty(n) = \Theta(\lg^2 n)$.

Now that we know the work and span of P-MATRIX-MULTIPLY-RECURSIVE, we can compute its parallelism as $M_1(n)/M_\infty(n) = \Theta(n^3/\lg^2 n)$, which is very high.

Multithreading Strassen's method

To multithread Strassen's algorithm, we follow the same general outline as on page 79, only using nested parallelism:

1. Divide the input matrices A and B and output matrix C into $n/2 \times n/2$ submatrices, as in equation (27.6). This step takes $\Theta(1)$ work and span by index calculation.

2. Create 10 matrices $S_1, S_2, \ldots, S_{10}$, each of which is $n/2 \times n/2$ and is the sum or difference of two matrices created in step 1. We can create all 10 matrices with $\Theta(n^2)$ work and $\Theta(\lg n)$ span by using doubly nested **parallel for** loops.

3. Using the submatrices created in step 1 and the 10 matrices created in step 2, recursively spawn the computation of seven $n/2 \times n/2$ matrix products $P_1, P_2, \dots, P_7$.

4. Compute the desired submatrices $C_{11}, C_{12}, C_{21}, C_{22}$ of the result matrix C by adding and subtracting various combinations of the P_i matrices, once again using doubly nested **parallel for** loops. We can compute all four submatrices with $\Theta(n^2)$ work and $\Theta(\lg n)$ span.

To analyze this algorithm, we first observe that since the serialization is the same as the original serial algorithm, the work is just the running time of the serialization, namely, $\Theta(n^{\lg 7})$. As for P-MATRIX-MULTIPLY-RECURSIVE, we can devise a recurrence for the span. In this case, seven recursive calls execute in parallel, but since they all operate on matrices of the same size, we obtain the same recurrence (27.7) as we did for P-MATRIX-MULTIPLY-RECURSIVE, which has solution $\Theta(\lg^2 n)$. Thus, the parallelism of multithreaded Strassen's method is $\Theta(n^{\lg 7}/\lg^2 n)$, which is high, though slightly less than the parallelism of P-MATRIX-MULTIPLY-RECURSIVE.

Exercises

27.2-1
Draw the computation dag for computing P-SQUARE-MATRIX-MULTIPLY on 2×2 matrices, labeling how the vertices in your diagram correspond to strands in the execution of the algorithm. Use the convention that spawn and call edges point downward, continuation edges point horizontally to the right, and return edges point upward. Assuming that each strand takes unit time, analyze the work, span, and parallelism of this computation.

27.2-2
Repeat Exercise 27.2-1 for P-MATRIX-MULTIPLY-RECURSIVE.

27.2-3
Give pseudocode for a multithreaded algorithm that multiplies two $n \times n$ matrices with work $\Theta(n^3)$ but span only $\Theta(\lg n)$. Analyze your algorithm.

27.2-4
Give pseudocode for an efficient multithreaded algorithm that multiplies a $p \times q$ matrix by a $q \times r$ matrix. Your algorithm should be highly parallel even if any of p, q, and r are 1. Analyze your algorithm.

27.2-5

Give pseudocode for an efficient multithreaded algorithm that transposes an $n \times n$ matrix in place by using divide-and-conquer and no **parallel for** loops to divide the matrix recursively into four $n/2 \times n/2$ submatrices. Analyze your algorithm.

27.2-6

Give pseudocode for an efficient multithreaded implementation of the Floyd-Warshall algorithm (see Section 25.2), which computes shortest paths between all pairs of vertices in an edge-weighted graph. Analyze your algorithm.

27.3   Multithreaded merge sort

We first saw serial merge sort in Section 2.3.1, and in Section 2.3.2 we analyzed its running time and showed it to be $\Theta(n \lg n)$. Because merge sort already uses the divide-and-conquer paradigm, it seems like a terrific candidate for multithreading using nested parallelism. We can easily modify the pseudocode so that the first recursive call is spawned:

MERGE-SORT$'(A, p, r)$

```
1  if p < r
2      q = ⌊(p + r)/2⌋
3      spawn MERGE-SORT'(A, p, q)
4      MERGE-SORT'(A, q + 1, r)
5      sync
6      MERGE(A, p, q, r)
```

Like its serial counterpart, MERGE-SORT$'$ sorts the subarray $A[p \mathrel{..} r]$. After the two recursive subroutines in lines 3 and 4 have completed, which is ensured by the **sync** statement in line 5, MERGE-SORT$'$ calls the same MERGE procedure as on page 31.

Let us analyze MERGE-SORT$'$. To do so, we first need to analyze MERGE. Recall that its serial running time to merge n elements is $\Theta(n)$. Because MERGE is serial, both its work and its span are $\Theta(n)$. Thus, the following recurrence characterizes the work $MS_1'(n)$ of MERGE-SORT$'$ on n elements:

$$
\begin{aligned}
MS_1'(n) &= 2\,MS_1'(n/2) + \Theta(n) \\
&= \Theta(n \lg n) \,,
\end{aligned}
$$

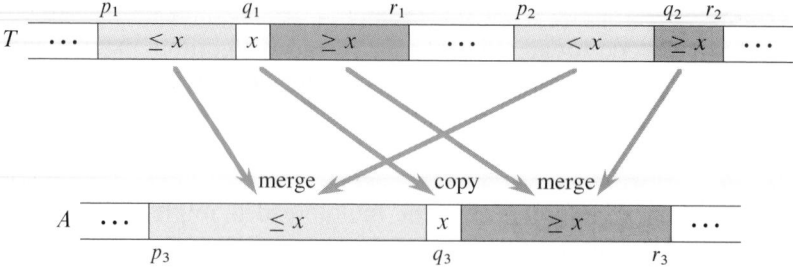

Figure 27.6 The idea behind the multithreaded merging of two sorted subarrays $T[p_1 \mathinner{\ldotp\ldotp} r_1]$ and $T[p_2 \mathinner{\ldotp\ldotp} r_2]$ into the subarray $A[p_3 \mathinner{\ldotp\ldotp} r_3]$. Letting $x = T[q_1]$ be the median of $T[p_1 \mathinner{\ldotp\ldotp} r_1]$ and q_2 be the place in $T[p_2 \mathinner{\ldotp\ldotp} r_2]$ such that x would fall between $T[q_2 - 1]$ and $T[q_2]$, every element in subarrays $T[p_1 \mathinner{\ldotp\ldotp} q_1 - 1]$ and $T[p_2 \mathinner{\ldotp\ldotp} q_2 - 1]$ (lightly shaded) is less than or equal to x, and every element in the subarrays $T[q_1 + 1 \mathinner{\ldotp\ldotp} r_1]$ and $T[q_2 + 1 \mathinner{\ldotp\ldotp} r_2]$ (heavily shaded) is at least x. To merge, we compute the index q_3 where x belongs in $A[p_3 \mathinner{\ldotp\ldotp} r_3]$, copy x into $A[q_3]$, and then recursively merge $T[p_1 \mathinner{\ldotp\ldotp} q_1 - 1]$ with $T[p_2 \mathinner{\ldotp\ldotp} q_2 - 1]$ into $A[p_3 \mathinner{\ldotp\ldotp} q_3 - 1]$ and $T[q_1 + 1 \mathinner{\ldotp\ldotp} r_1]$ with $T[q_2 \mathinner{\ldotp\ldotp} r_2]$ into $A[q_3 + 1 \mathinner{\ldotp\ldotp} r_3]$.

which is the same as the serial running time of merge sort. Since the two recursive calls of MERGE-SORT$'$ can run in parallel, the span MS'_∞ is given by the recurrence

$$
\begin{aligned}
MS'_\infty(n) &= MS'_\infty(n/2) + \Theta(n) \\
&= \Theta(n) \ .
\end{aligned}
$$

Thus, the parallelism of MERGE-SORT$'$ comes to $MS'_1(n)/MS'_\infty(n) = \Theta(\lg n)$, which is an unimpressive amount of parallelism. To sort 10 million elements, for example, it might achieve linear speedup on a few processors, but it would not scale up effectively to hundreds of processors.

You probably have already figured out where the parallelism bottleneck is in this multithreaded merge sort: the serial MERGE procedure. Although merging might initially seem to be inherently serial, we can, in fact, fashion a multithreaded version of it by using nested parallelism.

Our divide-and-conquer strategy for multithreaded merging, which is illustrated in Figure 27.6, operates on subarrays of an array T. Suppose that we are merging the two sorted subarrays $T[p_1 \mathinner{\ldotp\ldotp} r_1]$ of length $n_1 = r_1 - p_1 + 1$ and $T[p_2 \mathinner{\ldotp\ldotp} r_2]$ of length $n_2 = r_2 - p_2 + 1$ into another subarray $A[p_3 \mathinner{\ldotp\ldotp} r_3]$, of length $n_3 = r_3 - p_3 + 1 = n_1 + n_2$. Without loss of generality, we make the simplifying assumption that $n_1 \geq n_2$.

We first find the middle element $x = T[q_1]$ of the subarray $T[p_1 \mathinner{\ldotp\ldotp} r_1]$, where $q_1 = \lfloor (p_1 + r_1)/2 \rfloor$. Because the subarray is sorted, x is a median of $T[p_1 \mathinner{\ldotp\ldotp} r_1]$: every element in $T[p_1 \mathinner{\ldotp\ldotp} q_1 - 1]$ is no more than x, and every element in $T[q_1 + 1 \mathinner{\ldotp\ldotp} r_1]$ is no less than x. We then use binary search to find the

index q_2 in the subarray $T[p_2 \mathrel{..} r_2]$ so that the subarray would still be sorted if we inserted x between $T[q_2 - 1]$ and $T[q_2]$.

We next merge the original subarrays $T[p_1 \mathrel{..} r_1]$ and $T[p_2 \mathrel{..} r_2]$ into $A[p_3 \mathrel{..} r_3]$ as follows:

1. Set $q_3 = p_3 + (q_1 - p_1) + (q_2 - p_2)$.

2. Copy x into $A[q_3]$.

3. Recursively merge $T[p_1 \mathrel{..} q_1 - 1]$ with $T[p_2 \mathrel{..} q_2 - 1]$, and place the result into the subarray $A[p_3 \mathrel{..} q_3 - 1]$.

4. Recursively merge $T[q_1 + 1 \mathrel{..} r_1]$ with $T[q_2 \mathrel{..} r_2]$, and place the result into the subarray $A[q_3 + 1 \mathrel{..} r_3]$.

When we compute q_3, the quantity $q_1 - p_1$ is the number of elements in the subarray $T[p_1 \mathrel{..} q_1 - 1]$, and the quantity $q_2 - p_2$ is the number of elements in the subarray $T[p_2 \mathrel{..} q_2 - 1]$. Thus, their sum is the number of elements that end up before x in the subarray $A[p_3 \mathrel{..} r_3]$.

The base case occurs when $n_1 = n_2 = 0$, in which case we have no work to do to merge the two empty subarrays. Since we have assumed that the subarray $T[p_1 \mathrel{..} r_1]$ is at least as long as $T[p_2 \mathrel{..} r_2]$, that is, $n_1 \geq n_2$, we can check for the base case by just checking whether $n_1 = 0$. We must also ensure that the recursion properly handles the case when only one of the two subarrays is empty, which, by our assumption that $n_1 \geq n_2$, must be the subarray $T[p_2 \mathrel{..} r_2]$.

Now, let's put these ideas into pseudocode. We start with the binary search, which we express serially. The procedure $\textsc{Binary-Search}(x, T, p, r)$ takes a key x and a subarray $T[p \mathrel{..} r]$, and it returns one of the following:

- If $T[p \mathrel{..} r]$ is empty ($r < p$), then it returns the index p.

- If $x \leq T[p]$, and hence less than or equal to all the elements of $T[p \mathrel{..} r]$, then it returns the index p.

- If $x > T[p]$, then it returns the largest index q in the range $p < q \leq r + 1$ such that $T[q - 1] < x$.

Here is the pseudocode:

$\textsc{Binary-Search}(x, T, p, r)$

```
1  low = p
2  high = max(p, r + 1)
3  while low < high
4      mid = ⌊(low + high)/2⌋
5      if x ≤ T[mid]
6          high = mid
7      else low = mid + 1
8  return high
```

The call BINARY-SEARCH(x, T, p, r) takes $\Theta(\lg n)$ serial time in the worst case, where $n = r - p + 1$ is the size of the subarray on which it runs. (See Exercise 2.3-5.) Since BINARY-SEARCH is a serial procedure, its worst-case work and span are both $\Theta(\lg n)$.

We are now prepared to write pseudocode for the multithreaded merging procedure itself. Like the MERGE procedure on page 31, the P-MERGE procedure assumes that the two subarrays to be merged lie within the same array. Unlike MERGE, however, P-MERGE does not assume that the two subarrays to be merged are adjacent within the array. (That is, P-MERGE does not require that $p_2 = r_1 + 1$.) Another difference between MERGE and P-MERGE is that P-MERGE takes as an argument an output subarray A into which the merged values should be stored. The call P-MERGE$(T, p_1, r_1, p_2, r_2, A, p_3)$ merges the sorted subarrays $T[p_1 .. r_1]$ and $T[p_2 .. r_2]$ into the subarray $A[p_3 .. r_3]$, where $r_3 = p_3 + (r_1 - p_1 + 1) + (r_2 - p_2 + 1) - 1 = p_3 + (r_1 - p_1) + (r_2 - p_2) + 1$ and is not provided as an input.

P-MERGE$(T, p_1, r_1, p_2, r_2, A, p_3)$

```
 1   n₁ = r₁ - p₁ + 1
 2   n₂ = r₂ - p₂ + 1
 3   if n₁ < n₂                    // ensure that n₁ ≥ n₂
 4       exchange p₁ with p₂
 5       exchange r₁ with r₂
 6       exchange n₁ with n₂
 7   if n₁ == 0                    // both empty?
 8       return
 9   else q₁ = ⌊(p₁ + r₁)/2⌋
10       q₂ = BINARY-SEARCH(T[q₁], T, p₂, r₂)
11       q₃ = p₃ + (q₁ - p₁) + (q₂ - p₂)
12       A[q₃] = T[q₁]
13       spawn P-MERGE(T, p₁, q₁ - 1, p₂, q₂ - 1, A, p₃)
14       P-MERGE(T, q₁ + 1, r₁, q₂, r₂, A, q₃ + 1)
15       sync
```

The P-MERGE procedure works as follows. Lines 1–2 compute the lengths n_1 and n_2 of the subarrays $T[p_1 .. r_1]$ and $T[p_2 .. r_2]$, respectively. Lines 3–6 enforce the assumption that $n_1 \geq n_2$. Line 7 tests for the base case, where the subarray $T[p_1 .. r_1]$ is empty (and hence so is $T[p_2 .. r_2]$), in which case we simply return. Lines 9–15 implement the divide-and-conquer strategy. Line 9 computes the midpoint of $T[p_1 .. r_1]$, and line 10 finds the point q_2 in $T[p_2 .. r_2]$ such that all elements in $T[p_2 .. q_2 - 1]$ are less than $T[q_1]$ (which corresponds to x) and all the elements in $T[q_2 .. r_2]$ are at least as large as $T[q_1]$. Line 11 com-

putes the index q_3 of the element that divides the output subarray $A[p_3 .. r_3]$ into $A[p_3 .. q_3 - 1]$ and $A[q_3+1 .. r_3]$, and then line 12 copies $T[q_1]$ directly into $A[q_3]$.

Then, we recurse using nested parallelism. Line 13 spawns the first subproblem, while line 14 calls the second subproblem in parallel. The **sync** statement in line 15 ensures that the subproblems have completed before the procedure returns. (Since every procedure implicitly executes a **sync** before returning, we could have omitted the **sync** statement in line 15, but including it is good coding practice.) There is some cleverness in the coding to ensure that when the subarray $T[p_2 .. r_2]$ is empty, the code operates correctly. The way it works is that on each recursive call, a median element of $T[p_1 .. r_1]$ is placed into the output subarray, until $T[p_1 .. r_1]$ itself finally becomes empty, triggering the base case.

Analysis of multithreaded merging

We first derive a recurrence for the span $PM_\infty(n)$ of P-MERGE, where the two subarrays contain a total of $n = n_1 + n_2$ elements. Because the spawn in line 13 and the call in line 14 operate logically in parallel, we need examine only the costlier of the two calls. The key is to understand that in the worst case, the maximum number of elements in either of the recursive calls can be at most $3n/4$, which we see as follows. Because lines 3–6 ensure that $n_2 \leq n_1$, it follows that $n_2 = 2n_2/2 \leq (n_1 + n_2)/2 = n/2$. In the worst case, one of the two recursive calls merges $\lfloor n_1/2 \rfloor$ elements of $T[p_1 .. r_1]$ with all n_2 elements of $T[p_2 .. r_2]$, and hence the number of elements involved in the call is

$$
\begin{aligned}
\lfloor n_1/2 \rfloor + n_2 \ &\leq\ n_1/2 + n_2/2 + n_2/2 \\
&=\ (n_1 + n_2)/2 + n_2/2 \\
&\leq\ n/2 + n/4 \\
&=\ 3n/4 .
\end{aligned}
$$

Adding in the $\Theta(\lg n)$ cost of the call to BINARY-SEARCH in line 10, we obtain the following recurrence for the worst-case span:

$$PM_\infty(n) = PM_\infty(3n/4) + \Theta(\lg n) . \tag{27.8}$$

(For the base case, the span is $\Theta(1)$, since lines 1–8 execute in constant time.) This recurrence does not fall under any of the cases of the master theorem, but it meets the condition of Exercise 4.6-2. Therefore, the solution to recurrence (27.8) is $PM_\infty(n) = \Theta(\lg^2 n)$.

We now analyze the work $PM_1(n)$ of P-MERGE on n elements, which turns out to be $\Theta(n)$. Since each of the n elements must be copied from array T to array A, we have $PM_1(n) = \Omega(n)$. Thus, it remains only to show that $PM_1(n) = O(n)$.

We shall first derive a recurrence for the worst-case work. The binary search in line 10 costs $\Theta(\lg n)$ in the worst case, which dominates the other work outside

of the recursive calls. For the recursive calls, observe that although the recursive calls in lines 13 and 14 might merge different numbers of elements, together the two recursive calls merge at most n elements (actually $n - 1$ elements, since $T[q_1]$ does not participate in either recursive call). Moreover, as we saw in analyzing the span, a recursive call operates on at most $3n/4$ elements. We therefore obtain the recurrence

$$PM_1(n) = PM_1(\alpha n) + PM_1((1 - \alpha)n) + O(\lg n) , \qquad (27.9)$$

where α lies in the range $1/4 \leq \alpha \leq 3/4$, and where we understand that the actual value of α may vary for each level of recursion.

We prove that recurrence (27.9) has solution $PM_1 = O(n)$ via the substitution method. Assume that $PM_1(n) \leq c_1 n - c_2 \lg n$ for some positive constants c_1 and c_2. Substituting gives us

$$
\begin{aligned}
PM_1(n) &\leq (c_1 \alpha n - c_2 \lg(\alpha n)) + (c_1(1 - \alpha)n - c_2 \lg((1 - \alpha)n)) + \Theta(\lg n) \\
&= c_1(\alpha + (1 - \alpha))n - c_2(\lg(\alpha n) + \lg((1 - \alpha)n)) + \Theta(\lg n) \\
&= c_1 n - c_2(\lg \alpha + \lg n + \lg(1 - \alpha) + \lg n) + \Theta(\lg n) \\
&= c_1 n - c_2 \lg n - (c_2(\lg n + \lg(\alpha(1 - \alpha))) - \Theta(\lg n)) \\
&\leq c_1 n - c_2 \lg n ,
\end{aligned}
$$

since we can choose c_2 large enough that $c_2(\lg n + \lg(\alpha(1 - \alpha)))$ dominates the $\Theta(\lg n)$ term. Furthermore, we can choose c_1 large enough to satisfy the base conditions of the recurrence. Since the work $PM_1(n)$ of P-MERGE is both $\Omega(n)$ and $O(n)$, we have $PM_1(n) = \Theta(n)$.

The parallelism of P-MERGE is $PM_1(n)/PM_\infty(n) = \Theta(n/\lg^2 n)$.

Multithreaded merge sort

Now that we have a nicely parallelized multithreaded merging procedure, we can incorporate it into a multithreaded merge sort. This version of merge sort is similar to the MERGE-SORT′ procedure we saw earlier, but unlike MERGE-SORT′, it takes as an argument an output subarray B, which will hold the sorted result. In particular, the call P-MERGE-SORT(A, p, r, B, s) sorts the elements in $A[p \mathinner{..} r]$ and stores them in $B[s \mathinner{..} s + r - p]$.

P-MERGE-SORT(A, p, r, B, s)

```
 1  n = r − p + 1
 2  if n == 1
 3      B[s] = A[p]
 4  else let T[1 .. n] be a new array
 5      q = ⌊(p + r)/2⌋
 6      q′ = q − p + 1
 7      spawn P-MERGE-SORT(A, p, q, T, 1)
 8      P-MERGE-SORT(A, q + 1, r, T, q′ + 1)
 9      sync
10      P-MERGE(T, 1, q′, q′ + 1, n, B, s)
```

After line 1 computes the number n of elements in the input subarray $A[p .. r]$, lines 2–3 handle the base case when the array has only 1 element. Lines 4–6 set up for the recursive spawn in line 7 and call in line 8, which operate in parallel. In particular, line 4 allocates a temporary array T with n elements to store the results of the recursive merge sorting. Line 5 calculates the index q of $A[p .. r]$ to divide the elements into the two subarrays $A[p .. q]$ and $A[q + 1 .. r]$ that will be sorted recursively, and line 6 goes on to compute the number q' of elements in the first subarray $A[p .. q]$, which line 8 uses to determine the starting index in T of where to store the sorted result of $A[q + 1 .. r]$. At that point, the spawn and recursive call are made, followed by the **sync** in line 9, which forces the procedure to wait until the spawned procedure is done. Finally, line 10 calls P-MERGE to merge the sorted subarrays, now in $T[1 .. q']$ and $T[q' + 1 .. n]$, into the output subarray $B[s .. s + r − p]$.

Analysis of multithreaded merge sort

We start by analyzing the work $PMS_1(n)$ of P-MERGE-SORT, which is considerably easier than analyzing the work of P-MERGE. Indeed, the work is given by the recurrence

$$PMS_1(n) = 2\,PMS_1(n/2) + PM_1(n)$$
$$= 2\,PMS_1(n/2) + \Theta(n) .$$

This recurrence is the same as the recurrence (4.4) for ordinary MERGE-SORT from Section 2.3.1 and has solution $PMS_1(n) = \Theta(n \lg n)$ by case 2 of the master theorem.

We now derive and analyze a recurrence for the worst-case span $PMS_\infty(n)$. Because the two recursive calls to P-MERGE-SORT on lines 7 and 8 operate logically in parallel, we can ignore one of them, obtaining the recurrence

$$PMS_\infty(n) \;=\; PMS_\infty(n/2) + PM_\infty(n)$$
$$\;=\; PMS_\infty(n/2) + \Theta(\lg^2 n) \,. \tag{27.10}$$

As for recurrence (27.8), the master theorem does not apply to recurrence (27.10), but Exercise 4.6-2 does. The solution is $PMS_\infty(n) = \Theta(\lg^3 n)$, and so the span of P-MERGE-SORT is $\Theta(\lg^3 n)$.

Parallel merging gives P-MERGE-SORT a significant parallelism advantage over MERGE-SORT′. Recall that the parallelism of MERGE-SORT′, which calls the serial MERGE procedure, is only $\Theta(\lg n)$. For P-MERGE-SORT, the parallelism is

$$PMS_1(n)/PMS_\infty(n) \;=\; \Theta(n \lg n)/\Theta(\lg^3 n)$$
$$\;=\; \Theta(n/\lg^2 n) \,,$$

which is much better both in theory and in practice. A good implementation in practice would sacrifice some parallelism by coarsening the base case in order to reduce the constants hidden by the asymptotic notation. The straightforward way to coarsen the base case is to switch to an ordinary serial sort, perhaps quicksort, when the size of the array is sufficiently small.

Exercises

27.3-1
Explain how to coarsen the base case of P-MERGE.

27.3-2
Instead of finding a median element in the larger subarray, as P-MERGE does, consider a variant that finds a median element of all the elements in the two sorted subarrays using the result of Exercise 9.3-8. Give pseudocode for an efficient multithreaded merging procedure that uses this median-finding procedure. Analyze your algorithm.

27.3-3
Give an efficient multithreaded algorithm for partitioning an array around a pivot, as is done by the PARTITION procedure on page 171. You need not partition the array in place. Make your algorithm as parallel as possible. Analyze your algorithm. (*Hint:* You may need an auxiliary array and may need to make more than one pass over the input elements.)

27.3-4
Give a multithreaded version of RECURSIVE-FFT on page 911. Make your implementation as parallel as possible. Analyze your algorithm.

27.3-5 ★

Give a multithreaded version of RANDOMIZED-SELECT on page 216. Make your implementation as parallel as possible. Analyze your algorithm. (*Hint:* Use the partitioning algorithm from Exercise 27.3-3.)

27.3-6 ★

Show how to multithread SELECT from Section 9.3. Make your implementation as parallel as possible. Analyze your algorithm.

Problems

27-1   *Implementing parallel loops using nested parallelism*

Consider the following multithreaded algorithm for performing pairwise addition on n-element arrays $A[1 \ldots n]$ and $B[1 \ldots n]$, storing the sums in $C[1 \ldots n]$:

SUM-ARRAYS(A, B, C)

1   **parallel for** $i = 1$ **to** $A.length$
2       $C[i] = A[i] + B[i]$

a. Rewrite the parallel loop in SUM-ARRAYS using nested parallelism (**spawn** and **sync**) in the manner of MAT-VEC-MAIN-LOOP. Analyze the parallelism of your implementation.

Consider the following alternative implementation of the parallel loop, which contains a value *grain-size* to be specified:

SUM-ARRAYS'(A, B, C)

1   $n = A.length$
2   *grain-size* = ?   **//** to be determined
3   $r = \lceil n/grain\text{-}size \rceil$
4   **for** $k = 0$ **to** $r - 1$
5   **spawn** ADD-SUBARRAY($A, B, C, k \cdot grain\text{-}size + 1,$
                            $\min((k + 1) \cdot grain\text{-}size, n))$

6   **sync**

ADD-SUBARRAY(A, B, C, i, j)

1   **for** $k = i$ **to** j
2       $C[k] = A[k] + B[k]$

b. Suppose that we set *grain-size* $= 1$. What is the parallelism of this implementation?

c. Give a formula for the span of SUM-ARRAYS′ in terms of n and *grain-size*. Derive the best value for *grain-size* to maximize parallelism.

27-2   Saving temporary space in matrix multiplication

The P-MATRIX-MULTIPLY-RECURSIVE procedure has the disadvantage that it must allocate a temporary matrix T of size $n \times n$, which can adversely affect the constants hidden by the Θ-notation. The P-MATRIX-MULTIPLY-RECURSIVE procedure does have high parallelism, however. For example, ignoring the constants in the Θ-notation, the parallelism for multiplying 1000×1000 matrices comes to approximately $1000^3/10^2 = 10^7$, since $\lg 1000 \approx 10$. Most parallel computers have far fewer than 10 million processors.

a. Describe a recursive multithreaded algorithm that eliminates the need for the temporary matrix T at the cost of increasing the span to $\Theta(n)$. (*Hint:* Compute $C = C + AB$ following the general strategy of P-MATRIX-MULTIPLY-RECURSIVE, but initialize C in parallel and insert a **sync** in a judiciously chosen location.)

b. Give and solve recurrences for the work and span of your implementation.

c. Analyze the parallelism of your implementation. Ignoring the constants in the Θ-notation, estimate the parallelism on 1000×1000 matrices. Compare with the parallelism of P-MATRIX-MULTIPLY-RECURSIVE.

27-3   Multithreaded matrix algorithms

a. Parallelize the LU-DECOMPOSITION procedure on page 821 by giving pseudocode for a multithreaded version of this algorithm. Make your implementation as parallel as possible, and analyze its work, span, and parallelism.

b. Do the same for LUP-DECOMPOSITION on page 824.

c. Do the same for LUP-SOLVE on page 817.

d. Do the same for a multithreaded algorithm based on equation (28.13) for inverting a symmetric positive-definite matrix.

27-4   *Multithreading reductions and prefix computations*

A ⊗-*reduction* of an array $x[1 .. n]$, where $\otimes$ is an associative operator, is the value

$$y = x[1] \otimes x[2] \otimes \cdots \otimes x[n] \ .$$

The following procedure computes the $\otimes$-reduction of a subarray $x[i .. j]$ serially.

REDUCE(x, i, j)

1   $y = x[i]$
2   **for** $k = i + 1$ **to** j
3       $y = y \otimes x[k]$
4   **return** y

a. Use nested parallelism to implement a multithreaded algorithm P-REDUCE, which performs the same function with $\Theta(n)$ work and $\Theta(\lg n)$ span. Analyze your algorithm.

A related problem is that of computing a ⊗-*prefix computation*, sometimes called a ⊗-*scan*, on an array $x[1 .. n]$, where $\otimes$ is once again an associative operator. The $\otimes$-scan produces the array $y[1 .. n]$ given by

$$
\begin{aligned}
y[1] &= x[1] \,, \\
y[2] &= x[1] \otimes x[2] \,, \\
y[3] &= x[1] \otimes x[2] \otimes x[3] \,, \\
&\vdots \\
y[n] &= x[1] \otimes x[2] \otimes x[3] \otimes \cdots \otimes x[n] \,,
\end{aligned}
$$

that is, all prefixes of the array x "summed" using the $\otimes$ operator. The following serial procedure SCAN performs a $\otimes$-prefix computation:

SCAN(x)

1   $n = x.length$
2   let $y[1 .. n]$ be a new array
3   $y[1] = x[1]$
4   **for** $i = 2$ **to** n
5       $y[i] = y[i - 1] \otimes x[i]$
6   **return** y

Unfortunately, multithreading SCAN is not straightforward. For example, changing the **for** loop to a **parallel for** loop would create races, since each iteration of the loop body depends on the previous iteration. The following procedure P-SCAN-1 performs the $\otimes$-prefix computation in parallel, albeit inefficiently:

P-SCAN-1(x)

1 $n = x.length$
2 let $y[1 .. n]$ be a new array
3 P-SCAN-1-AUX($x, y, 1, n$)
4 **return** y

P-SCAN-1-AUX(x, y, i, j)

1 **parallel for** $l = i$ **to** j
2      $y[l] = $ P-REDUCE($x, 1, l$)

b. Analyze the work, span, and parallelism of P-SCAN-1.

By using nested parallelism, we can obtain a more efficient $\otimes$-prefix computation:

P-SCAN-2(x)

1 $n = x.length$
2 let $y[1 .. n]$ be a new array
3 P-SCAN-2-AUX($x, y, 1, n$)
4 **return** y

P-SCAN-2-AUX(x, y, i, j)

1 **if** $i == j$
2      $y[i] = x[i]$
3 **else** $k = \lfloor (i + j)/2 \rfloor$
4   **spawn** P-SCAN-2-AUX(x, y, i, k)
5   P-SCAN-2-AUX($x, y, k + 1, j$)
6   **sync**
7   **parallel for** $l = k + 1$ **to** j
8          $y[l] = y[k] \otimes y[l]$

c. Argue that P-SCAN-2 is correct, and analyze its work, span, and parallelism.

We can improve on both P-SCAN-1 and P-SCAN-2 by performing the $\otimes$-prefix computation in two distinct passes over the data. On the first pass, we gather the terms for various contiguous subarrays of x into a temporary array t, and on the second pass we use the terms in t to compute the final result y. The following pseudocode implements this strategy, but certain expressions have been omitted:

P-SCAN-3(x)

```
1   n = x.length
2   let y[1 .. n] and t[1 .. n] be new arrays
3   y[1] = x[1]
4   if n > 1
5       P-SCAN-UP(x, t, 2, n)
6       P-SCAN-DOWN(x[1], x, t, y, 2, n)
7   return y
```

P-SCAN-UP(x, t, i, j)

```
1   if i == j
2       return x[i]
3   else
4       k = ⌊(i + j)/2⌋
5       t[k] = spawn P-SCAN-UP(x, t, i, k)
6       right = P-SCAN-UP(x, t, k + 1, j)
7       sync
8       return _____              // fill in the blank
```

P-SCAN-DOWN(v, x, t, y, i, j)

```
1   if i == j
2       y[i] = v ⊗ x[i]
3   else
4       k = ⌊(i + j)/2⌋
5       spawn P-SCAN-DOWN(_____, x, t, y, i, k)   // fill in the blank
6       P-SCAN-DOWN(_____, x, t, y, k + 1, j)      // fill in the blank
7       sync
```

d. Fill in the three missing expressions in line 8 of P-SCAN-UP and lines 5 and 6 of P-SCAN-DOWN. Argue that with expressions you supplied, P-SCAN-3 is correct. (*Hint:* Prove that the value v passed to P-SCAN-DOWN(v, x, t, y, i, j) satisfies $v = x[1] \otimes x[2] \otimes \cdots \otimes x[i - 1]$.)

e. Analyze the work, span, and parallelism of P-SCAN-3.

27-5   *Multithreading a simple stencil calculation*

Computational science is replete with algorithms that require the entries of an array to be filled in with values that depend on the values of certain already computed neighboring entries, along with other information that does not change over the course of the computation. The pattern of neighboring entries does not change during the computation and is called a *stencil*. For example, Section 15.4 presents

a stencil algorithm to compute a longest common subsequence, where the value in entry $c[i, j]$ depends only on the values in $c[i - 1, j], c[i, j - 1]$, and $c[i - 1, j - 1]$, as well as the elements x_i and y_j within the two sequences given as inputs. The input sequences are fixed, but the algorithm fills in the two-dimensional array c so that it computes entry $c[i, j]$ after computing all three entries $c[i - 1, j], c[i, j - 1]$, and $c[i - 1, j - 1]$.

In this problem, we examine how to use nested parallelism to multithread a simple stencil calculation on an $n \times n$ array A in which, of the values in A, the value placed into entry $A[i, j]$ depends only on values in $A[i', j']$, where $i' \leq i$ and $j' \leq j$ (and of course, $i' \neq i$ or $j' \neq j$). In other words, the value in an entry depends only on values in entries that are above it and/or to its left, along with static information outside of the array. Furthermore, we assume throughout this problem that once we have filled in the entries upon which $A[i, j]$ depends, we can fill in $A[i, j]$ in $\Theta(1)$ time (as in the LCS-LENGTH procedure of Section 15.4).

We can partition the $n \times n$ array A into four $n/2 \times n/2$ subarrays as follows:

$$A = \begin{pmatrix} A_{11} & A_{12} \\ A_{21} & A_{22} \end{pmatrix}. \tag{27.11}$$

Observe now that we can fill in subarray A_{11} recursively, since it does not depend on the entries of the other three subarrays. Once A_{11} is complete, we can continue to fill in A_{12} and A_{21} recursively in parallel, because although they both depend on A_{11}, they do not depend on each other. Finally, we can fill in A_{22} recursively.

a. Give multithreaded pseudocode that performs this simple stencil calculation using a divide-and-conquer algorithm SIMPLE-STENCIL based on the decomposition (27.11) and the discussion above. (Don't worry about the details of the base case, which depends on the specific stencil.) Give and solve recurrences for the work and span of this algorithm in terms of n. What is the parallelism?

b. Modify your solution to part (a) to divide an $n \times n$ array into nine $n/3 \times n/3$ subarrays, again recursing with as much parallelism as possible. Analyze this algorithm. How much more or less parallelism does this algorithm have compared with the algorithm from part (a)?

c. Generalize your solutions to parts (a) and (b) as follows. Choose an integer $b \geq 2$. Divide an $n \times n$ array into b^2 subarrays, each of size $n/b \times n/b$, recursing with as much parallelism as possible. In terms of n and b, what are the work, span, and parallelism of your algorithm? Argue that, using this approach, the parallelism must be $o(n)$ for any choice of $b \geq 2$. (*Hint:* For this last argument, show that the exponent of n in the parallelism is strictly less than 1 for any choice of $b \geq 2$.)

d. Give pseudocode for a multithreaded algorithm for this simple stencil calculation that achieves $\Theta(n/\lg n)$ parallelism. Argue using notions of work and span that the problem, in fact, has $\Theta(n)$ inherent parallelism. As it turns out, the divide-and-conquer nature of our multithreaded pseudocode does not let us achieve this maximal parallelism.

27-6 *Randomized multithreaded algorithms*

Just as with ordinary serial algorithms, we sometimes want to implement randomized multithreaded algorithms. This problem explores how to adapt the various performance measures in order to handle the expected behavior of such algorithms. It also asks you to design and analyze a multithreaded algorithm for randomized quicksort.

a. Explain how to modify the work law (27.2), span law (27.3), and greedy scheduler bound (27.4) to work with expectations when T_P, T_1, and T_∞ are all random variables.

b. Consider a randomized multithreaded algorithm for which 1% of the time we have $T_1 = 10^4$ and $T_{10,000} = 1$, but for 99% of the time we have $T_1 = T_{10,000} = 10^9$. Argue that the *speedup* of a randomized multithreaded algorithm should be defined as $E[T_1]/E[T_P]$, rather than $E[T_1/T_P]$.

c. Argue that the *parallelism* of a randomized multithreaded algorithm should be defined as the ratio $E[T_1]/E[T_\infty]$.

d. Multithread the RANDOMIZED-QUICKSORT algorithm on page 179 by using nested parallelism. (Do not parallelize RANDOMIZED-PARTITION.) Give the pseudocode for your P-RANDOMIZED-QUICKSORT algorithm.

e. Analyze your multithreaded algorithm for randomized quicksort. (*Hint:* Review the analysis of RANDOMIZED-SELECT on page 216.)

Chapter notes

Parallel computers, models for parallel computers, and algorithmic models for parallel programming have been around in various forms for years. Prior editions of this book included material on sorting networks and the PRAM (Parallel Random-Access Machine) model. The data-parallel model [48, 168] is another popular algorithmic programming model, which features operations on vectors and matrices as primitives.

Graham [149] and Brent [55] showed that there exist schedulers achieving the bound of Theorem 27.1. Eager, Zahorjan, and Lazowska [98] showed that any greedy scheduler achieves this bound and proposed the methodology of using work and span (although not by those names) to analyze parallel algorithms. Blelloch [47] developed an algorithmic programming model based on work and span (which he called the "depth" of the computation) for data-parallel programming. Blumofe and Leiserson [52] gave a distributed scheduling algorithm for dynamic multi-threading based on randomized "work-stealing" and showed that it achieves the bound $E[T_P] \leq T_1/P + O(T_\infty)$. Arora, Blumofe, and Plaxton [19] and Blelloch, Gibbons, and Matias [49] also provided provably good algorithms for scheduling dynamic multithreaded computations.

The multithreaded pseudocode and programming model were heavily influenced by the Cilk [51, 118] project at MIT and the Cilk++ [71] extensions to C++ distributed by Cilk Arts, Inc. Many of the multithreaded algorithms in this chapter appeared in unpublished lecture notes by C. E. Leiserson and H. Prokop and have been implemented in Cilk or Cilk++. The multithreaded merge-sorting algorithm was inspired by an algorithm of Akl [12].

The notion of sequential consistency is due to Lamport [223].

28 Matrix Operations

Because operations on matrices lie at the heart of scientific computing, efficient algorithms for working with matrices have many practical applications. This chapter focuses on how to multiply matrices and solve sets of simultaneous linear equations. Appendix D reviews the basics of matrices.

Section 28.1 shows how to solve a set of linear equations using LUP decompositions. Then, Section 28.2 explores the close relationship between multiplying and inverting matrices. Finally, Section 28.3 discusses the important class of symmetric positive-definite matrices and shows how we can use them to find a least-squares solution to an overdetermined set of linear equations.

One important issue that arises in practice is *numerical stability*. Due to the limited precision of floating-point representations in actual computers, round-off errors in numerical computations may become amplified over the course of a computation, leading to incorrect results; we call such computations *numerically unstable*. Although we shall briefly consider numerical stability on occasion, we do not focus on it in this chapter. We refer you to the excellent book by Golub and Van Loan [144] for a thorough discussion of stability issues.

28.1 Solving systems of linear equations

Numerous applications need to solve sets of simultaneous linear equations. We can formulate a linear system as a matrix equation in which each matrix or vector element belongs to a field, typically the real numbers $\mathbb{R}$. This section discusses how to solve a system of linear equations using a method called LUP decomposition.

We start with a set of linear equations in n unknowns $x_1, x_2, \ldots, x_n$:

$$a_{11}x_1 + a_{12}x_2 + \cdots + a_{1n}x_n = b_1 \, ,$$
$$a_{21}x_1 + a_{22}x_2 + \cdots + a_{2n}x_n = b_2 \, ,$$
$$\vdots \qquad\qquad\qquad\qquad \tag{28.1}$$
$$a_{n1}x_1 + a_{n2}x_2 + \cdots + a_{nn}x_n = b_n \, .$$

A **solution** to the equations (28.1) is a set of values for $x_1, x_2, \ldots, x_n$ that satisfy all of the equations simultaneously. In this section, we treat only the case in which there are exactly n equations in n unknowns.

We can conveniently rewrite equations (28.1) as the matrix-vector equation

$$\begin{pmatrix} a_{11} & a_{12} & \cdots & a_{1n} \\ a_{21} & a_{22} & \cdots & a_{2n} \\ \vdots & \vdots & \ddots & \vdots \\ a_{n1} & a_{n2} & \cdots & a_{nn} \end{pmatrix} \begin{pmatrix} x_1 \\ x_2 \\ \vdots \\ x_n \end{pmatrix} = \begin{pmatrix} b_1 \\ b_2 \\ \vdots \\ b_n \end{pmatrix}$$

or, equivalently, letting $A = (a_{ij})$, $x = (x_i)$, and $b = (b_i)$, as

$$Ax = b \, . \tag{28.2}$$

If A is nonsingular, it possesses an inverse A^{-1}, and

$$x = A^{-1}b \tag{28.3}$$

is the solution vector. We can prove that x is the unique solution to equation (28.2) as follows. If there are two solutions, x and x', then $Ax = Ax' = b$ and, letting I denote an identity matrix,

$$\begin{aligned} x &= Ix \\ &= (A^{-1}A)x \\ &= A^{-1}(Ax) \\ &= A^{-1}(Ax') \\ &= (A^{-1}A)x' \\ &= x' \, . \end{aligned}$$

In this section, we shall be concerned predominantly with the case in which A is nonsingular or, equivalently (by Theorem D.1), the rank of A is equal to the number n of unknowns. There are other possibilities, however, which merit a brief discussion. If the number of equations is less than the number n of unknowns—or, more generally, if the rank of A is less than n—then the system is **underdetermined**. An underdetermined system typically has infinitely many solutions, although it may have no solutions at all if the equations are inconsistent. If the number of equations exceeds the number n of unknowns, the system is **overdetermined**, and there may not exist any solutions. Section 28.3 addresses the important

problem of finding good approximate solutions to overdetermined systems of linear equations.

Let us return to our problem of solving the system $Ax = b$ of n equations in n unknowns. We could compute A^{-1} and then, using equation (28.3), multiply b by A^{-1}, yielding $x = A^{-1}b$. This approach suffers in practice from numerical instability. Fortunately, another approach—LUP decomposition—is numerically stable and has the further advantage of being faster in practice.

Overview of LUP decomposition

The idea behind LUP decomposition is to find three $n \times n$ matrices L, U, and P such that

$$PA = LU \; , \tag{28.4}$$

where

- L is a unit lower-triangular matrix,

- U is an upper-triangular matrix, and

- P is a permutation matrix.

We call matrices L, U, and P satisfying equation (28.4) an ***LUP decomposition*** of the matrix A. We shall show that every nonsingular matrix A possesses such a decomposition.

Computing an LUP decomposition for the matrix A has the advantage that we can more easily solve linear systems when they are triangular, as is the case for both matrices L and U. Once we have found an LUP decomposition for A, we can solve equation (28.2), $Ax = b$, by solving only triangular linear systems, as follows. Multiplying both sides of $Ax = b$ by P yields the equivalent equation $PAx = Pb$, which, by Exercise D.1-4, amounts to permuting the equations (28.1). Using our decomposition (28.4), we obtain

$$LUx = Pb \; .$$

We can now solve this equation by solving two triangular linear systems. Let us define $y = Ux$, where x is the desired solution vector. First, we solve the lower-triangular system

$$Ly = Pb \tag{28.5}$$

for the unknown vector y by a method called "forward substitution." Having solved for y, we then solve the upper-triangular system

$$Ux = y \tag{28.6}$$

for the unknown x by a method called "back substitution." Because the permutation matrix P is invertible (Exercise D.2-3), multiplying both sides of equation (28.4) by P^{-1} gives $P^{-1}PA = P^{-1}LU$, so that

$$A = P^{-1}LU \ . \tag{28.7}$$

Hence, the vector x is our solution to $Ax = b$:

$$
\begin{aligned}
Ax &= P^{-1}LUx &&\text{(by equation (28.7))} \\
&= P^{-1}Ly &&\text{(by equation (28.6))} \\
&= P^{-1}Pb &&\text{(by equation (28.5))} \\
&= b \ .
\end{aligned}
$$

Our next step is to show how forward and back substitution work and then attack the problem of computing the LUP decomposition itself.

Forward and back substitution

Forward substitution can solve the lower-triangular system (28.5) in $\Theta(n^2)$ time, given L, P, and b. For convenience, we represent the permutation P compactly by an array $\pi[1 \mathinner{.\,.} n]$. For $i = 1, 2, \ldots, n$, the entry $\pi[i]$ indicates that $P_{i,\pi[i]} = 1$ and $P_{ij} = 0$ for $j \neq \pi[i]$. Thus, PA has $a_{\pi[i],j}$ in row i and column j, and Pb has $b_{\pi[i]}$ as its ith element. Since L is unit lower-triangular, we can rewrite equation (28.5) as

$$
\begin{aligned}
y_1 &= b_{\pi[1]} \ , \\
l_{21}y_1 + y_2 &= b_{\pi[2]} \ , \\
l_{31}y_1 + l_{32}y_2 + y_3 &= b_{\pi[3]} \ , \\
&\vdots \\
l_{n1}y_1 + l_{n2}y_2 + l_{n3}y_3 + \cdots + y_n &= b_{\pi[n]} \ .
\end{aligned}
$$

The first equation tells us that $y_1 = b_{\pi[1]}$. Knowing the value of y_1, we can substitute it into the second equation, yielding

$$y_2 = b_{\pi[2]} - l_{21}y_1 \ .$$

Now, we can substitute both y_1 and y_2 into the third equation, obtaining

$$y_3 = b_{\pi[3]} - (l_{31}y_1 + l_{32}y_2) \ .$$

In general, we substitute $y_1, y_2, \ldots, y_{i-1}$ "forward" into the ith equation to solve for y_i:

$$y_i = b_{\pi[i]} - \sum_{j=1}^{i-1} l_{ij} y_j .$$

Having solved for y, we solve for x in equation (28.6) using **_back substitution_**, which is similar to forward substitution. Here, we solve the nth equation first and work backward to the first equation. Like forward substitution, this process runs in $\Theta(n^2)$ time. Since U is upper-triangular, we can rewrite the system (28.6) as

$$
\begin{aligned}
u_{11}x_1 + u_{12}x_2 + \cdots + \quad u_{1,n-2}x_{n-2} + \quad u_{1,n-1}x_{n-1} + \quad u_{1n}x_n &= y_1 , \\
u_{22}x_2 + \cdots + \quad u_{2,n-2}x_{n-2} + \quad u_{2,n-1}x_{n-1} + \quad u_{2n}x_n &= y_2 , \\
&\vdots \\
u_{n-2,n-2}x_{n-2} + u_{n-2,n-1}x_{n-1} + u_{n-2,n}x_n &= y_{n-2} , \\
u_{n-1,n-1}x_{n-1} + u_{n-1,n}x_n &= y_{n-1} , \\
u_{n,n}x_n &= y_n .
\end{aligned}
$$

Thus, we can solve for $x_n, x_{n-1}, \ldots, x_1$ successively as follows:

$$
\begin{aligned}
x_n &= y_n/u_{n,n} , \\
x_{n-1} &= (y_{n-1} - u_{n-1,n}x_n)/u_{n-1,n-1} , \\
x_{n-2} &= (y_{n-2} - (u_{n-2,n-1}x_{n-1} + u_{n-2,n}x_n))/u_{n-2,n-2} , \\
&\vdots
\end{aligned}
$$

or, in general,

$$x_i = \left(y_i - \sum_{j=i+1}^{n} u_{ij}x_j \right) /u_{ii} .$$

Given P, L, U, and b, the procedure LUP-SOLVE solves for x by combining forward and back substitution. The pseudocode assumes that the dimension n appears in the attribute $L.rows$ and that the permutation matrix P is represented by the array π.

LUP-SOLVE(L, U, π, b)

```
1   n = L.rows
2   let x and y be new vectors of length n
3   for i = 1 to n
4       y_i = b_{π[i]} − Σ_{j=1}^{i−1} l_{ij} y_j
5   for i = n downto 1
6       x_i = (y_i − Σ_{j=i+1}^{n} u_{ij} x_j) / u_{ii}
7   return x
```

Procedure LUP-SOLVE solves for y using forward substitution in lines 3–4, and then it solves for x using backward substitution in lines 5–6. Since the summation within each of the **for** loops includes an implicit loop, the running time is $\Theta(n^2)$.

As an example of these methods, consider the system of linear equations defined by

$$\begin{pmatrix} 1 & 2 & 0 \\ 3 & 4 & 4 \\ 5 & 6 & 3 \end{pmatrix} x = \begin{pmatrix} 3 \\ 7 \\ 8 \end{pmatrix},$$

where

$$A = \begin{pmatrix} 1 & 2 & 0 \\ 3 & 4 & 4 \\ 5 & 6 & 3 \end{pmatrix},$$

$$b = \begin{pmatrix} 3 \\ 7 \\ 8 \end{pmatrix},$$

and we wish to solve for the unknown x. The LUP decomposition is

$$L = \begin{pmatrix} 1 & 0 & 0 \\ 0.2 & 1 & 0 \\ 0.6 & 0.5 & 1 \end{pmatrix},$$

$$U = \begin{pmatrix} 5 & 6 & 3 \\ 0 & 0.8 & -0.6 \\ 0 & 0 & 2.5 \end{pmatrix},$$

$$P = \begin{pmatrix} 0 & 0 & 1 \\ 1 & 0 & 0 \\ 0 & 1 & 0 \end{pmatrix}.$$

(You might want to verify that $PA = LU$.) Using forward substitution, we solve $Ly = Pb$ for y:

$$\begin{pmatrix} 1 & 0 & 0 \\ 0.2 & 1 & 0 \\ 0.6 & 0.5 & 1 \end{pmatrix} \begin{pmatrix} y_1 \\ y_2 \\ y_3 \end{pmatrix} = \begin{pmatrix} 8 \\ 3 \\ 7 \end{pmatrix},$$

obtaining

$$y = \begin{pmatrix} 8 \\ 1.4 \\ 1.5 \end{pmatrix}$$

by computing first y_1, then y_2, and finally y_3. Using back substitution, we solve $Ux = y$ for x:

$$\begin{pmatrix} 5 & 6 & 3 \\ 0 & 0.8 & -0.6 \\ 0 & 0 & 2.5 \end{pmatrix} \begin{pmatrix} x_1 \\ x_2 \\ x_3 \end{pmatrix} = \begin{pmatrix} 8 \\ 1.4 \\ 1.5 \end{pmatrix},$$

thereby obtaining the desired answer

$$x = \begin{pmatrix} -1.4 \\ 2.2 \\ 0.6 \end{pmatrix}$$

by computing first x_3, then x_2, and finally x_1.

Computing an LU decomposition

We have now shown that if we can create an LUP decomposition for a nonsingular matrix A, then forward and back substitution can solve the system $Ax = b$ of linear equations. Now we show how to efficiently compute an LUP decomposition for A. We start with the case in which A is an $n \times n$ nonsingular matrix and P is absent (or, equivalently, $P = I_n$). In this case, we factor $A = LU$. We call the two matrices L and U an **LU decomposition** of A.

We use a process known as **Gaussian elimination** to create an LU decomposition. We start by subtracting multiples of the first equation from the other equations in order to remove the first variable from those equations. Then, we subtract multiples of the second equation from the third and subsequent equations so that now the first and second variables are removed from them. We continue this process until the system that remains has an upper-triangular form—in fact, it is the matrix U. The matrix L is made up of the row multipliers that cause variables to be eliminated.

Our algorithm to implement this strategy is recursive. We wish to construct an LU decomposition for an $n \times n$ nonsingular matrix A. If $n = 1$, then we are done, since we can choose $L = I_1$ and $U = A$. For $n > 1$, we break A into four parts:

$$\begin{aligned} A &= \begin{pmatrix} a_{11} & a_{12} & \cdots & a_{1n} \\ a_{21} & a_{22} & \cdots & a_{2n} \\ \vdots & \vdots & \ddots & \vdots \\ a_{n1} & a_{n2} & \cdots & a_{nn} \end{pmatrix} \\ &= \begin{pmatrix} a_{11} & w^{\mathrm{T}} \\ v & A' \end{pmatrix}, \end{aligned}$$

where $v = (v_2, v_3, \ldots, v_n) = (a_{21}, a_{31}, \ldots, a_{n1})$ is a column $(n-1)$-vector, $w^{\mathrm{T}} = (w_2, w_3, \ldots, w_n)^{\mathrm{T}} = (a_{12}, a_{13}, \ldots, a_{1n})^{\mathrm{T}}$ is a row $(n-1)$-vector, and A' is an $(n-1) \times (n-1)$ matrix. Then, using matrix algebra (verify the equations by

simply multiplying through), we can factor A as

$$A = \begin{pmatrix} a_{11} & w^{\mathrm{T}} \\ v & A' \end{pmatrix}$$

$$= \begin{pmatrix} 1 & 0 \\ v/a_{11} & I_{n-1} \end{pmatrix} \begin{pmatrix} a_{11} & w^{\mathrm{T}} \\ 0 & A' - vw^{\mathrm{T}}/a_{11} \end{pmatrix}. \qquad (28.8)$$

The 0s in the first and second matrices of equation (28.8) are row and column $(n-1)$-vectors, respectively. The term vw^{T}/a_{11}, formed by taking the outer product of v and w and dividing each element of the result by a_{11}, is an $(n-1) \times (n-1)$ matrix, which conforms in size to the matrix A' from which it is subtracted. The resulting $(n-1) \times (n-1)$ matrix

$$A' - vw^{\mathrm{T}}/a_{11} \qquad (28.9)$$

is called the ***Schur complement*** of A with respect to a_{11}.

We claim that if A is nonsingular, then the Schur complement is nonsingular, too. Why? Suppose that the Schur complement, which is $(n-1) \times (n-1)$, is singular. Then by Theorem D.1, it has row rank strictly less than $n-1$. Because the bottom $n-1$ entries in the first column of the matrix

$$\begin{pmatrix} a_{11} & w^{\mathrm{T}} \\ 0 & A' - vw^{\mathrm{T}}/a_{11} \end{pmatrix}$$

are all 0, the bottom $n-1$ rows of this matrix must have row rank strictly less than $n-1$. The row rank of the entire matrix, therefore, is strictly less than n. Applying Exercise D.2-8 to equation (28.8), A has rank strictly less than n, and from Theorem D.1 we derive the contradiction that A is singular.

Because the Schur complement is nonsingular, we can now recursively find an LU decomposition for it. Let us say that

$$A' - vw^{\mathrm{T}}/a_{11} = L'U',$$

where L' is unit lower-triangular and U' is upper-triangular. Then, using matrix algebra, we have

$$A = \begin{pmatrix} 1 & 0 \\ v/a_{11} & I_{n-1} \end{pmatrix} \begin{pmatrix} a_{11} & w^{\mathrm{T}} \\ 0 & A' - vw^{\mathrm{T}}/a_{11} \end{pmatrix}$$

$$= \begin{pmatrix} 1 & 0 \\ v/a_{11} & I_{n-1} \end{pmatrix} \begin{pmatrix} a_{11} & w^{\mathrm{T}} \\ 0 & L'U' \end{pmatrix}$$

$$= \begin{pmatrix} 1 & 0 \\ v/a_{11} & L' \end{pmatrix} \begin{pmatrix} a_{11} & w^{\mathrm{T}} \\ 0 & U' \end{pmatrix}$$

$$= LU,$$

thereby providing our LU decomposition. (Note that because L' is unit lower-triangular, so is L, and because U' is upper-triangular, so is U.)

Of course, if $a_{11} = 0$, this method doesn't work, because it divides by 0. It also doesn't work if the upper leftmost entry of the Schur complement $A' - vw^T/a_{11}$ is 0, since we divide by it in the next step of the recursion. The elements by which we divide during LU decomposition are called *pivots*, and they occupy the diagonal elements of the matrix U. The reason we include a permutation matrix P during LUP decomposition is that it allows us to avoid dividing by 0. When we use permutations to avoid division by 0 (or by small numbers, which would contribute to numerical instability), we are *pivoting*.

An important class of matrices for which LU decomposition always works correctly is the class of symmetric positive-definite matrices. Such matrices require no pivoting, and thus we can employ the recursive strategy outlined above without fear of dividing by 0. We shall prove this result, as well as several others, in Section 28.3.

Our code for LU decomposition of a matrix A follows the recursive strategy, except that an iteration loop replaces the recursion. (This transformation is a standard optimization for a "tail-recursive" procedure—one whose last operation is a recursive call to itself. See Problem 7-4.) It assumes that the attribute $A.rows$ gives the dimension of A. We initialize the matrix U with 0s below the diagonal and matrix L with 1s on its diagonal and 0s above the diagonal. Each iteration works on a square submatrix, using its upper leftmost element as the pivot to compute the v and w vectors and the Schur complement, which becomes the square submatrix worked on by the next iteration.

LU-DECOMPOSITION(A)

```
 1   n = A.rows
 2   let L and U be new n × n matrices
 3   initialize U with 0s below the diagonal
 4   initialize L with 1s on the diagonal and 0s above the diagonal
 5   for k = 1 to n
 6       u_kk = a_kk
 7       for i = k + 1 to n
 8           l_ik = a_ik/a_kk          // a_ik holds v_i
 9           u_ki = a_ki               // a_ki holds w_i
10       for i = k + 1 to n
11           for j = k + 1 to n
12               a_ij = a_ij − l_ik u_kj
13   return L and U
```

The outer **for** loop beginning in line 5 iterates once for each recursive step. Within this loop, line 6 determines the pivot to be $u_{kk} = a_{kk}$. The **for** loop in lines 7–9 (which does not execute when $k = n$) uses the v and w vectors to update L and U.

$$
\begin{array}{cccc}
2 & 3 & 1 & 5 \\
6 & 13 & 5 & 19 \\
2 & 19 & 10 & 23 \\
4 & 10 & 11 & 31
\end{array}
\qquad
\begin{array}{c|ccc}
\textbf{2} & 3 & 1 & 5 \\
3 & 4 & 2 & 4 \\
1 & 16 & 9 & 18 \\
2 & 4 & 9 & 21
\end{array}
\qquad
\begin{array}{cc|cc}
2 & 3 & 1 & 5 \\
3 & \textbf{4} & 2 & 4 \\
1 & 4 & 1 & 2 \\
2 & 1 & 7 & 17
\end{array}
\qquad
\begin{array}{ccc|c}
2 & 3 & 1 & 5 \\
3 & 4 & 2 & 4 \\
1 & 4 & \textbf{1} & 2 \\
2 & 1 & 7 & 3
\end{array}
$$

$$
\qquad\text{(a)}\qquad\qquad\qquad\text{(b)}\qquad\qquad\qquad\text{(c)}\qquad\qquad\qquad\text{(d)}
$$

$$
\underbrace{\begin{pmatrix}
2 & 3 & 1 & 5 \\
6 & 13 & 5 & 19 \\
2 & 19 & 10 & 23 \\
4 & 10 & 11 & 31
\end{pmatrix}}_{A}
=
\underbrace{\begin{pmatrix}
1 & 0 & 0 & 0 \\
3 & 1 & 0 & 0 \\
1 & 4 & 1 & 0 \\
2 & 1 & 7 & 1
\end{pmatrix}}_{L}
\underbrace{\begin{pmatrix}
2 & 3 & 1 & 5 \\
0 & 4 & 2 & 4 \\
0 & 0 & 1 & 2 \\
0 & 0 & 0 & 3
\end{pmatrix}}_{U}
$$

$$
\text{(e)}
$$

Figure 28.1   The operation of LU-DECOMPOSITION. **(a)** The matrix A. **(b)** The element $a_{11} = 2$ in the black circle is the pivot, the shaded column is v/a_{11}, and the shaded row is w^{T}. The elements of U computed thus far are above the horizontal line, and the elements of L are to the left of the vertical line. The Schur complement matrix $A' - vw^{\mathrm{T}}/a_{11}$ occupies the lower right. **(c)** We now operate on the Schur complement matrix produced from part (b). The element $a_{22} = 4$ in the black circle is the pivot, and the shaded column and row are v/a_{22} and w^{T} (in the partitioning of the Schur complement), respectively. Lines divide the matrix into the elements of U computed so far (above), the elements of L computed so far (left), and the new Schur complement (lower right). **(d)** After the next step, the matrix A is factored. (The element 3 in the new Schur complement becomes part of U when the recursion terminates.) **(e)** The factorization $A = LU$.

Line 8 determines the below-diagonal elements of L, storing v_i/a_{kk} in l_{ik}, and line 9 computes the above-diagonal elements of U, storing w_i in u_{ki}. Finally, lines 10–12 compute the elements of the Schur complement and store them back into the matrix A. (We don't need to divide by a_{kk} in line 12 because we already did so when we computed l_{ik} in line 8.) Because line 12 is triply nested, LU-DECOMPOSITION runs in time $\Theta(n^3)$.

Figure 28.1 illustrates the operation of LU-DECOMPOSITION. It shows a standard optimization of the procedure in which we store the significant elements of L and U in place in the matrix A. That is, we can set up a correspondence between each element a_{ij} and either l_{ij} (if $i > j$) or u_{ij} (if $i \leq j$) and update the matrix A so that it holds both L and U when the procedure terminates. To obtain the pseudocode for this optimization from the above pseudocode, just replace each reference to l or u by a; you can easily verify that this transformation preserves correctness.

Computing an LUP decomposition

Generally, in solving a system of linear equations $Ax = b$, we must pivot on off-diagonal elements of A to avoid dividing by 0. Dividing by 0 would, of course, be disastrous. But we also want to avoid dividing by a small value—even if A is nonsingular—because numerical instabilities can result. We therefore try to pivot on a large value.

The mathematics behind LUP decomposition is similar to that of LU decomposition. Recall that we are given an $n \times n$ nonsingular matrix A, and we wish to find a permutation matrix P, a unit lower-triangular matrix L, and an upper-triangular matrix U such that $PA = LU$. Before we partition the matrix A, as we did for LU decomposition, we move a nonzero element, say a_{k1}, from somewhere in the first column to the $(1, 1)$ position of the matrix. For numerical stability, we choose a_{k1} as the element in the first column with the greatest absolute value. (The first column cannot contain only 0s, for then A would be singular, because its determinant would be 0, by Theorems D.4 and D.5.) In order to preserve the set of equations, we exchange row 1 with row k, which is equivalent to multiplying A by a permutation matrix Q on the left (Exercise D.1-4). Thus, we can write QA as

$$QA = \begin{pmatrix} a_{k1} & w^{\mathrm{T}} \\ v & A' \end{pmatrix},$$

where $v = (a_{21}, a_{31}, \ldots, a_{n1})$, except that a_{11} replaces a_{k1}; $w^{\mathrm{T}} = (a_{k2}, a_{k3}, \ldots, a_{kn})^{\mathrm{T}}$; and A' is an $(n - 1) \times (n - 1)$ matrix. Since $a_{k1} \neq 0$, we can now perform much the same linear algebra as for LU decomposition, but now guaranteeing that we do not divide by 0:

$$\begin{aligned} QA &= \begin{pmatrix} a_{k1} & w^{\mathrm{T}} \\ v & A' \end{pmatrix} \\ &= \begin{pmatrix} 1 & 0 \\ v/a_{k1} & I_{n-1} \end{pmatrix} \begin{pmatrix} a_{k1} & w^{\mathrm{T}} \\ 0 & A' - vw^{\mathrm{T}}/a_{k1} \end{pmatrix}. \end{aligned}$$

As we saw for LU decomposition, if A is nonsingular, then the Schur complement $A' - vw^{\mathrm{T}}/a_{k1}$ is nonsingular, too. Therefore, we can recursively find an LUP decomposition for it, with unit lower-triangular matrix L', upper-triangular matrix U', and permutation matrix P', such that

$$P'(A' - vw^{\mathrm{T}}/a_{k1}) = L'U'.$$

Define

$$P = \begin{pmatrix} 1 & 0 \\ 0 & P' \end{pmatrix} Q,$$

which is a permutation matrix, since it is the product of two permutation matrices (Exercise D.1-4). We now have

$$PA = \begin{pmatrix} 1 & 0 \\ 0 & P' \end{pmatrix} QA$$

$$= \begin{pmatrix} 1 & 0 \\ 0 & P' \end{pmatrix} \begin{pmatrix} 1 & 0 \\ v/a_{k1} & I_{n-1} \end{pmatrix} \begin{pmatrix} a_{k1} & w^{\mathrm{T}} \\ 0 & A' - vw^{\mathrm{T}}/a_{k1} \end{pmatrix}$$

$$= \begin{pmatrix} 1 & 0 \\ P'v/a_{k1} & P' \end{pmatrix} \begin{pmatrix} a_{k1} & w^{\mathrm{T}} \\ 0 & A' - vw^{\mathrm{T}}/a_{k1} \end{pmatrix}$$

$$= \begin{pmatrix} 1 & 0 \\ P'v/a_{k1} & I_{n-1} \end{pmatrix} \begin{pmatrix} a_{k1} & w^{\mathrm{T}} \\ 0 & P'(A' - vw^{\mathrm{T}}/a_{k1}) \end{pmatrix}$$

$$= \begin{pmatrix} 1 & 0 \\ P'v/a_{k1} & I_{n-1} \end{pmatrix} \begin{pmatrix} a_{k1} & w^{\mathrm{T}} \\ 0 & L'U' \end{pmatrix}$$

$$= \begin{pmatrix} 1 & 0 \\ P'v/a_{k1} & L' \end{pmatrix} \begin{pmatrix} a_{k1} & w^{\mathrm{T}} \\ 0 & U' \end{pmatrix}$$

$$= LU,$$

yielding the LUP decomposition. Because L' is unit lower-triangular, so is L, and because U' is upper-triangular, so is U.

Notice that in this derivation, unlike the one for LU decomposition, we must multiply both the column vector v/a_{k1} and the Schur complement $A' - vw^{\mathrm{T}}/a_{k1}$ by the permutation matrix P'. Here is the pseudocode for LUP decomposition:

LUP-DECOMPOSITION(A)

```
 1   n = A.rows
 2   let π[1..n] be a new array
 3   for i = 1 to n
 4       π[i] = i
 5   for k = 1 to n
 6       p = 0
 7       for i = k to n
 8           if |a_ik| > p
 9               p = |a_ik|
10               k' = i
11       if p == 0
12           error "singular matrix"
13       exchange π[k] with π[k']
14       for i = 1 to n
15           exchange a_ki with a_k'i
16       for i = k + 1 to n
17           a_ik = a_ik/a_kk
18           for j = k + 1 to n
19               a_ij = a_ij - a_ik a_kj
```

Like LU-DECOMPOSITION, our LUP-DECOMPOSITION procedure replaces the recursion with an iteration loop. As an improvement over a direct implementation of the recursion, we dynamically maintain the permutation matrix P as an array π, where $\pi[i] = j$ means that the ith row of P contains a 1 in column j. We also implement the code to compute L and U "in place" in the matrix A. Thus, when the procedure terminates,

$$a_{ij} = \begin{cases} l_{ij} & \text{if } i > j \text{ ,} \\ u_{ij} & \text{if } i \le j \text{ .} \end{cases}$$

Figure 28.2 illustrates how LUP-DECOMPOSITION factors a matrix. Lines 3–4 initialize the array π to represent the identity permutation. The outer **for** loop beginning in line 5 implements the recursion. Each time through the outer loop, lines 6–10 determine the element $a_{k'k}$ with largest absolute value of those in the current first column (column k) of the $(n - k + 1) \times (n - k + 1)$ matrix whose LUP decomposition we are finding. If all elements in the current first column are zero, lines 11–12 report that the matrix is singular. To pivot, we exchange $\pi[k']$ with $\pi[k]$ in line 13 and exchange the kth and k'th rows of A in lines 14–15, thereby making the pivot element a_{kk}. (The entire rows are swapped because in the derivation of the method above, not only is $A' - vw^{\mathrm{T}}/a_{k1}$ multiplied by P', but so is v/a_{k1}.) Finally, the Schur complement is computed by lines 16–19 in much the same way as it is computed by lines 7–12 of LU-DECOMPOSITION, except that here the operation is written to work in place.

Because of its triply nested loop structure, LUP-DECOMPOSITION has a running time of $\Theta(n^3)$, which is the same as that of LU-DECOMPOSITION. Thus, pivoting costs us at most a constant factor in time.

Exercises

28.1-1
Solve the equation

$$\begin{pmatrix} 1 & 0 & 0 \\ 4 & 1 & 0 \\ -6 & 5 & 1 \end{pmatrix} \begin{pmatrix} x_1 \\ x_2 \\ x_3 \end{pmatrix} = \begin{pmatrix} 3 \\ 14 \\ -7 \end{pmatrix}$$

by using forward substitution.

28.1-2
Find an LU decomposition of the matrix

$$\begin{pmatrix} 4 & -5 & 6 \\ 8 & -6 & 7 \\ 12 & -7 & 12 \end{pmatrix} .$$

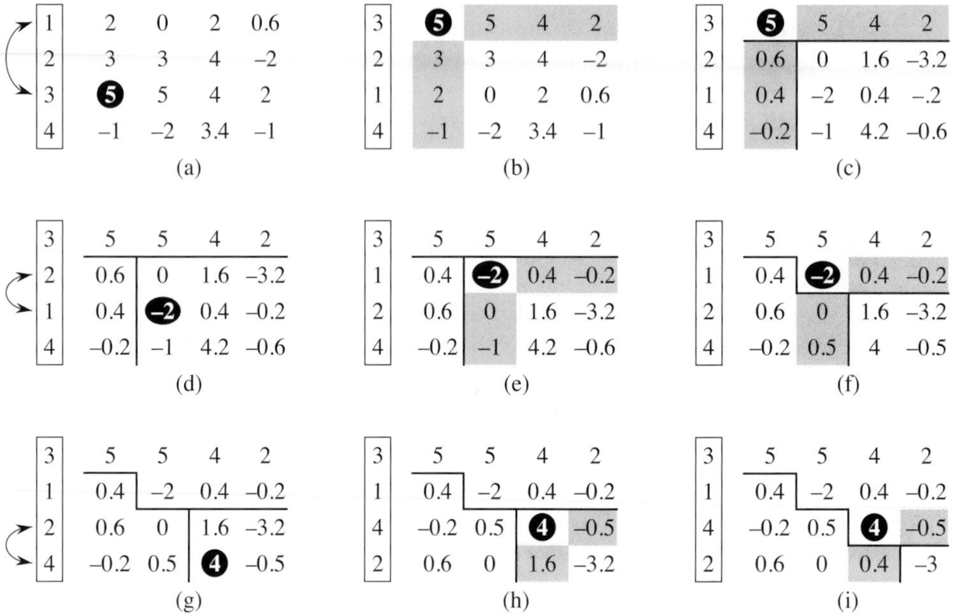

$$
\begin{pmatrix} 0 & 0 & 1 & 0 \\ 1 & 0 & 0 & 0 \\ 0 & 0 & 0 & 1 \\ 0 & 1 & 0 & 0 \end{pmatrix}
\begin{pmatrix} 2 & 0 & 2 & 0.6 \\ 3 & 3 & 4 & -2 \\ 5 & 5 & 4 & 2 \\ -1 & -2 & 3.4 & -1 \end{pmatrix}
=
\begin{pmatrix} 1 & 0 & 0 & 0 \\ 0.4 & 1 & 0 & 0 \\ -0.2 & 0.5 & 1 & 0 \\ 0.6 & 0 & 0.4 & 1 \end{pmatrix}
\begin{pmatrix} 5 & 5 & 4 & 2 \\ 0 & -2 & 0.4 & -0.2 \\ 0 & 0 & 4 & -0.5 \\ 0 & 0 & 0 & -3 \end{pmatrix}
$$

$$
\qquad\quad P \qquad\qquad\qquad A \qquad\qquad\qquad\qquad L \qquad\qquad\qquad\qquad U
$$

(j)

Figure 28.2 The operation of LUP-DECOMPOSITION. **(a)** The input matrix A with the identity permutation of the rows on the left. The first step of the algorithm determines that the element 5 in the black circle in the third row is the pivot for the first column. **(b)** Rows 1 and 3 are swapped and the permutation is updated. The shaded column and row represent v and w^{T}. **(c)** The vector v is replaced by $v/5$, and the lower right of the matrix is updated with the Schur complement. Lines divide the matrix into three regions: elements of U (above), elements of L (left), and elements of the Schur complement (lower right). **(d)–(f)** The second step. **(g)–(i)** The third step. No further changes occur on the fourth (final) step. **(j)** The LUP decomposition $PA = LU$.

28.1-3

Solve the equation

$$\begin{pmatrix} 1 & 5 & 4 \\ 2 & 0 & 3 \\ 5 & 8 & 2 \end{pmatrix} \begin{pmatrix} x_1 \\ x_2 \\ x_3 \end{pmatrix} = \begin{pmatrix} 12 \\ 9 \\ 5 \end{pmatrix}$$

by using an LUP decomposition.

28.1-4

Describe the LUP decomposition of a diagonal matrix.

28.1-5

Describe the LUP decomposition of a permutation matrix A, and prove that it is unique.

28.1-6

Show that for all $n \geq 1$, there exists a singular $n \times n$ matrix that has an LU decomposition.

28.1-7

In LU-DECOMPOSITION, is it necessary to perform the outermost **for** loop iteration when $k = n$? How about in LUP-DECOMPOSITION?

28.2 Inverting matrices

Although in practice we do not generally use matrix inverses to solve systems of linear equations, preferring instead to use more numerically stable techniques such as LUP decomposition, sometimes we need to compute a matrix inverse. In this section, we show how to use LUP decomposition to compute a matrix inverse. We also prove that matrix multiplication and computing the inverse of a matrix are equivalently hard problems, in that (subject to technical conditions) we can use an algorithm for one to solve the other in the same asymptotic running time. Thus, we can use Strassen's algorithm (see Section 4.2) for matrix multiplication to invert a matrix. Indeed, Strassen's original paper was motivated by the problem of showing that a set of a linear equations could be solved more quickly than by the usual method.

Computing a matrix inverse from an LUP decomposition

Suppose that we have an LUP decomposition of a matrix A in the form of three matrices L, U, and P such that $PA = LU$. Using LUP-SOLVE, we can solve an equation of the form $Ax = b$ in time $\Theta(n^2)$. Since the LUP decomposition depends on A but not b, we can run LUP-SOLVE on a second set of equations of the form $Ax = b'$ in additional time $\Theta(n^2)$. In general, once we have the LUP decomposition of A, we can solve, in time $\Theta(kn^2)$, k versions of the equation $Ax = b$ that differ only in b.

We can think of the equation

$$AX = I_n, \tag{28.10}$$

which defines the matrix X, the inverse of A, as a set of n distinct equations of the form $Ax = b$. To be precise, let X_i denote the ith column of X, and recall that the unit vector e_i is the ith column of I_n. We can then solve equation (28.10) for X by using the LUP decomposition for A to solve each equation

$$AX_i = e_i$$

separately for X_i. Once we have the LUP decomposition, we can compute each of the n columns X_i in time $\Theta(n^2)$, and so we can compute X from the LUP decomposition of A in time $\Theta(n^3)$. Since we can determine the LUP decomposition of A in time $\Theta(n^3)$, we can compute the inverse A^{-1} of a matrix A in time $\Theta(n^3)$.

Matrix multiplication and matrix inversion

We now show that the theoretical speedups obtained for matrix multiplication translate to speedups for matrix inversion. In fact, we prove something stronger: matrix inversion is equivalent to matrix multiplication, in the following sense. If $M(n)$ denotes the time to multiply two $n \times n$ matrices, then we can invert a nonsingular $n \times n$ matrix in time $O(M(n))$. Moreover, if $I(n)$ denotes the time to invert a nonsingular $n \times n$ matrix, then we can multiply two $n \times n$ matrices in time $O(I(n))$. We prove these results as two separate theorems.

Theorem 28.1 (Multiplication is no harder than inversion)
If we can invert an $n \times n$ matrix in time $I(n)$, where $I(n) = \Omega(n^2)$ and $I(n)$ satisfies the regularity condition $I(3n) = O(I(n))$, then we can multiply two $n \times n$ matrices in time $O(I(n))$.

Proof   Let A and B be $n \times n$ matrices whose matrix product C we wish to compute. We define the $3n \times 3n$ matrix D by

$$D = \begin{pmatrix} I_n & A & 0 \\ 0 & I_n & B \\ 0 & 0 & I_n \end{pmatrix}.$$

The inverse of D is

$$D^{-1} = \begin{pmatrix} I_n & -A & AB \\ 0 & I_n & -B \\ 0 & 0 & I_n \end{pmatrix},$$

and thus we can compute the product AB by taking the upper right $n \times n$ submatrix of D^{-1}.

We can construct matrix D in $\Theta(n^2)$ time, which is $O(I(n))$ because we assume that $I(n) = \Omega(n^2)$, and we can invert D in $O(I(3n)) = O(I(n))$ time, by the regularity condition on $I(n)$. We thus have $M(n) = O(I(n))$.   ∎

Note that $I(n)$ satisfies the regularity condition whenever $I(n) = \Theta(n^c \lg^d n)$ for any constants $c > 0$ and $d \geq 0$.

The proof that matrix inversion is no harder than matrix multiplication relies on some properties of symmetric positive-definite matrices that we will prove in Section 28.3.

Theorem 28.2 (Inversion is no harder than multiplication)
Suppose we can multiply two $n \times n$ real matrices in time $M(n)$, where $M(n) = \Omega(n^2)$ and $M(n)$ satisfies the two regularity conditions $M(n + k) = O(M(n))$ for any k in the range $0 \leq k \leq n$ and $M(n/2) \leq cM(n)$ for some constant $c < 1/2$. Then we can compute the inverse of any real nonsingular $n \times n$ matrix in time $O(M(n))$.

Proof   We prove the theorem here for real matrices. Exercise 28.2-6 asks you to generalize the proof for matrices whose entries are complex numbers.

We can assume that n is an exact power of 2, since we have

$$\begin{pmatrix} A & 0 \\ 0 & I_k \end{pmatrix}^{-1} = \begin{pmatrix} A^{-1} & 0 \\ 0 & I_k \end{pmatrix}$$

for any $k > 0$. Thus, by choosing k such that $n + k$ is a power of 2, we enlarge the matrix to a size that is the next power of 2 and obtain the desired answer A^{-1} from the answer to the enlarged problem. The first regularity condition on $M(n)$ ensures that this enlargement does not cause the running time to increase by more than a constant factor.

For the moment, let us assume that the $n \times n$ matrix A is symmetric and positive-definite. We partition each of A and its inverse A^{-1} into four $n/2 \times n/2$ submatrices:

$$A = \begin{pmatrix} B & C^{\mathrm{T}} \\ C & D \end{pmatrix} \quad \text{and} \quad A^{-1} = \begin{pmatrix} R & T \\ U & V \end{pmatrix}. \tag{28.11}$$

Then, if we let

$$S = D - CB^{-1}C^{\mathrm{T}} \tag{28.12}$$

be the Schur complement of A with respect to B (we shall see more about this form of Schur complement in Section 28.3), we have

$$A^{-1} = \begin{pmatrix} R & T \\ U & V \end{pmatrix} = \begin{pmatrix} B^{-1} + B^{-1}C^{\mathrm{T}}S^{-1}CB^{-1} & -B^{-1}C^{\mathrm{T}}S^{-1} \\ -S^{-1}CB^{-1} & S^{-1} \end{pmatrix}, \tag{28.13}$$

since $AA^{-1} = I_n$, as you can verify by performing the matrix multiplication. Because A is symmetric and positive-definite, Lemmas 28.4 and 28.5 in Section 28.3 imply that B and S are both symmetric and positive-definite. By Lemma 28.3 in Section 28.3, therefore, the inverses B^{-1} and S^{-1} exist, and by Exercise D.2-6, B^{-1} and S^{-1} are symmetric, so that $(B^{-1})^{\mathrm{T}} = B^{-1}$ and $(S^{-1})^{\mathrm{T}} = S^{-1}$. Therefore, we can compute the submatrices R, T, U, and V of A^{-1} as follows, where all matrices mentioned are $n/2 \times n/2$:

1. Form the submatrices B, C, C^{T}, and D of A.

2. Recursively compute the inverse B^{-1} of B.

3. Compute the matrix product $W = CB^{-1}$, and then compute its transpose W^{T}, which equals $B^{-1}C^{\mathrm{T}}$ (by Exercise D.1-2 and $(B^{-1})^{\mathrm{T}} = B^{-1}$).

4. Compute the matrix product $X = WC^{\mathrm{T}}$, which equals $CB^{-1}C^{\mathrm{T}}$, and then compute the matrix $S = D - X = D - CB^{-1}C^{\mathrm{T}}$.

5. Recursively compute the inverse S^{-1} of S, and set V to S^{-1}.

6. Compute the matrix product $Y = S^{-1}W$, which equals $S^{-1}CB^{-1}$, and then compute its transpose Y^{T}, which equals $B^{-1}C^{\mathrm{T}}S^{-1}$ (by Exercise D.1-2, $(B^{-1})^{\mathrm{T}} = B^{-1}$, and $(S^{-1})^{\mathrm{T}} = S^{-1}$). Set T to $-Y^{\mathrm{T}}$ and U to $-Y$.

7. Compute the matrix product $Z = W^{\mathrm{T}}Y$, which equals $B^{-1}C^{\mathrm{T}}S^{-1}CB^{-1}$, and set R to $B^{-1} + Z$.

Thus, we can invert an $n \times n$ symmetric positive-definite matrix by inverting two $n/2 \times n/2$ matrices in steps 2 and 5; performing four multiplications of $n/2 \times n/2$ matrices in steps 3, 4, 6, and 7; plus an additional cost of $O(n^2)$ for extracting submatrices from A, inserting submatrices into A^{-1}, and performing a constant number of additions, subtractions, and transposes on $n/2 \times n/2$ matrices. We get the recurrence

$$\begin{aligned} I(n) &\leq 2I(n/2) + 4M(n/2) + O(n^2) \\ &= 2I(n/2) + \Theta(M(n)) \\ &= O(M(n)). \end{aligned}$$

The second line holds because the second regularity condition in the statement of the theorem implies that $4M(n/2) < 2M(n)$ and because we assume that $M(n) = \Omega(n^2)$. The third line follows because the second regularity condition allows us to apply case 3 of the master theorem (Theorem 4.1).

It remains to prove that we can obtain the same asymptotic running time for matrix multiplication as for matrix inversion when A is invertible but not symmetric and positive-definite. The basic idea is that for any nonsingular matrix A, the matrix $A^{\mathrm{T}}A$ is symmetric (by Exercise D.1-2) and positive-definite (by Theorem D.6). The trick, then, is to reduce the problem of inverting A to the problem of inverting $A^{\mathrm{T}}A$.

The reduction is based on the observation that when A is an $n \times n$ nonsingular matrix, we have

$$A^{-1} = (A^{\mathrm{T}}A)^{-1}A^{\mathrm{T}},$$

since $((A^{\mathrm{T}}A)^{-1}A^{\mathrm{T}})A = (A^{\mathrm{T}}A)^{-1}(A^{\mathrm{T}}A) = I_n$ and a matrix inverse is unique. Therefore, we can compute A^{-1} by first multiplying A^{T} by A to obtain $A^{\mathrm{T}}A$, then inverting the symmetric positive-definite matrix $A^{\mathrm{T}}A$ using the above divide-and-conquer algorithm, and finally multiplying the result by A^{T}. Each of these three steps takes $O(M(n))$ time, and thus we can invert any nonsingular matrix with real entries in $O(M(n))$ time. ∎

The proof of Theorem 28.2 suggests a means of solving the equation $Ax = b$ by using LU decomposition without pivoting, so long as A is nonsingular. We multiply both sides of the equation by A^{T}, yielding $(A^{\mathrm{T}}A)x = A^{\mathrm{T}}b$. This transformation doesn't affect the solution x, since A^{T} is invertible, and so we can factor the symmetric positive-definite matrix $A^{\mathrm{T}}A$ by computing an LU decomposition. We then use forward and back substitution to solve for x with the right-hand side $A^{\mathrm{T}}b$. Although this method is theoretically correct, in practice the procedure LUP-DECOMPOSITION works much better. LUP decomposition requires fewer arithmetic operations by a constant factor, and it has somewhat better numerical properties.

Exercises

28.2-1
Let $M(n)$ be the time to multiply two $n \times n$ matrices, and let $S(n)$ denote the time required to square an $n \times n$ matrix. Show that multiplying and squaring matrices have essentially the same difficulty: an $M(n)$-time matrix-multiplication algorithm implies an $O(M(n))$-time squaring algorithm, and an $S(n)$-time squaring algorithm implies an $O(S(n))$-time matrix-multiplication algorithm.

28.2-2

Let $M(n)$ be the time to multiply two $n \times n$ matrices. Show that an $M(n)$-time matrix-multiplication algorithm implies an $O(M(n))$-time LUP-decomposition algorithm.

28.2-3

Let $M(n)$ be the time to multiply two $n \times n$ matrices, and let $D(n)$ denote the time required to find the determinant of an $n \times n$ matrix. Show that multiplying matrices and computing the determinant have essentially the same difficulty: an $M(n)$-time matrix-multiplication algorithm implies an $O(M(n))$-time determinant algorithm, and a $D(n)$-time determinant algorithm implies an $O(D(n))$-time matrix-multiplication algorithm.

28.2-4

Let $M(n)$ be the time to multiply two $n \times n$ boolean matrices, and let $T(n)$ be the time to find the transitive closure of an $n \times n$ boolean matrix. (See Section 25.2.) Show that an $M(n)$-time boolean matrix-multiplication algorithm implies an $O(M(n) \lg n)$-time transitive-closure algorithm, and a $T(n)$-time transitive-closure algorithm implies an $O(T(n))$-time boolean matrix-multiplication algorithm.

28.2-5

Does the matrix-inversion algorithm based on Theorem 28.2 work when matrix elements are drawn from the field of integers modulo 2? Explain.

28.2-6 ★

Generalize the matrix-inversion algorithm of Theorem 28.2 to handle matrices of complex numbers, and prove that your generalization works correctly. (*Hint:* Instead of the transpose of A, use the ***conjugate transpose*** A^*, which you obtain from the transpose of A by replacing every entry with its complex conjugate. Instead of symmetric matrices, consider ***Hermitian*** matrices, which are matrices A such that $A = A^*$.)

28.3   Symmetric positive-definite matrices and least-squares approximation

Symmetric positive-definite matrices have many interesting and desirable properties. For example, they are nonsingular, and we can perform LU decomposition on them without having to worry about dividing by 0. In this section, we shall

prove several other important properties of symmetric positive-definite matrices and show an interesting application to curve fitting by a least-squares approximation.

The first property we prove is perhaps the most basic.

Lemma 28.3
Any positive-definite matrix is nonsingular.

Proof   Suppose that a matrix A is singular. Then by Corollary D.3, there exists a nonzero vector x such that $Ax = 0$. Hence, $x^{T}Ax = 0$, and A cannot be positive-definite.   ∎

The proof that we can perform LU decomposition on a symmetric positive-definite matrix A without dividing by 0 is more involved. We begin by proving properties about certain submatrices of A. Define the kth ***leading submatrix*** of A to be the matrix A_k consisting of the intersection of the first k rows and first k columns of A.

Lemma 28.4
If A is a symmetric positive-definite matrix, then every leading submatrix of A is symmetric and positive-definite.

Proof   That each leading submatrix A_k is symmetric is obvious. To prove that A_k is positive-definite, we assume that it is not and derive a contradiction. If A_k is not positive-definite, then there exists a k-vector $x_k \neq 0$ such that $x_k^{T}A_k x_k \leq 0$. Let A be $n \times n$, and

$$A = \begin{pmatrix} A_k & B^{T} \\ B & C \end{pmatrix} \tag{28.14}$$

for submatrices B (which is $(n-k) \times k$) and C (which is $(n-k) \times (n-k)$). Define the n-vector $x = (\, x_k^{T} \quad 0\,)^{T}$, where $n - k$ 0s follow x_k. Then we have

$$
\begin{aligned}
x^{T}Ax &= (\, x_k^{T} \quad 0\,) \begin{pmatrix} A_k & B^{T} \\ B & C \end{pmatrix} \begin{pmatrix} x_k \\ 0 \end{pmatrix} \\
&= (\, x_k^{T} \quad 0\,) \begin{pmatrix} A_k x_k \\ B x_k \end{pmatrix} \\
&= x_k^{T} A_k x_k \\
&\leq 0\,,
\end{aligned}
$$

which contradicts A being positive-definite.   ∎

We now turn to some essential properties of the Schur complement. Let A be a symmetric positive-definite matrix, and let A_k be a leading $k \times k$ submatrix of A. Partition A once again according to equation (28.14). We generalize equation (28.9) to define the ***Schur complement*** S of A with respect to A_k as

$$S = C - BA_k^{-1}B^{\mathrm{T}} \,. \tag{28.15}$$

(By Lemma 28.4, A_k is symmetric and positive-definite; therefore, A_k^{-1} exists by Lemma 28.3, and S is well defined.) Note that our earlier definition (28.9) of the Schur complement is consistent with equation (28.15), by letting $k = 1$.

The next lemma shows that the Schur-complement matrices of symmetric positive-definite matrices are themselves symmetric and positive-definite. We used this result in Theorem 28.2, and we need its corollary to prove the correctness of LU decomposition for symmetric positive-definite matrices.

Lemma 28.5 (Schur complement lemma)
If A is a symmetric positive-definite matrix and A_k is a leading $k \times k$ submatrix of A, then the Schur complement S of A with respect to A_k is symmetric and positive-definite.

Proof   Because A is symmetric, so is the submatrix C. By Exercise D.2-6, the product $BA_k^{-1}B^{\mathrm{T}}$ is symmetric, and by Exercise D.1-1, S is symmetric.

It remains to show that S is positive-definite. Consider the partition of A given in equation (28.14). For any nonzero vector x, we have $x^{\mathrm{T}}Ax > 0$ by the assumption that A is positive-definite. Let us break x into two subvectors y and z compatible with A_k and C, respectively. Because A_k^{-1} exists, we have

$$
\begin{aligned}
x^{\mathrm{T}}Ax &= \begin{pmatrix} y^{\mathrm{T}} & z^{\mathrm{T}} \end{pmatrix} \begin{pmatrix} A_k & B^{\mathrm{T}} \\ B & C \end{pmatrix} \begin{pmatrix} y \\ z \end{pmatrix} \\
&= \begin{pmatrix} y^{\mathrm{T}} & z^{\mathrm{T}} \end{pmatrix} \begin{pmatrix} A_k y + B^{\mathrm{T}} z \\ By + Cz \end{pmatrix} \\
&= y^{\mathrm{T}}A_k y + y^{\mathrm{T}}B^{\mathrm{T}}z + z^{\mathrm{T}}By + z^{\mathrm{T}}Cz \\
&= (y + A_k^{-1}B^{\mathrm{T}}z)^{\mathrm{T}}A_k(y + A_k^{-1}B^{\mathrm{T}}z) + z^{\mathrm{T}}(C - BA_k^{-1}B^{\mathrm{T}})z \,, \tag{28.16}
\end{aligned}
$$

by matrix magic. (Verify by multiplying through.) This last equation amounts to "completing the square" of the quadratic form. (See Exercise 28.3-2.)

Since $x^{\mathrm{T}}Ax > 0$ holds for any nonzero x, let us pick any nonzero z and then choose $y = -A_k^{-1}B^{\mathrm{T}}z$, which causes the first term in equation (28.16) to vanish, leaving

$$z^{\mathrm{T}}(C - BA_k^{-1}B^{\mathrm{T}})z = z^{\mathrm{T}}Sz$$

as the value of the expression. For any $z \neq 0$, we therefore have $z^{\mathrm{T}}Sz = x^{\mathrm{T}}Ax > 0$, and thus S is positive-definite.   ∎

Corollary 28.6
LU decomposition of a symmetric positive-definite matrix never causes a division by 0.

Proof   Let A be a symmetric positive-definite matrix. We shall prove something stronger than the statement of the corollary: every pivot is strictly positive. The first pivot is a_{11}. Let e_1 be the first unit vector, from which we obtain $a_{11} = e_1^T A e_1 > 0$. Since the first step of LU decomposition produces the Schur complement of A with respect to $A_1 = (a_{11})$, Lemma 28.5 implies by induction that all pivots are positive.   ∎

Least-squares approximation

One important application of symmetric positive-definite matrices arises in fitting curves to given sets of data points. Suppose that we are given a set of m data points

$$(x_1, y_1), (x_2, y_2), \ldots, (x_m, y_m) \,,$$

where we know that the y_i are subject to measurement errors. We would like to determine a function $F(x)$ such that the approximation errors

$$\eta_i = F(x_i) - y_i \tag{28.17}$$

are small for $i = 1, 2, \ldots, m$. The form of the function F depends on the problem at hand. Here, we assume that it has the form of a linearly weighted sum,

$$F(x) = \sum_{j=1}^{n} c_j f_j(x) \,,$$

where the number of summands n and the specific ***basis functions*** f_j are chosen based on knowledge of the problem at hand. A common choice is $f_j(x) = x^{j-1}$, which means that

$$F(x) = c_1 + c_2 x + c_3 x^2 + \cdots + c_n x^{n-1}$$

is a polynomial of degree $n - 1$ in x. Thus, given m data points $(x_1, y_1), (x_2, y_2), \ldots, (x_m, y_m)$, we wish to calculate n coefficients $c_1, c_2, \ldots, c_n$ that minimize the approximation errors $\eta_1, \eta_2, \ldots, \eta_m$.

  By choosing $n = m$, we can calculate each y_i *exactly* in equation (28.17). Such a high-degree F "fits the noise" as well as the data, however, and generally gives poor results when used to predict y for previously unseen values of x. It is usually better to choose n significantly smaller than m and hope that by choosing the coefficients c_j well, we can obtain a function F that finds the significant patterns in the data points without paying undue attention to the noise. Some theoretical

principles exist for choosing n, but they are beyond the scope of this text. In any case, once we choose a value of n that is less than m, we end up with an overdetermined set of equations whose solution we wish to approximate. We now show how to do so.

Let

$$A = \begin{pmatrix} f_1(x_1) & f_2(x_1) & \cdots & f_n(x_1) \\ f_1(x_2) & f_2(x_2) & \cdots & f_n(x_2) \\ \vdots & \vdots & \ddots & \vdots \\ f_1(x_m) & f_2(x_m) & \cdots & f_n(x_m) \end{pmatrix}$$

denote the matrix of values of the basis functions at the given points; that is, $a_{ij} = f_j(x_i)$. Let $c = (c_k)$ denote the desired n-vector of coefficients. Then,

$$\begin{aligned} Ac &= \begin{pmatrix} f_1(x_1) & f_2(x_1) & \cdots & f_n(x_1) \\ f_1(x_2) & f_2(x_2) & \cdots & f_n(x_2) \\ \vdots & \vdots & \ddots & \vdots \\ f_1(x_m) & f_2(x_m) & \cdots & f_n(x_m) \end{pmatrix} \begin{pmatrix} c_1 \\ c_2 \\ \vdots \\ c_n \end{pmatrix} \\ &= \begin{pmatrix} F(x_1) \\ F(x_2) \\ \vdots \\ F(x_m) \end{pmatrix} \end{aligned}$$

is the m-vector of "predicted values" for y. Thus,

$$\eta = Ac - y$$

is the m-vector of ***approximation errors***.

To minimize approximation errors, we choose to minimize the norm of the error vector η, which gives us a ***least-squares solution***, since

$$\|\eta\| = \left(\sum_{i=1}^{m} \eta_i^2 \right)^{1/2} .$$

Because

$$\|\eta\|^2 = \|Ac - y\|^2 = \sum_{i=1}^{m} \left(\sum_{j=1}^{n} a_{ij} c_j - y_i \right)^2 ,$$

we can minimize $\|\eta\|$ by differentiating $\|\eta\|^2$ with respect to each c_k and then setting the result to 0:

$$\frac{d \, \|\eta\|^2}{dc_k} = \sum_{i=1}^{m} 2 \left(\sum_{j=1}^{n} a_{ij} c_j - y_i \right) a_{ik} = 0 . \tag{28.18}$$

The n equations (28.18) for $k = 1, 2, \ldots, n$ are equivalent to the single matrix equation

$$(Ac - y)^\mathrm{T} A = 0$$

or, equivalently (using Exercise D.1-2), to

$$A^\mathrm{T}(Ac - y) = 0 ,$$

which implies

$$A^\mathrm{T} Ac = A^\mathrm{T} y . \tag{28.19}$$

In statistics, this is called the ***normal equation***. The matrix $A^\mathrm{T} A$ is symmetric by Exercise D.1-2, and if A has full column rank, then by Theorem D.6, $A^\mathrm{T} A$ is positive-definite as well. Hence, $(A^\mathrm{T} A)^{-1}$ exists, and the solution to equation (28.19) is

$$
\begin{aligned}
c &= \left((A^\mathrm{T} A)^{-1} A^\mathrm{T} \right) y \\
&= A^+ y , \tag{28.20}
\end{aligned}
$$

where the matrix $A^+ = \left((A^\mathrm{T} A)^{-1} A^\mathrm{T} \right)$ is the ***pseudoinverse*** of the matrix A. The pseudoinverse naturally generalizes the notion of a matrix inverse to the case in which A is not square. (Compare equation (28.20) as the approximate solution to $Ac = y$ with the solution $A^{-1} b$ as the exact solution to $Ax = b$.)

As an example of producing a least-squares fit, suppose that we have five data points

$$
\begin{aligned}
(x_1, y_1) &= (-1, 2) , \\
(x_2, y_2) &= (1, 1) , \\
(x_3, y_3) &= (2, 1) , \\
(x_4, y_4) &= (3, 0) , \\
(x_5, y_5) &= (5, 3) ,
\end{aligned}
$$

shown as black dots in Figure 28.3. We wish to fit these points with a quadratic polynomial

$$F(x) = c_1 + c_2 x + c_3 x^2 .$$

We start with the matrix of basis-function values

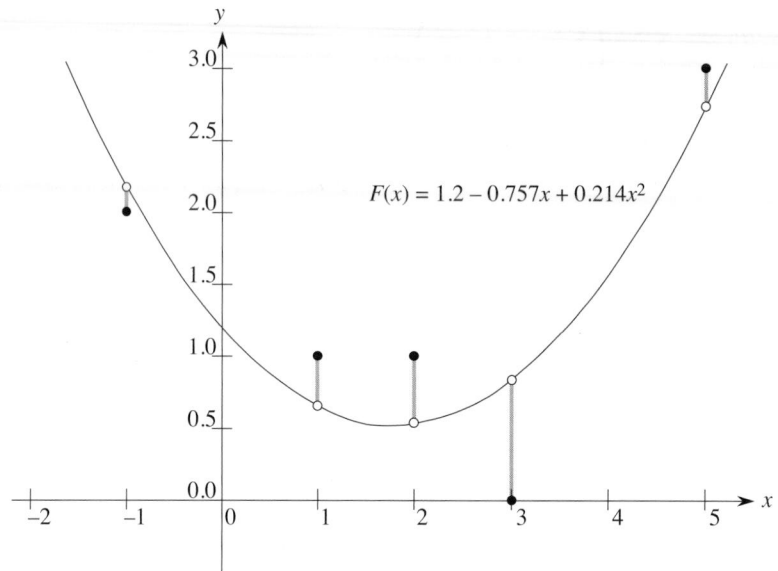

Figure 28.3 The least-squares fit of a quadratic polynomial to the set of five data points $\{(-1, 2), (1, 1), (2, 1), (3, 0), (5, 3)\}$. The black dots are the data points, and the white dots are their estimated values predicted by the polynomial $F(x) = 1.2 - 0.757x + 0.214x^2$, the quadratic polynomial that minimizes the sum of the squared errors. Each shaded line shows the error for one data point.

$$
A = \begin{pmatrix} 1 & x_1 & x_1^2 \\ 1 & x_2 & x_2^2 \\ 1 & x_3 & x_3^2 \\ 1 & x_4 & x_4^2 \\ 1 & x_5 & x_5^2 \end{pmatrix} = \begin{pmatrix} 1 & -1 & 1 \\ 1 & 1 & 1 \\ 1 & 2 & 4 \\ 1 & 3 & 9 \\ 1 & 5 & 25 \end{pmatrix} ,
$$

whose pseudoinverse is

$$
A^+ = \begin{pmatrix} 0.500 & 0.300 & 0.200 & 0.100 & -0.100 \\ -0.388 & 0.093 & 0.190 & 0.193 & -0.088 \\ 0.060 & -0.036 & -0.048 & -0.036 & 0.060 \end{pmatrix} .
$$

Multiplying y by A^+, we obtain the coefficient vector

$$
c = \begin{pmatrix} 1.200 \\ -0.757 \\ 0.214 \end{pmatrix} ,
$$

which corresponds to the quadratic polynomial

$$F(x) = 1.200 - 0.757x + 0.214x^2$$

as the closest-fitting quadratic to the given data, in a least-squares sense.

As a practical matter, we solve the normal equation (28.19) by multiplying y by A^T and then finding an LU decomposition of $A^T A$. If A has full rank, the matrix $A^T A$ is guaranteed to be nonsingular, because it is symmetric and positive-definite. (See Exercise D.1-2 and Theorem D.6.)

Exercises

28.3-1
Prove that every diagonal element of a symmetric positive-definite matrix is positive.

28.3-2
Let $A = \begin{pmatrix} a & b \\ b & c \end{pmatrix}$ be a 2×2 symmetric positive-definite matrix. Prove that its determinant $ac - b^2$ is positive by "completing the square" in a manner similar to that used in the proof of Lemma 28.5.

28.3-3
Prove that the maximum element in a symmetric positive-definite matrix lies on the diagonal.

28.3-4
Prove that the determinant of each leading submatrix of a symmetric positive-definite matrix is positive.

28.3-5
Let A_k denote the kth leading submatrix of a symmetric positive-definite matrix A. Prove that $\det(A_k)/\det(A_{k-1})$ is the kth pivot during LU decomposition, where, by convention, $\det(A_0) = 1$.

28.3-6
Find the function of the form

$$F(x) = c_1 + c_2 x \lg x + c_3 e^x$$

that is the best least-squares fit to the data points

$(1, 1), (2, 1), (3, 3), (4, 8)$.

28.3-7
Show that the pseudoinverse A^+ satisfies the following four equations:

$$\begin{aligned}
AA^+A &= A, \\
A^+AA^+ &= A^+, \\
(AA^+)^{\mathrm{T}} &= AA^+, \\
(A^+A)^{\mathrm{T}} &= A^+A.
\end{aligned}$$

Problems

28-1   Tridiagonal systems of linear equations
Consider the tridiagonal matrix

$$A = \begin{pmatrix}
1 & -1 & 0 & 0 & 0 \\
-1 & 2 & -1 & 0 & 0 \\
0 & -1 & 2 & -1 & 0 \\
0 & 0 & -1 & 2 & -1 \\
0 & 0 & 0 & -1 & 2
\end{pmatrix}.$$

a. Find an LU decomposition of A.

b. Solve the equation $Ax = \begin{pmatrix} 1 & 1 & 1 & 1 & 1 \end{pmatrix}^{\mathrm{T}}$ by using forward and back substitution.

c. Find the inverse of A.

d. Show how, for any $n \times n$ symmetric positive-definite, tridiagonal matrix A and any n-vector b, to solve the equation $Ax = b$ in $O(n)$ time by performing an LU decomposition. Argue that any method based on forming A^{-1} is asymptotically more expensive in the worst case.

e. Show how, for any $n \times n$ nonsingular, tridiagonal matrix A and any n-vector b, to solve the equation $Ax = b$ in $O(n)$ time by performing an LUP decomposition.

28-2   Splines
A practical method for interpolating a set of points with a curve is to use *cubic splines*. We are given a set $\{(x_i, y_i) : i = 0, 1, \ldots, n\}$ of $n + 1$ point-value pairs, where $x_0 < x_1 < \cdots < x_n$. We wish to fit a piecewise-cubic curve (spline) $f(x)$ to the points. That is, the curve $f(x)$ is made up of n cubic polynomials $f_i(x) = a_i + b_i x + c_i x^2 + d_i x^3$ for $i = 0, 1, \ldots, n - 1$, where if x falls in

the range $x_i \leq x \leq x_{i+1}$, then the value of the curve is given by $f(x) = f_i(x-x_i)$. The points x_i at which the cubic polynomials are "pasted" together are called **knots**. For simplicity, we shall assume that $x_i = i$ for $i = 0, 1, \ldots, n$.

To ensure continuity of $f(x)$, we require that

$$f(x_i) = f_i(0) = y_i \,,$$
$$f(x_{i+1}) = f_i(1) = y_{i+1}$$

for $i = 0, 1, \ldots, n - 1$. To ensure that $f(x)$ is sufficiently smooth, we also insist that the first derivative be continuous at each knot:

$$f'(x_{i+1}) = f_i'(1) = f_{i+1}'(0)$$

for $i = 0, 1, \ldots, n - 2$.

a. Suppose that for $i = 0, 1, \ldots, n$, we are given not only the point-value pairs $\{(x_i, y_i)\}$ but also the first derivatives $D_i = f'(x_i)$ at each knot. Express each coefficient a_i, b_i, c_i, and d_i in terms of the values y_i, y_{i+1}, D_i, and D_{i+1}. (Remember that $x_i = i$.) How quickly can we compute the $4n$ coefficients from the point-value pairs and first derivatives?

The question remains of how to choose the first derivatives of $f(x)$ at the knots. One method is to require the second derivatives to be continuous at the knots:

$$f''(x_{i+1}) = f_i''(1) = f_{i+1}''(0)$$

for $i = 0, 1, \ldots, n - 2$. At the first and last knots, we assume that $f''(x_0) = f_0''(0) = 0$ and $f''(x_n) = f_{n-1}''(1) = 0$; these assumptions make $f(x)$ a **natural** cubic spline.

b. Use the continuity constraints on the second derivative to show that for $i = 1, 2, \ldots, n - 1$,

$$D_{i-1} + 4D_i + D_{i+1} = 3(y_{i+1} - y_{i-1}) \,. \tag{28.21}$$

c. Show that

$$2D_0 + D_1 = 3(y_1 - y_0) \,, \tag{28.22}$$
$$D_{n-1} + 2D_n = 3(y_n - y_{n-1}) \,. \tag{28.23}$$

d. Rewrite equations (28.21)–(28.23) as a matrix equation involving the vector $D = \langle D_0, D_1, \ldots, D_n \rangle$ of unknowns. What attributes does the matrix in your equation have?

e. Argue that a natural cubic spline can interpolate a set of $n + 1$ point-value pairs in $O(n)$ time (see Problem 28-1).

f. Show how to determine a natural cubic spline that interpolates a set of $n + 1$ points (x_i, y_i) satisfying $x_0 < x_1 < \cdots < x_n$, even when x_i is not necessarily equal to i. What matrix equation must your method solve, and how quickly does your algorithm run?

Chapter notes

Many excellent texts describe numerical and scientific computation in much greater detail than we have room for here. The following are especially readable: George and Liu [132], Golub and Van Loan [144], Press, Teukolsky, Vetterling, and Flannery [283, 284], and Strang [323, 324].

Golub and Van Loan [144] discuss numerical stability. They show why $\det(A)$ is not necessarily a good indicator of the stability of a matrix A, proposing instead to use $\|A\|_\infty \|A^{-1}\|_\infty$, where $\|A\|_\infty = \max_{1 \le i \le n} \sum_{j=1}^{n} |a_{ij}|$. They also address the question of how to compute this value without actually computing A^{-1}.

Gaussian elimination, upon which the LU and LUP decompositions are based, was the first systematic method for solving linear systems of equations. It was also one of the earliest numerical algorithms. Although it was known earlier, its discovery is commonly attributed to C. F. Gauss (1777–1855). In his famous paper [325], Strassen showed that an $n \times n$ matrix can be inverted in $O(n^{\lg 7})$ time. Winograd [358] originally proved that matrix multiplication is no harder than matrix inversion, and the converse is due to Aho, Hopcroft, and Ullman [5].

Another important matrix decomposition is the *singular value decomposition*, or *SVD*. The SVD factors an $m \times n$ matrix A into $A = Q_1 \Sigma Q_2^{\mathrm{T}}$, where Σ is an $m \times n$ matrix with nonzero values only on the diagonal, Q_1 is $m \times m$ with mutually orthonormal columns, and Q_2 is $n \times n$, also with mutually orthonormal columns. Two vectors are *orthonormal* if their inner product is 0 and each vector has a norm of 1. The books by Strang [323, 324] and Golub and Van Loan [144] contain good treatments of the SVD.

Strang [324] has an excellent presentation of symmetric positive-definite matrices and of linear algebra in general.

29   Linear Programming

Many problems take the form of maximizing or minimizing an objective, given limited resources and competing constraints. If we can specify the objective as a linear function of certain variables, and if we can specify the constraints on resources as equalities or inequalities on those variables, then we have a *linear-programming problem*. Linear programs arise in a variety of practical applications. We begin by studying an application in electoral politics.

A political problem

Suppose that you are a politician trying to win an election. Your district has three different types of areas—urban, suburban, and rural. These areas have, respectively, 100,000, 200,000, and 50,000 registered voters. Although not all the registered voters actually go to the polls, you decide that to govern effectively, you would like at least half the registered voters in each of the three regions to vote for you. You are honorable and would never consider supporting policies in which you do not believe. You realize, however, that certain issues may be more effective in winning votes in certain places. Your primary issues are building more roads, gun control, farm subsidies, and a gasoline tax dedicated to improved public transit. According to your campaign staff's research, you can estimate how many votes you win or lose from each population segment by spending $1,000 on advertising on each issue. This information appears in the table of Figure 29.1. In this table, each entry indicates the number of thousands of either urban, suburban, or rural voters who would be won over by spending $1,000 on advertising in support of a particular issue. Negative entries denote votes that would be lost. Your task is to figure out the minimum amount of money that you need to spend in order to win 50,000 urban votes, 100,000 suburban votes, and 25,000 rural votes.

You could, by trial and error, devise a strategy that wins the required number of votes, but the strategy you come up with might not be the least expensive one. For example, you could devote $20,000 of advertising to building roads, $0 to gun control, $4,000 to farm subsidies, and $9,000 to a gasoline tax. In this case, you

policy	urban	suburban	rural
build roads	−2	5	3
gun control	8	2	−5
farm subsidies	0	0	10
gasoline tax	10	0	−2

Figure 29.1 The effects of policies on voters. Each entry describes the number of thousands of urban, suburban, or rural voters who could be won over by spending $1,000 on advertising support of a policy on a particular issue. Negative entries denote votes that would be lost.

would win $20(-2)+0(8)+4(0)+9(10) = 50$ thousand urban votes, $20(5)+0(2)+4(0)+9(0) = 100$ thousand suburban votes, and $20(3)+0(-5)+4(10)+9(-2) = 82$ thousand rural votes. You would win the exact number of votes desired in the urban and suburban areas and more than enough votes in the rural area. (In fact, in the rural area, you would receive more votes than there are voters.) In order to garner these votes, you would have paid for $20 + 0 + 4 + 9 = 33$ thousand dollars of advertising.

Naturally, you may wonder whether this strategy is the best possible. That is, could you achieve your goals while spending less on advertising? Additional trial and error might help you to answer this question, but wouldn't you rather have a systematic method for answering such questions? In order to develop one, we shall formulate this question mathematically. We introduce 4 variables:

- x_1 is the number of thousands of dollars spent on advertising on building roads,

- x_2 is the number of thousands of dollars spent on advertising on gun control,

- x_3 is the number of thousands of dollars spent on advertising on farm subsidies, and

- x_4 is the number of thousands of dollars spent on advertising on a gasoline tax.

We can write the requirement that we win at least 50,000 urban votes as

$$-2x_1 + 8x_2 + 0x_3 + 10x_4 \geq 50 . \tag{29.1}$$

Similarly, we can write the requirements that we win at least 100,000 suburban votes and 25,000 rural votes as

$$5x_1 + 2x_2 + 0x_3 + 0x_4 \geq 100 \tag{29.2}$$

and

$$3x_1 - 5x_2 + 10x_3 - 2x_4 \geq 25 . \tag{29.3}$$

Any setting of the variables x_1, x_2, x_3, x_4 that satisfies inequalities (29.1)–(29.3) yields a strategy that wins a sufficient number of each type of vote. In order to

keep costs as small as possible, you would like to minimize the amount spent on advertising. That is, you want to minimize the expression

$$x_1 + x_2 + x_3 + x_4 \, . \tag{29.4}$$

Although negative advertising often occurs in political campaigns, there is no such thing as negative-cost advertising. Consequently, we require that

$$x_1 \geq 0, \; x_2 \geq 0, \; x_3 \geq 0, \; \text{and} \; x_4 \geq 0 \, . \tag{29.5}$$

Combining inequalities (29.1)–(29.3) and (29.5) with the objective of minimizing (29.4), we obtain what is known as a "linear program." We format this problem as

$$
\begin{array}{llllllll}
\text{minimize} & x_1 & + & x_2 & + & x_3 & + & x_4 & & & (29.6) \\
\text{subject to} \\
& -2x_1 & + & 8x_2 & + & 0x_3 & + & 10x_4 & \geq & 50 & (29.7) \\
& 5x_1 & + & 2x_2 & + & 0x_3 & + & 0x_4 & \geq & 100 & (29.8) \\
& 3x_1 & - & 5x_2 & + & 10x_3 & - & 2x_4 & \geq & 25 & (29.9) \\
& & & x_1, x_2, x_3, x_4 & & & & & \geq & 0 \, . & (29.10)
\end{array}
$$

The solution of this linear program yields your optimal strategy.

General linear programs

In the general linear-programming problem, we wish to optimize a linear function subject to a set of linear inequalities. Given a set of real numbers $a_1, a_2, \ldots, a_n$ and a set of variables $x_1, x_2, \ldots, x_n$, we define a ***linear function*** f on those variables by

$$f(x_1, x_2, \ldots, x_n) = a_1 x_1 + a_2 x_2 + \cdots + a_n x_n = \sum_{j=1}^{n} a_j x_j \, .$$

If b is a real number and f is a linear function, then the equation

$$f(x_1, x_2, \ldots, x_n) = b$$

is a ***linear equality*** and the inequalities

$$f(x_1, x_2, \ldots, x_n) \leq b$$

and

$$f(x_1, x_2, \ldots, x_n) \geq b$$

are *linear inequalities*. We use the general term *linear constraints* to denote either linear equalities or linear inequalities. In linear programming, we do not allow strict inequalities. Formally, a *linear-programming problem* is the problem of either minimizing or maximizing a linear function subject to a finite set of linear constraints. If we are to minimize, then we call the linear program a *minimization linear program*, and if we are to maximize, then we call the linear program a *maximization linear program*.

The remainder of this chapter covers how to formulate and solve linear programs. Although several polynomial-time algorithms for linear programming have been developed, we will not study them in this chapter. Instead, we shall study the simplex algorithm, which is the oldest linear-programming algorithm. The simplex algorithm does not run in polynomial time in the worst case, but it is fairly efficient and widely used in practice.

An overview of linear programming

In order to describe properties of and algorithms for linear programs, we find it convenient to express them in canonical forms. We shall use two forms, *standard* and *slack*, in this chapter. We will define them precisely in Section 29.1. Informally, a linear program in standard form is the maximization of a linear function subject to linear *inequalities*, whereas a linear program in slack form is the maximization of a linear function subject to linear *equalities*. We shall typically use standard form for expressing linear programs, but we find it more convenient to use slack form when we describe the details of the simplex algorithm. For now, we restrict our attention to maximizing a linear function on n variables subject to a set of m linear inequalities.

Let us first consider the following linear program with two variables:

$$\text{maximize} \quad x_1 + x_2 \tag{29.11}$$

subject to

$$4x_1 - x_2 \le 8 \tag{29.12}$$
$$2x_1 + x_2 \le 10 \tag{29.13}$$
$$5x_1 - 2x_2 \ge -2 \tag{29.14}$$
$$x_1, x_2 \ge 0 \ . \tag{29.15}$$

We call any setting of the variables x_1 and x_2 that satisfies all the constraints (29.12)–(29.15) a *feasible solution* to the linear program. If we graph the constraints in the (x_1, x_2)-Cartesian coordinate system, as in Figure 29.2(a), we see

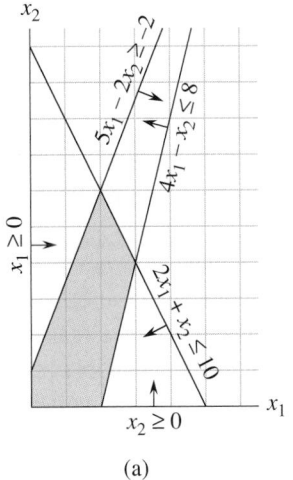
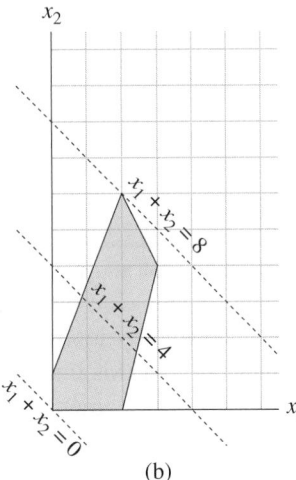

Figure 29.2 **(a)** The linear program given in (29.12)–(29.15). Each constraint is represented by a line and a direction. The intersection of the constraints, which is the feasible region, is shaded. **(b)** The dotted lines show, respectively, the points for which the objective value is 0, 4, and 8. The optimal solution to the linear program is $x_1 = 2$ and $x_2 = 6$ with objective value 8.

that the set of feasible solutions (shaded in the figure) forms a convex region[1] in the two-dimensional space. We call this convex region the ***feasible region*** and the function we wish to maximize the ***objective function***. Conceptually, we could evaluate the objective function $x_1 + x_2$ at each point in the feasible region; we call the value of the objective function at a particular point the ***objective value***. We could then identify a point that has the maximum objective value as an optimal solution. For this example (and for most linear programs), the feasible region contains an infinite number of points, and so we need to determine an efficient way to find a point that achieves the maximum objective value without explicitly evaluating the objective function at every point in the feasible region.

In two dimensions, we can optimize via a graphical procedure. The set of points for which $x_1 + x_2 = z$, for any z, is a line with a slope of -1. If we plot $x_1 + x_2 = 0$, we obtain the line with slope -1 through the origin, as in Figure 29.2(b). The intersection of this line and the feasible region is the set of feasible solutions that have an objective value of 0. In this case, that intersection of the line with the feasible region is the single point $(0, 0)$. More generally, for any z, the intersection

---

[1] An intuitive definition of a convex region is that it fulfills the requirement that for any two points in the region, all points on a line segment between them are also in the region.

of the line $x_1 + x_2 = z$ and the feasible region is the set of feasible solutions that have objective value z. Figure 29.2(b) shows the lines $x_1 + x_2 = 0$, $x_1 + x_2 = 4$, and $x_1 + x_2 = 8$. Because the feasible region in Figure 29.2 is bounded, there must be some maximum value z for which the intersection of the line $x_1 + x_2 = z$ and the feasible region is nonempty. Any point at which this occurs is an optimal solution to the linear program, which in this case is the point $x_1 = 2$ and $x_2 = 6$ with objective value 8.

It is no accident that an optimal solution to the linear program occurs at a vertex of the feasible region. The maximum value of z for which the line $x_1 + x_2 = z$ intersects the feasible region must be on the boundary of the feasible region, and thus the intersection of this line with the boundary of the feasible region is either a single vertex or a line segment. If the intersection is a single vertex, then there is just one optimal solution, and it is that vertex. If the intersection is a line segment, every point on that line segment must have the same objective value; in particular, both endpoints of the line segment are optimal solutions. Since each endpoint of a line segment is a vertex, there is an optimal solution at a vertex in this case as well.

Although we cannot easily graph linear programs with more than two variables, the same intuition holds. If we have three variables, then each constraint corresponds to a half-space in three-dimensional space. The intersection of these half-spaces forms the feasible region. The set of points for which the objective function obtains a given value z is now a plane (assuming no degenerate conditions). If all coefficients of the objective function are nonnegative, and if the origin is a feasible solution to the linear program, then as we move this plane away from the origin, in a direction normal to the objective function, we find points of increasing objective value. (If the origin is not feasible or if some coefficients in the objective function are negative, the intuitive picture becomes slightly more complicated.) As in two dimensions, because the feasible region is convex, the set of points that achieve the optimal objective value must include a vertex of the feasible region. Similarly, if we have n variables, each constraint defines a half-space in n-dimensional space. We call the feasible region formed by the intersection of these half-spaces a *simplex*. The objective function is now a hyperplane and, because of convexity, an optimal solution still occurs at a vertex of the simplex.

The *simplex algorithm* takes as input a linear program and returns an optimal solution. It starts at some vertex of the simplex and performs a sequence of iterations. In each iteration, it moves along an edge of the simplex from a current vertex to a neighboring vertex whose objective value is no smaller than that of the current vertex (and usually is larger.) The simplex algorithm terminates when it reaches a local maximum, which is a vertex from which all neighboring vertices have a smaller objective value. Because the feasible region is convex and the objective function is linear, this local optimum is actually a global optimum. In Section 29.4,

we shall use a concept called "duality" to show that the solution returned by the simplex algorithm is indeed optimal.

Although the geometric view gives a good intuitive view of the operations of the simplex algorithm, we shall not refer to it explicitly when developing the details of the simplex algorithm in Section 29.3. Instead, we take an algebraic view. We first write the given linear program in slack form, which is a set of linear equalities. These linear equalities express some of the variables, called "basic variables," in terms of other variables, called "nonbasic variables." We move from one vertex to another by making a basic variable become nonbasic and making a nonbasic variable become basic. We call this operation a "pivot" and, viewed algebraically, it is nothing more than rewriting the linear program in an equivalent slack form.

The two-variable example described above was particularly simple. We shall need to address several more details in this chapter. These issues include identifying linear programs that have no solutions, linear programs that have no finite optimal solution, and linear programs for which the origin is not a feasible solution.

Applications of linear programming

Linear programming has a large number of applications. Any textbook on operations research is filled with examples of linear programming, and linear programming has become a standard tool taught to students in most business schools. The election scenario is one typical example. Two more examples of linear programming are the following:

- An airline wishes to schedule its flight crews. The Federal Aviation Administration imposes many constraints, such as limiting the number of consecutive hours that each crew member can work and insisting that a particular crew work only on one model of aircraft during each month. The airline wants to schedule crews on all of its flights using as few crew members as possible.

- An oil company wants to decide where to drill for oil. Siting a drill at a particular location has an associated cost and, based on geological surveys, an expected payoff of some number of barrels of oil. The company has a limited budget for locating new drills and wants to maximize the amount of oil it expects to find, given this budget.

With linear programs, we also model and solve graph and combinatorial problems, such as those appearing in this textbook. We have already seen a special case of linear programming used to solve systems of difference constraints in Section 24.4. In Section 29.2, we shall study how to formulate several graph and network-flow problems as linear programs. In Section 35.4, we shall use linear programming as a tool to find an approximate solution to another graph problem.

Algorithms for linear programming

This chapter studies the simplex algorithm. This algorithm, when implemented carefully, often solves general linear programs quickly in practice. With some carefully contrived inputs, however, the simplex algorithm can require exponential time. The first polynomial-time algorithm for linear programming was the ***ellipsoid algorithm***, which runs slowly in practice. A second class of polynomial-time algorithms are known as ***interior-point methods***. In contrast to the simplex algorithm, which moves along the exterior of the feasible region and maintains a feasible solution that is a vertex of the simplex at each iteration, these algorithms move through the interior of the feasible region. The intermediate solutions, while feasible, are not necessarily vertices of the simplex, but the final solution is a vertex. For large inputs, interior-point algorithms can run as fast as, and sometimes faster than, the simplex algorithm. The chapter notes point you to more information about these algorithms.

If we add to a linear program the additional requirement that all variables take on integer values, we have an ***integer linear program***. Exercise 34.5-3 asks you to show that just finding a feasible solution to this problem is NP-hard; since no polynomial-time algorithms are known for any NP-hard problems, there is no known polynomial-time algorithm for integer linear programming. In contrast, we can solve a general linear-programming problem in polynomial time.

In this chapter, if we have a linear program with variables $x = (x_1, x_2, \ldots, x_n)$ and wish to refer to a particular setting of the variables, we shall use the notation $\bar{x} = (\bar{x}_1, \bar{x}_2, \ldots, \bar{x}_n)$.

29.1   Standard and slack forms

This section describes two formats, standard form and slack form, that are useful when we specify and work with linear programs. In standard form, all the constraints are inequalities, whereas in slack form, all constraints are equalities (except for those that require the variables to be nonnegative).

Standard form

In ***standard form***, we are given n real numbers $c_1, c_2, \ldots, c_n$; m real numbers $b_1, b_2, \ldots, b_m$; and mn real numbers a_{ij} for $i = 1, 2, \ldots, m$ and $j = 1, 2, \ldots, n$. We wish to find n real numbers $x_1, x_2, \ldots, x_n$ that

maximize $\displaystyle\sum_{j=1}^{n} c_j x_j$ (29.16)

subject to

$$\sum_{j=1}^{n} a_{ij} x_j \;\le\; b_i \quad \text{for } i = 1, 2, \ldots, m \qquad (29.17)$$

$$x_j \;\ge\; 0 \quad \text{for } j = 1, 2, \ldots, n\,. \qquad (29.18)$$

Generalizing the terminology we introduced for the two-variable linear program, we call expression (29.16) the ***objective function*** and the $n + m$ inequalities in lines (29.17) and (29.18) the ***constraints***. The n constraints in line (29.18) are the ***nonnegativity constraints***. An arbitrary linear program need not have nonnegativity constraints, but standard form requires them. Sometimes we find it convenient to express a linear program in a more compact form. If we create an $m \times n$ matrix $A = (a_{ij})$, an m-vector $b = (b_i)$, an n-vector $c = (c_j)$, and an n-vector $x = (x_j)$, then we can rewrite the linear program defined in (29.16)–(29.18) as

maximize $c^{\mathrm{T}} x$ (29.19)

subject to

$$A x \;\le\; b \qquad (29.20)$$

$$x \;\ge\; 0\,. \qquad (29.21)$$

In line (29.19), $c^{\mathrm{T}} x$ is the inner product of two vectors. In inequality (29.20), Ax is a matrix-vector product, and in inequality (29.21), $x \ge 0$ means that each entry of the vector x must be nonnegative. We see that we can specify a linear program in standard form by a tuple (A, b, c), and we shall adopt the convention that A, b, and c always have the dimensions given above.

We now introduce terminology to describe solutions to linear programs. We used some of this terminology in the earlier example of a two-variable linear program. We call a setting of the variables $\bar{x}$ that satisfies all the constraints a ***feasible solution***, whereas a setting of the variables $\bar{x}$ that fails to satisfy at least one constraint is an ***infeasible solution***. We say that a solution $\bar{x}$ has ***objective value*** $c^{\mathrm{T}} \bar{x}$. A feasible solution $\bar{x}$ whose objective value is maximum over all feasible solutions is an ***optimal solution***, and we call its objective value $c^{\mathrm{T}} \bar{x}$ the ***optimal objective value***. If a linear program has no feasible solutions, we say that the linear program is ***infeasible***; otherwise it is ***feasible***. If a linear program has some feasible solutions but does not have a finite optimal objective value, we say that the linear program is ***unbounded***. Exercise 29.1-9 asks you to show that a linear program can have a finite optimal objective value even if the feasible region is not bounded.

Converting linear programs into standard form

It is always possible to convert a linear program, given as minimizing or maximizing a linear function subject to linear constraints, into standard form. A linear program might not be in standard form for any of four possible reasons:

1. The objective function might be a minimization rather than a maximization.

2. There might be variables without nonnegativity constraints.

3. There might be *equality constraints*, which have an equal sign rather than a less-than-or-equal-to sign.

4. There might be *inequality constraints*, but instead of having a less-than-or-equal-to sign, they have a greater-than-or-equal-to sign.

When converting one linear program L into another linear program L', we would like the property that an optimal solution to L' yields an optimal solution to L. To capture this idea, we say that two maximization linear programs L and L' are *equivalent* if for each feasible solution $\bar{x}$ to L with objective value z, there is a corresponding feasible solution $\bar{x}'$ to L' with objective value z, and for each feasible solution $\bar{x}'$ to L' with objective value z, there is a corresponding feasible solution $\bar{x}$ to L with objective value z. (This definition does not imply a one-to-one correspondence between feasible solutions.) A minimization linear program L and a maximization linear program L' are equivalent if for each feasible solution $\bar{x}$ to L with objective value z, there is a corresponding feasible solution $\bar{x}'$ to L' with objective value $-z$, and for each feasible solution $\bar{x}'$ to L' with objective value z, there is a corresponding feasible solution $\bar{x}$ to L with objective value $-z$.

We now show how to remove, one by one, each of the possible problems in the list above. After removing each one, we shall argue that the new linear program is equivalent to the old one.

To convert a minimization linear program L into an equivalent maximization linear program L', we simply negate the coefficients in the objective function. Since L and L' have identical sets of feasible solutions and, for any feasible solution, the objective value in L is the negative of the objective value in L', these two linear programs are equivalent. For example, if we have the linear program

minimize $-2x_1 + 3x_2$

subject to

$$
\begin{array}{rcrcl}
x_1 & + & x_2 & = & 7 \\
x_1 & - & 2x_2 & \le & 4 \\
x_1 & & & \ge & 0 \ ,
\end{array}
$$

and we negate the coefficients of the objective function, we obtain

maximize $2x_1 \;-\; 3x_2$

subject to

$$
\begin{aligned}
x_1 + x_2 &= 7 \\
x_1 - 2x_2 &\le 4 \\
x_1 &\ge 0 .
\end{aligned}
$$

Next, we show how to convert a linear program in which some of the variables do not have nonnegativity constraints into one in which each variable has a non-negativity constraint. Suppose that some variable x_j does not have a nonnegativity constraint. Then, we replace each occurrence of x_j by $x_j' - x_j''$, and add the non-negativity constraints $x_j' \ge 0$ and $x_j'' \ge 0$. Thus, if the objective function has a term $c_j x_j$, we replace it by $c_j x_j' - c_j x_j''$, and if constraint i has a term $a_{ij} x_j$, we replace it by $a_{ij} x_j' - a_{ij} x_j''$. Any feasible solution $\hat{x}$ to the new linear program corresponds to a feasible solution $\bar{x}$ to the original linear program with $\bar{x}_j = \hat{x}_j' - \hat{x}_j''$ and with the same objective value. Also, any feasible solution $\bar{x}$ to the original linear program corresponds to a feasible solution $\hat{x}$ to the new linear program with $\hat{x}_j' = \bar{x}_j$ and $\hat{x}_j'' = 0$ if $\bar{x}_j \ge 0$, or with $\hat{x}_j'' = -\bar{x}_j$ and $\hat{x}_j' = 0$ if $\bar{x}_j < 0$. The two linear programs have the same objective value regardless of the sign of $\bar{x}_j$. Thus, the two linear programs are equivalent. We apply this conversion scheme to each variable that does not have a nonnegativity constraint to yield an equivalent linear program in which all variables have nonnegativity constraints.

Continuing the example, we want to ensure that each variable has a corresponding nonnegativity constraint. Variable x_1 has such a constraint, but variable x_2 does not. Therefore, we replace x_2 by two variables x_2' and x_2'', and we modify the linear program to obtain

maximize $2x_1 \;-\; 3x_2' \;+\; 3x_2''$

subject to

$$
\begin{aligned}
x_1 + x_2' - x_2'' &= 7 \\
x_1 - 2x_2' + 2x_2'' &\le 4 \\
x_1, x_2', x_2'' &\ge 0 .
\end{aligned}
\tag{29.22}
$$

Next, we convert equality constraints into inequality constraints. Suppose that a linear program has an equality constraint $f(x_1, x_2, \ldots, x_n) = b$. Since $x = y$ if and only if both $x \ge y$ and $x \le y$, we can replace this equality constraint by the pair of inequality constraints $f(x_1, x_2, \ldots, x_n) \le b$ and $f(x_1, x_2, \ldots, x_n) \ge b$. Repeating this conversion for each equality constraint yields a linear program in which all constraints are inequalities.

Finally, we can convert the greater-than-or-equal-to constraints to less-than-or-equal-to constraints by multiplying these constraints through by -1. That is, any inequality of the form

$$\sum_{j=1}^{n} a_{ij} x_j \geq b_i$$

is equivalent to

$$\sum_{j=1}^{n} -a_{ij} x_j \leq -b_i \ .$$

Thus, by replacing each coefficient a_{ij} by $-a_{ij}$ and each value b_i by $-b_i$, we obtain an equivalent less-than-or-equal-to constraint.

Finishing our example, we replace the equality in constraint (29.22) by two inequalities, obtaining

$$
\begin{array}{lrcrcrcl}
\text{maximize} & 2x_1 & - & 3x_2' & + & 3x_2'' \\
\text{subject to} \\
& x_1 & + & x_2' & - & x_2'' & \leq & 7 \\
& x_1 & + & x_2' & - & x_2'' & \geq & 7 \\
& x_1 & - & 2x_2' & + & 2x_2'' & \leq & 4 \\
& x_1, x_2', x_2'' & & & & & \geq & 0 \ .
\end{array}
\tag{29.23}
$$

Finally, we negate constraint (29.23). For consistency in variable names, we rename x_2' to x_2 and x_2'' to x_3, obtaining the standard form

$$
\begin{array}{lrcrcrcl}
\text{maximize} & 2x_1 & - & 3x_2 & + & 3x_3 & & & \tag{29.24}
\end{array}
$$

subject to

$$
\begin{array}{rcrcrcrl}
x_1 & + & x_2 & - & x_3 & \leq & 7 & \tag{29.25} \\
-x_1 & - & x_2 & + & x_3 & \leq & -7 & \tag{29.26} \\
x_1 & - & 2x_2 & + & 2x_3 & \leq & 4 & \tag{29.27} \\
x_1, x_2, x_3 & & & & & \geq & 0 \ . & \tag{29.28}
\end{array}
$$

Converting linear programs into slack form

To efficiently solve a linear program with the simplex algorithm, we prefer to express it in a form in which some of the constraints are equality constraints. More precisely, we shall convert it into a form in which the nonnegativity constraints are the only inequality constraints, and the remaining constraints are equalities. Let

$$\sum_{j=1}^{n} a_{ij} x_j \leq b_i \tag{29.29}$$

be an inequality constraint. We introduce a new variable s and rewrite inequality (29.29) as the two constraints

$$s = b_i - \sum_{j=1}^{n} a_{ij} x_j \, , \tag{29.30}$$

$$s \geq 0 \, . \tag{29.31}$$

We call s a **slack variable** because it measures the **slack**, or difference, between the left-hand and right-hand sides of equation (29.29). (We shall soon see why we find it convenient to write the constraint with only the slack variable on the left-hand side.) Because inequality (29.29) is true if and only if both equation (29.30) and inequality (29.31) are true, we can convert each inequality constraint of a linear program in this way to obtain an equivalent linear program in which the only inequality constraints are the nonnegativity constraints. When converting from standard to slack form, we shall use x_{n+i} (instead of s) to denote the slack variable associated with the ith inequality. The ith constraint is therefore

$$x_{n+i} = b_i - \sum_{j=1}^{n} a_{ij} x_j \, , \tag{29.32}$$

along with the nonnegativity constraint $x_{n+i} \geq 0$.

By converting each constraint of a linear program in standard form, we obtain a linear program in a different form. For example, for the linear program described in (29.24)–(29.28), we introduce slack variables x_4, x_5, and x_6, obtaining

$$\text{maximize} \qquad\qquad 2x_1 \quad - \quad 3x_2 \quad + \quad 3x_3 \tag{29.33}$$

subject to

$$
\begin{aligned}
x_4 &= 7 \;-\; x_1 \;-\; x_2 \;+\; x_3 & (29.34)\\
x_5 &= -7 \;+\; x_1 \;+\; x_2 \;-\; x_3 & (29.35)\\
x_6 &= 4 \;-\; x_1 \;+\; 2x_2 \;-\; 2x_3 & (29.36)\\
x_1, x_2, x_3, x_4, x_5, x_6 &\geq 0 \;. & (29.37)
\end{aligned}
$$

In this linear program, all the constraints except for the nonnegativity constraints are equalities, and each variable is subject to a nonnegativity constraint. We write each equality constraint with one of the variables on the left-hand side of the equality and all others on the right-hand side. Furthermore, each equation has the same set of variables on the right-hand side, and these variables are also the only ones that appear in the objective function. We call the variables on the left-hand side of the equalities **basic variables** and those on the right-hand side **nonbasic variables**.

For linear programs that satisfy these conditions, we shall sometimes omit the words "maximize" and "subject to," as well as the explicit nonnegativity constraints. We shall also use the variable z to denote the value of the objective func-

tion. We call the resulting format **slack form**. If we write the linear program given in (29.33)–(29.37) in slack form, we obtain

$$z \quad = \qquad\qquad 2x_1 \quad - \quad 3x_2 \quad + \quad 3x_3 \tag{29.38}$$

$$x_4 \quad = \quad 7 \quad - \quad x_1 \quad - \quad x_2 \quad + \quad x_3 \tag{29.39}$$

$$x_5 \quad = \quad -7 \quad + \quad x_1 \quad + \quad x_2 \quad - \quad x_3 \tag{29.40}$$

$$x_6 \quad = \quad 4 \quad - \quad x_1 \quad + \quad 2x_2 \quad - \quad 2x_3 \ . \tag{29.41}$$

As with standard form, we find it convenient to have a more concise notation for describing a slack form. As we shall see in Section 29.3, the sets of basic and nonbasic variables will change as the simplex algorithm runs. We use N to denote the set of indices of the nonbasic variables and B to denote the set of indices of the basic variables. We always have that $|N| = n$, $|B| = m$, and $N \cup B = \{1, 2, \ldots, n + m\}$. The equations are indexed by the entries of B, and the variables on the right-hand sides are indexed by the entries of N. As in standard form, we use b_i, c_j, and a_{ij} to denote constant terms and coefficients. We also use v to denote an optional constant term in the objective function. (We shall see a little later that including the constant term in the objective function makes it easy to determine the value of the objective function.) Thus we can concisely define a slack form by a tuple (N, B, A, b, c, v), denoting the slack form

$$z \quad = \quad v \quad + \quad \sum_{j \in N} c_j x_j \tag{29.42}$$

$$x_i \quad = \quad b_i \quad - \quad \sum_{j \in N} a_{ij} x_j \quad \text{for } i \in B \ , \tag{29.43}$$

in which all variables x are constrained to be nonnegative. Because we subtract the sum $\sum_{j \in N} a_{ij} x_j$ in (29.43), the values a_{ij} are actually the negatives of the coefficients as they "appear" in the slack form.

For example, in the slack form

$$z \quad = \quad 28 \quad - \quad \frac{x_3}{6} \quad - \quad \frac{x_5}{6} \quad - \quad \frac{2x_6}{3}$$

$$x_1 \quad = \quad 8 \quad + \quad \frac{x_3}{6} \quad + \quad \frac{x_5}{6} \quad - \quad \frac{x_6}{3}$$

$$x_2 \quad = \quad 4 \quad - \quad \frac{8x_3}{3} \quad - \quad \frac{2x_5}{3} \quad + \quad \frac{x_6}{3}$$

$$x_4 \quad = \quad 18 \quad - \quad \frac{x_3}{2} \quad + \quad \frac{x_5}{2} \ ,$$

we have $B = \{1, 2, 4\}$, $N = \{3, 5, 6\}$,

$$A = \begin{pmatrix} a_{13} & a_{15} & a_{16} \\ a_{23} & a_{25} & a_{26} \\ a_{43} & a_{45} & a_{46} \end{pmatrix} = \begin{pmatrix} -1/6 & -1/6 & 1/3 \\ 8/3 & 2/3 & -1/3 \\ 1/2 & -1/2 & 0 \end{pmatrix},$$

$$b = \begin{pmatrix} b_1 \\ b_2 \\ b_4 \end{pmatrix} = \begin{pmatrix} 8 \\ 4 \\ 18 \end{pmatrix},$$

$c = \begin{pmatrix} c_3 & c_5 & c_6 \end{pmatrix}^T = \begin{pmatrix} -1/6 & -1/6 & -2/3 \end{pmatrix}^T$, and $v = 28$. Note that the indices into A, b, and c are not necessarily sets of contiguous integers; they depend on the index sets B and N. As an example of the entries of A being the negatives of the coefficients as they appear in the slack form, observe that the equation for x_1 includes the term $x_3/6$, yet the coefficient a_{13} is actually $-1/6$ rather than $+1/6$.

Exercises

29.1-1
If we express the linear program in (29.24)–(29.28) in the compact notation of (29.19)–(29.21), what are n, m, A, b, and c?

29.1-2
Give three feasible solutions to the linear program in (29.24)–(29.28). What is the objective value of each one?

29.1-3
For the slack form in (29.38)–(29.41), what are N, B, A, b, c, and v?

29.1-4
Convert the following linear program into standard form:

$$\begin{array}{llll}
\text{minimize} & 2x_1 + 7x_2 + x_3 & & \\
\text{subject to} & & & \\
& x_1 \qquad\quad - \; x_3 & = & 7 \\
& 3x_1 + x_2 & \geq & 24 \\
& \quad\quad x_2 & \geq & 0 \\
& \qquad\qquad x_3 & \leq & 0 \; .
\end{array}$$

29.1-5
Convert the following linear program into slack form:

$$\text{maximize} \quad 2x_1 \quad - \quad 6x_3$$

subject to

$$
\begin{array}{rcrcrcr}
x_1 & + & x_2 & - & x_3 & \le & 7 \\
3x_1 & - & x_2 & & & \ge & 8 \\
-x_1 & + & 2x_2 & + & 2x_3 & \ge & 0 \\
& & x_1, x_2, x_3 & & & \ge & 0 \; .
\end{array}
$$

What are the basic and nonbasic variables?

29.1-6
Show that the following linear program is infeasible:

$$\text{maximize} \quad 3x_1 \quad - \quad 2x_2$$

subject to

$$
\begin{array}{rcrcr}
x_1 & + & x_2 & \le & 2 \\
-2x_1 & - & 2x_2 & \le & -10 \\
& & x_1, x_2 & \ge & 0 \; .
\end{array}
$$

29.1-7
Show that the following linear program is unbounded:

$$\text{maximize} \quad x_1 \quad - \quad x_2$$

subject to

$$
\begin{array}{rcrcr}
-2x_1 & + & x_2 & \le & -1 \\
-x_1 & - & 2x_2 & \le & -2 \\
& & x_1, x_2 & \ge & 0 \; .
\end{array}
$$

29.1-8
Suppose that we have a general linear program with n variables and m constraints, and suppose that we convert it into standard form. Give an upper bound on the number of variables and constraints in the resulting linear program.

29.1-9
Give an example of a linear program for which the feasible region is not bounded, but the optimal objective value is finite.

29.2   Formulating problems as linear programs

Although we shall focus on the simplex algorithm in this chapter, it is also important to be able to recognize when we can formulate a problem as a linear program. Once we cast a problem as a polynomial-sized linear program, we can solve it in polynomial time by the ellipsoid algorithm or interior-point methods. Several linear-programming software packages can solve problems efficiently, so that once the problem is in the form of a linear program, such a package can solve it.

We shall look at several concrete examples of linear-programming problems. We start with two problems that we have already studied: the single-source shortest-paths problem (see Chapter 24) and the maximum-flow problem (see Chapter 26). We then describe the minimum-cost-flow problem. Although the minimum-cost-flow problem has a polynomial-time algorithm that is not based on linear programming, we won't describe the algorithm. Finally, we describe the multicommodity-flow problem, for which the only known polynomial-time algorithm is based on linear programming.

When we solved graph problems in Part VI, we used attribute notation, such as $v.d$ and $(u, v).f$. Linear programs typically use subscripted variables rather than objects with attached attributes, however. Therefore, when we express variables in linear programs, we shall indicate vertices and edges through subscripts. For example, we denote the shortest-path weight for vertex v not by $v.d$ but by d_v. Similarly, we denote the flow from vertex u to vertex v not by $(u, v).f$ but by f_{uv}. For quantities that are given as inputs to problems, such as edge weights or capacities, we shall continue to use notations such as $w(u, v)$ and $c(u, v)$.

Shortest paths

We can formulate the single-source shortest-paths problem as a linear program. In this section, we shall focus on how to formulate the single-pair shortest-path problem, leaving the extension to the more general single-source shortest-paths problem as Exercise 29.2-3.

In the single-pair shortest-path problem, we are given a weighted, directed graph $G = (V, E)$, with weight function $w : E \rightarrow \mathbb{R}$ mapping edges to real-valued weights, a source vertex s, and destination vertex t. We wish to compute the value d_t, which is the weight of a shortest path from s to t. To express this problem as a linear program, we need to determine a set of variables and constraints that define when we have a shortest path from s to t. Fortunately, the Bellman-Ford algorithm does exactly this. When the Bellman-Ford algorithm terminates, it has computed, for each vertex v, a value d_v (using subscript notation here rather than attribute notation) such that for each edge $(u, v) \in E$, we have $d_v \leq d_u + w(u, v)$.

The source vertex initially receives a value $d_s = 0$, which never changes. Thus we obtain the following linear program to compute the shortest-path weight from s to t:

maximize d_t (29.44)

subject to

$$d_v \;\leq\; d_u + w(u, v) \quad \text{for each edge } (u, v) \in E \;,$$ (29.45)

$$d_s \;=\; 0 \;.$$ (29.46)

You might be surprised that this linear program maximizes an objective function when it is supposed to compute shortest paths. We do not want to minimize the objective function, since then setting $\bar{d}_v = 0$ for all $v \in V$ would yield an optimal solution to the linear program without solving the shortest-paths problem. We maximize because an optimal solution to the shortest-paths problem sets each $\bar{d}_v$ to $\min_{u:(u,v)\in E} \{\bar{d}_u + w(u, v)\}$, so that $\bar{d}_v$ is the largest value that is less than or equal to all of the values in the set $\{\bar{d}_u + w(u, v)\}$. We want to maximize d_v for all vertices v on a shortest path from s to t subject to these constraints on all vertices v, and maximizing d_t achieves this goal.

This linear program has $|V|$ variables d_v, one for each vertex $v \in V$. It also has $|E| + 1$ constraints: one for each edge, plus the additional constraint that the source vertex's shortest-path weight always has the value 0.

Maximum flow

Next, we express the maximum-flow problem as a linear program. Recall that we are given a directed graph $G = (V, E)$ in which each edge $(u, v) \in E$ has a nonnegative capacity $c(u, v) \geq 0$, and two distinguished vertices: a source s and a sink t. As defined in Section 26.1, a flow is a nonnegative real-valued function $f : V \times V \to \mathbb{R}$ that satisfies the capacity constraint and flow conservation. A maximum flow is a flow that satisfies these constraints and maximizes the flow value, which is the total flow coming out of the source minus the total flow into the source. A flow, therefore, satisfies linear constraints, and the value of a flow is a linear function. Recalling also that we assume that $c(u, v) = 0$ if $(u, v) \notin E$ and that there are no antiparallel edges, we can express the maximum-flow problem as a linear program:

maximize $\displaystyle\sum_{v \in V} f_{sv} \;-\; \sum_{v \in V} f_{vs}$ (29.47)

subject to

$$f_{uv} \;\leq\; c(u, v) \quad \text{for each } u, v \in V \;,$$ (29.48)

$$\sum_{v \in V} f_{vu} \;=\; \sum_{v \in V} f_{uv} \quad \text{for each } u \in V - \{s, t\} \;,$$ (29.49)

$$f_{uv} \;\geq\; 0 \qquad \text{for each } u, v \in V \;.$$ (29.50)

This linear program has $|V|^2$ variables, corresponding to the flow between each pair of vertices, and it has $2|V|^2 + |V| - 2$ constraints.

It is usually more efficient to solve a smaller-sized linear program. The linear program in (29.47)–(29.50) has, for ease of notation, a flow and capacity of 0 for each pair of vertices u, v with $(u, v) \notin E$. It would be more efficient to rewrite the linear program so that it has $O(V + E)$ constraints. Exercise 29.2-5 asks you to do so.

Minimum-cost flow

In this section, we have used linear programming to solve problems for which we already knew efficient algorithms. In fact, an efficient algorithm designed specifically for a problem, such as Dijkstra's algorithm for the single-source shortest-paths problem, or the push-relabel method for maximum flow, will often be more efficient than linear programming, both in theory and in practice.

The real power of linear programming comes from the ability to solve new problems. Recall the problem faced by the politician in the beginning of this chapter. The problem of obtaining a sufficient number of votes, while not spending too much money, is not solved by any of the algorithms that we have studied in this book, yet we can solve it by linear programming. Books abound with such real-world problems that linear programming can solve. Linear programming is also particularly useful for solving variants of problems for which we may not already know of an efficient algorithm.

Consider, for example, the following generalization of the maximum-flow problem. Suppose that, in addition to a capacity $c(u, v)$ for each edge (u, v), we are given a real-valued cost $a(u, v)$. As in the maximum-flow problem, we assume that $c(u, v) = 0$ if $(u, v) \notin E$, and that there are no antiparallel edges. If we send f_{uv} units of flow over edge (u, v), we incur a cost of $a(u, v) f_{uv}$. We are also given a flow demand d. We wish to send d units of flow from s to t while minimizing the total cost $\sum_{(u,v) \in E} a(u, v) f_{uv}$ incurred by the flow. This problem is known as the ***minimum-cost-flow problem***.

Figure 29.3(a) shows an example of the minimum-cost-flow problem. We wish to send 4 units of flow from s to t while incurring the minimum total cost. Any particular legal flow, that is, a function f satisfying constraints (29.48)–(29.50), incurs a total cost of $\sum_{(u,v) \in E} a(u, v) f_{uv}$. We wish to find the particular 4-unit flow that minimizes this cost. Figure 29.3(b) shows an optimal solution, with total cost $\sum_{(u,v) \in E} a(u, v) f_{uv} = (2 \cdot 2) + (5 \cdot 2) + (3 \cdot 1) + (7 \cdot 1) + (1 \cdot 3) = 27$.

There are polynomial-time algorithms specifically designed for the minimum-cost-flow problem, but they are beyond the scope of this book. We can, however, express the minimum-cost-flow problem as a linear program. The linear program looks similar to the one for the maximum-flow problem with the additional con-

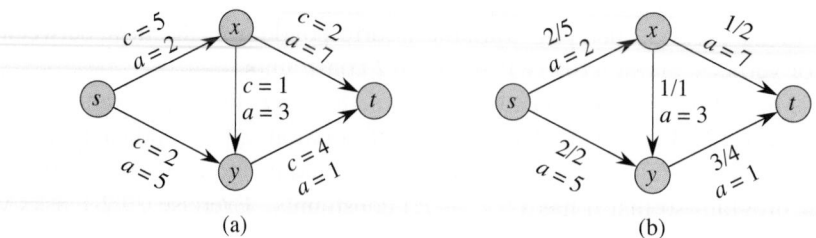

Figure 29.3   **(a)** An example of a minimum-cost-flow problem. We denote the capacities by c and the costs by a. Vertex s is the source and vertex t is the sink, and we wish to send 4 units of flow from s to t. **(b)** A solution to the minimum-cost flow problem in which 4 units of flow are sent from s to t. For each edge, the flow and capacity are written as flow/capacity.

straint that the value of the flow be exactly d units, and with the new objective function of minimizing the cost:

minimize $\displaystyle\sum_{(u,v)\in E} a(u,v) f_{uv}$ (29.51)

subject to

$$f_{uv} \leq c(u,v) \quad \text{for each } u, v \in V \,,$$

$$\sum_{v\in V} f_{vu} - \sum_{v\in V} f_{uv} = 0 \qquad \text{for each } u \in V - \{s,t\} \,,$$

$$\sum_{v\in V} f_{sv} - \sum_{v\in V} f_{vs} = d \,,$$

$$f_{uv} \geq 0 \qquad \text{for each } u, v \in V \,. \qquad (29.52)$$

Multicommodity flow

As a final example, we consider another flow problem. Suppose that the Lucky Puck company from Section 26.1 decides to diversify its product line and ship not only hockey pucks, but also hockey sticks and hockey helmets. Each piece of equipment is manufactured in its own factory, has its own warehouse, and must be shipped, each day, from factory to warehouse. The sticks are manufactured in Vancouver and must be shipped to Saskatoon, and the helmets are manufactured in Edmonton and must be shipped to Regina. The capacity of the shipping network does not change, however, and the different items, or ***commodities***, must share the same network.

This example is an instance of a ***multicommodity-flow problem***. In this problem, we are again given a directed graph $G = (V, E)$ in which each edge $(u, v) \in E$ has a nonnegative capacity $c(u, v) \geq 0$. As in the maximum-flow problem, we implicitly assume that $c(u, v) = 0$ for $(u, v) \notin E$, and that the graph has no antipar-

allel edges. In addition, we are given k different commodities, $K_1, K_2, \ldots, K_k$, where we specify commodity i by the triple $K_i = (s_i, t_i, d_i)$. Here, vertex s_i is the source of commodity i, vertex t_i is the sink of commodity i, and d_i is the demand for commodity i, which is the desired flow value for the commodity from s_i to t_i. We define a flow for commodity i, denoted by f_i, (so that f_{iuv} is the flow of commodity i from vertex u to vertex v) to be a real-valued function that satisfies the flow-conservation and capacity constraints. We now define f_{uv}, the **aggregate flow**, to be the sum of the various commodity flows, so that $f_{uv} = \sum_{i=1}^{k} f_{iuv}$. The aggregate flow on edge (u, v) must be no more than the capacity of edge (u, v). We are not trying to minimize any objective function in this problem; we need only determine whether such a flow exists. Thus, we write a linear program with a "null" objective function:

minimize $\qquad\qquad\qquad\qquad 0$

subject to

$$\sum_{i=1}^{k} f_{iuv} \;\le\; c(u, v) \quad \text{for each } u, v \in V\,,$$

$$\sum_{v \in V} f_{iuv} - \sum_{v \in V} f_{ivu} \;=\; 0 \qquad \begin{array}{l}\text{for each } i = 1, 2, \ldots, k \text{ and} \\ \text{for each } u \in V - \{s_i, t_i\}\,,\end{array}$$

$$\sum_{v \in V} f_{i,s_i,v} - \sum_{v \in V} f_{i,v,s_i} \;=\; d_i \qquad \text{for each } i = 1, 2, \ldots, k\,,$$

$$f_{iuv} \;\ge\; 0 \qquad \begin{array}{l}\text{for each } u, v \in V \text{ and} \\ \text{for each } i = 1, 2, \ldots, k\,.\end{array}$$

The only known polynomial-time algorithm for this problem expresses it as a linear program and then solves it with a polynomial-time linear-programming algorithm.

Exercises

29.2-1
Put the single-pair shortest-path linear program from (29.44)–(29.46) into standard form.

29.2-2
Write out explicitly the linear program corresponding to finding the shortest path from node s to node y in Figure 24.2(a).

29.2-3
In the single-source shortest-paths problem, we want to find the shortest-path weights from a source vertex s to all vertices $v \in V$. Given a graph G, write a

linear program for which the solution has the property that d_v is the shortest-path weight from s to v for each vertex $v \in V$.

29.2-4
Write out explicitly the linear program corresponding to finding the maximum flow in Figure 26.1(a).

29.2-5
Rewrite the linear program for maximum flow (29.47)–(29.50) so that it uses only $O(V + E)$ constraints.

29.2-6
Write a linear program that, given a bipartite graph $G = (V, E)$, solves the maximum-bipartite-matching problem.

29.2-7
In the ***minimum-cost multicommodity-flow problem***, we are given directed graph $G = (V, E)$ in which each edge $(u, v) \in E$ has a nonnegative capacity $c(u, v) \geq 0$ and a cost $a(u, v)$. As in the multicommodity-flow problem, we are given k different commodities, $K_1, K_2, \ldots, K_k$, where we specify commodity i by the triple $K_i = (s_i, t_i, d_i)$. We define the flow f_i for commodity i and the aggregate flow f_{uv} on edge (u, v) as in the multicommodity-flow problem. A feasible flow is one in which the aggregate flow on each edge (u, v) is no more than the capacity of edge (u, v). The cost of a flow is $\sum_{u,v \in V} a(u, v) f_{uv}$, and the goal is to find the feasible flow of minimum cost. Express this problem as a linear program.

29.3   The simplex algorithm

The simplex algorithm is the classical method for solving linear programs. In contrast to most of the other algorithms in this book, its running time is not polynomial in the worst case. It does yield insight into linear programs, however, and is often remarkably fast in practice.

In addition to having a geometric interpretation, described earlier in this chapter, the simplex algorithm bears some similarity to Gaussian elimination, discussed in Section 28.1. Gaussian elimination begins with a system of linear equalities whose solution is unknown. In each iteration, we rewrite this system in an equivalent form that has some additional structure. After some number of iterations, we have rewritten the system so that the solution is simple to obtain. The simplex algorithm proceeds in a similar manner, and we can view it as Gaussian elimination for inequalities.

We now describe the main idea behind an iteration of the simplex algorithm. Associated with each iteration will be a "basic solution" that we can easily obtain from the slack form of the linear program: set each nonbasic variable to 0 and compute the values of the basic variables from the equality constraints. An iteration converts one slack form into an equivalent slack form. The objective value of the associated basic feasible solution will be no less than that at the previous iteration, and usually greater. To achieve this increase in the objective value, we choose a nonbasic variable such that if we were to increase that variable's value from 0, then the objective value would increase, too. The amount by which we can increase the variable is limited by the other constraints. In particular, we raise it until some basic variable becomes 0. We then rewrite the slack form, exchanging the roles of that basic variable and the chosen nonbasic variable. Although we have used a particular setting of the variables to guide the algorithm, and we shall use it in our proofs, the algorithm does not explicitly maintain this solution. It simply rewrites the linear program until an optimal solution becomes "obvious."

An example of the simplex algorithm

We begin with an extended example. Consider the following linear program in standard form:

$$\text{maximize} \quad 3x_1 + x_2 + 2x_3 \tag{29.53}$$

subject to

$$x_1 + x_2 + 3x_3 \le 30 \tag{29.54}$$
$$2x_1 + 2x_2 + 5x_3 \le 24 \tag{29.55}$$
$$4x_1 + x_2 + 2x_3 \le 36 \tag{29.56}$$
$$x_1, x_2, x_3 \ge 0 \ . \tag{29.57}$$

In order to use the simplex algorithm, we must convert the linear program into slack form; we saw how to do so in Section 29.1. In addition to being an algebraic manipulation, slack is a useful algorithmic concept. Recalling from Section 29.1 that each variable has a corresponding nonnegativity constraint, we say that an equality constraint is ***tight*** for a particular setting of its nonbasic variables if they cause the constraint's basic variable to become 0. Similarly, a setting of the non-basic variables that would make a basic variable become negative ***violates*** that constraint. Thus, the slack variables explicitly maintain how far each constraint is from being tight, and so they help to determine how much we can increase values of nonbasic variables without violating any constraints.

Associating the slack variables x_4, x_5, and x_6 with inequalities (29.54)–(29.56), respectively, and putting the linear program into slack form, we obtain

$$z = \qquad 3x_1 + x_2 + 2x_3 \tag{29.58}$$

$$x_4 = 30 - x_1 - x_2 - 3x_3 \tag{29.59}$$

$$x_5 = 24 - 2x_1 - 2x_2 - 5x_3 \tag{29.60}$$

$$x_6 = 36 - 4x_1 - x_2 - 2x_3 \ . \tag{29.61}$$

The system of constraints (29.59)–(29.61) has 3 equations and 6 variables. Any setting of the variables x_1, x_2, and x_3 defines values for x_4, x_5, and x_6; therefore, we have an infinite number of solutions to this system of equations. A solution is feasible if all of $x_1, x_2, \ldots, x_6$ are nonnegative, and there can be an infinite number of feasible solutions as well. The infinite number of possible solutions to a system such as this one will be useful in later proofs. We focus on the ***basic solution***: set all the (nonbasic) variables on the right-hand side to 0 and then compute the values of the (basic) variables on the left-hand side. In this example, the basic solution is $(\bar{x}_1, \bar{x}_2, \ldots, \bar{x}_6) = (0, 0, 0, 30, 24, 36)$ and it has objective value $z = (3 \cdot 0) + (1 \cdot 0) + (2 \cdot 0) = 0$. Observe that this basic solution sets $\bar{x}_i = b_i$ for each $i \in B$. An iteration of the simplex algorithm rewrites the set of equations and the objective function so as to put a different set of variables on the right-hand side. Thus, a different basic solution is associated with the rewritten problem. We emphasize that the rewrite does not in any way change the underlying linear-programming problem; the problem at one iteration has the identical set of feasible solutions as the problem at the previous iteration. The problem does, however, have a different basic solution than that of the previous iteration.

If a basic solution is also feasible, we call it a ***basic feasible solution***. As we run the simplex algorithm, the basic solution is almost always a basic feasible solution. We shall see in Section 29.5, however, that for the first few iterations of the simplex algorithm, the basic solution might not be feasible.

Our goal, in each iteration, is to reformulate the linear program so that the basic solution has a greater objective value. We select a nonbasic variable x_e whose coefficient in the objective function is positive, and we increase the value of x_e as much as possible without violating any of the constraints. The variable x_e becomes basic, and some other variable x_l becomes nonbasic. The values of other basic variables and of the objective function may also change.

To continue the example, let's think about increasing the value of x_1. As we increase x_1, the values of x_4, x_5, and x_6 all decrease. Because we have a nonnegativity constraint for each variable, we cannot allow any of them to become negative. If x_1 increases above 30, then x_4 becomes negative, and x_5 and x_6 become negative when x_1 increases above 12 and 9, respectively. The third constraint (29.61) is the tightest constraint, and it limits how much we can increase x_1. Therefore, we switch the roles of x_1 and x_6. We solve equation (29.61) for x_1 and obtain

$$x_1 = 9 - \frac{x_2}{4} - \frac{x_3}{2} - \frac{x_6}{4} \ . \tag{29.62}$$

To rewrite the other equations with x_6 on the right-hand side, we substitute for x_1 using equation (29.62). Doing so for equation (29.59), we obtain

$$
\begin{aligned}
x_4 &= 30 - x_1 - x_2 - 3x_3 \\
&= 30 - \left(9 - \frac{x_2}{4} - \frac{x_3}{2} - \frac{x_6}{4} \right) - x_2 - 3x_3 \\
&= 21 - \frac{3x_2}{4} - \frac{5x_3}{2} + \frac{x_6}{4} .
\end{aligned} \tag{29.63}
$$

Similarly, we combine equation (29.62) with constraint (29.60) and with objective function (29.58) to rewrite our linear program in the following form:

$$
z = 27 + \frac{x_2}{4} + \frac{x_3}{2} - \frac{3x_6}{4} \tag{29.64}
$$

$$
x_1 = 9 - \frac{x_2}{4} - \frac{x_3}{2} - \frac{x_6}{4} \tag{29.65}
$$

$$
x_4 = 21 - \frac{3x_2}{4} - \frac{5x_3}{2} + \frac{x_6}{4} \tag{29.66}
$$

$$
x_5 = 6 - \frac{3x_2}{2} - 4x_3 + \frac{x_6}{2} . \tag{29.67}
$$

We call this operation a ***pivot***. As demonstrated above, a pivot chooses a nonbasic variable x_e, called the ***entering variable***, and a basic variable x_l, called the ***leaving variable***, and exchanges their roles.

The linear program described in equations (29.64)–(29.67) is equivalent to the linear program described in equations (29.58)–(29.61). We perform two operations in the simplex algorithm: rewrite equations so that variables move between the left-hand side and the right-hand side, and substitute one equation into another. The first operation trivially creates an equivalent problem, and the second, by elementary linear algebra, also creates an equivalent problem. (See Exercise 29.3-3.)

To demonstrate this equivalence, observe that our original basic solution $(0, 0, 0, 30, 24, 36)$ satisfies the new equations (29.65)–(29.67) and has objective value $27 + (1/4) \cdot 0 + (1/2) \cdot 0 - (3/4) \cdot 36 = 0$. The basic solution associated with the new linear program sets the nonbasic values to 0 and is $(9, 0, 0, 21, 6, 0)$, with objective value $z = 27$. Simple arithmetic verifies that this solution also satisfies equations (29.59)–(29.61) and, when plugged into objective function (29.58), has objective value $(3 \cdot 9) + (1 \cdot 0) + (2 \cdot 0) = 27$.

Continuing the example, we wish to find a new variable whose value we wish to increase. We do not want to increase x_6, since as its value increases, the objective value decreases. We can attempt to increase either x_2 or x_3; let us choose x_3. How far can we increase x_3 without violating any of the constraints? Constraint (29.65) limits it to 18, constraint (29.66) limits it to $42/5$, and constraint (29.67) limits it to $3/2$. The third constraint is again the tightest one, and therefore we rewrite the third constraint so that x_3 is on the left-hand side and x_5 is on the right-hand

side. We then substitute this new equation, $x_3 = 3/2 - 3x_2/8 - x_5/4 + x_6/8$, into equations (29.64)–(29.66) and obtain the new, but equivalent, system

$$z = \frac{111}{4} + \frac{x_2}{16} - \frac{x_5}{8} - \frac{11x_6}{16} \tag{29.68}$$

$$x_1 = \frac{33}{4} - \frac{x_2}{16} + \frac{x_5}{8} - \frac{5x_6}{16} \tag{29.69}$$

$$x_3 = \frac{3}{2} - \frac{3x_2}{8} - \frac{x_5}{4} + \frac{x_6}{8} \tag{29.70}$$

$$x_4 = \frac{69}{4} + \frac{3x_2}{16} + \frac{5x_5}{8} - \frac{x_6}{16} . \tag{29.71}$$

This system has the associated basic solution $(33/4, 0, 3/2, 69/4, 0, 0)$, with objective value $111/4$. Now the only way to increase the objective value is to increase x_2. The three constraints give upper bounds of 132, 4, and ∞, respectively. (We get an upper bound of ∞ from constraint (29.71) because, as we increase x_2, the value of the basic variable x_4 increases also. This constraint, therefore, places no restriction on how much we can increase x_2.) We increase x_2 to 4, and it becomes nonbasic. Then we solve equation (29.70) for x_2 and substitute in the other equations to obtain

$$z = 28 - \frac{x_3}{6} - \frac{x_5}{6} - \frac{2x_6}{3} \tag{29.72}$$

$$x_1 = 8 + \frac{x_3}{6} + \frac{x_5}{6} - \frac{x_6}{3} \tag{29.73}$$

$$x_2 = 4 - \frac{8x_3}{3} - \frac{2x_5}{3} + \frac{x_6}{3} \tag{29.74}$$

$$x_4 = 18 - \frac{x_3}{2} + \frac{x_5}{2} . \tag{29.75}$$

At this point, all coefficients in the objective function are negative. As we shall see later in this chapter, this situation occurs only when we have rewritten the linear program so that the basic solution is an optimal solution. Thus, for this problem, the solution $(8, 4, 0, 18, 0, 0)$, with objective value 28, is optimal. We can now return to our original linear program given in (29.53)–(29.57). The only variables in the original linear program are x_1, x_2, and x_3, and so our solution is $x_1 = 8$, $x_2 = 4$, and $x_3 = 0$, with objective value $(3 \cdot 8) + (1 \cdot 4) + (2 \cdot 0) = 28$. Note that the values of the slack variables in the final solution measure how much slack remains in each inequality. Slack variable x_4 is 18, and in inequality (29.54), the left-hand side, with value $8 + 4 + 0 = 12$, is 18 less than the right-hand side of 30. Slack variables x_5 and x_6 are 0 and indeed, in inequalities (29.55) and (29.56), the left-hand and right-hand sides are equal. Observe also that even though the coefficients in the original slack form are integral, the coefficients in the other linear programs are not necessarily integral, and the intermediate solutions are not

necessarily integral. Furthermore, the final solution to a linear program need not be integral; it is purely coincidental that this example has an integral solution.

Pivoting

We now formalize the procedure for pivoting. The procedure PIVOT takes as input a slack form, given by the tuple (N, B, A, b, c, v), the index l of the leaving variable x_l, and the index e of the entering variable x_e. It returns the tuple $(\widehat{N}, \widehat{B}, \widehat{A}, \widehat{b}, \widehat{c}, \widehat{v})$ describing the new slack form. (Recall again that the entries of the $m \times n$ matrices A and $\widehat{A}$ are actually the negatives of the coefficients that appear in the slack form.)

PIVOT(N, B, A, b, c, v, l, e)

```
 1   // Compute the coefficients of the equation for new basic variable xₑ.
 2   let Â be a new m × n matrix
 3   b̂ₑ = bₗ/aₗₑ
 4   for each j ∈ N − {e}
 5       âₑⱼ = aₗⱼ/aₗₑ
 6   âₑₗ = 1/aₗₑ
 7   // Compute the coefficients of the remaining constraints.
 8   for each i ∈ B − {l}
 9       b̂ᵢ = bᵢ − aᵢₑb̂ₑ
10       for each j ∈ N − {e}
11           âᵢⱼ = aᵢⱼ − aᵢₑâₑⱼ
12       âᵢₗ = −aᵢₑâₑₗ
13   // Compute the objective function.
14   v̂ = v + cₑb̂ₑ
15   for each j ∈ N − {e}
16       ĉⱼ = cⱼ − cₑâₑⱼ
17   ĉₗ = −cₑâₑₗ
18   // Compute new sets of basic and nonbasic variables.
19   N̂ = N − {e} ∪ {l}
20   B̂ = B − {l} ∪ {e}
21   return (N̂, B̂, Â, b̂, ĉ, v̂)
```

PIVOT works as follows. Lines 3–6 compute the coefficients in the new equation for x_e by rewriting the equation that has x_l on the left-hand side to instead have x_e on the left-hand side. Lines 8–12 update the remaining equations by substituting the right-hand side of this new equation for each occurrence of x_e. Lines 14–17 do the same substitution for the objective function, and lines 19 and 20 update the

sets of nonbasic and basic variables. Line 21 returns the new slack form. As given, if $a_{le} = 0$, PIVOT would cause an error by dividing by 0, but as we shall see in the proofs of Lemmas 29.2 and 29.12, we call PIVOT only when $a_{le} \neq 0$.

We now summarize the effect that PIVOT has on the values of the variables in the basic solution.

Lemma 29.1

Consider a call to $\text{PIVOT}(N, B, A, b, c, v, l, e)$ in which $a_{le} \neq 0$. Let the values returned from the call be $(\widehat{N}, \widehat{B}, \widehat{A}, \widehat{b}, \widehat{c}, \widehat{v})$, and let $\bar{x}$ denote the basic solution after the call. Then

1. $\bar{x}_j = 0$ for each $j \in \widehat{N}$.
2. $\bar{x}_e = b_l / a_{le}$.
3. $\bar{x}_i = b_i - a_{ie}\widehat{b}_e$ for each $i \in \widehat{B} - \{e\}$.

Proof   The first statement is true because the basic solution always sets all nonbasic variables to 0. When we set each nonbasic variable to 0 in a constraint

$$x_i = \widehat{b}_i - \sum_{j \in \widehat{N}} \widehat{a}_{ij} x_j \,,$$

we have that $\bar{x}_i = \widehat{b}_i$ for each $i \in \widehat{B}$. Since $e \in \widehat{B}$, line 3 of PIVOT gives

$$\bar{x}_e = \widehat{b}_e = b_l / a_{le} \,,$$

which proves the second statement. Similarly, using line 9 for each $i \in \widehat{B} - \{e\}$, we have

$$\bar{x}_i = \widehat{b}_i = b_i - a_{ie}\widehat{b}_e \,,$$

which proves the third statement.   ∎

The formal simplex algorithm

We are now ready to formalize the simplex algorithm, which we demonstrated by example. That example was a particularly nice one, and we could have had several other issues to address:

- How do we determine whether a linear program is feasible?
- What do we do if the linear program is feasible, but the initial basic solution is not feasible?
- How do we determine whether a linear program is unbounded?
- How do we choose the entering and leaving variables?

In Section 29.5, we shall show how to determine whether a problem is feasible, and if so, how to find a slack form in which the initial basic solution is feasible. Therefore, let us assume that we have a procedure INITIALIZE-SIMPLEX(A, b, c) that takes as input a linear program in standard form, that is, an $m \times n$ matrix $A = (a_{ij})$, an m-vector $b = (b_i)$, and an n-vector $c = (c_j)$. If the problem is infeasible, the procedure returns a message that the program is infeasible and then terminates. Otherwise, the procedure returns a slack form for which the initial basic solution is feasible.

The procedure SIMPLEX takes as input a linear program in standard form, as just described. It returns an n-vector $\bar{x} = (\bar{x}_j)$ that is an optimal solution to the linear program described in (29.19)–(29.21).

SIMPLEX(A, b, c)

```
 1   (N, B, A, b, c, v) = INITIALIZE-SIMPLEX(A, b, c)
 2   let Δ be a new vector of length m
 3   while some index j ∈ N has c_j > 0
 4        choose an index e ∈ N for which c_e > 0
 5        for each index i ∈ B
 6            if a_ie > 0
 7                Δ_i = b_i/a_ie
 8            else Δ_i = ∞
 9        choose an index l ∈ B that minimizes Δ_l
10        if Δ_l == ∞
11            return "unbounded"
12        else (N, B, A, b, c, v) = PIVOT(N, B, A, b, c, v, l, e)
13   for i = 1 to n
14        if i ∈ B
15            x̄_i = b_i
16        else x̄_i = 0
17   return (x̄_1, x̄_2, ..., x̄_n)
```

The SIMPLEX procedure works as follows. In line 1, it calls the procedure INITIALIZE-SIMPLEX(A, b, c), described above, which either determines that the linear program is infeasible or returns a slack form for which the basic solution is feasible. The **while** loop of lines 3–12 forms the main part of the algorithm. If all coefficients in the objective function are negative, then the **while** loop terminates. Otherwise, line 4 selects a variable x_e, whose coefficient in the objective function is positive, as the entering variable. Although we may choose any such variable as the entering variable, we assume that we use some prespecified deterministic rule. Next, lines 5–9 check each constraint and pick the one that most severely limits the amount by which we can increase x_e without violating any of the nonnegativ-

ity constraints; the basic variable associated with this constraint is x_l. Again, we are free to choose one of several variables as the leaving variable, but we assume that we use some prespecified deterministic rule. If none of the constraints limits the amount by which the entering variable can increase, the algorithm returns "unbounded" in line 11. Otherwise, line 12 exchanges the roles of the entering and leaving variables by calling PIVOT(N, B, A, b, c, v, l, e), as described above. Lines 13–16 compute a solution $\bar{x}_1, \bar{x}_2, \ldots, \bar{x}_n$ for the original linear-programming variables by setting all the nonbasic variables to 0 and each basic variable $\bar{x}_i$ to b_i, and line 17 returns these values.

To show that SIMPLEX is correct, we first show that if SIMPLEX has an initial feasible solution and eventually terminates, then it either returns a feasible solution or determines that the linear program is unbounded. Then, we show that SIMPLEX terminates. Finally, in Section 29.4 (Theorem 29.10) we show that the solution returned is optimal.

Lemma 29.2
Given a linear program (A, b, c), suppose that the call to INITIALIZE-SIMPLEX in line 1 of SIMPLEX returns a slack form for which the basic solution is feasible. Then if SIMPLEX returns a solution in line 17, that solution is a feasible solution to the linear program. If SIMPLEX returns "unbounded" in line 11, the linear program is unbounded.

Proof   We use the following three-part loop invariant:

At the start of each iteration of the **while** loop of lines 3–12,

1. the slack form is equivalent to the slack form returned by the call of INITIALIZE-SIMPLEX,
2. for each $i \in B$, we have $b_i \geq 0$, and
3. the basic solution associated with the slack form is feasible.

Initialization: The equivalence of the slack forms is trivial for the first iteration. We assume, in the statement of the lemma, that the call to INITIALIZE-SIMPLEX in line 1 of SIMPLEX returns a slack form for which the basic solution is feasible. Thus, the third part of the invariant is true. Because the basic solution is feasible, each basic variable x_i is nonnegative. Furthermore, since the basic solution sets each basic variable x_i to b_i, we have that $b_i \geq 0$ for all $i \in B$. Thus, the second part of the invariant holds.

Maintenance: We shall show that each iteration of the **while** loop maintains the loop invariant, assuming that the **return** statement in line 11 does not execute. We shall handle the case in which line 11 executes when we discuss termination.

An iteration of the **while** loop exchanges the role of a basic and a nonbasic variable by calling the PIVOT procedure. By Exercise 29.3-3, the slack form is equivalent to the one from the previous iteration which, by the loop invariant, is equivalent to the initial slack form.

We now demonstrate the second part of the loop invariant. We assume that at the start of each iteration of the **while** loop, $b_i \geq 0$ for each $i \in B$, and we shall show that these inequalities remain true after the call to PIVOT in line 12. Since the only changes to the variables b_i and the set B of basic variables occur in this assignment, it suffices to show that line 12 maintains this part of the invariant. We let b_i, a_{ij}, and B refer to values before the call of PIVOT, and $\widehat{b}_i$ refer to values returned from PIVOT.

First, we observe that $\widehat{b}_e \geq 0$ because $b_l \geq 0$ by the loop invariant, $a_{le} > 0$ by lines 6 and 9 of SIMPLEX, and $\widehat{b}_e = b_l / a_{le}$ by line 3 of PIVOT.

For the remaining indices $i \in B - \{l\}$, we have that

$$
\begin{aligned}
\widehat{b}_i &= b_i - a_{ie}\widehat{b}_e && \text{(by line 9 of PIVOT)} \\
&= b_i - a_{ie}(b_l / a_{le}) && \text{(by line 3 of PIVOT) .}
\end{aligned}
\tag{29.76}
$$

We have two cases to consider, depending on whether $a_{ie} > 0$ or $a_{ie} \leq 0$. If $a_{ie} > 0$, then since we chose l such that

$$
b_l / a_{le} \leq b_i / a_{ie} \quad \text{for all } i \in B ,
\tag{29.77}
$$

we have

$$
\begin{aligned}
\widehat{b}_i &= b_i - a_{ie}(b_l / a_{le}) && \text{(by equation (29.76))} \\
&\geq b_i - a_{ie}(b_i / a_{ie}) && \text{(by inequality (29.77))} \\
&= b_i - b_i \\
&= 0 ,
\end{aligned}
$$

and thus $\widehat{b}_i \geq 0$. If $a_{ie} \leq 0$, then because a_{le}, b_i, and b_l are all nonnegative, equation (29.76) implies that $\widehat{b}_i$ must be nonnegative, too.

We now argue that the basic solution is feasible, i.e., that all variables have nonnegative values. The nonbasic variables are set to 0 and thus are nonnegative. Each basic variable x_i is defined by the equation

$$
x_i = b_i - \sum_{j \in N} a_{ij} x_j .
$$

The basic solution sets $\bar{x}_i = b_i$. Using the second part of the loop invariant, we conclude that each basic variable $\bar{x}_i$ is nonnegative.

Termination: The **while** loop can terminate in one of two ways. If it terminates because of the condition in line 3, then the current basic solution is feasible and line 17 returns this solution. The other way it terminates is by returning "unbounded" in line 11. In this case, for each iteration of the **for** loop in lines 5–8, when line 6 is executed, we find that $a_{ie} \leq 0$. Consider the solution $\bar{x}$ defined as

$$
\bar{x}_i = \begin{cases} \infty & \text{if } i = e, \\ 0 & \text{if } i \in N - \{e\}, \\ b_i - \sum_{j \in N} a_{ij} \bar{x}_j & \text{if } i \in B. \end{cases}
$$

We now show that this solution is feasible, i.e., that all variables are nonnegative. The nonbasic variables other than $\bar{x}_e$ are 0, and $\bar{x}_e = \infty > 0$; thus all nonbasic variables are nonnegative. For each basic variable $\bar{x}_i$, we have

$$
\begin{aligned}
\bar{x}_i &= b_i - \sum_{j \in N} a_{ij} \bar{x}_j \\
&= b_i - a_{ie} \bar{x}_e .
\end{aligned}
$$

The loop invariant implies that $b_i \geq 0$, and we have $a_{ie} \leq 0$ and $\bar{x}_e = \infty > 0$. Thus, $\bar{x}_i \geq 0$.

Now we show that the objective value for the solution $\bar{x}$ is unbounded. From equation (29.42), the objective value is

$$
\begin{aligned}
z &= v + \sum_{j \in N} c_j \bar{x}_j \\
&= v + c_e \bar{x}_e .
\end{aligned}
$$

Since $c_e > 0$ (by line 4 of SIMPLEX) and $\bar{x}_e = \infty$, the objective value is ∞, and thus the linear program is unbounded. ∎

It remains to show that SIMPLEX terminates, and when it does terminate, the solution it returns is optimal. Section 29.4 will address optimality. We now discuss termination.

Termination

In the example given in the beginning of this section, each iteration of the simplex algorithm increased the objective value associated with the basic solution. As Exercise 29.3-2 asks you to show, no iteration of SIMPLEX can decrease the objective value associated with the basic solution. Unfortunately, it is possible that an iteration leaves the objective value unchanged. This phenomenon is called **_degeneracy_**, and we shall now study it in greater detail.

The assignment in line 14 of PIVOT, $\hat{v} = v + c_e \hat{b}_e$, changes the objective value. Since SIMPLEX calls PIVOT only when $c_e > 0$, the only way for the objective value to remain unchanged (i.e., $\hat{v} = v$) is for $\hat{b}_e$ to be 0. This value is assigned as $\hat{b}_e = b_l / a_{le}$ in line 3 of PIVOT. Since we always call PIVOT with $a_{le} \neq 0$, we see that for $\hat{b}_e$ to equal 0, and hence the objective value to be unchanged, we must have $b_l = 0$.

Indeed, this situation can occur. Consider the linear program

$$
\begin{aligned}
z &= & x_1 &+ x_2 &+ x_3 \\
x_4 &= 8 &- x_1 &- x_2 & \\
x_5 &= & & x_2 &- x_3 \ .
\end{aligned}
$$

Suppose that we choose x_1 as the entering variable and x_4 as the leaving variable. After pivoting, we obtain

$$
\begin{aligned}
z &= 8 & &+ x_3 &- x_4 \\
x_1 &= 8 &- x_2 & &- x_4 \\
x_5 &= & x_2 &- x_3 & \ .
\end{aligned}
$$

At this point, our only choice is to pivot with x_3 entering and x_5 leaving. Since $b_5 = 0$, the objective value of 8 remains unchanged after pivoting:

$$
\begin{aligned}
z &= 8 &+ x_2 &- x_4 &- x_5 \\
x_1 &= 8 &- x_2 &- x_4 & \\
x_3 &= & x_2 & &- x_5 \ .
\end{aligned}
$$

The objective value has not changed, but our slack form has. Fortunately, if we pivot again, with x_2 entering and x_1 leaving, the objective value increases (to 16), and the simplex algorithm can continue.

Degeneracy can prevent the simplex algorithm from terminating, because it can lead to a phenomenon known as *cycling*: the slack forms at two different iterations of SIMPLEX are identical. Because of degeneracy, SIMPLEX could choose a sequence of pivot operations that leave the objective value unchanged but repeat a slack form within the sequence. Since SIMPLEX is a deterministic algorithm, if it cycles, then it will cycle through the same series of slack forms forever, never terminating.

Cycling is the only reason that SIMPLEX might not terminate. To show this fact, we must first develop some additional machinery.

At each iteration, SIMPLEX maintains A, b, c, and v in addition to the sets N and B. Although we need to explicitly maintain A, b, c, and v in order to implement the simplex algorithm efficiently, we can get by without maintaining them. In other words, the sets of basic and nonbasic variables suffice to uniquely determine the slack form. Before proving this fact, we prove a useful algebraic lemma.

Lemma 29.3

Let I be a set of indices. For each $j \in I$, let α_j and β_j be real numbers, and let x_j be a real-valued variable. Let γ be any real number. Suppose that for any settings of the x_j, we have

$$\sum_{j \in I} \alpha_j x_j = \gamma + \sum_{j \in I} \beta_j x_j \ . \tag{29.78}$$

Then $\alpha_j = \beta_j$ for each $j \in I$, and $\gamma = 0$.

Proof Since equation (29.78) holds for any values of the x_j, we can use particular values to draw conclusions about α, β, and γ. If we let $x_j = 0$ for each $j \in I$, we conclude that $\gamma = 0$. Now pick an arbitrary index $j \in I$, and set $x_j = 1$ and $x_k = 0$ for all $k \neq j$. Then we must have $\alpha_j = \beta_j$. Since we picked j as any index in I, we conclude that $\alpha_j = \beta_j$ for each $j \in I$. ■

A particular linear program has many different slack forms; recall that each slack form has the same set of feasible and optimal solutions as the original linear program. We now show that the slack form of a linear program is uniquely determined by the set of basic variables. That is, given the set of basic variables, a unique slack form (unique set of coefficients and right-hand sides) is associated with those basic variables.

Lemma 29.4

Let (A, b, c) be a linear program in standard form. Given a set B of basic variables, the associated slack form is uniquely determined.

Proof Assume for the purpose of contradiction that there are two different slack forms with the same set B of basic variables. The slack forms must also have identical sets $N = \{1, 2, \ldots, n + m\} - B$ of nonbasic variables. We write the first slack form as

$$z = v + \sum_{j \in N} c_j x_j \tag{29.79}$$

$$x_i = b_i - \sum_{j \in N} a_{ij} x_j \quad \text{for } i \in B \ , \tag{29.80}$$

and the second as

$$z = v' + \sum_{j \in N} c'_j x_j \tag{29.81}$$

$$x_i = b'_i - \sum_{j \in N} a'_{ij} x_j \quad \text{for } i \in B \ . \tag{29.82}$$

Consider the system of equations formed by subtracting each equation in line (29.82) from the corresponding equation in line (29.80). The resulting system is

$$0 = (b_i - b_i') - \sum_{j \in N}(a_{ij} - a_{ij}')x_j \quad \text{for } i \in B$$

or, equivalently,

$$\sum_{j \in N} a_{ij}x_j = (b_i - b_i') + \sum_{j \in N} a_{ij}'x_j \quad \text{for } i \in B \ .$$

Now, for each $i \in B$, apply Lemma 29.3 with $\alpha_j = a_{ij}, \beta_j = a_{ij}', \gamma = b_i - b_i'$, and $I = N$. Since $\alpha_j = \beta_j$, we have that $a_{ij} = a_{ij}'$ for each $j \in N$, and since $\gamma = 0$, we have that $b_i = b_i'$. Thus, for the two slack forms, A and b are identical to A' and b'. Using a similar argument, Exercise 29.3-1 shows that it must also be the case that $c = c'$ and $\nu = \nu'$, and hence that the slack forms must be identical. ∎

We can now show that cycling is the only possible reason that SIMPLEX might not terminate.

Lemma 29.5
If SIMPLEX fails to terminate in at most $\binom{n+m}{m}$ iterations, then it cycles.

Proof   By Lemma 29.4, the set B of basic variables uniquely determines a slack form. There are $n + m$ variables and $|B| = m$, and therefore, there are at most $\binom{n+m}{m}$ ways to choose B. Thus, there are only at most $\binom{n+m}{m}$ unique slack forms. Therefore, if SIMPLEX runs for more than $\binom{n+m}{m}$ iterations, it must cycle. ∎

Cycling is theoretically possible, but extremely rare. We can prevent it by choosing the entering and leaving variables somewhat more carefully. One option is to perturb the input slightly so that it is impossible to have two solutions with the same objective value. Another option is to break ties by always choosing the variable with the smallest index, a strategy known as ***Bland's rule***. We omit the proof that these strategies avoid cycling.

Lemma 29.6
If lines 4 and 9 of SIMPLEX always break ties by choosing the variable with the smallest index, then SIMPLEX must terminate. ∎

We conclude this section with the following lemma.

Lemma 29.7

Assuming that INITIALIZE-SIMPLEX returns a slack form for which the basic solution is feasible, SIMPLEX either reports that a linear program is unbounded, or it terminates with a feasible solution in at most $\binom{n+m}{m}$ iterations.

Proof Lemmas 29.2 and 29.6 show that if INITIALIZE-SIMPLEX returns a slack form for which the basic solution is feasible, SIMPLEX either reports that a linear program is unbounded, or it terminates with a feasible solution. By the contrapositive of Lemma 29.5, if SIMPLEX terminates with a feasible solution, then it terminates in at most $\binom{n+m}{m}$ iterations. ∎

Exercises

29.3-1
Complete the proof of Lemma 29.4 by showing that it must be the case that $c = c'$ and $v = v'$.

29.3-2
Show that the call to PIVOT in line 12 of SIMPLEX never decreases the value of v.

29.3-3
Prove that the slack form given to the PIVOT procedure and the slack form that the procedure returns are equivalent.

29.3-4
Suppose we convert a linear program (A, b, c) in standard form to slack form. Show that the basic solution is feasible if and only if $b_i \geq 0$ for $i = 1, 2, \ldots, m$.

29.3-5
Solve the following linear program using SIMPLEX:

$$
\begin{array}{lrcrcl}
\text{maximize} & 18x_1 & + & 12.5x_2 \\
\text{subject to} \\
& x_1 & + & x_2 & \leq & 20 \\
& x_1 & & & \leq & 12 \\
& & & x_2 & \leq & 16 \\
& x_1, x_2 & & & \geq & 0 \ .
\end{array}
$$

29.3-6
Solve the following linear program using SIMPLEX:

maximize $5x_1 \;-\; 3x_2$

subject to

$$
\begin{aligned}
x_1 \;-\;\; x_2 &\;\le\; 1 \\
2x_1 \;+\;\; x_2 &\;\le\; 2 \\
x_1, x_2 &\;\ge\; 0 \;.
\end{aligned}
$$

29.3-7
Solve the following linear program using SIMPLEX:

minimize $x_1 \;+\; x_2 \;+\; x_3$

subject to

$$
\begin{aligned}
2x_1 \;+\; 7.5x_2 \;+\; 3x_3 &\;\ge\; 10000 \\
20x_1 \;+\; 5x_2 \;+\; 10x_3 &\;\ge\; 30000 \\
x_1, x_2, x_3 &\;\ge\; 0 \;.
\end{aligned}
$$

29.3-8
In the proof of Lemma 29.5, we argued that there are at most $\binom{m+n}{n}$ ways to choose a set B of basic variables. Give an example of a linear program in which there are strictly fewer than $\binom{m+n}{n}$ ways to choose the set B.

29.4   Duality

We have proven that, under certain assumptions, SIMPLEX terminates. We have not yet shown that it actually finds an optimal solution to a linear program, however. In order to do so, we introduce a powerful concept called *linear-programming duality*.

Duality enables us to prove that a solution is indeed optimal. We saw an example of duality in Chapter 26 with Theorem 26.6, the max-flow min-cut theorem. Suppose that, given an instance of a maximum-flow problem, we find a flow f with value $|f|$. How do we know whether f is a maximum flow? By the max-flow min-cut theorem, if we can find a cut whose value is also $|f|$, then we have verified that f is indeed a maximum flow. This relationship provides an example of duality: given a maximization problem, we define a related minimization problem such that the two problems have the same optimal objective values.

Given a linear program in which the objective is to maximize, we shall describe how to formulate a *dual* linear program in which the objective is to minimize and

whose optimal value is identical to that of the original linear program. When referring to dual linear programs, we call the original linear program the ***primal***.

Given a primal linear program in standard form, as in (29.16)–(29.18), we define
the dual linear program as

$$\text{minimize} \quad \sum_{i=1}^{m} b_i y_i \tag{29.83}$$

subject to

$$\sum_{i=1}^{m} a_{ij} y_i \geq c_j \quad \text{for } j = 1, 2, \ldots, n, \tag{29.84}$$

$$y_i \geq 0 \quad \text{for } i = 1, 2, \ldots, m. \tag{29.85}$$

To form the dual, we change the maximization to a minimization, exchange the
roles of coefficients on the right-hand sides and the objective function, and replace
each less-than-or-equal-to by a greater-than-or-equal-to. Each of the m constraints
in the primal has an associated variable y_i in the dual, and each of the n constraints
in the dual has an associated variable x_j in the primal. For example, consider the
linear program given in (29.53)–(29.57). The dual of this linear program is

$$\text{minimize} \quad 30y_1 + 24y_2 + 36y_3 \tag{29.86}$$

subject to

$$y_1 + 2y_2 + 4y_3 \geq 3 \tag{29.87}$$

$$y_1 + 2y_2 + y_3 \geq 1 \tag{29.88}$$

$$3y_1 + 5y_2 + 2y_3 \geq 2 \tag{29.89}$$

$$y_1, y_2, y_3 \geq 0. \tag{29.90}$$

We shall show in Theorem 29.10 that the optimal value of the dual linear program is always equal to the optimal value of the primal linear program. Furthermore, the simplex algorithm actually implicitly solves both the primal and the dual
linear programs simultaneously, thereby providing a proof of optimality.

We begin by demonstrating ***weak duality***, which states that any feasible solution to the primal linear program has a value no greater than that of any feasible
solution to the dual linear program.

Lemma 29.8 (Weak linear-programming duality)
Let $\bar{x}$ be any feasible solution to the primal linear program in (29.16)–(29.18) and
let $\bar{y}$ be any feasible solution to the dual linear program in (29.83)–(29.85). Then,
we have

$$\sum_{j=1}^{n} c_j \bar{x}_j \leq \sum_{i=1}^{m} b_i \bar{y}_i.$$

Proof We have

$$
\begin{aligned}
\sum_{j=1}^{n} c_j \bar{x}_j &\le \sum_{j=1}^{n} \left(\sum_{i=1}^{m} a_{ij} \bar{y}_i \right) \bar{x}_j \quad \text{(by inequalities (29.84))} \\
&= \sum_{i=1}^{m} \left(\sum_{j=1}^{n} a_{ij} \bar{x}_j \right) \bar{y}_i \\
&\le \sum_{i=1}^{m} b_i \bar{y}_i \qquad\qquad \text{(by inequalities (29.17))} .
\end{aligned}
$$
■

Corollary 29.9

Let $\bar{x}$ be a feasible solution to a primal linear program (A, b, c), and let $\bar{y}$ be a feasible solution to the corresponding dual linear program. If

$$
\sum_{j=1}^{n} c_j \bar{x}_j = \sum_{i=1}^{m} b_i \bar{y}_i \ ,
$$

then $\bar{x}$ and $\bar{y}$ are optimal solutions to the primal and dual linear programs, respectively.

Proof By Lemma 29.8, the objective value of a feasible solution to the primal cannot exceed that of a feasible solution to the dual. The primal linear program is a maximization problem and the dual is a minimization problem. Thus, if feasible solutions $\bar{x}$ and $\bar{y}$ have the same objective value, neither can be improved. ■

Before proving that there always is a dual solution whose value is equal to that of an optimal primal solution, we describe how to find such a solution. When we ran the simplex algorithm on the linear program in (29.53)–(29.57), the final iteration yielded the slack form (29.72)–(29.75) with objective $z = 28 - x_3/6 - x_5/6 - 2x_6/3$, $B = \{1, 2, 4\}$, and $N = \{3, 5, 6\}$. As we shall show below, the basic solution associated with the final slack form is indeed an optimal solution to the linear program; an optimal solution to linear program (29.53)–(29.57) is therefore $(\bar{x}_1, \bar{x}_2, \bar{x}_3) = (8, 4, 0)$, with objective value $(3 \cdot 8) + (1 \cdot 4) + (2 \cdot 0) = 28$. As we also show below, we can read off an optimal dual solution: the negatives of the coefficients of the primal objective function are the values of the dual variables. More precisely, suppose that the last slack form of the primal is

$$
\begin{aligned}
z &= v' + \sum_{j \in N} c'_j x_j \\
x_i &= b'_i - \sum_{j \in N} a'_{ij} x_j \quad \text{for } i \in B \ .
\end{aligned}
$$

Then, to produce an optimal dual solution, we set

$$\bar{y}_i = \begin{cases} -c'_{n+i} & \text{if } (n+i) \in N \ , \\ 0 & \text{otherwise} \ . \end{cases} \tag{29.91}$$

Thus, an optimal solution to the dual linear program defined in (29.86)–(29.90) is $\bar{y}_1 = 0$ (since $n+1 = 4 \in B$), $\bar{y}_2 = -c'_5 = 1/6$, and $\bar{y}_3 = -c'_6 = 2/3$. Evaluating the dual objective function (29.86), we obtain an objective value of $(30 \cdot 0) + (24 \cdot (1/6)) + (36 \cdot (2/3)) = 28$, which confirms that the objective value of the primal is indeed equal to the objective value of the dual. Combining these calculations with Lemma 29.8 yields a proof that the optimal objective value of the primal linear program is 28. We now show that this approach applies in general: we can find an optimal solution to the dual and simultaneously prove that a solution to the primal is optimal.

Theorem 29.10 (Linear-programming duality)
Suppose that SIMPLEX returns values $\bar{x} = (\bar{x}_1, \bar{x}_2, \ldots, \bar{x}_n)$ for the primal linear program (A, b, c). Let N and B denote the nonbasic and basic variables for the final slack form, let c' denote the coefficients in the final slack form, and let $\bar{y} = (\bar{y}_1, \bar{y}_2, \ldots, \bar{y}_m)$ be defined by equation (29.91). Then $\bar{x}$ is an optimal solution to the primal linear program, $\bar{y}$ is an optimal solution to the dual linear program, and

$$\sum_{j=1}^{n} c_j \bar{x}_j = \sum_{i=1}^{m} b_i \bar{y}_i \ . \tag{29.92}$$

Proof By Corollary 29.9, if we can find feasible solutions $\bar{x}$ and $\bar{y}$ that satisfy equation (29.92), then $\bar{x}$ and $\bar{y}$ must be optimal primal and dual solutions. We shall now show that the solutions $\bar{x}$ and $\bar{y}$ described in the statement of the theorem satisfy equation (29.92).

Suppose that we run SIMPLEX on a primal linear program, as given in lines (29.16)–(29.18). The algorithm proceeds through a series of slack forms until it terminates with a final slack form with objective function

$$z = v' + \sum_{j \in N} c'_j x_j \ . \tag{29.93}$$

Since SIMPLEX terminated with a solution, by the condition in line 3 we know that

$$c'_j \le 0 \quad \text{for all } j \in N \ . \tag{29.94}$$

If we define

$$c'_j = 0 \quad \text{for all } j \in B ,\tag{29.95}$$

we can rewrite equation (29.93) as

$$
\begin{aligned}
z &= v' + \sum_{j \in N} c'_j x_j \\
&= v' + \sum_{j \in N} c'_j x_j + \sum_{j \in B} c'_j x_j \quad \text{(because } c'_j = 0 \text{ if } j \in B) \\
&= v' + \sum_{j=1}^{n+m} c'_j x_j \qquad \text{(because } N \cup B = \{1, 2, \dots, n+m\}) . \tag{29.96}
\end{aligned}
$$

For the basic solution $\bar{x}$ associated with this final slack form, $\bar{x}_j = 0$ for all $j \in N$, and $z = v'$. Since all slack forms are equivalent, if we evaluate the original objective function on $\bar{x}$, we must obtain the same objective value:

$$
\begin{aligned}
\sum_{j=1}^{n} c_j \bar{x}_j &= v' + \sum_{j=1}^{n+m} c'_j \bar{x}_j \tag{29.97} \\
&= v' + \sum_{j \in N} c'_j \bar{x}_j + \sum_{j \in B} c'_j \bar{x}_j \\
&= v' + \sum_{j \in N} (c'_j \cdot 0) + \sum_{j \in B} (0 \cdot \bar{x}_j) \tag{29.98} \\
&= v' .
\end{aligned}
$$

We shall now show that $\bar{y}$, defined by equation (29.91), is feasible for the dual linear program and that its objective value $\sum_{i=1}^{m} b_i \bar{y}_i$ equals $\sum_{j=1}^{n} c_j \bar{x}_j$. Equation (29.97) says that the first and last slack forms, evaluated at $\bar{x}$, are equal. More generally, the equivalence of all slack forms implies that for *any* set of values $x = (x_1, x_2, \dots, x_n)$, we have

$$\sum_{j=1}^{n} c_j x_j = v' + \sum_{j=1}^{n+m} c'_j x_j .$$

Therefore, for any particular set of values $\bar{x} = (\bar{x}_1, \bar{x}_2, \dots, \bar{x}_n)$, we have

$$\sum_{j=1}^{n} c_j \bar{x}_j$$

$$= v' + \sum_{j=1}^{n+m} c'_j \bar{x}_j$$

$$= v' + \sum_{j=1}^{n} c'_j \bar{x}_j + \sum_{j=n+1}^{n+m} c'_j \bar{x}_j$$

$$= v' + \sum_{j=1}^{n} c'_j \bar{x}_j + \sum_{i=1}^{m} c'_{n+i} \bar{x}_{n+i}$$

$$= v' + \sum_{j=1}^{n} c'_j \bar{x}_j + \sum_{i=1}^{m} (-\bar{y}_i) \bar{x}_{n+i} \qquad \text{(by equations (29.91) and (29.95))}$$

$$= v' + \sum_{j=1}^{n} c'_j \bar{x}_j + \sum_{i=1}^{m} (-\bar{y}_i) \left(b_i - \sum_{j=1}^{n} a_{ij} \bar{x}_j \right) \quad \text{(by equation (29.32))}$$

$$= v' + \sum_{j=1}^{n} c'_j \bar{x}_j - \sum_{i=1}^{m} b_i \bar{y}_i + \sum_{i=1}^{m} \sum_{j=1}^{n} (a_{ij} \bar{x}_j) \bar{y}_i$$

$$= v' + \sum_{j=1}^{n} c'_j \bar{x}_j - \sum_{i=1}^{m} b_i \bar{y}_i + \sum_{j=1}^{n} \sum_{i=1}^{m} (a_{ij} \bar{y}_i) \bar{x}_j$$

$$= \left(v' - \sum_{i=1}^{m} b_i \bar{y}_i \right) + \sum_{j=1}^{n} \left(c'_j + \sum_{i=1}^{m} a_{ij} \bar{y}_i \right) \bar{x}_j ,$$

so that

$$\sum_{j=1}^{n} c_j \bar{x}_j = \left(v' - \sum_{i=1}^{m} b_i \bar{y}_i \right) + \sum_{j=1}^{n} \left(c'_j + \sum_{i=1}^{m} a_{ij} \bar{y}_i \right) \bar{x}_j . \qquad (29.99)$$

Applying Lemma 29.3 to equation (29.99), we obtain

$$v' - \sum_{i=1}^{m} b_i \bar{y}_i = 0 , \qquad (29.100)$$

$$c'_j + \sum_{i=1}^{m} a_{ij} \bar{y}_i = c_j \quad \text{for } j = 1, 2, \ldots, n . \qquad (29.101)$$

By equation (29.100), we have that $\sum_{i=1}^{m} b_i \bar{y}_i = v'$, and hence the objective value of the dual $\left(\sum_{i=1}^{m} b_i \bar{y}_i \right)$ is equal to that of the primal (v'). It remains to show

that the solution $\bar{y}$ is feasible for the dual problem. From inequalities (29.94) and equations (29.95), we have that $c'_j \leq 0$ for all $j = 1, 2, \ldots, n + m$. Hence, for any $j = 1, 2, \ldots, n$, equations (29.101) imply that

$$
\begin{aligned}
c_j &= c'_j + \sum_{i=1}^{m} a_{ij} \bar{y}_i \\
&\leq \sum_{i=1}^{m} a_{ij} \bar{y}_i \ ,
\end{aligned}
$$

which satisfies the constraints (29.84) of the dual. Finally, since $c'_j \leq 0$ for each $j \in N \cup B$, when we set $\bar{y}$ according to equation (29.91), we have that each $\bar{y}_i \geq 0$, and so the nonnegativity constraints are satisfied as well. ∎

We have shown that, given a feasible linear program, if INITIALIZE-SIMPLEX returns a feasible solution, and if SIMPLEX terminates without returning "unbounded," then the solution returned is indeed an optimal solution. We have also shown how to construct an optimal solution to the dual linear program.

Exercises

29.4-1
Formulate the dual of the linear program given in Exercise 29.3-5.

29.4-2
Suppose that we have a linear program that is not in standard form. We could produce the dual by first converting it to standard form, and then taking the dual. It would be more convenient, however, to be able to produce the dual directly. Explain how we can directly take the dual of an arbitrary linear program.

29.4-3
Write down the dual of the maximum-flow linear program, as given in lines (29.47)–(29.50) on page 860. Explain how to interpret this formulation as a minimum-cut problem.

29.4-4
Write down the dual of the minimum-cost-flow linear program, as given in lines (29.51)–(29.52) on page 862. Explain how to interpret this problem in terms of graphs and flows.

29.4-5
Show that the dual of the dual of a linear program is the primal linear program.

29.4-6

Which result from Chapter 26 can be interpreted as weak duality for the maximum-flow problem?

29.5   The initial basic feasible solution

In this section, we first describe how to test whether a linear program is feasible, and if it is, how to produce a slack form for which the basic solution is feasible. We conclude by proving the fundamental theorem of linear programming, which says that the SIMPLEX procedure always produces the correct result.

Finding an initial solution

In Section 29.3, we assumed that we had a procedure INITIALIZE-SIMPLEX that determines whether a linear program has any feasible solutions, and if it does, gives a slack form for which the basic solution is feasible. We describe this procedure here.

A linear program can be feasible, yet the initial basic solution might not be feasible. Consider, for example, the following linear program:

$$\text{maximize} \quad 2x_1 \ - \ x_2 \quad\quad\quad\quad\quad\quad\quad\quad\quad (29.102)$$

subject to

$$2x_1 \ - \ x_2 \ \le \ 2 \quad\quad\quad\quad\quad (29.103)$$
$$x_1 \ - \ 5x_2 \ \le \ -4 \quad\quad\quad\quad (29.104)$$
$$x_1, x_2 \ \ge \ 0 \ . \quad\quad\quad\quad\quad (29.105)$$

If we were to convert this linear program to slack form, the basic solution would set $x_1 = 0$ and $x_2 = 0$. This solution violates constraint (29.104), and so it is not a feasible solution. Thus, INITIALIZE-SIMPLEX cannot just return the obvious slack form. In order to determine whether a linear program has any feasible solutions, we will formulate an ***auxiliary linear program***. For this auxiliary linear program, we can find (with a little work) a slack form for which the basic solution is feasible. Furthermore, the solution of this auxiliary linear program determines whether the initial linear program is feasible and if so, it provides a feasible solution with which we can initialize SIMPLEX.

Lemma 29.11

Let L be a linear program in standard form, given as in (29.16)–(29.18). Let x_0 be a new variable, and let L_{aux} be the following linear program with $n + 1$ variables:

maximize $-x_0$ (29.106)

subject to

$$\sum_{j=1}^{n} a_{ij} x_j - x_0 \leq b_i \quad \text{for } i = 1, 2, \ldots, m ,$$ (29.107)

$$x_j \geq 0 \quad \text{for } j = 0, 1, \ldots, n .$$ (29.108)

Then L is feasible if and only if the optimal objective value of L_{aux} is 0.

Proof   Suppose that L has a feasible solution $\bar{x} = (\bar{x}_1, \bar{x}_2, \ldots, \bar{x}_n)$. Then the solution $\bar{x}_0 = 0$ combined with $\bar{x}$ is a feasible solution to L_{aux} with objective value 0. Since $x_0 \geq 0$ is a constraint of L_{aux} and the objective function is to maximize $-x_0$, this solution must be optimal for L_{aux}.

Conversely, suppose that the optimal objective value of L_{aux} is 0. Then $\bar{x}_0 = 0$, and the remaining solution values of $\bar{x}$ satisfy the constraints of L.   ∎

We now describe our strategy to find an initial basic feasible solution for a linear program L in standard form:

INITIALIZE-SIMPLEX(A, b, c)

```
 1   let k be the index of the minimum b_i
 2   if b_k ≥ 0                          // is the initial basic solution feasible?
 3       return ({1, 2, …, n}, {n + 1, n + 2, …, n + m}, A, b, c, 0)
 4   form L_aux by adding −x_0 to the left-hand side of each constraint
             and setting the objective function to −x_0
 5   let (N, B, A, b, c, v) be the resulting slack form for L_aux
 6   l = n + k
 7   // L_aux has n + 1 nonbasic variables and m basic variables.
 8   (N, B, A, b, c, v) = PIVOT(N, B, A, b, c, v, l, 0)
 9   // The basic solution is now feasible for L_aux.
10   iterate the while loop of lines 3–12 of SIMPLEX until an optimal solution
             to L_aux is found
11   if the optimal solution to L_aux sets x̄_0 to 0
12       if x̄_0 is basic
13           perform one (degenerate) pivot to make it nonbasic
14       from the final slack form of L_aux, remove x_0 from the constraints and
             restore the original objective function of L, but replace each basic
             variable in this objective function by the right-hand side of its
             associated constraint
15       return the modified final slack form
16   else return "infeasible"
```

INITIALIZE-SIMPLEX works as follows. In lines 1–3, we implicitly test the basic solution to the initial slack form for L given by $N = \{1, 2, \ldots, n\}$, $B = \{n+1, n+2, \ldots, n+m\}$, $\bar{x}_i = b_i$ for all $i \in B$, and $\bar{x}_j = 0$ for all $j \in N$. (Creating the slack form requires no explicit effort, as the values of A, b, and c are the same in both slack and standard forms.) If line 2 finds this basic solution to be feasible—that is, $\bar{x}_i \geq 0$ for all $i \in N \cup B$—then line 3 returns the slack form. Otherwise, in line 4, we form the auxiliary linear program L_{aux} as in Lemma 29.11. Since the initial basic solution to L is not feasible, the initial basic solution to the slack form for L_{aux} cannot be feasible either. To find a basic feasible solution, we perform a single pivot operation. Line 6 selects $l = n+k$ as the index of the basic variable that will be the leaving variable in the upcoming pivot operation. Since the basic variables are $x_{n+1}, x_{n+2}, \ldots, x_{n+m}$, the leaving variable x_l will be the one with the most negative value. Line 8 performs that call of PIVOT, with x_0 entering and x_l leaving. We shall see shortly that the basic solution resulting from this call of PIVOT will be feasible. Now that we have a slack form for which the basic solution is feasible, we can, in line 10, repeatedly call PIVOT to fully solve the auxiliary linear program. As the test in line 11 demonstrates, if we find an optimal solution to L_{aux} with objective value 0, then in lines 12–14, we create a slack form for L for which the basic solution is feasible. To do so, we first, in lines 12–13, handle the degenerate case in which x_0 may still be basic with value $\bar{x}_0 = 0$. In this case, we perform a pivot step to remove x_0 from the basis, using any $e \in N$ such that $a_{0e} \neq 0$ as the entering variable. The new basic solution remains feasible; the degenerate pivot does not change the value of any variable. Next we delete all x_0 terms from the constraints and restore the original objective function for L. The original objective function may contain both basic and nonbasic variables. Therefore, in the objective function we replace each basic variable by the right-hand side of its associated constraint. Line 15 then returns this modified slack form. If, on the other hand, line 11 discovers that the original linear program L is infeasible, then line 16 returns this information.

We now demonstrate the operation of INITIALIZE-SIMPLEX on the linear program (29.102)–(29.105). This linear program is feasible if we can find nonnegative values for x_1 and x_2 that satisfy inequalities (29.103) and (29.104). Using Lemma 29.11, we formulate the auxiliary linear program

$$\text{maximize} \qquad\qquad\qquad -x_0 \qquad\qquad\qquad\qquad (29.109)$$

subject to

$$2x_1 \;-\; x_2 \;-\; x_0 \;\leq\; 2 \qquad\qquad (29.110)$$
$$x_1 \;-\; 5x_2 \;-\; x_0 \;\leq\; -4 \qquad\qquad (29.111)$$
$$x_1, x_2, x_0 \;\geq\; 0 \;.$$

By Lemma 29.11, if the optimal objective value of this auxiliary linear program is 0, then the original linear program has a feasible solution. If the optimal objective

value of this auxiliary linear program is negative, then the original linear program does not have a feasible solution.

We write this linear program in slack form, obtaining

$$
\begin{aligned}
z &= && && && && - && x_0 \\
x_3 &= && 2 &- &2x_1 &+ &x_2 &+ &x_0 \\
x_4 &= && -4 &- &x_1 &+ &5x_2 &+ &x_0 \ .
\end{aligned}
$$

We are not out of the woods yet, because the basic solution, which would set $x_4 = -4$, is not feasible for this auxiliary linear program. We can, however, with one call to PIVOT, convert this slack form into one in which the basic solution is feasible. As line 8 indicates, we choose x_0 to be the entering variable. In line 6, we choose as the leaving variable x_4, which is the basic variable whose value in the basic solution is most negative. After pivoting, we have the slack form

$$
\begin{aligned}
z &= -4 &- &x_1 &+ &5x_2 &- &x_4 \\
x_0 &= 4 &+ &x_1 &- &5x_2 &+ &x_4 \\
x_3 &= 6 &- &x_1 &- &4x_2 &+ &x_4 \ .
\end{aligned}
$$

The associated basic solution is $(\bar{x}_0, \bar{x}_1, \bar{x}_2, \bar{x}_3, \bar{x}_4) = (4, 0, 0, 6, 0)$, which is feasible. We now repeatedly call PIVOT until we obtain an optimal solution to L_{aux}. In this case, one call to PIVOT with x_2 entering and x_0 leaving yields

$$
\begin{aligned}
z &= && && &- &x_0 \\
x_2 &= \frac{4}{5} &- &\frac{x_0}{5} &+ &\frac{x_1}{5} &+ &\frac{x_4}{5} \\
x_3 &= \frac{14}{5} &+ &\frac{4x_0}{5} &- &\frac{9x_1}{5} &+ &\frac{x_4}{5} \ .
\end{aligned}
$$

This slack form is the final solution to the auxiliary problem. Since this solution has $x_0 = 0$, we know that our initial problem was feasible. Furthermore, since $x_0 = 0$, we can just remove it from the set of constraints. We then restore the original objective function, with appropriate substitutions made to include only nonbasic variables. In our example, we get the objective function

$$
2x_1 - x_2 = 2x_1 - \left(\frac{4}{5} - \frac{x_0}{5} + \frac{x_1}{5} + \frac{x_4}{5} \right) \ .
$$

Setting $x_0 = 0$ and simplifying, we get the objective function

$$
-\frac{4}{5} + \frac{9x_1}{5} - \frac{x_4}{5} \ ,
$$

and the slack form

$$z = -\frac{4}{5} + \frac{9x_1}{5} - \frac{x_4}{5}$$

$$x_2 = \frac{4}{5} + \frac{x_1}{5} + \frac{x_4}{5}$$

$$x_3 = \frac{14}{5} - \frac{9x_1}{5} + \frac{x_4}{5} .$$

This slack form has a feasible basic solution, and we can return it to procedure SIMPLEX.

We now formally show the correctness of INITIALIZE-SIMPLEX.

Lemma 29.12

If a linear program L has no feasible solution, then INITIALIZE-SIMPLEX returns "infeasible." Otherwise, it returns a valid slack form for which the basic solution is feasible.

Proof First suppose that the linear program L has no feasible solution. Then by Lemma 29.11, the optimal objective value of L_{aux}, defined in (29.106)–(29.108), is nonzero, and by the nonnegativity constraint on x_0, the optimal objective value must be negative. Furthermore, this objective value must be finite, since setting $x_i = 0$, for $i = 1, 2, \ldots, n$, and $x_0 = |\min_{i=1}^{m}\{b_i\}|$ is feasible, and this solution has objective value $-|\min_{i=1}^{m}\{b_i\}|$. Therefore, line 10 of INITIALIZE-SIMPLEX finds a solution with a nonpositive objective value. Let $\bar{x}$ be the basic solution associated with the final slack form. We cannot have $\bar{x}_0 = 0$, because then L_{aux} would have objective value 0, which contradicts that the objective value is negative. Thus the test in line 11 results in line 16 returning "infeasible."

Suppose now that the linear program L does have a feasible solution. From Exercise 29.3-4, we know that if $b_i \geq 0$ for $i = 1, 2, \ldots, m$, then the basic solution associated with the initial slack form is feasible. In this case, lines 2–3 return the slack form associated with the input. (Converting the standard form to slack form is easy, since A, b, and c are the same in both.)

In the remainder of the proof, we handle the case in which the linear program is feasible but we do not return in line 3. We argue that in this case, lines 4–10 find a feasible solution to L_{aux} with objective value 0. First, by lines 1–2, we must have

$$b_k < 0 ,$$

and

$$b_k \leq b_i \quad \text{for each } i \in B . \tag{29.112}$$

In line 8, we perform one pivot operation in which the leaving variable x_l (recall that $l = n + k$, so that $b_l < 0$) is the left-hand side of the equation with minimum b_i, and the entering variable is x_0, the extra added variable. We now show

that after this pivot, all entries of b are nonnegative, and hence the basic solution to L_{aux} is feasible. Letting $\bar{x}$ be the basic solution after the call to PIVOT, and letting $\hat{b}$ and $\hat{B}$ be values returned by PIVOT, Lemma 29.1 implies that

$$\bar{x}_i = \begin{cases} b_i - a_{ie}\hat{b}_e & \text{if } i \in \hat{B} - \{e\}, \\ b_l/a_{le} & \text{if } i = e. \end{cases} \tag{29.113}$$

The call to PIVOT in line 8 has $e = 0$. If we rewrite inequalities (29.107), to include coefficients a_{i0},

$$\sum_{j=0}^{n} a_{ij}x_j \leq b_i \quad \text{for } i = 1, 2, \ldots, m, \tag{29.114}$$

then

$$a_{i0} = a_{ie} = -1 \quad \text{for each } i \in B. \tag{29.115}$$

(Note that a_{i0} is the coefficient of x_0 as it appears in inequalities (29.114), not the negation of the coefficient, because L_{aux} is in standard rather than slack form.) Since $l \in B$, we also have that $a_{le} = -1$. Thus, $b_l/a_{le} > 0$, and so $\bar{x}_e > 0$. For the remaining basic variables, we have

$$
\begin{aligned}
\bar{x}_i &= b_i - a_{ie}\hat{b}_e && \text{(by equation (29.113))} \\
&= b_i - a_{ie}(b_l/a_{le}) && \text{(by line 3 of PIVOT)} \\
&= b_i - b_l && \text{(by equation (29.115) and } a_{le} = -1\text{)} \\
&\geq 0 && \text{(by inequality (29.112))} ,
\end{aligned}
$$

which implies that each basic variable is now nonnegative. Hence the basic solution after the call to PIVOT in line 8 is feasible. We next execute line 10, which solves L_{aux}. Since we have assumed that L has a feasible solution, Lemma 29.11 implies that L_{aux} has an optimal solution with objective value 0. Since all the slack forms are equivalent, the final basic solution to L_{aux} must have $\bar{x}_0 = 0$, and after removing x_0 from the linear program, we obtain a slack form that is feasible for L. Line 15 then returns this slack form.   ∎

Fundamental theorem of linear programming

We conclude this chapter by showing that the SIMPLEX procedure works. In particular, any linear program either is infeasible, is unbounded, or has an optimal solution with a finite objective value. In each case, SIMPLEX acts appropriately.

Theorem 29.13 (Fundamental theorem of linear programming)
Any linear program L, given in standard form, either

1. has an optimal solution with a finite objective value,

2. is infeasible, or

3. is unbounded.

If L is infeasible, SIMPLEX returns "infeasible." If L is unbounded, SIMPLEX returns "unbounded." Otherwise, SIMPLEX returns an optimal solution with a finite objective value.

Proof   By Lemma 29.12, if linear program L is infeasible, then SIMPLEX returns "infeasible." Now suppose that the linear program L is feasible. By Lemma 29.12, INITIALIZE-SIMPLEX returns a slack form for which the basic solution is feasible. By Lemma 29.7, therefore, SIMPLEX either returns "unbounded" or terminates with a feasible solution. If it terminates with a finite solution, then Theorem 29.10 tells us that this solution is optimal. On the other hand, if SIMPLEX returns "unbounded," Lemma 29.2 tells us the linear program L is indeed unbounded. Since SIMPLEX always terminates in one of these ways, the proof is complete.   ∎

Exercises

29.5-1
Give detailed pseudocode to implement lines 5 and 14 of INITIALIZE-SIMPLEX.

29.5-2
Show that when the main loop of SIMPLEX is run by INITIALIZE-SIMPLEX, it can never return "unbounded."

29.5-3
Suppose that we are given a linear program L in standard form, and suppose that for both L and the dual of L, the basic solutions associated with the initial slack forms are feasible. Show that the optimal objective value of L is 0.

29.5-4
Suppose that we allow strict inequalities in a linear program. Show that in this case, the fundamental theorem of linear programming does not hold.

29.5-5
Solve the following linear program using SIMPLEX:

maximize $\quad x_1 \;+\; 3x_2$

subject to

$$
\begin{array}{rcrcr}
x_1 & - & x_2 & \le & 8 \\
-x_1 & - & x_2 & \le & -3 \\
-x_1 & + & 4x_2 & \le & 2 \\
x_1, x_2 & & & \ge & 0 \,.
\end{array}
$$

29.5-6
Solve the following linear program using SIMPLEX:

maximize $\quad x_1 \;-\; 2x_2$

subject to

$$
\begin{array}{rcrcr}
x_1 & + & 2x_2 & \le & 4 \\
-2x_1 & - & 6x_2 & \le & -12 \\
& & x_2 & \le & 1 \\
x_1, x_2 & & & \ge & 0 \,.
\end{array}
$$

29.5-7
Solve the following linear program using SIMPLEX:

maximize $\quad x_1 \;+\; 3x_2$

subject to

$$
\begin{array}{rcrcr}
-x_1 & + & x_2 & \le & -1 \\
-x_1 & - & x_2 & \le & -3 \\
-x_1 & + & 4x_2 & \le & 2 \\
x_1, x_2 & & & \ge & 0 \,.
\end{array}
$$

29.5-8
Solve the linear program given in (29.6)–(29.10).

29.5-9
Consider the following 1-variable linear program, which we call P:

maximize $\quad tx$

subject to

$$
\begin{array}{rcr}
rx & \le & s \\
x & \ge & 0 \,,
\end{array}
$$

where r, s, and t are arbitrary real numbers. Let D be the dual of P.

State for which values of r, s, and t you can assert that

1. Both P and D have optimal solutions with finite objective values.
2. P is feasible, but D is infeasible.
3. D is feasible, but P is infeasible.
4. Neither P nor D is feasible.

Problems

29-1 *Linear-inequality feasibility*

Given a set of m linear inequalities on n variables $x_1, x_2, \ldots, x_n$, the *linear-inequality feasibility problem* asks whether there is a setting of the variables that simultaneously satisfies each of the inequalities.

a. Show that if we have an algorithm for linear programming, we can use it to solve a linear-inequality feasibility problem. The number of variables and constraints that you use in the linear-programming problem should be polynomial in n and m.

b. Show that if we have an algorithm for the linear-inequality feasibility problem, we can use it to solve a linear-programming problem. The number of variables and linear inequalities that you use in the linear-inequality feasibility problem should be polynomial in n and m, the number of variables and constraints in the linear program.

29-2 *Complementary slackness*

Complementary slackness describes a relationship between the values of primal variables and dual constraints and between the values of dual variables and primal constraints. Let $\bar{x}$ be a feasible solution to the primal linear program given in (29.16)–(29.18), and let $\bar{y}$ be a feasible solution to the dual linear program given in (29.83)–(29.85). Complementary slackness states that the following conditions are necessary and sufficient for $\bar{x}$ and $\bar{y}$ to be optimal:

$$\sum_{i=1}^{m} a_{ij} \bar{y}_i = c_j \text{ or } \bar{x}_j = 0 \quad \text{for } j = 1, 2, \ldots, n$$

and

$$\sum_{j=1}^{n} a_{ij} \bar{x}_j = b_i \text{ or } \bar{y}_i = 0 \quad \text{for } i = 1, 2, \ldots, m .$$

a. Verify that complementary slackness holds for the linear program in lines (29.53)–(29.57).

b. Prove that complementary slackness holds for any primal linear program and its corresponding dual.

c. Prove that a feasible solution $\bar{x}$ to a primal linear program given in lines (29.16)–(29.18) is optimal if and only if there exist values $\bar{y} = (\bar{y}_1, \bar{y}_2, \ldots, \bar{y}_m)$ such that

1. $\bar{y}$ is a feasible solution to the dual linear program given in (29.83)–(29.85),
2. $\sum_{i=1}^{m} a_{ij} \bar{y}_i = c_j$ for all j such that $\bar{x}_j > 0$, and
3. $\bar{y}_i = 0$ for all i such that $\sum_{j=1}^{n} a_{ij} \bar{x}_j < b_i$.

29-3 Integer linear programming

An *integer linear-programming problem* is a linear-programming problem with the additional constraint that the variables x must take on integral values. Exercise 34.5-3 shows that just determining whether an integer linear program has a feasible solution is NP-hard, which means that there is no known polynomial-time algorithm for this problem.

a. Show that weak duality (Lemma 29.8) holds for an integer linear program.

b. Show that duality (Theorem 29.10) does not always hold for an integer linear program.

c. Given a primal linear program in standard form, let us define P to be the optimal objective value for the primal linear program, D to be the optimal objective value for its dual, IP to be the optimal objective value for the integer version of the primal (that is, the primal with the added constraint that the variables take on integer values), and ID to be the optimal objective value for the integer version of the dual. Assuming that both the primal integer program and the dual integer program are feasible and bounded, show that

$$IP \le P = D \le ID .$$

29-4 Farkas's lemma

Let A be an $m \times n$ matrix and c be an n-vector. Then Farkas's lemma states that exactly one of the systems

$$Ax \leq 0,$$
$$c^{\mathrm{T}}x > 0$$

and

$$A^{\mathrm{T}}y = c,$$
$$y \geq 0$$

is solvable, where x is an n-vector and y is an m-vector. Prove Farkas's lemma.

29-5   *Minimum-cost circulation*

In this problem, we consider a variant of the minimum-cost-flow problem from Section 29.2 in which we are not given a demand, a source, or a sink. Instead, we are given, as before, a flow network and edge costs $a(u, v)$. A flow is feasible if it satisfies the capacity constraint on every edge and flow conservation at *every* vertex. The goal is to find, among all feasible flows, the one of minimum cost. We call this problem the ***minimum-cost-circulation problem.***

a. Formulate the minimum-cost-circulation problem as a linear program.

b. Suppose that for all edges $(u, v) \in E$, we have $a(u, v) > 0$. Characterize an optimal solution to the minimum-cost-circulation problem.

c. Formulate the maximum-flow problem as a minimum-cost-circulation problem linear program. That is given a maximum-flow problem instance $G = (V, E)$ with source s, sink t and edge capacities c, create a minimum-cost-circulation problem by giving a (possibly different) network $G' = (V', E')$ with edge capacities c' and edge costs a' such that you can discern a solution to the maximum-flow problem from a solution to the minimum-cost-circulation problem.

d. Formulate the single-source shortest-path problem as a minimum-cost-circulation problem linear program.

Chapter notes

This chapter only begins to study the wide field of linear programming. A number of books are devoted exclusively to linear programming, including those by Chvátal [69], Gass [130], Karloff [197], Schrijver [303], and Vanderbei [344]. Many other books give a good coverage of linear programming, including those by Papadimitriou and Steiglitz [271] and Ahuja, Magnanti, and Orlin [7]. The coverage in this chapter draws on the approach taken by Chvátal.

The simplex algorithm for linear programming was invented by G. Dantzig in 1947. Shortly after, researchers discovered how to formulate a number of problems in a variety of fields as linear programs and solve them with the simplex algorithm. As a result, applications of linear programming flourished, along with several algorithms. Variants of the simplex algorithm remain the most popular methods for solving linear-programming problems. This history appears in a number of places, including the notes in [69] and [197].

The ellipsoid algorithm was the first polynomial-time algorithm for linear programming and is due to L. G. Khachian in 1979; it was based on earlier work by N. Z. Shor, D. B. Judin, and A. S. Nemirovskii. Grötschel, Lovász, and Schrijver [154] describe how to use the ellipsoid algorithm to solve a variety of problems in combinatorial optimization. To date, the ellipsoid algorithm does not appear to be competitive with the simplex algorithm in practice.

Karmarkar's paper [198] includes a description of the first interior-point algorithm. Many subsequent researchers designed interior-point algorithms. Good surveys appear in the article of Goldfarb and Todd [141] and the book by Ye [361].

Analysis of the simplex algorithm remains an active area of research. V. Klee and G. J. Minty constructed an example on which the simplex algorithm runs through $2^n - 1$ iterations. The simplex algorithm usually performs very well in practice and many researchers have tried to give theoretical justification for this empirical observation. A line of research begun by K. H. Borgwardt, and carried on by many others, shows that under certain probabilistic assumptions on the input, the simplex algorithm converges in expected polynomial time. Spielman and Teng [322] made progress in this area, introducing the "smoothed analysis of algorithms" and applying it to the simplex algorithm.

The simplex algorithm is known to run efficiently in certain special cases. Particularly noteworthy is the network-simplex algorithm, which is the simplex algorithm, specialized to network-flow problems. For certain network problems, including the shortest-paths, maximum-flow, and minimum-cost-flow problems, variants of the network-simplex algorithm run in polynomial time. See, for example, the article by Orlin [268] and the citations therein.

30 Polynomials and the FFT

The straightforward method of adding two polynomials of degree n takes $\Theta(n)$ time, but the straightforward method of multiplying them takes $\Theta(n^2)$ time. In this chapter, we shall show how the fast Fourier transform, or FFT, can reduce the time to multiply polynomials to $\Theta(n \lg n)$.

The most common use for Fourier transforms, and hence the FFT, is in signal processing. A signal is given in the *time domain*: as a function mapping time to amplitude. Fourier analysis allows us to express the signal as a weighted sum of phase-shifted sinusoids of varying frequencies. The weights and phases associated with the frequencies characterize the signal in the *frequency domain*. Among the many everyday applications of FFT's are compression techniques used to encode digital video and audio information, including MP3 files. Several fine books delve into the rich area of signal processing; the chapter notes reference a few of them.

Polynomials

A *polynomial* in the variable x over an algebraic field F represents a function $A(x)$ as a formal sum:

$$A(x) = \sum_{j=0}^{n-1} a_j x^j .$$

We call the values $a_0, a_1, \ldots, a_{n-1}$ the *coefficients* of the polynomial. The coefficients are drawn from a field F, typically the set $\mathbb{C}$ of complex numbers. A polynomial $A(x)$ has *degree* k if its highest nonzero coefficient is a_k; we write that degree$(A) = k$. Any integer strictly greater than the degree of a polynomial is a *degree-bound* of that polynomial. Therefore, the degree of a polynomial of degree-bound n may be any integer between 0 and $n - 1$, inclusive.

We can define a variety of operations on polynomials. For *polynomial addition*, if $A(x)$ and $B(x)$ are polynomials of degree-bound n, their *sum* is a polyno-

mial $C(x)$, also of degree-bound n, such that $C(x) = A(x) + B(x)$ for all x in the underlying field. That is, if

$$A(x) = \sum_{j=0}^{n-1} a_j x^j$$

and

$$B(x) = \sum_{j=0}^{n-1} b_j x^j \ ,$$

then

$$C(x) = \sum_{j=0}^{n-1} c_j x^j \ ,$$

where $c_j = a_j + b_j$ for $j = 0, 1, \ldots, n - 1$. For example, if we have the polynomials $A(x) = 6x^3 + 7x^2 - 10x + 9$ and $B(x) = -2x^3 + 4x - 5$, then $C(x) = 4x^3 + 7x^2 - 6x + 4$.

For ***polynomial multiplication***, if $A(x)$ and $B(x)$ are polynomials of degree-bound n, their ***product*** $C(x)$ is a polynomial of degree-bound $2n - 1$ such that $C(x) = A(x)B(x)$ for all x in the underlying field. You probably have multiplied polynomials before, by multiplying each term in $A(x)$ by each term in $B(x)$ and then combining terms with equal powers. For example, we can multiply $A(x) = 6x^3 + 7x^2 - 10x + 9$ and $B(x) = -2x^3 + 4x - 5$ as follows:

$$
\begin{array}{r}
6x^3 + 7x^2 - 10x + 9 \\
- 2x^3 + 4x - 5 \\
\hline
- 30x^3 - 35x^2 + 50x - 45 \\
24x^4 + 28x^3 - 40x^2 + 36x \\
- 12x^6 - 14x^5 + 20x^4 - 18x^3 \\
\hline
- 12x^6 - 14x^5 + 44x^4 - 20x^3 - 75x^2 + 86x - 45
\end{array}
$$

Another way to express the product $C(x)$ is

$$C(x) = \sum_{j=0}^{2n-2} c_j x^j \ , \tag{30.1}$$

where

$$c_j = \sum_{k=0}^{j} a_k b_{j-k} \ . \tag{30.2}$$

Note that $\text{degree}(C) = \text{degree}(A) + \text{degree}(B)$, implying that if A is a polynomial of degree-bound n_a and B is a polynomial of degree-bound n_b, then C is a polynomial of degree-bound $n_a + n_b - 1$. Since a polynomial of degree-bound k is also a polynomial of degree-bound $k + 1$, we will normally say that the product polynomial C is a polynomial of degree-bound $n_a + n_b$.

Chapter outline

Section 30.1 presents two ways to represent polynomials: the coefficient representation and the point-value representation. The straightforward method for multiplying polynomials—equations (30.1) and (30.2)—takes $\Theta(n^2)$ time when we represent polynomials in coefficient form, but only $\Theta(n)$ time when we represent them in point-value form. We can, however, multiply polynomials using the coefficient representation in only $\Theta(n \lg n)$ time by converting between the two representations. To see why this approach works, we must first study complex roots of unity, which we do in Section 30.2. Then, we use the FFT and its inverse, also described in Section 30.2, to perform the conversions. Section 30.3 shows how to implement the FFT quickly in both serial and parallel models.

This chapter uses complex numbers extensively, and within this chapter we use the symbol i exclusively to denote $\sqrt{-1}$.

30.1   Representing polynomials

The coefficient and point-value representations of polynomials are in a sense equivalent; that is, a polynomial in point-value form has a unique counterpart in coefficient form. In this section, we introduce the two representations and show how to combine them so that we can multiply two degree-bound n polynomials in $\Theta(n \lg n)$ time.

Coefficient representation

A *coefficient representation* of a polynomial $A(x) = \sum_{j=0}^{n-1} a_j x^j$ of degree-bound n is a vector of coefficients $a = (a_0, a_1, \ldots, a_{n-1})$. In matrix equations in this chapter, we shall generally treat vectors as column vectors.

The coefficient representation is convenient for certain operations on polynomials. For example, the operation of *evaluating* the polynomial $A(x)$ at a given point x_0 consists of computing the value of $A(x_0)$. We can evaluate a polynomial in $\Theta(n)$ time using *Horner's rule*:

$$A(x_0) = a_0 + x_0(a_1 + x_0(a_2 + \cdots + x_0(a_{n-2} + x_0(a_{n-1})) \cdots)) \, .$$

Similarly, adding two polynomials represented by the coefficient vectors $a = (a_0, a_1, \ldots, a_{n-1})$ and $b = (b_0, b_1, \ldots, b_{n-1})$ takes $\Theta(n)$ time: we just produce the coefficient vector $c = (c_0, c_1, \ldots, c_{n-1})$, where $c_j = a_j + b_j$ for $j = 0, 1, \ldots, n - 1$.

Now, consider multiplying two degree-bound n polynomials $A(x)$ and $B(x)$ represented in coefficient form. If we use the method described by equations (30.1) and (30.2), multiplying polynomials takes time $\Theta(n^2)$, since we must multiply each coefficient in the vector a by each coefficient in the vector b. The operation of multiplying polynomials in coefficient form seems to be considerably more difficult than that of evaluating a polynomial or adding two polynomials. The resulting coefficient vector c, given by equation (30.2), is also called the **convolution** of the input vectors a and b, denoted $c = a \otimes b$. Since multiplying polynomials and computing convolutions are fundamental computational problems of considerable practical importance, this chapter concentrates on efficient algorithms for them.

Point-value representation

A *point-value representation* of a polynomial $A(x)$ of degree-bound n is a set of n *point-value pairs*

$$\{(x_0, y_0), (x_1, y_1), \ldots, (x_{n-1}, y_{n-1})\}$$

such that all of the x_k are distinct and

$$y_k = A(x_k) \tag{30.3}$$

for $k = 0, 1, \ldots, n - 1$. A polynomial has many different point-value representations, since we can use any set of n distinct points $x_0, x_1, \ldots, x_{n-1}$ as a basis for the representation.

Computing a point-value representation for a polynomial given in coefficient form is in principle straightforward, since all we have to do is select n distinct points $x_0, x_1, \ldots, x_{n-1}$ and then evaluate $A(x_k)$ for $k = 0, 1, \ldots, n - 1$. With Horner's method, evaluating a polynomial at n points takes time $\Theta(n^2)$. We shall see later that if we choose the points x_k cleverly, we can accelerate this computation to run in time $\Theta(n \lg n)$.

The inverse of evaluation—determining the coefficient form of a polynomial from a point-value representation—is *interpolation*. The following theorem shows that interpolation is well defined when the desired interpolating polynomial must have a degree-bound equal to the given number of point-value pairs.

Theorem 30.1 (Uniqueness of an interpolating polynomial)
For any set $\{(x_0, y_0), (x_1, y_1), \ldots, (x_{n-1}, y_{n-1})\}$ of n point-value pairs such that all the x_k values are distinct, there is a unique polynomial $A(x)$ of degree-bound n such that $y_k = A(x_k)$ for $k = 0, 1, \ldots, n - 1$.

Proof   The proof relies on the existence of the inverse of a certain matrix. Equation (30.3) is equivalent to the matrix equation

$$
\begin{pmatrix}
1 & x_0 & x_0^2 & \cdots & x_0^{n-1} \\
1 & x_1 & x_1^2 & \cdots & x_1^{n-1} \\
\vdots & \vdots & \vdots & \ddots & \vdots \\
1 & x_{n-1} & x_{n-1}^2 & \cdots & x_{n-1}^{n-1}
\end{pmatrix}
\begin{pmatrix}
a_0 \\
a_1 \\
\vdots \\
a_{n-1}
\end{pmatrix}
=
\begin{pmatrix}
y_0 \\
y_1 \\
\vdots \\
y_{n-1}
\end{pmatrix} .
\tag{30.4}
$$

The matrix on the left is denoted $V(x_0, x_1, \ldots, x_{n-1})$ and is known as a Vandermonde matrix. By Problem D-1, this matrix has determinant

$$
\prod_{0 \le j < k \le n-1} (x_k - x_j) ,
$$

and therefore, by Theorem D.5, it is invertible (that is, nonsingular) if the x_k are distinct. Thus, we can solve for the coefficients a_j uniquely given the point-value representation:

$$
a = V(x_0, x_1, \ldots, x_{n-1})^{-1} y .
$$ ∎

The proof of Theorem 30.1 describes an algorithm for interpolation based on solving the set (30.4) of linear equations. Using the LU decomposition algorithms of Chapter 28, we can solve these equations in time $O(n^3)$.

A faster algorithm for n-point interpolation is based on ***Lagrange's formula***:

$$
A(x) = \sum_{k=0}^{n-1} y_k \frac{\displaystyle\prod_{j \ne k} (x - x_j)}{\displaystyle\prod_{j \ne k} (x_k - x_j)} .
\tag{30.5}
$$

You may wish to verify that the right-hand side of equation (30.5) is a polynomial of degree-bound n that satisfies $A(x_k) = y_k$ for all k. Exercise 30.1-5 asks you how to compute the coefficients of A using Lagrange's formula in time $\Theta(n^2)$.

Thus, n-point evaluation and interpolation are well-defined inverse operations that transform between the coefficient representation of a polynomial and a point-value representation.[1]   The algorithms described above for these problems take time $\Theta(n^2)$.

The point-value representation is quite convenient for many operations on polynomials. For addition, if $C(x) = A(x) + B(x)$, then $C(x_k) = A(x_k) + B(x_k)$ for any point x_k. More precisely, if we have a point-value representation for A,

---

[1] Interpolation is a notoriously tricky problem from the point of view of numerical stability. Although the approaches described here are mathematically correct, small differences in the inputs or round-off errors during computation can cause large differences in the result.

$$\{(x_0, y_0), (x_1, y_1), \ldots, (x_{n-1}, y_{n-1})\} \ ,$$

and for B,

$$\{(x_0, y_0'), (x_1, y_1'), \ldots, (x_{n-1}, y_{n-1}')\}$$

(note that A and B are evaluated at the *same* n points), then a point-value representation for C is

$$\{(x_0, y_0 + y_0'), (x_1, y_1 + y_1'), \ldots, (x_{n-1}, y_{n-1} + y_{n-1}')\} \ .$$

Thus, the time to add two polynomials of degree-bound n in point-value form is $\Theta(n)$.

Similarly, the point-value representation is convenient for multiplying polynomials. If $C(x) = A(x)B(x)$, then $C(x_k) = A(x_k)B(x_k)$ for any point x_k, and we can pointwise multiply a point-value representation for A by a point-value representation for B to obtain a point-value representation for C. We must face the problem, however, that $\text{degree}(C) = \text{degree}(A) + \text{degree}(B)$; if A and B are of degree-bound n, then C is of degree-bound $2n$. A standard point-value representation for A and B consists of n point-value pairs for each polynomial. When we multiply these together, we get n point-value pairs, but we need $2n$ pairs to interpolate a unique polynomial C of degree-bound $2n$. (See Exercise 30.1-4.) We must therefore begin with "extended" point-value representations for A and for B consisting of $2n$ point-value pairs each. Given an extended point-value representation for A,

$$\{(x_0, y_0), (x_1, y_1), \ldots, (x_{2n-1}, y_{2n-1})\} \ ,$$

and a corresponding extended point-value representation for B,

$$\{(x_0, y_0'), (x_1, y_1'), \ldots, (x_{2n-1}, y_{2n-1}')\} \ ,$$

then a point-value representation for C is

$$\{(x_0, y_0 y_0'), (x_1, y_1 y_1'), \ldots, (x_{2n-1}, y_{2n-1} y_{2n-1}')\} \ .$$

Given two input polynomials in extended point-value form, we see that the time to multiply them to obtain the point-value form of the result is $\Theta(n)$, much less than the time required to multiply polynomials in coefficient form.

Finally, we consider how to evaluate a polynomial given in point-value form at a new point. For this problem, we know of no simpler approach than converting the polynomial to coefficient form first, and then evaluating it at the new point.

Fast multiplication of polynomials in coefficient form

Can we use the linear-time multiplication method for polynomials in point-value form to expedite polynomial multiplication in coefficient form? The answer hinges

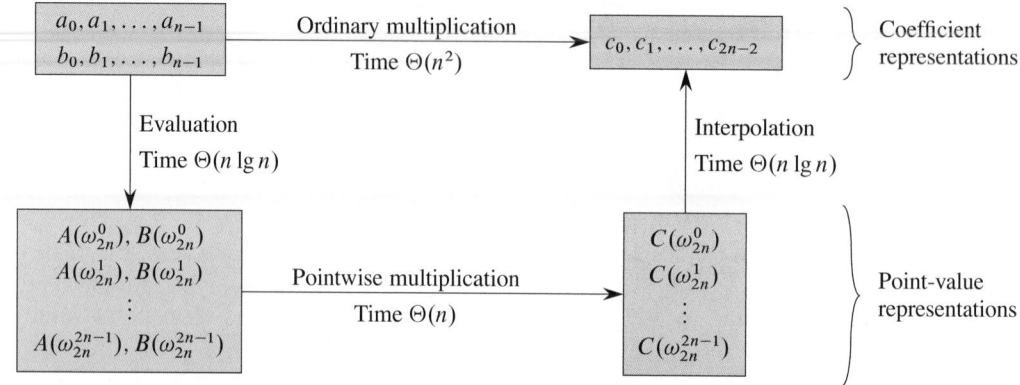

Figure 30.1 A graphical outline of an efficient polynomial-multiplication process. Representations on the top are in coefficient form, while those on the bottom are in point-value form. The arrows from left to right correspond to the multiplication operation. The ω_{2n} terms are complex $(2n)$th roots of unity.

on whether we can convert a polynomial quickly from coefficient form to point-value form (evaluate) and vice versa (interpolate).

We can use any points we want as evaluation points, but by choosing the evaluation points carefully, we can convert between representations in only $\Theta(n \lg n)$ time. As we shall see in Section 30.2, if we choose "complex roots of unity" as the evaluation points, we can produce a point-value representation by taking the discrete Fourier transform (or DFT) of a coefficient vector. We can perform the inverse operation, interpolation, by taking the "inverse DFT" of point-value pairs, yielding a coefficient vector. Section 30.2 will show how the FFT accomplishes the DFT and inverse DFT operations in $\Theta(n \lg n)$ time.

Figure 30.1 shows this strategy graphically. One minor detail concerns degree-bounds. The product of two polynomials of degree-bound n is a polynomial of degree-bound $2n$. Before evaluating the input polynomials A and B, therefore, we first double their degree-bounds to $2n$ by adding n high-order coefficients of 0. Because the vectors have $2n$ elements, we use "complex $(2n)$th roots of unity," which are denoted by the ω_{2n} terms in Figure 30.1.

Given the FFT, we have the following $\Theta(n \lg n)$-time procedure for multiplying two polynomials $A(x)$ and $B(x)$ of degree-bound n, where the input and output representations are in coefficient form. We assume that n is a power of 2; we can always meet this requirement by adding high-order zero coefficients.

1. *Double degree-bound:* Create coefficient representations of $A(x)$ and $B(x)$ as degree-bound $2n$ polynomials by adding n high-order zero coefficients to each.

2. *Evaluate:* Compute point-value representations of $A(x)$ and $B(x)$ of length $2n$ by applying the FFT of order $2n$ on each polynomial. These representations contain the values of the two polynomials at the $(2n)$th roots of unity.

3. *Pointwise multiply:* Compute a point-value representation for the polynomial $C(x) = A(x)B(x)$ by multiplying these values together pointwise. This representation contains the value of $C(x)$ at each $(2n)$th root of unity.

4. *Interpolate:* Create the coefficient representation of the polynomial $C(x)$ by applying the FFT on $2n$ point-value pairs to compute the inverse DFT.

Steps (1) and (3) take time $\Theta(n)$, and steps (2) and (4) take time $\Theta(n \lg n)$. Thus, once we show how to use the FFT, we will have proven the following.

Theorem 30.2
We can multiply two polynomials of degree-bound n in time $\Theta(n \lg n)$, with both the input and output representations in coefficient form. ∎

Exercises

30.1-1
Multiply the polynomials $A(x) = 7x^3 - x^2 + x - 10$ and $B(x) = 8x^3 - 6x + 3$ using equations (30.1) and (30.2).

30.1-2
Another way to evaluate a polynomial $A(x)$ of degree-bound n at a given point x_0 is to divide $A(x)$ by the polynomial $(x - x_0)$, obtaining a quotient polynomial $q(x)$ of degree-bound $n - 1$ and a remainder r, such that

$$A(x) = q(x)(x - x_0) + r \ .$$

Clearly, $A(x_0) = r$. Show how to compute the remainder r and the coefficients of $q(x)$ in time $\Theta(n)$ from x_0 and the coefficients of A.

30.1-3
Derive a point-value representation for $A^{\text{rev}}(x) = \sum_{j=0}^{n-1} a_{n-1-j} x^j$ from a point-value representation for $A(x) = \sum_{j=0}^{n-1} a_j x^j$, assuming that none of the points is 0.

30.1-4
Prove that n distinct point-value pairs are necessary to uniquely specify a polynomial of degree-bound n, that is, if fewer than n distinct point-value pairs are given, they fail to specify a unique polynomial of degree-bound n. (*Hint:* Using Theorem 30.1, what can you say about a set of $n - 1$ point-value pairs to which you add one more arbitrarily chosen point-value pair?)

30.1-5

Show how to use equation (30.5) to interpolate in time $\Theta(n^2)$. (*Hint:* First compute the coefficient representation of the polynomial $\prod_j (x - x_j)$ and then divide by $(x - x_k)$ as necessary for the numerator of each term; see Exercise 30.1-2. You can compute each of the n denominators in time $O(n)$.)

30.1-6

Explain what is wrong with the "obvious" approach to polynomial division using a point-value representation, i.e., dividing the corresponding y values. Discuss separately the case in which the division comes out exactly and the case in which it doesn't.

30.1-7

Consider two sets A and B, each having n integers in the range from 0 to $10n$. We wish to compute the ***Cartesian sum*** of A and B, defined by

$$C = \{x + y : x \in A \text{ and } y \in B\} \ .$$

Note that the integers in C are in the range from 0 to $20n$. We want to find the elements of C and the number of times each element of C is realized as a sum of elements in A and B. Show how to solve the problem in $O(n \lg n)$ time. (*Hint:* Represent A and B as polynomials of degree at most $10n$.)

30.2   The DFT and FFT

In Section 30.1, we claimed that if we use complex roots of unity, we can evaluate and interpolate polynomials in $\Theta(n \lg n)$ time. In this section, we define complex roots of unity and study their properties, define the DFT, and then show how the FFT computes the DFT and its inverse in $\Theta(n \lg n)$ time.

Complex roots of unity

A ***complex nth root of unity*** is a complex number ω such that

$$\omega^n = 1 \ .$$

There are exactly n complex nth roots of unity: $e^{2\pi i k/n}$ for $k = 0, 1, \ldots, n - 1$. To interpret this formula, we use the definition of the exponential of a complex number:

$$e^{iu} = \cos(u) + i \sin(u) \ .$$

Figure 30.2 shows that the n complex roots of unity are equally spaced around the circle of unit radius centered at the origin of the complex plane. The value

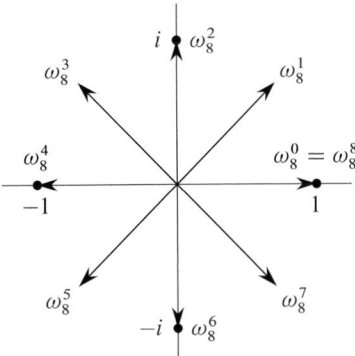

Figure 30.2   The values of $\omega_8^0, \omega_8^1, \ldots, \omega_8^7$ in the complex plane, where $\omega_8 = e^{2\pi i/8}$ is the principal 8th root of unity.

$$\omega_n = e^{2\pi i/n} \tag{30.6}$$

is the ***principal nth root of unity***;[2] all other complex nth roots of unity are powers of ω_n.

The n complex nth roots of unity,

$$\omega_n^0, \omega_n^1, \ldots, \omega_n^{n-1} ,$$

form a group under multiplication (see Section 31.3). This group has the same structure as the additive group $(\mathbb{Z}_n, +)$ modulo n, since $\omega_n^n = \omega_n^0 = 1$ implies that $\omega_n^j \omega_n^k = \omega_n^{j+k} = \omega_n^{(j+k) \bmod n}$. Similarly, $\omega_n^{-1} = \omega_n^{n-1}$. The following lemmas furnish some essential properties of the complex nth roots of unity.

Lemma 30.3 (Cancellation lemma)
For any integers $n \geq 0, k \geq 0$, and $d > 0$,

$$\omega_{dn}^{dk} = \omega_n^k . \tag{30.7}$$

Proof   The lemma follows directly from equation (30.6), since

$$\begin{aligned}
\omega_{dn}^{dk} &= \left(e^{2\pi i/dn}\right)^{dk} \\
&= \left(e^{2\pi i/n}\right)^{k} \\
&= \omega_n^k .
\end{aligned}$$

$\blacksquare$

---

[2]Many other authors define ω_n differently: $\omega_n = e^{-2\pi i/n}$. This alternative definition tends to be used for signal-processing applications. The underlying mathematics is substantially the same with either definition of ω_n.

Corollary 30.4
For any even integer $n > 0$,

$$\omega_n^{n/2} = \omega_2 = -1 \ .$$

Proof   The proof is left as Exercise 30.2-1.   ∎

Lemma 30.5 (Halving lemma)
If $n > 0$ is even, then the squares of the n complex nth roots of unity are the $n/2$ complex $(n/2)$th roots of unity.

Proof   By the cancellation lemma, we have $(\omega_n^k)^2 = \omega_{n/2}^k$, for any nonnegative integer k. Note that if we square all of the complex nth roots of unity, then we obtain each $(n/2)$th root of unity exactly twice, since

$$
\begin{aligned}
(\omega_n^{k+n/2})^2 &= \omega_n^{2k+n} \\
&= \omega_n^{2k} \omega_n^{n} \\
&= \omega_n^{2k} \\
&= (\omega_n^k)^2 \ .
\end{aligned}
$$

Thus, ω_n^k and $\omega_n^{k+n/2}$ have the same square. We could also have used Corollary 30.4 to prove this property, since $\omega_n^{n/2} = -1$ implies $\omega_n^{k+n/2} = -\omega_n^k$, and thus $(\omega_n^{k+n/2})^2 = (\omega_n^k)^2$.   ∎

As we shall see, the halving lemma is essential to our divide-and-conquer approach for converting between coefficient and point-value representations of polynomials, since it guarantees that the recursive subproblems are only half as large.

Lemma 30.6 (Summation lemma)
For any integer $n \geq 1$ and nonzero integer k not divisible by n,

$$\sum_{j=0}^{n-1} \left(\omega_n^k\right)^j = 0 \ .$$

Proof   Equation (A.5) applies to complex values as well as to reals, and so we have

$$\sum_{j=0}^{n-1} \left(\omega_n^k\right)^j = \frac{(\omega_n^k)^n - 1}{\omega_n^k - 1}$$

$$= \frac{(\omega_n^n)^k - 1}{\omega_n^k - 1}$$

$$= \frac{(1)^k - 1}{\omega_n^k - 1}$$

$$= 0 \, .$$

Because we require that k is not divisible by n, and because $\omega_n^k = 1$ only when k is divisible by n, we ensure that the denominator is not 0. ∎

The DFT

Recall that we wish to evaluate a polynomial

$$A(x) = \sum_{j=0}^{n-1} a_j x^j$$

of degree-bound n at $\omega_n^0, \omega_n^1, \omega_n^2, \ldots, \omega_n^{n-1}$ (that is, at the n complex nth roots of unity).[3] We assume that A is given in coefficient form: $a = (a_0, a_1, \ldots, a_{n-1})$. Let us define the results y_k, for $k = 0, 1, \ldots, n-1$, by

$$y_k = A(\omega_n^k)$$

$$= \sum_{j=0}^{n-1} a_j \omega_n^{kj} \, . \tag{30.8}$$

The vector $y = (y_0, y_1, \ldots, y_{n-1})$ is the **discrete Fourier transform (DFT)** of the coefficient vector $a = (a_0, a_1, \ldots, a_{n-1})$. We also write $y = \text{DFT}_n(a)$.

The FFT

By using a method known as the **fast Fourier transform (FFT)**, which takes advantage of the special properties of the complex roots of unity, we can compute $\text{DFT}_n(a)$ in time $\Theta(n \lg n)$, as opposed to the $\Theta(n^2)$ time of the straightforward method. We assume throughout that n is an exact power of 2. Although strategies

---

[3]The length n is actually what we referred to as $2n$ in Section 30.1, since we double the degree-bound of the given polynomials prior to evaluation. In the context of polynomial multiplication, therefore, we are actually working with complex $(2n)$th roots of unity.

for dealing with non-power-of-2 sizes are known, they are beyond the scope of this book.

The FFT method employs a divide-and-conquer strategy, using the even-indexed and odd-indexed coefficients of $A(x)$ separately to define the two new polynomials $A^{[0]}(x)$ and $A^{[1]}(x)$ of degree-bound $n/2$:

$$A^{[0]}(x) = a_0 + a_2 x + a_4 x^2 + \cdots + a_{n-2} x^{n/2-1} ,$$
$$A^{[1]}(x) = a_1 + a_3 x + a_5 x^2 + \cdots + a_{n-1} x^{n/2-1} .$$

Note that $A^{[0]}$ contains all the even-indexed coefficients of A (the binary representation of the index ends in 0) and $A^{[1]}$ contains all the odd-indexed coefficients (the binary representation of the index ends in 1). It follows that

$$A(x) = A^{[0]}(x^2) + x A^{[1]}(x^2) , \tag{30.9}$$

so that the problem of evaluating $A(x)$ at $\omega_n^0, \omega_n^1, \ldots, \omega_n^{n-1}$ reduces to

1. evaluating the degree-bound $n/2$ polynomials $A^{[0]}(x)$ and $A^{[1]}(x)$ at the points

$$(\omega_n^0)^2, (\omega_n^1)^2, \ldots, (\omega_n^{n-1})^2 , \tag{30.10}$$

   and then

2. combining the results according to equation (30.9).

By the halving lemma, the list of values (30.10) consists not of n distinct values but only of the $n/2$ complex $(n/2)$th roots of unity, with each root occurring exactly twice. Therefore, we recursively evaluate the polynomials $A^{[0]}$ and $A^{[1]}$ of degree-bound $n/2$ at the $n/2$ complex $(n/2)$th roots of unity. These subproblems have exactly the same form as the original problem, but are half the size. We have now successfully divided an n-element DFT_n computation into two $n/2$-element $\text{DFT}_{n/2}$ computations. This decomposition is the basis for the following recursive FFT algorithm, which computes the DFT of an n-element vector $a = (a_0, a_1, \ldots, a_{n-1})$, where n is a power of 2.

RECURSIVE-FFT(a)

```
 1   n = a.length                    // n is a power of 2
 2   if n == 1
 3        return a
 4   ωₙ = e^{2πi/n}
 5   ω = 1
 6   a^{[0]} = (a₀, a₂, ..., a_{n-2})
 7   a^{[1]} = (a₁, a₃, ..., a_{n-1})
 8   y^{[0]} = RECURSIVE-FFT(a^{[0]})
 9   y^{[1]} = RECURSIVE-FFT(a^{[1]})
10   for k = 0 to n/2 - 1
11        y_k = y_k^{[0]} + ω y_k^{[1]}
12        y_{k+(n/2)} = y_k^{[0]} - ω y_k^{[1]}
13        ω = ω ωₙ
14   return y                        // y is assumed to be a column vector
```

The RECURSIVE-FFT procedure works as follows. Lines 2–3 represent the basis of the recursion; the DFT of one element is the element itself, since in this case

$$
\begin{aligned}
y_0 &= a_0 \, \omega_1^0 \\
    &= a_0 \cdot 1 \\
    &= a_0 \, .
\end{aligned}
$$

Lines 6–7 define the coefficient vectors for the polynomials $A^{[0]}$ and $A^{[1]}$. Lines 4, 5, and 13 guarantee that ω is updated properly so that whenever lines 11–12 are executed, we have $\omega = \omega_n^k$. (Keeping a running value of ω from iteration to iteration saves time over computing ω_n^k from scratch each time through the **for** loop.) Lines 8–9 perform the recursive $\text{DFT}_{n/2}$ computations, setting, for $k = 0, 1, \ldots, n/2 - 1$,

$$
\begin{aligned}
y_k^{[0]} &= A^{[0]}(\omega_{n/2}^k) \, , \\
y_k^{[1]} &= A^{[1]}(\omega_{n/2}^k) \, ,
\end{aligned}
$$

or, since $\omega_{n/2}^k = \omega_n^{2k}$ by the cancellation lemma,

$$
\begin{aligned}
y_k^{[0]} &= A^{[0]}(\omega_n^{2k}) \, , \\
y_k^{[1]} &= A^{[1]}(\omega_n^{2k}) \, .
\end{aligned}
$$

Lines 11–12 combine the results of the recursive $\mathrm{DFT}_{n/2}$ calculations. For $y_0, y_1,$ $\ldots, y_{n/2-1}$, line 11 yields

$$
\begin{aligned}
y_k &= y_k^{[0]} + \omega_n^k y_k^{[1]} \\
&= A^{[0]}(\omega_n^{2k}) + \omega_n^k A^{[1]}(\omega_n^{2k}) \\
&= A(\omega_n^k) \qquad\qquad \text{(by equation (30.9))} .
\end{aligned}
$$

For $y_{n/2}, y_{n/2+1}, \ldots, y_{n-1}$, letting $k = 0, 1, \ldots, n/2 - 1$, line 12 yields

$$
\begin{aligned}
y_{k+(n/2)} &= y_k^{[0]} - \omega_n^k y_k^{[1]} \\
&= y_k^{[0]} + \omega_n^{k+(n/2)} y_k^{[1]} & \text{(since } \omega_n^{k+(n/2)} = -\omega_n^k) \\
&= A^{[0]}(\omega_n^{2k}) + \omega_n^{k+(n/2)} A^{[1]}(\omega_n^{2k}) \\
&= A^{[0]}(\omega_n^{2k+n}) + \omega_n^{k+(n/2)} A^{[1]}(\omega_n^{2k+n}) & \text{(since } \omega_n^{2k+n} = \omega_n^{2k}) \\
&= A(\omega_n^{k+(n/2)}) & \text{(by equation (30.9))} .
\end{aligned}
$$

Thus, the vector y returned by RECURSIVE-FFT is indeed the DFT of the input vector a.

Lines 11 and 12 multiply each value $y_k^{[1]}$ by ω_n^k, for $k = 0, 1, \ldots, n/2 - 1$. Line 11 adds this product to $y_k^{[0]}$, and line 12 subtracts it. Because we use each factor ω_n^k in both its positive and negative forms, we call the factors ω_n^k ***twiddle factors***.

To determine the running time of procedure RECURSIVE-FFT, we note that exclusive of the recursive calls, each invocation takes time $\Theta(n)$, where n is the length of the input vector. The recurrence for the running time is therefore

$$
\begin{aligned}
T(n) &= 2T(n/2) + \Theta(n) \\
&= \Theta(n \lg n) .
\end{aligned}
$$

Thus, we can evaluate a polynomial of degree-bound n at the complex nth roots of unity in time $\Theta(n \lg n)$ using the fast Fourier transform.

Interpolation at the complex roots of unity

We now complete the polynomial multiplication scheme by showing how to interpolate the complex roots of unity by a polynomial, which enables us to convert from point-value form back to coefficient form. We interpolate by writing the DFT as a matrix equation and then looking at the form of the matrix inverse.

From equation (30.4), we can write the DFT as the matrix product $y = V_n a$, where V_n is a Vandermonde matrix containing the appropriate powers of ω_n:

$$
\begin{pmatrix} y_0 \\ y_1 \\ y_2 \\ y_3 \\ \vdots \\ y_{n-1} \end{pmatrix} = \begin{pmatrix} 1 & 1 & 1 & 1 & \cdots & 1 \\ 1 & \omega_n & \omega_n^2 & \omega_n^3 & \cdots & \omega_n^{n-1} \\ 1 & \omega_n^2 & \omega_n^4 & \omega_n^6 & \cdots & \omega_n^{2(n-1)} \\ 1 & \omega_n^3 & \omega_n^6 & \omega_n^9 & \cdots & \omega_n^{3(n-1)} \\ \vdots & \vdots & \vdots & \vdots & \ddots & \vdots \\ 1 & \omega_n^{n-1} & \omega_n^{2(n-1)} & \omega_n^{3(n-1)} & \cdots & \omega_n^{(n-1)(n-1)} \end{pmatrix} \begin{pmatrix} a_0 \\ a_1 \\ a_2 \\ a_3 \\ \vdots \\ a_{n-1} \end{pmatrix} .
$$

The (k, j) entry of V_n is ω_n^{kj}, for $j, k = 0, 1, \ldots, n - 1$. The exponents of the entries of V_n form a multiplication table.

For the inverse operation, which we write as $a = \mathrm{DFT}_n^{-1}(y)$, we proceed by multiplying y by the matrix V_n^{-1}, the inverse of V_n.

Theorem 30.7
For $j, k = 0, 1, \ldots, n - 1$, the (j, k) entry of V_n^{-1} is ω_n^{-kj} / n.

Proof   We show that $V_n^{-1} V_n = I_n$, the $n \times n$ identity matrix. Consider the (j, j') entry of $V_n^{-1} V_n$:

$$
\begin{aligned}
[V_n^{-1} V_n]_{jj'} &= \sum_{k=0}^{n-1} (\omega_n^{-kj} / n)(\omega_n^{kj'}) \\
&= \sum_{k=0}^{n-1} \omega_n^{k(j'-j)} / n .
\end{aligned}
$$

This summation equals 1 if $j' = j$, and it is 0 otherwise by the summation lemma (Lemma 30.6). Note that we rely on $-(n - 1) \le j' - j \le n - 1$, so that $j' - j$ is not divisible by n, in order for the summation lemma to apply.   ∎

Given the inverse matrix V_n^{-1}, we have that $\mathrm{DFT}_n^{-1}(y)$ is given by

$$
a_j = \frac{1}{n} \sum_{k=0}^{n-1} y_k \omega_n^{-kj} \tag{30.11}
$$

for $j = 0, 1, \ldots, n - 1$. By comparing equations (30.8) and (30.11), we see that by modifying the FFT algorithm to switch the roles of a and y, replace ω_n by ω_n^{-1}, and divide each element of the result by n, we compute the inverse DFT (see Exercise 30.2-4). Thus, we can compute DFT_n^{-1} in $\Theta(n \lg n)$ time as well.

We see that, by using the FFT and the inverse FFT, we can transform a polynomial of degree-bound n back and forth between its coefficient representation and a point-value representation in time $\Theta(n \lg n)$. In the context of polynomial multiplication, we have shown the following.

Theorem 30.8 (Convolution theorem)
For any two vectors a and b of length n, where n is a power of 2,

$$a \otimes b = \text{DFT}_{2n}^{-1}(\text{DFT}_{2n}(a) \cdot \text{DFT}_{2n}(b)) ,$$

where the vectors a and b are padded with 0s to length $2n$ and $\cdot$ denotes the componentwise product of two $2n$-element vectors. ∎

Exercises

30.2-1
Prove Corollary 30.4.

30.2-2
Compute the DFT of the vector $(0, 1, 2, 3)$.

30.2-3
Do Exercise 30.1-1 by using the $\Theta(n \lg n)$-time scheme.

30.2-4
Write pseudocode to compute DFT_n^{-1} in $\Theta(n \lg n)$ time.

30.2-5
Describe the generalization of the FFT procedure to the case in which n is a power of 3. Give a recurrence for the running time, and solve the recurrence.

30.2-6 ★
Suppose that instead of performing an n-element FFT over the field of complex numbers (where n is even), we use the ring $\mathbb{Z}_m$ of integers modulo m, where $m = 2^{tn/2} + 1$ and t is an arbitrary positive integer. Use $\omega = 2^t$ instead of ω_n as a principal nth root of unity, modulo m. Prove that the DFT and the inverse DFT are well defined in this system.

30.2-7
Given a list of values $z_0, z_1, \ldots, z_{n-1}$ (possibly with repetitions), show how to find the coefficients of a polynomial $P(x)$ of degree-bound $n + 1$ that has zeros only at $z_0, z_1, \ldots, z_{n-1}$ (possibly with repetitions). Your procedure should run in time $O(n \lg^2 n)$. (*Hint:* The polynomial $P(x)$ has a zero at z_j if and only if $P(x)$ is a multiple of $(x - z_j)$.)

30.2-8 ★
The *chirp transform* of a vector $a = (a_0, a_1, \ldots, a_{n-1})$ is the vector $y = (y_0, y_1, \ldots, y_{n-1})$, where $y_k = \sum_{j=0}^{n-1} a_j z^{kj}$ and z is any complex number. The

DFT is therefore a special case of the chirp transform, obtained by taking $z = \omega_n$. Show how to evaluate the chirp transform in time $O(n \lg n)$ for any complex number z. (*Hint:* Use the equation

$$y_k = z^{k^2/2} \sum_{j=0}^{n-1} \left(a_j z^{j^2/2} \right) \left(z^{-(k-j)^2/2} \right)$$

to view the chirp transform as a convolution.)

30.3 Efficient FFT implementations

Since the practical applications of the DFT, such as signal processing, demand the utmost speed, this section examines two efficient FFT implementations. First, we shall examine an iterative version of the FFT algorithm that runs in $\Theta(n \lg n)$ time but can have a lower constant hidden in the Θ-notation than the recursive version in Section 30.2. (Depending on the exact implementation, the recursive version may use the hardware cache more efficiently.) Then, we shall use the insights that led us to the iterative implementation to design an efficient parallel FFT circuit.

An iterative FFT implementation

We first note that the **for** loop of lines 10–13 of RECURSIVE-FFT involves computing the value $\omega_n^k y_k^{[1]}$ twice. In compiler terminology, we call such a value a **common subexpression**. We can change the loop to compute it only once, storing it in a temporary variable t.

$$
\begin{aligned}
&\textbf{for } k = 0 \textbf{ to } n/2 - 1 \\
&\quad t = \omega \, y_k^{[1]} \\
&\quad y_k = y_k^{[0]} + t \\
&\quad y_{k+(n/2)} = y_k^{[0]} - t \\
&\quad \omega = \omega \, \omega_n
\end{aligned}
$$

The operation in this loop, multiplying the twiddle factor $\omega = \omega_n^k$ by $y_k^{[1]}$, storing the product into t, and adding and subtracting t from $y_k^{[0]}$, is known as a **butterfly operation** and is shown schematically in Figure 30.3.

We now show how to make the FFT algorithm iterative rather than recursive in structure. In Figure 30.4, we have arranged the input vectors to the recursive calls in an invocation of RECURSIVE-FFT in a tree structure, where the initial call is for $n = 8$. The tree has one node for each call of the procedure, labeled

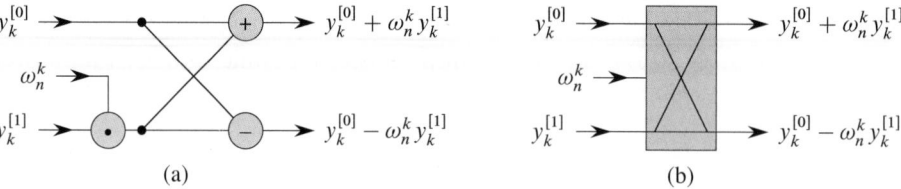

Figure 30.3 A butterfly operation. **(a)** The two input values enter from the left, the twiddle factor ω_n^k is multiplied by $y_k^{[1]}$, and the sum and difference are output on the right. **(b)** A simplified drawing of a butterfly operation. We will use this representation in a parallel FFT circuit.

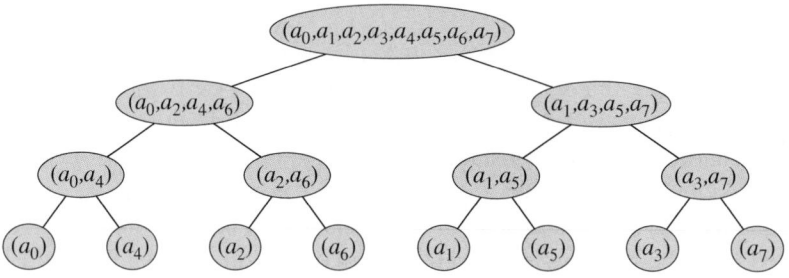

Figure 30.4 The tree of input vectors to the recursive calls of the RECURSIVE-FFT procedure. The initial invocation is for $n = 8$.

by the corresponding input vector. Each RECURSIVE-FFT invocation makes two recursive calls, unless it has received a 1-element vector. The first call appears in the left child, and the second call appears in the right child.

Looking at the tree, we observe that if we could arrange the elements of the initial vector a into the order in which they appear in the leaves, we could trace the execution of the RECURSIVE-FFT procedure, but bottom up instead of top down. First, we take the elements in pairs, compute the DFT of each pair using one butterfly operation, and replace the pair with its DFT. The vector then holds $n/2$ 2-element DFTs. Next, we take these $n/2$ DFTs in pairs and compute the DFT of the four vector elements they come from by executing two butterfly operations, replacing two 2-element DFTs with one 4-element DFT. The vector then holds $n/4$ 4-element DFTs. We continue in this manner until the vector holds two $(n/2)$-element DFTs, which we combine using $n/2$ butterfly operations into the final n-element DFT.

To turn this bottom-up approach into code, we use an array $A[0 \mathinner{\ldotp\ldotp} n-1]$ that initially holds the elements of the input vector a in the order in which they appear

in the leaves of the tree of Figure 30.4. (We shall show later how to determine this order, which is known as a bit-reversal permutation.) Because we have to combine DFTs on each level of the tree, we introduce a variable s to count the levels, ranging from 1 (at the bottom, when we are combining pairs to form 2-element DFTs) to $\lg n$ (at the top, when we are combining two $(n/2)$-element DFTs to produce the final result). The algorithm therefore has the following structure:

```
1   for s = 1 to lg n
2       for k = 0 to n − 1 by 2^s
3           combine the two 2^{s−1}-element DFTs in
                A[k .. k + 2^{s−1} − 1] and A[k + 2^{s−1} .. k + 2^s − 1]
                into one 2^s-element DFT in A[k .. k + 2^s − 1]
```

We can express the body of the loop (line 3) as more precise pseudocode. We copy the **for** loop from the RECURSIVE-FFT procedure, identifying $y^{[0]}$ with $A[k .. k + 2^{s-1} - 1]$ and $y^{[1]}$ with $A[k + 2^{s-1} .. k + 2^s - 1]$. The twiddle factor used in each butterfly operation depends on the value of s; it is a power of ω_m, where $m = 2^s$. (We introduce the variable m solely for the sake of readability.) We introduce another temporary variable u that allows us to perform the butterfly operation in place. When we replace line 3 of the overall structure by the loop body, we get the following pseudocode, which forms the basis of the parallel implementation we shall present later. The code first calls the auxiliary procedure BIT-REVERSE-COPY(a, A) to copy vector a into array A in the initial order in which we need the values.

ITERATIVE-FFT(a)

```
 1   BIT-REVERSE-COPY(a, A)
 2   n = a.length          // n is a power of 2
 3   for s = 1 to lg n
 4       m = 2^s
 5       ω_m = e^{2πi/m}
 6       for k = 0 to n − 1 by m
 7           ω = 1
 8           for j = 0 to m/2 − 1
 9               t = ω A[k + j + m/2]
10               u = A[k + j]
11               A[k + j] = u + t
12               A[k + j + m/2] = u − t
13               ω = ω ω_m
14   return A
```

How does BIT-REVERSE-COPY get the elements of the input vector a into the desired order in the array A? The order in which the leaves appear in Figure 30.4

is a ***bit-reversal permutation***. That is, if we let $\text{rev}(k)$ be the $\lg n$-bit integer formed by reversing the bits of the binary representation of k, then we want to place vector element a_k in array position $A[\text{rev}(k)]$. In Figure 30.4, for example, the leaves appear in the order $0, 4, 2, 6, 1, 5, 3, 7$; this sequence in binary is $000, 100, 010, 110, 001, 101, 011, 111$, and when we reverse the bits of each value we get the sequence $000, 001, 010, 011, 100, 101, 110, 111$. To see that we want a bit-reversal permutation in general, we note that at the top level of the tree, indices whose low-order bit is 0 go into the left subtree and indices whose low-order bit is 1 go into the right subtree. Stripping off the low-order bit at each level, we continue this process down the tree, until we get the order given by the bit-reversal permutation at the leaves.

Since we can easily compute the function $\text{rev}(k)$, the BIT-REVERSE-COPY procedure is simple:

BIT-REVERSE-COPY(a, A)

1   $n = a.length$
2   **for** $k = 0$ **to** $n - 1$
3       $A[\text{rev}(k)] = a_k$

The iterative FFT implementation runs in time $\Theta(n \lg n)$. The call to BIT-REVERSE-COPY(a, A) certainly runs in $O(n \lg n)$ time, since we iterate n times and can reverse an integer between 0 and $n - 1$, with $\lg n$ bits, in $O(\lg n)$ time. (In practice, because we usually know the initial value of n in advance, we would probably code a table mapping k to $\text{rev}(k)$, making BIT-REVERSE-COPY run in $\Theta(n)$ time with a low hidden constant. Alternatively, we could use the clever amortized reverse binary counter scheme described in Problem 17-1.) To complete the proof that ITERATIVE-FFT runs in time $\Theta(n \lg n)$, we show that $L(n)$, the number of times the body of the innermost loop (lines 8–13) executes, is $\Theta(n \lg n)$. The **for** loop of lines 6–13 iterates $n/m = n/2^s$ times for each value of s, and the innermost loop of lines 8–13 iterates $m/2 = 2^{s-1}$ times. Thus,

$$
\begin{aligned}
L(n) &= \sum_{s=1}^{\lg n} \frac{n}{2^s} \cdot 2^{s-1} \\
&= \sum_{s=1}^{\lg n} \frac{n}{2} \\
&= \Theta(n \lg n) .
\end{aligned}
$$

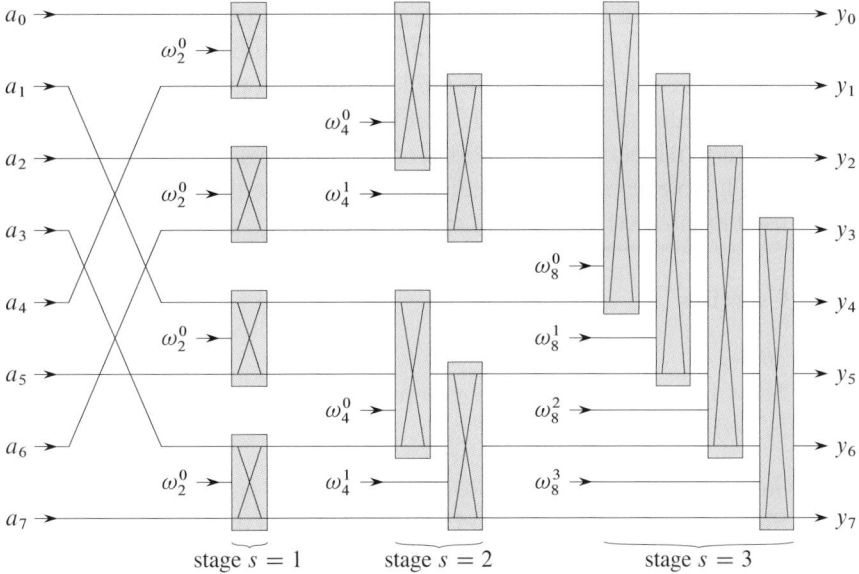

Figure 30.5 A circuit that computes the FFT in parallel, here shown on $n = 8$ inputs. Each butterfly operation takes as input the values on two wires, along with a twiddle factor, and it produces as outputs the values on two wires. The stages of butterflies are labeled to correspond to iterations of the outermost loop of the ITERATIVE-FFT procedure. Only the top and bottom wires passing through a butterfly interact with it; wires that pass through the middle of a butterfly do not affect that butterfly, nor are their values changed by that butterfly. For example, the top butterfly in stage 2 has nothing to do with wire 1 (the wire whose output is labeled y_1); its inputs and outputs are only on wires 0 and 2 (labeled y_0 and y_2, respectively). This circuit has depth $\Theta(\lg n)$ and performs $\Theta(n \lg n)$ butterfly operations altogether.

A parallel FFT circuit

We can exploit many of the properties that allowed us to implement an efficient iterative FFT algorithm to produce an efficient parallel algorithm for the FFT. We will express the parallel FFT algorithm as a circuit. Figure 30.5 shows a parallel FFT circuit, which computes the FFT on n inputs, for $n = 8$. The circuit begins with a bit-reverse permutation of the inputs, followed by $\lg n$ stages, each stage consisting of $n/2$ butterflies executed in parallel. The **depth** of the circuit—the maximum number of computational elements between any output and any input that can reach it—is therefore $\Theta(\lg n)$.

The leftmost part of the parallel FFT circuit performs the bit-reverse permutation, and the remainder mimics the iterative ITERATIVE-FFT procedure. Because each iteration of the outermost **for** loop performs $n/2$ independent butterfly operations, the circuit performs them in parallel. The value of s in each iteration within

ITERATIVE-FFT corresponds to a stage of butterflies shown in Figure 30.5. For $s = 1, 2, \ldots, \lg n$, stage s consists of $n/2^s$ groups of butterflies (corresponding to each value of k in ITERATIVE-FFT), with 2^{s-1} butterflies per group (corresponding to each value of j in ITERATIVE-FFT). The butterflies shown in Figure 30.5 correspond to the butterfly operations of the innermost loop (lines 9–12 of ITERATIVE-FFT). Note also that the twiddle factors used in the butterflies correspond to those used in ITERATIVE-FFT: in stage s, we use $\omega_m^0, \omega_m^1, \ldots, \omega_m^{m/2-1}$, where $m = 2^s$.

Exercises

30.3-1
Show how ITERATIVE-FFT computes the DFT of the input vector $(0, 2, 3, -1, 4, 5, 7, 9)$.

30.3-2
Show how to implement an FFT algorithm with the bit-reversal permutation occurring at the end, rather than at the beginning, of the computation. (*Hint:* Consider the inverse DFT.)

30.3-3
How many times does ITERATIVE-FFT compute twiddle factors in each stage? Rewrite ITERATIVE-FFT to compute twiddle factors only 2^{s-1} times in stage s.

30.3-4 ★
Suppose that the adders within the butterfly operations of the FFT circuit sometimes fail in such a manner that they always produce a zero output, independent of their inputs. Suppose that exactly one adder has failed, but that you don't know which one. Describe how you can identify the failed adder by supplying inputs to the overall FFT circuit and observing the outputs. How efficient is your method?

Problems

30-1   Divide-and-conquer multiplication
a. Show how to multiply two linear polynomials $ax + b$ and $cx + d$ using only three multiplications. (*Hint:* One of the multiplications is $(a + b) \cdot (c + d)$.)

b. Give two divide-and-conquer algorithms for multiplying two polynomials of degree-bound n in $\Theta(n^{\lg 3})$ time. The first algorithm should divide the input polynomial coefficients into a high half and a low half, and the second algorithm should divide them according to whether their index is odd or even.

c. Show how to multiply two n-bit integers in $O(n^{\lg 3})$ steps, where each step operates on at most a constant number of 1-bit values.

30-2 Toeplitz matrices

A **Toeplitz matrix** is an $n \times n$ matrix $A = (a_{ij})$ such that $a_{ij} = a_{i-1,j-1}$ for $i = 2, 3, \ldots, n$ and $j = 2, 3, \ldots, n$.

a. Is the sum of two Toeplitz matrices necessarily Toeplitz? What about the product?

b. Describe how to represent a Toeplitz matrix so that you can add two $n \times n$ Toeplitz matrices in $O(n)$ time.

c. Give an $O(n \lg n)$-time algorithm for multiplying an $n \times n$ Toeplitz matrix by a vector of length n. Use your representation from part (b).

d. Give an efficient algorithm for multiplying two $n \times n$ Toeplitz matrices. Analyze its running time.

30-3 Multidimensional fast Fourier transform

We can generalize the 1-dimensional discrete Fourier transform defined by equation (30.8) to d dimensions. The input is a d-dimensional array $A = (a_{j_1, j_2, \ldots, j_d})$ whose dimensions are $n_1, n_2, \ldots, n_d$, where $n_1 n_2 \cdots n_d = n$. We define the d-dimensional discrete Fourier transform by the equation

$$y_{k_1, k_2, \ldots, k_d} = \sum_{j_1=0}^{n_1-1} \sum_{j_2=0}^{n_2-1} \cdots \sum_{j_d=0}^{n_d-1} a_{j_1, j_2, \ldots, j_d} \, \omega_{n_1}^{j_1 k_1} \omega_{n_2}^{j_2 k_2} \cdots \omega_{n_d}^{j_d k_d}$$

for $0 \le k_1 < n_1, 0 \le k_2 < n_2, \ldots, 0 \le k_d < n_d$.

a. Show that we can compute a d-dimensional DFT by computing 1-dimensional DFTs on each dimension in turn. That is, we first compute n/n_1 separate 1-dimensional DFTs along dimension 1. Then, using the result of the DFTs along dimension 1 as the input, we compute n/n_2 separate 1-dimensional DFTs along dimension 2. Using this result as the input, we compute n/n_3 separate 1-dimensional DFTs along dimension 3, and so on, through dimension d.

b. Show that the ordering of dimensions does not matter, so that we can compute a d-dimensional DFT by computing the 1-dimensional DFTs in any order of the d dimensions.

c. Show that if we compute each 1-dimensional DFT by computing the fast Fourier transform, the total time to compute a d-dimensional DFT is $O(n \lg n)$, independent of d.

30-4   *Evaluating all derivatives of a polynomial at a point*

Given a polynomial $A(x)$ of degree-bound n, we define its tth derivative by

$$A^{(t)}(x) = \begin{cases} A(x) & \text{if } t = 0 , \\ \frac{d}{dx} A^{(t-1)}(x) & \text{if } 1 \le t \le n - 1 , \\ 0 & \text{if } t \ge n . \end{cases}$$

From the coefficient representation $(a_0, a_1, \ldots, a_{n-1})$ of $A(x)$ and a given point x_0, we wish to determine $A^{(t)}(x_0)$ for $t = 0, 1, \ldots, n - 1$.

a. Given coefficients $b_0, b_1, \ldots, b_{n-1}$ such that

$$A(x) = \sum_{j=0}^{n-1} b_j (x - x_0)^j ,$$

show how to compute $A^{(t)}(x_0)$, for $t = 0, 1, \ldots, n - 1$, in $O(n)$ time.

b. Explain how to find $b_0, b_1, \ldots, b_{n-1}$ in $O(n \lg n)$ time, given $A(x_0 + \omega_n^k)$ for $k = 0, 1, \ldots, n - 1$.

c. Prove that

$$A(x_0 + \omega_n^k) = \sum_{r=0}^{n-1} \left(\frac{\omega_n^{kr}}{r!} \sum_{j=0}^{n-1} f(j) g(r - j) \right) ,$$

where $f(j) = a_j \cdot j!$ and

$$g(l) = \begin{cases} x_0^{-l}/(-l)! & \text{if } -(n - 1) \le l \le 0 , \\ 0 & \text{if } 1 \le l \le n - 1 . \end{cases}$$

d. Explain how to evaluate $A(x_0 + \omega_n^k)$ for $k = 0, 1, \ldots, n - 1$ in $O(n \lg n)$ time. Conclude that we can evaluate all nontrivial derivatives of $A(x)$ at x_0 in $O(n \lg n)$ time.

30-5 *Polynomial evaluation at multiple points*

We have seen how to evaluate a polynomial of degree-bound n at a single point in $O(n)$ time using Horner's rule. We have also discovered how to evaluate such a polynomial at all n complex roots of unity in $O(n \lg n)$ time using the FFT. We shall now show how to evaluate a polynomial of degree-bound n at n arbitrary points in $O(n \lg^2 n)$ time.

To do so, we shall assume that we can compute the polynomial remainder when one such polynomial is divided by another in $O(n \lg n)$ time, a result that we state without proof. For example, the remainder of $3x^3 + x^2 - 3x + 1$ when divided by $x^2 + x + 2$ is

$$(3x^3 + x^2 - 3x + 1) \bmod (x^2 + x + 2) = -7x + 5 .$$

Given the coefficient representation of a polynomial $A(x) = \sum_{k=0}^{n-1} a_k x^k$ and n points $x_0, x_1, \ldots, x_{n-1}$, we wish to compute the n values $A(x_0), A(x_1), \ldots, A(x_{n-1})$. For $0 \leq i \leq j \leq n-1$, define the polynomials $P_{ij}(x) = \prod_{k=i}^{j} (x - x_k)$ and $Q_{ij}(x) = A(x) \bmod P_{ij}(x)$. Note that $Q_{ij}(x)$ has degree at most $j - i$.

a. Prove that $A(x) \bmod (x - z) = A(z)$ for any point z.

b. Prove that $Q_{kk}(x) = A(x_k)$ and that $Q_{0,n-1}(x) = A(x)$.

c. Prove that for $i \leq k \leq j$, we have $Q_{ik}(x) = Q_{ij}(x) \bmod P_{ik}(x)$ and $Q_{kj}(x) = Q_{ij}(x) \bmod P_{kj}(x)$.

d. Give an $O(n \lg^2 n)$-time algorithm to evaluate $A(x_0), A(x_1), \ldots, A(x_{n-1})$.

30-6 *FFT using modular arithmetic*

As defined, the discrete Fourier transform requires us to compute with complex numbers, which can result in a loss of precision due to round-off errors. For some problems, the answer is known to contain only integers, and by using a variant of the FFT based on modular arithmetic, we can guarantee that the answer is calculated exactly. An example of such a problem is that of multiplying two polynomials with integer coefficients. Exercise 30.2-6 gives one approach, using a modulus of length $\Omega(n)$ bits to handle a DFT on n points. This problem gives another approach, which uses a modulus of the more reasonable length $O(\lg n)$; it requires that you understand the material of Chapter 31. Let n be a power of 2.

a. Suppose that we search for the smallest k such that $p = kn + 1$ is prime. Give a simple heuristic argument why we might expect k to be approximately $\ln n$. (The value of k might be much larger or smaller, but we can reasonably expect to examine $O(\lg n)$ candidate values of k on average.) How does the expected length of p compare to the length of n?

Let g be a generator of $\mathbb{Z}_p^*$, and let $w = g^k \bmod p$.

b. Argue that the DFT and the inverse DFT are well-defined inverse operations modulo p, where w is used as a principal nth root of unity.

c. Show how to make the FFT and its inverse work modulo p in time $O(n \lg n)$, where operations on words of $O(\lg n)$ bits take unit time. Assume that the algorithm is given p and w.

d. Compute the DFT modulo $p = 17$ of the vector $(0, 5, 3, 7, 7, 2, 1, 6)$. Note that $g = 3$ is a generator of $\mathbb{Z}_{17}^*$.

Chapter notes

Van Loan's book [343] provides an outstanding treatment of the fast Fourier transform. Press, Teukolsky, Vetterling, and Flannery [283, 284] have a good description of the fast Fourier transform and its applications. For an excellent introduction to signal processing, a popular FFT application area, see the texts by Oppenheim and Schafer [266] and Oppenheim and Willsky [267]. The Oppenheim and Schafer book also shows how to handle cases in which n is not an integer power of 2.

Fourier analysis is not limited to 1-dimensional data. It is widely used in image processing to analyze data in 2 or more dimensions. The books by Gonzalez and Woods [146] and Pratt [281] discuss multidimensional Fourier transforms and their use in image processing, and books by Tolimieri, An, and Lu [338] and Van Loan [343] discuss the mathematics of multidimensional fast Fourier transforms.

Cooley and Tukey [76] are widely credited with devising the FFT in the 1960s. The FFT had in fact been discovered many times previously, but its importance was not fully realized before the advent of modern digital computers. Although Press, Teukolsky, Vetterling, and Flannery attribute the origins of the method to Runge and König in 1924, an article by Heideman, Johnson, and Burrus [163] traces the history of the FFT as far back as C. F. Gauss in 1805.

Frigo and Johnson [117] developed a fast and flexible implementation of the FFT, called FFTW ("fastest Fourier transform in the West"). FFTW is designed for situations requiring multiple DFT computations on the same problem size. Before actually computing the DFTs, FFTW executes a "planner," which, by a series of trial runs, determines how best to decompose the FFT computation for the given problem size on the host machine. FFTW adapts to use the hardware cache efficiently, and once subproblems are small enough, FFTW solves them with optimized, straight-line code. Furthermore, FFTW has the unusual advantage of taking $\Theta(n \lg n)$ time for any problem size n, even when n is a large prime.

Although the standard Fourier transform assumes that the input represents points that are uniformly spaced in the time domain, other techniques can approximate the FFT on "nonequispaced" data. The article by Ware [348] provides an overview.

31 Number-Theoretic Algorithms

Number theory was once viewed as a beautiful but largely useless subject in pure mathematics. Today number-theoretic algorithms are used widely, due in large part to the invention of cryptographic schemes based on large prime numbers. These schemes are feasible because we can find large primes easily, and they are secure because we do not know how to factor the product of large primes (or solve related problems, such as computing discrete logarithms) efficiently. This chapter presents some of the number theory and related algorithms that underlie such applications.

Section 31.1 introduces basic concepts of number theory, such as divisibility, modular equivalence, and unique factorization. Section 31.2 studies one of the world's oldest algorithms: Euclid's algorithm for computing the greatest common divisor of two integers. Section 31.3 reviews concepts of modular arithmetic. Section 31.4 then studies the set of multiples of a given number a, modulo n, and shows how to find all solutions to the equation $ax \equiv b \pmod{n}$ by using Euclid's algorithm. The Chinese remainder theorem is presented in Section 31.5. Section 31.6 considers powers of a given number a, modulo n, and presents a repeated-squaring algorithm for efficiently computing $a^b \bmod n$, given a, b, and n. This operation is at the heart of efficient primality testing and of much modern cryptography. Section 31.7 then describes the RSA public-key cryptosystem. Section 31.8 examines a randomized primality test. We can use this test to find large primes efficiently, which we need to do in order to create keys for the RSA cryptosystem. Finally, Section 31.9 reviews a simple but effective heuristic for factoring small integers. It is a curious fact that factoring is one problem people may wish to be intractable, since the security of RSA depends on the difficulty of factoring large integers.

Size of inputs and cost of arithmetic computations

Because we shall be working with large integers, we need to adjust how we think about the size of an input and about the cost of elementary arithmetic operations.

In this chapter, a "large input" typically means an input containing "large integers" rather than an input containing "many integers" (as for sorting). Thus,

we shall measure the size of an input in terms of the *number of bits* required to represent that input, not just the number of integers in the input. An algorithm with integer inputs $a_1, a_2, \ldots, a_k$ is a ***polynomial-time algorithm*** if it runs in time polynomial in $\lg a_1, \lg a_2, \ldots, \lg a_k$, that is, polynomial in the lengths of its binary-encoded inputs.

In most of this book, we have found it convenient to think of the elementary arithmetic operations (multiplications, divisions, or computing remainders) as primitive operations that take one unit of time. By counting the number of such arithmetic operations that an algorithm performs, we have a basis for making a reasonable estimate of the algorithm's actual running time on a computer. Elementary operations can be time-consuming, however, when their inputs are large. It thus becomes convenient to measure how many ***bit operations*** a number-theoretic algorithm requires. In this model, multiplying two β-bit integers by the ordinary method uses $\Theta(\beta^2)$ bit operations. Similarly, we can divide a β-bit integer by a shorter integer or take the remainder of a β-bit integer when divided by a shorter integer in time $\Theta(\beta^2)$ by simple algorithms. (See Exercise 31.1-12.) Faster methods are known. For example, a simple divide-and-conquer method for multiplying two β-bit integers has a running time of $\Theta(\beta^{\lg 3})$, and the fastest known method has a running time of $\Theta(\beta \lg \beta \lg \lg \beta)$. For practical purposes, however, the $\Theta(\beta^2)$ algorithm is often best, and we shall use this bound as a basis for our analyses.

We shall generally analyze algorithms in this chapter in terms of both the number of arithmetic operations and the number of bit operations they require.

31.1   Elementary number-theoretic notions

This section provides a brief review of notions from elementary number theory concerning the set $\mathbb{Z} = \{\ldots, -2, -1, 0, 1, 2, \ldots\}$ of integers and the set $\mathbb{N} = \{0, 1, 2, \ldots\}$ of natural numbers.

Divisibility and divisors

The notion of one integer being divisible by another is key to the theory of numbers. The notation $d \mid a$ (read "d ***divides*** a") means that $a = kd$ for some integer k. Every integer divides 0. If $a > 0$ and $d \mid a$, then $|d| \leq |a|$. If $d \mid a$, then we also say that a is a ***multiple*** of d. If d does not divide a, we write $d \nmid a$.

If $d \mid a$ and $d \geq 0$, we say that d is a ***divisor*** of a. Note that $d \mid a$ if and only if $-d \mid a$, so that no generality is lost by defining the divisors to be nonnegative, with the understanding that the negative of any divisor of a also divides a. A

divisor of a nonzero integer a is at least 1 but not greater than $|a|$. For example, the divisors of 24 are 1, 2, 3, 4, 6, 8, 12, and 24.

Every positive integer a is divisible by the **trivial divisors** 1 and a. The nontrivial divisors of a are the **factors** of a. For example, the factors of 20 are 2, 4, 5, and 10.

Prime and composite numbers

An integer $a > 1$ whose only divisors are the trivial divisors 1 and a is a **prime number** or, more simply, a **prime**. Primes have many special properties and play a critical role in number theory. The first 20 primes, in order, are

$$2, \ 3, \ 5, \ 7, \ 11, \ 13, \ 17, \ 19, \ 23, \ 29, \ 31, \ 37, \ 41, \ 43, \ 47, \ 53, \ 59, \ 61, \ 67, \ 71 \ .$$

Exercise 31.1-2 asks you to prove that there are infinitely many primes. An integer $a > 1$ that is not prime is a **composite number** or, more simply, a **composite**. For example, 39 is composite because $3 \mid 39$. We call the integer 1 a **unit**, and it is neither prime nor composite. Similarly, the integer 0 and all negative integers are neither prime nor composite.

The division theorem, remainders, and modular equivalence

Given an integer n, we can partition the integers into those that are multiples of n and those that are not multiples of n. Much number theory is based upon refining this partition by classifying the nonmultiples of n according to their remainders when divided by n. The following theorem provides the basis for this refinement. We omit the proof (but see, for example, Niven and Zuckerman [265]).

Theorem 31.1 (Division theorem)
For any integer a and any positive integer n, there exist unique integers q and r such that $0 \le r < n$ and $a = qn + r$.   ∎

The value $q = \lfloor a/n \rfloor$ is the **quotient** of the division. The value $r = a \bmod n$ is the **remainder** (or **residue**) of the division. We have that $n \mid a$ if and only if $a \bmod n = 0$.

We can partition the integers into n equivalence classes according to their remainders modulo n. The **equivalence class modulo n** containing an integer a is

$$[a]_n = \{a + kn : k \in \mathbb{Z}\} \ .$$

For example, $[3]_7 = \{\ldots, -11, -4, 3, 10, 17, \ldots\}$; we can also denote this set by $[-4]_7$ and $[10]_7$. Using the notation defined on page 54, we can say that writing $a \in [b]_n$ is the same as writing $a \equiv b \pmod{n}$. The set of all such equivalence classes is

$$\mathbb{Z}_n = \{[a]_n : 0 \leq a \leq n-1\} \ . \tag{31.1}$$

When you see the definition

$$\mathbb{Z}_n = \{0, 1, \ldots, n-1\} \ , \tag{31.2}$$

you should read it as equivalent to equation (31.1) with the understanding that 0 represents $[0]_n$, 1 represents $[1]_n$, and so on; each class is represented by its smallest nonnegative element. You should keep the underlying equivalence classes in mind, however. For example, if we refer to -1 as a member of $\mathbb{Z}_n$, we are really referring to $[n-1]_n$, since $-1 \equiv n-1 \pmod{n}$.

Common divisors and greatest common divisors

If d is a divisor of a and d is also a divisor of b, then d is a **common divisor** of a and b. For example, the divisors of 30 are 1, 2, 3, 5, 6, 10, 15, and 30, and so the common divisors of 24 and 30 are 1, 2, 3, and 6. Note that 1 is a common divisor of any two integers.

An important property of common divisors is that

$$d \mid a \text{ and } d \mid b \text{ implies } d \mid (a+b) \text{ and } d \mid (a-b) \ . \tag{31.3}$$

More generally, we have that

$$d \mid a \text{ and } d \mid b \text{ implies } d \mid (ax+by) \tag{31.4}$$

for any integers x and y. Also, if $a \mid b$, then either $|a| \leq |b|$ or $b = 0$, which implies that

$$a \mid b \text{ and } b \mid a \text{ implies } a = \pm b \ . \tag{31.5}$$

The **greatest common divisor** of two integers a and b, not both zero, is the largest of the common divisors of a and b; we denote it by $\gcd(a, b)$. For example, $\gcd(24, 30) = 6$, $\gcd(5, 7) = 1$, and $\gcd(0, 9) = 9$. If a and b are both nonzero, then $\gcd(a, b)$ is an integer between 1 and $\min(|a|, |b|)$. We define $\gcd(0, 0)$ to be 0; this definition is necessary to make standard properties of the gcd function (such as equation (31.9) below) universally valid.

The following are elementary properties of the gcd function:

$$
\begin{aligned}
\gcd(a, b) &= \gcd(b, a) \ , & (31.6) \\
\gcd(a, b) &= \gcd(-a, b) \ , & (31.7) \\
\gcd(a, b) &= \gcd(|a|, |b|) \ , & (31.8) \\
\gcd(a, 0) &= |a| \ , & (31.9) \\
\gcd(a, ka) &= |a| \qquad \text{for any } k \in \mathbb{Z} \ . & (31.10)
\end{aligned}
$$

The following theorem provides an alternative and useful characterization of $\gcd(a, b)$.

Theorem 31.2
If a and b are any integers, not both zero, then $\gcd(a, b)$ is the smallest positive element of the set $\{ax + by : x, y \in \mathbb{Z}\}$ of linear combinations of a and b.

Proof Let s be the smallest positive such linear combination of a and b, and let $s = ax + by$ for some $x, y \in \mathbb{Z}$. Let $q = \lfloor a/s \rfloor$. Equation (3.8) then implies

$$
\begin{aligned}
a \bmod s &= a - qs \\
&= a - q(ax + by) \\
&= a(1 - qx) + b(-qy) \,,
\end{aligned}
$$

and so $a \bmod s$ is a linear combination of a and b as well. But, since $0 \le a \bmod s < s$, we have that $a \bmod s = 0$, because s is the smallest positive such linear combination. Therefore, we have that $s \mid a$ and, by analogous reasoning, $s \mid b$. Thus, s is a common divisor of a and b, and so $\gcd(a, b) \ge s$. Equation (31.4) implies that $\gcd(a, b) \mid s$, since $\gcd(a, b)$ divides both a and b and s is a linear combination of a and b. But $\gcd(a, b) \mid s$ and $s > 0$ imply that $\gcd(a, b) \le s$. Combining $\gcd(a, b) \ge s$ and $\gcd(a, b) \le s$ yields $\gcd(a, b) = s$. We conclude that s is the greatest common divisor of a and b.   ■

Corollary 31.3
For any integers a and b, if $d \mid a$ and $d \mid b$, then $d \mid \gcd(a, b)$.

Proof This corollary follows from equation (31.4), because $\gcd(a, b)$ is a linear combination of a and b by Theorem 31.2.   ■

Corollary 31.4
For all integers a and b and any nonnegative integer n,

$$
\gcd(an, bn) = n \gcd(a, b) \,.
$$

Proof If $n = 0$, the corollary is trivial. If $n > 0$, then $\gcd(an, bn)$ is the smallest positive element of the set $\{anx + bny : x, y \in \mathbb{Z}\}$, which is n times the smallest positive element of the set $\{ax + by : x, y \in \mathbb{Z}\}$.   ■

Corollary 31.5
For all positive integers n, a, and b, if $n \mid ab$ and $\gcd(a, n) = 1$, then $n \mid b$.

Proof We leave the proof as Exercise 31.1-5.   ■

Relatively prime integers

Two integers a and b are **relatively prime** if their only common divisor is 1, that is, if $\gcd(a, b) = 1$. For example, 8 and 15 are relatively prime, since the divisors of 8 are 1, 2, 4, and 8, and the divisors of 15 are 1, 3, 5, and 15. The following theorem states that if two integers are each relatively prime to an integer p, then their product is relatively prime to p.

Theorem 31.6
For any integers a, b, and p, if both $\gcd(a, p) = 1$ and $\gcd(b, p) = 1$, then $\gcd(ab, p) = 1$.

Proof It follows from Theorem 31.2 that there exist integers x, y, x', and y' such that

$$
\begin{aligned}
ax + py &= 1, \\
bx' + py' &= 1.
\end{aligned}
$$

Multiplying these equations and rearranging, we have

$$ab(xx') + p(ybx' + y'ax + pyy') = 1.$$

Since 1 is thus a positive linear combination of ab and p, an appeal to Theorem 31.2 completes the proof. ∎

Integers $n_1, n_2, \ldots, n_k$ are **pairwise relatively prime** if, whenever $i \neq j$, we have $\gcd(n_i, n_j) = 1$.

Unique factorization

An elementary but important fact about divisibility by primes is the following.

Theorem 31.7
For all primes p and all integers a and b, if $p \mid ab$, then $p \mid a$ or $p \mid b$ (or both).

Proof Assume for the purpose of contradiction that $p \mid ab$, but that $p \nmid a$ and $p \nmid b$. Thus, $\gcd(a, p) = 1$ and $\gcd(b, p) = 1$, since the only divisors of p are 1 and p, and we assume that p divides neither a nor b. Theorem 31.6 then implies that $\gcd(ab, p) = 1$, contradicting our assumption that $p \mid ab$, since $p \mid ab$ implies $\gcd(ab, p) = p$. This contradiction completes the proof. ∎

A consequence of Theorem 31.7 is that we can uniquely factor any composite integer into a product of primes.

Theorem 31.8 (Unique factorization)
There is exactly one way to write any composite integer a as a product of the form

$$a = p_1^{e_1} p_2^{e_2} \cdots p_r^{e_r} \, ,$$

where the p_i are prime, $p_1 < p_2 < \cdots < p_r$, and the e_i are positive integers.

Proof   We leave the proof as Exercise 31.1-11.   ∎

As an example, the number 6000 is uniquely factored into primes as $2^4 \cdot 3 \cdot 5^3$.

Exercises

31.1-1
Prove that if $a > b > 0$ and $c = a + b$, then $c \bmod a = b$.

31.1-2
Prove that there are infinitely many primes. (*Hint:* Show that none of the primes $p_1, p_2, \ldots, p_k$ divide $(p_1 p_2 \cdots p_k) + 1$.)

31.1-3
Prove that if $a \mid b$ and $b \mid c$, then $a \mid c$.

31.1-4
Prove that if p is prime and $0 < k < p$, then $\gcd(k, p) = 1$.

31.1-5
Prove Corollary 31.5.

31.1-6
Prove that if p is prime and $0 < k < p$, then $p \mid \binom{p}{k}$. Conclude that for all integers a and b and all primes p,

$$(a + b)^p \equiv a^p + b^p \pmod{p} \, .$$

31.1-7
Prove that if a and b are any positive integers such that $a \mid b$, then

$$(x \bmod b) \bmod a = x \bmod a$$

for any x. Prove, under the same assumptions, that

$$x \equiv y \pmod{b} \text{ implies } x \equiv y \pmod{a}$$

for any integers x and y.

31.1-8

For any integer $k > 0$, an integer n is a ***kth power*** if there exists an integer a such that $a^k = n$. Furthermore, $n > 1$ is a ***nontrivial power*** if it is a kth power for some integer $k > 1$. Show how to determine whether a given β-bit integer n is a nontrivial power in time polynomial in β.

31.1-9

Prove equations (31.6)–(31.10).

31.1-10

Show that the gcd operator is associative. That is, prove that for all integers a, b, and c,

$$\gcd(a, \gcd(b, c)) = \gcd(\gcd(a, b), c) \, .$$

31.1-11 ★

Prove Theorem 31.8.

31.1-12

Give efficient algorithms for the operations of dividing a β-bit integer by a shorter integer and of taking the remainder of a β-bit integer when divided by a shorter integer. Your algorithms should run in time $\Theta(\beta^2)$.

31.1-13

Give an efficient algorithm to convert a given β-bit (binary) integer to a decimal representation. Argue that if multiplication or division of integers whose length is at most β takes time $M(\beta)$, where $M(\beta) = \Omega(\beta)$, then you can convert binary to decimal in time $O(M(\beta) \lg \beta)$. (*Hint:* Use a divide-and-conquer approach, obtaining the top and bottom halves of the result with separate recursions.)

31.2   Greatest common divisor

In this section, we describe Euclid's algorithm for efficiently computing the greatest common divisor of two integers. When we analyze the running time, we shall see a surprising connection with the Fibonacci numbers, which yield a worst-case input for Euclid's algorithm.

We restrict ourselves in this section to nonnegative integers. This restriction is justified by equation (31.8), which states that $\gcd(a, b) = \gcd(|a|, |b|)$.

In principle, we can compute $\gcd(a, b)$ for positive integers a and b from the prime factorizations of a and b. Indeed, if

$$a = p_1^{e_1} p_2^{e_2} \cdots p_r^{e_r},$$ (31.11)

$$b = p_1^{f_1} p_2^{f_2} \cdots p_r^{f_r},$$ (31.12)

with zero exponents being used to make the set of primes $p_1, p_2, \ldots, p_r$ the same for both a and b, then, as Exercise 31.2-1 asks you to show,

$$\gcd(a, b) = p_1^{\min(e_1, f_1)} p_2^{\min(e_2, f_2)} \cdots p_r^{\min(e_r, f_r)}.$$ (31.13)

As we shall show in Section 31.9, however, the best algorithms to date for factoring do not run in polynomial time. Thus, this approach to computing greatest common divisors seems unlikely to yield an efficient algorithm.

Euclid's algorithm for computing greatest common divisors relies on the following theorem.

Theorem 31.9 (GCD recursion theorem)

For any nonnegative integer a and any positive integer b,

$$\gcd(a, b) = \gcd(b, a \bmod b).$$

Proof   We shall show that $\gcd(a, b)$ and $\gcd(b, a \bmod b)$ divide each other, so that by equation (31.5) they must be equal (since they are both nonnegative).

We first show that $\gcd(a, b) \mid \gcd(b, a \bmod b)$. If we let $d = \gcd(a, b)$, then $d \mid a$ and $d \mid b$. By equation (3.8), $a \bmod b = a - qb$, where $q = \lfloor a/b \rfloor$. Since $a \bmod b$ is thus a linear combination of a and b, equation (31.4) implies that $d \mid (a \bmod b)$. Therefore, since $d \mid b$ and $d \mid (a \bmod b)$, Corollary 31.3 implies that $d \mid \gcd(b, a \bmod b)$ or, equivalently, that

$$\gcd(a, b) \mid \gcd(b, a \bmod b).$$ (31.14)

Showing that $\gcd(b, a \bmod b) \mid \gcd(a, b)$ is almost the same. If we now let $d = \gcd(b, a \bmod b)$, then $d \mid b$ and $d \mid (a \bmod b)$. Since $a = qb + (a \bmod b)$, where $q = \lfloor a/b \rfloor$, we have that a is a linear combination of b and $(a \bmod b)$. By equation (31.4), we conclude that $d \mid a$. Since $d \mid b$ and $d \mid a$, we have that $d \mid \gcd(a, b)$ by Corollary 31.3 or, equivalently, that

$$\gcd(b, a \bmod b) \mid \gcd(a, b).$$ (31.15)

Using equation (31.5) to combine equations (31.14) and (31.15) completes the proof.   ∎

Euclid's algorithm

The *Elements* of Euclid (circa 300 B.C.) describes the following gcd algorithm, although it may be of even earlier origin. We express Euclid's algorithm as a recursive program based directly on Theorem 31.9. The inputs a and b are arbitrary nonnegative integers.

EUCLID(a, b)

1 **if** $b == 0$
2   **return** a
3 **else return** EUCLID$(b, a \bmod b)$

As an example of the running of EUCLID, consider the computation of $\gcd(30, 21)$:

$$
\begin{aligned}
\text{EUCLID}(30, 21) &= \text{EUCLID}(21, 9) \\
&= \text{EUCLID}(9, 3) \\
&= \text{EUCLID}(3, 0) \\
&= 3 .
\end{aligned}
$$

This computation calls EUCLID recursively three times.

The correctness of EUCLID follows from Theorem 31.9 and the property that if the algorithm returns a in line 2, then $b = 0$, so that equation (31.9) implies that $\gcd(a, b) = \gcd(a, 0) = a$. The algorithm cannot recurse indefinitely, since the second argument strictly decreases in each recursive call and is always nonnegative. Therefore, EUCLID always terminates with the correct answer.

The running time of Euclid's algorithm

We analyze the worst-case running time of EUCLID as a function of the size of a and b. We assume with no loss of generality that $a > b \geq 0$. To justify this assumption, observe that if $b > a \geq 0$, then EUCLID(a, b) immediately makes the recursive call EUCLID(b, a). That is, if the first argument is less than the second argument, EUCLID spends one recursive call swapping its arguments and then proceeds. Similarly, if $b = a > 0$, the procedure terminates after one recursive call, since $a \bmod b = 0$.

The overall running time of EUCLID is proportional to the number of recursive calls it makes. Our analysis makes use of the Fibonacci numbers F_k, defined by the recurrence (3.22).

Lemma 31.10
If $a > b \geq 1$ and the call EUCLID(a, b) performs $k \geq 1$ recursive calls, then $a \geq F_{k+2}$ and $b \geq F_{k+1}$.

Proof The proof proceeds by induction on k. For the basis of the induction, let $k = 1$. Then, $b \geq 1 = F_2$, and since $a > b$, we must have $a \geq 2 = F_3$. Since $b > (a \bmod b)$, in each recursive call the first argument is strictly larger than the second; the assumption that $a > b$ therefore holds for each recursive call.

Assume inductively that the lemma holds if $k - 1$ recursive calls are made; we shall then prove that the lemma holds for k recursive calls. Since $k > 0$, we have $b > 0$, and EUCLID(a, b) calls EUCLID$(b, a \bmod b)$ recursively, which in turn makes $k - 1$ recursive calls. The inductive hypothesis then implies that $b \geq F_{k+1}$ (thus proving part of the lemma), and $a \bmod b \geq F_k$. We have

$$
\begin{aligned}
b + (a \bmod b) &= b + (a - b \lfloor a/b \rfloor) \\
&\leq a,
\end{aligned}
$$

since $a > b > 0$ implies $\lfloor a/b \rfloor \geq 1$. Thus,

$$
\begin{aligned}
a &\geq b + (a \bmod b) \\
&\geq F_{k+1} + F_k \\
&= F_{k+2}.
\end{aligned}
$$

∎

The following theorem is an immediate corollary of this lemma.

Theorem 31.11 (Lamé's theorem)
For any integer $k \geq 1$, if $a > b \geq 1$ and $b < F_{k+1}$, then the call EUCLID(a, b) makes fewer than k recursive calls. ∎

We can show that the upper bound of Theorem 31.11 is the best possible by showing that the call EUCLID(F_{k+1}, F_k) makes exactly $k - 1$ recursive calls when $k \geq 2$. We use induction on k. For the base case, $k = 2$, and the call EUCLID(F_3, F_2) makes exactly one recursive call, to EUCLID$(1, 0)$. (We have to start at $k = 2$, because when $k = 1$ we do not have $F_2 > F_1$.) For the inductive step, assume that EUCLID(F_k, F_{k-1}) makes exactly $k - 2$ recursive calls. For $k > 2$, we have $F_k > F_{k-1} > 0$ and $F_{k+1} = F_k + F_{k-1}$, and so by Exercise 31.1-1, we have $F_{k+1} \bmod F_k = F_{k-1}$. Thus, we have

$$
\begin{aligned}
\gcd(F_{k+1}, F_k) &= \gcd(F_k, F_{k+1} \bmod F_k) \\
&= \gcd(F_k, F_{k-1}).
\end{aligned}
$$

Therefore, the call EUCLID(F_{k+1}, F_k) recurses one time more than the call EUCLID(F_k, F_{k-1}), or exactly $k - 1$ times, meeting the upper bound of Theorem 31.11.

Since F_k is approximately $\phi^k / \sqrt{5}$, where ϕ is the golden ratio $(1 + \sqrt{5})/2$ defined by equation (3.24), the number of recursive calls in EUCLID is $O(\lg b)$. (See

a	b	$\lfloor a/b \rfloor$	d	x	y
99	78	1	3	−11	14
78	21	3	3	3	−11
21	15	1	3	−2	3
15	6	2	3	1	−2
6	3	2	3	0	1
3	0	—	3	1	0

Figure 31.1 How EXTENDED-EUCLID computes gcd(99, 78). Each line shows one level of the recursion: the values of the inputs a and b, the computed value $\lfloor a/b \rfloor$, and the values d, x, and y returned. The triple (d, x, y) returned becomes the triple (d', x', y') used at the next higher level of recursion. The call EXTENDED-EUCLID(99, 78) returns $(3, -11, 14)$, so that $\gcd(99, 78) = 3 = 99 \cdot (-11) + 78 \cdot 14$.

Exercise 31.2-5 for a tighter bound.) Therefore, if we call EUCLID on two β-bit numbers, then it performs $O(\beta)$ arithmetic operations and $O(\beta^3)$ bit operations (assuming that multiplication and division of β-bit numbers take $O(\beta^2)$ bit operations). Problem 31-2 asks you to show an $O(\beta^2)$ bound on the number of bit operations.

The extended form of Euclid's algorithm

We now rewrite Euclid's algorithm to compute additional useful information. Specifically, we extend the algorithm to compute the integer coefficients x and y such that

$$d = \gcd(a, b) = ax + by \;. \tag{31.16}$$

Note that x and y may be zero or negative. We shall find these coefficients useful later for computing modular multiplicative inverses. The procedure EXTENDED-EUCLID takes as input a pair of nonnegative integers and returns a triple of the form (d, x, y) that satisfies equation (31.16).

EXTENDED-EUCLID(a, b)

```
1  if b == 0
2      return (a, 1, 0)
3  else (d′, x′, y′) = EXTENDED-EUCLID(b, a mod b)
4      (d, x, y) = (d′, y′, x′ − ⌊a/b⌋ y′)
5      return (d, x, y)
```

Figure 31.1 illustrates how EXTENDED-EUCLID computes gcd(99, 78).

The EXTENDED-EUCLID procedure is a variation of the EUCLID procedure. Line 1 is equivalent to the test "$b == 0$" in line 1 of EUCLID. If $b = 0$, then

EXTENDED-EUCLID returns not only $d = a$ in line 2, but also the coefficients $x = 1$ and $y = 0$, so that $a = ax + by$. If $b \neq 0$, EXTENDED-EUCLID first computes (d', x', y') such that $d' = \gcd(b, a \bmod b)$ and

$$d' = bx' + (a \bmod b)y' . \tag{31.17}$$

As for EUCLID, we have in this case $d = \gcd(a, b) = d' = \gcd(b, a \bmod b)$. To obtain x and y such that $d = ax + by$, we start by rewriting equation (31.17) using the equation $d = d'$ and equation (3.8):

$$
\begin{aligned}
d &= bx' + (a - b \lfloor a/b \rfloor)y' \\
  &= ay' + b(x' - \lfloor a/b \rfloor y') .
\end{aligned}
$$

Thus, choosing $x = y'$ and $y = x' - \lfloor a/b \rfloor y'$ satisfies the equation $d = ax + by$, proving the correctness of EXTENDED-EUCLID.

Since the number of recursive calls made in EUCLID is equal to the number of recursive calls made in EXTENDED-EUCLID, the running times of EUCLID and EXTENDED-EUCLID are the same, to within a constant factor. That is, for $a > b > 0$, the number of recursive calls is $O(\lg b)$.

Exercises

31.2-1
Prove that equations (31.11) and (31.12) imply equation (31.13).

31.2-2
Compute the values (d, x, y) that the call EXTENDED-EUCLID$(899, 493)$ returns.

31.2-3
Prove that for all integers a, k, and n,

$$\gcd(a, n) = \gcd(a + kn, n) .$$

31.2-4
Rewrite EUCLID in an iterative form that uses only a constant amount of memory (that is, stores only a constant number of integer values).

31.2-5
If $a > b \geq 0$, show that the call EUCLID(a, b) makes at most $1 + \log_\phi b$ recursive calls. Improve this bound to $1 + \log_\phi(b/ \gcd(a, b))$.

31.2-6
What does EXTENDED-EUCLID(F_{k+1}, F_k) return? Prove your answer correct.

31.2-7
Define the gcd function for more than two arguments by the recursive equation $\gcd(a_0, a_1, \ldots, a_n) = \gcd(a_0, \gcd(a_1, a_2, \ldots, a_n))$. Show that the gcd function returns the same answer independent of the order in which its arguments are specified. Also show how to find integers $x_0, x_1, \ldots, x_n$ such that $\gcd(a_0, a_1, \ldots, a_n) = a_0 x_0 + a_1 x_1 + \cdots + a_n x_n$. Show that the number of divisions performed by your algorithm is $O(n + \lg(\max\{a_0, a_1, \ldots, a_n\}))$.

31.2-8
Define $\mathrm{lcm}(a_1, a_2, \ldots, a_n)$ to be the ***least common multiple*** of the n integers $a_1, a_2, \ldots, a_n$, that is, the smallest nonnegative integer that is a multiple of each a_i. Show how to compute $\mathrm{lcm}(a_1, a_2, \ldots, a_n)$ efficiently using the (two-argument) gcd operation as a subroutine.

31.2-9
Prove that n_1, n_2, n_3, and n_4 are pairwise relatively prime if and only if

$$\gcd(n_1 n_2, n_3 n_4) = \gcd(n_1 n_3, n_2 n_4) = 1 .$$

More generally, show that $n_1, n_2, \ldots, n_k$ are pairwise relatively prime if and only if a set of $\lceil \lg k \rceil$ pairs of numbers derived from the n_i are relatively prime.

31.3 Modular arithmetic

Informally, we can think of modular arithmetic as arithmetic as usual over the integers, except that if we are working modulo n, then every result x is replaced by the element of $\{0, 1, \ldots, n - 1\}$ that is equivalent to x, modulo n (that is, x is replaced by $x \bmod n$). This informal model suffices if we stick to the operations of addition, subtraction, and multiplication. A more formal model for modular arithmetic, which we now give, is best described within the framework of group theory.

Finite groups

A ***group*** $(S, \oplus)$ is a set S together with a binary operation $\oplus$ defined on S for which the following properties hold:

1. **Closure:** For all $a, b \in S$, we have $a \oplus b \in S$.

2. **Identity:** There exists an element $e \in S$, called the ***identity*** of the group, such that $e \oplus a = a \oplus e = a$ for all $a \in S$.

3. **Associativity:** For all $a, b, c \in S$, we have $(a \oplus b) \oplus c = a \oplus (b \oplus c)$.

4. **Inverses:** For each $a \in S$, there exists a unique element $b \in S$, called the *inverse* of a, such that $a \oplus b = b \oplus a = e$.

As an example, consider the familiar group $(\mathbb{Z}, +)$ of the integers $\mathbb{Z}$ under the operation of addition: 0 is the identity, and the inverse of a is $-a$. If a group $(S, \oplus)$ satisfies the *commutative law* $a \oplus b = b \oplus a$ for all $a, b \in S$, then it is an *abelian group*. If a group $(S, \oplus)$ satisfies $|S| < \infty$, then it is a *finite group*.

The groups defined by modular addition and multiplication

We can form two finite abelian groups by using addition and multiplication modulo n, where n is a positive integer. These groups are based on the equivalence classes of the integers modulo n, defined in Section 31.1.

To define a group on $\mathbb{Z}_n$, we need to have suitable binary operations, which we obtain by redefining the ordinary operations of addition and multiplication. We can easily define addition and multiplication operations for $\mathbb{Z}_n$, because the equivalence class of two integers uniquely determines the equivalence class of their sum or product. That is, if $a \equiv a' \pmod{n}$ and $b \equiv b' \pmod{n}$, then

$$a + b \equiv a' + b' \pmod{n},$$
$$ab \equiv a'b' \pmod{n}.$$

Thus, we define addition and multiplication modulo n, denoted $+_n$ and $\cdot_n$, by

$$[a]_n +_n [b]_n = [a + b]_n, \tag{31.18}$$
$$[a]_n \cdot_n [b]_n = [ab]_n.$$

(We can define subtraction similarly on $\mathbb{Z}_n$ by $[a]_n -_n [b]_n = [a - b]_n$, but division is more complicated, as we shall see.) These facts justify the common and convenient practice of using the smallest nonnegative element of each equivalence class as its representative when performing computations in $\mathbb{Z}_n$. We add, subtract, and multiply as usual on the representatives, but we replace each result x by the representative of its class, that is, by $x \bmod n$.

Using this definition of addition modulo n, we define the *additive group modulo n* as $(\mathbb{Z}_n, +_n)$. The size of the additive group modulo n is $|\mathbb{Z}_n| = n$. Figure 31.2(a) gives the operation table for the group $(\mathbb{Z}_6, +_6)$.

Theorem 31.12
The system $(\mathbb{Z}_n, +_n)$ is a finite abelian group.

Proof Equation (31.18) shows that $(\mathbb{Z}_n, +_n)$ is closed. Associativity and commutativity of $+_n$ follow from the associativity and commutativity of $+$:

$+_6$	0	1	2	3	4	5
0	0	1	2	3	4	5
1	1	2	3	4	5	0
2	2	3	4	5	0	1
3	3	4	5	0	1	2
4	4	5	0	1	2	3
5	5	0	1	2	3	4

$\cdot_{15}$	1	2	4	7	8	11	13	14
1	1	2	4	7	8	11	13	14
2	2	4	8	14	1	7	11	13
4	4	8	1	13	2	14	7	11
7	7	14	13	4	11	2	1	8
8	8	1	2	11	4	13	14	7
11	11	7	14	2	13	1	8	4
13	13	11	7	1	14	8	4	2
14	14	13	11	8	7	4	2	1

(a)   (b)

Figure 31.2 Two finite groups. Equivalence classes are denoted by their representative elements. **(a)** The group $(\mathbb{Z}_6, +_6)$. **(b)** The group $(\mathbb{Z}_{15}^*, \cdot_{15})$.

$$
\begin{aligned}
([a]_n +_n [b]_n) +_n [c]_n &= [a+b]_n +_n [c]_n \\
&= [(a+b)+c]_n \\
&= [a+(b+c)]_n \\
&= [a]_n +_n [b+c]_n \\
&= [a]_n +_n ([b]_n +_n [c]_n) ,
\end{aligned}
$$

$$
\begin{aligned}
[a]_n +_n [b]_n &= [a+b]_n \\
&= [b+a]_n \\
&= [b]_n +_n [a]_n .
\end{aligned}
$$

The identity element of $(\mathbb{Z}_n, +_n)$ is 0 (that is, $[0]_n$). The (additive) inverse of an element a (that is, of $[a]_n$) is the element $-a$ (that is, $[-a]_n$ or $[n-a]_n$), since $[a]_n +_n [-a]_n = [a-a]_n = [0]_n$. ∎

Using the definition of multiplication modulo n, we define the ***multiplicative group modulo n*** as $(\mathbb{Z}_n^*, \cdot_n)$. The elements of this group are the set $\mathbb{Z}_n^*$ of elements in $\mathbb{Z}_n$ that are relatively prime to n, so that each one has a unique inverse, modulo n:

$$\mathbb{Z}_n^* = \{[a]_n \in \mathbb{Z}_n : \gcd(a,n) = 1\} .$$

To see that $\mathbb{Z}_n^*$ is well defined, note that for $0 \le a < n$, we have $a \equiv (a+kn)$ (mod n) for all integers k. By Exercise 31.2-3, therefore, $\gcd(a,n) = 1$ implies $\gcd(a+kn,n) = 1$ for all integers k. Since $[a]_n = \{a+kn : k \in \mathbb{Z}\}$, the set $\mathbb{Z}_n^*$ is well defined. An example of such a group is

$$\mathbb{Z}_{15}^* = \{1,2,4,7,8,11,13,14\} ,$$

where the group operation is multiplication modulo 15. (Here we denote an element $[a]_{15}$ as a; for example, we denote $[7]_{15}$ as 7.) Figure 31.2(b) shows the group $(\mathbb{Z}_{15}^*, \cdot_{15})$. For example, $8 \cdot 11 \equiv 13 \pmod{15}$, working in $\mathbb{Z}_{15}^*$. The identity for this group is 1.

Theorem 31.13
The system $(\mathbb{Z}_n^*, \cdot_n)$ is a finite abelian group.

Proof   Theorem 31.6 implies that $(\mathbb{Z}_n^*, \cdot_n)$ is closed. Associativity and commutativity can be proved for $\cdot_n$ as they were for $+_n$ in the proof of Theorem 31.12. The identity element is $[1]_n$. To show the existence of inverses, let a be an element of $\mathbb{Z}_n^*$ and let (d, x, y) be returned by EXTENDED-EUCLID(a, n). Then, $d = 1$, since $a \in \mathbb{Z}_n^*$, and

$$ax + ny = 1 \tag{31.19}$$

or, equivalently,

$$ax \equiv 1 \pmod{n} .$$

Thus, $[x]_n$ is a multiplicative inverse of $[a]_n$, modulo n. Furthermore, we claim that $[x]_n \in \mathbb{Z}_n^*$. To see why, equation (31.19) demonstrates that the smallest positive linear combination of x and n must be 1. Therefore, Theorem 31.2 implies that $\gcd(x, n) = 1$. We defer the proof that inverses are uniquely defined until Corollary 31.26.   ∎

As an example of computing multiplicative inverses, suppose that $a = 5$ and $n = 11$. Then EXTENDED-EUCLID(a, n) returns $(d, x, y) = (1, -2, 1)$, so that $1 = 5 \cdot (-2) + 11 \cdot 1$. Thus, $[-2]_{11}$ (i.e., $[9]_{11}$) is the multiplicative inverse of $[5]_{11}$.

When working with the groups $(\mathbb{Z}_n, +_n)$ and $(\mathbb{Z}_n^*, \cdot_n)$ in the remainder of this chapter, we follow the convenient practice of denoting equivalence classes by their representative elements and denoting the operations $+_n$ and $\cdot_n$ by the usual arithmetic notations $+$ and $\cdot$ (or juxtaposition, so that $ab = a \cdot b$) respectively. Also, equivalences modulo n may also be interpreted as equations in $\mathbb{Z}_n$. For example, the following two statements are equivalent:

$$\begin{aligned} ax &\equiv b \pmod{n} , \\ [a]_n \cdot_n [x]_n &= [b]_n . \end{aligned}$$

As a further convenience, we sometimes refer to a group $(S, \oplus)$ merely as S when the operation $\oplus$ is understood from context. We may thus refer to the groups $(\mathbb{Z}_n, +_n)$ and $(\mathbb{Z}_n^*, \cdot_n)$ as $\mathbb{Z}_n$ and $\mathbb{Z}_n^*$, respectively.

We denote the (multiplicative) inverse of an element a by $(a^{-1} \bmod n)$. Division in $\mathbb{Z}_n^*$ is defined by the equation $a/b \equiv ab^{-1} \pmod{n}$. For example, in $\mathbb{Z}_{15}^*$

we have that $7^{-1} \equiv 13 \pmod{15}$, since $7 \cdot 13 = 91 \equiv 1 \pmod{15}$, so that $4/7 \equiv 4 \cdot 13 \equiv 7 \pmod{15}$.

The size of $\mathbb{Z}_n^*$ is denoted $\phi(n)$. This function, known as *Euler's phi function*, satisfies the equation

$$\phi(n) = n \prod_{p \,:\, p \text{ is prime and } p \,|\, n} \left(1 - \frac{1}{p} \right), \tag{31.20}$$

so that p runs over all the primes dividing n (including n itself, if n is prime). We shall not prove this formula here. Intuitively, we begin with a list of the n remainders $\{0, 1, \ldots, n - 1\}$ and then, for each prime p that divides n, cross out every multiple of p in the list. For example, since the prime divisors of 45 are 3 and 5,

$$\begin{aligned} \phi(45) &= 45 \left(1 - \frac{1}{3} \right) \left(1 - \frac{1}{5} \right) \\ &= 45 \left(\frac{2}{3} \right) \left(\frac{4}{5} \right) \\ &= 24 \,. \end{aligned}$$

If p is prime, then $\mathbb{Z}_p^* = \{1, 2, \ldots, p - 1\}$, and

$$\begin{aligned} \phi(p) &= p \left(1 - \frac{1}{p} \right) \\ &= p - 1 \,. \end{aligned} \tag{31.21}$$

If n is composite, then $\phi(n) < n - 1$, although it can be shown that

$$\phi(n) > \frac{n}{e^\gamma \ln \ln n + \frac{3}{\ln \ln n}} \tag{31.22}$$

for $n \geq 3$, where $\gamma = 0.5772156649\ldots$ is *Euler's constant*. A somewhat simpler (but looser) lower bound for $n > 5$ is

$$\phi(n) > \frac{n}{6 \ln \ln n} \,. \tag{31.23}$$

The lower bound (31.22) is essentially the best possible, since

$$\liminf_{n \to \infty} \frac{\phi(n)}{n / \ln \ln n} = e^{-\gamma} \,. \tag{31.24}$$

Subgroups

If $(S, \oplus)$ is a group, $S' \subseteq S$, and $(S', \oplus)$ is also a group, then $(S', \oplus)$ is a *subgroup* of $(S, \oplus)$. For example, the even integers form a subgroup of the integers under the operation of addition. The following theorem provides a useful tool for recognizing subgroups.

Theorem 31.14 (A nonempty closed subset of a finite group is a subgroup)

If $(S, \oplus)$ is a finite group and S' is any nonempty subset of S such that $a \oplus b \in S'$ for all $a, b \in S'$, then $(S', \oplus)$ is a subgroup of $(S, \oplus)$.

Proof   We leave the proof as Exercise 31.3-3.   ∎

For example, the set $\{0, 2, 4, 6\}$ forms a subgroup of $\mathbb{Z}_8$, since it is nonempty and closed under the operation $+$ (that is, it is closed under $+_8$).

The following theorem provides an extremely useful constraint on the size of a subgroup; we omit the proof.

Theorem 31.15 (Lagrange's theorem)

If $(S, \oplus)$ is a finite group and $(S', \oplus)$ is a subgroup of $(S, \oplus)$, then $|S'|$ is a divisor of $|S|$.   ∎

A subgroup S' of a group S is a **proper** subgroup if $S' \neq S$. We shall use the following corollary in our analysis in Section 31.8 of the Miller-Rabin primality test procedure.

Corollary 31.16

If S' is a proper subgroup of a finite group S, then $|S'| \leq |S| / 2$.   ∎

Subgroups generated by an element

Theorem 31.14 gives us an easy way to produce a subgroup of a finite group $(S, \oplus)$: choose an element a and take all elements that can be generated from a using the group operation. Specifically, define $a^{(k)}$ for $k \geq 1$ by

$$a^{(k)} = \bigoplus_{i=1}^{k} a = \underbrace{a \oplus a \oplus \cdots \oplus a}_{k} \; .$$

For example, if we take $a = 2$ in the group $\mathbb{Z}_6$, the sequence $a^{(1)}, a^{(2)}, a^{(3)}, \ldots$ is

$$2, 4, 0, 2, 4, 0, 2, 4, 0, \ldots \; .$$

In the group $\mathbb{Z}_n$, we have $a^{(k)} = ka \bmod n$, and in the group $\mathbb{Z}_n^*$, we have $a^{(k)} = a^k \bmod n$. We define the **subgroup generated by** a, denoted $\langle a \rangle$ or $(\langle a \rangle, \oplus)$, by

$$\langle a \rangle = \{a^{(k)} : k \geq 1\} \; .$$

We say that a **generates** the subgroup $\langle a \rangle$ or that a is a **generator** of $\langle a \rangle$. Since S is finite, $\langle a \rangle$ is a finite subset of S, possibly including all of S. Since the associativity of $\oplus$ implies

$$a^{(i)} \oplus a^{(j)} = a^{(i+j)} \, ,$$

$\langle a \rangle$ is closed and therefore, by Theorem 31.14, $\langle a \rangle$ is a subgroup of S. For example, in $\mathbb{Z}_6$, we have

$$\langle 0 \rangle \quad = \quad \{0\} \, ,$$
$$\langle 1 \rangle \quad = \quad \{0, 1, 2, 3, 4, 5\} \, ,$$
$$\langle 2 \rangle \quad = \quad \{0, 2, 4\} \, .$$

Similarly, in $\mathbb{Z}_7^*$, we have

$$\langle 1 \rangle \quad = \quad \{1\} \, ,$$
$$\langle 2 \rangle \quad = \quad \{1, 2, 4\} \, ,$$
$$\langle 3 \rangle \quad = \quad \{1, 2, 3, 4, 5, 6\} \, .$$

The **order** of a (in the group S), denoted ord(a), is defined as the smallest positive integer t such that $a^{(t)} = e$.

Theorem 31.17
For any finite group $(S, \oplus)$ and any $a \in S$, the order of a is equal to the size of the subgroup it generates, or ord(a) = $|\langle a \rangle|$.

Proof Let $t = \text{ord}(a)$. Since $a^{(t)} = e$ and $a^{(t+k)} = a^{(t)} \oplus a^{(k)} = a^{(k)}$ for $k \geq 1$, if $i > t$, then $a^{(i)} = a^{(j)}$ for some $j < i$. Thus, as we generate elements by a, we see no new elements after $a^{(t)}$. Thus, $\langle a \rangle = \{a^{(1)}, a^{(2)}, \ldots, a^{(t)}\}$, and so $|\langle a \rangle| \leq t$. To show that $|\langle a \rangle| \geq t$, we show that each element of the sequence $a^{(1)}, a^{(2)}, \ldots, a^{(t)}$ is distinct. Suppose for the purpose of contradiction that $a^{(i)} = a^{(j)}$ for some i and j satisfying $1 \leq i < j \leq t$. Then, $a^{(i+k)} = a^{(j+k)}$ for $k \geq 0$. But this equality implies that $a^{(i+(t-j))} = a^{(j+(t-j))} = e$, a contradiction, since $i + (t - j) < t$ but t is the least positive value such that $a^{(t)} = e$. Therefore, each element of the sequence $a^{(1)}, a^{(2)}, \ldots, a^{(t)}$ is distinct, and $|\langle a \rangle| \geq t$. We conclude that ord($a$) = $|\langle a \rangle|$. ∎

Corollary 31.18
The sequence $a^{(1)}, a^{(2)}, \ldots$ is periodic with period $t = \text{ord}(a)$; that is, $a^{(i)} = a^{(j)}$ if and only if $i \equiv j \pmod{t}$. ∎

Consistent with the above corollary, we define $a^{(0)}$ as e and $a^{(i)}$ as $a^{(i \bmod t)}$, where $t = \text{ord}(a)$, for all integers i.

Corollary 31.19
If $(S, \oplus)$ is a finite group with identity e, then for all $a \in S$,

$$a^{(|S|)} = e \, .$$

Proof Lagrange's theorem (Theorem 31.15) implies that $\mathrm{ord}(a) \mid |S|$, and so $|S| \equiv 0 \pmod{t}$, where $t = \mathrm{ord}(a)$. Therefore, $a^{(|S|)} = a^{(0)} = e$. ∎

Exercises

31.3-1
Draw the group operation tables for the groups $(\mathbb{Z}_4, +_4)$ and $(\mathbb{Z}_5^*, \cdot_5)$. Show that these groups are isomorphic by exhibiting a one-to-one correspondence α between their elements such that $a + b \equiv c \pmod{4}$ if and only if $\alpha(a) \cdot \alpha(b) \equiv \alpha(c) \pmod{5}$.

31.3-2
List all subgroups of $\mathbb{Z}_9$ and of $\mathbb{Z}_{13}^*$.

31.3-3
Prove Theorem 31.14.

31.3-4
Show that if p is prime and e is a positive integer, then

$$\phi(p^e) = p^{e-1}(p-1) \, .$$

31.3-5
Show that for any integer $n > 1$ and for any $a \in \mathbb{Z}_n^*$, the function $f_a : \mathbb{Z}_n^* \to \mathbb{Z}_n^*$ defined by $f_a(x) = ax \bmod n$ is a permutation of $\mathbb{Z}_n^*$.

31.4   Solving modular linear equations

We now consider the problem of finding solutions to the equation

$$ax \equiv b \pmod{n} \, , \tag{31.25}$$

where $a > 0$ and $n > 0$. This problem has several applications; for example, we shall use it as part of the procedure for finding keys in the RSA public-key cryptosystem in Section 31.7. We assume that a, b, and n are given, and we wish to find all values of x, modulo n, that satisfy equation (31.25). The equation may have zero, one, or more than one such solution.

Let $\langle a \rangle$ denote the subgroup of $\mathbb{Z}_n$ generated by a. Since $\langle a \rangle = \{a^{(x)} : x > 0\} = \{ax \bmod n : x > 0\}$, equation (31.25) has a solution if and only if $[b] \in \langle a \rangle$. Lagrange's theorem (Theorem 31.15) tells us that $|\langle a \rangle|$ must be a divisor of n. The following theorem gives us a precise characterization of $\langle a \rangle$.

Theorem 31.20
For any positive integers a and n, if $d = \gcd(a, n)$, then

$$\langle a \rangle = \langle d \rangle = \{0, d, 2d, \ldots, ((n/d) - 1)d\} \tag{31.26}$$

in $\mathbb{Z}_n$, and thus

$$|\langle a \rangle| = n/d \ .$$

Proof We begin by showing that $d \in \langle a \rangle$. Recall that EXTENDED-EUCLID(a, n) produces integers x' and y' such that $ax' + ny' = d$. Thus, $ax' \equiv d \pmod{n}$, so that $d \in \langle a \rangle$. In other words, d is a multiple of a in $\mathbb{Z}_n$.

Since $d \in \langle a \rangle$, it follows that every multiple of d belongs to $\langle a \rangle$, because any multiple of a multiple of a is itself a multiple of a. Thus, $\langle a \rangle$ contains every element in $\{0, d, 2d, \ldots, ((n/d) - 1)d\}$. That is, $\langle d \rangle \subseteq \langle a \rangle$.

We now show that $\langle a \rangle \subseteq \langle d \rangle$. If $m \in \langle a \rangle$, then $m = ax \bmod n$ for some integer x, and so $m = ax + ny$ for some integer y. However, $d \mid a$ and $d \mid n$, and so $d \mid m$ by equation (31.4). Therefore, $m \in \langle d \rangle$.

Combining these results, we have that $\langle a \rangle = \langle d \rangle$. To see that $|\langle a \rangle| = n/d$, observe that there are exactly n/d multiples of d between 0 and $n - 1$, inclusive. ∎

Corollary 31.21
The equation $ax \equiv b \pmod{n}$ is solvable for the unknown x if and only if $d \mid b$, where $d = \gcd(a, n)$.

Proof The equation $ax \equiv b \pmod{n}$ is solvable if and only if $[b] \in \langle a \rangle$, which is the same as saying

$$(b \bmod n) \in \{0, d, 2d, \ldots, ((n/d) - 1)d\} \ ,$$

by Theorem 31.20. If $0 \le b < n$, then $b \in \langle a \rangle$ if and only if $d \mid b$, since the members of $\langle a \rangle$ are precisely the multiples of d. If $b < 0$ or $b \ge n$, the corollary then follows from the observation that $d \mid b$ if and only if $d \mid (b \bmod n)$, since b and $b \bmod n$ differ by a multiple of n, which is itself a multiple of d. ∎

Corollary 31.22
The equation $ax \equiv b \pmod{n}$ either has d distinct solutions modulo n, where $d = \gcd(a, n)$, or it has no solutions.

Proof If $ax \equiv b \pmod{n}$ has a solution, then $b \in \langle a \rangle$. By Theorem 31.17, $\text{ord}(a) = |\langle a \rangle|$, and so Corollary 31.18 and Theorem 31.20 imply that the sequence $ai \bmod n$, for $i = 0, 1, \ldots$, is periodic with period $|\langle a \rangle| = n/d$. If $b \in \langle a \rangle$, then b appears exactly d times in the sequence $ai \bmod n$, for $i = 0, 1, \ldots, n - 1$, since

the length-(n/d) block of values $\langle a \rangle$ repeats exactly d times as i increases from 0 to $n-1$. The indices x of the d positions for which $ax \bmod n = b$ are the solutions of the equation $ax \equiv b \pmod{n}$. ∎

Theorem 31.23

Let $d = \gcd(a, n)$, and suppose that $d = ax' + ny'$ for some integers x' and y' (for example, as computed by EXTENDED-EUCLID). If $d \mid b$, then the equation $ax \equiv b \pmod{n}$ has as one of its solutions the value x_0, where

$$x_0 = x'(b/d) \bmod n .$$

Proof We have

$$
\begin{aligned}
ax_0 &\equiv ax'(b/d) &&\pmod{n} \\
&\equiv d(b/d) &&\pmod{n} &&(\text{because } ax' \equiv d \pmod{n}) \\
&\equiv b &&\pmod{n} ,
\end{aligned}
$$

and thus x_0 is a solution to $ax \equiv b \pmod{n}$. ∎

Theorem 31.24

Suppose that the equation $ax \equiv b \pmod{n}$ is solvable (that is, $d \mid b$, where $d = \gcd(a, n)$) and that x_0 is any solution to this equation. Then, this equation has exactly d distinct solutions, modulo n, given by $x_i = x_0 + i(n/d)$ for $i = 0, 1, \ldots, d - 1$.

Proof Because $n/d > 0$ and $0 \leq i(n/d) < n$ for $i = 0, 1, \ldots, d - 1$, the values $x_0, x_1, \ldots, x_{d-1}$ are all distinct, modulo n. Since x_0 is a solution of $ax \equiv b \pmod{n}$, we have $ax_0 \bmod n \equiv b \pmod{n}$. Thus, for $i = 0, 1, \ldots, d - 1$, we have

$$
\begin{aligned}
ax_i \bmod n &= a(x_0 + in/d) \bmod n \\
&= (ax_0 + ain/d) \bmod n \\
&= ax_0 \bmod n \quad (\text{because } d \mid a \text{ implies that } ain/d \text{ is a multiple of } n) \\
&\equiv b \pmod{n} ,
\end{aligned}
$$

and hence $ax_i \equiv b \pmod{n}$, making x_i a solution, too. By Corollary 31.22, the equation $ax \equiv b \pmod{n}$ has exactly d solutions, so that $x_0, x_1, \ldots, x_{d-1}$ must be all of them. ∎

We have now developed the mathematics needed to solve the equation $ax \equiv b \pmod{n}$; the following algorithm prints all solutions to this equation. The inputs a and n are arbitrary positive integers, and b is an arbitrary integer.

MODULAR-LINEAR-EQUATION-SOLVER (a, b, n)

```
1  (d, x', y') = EXTENDED-EUCLID(a, n)
2  if d | b
3      x₀ = x'(b/d) mod n
4      for i = 0 to d − 1
5          print (x₀ + i(n/d)) mod n
6  else print "no solutions"
```

As an example of the operation of this procedure, consider the equation $14x \equiv 30 \pmod{100}$ (here, $a = 14$, $b = 30$, and $n = 100$). Calling EXTENDED-EUCLID in line 1, we obtain $(d, x', y') = (2, -7, 1)$. Since $2 \mid 30$, lines 3–5 execute. Line 3 computes $x_0 = (-7)(15) \bmod 100 = 95$. The loop on lines 4–5 prints the two solutions 95 and 45.

The procedure MODULAR-LINEAR-EQUATION-SOLVER works as follows. Line 1 computes $d = \gcd(a, n)$, along with two values x' and y' such that $d = ax' + ny'$, demonstrating that x' is a solution to the equation $ax' \equiv d \pmod{n}$. If d does not divide b, then the equation $ax \equiv b \pmod{n}$ has no solution, by Corollary 31.21. Line 2 checks to see whether $d \mid b$; if not, line 6 reports that there are no solutions. Otherwise, line 3 computes a solution x_0 to $ax \equiv b \pmod{n}$, in accordance with Theorem 31.23. Given one solution, Theorem 31.24 states that adding multiples of (n/d), modulo n, yields the other $d - 1$ solutions. The **for** loop of lines 4–5 prints out all d solutions, beginning with x_0 and spaced n/d apart, modulo n.

MODULAR-LINEAR-EQUATION-SOLVER performs $O(\lg n + \gcd(a, n))$ arithmetic operations, since EXTENDED-EUCLID performs $O(\lg n)$ arithmetic operations, and each iteration of the **for** loop of lines 4–5 performs a constant number of arithmetic operations.

The following corollaries of Theorem 31.24 give specializations of particular interest.

Corollary 31.25
For any $n > 1$, if $\gcd(a, n) = 1$, then the equation $ax \equiv b \pmod{n}$ has a unique solution, modulo n. ∎

If $b = 1$, a common case of considerable interest, the x we are looking for is a *multiplicative inverse* of a, modulo n.

Corollary 31.26
For any $n > 1$, if $\gcd(a, n) = 1$, then the equation $ax \equiv 1 \pmod{n}$ has a unique solution, modulo n. Otherwise, it has no solution. ∎

Thanks to Corollary 31.26, we can use the notation $a^{-1} \bmod n$ to refer to *the* multiplicative inverse of a, modulo n, when a and n are relatively prime. If $\gcd(a, n) = 1$, then the unique solution to the equation $ax \equiv 1 \pmod{n}$ is the integer x returned by EXTENDED-EUCLID, since the equation

$$\gcd(a, n) = 1 = ax + ny$$

implies $ax \equiv 1 \pmod{n}$. Thus, we can compute $a^{-1} \bmod n$ efficiently using EXTENDED-EUCLID.

Exercises

31.4-1
Find all solutions to the equation $35x \equiv 10 \pmod{50}$.

31.4-2
Prove that the equation $ax \equiv ay \pmod{n}$ implies $x \equiv y \pmod{n}$ whenever $\gcd(a, n) = 1$. Show that the condition $\gcd(a, n) = 1$ is necessary by supplying a counterexample with $\gcd(a, n) > 1$.

31.4-3
Consider the following change to line 3 of the procedure MODULAR-LINEAR-EQUATION-SOLVER:

3      $x_0 = x'(b/d) \bmod (n/d)$

Will this work? Explain why or why not.

31.4-4   ★
Let p be prime and $f(x) \equiv f_0 + f_1 x + \cdots + f_t x^t \pmod{p}$ be a polynomial of degree t, with coefficients f_i drawn from $\mathbb{Z}_p$. We say that $a \in \mathbb{Z}_p$ is a *zero* of f if $f(a) \equiv 0 \pmod{p}$. Prove that if a is a zero of f, then $f(x) \equiv (x - a)g(x) \pmod{p}$ for some polynomial $g(x)$ of degree $t - 1$. Prove by induction on t that if p is prime, then a polynomial $f(x)$ of degree t can have at most t distinct zeros modulo p.

31.5   The Chinese remainder theorem

Around A.D. 100, the Chinese mathematician Sun-Tsŭ solved the problem of finding those integers x that leave remainders 2, 3, and 2 when divided by 3, 5, and 7 respectively. One such solution is $x = 23$; all solutions are of the form $23 + 105k$

for arbitrary integers k. The "Chinese remainder theorem" provides a correspondence between a system of equations modulo a set of pairwise relatively prime moduli (for example, 3, 5, and 7) and an equation modulo their product (for example, 105).

The Chinese remainder theorem has two major applications. Let the integer n be factored as $n = n_1 n_2 \cdots n_k$, where the factors n_i are pairwise relatively prime. First, the Chinese remainder theorem is a descriptive "structure theorem" that describes the structure of $\mathbb{Z}_n$ as identical to that of the Cartesian product $\mathbb{Z}_{n_1} \times \mathbb{Z}_{n_2} \times \cdots \times \mathbb{Z}_{n_k}$ with componentwise addition and multiplication modulo n_i in the ith component. Second, this description helps us to design efficient algorithms, since working in each of the systems $\mathbb{Z}_{n_i}$ can be more efficient (in terms of bit operations) than working modulo n.

Theorem 31.27 (Chinese remainder theorem)

Let $n = n_1 n_2 \cdots n_k$, where the n_i are pairwise relatively prime. Consider the correspondence

$$a \leftrightarrow (a_1, a_2, \ldots, a_k), \qquad (31.27)$$

where $a \in \mathbb{Z}_n$, $a_i \in \mathbb{Z}_{n_i}$, and

$$a_i = a \bmod n_i$$

for $i = 1, 2, \ldots, k$. Then, mapping (31.27) is a one-to-one correspondence (bijection) between $\mathbb{Z}_n$ and the Cartesian product $\mathbb{Z}_{n_1} \times \mathbb{Z}_{n_2} \times \cdots \times \mathbb{Z}_{n_k}$. Operations performed on the elements of $\mathbb{Z}_n$ can be equivalently performed on the corresponding k-tuples by performing the operations independently in each coordinate position in the appropriate system. That is, if

$$
\begin{aligned}
a &\leftrightarrow (a_1, a_2, \ldots, a_k), \\
b &\leftrightarrow (b_1, b_2, \ldots, b_k),
\end{aligned}
$$

then

$$(a + b) \bmod n \leftrightarrow ((a_1 + b_1) \bmod n_1, \ldots, (a_k + b_k) \bmod n_k), \qquad (31.28)$$

$$(a - b) \bmod n \leftrightarrow ((a_1 - b_1) \bmod n_1, \ldots, (a_k - b_k) \bmod n_k), \qquad (31.29)$$

$$(ab) \bmod n \leftrightarrow (a_1 b_1 \bmod n_1, \ldots, a_k b_k \bmod n_k). \qquad (31.30)$$

Proof Transforming between the two representations is fairly straightforward. Going from a to $(a_1, a_2, \ldots, a_k)$ is quite easy and requires only k "mod" operations.

Computing a from inputs $(a_1, a_2, \ldots, a_k)$ is a bit more complicated. We begin by defining $m_i = n/n_i$ for $i = 1, 2, \ldots, k$; thus m_i is the product of all of the n_j's other than n_i: $m_i = n_1 n_2 \cdots n_{i-1} n_{i+1} \cdots n_k$. We next define

$$c_i = m_i(m_i^{-1} \bmod n_i) \tag{31.31}$$

for $i = 1, 2, \ldots, k$. Equation (31.31) is always well defined: since m_i and n_i are relatively prime (by Theorem 31.6), Corollary 31.26 guarantees that $m_i^{-1} \bmod n_i$ exists. Finally, we can compute a as a function of $a_1, a_2, \ldots, a_k$ as follows:

$$a \equiv (a_1 c_1 + a_2 c_2 + \cdots + a_k c_k) \pmod{n} . \tag{31.32}$$

We now show that equation (31.32) ensures that $a \equiv a_i \pmod{n_i}$ for $i = 1, 2, \ldots, k$. Note that if $j \neq i$, then $m_j \equiv 0 \pmod{n_i}$, which implies that $c_j \equiv m_j \equiv 0 \pmod{n_i}$. Note also that $c_i \equiv 1 \pmod{n_i}$, from equation (31.31). We thus have the appealing and useful correspondence

$$c_i \leftrightarrow (0, 0, \ldots, 0, 1, 0, \ldots, 0) ,$$

a vector that has 0s everywhere except in the ith coordinate, where it has a 1; the c_i thus form a "basis" for the representation, in a certain sense. For each i, therefore, we have

$$
\begin{aligned}
a &\equiv a_i c_i & \pmod{n_i} \\
&\equiv a_i m_i(m_i^{-1} \bmod n_i) & \pmod{n_i} \\
&\equiv a_i & \pmod{n_i} ,
\end{aligned}
$$

which is what we wished to show: our method of computing a from the a_i's produces a result a that satisfies the constraints $a \equiv a_i \pmod{n_i}$ for $i = 1, 2, \ldots, k$. The correspondence is one-to-one, since we can transform in both directions. Finally, equations (31.28)–(31.30) follow directly from Exercise 31.1-7, since $x \bmod n_i = (x \bmod n) \bmod n_i$ for any x and $i = 1, 2, \ldots, k$. ∎

We shall use the following corollaries later in this chapter.

Corollary 31.28

If $n_1, n_2, \ldots, n_k$ are pairwise relatively prime and $n = n_1 n_2 \cdots n_k$, then for any integers $a_1, a_2, \ldots, a_k$, the set of simultaneous equations

$$x \equiv a_i \pmod{n_i} ,$$

for $i = 1, 2, \ldots, k$, has a unique solution modulo n for the unknown x. ∎

Corollary 31.29

If $n_1, n_2, \ldots, n_k$ are pairwise relatively prime and $n = n_1 n_2 \cdots n_k$, then for all integers x and a,

$$x \equiv a \pmod{n_i}$$

for $i = 1, 2, \ldots, k$ if and only if

$$x \equiv a \pmod{n} .$$ ∎

	0	1	2	3	4	5	6	7	8	9	10	11	12
0	0	40	15	55	30	5	45	20	60	35	10	50	25
1	26	1	41	16	56	31	6	46	21	61	36	11	51
2	52	27	2	42	17	57	32	7	47	22	62	37	12
3	13	53	28	3	43	18	58	33	8	48	23	63	38
4	39	14	54	29	4	44	19	59	34	9	49	24	64

Figure 31.3   An illustration of the Chinese remainder theorem for $n_1 = 5$ and $n_2 = 13$. For this example, $c_1 = 26$ and $c_2 = 40$. In row i, column j is shown the value of a, modulo 65, such that $a \bmod 5 = i$ and $a \bmod 13 = j$. Note that row 0, column 0 contains a 0. Similarly, row 4, column 12 contains a 64 (equivalent to -1). Since $c_1 = 26$, moving down a row increases a by 26. Similarly, $c_2 = 40$ means that moving right by a column increases a by 40. Increasing a by 1 corresponds to moving diagonally downward and to the right, wrapping around from the bottom to the top and from the right to the left.

As an example of the application of the Chinese remainder theorem, suppose we are given the two equations

$$a \equiv 2 \pmod 5,$$
$$a \equiv 3 \pmod{13},$$

so that $a_1 = 2$, $n_1 = m_2 = 5$, $a_2 = 3$, and $n_2 = m_1 = 13$, and we wish to compute $a \bmod 65$, since $n = n_1 n_2 = 65$. Because $13^{-1} \equiv 2 \pmod 5$ and $5^{-1} \equiv 8 \pmod{13}$, we have

$$c_1 = 13(2 \bmod 5) = 26,$$
$$c_2 = 5(8 \bmod 13) = 40,$$

and

$$
\begin{aligned}
a &\equiv 2 \cdot 26 + 3 \cdot 40 &&\pmod{65}\\
&\equiv 52 + 120 &&\pmod{65}\\
&\equiv 42 &&\pmod{65}.
\end{aligned}
$$

See Figure 31.3 for an illustration of the Chinese remainder theorem, modulo 65.

Thus, we can work modulo n by working modulo n directly or by working in the transformed representation using separate modulo n_i computations, as convenient. The computations are entirely equivalent.

Exercises

31.5-1
Find all solutions to the equations $x \equiv 4 \pmod 5$ and $x \equiv 5 \pmod{11}$.

31.5-2
Find all integers x that leave remainders $1, 2, 3$ when divided by $9, 8, 7$ respectively.

31.5-3
Argue that, under the definitions of Theorem 31.27, if $\gcd(a, n) = 1$, then

$$(a^{-1} \bmod n) \leftrightarrow ((a_1^{-1} \bmod n_1), (a_2^{-1} \bmod n_2), \ldots, (a_k^{-1} \bmod n_k)) \ .$$

31.5-4
Under the definitions of Theorem 31.27, prove that for any polynomial f, the number of roots of the equation $f(x) \equiv 0 \pmod{n}$ equals the product of the number of roots of each of the equations $f(x) \equiv 0 \pmod{n_1}$, $f(x) \equiv 0 \pmod{n_2}$, ..., $f(x) \equiv 0 \pmod{n_k}$.

31.6   Powers of an element

Just as we often consider the multiples of a given element a, modulo n, we consider the sequence of powers of a, modulo n, where $a \in \mathbb{Z}_n^*$:

$$a^0, a^1, a^2, a^3, \ldots, \tag{31.33}$$

modulo n. Indexing from 0, the 0th value in this sequence is $a^0 \bmod n = 1$, and the ith value is $a^i \bmod n$. For example, the powers of 3 modulo 7 are

i	0	1	2	3	4	5	6	7	8	9	10	11	$\cdots$
$3^i \bmod 7$	1	3	2	6	4	5	1	3	2	6	4	5	$\cdots$

whereas the powers of 2 modulo 7 are

i	0	1	2	3	4	5	6	7	8	9	10	11	$\cdots$
$2^i \bmod 7$	1	2	4	1	2	4	1	2	4	1	2	4	$\cdots$

In this section, let $\langle a \rangle$ denote the subgroup of $\mathbb{Z}_n^*$ generated by a by repeated multiplication, and let $\mathrm{ord}_n(a)$ (the "order of a, modulo n") denote the order of a in $\mathbb{Z}_n^*$. For example, $\langle 2 \rangle = \{1, 2, 4\}$ in $\mathbb{Z}_7^*$, and $\mathrm{ord}_7(2) = 3$. Using the definition of the Euler phi function $\phi(n)$ as the size of $\mathbb{Z}_n^*$ (see Section 31.3), we now translate Corollary 31.19 into the notation of $\mathbb{Z}_n^*$ to obtain Euler's theorem and specialize it to $\mathbb{Z}_p^*$, where p is prime, to obtain Fermat's theorem.

Theorem 31.30 (Euler's theorem)
For any integer $n > 1$,

$$a^{\phi(n)} \equiv 1 \pmod{n} \text{ for all } a \in \mathbb{Z}_n^* \ . \qquad \blacksquare$$

Theorem 31.31 (Fermat's theorem)
If p is prime, then

$$a^{p-1} \equiv 1 \pmod{p} \text{ for all } a \in \mathbb{Z}_p^*.$$

Proof By equation (31.21), $\phi(p) = p - 1$ if p is prime. ∎

Fermat's theorem applies to every element in $\mathbb{Z}_p$ except 0, since $0 \notin \mathbb{Z}_p^*$. For all $a \in \mathbb{Z}_p$, however, we have $a^p \equiv a \pmod{p}$ if p is prime.

If $\mathrm{ord}_n(g) = |\mathbb{Z}_n^*|$, then every element in $\mathbb{Z}_n^*$ is a power of g, modulo n, and g is a ***primitive root*** or a ***generator*** of $\mathbb{Z}_n^*$. For example, 3 is a primitive root, modulo 7, but 2 is not a primitive root, modulo 7. If $\mathbb{Z}_n^*$ possesses a primitive root, the group $\mathbb{Z}_n^*$ is ***cyclic***. We omit the proof of the following theorem, which is proven by Niven and Zuckerman [265].

Theorem 31.32
The values of $n > 1$ for which $\mathbb{Z}_n^*$ is cyclic are 2, 4, p^e, and $2p^e$, for all primes $p > 2$ and all positive integers e. ∎

If g is a primitive root of $\mathbb{Z}_n^*$ and a is any element of $\mathbb{Z}_n^*$, then there exists a z such that $g^z \equiv a \pmod{n}$. This z is a ***discrete logarithm*** or an ***index*** of a, modulo n, to the base g; we denote this value as $\mathrm{ind}_{n,g}(a)$.

Theorem 31.33 (Discrete logarithm theorem)
If g is a primitive root of $\mathbb{Z}_n^*$, then the equation $g^x \equiv g^y \pmod{n}$ holds if and only if the equation $x \equiv y \pmod{\phi(n)}$ holds.

Proof Suppose first that $x \equiv y \pmod{\phi(n)}$. Then, $x = y + k\phi(n)$ for some integer k. Therefore,

$$
\begin{aligned}
g^x &\equiv g^{y+k\phi(n)} & \pmod{n} \\
&\equiv g^y \cdot (g^{\phi(n)})^k & \pmod{n} \\
&\equiv g^y \cdot 1^k & \pmod{n} & \quad \text{(by Euler's theorem)} \\
&\equiv g^y & \pmod{n}.
\end{aligned}
$$

Conversely, suppose that $g^x \equiv g^y \pmod{n}$. Because the sequence of powers of g generates every element of $\langle g \rangle$ and $|\langle g \rangle| = \phi(n)$, Corollary 31.18 implies that the sequence of powers of g is periodic with period $\phi(n)$. Therefore, if $g^x \equiv g^y \pmod{n}$, then we must have $x \equiv y \pmod{\phi(n)}$. ∎

We now turn our attention to the square roots of 1, modulo a prime power. The following theorem will be useful in our development of a primality-testing algorithm in Section 31.8.

Theorem 31.34

If p is an odd prime and $e \geq 1$, then the equation

$$x^2 \equiv 1 \pmod{p^e} \tag{31.34}$$

has only two solutions, namely $x = 1$ and $x = -1$.

Proof Equation (31.34) is equivalent to

$$p^e \mid (x-1)(x+1) .$$

Since $p > 2$, we can have $p \mid (x-1)$ or $p \mid (x+1)$, but not both. (Otherwise, by property (31.3), p would also divide their difference $(x+1) - (x-1) = 2$.) If $p \nmid (x-1)$, then $\gcd(p^e, x-1) = 1$, and by Corollary 31.5, we would have $p^e \mid (x+1)$. That is, $x \equiv -1 \pmod{p^e}$. Symmetrically, if $p \nmid (x+1)$, then $\gcd(p^e, x+1) = 1$, and Corollary 31.5 implies that $p^e \mid (x-1)$, so that $x \equiv 1 \pmod{p^e}$. Therefore, either $x \equiv -1 \pmod{p^e}$ or $x \equiv 1 \pmod{p^e}$. ∎

A number x is a ***nontrivial square root of 1, modulo n***, if it satisfies the equation $x^2 \equiv 1 \pmod{n}$ but x is equivalent to neither of the two "trivial" square roots: 1 or -1, modulo n. For example, 6 is a nontrivial square root of 1, modulo 35. We shall use the following corollary to Theorem 31.34 in the correctness proof in Section 31.8 for the Miller-Rabin primality-testing procedure.

Corollary 31.35

If there exists a nontrivial square root of 1, modulo n, then n is composite.

Proof By the contrapositive of Theorem 31.34, if there exists a nontrivial square root of 1, modulo n, then n cannot be an odd prime or a power of an odd prime. If $x^2 \equiv 1 \pmod{2}$, then $x \equiv 1 \pmod{2}$, and so all square roots of 1, modulo 2, are trivial. Thus, n cannot be prime. Finally, we must have $n > 1$ for a nontrivial square root of 1 to exist. Therefore, n must be composite. ∎

Raising to powers with repeated squaring

A frequently occurring operation in number-theoretic computations is raising one number to a power modulo another number, also known as ***modular exponentiation***. More precisely, we would like an efficient way to compute $a^b \bmod n$, where a and b are nonnegative integers and n is a positive integer. Modular exponentiation is an essential operation in many primality-testing routines and in the RSA public-key cryptosystem. The method of ***repeated squaring*** solves this problem efficiently using the binary representation of b.

Let $\langle b_k, b_{k-1}, \ldots, b_1, b_0 \rangle$ be the binary representation of b. (That is, the binary representation is $k + 1$ bits long, b_k is the most significant bit, and b_0 is the least

i	9	8	7	6	5	4	3	2	1	0
b_i	1	0	0	0	1	1	0	0	0	0
c	1	2	4	8	17	35	70	140	280	560
d	7	49	157	526	160	241	298	166	67	1

Figure 31.4 The results of MODULAR-EXPONENTIATION when computing a^b (mod n), where $a = 7, b = 560 = \langle 1000110000 \rangle$, and $n = 561$. The values are shown after each execution of the **for** loop. The final result is 1.

significant bit.) The following procedure computes a^c mod n as c is increased by doublings and incrementations from 0 to b.

MODULAR-EXPONENTIATION(a, b, n)

```
1   c = 0
2   d = 1
3   let ⟨b_k, b_{k-1}, ..., b_0⟩ be the binary representation of b
4   for i = k downto 0
5       c = 2c
6       d = (d · d) mod n
7       if b_i == 1
8           c = c + 1
9           d = (d · a) mod n
10  return d
```

The essential use of squaring in line 6 of each iteration explains the name "repeated squaring." As an example, for $a = 7$, $b = 560$, and $n = 561$, the algorithm computes the sequence of values modulo 561 shown in Figure 31.4; the sequence of exponents used appears in the row of the table labeled by c.

The variable c is not really needed by the algorithm but is included for the following two-part loop invariant:

Just prior to each iteration of the **for** loop of lines 4–9,

1. The value of c is the same as the prefix $\langle b_k, b_{k-1}, \ldots, b_{i+1} \rangle$ of the binary representation of b, and

2. $d = a^c \bmod n$.

We use this loop invariant as follows:

Initialization: Initially, $i = k$, so that the prefix $\langle b_k, b_{k-1}, \ldots, b_{i+1} \rangle$ is empty, which corresponds to $c = 0$. Moreover, $d = 1 = a^0 \bmod n$.

Maintenance: Let c' and d' denote the values of c and d at the end of an iteration of the **for** loop, and thus the values prior to the next iteration. Each iteration updates $c' = 2c$ (if $b_i = 0$) or $c' = 2c + 1$ (if $b_i = 1$), so that c will be correct prior to the next iteration. If $b_i = 0$, then $d' = d^2 \bmod n = (a^c)^2 \bmod n = a^{2c} \bmod n = a^{c'} \bmod n$. If $b_i = 1$, then $d' = d^2 a \bmod n = (a^c)^2 a \bmod n = a^{2c+1} \bmod n = a^{c'} \bmod n$. In either case, $d = a^c \bmod n$ prior to the next iteration.

Termination: At termination, $i = -1$. Thus, $c = b$, since c has the value of the prefix $\langle b_k, b_{k-1}, \ldots, b_0 \rangle$ of b's binary representation. Hence $d = a^c \bmod n = a^b \bmod n$.

If the inputs a, b, and n are β-bit numbers, then the total number of arithmetic operations required is $O(\beta)$ and the total number of bit operations required is $O(\beta^3)$.

Exercises

31.6-1
Draw a table showing the order of every element in $\mathbb{Z}_{11}^*$. Pick the smallest primitive root g and compute a table giving $\text{ind}_{11,g}(x)$ for all $x \in \mathbb{Z}_{11}^*$.

31.6-2
Give a modular exponentiation algorithm that examines the bits of b from right to left instead of left to right.

31.6-3
Assuming that you know $\phi(n)$, explain how to compute $a^{-1} \bmod n$ for any $a \in \mathbb{Z}_n^*$ using the procedure MODULAR-EXPONENTIATION.

31.7   The RSA public-key cryptosystem

With a public-key cryptosystem, we can encrypt messages sent between two communicating parties so that an eavesdropper who overhears the encrypted messages will not be able to decode them. A public-key cryptosystem also enables a party to append an unforgeable "digital signature" to the end of an electronic message. Such a signature is the electronic version of a handwritten signature on a paper document. It can be easily checked by anyone, forged by no one, yet loses its validity if any bit of the message is altered. It therefore provides authentication of both the identity of the signer and the contents of the signed message. It is the perfect tool

for electronically signed business contracts, electronic checks, electronic purchase orders, and other electronic communications that parties wish to authenticate.

The RSA public-key cryptosystem relies on the dramatic difference between the ease of finding large prime numbers and the difficulty of factoring the product of two large prime numbers. Section 31.8 describes an efficient procedure for finding large prime numbers, and Section 31.9 discusses the problem of factoring large integers.

Public-key cryptosystems

In a public-key cryptosystem, each participant has both a ***public key*** and a ***secret key***. Each key is a piece of information. For example, in the RSA cryptosystem, each key consists of a pair of integers. The participants "Alice" and "Bob" are traditionally used in cryptography examples; we denote their public and secret keys as P_A, S_A for Alice and P_B, S_B for Bob.

Each participant creates his or her own public and secret keys. Secret keys are kept secret, but public keys can be revealed to anyone or even published. In fact, it is often convenient to assume that everyone's public key is available in a public directory, so that any participant can easily obtain the public key of any other participant.

The public and secret keys specify functions that can be applied to any message. Let $\mathcal{D}$ denote the set of permissible messages. For example, $\mathcal{D}$ might be the set of all finite-length bit sequences. In the simplest, and original, formulation of public-key cryptography, we require that the public and secret keys specify one-to-one functions from $\mathcal{D}$ to itself. We denote the function corresponding to Alice's public key P_A by $P_A()$ and the function corresponding to her secret key S_A by $S_A()$. The functions $P_A()$ and $S_A()$ are thus permutations of $\mathcal{D}$. We assume that the functions $P_A()$ and $S_A()$ are efficiently computable given the corresponding key P_A or S_A.

The public and secret keys for any participant are a "matched pair" in that they specify functions that are inverses of each other. That is,

$$M = S_A(P_A(M)), \tag{31.35}$$
$$M = P_A(S_A(M)) \tag{31.36}$$

for any message $M \in \mathcal{D}$. Transforming M with the two keys P_A and S_A successively, in either order, yields the message M back.

In a public-key cryptosystem, we require that no one but Alice be able to compute the function $S_A()$ in any practical amount of time. This assumption is crucial to keeping encrypted mail sent to Alice private and to knowing that Alice's digital signatures are authentic. Alice must keep S_A secret; if she does not, she loses her uniqueness and the cryptosystem cannot provide her with unique capabilities. The assumption that only Alice can compute $S_A()$ must hold even though everyone

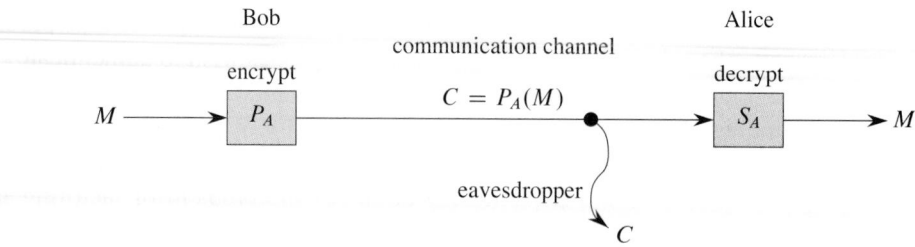

Figure 31.5   Encryption in a public key system. Bob encrypts the message M using Alice's public key P_A and transmits the resulting ciphertext $C = P_A(M)$ over a communication channel to Alice. An eavesdropper who captures the transmitted ciphertext gains no information about M. Alice receives C and decrypts it using her secret key to obtain the original message $M = S_A(C)$.

knows P_A and can compute $P_A()$, the inverse function to $S_A()$, efficiently. In order to design a workable public-key cryptosystem, we must figure out how to create a system in which we can reveal a transformation $P_A()$ without thereby revealing how to compute the corresponding inverse transformation $S_A()$. This task appears formidable, but we shall see how to accomplish it.

In a public-key cryptosystem, encryption works as shown in Figure 31.5. Suppose Bob wishes to send Alice a message M encrypted so that it will look like unintelligible gibberish to an eavesdropper. The scenario for sending the message goes as follows.

- Bob obtains Alice's public key P_A (from a public directory or directly from Alice).

- Bob computes the ***ciphertext*** $C = P_A(M)$ corresponding to the message M and sends C to Alice.

- When Alice receives the ciphertext C, she applies her secret key S_A to retrieve the original message: $S_A(C) = S_A(P_A(M)) = M$.

Because $S_A()$ and $P_A()$ are inverse functions, Alice can compute M from C. Because only Alice is able to compute $S_A()$, Alice is the only one who can compute M from C. Because Bob encrypts M using $P_A()$, only Alice can understand the transmitted message.

We can just as easily implement digital signatures within our formulation of a public-key cryptosystem. (There are other ways of approaching the problem of constructing digital signatures, but we shall not go into them here.) Suppose now that Alice wishes to send Bob a digitally signed response M'. Figure 31.6 shows how the digital-signature scenario proceeds.

- Alice computes her ***digital signature*** σ for the message M' using her secret key S_A and the equation $\sigma = S_A(M')$.

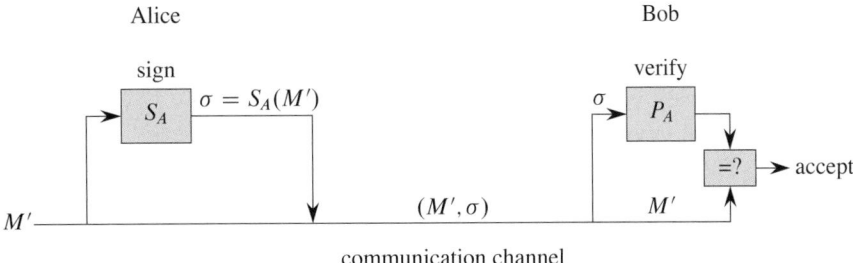

Figure 31.6 Digital signatures in a public-key system. Alice signs the message M' by appending her digital signature $\sigma = S_A(M')$ to it. She transmits the message/signature pair (M', σ) to Bob, who verifies it by checking the equation $M' = P_A(\sigma)$. If the equation holds, he accepts (M', σ) as a message that Alice has signed.

- Alice sends the message/signature pair (M', σ) to Bob.

- When Bob receives (M', σ), he can verify that it originated from Alice by us-ing Alice's public key to verify the equation $M' = P_A(\sigma)$. (Presumably, M' contains Alice's name, so Bob knows whose public key to use.) If the equation holds, then Bob concludes that the message M' was actually signed by Alice. If the equation fails to hold, Bob concludes either that the message M' or the digital signature σ was corrupted by transmission errors or that the pair (M', σ) is an attempted forgery.

Because a digital signature provides both authentication of the signer's identity and authentication of the contents of the signed message, it is analogous to a handwrit-ten signature at the end of a written document.

A digital signature must be verifiable by anyone who has access to the signer's public key. A signed message can be verified by one party and then passed on to other parties who can also verify the signature. For example, the message might be an electronic check from Alice to Bob. After Bob verifies Alice's signature on the check, he can give the check to his bank, who can then also verify the signature and effect the appropriate funds transfer.

A signed message is not necessarily encrypted; the message can be "in the clear" and not protected from disclosure. By composing the above protocols for encryp-tion and for signatures, we can create messages that are both signed and encrypted. The signer first appends his or her digital signature to the message and then en-crypts the resulting message/signature pair with the public key of the intended re-cipient. The recipient decrypts the received message with his or her secret key to obtain both the original message and its digital signature. The recipient can then verify the signature using the public key of the signer. The corresponding com-bined process using paper-based systems would be to sign the paper document and

then seal the document inside a paper envelope that is opened only by the intended recipient.

The RSA cryptosystem

In the **RSA public-key cryptosystem**, a participant creates his or her public and secret keys with the following procedure:

1. Select at random two large prime numbers p and q such that $p \neq q$. The primes p and q might be, say, 1024 bits each.

2. Compute $n = pq$.

3. Select a small odd integer e that is relatively prime to $\phi(n)$, which, by equation (31.20), equals $(p-1)(q-1)$.

4. Compute d as the multiplicative inverse of e, modulo $\phi(n)$. (Corollary 31.26 guarantees that d exists and is uniquely defined. We can use the technique of Section 31.4 to compute d, given e and $\phi(n)$.)

5. Publish the pair $P = (e, n)$ as the participant's **RSA public key**.

6. Keep secret the pair $S = (d, n)$ as the participant's **RSA secret key**.

For this scheme, the domain $\mathcal{D}$ is the set $\mathbb{Z}_n$. To transform a message M associated with a public key $P = (e, n)$, compute

$$P(M) = M^e \bmod n . \tag{31.37}$$

To transform a ciphertext C associated with a secret key $S = (d, n)$, compute

$$S(C) = C^d \bmod n . \tag{31.38}$$

These equations apply to both encryption and signatures. To create a signature, the signer applies his or her secret key to the message to be signed, rather than to a ciphertext. To verify a signature, the public key of the signer is applied to it, rather than to a message to be encrypted.

We can implement the public-key and secret-key operations using the procedure MODULAR-EXPONENTIATION described in Section 31.6. To analyze the running time of these operations, assume that the public key (e, n) and secret key (d, n) satisfy $\lg e = O(1)$, $\lg d \leq \beta$, and $\lg n \leq \beta$. Then, applying a public key requires $O(1)$ modular multiplications and uses $O(\beta^2)$ bit operations. Applying a secret key requires $O(\beta)$ modular multiplications, using $O(\beta^3)$ bit operations.

Theorem 31.36 (Correctness of RSA)
The RSA equations (31.37) and (31.38) define inverse transformations of $\mathbb{Z}_n$ satisfying equations (31.35) and (31.36).

Proof   From equations (31.37) and (31.38), we have that for any $M \in \mathbb{Z}_n$,

$$P(S(M)) = S(P(M)) = M^{ed} \pmod{n}.$$

Since e and d are multiplicative inverses modulo $\phi(n) = (p-1)(q-1)$,

$$ed = 1 + k(p-1)(q-1)$$

for some integer k. But then, if $M \not\equiv 0 \pmod{p}$, we have

$$
\begin{aligned}
M^{ed} &\equiv M(M^{p-1})^{k(q-1)} & \pmod{p} \\
&\equiv M((M \bmod p)^{p-1})^{k(q-1)} & \pmod{p} \\
&\equiv M(1)^{k(q-1)} & \pmod{p} \quad \text{(by Theorem 31.31)} \\
&\equiv M & \pmod{p}.
\end{aligned}
$$

Also, $M^{ed} \equiv M \pmod{p}$ if $M \equiv 0 \pmod{p}$. Thus,

$$M^{ed} \equiv M \pmod{p}$$

for all M. Similarly,

$$M^{ed} \equiv M \pmod{q}$$

for all M. Thus, by Corollary 31.29 to the Chinese remainder theorem,

$$M^{ed} \equiv M \pmod{n}$$

for all M.   ∎

The security of the RSA cryptosystem rests in large part on the difficulty of factoring large integers. If an adversary can factor the modulus n in a public key, then the adversary can derive the secret key from the public key, using the knowledge of the factors p and q in the same way that the creator of the public key used them. Therefore, if factoring large integers is easy, then breaking the RSA cryptosystem is easy. The converse statement, that if factoring large integers is hard, then breaking RSA is hard, is unproven. After two decades of research, however, no easier method has been found to break the RSA public-key cryptosystem than to factor the modulus n. And as we shall see in Section 31.9, factoring large integers is surprisingly difficult. By randomly selecting and multiplying together two 1024-bit primes, we can create a public key that cannot be "broken" in any feasible amount of time with current technology. In the absence of a fundamental breakthrough in the design of number-theoretic algorithms, and when implemented with care following recommended standards, the RSA cryptosystem is capable of providing a high degree of security in applications.

In order to achieve security with the RSA cryptosystem, however, we should use integers that are quite long—hundreds or even more than one thousand bits

long—to resist possible advances in the art of factoring. At the time of this writing (2009), RSA moduli were commonly in the range of 768 to 2048 bits. To create moduli of such sizes, we must be able to find large primes efficiently. Section 31.8 addresses this problem.

For efficiency, RSA is often used in a "hybrid" or "key-management" mode with fast non-public-key cryptosystems. With such a system, the encryption and decryption keys are identical. If Alice wishes to send a long message M to Bob privately, she selects a random key K for the fast non-public-key cryptosystem and encrypts M using K, obtaining ciphertext C. Here, C is as long as M, but K is quite short. Then, she encrypts K using Bob's public RSA key. Since K is short, computing $P_B(K)$ is fast (much faster than computing $P_B(M)$). She then transmits $(C, P_B(K))$ to Bob, who decrypts $P_B(K)$ to obtain K and then uses K to decrypt C, obtaining M.

We can use a similar hybrid approach to make digital signatures efficiently. This approach combines RSA with a public *collision-resistant hash function* h—a function that is easy to compute but for which it is computationally infeasible to find two messages M and M' such that $h(M) = h(M')$. The value $h(M)$ is a short (say, 256-bit) "fingerprint" of the message M. If Alice wishes to sign a message M, she first applies h to M to obtain the fingerprint $h(M)$, which she then encrypts with her secret key. She sends $(M, S_A(h(M)))$ to Bob as her signed version of M. Bob can verify the signature by computing $h(M)$ and verifying that P_A applied to $S_A(h(M))$ as received equals $h(M)$. Because no one can create two messages with the same fingerprint, it is computationally infeasible to alter a signed message and preserve the validity of the signature.

Finally, we note that the use of *certificates* makes distributing public keys much easier. For example, assume there is a "trusted authority" T whose public key is known by everyone. Alice can obtain from T a signed message (her certificate) stating that "Alice's public key is P_A." This certificate is "self-authenticating" since everyone knows P_T. Alice can include her certificate with her signed messages, so that the recipient has Alice's public key immediately available in order to verify her signature. Because her key was signed by T, the recipient knows that Alice's key is really Alice's.

Exercises

31.7-1
Consider an RSA key set with $p = 11$, $q = 29$, $n = 319$, and $e = 3$. What value of d should be used in the secret key? What is the encryption of the message $M = 100$?

31.7-2
Prove that if Alice's public exponent e is 3 and an adversary obtains Alice's secret exponent d, where $0 < d < \phi(n)$, then the adversary can factor Alice's modulus n in time polynomial in the number of bits in n. (Although you are not asked to prove it, you may be interested to know that this result remains true even if the condition $e = 3$ is removed. See Miller [255].)

31.7-3 ★
Prove that RSA is multiplicative in the sense that

$$P_A(M_1)P_A(M_2) \equiv P_A(M_1M_2) \pmod{n} .$$

Use this fact to prove that if an adversary had a procedure that could efficiently decrypt 1 percent of messages from $\mathbb{Z}_n$ encrypted with P_A, then he could employ a probabilistic algorithm to decrypt every message encrypted with P_A with high probability.

★ **31.8 Primality testing**

In this section, we consider the problem of finding large primes. We begin with a discussion of the density of primes, proceed to examine a plausible, but incomplete, approach to primality testing, and then present an effective randomized primality test due to Miller and Rabin.

The density of prime numbers

For many applications, such as cryptography, we need to find large "random" primes. Fortunately, large primes are not too rare, so that it is feasible to test random integers of the appropriate size until we find a prime. The *prime distribution function* $\pi(n)$ specifies the number of primes that are less than or equal to n. For example, $\pi(10) = 4$, since there are 4 prime numbers less than or equal to 10, namely, 2, 3, 5, and 7. The prime number theorem gives a useful approximation to $\pi(n)$.

Theorem 31.37 (Prime number theorem)
$$\lim_{n \to \infty} \frac{\pi(n)}{n/\ln n} = 1 .$$ ∎

The approximation $n/\ln n$ gives reasonably accurate estimates of $\pi(n)$ even for small n. For example, it is off by less than 6% at $n = 10^9$, where $\pi(n) =$

50,847,534 and $n/\ln n \approx 48,254,942$. (To a number theorist, 10^9 is a small number.)

We can view the process of randomly selecting an integer n and determining whether it is prime as a Bernoulli trial (see Section C.4). By the prime number theorem, the probability of a success—that is, the probability that n is prime—is approximately $1/\ln n$. The geometric distribution tells us how many trials we need to obtain a success, and by equation (C.32), the expected number of trials is approximately $\ln n$. Thus, we would expect to examine approximately $\ln n$ integers chosen randomly near n in order to find a prime that is of the same length as n. For example, we expect that finding a 1024-bit prime would require testing approximately $\ln 2^{1024} \approx 710$ randomly chosen 1024-bit numbers for primality. (Of course, we can cut this figure in half by choosing only odd integers.)

In the remainder of this section, we consider the problem of determining whether or not a large odd integer n is prime. For notational convenience, we assume that n has the prime factorization

$$n = p_1^{e_1} p_2^{e_2} \cdots p_r^{e_r} \, , \tag{31.39}$$

where $r \geq 1$, $p_1, p_2, \ldots, p_r$ are the prime factors of n, and $e_1, e_2, \ldots, e_r$ are positive integers. The integer n is prime if and only if $r = 1$ and $e_1 = 1$.

One simple approach to the problem of testing for primality is ***trial division***. We try dividing n by each integer $2, 3, \ldots, \lfloor \sqrt{n} \rfloor$. (Again, we may skip even integers greater than 2.) It is easy to see that n is prime if and only if none of the trial divisors divides n. Assuming that each trial division takes constant time, the worst-case running time is $\Theta(\sqrt{n})$, which is exponential in the length of n. (Recall that if n is encoded in binary using β bits, then $\beta = \lceil \lg(n + 1) \rceil$, and so $\sqrt{n} = \Theta(2^{\beta/2})$.) Thus, trial division works well only if n is very small or happens to have a small prime factor. When it works, trial division has the advantage that it not only determines whether n is prime or composite, but also determines one of n's prime factors if n is composite.

In this section, we are interested only in finding out whether a given number n is prime; if n is composite, we are not concerned with finding its prime factorization. As we shall see in Section 31.9, computing the prime factorization of a number is computationally expensive. It is perhaps surprising that it is much easier to tell whether or not a given number is prime than it is to determine the prime factorization of the number if it is not prime.

Pseudoprimality testing

We now consider a method for primality testing that "almost works" and in fact is good enough for many practical applications. Later on, we shall present a re-

finement of this method that removes the small defect. Let $\mathbb{Z}_n^+$ denote the nonzero elements of $\mathbb{Z}_n$:

$$\mathbb{Z}_n^+ = \{1, 2, \ldots, n - 1\} \ .$$

If n is prime, then $\mathbb{Z}_n^+ = \mathbb{Z}_n^*$.

We say that n is a ***base-a pseudoprime*** if n is composite and

$$a^{n-1} \equiv 1 \pmod{n} \ . \tag{31.40}$$

Fermat's theorem (Theorem 31.31) implies that if n is prime, then n satisfies equation (31.40) for every a in $\mathbb{Z}_n^+$. Thus, if we can find any $a \in \mathbb{Z}_n^+$ such that n does *not* satisfy equation (31.40), then n is certainly composite. Surprisingly, the converse *almost* holds, so that this criterion forms an almost perfect test for primality. We test to see whether n satisfies equation (31.40) for $a = 2$. If not, we declare n to be composite by returning COMPOSITE. Otherwise, we return PRIME, guessing that n is prime (when, in fact, all we know is that n is either prime or a base-2 pseudoprime).

The following procedure pretends in this manner to be checking the primality of n. It uses the procedure MODULAR-EXPONENTIATION from Section 31.6. We assume that the input n is an odd integer greater than 2.

PSEUDOPRIME(n)

```
1   if MODULAR-EXPONENTIATION(2, n − 1, n) ≢ 1  (mod n)
2       return COMPOSITE        // definitely
3   else return PRIME           // we hope!
```

This procedure can make errors, but only of one type. That is, if it says that n is composite, then it is always correct. If it says that n is prime, however, then it makes an error only if n is a base-2 pseudoprime.

How often does this procedure err? Surprisingly rarely. There are only 22 values of n less than 10,000 for which it errs; the first four such values are 341, 561, 645, and 1105. We won't prove it, but the probability that this program makes an error on a randomly chosen β-bit number goes to zero as $\beta \rightarrow \infty$. Using more precise estimates due to Pomerance [279] of the number of base-2 pseudoprimes of a given size, we may estimate that a randomly chosen 512-bit number that is called prime by the above procedure has less than one chance in 10^{20} of being a base-2 pseudoprime, and a randomly chosen 1024-bit number that is called prime has less than one chance in 10^{41} of being a base-2 pseudoprime. So if you are merely trying to find a large prime for some application, for all practical purposes you almost never go wrong by choosing large numbers at random until one of them causes PSEUDOPRIME to return PRIME. But when the numbers being tested for primality are not randomly chosen, we need a better approach for testing primality.

As we shall see, a little more cleverness, and some randomization, will yield a primality-testing routine that works well on all inputs.

Unfortunately, we cannot entirely eliminate all the errors by simply checking equation (31.40) for a second base number, say $a = 3$, because there exist composite integers n, known as ***Carmichael numbers***, that satisfy equation (31.40) for *all* $a \in \mathbb{Z}_n^*$. (We note that equation (31.40) does fail when $\gcd(a, n) > 1$—that is, when $a \notin \mathbb{Z}_n^*$—but hoping to demonstrate that n is composite by finding such an a can be difficult if n has only large prime factors.) The first three Carmichael numbers are 561, 1105, and 1729. Carmichael numbers are extremely rare; there are, for example, only 255 of them less than 100,000,000. Exercise 31.8-2 helps explain why they are so rare.

We next show how to improve our primality test so that it won't be fooled by Carmichael numbers.

The Miller-Rabin randomized primality test

The Miller-Rabin primality test overcomes the problems of the simple test PSEU-DOPRIME with two modifications:

- It tries several randomly chosen base values a instead of just one base value.

- While computing each modular exponentiation, it looks for a nontrivial square root of 1, modulo n, during the final set of squarings. If it finds one, it stops and returns COMPOSITE. Corollary 31.35 from Section 31.6 justifies detecting composites in this manner.

The pseudocode for the Miller-Rabin primality test follows. The input $n > 2$ is the odd number to be tested for primality, and s is the number of randomly chosen base values from $\mathbb{Z}_n^+$ to be tried. The code uses the random-number generator RANDOM described on page 117: RANDOM$(1, n - 1)$ returns a randomly chosen integer a satisfying $1 \le a \le n-1$. The code uses an auxiliary procedure WITNESS such that WITNESS(a, n) is TRUE if and only if a is a "witness" to the compositeness of n—that is, if it is possible using a to prove (in a manner that we shall see) that n is composite. The test WITNESS(a, n) is an extension of, but more effective than, the test

$$a^{n-1} \not\equiv 1 \pmod{n}$$

that formed the basis (using $a = 2$) for PSEUDOPRIME. We first present and justify the construction of WITNESS, and then we shall show how we use it in the Miller-Rabin primality test. Let $n - 1 = 2^t u$ where $t \ge 1$ and u is odd; i.e., the binary representation of $n - 1$ is the binary representation of the odd integer u followed by exactly t zeros. Therefore, $a^{n-1} \equiv (a^u)^{2^t} \pmod{n}$, so that we can

compute $a^{n-1} \bmod n$ by first computing $a^u \bmod n$ and then squaring the result t times successively.

WITNESS(a, n)

1   let t and u be such that $t \geq 1$, u is odd, and $n - 1 = 2^t u$
2   $x_0 = $ MODULAR-EXPONENTIATION(a, u, n)
3   **for** $i = 1$ **to** t
4       $x_i = x_{i-1}^2 \bmod n$
5   **if** $x_i == 1$ and $x_{i-1} \neq 1$ and $x_{i-1} \neq n - 1$
6   **return** TRUE
7   **if** $x_t \neq 1$
8   **return** TRUE
9   **return** FALSE

This pseudocode for WITNESS computes $a^{n-1} \bmod n$ by first computing the value $x_0 = a^u \bmod n$ in line 2 and then squaring the result t times in a row in the **for** loop of lines 3–6. By induction on i, the sequence $x_0, x_1, \ldots, x_t$ of values computed satisfies the equation $x_i \equiv a^{2^i u} \pmod{n}$ for $i = 0, 1, \ldots, t$, so that in particular $x_t \equiv a^{n-1} \pmod{n}$. After line 4 performs a squaring step, however, the loop may terminate early if lines 5–6 detect that a nontrivial square root of 1 has just been discovered. (We shall explain these tests shortly.) If so, the algorithm stops and returns TRUE. Lines 7–8 return TRUE if the value computed for $x_t \equiv a^{n-1} \pmod{n}$ is not equal to 1, just as the PSEUDOPRIME procedure returns COMPOSITE in this case. Line 9 returns FALSE if we haven't returned TRUE in lines 6 or 8.

We now argue that if WITNESS(a, n) returns TRUE, then we can construct a proof that n is composite using a as a witness.

If WITNESS returns TRUE from line 8, then it has discovered that $x_t = a^{n-1} \bmod n \neq 1$. If n is prime, however, we have by Fermat's theorem (Theorem 31.31) that $a^{n-1} \equiv 1 \pmod{n}$ for all $a \in \mathbb{Z}_n^+$. Therefore, n cannot be prime, and the equation $a^{n-1} \bmod n \neq 1$ proves this fact.

If WITNESS returns TRUE from line 6, then it has discovered that x_{i-1} is a nontrivial square root of 1, modulo n, since we have that $x_{i-1} \not\equiv \pm 1 \pmod{n}$ yet $x_i \equiv x_{i-1}^2 \equiv 1 \pmod{n}$. Corollary 31.35 states that only if n is composite can there exist a nontrivial square root of 1 modulo n, so that demonstrating that x_{i-1} is a nontrivial square root of 1 modulo n proves that n is composite.

This completes our proof of the correctness of WITNESS. If we find that the call WITNESS(a, n) returns TRUE, then n is surely composite, and the witness a, along with the reason that the procedure returns TRUE (did it return from line 6 or from line 8?), provides a proof that n is composite.

At this point, we briefly present an alternative description of the behavior of WITNESS as a function of the sequence $X = \langle x_0, x_1, \ldots, x_t \rangle$, which we shall find useful later on, when we analyze the efficiency of the Miller-Rabin primality test. Note that if $x_i = 1$ for some $0 \leq i < t$, WITNESS might not compute the rest of the sequence. If it were to do so, however, each value $x_{i+1}, x_{i+2}, \ldots, x_t$ would be 1, and we consider these positions in the sequence X as being all 1s. We have four cases:

1. $X = \langle \ldots, d \rangle$, where $d \neq 1$: the sequence X does not end in 1. Return TRUE in line 8; a is a witness to the compositeness of n (by Fermat's Theorem).

2. $X = \langle 1, 1, \ldots, 1 \rangle$: the sequence X is all 1s. Return FALSE; a is not a witness to the compositeness of n.

3. $X = \langle \ldots, -1, 1, \ldots, 1 \rangle$: the sequence X ends in 1, and the last non-1 is equal to -1. Return FALSE; a is not a witness to the compositeness of n.

4. $X = \langle \ldots, d, 1, \ldots, 1 \rangle$, where $d \neq \pm 1$: the sequence X ends in 1, but the last non-1 is not -1. Return TRUE in line 6; a is a witness to the compositeness of n, since d is a nontrivial square root of 1.

We now examine the Miller-Rabin primality test based on the use of WITNESS. Again, we assume that n is an odd integer greater than 2.

MILLER-RABIN(n, s)

```
1   for j = 1 to s
2       a = RANDOM(1, n − 1)
3       if WITNESS(a, n)
4           return COMPOSITE        // definitely
5   return PRIME                    // almost surely
```

The procedure MILLER-RABIN is a probabilistic search for a proof that n is composite. The main loop (beginning on line 1) picks up to s random values of a from $\mathbb{Z}_n^+$ (line 2). If one of the a's picked is a witness to the compositeness of n, then MILLER-RABIN returns COMPOSITE on line 4. Such a result is always correct, by the correctness of WITNESS. If MILLER-RABIN finds no witness in s trials, then the procedure assumes that this is because no witnesses exist, and therefore it assumes that n is prime. We shall see that this result is likely to be correct if s is large enough, but that there is still a tiny chance that the procedure may be unlucky in its choice of a's and that witnesses do exist even though none has been found.

To illustrate the operation of MILLER-RABIN, let n be the Carmichael number 561, so that $n - 1 = 560 = 2^4 \cdot 35$, $t = 4$, and $u = 35$. If the procedure chooses $a = 7$ as a base, Figure 31.4 in Section 31.6 shows that WITNESS computes $x_0 \equiv a^{35} \equiv 241 \pmod{561}$ and thus computes the sequence

$X = \langle 241, 298, 166, 67, 1 \rangle$. Thus, WITNESS discovers a nontrivial square root of 1 in the last squaring step, since $a^{280} \equiv 67 \pmod{n}$ and $a^{560} \equiv 1 \pmod{n}$. Therefore, $a = 7$ is a witness to the compositeness of n, WITNESS$(7, n)$ returns TRUE, and MILLER-RABIN returns COMPOSITE.

If n is a β-bit number, MILLER-RABIN requires $O(s\beta)$ arithmetic operations and $O(s\beta^3)$ bit operations, since it requires asymptotically no more work than s modular exponentiations.

Error rate of the Miller-Rabin primality test

If MILLER-RABIN returns PRIME, then there is a very slim chance that it has made an error. Unlike PSEUDOPRIME, however, the chance of error does not depend on n; there are no bad inputs for this procedure. Rather, it depends on the size of s and the "luck of the draw" in choosing base values a. Moreover, since each test is more stringent than a simple check of equation (31.40), we can expect on general principles that the error rate should be small for randomly chosen integers n. The following theorem presents a more precise argument.

Theorem 31.38
If n is an odd composite number, then the number of witnesses to the compositeness of n is at least $(n - 1)/2$.

Proof The proof shows that the number of nonwitnesses is at most $(n - 1)/2$, which implies the theorem.

We start by claiming that any nonwitness must be a member of $\mathbb{Z}_n^*$. Why? Consider any nonwitness a. It must satisfy $a^{n-1} \equiv 1 \pmod{n}$ or, equivalently, $a \cdot a^{n-2} \equiv 1 \pmod{n}$. Thus, the equation $ax \equiv 1 \pmod{n}$ has a solution, namely a^{n-2}. By Corollary 31.21, $\gcd(a, n) \mid 1$, which in turn implies that $\gcd(a, n) = 1$. Therefore, a is a member of $\mathbb{Z}_n^*$; all nonwitnesses belong to $\mathbb{Z}_n^*$.

To complete the proof, we show that not only are all nonwitnesses contained in $\mathbb{Z}_n^*$, they are all contained in a proper subgroup B of $\mathbb{Z}_n^*$ (recall that we say B is a *proper* subgroup of $\mathbb{Z}_n^*$ when B is subgroup of $\mathbb{Z}_n^*$ but B is not equal to $\mathbb{Z}_n^*$). By Corollary 31.16, we then have $|B| \leq |\mathbb{Z}_n^*|/2$. Since $|\mathbb{Z}_n^*| \leq n - 1$, we obtain $|B| \leq (n - 1)/2$. Therefore, the number of nonwitnesses is at most $(n - 1)/2$, so that the number of witnesses must be at least $(n - 1)/2$.

We now show how to find a proper subgroup B of $\mathbb{Z}_n^*$ containing all of the nonwitnesses. We break the proof into two cases.

Case 1: There exists an $x \in \mathbb{Z}_n^*$ such that

$$x^{n-1} \not\equiv 1 \pmod{n}.$$

In other words, n is not a Carmichael number. Because, as we noted earlier, Carmichael numbers are extremely rare, case 1 is the main case that arises "in practice" (e.g., when n has been chosen randomly and is being tested for primality).

Let $B = \{b \in \mathbb{Z}_n^* : b^{n-1} \equiv 1 \pmod{n}\}$. Clearly, B is nonempty, since $1 \in B$. Since B is closed under multiplication modulo n, we have that B is a subgroup of $\mathbb{Z}_n^*$ by Theorem 31.14. Note that every nonwitness belongs to B, since a nonwitness a satisfies $a^{n-1} \equiv 1 \pmod{n}$. Since $x \in \mathbb{Z}_n^* - B$, we have that B is a proper subgroup of $\mathbb{Z}_n^*$.

Case 2: For all $x \in \mathbb{Z}_n^*$,

$$x^{n-1} \equiv 1 \pmod{n} . \tag{31.41}$$

In other words, n is a Carmichael number. This case is extremely rare in practice. However, the Miller-Rabin test (unlike a pseudo-primality test) can efficiently determine that Carmichael numbers are composite, as we now show.

In this case, n cannot be a prime power. To see why, let us suppose to the contrary that $n = p^e$, where p is a prime and $e > 1$. We derive a contradiction as follows. Since we assume that n is odd, p must also be odd. Theorem 31.32 implies that $\mathbb{Z}_n^*$ is a cyclic group: it contains a generator g such that $\mathrm{ord}_n(g) = |\mathbb{Z}_n^*| = \phi(n) = p^e(1 - 1/p) = (p-1)p^{e-1}$. (The formula for $\phi(n)$ comes from equation (31.20).) By equation (31.41), we have $g^{n-1} \equiv 1 \pmod{n}$. Then the discrete logarithm theorem (Theorem 31.33, taking $y = 0$) implies that $n - 1 \equiv 0 \pmod{\phi(n)}$, or

$$(p-1)p^{e-1} \mid p^e - 1 .$$

This is a contradiction for $e > 1$, since $(p-1)p^{e-1}$ is divisible by the prime p but $p^e - 1$ is not. Thus, n is not a prime power.

Since the odd composite number n is not a prime power, we decompose it into a product $n_1 n_2$, where n_1 and n_2 are odd numbers greater than 1 that are relatively prime to each other. (There may be several ways to decompose n, and it does not matter which one we choose. For example, if $n = p_1^{e_1} p_2^{e_2} \cdots p_r^{e_r}$, then we can choose $n_1 = p_1^{e_1}$ and $n_2 = p_2^{e_2} p_3^{e_3} \cdots p_r^{e_r}$.)

Recall that we define t and u so that $n - 1 = 2^t u$, where $t \geq 1$ and u is odd, and that for an input a, the procedure WITNESS computes the sequence

$$X = \langle a^u, a^{2u}, a^{2^2 u}, \ldots, a^{2^t u} \rangle$$

(all computations are performed modulo n).

Let us call a pair (v, j) of integers *acceptable* if $v \in \mathbb{Z}_n^*$, $j \in \{0, 1, \ldots, t\}$, and

$$v^{2^j u} \equiv -1 \pmod{n} .$$

Acceptable pairs certainly exist since u is odd; we can choose $v = n - 1$ and $j = 0$, so that $(n - 1, 0)$ is an acceptable pair. Now pick the largest possible j such that there exists an acceptable pair (v, j), and fix v so that (v, j) is an acceptable pair. Let

$$B = \{x \in \mathbb{Z}_n^* : x^{2^j u} \equiv \pm 1 \pmod{n}\} .$$

Since B is closed under multiplication modulo n, it is a subgroup of $\mathbb{Z}_n^*$. By Theorem 31.15, therefore, $|B|$ divides $|\mathbb{Z}_n^*|$. Every nonwitness must be a member of B, since the sequence X produced by a nonwitness must either be all 1s or else contain a -1 no later than the jth position, by the maximality of j. (If (a, j') is acceptable, where a is a nonwitness, we must have $j' \le j$ by how we chose j.)

We now use the existence of v to demonstrate that there exists a $w \in \mathbb{Z}_n^* - B$, and hence that B is a proper subgroup of $\mathbb{Z}_n^*$. Since $v^{2^j u} \equiv -1 \pmod{n}$, we have $v^{2^j u} \equiv -1 \pmod{n_1}$ by Corollary 31.29 to the Chinese remainder theorem. By Corollary 31.28, there exists a w simultaneously satisfying the equations

$$w \equiv v \pmod{n_1} ,$$
$$w \equiv 1 \pmod{n_2} .$$

Therefore,

$$w^{2^j u} \equiv -1 \pmod{n_1} ,$$
$$w^{2^j u} \equiv 1 \pmod{n_2} .$$

By Corollary 31.29, $w^{2^j u} \not\equiv 1 \pmod{n_1}$ implies $w^{2^j u} \not\equiv 1 \pmod{n}$, and $w^{2^j u} \not\equiv -1 \pmod{n_2}$ implies $w^{2^j u} \not\equiv -1 \pmod{n}$. Hence, we conclude that $w^{2^j u} \not\equiv \pm 1 \pmod{n}$, and so $w \notin B$.

It remains to show that $w \in \mathbb{Z}_n^*$, which we do by first working separately modulo n_1 and modulo n_2. Working modulo n_1, we observe that since $v \in \mathbb{Z}_n^*$, we have that $\gcd(v, n) = 1$, and so also $\gcd(v, n_1) = 1$; if v does not have any common divisors with n, then it certainly does not have any common divisors with n_1. Since $w \equiv v \pmod{n_1}$, we see that $\gcd(w, n_1) = 1$. Working modulo n_2, we observe that $w \equiv 1 \pmod{n_2}$ implies $\gcd(w, n_2) = 1$. To combine these results, we use Theorem 31.6, which implies that $\gcd(w, n_1 n_2) = \gcd(w, n) = 1$. That is, $w \in \mathbb{Z}_n^*$.

Therefore $w \in \mathbb{Z}_n^* - B$, and we finish case 2 with the conclusion that B is a proper subgroup of $\mathbb{Z}_n^*$.

In either case, we see that the number of witnesses to the compositeness of n is at least $(n - 1)/2$.   ■

Theorem 31.39
For any odd integer $n > 2$ and positive integer s, the probability that MILLER-RABIN(n, s) errs is at most 2^{-s}.

Proof   Using Theorem 31.38, we see that if n is composite, then each execution of the **for** loop of lines 1–4 has a probability of at least $1/2$ of discovering a witness x to the compositeness of n. MILLER-RABIN makes an error only if it is so unlucky as to miss discovering a witness to the compositeness of n on each of the s iterations of the main loop. The probability of such a sequence of misses is at most 2^{-s}.   ∎

If n is prime, MILLER-RABIN always reports PRIME, and if n is composite, the chance that MILLER-RABIN reports PRIME is at most 2^{-s}.

When applying MILLER-RABIN to a large randomly chosen integer n, however, we need to consider as well the prior probability that n is prime, in order to correctly interpret MILLER-RABIN's result. Suppose that we fix a bit length β and choose at random an integer n of length β bits to be tested for primality. Let A denote the event that n is prime. By the prime number theorem (Theorem 31.37), the probability that n is prime is approximately

$$\Pr\{A\} \approx 1/\ln n$$
$$\approx 1.443/\beta .$$

Now let B denote the event that MILLER-RABIN returns PRIME. We have that $\Pr\{\overline{B} \mid A\} = 0$ (or equivalently, that $\Pr\{B \mid A\} = 1$) and $\Pr\{B \mid \overline{A}\} \le 2^{-s}$ (or equivalently, that $\Pr\{\overline{B} \mid \overline{A}\} > 1 - 2^{-s}$).

But what is $\Pr\{A \mid B\}$, the probability that n is prime, given that MILLER-RABIN has returned PRIME? By the alternate form of Bayes's theorem (equation (C.18)) we have

$$\Pr\{A \mid B\} = \frac{\Pr\{A\}\Pr\{B \mid A\}}{\Pr\{A\}\Pr\{B \mid A\} + \Pr\{\overline{A}\}\Pr\{B \mid \overline{A}\}}$$
$$\approx \frac{1}{1 + 2^{-s}(\ln n - 1)} .$$

This probability does not exceed $1/2$ until s exceeds $\lg(\ln n - 1)$. Intuitively, that many initial trials are needed just for the confidence derived from failing to find a witness to the compositeness of n to overcome the prior bias in favor of n being composite. For a number with $\beta = 1024$ bits, this initial testing requires about

$$\lg(\ln n - 1) \approx \lg(\beta/1.443)$$
$$\approx 9$$

trials. In any case, choosing $s = 50$ should suffice for almost any imaginable application.

In fact, the situation is much better. If we are trying to find large primes by applying MILLER-RABIN to large randomly chosen odd integers, then choosing a small value of s (say 3) is very unlikely to lead to erroneous results, though

we won't prove it here. The reason is that for a randomly chosen odd composite integer n, the expected number of nonwitnesses to the compositeness of n is likely to be very much smaller than $(n-1)/2$.

If the integer n is not chosen randomly, however, the best that can be proven is that the number of nonwitnesses is at most $(n-1)/4$, using an improved version of Theorem 31.38. Furthermore, there do exist integers n for which the number of nonwitnesses is $(n-1)/4$.

Exercises

31.8-1
Prove that if an odd integer $n > 1$ is not a prime or a prime power, then there exists a nontrivial square root of 1 modulo n.

31.8-2 ★
It is possible to strengthen Euler's theorem slightly to the form

$$a^{\lambda(n)} \equiv 1 \pmod{n} \text{ for all } a \in \mathbb{Z}_n^* \,,$$

where $n = p_1^{e_1} \cdots p_r^{e_r}$ and $\lambda(n)$ is defined by

$$\lambda(n) = \text{lcm}(\phi(p_1^{e_1}), \ldots, \phi(p_r^{e_r})) \,. \tag{31.42}$$

Prove that $\lambda(n) \mid \phi(n)$. A composite number n is a Carmichael number if $\lambda(n) \mid n-1$. The smallest Carmichael number is $561 = 3 \cdot 11 \cdot 17$; here, $\lambda(n) = \text{lcm}(2, 10, 16) = 80$, which divides 560. Prove that Carmichael numbers must be both "square-free" (not divisible by the square of any prime) and the product of at least three primes. (For this reason, they are not very common.)

31.8-3
Prove that if x is a nontrivial square root of 1, modulo n, then $\gcd(x-1, n)$ and $\gcd(x+1, n)$ are both nontrivial divisors of n.

★ 31.9 Integer factorization

Suppose we have an integer n that we wish to **factor**, that is, to decompose into a product of primes. The primality test of the preceding section may tell us that n is composite, but it does not tell us the prime factors of n. Factoring a large integer n seems to be much more difficult than simply determining whether n is prime or composite. Even with today's supercomputers and the best algorithms to date, we cannot feasibly factor an arbitrary 1024-bit number.

Pollard's rho heuristic

Trial division by all integers up to R is guaranteed to factor completely any number up to R^2. For the same amount of work, the following procedure, POLLARD-RHO, factors any number up to R^4 (unless we are unlucky). Since the procedure is only a heuristic, neither its running time nor its success is guaranteed, although the procedure is highly effective in practice. Another advantage of the POLLARD-RHO procedure is that it uses only a constant number of memory locations. (If you wanted to, you could easily implement POLLARD-RHO on a programmable pocket calculator to find factors of small numbers.)

POLLARD-RHO(n)

```
 1  i = 1
 2  x₁ = RANDOM(0, n − 1)
 3  y = x₁
 4  k = 2
 5  while TRUE
 6      i = i + 1
 7      xᵢ = (x²ᵢ₋₁ − 1) mod n
 8      d = gcd(y − xᵢ, n)
 9      if d ≠ 1 and d ≠ n
10          print d
11      if i == k
12          y = xᵢ
13          k = 2k
```

The procedure works as follows. Lines 1–2 initialize i to 1 and x_1 to a randomly chosen value in $\mathbb{Z}_n$. The **while** loop beginning on line 5 iterates forever, searching for factors of n. During each iteration of the **while** loop, line 7 uses the recurrence

$$x_i = (x_{i-1}^2 - 1) \bmod n \tag{31.43}$$

to produce the next value of x_i in the infinite sequence

$$x_1, x_2, x_3, x_4, \ldots , \tag{31.44}$$

with line 6 correspondingly incrementing i. The pseudocode is written using subscripted variables x_i for clarity, but the program works the same if all of the subscripts are dropped, since only the most recent value of x_i needs to be maintained. With this modification, the procedure uses only a constant number of memory locations.

Every so often, the program saves the most recently generated x_i value in the variable y. Specifically, the values that are saved are the ones whose subscripts are powers of 2:

$$x_1, x_2, x_4, x_8, x_{16}, \ldots .$$

Line 3 saves the value x_1, and line 12 saves x_k whenever i is equal to k. The variable k is initialized to 2 in line 4, and line 13 doubles it whenever line 12 updates y. Therefore, k follows the sequence $2, 4, 8, 16 \ldots$ and always gives the subscript of the next value x_k to be saved in y.

Lines 8–10 try to find a factor of n, using the saved value of y and the current value of x_i. Specifically, line 8 computes the greatest common divisor $d = \gcd(y - x_i, n)$. If line 9 finds d to be a nontrivial divisor of n, then line 10 prints d.

This procedure for finding a factor may seem somewhat mysterious at first. Note, however, that POLLARD-RHO never prints an incorrect answer; any number it prints is a nontrivial divisor of n. POLLARD-RHO might not print anything at all, though; it comes with no guarantee that it will print any divisors. We shall see, however, that we have good reason to expect POLLARD-RHO to print a factor p of n after $\Theta(\sqrt{p})$ iterations of the **while** loop. Thus, if n is composite, we can expect this procedure to discover enough divisors to factor n completely after approximately $n^{1/4}$ updates, since every prime factor p of n except possibly the largest one is less than $\sqrt{n}$.

We begin our analysis of how this procedure behaves by studying how long it takes a random sequence modulo n to repeat a value. Since $\mathbb{Z}_n$ is finite, and since each value in the sequence (31.44) depends only on the previous value, the sequence (31.44) eventually repeats itself. Once we reach an x_i such that $x_i = x_j$ for some $j < i$, we are in a cycle, since $x_{i+1} = x_{j+1}, x_{i+2} = x_{j+2}$, and so on. The reason for the name "rho heuristic" is that, as Figure 31.7 shows, we can draw the sequence $x_1, x_2, \ldots, x_{j-1}$ as the "tail" of the rho and the cycle $x_j, x_{j+1}, \ldots, x_i$ as the "body" of the rho.

Let us consider the question of how long it takes for the sequence of x_i to repeat. This information is not exactly what we need, but we shall see later how to modify the argument. For the purpose of this estimation, let us assume that the function

$$f_n(x) = (x^2 - 1) \bmod n$$

behaves like a "random" function. Of course, it is not really random, but this assumption yields results consistent with the observed behavior of POLLARD-RHO. We can then consider each x_i to have been independently drawn from $\mathbb{Z}_n$ according to a uniform distribution on $\mathbb{Z}_n$. By the birthday-paradox analysis of Section 5.4.1, we expect $\Theta(\sqrt{n})$ steps to be taken before the sequence cycles.

Now for the required modification. Let p be a nontrivial factor of n such that $\gcd(p, n/p) = 1$. For example, if n has the factorization $n = p_1^{e_1} p_2^{e_2} \cdots p_r^{e_r}$, then we may take p to be $p_1^{e_1}$. (If $e_1 = 1$, then p is just the smallest prime factor of n, a good example to keep in mind.)

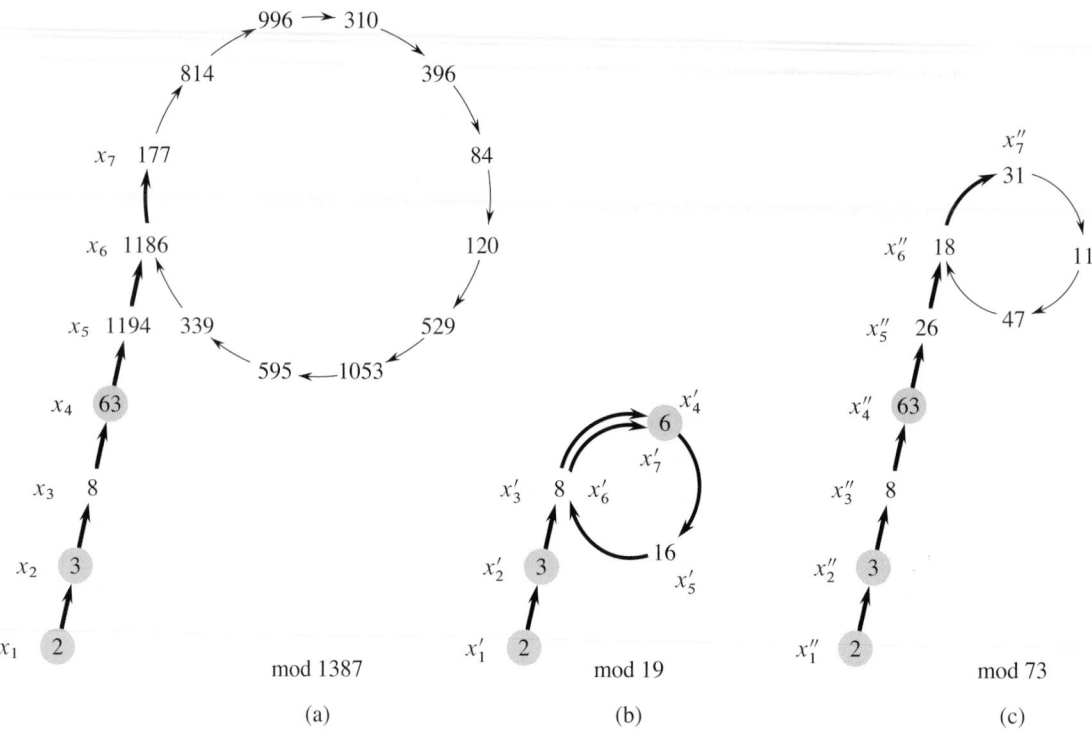

Figure 31.7 Pollard's rho heuristic. **(a)** The values produced by the recurrence $x_{i+1} = (x_i^2 - 1) \bmod 1387$, starting with $x_1 = 2$. The prime factorization of 1387 is $19 \cdot 73$. The heavy arrows indicate the iteration steps that are executed before the factor 19 is discovered. The light arrows point to unreached values in the iteration, to illustrate the "rho" shape. The shaded values are the y values stored by POLLARD-RHO. The factor 19 is discovered upon reaching $x_7 = 177$, when $\gcd(63 - 177, 1387) = 19$ is computed. The first x value that would be repeated is 1186, but the factor 19 is discovered before this value is repeated. **(b)** The values produced by the same recurrence, modulo 19. Every value x_i given in part (a) is equivalent, modulo 19, to the value x_i' shown here. For example, both $x_4 = 63$ and $x_7 = 177$ are equivalent to 6, modulo 19. **(c)** The values produced by the same recurrence, modulo 73. Every value x_i given in part (a) is equivalent, modulo 73, to the value x_i'' shown here. By the Chinese remainder theorem, each node in part (a) corresponds to a pair of nodes, one from part (b) and one from part (c).

The sequence $\langle x_i \rangle$ induces a corresponding sequence $\langle x_i' \rangle$ modulo p, where

$$x_i' = x_i \bmod p$$

for all i.

Furthermore, because f_n is defined using only arithmetic operations (squaring and subtraction) modulo n, we can compute x_{i+1}' from x_i'; the "modulo p" view of

the sequence is a smaller version of what is happening modulo n:

$$
\begin{aligned}
x'_{i+1} &= x_{i+1} \bmod p \\
&= f_n(x_i) \bmod p \\
&= ((x_i^2 - 1) \bmod n) \bmod p \\
&= (x_i^2 - 1) \bmod p \qquad \text{(by Exercise 31.1-7)} \\
&= ((x_i \bmod p)^2 - 1) \bmod p \\
&= ((x'_i)^2 - 1) \bmod p \\
&= f_p(x'_i) \,.
\end{aligned}
$$

Thus, although we are not explicitly computing the sequence $\langle x'_i \rangle$, this sequence is well defined and obeys the same recurrence as the sequence $\langle x_i \rangle$.

Reasoning as before, we find that the expected number of steps before the sequence $\langle x'_i \rangle$ repeats is $\Theta(\sqrt{p})$. If p is small compared to n, the sequence $\langle x'_i \rangle$ might repeat much more quickly than the sequence $\langle x_i \rangle$. Indeed, as parts (b) and (c) of Figure 31.7 show, the $\langle x'_i \rangle$ sequence repeats as soon as two elements of the sequence $\langle x_i \rangle$ are merely equivalent modulo p, rather than equivalent modulo n.

Let t denote the index of the first repeated value in the $\langle x'_i \rangle$ sequence, and let $u > 0$ denote the length of the cycle that has been thereby produced. That is, t and $u > 0$ are the smallest values such that $x'_{t+i} = x'_{t+u+i}$ for all $i \geq 0$. By the above arguments, the expected values of t and u are both $\Theta(\sqrt{p})$. Note that if $x'_{t+i} = x'_{t+u+i}$, then $p \mid (x_{t+u+i} - x_{t+i})$. Thus, $\gcd(x_{t+u+i} - x_{t+i}, n) > 1$.

Therefore, once POLLARD-RHO has saved as y any value x_k such that $k \geq t$, then $y \bmod p$ is always on the cycle modulo p. (If a new value is saved as y, that value is also on the cycle modulo p.) Eventually, k is set to a value that is greater than u, and the procedure then makes an entire loop around the cycle modulo p without changing the value of y. The procedure then discovers a factor of n when x_i "runs into" the previously stored value of y, modulo p, that is, when $x_i \equiv y \pmod{p}$.

Presumably, the factor found is the factor p, although it may occasionally happen that a multiple of p is discovered. Since the expected values of both t and u are $\Theta(\sqrt{p})$, the expected number of steps required to produce the factor p is $\Theta(\sqrt{p})$.

This algorithm might not perform quite as expected, for two reasons. First, the heuristic analysis of the running time is not rigorous, and it is possible that the cycle of values, modulo p, could be much larger than $\sqrt{p}$. In this case, the algorithm performs correctly but much more slowly than desired. In practice, this issue seems to be moot. Second, the divisors of n produced by this algorithm might always be one of the trivial divisors 1 or n. For example, suppose that $n = pq$, where p and q are prime. It can happen that the values of t and u for p are identical with the values of t and u for q, and thus the factor p is always revealed in the same gcd operation that reveals the factor q. Since both factors are revealed at the same

time, the trivial divisor $pq = n$ is revealed, which is useless. Again, this problem seems to be insignificant in practice. If necessary, we can restart the heuristic with a different recurrence of the form $x_{i+1} = (x_i^2 - c) \bmod n$. (We should avoid the values $c = 0$ and $c = 2$ for reasons we will not go into here, but other values are fine.)

Of course, this analysis is heuristic and not rigorous, since the recurrence is not really "random." Nonetheless, the procedure performs well in practice, and it seems to be as efficient as this heuristic analysis indicates. It is the method of choice for finding small prime factors of a large number. To factor a β-bit composite number n completely, we only need to find all prime factors less than $\lfloor n^{1/2} \rfloor$, and so we expect POLLARD-RHO to require at most $n^{1/4} = 2^{\beta/4}$ arithmetic operations and at most $n^{1/4}\beta^2 = 2^{\beta/4}\beta^2$ bit operations. POLLARD-RHO's ability to find a small factor p of n with an expected number $\Theta(\sqrt{p})$ of arithmetic operations is often its most appealing feature.

Exercises

31.9-1
Referring to the execution history shown in Figure 31.7(a), when does POLLARD-RHO print the factor 73 of 1387?

31.9-2
Suppose that we are given a function $f : \mathbb{Z}_n \rightarrow \mathbb{Z}_n$ and an initial value $x_0 \in \mathbb{Z}_n$. Define $x_i = f(x_{i-1})$ for $i = 1, 2, \ldots$. Let t and $u > 0$ be the smallest values such that $x_{t+i} = x_{t+u+i}$ for $i = 0, 1, \ldots$. In the terminology of Pollard's rho algorithm, t is the length of the tail and u is the length of the cycle of the rho. Give an efficient algorithm to determine t and u exactly, and analyze its running time.

31.9-3
How many steps would you expect POLLARD-RHO to require to discover a factor of the form p^e, where p is prime and $e > 1$?

31.9-4 ★
One disadvantage of POLLARD-RHO as written is that it requires one gcd computation for each step of the recurrence. Instead, we could batch the gcd computations by accumulating the product of several x_i values in a row and then using this product instead of x_i in the gcd computation. Describe carefully how you would implement this idea, why it works, and what batch size you would pick as the most effective when working on a β-bit number n.

Problems

31-1 Binary gcd algorithm

Most computers can perform the operations of subtraction, testing the parity (odd or even) of a binary integer, and halving more quickly than computing remainders. This problem investigates the **binary gcd algorithm**, which avoids the remainder computations used in Euclid's algorithm.

a. Prove that if a and b are both even, then $\gcd(a, b) = 2 \cdot \gcd(a/2, b/2)$.

b. Prove that if a is odd and b is even, then $\gcd(a, b) = \gcd(a, b/2)$.

c. Prove that if a and b are both odd, then $\gcd(a, b) = \gcd((a - b)/2, b)$.

d. Design an efficient binary gcd algorithm for input integers a and b, where $a \geq b$, that runs in $O(\lg a)$ time. Assume that each subtraction, parity test, and halving takes unit time.

31-2 Analysis of bit operations in Euclid's algorithm

a. Consider the ordinary "paper and pencil" algorithm for long division: dividing a by b, which yields a quotient q and remainder r. Show that this method requires $O((1 + \lg q) \lg b)$ bit operations.

b. Define $\mu(a, b) = (1 + \lg a)(1 + \lg b)$. Show that the number of bit operations performed by EUCLID in reducing the problem of computing $\gcd(a, b)$ to that of computing $\gcd(b, a \bmod b)$ is at most $c(\mu(a, b) - \mu(b, a \bmod b))$ for some sufficiently large constant $c > 0$.

c. Show that $\text{EUCLID}(a, b)$ requires $O(\mu(a, b))$ bit operations in general and $O(\beta^2)$ bit operations when applied to two β-bit inputs.

31-3 Three algorithms for Fibonacci numbers

This problem compares the efficiency of three methods for computing the nth Fibonacci number F_n, given n. Assume that the cost of adding, subtracting, or multiplying two numbers is $O(1)$, independent of the size of the numbers.

a. Show that the running time of the straightforward recursive method for computing F_n based on recurrence (3.22) is exponential in n. (See, for example, the FIB procedure on page 775.)

b. Show how to compute F_n in $O(n)$ time using memoization.

c. Show how to compute F_n in $O(\lg n)$ time using only integer addition and multiplication. (*Hint:* Consider the matrix

$$\begin{pmatrix} 0 & 1 \\ 1 & 1 \end{pmatrix}$$

and its powers.)

d. Assume now that adding two β-bit numbers takes $\Theta(\beta)$ time and that multiplying two β-bit numbers takes $\Theta(\beta^2)$ time. What is the running time of these three methods under this more reasonable cost measure for the elementary arithmetic operations?

31-4 *Quadratic residues*

Let p be an odd prime. A number $a \in Z_p^*$ is a **quadratic residue** if the equation $x^2 = a \pmod{p}$ has a solution for the unknown x.

a. Show that there are exactly $(p-1)/2$ quadratic residues, modulo p.

b. If p is prime, we define the **Legendre symbol** $\left(\frac{a}{p}\right)$, for $a \in \mathbb{Z}_p^*$, to be 1 if a is a quadratic residue modulo p and -1 otherwise. Prove that if $a \in \mathbb{Z}_p^*$, then

$$\left(\frac{a}{p}\right) \equiv a^{(p-1)/2} \pmod{p} .$$

Give an efficient algorithm that determines whether a given number a is a quadratic residue modulo p. Analyze the efficiency of your algorithm.

c. Prove that if p is a prime of the form $4k+3$ and a is a quadratic residue in $\mathbb{Z}_p^*$, then $a^{k+1} \bmod p$ is a square root of a, modulo p. How much time is required to find the square root of a quadratic residue a modulo p?

d. Describe an efficient randomized algorithm for finding a nonquadratic residue, modulo an arbitrary prime p, that is, a member of $\mathbb{Z}_p^*$ that is not a quadratic residue. How many arithmetic operations does your algorithm require on average?

Chapter notes

Niven and Zuckerman [265] provide an excellent introduction to elementary number theory. Knuth [210] contains a good discussion of algorithms for finding the

greatest common divisor, as well as other basic number-theoretic algorithms. Bach [30] and Riesel [295] provide more recent surveys of computational number theory. Dixon [91] gives an overview of factorization and primality testing. The conference proceedings edited by Pomerance [280] contains several excellent survey articles. More recently, Bach and Shallit [31] have provided an exceptional overview of the basics of computational number theory.

Knuth [210] discusses the origin of Euclid's algorithm. It appears in Book 7, Propositions 1 and 2, of the Greek mathematician Euclid's *Elements*, which was written around 300 B.C. Euclid's description may have been derived from an algorithm due to Eudoxus around 375 B.C. Euclid's algorithm may hold the honor of being the oldest nontrivial algorithm; it is rivaled only by an algorithm for multiplication known to the ancient Egyptians. Shallit [312] chronicles the history of the analysis of Euclid's algorithm.

Knuth attributes a special case of the Chinese remainder theorem (Theorem 31.27) to the Chinese mathematician Sun-Tsǔ, who lived sometime between 200 B.C. and A.D. 200—the date is quite uncertain. The same special case was given by the Greek mathematician Nichomachus around A.D. 100. It was generalized by Chhin Chiu-Shao in 1247. The Chinese remainder theorem was finally stated and proved in its full generality by L. Euler in 1734.

The randomized primality-testing algorithm presented here is due to Miller [255] and Rabin [289]; it is the fastest randomized primality-testing algorithm known, to within constant factors. The proof of Theorem 31.39 is a slight adaptation of one suggested by Bach [29]. A proof of a stronger result for MILLER-RABIN was given by Monier [258, 259]. For many years primality-testing was the classic example of a problem where randomization appeared to be necessary to obtain an efficient (polynomial-time) algorithm. In 2002, however, Agrawal, Kayal, and Saxena [4] surprised everyone with their deterministic polynomial-time primality-testing algorithm. Until then, the fastest deterministic primality testing algorithm known, due to Cohen and Lenstra [73], ran in time $(\lg n)^{O(\lg \lg \lg n)}$ on input n, which is just slightly superpolynomial. Nonetheless, for practical purposes randomized primality-testing algorithms remain more efficient and are preferred.

The problem of finding large "random" primes is nicely discussed in an article by Beauchemin, Brassard, Crépeau, Goutier, and Pomerance [36].

The concept of a public-key cryptosystem is due to Diffie and Hellman [87]. The RSA cryptosystem was proposed in 1977 by Rivest, Shamir, and Adleman [296]. Since then, the field of cryptography has blossomed. Our understanding of the RSA cryptosystem has deepened, and modern implementations use significant refinements of the basic techniques presented here. In addition, many new techniques have been developed for proving cryptosystems to be secure. For example, Goldwasser and Micali [142] show that randomization can be an effective tool in the design of secure public-key encryption schemes. For signature schemes,

Goldwasser, Micali, and Rivest [143] present a digital-signature scheme for which every conceivable type of forgery is provably as difficult as factoring. Menezes, van Oorschot, and Vanstone [254] provide an overview of applied cryptography.

The rho heuristic for integer factorization was invented by Pollard [277]. The version presented here is a variant proposed by Brent [56].

The best algorithms for factoring large numbers have a running time that grows roughly exponentially with the cube root of the length of the number n to be factored. The general number-field sieve factoring algorithm (as developed by Buhler, Lenstra, and Pomerance [57] as an extension of the ideas in the number-field sieve factoring algorithm by Pollard [278] and Lenstra et al. [232] and refined by Coppersmith [77] and others) is perhaps the most efficient such algorithm in general for large inputs. Although it is difficult to give a rigorous analysis of this algorithm, under reasonable assumptions we can derive a running-time estimate of $L(1/3, n)^{1.902+o(1)}$, where $L(\alpha, n) = e^{(\ln n)^\alpha (\ln \ln n)^{1-\alpha}}$.

The elliptic-curve method due to Lenstra [233] may be more effective for some inputs than the number-field sieve method, since, like Pollard's rho method, it can find a small prime factor p quite quickly. With this method, the time to find p is estimated to be $L(1/2, p)^{\sqrt{2}+o(1)}$.

32 String Matching

Text-editing programs frequently need to find all occurrences of a pattern in the text. Typically, the text is a document being edited, and the pattern searched for is a particular word supplied by the user. Efficient algorithms for this problem—called "string matching"—can greatly aid the responsiveness of the text-editing program. Among their many other applications, string-matching algorithms search for particular patterns in DNA sequences. Internet search engines also use them to find Web pages relevant to queries.

We formalize the string-matching problem as follows. We assume that the text is an array $T[1 \mathinner{\ldotp\ldotp} n]$ of length n and that the pattern is an array $P[1 \mathinner{\ldotp\ldotp} m]$ of length $m \leq n$. We further assume that the elements of P and T are characters drawn from a finite alphabet Σ. For example, we may have $\Sigma = \{0,1\}$ or $\Sigma = \{a, b, \ldots, z\}$. The character arrays P and T are often called *strings* of characters.

Referring to Figure 32.1, we say that pattern P *occurs with shift s* in text T (or, equivalently, that pattern P *occurs beginning at position $s + 1$* in text T) if $0 \leq s \leq n - m$ and $T[s + 1 \mathinner{\ldotp\ldotp} s + m] = P[1 \mathinner{\ldotp\ldotp} m]$ (that is, if $T[s + j] = P[j]$, for $1 \leq j \leq m$). If P occurs with shift s in T, then we call s a *valid shift*; otherwise, we call s an *invalid shift*. The *string-matching problem* is the problem of finding all valid shifts with which a given pattern P occurs in a given text T.

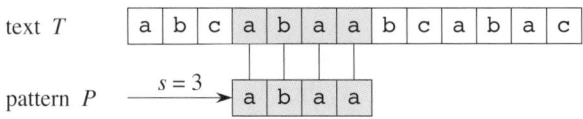

Figure 32.1 An example of the string-matching problem, where we want to find all occurrences of the pattern $P = \mathtt{abaa}$ in the text $T = \mathtt{abcabaabcabac}$. The pattern occurs only once in the text, at shift $s = 3$, which we call a valid shift. A vertical line connects each character of the pattern to its matching character in the text, and all matched characters are shaded.

Algorithm	Preprocessing time	Matching time
Naive	0	$O((n - m + 1)m)$
Rabin-Karp	$\Theta(m)$	$O((n - m + 1)m)$
Finite automaton	$O(m \lvert \Sigma \rvert)$	$\Theta(n)$
Knuth-Morris-Pratt	$\Theta(m)$	$\Theta(n)$

Figure 32.2   The string-matching algorithms in this chapter and their preprocessing and matching times.

Except for the naive brute-force algorithm, which we review in Section 32.1, each string-matching algorithm in this chapter performs some preprocessing based on the pattern and then finds all valid shifts; we call this latter phase "matching." Figure 32.2 shows the preprocessing and matching times for each of the algorithms in this chapter. The total running time of each algorithm is the sum of the preprocessing and matching times. Section 32.2 presents an interesting string-matching algorithm, due to Rabin and Karp. Although the $\Theta((n - m + 1)m)$ worst-case running time of this algorithm is no better than that of the naive method, it works much better on average and in practice. It also generalizes nicely to other pattern-matching problems. Section 32.3 then describes a string-matching algorithm that begins by constructing a finite automaton specifically designed to search for occurrences of the given pattern P in a text. This algorithm takes $O(m \lvert \Sigma \rvert)$ preprocessing time, but only $\Theta(n)$ matching time. Section 32.4 presents the similar, but much cleverer, Knuth-Morris-Pratt (or KMP) algorithm; it has the same $\Theta(n)$ matching time, and it reduces the preprocessing time to only $\Theta(m)$.

Notation and terminology

We denote by Σ^* (read "sigma-star") the set of all finite-length strings formed using characters from the alphabet Σ. In this chapter, we consider only finite-length strings. The zero-length *empty string*, denoted ε, also belongs to Σ^*. The length of a string x is denoted $\lvert x \rvert$. The *concatenation* of two strings x and y, denoted xy, has length $\lvert x \rvert + \lvert y \rvert$ and consists of the characters from x followed by the characters from y.

We say that a string w is a *prefix* of a string x, denoted $w \sqsubset x$, if $x = wy$ for some string $y \in \Sigma^*$. Note that if $w \sqsubset x$, then $\lvert w \rvert \leq \lvert x \rvert$. Similarly, we say that a string w is a *suffix* of a string x, denoted $w \sqsupset x$, if $x = yw$ for some $y \in \Sigma^*$. As with a prefix, $w \sqsupset x$ implies $\lvert w \rvert \leq \lvert x \rvert$. For example, we have $\mathtt{ab} \sqsubset \mathtt{abcca}$ and $\mathtt{cca} \sqsupset \mathtt{abcca}$. The empty string ε is both a suffix and a prefix of every string. For any strings x and y and any character a, we have $x \sqsupset y$ if and only if $xa \sqsupset ya$.

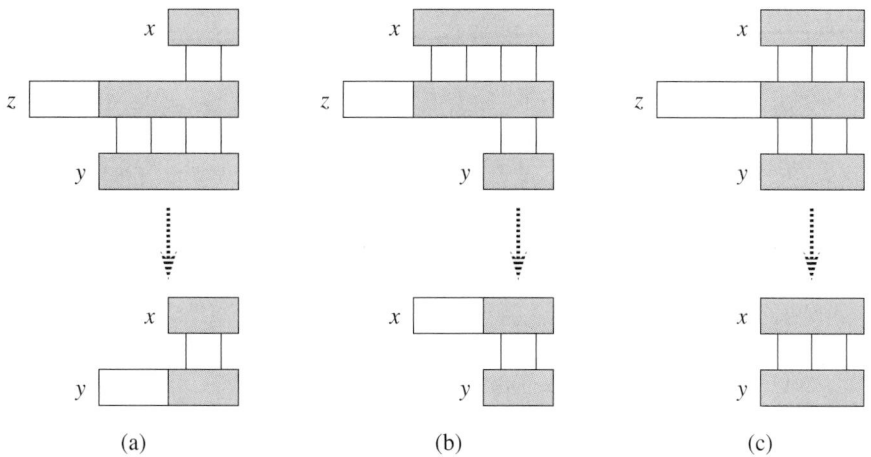

Figure 32.3 A graphical proof of Lemma 32.1. We suppose that $x \sqsupset z$ and $y \sqsupset z$. The three parts of the figure illustrate the three cases of the lemma. Vertical lines connect matching regions (shown shaded) of the strings. **(a)** If $|x| \le |y|$, then $x \sqsupset y$. **(b)** If $|x| \ge |y|$, then $y \sqsupset x$. **(c)** If $|x| = |y|$, then $x = y$.

Also note that $\sqsubset$ and $\sqsupset$ are transitive relations. The following lemma will be useful later.

Lemma 32.1 (Overlapping-suffix lemma)
Suppose that x, y, and z are strings such that $x \sqsupset z$ and $y \sqsupset z$. If $|x| \le |y|$, then $x \sqsupset y$. If $|x| \ge |y|$, then $y \sqsupset x$. If $|x| = |y|$, then $x = y$.

Proof   See Figure 32.3 for a graphical proof.   ∎

For brevity of notation, we denote the k-character prefix $P[1 \mathinner{.\,.} k]$ of the pattern $P[1 \mathinner{.\,.} m]$ by P_k. Thus, $P_0 = \varepsilon$ and $P_m = P = P[1 \mathinner{.\,.} m]$. Similarly, we denote the k-character prefix of the text T by T_k. Using this notation, we can state the string-matching problem as that of finding all shifts s in the range $0 \le s \le n - m$ such that $P \sqsupset T_{s+m}$.

In our pseudocode, we allow two equal-length strings to be compared for equality as a primitive operation. If the strings are compared from left to right and the comparison stops when a mismatch is discovered, we assume that the time taken by such a test is a linear function of the number of matching characters discovered. To be precise, the test "$x == y$" is assumed to take time $\Theta(t + 1)$, where t is the length of the longest string z such that $z \sqsubset x$ and $z \sqsubset y$. (We write $\Theta(t + 1)$ rather than $\Theta(t)$ to handle the case in which $t = 0$; the first characters compared do not match, but it takes a positive amount of time to perform this comparison.)

32.1   The naive string-matching algorithm

The naive algorithm finds all valid shifts using a loop that checks the condition $P[1..m] = T[s + 1..s + m]$ for each of the $n - m + 1$ possible values of s.

NAIVE-STRING-MATCHER(T, P)

1 $n = T.length$
2 $m = P.length$
3 **for** $s = 0$ **to** $n - m$
4   **if** $P[1..m] == T[s + 1..s + m]$
5   print "Pattern occurs with shift" s

Figure 32.4 portrays the naive string-matching procedure as sliding a "template" containing the pattern over the text, noting for which shifts all of the characters on the template equal the corresponding characters in the text. The **for** loop of lines 3–5 considers each possible shift explicitly. The test in line 4 determines whether the current shift is valid; this test implicitly loops to check corresponding character positions until all positions match successfully or a mismatch is found. Line 5 prints out each valid shift s.

Procedure NAIVE-STRING-MATCHER takes time $O((n - m + 1)m)$, and this bound is tight in the worst case. For example, consider the text string a^n (a string of n a's) and the pattern a^m. For each of the $n - m + 1$ possible values of the shift s, the implicit loop on line 4 to compare corresponding characters must execute m times to validate the shift. The worst-case running time is thus $\Theta((n - m + 1)m)$, which is $\Theta(n^2)$ if $m = \lfloor n/2 \rfloor$. Because it requires no preprocessing, NAIVE-STRING-MATCHER's running time equals its matching time.

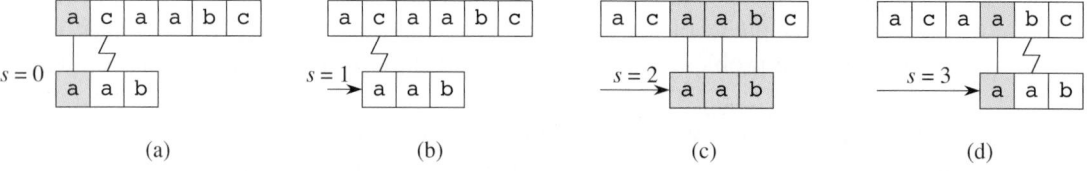

(a)   (b)   (c)   (d)

Figure 32.4 The operation of the naive string matcher for the pattern $P =$ aab and the text $T =$ acaabc. We can imagine the pattern P as a template that we slide next to the text. **(a)–(d)** The four successive alignments tried by the naive string matcher. In each part, vertical lines connect corresponding regions found to match (shown shaded), and a jagged line connects the first mismatched character found, if any. The algorithm finds one occurrence of the pattern, at shift $s = 2$, shown in part (c).

As we shall see, NAIVE-STRING-MATCHER is not an optimal procedure for this problem. Indeed, in this chapter we shall see that the Knuth-Morris-Pratt algorithm is much better in the worst case. The naive string-matcher is inefficient because it entirely ignores information gained about the text for one value of s when it considers other values of s. Such information can be quite valuable, however. For example, if $P = \mathtt{aaab}$ and we find that $s = 0$ is valid, then none of the shifts $1, 2$, or 3 are valid, since $T[4] = \mathtt{b}$. In the following sections, we examine several ways to make effective use of this sort of information.

Exercises

32.1-1
Show the comparisons the naive string matcher makes for the pattern $P = \mathtt{0001}$ in the text $T = \mathtt{000010001010001}$.

32.1-2
Suppose that all characters in the pattern P are different. Show how to accelerate NAIVE-STRING-MATCHER to run in time $O(n)$ on an n-character text T.

32.1-3
Suppose that pattern P and text T are *randomly* chosen strings of length m and n, respectively, from the d-ary alphabet $\Sigma_d = \{0, 1, \ldots, d-1\}$, where $d \geq 2$. Show that the *expected* number of character-to-character comparisons made by the implicit loop in line 4 of the naive algorithm is

$$(n - m + 1)\frac{1 - d^{-m}}{1 - d^{-1}} \leq 2(n - m + 1)$$

over all executions of this loop. (Assume that the naive algorithm stops comparing characters for a given shift once it finds a mismatch or matches the entire pattern.) Thus, for randomly chosen strings, the naive algorithm is quite efficient.

32.1-4
Suppose we allow the pattern P to contain occurrences of a ***gap character*** $\diamond$ that can match an *arbitrary* string of characters (even one of zero length). For example, the pattern $\mathtt{ab}\diamond\mathtt{ba}\diamond\mathtt{c}$ occurs in the text $\mathtt{cabccbacbacab}$ as

```
c ab cc ba cba c ab
  ab  ◇  ba  ◇   c
```

and as

```
c ab ccbac ba    c ab .
  ab   ◇    ba ◇  c
```

Note that the gap character may occur an arbitrary number of times in the pattern but not at all in the text. Give a polynomial-time algorithm to determine whether such a pattern P occurs in a given text T, and analyze the running time of your algorithm.

32.2   The Rabin-Karp algorithm

Rabin and Karp proposed a string-matching algorithm that performs well in practice and that also generalizes to other algorithms for related problems, such as two-dimensional pattern matching. The Rabin-Karp algorithm uses $\Theta(m)$ preprocessing time, and its worst-case running time is $\Theta((n-m+1)m)$. Based on certain assumptions, however, its average-case running time is better.

This algorithm makes use of elementary number-theoretic notions such as the equivalence of two numbers modulo a third number. You might want to refer to Section 31.1 for the relevant definitions.

For expository purposes, let us assume that $\Sigma = \{0, 1, 2, \ldots, 9\}$, so that each character is a decimal digit. (In the general case, we can assume that each character is a digit in radix-d notation, where $d = |\Sigma|$.) We can then view a string of k consecutive characters as representing a length-k decimal number. The character string 31415 thus corresponds to the decimal number $31{,}415$. Because we interpret the input characters as both graphical symbols and digits, we find it convenient in this section to denote them as we would digits, in our standard text font.

Given a pattern $P[1 \mathrel{..} m]$, let p denote its corresponding decimal value. In a similar manner, given a text $T[1 \mathrel{..} n]$, let t_s denote the decimal value of the length-m substring $T[s + 1 \mathrel{..} s + m]$, for $s = 0, 1, \ldots, n - m$. Certainly, $t_s = p$ if and only if $T[s + 1 \mathrel{..} s + m] = P[1 \mathrel{..} m]$; thus, s is a valid shift if and only if $t_s = p$. If we could compute p in time $\Theta(m)$ and all the t_s values in a total of $\Theta(n - m + 1)$ time,[1] then we could determine all valid shifts s in time $\Theta(m) + \Theta(n - m + 1) = \Theta(n)$ by comparing p with each of the t_s values. (For the moment, let's not worry about the possibility that p and the t_s values might be very large numbers.)

We can compute p in time $\Theta(m)$ using Horner's rule (see Section 30.1):

$$p = P[m] + 10\,(P[m - 1] + 10(P[m - 2] + \cdots + 10(P[2] + 10P[1])\cdots))\,.$$

Similarly, we can compute t_0 from $T[1 \mathrel{..} m]$ in time $\Theta(m)$.

---

[1] We write $\Theta(n - m + 1)$ instead of $\Theta(n - m)$ because s takes on $n - m + 1$ different values. The "$+1$" is significant in an asymptotic sense because when $m = n$, computing the lone t_s value takes $\Theta(1)$ time, not $\Theta(0)$ time.

To compute the remaining values $t_1, t_2, \ldots, t_{n-m}$ in time $\Theta(n - m)$, we observe that we can compute t_{s+1} from t_s in constant time, since

$$t_{s+1} = 10(t_s - 10^{m-1} T[s + 1]) + T[s + m + 1] \, . \tag{32.1}$$

Subtracting $10^{m-1} T[s + 1]$ removes the high-order digit from t_s, multiplying the result by 10 shifts the number left by one digit position, and adding $T[s + m + 1]$ brings in the appropriate low-order digit. For example, if $m = 5$ and $t_s = 31415$, then we wish to remove the high-order digit $T[s + 1] = 3$ and bring in the new low-order digit (suppose it is $T[s + 5 + 1] = 2$) to obtain

$$
\begin{aligned}
t_{s+1} &= 10(31415 - 10000 \cdot 3) + 2 \\
        &= 14152 \, .
\end{aligned}
$$

If we precompute the constant 10^{m-1} (which we can do in time $O(\lg m)$ using the techniques of Section 31.6, although for this application a straightforward $O(m)$-time method suffices), then each execution of equation (32.1) takes a constant number of arithmetic operations. Thus, we can compute p in time $\Theta(m)$, and we can compute all of $t_0, t_1, \ldots, t_{n-m}$ in time $\Theta(n - m + 1)$. Therefore, we can find all occurrences of the pattern $P[1 \ldots m]$ in the text $T[1 \ldots n]$ with $\Theta(m)$ preprocessing time and $\Theta(n - m + 1)$ matching time.

Until now, we have intentionally overlooked one problem: p and t_s may be too large to work with conveniently. If P contains m characters, then we cannot reasonably assume that each arithmetic operation on p (which is m digits long) takes "constant time." Fortunately, we can solve this problem easily, as Figure 32.5 shows: compute p and the t_s values modulo a suitable modulus q. We can compute p modulo q in $\Theta(m)$ time and all the t_s values modulo q in $\Theta(n - m + 1)$ time. If we choose the modulus q as a prime such that $10q$ just fits within one computer word, then we can perform all the necessary computations with single-precision arithmetic. In general, with a d-ary alphabet $\{0, 1, \ldots, d - 1\}$, we choose q so that dq fits within a computer word and adjust the recurrence equation (32.1) to work modulo q, so that it becomes

$$t_{s+1} = (d(t_s - T[s + 1]h) + T[s + m + 1]) \bmod q \, , \tag{32.2}$$

where $h \equiv d^{m-1} \pmod{q}$ is the value of the digit "1" in the high-order position of an m-digit text window.

The solution of working modulo q is not perfect, however: $t_s \equiv p \pmod{q}$ does not imply that $t_s = p$. On the other hand, if $t_s \not\equiv p \pmod{q}$, then we definitely have that $t_s \ne p$, so that shift s is invalid. We can thus use the test $t_s \equiv p \pmod{q}$ as a fast heuristic test to rule out invalid shifts s. Any shift s for which $t_s \equiv p \pmod{q}$ must be tested further to see whether s is really valid or we just have a *spurious hit*. This additional test explicitly checks the condition

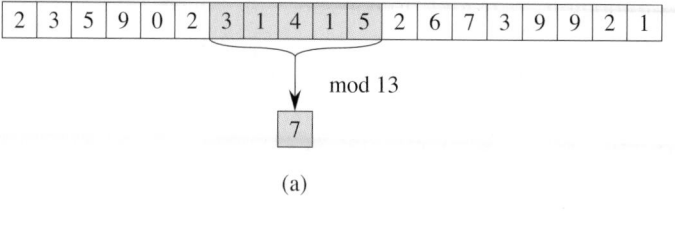

(a)

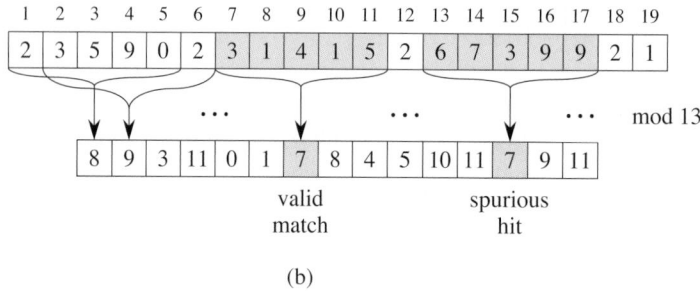

(b)

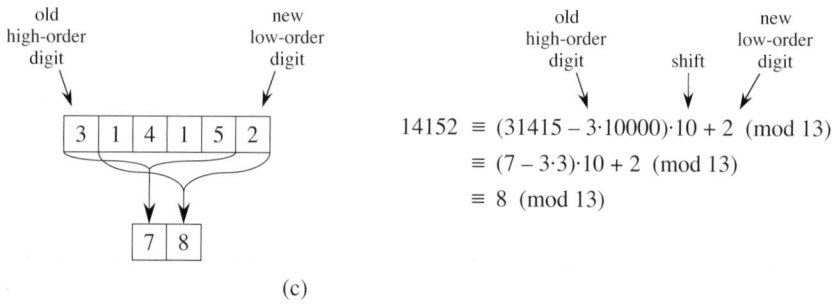

(c)

Figure 32.5 The Rabin-Karp algorithm. Each character is a decimal digit, and we compute values modulo 13. **(a)** A text string. A window of length 5 is shown shaded. The numerical value of the shaded number, computed modulo 13, yields the value 7. **(b)** The same text string with values computed modulo 13 for each possible position of a length-5 window. Assuming the pattern $P = 31415$, we look for windows whose value modulo 13 is 7, since $31415 \equiv 7 \pmod{13}$. The algorithm finds two such windows, shown shaded in the figure. The first, beginning at text position 7, is indeed an occurrence of the pattern, while the second, beginning at text position 13, is a spurious hit. **(c)** How to compute the value for a window in constant time, given the value for the previous window. The first window has value 31415. Dropping the high-order digit 3, shifting left (multiplying by 10), and then adding in the low-order digit 2 gives us the new value 14152. Because all computations are performed modulo 13, the value for the first window is 7, and the value for the new window is 8.

$P[1 . . m] = T[s + 1 . . s + m]$. If q is large enough, then we hope that spurious hits occur infrequently enough that the cost of the extra checking is low.

The following procedure makes these ideas precise. The inputs to the procedure are the text T, the pattern P, the radix d to use (which is typically taken to be $|\Sigma|$), and the prime q to use.

RABIN-KARP-MATCHER(T, P, d, q)

```
 1  n = T.length
 2  m = P.length
 3  h = d^{m-1} mod q
 4  p = 0
 5  t_0 = 0
 6  for i = 1 to m                  // preprocessing
 7      p = (dp + P[i]) mod q
 8      t_0 = (dt_0 + T[i]) mod q
 9  for s = 0 to n - m              // matching
10      if p == t_s
11          if P[1 . . m] == T[s + 1 . . s + m]
12              print "Pattern occurs with shift" s
13      if s < n - m
14          t_{s+1} = (d(t_s - T[s + 1]h) + T[s + m + 1]) mod q
```

The procedure RABIN-KARP-MATCHER works as follows. All characters are interpreted as radix-d digits. The subscripts on t are provided only for clarity; the program works correctly if all the subscripts are dropped. Line 3 initializes h to the value of the high-order digit position of an m-digit window. Lines 4–8 compute p as the value of $P[1 . . m] \bmod q$ and t_0 as the value of $T[1 . . m] \bmod q$. The **for** loop of lines 9–14 iterates through all possible shifts s, maintaining the following invariant:

> Whenever line 10 is executed, $t_s = T[s + 1 . . s + m] \bmod q$.

If $p = t_s$ in line 10 (a "hit"), then line 11 checks to see whether $P[1 . . m] = T[s + 1 . . s + m]$ in order to rule out the possibility of a spurious hit. Line 12 prints out any valid shifts that are found. If $s < n - m$ (checked in line 13), then the **for** loop will execute at least one more time, and so line 14 first executes to ensure that the loop invariant holds when we get back to line 10. Line 14 computes the value of $t_{s+1} \bmod q$ from the value of $t_s \bmod q$ in constant time using equation (32.2) directly.

RABIN-KARP-MATCHER takes $\Theta(m)$ preprocessing time, and its matching time is $\Theta((n - m + 1)m)$ in the worst case, since (like the naive string-matching algorithm) the Rabin-Karp algorithm explicitly verifies every valid shift. If $P = \mathsf{a}^m$

and $T = \text{a}^n$, then verifying takes time $\Theta((n-m+1)m)$, since each of the $n-m+1$ possible shifts is valid.

In many applications, we expect few valid shifts—perhaps some constant c of them. In such applications, the expected matching time of the algorithm is only $O((n-m+1)+cm) = O(n+m)$, plus the time required to process spurious hits. We can base a heuristic analysis on the assumption that reducing values modulo q acts like a random mapping from Σ^* to $\mathbb{Z}_q$. (See the discussion on the use of division for hashing in Section 11.3.1. It is difficult to formalize and prove such an assumption, although one viable approach is to assume that q is chosen randomly from integers of the appropriate size. We shall not pursue this formalization here.) We can then expect that the number of spurious hits is $O(n/q)$, since we can estimate the chance that an arbitrary t_s will be equivalent to p, modulo q, as $1/q$. Since there are $O(n)$ positions at which the test of line 10 fails and we spend $O(m)$ time for each hit, the expected matching time taken by the Rabin-Karp algorithm is

$$O(n) + O(m(v + n/q)),$$

where v is the number of valid shifts. This running time is $O(n)$ if $v = O(1)$ and we choose $q \geq m$. That is, if the expected number of valid shifts is small $(O(1))$ and we choose the prime q to be larger than the length of the pattern, then we can expect the Rabin-Karp procedure to use only $O(n+m)$ matching time. Since $m \leq n$, this expected matching time is $O(n)$.

Exercises

32.2-1
Working modulo $q = 11$, how many spurious hits does the Rabin-Karp matcher encounter in the text $T = 3141592653589793$ when looking for the pattern $P = 26$?

32.2-2
How would you extend the Rabin-Karp method to the problem of searching a text string for an occurrence of any one of a given set of k patterns? Start by assuming that all k patterns have the same length. Then generalize your solution to allow the patterns to have different lengths.

32.2-3
Show how to extend the Rabin-Karp method to handle the problem of looking for a given $m \times m$ pattern in an $n \times n$ array of characters. (The pattern may be shifted vertically and horizontally, but it may not be rotated.)

32.2-4

Alice has a copy of a long n-bit file $A = \langle a_{n-1}, a_{n-2}, \ldots, a_0 \rangle$, and Bob similarly has an n-bit file $B = \langle b_{n-1}, b_{n-2}, \ldots, b_0 \rangle$. Alice and Bob wish to know if their files are identical. To avoid transmitting all of A or B, they use the following fast probabilistic check. Together, they select a prime $q > 1000n$ and randomly select an integer x from $\{0, 1, \ldots, q - 1\}$. Then, Alice evaluates

$$A(x) = \left(\sum_{i=0}^{n-1} a_i x^i \right) \bmod q$$

and Bob similarly evaluates $B(x)$. Prove that if $A \neq B$, there is at most one chance in 1000 that $A(x) = B(x)$, whereas if the two files are the same, $A(x)$ is necessarily the same as $B(x)$. (*Hint:* See Exercise 31.4-4.)

32.3   String matching with finite automata

Many string-matching algorithms build a finite automaton—a simple machine for processing information—that scans the text string T for all occurrences of the pattern P. This section presents a method for building such an automaton. These string-matching automata are very efficient: they examine each text character *exactly once*, taking constant time per text character. The matching time used—after preprocessing the pattern to build the automaton—is therefore $\Theta(n)$. The time to build the automaton, however, can be large if Σ is large. Section 32.4 describes a clever way around this problem.

We begin this section with the definition of a finite automaton. We then examine a special string-matching automaton and show how to use it to find occurrences of a pattern in a text. Finally, we shall show how to construct the string-matching automaton for a given input pattern.

Finite automata

A *finite automaton M*, illustrated in Figure 32.6, is a 5-tuple $(Q, q_0, A, \Sigma, \delta)$, where

* Q is a finite set of **states**,

* $q_0 \in Q$ is the **start state**,

* $A \subseteq Q$ is a distinguished set of **accepting states**,

* Σ is a finite **input alphabet**,

* δ is a function from $Q \times \Sigma$ into Q, called the **transition function** of M.

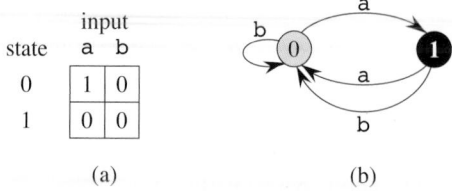

<table>
<tr><td></td><td colspan="2">input</td></tr>
<tr><td>state</td><td>a</td><td>b</td></tr>
<tr><td>0</td><td>1</td><td>0</td></tr>
<tr><td>1</td><td>0</td><td>0</td></tr>
</table>

state	input a	input b
0	1	0
1	0	0

(a)   (b)

Figure 32.6 A simple two-state finite automaton with state set $Q = \{0, 1\}$, start state $q_0 = 0$, and input alphabet $\Sigma = \{a, b\}$. **(a)** A tabular representation of the transition function δ. **(b)** An equivalent state-transition diagram. State 1, shown blackened, is the only accepting state. Directed edges represent transitions. For example, the edge from state 1 to state 0 labeled b indicates that $\delta(1, b) = 0$. This automaton accepts those strings that end in an odd number of a's. More precisely, it accepts a string x if and only if $x = yz$, where $y = \varepsilon$ or y ends with a b, and $z = a^k$, where k is odd. For example, on input abaaa, including the start state, this automaton enters the sequence of states $\langle 0, 1, 0, 1, 0, 1 \rangle$, and so it accepts this input. For input abbaa, it enters the sequence of states $\langle 0, 1, 0, 0, 1, 0 \rangle$, and so it rejects this input.

The finite automaton begins in state q_0 and reads the characters of its input string one at a time. If the automaton is in state q and reads input character a, it moves ("makes a transition") from state q to state $\delta(q, a)$. Whenever its current state q is a member of A, the machine M has **accepted** the string read so far. An input that is not accepted is **rejected**.

A finite automaton M induces a function ϕ, called the **final-state function**, from Σ^* to Q such that $\phi(w)$ is the state M ends up in after scanning the string w. Thus, M accepts a string w if and only if $\phi(w) \in A$. We define the function ϕ recursively, using the transition function:

$$\phi(\varepsilon) = q_0 ,$$
$$\phi(wa) = \delta(\phi(w), a) \quad \text{for } w \in \Sigma^*, a \in \Sigma .$$

String-matching automata

For a given pattern P, we construct a string-matching automaton in a preprocessing step before using it to search the text string. Figure 32.7 illustrates the automaton for the pattern $P = $ ababaca. From now on, we shall assume that P is a given fixed pattern string; for brevity, we shall not indicate the dependence upon P in our notation.

In order to specify the string-matching automaton corresponding to a given pattern $P[1 .. m]$, we first define an auxiliary function σ, called the **suffix function** corresponding to P. The function σ maps Σ^* to $\{0, 1, \ldots, m\}$ such that $\sigma(x)$ is the length of the longest prefix of P that is also a suffix of x:

$$\sigma(x) = \max \{k : P_k \sqsupset x\} . \tag{32.3}$$

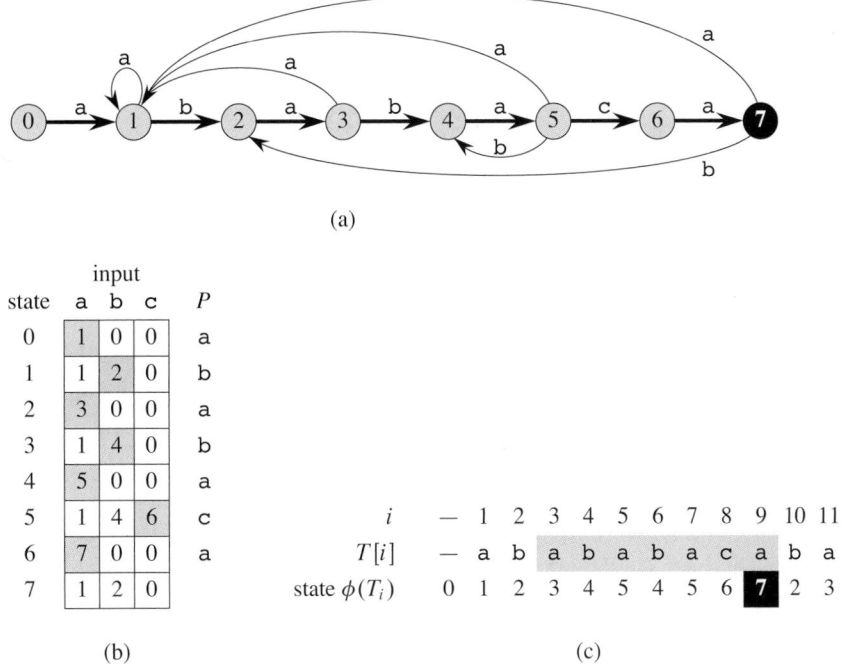

Figure 32.7 **(a)** A state-transition diagram for the string-matching automaton that accepts all strings ending in the string ababaca. State 0 is the start state, and state 7 (shown blackened) is the only accepting state. The transition function δ is defined by equation (32.4), and a directed edge from state i to state j labeled a represents $\delta(i, a) = j$. The right-going edges forming the "spine" of the automaton, shown heavy in the figure, correspond to successful matches between pattern and input characters. Except for the edges from state 7 to states 1 and 2, the left-going edges correspond to mismatches. Some edges corresponding to mismatches are omitted; by convention, if a state i has no outgoing edge labeled a for some $a \in \Sigma$, then $\delta(i, a) = 0$. **(b)** The corresponding transition function δ, and the pattern string $P = $ ababaca. The entries corresponding to successful matches between pattern and input characters are shown shaded. **(c)** The operation of the automaton on the text $T = $ abababacaba. Under each text character $T[i]$ appears the state $\phi(T_i)$ that the automaton is in after processing the prefix T_i. The automaton finds one occurrence of the pattern, ending in position 9.

The suffix function σ is well defined since the empty string $P_0 = \varepsilon$ is a suffix of every string. As examples, for the pattern $P = $ ab, we have $\sigma(\varepsilon) = 0$, $\sigma(\text{ccaca}) = 1$, and $\sigma(\text{ccab}) = 2$. For a pattern P of length m, we have $\sigma(x) = m$ if and only if $P \sqsupset x$. From the definition of the suffix function, $x \sqsupset y$ implies $\sigma(x) \leq \sigma(y)$.

We define the string-matching automaton that corresponds to a given pattern $P[1 .. m]$ as follows:

- The state set Q is $\{0, 1, \ldots, m\}$. The start state q_0 is state 0, and state m is the only accepting state.

- The transition function δ is defined by the following equation, for any state q and character a:

$$\delta(q, a) = \sigma(P_q a) \,. \tag{32.4}$$

We define $\delta(q, a) = \sigma(P_q a)$ because we want to keep track of the longest prefix of the pattern P that has matched the text string T so far. We consider the most recently read characters of T. In order for a substring of T—let's say the substring ending at $T[i]$—to match some prefix P_j of P, this prefix P_j must be a suffix of T_i. Suppose that $q = \phi(T_i)$, so that after reading T_i, the automaton is in state q. We design the transition function δ so that this state number, q, tells us the length of the longest prefix of P that matches a suffix of T_i. That is, in state q, $P_q \sqsupset T_i$ and $q = \sigma(T_i)$. (Whenever $q = m$, all m characters of P match a suffix of T_i, and so we have found a match.) Thus, since $\phi(T_i)$ and $\sigma(T_i)$ both equal q, we shall see (in Theorem 32.4, below) that the automaton maintains the following invariant:

$$\phi(T_i) = \sigma(T_i) \,. \tag{32.5}$$

If the automaton is in state q and reads the next character $T[i + 1] = a$, then we want the transition to lead to the state corresponding to the longest prefix of P that is a suffix of $T_i a$, and that state is $\sigma(T_i a)$. Because P_q is the longest prefix of P that is a suffix of T_i, the longest prefix of P that is a suffix of $T_i a$ is not only $\sigma(T_i a)$, but also $\sigma(P_q a)$. (Lemma 32.3, on page 1000, proves that $\sigma(T_i a) = \sigma(P_q a)$.) Thus, when the automaton is in state q, we want the transition function on character a to take the automaton to state $\sigma(P_q a)$.

There are two cases to consider. In the first case, $a = P[q + 1]$, so that the character a continues to match the pattern; in this case, because $\delta(q, a) = q + 1$, the transition continues to go along the "spine" of the automaton (the heavy edges in Figure 32.7). In the second case, $a \neq P[q + 1]$, so that a does not continue to match the pattern. Here, we must find a smaller prefix of P that is also a suffix of T_i. Because the preprocessing step matches the pattern against itself when creating the string-matching automaton, the transition function quickly identifies the longest such smaller prefix of P.

Let's look at an example. The string-matching automaton of Figure 32.7 has $\delta(5, \text{c}) = 6$, illustrating the first case, in which the match continues. To illustrate the second case, observe that the automaton of Figure 32.7 has $\delta(5, \text{b}) = 4$. We make this transition because if the automaton reads a b in state $q = 5$, then $P_q \text{b} = \text{ababab}$, and the longest prefix of P that is also a suffix of ababab is $P_4 = \text{abab}$.

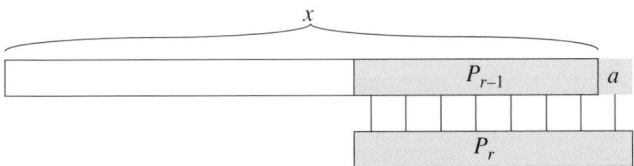

Figure 32.8 An illustration for the proof of Lemma 32.2. The figure shows that $r \leq \sigma(x) + 1$, where $r = \sigma(xa)$.

To clarify the operation of a string-matching automaton, we now give a simple, efficient program for simulating the behavior of such an automaton (represented by its transition function δ) in finding occurrences of a pattern P of length m in an input text $T[1 \mathinner{.\,.} n]$. As for any string-matching automaton for a pattern of length m, the state set Q is $\{0, 1, \ldots, m\}$, the start state is 0, and the only accepting state is state m.

FINITE-AUTOMATON-MATCHER(T, δ, m)

```
1  n = T.length
2  q = 0
3  for i = 1 to n
4      q = δ(q, T[i])
5      if q == m
6          print "Pattern occurs with shift" i − m
```

From the simple loop structure of FINITE-AUTOMATON-MATCHER, we can easily see that its matching time on a text string of length n is $\Theta(n)$. This matching time, however, does not include the preprocessing time required to compute the transition function δ. We address this problem later, after first proving that the procedure FINITE-AUTOMATON-MATCHER operates correctly.

Consider how the automaton operates on an input text $T[1 \mathinner{.\,.} n]$. We shall prove that the automaton is in state $\sigma(T_i)$ after scanning character $T[i]$. Since $\sigma(T_i) = m$ if and only if $P \sqsupset T_i$, the machine is in the accepting state m if and only if it has just scanned the pattern P. To prove this result, we make use of the following two lemmas about the suffix function σ.

Lemma 32.2 (Suffix-function inequality)
For any string x and character a, we have $\sigma(xa) \leq \sigma(x) + 1$.

Proof Referring to Figure 32.8, let $r = \sigma(xa)$. If $r = 0$, then the conclusion $\sigma(xa) = r \leq \sigma(x) + 1$ is trivially satisfied, by the nonnegativity of $\sigma(x)$. Now assume that $r > 0$. Then, $P_r \sqsupset xa$, by the definition of σ. Thus, $P_{r-1} \sqsupset x$, by

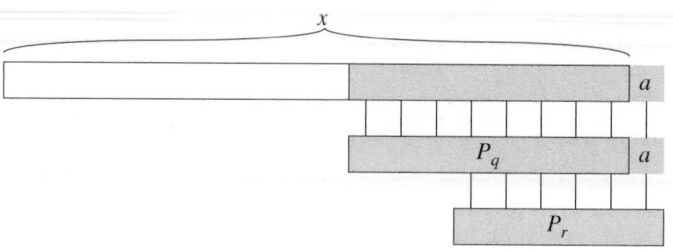

Figure 32.9 An illustration for the proof of Lemma 32.3. The figure shows that $r = \sigma(P_q a)$, where $q = \sigma(x)$ and $r = \sigma(xa)$.

dropping the a from the end of P_r and from the end of xa. Therefore, $r-1 \leq \sigma(x)$, since $\sigma(x)$ is the largest k such that $P_k \sqsupset x$, and thus $\sigma(xa) = r \leq \sigma(x) + 1$. ∎

Lemma 32.3 (Suffix-function recursion lemma)
For any string x and character a, if $q = \sigma(x)$, then $\sigma(xa) = \sigma(P_q a)$.

Proof From the definition of σ, we have $P_q \sqsupset x$. As Figure 32.9 shows, we also have $P_q a \sqsupset xa$. If we let $r = \sigma(xa)$, then $P_r \sqsupset xa$ and, by Lemma 32.2, $r \leq q + 1$. Thus, we have $|P_r| = r \leq q + 1 = |P_q a|$. Since $P_q a \sqsupset xa$, $P_r \sqsupset xa$, and $|P_r| \leq |P_q a|$, Lemma 32.1 implies that $P_r \sqsupset P_q a$. Therefore, $r \leq \sigma(P_q a)$, that is, $\sigma(xa) \leq \sigma(P_q a)$. But we also have $\sigma(P_q a) \leq \sigma(xa)$, since $P_q a \sqsupset xa$. Thus, $\sigma(xa) = \sigma(P_q a)$. ∎

We are now ready to prove our main theorem characterizing the behavior of a string-matching automaton on a given input text. As noted above, this theorem shows that the automaton is merely keeping track, at each step, of the longest prefix of the pattern that is a suffix of what has been read so far. In other words, the automaton maintains the invariant (32.5).

Theorem 32.4
If ϕ is the final-state function of a string-matching automaton for a given pattern P and $T[1 \mathinner{.\,.} n]$ is an input text for the automaton, then

$$\phi(T_i) = \sigma(T_i)$$

for $i = 0, 1, \ldots, n$.

Proof The proof is by induction on i. For $i = 0$, the theorem is trivially true, since $T_0 = \varepsilon$. Thus, $\phi(T_0) = 0 = \sigma(T_0)$.

Now, we assume that $\phi(T_i) = \sigma(T_i)$ and prove that $\phi(T_{i+1}) = \sigma(T_{i+1})$. Let q denote $\phi(T_i)$, and let a denote $T[i+1]$. Then,

$$
\begin{aligned}
\phi(T_{i+1}) &= \phi(T_i a) && \text{(by the definitions of } T_{i+1} \text{ and } a) \\
&= \delta(\phi(T_i), a) && \text{(by the definition of } \phi) \\
&= \delta(q, a) && \text{(by the definition of } q) \\
&= \sigma(P_q a) && \text{(by the definition (32.4) of } \delta) \\
&= \sigma(T_i a) && \text{(by Lemma 32.3 and induction)} \\
&= \sigma(T_{i+1}) && \text{(by the definition of } T_{i+1}) \ .
\end{aligned}
$$

$\blacksquare$

By Theorem 32.4, if the machine enters state q on line 4, then q is the largest value such that $P_q \sqsupseteq T_i$. Thus, we have $q = m$ on line 5 if and only if the machine has just scanned an occurrence of the pattern P. We conclude that FINITE-AUTOMATON-MATCHER operates correctly.

Computing the transition function

The following procedure computes the transition function δ from a given pattern $P[1..m]$.

COMPUTE-TRANSITION-FUNCTION(P, Σ)

```
1   m = P.length
2   for q = 0 to m
3       for each character a ∈ Σ
4           k = min(m + 1, q + 2)
5           repeat
6               k = k - 1
7           until P_k ⊐ P_q a
8           δ(q, a) = k
9   return δ
```

This procedure computes $\delta(q, a)$ in a straightforward manner according to its definition in equation (32.4). The nested loops beginning on lines 2 and 3 consider all states q and all characters a, and lines 4–8 set $\delta(q, a)$ to be the largest k such that $P_k \sqsupseteq P_q a$. The code starts with the largest conceivable value of k, which is $\min(m, q + 1)$. It then decreases k until $P_k \sqsupseteq P_q a$, which must eventually occur, since $P_0 = \varepsilon$ is a suffix of every string.

The running time of COMPUTE-TRANSITION-FUNCTION is $O(m^3 |\Sigma|)$, because the outer loops contribute a factor of $m |\Sigma|$, the inner **repeat** loop can run at most $m + 1$ times, and the test $P_k \sqsupseteq P_q a$ on line 7 can require comparing up

to m characters. Much faster procedures exist; by utilizing some cleverly computed information about the pattern P (see Exercise 32.4-8), we can improve the time required to compute δ from P to $O(m\,|\Sigma|)$. With this improved procedure for computing δ, we can find all occurrences of a length-m pattern in a length-n text over an alphabet Σ with $O(m\,|\Sigma|)$ preprocessing time and $\Theta(n)$ matching time.

Exercises

32.3-1
Construct the string-matching automaton for the pattern $P = \text{aabab}$ and illustrate its operation on the text string $T = \text{aaababaabaabababaab}$.

32.3-2
Draw a state-transition diagram for a string-matching automaton for the pattern ababbabbababbababbabb over the alphabet $\Sigma = \{\text{a}, \text{b}\}$.

32.3-3
We call a pattern P *nonoverlappable* if $P_k \sqsupset P_q$ implies $k = 0$ or $k = q$. Describe the state-transition diagram of the string-matching automaton for a nonoverlappable pattern.

32.3-4 ★
Given two patterns P and P', describe how to construct a finite automaton that determines all occurrences of *either* pattern. Try to minimize the number of states in your automaton.

32.3-5
Given a pattern P containing gap characters (see Exercise 32.1-4), show how to build a finite automaton that can find an occurrence of P in a text T in $O(n)$ matching time, where $n = |T|$.

★ 32.4 The Knuth-Morris-Pratt algorithm

We now present a linear-time string-matching algorithm due to Knuth, Morris, and Pratt. This algorithm avoids computing the transition function δ altogether, and its matching time is $\Theta(n)$ using just an auxiliary function π, which we precompute from the pattern in time $\Theta(m)$ and store in an array $\pi[1 \mathinner{.\,.} m]$. The array π allows us to compute the transition function δ efficiently (in an amortized sense) "on the fly" as needed. Loosely speaking, for any state $q = 0, 1, \ldots, m$ and any character

$a \in \Sigma$, the value $\pi[q]$ contains the information we need to compute $\delta(q, a)$ but that does not depend on a. Since the array π has only m entries, whereas δ has $\Theta(m |\Sigma|)$ entries, we save a factor of $|\Sigma|$ in the preprocessing time by computing π rather than δ.

The prefix function for a pattern

The prefix function π for a pattern encapsulates knowledge about how the pattern matches against shifts of itself. We can take advantage of this information to avoid testing useless shifts in the naive pattern-matching algorithm and to avoid precomputing the full transition function δ for a string-matching automaton.

Consider the operation of the naive string matcher. Figure 32.10(a) shows a particular shift s of a template containing the pattern $P = \mathtt{ababaca}$ against a text T. For this example, $q = 5$ of the characters have matched successfully, but the 6th pattern character fails to match the corresponding text character. The information that q characters have matched successfully determines the corresponding text characters. Knowing these q text characters allows us to determine immediately that certain shifts are invalid. In the example of the figure, the shift $s + 1$ is necessarily invalid, since the first pattern character (a) would be aligned with a text character that we know does not match the first pattern character, but does match the second pattern character (b). The shift $s' = s + 2$ shown in part (b) of the figure, however, aligns the first three pattern characters with three text characters that must necessarily match. In general, it is useful to know the answer to the following question:

> Given that pattern characters $P[1 .. q]$ match text characters $T[s+1 .. s+q]$, what is the least shift $s' > s$ such that for some $k < q$,
>
> $$P[1 .. k] = T[s' + 1 .. s' + k], \tag{32.6}$$
>
> where $s' + k = s + q$?

In other words, knowing that $P_q \sqsupset T_{s+q}$, we want the longest proper prefix P_k of P_q that is also a suffix of T_{s+q}. (Since $s' + k = s + q$, if we are given s and q, then finding the smallest shift s' is tantamount to finding the longest prefix length k.) We add the difference $q - k$ in the lengths of these prefixes of P to the shift s to arrive at our new shift s', so that $s' = s + (q - k)$. In the best case, $k = 0$, so that $s' = s + q$, and we immediately rule out shifts $s + 1, s + 2, \ldots, s + q - 1$. In any case, at the new shift s' we don't need to compare the first k characters of P with the corresponding characters of T, since equation (32.6) guarantees that they match.

We can precompute the necessary information by comparing the pattern against itself, as Figure 32.10(c) demonstrates. Since $T[s' + 1 .. s' + k]$ is part of the

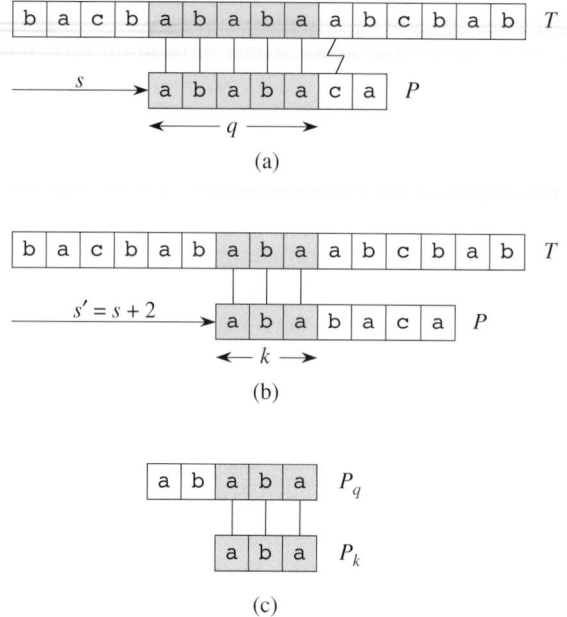

Figure 32.10 The prefix function π. **(a)** The pattern $P = \text{ababaca}$ aligns with a text T so that the first $q = 5$ characters match. Matching characters, shown shaded, are connected by vertical lines. **(b)** Using only our knowledge of the 5 matched characters, we can deduce that a shift of $s + 1$ is invalid, but that a shift of $s' = s+2$ is consistent with everything we know about the text and therefore is potentially valid. **(c)** We can precompute useful information for such deductions by comparing the pattern with itself. Here, we see that the longest prefix of P that is also a proper suffix of P_5 is P_3. We represent this precomputed information in the array π, so that $\pi[5] = 3$. Given that q characters have matched successfully at shift s, the next potentially valid shift is at $s' = s + (q - \pi[q])$ as shown in part (b).

known portion of the text, it is a suffix of the string P_q. Therefore, we can interpret equation (32.6) as asking for the greatest $k < q$ such that $P_k \sqsupset P_q$. Then, the new shift $s' = s + (q - k)$ is the next potentially valid shift. We will find it convenient to store, for each value of q, the number k of matching characters at the new shift s', rather than storing, say, $s' - s$.

We formalize the information that we precompute as follows. Given a pattern $P[1 \mathinner{.\,.} m]$, the ***prefix function*** for the pattern P is the function $\pi : \{1, 2, \ldots, m\} \rightarrow \{0, 1, \ldots, m - 1\}$ such that

$$\pi[q] = \max \{k : k < q \text{ and } P_k \sqsupset P_q\} \; .$$

That is, $\pi[q]$ is the length of the longest prefix of P that is a proper suffix of P_q. Figure 32.11(a) gives the complete prefix function π for the pattern ababaca.

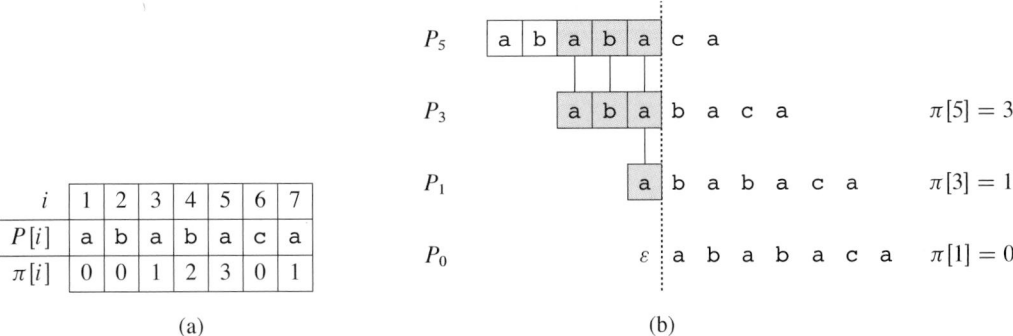

i	1	2	3	4	5	6	7
$P[i]$	a	b	a	b	a	c	a
$\pi[i]$	0	0	1	2	3	0	1

(a)   (b)

Figure 32.11 An illustration of Lemma 32.5 for the pattern $P = \mathtt{ababaca}$ and $q = 5$. **(a)** The π function for the given pattern. Since $\pi[5] = 3$, $\pi[3] = 1$, and $\pi[1] = 0$, by iterating π we obtain $\pi^*[5] = \{3, 1, 0\}$. **(b)** We slide the template containing the pattern P to the right and note when some prefix P_k of P matches up with some proper suffix of P_5; we get matches when $k = 3, 1$, and 0. In the figure, the first row gives P, and the dotted vertical line is drawn just after P_5. Successive rows show all the shifts of P that cause some prefix P_k of P to match some suffix of P_5. Successfully matched characters are shown shaded. Vertical lines connect aligned matching characters. Thus, $\{k : k < 5 \text{ and } P_k \sqsupset P_5\} = \{3, 1, 0\}$. Lemma 32.5 claims that $\pi^*[q] = \{k : k < q \text{ and } P_k \sqsupset P_q\}$ for all q.

The pseudocode below gives the Knuth-Morris-Pratt matching algorithm as the procedure KMP-MATCHER. For the most part, the procedure follows from FINITE-AUTOMATON-MATCHER, as we shall see. KMP-MATCHER calls the auxiliary procedure COMPUTE-PREFIX-FUNCTION to compute π.

KMP-MATCHER(T, P)

```
 1  n = T.length
 2  m = P.length
 3  π = COMPUTE-PREFIX-FUNCTION(P)
 4  q = 0                              // number of characters matched
 5  for i = 1 to n                     // scan the text from left to right
 6      while q > 0 and P[q + 1] ≠ T[i]
 7          q = π[q]                    // next character does not match
 8      if P[q + 1] == T[i]
 9          q = q + 1                   // next character matches
10      if q == m                       // is all of P matched?
11          print "Pattern occurs with shift" i − m
12          q = π[q]                     // look for the next match
```

COMPUTE-PREFIX-FUNCTION(P)

```
 1  m = P.length
 2  let π[1..m] be a new array
 3  π[1] = 0
 4  k = 0
 5  for q = 2 to m
 6      while k > 0 and P[k + 1] ≠ P[q]
 7          k = π[k]
 8      if P[k + 1] == P[q]
 9          k = k + 1
10      π[q] = k
11  return π
```

These two procedures have much in common, because both match a string against the pattern P: KMP-MATCHER matches the text T against P, and COMPUTE-PREFIX-FUNCTION matches P against itself.

We begin with an analysis of the running times of these procedures. Proving these procedures correct will be more complicated.

Running-time analysis

The running time of COMPUTE-PREFIX-FUNCTION is $\Theta(m)$, which we show by using the aggregate method of amortized analysis (see Section 17.1). The only tricky part is showing that the **while** loop of lines 6–7 executes $O(m)$ times altogether. We shall show that it makes at most $m - 1$ iterations. We start by making some observations about k. First, line 4 starts k at 0, and the only way that k increases is by the increment operation in line 9, which executes at most once per iteration of the **for** loop of lines 5–10. Thus, the total increase in k is at most $m - 1$. Second, since $k < q$ upon entering the **for** loop and each iteration of the loop increments q, we always have $k < q$. Therefore, the assignments in lines 3 and 10 ensure that $\pi[q] < q$ for all $q = 1, 2, \ldots, m$, which means that each iteration of the **while** loop decreases k. Third, k never becomes negative. Putting these facts together, we see that the total decrease in k from the **while** loop is bounded from above by the total increase in k over all iterations of the **for** loop, which is $m - 1$. Thus, the **while** loop iterates at most $m - 1$ times in all, and COMPUTE-PREFIX-FUNCTION runs in time $\Theta(m)$.

Exercise 32.4-4 asks you to show, by a similar aggregate analysis, that the matching time of KMP-MATCHER is $\Theta(n)$.

Compared with FINITE-AUTOMATON-MATCHER, by using π rather than δ, we have reduced the time for preprocessing the pattern from $O(m |\Sigma|)$ to $\Theta(m)$, while keeping the actual matching time bounded by $\Theta(n)$.

Correctness of the prefix-function computation

We shall see a little later that the prefix function π helps us simulate the transition function δ in a string-matching automaton. But first, we need to prove that the procedure COMPUTE-PREFIX-FUNCTION does indeed compute the prefix function correctly. In order to do so, we will need to find all prefixes P_k that are proper suffixes of a given prefix P_q. The value of $\pi[q]$ gives us the longest such prefix, but the following lemma, illustrated in Figure 32.11, shows that by iterating the prefix function π, we can indeed enumerate all the prefixes P_k that are proper suffixes of P_q. Let

$$\pi^*[q] = \{\pi[q], \pi^{(2)}[q], \pi^{(3)}[q], \ldots, \pi^{(t)}[q]\} \,,$$

where $\pi^{(i)}[q]$ is defined in terms of functional iteration, so that $\pi^{(0)}[q] = q$ and $\pi^{(i)}[q] = \pi[\pi^{(i-1)}[q]]$ for $i \geq 1$, and where the sequence in $\pi^*[q]$ stops upon reaching $\pi^{(t)}[q] = 0$.

Lemma 32.5 (Prefix-function iteration lemma)
Let P be a pattern of length m with prefix function π. Then, for $q = 1, 2, \ldots, m$, we have $\pi^*[q] = \{k : k < q \text{ and } P_k \sqsupset P_q\}$.

Proof   We first prove that $\pi^*[q] \subseteq \{k : k < q \text{ and } P_k \sqsupset P_q\}$ or, equivalently,

$$i \in \pi^*[q] \text{ implies } P_i \sqsupset P_q \,. \tag{32.7}$$

If $i \in \pi^*[q]$, then $i = \pi^{(u)}[q]$ for some $u > 0$. We prove equation (32.7) by induction on u. For $u = 1$, we have $i = \pi[q]$, and the claim follows since $i < q$ and $P_{\pi[q]} \sqsupset P_q$ by the definition of π. Using the relations $\pi[i] < i$ and $P_{\pi[i]} \sqsupset P_i$ and the transitivity of $<$ and $\sqsupset$ establishes the claim for all i in $\pi^*[q]$. Therefore, $\pi^*[q] \subseteq \{k : k < q \text{ and } P_k \sqsupset P_q\}$.

We now prove that $\{k : k < q \text{ and } P_k \sqsupset P_q\} \subseteq \pi^*[q]$ by contradiction. Suppose to the contrary that the set $\{k : k < q \text{ and } P_k \sqsupset P_q\} - \pi^*[q]$ is nonempty, and let j be the largest number in the set. Because $\pi[q]$ is the largest value in $\{k : k < q \text{ and } P_k \sqsupset P_q\}$ and $\pi[q] \in \pi^*[q]$, we must have $j < \pi[q]$, and so we let j' denote the smallest integer in $\pi^*[q]$ that is greater than j. (We can choose $j' = \pi[q]$ if no other number in $\pi^*[q]$ is greater than j.) We have $P_j \sqsupset P_q$ because $j \in \{k : k < q \text{ and } P_k \sqsupset P_q\}$, and from $j' \in \pi^*[q]$ and equation (32.7), we have $P_{j'} \sqsupset P_q$. Thus, $P_j \sqsupset P_{j'}$ by Lemma 32.1, and j is the largest value less than j' with this property. Therefore, we must have $\pi[j'] = j$ and, since $j' \in \pi^*[q]$, we must have $j \in \pi^*[q]$ as well. This contradiction proves the lemma.   ■

The algorithm COMPUTE-PREFIX-FUNCTION computes $\pi[q]$, in order, for $q = 1, 2, \ldots, m$. Setting $\pi[1]$ to 0 in line 3 of COMPUTE-PREFIX-FUNCTION is certainly correct, since $\pi[q] < q$ for all q. We shall use the following lemma and

its corollary to prove that COMPUTE-PREFIX-FUNCTION computes $\pi[q]$ correctly for $q > 1$.

Lemma 32.6

Let P be a pattern of length m, and let π be the prefix function for P. For $q = 1, 2, \ldots, m$, if $\pi[q] > 0$, then $\pi[q] - 1 \in \pi^*[q - 1]$.

Proof Let $r = \pi[q] > 0$, so that $r < q$ and $P_r \sqsupset P_q$; thus, $r - 1 < q - 1$ and $P_{r-1} \sqsupset P_{q-1}$ (by dropping the last character from P_r and P_q, which we can do because $r > 0$). By Lemma 32.5, therefore, $r - 1 \in \pi^*[q - 1]$. Thus, we have $\pi[q] - 1 = r - 1 \in \pi^*[q - 1]$. ∎

For $q = 2, 3, \ldots, m$, define the subset $E_{q-1} \subseteq \pi^*[q - 1]$ by

$$
\begin{aligned}
E_{q-1} &= \{k \in \pi^*[q - 1] : P[k + 1] = P[q]\} \\
&= \{k : k < q - 1 \text{ and } P_k \sqsupset P_{q-1} \text{ and } P[k + 1] = P[q]\} \text{ (by Lemma 32.5)} \\
&= \{k : k < q - 1 \text{ and } P_{k+1} \sqsupset P_q\} \ .
\end{aligned}
$$

The set E_{q-1} consists of the values $k < q - 1$ for which $P_k \sqsupset P_{q-1}$ and for which, because $P[k + 1] = P[q]$, we have $P_{k+1} \sqsupset P_q$. Thus, E_{q-1} consists of those values $k \in \pi^*[q - 1]$ such that we can extend P_k to P_{k+1} and get a proper suffix of P_q.

Corollary 32.7

Let P be a pattern of length m, and let π be the prefix function for P. For $q = 2, 3, \ldots, m$,

$$
\pi[q] = \begin{cases} 0 & \text{if } E_{q-1} = \emptyset, \\ 1 + \max\{k \in E_{q-1}\} & \text{if } E_{q-1} \neq \emptyset. \end{cases}
$$

Proof If E_{q-1} is empty, there is no $k \in \pi^*[q - 1]$ (including $k = 0$) for which we can extend P_k to P_{k+1} and get a proper suffix of P_q. Therefore $\pi[q] = 0$.

If E_{q-1} is nonempty, then for each $k \in E_{q-1}$ we have $k + 1 < q$ and $P_{k+1} \sqsupset P_q$. Therefore, from the definition of $\pi[q]$, we have

$$\pi[q] \geq 1 + \max\{k \in E_{q-1}\} \ . \tag{32.8}$$

Note that $\pi[q] > 0$. Let $r = \pi[q] - 1$, so that $r + 1 = \pi[q]$ and therefore $P_{r+1} \sqsupset P_q$. Since $r + 1 > 0$, we have $P[r + 1] = P[q]$. Furthermore, by Lemma 32.6, we have $r \in \pi^*[q - 1]$. Therefore, $r \in E_{q-1}$, and so $r \leq \max\{k \in E_{q-1}\}$ or, equivalently,

$$\pi[q] \leq 1 + \max\{k \in E_{q-1}\} \ . \tag{32.9}$$

Combining equations (32.8) and (32.9) completes the proof. ∎

We now finish the proof that COMPUTE-PREFIX-FUNCTION computes π correctly. In the procedure COMPUTE-PREFIX-FUNCTION, at the start of each iteration of the **for** loop of lines 5–10, we have that $k = \pi[q-1]$. This condition is enforced by lines 3 and 4 when the loop is first entered, and it remains true in each successive iteration because of line 10. Lines 6–9 adjust k so that it becomes the correct value of $\pi[q]$. The **while** loop of lines 6–7 searches through all values $k \in \pi^*[q-1]$ until it finds a value of k for which $P[k+1] = P[q]$; at that point, k is the largest value in the set E_{q-1}, so that, by Corollary 32.7, we can set $\pi[q]$ to $k + 1$. If the **while** loop cannot find a $k \in \pi^*[q-1]$ such that $P[k+1] = P[q]$, then k equals 0 at line 8. If $P[1] = P[q]$, then we should set both k and $\pi[q]$ to 1; otherwise we should leave k alone and set $\pi[q]$ to 0. Lines 8–10 set k and $\pi[q]$ correctly in either case. This completes our proof of the correctness of COMPUTE-PREFIX-FUNCTION.

Correctness of the Knuth-Morris-Pratt algorithm

We can think of the procedure KMP-MATCHER as a reimplemented version of the procedure FINITE-AUTOMATON-MATCHER, but using the prefix function π to compute state transitions. Specifically, we shall prove that in the ith iteration of the **for** loops of both KMP-MATCHER and FINITE-AUTOMATON-MATCHER, the state q has the same value when we test for equality with m (at line 10 in KMP-MATCHER and at line 5 in FINITE-AUTOMATON-MATCHER). Once we have argued that KMP-MATCHER simulates the behavior of FINITE-AUTOMATON-MATCHER, the correctness of KMP-MATCHER follows from the correctness of FINITE-AUTOMATON-MATCHER (though we shall see a little later why line 12 in KMP-MATCHER is necessary).

Before we formally prove that KMP-MATCHER correctly simulates FINITE-AUTOMATON-MATCHER, let's take a moment to understand how the prefix function π replaces the δ transition function. Recall that when a string-matching automaton is in state q and it scans a character $a = T[i]$, it moves to a new state $\delta(q,a)$. If $a = P[q+1]$, so that a continues to match the pattern, then $\delta(q,a) = q + 1$. Otherwise, $a \neq P[q+1]$, so that a does not continue to match the pattern, and $0 \leq \delta(q,a) \leq q$. In the first case, when a continues to match, KMP-MATCHER moves to state $q + 1$ without referring to the π function: the **while** loop test in line 6 comes up false the first time, the test in line 8 comes up true, and line 9 increments q.

The π function comes into play when the character a does not continue to match the pattern, so that the new state $\delta(q,a)$ is either q or to the left of q along the spine of the automaton. The **while** loop of lines 6–7 in KMP-MATCHER iterates through the states in $\pi^*[q]$, stopping either when it arrives in a state, say q', such that a matches $P[q'+1]$ or q' has gone all the way down to 0. If a matches $P[q'+1]$,

then line 9 sets the new state to $q' + 1$, which should equal $\delta(q, a)$ for the simulation to work correctly. In other words, the new state $\delta(q, a)$ should be either state 0 or one greater than some state in $\pi^*[q]$.

Let's look at the example in Figures 32.7 and 32.11, which are for the pattern $P = \texttt{ababaca}$. Suppose that the automaton is in state $q = 5$; the states in $\pi^*[5]$ are, in descending order, 3, 1, and 0. If the next character scanned is $\texttt{c}$, then we can easily see that the automaton moves to state $\delta(5, \texttt{c}) = 6$ in both FINITE-AUTOMATON-MATCHER and KMP-MATCHER. Now suppose that the next character scanned is instead $\texttt{b}$, so that the automaton should move to state $\delta(5, \texttt{b}) = 4$. The **while** loop in KMP-MATCHER exits having executed line 7 once, and it arrives in state $q' = \pi[5] = 3$. Since $P[q' + 1] = P[4] = \texttt{b}$, the test in line 8 comes up true, and KMP-MATCHER moves to the new state $q' + 1 = 4 = \delta(5, \texttt{b})$. Finally, suppose that the next character scanned is instead $\texttt{a}$, so that the automaton should move to state $\delta(5, \texttt{a}) = 1$. The first three times that the test in line 6 executes, the test comes up true. The first time, we find that $P[6] = \texttt{c} \neq \texttt{a}$, and KMP-MATCHER moves to state $\pi[5] = 3$ (the first state in $\pi^*[5]$). The second time, we find that $P[4] = \texttt{b} \neq \texttt{a}$ and move to state $\pi[3] = 1$ (the second state in $\pi^*[5]$). The third time, we find that $P[2] = \texttt{b} \neq \texttt{a}$ and move to state $\pi[1] = 0$ (the last state in $\pi^*[5]$). The **while** loop exits once it arrives in state $q' = 0$. Now, line 8 finds that $P[q' + 1] = P[1] = \texttt{a}$, and line 9 moves the automaton to the new state $q' + 1 = 1 = \delta(5, \texttt{a})$.

Thus, our intuition is that KMP-MATCHER iterates through the states in $\pi^*[q]$ in decreasing order, stopping at some state q' and then possibly moving to state $q' + 1$. Although that might seem like a lot of work just to simulate computing $\delta(q, a)$, bear in mind that asymptotically, KMP-MATCHER is no slower than FINITE-AUTOMATON-MATCHER.

We are now ready to formally prove the correctness of the Knuth-Morris-Pratt algorithm. By Theorem 32.4, we have that $q = \sigma(T_i)$ after each time we execute line 4 of FINITE-AUTOMATON-MATCHER. Therefore, it suffices to show that the same property holds with regard to the **for** loop in KMP-MATCHER. The proof proceeds by induction on the number of loop iterations. Initially, both procedures set q to 0 as they enter their respective **for** loops for the first time. Consider iteration i of the **for** loop in KMP-MATCHER, and let q' be state at the start of this loop iteration. By the inductive hypothesis, we have $q' = \sigma(T_{i-1})$. We need to show that $q = \sigma(T_i)$ at line 10. (Again, we shall handle line 12 separately.)

When we consider the character $T[i]$, the longest prefix of P that is a suffix of T_i is either $P_{q'+1}$ (if $P[q' + 1] = T[i]$) or some prefix (not necessarily proper, and possibly empty) of $P_{q'}$. We consider separately the three cases in which $\sigma(T_i) = 0$, $\sigma(T_i) = q' + 1$, and $0 < \sigma(T_i) \leq q'$.

- If $\sigma(T_i) = 0$, then $P_0 = \varepsilon$ is the only prefix of P that is a suffix of T_i. The **while** loop of lines 6–7 iterates through the values in $\pi^*[q']$, but although $P_q \sqsupset T_{i-1}$ for every $q \in \pi^*[q']$, the loop never finds a q such that $P[q+1] = T[i]$. The loop terminates when q reaches 0, and of course line 9 does not execute. Therefore, $q = 0$ at line 10, so that $q = \sigma(T_i)$.

- If $\sigma(T_i) = q' + 1$, then $P[q'+1] = T[i]$, and the **while** loop test in line 6 fails the first time through. Line 9 executes, incrementing q so that afterward we have $q = q' + 1 = \sigma(T_i)$.

- If $0 < \sigma(T_i) \le q'$, then the **while** loop of lines 6–7 iterates at least once, checking in decreasing order each value $q \in \pi^*[q']$ until it stops at some $q < q'$. Thus, P_q is the longest prefix of $P_{q'}$ for which $P[q+1] = T[i]$, so that when the **while** loop terminates, $q + 1 = \sigma(P_{q'}T[i])$. Since $q' = \sigma(T_{i-1})$, Lemma 32.3 implies that $\sigma(T_{i-1}T[i]) = \sigma(P_{q'}T[i])$. Thus, we have

$$
\begin{aligned}
q + 1 &= \sigma(P_{q'}T[i]) \\
&= \sigma(T_{i-1}T[i]) \\
&= \sigma(T_i)
\end{aligned}
$$

when the **while** loop terminates. After line 9 increments q, we have $q = \sigma(T_i)$.

Line 12 is necessary in KMP-MATCHER, because otherwise, we might reference $P[m+1]$ on line 6 after finding an occurrence of P. (The argument that $q = \sigma(T_{i-1})$ upon the next execution of line 6 remains valid by the hint given in Exercise 32.4-8: $\delta(m, a) = \delta(\pi[m], a)$ or, equivalently, $\sigma(Pa) = \sigma(P_{\pi[m]}a)$ for any $a \in \Sigma$.) The remaining argument for the correctness of the Knuth-Morris-Pratt algorithm follows from the correctness of FINITE-AUTOMATON-MATCHER, since we have shown that KMP-MATCHER simulates the behavior of FINITE-AUTOMATON-MATCHER.

Exercises

32.4-1
Compute the prefix function π for the pattern `ababbabbabbababbbabb`.

32.4-2
Give an upper bound on the size of $\pi^*[q]$ as a function of q. Give an example to show that your bound is tight.

32.4-3
Explain how to determine the occurrences of pattern P in the text T by examining the π function for the string PT (the string of length $m+n$ that is the concatenation of P and T).

32.4-4
Use an aggregate analysis to show that the running time of KMP-MATCHER is $\Theta(n)$.

32.4-5
Use a potential function to show that the running time of KMP-MATCHER is $\Theta(n)$.

32.4-6
Show how to improve KMP-MATCHER by replacing the occurrence of π in line 7 (but not line 12) by π', where π' is defined recursively for $q = 1, 2, \ldots, m - 1$ by the equation

$$
\pi'[q] = \begin{cases}
0 & \text{if } \pi[q] = 0, \\
\pi'[\pi[q]] & \text{if } \pi[q] \neq 0 \text{ and } P[\pi[q] + 1] = P[q + 1], \\
\pi[q] & \text{if } \pi[q] \neq 0 \text{ and } P[\pi[q] + 1] \neq P[q + 1].
\end{cases}
$$

Explain why the modified algorithm is correct, and explain in what sense this change constitutes an improvement.

32.4-7
Give a linear-time algorithm to determine whether a text T is a cyclic rotation of another string T'. For example, `arc` and `car` are cyclic rotations of each other.

32.4-8 ★
Give an $O(m |\Sigma|)$-time algorithm for computing the transition function δ for the string-matching automaton corresponding to a given pattern P. (*Hint:* Prove that $\delta(q, a) = \delta(\pi[q], a)$ if $q = m$ or $P[q + 1] \neq a$.)

Problems

32-1   *String matching based on repetition factors*
Let y^i denote the concatenation of string y with itself i times. For example, $(\texttt{ab})^3 = \texttt{ababab}$. We say that a string $x \in \Sigma^*$ has ***repetition factor*** r if $x = y^r$ for some string $y \in \Sigma^*$ and some $r > 0$. Let $\rho(x)$ denote the largest r such that x has repetition factor r.

a. Give an efficient algorithm that takes as input a pattern $P[1 \mathinner{\ldotp\ldotp} m]$ and computes the value $\rho(P_i)$ for $i = 1, 2, \ldots, m$. What is the running time of your algorithm?

b. For any pattern $P[1 \mathinner{.\,.} m]$, let $\rho^*(P)$ be defined as $\max_{1 \le i \le m} \rho(P_i)$. Prove that if the pattern P is chosen randomly from the set of all binary strings of length m, then the expected value of $\rho^*(P)$ is $O(1)$.

c. Argue that the following string-matching algorithm correctly finds all occurrences of pattern P in a text $T[1 \mathinner{.\,.} n]$ in time $O(\rho^*(P)n + m)$:

REPETITION-MATCHER(P, T)

```
 1  m = P.length
 2  n = T.length
 3  k = 1 + ρ*(P)
 4  q = 0
 5  s = 0
 6  while s ≤ n − m
 7      if T[s + q + 1] == P[q + 1]
 8          q = q + 1
 9          if q == m
10              print "Pattern occurs with shift" s
11      if q == m or T[s + q + 1] ≠ P[q + 1]
12          s = s + max(1, ⌈q/k⌉)
13          q = 0
```

This algorithm is due to Galil and Seiferas. By extending these ideas greatly, they obtained a linear-time string-matching algorithm that uses only $O(1)$ storage beyond what is required for P and T.

Chapter notes

The relation of string matching to the theory of finite automata is discussed by Aho, Hopcroft, and Ullman [5]. The Knuth-Morris-Pratt algorithm [214] was invented independently by Knuth and Pratt and by Morris; they published their work jointly. Reingold, Urban, and Gries [294] give an alternative treatment of the Knuth-Morris-Pratt algorithm. The Rabin-Karp algorithm was proposed by Karp and Rabin [201]. Galil and Seiferas [126] give an interesting deterministic linear-time string-matching algorithm that uses only $O(1)$ space beyond that required to store the pattern and text.

33   Computational Geometry

Computational geometry is the branch of computer science that studies algorithms for solving geometric problems. In modern engineering and mathematics, computational geometry has applications in such diverse fields as computer graphics, robotics, VLSI design, computer-aided design, molecular modeling, metallurgy, manufacturing, textile layout, forestry, and statistics. The input to a computational-geometry problem is typically a description of a set of geometric objects, such as a set of points, a set of line segments, or the vertices of a polygon in counterclockwise order. The output is often a response to a query about the objects, such as whether any of the lines intersect, or perhaps a new geometric object, such as the convex hull (smallest enclosing convex polygon) of the set of points.

In this chapter, we look at a few computational-geometry algorithms in two dimensions, that is, in the plane. We represent each input object by a set of points $\{p_1, p_2, p_3, \ldots\}$, where each $p_i = (x_i, y_i)$ and $x_i, y_i \in \mathbb{R}$. For example, we represent an n-vertex polygon P by a sequence $\langle p_0, p_1, p_2, \ldots, p_{n-1} \rangle$ of its vertices in order of their appearance on the boundary of P. Computational geometry can also apply to three dimensions, and even higher-dimensional spaces, but such problems and their solutions can be very difficult to visualize. Even in two dimensions, however, we can see a good sample of computational-geometry techniques.

Section 33.1 shows how to answer basic questions about line segments efficiently and accurately: whether one segment is clockwise or counterclockwise from another that shares an endpoint, which way we turn when traversing two adjoining line segments, and whether two line segments intersect. Section 33.2 presents a technique called "sweeping" that we use to develop an $O(n \lg n)$-time algorithm for determining whether a set of n line segments contains any intersections. Section 33.3 gives two "rotational-sweep" algorithms that compute the convex hull (smallest enclosing convex polygon) of a set of n points: Graham's scan, which runs in time $O(n \lg n)$, and Jarvis's march, which takes $O(nh)$ time, where h is the number of vertices of the convex hull. Finally, Section 33.4 gives

an $O(n \lg n)$-time divide-and-conquer algorithm for finding the closest pair of points in a set of n points in the plane.

33.1   Line-segment properties

Several of the computational-geometry algorithms in this chapter require answers to questions about the properties of line segments. A ***convex combination*** of two distinct points $p_1 = (x_1, y_1)$ and $p_2 = (x_2, y_2)$ is any point $p_3 = (x_3, y_3)$ such that for some α in the range $0 \le \alpha \le 1$, we have $x_3 = \alpha x_1 + (1 - \alpha)x_2$ and $y_3 = \alpha y_1 + (1 - \alpha)y_2$. We also write that $p_3 = \alpha p_1 + (1 - \alpha)p_2$. Intuitively, p_3 is any point that is on the line passing through p_1 and p_2 and is on or between p_1 and p_2 on the line. Given two distinct points p_1 and p_2, the ***line segment*** $\overline{p_1 p_2}$ is the set of convex combinations of p_1 and p_2. We call p_1 and p_2 the ***endpoints*** of segment $\overline{p_1 p_2}$. Sometimes the ordering of p_1 and p_2 matters, and we speak of the ***directed segment*** $\overrightarrow{p_1 p_2}$. If p_1 is the ***origin*** $(0, 0)$, then we can treat the directed segment $\overrightarrow{p_1 p_2}$ as the ***vector*** p_2.

In this section, we shall explore the following questions:

1. Given two directed segments $\overrightarrow{p_0 p_1}$ and $\overrightarrow{p_0 p_2}$, is $\overrightarrow{p_0 p_1}$ clockwise from $\overrightarrow{p_0 p_2}$ with respect to their common endpoint p_0?

2. Given two line segments $\overline{p_0 p_1}$ and $\overline{p_1 p_2}$, if we traverse $\overline{p_0 p_1}$ and then $\overline{p_1 p_2}$, do we make a left turn at point p_1?

3. Do line segments $\overline{p_1 p_2}$ and $\overline{p_3 p_4}$ intersect?

There are no restrictions on the given points.

We can answer each question in $O(1)$ time, which should come as no surprise since the input size of each question is $O(1)$. Moreover, our methods use only additions, subtractions, multiplications, and comparisons. We need neither division nor trigonometric functions, both of which can be computationally expensive and prone to problems with round-off error. For example, the "straightforward" method of determining whether two segments intersect—compute the line equation of the form $y = mx + b$ for each segment (m is the slope and b is the y-intercept), find the point of intersection of the lines, and check whether this point is on both segments—uses division to find the point of intersection. When the segments are nearly parallel, this method is very sensitive to the precision of the division operation on real computers. The method in this section, which avoids division, is much more accurate.

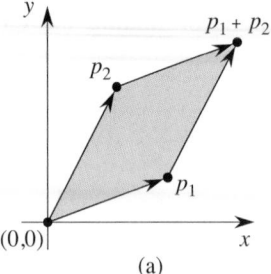
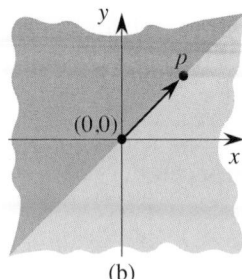

Figure 33.1 (a) The cross product of vectors p_1 and p_2 is the signed area of the parallelogram. (b) The lightly shaded region contains vectors that are clockwise from p. The darkly shaded region contains vectors that are counterclockwise from p.

Cross products

Computing cross products lies at the heart of our line-segment methods. Consider vectors p_1 and p_2, shown in Figure 33.1(a). We can interpret the ***cross product*** $p_1 \times p_2$ as the signed area of the parallelogram formed by the points $(0, 0)$, p_1, p_2, and $p_1 + p_2 = (x_1 + x_2, y_1 + y_2)$. An equivalent, but more useful, definition gives the cross product as the determinant of a matrix:[1]

$$
\begin{aligned}
p_1 \times p_2 &= \det \begin{pmatrix} x_1 & x_2 \\ y_1 & y_2 \end{pmatrix} \\
&= x_1 y_2 - x_2 y_1 \\
&= -p_2 \times p_1 .
\end{aligned}
$$

If $p_1 \times p_2$ is positive, then p_1 is clockwise from p_2 with respect to the origin $(0, 0)$; if this cross product is negative, then p_1 is counterclockwise from p_2. (See Exercise 33.1-1.) Figure 33.1(b) shows the clockwise and counterclockwise regions relative to a vector p. A boundary condition arises if the cross product is 0; in this case, the vectors are ***colinear***, pointing in either the same or opposite directions.

To determine whether a directed segment $\overrightarrow{p_0 p_1}$ is closer to a directed segment $\overrightarrow{p_0 p_2}$ in a clockwise direction or in a counterclockwise direction with respect to their common endpoint p_0, we simply translate to use p_0 as the origin. That is, we let $p_1 - p_0$ denote the vector $p_1' = (x_1', y_1')$, where $x_1' = x_1 - x_0$ and $y_1' = y_1 - y_0$, and we define $p_2 - p_0$ similarly. We then compute the cross product

---

[1] Actually, the cross product is a three-dimensional concept. It is a vector that is perpendicular to both p_1 and p_2 according to the "right-hand rule" and whose magnitude is $|x_1 y_2 - x_2 y_1|$. In this chapter, however, we find it convenient to treat the cross product simply as the value $x_1 y_2 - x_2 y_1$.

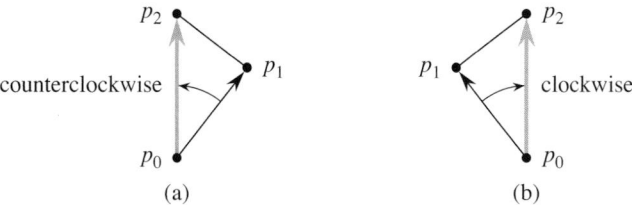

Figure 33.2   Using the cross product to determine how consecutive line segments $\overline{p_0p_1}$ and $\overline{p_1p_2}$ turn at point p_1. We check whether the directed segment $\overrightarrow{p_0p_2}$ is clockwise or counterclockwise relative to the directed segment $\overrightarrow{p_0p_1}$. **(a)** If counterclockwise, the points make a left turn. **(b)** If clockwise, they make a right turn.

$$(p_1 - p_0) \times (p_2 - p_0) = (x_1 - x_0)(y_2 - y_0) - (x_2 - x_0)(y_1 - y_0) \;.$$

If this cross product is positive, then $\overrightarrow{p_0p_1}$ is clockwise from $\overrightarrow{p_0p_2}$; if negative, it is counterclockwise.

Determining whether consecutive segments turn left or right

Our next question is whether two consecutive line segments $\overline{p_0p_1}$ and $\overline{p_1p_2}$ turn left or right at point p_1. Equivalently, we want a method to determine which way a given angle $\angle p_0p_1p_2$ turns. Cross products allow us to answer this question without computing the angle. As Figure 33.2 shows, we simply check whether directed segment $\overrightarrow{p_0p_2}$ is clockwise or counterclockwise relative to directed segment $\overrightarrow{p_0p_1}$. To do so, we compute the cross product $(p_2 - p_0) \times (p_1 - p_0)$. If the sign of this cross product is negative, then $\overrightarrow{p_0p_2}$ is counterclockwise with respect to $\overrightarrow{p_0p_1}$, and thus we make a left turn at p_1. A positive cross product indicates a clockwise orientation and a right turn. A cross product of 0 means that points p_0, p_1, and p_2 are colinear.

Determining whether two line segments intersect

To determine whether two line segments intersect, we check whether each segment straddles the line containing the other. A segment $\overline{p_1p_2}$ ***straddles*** a line if point p_1 lies on one side of the line and point p_2 lies on the other side. A boundary case arises if p_1 or p_2 lies directly on the line. Two line segments intersect if and only if either (or both) of the following conditions holds:

1. Each segment straddles the line containing the other.

2. An endpoint of one segment lies on the other segment. (This condition comes from the boundary case.)

The following procedures implement this idea. SEGMENTS-INTERSECT returns TRUE if segments $\overline{p_1 p_2}$ and $\overline{p_3 p_4}$ intersect and FALSE if they do not. It calls the subroutines DIRECTION, which computes relative orientations using the cross-product method above, and ON-SEGMENT, which determines whether a point known to be colinear with a segment lies on that segment.

SEGMENTS-INTERSECT(p_1, p_2, p_3, p_4)

```
1   d₁ = DIRECTION(p₃, p₄, p₁)
2   d₂ = DIRECTION(p₃, p₄, p₂)
3   d₃ = DIRECTION(p₁, p₂, p₃)
4   d₄ = DIRECTION(p₁, p₂, p₄)
5   if ((d₁ > 0 and d₂ < 0) or (d₁ < 0 and d₂ > 0)) and
          ((d₃ > 0 and d₄ < 0) or (d₃ < 0 and d₄ > 0))
6       return TRUE
7   elseif d₁ == 0 and ON-SEGMENT(p₃, p₄, p₁)
8       return TRUE
9   elseif d₂ == 0 and ON-SEGMENT(p₃, p₄, p₂)
10      return TRUE
11  elseif d₃ == 0 and ON-SEGMENT(p₁, p₂, p₃)
12      return TRUE
13  elseif d₄ == 0 and ON-SEGMENT(p₁, p₂, p₄)
14      return TRUE
15  else return FALSE
```

DIRECTION(p_i, p_j, p_k)

```
1   return (pₖ − pᵢ) × (pⱼ − pᵢ)
```

ON-SEGMENT(p_i, p_j, p_k)

```
1   if min(xᵢ, xⱼ) ≤ xₖ ≤ max(xᵢ, xⱼ) and min(yᵢ, yⱼ) ≤ yₖ ≤ max(yᵢ, yⱼ)
2       return TRUE
3   else return FALSE
```

SEGMENTS-INTERSECT works as follows. Lines 1–4 compute the relative orientation d_i of each endpoint p_i with respect to the other segment. If all the relative orientations are nonzero, then we can easily determine whether segments $\overline{p_1 p_2}$ and $\overline{p_3 p_4}$ intersect, as follows. Segment $\overline{p_1 p_2}$ straddles the line containing segment $\overline{p_3 p_4}$ if directed segments $\overrightarrow{p_3 p_1}$ and $\overrightarrow{p_3 p_2}$ have opposite orientations relative to $\overrightarrow{p_3 p_4}$. In this case, the signs of d_1 and d_2 differ. Similarly, $\overline{p_3 p_4}$ straddles the line containing $\overline{p_1 p_2}$ if the signs of d_3 and d_4 differ. If the test of line 5 is true, then the segments straddle each other, and SEGMENTS-INTERSECT returns TRUE. Figure 33.3(a) shows this case. Otherwise, the segments do not straddle

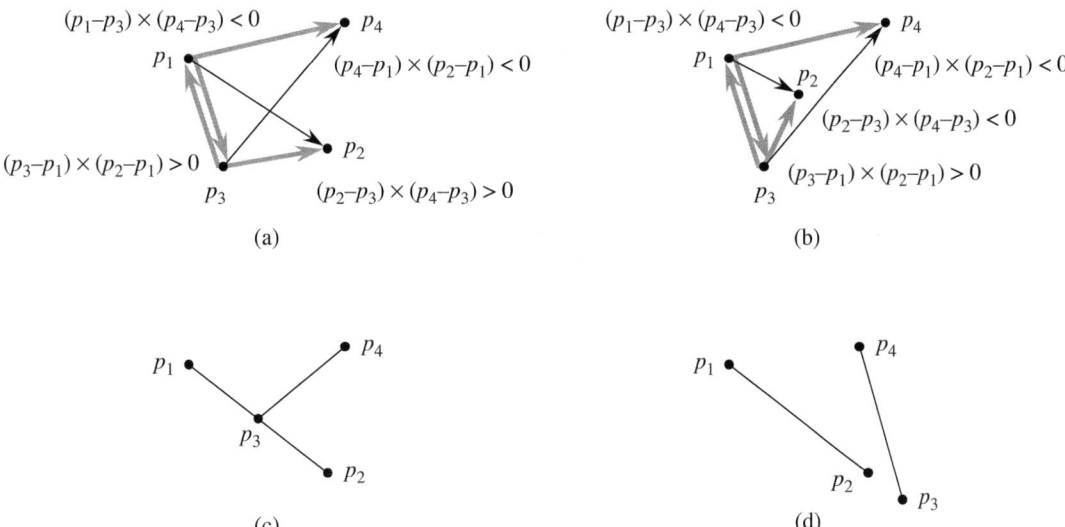

Figure 33.3   Cases in the procedure SEGMENTS-INTERSECT. **(a)** The segments $\overline{p_1 p_2}$ and $\overline{p_3 p_4}$ straddle each other's lines. Because $\overline{p_3 p_4}$ straddles the line containing $\overline{p_1 p_2}$, the signs of the cross products $(p_3 - p_1) \times (p_2 - p_1)$ and $(p_4 - p_1) \times (p_2 - p_1)$ differ. Because $\overline{p_1 p_2}$ straddles the line containing $\overline{p_3 p_4}$, the signs of the cross products $(p_1 - p_3) \times (p_4 - p_3)$ and $(p_2 - p_3) \times (p_4 - p_3)$ differ. **(b)** Segment $\overline{p_3 p_4}$ straddles the line containing $\overline{p_1 p_2}$, but $\overline{p_1 p_2}$ does not straddle the line containing $\overline{p_3 p_4}$. The signs of the cross products $(p_1 - p_3) \times (p_4 - p_3)$ and $(p_2 - p_3) \times (p_4 - p_3)$ are the same. **(c)** Point p_3 is colinear with $\overline{p_1 p_2}$ and is between p_1 and p_2. **(d)** Point p_3 is colinear with $\overline{p_1 p_2}$, but it is not between p_1 and p_2. The segments do not intersect.

each other's lines, although a boundary case may apply. If all the relative orientations are nonzero, no boundary case applies. All the tests against 0 in lines 7–13 then fail, and SEGMENTS-INTERSECT returns FALSE in line 15. Figure 33.3(b) shows this case.

A boundary case occurs if any relative orientation d_k is 0. Here, we know that p_k is colinear with the other segment. It is directly on the other segment if and only if it is between the endpoints of the other segment. The procedure ON-SEGMENT returns whether p_k is between the endpoints of segment $\overline{p_i p_j}$, which will be the other segment when called in lines 7–13; the procedure assumes that p_k is colinear with segment $\overline{p_i p_j}$. Figures 33.3(c) and (d) show cases with colinear points. In Figure 33.3(c), p_3 is on $\overline{p_1 p_2}$, and so SEGMENTS-INTERSECT returns TRUE in line 12. No endpoints are on other segments in Figure 33.3(d), and so SEGMENTS-INTERSECT returns FALSE in line 15.

Other applications of cross products

Later sections of this chapter introduce additional uses for cross products. In Section 33.3, we shall need to sort a set of points according to their polar angles with respect to a given origin. As Exercise 33.1-3 asks you to show, we can use cross products to perform the comparisons in the sorting procedure. In Section 33.2, we shall use red-black trees to maintain the vertical ordering of a set of line segments. Rather than keeping explicit key values which we compare to each other in the red-black tree code, we shall compute a cross-product to determine which of two segments that intersect a given vertical line is above the other.

Exercises

33.1-1
Prove that if $p_1 \times p_2$ is positive, then vector p_1 is clockwise from vector p_2 with respect to the origin $(0, 0)$ and that if this cross product is negative, then p_1 is counterclockwise from p_2.

33.1-2
Professor van Pelt proposes that only the x-dimension needs to be tested in line 1 of ON-SEGMENT. Show why the professor is wrong.

33.1-3
The *polar angle* of a point p_1 with respect to an origin point p_0 is the angle of the vector $p_1 - p_0$ in the usual polar coordinate system. For example, the polar angle of $(3, 5)$ with respect to $(2, 4)$ is the angle of the vector $(1, 1)$, which is 45 degrees or $\pi/4$ radians. The polar angle of $(3, 3)$ with respect to $(2, 4)$ is the angle of the vector $(1, -1)$, which is 315 degrees or $7\pi/4$ radians. Write pseudocode to sort a sequence $\langle p_1, p_2, \ldots, p_n \rangle$ of n points according to their polar angles with respect to a given origin point p_0. Your procedure should take $O(n \lg n)$ time and use cross products to compare angles.

33.1-4
Show how to determine in $O(n^2 \lg n)$ time whether any three points in a set of n points are colinear.

33.1-5
A *polygon* is a piecewise-linear, closed curve in the plane. That is, it is a curve ending on itself that is formed by a sequence of straight-line segments, called the *sides* of the polygon. A point joining two consecutive sides is a *vertex* of the polygon. If the polygon is *simple*, as we shall generally assume, it does not cross itself. The set of points in the plane enclosed by a simple polygon forms the *interior* of

the polygon, the set of points on the polygon itself forms its **boundary**, and the set
of points surrounding the polygon forms its **exterior**. A simple polygon is **convex**
if, given any two points on its boundary or in its interior, all points on the line
segment drawn between them are contained in the polygon's boundary or interior.
A vertex of a convex polygon cannot be expressed as a convex combination of any
two distinct points on the boundary or in the interior of the polygon.

Professor Amundsen proposes the following method to determine whether a se-
quence $\langle p_0, p_1, \ldots, p_{n-1} \rangle$ of n points forms the consecutive vertices of a convex
polygon. Output "yes" if the set $\{\angle p_i\, p_{i+1}\, p_{i+2} : i = 0, 1, \ldots, n - 1\}$, where subscript addition is performed modulo n, does not contain both left turns and right
turns; otherwise, output "no." Show that although this method runs in linear time,
it does not always produce the correct answer. Modify the professor's method so
that it always produces the correct answer in linear time.

33.1-6
Given a point $p_0 = (x_0, y_0)$, the ***right horizontal ray*** from p_0 is the set of points
$\{p_i = (x_i, y_i) : x_i \geq x_0 \text{ and } y_i = y_0\}$, that is, it is the set of points due right of p_0
along with p_0 itself. Show how to determine whether a given right horizontal ray
from p_0 intersects a line segment $\overline{p_1 p_2}$ in $O(1)$ time by reducing the problem to
that of determining whether two line segments intersect.

33.1-7
One way to determine whether a point p_0 is in the interior of a simple, but not
necessarily convex, polygon P is to look at any ray from p_0 and check that the ray
intersects the boundary of P an odd number of times but that p_0 itself is not on
the boundary of P. Show how to compute in $\Theta(n)$ time whether a point p_0 is in
the interior of an n-vertex polygon P. (*Hint:* Use Exercise 33.1-6. Make sure your
algorithm is correct when the ray intersects the polygon boundary at a vertex and
when the ray overlaps a side of the polygon.)

33.1-8
Show how to compute the area of an n-vertex simple, but not necessarily convex,
polygon in $\Theta(n)$ time. (See Exercise 33.1-5 for definitions pertaining to polygons.)

33.2   Determining whether any pair of segments intersects

This section presents an algorithm for determining whether any two line segments
in a set of segments intersect. The algorithm uses a technique known as "sweeping," which is common to many computational-geometry algorithms. Moreover, as

the exercises at the end of this section show, this algorithm, or simple variations of it, can help solve other computational-geometry problems.

The algorithm runs in $O(n \lg n)$ time, where n is the number of segments we are given. It determines only whether or not any intersection exists; it does not print all the intersections. (By Exercise 33.2-1, it takes $\Omega(n^2)$ time in the worst case to find *all* the intersections in a set of n line segments.)

In *sweeping*, an imaginary vertical *sweep line* passes through the given set of geometric objects, usually from left to right. We treat the spatial dimension that the sweep line moves across, in this case the x-dimension, as a dimension of time. Sweeping provides a method for ordering geometric objects, usually by placing them into a dynamic data structure, and for taking advantage of relationships among them. The line-segment-intersection algorithm in this section considers all the line-segment endpoints in left-to-right order and checks for an intersection each time it encounters an endpoint.

To describe and prove correct our algorithm for determining whether any two of n line segments intersect, we shall make two simplifying assumptions. First, we assume that no input segment is vertical. Second, we assume that no three input segments intersect at a single point. Exercises 33.2-8 and 33.2-9 ask you to show that the algorithm is robust enough that it needs only a slight modification to work even when these assumptions do not hold. Indeed, removing such simplifying assumptions and dealing with boundary conditions often present the most difficult challenges when programming computational-geometry algorithms and proving their correctness.

Ordering segments

Because we assume that there are no vertical segments, we know that any input segment intersecting a given vertical sweep line intersects it at a single point. Thus, we can order the segments that intersect a vertical sweep line according to the y-coordinates of the points of intersection.

To be more precise, consider two segments s_1 and s_2. We say that these segments are *comparable* at x if the vertical sweep line with x-coordinate x intersects both of them. We say that s_1 is *above* s_2 at x, written $s_1 \succeq_x s_2$, if s_1 and s_2 are comparable at x and the intersection of s_1 with the sweep line at x is higher than the intersection of s_2 with the same sweep line, or if s_1 and s_2 intersect at the sweep line. In Figure 33.4(a), for example, we have the relationships $a \succeq_r c$, $a \succeq_t b$, $b \succeq_t c$, $a \succeq_t c$, and $b \succeq_u c$. Segment d is not comparable with any other segment.

For any given x, the relation "$\succeq_x$" is a total preorder (see Section B.2) for all segments that intersect the sweep line at x. That is, the relation is transitive, and if segments s_1 and s_2 each intersect the sweep line at x, then either $s_1 \succeq_x s_2$ or $s_2 \succeq_x s_1$, or both (if s_1 and s_2 intersect at the sweep line). (The relation $\succeq_x$ is

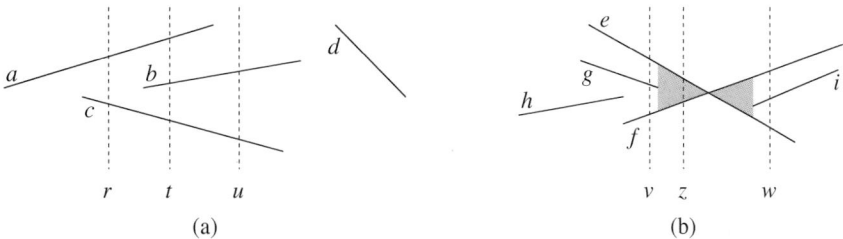

Figure 33.4 The ordering among line segments at various vertical sweep lines. **(a)** We have $a \succeq_r c$, $a \succeq_t b$, $b \succeq_t c$, $a \succeq_t c$, and $b \succeq_u c$. Segment d is comparable with no other segment shown. **(b)** When segments e and f intersect, they reverse their orders: we have $e \succeq_v f$ but $f \succeq_w e$. Any sweep line (such as z) that passes through the shaded region has e and f consecutive in the ordering given by the relation $\succeq_z$.

also reflexive, but neither symmetric nor antisymmetric.) The total preorder may differ for differing values of x, however, as segments enter and leave the ordering. A segment enters the ordering when its left endpoint is encountered by the sweep, and it leaves the ordering when its right endpoint is encountered.

What happens when the sweep line passes through the intersection of two segments? As Figure 33.4(b) shows, the segments reverse their positions in the total preorder. Sweep lines v and w are to the left and right, respectively, of the point of intersection of segments e and f, and we have $e \succeq_v f$ and $f \succeq_w e$. Note that because we assume that no three segments intersect at the same point, there must be some vertical sweep line x for which intersecting segments e and f are *consecutive* in the total preorder $\succeq_x$. Any sweep line that passes through the shaded region of Figure 33.4(b), such as z, has e and f consecutive in its total preorder.

Moving the sweep line

Sweeping algorithms typically manage two sets of data:

1. The ***sweep-line status*** gives the relationships among the objects that the sweep line intersects.

2. The ***event-point schedule*** is a sequence of points, called ***event points***, which we order from left to right according to their x-coordinates. As the sweep progresses from left to right, whenever the sweep line reaches the x-coordinate of an event point, the sweep halts, processes the event point, and then resumes. Changes to the sweep-line status occur only at event points.

For some algorithms (the algorithm asked for in Exercise 33.2-7, for example), the event-point schedule develops dynamically as the algorithm progresses. The algorithm at hand, however, determines all the event points before the sweep, based

solely on simple properties of the input data. In particular, each segment endpoint is an event point. We sort the segment endpoints by increasing x-coordinate and proceed from left to right. (If two or more endpoints are *covertical*, i.e., they have the same x-coordinate, we break the tie by putting all the covertical left endpoints before the covertical right endpoints. Within a set of covertical left endpoints, we put those with lower y-coordinates first, and we do the same within a set of covertical right endpoints.) When we encounter a segment's left endpoint, we insert the segment into the sweep-line status, and we delete the segment from the sweep-line status upon encountering its right endpoint. Whenever two segments first become consecutive in the total preorder, we check whether they intersect.

The sweep-line status is a total preorder T, for which we require the following operations:

- INSERT(T, s): insert segment s into T.

- DELETE(T, s): delete segment s from T.

- ABOVE(T, s): return the segment immediately above segment s in T.

- BELOW(T, s): return the segment immediately below segment s in T.

It is possible for segments s_1 and s_2 to be mutually above each other in the total preorder T; this situation can occur if s_1 and s_2 intersect at the sweep line whose total preorder is given by T. In this case, the two segments may appear in either order in T.

If the input contains n segments, we can perform each of the operations INSERT, DELETE, ABOVE, and BELOW in $O(\lg n)$ time using red-black trees. Recall that the red-black-tree operations in Chapter 13 involve comparing keys. We can replace the key comparisons by comparisons that use cross products to determine the relative ordering of two segments (see Exercise 33.2-2).

Segment-intersection pseudocode

The following algorithm takes as input a set S of n line segments, returning the boolean value TRUE if any pair of segments in S intersects, and FALSE otherwise. A red-black tree maintains the total preorder T.

ANY-SEGMENTS-INTERSECT(*S*)

```
 1  T = ∅
 2  sort the endpoints of the segments in S from left to right,
            breaking ties by putting left endpoints before right endpoints
            and breaking further ties by putting points with lower
            y-coordinates first
 3  for each point p in the sorted list of endpoints
 4      if p is the left endpoint of a segment s
 5          INSERT(T, s)
 6          if (ABOVE(T, s) exists and intersects s)
                or (BELOW(T, s) exists and intersects s)
 7              return TRUE
 8      if p is the right endpoint of a segment s
 9          if both ABOVE(T, s) and BELOW(T, s) exist
                and ABOVE(T, s) intersects BELOW(T, s)
10              return TRUE
11          DELETE(T, s)
12  return FALSE
```

Figure 33.5 illustrates how the algorithm works. Line 1 initializes the total preorder to be empty. Line 2 determines the event-point schedule by sorting the $2n$ segment endpoints from left to right, breaking ties as described above. One way to perform line 2 is by lexicographically sorting the endpoints on (x, e, y), where x and y are the usual coordinates, $e = 0$ for a left endpoint, and $e = 1$ for a right endpoint.

Each iteration of the **for** loop of lines 3–11 processes one event point p. If p is the left endpoint of a segment s, line 5 adds s to the total preorder, and lines 6–7 return TRUE if s intersects either of the segments it is consecutive with in the total preorder defined by the sweep line passing through p. (A boundary condition occurs if p lies on another segment s'. In this case, we require only that s and s' be placed consecutively into T.) If p is the right endpoint of a segment s, then we need to delete s from the total preorder. But first, lines 9–10 return TRUE if there is an intersection between the segments surrounding s in the total preorder defined by the sweep line passing through p. If these segments do not intersect, line 11 deletes segment s from the total preorder. If the segments surrounding segment s intersect, they would have become consecutive after deleting s had the **return** statement in line 10 not prevented line 11 from executing. The correctness argument, which follows, will make it clear why it suffices to check the segments surrounding s. Finally, if we never find any intersections after having processed all $2n$ event points, line 12 returns FALSE.

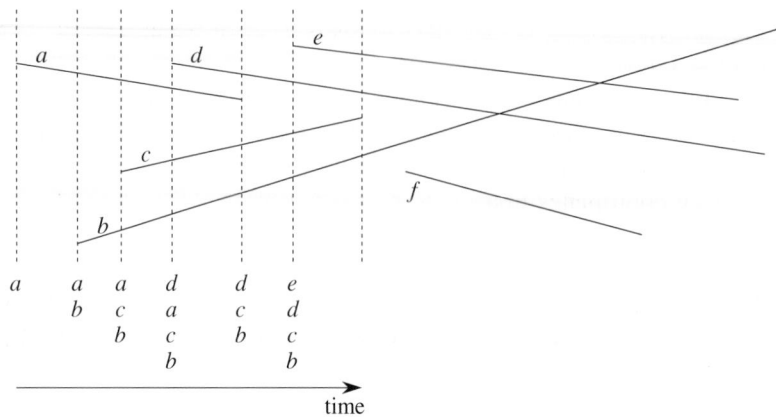

$$a \qquad a \qquad a \qquad d \qquad d \qquad e$$
$$ \qquad b \qquad c \qquad a \qquad c \qquad d$$
$$ \qquad \qquad b \qquad c \qquad b \qquad c$$
$$ \qquad \qquad \qquad b \qquad \qquad b$$

time

Figure 33.5   The execution of ANY-SEGMENTS-INTERSECT. Each dashed line is the sweep line at an event point. Except for the rightmost sweep line, the ordering of segment names below each sweep line corresponds to the total preorder T at the end of the **for** loop processing the corresponding event point. The rightmost sweep line occurs when processing the right endpoint of segment c; because segments d and b surround c and intersect each other, the procedure returns TRUE.

Correctness

To show that ANY-SEGMENTS-INTERSECT is correct, we will prove that the call ANY-SEGMENTS-INTERSECT(S) returns TRUE if and only if there is an intersection among the segments in S.

It is easy to see that ANY-SEGMENTS-INTERSECT returns TRUE (on lines 7 and 10) only if it finds an intersection between two of the input segments. Hence, if it returns TRUE, there is an intersection.

We also need to show the converse: that if there is an intersection, then ANY-SEGMENTS-INTERSECT returns TRUE. Let us suppose that there is at least one intersection. Let p be the leftmost intersection point, breaking ties by choosing the point with the lowest y-coordinate, and let a and b be the segments that intersect at p. Since no intersections occur to the left of p, the order given by T is correct at all points to the left of p. Because no three segments intersect at the same point, a and b become consecutive in the total preorder at some sweep line z.[2] Moreover, z is to the left of p or goes through p. Some segment endpoint q on sweep line z

---

[2]If we allow three segments to intersect at the same point, there may be an intervening segment c that intersects both a and b at point p. That is, we may have $a \succeq_w c$ and $c \succeq_w b$ for all sweep lines w to the left of p for which $a \succeq_w b$. Exercise 33.2-8 asks you to show that ANY-SEGMENTS-INTERSECT is correct even if three segments do intersect at the same point.

is the event point at which a and b become consecutive in the total preorder. If p is on sweep line z, then $q = p$. If p is not on sweep line z, then q is to the left of p. In either case, the order given by T is correct just before encountering q. (Here is where we use the lexicographic order in which the algorithm processes event points. Because p is the lowest of the leftmost intersection points, even if p is on sweep line z and some other intersection point p' is on z, event point $q = p$ is processed before the other intersection p' can interfere with the total preorder T. Moreover, even if p is the left endpoint of one segment, say a, and the right endpoint of the other segment, say b, because left endpoint events occur before right endpoint events, segment b is in T upon first encountering segment a.) Either event point q is processed by ANY-SEGMENTS-INTERSECT or it is not processed.

If q is processed by ANY-SEGMENTS-INTERSECT, only two possible actions may occur:

1. Either a or b is inserted into T, and the other segment is above or below it in the total preorder. Lines 4–7 detect this case.

2. Segments a and b are already in T, and a segment between them in the total preorder is deleted, making a and b become consecutive. Lines 8–11 detect this case.

In either case, we find the intersection p and ANY-SEGMENTS-INTERSECT returns TRUE.

If event point q is not processed by ANY-SEGMENTS-INTERSECT, the procedure must have returned before processing all event points. This situation could have occurred only if ANY-SEGMENTS-INTERSECT had already found an intersection and returned TRUE.

Thus, if there is an intersection, ANY-SEGMENTS-INTERSECT returns TRUE. As we have already seen, if ANY-SEGMENTS-INTERSECT returns TRUE, there is an intersection. Therefore, ANY-SEGMENTS-INTERSECT always returns a correct answer.

Running time

If set S contains n segments, then ANY-SEGMENTS-INTERSECT runs in time $O(n \lg n)$. Line 1 takes $O(1)$ time. Line 2 takes $O(n \lg n)$ time, using merge sort or heapsort. The **for** loop of lines 3–11 iterates at most once per event point, and so with $2n$ event points, the loop iterates at most $2n$ times. Each iteration takes $O(\lg n)$ time, since each red-black-tree operation takes $O(\lg n)$ time and, using the method of Section 33.1, each intersection test takes $O(1)$ time. The total time is thus $O(n \lg n)$.

Exercises

33.2-1
Show that a set of n line segments may contain $\Theta(n^2)$ intersections.

33.2-2
Given two segments a and b that are comparable at x, show how to determine in $O(1)$ time which of $a \succeq_x b$ or $b \succeq_x a$ holds. Assume that neither segment is vertical. (*Hint:* If a and b do not intersect, you can just use cross products. If a and b intersect—which you can of course determine using only cross products—you can still use only addition, subtraction, and multiplication, avoiding division. Of course, in the application of the $\succeq_x$ relation used here, if a and b intersect, we can just stop and declare that we have found an intersection.)

33.2-3
Professor Mason suggests that we modify ANY-SEGMENTS-INTERSECT so that instead of returning upon finding an intersection, it prints the segments that intersect and continues on to the next iteration of the **for** loop. The professor calls the resulting procedure PRINT-INTERSECTING-SEGMENTS and claims that it prints all intersections, from left to right, as they occur in the set of line segments. Professor Dixon disagrees, claiming that Professor Mason's idea is incorrect. Which professor is right? Will PRINT-INTERSECTING-SEGMENTS always find the leftmost intersection first? Will it always find all the intersections?

33.2-4
Give an $O(n \lg n)$-time algorithm to determine whether an n-vertex polygon is simple.

33.2-5
Give an $O(n \lg n)$-time algorithm to determine whether two simple polygons with a total of n vertices intersect.

33.2-6
A *disk* consists of a circle plus its interior and is represented by its center point and radius. Two disks intersect if they have any point in common. Give an $O(n \lg n)$-time algorithm to determine whether any two disks in a set of n intersect.

33.2-7
Given a set of n line segments containing a total of k intersections, show how to output all k intersections in $O((n + k) \lg n)$ time.

33.2-8

Argue that ANY-SEGMENTS-INTERSECT works correctly even if three or more segments intersect at the same point.

33.2-9

Show that ANY-SEGMENTS-INTERSECT works correctly in the presence of vertical segments if we treat the bottom endpoint of a vertical segment as if it were a left endpoint and the top endpoint as if it were a right endpoint. How does your answer to Exercise 33.2-2 change if we allow vertical segments?

33.3   Finding the convex hull

The *convex hull* of a set Q of points, denoted by CH(Q), is the smallest convex polygon P for which each point in Q is either on the boundary of P or in its interior. (See Exercise 33.1-5 for a precise definition of a convex polygon.) We implicitly assume that all points in the set Q are unique and that Q contains at least three points which are not colinear. Intuitively, we can think of each point in Q as being a nail sticking out from a board. The convex hull is then the shape formed by a tight rubber band that surrounds all the nails. Figure 33.6 shows a set of points and its convex hull.

In this section, we shall present two algorithms that compute the convex hull of a set of n points. Both algorithms output the vertices of the convex hull in counterclockwise order. The first, known as Graham's scan, runs in $O(n \lg n)$ time. The second, called Jarvis's march, runs in $O(nh)$ time, where h is the number of vertices of the convex hull. As Figure 33.6 illustrates, every vertex of CH(Q) is a

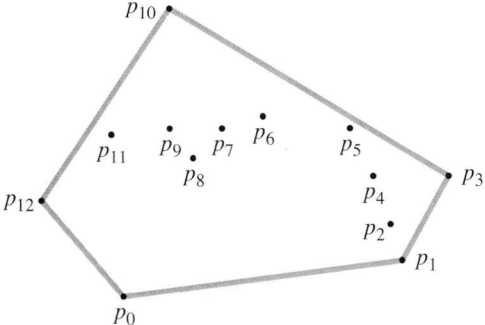

Figure 33.6   A set of points $Q = \{p_0, p_1, \ldots, p_{12}\}$ with its convex hull CH(Q) in gray.

point in Q. Both algorithms exploit this property, deciding which vertices in Q to keep as vertices of the convex hull and which vertices in Q to reject.

We can compute convex hulls in $O(n \lg n)$ time by any one of several methods. Both Graham's scan and Jarvis's march use a technique called "rotational sweep," processing vertices in the order of the polar angles they form with a reference vertex. Other methods include the following:

- In the ***incremental method***, we first sort the points from left to right, yielding a sequence $\langle p_1, p_2, \ldots, p_n \rangle$. At the ith stage, we update the convex hull of the $i - 1$ leftmost points, $CH(\{p_1, p_2, \ldots, p_{i-1}\})$, according to the ith point from the left, thus forming $CH(\{p_1, p_2, \ldots, p_i\})$. Exercise 33.3-6 asks you how to implement this method to take a total of $O(n \lg n)$ time.

- In the ***divide-and-conquer method***, we divide the set of n points in $\Theta(n)$ time into two subsets, one containing the leftmost $\lceil n/2 \rceil$ points and one containing the rightmost $\lfloor n/2 \rfloor$ points, recursively compute the convex hulls of the subsets, and then, by means of a clever method, combine the hulls in $O(n)$ time. The running time is described by the familiar recurrence $T(n) = 2T(n/2) + O(n)$, and so the divide-and-conquer method runs in $O(n \lg n)$ time.

- The ***prune-and-search method*** is similar to the worst-case linear-time median algorithm of Section 9.3. With this method, we find the upper portion (or "upper chain") of the convex hull by repeatedly throwing out a constant fraction of the remaining points until only the upper chain of the convex hull remains. We then do the same for the lower chain. This method is asymptotically the fastest: if the convex hull contains h vertices, it runs in only $O(n \lg h)$ time.

Computing the convex hull of a set of points is an interesting problem in its own right. Moreover, algorithms for some other computational-geometry problems start by computing a convex hull. Consider, for example, the two-dimensional ***farthest-pair problem***: we are given a set of n points in the plane and wish to find the two points whose distance from each other is maximum. As Exercise 33.3-3 asks you to prove, these two points must be vertices of the convex hull. Although we won't prove it here, we can find the farthest pair of vertices of an n-vertex convex polygon in $O(n)$ time. Thus, by computing the convex hull of the n input points in $O(n \lg n)$ time and then finding the farthest pair of the resulting convex-polygon vertices, we can find the farthest pair of points in any set of n points in $O(n \lg n)$ time.

Graham's scan

Graham's scan solves the convex-hull problem by maintaining a stack S of candidate points. It pushes each point of the input set Q onto the stack one time,

and it eventually pops from the stack each point that is not a vertex of CH(Q). When the algorithm terminates, stack S contains exactly the vertices of CH(Q), in counterclockwise order of their appearance on the boundary.

The procedure GRAHAM-SCAN takes as input a set Q of points, where $|Q| \geq 3$. It calls the functions TOP(S), which returns the point on top of stack S without changing S, and NEXT-TO-TOP(S), which returns the point one entry below the top of stack S without changing S. As we shall prove in a moment, the stack S returned by GRAHAM-SCAN contains, from bottom to top, exactly the vertices of CH(Q) in counterclockwise order.

GRAHAM-SCAN(Q)

```
 1   let p₀ be the point in Q with the minimum y-coordinate,
          or the leftmost such point in case of a tie
 2   let ⟨p₁, p₂, ..., pₘ⟩ be the remaining points in Q,
          sorted by polar angle in counterclockwise order around p₀
          (if more than one point has the same angle, remove all but
          the one that is farthest from p₀)
 3   if m < 2
 4       return "convex hull is empty"
 5   else let S be an empty stack
 6       PUSH(S, p₀)
 7       PUSH(S, p₁)
 8       PUSH(S, p₂)
 9       for i = 3 to m
10           while the angle formed by points NEXT-TO-TOP(S), TOP(S),
                      and pᵢ makes a nonleft turn
11               POP(S)
12           PUSH(S, pᵢ)
13       return S
```

Figure 33.7 illustrates the progress of GRAHAM-SCAN. Line 1 chooses point p_0 as the point with the lowest y-coordinate, picking the leftmost such point in case of a tie. Since there is no point in Q that is below p_0 and any other points with the same y-coordinate are to its right, p_0 must be a vertex of CH(Q). Line 2 sorts the remaining points of Q by polar angle relative to p_0, using the same method—comparing cross products—as in Exercise 33.1-3. If two or more points have the same polar angle relative to p_0, all but the farthest such point are convex combinations of p_0 and the farthest point, and so we remove them entirely from consideration. We let m denote the number of points other than p_0 that remain. The polar angle, measured in radians, of each point in Q relative to p_0 is in the half-open interval $[0, \pi)$. Since the points are sorted according to polar angles, they are sorted in counterclockwise order relative to p_0. We designate this sorted

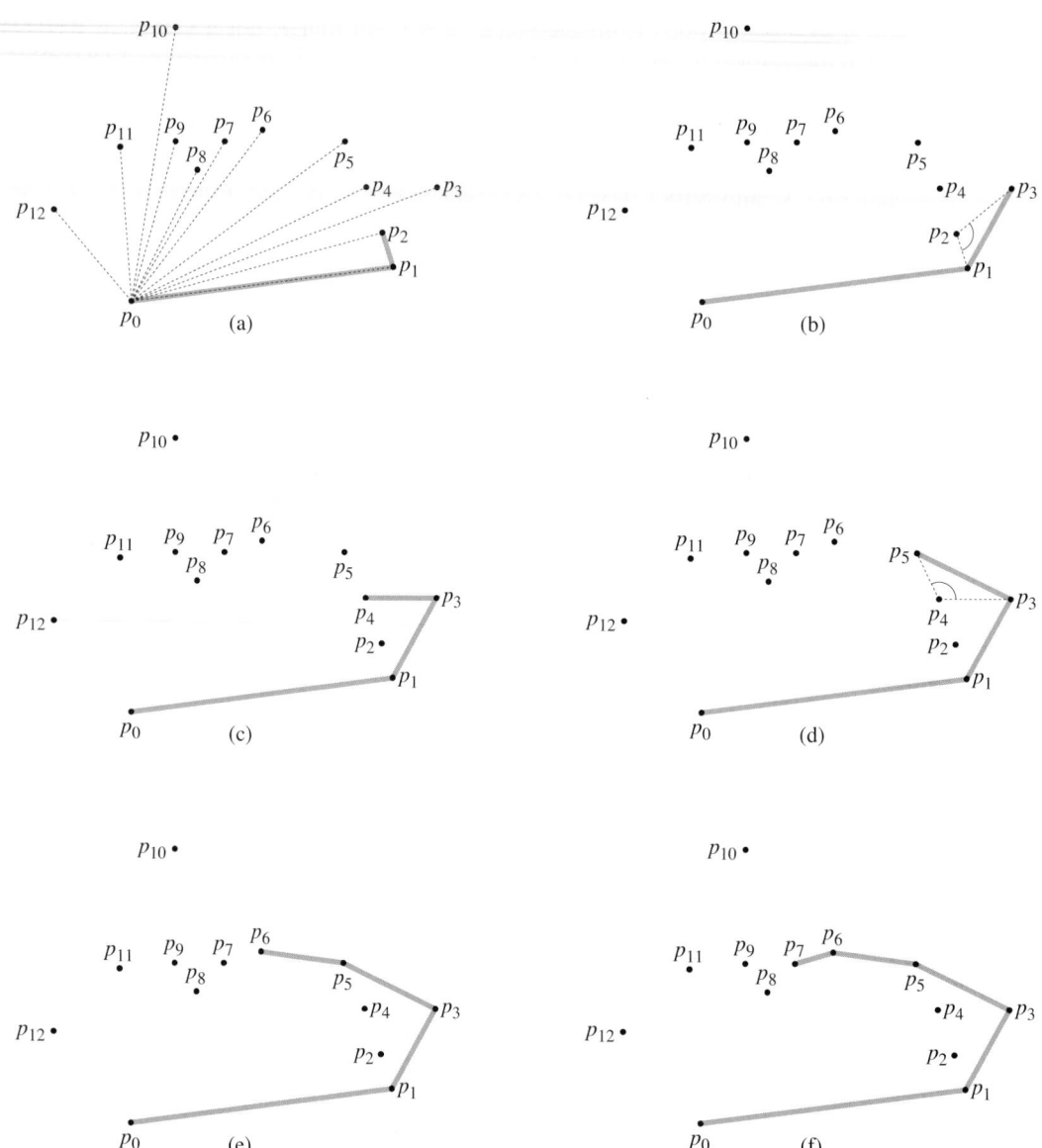

Figure 33.7 The execution of GRAHAM-SCAN on the set Q of Figure 33.6. The current convex hull contained in stack S is shown in gray at each step. **(a)** The sequence $\langle p_1, p_2, \ldots, p_{12} \rangle$ of points numbered in order of increasing polar angle relative to p_0, and the initial stack S containing p_0, p_1, and p_2. **(b)–(k)** Stack S after each iteration of the **for** loop of lines 9–12. Dashed lines show nonleft turns, which cause points to be popped from the stack. In part (h), for example, the right turn at angle $\angle p_7 p_8 p_9$ causes p_8 to be popped, and then the right turn at angle $\angle p_6 p_7 p_9$ causes p_7 to be popped.

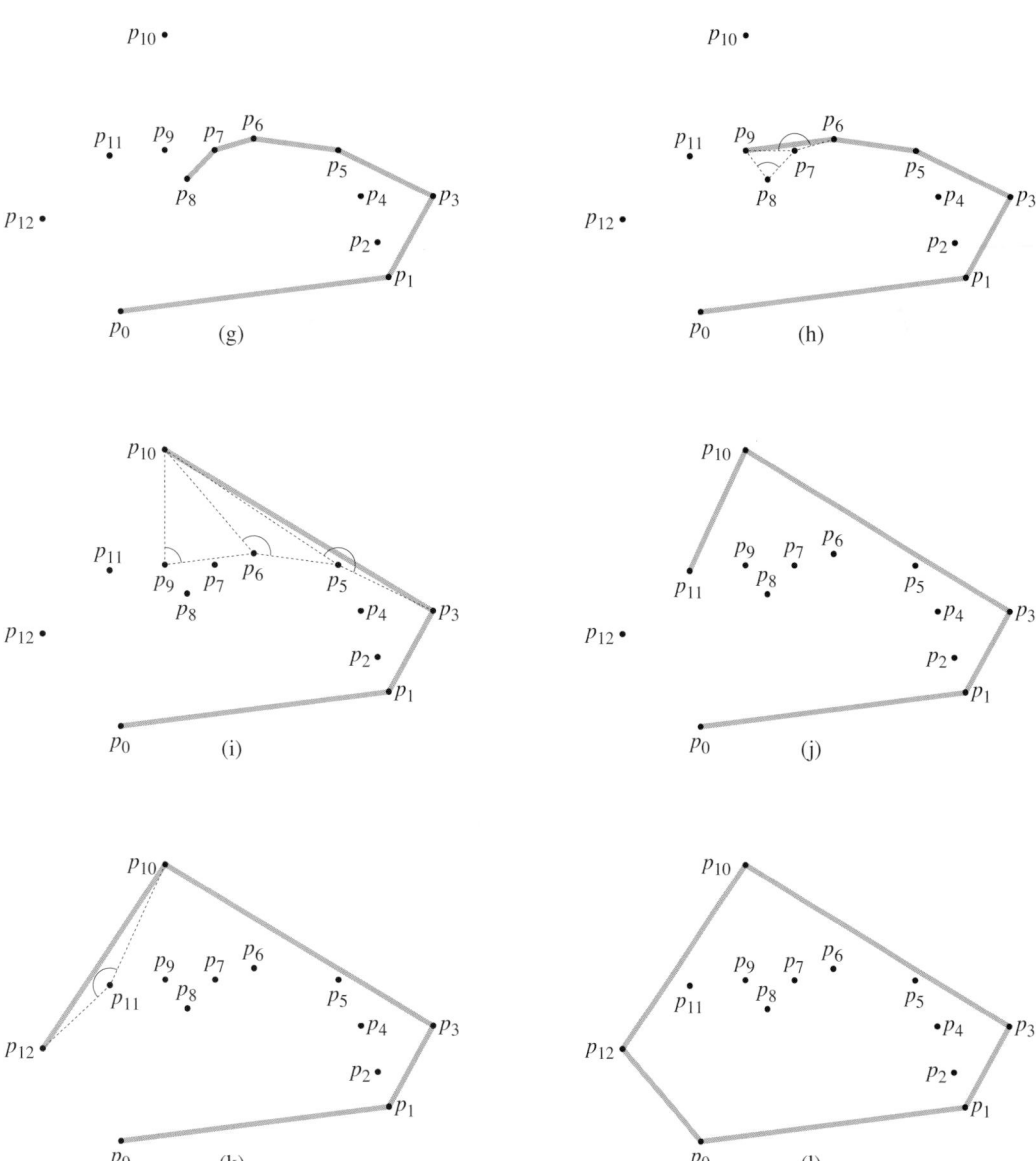

Figure 33.7, continued   **(l)** The convex hull returned by the procedure, which matches that of Figure 33.6.

sequence of points by $\langle p_1, p_2, \ldots, p_m \rangle$. Note that points p_1 and p_m are vertices of CH(Q) (see Exercise 33.3-1). Figure 33.7(a) shows the points of Figure 33.6 sequentially numbered in order of increasing polar angle relative to p_0.

The remainder of the procedure uses the stack S. Lines 5–8 initialize the stack to contain, from bottom to top, the first three points p_0, p_1, and p_2. Figure 33.7(a) shows the initial stack S. The **for** loop of lines 9–12 iterates once for each point in the subsequence $\langle p_3, p_4, \ldots, p_m \rangle$. We shall see that after processing point p_i, stack S contains, from bottom to top, the vertices of CH($\{p_0, p_1, \ldots, p_i\}$) in counterclockwise order. The **while** loop of lines 10–11 removes points from the stack if we find them not to be vertices of the convex hull. When we traverse the convex hull counterclockwise, we should make a left turn at each vertex. Thus, each time the **while** loop finds a vertex at which we make a nonleft turn, we pop the vertex from the stack. (By checking for a nonleft turn, rather than just a right turn, this test precludes the possibility of a straight angle at a vertex of the resulting convex hull. We want no straight angles, since no vertex of a convex polygon may be a convex combination of other vertices of the polygon.) After we pop all vertices that have nonleft turns when heading toward point p_i, we push p_i onto the stack. Figures 33.7(b)–(k) show the state of the stack S after each iteration of the **for** loop. Finally, GRAHAM-SCAN returns the stack S in line 13. Figure 33.7(l) shows the corresponding convex hull.

The following theorem formally proves the correctness of GRAHAM-SCAN.

Theorem 33.1 (Correctness of Graham's scan)
If GRAHAM-SCAN executes on a set Q of points, where $|Q| \geq 3$, then at termination, the stack S consists of, from bottom to top, exactly the vertices of CH(Q) in counterclockwise order.

Proof After line 2, we have the sequence of points $\langle p_1, p_2, \ldots, p_m \rangle$. Let us define, for $i = 2, 3, \ldots, m$, the subset of points $Q_i = \{p_0, p_1, \ldots, p_i\}$. The points in $Q - Q_m$ are those that were removed because they had the same polar angle relative to p_0 as some point in Q_m; these points are not in CH(Q), and so CH(Q_m) = CH(Q). Thus, it suffices to show that when GRAHAM-SCAN terminates, the stack S consists of the vertices of CH(Q_m) in counterclockwise order, when listed from bottom to top. Note that just as p_0, p_1, and p_m are vertices of CH(Q), the points p_0, p_1, and p_i are all vertices of CH(Q_i).

The proof uses the following loop invariant:

> At the start of each iteration of the **for** loop of lines 9–12, stack S consists of, from bottom to top, exactly the vertices of CH(Q_{i-1}) in counterclockwise order.

Initialization: The invariant holds the first time we execute line 9, since at that time, stack S consists of exactly the vertices of $Q_2 = Q_{i-1}$, and this set of three

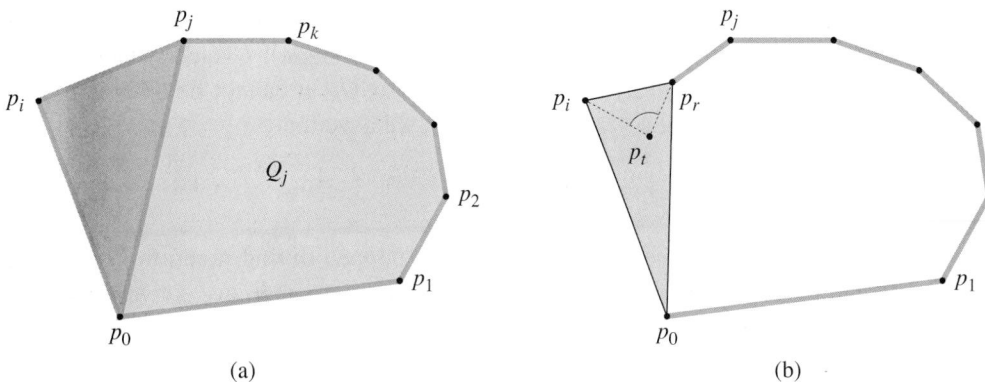

Figure 33.8 The proof of correctness of GRAHAM-SCAN. **(a)** Because p_i's polar angle relative to p_0 is greater than p_j's polar angle, and because the angle $\angle p_k p_j p_i$ makes a left turn, adding p_i to $CH(Q_j)$ gives exactly the vertices of $CH(Q_j \cup \{p_i\})$. **(b)** If the angle $\angle p_r p_t p_i$ makes a nonleft turn, then p_t is either in the interior of the triangle formed by p_0, p_r, and p_i or on a side of the triangle, which means that it cannot be a vertex of $CH(Q_i)$.

vertices forms its own convex hull. Moreover, they appear in counterclockwise order from bottom to top.

Maintenance: Entering an iteration of the **for** loop, the top point on stack S is p_{i-1}, which was pushed at the end of the previous iteration (or before the first iteration, when $i = 3$). Let p_j be the top point on S after executing the while loop of lines 10–11 but before line 12 pushes p_i, and let p_k be the point just below p_j on S. At the moment that p_j is the top point on S and we have not yet pushed p_i, stack S contains exactly the same points it contained after iteration j of the **for** loop. By the loop invariant, therefore, S contains exactly the vertices of $CH(Q_j)$ at that moment, and they appear in counterclockwise order from bottom to top.

Let us continue to focus on this moment just before pushing p_i. We know that p_i's polar angle relative to p_0 is greater than p_j's polar angle and that the angle $\angle p_k p_j p_i$ makes a left turn (otherwise we would have popped p_j). Therefore, because S contains exactly the vertices of $CH(Q_j)$, we see from Figure 33.8(a) that once we push p_i, stack S will contain exactly the vertices of $CH(Q_j \cup \{p_i\})$, still in counterclockwise order from bottom to top.

We now show that $CH(Q_j \cup \{p_i\})$ is the same set of points as $CH(Q_i)$. Consider any point p_t that was popped during iteration i of the **for** loop, and let p_r be the point just below p_t on stack S at the time p_t was popped (p_r might be p_j). The angle $\angle p_r p_t p_i$ makes a nonleft turn, and the polar angle of p_t relative to p_0 is greater than the polar angle of p_r. As Figure 33.8(b) shows, p_t must

be either in the interior of the triangle formed by p_0, p_r, and p_i or on a side of this triangle (but it is not a vertex of the triangle). Clearly, since p_t is within a triangle formed by three other points of Q_i, it cannot be a vertex of $CH(Q_i)$. Since p_t is not a vertex of $CH(Q_i)$, we have that

$$CH(Q_i - \{p_t\}) = CH(Q_i) \ . \tag{33.1}$$

Let P_i be the set of points that were popped during iteration i of the **for** loop. Since the equality (33.1) applies for all points in P_i, we can apply it repeatedly to show that $CH(Q_i - P_i) = CH(Q_i)$. But $Q_i - P_i = Q_j \cup \{p_i\}$, and so we conclude that $CH(Q_j \cup \{p_i\}) = CH(Q_i - P_i) = CH(Q_i)$.

We have shown that once we push p_i, stack S contains exactly the vertices of $CH(Q_i)$ in counterclockwise order from bottom to top. Incrementing i will then cause the loop invariant to hold for the next iteration.

Termination: When the loop terminates, we have $i = m + 1$, and so the loop invariant implies that stack S consists of exactly the vertices of $CH(Q_m)$, which is $CH(Q)$, in counterclockwise order from bottom to top. This completes the proof.   ∎

We now show that the running time of GRAHAM-SCAN is $O(n \lg n)$, where $n = |Q|$. Line 1 takes $\Theta(n)$ time. Line 2 takes $O(n \lg n)$ time, using merge sort or heapsort to sort the polar angles and the cross-product method of Section 33.1 to compare angles. (We can remove all but the farthest point with the same polar angle in total of $O(n)$ time over all n points.) Lines 5–8 take $O(1)$ time. Because $m \leq n - 1$, the **for** loop of lines 9–12 executes at most $n - 3$ times. Since PUSH takes $O(1)$ time, each iteration takes $O(1)$ time exclusive of the time spent in the **while** loop of lines 10–11, and thus overall the **for** loop takes $O(n)$ time exclusive of the nested **while** loop.

We use aggregate analysis to show that the **while** loop takes $O(n)$ time overall. For $i = 0, 1, \ldots, m$, we push each point p_i onto stack S exactly once. As in the analysis of the MULTIPOP procedure of Section 17.1, we observe that we can pop at most the number of items that we push. At least three points—p_0, p_1, and p_m—are never popped from the stack, so that in fact at most $m - 2$ POP operations are performed in total. Each iteration of the **while** loop performs one POP, and so there are at most $m - 2$ iterations of the **while** loop altogether. Since the test in line 10 takes $O(1)$ time, each call of POP takes $O(1)$ time, and $m \leq n - 1$, the total time taken by the **while** loop is $O(n)$. Thus, the running time of GRAHAM-SCAN is $O(n \lg n)$.

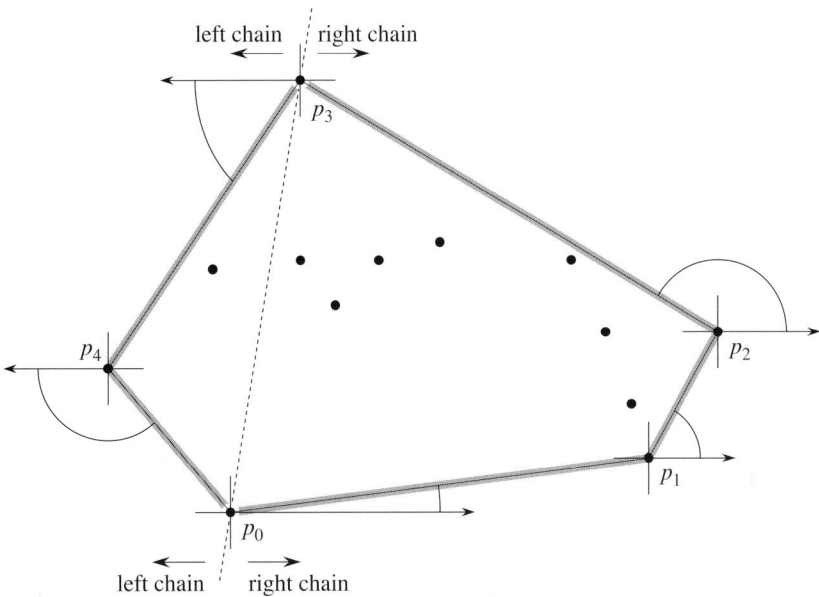

Figure 33.9 The operation of Jarvis's march. We choose the first vertex as the lowest point p_0. The next vertex, p_1, has the smallest polar angle of any point with respect to p_0. Then, p_2 has the smallest polar angle with respect to p_1. The right chain goes as high as the highest point p_3. Then, we construct the left chain by finding smallest polar angles with respect to the negative x-axis.

Jarvis's march

Jarvis's march computes the convex hull of a set Q of points by a technique known as ***package wrapping*** (or ***gift wrapping***). The algorithm runs in time $O(nh)$, where h is the number of vertices of $\mathrm{CH}(Q)$. When h is $o(\lg n)$, Jarvis's march is asymptotically faster than Graham's scan.

Intuitively, Jarvis's march simulates wrapping a taut piece of paper around the set Q. We start by taping the end of the paper to the lowest point in the set, that is, to the same point p_0 with which we start Graham's scan. We know that this point must be a vertex of the convex hull. We pull the paper to the right to make it taut, and then we pull it higher until it touches a point. This point must also be a vertex of the convex hull. Keeping the paper taut, we continue in this way around the set of vertices until we come back to our original point p_0.

More formally, Jarvis's march builds a sequence $H = \langle p_0, p_1, \ldots, p_{h-1} \rangle$ of the vertices of $\mathrm{CH}(Q)$. We start with p_0. As Figure 33.9 shows, the next vertex p_1 in the convex hull has the smallest polar angle with respect to p_0. (In case of ties, we choose the point farthest from p_0.) Similarly, p_2 has the smallest polar angle

with respect to p_1, and so on. When we reach the highest vertex, say p_k (breaking ties by choosing the farthest such vertex), we have constructed, as Figure 33.9 shows, the **right chain** of CH(Q). To construct the **left chain**, we start at p_k and choose p_{k+1} as the point with the smallest polar angle with respect to p_k, but *from the negative x-axis*. We continue on, forming the left chain by taking polar angles from the negative x-axis, until we come back to our original vertex p_0.

We could implement Jarvis's march in one conceptual sweep around the convex hull, that is, without separately constructing the right and left chains. Such implementations typically keep track of the angle of the last convex-hull side chosen and require the sequence of angles of hull sides to be strictly increasing (in the range of 0 to 2π radians). The advantage of constructing separate chains is that we need not explicitly compute angles; the techniques of Section 33.1 suffice to compare angles.

If implemented properly, Jarvis's march has a running time of $O(nh)$. For each of the h vertices of CH(Q), we find the vertex with the minimum polar angle. Each comparison between polar angles takes $O(1)$ time, using the techniques of Section 33.1. As Section 9.1 shows, we can compute the minimum of n values in $O(n)$ time if each comparison takes $O(1)$ time. Thus, Jarvis's march takes $O(nh)$ time.

Exercises

33.3-1
Prove that in the procedure GRAHAM-SCAN, points p_1 and p_m must be vertices of CH(Q).

33.3-2
Consider a model of computation that supports addition, comparison, and multiplication and for which there is a lower bound of $\Omega(n \lg n)$ to sort n numbers. Prove that $\Omega(n \lg n)$ is a lower bound for computing, in order, the vertices of the convex hull of a set of n points in such a model.

33.3-3
Given a set of points Q, prove that the pair of points farthest from each other must be vertices of CH(Q).

33.3-4
For a given polygon P and a point q on its boundary, the **shadow** of q is the set of points r such that the segment $\overline{qr}$ is entirely on the boundary or in the interior of P. As Figure 33.10 illustrates, a polygon P is **star-shaped** if there exists a point p in the interior of P that is in the shadow of every point on the boundary of P. The set of all such points p is called the **kernel** of P. Given an n-vertex,

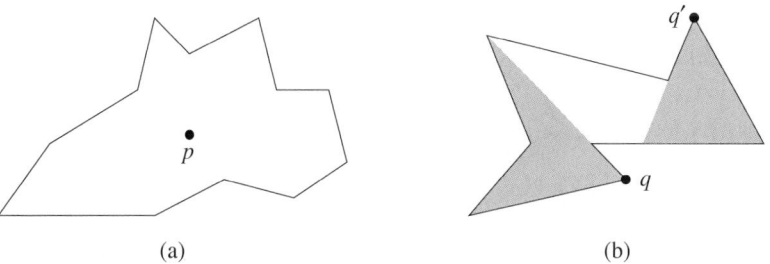

(a)   (b)

Figure 33.10   The definition of a star-shaped polygon, for use in Exercise 33.3-4. **(a)** A star-shaped polygon. The segment from point p to any point q on the boundary intersects the boundary only at q. **(b)** A non-star-shaped polygon. The shaded region on the left is the shadow of q, and the shaded region on the right is the shadow of q'. Since these regions are disjoint, the kernel is empty.

star-shaped polygon P specified by its vertices in counterclockwise order, show how to compute $CH(P)$ in $O(n)$ time.

33.3-5
In the **on-line convex-hull problem**, we are given the set Q of n points one point at a time. After receiving each point, we compute the convex hull of the points seen so far. Obviously, we could run Graham's scan once for each point, with a total running time of $O(n^2 \lg n)$. Show how to solve the on-line convex-hull problem in a total of $O(n^2)$ time.

33.3-6 ★
Show how to implement the incremental method for computing the convex hull of n points so that it runs in $O(n \lg n)$ time.

33.4 Finding the closest pair of points

We now consider the problem of finding the closest pair of points in a set Q of $n \geq 2$ points. "Closest" refers to the usual euclidean distance: the distance between points $p_1 = (x_1, y_1)$ and $p_2 = (x_2, y_2)$ is $\sqrt{(x_1 - x_2)^2 + (y_1 - y_2)^2}$. Two points in set Q may be coincident, in which case the distance between them is zero. This problem has applications in, for example, traffic-control systems. A system for controlling air or sea traffic might need to identify the two closest vehicles in order to detect potential collisions.

A brute-force closest-pair algorithm simply looks at all the $\binom{n}{2} = \Theta(n^2)$ pairs of points. In this section, we shall describe a divide-and-conquer algorithm for

this problem, whose running time is described by the familiar recurrence $T(n) = 2T(n/2) + O(n)$. Thus, this algorithm uses only $O(n \lg n)$ time.

The divide-and-conquer algorithm

Each recursive invocation of the algorithm takes as input a subset $P \subseteq Q$ and arrays X and Y, each of which contains all the points of the input subset P. The points in array X are sorted so that their x-coordinates are monotonically increasing. Similarly, array Y is sorted by monotonically increasing y-coordinate. Note that in order to attain the $O(n \lg n)$ time bound, we cannot afford to sort in each recursive call; if we did, the recurrence for the running time would be $T(n) = 2T(n/2) + O(n \lg n)$, whose solution is $T(n) = O(n \lg^2 n)$. (Use the version of the master method given in Exercise 4.6-2.) We shall see a little later how to use "presorting" to maintain this sorted property without actually sorting in each recursive call.

A given recursive invocation with inputs P, X, and Y first checks whether $|P| \leq 3$. If so, the invocation simply performs the brute-force method described above: try all $\binom{|P|}{2}$ pairs of points and return the closest pair. If $|P| > 3$, the recursive invocation carries out the divide-and-conquer paradigm as follows.

Divide: Find a vertical line l that bisects the point set P into two sets P_L and P_R such that $|P_L| = \lceil |P|/2 \rceil$, $|P_R| = \lfloor |P|/2 \rfloor$, all points in P_L are on or to the left of line l, and all points in P_R are on or to the right of l. Divide the array X into arrays X_L and X_R, which contain the points of P_L and P_R respectively, sorted by monotonically increasing x-coordinate. Similarly, divide the array Y into arrays Y_L and Y_R, which contain the points of P_L and P_R respectively, sorted by monotonically increasing y-coordinate.

Conquer: Having divided P into P_L and P_R, make two recursive calls, one to find the closest pair of points in P_L and the other to find the closest pair of points in P_R. The inputs to the first call are the subset P_L and arrays X_L and Y_L; the second call receives the inputs P_R, X_R, and Y_R. Let the closest-pair distances returned for P_L and P_R be δ_L and δ_R, respectively, and let $\delta = \min(\delta_L, \delta_R)$.

Combine: The closest pair is either the pair with distance δ found by one of the recursive calls, or it is a pair of points with one point in P_L and the other in P_R. The algorithm determines whether there is a pair with one point in P_L and the other point in P_R and whose distance is less than δ. Observe that if a pair of points has distance less than δ, both points of the pair must be within δ units of line l. Thus, as Figure 33.11(a) shows, they both must reside in the 2δ-wide vertical strip centered at line l. To find such a pair, if one exists, we do the following:

1. Create an array Y', which is the array Y with all points not in the 2δ-wide vertical strip removed. The array Y' is sorted by y-coordinate, just as Y is.

2. For each point p in the array Y', try to find points in Y' that are within δ units of p. As we shall see shortly, only the 7 points in Y' that follow p need be considered. Compute the distance from p to each of these 7 points, and keep track of the closest-pair distance δ' found over all pairs of points in Y'.

3. If $\delta' < \delta$, then the vertical strip does indeed contain a closer pair than the recursive calls found. Return this pair and its distance δ'. Otherwise, return the closest pair and its distance δ found by the recursive calls.

The above description omits some implementation details that are necessary to achieve the $O(n \lg n)$ running time. After proving the correctness of the algorithm, we shall show how to implement the algorithm to achieve the desired time bound.

Correctness

The correctness of this closest-pair algorithm is obvious, except for two aspects. First, by bottoming out the recursion when $|P| \leq 3$, we ensure that we never try to solve a subproblem consisting of only one point. The second aspect is that we need only check the 7 points following each point p in array Y'; we shall now prove this property.

Suppose that at some level of the recursion, the closest pair of points is $p_L \in P_L$ and $p_R \in P_R$. Thus, the distance δ' between p_L and p_R is strictly less than δ. Point p_L must be on or to the left of line l and less than δ units away. Similarly, p_R is on or to the right of l and less than δ units away. Moreover, p_L and p_R are within δ units of each other vertically. Thus, as Figure 33.11(a) shows, p_L and p_R are within a $\delta \times 2\delta$ rectangle centered at line l. (There may be other points within this rectangle as well.)

We next show that at most 8 points of P can reside within this $\delta \times 2\delta$ rectangle. Consider the $\delta \times \delta$ square forming the left half of this rectangle. Since all points within P_L are at least δ units apart, at most 4 points can reside within this square; Figure 33.11(b) shows how. Similarly, at most 4 points in P_R can reside within the $\delta \times \delta$ square forming the right half of the rectangle. Thus, at most 8 points of P can reside within the $\delta \times 2\delta$ rectangle. (Note that since points on line l may be in either P_L or P_R, there may be up to 4 points on l. This limit is achieved if there are two pairs of coincident points such that each pair consists of one point from P_L and one point from P_R, one pair is at the intersection of l and the top of the rectangle, and the other pair is where l intersects the bottom of the rectangle.)

Having shown that at most 8 points of P can reside within the rectangle, we can easily see why we need to check only the 7 points following each point in the array Y'. Still assuming that the closest pair is p_L and p_R, let us assume without

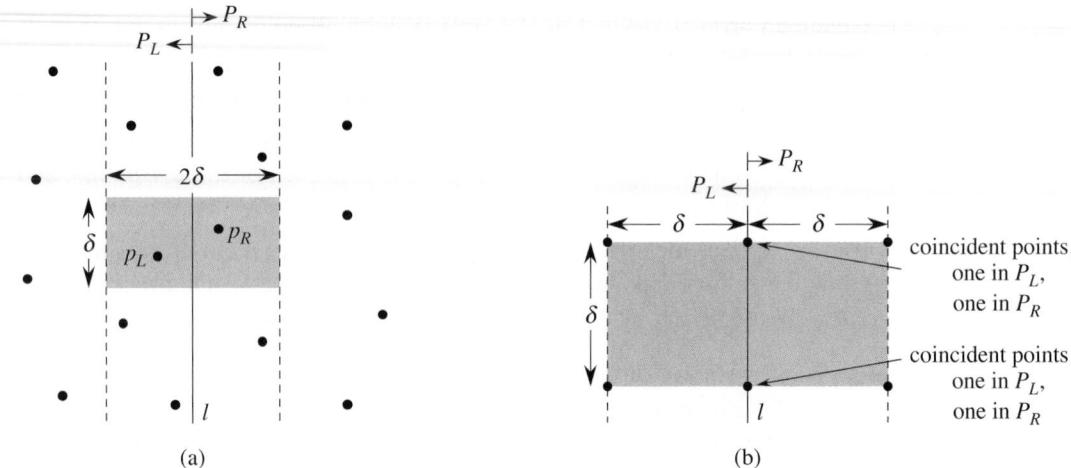

Figure 33.11   Key concepts in the proof that the closest-pair algorithm needs to check only 7 points following each point in the array Y'. **(a)** If $p_L \in P_L$ and $p_R \in P_R$ are less than δ units apart, they must reside within a $\delta \times 2\delta$ rectangle centered at line l. **(b)** How 4 points that are pairwise at least δ units apart can all reside within a $\delta \times \delta$ square. On the left are 4 points in P_L, and on the right are 4 points in P_R. The $\delta \times 2\delta$ rectangle can contain 8 points if the points shown on line l are actually pairs of coincident points with one point in P_L and one in P_R.

loss of generality that p_L precedes p_R in array Y'. Then, even if p_L occurs as early as possible in Y' and p_R occurs as late as possible, p_R is in one of the 7 positions following p_L. Thus, we have shown the correctness of the closest-pair algorithm.

Implementation and running time

As we have noted, our goal is to have the recurrence for the running time be $T(n) = 2T(n/2) + O(n)$, where $T(n)$ is the running time for a set of n points. The main difficulty comes from ensuring that the arrays X_L, X_R, Y_L, and Y_R, which are passed to recursive calls, are sorted by the proper coordinate and also that the array Y' is sorted by y-coordinate. (Note that if the array X that is received by a recursive call is already sorted, then we can easily divide set P into P_L and P_R in linear time.)

The key observation is that in each call, we wish to form a sorted subset of a sorted array. For example, a particular invocation receives the subset P and the array Y, sorted by y-coordinate. Having partitioned P into P_L and P_R, it needs to form the arrays Y_L and Y_R, which are sorted by y-coordinate, in linear time. We can view the method as the opposite of the MERGE procedure from merge sort in

Section 2.3.1: we are splitting a sorted array into two sorted arrays. The following pseudocode gives the idea.

```
1   let Y_L[1 .. Y.length] and Y_R[1 .. Y.length] be new arrays
2   Y_L.length = Y_R.length = 0
3   for i = 1 to Y.length
4        if Y[i] ∈ P_L
5             Y_L.length = Y_L.length + 1
6             Y_L[Y_L.length] = Y[i]
7        else Y_R.length = Y_R.length + 1
8             Y_R[Y_R.length] = Y[i]
```

We simply examine the points in array Y in order. If a point $Y[i]$ is in P_L, we append it to the end of array Y_L; otherwise, we append it to the end of array Y_R. Similar pseudocode works for forming arrays X_L, X_R, and Y'.

The only remaining question is how to get the points sorted in the first place. We *presort* them; that is, we sort them once and for all *before* the first recursive call. We pass these sorted arrays into the first recursive call, and from there we whittle them down through the recursive calls as necessary. Presorting adds an additional $O(n \lg n)$ term to the running time, but now each step of the recursion takes linear time exclusive of the recursive calls. Thus, if we let $T(n)$ be the running time of each recursive step and $T'(n)$ be the running time of the entire algorithm, we get $T'(n) = T(n) + O(n \lg n)$ and

$$T(n) = \begin{cases} 2T(n/2) + O(n) & \text{if } n > 3, \\ O(1) & \text{if } n \leq 3. \end{cases}$$

Thus, $T(n) = O(n \lg n)$ and $T'(n) = O(n \lg n)$.

Exercises

33.4-1
Professor Williams comes up with a scheme that allows the closest-pair algorithm to check only 5 points following each point in array Y'. The idea is always to place points on line l into set P_L. Then, there cannot be pairs of coincident points on line l with one point in P_L and one in P_R. Thus, at most 6 points can reside in the $\delta \times 2\delta$ rectangle. What is the flaw in the professor's scheme?

33.4-2
Show that it actually suffices to check only the points in the 5 array positions following each point in the array Y'.

33.4-3

We can define the distance between two points in ways other than euclidean. In the plane, the L_m-*distance* between points p_1 and p_2 is given by the expression $(|x_1 - x_2|^m + |y_1 - y_2|^m)^{1/m}$. Euclidean distance, therefore, is L_2-distance. Modify the closest-pair algorithm to use the L_1-distance, which is also known as the *Manhattan distance*.

33.4-4

Given two points p_1 and p_2 in the plane, the L_∞-distance between them is given by $\max(|x_1 - x_2|, |y_1 - y_2|)$. Modify the closest-pair algorithm to use the L_∞-distance.

33.4-5

Suppose that $\Omega(n)$ of the points given to the closest-pair algorithm are covertical. Show how to determine the sets P_L and P_R and how to determine whether each point of Y is in P_L or P_R so that the running time for the closest-pair algorithm remains $O(n \lg n)$.

33.4-6

Suggest a change to the closest-pair algorithm that avoids presorting the Y array but leaves the running time as $O(n \lg n)$. (*Hint:* Merge sorted arrays Y_L and Y_R to form the sorted array Y.)

Problems

33-1   *Convex layers*

Given a set Q of points in the plane, we define the *convex layers* of Q inductively. The first convex layer of Q consists of those points in Q that are vertices of $\text{CH}(Q)$. For $i > 1$, define Q_i to consist of the points of Q with all points in convex layers $1, 2, \ldots, i-1$ removed. Then, the ith convex layer of Q is $\text{CH}(Q_i)$ if $Q_i \neq \emptyset$ and is undefined otherwise.

a. Give an $O(n^2)$-time algorithm to find the convex layers of a set of n points.

b. Prove that $\Omega(n \lg n)$ time is required to compute the convex layers of a set of n points with any model of computation that requires $\Omega(n \lg n)$ time to sort n real numbers.

33-2 Maximal layers

Let Q be a set of n points in the plane. We say that point (x, y) **dominates** point (x', y') if $x \geq x'$ and $y \geq y'$. A point in Q that is dominated by no other points in Q is said to be **maximal**. Note that Q may contain many maximal points, which can be organized into **maximal layers** as follows. The first maximal layer L_1 is the set of maximal points of Q. For $i > 1$, the ith maximal layer L_i is the set of maximal points in $Q - \bigcup_{j=1}^{i-1} L_j$.

Suppose that Q has k nonempty maximal layers, and let y_i be the y-coordinate of the leftmost point in L_i for $i = 1, 2, \ldots, k$. For now, assume that no two points in Q have the same x- or y-coordinate.

a. Show that $y_1 > y_2 > \cdots > y_k$.

Consider a point (x, y) that is to the left of any point in Q and for which y is distinct from the y-coordinate of any point in Q. Let $Q' = Q \cup \{(x, y)\}$.

b. Let j be the minimum index such that $y_j < y$, unless $y < y_k$, in which case we let $j = k + 1$. Show that the maximal layers of Q' are as follows:

- If $j \leq k$, then the maximal layers of Q' are the same as the maximal layers of Q, except that L_j also includes (x, y) as its new leftmost point.
- If $j = k + 1$, then the first k maximal layers of Q' are the same as for Q, but in addition, Q' has a nonempty $(k + 1)$st maximal layer: $L_{k+1} = \{(x, y)\}$.

c. Describe an $O(n \lg n)$-time algorithm to compute the maximal layers of a set Q of n points. (*Hint:* Move a sweep line from right to left.)

d. Do any difficulties arise if we now allow input points to have the same x- or y-coordinate? Suggest a way to resolve such problems.

33-3 Ghostbusters and ghosts

A group of n Ghostbusters is battling n ghosts. Each Ghostbuster carries a proton pack, which shoots a stream at a ghost, eradicating it. A stream goes in a straight line and terminates when it hits the ghost. The Ghostbusters decide upon the following strategy. They will pair off with the ghosts, forming n Ghostbuster-ghost pairs, and then simultaneously each Ghostbuster will shoot a stream at his chosen ghost. As we all know, it is *very* dangerous to let streams cross, and so the Ghostbusters must choose pairings for which no streams will cross.

Assume that the position of each Ghostbuster and each ghost is a fixed point in the plane and that no three positions are colinear.

a. Argue that there exists a line passing through one Ghostbuster and one ghost such that the number of Ghostbusters on one side of the line equals the number of ghosts on the same side. Describe how to find such a line in $O(n \lg n)$ time.

b. Give an $O(n^2 \lg n)$-time algorithm to pair Ghostbusters with ghosts in such a way that no streams cross.

33-4   *Picking up sticks*

Professor Charon has a set of n sticks, which are piled up in some configuration. Each stick is specified by its endpoints, and each endpoint is an ordered triple giving its (x, y, z) coordinates. No stick is vertical. He wishes to pick up all the sticks, one at a time, subject to the condition that he may pick up a stick only if there is no other stick on top of it.

a. Give a procedure that takes two sticks a and b and reports whether a is above, below, or unrelated to b.

b. Describe an efficient algorithm that determines whether it is possible to pick up all the sticks, and if so, provides a legal order in which to pick them up.

33-5   *Sparse-hulled distributions*

Consider the problem of computing the convex hull of a set of points in the plane that have been drawn according to some known random distribution. Sometimes, the number of points, or size, of the convex hull of n points drawn from such a distribution has expectation $O(n^{1-\epsilon})$ for some constant $\epsilon > 0$. We call such a distribution *sparse-hulled*. Sparse-hulled distributions include the following:

- Points drawn uniformly from a unit-radius disk. The convex hull has expected size $\Theta(n^{1/3})$.

- Points drawn uniformly from the interior of a convex polygon with k sides, for any constant k. The convex hull has expected size $\Theta(\lg n)$.

- Points drawn according to a two-dimensional normal distribution. The convex hull has expected size $\Theta(\sqrt{\lg n})$.

a. Given two convex polygons with n_1 and n_2 vertices respectively, show how to compute the convex hull of all $n_1 + n_2$ points in $O(n_1 + n_2)$ time. (The polygons may overlap.)

b. Show how to compute the convex hull of a set of n points drawn independently according to a sparse-hulled distribution in $O(n)$ average-case time. (*Hint:* Recursively find the convex hulls of the first $n/2$ points and the second $n/2$ points, and then combine the results.)

Chapter notes

This chapter barely scratches the surface of computational-geometry algorithms and techniques. Books on computational geometry include those by Preparata and Shamos [282], Edelsbrunner [99], and O'Rourke [269].

Although geometry has been studied since antiquity, the development of algorithms for geometric problems is relatively new. Preparata and Shamos note that the earliest notion of the complexity of a problem was given by E. Lemoine in 1902. He was studying euclidean constructions—those using a compass and a ruler—and devised a set of five primitives: placing one leg of the compass on a given point, placing one leg of the compass on a given line, drawing a circle, passing the ruler's edge through a given point, and drawing a line. Lemoine was interested in the number of primitives needed to effect a given construction; he called this amount the "simplicity" of the construction.

The algorithm of Section 33.2, which determines whether any segments intersect, is due to Shamos and Hoey [313].

The original version of Graham's scan is given by Graham [150]. The package-wrapping algorithm is due to Jarvis [189]. Using a decision-tree model of computation, Yao [359] proved a worst-case lower bound of $\Omega(n \lg n)$ for the running time of any convex-hull algorithm. When the number of vertices h of the convex hull is taken into account, the prune-and-search algorithm of Kirkpatrick and Seidel [206], which takes $O(n \lg h)$ time, is asymptotically optimal.

The $O(n \lg n)$-time divide-and-conquer algorithm for finding the closest pair of points is by Shamos and appears in Preparata and Shamos [282]. Preparata and Shamos also show that the algorithm is asymptotically optimal in a decision-tree model.

34   NP-Completeness

Almost all the algorithms we have studied thus far have been ***polynomial-time algorithms***: on inputs of size n, their worst-case running time is $O(n^k)$ for some constant k. You might wonder whether *all* problems can be solved in polynomial time. The answer is no. For example, there are problems, such as Turing's famous "Halting Problem," that cannot be solved by any computer, no matter how much time we allow. There are also problems that can be solved, but not in time $O(n^k)$ for any constant k. Generally, we think of problems that are solvable by polynomial-time algorithms as being tractable, or easy, and problems that require superpolynomial time as being intractable, or hard.

The subject of this chapter, however, is an interesting class of problems, called the "NP-complete" problems, whose status is unknown. No polynomial-time algorithm has yet been discovered for an NP-complete problem, nor has anyone yet been able to prove that no polynomial-time algorithm can exist for any one of them. This so-called P $\neq$ NP question has been one of the deepest, most perplexing open research problems in theoretical computer science since it was first posed in 1971.

Several NP-complete problems are particularly tantalizing because they seem on the surface to be similar to problems that we know how to solve in polynomial time. In each of the following pairs of problems, one is solvable in polynomial time and the other is NP-complete, but the difference between problems appears to be slight:

Shortest vs. longest simple paths: In Chapter 24, we saw that even with negative edge weights, we can find *shortest* paths from a single source in a directed graph $G = (V, E)$ in $O(VE)$ time. Finding a *longest* simple path between two vertices is difficult, however. Merely determining whether a graph contains a simple path with at least a given number of edges is NP-complete.

Euler tour vs. hamiltonian cycle: An ***Euler tour*** of a strongly connected, directed graph $G = (V, E)$ is a cycle that traverses each *edge* of G exactly once, although it is allowed to visit each vertex more than once. By Problem 22-3, we can determine whether a graph has an Euler tour in only $O(E)$ time and, in

fact, we can find the edges of the Euler tour in $O(E)$ time. A **hamiltonian cycle** of a directed graph $G = (V, E)$ is a simple cycle that contains each *vertex* in V. Determining whether a directed graph has a hamiltonian cycle is NP-complete. (Later in this chapter, we shall prove that determining whether an *undirected* graph has a hamiltonian cycle is NP-complete.)

2-CNF satisfiability vs. 3-CNF satisfiability: A boolean formula contains variables whose values are 0 or 1; boolean connectives such as $\land$ (AND), $\lor$ (OR), and $\lnot$ (NOT); and parentheses. A boolean formula is **satisfiable** if there exists some assignment of the values 0 and 1 to its variables that causes it to evaluate to 1. We shall define terms more formally later in this chapter, but informally, a boolean formula is in **k-conjunctive normal form**, or k-CNF, if it is the AND of clauses of ORs of exactly k variables or their negations. For example, the boolean formula $(x_1 \lor \lnot x_2) \land (\lnot x_1 \lor x_3) \land (\lnot x_2 \lor \lnot x_3)$ is in 2-CNF. (It has the satisfying assignment $x_1 = 1, x_2 = 0, x_3 = 1$.) Although we can determine in polynomial time whether a 2-CNF formula is satisfiable, we shall see later in this chapter that determining whether a 3-CNF formula is satisfiable is NP-complete.

NP-completeness and the classes P and NP

Throughout this chapter, we shall refer to three classes of problems: P, NP, and NPC, the latter class being the NP-complete problems. We describe them informally here, and we shall define them more formally later on.

The class P consists of those problems that are solvable in polynomial time. More specifically, they are problems that can be solved in time $O(n^k)$ for some constant k, where n is the size of the input to the problem. Most of the problems examined in previous chapters are in P.

The class NP consists of those problems that are "verifiable" in polynomial time. What do we mean by a problem being verifiable? If we were somehow given a "certificate" of a solution, then we could verify that the certificate is correct in time polynomial in the size of the input to the problem. For example, in the hamiltonian-cycle problem, given a directed graph $G = (V, E)$, a certificate would be a sequence $\langle v_1, v_2, v_3, \ldots, v_{|V|} \rangle$ of $|V|$ vertices. We could easily check in polynomial time that $(v_i, v_{i+1}) \in E$ for $i = 1, 2, 3, \ldots, |V| - 1$ and that $(v_{|V|}, v_1) \in E$ as well. As another example, for 3-CNF satisfiability, a certificate would be an assignment of values to variables. We could check in polynomial time that this assignment satisfies the boolean formula.

Any problem in P is also in NP, since if a problem is in P then we can solve it in polynomial time without even being supplied a certificate. We shall formalize this notion later in this chapter, but for now we can believe that $P \subseteq NP$. The open question is whether or not P is a proper subset of NP.

Informally, a problem is in the class NPC—and we refer to it as being **NP-complete**—if it is in NP and is as "hard" as any problem in NP. We shall formally define what it means to be as hard as any problem in NP later in this chapter. In the meantime, we will state without proof that if *any* NP-complete problem can be solved in polynomial time, then *every* problem in NP has a polynomial-time algorithm. Most theoretical computer scientists believe that the NP-complete problems are intractable, since given the wide range of NP-complete problems that have been studied to date—without anyone having discovered a polynomial-time solution to any of them—it would be truly astounding if all of them could be solved in polynomial time. Yet, given the effort devoted thus far to proving that NP-complete problems are intractable—without a conclusive outcome—we cannot rule out the possibility that the NP-complete problems are in fact solvable in polynomial time.

To become a good algorithm designer, you must understand the rudiments of the theory of NP-completeness. If you can establish a problem as NP-complete, you provide good evidence for its intractability. As an engineer, you would then do better to spend your time developing an approximation algorithm (see Chapter 35) or solving a tractable special case, rather than searching for a fast algorithm that solves the problem exactly. Moreover, many natural and interesting problems that on the surface seem no harder than sorting, graph searching, or network flow are in fact NP-complete. Therefore, you should become familiar with this remarkable class of problems.

Overview of showing problems to be NP-complete

The techniques we use to show that a particular problem is NP-complete differ fundamentally from the techniques used throughout most of this book to design and analyze algorithms. When we demonstrate that a problem is NP-complete, we are making a statement about how hard it is (or at least how hard we think it is), rather than about how easy it is. We are not trying to prove the existence of an efficient algorithm, but instead that no efficient algorithm is likely to exist. In this way, NP-completeness proofs bear some similarity to the proof in Section 8.1 of an $\Omega(n \lg n)$-time lower bound for any comparison sort algorithm; the specific techniques used for showing NP-completeness differ from the decision-tree method used in Section 8.1, however.

We rely on three key concepts in showing a problem to be NP-complete:

Decision problems vs. optimization problems

Many problems of interest are *optimization problems*, in which each feasible (i.e., "legal") solution has an associated value, and we wish to find a feasible solution with the best value. For example, in a problem that we call SHORTEST-PATH,

we are given an undirected graph G and vertices u and v, and we wish to find a path from u to v that uses the fewest edges. In other words, SHORTEST-PATH is the single-pair shortest-path problem in an unweighted, undirected graph. NP-completeness applies directly not to optimization problems, however, but to ***decision problems***, in which the answer is simply "yes" or "no" (or, more formally, "1" or "0").

Although NP-complete problems are confined to the realm of decision problems, we can take advantage of a convenient relationship between optimization problems and decision problems. We usually can cast a given optimization problem as a related decision problem by imposing a bound on the value to be optimized. For example, a decision problem related to SHORTEST-PATH is PATH: given an undirected graph G, vertices u and v, and an integer k, does a path exist from u to v consisting of at most k edges?

The relationship between an optimization problem and its related decision problem works in our favor when we try to show that the optimization problem is "hard." That is because the decision problem is in a sense "easier," or at least "no harder." As a specific example, we can solve PATH by solving SHORTEST-PATH and then comparing the number of edges in the shortest path found to the value of the decision-problem parameter k. In other words, if an optimization problem is easy, its related decision problem is easy as well. Stated in a way that has more relevance to NP-completeness, if we can provide evidence that a decision problem is hard, we also provide evidence that its related optimization problem is hard. Thus, even though it restricts attention to decision problems, the theory of NP-completeness often has implications for optimization problems as well.

Reductions

The above notion of showing that one problem is no harder or no easier than another applies even when both problems are decision problems. We take advantage of this idea in almost every NP-completeness proof, as follows. Let us consider a decision problem A, which we would like to solve in polynomial time. We call the input to a particular problem an ***instance*** of that problem; for example, in PATH, an instance would be a particular graph G, particular vertices u and v of G, and a particular integer k. Now suppose that we already know how to solve a different decision problem B in polynomial time. Finally, suppose that we have a procedure that transforms any instance α of A into some instance β of B with the following characteristics:

• The transformation takes polynomial time.

• The answers are the same. That is, the answer for α is "yes" if and only if the answer for β is also "yes."

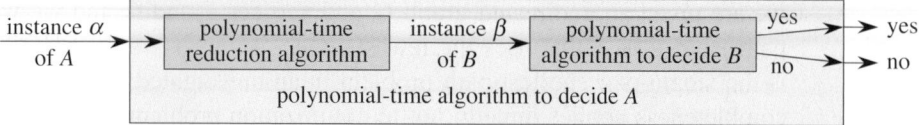

Figure 34.1 How to use a polynomial-time reduction algorithm to solve a decision problem A in polynomial time, given a polynomial-time decision algorithm for another problem B. In polynomial time, we transform an instance α of A into an instance β of B, we solve B in polynomial time, and we use the answer for β as the answer for α.

We call such a procedure a polynomial-time ***reduction algorithm*** and, as Figure 34.1 shows, it provides us a way to solve problem A in polynomial time:

1. Given an instance α of problem A, use a polynomial-time reduction algorithm to transform it to an instance β of problem B.

2. Run the polynomial-time decision algorithm for B on the instance β.

3. Use the answer for β as the answer for α.

As long as each of these steps takes polynomial time, all three together do also, and so we have a way to decide on α in polynomial time. In other words, by "reducing" solving problem A to solving problem B, we use the "easiness" of B to prove the "easiness" of A.

Recalling that NP-completeness is about showing how hard a problem is rather than how easy it is, we use polynomial-time reductions in the opposite way to show that a problem is NP-complete. Let us take the idea a step further, and show how we could use polynomial-time reductions to show that no polynomial-time algorithm can exist for a particular problem B. Suppose we have a decision problem A for which we already know that no polynomial-time algorithm can exist. (Let us not concern ourselves for now with how to find such a problem A.) Suppose further that we have a polynomial-time reduction transforming instances of A to instances of B. Now we can use a simple proof by contradiction to show that no polynomial-time algorithm can exist for B. Suppose otherwise; i.e., suppose that B has a polynomial-time algorithm. Then, using the method shown in Figure 34.1, we would have a way to solve problem A in polynomial time, which contradicts our assumption that there is no polynomial-time algorithm for A.

For NP-completeness, we cannot assume that there is absolutely no polynomial-time algorithm for problem A. The proof methodology is similar, however, in that we prove that problem B is NP-complete on the assumption that problem A is also NP-complete.

A first NP-complete problem

Because the technique of reduction relies on having a problem already known to be NP-complete in order to prove a different problem NP-complete, we need a "first" NP-complete problem. The problem we shall use is the circuit-satisfiability problem, in which we are given a boolean combinational circuit composed of AND, OR, and NOT gates, and we wish to know whether there exists some set of boolean inputs to this circuit that causes its output to be 1. We shall prove that this first problem is NP-complete in Section 34.3.

Chapter outline

This chapter studies the aspects of NP-completeness that bear most directly on the analysis of algorithms. In Section 34.1, we formalize our notion of "problem" and define the complexity class P of polynomial-time solvable decision problems. We also see how these notions fit into the framework of formal-language theory. Section 34.2 defines the class NP of decision problems whose solutions are verifiable in polynomial time. It also formally poses the $P \neq NP$ question.

Section 34.3 shows we can relate problems via polynomial-time "reductions." It defines NP-completeness and sketches a proof that one problem, called "circuit satisfiability," is NP-complete. Having found one NP-complete problem, we show in Section 34.4 how to prove other problems to be NP-complete much more simply by the methodology of reductions. We illustrate this methodology by showing that two formula-satisfiability problems are NP-complete. With additional reductions, we show in Section 34.5 a variety of other problems to be NP-complete.

34.1 Polynomial time

We begin our study of NP-completeness by formalizing our notion of polynomial-time solvable problems. We generally regard these problems as tractable, but for philosophical, not mathematical, reasons. We can offer three supporting arguments.

First, although we may reasonably regard a problem that requires time $\Theta(n^{100})$ to be intractable, very few practical problems require time on the order of such a high-degree polynomial. The polynomial-time computable problems encountered in practice typically require much less time. Experience has shown that once the first polynomial-time algorithm for a problem has been discovered, more efficient algorithms often follow. Even if the current best algorithm for a problem has a running time of $\Theta(n^{100})$, an algorithm with a much better running time will likely soon be discovered.

Second, for many reasonable models of computation, a problem that can be solved in polynomial time in one model can be solved in polynomial time in another. For example, the class of problems solvable in polynomial time by the serial random-access machine used throughout most of this book is the same as the class of problems solvable in polynomial time on abstract Turing machines.[1] It is also the same as the class of problems solvable in polynomial time on a parallel computer when the number of processors grows polynomially with the input size.

Third, the class of polynomial-time solvable problems has nice closure properties, since polynomials are closed under addition, multiplication, and composition. For example, if the output of one polynomial-time algorithm is fed into the input of another, the composite algorithm is polynomial. Exercise 34.1-5 asks you to show that if an algorithm makes a constant number of calls to polynomial-time subroutines and performs an additional amount of work that also takes polynomial time, then the running time of the composite algorithm is polynomial.

Abstract problems

To understand the class of polynomial-time solvable problems, we must first have a formal notion of what a "problem" is. We define an ***abstract problem*** Q to be a binary relation on a set I of problem ***instances*** and a set S of problem ***solutions***. For example, an instance for SHORTEST-PATH is a triple consisting of a graph and two vertices. A solution is a sequence of vertices in the graph, with perhaps the empty sequence denoting that no path exists. The problem SHORTEST-PATH itself is the relation that associates each instance of a graph and two vertices with a shortest path in the graph that connects the two vertices. Since shortest paths are not necessarily unique, a given problem instance may have more than one solution.

This formulation of an abstract problem is more general than we need for our purposes. As we saw above, the theory of NP-completeness restricts attention to ***decision problems***: those having a yes/no solution. In this case, we can view an abstract decision problem as a function that maps the instance set I to the solution set $\{0, 1\}$. For example, a decision problem related to SHORTEST-PATH is the problem PATH that we saw earlier. If $i = \langle G, u, v, k \rangle$ is an instance of the decision problem PATH, then PATH$(i) = 1$ (yes) if a shortest path from u to v has at most k edges, and PATH$(i) = 0$ (no) otherwise. Many abstract problems are not decision problems, but rather ***optimization problems***, which require some value to be minimized or maximized. As we saw above, however, we can usually recast an optimization problem as a decision problem that is no harder.

---

[1]See Hopcroft and Ullman [180] or Lewis and Papadimitriou [236] for a thorough treatment of the Turing-machine model.

Encodings

In order for a computer program to solve an abstract problem, we must represent problem instances in a way that the program understands. An ***encoding*** of a set S of abstract objects is a mapping e from S to the set of binary strings.[2] For example, we are all familiar with encoding the natural numbers $\mathbb{N} = \{0, 1, 2, 3, 4, \ldots\}$ as the strings $\{0, 1, 10, 11, 100, \ldots\}$. Using this encoding, $e(17) = 10001$. If you have looked at computer representations of keyboard characters, you probably have seen the ASCII code, where, for example, the encoding of A is 1000001. We can encode a compound object as a binary string by combining the representations of its constituent parts. Polygons, graphs, functions, ordered pairs, programs—all can be encoded as binary strings.

Thus, a computer algorithm that "solves" some abstract decision problem actually takes an encoding of a problem instance as input. We call a problem whose instance set is the set of binary strings a ***concrete problem***. We say that an algorithm ***solves*** a concrete problem in time $O(T(n))$ if, when it is provided a problem instance i of length $n = |i|$, the algorithm can produce the solution in $O(T(n))$ time.[3] A concrete problem is ***polynomial-time solvable***, therefore, if there exists an algorithm to solve it in time $O(n^k)$ for some constant k.

We can now formally define the ***complexity class*** **P** as the set of concrete decision problems that are polynomial-time solvable.

We can use encodings to map abstract problems to concrete problems. Given an abstract decision problem Q mapping an instance set I to $\{0, 1\}$, an encoding $e : I \to \{0, 1\}^*$ can induce a related concrete decision problem, which we denote by $e(Q)$.[4] If the solution to an abstract-problem instance $i \in I$ is $Q(i) \in \{0, 1\}$, then the solution to the concrete-problem instance $e(i) \in \{0, 1\}^*$ is also $Q(i)$. As a technicality, some binary strings might represent no meaningful abstract-problem instance. For convenience, we shall assume that any such string maps arbitrarily to 0. Thus, the concrete problem produces the same solutions as the abstract problem on binary-string instances that represent the encodings of abstract-problem instances.

We would like to extend the definition of polynomial-time solvability from concrete problems to abstract problems by using encodings as the bridge, but we would

---

[2] The codomain of e need not be *binary* strings; any set of strings over a finite alphabet having at least 2 symbols will do.

[3] We assume that the algorithm's output is separate from its input. Because it takes at least one time step to produce each bit of the output and the algorithm takes $O(T(n))$ time steps, the size of the output is $O(T(n))$.

[4] We denote by $\{0, 1\}^*$ the set of all strings composed of symbols from the set $\{0, 1\}$.

like the definition to be independent of any particular encoding. That is, the efficiency of solving a problem should not depend on how the problem is encoded. Unfortunately, it depends quite heavily on the encoding. For example, suppose that an integer k is to be provided as the sole input to an algorithm, and suppose that the running time of the algorithm is $\Theta(k)$. If the integer k is provided in *unary*—a string of k 1s—then the running time of the algorithm is $O(n)$ on length-n inputs, which is polynomial time. If we use the more natural binary representation of the integer k, however, then the input length is $n = \lfloor \lg k \rfloor + 1$. In this case, the running time of the algorithm is $\Theta(k) = \Theta(2^n)$, which is exponential in the size of the input. Thus, depending on the encoding, the algorithm runs in either polynomial or superpolynomial time.

How we encode an abstract problem matters quite a bit to how we understand polynomial time. We cannot really talk about solving an abstract problem without first specifying an encoding. Nevertheless, in practice, if we rule out "expensive" encodings such as unary ones, the actual encoding of a problem makes little difference to whether the problem can be solved in polynomial time. For example, representing integers in base 3 instead of binary has no effect on whether a problem is solvable in polynomial time, since we can convert an integer represented in base 3 to an integer represented in base 2 in polynomial time.

We say that a function $f : \{0, 1\}^* \rightarrow \{0, 1\}^*$ is *polynomial-time computable* if there exists a polynomial-time algorithm A that, given any input $x \in \{0, 1\}^*$, produces as output $f(x)$. For some set I of problem instances, we say that two encodings e_1 and e_2 are *polynomially related* if there exist two polynomial-time computable functions f_{12} and f_{21} such that for any $i \in I$, we have $f_{12}(e_1(i)) = e_2(i)$ and $f_{21}(e_2(i)) = e_1(i)$.[5] That is, a polynomial-time algorithm can compute the encoding $e_2(i)$ from the encoding $e_1(i)$, and vice versa. If two encodings e_1 and e_2 of an abstract problem are polynomially related, whether the problem is polynomial-time solvable or not is independent of which encoding we use, as the following lemma shows.

Lemma 34.1

Let Q be an abstract decision problem on an instance set I, and let e_1 and e_2 be polynomially related encodings on I. Then, $e_1(Q) \in \text{P}$ if and only if $e_2(Q) \in \text{P}$.

---

[5]Technically, we also require the functions f_{12} and f_{21} to "map noninstances to noninstances." A *noninstance* of an encoding e is a string $x \in \{0, 1\}^*$ such that there is no instance i for which $e(i) = x$. We require that $f_{12}(x) = y$ for every noninstance x of encoding e_1, where y is some noninstance of e_2, and that $f_{21}(x') = y'$ for every noninstance x' of e_2, where y' is some noninstance of e_1.

Proof   We need only prove the forward direction, since the backward direction is symmetric. Suppose, therefore, that $e_1(Q)$ can be solved in time $O(n^k)$ for some constant k. Further, suppose that for any problem instance i, the encoding $e_1(i)$ can be computed from the encoding $e_2(i)$ in time $O(n^c)$ for some constant c, where $n = |e_2(i)|$. To solve problem $e_2(Q)$, on input $e_2(i)$, we first compute $e_1(i)$ and then run the algorithm for $e_1(Q)$ on $e_1(i)$. How long does this take? Converting encodings takes time $O(n^c)$, and therefore $|e_1(i)| = O(n^c)$, since the output of a serial computer cannot be longer than its running time. Solving the problem on $e_1(i)$ takes time $O(|e_1(i)|^k) = O(n^{ck})$, which is polynomial since both c and k are constants.   ∎

Thus, whether an abstract problem has its instances encoded in binary or base 3 does not affect its "complexity," that is, whether it is polynomial-time solvable or not; but if instances are encoded in unary, its complexity may change. In order to be able to converse in an encoding-independent fashion, we shall generally assume that problem instances are encoded in any reasonable, concise fashion, unless we specifically say otherwise. To be precise, we shall assume that the encoding of an integer is polynomially related to its binary representation, and that the encoding of a finite set is polynomially related to its encoding as a list of its elements, enclosed in braces and separated by commas. (ASCII is one such encoding scheme.) With such a "standard" encoding in hand, we can derive reasonable encodings of other mathematical objects, such as tuples, graphs, and formulas. To denote the standard encoding of an object, we shall enclose the object in angle braces. Thus, $\langle G \rangle$ denotes the standard encoding of a graph G.

As long as we implicitly use an encoding that is polynomially related to this standard encoding, we can talk directly about abstract problems without reference to any particular encoding, knowing that the choice of encoding has no effect on whether the abstract problem is polynomial-time solvable. Henceforth, we shall generally assume that all problem instances are binary strings encoded using the standard encoding, unless we explicitly specify the contrary. We shall also typically neglect the distinction between abstract and concrete problems. You should watch out for problems that arise in practice, however, in which a standard encoding is not obvious and the encoding does make a difference.

A formal-language framework

By focusing on decision problems, we can take advantage of the machinery of formal-language theory. Let's review some definitions from that theory. An ***alphabet*** Σ is a finite set of symbols. A ***language*** L over Σ is any set of strings made up of symbols from Σ. For example, if $\Sigma = \{0, 1\}$, the set $L = \{10, 11, 101, 111, 1011, 1101, 10001, \ldots\}$ is the language of binary represen-

tations of prime numbers. We denote the ***empty string*** by ε, the ***empty language*** by $\emptyset$, and the language of all strings over Σ by Σ^*. For example, if $\Sigma = \{0, 1\}$, then $\Sigma^* = \{\varepsilon, 0, 1, 00, 01, 10, 11, 000, \ldots\}$ is the set of all binary strings. Every language L over Σ is a subset of Σ^*.

We can perform a variety of operations on languages. Set-theoretic operations, such as ***union*** and ***intersection***, follow directly from the set-theoretic definitions. We define the ***complement*** of L by $\overline{L} = \Sigma^* - L$. The ***concatenation*** $L_1 L_2$ of two languages L_1 and L_2 is the language

$$L = \{x_1 x_2 : x_1 \in L_1 \text{ and } x_2 \in L_2\} .$$

The ***closure*** or ***Kleene star*** of a language L is the language

$$L^* = \{\varepsilon\} \cup L \cup L^2 \cup L^3 \cup \cdots ,$$

where L^k is the language obtained by concatenating L to itself k times.

From the point of view of language theory, the set of instances for any decision problem Q is simply the set Σ^*, where $\Sigma = \{0, 1\}$. Since Q is entirely characterized by those problem instances that produce a 1 (yes) answer, we can view Q as a language L over $\Sigma = \{0, 1\}$, where

$$L = \{x \in \Sigma^* : Q(x) = 1\} .$$

For example, the decision problem PATH has the corresponding language

$$
\begin{aligned}
\text{PATH} = \{ \langle G, u, v, k \rangle : \ & G = (V, E) \text{ is an undirected graph,} \\
& u, v \in V, \\
& k \geq 0 \text{ is an integer, and} \\
& \text{there exists a path from } u \text{ to } v \text{ in } G \\
& \text{consisting of at most } k \text{ edges}\} .
\end{aligned}
$$

(Where convenient, we shall sometimes use the same name—PATH in this case—to refer to both a decision problem and its corresponding language.)

The formal-language framework allows us to express concisely the relation between decision problems and algorithms that solve them. We say that an algorithm A ***accepts*** a string $x \in \{0, 1\}^*$ if, given input x, the algorithm's output $A(x)$ is 1. The language ***accepted*** by an algorithm A is the set of strings $L = \{x \in \{0, 1\}^* : A(x) = 1\}$, that is, the set of strings that the algorithm accepts. An algorithm A ***rejects*** a string x if $A(x) = 0$.

Even if language L is accepted by an algorithm A, the algorithm will not necessarily reject a string $x \notin L$ provided as input to it. For example, the algorithm may loop forever. A language L is ***decided*** by an algorithm A if every binary string in L is accepted by A and every binary string not in L is rejected by A. A language L is ***accepted in polynomial time*** by an algorithm A if it is accepted by A and if in addition there exists a constant k such that for any length-n string $x \in L$,

algorithm A accepts x in time $O(n^k)$. A language L is ***decided in polynomial time*** by an algorithm A if there exists a constant k such that for any length-n string $x \in \{0, 1\}^*$, the algorithm correctly decides whether $x \in L$ in time $O(n^k)$. Thus, to accept a language, an algorithm need only produce an answer when provided a string in L, but to decide a language, it must correctly accept or reject every string in $\{0, 1\}^*$.

As an example, the language PATH can be accepted in polynomial time. One polynomial-time accepting algorithm verifies that G encodes an undirected graph, verifies that u and v are vertices in G, uses breadth-first search to compute a shortest path from u to v in G, and then compares the number of edges on the shortest path obtained with k. If G encodes an undirected graph and the path found from u to v has at most k edges, the algorithm outputs 1 and halts. Otherwise, the algorithm runs forever. This algorithm does not decide PATH, however, since it does not explicitly output 0 for instances in which a shortest path has more than k edges. A decision algorithm for PATH must explicitly reject binary strings that do not belong to PATH. For a decision problem such as PATH, such a decision algorithm is easy to design: instead of running forever when there is not a path from u to v with at most k edges, it outputs 0 and halts. (It must also output 0 and halt if the input encoding is faulty.) For other problems, such as Turing's Halting Problem, there exists an accepting algorithm, but no decision algorithm exists.

We can informally define a ***complexity class*** as a set of languages, membership in which is determined by a ***complexity measure***, such as running time, of an algorithm that determines whether a given string x belongs to language L. The actual definition of a complexity class is somewhat more technical.[6]

Using this language-theoretic framework, we can provide an alternative definition of the complexity class P:

$$P = \{L \subseteq \{0, 1\}^* : \text{there exists an algorithm } A \text{ that decides } L \text{ in polynomial time}\} \,.$$

In fact, P is also the class of languages that can be accepted in polynomial time.

Theorem 34.2
$P = \{L : L \text{ is accepted by a polynomial-time algorithm}\} \,.$

Proof Because the class of languages decided by polynomial-time algorithms is a subset of the class of languages accepted by polynomial-time algorithms, we need only show that if L is accepted by a polynomial-time algorithm, it is decided by a polynomial-time algorithm. Let L be the language accepted by some

---

[6]For more on complexity classes, see the seminal paper by Hartmanis and Stearns [162].

polynomial-time algorithm A. We shall use a classic "simulation" argument to construct another polynomial-time algorithm A' that decides L. Because A accepts L in time $O(n^k)$ for some constant k, there also exists a constant c such that A accepts L in at most cn^k steps. For any input string x, the algorithm A' simulates cn^k steps of A. After simulating cn^k steps, algorithm A' inspects the behavior of A. If A has accepted x, then A' accepts x by outputting a 1. If A has not accepted x, then A' rejects x by outputting a 0. The overhead of A' simulating A does not increase the running time by more than a polynomial factor, and thus A' is a polynomial-time algorithm that decides L.   ■

Note that the proof of Theorem 34.2 is nonconstructive. For a given language $L \in P$, we may not actually know a bound on the running time for the algorithm A that accepts L. Nevertheless, we know that such a bound exists, and therefore, that an algorithm A' exists that can check the bound, even though we may not be able to find the algorithm A' easily.

Exercises

34.1-1
Define the optimization problem LONGEST-PATH-LENGTH as the relation that associates each instance of an undirected graph and two vertices with the number of edges in a longest simple path between the two vertices. Define the decision problem LONGEST-PATH $= \{\langle G, u, v, k \rangle : G = (V, E)$ is an undirected graph, $u, v \in V$, $k \geq 0$ is an integer, and there exists a simple path from u to v in G consisting of at least k edges$\}$. Show that the optimization problem LONGEST-PATH-LENGTH can be solved in polynomial time if and only if LONGEST-PATH $\in P$.

34.1-2
Give a formal definition for the problem of finding the longest simple cycle in an undirected graph. Give a related decision problem. Give the language corresponding to the decision problem.

34.1-3
Give a formal encoding of directed graphs as binary strings using an adjacency-matrix representation. Do the same using an adjacency-list representation. Argue that the two representations are polynomially related.

34.1-4
Is the dynamic-programming algorithm for the 0-1 knapsack problem that is asked for in Exercise 16.2-2 a polynomial-time algorithm? Explain your answer.

34.1-5
Show that if an algorithm makes at most a constant number of calls to polynomial-time subroutines and performs an additional amount of work that also takes polynomial time, then it runs in polynomial time. Also show that a polynomial number of calls to polynomial-time subroutines may result in an exponential-time algorithm.

34.1-6
Show that the class P, viewed as a set of languages, is closed under union, intersection, concatenation, complement, and Kleene star. That is, if $L_1, L_2 \in P$, then $L_1 \cup L_2 \in P$, $L_1 \cap L_2 \in P$, $L_1 L_2 \in P$, $\overline{L_1} \in P$, and $L_1^* \in P$.

34.2 Polynomial-time verification

We now look at algorithms that verify membership in languages. For example, suppose that for a given instance $\langle G, u, v, k \rangle$ of the decision problem PATH, we are also given a path p from u to v. We can easily check whether p is a path in G and whether the length of p is at most k, and if so, we can view p as a "certificate" that the instance indeed belongs to PATH. For the decision problem PATH, this certificate doesn't seem to buy us much. After all, PATH belongs to P—in fact, we can solve PATH in linear time—and so verifying membership from a given certificate takes as long as solving the problem from scratch. We shall now examine a problem for which we know of no polynomial-time decision algorithm and yet, given a certificate, verification is easy.

Hamiltonian cycles

The problem of finding a hamiltonian cycle in an undirected graph has been studied for over a hundred years. Formally, a *hamiltonian cycle* of an undirected graph $G = (V, E)$ is a simple cycle that contains each vertex in V. A graph that contains a hamiltonian cycle is said to be *hamiltonian*; otherwise, it is *nonhamiltonian*. The name honors W. R. Hamilton, who described a mathematical game on the dodecahedron (Figure 34.2(a)) in which one player sticks five pins in any five consecutive vertices and the other player must complete the path to form a cycle

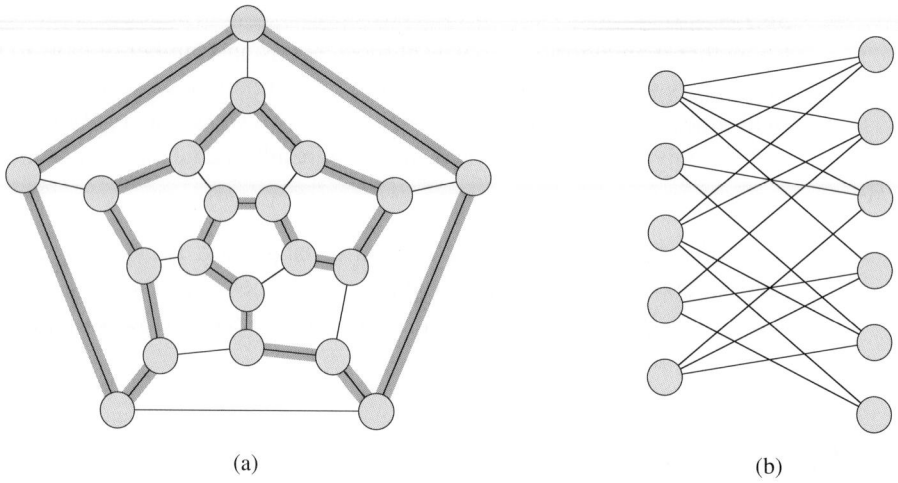

Figure 34.2 (a) A graph representing the vertices, edges, and faces of a dodecahedron, with a hamiltonian cycle shown by shaded edges. (b) A bipartite graph with an odd number of vertices. Any such graph is nonhamiltonian.

containing all the vertices.[7] The dodecahedron is hamiltonian, and Figure 34.2(a) shows one hamiltonian cycle. Not all graphs are hamiltonian, however. For example, Figure 34.2(b) shows a bipartite graph with an odd number of vertices. Exercise 34.2-2 asks you to show that all such graphs are nonhamiltonian.

We can define the ***hamiltonian-cycle problem***, "Does a graph G have a hamiltonian cycle?" as a formal language:

HAM-CYCLE $= \{\langle G \rangle : G$ is a hamiltonian graph$\}$.

How might an algorithm decide the language HAM-CYCLE? Given a problem instance $\langle G \rangle$, one possible decision algorithm lists all permutations of the vertices of G and then checks each permutation to see if it is a hamiltonian cycle. What is the running time of this algorithm? If we use the "reasonable" encoding of a graph as its adjacency matrix, the number m of vertices in the graph is $\Omega(\sqrt{n})$, where $n = |\langle G \rangle|$ is the length of the encoding of G. There are $m!$ possible permutations

---

[7]In a letter dated 17 October 1856 to his friend John T. Graves, Hamilton [157, p. 624] wrote, "I have found that some young persons have been much amused by trying a new mathematical game which the Icosion furnishes, one person sticking five pins in any five consecutive points ...and the other player then aiming to insert, which by the theory in this letter can always be done, fifteen other pins, in cyclical succession, so as to cover all the other points, and to end in immediate proximity to the pin wherewith his antagonist had begun."

of the vertices, and therefore the running time is $\Omega(m!) = \Omega(\sqrt{n}!) = \Omega(2^{\sqrt{n}})$, which is not $O(n^k)$ for any constant k. Thus, this naive algorithm does not run in polynomial time. In fact, the hamiltonian-cycle problem is NP-complete, as we shall prove in Section 34.5.

Verification algorithms

Consider a slightly easier problem. Suppose that a friend tells you that a given graph G is hamiltonian, and then offers to prove it by giving you the vertices in order along the hamiltonian cycle. It would certainly be easy enough to verify the proof: simply verify that the provided cycle is hamiltonian by checking whether it is a permutation of the vertices of V and whether each of the consecutive edges along the cycle actually exists in the graph. You could certainly implement this verification algorithm to run in $O(n^2)$ time, where n is the length of the encoding of G. Thus, a proof that a hamiltonian cycle exists in a graph can be verified in polynomial time.

We define a ***verification algorithm*** as being a two-argument algorithm A, where one argument is an ordinary input string x and the other is a binary string y called a ***certificate***. A two-argument algorithm A ***verifies*** an input string x if there exists a certificate y such that $A(x, y) = 1$. The ***language verified*** by a verification algorithm A is

$$L = \{x \in \{0, 1\}^* : \text{there exists } y \in \{0, 1\}^* \text{ such that } A(x, y) = 1\} \ .$$

Intuitively, an algorithm A verifies a language L if for any string $x \in L$, there exists a certificate y that A can use to prove that $x \in L$. Moreover, for any string $x \notin L$, there must be no certificate proving that $x \in L$. For example, in the hamiltonian-cycle problem, the certificate is the list of vertices in some hamiltonian cycle. If a graph is hamiltonian, the hamiltonian cycle itself offers enough information to verify this fact. Conversely, if a graph is not hamiltonian, there can be no list of vertices that fools the verification algorithm into believing that the graph is hamiltonian, since the verification algorithm carefully checks the proposed "cycle" to be sure.

The complexity class NP

The *complexity class* **NP** is the class of languages that can be verified by a polynomial-time algorithm.[8] More precisely, a language L belongs to NP if and only if there exist a two-input polynomial-time algorithm A and a constant c such that

$$L = \{x \in \{0, 1\}^* : \text{there exists a certificate } y \text{ with } |y| = O(|x|^c) \\ \text{such that } A(x, y) = 1\} \, .$$

We say that algorithm A *verifies* language L *in polynomial time*.

From our earlier discussion on the hamiltonian-cycle problem, we now see that HAM-CYCLE $\in$ NP. (It is always nice to know that an important set is nonempty.) Moreover, if $L \in$ P, then $L \in$ NP, since if there is a polynomial-time algorithm to decide L, the algorithm can be easily converted to a two-argument verification algorithm that simply ignores any certificate and accepts exactly those input strings it determines to be in L. Thus, P $\subseteq$ NP.

It is unknown whether P $=$ NP, but most researchers believe that P and NP are not the same class. Intuitively, the class P consists of problems that can be solved quickly. The class NP consists of problems for which a solution can be verified quickly. You may have learned from experience that it is often more difficult to solve a problem from scratch than to verify a clearly presented solution, especially when working under time constraints. Theoretical computer scientists generally believe that this analogy extends to the classes P and NP, and thus that NP includes languages that are not in P.

There is more compelling, though not conclusive, evidence that P $\neq$ NP—the existence of languages that are "NP-complete." We shall study this class in Section 34.3.

Many other fundamental questions beyond the P $\neq$ NP question remain unresolved. Figure 34.3 shows some possible scenarios. Despite much work by many researchers, no one even knows whether the class NP is closed under complement. That is, does $L \in$ NP imply $\overline{L} \in$ NP? We can define the *complexity class* **co-NP** as the set of languages L such that $\overline{L} \in$ NP. We can restate the question of whether NP is closed under complement as whether NP $=$ co-NP. Since P is closed under complement (Exercise 34.1-6), it follows from Exercise 34.2-9 that P $\subseteq$ NP $\cap$ co-NP. Once again, however, no one knows whether P $=$ NP $\cap$ co-NP or whether there is some language in NP $\cap$ co-NP $-$ P.

---

[8]The name "NP" stands for "nondeterministic polynomial time." The class NP was originally studied in the context of nondeterminism, but this book uses the somewhat simpler yet equivalent notion of verification. Hopcroft and Ullman [180] give a good presentation of NP-completeness in terms of nondeterministic models of computation.

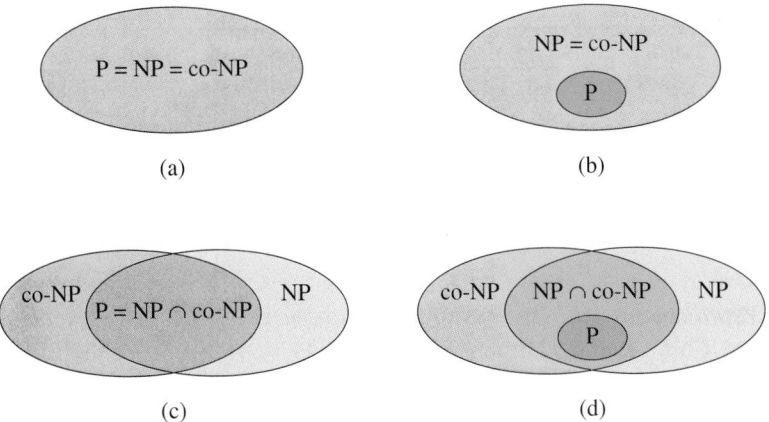

Figure 34.3 Four possibilities for relationships among complexity classes. In each diagram, one region enclosing another indicates a proper-subset relation. (**a**) P = NP = co-NP. Most researchers regard this possibility as the most unlikely. (**b**) If NP is closed under complement, then NP = co-NP, but it need not be the case that P = NP. (**c**) P = NP∩co-NP, but NP is not closed under complement. (**d**) NP ≠ co-NP and P ≠ NP ∩ co-NP. Most researchers regard this possibility as the most likely.

Thus, our understanding of the precise relationship between P and NP is woefully incomplete. Nevertheless, even though we might not be able to prove that a particular problem is intractable, if we can prove that it is NP-complete, then we have gained valuable information about it.

Exercises

34.2-1
Consider the language GRAPH-ISOMORPHISM = $\{\langle G_1, G_2 \rangle : G_1$ and G_2 are isomorphic graphs$\}$. Prove that GRAPH-ISOMORPHISM ∈ NP by describing a polynomial-time algorithm to verify the language.

34.2-2
Prove that if G is an undirected bipartite graph with an odd number of vertices, then G is nonhamiltonian.

34.2-3
Show that if HAM-CYCLE ∈ P, then the problem of listing the vertices of a hamiltonian cycle, in order, is polynomial-time solvable.

34.2-4

Prove that the class NP of languages is closed under union, intersection, concatenation, and Kleene star. Discuss the closure of NP under complement.

34.2-5

Show that any language in NP can be decided by an algorithm running in time $2^{O(n^k)}$ for some constant k.

34.2-6

A ***hamiltonian path*** in a graph is a simple path that visits every vertex exactly once. Show that the language HAM-PATH $= \{\langle G, u, v \rangle :$ there is a hamiltonian path from u to v in graph $G\}$ belongs to NP.

34.2-7

Show that the hamiltonian-path problem from Exercise 34.2-6 can be solved in polynomial time on directed acyclic graphs. Give an efficient algorithm for the problem.

34.2-8

Let ϕ be a boolean formula constructed from the boolean input variables $x_1, x_2,$ $\dots, x_k$, negations ($\neg$), ANDs ($\wedge$), ORs ($\vee$), and parentheses. The formula ϕ is a ***tautology*** if it evaluates to 1 for every assignment of 1 and 0 to the input variables. Define TAUTOLOGY as the language of boolean formulas that are tautologies. Show that TAUTOLOGY $\in$ co-NP.

34.2-9

Prove that P $\subseteq$ co-NP.

34.2-10

Prove that if NP $\neq$ co-NP, then P $\neq$ NP.

34.2-11

Let G be a connected, undirected graph with at least 3 vertices, and let G^3 be the graph obtained by connecting all pairs of vertices that are connected by a path in G of length at most 3. Prove that G^3 is hamiltonian. (*Hint:* Construct a spanning tree for G, and use an inductive argument.)

34.3 NP-completeness and reducibility

Perhaps the most compelling reason why theoretical computer scientists believe that P $\neq$ NP comes from the existence of the class of "NP-complete" problems. This class has the intriguing property that if *any* NP-complete problem can be solved in polynomial time, then *every* problem in NP has a polynomial-time solution, that is, P = NP. Despite years of study, though, no polynomial-time algorithm has ever been discovered for any NP-complete problem.

The language HAM-CYCLE is one NP-complete problem. If we could decide HAM-CYCLE in polynomial time, then we could solve every problem in NP in polynomial time. In fact, if NP $-$ P should turn out to be nonempty, we could say with certainty that HAM-CYCLE $\in$ NP $-$ P.

The NP-complete languages are, in a sense, the "hardest" languages in NP. In this section, we shall show how to compare the relative "hardness" of languages using a precise notion called "polynomial-time reducibility." Then we formally define the NP-complete languages, and we finish by sketching a proof that one such language, called CIRCUIT-SAT, is NP-complete. In Sections 34.4 and 34.5, we shall use the notion of reducibility to show that many other problems are NP-complete.

Reducibility

Intuitively, a problem Q can be reduced to another problem Q' if any instance of Q can be "easily rephrased" as an instance of Q', the solution to which provides a solution to the instance of Q. For example, the problem of solving linear equations in an indeterminate x reduces to the problem of solving quadratic equations. Given a linear-equation instance $ax + b = 0$ (with solution $x = -b/a$), we transform it to the quadratic equation $ax^2 + bx + 0 = 0$, whose solutions are $x = 0$ and $x = -b/a$, thereby providing a solution to $ax + b = 0$. Thus, if a problem Q reduces to another problem Q', then Q is, in a sense, "no harder to solve" than Q'.

Returning to our formal-language framework for decision problems, we say that a language L_1 is ***polynomial-time reducible*** to a language L_2, written $L_1 \leq_P L_2$, if there exists a polynomial-time computable function $f : \{0, 1\}^* \rightarrow \{0, 1\}^*$ such that for all $x \in \{0, 1\}^*$,

$$x \in L_1 \text{ if and only if } f(x) \in L_2 . \tag{34.1}$$

We call the function f the ***reduction function***, and a polynomial-time algorithm F that computes f is a ***reduction algorithm***.

Figure 34.4 illustrates the idea of a polynomial-time reduction from a language L_1 to another language L_2. Each language is a subset of $\{0, 1\}^*$. The reduction function f provides a polynomial-time mapping such that if $x \in L_1$,

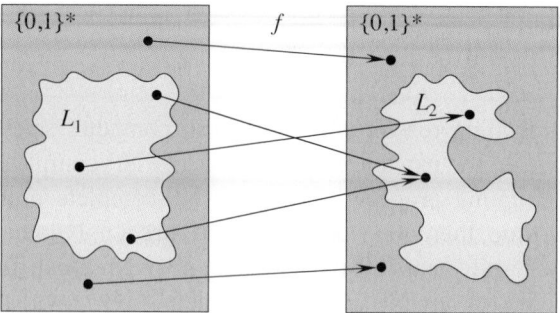

Figure 34.4 An illustration of a polynomial-time reduction from a language L_1 to a language L_2 via a reduction function f. For any input $x \in \{0, 1\}^*$, the question of whether $x \in L_1$ has the same answer as the question of whether $f(x) \in L_2$.

then $f(x) \in L_2$. Moreover, if $x \notin L_1$, then $f(x) \notin L_2$. Thus, the reduction function maps any instance x of the decision problem represented by the language L_1 to an instance $f(x)$ of the problem represented by L_2. Providing an answer to whether $f(x) \in L_2$ directly provides the answer to whether $x \in L_1$.

Polynomial-time reductions give us a powerful tool for proving that various languages belong to P.

Lemma 34.3
If $L_1, L_2 \subseteq \{0, 1\}^*$ are languages such that $L_1 \leq_P L_2$, then $L_2 \in$ P implies $L_1 \in$ P.

Proof Let A_2 be a polynomial-time algorithm that decides L_2, and let F be a polynomial-time reduction algorithm that computes the reduction function f. We shall construct a polynomial-time algorithm A_1 that decides L_1.

Figure 34.5 illustrates how we construct A_1. For a given input $x \in \{0, 1\}^*$, algorithm A_1 uses F to transform x into $f(x)$, and then it uses A_2 to test whether $f(x) \in L_2$. Algorithm A_1 takes the output from algorithm A_2 and produces that answer as its own output.

The correctness of A_1 follows from condition (34.1). The algorithm runs in polynomial time, since both F and A_2 run in polynomial time (see Exercise 34.1-5). ∎

NP-completeness

Polynomial-time reductions provide a formal means for showing that one problem is at least as hard as another, to within a polynomial-time factor. That is, if $L_1 \leq_P L_2$, then L_1 is not more than a polynomial factor harder than L_2, which is

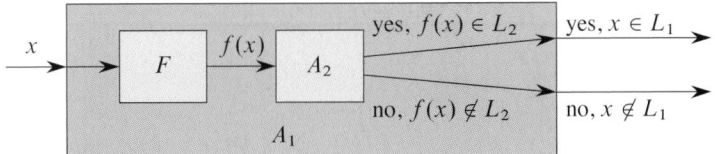

Figure 34.5 The proof of Lemma 34.3. The algorithm F is a reduction algorithm that computes the reduction function f from L_1 to L_2 in polynomial time, and A_2 is a polynomial-time algorithm that decides L_2. Algorithm A_1 decides whether $x \in L_1$ by using F to transform any input x into $f(x)$ and then using A_2 to decide whether $f(x) \in L_2$.

why the "less than or equal to" notation for reduction is mnemonic. We can now define the set of NP-complete languages, which are the hardest problems in NP.

A language $L \subseteq \{0, 1\}^*$ is **NP-complete** if

1. $L \in$ NP, and

2. $L' \le_P L$ for every $L' \in$ NP.

If a language L satisfies property 2, but not necessarily property 1, we say that L is **NP-hard**. We also define NPC to be the class of NP-complete languages.

As the following theorem shows, NP-completeness is at the crux of deciding whether P is in fact equal to NP.

Theorem 34.4
If any NP-complete problem is polynomial-time solvable, then P = NP. Equivalently, if any problem in NP is not polynomial-time solvable, then no NP-complete problem is polynomial-time solvable.

Proof Suppose that $L \in$ P and also that $L \in$ NPC. For any $L' \in$ NP, we have $L' \le_P L$ by property 2 of the definition of NP-completeness. Thus, by Lemma 34.3, we also have that $L' \in$ P, which proves the first statement of the theorem.

To prove the second statement, note that it is the contrapositive of the first statement. ∎

It is for this reason that research into the P $\ne$ NP question centers around the NP-complete problems. Most theoretical computer scientists believe that P $\ne$ NP, which leads to the relationships among P, NP, and NPC shown in Figure 34.6. But, for all we know, someone may yet come up with a polynomial-time algorithm for an NP-complete problem, thus proving that P = NP. Nevertheless, since no polynomial-time algorithm for any NP-complete problem has yet been discov-

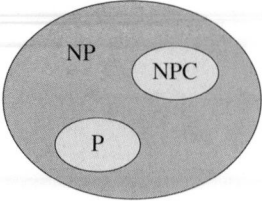

Figure 34.6 How most theoretical computer scientists view the relationships among P, NP, and NPC. Both P and NPC are wholly contained within NP, and P ∩ NPC = ∅.

ered, a proof that a problem is NP-complete provides excellent evidence that it is intractable.

Circuit satisfiability

We have defined the notion of an NP-complete problem, but up to this point, we have not actually proved that any problem is NP-complete. Once we prove that at least one problem is NP-complete, we can use polynomial-time reducibility as a tool to prove other problems to be NP-complete. Thus, we now focus on demonstrating the existence of an NP-complete problem: the circuit-satisfiability problem.

Unfortunately, the formal proof that the circuit-satisfiability problem is NP-complete requires technical detail beyond the scope of this text. Instead, we shall informally describe a proof that relies on a basic understanding of boolean combinational circuits.

Boolean combinational circuits are built from boolean combinational elements that are interconnected by wires. A *boolean combinational element* is any circuit element that has a constant number of boolean inputs and outputs and that performs a well-defined function. Boolean values are drawn from the set $\{0, 1\}$, where 0 represents FALSE and 1 represents TRUE.

The boolean combinational elements that we use in the circuit-satisfiability problem compute simple boolean functions, and they are known as *logic gates*. Figure 34.7 shows the three basic logic gates that we use in the circuit-satisfiability problem: the *NOT gate* (or *inverter*), the *AND gate*, and the *OR gate*. The NOT gate takes a single binary *input* x, whose value is either 0 or 1, and produces a binary *output* z whose value is opposite that of the input value. Each of the other two gates takes two binary inputs x and y and produces a single binary output z.

We can describe the operation of each gate, and of any boolean combinational element, by a *truth table*, shown under each gate in Figure 34.7. A truth table gives the outputs of the combinational element for each possible setting of the inputs. For

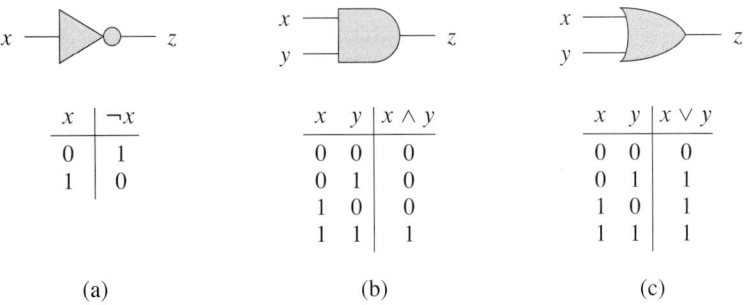

x	$\neg x$
0	1
1	0

x	y	$x \wedge y$
0	0	0
0	1	0
1	0	0
1	1	1

x	y	$x \vee y$
0	0	0
0	1	1
1	0	1
1	1	1

(a) (b) (c)

Figure 34.7 Three basic logic gates, with binary inputs and outputs. Under each gate is the truth table that describes the gate's operation. **(a)** The NOT gate. **(b)** The AND gate. **(c)** The OR gate.

example, the truth table for the OR gate tells us that when the inputs are $x = 0$ and $y = 1$, the output value is $z = 1$. We use the symbols $\neg$ to denote the NOT function, $\wedge$ to denote the AND function, and $\vee$ to denote the OR function. Thus, for example, $0 \vee 1 = 1$.

We can generalize AND and OR gates to take more than two inputs. An AND gate's output is 1 if all of its inputs are 1, and its output is 0 otherwise. An OR gate's output is 1 if any of its inputs are 1, and its output is 0 otherwise.

A *boolean combinational circuit* consists of one or more boolean combinational elements interconnected by *wires*. A wire can connect the output of one element to the input of another, thereby providing the output value of the first element as an input value of the second. Figure 34.8 shows two similar boolean combinational circuits, differing in only one gate. Part (a) of the figure also shows the values on the individual wires, given the input $\langle x_1 = 1, x_2 = 1, x_3 = 0 \rangle$. Although a single wire may have no more than one combinational-element output connected to it, it can feed several element inputs. The number of element inputs fed by a wire is called the *fan-out* of the wire. If no element output is connected to a wire, the wire is a *circuit input*, accepting input values from an external source. If no element input is connected to a wire, the wire is a *circuit output*, providing the results of the circuit's computation to the outside world. (An internal wire can also fan out to a circuit output.) For the purpose of defining the circuit-satisfiability problem, we limit the number of circuit outputs to 1, though in actual hardware design, boolean combinational circuit may have multiple outputs.

Boolean combinational circuits contain no cycles. In other words, sup' create a directed graph $G = (V, E)$ with one vertex for each combinatio' and with k directed edges for each wire whose fan-out is k; the g a directed edge (u, v) if a wire connects the output of element u t element v. Then G must be acyclic.

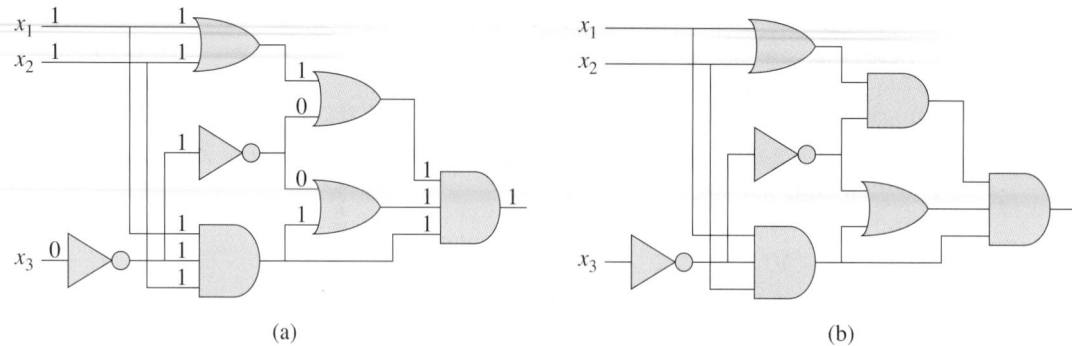

Figure 34.8 Two instances of the circuit-satisfiability problem. **(a)** The assignment $\langle x_1 = 1,$ $x_2 = 1, x_3 = 0\rangle$ to the inputs of this circuit causes the output of the circuit to be 1. The circuit is therefore satisfiable. **(b)** No assignment to the inputs of this circuit can cause the output of the circuit to be 1. The circuit is therefore unsatisfiable.

A ***truth assignment*** for a boolean combinational circuit is a set of boolean input values. We say that a one-output boolean combinational circuit is ***satisfiable*** if it has a ***satisfying assignment***: a truth assignment that causes the output of the circuit to be 1. For example, the circuit in Figure 34.8(a) has the satisfying assignment $\langle x_1 = 1, x_2 = 1, x_3 = 0\rangle$, and so it is satisfiable. As Exercise 34.3-1 asks you to show, no assignment of values to x_1, x_2, and x_3 causes the circuit in Figure 34.8(b) to produce a 1 output; it always produces 0, and so it is unsatisfiable.

The ***circuit-satisfiability problem*** is, "Given a boolean combinational circuit composed of AND, OR, and NOT gates, is it satisfiable?" In order to pose this question formally, however, we must agree on a standard encoding for circuits. The ***size*** of a boolean combinational circuit is the number of boolean combinational elements plus the number of wires in the circuit. We could devise a graphlike encoding that maps any given circuit C into a binary string $\langle C \rangle$ whose length is polynomial in the size of the circuit itself. As a formal language, we can therefore define

CIRCUIT-SAT $= \{\langle C \rangle : C$ is a satisfiable boolean combinational circuit$\}$.

The circuit-satisfiability problem arises in the area of computer-aided hardware optimization. If a subcircuit always produces 0, that subcircuit is unnecessary; the designer can replace it by a simpler subcircuit that omits all logic gates and provides the constant 0 value as its output. You can see why we would like to have a polynomial-time algorithm for this problem.

Given a circuit C, we might attempt to determine whether it is satisfiable by simply checking all possible assignments to the inputs. Unfortunately, if the circuit has k inputs, then we would have to check up to 2^k possible assignments. When

the size of C is polynomial in k, checking each one takes $\Omega(2^k)$ time, which is superpolynomial in the size of the circuit.[9] In fact, as we have claimed, there is strong evidence that no polynomial-time algorithm exists that solves the circuit-satisfiability problem because circuit satisfiability is NP-complete. We break the proof of this fact into two parts, based on the two parts of the definition of NP-completeness.

Lemma 34.5
The circuit-satisfiability problem belongs to the class NP.

Proof   We shall provide a two-input, polynomial-time algorithm A that can verify CIRCUIT-SAT. One of the inputs to A is (a standard encoding of) a boolean combinational circuit C. The other input is a certificate corresponding to an assignment of boolean values to the wires in C. (See Exercise 34.3-4 for a smaller certificate.)

We construct the algorithm A as follows. For each logic gate in the circuit, it checks that the value provided by the certificate on the output wire is correctly computed as a function of the values on the input wires. Then, if the output of the entire circuit is 1, the algorithm outputs 1, since the values assigned to the inputs of C provide a satisfying assignment. Otherwise, A outputs 0.

Whenever a satisfiable circuit C is input to algorithm A, there exists a certificate whose length is polynomial in the size of C and that causes A to output a 1. Whenever an unsatisfiable circuit is input, no certificate can fool A into believing that the circuit is satisfiable. Algorithm A runs in polynomial time: with a good implementation, linear time suffices. Thus, we can verify CIRCUIT-SAT in polynomial time, and CIRCUIT-SAT $\in$ NP.   ■

The second part of proving that CIRCUIT-SAT is NP-complete is to show that the language is NP-hard. That is, we must show that every language in NP is polynomial-time reducible to CIRCUIT-SAT. The actual proof of this fact is full of technical intricacies, and so we shall settle for a sketch of the proof based on some understanding of the workings of computer hardware.

A computer program is stored in the computer memory as a sequence of instructions. A typical instruction encodes an operation to be performed, addresses of operands in memory, and an address where the result is to be stored. A special memory location, called the ***program counter***, keeps track of which instruc-

---

[9]On the other hand, if the size of the circuit C is $\Theta(2^k)$, then an algorithm whose running time is $O(2^k)$ has a running time that is polynomial in the circuit size. Even if P $\neq$ NP, this situation would not contradict the NP-completeness of the problem; the existence of a polynomial-time algorithm for a special case does not imply that there is a polynomial-time algorithm for all cases.

tion is to be executed next. The program counter automatically increments upon fetching each instruction, thereby causing the computer to execute instructions sequentially. The execution of an instruction can cause a value to be written to the program counter, however, which alters the normal sequential execution and allows the computer to loop and perform conditional branches.

At any point during the execution of a program, the computer's memory holds the entire state of the computation. (We take the memory to include the program itself, the program counter, working storage, and any of the various bits of state that a computer maintains for bookkeeping.) We call any particular state of computer memory a **configuration**. We can view the execution of an instruction as mapping one configuration to another. The computer hardware that accomplishes this mapping can be implemented as a boolean combinational circuit, which we denote by M in the proof of the following lemma.

Lemma 34.6
The circuit-satisfiability problem is NP-hard.

Proof   Let L be any language in NP. We shall describe a polynomial-time algorithm F computing a reduction function f that maps every binary string x to a circuit $C = f(x)$ such that $x \in L$ if and only if $C \in \text{CIRCUIT-SAT}$.

Since $L \in \text{NP}$, there must exist an algorithm A that verifies L in polynomial time. The algorithm F that we shall construct uses the two-input algorithm A to compute the reduction function f.

Let $T(n)$ denote the worst-case running time of algorithm A on length-n input strings, and let $k \geq 1$ be a constant such that $T(n) = O(n^k)$ and the length of the certificate is $O(n^k)$. (The running time of A is actually a polynomial in the total input size, which includes both an input string and a certificate, but since the length of the certificate is polynomial in the length n of the input string, the running time is polynomial in n.)

The basic idea of the proof is to represent the computation of A as a sequence of configurations. As Figure 34.9 illustrates, we can break each configuration into parts consisting of the program for A, the program counter and auxiliary machine state, the input x, the certificate y, and working storage. The combinational circuit M, which implements the computer hardware, maps each configuration c_i to the next configuration c_{i+1}, starting from the initial configuration c_0. Algorithm A writes its output—0 or 1—to some designated location by the time it finishes executing, and if we assume that thereafter A halts, the value never changes. Thus, if the algorithm runs for at most $T(n)$ steps, the output appears as one of the bits in $c_{T(n)}$.

The reduction algorithm F constructs a single combinational circuit that computes all configurations produced by a given initial configuration. The idea is to

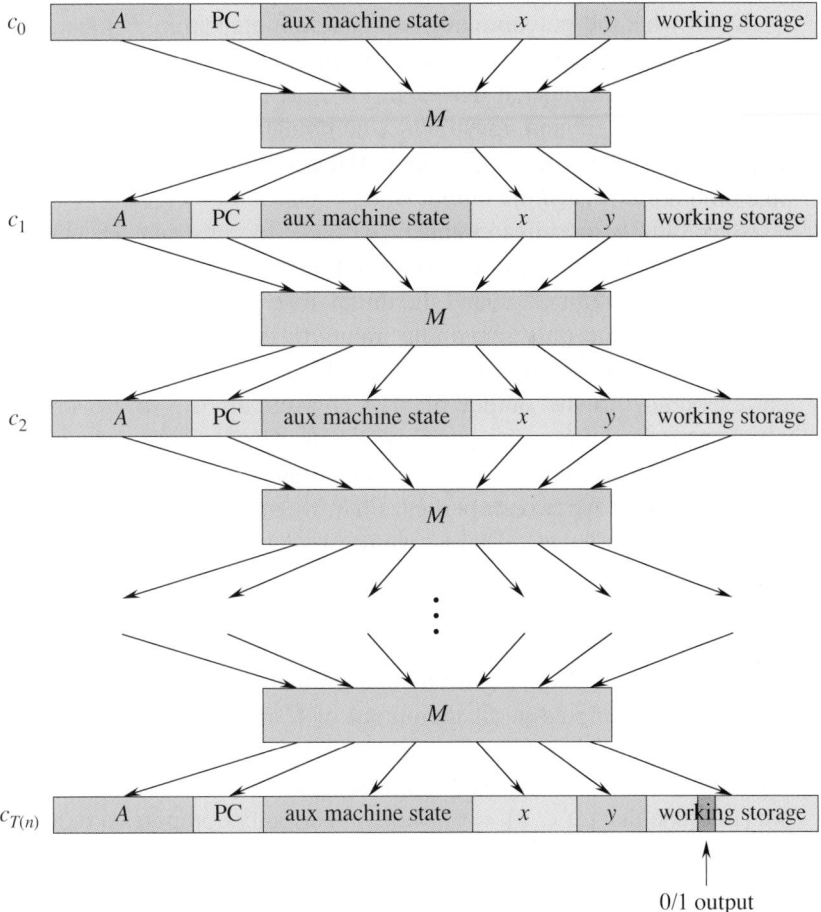

Figure 34.9 The sequence of configurations produced by an algorithm A running on an input x and certificate y. Each configuration represents the state of the computer for one step of the computation and, besides A, x, and y, includes the program counter (PC), auxiliary machine state, and working storage. Except for the certificate y, the initial configuration c_0 is constant. A boolean combinational circuit M maps each configuration to the next configuration. The output is a distinguished bit in the working storage.

paste together $T(n)$ copies of the circuit M. The output of the ith circuit, which produces configuration c_i, feeds directly into the input of the $(i+1)$st circuit. Thus, the configurations, rather than being stored in the computer's memory, simply reside as values on the wires connecting copies of M.

Recall what the polynomial-time reduction algorithm F must do. Given an input x, it must compute a circuit $C = f(x)$ that is satisfiable if and only if there exists a certificate y such that $A(x, y) = 1$. When F obtains an input x, it first computes $n = |x|$ and constructs a combinational circuit C' consisting of $T(n)$ copies of M. The input to C' is an initial configuration corresponding to a computation on $A(x, y)$, and the output is the configuration $c_{T(n)}$.

Algorithm F modifies circuit C' slightly to construct the circuit $C = f(x)$. First, it wires the inputs to C' corresponding to the program for A, the initial program counter, the input x, and the initial state of memory directly to these known values. Thus, the only remaining inputs to the circuit correspond to the certificate y. Second, it ignores all outputs from C', except for the one bit of $c_{T(n)}$ corresponding to the output of A. This circuit C, so constructed, computes $C(y) = A(x, y)$ for any input y of length $O(n^k)$. The reduction algorithm F, when provided an input string x, computes such a circuit C and outputs it.

We need to prove two properties. First, we must show that F correctly computes a reduction function f. That is, we must show that C is satisfiable if and only if there exists a certificate y such that $A(x, y) = 1$. Second, we must show that F runs in polynomial time.

To show that F correctly computes a reduction function, let us suppose that there exists a certificate y of length $O(n^k)$ such that $A(x, y) = 1$. Then, if we apply the bits of y to the inputs of C, the output of C is $C(y) = A(x, y) = 1$. Thus, if a certificate exists, then C is satisfiable. For the other direction, suppose that C is satisfiable. Hence, there exists an input y to C such that $C(y) = 1$, from which we conclude that $A(x, y) = 1$. Thus, F correctly computes a reduction function.

To complete the proof sketch, we need only show that F runs in time polynomial in $n = |x|$. The first observation we make is that the number of bits required to represent a configuration is polynomial in n. The program for A itself has constant size, independent of the length of its input x. The length of the input x is n, and the length of the certificate y is $O(n^k)$. Since the algorithm runs for at most $O(n^k)$ steps, the amount of working storage required by A is polynomial in n as well. (We assume that this memory is contiguous; Exercise 34.3-5 asks you to extend the argument to the situation in which the locations accessed by A are scattered across a much larger region of memory and the particular pattern of scattering can differ for each input x.)

The combinational circuit M implementing the computer hardware has size polynomial in the length of a configuration, which is $O(n^k)$; hence, the size of M is polynomial in n. (Most of this circuitry implements the logic of the memory

system.) The circuit C consists of at most $t = O(n^k)$ copies of M, and hence it has size polynomial in n. The reduction algorithm F can construct C from x in polynomial time, since each step of the construction takes polynomial time.   ∎

The language CIRCUIT-SAT is therefore at least as hard as any language in NP, and since it belongs to NP, it is NP-complete.

Theorem 34.7
The circuit-satisfiability problem is NP-complete.

Proof   Immediate from Lemmas 34.5 and 34.6 and from the definition of NP-completeness.   ∎

Exercises

34.3-1
Verify that the circuit in Figure 34.8(b) is unsatisfiable.

34.3-2
Show that the $\leq_P$ relation is a transitive relation on languages. That is, show that if $L_1 \leq_P L_2$ and $L_2 \leq_P L_3$, then $L_1 \leq_P L_3$.

34.3-3
Prove that $L \leq_P \overline{L}$ if and only if $\overline{L} \leq_P L$.

34.3-4
Show that we could have used a satisfying assignment as a certificate in an alternative proof of Lemma 34.5. Which certificate makes for an easier proof?

34.3-5
The proof of Lemma 34.6 assumes that the working storage for algorithm A occupies a contiguous region of polynomial size. Where in the proof do we exploit this assumption? Argue that this assumption does not involve any loss of generality.

34.3-6
A language L is **complete** for a language class C with respect to polynomial-time reductions if $L \in C$ and $L' \leq_P L$ for all $L' \in C$. Show that $\emptyset$ and $\{0, 1\}^*$ are the only languages in P that are not complete for P with respect to polynomial-time reductions.

34.3-7

Show that, with respect to polynomial-time reductions (see Exercise 34.3-6), L is complete for NP if and only if $\overline{L}$ is complete for co-NP.

34.3-8

The reduction algorithm F in the proof of Lemma 34.6 constructs the circuit $C = f(x)$ based on knowledge of x, A, and k. Professor Sartre observes that the string x is input to F, but only the existence of A, k, and the constant factor implicit in the $O(n^k)$ running time is known to F (since the language L belongs to NP), not their actual values. Thus, the professor concludes that F can't possibly construct the circuit C and that the language CIRCUIT-SAT is not necessarily NP-hard. Explain the flaw in the professor's reasoning.

34.4   NP-completeness proofs

We proved that the circuit-satisfiability problem is NP-complete by a direct proof that $L \leq_P$ CIRCUIT-SAT for every language $L \in$ NP. In this section, we shall show how to prove that languages are NP-complete without directly reducing *every* language in NP to the given language. We shall illustrate this methodology by proving that various formula-satisfiability problems are NP-complete. Section 34.5 provides many more examples of the methodology.

The following lemma is the basis of our method for showing that a language is NP-complete.

Lemma 34.8

If L is a language such that $L' \leq_P L$ for some $L' \in$ NPC, then L is NP-hard. If, in addition, $L \in$ NP, then $L \in$ NPC.

Proof   Since L' is NP-complete, for all $L'' \in$ NP, we have $L'' \leq_P L'$. By supposition, $L' \leq_P L$, and thus by transitivity (Exercise 34.3-2), we have $L'' \leq_P L$, which shows that L is NP-hard. If $L \in$ NP, we also have $L \in$ NPC.   ■

In other words, by reducing a known NP-complete language L' to L, we implicitly reduce every language in NP to L. Thus, Lemma 34.8 gives us a method for proving that a language L is NP-complete:

1. Prove $L \in$ NP.

2. Select a known NP-complete language L'.

3. Describe an algorithm that computes a function f mapping every instance $x \in \{0, 1\}^*$ of L' to an instance $f(x)$ of L.

4. Prove that the function f satisfies $x \in L'$ if and only if $f(x) \in L$ for all $x \in \{0, 1\}^*$.

5. Prove that the algorithm computing f runs in polynomial time.

(Steps 2–5 show that L is NP-hard.) This methodology of reducing from a single known NP-complete language is far simpler than the more complicated process of showing directly how to reduce from every language in NP. Proving CIRCUIT-SAT $\in$ NPC has given us a "foot in the door." Because we know that the circuit-satisfiability problem is NP-complete, we now can prove much more easily that other problems are NP-complete. Moreover, as we develop a catalog of known NP-complete problems, we will have more and more choices for languages from which to reduce.

Formula satisfiability

We illustrate the reduction methodology by giving an NP-completeness proof for the problem of determining whether a boolean formula, not a circuit, is satisfiable. This problem has the historical honor of being the first problem ever shown to be NP-complete.

We formulate the *(formula) satisfiability* problem in terms of the language SAT as follows. An instance of SAT is a boolean formula ϕ composed of

1. n boolean variables: $x_1, x_2, \ldots, x_n$;

2. m boolean connectives: any boolean function with one or two inputs and one output, such as $\wedge$ (AND), $\vee$ (OR), $\neg$ (NOT), $\rightarrow$ (implication), $\leftrightarrow$ (if and only if); and

3. parentheses. (Without loss of generality, we assume that there are no redundant parentheses, i.e., a formula contains at most one pair of parentheses per boolean connective.)

We can easily encode a boolean formula ϕ in a length that is polynomial in $n + m$. As in boolean combinational circuits, a *truth assignment* for a boolean formula ϕ is a set of values for the variables of ϕ, and a *satisfying assignment* is a truth assignment that causes it to evaluate to 1. A formula with a satisfying assignment is a *satisfiable* formula. The satisfiability problem asks whether a given boolean formula is satisfiable; in formal-language terms,

$$\text{SAT} = \{\langle \phi \rangle : \phi \text{ is a satisfiable boolean formula}\} .$$

As an example, the formula

$$\phi = ((x_1 \rightarrow x_2) \vee \neg((\neg x_1 \leftrightarrow x_3) \vee x_4)) \wedge \neg x_2$$

has the satisfying assignment $\langle x_1 = 0, x_2 = 0, x_3 = 1, x_4 = 1 \rangle$, since

$$
\begin{aligned}
\phi &= ((0 \rightarrow 0) \vee \neg((\neg 0 \leftrightarrow 1) \vee 1)) \wedge \neg 0 \qquad\qquad (34.2)\\
&= (1 \vee \neg(1 \vee 1)) \wedge 1 \\
&= (1 \vee 0) \wedge 1 \\
&= 1 ,
\end{aligned}
$$

and thus this formula ϕ belongs to SAT.

The naive algorithm to determine whether an arbitrary boolean formula is satisfiable does not run in polynomial time. A formula with n variables has 2^n possible assignments. If the length of $\langle \phi \rangle$ is polynomial in n, then checking every assignment requires $\Omega(2^n)$ time, which is superpolynomial in the length of $\langle \phi \rangle$. As the following theorem shows, a polynomial-time algorithm is unlikely to exist.

Theorem 34.9
Satisfiability of boolean formulas is NP-complete.

Proof We start by arguing that SAT $\in$ NP. Then we prove that SAT is NP-hard by showing that CIRCUIT-SAT $\leq_\mathrm{P}$ SAT; by Lemma 34.8, this will prove the theorem.

To show that SAT belongs to NP, we show that a certificate consisting of a satisfying assignment for an input formula ϕ can be verified in polynomial time. The verifying algorithm simply replaces each variable in the formula with its corresponding value and then evaluates the expression, much as we did in equation (34.2) above. This task is easy to do in polynomial time. If the expression evaluates to 1, then the algorithm has verified that the formula is satisfiable. Thus, SAT is in NP.

To prove that SAT is NP-hard, we show that CIRCUIT-SAT $\leq_\mathrm{P}$ SAT. In other words, we need to show how to reduce any instance of circuit satisfiability to an instance of formula satisfiability in polynomial time. We can use induction to express any boolean combinational circuit as a boolean formula. We simply look at the gate that produces the circuit output and inductively express each of the gate's inputs as formulas. We then obtain the formula for the circuit by writing an expression that applies the gate's function to its inputs' formulas.

Unfortunately, this straightforward method does not amount to a polynomial-time reduction. As Exercise 34.4-1 asks you to show, shared subformulas—which arise from gates whose output wires have fan-out of 2 or more—can cause the size of the generated formula to grow exponentially. Thus, the reduction algorithm must be somewhat more clever.

Figure 34.10 illustrates how we overcome this problem, using as an example the circuit from Figure 34.8(a). For each wire x_i in the circuit C, the formula ϕ

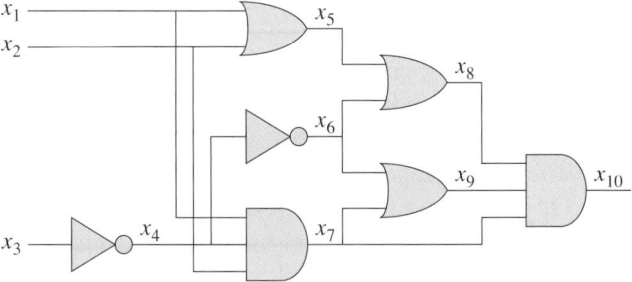

Figure 34.10 Reducing circuit satisfiability to formula satisfiability. The formula produced by the reduction algorithm has a variable for each wire in the circuit.

has a variable x_i. We can now express how each gate operates as a small formula involving the variables of its incident wires. For example, the operation of the output AND gate is $x_{10} \leftrightarrow (x_7 \wedge x_8 \wedge x_9)$. We call each of these small formulas a **clause**.

The formula ϕ produced by the reduction algorithm is the AND of the circuit-output variable with the conjunction of clauses describing the operation of each gate. For the circuit in the figure, the formula is

$$\phi = x_{10} \wedge (x_4 \leftrightarrow \neg x_3)$$
$$\wedge (x_5 \leftrightarrow (x_1 \vee x_2))$$
$$\wedge (x_6 \leftrightarrow \neg x_4)$$
$$\wedge (x_7 \leftrightarrow (x_1 \wedge x_2 \wedge x_4))$$
$$\wedge (x_8 \leftrightarrow (x_5 \vee x_6))$$
$$\wedge (x_9 \leftrightarrow (x_6 \vee x_7))$$
$$\wedge (x_{10} \leftrightarrow (x_7 \wedge x_8 \wedge x_9)) \ .$$

Given a circuit C, it is straightforward to produce such a formula ϕ in polynomial time.

Why is the circuit C satisfiable exactly when the formula ϕ is satisfiable? If C has a satisfying assignment, then each wire of the circuit has a well-defined value, and the output of the circuit is 1. Therefore, when we assign wire values to variables in ϕ, each clause of ϕ evaluates to 1, and thus the conjunction of all evaluates to 1. Conversely, if some assignment causes ϕ to evaluate to 1, the circuit C is satisfiable by an analogous argument. Thus, we have shown that CIRCUIT-SAT $\leq_P$ SAT, which completes the proof. ∎

3-CNF satisfiability

We can prove many problems NP-complete by reducing from formula satisfiability. The reduction algorithm must handle any input formula, though, and this requirement can lead to a huge number of cases that we must consider. We often prefer to reduce from a restricted language of boolean formulas, so that we need to consider fewer cases. Of course, we must not restrict the language so much that it becomes polynomial-time solvable. One convenient language is 3-CNF satisfiability, or 3-CNF-SAT.

We define 3-CNF satisfiability using the following terms. A *literal* in a boolean formula is an occurrence of a variable or its negation. A boolean formula is in *conjunctive normal form*, or *CNF*, if it is expressed as an AND of *clauses*, each of which is the OR of one or more literals. A boolean formula is in *3-conjunctive normal form*, or *3-CNF*, if each clause has exactly three distinct literals.

For example, the boolean formula

$$(x_1 \vee \neg x_1 \vee \neg x_2) \wedge (x_3 \vee x_2 \vee x_4) \wedge (\neg x_1 \vee \neg x_3 \vee \neg x_4)$$

is in 3-CNF. The first of its three clauses is $(x_1 \vee \neg x_1 \vee \neg x_2)$, which contains the three literals x_1, $\neg x_1$, and $\neg x_2$.

In 3-CNF-SAT, we are asked whether a given boolean formula ϕ in 3-CNF is satisfiable. The following theorem shows that a polynomial-time algorithm that can determine the satisfiability of boolean formulas is unlikely to exist, even when they are expressed in this simple normal form.

Theorem 34.10
Satisfiability of boolean formulas in 3-conjunctive normal form is NP-complete.

Proof   The argument we used in the proof of Theorem 34.9 to show that SAT $\in$ NP applies equally well here to show that 3-CNF-SAT $\in$ NP. By Lemma 34.8, therefore, we need only show that SAT $\leq_P$ 3-CNF-SAT.

We break the reduction algorithm into three basic steps. Each step progressively transforms the input formula ϕ closer to the desired 3-conjunctive normal form.

The first step is similar to the one used to prove CIRCUIT-SAT $\leq_P$ SAT in Theorem 34.9. First, we construct a binary "parse" tree for the input formula ϕ, with literals as leaves and connectives as internal nodes. Figure 34.11 shows such a parse tree for the formula

$$\phi = ((x_1 \rightarrow x_2) \vee \neg((\neg x_1 \leftrightarrow x_3) \vee x_4)) \wedge \neg x_2 . \tag{34.3}$$

Should the input formula contain a clause such as the OR of several literals, we use associativity to parenthesize the expression fully so that every internal node in the resulting tree has 1 or 2 children. We can now think of the binary parse tree as a circuit for computing the function.

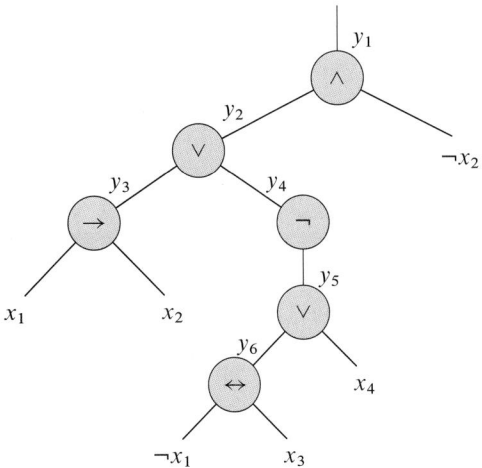

Figure 34.11 The tree corresponding to the formula $\phi = ((x_1 \rightarrow x_2) \vee \neg((\neg x_1 \leftrightarrow x_3) \vee x_4)) \wedge \neg x_2$.

Mimicking the reduction in the proof of Theorem 34.9, we introduce a variable y_i for the output of each internal node. Then, we rewrite the original formula ϕ as the AND of the root variable and a conjunction of clauses describing the operation of each node. For the formula (34.3), the resulting expression is

$$
\begin{aligned}
\phi' = \ & y_1 \wedge (y_1 \leftrightarrow (y_2 \wedge \neg x_2)) \\
& \wedge (y_2 \leftrightarrow (y_3 \vee y_4)) \\
& \wedge (y_3 \leftrightarrow (x_1 \rightarrow x_2)) \\
& \wedge (y_4 \leftrightarrow \neg y_5) \\
& \wedge (y_5 \leftrightarrow (y_6 \vee x_4)) \\
& \wedge (y_6 \leftrightarrow (\neg x_1 \leftrightarrow x_3)) \ .
\end{aligned}
$$

Observe that the formula ϕ' thus obtained is a conjunction of clauses ϕ'_i, each of which has at most 3 literals. The only requirement that we might fail to meet is that each clause has to be an OR of 3 literals.

The second step of the reduction converts each clause ϕ'_i into conjunctive normal form. We construct a truth table for ϕ'_i by evaluating all possible assignments to its variables. Each row of the truth table consists of a possible assignment of the variables of the clause, together with the value of the clause under that assignment. Using the truth-table entries that evaluate to 0, we build a formula in **disjunctive normal form** (or **DNF**)—an OR of ANDs—that is equivalent to $\neg\phi'_i$. We then negate this formula and convert it into a CNF formula ϕ''_i by using **DeMorgan's**

y_1	y_2	x_2	$(y_1 \leftrightarrow (y_2 \wedge \neg x_2))$
1	1	1	0
1	1	0	1
1	0	1	0
1	0	0	0
0	1	1	1
0	1	0	0
0	0	1	1
0	0	0	1

Figure 34.12   The truth table for the clause $(y_1 \leftrightarrow (y_2 \wedge \neg x_2))$.

laws for propositional logic,

$$\neg(a \wedge b) = \neg a \vee \neg b ,$$
$$\neg(a \vee b) = \neg a \wedge \neg b ,$$

to complement all literals, change ORs into ANDs, and change ANDs into ORs.

In our example, we convert the clause $\phi_1' = (y_1 \leftrightarrow (y_2 \wedge \neg x_2))$ into CNF as follows. The truth table for ϕ_1' appears in Figure 34.12. The DNF formula equivalent to $\neg\phi_1'$ is

$$(y_1 \wedge y_2 \wedge x_2) \vee (y_1 \wedge \neg y_2 \wedge x_2) \vee (y_1 \wedge \neg y_2 \wedge \neg x_2) \vee (\neg y_1 \wedge y_2 \wedge \neg x_2) .$$

Negating and applying DeMorgan's laws, we get the CNF formula

$$\begin{aligned}
\phi_1'' = {} & (\neg y_1 \vee \neg y_2 \vee \neg x_2) \wedge (\neg y_1 \vee y_2 \vee \neg x_2) \\
& \wedge (\neg y_1 \vee y_2 \vee x_2) \wedge (y_1 \vee \neg y_2 \vee x_2) ,
\end{aligned}$$

which is equivalent to the original clause ϕ_1'.

At this point, we have converted each clause ϕ_i' of the formula ϕ' into a CNF formula ϕ_i'', and thus ϕ' is equivalent to the CNF formula ϕ'' consisting of the conjunction of the ϕ_i''. Moreover, each clause of ϕ'' has at most 3 literals.

The third and final step of the reduction further transforms the formula so that each clause has *exactly* 3 distinct literals. We construct the final 3-CNF formula ϕ''' from the clauses of the CNF formula ϕ''. The formula ϕ''' also uses two auxiliary variables that we shall call p and q. For each clause C_i of ϕ'', we include the following clauses in ϕ''':

- If C_i has 3 distinct literals, then simply include C_i as a clause of ϕ'''.

- If C_i has 2 distinct literals, that is, if $C_i = (l_1 \vee l_2)$, where l_1 and l_2 are literals, then include $(l_1 \vee l_2 \vee p) \wedge (l_1 \vee l_2 \vee \neg p)$ as clauses of ϕ'''. The literals p and $\neg p$ merely fulfill the syntactic requirement that each clause of ϕ''' has

exactly 3 distinct literals. Whether $p = 0$ or $p = 1$, one of the clauses is equivalent to $l_1 \vee l_2$, and the other evaluates to 1, which is the identity for AND.

- If C_i has just 1 distinct literal l, then include $(l \vee p \vee q) \wedge (l \vee p \vee \neg q) \wedge (l \vee \neg p \vee q) \wedge (l \vee \neg p \vee \neg q)$ as clauses of ϕ'''. Regardless of the values of p and q, one of the four clauses is equivalent to l, and the other 3 evaluate to 1.

We can see that the 3-CNF formula ϕ''' is satisfiable if and only if ϕ is satisfiable by inspecting each of the three steps. Like the reduction from CIRCUIT-SAT to SAT, the construction of ϕ' from ϕ in the first step preserves satisfiability. The second step produces a CNF formula ϕ'' that is algebraically equivalent to ϕ'. The third step produces a 3-CNF formula ϕ''' that is effectively equivalent to ϕ'', since any assignment to the variables p and q produces a formula that is algebraically equivalent to ϕ''.

We must also show that the reduction can be computed in polynomial time. Constructing ϕ' from ϕ introduces at most 1 variable and 1 clause per connective in ϕ. Constructing ϕ'' from ϕ' can introduce at most 8 clauses into ϕ'' for each clause from ϕ', since each clause of ϕ' has at most 3 variables, and the truth table for each clause has at most $2^3 = 8$ rows. The construction of ϕ''' from ϕ'' introduces at most 4 clauses into ϕ''' for each clause of ϕ''. Thus, the size of the resulting formula ϕ''' is polynomial in the length of the original formula. Each of the constructions can easily be accomplished in polynomial time.   ■

Exercises

34.4-1
Consider the straightforward (nonpolynomial-time) reduction in the proof of Theorem 34.9. Describe a circuit of size n that, when converted to a formula by this method, yields a formula whose size is exponential in n.

34.4-2
Show the 3-CNF formula that results when we use the method of Theorem 34.10 on the formula (34.3).

34.4-3
Professor Jagger proposes to show that SAT $\leq_P$ 3-CNF-SAT by using only the truth-table technique in the proof of Theorem 34.10, and not the other steps. That is, the professor proposes to take the boolean formula ϕ, form a truth table for its variables, derive from the truth table a formula in 3-DNF that is equivalent to $\neg \phi$, and then negate and apply DeMorgan's laws to produce a 3-CNF formula equivalent to ϕ. Show that this strategy does not yield a polynomial-time reduction.

34.4-4

Show that the problem of determining whether a boolean formula is a tautology is complete for co-NP. (*Hint:* See Exercise 34.3-7.)

34.4-5

Show that the problem of determining the satisfiability of boolean formulas in disjunctive normal form is polynomial-time solvable.

34.4-6

Suppose that someone gives you a polynomial-time algorithm to decide formula satisfiability. Describe how to use this algorithm to find satisfying assignments in polynomial time.

34.4-7

Let 2-CNF-SAT be the set of satisfiable boolean formulas in CNF with exactly 2 literals per clause. Show that 2-CNF-SAT $\in$ P. Make your algorithm as efficient as possible. (*Hint:* Observe that $x \vee y$ is equivalent to $\neg x \rightarrow y$. Reduce 2-CNF-SAT to an efficiently solvable problem on a directed graph.)

34.5   NP-complete problems

NP-complete problems arise in diverse domains: boolean logic, graphs, arithmetic, network design, sets and partitions, storage and retrieval, sequencing and scheduling, mathematical programming, algebra and number theory, games and puzzles, automata and language theory, program optimization, biology, chemistry, physics, and more. In this section, we shall use the reduction methodology to provide NP-completeness proofs for a variety of problems drawn from graph theory and set partitioning.

Figure 34.13 outlines the structure of the NP-completeness proofs in this section and Section 34.4. We prove each language in the figure to be NP-complete by reduction from the language that points to it. At the root is CIRCUIT-SAT, which we proved NP-complete in Theorem 34.7.

34.5.1   The clique problem

A *clique* in an undirected graph $G = (V, E)$ is a subset $V' \subseteq V$ of vertices, each pair of which is connected by an edge in E. In other words, a clique is a complete subgraph of G. The *size* of a clique is the number of vertices it contains. The *clique problem* is the optimization problem of finding a clique of maximum size in

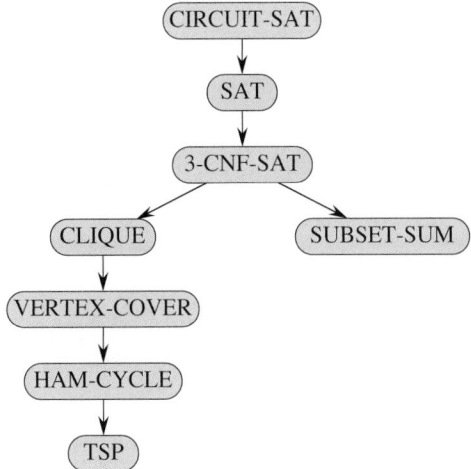

Figure 34.13   The structure of NP-completeness proofs in Sections 34.4 and 34.5. All proofs ultimately follow by reduction from the NP-completeness of CIRCUIT-SAT.

a graph. As a decision problem, we ask simply whether a clique of a given size k exists in the graph. The formal definition is

$$\text{CLIQUE} = \{\langle G, k \rangle : G \text{ is a graph containing a clique of size } k\} \ .$$

A naive algorithm for determining whether a graph $G = (V, E)$ with $|V|$ vertices has a clique of size k is to list all k-subsets of V, and check each one to see whether it forms a clique. The running time of this algorithm is $\Omega(k^2 \binom{|V|}{k})$, which is polynomial if k is a constant. In general, however, k could be near $|V|/2$, in which case the algorithm runs in superpolynomial time. Indeed, an efficient algorithm for the clique problem is unlikely to exist.

Theorem 34.11
The clique problem is NP-complete.

Proof   To show that CLIQUE $\in$ NP, for a given graph $G = (V, E)$, we use the set $V' \subseteq V$ of vertices in the clique as a certificate for G. We can check whether V' is a clique in polynomial time by checking whether, for each pair $u, v \in V'$, the edge (u, v) belongs to E.

We next prove that 3-CNF-SAT $\leq_P$ CLIQUE, which shows that the clique problem is NP-hard. You might be surprised that we should be able to prove such a result, since on the surface logical formulas seem to have little to do with graphs.

The reduction algorithm begins with an instance of 3-CNF-SAT. Let $\phi = C_1 \wedge C_2 \wedge \cdots \wedge C_k$ be a boolean formula in 3-CNF with k clauses. For $r =$

$$C_1 = x_1 \vee \neg x_2 \vee \neg x_3$$

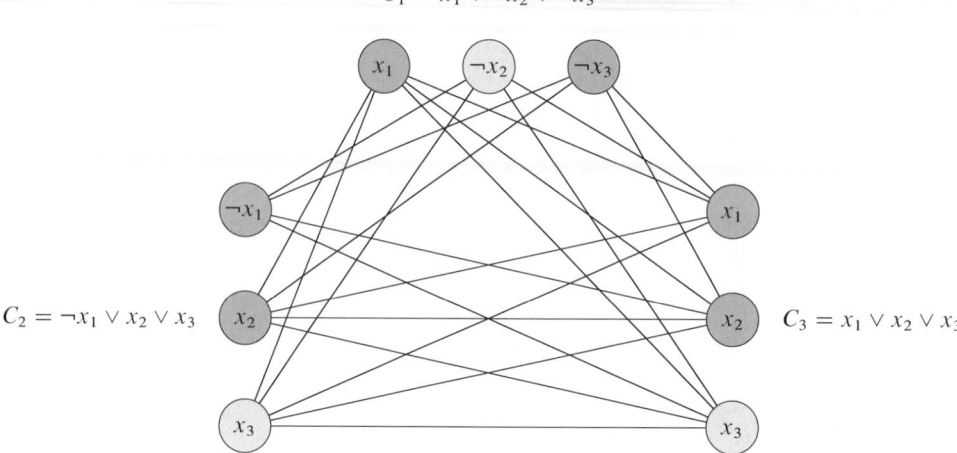

Figure 34.14 The graph G derived from the 3-CNF formula $\phi = C_1 \wedge C_2 \wedge C_3$, where $C_1 = (x_1 \vee \neg x_2 \vee \neg x_3)$, $C_2 = (\neg x_1 \vee x_2 \vee x_3)$, and $C_3 = (x_1 \vee x_2 \vee x_3)$, in reducing 3-CNF-SAT to CLIQUE. A satisfying assignment of the formula has $x_2 = 0$, $x_3 = 1$, and x_1 either 0 or 1. This assignment satisfies C_1 with $\neg x_2$, and it satisfies C_2 and C_3 with x_3, corresponding to the clique with lightly shaded vertices.

$1, 2, \ldots, k$, each clause C_r has exactly three distinct literals l_1^r, l_2^r, and l_3^r. We shall construct a graph G such that ϕ is satisfiable if and only if G has a clique of size k.

We construct the graph $G = (V, E)$ as follows. For each clause $C_r = (l_1^r \vee l_2^r \vee l_3^r)$ in ϕ, we place a triple of vertices v_1^r, v_2^r, and v_3^r into V. We put an edge between two vertices v_i^r and v_j^s if both of the following hold:

- v_i^r and v_j^s are in different triples, that is, $r \neq s$, and

- their corresponding literals are **consistent**, that is, l_i^r is not the negation of l_j^s.

We can easily build this graph from ϕ in polynomial time. As an example of this construction, if we have

$$\phi = (x_1 \vee \neg x_2 \vee \neg x_3) \wedge (\neg x_1 \vee x_2 \vee x_3) \wedge (x_1 \vee x_2 \vee x_3) \,,$$

then G is the graph shown in Figure 34.14.

We must show that this transformation of ϕ into G is a reduction. First, suppose that ϕ has a satisfying assignment. Then each clause C_r contains at least one literal l_i^r that is assigned 1, and each such literal corresponds to a vertex v_i^r. Picking one such "true" literal from each clause yields a set V' of k vertices. We claim that V' is a clique. For any two vertices $v_i^r, v_j^s \in V'$, where $r \neq s$, both corresponding literals l_i^r and l_j^s map to 1 by the given satisfying assignment, and thus the literals

cannot be complements. Thus, by the construction of G, the edge (v_i^r, v_j^s) belongs to E.

Conversely, suppose that G has a clique V' of size k. No edges in G connect vertices in the same triple, and so V' contains exactly one vertex per triple. We can assign 1 to each literal l_i^r such that $v_i^r \in V'$ without fear of assigning 1 to both a literal and its complement, since G contains no edges between inconsistent literals. Each clause is satisfied, and so ϕ is satisfied. (Any variables that do not correspond to a vertex in the clique may be set arbitrarily.) ∎

In the example of Figure 34.14, a satisfying assignment of ϕ has $x_2 = 0$ and $x_3 = 1$. A corresponding clique of size $k = 3$ consists of the vertices corresponding to $\neg x_2$ from the first clause, x_3 from the second clause, and x_3 from the third clause. Because the clique contains no vertices corresponding to either x_1 or $\neg x_1$, we can set x_1 to either 0 or 1 in this satisfying assignment.

Observe that in the proof of Theorem 34.11, we reduced an arbitrary instance of 3-CNF-SAT to an instance of CLIQUE with a particular structure. You might think that we have shown only that CLIQUE is NP-hard in graphs in which the vertices are restricted to occur in triples and in which there are no edges between vertices in the same triple. Indeed, we have shown that CLIQUE is NP-hard only in this restricted case, but this proof suffices to show that CLIQUE is NP-hard in general graphs. Why? If we had a polynomial-time algorithm that solved CLIQUE on general graphs, it would also solve CLIQUE on restricted graphs.

The opposite approach—reducing instances of 3-CNF-SAT with a special structure to general instances of CLIQUE—would not have sufficed, however. Why not? Perhaps the instances of 3-CNF-SAT that we chose to reduce from were "easy," and so we would not have reduced an NP-hard problem to CLIQUE.

Observe also that the reduction used the instance of 3-CNF-SAT, but not the solution. We would have erred if the polynomial-time reduction had relied on knowing whether the formula ϕ is satisfiable, since we do not know how to decide whether ϕ is satisfiable in polynomial time.

34.5.2 The vertex-cover problem

A *vertex cover* of an undirected graph $G = (V, E)$ is a subset $V' \subseteq V$ such that if $(u, v) \in E$, then $u \in V'$ or $v \in V'$ (or both). That is, each vertex "covers" its incident edges, and a vertex cover for G is a set of vertices that covers all the edges in E. The *size* of a vertex cover is the number of vertices in it. For example, the graph in Figure 34.15(b) has a vertex cover $\{w, z\}$ of size 2.

The *vertex-cover problem* is to find a vertex cover of minimum size in a given graph. Restating this optimization problem as a decision problem, we wish to

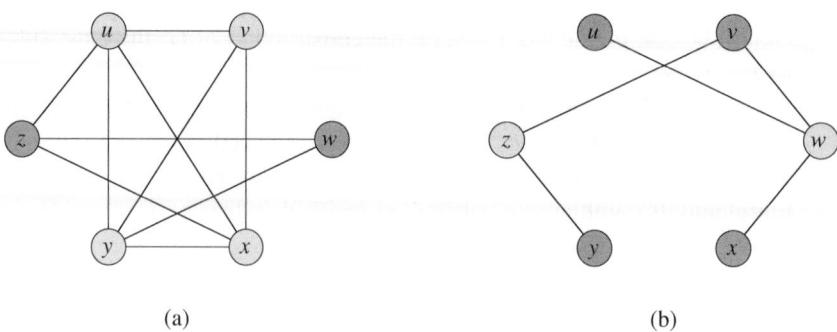

Figure 34.15   Reducing CLIQUE to VERTEX-COVER. **(a)** An undirected graph $G = (V, E)$ with clique $V' = \{u, v, x, y\}$. **(b)** The graph $\overline{G}$ produced by the reduction algorithm that has vertex cover $V - V' = \{w, z\}$.

determine whether a graph has a vertex cover of a given size k. As a language, we define

VERTEX-COVER $= \{\langle G, k \rangle : \text{graph } G \text{ has a vertex cover of size } k\}$.

The following theorem shows that this problem is NP-complete.

Theorem 34.12
The vertex-cover problem is NP-complete.

Proof   We first show that VERTEX-COVER $\in$ NP. Suppose we are given a graph $G = (V, E)$ and an integer k. The certificate we choose is the vertex cover $V' \subseteq V$ itself. The verification algorithm affirms that $|V'| = k$, and then it checks, for each edge $(u, v) \in E$, that $u \in V'$ or $v \in V'$. We can easily verify the certificate in polynomial time.

We prove that the vertex-cover problem is NP-hard by showing that CLIQUE $\leq_P$ VERTEX-COVER. This reduction relies on the notion of the "complement" of a graph. Given an undirected graph $G = (V, E)$, we define the ***complement*** of G as $\overline{G} = (V, \overline{E})$, where $\overline{E} = \{(u, v) : u, v \in V, u \neq v, \text{ and } (u, v) \notin E\}$. In other words, $\overline{G}$ is the graph containing exactly those edges that are not in G. Figure 34.15 shows a graph and its complement and illustrates the reduction from CLIQUE to VERTEX-COVER.

The reduction algorithm takes as input an instance $\langle G, k \rangle$ of the clique problem. It computes the complement $\overline{G}$, which we can easily do in polynomial time. The output of the reduction algorithm is the instance $\langle \overline{G}, |V| - k \rangle$ of the vertex-cover problem. To complete the proof, we show that this transformation is indeed a

reduction: the graph G has a clique of size k if and only if the graph $\overline{G}$ has a vertex cover of size $|V| - k$.

Suppose that G has a clique $V' \subseteq V$ with $|V'| = k$. We claim that $V - V'$ is a vertex cover in $\overline{G}$. Let (u, v) be any edge in $\overline{E}$. Then, $(u, v) \notin E$, which implies that at least one of u or v does not belong to V', since every pair of vertices in V' is connected by an edge of E. Equivalently, at least one of u or v is in $V - V'$, which means that edge (u, v) is covered by $V - V'$. Since (u, v) was chosen arbitrarily from $\overline{E}$, every edge of $\overline{E}$ is covered by a vertex in $V - V'$. Hence, the set $V - V'$, which has size $|V| - k$, forms a vertex cover for $\overline{G}$.

Conversely, suppose that $\overline{G}$ has a vertex cover $V' \subseteq V$, where $|V'| = |V| - k$. Then, for all $u, v \in V$, if $(u, v) \in \overline{E}$, then $u \in V'$ or $v \in V'$ or both. The contrapositive of this implication is that for all $u, v \in V$, if $u \notin V'$ and $v \notin V'$, then $(u, v) \in E$. In other words, $V - V'$ is a clique, and it has size $|V| - |V'| = k$. ∎

Since VERTEX-COVER is NP-complete, we don't expect to find a polynomial-time algorithm for finding a minimum-size vertex cover. Section 35.1 presents a polynomial-time "approximation algorithm," however, which produces "approximate" solutions for the vertex-cover problem. The size of a vertex cover produced by the algorithm is at most twice the minimum size of a vertex cover.

Thus, we shouldn't give up hope just because a problem is NP-complete. We may be able to design a polynomial-time approximation algorithm that obtains near-optimal solutions, even though finding an optimal solution is NP-complete. Chapter 35 gives several approximation algorithms for NP-complete problems.

34.5.3 The hamiltonian-cycle problem

We now return to the hamiltonian-cycle problem defined in Section 34.2.

Theorem 34.13
The hamiltonian cycle problem is NP-complete.

Proof We first show that HAM-CYCLE belongs to NP. Given a graph $G = (V, E)$, our certificate is the sequence of $|V|$ vertices that makes up the hamiltonian cycle. The verification algorithm checks that this sequence contains each vertex in V exactly once and that with the first vertex repeated at the end, it forms a cycle in G. That is, it checks that there is an edge between each pair of consecutive vertices and between the first and last vertices. We can verify the certificate in polynomial time.

We now prove that VERTEX-COVER $\leq_P$ HAM-CYCLE, which shows that HAM-CYCLE is NP-complete. Given an undirected graph $G = (V, E)$ and an

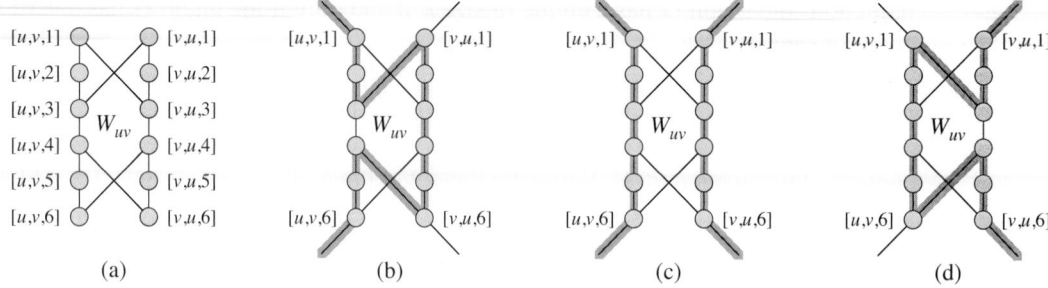

Figure 34.16   The widget used in reducing the vertex-cover problem to the hamiltonian-cycle problem. An edge (u, v) of graph G corresponds to widget W_{uv} in the graph G' created in the reduction. **(a)** The widget, with individual vertices labeled. **(b)–(d)** The shaded paths are the only possible ones through the widget that include all vertices, assuming that the only connections from the widget to the remainder of G' are through vertices $[u, v, 1], [u, v, 6], [v, u, 1],$ and $[v, u, 6]$.

integer k, we construct an undirected graph $G' = (V', E')$ that has a hamiltonian cycle if and only if G has a vertex cover of size k.

Our construction uses a ***widget***, which is a piece of a graph that enforces certain properties. Figure 34.16(a) shows the widget we use. For each edge $(u, v) \in E$, the graph G' that we construct will contain one copy of this widget, which we denote by W_{uv}. We denote each vertex in W_{uv} by $[u, v, i]$ or $[v, u, i]$, where $1 \le i \le 6$, so that each widget W_{uv} contains 12 vertices. Widget W_{uv} also contains the 14 edges shown in Figure 34.16(a).

Along with the internal structure of the widget, we enforce the properties we want by limiting the connections between the widget and the remainder of the graph G' that we construct. In particular, only vertices $[u, v, 1], [u, v, 6], [v, u, 1],$ and $[v, u, 6]$ will have edges incident from outside W_{uv}. Any hamiltonian cycle of G' must traverse the edges of W_{uv} in one of the three ways shown in Figures 34.16(b)–(d). If the cycle enters through vertex $[u, v, 1]$, it must exit through vertex $[u, v, 6]$, and it either visits all 12 of the widget's vertices (Figure 34.16(b)) or the six vertices $[u, v, 1]$ through $[u, v, 6]$ (Figure 34.16(c)). In the latter case, the cycle will have to reenter the widget to visit vertices $[v, u, 1]$ through $[v, u, 6]$. Similarly, if the cycle enters through vertex $[v, u, 1]$, it must exit through vertex $[v, u, 6]$, and it either visits all 12 of the widget's vertices (Figure 34.16(d)) or the six vertices $[v, u, 1]$ through $[v, u, 6]$ (Figure 34.16(c)). No other paths through the widget that visit all 12 vertices are possible. In particular, it is impossible to construct two vertex-disjoint paths, one of which connects $[u, v, 1]$ to $[v, u, 6]$ and the other of which connects $[v, u, 1]$ to $[u, v, 6]$, such that the union of the two paths contains all of the widget's vertices.

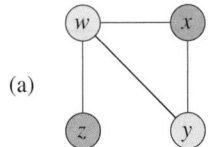

(a)

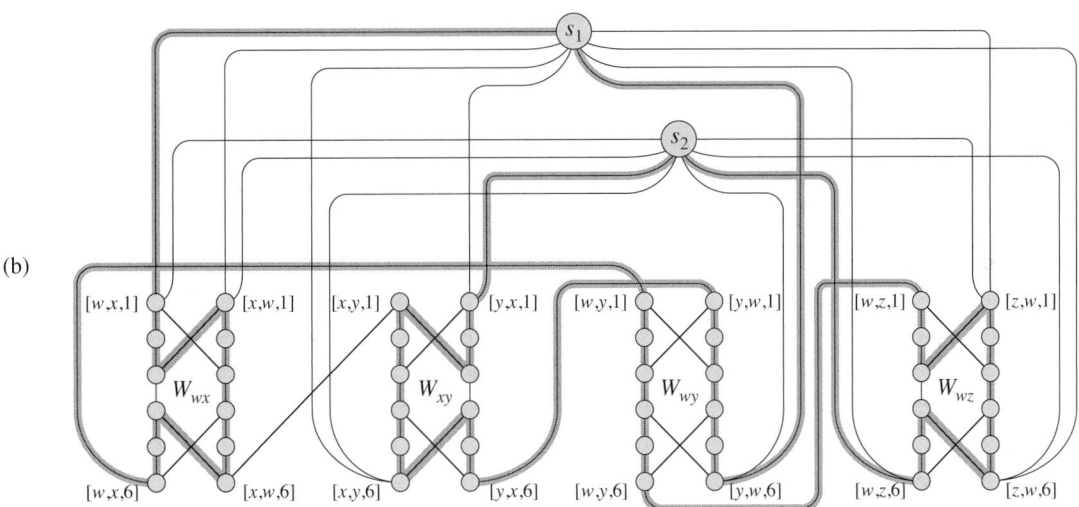

(b)

Figure 34.17 Reducing an instance of the vertex-cover problem to an instance of the hamiltonian-cycle problem. **(a)** An undirected graph G with a vertex cover of size 2, consisting of the lightly shaded vertices w and y. **(b)** The undirected graph G' produced by the reduction, with the hamiltonian cycle corresponding to the vertex cover shaded. The vertex cover $\{w, y\}$ corresponds to edges $(s_1, [w, x, 1])$ and $(s_2, [y, x, 1])$ appearing in the hamiltonian cycle.

The only other vertices in V' other than those of widgets are **selector vertices** $s_1, s_2, \ldots, s_k$. We use edges incident on selector vertices in G' to select the k vertices of the cover in G.

In addition to the edges in widgets, E' contains two other types of edges, which Figure 34.17 shows. First, for each vertex $u \in V$, we add edges to join pairs of widgets in order to form a path containing all widgets corresponding to edges incident on u in G. We arbitrarily order the vertices adjacent to each vertex $u \in V$ as $u^{(1)}, u^{(2)}, \ldots, u^{(\text{degree}(u))}$, where degree$(u)$ is the number of vertices adjacent to u. We create a path in G' through all the widgets corresponding to edges incident on u by adding to E' the edges $\{([u, u^{(i)}, 6], [u, u^{(i+1)}, 1]) : 1 \leq i \leq \text{degree}(u) - 1\}$. In Figure 34.17, for example, we order the vertices adjacent to w as x, y, z, and so graph G' in part (b) of the figure includes the edges

$([w, x, 6], [w, y, 1])$ and $([w, y, 6], [w, z, 1])$. For each vertex $u \in V$, these edges in G' fill in a path containing all widgets corresponding to edges incident on u in G.

The intuition behind these edges is that if we choose a vertex $u \in V$ in the vertex cover of G, we can construct a path from $[u, u^{(1)}, 1]$ to $[u, u^{(\text{degree}(u))}, 6]$ in G' that "covers" all widgets corresponding to edges incident on u. That is, for each of these widgets, say $W_{u, u^{(i)}}$, the path either includes all 12 vertices (if u is in the vertex cover but $u^{(i)}$ is not) or just the six vertices $[u, u^{(i)}, 1], [u, u^{(i)}, 2], \ldots, [u, u^{(i)}, 6]$ (if both u and $u^{(i)}$ are in the vertex cover).

The final type of edge in E' joins the first vertex $[u, u^{(1)}, 1]$ and the last vertex $[u, u^{(\text{degree}(u))}, 6]$ of each of these paths to each of the selector vertices. That is, we include the edges

$$\{(s_j, [u, u^{(1)}, 1]) : u \in V \text{ and } 1 \leq j \leq k\}$$
$$\cup \{(s_j, [u, u^{(\text{degree}(u))}, 6]) : u \in V \text{ and } 1 \leq j \leq k\} .$$

Next, we show that the size of G' is polynomial in the size of G, and hence we can construct G' in time polynomial in the size of G. The vertices of G' are those in the widgets, plus the selector vertices. With 12 vertices per widget, plus $k \leq |V|$ selector vertices, we have a total of

$$
\begin{aligned}
|V'| &= 12 |E| + k \\
&\leq 12 |E| + |V|
\end{aligned}
$$

vertices. The edges of G' are those in the widgets, those that go between widgets, and those connecting selector vertices to widgets. Each widget contains 14 edges, totaling $14 |E|$ in all widgets. For each vertex $u \in V$, graph G' has $\text{degree}(u) - 1$ edges going between widgets, so that summed over all vertices in V,

$$\sum_{u \in V} (\text{degree}(u) - 1) = 2 |E| - |V|$$

edges go between widgets. Finally, G' has two edges for each pair consisting of a selector vertex and a vertex of V, totaling $2k |V|$ such edges. The total number of edges of G' is therefore

$$
\begin{aligned}
|E'| &= (14 |E|) + (2 |E| - |V|) + (2k |V|) \\
&= 16 |E| + (2k - 1) |V| \\
&\leq 16 |E| + (2 |V| - 1) |V| .
\end{aligned}
$$

Now we show that the transformation from graph G to G' is a reduction. That is, we must show that G has a vertex cover of size k if and only if G' has a hamiltonian cycle.

Suppose that $G = (V, E)$ has a vertex cover $V^* \subseteq V$ of size k. Let $V^* = \{u_1, u_2, \ldots, u_k\}$. As Figure 34.17 shows, we form a hamiltonian cycle in G' by including the following edges[10] for each vertex $u_j \in V^*$. Include edges $\{([u_j, u_j^{(i)}, 6], [u_j, u_j^{(i+1)}, 1]) : 1 \leq i \leq \text{degree}(u_j) - 1\}$, which connect all widgets corresponding to edges incident on u_j. We also include the edges within these widgets as Figures 34.16(b)–(d) show, depending on whether the edge is covered by one or two vertices in V^*. The hamiltonian cycle also includes the edges

$$\{(s_j, [u_j, u_j^{(1)}, 1]) : 1 \leq j \leq k\}$$
$$\cup \{(s_{j+1}, [u_j, u_j^{(\text{degree}(u_j))}, 6]) : 1 \leq j \leq k - 1\}$$
$$\cup \{(s_1, [u_k, u_k^{(\text{degree}(u_k))}, 6])\} .$$

By inspecting Figure 34.17, you can verify that these edges form a cycle. The cycle starts at s_1, visits all widgets corresponding to edges incident on u_1, then visits s_2, visits all widgets corresponding to edges incident on u_2, and so on, until it returns to s_1. The cycle visits each widget either once or twice, depending on whether one or two vertices of V^* cover its corresponding edge. Because V^* is a vertex cover for G, each edge in E is incident on some vertex in V^*, and so the cycle visits each vertex in each widget of G'. Because the cycle also visits every selector vertex, it is hamiltonian.

Conversely, suppose that $G' = (V', E')$ has a hamiltonian cycle $C \subseteq E'$. We claim that the set

$$V^* = \{u \in V : (s_j, [u, u^{(1)}, 1]) \in C \text{ for some } 1 \leq j \leq k\} \tag{34.4}$$

is a vertex cover for G. To see why, partition C into maximal paths that start at some selector vertex s_i, traverse an edge $(s_i, [u, u^{(1)}, 1])$ for some $u \in V$, and end at a selector vertex s_j without passing through any other selector vertex. Let us call each such path a "cover path." From how G' is constructed, each cover path must start at some s_i, take the edge $(s_i, [u, u^{(1)}, 1])$ for some vertex $u \in V$, pass through all the widgets corresponding to edges in E incident on u, and then end at some selector vertex s_j. We refer to this cover path as p_u, and by equation (34.4), we put u into V^*. Each widget visited by p_u must be W_{uv} or W_{vu} for some $v \in V$. For each widget visited by p_u, its vertices are visited by either one or two cover paths. If they are visited by one cover path, then edge $(u, v) \in E$ is covered in G by vertex u. If two cover paths visit the widget, then the other cover path must be p_v, which implies that $v \in V^*$, and edge $(u, v) \in E$ is covered by both u and v.

---

[10]Technically, we define a cycle in terms of vertices rather than edges (see Section B.4). In the interest of clarity, we abuse notation here and define the hamiltonian cycle in terms of edges.

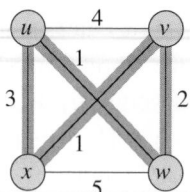

Figure 34.18   An instance of the traveling-salesman problem. Shaded edges represent a minimum-cost tour, with cost 7.

Because each vertex in each widget is visited by some cover path, we see that each edge in E is covered by some vertex in V^*.   ∎

34.5.4   The traveling-salesman problem

In the ***traveling-salesman problem***, which is closely related to the hamiltonian-cycle problem, a salesman must visit n cities. Modeling the problem as a complete graph with n vertices, we can say that the salesman wishes to make a ***tour***, or hamiltonian cycle, visiting each city exactly once and finishing at the city he starts from. The salesman incurs a nonnegative integer cost $c(i, j)$ to travel from city i to city j, and the salesman wishes to make the tour whose total cost is minimum, where the total cost is the sum of the individual costs along the edges of the tour. For example, in Figure 34.18, a minimum-cost tour is $\langle u, w, v, x, u \rangle$, with cost 7. The formal language for the corresponding decision problem is

$$\text{TSP} = \{\langle G, c, k \rangle : \ G = (V, E) \text{ is a complete graph,}$$
$$c \text{ is a function from } V \times V \to \mathbb{N},$$
$$k \in \mathbb{N}, \text{ and}$$
$$G \text{ has a traveling-salesman tour with cost at most } k\} \ .$$

The following theorem shows that a fast algorithm for the traveling-salesman problem is unlikely to exist.

Theorem 34.14
The traveling-salesman problem is NP-complete.

Proof   We first show that TSP belongs to NP. Given an instance of the problem, we use as a certificate the sequence of n vertices in the tour. The verification algorithm checks that this sequence contains each vertex exactly once, sums up the edge costs, and checks whether the sum is at most k. This process can certainly be done in polynomial time.

To prove that TSP is NP-hard, we show that HAM-CYCLE $\leq_P$ TSP. Let $G = (V, E)$ be an instance of HAM-CYCLE. We construct an instance of TSP as follows. We form the complete graph $G' = (V, E')$, where $E' = \{(i, j) : i, j \in V \text{ and } i \neq j\}$, and we define the cost function c by

$$c(i, j) = \begin{cases} 0 & \text{if } (i, j) \in E, \\ 1 & \text{if } (i, j) \notin E. \end{cases}$$

(Note that because G is undirected, it has no self-loops, and so $c(v, v) = 1$ for all vertices $v \in V$.) The instance of TSP is then $\langle G', c, 0 \rangle$, which we can easily create in polynomial time.

We now show that graph G has a hamiltonian cycle if and only if graph G' has a tour of cost at most 0. Suppose that graph G has a hamiltonian cycle h. Each edge in h belongs to E and thus has cost 0 in G'. Thus, h is a tour in G' with cost 0. Conversely, suppose that graph G' has a tour h' of cost at most 0. Since the costs of the edges in E' are 0 and 1, the cost of tour h' is exactly 0 and each edge on the tour must have cost 0. Therefore, h' contains only edges in E. We conclude that h' is a hamiltonian cycle in graph G.   ■

34.5.5 The subset-sum problem

We next consider an arithmetic NP-complete problem. In the *subset-sum problem*, we are given a finite set S of positive integers and an integer *target* $t > 0$. We ask whether there exists a subset $S' \subseteq S$ whose elements sum to t. For example, if $S = \{1, 2, 7, 14, 49, 98, 343, 686, 2409, 2793, 16808, 17206, 117705, 117993\}$ and $t = 138457$, then the subset $S' = \{1, 2, 7, 98, 343, 686, 2409, 17206, 117705\}$ is a solution.

As usual, we define the problem as a language:

SUBSET-SUM $= \{\langle S, t \rangle :$ there exists a subset $S' \subseteq S$ such that $t = \sum_{s \in S'} s\}$.

As with any arithmetic problem, it is important to recall that our standard encoding assumes that the input integers are coded in binary. With this assumption in mind, we can show that the subset-sum problem is unlikely to have a fast algorithm.

Theorem 34.15
The subset-sum problem is NP-complete.

Proof   To show that SUBSET-SUM is in NP, for an instance $\langle S, t \rangle$ of the problem, we let the subset S' be the certificate. A verification algorithm can check whether $t = \sum_{s \in S'} s$ in polynomial time.

We now show that 3-CNF-SAT $\leq_P$ SUBSET-SUM. Given a 3-CNF formula ϕ over variables $x_1, x_2, \ldots, x_n$ with clauses $C_1, C_2, \ldots, C_k$, each containing exactly

three distinct literals, the reduction algorithm constructs an instance $\langle S, t \rangle$ of the subset-sum problem such that ϕ is satisfiable if and only if there exists a subset of S whose sum is exactly t. Without loss of generality, we make two simplifying assumptions about the formula ϕ. First, no clause contains both a variable and its negation, for such a clause is automatically satisfied by any assignment of values to the variables. Second, each variable appears in at least one clause, because it does not matter what value is assigned to a variable that appears in no clauses.

The reduction creates two numbers in set S for each variable x_i and two numbers in S for each clause C_j. We shall create numbers in base 10, where each number contains $n + k$ digits and each digit corresponds to either one variable or one clause. Base 10 (and other bases, as we shall see) has the property we need of preventing carries from lower digits to higher digits.

As Figure 34.19 shows, we construct set S and target t as follows. We label each digit position by either a variable or a clause. The least significant k digits are labeled by the clauses, and the most significant n digits are labeled by variables.

- The target t has a 1 in each digit labeled by a variable and a 4 in each digit labeled by a clause.

- For each variable x_i, set S contains two integers v_i and v_i'. Each of v_i and v_i' has a 1 in the digit labeled by x_i and 0s in the other variable digits. If literal x_i appears in clause C_j, then the digit labeled by C_j in v_i contains a 1. If literal $\neg x_i$ appears in clause C_j, then the digit labeled by C_j in v_i' contains a 1. All other digits labeled by clauses in v_i and v_i' are 0.

  All v_i and v_i' values in set S are unique. Why? For $l \neq i$, no v_l or v_l' values can equal v_i and v_i' in the most significant n digits. Furthermore, by our simplifying assumptions above, no v_i and v_i' can be equal in all k least significant digits. If v_i and v_i' were equal, then x_i and $\neg x_i$ would have to appear in exactly the same set of clauses. But we assume that no clause contains both x_i and $\neg x_i$ and that either x_i or $\neg x_i$ appears in some clause, and so there must be some clause C_j for which v_i and v_i' differ.

- For each clause C_j, set S contains two integers s_j and s_j'. Each of s_j and s_j' has 0s in all digits other than the one labeled by C_j. For s_j, there is a 1 in the C_j digit, and s_j' has a 2 in this digit. These integers are "slack variables," which we use to get each clause-labeled digit position to add to the target value of 4.

  Simple inspection of Figure 34.19 demonstrates that all s_j and s_j' values in S are unique in set S.

Note that the greatest sum of digits in any one digit position is 6, which occurs in the digits labeled by clauses (three 1s from the v_i and v_i' values, plus 1 and 2 from

		x_1	x_2	x_3	C_1	C_2	C_3	C_4
v_1	=	1	0	0	1	0	0	1
v_1'	=	1	0	0	0	1	1	0
v_2	=	0	1	0	0	0	0	1
v_2'	=	0	1	0	1	1	1	0
v_3	=	0	0	1	0	0	1	1
v_3'	=	0	0	1	1	1	0	0
s_1	=	0	0	0	1	0	0	0
s_1'	=	0	0	0	2	0	0	0
s_2	=	0	0	0	0	1	0	0
s_2'	=	0	0	0	0	2	0	0
s_3	=	0	0	0	0	0	1	0
s_3'	=	0	0	0	0	0	2	0
s_4	=	0	0	0	0	0	0	1
s_4'	=	0	0	0	0	0	0	2
t	=	1	1	1	4	4	4	4

Figure 34.19 The reduction of 3-CNF-SAT to SUBSET-SUM. The formula in 3-CNF is $\phi = C_1 \wedge C_2 \wedge C_3 \wedge C_4$, where $C_1 = (x_1 \vee \neg x_2 \vee \neg x_3), C_2 = (\neg x_1 \vee \neg x_2 \vee \neg x_3), C_3 = (\neg x_1 \vee \neg x_2 \vee x_3)$, and $C_4 = (x_1 \vee x_2 \vee x_3)$. A satisfying assignment of ϕ is $\langle x_1 = 0, x_2 = 0, x_3 = 1 \rangle$. The set S produced by the reduction consists of the base-10 numbers shown; reading from top to bottom, $S = \{1001001, 1000110, 100001, 101110, 10011, 11100, 1000, 2000, 100, 200, 10, 20, 1, 2\}$. The target t is 1114444. The subset $S' \subseteq S$ is lightly shaded, and it contains v_1', v_2', and v_3, corresponding to the satisfying assignment. It also contains slack variables $s_1, s_1', s_2', s_3, s_4$, and s_4' to achieve the target value of 4 in the digits labeled by C_1 through C_4.

the s_j and s_j' values). Interpreting these numbers in base 10, therefore, no carries can occur from lower digits to higher digits.[11]

We can perform the reduction in polynomial time. The set S contains $2n + 2k$ values, each of which has $n + k$ digits, and the time to produce each digit is polynomial in $n + k$. The target t has $n + k$ digits, and the reduction produces each in constant time.

We now show that the 3-CNF formula ϕ is satisfiable if and only if there exists a subset $S' \subseteq S$ whose sum is t. First, suppose that ϕ has a satisfying assignment. For $i = 1, 2, \ldots, n$, if $x_i = 1$ in this assignment, then include v_i in S'. Otherwise, include v_i'. In other words, we include in S' exactly the v_i and v_i' values that cor-

---

[11] In fact, any base b, where $b \geq 7$, would work. The instance at the beginning of this subsection is the set S and target t in Figure 34.19 interpreted in base 7, with S listed in sorted order.

respond to literals with the value 1 in the satisfying assignment. Having included either v_i or v_i', but not both, for all i, and having put 0 in the digits labeled by variables in all s_j and s_j', we see that for each variable-labeled digit, the sum of the values of S' must be 1, which matches those digits of the target t. Because each clause is satisfied, the clause contains some literal with the value 1. Therefore, each digit labeled by a clause has at least one 1 contributed to its sum by a v_i or v_i' value in S'. In fact, 1, 2, or 3 literals may be 1 in each clause, and so each clause-labeled digit has a sum of 1, 2, or 3 from the v_i and v_i' values in S'. In Figure 34.19 for example, literals $\neg x_1, \neg x_2$, and x_3 have the value 1 in a satisfying assignment. Each of clauses C_1 and C_4 contains exactly one of these literals, and so together v_1', v_2', and v_3 contribute 1 to the sum in the digits for C_1 and C_4. Clause C_2 contains two of these literals, and v_1', v_2', and v_3 contribute 2 to the sum in the digit for C_2. Clause C_3 contains all three of these literals, and v_1', v_2', and v_3 contribute 3 to the sum in the digit for C_3. We achieve the target of 4 in each digit labeled by clause C_j by including in S' the appropriate nonempty subset of slack variables $\{s_j, s_j'\}$. In Figure 34.19, S' includes $s_1, s_1', s_2', s_3, s_4$, and s_4'. Since we have matched the target in all digits of the sum, and no carries can occur, the values of S' sum to t.

Now, suppose that there is a subset $S' \subseteq S$ that sums to t. The subset S' must include exactly one of v_i and v_i' for each $i = 1, 2, \ldots, n$, for otherwise the digits labeled by variables would not sum to 1. If $v_i \in S'$, we set $x_i = 1$. Otherwise, $v_i' \in S'$, and we set $x_i = 0$. We claim that every clause C_j, for $j = 1, 2, \ldots, k$, is satisfied by this assignment. To prove this claim, note that to achieve a sum of 4 in the digit labeled by C_j, the subset S' must include at least one v_i or v_i' value that has a 1 in the digit labeled by C_j, since the contributions of the slack variables s_j and s_j' together sum to at most 3. If S' includes a v_i that has a 1 in C_j's position, then the literal x_i appears in clause C_j. Since we have set $x_i = 1$ when $v_i \in S'$, clause C_j is satisfied. If S' includes a v_i' that has a 1 in that position, then the literal $\neg x_i$ appears in C_j. Since we have set $x_i = 0$ when $v_i' \in S'$, clause C_j is again satisfied. Thus, all clauses of ϕ are satisfied, which completes the proof. ∎

Exercises

34.5-1
The ***subgraph-isomorphism problem*** takes two undirected graphs G_1 and G_2, and it asks whether G_1 is isomorphic to a subgraph of G_2. Show that the subgraph-isomorphism problem is NP-complete.

34.5-2
Given an integer $m \times n$ matrix A and an integer m-vector b, the ***0-1 integer-programming problem*** asks whether there exists an integer n-vector x with ele-

ments in the set $\{0, 1\}$ such that $Ax \leq b$. Prove that 0-1 integer programming is NP-complete. (*Hint:* Reduce from 3-CNF-SAT.)

34.5-3

The ***integer linear-programming problem*** is like the 0-1 integer-programming problem given in Exercise 34.5-2, except that the values of the vector x may be any integers rather than just 0 or 1. Assuming that the 0-1 integer-programming problem is NP-hard, show that the integer linear-programming problem is NP-complete.

34.5-4

Show how to solve the subset-sum problem in polynomial time if the target value t is expressed in unary.

34.5-5

The ***set-partition problem*** takes as input a set S of numbers. The question is whether the numbers can be partitioned into two sets A and $\overline{A} = S - A$ such that $\sum_{x \in A} x = \sum_{x \in \overline{A}} x$. Show that the set-partition problem is NP-complete.

34.5-6

Show that the hamiltonian-path problem is NP-complete.

34.5-7

The ***longest-simple-cycle problem*** is the problem of determining a simple cycle (no repeated vertices) of maximum length in a graph. Formulate a related decision problem, and show that the decision problem is NP-complete.

34.5-8

In the ***half 3-CNF satisfiability*** problem, we are given a 3-CNF formula ϕ with n variables and m clauses, where m is even. We wish to determine whether there exists a truth assignment to the variables of ϕ such that exactly half the clauses evaluate to 0 and exactly half the clauses evaluate to 1. Prove that the half 3-CNF satisfiability problem is NP-complete.

Problems

34-1 *Independent set*

An ***independent set*** of a graph $G = (V, E)$ is a subset $V' \subseteq V$ of vertices such that each edge in E is incident on at most one vertex in V'. The ***independent-set problem*** is to find a maximum-size independent set in G.

a. Formulate a related decision problem for the independent-set problem, and prove that it is NP-complete. (*Hint:* Reduce from the clique problem.)

b. Suppose that you are given a "black-box" subroutine to solve the decision problem you defined in part (a). Give an algorithm to find an independent set of maximum size. The running time of your algorithm should be polynomial in $|V|$ and $|E|$, counting queries to the black box as a single step.

Although the independent-set decision problem is NP-complete, certain special cases are polynomial-time solvable.

c. Give an efficient algorithm to solve the independent-set problem when each vertex in G has degree 2. Analyze the running time, and prove that your algorithm works correctly.

d. Give an efficient algorithm to solve the independent-set problem when G is bipartite. Analyze the running time, and prove that your algorithm works correctly. (*Hint:* Use the results of Section 26.3.)

34-2   *Bonnie and Clyde*

Bonnie and Clyde have just robbed a bank. They have a bag of money and want to divide it up. For each of the following scenarios, either give a polynomial-time algorithm, or prove that the problem is NP-complete. The input in each case is a list of the n items in the bag, along with the value of each.

a. The bag contains n coins, but only 2 different denominations: some coins are worth x dollars, and some are worth y dollars. Bonnie and Clyde wish to divide the money exactly evenly.

b. The bag contains n coins, with an arbitrary number of different denominations, but each denomination is a nonnegative integer power of 2, i.e., the possible denominations are 1 dollar, 2 dollars, 4 dollars, etc. Bonnie and Clyde wish to divide the money exactly evenly.

c. The bag contains n checks, which are, in an amazing coincidence, made out to "Bonnie or Clyde." They wish to divide the checks so that they each get the exact same amount of money.

d. The bag contains n checks as in part (c), but this time Bonnie and Clyde are willing to accept a split in which the difference is no larger than 100 dollars.

34-3 *Graph coloring*

Mapmakers try to use as few colors as possible when coloring countries on a map, as long as no two countries that share a border have the same color. We can model this problem with an undirected graph $G = (V, E)$ in which each vertex represents a country and vertices whose respective countries share a border are adjacent. Then, a ***k-coloring*** is a function $c : V \rightarrow \{1, 2, \ldots, k\}$ such that $c(u) \neq c(v)$ for every edge $(u, v) \in E$. In other words, the numbers $1, 2, \ldots, k$ represent the k colors, and adjacent vertices must have different colors. The ***graph-coloring problem*** is to determine the minimum number of colors needed to color a given graph.

a. Give an efficient algorithm to determine a 2-coloring of a graph, if one exists.

b. Cast the graph-coloring problem as a decision problem. Show that your decision problem is solvable in polynomial time if and only if the graph-coloring problem is solvable in polynomial time.

c. Let the language 3-COLOR be the set of graphs that can be 3-colored. Show that if 3-COLOR is NP-complete, then your decision problem from part (b) is NP-complete.

To prove that 3-COLOR is NP-complete, we use a reduction from 3-CNF-SAT. Given a formula ϕ of m clauses on n variables $x_1, x_2, \ldots, x_n$, we construct a graph $G = (V, E)$ as follows. The set V consists of a vertex for each variable, a vertex for the negation of each variable, 5 vertices for each clause, and 3 special vertices: TRUE, FALSE, and RED. The edges of the graph are of two types: "literal" edges that are independent of the clauses and "clause" edges that depend on the clauses. The literal edges form a triangle on the special vertices and also form a triangle on x_i, $\neg x_i$, and RED for $i = 1, 2, \ldots, n$.

d. Argue that in any 3-coloring c of a graph containing the literal edges, exactly one of a variable and its negation is colored $c(\text{TRUE})$ and the other is colored $c(\text{FALSE})$. Argue that for any truth assignment for ϕ, there exists a 3-coloring of the graph containing just the literal edges.

The widget shown in Figure 34.20 helps to enforce the condition corresponding to a clause $(x \vee y \vee z)$. Each clause requires a unique copy of the 5 vertices that are heavily shaded in the figure; they connect as shown to the literals of the clause and the special vertex TRUE.

e. Argue that if each of x, y, and z is colored $c(\text{TRUE})$ or $c(\text{FALSE})$, then the widget is 3-colorable if and only if at least one of x, y, or z is colored $c(\text{TRUE})$.

f. Complete the proof that 3-COLOR is NP-complete.

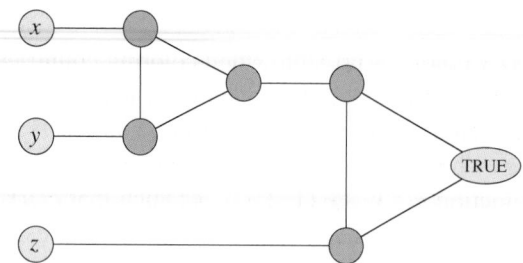

Figure 34.20   The widget corresponding to a clause $(x \vee y \vee z)$, used in Problem 34-3.

34-4   *Scheduling with profits and deadlines*

Suppose that we have one machine and a set of n tasks $a_1, a_2, \ldots, a_n$, each of which requires time on the machine. Each task a_j requires t_j time units on the machine (its processing time), yields a profit of p_j, and has a deadline d_j. The machine can process only one task at a time, and task a_j must run without interruption for t_j consecutive time units. If we complete task a_j by its deadline d_j, we receive a profit p_j, but if we complete it after its deadline, we receive no profit. As an optimization problem, we are given the processing times, profits, and deadlines for a set of n tasks, and we wish to find a schedule that completes all the tasks and returns the greatest amount of profit. The processing times, profits, and deadlines are all nonnegative numbers.

a. State this problem as a decision problem.

b. Show that the decision problem is NP-complete.

c. Give a polynomial-time algorithm for the decision problem, assuming that all processing times are integers from 1 to n. (*Hint:* Use dynamic programming.)

d. Give a polynomial-time algorithm for the optimization problem, assuming that all processing times are integers from 1 to n.

Chapter notes

The book by Garey and Johnson [129] provides a wonderful guide to NP-completeness, discussing the theory at length and providing a catalogue of many problems that were known to be NP-complete in 1979. The proof of Theorem 34.13 is adapted from their book, and the list of NP-complete problem domains at the beginning of Section 34.5 is drawn from their table of contents. Johnson wrote a series

of 23 columns in the *Journal of Algorithms* between 1981 and 1992 reporting new developments in NP-completeness. Hopcroft, Motwani, and Ullman [177], Lewis and Papadimitriou [236], Papadimitriou [270], and Sipser [317] have good treatments of NP-completeness in the context of complexity theory. NP-completeness and several reductions also appear in books by Aho, Hopcroft, and Ullman [5]; Dasgupta, Papadimitriou, and Vazirani [82]; Johnsonbaugh and Schaefer [193]; and Kleinberg and Tardos [208].

The class P was introduced in 1964 by Cobham [72] and, independently, in 1965 by Edmonds [100], who also introduced the class NP and conjectured that $P \neq NP$. The notion of NP-completeness was proposed in 1971 by Cook [75], who gave the first NP-completeness proofs for formula satisfiability and 3-CNF satisfiability. Levin [234] independently discovered the notion, giving an NP-completeness proof for a tiling problem. Karp [199] introduced the methodology of reductions in 1972 and demonstrated the rich variety of NP-complete problems. Karp's paper included the original NP-completeness proofs of the clique, vertex-cover, and hamiltonian-cycle problems. Since then, thousands of problems have been proven to be NP-complete by many researchers. In a talk at a meeting celebrating Karp's 60th birthday in 1995, Papadimitriou remarked, "about 6000 papers each year have the term 'NP-complete' on their title, abstract, or list of keywords. This is more than each of the terms 'compiler,' 'database,' 'expert,' 'neural network,' or 'operating system.' "

Recent work in complexity theory has shed light on the complexity of computing approximate solutions. This work gives a new definition of NP using "probabilistically checkable proofs." This new definition implies that for problems such as clique, vertex cover, the traveling-salesman problem with the triangle inequality, and many others, computing good approximate solutions is NP-hard and hence no easier than computing optimal solutions. An introduction to this area can be found in Arora's thesis [20]; a chapter by Arora and Lund in Hochbaum [172]; a survey article by Arora [21]; a book edited by Mayr, Prömel, and Steger [246]; and a survey article by Johnson [191].

35 Approximation Algorithms

Many problems of practical significance are NP-complete, yet they are too important to abandon merely because we don't know how to find an optimal solution in polynomial time. Even if a problem is NP-complete, there may be hope. We have at least three ways to get around NP-completeness. First, if the actual inputs are small, an algorithm with exponential running time may be perfectly satisfactory. Second, we may be able to isolate important special cases that we can solve in polynomial time. Third, we might come up with approaches to find *near-optimal* solutions in polynomial time (either in the worst case or the expected case). In practice, near-optimality is often good enough. We call an algorithm that returns near-optimal solutions an ***approximation algorithm***. This chapter presents polynomial-time approximation algorithms for several NP-complete problems.

Performance ratios for approximation algorithms

Suppose that we are working on an optimization problem in which each potential solution has a positive cost, and we wish to find a near-optimal solution. Depending on the problem, we may define an optimal solution as one with maximum possible cost or one with minimum possible cost; that is, the problem may be either a maximization or a minimization problem.

We say that an algorithm for a problem has an ***approximation ratio*** of $\rho(n)$ if, for any input of size n, the cost C of the solution produced by the algorithm is within a factor of $\rho(n)$ of the cost C^* of an optimal solution:

$$\max \left(\frac{C}{C^*}, \frac{C^*}{C} \right) \leq \rho(n) . \tag{35.1}$$

If an algorithm achieves an approximation ratio of $\rho(n)$, we call it a ***$\rho(n)$-approximation algorithm***. The definitions of the approximation ratio and of a $\rho(n)$-approximation algorithm apply to both minimization and maximization problems. For a maximization problem, $0 < C \leq C^*$, and the ratio C^*/C gives the factor by which the cost of an optimal solution is larger than the cost of the approximate

solution. Similarly, for a minimization problem, $0 < C^* \le C$, and the ratio C/C^* gives the factor by which the cost of the approximate solution is larger than the cost of an optimal solution. Because we assume that all solutions have positive cost, these ratios are always well defined. The approximation ratio of an approximation algorithm is never less than 1, since $C/C^* \le 1$ implies $C^*/C \ge 1$. Therefore, a 1-approximation algorithm[1] produces an optimal solution, and an approximation algorithm with a large approximation ratio may return a solution that is much worse than optimal.

For many problems, we have polynomial-time approximation algorithms with small constant approximation ratios, although for other problems, the best known polynomial-time approximation algorithms have approximation ratios that grow as functions of the input size n. An example of such a problem is the set-cover problem presented in Section 35.3.

Some NP-complete problems allow polynomial-time approximation algorithms that can achieve increasingly better approximation ratios by using more and more computation time. That is, we can trade computation time for the quality of the approximation. An example is the subset-sum problem studied in Section 35.5. This situation is important enough to deserve a name of its own.

An ***approximation scheme*** for an optimization problem is an approximation algorithm that takes as input not only an instance of the problem, but also a value $\epsilon > 0$ such that for any fixed ϵ, the scheme is a $(1 + \epsilon)$-approximation algorithm. We say that an approximation scheme is a ***polynomial-time approximation scheme*** if for any fixed $\epsilon > 0$, the scheme runs in time polynomial in the size n of its input instance.

The running time of a polynomial-time approximation scheme can increase very rapidly as ϵ decreases. For example, the running time of a polynomial-time approximation scheme might be $O(n^{2/\epsilon})$. Ideally, if ϵ decreases by a constant factor, the running time to achieve the desired approximation should not increase by more than a constant factor (though not necessarily the same constant factor by which ϵ decreased).

We say that an approximation scheme is a ***fully polynomial-time approximation scheme*** if it is an approximation scheme and its running time is polynomial in both $1/\epsilon$ and the size n of the input instance. For example, the scheme might have a running time of $O((1/\epsilon)^2 n^3)$. With such a scheme, any constant-factor decrease in ϵ comes with a corresponding constant-factor increase in the running time.

---

[1] When the approximation ratio is independent of n, we use the terms "approximation ratio of ρ" and "ρ-approximation algorithm," indicating no dependence on n.

Chapter outline

The first four sections of this chapter present some examples of polynomial-time approximation algorithms for NP-complete problems, and the fifth section presents a fully polynomial-time approximation scheme. Section 35.1 begins with a study of the vertex-cover problem, an NP-complete minimization problem that has an approximation algorithm with an approximation ratio of 2. Section 35.2 presents an approximation algorithm with an approximation ratio of 2 for the case of the traveling-salesman problem in which the cost function satisfies the triangle inequality. It also shows that without the triangle inequality, for any constant $\rho \geq 1$, a ρ-approximation algorithm cannot exist unless P = NP. In Section 35.3, we show how to use a greedy method as an effective approximation algorithm for the set-covering problem, obtaining a covering whose cost is at worst a logarithmic factor larger than the optimal cost. Section 35.4 presents two more approximation algorithms. First we study the optimization version of 3-CNF satisfiability and give a simple randomized algorithm that produces a solution with an expected approximation ratio of 8/7. Then we examine a weighted variant of the vertex-cover problem and show how to use linear programming to develop a 2-approximation algorithm. Finally, Section 35.5 presents a fully polynomial-time approximation scheme for the subset-sum problem.

35.1   The vertex-cover problem

Section 34.5.2 defined the vertex-cover problem and proved it NP-complete. Recall that a ***vertex cover*** of an undirected graph $G = (V, E)$ is a subset $V' \subseteq V$ such that if (u, v) is an edge of G, then either $u \in V'$ or $v \in V'$ (or both). The size of a vertex cover is the number of vertices in it.

The ***vertex-cover problem*** is to find a vertex cover of minimum size in a given undirected graph. We call such a vertex cover an ***optimal vertex cover***. This problem is the optimization version of an NP-complete decision problem.

Even though we don't know how to find an optimal vertex cover in a graph G in polynomial time, we can efficiently find a vertex cover that is near-optimal. The following approximation algorithm takes as input an undirected graph G and returns a vertex cover whose size is guaranteed to be no more than twice the size of an optimal vertex cover.

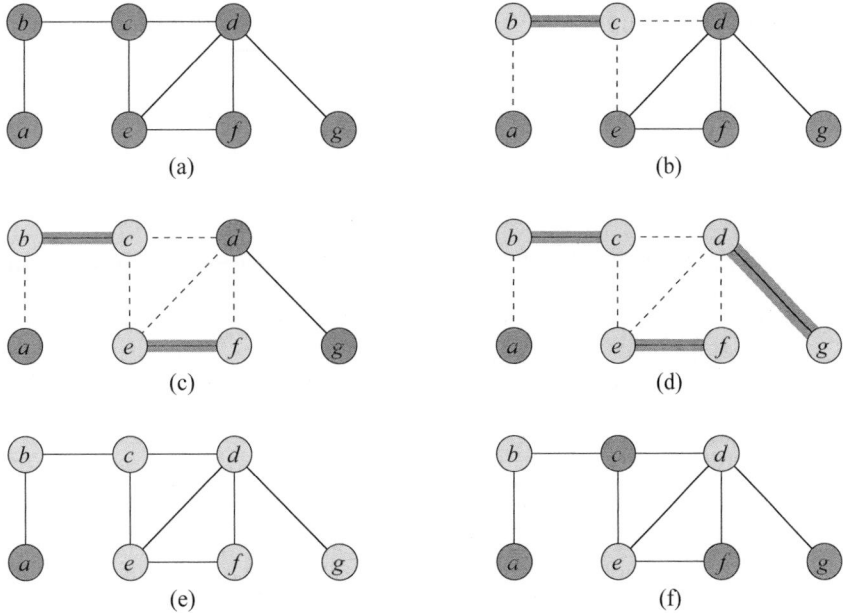

Figure 35.1   The operation of APPROX-VERTEX-COVER. **(a)** The input graph G, which has 7 vertices and 8 edges. **(b)** The edge (b, c), shown heavy, is the first edge chosen by APPROX-VERTEX-COVER. Vertices b and c, shown lightly shaded, are added to the set C containing the vertex cover being created. Edges (a, b), (c, e), and (c, d), shown dashed, are removed since they are now covered by some vertex in C. **(c)** Edge (e, f) is chosen; vertices e and f are added to C. **(d)** Edge (d, g) is chosen; vertices d and g are added to C. **(e)** The set C, which is the vertex cover produced by APPROX-VERTEX-COVER, contains the six vertices b, c, d, e, f, g. **(f)** The optimal vertex cover for this problem contains only three vertices: b, d, and e.

APPROX-VERTEX-COVER(G)

1   $C = \emptyset$
2   $E' = G.E$
3   **while** $E' \neq \emptyset$
4   let (u, v) be an arbitrary edge of E'
5       $C = C \cup \{u, v\}$
6   remove from E' edge (u, v) and every edge incident on either u or v
7   **return** C

Figure 35.1 illustrates how APPROX-VERTEX-COVER operates on an example graph. The variable C contains the vertex cover being constructed. Line 1 initializes C to the empty set. Line 2 sets E' to be a copy of the edge set $G.E$ of the graph. The loop of lines 3–6 repeatedly picks an edge (u, v) from E', adds its

endpoints u and v to C, and deletes all edges in E' that are covered by either u or v. Finally, line 7 returns the vertex cover C. The running time of this algorithm is $O(V + E)$, using adjacency lists to represent E'.

Theorem 35.1
APPROX-VERTEX-COVER is a polynomial-time 2-approximation algorithm.

Proof   We have already shown that APPROX-VERTEX-COVER runs in polynomial time.

The set C of vertices that is returned by APPROX-VERTEX-COVER is a vertex cover, since the algorithm loops until every edge in $G.E$ has been covered by some vertex in C.

To see that APPROX-VERTEX-COVER returns a vertex cover that is at most twice the size of an optimal cover, let A denote the set of edges that line 4 of APPROX-VERTEX-COVER picked. In order to cover the edges in A, any vertex cover—in particular, an optimal cover C^*—must include at least one endpoint of each edge in A. No two edges in A share an endpoint, since once an edge is picked in line 4, all other edges that are incident on its endpoints are deleted from E' in line 6. Thus, no two edges in A are covered by the same vertex from C^*, and we have the lower bound

$$|C^*| \geq |A| \tag{35.2}$$

on the size of an optimal vertex cover. Each execution of line 4 picks an edge for which neither of its endpoints is already in C, yielding an upper bound (an exact upper bound, in fact) on the size of the vertex cover returned:

$$|C| = 2|A| . \tag{35.3}$$

Combining equations (35.2) and (35.3), we obtain

$$\begin{aligned} |C| &= 2|A| \\ &\leq 2|C^*| , \end{aligned}$$

thereby proving the theorem.   ∎

Let us reflect on this proof. At first, you might wonder how we can possibly prove that the size of the vertex cover returned by APPROX-VERTEX-COVER is at most twice the size of an optimal vertex cover, when we do not even know the size of an optimal vertex cover. Instead of requiring that we know the exact size of an optimal vertex cover, we rely on a lower bound on the size. As Exercise 35.1-2 asks you to show, the set A of edges that line 4 of APPROX-VERTEX-COVER selects is actually a maximal matching in the graph G. (A ***maximal matching*** is a matching that is not a proper subset of any other matching.) The size of a maximal matching

is, as we argued in the proof of Theorem 35.1, a lower bound on the size of an optimal vertex cover. The algorithm returns a vertex cover whose size is at most twice the size of the maximal matching A. By relating the size of the solution returned to the lower bound, we obtain our approximation ratio. We will use this methodology in later sections as well.

Exercises

35.1-1
Give an example of a graph for which APPROX-VERTEX-COVER always yields a suboptimal solution.

35.1-2
Prove that the set of edges picked in line 4 of APPROX-VERTEX-COVER forms a maximal matching in the graph G.

35.1-3   ★
Professor Bündchen proposes the following heuristic to solve the vertex-cover problem. Repeatedly select a vertex of highest degree, and remove all of its incident edges. Give an example to show that the professor's heuristic does not have an approximation ratio of 2. (*Hint:* Try a bipartite graph with vertices of uniform degree on the left and vertices of varying degree on the right.)

35.1-4
Give an efficient greedy algorithm that finds an optimal vertex cover for a tree in linear time.

35.1-5
From the proof of Theorem 34.12, we know that the vertex-cover problem and the NP-complete clique problem are complementary in the sense that an optimal vertex cover is the complement of a maximum-size clique in the complement graph. Does this relationship imply that there is a polynomial-time approximation algorithm with a constant approximation ratio for the clique problem? Justify your answer.

35.2   The traveling-salesman problem

In the traveling-salesman problem introduced in Section 34.5.4, we are given a complete undirected graph $G = (V, E)$ that has a nonnegative integer cost $c(u, v)$ associated with each edge $(u, v) \in E$, and we must find a hamiltonian cycle (a tour) of G with minimum cost. As an extension of our notation, let $c(A)$ denote the total cost of the edges in the subset $A \subseteq E$:

$$c(A) = \sum_{(u,v) \in A} c(u, v) .$$

In many practical situations, the least costly way to go from a place u to a place w is to go directly, with no intermediate steps. Put another way, cutting out an intermediate stop never increases the cost. We formalize this notion by saying that the cost function c satisfies the ***triangle inequality*** if, for all vertices $u, v, w \in V$,

$$c(u, w) \leq c(u, v) + c(v, w) .$$

The triangle inequality seems as though it should naturally hold, and it is automatically satisfied in several applications. For example, if the vertices of the graph are points in the plane and the cost of traveling between two vertices is the ordinary euclidean distance between them, then the triangle inequality is satisfied. Furthermore, many cost functions other than euclidean distance satisfy the triangle inequality.

As Exercise 35.2-2 shows, the traveling-salesman problem is NP-complete even if we require that the cost function satisfy the triangle inequality. Thus, we should not expect to find a polynomial-time algorithm for solving this problem exactly. Instead, we look for good approximation algorithms.

In Section 35.2.1, we examine a 2-approximation algorithm for the traveling-salesman problem with the triangle inequality. In Section 35.2.2, we show that without the triangle inequality, a polynomial-time approximation algorithm with a constant approximation ratio does not exist unless P = NP.

35.2.1   The traveling-salesman problem with the triangle inequality

Applying the methodology of the previous section, we shall first compute a structure—a minimum spanning tree—whose weight gives a lower bound on the length of an optimal traveling-salesman tour. We shall then use the minimum spanning tree to create a tour whose cost is no more than twice that of the minimum spanning tree's weight, as long as the cost function satisfies the triangle inequality. The following algorithm implements this approach, calling the minimum-spanning-tree algorithm MST-PRIM from Section 23.2 as a subroutine. The parameter G is a complete undirected graph, and the cost function c satisfies the triangle inequality.

APPROX-TSP-TOUR(G, c)

1   select a vertex $r \in G.V$ to be a "root" vertex
2   compute a minimum spanning tree T for G from root r
         using MST-PRIM(G, c, r)
3   let H be a list of vertices, ordered according to when they are first visited
         in a preorder tree walk of T
4   **return** the hamiltonian cycle H

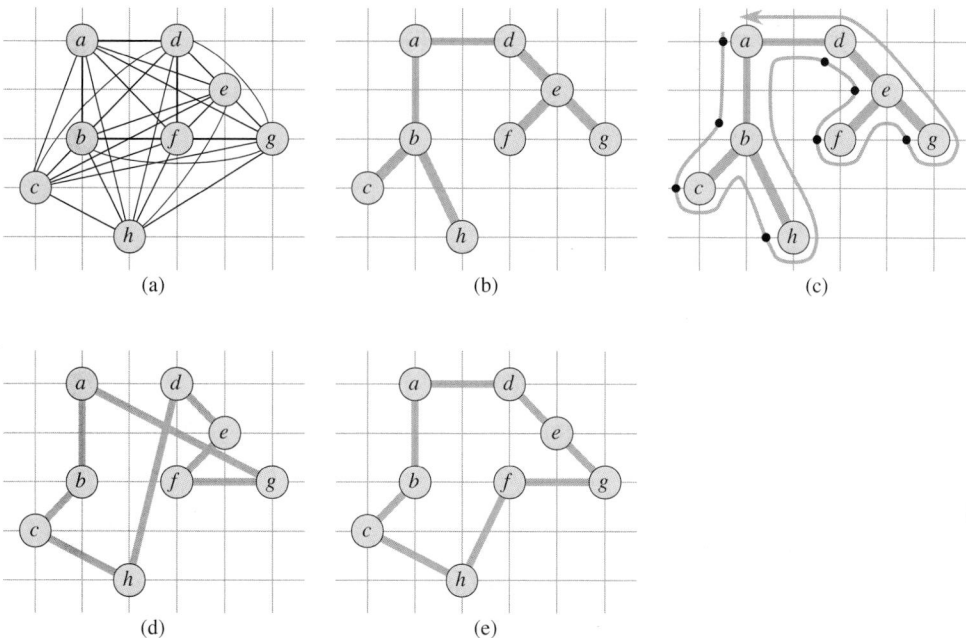

Figure 35.2   The operation of APPROX-TSP-TOUR. **(a)** A complete undirected graph. Vertices lie on intersections of integer grid lines. For example, f is one unit to the right and two units up from h. The cost function between two points is the ordinary euclidean distance. **(b)** A minimum spanning tree T of the complete graph, as computed by MST-PRIM. Vertex a is the root vertex. Only edges in the minimum spanning tree are shown. The vertices happen to be labeled in such a way that they are added to the main tree by MST-PRIM in alphabetical order. **(c)** A walk of T, starting at a. A full walk of the tree visits the vertices in the order $a, b, c, b, h, b, a, d, e, f, e, g, e, d, a$. A preorder walk of T lists a vertex just when it is first encountered, as indicated by the dot next to each vertex, yielding the ordering a, b, c, h, d, e, f, g. **(d)** A tour obtained by visiting the vertices in the order given by the preorder walk, which is the tour H returned by APPROX-TSP-TOUR. Its total cost is approximately 19.074. **(e)** An optimal tour H^* for the original complete graph. Its total cost is approximately 14.715.

Recall from Section 12.1 that a preorder tree walk recursively visits every vertex in the tree, listing a vertex when it is first encountered, before visiting any of its children.

Figure 35.2 illustrates the operation of APPROX-TSP-TOUR. Part (a) of the figure shows a complete undirected graph, and part (b) shows the minimum spanning tree T grown from root vertex a by MST-PRIM. Part (c) shows how a preorder walk of T visits the vertices, and part (d) displays the corresponding tour, which is the tour returned by APPROX-TSP-TOUR. Part (e) displays an optimal tour, which is about 23% shorter.

By Exercise 23.2-2, even with a simple implementation of MST-PRIM, the running time of APPROX-TSP-TOUR is $\Theta(V^2)$. We now show that if the cost function for an instance of the traveling-salesman problem satisfies the triangle inequality, then APPROX-TSP-TOUR returns a tour whose cost is not more than twice the cost of an optimal tour.

Theorem 35.2
APPROX-TSP-TOUR is a polynomial-time 2-approximation algorithm for the traveling-salesman problem with the triangle inequality.

Proof We have already seen that APPROX-TSP-TOUR runs in polynomial time.

Let H^* denote an optimal tour for the given set of vertices. We obtain a spanning tree by deleting any edge from a tour, and each edge cost is nonnegative. Therefore, the weight of the minimum spanning tree T computed in line 2 of APPROX-TSP-TOUR provides a lower bound on the cost of an optimal tour:

$$c(T) \leq c(H^*) . \tag{35.4}$$

A ***full walk*** of T lists the vertices when they are first visited and also whenever they are returned to after a visit to a subtree. Let us call this full walk W. The full walk of our example gives the order

$$a, b, c, b, h, b, a, d, e, f, e, g, e, d, a .$$

Since the full walk traverses every edge of T exactly twice, we have (extending our definition of the cost c in the natural manner to handle multisets of edges)

$$c(W) = 2c(T) . \tag{35.5}$$

Inequality (35.4) and equation (35.5) imply that

$$c(W) \leq 2c(H^*) , \tag{35.6}$$

and so the cost of W is within a factor of 2 of the cost of an optimal tour.

Unfortunately, the full walk W is generally not a tour, since it visits some vertices more than once. By the triangle inequality, however, we can delete a visit to any vertex from W and the cost does not increase. (If we delete a vertex v from W between visits to u and w, the resulting ordering specifies going directly from u to w.) By repeatedly applying this operation, we can remove from W all but the first visit to each vertex. In our example, this leaves the ordering

$$a, b, c, h, d, e, f, g .$$

This ordering is the same as that obtained by a preorder walk of the tree T. Let H be the cycle corresponding to this preorder walk. It is a hamiltonian cycle, since ev-

ery vertex is visited exactly once, and in fact it is the cycle computed by APPROX-TSP-TOUR. Since H is obtained by deleting vertices from the full walk W, we have

$$c(H) \leq c(W) \,. \tag{35.7}$$

Combining inequalities (35.6) and (35.7) gives $c(H) \leq 2c(H^*)$, which completes the proof. ∎

In spite of the nice approximation ratio provided by Theorem 35.2, APPROX-TSP-TOUR is usually not the best practical choice for this problem. There are other approximation algorithms that typically perform much better in practice. (See the references at the end of this chapter.)

35.2.2 The general traveling-salesman problem

If we drop the assumption that the cost function c satisfies the triangle inequality, then we cannot find good approximate tours in polynomial time unless $P = NP$.

Theorem 35.3
If $P \neq NP$, then for any constant $\rho \geq 1$, there is no polynomial-time approximation algorithm with approximation ratio ρ for the general traveling-salesman problem.

Proof The proof is by contradiction. Suppose to the contrary that for some number $\rho \geq 1$, there is a polynomial-time approximation algorithm A with approximation ratio ρ. Without loss of generality, we assume that ρ is an integer, by rounding it up if necessary. We shall then show how to use A to solve instances of the hamiltonian-cycle problem (defined in Section 34.2) in polynomial time. Since Theorem 34.13 tells us that the hamiltonian-cycle problem is NP-complete, Theorem 34.4 implies that if we can solve it in polynomial time, then $P = NP$.

Let $G = (V, E)$ be an instance of the hamiltonian-cycle problem. We wish to determine efficiently whether G contains a hamiltonian cycle by making use of the hypothesized approximation algorithm A. We turn G into an instance of the traveling-salesman problem as follows. Let $G' = (V, E')$ be the complete graph on V; that is,

$$E' = \{(u, v) : u, v \in V \text{ and } u \neq v\} \,.$$

Assign an integer cost to each edge in E' as follows:

$$c(u, v) = \begin{cases} 1 & \text{if } (u, v) \in E \,, \\ \rho |V| + 1 & \text{otherwise} \,. \end{cases}$$

We can create representations of G' and c from a representation of G in time polynomial in $|V|$ and $|E|$.

Now, consider the traveling-salesman problem (G', c). If the original graph G has a hamiltonian cycle H, then the cost function c assigns to each edge of H a cost of 1, and so (G', c) contains a tour of cost $|V|$. On the other hand, if G does not contain a hamiltonian cycle, then any tour of G' must use some edge not in E. But any tour that uses an edge not in E has a cost of at least

$$
\begin{aligned}
(\rho |V| + 1) + (|V| - 1) \;&=\; \rho |V| + |V| \\
&>\; \rho |V| \; .
\end{aligned}
$$

Because edges not in G are so costly, there is a gap of at least $\rho |V|$ between the cost of a tour that is a hamiltonian cycle in G (cost $|V|$) and the cost of any other tour (cost at least $\rho |V| + |V|$). Therefore, the cost of a tour that is not a hamiltonian cycle in G is at least a factor of $\rho + 1$ greater than the cost of a tour that is a hamiltonian cycle in G.

Now, suppose that we apply the approximation algorithm A to the traveling-salesman problem (G', c). Because A is guaranteed to return a tour of cost no more than ρ times the cost of an optimal tour, if G contains a hamiltonian cycle, then A must return it. If G has no hamiltonian cycle, then A returns a tour of cost more than $\rho |V|$. Therefore, we can use A to solve the hamiltonian-cycle problem in polynomial time. ∎

The proof of Theorem 35.3 serves as an example of a general technique for proving that we cannot approximate a problem very well. Suppose that given an NP-hard problem X, we can produce in polynomial time a minimization problem Y such that "yes" instances of X correspond to instances of Y with value at most k (for some k), but that "no" instances of X correspond to instances of Y with value greater than ρk. Then, we have shown that, unless P = NP, there is no polynomial-time ρ-approximation algorithm for problem Y.

Exercises

35.2-1
Suppose that a complete undirected graph $G = (V, E)$ with at least 3 vertices has a cost function c that satisfies the triangle inequality. Prove that $c(u, v) \geq 0$ for all $u, v \in V$.

35.2-2
Show how in polynomial time we can transform one instance of the traveling-salesman problem into another instance whose cost function satisfies the triangle inequality. The two instances must have the same set of optimal tours. Explain why such a polynomial-time transformation does not contradict Theorem 35.3, assuming that P $\neq$ NP.

35.2-3

Consider the following ***closest-point heuristic*** for building an approximate traveling-salesman tour whose cost function satisfies the triangle inequality. Begin with a trivial cycle consisting of a single arbitrarily chosen vertex. At each step, identify the vertex u that is not on the cycle but whose distance to any vertex on the cycle is minimum. Suppose that the vertex on the cycle that is nearest u is vertex v. Extend the cycle to include u by inserting u just after v. Repeat until all vertices are on the cycle. Prove that this heuristic returns a tour whose total cost is not more than twice the cost of an optimal tour.

35.2-4

In the ***bottleneck traveling-salesman problem***, we wish to find the hamiltonian cycle that minimizes the cost of the most costly edge in the cycle. Assuming that the cost function satisfies the triangle inequality, show that there exists a polynomial-time approximation algorithm with approximation ratio 3 for this problem. (*Hint:* Show recursively that we can visit all the nodes in a bottleneck spanning tree, as discussed in Problem 23-3, exactly once by taking a full walk of the tree and skipping nodes, but without skipping more than two consecutive intermediate nodes. Show that the costliest edge in a bottleneck spanning tree has a cost that is at most the cost of the costliest edge in a bottleneck hamiltonian cycle.)

35.2-5

Suppose that the vertices for an instance of the traveling-salesman problem are points in the plane and that the cost $c(u, v)$ is the euclidean distance between points u and v. Show that an optimal tour never crosses itself.

35.3   The set-covering problem

The set-covering problem is an optimization problem that models many problems that require resources to be allocated. Its corresponding decision problem generalizes the NP-complete vertex-cover problem and is therefore also NP-hard. The approximation algorithm developed to handle the vertex-cover problem doesn't apply here, however, and so we need to try other approaches. We shall examine a simple greedy heuristic with a logarithmic approximation ratio. That is, as the size of the instance gets larger, the size of the approximate solution may grow, relative to the size of an optimal solution. Because the logarithm function grows rather slowly, however, this approximation algorithm may nonetheless give useful results.

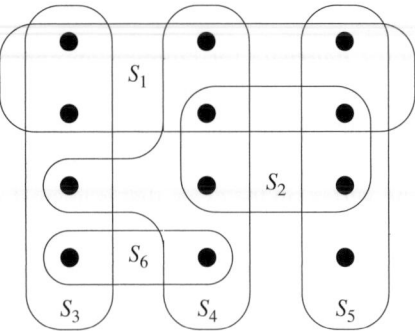

Figure 35.3 An instance $(X, \mathcal{F})$ of the set-covering problem, where X consists of the 12 black points and $\mathcal{F} = \{S_1, S_2, S_3, S_4, S_5, S_6\}$. A minimum-size set cover is $\mathcal{C} = \{S_3, S_4, S_5\}$, with size 3. The greedy algorithm produces a cover of size 4 by selecting either the sets S_1, S_4, S_5, and S_3 or the sets S_1, S_4, S_5, and S_6, in order.

An instance $(X, \mathcal{F})$ of the ***set-covering problem*** consists of a finite set X and a family $\mathcal{F}$ of subsets of X, such that every element of X belongs to at least one subset in $\mathcal{F}$:

$$X = \bigcup_{S \in \mathcal{F}} S \,.$$

We say that a subset $S \in \mathcal{F}$ ***covers*** its elements. The problem is to find a minimum-size subset $\mathcal{C} \subseteq \mathcal{F}$ whose members cover all of X:

$$X = \bigcup_{S \in \mathcal{C}} S \,. \tag{35.8}$$

We say that any $\mathcal{C}$ satisfying equation (35.8) ***covers*** X. Figure 35.3 illustrates the set-covering problem. The size of $\mathcal{C}$ is the number of sets it contains, rather than the number of individual elements in these sets, since every subset $\mathcal{C}$ that covers X must contain all $|X|$ individual elements. In Figure 35.3, the minimum set cover has size 3.

The set-covering problem abstracts many commonly arising combinatorial problems. As a simple example, suppose that X represents a set of skills that are needed to solve a problem and that we have a given set of people available to work on the problem. We wish to form a committee, containing as few people as possible, such that for every requisite skill in X, at least one member of the committee has that skill. In the decision version of the set-covering problem, we ask whether a covering exists with size at most k, where k is an additional parameter specified in the problem instance. The decision version of the problem is NP-complete, as Exercise 35.3-2 asks you to show.

A greedy approximation algorithm

The greedy method works by picking, at each stage, the set S that covers the greatest number of remaining elements that are uncovered.

GREEDY-SET-COVER$(X, \mathcal{F})$

```
1   U = X
2   𝒞 = ∅
3   while U ≠ ∅
4       select an S ∈ 𝓕 that maximizes |S ∩ U|
5       U = U − S
6       𝒞 = 𝒞 ∪ {S}
7   return 𝒞
```

In the example of Figure 35.3, GREEDY-SET-COVER adds to $\mathcal{C}$, in order, the sets S_1, S_4, and S_5, followed by either S_3 or S_6.

The algorithm works as follows. The set U contains, at each stage, the set of remaining uncovered elements. The set $\mathcal{C}$ contains the cover being constructed. Line 4 is the greedy decision-making step, choosing a subset S that covers as many uncovered elements as possible (breaking ties arbitrarily). After S is selected, line 5 removes its elements from U, and line 6 places S into $\mathcal{C}$. When the algorithm terminates, the set $\mathcal{C}$ contains a subfamily of $\mathcal{F}$ that covers X.

We can easily implement GREEDY-SET-COVER to run in time polynomial in $|X|$ and $|\mathcal{F}|$. Since the number of iterations of the loop on lines 3–6 is bounded from above by $\min(|X|, |\mathcal{F}|)$, and we can implement the loop body to run in time $O(|X| |\mathcal{F}|)$, a simple implementation runs in time $O(|X| |\mathcal{F}| \min(|X|, |\mathcal{F}|))$. Exercise 35.3-3 asks for a linear-time algorithm.

Analysis

We now show that the greedy algorithm returns a set cover that is not too much larger than an optimal set cover. For convenience, in this chapter we denote the dth harmonic number $H_d = \sum_{i=1}^{d} 1/i$ (see Section A.1) by $H(d)$. As a boundary condition, we define $H(0) = 0$.

Theorem 35.4
GREEDY-SET-COVER is a polynomial-time $\rho(n)$-approximation algorithm, where

$$\rho(n) = H(\max\{|S| : S \in \mathcal{F}\}) .$$

Proof   We have already shown that GREEDY-SET-COVER runs in polynomial time.

To show that GREEDY-SET-COVER is a $\rho(n)$-approximation algorithm, we assign a cost of 1 to each set selected by the algorithm, distribute this cost over the elements covered for the first time, and then use these costs to derive the desired relationship between the size of an optimal set cover $\mathcal{C}^*$ and the size of the set cover $\mathcal{C}$ returned by the algorithm. Let S_i denote the ith subset selected by GREEDY-SET-COVER; the algorithm incurs a cost of 1 when it adds S_i to $\mathcal{C}$. We spread this cost of selecting S_i evenly among the elements covered for the first time by S_i. Let c_x denote the cost allocated to element x, for each $x \in X$. Each element is assigned a cost only once, when it is covered for the first time. If x is covered for the first time by S_i, then

$$c_x = \frac{1}{|S_i - (S_1 \cup S_2 \cup \cdots \cup S_{i-1})|} \ .$$

Each step of the algorithm assigns 1 unit of cost, and so

$$|\mathcal{C}| = \sum_{x \in X} c_x \ . \tag{35.9}$$

Each element $x \in X$ is in at least one set in the optimal cover $\mathcal{C}^*$, and so we have

$$\sum_{S \in \mathcal{C}^*} \sum_{x \in S} c_x \geq \sum_{x \in X} c_x \ . \tag{35.10}$$

Combining equation (35.9) and inequality (35.10), we have that

$$|\mathcal{C}| \leq \sum_{S \in \mathcal{C}^*} \sum_{x \in S} c_x \ . \tag{35.11}$$

The remainder of the proof rests on the following key inequality, which we shall prove shortly. For any set S belonging to the family $\mathcal{F}$,

$$\sum_{x \in S} c_x \leq H(|S|) \ . \tag{35.12}$$

From inequalities (35.11) and (35.12), it follows that

$$\begin{aligned} |\mathcal{C}| &\leq \sum_{S \in \mathcal{C}^*} H(|S|) \\ &\leq |\mathcal{C}^*| \cdot H(\max\{|S| : S \in \mathcal{F}\}) \ , \end{aligned}$$

thus proving the theorem.

All that remains is to prove inequality (35.12). Consider any set $S \in \mathcal{F}$ and any $i = 1, 2, \ldots, |\mathcal{C}|$, and let

$$u_i = |S - (S_1 \cup S_2 \cup \cdots \cup S_i)|$$

be the number of elements in S that remain uncovered after the algorithm has selected sets $S_1, S_2, \ldots, S_i$. We define $u_0 = |S|$ to be the number of elements

of S, which are all initially uncovered. Let k be the least index such that $u_k = 0$, so that every element in S is covered by at least one of the sets $S_1, S_2, \ldots, S_k$ and some element in S is uncovered by $S_1 \cup S_2 \cup \cdots \cup S_{k-1}$. Then, $u_{i-1} \geq u_i$, and $u_{i-1} - u_i$ elements of S are covered for the first time by S_i, for $i = 1, 2, \ldots, k$. Thus,

$$\sum_{x \in S} c_x = \sum_{i=1}^{k} (u_{i-1} - u_i) \cdot \frac{1}{|S_i - (S_1 \cup S_2 \cup \cdots \cup S_{i-1})|} \, .$$

Observe that

$$|S_i - (S_1 \cup S_2 \cup \cdots \cup S_{i-1})| \geq |S - (S_1 \cup S_2 \cup \cdots \cup S_{i-1})|$$
$$= u_{i-1} \, ,$$

because the greedy choice of S_i guarantees that S cannot cover more new elements than S_i does (otherwise, the algorithm would have chosen S instead of S_i). Consequently, we obtain

$$\sum_{x \in S} c_x \leq \sum_{i=1}^{k} (u_{i-1} - u_i) \cdot \frac{1}{u_{i-1}} \, .$$

We now bound this quantity as follows:

$$\sum_{x \in S} c_x \leq \sum_{i=1}^{k} (u_{i-1} - u_i) \cdot \frac{1}{u_{i-1}}$$

$$= \sum_{i=1}^{k} \sum_{j=u_i+1}^{u_{i-1}} \frac{1}{u_{i-1}}$$

$$\leq \sum_{i=1}^{k} \sum_{j=u_i+1}^{u_{i-1}} \frac{1}{j} \qquad \text{(because } j \leq u_{i-1})$$

$$= \sum_{i=1}^{k} \left(\sum_{j=1}^{u_{i-1}} \frac{1}{j} - \sum_{j=1}^{u_i} \frac{1}{j} \right)$$

$$= \sum_{i=1}^{k} (H(u_{i-1}) - H(u_i))$$

$$= H(u_0) - H(u_k) \qquad \text{(because the sum telescopes)}$$

$$= H(u_0) - H(0)$$

$$= H(u_0) \qquad \text{(because } H(0) = 0)$$

$$= H(|S|) \, ,$$

which completes the proof of inequality (35.12).   ∎

Corollary 35.5
GREEDY-SET-COVER is a polynomial-time $(\ln |X| + 1)$-approximation algorithm.

Proof   Use inequality (A.14) and Theorem 35.4.   ∎

In some applications, $\max \{|S| : S \in \mathcal{F}\}$ is a small constant, and so the solution returned by GREEDY-SET-COVER is at most a small constant times larger than optimal. One such application occurs when this heuristic finds an approximate vertex cover for a graph whose vertices have degree at most 3. In this case, the solution found by GREEDY-SET-COVER is not more than $H(3) = 11/6$ times as large as an optimal solution, a performance guarantee that is slightly better than that of APPROX-VERTEX-COVER.

Exercises

35.3-1
Consider each of the following words as a set of letters: {`arid`, `dash`, `drain`, `heard`, `lost`, `nose`, `shun`, `slate`, `snare`, `thread`}. Show which set cover GREEDY-SET-COVER produces when we break ties in favor of the word that appears first in the dictionary.

35.3-2
Show that the decision version of the set-covering problem is NP-complete by reducing it from the vertex-cover problem.

35.3-3
Show how to implement GREEDY-SET-COVER in such a way that it runs in time
$$O\left(\sum_{S \in \mathcal{F}} |S|\right).$$

35.3-4
Show that the following weaker form of Theorem 35.4 is trivially true:
$$|\mathcal{C}| \leq |\mathcal{C}^*| \max \{|S| : S \in \mathcal{F}\} .$$

35.3-5
GREEDY-SET-COVER can return a number of different solutions, depending on how we break ties in line 4. Give a procedure BAD-SET-COVER-INSTANCE(n) that returns an n-element instance of the set-covering problem for which, depending on how we break ties in line 4, GREEDY-SET-COVER can return a number of different solutions that is exponential in n.

35.4 Randomization and linear programming

In this section, we study two useful techniques for designing approximation algorithms: randomization and linear programming. We shall give a simple randomized algorithm for an optimization version of 3-CNF satisfiability, and then we shall use linear programming to help design an approximation algorithm for a weighted version of the vertex-cover problem. This section only scratches the surface of these two powerful techniques. The chapter notes give references for further study of these areas.

A randomized approximation algorithm for MAX-3-CNF satisfiability

Just as some randomized algorithms compute exact solutions, some randomized algorithms compute approximate solutions. We say that a randomized algorithm for a problem has an ***approximation ratio*** of $\rho(n)$ if, for any input of size n, the *expected* cost C of the solution produced by the randomized algorithm is within a factor of $\rho(n)$ of the cost C^* of an optimal solution:

$$\max\left(\frac{C}{C^*}, \frac{C^*}{C}\right) \le \rho(n) . \tag{35.13}$$

We call a randomized algorithm that achieves an approximation ratio of $\rho(n)$ a ***randomized $\rho(n)$-approximation algorithm.*** In other words, a randomized approximation algorithm is like a deterministic approximation algorithm, except that the approximation ratio is for an expected cost.

A particular instance of 3-CNF satisfiability, as defined in Section 34.4, may or may not be satisfiable. In order to be satisfiable, there must exist an assignment of the variables so that every clause evaluates to 1. If an instance is not satisfiable, we may want to compute how "close" to satisfiable it is, that is, we may wish to find an assignment of the variables that satisfies as many clauses as possible. We call the resulting maximization problem ***MAX-3-CNF satisfiability***. The input to MAX-3-CNF satisfiability is the same as for 3-CNF satisfiability, and the goal is to return an assignment of the variables that maximizes the number of clauses evaluating to 1. We now show that randomly setting each variable to 1 with probability $1/2$ and to 0 with probability $1/2$ yields a randomized 8/7-approximation algorithm. According to the definition of 3-CNF satisfiability from Section 34.4, we require each clause to consist of exactly three distinct literals. We further assume that no clause contains both a variable and its negation. (Exercise 35.4-1 asks you to remove this last assumption.)

Theorem 35.6
Given an instance of MAX-3-CNF satisfiability with n variables $x_1, x_2, \ldots, x_n$ and m clauses, the randomized algorithm that independently sets each variable to 1 with probability $1/2$ and to 0 with probability $1/2$ is a randomized 8/7-approximation algorithm.

Proof Suppose that we have independently set each variable to 1 with probability $1/2$ and to 0 with probability $1/2$. For $i = 1, 2, \ldots, m$, we define the indicator random variable

$$Y_i = I\{\text{clause } i \text{ is satisfied}\} \, ,$$

so that $Y_i = 1$ as long as we have set at least one of the literals in the ith clause to 1. Since no literal appears more than once in the same clause, and since we have assumed that no variable and its negation appear in the same clause, the settings of the three literals in each clause are independent. A clause is not satisfied only if all three of its literals are set to 0, and so $\Pr\{\text{clause } i \text{ is not satisfied}\} = (1/2)^3 = 1/8$. Thus, we have $\Pr\{\text{clause } i \text{ is satisfied}\} = 1 - 1/8 = 7/8$, and by Lemma 5.1, we have $\mathrm{E}[Y_i] = 7/8$. Let Y be the number of satisfied clauses overall, so that $Y = Y_1 + Y_2 + \cdots + Y_m$. Then, we have

$$
\begin{aligned}
\mathrm{E}[Y] &= \mathrm{E}\left[\sum_{i=1}^{m} Y_i\right] \\
&= \sum_{i=1}^{m} \mathrm{E}[Y_i] \qquad \text{(by linearity of expectation)} \\
&= \sum_{i=1}^{m} 7/8 \\
&= 7m/8 \, .
\end{aligned}
$$

Clearly, m is an upper bound on the number of satisfied clauses, and hence the approximation ratio is at most $m/(7m/8) = 8/7$.   ∎

Approximating weighted vertex cover using linear programming

In the ***minimum-weight vertex-cover problem***, we are given an undirected graph $G = (V, E)$ in which each vertex $v \in V$ has an associated positive weight $w(v)$. For any vertex cover $V' \subseteq V$, we define the weight of the vertex cover $w(V') = \sum_{v \in V'} w(v)$. The goal is to find a vertex cover of minimum weight.

We cannot apply the algorithm used for unweighted vertex cover, nor can we use a random solution; both methods may return solutions that are far from optimal. We shall, however, compute a lower bound on the weight of the minimum-weight

vertex cover, by using a linear program. We shall then "round" this solution and use it to obtain a vertex cover.

Suppose that we associate a variable $x(v)$ with each vertex $v \in V$, and let us require that $x(v)$ equals either 0 or 1 for each $v \in V$. We put v into the vertex cover if and only if $x(v) = 1$. Then, we can write the constraint that for any edge (u, v), at least one of u and v must be in the vertex cover as $x(u) + x(v) \geq 1$. This view gives rise to the following **0-1 integer program** for finding a minimum-weight vertex cover:

$$\text{minimize} \quad \sum_{v \in V} w(v) \, x(v) \tag{35.14}$$

subject to

$$
\begin{align}
x(u) + x(v) &\geq 1 && \text{for each } (u, v) \in E \tag{35.15} \\
x(v) &\in \{0, 1\} && \text{for each } v \in V . \tag{35.16}
\end{align}
$$

In the special case in which all the weights $w(v)$ are equal to 1, this formulation is the optimization version of the NP-hard vertex-cover problem. Suppose, however, that we remove the constraint that $x(v) \in \{0, 1\}$ and replace it by $0 \leq x(v) \leq 1$. We then obtain the following linear program, which is known as the **linear-programming relaxation**:

$$\text{minimize} \quad \sum_{v \in V} w(v) \, x(v) \tag{35.17}$$

subject to

$$
\begin{align}
x(u) + x(v) &\geq 1 && \text{for each } (u, v) \in E \tag{35.18} \\
x(v) &\leq 1 && \text{for each } v \in V \tag{35.19} \\
x(v) &\geq 0 && \text{for each } v \in V . \tag{35.20}
\end{align}
$$

Any feasible solution to the 0-1 integer program in lines (35.14)–(35.16) is also a feasible solution to the linear program in lines (35.17)–(35.20). Therefore, the value of an optimal solution to the linear program gives a lower bound on the value of an optimal solution to the 0-1 integer program, and hence a lower bound on the optimal weight in the minimum-weight vertex-cover problem.

The following procedure uses the solution to the linear-programming relaxation to construct an approximate solution to the minimum-weight vertex-cover problem:

APPROX-MIN-WEIGHT-VC(G, w)

1   $C = \emptyset$
2   compute $\bar{x}$, an optimal solution to the linear program in lines (35.17)–(35.20)
3   **for** each $v \in V$
4   **if** $\bar{x}(v) \geq 1/2$
5           $C = C \cup \{v\}$
6   **return** C

The APPROX-MIN-WEIGHT-VC procedure works as follows. Line 1 initial-izes the vertex cover to be empty. Line 2 formulates the linear program in lines (35.17)–(35.20) and then solves this linear program. An optimal solution gives each vertex v an associated value $\bar{x}(v)$, where $0 \leq \bar{x}(v) \leq 1$. We use this value to guide the choice of which vertices to add to the vertex cover C in lines 3–5. If $\bar{x}(v) \geq 1/2$, we add v to C; otherwise we do not. In effect, we are "rounding" each fractional variable in the solution to the linear program to 0 or 1 in order to obtain a solution to the 0-1 integer program in lines (35.14)–(35.16). Finally, line 6 returns the vertex cover C.

Theorem 35.7
Algorithm APPROX-MIN-WEIGHT-VC is a polynomial-time 2-approximation al-gorithm for the minimum-weight vertex-cover problem.

Proof   Because there is a polynomial-time algorithm to solve the linear program in line 2, and because the **for** loop of lines 3–5 runs in polynomial time, APPROX-MIN-WEIGHT-VC is a polynomial-time algorithm.

Now we show that APPROX-MIN-WEIGHT-VC is a 2-approximation algo-rithm. Let C^* be an optimal solution to the minimum-weight vertex-cover prob-lem, and let z^* be the value of an optimal solution to the linear program in lines (35.17)–(35.20). Since an optimal vertex cover is a feasible solution to the linear program, z^* must be a lower bound on $w(C^*)$, that is,

$$z^* \leq w(C^*) . \tag{35.21}$$

Next, we claim that by rounding the fractional values of the variables $\bar{x}(v)$, we produce a set C that is a vertex cover and satisfies $w(C) \leq 2z^*$. To see that C is a vertex cover, consider any edge $(u, v) \in E$. By constraint (35.18), we know that $x(u) + x(v) \geq 1$, which implies that at least one of $\bar{x}(u)$ and $\bar{x}(v)$ is at least $1/2$. Therefore, at least one of u and v is included in the vertex cover, and so every edge is covered.

Now, we consider the weight of the cover. We have

$$
\begin{aligned}
z^* &= \sum_{v \in V} w(v)\, \bar{x}(v) \\
&\geq \sum_{v \in V : \bar{x}(v) \geq 1/2} w(v)\, \bar{x}(v) \\
&\geq \sum_{v \in V : \bar{x}(v) \geq 1/2} w(v) \cdot \frac{1}{2} \\
&= \sum_{v \in C} w(v) \cdot \frac{1}{2} \\
&= \frac{1}{2} \sum_{v \in C} w(v) \\
&= \frac{1}{2} w(C) \,.
\end{aligned}
\tag{35.22}
$$

Combining inequalities (35.21) and (35.22) gives

$$
w(C) \leq 2z^* \leq 2w(C^*) \,,
$$

and hence APPROX-MIN-WEIGHT-VC is a 2-approximation algorithm.   ∎

Exercises

35.4-1
Show that even if we allow a clause to contain both a variable and its negation, randomly setting each variable to 1 with probability $1/2$ and to 0 with probability $1/2$ still yields a randomized 8/7-approximation algorithm.

35.4-2
The *MAX-CNF satisfiability problem* is like the MAX-3-CNF satisfiability problem, except that it does not restrict each clause to have exactly 3 literals. Give a randomized 2-approximation algorithm for the MAX-CNF satisfiability problem.

35.4-3
In the MAX-CUT problem, we are given an unweighted undirected graph $G = (V, E)$. We define a cut $(S, V - S)$ as in Chapter 23 and the *weight* of a cut as the number of edges crossing the cut. The goal is to find a cut of maximum weight. Suppose that for each vertex v, we randomly and independently place v in S with probability $1/2$ and in $V - S$ with probability $1/2$. Show that this algorithm is a randomized 2-approximation algorithm.

35.4-4

Show that the constraints in line (35.19) are redundant in the sense that if we remove them from the linear program in lines (35.17)–(35.20), any optimal solution to the resulting linear program must satisfy $x(v) \leq 1$ for each $v \in V$.

35.5   The subset-sum problem

Recall from Section 34.5.5 that an instance of the subset-sum problem is a pair (S, t), where S is a set $\{x_1, x_2, \ldots, x_n\}$ of positive integers and t is a positive integer. This decision problem asks whether there exists a subset of S that adds up exactly to the target value t. As we saw in Section 34.5.5, this problem is NP-complete.

The optimization problem associated with this decision problem arises in practical applications. In the optimization problem, we wish to find a subset of $\{x_1, x_2, \ldots, x_n\}$ whose sum is as large as possible but not larger than t. For example, we may have a truck that can carry no more than t pounds, and n different boxes to ship, the ith of which weighs x_i pounds. We wish to fill the truck with as heavy a load as possible without exceeding the given weight limit.

In this section, we present an exponential-time algorithm that computes the optimal value for this optimization problem, and then we show how to modify the algorithm so that it becomes a fully polynomial-time approximation scheme. (Recall that a fully polynomial-time approximation scheme has a running time that is polynomial in $1/\epsilon$ as well as in the size of the input.)

An exponential-time exact algorithm

Suppose that we computed, for each subset S' of S, the sum of the elements in S', and then we selected, among the subsets whose sum does not exceed t, the one whose sum was closest to t. Clearly this algorithm would return the optimal solution, but it could take exponential time. To implement this algorithm, we could use an iterative procedure that, in iteration i, computes the sums of all subsets of $\{x_1, x_2, \ldots, x_i\}$, using as a starting point the sums of all subsets of $\{x_1, x_2, \ldots, x_{i-1}\}$. In doing so, we would realize that once a particular subset S' had a sum exceeding t, there would be no reason to maintain it, since no superset of S' could be the optimal solution. We now give an implementation of this strategy.

The procedure EXACT-SUBSET-SUM takes an input set $S = \{x_1, x_2, \ldots, x_n\}$ and a target value t; we'll see its pseudocode in a moment. This procedure it-

eratively computes L_i, the list of sums of all subsets of $\{x_1, \ldots, x_i\}$ that do not exceed t, and then it returns the maximum value in L_n.

If L is a list of positive integers and x is another positive integer, then we let $L + x$ denote the list of integers derived from L by increasing each element of L by x. For example, if $L = \langle 1, 2, 3, 5, 9 \rangle$, then $L + 2 = \langle 3, 4, 5, 7, 11 \rangle$. We also use this notation for sets, so that

$$S + x = \{s + x : s \in S\} \ .$$

We also use an auxiliary procedure MERGE-LISTS(L, L'), which returns the sorted list that is the merge of its two sorted input lists L and L' with duplicate values removed. Like the MERGE procedure we used in merge sort (Section 2.3.1), MERGE-LISTS runs in time $O(|L| + |L'|)$. We omit the pseudocode for MERGE-LISTS.

EXACT-SUBSET-SUM(S, t)

```
1  n = |S|
2  L_0 = ⟨0⟩
3  for i = 1 to n
4      L_i = MERGE-LISTS(L_{i-1}, L_{i-1} + x_i)
5      remove from L_i every element that is greater than t
6  return the largest element in L_n
```

To see how EXACT-SUBSET-SUM works, let P_i denote the set of all values obtained by selecting a (possibly empty) subset of $\{x_1, x_2, \ldots, x_i\}$ and summing its members. For example, if $S = \{1, 4, 5\}$, then

$$P_1 = \{0, 1\} \ ,$$
$$P_2 = \{0, 1, 4, 5\} \ ,$$
$$P_3 = \{0, 1, 4, 5, 6, 9, 10\} \ .$$

Given the identity

$$P_i = P_{i-1} \cup (P_{i-1} + x_i) \ , \tag{35.23}$$

we can prove by induction on i (see Exercise 35.5-1) that the list L_i is a sorted list containing every element of P_i whose value is not more than t. Since the length of L_i can be as much as 2^i, EXACT-SUBSET-SUM is an exponential-time algorithm in general, although it is a polynomial-time algorithm in the special cases in which t is polynomial in $|S|$ or all the numbers in S are bounded by a polynomial in $|S|$.

A fully polynomial-time approximation scheme

We can derive a fully polynomial-time approximation scheme for the subset-sum problem by "trimming" each list L_i after it is created. The idea behind trimming is

that if two values in L are close to each other, then since we want just an approximate solution, we do not need to maintain both of them explicitly. More precisely, we use a trimming parameter δ such that $0 < \delta < 1$. When we **trim** a list L by δ, we remove as many elements from L as possible, in such a way that if L' is the result of trimming L, then for every element y that was removed from L, there is an element z still in L' that approximates y, that is,

$$\frac{y}{1+\delta} \le z \le y . \tag{35.24}$$

We can think of such a z as "representing" y in the new list L'. Each removed element y is represented by a remaining element z satisfying inequality (35.24). For example, if $\delta = 0.1$ and

$$L = \langle 10, 11, 12, 15, 20, 21, 22, 23, 24, 29 \rangle ,$$

then we can trim L to obtain

$$L' = \langle 10, 12, 15, 20, 23, 29 \rangle ,$$

where the deleted value 11 is represented by 10, the deleted values 21 and 22 are represented by 20, and the deleted value 24 is represented by 23. Because every element of the trimmed version of the list is also an element of the original version of the list, trimming can dramatically decrease the number of elements kept while keeping a close (and slightly smaller) representative value in the list for each deleted element.

The following procedure trims list $L = \langle y_1, y_2, \ldots, y_m \rangle$ in time $\Theta(m)$, given L and δ, and assuming that L is sorted into monotonically increasing order. The output of the procedure is a trimmed, sorted list.

TRIM(L, δ)

```
1   let m be the length of L
2   L' = ⟨y₁⟩
3   last = y₁
4   for i = 2 to m
5       if yᵢ > last · (1 + δ)        // yᵢ ≥ last because L is sorted
6           append yᵢ onto the end of L'
7           last = yᵢ
8   return L'
```

The procedure scans the elements of L in monotonically increasing order. A number is appended onto the returned list L' only if it is the first element of L or if it cannot be represented by the most recent number placed into L'.

Given the procedure TRIM, we can construct our approximation scheme as follows. This procedure takes as input a set $S = \{x_1, x_2, \ldots, x_n\}$ of n integers (in arbitrary order), a target integer t, and an "approximation parameter" ϵ, where

$$0 < \epsilon < 1 . \tag{35.25}$$

It returns a value z whose value is within a $1 + \epsilon$ factor of the optimal solution.

APPROX-SUBSET-SUM(S, t, ϵ)

```
1   n = |S|
2   L₀ = ⟨0⟩
3   for i = 1 to n
4       Lᵢ = MERGE-LISTS(Lᵢ₋₁, Lᵢ₋₁ + xᵢ)
5       Lᵢ = TRIM(Lᵢ, ε/2n)
6       remove from Lᵢ every element that is greater than t
7   let z* be the largest value in Lₙ
8   return z*
```

Line 2 initializes the list L_0 to be the list containing just the element 0. The **for** loop in lines 3–6 computes L_i as a sorted list containing a suitably trimmed version of the set P_i, with all elements larger than t removed. Since we create L_i from L_{i-1}, we must ensure that the repeated trimming doesn't introduce too much compounded inaccuracy. In a moment, we shall see that APPROX-SUBSET-SUM returns a correct approximation if one exists.

As an example, suppose we have the instance

$$S = \langle 104, 102, 201, 101 \rangle$$

with $t = 308$ and $\epsilon = 0.40$. The trimming parameter δ is $\epsilon/8 = 0.05$. APPROX-SUBSET-SUM computes the following values on the indicated lines:

line 2: $L_0 = \langle 0 \rangle$,

line 4: $L_1 = \langle 0, 104 \rangle$,
line 5: $L_1 = \langle 0, 104 \rangle$,
line 6: $L_1 = \langle 0, 104 \rangle$,

line 4: $L_2 = \langle 0, 102, 104, 206 \rangle$,
line 5: $L_2 = \langle 0, 102, 206 \rangle$,
line 6: $L_2 = \langle 0, 102, 206 \rangle$,

line 4: $L_3 = \langle 0, 102, 201, 206, 303, 407 \rangle$,
line 5: $L_3 = \langle 0, 102, 201, 303, 407 \rangle$,
line 6: $L_3 = \langle 0, 102, 201, 303 \rangle$,

line 4: $L_4 = \langle 0, 101, 102, 201, 203, 302, 303, 404 \rangle$,
line 5: $L_4 = \langle 0, 101, 201, 302, 404 \rangle$,
line 6: $L_4 = \langle 0, 101, 201, 302 \rangle$.

The algorithm returns $z^* = 302$ as its answer, which is well within $\epsilon = 40\%$ of the optimal answer $307 = 104 + 102 + 101$; in fact, it is within 2%.

Theorem 35.8
APPROX-SUBSET-SUM is a fully polynomial-time approximation scheme for the subset-sum problem.

Proof The operations of trimming L_i in line 5 and removing from L_i every element that is greater than t maintain the property that every element of L_i is also a member of P_i. Therefore, the value z^* returned in line 8 is indeed the sum of some subset of S. Let $y^* \in P_n$ denote an optimal solution to the subset-sum problem. Then, from line 6, we know that $z^* \leq y^*$. By inequality (35.1), we need to show that $y^*/z^* \leq 1 + \epsilon$. We must also show that the running time of this algorithm is polynomial in both $1/\epsilon$ and the size of the input.

As Exercise 35.5-2 asks you to show, for every element y in P_i that is at most t, there exists an element $z \in L_i$ such that

$$\frac{y}{(1 + \epsilon/2n)^i} \leq z \leq y . \tag{35.26}$$

Inequality (35.26) must hold for $y^* \in P_n$, and therefore there exists an element $z \in L_n$ such that

$$\frac{y^*}{(1 + \epsilon/2n)^n} \leq z \leq y^* ,$$

and thus

$$\frac{y^*}{z} \leq \left(1 + \frac{\epsilon}{2n}\right)^n . \tag{35.27}$$

Since there exists an element $z \in L_n$ fulfilling inequality (35.27), the inequality must hold for z^*, which is the largest value in L_n; that is,

$$\frac{y^*}{z^*} \leq \left(1 + \frac{\epsilon}{2n}\right)^n . \tag{35.28}$$

Now, we show that $y^*/z^* \leq 1 + \epsilon$. We do so by showing that $(1 + \epsilon/2n)^n \leq 1 + \epsilon$. By equation (3.14), we have $\lim_{n \to \infty} (1 + \epsilon/2n)^n = e^{\epsilon/2}$. Exercise 35.5-3 asks you to show that

$$\frac{d}{dn} \left(1 + \frac{\epsilon}{2n}\right)^n > 0 . \tag{35.29}$$

Therefore, the function $(1 + \epsilon/2n)^n$ increases with n as it approaches its limit of $e^{\epsilon/2}$, and we have

$$\left(1 + \frac{\epsilon}{2n}\right)^n \;\le\; e^{\epsilon/2}$$

$$\le\; 1 + \epsilon/2 + (\epsilon/2)^2 \quad \text{(by inequality (3.13))}$$

$$\le\; 1 + \epsilon \qquad\qquad\quad \text{(by inequality (35.25))} \;. \tag{35.30}$$

Combining inequalities (35.28) and (35.30) completes the analysis of the approximation ratio.

To show that APPROX-SUBSET-SUM is a fully polynomial-time approximation scheme, we derive a bound on the length of L_i. After trimming, successive elements z and z' of L_i must have the relationship $z'/z > 1+\epsilon/2n$. That is, they must differ by a factor of at least $1 + \epsilon/2n$. Each list, therefore, contains the value 0, possibly the value 1, and up to $\lfloor \log_{1+\epsilon/2n} t \rfloor$ additional values. The number of elements in each list L_i is at most

$$\log_{1+\epsilon/2n} t + 2 \;=\; \frac{\ln t}{\ln(1 + \epsilon/2n)} + 2$$

$$\le\; \frac{2n(1 + \epsilon/2n)\ln t}{\epsilon} + 2 \quad \text{(by inequality (3.17))}$$

$$<\; \frac{3n \ln t}{\epsilon} + 2 \qquad\qquad \text{(by inequality (35.25))} \;.$$

This bound is polynomial in the size of the input—which is the number of bits $\lg t$ needed to represent t plus the number of bits needed to represent the set S, which is in turn polynomial in n—and in $1/\epsilon$. Since the running time of APPROX-SUBSET-SUM is polynomial in the lengths of the L_i, we conclude that APPROX-SUBSET-SUM is a fully polynomial-time approximation scheme.   ■

Exercises

35.5-1
Prove equation (35.23). Then show that after executing line 5 of EXACT-SUBSET-SUM, L_i is a sorted list containing every element of P_i whose value is not more than t.

35.5-2
Using induction on i, prove inequality (35.26).

35.5-3
Prove inequality (35.29).

35.5-4

How would you modify the approximation scheme presented in this section to find a good approximation to the smallest value not less than t that is a sum of some subset of the given input list?

35.5-5

Modify the APPROX-SUBSET-SUM procedure to also return the subset of S that sums to the value z^*.

Problems

35-1   *Bin packing*

Suppose that we are given a set of n objects, where the size s_i of the ith object satisfies $0 < s_i < 1$. We wish to pack all the objects into the minimum number of unit-size bins. Each bin can hold any subset of the objects whose total size does not exceed 1.

a. Prove that the problem of determining the minimum number of bins required is NP-hard. (*Hint:* Reduce from the subset-sum problem.)

The *first-fit* heuristic takes each object in turn and places it into the first bin that can accommodate it. Let $S = \sum_{i=1}^{n} s_i$.

b. Argue that the optimal number of bins required is at least $\lceil S \rceil$.

c. Argue that the first-fit heuristic leaves at most one bin less than half full.

d. Prove that the number of bins used by the first-fit heuristic is never more than $\lceil 2S \rceil$.

e. Prove an approximation ratio of 2 for the first-fit heuristic.

f. Give an efficient implementation of the first-fit heuristic, and analyze its running time.

35-2   *Approximating the size of a maximum clique*

Let $G = (V, E)$ be an undirected graph. For any $k \geq 1$, define $G^{(k)}$ to be the undirected graph $(V^{(k)}, E^{(k)})$, where $V^{(k)}$ is the set of all ordered k-tuples of vertices from V and $E^{(k)}$ is defined so that $(v_1, v_2, \ldots, v_k)$ is adjacent to $(w_1, w_2, \ldots, w_k)$ if and only if for $i = 1, 2, \ldots, k$, either vertex v_i is adjacent to w_i in G, or else $v_i = w_i$.

a. Prove that the size of the maximum clique in $G^{(k)}$ is equal to the kth power of the size of the maximum clique in G.

b. Argue that if there is an approximation algorithm that has a constant approximation ratio for finding a maximum-size clique, then there is a polynomial-time approximation scheme for the problem.

35-3 *Weighted set-covering problem*

Suppose that we generalize the set-covering problem so that each set S_i in the family $\mathcal{F}$ has an associated weight w_i and the weight of a cover $\mathcal{C}$ is $\sum_{S_i \in \mathcal{C}} w_i$. We wish to determine a minimum-weight cover. (Section 35.3 handles the case in which $w_i = 1$ for all i.)

Show how to generalize the greedy set-covering heuristic in a natural manner to provide an approximate solution for any instance of the weighted set-covering problem. Show that your heuristic has an approximation ratio of $H(d)$, where d is the maximum size of any set S_i.

35-4 *Maximum matching*

Recall that for an undirected graph G, a matching is a set of edges such that no two edges in the set are incident on the same vertex. In Section 26.3, we saw how to find a maximum matching in a bipartite graph. In this problem, we will look at matchings in undirected graphs in general (i.e., the graphs are not required to be bipartite).

a. A ***maximal matching*** is a matching that is not a proper subset of any other matching. Show that a maximal matching need not be a maximum matching by exhibiting an undirected graph G and a maximal matching M in G that is not a maximum matching. (*Hint:* You can find such a graph with only four vertices.)

b. Consider an undirected graph $G = (V, E)$. Give an $O(E)$-time greedy algorithm to find a maximal matching in G.

In this problem, we shall concentrate on a polynomial-time approximation algorithm for maximum matching. Whereas the fastest known algorithm for maximum matching takes superlinear (but polynomial) time, the approximation algorithm here will run in linear time. You will show that the linear-time greedy algorithm for maximal matching in part (b) is a 2-approximation algorithm for maximum matching.

c. Show that the size of a maximum matching in G is a lower bound on the size of any vertex cover for G.

d. Consider a maximal matching M in $G = (V, E)$. Let

$$T = \{v \in V : \text{some edge in } M \text{ is incident on } v\} \ .$$

What can you say about the subgraph of G induced by the vertices of G that are not in T?

e. Conclude from part (d) that $2|M|$ is the size of a vertex cover for G.

f. Using parts (c) and (e), prove that the greedy algorithm in part (b) is a 2-approximation algorithm for maximum matching.

35-5   *Parallel machine scheduling*

In the ***parallel-machine-scheduling problem***, we are given n jobs, $J_1, J_2, \ldots, J_n$, where each job J_k has an associated nonnegative processing time of p_k. We are also given m identical machines, $M_1, M_2, \ldots, M_m$. Any job can run on any machine. A ***schedule*** specifies, for each job J_k, the machine on which it runs and the time period during which it runs. Each job J_k must run on some machine M_i for p_k consecutive time units, and during that time period no other job may run on M_i. Let C_k denote the ***completion time*** of job J_k, that is, the time at which job J_k completes processing. Given a schedule, we define $C_{\max} = \max_{1 \leq j \leq n} C_j$ to be the ***makespan*** of the schedule. The goal is to find a schedule whose makespan is minimum.

For example, suppose that we have two machines M_1 and M_2 and that we have four jobs J_1, J_2, J_3, J_4, with $p_1 = 2$, $p_2 = 12$, $p_3 = 4$, and $p_4 = 5$. Then one possible schedule runs, on machine M_1, job J_1 followed by job J_2, and on machine M_2, it runs job J_4 followed by job J_3. For this schedule, $C_1 = 2, C_2 = 14$, $C_3 = 9, C_4 = 5$, and $C_{\max} = 14$. An optimal schedule runs J_2 on machine M_1, and it runs jobs J_1, J_3, and J_4 on machine M_2. For this schedule, $C_1 = 2, C_2 = 12$, $C_3 = 6, C_4 = 11$, and $C_{\max} = 12$.

Given a parallel-machine-scheduling problem, we let $C^*_{\max}$ denote the makespan of an optimal schedule.

a. Show that the optimal makespan is at least as large as the greatest processing time, that is,

$$C^*_{\max} \geq \max_{1 \leq k \leq n} p_k \ .$$

b. Show that the optimal makespan is at least as large as the average machine load, that is,

$$C^*_{\max} \geq \frac{1}{m} \sum_{1 \leq k \leq n} p_k \ .$$

Suppose that we use the following greedy algorithm for parallel machine scheduling: whenever a machine is idle, schedule any job that has not yet been scheduled.

c. Write pseudocode to implement this greedy algorithm. What is the running time of your algorithm?

d. For the schedule returned by the greedy algorithm, show that

$$C_{\max} \leq \frac{1}{m} \sum_{1 \leq k \leq n} p_k + \max_{1 \leq k \leq n} p_k \,.$$

Conclude that this algorithm is a polynomial-time 2-approximation algorithm.

35-6 *Approximating a maximum spanning tree*

Let $G = (V, E)$ be an undirected graph with distinct edge weights $w(u, v)$ on each edge $(u, v) \in E$. For each vertex $v \in V$, let $\max(v) = \operatorname{argmax}_{(u,v) \in E} \{w(u, v)\}$ be the maximum-weight edge incident on that vertex. Let $S_G = \{\max(v) : v \in V\}$ be the set of maximum-weight edges incident on each vertex, and let T_G be the maximum-weight spanning tree of G, that is, the spanning tree of maximum total weight. For any subset of edges $E' \subseteq E$, define $w(E') = \sum_{(u,v) \in E'} w(u, v)$.

a. Give an example of a graph with at least 4 vertices for which $S_G = T_G$.

b. Give an example of a graph with at least 4 vertices for which $S_G \neq T_G$.

c. Prove that $S_G \subseteq T_G$ for any graph G.

d. Prove that $w(S_G) \geq w(T_G)/2$ for any graph G.

e. Give an $O(V + E)$-time algorithm to compute a 2-approximation to the maximum spanning tree.

35-7 *An approximation algorithm for the 0-1 knapsack problem*

Recall the knapsack problem from Section 16.2. There are n items, where the ith item is worth v_i dollars and weighs w_i pounds. We are also given a knapsack that can hold at most W pounds. Here, we add the further assumptions that each weight w_i is at most W and that the items are indexed in monotonically decreasing order of their values: $v_1 \geq v_2 \geq \cdots \geq v_n$.

In the 0-1 knapsack problem, we wish to find a subset of the items whose total weight is at most W and whose total value is maximum. The fractional knapsack problem is like the 0-1 knapsack problem, except that we are allowed to take a fraction of each item, rather than being restricted to taking either all or none of

each item. If we take a fraction x_i of item i, where $0 \le x_i \le 1$, we contribute $x_i w_i$ to the weight of the knapsack and receive value $x_i v_i$. Our goal is to develop a polynomial-time 2-approximation algorithm for the 0-1 knapsack problem.

In order to design a polynomial-time algorithm, we consider restricted instances of the 0-1 knapsack problem. Given an instance I of the knapsack problem, we form restricted instances I_j, for $j = 1, 2, \ldots, n$, by removing items $1, 2, \ldots, j-1$ and requiring the solution to include item j (all of item j in both the fractional and 0-1 knapsack problems). No items are removed in instance I_1. For instance I_j, let P_j denote an optimal solution to the 0-1 problem and Q_j denote an optimal solution to the fractional problem.

a. Argue that an optimal solution to instance I of the 0-1 knapsack problem is one of $\{P_1, P_2, \ldots, P_n\}$.

b. Prove that we can find an optimal solution Q_j to the fractional problem for instance I_j by including item j and then using the greedy algorithm in which at each step, we take as much as possible of the unchosen item in the set $\{j+1, j+2, \ldots, n\}$ with maximum value per pound v_i / w_i.

c. Prove that we can always construct an optimal solution Q_j to the fractional problem for instance I_j that includes at most one item fractionally. That is, for all items except possibly one, we either include all of the item or none of the item in the knapsack.

d. Given an optimal solution Q_j to the fractional problem for instance I_j, form solution R_j from Q_j by deleting any fractional items from Q_j. Let $v(S)$ denote the total value of items taken in a solution S. Prove that $v(R_j) \ge v(Q_j)/2 \ge v(P_j)/2$.

e. Give a polynomial-time algorithm that returns a maximum-value solution from the set $\{R_1, R_2, \ldots, R_n\}$, and prove that your algorithm is a polynomial-time 2-approximation algorithm for the 0-1 knapsack problem.

Chapter notes

Although methods that do not necessarily compute exact solutions have been known for thousands of years (for example, methods to approximate the value of π), the notion of an approximation algorithm is much more recent. Hochbaum [172] credits Garey, Graham, and Ullman [128] and Johnson [190] with formalizing the concept of a polynomial-time approximation algorithm. The first such algorithm is often credited to Graham [149].

Since this early work, thousands of approximation algorithms have been designed for a wide range of problems, and there is a wealth of literature on this field. Recent texts by Ausiello et al. [26], Hochbaum [172], and Vazirani [345] deal exclusively with approximation algorithms, as do surveys by Shmoys [315] and Klein and Young [207]. Several other texts, such as Garey and Johnson [129] and Papadimitriou and Steiglitz [271], have significant coverage of approximation algorithms as well. Lawler, Lenstra, Rinnooy Kan, and Shmoys [225] provide an extensive treatment of approximation algorithms for the traveling-salesman problem.

Papadimitriou and Steiglitz attribute the algorithm APPROX-VERTEX-COVER to F. Gavril and M. Yannakakis. The vertex-cover problem has been studied extensively (Hochbaum [172] lists 16 different approximation algorithms for this problem), but all the approximation ratios are at least $2 - o(1)$.

The algorithm APPROX-TSP-TOUR appears in a paper by Rosenkrantz, Stearns, and Lewis [298]. Christofides improved on this algorithm and gave a $3/2$-approximation algorithm for the traveling-salesman problem with the triangle inequality. Arora [22] and Mitchell [257] have shown that if the points are in the euclidean plane, there is a polynomial-time approximation scheme. Theorem 35.3 is due to Sahni and Gonzalez [301].

The analysis of the greedy heuristic for the set-covering problem is modeled after the proof published by Chvátal [68] of a more general result; the basic result as presented here is due to Johnson [190] and Lovász [238].

The algorithm APPROX-SUBSET-SUM and its analysis are loosely modeled after related approximation algorithms for the knapsack and subset-sum problems by Ibarra and Kim [187].

Problem 35-7 is a combinatorial version of a more general result on approximating knapsack-type integer programs by Bienstock and McClosky [45].

The randomized algorithm for MAX-3-CNF satisfiability is implicit in the work of Johnson [190]. The weighted vertex-cover algorithm is by Hochbaum [171]. Section 35.4 only touches on the power of randomization and linear programming in the design of approximation algorithms. A combination of these two ideas yields a technique called "randomized rounding," which formulates a problem as an integer linear program, solves the linear-programming relaxation, and interprets the variables in the solution as probabilities. These probabilities then help guide the solution of the original problem. This technique was first used by Raghavan and Thompson [290], and it has had many subsequent uses. (See Motwani, Naor, and Raghavan [261] for a survey.) Several other notable recent ideas in the field of approximation algorithms include the primal-dual method (see Goemans and Williamson [135] for a survey), finding sparse cuts for use in divide-and-conquer algorithms [229], and the use of semidefinite programming [134].

As mentioned in the chapter notes for Chapter 34, recent results in probabilistically checkable proofs have led to lower bounds on the approximability of many problems, including several in this chapter. In addition to the references there, the chapter by Arora and Lund [23] contains a good description of the relationship between probabilistically checkable proofs and the hardness of approximating various problems.

VIII   Appendix: Mathematical Background

Introduction

When we analyze algorithms, we often need to draw upon a body of mathematical tools. Some of these tools are as simple as high-school algebra, but others may be new to you. In Part I, we saw how to manipulate asymptotic notations and solve recurrences. This appendix comprises a compendium of several other concepts and methods we use to analyze algorithms. As noted in the introduction to Part I, you may have seen much of the material in this appendix before having read this book (although the specific notational conventions we use might occasionally differ from those you have seen elsewhere). Hence, you should treat this appendix as reference material. As in the rest of this book, however, we have included exercises and problems, in order for you to improve your skills in these areas.

Appendix A offers methods for evaluating and bounding summations, which occur frequently in the analysis of algorithms. Many of the formulas here appear in any calculus text, but you will find it convenient to have these methods compiled in one place.

Appendix B contains basic definitions and notations for sets, relations, functions, graphs, and trees. It also gives some basic properties of these mathematical objects.

Appendix C begins with elementary principles of counting: permutations, combinations, and the like. The remainder contains definitions and properties of basic probability. Most of the algorithms in this book require no probability for their analysis, and thus you can easily omit the latter sections of the chapter on a first reading, even without skimming them. Later, when you encounter a probabilistic analysis that you want to understand better, you will find Appendix C well organized for reference purposes.

Appendix D defines matrices, their operations, and some of their basic properties. You have probably seen most of this material already if you have taken a course in linear algebra, but you might find it helpful to have one place to look for our notation and definitions.

A   Summations

When an algorithm contains an iterative control construct such as a **while** or **for** loop, we can express its running time as the sum of the times spent on each execution of the body of the loop. For example, we found in Section 2.2 that the jth iteration of insertion sort took time proportional to j in the worst case. By adding up the time spent on each iteration, we obtained the summation (or series)

$$\sum_{j=2}^{n} j \ .$$

When we evaluated this summation, we attained a bound of $\Theta(n^2)$ on the worst-case running time of the algorithm. This example illustrates why you should know how to manipulate and bound summations.

Section A.1 lists several basic formulas involving summations. Section A.2 offers useful techniques for bounding summations. We present the formulas in Section A.1 without proof, though proofs for some of them appear in Section A.2 to illustrate the methods of that section. You can find most of the other proofs in any calculus text.

A.1   Summation formulas and properties

Given a sequence $a_1, a_2, \ldots, a_n$ of numbers, where n is a nonnegative integer, we can write the finite sum $a_1 + a_2 + \cdots + a_n$ as

$$\sum_{k=1}^{n} a_k \ .$$

If $n = 0$, the value of the summation is defined to be 0. The value of a finite series is always well defined, and we can add its terms in any order.

Given an infinite sequence $a_1, a_2, \ldots$ of numbers, we can write the infinite sum $a_1 + a_2 + \cdots$ as

$$\sum_{k=1}^{\infty} a_k \, ,$$

which we interpret to mean

$$\lim_{n \to \infty} \sum_{k=1}^{n} a_k \, .$$

If the limit does not exist, the series **diverges**; otherwise, it **converges**. The terms of a convergent series cannot always be added in any order. We can, however, rearrange the terms of an **absolutely convergent series**, that is, a series $\sum_{k=1}^{\infty} a_k$ for which the series $\sum_{k=1}^{\infty} |a_k|$ also converges.

Linearity

For any real number c and any finite sequences $a_1, a_2, \ldots, a_n$ and $b_1, b_2, \ldots, b_n$,

$$\sum_{k=1}^{n} (c a_k + b_k) = c \sum_{k=1}^{n} a_k + \sum_{k=1}^{n} b_k \, .$$

The linearity property also applies to infinite convergent series.

We can exploit the linearity property to manipulate summations incorporating asymptotic notation. For example,

$$\sum_{k=1}^{n} \Theta(f(k)) = \Theta \left(\sum_{k=1}^{n} f(k) \right) .$$

In this equation, the Θ-notation on the left-hand side applies to the variable k, but on the right-hand side, it applies to n. We can also apply such manipulations to infinite convergent series.

Arithmetic series

The summation

$$\sum_{k=1}^{n} k = 1 + 2 + \cdots + n \, ,$$

is an **arithmetic series** and has the value

$$\sum_{k=1}^{n} k \;=\; \frac{1}{2} n(n + 1) \tag{A.1}$$

$$\;=\; \Theta(n^2) \, . \tag{A.2}$$

Sums of squares and cubes

We have the following summations of squares and cubes:

$$\sum_{k=0}^{n} k^2 = \frac{n(n+1)(2n+1)}{6} ,$$ (A.3)

$$\sum_{k=0}^{n} k^3 = \frac{n^2(n+1)^2}{4} .$$ (A.4)

Geometric series

For real $x \neq 1$, the summation

$$\sum_{k=0}^{n} x^k = 1 + x + x^2 + \cdots + x^n$$

is a *geometric* or *exponential series* and has the value

$$\sum_{k=0}^{n} x^k = \frac{x^{n+1} - 1}{x - 1} .$$ (A.5)

When the summation is infinite and $|x| < 1$, we have the infinite decreasing geometric series

$$\sum_{k=0}^{\infty} x^k = \frac{1}{1 - x} .$$ (A.6)

Because we assume that $0^0 = 1$, these formulas apply even when $x = 0$.

Harmonic series

For positive integers n, the nth *harmonic number* is

$$\begin{aligned} H_n &= 1 + \frac{1}{2} + \frac{1}{3} + \frac{1}{4} + \cdots + \frac{1}{n} \\ &= \sum_{k=1}^{n} \frac{1}{k} \\ &= \ln n + O(1) . \end{aligned}$$ (A.7)

(We shall prove a related bound in Section A.2.)

Integrating and differentiating series

By integrating or differentiating the formulas above, additional formulas arise. For example, by differentiating both sides of the infinite geometric series (A.6) and multiplying by x, we get

$$\sum_{k=0}^{\infty} k x^k = \frac{x}{(1-x)^2} \tag{A.8}$$

for $|x| < 1$.

Telescoping series

For any sequence $a_0, a_1, \ldots, a_n$,

$$\sum_{k=1}^{n} (a_k - a_{k-1}) = a_n - a_0 , \tag{A.9}$$

since each of the terms $a_1, a_2, \ldots, a_{n-1}$ is added in exactly once and subtracted out exactly once. We say that the sum **telescopes**. Similarly,

$$\sum_{k=0}^{n-1} (a_k - a_{k+1}) = a_0 - a_n .$$

As an example of a telescoping sum, consider the series

$$\sum_{k=1}^{n-1} \frac{1}{k(k+1)} .$$

Since we can rewrite each term as

$$\frac{1}{k(k+1)} = \frac{1}{k} - \frac{1}{k+1} ,$$

we get

$$
\begin{aligned}
\sum_{k=1}^{n-1} \frac{1}{k(k+1)} &= \sum_{k=1}^{n-1} \left(\frac{1}{k} - \frac{1}{k+1} \right) \\
&= 1 - \frac{1}{n} .
\end{aligned}
$$

Products

We can write the finite product $a_1 a_2 \cdots a_n$ as

$$\prod_{k=1}^{n} a_k .$$

If $n = 0$, the value of the product is defined to be 1. We can convert a formula with a product to a formula with a summation by using the identity

$$\lg \left(\prod_{k=1}^{n} a_k \right) = \sum_{k=1}^{n} \lg a_k .$$

Exercises

A.1-1
Find a simple formula for $\sum_{k=1}^{n}(2k-1)$.

A.1-2   ★
Show that $\sum_{k=1}^{n} 1/(2k-1) = \ln(\sqrt{n}) + O(1)$ by manipulating the harmonic series.

A.1-3
Show that $\sum_{k=0}^{\infty} k^2 x^k = x(1+x)/(1-x)^3$ for $|x| < 1$.

A.1-4   ★
Show that $\sum_{k=0}^{\infty}(k-1)/2^k = 0$.

A.1-5   ★
Evaluate the sum $\sum_{k=1}^{\infty}(2k+1)x^{2k}$ for $|x| < 1$.

A.1-6
Prove that $\sum_{k=1}^{n} O(f_k(i)) = O\left(\sum_{k=1}^{n} f_k(i)\right)$ by using the linearity property of summations.

A.1-7
Evaluate the product $\prod_{k=1}^{n} 2 \cdot 4^k$.

A.1-8   ★
Evaluate the product $\prod_{k=2}^{n}(1 - 1/k^2)$.

A.2   Bounding summations

We have many techniques at our disposal for bounding the summations that describe the running times of algorithms. Here are some of the most frequently used methods.

Mathematical induction

The most basic way to evaluate a series is to use mathematical induction. As an example, let us prove that the arithmetic series $\sum_{k=1}^{n} k$ evaluates to $\frac{1}{2}n(n+1)$. We can easily verify this assertion for $n = 1$. We make the inductive assumption that

it holds for n, and we prove that it holds for $n + 1$. We have

$$
\begin{aligned}
\sum_{k=1}^{n+1} k &= \sum_{k=1}^{n} k + (n + 1) \\
&= \frac{1}{2} n(n + 1) + (n + 1) \\
&= \frac{1}{2} (n + 1)(n + 2) \ .
\end{aligned}
$$

You don't always need to guess the exact value of a summation in order to use mathematical induction. Instead, you can use induction to prove a bound on a summation. As an example, let us prove that the geometric series $\sum_{k=0}^{n} 3^k$ is $O(3^n)$. More specifically, let us prove that $\sum_{k=0}^{n} 3^k \leq c3^n$ for some constant c. For the initial condition $n = 0$, we have $\sum_{k=0}^{0} 3^k = 1 \leq c \cdot 1$ as long as $c \geq 1$. Assuming that the bound holds for n, let us prove that it holds for $n + 1$. We have

$$
\begin{aligned}
\sum_{k=0}^{n+1} 3^k &= \sum_{k=0}^{n} 3^k + 3^{n+1} \\
&\leq c3^n + 3^{n+1} \qquad \text{(by the inductive hypothesis)} \\
&= \left(\frac{1}{3} + \frac{1}{c} \right) c3^{n+1} \\
&\leq c3^{n+1}
\end{aligned}
$$

as long as $(1/3 + 1/c) \leq 1$ or, equivalently, $c \geq 3/2$. Thus, $\sum_{k=0}^{n} 3^k = O(3^n)$, as we wished to show.

We have to be careful when we use asymptotic notation to prove bounds by induction. Consider the following fallacious proof that $\sum_{k=1}^{n} k = O(n)$. Certainly, $\sum_{k=1}^{1} k = O(1)$. Assuming that the bound holds for n, we now prove it for $n + 1$:

$$
\begin{aligned}
\sum_{k=1}^{n+1} k &= \sum_{k=1}^{n} k + (n + 1) \\
&= O(n) + (n + 1) \qquad \Longleftarrow \textit{wrong!!} \\
&= O(n + 1) \ .
\end{aligned}
$$

The bug in the argument is that the "constant" hidden by the "big-oh" grows with n and thus is not constant. We have not shown that the same constant works for *all* n.

Bounding the terms

We can sometimes obtain a good upper bound on a series by bounding each term of the series, and it often suffices to use the largest term to bound the others. For

example, a quick upper bound on the arithmetic series (A.1) is

$$\sum_{k=1}^{n} k \leq \sum_{k=1}^{n} n$$

$$= n^2 \, .$$

In general, for a series $\sum_{k=1}^{n} a_k$, if we let $a_{\max} = \max_{1 \leq k \leq n} a_k$, then

$$\sum_{k=1}^{n} a_k \leq n \cdot a_{\max} \, .$$

The technique of bounding each term in a series by the largest term is a weak method when the series can in fact be bounded by a geometric series. Given the series $\sum_{k=0}^{n} a_k$, suppose that $a_{k+1}/a_k \leq r$ for all $k \geq 0$, where $0 < r < 1$ is a constant. We can bound the sum by an infinite decreasing geometric series, since $a_k \leq a_0 r^k$, and thus

$$\sum_{k=0}^{n} a_k \leq \sum_{k=0}^{\infty} a_0 r^k$$

$$= a_0 \sum_{k=0}^{\infty} r^k$$

$$= a_0 \frac{1}{1 - r} \, .$$

We can apply this method to bound the summation $\sum_{k=1}^{\infty} (k/3^k)$. In order to start the summation at $k = 0$, we rewrite it as $\sum_{k=0}^{\infty} ((k + 1)/3^{k+1})$. The first term ($a_0$) is $1/3$, and the ratio (r) of consecutive terms is

$$\frac{(k + 2)/3^{k+2}}{(k + 1)/3^{k+1}} = \frac{1}{3} \cdot \frac{k + 2}{k + 1}$$

$$\leq \frac{2}{3}$$

for all $k \geq 0$. Thus, we have

$$\sum_{k=1}^{\infty} \frac{k}{3^k} = \sum_{k=0}^{\infty} \frac{k + 1}{3^{k+1}}$$

$$\leq \frac{1}{3} \cdot \frac{1}{1 - 2/3}$$

$$= 1 \, .$$

A common bug in applying this method is to show that the ratio of consecutive terms is less than 1 and then to assume that the summation is bounded by a geometric series. An example is the infinite harmonic series, which diverges since

$$\sum_{k=1}^{\infty} \frac{1}{k} = \lim_{n \to \infty} \sum_{k=1}^{n} \frac{1}{k}$$
$$= \lim_{n \to \infty} \Theta(\lg n)$$
$$= \infty .$$

The ratio of the $(k+1)$st and kth terms in this series is $k/(k+1) < 1$, but the series is not bounded by a decreasing geometric series. To bound a series by a geometric series, we must show that there is an $r < 1$, which is a *constant*, such that the ratio of all pairs of consecutive terms never exceeds r. In the harmonic series, no such r exists because the ratio becomes arbitrarily close to 1.

Splitting summations

One way to obtain bounds on a difficult summation is to express the series as the sum of two or more series by partitioning the range of the index and then to bound each of the resulting series. For example, suppose we try to find a lower bound on the arithmetic series $\sum_{k=1}^{n} k$, which we have already seen has an upper bound of n^2. We might attempt to bound each term in the summation by the smallest term, but since that term is 1, we get a lower bound of n for the summation — far off from our upper bound of n^2.

We can obtain a better lower bound by first splitting the summation. Assume for convenience that n is even. We have

$$\sum_{k=1}^{n} k = \sum_{k=1}^{n/2} k + \sum_{k=n/2+1}^{n} k$$
$$\geq \sum_{k=1}^{n/2} 0 + \sum_{k=n/2+1}^{n} (n/2)$$
$$= (n/2)^2$$
$$= \Omega(n^2) ,$$

which is an asymptotically tight bound, since $\sum_{k=1}^{n} k = O(n^2)$.

For a summation arising from the analysis of an algorithm, we can often split the summation and ignore a constant number of the initial terms. Generally, this technique applies when each term a_k in a summation $\sum_{k=0}^{n} a_k$ is independent of n.

Then for any constant $k_0 > 0$, we can write

$$\sum_{k=0}^{n} a_k = \sum_{k=0}^{k_0-1} a_k + \sum_{k=k_0}^{n} a_k$$

$$= \Theta(1) + \sum_{k=k_0}^{n} a_k \, ,$$

since the initial terms of the summation are all constant and there are a constant number of them. We can then use other methods to bound $\sum_{k=k_0}^{n} a_k$. This technique applies to infinite summations as well. For example, to find an asymptotic upper bound on

$$\sum_{k=0}^{\infty} \frac{k^2}{2^k} \, ,$$

we observe that the ratio of consecutive terms is

$$\frac{(k+1)^2/2^{k+1}}{k^2/2^k} = \frac{(k+1)^2}{2k^2}$$

$$\leq \frac{8}{9}$$

if $k \geq 3$. Thus, the summation can be split into

$$\sum_{k=0}^{\infty} \frac{k^2}{2^k} = \sum_{k=0}^{2} \frac{k^2}{2^k} + \sum_{k=3}^{\infty} \frac{k^2}{2^k}$$

$$\leq \sum_{k=0}^{2} \frac{k^2}{2^k} + \frac{9}{8} \sum_{k=0}^{\infty} \left(\frac{8}{9}\right)^k$$

$$= O(1) \, ,$$

since the first summation has a constant number of terms and the second summation is a decreasing geometric series.

The technique of splitting summations can help us determine asymptotic bounds in much more difficult situations. For example, we can obtain a bound of $O(\lg n)$ on the harmonic series (A.7):

$$H_n = \sum_{k=1}^{n} \frac{1}{k} \, .$$

We do so by splitting the range 1 to n into $\lfloor \lg n \rfloor + 1$ pieces and upper-bounding the contribution of each piece by 1. For $i = 0, 1, \ldots, \lfloor \lg n \rfloor$, the i th piece consists

of the terms starting at $1/2^i$ and going up to but not including $1/2^{i+1}$. The last piece might contain terms not in the original harmonic series, and thus we have

$$
\begin{aligned}
\sum_{k=1}^{n} \frac{1}{k} &\leq \sum_{i=0}^{\lfloor \lg n \rfloor} \sum_{j=0}^{2^i-1} \frac{1}{2^i + j} \\
&\leq \sum_{i=0}^{\lfloor \lg n \rfloor} \sum_{j=0}^{2^i-1} \frac{1}{2^i} \\
&= \sum_{i=0}^{\lfloor \lg n \rfloor} 1 \\
&\leq \lg n + 1 \, .
\end{aligned}
\tag{A.10}
$$

Approximation by integrals

When a summation has the form $\sum_{k=m}^{n} f(k)$, where $f(k)$ is a monotonically increasing function, we can approximate it by integrals:

$$
\int_{m-1}^{n} f(x)\,dx \leq \sum_{k=m}^{n} f(k) \leq \int_{m}^{n+1} f(x)\,dx \, .
\tag{A.11}
$$

Figure A.1 justifies this approximation. The summation is represented as the area of the rectangles in the figure, and the integral is the shaded region under the curve. When $f(k)$ is a monotonically decreasing function, we can use a similar method to provide the bounds

$$
\int_{m}^{n+1} f(x)\,dx \leq \sum_{k=m}^{n} f(k) \leq \int_{m-1}^{n} f(x)\,dx \, .
\tag{A.12}
$$

The integral approximation (A.12) gives a tight estimate for the nth harmonic number. For a lower bound, we obtain

$$
\begin{aligned}
\sum_{k=1}^{n} \frac{1}{k} &\geq \int_{1}^{n+1} \frac{dx}{x} \\
&= \ln(n+1) \, .
\end{aligned}
\tag{A.13}
$$

For the upper bound, we derive the inequality

$$
\begin{aligned}
\sum_{k=2}^{n} \frac{1}{k} &\leq \int_{1}^{n} \frac{dx}{x} \\
&= \ln n \, ,
\end{aligned}
$$

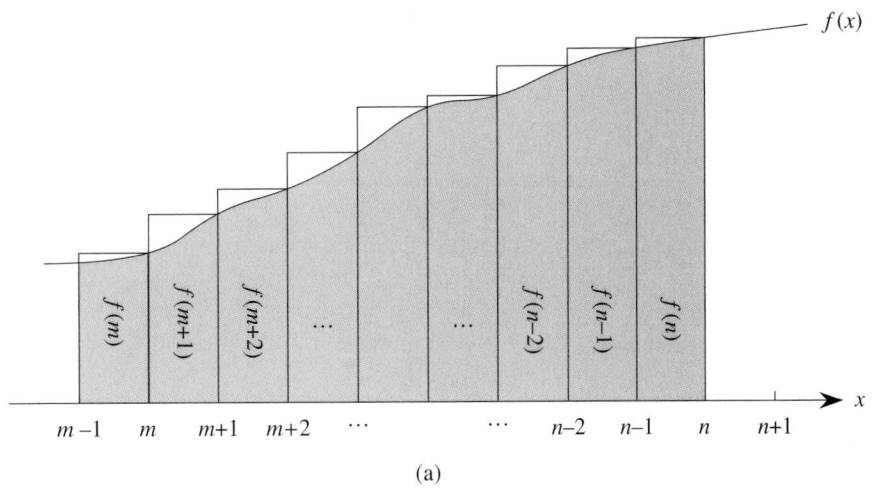

(a)

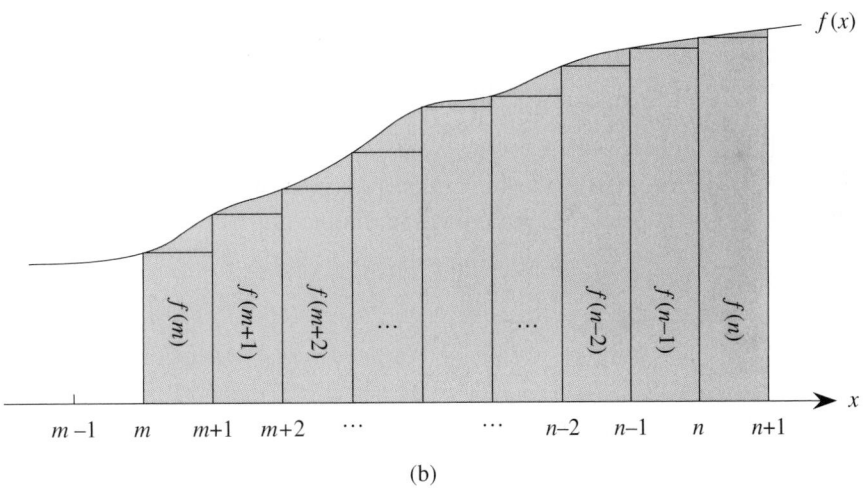

(b)

Figure A.1 Approximation of $\sum_{k=m}^{n} f(k)$ by integrals. The area of each rectangle is shown within the rectangle, and the total rectangle area represents the value of the summation. The integral is represented by the shaded area under the curve. By comparing areas in **(a)**, we get $\int_{m-1}^{n} f(x)\,dx \leq \sum_{k=m}^{n} f(k)$, and then by shifting the rectangles one unit to the right, we get $\sum_{k=m}^{n} f(k) \leq \int_{m}^{n+1} f(x)\,dx$ in **(b)**.

which yields the bound

$$\sum_{k=1}^{n} \frac{1}{k} \leq \ln n + 1 \ . \tag{A.14}$$

Exercises

A.2-1
Show that $\sum_{k=1}^{n} 1/k^2$ is bounded above by a constant.

A.2-2
Find an asymptotic upper bound on the summation

$$\sum_{k=0}^{\lfloor \lg n \rfloor} \lceil n/2^k \rceil \ .$$

A.2-3
Show that the nth harmonic number is $\Omega(\lg n)$ by splitting the summation.

A.2-4
Approximate $\sum_{k=1}^{n} k^3$ with an integral.

A.2-5
Why didn't we use the integral approximation (A.12) directly on $\sum_{k=1}^{n} 1/k$ to obtain an upper bound on the nth harmonic number?

Problems

A-1   Bounding summations
Give asymptotically tight bounds on the following summations. Assume that $r \geq 0$ and $s \geq 0$ are constants.

a. $\displaystyle\sum_{k=1}^{n} k^r$.

b. $\displaystyle\sum_{k=1}^{n} \lg^s k$.

$$c. \ \sum_{k=1}^{n} k^r \lg^s k.$$

Appendix notes

Knuth [209] provides an excellent reference for the material presented here. You can find basic properties of series in any good calculus book, such as Apostol [18] or Thomas et al. [334].

B   Sets, Etc.

Many chapters of this book touch on the elements of discrete mathematics. This appendix reviews more completely the notations, definitions, and elementary properties of sets, relations, functions, graphs, and trees. If you are already well versed in this material, you can probably just skim this chapter.

B.1   Sets

A *set* is a collection of distinguishable objects, called its *members* or *elements*. If an object x is a member of a set S, we write $x \in S$ (read "x is a member of S" or, more briefly, "x is in S"). If x is not a member of S, we write $x \notin S$. We can describe a set by explicitly listing its members as a list inside braces. For example, we can define a set S to contain precisely the numbers 1, 2, and 3 by writing $S = \{1, 2, 3\}$. Since 2 is a member of the set S, we can write $2 \in S$, and since 4 is not a member, we have $4 \notin S$. A set cannot contain the same object more than once,[1] and its elements are not ordered. Two sets A and B are *equal*, written $A = B$, if they contain the same elements. For example, $\{1, 2, 3, 1\} = \{1, 2, 3\} = \{3, 2, 1\}$.

We adopt special notations for frequently encountered sets:

- $\emptyset$ denotes the *empty set*, that is, the set containing no members.

- $\mathbb{Z}$ denotes the set of *integers*, that is, the set $\{\ldots, -2, -1, 0, 1, 2, \ldots\}$.

- $\mathbb{R}$ denotes the set of *real numbers*.

- $\mathbb{N}$ denotes the set of *natural numbers*, that is, the set $\{0, 1, 2, \ldots\}$.[2]

---

[1] A variation of a set, which can contain the same object more than once, is called a *multiset*.

[2] Some authors start the natural numbers with 1 instead of 0. The modern trend seems to be to start with 0.

If all the elements of a set A are contained in a set B, that is, if $x \in A$ implies $x \in B$, then we write $A \subseteq B$ and say that A is a *subset* of B. A set A is a *proper subset* of B, written $A \subset B$, if $A \subseteq B$ but $A \neq B$. (Some authors use the symbol "$\subset$" to denote the ordinary subset relation, rather than the proper-subset relation.) For any set A, we have $A \subseteq A$. For two sets A and B, we have $A = B$ if and only if $A \subseteq B$ and $B \subseteq A$. For any three sets A, B, and C, if $A \subseteq B$ and $B \subseteq C$, then $A \subseteq C$. For any set A, we have $\emptyset \subseteq A$.

We sometimes define sets in terms of other sets. Given a set A, we can define a set $B \subseteq A$ by stating a property that distinguishes the elements of B. For example, we can define the set of even integers by $\{x : x \in \mathbb{Z} \text{ and } x/2 \text{ is an integer}\}$. The colon in this notation is read "such that." (Some authors use a vertical bar in place of the colon.)

Given two sets A and B, we can also define new sets by applying *set operations*:

- The *intersection* of sets A and B is the set

$$A \cap B = \{x : x \in A \text{ and } x \in B\} \ .$$

- The *union* of sets A and B is the set

$$A \cup B = \{x : x \in A \text{ or } x \in B\} \ .$$

- The *difference* between two sets A and B is the set

$$A - B = \{x : x \in A \text{ and } x \notin B\} \ .$$

Set operations obey the following laws:

Empty set laws:

$$
\begin{aligned}
A \cap \emptyset &= \emptyset \ , \\
A \cup \emptyset &= A \ .
\end{aligned}
$$

Idempotency laws:

$$
\begin{aligned}
A \cap A &= A \ , \\
A \cup A &= A \ .
\end{aligned}
$$

Commutative laws:

$$
\begin{aligned}
A \cap B &= B \cap A \ , \\
A \cup B &= B \cup A \ .
\end{aligned}
$$

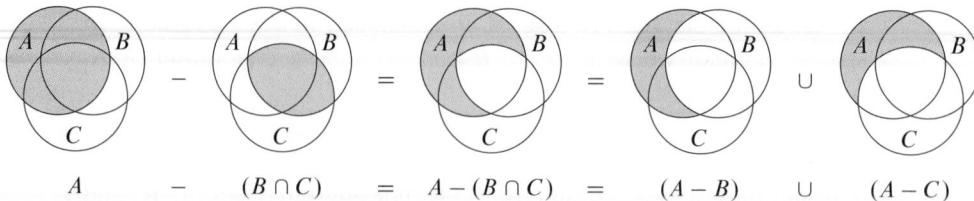

$$A \quad - \quad (B \cap C) \quad = \quad A - (B \cap C) \quad = \quad (A - B) \quad \cup \quad (A - C)$$

Figure B.1   A Venn diagram illustrating the first of DeMorgan's laws (B.2). Each of the sets A, B, and C is represented as a circle.

Associative laws:

$$A \cap (B \cap C) = (A \cap B) \cap C ,$$
$$A \cup (B \cup C) = (A \cup B) \cup C .$$

Distributive laws:

$$A \cap (B \cup C) = (A \cap B) \cup (A \cap C) ,$$
$$A \cup (B \cap C) = (A \cup B) \cap (A \cup C) . \qquad \text{(B.1)}$$

Absorption laws:

$$A \cap (A \cup B) = A ,$$
$$A \cup (A \cap B) = A .$$

DeMorgan's laws:

$$A - (B \cap C) = (A - B) \cup (A - C) ,$$
$$A - (B \cup C) = (A - B) \cap (A - C) . \qquad \text{(B.2)}$$

Figure B.1 illustrates the first of DeMorgan's laws, using a ***Venn diagram***: a graphical picture in which sets are represented as regions of the plane.

Often, all the sets under consideration are subsets of some larger set U called the ***universe***. For example, if we are considering various sets made up only of integers, the set $\mathbb{Z}$ of integers is an appropriate universe. Given a universe U, we define the ***complement*** of a set A as $\overline{A} = U - A = \{x : x \in U \text{ and } x \notin A\}$. For any set $A \subseteq U$, we have the following laws:

$$\overline{\overline{A}} = A ,$$
$$A \cap \overline{A} = \emptyset ,$$
$$A \cup \overline{A} = U .$$

We can rewrite DeMorgan's laws (B.2) with set complements. For any two sets $B, C \subseteq U$, we have

$$\overline{B \cap C} = \overline{B} \cup \overline{C},$$
$$\overline{B \cup C} = \overline{B} \cap \overline{C}.$$

Two sets A and B are *disjoint* if they have no elements in common, that is, if $A \cap B = \emptyset$. A collection $\mathcal{S} = \{S_i\}$ of nonempty sets forms a *partition* of a set S if

- the sets are *pairwise disjoint*, that is, $S_i, S_j \in \mathcal{S}$ and $i \neq j$ imply $S_i \cap S_j = \emptyset$, and

- their union is S, that is,

$$S = \bigcup_{S_i \in \mathcal{S}} S_i.$$

In other words, $\mathcal{S}$ forms a partition of S if each element of S appears in exactly one $S_i \in \mathcal{S}$.

The number of elements in a set is the *cardinality* (or *size*) of the set, denoted $|S|$. Two sets have the same cardinality if their elements can be put into a one-to-one correspondence. The cardinality of the empty set is $|\emptyset| = 0$. If the cardinality of a set is a natural number, we say the set is *finite*; otherwise, it is *infinite*. An infinite set that can be put into a one-to-one correspondence with the natural numbers $\mathbb{N}$ is *countably infinite*; otherwise, it is *uncountable*. For example, the integers $\mathbb{Z}$ are countable, but the reals $\mathbb{R}$ are uncountable.

For any two finite sets A and B, we have the identity

$$|A \cup B| = |A| + |B| - |A \cap B|, \tag{B.3}$$

from which we can conclude that

$$|A \cup B| \leq |A| + |B|.$$

If A and B are disjoint, then $|A \cap B| = 0$ and thus $|A \cup B| = |A| + |B|$. If $A \subseteq B$, then $|A| \leq |B|$.

A finite set of n elements is sometimes called an *n-set*. A 1-set is called a *singleton*. A subset of k elements of a set is sometimes called a *k-subset*.

We denote the set of all subsets of a set S, including the empty set and S itself, by 2^S; we call 2^S the *power set* of S. For example, $2^{\{a,b\}} = \{\emptyset, \{a\}, \{b\}, \{a,b\}\}$. The power set of a finite set S has cardinality $2^{|S|}$ (see Exercise B.1-5).

We sometimes care about setlike structures in which the elements are ordered. An *ordered pair* of two elements a and b is denoted (a, b) and is defined formally as the set $(a, b) = \{a, \{a, b\}\}$. Thus, the ordered pair (a, b) is *not* the same as the ordered pair (b, a).

The ***Cartesian product*** of two sets A and B, denoted $A \times B$, is the set of all ordered pairs such that the first element of the pair is an element of A and the second is an element of B. More formally,

$$A \times B = \{(a,b) : a \in A \text{ and } b \in B\} \ .$$

For example, $\{a,b\} \times \{a,b,c\} = \{(a,a),(a,b),(a,c),(b,a),(b,b),(b,c)\}$. When A and B are finite sets, the cardinality of their Cartesian product is

$$|A \times B| = |A| \cdot |B| \ . \tag{B.4}$$

The Cartesian product of n sets $A_1, A_2, \ldots, A_n$ is the set of ***n-tuples***

$$A_1 \times A_2 \times \cdots \times A_n = \{(a_1, a_2, \ldots, a_n) : a_i \in A_i \text{ for } i = 1, 2, \ldots, n\} \ ,$$

whose cardinality is

$$|A_1 \times A_2 \times \cdots \times A_n| = |A_1| \cdot |A_2| \cdots |A_n|$$

if all sets are finite. We denote an n-fold Cartesian product over a single set A by the set

$$A^n = A \times A \times \cdots \times A \ ,$$

whose cardinality is $|A^n| = |A|^n$ if A is finite. We can also view an n-tuple as a finite sequence of length n (see page 1166).

Exercises

B.1-1
Draw Venn diagrams that illustrate the first of the distributive laws (B.1).

B.1-2
Prove the generalization of DeMorgan's laws to any finite collection of sets:

$$\overline{A_1 \cap A_2 \cap \cdots \cap A_n} = \overline{A_1} \cup \overline{A_2} \cup \cdots \cup \overline{A_n} \ ,$$
$$\overline{A_1 \cup A_2 \cup \cdots \cup A_n} = \overline{A_1} \cap \overline{A_2} \cap \cdots \cap \overline{A_n} \ .$$

B.1-3 ★

Prove the generalization of equation (B.3), which is called the ***principle of inclusion and exclusion***:

$$|A_1 \cup A_2 \cup \cdots \cup A_n| =$$
$$|A_1| + |A_2| + \cdots + |A_n|$$
$$- |A_1 \cap A_2| - |A_1 \cap A_3| - \cdots \qquad \text{(all pairs)}$$
$$+ |A_1 \cap A_2 \cap A_3| + \cdots \qquad \text{(all triples)}$$
$$\vdots$$
$$+ (-1)^{n-1} |A_1 \cap A_2 \cap \cdots \cap A_n| \ .$$

B.1-4

Show that the set of odd natural numbers is countable.

B.1-5

Show that for any finite set S, the power set 2^S has $2^{|S|}$ elements (that is, there are $2^{|S|}$ distinct subsets of S).

B.1-6

Give an inductive definition for an n-tuple by extending the set-theoretic definition for an ordered pair.

B.2 Relations

A ***binary relation*** R on two sets A and B is a subset of the Cartesian product $A \times B$. If $(a, b) \in R$, we sometimes write $a \ R \ b$. When we say that R is a binary relation on a set A, we mean that R is a subset of $A \times A$. For example, the "less than" relation on the natural numbers is the set $\{(a, b) : a, b \in \mathbb{N} \text{ and } a < b\}$. An n-ary relation on sets $A_1, A_2, \ldots, A_n$ is a subset of $A_1 \times A_2 \times \cdots \times A_n$.

A binary relation $R \subseteq A \times A$ is ***reflexive*** if

$$a \ R \ a$$

for all $a \in A$. For example, "=" and "$\leq$" are reflexive relations on $\mathbb{N}$, but "$<$" is not. The relation R is ***symmetric*** if

$$a \ R \ b \text{ implies } b \ R \ a$$

for all $a, b \in A$. For example, "=" is symmetric, but "$<$" and "$\leq$" are not. The relation R is ***transitive*** if

$$a \ R \ b \text{ and } b \ R \ c \text{ imply } a \ R \ c$$

for all $a, b, c \in A$. For example, the relations "$<$," "$\leq$," and "$=$" are transitive, but the relation $R = \{(a, b) : a, b \in \mathbb{N} \text{ and } a = b - 1\}$ is not, since $3\ R\ 4$ and $4\ R\ 5$ do not imply $3\ R\ 5$.

A relation that is reflexive, symmetric, and transitive is an ***equivalence relation***. For example, "$=$" is an equivalence relation on the natural numbers, but "$<$" is not. If R is an equivalence relation on a set A, then for $a \in A$, the ***equivalence class*** of a is the set $[a] = \{b \in A : a\ R\ b\}$, that is, the set of all elements equivalent to a. For example, if we define $R = \{(a, b) : a, b \in \mathbb{N} \text{ and } a + b \text{ is an even number}\}$, then R is an equivalence relation, since $a + a$ is even (reflexive), $a + b$ is even implies $b + a$ is even (symmetric), and $a + b$ is even and $b + c$ is even imply $a + c$ is even (transitive). The equivalence class of 4 is $[4] = \{0, 2, 4, 6, \ldots\}$, and the equivalence class of 3 is $[3] = \{1, 3, 5, 7, \ldots\}$. A basic theorem of equivalence classes is the following.

Theorem B.1 (An equivalence relation is the same as a partition)
The equivalence classes of any equivalence relation R on a set A form a partition of A, and any partition of A determines an equivalence relation on A for which the sets in the partition are the equivalence classes.

Proof   For the first part of the proof, we must show that the equivalence classes of R are nonempty, pairwise-disjoint sets whose union is A. Because R is reflexive, $a \in [a]$, and so the equivalence classes are nonempty; moreover, since every element $a \in A$ belongs to the equivalence class $[a]$, the union of the equivalence classes is A. It remains to show that the equivalence classes are pairwise disjoint, that is, if two equivalence classes $[a]$ and $[b]$ have an element c in common, then they are in fact the same set. Suppose that $a\ R\ c$ and $b\ R\ c$. By symmetry, $c\ R\ b$, and by transitivity, $a\ R\ b$. Thus, for any arbitrary element $x \in [a]$, we have $x\ R\ a$ and, by transitivity, $x\ R\ b$, and thus $[a] \subseteq [b]$. Similarly, $[b] \subseteq [a]$, and thus $[a] = [b]$.

For the second part of the proof, let $\mathcal{A} = \{A_i\}$ be a partition of A, and define $R = \{(a, b) : \text{there exists } i \text{ such that } a \in A_i \text{ and } b \in A_i\}$. We claim that R is an equivalence relation on A. Reflexivity holds, since $a \in A_i$ implies $a\ R\ a$. Symmetry holds, because if $a\ R\ b$, then a and b are in the same set A_i, and hence $b\ R\ a$. If $a\ R\ b$ and $b\ R\ c$, then all three elements are in the same set A_i, and thus $a\ R\ c$ and transitivity holds. To see that the sets in the partition are the equivalence classes of R, observe that if $a \in A_i$, then $x \in [a]$ implies $x \in A_i$, and $x \in A_i$ implies $x \in [a]$. ∎

A binary relation R on a set A is ***antisymmetric*** if

$$a\ R\ b \text{ and } b\ R\ a \text{ imply } a = b.$$

For example, the "$\leq$" relation on the natural numbers is antisymmetric, since $a \leq b$ and $b \leq a$ imply $a = b$. A relation that is reflexive, antisymmetric, and transitive is a ***partial order***, and we call a set on which a partial order is defined a ***partially ordered set***. For example, the relation "is a descendant of" is a partial order on the set of all people (if we view individuals as being their own descendants).

In a partially ordered set A, there may be no single "maximum" element a such that $b R a$ for all $b \in A$. Instead, the set may contain several ***maximal*** elements a such that for no $b \in A$, where $b \neq a$, is it the case that $a R b$. For example, a collection of different-sized boxes may contain several maximal boxes that don't fit inside any other box, yet it has no single "maximum" box into which any other box will fit.[3]

A relation R on a set A is a ***total relation*** if for all $a, b \in A$, we have $a R b$ or $b R a$ (or both), that is, if every pairing of elements of A is related by R. A partial order that is also a total relation is a ***total order*** or ***linear order***. For example, the relation "$\leq$" is a total order on the natural numbers, but the "is a descendant of" relation is not a total order on the set of all people, since there are individuals neither of whom is descended from the other. A total relation that is transitive, but not necessarily either symmetric or antisymmetric, is a ***total preorder***.

Exercises

B.2-1
Prove that the subset relation "$\subseteq$" on all subsets of $\mathbb{Z}$ is a partial order but not a total order.

B.2-2
Show that for any positive integer n, the relation "equivalent modulo n" is an equivalence relation on the integers. (We say that $a \equiv b \pmod{n}$ if there exists an integer q such that $a - b = qn$.) Into what equivalence classes does this relation partition the integers?

B.2-3
Give examples of relations that are

a. reflexive and symmetric but not transitive,

b. reflexive and transitive but not symmetric,

c. symmetric and transitive but not reflexive.

---

[3]To be precise, in order for the "fit inside" relation to be a partial order, we need to view a box as fitting inside itself.

B.2-4

Let S be a finite set, and let R be an equivalence relation on $S \times S$. Show that if in addition R is antisymmetric, then the equivalence classes of S with respect to R are singletons.

B.2-5

Professor Narcissus claims that if a relation R is symmetric and transitive, then it is also reflexive. He offers the following proof. By symmetry, $a \, R \, b$ implies $b \, R \, a$. Transitivity, therefore, implies $a \, R \, a$. Is the professor correct?

B.3   Functions

Given two sets A and B, a **function** f is a binary relation on A and B such that for all $a \in A$, there exists precisely one $b \in B$ such that $(a, b) \in f$. The set A is called the **domain** of f, and the set B is called the **codomain** of f. We sometimes write $f : A \rightarrow B$; and if $(a, b) \in f$, we write $b = f(a)$, since b is uniquely determined by the choice of a.

Intuitively, the function f assigns an element of B to each element of A. No element of A is assigned two different elements of B, but the same element of B can be assigned to two different elements of A. For example, the binary relation

$$f = \{(a, b) : a, b \in \mathbb{N} \text{ and } b = a \bmod 2\}$$

is a function $f : \mathbb{N} \rightarrow \{0, 1\}$, since for each natural number a, there is exactly one value b in $\{0, 1\}$ such that $b = a \bmod 2$. For this example, $0 = f(0), 1 = f(1), 0 = f(2)$, etc. In contrast, the binary relation

$$g = \{(a, b) : a, b \in \mathbb{N} \text{ and } a + b \text{ is even}\}$$

is not a function, since $(1, 3)$ and $(1, 5)$ are both in g, and thus for the choice $a = 1$, there is not precisely one b such that $(a, b) \in g$.

Given a function $f : A \rightarrow B$, if $b = f(a)$, we say that a is the **argument** of f and that b is the **value** of f at a. We can define a function by stating its value for every element of its domain. For example, we might define $f(n) = 2n$ for $n \in \mathbb{N}$, which means $f = \{(n, 2n) : n \in \mathbb{N}\}$. Two functions f and g are **equal** if they have the same domain and codomain and if, for all a in the domain, $f(a) = g(a)$.

A **finite sequence** of length n is a function f whose domain is the set of n integers $\{0, 1, \ldots, n - 1\}$. We often denote a finite sequence by listing its values: $\langle f(0), f(1), \ldots, f(n - 1) \rangle$. An **infinite sequence** is a function whose domain is the set $\mathbb{N}$ of natural numbers. For example, the Fibonacci sequence, defined by recurrence (3.22), is the infinite sequence $\langle 0, 1, 1, 2, 3, 5, 8, 13, 21, \ldots \rangle$.

When the domain of a function f is a Cartesian product, we often omit the extra parentheses surrounding the argument of f. For example, if we had a function $f : A_1 \times A_2 \times \cdots \times A_n \to B$, we would write $b = f(a_1, a_2, \ldots, a_n)$ instead of $b = f((a_1, a_2, \ldots, a_n))$. We also call each a_i an **argument** to the function f, though technically the (single) argument to f is the n-tuple $(a_1, a_2, \ldots, a_n)$.

If $f : A \to B$ is a function and $b = f(a)$, then we sometimes say that b is the **image** of a under f. The image of a set $A' \subseteq A$ under f is defined by

$$f(A') = \{b \in B : b = f(a) \text{ for some } a \in A'\} \ .$$

The **range** of f is the image of its domain, that is, $f(A)$. For example, the range of the function $f : \mathbb{N} \to \mathbb{N}$ defined by $f(n) = 2n$ is $f(\mathbb{N}) = \{m : m = 2n \text{ for some } n \in \mathbb{N}\}$, in other words, the set of nonnegative even integers.

A function is a **surjection** if its range is its codomain. For example, the function $f(n) = \lfloor n/2 \rfloor$ is a surjective function from $\mathbb{N}$ to $\mathbb{N}$, since every element in $\mathbb{N}$ appears as the value of f for some argument. In contrast, the function $f(n) = 2n$ is not a surjective function from $\mathbb{N}$ to $\mathbb{N}$, since no argument to f can produce 3 as a value. The function $f(n) = 2n$ is, however, a surjective function from the natural numbers to the even numbers. A surjection $f : A \to B$ is sometimes described as mapping A **onto** B. When we say that f is onto, we mean that it is surjective.

A function $f : A \to B$ is an **injection** if distinct arguments to f produce distinct values, that is, if $a \neq a'$ implies $f(a) \neq f(a')$. For example, the function $f(n) = 2n$ is an injective function from $\mathbb{N}$ to $\mathbb{N}$, since each even number b is the image under f of at most one element of the domain, namely $b/2$. The function $f(n) = \lfloor n/2 \rfloor$ is not injective, since the value 1 is produced by two arguments: 2 and 3. An injection is sometimes called a **one-to-one** function.

A function $f : A \to B$ is a **bijection** if it is injective and surjective. For example, the function $f(n) = (-1)^n \lceil n/2 \rceil$ is a bijection from $\mathbb{N}$ to $\mathbb{Z}$:

$$
\begin{array}{ccc}
0 & \to & 0 \,, \\
1 & \to & -1 \,, \\
2 & \to & 1 \,, \\
3 & \to & -2 \,, \\
4 & \to & 2 \,, \\
& \vdots &
\end{array}
$$

The function is injective, since no element of $\mathbb{Z}$ is the image of more than one element of $\mathbb{N}$. It is surjective, since every element of $\mathbb{Z}$ appears as the image of some element of $\mathbb{N}$. Hence, the function is bijective. A bijection is sometimes called a **one-to-one correspondence**, since it pairs elements in the domain and codomain. A bijection from a set A to itself is sometimes called a **permutation**.

When a function f is bijective, we define its **inverse** f^{-1} as

$$f^{-1}(b) = a \text{ if and only if } f(a) = b \ .$$

For example, the inverse of the function $f(n) = (-1)^n \lceil n/2 \rceil$ is

$$
f^{-1}(m) = \begin{cases} 2m & \text{if } m \geq 0 , \\ -2m - 1 & \text{if } m < 0 . \end{cases}
$$

Exercises

B.3-1
Let A and B be finite sets, and let $f : A \to B$ be a function. Show that

a. if f is injective, then $|A| \leq |B|$;

b. if f is surjective, then $|A| \geq |B|$.

B.3-2
Is the function $f(x) = x + 1$ bijective when the domain and the codomain are $\mathbb{N}$? Is it bijective when the domain and the codomain are $\mathbb{Z}$?

B.3-3
Give a natural definition for the inverse of a binary relation such that if a relation is in fact a bijective function, its relational inverse is its functional inverse.

B.3-4   ★
Give a bijection from $\mathbb{Z}$ to $\mathbb{Z} \times \mathbb{Z}$.

B.4   Graphs

This section presents two kinds of graphs: directed and undirected. Certain definitions in the literature differ from those given here, but for the most part, the differences are slight. Section 22.1 shows how we can represent graphs in computer memory.

A ***directed graph*** (or ***digraph***) G is a pair (V, E), where V is a finite set and E is a binary relation on V. The set V is called the ***vertex set*** of G, and its elements are called ***vertices*** (singular: ***vertex***). The set E is called the ***edge set*** of G, and its elements are called ***edges***. Figure B.2(a) is a pictorial representation of a directed graph on the vertex set $\{1, 2, 3, 4, 5, 6\}$. Vertices are represented by circles in the figure, and edges are represented by arrows. Note that ***self-loops***—edges from a vertex to itself—are possible.

In an ***undirected graph*** $G = (V, E)$, the edge set E consists of *unordered* pairs of vertices, rather than ordered pairs. That is, an edge is a set $\{u, v\}$, where

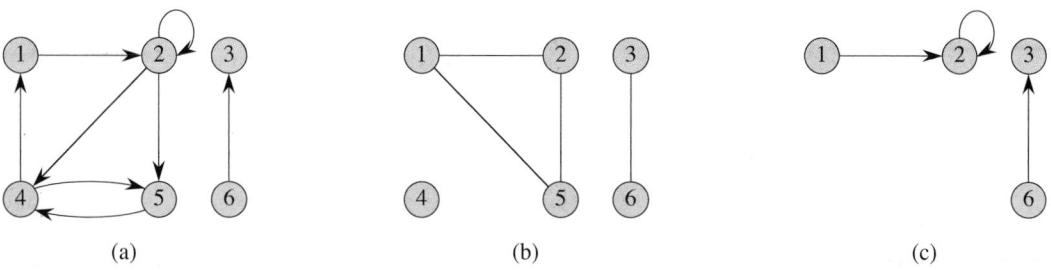

Figure B.2 Directed and undirected graphs. **(a)** A directed graph $G = (V, E)$, where $V = \{1, 2, 3, 4, 5, 6\}$ and $E = \{(1, 2), (2, 2), (2, 4), (2, 5), (4, 1), (4, 5), (5, 4), (6, 3)\}$. The edge $(2, 2)$ is a self-loop. **(b)** An undirected graph $G = (V, E)$, where $V = \{1, 2, 3, 4, 5, 6\}$ and $E = \{(1, 2), (1, 5), (2, 5), (3, 6)\}$. The vertex 4 is isolated. **(c)** The subgraph of the graph in part (a) induced by the vertex set $\{1, 2, 3, 6\}$.

$u, v \in V$ and $u \neq v$. By convention, we use the notation (u, v) for an edge, rather than the set notation $\{u, v\}$, and we consider (u, v) and (v, u) to be the same edge. In an undirected graph, self-loops are forbidden, and so every edge consists of two distinct vertices. Figure B.2(b) is a pictorial representation of an undirected graph on the vertex set $\{1, 2, 3, 4, 5, 6\}$.

Many definitions for directed and undirected graphs are the same, although certain terms have slightly different meanings in the two contexts. If (u, v) is an edge in a directed graph $G = (V, E)$, we say that (u, v) is ***incident from*** or ***leaves*** vertex u and is ***incident to*** or ***enters*** vertex v. For example, the edges leaving vertex 2 in Figure B.2(a) are $(2, 2)$, $(2, 4)$, and $(2, 5)$. The edges entering vertex 2 are $(1, 2)$ and $(2, 2)$. If (u, v) is an edge in an undirected graph $G = (V, E)$, we say that (u, v) is ***incident on*** vertices u and v. In Figure B.2(b), the edges incident on vertex 2 are $(1, 2)$ and $(2, 5)$.

If (u, v) is an edge in a graph $G = (V, E)$, we say that vertex v is ***adjacent*** to vertex u. When the graph is undirected, the adjacency relation is symmetric. When the graph is directed, the adjacency relation is not necessarily symmetric. If v is adjacent to u in a directed graph, we sometimes write $u \rightarrow v$. In parts (a) and (b) of Figure B.2, vertex 2 is adjacent to vertex 1, since the edge $(1, 2)$ belongs to both graphs. Vertex 1 is *not* adjacent to vertex 2 in Figure B.2(a), since the edge $(2, 1)$ does not belong to the graph.

The ***degree*** of a vertex in an undirected graph is the number of edges incident on it. For example, vertex 2 in Figure B.2(b) has degree 2. A vertex whose degree is 0, such as vertex 4 in Figure B.2(b), is ***isolated***. In a directed graph, the ***out-degree*** of a vertex is the number of edges leaving it, and the ***in-degree*** of a vertex is the number of edges entering it. The ***degree*** of a vertex in a directed graph is its in-

degree plus its out-degree. Vertex 2 in Figure B.2(a) has in-degree 2, out-degree 3, and degree 5.

A **path** of **length** k from a vertex u to a vertex u' in a graph $G = (V, E)$ is a sequence $\langle v_0, v_1, v_2, \ldots, v_k \rangle$ of vertices such that $u = v_0$, $u' = v_k$, and $(v_{i-1}, v_i) \in E$ for $i = 1, 2, \ldots, k$. The length of the path is the number of edges in the path. The path **contains** the vertices $v_0, v_1, \ldots, v_k$ and the edges $(v_0, v_1), (v_1, v_2), \ldots, (v_{k-1}, v_k)$. (There is always a 0-length path from u to u.) If there is a path p from u to u', we say that u' is **reachable** from u via p, which we sometimes write as $u \overset{p}{\leadsto} u'$ if G is directed. A path is **simple** [4] if all vertices in the path are distinct. In Figure B.2(a), the path $\langle 1, 2, 5, 4 \rangle$ is a simple path of length 3. The path $\langle 2, 5, 4, 5 \rangle$ is not simple.

A **subpath** of path $p = \langle v_0, v_1, \ldots, v_k \rangle$ is a contiguous subsequence of its vertices. That is, for any $0 \le i \le j \le k$, the subsequence of vertices $\langle v_i, v_{i+1}, \ldots, v_j \rangle$ is a subpath of p.

In a directed graph, a path $\langle v_0, v_1, \ldots, v_k \rangle$ forms a **cycle** if $v_0 = v_k$ and the path contains at least one edge. The cycle is **simple** if, in addition, $v_1, v_2, \ldots, v_k$ are distinct. A self-loop is a cycle of length 1. Two paths $\langle v_0, v_1, v_2, \ldots, v_{k-1}, v_0 \rangle$ and $\langle v_0', v_1', v_2', \ldots, v_{k-1}', v_0' \rangle$ form the same cycle if there exists an integer j such that $v_i' = v_{(i+j) \bmod k}$ for $i = 0, 1, \ldots, k - 1$. In Figure B.2(a), the path $\langle 1, 2, 4, 1 \rangle$ forms the same cycle as the paths $\langle 2, 4, 1, 2 \rangle$ and $\langle 4, 1, 2, 4 \rangle$. This cycle is simple, but the cycle $\langle 1, 2, 4, 5, 4, 1 \rangle$ is not. The cycle $\langle 2, 2 \rangle$ formed by the edge $(2, 2)$ is a self-loop. A directed graph with no self-loops is **simple**. In an undirected graph, a path $\langle v_0, v_1, \ldots, v_k \rangle$ forms a **cycle** if $k > 0$, $v_0 = v_k$, and all edges on the path are distinct; the cycle is **simple** if $v_1, v_2, \ldots, v_k$ are distinct. For example, in Figure B.2(b), the path $\langle 1, 2, 5, 1 \rangle$ is a simple cycle. A graph with no simple cycles is **acyclic**.

An undirected graph is **connected** if every vertex is reachable from all other vertices. The **connected components** of an undirected graph are the equivalence classes of vertices under the "is reachable from" relation. The graph in Figure B.2(b) has three connected components: $\{1, 2, 5\}$, $\{3, 6\}$, and $\{4\}$. Every vertex in $\{1, 2, 5\}$ is reachable from every other vertex in $\{1, 2, 5\}$. An undirected graph is connected if it has exactly one connected component. The edges of a connected component are those that are incident on only the vertices of the component; in other words, edge (u, v) is an edge of a connected component only if both u and v are vertices of the component.

---

[4]Some authors refer to what we call a path as a "walk" and to what we call a simple path as just a "path." We use the terms "path" and "simple path" throughout this book in a manner consistent with their definitions.

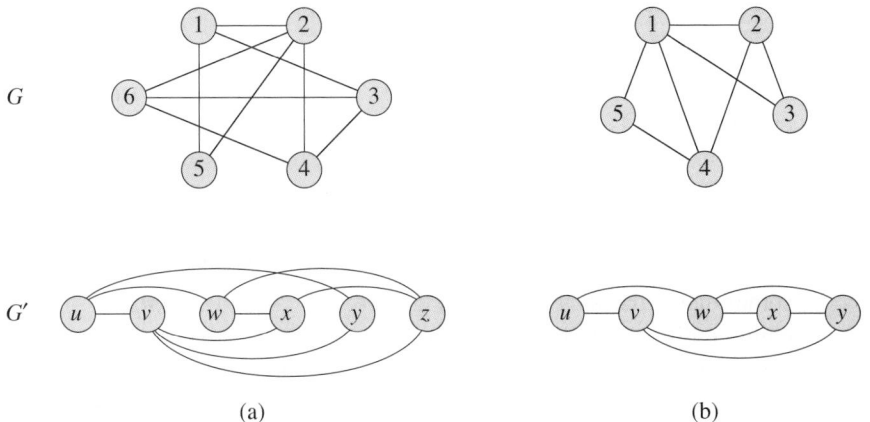

G

G'

(a)   (b)

Figure B.3 **(a)** A pair of isomorphic graphs. The vertices of the top graph are mapped to the vertices of the bottom graph by $f(1) = u$, $f(2) = v$, $f(3) = w$, $f(4) = x$, $f(5) = y$, $f(6) = z$. **(b)** Two graphs that are not isomorphic, since the top graph has a vertex of degree 4 and the bottom graph does not.

A directed graph is **strongly connected** if every two vertices are reachable from each other. The **strongly connected components** of a directed graph are the equivalence classes of vertices under the "are mutually reachable" relation. A directed graph is strongly connected if it has only one strongly connected component. The graph in Figure B.2(a) has three strongly connected components: $\{1, 2, 4, 5\}$, $\{3\}$, and $\{6\}$. All pairs of vertices in $\{1, 2, 4, 5\}$ are mutually reachable. The vertices $\{3, 6\}$ do not form a strongly connected component, since vertex 6 cannot be reached from vertex 3.

Two graphs $G = (V, E)$ and $G' = (V', E')$ are **isomorphic** if there exists a bijection $f : V \rightarrow V'$ such that $(u, v) \in E$ if and only if $(f(u), f(v)) \in E'$. In other words, we can relabel the vertices of G to be vertices of G', maintaining the corresponding edges in G and G'. Figure B.3(a) shows a pair of isomorphic graphs G and G' with respective vertex sets $V = \{1, 2, 3, 4, 5, 6\}$ and $V' = \{u, v, w, x, y, z\}$. The mapping from V to V' given by $f(1) = u$, $f(2) = v$, $f(3) = w$, $f(4) = x$, $f(5) = y$, $f(6) = z$ provides the required bijective function. The graphs in Figure B.3(b) are not isomorphic. Although both graphs have 5 vertices and 7 edges, the top graph has a vertex of degree 4 and the bottom graph does not.

We say that a graph $G' = (V', E')$ is a **subgraph** of $G = (V, E)$ if $V' \subseteq V$ and $E' \subseteq E$. Given a set $V' \subseteq V$, the subgraph of G **induced** by V' is the graph $G' = (V', E')$, where

$$E' = \{(u, v) \in E : u, v \in V'\} \ .$$

The subgraph induced by the vertex set $\{1, 2, 3, 6\}$ in Figure B.2(a) appears in Figure B.2(c) and has the edge set $\{(1, 2), (2, 2), (6, 3)\}$.

Given an undirected graph $G = (V, E)$, the ***directed version*** of G is the directed graph $G' = (V, E')$, where $(u, v) \in E'$ if and only if $(u, v) \in E$. That is, we replace each undirected edge (u, v) in G by the two directed edges (u, v) and (v, u) in the directed version. Given a directed graph $G = (V, E)$, the ***undirected version*** of G is the undirected graph $G' = (V, E')$, where $(u, v) \in E'$ if and only if $u \neq v$ and E contains at least one of the edges (u, v) and (v, u). That is, the undirected version contains the edges of G "with their directions removed" and with self-loops eliminated. (Since (u, v) and (v, u) are the same edge in an undirected graph, the undirected version of a directed graph contains it only once, even if the directed graph contains both edges (u, v) and (v, u).) In a directed graph $G = (V, E)$, a ***neighbor*** of a vertex u is any vertex that is adjacent to u in the undirected version of G. That is, v is a neighbor of u if $u \neq v$ and either $(u, v) \in E$ or $(v, u) \in E$. In an undirected graph, u and v are neighbors if they are adjacent.

Several kinds of graphs have special names. A ***complete graph*** is an undirected graph in which every pair of vertices is adjacent. A ***bipartite graph*** is an undirected graph $G = (V, E)$ in which V can be partitioned into two sets V_1 and V_2 such that $(u, v) \in E$ implies either $u \in V_1$ and $v \in V_2$ or $u \in V_2$ and $v \in V_1$. That is, all edges go between the two sets V_1 and V_2. An acyclic, undirected graph is a ***forest***, and a connected, acyclic, undirected graph is a ***(free) tree*** (see Section B.5). We often take the first letters of "directed acyclic graph" and call such a graph a ***dag***.

There are two variants of graphs that you may occasionally encounter. A ***multi-graph*** is like an undirected graph, but it can have both multiple edges between vertices and self-loops. A ***hypergraph*** is like an undirected graph, but each ***hyperedge***, rather than connecting two vertices, connects an arbitrary subset of vertices. Many algorithms written for ordinary directed and undirected graphs can be adapted to run on these graphlike structures.

The ***contraction*** of an undirected graph $G = (V, E)$ by an edge $e = (u, v)$ is a graph $G' = (V', E')$, where $V' = V - \{u, v\} \cup \{x\}$ and x is a new vertex. The set of edges E' is formed from E by deleting the edge (u, v) and, for each vertex w adjacent to u or v, deleting whichever of (u, w) and (v, w) is in E and adding the new edge (x, w). In effect, u and v are "contracted" into a single vertex.

Exercises

B.4-1

Attendees of a faculty party shake hands to greet each other, and each professor remembers how many times he or she shook hands. At the end of the party, the department head adds up the number of times that each professor shook hands.

Show that the result is even by proving the *handshaking lemma*: if $G = (V, E)$ is an undirected graph, then

$$\sum_{v \in V} \text{degree}(v) = 2|E| \ .$$

B.4-2
Show that if a directed or undirected graph contains a path between two vertices u and v, then it contains a simple path between u and v. Show that if a directed graph contains a cycle, then it contains a simple cycle.

B.4-3
Show that any connected, undirected graph $G = (V, E)$ satisfies $|E| \geq |V| - 1$.

B.4-4
Verify that in an undirected graph, the "is reachable from" relation is an equivalence relation on the vertices of the graph. Which of the three properties of an equivalence relation hold in general for the "is reachable from" relation on the vertices of a directed graph?

B.4-5
What is the undirected version of the directed graph in Figure B.2(a)? What is the directed version of the undirected graph in Figure B.2(b)?

B.4-6 ★
Show that we can represent a hypergraph by a bipartite graph if we let incidence in the hypergraph correspond to adjacency in the bipartite graph. (*Hint:* Let one set of vertices in the bipartite graph correspond to vertices of the hypergraph, and let the other set of vertices of the bipartite graph correspond to hyperedges.)

B.5 Trees

As with graphs, there are many related, but slightly different, notions of trees. This section presents definitions and mathematical properties of several kinds of trees. Sections 10.4 and 22.1 describe how we can represent trees in computer memory.

B.5.1 Free trees

As defined in Section B.4, a *free tree* is a connected, acyclic, undirected graph. We often omit the adjective "free" when we say that a graph is a tree. If an undirected graph is acyclic but possibly disconnected, it is a *forest*. Many algorithms that work

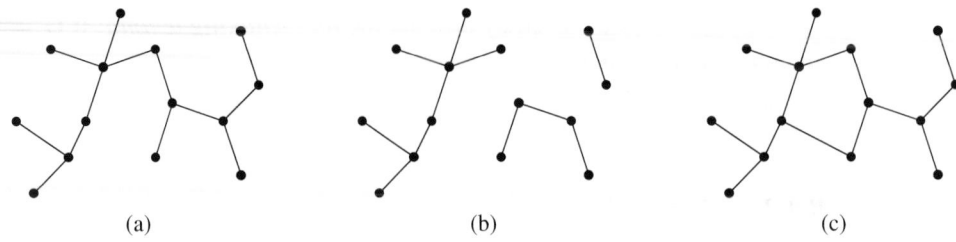

(a)   (b)   (c)

Figure B.4   **(a)** A free tree. **(b)** A forest. **(c)** A graph that contains a cycle and is therefore neither a tree nor a forest.

for trees also work for forests. Figure B.4(a) shows a free tree, and Figure B.4(b) shows a forest. The forest in Figure B.4(b) is not a tree because it is not connected. The graph in Figure B.4(c) is connected but neither a tree nor a forest, because it contains a cycle.

The following theorem captures many important facts about free trees.

Theorem B.2 (Properties of free trees)
Let $G = (V, E)$ be an undirected graph. The following statements are equivalent.

1. G is a free tree.

2. Any two vertices in G are connected by a unique simple path.

3. G is connected, but if any edge is removed from E, the resulting graph is disconnected.

4. G is connected, and $|E| = |V| - 1$.

5. G is acyclic, and $|E| = |V| - 1$.

6. G is acyclic, but if any edge is added to E, the resulting graph contains a cycle.

Proof   (1) $\Rightarrow$ (2): Since a tree is connected, any two vertices in G are connected by at least one simple path. Suppose, for the sake of contradiction, that vertices u and v are connected by two distinct simple paths p_1 and p_2, as shown in Figure B.5. Let w be the vertex at which the paths first diverge; that is, w is the first vertex on both p_1 and p_2 whose successor on p_1 is x and whose successor on p_2 is y, where $x \neq y$. Let z be the first vertex at which the paths reconverge; that is, z is the first vertex following w on p_1 that is also on p_2. Let p' be the subpath of p_1 from w through x to z, and let p'' be the subpath of p_2 from w through y to z. Paths p' and p'' share no vertices except their endpoints. Thus, the path obtained by concatenating p' and the reverse of p'' is a cycle, which contradicts our assumption

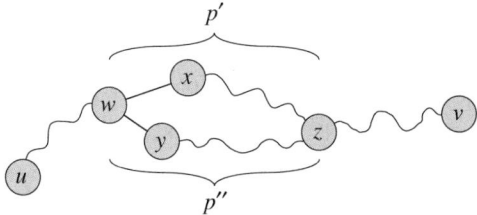

Figure B.5 A step in the proof of Theorem B.2: if (1) G is a free tree, then (2) any two vertices in G are connected by a unique simple path. Assume for the sake of contradiction that vertices u and v are connected by two distinct simple paths p_1 and p_2. These paths first diverge at vertex w, and they first reconverge at vertex z. The path p' concatenated with the reverse of the path p'' forms a cycle, which yields the contradiction.

that G is a tree. Thus, if G is a tree, there can be at most one simple path between two vertices.

(2) $\Rightarrow$ (3): If any two vertices in G are connected by a unique simple path, then G is connected. Let (u, v) be any edge in E. This edge is a path from u to v, and so it must be the unique path from u to v. If we remove (u, v) from G, there is no path from u to v, and hence its removal disconnects G.

(3) $\Rightarrow$ (4): By assumption, the graph G is connected, and by Exercise B.4-3, we have $|E| \geq |V| - 1$. We shall prove $|E| \leq |V| - 1$ by induction. A connected graph with $n = 1$ or $n = 2$ vertices has $n - 1$ edges. Suppose that G has $n \geq 3$ vertices and that all graphs satisfying (3) with fewer than n vertices also satisfy $|E| \leq |V| - 1$. Removing an arbitrary edge from G separates the graph into $k \geq 2$ connected components (actually $k = 2$). Each component satisfies (3), or else G would not satisfy (3). If we view each connected component V_i, with edge set E_i, as its own free tree, then because each component has fewer than $|V|$ vertices, by the inductive hypothesis we have $|E_i| \leq |V_i| - 1$. Thus, the number of edges in all components combined is at most $|V| - k \leq |V| - 2$. Adding in the removed edge yields $|E| \leq |V| - 1$.

(4) $\Rightarrow$ (5): Suppose that G is connected and that $|E| = |V| - 1$. We must show that G is acyclic. Suppose that G has a cycle containing k vertices $v_1, v_2, \ldots, v_k$, and without loss of generality assume that this cycle is simple. Let $G_k = (V_k, E_k)$ be the subgraph of G consisting of the cycle. Note that $|V_k| = |E_k| = k$. If $k < |V|$, there must be a vertex $v_{k+1} \in V - V_k$ that is adjacent to some vertex $v_i \in V_k$, since G is connected. Define $G_{k+1} = (V_{k+1}, E_{k+1})$ to be the subgraph of G with $V_{k+1} = V_k \cup \{v_{k+1}\}$ and $E_{k+1} = E_k \cup \{(v_i, v_{k+1})\}$. Note that $|V_{k+1}| = |E_{k+1}| = k + 1$. If $k + 1 < |V|$, we can continue, defining G_{k+2} in the same manner, and so forth, until we obtain $G_n = (V_n, E_n)$, where $n = |V|$,

$V_n = V$, and $|E_n| = |V_n| = |V|$. Since G_n is a subgraph of G, we have $E_n \subseteq E$, and hence $|E| \geq |V|$, which contradicts the assumption that $|E| = |V| - 1$. Thus, G is acyclic.

$(5) \Rightarrow (6)$: Suppose that G is acyclic and that $|E| = |V| - 1$. Let k be the number of connected components of G. Each connected component is a free tree by definition, and since (1) implies (5), the sum of all edges in all connected components of G is $|V| - k$. Consequently, we must have $k = 1$, and G is in fact a tree. Since (1) implies (2), any two vertices in G are connected by a unique simple path. Thus, adding any edge to G creates a cycle.

$(6) \Rightarrow (1)$: Suppose that G is acyclic but that adding any edge to E creates a cycle. We must show that G is connected. Let u and v be arbitrary vertices in G. If u and v are not already adjacent, adding the edge (u, v) creates a cycle in which all edges but (u, v) belong to G. Thus, the cycle minus edge (u, v) must contain a path from u to v, and since u and v were chosen arbitrarily, G is connected.   ∎

B.5.2   Rooted and ordered trees

A *rooted tree* is a free tree in which one of the vertices is distinguished from the others. We call the distinguished vertex the *root* of the tree. We often refer to a vertex of a rooted tree as a *node*[5] of the tree. Figure B.6(a) shows a rooted tree on a set of 12 nodes with root 7.

Consider a node x in a rooted tree T with root r. We call any node y on the unique simple path from r to x an *ancestor* of x. If y is an ancestor of x, then x is a *descendant* of y. (Every node is both an ancestor and a descendant of itself.) If y is an ancestor of x and $x \neq y$, then y is a *proper ancestor* of x and x is a *proper descendant* of y. The *subtree rooted at x* is the tree induced by descendants of x, rooted at x. For example, the subtree rooted at node 8 in Figure B.6(a) contains nodes 8, 6, 5, and 9.

If the last edge on the simple path from the root r of a tree T to a node x is (y, x), then y is the *parent* of x, and x is a *child* of y. The root is the only node in T with no parent. If two nodes have the same parent, they are *siblings*. A node with no children is a *leaf* or *external node*. A nonleaf node is an *internal node*.

---

[5]The term "node" is often used in the graph theory literature as a synonym for "vertex." We reserve the term "node" to mean a vertex of a rooted tree.

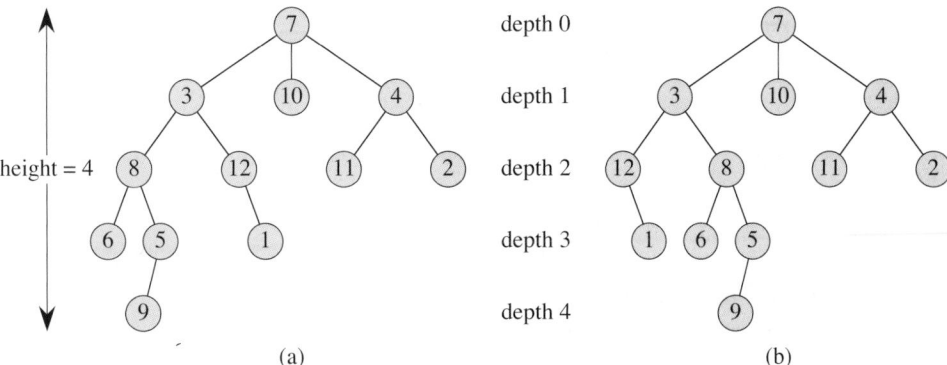

Figure B.6 Rooted and ordered trees. **(a)** A rooted tree with height 4. The tree is drawn in a standard way: the root (node 7) is at the top, its children (nodes with depth 1) are beneath it, their children (nodes with depth 2) are beneath them, and so forth. If the tree is ordered, the relative left-to-right order of the children of a node matters; otherwise it doesn't. **(b)** Another rooted tree. As a rooted tree, it is identical to the tree in (a), but as an ordered tree it is different, since the children of node 3 appear in a different order.

The number of children of a node x in a rooted tree T equals the ***degree*** of x.[6] The length of the simple path from the root r to a node x is the ***depth*** of x in T. A ***level*** of a tree consists of all nodes at the same depth. The ***height*** of a node in a tree is the number of edges on the longest simple downward path from the node to a leaf, and the height of a tree is the height of its root. The height of a tree is also equal to the largest depth of any node in the tree.

An ***ordered tree*** is a rooted tree in which the children of each node are ordered. That is, if a node has k children, then there is a first child, a second child, ..., and a kth child. The two trees in Figure B.6 are different when considered to be ordered trees, but the same when considered to be just rooted trees.

B.5.3 Binary and positional trees

We define binary trees recursively. A ***binary tree*** T is a structure defined on a finite set of nodes that either

* contains no nodes, or

---

[6]Notice that the degree of a node depends on whether we consider T to be a rooted tree or a free tree. The degree of a vertex in a free tree is, as in any undirected graph, the number of adjacent vertices. In a rooted tree, however, the degree is the number of children—the parent of a node does not count toward its degree.

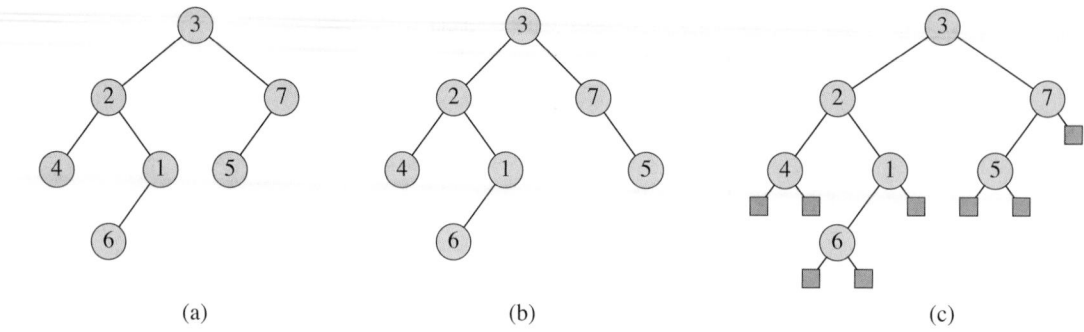

Figure B.7 Binary trees. **(a)** A binary tree drawn in a standard way. The left child of a node is drawn beneath the node and to the left. The right child is drawn beneath and to the right. **(b)** A binary tree different from the one in (a). In (a), the left child of node 7 is 5 and the right child is absent. In (b), the left child of node 7 is absent and the right child is 5. As ordered trees, these trees are the same, but as binary trees, they are distinct. **(c)** The binary tree in (a) represented by the internal nodes of a full binary tree: an ordered tree in which each internal node has degree 2. The leaves in the tree are shown as squares.

- is composed of three disjoint sets of nodes: a ***root*** node, a binary tree called its ***left subtree***, and a binary tree called its ***right subtree***.

The binary tree that contains no nodes is called the ***empty tree*** or ***null tree***, sometimes denoted NIL. If the left subtree is nonempty, its root is called the ***left child*** of the root of the entire tree. Likewise, the root of a nonnull right subtree is the ***right child*** of the root of the entire tree. If a subtree is the null tree NIL, we say that the child is ***absent*** or ***missing***. Figure B.7(a) shows a binary tree.

A binary tree is not simply an ordered tree in which each node has degree at most 2. For example, in a binary tree, if a node has just one child, the position of the child—whether it is the ***left child*** or the ***right child***—matters. In an ordered tree, there is no distinguishing a sole child as being either left or right. Figure B.7(b) shows a binary tree that differs from the tree in Figure B.7(a) because of the position of one node. Considered as ordered trees, however, the two trees are identical.

We can represent the positioning information in a binary tree by the internal nodes of an ordered tree, as shown in Figure B.7(c). The idea is to replace each missing child in the binary tree with a node having no children. These leaf nodes are drawn as squares in the figure. The tree that results is a ***full binary tree***: each node is either a leaf or has degree exactly 2. There are no degree-1 nodes. Consequently, the order of the children of a node preserves the position information.

We can extend the positioning information that distinguishes binary trees from ordered trees to trees with more than 2 children per node. In a ***positional tree***, the

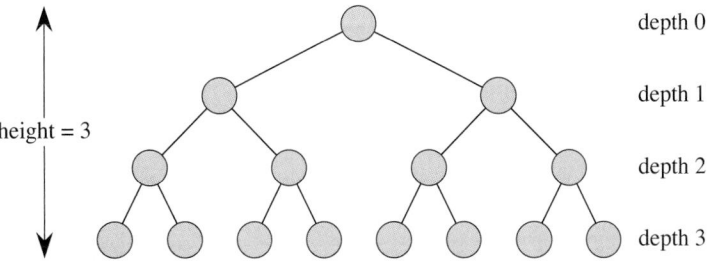

Figure B.8   A complete binary tree of height 3 with 8 leaves and 7 internal nodes.

children of a node are labeled with distinct positive integers. The ith child of a node is **absent** if no child is labeled with integer i. A **k-ary** tree is a positional tree in which for every node, all children with labels greater than k are missing. Thus, a binary tree is a k-ary tree with $k = 2$.

A **complete k-ary tree** is a k-ary tree in which all leaves have the same depth and all internal nodes have degree k. Figure B.8 shows a complete binary tree of height 3. How many leaves does a complete k-ary tree of height h have? The root has k children at depth 1, each of which has k children at depth 2, etc. Thus, the number of leaves at depth h is k^h. Consequently, the height of a complete k-ary tree with n leaves is $\log_k n$. The number of internal nodes of a complete k-ary tree of height h is

$$
\begin{aligned}
1 + k + k^2 + \cdots + k^{h-1} &= \sum_{i=0}^{h-1} k^i \\
&= \frac{k^h - 1}{k - 1}
\end{aligned}
$$

by equation (A.5). Thus, a complete binary tree has $2^h - 1$ internal nodes.

Exercises

B.5-1
Draw all the free trees composed of the three vertices x, y, and z. Draw all the rooted trees with nodes x, y, and z with x as the root. Draw all the ordered trees with nodes x, y, and z with x as the root. Draw all the binary trees with nodes x, y, and z with x as the root.

B.5-2

Let $G = (V, E)$ be a directed acyclic graph in which there is a vertex $v_0 \in V$ such that there exists a unique path from v_0 to every vertex $v \in V$. Prove that the undirected version of G forms a tree.

B.5-3

Show by induction that the number of degree-2 nodes in any nonempty binary tree is 1 fewer than the number of leaves. Conclude that the number of internal nodes in a full binary tree is 1 fewer than the number of leaves.

B.5-4

Use induction to show that a nonempty binary tree with n nodes has height at least $\lfloor \lg n \rfloor$.

B.5-5 ★

The ***internal path length*** of a full binary tree is the sum, taken over all internal nodes of the tree, of the depth of each node. Likewise, the ***external path length*** is the sum, taken over all leaves of the tree, of the depth of each leaf. Consider a full binary tree with n internal nodes, internal path length i, and external path length e. Prove that $e = i + 2n$.

B.5-6 ★

Let us associate a "weight" $w(x) = 2^{-d}$ with each leaf x of depth d in a binary tree T, and let L be the set of leaves of T. Prove that $\sum_{x \in L} w(x) \leq 1$. (This is known as the ***Kraft inequality***.)

B.5-7 ★

Show that if $L \geq 2$, then every binary tree with L leaves contains a subtree having between $L/3$ and $2L/3$ leaves, inclusive.

Problems

B-1 *Graph coloring*

Given an undirected graph $G = (V, E)$, a ***k-coloring*** of G is a function $c : V \to \{0, 1, \ldots, k-1\}$ such that $c(u) \neq c(v)$ for every edge $(u, v) \in E$. In other words, the numbers $0, 1, \ldots, k-1$ represent the k colors, and adjacent vertices must have different colors.

a. Show that any tree is 2-colorable.

b. Show that the following are equivalent:

1. G is bipartite.
2. G is 2-colorable.
3. G has no cycles of odd length.

c. Let d be the maximum degree of any vertex in a graph G. Prove that we can color G with $d + 1$ colors.

d. Show that if G has $O(|V|)$ edges, then we can color G with $O(\sqrt{|V|})$ colors.

B-2 Friendly graphs
Reword each of the following statements as a theorem about undirected graphs, and then prove it. Assume that friendship is symmetric but not reflexive.

a. Any group of at least two people contains at least two people with the same number of friends in the group.

b. Every group of six people contains either at least three mutual friends or at least three mutual strangers.

c. Any group of people can be partitioned into two subgroups such that at least half the friends of each person belong to the subgroup of which that person is *not* a member.

d. If everyone in a group is the friend of at least half the people in the group, then the group can be seated around a table in such a way that everyone is seated between two friends.

B-3 Bisecting trees
Many divide-and-conquer algorithms that operate on graphs require that the graph be bisected into two nearly equal-sized subgraphs, which are induced by a partition of the vertices. This problem investigates bisections of trees formed by removing a small number of edges. We require that whenever two vertices end up in the same subtree after removing edges, then they must be in the same partition.

a. Show that we can partition the vertices of any n-vertex binary tree into two sets A and B, such that $|A| \le 3n/4$ and $|B| \le 3n/4$, by removing a single edge.

b. Show that the constant $3/4$ in part (a) is optimal in the worst case by giving an example of a simple binary tree whose most evenly balanced partition upon removal of a single edge has $|A| = 3n/4$.

c. Show that by removing at most $O(\lg n)$ edges, we can partition the vertices of any n-vertex binary tree into two sets A and B such that $|A| = \lfloor n/2 \rfloor$ and $|B| = \lceil n/2 \rceil$.

Appendix notes

G. Boole pioneered the development of symbolic logic, and he introduced many of the basic set notations in a book published in 1854. Modern set theory was created by G. Cantor during the period 1874–1895. Cantor focused primarily on sets of infinite cardinality. The term "function" is attributed to G. W. Leibniz, who used it to refer to several kinds of mathematical formulas. His limited definition has been generalized many times. Graph theory originated in 1736, when L. Euler proved that it was impossible to cross each of the seven bridges in the city of Königsberg exactly once and return to the starting point.

The book by Harary [160] provides a useful compendium of many definitions and results from graph theory.

C Counting and Probability

This appendix reviews elementary combinatorics and probability theory. If you have a good background in these areas, you may want to skim the beginning of this appendix lightly and concentrate on the later sections. Most of this book's chapters do not require probability, but for some chapters it is essential.

Section C.1 reviews elementary results in counting theory, including standard formulas for counting permutations and combinations. The axioms of probability and basic facts concerning probability distributions form Section C.2. Random variables are introduced in Section C.3, along with the properties of expectation and variance. Section C.4 investigates the geometric and binomial distributions that arise from studying Bernoulli trials. The study of the binomial distribution continues in Section C.5, an advanced discussion of the "tails" of the distribution.

C.1 Counting

Counting theory tries to answer the question "How many?" without actually enumerating all the choices. For example, we might ask, "How many different n-bit numbers are there?" or "How many orderings of n distinct elements are there?" In this section, we review the elements of counting theory. Since some of the material assumes a basic understanding of sets, you might wish to start by reviewing the material in Section B.1.

Rules of sum and product

We can sometimes express a set of items that we wish to count as a union of disjoint sets or as a Cartesian product of sets.

The **rule of sum** says that the number of ways to choose one element from one of two *disjoint* sets is the sum of the cardinalities of the sets. That is, if A and B are two finite sets with no members in common, then $|A \cup B| = |A| + |B|$, which

follows from equation (B.3). For example, each position on a car's license plate is a letter or a digit. The number of possibilities for each position is therefore $26 + 10 = 36$, since there are 26 choices if it is a letter and 10 choices if it is a digit.

The ***rule of product*** says that the number of ways to choose an ordered pair is the number of ways to choose the first element times the number of ways to choose the second element. That is, if A and B are two finite sets, then $|A \times B| = |A| \cdot |B|$, which is simply equation (B.4). For example, if an ice-cream parlor offers 28 flavors of ice cream and 4 toppings, the number of possible sundaes with one scoop of ice cream and one topping is $28 \cdot 4 = 112$.

Strings

A ***string*** over a finite set S is a sequence of elements of S. For example, there are 8 binary strings of length 3:

$$000, 001, 010, 011, 100, 101, 110, 111 .$$

We sometimes call a string of length k a ***k-string***. A ***substring*** s' of a string s is an ordered sequence of consecutive elements of s. A ***k-substring*** of a string is a substring of length k. For example, 010 is a 3-substring of 01101001 (the 3-substring that begins in position 4), but 111 is not a substring of 01101001.

We can view a k-string over a set S as an element of the Cartesian product S^k of k-tuples; thus, there are $|S|^k$ strings of length k. For example, the number of binary k-strings is 2^k. Intuitively, to construct a k-string over an n-set, we have n ways to pick the first element; for each of these choices, we have n ways to pick the second element; and so forth k times. This construction leads to the k-fold product $n \cdot n \cdots n = n^k$ as the number of k-strings.

Permutations

A ***permutation*** of a finite set S is an ordered sequence of all the elements of S, with each element appearing exactly once. For example, if $S = \{a, b, c\}$, then S has 6 permutations:

$$abc, acb, bac, bca, cab, cba .$$

There are $n!$ permutations of a set of n elements, since we can choose the first element of the sequence in n ways, the second in $n - 1$ ways, the third in $n - 2$ ways, and so on.

A ***k-permutation*** of S is an ordered sequence of k elements of S, with no element appearing more than once in the sequence. (Thus, an ordinary permutation is an n-permutation of an n-set.) The twelve 2-permutations of the set $\{a, b, c, d\}$ are

$ab, ac, ad, ba, bc, bd, ca, cb, cd, da, db, dc$.

The number of k-permutations of an n-set is

$$n(n-1)(n-2)\cdots(n-k+1) = \frac{n!}{(n-k)!} , \tag{C.1}$$

since we have n ways to choose the first element, $n-1$ ways to choose the second element, and so on, until we have selected k elements, the last being a selection from the remaining $n-k+1$ elements.

Combinations

A **k-combination** of an n-set S is simply a k-subset of S. For example, the 4-set $\{a, b, c, d\}$ has six 2-combinations:

ab, ac, ad, bc, bd, cd .

(Here we use the shorthand of denoting the 2-subset $\{a, b\}$ by ab, and so on.) We can construct a k-combination of an n-set by choosing k distinct (different) elements from the n-set. The order in which we select the elements does not matter.

We can express the number of k-combinations of an n-set in terms of the number of k-permutations of an n-set. Every k-combination has exactly $k!$ permutations of its elements, each of which is a distinct k-permutation of the n-set. Thus, the number of k-combinations of an n-set is the number of k-permutations divided by $k!$; from equation (C.1), this quantity is

$$\frac{n!}{k!\,(n-k)!} . \tag{C.2}$$

For $k = 0$, this formula tells us that the number of ways to choose 0 elements from an n-set is 1 (not 0), since $0! = 1$.

Binomial coefficients

The notation $\binom{n}{k}$ (read "n choose k") denotes the number of k-combinations of an n-set. From equation (C.2), we have

$$\binom{n}{k} = \frac{n!}{k!\,(n-k)!} .$$

This formula is symmetric in k and $n-k$:

$$\binom{n}{k} = \binom{n}{n-k} . \tag{C.3}$$

These numbers are also known as ***binomial coefficients***, due to their appearance in the ***binomial expansion***:

$$(x + y)^n = \sum_{k=0}^{n} \binom{n}{k} x^k y^{n-k} \ . \tag{C.4}$$

A special case of the binomial expansion occurs when $x = y = 1$:

$$2^n = \sum_{k=0}^{n} \binom{n}{k} \ .$$

This formula corresponds to counting the 2^n binary n-strings by the number of 1s they contain: $\binom{n}{k}$ binary n-strings contain exactly k 1s, since we have $\binom{n}{k}$ ways to choose k out of the n positions in which to place the 1s.

Many identities involve binomial coefficients. The exercises at the end of this section give you the opportunity to prove a few.

Binomial bounds

We sometimes need to bound the size of a binomial coefficient. For $1 \leq k \leq n$, we have the lower bound

$$\binom{n}{k} = \frac{n(n-1)\cdots(n-k+1)}{k(k-1)\cdots 1}$$

$$= \left(\frac{n}{k}\right)\left(\frac{n-1}{k-1}\right)\cdots\left(\frac{n-k+1}{1}\right)$$

$$\geq \left(\frac{n}{k}\right)^k \ .$$

Taking advantage of the inequality $k! \geq (k/e)^k$ derived from Stirling's approximation (3.18), we obtain the upper bounds

$$\binom{n}{k} = \frac{n(n-1)\cdots(n-k+1)}{k(k-1)\cdots 1}$$

$$\leq \frac{n^k}{k!}$$

$$\leq \left(\frac{en}{k}\right)^k \ . \tag{C.5}$$

For all integers k such that $0 \leq k \leq n$, we can use induction (see Exercise C.1-12) to prove the bound

$$\binom{n}{k} \le \frac{n^n}{k^k (n-k)^{n-k}} \,,$$ (C.6)

where for convenience we assume that $0^0 = 1$. For $k = \lambda n$, where $0 \le \lambda \le 1$, we can rewrite this bound as

$$
\begin{aligned}
\binom{n}{\lambda n} &\le \frac{n^n}{(\lambda n)^{\lambda n}((1-\lambda)n)^{(1-\lambda)n}} \\
&= \left(\left(\frac{1}{\lambda} \right)^\lambda \left(\frac{1}{1-\lambda} \right)^{1-\lambda} \right)^n \\
&= 2^{n\,H(\lambda)} \,,
\end{aligned}
$$

where

$$H(\lambda) = -\lambda \lg \lambda - (1-\lambda)\lg(1-\lambda)$$ (C.7)

is the *(binary) entropy function* and where, for convenience, we assume that $0 \lg 0 = 0$, so that $H(0) = H(1) = 0$.

Exercises

C.1-1

How many k-substrings does an n-string have? (Consider identical k-substrings at different positions to be different.) How many substrings does an n-string have in total?

C.1-2

An n-input, m-output *boolean function* is a function from $\{\text{TRUE}, \text{FALSE}\}^n$ to $\{\text{TRUE}, \text{FALSE}\}^m$. How many n-input, 1-output boolean functions are there? How many n-input, m-output boolean functions are there?

C.1-3

In how many ways can n professors sit around a circular conference table? Consider two seatings to be the same if one can be rotated to form the other.

C.1-4

In how many ways can we choose three distinct numbers from the set $\{1, 2, \ldots, 99\}$ so that their sum is even?

C.1-5

Prove the identity

$$\binom{n}{k} = \frac{n}{k}\binom{n-1}{k-1} \qquad\qquad\qquad (\text{C.8})$$

for $0 < k \le n$.

C.1-6

Prove the identity

$$\binom{n}{k} = \frac{n}{n-k}\binom{n-1}{k}$$

for $0 \le k < n$.

C.1-7

To choose k objects from n, you can make one of the objects distinguished and consider whether the distinguished object is chosen. Use this approach to prove that

$$\binom{n}{k} = \binom{n-1}{k} + \binom{n-1}{k-1}.$$

C.1-8

Using the result of Exercise C.1-7, make a table for $n = 0, 1, \ldots, 6$ and $0 \le k \le n$ of the binomial coefficients $\binom{n}{k}$ with $\binom{0}{0}$ at the top, $\binom{1}{0}$ and $\binom{1}{1}$ on the next line, and so forth. Such a table of binomial coefficients is called **_Pascal's triangle_**.

C.1-9

Prove that

$$\sum_{i=1}^{n} i = \binom{n+1}{2}.$$

C.1-10

Show that for any integers $n \ge 0$ and $0 \le k \le n$, the expression $\binom{n}{k}$ achieves its maximum value when $k = \lfloor n/2 \rfloor$ or $k = \lceil n/2 \rceil$.

C.1-11 ★

Argue that for any integers $n \ge 0$, $j \ge 0$, $k \ge 0$, and $j + k \le n$,

$$\binom{n}{j+k} \le \binom{n}{j}\binom{n-j}{k}. \qquad\qquad\qquad (\text{C.9})$$

Provide both an algebraic proof and an argument based on a method for choosing $j + k$ items out of n. Give an example in which equality does not hold.

C.1-12   ★
Use induction on all integers k such that $0 \leq k \leq n/2$ to prove inequality (C.6), and use equation (C.3) to extend it to all integers k such that $0 \leq k \leq n$.

C.1-13   ★
Use Stirling's approximation to prove that

$$\binom{2n}{n} = \frac{2^{2n}}{\sqrt{\pi n}}(1 + O(1/n)) . \tag{C.10}$$

C.1-14   ★
By differentiating the entropy function $H(\lambda)$, show that it achieves its maximum value at $\lambda = 1/2$. What is $H(1/2)$?

C.1-15   ★
Show that for any integer $n \geq 0$,

$$\sum_{k=0}^{n} \binom{n}{k} k = n2^{n-1} . \tag{C.11}$$

C.2   Probability

Probability is an essential tool for the design and analysis of probabilistic and randomized algorithms. This section reviews basic probability theory.

We define probability in terms of a ***sample space*** S, which is a set whose elements are called ***elementary events***. We can think of each elementary event as a possible outcome of an experiment. For the experiment of flipping two distinguishable coins, with each individual flip resulting in a head (H) or a tail (T), we can view the sample space as consisting of the set of all possible 2-strings over {H, T}:

$$S = \{HH, HT, TH, TT\} .$$

An **event** is a subset[1] of the sample space S. For example, in the experiment of flipping two coins, the event of obtaining one head and one tail is $\{HT, TH\}$. The event S is called the **certain event**, and the event $\emptyset$ is called the **null event**. We say that two events A and B are **mutually exclusive** if $A \cap B = \emptyset$. We sometimes treat an elementary event $s \in S$ as the event $\{s\}$. By definition, all elementary events are mutually exclusive.

Axioms of probability

A **probability distribution** $\Pr\{\}$ on a sample space S is a mapping from events of S to real numbers satisfying the following **probability axioms**:

1. $\Pr\{A\} \geq 0$ for any event A.

2. $\Pr\{S\} = 1$.

3. $\Pr\{A \cup B\} = \Pr\{A\} + \Pr\{B\}$ for any two mutually exclusive events A and B. More generally, for any (finite or countably infinite) sequence of events $A_1, A_2, \ldots$ that are pairwise mutually exclusive,

$$\Pr\left\{\bigcup_i A_i\right\} = \sum_i \Pr\{A_i\} \ .$$

We call $\Pr\{A\}$ the **probability** of the event A. We note here that axiom 2 is a normalization requirement: there is really nothing fundamental about choosing 1 as the probability of the certain event, except that it is natural and convenient.

Several results follow immediately from these axioms and basic set theory (see Section B.1). The null event $\emptyset$ has probability $\Pr\{\emptyset\} = 0$. If $A \subseteq B$, then $\Pr\{A\} \leq \Pr\{B\}$. Using $\overline{A}$ to denote the event $S - A$ (the **complement** of A), we have $\Pr\{\overline{A}\} = 1 - \Pr\{A\}$. For any two events A and B,

$$\begin{aligned}
\Pr\{A \cup B\} &= \Pr\{A\} + \Pr\{B\} - \Pr\{A \cap B\} & \text{(C.12)} \\
&\leq \Pr\{A\} + \Pr\{B\} \ . & \text{(C.13)}
\end{aligned}$$

---

[1]For a general probability distribution, there may be some subsets of the sample space S that are not considered to be events. This situation usually arises when the sample space is uncountably infinite. The main requirement for what subsets are events is that the set of events of a sample space be closed under the operations of taking the complement of an event, forming the union of a finite or countable number of events, and taking the intersection of a finite or countable number of events. Most of the probability distributions we shall see are over finite or countable sample spaces, and we shall generally consider all subsets of a sample space to be events. A notable exception is the continuous uniform probability distribution, which we shall see shortly.

In our coin-flipping example, suppose that each of the four elementary events has probability $1/4$. Then the probability of getting at least one head is

$$\begin{aligned}
\Pr\{\text{HH}, \text{HT}, \text{TH}\} &= \Pr\{\text{HH}\} + \Pr\{\text{HT}\} + \Pr\{\text{TH}\} \\
&= 3/4 \,.
\end{aligned}$$

Alternatively, since the probability of getting strictly less than one head is $\Pr\{\text{TT}\} = 1/4$, the probability of getting at least one head is $1 - 1/4 = 3/4$.

Discrete probability distributions

A probability distribution is ***discrete*** if it is defined over a finite or countably infinite sample space. Let S be the sample space. Then for any event A,

$$\Pr\{A\} = \sum_{s \in A} \Pr\{s\} \,,$$

since elementary events, specifically those in A, are mutually exclusive. If S is finite and every elementary event $s \in S$ has probability

$$\Pr\{s\} = 1/\lvert S \rvert \,,$$

then we have the ***uniform probability distribution*** on S. In such a case the experiment is often described as "picking an element of S at random."

As an example, consider the process of flipping a ***fair coin***, one for which the probability of obtaining a head is the same as the probability of obtaining a tail, that is, $1/2$. If we flip the coin n times, we have the uniform probability distribution defined on the sample space $S = \{\text{H}, \text{T}\}^n$, a set of size 2^n. We can represent each elementary event in S as a string of length n over $\{\text{H}, \text{T}\}$, each string occurring with probability $1/2^n$. The event

$$A = \{\text{exactly } k \text{ heads and exactly } n - k \text{ tails occur}\}$$

is a subset of S of size $\lvert A \rvert = \binom{n}{k}$, since $\binom{n}{k}$ strings of length n over $\{\text{H}, \text{T}\}$ contain exactly k H's. The probability of event A is thus $\Pr\{A\} = \binom{n}{k}/2^n$.

Continuous uniform probability distribution

The continuous uniform probability distribution is an example of a probability distribution in which not all subsets of the sample space are considered to be events. The continuous uniform probability distribution is defined over a closed interval $[a, b]$ of the reals, where $a < b$. Our intuition is that each point in the interval $[a, b]$ should be "equally likely." There are an uncountable number of points, however, so if we give all points the same finite, positive probability, we cannot simultaneously satisfy axioms 2 and 3. For this reason, we would like to associate a

probability only with *some* of the subsets of S, in such a way that the axioms are satisfied for these events.

For any closed interval $[c, d]$, where $a \leq c \leq d \leq b$, the **continuous uniform probability distribution** defines the probability of the event $[c, d]$ to be

$$\Pr\{[c, d]\} = \frac{d - c}{b - a} .$$

Note that for any point $x = [x, x]$, the probability of x is 0. If we remove the endpoints of an interval $[c, d]$, we obtain the open interval (c, d). Since $[c, d] = [c, c] \cup (c, d) \cup [d, d]$, axiom 3 gives us $\Pr\{[c, d]\} = \Pr\{(c, d)\}$. Generally, the set of events for the continuous uniform probability distribution contains any subset of the sample space $[a, b]$ that can be obtained by a finite or countable union of open and closed intervals, as well as certain more complicated sets.

Conditional probability and independence

Sometimes we have some prior partial knowledge about the outcome of an experiment. For example, suppose that a friend has flipped two fair coins and has told you that at least one of the coins showed a head. What is the probability that both coins are heads? The information given eliminates the possibility of two tails. The three remaining elementary events are equally likely, so we infer that each occurs with probability $1/3$. Since only one of these elementary events shows two heads, the answer to our question is $1/3$.

Conditional probability formalizes the notion of having prior partial knowledge of the outcome of an experiment. The **conditional probability** of an event A given that another event B occurs is defined to be

$$\Pr\{A \mid B\} = \frac{\Pr\{A \cap B\}}{\Pr\{B\}} \tag{C.14}$$

whenever $\Pr\{B\} \neq 0$. (We read "$\Pr\{A \mid B\}$" as "the probability of A given B.") Intuitively, since we are given that event B occurs, the event that A also occurs is $A \cap B$. That is, $A \cap B$ is the set of outcomes in which both A and B occur. Because the outcome is one of the elementary events in B, we normalize the probabilities of all the elementary events in B by dividing them by $\Pr\{B\}$, so that they sum to 1. The conditional probability of A given B is, therefore, the ratio of the probability of event $A \cap B$ to the probability of event B. In the example above, A is the event that both coins are heads, and B is the event that at least one coin is a head. Thus, $\Pr\{A \mid B\} = (1/4)/(3/4) = 1/3$.

Two events are **independent** if

$$\Pr\{A \cap B\} = \Pr\{A\} \Pr\{B\} , \tag{C.15}$$

which is equivalent, if $\Pr\{B\} \neq 0$, to the condition

$\Pr\{A \mid B\} = \Pr\{A\}$.

For example, suppose that we flip two fair coins and that the outcomes are independent. Then the probability of two heads is $(1/2)(1/2) = 1/4$. Now suppose that one event is that the first coin comes up heads and the other event is that the coins come up differently. Each of these events occurs with probability $1/2$, and the probability that both events occur is $1/4$; thus, according to the definition of independence, the events are independent—even though you might think that both events depend on the first coin. Finally, suppose that the coins are welded together so that they both fall heads or both fall tails and that the two possibilities are equally likely. Then the probability that each coin comes up heads is $1/2$, but the probability that they both come up heads is $1/2 \neq (1/2)(1/2)$. Consequently, the event that one comes up heads and the event that the other comes up heads are not independent.

A collection $A_1, A_2, \ldots, A_n$ of events is said to be **pairwise independent** if

$$\Pr\{A_i \cap A_j\} = \Pr\{A_i\}\Pr\{A_j\}$$

for all $1 \le i < j \le n$. We say that the events of the collection are **(mutually) independent** if every k-subset $A_{i_1}, A_{i_2}, \ldots, A_{i_k}$ of the collection, where $2 \le k \le n$ and $1 \le i_1 < i_2 < \cdots < i_k \le n$, satisfies

$$\Pr\{A_{i_1} \cap A_{i_2} \cap \cdots \cap A_{i_k}\} = \Pr\{A_{i_1}\}\Pr\{A_{i_2}\}\cdots\Pr\{A_{i_k}\} \ .$$

For example, suppose we flip two fair coins. Let A_1 be the event that the first coin is heads, let A_2 be the event that the second coin is heads, and let A_3 be the event that the two coins are different. We have

$$
\begin{aligned}
\Pr\{A_1\} &= 1/2 \ , \\
\Pr\{A_2\} &= 1/2 \ , \\
\Pr\{A_3\} &= 1/2 \ , \\
\Pr\{A_1 \cap A_2\} &= 1/4 \ , \\
\Pr\{A_1 \cap A_3\} &= 1/4 \ , \\
\Pr\{A_2 \cap A_3\} &= 1/4 \ , \\
\Pr\{A_1 \cap A_2 \cap A_3\} &= 0 \ .
\end{aligned}
$$

Since for $1 \le i < j \le 3$, we have $\Pr\{A_i \cap A_j\} = \Pr\{A_i\}\Pr\{A_j\} = 1/4$, the events A_1, A_2, and A_3 are pairwise independent. The events are not mutually independent, however, because $\Pr\{A_1 \cap A_2 \cap A_3\} = 0$ and $\Pr\{A_1\}\Pr\{A_2\}\Pr\{A_3\} = 1/8 \neq 0$.

Bayes's theorem

From the definition of conditional probability (C.14) and the commutative law $A \cap B = B \cap A$, it follows that for two events A and B, each with nonzero probability,

$$\Pr\{A \cap B\} = \Pr\{B\}\Pr\{A \mid B\} \tag{C.16}$$
$$= \Pr\{A\}\Pr\{B \mid A\} \ .$$

Solving for $\Pr\{A \mid B\}$, we obtain

$$\Pr\{A \mid B\} = \frac{\Pr\{A\}\Pr\{B \mid A\}}{\Pr\{B\}} \ , \tag{C.17}$$

which is known as **Bayes's theorem**. The denominator $\Pr\{B\}$ is a normalizing constant, which we can reformulate as follows. Since $B = (B \cap A) \cup (B \cap \overline{A})$, and since $B \cap A$ and $B \cap \overline{A}$ are mutually exclusive events,

$$\Pr\{B\} = \Pr\{B \cap A\} + \Pr\{B \cap \overline{A}\}$$
$$= \Pr\{A\}\Pr\{B \mid A\} + \Pr\{\overline{A}\}\Pr\{B \mid \overline{A}\} \ .$$

Substituting into equation (C.17), we obtain an equivalent form of Bayes's theorem:

$$\Pr\{A \mid B\} = \frac{\Pr\{A\}\Pr\{B \mid A\}}{\Pr\{A\}\Pr\{B \mid A\} + \Pr\{\overline{A}\}\Pr\{B \mid \overline{A}\}} \ . \tag{C.18}$$

Bayes's theorem can simplify the computing of conditional probabilities. For example, suppose that we have a fair coin and a biased coin that always comes up heads. We run an experiment consisting of three independent events: we choose one of the two coins at random, we flip that coin once, and then we flip it again. Suppose that the coin we have chosen comes up heads both times. What is the probability that it is biased?

We solve this problem using Bayes's theorem. Let A be the event that we choose the biased coin, and let B be the event that the chosen coin comes up heads both times. We wish to determine $\Pr\{A \mid B\}$. We have $\Pr\{A\} = 1/2$, $\Pr\{B \mid A\} = 1$, $\Pr\{\overline{A}\} = 1/2$, and $\Pr\{B \mid \overline{A}\} = 1/4$; hence,

$$\Pr\{A \mid B\} = \frac{(1/2) \cdot 1}{(1/2) \cdot 1 + (1/2) \cdot (1/4)}$$
$$= 4/5 \ .$$

Exercises

C.2-1

Professor Rosencrantz flips a fair coin once. Professor Guildenstern flips a fair coin twice. What is the probability that Professor Rosencrantz obtains more heads than Professor Guildenstern?

C.2-2

Prove **Boole's inequality**: For any finite or countably infinite sequence of events $A_1, A_2, \ldots,$

$$\Pr\{A_1 \cup A_2 \cup \cdots\} \leq \Pr\{A_1\} + \Pr\{A_2\} + \cdots . \qquad (C.19)$$

C.2-3

Suppose we shuffle a deck of 10 cards, each bearing a distinct number from 1 to 10, to mix the cards thoroughly. We then remove three cards, one at a time, from the deck. What is the probability that we select the three cards in sorted (increasing) order?

C.2-4

Prove that

$$\Pr\{A \mid B\} + \Pr\{\overline{A} \mid B\} = 1 .$$

C.2-5

Prove that for any collection of events $A_1, A_2, \ldots, A_n$,

$$\Pr\{A_1 \cap A_2 \cap \cdots \cap A_n\} = \Pr\{A_1\} \cdot \Pr\{A_2 \mid A_1\} \cdot \Pr\{A_3 \mid A_1 \cap A_2\} \cdots$$
$$\Pr\{A_n \mid A_1 \cap A_2 \cap \cdots \cap A_{n-1}\} .$$

C.2-6   ⋆

Describe a procedure that takes as input two integers a and b such that $0 < a < b$ and, using fair coin flips, produces as output heads with probability a/b and tails with probability $(b - a)/b$. Give a bound on the expected number of coin flips, which should be $O(1)$. (*Hint:* Represent a/b in binary.)

C.2-7   ⋆

Show how to construct a set of n events that are pairwise independent but such that no subset of $k > 2$ of them is mutually independent.

C.2-8   ⋆

Two events A and B are **conditionally independent**, given C, if

$$\Pr\{A \cap B \mid C\} = \Pr\{A \mid C\} \cdot \Pr\{B \mid C\} .$$

Give a simple but nontrivial example of two events that are not independent but are conditionally independent given a third event.

C.2-9   ⋆

You are a contestant in a game show in which a prize is hidden behind one of three curtains. You will win the prize if you select the correct curtain. After you

have picked one curtain but before the curtain is lifted, the emcee lifts one of the other curtains, knowing that it will reveal an empty stage, and asks if you would like to switch from your current selection to the remaining curtain. How would your chances change if you switch? (This question is the celebrated **Monty Hall problem**, named after a game-show host who often presented contestants with just this dilemma.)

C.2-10 ★

A prison warden has randomly picked one prisoner among three to go free. The other two will be executed. The guard knows which one will go free but is forbidden to give any prisoner information regarding his status. Let us call the prisoners X, Y, and Z. Prisoner X asks the guard privately which of Y or Z will be executed, arguing that since he already knows that at least one of them must die, the guard won't be revealing any information about his own status. The guard tells X that Y is to be executed. Prisoner X feels happier now, since he figures that either he or prisoner Z will go free, which means that his probability of going free is now $1/2$. Is he right, or are his chances still $1/3$? Explain.

C.3   Discrete random variables

A **(discrete) random variable** X is a function from a finite or countably infinite sample space S to the real numbers. It associates a real number with each possible outcome of an experiment, which allows us to work with the probability distribution induced on the resulting set of numbers. Random variables can also be defined for uncountably infinite sample spaces, but they raise technical issues that are unnecessary to address for our purposes. Henceforth, we shall assume that random variables are discrete.

For a random variable X and a real number x, we define the event $X = x$ to be $\{s \in S : X(s) = x\}$; thus,

$$\Pr\{X = x\} = \sum_{s \in S : X(s) = x} \Pr\{s\} \; .$$

The function

$$f(x) = \Pr\{X = x\}$$

is the **probability density function** of the random variable X. From the probability axioms, $\Pr\{X = x\} \geq 0$ and $\sum_x \Pr\{X = x\} = 1$.

As an example, consider the experiment of rolling a pair of ordinary, 6-sided dice. There are 36 possible elementary events in the sample space. We assume

that the probability distribution is uniform, so that each elementary event $s \in S$ is equally likely: $\Pr\{s\} = 1/36$. Define the random variable X to be the *maximum* of the two values showing on the dice. We have $\Pr\{X = 3\} = 5/36$, since X assigns a value of 3 to 5 of the 36 possible elementary events, namely, $(1, 3), (2, 3), (3, 3),$ $(3, 2),$ and $(3, 1)$.

We often define several random variables on the same sample space. If X and Y are random variables, the function

$$f(x, y) = \Pr\{X = x \text{ and } Y = y\}$$

is the *joint probability density function* of X and Y. For a fixed value y,

$$\Pr\{Y = y\} = \sum_{x} \Pr\{X = x \text{ and } Y = y\} ,$$

and similarly, for a fixed value x,

$$\Pr\{X = x\} = \sum_{y} \Pr\{X = x \text{ and } Y = y\} .$$

Using the definition (C.14) of conditional probability, we have

$$\Pr\{X = x \mid Y = y\} = \frac{\Pr\{X = x \text{ and } Y = y\}}{\Pr\{Y = y\}} .$$

We define two random variables X and Y to be *independent* if for all x and y, the events $X = x$ and $Y = y$ are independent or, equivalently, if for all x and y, we have $\Pr\{X = x \text{ and } Y = y\} = \Pr\{X = x\} \Pr\{Y = y\}$.

Given a set of random variables defined over the same sample space, we can define new random variables as sums, products, or other functions of the original variables.

Expected value of a random variable

The simplest and most useful summary of the distribution of a random variable is the "average" of the values it takes on. The *expected value* (or, synonymously, *expectation* or *mean*) of a discrete random variable X is

$$E[X] = \sum_{x} x \cdot \Pr\{X = x\} , \tag{C.20}$$

which is well defined if the sum is finite or converges absolutely. Sometimes the expectation of X is denoted by μ_X or, when the random variable is apparent from context, simply by μ.

Consider a game in which you flip two fair coins. You earn \$3 for each head but lose \$2 for each tail. The expected value of the random variable X representing

your earnings is

$$
\begin{aligned}
E[X] &= 6 \cdot \Pr\{2 \text{ H's}\} + 1 \cdot \Pr\{1 \text{ H}, 1 \text{ T}\} - 4 \cdot \Pr\{2 \text{ T's}\} \\
&= 6(1/4) + 1(1/2) - 4(1/4) \\
&= 1 .
\end{aligned}
$$

The expectation of the sum of two random variables is the sum of their expectations, that is,

$$
E[X + Y] = E[X] + E[Y] , \tag{C.21}
$$

whenever $E[X]$ and $E[Y]$ are defined. We call this property *linearity of expectation*, and it holds even if X and Y are not independent. It also extends to finite and absolutely convergent summations of expectations. Linearity of expectation is the key property that enables us to perform probabilistic analyses by using indicator random variables (see Section 5.2).

If X is any random variable, any function $g(x)$ defines a new random variable $g(X)$. If the expectation of $g(X)$ is defined, then

$$
E[g(X)] = \sum_x g(x) \cdot \Pr\{X = x\} .
$$

Letting $g(x) = ax$, we have for any constant a,

$$
E[aX] = aE[X] . \tag{C.22}
$$

Consequently, expectations are linear: for any two random variables X and Y and any constant a,

$$
E[aX + Y] = aE[X] + E[Y] . \tag{C.23}
$$

When two random variables X and Y are independent and each has a defined expectation,

$$
\begin{aligned}
E[XY] &= \sum_x \sum_y xy \cdot \Pr\{X = x \text{ and } Y = y\} \\
&= \sum_x \sum_y xy \cdot \Pr\{X = x\}\Pr\{Y = y\} \\
&= \left(\sum_x x \cdot \Pr\{X = x\}\right) \left(\sum_y y \cdot \Pr\{Y = y\}\right) \\
&= E[X]E[Y] .
\end{aligned}
$$

In general, when n random variables $X_1, X_2, \ldots, X_n$ are mutually independent,

$$
E[X_1 X_2 \cdots X_n] = E[X_1]E[X_2] \cdots E[X_n] . \tag{C.24}
$$

When a random variable X takes on values from the set of natural numbers $\mathbb{N} = \{0, 1, 2, \ldots\}$, we have a nice formula for its expectation:

$$
\begin{aligned}
E[X] &= \sum_{i=0}^{\infty} i \cdot \Pr\{X = i\} \\
&= \sum_{i=0}^{\infty} i (\Pr\{X \geq i\} - \Pr\{X \geq i + 1\}) \\
&= \sum_{i=1}^{\infty} \Pr\{X \geq i\} ,
\end{aligned}
\tag{C.25}
$$

since each term $\Pr\{X \geq i\}$ is added in i times and subtracted out $i - 1$ times (except $\Pr\{X \geq 0\}$, which is added in 0 times and not subtracted out at all).

When we apply a convex function $f(x)$ to a random variable X, *Jensen's inequality* gives us

$$
E[f(X)] \geq f(E[X]) ,
\tag{C.26}
$$

provided that the expectations exist and are finite. (A function $f(x)$ is *convex* if for all x and y and for all $0 \leq \lambda \leq 1$, we have $f(\lambda x + (1 - \lambda) y) \leq \lambda f(x) + (1 - \lambda) f(y)$.)

Variance and standard deviation

The expected value of a random variable does not tell us how "spread out" the variable's values are. For example, if we have random variables X and Y for which $\Pr\{X = 1/4\} = \Pr\{X = 3/4\} = 1/2$ and $\Pr\{Y = 0\} = \Pr\{Y = 1\} = 1/2$, then both $E[X]$ and $E[Y]$ are $1/2$, yet the actual values taken on by Y are farther from the mean than the actual values taken on by X.

The notion of variance mathematically expresses how far from the mean a random variable's values are likely to be. The *variance* of a random variable X with mean $E[X]$ is

$$
\begin{aligned}
\text{Var}[X] &= E\left[(X - E[X])^2\right] \\
&= E\left[X^2 - 2X E[X] + E^2[X]\right] \\
&= E\left[X^2\right] - 2E[X E[X]] + E^2[X] \\
&= E\left[X^2\right] - 2E^2[X] + E^2[X] \\
&= E\left[X^2\right] - E^2[X] .
\end{aligned}
\tag{C.27}
$$

To justify the equality $E[E^2[X]] = E^2[X]$, note that because $E[X]$ is a real number and not a random variable, so is $E^2[X]$. The equality $E[X E[X]] = E^2[X]$

follows from equation (C.22), with $a = \mathrm{E}[X]$. Rewriting equation (C.27) yields an expression for the expectation of the square of a random variable:

$$\mathrm{E}\left[X^2\right] = \mathrm{Var}[X] + \mathrm{E}^2[X] \ . \tag{C.28}$$

The variance of a random variable X and the variance of aX are related (see Exercise C.3-10):

$$\mathrm{Var}[aX] = a^2\mathrm{Var}[X] \ .$$

When X and Y are independent random variables,

$$\mathrm{Var}[X + Y] = \mathrm{Var}[X] + \mathrm{Var}[Y] \ .$$

In general, if n random variables $X_1, X_2, \ldots, X_n$ are pairwise independent, then

$$\mathrm{Var}\left[\sum_{i=1}^{n} X_i\right] = \sum_{i=1}^{n} \mathrm{Var}[X_i] \ . \tag{C.29}$$

The **standard deviation** of a random variable X is the nonnegative square root of the variance of X. The standard deviation of a random variable X is sometimes denoted σ_X or simply σ when the random variable X is understood from context. With this notation, the variance of X is denoted σ^2.

Exercises

C.3-1
Suppose we roll two ordinary, 6-sided dice. What is the expectation of the sum of the two values showing? What is the expectation of the maximum of the two values showing?

C.3-2
An array $A[1 .. n]$ contains n distinct numbers that are randomly ordered, with each permutation of the n numbers being equally likely. What is the expectation of the index of the maximum element in the array? What is the expectation of the index of the minimum element in the array?

C.3-3
A carnival game consists of three dice in a cage. A player can bet a dollar on any of the numbers 1 through 6. The cage is shaken, and the payoff is as follows. If the player's number doesn't appear on any of the dice, he loses his dollar. Otherwise, if his number appears on exactly k of the three dice, for $k = 1, 2, 3$, he keeps his dollar and wins k more dollars. What is his expected gain from playing the carnival game once?

C.3-4
Argue that if X and Y are nonnegative random variables, then

$$\mathrm{E}\left[\max(X, Y)\right] \leq \mathrm{E}\left[X\right] + \mathrm{E}\left[Y\right] .$$

C.3-5 ⋆
Let X and Y be independent random variables. Prove that $f(X)$ and $g(Y)$ are independent for any choice of functions f and g.

C.3-6 ⋆
Let X be a nonnegative random variable, and suppose that $\mathrm{E}\left[X\right]$ is well defined. Prove ***Markov's inequality***:

$$\Pr\{X \geq t\} \leq \mathrm{E}\left[X\right]/t \tag{C.30}$$

for all $t > 0$.

C.3-7 ⋆
Let S be a sample space, and let X and X' be random variables such that $X(s) \geq X'(s)$ for all $s \in S$. Prove that for any real constant t,

$$\Pr\{X \geq t\} \geq \Pr\{X' \geq t\} .$$

C.3-8
Which is larger: the expectation of the square of a random variable, or the square of its expectation?

C.3-9
Show that for any random variable X that takes on only the values 0 and 1, we have $\mathrm{Var}\left[X\right] = \mathrm{E}\left[X\right]\mathrm{E}\left[1 - X\right]$.

C.3-10
Prove that $\mathrm{Var}\left[aX\right] = a^2\mathrm{Var}\left[X\right]$ from the definition (C.27) of variance.

C.4 The geometric and binomial distributions

We can think of a coin flip as an instance of a ***Bernoulli trial***, which is an experiment with only two possible outcomes: ***success***, which occurs with probability p, and ***failure***, which occurs with probability $q = 1 - p$. When we speak of ***Bernoulli trials*** collectively, we mean that the trials are mutually independent and, unless we specifically say otherwise, that each has the same probability p for success. Two

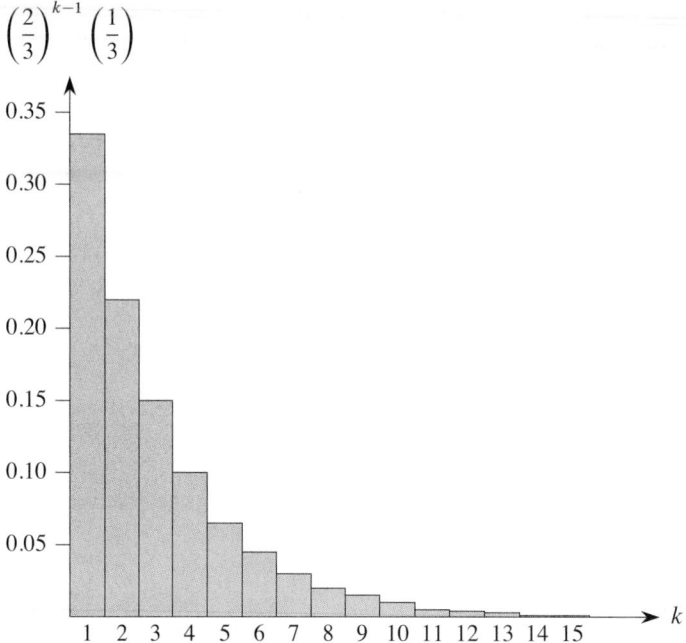

$$\left(\frac{2}{3}\right)^{k-1}\left(\frac{1}{3}\right)$$

Figure C.1   A geometric distribution with probability $p = 1/3$ of success and a probability $q = 1 - p$ of failure. The expectation of the distribution is $1/p = 3$.

important distributions arise from Bernoulli trials: the geometric distribution and the binomial distribution.

The geometric distribution

Suppose we have a sequence of Bernoulli trials, each with a probability p of success and a probability $q = 1 - p$ of failure. How many trials occur before we obtain a success? Let us define the random variable X be the number of trials needed to obtain a success. Then X has values in the range $\{1, 2, \ldots\}$, and for $k \geq 1$,

$$\Pr\{X = k\} = q^{k-1}p \,, \tag{C.31}$$

since we have $k - 1$ failures before the one success. A probability distribution satisfying equation (C.31) is said to be a ***geometric distribution***. Figure C.1 illustrates such a distribution.

Assuming that $q < 1$, we can calculate the expectation of a geometric distribution using identity (A.8):

$$
\begin{aligned}
\mathrm{E}[X] &= \sum_{k=1}^{\infty} k q^{k-1} p \\
&= \frac{p}{q} \sum_{k=0}^{\infty} k q^k \\
&= \frac{p}{q} \cdot \frac{q}{(1-q)^2} \\
&= \frac{p}{q} \cdot \frac{q}{p^2} \\
&= 1/p .
\end{aligned}
\tag{C.32}
$$

Thus, on average, it takes $1/p$ trials before we obtain a success, an intuitive result. The variance, which can be calculated similarly, but using Exercise A.1-3, is

$$
\mathrm{Var}[X] = q/p^2 .
\tag{C.33}
$$

As an example, suppose we repeatedly roll two dice until we obtain either a seven or an eleven. Of the 36 possible outcomes, 6 yield a seven and 2 yield an eleven. Thus, the probability of success is $p = 8/36 = 2/9$, and we must roll $1/p = 9/2 = 4.5$ times on average to obtain a seven or eleven.

The binomial distribution

How many successes occur during n Bernoulli trials, where a success occurs with probability p and a failure with probability $q = 1 - p$? Define the random variable X to be the number of successes in n trials. Then X has values in the range $\{0, 1, \ldots, n\}$, and for $k = 0, 1, \ldots, n$,

$$
\Pr\{X = k\} = \binom{n}{k} p^k q^{n-k} ,
\tag{C.34}
$$

since there are $\binom{n}{k}$ ways to pick which k of the n trials are successes, and the probability that each occurs is $p^k q^{n-k}$. A probability distribution satisfying equation (C.34) is said to be a ***binomial distribution***. For convenience, we define the family of binomial distributions using the notation

$$
b(k; n, p) = \binom{n}{k} p^k (1 - p)^{n-k} .
\tag{C.35}
$$

Figure C.2 illustrates a binomial distribution. The name "binomial" comes from the right-hand side of equation (C.34) being the kth term of the expansion of $(p + q)^n$. Consequently, since $p + q = 1$,

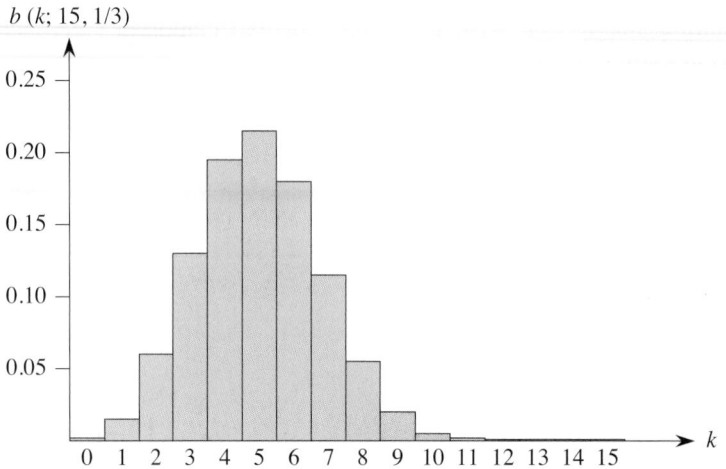

$b\,(k;\,15,\,1/3)$

Figure C.2   The binomial distribution $b(k; 15, 1/3)$ resulting from $n = 15$ Bernoulli trials, each with probability $p = 1/3$ of success. The expectation of the distribution is $np = 5$.

$$\sum_{k=0}^{n} b(k; n, p) = 1 \,, \tag{C.36}$$

as axiom 2 of the probability axioms requires.

   We can compute the expectation of a random variable having a binomial distribution from equations (C.8) and (C.36). Let X be a random variable that follows the binomial distribution $b(k; n, p)$, and let $q = 1 - p$. By the definition of expectation, we have

$$
\begin{aligned}
\mathrm{E}\,[X] &= \sum_{k=0}^{n} k \cdot \Pr\{X = k\} \\
&= \sum_{k=0}^{n} k \cdot b(k; n, p) \\
&= \sum_{k=1}^{n} k \binom{n}{k} p^{k} q^{n-k} \\
&= np \sum_{k=1}^{n} \binom{n-1}{k-1} p^{k-1} q^{n-k} \qquad \text{(by equation (C.8))} \\
&= np \sum_{k=0}^{n-1} \binom{n-1}{k} p^{k} q^{(n-1)-k}
\end{aligned}
$$

$$= np \sum_{k=0}^{n-1} b(k; n-1, p)$$

$$= np \qquad \qquad \text{(by equation (C.36))} \ . \qquad \qquad (C.37)$$

By using the linearity of expectation, we can obtain the same result with substantially less algebra. Let X_i be the random variable describing the number of successes in the ith trial. Then $E[X_i] = p \cdot 1 + q \cdot 0 = p$, and by linearity of expectation (equation (C.21)), the expected number of successes for n trials is

$$E[X] = E\left[\sum_{i=1}^{n} X_i\right]$$

$$= \sum_{i=1}^{n} E[X_i]$$

$$= \sum_{i=1}^{n} p$$

$$= np \ . \qquad \qquad (C.38)$$

We can use the same approach to calculate the variance of the distribution. Using equation (C.27), we have $\text{Var}[X_i] = E[X_i^2] - E^2[X_i]$. Since X_i only takes on the values 0 and 1, we have $X_i^2 = X_i$, which implies $E[X_i^2] = E[X_i] = p$. Hence,

$$\text{Var}[X_i] = p - p^2 = p(1-p) = pq \ . \qquad \qquad (C.39)$$

To compute the variance of X, we take advantage of the independence of the n trials; thus, by equation (C.29),

$$\text{Var}[X] = \text{Var}\left[\sum_{i=1}^{n} X_i\right]$$

$$= \sum_{i=1}^{n} \text{Var}[X_i]$$

$$= \sum_{i=1}^{n} pq$$

$$= npq \ . \qquad \qquad (C.40)$$

As Figure C.2 shows, the binomial distribution $b(k; n, p)$ increases with k until it reaches the mean np, and then it decreases. We can prove that the distribution always behaves in this manner by looking at the ratio of successive terms:

$$\frac{b(k;n,p)}{b(k-1;n,p)} = \frac{\binom{n}{k}p^k q^{n-k}}{\binom{n}{k-1}p^{k-1}q^{n-k+1}}$$

$$= \frac{n!(k-1)!(n-k+1)!p}{k!(n-k)!n!q}$$

$$= \frac{(n-k+1)p}{kq} \tag{C.41}$$

$$= 1 + \frac{(n+1)p-k}{kq} .$$

This ratio is greater than 1 precisely when $(n+1)p-k$ is positive. Consequently, $b(k;n,p) > b(k-1;n,p)$ for $k < (n+1)p$ (the distribution increases), and $b(k;n,p) < b(k-1;n,p)$ for $k > (n+1)p$ (the distribution decreases). If $k = (n+1)p$ is an integer, then $b(k;n,p) = b(k-1;n,p)$, and so the distribution then has two maxima: at $k = (n+1)p$ and at $k-1 = (n+1)p-1 = np-q$. Otherwise, it attains a maximum at the unique integer k that lies in the range $np-q < k < (n+1)p$.

The following lemma provides an upper bound on the binomial distribution.

Lemma C.1
Let $n \geq 0$, let $0 < p < 1$, let $q = 1 - p$, and let $0 \leq k \leq n$. Then

$$b(k;n,p) \leq \left(\frac{np}{k}\right)^k \left(\frac{nq}{n-k}\right)^{n-k} .$$

Proof   Using equation (C.6), we have

$$b(k;n,p) = \binom{n}{k}p^k q^{n-k}$$

$$\leq \left(\frac{n}{k}\right)^k \left(\frac{n}{n-k}\right)^{n-k} p^k q^{n-k}$$

$$= \left(\frac{np}{k}\right)^k \left(\frac{nq}{n-k}\right)^{n-k} . \qquad \blacksquare$$

Exercises

C.4-1
Verify axiom 2 of the probability axioms for the geometric distribution.

C.4-2
How many times on average must we flip 6 fair coins before we obtain 3 heads and 3 tails?

C.4-3
Show that $b(k;n,p) = b(n-k;n,q)$, where $q = 1 - p$.

C.4-4
Show that value of the maximum of the binomial distribution $b(k;n,p)$ is approximately $1/\sqrt{2\pi npq}$, where $q = 1 - p$.

C.4-5 ★
Show that the probability of no successes in n Bernoulli trials, each with probability $p = 1/n$, is approximately $1/e$. Show that the probability of exactly one success is also approximately $1/e$.

C.4-6 ★
Professor Rosencrantz flips a fair coin n times, and so does Professor Guildenstern. Show that the probability that they get the same number of heads is $\binom{2n}{n}/4^n$. (*Hint:* For Professor Rosencrantz, call a head a success; for Professor Guildenstern, call a tail a success.) Use your argument to verify the identity

$$\sum_{k=0}^{n}\binom{n}{k}^2 = \binom{2n}{n}.$$

C.4-7 ★
Show that for $0 \le k \le n$,

$$b(k;n,1/2) \le 2^{n\,H(k/n)-n},$$

where $H(x)$ is the entropy function (C.7).

C.4-8 ★
Consider n Bernoulli trials, where for $i = 1, 2, \ldots, n$, the ith trial has probability p_i of success, and let X be the random variable denoting the total number of successes. Let $p \ge p_i$ for all $i = 1, 2, \ldots, n$. Prove that for $1 \le k \le n$,

$$\Pr\{X < k\} \ge \sum_{i=0}^{k-1} b(i;n,p).$$

C.4-9 ★
Let X be the random variable for the total number of successes in a set A of n Bernoulli trials, where the ith trial has a probability p_i of success, and let X' be the random variable for the total number of successes in a second set A' of n Bernoulli trials, where the ith trial has a probability $p'_i \ge p_i$ of success. Prove that for $0 \le k \le n$,

$$\Pr\{X' \geq k\} \geq \Pr\{X \geq k\} \ .$$

(*Hint:* Show how to obtain the Bernoulli trials in A' by an experiment involving the trials of A, and use the result of Exercise C.3-7.)

★ C.5   The tails of the binomial distribution

The probability of having at least, or at most, k successes in n Bernoulli trials, each with probability p of success, is often of more interest than the probability of having exactly k successes. In this section, we investigate the **tails** of the binomial distribution: the two regions of the distribution $b(k; n, p)$ that are far from the mean np. We shall prove several important bounds on (the sum of all terms in) a tail.

We first provide a bound on the right tail of the distribution $b(k; n, p)$. We can determine bounds on the left tail by inverting the roles of successes and failures.

Theorem C.2
Consider a sequence of n Bernoulli trials, where success occurs with probability p. Let X be the random variable denoting the total number of successes. Then for $0 \leq k \leq n$, the probability of at least k successes is

$$\Pr\{X \geq k\} = \sum_{i=k}^{n} b(i; n, p)$$

$$\leq \binom{n}{k} p^k \ .$$

Proof   For $S \subseteq \{1, 2, \ldots, n\}$, we let A_S denote the event that the ith trial is a success for every $i \in S$. Clearly $\Pr\{A_S\} = p^k$ if $|S| = k$. We have

$$\Pr\{X \geq k\} = \Pr\{\text{there exists } S \subseteq \{1, 2, \ldots, n\} : |S| = k \text{ and } A_S\}$$

$$= \Pr\left\{ \bigcup_{S \subseteq \{1,2,\ldots,n\}:|S|=k} A_S \right\}$$

$$\leq \sum_{S \subseteq \{1,2,\ldots,n\}:|S|=k} \Pr\{A_S\} \qquad \text{(by inequality (C.19))}$$

$$= \binom{n}{k} p^k \ . \qquad \blacksquare$$

The following corollary restates the theorem for the left tail of the binomial distribution. In general, we shall leave it to you to adapt the proofs from one tail to the other.

Corollary C.3

Consider a sequence of n Bernoulli trials, where success occurs with probability p. If X is the random variable denoting the total number of successes, then for $0 \leq k \leq n$, the probability of at most k successes is

$$
\begin{aligned}
\Pr\{X \leq k\} &= \sum_{i=0}^{k} b(i; n, p) \\
&\leq \binom{n}{n-k}(1-p)^{n-k} \\
&= \binom{n}{k}(1-p)^{n-k} .
\end{aligned}
$$

■

Our next bound concerns the left tail of the binomial distribution. Its corollary shows that, far from the mean, the left tail diminishes exponentially.

Theorem C.4

Consider a sequence of n Bernoulli trials, where success occurs with probability p and failure with probability $q = 1 - p$. Let X be the random variable denoting the total number of successes. Then for $0 < k < np$, the probability of fewer than k successes is

$$
\begin{aligned}
\Pr\{X < k\} &= \sum_{i=0}^{k-1} b(i; n, p) \\
&< \frac{kq}{np - k} b(k; n, p) .
\end{aligned}
$$

Proof   We bound the series $\sum_{i=0}^{k-1} b(i; n, p)$ by a geometric series using the technique from Section A.2, page 1151. For $i = 1, 2, \ldots, k$, we have from equation (C.41),

$$
\begin{aligned}
\frac{b(i-1; n, p)}{b(i; n, p)} &= \frac{iq}{(n-i+1)p} \\
&< \frac{iq}{(n-i)p} \\
&\leq \frac{kq}{(n-k)p} .
\end{aligned}
$$

If we let

$$x = \frac{kq}{(n-k)p}$$

$$< \frac{kq}{(n-np)p}$$

$$= \frac{kq}{nqp}$$

$$= \frac{k}{np}$$

$$< 1,$$

it follows that

$$b(i-1;n,p) < x\, b(i;n,p)$$

for $0 < i \le k$. Iteratively applying this inequality $k-i$ times, we obtain

$$b(i;n,p) < x^{k-i}\, b(k;n,p)$$

for $0 \le i < k$, and hence

$$\sum_{i=0}^{k-1} b(i;n,p) \;<\; \sum_{i=0}^{k-1} x^{k-i} b(k;n,p)$$

$$< \; b(k;n,p) \sum_{i=1}^{\infty} x^i$$

$$= \; \frac{x}{1-x} b(k;n,p)$$

$$= \; \frac{kq}{np-k} b(k;n,p) \,. \qquad \blacksquare$$

Corollary C.5

Consider a sequence of n Bernoulli trials, where success occurs with probability p and failure with probability $q = 1-p$. Then for $0 < k \le np/2$, the probability of fewer than k successes is less than one half of the probability of fewer than $k+1$ successes.

Proof   Because $k \le np/2$, we have

$$\frac{kq}{np-k} \;\le\; \frac{(np/2)q}{np-(np/2)}$$

$$
\begin{aligned}
&= \frac{(np/2)q}{np/2} \\
&\leq 1,
\end{aligned}
\tag{C.42}
$$

since $q \leq 1$. Letting X be the random variable denoting the number of successes, Theorem C.4 and inequality (C.42) imply that the probability of fewer than k successes is

$$
\Pr\{X < k\} = \sum_{i=0}^{k-1} b(i;n,p) < b(k;n,p) .
$$

Thus we have

$$
\begin{aligned}
\frac{\Pr\{X < k\}}{\Pr\{X < k+1\}}
&= \frac{\sum_{i=0}^{k-1} b(i;n,p)}{\sum_{i=0}^{k} b(i;n,p)} \\
&= \frac{\sum_{i=0}^{k-1} b(i;n,p)}{\sum_{i=0}^{k-1} b(i;n,p) + b(k;n,p)} \\
&< 1/2 ,
\end{aligned}
$$

since $\sum_{i=0}^{k-1} b(i;n,p) < b(k;n,p)$. ∎

Bounds on the right tail follow similarly. Exercise C.5-2 asks you to prove them.

Corollary C.6
Consider a sequence of n Bernoulli trials, where success occurs with probability p. Let X be the random variable denoting the total number of successes. Then for $np < k < n$, the probability of more than k successes is

$$
\begin{aligned}
\Pr\{X > k\} &= \sum_{i=k+1}^{n} b(i;n,p) \\
&< \frac{(n-k)p}{k - np} b(k;n,p) .
\end{aligned}
$$
∎

Corollary C.7
Consider a sequence of n Bernoulli trials, where success occurs with probability p and failure with probability $q = 1 - p$. Then for $(np + n)/2 < k < n$, the probability of more than k successes is less than one half of the probability of more than $k - 1$ successes. ∎

The next theorem considers n Bernoulli trials, each with a probability p_i of success, for $i = 1, 2, \ldots, n$. As the subsequent corollary shows, we can use the

theorem to provide a bound on the right tail of the binomial distribution by setting $p_i = p$ for each trial.

Theorem C.8

Consider a sequence of n Bernoulli trials, where in the ith trial, for $i = 1, 2, \ldots, n$, success occurs with probability p_i and failure occurs with probability $q_i = 1 - p_i$. Let X be the random variable describing the total number of successes, and let $\mu = \mathrm{E}[X]$. Then for $r > \mu$,

$$\Pr\{X - \mu \geq r\} \leq \left(\frac{\mu e}{r}\right)^r .$$

Proof   Since for any $\alpha > 0$, the function $e^{\alpha x}$ is strictly increasing in x,

$$\Pr\{X - \mu \geq r\} = \Pr\{e^{\alpha(X-\mu)} \geq e^{\alpha r}\} , \tag{C.43}$$

where we will determine α later. Using Markov's inequality (C.30), we obtain

$$\Pr\{e^{\alpha(X-\mu)} \geq e^{\alpha r}\} \leq \mathrm{E}\left[e^{\alpha(X-\mu)}\right] e^{-\alpha r} . \tag{C.44}$$

The bulk of the proof consists of bounding $\mathrm{E}\left[e^{\alpha(X-\mu)}\right]$ and substituting a suitable value for α in inequality (C.44). First, we evaluate $\mathrm{E}\left[e^{\alpha(X-\mu)}\right]$. Using the technique of indicator random variables (see Section 5.2), let $X_i = \mathrm{I}\{$the ith Bernoulli trial is a success$\}$ for $i = 1, 2, \ldots, n$; that is, X_i is the random variable that is 1 if the ith Bernoulli trial is a success and 0 if it is a failure. Thus,

$$X = \sum_{i=1}^{n} X_i ,$$

and by linearity of expectation,

$$\mu = \mathrm{E}[X] = \mathrm{E}\left[\sum_{i=1}^{n} X_i\right] = \sum_{i=1}^{n} \mathrm{E}[X_i] = \sum_{i=1}^{n} p_i ,$$

which implies

$$X - \mu = \sum_{i=1}^{n} (X_i - p_i) .$$

To evaluate $\mathrm{E}\left[e^{\alpha(X-\mu)}\right]$, we substitute for $X - \mu$, obtaining

$$\begin{aligned}
\mathrm{E}\left[e^{\alpha(X-\mu)}\right] &= \mathrm{E}\left[e^{\alpha \sum_{i=1}^{n}(X_i - p_i)}\right] \\
&= \mathrm{E}\left[\prod_{i=1}^{n} e^{\alpha(X_i - p_i)}\right] \\
&= \prod_{i=1}^{n} \mathrm{E}\left[e^{\alpha(X_i - p_i)}\right] ,
\end{aligned}$$

which follows from (C.24), since the mutual independence of the random variables X_i implies the mutual independence of the random variables $e^{\alpha(X_i - p_i)}$ (see Exercise C.3-5). By the definition of expectation,

$$
\begin{aligned}
\mathrm{E}\left[e^{\alpha(X_i - p_i)}\right] &= e^{\alpha(1-p_i)}p_i + e^{\alpha(0-p_i)}q_i \\
&= p_i e^{\alpha q_i} + q_i e^{-\alpha p_i} \\
&\leq p_i e^{\alpha} + 1 \\
&\leq \exp(p_i e^{\alpha}),
\end{aligned}
\tag{C.45}
$$

where $\exp(x)$ denotes the exponential function: $\exp(x) = e^x$. (Inequality (C.45) follows from the inequalities $\alpha > 0$, $q_i \leq 1$, $e^{\alpha q_i} \leq e^{\alpha}$, and $e^{-\alpha p_i} \leq 1$, and the last line follows from inequality (3.12).) Consequently,

$$
\begin{aligned}
\mathrm{E}\left[e^{\alpha(X - \mu)}\right] &= \prod_{i=1}^{n} \mathrm{E}\left[e^{\alpha(X_i - p_i)}\right] \\
&\leq \prod_{i=1}^{n} \exp(p_i e^{\alpha}) \\
&= \exp\left(\sum_{i=1}^{n} p_i e^{\alpha}\right) \\
&= \exp(\mu e^{\alpha}),
\end{aligned}
\tag{C.46}
$$

since $\mu = \sum_{i=1}^{n} p_i$. Therefore, from equation (C.43) and inequalities (C.44) and (C.46), it follows that

$$
\Pr\{X - \mu \geq r\} \leq \exp(\mu e^{\alpha} - \alpha r).
\tag{C.47}
$$

Choosing $\alpha = \ln(r/\mu)$ (see Exercise C.5-7), we obtain

$$
\begin{aligned}
\Pr\{X - \mu \geq r\} &\leq \exp(\mu e^{\ln(r/\mu)} - r\ln(r/\mu)) \\
&= \exp(r - r\ln(r/\mu)) \\
&= \frac{e^r}{(r/\mu)^r} \\
&= \left(\frac{\mu e}{r}\right)^r.
\end{aligned}
$$
$\blacksquare$

When applied to Bernoulli trials in which each trial has the same probability of success, Theorem C.8 yields the following corollary bounding the right tail of a binomial distribution.

Corollary C.9

Consider a sequence of n Bernoulli trials, where in each trial success occurs with probability p and failure occurs with probability $q = 1 - p$. Then for $r > np$,

$$
\begin{aligned}
\Pr\{X - np \geq r\} &= \sum_{k=\lceil np+r \rceil}^{n} b(k;n,p) \\
&\leq \left(\frac{npe}{r}\right)^r .
\end{aligned}
$$

Proof   By equation (C.37), we have $\mu = \mathrm{E}[X] = np$.   ■

Exercises

C.5-1   ★
Which is less likely: obtaining no heads when you flip a fair coin n times, or obtaining fewer than n heads when you flip the coin $4n$ times?

C.5-2   ★
Prove Corollaries C.6 and C.7.

C.5-3   ★
Show that

$$
\sum_{i=0}^{k-1} \binom{n}{i} a^i < (a+1)^n \frac{k}{na - k(a+1)} b(k;n,a/(a+1))
$$

for all $a > 0$ and all k such that $0 < k < na/(a+1)$.

C.5-4   ★
Prove that if $0 < k < np$, where $0 < p < 1$ and $q = 1 - p$, then

$$
\sum_{i=0}^{k-1} p^i q^{n-i} < \frac{kq}{np-k} \left(\frac{np}{k}\right)^k \left(\frac{nq}{n-k}\right)^{n-k} .
$$

C.5-5   ★
Use Theorem C.8 to show that

$$
\Pr\{\mu - X \geq r\} \leq \left(\frac{(n-\mu)e}{r}\right)^r
$$

for $r > n - \mu$. Similarly, use Corollary C.9 to show that

$$
\Pr\{np - X \geq r\} \leq \left(\frac{nqe}{r}\right)^r
$$

for $r > n - np$.

C.5-6 ★

Consider a sequence of n Bernoulli trials, where in the ith trial, for $i = 1, 2, \ldots, n$, success occurs with probability p_i and failure occurs with probability $q_i = 1 - p_i$. Let X be the random variable describing the total number of successes, and let $\mu = \mathrm{E}[X]$. Show that for $r \geq 0$,

$$\Pr\{X - \mu \geq r\} \leq e^{-r^2/2n} .$$

(*Hint:* Prove that $p_i e^{\alpha q_i} + q_i e^{-\alpha p_i} \leq e^{\alpha^2/2}$. Then follow the outline of the proof of Theorem C.8, using this inequality in place of inequality (C.45).)

C.5-7 ★

Show that choosing $\alpha = \ln(r/\mu)$ minimizes the right-hand side of inequality (C.47).

Problems

C-1   Balls and bins

In this problem, we investigate the effect of various assumptions on the number of ways of placing n balls into b distinct bins.

a. Suppose that the n balls are distinct and that their order within a bin does not matter. Argue that the number of ways of placing the balls in the bins is b^n.

b. Suppose that the balls are distinct and that the balls in each bin are ordered. Prove that there are exactly $(b + n - 1)!/(b - 1)!$ ways to place the balls in the bins. (*Hint:* Consider the number of ways of arranging n distinct balls and $b - 1$ indistinguishable sticks in a row.)

c. Suppose that the balls are identical, and hence their order within a bin does not matter. Show that the number of ways of placing the balls in the bins is $\binom{b+n-1}{n}$. (*Hint:* Of the arrangements in part (b), how many are repeated if the balls are made identical?)

d. Suppose that the balls are identical and that no bin may contain more than one ball, so that $n \leq b$. Show that the number of ways of placing the balls is $\binom{b}{n}$.

e. Suppose that the balls are identical and that no bin may be left empty. Assuming that $n \geq b$, show that the number of ways of placing the balls is $\binom{n-1}{b-1}$.

Appendix notes

The first general methods for solving probability problems were discussed in a famous correspondence between B. Pascal and P. de Fermat, which began in 1654, and in a book by C. Huygens in 1657. Rigorous probability theory began with the work of J. Bernoulli in 1713 and A. De Moivre in 1730. Further developments of the theory were provided by P.-S. Laplace, S.-D. Poisson, and C. F. Gauss.

Sums of random variables were originally studied by P. L. Chebyshev and A. A. Markov. A. N. Kolmogorov axiomatized probability theory in 1933. Chernoff [66] and Hoeffding [173] provided bounds on the tails of distributions. Seminal work in random combinatorial structures was done by P. Erdős.

Knuth [209] and Liu [237] are good references for elementary combinatorics and counting. Standard textbooks such as Billingsley [46], Chung [67], Drake [95], Feller [104], and Rozanov [300] offer comprehensive introductions to probability.

D   Matrices

Matrices arise in numerous applications, including, but by no means limited to, scientific computing. If you have seen matrices before, much of the material in this appendix will be familiar to you, but some of it might be new. Section D.1 covers basic matrix definitions and operations, and Section D.2 presents some basic matrix properties.

D.1   Matrices and matrix operations

In this section, we review some basic concepts of matrix theory and some fundamental properties of matrices.

Matrices and vectors

A *matrix* is a rectangular array of numbers. For example,

$$
\begin{aligned}
A &= \begin{pmatrix} a_{11} & a_{12} & a_{13} \\ a_{21} & a_{22} & a_{23} \end{pmatrix} \\
&= \begin{pmatrix} 1 & 2 & 3 \\ 4 & 5 & 6 \end{pmatrix}
\end{aligned}
\tag{D.1}
$$

is a 2×3 matrix $A = (a_{ij})$, where for $i = 1, 2$ and $j = 1, 2, 3$, we denote the element of the matrix in row i and column j by a_{ij}. We use uppercase letters to denote matrices and corresponding subscripted lowercase letters to denote their elements. We denote the set of all $m \times n$ matrices with real-valued entries by $\mathbb{R}^{m \times n}$ and, in general, the set of $m \times n$ matrices with entries drawn from a set S by $S^{m \times n}$.

The *transpose* of a matrix A is the matrix A^{T} obtained by exchanging the rows and columns of A. For the matrix A of equation (D.1),

$$A^{\mathrm{T}} = \begin{pmatrix} 1 & 4 \\ 2 & 5 \\ 3 & 6 \end{pmatrix}.$$

A *vector* is a one-dimensional array of numbers. For example,

$$x = \begin{pmatrix} 2 \\ 3 \\ 5 \end{pmatrix}$$

is a vector of size 3. We sometimes call a vector of length n an ***n-vector***. We use lowercase letters to denote vectors, and we denote the ith element of a size-n vector x by x_i, for $i = 1, 2, \ldots, n$. We take the standard form of a vector to be as a ***column vector*** equivalent to an $n \times 1$ matrix; the corresponding ***row vector*** is obtained by taking the transpose:

$$x^{\mathrm{T}} = (2 \quad 3 \quad 5).$$

The ***unit vector*** e_i is the vector whose ith element is 1 and all of whose other elements are 0. Usually, the size of a unit vector is clear from the context.

A ***zero matrix*** is a matrix all of whose entries are 0. Such a matrix is often denoted 0, since the ambiguity between the number 0 and a matrix of 0s is usually easily resolved from context. If a matrix of 0s is intended, then the size of the matrix also needs to be derived from the context.

Square matrices

Square $n \times n$ matrices arise frequently. Several special cases of square matrices are of particular interest:

1. A ***diagonal matrix*** has $a_{ij} = 0$ whenever $i \neq j$. Because all of the off-diagonal elements are zero, we can specify the matrix by listing the elements along the diagonal:

$$\mathrm{diag}(a_{11}, a_{22}, \ldots, a_{nn}) = \begin{pmatrix} a_{11} & 0 & \ldots & 0 \\ 0 & a_{22} & \ldots & 0 \\ \vdots & \vdots & \ddots & \vdots \\ 0 & 0 & \ldots & a_{nn} \end{pmatrix}.$$

2. The $n \times n$ ***identity matrix*** I_n is a diagonal matrix with 1s along the diagonal:

$$\begin{aligned} I_n &= \mathrm{diag}(1, 1, \ldots, 1) \\ &= \begin{pmatrix} 1 & 0 & \ldots & 0 \\ 0 & 1 & \ldots & 0 \\ \vdots & \vdots & \ddots & \vdots \\ 0 & 0 & \ldots & 1 \end{pmatrix}. \end{aligned}$$

When I appears without a subscript, we derive its size from the context. The ith column of an identity matrix is the unit vector e_i.

3. A ***tridiagonal matrix*** T is one for which $t_{ij} = 0$ if $|i - j| > 1$. Nonzero entries appear only on the main diagonal, immediately above the main diagonal ($t_{i,i+1}$ for $i = 1, 2, \ldots, n - 1$), or immediately below the main diagonal ($t_{i+1,i}$ for $i = 1, 2, \ldots, n - 1$):

$$T = \begin{pmatrix} t_{11} & t_{12} & 0 & 0 & \cdots & 0 & 0 & 0 \\ t_{21} & t_{22} & t_{23} & 0 & \cdots & 0 & 0 & 0 \\ 0 & t_{32} & t_{33} & t_{34} & \cdots & 0 & 0 & 0 \\ \vdots & \vdots & \vdots & \vdots & \ddots & \vdots & \vdots & \vdots \\ 0 & 0 & 0 & 0 & \cdots & t_{n-2,n-2} & t_{n-2,n-1} & 0 \\ 0 & 0 & 0 & 0 & \cdots & t_{n-1,n-2} & t_{n-1,n-1} & t_{n-1,n} \\ 0 & 0 & 0 & 0 & \cdots & 0 & t_{n,n-1} & t_{nn} \end{pmatrix}.$$

4. An ***upper-triangular matrix*** U is one for which $u_{ij} = 0$ if $i > j$. All entries below the diagonal are zero:

$$U = \begin{pmatrix} u_{11} & u_{12} & \cdots & u_{1n} \\ 0 & u_{22} & \cdots & u_{2n} \\ \vdots & \vdots & \ddots & \vdots \\ 0 & 0 & \cdots & u_{nn} \end{pmatrix}.$$

An upper-triangular matrix is ***unit upper-triangular*** if it has all 1s along the diagonal.

5. A ***lower-triangular matrix*** L is one for which $l_{ij} = 0$ if $i < j$. All entries above the diagonal are zero:

$$L = \begin{pmatrix} l_{11} & 0 & \cdots & 0 \\ l_{21} & l_{22} & \cdots & 0 \\ \vdots & \vdots & \ddots & \vdots \\ l_{n1} & l_{n2} & \cdots & l_{nn} \end{pmatrix}.$$

A lower-triangular matrix is ***unit lower-triangular*** if it has all 1s along the diagonal.

6. A ***permutation matrix*** P has exactly one 1 in each row or column, and 0s elsewhere. An example of a permutation matrix is

$$
P = \begin{pmatrix}
0 & 1 & 0 & 0 & 0 \\
0 & 0 & 0 & 1 & 0 \\
1 & 0 & 0 & 0 & 0 \\
0 & 0 & 0 & 0 & 1 \\
0 & 0 & 1 & 0 & 0
\end{pmatrix} .
$$

Such a matrix is called a permutation matrix because multiplying a vector x by a permutation matrix has the effect of permuting (rearranging) the elements of x. Exercise D.1-4 explores additional properties of permutation matrices.

7. A ***symmetric matrix*** A satisfies the condition $A = A^{\mathrm{T}}$. For example,

$$
\begin{pmatrix}
1 & 2 & 3 \\
2 & 6 & 4 \\
3 & 4 & 5
\end{pmatrix}
$$

is a symmetric matrix.

Basic matrix operations

The elements of a matrix or vector are numbers from a number system, such as the real numbers, the complex numbers, or integers modulo a prime. The number system defines how to add and multiply numbers. We can extend these definitions to encompass addition and multiplication of matrices.

We define ***matrix addition*** as follows. If $A = (a_{ij})$ and $B = (b_{ij})$ are $m \times n$ matrices, then their matrix sum $C = (c_{ij}) = A + B$ is the $m \times n$ matrix defined by

$$
c_{ij} = a_{ij} + b_{ij}
$$

for $i = 1, 2, \ldots, m$ and $j = 1, 2, \ldots, n$. That is, matrix addition is performed componentwise. A zero matrix is the identity for matrix addition:

$$
A + 0 = A = 0 + A .
$$

If λ is a number and $A = (a_{ij})$ is a matrix, then $\lambda A = (\lambda a_{ij})$ is the ***scalar multiple*** of A obtained by multiplying each of its elements by λ. As a special case, we define the ***negative*** of a matrix $A = (a_{ij})$ to be $-1 \cdot A = -A$, so that the ijth entry of $-A$ is $-a_{ij}$. Thus,

$$
A + (-A) = 0 = (-A) + A .
$$

We use the negative of a matrix to define ***matrix subtraction***: $A - B = A + (-B)$.

We define ***matrix multiplication*** as follows. We start with two matrices A and B that are ***compatible*** in the sense that the number of columns of A equals the number of rows of B. (In general, an expression containing a matrix product AB is always assumed to imply that matrices A and B are compatible.) If $A = (a_{ik})$ is an $m \times n$ matrix and $B = (b_{kj})$ is an $n \times p$ matrix, then their matrix product $C = AB$ is the $m \times p$ matrix $C = (c_{ij})$, where

$$c_{ij} = \sum_{k=1}^{n} a_{ik}b_{kj} \tag{D.2}$$

for $i = 1, 2, \ldots, m$ and $j = 1, 2, \ldots, p$. The procedure SQUARE-MATRIX-MULTIPLY in Section 4.2 implements matrix multiplication in the straightforward manner based on equation (D.2), assuming that the matrices are square: $m = n = p$. To multiply $n \times n$ matrices, SQUARE-MATRIX-MULTIPLY performs n^3 multiplications and $n^2(n-1)$ additions, and so its running time is $\Theta(n^3)$.

Matrices have many (but not all) of the algebraic properties typical of numbers. Identity matrices are identities for matrix multiplication:

$$I_m A = A I_n = A$$

for any $m \times n$ matrix A. Multiplying by a zero matrix gives a zero matrix:

$$A 0 = 0 .$$

Matrix multiplication is associative:

$$A(BC) = (AB)C$$

for compatible matrices A, B, and C. Matrix multiplication distributes over addition:

$$
\begin{aligned}
A(B + C) &= AB + AC , \\
(B + C)D &= BD + CD .
\end{aligned}
$$

For $n > 1$, multiplication of $n \times n$ matrices is not commutative. For example, if $A = \begin{pmatrix} 0 & 1 \\ 0 & 0 \end{pmatrix}$ and $B = \begin{pmatrix} 0 & 0 \\ 1 & 0 \end{pmatrix}$, then

$$AB = \begin{pmatrix} 1 & 0 \\ 0 & 0 \end{pmatrix}$$

and

$$BA = \begin{pmatrix} 0 & 0 \\ 0 & 1 \end{pmatrix} .$$

We define matrix-vector products or vector-vector products as if the vector were the equivalent $n \times 1$ matrix (or a $1 \times n$ matrix, in the case of a row vector). Thus, if A is an $m \times n$ matrix and x is an n-vector, then Ax is an m-vector. If x and y are n-vectors, then

$$x^{\mathrm{T}} y = \sum_{i=1}^{n} x_i y_i$$

is a number (actually a 1×1 matrix) called the ***inner product*** of x and y. The matrix xy^{T} is an $n \times n$ matrix Z called the ***outer product*** of x and y, with $z_{ij} = x_i y_j$. The ***(euclidean) norm*** $\|x\|$ of an n-vector x is defined by

$$\begin{aligned}
\|x\| &= (x_1^2 + x_2^2 + \cdots + x_n^2)^{1/2} \\
&= (x^{\mathrm{T}} x)^{1/2}.
\end{aligned}$$

Thus, the norm of x is its length in n-dimensional euclidean space.

Exercises

D.1-1
Show that if A and B are symmetric $n \times n$ matrices, then so are $A + B$ and $A - B$.

D.1-2
Prove that $(AB)^{\mathrm{T}} = B^{\mathrm{T}} A^{\mathrm{T}}$ and that $A^{\mathrm{T}} A$ is always a symmetric matrix.

D.1-3
Prove that the product of two lower-triangular matrices is lower-triangular.

D.1-4
Prove that if P is an $n \times n$ permutation matrix and A is an $n \times n$ matrix, then the matrix product PA is A with its rows permuted, and the matrix product AP is A with its columns permuted. Prove that the product of two permutation matrices is a permutation matrix.

D.2   Basic matrix properties

In this section, we define some basic properties pertaining to matrices: inverses, linear dependence and independence, rank, and determinants. We also define the class of positive-definite matrices.

Matrix inverses, ranks, and determinants

We define the *inverse* of an $n \times n$ matrix A to be the $n \times n$ matrix, denoted A^{-1} (if it exists), such that $AA^{-1} = I_n = A^{-1}A$. For example,

$$\begin{pmatrix} 1 & 1 \\ 1 & 0 \end{pmatrix}^{-1} = \begin{pmatrix} 0 & 1 \\ 1 & -1 \end{pmatrix}.$$

Many nonzero $n \times n$ matrices do not have inverses. A matrix without an inverse is called *noninvertible*, or *singular*. An example of a nonzero singular matrix is

$$\begin{pmatrix} 1 & 0 \\ 1 & 0 \end{pmatrix}.$$

If a matrix has an inverse, it is called *invertible*, or *nonsingular*. Matrix inverses, when they exist, are unique. (See Exercise D.2-1.) If A and B are nonsingular $n \times n$ matrices, then

$$(BA)^{-1} = A^{-1}B^{-1}.$$

The inverse operation commutes with the transpose operation:

$$(A^{-1})^{\mathrm{T}} = (A^{\mathrm{T}})^{-1}.$$

The vectors $x_1, x_2, \ldots, x_n$ are *linearly dependent* if there exist coefficients $c_1, c_2, \ldots, c_n$, not all of which are zero, such that $c_1 x_1 + c_2 x_2 + \cdots + c_n x_n = 0$. The row vectors $x_1 = (1 \quad 2 \quad 3)$, $x_2 = (2 \quad 6 \quad 4)$, and $x_3 = (4 \quad 11 \quad 9)$ are linearly dependent, for example, since $2x_1 + 3x_2 - 2x_3 = 0$. If vectors are not linearly dependent, they are *linearly independent*. For example, the columns of an identity matrix are linearly independent.

The *column rank* of a nonzero $m \times n$ matrix A is the size of the largest set of linearly independent columns of A. Similarly, the *row rank* of A is the size of the largest set of linearly independent rows of A. A fundamental property of any matrix A is that its row rank always equals its column rank, so that we can simply refer to the *rank* of A. The rank of an $m \times n$ matrix is an integer between 0 and $\min(m, n)$, inclusive. (The rank of a zero matrix is 0, and the rank of an $n \times n$ identity matrix is n.) An alternate, but equivalent and often more useful, definition is that the rank of a nonzero $m \times n$ matrix A is the smallest number r such that there exist matrices B and C of respective sizes $m \times r$ and $r \times n$ such that

$$A = BC.$$

A square $n \times n$ matrix has *full rank* if its rank is n. An $m \times n$ matrix has *full column rank* if its rank is n. The following theorem gives a fundamental property of ranks.

Theorem D.1
A square matrix has full rank if and only if it is nonsingular.   ∎

A **null vector** for a matrix A is a nonzero vector x such that $Ax = 0$. The following theorem (whose proof is left as Exercise D.2-7) and its corollary relate the notions of column rank and singularity to null vectors.

Theorem D.2
A matrix A has full column rank if and only if it does not have a null vector.   ∎

Corollary D.3
A square matrix A is singular if and only if it has a null vector.   ∎

The ijth **minor** of an $n \times n$ matrix A, for $n > 1$, is the $(n-1) \times (n-1)$ matrix $A_{[ij]}$ obtained by deleting the ith row and jth column of A. We define the **determinant** of an $n \times n$ matrix A recursively in terms of its minors by

$$\det(A) = \begin{cases} a_{11} & \text{if } n = 1, \\ \displaystyle\sum_{j=1}^{n} (-1)^{1+j} a_{1j} \det(A_{[1j]}) & \text{if } n > 1. \end{cases}$$

The term $(-1)^{i+j} \det(A_{[ij]})$ is known as the **cofactor** of the element a_{ij}.

The following theorems, whose proofs are omitted here, express fundamental properties of the determinant.

Theorem D.4 (Determinant properties)
The determinant of a square matrix A has the following properties:

- If any row or any column of A is zero, then $\det(A) = 0$.

- The determinant of A is multiplied by λ if the entries of any one row (or any one column) of A are all multiplied by λ.

- The determinant of A is unchanged if the entries in one row (respectively, column) are added to those in another row (respectively, column).

- The determinant of A equals the determinant of A^{T}.

- The determinant of A is multiplied by -1 if any two rows (or any two columns) are exchanged.

Also, for any square matrices A and B, we have $\det(AB) = \det(A)\det(B)$.   ∎

Theorem D.5
An $n \times n$ matrix A is singular if and only if $\det(A) = 0$.   ∎

Positive-definite matrices

Positive-definite matrices play an important role in many applications. An $n \times n$ matrix A is ***positive-definite*** if $x^T A x > 0$ for all n-vectors $x \neq 0$. For example, the identity matrix is positive-definite, since for any nonzero vector $x = (\ x_1 \ \ x_2 \ \ \cdots \ \ x_n\ )^T$,

$$x^T I_n x \ = \ x^T x$$
$$= \ \sum_{i=1}^{n} x_i^2$$
$$> \ 0\ .$$

Matrices that arise in applications are often positive-definite due to the following theorem.

Theorem D.6
For any matrix A with full column rank, the matrix $A^T A$ is positive-definite.

Proof   We must show that $x^T (A^T A) x > 0$ for any nonzero vector x. For any vector x,

$$x^T (A^T A) x \ = \ (Ax)^T (Ax) \quad \text{(by Exercise D.1-2)}$$
$$= \ \|Ax\|^2\ .$$

Note that $\|Ax\|^2$ is just the sum of the squares of the elements of the vector Ax. Therefore, $\|Ax\|^2 \geq 0$. If $\|Ax\|^2 = 0$, every element of Ax is 0, which is to say $Ax = 0$. Since A has full column rank, $Ax = 0$ implies $x = 0$, by Theorem D.2. Hence, $A^T A$ is positive-definite.   ∎

Section 28.3 explores other properties of positive-definite matrices.

Exercises

D.2-1
Prove that matrix inverses are unique, that is, if B and C are inverses of A, then $B = C$.

D.2-2
Prove that the determinant of a lower-triangular or upper-triangular matrix is equal to the product of its diagonal elements. Prove that the inverse of a lower-triangular matrix, if it exists, is lower-triangular.

D.2-3

Prove that if P is a permutation matrix, then P is invertible, its inverse is P^{T}, and P^{T} is a permutation matrix.

D.2-4

Let A and B be $n \times n$ matrices such that $AB = I$. Prove that if A' is obtained from A by adding row j into row i, where $i \neq j$, then subtracting column i from column j of B yields the inverse B' of A'.

D.2-5

Let A be a nonsingular $n \times n$ matrix with complex entries. Show that every entry of A^{-1} is real if and only if every entry of A is real.

D.2-6

Show that if A is a nonsingular, symmetric, $n \times n$ matrix, then A^{-1} is symmetric. Show that if B is an arbitrary $m \times n$ matrix, then the $m \times m$ matrix given by the product BAB^{T} is symmetric.

D.2-7

Prove Theorem D.2. That is, show that a matrix A has full column rank if and only if $Ax = 0$ implies $x = 0$. (*Hint:* Express the linear dependence of one column on the others as a matrix-vector equation.)

D.2-8

Prove that for any two compatible matrices A and B,

$$\mathrm{rank}(AB) \leq \min(\mathrm{rank}(A), \mathrm{rank}(B)) \,,$$

where equality holds if either A or B is a nonsingular square matrix. (*Hint:* Use the alternate definition of the rank of a matrix.)

Problems

D-1   *Vandermonde matrix*

Given numbers $x_0, x_1, \ldots, x_{n-1}$, prove that the determinant of the **Vandermonde matrix**

$$V(x_0, x_1, \ldots, x_{n-1}) = \begin{pmatrix} 1 & x_0 & x_0^2 & \cdots & x_0^{n-1} \\ 1 & x_1 & x_1^2 & \cdots & x_1^{n-1} \\ \vdots & \vdots & \vdots & \ddots & \vdots \\ 1 & x_{n-1} & x_{n-1}^2 & \cdots & x_{n-1}^{n-1} \end{pmatrix}$$

is

$$\det(V(x_0, x_1, \ldots, x_{n-1})) = \prod_{0 \le j < k \le n-1} (x_k - x_j) .$$

(*Hint:* Multiply column i by $-x_0$ and add it to column $i + 1$ for $i = n - 1$, $n - 2, \ldots, 1$, and then use induction.)

D-2 Permutations defined by matrix-vector multiplication over $GF(2)$

One class of permutations of the integers in the set $S_n = \{0, 1, 2, \ldots, 2^n - 1\}$ is defined by matrix multiplication over $GF(2)$. For each integer x in S_n, we view its binary representation as an n-bit vector

$$\begin{pmatrix} x_0 \\ x_1 \\ x_2 \\ \vdots \\ x_{n-1} \end{pmatrix},$$

where $x = \sum_{i=0}^{n-1} x_i 2^i$. If A is an $n \times n$ matrix in which each entry is either 0 or 1, then we can define a permutation mapping each value x in S_n to the number whose binary representation is the matrix-vector product Ax. Here, we perform all arithmetic over $GF(2)$: all values are either 0 or 1, and with one exception the usual rules of addition and multiplication apply. The exception is that $1 + 1 = 0$. You can think of arithmetic over $GF(2)$ as being just like regular integer arithmetic, except that you use only the least significant bit.

As an example, for $S_2 = \{0, 1, 2, 3\}$, the matrix

$$A = \begin{pmatrix} 1 & 0 \\ 1 & 1 \end{pmatrix}$$

defines the following permutation π_A: $\pi_A(0) = 0$, $\pi_A(1) = 3$, $\pi_A(2) = 2$, $\pi_A(3) = 1$. To see why $\pi_A(3) = 1$, observe that, working in $GF(2)$,

$$\begin{aligned} \pi_A(3) &= \begin{pmatrix} 1 & 0 \\ 1 & 1 \end{pmatrix} \begin{pmatrix} 1 \\ 1 \end{pmatrix} \\ &= \begin{pmatrix} 1 \cdot 1 + 0 \cdot 1 \\ 1 \cdot 1 + 1 \cdot 1 \end{pmatrix} \\ &= \begin{pmatrix} 1 \\ 0 \end{pmatrix}, \end{aligned}$$

which is the binary representation of 1.

For the remainder of this problem, we work over $GF(2)$, and all matrix and vector entries are 0 or 1. We define the rank of a 0-1 matrix (a matrix for which each entry is either 0 or 1) over $GF(2)$ the same as for a regular matrix, but with all arithmetic that determines linear independence performed over $GF(2)$. We define the **range** of an $n \times n$ 0-1 matrix A by

$$R(A) = \{y : y = Ax \text{ for some } x \in S_n\} \;,$$

so that $R(A)$ is the set of numbers in S_n that we can produce by multiplying each value x in S_n by A.

a. If r is the rank of matrix A, prove that $|R(A)| = 2^r$. Conclude that A defines a permutation on S_n only if A has full rank.

For a given $n \times n$ matrix A and a given value $y \in R(A)$, we define the **preimage** of y by

$$P(A, y) = \{x : Ax = y\} \;,$$

so that $P(A, y)$ is the set of values in S_n that map to y when multiplied by A.

b. If r is the rank of $n \times n$ matrix A and $y \in R(A)$, prove that $|P(A, y)| = 2^{n-r}$.

Let $0 \leq m \leq n$, and suppose we partition the set S_n into blocks of consecutive numbers, where the ith block consists of the 2^m numbers $i2^m, i2^m + 1, i2^m + 2, \ldots, (i + 1)2^m - 1$. For any subset $S \subseteq S_n$, define $B(S, m)$ to be the set of size-2^m blocks of S_n containing some element of S. As an example, when $n = 3, m = 1$, and $S = \{1, 4, 5\}$, then $B(S, m)$ consists of blocks 0 (since 1 is in the 0th block) and 2 (since both 4 and 5 are in block 2).

c. Let r be the rank of the lower left $(n - m) \times m$ submatrix of A, that is, the matrix formed by taking the intersection of the bottom $n - m$ rows and the leftmost m columns of A. Let S be any size-2^m block of S_n, and let $S' = \{y : y = Ax \text{ for some } x \in S\}$. Prove that $|B(S', m)| = 2^r$ and that for each block in $B(S', m)$, exactly 2^{m-r} numbers in S map to that block.

Because multiplying the zero vector by any matrix yields a zero vector, the set of permutations of S_n defined by multiplying by $n \times n$ 0-1 matrices with full rank over $GF(2)$ cannot include all permutations of S_n. Let us extend the class of permutations defined by matrix-vector multiplication to include an additive term, so that $x \in S_n$ maps to $Ax + c$, where c is an n-bit vector and addition is performed over $GF(2)$. For example, when

$$A = \begin{pmatrix} 1 & 0 \\ 1 & 1 \end{pmatrix}$$

and

$$c = \begin{pmatrix} 0 \\ 1 \end{pmatrix},$$

we get the following permutation $\pi_{A,c}$: $\pi_{A,c}(0) = 2$, $\pi_{A,c}(1) = 1$, $\pi_{A,c}(2) = 0$, $\pi_{A,c}(3) = 3$. We call any permutation that maps $x \in S_n$ to $Ax + c$, for some $n \times n$ 0-1 matrix A with full rank and some n-bit vector c, a **linear permutation**.

d. Use a counting argument to show that the number of linear permutations of S_n is much less than the number of permutations of S_n.

e. Give an example of a value of n and a permutation of S_n that cannot be achieved by any linear permutation. (*Hint:* For a given permutation, think about how multiplying a matrix by a unit vector relates to the columns of the matrix.)

Appendix notes

Linear-algebra textbooks provide plenty of background information on matrices. The books by Strang [323, 324] are particularly good.

Bibliography

[1] Milton Abramowitz and Irene A. Stegun, editors. *Handbook of Mathematical Functions*. Dover, 1965.

[2] G. M. Adel'son-Vel'skiĭ and E. M. Landis. An algorithm for the organization of information. *Soviet Mathematics Doklady*, 3(5):1259–1263, 1962.

[3] Alok Aggarwal and Jeffrey Scott Vitter. The input/output complexity of sorting and related problems. *Communications of the ACM*, 31(9):1116–1127, 1988.

[4] Manindra Agrawal, Neeraj Kayal, and Nitin Saxena. PRIMES is in P. *Annals of Mathematics*, 160(2):781–793, 2004.

[5] Alfred V. Aho, John E. Hopcroft, and Jeffrey D. Ullman. *The Design and Analysis of Computer Algorithms*. Addison-Wesley, 1974.

[6] Alfred V. Aho, John E. Hopcroft, and Jeffrey D. Ullman. *Data Structures and Algorithms*. Addison-Wesley, 1983.

[7] Ravindra K. Ahuja, Thomas L. Magnanti, and James B. Orlin. *Network Flows: Theory, Algorithms, and Applications*. Prentice Hall, 1993.

[8] Ravindra K. Ahuja, Kurt Mehlhorn, James B. Orlin, and Robert E. Tarjan. Faster algorithms for the shortest path problem. *Journal of the ACM*, 37(2):213–223, 1990.

[9] Ravindra K. Ahuja and James B. Orlin. A fast and simple algorithm for the maximum flow problem. *Operations Research*, 37(5):748–759, 1989.

[10] Ravindra K. Ahuja, James B. Orlin, and Robert E. Tarjan. Improved time bounds for the maximum flow problem. *SIAM Journal on Computing*, 18(5):939–954, 1989.

[11] Miklós Ajtai, Nimrod Megiddo, and Orli Waarts. Improved algorithms and analysis for secretary problems and generalizations. In *Proceedings of the 36th Annual Symposium on Foundations of Computer Science*, pages 473–482, 1995.

[12] Selim G. Akl. *The Design and Analysis of Parallel Algorithms*. Prentice Hall, 1989.

[13] Mohamad Akra and Louay Bazzi. On the solution of linear recurrence equations. *Computational Optimization and Applications*, 10(2):195–210, 1998.

[14] Noga Alon. Generating pseudo-random permutations and maximum flow algorithms. *Information Processing Letters*, 35:201–204, 1990.

[15] Arne Andersson. Balanced search trees made simple. In *Proceedings of the Third Workshop on Algorithms and Data Structures*, volume 709 of *Lecture Notes in Computer Science*, pages 60–71. Springer, 1993.

[16] Arne Andersson. Faster deterministic sorting and searching in linear space. In *Proceedings of the 37th Annual Symposium on Foundations of Computer Science*, pages 135–141, 1996.

[17] Arne Andersson, Torben Hagerup, Stefan Nilsson, and Rajeev Raman. Sorting in linear time? *Journal of Computer and System Sciences*, 57:74–93, 1998.

[18] Tom M. Apostol. *Calculus*, volume 1. Blaisdell Publishing Company, second edition, 1967.

[19] Nimar S. Arora, Robert D. Blumofe, and C. Greg Plaxton. Thread scheduling for multiprogrammed multiprocessors. In *Proceedings of the 10th Annual ACM Symposium on Parallel Algorithms and Architectures*, pages 119–129, 1998.

[20] Sanjeev Arora. *Probabilistic checking of proofs and the hardness of approximation problems*. PhD thesis, University of California, Berkeley, 1994.

[21] Sanjeev Arora. The approximability of NP-hard problems. In *Proceedings of the 30th Annual ACM Symposium on Theory of Computing*, pages 337–348, 1998.

[22] Sanjeev Arora. Polynomial time approximation schemes for euclidean traveling salesman and other geometric problems. *Journal of the ACM*, 45(5):753–782, 1998.

[23] Sanjeev Arora and Carsten Lund. Hardness of approximations. In Dorit S. Hochbaum, editor, *Approximation Algorithms for NP-Hard Problems*, pages 399–446. PWS Publishing Company, 1997.

[24] Javed A. Aslam. A simple bound on the expected height of a randomly built binary search tree. Technical Report TR2001-387, Dartmouth College Department of Computer Science, 2001.

[25] Mikhail J. Atallah, editor. *Algorithms and Theory of Computation Handbook*. CRC Press, 1999.

[26] G. Ausiello, P. Crescenzi, G. Gambosi, V. Kann, A. Marchetti-Spaccamela, and M. Protasi. *Complexity and Approximation: Combinatorial Optimization Problems and Their Approximability Properties*. Springer, 1999.

[27] Shai Avidan and Ariel Shamir. Seam carving for content-aware image resizing. *ACM Transactions on Graphics*, 26(3), article 10, 2007.

[28] Sara Baase and Allen Van Gelder. *Computer Algorithms: Introduction to Design and Analysis*. Addison-Wesley, third edition, 2000.

[29] Eric Bach. Private communication, 1989.

[30] Eric Bach. Number-theoretic algorithms. In *Annual Review of Computer Science*, volume 4, pages 119–172. Annual Reviews, Inc., 1990.

[31] Eric Bach and Jeffrey Shallit. *Algorithmic Number Theory—Volume I: Efficient Algorithms*. The MIT Press, 1996.

[32] David H. Bailey, King Lee, and Horst D. Simon. Using Strassen's algorithm to accelerate the solution of linear systems. *The Journal of Supercomputing*, 4(4):357–371, 1990.

[33] Surender Baswana, Ramesh Hariharan, and Sandeep Sen. Improved decremental algorithms for maintaining transitive closure and all-pairs shortest paths. *Journal of Algorithms*, 62(2):74–92, 2007.

[34] R. Bayer. Symmetric binary B-trees: Data structure and maintenance algorithms. *Acta Informatica*, 1(4):290–306, 1972.

[35] R. Bayer and E. M. McCreight. Organization and maintenance of large ordered indexes. *Acta Informatica*, 1(3):173–189, 1972.

[36] Pierre Beauchemin, Gilles Brassard, Claude Crépeau, Claude Goutier, and Carl Pomerance. The generation of random numbers that are probably prime. *Journal of Cryptology*, 1(1):53–64, 1988.

[37] Richard Bellman. *Dynamic Programming*. Princeton University Press, 1957.

[38] Richard Bellman. On a routing problem. *Quarterly of Applied Mathematics*, 16(1):87–90, 1958.

[39] Michael Ben-Or. Lower bounds for algebraic computation trees. In *Proceedings of the Fifteenth Annual ACM Symposium on Theory of Computing*, pages 80–86, 1983.

[40] Michael A. Bender, Erik D. Demaine, and Martin Farach-Colton. Cache-oblivious B-trees. In *Proceedings of the 41st Annual Symposium on Foundations of Computer Science*, pages 399–409, 2000.

[41] Samuel W. Bent and John W. John. Finding the median requires $2n$ comparisons. In *Proceedings of the Seventeenth Annual ACM Symposium on Theory of Computing*, pages 213–216, 1985.

[42] Jon L. Bentley. *Writing Efficient Programs*. Prentice Hall, 1982.

[43] Jon L. Bentley. *Programming Pearls*. Addison-Wesley, 1986.

[44] Jon L. Bentley, Dorothea Haken, and James B. Saxe. A general method for solving divide-and-conquer recurrences. *SIGACT News*, 12(3):36–44, 1980.

[45] Daniel Bienstock and Benjamin McClosky. Tightening simplex mixed-integer sets with guaranteed bounds. *Optimization Online*, July 2008.

[46] Patrick Billingsley. *Probability and Measure*. John Wiley & Sons, second edition, 1986.

[47] Guy E. Blelloch. *Scan Primitives and Parallel Vector Models*. PhD thesis, Department of Electrical Engineering and Computer Science, MIT, 1989. Available as MIT Laboratory for Computer Science Technical Report MIT/LCS/TR-463.

[48] Guy E. Blelloch. Programming parallel algorithms. *Communications of the ACM*, 39(3):85–97, 1996.

[49] Guy E. Blelloch, Phillip B. Gibbons, and Yossi Matias. Provably efficient scheduling for languages with fine-grained parallelism. In *Proceedings of the 7th Annual ACM Symposium on Parallel Algorithms and Architectures*, pages 1–12, 1995.

[50] Manuel Blum, Robert W. Floyd, Vaughan Pratt, Ronald L. Rivest, and Robert E. Tarjan. Time bounds for selection. *Journal of Computer and System Sciences*, 7(4):448–461, 1973.

[51] Robert D. Blumofe, Christopher F. Joerg, Bradley C. Kuszmaul, Charles E. Leiserson, Keith H. Randall, and Yuli Zhou. Cilk: An efficient multithreaded runtime system. *Journal of Parallel and Distributed Computing*, 37(1):55–69, 1996.

[52] Robert D. Blumofe and Charles E. Leiserson. Scheduling multithreaded computations by work stealing. *Journal of the ACM*, 46(5):720–748, 1999.

[53] Béla Bollobás. *Random Graphs*. Academic Press, 1985.

[54] Gilles Brassard and Paul Bratley. *Fundamentals of Algorithmics*. Prentice Hall, 1996.

[55] Richard P. Brent. The parallel evaluation of general arithmetic expressions. *Journal of the ACM*, 21(2):201–206, 1974.

[56] Richard P. Brent. An improved Monte Carlo factorization algorithm. *BIT*, 20(2):176–184, 1980.

[57] J. P. Buhler, H. W. Lenstra, Jr., and Carl Pomerance. Factoring integers with the number field sieve. In A. K. Lenstra and H. W. Lenstra, Jr., editors, *The Development of the Number Field Sieve*, volume 1554 of *Lecture Notes in Mathematics*, pages 50–94. Springer, 1993.

[58] J. Lawrence Carter and Mark N. Wegman. Universal classes of hash functions. *Journal of Computer and System Sciences*, 18(2):143–154, 1979.

[59] Barbara Chapman, Gabriele Jost, and Ruud van der Pas. *Using OpenMP: Portable Shared Memory Parallel Programming*. The MIT Press, 2007.

[60] Bernard Chazelle. A minimum spanning tree algorithm with inverse-Ackermann type complexity. *Journal of the ACM*, 47(6):1028–1047, 2000.

[61] Joseph Cheriyan and Torben Hagerup. A randomized maximum-flow algorithm. *SIAM Journal on Computing*, 24(2):203–226, 1995.

[62] Joseph Cheriyan and S. N. Maheshwari. Analysis of preflow push algorithms for maximum network flow. *SIAM Journal on Computing*, 18(6):1057–1086, 1989.

[63] Boris V. Cherkassky and Andrew V. Goldberg. On implementing the push-relabel method for the maximum flow problem. *Algorithmica*, 19(4):390–410, 1997.

[64] Boris V. Cherkassky, Andrew V. Goldberg, and Tomasz Radzik. Shortest paths algorithms: Theory and experimental evaluation. *Mathematical Programming*, 73(2):129–174, 1996.

[65] Boris V. Cherkassky, Andrew V. Goldberg, and Craig Silverstein. Buckets, heaps, lists and monotone priority queues. *SIAM Journal on Computing*, 28(4):1326–1346, 1999.

[66] H. Chernoff. A measure of asymptotic efficiency for tests of a hypothesis based on the sum of observations. *Annals of Mathematical Statistics*, 23(4):493–507, 1952.

[67] Kai Lai Chung. *Elementary Probability Theory with Stochastic Processes*. Springer, 1974.

[68] V. Chvátal. A greedy heuristic for the set-covering problem. *Mathematics of Operations Research*, 4(3):233–235, 1979.

[69] V. Chvátal. *Linear Programming*. W. H. Freeman and Company, 1983.

[70] V. Chvátal, D. A. Klarner, and D. E. Knuth. Selected combinatorial research problems. Technical Report STAN-CS-72-292, Computer Science Department, Stanford University, 1972.

[71] Cilk Arts, Inc., Burlington, Massachusetts. *Cilk++ Programmer's Guide*, 2008. Available at http://www.cilk.com/archive/docs/cilk1guide.

[72] Alan Cobham. The intrinsic computational difficulty of functions. In *Proceedings of the 1964 Congress for Logic, Methodology, and the Philosophy of Science*, pages 24–30. North-Holland, 1964.

[73] H. Cohen and H. W. Lenstra, Jr. Primality testing and Jacobi sums. *Mathematics of Computation*, 42(165):297–330, 1984.

[74] Douglas Comer. The ubiquitous B-tree. *ACM Computing Surveys*, 11(2):121–137, 1979.

[75] Stephen Cook. The complexity of theorem proving procedures. In *Proceedings of the Third Annual ACM Symposium on Theory of Computing*, pages 151–158, 1971.

[76] James W. Cooley and John W. Tukey. An algorithm for the machine calculation of complex Fourier series. *Mathematics of Computation*, 19(90):297–301, 1965.

[77] Don Coppersmith. Modifications to the number field sieve. *Journal of Cryptology*, 6(3):169–180, 1993.

[78] Don Coppersmith and Shmuel Winograd. Matrix multiplication via arithmetic progression. *Journal of Symbolic Computation*, 9(3):251–280, 1990.

[79] Thomas H. Cormen, Thomas Sundquist, and Leonard F. Wisniewski. Asymptotically tight bounds for performing BMMC permutations on parallel disk systems. *SIAM Journal on Computing*, 28(1):105–136, 1998.

[80] Don Dailey and Charles E. Leiserson. Using Cilk to write multiprocessor chess programs. In H. J. van den Herik and B. Monien, editors, *Advances in Computer Games*, volume 9, pages 25–52. University of Maastricht, Netherlands, 2001.

[81] Paolo D'Alberto and Alexandru Nicolau. Adaptive Strassen's matrix multiplication. In *Proceedings of the 21st Annual International Conference on Supercomputing*, pages 284–292, June 2007.

[82] Sanjoy Dasgupta, Christos Papadimitriou, and Umesh Vazirani. *Algorithms*. McGraw-Hill, 2008.

[83] Roman Dementiev, Lutz Kettner, Jens Mehnert, and Peter Sanders. Engineering a sorted list data structure for 32 bit keys. In *Proceedings of the Sixth Workshop on Algorithm Engineering and Experiments and the First Workshop on Analytic Algorithmics and Combinatorics*, pages 142–151, January 2004.

[84] Camil Demetrescu and Giuseppe F. Italiano. Fully dynamic all pairs shortest paths with real edge weights. *Journal of Computer and System Sciences*, 72(5):813–837, 2006.

[85] Eric V. Denardo and Bennett L. Fox. Shortest-route methods: 1. Reaching, pruning, and buckets. *Operations Research*, 27(1):161–186, 1979.

[86] Martin Dietzfelbinger, Anna Karlin, Kurt Mehlhorn, Friedhelm Meyer auf der Heide, Hans Rohnert, and Robert E. Tarjan. Dynamic perfect hashing: Upper and lower bounds. *SIAM Journal on Computing*, 23(4):738–761, 1994.

[87] Whitfield Diffie and Martin E. Hellman. New directions in cryptography. *IEEE Transactions on Information Theory*, IT-22(6):644–654, 1976.

[88] E. W. Dijkstra. A note on two problems in connexion with graphs. *Numerische Mathematik*, 1(1):269–271, 1959.

[89] E. A. Dinic. Algorithm for solution of a problem of maximum flow in a network with power estimation. *Soviet Mathematics Doklady*, 11(5):1277–1280, 1970.

[90] Brandon Dixon, Monika Rauch, and Robert E. Tarjan. Verification and sensitivity analysis of minimum spanning trees in linear time. *SIAM Journal on Computing*, 21(6):1184–1192, 1992.

[91] John D. Dixon. Factorization and primality tests. *The American Mathematical Monthly*, 91(6):333–352, 1984.

[92] Dorit Dor, Johan Håstad, Staffan Ulfberg, and Uri Zwick. On lower bounds for selecting the median. *SIAM Journal on Discrete Mathematics*, 14(3):299–311, 2001.

[93] Dorit Dor and Uri Zwick. Selecting the median. *SIAM Journal on Computing*, 28(5):1722–1758, 1999.

[94] Dorit Dor and Uri Zwick. Median selection requires $(2 + \epsilon)n$ comparisons. *SIAM Journal on Discrete Mathematics*, 14(3):312–325, 2001.

[95] Alvin W. Drake. *Fundamentals of Applied Probability Theory*. McGraw-Hill, 1967.

[96] James R. Driscoll, Harold N. Gabow, Ruth Shrairman, and Robert E. Tarjan. Relaxed heaps: An alternative to Fibonacci heaps with applications to parallel computation. *Communications of the ACM*, 31(11):1343–1354, 1988.

[97] James R. Driscoll, Neil Sarnak, Daniel D. Sleator, and Robert E. Tarjan. Making data structures persistent. *Journal of Computer and System Sciences*, 38(1):86–124, 1989.

[98] Derek L. Eager, John Zahorjan, and Edward D. Lazowska. Speedup versus efficiency in parallel systems. *IEEE Transactions on Computers*, 38(3):408–423, 1989.

[99] Herbert Edelsbrunner. *Algorithms in Combinatorial Geometry*, volume 10 of *EATCS Monographs on Theoretical Computer Science*. Springer, 1987.

[100] Jack Edmonds. Paths, trees, and flowers. *Canadian Journal of Mathematics*, 17:449–467, 1965.

[101] Jack Edmonds. Matroids and the greedy algorithm. *Mathematical Programming*, 1(1):127–136, 1971.

[102] Jack Edmonds and Richard M. Karp. Theoretical improvements in the algorithmic efficiency for network flow problems. *Journal of the ACM*, 19(2):248–264, 1972.

[103] Shimon Even. *Graph Algorithms*. Computer Science Press, 1979.

[104] William Feller. *An Introduction to Probability Theory and Its Applications*. John Wiley & Sons, third edition, 1968.

[105] Robert W. Floyd. Algorithm 97 (SHORTEST PATH). *Communications of the ACM*, 5(6):345, 1962.

[106] Robert W. Floyd. Algorithm 245 (TREESORT). *Communications of the ACM*, 7(12):701, 1964.

[107] Robert W. Floyd. Permuting information in idealized two-level storage. In Raymond E. Miller and James W. Thatcher, editors, *Complexity of Computer Computations*, pages 105–109. Plenum Press, 1972.

[108] Robert W. Floyd and Ronald L. Rivest. Expected time bounds for selection. *Communications of the ACM*, 18(3):165–172, 1975.

[109] Lestor R. Ford, Jr. and D. R. Fulkerson. *Flows in Networks*. Princeton University Press, 1962.

[110] Lestor R. Ford, Jr. and Selmer M. Johnson. A tournament problem. *The American Mathematical Monthly*, 66(5):387–389, 1959.

[111] Michael L. Fredman. New bounds on the complexity of the shortest path problem. *SIAM Journal on Computing*, 5(1):83–89, 1976.

[112] Michael L. Fredman, János Komlós, and Endre Szemerédi. Storing a sparse table with $O(1)$ worst case access time. *Journal of the ACM*, 31(3):538–544, 1984.

[113] Michael L. Fredman and Michael E. Saks. The cell probe complexity of dynamic data structures. In *Proceedings of the Twenty First Annual ACM Symposium on Theory of Computing*, pages 345–354, 1989.

[114] Michael L. Fredman and Robert E. Tarjan. Fibonacci heaps and their uses in improved network optimization algorithms. *Journal of the ACM*, 34(3):596–615, 1987.

[115] Michael L. Fredman and Dan E. Willard. Surpassing the information theoretic bound with fusion trees. *Journal of Computer and System Sciences*, 47(3):424–436, 1993.

[116] Michael L. Fredman and Dan E. Willard. Trans-dichotomous algorithms for minimum spanning trees and shortest paths. *Journal of Computer and System Sciences*, 48(3):533–551, 1994.

[117] Matteo Frigo and Steven G. Johnson. The design and implementation of FFTW3. *Proceedings of the IEEE*, 93(2):216–231, 2005.

[118] Matteo Frigo, Charles E. Leiserson, and Keith H. Randall. The implementation of the Cilk-5 multithreaded language. In *Proceedings of the 1998 ACM SIGPLAN Conference on Programming Language Design and Implementation*, pages 212–223, 1998.

[119] Harold N. Gabow. Path-based depth-first search for strong and biconnected components. *Information Processing Letters*, 74(3–4):107–114, 2000.

[120] Harold N. Gabow, Z. Galil, T. Spencer, and Robert E. Tarjan. Efficient algorithms for finding minimum spanning trees in undirected and directed graphs. *Combinatorica*, 6(2):109–122, 1986.

[121] Harold N. Gabow and Robert E. Tarjan. A linear-time algorithm for a special case of disjoint set union. *Journal of Computer and System Sciences*, 30(2):209–221, 1985.

[122] Harold N. Gabow and Robert E. Tarjan. Faster scaling algorithms for network problems. *SIAM Journal on Computing*, 18(5):1013–1036, 1989.

[123] Zvi Galil and Oded Margalit. All pairs shortest distances for graphs with small integer length edges. *Information and Computation*, 134(2):103–139, 1997.

[124] Zvi Galil and Oded Margalit. All pairs shortest paths for graphs with small integer length edges. *Journal of Computer and System Sciences*, 54(2):243–254, 1997.

[125] Zvi Galil and Kunsoo Park. Dynamic programming with convexity, concavity and sparsity. *Theoretical Computer Science*, 92(1):49–76, 1992.

[126] Zvi Galil and Joel Seiferas. Time-space-optimal string matching. *Journal of Computer and System Sciences*, 26(3):280–294, 1983.

[127] Igal Galperin and Ronald L. Rivest. Scapegoat trees. In *Proceedings of the 4th ACM-SIAM Symposium on Discrete Algorithms*, pages 165–174, 1993.

[128] Michael R. Garey, R. L. Graham, and J. D. Ullman. Worst-case analyis of memory allocation algorithms. In *Proceedings of the Fourth Annual ACM Symposium on Theory of Computing*, pages 143–150, 1972.

[129] Michael R. Garey and David S. Johnson. *Computers and Intractability: A Guide to the Theory of NP-Completeness*. W. H. Freeman, 1979.

[130] Saul Gass. *Linear Programming: Methods and Applications*. International Thomson Publishing, fourth edition, 1975.

[131] Fănică Gavril. Algorithms for minimum coloring, maximum clique, minimum covering by cliques, and maximum independent set of a chordal graph. *SIAM Journal on Computing*, 1(2):180–187, 1972.

[132] Alan George and Joseph W-H Liu. *Computer Solution of Large Sparse Positive Definite Systems*. Prentice Hall, 1981.

[133] E. N. Gilbert and E. F. Moore. Variable-length binary encodings. *Bell System Technical Journal*, 38(4):933–967, 1959.

[134] Michel X. Goemans and David P. Williamson. Improved approximation algorithms for maximum cut and satisfiability problems using semidefinite programming. *Journal of the ACM*, 42(6):1115–1145, 1995.

[135] Michel X. Goemans and David P. Williamson. The primal-dual method for approximation algorithms and its application to network design problems. In Dorit S. Hochbaum, editor, *Approximation Algorithms for NP-Hard Problems*, pages 144–191. PWS Publishing Company, 1997.

[136] Andrew V. Goldberg. *Efficient Graph Algorithms for Sequential and Parallel Computers*. PhD thesis, Department of Electrical Engineering and Computer Science, MIT, 1987.

[137] Andrew V. Goldberg. Scaling algorithms for the shortest paths problem. *SIAM Journal on Computing*, 24(3):494–504, 1995.

[138] Andrew V. Goldberg and Satish Rao. Beyond the flow decomposition barrier. *Journal of the ACM*, 45(5):783–797, 1998.

[139] Andrew V. Goldberg, Éva Tardos, and Robert E. Tarjan. Network flow algorithms. In Bernhard Korte, László Lovász, Hans Jürgen Prömel, and Alexander Schrijver, editors, *Paths, Flows, and VLSI-Layout*, pages 101–164. Springer, 1990.

[140] Andrew V. Goldberg and Robert E. Tarjan. A new approach to the maximum flow problem. *Journal of the ACM*, 35(4):921–940, 1988.

[141] D. Goldfarb and M. J. Todd. Linear programming. In G. L. Nemhauser, A. H. G. Rinnooy-Kan, and M. J. Todd, editors, *Handbook in Operations Research and Management Science, Vol. 1, Optimization*, pages 73–170. Elsevier Science Publishers, 1989.

[142] Shafi Goldwasser and Silvio Micali. Probabilistic encryption. *Journal of Computer and System Sciences*, 28(2):270–299, 1984.

[143] Shafi Goldwasser, Silvio Micali, and Ronald L. Rivest. A digital signature scheme secure against adaptive chosen-message attacks. *SIAM Journal on Computing*, 17(2):281–308, 1988.

[144] Gene H. Golub and Charles F. Van Loan. *Matrix Computations*. The Johns Hopkins University Press, third edition, 1996.

[145] G. H. Gonnet. *Handbook of Algorithms and Data Structures*. Addison-Wesley, 1984.

[146] Rafael C. Gonzalez and Richard E. Woods. *Digital Image Processing*. Addison-Wesley, 1992.

[147] Michael T. Goodrich and Roberto Tamassia. *Data Structures and Algorithms in Java*. John Wiley & Sons, 1998.

[148] Michael T. Goodrich and Roberto Tamassia. *Algorithm Design: Foundations, Analysis, and Internet Examples*. John Wiley & Sons, 2001.

[149] Ronald L. Graham. Bounds for certain multiprocessor anomalies. *Bell System Technical Journal*, 45(9):1563–1581, 1966.

[150] Ronald L. Graham. An efficient algorithm for determining the convex hull of a finite planar set. *Information Processing Letters*, 1(4):132–133, 1972.

[151] Ronald L. Graham and Pavol Hell. On the history of the minimum spanning tree problem. *Annals of the History of Computing*, 7(1):43–57, 1985.

[152] Ronald L. Graham, Donald E. Knuth, and Oren Patashnik. *Concrete Mathematics*. Addison-Wesley, second edition, 1994.

[153] David Gries. *The Science of Programming*. Springer, 1981.

[154] M. Grötschel, László Lovász, and Alexander Schrijver. *Geometric Algorithms and Combinatorial Optimization*. Springer, 1988.

[155] Leo J. Guibas and Robert Sedgewick. A dichromatic framework for balanced trees. In *Proceedings of the 19th Annual Symposium on Foundations of Computer Science*, pages 8–21, 1978.

[156] Dan Gusfield. *Algorithms on Strings, Trees, and Sequences: Computer Science and Computational Biology*. Cambridge University Press, 1997.

[157] H. Halberstam and R. E. Ingram, editors. *The Mathematical Papers of Sir William Rowan Hamilton*, volume III (Algebra). Cambridge University Press, 1967.

[158] Yijie Han. Improved fast integer sorting in linear space. In *Proceedings of the 12th ACM-SIAM Symposium on Discrete Algorithms*, pages 793–796, 2001.

[159] Yijie Han. An $O(n^3(\log \log n/\log n)^{5/4})$ time algorithm for all pairs shortest path. *Algorithmica*, 51(4):428–434, 2008.

[160] Frank Harary. *Graph Theory*. Addison-Wesley, 1969.

[161] Gregory C. Harfst and Edward M. Reingold. A potential-based amortized analysis of the union-find data structure. *SIGACT News*, 31(3):86–95, 2000.

[162] J. Hartmanis and R. E. Stearns. On the computational complexity of algorithms. *Transactions of the American Mathematical Society*, 117:285–306, May 1965.

[163] Michael T. Heideman, Don H. Johnson, and C. Sidney Burrus. Gauss and the history of the Fast Fourier Transform. *IEEE ASSP Magazine*, 1(4):14–21, 1984.

[164] Monika R. Henzinger and Valerie King. Fully dynamic biconnectivity and transitive closure. In *Proceedings of the 36th Annual Symposium on Foundations of Computer Science*, pages 664–672, 1995.

[165] Monika R. Henzinger and Valerie King. Randomized fully dynamic graph algorithms with polylogarithmic time per operation. *Journal of the ACM*, 46(4):502–516, 1999.

[166] Monika R. Henzinger, Satish Rao, and Harold N. Gabow. Computing vertex connectivity: New bounds from old techniques. *Journal of Algorithms*, 34(2):222–250, 2000.

[167] Nicholas J. Higham. Exploiting fast matrix multiplication within the level 3 BLAS. *ACM Transactions on Mathematical Software*, 16(4):352–368, 1990.

[168] W. Daniel Hillis and Jr. Guy L. Steele. Data parallel algorithms. *Communications of the ACM*, 29(12):1170–1183, 1986.

[169] C. A. R. Hoare. Algorithm 63 (PARTITION) and algorithm 65 (FIND). *Communications of the ACM*, 4(7):321–322, 1961.

[170] C. A. R. Hoare. Quicksort. *The Computer Journal*, 5(1):10–15, 1962.

[171] Dorit S. Hochbaum. Efficient bounds for the stable set, vertex cover and set packing problems. *Discrete Applied Mathematics*, 6(3):243–254, 1983.

[172] Dorit S. Hochbaum, editor. *Approximation Algorithms for NP-Hard Problems*. PWS Publishing Company, 1997.

[173] W. Hoeffding. On the distribution of the number of successes in independent trials. *Annals of Mathematical Statistics*, 27(3):713–721, 1956.

[174] Micha Hofri. *Probabilistic Analysis of Algorithms*. Springer, 1987.

[175] Micha Hofri. *Analysis of Algorithms*. Oxford University Press, 1995.

[176] John E. Hopcroft and Richard M. Karp. An $n^{5/2}$ algorithm for maximum matchings in bipartite graphs. *SIAM Journal on Computing*, 2(4):225–231, 1973.

[177] John E. Hopcroft, Rajeev Motwani, and Jeffrey D. Ullman. *Introduction to Automata Theory, Languages, and Computation*. Addison Wesley, third edition, 2006.

[178] John E. Hopcroft and Robert E. Tarjan. Efficient algorithms for graph manipulation. *Communications of the ACM*, 16(6):372–378, 1973.

[179] John E. Hopcroft and Jeffrey D. Ullman. Set merging algorithms. *SIAM Journal on Computing*, 2(4):294–303, 1973.

[180] John E. Hopcroft and Jeffrey D. Ullman. *Introduction to Automata Theory, Languages, and Computation*. Addison-Wesley, 1979.

[181] Ellis Horowitz, Sartaj Sahni, and Sanguthevar Rajasekaran. *Computer Algorithms*. Computer Science Press, 1998.

[182] T. C. Hu and M. T. Shing. Computation of matrix chain products. Part I. *SIAM Journal on Computing*, 11(2):362–373, 1982.

[183] T. C. Hu and M. T. Shing. Computation of matrix chain products. Part II. *SIAM Journal on Computing*, 13(2):228–251, 1984.

[184] T. C. Hu and A. C. Tucker. Optimal computer search trees and variable-length alphabetic codes. *SIAM Journal on Applied Mathematics*, 21(4):514–532, 1971.

[185] David A. Huffman. A method for the construction of minimum-redundancy codes. *Proceedings of the IRE*, 40(9):1098–1101, 1952.

[186] Steven Huss-Lederman, Elaine M. Jacobson, Jeremy R. Johnson, Anna Tsao, and Thomas Turnbull. Implementation of Strassen's algorithm for matrix multiplication. In *Proceedings of the 1996 ACM/IEEE Conference on Supercomputing*, article 32, 1996.

[187] Oscar H. Ibarra and Chul E. Kim. Fast approximation algorithms for the knapsack and sum of subset problems. *Journal of the ACM*, 22(4):463–468, 1975.

[188] E. J. Isaac and R. C. Singleton. Sorting by address calculation. *Journal of the ACM*, 3(3):169–174, 1956.

[189] R. A. Jarvis. On the identification of the convex hull of a finite set of points in the plane. *Information Processing Letters*, 2(1):18–21, 1973.

[190] David S. Johnson. Approximation algorithms for combinatorial problems. *Journal of Computer and System Sciences*, 9(3):256–278, 1974.

[191] David S. Johnson. The NP-completeness column: An ongoing guide—The tale of the second prover. *Journal of Algorithms*, 13(3):502–524, 1992.

[192] Donald B. Johnson. Efficient algorithms for shortest paths in sparse networks. *Journal of the ACM*, 24(1):1–13, 1977.

[193] Richard Johnsonbaugh and Marcus Schaefer. *Algorithms*. Pearson Prentice Hall, 2004.

[194] A. Karatsuba and Yu. Ofman. Multiplication of multidigit numbers on automata. *Soviet Physics—Doklady*, 7(7):595–596, 1963. Translation of an article in *Doklady Akademii Nauk SSSR*, 145(2), 1962.

[195] David R. Karger, Philip N. Klein, and Robert E. Tarjan. A randomized linear-time algorithm to find minimum spanning trees. *Journal of the ACM*, 42(2):321–328, 1995.

[196] David R. Karger, Daphne Koller, and Steven J. Phillips. Finding the hidden path: Time bounds for all-pairs shortest paths. *SIAM Journal on Computing*, 22(6):1199–1217, 1993.

[197] Howard Karloff. *Linear Programming*. Birkhäuser, 1991.

[198] N. Karmarkar. A new polynomial-time algorithm for linear programming. *Combinatorica*, 4(4):373–395, 1984.

[199] Richard M. Karp. Reducibility among combinatorial problems. In Raymond E. Miller and James W. Thatcher, editors, *Complexity of Computer Computations*, pages 85–103. Plenum Press, 1972.

[200] Richard M. Karp. An introduction to randomized algorithms. *Discrete Applied Mathematics*, 34(1–3):165–201, 1991.

[201] Richard M. Karp and Michael O. Rabin. Efficient randomized pattern-matching algorithms. *IBM Journal of Research and Development*, 31(2):249–260, 1987.

[202] A. V. Karzanov. Determining the maximal flow in a network by the method of preflows. *Soviet Mathematics Doklady*, 15(2):434–437, 1974.

[203] Valerie King. A simpler minimum spanning tree verification algorithm. *Algorithmica*, 18(2):263–270, 1997.

[204] Valerie King, Satish Rao, and Robert E. Tarjan. A faster deterministic maximum flow algorithm. *Journal of Algorithms*, 17(3):447–474, 1994.

[205] Jeffrey H. Kingston. *Algorithms and Data Structures: Design, Correctness, Analysis*. Addison-Wesley, second edition, 1997.

[206] D. G. Kirkpatrick and R. Seidel. The ultimate planar convex hull algorithm? *SIAM Journal on Computing*, 15(2):287–299, 1986.

[207] Philip N. Klein and Neal E. Young. Approximation algorithms for NP-hard optimization problems. In *CRC Handbook on Algorithms*, pages 34-1–34-19. CRC Press, 1999.

[208] Jon Kleinberg and Éva Tardos. *Algorithm Design*. Addison-Wesley, 2006.

[209] Donald E. Knuth. *Fundamental Algorithms*, volume 1 of *The Art of Computer Programming*. Addison-Wesley, 1968. Third edition, 1997.

[210] Donald E. Knuth. *Seminumerical Algorithms*, volume 2 of *The Art of Computer Programming*. Addison-Wesley, 1969. Third edition, 1997.

[211] Donald E. Knuth. *Sorting and Searching*, volume 3 of *The Art of Computer Programming*. Addison-Wesley, 1973. Second edition, 1998.

[212] Donald E. Knuth. Optimum binary search trees. *Acta Informatica*, 1(1):14–25, 1971.

[213] Donald E. Knuth. Big omicron and big omega and big theta. *SIGACT News*, 8(2):18–23, 1976.

[214] Donald E. Knuth, James H. Morris, Jr., and Vaughan R. Pratt. Fast pattern matching in strings. *SIAM Journal on Computing*, 6(2):323–350, 1977.

[215] J. Komlós. Linear verification for spanning trees. *Combinatorica*, 5(1):57–65, 1985.

[216] Bernhard Korte and László Lovász. Mathematical structures underlying greedy algorithms. In F. Gecseg, editor, *Fundamentals of Computation Theory*, volume 117 of *Lecture Notes in Computer Science*, pages 205–209. Springer, 1981.

[217] Bernhard Korte and László Lovász. Structural properties of greedoids. *Combinatorica*, 3(3–4):359–374, 1983.

[218] Bernhard Korte and László Lovász. Greedoids—A structural framework for the greedy algorithm. In W. Pulleybank, editor, *Progress in Combinatorial Optimization*, pages 221–243. Academic Press, 1984.

[219] Bernhard Korte and László Lovász. Greedoids and linear objective functions. *SIAM Journal on Algebraic and Discrete Methods*, 5(2):229–238, 1984.

[220] Dexter C. Kozen. *The Design and Analysis of Algorithms*. Springer, 1992.

[221] David W. Krumme, George Cybenko, and K. N. Venkataraman. Gossiping in minimal time. *SIAM Journal on Computing*, 21(1):111–139, 1992.

[222] Joseph B. Kruskal, Jr. On the shortest spanning subtree of a graph and the traveling salesman problem. *Proceedings of the American Mathematical Society*, 7(1):48–50, 1956.

[223] Leslie Lamport. How to make a multiprocessor computer that correctly executes multiprocess programs. *IEEE Transactions on Computers*, C-28(9):690–691, 1979.

[224] Eugene L. Lawler. *Combinatorial Optimization: Networks and Matroids*. Holt, Rinehart, and Winston, 1976.

[225] Eugene L. Lawler, J. K. Lenstra, A. H. G. Rinnooy Kan, and D. B. Shmoys, editors. *The Traveling Salesman Problem*. John Wiley & Sons, 1985.

[226] C. Y. Lee. An algorithm for path connection and its applications. *IRE Transactions on Electronic Computers*, EC-10(3):346–365, 1961.

[227] Tom Leighton. Tight bounds on the complexity of parallel sorting. *IEEE Transactions on Computers*, C-34(4):344–354, 1985.

[228] Tom Leighton. Notes on better master theorems for divide-and-conquer recurrences. Class notes. Available at http://citeseer.ist.psu.edu/252350.html, October 1996.

[229] Tom Leighton and Satish Rao. Multicommodity max-flow min-cut theorems and their use in designing approximation algorithms. *Journal of the ACM*, 46(6):787–832, 1999.

[230] Daan Leijen and Judd Hall. Optimize managed code for multi-core machines. *MSDN Magazine*, October 2007.

[231] Debra A. Lelewer and Daniel S. Hirschberg. Data compression. *ACM Computing Surveys*, 19(3):261–296, 1987.

[232] A. K. Lenstra, H. W. Lenstra, Jr., M. S. Manasse, and J. M. Pollard. The number field sieve. In A. K. Lenstra and H. W. Lenstra, Jr., editors, *The Development of the Number Field Sieve*, volume 1554 of *Lecture Notes in Mathematics*, pages 11–42. Springer, 1993.

[233] H. W. Lenstra, Jr. Factoring integers with elliptic curves. *Annals of Mathematics*, 126(3):649–673, 1987.

[234] L. A. Levin. Universal sorting problems. *Problemy Peredachi Informatsii*, 9(3):265–266, 1973. In Russian.

[235] Anany Levitin. *Introduction to the Design & Analysis of Algorithms*. Addison-Wesley, 2007.

[236] Harry R. Lewis and Christos H. Papadimitriou. *Elements of the Theory of Computation*. Prentice Hall, second edition, 1998.

[237] C. L. Liu. *Introduction to Combinatorial Mathematics*. McGraw-Hill, 1968.

[238] László Lovász. On the ratio of optimal integral and fractional covers. *Discrete Mathematics*, 13(4):383–390, 1975.

[239] László Lovász and Michael D. Plummer. *Matching Theory*, volume 121 of *Annals of Discrete Mathematics*. North Holland, 1986.

[240] Bruce M. Maggs and Serge A. Plotkin. Minimum-cost spanning tree as a path-finding problem. *Information Processing Letters*, 26(6):291–293, 1988.

[241] Michael Main. *Data Structures and Other Objects Using Java*. Addison-Wesley, 1999.

[242] Udi Manber. *Introduction to Algorithms: A Creative Approach*. Addison-Wesley, 1989.

[243] Conrado Martínez and Salvador Roura. Randomized binary search trees. *Journal of the ACM*, 45(2):288–323, 1998.

[244] William J. Masek and Michael S. Paterson. A faster algorithm computing string edit distances. *Journal of Computer and System Sciences*, 20(1):18–31, 1980.

[245] H. A. Maurer, Th. Ottmann, and H.-W. Six. Implementing dictionaries using binary trees of very small height. *Information Processing Letters*, 5(1):11–14, 1976.

[246] Ernst W. Mayr, Hans Jürgen Prömel, and Angelika Steger, editors. *Lectures on Proof Verification and Approximation Algorithms*, volume 1367 of *Lecture Notes in Computer Science*. Springer, 1998.

[247] C. C. McGeoch. All pairs shortest paths and the essential subgraph. *Algorithmica*, 13(5):426–441, 1995.

[248] M. D. McIlroy. A killer adversary for quicksort. *Software—Practice and Experience*, 29(4):341–344, 1999.

[249] Kurt Mehlhorn. *Sorting and Searching*, volume 1 of *Data Structures and Algorithms*. Springer, 1984.

[250] Kurt Mehlhorn. *Graph Algorithms and NP-Completeness*, volume 2 of *Data Structures and Algorithms*. Springer, 1984.

[251] Kurt Mehlhorn. *Multidimensional Searching and Computational Geometry*, volume 3 of *Data Structures and Algorithms*. Springer, 1984.

[252] Kurt Mehlhorn and Stefan Näher. Bounded ordered dictionaries in $O(\log \log N)$ time and $O(n)$ space. *Information Processing Letters*, 35(4):183–189, 1990.

[253] Kurt Mehlhorn and Stefan Näher. *LEDA: A Platform for Combinatorial and Geometric Computing*. Cambridge University Press, 1999.

[254] Alfred J. Menezes, Paul C. van Oorschot, and Scott A. Vanstone. *Handbook of Applied Cryptography*. CRC Press, 1997.

[255] Gary L. Miller. Riemann's hypothesis and tests for primality. *Journal of Computer and System Sciences*, 13(3):300–317, 1976.

[256] John C. Mitchell. *Foundations for Programming Languages*. The MIT Press, 1996.

[257] Joseph S. B. Mitchell. Guillotine subdivisions approximate polygonal subdivisions: A simple polynomial-time approximation scheme for geometric TSP, k-MST, and related problems. *SIAM Journal on Computing*, 28(4):1298–1309, 1999.

[258] Louis Monier. *Algorithmes de Factorisation D'Entiers*. PhD thesis, L'Université Paris-Sud, 1980.

[259] Louis Monier. Evaluation and comparison of two efficient probabilistic primality testing algorithms. *Theoretical Computer Science*, 12(1):97–108, 1980.

[260] Edward F. Moore. The shortest path through a maze. In *Proceedings of the International Symposium on the Theory of Switching*, pages 285–292. Harvard University Press, 1959.

[261] Rajeev Motwani, Joseph (Seffi) Naor, and Prabhakar Raghavan. Randomized approximation algorithms in combinatorial optimization. In Dorit Hochbaum, editor, *Approximation Algorithms for NP-Hard Problems*, chapter 11, pages 447–481. PWS Publishing Company, 1997.

[262] Rajeev Motwani and Prabhakar Raghavan. *Randomized Algorithms*. Cambridge University Press, 1995.

[263] J. I. Munro and V. Raman. Fast stable in-place sorting with $O(n)$ data moves. *Algorithmica*, 16(2):151–160, 1996.

[264] J. Nievergelt and E. M. Reingold. Binary search trees of bounded balance. *SIAM Journal on Computing*, 2(1):33–43, 1973.

[265] Ivan Niven and Herbert S. Zuckerman. *An Introduction to the Theory of Numbers*. John Wiley & Sons, fourth edition, 1980.

[266] Alan V. Oppenheim and Ronald W. Schafer, with John R. Buck. *Discrete-Time Signal Processing*. Prentice Hall, second edition, 1998.

[267] Alan V. Oppenheim and Alan S. Willsky, with S. Hamid Nawab. *Signals and Systems*. Prentice Hall, second edition, 1997.

[268] James B. Orlin. A polynomial time primal network simplex algorithm for minimum cost flows. *Mathematical Programming*, 78(1):109–129, 1997.

[269] Joseph O'Rourke. *Computational Geometry in C*. Cambridge University Press, second edition, 1998.

[270] Christos H. Papadimitriou. *Computational Complexity*. Addison-Wesley, 1994.

[271] Christos H. Papadimitriou and Kenneth Steiglitz. *Combinatorial Optimization: Algorithms and Complexity*. Prentice Hall, 1982.

[272] Michael S. Paterson. Progress in selection. In *Proceedings of the Fifth Scandinavian Workshop on Algorithm Theory*, pages 368–379, 1996.

[273] Mihai Pătraşcu and Mikkel Thorup. Time-space trade-offs for predecessor search. In *Proceedings of the 38th Annual ACM Symposium on Theory of Computing*, pages 232–240, 2006.

[274] Mihai Pătraşcu and Mikkel Thorup. Randomization does not help searching predecessors. In *Proceedings of the 18th ACM-SIAM Symposium on Discrete Algorithms*, pages 555–564, 2007.

[275] Pavel A. Pevzner. *Computational Molecular Biology: An Algorithmic Approach*. The MIT Press, 2000.

[276] Steven Phillips and Jeffery Westbrook. Online load balancing and network flow. In *Proceedings of the 25th Annual ACM Symposium on Theory of Computing*, pages 402–411, 1993.

[277] J. M. Pollard. A Monte Carlo method for factorization. *BIT*, 15(3):331–334, 1975.

[278] J. M. Pollard. Factoring with cubic integers. In A. K. Lenstra and H. W. Lenstra, Jr., editors, *The Development of the Number Field Sieve*, volume 1554 of *Lecture Notes in Mathematics*, pages 4–10. Springer, 1993.

[279] Carl Pomerance. On the distribution of pseudoprimes. *Mathematics of Computation*, 37(156):587–593, 1981.

[280] Carl Pomerance, editor. *Proceedings of the AMS Symposia in Applied Mathematics: Computational Number Theory and Cryptography*. American Mathematical Society, 1990.

[281] William K. Pratt. *Digital Image Processing*. John Wiley & Sons, fourth edition, 2007.

[282] Franco P. Preparata and Michael Ian Shamos. *Computational Geometry: An Introduction*. Springer, 1985.

[283] William H. Press, Saul A. Teukolsky, William T. Vetterling, and Brian P. Flannery. *Numerical Recipes in C++: The Art of Scientific Computing*. Cambridge University Press, second edition, 2002.

[284] William H. Press, Saul A. Teukolsky, William T. Vetterling, and Brian P. Flannery. *Numerical Recipes: The Art of Scientific Computing*. Cambridge University Press, third edition, 2007.

[285] R. C. Prim. Shortest connection networks and some generalizations. *Bell System Technical Journal*, 36(6):1389–1401, 1957.

[286] William Pugh. Skip lists: A probabilistic alternative to balanced trees. *Communications of the ACM*, 33(6):668–676, 1990.

[287] Paul W. Purdom, Jr. and Cynthia A. Brown. *The Analysis of Algorithms*. Holt, Rinehart, and Winston, 1985.

[288] Michael O. Rabin. Probabilistic algorithms. In J. F. Traub, editor, *Algorithms and Complexity: New Directions and Recent Results*, pages 21–39. Academic Press, 1976.

[289] Michael O. Rabin. Probabilistic algorithm for testing primality. *Journal of Number Theory*, 12(1):128–138, 1980.

[290] P. Raghavan and C. D. Thompson. Randomized rounding: A technique for provably good algorithms and algorithmic proofs. *Combinatorica*, 7(4):365–374, 1987.

[291] Rajeev Raman. Recent results on the single-source shortest paths problem. *SIGACT News*, 28(2):81–87, 1997.

[292] James Reinders. *Intel Threading Building Blocks: Outfitting C++ for Multi-core Processor Parallelism*. O'Reilly Media, Inc., 2007.

[293] Edward M. Reingold, Jürg Nievergelt, and Narsingh Deo. *Combinatorial Algorithms: Theory and Practice*. Prentice Hall, 1977.

[294] Edward M. Reingold, Kenneth J. Urban, and David Gries. K-M-P string matching revisited. *Information Processing Letters*, 64(5):217–223, 1997.

[295] Hans Riesel. *Prime Numbers and Computer Methods for Factorization*, volume 126 of *Progress in Mathematics*. Birkhäuser, second edition, 1994.

[296] Ronald L. Rivest, Adi Shamir, and Leonard M. Adleman. A method for obtaining digital signatures and public-key cryptosystems. *Communications of the ACM*, 21(2):120–126, 1978. See also U.S. Patent 4,405,829.

[297] Herbert Robbins. A remark on Stirling's formula. *American Mathematical Monthly*, 62(1):26–29, 1955.

[298] D. J. Rosenkrantz, R. E. Stearns, and P. M. Lewis. An analysis of several heuristics for the traveling salesman problem. *SIAM Journal on Computing*, 6(3):563–581, 1977.

[299] Salvador Roura. An improved master theorem for divide-and-conquer recurrences. In *Proceedings of Automata, Languages and Programming, 24th International Colloquium, ICALP'97*, volume 1256 of *Lecture Notes in Computer Science*, pages 449–459. Springer, 1997.

[300] Y. A. Rozanov. *Probability Theory: A Concise Course*. Dover, 1969.

[301] S. Sahni and T. Gonzalez. P-complete approximation problems. *Journal of the ACM*, 23(3):555–565, 1976.

[302] A. Schönhage, M. Paterson, and N. Pippenger. Finding the median. *Journal of Computer and System Sciences*, 13(2):184–199, 1976.

[303] Alexander Schrijver. *Theory of Linear and Integer Programming*. John Wiley & Sons, 1986.

[304] Alexander Schrijver. Paths and flows—A historical survey. *CWI Quarterly*, 6(3):169–183, 1993.

[305] Robert Sedgewick. Implementing quicksort programs. *Communications of the ACM*, 21(10):847–857, 1978.

[306] Robert Sedgewick. *Algorithms*. Addison-Wesley, second edition, 1988.

[307] Robert Sedgewick and Philippe Flajolet. *An Introduction to the Analysis of Algorithms*. Addison-Wesley, 1996.

[308] Raimund Seidel. On the all-pairs-shortest-path problem in unweighted undirected graphs. *Journal of Computer and System Sciences*, 51(3):400–403, 1995.

[309] Raimund Seidel and C. R. Aragon. Randomized search trees. *Algorithmica*, 16(4–5):464–497, 1996.

[310] João Setubal and João Meidanis. *Introduction to Computational Molecular Biology*. PWS Publishing Company, 1997.

[311] Clifford A. Shaffer. *A Practical Introduction to Data Structures and Algorithm Analysis*. Prentice Hall, second edition, 2001.

[312] Jeffrey Shallit. Origins of the analysis of the Euclidean algorithm. *Historia Mathematica*, 21(4):401–419, 1994.

[313] Michael I. Shamos and Dan Hoey. Geometric intersection problems. In *Proceedings of the 17th Annual Symposium on Foundations of Computer Science*, pages 208–215, 1976.

[314] M. Sharir. A strong-connectivity algorithm and its applications in data flow analysis. *Computers and Mathematics with Applications*, 7(1):67–72, 1981.

[315] David B. Shmoys. Computing near-optimal solutions to combinatorial optimization problems. In William Cook, László Lovász, and Paul Seymour, editors, *Combinatorial Optimization*, volume 20 of *DIMACS Series in Discrete Mathematics and Theoretical Computer Science*. American Mathematical Society, 1995.

[316] Avi Shoshan and Uri Zwick. All pairs shortest paths in undirected graphs with integer weights. In *Proceedings of the 40th Annual Symposium on Foundations of Computer Science*, pages 605–614, 1999.

[317] Michael Sipser. *Introduction to the Theory of Computation*. Thomson Course Technology, second edition, 2006.

[318] Steven S. Skiena. *The Algorithm Design Manual*. Springer, second edition, 1998.

[319] Daniel D. Sleator and Robert E. Tarjan. A data structure for dynamic trees. *Journal of Computer and System Sciences*, 26(3):362–391, 1983.

[320] Daniel D. Sleator and Robert E. Tarjan. Self-adjusting binary search trees. *Journal of the ACM*, 32(3):652–686, 1985.

[321] Joel Spencer. *Ten Lectures on the Probabilistic Method*, volume 64 of *CBMS-NSF Regional Conference Series in Applied Mathematics*. Society for Industrial and Applied Mathematics, 1993.

[322] Daniel A. Spielman and Shang-Hua Teng. Smoothed analysis of algorithms: Why the simplex algorithm usually takes polynomial time. *Journal of the ACM*, 51(3):385–463, 2004.

[323] Gilbert Strang. *Introduction to Applied Mathematics*. Wellesley-Cambridge Press, 1986.

[324] Gilbert Strang. *Linear Algebra and Its Applications*. Thomson Brooks/Cole, fourth edition, 2006.

[325] Volker Strassen. Gaussian elimination is not optimal. *Numerische Mathematik*, 14(3):354–356, 1969.

[326] T. G. Szymanski. A special case of the maximal common subsequence problem. Technical Report TR-170, Computer Science Laboratory, Princeton University, 1975.

[327] Robert E. Tarjan. Depth first search and linear graph algorithms. *SIAM Journal on Computing*, 1(2):146–160, 1972.

[328] Robert E. Tarjan. Efficiency of a good but not linear set union algorithm. *Journal of the ACM*, 22(2):215–225, 1975.

[329] Robert E. Tarjan. A class of algorithms which require nonlinear time to maintain disjoint sets. *Journal of Computer and System Sciences*, 18(2):110–127, 1979.

[330] Robert E. Tarjan. *Data Structures and Network Algorithms*. Society for Industrial and Applied Mathematics, 1983.

[331] Robert E. Tarjan. Amortized computational complexity. *SIAM Journal on Algebraic and Discrete Methods*, 6(2):306–318, 1985.

[332] Robert E. Tarjan. Class notes: Disjoint set union. COS 423, Princeton University, 1999.

[333] Robert E. Tarjan and Jan van Leeuwen. Worst-case analysis of set union algorithms. *Journal of the ACM*, 31(2):245–281, 1984.

[334] George B. Thomas, Jr., Maurice D. Weir, Joel Hass, and Frank R. Giordano. *Thomas' Calculus*. Addison-Wesley, eleventh edition, 2005.

[335] Mikkel Thorup. Faster deterministic sorting and priority queues in linear space. In *Proceedings of the 9th ACM-SIAM Symposium on Discrete Algorithms*, pages 550–555, 1998.

[336] Mikkel Thorup. Undirected single-source shortest paths with positive integer weights in linear time. *Journal of the ACM*, 46(3):362–394, 1999.

[337] Mikkel Thorup. On RAM priority queues. *SIAM Journal on Computing*, 30(1):86–109, 2000.

[338] Richard Tolimieri, Myoung An, and Chao Lu. *Mathematics of Multidimensional Fourier Transform Algorithms*. Springer, second edition, 1997.

[339] P. van Emde Boas. Preserving order in a forest in less than logarithmic time. In *Proceedings of the 16th Annual Symposium on Foundations of Computer Science*, pages 75–84, 1975.

[340] P. van Emde Boas. Preserving order in a forest in less than logarithmic time and linear space. *Information Processing Letters*, 6(3):80–82, 1977.

[341] P. van Emde Boas, R. Kaas, and E. Zijlstra. Design and implementation of an efficient priority queue. *Mathematical Systems Theory*, 10(1):99–127, 1976.

[342] Jan van Leeuwen, editor. *Handbook of Theoretical Computer Science, Volume A: Algorithms and Complexity*. Elsevier Science Publishers and the MIT Press, 1990.

[343] Charles Van Loan. *Computational Frameworks for the Fast Fourier Transform*. Society for Industrial and Applied Mathematics, 1992.

[344] Robert J. Vanderbei. *Linear Programming: Foundations and Extensions*. Kluwer Academic Publishers, 1996.

[345] Vijay V. Vazirani. *Approximation Algorithms*. Springer, 2001.

[346] Rakesh M. Verma. General techniques for analyzing recursive algorithms with applications. *SIAM Journal on Computing*, 26(2):568–581, 1997.

[347] Hao Wang and Bill Lin. Pipelined van Emde Boas tree: Algorithms, analysis, and applications. In *26th IEEE International Conference on Computer Communications*, pages 2471–2475, 2007.

[348] Antony F. Ware. Fast approximate Fourier transforms for irregularly spaced data. *SIAM Review*, 40(4):838–856, 1998.

[349] Stephen Warshall. A theorem on boolean matrices. *Journal of the ACM*, 9(1):11–12, 1962.

[350] Michael S. Waterman. *Introduction to Computational Biology, Maps, Sequences and Genomes*. Chapman & Hall, 1995.

[351] Mark Allen Weiss. *Data Structures and Problem Solving Using C++*. Addison-Wesley, second edition, 2000.

[352] Mark Allen Weiss. *Data Structures and Problem Solving Using Java*. Addison-Wesley, third edition, 2006.

[353] Mark Allen Weiss. *Data Structures and Algorithm Analysis in C++*. Addison-Wesley, third edition, 2007.

[354] Mark Allen Weiss. *Data Structures and Algorithm Analysis in Java*. Addison-Wesley, second edition, 2007.

[355] Hassler Whitney. On the abstract properties of linear dependence. *American Journal of Mathematics*, 57(3):509–533, 1935.

[356] Herbert S. Wilf. *Algorithms and Complexity*. A K Peters, second edition, 2002.

[357] J. W. J. Williams. Algorithm 232 (HEAPSORT). *Communications of the ACM*, 7(6):347–348, 1964.

[358] Shmuel Winograd. On the algebraic complexity of functions. In *Actes du Congrès International des Mathématiciens*, volume 3, pages 283–288, 1970.

[359] Andrew C.-C. Yao. A lower bound to finding convex hulls. *Journal of the ACM*, 28(4):780–787, 1981.

[360] Chee Yap. A real elementary approach to the master recurrence and generalizations. Unpublished manuscript. Available at http://cs.nyu.edu/yap/papers/, July 2008.

[361] Yinyu Ye. *Interior Point Algorithms: Theory and Analysis*. John Wiley & Sons, 1997.

[362] Daniel Zwillinger, editor. *CRC Standard Mathematical Tables and Formulae*. Chapman & Hall/CRC Press, 31st edition, 2003.

Index

This index uses the following conventions. Numbers are alphabetized as if spelled out; for example, "2-3-4 tree" is indexed as if it were "two-three-four tree." When an entry refers to a place other than the main text, the page number is followed by a tag: ex. for exercise, pr. for problem, fig. for figure, and n. for footnote. A tagged page number often indicates the first page of an exercise or problem, which is not necessarily the page on which the reference actually appears.

$\alpha(n)$, 574

ϕ (golden ratio), 59, 108 pr.

$\hat{\phi}$ (conjugate of the golden ratio), 59

$\phi(n)$ (Euler's phi function), 943

$\rho(n)$-approximation algorithm, 1106, 1123

o-notation, 50–51, 64

O-notation, 45 fig., 47–48, 64

O'-notation, 62 pr.

$\widetilde{O}$-notation, 62 pr.

ω-notation, 51

Ω-notation, 45 fig., 48–49, 64

$\overset{\infty}{\Omega}$-notation, 62 pr.

$\widetilde{\Omega}$-notation, 62 pr.

Θ-notation, 44–47, 45 fig., 64

$\widetilde{\Theta}$-notation, 62 pr.

{ } (set), 1158

$\in$ (set member), 1158

$\notin$ (not a set member), 1158

$\emptyset$

   (empty language), 1058

   (empty set), 1158

$\subseteq$ (subset), 1159

$\subset$ (proper subset), 1159

: (such that), 1159

$\cap$ (set intersection), 1159

$\cup$ (set union), 1159

$-$ (set difference), 1159

$| \, |$

   (flow value), 710

   (length of a string), 986

   (set cardinality), 1161

$\times$

   (Cartesian product), 1162

   (cross product), 1016

$\langle\,\rangle$

   (sequence), 1166

   (standard encoding), 1057

$\binom{n}{k}$ (choose), 1185

$\|\;\|$ (euclidean norm), 1222

! (factorial), 57

$\lceil\;\rceil$ (ceiling), 54

$\lfloor\;\rfloor$ (floor), 54

$\sqrt[\downarrow]{\;}$ (lower square root), 546

$\sqrt[\uparrow]{\;}$ (upper square root), 546

$\sum$ (sum), 1145

$\prod$ (product), 1148

$\rightarrow$ (adjacency relation), 1169

$\rightsquigarrow$ (reachability relation), 1170

$\wedge$ (AND), 697, 1071

$\neg$ (NOT), 1071

$\vee$ (OR), 697, 1071

$\oplus$ (group operator), 939

$\otimes$ (convolution operator), 901

* (closure operator), 1058

| (divides relation), 927

∤ (does-not-divide relation), 927

≡ (equivalent modulo n), 54, 1165 ex.

≢ (not equivalent modulo n), 54

$[a]_n$ (equivalence class modulo n), 928

$+_n$ (addition modulo n), 940

$\cdot_n$ (multiplication modulo n), 940

$(\frac{a}{p})$ (Legendre symbol), 982 pr.

ε (empty string), 986, 1058

⊏ (prefix relation), 986

⊐ (suffix relation), 986

$\succeq_x$ (above relation), 1022

// (comment symbol), 21

≫ (much-greater-than relation), 574

≪ (much-less-than relation), 783

$\leq_P$ (polynomial-time reducibility relation), 1067, 1077 ex.

AA-tree, 338

abelian group, 940

ABOVE, 1024

above relation ($\succeq_x$), 1022

absent child, 1178

absolutely convergent series, 1146

absorption laws for sets, 1160

abstract problem, 1054

acceptable pair of integers, 972

acceptance

  by an algorithm, 1058

  by a finite automaton, 996

accepting state, 995

accounting method, 456–459

  for binary counters, 458

  for dynamic tables, 465–466

  for stack operations, 457–458, 458 ex.

Ackermann's function, 585

activity-selection problem, 415–422, 450

acyclic graph, 1170

  relation to matroids, 448 pr.

add instruction, 23

addition

  of binary integers, 22 ex.

  of matrices, 1220

  modulo n ($+_n$), 940

  of polynomials, 898

additive group modulo n, 940

addressing, open, *see* open-address hash table

ADD-SUBARRAY, 805 pr.

adjacency-list representation, 590

  replaced by a hash table, 593 ex.

adjacency-matrix representation, 591

adjacency relation (→), 1169

adjacent vertices, 1169

admissible edge, 749

admissible network, 749–750

adversary, 190

aggregate analysis, 452–456

  for binary counters, 454–455

  for breadth-first search, 597

  for depth-first search, 606

  for Dijkstra's algorithm, 661

  for disjoint-set data structures, 566–567, 568 ex.

  for dynamic tables, 465

  for Fibonacci heaps, 518, 522 ex.

  for Graham's scan, 1036

  for the Knuth-Morris-Pratt algorithm, 1006

  for Prim's algorithm, 636

  for rod-cutting, 367

  for shortest paths in a dag, 655

  for stack operations, 452–454

aggregate flow, 863

Akra-Bazzi method for solving a recurrence, 112–113

algorithm, 5

  correctness of, 6

  origin of word, 42

  running time of, 25

  as a technology, 13

Alice, 959

ALLOCATE-NODE, 492

ALLOCATE-OBJECT, 244

allocation of objects, 243–244

all-pairs shortest paths, 644, 684–707

  in dynamic graphs, 707

  in ϵ-dense graphs, 706 pr.

  Floyd-Warshall algorithm for, 693–697, 706

  Johnson's algorithm for, 700–706

  by matrix multiplication, 686–693, 706–707

  by repeated squaring, 689–691

alphabet, 995, 1057

$\alpha(n)$, 574

amortized analysis, 451–478

  accounting method of, 456–459

  aggregate analysis, 367, 452–456

for bit-reversal permutation, 472 pr.
for breadth-first search, 597
for depth-first search, 606
for Dijkstra's algorithm, 661
for disjoint-set data structures, 566–567,
  568 ex., 572 ex., 575–581, 581–582 ex.
for dynamic tables, 463–471
for Fibonacci heaps, 509–512, 517–518,
  520–522, 522 ex.
for the generic push-relabel algorithm, 746
for Graham's scan, 1036
for the Knuth-Morris-Pratt algorithm, 1006
for making binary search dynamic, 473 pr.
potential method of, 459–463
for restructuring red-black trees, 474 pr.
for self-organizing lists with move-to-front,
  476 pr.
for shortest paths in a dag, 655
for stacks on secondary storage, 502 pr.
for weight-balanced trees, 473 pr.
amortized cost
  in the accounting method, 456
  in aggregate analysis, 452
  in the potential method, 459
ancestor, 1176
  least common, 584 pr.
AND function ($\wedge$), 697, 1071
AND gate, 1070
and, in pseudocode, 22
antiparallel edges, 711–712
antisymmetric relation, 1164
ANY-SEGMENTS-INTERSECT, 1025
approximation
  by least squares, 835–839
  of summation by integrals, 1154–1156
approximation algorithm, 10, 1105–1140
  for bin packing, 1134 pr.
  for MAX-CNF satisfiability, 1127 ex.
  for maximum clique, 1111 ex., 1134 pr.
  for maximum matching, 1135 pr.
  for maximum spanning tree, 1137 pr.
  for maximum-weight cut, 1127 ex.
  for MAX-3-CNF satisfiability, 1123–1124,
    1139
  for minimum-weight vertex cover,
    1124–1127, 1139
  for parallel machine scheduling, 1136 pr.
  randomized, 1123

for set cover, 1117–1122, 1139
for subset sum, 1128–1134, 1139
for traveling-salesman problem, 1111–1117,
  1139
for vertex cover, 1108–1111, 1139
for weighted set cover, 1135 pr.
for 0-1 knapsack problem, 1137 pr., 1139
approximation error, 836
approximation ratio, 1106, 1123
approximation scheme, 1107
APPROX-MIN-WEIGHT-VC, 1126
APPROX-SUBSET-SUM, 1131
APPROX-TSP-TOUR, 1112
APPROX-VERTEX-COVER, 1109
arbitrage, 679 pr.
arc, *see* edge
argument of a function, 1166–1167
arithmetic instructions, 23
arithmetic, modular, 54, 939–946
arithmetic series, 1146
arithmetic with infinities, 650
arm, 485
array, 21
  Monge, 110 pr.
  passing as a parameter, 21
articulation point, 621 pr.
assignment
  multiple, 21
  satisfying, 1072, 1079
  truth, 1072, 1079
associative laws for sets, 1160
associative operation, 939
asymptotically larger, 52
asymptotically nonnegative, 45
asymptotically positive, 45
asymptotically smaller, 52
asymptotically tight bound, 45
asymptotic efficiency, 43
asymptotic lower bound, 48
asymptotic notation, 43–53, 62 pr.
  and graph algorithms, 588
  and linearity of summations, 1146
asymptotic upper bound, 47
attribute of an object, 21
augmentation of a flow, 716
augmenting data structures, 339–355
augmenting path, 719–720, 763 pr.
authentication, 284 pr., 960–961, 964

automaton
  finite, 995
  string-matching, 996–1002
auxiliary hash function, 272
auxiliary linear program, 886
average-case running time, 28, 116
AVL-INSERT, 333 pr.
AVL tree, 333 pr., 337
axioms, for probability, 1190

babyface, 602 ex.
back edge, 609, 613
back substitution, 817
BAD-SET-COVER-INSTANCE, 1122 ex.
BALANCE, 333 pr.
balanced search tree
  AA-trees, 338
  AVL trees, 333 pr., 337
  B-trees, 484–504
  k-neighbor trees, 338
  red-black trees, 308–338
  scapegoat trees, 338
  splay trees, 338, 482
  treaps, 333 pr., 338
  2-3-4 trees, 489, 503 pr.
  2-3 trees, 337, 504
  weight-balanced trees, 338, 473 pr.
balls and bins, 133–134, 1215 pr.
base-a pseudoprime, 967
base case, 65, 84
base, in DNA, 391
basic feasible solution, 866
basic solution, 866
basic variable, 855
basis function, 835
Bayes's theorem, 1194
BELLMAN-FORD, 651
Bellman-Ford algorithm, 651–655, 682
  for all-pairs shortest paths, 684
  in Johnson's algorithm, 702–704
  and objective functions, 670 ex.
  to solve systems of difference constraints,
    668
  Yen's improvement to, 678 pr.
BELOW, 1024
Bernoulli trial, 1201
  and balls and bins, 133–134
  and streaks, 135–139

best-case running time, 29 ex., 49
BFS, 595
BIASED-RANDOM, 117 ex.
biconnected component, 621 pr.
big-oh notation, 45 fig., 47–48, 64
big-omega notation, 45 fig., 48–49, 64
bijective function, 1167
binary character code, 428
binary counter
  analyzed by accounting method, 458
  analyzed by aggregate analysis, 454–455
  analyzed by potential method, 461–462
  bit-reversed, 472 pr.
binary entropy function, 1187
binary gcd algorithm, 981 pr.
binary heap, *see* heap
binary relation, 1163
binary search, 39 ex.
  with fast insertion, 473 pr.
  in insertion sort, 39 ex.
  in multithreaded merging, 799–800
  in searching B-trees, 499 ex.
BINARY-SEARCH, 799
binary search tree, 286–307
  AA-trees, 338
  AVL trees, 333 pr., 337
  deletion from, 295–298, 299 ex.
  with equal keys, 303 pr.
  insertion into, 294–295
  k-neighbor trees, 338
  maximum key of, 291
  minimum key of, 291
  optimal, 397–404, 413
  predecessor in, 291–292
  querying, 289–294
  randomly built, 299–303, 304 pr.
  right-converting of, 314 ex.
  scapegoat trees, 338
  searching, 289–291
  for sorting, 299 ex.
  splay trees, 338
  successor in, 291–292
  and treaps, 333 pr.
  weight-balanced trees, 338
  see also red-black tree
binary-search-tree property, 287
  in treaps, 333 pr.
  vs. min-heap property, 289 ex.

binary tree, 1177
  full, 1178
  number of different ones, 306 pr.
  representation of, 246
  superimposed upon a bit vector, 533–534
  see also binary search tree
binomial coefficient, 1186–1187
binomial distribution, 1203–1206
  and balls and bins, 133
  maximum value of, 1207 ex.
  tails of, 1208–1215
binomial expansion, 1186
binomial heap, 527 pr.
binomial tree, 527 pr.
bin packing, 1134 pr.
bipartite graph, 1172
  corresponding flow network of, 732
  d-regular, 736 ex.
  and hypergraphs, 1173 ex.
bipartite matching, 530, 732–736, 747 ex., 766
  Hopcroft-Karp algorithm for, 763 pr.
birthday paradox, 130–133, 142 ex.
bisection of a tree, 1181 pr.
bitonic euclidean traveling-salesman problem, 405 pr.
bitonic sequence, 682 pr.
bitonic tour, 405 pr.
bit operation, 927
  in Euclid's algorithm, 981 pr.
bit-reversal permutation, 472 pr., 918
BIT-REVERSE-COPY, 918
bit-reversed binary counter, 472 pr.
BIT-REVERSED-INCREMENT, 472 pr.
bit vector, 255 ex., 532–536
black-height, 309
black vertex, 594, 603
blocking flow, 765
block structure in pseudocode, 20
Bob, 959
Boole's inequality, 1195 ex.
boolean combinational circuit, 1071
boolean combinational element, 1070
boolean connective, 1079
boolean formula, 1049, 1066 ex., 1079, 1086 ex.
boolean function, 1187 ex.
boolean matrix multiplication, 832 ex.
Borůvka's algorithm, 641

bottleneck spanning tree, 640 pr.
bottleneck traveling-salesman problem, 1117 ex.
bottom of a stack, 233
BOTTOM-UP-CUT-ROD, 366
bottom-up method, for dynamic programming, 365
bound
  asymptotically tight, 45
  asymptotic lower, 48
  asymptotic upper, 47
  on binomial coefficients, 1186–1187
  on binomial distributions, 1206
  polylogarithmic, 57
  on the tails of a binomial distribution, 1208–1215
  see also lower bounds
boundary condition, in a recurrence, 67, 84
boundary of a polygon, 1020 ex.
bounding a summation, 1149–1156
box, nesting, 678 pr.
B^+-tree, 488
branching factor, in B-trees, 487
branch instructions, 23
breadth-first search, 594–602, 623
  in maximum flow, 727–730, 766
  and shortest paths, 597–600, 644
  similarity to Dijkstra's algorithm, 662, 663 ex.
breadth-first tree, 594, 600
bridge, 621 pr.
B^*-tree, 489 n.
B-tree, 484–504
  compared with red-black trees, 484, 490
  creating, 492
  deletion from, 499–502
  full node in, 489
  height of, 489–490
  insertion into, 493–497
  minimum degree of, 489
  minimum key of, 497 ex.
  properties of, 488–491
  searching, 491–492
  splitting a node in, 493–495
  2-3-4 trees, 489
B-TREE-CREATE, 492
B-TREE-DELETE, 499
B-TREE-INSERT, 495

B-Tree-Insert-Nonfull, 496
B-Tree-Search, 492, 499 ex.
B-Tree-Split-Child, 494
Bubblesort, 40 pr.
bucket, 200
bucket sort, 200–204
Bucket-Sort, 201
Build-Max-Heap, 157
Build-Max-Heap′, 167 pr.
Build-Min-Heap, 159
butterfly operation, 915
by, in pseudocode, 21

cache, 24, 449 pr.
cache hit, 449 pr.
cache miss, 449 pr.
cache obliviousness, 504
caching, off-line, 449 pr.
call
    in a multithreaded computation, 776
    of a subroutine, 23, 25 n.
    by value, 21
call edge, 778
cancellation lemma, 907
cancellation of flow, 717
canonical form for task scheduling, 444
capacity
    of a cut, 721
    of an edge, 709
    residual, 716, 719
    of a vertex, 714 ex.
capacity constraint, 709–710
cardinality of a set ($|\ |$), 1161
Carmichael number, 968, 975 ex.
Cartesian product ($\times$), 1162
Cartesian sum, 906 ex.
cascading cut, 520
Cascading-Cut, 519
Catalan numbers, 306 pr., 372
ceiling function ($\lceil\ \rceil$), 54
    in master theorem, 103–106
ceiling instruction, 23
certain event, 1190
certificate
    in a cryptosystem, 964
    for verification algorithms, 1063
Chained-Hash-Delete, 258
Chained-Hash-Insert, 258

Chained-Hash-Search, 258
chaining, 257–260, 283 pr.
chain of a convex hull, 1038
changing a key, in a Fibonacci heap, 529 pr.
changing variables, in the substitution method, 86–87
character code, 428
chess-playing program, 790–791
child
    in a binary tree, 1178
    in a multithreaded computation, 776
    in a rooted tree, 1176
child list in a Fibonacci heap, 507
Chinese remainder theorem, 950–954, 983
chip multiprocessor, 772
chirp transform, 914 ex.
choose ($\binom{n}{k}$), 1185
chord, 345 ex.
Cilk, 774, 812
Cilk++, 774, 812
ciphertext, 960
circuit
    boolean combinational, 1071
    depth of, 919
    for fast Fourier transform, 919–920
CIRCUIT-SAT, 1072
circuit satisfiability, 1070–1077
circular, doubly linked list with a sentinel, 239
circular linked list, 236
    see also linked list
class
    complexity, 1059
    equivalence, 1164
classification of edges
    in breadth-first search, 621 pr.
    in depth-first search, 609–610, 611 ex.
    in a multithreaded dag, 778–779
clause, 1081–1082
clean area, 208 pr.
clique, 1086–1089, 1105
    approximation algorithm for, 1111 ex., 1134 pr.
CLIQUE, 1087
closed interval, 348
closed semiring, 707
closest pair, finding, 1039–1044, 1047
closest-point heuristic, 1117 ex.

closure
  group property, 939
  of a language, 1058
  operator (*), 1058
  transitive, *see* transitive closure
cluster
  in a bit vector with a superimposed tree of
    constant height, 534
  for parallel computing, 772
  in proto van Emde Boas structures, 538
  in van Emde Boas trees, 546
clustering, 272
CNF (conjunctive normal form), 1049, 1082
CNF satisfiability, 1127 ex.
coarsening leaves of recursion
  in merge sort, 39 pr.
  when recursively spawning, 787
code, 428–429
  Huffman, 428–437, 450
codeword, 429
codomain, 1166
coefficient
  binomial, 1186
  of a polynomial, 55, 898
  in slack form, 856
coefficient representation, 900
  and fast multiplication, 903–905
cofactor, 1224
coin changing, 446 pr.
colinearity, 1016
collision, 257
  resolution by chaining, 257–260
  resolution by open addressing, 269–277
collision-resistant hash function, 964
coloring, 1103 pr., 1180 pr.
color, of a red-black-tree node, 308
column-major order, 208 pr.
column rank, 1223
columnsort, 208 pr.
column vector, 1218
combination, 1185
combinational circuit, 1071
combinational element, 1070
combine step, in divide-and-conquer, 30, 65
comment, in pseudocode (//), 21
commodity, 862
common divisor, 929
  greatest, *see* greatest common divisor

common multiple, 939 ex.
common subexpression, 915
common subsequence, 7, 391
  longest, 7, 390–397, 413
commutative laws for sets, 1159
commutative operation, 940
COMPACTIFY-LIST, 245 ex.
compact list, 250 pr.
COMPACT-LIST-SEARCH, 250 pr.
COMPACT-LIST-SEARCH′, 251 pr.
comparable line segments, 1022
COMPARE-EXCHANGE, 208 pr.
compare-exchange operation, 208 pr.
comparison sort, 191
  and binary search trees, 289 ex.
  randomized, 205 pr.
  and selection, 222
compatible activities, 415
compatible matrices, 371, 1221
competitive analysis, 476 pr.
complement
  of an event, 1190
  of a graph, 1090
  of a language, 1058
  Schur, 820, 834
  of a set, 1160
complementary slackness, 894 pr.
complete graph, 1172
complete k-ary tree, 1179
  see also heap
completeness of a language, 1077 ex.
complete step, 782
completion time, 447 pr., 1136 pr.
complexity class, 1059
  co-NP, 1064
  NP, 1049, 1064
  NPC, 1050, 1069
  P, 1049, 1055
complexity measure, 1059
complex numbers
  inverting matrices of, 832 ex.
  multiplication of, 83 ex.
complex root of unity, 906
  interpolation at, 912–913
component
  biconnected, 621 pr.
  connected, 1170
  strongly connected, 1171

component graph, 617

composite number, 928

   witness to, 968

composition, of multithreaded computations, 784 fig.

computational depth, 812

computational geometry, 1014–1047

computational problem, 5–6

computation dag, 777

computation, multithreaded, 777

COMPUTE-PREFIX-FUNCTION, 1006

COMPUTE-TRANSITION-FUNCTION, 1001

concatenation

   of languages, 1058

   of strings, 986

concrete problem, 1055

concurrency keywords, 774, 776, 785

concurrency platform, 773

conditional branch instruction, 23

conditional independence, 1195 ex.

conditional probability, 1192, 1194

configuration, 1074

conjugate of the golden ratio ($\hat{\phi}$), 59

conjugate transpose, 832 ex.

conjunctive normal form, 1049, 1082

connected component, 1170–1171

   identified using depth-first search, 612 ex.

   identified using disjoint-set data structures, 562–564

CONNECTED-COMPONENTS, 563

connected graph, 1170

connective, 1079

co-NP (complexity class), 1064

conquer step, in divide-and-conquer, 30, 65

conservation of flow, 709–710

consistency

   of literals, 1088

   sequential, 779, 812

CONSOLIDATE, 516

consolidating a Fibonacci-heap root list, 513–517

constraint, 851

   difference, 665

   equality, 670 ex., 852–853

   inequality, 852–853

   linear, 846

   nonnegativity, 851, 853

   tight, 865

   violation of, 865

constraint graph, 666–668

contain, in a path, 1170

continuation edge, 778

continuous uniform probability distribution, 1192

contraction

   of a dynamic table, 467–471

   of a matroid, 442

   of an undirected graph by an edge, 1172

control instructions, 23

convergence property, 650, 672–673

convergent series, 1146

converting binary to decimal, 933 ex.

convex combination of points, 1015

convex function, 1199

convex hull, 8, 1029–1039, 1046 pr.

convex layers, 1044 pr.

convex polygon, 1020 ex.

convex set, 714 ex.

convolution ($\otimes$), 901

convolution theorem, 913

copy instruction, 23

correctness of an algorithm, 6

corresponding flow network for bipartite matching, 732

countably infinite set, 1161

counter, *see* binary counter

counting, 1183–1189

   probabilistic, 143 pr.

counting sort, 194–197

   in radix sort, 198

COUNTING-SORT, 195

coupon collector's problem, 134

cover

   path, 761 pr.

   by a subset, 1118

   vertex, 1089, 1108, 1124–1127, 1139

covertical, 1024

CREATE-NEW-RS-VEB-TREE, 557 pr.

credit, 456

critical edge, 729

critical path

   of a dag, 657

   of a multithreaded computation, 779

cross a cut, 626

cross edge, 609

cross product ($\times$), 1016

cryptosystem, 958–965, 983
cubic spline, 840 pr.
currency exchange, 390 ex., 679 pr.
curve fitting, 835–839
cut
   capacity of, 721
   cascading, 520
   of a flow network, 720–724
   minimum, 721, 731 ex.
   net flow across, 720
   of an undirected graph, 626
   weight of, 1127 ex.
CUT, 519
CUT-ROD, 363
cutting, in a Fibonacci heap, 519
cycle of a graph, 1170
   hamiltonian, 1049, 1061
   minimum mean-weight, 680 pr.
   negative-weight, *see* negative-weight cycle
   and shortest paths, 646–647
cyclic group, 955
cyclic rotation, 1012 ex.
cycling, of simplex algorithm, 875

dag, *see* directed acyclic graph
DAG-SHORTEST-PATHS, 655
d-ary heap, 167 pr.
   in shortest-paths algorithms, 706 pr.
data-movement instructions, 23
data-parallel model, 811
data structure, 9, 229–355, 481–585
   AA-trees, 338
   augmentation of, 339–355
   AVL trees, 333 pr., 337
   binary search trees, 286–307
   binomial heaps, 527 pr.
   bit vectors, 255 ex., 532–536
   B-trees, 484–504
   deques, 236 ex.
   dictionaries, 229
   direct-address tables, 254–255
   for disjoint sets, 561–585
   for dynamic graphs, 483
   dynamic sets, 229–231
   dynamic trees, 482
   exponential search trees, 212, 483
   Fibonacci heaps, 505–530
   fusion trees, 212, 483

hash tables, 256–261
heaps, 151–169
interval trees, 348–354
k-neighbor trees, 338
linked lists, 236–241
mergeable heap, 505
order-statistic trees, 339–345
persistent, 331 pr., 482
potential of, 459
priority queues, 162–166
proto van Emde Boas structures, 538–545
queues, 232, 234–235
radix trees, 304 pr.
red-black trees, 308–338
relaxed heaps, 530
rooted trees, 246–249
scapegoat trees, 338
on secondary storage, 484–487
skip lists, 338
splay trees, 338, 482
stacks, 232–233
treaps, 333 pr., 338
2-3-4 heaps, 529 pr.
2-3-4 trees, 489, 503 pr.
2-3 trees, 337, 504
van Emde Boas trees, 531–560
weight-balanced trees, 338
data type, 23
deadline, 444
deallocation of objects, 243–244
decision by an algorithm, 1058–1059
decision problem, 1051, 1054
   and optimization problems, 1051
decision tree, 192–193
DECREASE-KEY, 162, 505
decreasing a key
   in Fibonacci heaps, 519–522
   in 2-3-4 heaps, 529 pr.
DECREMENT, 456 ex.
degeneracy, 874
degree
   of a binomial-tree root, 527 pr.
   maximum, of a Fibonacci heap, 509,
      523–526
   minimum, of a B-tree, 489
   of a node, 1177
   of a polynomial, 55, 898
   of a vertex, 1169

degree-bound, 898
DELETE, 230, 505
DELETE-LARGER-HALF, 463 ex.
deletion
    from binary search trees, 295–298, 299 ex.
    from a bit vector with a superimposed binary
        tree, 534
    from a bit vector with a superimposed tree of
        constant height, 535
    from B-trees, 499–502
    from chained hash tables, 258
    from direct-address tables, 254
    from dynamic tables, 467–471
    from Fibonacci heaps, 522, 526 pr.
    from heaps, 166 ex.
    from interval trees, 349
    from linked lists, 238
    from open-address hash tables, 271
    from order-statistic trees, 343–344
    from proto van Emde Boas structures, 544
    from queues, 234
    from red-black trees, 323–330
    from stacks, 232
    from sweep-line statuses, 1024
    from 2-3-4 heaps, 529 pr.
    from van Emde Boas trees, 554–556
DeMorgan's laws
    for propositional logic, 1083
    for sets, 1160, 1162 ex.
dense graph, 589
    ϵ-dense, 706 pr.
density
    of prime numbers, 965–966
    of a rod, 370 ex.
dependence
    and indicator random variables, 119
    linear, 1223
    see also independence
depth
    average, of a node in a randomly built binary
        search tree, 304 pr.
    of a circuit, 919
    of a node in a rooted tree, 1177
    of quicksort recursion tree, 178 ex.
    of a stack, 188 pr.
depth-determination problem, 583 pr.
depth-first forest, 603
depth-first search, 603–612, 623

    in finding articulation points, bridges, and
        biconnected components, 621 pr.
    in finding strongly connected components,
        615–621, 623
    in topological sorting, 612–615
depth-first tree, 603
deque, 236 ex.
DEQUEUE, 235
derivative of a series, 1147
descendant, 1176
destination vertex, 644
det, *see* determinant
determinacy race, 788
determinant, 1224–1225
    and matrix multiplication, 832 ex.
deterministic algorithm, 123
    multithreaded, 787
DETERMINISTIC-SEARCH, 143 pr.
DFS, 604
DFS-VISIT, 604
DFT (discrete Fourier transform), 9, 909
diagonal matrix, 1218
    LUP decomposition of, 827 ex.
diameter of a tree, 602 ex.
dictionary, 229
difference constraints, 664–670
difference equation, *see* recurrence
difference of sets ($-$), 1159
    symmetric, 763 pr.
differentiation of a series, 1147
digital signature, 960
digraph, *see* directed graph
DIJKSTRA, 658
Dijkstra's algorithm, 658–664, 682
    for all-pairs shortest paths, 684, 704
    implemented with a Fibonacci heap, 662
    implemented with a min-heap, 662
    with integer edge weights, 664 ex.
    in Johnson's algorithm, 702
    similarity to breadth-first search, 662,
        663 ex.
    similarity to Prim's algorithm, 634, 662
DIRECT-ADDRESS-DELETE, 254
direct addressing, 254–255, 532–536
DIRECT-ADDRESS-INSERT, 254
DIRECT-ADDRESS-SEARCH, 254
direct-address table, 254–255
directed acyclic graph (dag), 1172

and back edges, 613
and component graphs, 617
and hamiltonian paths, 1066 ex.
longest simple path in, 404 pr.
for representing a multithreaded
    computation, 777
single-source shortest-paths algorithm for,
    655–658
topological sort of, 612–615, 623
directed graph, 1168
    all-pairs shortest paths in, 684–707
    constraint graph, 666
    Euler tour of, 623 pr., 1048
    hamiltonian cycle of, 1049
    and longest paths, 1048
    path cover of, 761 pr.
    PERT chart, 657, 657 ex.
    semiconnected, 621 ex.
    shortest path in, 643
    single-source shortest paths in, 643–683
    singly connected, 612 ex.
    square of, 593 ex.
    transitive closure of, 697
    transpose of, 592 ex.
    universal sink in, 593 ex.
    see also directed acyclic graph, graph,
        network
directed segment, 1015–1017
directed version of an undirected graph, 1172
DIRECTION, 1018
dirty area, 208 pr.
DISCHARGE, 751
discharge of an overflowing vertex, 751
discovered vertex, 594, 603
discovery time, in depth-first search, 605
discrete Fourier transform, 9, 909
discrete logarithm, 955
discrete logarithm theorem, 955
discrete probability distribution, 1191
discrete random variable, 1196–1201
disjoint-set data structure, 561–585
    analysis of, 575–581, 581 ex.
    in connected components, 562–564
    in depth determination, 583 pr.
    disjoint-set-forest implementation of,
        568–572
    in Kruskal's algorithm, 631
    linear-time special case of, 585

linked-list implementation of, 564–568
    in off-line least common ancestors, 584 pr.
    in off-line minimum, 582 pr.
    in task scheduling, 448 pr.
disjoint-set forest, 568–572
    analysis of, 575–581, 581 ex.
    rank properties of, 575, 581 ex.
    see also disjoint-set data structure
disjoint sets, 1161
disjunctive normal form, 1083
disk, 1028 ex.
disk drive, 485–487
    see also secondary storage
DISK-READ, 487
DISK-WRITE, 487
distance
    edit, 406 pr.
    euclidean, 1039
    L_m, 1044 ex.
    Manhattan, 225 pr., 1044 ex.
    of a shortest path, 597
distributed memory, 772
distribution
    binomial, 1203–1206
    continuous uniform, 1192
    discrete, 1191
    geometric, 1202–1203
    of inputs, 116, 122
    of prime numbers, 965
    probability, 1190
    sparse-hulled, 1046 pr.
    uniform, 1191
distributive laws for sets, 1160
divergent series, 1146
divide-and-conquer method, 30–35, 65
    analysis of, 34–35
    for binary search, 39 ex.
    for conversion of binary to decimal, 933 ex.
    for fast Fourier transform, 909–912
    for finding the closest pair of points,
        1040–1043
    for finding the convex hull, 1030
    for matrix inversion, 829–831
    for matrix multiplication, 76–83, 792–797
    for maximum-subarray problem, 68–75
    for merge sort, 30–37, 797–805
    for multiplication, 920 pr.

for multithreaded matrix multiplication, 792–797

for multithreaded merge sort, 797–805

for quicksort, 170–190

relation to dynamic programming, 359

for selection, 215–224

solving recurrences for, 83–106, 112–113

for Strassen's algorithm, 79–83

divide instruction, 23

divides relation ($|$), 927

divide step, in divide-and-conquer, 30, 65

division method, 263, 268–269 ex.

division theorem, 928

divisor, 927–928

common, 929

see also greatest common divisor

DNA, 6–7, 390–391, 406 pr.

DNF (disjunctive normal form), 1083

does-not-divide relation ($\nmid$), 927

domain, 1166

dominates relation, 1045 pr.

double hashing, 272–274, 277 ex.

doubly linked list, 236

see also linked list

downto, in pseudocode, 21

d-regular graph, 736 ex.

duality, 879–886, 895 pr.

weak, 880–881, 886 ex.

dual linear program, 879

dummy key, 397

dynamic graph, 562 n.

all-pairs shortest paths algorithms for, 707

data structures for, 483

minimum-spanning-tree algorithm for, 637 ex.

transitive closure of, 705 pr., 707

dynamic multithreaded algorithm, *see* multithreaded algorithm

dynamic multithreading, 773

dynamic order statistics, 339–345

dynamic-programming method, 359–413

for activity selection, 421 ex.

for all-pairs shortest paths, 686–697

for bitonic euclidean traveling-salesman problem, 405 pr.

bottom-up, 365

for breaking a string, 410 pr.

compared with greedy algorithms, 381, 390 ex., 418, 423–427

for edit distance, 406 pr.

elements of, 378–390

for Floyd-Warshall algorithm, 693–697

for inventory planning, 411 pr.

for longest common subsequence, 390–397

for longest palindrome subsequence, 405 pr.

for longest simple path in a weighted directed acyclic graph, 404 pr.

for matrix-chain multiplication, 370–378

and memoization, 387–389

for optimal binary search trees, 397–404

optimal substructure in, 379–384

overlapping subproblems in, 384–386

for printing neatly, 405 pr.

reconstructing an optimal solution in, 387

relation to divide-and-conquer, 359

for rod-cutting, 360–370

for seam carving, 409 pr.

for signing free agents, 411 pr.

top-down with memoization, 365

for transitive closure, 697–699

for Viterbi algorithm, 408 pr.

for 0-1 knapsack problem, 427 ex.

dynamic set, 229–231

see also data structure

dynamic table, 463–471

analyzed by accounting method, 465–466

analyzed by aggregate analysis, 465

analyzed by potential method, 466–471

load factor of, 463

dynamic tree, 482

e, 55

E [ ] (expected value), 1197

early-first form, 444

early task, 444

edge, 1168

admissible, 749

antiparallel, 711–712

attributes of, 592

back, 609

bridge, 621 pr.

call, 778

capacity of, 709

classification in breadth-first search, 621 pr.

classification in depth-first search, 609–610

continuation, 778
critical, 729
cross, 609
forward, 609
inadmissible, 749
light, 626
negative-weight, 645–646
residual, 716
return, 779
safe, 626
saturated, 739
spawn, 778
tree, 601, 603, 609
weight of, 591
edge connectivity, 731 ex.
edge set, 1168
edit distance, 406 pr.
Edmonds-Karp algorithm, 727–730
elementary event, 1189
elementary insertion, 465
element of a set ($\in$), 1158
ellipsoid algorithm, 850, 897
elliptic-curve factorization method, 984
elseif, in pseudocode, 20 n.
else, in pseudocode, 20
empty language ($\emptyset$), 1058
empty set ($\emptyset$), 1158
empty set laws, 1159
empty stack, 233
empty string (ε), 986, 1058
empty tree, 1178
encoding of problem instances, 1055–1057
endpoint
    of an interval, 348
    of a line segment, 1015
ENQUEUE, 235
entering a vertex, 1169
entering variable, 867
entropy function, 1187
ϵ-dense graph, 706 pr.
ϵ-universal hash function, 269 ex.
equality
    of functions, 1166
    linear, 845
    of sets, 1158
equality constraint, 670 ex., 852
    and inequality constraints, 853
    tight, 865

violation of, 865
equation
    and asymptotic notation, 49–50
    normal, 837
    recurrence, *see* recurrence
equivalence class, 1164
    modulo n ($[a]_n$), 928
equivalence, modular ($\equiv$), 54, 1165 ex.
equivalence relation, 1164
    and modular equivalence, 1165 ex.
equivalent linear programs, 852
error, in pseudocode, 22
escape problem, 760 pr.
EUCLID, 935
Euclid's algorithm, 933–939, 981 pr., 983
euclidean distance, 1039
euclidean norm ($\| \|$), 1222
Euler's constant, 943
Euler's phi function, 943
Euler's theorem, 954, 975 ex.
Euler tour, 623 pr., 1048
    and hamiltonian cycles, 1048
evaluation of a polynomial, 41 pr., 900, 905 ex.
    derivatives of, 922 pr.
    at multiple points, 923 pr.
event, 1190
event point, 1023
event-point schedule, 1023
EXACT-SUBSET-SUM, 1129
excess flow, 736
exchange property, 437
exclusion and inclusion, 1163 ex.
execute a subroutine, 25 n.
expansion of a dynamic table, 464–467
expectation, *see* expected value
expected running time, 28, 117
expected value, 1197–1199
    of a binomial distribution, 1204
    of a geometric distribution, 1202
    of an indicator random variable, 118
explored vertex, 605
exponential function, 55–56
exponential height, 300
exponential search tree, 212, 483
exponential series, 1147
exponentiation instruction, 24
exponentiation, modular, 956
EXTENDED-BOTTOM-UP-CUT-ROD, 369

EXTENDED-EUCLID, 937
EXTEND-SHORTEST-PATHS, 688
extension of a set, 438
exterior of a polygon, 1020 ex.
external node, 1176
external path length, 1180 ex.
extracting the maximum key
    from d-ary heaps, 167 pr.
    from max-heaps, 163
extracting the minimum key
    from Fibonacci heaps, 512–518
    from 2-3-4 heaps, 529 pr.
    from Young tableaus, 167 pr.
EXTRACT-MAX, 162–163
EXTRACT-MIN, 162, 505

factor, 928
    twiddle, 912
factorial function (!), 57–58
factorization, 975–980, 984
    unique, 931
failure, in a Bernoulli trial, 1201
fair coin, 1191
fan-out, 1071
Farkas's lemma, 895 pr.
farthest-pair problem, 1030
FASTER-ALL-PAIRS-SHORTEST-PATHS, 691,
    692 ex.
fast Fourier transform (FFT), 898–925
    circuit for, 919–920
    iterative implementation of, 915–918
    multidimensional, 921 pr.
    multithreaded algorithm for, 804 ex.
    recursive implementation of, 909–912
    using modular arithmetic, 923 pr.
feasibility problem, 665, 894 pr.
feasible linear program, 851
feasible region, 847
feasible solution, 665, 846, 851
Fermat's theorem, 954
FFT, see fast Fourier transform
FFTW, 924
FIB, 775
FIB-HEAP-CHANGE-KEY, 529 pr.
FIB-HEAP-DECREASE-KEY, 519
FIB-HEAP-DELETE, 522
FIB-HEAP-EXTRACT-MIN, 513
FIB-HEAP-INSERT, 510

FIB-HEAP-LINK, 516
FIB-HEAP-PRUNE, 529 pr.
FIB-HEAP-UNION, 512
Fibonacci heap, 505–530
    changing a key in, 529 pr.
    compared with binary heaps, 506–507
    creating, 510
    decreasing a key in, 519–522
    deletion from, 522, 526 pr.
    in Dijkstra's algorithm, 662
    extracting the minimum key from, 512–518
    insertion into, 510–511
    in Johnson's algorithm, 704
    maximum degree of, 509, 523–526
    minimum key of, 511
    potential function for, 509
    in Prim's algorithm, 636
    pruning, 529 pr.
    running times of operations on, 506 fig.
    uniting, 511–512
Fibonacci numbers, 59–60, 108 pr., 523
    computation of, 774–780, 981 pr.
FIFO (first-in, first-out), 232
    see also queue
final-state function, 996
final strand, 779
FIND-DEPTH, 583 pr.
FIND-MAX-CROSSING-SUBARRAY, 71
FIND-MAXIMUM-SUBARRAY, 72
find path, 569
FIND-SET, 562
    disjoint-set-forest implementation of, 571,
        585
    linked-list implementation of, 564
finished vertex, 603
finishing time, in depth-first search, 605
    and strongly connected components, 618
finish time, in activity selection, 415
finite automaton, 995
    for string matching, 996–1002
FINITE-AUTOMATON-MATCHER, 999
finite group, 940
finite sequence, 1166
finite set, 1161
first-fit heuristic, 1134 pr.
first-in, first-out, 232
    see also queue
fixed-length code, 429

floating-point data type, 23
floor function ($\lfloor \ \rfloor$), 54
   in master theorem, 103–106
floor instruction, 23
flow, 709–714
   aggregate, 863
   augmentation of, 716
   blocking, 765
   cancellation of, 717
   excess, 736
   integer-valued, 733
   net, across a cut, 720
   value of, 710
flow conservation, 709–710
flow network, 709–714
   corresponding to a bipartite graph, 732
   cut of, 720–724
   with multiple sources and sinks, 712
FLOYD-WARSHALL, 695
FLOYD-WARSHALL$'$, 699 ex.
Floyd-Warshall algorithm, 693–697,
    699–700 ex., 706
   multithreaded, 797 ex.
FORD-FULKERSON, 724
Ford-Fulkerson method, 714–731, 765
FORD-FULKERSON-METHOD, 715
forest, 1172–1173
   depth-first, 603
   disjoint-set, 568–572
for, in pseudocode, 20–21
   and loop invariants, 19 n.
formal power series, 108 pr.
formula satisfiability, 1079–1081, 1105
forward edge, 609
forward substitution, 816–817
Fourier transform, *see* discrete Fourier
    transform, fast Fourier transform
fractional knapsack problem, 426, 428 ex.
free agent, 411 pr.
freeing of objects, 243–244
free list, 243
FREE-OBJECT, 244
free tree, 1172–1176
frequency domain, 898
full binary tree, 1178, 1180 ex.
   relation to optimal code, 430
full node, 489
full rank, 1223

full walk of a tree, 1114
fully parenthesized matrix-chain product, 370
fully polynomial-time approximation scheme,
    1107
   for subset sum, 1128–1134, 1139
function, 1166–1168
   Ackermann's, 585
   basis, 835
   convex, 1199
   final-state, 996
   hash, *see* hash function
   linear, 26, 845
   objective, 664, 847, 851
   potential, 459
   prefix, 1003–1004
   quadratic, 27
   reduction, 1067
   suffix, 996
   transition, 995, 1001–1002, 1012 ex.
functional iteration, 58
fundamental theorem of linear programming,
    892
furthest-in-future strategy, 449 pr.
fusion tree, 212, 483
fuzzy sorting, 189 pr.

Gabow's scaling algorithm for single-source
    shortest paths, 679 pr.
gap character, 989 ex., 1002 ex.
gap heuristic, 760 ex., 766
garbage collection, 151, 243
gate, 1070
Gaussian elimination, 819, 842
gcd, *see* greatest common divisor
general number-field sieve, 984
generating function, 108 pr.
generator
   of a subgroup, 944
   of $\mathbb{Z}_n^*$, 955
GENERIC-MST, 626
GENERIC-PUSH-RELABEL, 741
generic push-relabel algorithm, 740–748
geometric distribution, 1202–1203
   and balls and bins, 134
geometric series, 1147
geometry, computational, 1014–1047
$GF(2)$, 1227 pr.
gift wrapping, 1037, 1047

global variable, 21
Goldberg's algorithm, *see* push-relabel
    algorithm
golden ratio (ϕ), 59, 108 pr.
gossiping, 478
GRAFT, 583 pr.
Graham's scan, 1030–1036, 1047
GRAHAM-SCAN, 1031
graph, 1168–1173
    adjacency-list representation of, 590
    adjacency-matrix representation of, 591
    algorithms for, 587–766
    and asymptotic notation, 588
    attributes of, 588, 592
    breadth-first search of, 594–602, 623
    coloring of, 1103 pr.
    complement of, 1090
    component, 617
    constraint, 666–668
    dense, 589
    depth-first search of, 603–612, 623
    dynamic, 562 n.
    ϵ-dense, 706 pr.
    hamiltonian, 1061
    incidence matrix of, 448 pr., 593 ex.
    interval, 422 ex.
    nonhamiltonian, 1061
    shortest path in, 597
    singly connected, 612 ex.
    sparse, 589
    static, 562 n.
    subproblem, 367–368
    tour of, 1096
    weighted, 591
    see also directed acyclic graph, directed
        graph, flow network, undirected graph,
        tree
graphic matroid, 437–438, 642
GRAPH-ISOMORPHISM, 1065 ex.
gray vertex, 594, 603
greatest common divisor (gcd), 929–930,
    933 ex.
    binary gcd algorithm for, 981 pr.
    Euclid's algorithm for, 933–939, 981 pr., 983
    with more than two arguments, 939 ex.
    recursion theorem for, 934
greedoid, 450
GREEDY, 440

GREEDY-ACTIVITY-SELECTOR, 421
greedy algorithm, 414–450
    for activity selection, 415–422
    for coin changing, 446 pr.
    compared with dynamic programming, 381,
        390 ex., 418, 423–427
    Dijkstra's algorithm, 658–664
    elements of, 423–428
    for fractional knapsack problem, 426
    greedy-choice property in, 424–425
    for Huffman code, 428–437
    Kruskal's algorithm, 631–633
    and matroids, 437–443
    for minimum spanning tree, 631–638
    for multithreaded scheduling, 781–783
    for off-line caching, 449 pr.
    optimal substructure in, 425
    Prim's algorithm, 634–636
    for set cover, 1117–1122, 1139
    for task scheduling, 443–446, 447–448 pr.
    on a weighted matroid, 439–442
    for weighted set cover, 1135 pr.
greedy-choice property, 424–425
    of activity selection, 417–418
    of Huffman codes, 433–434
    of a weighted matroid, 441
greedy scheduler, 782
GREEDY-SET-COVER, 1119
grid, 760 pr.
group, 939–946
    cyclic, 955
    operator ($\oplus$), 939
guessing the solution, in the substitution
    method, 84–85

half 3-CNF satisfiability, 1101 ex.
half-open interval, 348
Hall's theorem, 735 ex.
halting problem, 1048
halving lemma, 908
HAM-CYCLE, 1062
hamiltonian cycle, 1049, 1061, 1091–1096,
    1105
hamiltonian graph, 1061
hamiltonian path, 1066 ex., 1101 ex.
HAM-PATH, 1066 ex.
handle, 163, 507
handshaking lemma, 1172 ex.

harmonic number, 1147, 1153–1154
harmonic series, 1147, 1153–1154
HASH-DELETE, 277 ex.
hash function, 256, 262–269
    auxiliary, 272
    collision-resistant, 964
    division method for, 263, 268–269 ex.
    ϵ-universal, 269 ex.
    multiplication method for, 263–264
    universal, 265–268
hashing, 253–285
    with chaining, 257–260, 283 pr.
    double, 272–274, 277 ex.
    k-universal, 284 pr.
    in memoization, 365, 387
    with open addressing, 269–277
    perfect, 277–282, 285
    to replace adjacency lists, 593 ex.
    universal, 265–268
HASH-INSERT, 270, 277 ex.
HASH-SEARCH, 271, 277 ex.
hash table, 256–261
    dynamic, 471 ex.
    secondary, 278
    see also hashing
hash value, 256
hat-check problem, 122 ex.
head
    in a disk drive, 485
    of a linked list, 236
    of a queue, 234
heap, 151–169
    analyzed by potential method, 462 ex.
    binomial, 527 pr.
    building, 156–159, 166 pr.
    compared with Fibonacci heaps, 506–507
    d-ary, 167 pr., 706 pr.
    deletion from, 166 ex.
    in Dijkstra's algorithm, 662
    extracting the maximum key from, 163
    Fibonacci, *see* Fibonacci heap
    as garbage-collected storage, 151
    height of, 153
    in Huffman's algorithm, 433
    to implement a mergeable heap, 506
    increasing a key in, 163–164
    insertion into, 164
    in Johnson's algorithm, 704

max-heap, 152
maximum key of, 163
mergeable, *see* mergeable heap
min-heap, 153
    in Prim's algorithm, 636
    as a priority queue, 162–166
    relaxed, 530
    running times of operations on, 506 fig.
    and treaps, 333 pr.
    2-3-4, 529 pr.
HEAP-DECREASE-KEY, 165 ex.
HEAP-DELETE, 166 ex.
HEAP-EXTRACT-MAX, 163
HEAP-EXTRACT-MIN, 165 ex.
HEAP-INCREASE-KEY, 164
HEAP-MAXIMUM, 163
HEAP-MINIMUM, 165 ex.
heap property, 152
    maintenance of, 154–156
    vs. binary-search-tree property, 289 ex.
heapsort, 151–169
HEAPSORT, 160
heel, 602 ex.
height
    of a binomial tree, 527 pr.
    black-, 309
    of a B-tree, 489–490
    of a d-ary heap, 167 pr.
    of a decision tree, 193
    exponential, 300
    of a heap, 153
    of a node in a heap, 153, 159 ex.
    of a node in a tree, 1177
    of a red-black tree, 309
    of a tree, 1177
height-balanced tree, 333 pr.
height function, in push-relabel algorithms, 738
hereditary family of subsets, 437
Hermitian matrix, 832 ex.
high endpoint of an interval, 348
high function, 537, 546
HIRE-ASSISTANT, 115
hiring problem, 114–115, 123–124, 145
    on-line, 139–141
    probabilistic analysis of, 120–121
hit
    cache, 449 pr.
    spurious, 991

HOARE-PARTITION, 185 pr.
HOPCROFT-KARP, 764 pr.
Hopcroft-Karp bipartite matching algorithm,
    763 pr.
horizontal ray, 1021 ex.
Horner's rule, 41 pr., 900
    in the Rabin-Karp algorithm, 990
HUFFMAN, 431
Huffman code, 428–437, 450
hull, convex, 8, 1029–1039, 1046 pr.
Human Genome Project, 6
hyperedge, 1172
hypergraph, 1172
    and bipartite graphs, 1173 ex.

ideal parallel computer, 779
idempotency laws for sets, 1159
identity, 939
identity matrix, 1218
if, in pseudocode, 20
image, 1167
image compression, 409 pr., 413
inadmissible edge, 749
incidence, 1169
incidence matrix
    and difference constraints, 666
    of a directed graph, 448 pr., 593 ex.
    of an undirected graph, 448 pr.
inclusion and exclusion, 1163 ex.
incomplete step, 782
INCREASE-KEY, 162
increasing a key, in a max-heap, 163–164
INCREMENT, 454
incremental design method, 29
    for finding the convex hull, 1030
in-degree, 1169
indentation in pseudocode, 20
independence
    of events, 1192–1193, 1195 ex.
    of random variables, 1197
    of subproblems in dynamic programming,
        383–384
independent family of subsets, 437
independent set, 1101 pr.
    of tasks, 444
independent strands, 789
index function, 537, 546
index of an element of $\mathbb{Z}_n^*$, 955

indicator random variable, 118–121
    in analysis of expected height of a randomly
        built binary search tree, 300–303
    in analysis of inserting into a treap, 333 pr.
    in analysis of streaks, 138–139
    in analysis of the birthday paradox, 132–133
    in approximation algorithm for
        MAX-3-CNF satisfiability, 1124
    in bounding the right tail of the binomial
        distribution, 1212–1213
    in bucket sort analysis, 202–204
    expected value of, 118
    in hashing analysis, 259–260
    in hiring-problem analysis, 120–121
    and linearity of expectation, 119
    in quicksort analysis, 182–184, 187 pr.
    in randomized-selection analysis, 217–219,
        226 pr.
    in universal-hashing analysis, 265–266
induced subgraph, 1171
inequality constraint, 852
    and equality constraints, 853
inequality, linear, 846
infeasible linear program, 851
infeasible solution, 851
infinite sequence, 1166
infinite set, 1161
infinite sum, 1145
infinity, arithmetic with, 650
INITIALIZE-PREFLOW, 740
INITIALIZE-SIMPLEX, 871, 887
INITIALIZE-SINGLE-SOURCE, 648
initial strand, 779
injective function, 1167
inner product, 1222
inorder tree walk, 287, 293 ex., 342
INORDER-TREE-WALK, 288
in-place sorting, 17, 148, 206 pr.
input
    to an algorithm, 5
    to a combinational circuit, 1071
    distribution of, 116, 122
    to a logic gate, 1070
    size of, 25
input alphabet, 995
INSERT, 162, 230, 463 ex., 505
insertion
    into binary search trees, 294–295

into a bit vector with a superimposed binary tree, 534
into a bit vector with a superimposed tree of constant height, 534
into B-trees, 493–497
into chained hash tables, 258
into d-ary heaps, 167 pr.
into direct-address tables, 254
into dynamic tables, 464–467
elementary, 465
into Fibonacci heaps, 510–511
into heaps, 164
into interval trees, 349
into linked lists, 237–238
into open-address hash tables, 270
into order-statistic trees, 343
into proto van Emde Boas structures, 544
into queues, 234
into red-black trees, 315–323
into stacks, 232
into sweep-line statuses, 1024
into treaps, 333 pr.
into 2-3-4 heaps, 529 pr.
into van Emde Boas trees, 552–554
into Young tableaus, 167 pr.
insertion sort, 12, 16–20, 25–27
in bucket sort, 201–204
compared with merge sort, 14 ex.
compared with quicksort, 178 ex.
decision tree for, 192 fig.
in merge sort, 39 pr.
in quicksort, 185 ex.
using binary search, 39 ex.
INSERTION-SORT, 18, 26, 208 pr.
instance
of an abstract problem, 1051, 1054
of a problem, 5
instructions of the RAM model, 23
integer data type, 23
integer linear programming, 850, 895 pr., 1101 ex.
integers ($\mathbb{Z}$), 1158
integer-valued flow, 733
integrality theorem, 734
integral, to approximate summations, 1154–1156
integration of a series, 1147
interior of a polygon, 1020 ex.

interior-point method, 850, 897
intermediate vertex, 693
internal node, 1176
internal path length, 1180 ex.
interpolation by a cubic spline, 840 pr.
interpolation by a polynomial, 901, 906 ex.
at complex roots of unity, 912–913
intersection
of chords, 345 ex.
determining, for a set of line segments, 1021–1029, 1047
determining, for two line segments, 1017–1019
of languages, 1058
of sets ($\cap$), 1159
interval, 348
fuzzy sorting of, 189 pr.
INTERVAL-DELETE, 349
interval graph, 422 ex.
INTERVAL-INSERT, 349
INTERVAL-SEARCH, 349, 351
INTERVAL-SEARCH-EXACTLY, 354 ex.
interval tree, 348–354
interval trichotomy, 348
intractability, 1048
invalid shift, 985
inventory planning, 411 pr.
inverse
of a bijective function, 1167
in a group, 940
of a matrix, 827–831, 842, 1223, 1225 ex.
multiplicative, modulo n, 949
inversion
in a self-organizing list, 476 pr.
in a sequence, 41 pr., 122 ex., 345 ex.
inverter, 1070
invertible matrix, 1223
isolated vertex, 1169
isomorphic graphs, 1171
iterated function, 63 pr.
iterated logarithm function, 58–59
ITERATIVE-FFT, 917
ITERATIVE-TREE-SEARCH, 291
iter function, 577

Jarvis's march, 1037–1038, 1047
Jensen's inequality, 1199
JOHNSON, 704

Johnson's algorithm, 700–706
joining
    of red-black trees, 332 pr.
    of 2-3-4 trees, 503 pr.
joint probability density function, 1197
Josephus permutation, 355 pr.

Karmarkar's algorithm, 897
Karp's minimum mean-weight cycle algorithm,
    680 pr.
k-ary tree, 1179
k-CNF, 1049
k-coloring, 1103 pr., 1180 pr.
k-combination, 1185
k-conjunctive normal form, 1049
kernel of a polygon, 1038 ex.
key, 16, 147, 162, 229
    dummy, 397
    interpreted as a natural number, 263
    median, of a B-tree node, 493
    public, 959, 962
    secret, 959, 962
    static, 277
keywords, in pseudocode, 20–22
    multithreaded, 774, 776–777, 785–786
"killer adversary" for quicksort, 190
Kirchhoff's current law, 708
Kleene star (*), 1058
KMP algorithm, 1002–1013
KMP-MATCHER, 1005
knapsack problem
    fractional, 426, 428 ex.
    0-1, 425, 427 ex., 1137 pr., 1139
k-neighbor tree, 338
knot, of a spline, 840 pr.
Knuth-Morris-Pratt algorithm, 1002–1013
k-permutation, 126, 1184
Kraft inequality, 1180 ex.
Kruskal's algorithm, 631–633, 642
    with integer edge weights, 637 ex.
k-sorted, 207 pr.
k-string, 1184
k-subset, 1161
k-substring, 1184
kth power, 933 ex.
k-universal hashing, 284 pr.

Lagrange's formula, 902

Lagrange's theorem, 944
Lamé's theorem, 936
language, 1057
    completeness of, 1077 ex.
    proving NP-completeness of, 1078–1079
    verification of, 1063
last-in, first-out, 232
    see also stack
late task, 444
layers
    convex, 1044 pr.
    maximal, 1045 pr.
LCA, 584 pr.
lcm (least common multiple), 939 ex.
LCS, 7, 390–397, 413
LCS-LENGTH, 394
leading submatrix, 833, 839 ex.
leaf, 1176
least common ancestor, 584 pr.
least common multiple, 939 ex.
least-squares approximation, 835–839
leaving a vertex, 1169
leaving variable, 867
LEFT, 152
left child, 1178
left-child, right-sibling representation, 246,
    249 ex.
LEFT-ROTATE, 313, 353 ex.
left rotation, 312
left spine, 333 pr.
left subtree, 1178
Legendre symbol ($\frac{a}{p}$), 982 pr.
length
    of a path, 1170
    of a sequence, 1166
    of a spine, 333 pr.
    of a string, 986, 1184
level
    of a function, 573
    of a tree, 1177
level function, 576
lexicographically less than, 304 pr.
lexicographic sorting, 304 pr.
lg (binary logarithm), 56
lg* (iterated logarithm function), 58–59
lg^k (exponentiation of logarithms), 56
lg lg (composition of logarithms), 56
LIFO (last-in, first-out), 232

see also stack
light edge, 626
linear constraint, 846
linear dependence, 1223
linear equality, 845
linear equations
    solving modular, 946–950
    solving systems of, 813–827
    solving tridiagonal systems of, 840 pr.
linear function, 26, 845
linear independence, 1223
linear inequality, 846
linear-inequality feasibility problem, 894 pr.
linearity of expectation, 1198
    and indicator random variables, 119
linearity of summations, 1146
linear order, 1165
linear permutation, 1229 pr.
linear probing, 272
linear programming, 7, 843–897
    algorithms for, 850
    applications of, 849
    duality in, 879–886
    ellipsoid algorithm for, 850, 897
    finding an initial solution in, 886–891
    fundamental theorem of, 892
    interior-point methods for, 850, 897
    Karmarkar's algorithm for, 897
    and maximum flow, 860–861
    and minimum-cost circulation, 896 pr.
    and minimum-cost flow, 861–862
    and minimum-cost multicommodity flow,
        864 ex.
    and multicommodity flow, 862–863
    simplex algorithm for, 864–879, 896
    and single-pair shortest path, 859–860
    and single-source shortest paths, 664–670,
        863 ex.
    slack form for, 854–857
    standard form for, 850–854
    see also integer linear programming, 0-1
        integer programming
linear-programming relaxation, 1125
linear search, 22 ex.
linear speedup, 780
line segment, 1015
    comparable, 1022
    determining turn of, 1017

determining whether any intersect,
    1021–1029, 1047
determining whether two intersect,
    1017–1019
link
    of binomial trees, 527 pr.
    of Fibonacci-heap roots, 513
    of trees in a disjoint-set forest, 570–571
LINK, 571
linked list, 236–241
    compact, 245 ex., 250 pr.
    deletion from, 238
    to implement disjoint sets, 564–568
    insertion into, 237–238
    neighbor list, 750
    searching, 237, 268 ex.
    self-organizing, 476 pr.
list, *see* linked list
LIST-DELETE, 238
LIST-DELETE$'$, 238
LIST-INSERT, 238
LIST-INSERT$'$, 240
LIST-SEARCH, 237
LIST-SEARCH$'$, 239
literal, 1082
little-oh notation, 50–51, 64
little-omega notation, 51
L_m-distance, 1044 ex.
ln (natural logarithm), 56
load factor
    of a dynamic table, 463
    of a hash table, 258
load instruction, 23
local variable, 21
logarithm function (log), 56–57
    discrete, 955
    iterated ($\lg^*$), 58–59
logical parallelism, 777
logic gate, 1070
longest common subsequence, 7, 390–397, 413
longest palindrome subsequence, 405 pr.
LONGEST-PATH, 1060 ex.
LONGEST-PATH-LENGTH, 1060 ex.
longest simple cycle, 1101 ex.
longest simple path, 1048
    in an unweighted graph, 382
    in a weighted directed acyclic graph, 404 pr.
LOOKUP-CHAIN, 388

loop, in pseudocode, 20
  parallel, 785–787
loop invariant, 18–19
  for breadth-first search, 595
  for building a heap, 157
  for consolidating the root list of a Fibonacci
    heap, 517
  for determining the rank of an element in an
    order-statistic tree, 342
  for Dijkstra's algorithm, 660
  and **for** loops, 19 n.
  for the generic minimum-spanning-tree
    method, 625
  for the generic push-relabel algorithm, 743
  for Graham's scan, 1034
  for heapsort, 160 ex.
  for Horner's rule, 41 pr.
  for increasing a key in a heap, 166 ex.
  initialization of, 19
  for insertion sort, 18
  maintenance of, 19
  for merging, 32
  for modular exponentiation, 957
  origin of, 42
  for partitioning, 171
  for Prim's algorithm, 636
  for the Rabin-Karp algorithm, 993
  for randomly permuting an array, 127,
    128 ex.
  for red-black tree insertion, 318
  for the relabel-to-front algorithm, 755
  for searching an interval tree, 352
  for the simplex algorithm, 872
  for string-matching automata, 998, 1000
  and termination, 19
low endpoint of an interval, 348
lower bounds
  on approximations, 1140
  asymptotic, 48
  for average sorting, 207 pr.
  on binomial coefficients, 1186
  for comparting water jugs, 206 pr.
  for convex hull, 1038 ex., 1047
  for disjoint-set data structures, 585
  for finding the minimum, 214
  for finding the predecessor, 560
  for length of an optimal traveling-salesman
    tour, 1112–1115

for median finding, 227
  for merging, 208 pr.
  for minimum-weight vertex cover,
    1124–1126
  for multithreaded computations, 780
  and potential functions, 478
  for priority-queue operations, 531
  and recurrences, 67
  for simultaneous minimum and maximum,
    215 ex.
  for size of an optimal vertex cover, 1110,
    1135 pr.
  for sorting, 191–194, 205 pr., 211, 531
  for streaks, 136–138, 142 ex.
  on summations, 1152, 1154
lower median, 213
lower square root $(\sqrt[1]{})$, 546
lower-triangular matrix, 1219, 1222 ex.,
    1225 ex.
low function, 537, 546
LU decomposition, 806 pr., 819–822
LU-DECOMPOSITION, 821
LUP decomposition, 806 pr., 815
  computation of, 823–825
  of a diagonal matrix, 827 ex.
  in matrix inversion, 828
  and matrix multiplication, 832 ex.
  of a permutation matrix, 827 ex.
  use of, 815–819
LUP-DECOMPOSITION, 824
LUP-SOLVE, 817

main memory, 484
MAKE-HEAP, 505
MAKE-SET, 561
  disjoint-set-forest implementation of, 571
  linked-list implementation of, 564
makespan, 1136 pr.
MAKE-TREE, 583 pr.
Manhattan distance, 225 pr., 1044 ex.
marked node, 508, 519–520
Markov's inequality, 1201 ex.
master method for solving a recurrence, 93–97
master theorem, 94
  proof of, 97–106
matched vertex, 732
matching
  bipartite, 732, 763 pr.

maximal, 1110, 1135 pr.
maximum, 1135 pr.
and maximum flow, 732–736, 747 ex.
perfect, 735 ex.
of strings, 985–1013
weighted bipartite, 530
matric matroid, 437
matrix, 1217–1229
addition of, 1220
adjacency, 591
conjugate transpose of, 832 ex.
determinant of, 1224–1225
diagonal, 1218
Hermitian, 832 ex.
identity, 1218
incidence, 448 pr., 593 ex.
inversion of, 806 pr., 827–831, 842
lower-triangular, 1219, 1222 ex., 1225 ex.
multiplication of, *see* matrix multiplication
negative of, 1220
permutation, 1220, 1222 ex.
predecessor, 685
product of, with a vector, 785–787, 790, 792 ex.
pseudoinverse of, 837
scalar multiple of, 1220
subtraction of, 1221
symmetric, 1220
symmetric positive-definite, 832–835, 842
Toeplitz, 921 pr.
transpose of, 797 ex., 1217
transpose of, multithreaded, 792 ex.
tridiagonal, 1219
unit lower-triangular, 1219
unit upper-triangular, 1219
upper-triangular, 1219, 1225 ex.
Vandermonde, 902, 1226 pr.
matrix-chain multiplication, 370–378
MATRIX-CHAIN-MULTIPLY
MATRIX-CHAIN-ORDER, 375
matrix multiplication, 75–83, 1221
for all-pairs shortest paths, 686–693, 706–707
boolean, 832 ex.
and computing the determinant, 832 ex.
divide-and-conquer method for, 76–83
and LUP decomposition, 832 ex.
and matrix inversion, 828–831, 842

multithreaded algorithm for, 792–797, 806 pr.
Pan's method for, 82 ex.
Strassen's algorithm for, 79–83, 111–112
MATRIX-MULTIPLY, 371
matrix-vector multiplication, multithreaded, 785–787, 792 ex.
with race, 790
matroid, 437–443, 448 pr., 450, 642
for task scheduling, 443–446
MAT-VEC, 785
MAT-VEC-MAIN-LOOP, 786
MAT-VEC-WRONG, 790
MAX-CNF satisfiability, 1127 ex.
MAX-CUT problem, 1127 ex.
MAX-FLOW-BY-SCALING, 763 pr.
max-flow min-cut theorem, 723
max-heap, 152
building, 156–159
d-ary, 167 pr.
deletion from, 166 ex.
extracting the maximum key from, 163
in heapsort, 159–162
increasing a key in, 163–164
insertion into, 164
maximum key of, 163
as a max-priority queue, 162–166
mergeable, 250 n., 481 n., 505 n.
MAX-HEAPIFY, 154
MAX-HEAP-INSERT, 164
building a heap with, 166 pr.
max-heap property, 152
maintenance of, 154–156
maximal element, of a partially ordered set, 1165
maximal layers, 1045 pr.
maximal matching, 1110, 1135 pr.
maximal point, 1045 pr.
maximal subset, in a matroid, 438
maximization linear program, 846
and minimization linear programs, 852
maximum, 213
in binary search trees, 291
of a binomial distribution, 1207 ex.
in a bit vector with a superimposed binary tree, 533
in a bit vector with a superimposed tree of constant height, 535

finding, 214–215
  in heaps, 163
  in order-statistic trees, 347 ex.
  in proto van Emde Boas structures, 544 ex.
  in red-black trees, 311
  in van Emde Boas trees, 550
MAXIMUM, 162–163, 230
maximum bipartite matching, 732–736,
      747 ex., 766
  Hopcroft-Karp algorithm for, 763 pr.
maximum degree, in a Fibonacci heap, 509,
      523–526
maximum flow, 708–766
  Edmonds-Karp algorithm for, 727–730
  Ford-Fulkerson method for, 714–731, 765
  as a linear program, 860–861
  and maximum bipartite matching, 732–736,
      747 ex.
  push-relabel algorithms for, 736–760, 765
  relabel-to-front algorithm for, 748–760
  scaling algorithm for, 762 pr., 765
  updating, 762 pr.
maximum matching, 1135 pr.
maximum spanning tree, 1137 pr.
maximum-subarray problem, 68–75, 111
max-priority queue, 162
MAX-3-CNF satisfiability, 1123–1124, 1139
MAYBE-MST-A, 641 pr.
MAYBE-MST-B, 641 pr.
MAYBE-MST-C, 641 pr.
mean, *see* expected value
mean weight of a cycle, 680 pr.
median, 213–227
  multithreaded algorithm for, 805 ex.
  of sorted lists, 223 ex.
  of two sorted lists, 804 ex.
  weighted, 225 pr.
median key, of a B-tree node, 493
median-of-3 method, 188 pr.
member of a set ($\in$), 1158
membership
  in proto van Emde Boas structures, 540–541
  in Van Emde Boas trees, 550
memoization, 365, 387–389
MEMOIZED-CUT-ROD, 365
MEMOIZED-CUT-ROD-AUX, 366
MEMOIZED-MATRIX-CHAIN, 388
memory, 484

memory hierarchy, 24
MERGE, 31
mergeable heap, 481, 505
  binomial heaps, 527 pr.
  linked-list implementation of, 250 pr.
  relaxed heaps, 530
  running times of operations on, 506 fig.
  2-3-4 heaps, 529 pr.
  see also Fibonacci heap
mergeable max-heap, 250 n., 481 n., 505 n.
mergeable min-heap, 250 n., 481 n., 505
MERGE-LISTS, 1129
merge sort, 12, 30–37
  compared with insertion sort, 14 ex.
  multithreaded algorithm for, 797–805, 812
  use of insertion sort in, 39 pr.
MERGE-SORT, 34
MERGE-SORT', 797
merging
  of k sorted lists, 166 ex.
  lower bounds for, 208 pr.
  multithreaded algorithm for, 798–801
  of two sorted arrays, 30
MILLER-RABIN, 970
Miller-Rabin primality test, 968–975, 983
MIN-GAP, 354 ex.
min-heap, 153
  analyzed by potential method, 462 ex.
  building, 156–159
  d-ary, 706 pr.
  in Dijkstra's algorithm, 662
  in Huffman's algorithm, 433
  in Johnson's algorithm, 704
  mergeable, 250 n., 481 n., 505
  as a min-priority queue, 165 ex.
  in Prim's algorithm, 636
MIN-HEAPIFY, 156 ex.
MIN-HEAP-INSERT, 165 ex.
min-heap ordering, 507
min-heap property, 153, 507
  maintenance of, 156 ex.
  in treaps, 333 pr.
  vs. binary-search-tree property, 289 ex.
minimization linear program, 846
  and maximization linear programs, 852
minimum, 213
  in binary search trees, 291

in a bit vector with a superimposed binary tree, 533

in a bit vector with a superimposed tree of constant height, 535

in B-trees, 497 ex.

in Fibonacci heaps, 511

finding, 214–215

off-line, 582 pr.

in order-statistic trees, 347 ex.

in proto van Emde Boas structures, 541–542

in red-black trees, 311

in 2-3-4 heaps, 529 pr.

in van Emde Boas trees, 550

MINIMUM, 162, 214, 230, 505

minimum-cost circulation, 896 pr.

minimum-cost flow, 861–862

minimum-cost multicommodity flow, 864 ex.

minimum-cost spanning tree, *see* minimum spanning tree

minimum cut, 721, 731 ex.

minimum degree, of a B-tree, 489

minimum mean-weight cycle, 680 pr.

minimum node, of a Fibonacci heap, 508

minimum path cover, 761 pr.

minimum spanning tree, 624–642

    in approximation algorithm for traveling-salesman problem, 1112

    Borůvka's algorithm for, 641

    on dynamic graphs, 637 ex.

    generic method for, 625–630

    Kruskal's algorithm for, 631–633

    Prim's algorithm for, 634–636

    relation to matroids, 437, 439–440

    second-best, 638 pr.

minimum-weight spanning tree, *see* minimum spanning tree

minimum-weight vertex cover, 1124–1127, 1139

minor of a matrix, 1224

min-priority queue, 162

    in constructing Huffman codes, 431

    in Dijkstra's algorithm, 661

    in Prim's algorithm, 634, 636

miss, 449 pr.

missing child, 1178

mod, 54, 928

modifying operation, 230

modular arithmetic, 54, 923 pr., 939–946

modular equivalence, 54, 1165 ex.

modular exponentiation, 956

MODULAR-EXPONENTIATION, 957

modular linear equations, 946–950

MODULAR-LINEAR-EQUATION-SOLVER, 949

modulo, 54, 928

Monge array, 110 pr.

monotone sequence, 168

monotonically decreasing, 53

monotonically increasing, 53

Monty Hall problem, 1195 ex.

move-to-front heuristic, 476 pr., 478

MST-KRUSKAL, 631

MST-PRIM, 634

MST-REDUCE, 639 pr.

much-greater-than ($\gg$), 574

much-less-than ($\ll$), 783

multicommodity flow, 862–863

    minimum-cost, 864 ex.

multicore computer, 772

multidimensional fast Fourier transform, 921 pr.

multigraph, 1172

    converting to equivalent undirected graph, 593 ex.

multiple, 927

    of an element modulo n, 946–950

    least common, 939 ex.

    scalar, 1220

multiple assignment, 21

multiple sources and sinks, 712

multiplication

    of complex numbers, 83 ex.

    divide-and-conquer method for, 920 pr.

    of matrices, *see* matrix multiplication

    of a matrix chain, 370–378

    matrix-vector, multithreaded, 785–787, 790, 792 ex.

    modulo n ($\cdot_n$), 940

    of polynomials, 899

multiplication method, 263–264

multiplicative group modulo n, 941

multiplicative inverse, modulo n, 949

multiply instruction, 23

MULTIPOP, 453

multiprocessor, 772

MULTIPUSH, 456 ex.

multiset, 1158 n.
multithreaded algorithm, 10, 772–812
  for computing Fibonacci numbers, 774–780
  for fast Fourier transform, 804 ex.
  Floyd-Warshall algorithm, 797 ex.
  for LU decomposition, 806 pr.
  for LUP decomposition, 806 pr.
  for matrix inversion, 806 pr.
  for matrix multiplication, 792–797, 806 pr.
  for matrix transpose, 792 ex., 797 ex.
  for matrix-vector product, 785–787, 790, 792 ex.
  for median, 805 ex.
  for merge sorting, 797–805, 812
  for merging, 798–801
  for order statistics, 805 ex.
  for partitioning, 804 ex.
  for prefix computation, 807 pr.
  for quicksort, 811 pr.
  for reduction, 807 pr.
  for a simple stencil calculation, 809 pr.
  for solving systems of linear equations, 806 pr.
  Strassen's algorithm, 795–796
multithreaded composition, 784 fig.
multithreaded computation, 777
multithreaded scheduling, 781–783
mutually exclusive events, 1190
mutually independent events, 1193

$\mathbb{N}$ (set of natural numbers), 1158
naive algorithm, for string matching, 988–990
NAIVE-STRING-MATCHER, 988
natural cubic spline, 840 pr.
natural numbers ($\mathbb{N}$), 1158
  keys interpreted as, 263
negative of a matrix, 1220
negative-weight cycle
  and difference constraints, 667
  and relaxation, 677 ex.
  and shortest paths, 645, 653–654, 692 ex., 700 ex.
negative-weight edges, 645–646
neighbor, 1172
neighborhood, 735 ex.
neighbor list, 750
nested parallelism, 776, 805 pr.
nesting boxes, 678 pr.

net flow across a cut, 720
network
  admissible, 749–750
  flow, *see* flow network
  residual, 715–719
  for sorting, 811
new, in pseudocode, 785
NEXT-TO-TOP, 1031
NIL, 21
node, 1176
  see also vertex
nonbasic variable, 855
nondeterministic multithreaded algorithm, 787
nondeterministic polynomial time, 1064 n.
  see also NP
nonhamiltonian graph, 1061
noninstance, 1056 n.
noninvertible matrix, 1223
nonnegativity constraint, 851, 853
nonoverlappable string pattern, 1002 ex.
nonsaturating push, 739, 745
nonsingular matrix, 1223
nontrivial power, 933 ex.
nontrivial square root of 1, modulo n, 956
no-path property, 650, 672
normal equation, 837
norm of a vector, 1222
NOT function ($\neg$), 1071
not a set member ($\notin$), 1158
not equivalent ($\not\equiv$), 54
NOT gate, 1070
NP (complexity class), 1049, 1064, 1066 ex., 1105
NPC (complexity class), 1050, 1069
NP-complete, 1050, 1069
NP-completeness, 9–10, 1048–1105
  of the circuit-satisfiability problem, 1070–1077
  of the clique problem, 1086–1089, 1105
  of determining whether a boolean formula is a tautology, 1086 ex.
  of the formula-satisfiability problem, 1079–1081, 1105
  of the graph-coloring problem, 1103 pr.
  of the half 3-CNF satisfiability problem, 1101 ex.
  of the hamiltonian-cycle problem, 1091–1096, 1105

of the hamiltonian-path problem, 1101 ex.
of the independent-set problem, 1101 pr.
of integer linear programming, 1101 ex.
of the longest-simple-cycle problem,
    1101 ex.
    proving, of a language, 1078–1079
of scheduling with profits and deadlines,
    1104 pr.
of the set-covering problem, 1122 ex.
of the set-partition problem, 1101 ex.
of the subgraph-isomorphism problem,
    1100 ex.
of the subset-sum problem, 1097–1100
of the 3-CNF-satisfiability problem,
    1082–1085, 1105
of the traveling-salesman problem,
    1096–1097
of the vertex-cover problem, 1089–1091,
    1105
of 0-1 integer programming, 1100 ex.
NP-hard, 1069
n-set, 1161
n-tuple, 1162
null event, 1190
null tree, 1178
null vector, 1224
number-field sieve, 984
numerical stability, 813, 815, 842
n-vector, 1218

o-notation, 50–51, 64
O-notation, 45 fig., 47–48, 64
O'-notation, 62 pr.
$\widetilde{O}$-notation, 62 pr.
object, 21
    allocation and freeing of, 243–244
    array implementation of, 241–246
    passing as parameter, 21
objective function, 664, 847, 851
objective value, 847, 851
oblivious compare-exchange algorithm, 208 pr.
occurrence of a pattern, 985
OFF-LINE-MINIMUM, 583 pr.
off-line problem
    caching, 449 pr.
    least common ancestors, 584 pr.
    minimum, 582 pr.
Omega-notation, 45 fig., 48–49, 64

1-approximation algorithm, 1107
one-pass method, 585
one-to-one correspondence, 1167
one-to-one function, 1167
on-line convex-hull problem, 1039 ex.
on-line hiring problem, 139–141
ON-LINE-MAXIMUM, 140
on-line multithreaded scheduler, 781
ON-SEGMENT, 1018
onto function, 1167
open-address hash table, 269–277
    with double hashing, 272–274, 277 ex.
    with linear probing, 272
    with quadratic probing, 272, 283 pr.
open interval, 348
OpenMP, 774
optimal binary search tree, 397–404, 413
OPTIMAL-BST, 402
optimal objective value, 851
optimal solution, 851
optimal subset, of a matroid, 439
optimal substructure
    of activity selection, 416
    of binary search trees, 399–400
    in dynamic programming, 379–384
    of the fractional knapsack problem, 426
    in greedy algorithms, 425
    of Huffman codes, 435
    of longest common subsequences, 392–393
    of matrix-chain multiplication, 373
    of rod-cutting, 362
    of shortest paths, 644–645, 687, 693–694
    of unweighted shortest paths, 382
    of weighted matroids, 442
    of the 0-1 knapsack problem, 426
optimal vertex cover, 1108
optimization problem, 359, 1050, 1054
    approximation algorithms for, 10,
        1106–1140
    and decision problems, 1051
OR function ($\vee$), 697, 1071
order
    of a group, 945
    linear, 1165
    partial, 1165
    total, 1165
ordered pair, 1161
ordered tree, 1177

order of growth, 28
order statistics, 213–227
    dynamic, 339–345
    multithreaded algorithm for, 805 ex.
order-statistic tree, 339–345
    querying, 347 ex.
OR gate, 1070
origin, 1015
or, in pseudocode, 22
orthonormal, 842
OS-KEY-RANK, 344 ex.
OS-RANK, 342
OS-SELECT, 341
out-degree, 1169
outer product, 1222
output
    of an algorithm, 5
    of a combinational circuit, 1071
    of a logic gate, 1070
overdetermined system of linear equations, 814
overflow
    of a queue, 235
    of a stack, 233
overflowing vertex, 736
    discharge of, 751
overlapping intervals, 348
    finding all, 354 ex.
    point of maximum overlap, 354 pr.
overlapping rectangles, 354 ex.
overlapping subproblems, 384–386
overlapping-suffix lemma, 987

P (complexity class), 1049, 1055, 1059,
    1061 ex., 1105
package wrapping, 1037, 1047
page on a disk, 486, 499 ex., 502 pr.
pair, ordered, 1161
pairwise disjoint sets, 1161
pairwise independence, 1193
pairwise relatively prime, 931
palindrome, 405 pr.
Pan's method for matrix multiplication, 82 ex.
parallel algorithm, 10, 772
    see also multithreaded algorithm
parallel computer, 772
    ideal, 779
parallel for, in pseudocode, 785–786
parallelism

logical, 777
    of a multithreaded computation, 780
    nested, 776
    of a randomized multithreaded algorithm,
        811 pr.
parallel loop, 785–787, 805 pr.
parallel-machine-scheduling problem, 1136 pr.
parallel prefix, 807 pr.
parallel random-access machine, 811
parallel slackness, 781
    rule of thumb, 783
parallel, strands being logically in, 778
parameter, 21
    costs of passing, 107 pr.
parent
    in a breadth-first tree, 594
    in a multithreaded computation, 776
    in a rooted tree, 1176
PARENT, 152
parenthesis structure of depth-first search, 606
parenthesis theorem, 606
parenthesization of a matrix-chain product, 370
parse tree, 1082
partially ordered set, 1165
partial order, 1165
PARTITION, 171
PARTITION', 186 pr.
partition function, 361 n.
partitioning, 171–173
    around median of 3 elements, 185 ex.
    Hoare's method for, 185 pr.
    multithreaded algorithm for, 804 ex.
    randomized, 179
partition of a set, 1161, 1164
Pascal's triangle, 1188 ex.
path, 1170
    augmenting, 719–720, 763 pr.
    critical, 657
    find, 569
    hamiltonian, 1066 ex.
    longest, 382, 1048
    shortest, *see* shortest paths
    simple, 1170
    weight of, 643
PATH, 1051, 1058
path compression, 569
path cover, 761 pr.
path length, of a tree, 304 pr., 1180 ex.

path-relaxation property, 650, 673
pattern, in string matching, 985
  nonoverlappable, 1002 ex.
pattern matching, *see* string matching
penalty, 444
perfect hashing, 277–282, 285
perfect linear speedup, 780
perfect matching, 735 ex.
permutation, 1167
  bit-reversal, 472 pr., 918
  Josephus, 355 pr.
  k-permutation, 126, 1184
  linear, 1229 pr.
  in place, 126
  random, 124–128
  of a set, 1184
  uniform random, 116, 125
permutation matrix, 1220, 1222 ex., 1226 ex.
  LUP decomposition of, 827 ex.
PERMUTE-BY-CYCLIC, 129 ex.
PERMUTE-BY-SORTING, 125
PERMUTE-WITH-ALL, 129 ex.
PERMUTE-WITHOUT-IDENTITY, 128 ex.
persistent data structure, 331 pr., 482
PERSISTENT-TREE-INSERT, 331 pr.
PERT chart, 657, 657 ex.
P-FIB, 776
phase, of the relabel-to-front algorithm, 758
phi function ($\phi(n)$), 943
PISANO-DELETE, 526 pr.
pivot
  in linear programming, 867, 869–870,
    878 ex.
  in LU decomposition, 821
  in quicksort, 171
PIVOT, 869
platter, 485
P-MATRIX-MULTIPLY-RECURSIVE, 794
P-MERGE, 800
P-MERGE-SORT, 803
pointer, 21
  array implementation of, 241–246
  trailing, 295
point-value representation, 901
polar angle, 1020 ex.
Pollard's rho heuristic, 976–980, 980 ex., 984
POLLARD-RHO, 976
polygon, 1020 ex.

kernel of, 1038 ex.
  star-shaped, 1038 ex.
polylogarithmically bounded, 57
polynomial, 55, 898
  addition of, 898
  asymptotic behavior of, 61 pr.
  coefficient representation of, 900
  derivatives of, 922 pr.
  evaluation of, 41 pr., 900, 905 ex., 923 pr.
  interpolation by, 901, 906 ex.
  multiplication of, 899, 903–905, 920 pr.
  point-value representation of, 901
polynomial-growth condition, 113
polynomially bounded, 55
polynomially related, 1056
polynomial-time acceptance, 1058
polynomial-time algorithm, 927, 1048
polynomial-time approximation scheme, 1107
  for maximum clique, 1134 pr.
polynomial-time computability, 1056
polynomial-time decision, 1059
polynomial-time reducibility ($\leq_P$), 1067,
    1077 ex.
polynomial-time solvability, 1055
polynomial-time verification, 1061–1066
POP, 233, 452
pop from a run-time stack, 188 pr.
positional tree, 1178
positive-definite matrix, 1225
post-office location problem, 225 pr.
postorder tree walk, 287
potential function, 459
  for lower bounds, 478
potential method, 459–463
  for binary counters, 461–462
  for disjoint-set data structures, 575–581,
    582 ex.
  for dynamic tables, 466–471
  for Fibonacci heaps, 509–512, 517–518,
    520–522
  for the generic push-relabel algorithm, 746
  for min-heaps, 462 ex.
  for restructuring red-black trees, 474 pr.
  for self-organizing lists with move-to-front,
    476 pr.
  for stack operations, 460–461
potential, of a data structure, 459
power

of an element, modulo n, 954–958
kth, 933 ex.
nontrivial, 933 ex.
power series, 108 pr.
power set, 1161
Pr { } (probability distribution), 1190
PRAM, 811
predecessor
in binary search trees, 291–292
in a bit vector with a superimposed binary
tree, 534
in a bit vector with a superimposed tree of
constant height, 535
in breadth-first trees, 594
in B-trees, 497 ex.
in linked lists, 236
in order-statistic trees, 347 ex.
in proto van Emde Boas structures, 544 ex.
in red-black trees, 311
in shortest-paths trees, 647
in Van Emde Boas trees, 551–552
PREDECESSOR, 230
predecessor matrix, 685
predecessor subgraph
in all-pairs shortest paths, 685
in breadth-first search, 600
in depth-first search, 603
in single-source shortest paths, 647
predecessor-subgraph property, 650, 676
preemption, 447 pr.
prefix
of a sequence, 392
of a string ($\sqsubset$), 986
prefix code, 429
prefix computation, 807 pr.
prefix function, 1003–1004
prefix-function iteration lemma, 1007
preflow, 736, 765
preimage of a matrix, 1228 pr.
preorder, total, 1165
preorder tree walk, 287
presorting, 1043
Prim's algorithm, 634–636, 642
with an adjacency matrix, 637 ex.
in approximation algorithm for
traveling-salesman problem, 1112
implemented with a Fibonacci heap, 636
implemented with a min-heap, 636

with integer edge weights, 637 ex.
similarity to Dijkstra's algorithm, 634, 662
for sparse graphs, 638 pr.
primality testing, 965–975, 983
Miller-Rabin test, 968–975, 983
pseudoprimality testing, 966–968
primal linear program, 880
primary clustering, 272
primary memory, 484
prime distribution function, 965
prime number, 928
density of, 965–966
prime number theorem, 965
primitive root of $\mathbb{Z}_n^*$, 955
principal root of unity, 907
principle of inclusion and exclusion, 1163 ex.
PRINT-ALL-PAIRS-SHORTEST-PATH, 685
PRINT-CUT-ROD-SOLUTION, 369
PRINT-INTERSECTING-SEGMENTS, 1028 ex.
PRINT-LCS, 395
PRINT-OPTIMAL-PARENS, 377
PRINT-PATH, 601
PRINT-SET, 572 ex.
priority queue, 162–166
in constructing Huffman codes, 431
in Dijkstra's algorithm, 661
heap implementation of, 162–166
lower bounds for, 531
max-priority queue, 162
min-priority queue, 162, 165 ex.
with monotone extractions, 168
in Prim's algorithm, 634, 636
proto van Emde Boas structure
implementation of, 538–545
van Emde Boas tree implementation of,
531–560
see also binary search tree, binomial heap,
Fibonacci heap
probabilistically checkable proof, 1105, 1140
probabilistic analysis, 115–116, 130–142
of approximation algorithm for
MAX-3-CNF satisfiability, 1124
and average inputs, 28
of average node depth in a randomly built
binary search tree, 304 pr.
of balls and bins, 133–134
of birthday paradox, 130–133
of bucket sort, 201–204, 204 ex.

of collisions, 261 ex., 282 ex.
of convex hull over a sparse-hulled
   distribution, 1046 pr.
of file comparison, 995 ex.
of fuzzy sorting of intervals, 189 pr.
of hashing with chaining, 258–260
of height of a randomly built binary search
   tree, 299–303
of hiring problem, 120–121, 139–141
of insertion into a binary search tree with
   equal keys, 303 pr.
of longest-probe bound for hashing, 282 pr.
of lower bound for sorting, 205 pr.
of Miller-Rabin primality test, 971–975
and multithreaded algorithms, 811 pr.
of on-line hiring problem, 139–141
of open-address hashing, 274–276, 277 ex.
of partitioning, 179 ex., 185 ex., 187–188 pr.
of perfect hashing, 279–282
of Pollard's rho heuristic, 977–980
of probabilistic counting, 143 pr.
of quicksort, 181–184, 187–188 pr., 303 ex.
of Rabin-Karp algorithm, 994
and randomized algorithms, 123–124
of randomized selection, 217–219, 226 pr.
of searching a compact list, 250 pr.
of slot-size bound for chaining, 283 pr.
of sorting points by distance from origin,
   204 ex.
of streaks, 135–139
of universal hashing, 265–268
probabilistic counting, 143 pr.
probability, 1189–1196
probability density function, 1196
probability distribution, 1190
probability distribution function, 204 ex.
probe sequence, 270
probing, 270, 282 pr.
   see also linear probing, quadratic probing,
     double hashing
problem
   abstract, 1054
   computational, 5–6
   concrete, 1055
   decision, 1051, 1054
   intractable, 1048
   optimization, 359, 1050, 1054
   solution to, 6, 1054–1055

tractable, 1048
procedure, 6, 16–17
product ($\prod$), 1148
   Cartesian, 1162
   cross, 1016
   inner, 1222
   of matrices, 1221, 1226 ex.
   outer, 1222
   of polynomials, 899
   rule of, 1184
   scalar flow, 714 ex.
professional wrestler, 602 ex.
program counter, 1073
programming, *see* dynamic programming,
   linear programming
proper ancestor, 1176
proper descendant, 1176
proper subgroup, 944
proper subset ($\subset$), 1159
proto van Emde Boas structure, 538–545
   cluster in, 538
   compared with van Emde Boas trees, 547
   deletion from, 544
   insertion into, 544
   maximum in, 544 ex.
   membership in, 540–541
   minimum in, 541–542
   predecessor in, 544 ex.
   successor in, 543–544
   summary in, 540
PROTO-VEB-INSERT, 544
PROTO-VEB-MEMBER, 541
PROTO-VEB-MINIMUM, 542
proto-vEB structure, *see* proto van Emde Boas
   structure
PROTO-VEB-SUCCESSOR, 543
prune-and-search method, 1030
pruning a Fibonacci heap, 529 pr.
P-SCAN-1, 808 pr.
P-SCAN-2, 808 pr.
P-SCAN-3, 809 pr.
P-SCAN-DOWN, 809 pr.
P-SCAN-UP, 809 pr.
pseudocode, 16, 20–22
pseudoinverse, 837
pseudoprime, 966–968
PSEUDOPRIME, 967
pseudorandom-number generator, 117

P-Square-Matrix-Multiply, 793
P-Transpose, 792 ex.
public key, 959, 962
public-key cryptosystem, 958–965, 983
Push
  push-relabel operation, 739
  stack operation, 233, 452
push onto a run-time stack, 188 pr.
push operation (in push-relabel algorithms),
    738–739
  nonsaturating, 739, 745
  saturating, 739, 745
push-relabel algorithm, 736–760, 765
  basic operations in, 738–740
  by discharging an overflowing vertex of
    maximum height, 760 ex.
  to find a maximum bipartite matching,
    747 ex.
  gap heuristic for, 760 ex., 766
  generic algorithm, 740–748
  with a queue of overflowing vertices, 759 ex.
  relabel-to-front algorithm, 748–760

quadratic function, 27
quadratic probing, 272, 283 pr.
quadratic residue, 982 pr.
quantile, 223 ex.
query, 230
queue, 232, 234–235
  in breadth-first search, 595
  implemented by stacks, 236 ex.
  linked-list implementation of, 240 ex.
  priority, *see* priority queue
  in push-relabel algorithms, 759 ex.
quicksort, 170–190
  analysis of, 174–185
  average-case analysis of, 181–184
  compared with insertion sort, 178 ex.
  compared with radix sort, 199
  with equal element values, 186 pr.
  good worst-case implementation of, 223 ex.
  "killer adversary" for, 190
  with median-of-3 method, 188 pr.
  multithreaded algorithm for, 811 pr.
  randomized version of, 179–180, 187 pr.
  stack depth of, 188 pr.
  tail-recursive version of, 188 pr.
  use of insertion sort in, 185 ex.

worst-case analysis of, 180–181
Quicksort, 171
Quicksort', 186 pr.
quotient, 928

$\mathbb{R}$ (set of real numbers), 1158
Rabin-Karp algorithm, 990–995, 1013
Rabin-Karp-Matcher, 993
race, 787–790
Race-Example, 788
radix sort, 197–200
  compared with quicksort, 199
Radix-Sort, 198
radix tree, 304 pr.
RAM, 23–24
Random, 117
random-access machine, 23–24
  parallel, 811
randomized algorithm, 116–117, 122–130
  and average inputs, 28
  comparison sort, 205 pr.
  for fuzzy sorting of intervals, 189 pr.
  for hiring problem, 123–124
  for insertion into a binary search tree with
    equal keys, 303 pr.
  for MAX-3-CNF satisfiability, 1123–1124,
    1139
  Miller-Rabin primality test, 968–975, 983
  multithreaded, 811 pr.
  for partitioning, 179, 185 ex., 187–188 pr.
  for permuting an array, 124–128
  Pollard's rho heuristic, 976–980, 980 ex.,
    984
  and probabilistic analysis, 123–124
  quicksort, 179–180, 185 ex., 187–188 pr.
  randomized rounding, 1139
  for searching a compact list, 250 pr.
  for selection, 215–220
  universal hashing, 265–268
  worst-case performance of, 180 ex.
Randomized-Hire-Assistant, 124
Randomized-Partition, 179
Randomized-Quicksort, 179, 303 ex.
  relation to randomly built binary search
    trees, 304 pr.
randomized rounding, 1139
Randomized-Select, 216
Randomize-In-Place, 126

randomly built binary search tree, 299–303, 304 pr.

random-number generator, 117

random permutation, 124–128

   uniform, 116, 125

RANDOM-SAMPLE, 130 ex.

random sampling, 129 ex., 179

RANDOM-SEARCH, 143 pr.

random variable, 1196–1201

   indicator, *see* indicator random variable

range, 1167

   of a matrix, 1228 pr.

rank

   column, 1223

   full, 1223

   of a matrix, 1223, 1226 ex.

   of a node in a disjoint-set forest, 569, 575, 581 ex.

   of a number in an ordered set, 300, 339

   in order-statistic trees, 341–343, 344–345 ex.

   row, 1223

rate of growth, 28

ray, 1021 ex.

RB-DELETE, 324

RB-DELETE-FIXUP, 326

RB-ENUMERATE, 348 ex.

RB-INSERT, 315

RB-INSERT-FIXUP, 316

RB-JOIN, 332 pr.

RB-TRANSPLANT, 323

reachability in a graph ($\rightsquigarrow$), 1170

real numbers ($\mathbb{R}$), 1158

reconstructing an optimal solution, in dynamic programming, 387

record, 147

rectangle, 354 ex.

recurrence, 34, 65–67, 83–113

   solution by Akra-Bazzi method, 112–113

   solution by master method, 93–97

   solution by recursion-tree method, 88–93

   solution by substitution method, 83–88

recurrence equation, *see* recurrence

recursion, 30

recursion tree, 37, 88–93

   in proof of master theorem, 98–100

   and the substitution method, 91–92

RECURSIVE-ACTIVITY-SELECTOR, 419

recursive case, 65

RECURSIVE-FFT, 911

RECURSIVE-MATRIX-CHAIN, 385

red-black tree, 308–338

   augmentation of, 346–347

   compared with B-trees, 484, 490

   deletion from, 323–330

   in determining whether any line segments intersect, 1024

   for enumerating keys in a range, 348 ex.

   height of, 309

   insertion into, 315–323

   joining of, 332 pr.

   maximum key of, 311

   minimum key of, 311

   predecessor in, 311

   properties of, 308–312

   relaxed, 311 ex.

   restructuring, 474 pr.

   rotation in, 312–314

   searching in, 311

   successor in, 311

   see also interval tree, order-statistic tree

REDUCE, 807 pr.

reduced-space van Emde Boas tree, 557 pr.

reducibility, 1067–1068

reduction algorithm, 1052, 1067

reduction function, 1067

reduction, of an array, 807 pr.

reflexive relation, 1163

reflexivity of asymptotic notation, 51

region, feasible, 847

regularity condition, 95

rejection

   by an algorithm, 1058

   by a finite automaton, 996

RELABEL, 740

relabeled vertex, 740

relabel operation, in push-relabel algorithms, 740, 745

RELABEL-TO-FRONT, 755

relabel-to-front algorithm, 748–760

   phase of, 758

relation, 1163–1166

relatively prime, 931

RELAX, 649

relaxation

   of an edge, 648–650

   linear programming, 1125

relaxed heap, 530
relaxed red-black tree, 311 ex.
release time, 447 pr.
remainder, 54, 928
remainder instruction, 23
repeated squaring
    for all-pairs shortest paths, 689–691
    for raising a number to a power, 956
repeat, in pseudocode, 20
repetition factor, of a string, 1012 pr.
REPETITION-MATCHER, 1013 pr.
representative of a set, 561
RESET, 459 ex.
residual capacity, 716, 719
residual edge, 716
residual network, 715–719
residue, 54, 928, 982 pr.
respecting a set of edges, 626
return edge, 779
return, in pseudocode, 22
return instruction, 23
reweighting
    in all-pairs shortest paths, 700–702
    in single-source shortest paths, 679 pr.
rho heuristic, 976–980, 980 ex., 984
$\rho(n)$-approximation algorithm, 1106, 1123
RIGHT, 152
right child, 1178
right-conversion, 314 ex.
right horizontal ray, 1021 ex.
RIGHT-ROTATE, 313
right rotation, 312
right spine, 333 pr.
right subtree, 1178
rod-cutting, 360–370, 390 ex.
root
    of a tree, 1176
    of unity, 906–907
    of $\mathbb{Z}_n^*$, 955
rooted tree, 1176
    representation of, 246–249
root list, of a Fibonacci heap, 509
rotation
    cyclic, 1012 ex.
    in a red-black tree, 312–314
rotational sweep, 1030–1038
rounding, 1126
    randomized, 1139

row-major order, 394
row rank, 1223
row vector, 1218
RSA public-key cryptosystem, 958–965, 983
RS-vEB tree, 557 pr.
rule of product, 1184
rule of sum, 1183
running time, 25
    average-case, 28, 116
    best-case, 29 ex., 49
    expected, 28, 117
    of a graph algorithm, 588
    and multithreaded computation, 779–780
    order of growth, 28
    rate of growth, 28
    worst-case, 27, 49

sabermetrics, 412 n.
safe edge, 626
SAME-COMPONENT, 563
sample space, 1189
sampling, 129 ex., 179
SAT, 1079
satellite data, 147, 229
satisfiability, 1072, 1079–1081, 1105,
    1123–1124, 1127 ex., 1139
satisfiable formula, 1049, 1079
satisfying assignment, 1072, 1079
saturated edge, 739
saturating push, 739, 745
scalar flow product, 714 ex.
scalar multiple, 1220
scaling
    in maximum flow, 762 pr., 765
    in single-source shortest paths, 679 pr.
scan, 807 pr.
SCAN, 807 pr.
scapegoat tree, 338
schedule, 444, 1136 pr.
    event-point, 1023
scheduler, for multithreaded computations,
    777, 781–783, 812
    centralized, 782
    greedy, 782
    work-stealing algorithm for, 812
scheduling, 443–446, 447 pr., 450, 1104 pr.,
    1136 pr.
Schur complement, 820, 834

Schur complement lemma, 834
SCRAMBLE-SEARCH, 143 pr.
seam carving, 409 pr., 413
SEARCH, 230
searching, 22 ex.
    binary search, 39 ex., 799–800
    in binary search trees, 289–291
    in B-trees, 491–492
    in chained hash tables, 258
    in compact lists, 250 pr.
    in direct-address tables, 254
    for an exact interval, 354 ex.
    in interval trees, 350–353
    linear search, 22 ex.
    in linked lists, 237
    in open-address hash tables, 270–271
    in proto van Emde Boas structures, 540–541
    in red-black trees, 311
    in an unsorted array, 143 pr.
    in Van Emde Boas trees, 550
search tree, *see* balanced search tree, binary
        search tree, B-tree, exponential search
        tree, interval tree, optimal binary search
        tree, order-statistic tree, red-black tree,
        splay tree, 2-3 tree, 2-3-4 tree
secondary clustering, 272
secondary hash table, 278
secondary storage
    search tree for, 484–504
    stacks on, 502 pr.
second-best minimum spanning tree, 638 pr.
secret key, 959, 962
segment, *see* directed segment, line segment
SEGMENTS-INTERSECT, 1018
SELECT, 220
selection, 213
    of activities, 415–422, 450
    and comparison sorts, 222
    in expected linear time, 215–220
    multithreaded, 805 ex.
    in order-statistic trees, 340–341
    in worst-case linear time, 220–224
selection sort, 29 ex.
selector vertex, 1093
self-loop, 1168
self-organizing list, 476 pr., 478
semiconnected graph, 621 ex.
sentinel, 31, 238–240, 309

sequence ($\langle \, \rangle$)
    bitonic, 682 pr.
    finite, 1166
    infinite, 1166
    inversion in, 41 pr., 122 ex., 345 ex.
    probe, 270
sequential consistency, 779, 812
serial algorithm versus parallel algorithm, 772
serialization, of a multithreaded algorithm,
        774, 776
series, 108 pr., 1146–1148
    strands being logically in, 778
set ($\{ \, \}$), 1158–1163
    cardinality ($| \, |$), 1161
    convex, 714 ex.
    difference ($-$), 1159
    independent, 1101 pr.
    intersection ($\cap$), 1159
    member ($\in$), 1158
    not a member ($\notin$), 1158
    union ($\cup$), 1159
set-covering problem, 1117–1122, 1139
    weighted, 1135 pr.
set-partition problem, 1101 ex.
shadow of a point, 1038 ex.
shared memory, 772
Shell's sort, 42
shift, in string matching, 985
shift instruction, 24
short-circuiting operator, 22
SHORTEST-PATH, 1050
shortest paths, 7, 643–707
    all-pairs, 644, 684–707
    Bellman-Ford algorithm for, 651–655
    with bitonic paths, 682 pr.
    and breadth-first search, 597–600, 644
    convergence property of, 650, 672–673
    and difference constraints, 664–670
    Dijkstra's algorithm for, 658–664
    in a directed acyclic graph, 655–658
    in ϵ-dense graphs, 706 pr.
    estimate of, 648
    Floyd-Warshall algorithm for, 693–697,
        700 ex., 706
    Gabow's scaling algorithm for, 679 pr.
    Johnson's algorithm for, 700–706
    as a linear program, 859–860
    and longest paths, 1048

by matrix multiplication, 686–693, 706–707
and negative-weight cycles, 645, 653–654,
    692 ex., 700 ex.
with negative-weight edges, 645–646
no-path property of, 650, 672
optimal substructure of, 644–645, 687,
    693–694
path-relaxation property of, 650, 673
predecessor-subgraph property of, 650, 676
problem variants, 644
and relaxation, 648–650
by repeated squaring, 689–691
single-destination, 644
single-pair, 381, 644
single-source, 643–683
tree of, 647–648, 673–676
triangle inequality of, 650, 671
in an unweighted graph, 381, 597
upper-bound property of, 650, 671–672
in a weighted graph, 643
sibling, 1176
side of a polygon, 1020 ex.
signature, 960
simple cycle, 1170
simple graph, 1170
simple path, 1170
    longest, 382, 1048
simple polygon, 1020 ex.
simple stencil calculation, 809 pr.
simple uniform hashing, 259
simplex, 848
SIMPLEX, 871
simplex algorithm, 848, 864–879, 896–897
single-destination shortest paths, 644
single-pair shortest path, 381, 644
    as a linear program, 859–860
single-source shortest paths, 643–683
    Bellman-Ford algorithm for, 651–655
    with bitonic paths, 682 pr.
    and difference constraints, 664–670
    Dijkstra's algorithm for, 658–664
    in a directed acyclic graph, 655–658
    in ϵ-dense graphs, 706 pr.
    Gabow's scaling algorithm for, 679 pr.
    as a linear program, 863 ex.
    and longest paths, 1048
singleton, 1161
singly connected graph, 612 ex.

singly linked list, 236
    see also linked list
singular matrix, 1223
singular value decomposition, 842
sink vertex, 593 ex., 709, 712
size
    of an algorithm's input, 25, 926–927,
        1055–1057
    of a binomial tree, 527 pr.
    of a boolean combinational circuit, 1072
    of a clique, 1086
    of a set, 1161
    of a subtree in a Fibonacci heap, 524
    of a vertex cover, 1089, 1108
skip list, 338
slack, 855
slack form, 846, 854–857
    uniqueness of, 876
slackness
    complementary, 894 pr.
    parallel, 781
slack variable, 855
slot
    of a direct-access table, 254
    of a hash table, 256
SLOW-ALL-PAIRS-SHORTEST-PATHS, 689
smoothed analysis, 897
⋆Socrates, 790
solution
    to an abstract problem, 1054
    basic, 866
    to a computational problem, 6
    to a concrete problem, 1055
    feasible, 665, 846, 851
    infeasible, 851
    optimal, 851
    to a system of linear equations, 814
sorted linked list, 236
    see also linked list
sorting, 5, 16–20, 30–37, 147–212, 797–805
    bubblesort, 40 pr.
    bucket sort, 200–204
    columnsort, 208 pr.
    comparison sort, 191
    counting sort, 194–197
    fuzzy, 189 pr.
    heapsort, 151–169
    insertion sort, 12, 16–20

k-sorting, 207 pr.

lexicographic, 304 pr.

in linear time, 194–204, 206 pr.

lower bounds for, 191–194, 211, 531

merge sort, 12, 30–37, 797–805

by oblivious compare-exchange algorithms, 208 pr.

in place, 17, 148, 206 pr.

of points by polar angle, 1020 ex.

probabilistic lower bound for, 205 pr.

quicksort, 170–190

radix sort, 197–200

selection sort, 29 ex.

Shell's sort, 42

stable, 196

table of running times, 149

topological, 8, 612–615, 623

using a binary search tree, 299 ex.

with variable-length items, 206 pr.

0-1 sorting lemma, 208 pr.

sorting network, 811

source vertex, 594, 644, 709, 712

span law, 780

spanning tree, 439, 624

bottleneck, 640 pr.

maximum, 1137 pr.

verification of, 642

see also minimum spanning tree

span, of a multithreaded computation, 779

sparse graph, 589

all-pairs shortest paths for, 700–705

and Prim's algorithm, 638 pr.

sparse-hulled distribution, 1046 pr.

spawn, in pseudocode, 776–777

spawn edge, 778

speedup, 780

of a randomized multithreaded algorithm, 811 pr.

spindle, 485

spine

of a string-matching automaton, 997 fig.

of a treap, 333 pr.

splay tree, 338, 482

spline, 840 pr.

splitting

of B-tree nodes, 493–495

of 2-3-4 trees, 503 pr.

splitting summations, 1152–1154

spurious hit, 991

square matrix, 1218

SQUARE-MATRIX-MULTIPLY, 75, 689

SQUARE-MATRIX-MULTIPLY-RECURSIVE, 77

square of a directed graph, 593 ex.

square root, modulo a prime, 982 pr.

squaring, repeated

for all-pairs shortest paths, 689–691

for raising a number to a power, 956

stability

numerical, 813, 815, 842

of sorting algorithms, 196, 200 ex.

stack, 232–233

in Graham's scan, 1030

implemented by queues, 236 ex.

linked-list implementation of, 240 ex.

operations analyzed by accounting method, 457–458

operations analyzed by aggregate analysis, 452–454

operations analyzed by potential method, 460–461

for procedure execution, 188 pr.

on secondary storage, 502 pr.

STACK-EMPTY, 233

standard deviation, 1200

standard encoding ($\langle\ \rangle$), 1057

standard form, 846, 850–854

star-shaped polygon, 1038 ex.

start state, 995

start time, 415

state of a finite automaton, 995

static graph, 562 n.

static set of keys, 277

static threading, 773

stencil, 809 pr.

stencil calculation, 809 pr.

Stirling's approximation, 57

storage management, 151, 243–244, 245 ex., 261 ex.

store instruction, 23

straddle, 1017

strand, 777

final, 779

independent, 789

initial, 779

logically in parallel, 778

logically in series, 778

Strassen's algorithm, 79–83, 111–112
  multithreaded, 795–796

streaks, 135–139

strictly decreasing, 53

strictly increasing, 53

string, 985, 1184

string matching, 985–1013
  based on repetition factors, 1012 pr.
  by finite automata, 995–1002
  with gap characters, 989 ex., 1002 ex.
  Knuth-Morris-Pratt algorithm for, 1002–1013
  naive algorithm for, 988–990
  Rabin-Karp algorithm for, 990–995, 1013

string-matching automaton, 996–1002, 1002 ex.

strongly connected component, 1171
  decomposition into, 615–621, 623

STRONGLY-CONNECTED-COMPONENTS, 617

strongly connected graph, 1171

subgraph, 1171
  predecessor, *see* predecessor subgraph

subgraph-isomorphism problem, 1100 ex.

subgroup, 943–946

subpath, 1170

subproblem graph, 367–368

subroutine
  calling, 21, 23, 25 n.
  executing, 25 n.

subsequence, 391

subset (⊆), 1159, 1161
  hereditary family of, 437
  independent family of, 437

SUBSET-SUM, 1097

subset-sum problem
  approximation algorithm for, 1128–1134, 1139
  NP-completeness of, 1097–1100
  with unary target, 1101 ex.

substitution method, 83–88
  and recursion trees, 91–92

substring, 1184

subtract instruction, 23

subtraction of matrices, 1221

subtree, 1176
  maintaining sizes of, in order-statistic trees, 343–344

success, in a Bernoulli trial, 1201

successor
  in binary search trees, 291–292
  in a bit vector with a superimposed binary tree, 533
  in a bit vector with a superimposed tree of constant height, 535
  finding *i*th, of a node in an order-statistic tree, 344 ex.
  in linked lists, 236
  in order-statistic trees, 347 ex.
  in proto van Emde Boas structures, 543–544
  in red-black trees, 311
  in Van Emde Boas trees, 550–551

SUCCESSOR, 230

such that (:), 1159

suffix (⊐), 986

suffix function, 996

suffix-function inequality, 999

suffix-function recursion lemma, 1000

sum ($\sum$), 1145
  Cartesian, 906 ex.
  infinite, 1145
  of matrices, 1220
  of polynomials, 898
  rule of, 1183
  telescoping, 1148

SUM-ARRAYS, 805 pr.

SUM-ARRAYS', 805 pr.

summary
  in a bit vector with a superimposed tree of constant height, 534
  in proto van Emde Boas structures, 540
  in van Emde Boas trees, 546

summation, 1145–1157
  in asymptotic notation, 49–50, 1146
  bounding, 1149–1156
  formulas and properties of, 1145–1149
  linearity of, 1146

summation lemma, 908

supercomputer, 772

superpolynomial time, 1048

supersink, 712

supersource, 712

surjection, 1167

SVD, 842

sweeping, 1021–1029, 1045 pr.
  rotational, 1030–1038

sweep line, 1022
sweep-line status, 1023–1024
symbol table, 253, 262, 265
symmetric difference, 763 pr.
symmetric matrix, 1220, 1222 ex., 1226 ex.
symmetric positive-definite matrix, 832–835, 842
symmetric relation, 1163
symmetry of Θ-notation, 52
sync, in pseudocode, 776–777
system of difference constraints, 664–670
system of linear equations, 806 pr., 813–827, 840 pr.

TABLE-DELETE, 468
TABLE-INSERT, 464
tail
    of a binomial distribution, 1208–1215
    of a linked list, 236
    of a queue, 234
tail recursion, 188 pr., 419
TAIL-RECURSIVE-QUICKSORT, 188 pr.
target, 1097
Tarjan's off-line least-common-ancestors
    algorithm, 584 pr.
task, 443
Task Parallel Library, 774
task scheduling, 443–446, 448 pr., 450
tautology, 1066 ex., 1086 ex.
Taylor series, 306 pr.
telescoping series, 1148
telescoping sum, 1148
testing
    of primality, 965–975, 983
    of pseudoprimality, 966–968
text, in string matching, 985
then clause, 20 n.
Theta-notation, 44–47, 64
thread, 773
Threading Building Blocks, 774
3-CNF, 1082
3-CNF-SAT, 1082
3-CNF satisfiability, 1082–1085, 1105
    approximation algorithm for, 1123–1124, 1139
    and 2-CNF satisfiability, 1049
3-COLOR, 1103 pr.
3-conjunctive normal form, 1082

tight constraint, 865
time, *see* running time
time domain, 898
time-memory trade-off, 365
timestamp, 603, 611 ex.
Toeplitz matrix, 921 pr.
to, in pseudocode, 20
TOP, 1031
top-down method, for dynamic programming, 365
top of a stack, 232
topological sort, 8, 612–615, 623
    in computing single-source shortest paths in a dag, 655
TOPOLOGICAL-SORT, 613
total order, 1165
total path length, 304 pr.
total preorder, 1165
total relation, 1165
tour
    bitonic, 405 pr.
    Euler, 623 pr., 1048
    of a graph, 1096
track, 486
tractability, 1048
trailing pointer, 295
transition function, 995, 1001–1002, 1012 ex.
transitive closure, 697–699
    and boolean matrix multiplication, 832 ex.
    of dynamic graphs, 705 pr., 707
TRANSITIVE-CLOSURE, 698
transitive relation, 1163
transitivity of asymptotic notation, 51
TRANSPLANT, 296, 323
transpose
    conjugate, 832 ex.
    of a directed graph, 592 ex.
    of a matrix, 1217
    of a matrix, multithreaded, 792 ex.
transpose symmetry of asymptotic notation, 52
traveling-salesman problem
    approximation algorithm for, 1111–1117, 1139
    bitonic euclidean, 405 pr.
    bottleneck, 1117 ex.
    NP-completeness of, 1096–1097
    with the triangle inequality, 1112–1115
    without the triangle inequality, 1115–1116

traversal of a tree, 287, 293 ex., 342, 1114

treap, 333 pr., 338

TREAP-INSERT, 333 pr.

tree, 1173–1180

  AA-trees, 338

  AVL, 333 pr., 337

  binary, *see* binary tree

  binomial, 527 pr.

  bisection of, 1181 pr.

  breadth-first, 594, 600

  B-trees, 484–504

  decision, 192–193

  depth-first, 603

  diameter of, 602 ex.

  dynamic, 482

  free, 1172–1176

  full walk of, 1114

  fusion, 212, 483

  heap, 151–169

  height-balanced, 333 pr.

  height of, 1177

  interval, 348–354

  k-neighbor, 338

  minimum spanning, *see* minimum spanning
    tree

  optimal binary search, 397–404, 413

  order-statistic, 339–345

  parse, 1082

  recursion, 37, 88–93

  red-black, *see* red-black tree

  rooted, 246–249, 1176

  scapegoat, 338

  search, *see* search tree

  shortest-paths, 647–648, 673–676

  spanning, *see* minimum spanning tree,
    spanning tree

  splay, 338, 482

  treap, 333 pr., 338

  2-3, 337, 504

  2-3-4, 489, 503 pr.

  van Emde Boas, 531–560

  walk of, 287, 293 ex., 342, 1114

  weight-balanced trees, 338

TREE-DELETE, 298, 299 ex., 323–324

tree edge, 601, 603, 609

TREE-INSERT, 294, 315

TREE-MAXIMUM, 291

TREE-MINIMUM, 291

TREE-PREDECESSOR, 292

TREE-SEARCH, 290

TREE-SUCCESSOR, 292

tree walk, 287, 293 ex., 342, 1114

trial, Bernoulli, 1201

trial division, 966

triangle inequality, 1112

  for shortest paths, 650, 671

triangular matrix, 1219, 1222 ex., 1225 ex.

trichotomy, interval, 348

trichotomy property of real numbers, 52

tridiagonal linear systems, 840 pr.

tridiagonal matrix, 1219

trie (radix tree), 304 pr.

  y-fast, 558 pr.

TRIM, 1130

trimming a list, 1130

trivial divisor, 928

truth assignment, 1072, 1079

truth table, 1070

TSP, 1096

tuple, 1162

twiddle factor, 912

2-CNF-SAT, 1086 ex.

2-CNF satisfiability, 1086 ex.

  and 3-CNF satisfiability, 1049

two-pass method, 571

2-3-4 heap, 529 pr.

2-3-4 tree, 489

  joining, 503 pr.

  splitting, 503 pr.

2-3 tree, 337, 504

unary, 1056

unbounded linear program, 851

unconditional branch instruction, 23

uncountable set, 1161

underdetermined system of linear equations,
    814

underflow

  of a queue, 234

  of a stack, 233

undirected graph, 1168

  articulation point of, 621 pr.

  biconnected component of, 621 pr.

  bridge of, 621 pr.

  clique in, 1086

  coloring of, 1103 pr., 1180 pr.

computing a minimum spanning tree in, 624–642
converting to, from a multigraph, 593 ex.
d-regular, 736 ex.
grid, 760 pr.
hamiltonian, 1061
independent set of, 1101 pr.
matching of, 732
nonhamiltonian, 1061
vertex cover of, 1089, 1108
see also graph
undirected version of a directed graph, 1172
uniform hashing, 271
uniform probability distribution, 1191–1192
uniform random permutation, 116, 125
union
of dynamic sets, *see* uniting
of languages, 1058
of sets ($\cup$), 1159
UNION, 505, 562
disjoint-set-forest implementation of, 571
linked-list implementation of, 565–567, 568 ex.
union by rank, 569
unique factorization of integers, 931
unit (1), 928
uniting
of Fibonacci heaps, 511–512
of heaps, 506
of linked lists, 241 ex.
of 2-3-4 heaps, 529 pr.
unit lower-triangular matrix, 1219
unit-time task, 443
unit upper-triangular matrix, 1219
unit vector, 1218
universal collection of hash functions, 265
universal hashing, 265–268
universal sink, 593 ex.
universe, 1160
of keys in van Emde Boas trees, 532
universe size, 532
unmatched vertex, 732
unsorted linked list, 236
see also linked list
until, in pseudocode, 20
unweighted longest simple paths, 382
unweighted shortest paths, 381
upper bound, 47

upper-bound property, 650, 671–672
upper median, 213
upper square root ($\sqrt[\uparrow]{\ }$), 546
upper-triangular matrix, 1219, 1225 ex.

valid shift, 985
value
of a flow, 710
of a function, 1166
objective, 847, 851
value over replacement player, 411 pr.
Vandermonde matrix, 902, 1226 pr.
van Emde Boas tree, 531–560
cluster in, 546
compared with proto van Emde Boas structures, 547
deletion from, 554–556
insertion into, 552–554
maximum in, 550
membership in, 550
minimum in, 550
predecessor in, 551–552
with reduced space, 557 pr.
successor in, 550–551
summary in, 546
Var[ ] (variance), 1199
variable
basic, 855
entering, 867
leaving, 867
nonbasic, 855
in pseudocode, 21
random, 1196–1201
slack, 855
see also indicator random variable
variable-length code, 429
variance, 1199
of a binomial distribution, 1205
of a geometric distribution, 1203
VEB-EMPTY-TREE-INSERT, 553
vEB tree, *see* van Emde Boas tree
VEB-TREE-DELETE, 554
VEB-TREE-INSERT, 553
VEB-TREE-MAXIMUM, 550
VEB-TREE-MEMBER, 550
VEB-TREE-MINIMUM, 550
VEB-TREE-PREDECESSOR, 552
VEB-TREE-SUCCESSOR, 551

vector, 1218, 1222–1224
    convolution of, 901
    cross product of, 1016
    orthonormal, 842
    in the plane, 1015
Venn diagram, 1160
verification, 1061–1066
    of spanning trees, 642
verification algorithm, 1063
vertex
    articulation point, 621 pr.
    attributes of, 592
    capacity of, 714 ex.
    in a graph, 1168
    intermediate, 693
    isolated, 1169
    overflowing, 736
    of a polygon, 1020 ex.
    relabeled, 740
    selector, 1093
vertex cover, 1089, 1108, 1124–1127, 1139
VERTEX-COVER, 1090
vertex-cover problem
    approximation algorithm for, 1108–1111,
        1139
    NP-completeness of, 1089–1091, 1105
vertex set, 1168
violation, of an equality constraint, 865
virtual memory, 24
Viterbi algorithm, 408 pr.
VORP, 411 pr.

walk of a tree, 287, 293 ex., 342, 1114
weak duality, 880–881, 886 ex., 895 pr.
weight
    of a cut, 1127 ex.
    of an edge, 591
    mean, 680 pr.
    of a path, 643
weight-balanced tree, 338, 473 pr.
weighted bipartite matching, 530
weighted matroid, 439–442
weighted median, 225 pr.
weighted set-covering problem, 1135 pr.
weighted-union heuristic, 566
weighted vertex cover, 1124–1127, 1139
weight function
    for a graph, 591

    in a weighted matroid, 439
while, in pseudocode, 20
white-path theorem, 608
white vertex, 594, 603
widget, 1092
wire, 1071
WITNESS, 969
witness, to the compositeness of a number, 968
work law, 780
work, of a multithreaded computation, 779
work-stealing scheduling algorithm, 812
worst-case running time, 27, 49

Yen's improvement to the Bellman-Ford
        algorithm, 678 pr.
y-fast trie, 558 pr.
Young tableau, 167 pr.

$\mathbb{Z}$ (set of integers), 1158
$\mathbb{Z}_n$ (equivalence classes modulo n), 928
$\mathbb{Z}_n^*$ (elements of multiplicative group
        modulo n), 941
$\mathbb{Z}_n^+$ (nonzero elements of $\mathbb{Z}_n$), 967
zero matrix, 1218
zero of a polynomial modulo a prime, 950 ex.
0-1 integer programming, 1100 ex., 1125
0-1 knapsack problem, 425, 427 ex., 1137 pr.,
        1139
0-1 sorting lemma, 208 pr.
zonk, 1195 ex.

He was a shrewd and faithful tyke
As ever leapt a gate or dyke;
His honest, jolly, brindled face
Won him good friends in every place.
His breast was white, his shaggy back
Well clad with coat of glossy black;
His bushy tail, with upward curl,
Hung o'er his haunches in a swirl.

No doubt but each was fond of t'other
And warmly intimate together;
With social nose they ran and snuffed
For moles or mice at mound and tuft;
At times scoured off on long excursion,
Or rolled each other for diversion;
Until, with larking weary grown,
Upon a knoll they sat them down,
And there began a long digression
About the lords of the creation.

CAESAR

I've often wondered, honest Luath,
What sort of life poor dogs like you have;
And when the gentry's life I mark,
How fare the poor who live by work.
  Our Laird gets in his rents and sums,
His coal, his produce, all his claims;
He rises when he thinks he will;
His flunkeys answer to his bell:
He calls his coach; he calls his horse;
He draws a well-filled silken purse
Long as my tail, where, through the stitches
I see his golden guinea riches.
  From morn to night it's nought but toiling
At baking, roasting, frying, boiling,
And though the gentry cram and swill
Yet all the servants take their fill
Of sauce, ragouts and spicy hash
That's nothing more than wasteful trash.
Our lap-dog, that small withered wonder,
Eats bigger dinners, yes, by thunder!

175

Than any honest tenant eats
In all his Honour's wide estates.
What the poor cotters fill their paunch on
I own is past my comprehension.

LUATH

Caesar, you're right; they're tried enough;
A labourer digging hard and rough
In sodden ditch and stony dyke,
Laying bare quarries and suchlike;
He and his wife he just sustains,
Besides a troop of ragged bairns,
And nought but his strong hands to keep
Them right and tight in food and sleep.
    And when they meet with black disaster,
Like loss of health, or lack of masters,
You'd almost think, a little longer
And they must starve of cold and hunger;
But yet—I never understand it!—
They're mostly wonderful contented;
And strapping lads and clever hussies
Are bred just such a way as this is.

CAESAR

But look, my friend, how you're neglected,
How huffed and cuffed and disrespected!
Lord, man! our gentry care so little
For ploughmen, ditchers and such cattle;
They go as scornful past a hedger
As I would by a stinking badger.
    I've noticed, on our Laird's court-day,
And many a time with sore dismay,
Poor tenants, late with rents and dues,
Taking the factor's harsh abuse;
He'll stamp and threaten, curse and swear
He'll jail them and distrain their gear;
While they must stand with aspect humble,
And hear it all, and fear and tremble!
I see how folk live that have riches;
But surely poor folk must be wretches!

176

They're not so wretched as you'd think,
Though always on privation's brink;
They're so accustomed to the sight,
The view it gives them little fright.

Then chance and fortune are so guided
They're always more or less provided;
And though fatigued with close employment,
A spell of rest's a sweet enjoyment.

The dearest comfort of their lives,
Their thriving brood and faithful wives;
The prattling things are just their pride,
That sweeten board and fireside.

And then, twelvepenny-worth of ale
Will always over care prevail;
They lay aside their private cares
To canvass Church and State affairs:
They'll talk of patronage and priests
With kindling fury in their breasts;
Or tell what new taxation's coming,
And hear the news from London humming.

As bleak-faced Hallowmass returns
They hear the jolly rattling churns,
When rural life of every station
Unite in common recreation;
Love smiles, Wit sparkles, social Mirth
Forgets there's trouble on the earth.

That merry day the year begins
They bar the door on frosty winds;
The strong ale wreathes with mantling cream
And gives a heart-inspiring steam;
The treasured pipe and snuffbox full
Are handed round with right goodwill;
The cheerful elders talk and browse,
The young go romping through the house—
My heart has been so glad to see them
That I for joy ran barking with them.

Still, it's too true what you have said:
That game is far too often played.
There's many a creditable stock
Of decent, honest, kindly folk,

Are bundled out both root and branch,
Some rascal's greedy pride to quench,
Who thinks to knit himself the faster
In favour with his absent master,
Who, maybe, is a-parliamenting,
For Britain's good his soul indenting—

CAESAR

Faith, lad, you little know about it;
For Britain's good!—good faith! I doubt it!
Say rather, going as premiers lead him,
With Aye or No just as they bid him!
At operas and plays parading,
Mortgaging, gambling, masquerading.
Or maybe, in a frolic daft,
For Hague or Calais boards a craft,
To make a tour, by pleasure swirled,
To learn *bon ton* and see the world.
    There, at Vienna or Versailles,
He breaks his father's old entails,
Or to Madrid diverts his route
To strum guitars or fight with nought;
Or down Italian vistas hurtles,
Whore-hunting among groves of myrtles;
Then boozes muddy German water
To make himself look fair and fatter
And clear the consequential sorrows—
Love-gifts of carnival signoras.
For Britain's good!—for her destruction!
With dissipation, feud and faction!

LUATH

Well, well! dear sirs! is that the way
So many great estates decay?
Are we so goaded, cramped and pressed
For wealth to go that way at last?
    O, if they'd stay away from courts
And please themselves with country sports,
It would for everyone be better,
The laird, the tenant and the cotter!

178

For these wild, noisy, rambling sparks,
They're not ill-natured in their larks:
Except for stripping ancient glades,
Or speaking lightly of their jades,
Or shooting of a hare or moorcock,
They little harm the simple poor folk.

But will you tell me, Master Caesar,
Sure, great folks live a life of pleasure?
No cold nor hunger's grip can press them,
The very thought need not distress them.

CAESAR

Lord, man, you'd never envy them
If you were sometimes where I am.

It's true, they needn't starve or sweat
Through winter's cold or summer's heat;
They've no hard work to cramp their bones
And fill old age with aches and groans:
But human beings are such fools,
For all their colleges and schools,
That when no present ills perplex them
They make enough themselves to vex them;
The less they have to disconcert them
In like proportion less will hurt them.
A country fellow at the plough,
His acres tilled, his heart's aglow;
A country lassie at her wheel,
Her dozens done, she's fine and well;
But gentlemen, and ladies worst,
At dusk with idleness are cursed.
They loiter, lounging, lank and lazy;
Though nothing ails them, yet uneasy;
Their days insipid, dull and tasteless;
Their nights unquiet, long and restless.
And even sports, their balls and races,
Their galloping through public places,
Are such parades of pomp and art,
The joy can scarcely reach the heart.
The men fall out in party matches,
Then make it up in wild debauches:

One night they're mad with drink and whoring,
Next day their life is past enduring.
The ladies arm-in-arm, in clusters,
Are great and gracious all as sisters;
But hear their thoughts of one another,
They're downright devils all together.
And then, with eggshell cup and platie,
They sip the scandal-brew so pretty,
Or through long nights, with acid looks,
Pore on the devil's picture books;
Stake on a chance a farmer's stackyard,
And cheat like any unhanged blackguard.
    There are exceptions, man and woman;
But this is gentry's life in common.

    By this the sun was out of sight
And twilight darkening brought the night;
A beetle hummed with lazy drone,
The cows stood lowing in the lane;
When up they got with friendly shrugs,
Rejoiced they were not men but dogs;
And each took off his homeward way,
Resolved to meet some other day.

GEORGE GORDON BYRON

GEORGE GORDON BYRON (English, 1788-1824). The most gifted showman
of English Romanticism. Suffered handicap of clubfoot. *Childe Harold's
Pilgrimage* brought early fame and acclaim of English society, despite scandalous private life. Settled in Italy, where he wrote greatest work, the
satirical *Don Juan*. Joined Greek rebels in 1823, died of fever a year later.
    Poetry expresses the essence of romantic melancholy and pessimism.

SHE WALKS IN BEAUTY

SHE walks in beauty, like the night
  Of cloudless climes and starry skies;
And all that's best of dark and bright
  Meet in her aspect and her eyes:
Thus mellowed to that tender light
  Which heaven to gaudy day denies.

One shade the more, one ray the less,
    Had half impaired the nameless grace
Which waves in every raven tress,
    Or softly lightens o'er her face;
Where thoughts serenely sweet express
    How pure, how dear their dwelling-place.

And on that cheek, and o'er that brow,
    So soft, so calm, yet eloquent,
The smiles that win, the tints that glow,
    But tell of days in goodness spent,
A mind at peace with all below,
    A heart whose love is innocent!

SO, WE'LL GO NO MORE A-ROVING

So, we'll go no more a-roving
    So late into the night,
Though the heart be still as loving,
    And the moon be still as bright.

For the sword outwears its sheath,
    And the soul wears out the breast,
And the heart must pause to breathe,
    And Love itself have rest.

Though the night was made for loving,
    And the day returns too soon,
Yet we'll go no more a-roving
    By the light of the moon.

THE ISLES OF GREECE

The isles of Greece! the isles of Greece
    Where burning Sappho loved and sung,
Where grew the arts of war and peace,
    Where Delos rose, and Phœbus sprung!
Eternal summer gilds them yet,
But all, except their sun, is set.

The Scian and the Teian muse,
  The hero's harp, the lover's lute,
Have found the fame your shores refuse;
  Their place of birth alone is mute
To sounds which echo further west
Than your sires' "Islands of the Blest."

The mountains look on Marathon—
  And Marathon looks on the sea;
And musing there an hour alone,
  I dreamed that Greece might still be free;
For standing on the Persians' grave,
I could not deem myself a slave.

A king sate on the rocky brow
  Which looks o'er sea-born Salamis;
And ships, by thousands, lay below,
  And men in nations—all were his!
He counted them at break of day—
And when the sun set, where were they?

And where are they? and where art thou,
  My country? On thy voiceless shore
The heroic lay is tuneless now—
  The heroic bosom beats no more!
And must thy lyre, so long divine,
Degenerate into hands like mine?

'Tis something in the dearth of fame,
  Though linked among a fettered race,
To feel at least a patriot's shame,
  Even as I sing, suffuse my face;
For what is left the poet here?
For Greeks a blush—for Greece a tear.

Must *we* but weep o'er days more blest?
  Must *we* but blush?—Our fathers bled.
Earth! render back from out thy breast
  A remnant of our Spartan dead!
Of the three hundred grant but three,
To make a new Thermopylae!

182

What, silent still? and silent all?
   Ah! no— the voices of the dead
Sound like a distant torrent's fall,
   And answer, "Let one living head,
But one, arise—we come, we come!"
'Tis but the living who are dumb.

In vain—in vain; strike other chords;
   Fill high the cup with Samian wine!
Leave battles to the Turkish hordes,
   And shed the blood of Scio's vine!
Hark! rising to the ignoble call—
How answers each bold Bacchanal!

You have the Pyrric dance as yet;
   Where is the Pyrric phalanx gone?
Of two such lessons, why forget
   The nobler and the manlier one?
You have the letters Cadmus gave—
Think ye he meant them for a slave?

Fill high the bowl with Samian wine!
   We will not think of themes like these!
It made Anacreon's song divine.
   He served—but served Polycrates—
A tyrant; but our masters then
Were still, at least, our countrymen.

The tyrant of the Chersonese
   Was freedom's best and bravest friend;
That tyrant was Miltiades!
   O that the present hour would lend
Another despot of the kind!
Such chains as his were sure to bind.

Fill high the bowl with Samian wine!
   On Suli's rock, and Parga's shore,
Exists the remnant of a line
   Such as the Doric mothers bore;
And there, perhaps, some seed is sown,
The Heracleidan blood might own.

183

Trust not for freedom to the Franks—
  They have a king who buys and sells;
In native swords and native ranks
  The only hope of courage dwells.
But Turkish force and Latin fraud
Would break your shield, however broad.

Fill high the bowl with Samian wine!
  Our virgins dance beneath the shade—
I see their glorious black eyes shine;
  But gazing on each glowing maid,
My own the burning teardrop laves,
To think such breasts must suckle slaves.

Place me on Sunium's marbled steep,
  Where nothing, save the waves and I,
May hear our mutual murmurs sweep;
  There, swan-like, let me sing and die.
A land of slaves shall ne'er be mine—
Dash down yon cup of Samian wine!

WHEN WE TWO PARTED

When we two parted
  In silence and tears,
Half broken-hearted,
  To sever for years,
Pale grew thy cheek and cold,
  Colder thy kiss;
Truly that hour foretold
  Sorrow to this!

The dew of the morning
  Sunk chill on my brow;
It felt like the waning
  Of what I feel now.
Thy vows are all broken,
  And light is thy fame:
I hear thy name spoken
  And share in its shame.

They name thee before me,
  A knell to mine ear;
A shudder comes o'er me—
  Why wert thou so dear?
They knew not I knew thee
  Who knew thee too well:
Long, long shall I rue thee
  Too deeply to tell.

In secret we met:
  In silence I grieve
That thy heart could forget,
  Thy spirit deceive.
If I should meet thee
  After long years,
How should I greet thee?
  With silence and tears.

ELEGY ON THYRZA

And thou art dead, as young and fair
  As aught of mortal birth;
And form so soft and charms so rare
  Too soon return'd to Earth!
Though Earth received them in her bed,
And o'er the spot the crowd may tread
  In carelessness or mirth,
There is an eye which could not brook
A moment on that grave to look.

I will not ask where thou liest low,
  Nor gaze upon the spot;
There flowers or weeds at will may grow,
  So I behold them not:
It is enough for me to prove
That what I loved and long must love
  Like common earth can rot;
To me there needs no stone to tell
'Tis Nothing that I loved so well.

185

Yet did I love thee to the last,
  As fervently as thou,
Who didst not change through all the past
  And canst not alter now.
The love where Death has set his seal
Nor age can chill, nor rival steal,
  Nor falsehood disavow:
And, what were worse, thou canst not see
Or wrong, or change, or fault in me.

The better days of life were ours;
  The worst can be but mine:
The sun that cheers, the storm that lours,
  Shall never more be thine.
The silence of that dreamless sleep
I envy now too much to weep;
  Nor need I to repine.
That all those charms have pass'd away
I might have watch'd through long decay.

The flower in ripen'd bloom unmatch'd
  Must fall the earliest prey;
Though by no hand untimely snatch'd,
  The leaves must drop away.
And yet it were a greater grief
To watch it withering, leaf by leaf,
  Than see it pluck'd to-day;
Since earthly eye but ill can bear
To trace the change to foul from fair.

I know not if I could have borne
  To see thy beauties fade;
The night that follow'd such a morn
  Had worn a deeper shade:
Thy day without a cloud hath past,
  And thou wert lovely to the last,
    Extinguish'd, not decay'd;
As stars that shoot along the sky
Shine brightest as they fall from high.

As once I wept, if I could weep,
  My tears might well be shed,
To think I was not near, to keep
  One vigil o'er thy bed:
To gaze, how fondly! on thy face,
To fold thee in a faint embrace,
  Uphold thy drooping head;
And show that love, however vain,
Nor thou nor I can feel again.

Yet how much less it were to gain,
  Though thou hast left me free,
The loveliest things that still remain
  Than thus remember thee!
The all of thine that cannot die
Through dark and dread Eternity
  Returns again to me,
And more thy buried love endears
Than aught except its living years.

C

PEDRO CALDERON DE LA BARCA

PEDRO CALDERON DE LA BARCA (Spanish, 1600-1681). Baroque and Catholic playwright and poet. Won early fame as dramatist. After service in Spanish army, became priest at 50. Wrote 120 plays, notable for elaborate construction and philosophic content, and many *autos* (religious mysteries). Among them: *La vida es sueño, El alcalde de Zalamea, El médico de Su Honra.*

SEGISMUND'S DREAM

(The King of Poland, frightened by an omen at his son's birth, which the soothsayers have interpreted to mean that the boy will grow up a mere wild beast, bringing fire and slaughter on the country if he succeeds to power, has imprisoned him in a tower till he shall come of age, with a faithful officer for guard. He then has him released—to see if the oracle has been mistaken!—and told that all this confinement and misery has been a dream—as in the "Induction" to the "Taming of the Shrew.")

    Segismund (within)—
Forbear! I stifle with your perfume! cease
Your crazy salutations! peace, I say—
Begone, or let me go, ere I go mad
With all this babble, mummery, and glare,
For I am growing dangerous—Air! room! air!—
    (*He rushes in. Music ceases.*)
Oh but to save the reeling brain from wreck
With its bewildered senses!—
    (*He covers his eyes for a while.*)
    (*After looking in the mirror.*)
What, this fantastic Segismund the same

188

Who last night, as for all his nights before,
Lay down to sleep in wolfskin on the ground
In a black turret which the wolf howled round.
And woke again upon a golden bed,
Round which as clouds about a rising sun,
In scarce less glittering caparison,
Gathered gay shapes that, underneath a breeze
Of music, handed him upon their knees
The wine of heaven in a cup of gold,
And still in soft melodious undersong
Hailing me Prince of Poland!—"Segismund,"
They said, "Our Prince! The Prince of Poland!" and
Again, "Oh, welcome, welcome, to his own
Our own Prince Segismund—"

If reason, sense, and self-identity
Obliterated from a worn-out brain,
Art thou not maddest striving to be sane,
And catching at that Self of yesterday
That, like a leper's rags, best flung away!
Or if not mad, then dreaming—dreaming?—well—
Dreaming then—Or, if self to self be true,
Not mocked by that, but as poor souls have been
By those who wronged them, to give wrong new relish?
Or have those stars indeed they told me of
As masters of my wretched life of old,
Into some happier constellation rolled,
And brought my better fortune out on earth
Clear as themselves in heav'n!—

(The great officers of state crowd around him with protestations of
fidelity; Clotaldo, his old warder, comes, and after attempts at
explaining and justifying the situation, Segismund in a fury attempts
to strike his head off; the Princess Estrella, betrothed to the Duke
of Muscovy, enters, and Segismund claims her for his own and
attempts to throttle the Duke; the King is called in, and after a
storm of reproaches which the King parries on the ground of good
intentions, Segismund closes as follows:)

Be assured your Savage, once let loose,
Will not be caged again so quickly; not
By threat or adulation to be tamed,

Till he have had his quarrel out with those
Who made him what he is.
    King—
Beware! Beware!
Subdue the kindled Tiger in your eye,
Nor dream that it was sheer necessity
Made me thus far relax the bond of fate,
And, with far more of terror than of hope
Threaten myself, my people, and the State.
Know that, if old, I yet have vigor left
To wield the sword as well as wear the crown;
And if my more immediate issue fail,
Not wanting scions of collateral blood,
Whose wholesome growth shall more than compensate
For all the loss of a distorted stem.
    Segismund—
That will I straightway bring to trial—Oh,
After a revelation such as this,
The Last Day shall have little left to show
Of righted wrong and villainy requited!
Nay, Judgment now beginning upon earth,
Myself, methinks, in right of all my wrongs,
Appointed heav'n's avenging minister,
Accuser, judge, and executioner,
Sword in hand, cite the guilty—First, as worst,
The usurper of his son's inheritance;
Him and his old accomplice, time and crime
Inveterate, and unable to repay
The golden years of life they stole away.
What, does he yet maintain his state, and keep
The throne he should be judged from? Down with him,
That I may trample on the false white head
So long has worn my crown! Where are my soldiers?
Of all my subjects and my vassals here
Not one to do my bidding? Hark! A trumpet!
The trumpet—
(*He pauses as the trumpet sounds as in Act I., and masked Soldiers
gradually fill in behind the throne.*)
    King (*rising before his throne*)—
Aye, indeed, the trumpet blows

A memorable note, to summon those
Who, if forthwith you fall not at the feet
Of him whose head you threaten with the dust,
Forthwith shall draw the curtain of the Past
About you; and this momentary gleam
Of glory, that you think to hold life-fast,
So coming, so shall vanish, as a dream.

   Segismund—
He prophesies; the old man prophesies;
And, at his trumpet's summons, from the tower
The leash-bound shadows loosened after me
My rising glory reach and overlour—
But, reach not I my height, he shall not hold,
But with me back to his own darkness!

   (*He dashes toward the throne and is inclosed by the soldiers.*)
Traitors!
Hold off! Unhand me! Am not I your king?
And you would strangle him!
But I am breaking with an inward Fire
Shall scorch you off, and wrap me on the wings
Of conflagration from a kindled pyre
Of lying prophecies and prophet kings
Above the extinguished stars—Reach me the sword
He flung me—Fill me such a bowl of wine
As that you woke the day with—

   King—
And shall close,—
But of the vintage that Clotaldo knows.

(He is drugged, returned to the tower, and on waking assured that
the recent taste of freedom and kingship was all a dream, and his
former life in the tower the reality.)

   Segismund—
You know
'Tis nothing but a dream?
   Clotaldo—
Nay, you yourself
Know best how lately you awoke from that
You know you went to sleep on?
Why, have you never dreamt the like before?

Segismund—
Never, to such reality.
   Clotaldo—
Such dreams
Are oftentimes the sleeping exhalations
Of that ambition that lies smoldering
Under the ashes of the lowest fortune;
By which, when reason slumbers, or has lost
The reins of sensible comparison,
We fly at something higher than we are—
Scarce ever dive to lower—to be kings,
Or conquerors, crowned with laurel or with gold,
Nay, mounting heav'n itself on eagle wings.
Which, by the way, now that I think of it,
May furnish us the key to this high flight—
That royal Eagle we were watching, and
Talking of as you went to sleep last night.
   Segismund—
Last night? Last night?
   Clotaldo—
Aye, do you not remember
Envying his immunity of flight,
As, rising from his throne of rock, he sailed
Above the mountains far into the West
That burned about him, while with poising wings
He darkled in it as a burning brand
Is seen to smolder in the fire it feeds?
   Segismund—
Last night—last night—Oh, what a day was that
Between that last night and this sad To-day!
   Clotaldo—
And yet, perhaps,
Only some few dark moments, into which
Imagination, once lit up within
And unconditional of time and space,
Can pour infinities.
   Segismund—
And I remember
How the old man they called the King, who wore
The crown of gold about his silver hair,
And a mysterious girdle round his waist,

Just when my rage was roaring at its height,
And after which it was all dark again,
Bid me beware lest all should be a dream.

   Clotaldo—
Aye, there another specialty of dreams,
That once the dreamer 'gins to dream he dreams.
His foot is on the very verge of waking.

   Segismund—
Would it had been upon the verge of death
That knows no waking—
Lifting me up to glory, to fall back,
Stunned, crippled—wretcheder than ev'n before.

   Clotaldo—
Yet not so glorious, Segismund, if you
Your visionary honor wore so ill
As to work murder and revenge on those
Who meant you well.

   Segismund—
Who meant me!—me! their Prince
Chained like a felon—

   Clotaldo—
Stay, stay—Not so fast,
You dreamed the Prince, remember.

   Segismund—
Then in dream
Revenged it only.
True. But as they say
Dreams are rough copies of the waking soul
Yet uncorrected of the higher Will,
So that men sometimes in their dreams confess
An unsuspected, or forgotten, self;
One must beware to check—aye, if one may,
Stifle ere born, such passion in ourselves
As makes, we see, such havoc with our sleep,
And ill reacts upon the waking day.
And, by the bye, for one test, Segismund,
Between such swearable realities—
Since Dreaming, Madness, Passion, are akin
In missing each that salutary rein
Of reason, and the guiding will of man:
One test, I think, of waking sanity

193

Shall be that conscious power of self-control,
To curb all passion, but much most of all
That evil and vindictive, that ill squares
With human, and with holy canon less,
Which bids us pardon ev'n our enemies,
And much more those who, out of no ill will,
Mistakenly have taken up the rod
Which heav'n, they think, has put into their hands.
   Segismund—
I think I soon shall have to try again—
Sleep has not yet done with me.
   Clotaldo—
Such a sleep.
Take my advice—'tis early yet—the sun
Scarce up above the mountain; go within,
And if the night deceived you, try anew
With morning; morning dreams they say come true.
   Segismund—
Oh, rather pray for me a sleep so fast
As shall obliterate dream and waking too.
   (*Exit into the tower.*)
   Clotaldo—
So sleep; sleep fast: and sleep away those two
Night potions, and the waking dream between
Which dream thou must believe; and, if to see
Again, poor Segismund! that dream must be.
And yet, and yet, in these our ghostly lives,
Half night, half day, half sleeping, half awake,
How if our working life, like that of sleep,
Be all a dream in that eternal life
To which we wake not till we sleep in death?
How if, I say, the senses we now trust
For date of sensible comparison,—
Aye, ev'n the Reason's self that dates with them,
Should be in essence or intensity
Hereafter so transcended, and awoke
To a perceptive subtlety so keen
As to confess themselves befooled before,
In all that now they will avouch for most?
One man—like this—but only so much longer
As life is longer than a summer's day,

194

Believed himself a king upon his throne,
And played at hazard with his fellows' lives,
Who cheaply dreamed away their lives to him.
The sailor dreamed of tossing on the flood:
The soldier of his laurels grown in blood:
The lover of the beauty that he knew
Must yet dissolve to dusty residue:
The merchant and the miser of his bags
Of fingered gold; the beggar of his rags:
And all this stage of earth on which we seem
Such busy actors, and the parts we played,
Substantial as the shadow of a shade,
And Dreaming but a dream within a dream.

   Fife—
Was it not said, sir,
By some philosopher as yet unborn
That any chimney sweep who for twelve hours
Dreams himself king is happy as the king
Who dreams himself twelve hours a chimney-sweep?

   Clotaldo—
A theme indeed for wiser heads than yours
To moralize upon.

(An insurrection breaking out to reinstate Segismund, a band of
soldiers bring him, asleep, from the tower.)

   Captain—
O Royal Segismund, our Prince and King,
Look on us—listen to us—answer us,
Your faithful soldiery and subjects, now
About you kneeling, but on fire to rise
And cleave a passage through your enemies,
Until we seat you on your lawful throne.
For though your father, King Basilio,
Now King of Poland, jealous of the stars
That prophesy his setting with your rise,
Here holds you ignominiously eclipsed,
And would Astolfo, Duke of Muscovy,
Mount to the throne of Poland after him;
So will not we, your loyal soldiery

195

And subjects; neither those of us now first
Apprised of your existence and your right:
Nor those that hitherto deluded by
Allegiance false, their vizors now fling down,
And craving pardon on their knees with us
For that unconscious disloyalty,
Offer with us the service of their blood;
Not only we and they; but at our heels
The heart, if not the bulk, of Poland follows
To join their voices and their arms with ours,
In vindicating with our lives our own
Prince Segismund to Poland and her throne.

    Soldiers—
Segismund, Segismund, Prince Segismund!
Our own King Segismund, etc.

    (*They all arise.*)

    Segismund—
Again? So soon?—What, not yet done with me?
The sun is little higher up, I think,
Than when I last lay down,
To bury in the depth of your own sea
You that infest its shallows.

    Captain—
Sir!

    Segismund—
And now,
Not in a palace, not in the fine clothes
We all were in; but here, in the old place,
And in your old accounterment—
Only your vizors off, and lips unlockt
To mock me with that idle title—

    Captain—
Nay,
Indeed no idle title, but your own,
Then, now, and now forever. For, behold,
Ev'n as I speak. the mountain passes fill
And bristle with the advancing soldiery
That glitters in your rising glory, sir;
And, at our signal, echo to our cry,
"Segismund, King of Poland!"

    (*Shouts, trumpets, etc.*)

196

Segismund—
Oh, how cheap
The muster of a countless host of shadows,
As impotent to do with as to keep!
All this they said before—to softer music.
   Captain—
Soft music, sir, to what indeed were shadows,
That, following the sunshine of a Court,
Shall back be brought with it—if shadows still,
Yet to substantial reckoning.
   Segismund—
They shall?
The white-haired and white-wandel chamberlain,
So busy with his wand too—the old King
That I was somewhat hard on—he had been
Hard upon me—and the fine feathered Prince
Who crowed so loud—my cousin,—and another,
Another cousin, we will not bear hard on—
And—but Clotaldo?
   Captain—
Fled, my Lord, but close
Pursued; and then—
   Segismund—
Then, as he fled before,
And after he had sworn it on his knees,
Came back to take me—where I am!—No more,
No more of this! Away with you! Begone!
Whether but visions of ambitious night
That morning ought to scatter, or grown out
Of night's proportions you invade the day
To scare me from my little wits yet left,
Begone! I know I must be near awake,
Knowing I dream; or, if not at my voice,
Then vanish at the clapping of my hands,
Or take this foolish fellow for your sport:
Dressing me up in visionary glories,
Which the first air of waking consciousness
Scatters as fast as from the alamander—
That, waking one fine morning in full flower,
One rougher insurrection of the breeze
Of all her sudden honor disadorns

197

To the last blossom, and she stands again
The winter-naked scarecrow that she was!
        (*Shouts, trumpets, etc.*)
    A Soldier—
Challenging King Basilio's now in sight,
And bearing down upon us.
    Captain—
Sir, you hear;
A little hesitation and delay,
And all is lost—your own right, and the lives
Of those who now maintain it at that cost;
With you all saved and won; without, all lost.
That former recognition of your right
Grant but a dream, if you will have it so;
Great things forecast themselves by shadows great:
Or will you have it, this like that dream too,
People, and place, and time itself, all dream—
Yet, being in't, and as the shadows come
Quicker and thicker than you can escape,
Adopt your visionary soldiery,
Who, having struck a solid chain away,
Now put an airy sword into your hand,
And harnessing you piecemeal till you stand
Amidst us all complete in glittering,
If unsubstantial, steel—

(A battle is fought, in which Segismund is victorious; taught by his
former experience, he resolves to be wise and temperate, and closes
with the following moralizing:)

    You stare upon me all, amazed to hear
The word of civil justice from such lips
As never yet seemed tuned to such discourse.
But listen—In that same enchanted tower,
Not long ago, I learned it from a dream
Expounded by this ancient prophet here;
And which he told me, should it come again,
How I should bear myself beneath it; not
As then with angry passion all on fire,
Arguing and making a distempered soul;
But ev'n with justice, mercy, self-control,

As if the dream I walked in were no dream,
And conscience one day to account for it.
A dream it was in which I thought myself,
And you that hailed me now then hailed me King,
In a brave palace that was all my own,
Within, and all without it, mine; until,
Drunk with excess of majesty and pride,
Methought I towered so high and swelled so wide,
That of myself I burst the glittering bubble,
That my ambition had about me blown,
And all again was darkness. Such a dream
As this in which I may be walking now;
Dispensing solemn justice to you shadows,
Who make believe to listen; but anon,
With all your glittering arms and equipage,
Kings, princes, captains, warriors, plume and steel,
Aye, ev'n with all your airy theater,
May flit into air you seem to rend
With acclamation, leaving me to wake
In the dark tower; or dreaming that I wake
From this that waking is; or this and that
Both waking or both dreaming; such a doubt
Confounds and clouds our mortal life about.
And, whether wake or dreaming; this I know,
How dream-wise human glories come and go;
Whose momentary tenure not to break,
Walking as one who knows he soon may wake
So fairly carry the full cup, so well
Disordered insolence and passion quell,
That there be nothing after to upbraid
Dreamer or doer in the part he played,
Whether To-morrow's dawn shall break the spell,
Or the Last Trumpet of the eternal Day,
When Dreaming with the Night shall pass away.

(*Exeunt.*)

199

KAREL CAPEK

KAREL CAPEK (Czech, 1890-1938). Most widely known Czech writer, through plays, *R.U.R.* and *The Life of the Insects.* Also author of six novels, short story collections, travel books. Ardent humanitarian, fond of utopian themes. Like his friend Masaryk, strongly under influence of American ideas. Said to have died "of the death of his country."

THE ISLAND

AT one time there lived in Lisbon a certain Dom Luiz de Faria who later sailed away in order to see the world, and having visited the greater part of it, died on an island as remote as one's imagination can picture. During his life in Lisbon he was a man full of wisdom and judgment. He lived as such men usually do, in a way to gratify his own desires without doing harm to others, and he occupied a position in affairs commensurate with his innate pride. But even that life eventually bored him and became a burden to him. Therefore he exchanged his property for money and sailed away on the first ship out into the world.

On this ship he sailed first to Cadiz and then to Palermo, Constantinople and Beiruth, to Palestine, Egypt and around Arabia clear up to Ceylon. Then they sailed around lower India and the islands including Java whence they struck for the open sea again heading towards the east and south. Sometimes they met fellow countrymen who were homeward bound and who wept with joy when they asked questions about their native land.

In all the countries they visited Dom Luiz saw so many things that were extraordinary and well-nigh marvellous, that he felt as if he had forgotten all his former life.

While they sailed thus over the wide sea, the stormy season overtook them and their boat tossed on the waves like a cork which has neither a goal nor anchor. For three days the storm increased in violence. The third night the ship struck a coral reef.

Dom Luiz during the terrific crash felt himself lifted to a great height and then plunged down into the water. But the water hurled him back and pitched him unconscious on a broken timber.

When he recovered consciousness, he realised that it was bright noon and that he was drifting on a pile of shattered beams wholly alone on a calm sea. At that instant he felt for the first time a real joy in being alive.

He floated thus until evening and throughout the night and the entire succeeding day, but not a glimpse of land did he have. Besides, the pile of rafters on which he floated was becoming loosened by the action of the water, and piece after piece detached itself, Dom Luiz vainly trying to tie them together with strips of his own clothing. At last only three weak timbers remained to him and he sank back in weariness. With a feeling of being utterly forsaken, Dom Luiz made his adieu to life and resigned himself to the will of God.

The third day at dawn he saw that the waves were bearing him to a beautiful island of charming groves and green thickets which seemed to be floating on the bosom of the ocean.

Finally, covered with salt and foam he stepped out on the land. At that instant several savages emerged from the forest, but Dom Luiz gave utterance to an unfriendly shout for he was afraid of them. Then he knelt down to pray, sank to the earth and fell asleep on the shore of the ocean.

When the sun was setting, he was awakened by a great hunger. The sand all around him was marked by the prints of bare flat feet. Dom Luiz was much rejoiced for he realised that around him had walked and sat many savages who had discussed and wondered about him but had done him no injury. Forthwith he went to seek food but it had already grown dark. When he had passed to the other side of the cliff, he beheld the savages sitting in a circle eating their supper. He saw men, women and children in that circle, but he took a position at some distance, not being bold enough to go closer, as if he were a beggar from some far-off province.

A young female of the savage group arose from her place and brought him a flat basket full of fruit. Luiz flung himself upon the basket and devoured bananas, figs, both dried and fresh, other fruits and fresh clams, meat dried in the sun and sweet bread of a very different sort from ours. The girl also brought him a pitcher of spring water and, seating herself in a squat position, she watched him eat and drink. When Luiz had had his fill, he felt a great relief in his whole body and began to thank the girl aloud for her gifts and for the water, for her kind-heartedness and for the mercifulness of all the others. As he spoke thus, a deep gratitude like the sweet anguish of an overflowing heart grew in him and poured itself out in beautiful words which he had never before been able to utter so well. The savage girl sat in front of him and listened.

The following day he continued his inspection, encircling the

Dom Luiz felt that he must repeat his gratitude in a way to make her understand and so he thanked her as fervently as if he were praying. In the meantime the savages had all gone away into the forest and Luiz was afraid that he would remain alone in the unfamiliar place with this great joy in his heart. So he began to relate things to the girl to detain her—telling her where he came from, how the ship was wrecked and what sufferings he had endured on the sea. All the while the savage maid lay before him flat on her stomach and listened silently. Then Luiz observed that she had fallen asleep with her face on the earth. Seating himself at some distance, he gazed at the heavenly stars and listened to the murmur of the sea until sleep overcame him.

When he awoke in the morning, he looked for the maid but she had vanished. Only the impression of her entire body—straight and long like a green twig—remained in the sand. And when Luiz stepped into the hollow, it was warm and sun-heated. Then he followed the shoreline to inspect the island. Sometimes he had to go through forests or underbrush; often he had to skirt swamps and climb over boulders. At times he met groups of savages but he was not afraid of them. He noted that the ocean was a more beautiful blue than anywhere else in the world and that there were blossoming trees and unusual loveliness of vegetation. Thus he journeyed all day long enjoying the beauty of the island which was the most pleasing of any he had ever seen. Even the natives, he observed, were far more handsome than other savage tribes.

The following day he continued his inspection, encircling the entire island which was of an undulating surface blessed with streams and flowering verdure, just as one would picture paradise. By evening he reached the spot on the shore where he had landed from the sea and there sat the young savage girl all alone braiding her hair. At her feet lay the timbers on which he had floated hither. The waves of the impassable sea splashed up as far as the rafters so that he could advance no farther. Here Dom Luiz seated himself beside her and gazed at the sweep of the water bearing off his thoughts wave on wave. After many hundreds of waves had thus come and gone, his heart overflowed with an immeasurable sorrow and he began to pour out his grief, telling how he had journeyed for two days making a complete circumference of the island but that nowhere had he found a city or a harbour or a human being resembling himself. He told how all his comrades had perished at sea and that he had been cast up on an island from

which there was no return; that he was left alone among low savage beings who spoke another language in which it was impossible to distinguish words or sense. Thus he complained bitterly and the savage maid listened to him lying on the sand until she fell asleep as if rocked to slumber by the grievous lullaby of his tribulations. Then Luiz became silent and breathed softly.

In the morning they sat together on the rock overlooking the sea giving a view of the entire horizon. There Dom Luiz reviewed his whole life, the elegance and splendour of Lisbon, his love affairs, his voyages and all that he had seen in the world and he closed his eyes to vision more clearly the beautiful scenes in his own life. When he again opened his eyes, he saw the savage girl sitting on her heels and looking before her with a somewhat unintelligent gaze. He saw that she was lovely, with a small body and slender limbs, as brown as the earth, and finely erect.

After that he sat often on the rock looking out for a possible passing ship. He saw the sun rise up from the ocean and sink in its depths and he became accustomed to this just as he did to all else. He learned day by day more of the pleasant sweetness of the island and its climate. It was like an isle of love. Sometimes the savages came to him and gazed on him with respect as they squatted in a circle about him like penguins. Among them were tattooed men and venerable ancients and these brought him portions of food that he might live.

When the rainy season came, Dom Luiz took up his abode in the young savage girl's hut. Thus he lived among the wild natives and went naked just as they did but he felt scorn for them and did not learn a single word of their language. He did not know what name they gave to the island on which he lived, to the roof which covered his head or to the woman who in the eyes of God was his only mate. Whenever he returned to the hut, he found there food prepared for him, a couch and the quiet embrace of his brown wife. Although he regarded her as not really or wholly a human being, but rather more nearly like other animals, nevertheless he treated her as if she understood him, telling her everything in his own language and feeling fully satisfied because she listened to him attentively. He narrated to her everything that occupied his mind—events of his former life in Lisbon, things about his home, details of his travels. At first it grieved him that the savage maiden neither understood his words nor the significance of what he was saying but he became accustomed even to that and continued to recount everything in the

same phrases and also with variations and always afterward he took her into his arms.

But in the course of time his narrations grew shorter and more interrupted. The adventures he had had slipped the memory of Dom Luiz just as if they hadn't happened or as if nothing had ever happened. For whole days he would lie on his couch lost in thought and silence. He became accustomed to his new life and continued to sit on his rock but he no longer kept a lookout for passing ships. Thus many years passed and Luiz forgot about returning, forgot the past, even his own native speech, and his mind was as mute as his tongue. Always at night he returned to his hut but he never learned to know the natives any more intimately than he had the day he arrived on the island.

Once in the summer he was deep in the forest when such a strange unrest overwhelmed him suddenly that he ran out of the wood to behold out on the ocean a beautiful ship at anchor. With violently beating heart he rushed to the shore to mount his boulder and when he reached it, he saw on the beach a group of sailors and officers. He concealed himself behind the rock like a savage and listened. Their words touched the margin of his memory and he then realised that the newcomers were speaking his native tongue. He rose then and tried to address them but he only gave utterance to a loud shout. The new arrivals were frightened and he gave a second outcry. They raised their carbines but in that instant his tongue became untangled and he cried out, "Seignors,—have mercy!" All of them cried out in joy and hastened forward to him. But Luiz was seized by a savage instinct to flee before them. They, however, had completely surrounded him and one after another embraced him and overwhelmed him with questions. Thus he stood in the midst of the group—naked and full of anguish, looking in every direction for a loophole of escape.

"Don't be afraid," an elderly officer said to him. "Just recall that you are a human being. Bring him meat and wine for he looks thin and miserable. And you—sit down here among us and rest while you get accustomed again to the speech of human beings instead of to screeches which no doubt apes employ as speech."

They brought Dom Luiz sweet wine, prepared meats and biscuits. He sat among them as if in a dream and ate and gradually began to feel his memory returning. The others also ate and drank and conversed merrily rejoicing that they had found a fellow countryman. When Luiz had partaken of some of the food, a delicious feeling

of gratitude filled him just as that time when the savage maiden had fed him but in addition he now felt a joy in the beautiful speech which he heard and understood and in the companionable people who addressed him as a brother. The words now came to his tongue of themselves and he expressed his thanks to them as best he could.

"Rest a little longer," the old officer said to him, "and then you can tell us who you are and how you got here. Then the precious gift of language will return to you for there is nothing more beautiful than the power of speech which permits a man to talk, to relate his adventures and to pour out his feelings."

While he was speaking a young sailor tuned up and began softly to sing a song about a man who went away beyond the sea while his sweetheart implores the sea and the winds and the sky to restore him to her, the pleading grief of the maiden being expressed in the most touching words one could find anywhere. After him others sang or recited other poems of similar content, each of them a little sadder in strain. All the songs gave voice to the longing for a loved one; they told of ships sailing to far distant lands and of the ever changeful sea. At the last everyone was filled with memories of home and of all whom they had left behind. Dom Luiz wept copious tears, painfully happy in the afflictions he had suffered and in their joyous solution, when after having become unused to civilized speech he now heard the beautiful music of poetry. He wept because it was all like a dream which he feared could not be real.

Finally the old officer arose and said, "Children, now we will inspect the island which we found here in the ocean and before the sun sets we will gather here to row back to the ship. At night we will lift anchor and under God's protection, we will sail back. You, my friend," he turned to Luiz, "if you have anything that is yours and that you want to take with you as a souvenir, bring it here and wait for us till just before sunset."

The sailors scattered over the island shore and Dom Luiz betook himself to the savage woman's hut. The farther he advanced the more he loitered, turning over in his mind just how he should tell the savage that he must go away and forsake her. He sat down on a stone and debated with himself for he could not run away without any show of gratitude when he had lived with her for ten years. He recalled all the things she had done for him, how she had provided his food and shelter and had served him with her body and by her labours. Then he entered her hut, sat down beside her and talked a great deal and very hurriedly as if thus he could the better convince

205

her. He told her that they had come for him and that he must now sail away to attend to very necessary affairs of which he conjured up a great quantity. Then he took her in his arms and thanked her for everything that she had done for him and he promised her that he would soon return, accompanying his promises with solemn vows and protestations. When he had talked a long time, he noticed that she was listening to him without the faintest understanding or comprehension. This angered him and, losing his patience, he repeated all his arguments as emphatically as possible and he stamped his feet in his irritability. It suddenly occurred to him that the sailors were probably pushing off, not waiting for him, and he rushed out from the hut in the middle of his speech and hastened to the shore. But as yet no one was there so he sat down to wait. But the thought worried him that in all likelihood the savage woman had not thoroughly understood what he had said to her about being compelled to go away. That seemed such a terrible thing to him that he suddenly started back on a run to explain everything to her once more. However, he did not step into her hut but looked through a crack to see what she was doing. He saw that she had gathered fresh grass to make a soft bed for him for the night; he saw her placing fruit for him to eat and he noted for the first time that she herself ate only the poorer specimens—those that were dwarfed or spotted and for him she selected the most beautiful—all the large and perfect samples of fruit. Then she sat down as immovable as a statue and waited for him. Of a sudden Dom Luis comprehended clearly that he must yet eat the fruit set out for him and lie down on the couch prepared so carefully and complete her expectations before he could depart.

Meanwhile the sun was setting and the sailors gathered on the shore to push off to the ship. Only Dom Luiz was missing and so they called out to him, "Seignor! Seignor!" When he did not come, they scattered in various directions on the edge of the forest to seek him, all the time continuing to call out to him. Two of the seamen ran quite close to him, calling him all the while but he hid among the shrubbery, his heart pounding in his breast for fear they would find him. Then all the voices died down, and the darkness came. Splashing the oars, the seamen rowed to the vessel loudly lamenting the lost survivor of the wreck. Then absolute quiet ensued and Dom Luiz emerged from the underbrush and returned to the hut. The savage woman sat there unmoved and patient. Dom Luiz ate the fruit, lay down on the freshly made couch with her beside him.

When dawn was breaking Dom Luiz lay sleepless and gazed out through the door of the hut where beyond the trees of the forest could be seen the sunlit sea—that sea on which the beautiful ship was just sailing away from the island. The savage woman lay beside him asleep but she was no longer attractive as in former years but ugly and terrible to look upon. Tear after tear rolled down on her bosom while Dom Luiz, in a whisper, lest she might hear, repeated beautiful words, wonderful poems describing the sorrow of longing and of vain eternal yearning.

Then the ship disappeared beyond the horizon and Dom Luiz remained on the island but he never uttered a single word from that day during all the years that preceded his death.

GIOSUE CARDUCCI

GIOSUÈ CARDUCCI (Italian, 1835-1907). Protagonist of the Italian classics in post-Risorgimento literature. Favored return to early literary forms, Roman paganism and imperialism. Opposed to Romanticism and Christianity. Poetry preoccupied with history and landscape of Italy: *Iams and Epodes, Barbarian Odes*. Critical works created great stir in their time.

SONNET

Alone my vessel passes, mid the cry
Of halycons, on the stormy waters borne,
Swept on, by thunder of the billows torn,
Beneath the clamours of the lightening sky.
All Memories turn to that far shore gone by
Their faces wet with tears and sorrow-worn,
And all fair Hopes o'erthrown their glances forlorn
Cast on the splintered oars that broken lie.

Yet at the stern still doth my Genius stand,
While to the creaking masts he hearkeneth,
And cries o'er sea and sky his loud command:
'Row on! row on! O guides of desperate breath,
Toward cloudy ports of the forgetful land.
Toward whitening breakers of the reefs of death.'

PANTHEISM

I told it not, O vigilant stars, to you;
To thee, all-seeing sun, I made no moan;
Her name, the flower of all things fair and true,
Was echoed in my silent heart alone.

Yet now my secret star tells unto star,
Through the brown night, to some vague sphery tune;
The great sun smiles at it, when, sinking far,
He whispers love to the white and rising moon.

On shadowy hills, on shores where life is gay,
Each bush repeats it to each flower that blows;
The flitting birds sing, 'Poet grim and grey,
At last Love's honeyed dreams thy spirit knows.'

I told it not, yet heaven and earth repeat
The name beloved in sounds divine that swell,
And mid the acacia-blossom's perfume sweet
Murmurs the Spirit of All—'She loves thee well.'

SNOWFALL

Slowly flutters the snow from ash-coloured heavens in silence;
Sound or tumult of life rises not up from the town;

Not of herbseller the cry, nor rumorous rattle of wagons,
Not love's passionate song joyous in musical youth.

But, from the belfry swaying, hoarsely the hours thro' the evening
Moan like sighs from a world far from the light of our day.

Wandering song-birds beat at my tarnished window panes; friendly
Spirits returning are they, seeking and calling for me.

Soon, O belovèd ones, soon—be calm, heart ever undaunted—
Soon to the silence I come, soon in the shades to repose.

MIGUEL DE CERVANTES Y SAAVEDRA

MIGUEL DE CERVANTES Y SAAVEDRA (Spanish, 1547-1616). Spain's greatest writer and one of foremost in world literature. Wrote poetry and plays, but greatest triumph was novel, *Don Quixote*. Like *Hamlet* and *Faust*, *Quixote* reveals the many contradictions in man's nature. Imbued with deep humanism and gentle humor, Cervantes died same day as his great contemporary, Shakespeare.

SANCHO PANZA IN HIS ISLAND

SANCHO, with all his attendants, came to a town that had about a thousand inhabitants, and was one of the best where the duke had any power. They gave him to understand that the name of the place was the Island of Barataria, either because the town was called Barataria, or because the government cost him so cheap. As soon as he came to the gates (for it was walled) the chief officers and inhabitants, in their formalities, came out to receive him, the bells rung, and all the people gave general demonstrations of their joy. The new governor was then carried in mighty pomp to the great church, to give Heaven thanks: and, after some ridiculous ceremonies, they delivered him the keys of the gates, and received him as perpetual governor of the Island of Barataria. In the meantime, the garb, the port, the huge beard, and the short and thick shape of the new governor, made everyone who knew nothing of the jest wonder: and even those who were privy to the plot, who were many. were not a little surprised.

In short, from the church they carried him to the court of justice; where, when they had placed him in his seat, "My lord governor," said the duke's steward to him, "it is an ancient custom here, that he who takes possession of this famous island must answer to some difficult and intricate question that is propounded to him; and by the return he makes the people feel the pulse of his understanding, and by an estimate of his abilities, judge whether they ought to rejoice or to be sorry for his coming."

All the while the steward was speaking, Sancho was staring on an inscription in large characters on the wall over against his seat; and, as he could not read, he asked what was the meaning of that which he saw painted there upon the wall. "Sir," said they, "it is an account of the day when your lordship took possession of this island; and the inscription runs thus: 'This day, being such a day

of this month, in such a year, the Lord Don Sancho Panza took possession of this island, which may he long enjoy.' " "And who is he?" asked Sancho. "Your lordship," answered the steward; "for we know of no other Panza in the island but yourself, who now sit in this chair." "Well, friend," said Sancho, "pray take notice that Don does not belong to me, nor was it borne by any of my family before me. Plain Sancho Panza is my name; my father was called Sancho, my grandfather Sancho, and all of us have been Panzas, without any Don or Donna added to our name. Now do I already guess your Dons are as thick as stones in this island. But it is enough that Heaven knows my meaning; if my government happens to last but four days to an end, it shall go hard but I will clear the island of these swarms of Dons, that must needs be as troublesome as so many flesh-flies. Come, now for your question, good Mr. Steward, and I will answer it as well as I can, whether the town be sorry or pleased."

At the same instant two men came into the court, the one dressed like a country fellow, the other looked like a tailor, with a pair of shears in his hand. "If it please you, my lord," cried the tailor, "I and this farmer here are come before your worship. This honest man came to my shop yesterday, for, saving your presence, I am a tailor, and, Heaven be praised, free of my company; so, my lord, he showed me a piece of cloth. 'Sir,' quoth he, 'is there enough of this to make a cap?' Whereupon I measured the stuff, and answered him, 'Yes,' if it like your worship. Now, as I imagined, do you see, he could not but imagine (and perhaps he imagined right enough) that I had a mind to cabbage some of his cloth, judging hard of us honest tailors. 'Pr'ythee,' quoth he, 'look there be not enough for two caps?' Now I smelt him out, and told him there was. Whereupon the old knave, (if it like your worship,) going on to the tune, bid me look again, and see whether it would not make three. And at last, if it would not make five. I was resolved to humour my customer, and said it might: so we struck a bargain.

"Just now the man is come for his caps, which I gave him; but when I asked him for my money he will have me give him his cloth again, or pay him for it."—"Is this true, honest man?" said Sancho to the farmer. "Yes, if it please you," answered the fellow; "but pray let him show the five caps he has made me." "With all my heart," cried the tailor; and with that, pulling his hand from under his cloak, he held up five little tiny caps, hanging upon his four fingers and thumb, as upon so many pins. "There," quoth he, "you

see the five caps this good gaffer asks for; and may I never whip a stitch more if I have wronged him of the least snip of his cloth, and let any workman be judge." The sight of the caps, and the oddness of the cause, set the whole court a laughing. Only Sancho sat gravely considering a while, and then, "Methinks," said he, "this suit here needs not be long depending, but may be decided without any more ado, with a great deal of equity; and, therefore, the judgment of the court is, that the tailor shall lose his making, and the countryman his cloth, and that the caps be given to the poor prisoners, and so let there be an end of the business."

If this sentence provoked the laughter of the whole court, the next no less raised their admiration. For, after the governor's order was executed, two old men appeared before him, one of them with a large cane in his hand, which he used as a staff. "My lord," said the other, who had none, "some time ago I lent this man ten gold crowns to do him a kindness, which money he was to repay me on demand. I did not ask him for it again in a good while, lest it should prove a greater inconvenience to him to repay me than he laboured under when he borrowed it. However, perceiving that he took no care to pay me, I have asked him for my due; nay, I have been forced to dun him hard for it. But still he did not only refuse to pay me again, but denied he owed me anything, and said, that if I lent him so much money he certainly returned it. Now, because I have no witnesses of the loan, nor he of the pretended payment, I beseech your lordship to put him to his oath, and if he will swear he has paid me, I will freely forgive him before God and the world." "What say you to this, old gentleman with the staff?" asked Sancho. "Sir," answered the old man, "I own he lent me the gold; and since he requires my oath, I beg you will be pleased to hold down your rod of justice, that I may swear upon it how I have honestly and truly returned him his money." Thereupon the governor held down his rod, and in the meantime the defendant gave his cane to the plaintiff to hold, as if it hindered him, while he was to make a cross and swear over the judge's rod: this done, he declared that it was true the other had lent him ten crowns, but that he had really returned him the same sum into his own hands; and that, because he supposed the plaintiff had forgotten it, he was continually asking him for it. The great governor, hearing this, asked the creditor what he had to reply. He made answer, that since his adversary had sworn it he was satisfied; for he believed him to be a better Christian than to offer to forswear himself, and that perhaps he had forgotten he had

211

been repaid. Then the defendant took his cane again, and, having made a low obeisance to the judge, was immediately leaving the court; which, when Sancho perceived, reflecting on the passage of the cane, and admiring the creditor's patience, after he had studied a while with his head leaning over his stomach, and his forefinger on his nose, on a sudden he ordered the old man with the staff to be called back. When he was returned, "Honest man," said Sancho, "let me see that cane a little, I have a use for it." "With all my heart," answered the other; "sir, here it is," and with that he gave it him. Sancho took it, and giving it to the other old man, "There," said he, "go your ways, and Heaven be with you, for now you are paid." "How so, my lord?" cried the old man; "do you judge this cane to be worth ten gold crowns?" "Certainly," said the governor, "or else I am the greatest dunce in the world. And now you shall see whether I have not a headpiece fit to govern a whole kingdom upon a shift." This said, he ordered the cane to be broken in open court, which was no sooner done, than out dropped the ten crowns. All the spectators were amazed, and began to look on their governor as a second Solomon. They asked him how he could conjecture that the ten crowns were in the cane? He told them that having observed how the defendant gave it to the plaintiff to hold while he took his oath, and then swore that he had truly returned him the money into his own hands, after which he took his cane again from the plaintiff —this considered, it came into his head that the money was lodged within the reed; from whence may be learned, that though sometimes those that govern are destitute of sense, yet it often pleases God to direct them in their judgment. Besides, he had heard the curate of his parish tell of such another business, and he had so special a memory, that were it not that he was so unlucky as to forget all he had a mind to remember, there could not have been a better in the whole island. At last the two old men went away, the one to his satisfaction, the other with eternal shame and disgrace: and the beholders were astonished; insomuch, that the person who was commissioned to register Sancho's words and actions, and observe his behaviour, was not able to determine whether he should not give him the character of a wise man, instead of that of a fool, which he had been thought to deserve.

* * * *

The history informs us that Sancho was conducted from the court of justice to a sumptuous palace, where, in a spacious room,

he found the cloth laid, and a most neat and magnificent entertainment prepared. As soon as he entered, the wind-music played, and four pages waited on him, in order to the washing his hands, which he did with a great deal of gravity. And now, the instruments ceasing, Sancho sat down at the upper end of the table, for there was no seat but there, and the cloth was only laid for one. A certain personage, who afterwards appeared to be a physician, came and stood at his elbow, with a whalebone wand in his hand. Then they took off a curious white cloth that lay over the dishes on the table, and discovered great variety of fruit and other eatables. One that looked like a student said grace: a page put a laced bib under Sancho's chin, and another, who did the office of sewer, set a dish of fruit before him. But he had hardly put one bit into his mouth, before the physician touched the dish with his wand, and then it was taken away by a page in an instant. Immediately another, with meat, was clapped in the place; but Sancho no sooner offered to taste it, than the doctor, with the wand, conjured it away as fast as the fruit. Sancho was annoyed at this sudden removal, and, looking about him on the company, asked them whether they used to tantalise people at that rate, feeding their eyes, and starving their bellies? "My lord governor," answered the physician, "you are to eat here no otherwise than according to the use and custom of other islands where there are governors. I am a doctor of physic, my lord, and have a salary allowed me in this island for taking charge of the governor's health, and I am more careful of it than of my own, studying night and day his constitution, that I may know what to prescribe when he falls sick. Now, the chief thing I do is to attend him always at his meals, to let him eat what I think convenient for him, and to prevent his eating what I imagine to be prejudicial to his health and offensive to his stomach. Therefore, I now ordered the fruit to be taken away because it was too cold and moist: and the other dish, because it is as much too hot, and over seasoned with spices, which are apt to increase thirst, and he that drinks much destroys and consumes the radical moisture, which is the fuel of life." "So, then," quoth Sancho, "this dish of roasted partridges here can do me no manner of harm." "Hold," said the physician, "the lord governor shall not eat of them while I live to prevent it." "Why so?" cried Sancho. "Because," answered the doctor, "our great master, Hippocrates, the north star and luminary of physic, says in one of his aphorisms, *Omnis saturatio mala, perdricis autem pessima*; that is, 'All repletion is bad, but that of

213

partridges is worst of all!' " "If it be so," said Sancho, "let Mr. Doctor see which of all these dishes on the table will do me the most good, and least harm, and let me eat my bellyful of that, without having it whisked away with his wand. For, by my hopes, and the pleasures of government, as I live, I am ready to die with hunger; and, not to allow me to eat any victuals, (let Mr. Doctor say what he will,) is the way to shorten my life, and not to lengthen it." "Very true, my lord," replied the physician; "however, I am of opinion you ought not to eat of these rabbits, as being a hairy, furry sort of food; nor would I have you taste that veal. Indeed, if it were neither roasted nor par boiled, something might be said; but, as it is, it must not be." "Well, then," said Sancho, "what think you of that huge dish yonder that smokes so? I take it to be an olla podrida, and, that being a hodge-podge of so many sorts of victuals, sure I cannot but light upon something there that will nick me, and be both wholesome and toothsome." "*Absit*," cried the doctor, "far be such an ill thought from us; no diet in the world yields worse nutriment than those wish-washes do. No, leave that luxurious compound to your rich monks and prebendaries, your masters of colleges, and lusty feeders at country weddings; but let them not encumber the tables of governors, where nothing but delicate unmixed viands, in their prime, ought to make their appearance. The reason is, that simple medicines are generally allowed to be better than compounds; for, in a composition, there may happen a mistake by an unequal proportion of the ingredients; but simples are not subject to that accident. Therefore, what I would advise at present, as a fit diet for the governor, for the preservation and support of his health, is a hundred of small wafers, and a few thin slices of marmalade, to strengthen his stomach and help digestion." Sancho, hearing this, leaned back upon his chair, and, looking earnestly in the doctor's face, very seriously asked him what his name was, and where he had studied. "My lord," answered he, "I am called Doctor Pedro Rezio de Augero. The name of the place where I was born is Tirteafuera, and lies between Caraquel and Almodabar del Campo, on the right hand; and I took my degree of Doctor in the University of Ossuna." "Hark you," said Sancho, in a mighty chafe, "Mr. Doctor Pedro Rezio de Augero, born at Tirteafuera, that lies between Caraquel and Almodabar del Campo, on the right hand, and who took your degree of Doctor at the University of Ossuna, and so forth, take yourself away! Avoid the room this moment, or, by the sun's light, I'll get me a good cudgel, and, beginning with

214

your carcase, will so belabour and rib-roast all the physicmongers in the island, that I will not leave therein one of the tribe, of those, I mean, that are ignorant quacks; for, as for learned and wise physicians, I will make much of them, and honour them like so many angels. Once more, Pedro Rezio, I say, get out of my presence. Avaunt! or I will take the chair I sit upon, and comb your head with it to some purpose, and let me be called to an account about it when I give up my office; I do not care, I will clear myself by saying I did the world good service in ridding it of a bad physician, the plague of the commonwealth. Body of me! let me eat, or let them take their government again; for an office that will not afford a man victuals is not worth two horsebeans."

ADALBERT VON CHAMISSO

ADALBERT VON CHAMISSO (German, 1781-1838). French-born, fled the Revolution with his parents and became page to Queen of Prussia at age of nine. Botanist on round-the-world scientific voyage. Author of romantic poems and the tale of Peter Schlemihl, so widely read it has become an international legend.

PETER SCHLEMIHL, THE SHADOWLESS MAN

I. THE GREY MAN

HAVING safely landed after a fatiguing journey, I took my modest belongings to the nearest cheap inn, engaged a garret room, washed, put on my newly-turned black coat, and proceeded to find Mr. Thomas John's mansion. After a severe cross-examination on the part of the hall-porter, I had the honour of being shown into the park where Mr. John was entertaining a party. He graciously took my letter of introduction, continuing the while to talk to his guests. Then he broke the seal, still joining in the conversation, which turned upon wealth. "Anyone," he remarked, "who has not at least a million is, pardon the word, a rogue." "How true," I exclaimed; which pleased him, for he asked me to stay. Then, offering his arm to a fair lady, he led the party to the rose-clad hill. Everybody was very jolly; and I followed behind, so as not to make myself a nuisance.

The beautiful Fanny, who seemed to be the queen of the day, in trying to pick a rose, had scratched her finger, which caused much commotion. She asked for some plaster, and a quiet, lean, tall, elderly man, dressed in grey, who walked by my side, put his hand in his coat pocket, pulled out a pocket-book, and, with a deep bow, handed the lady what she wanted. She took it without thanks, and we all continued to ascend the hill.

Arrived at the top, Mr. John, espying a light spot on the horizon, called for a telescope. Before the servants had time to move, the grey man, bowing modestly, had put his hand in his pocket and pulled out a beautiful telescope, which passed from hand to hand without being returned to its owner. Nobody seemed surprised at the huge instrument issuing from a tiny pocket, and nobody took any more notice of the grey man than of myself.

The ground was damp, and somebody suggested how fine it would be to spread some Turkey carpets. Scarcely had the wish been expressed, when the grey man again put his hand into his pocket, and, with a modest, humble gesture, pulled out a rich Turkey carpet, some twenty yards by ten, which was spread out by the servants without anybody appearing to be surprised. I asked a young gentleman who the obliging man might be. He did not know.

The sun began to get troublesome, and Fanny casually asked the grey man if he might happen to have a tent by him. He bowed deeply, and began to pull out of his pocket canvas, and bars, and ropes, and everything needed for the tent, which was promptly put up. Again nobody seemed surprised. I felt uncanny; especially when, at the next expressed desire, I saw him pull out of his pocket three fine large horses with saddles and trappings! You would not believe it if I did not tell you that I saw it with my own eyes.

It was gruesome. I sneaked away, and had already reached the foot of the hill, when, to my horror, I noticed the grey man approaching. He took off his hat, bowed humbly, and addressed me.

"Forgive my impertinence, sir, but during the short time I have had the happiness to be near you I have been able to look with indescribable admiration upon that beautiful shadow of yours, which you throw from you contemptuously, as it were. Pardon me, but would you feel inclined to sell it?"

I thought he was mad. "Is your own shadow not enough for you? What a strange bargain!"

"No price is too high for this invaluable shadow. I have many a

216

precious thing in my pocket, which you may choose—a mandrake, the dish-cloth of Roland's page, Fortunati's purse——"

"What! Fortunati's purse?"

"Will you condescend to try it?" he said, handing me a money-bag of moderate size, from which I drew ten gold pieces, and another ten, and yet another ten.

I extended my hand, and exclaimed, "A bargain! For this purse you can have my shadow." He seized my hand, knelt down, cleverly detached my shadow from the lawn, rolled it up, folded it, and put it in his pocket. Then he bowed and retired behind the rose-hedge, chuckling gently.

I hurried back to my inn, after having tied the bag around my neck, under my waistcoat. As I went along the sunny street, I heard an old woman's voice, "Heigh, young man, you have lost your shadow!"

"Thank you," I said, threw her a gold piece, and sought the shade of the trees. But I had to cross a broad street again, just as a group of boys were leaving school. They shouted at me, jeered, and threw mud at me. To keep them away I threw a handful of gold among them, and jumped into a carriage. Now I began to feel what I had sacrificed. What was to become of me?

At the inn I sent for my things, and then made the driver take me to the best hotel, where I engaged the state rooms and locked myself up. And what, my dear Chamisso, do you think I did then? I pulled masses of gold out of the bag, covered the floor of the room with ducats, threw myself upon them, made them tinkle, rolled over them, buried my hands in them, until I was exhausted and fell to sleep. Next morning I had to cart all these coins into a cupboard, leaving only just a few handfuls. Then, with the help of the host, I engaged some servants, a certain Bendel, a good, faithful soul, being specially recommended to me as a valet. I spent the whole day with tailors, bootmakers, jewellers, merchants, and bought a heap of precious things, just to get rid of the heaps of gold.

I never ventured out in daytime; and even at night when I happened to step out into the moonlight, I had to suffer untold anguish from the contemptuous sneers of men, the deep pity of women, the shuddering fear of fair maidens. Then I sent Bendel to search for the grey man, giving him every possible indication. He came back late, and told me that none of Mr. John's servants or guests remembered the stranger, and that he could find no trace of him. "By the

way," he concluded, "a gentleman whom I met just as I went out, bid me tell you that he was on the point of leaving the country, and that in a year and a day he would call on you to propose new business. He said you would know who he was."

"How did he look?" Bendel described the man in the grey coat! He was in despair when I told him that this was the very person I wanted. But it was too late; he had gone without leaving a trace.

A famous artist for whom I sent to ask him whether he could paint me a shadow, told me that he might, but I should be bound to lose it again at the slightest movement.

"How did you manage to lose yours?" he asked. I had to lie. "When I was travelling in Russia it froze so firmly to the ground that I could not get it off again."

"The best thing you can do is not to walk in the sun," the artist retorted with a piercing look, and walked out.

I confessed my misfortune to Bendel, and the sympathetic lad, after a terrible struggle with his conscience, decided to remain in my service. From that day he was always with me, ever trying to throw his broad shadow over me to conceal my affliction from the world. Nevertheless, the fair Fanny, whom I often met in the hours of dusk and evening, and who had begun to show me marked favour, discovered my terrible secret one night, as the moon suddenly rose from behind a cloud, and fainted with terror.

There was nothing left for me but to leave the town. I sent for horses, took only Bendel and another servant, a rogue named Gauner, with me, and covered thirty miles during the night. Then we continued our journey across the mountains to a little-frequented watering-place, where I was anxious to seek rest from my troubles.

II. A SOUL FOR A SHADOW

Bendel preceded me to prepare a house for my reception, and spent money so lavishly that the rumour spread the King of Prussia was coming incognito. A grand reception was prepared by the townsfolk, with music and flowers and a chorus of maidens in white, led by a girl of wonderful beauty. And all this in broad sunlight! I did not move in my carriage, and Bendel tried to explain that there must be a mistake, which made the good folk believe that I wanted to remain incognito. Bendel handed a diamond tiara to the beautiful maiden, and we drove on amid cheering and firing of guns.

I became known as Count Peter, and when it was found out that

218

the King of Prussia was elsewhere, they all thought I must be some other king. I gave a grand fête, Bendel taking good care to have such lavish illuminations all round that no one should notice the absence of my shadow. I had masses of gold coins thrown among the people in the street, and gave Mina, the beautiful girl who headed the chorus at my arrival, all the jewels I had brought with me, for distribution among her friends. She was the daughter of the verdurer, and I lost no time in making friends with her parents, and succeeded in gaining Mina's affection.

Continuing to spend money with regal lavishness, I myself led a simple and retired life, never leaving my rooms in daylight. Bendel warned me of Gauner's extensive thefts; but I did not mind. Why should I grudge him the money, of which I had an inexhaustible store? In the evenings I used to meet Mina in her garden, and always found her loving, though awed by my wealth and supposed rank. Yet, conscious of my dreadful secret, I dared not ask for her hand. But the year was nearly up since I had made the fateful bargain, and I look forward to the promised visit of the grey man, whom I hoped to persuade to take back his bag for my shadow. In fact, I told the verdurer that on the first of the next month I should ask him for his daughter's hand.

The anniversary arrived—midday, evening, midnight. I waited through the long hours, heard the clock strike twelve; but the grey man did not come! Towards morning I fell into a fitful slumber. I was awakened by angry voices. Gauner forced his way into my room, which was defended by the faithful Bendel.

"What do you want, you rogue?"

"Only to see your shadow, with your lordship's permission."

"How dare you——"

"I am not going to serve a man without a shadow. Either you show it to me, or I go."

I wanted to offer him money; but he, who had stolen millions, refused to accept money from a man without a shadow. He put on his hat, and left the room whistling.

When at dark I went, with a heavy heart, to Mina's bower, I found her, pale and beautiful, and her father with a letter in his hand. He looked at the letter, then scrutinised me, and said, "Do you happen to know, my lord, a certain Peter Schlemihl, who lost his shadow?"

"Oh, my foreboding!" cried Mina. "I knew it; he has no shadow!"

"And you dared," continued the verdurer, "to deceive us? See how she sobs! Confess now how you lost your shadow."

Again I was forced to lie. "Some time ago a man stepped so clumsily into my shadow that he made a big hole. I sent it to be mended, and was promised to have it back yesterday."

"Very well. Either you present yourself within three days with a well-fitting shadow, or, on the next day, my daughter will be another man's wife."

I rushed away, half conscious, groaning and raving. I do not know how long and how far I ran, but I found myself on a sunny heath, when somebody suddenly pulled my sleeve. I turned round. It was the man in the grey coat!

"I announced my visit for to-day. You made a mistake in your impatience. All is well. You buy your shadow back and you will be welcomed by your bride. As for Gauner, who has betrayed you and has asked for Mina's hand—he is ripe for me."

I groped for the bag but the stranger stopped me.

"No, my lord, you keep this; I only want a little souvenir. Be good enough and sign this scrap." On the parchment was written: "I herewith assign to bearer my soul after its natural separation from my body."

I sternly refused. "I am not inclined to stake my soul for my shadow."

He continued to urge, giving the most plausible reasons why I should sign. But I was firm. He even tried to tempt me by unrolling my shadow on the heath. "A line of your pen, and you save your Mina from that rogue's clutches."

At that moment Bendel arrived on the scene, saw me in tears, my shadow on the ground apparently in the stranger's power, and set upon the man with his stick. The grey man walked away, and Bendel followed him, raining blows upon his shoulders, till they disappeared from sight.

I was left with my despair, and spent the day and night on the heath. I was resolved not to return among men, and wandered about for three days, feeding on wild fruit and spring-water. On the morning of the fourth day I suddenly heard a sound, but could see nobody—only a shadow, not unlike my own, but without body. I determined to seize it, and rushed after it. Gradually I gained on it; with a final rush I made for it—and met unexpectedly bodily resistance. We fell on the ground, and a man became visible under me. I understood at once. The man must have had the invisible

220

bird's nest, which he dropped in the struggle, thus becoming visible himself.

The nest being invisible, I looked for its shadow, found it, seized it quickly, and, of course, disappeared from the man's sight. I left him tearing his hair in despair; and I rejoiced at being able to go again among men. Quickly I proceeded to Mina's garden, which was still empty, although I imagined I heard steps following me. I sat down on a bench, and watched the verdurer leaving the house. Then a fog seemed to pass over my head. I looked around, and— oh, horror!—beheld the grey man sitting by my side. He had pulled his magic cap over my head, at his feet was his shadow and my own, and his hand played with the parchment.

"So we are both under the same cap," he began; "now please give me back my bird's nest. Thanks! You see, sometimes we are forced to do what we refuse when asked kindly. I think you had better buy that shadow back. I'll throw in the magic cap."

Meanwhile, Mina's mother had joined the verdurer, and they began to discuss Mina's approaching marriage and Gauner's wealth, which amounted to ten millions. Then Mina joined them. She was urged to consent, and finally said, sobbingly, "I have no further wish on earth. Do with me as you please." At this moment Gauner approached, and Mina fainted.

"Can you endure this?" asked my companion. "Have you no blood in your veins?" He rapidly scratched a slight wound in my hand, and dipped a pen in the blood. "To be sure, red blood! Then sign." And I took the pen and parchment.

I had scarcely touched food for days, and the excitement of this last hour had completely exhausted my strength. Before I had time to sign I swooned away. When I awoke it was dark. My hateful companion was in a towering rage. The sound of festive music came from the brightly illuminated house; groups of people strolled through the garden, talking of Mina's marriage with the wealthy Mr. Gauner, which had taken place this morning.

Disengaging myself from the magic cap, which act made my companion disappear from my view, I made for the garden gate. But the invisible wretch followed me with his taunts. He only left me at the door of my house, with a mocking "au revoir." The place had been wrecked by the mob and was deserted. Only the faithful Bendel was there to receive me with tears of mingled grief and joy. I pressed him to my heart, and bid him leave me to my misery. I told him to keep a few boxes filled with gold, that were still in

the house, made him saddle my horse, and departed, leaving the choice of the road to the animal, for I had neither aim, nor wish, nor hope.

A pedestrian joined me on the sad journey. After tramping along for a while, he asked permission to put his cloak on my horse. I consented; he thanked me, and then, in a kind of soliloquy, began to praise the power of wealth, and to speak cleverly of metaphysics. Meanwhile, day was dawning; the sun was about to rise, the shadows to spread their splendour—and I was not alone! I looked at my companion—it was the man with the grey coat!

He smiled at my surprise, and continued to converse amiably. In fact, he not only offered to replace for the time being my former servant Bendel, but actually lent me my shadow for the journey. The temptation was great. I suddenly gave my horse the spurs and galloped off at full speed; but, alas! my shadow remained behind and I had to turn back shamefacedly.

"You can't escape me," said my compainion, "I hold you by your shadow." And all the time, hour by hour, day by day, he continued his urging. At last we quarrelled seriously, and he decided to leave me. "If ever you want me, you have only to shake your bag. You hold me by my gold. You know I can be useful, especially to the wealthy; and you have seen it."

I thought of the past and asked him quickly, "Did you get Mr. John's signature?" He smiled. "With so good a friend, the formality was not necessary."

"Where is he? I want to know."

He hesitated, then put his hand into his pocket, and pulled out Mr. John's livid body; the blue lips of the corpse moved, and uttered painfully the words: *"Justo judico Dei judicatus sum; justo judicio Dei condemnatus sum."*

Seized with horror, I threw the inexhaustible moneybag into the abyss, and then spoke the final words. "You fiend, I exorcise you in the name of God! Be off, and never show yourself before mine eyes again!"

He glared at me furiously and disappeared instantly.

III. THE WANDERER

Left now without shadow and without money, save for the few gold pieces still in my pocket, I could almost have been happy, had it not been for the loss of my love. My horse was down below at

the inn; I decided to leave it there and to wander on on foot. In the forest I encountered a peasant, from whom I obtained information about the district and its inhabitants. He was an intelligent man, and I quite enjoyed the talk. When we approached the wide bed of a mountain stream, I made him walk in front, but he turned round to speak to me. Suddenly he broke off—"But how is that? You have no shadow!"

Unfortunately!" I said, with a sigh. "During an illness I lost my hair, nails, and shadow. The hair and nails have grown again, but the shadow won't."

"That must have been a bad illness," said the peasant, and walked on in silence till we reached the nearest side-road, when he turned off without saying another word. I wept bitter tears, and my good spirits had vanished. And so I wandered on sadly, avoiding all villages till nightfall, and often waiting for hours to pass a sunny patch unobserved. I wanted to find work in a mine to save me from my thoughts.

My boots began to be worn out. My slender means made me decide to buy a strong pair that had already been used; new ones were too dear. I put them on at once, and walked out of the village, scarcely noticing the way, since I was thinking deeply of the mine I hoped to reach the same night, and of the manner in which I was to obtain employment. I had scarcely walked two hundred steps, when I noticed that I had lost the road. I was in a wild virginal forest. Another few steps and I was on an endless ice-field. The cold was unbearable, and I had to hasten my steps. I ran for a few minutes, and found myself in rice-fields where Chinese labourers were working. There could be no doubt; I had seven-league boots on my feet!

I fell on my knees, shedding tears of gratitude. Now my future was clear. Excluded from society, study and science were to be my future strength and hope. I wandered through the whole world from east to west, from north to south, comparing the fauna and flora of the different regions. To reduce the speed of my progress, I found I had only to pull a pair of slippers over my boots. When I wanted money, I just took an ivory tusk to sell in London. And finally I made a home in the ancient caves of the desert near Thebes.

Once in the far north I encountered a polar bear. Throwing off my slippers, I wanted to step upon an island facing me. I firmly placed my foot on it, but on the other side I fell into the sea, as the slipper had not come off my boot. I saved my life and hurried to

the Libyan desert to cure my cold in the sun; but the heat made me ill. I lost consciousness, and when I awoke again I was in a comfortable bed among other beds, and on the wall facing me I saw inscribed in golden letters my own name.

To cut things short—the institution which had received me had been founded by Bendel and the widowed Mina with my money, and in my honour had been called the Schlemihlium. As soon as I felt strong enough, I returned to my desert cave, and thus I live to this day.

You, my dear Chamisso, are to be the keeper of my strange history, which may contain useful advice for many. You, if you will live among men, honour first the shadow, then the money. But, if you live only for your better self, you will need no advice.

FRANCOIS-RENE DE CHATEAUBRIAND

FRANÇOIS-RENÉ DE CHATEAUBRIAND (French, 1768-1848). Father of the Romantic Movement in France. Had active, stormy career, both as writer and statesman. Travels in America reflected in *Atala* and *René*, epic romances of "the noble savage." Other major works: *Genius of Christianity* and *The Martyrs*, pleas for Catholicism, and colorful autobiography, *Mémoires d'Outre-Tombe*.

CHACTAS RELATES THE DEATH OF ATALA

The heroine of "Atala" is the daughter of a white man and a Christianized Indian. By her mother's command she took a vow of virginity, but later fell in love with Chactas, a young Indian. When she was tempted by this passion to break her vow she took poison.

As the last rays of light calm the winds and restore serenity to the sky, so the tender words of the hermit appeased the troubles that agitated the breast of my beloved. Her thoughts now rested only upon my grief, which she endeavored to alleviate; and, to fortify my mind to bear the loss, sometimes she told me that she should die happy, if I would dry up my tears; sometimes she talked of my mother, or my native country; seeking to distract my mind from my present sorrow, by awaking other remembrances, she exhorted me to patience and virtue. "Thou wilt not always be unhappy," said she; "if Heaven sends you this severe trial now, it is only to

224

render you more compassionate to the misfortunes of others. The heart, O Chactas, resembles those trees, which yield a balm to heal the wounds of man only when they are wounded by a knife." When she had thus spoken she turned towards the missionary for that comfort which she had administered unto me; and alternately consoling and consoled, she gave and received the word of life upon the couch of death.

The hermit's zeal seemed to increase; his aged limbs were re-animated by the ardor of his charity. He was constantly preparing drugs, re-kindling the fire, attending the couch, and making pious exhortations on God and the happiness of the just. With the torch of religion in his hand, he showed the way to future regions. The humble cell was filled with the splendor of her Christian death; and the celestial spirits, no doubt, attended the edifying scene, where religion struggled with love, youth, and death.

Divine religion triumphed; and the pious melancholy that succeeded in our hearts, to the transports of passion, was the trophy of her victory. Towards the middle of the night, Atala seemed sufficiently revived to repeat the prayers of the holy priest; rising from the side of her couch a short time after, she extended her hand toward me, and in a trembling voice said, "O son of Outalissi, dost thou remember the first night when thou didst take me for the virgin of the last love! Oh! wonderful omen of our future fate." She then stopped, then resumed, "When I think that I am about to leave thee for ever, my heart makes such efforts to revive, that love seems almost to render me immortal; but God, thy will be done." After a short pause, she added, "It now only remains for me to ask your forgiveness for all the uneasiness that I have caused you. I have made you unhappy by my pride and my caprices. Chactas, a little earth will soon separate us, and deliver you from all my misfortunes." "Forgive you," replied I, bathed in tears; "is it not I who have caused your misfortunes?" "Beloved friend," said she, interrupting me, "you have rendered me very happy, and had I to begin life again, I should prefer the happiness of our short love in exile, to a life of tranquillity in my native country."

Here Atala's voice faltered; the films of death covered her glassy eyes and mouth; her wandering hands seemed to seek the shroud, and she whispered to the invisible spirits; then making an effort, she endeavored, but in vain, to untie the golden crucifix that was suspended around her neck; she begged of me to take it off, and in a low voice said, "When I spoke to thee the first time, near the pile,

thou observedst this cross by the light of the fire: it is the only property which Atala possesses. Lopez, thy father and mine, sent it to my mother at my birth. Receive it from me as thine inheritance, preserve it as a memorial of our misfortunes: thou wilt doubtless implore the God of the unfortunate, as thou goest through this life of trouble. O Chactas, I have one last request to make to thee: O my dearest friend, our union on this earth could have been but short, but there is a future state which will be more durable; it is everlasting; and how dreadful to be separated forever. I only precede and wait thy arrival in the celestial regions: if thou lovest me, embrace the Christian religion, which will procure for us an eternal reunion. That divine religion performs a great miracle, since it enables me to quit thee without despair. O Chactas! I only wish to exact one single promise from thee. I know too well the consequence of a rash vow. It might deprive thee of some other woman more happy than myself. O my mother! forgive thy distracted child; O Virgin, take pity on me! I fall again into my former weakness, I avert my thoughts from Thee, O God! when they should all be applied in imploring Thy mercy."

Overwhelmed with grief and sobbing, my heart was ready to burst. I promised Atala that one day I would embrace the Christian religion. At these words, the priest rising as if inspired, extended his arms towards the vault of the cell, and exclaimed, "It is time to call here the presence of the Omnipotent."

As he spoke, methought an invisible hand forced me to prostrate myself at the side of Atala's couch. The priest then opened a secret recess, where a golden urn was concealed, covered by a silk veil; he fell on his knees in devout adoration; the whole cell seemed suddenly illuminated by it. Methought I heard the voices of angels, and the sounds of celestial harps. When the hallowed hermit took the sacred urn from the tabernacle, to me it seemed as if I saw the Great Spirit emerging from the rock.

The priest uncovered the chalice, took a wafer as white as snow between his fingers, and approached Atala, pronouncing mysterious words. She raised her eyes towards Heaven, and was in rapture: all her pains subsided: departing life seemed as if collecting on her faded lips; and her mouth, half opened, received the God concealed under the mystic bread: the holy divine then dipped some cotton in consecrated oil, and anointed her forehead, and after looking a few minutes upon Atala, he suddenly uttered these solemn words: "Depart, Christian soul; go and rejoin thy Creator." Then raising

226

my drooping head, and steadfastly looking at the vase which contained the consecrated oil, I exclaimed, "Will that remedy restore life to Atala?" "Yes, my son," said the pious anchoret, falling in my arms, "to life eternal." Atala had just expired.——

Here Chactas was again obliged to interrupt his narration; his tears fell; sobs stifled his utterance. The blind sachem uncovered his bosom, and taking out Atala's crucifix, "Here," said he, "this is the pledge of love and misery; René, my son, thou canst behold it—but I,—no more; tell me after so many years is not the gold changed; have not my tears left some traces on it? Couldst thou perceive a place where a saint pressed it to her lips? Why is not old Chactas a Christian? What frivolous reasons of policy could make me still adhere to the idolatry of my forefathers? No! I will delay it no longer: the earth cries to me aloud, When wilt thou descend to the grave? and what do you wait for to embrace this divine religion? O earth, thou wilt not wait long. As soon as a priest shall have renovated by the baptismal flood a head grown white with age and sorrow, I hope to be united to Atala."—But to continue our narration.

I cannot now, O René, describe the despair that seized my soul when Atala had breathed her last; such a description would require more warmth than remains to my grief-worn spirits. Yes, the moon that spreads her silvery rays around our heads, and over the vast plains of Kentucky shall cease to shine, and the rivers to flow, before my tears for Atala shall be dried up. For two days I was insensible to the advice of the hermit. In endeavoring to calm my distress, this holy man did not use vain and worldly arguments; he only said, "My son, the will of God be done;" and clasped me in his arms. Had I not felt, I never should have thought there could have been so much comfort in those few words of a resigned Christian. The tenderness, compassion, and unalterable affection, of the pious servant of the Most High, conquered my obstinate grief. Ashamed of the tears he had shed on my account, "O father," said I, "let not the passions of a miserable youth disturb thy aged breast; let me take the sad remains of my beloved; I will bury them in some remote corner of the desert, and if I am condemned to live, I shall endeavor to render myself worthy of those eternal nuptials promised by Atala."

The hermit was delighted with my returning fortitude, and enthusiastically exclaimed, "May the blood of Jesus Christ, our divine master, which was shed in compassion to our miseries, have

227

mercy upon this young man; increase his courage, and restore peace to his troubled mind, and only leave in it a useful and humble recollection of his misfortunes."

The holy priest refused to give up the corpse of the daughter of Lopez, but he offered to assemble the inhabitants of the village and to inter her with all Christian pomp, but I refused, saying, "The misfortunes and virtues of Atala are unknown to the rest of mankind; let a solitary grave be dug by our hands to share their obscurity." We agreed to set out the next day by sunrise to inter Atala, at the foot of the natural bridge, and in the entrance to the groves of death.

Towards night we carried the precious remains of this pious saint to the entrance of the cell on the north side. The hermit had enveloped her in a piece of linen cloth of his mother's spinning —the only thing that he had preserved from Europe, and which he intended for his own shroud. Atala lay stretched on a couch of sensitive plants; her feet, head, and shoulders were uncovered, and her hair was adorned with a flower of a magnolia; it was the sensitive flower which I had placed upon the maiden's head. Her lips, that were like a withered rose, seemed endeavoring to smile: dark blue veins appeared upon her marble cheeks, her beauteous eyelids were closed, her feet were joined, and her alabaster hands pressed an ebony crucifix to her heart; the fatal scapulary was suspended on her bosom; she looked as if enchanted by the spirit of melancholy, and resting in the double sleep of innocence and death. Her appearance was quite celestial, and had any one seen her, and been ignorant that she had possessed animation, he would have supposed her the statue of virginity.

The pious anchoret ceased not to pray during the whole night. I sat in silence at the top of Atala's funeral couch: how often had I supported her sleeping head upon my knees, and how often had I bent over her beauteous form listening to her and inhaling her perfumed breath; but now no soft murmur issued from her motionless bosom, and it was in vain that I waited for my beloved to awake. The moon supplied her pale light to the funeral eve: she rose at midnight, as a fair virgin that weeps over the bier of a departed friend: it covered the whole scene with a deep melancholy, displaying the aged oaks and flowing rivers. From time to time the cenobite plunged a bunch of flowers into consecrated water, and bathed the couch of death with the heavenly dew, repeating in a solemn voice some verses from the ancient poet Job.

"Man cometh forth like a flower, and is cut down; he fleeth also as a shadow, and continueth not.

"Wherefore is light given to him that is in misery? and life unto the bitter in soul?"

Thus did the venerable missionary sing; his grave and tremulous voice was re-echoed in the silent woods, and the name of God and the grave was resounded by the neighboring torrents and mountains: the sad warbling of the Virginia dove, the roaring of the waves, and the bell that called travelers, mixed with these funeral chants, and methought I heard in the groves of death the departed spirits join the hermit's voice in mournful chorus. The eastern horizon was now fringed with gold: sparrow-hawks shrieked on the cliffs, and the squirrels hastened into the crevices of old elms: it was the time appointed for Atala's funeral. I carried the corpse upon my shoulders, the hermit preceding me with a spade in his hand. We descended from one mountain to another: old age and death equally retarded our steps. At the sight of the dog which had discovered us in the forest, and who now leaping with joy followed us another road, I could not refrain from tears. Often did the golden tresses of Atala, fanned by the morning gale obscure my eyes, and often was I obliged to deposit my sacred load upon the grass to recover my strength. At last we arrived at the sad spot: we descended under the bridge. O my dear son, what a melancholy sight to see a young savage and an old hermit kneeling opposite each other busily engaged in digging a grave for an innocent virgin, whose corpse lay stretched in a dried ravine.

When we had finished our dismal task we placed the beauteous virgin in her earthly bed: alas! I had hoped to have prepared another couch for her. Then taking a little dust in my hand, and maintaining the most profound silence I scattered it, and for the last time looked at the remains of my beloved; then I spread the earth on a face of eighteen years. I saw the lovely features and graceful form of my sister gradually disappear behind the curtain of eternity. Her snowy bosom appeared rising under the black clay as a lily that lifts its fair head from the dark mold. "Lopez!" I exclaimed, "behold thy son, burying his sister!" and I entirely covered Atala with the earth of sleep. We returned to the cell, when I informed the priest of the project that I had formed of settling near him. The saint, who was thoroughly acquainted with the heart of man, discovered that my thoughts were the effects of

sorrow. He said, "O, Chactas, son of Outalissi, whilst Atala lived, I entreated you to remain here, but now that your destiny is altered, you owe yourself to your native land; believe me, my dear son, grief is not eternal; it will sooner or later forsake the heart of man. Return to Meschacébé [Mississippi], and console your mother, who daily weeps and wants your support.

"Be instructed in the religion of your beloved Atala, and never forget the promise you made her to follow the paths of virtue, and to embrace the Christian religion: I will guard the tomb of your sister. Depart my son; God, the soul of Atala, and the heart of your old friend, will follow you."

Such were the words of the hermit of the rock. His authority was so great, and his wisdom so profound, that it was impossible to disobey him. The next day I quitted my venerable host, who, as he clasped me to his arms, gave me his last counsel and benediction, accompanied with tears. I went to the grave of my Atala, I was surprised to see upon it a little cross, that looked like the top-mast of a wrecked ship seen at a distance. I guessed that the priest had come to pray at the tomb, during the night; this mark of friendship and religion filled my eyes with tears, I felt almost tempted to open the grave, that I might once more behold my beloved Atala; I sat on the earth newly turned, my elbows resting upon my knees, my head supported by my hands; I remained buried in deep and sorrowful meditation. Then for the first time I made the most serious reflections upon the vanity of mankind, and the still greater vanity of human projects.

BANKIM CHANDRA CHATTERJEE

BANKIM CHANDRA CHATTERJEE (Indian, 1838-1894). Leading Bengali novelist and literary pioneer. Historical romances, strongly influenced by Walter Scott: *Ānanda Math, Sitārām, Mrinalinī*. His goal was revival of national pride in protest against foreign rule. Also wrote contemporary social novels and *Krishna Charita*, exposition of religious views.

THE BRIDE'S ARRIVAL

No SOONER had Prafulla's boat put in at Bhutnath landing than the news spread through the village that Brajeswar had again brought

home a wife; it was whispered she was full-grown, even old. People came running from all directions to see the bride, the young, the old, the blind, the lame, everybody. The cook left her pots and ran; the cutter of fish turned her basket upside down over her fish and ran; the bather came running in wet clothes. The diner went half-hungry. The disputer suddenly agreed with her opponent. The woman spanking her child spared him for once. Off he went in his mother's arms to see the old bride. When the news came a husband was eating. The curry and dhal had been served but not the fish; he had to do without fish that day. An old woman complained to her granddaughter, "How can I go to the pond unless you take me?" At the news of the bride's coming the girl abandoned the old woman and dashed off. The old woman managed somehow to get there too. A young woman, having just been scolded by her mother, was promising not to leave the house again when she heard the news. Her promise was at once forgotten; away she went towards the bride's house. A mother left her baby and ran; the baby toddled after her, crying. A young wife veiled her face and passed shamelessly in front of her seated husband and his elder brother. Running loosened the young women's clothes but they had no time to set them right. Their hair fell down but they did not stop to twist it up again. In their excitement they did not notice what they pulled where. There was an uproar. The goddess of modesty fled in shame.

The bride and bridegroom were standing on a low stool while his mother went through the formalities of reception. People leaned forward to get a look at the bride. She did not relax proprieties and kept her veil three-fourths of a yard long. No one could see her face. During the ceremony her mother-in-law raised the veil once to look at her. She started a little but said nothing, merely murmuring, "The bride is nice." There were tears in her eyes.

The reception over, her mother-in-law took the bride to her room and then addressed the assembled neighbours: "Mothers! My son's wife has come a long way. She is hungry and thirsty. I am going to give them their food immediately. Our daughter-in-law will stay here in our house. You will see her all the time. Go home now and take your own meals."

Disappointed, the village women went away finding fault. The offence was the mother-in-law's but the bride got most of the blame because no one had seen her face. They all expressed their disgust at an old bride. Again they all opined that such were to be found

231

in Kulin families. Then whoever had seen an old bride in a Kulin home began to tell about it. Govinda Mukerjee had married a woman fifty-five years old. Hari Chatterjee had brought a seventy-year-old maiden wife home. Manu Banerjee married an old woman after she had been brought down to the bank of the Ganges to die. All such tales with embellishments grew familiar on the way. Venting itself in this fashion, the village gradually grew quiet.

GEOFFREY CHAUCER

GEOFFREY CHAUCER (English, *ca.* 1340-1400). The Father of English poetry, whose choice of London dialect determined standard speech. Had full, rich life and sound, practical philosophy. *The Canterbury Tales* shows influence of Boccaccio, Petrarch, and others. Remarkable storyteller, creator of character, humorist. Other works: *Troilus and Criseyde, The Legend of Good Women.*

THE PARDONER'S TALE

THERE dwelt one time in Flanders a company of young folk who followed such folly as riotous living and gaming in stews and taverns, where with harps, lutes and citerns they danced and played at dice both day and night, and ate and drank without restraint. Thus they served the Devil in cursed fashion within those Devil's temples by abominable superfluity.

These rioters, three, of whom I speak, long ere any bell had rung for prime had sat down in a tavern to drink. And as they sat, they heard the tinkle of a bell that was carried before a corpse to his grave. One of them called to his boy. 'Be off with you, and ask straightway what corpse is passing by; and mind you report his name aright.'

'Sir,' quoth the boy, 'that needs not be. It was told me two hours before you came here; he was an old fellow of yours, by God, and he was suddenly slain tonight, as he sat very drunk on his bench. There came a privy thief men call death, that slays all people in this countryside, and with his spear he smote his heart in two, and went his way without a word. A thousand he has slain in this pestilence; and master, ere you come into his presence, methinks

232

it were best to be warned of such an adversary. Be ready to meet him ever; thus my mother taught me, I say no more.'

'By St. Mary,' said the taverner, 'the child speaks truth, for over a mile hence, in a large village, he has slain both woman, child, servant and knave. I trow his habitation be there. It were great wisdom to be advised ere he do injure a man.'

'Yea, God's arms!' quoth this rioter, 'is it such peril to meet with him? I will seek him in the highways and byways, I vow by God's bones. Hearken, fellows, we three be like; let each hold up his hand to the other and become the other's brother, and we will slay this false traitor, Death. He that slays so many shall be slain ere night, by God's Dignity!'

Together these three plighted their troth each to live and die for the rest as though he were their sworn brother, and up they then started in this drunken rage, and forth they went toward that village of which the taverner had spoken; and many a grisly oath they swore, and rent Christ's blessed body. —'Death shall be dead if they can but catch him.'

When they had gone not quite a mile just as they were about to go over a stile, an old man and poor met them and greeted them full meekly, and said, 'Lordings, God be with you!'

The proudest of the three rioters answered, 'What, churl, bad luck to you! Why are you all wrapped up save your face? Why live you so long to so great an age?'

This old man began to peer into his visage, and said, 'Because I cannot find a man, though I walked to India, neither in hamlet nor in city, who will change his youth for mine age. And therefore must I keep mine old age as long as it is God's will. Death, alas will not have me! Thus I walk like a restless caitiff, and early and late I knock with my staff upon the ground which is my mother's gate, and say, "Beloved Mother, let me in. Lo, how I wane away, flesh and blood and skin! Alas when shall my bones be at rest? Mother, with you I would exchange my chest, that has been long time in my chamber, yea for an hair-cloth to wrap me in!" But yet she will not do me that favour; wherefore my face is full pale and withered.—But sirs, it is not courteous to speak churlishly to an old man, unless he trespass in word or deed. You may yourselves read in Holy Writ, "Before an old hoary-head man ye shall arise;" wherefore I counsel you, do no harm now to an old man, no more than you would that men did to you in your old age if it be that

you abide so long. And God be with you, wherever you go or be; I must go whither I have to go.'

'Nay old churl, you shall not go, by God,' said the second gamester straightway. 'You part not so lightly by St. John! You spoke right now of that traitor Death who slays all our friends in this country side. By my troth, you are his spy! Tell where he is, or by God and the Holy Sacrament you shall die. Truly you are of his consent to slay us young folk, false thief!'

'Now, sirs,' quoth he, 'If you be so lief to find Death, turn up this crooked way; for by my faith I left him in that grove under a tree, and there he will abide, nor for all your boasting will he hide him. See you that oak? Right here you shall find him. May God, Who redeemed mankind, save you and amend you!' Thus said this old man.

And each of these rioters ran till he came to the tree, and there they found florins coined of fine round gold well nigh seven bushels, as they thought. No longer sought they then after Death, but each was so glad at the sight that they sat them down by the precious hoard. The worst of them spoke the first word. 'Brethren,' he said, 'heed what I say; my wit is great, though I jest oft and play. This treasure has been given us by Fortune that we may live our lives in mirth and jollity, and lightly as it comes, so we will spend it. Eh! God's precious dignity! Who would have weened today that we should have so fair a grace! But could this gold be carried to my house or else to yours,—for you know well all this gold is ours,—then were we in high felicity! But truly by day it may not be done. Men would say we were sturdy thieves and hang us for our treasure. This treasure must be carried by night, as wisely and as slyly as may be. Wherefore I advise that we draw cuts amongst us all, and he that draws the shortest shall run with a blithe heart to the town and that full swift and privily bring us bread and wine. And two of us shall cunningly guard this treasure, and at night, if he will not tarry, we will carry it where we all agree is safest.'

One of them brought the cuts in his fist and bade them draw and look where the lot should fall. It fell to the youngest of them and he went forth toward the town at once. So soon as he was gone one said to the other, 'You well know you are my sworn brother, and you will profit by what I tell you. Here is gold and plenty of it, to be divided amongst us three. You know well our fellow is gone. If I can shape it so that it be divided betwixt us two, had I not done you a friendly turn?'

The other answered, 'I wot not how that may be. He knows well the gold is with us two. What shall we do? What shall we say?'

'Shall it be a secret?' said the first wicked fellow. 'I shall tell you in a few words what we shall do to bring it about.'

'I agree,' quoth the other, 'not to betray you, by my troth.'

'Now,' quoth the first, 'you know well we be two and that two should be stronger than one. Look when he is set down; do you arise as though you would play with him, and I will rive him through the two sides while you struggle with him as in sport; and look that you do the same with your dagger. And then shall all this gold be shared, dear friend, betwixt you and me. Then may we both fulfil all our lusts, and play at dice at our will.' And thus, as you heard me say, were these two villains accorded to slay the third.

The youngest, who went to town, revolved full often in his heart the beauty of those bright new florins. 'Oh Lord,' quoth he, 'if so be I could have all this gold to myself, no man living under God's throne should live so merry as I!' And at last the fiend, our enemy, put it into his thought to buy poison with which he might slay his two fellows; for the fiend found him in such a way of life that he had leave to bring him to sorrow, for this was his full intention namely to slay them both and never to repent. And forth he went without tarrying into the town to an apothecary, and prayed him to sell him some poison that he might kill his rats; and there was also a pole-cat in his yard, which he said, had killed his capons and he would fain wreak him upon the vermin that destroyed him by night. The apothecary answered, 'And you shall have such a thing, that, so may God save my soul, no creature in all this world can eat or drink of this composition the amount of a grain of wheat, but he shall at once forfeit his life. Yea, die he shall, and that in less time than you can walk a mile, this poison is so strong and violent.'

This cursed man clutched the box of poison in his hand and then ran into the next street to a man and borrowed of him three large bottles. Into two of them he poured his poison, but the third he kept clean for his drink, for all night long he planned to labour in carrying away his gold. And when this rioter, the Devil take him! had filled his three great bottles with wine, he repaired again to his fellows.

What need to speak about it more? for just as they had planned his death, even so they slew him, and that anon. And when this was done, one spake thus, 'Now let us sit and drink and make merry,

and then we will bury his body.' And then by chance, he took one of the bottles where the poison was, and he drank and gave his fellow to drink also. Wherefore anon they both died. And certes, Avicenna wrote never in any canon or any chapter more wondrous sufferings of empoisoning than these two wretches showed ere they died. Thus ended these two murderers as well as the poisoner.

ANTON CHEKHOV

ANTON CHEKHOV (Russian, 1860-1904). Great master of Russian short story, whose style heavily influenced modern writing. Meticulously wrought tales, concerned with introspective, inarticulate emotions rather than with outward events. Grandson of a serf, became the artist of twilight Czarist Russia. His great plays, *The Cherry Orchard, The Sea Gull, Three Sisters, Uncle Vanya,* left indelible mark on modern theater, but never successfully imitated.

THE SLANDERER

SERGEY KAPITONICH AKHINEYEV, the teacher of calligraphy, gave his daughter Natalya in marriage to the teacher of history and geography, Ivan Petrovich Loshadinikh. The wedding feast went on swimmingly. They sang, played, and danced in the parlor. Waiters, hired for the occasion from the club, bustled about hither and thither like madmen, in black frock coats and soiled white neckties. A loud noise of voices smote the air. From the outside people looked in at the windows—their social standing gave them no right to enter.

Just at midnight the host, Akhineyev, made his way to the kitchen to see whether everything was ready for the supper. The kitchen was filled with smoke from the floor to the ceiling; the smoke reeked with the odors of geese, ducks, and many other things. Victuals and beverages were scattered about on two tables in artistic disorder. Marfa, the cook, a stout, red-faced woman, was busying herself near the loaded tables.

"Show me the sturgeon, dear," said Akhineyev, rubbing his hands and licking his lips. "What a fine odor! I could just devour the whole kitchen! Well, let me see the sturgeon!"

Marfa walked up to one of the benches and carefully lifted a

236

greasy newspaper. Beneath that paper, in a huge dish, lay a big fat sturgeon, amid capers, olives, and carrots. Akhineyev glanced at the sturgeon and heaved a sigh of relief. His face became radiant, his eyes rolled. He bent down, and, smacking his lips, gave vent to a sound like a creaking wheel. He stood a while, then snapped his fingers for pleasure, and smacked his lips once more.

"Bah! The sound of a hearty kiss. Whom have you been kissing there, Marfusha?" some one's voice was heard from the adjoining room, and soon the closely cropped head of Vankin, the assistant school instructor, appeared in the doorway. "Whom have you been kissing here? A-a-ah! Very good! Sergey Kapitonich! A fine old man indeed! With the female sex tête-à-tête!"

"I wasn't kissing at all," said Akhineyev, confused; "who told you, you fool? I only—smacked my lips on account of—in consideration of my pleasure—at the sight of the fish."

"Tell that to some one else, not to me!" exclaimed Vankin, whose face expanded into a broad smile as he disappeared behind the door. Akhineyev blushed.

"The devil knows what may be the outcome of this!" he thought. "He'll go about tale-bearing now, the rascal. He'll disgrace me before the whole town, the brute!"

Akhineyev entered the parlor timidly and cast furtive glances to see what Vankin was doing. Vankin stood near the piano and, deftly bending down, whispered something to the inspector's sister-in-law, who was laughing.

"That's about me!" thought Akhineyev. "About me, the devil take him! She believes him, she's laughing. My God! No, that mustn't be left like that. No. I'll have to fix it so that no one shall believe him. I'll speak to all of them, and he'll remain a foolish gossip in the end."

Akhineyev scratched his head, and, still confused, walked up to Padekoi.

"I was in the kitchen a little while ago, arranging things there for the supper," he said to the Frenchman. "You like fish, I know, and I have a sturgeon just so big. About two yards. Ha, ha, ha! Yes, by the way, I have almost forgotten. There was a real anecdote about that sturgeon in the kitchen. I entered the kitchen a little while ago and wanted to examine the food. I glanced at the sturgeon and for pleasure, I smacked my lips—it was so piquant! And just at that moment the fool Vankin entered and says—ha, ha, ha—and says: 'A-a! A-a-ah! You have been kissing here?'—with Marfa;

just think of it—with the cook! What a piece of invention, that blockhead. The woman is ugly, she looks like a monkey, and he says we were kissing. What a queer fellow!"

"Who's a queer fellow?" asked Tarantulov, as he approached them.

"I refer to Vankin. I went out into the kitchen—"
The story of Marfa and the sturgeon was repeated.

"That makes me laugh. What a queer fellow he is. In my opinion it is more pleasant to kiss the dog than to kiss Marfa," added Akhineyev, and, turning around, he noticed Mzda.

"We have been speaking about Vankin," he said to him. "What a queer fellow. He entered the kitchen and noticed me standing beside Marfa, and immediately he began to invent different stories. 'What?' he says, 'you have been kissing each other!' He was drunk, so he must have been dreaming. 'And I,' I said, 'I would rather kiss a duck than kiss Marfa. And I have a wife,' said I, 'you fool.' He made me appear ridiculous."

"Who made you appear ridiculous?" inquired the teacher of religion, addressing Akhineyev.

"Vankin. I was standing in the kitchen, you know, and looking at the sturgeon—" And so forth. In about half an hour all the guests knew the story about Vankin and the sturgeon.

"Now let him tell," thought Akhineyev, rubbing his hands. "Let him do it. He'll start to tell them, and they'll cut him short: 'Don't talk nonsense, you fool! We know all about it.'"

And Akhineyev felt so much appeased that, for joy, he drank four glasses of brandy over and above his fill. Having escorted his daughter to her room, he went to his own and soon slept the sleep of an innocent child, and on the following day he no longer remembered the story of the sturgeon. But, alas! Man proposes and God disposes. The evil tongue does its wicked work, and even Akhineyev's cunning did not do him any good. One week later, on a Wednesday, after the third lesson, when Akhineyev stood in the teachers' room and discussed the vicious inclinations of the pupil Visyekin, the director approached him, and, beckoning to him, called him aside.

"See here, Sergey Kapitonich," said the director. "Pardon me. It isn't my affair, yet I must make it clear to you, nevertheless. It is my duty— You see, rumors are on foot that you are on intimate terms with that woman—with your cook— It isn't my affair, but— You may be on intimate terms with her, you may kiss

238

her— You may do whatever you like, but, please, don't do it so openly! I beg of you. Don't forget that you are a pedagogue."

Akhineyev stood as though frozen and petrified. Like one stung by a swarm of bees and scalded with boiling water, he went home. On his way it seemed to him as though the whole town stared at him as at one besmeared with tar— At home new troubles awaited him.

"Why don't you eat anything?" asked his wife at their dinner. "What are you thinking about? Are you thinking about Cupid, eh? You are longing for Marfushka. I know everything already, you Mahomet. Kind people have opened my eyes, you barbarian!"

And she slapped him on the cheek.

He rose from the table, and staggering, without cap or coat, directed his footsteps toward Vankin. The latter was at home.

"You rascal!" he said to Vankin. "Why have you covered me with mud before the whole world? Why have you slandered me?"

"How; what slander? What are you inventing?"

"And who told everybody that I was kissing Marfa? Not you, perhaps? Not you, you murderer?"

Vankin began to blink his eyes, and all the fibres of his face began to quiver. He lifted his eyes toward the image and ejaculated:

"May God punish me, may I lose my eyesight and die, if I said even a single word about you to any one! May I have neither house nor home!"

Vankin's sincerity admitted of no doubt. It was evident that it was not he who had gossiped.

"But who was it? Who?" Akhineyev asked himself, going over in his mind all his acquaintances, and striking his chest. "Who was it?"

CHIKAMATSU MONZAEMON

CHIKAMATSU MONZAEMON (Japanese, 1653-1725). The Shakespeare of Japan. Wrote for Kabuki theater, also for puppet theater. Author of numerous plays, mostly historical or domestic dramas. Due to conventions of puppet theater, and allusiveness of writing, plays extremely difficult to translate.

Most popular: *Battles of Kokusenya, The Double Suicide of Sonezaki.*

ADVENTURES OF THE HAKATA DAMSEL

FOUR days after leaving the capital Soshichi and Kojoro found themselves at Seki, a post-town in the province of Isé. There the

foot-worn travellers halted before a stone image of Jizo, a guardian god of children. Fervently were they praying to the deity that he might soften Sozaémon toward them when palanquin bearers accosted them.

"Cannot we serve you, sir?"

"That may be. We are going to the province of Owari. How much will you charge to carry us to the next stage?"

"It is five miles to Ishiyakushi, the next stage, so we ask you for *korori*."

Soshichi was startled.

"I don't know how much *korori* is."

"A hundred *mon*, sir."

"Too much. Come down to seventy."

"Very good, sir."

With the care-worn fugitives within their palanquins the bearers presently began a rapid march, keeping in time in their steps to the cries: *"Sokosei!"—"Katasei!"—"Makkasei!"* Mile succeeded mile, until Oiwaki was reached, where it was customary to change palanquins and bearers. The carriers therefore stopped. Kojoro stepped out promptly, but Soshichi would not get down, so great was his fear lest the bearers' sign *"korori"* should prove a bad omen. His mind might be said to be fettered with apprehension ere his body was tied to the detective's cord.

"Well, Kojoro," said Soshichi, "you had better change palanquins and go ahead of me."

"I will."

"And wait for me at a place called Yokkaichi."

"I will, my husband."

Kojoro, all unaware of Soshichi's fears, changed palanquins and let herself be carried ahead. A few minutes later a palanquin arrived from the next stage. The newcomers addressed Soshichi's bearers.

"Isn't your passenger the companion of the young woman who's just gone on? Let us exchange passengers."

"That'll suit us nicely. Now, sir, we're going to do an exchange. Please descend."

The bearers lifted the blind of the palanquin for Soshichi. The passenger of the other palanquin had already stepped out. He was lightly dressed in drawers and leggings, carried a packet in his hand and a *hayanawa* in his belt. Soshochi but glimpsed at him

240

and shuddered. He turned his face away and covered his head with a *tenugui*. Hurriedly he descended and with a brief "Thank you, bearers", stepped into the other palanquin and quickly pulled down the blind.

"I'm in a hurry," he said in a tremulous voice. "I'll give you extra; start quickly."

He had hardly uttered these words when a shrill voice cried, "We arrest Komachiya Soshichi!"

The next moment a strong hempen cord had been wound round his palanquin. The terror-stricken captive struggled in the palanquin but to no purpose; and he could but cry like a caged bird. Armed detectives, lying in ambush, emerged and surrounded him.

"Prisoner, you know what charge we arrest you on. The official information asserts that there are eight in your gang. We have come to arrest you. Do you permit yourself to be arrested, or shall we have to bind you by force?"

To this the prisoner made no reply, but was heard to address a plaintive prayer to Amida Buddha.

"No," said the first detective, "let us take him as he is to the next stage and bind him when we get there. That's more convenient. Now, bearers, move off."

"Certainly, sir, but inasmuch as he can't escape death, why don't you bind him here?"

So murmuring, the bearers approached the palanquin and lifted it, when, to their amazement, blood dribbled down *gaba-gaba* from it, instantaneously forming a scarlet patch upon the ground. The occupant uttered a groan of pain. The affrighted coolies cried, "The prisoner has killed himself in the palanquin! Come and look!"

The palanquin was hastily set to earth. The bearers drew apart. The detectives unwound the cord from the palanquin and raised its blind. Soshichi, with fixed eyes, was gasping after a mortal fashion. The long blade plunged in his right side was buried to the hilt. Its point protruded from his left. The detectives were speechless with terror and dismay.

Kojoro, bound, was brought back. Seeing her husband's plight she was struck with unspeakable grief. She trod the tide of blood. She thrust her face into the palanquin.

"I am here, Soshichi San. Kojoro is here, Soshichi. I was bound a few minutes ago. Till last night we slept together. We had a vow to die in the same hour. And now, despite our vows, you have

died alone, leaving me behind to suffer by myself. That is selfish of you. But never mind that now. You must be in pain; I see you are in great pain."

With these words she wept and, sinking down, placed her face in the dying man's lap. Intelligence returned to the eyes of Soshichi.

"Ah, Kojoro," he gasped, "are you bound? I am a wicked man who has broken the national laws and disobeyed my father. I have so narrowed the compass of the wide world that my own home could no longer be a home to me and have wandered to this place till at last I am caught in a heavenly net—quite naturally and justly. Were I brought to my home and there executed I should bring disgrace on all my relatives and prove doubly undutiful to my father. With this thought in my mind I have done the deed you see. This is just retribution I now receive for having joined Kezori Kuémon's gang of smugglers and having lived above my station. And since in the eye of the law a wife cannot escape connection with her husband's crime, you are bound, undergo dishonour and are made to suffer—all of which is caused by my own wicked nature. But for Soshichi you would not have suffered thus. Poor girl? How great must be your grief! You have to sacrifice your life on account of the man with whom you have lived for but a short space of time. Pray forgive me, Kojoro."

Soshichi breathed with difficulty. Death second by second drew nearer. The stern detectives, taking pity upon the sorrowful pair, spoke gently. "When you reach prison you will not be suffered to see each other. Man must help man. Take your fill of speech now."

The more Kojoro listened to Soshichi's kind words the more sorrowful she grew.

"Soshichi San, my dear, you are not to blame. For whose sake is it you have done what you have done? Out of eagerness to prevent Kojoro passing into another's hands you joined Kuémon and forsook even your father. At the risk of your life you became my husband, so dearly have you loved me. So overcome am I at your goodness to me that I cannot find even in Chinese or Hindoo, still less in Japanese, fit words to express my gratitude. Were my hands but unbound I would prostrate myself before you ere I die."

Anguish took her. She wept so bitterly that she seemed almost to lose consciousness.

"Now," gasped Soshichi, "now comes the last moment we behold each other in this life. In the next world, remember, we shall be husband and wife. Namu Amida Buddha."

The voice that prayed was faint. Then he drew the sword from his side and almost in the same moment ceased to breathe. Piteous was Kojoro's cry. "Husband, stay for me a moment! I would accompany you! Sooner or later I shall be slain. Officers, have mercy! Slay me here—slay me, I entreat you!"

She wailed and rushed hither and thither in the frenzy of madness. At this moment a police superintendent and his underlings arrived, convoying Kezori Kuémon, his followers and their respective courtesans. All were bound. All had been captured in one place or another. The leader of the party unrolled a scroll and read as follows:

"Prisoners, I read you an Imperial mandate. Listen to it with gratitude. Forasmuch as you have committed the crime of smuggling in connection with great ships in the offing in defiance of the national laws, you richly deserve capital punishment. But in honour of his coronation, His Majesty the Emperor is graciously pleased to pardon you and to release you from such a penalty."

The gratitude of the prisoners knew no bounds. They cried out for joy. The police superintendent addressed the courtesans.

"Forasmuch as your profession compelled you to become the companions of these men you are guilty of no crime. Henceforward you can go whither you choose. Now, men, set these women free."

The constables released the women. The courtesans caressed the abrasions the cords had caused.

"The power of His Majesty the Emperor," they exclaimed, "is great indeed! Our hands are freed from the cords. We feel like birds escaped from their cages."

But Kojoro, albeit set at freedom like her companions, continued to weep. At length she lifted her head.

"Sorrow it is that my husband Soshichi has forsaken me and his soul winged its way to the other world or ever the compassion of this edict could be made known to him. This life is not now worth while the living for this 'Kojoro of Hakata', who is just like a bird which has lost its mate by death. Officers, have mercy! Slay me!"

The bitter tears fell.

"Your grief is natural," said the sympathetic superintendent. "Though your husband was one of a gang of ruffians, he joined them out of youthful folly and infatuation. It follows therefore that his offence was small. We regret that his impetuosity should have led to his suicide. We grieve on your behalf, but nothing is to be done. Your best course will be to serve your father-in-law in

243

Soshichi's place and busy yourself in prayers for the peace of the departed soul. Now, my men, treat the prisoners as the Imperial edict commands."

Of the smugglers who had escaped death, some were branded or tattooed upon the face, others had their ears or noses cut off that they might not repeat their offences. Then they were set free.

The rumour of the adventures of the hapless Hakata damsel did not take long to spread far and wide. It remained a topic of conversation for generations afterwards.

CH'U YUAN

CH'U YUAN (Chinese, *ca.* 343-277 B.C.). Greatest poet of ancient China. According to legend, a loyal minister who drowned self when he lost emperor's favor. Poems, though personal, are still close to ritual song. The *Li Sao* one of most famous long poems in Chinese.

STRAY THOUGHTS

My Heart with Grief is heavy,
  I sigh with Head down hung.
My Thoughts are like a tangled Skein,
  And yet the Night is young.

In Autumn all Things wither,
  The World is full of Hate,
My Prince is easily enraged,
  And my Affliction great.

The People's Suff'rings move my Heart,
  Our Land I cannot leave.
Here for my Loved One my stray Thoughts
  Into a Song I weave.
Oh, once you gave your Promise,
  At Dusk we two should meet;
But then you went back on your Word,
  For such was your Deceit.

244

You praise another's Beauty,
    Admire another's Grace,
Forswear your former Pledge to me,
    And turn an angry Face.
I longed for Reconcilement,
    But kept by Fear apart,
I dare no more draw near to you,
    So Grief besets my Heart.

I put my Thought in Verses
    My Prince disdains to hear,
I know true Worth no Favour wins,
    And Enemies will sneer.

All that I said was truthful,
    How could the Prince forget?
By honest Counsel I would make
    Him more illustrious yet.

I take a Sage as Model,
    And in his Steps would tread.
I strive for Excellence so that
    My Prince's Fame may spread.

Virtue is not outside us,
    Fame springs from noble Deeds,
All Reputations must be won,
    As Fruit must grow from Seeds.

Interlude

So I plead before my Love,
But his Heart I cannot move.
He approves another's Grace.
In his Heart I have no Place.

Chorus

A Bird flies from the South once more
To the great Stream's northern Shore.
In fair Splendour see him stand,
All alone in a far-off Land;

245

None to befriend him beneath the Sun,
For Mediators here are none.
Departed Long and in Disgrace,
I have no Way to plead my Case.
Beside the Northern Hill I sigh,
My Tears drop where the Stream flows by,
The short Midsummer Nights are here,
Yet each seems long as one whole Year.
The Capital is far away,
But there each Night in Thought I stray.
By narrow winding Track or wide,
Southward, with Moon and Stars my Guide,
Forward I press, but all in Vain:
My Soul is weary of such Pain!
Yet still my Nature is too Proud
To change or flatter like the Crowd!
For me no one will mediate,
None knows or cares for my sad Fate.

Refrain

Long the Bay and strong the Tide,
　　As up the Stream I go.
I make my Journey southward still,
　　In Hope to ease my Woe.
The Journey here is hard when Cliffs
　　Reach steeply to the Sky,
And hard it is to climb or cross
　　The Mountain Paths so high.
Brought to a Halt I hesitate,
　　And rest here for the Night.
My Mind is clouded, and there seems
　　To be no End in Sight.
My Thoughts have travelled far afield,
　　In Grief I heave a Sigh,
This Place is strange and desolate,
　　No Go-between have I!
My Thoughts in Verses I have set,
　　Some Ease of Mind to seek;
But still my Grief is unassuaged,
　　For who will hear me speak?

THOUGHTS BEFORE DROWNING

In balmy early Summer Days,
　　When Trees and Grasses teem,
With lonely and dejected Heart
　　I reach the southern Stream.

Now all around appears forlorn,
　　So silent and so still,
While sad and melancholy Thoughts
　　Upon me cast a Chill.

Once more I recollect the Past,
　　And Wrongs of former Days.
Let Others stoop some Gain to win,
　　But I'll not change my Ways.

Such Men as change for selfish Gain
　　I always have despised;
But hold the Principles of Old,
　　The former Rules have prized.

With Sternness and Benevolence
　　An upright Man is filled.
If Craftsmen will not ply the Axe,
　　Men doubt that they are skilled.

You see a Picture in the Night,
　　And black the Colours find.
If skillful Craftsmen squint to see,
　　You need not think them blind.

Now Darkness is construed as Light,
　　And Fair to Foul is turned,
Now Hens and Geese can fly on high,
　　While Phoenixes are spurned.

Now Good and Bad are thought the same,
　　And Jade confused with Stone.
To Men made blind by Prejudice,
　　My Virtues are unknown.

I feel my Task too hard for me;
  Despairing of Success,
I do not know to whom to show
  The Jewels I possess.

The country Dogs bark savagely
  At One they do not know.
And Fools suspect all Men of Worth,
  And slavish Envy show.

They will not see my Dignity,
  My Learning or my Grace,
And all my subtle Scholarship
  Endeavour to abase.

I double my Benevolence,
  To Honesty I hold;
But who can understand my Worth,
  Since dead the Sage of Old?

How is it that for such long Years
  The Good remain apart?
The ancient Kings are too long gone
  To hold them in our Heart.

I curb my Indignation now,
  My Anger I repress;
I shall not change or hesitate
  In Danger or Distress.

I journey on and take no Rest
  Till darkly sinks the Sun.
But now I ease my heavy Heart—
  My Race will soon be done.

Refrain

On and on the Rivers slow
Down their several Courses flow.
Dark the Way and overgrown,
And the Future all unknown.

All my Time in Anguish spent,
No End set to my Lament,
By the World misunderstood,
With no Friend or Kinsman good.

Though my Conscience is quite clear,
I can find no Witness here.
Gone the Charioteer so prized,
The swift Horses are despised.

Sad or happy, each Man's Fate
Overtakes him soon or late.
If I keep a steadfast Heart,
Fear in me can have no Part.

Death, I know, must come to All,
Nor for Mercy would I call.
Saints, I follow in your Wake!
Your Example shall I take!

CONFUCIUS

CONFUCIUS (Chinese, ca. 551-479 B.C.). Great poet and philosopher, source
of Chinese wisdom for twenty centuries. His *Shih Ching (Book of Odes)*
laid foundation of Chinese literature. Authorship of other extensive collections
is disputed, probably legendary. His work glorifies the moral virtues: loyalty,
brotherhood, truth, justice, tolerance, etc.

A CHALLENGE

If, boy, thy thoughts of me were kind,
    I'd lift my skirts and wade the Tsin;
But if thou be of other mind,
    Is there none else my love would win?
        O craziest of crazy boys!

Ay, if thy thoughts of me were kind,
    I'd lift my skirts and wade the Wei;
But if thy thoughts are else inclined,
    Is there none other gallant nigh?
        O craziest of crazy boys!

THE ABSENT HUSBAND

I picked and picked the mouse ears,
    Nor gained one basket load;
My heart was with my husband:
    I flung them on the road.

I climbed yon rugged mountain,
    My ponies all broke down;
I filled my golden goblet
    Long anxious thought to drown.

I climbed yon lofty ridges,
    With my ponies black and bay;
I filled for me my horn cup
    Long torture to allay.

I climbed yon craggy uplands,
    My steeds grew weak and ill;
My footmen were exhausted;—
    And here I sorrow still!

LAMENT OF A DISCARDED WIFE

When east winds blow unceasingly,
    They bring but gloominess and rain.
Strive, strive to live unitedly,
    And every angry thought restrain.
Some plants we gather for their leaves,
    But leave the roots untouched beneath;
So, while unsullied was my name,
    I should have lived with you till death.

With slow, slow step I took the road,
    My inmost heart rebelling sore,
You came not far with me, indeed,
    You only saw me to the door.
Who calls the lettuce bitter fare,
    The cress is not a whit more sweet.
Ay, feast there with your new-found bride,
    Well pleased, as when fond brothers meet.

250

The Wei, made turbid by the king,
    Grows limpid by the islets there.
There, feasting with your new-found bride
    For me no longer now you care.
Yet leave to me my fishing dam;
    My wicker nets, remove them not.
My person spurned—some vacant hour
    May bring compassion for my lot.

Where ran the river full and deep,
    With raft or boat I paddled o'er;
And where it flowed in shallower stream,
    I dived or swam from shore to shore.
And what we had, or what we lost,
    For that I strained my every nerve;
When other folks had loss, I'd crawl
    Upon my knees, if aught 'twould serve.

And you can show me no kind care,
    Nay, treated like a foe am I!
My virtue stood but in your way,
    Like traders' goods that none will buy.
Once it was feared we could not live;
    In your reverses then I shared:
And now, when fortune smiles on you,
    To very poison I'm compared.

I have laid by a goodly store,—
    For winter's use it was to be;—
Feast on there with your new-found bride,—
    I was for use in poverty!
Rude fits of anger you have shown,
    Now left me to be sorely tried.
Ah, you forget those days gone by,
    When you came nestling to my side!

COMRADES IN WAR TIME

How say we have no clothes?
    One plaid for both will do.
Let but the king, in raising men,
    Our spears and pikes renew,—
    We'll fight as one, we two!

251

How say we have no clothes?
    One skirt our limbs shall hide.
Let but the king, in raising men,
    Halberd and lance provide,—
    We'll do it, side by side!

How say we have no clothes?
    My kirtle thou shalt wear.
Let but the king, in raising men,
    Armor and arms prepare,
    The toils of war we'll share.

TRUST THY LAST FRIEND AGAINST THE WORLD

A babbling current fails
To float a load of thorns away,—
Of brothers, few are left us now,
Yet we remain, myself and thou:
    Believe not others' tales,
Others will lead thee far astray.

The babbling current fails
To float the firewood fagots far.—
Of brothers there are left but few,
Yet I and thou remain, we two:
    Believe not others' tales,
For verily untrue they are!

JOSEPH CONRAD

JOSEPH CONRAD (English, 1857-1924). Polish-born novelist, who went early to sea on English ships. Retiring from navy, became British subject, taught self to write English, and became greatest writer of sea stories in the language. Most-praised novel: *Lord Jim*. Others: *Nostromo, Victory, Youth, The Secret Agent, The Nigger of the Narcissus*.

THE LAGOON

THE white man, leaning with both arms over the roof of the little house in the stern of the boat, said to the steersman—
    "We will pass the night in Arsat's clearing. It is late."

The Malay only grunted, and went on looking fixedly at the river. The white man rested his chin on his crossed arms and gazed at the wake of the boat. At the end of the straight avenue of forests cut by the intense glitter of the river, the sun appeared unclouded and dazzling, poised low over the water that shone smoothly like a band of metal. The forests, somber and dull, stood motionless and silent on each side of the broad stream. At the foot of big, towering trees, trunkless nipa palms rose from the mud of the bank, in bunches of leaves enormous and heavy, that hung unstirring over the brown swirl of eddies. In the stillness of the air every tree, every leaf, every bough, every tendril of creeper and every petal of minute blossoms seemed to have been bewitched into an immobility perfect and final. Nothing moved on the river but the eight paddles that rose flashing regularly, dipped together with a single splash; while the steersman swept right and left with a periodic and sudden flourish of his blade describing a glinting semicircle above his head. The churned-up water frothed alongside with a confused murmer. And the white man's canoe, advancing upstream in the short-lived disturbance of its own making, seemed to enter the portals of a land from which the very memory of motion had forever departed.

The white man, turning his back upon the setting sun, looked along the empty and broad expanse of the sea-reach. For the last three miles of its course the wandering, hesitating river, as if enticed irresistibly by the freedom of an open horizon, flows straight into the sea, flows straight to the east—to the east that harbors both light and darkness. Astern of the boat the repeated call of some bird, a cry discordant and feeble, skipped along over the smooth water and lost itself, before it could reach the other shore, in the breathless silence of the world.

The steersman dug his paddle into the stream, and held hard with stiffened arms, his body thrown forward. The water gurgled aloud; and suddenly the long straight reach seemed to pivot on its center, the forests swung in a semicircle, and the slanting beams of sunset touched the broadside of the canoe with a fiery glow, throwing the slender and distorted shadows of its crew upon the streaked glitter of the river. The white man turned to look ahead. The course of the boat had been altered at right angles to the stream, and the carved dragon-head of its prow was pointing now at a gap in the fringing bushes of the bank. It glided through, brushing the overhanging twigs, and disappeared from the river like some slim and amphibious creature leaving the water for its lair in the forests.

The narrow creek was like a ditch: tortuous, fabulously deep; filled with gloom under the thin strip of pure and shining blue of the heaven. Immense trees soared up, invisible behind the festooned draperies of creepers. Here and there, near the glistening blackness of the water, a twisted root of some tall tree showed amongst the tracery of small ferns, black and dull, writhing and motionless, like an arrested snake. The short words of the paddlers reverberated, loudly between the thick and somber walls of vegetation. Darkness oozed out from between the trees, through the tangled maze of the creepers, from behind the great fantastic and unstirring leaves; the darkness, mysterious and invincible; the darkness scented and poisonous of impenetrable forests.

The men poled in the shoaling water. The creek broadened, opening out into a wide sweep of a stagnant lagoon. The forests receded from the marshy bank, leaving a level strip of bright green, reedy grass to frame the reflected blueness of the sky. A fleecy pink cloud drifted high above, trailing the delicate coloring of its image under the floating leaves and the silvery blossoms of the lotus. A little house, perched on high piles, appeared black in the distance. Near it, two tall nibong palms, that seemed to have come out of the forests in the background, leaned slightly over the ragged roof, with a suggestion of sad tenderness and care in the droop of their leafy and soaring heads.

The steersman, pointing with his paddle, said, "Arsat is there. I see his canoe fast between the piles."

The polers ran along the sides of the boat glancing over their shoulders at the end of the day's journey. They would have preferred to spend the night somewhere else than on this lagoon of weird aspect and ghostly reputation. Moreover, they disliked Arsat, first as a stranger, and also because he who repairs a ruined house, and dwells in it, proclaims that he is not afraid to live amongst the spirits that haunt the places abandoned by mankind. Such a man can disturb the course of fate by glances or words; while his familiar ghosts are not easy to propitiate by casual wayfarers upon whom they long to wreak the malice of their human master. White men care not for such things, being unbelievers and in league with the Father of Evil, who leads them unharmed through the invisible dangers of this world. To the warnings of the righteous they oppose an offensive pretense of disbelief. What is there to be done?

So they thought, throwing their weight on the end of their long poles. The big canoe glided on swiftly, noiselessly, and smoothly,

towards Arsat's clearing, till, in a great rattling of poles thrown down, and the loud murmurs of "Allah be praised!" it came with a gentle knock against the crooked piles below the house.

The boatmen with uplifted faces shouted discordantly, "Arsat! O Arsat!" Nobody came. The white man began to climb the rude ladder giving access to the bamboo platform before the house. The juragan of the boat said sulkily, "We will cook in the sampan, and sleep on the water."

"Pass my blankets and the basket," said the white man, curtly.

He knelt on the edge of the platform to receive the bundle. Then the boat shoved off, and the white man, standing up, confronted Arsat, who had come out through the low door of his hut. He was a man young, powerful, with broad chest and muscular arms. He had nothing on but his sarong. His head was bare. His big, soft eyes stared eagerly at the white man, but his voice and demeanor were composed as he asked, without any words of greeting—

"Have you medicine, Tuan?"

"No," said the visitor in a startled tone. "No. Why? Is there sickness in the house?"

"Enter and see," replied Arsat, in the same calm manner, and turning short round, passed again through the small doorway. The white man, dropping his bundles, followed.

In the dim light of the dwelling he made out on a couch of bamboos a woman stretched on her back under a broad sheet of red cotton cloth. She lay still, as if dead; but her big eyes, wide open, glittered in the gloom, staring upwards at the slender rafters, motionless and unseeing. She was in a high fever, and evidently unconscious. Her cheeks were sunk slightly, her lips were partly open, and on the young face there was the ominous and fixed expression—the absorbed, contemplating expression of the unconscious who are going to die. The two men stood looking down at her in silence.

"Has she been long ill?" asked the traveler.

"I have not slept for five nights," answered the Malay, in a deliberate tone. "At first she heard voices calling her from the water and struggled against me who held her. But since the sun of today rose she hears nothing—she hears not me. She sees nothing. She sees not me—me!"

He remained silent for a minute, then asked softly—

"Tuan, will she die?"

"I fear so," said the white man, sorrowfully. He had known Arsat

255

years ago, in a far country in times of trouble and danger, when no friendship is to be despised. And since his Malay friend had come unexpectedly to dwell in the hut on the lagoon with a strange woman, he had slept many times there, in his journeys up and down the river. He liked the man who knew how to keep faith in council and how to fight without fear by the side of his white friend. He liked him—not so much perhaps as a man likes his favorite dog—but still he liked him well enough to help and ask no questions, to think sometimes vaguely and hazily in the midst of his own pursuits, about the lonely man and the long-haired woman with audacious face and triumphant eyes, who lived together hidden by the forests—alone and feared.

The white man came out of the hut in time to see the enormous conflagration of sunset put out by the swift and stealthy shadows that, rising like a black and impalpable vapor above the tree-tops, spread over the heaven, extinguishing the crimson glow of floating clouds and the red brilliance of departing daylight. In a few moments all the stars came out above the intense blackness of the earth and the great lagoon gleaming suddenly with reflected lights resembled an oval patch of night sky flung down into the hopeless and abysmal night of the wilderness. The white man had some supper out of the basket, then collecting a few sticks that lay about the platform, made up a small fire, not for warmth, but for the sake of the smoke, which would keep off the mosquitos. He wrapped himself in the blankets and sat with his back against the reed wall of the house, smoking thoughtfully.

Arsat came through the doorway with noiseless steps and squatted down by the fire. The white man moved his outstretched legs a little.

"She breathes," said Arsat in a low voice, anticipating the expected question. "She breathes and burns as if with a great fire. She speaks not; she hears not—and burns!"

He paused for a moment, then asked in a quiet, incurious tone—

"Tuan . . . will she die?"

The white man moved his shoulders uneasily and muttered in a hesitating manner—

"If such is her fate."

"No, Tuan," said Arsat, calmly. "If such is my fate. I hear, I see, I wait. I remember . . . Tuan, do you remember the old days? Do you remember my brother?"

"Yes," said the white man. The Malay rose suddenly and went in.

256

The other, sitting still outside, could hear the voice in the hut. Arsat said: "Hear me! Speak!" His words were succeeded by a complete silence. "O Diamelen!" he cried, suddenly. After that cry there was a deep sigh. Arsat came out and sank down again in his old place.

They sat in silence before the fire. There was no sound within the house, there was no sound near them; but far away on the lagoon they could hear the voices of the boatmen ringing fitful and distinct on the calm water. The fire in the bows of the sampan shone faintly in the distance with a hazy red glow. Then it died out. The voices ceased. The land and the water slept invisible, unstirring and mute. It was as though there had been nothing left in the world but the glitter of stars streaming, ceaseless and vain, through the black stillness of the night.

The white man gazed straight before him into the darkness with wide-open eyes. The fear and fascination, the inspiration and the wonder of death—of death near, unavoidable, and unseen, soothed the unrest of his race and stirred the most indistinct, the most intimate of his thoughts. The ever-ready suspicion of evil, the gnawing suspicion that lurks in our hearts, flowed out into the stillness round him—into the stillness profound and dumb, and made it appear untrustworthy and infamous, like the placid and impenetrable mask of an unjustifiable violence. In that fleeting and powerful disturbance of his being the earth enfolded in the starlight peace became a shadowy country of inhuman strife, a battle-field of phantoms terrible and charming, august or ignoble, struggling ardently for the possession of our helpless hearts. An unquiet and mysterious country of inextinguishable desires and fears.

A plaintive murmur rose in the night; a murmur saddening and startling, as if the great solitudes of surrounding woods had tried to whisper into his ear the wisdom of their immense and lofty indifference. Sounds hesitating and vague floated in the air round him, shaped themselves slowly into words; and at last flowed on gently in a murmuring stream of soft and monotonous sentences. He stirred like a man waking up and changed his position slightly. Arsat, motionless and shadowy, sitting with bowed head under the stars, was speaking in a low and dreamy tone—

". . . for where can we lay down the heaviness of our trouble but in a friend's heart? A man must speak of war and of love. You, Tuan, know what war is, and you have seen me in time of danger seek death as other men seek life! A writing may be lost; a lie may

be written; but what the eye has seen is truth and remains in the mind!"

"I remember," said the white man, quietly. Arsat went on with mournful composure—

"Therefore I shall speak to you of love. Speak in the night. Speak before both night and love are gone—and the eye of day looks upon my sorrow and my shame; upon my blackened face; upon my burnt-up heart."

A sigh, short and faint, marked an almost imperceptible pause, and then his words flowed on, without a stir, without a gesture.

"After the time of trouble and war was over and you went away from my country in the pursuit of your desires, which we, men of the islands, cannot understand, I and my brother became again, as we had been before, the sword-bearers of the Ruler. You know we were men of family, belonging to a ruling race, and more fit than any to carry on our right shoulder the emblem of power. And in the time of prosperity Si Dendring showed us favor, as we, in time of sorrow, had showed to him the faithfulness of our courage. It was a time of peace. A time of deer-hunts and cock-fights; of idle talks and foolish squabbles between men whose bellies are full and weapons are rusty. But the sower watched the young rice-shoots grow up without fear, and the traders came and went, departed lean and returned fat into the river of peace. They brought news, too. Brought lies and truth mixed together, so that no man knew when to rejoice and when to be sorry. We heard from them about you also. They had seen you here and had seen you there. And I was glad to hear, for I remembered the stirring times, and I always remembered you, Tuan, till the time came when my eyes could see nothing in the past, because they had looked upon the one who is dying there—in the house."

He stopped to exclaim in an intense whisper, "O Mara bahia! O Calamity!" then went on speaking a little louder:

"There's no worse enemy and no better friend than a brother, Tuan, for one brother knows another, and in perfect knowledge is strength for good or evil. I loved my brother. I went to him and told him that I could see nothing but one face, hear nothing but one voice. He told me: 'Open your heart so that she can see what is in it—and wait. Patience is wisdom. Inchi Midah may die or our Ruler may throw off his fear of a woman!' . . . I waited! . . . You remember the lady with the veiled face, Tuan, and the fear of our

258

Ruler before her cunning and temper. And if she wanted her servant, what could I do? But I fed the hunger of my heart on short glances and stealthy words. I loitered on the path to the bath-houses in the daytime, and when the sun had fallen behind the forest I crept along the jasmine hedges of the women's courtyard. Unseeing, we spoke to one another through the scent of flowers, through the veil of leaves, through the blades of long grass that stood still before our lips; so great was our prudence, so faint was the murmur of our great longing. The time passed swiftly . . . and there were whispers amongst women—and our enemies watched—my brother was gloomy, and I began to think of killing and of a fierce death. . . . We are of a people who take what they want—like you whites. There is a time when a man should forget loyalty and respect. Might and authority are given to rulers, but to all men is given love and strength and courage. My brother said, 'You shall take her from their midst. We are two who are like one.' And I answered, 'Let it be soon, for I find no warmth in sunlight that does not shine upon her.' Our time came when the Ruler and all the great people went to the mouth of the river to fish by torchlight. There were hundreds of boats, and on the white sand, between the water and the forests, dwellings of leaves were built for the households of the Rajahs. The smoke of cooking-fires was like a blue mist of the evening, and many voices rang in it joyfully. While they were making the boats ready to beat up the fish, my brother came to me and said, 'Tonight!' I looked to my weapons, and when the time came our canoe took its place in the circle of boats carrying the torches. The lights blazed on the water, but behind the boats there was darkness. When the shouting began and the excitement made them like mad we dropped out. The water swallowed our fire, and we floated back to the shore that was dark with only here and there the glimmer of embers. We could hear the talk of slave-girls amongst the sheds. Then we found a place deserted and silent. We waited there. She came. She came running along the shore, rapid and leaving no trace, like a leaf driven by the wind into the sea. My brother said gloomily, 'Go and take her; carry her into our boat.' I lifted her in my arms. She panted. Her heart was beating against my breast. I said, 'I take you from those people. You came to the cry of my heart, but my arms take you into my boat against the will of the great!' 'It is right,' said my brother. 'We are men who take what we want and can hold it against many. We should have taken her

in daylight.' I said, 'Let us be off'; for since she was in my boat I began to think of our Ruler's many men. 'Yes. Let us be off,' said my brother. 'We are cast out and this boat is our country now—and the sea is our refuge.' He lingered with his foot on the shore, and I entreated him to hasten, for I remembered the strokes of her heart against my breast and thought that two men cannot withstand a hundred. We left, paddling downstream close to the bank; and as we passed by the creek where they were fishing, the great shouting had ceased, but the murmur of voices was loud like the humming of insects flying at noonday. The boats floated, clustered together, in the red light of torches, under a black roof of smoke; and men talked of their sport. Men that boasted, and praised, and jeered—men that would have been our friends in the morning, but on that night were already our enemies. We paddled swiftly past. We had no more friends in the country of our birth. She sat in the middle of the canoe with covered face; silent as she is now; unseeing as she is now—and I had no regret at what I was leaving because I could hear her breathing close to me—as I can hear her now."

He paused, listened with his ear turned to the doorway, then shook his head and went on:

"My brother wanted to shout the cry of challenge—one cry only —to let the people know we were freeborn robbers who trusted our arms and the great sea. And again I begged him in the name of our love to be silent. Could I not hear her breathing close to me? I knew the pursuit would come quick enough. My brother loved me. He dipped his paddle without a splash. He only said, 'There is a half a man in you now—the other half is in that woman. I can wait. When you are a whole man again, you will come back with me here to shout defiance. We are sons of the same mother.' I made no answer. All my strength and all my spirit were in my hands that held the paddle—for I longed to be with her in a safe place beyond the reach of men's anger and of women's spite. My love was so great, that I thought it could guide me to a country where death was unknown, if I could only escape from Inchi Midah's fury and from our Ruler's sword. We paddled with haste, breathing through our teeth. The blades bit deep into the smooth water. We passed out of the river; we flew in clear channels amongst the shallows. We skirted the black coast; we skirted the sand beaches where the sea speaks in whispers to the land; and the gleam of white sand flashed back past our boat, so swiftly she ran upon the water. We

spoke not. Only once I said, 'Sleep, Diamelen, for soon you may want all your strength.' I heard the sweetness of her voice, but I never turned my head. The sun rose and still we went on. Water fell from my face like rain from a cloud. We flew in the light and heat. I never looked back, but I knew that my brother's eyes, behind me, were looking steadily ahead, for the boat went as straight as a bushman's dart, when it leaves the end of the sumpitan. There was no better paddler, no better steersman than my brother. Many times, together, we had won races in that canoe. But we never had put out our strength as we did then—then, when for the last time we paddled together! There was no braver or stronger man in our country than my brother. I could not spare the strength to turn my head and look at him, but every moment I heard the hiss of his breath getting louder behind me. Still he did not speak. The sun was high. The heat clung to my back like a flame of fire. My ribs were ready to burst, but I could no longer get enough air into my chest. And then I felt I must cry out with my last breath, 'Let us rest!' . . . 'Good!' he answered; and his voice was firm. He was strong. He was brave. He knew not fear and no fatigue . . . My brother!"

A murmur powerful and gentle, a murmur vast and faint; the murmur of trembling leaves, of stirring boughs, ran through the tangled depths of the forests, ran over the starry smoothness of the lagoon, and the water between the piles lapped the slimy timber once with a sudden splash. A breath of warm air touched the two men's faces and passed on with a mournful sound—a breath loud and short like an uneasy sigh of the dreaming earth.

Arsat went on in an even, low voice.

"We ran our canoe on the white beach of a little bay close to a long tongue of land that seemed to bar our road; a long wooded cape going far into the sea. My brother knew that place. Beyond the cape a river has its entrance, and through the jungle of that land there is a narrow path. We made a fire and cooked rice. Then we lay down to sleep on the soft sand in the shade of our canoe, while she watched. No sooner had I closed my eyes than I heard her cry of alarm. We leaped up. The sun was halfway down the sky already, and coming in sight in the opening of the bay we saw a prau manned by many paddlers. We knew it at once; it was one of our Rajah's praus. They were watching the shore, and saw us. They beat the gong, and turned the head of the prau into the bay.

261

I felt my heart become weak within my breast. Diamelen sat on the sand and covered her face. There was no escape by sea. My brother laughed. He had the gun you had given him, Tuan, before you went away, but there was only a handful of powder. He spoke to me quickly: 'Run with her along the path. I shall keep them back, for they have no firearms, and landing in the face of a man with a gun is certain death for some. Run with her. On the other side of that wood there is a fisherman's house—and a canoe. When I have fired all the shots I will follow. I am a great runner, and before they can come up we shall be gone. I will hold out as long as I can, for she is but a woman—that can neither run nor fight, but she has your heart in her weak hands.' He dropped behind the canoe. The prau was coming. She and I ran, and as we rushed along the path I heard shots. My brother fired—once—twice—and the booming of the gong ceased. There was silence behind us. That neck of land is narrow. Before I heard my brother fire the third shot I saw the shelving shore, and I saw the water again; the mouth of a broad river. We crossed a grassy glade. We ran down to the water. I saw a low hut above the black mud, and a small canoe hauled up. I heard another shot behind me. I thought, 'That is his last charge.' We rushed down to the canoe; a man came running from the hut, but I leaped on him, and we rolled together in the mud. Then I got up, and he lay still at my feet. I don't know whether I had killed him or not. I and Diamelen pushed the canoe afloat. I heard yells behind me, and I saw my brother run across the glade. Many men were bounding after him. I took her in my arms and threw her into the boat, then leaped in myself. When I looked back I saw that my brother had fallen. He fell and was up again, but the men were closing round him. He shouted, 'I am coming!' The men were close to him. I looked. Many men. Then I looked at her. Tuan, I pushed the canoe! I pushed it into deep water. She was kneeling forward looking at me, and I said, "Take your paddle,' while I struck the water with mine. Tuan, I heard him cry. I heard him cry my name twice; and I heard voices shouting, 'Kill! Strike!' I never turned back. I heard him calling my name again with a great shriek, as when life is going out together with the voice—and I never turned my head. My own name! . . . My brother; Three times he called—but I was not afraid of life. Was she not there in that canoe? And could I not with her find a country where death is forgotten—where death is unknown!"

The white man sat up. Arsat rose and stood, an indistinct and silent figure above the dying embers of the fire. Over the lagoon a mist drifting and low had crept, erasing slowly the glittering images of the stars. And now a great expanse of white vapor covered the land: it flowed cold and gray in the darkness, eddied in noiseless whirls round the tree-trunks and about the platform of the house, which seemed to float upon a restless and impalpable illusion of a sea. Only far away the tops of the trees stood outlined on the twinkle of heaven, like a somber and forbidding shore—a coast deceptive, pitiless and black.

Arsat's voice vibrated loudly in the profound peace.

"I had her there! I had her! To get her I would have faced all mankind. But I had her—and—"

His words went out ringing into the empty distances. He paused, and seemed to listen to them dying away very far—beyond help and beyond recall. Then he said quietly—

"Tuan, I loved my brother."

A breath of wind made him shiver. High above his head, high above the silent sea of mist the drooping leaves of the palms rattled together with a mournful and expiring sound. The white man stretched his legs. His chin rested on his chest, and he murmured sadly without lifting his head—

"We all love our brothers."

Arsat burst out with an intense whispering violence—

"What did I care who died? I wanted peace in my own heart."

He seemed to hear a stir in the house—listened—then stepped in noiselessly. The white man stood up. A breeze was coming in fitful puffs. The stars shone paler as if they had retreated into the frozen depths of immense space. After a chill gust of wind there were a few seconds of perfect calm and absolute silence. Then from behind the black and wavy line of the forest a column of golden light shot up into the heavens and spread over the semicircle of the eastern horizon. The sun had risen. The mist lifted, broke into drifting patches, vanished into thin flying wreaths; and the unveiled lagoon lay, polished and black, in the heavy shadows at the foot of the wall of trees. A white eagle rose over it with a slanting and ponderous flight, reached the clear sunshine and appeared dazzlingly brilliant for a moment, then soaring higher, became a dark and motionless speck before it vanished into the blue as if it had left the earth forever. The white man, standing gazing upwards before

the doorway, heard in the hut a confused and broken murmur of distracted words ending with a loud groan. Suddenly Arsat stumbled out with outstretched hands, shivered, and stood still for some time with fixed eyes. Then he said—

"She burns no more."

Before his face the sun showed its edge above the tree-tops rising steadily. The breeze freshened; a great brilliance burst upon the lagoon, sparkled on the rippling water. The forests came out of the clear shadows of the morning, became distinct, as if they had rushed nearer—to stop short in a great stir of leaves, of nodding boughs, of swaying branches. In the merciless sunshine the whisper of unconscious life grew louder, speaking in an incomprehensible voice round the dumb darkness of that human sorrow. Arsat's eyes wandered slowly, then stared at the rising sun.

"I can see nothing," he said half aloud to himself.

"There is nothing," said the white man, moving to the edge of the platform and waving his hand to his boat. A shout came faintly over the lagoon and the sampan began to glide towards the abode of the friend of ghosts.

"If you want to come with me, I will wait all the morning," said the white man, looking away upon the water.

"No, Tuan," said Arsat, softly. "I shall not eat or sleep in this house, but I must first see my road. Now I can see nothing—see nothing! There is no light and no peace in the world; but there is death—death for many. We are sons of the same mother—and I left him in the midst of enemies; but I am going back now."

He drew a long breath and went on in a dreamy tone:

"In a little while I shall see clear enough to strike—to strike. But she has died, and . . . now . . . darkness."

He flung his arms wide open, let them fall along his body, then stood still with unmoved face and stony eyes, staring at the sun. The white man got down into his canoe. The poles ran smartly along the sides of the boat, looking over their shoulders at the beginning of a weary journey. High in the stern, his head muffled up in white rags, the juragan sat moody, letting his paddle trail in the water. The white man, leaning with both arms over the grass roof of the little cabin, looked back at the shining ripple of the boat's wake. Before the sampan passed out of the lagoon into the creek he lifted his eyes. Arsat had not moved. He stood lonely in the searching sunshine; and he looked beyond the great light of a cloudless day into the darkness of a world of illusions.

JAMES FENIMORE COOPER

JAMES FENIMORE COOPER (American, 1789-1851). The great romancer of the American frontier. Produced more than 50 books: novels, travel sketches, social criticism. Popular reputation rests on sea stories (*The Pilot*), and Leatherstocking tales (*The Last of the Mohicans, The Pathfinder, The Deerslayer*). Labored zealously in 19th century to further international understanding of American democracy.

THE ARIEL ON THE SHOALS

THE SEA was becoming more agitated, and the violence of the wind was gradually increasing. The latter no longer whistled amid the cordage of the vessel, but it seemed to howl surlily as it passed the complicated machinery that the frigate obtruded on its path. An endless succession of white surges rose above the heavy billows, and the very air was glittering with the light that was disengaged from the ocean. The ship yielded each moment more and more before the storm, and, in less than half an hour from the time that she had lifted her anchor, she was driven along with tremendous fury by the full power of a gale of wind. Still, the hardy and experienced mariners who directed her movements, held her to the course that was necessary to their preservation, and still Griffith gave forth, when directed by their unknown pilot, those orders that turned her in the narrow channel where safety was alone to be found.

So far the performance of his duty appeared easy to the stranger, and he gave the required directions in those still, calm tones that formed so remarkable a contrast to the responsibility of his situation. But when the land was becoming dim, in distance as well as darkness, and the agitated sea was only to be discovered as it swept by them in foam, he broke in upon the monotonous roaring of the tempest with the sounds of his voice, seeming to shake off his apathy and rouse himself to the occasion.

"Now is the time to watch her closely, Mr. Griffith," he cried; "here we get the true tide and the real danger. Place the best quarter-master of your ship in those chains, and let an officer stand by him and see that he gives us the right water."

"I will take that office on myself," said the captain; "pass a light into the weather main-chains."

"Stand by your braces!" exclaimed the pilot with startling quickness. "Heave away that lead!"

These preparations taught the crew to expect the crisis, and every officer and man stood in fearful silence at his assigned station awaiting the issue of the trial. Even the quarter-master at the cun gave out his orders to the men at the wheel in deeper and hoarser tones than usual, as if anxious not to disturb the quiet and order of the vessel.

While this deep expectation pervaded the frigate, the piercing cry of the leadsman, as he called, "By the mark seven!" rose above the tempest, crossed over the decks, and appeared to pass away to leeward, borne on the blast like the warnings of some water-spirit.

" 'Tis well," returned the pilot, calmly; "try it again."

The short pause was succeeded by another cry, "and a half-five!"

"She shoals! she shoals!" exclaimed Griffith; "keep her a good full."

"Ay! you must hold the vessel in command, now," said the pilot, with those cool tones that are most appalling in critical moments, because they seem to denote most preparation and care.

The third call of "By the deep four!" was followed by a prompt direction from the stranger to tack.

Griffith seemed to emulate the coolness of the pilot, in issuing the necessary orders to execute this manœuvre.

The vessel rose slowly from the inclined position into which she had been forced by the tempest, and the sails were shaking violently, as if to release themselves from their confinement while the ship stemmed the billows, when the well-known voice of the sailing-master was heard shouting from the forecastle—"Breakers! breakers, dead ahead!"

This appalling sound seemed yet to be lingering about the ship, when a second voice cried—"Breakers on our lee-bow!"

"We are in a bight of the shoals, Mr. Gray," said the commander. "She loses her way; perhaps an anchor might hold her."

"Clear away that best-bower!" shouted Griffith through his trumpet.

"Hold on!" cried the pilot, in a voice that reached the very hearts of all who heard him; "hold on every thing."

The young man turned fiercely to the daring stranger who thus defied the discipline of his vessel, and at once demanded—"Who is it that dares to countermand my orders?—is it not enough that you run the ship into danger, but you must interfere to keep her there? If another word—"

"Peace, Mr. Griffith," interrupted the captain, bending from the rigging, his gray locks blowing about in the wind, and adding a look of wildness to the haggard face that he exhibited by the light of his lantern; "yield the trumpet to Mr. Gray; he alone can save us."

Griffith threw his speaking-trumpet on the deck, and as he walked proudly away, muttered in bitterness of feeling—"Then all is lost, indeed, and, among the rest, the foolish hopes with which I visited this coast."

There was, however, no time for reply; the ship had been rapidly running into the wind, and, as the efforts of the crew were paralyzed by the contradictory orders they had heard, she gradually lost her way, and in a few seconds all her sails were taken aback.

Before the crew understood their situation, the pilot had applied the trumpet to his mouth, and, in a voice that rose above the tempest, he thundered forth his orders. Each command was given distinctly, and with a precision that showed him to be master of his profession. The helm was kept fast, the head yards swung up heavily against the wind, and the vessel was soon whirling round on her heel with a retrograde movement.

Griffith was too much of a seaman not to perceive that the pilot had seized, with a perception almost intuitive, the only method that promised to extricate the vessel from her situation. He was young, impetuous and proud, but he was also generous. Forgetting his resentment and his mortification, he rushed forward among the men, and, by his presence and example, added certainty to the experiment. The ship fell off slowly before the gale, and bowed her yards nearly to the water, as she felt the blast pouring its fury on her broadsides while the surly waves beat violently against her stern, as if in reproach at departing from her usual manner of moving.

The voice of the pilot, however, was still heard, steady and calm, and yet so clear and high as to reach every ear; and the obedient seamen whirled the yards at his bidding in despite of the tempest, as if they handled the toys of their childhood. When the ship had fallen off dead before the wind, her head sails were shaken, her aft-yards trimmed, and her helm shifted before she had time to run upon the danger that had threatened, as well to leeward as to windward. The beautiful fabric, obedient to her government, threw her bows up gracefully toward the wind again, and, as her sails were trimmed, moved out from amongst the dangerous shoals in

which she had been embayed, as steadily and swiftly as she had approached them.

A moment of breathless astonishment succeeded the accomplishment of this nice manœuvre, but there was no time for the usual expressions of surprise. The stranger still held the trumpet, and continued to lift his voice amid the howlings of the blast, whenever prudence or skill directed any change in the management of the ship. For an hour longer there was a fearful struggle for their preservation, the channel becoming at each step more complicated, and the shoals thickening around the mariners on every side. The lead was cast rapidly, and the quick eye of the pilot seemed to pierce the darkness with a keenness of vision that exceeded human power. It was apparent to all in the vessel, that they were under the guidance of one who understood the navigation thoroughly, and their exertions kept pace with their reviving confidence. Again and again the frigate appeared to be rushing blindly on shoals, where the sea was covered with foam, and where destruction would have been as sudden as it was certain, when the clear voice of the stranger was heard warning them of the danger and inciting them to their duty. The vessel was implicitly yielding to his government, and during those anxious moments, when she was dashing the waters aside, throwing the spray over her enormous yards, each ear would listen eagerly for those sounds that had obtained a command over the crew that can only be acquired, under such circumstances, by great steadiness and consummate skill. The ship was recovering from the inaction of changing her course in one of those critical tacks that she had made so often when the pilot for the first time addressed the commander of the frigate, who still continued to superintend the all-important duty of the leadsman.

"Now is the pinch," he said; "and if the ship behaves well, we are safe—but if otherwise, all we have yet done will be useless."

The veteran seaman whom he addressed left the chains at this portentous notice, and, calling to his first lieutenant, required of the stranger an explanation of his warning.

"See you yon light on the southern headland?" returned the pilot; "you may know it from the star near it by its sinking, at times, in the ocean. Now observe the hummock a little north of it, looking like a shadow on the horizon—'tis a hill far inland. If we keep that light open from the hill, we shall do well—but if not, we surely go to pieces."

"Let us tack again!" exclaimed the lieutenant.

The pilot shook his head, as he replied—"There is no more tacking or box-hauling to be done to-night. We have barely room to pass out of the shoals on this course, and if we can weather the 'Devil's Grip,' we clear their outermost point—but if not, as I said before, there is but an alternative."

"If we had beaten out the way we entered," exclaimed Griffith, "we should have done well."

"Say, also, if the tide would have let us do so," returned the pilot calmly. "Gentlemen, we must be prompt; we have but a mile to go, and the ship appears to fly. That topsail is not enough to keep her up to the wind; we want both jib and mainsail."

" 'Tis a perilous thing to loosen canvas in such a tempest!" observed the doubtful captain.

"It must be done," returned the collected stranger; "we perish without—see! the light already touches the edge of the hummock; the sea casts us to leeward!"

"It shall be done!" cried Griffith, seizing the trumpet from the hand of the pilot.

The orders of the lieutenant were executed almost as soon as issued, and, every thing being ready, the enormous folds of the mainsail were trusted loose to the blast. There was an instant when the result was doubtful; the tremendous threshing of the heavy sails seeming to bid defiance to all restraint, shaking the ship to her centre; but art and strength prevailed, and gradually the canvas was distended, and, bellying as it filled, was drawn down to its usual place by the power of a hundred men. The vessel yielded to this immense addition of force, and bowed before it like a reed bending to a breeze. But the success of the measure was announced by a joyful cry from the stranger that seemed to burst from his inmost soul.

"She feels it! she springs her luff! observe," he said, "the light opens from the hummock already; if she will only bear her canvas, we shall go clear!"

A report like that of a cannon interrupted his exclamation, and something resembling a white cloud was seen drifting before the wind from the head of the ship, till it was driven into the gloom far to leeward.

" 'Tis the jib blown from the bolt-ropes," said the commander of the frigate. "This is no time to spread light duck—but the mainsail may stand it yet."

269

"The sail would laugh at a tornado," returned the lieutenant; "but that mast springs like a piece of steel."

"Silence all!" cried the pilot. "Now, gentlemen, we shall soon know our fate. Let her luff—luff you can!"

This warning effectually closed all discourse, and the hardy mariners, knowing that they had already done all in the power of man to insure their safety, stood in breathless anxiety awaiting the result. At a short distance ahead of them, the whole ocean was white with foam, and the waves, instead of rolling on in regular succession, appeared to be tossing about in mad gambols. A single streak of dark billows, not half a cable's length in width, could be discerned running into this chaos of water; but it was soon lost to the eye amid the confusion of the disturbed element. Along this narrow path the vessel moved more heavily than before, being brought so near the wind as to keep her sails touching. The pilot silently proceeded to the wheel, and with his own hands he undertook the steerage of the ship. No noise proceeded from the frigate to interrupt the horrid tumult of the ocean, and she entered the channel among the breakers with the silence of a desperate calmness. Twenty times, as the foam rolled away to leeward, the crew were on the eve of uttering their joy, as they supposed the vessel past the danger; but breaker after breaker would still rise before them, following each other into the general mass to check their exultation. Occasionally the fluttering of the sails would be heard; and when the looks of the startled seamen were turned to the wheel, they beheld the stranger grasping its spokes, with his quick eye glancing from the water to the canvas. At length the ship reached a point where she appeared to be rushing directly into the jaws of destruction, when suddenly her course was changed, and her head receded rapidly from the wind. At the same instant the voice of the pilot was heard shouting—"Square away the yards!—in mainsail!"

A general burst from the crew echoed, "Square away the yards!" and quick as thought the frigate was seen gliding along the channel before the wind. The eye had hardly time to dwell on the foam, which seemed like clouds driving in the heavens, and directly the gallant vessel issued from her perils, and rose and fell on the heavy waves of the open sea.

STEPHEN CRANE

STEPHEN CRANE (American, 1871-1900). Great realistic writer, who died
of tuberculosis at 28, after writing greatest Civil War novel—*The Red Badge
of Courage.* Brief life filled with illness and trouble; he was much maligned
as journalist and foreign correspondent. Other masterpieces of realism:
The Open Boat and *Maggie: A Girl of the Streets,* works far in advance of
their time.

THE BRIDE COMES TO YELLOW SKY

I

THE great pullman was whirling onward with such dignity of
motion that a glance from the window seemed simply to prove
that the plains of Texas were pouring eastward. Vast flats of green
grass, dull-hued spaces of mesquit and cactus, little groups of frame
houses, woods of light and tender trees, all were sweeping into
the east, sweeping over the horizon, a precipice.

A newly married pair had boarded this coach at San Antonio.
The man's face was reddened from many days in the wind and
sun, and a direct result of his new black clothes was that his brick-
coloured hands were constantly performing in a most conscious
fashion. From time to time he looked down respectfully at his attire.
He sat with a hand on each knee, like a man waiting in a barber's
shop. The glances he devoted to other passengers were furtive and
shy.

The bride was not pretty, nor was she very young. She wore a
dress of blue cashmere, with small reservations of velvet here and
there, and with steel buttons abounding. She continually twisted
her head to regard her puff sleeves, very stiff, straight, and high.
They embarrassed her. It was quite apparent that she had cooked,
and that she expected to cook, dutifully. The blushes caused by the
careless scrutiny of some passengers as she had entered the car
were strange to see upon this plain, under-class countenance, which
was drawn in placid, almost emotionless lines.

They were evidently very happy. "Ever been in a parlour-car
before?" he asked, smiling with delight.

"No," she answered; "I never was. It's fine, ain't it?"

"Great! And then after a while we'll go forward to the diner,
and get a big lay-out. Finest meal in the world. Charge a dollar."

"Oh, do they?" cried the bride. "Charge a dollar? Why, that's
too much—for us—ain't it, Jack?"

"Not this trip, anyhow," he answered bravely. "We're going to go the whole thing."

Later he explained to her about the trains. "You see, it's a thousand miles from one end of Texas to the other; and this train runs right across it, and never stops but four times." He had the pride of an owner. He pointed out to her the dazzling fittings of the coach; and in truth her eyes opened wider as she contemplated the sea-green figured velvet, the shining brass, silver, and glass, the wood that gleamed as darkly brilliant as the surface of a pool of oil. At one end a bronze figure sturdily held a support for a separated chamber, and at convenient places on the ceiling were frescos in olive and silver.

To the minds of the pair, their surroundings reflected the glory of their marriage that morning in San Antonio; this was the environment of their new estate; and the man's face in particular beamed with an elation that made him appear ridiculous to the negro porter. This individual at times surveyed them from afar with an amused and superior grin. On other occasions he bullied them with skill in ways that did not make it exactly plain to them that they were being bullied. He subtly used all the manners of the most unconquerable kind of snobbery. He oppressed them; but of this oppression they had small knowledge, and they speedily forgot that infrequently a number of travellers covered them with stares of derisive enjoyment. Historically there was supposed to be something infinitely humorous in their situation.

"We are due in Yellow Sky at 3:42," he said, looking tenderly into her eyes.

"Oh, are we?" she said, as if she had not been aware of it. To evince surprise at her husband's statement was part of her wifely amiability. She took from a pocket a little silver watch; and as she held it before her, and stared at it with a frown of attention, the new husband's face shone.

"I bought it in San Anton' from a friend of mine," he told her gleefully.

"It's seventeen minutes past twelve," she said, looking up at him with a kind of shy and clumsy coquetry. A passenger, noting this play, grew excessively sardonic, and winked at himself in one of the numerous mirrors.

At last they went to the dining-car. Two rows of negro waiters, in glowing white suits, surveyed their entrance with the interest, and also the equanimity, of men who had been forewarned. The

272

pair fell to the lot of a waiter who happened to feel pleasure in steering them through their meal. He viewed them with the manner of a fatherly pilot, his countenance radiant with benevolence. The patronage, entwined with the ordinary deference, was not plain to them. And yet, as they returned to their coach, they showed in their faces a sense of escape.

To the left, miles down a long purple slope, was a little ribbon of mist where moved the keening Rio Grande. The train was approaching it at an angle, and the apex was Yellow Sky. Presently it was apparent that, as the distance from Yellow Sky grew shorter, the husband became commensurately restless. His brick-red hands were more insistent in their prominence. Occasionally he was even rather absent-minded and far-away when the bride leaned forward and addressed him.

As a matter of truth, Jack Potter was beginning to find the shadow of a deed weigh upon him like a leaden slab. He, the town marshal of Yellow Sky, a man known, liked, and feared in his corner, a prominent person, had gone to San Antonio to meet a girl he believed he loved, and there, after the usual prayers, had actually induced her to marry him, without consulting Yellow Sky for any part of the transaction. He was now bringing his bride before an innocent and unsuspecting community.

Of course people in Yellow Sky married as it pleased them, in accordance with a general custom; but such was Potter's thought of his duty to his friends, or of their idea of his duty, or of an unspoken form which does not control men in these matters, that he felt he was heinous. He had committed an extraordinary crime. Face to face with this girl in San Antonio, and spurred by his sharp impulse, he had gone headlong over all the social hedges. At San Antonio he was like a man hidden in the dark. A knife to sever any friendly duty, any form, was easy to his hand in that remote city. But the hour of Yellow Sky—the hour of daylight—was approaching.

He knew full well that his marriage was an important thing to his town. It could only be exceeded by the burning of the new hotel. His friends could not forgive him. Frequently he had reflected on the advisability of telling them by telegraph, but a new cowardice had been upon him. He feared to do it. And now the train was hurrying him toward a scene of amazement, glee, and reproach. He glanced out of the window at the line of haze swinging slowly in toward the train.

Yellow Sky had a kind of brass band, which played painfully, to the delight of the populace. He laughed without heart as he thought of it. If the citizens could dream of his prospective arrival with his bride, they would parade the band at the station and escort them, amid cheers and laughing congratulations, to his adobe home.

He resolved that he would use all the devices of speed and plains-craft in making the journey from the station to his house. Once within that safe citadel, he could issue some sort of vocal bulletin, and then not go among the citizens until they had time to wear off a little of their enthusiasm.

The bride looked anxiously at him. "What's worrying you, Jack?"

He laughed again. "I'm not worrying, girl; I'm only thinking of Yellow Sky."

She flushed in comprehension.

A sense of mutual guilt invaded their minds and developed a finer tenderness. They looked at each other with eyes softly aglow. But Potter often laughed the same nervous laugh; the flush upon the bride's face seemed quite permanent.

The traitor to the feelings of Yellow Sky narrowly watched the speeding landscape. "We're nearly there," he said.

Presently the porter came and announced the proximity of Potter's home. He held a brush in his hand, and, with all his airy superiority gone, he brushed Potter's new clothes as the latter slowly turned this way and that way. Potter fumbled out a coin and gave it to the porter, as he had seen others do. It was a heavy and muscle-bound business, as that of a man shoeing his first horse.

The porter took their bag, and as the train began to slow they moved forward to the hooded platform of the car. Presently the two engines and their long string of coaches rushed into the station of Yellow Sky.

"They have to take water here," said Potter, from a constricted throat and in mournful cadence, as one announcing death. Before the train stopped his eye had swept the length of the platform, and he was glad and astonished to see there was none upon it but the station-agent, who, with a slightly hurried and anxious air, was walking toward the water-tanks. When the train had halted, the porter alighted first, and placed in position a little temporary step.

"Come on, girl," said Potter, hoarsely. As he helped her down they each laughed on a false note. He took the bag from the negro,

and bade his wife cling to his arm. As they slunk rapidly away, his hang-dog glance perceived that they were unloading the two trunks, and also that the station-agent, far ahead near the baggage-car, had turned and was running toward him, making gestures. He laughed, and groaned as he laughed, when he noted the first effect of his marital bliss upon Yellow Sky. He gripped his wife's arm firmly to his side, and they fled. Behind them the porter stood, chuckling fatuously.

II

The California express on the Southern Railway was due at Yellow Sky in twenty-one minutes. There were six men at the bar of the Weary Gentleman saloon. One was a drummer who talked a great deal and rapidly; three were Texans who did not care to talk at that time; and two were Mexican sheep-herders, who did not talk as a general practice in the Weary Gentleman saloon. The barkeeper's dog lay on the board walk that crossed in front of the door. His head was on his paws, and he glanced drowsily here and there with the constant vigilance of a dog that is kicked on occasion. Across the sandy street were some vivid green grass-plots, so wonderful in appearance, amid the sands that burned near them in a blazing sun, that they caused a doubt in the mind. They exactly resembled the grass mats used to represent lawns on the stage. At the cooler end of the railway station, a man without a coat sat in a tilted chair and smoked his pipe. The fresh-cut bank of the Rio Grande circled near the town, and there could be seen beyond it a great plum-coloured plain of mesquit.

Save for the busy drummer and his companions in the saloon, Yellow Sky was dozing. The new-comer leaned gracefully upon the bar, and recited many tales with the confidence of a bard who has come upon a new field.

"—and at the moment that the old man fell downstairs with the bureau in his arms, the old woman was coming up with two scuttles of coal, and of course—"

The drummer's tale was interrupted by a young man who suddenly appeared in the open door. He cried: "Scratchy Wilson's drunk, and has turned loose with both hands." The two Mexicans at once set down their glasses and faded out of the rear entrance of the saloon.

275

The drummer, innocent and jocular, answered: "All right, old man. S'pose he has? Come in and have a drink, anyhow."

But the information had made such an obvious cleft in every skull in the room that the drummer was obliged to see its importance. All had become instantly solemn. "Say," said he, mystified, "what is this?" His three companions made the introductory gesture of eloquent speech; but the young man at the door forestalled them.

"It means, my friend," he answered, as he came into the saloon, "that for the next two hours this town won't be a health resort."

The barkeeper went to the door, and locked and barred it; reaching out of the window, he pulled in heavy wooden shutters, and barred them. Immediately a solemn, chapellike gloom was upon the place. The drummer was looking from one to another.

"But say," he cried, "what is this, anyhow? You don't mean there is going to be a gun-fight?"

"Don't know whether there'll be a fight or not," answered one man, grimly; "but there'll be some shootin'—some good shootin'."

The young man who had warned them waved his hand. "Oh, there'll be a fight fast enough, if any one wants it. Anybody can get a fight out there in the street. There's a fight just waiting."

The drummer seemed to be swayed between the interest of a foreigner and a perception of personal danger.

"What did you say his name was?" he asked.

"Scratchy Wilson," they answered in chorus.

"And will he kill anybody? What are you going to do? Does this happen often? Does he rampage around like this once a week or so? Can he break in that door?"

"No; he can't break down that door," replied the barkeeper. "He's tried it three times. But when he comes you'd better lay down on the floor, stranger. He's dead sure to shoot at it, and a bullet may come through."

Thereafter the drummer kept a strict eye upon the door. The time had not yet been called for him to hug the floor, but, as a minor precaution, he sidled near to the wall. "Will he kill anybody?" he said again.

The men laughed low and scornfully at the question.

"He's out to shoot, and he's out for trouble. Don't see any good in experimentin' with him."

"But what do you do in a case like this? What do you do?"

A man responded: "Why, he and Jack Potter—"

"But," in chorus the other men interrupted, "Jack Potter's in San Anton'."

"Well, who is he? What's he got to do with it?"

"Oh, he's the town marshal. He goes out and fights Scratchy when he gets on one of these tears."

"Wow!" said the drummer, mopping his brow. "Nice job he's got."

The voices had toned away to mere whisperings. The drummer wished to ask further questions, which were born of an increasing anxiety and bewilderment; but when he attempted them, the men merely looked at him in irritation and motioned him to remain silent. A tense waiting hush was upon them. In the deep shadows of the room their eyes shone as they listened for sounds from the street. One man made three gestures at the barkeeper; and the latter, moving like a ghost, handed him a glass and a bottle. The man poured a full glass of whisky in a swallow, and turned again toward the door in immovable silence. The drummer saw that the barkeeper, without a sound, had taken a Winchester from beneath the bar. Later he saw this individual beckoning to him, so he tiptoed across the room.

"You better come with me back of the bar."

"No, thanks," said the drummer, perspiring; "I'd rather be where I can make a break for the back door."

Whereupon the man of bottles made a kindly but peremptory gesture. The drummer obeyed it, and, finding himself seated on a box with his head below the level of the bar, balm was laid upon his soul at sight of various zinc and copper fittings that bore a resemblance to armour-plate. The barkeeper took a seat comfortably upon an adjacent box.

"You see," he whispered, "this here Scratchy Wilson is a wonder with a gun—a perfect wonder; and when he goes on the war-trail, we hunt our holes—naturally. He's about the last one of the old gang that used to hang out along the river here. He's a terror when he's drunk. When he's sober he's all right—kind of simple—wouldn't hurt a fly—nicest fellow in town. But when he's drunk—whoo!"

There were periods of stillness. "I wish Jack Potter was back from San Anton'," said the barkeeper. "He shot Wilson up once—in the leg—and he would sail in and pull out the kinks in this thing."

Presently they heard from a distance the sound of a shot, followed by three wild yowls. It instantly removed a bond from the men in the darkened saloon. There was a shuffling of feet. They looked at each other. "Here he comes," they said.

III

A man in a maroon-coloured flannel shirt, which had been purchased for purposes of decoration, and made principally by some Jewish women on the East Side of New York, rounded a corner and walked into the middle of the main street of Yellow Sky. In either hand the man held a long, heavy, blue-black revolver. Often he yelled, and these cries rang through a semblance of a deserted village, shrilly flying over the roofs in a volume that seemed to have no relation to the ordinary vocal strength of a man. It was as if the surrounding stillness formed the arch of a tomb over him. These cries of ferocious challenge rang against walls of silence. And his boots had red tops with gilded imprints, of the kind beloved in winter by little sledding boys on the hillsides of New England.

The man's face flamed in a rage begot of whisky. His eyes, rolling, and yet keen for ambush, hunted the still doorways and windows. He walked with the creeping movement of the midnight cat. As it occurred to him, he roared menacing information. The long revolvers in his hands were as easy as straws; they were moved with an electric swiftness. The little fingers of each hand played sometimes in a musician's way. Plain from the low collar of the shirt, the cords of his neck straightened and sank, straightened and sank, as passion moved him. The only sounds were his terrible invitations. The calm adobes preserved their demeanour at the passing of this small thing in the middle of the street.

There was no offer of fight—no offer of fight. The man called to the sky. There were no attractions. He bellowed and fumed and swayed his revolvers here and everywhere.

The dog of the barkeeper of the Weary Gentleman saloon had not appreciated the advance of events. He yet lay dozing in front of his master's door. At sight of the dog, the man paused and raised his revolver humorously. At sight of the man, the dog sprang up and walked diagonally away, with a sullen head, and growling. The man yelled, and the dog broke into a gallop. As it was about to enter an alley, there was a loud noise, a whistling, and something spat the ground directly before it. The dog screamed, and, wheeling in terror, galloped headlong in a new direction. Again there was

a noise, a whistling, and sand was kicked viciously before it. Fear-stricken, the dog turned and flurried like an animal in a pen. The man stood laughing, his weapons at his hips.

Ultimately the man was attracted by the closed door of the Weary Gentleman saloon. He went to it and, hammering with a revolver, demanded drink.

The door remaining imperturbable, he picked a bit of paper from the walk, and nailed it to the framework with a knife. He then turned his back contemptuously upon this popular resort and, walking to the opposite side of the street and spinning there on his heel quickly and lithely, fired at the bit of paper. He missed it by a half-inch. He swore at himself, and went away. Later he comfortably fusilladed the windows of his most intimate friend. The man was playing with this town; it was a toy for him.

But still there was no offer of fight. The name of Jack Potter, his ancient antagonist, entered his mind, and he concluded that it would be a glad thing if he should go to Potter's house, and by bombardment induce him to come out and fight. He moved in the direction of his desire, chanting Apache scalp-music.

When he arrived at it, Potter's house presented the same still front as had the other adobes. Taking up a strategic position, the man howled a challenge. But this house regarded him as might a great stone god. It gave no sign. After a decent wait, the man howled further challenges, mingling with them wonderful epithets.

Presently there came the spectacle of a man churning himself into deepest rage over the immobility of a house. He fumed at it as the winter wind attacks a prairie cabin in the North. To the distance there should have gone the sound of a tumult like the fighting of two hundred Mexicans. As necessity bade him, he paused for breath or to reload his revolvers.

IV

Potter and his bride walked sheepishly and with speed. Sometimes they laughed together shamefacedly and low.

"Next corner, dear," he said finally.

They put forth the efforts of a pair walking bowed against a strong wind. Potter was about to raise a finger to point the first appearance of the new home when, as they circled the corner, they came face to face with a man in a maroon-coloured shirt, who was feverishly pushing cartridges into a large revolver. Upon the instant the man dropped his revolver to the ground and, like lightning,

279

whipped another from its holster. The second weapon was aimed at the bridegroom's chest.

There was a silence. Potter's mouth seemed to be merely a grave for his tongue. He exhibited an instinct to at once loosen his arm from the woman's grip, and he dropped the bag to the sand. As for the bride, her face had gone as yellow as old cloth. She was a slave to hideous rites, gazing at the apparitional snake.

The two men faced each other at a distance of three paces. He of the revolver smiled with a new and quiet ferocity.

"Tried to sneak up on me," he said. "Tried to sneak up on me!" His eyes grew more baleful. As Potter made a slight movement, the man thrust his revolver venomously forward. "No; don't you do it, Jack Potter. Don't you move a finger toward a gun just yet. Don't you move an eyelash. The time has come for me to settle with you, and I'm goin' to do it my own way, and loaf along with no interferin'. So if you don't want a gun bent on you, just mind what I tell you."

Potter looked at his enemy, "I ain't got a gun on me, Scratchy," he said. "Honest, I ain't." He was stiffening and steadying, but yet somewhere at the back of his mind a vision of the Pullman floated: the sea-green figured velvet, the shining brass, silver, and glass, the wood that gleamed as darkly brilliant as the surface of a pool of oil—all the glory of the marriage, the environment of the new estate. "You know I fight when it comes to fighting, Scratchy Wilson; but I ain't got a gun on me. You'll have to do all the shootin' yourself."

His enemy's face went livid. He stepped forward, and lashed his weapon to and fro before Potter's chest. "Don't you tell me you ain't got no gun on you, you whelp. Don't tell me no lie like that. There ain't a man in Texas ever seen you without no gun. Don't take me for no kid." His eyes blazed with light, and his throat worked like a pump.

"I ain't takin' you for no kid," answered Potter. His heels had not moved an inch backward. "I'm takin' you for a damn fool. I tell you I ain't got a gun, and I ain't. If you're goin' to shoot me up, you better begin now; you'll never get a chance like this again."

So much enforced reasoning had told on Wilson's rage; he was calmer. "If you ain't got a gun, why ain't you got a gun?" he sneered. "Been to Sunday-school?"

"I ain't got a gun because I've just come from San Anton' with my wife. I'm married," said Potter. "And if I'd thought there was

going to be any galoots like you prowling around when I brought my wife home, I'd had a gun, and don't you forget it."

"Married!" said Scratchy, not at all comprehending.

"Yes, married. I'm married," said Potter, distinctly.

"Married?" said Scratchy. Seemingly for the first time, he saw the drooping, drowning woman at the other man's side. "No!" he said. He was like a creature allowed a glimpse of another world. He moved a pace backward, and his arm, with the revolver, dropped to his side. "Is this the lady?" he asked.

"Yes; this is the lady," answered Potter.

There was another period of silence.

"Well," said Wilson at last, slowly, "I s'pose it's all off now."

"It's all off if you say so, Scratchy. You know I didn't make the trouble." Potter lifted his valise.

"Well, I 'low it's off, Jack," said Wilson. He was looking at the ground. "Married!" He was not a student of chivalry; it was merely that in the presence of this foreign condition he was a simple child of the earlier plains. He picked up his starboard revolver, and, placing both weapons in their holsters, he went away. His feet made funnel-shaped tracks in the heavy sand.

D

DANDIN

DANDIN (Sanskrit, *ca.* 7th century A.D.). Colorful and picturesque Sanskrit author of a picaresque novel, *Dasakumāracharita (The Adventures of the Ten Princes)*. The play *Mricchakatika* is attributed to him by some.

THE COURTESAN'S MOTHER

THESE are the aspects on which a courtesan's mother has to concentrate her attention in rearing up her child, namely, to apply perfumed cosmetics to the limbs of the girl even from her childhood; to put her on such nutritious diet as would supply her with enough bodily radiance, strength, complexion and wits as well as her normal appetite and digestion; to keep even the man who gave her life from visiting her frequently after her fifth year of life; to celebrate her birthdays and other events of her life in adequate style; to initiate her into the arts of love-making with all their accessory aids; to familiarise her with the secrets of the arts of dancing, music, instrumental play, histrionics, painting and the culinary art; to teach her how to prepare sandal paste and flower pigments as well as to gain efficiency in calligraphy and conversational graces; to supply her with that amount of acquaintance of the Sastras such as grammar, logic and philosophy so as to enable her to carry on discussions without showing want of information; to guide her in the science of living; to teach her knowledge of games and dice-throwing as well as equip her with the necessary zest for watching cock- and bull-fights; to induce her to learn from adept and experienced gallants the trick of amorous wooing; to decorate her person attractively on occasions of festival and public carnival and to send her out attended upon by a proper retinue; to make her ingratiate herself in the favour of men of influence and rank in order to suc-

282

ceed in her performances before audiences; to propitiate the virtuosos in the various arts in order to gain a favourable atmosphere for
her own excursions into them; to make astrologers and palmists
spread her prospective fame from a reading of her chart; to gather
from that group who visit dancing girls enough of appreciation for
her good looks, qualities, wit and figure; to give her away to anyone blindly in love with her in case he is rich and independent also;
otherwise, to yield her up to one who has high intellectual attainments though poorly equipped with worldly materials; to persuade
her to live with one by Gandharva wedding but later on to extort
money from him and finally, if need be, to resort to courts of law
for recovering her money claims.

GABRIELE D'ANNUNZIO

GABRIELE D'ANNUNZIO (Italian, 1863-1938). Flamboyant, romantic poet
and dramatist. Influential in early 20th century Italy. Pushed anti-religious,
anti-democratic ideas of Carducci to grotesque extremes. Attracted by themes
of violence, illness, erotic decadence. Most widely read novel: *The Triumph
of Death*. Plays include *La Gioconda, Francesca da Rimini*.

FOUR SONNETS

I

He was a love-child. In his gloomy eye
   Burned flames of desperate hatred, prompt to glow,
   Like lurid gleams of sunset from the sky
   Fallen in foul waters of a ditch below;
   Pale, lean he was: his red hair stood up high
   Over his head deformed and marked with woe,
   And his misshapen body made awry
   As if from stone hewn by an axe's blow.

And yet—! None knew his heart-beats in the night,
   None saw his burning tears, none heard him weep
   Tears breaking his poor heart, in youth's despite,
   When o'er the deck broke from the odorous deep
   Vast waves of perfume 'neath the full moonlight,
   And nought was heard save long-drawn breaths of sleep.

283

II

Ah, none! She passes o'er the sands of gold,
    Singing a song, and with the sunlight crowned;
    Given to the Loves her ample breasts unfold,
    Given to the winds her tresses flow unbound.
    Joyous with youth her honest eyes and bold,
    Blue like the tropic skies, seek all around
    Fancies and dreams, while to the heavens out-rolled
O'er the opal sea her joyous songs resound.

He breathless, quivering with passions vain,
    Crouched in the boat along the swaying keel,
    Holds in his hands his temples filled with pain—
'See to the nets!' the skipper's orders peal,
    As he kicks him where he lies. And o'er the main
    Her jocund songs arise, rebound and wheel.

III

The song said: 'Sea-weeds! flowers o' the ample sea!
    Down in the waters green the mermaids dwell
    In gardens coralline, where mansions be,
Built for fair maids who love their sweethearts well.'
The song said: 'Flower of may on the hawthorn tree!
    There is a grotto made of many a shell,
    Deep in the waters blue, a home of glee
Built for fair maids who love's sweet story tell.'

And Rufus thought to himelf: 'I am a cur!
    For me there is no smile for dear love's sake,
And never a kiss for me! I am a cur!
    Up! draw the bridle tight! I work and ache;
My blood I sell for bread, while none demur:
    Yet—if one day the worn-out cord should break?'

IV

The murderer climbed the cliff with hurrying feet,
    With pale and anxious face, with aching head,
    Like a wild beast struck mad in the summer heat,
Grasping the guilty knife still dripping red.

The angry sea-gulls in battalions fleet
Raised o'er the crags their clamorous shout, and fled;
And the death-cry shook far off a lugger's sheet
As he hurled himself to the wave that onward sped.

Far echoed o'er the golden sands the sound
Of human labour: mournful and unblest,
Voices of women surged along the ground;
And tossed upon the sea's sublime unrest,
On emerald deeps with zones of glory crowned,
A corpse turned to the sun its shattered breast.

DANTE ALIGHIERI

DANTE ALIGHIERI (Italian, 1265-1321). One of world's great poets, and
Italy's supreme literary figure. Dabbled in politics, banished from Florence,
lived in bitter exile. Love for Beatrice de' Portinari glorified in *The Divine
Comedy*, philosophical-political allegory of 100 cantos, and in *La Vita Nuovo*,
collection of 31 love poems. His writing important in shaping Italian into a
literary language.

THE DIVINE COMEDY

"Through me ye enter the abode of woe:
  Through me to endless sorrow are ye brought:
  Through me amid the souls accurst ye go.
Justice did first my lofty Maker move;
  By power Almighty was my fabric wrought,
  By highest Wisdom, and by Primal Love.
Ere I was form'd, no things created were,
  Save those eternal—I eternal last:
  All hope abandon—ye who enter here."
These words, inscribed in colour dark, I saw
  High on the summit of a portal vast;
  Whereat I cried: "O master! with deep awe
Their sense I mark." Like one prepared, he said,
  "Here from thy soul must doubt be cast away;
  Here must each thought of cowardice be dead.—
Now, at that place I told thee of, arrived,
  The melancholy shades shalt thou survey,
  Of God—the mind's supremest good—deprived."

285

Then, as he clasp'd my hand with joyful mien,
    That comfort gave, and bade me cease to fear,
    He led me down into the world unseen.
There sobs, and wailings, and heart-rending cries,
    Resounded through the starless atmosphere,
    Whence tears began to gather in mine eyes.
Harsh tongues discordant—horrible discourse—
    Words of despair—fierce accents of despite—
    Striking of hands—with curses deep and hoarse,
Raised a loud tumult, which unceasing whirl'd
    Throughout that gloom of everlasting night,
    Like to the sand in circling eddies hurl'd.
Then (horror compassing my head around)
    I cried: "O master, what is this I hear?
    And who are these so plunged in grief profound?"
He answered me: "The groans which thou hast heard
    Proceed from those, who, when on earth they were,
    Nor praise deserved, nor infamy incurr'd.
Here with those caitiff angels they abide,
    Who stood aloof in heaven—to God untrue,
    Yet wanting courage with His foes to side.
Heaven drove them forth, its beauty not to stain:
    And Hell refuses to receive them too:—
    From them no glory could the damn'd obtain."
"O master, what infliction do they bear,"
    I said, "which makes them raise such shrieks of woe?
    He answer'd: "That I will in brief declare.
No hope of death have this unhappy crew;
    And their degraded life is sunk so low,
    With envy every other state they view.
No record hath the world of this vile class,
    Alike by Justice and by Pity spurn'd:
    Speak we no more of them—but look—and pass."
And as I look'd, a banner I beheld,
    That seemed incapable of rest, and turn'd,
    In one unvaried round for aye impell'd;
While shades were following in so long a train,
    I ne'er forsooth could have believed it true
    That Death such myriads of mankind had slain

286

And when I had examined many a shade,
  Behold! that abject one appear'd in view,
  Who, mean of soul, the grand refusal made.
Straight I perceived, and distant recognised,
  In that vast concourse the assembly vile
  Of those by God and by His foes despised.
These wretched ones, who never were alive,
  All naked stood, for sorely stung the while
  By wasps and hornets that around them drive.
The cruel swarm bedew'd their cheeks with blood
  Which trickled to their feet with many a tear,
  While worms disgusting drank the mingled flood.
Then, onward as I stretch'd mine eye, I saw
  A mighty stream, with numbers standing near;
  Whereat I said: "O master! by what law
Do these sad souls, whose state I fain would learn,
  So eagerly to cross the river haste,
  As by the doubtful twilight I discern?"
"These things," he answer'd me, "shall all be told
  Soon as our feet upon the bank are placed
  Of Acheron, that mournful river old."
Mine eyes cast down, my looks o'erwhelm'd with shame
  Fearing my questions had oppress'd the sage,
  I spake not till beside the stream we came.
Lo! in a vessel o'er the gloomy tide
  An old man comes—his locks all white with age:—
  "Woe, woe to you, ye guilty souls!" he cried;
"Hope not that heaven shall ever bless your sight;
  I come to bear you to the other shore,—
  To ice, and fire, in realms of endless night:
And thou—who breathest still the vital air—
  Begone—nor stay with these who live no more."
  But when he saw that yet I linger'd there—
"By other port," he said, "by other way,
  And not by this, a passage must thou find;
  Thee a far lighter vessel shall convey."
"Charon," my guide return'd, "thy wrath restrain,
  Thus is it will'd where will and power are join'd;
  Therefore submit, nor question us again."

The dark lake's pilot heard;—and at the sound
    Fell instant his rough cheeks, while flashing raged
    His angry eyes in flaming circles round.

But they—soon as these threatenings met their ear—
    Poor, naked, weary souls—their colour changed;
    And their teeth chatter'd through excess of fear.

God they blasphemed, their parents, man's whole race,
    The hour, the spot,—and e'en the very seed
    To which their miserable life they trace:

Then, while full bitterly their sorrows flow'd,
    They gather'd to that evil strand, decreed
    To all who live not in the fear of God.

Charon, the fiend, with eyes of living coal,
    Beckoning the mournful troop, collects them there,
    And with his oar strikes each reluctant soul.

As leaves in Autumn, borne before the wind,
    Drop one by one, until the branch, laid bare.
    Sees all its honours to the earth consign'd:

So cast them downward at his summons all
    The guilty race of Adam from that strand,—
    Each, as a falcon, answering to the call,

Thus pass they slowly o'er the water brown;
    And ere on the opposing bank they land,
    Fresh numbers to this shore come crowding down.

"All those, my son," exclaim'd the courteous guide,
    "Who in the wrath of the Almighty die,
    Are gather'd here from every region wide:

Goaded by Heavenly Justice in its ire,
    To pass the stream they rush thus hastily;
    So that their fear is turn'd into desire.

By virtuous soul this wave is never cross'd;
    Wherefore, if Charon warn thee to depart,
    The meaning of his words will not be lost."

This converse closed—the dusky region dread
    Trembled so awfully, that o'er my heart
    Doth terror still a chilly moisture shed.

Sent forth a blast that melancholy realm,
    Which flashing a vermilion light around,
    At once did all my senses overwhelm;
And down I sank like one in slumber bound.

ALPHONSE DAUDET

ALPHONSE DAUDET (French, 1840-1897). Associated with French natural-
ists, but essentially a romanticist. Creator of gentle satires and sentimental
stories. Gave up teaching to write, gained early fame and popularity. Best-
known stories in *Lettres de mon Moulin*. Best-known novel: *Sapho*.

THE DEATH OF THE DAUPHIN

THE little Dauphin is ill; the little Dauphin is dying. In all the
churches of the kingdom the Holy Sacrament remains exposed night
and day, and great tapers burn, for the recovery of the royal child.
The streets of the old capital are sad and silent, the bells ring no
more, the carriages slacken their pace. In the neighborhood of the
palace the curious towns-people gaze through the railings upon the
beadles with gilded paunches, who converse in the courts and put
on important airs.

All the castle is in a flutter. Chamberlains and major-domos run
up and down the marble stair-ways. The galleries are full of pages
and of courtiers in silken apparel, who hurry from one group to
another, begging in low tones for news. Upon the wide perrons the
maids of honor, in tears, exchange low courtesies and wipe their
eyes with daintily embroidered handkerchiefs.

A large assemblage of robed physicians has gathered in the Or-
angery. They can be seen through the panes waving their long black
sleeves and inclining their periwigs with professional gestures. The
governor and the equerry of the little Dauphin walk up and down
before the door awaiting the decision of the Faculty. Scullions pass
by without saluting them. The equerry swears like a pagan; the
governor quotes verses from Horace.

And meanwhile, over there, in the direction of the stables, is
heard a long and plaintive neighing; it is the little Dauphin's sorrel,
forgotten by the hostlers, and calling sadly before his empty manger.

And the King? Where is his Highness the King? The King has
locked himself up in a room at the other end of the castle. Majesties
do not like to be seen weeping. For the Queen it is different. Sitting
by the bedside of the little Dauphin, she bows her fair face, bathed
in tears, and sobs very loudly before everybody, like a mere draper's
wife.

On the bed embroidered with lace the little Dauphin, whiter than
the pillows on which he is extended, lies with closed eyes. They think

289

that he is asleep; but no, the little Dauphin is not asleep. He turns towards his mother, and seeing her tears, he asks:

"Madame la Reine, why do you weep? Do you really believe that I am going to die?"

The Queen tries to answer. Sobs prevent her from speaking.

"Do not weep, Madame la Reine. You forget that I am the Dauphin, and that Dauphins cannot die thus."

The Queen sobs more violently, and the little Dauphin begins to feel frightened.

"Holloa!" says he, "I do not want Death to come and take me away, and I know how to prevent him from coming here. Order up on the spot forty of the strongest lansquenets to keep guard around our bed! Have a hundred big cannons watch day and night, with lighted fuses, under our windows! And woe to Death if he dares to come near us!"

In order to humor the royal child, the Queen makes a sign. On the spot the great cannons are heard rolling in the courts, and forty tall lansquenets, with halberds in their fists, draw up around the room. They are all veterans, with grizzly mustaches. The little Dauphin claps his hands on seeing them. He recognizes one, and calls,

"Lorrain! Lorrain!"

The veteran makes a step towards the bed.

"I love you well, my old Lorrain. Let me see your big sword. If Death wants to fetch me, you will kill him, won't you?"

Lorrain answers:

"Yes, Monseigneur."

And two great tears roll down his tanned cheeks.

At that moment the chaplain approaches the little Dauphin, and pointing to the crucifix, talks to him in low tones. The little Dauphin listens with astonished air; then, suddenly interrupting him,

"I understand well what you are saying, Monsieur l'Abbé; but still, couldn't my little friend Beppo die in my place, if I gave him plenty of money?"

The chaplain continues to talk to him in low tones, and the little Dauphin looks more and more astonished.

When the chaplain has finished, the little Dauphin resumes, with a heavy sigh:

"What you have said is all very sad, Monsieur l'Abbé; but one thing consoles me, and that is that up there, in the Paradise of the stars, I shall still be the Dauphin. I know that the good God is my cousin, and cannot fail to treat me according to my rank."

Then he adds, turning towards his mother:

"Bring me my fairest clothes, my doublet of white ermine, and my pumps of velvet! I wish to look brave to the angels, and to enter Paradise in the dress of a Dauphin."

A third time the chaplain bends over the little Dauphin, and talks to him in low tones. In the midst of his discourse the royal child interrupts him angrily.

"Why, then," he cries, "to be Dauphin is nothing at all!"

And refusing to listen to anything more, the little Dauphin turns towards the wall and weeps bitterly.

DAVID

DAVID (Hebrew, ca. 1000 B.C.). The kingly harpist. King of Judea and
Israel. Famous as a poet and warrior.

PSALM XXXVII

FRET not thyself because of evil doers, neither be thou envious against the workers of iniquity.

For they shall soon be cut down like the grass, and wither as the green herb.

Trust in the Lord, and do good; *so* shall thou dwell in the land, and verily thou shalt be fed.

Delight thyself also in the Lord; and he shall give thee the desires of thy heart.

Commit thy way unto the Lord; trust also in him; and he shall bring *it* to pass.

And he shall bring forth thy righteousness as the light, and thy judgement as the noon-day.

Rest in the Lord, and wait patiently for him: fret not thyself because of him who prospereth in his way, because of the man who bringeth wicked devices to pass.

Cease from anger, and forsake wrath: fret not thyself in any wise to do evil.

For evil doers shall be cut off: but those that wait upon the Lord, they shall inherit the earth.

For yet a little while, and the wicked *shall* not *be:* yea, thou shalt diligently consider his place, and it *shall* not *be.*

291

But the meek shall inherit the earth; and shall delight themselves in the abundance of peace.

The wicked plotteth against the just, and gnasheth upon him with his teeth.

The Lord shall laugh at him: for he seeth that his day is coming.

The wicked have drawn out the sword, and have bent their bow, to cast down the poor and needy, *and* to slay such as be of upright conversation.

Their sword shall enter into their own heart, and their bows shall be broken.

A little that a righteous man hath *is* better than the riches of many wicked.

For the arms of the wicked shall be broken: but the Lord upholdeth the righteous.

The Lord knoweth the days of the upright: and their inheritance shall be forever.

They shall not be ashamed in the evil time: and in the days of famine they shall be satisfied.

But the wicked shall perish, and the enemies of the Lord *shall be* as the fat of lambs: they shall consume; into smoke shall they consume away.

The wicked borroweth, and payeth not again: but the righteous showeth mercy, and giveth.

For *such as be* blessed of him shall inherit the earth; and *they that be* cursed of him shall be cut off.

The steps of a *good* man are ordered by the Lord: and he delighteth in his way.

Though he fall, he shall not be utterly cast down: for the Lord upholdeth *him with* his hand.

I have been young, and *now* am old; yet have I not seen the righteous forsaken, nor his seed begging bread.

He is ever merciful, and lendeth; and his seed *is* blessed.

Depart from evil, and do good; and dwell for evermore.

For the Lord loveth judgement, and forsaketh not his saints; they are preserved for ever: but the seed of the wicked shall be cut off.

The righteous shall inherit the land and dwell therein for ever.

The mouth of the righteous speaketh wisdom, and his tongue talketh of judgement.

The law of his God *is* in his heart; none of his steps shall slide.

The wicked watcheth the righteous, and seeketh to slay him.

The Lord will not leave him in his hand, nor condemn him when he is judged.

Wait on the Lord, and keep his way, and he shall exalt thee to inherit the land: when the wicked are cut off, thou shalt see *it*.

I have seen the wicked in great power, and spreading himself like a green bay-tree.

Yet he passed away, and lo, he *was* not: yea, I sought him, but he could not be found.

Mark the perfect *man*, and behold the upright: for the end of *that* man *is* peace.

But the transgressors shall be destroyed together: the end of the wicked shall be cut off.

But the salvation of the righteous *is* of the Lord: *he is* their strength in the time of trouble.

And the Lord shall help them, and deliver them: he shall deliver them from the wicked, and save them, because they trust in him.

DANIEL DEFOE

DANIEL DEFOE (English, *ca.* 1660-1731). Most celebrated for *The Surprising Adventures of Robinson Crusoe,* now a children's classic, but primarily a journalist and politician. Served two years in jail for political dissent. Fore-runners of the early novel and modern realism: *Moll Flanders, Journal of the Plague Year, Roxana.*

IN DEFENCE OF HIS RIGHT

A GENTLEMAN of a very good estate married a lady of also a good fortune, and had one son by her, and one daughter, and no more, and after a few years his lady died. He soon married a second venter; and his second wife, though of an inferior quality and fortune to the former, took upon her to discourage and discountenance his children by his first lady, and made the family very uncomfortable, both to the children and to their father also.

The first thing of consequence which this conduct of the mother-in-law produced in the family, was that the son, who began to be a man, asked the father's leave to go abroad to travel. The mother-in-law, though willing enough to be rid of the young man, yet

because it would require something considerable to support his expenses abroad, violently opposed it, and brought his father also to refuse him after he had freely given him his consent.

This so affected the young gentleman, that after using all the dutiful applications to his father that he could possibly do, as well by himself as by some other relations, but to no purpose; and being a little encouraged by an uncle, who was brother to his mother, his father's first lady, he resolved to go abroad without leave, and accordingly did so.

What part of the world he travelled into I do not remember; it seems his father had constantly intelligence from him for some time, and was prevailed with to make him a reasonable allowance for his subsistence, which the young gentleman always drew bills for, and they were honourably paid; but after some time, the mother-in-law prevailing at home, one of his bills of exchange was refused, and being protested, was sent back without acceptance; upon which he drew no more, nor did he write any more letters, or his father hear anything from him for upwards of four years, or thereabout.

Upon this long silence, the mother-in-law made her advantage several ways; she first intimated to his father that he must needs be dead; and consequently, his estate should be settled upon her eldest son (for she had several children). His father withstood the motion very firmly, but the wife harassed him with her importunities; and she argued upon two points against him, I mean the son.

First, if he was dead, then there was no room to object, her son being heir at law.

Secondly, if he was not dead, his behaviour to his father in not writing for so long a time was inexcusable, and he ought to resent it, and settle the estate as if he were dead; that nothing could be more disobliging, and his father ought to depend upon it that he was dead, and treat him as if he was so; for he that would use a father so, should be taken for one dead, as to his filial relation, and be treated accordingly.

His father, however, stood out a long time, and told her that he could not answer it to his conscience; that there might happen many things in the world, which might render his son unable to write; that he might be taken by the Turks, and carried into slavery; or he might be among the Persians or Arabians (which it seems was the case), and so could not get any letters conveyed; and that he could not be satisfied to disinherit him, till he knew whether he had reason for it or no, or whether his son had offended him or no.

These answers, however just, were far from stopping her importunities, which she carried on so far, that she gave him no rest, and it made an unquiet family; she carried it very ill to him, and in a word, made her children do so too; and the gentleman was so wearied out with it, that once or twice he came to a kind of consent to do it, but his heart failed him, and then he fell back again and refused.

However, her having brought him so near it, was an encouragement to her to go on with her restless solicitations, till at last he came thus far to a provisional agreement, that if he did not hear from his son by such a time, or before it, he would consent to a re-settling the estate.

She was not well satisfied with the conditional agreement, but being able to obtain no other, she was obliged to accept of it as it was; though, as she often told him, she was far from being satisfied with it as to the time, for he had fixed it for four years, as above.

He grew angry at her telling him so, and answered, that she ought to be very well satisfied with it, for that it was time little enough, as his son's circumstances might be.

Well, she teased him however so continually, that at last she brought him down to one year: but before she brought him to that, she told him one day in heat, that she hoped his ghost would one time or other appear to him, and tell him that he was dead, and that he ought to do justice to his other children, for he should never come to claim the estate.

When he came, so much against his will, to consent to shorten the time to one year, he told her that he hoped his son's ghost, though he was not dead, would come to her, and tell her he was alive, before the time expired. "For why," says he, "may not injured souls walk while embodied, as well as afterwards?"

It happened one evening after this, that they had a most violent family quarrel upon this subject, when on a sudden a hand appeared at a casement, endeavouring to open it; but as all the iron casements used in former times opened outward, but hasped and fastened themselves in the inside, so the hand seemed to try to open the casement, but could not. The gentleman did not see it, but his wife did, and she presently started up, as if she was frightened, and, forgetting the quarrel they had upon their hands: "Lord bless me!" says she, "there are thieves in the garden." Her husband ran immediately to the door of the room they sat in, and opening it, looked out.

295

"There's nobody in the garden," says he; so he clapped the door to again, and came back.

"I am sure," says she, "I saw a man there."

"It must be the devil then," says he, "for I'm sure there's nobody in the garden."

"I'll swear," says she, "I saw a man put his hand up to open the casement; but finding it fast, and I suppose," adds she, "seeing us in the room, he walked off."

"It is impossible he could be gone," says he; "did not I run to the door immediately? and you know the garden walls on both sides hinder him going."

"Pry'thee," says she angrily, "I an't drunk nor in a dream, I know a man when I see him, and 'tis not dark, the sun is not quite down."

"You're only frighted with shadows," says he (very full of ill-nature): "folks generally are so that are haunted with an evil conscience: it may be 'twas the devil."

"No, no, I'm not soon frightened," says she; "if 'twas the devil, 'twas the ghost of your son: it may be come to tell you he was gone to the devil, and you might give your estate to your eldest bastard, since you won't settle it on the lawful heir."

"If it was my son," says he, "he's come to tell us he's alive, I warrant you, and to ask how you can be so much a devil to desire me to disinherit him;" and with these words: "Alexander," says he aloud, repeating it twice, starting up out of his chair, "if you are alive, show yourself, and don't let me be insulted thus every day with your being dead."

At those very words, the casement which the hand had been seen at by the mother, opened of itself, and his son Alexander looked in with a full face and staring directly upon the mother with an angry countenance, cried "Here," and then vanished in a moment.

The woman that was so stout before, shrieked out in a most dismal manner, so that the whole house was alarmed; her maid ran into the parlour, to see what was the matter, but her mistress was fainted away in her chair.

She was not fallen upon the ground, because it being a great easy chair, she sunk a little back against the side of the chair, and help coming immediately in, they kept her up; but it was not till a great while after, that she recovered enough to be sensible of anything.

Her husband ran immediately to the parlour door, and opening

it, went into the garden, but there was nothing; and after that he ran to another door that opened from the house into the garden, and then to two other doors which opened out of his garden, one into the stable-yard, and another into the field beyond the garden, but found them all fast shut and barred; but on one side was his gardener, and a boy, drawing the rolling-stone: he asked them if anybody else had been in the garden, but they both constantly affirmed nobody had been there; and they were both rolling a gravel-walk near the house.

Upon this he comes back into the room, sits him down again, and said not one word for a good while; the woman and servants being busy all the while, and in a hurry, endeavouring to recover his wife.

After some time she recovered so far as to speak, and the first words she said, were:

"L—d bless me! what was it?"

"Nay," says her husband, "it was Alexander, to be sure."

With that she fell into a fit, and screamed and shrieked out again most terribly.

Her husband not thinking that would have affected her, did what he could to persuade her out of it again; but that would not do, and they were obliged to carry her to bed, and get some help to her; but she continued ill for several days after.

However, this put an end for some considerable time to her solicitations about his disinheriting her son-in-law.

But time, that hardens the mind in cases of a worse nature, wore this off also by degrees, and she began to revive the old cause again, though not at first so eagerly as before.

Nay, he used her a little hardly upon it too, and if ever they had any words about it he would bid her hold her tongue, or that if she talked any more upon that subject, he would call Alexander again to open the casement.

This aggravated things much; and though it terrified her a great while, yet at length she was so exasperated, that she told him she believed he dealt with the devil, and that he had sold himself to the devil only to be able to fright his wife.

He jested with her, and told her any man would be beholden to the devil to hush a noisy woman, and that he was very glad he had found the way to do it, whatever it cost him.

She was so exasperated at this, that she threatened him if he played any more of his hellish arts with her she would have him

297

indicted for a wizard, and having a familiar; and she could prove it, she said, plain enough, for that he had raised the devil on purpose to fright his wife.

The fray parted that night with ill words and ill nature enough, but he little thought she intended as she said, and the next day he had forgot it all, and was as good-humoured as if nothing had happened.

But he found his wife chagrined and disturbed very much, full of resentment, and threatening him with what she resolved to do.

However, he little thought she intended him the mischief she had in her head, offering to talk friendly to her; but she rejected it with scorn, and told him she would be as good as her word, for she would not live with a man that should bring the devil into the room as often as he thought fit, to murder his wife.

He strove to pacify her by fair words, but she told him she was in earnest with him: and, in a word, she was in earnest; for she goes away to a justce, and making an affidavit that her husband had a familiar spirit, and that she went in danger of her life, she obtained a warrant for him to be apprehended.

In short, she brought home the warrant, showed it to him, and told him she had not given it into the hands of an officer, because he should have the liberty to go voluntarily before the justice of the peace, and if he thought fit to let her know when he would be ready, she would be so too, and would get some of her own friends to go along with her.

He was surprised at this, for he little thought she had been in earnest with him, and endeavoured to pacify her by all the ways possible; but she found she had frightened him heartily, and so indeed she had, for though the thing had nothing in it of guilt, yet he found it might expose him very much, and being loath to have such a thing brought upon the stage against him, he used all the entreaties with her that he was able, and begged her not to do it.

But the more he humbled himself the more she triumphed over him; and carrying things to an unsufferable height of insolence, she told him at last, she would make him do justice, as she called it; that she was sure she could have him punished if he continued obstinate, and she would not be exposed to witchcraft and sorcery; for she did not know to what length he might carry it.

To bring the story to a conclusion; she got the better of him to such a degree, that he offered to refer the thing to indifferent persons, friends on both sides; and they met several times, but could

bring it to no conclusion. His friends said there was nothing in it, and they would not have him comply with anything upon the pretence of it; that he called for his son, and somebody opened the casement and cried, "Here"; that there was not the least evidence of witchcraft in that, and insisted that she could make nothing of it.

Her friends carried it high, instructed by her: she offered to swear that he had threatened her before with his son's ghost; that now he visibly raised a spectre; for that calling upon his son, who was dead to be sure, the ghost immediately appeared; that he could not have called up the devil thus to personate his son, if he had not dealt with the devil himself, and had a familiar spirit, and that this was of dangerous consequence to her.

Upon the whole, the man wanted courage to stand it, and was afraid of being exposed; so that he was grievously perplexed, and knew not what to do.

When she found him humbled as much as she could desire, she told him, if he would do her justice, as she called it (that is to say, settle his estate upon her son), she would put it up, on condition that he should promise to fright her no more with raising the devil.

That part of her proposal exasperated him again, and he upbraided her with the slander of it, and told her he defied her, and she might do her worst.

Thus it broke off all treaty, and she began to threaten him again; however, at length she brought him to comply, and he gives a writing under his hand to her, some of her friends being by, promising that he would comply if his son did not arrive, or send an account of himself, within four months.

She was satisfied with this, and they were all made friends again, and accordingly he gave the writing; but when he delivered it to her in presence of her two arbitrators, he took the liberty to say to her, with a grave and solemn kind of speech:

"Look you," says he, "you have worried me into this agreement by your fiery temper, and I have signed it against justice, conscience, and reason; but depend upon it, I shall never perform it."

One of the arbitrators said, "Why, sir, this is doing nothing; for if you resolve not to perform it, what signifies the writing? why do you promise what you do not intend shall be done? This will but kindle a new flame to begin with, when the time fixed expires."

"Why," says he, "I am satisfied in my mind that my son is alive."

"Come, come," says his wife, speaking to the gentleman that had argued with her husband, "let him sign the agreement, and let me alone to make him perform the conditions."

"Well," says her husband, "you shall have the writing, and you shall be let alone; but I am satisfied you will never ask me to perform it; and yet I am no wizard," adds he, "as you have wickedly suggested."

She replied, that she would prove that he dealt with the devil, for that he raised an evil spirit by only calling his son by name; and so began to tell the story of the hand and the casement.

"Come," says the man to the gentleman that was her friend, "give me the pen; I never dealt with but one devil in my life, and there it sits," turning to his wife; "and now I have made an agreement with her that none but the devil would desire any man to sign, and I will sign it; I say, give me the pen, but she nor all the devils in hell will ever be able to get it executed; remember I say so."

She began to open at him, and so a new flame would have been kindled, but the gentlemen moderated between them, and her husband setting his hand to the writing put an end to the fray at that time.

At the end of four months she challenged the performance, and a day was appointed, and her two friends that had been the arbitrators were invited to dinner upon this occasion, believing that her husband would have executed the deeds; and accordingly the writings were brought all forth, engrossed, and read over; and some old writings, which at her marriage were signed by her trustees, in order to her quitting some part of the estate to her son, were also brought to be cancelled: the husband being brought over, by fair means or foul, I know not whether, to be in a humour, for peace' sake, to execute the deeds, and disinherit his son; alleging that, indeed, if he was dead it was no wrong to him, and if he was alive, he was very unkind and undutiful to his father, in not letting him hear from him in all that time.

Besides, it was urged that if he should at any time afterwards appear to be alive, his father (who had very much increased, it seems, in his wealth) was able to give him another fortune, and to make him a just satisfaction for the loss he should sustain by the paternal estate.

Upon these considerations, I say, they had brought over the poor

low-spirited husband to be almost willing to comply; or, at least, willing or unwilling, it was done, and, as above, they met accordingly.

When they had discoursed upon all the particulars, and, as above, the new deeds were read over, she or her husband took the old writings up to cancel them; I think the story says it was the wife, not her husband, that was just going to tear off the seal, when on a sudden they heard a rushing noise in the parlour where they sat, as if somebody had come in at the door of the room which opened from the hall, and went through the room towards the garden door, which was shut.

They were all surprised at it, for it was very distinct, but they saw nothing. The woman turned pale, and was in a terrible fright; however, as nothing was seen, she recovered a little, but began to ruffle her husband again.

"What," says she, "have you laid your plot to bring up more devils again?"

The man sat composed, though he was under no little surprise too.

One of her gentlemen said to him, "What is the meaning of all this?"

"I protest, sir," says he, "I know no more of it than you do."

"What can it be then?" said the other gentleman.

"I cannot conceive," says he, "for I am utterly unacquainted with such things."

"Have you heard nothing from your son?" says the gentleman.

"Not one word," says the father; "no, not the least word these five years."

"Have you wrote nothing to him," says the gentleman, "about this transaction?"

"Not a word," says he; "for I know not where to direct a letter to him."

"Sir," says the gentleman, "I have heard much of apparitions, but I never saw them in my life, nor did I ever believe there was anything of reality in them; and, indeed, I saw nothing now; but the passing of some body, or spirit, or something, across the room just now is plain; I heard it distinctly. I believe there is some unseen thing in the room, as much as if I saw it."

"Nay," says the other arbitrator, "I felt the wind of it as it

301

passed by me. Pray," adds he, turning to the husband, "do you see nothing yourself?"

"No, upon my word," says he, "not the least appearance in the world."

"I have been told," says the first arbitrator, "and have read, that an apparition may be seen by some people and be invisible to others, though all in the same room together."

However, the husband solemnly protested to them all that he saw nothing.

"Pray, sir," says the first arbitrator, "have you seen anything at any other time, or heard any voices or noises, or had any dreams about this matter?"

"Indeed," says he, "I have several times dreamed my son is alive, and that I had spoken with him; and once that I asked him why he was so undutiful, and slighted me so, as not to let me hear of him in so many years, seeing he knew it was in my power to disinherit him."

"Well, sir, and what answer did he give?"

"I never dreamed so far on as to have him answer; it always waked me."

"And what do you think of it yourself," says the arbitrator; "do you think he's dead?"

"No, indeed," says the father, "I do believe in my conscience he's alive, as much as I believe I am alive myself; and I am going to do as wicked a thing of its kind as ever any man did."

"Truly," says the second arbitrator, "it begins to shock me, I don't know what to say to it; I don't care to meddle any more with it, I don't like driving men to act against their consciences."

With this the wife, who, as I said, having a little recovered her spirits, and especially encouraged because she saw nothing, started up: "What's all this discourse to the purpose," says she; "is it not all agreed already? what do we come here for?"

"Nay," says the first arbitrator, "I think we meet now not to inquire into why it is done, but to execute things according to agreement, and what are we frighted at?"

"I'm not frighted," says the wife, "not I; come," says she to her husband, haughtily, "sign the deed; I'll cancel the old writings if forty devils were in the room;" and with that she takes up one of the deeds, and went to tear off the seal.

That moment the same casement flew open again, though it was

302

fast in the inside, just as it was before; and the shadow of a body was seen, as standing in the garden without, and the head reaching up to the casement, the face looking into the room, and staring directly at the woman with a stern and an angry countenance: "Hold," said the spectre, as if speaking to the woman, and immediately clapped the casement to again, and vanished.

It is impossible to describe here the consternation this second apparition put the whole company into; the wife, who was so bold just before, that she would do it though forty devils were in the room, screamed out like a woman in fits, and let the writing fall out of her hands: the two arbitrators were exceedingly terrified, but not so much as the rest; but one of them took up the award which they had signed, in which they awarded the husband to execute the deed to dispose of the estate from the son.

. "I dare say," said he, "be the spirit a good spirit or a bad, it will not be against cancelling this;" so he tore his name out of the award, and so did the other, by his example, and both of them got up from their seats, and said they would have no more to do in it.

But that which was most unexpected of all was that the man himself was so frighted, that he fainted away; notwithstanding it was, as it might be said, in his favour.

This put an end to the whole affair at that time; and, as I understand by the sequel, it did so for ever.

The story has many particulars more in it, too long to trouble you with: but two particulars, which are to the purpose, I must not omit, viz.:

1. That in about four or five months more after this second apparition, the man's son arrived from the East Indies, whither he had gone four years before in a Portuguese ship from Lisbon.

2. That upon being particularly inquired of about these things, and especially whether he had any knowlededge of them, or any apparition to him, or voices, or other intimation as to what was doing in England, relating to him; he affirmed constantly that he had not, except that once he dreamed his father had written him an angry letter, threatening him that if he did not come home he would disinherit him and leave him not one shilling. But he added, that he never did receive any such letter from his father in his life, or from any one else.

RICHARD DEHMEL

RICHARD DEHMEL (German, 1863-1920). Ardent anti-traditionalist, who went to extremes opposing prejudice and convention. A virtuoso in poetry (*Zwei Menschen*), theater (*Die Menschenfreunde*), and the essay (*Gott und die Welt*).

THE SILENT TOWN

A town lies in the valley,
A pale day fades and dies;
And it will not be long before
Neither moon nor starlight,
Night only fills the skies.

From all the mountain ridges
Creeps mist, and swathes the town;
No farm, no house, no wet red roof
Can pierce the thickly woven woof,
And scarce even spires and bridges.

But as the wanderer shudders,
Deep down a streak of light rejoices
His heart; and, through the smoke and haze,
Children's voices
Begin a gentle hymn of praise.

HELPLESSNESS

But when thou hadst departed,
I grew so lonely-hearted,
    I longed for thee so sore.
I stood with fingers aching,
As though I should lose thee shaking
    The handle of thy barred and bolted door.

And through the panes between us
I begged with eyes as keen as
    A beggar's in the South;
But up the steps thou wentest,
No backward look thou bentest,
    Thou didst not call me back unto thy mouth.

With senses stunned I hearkened,
Heard but in the passage darkened
   The rattling of thy keys;
And then the shadows caught me,
That in the park had sought me,
   When we two saw the moon sink o'er the trees.

ANGRY SEA

Thus once again! Through fog and howling squall:
   The sails shook, and the sailors shouted loudly;
At the bowsprit stood the water like a tall
    Tower: I felt your fear in my knees: and proudly
Your unknown face beside me gloomed.

Yet once again your eye upon me frowned,
   Your hair was like a flame behind you sweeping,
While wrestled in the waves a sound
    As of a little child that will be weeping—
You warded me no more.

You let my arms around your shoulder lie,
   Your wild wet hair my greedy mouth was lashing,
Our kiss was wonderfully sweetened by
    The foam of great salt waves about us crashing—
Then I in joy cried out.

Thus once again! What shadow chills thy brow?
   Or does the open ocean make thee craven?
The sea will whip thee warm! Come soon, come now!
    The ferry is dancing in the foggy haven—
Out! To the heights!

FROM A SAD BREAST

The roses still are like a flame,
   The dark leaves gently shake;
   I in the grass am grown awake,
O that you came,
   For the deep midnight's sake.

The moon is hid by the garden door,
  O'er which its light is shed
On the lake with willow-shadowed shore,
  In the moist clover I bury my head;
I never loved you so before!

As now I know I have not known,
  For all that ever I caressed
  Your neck, and blind your secretest
Being enjoyed, why you would groan,
  When I o'erflowed, from your sad breast.

Had you but seen yon glowworms glide,
  Two glowworms and their light the same!
Never again will I leave your side!
  O that you came!
  The roses still are like a flame.

KNOW'ST THOU YET?

Know'st thou yet, how pale, how white,
When I lay in eves of Maytime,
After kisses of the daytime,
Poured out at thy feet before thee,
Daffodillies trembled o'er me?

Then in deep June's azure night,
Know'st thou yet, how soft and seething,
When we, tired of wild caresses,
Wove around us thy wild tresses,
Daffodillies scents were breathing?

At thy feet again are gleaming,
When the silvery gloamings shimmer,
When the nights of azure glimmer,
Daffodillies scents are streaming.
Know'st thou yet, how hot? how white?

A GRAVE

These are the evenings prematurely pale.
  The dahlias that in the sunlight shone
Like last frail roses, now are standing stale,
  Rosettes of stone whose colour has grown wan.
The swaths of mist across the churchyard trail.

Come, sister. Yonder hedge of brass you see
   Rails round a lady withered in her spring.
   She loved me well. Come home, I am shivering.
Life gave her nothing but her own heart: she
Did good in silence, suffering silently.

THE LABORER

We have a bed, and a baby too,
My wife!
We have work besides, we have work for two,
And we have the sun, and the wind, and the rain,
And we only need one little thing more,
To be as free as the birds that soar:
Only time.

When we go through the fields on the Sunday morn,
My child,
And far and away o'er the bending corn,
We see the swarming swallows flash,
Then we only need a bit of a dress,
To have the birds' bright loveliness:
Only time.

The storm is gathering black as jet,
Feel the poor.
Only a little eternity yet;
We need nothing else, my wife, my child,
Except all things through us that thrive,
To be bold as the birds through the air that drive:
Only time!

HARVEST SONG

There stands a field of golden sheaves,
To the very edge of the world it heaves.
   Grind, mill, grind!

The wind falls in the wide land,
Many mills at the sky-edge stand.
   Grind, mill, grind!

There comes a sunset dark and red,
Many poor people are crying for bread.
        Grind, mill, grind!

The night holds in its lap the storm,
To-morrow the men to work will swarm.
        Grind, mill, grind!

Clean are the fields swept, never again
A man shall cry in hunger-pain.
        Grind, mill, grind!

THREATENING PROSPECT

The sky is whirling, the land flies fast;
    And while, by the express shocked and shaken,
Furrow on furrow whizzes past,
        Thee thy shivering limbs awaken:
            The sun of morning comes.

Through the hung mist with toiling wings
    Break herded crows that autumn is thinning,
While thick upon the dunged field clings
        The smoke of workshops just beginning;
            The sun of morning comes.

Under the trailing gray crape lies
    A chain of slag-heaps filling acres,
Chimney on chimney scales the skies,
        Standing by coffins fearsome wakers;
            The sun of morning comes.

Along the rapid landscape rolls
    A pair of road-dikes from the horizon,
Framed in by gnarled and weathered boles
        Of apple-trees a pale sheen lies on;
            The sun of morning comes.

Now sweeps thy gaze the opposite verge,
    Where boughs, of fruit despoiled, are showing,
And suddenly tree on tree they surge,
        With crumpled leafage fire-red glowing:
            The day is there.

GRAZIA DELEDDA

GRAZIA DELEDDA (Italian, 1875-1936). Considered by many Italy's greatest
woman novelist. Nobel Prize winner, 1926. Regionalist of the island of
Sardinia. A woman of great sympathy and understanding for the psychology
of the little people. Has been compared with Thomas Hardy. Novels: *Elias
Portolu, Cenere, Nostalgie.*

THE OPEN DOOR

On holy Wednesday Simon Barca went to confession. He was
desperate, and a desperate man is glad to remember God, as an
ill man the doctor.

So Simon went to the Basilica, a national monument which still
lends a richness to the once prosperous countryside, and where at
that hour of the morning, only a few monks from the nearby
monastery were celebrating Mass, in chapels where the damp had
spread a green film over the ancient frescoes. The peasant women,
with hoods over their heads and coarse skirts swathed tightly round
them and laced up with thin silver chains, were singing the Rosary
in their Latin dialect: their voices faded away in the airy depths
of the Basilica as amongst the ruins of a temple; through the wide
open doors a wild fragrance of spurge and budding alder trees
wafted in from the valley. Simon went to confess himself to the
prior, who filled the little confessional with his huge body, snoring
and puffing away in there like a bear in a cage.

"Father, I'm a lost man: I want to kill some fellow Christian, I
feel so desperate. I have committed the worst sins. Until a little
time ago I was the dutiful son of a family, the only son, Father.
At twenty I still slept with my mother; but she was hardly dead
when bad companions gathered round me like flies round a raisin
pip; and my uncle, priest though he is, turned me out of the house
instead of helping me, and now when he sees me he looks the
other way. Yes, I have committed the very worst sins: I have gam-
bled, drunk, gone with bad women, consulted witches, blasphemed,
wished my neighbour ill, coveted others' belongings, committed
. . . yes, Father . . . I forged a signature, and the bill of exchange
falls due in a few days . . . and I shall have to go to prison and I
shall be dishonoured. . . . It is all the fault of bad companions, and
they have deserted me now: and every door is closed against me
. . there is not one open door, now, for me! But I'm repentant,

Father, and will go to prison and atone, but give me the good Lord's absolution, so that I may fulfil the Easter duties and suffer innocent like Christ our Saviour."

The prior wheezed on and made no answer. Simon, his thin, dark rogue's face in his hands, breathed hard too, and thought:

"Perhaps he's scandalised: perhaps he is pleased to hear that the real cause of my ruin is my uncle Barca the priest. Monks and priests can't bear the sight of each other. Perhaps, to spite my uncle, he'll give me the money to pay the bill."

But the prior snored and said nothing: his warm breath blew on Simon's face. Tired of waiting, the penitent roused himself from his dream of expiation and his malicious thoughts; his big eyes, dark and childish, contracted, and a bitter smile deepened the hallows in his shaven cheeks. The prior was asleep. Ah, even God is deaf to the cries of a despairing sinner.

* * *

Simon stole away very quietly, his heart sad, his mind a ferment of ugly thoughts. The proceedings of the day were starting round the great altar, and the priest Barca's mobile voice could already be heard chanting with trills and shakes. People were coming and going: now men were arriving too; they were tall, with long square beards as in Moses' time, dressed in leather jackets and short serge trousers, full like skirts. Some seemed like prophets, they were so solemn, calm and unaffected; others were small, lean as our Simon, hardened by the wind and by evil thoughts.

The women, too, recalled those in the Bible. Simon met one in the court of the Basilica, a tall dry widow, with an olive face and huge greenish eyes, swathed in her almost priestly clothes as in a black sheath, and she only wanted a bunch of ears of corn to be a second mother-in-law of Boaz. Simon shuddered when he saw her; he shuddered with hatred, for the woman was a kind of housekeeper for Barca, and he shuddered at the sudden thought that at that moment there was no one in his uncle's house: and as if night had suddenly fallen, he began to see things and people in a mist, and he stalked along by the walls, stumbling against the stones which lay about the rough roads. So he found himself before his house, like a surviving bit of a tower, and only then the light seemed to flood back all around him.

He went in, and soon after, at the little window of the first and only storey, his face appeared, pensive as that of a general forming

310

a plan of battle from the height of a fortress. Simon's field of battle was the limited picture spread beneath him: it consisted of the country road crossed by a stream, where rushes and grass grew as in open country; the widow's little house opposite his; the big, dark house of his uncle the priest, and its yard, beside the widow's, shut in by a little chapel with a kitchen garden so overgrown with weeds and shaded by cypress trees that it seemed the corner of a cemetery. Simon thought how he had spent his childhood and his youth jumping the wall between his uncle's yard and the chapel's garden; he wondered if the time had come for repeating the feat, only the other way about, from the church garden into his uncle's yard. No one else was so familiar with the hidden corners, the passages, the twistings and turnings.

He shut his eyes, and saw the jutting out piece of the ground floor wall where the priest Barca used to put the big key of his room before going out; he opened them again, and, agitated, remembered that vast, rather mysterious room, lighted by a tiny lamp, filled with sacred images and bound books. Here, as a child, he had more than once surprised his uncle, in shirt and skull-cap, counting over gold pieces like a wizard, or skilfully piercing his name on bank-notes with a pin. One day, crawling on the floor, crouching down to imitate a wild-boar, Simon had moved one of the floor blocks, and under it had found a box full of money. Now he recalled those times as a prisoner remembers his days of freedom . . . . .

For three days he remained almost continually at the window, only leaving it to eat a mouthful of rye bread and some goat's cheese. Yes, while his uncle stored his money under the floor-blocks, he had to live like a poor shepherd; his house was empty, deserted, without furniture (he had sold it), even without doors (sold as well), and the spiders spun their webs over the rough boar's skin trunk in which he kept his poor mother's wedding dress and widow's weeds.

To console himself he would drink a small glass of brandy and go back to the window.

From below he smelt the fragrance of the cakes the women were getting ready for Easter, and he saw the smoke rise from wood or tiled roofs. Already a nightingale was singing in the valley, and the fluffy April clouds floated by over the chapel garden, white as bits of girls' clothing blown off some hedge by the wind.

On Holy Thursday the widow left his uncle's house and opened

311

the chapel, usually closed. Helped by the other women of the neighbourhood she pulled down the Christ, laid it on the ground between four lights and four dishes of sprouting corn, and so formed the Sepulchre. But everyone was going to the Basilica, where they were celebrating the Passion and two real thieves (at least they had once been condemned for theft) were tied to the cross beside Christ. From his window Simon saw his uncle himself, short, fat, prancing, and the tall widow, dry and stiff, walk one after the other towards the Basilica. He went down, but once in the street he leant his shoulder against the wall and stood for a long time motionless and pensive, listening to the far-off chanting of the procession. It was dusk; the new moon was sinking behind the violet tinted hills, in a greenish sky, and the evening star was rising, and seemed as if it would come along the streets of the village like Mary and Christ.

"In a few moments the procession will be here," thought Simon, and moved; but he walked close by the wall; he was afraid of going past the dead Christ stretched on the floor between the lights and the corn shoots.

Suddenly, coming to his uncle's door, he shivered. The door was open; someone must be in the house and it was useless to go on. He turned back and once more leant against the wall. But who could be in his uncle's house? The servants, peasants and shepherds, only came back on Saturday evening; the priest and the widow were in the procession. He went forward again to the door, knocked, called: "Basila! Basila!"

His voice lost itself inside the already dark house as in a cave. He went in, closed the door, flung himself up the stairs, traversed the narrow passages, found the jutting-out wall, found the key, opened, and was in his uncle's room. He seemed to be in a dream. The window was shut; a light like those round the dead Christ was burning before the picture of the Holy Martyrs. There was a crowd of them, men, women, old people, children, but all looking up with gentle faces, and Simon was not afraid of them. By the greenish glow of the light he bent and began to feel the floor blocks one by one, like a bricklayer with the job of mending the floor; but not one of the bricks moved, and he stood up and passed his hand across his forehead, wet with cold sweat.

The chanting of the procession reached his ears, and he shivered all over. He leant against his uncle's old bed, and the bed moved aside, creaking and shaking as if seized by the robber's own terror and perturbation. Then Simon looked at the block under the foot

312

of the bed, and it seemed to him that it moved: he bent and pulled it up with his nails, and in the space beneath, buried in the dust, he found an iron box with two thousand lire notes in it.

* * *

On Easter Day Barca the priest discharged the widow Basila, and immediately scandalous tales spread over the whole country. It was common knowledge that Barca had lost many thousand lire, some said two, some three, some twenty; and that Basila had forgotten and left his house door open on Good Friday. The police officer went to the priest's house; but the priest tried to appear unconcerned, clapped his hands and said:

"Trifles! miserable trifles!"

On Tuesday the widow's little house was searched with care, and she was arrested and set free again the next day. There was no evidence against her; but the inhabitants or rather the families in the district split into two parties; the men defended Basila saying that perhaps she had really forgotten the open door, so making it easy for any thief to go in; the women sneered: "And in a few short minutes the robber made himself at home and helped himself?"

Finally people stopped this talk; but the widow was looked down on by everyone. She was given no more work; she stopped going to church and lived in poverty in her wretched house. Simon used to see her, always upright on the threshold, her face pale and sad, but her great greenish eyes turned upwards like those of the Holy Martyrs.

* * *

Simon paid the false bill of exchange and bought back his doors and his cloak. No one was surprised, for like every gambler, he often had these ups and downs of fortune, and only his creditor knew about the bill. What astonished everyone was to see him suddenly change his way of living. He stopped going with bad women and gave up his disreputable companions, he went to church and nodded to his uncle. But his uncle persisted in turning away when he saw him, and one day when Simon went up to him determined to stop him and kiss his hand, he not only ignored his greeting but literally turned his back on him.

Simon stood petrified. He leant against the wall and remained fixed there, overcome by a terrible thought.

"He knows!"

313

Then he went to the widow Basila and said to her:

"Do you think you could bake, and wash, and mend my clothes for me? Fix your own wage."

The widow was standing up before a dead fire combing her hair; it was thick and very long, of a golden chestnut colour, and made a halo of martyrdom round her olive face; but when she saw Simon she covered her cheeks and breast with it like a veil, and shook her head in a threatening way, whilst her greenish eyes flashed beneath her knitted eyebrows, thick and black.

"You have someone already to bake and wash for you! Get out of here!"

He went like a whipped dog and leant against his wall again.

"She knows!"

He spent the days in this way, leaning against the wall, often whittling with a little knife at his walnut stick, or some plug of straw, but more often doing nothing at all. Never before, even at his worst times, had he lived so aimlessly. He was haunted by the widow's threatening eyes, and felt an almost physical ill when he thought that Basila had fallen into poverty and ill-repute through his fault; some nights he had fearsome dreams; the trunk with his mother's clothes in it seemed a live boar, and fixed staring eyes on the doors bought back with that money.

The summer passed, and in the autumn he moved his seat along the wall, seeking the sun. From the new place he saw the widow Basila more clearly, seated too in the sun spinning or sewing, barefooted, and sad as a slave.

The winter was long and severe. The poor people suffered much from hunger, and Barca and a lady who lived in the neighbourhood sent bread and vegetables to all the needy except the widow. For Christmas a lady with whom Simon had often wandered about, sent him a present of a ram's leg. He already had a little pig and a lamb: and thinking that Basila had nothing but potatoes, sent her the ram's leg, and to his astonishment found that she did not refuse the gift. Then all the rest of the winter, seized by a mania for expiation, he went on sending her gifts, often depriving himself of some real necessity.

Spring came again: once more the women put bowls of corn to sprout in cupboards, to adorn the sepulchres. Holy Friday evening Simon went to the procession and afterwards stood for some time in the usual spot, beside the wall, in the warm, whisper-filled evening. A yellowish glow was coming from the crack of Basila's door,

and Simon stared with queer eyes at that light which seemed mysterious to him. Suddenly he went and knocked and asked the woman if she would marry him.

*   *   *

People talked, then stopped talking, After all, Basila was only ten years older than Simon, and a good housewife: indeed, before long the young man's house was transformed, clean, with the stove always alight and the little yard swarming with fowls. Simon was seen on a horse again, as in the time when his mother was alive; they all said that he had married Basila to spite his uncle.

He was not in love with his wife, but he followed her advice and was glad at having lifted a weight off his conscience, and married a wise woman. The latter went to church again and talked in a brief manner, and it seemed to Simon that he had gone back to the happy times with his mother when he, still innocent at twenty, went to bed with her and repeated the prayers she suggested to him.

One day, several months after his marriage, the woman who had sent him the ram's leg called him as he was passing by her door, and asked him to lend her a hundred crowns.

He began to laugh: "If I had a hundred crowns I should set out to go round the world."

"I'll pay you the interest, Simon Barca! I can pay; I'll give you twenty per cent, like the others."

"You are going mad, Mallena Porceu!"

"What, mad? Tell me you don't trust me, Simon Barca, but don't insult me. You and your wife have lent money for interest, at twenty per cent., to certain people. Why can't you give me some too? Or is it true what your uncle Barca says? That your wife gives the money without you knowing?"

Simon grew pale, but answered:

"My uncle's in his second childhood, and you're what you are!"

The following days he was seen again leaning against the wall, as in his dark times. He was asking himself ceaselessly: "Why was the door open?" and his brain was toiling and toiling, digging down deep into a black chasm, seeking the truth as the miner seeks gold in the bowels of the earth.

"She must have taken a good part of the money, and left the door open to make people think some robber had gone in. Oh, the sly old cat! . . ." he thought furiously. But before believing his own idea he wanted to make sure with his eyes themselves.

Again it was Good Friday evening, and Basila had gone to

315

church. Simon waited for that time so as to be free to search the whole house; but hunt as he might, in drawers, in lockers, in the mattresses, he found nothing.

He looked round, tired of searching and in the half-light the trunk which still contained his mother's clothes seemed again like a live boar. He tried to open it, but could not. Then he remembered that Basila always kept the key with her. He went down to the kitchen, came back with an axe and began to strike at the trunk as if it were really a fierce boar. The lid came open. Simon knelt down and began to search; he found Basila's widow's clothes, and out of her black hood fluttered, silently, two, three, many bank-notes red, green, yellowish, like withered walnut leaves. Amongst the others was one of a thousand: he took it up, held it against the candle light and read Barca's name pierced on it with a pin. Then he began to curse and batter his head.

"But why did it happen to me?, why me of all people?" he cried aloud.

Suddenly a sad, sweet song like a murmuring wood floated in from the road. Simon grew quiet and stood listening, his head bent and his eyes wide open, and as the procession approached, he shook and sweated as when he had leant against his uncle's old bed.

CHARLES DICKENS

CHARLES DICKENS (English, 1812-1870). Sentimental-realistic novelist, one of the great Victorians. Despised greed and injustice, chose his material from lower classes, usually with some object of reform. Prejudiced but influential. Most prolific, his characters famous in English-speaking world. *David Copperfield, A Tale of Two Cities, Great Expectations, Oliver Twist, Pickwick Papers, A Christmas Carol.*

THE CONVICT IN THE MARSHES

MY FATHER's family name being Pirrip and my Christian name Philip, my infant tongue could make of both names nothing longer or more explicit than Pip. So I called myself Pip, and came to be called Pip.

I give Pirrip as my father's family name, on the authority of his

tombstone and my sister—Mrs. Joe Gargery, who married the black-smith. As I never saw my father or my mother, and never saw any likeness of either of them (for their days were long before the days of photographs), my first fancies regarding what they were like were unreasonably derived from their tombstones. The shape of the letters on my father's gave me an odd idea that he was a square, stout, dark man, with curly black hair. From the character and turn of the inscription, "*Also Georgiana, Wife of the Above,*" I drew a childish conclusion that my mother was freckled and sickly. To five little stone lozenges, each about a foot and a half long, which were arranged in a neat row beside their grave, and were sacred to the memory of five little brothers of mine—who gave up trying to get a living exceedingly early in that universal struggle—I am indebted for a belief I religiously entertained that they had all been born on their backs with their hands in their trousers pockets, and had never taken them out in this state of existence.

Ours was the marsh country, down by the river, within, as the river wound, twenty miles of the sea. My first most vivid and broad impression of the identity of things seems to me to have been gained on a memorable raw afternoon towards evening. At such a time I found out for certain that this bleak place overgrown with nettles was the churchyard; and that Philip Pirrip, late of this parish, and also Georgiana, wife of the above, were dead and buried; and that Alexander, Bartholomew, Abraham, Tobias, and Roger, infant child-ren of the aforesaid, were also dead and buried; and that the dark flat wilderness beyond the churchyard, intersected with dikes and mounds and gates, with scattered cattle feeding on it, was the marshes; and that the low leaden line beyond was the river; and that the distant savage lair from which the wind was rushing was the sea; and that the small bundle of shivers growing afraid of it all and beginning to cry was Pip.

"Hold your noise!" cried a terrible voice, as a man started up from among the graves at the side of the church porch. "Keep still, you little devil, or I'll cut your throat!"

A fearful man, all in coarse gray, with a great iron on his leg. A man with no hat, and with broken shoes, and with an old rag tied round his head. A man who had been soaked in water, and smoth-ered in mud, and lamed by stones, and cut by flints, and stung by nettles and torn by briers; who limped, and shivered, and glared, and growled; and whose teeth chattered in his head as he seized me by the chin.

317

"Oh! Don't cut my throat, sir," I pleaded in terror. "Pray don't do it, sir."

"Tell us your name!" said the man. "Quick!"

"Pip, sir."

"Once more," said the man, staring at me. "Give it mouth!"

"Pip. Pip, sir."

"Show us where you live," said the man. "Pint out the place!"

I pointed to where our village lay, on the flat inshore among the alder trees and pollards, a mile or more from the church.

The man, after looking at me for a moment, turned me upside down and emptied my pockets. There was nothing in them but a piece of bread. When the church came to itself—for he was so sudden and strong that he made it go head over heels before me, and I saw the steeple under my feet—when the church came to itself, I say, I was seated on a high tombstone, trembling, while he ate the bread ravenously.

"You young dog," said the man, licking his lips, "what fat cheeks you ha' got."

I believed they were fat, though I was at that time undersized for my years, and not strong.

"Darn me if I couldn't eat 'em," said the man, with a threatening shake of his head, "and if I han't half a mind to't!"

I earnestly expressed my hope that he wouldn't, and held tighter to the tombstone on which he had put me; partly to keep myself upon it; partly to keep myself from crying.

"Now lookee here!" said the man. "Where's your mother?"

"There, sir!" said I.

He started, made a short run, and stopped and looked over his shoulder.

"There, sir!" I timidly explained. "Also Georgiana. That's my mother."

"Oh!" said he, coming back. "And is that your father alonger your mother?"

"Yes, sir," said I; "him too; late of this parish."

"Ha!" he muttered then, considering. "Who d'ye live with—supposing you're kindly let to live, which I han't made up my mind about?"

"My sister, sir—Mrs. Joe Gargery—wife of Joe Gargery, tne blacksmith, sir."

"Blacksmith, eh?" said he. And looked down at his leg.

After darkly looking at his leg and at me several times, he ⸗ ⸗

closer to my tombstone, took me by both arms, and tilted me back as far as he could hold me; so that his eyes looked most powerfully down into mine, and mine looked most helplessly up into his.

"Now lookee here," he said, "the question being whether you're to be let to live. You know what a file is?"

"Yes, sir."

"And you know what wittles is?"

"Yes, sir."

After each question he tilted me over a little more, so as to give me a greater sense of helplessness and danger.

"You get me a file." He tilted me again. "And you get me wittles." He tilted me again. "You bring 'em both to me." He tilted me again. "Or I'll have your heart and liver out." He tilted me again.

I was dreadfully frightened, and so giddy that I clung to him with both hands, and said, "If you would kindly please to let me keep upright, sir, perhaps I shouldn't be sick, and perhaps I could attend more."

He gave me a most tremendous dip and roll, so that the church jumped over its own weathercock. Then, he held me by the arms in an upright position on the top of the stone, and went on in these fearful terms:—

"You bring me, to-morrow morning early, that file and them wittles. You bring the lot to me, at that old Battery over yonder. You do it, and you never dare to say a word or dare to make a sign concerning your having seen such a person as me, or any person sumever, and you shall be let to live. You fail, or you go from my words in any partickler, no matter how small it is, and your heart and your liver shall be tore out, roasted and ate. Now, I ain't alone, as you may think I am. There's a young man hid with me, in comparison with which young man I am a Angel. That young man hears the words I speak. That young man has a secret way pecooliar to himself of getting at a boy, and at his heart, and at his liver. It is in wain for a boy to attempt to hide himself from that young man. A boy may lock his door, may be warm in bed, may tuck himself up, may draw the clothes over his head, may think himself comfortable and safe, but that young man will softly creep and creep his way to him and tear him open. I am a keeping that young man from harming of you at the present moment, with great difficulty. I find it wery hard to hold that young man off of your inside. Now what do you say?"

319

I said that I would get him the file, and I would get him what broken bits of food I could, and I would come to him at the Battery, early in the morning.

"Say, Lord strike you dead if you don't!" said the man.

I said so, and he took me down.

"Now," he pursued, "you remember what you've undertook, and you remember that young man, and you get home!"

"Goo-good night, sir," I faltered.

"Much of that!" said he, glancing about him over the cold, wet flat. "I wish I was a frog. Or a eel!"

At the same time he hugged his shuddering body in both his arms—clasping himself, as if to hold himself together—and limped towards the low church wall. As I saw him go, picking his way among the nettles, and among the brambles that bound the green mounds, he looked in my young eyes as if he were eluding the hands of the dead people, stretching up cautiously out of their graves, to get a twist upon his ankle and pull him in.

When he came to the low church wall, he got over it, like a man whose legs were numbed and stiff, and then turned round to look for me. When I saw him turning, I set my face towards home, and made the best use of my legs. But presently I looked over my shoulder, and saw him going on again towards the river, still hugging himself in both arms, and picking his way with his sore feet among the great stones dropped into the marshes here and there for stepping places when the rains were heavy, or the tide was in.

The marshes were just a long black horizontal line then, as I stopped to look after him; and the river was just another horizontal line, not nearly so broad nor yet so black; and the sky was just a row of long angry red lines and dense black lines intermixed. On the edge of the river I could faintly make out the only two black things in all the prospect that seemed to be standing upright: one of these was the beacon by which the sailors steered,—like an unhooped cask upon a pole,—an ugly thing when you were near it; the other a gibbet, with some chains hanging to it which had once held a pirate. The man was limping on towards this latter, as if he were the pirate come to life, and come down, and going back to hook himself up again. It gave me a terrible turn when I thought so; and as I saw the cattle lifting their heads to gaze after him, I wondered whether they thought so too. I looked all round for the horrible young man, and could see no signs of him. But now I was frightened again, and ran home without stopping.

EMILY DICKINSON

EMILY DICKINSON (American, 1830-1886). The greatest American woman poet, whose reputation emerged 40 years after her death. During life, a gentle recluse intimate with nature and private tragedy. Her poetry remarkable for its economy of means, whimsey of imagery, intensity of feeling.

THE SOUL SELECTS

The soul selects her own society,
Then shuts the door;
On her divine majority
Obtrude no more.

Unmoved, she notes the chariots pausing
At her low gate;
Unmoved, an emperor is kneeling
Upon her mat.

I've known her from an ample nation
Choose one;
Then close the valves of her attention
Like stone.

MY LIFE CLOSED TWICE

My life closed twice before its close;
It yet remains to see
If Immortality unveil
A third event to me,

So huge, so hopeless to conceive,
As these that twice befell.
Parting is all we know of heaven,
And all we need of hell.

OF ALL THE SOULS THAT STAND CREATE

Of all the souls that stand create
I have elected one.
When sense from spirit files away,
And subterfuge is done;

When that which is and that which was
Apart, intrinsic, stand,
And this brief tragedy of flesh
Is shifted like a sand;

When figures show their royal front
And mists are carved away—
Behold the atom I preferred
To all the lists of clay!

THE MOUNTAINS GROW UNNOTICED

The mountains grow unnoticed,
Their purple figures rise
Without attempt, exhaustion,
Assistance or applause.

In their eternal faces
The sun with broad delight
Looks long—and last—and golden,
For fellowship at night.

I NEVER SAW A MOOR

I never saw a moor,
I never saw the sea;
Yet know I how the heather looks,
And what a wave must be.

I never spoke with God,
Nor visited in Heaven;
Yet certain am I of the spot
As if the chart were given.

APPARENTLY WITH NO SURPRISE

Apparently with no surprise
To any happy flower,
The frost beheads it at its play
In accidental power.

The blond assassin passes on;
The sun proceeds unmoved
To measure off another day
For an approving God.

322

THE HEART ASKS PLEASURE FIRST

The heart asks pleasure first;
And then, excuse from pain;
And then, those little anodynes
That deaden suffering;

And then, to go to sleep;
And then, if it should be
The will of its Inquisitor,
The liberty to die.

THERE IS NO FRIGATE LIKE A BOOK

There is no frigate like a book
    To take us lands away,
Nor any courses like a page
    Of prancing poetry.

This traverse may the poorest take
    Without oppress of toll;
How frugal is the chariot
    That bears a human soul!

THE CHARIOT

Because I could not stop for Death,
He kindly stopped for me;
The carriage held but just ourselves,
And Immortality.

We slowly drove, he knew no haste,
And I had put away
My labor and my leisure, too,
For his civility.

We passed the school where children played,
Their lessons scarcely done;
We passed the fields of gazing grain,
We passed the setting sun.

We paused before a house that seemed
A swelling of the ground:
The roof was scarcely visible,
The cornice but a mound.

Since then, 'tis centuries; but each
Feels shorter than the day
I first surmised the horses' heads
Were toward eternity.

DEATH

Death is a dialogue between
The spirit and the dust.
"Dissolve," says Death; the spirit, "Sir,
I have another trust."
Death doubts it, argues from the ground.
The spirit turns away,
Just laying off, for evidence,
An overcoat of clay.

DEATH

The bustle in the house
The morning after death
Is solemnest of industries
Enacted upon earth;—

The sweeping up the heart
And putting love away
We shall not want to use again
Until eternity.

RESURGAM

At last to be identified!
At last, the lamps upon thy side
The rest of life to see!
Past midnight, past the morning star!
Past sunrise! Ah! what leagues there are
Between our feet and day!

We thirst at first,—'tis nature's act;
   And, later, when we die
A little water supplicate
   Of fingers going by.

It intimates the finer wants
   Whose adequate supply
Is that great water in the West,
   Termed Immortality.

JOHN DONNE

JOHN DONNE (English, 1572-1631). Famed as preacher and metaphysical poet. Left Catholic Church for Church of England, became Dean of St. Paul's. Turned the English lyric to new subtleties of expression. Early love poems frankly sensuous. Later religious verse sometimes obscure but always noble. One of the idols of modern poets.

SONG

Go, and catch a falling star,
   Get with child a mandrake root,
Tell me, where all past years are,
   Or who cleft the Devil's foot,
Teach me to hear Mermaids singing,
   Or to keep off envy's stinging,
         And find
         What wind
Serves to advance an honest mind.

If thou be'st born to strange sights,
   Things invisible to see,
Ride ten thousand days and nights,
   Till age snow white hairs on thee,
Thou, when thou return'st, wilt tell me
All strange wonders that befell thee,
         And swear
         No where
Lives a woman true, and fair.

If thou find'st one, let me know,
  Such a Pilgrimage were sweet;
Yet do not, I would not go,
  Though at next door we might meet,
Though she were true, when you met her,
And last, till you write your letter,
      Yet she
      Will be
False, ere I come, to two, or three.

THE SUN RISING

  Busy old fool, unruly sun,
    Why dost thou thus
Through windows and through curtains call on us?
Must to thy motions lovers' seasons run?
    Saucy pedantic wretch, go chide
    Late schoolboys and sour prentices,
  Go tell court-huntsmen that the King will ride,
  Call country ants to harvest offices;
Love, all alike, no season knows, nor clime,
Nor hours, days, months, which are the rags of time.

  Thy beams, so reverend and strong
    Why shouldst thou think?
I could eclipse and cloud them with a wink,
But that I would not lose her sight so long;
    If her eyes have not blinded thine,
    Look, and tomorrow late tell me
  Whether both the Indias of spice and mine
  Be where thou left'st them, or lie here with me.
Ask for those kings whom thou saw'st yesterday,
And thou shalt hear, all here in one bed lay.

  She is all states, and all princes I;
    Nothing else is.
Princes do but play us; compared to this,
All honour's mimic, all wealth alchemy.
    Thou, sun, art half as happy as we,
    In that the world's contracted thus;

Thine age asks ease, and since thy duties be
To warm the world, that's done in warming us.
Shine here to us, and thou art everywhere;
This bed thy center is, these walls thy sphere.

THE ECSTASY

Where, like a pillow on a bed,
   A pregnant bank swelled up to rest
The violet's reclining head,
   Sat we two, one another's best.
Our hands were firmly cemented
   With a fast balm, which thence did spring;
Our eye-beams twisted, and did thread
   Our eyes upon one double string;
So to entergraft our hands, as yet
   Was all the means to make us one,
And pictures in our eyes to get
   Was all our propagation.

SEND BACK MY LONG-STRAY'D EYES
TO ME

Send back my long-stray'd eyes to me,
Which, O! too long have dwelt on thee:
But if from you they've learnt such ill,
   To sweetly smile,
   And then beguile,
Keep the deceivers, keep them still.

Send home my harmless heart again,
Which no unworthy thought could stain;
But if it has been taught by thine
   To forfeit both
   Its word and oath,
Keep it, for then 'tis none of mine.

Yet send me back my heart and eyes,
For I'll know all thy falsities;
That I one day may laugh, when thou
   Shalt grieve and mourn—
   Of one the scorn,
Who proves as false as thou art now.

327

THE GOOD MORROW

I wonder, by my troth, what thou and I
Did, till we loved? were we not weaned till then?
But sucked on country pleasures, childishly?
Or snorted we in the Seven Sleepers' den?
'Twas so; but this, all pleasures fancies be;
If ever any beauty I did see,
Which I desired, and got, 'twas but a dream of thee.

And now good morrow to our waking souls,
Which watch not one another out of fear;
For love all love of other sights controls,
And makes one little room an everywhere.
Let sea-discoverers to new worlds have gone;
Let maps to other, worlds on worlds have shown;
Let us possess one world; each hath one, and is one.

My face in thine eye, thine in mine appears,
And true plain hearts do in the faces rest;
Where can we find two better hemispheres
Without sharp north, without declining west?
Whatever dies, was not mix'd equally;
If our two loves be one, or thou and I
Love so alike that none can slacken, none can die.

THE LEGACY

When last I died, and, dear, I die
    As often as from thee I go,
    Though it be but an hour ago
—And lovers' hours be full eternity—
I can remember yet, that I
    Something did say, and something did bestow;
Though I be dead, which sent me, I might be
Mine own executor, and legacy.

I heard me say, "Tell her anon,
    That myself," that is you, not I,
    "Did kill me," and when I felt me die,
I bid me send my heart, when I was gone;

328

But I alas! could there find none;
   When I had ripp'd, and search'd where hearts should lie,
It kill'd me again, that I who still was true
In life, in my last will should cozen you.

Yet I found something like a heart,
   But colors it and corners had;
   It was not good, it was not bad,
It was entire to none, and few had part;
As good as could be made by art
   It seemed, and therefore for our loss be sad.
I meant to send that heart instead of mine,
But O! no man could hold it, for 'twas thine.

FEODOR MIKHAYLOVICH DOSTOYEVSKY

FEODOR MIKHAYLOVICH DOSTOYEVSKY (Russian, 1821-1881). Master of the psychological novel. Spokesman for the downtrodden little people of Czarist Russia. Important factors in life: epilepsy, penal servitude in Siberia, passion for gambling. Novels concerned with mystery of human personality, good and evil, God and immortality. Character analysis foreshadows modern psychology. His four masterpieces: *The Brothers Karamazov, Crime and Punishment, The Idiot, The Possessed.*

THE MURDERER'S CONFESSION TO SONIA

RASKOLNIKOFF wished to smile, but, do what he would, his countenance retained its sorrow-stricken look. He lowered his head, covering his face with his hands. All at once, he fancied that he was beginning to hate Sonia. Surprised, frightened even, at so strange a discovery, he suddenly raised his head and attentively considered the girl, who, in her turn, fixed on him a look of anxious love. Hatred fled from Raskolnikoff's heart. It was not that; he had only mistaken the nature of the sentiment he had experienced. It signified that the fatal moment had come. Once more he hid his face in his hands and bowed his head. Suddenly he grew pale, rose, and, after looking at Sonia, he mechanically went and sat on her bed, without uttering a single word. Raskolnikoff's impression was the very same he had experienced when standing behind the old wo-

man—he had loosened the hatchet from the loop, and said to himself: "There is not a moment to be lost!"

"What is the matter?" asked Sonia, in bewilderment.

No reply. Raskolnikoff had relied on making explanations under quite different conditions, and did not himself understand what was now at work within him. She gently approached him, sat on the bed by his side, and waited, without taking her eyes from his face. Her heart beat as if it would break. The situation was becoming unbearable; he turned towards the girl his lividly-pale face, his lips twitched with an effort to speak. Fear had seized upon Sonia.

"What is the matter with you?" she repeated, moving slightly away from him.

"Nothing, Sonia; don't be afraid. It is not worth while; it is all nonsense!" he murmured, like a man absent in mind. "Only, why can I have come to torment you?" added he all at once, looking at his interlocutress. "Yes, why? I keep on asking myself this question, Sonia."

Perhaps he had done so a quarter of an hour before, but at this moment his weakness was such that he scarcely retained consciousness; a continued trembling shook his whole frame.

"Oh! how you suffer!" said she, in a voice full of emotion, whilst looking at him.

"It is nothing! But this is the matter in question, Sonia." (For a moment or so, a pale smile hovered on his lips.) "You remember what I wished to tell you yesterday?" Sonia waited anxiously. "I told you, on parting, that I was, perhaps, bidding you farewell for ever, but that if I should come to-day, I would tell you who it was that killed Elizabeth." She began to tremble in every limb. "Well, then, that is why I have come."

"I know you told me that yesterday," she went on in a shaky voice. "How do you know that?" she added vivaciously. Sonia breathed with an effort. Her face grew more and more pale.

"I know it."

"Has *he* been discovered?" she asked, timidly, after a moment's silence.

"No, *he* has not been discovered."

For another moment she remained silent. "Then how do you know it?" she at length asked, in an almost unintelligible voice.

He turned towards the girl, and looked at her with a singular rigidity, whilst a feeble smile fluttered on his lips. "Guess!" he said.

Sonia felt on the point of being seized with convulsions. "But

330

you—why frighten me like this?" she asked, with a childlike smile.

"I know it, because I am very intimate with *him!*" went on Raskolnikoff, whose look remained fixed on her, as if he had not strength to turn his eyes aside. "Elizabeth—he had no wish to murder her— he killed her without premeditation. He only intended to kill the old woman, when he should find her alone. He went to her house —but at the very moment Elizabeth came in—he was there—and he killed her."

A painful silence followed upon these words. For a moment both continued to look at one another. "And so you can't guess?" he asked abruptly, feeling like a man on the point of throwing himself from the top of a steeple.

"No," stammered Sonia, in a scarcely audible voice.

"Try again."

At the moment he pronounced these words, Raskolnikoff experienced afresh, in his heart-of-hearts, that feeling of chilliness he knew so well. He looked at Sonia, and suddenly read on her face the same expression as on that of Elizabeth, when the wretched woman recoiled from the murderer advancing towards he, hatchet in hand. In that supreme moment Elizabeth had raised her arm, as children do when they begin to be afraid, and ready to weep, fix a glaring immovable glance on the object which frightens them. In the same way Sonia's face expressed indescribable fear. She also raised her arm, and gently pushed Raskolnikoff aside, whilst touching his breast with her hand, and then gradually drew back without ceasing to look hard at him. Her fear affected the young man, who, for his part, began to gaze on her with a scared expression.

"Have you guessed?" he murmured at last.

"My God!" exclaimed Sonia.

Then she sank exhausted on the bed, and buried her face in the pillows; a moment after, however, she rose with a rapid movement, approached him, and, seizing him by both hands, which her slender fingers clutched like nippers, she fixed on him a long look. Had he made a mistake? She hoped so, but she had no sooner cast a look on Raskolnikoff's face than the suspicion which had flashed on her mind became certainty.

"Enough, Sonia! enough! Spare me!" he implored in a plaintive voice. The event upset all his calculations, for it certainly was not *thus* that he had intended to confess his crime.

Sonia seemed beside herself; she jumped from her bed, went to the middle of the room wringing her hands, she then quickly re-

turned in the same way, sat once more by the young man's side, almost touching him with her shoulder. Suddenly she shivered, uttered a cry, and, without knowing why, fell on her knees before Raskolnikoff. "You are lost!" she exclaimed, with an accent of despair. And, rising suddenly, she threw herself on his neck, and kissed him, whilst lavishing on him tokens of tenderness.

Raskolnikoff broke away, and, with a sad smile, looked at the girl: "I do not understand you, Sonia. You kiss me after I told you *that*—. You cannot be conscious of what you are doing."

She did not hear the remark. "No, at this moment there cannot be a more wretched man on earth than you are!" she exclaimed with a transport of passion, whilst bursting into sobs.

Raskolnikoff felt his heart grow soft under the influence of a sentiment which for some time past he had not felt. He did not try to fight against the feeling; two tears spurted from his eyes and remained on the lashes. "Then you will not forsake me, Sonia?" said he with an almost suppliant look.

"No, no; never, nowhere!" she cried, "I shall follow you, shall follow you everywhere! Heaven! Wretch that I am! And why have I not known you sooner? Why did you not come before? Heaven!"

"You see I have come."

"Now? What is to be done now? Together, together," she went on, with a kind of exaltation, and once more she kissed the young man. "Yes, I will go with you to the galleys!"

These words caused Raskolnikoff a painful feeling; a bitter and almost haughty smile appeared on his lips. "Perhaps I may not yet wish to go to the galleys, Sonia," said he.

The girl rapidly turned her eyes on him. She had up to the present experienced no more than immense pity for an unhappy man. This statement, and the tone of voice in which it was pronounced, suddenly recalled to the girl that the wretched man was an assassin. She cast on him an astonished look. As yet, she did not know how nor why he had become a criminal. At this moment, these questions suggested themselves to her, and, once more doubting, she asked herself: "He, he a murderer? Is such a thing possible? But no, it cannot be true! Where am I?" she asked herself, as if she could have believed herself the sport of a dream. "How is it possible that you, being what you are, can have thought of such a thing? Oh! why?"

"To steal, if you wish to know. Cease, Sonia!" he replied in wearied and rather vexed accents.

Sonia remained stupefied; suddenly a cry escaped her: "Were you hungry? Did you do so to help your mother? Speak!"

"No, Sonia! no!" he stammered, drooping his head. "I was not so poor as all that. It is true I wanted to help my mother, but that was not the real reason.—Do not torment me, Sonia!"

The girl beat her hands together. "Is it possible that such a thing can be real? Heaven! is it possible? How can I believe such a thing? You say you killed to rob; you, who deprive yourself of all for the sake of others! Ah!" she cried suddenly. "That money you gave to Catherine Ivanovna! — that money! Heavens! can it be that?"

"No, Sonia!" he interrupted somewhat sharply. "This money comes from another source, I assure you. It was my mother who sent it to me during my sickness, through the intervention of a merchant, and I had just received it when I gave it. Razoumikin saw it himself, he even went so far as to receive it for me. The money was really my own property." Sonia listened in perplexity, and strove to understand. "As for the old woman's money, to tell the truth, I really do not know whether there was any money at all," he went on hesitatingly. "I took from her neck a well-filled chamois-leather purse. But I never examined the contents, probably because I had no time to do so. I took different things, sleeve-links, watch-chains. These things I hid, in the same way as the purse, on the following day, under a large stone in a yard which looks out on the V—— Prospect. Everything is still there."

Sonia listened with avidity. "But why did you take nothing, since, as you tell me, you committed murder to steal?" she went on, cling-ing to a last and very vague hope.

"I don't know—as yet I am undecided whether to take this money or not," replied Raskolnikoff in the same hesitating voice; then he smiled. "What silly tale have I been telling you?"

"Can he be mad?" Sonia asked herself, but she soon dispelled such an idea; no, it was something else, which she most certainly did not understand.

"Do you know what I am going to tell you, Sonia?" he went on in a convinced tone: "If nothing but need had urged me to com-mit a murder," laying stress on every word, and his look, although frank was more or less puzzling, "I should now be *happy!* Let me tell you that! And what can the motive be to you, since I told you just now that I had acted badly?" he cried despairingly, a moment afterwards. "What was the good of this foolish triumph over my-

333

self? Ah! Sonia, was it for that I came to you?" She once more wished to speak, but remained silent. "Yesterday, I made a proposal to you that we should both of us depart together, because you are all that is left to me."

"Why did you wish me to accompany you?" asked the girl timidly.

"Not to rob or to kill, I assure you," answered Raskolnikoff, with a caustic smile. "We are not of the same way of thinking. And—do you know, Sonia?—it is only of late that I have known why I asked you yesterday to accompany me. When I asked you to do so, I did not as yet know what it would lead to. I see it now. I have but one wish—it is that you should not leave me. You will not do so, will you, Sonia?" She clasped his hand. "And why have I told her this? Why make such a confession?" he exclaimed, a moment afterwards. He looked at her with infinite compassion, whilst his voice expressed the most profound despair. "I see, Sonia, that you are waiting for some kind of explanation, but what am I to say? You understand nothing about the matter, and I should only be causing you additional pain. I see you are once more commencing to weep and embrace me. Why do so at all? Because, failing in courage to bear my own burden, I have imposed it on another—because I seek in the anguish of others some mitigation for my own. And you can love a coward like that?"

"But you are likewise suffering!" exclaimed Sonia.

For a moment he experienced a new feeling of tenderness. "Sonia, my disposition is a bad one, and that can explain much. I have come because I am bad. Some would not have done so. But I am an infamous coward. Why, once more, have I come? I shall never forgive myself for that!"

"No, no!—on the contrary, you have done well to come," cried Sonia; "it is better, much better, I should know all!"

Raskolnikoff looked at her with sorrowful eye. "I was ambitious to become another Napoleon; that was why I committed a murder. Can you understand it now?"

"No," answered Sonia, naïvely and in a timid voice. "But speak! speak! I shall understand it all!"

"You will, say you? God! we shall see!" For some time Raskolnikoff collected his ideas. "That fact is that, one day, I asked myself the following question: 'Supposing Napoleon to have been in my place, supposing that to commence his career he had neither had Toulon, nor Egypt, nor the crossing of Mont Blanc, but, in lieu of

all these brilliant exploits, he was on the point of committing a murder with a view to secure his future, would he have recoiled at the idea of killing an old woman, and of robbing her of three thousand roubles? Would he have agreed that such a deed was too much wanting in prestige and much too—criminal a one?' For a long time I have split my head on that question, and could not help experiencing a feeling of shame when I finally came to the conclusion that he not only would not have hesitated, but that he would not have understood the possibility of such a thing. Every other expedient being out of his reach, he would not have flinched, he would have done so without the smallest scruple. Hence, I ought not to hesitate—being justified on the authority of Napoleon!"

JOHN DRYDEN

JOHN DRYDEN (English, 1631-1700). Dominant literary figure of the Restoration. Dramatist, poet, essayist, critic. Influential in establishing heroic couplet, which dominated English poetry for a century. Best-known poem: "Alexander's Feast." Drama: *All for Love.* Prose: *An Essay of Dramatic Poesy.*

ZEGRI AND ABENCERRAGE

Scene: *Granada, and the Christian Camp besieging it.* Present: Boabdelin, Abenamar, Abdelmelech, *and* Guards.

Boabdelin—
The alarm-bell rings from our Alhambra walls,
And from the streets sound drums and atabals.
          (Within, a bell, drums, and trumpets.)
   Enter a Messenger.
How now? from whence proceed these new alarms?
Messenger—
The two fierce factions are again in arms;
And changing into blood the day's delight,
The Zegrys with the the Abencerrages fight;
On each side their allies and friends appear;
The Macas here, the Alabezes there;
The Gazuls with the Bencerrages join,
And, with the Zegrys, all great Gomel's line.

335

Boabdelin—

Draw up behind the Vivarambla place;
Double my guards,—these factions I will face;
And try if all the fury they can bring
Be proof against the presence of their king.
        (Exit Boabdelin.)
The Factions appear: At the head of the Abencerrages, Ozmyn; *at
    the head of the Zegrys,* Zulema, Hamet, Gomel, *and* Selin; Aben-
    amar *and* Abdelmelech *join with the Abencerrages.*

Zulema—

The faint Abencerrages quit their ground:
Press them; put home your thrusts to every wound.

Abdelmelech—

Zegry, on manly force our line relies;
Thine poorly takes the advantage of surprise:
Unarmed and much outnumbered we retreat;
You gain no fame, when basely you defeat.
If thou art brave, seek nobler victory;
Save Moorish blood; and, while our bands stand by,
Let two and two an equal combat try.

Hamet—

'Tis not for fear the combat we refuse.
But we our gained advantage will not lose.

Zulema—

In combating, but two of you will fall;
And we resolve we will despatch you all.

Ozmyn—

We'll double yet the exchange before we die,
And each of ours two lives of yours shall buy.
    Almanzor *enters betwixt them, as they stand ready to engage.*

Almanzor—

I cannot stay to ask which cause is best:
But this is so to me, because opprest.
                    (Goes to the Abencerrages.)
    To them Boabdelin *and his* Guards, *going betwixt them.*

Boabdelin—

On your allegiance, I command you stay;
Who passes here, through me must make his way;
My life's the Isthmus; through this narrow line
You first must cut, before those seas can join.
What fury, Zegrys, has possessed your minds?

336

What rage the brave Abencerrages blinds?
If of your courage you new proofs would show,
Without much travel you may find a foe.
Those foes are neither so remote nor few
That you should need each other to pursue.
Lean times and foreign wars should minds unite;
When poor men mutter, but they seldom fight.
O holy Allah! that I live to see
Thy Granadines assist their enemy!
You fight the Christians' battles; every life
You lavish thus, in this intestine strife,
Does from our weak foundations take one prop,
Which helped to hold our sinking country up.

Ozmyn—

'Tis fit our private enmity should cease;
Though injured first, yet I will first seek peace.

Zulema—

No, murderer, no; I never will be won
To peace with him, whose hand has slain my son.

Ozmyn—

Our phrophet's curse
On me and all the Abencerrages light,
If unprovoked I with your son did fight.

Abdelmelech—

A band of Zegrys ran within the place,
Matched with a troop of thirty of our race.
Your son and Ozmyn the first squadrons led,
Which, ten by ten, like Parthians, charged and fled,
The ground was strowed with canes where we did meet,
Which crackled underneath our coursers' feet;
When Tarifa (I saw him ride apart)
Changed his blunt cane for a steel-pointed dart,
And, meeting Ozmyn next—
Who wanted time for treason to provide,—
He basely threw it at him, undefied.

Ozmyn (showing his arms)—

Witness this blood—which when by treason sought,
That followed, sir, which to myself I ought.

Zulema—

His hate to thee was grounded on a grudge,
Which all our generous Zegrys just did judge:

Thy villain-blood thou openly didst place
Above the purple of our kingly race.

Boabdelin—

From equal stems their blood both houses draw,
They from Morocco, you from Cordova.

Hamet—

Their mongrel race is mixed with Christian breed;
Hence 'tis that they those dogs in prisons feed.

Abdelmelech—

Our holy prophet wills, that charity
Should even to birds and beast extended be:
None knows what fate is for himself designed;
The thought of human chance should make us kind.

Gomel—

We waste that time we to revenge should give:
Fall on; let no Abencerrage live.

Advances before the rest of his party. Almanzor *advances on the
other side, and describes a line with his sword.*

Almanzor—

Upon thy life pass not this middle space:
Sure death stands guarding the forbidden place.

Gomel—

To dare that death, I will approach yet nigher:
Thus,—wert thou compassed in with circling fire.
    (They fight.)

Boabdelin—

Disarm them both; if they resist you, kill.

Almanzor, *in the midst of the guards, kills* Gomel, *and then is
    disarmed.*

Almanzor—

Now you have but the leavings of my will.

Boabdelin—

Kill him! this insolent unknown shall fall,
And be the victim to atone you all.

Ozmyn—

If he must die, not one of us will live:
That life he gave for us, for him we give.

Boabdelin—

It was a traitor's voice that spoke those words;
So are you all, who do not sheathe your swords.

Zulema—
　　Outrage unpunished, when a prince is by,
　　Forfeits to scorn the rights of majesty:
　　No subject his protection can expect,
　　Who what he owes himself does first neglect.

Abenamar—
　　This stranger, sir, is he,
　　Who lately in the Vivarambla place
　　Did, with so loud applause, your triumphs grace.

Boabdelin—
　　The word which I have given, I'll not revoke;
　　If he be brave, he's ready for the stroke.

Almanzor—
　　No man has more contempt than I of breath,
　　But whence hast thou the right to give me death?
　　Obeyed as sovereign by thy subjects be,
　　But know, that I alone am king of me.
　　I am as free as nature first made man,
　　Ere the base laws of servitude began,
　　When wild in woods the noble savage ran.

Boabdelin—
　　Since, then, no power above your own you know,
　　Mankind should use you like a common foe;
　　You should be hunted like a beast of prey:
　　By your own law I take your life away.

Almanzor—
　　My laws are made but only for my sake;
　　No king against himself a law can make.
　　If thou pretend'st to be a prince like me,
　　Blame not an act which should thy pattern be.
　　I saw the oppressed, and thought it did belong
　　To a king's office to redress the wrong:
　　I brought that succor which thou ought'st to bring,
　　And so, in nature, am thy subjects' king.

Boabdelin—
　　I do not want your counsel to direct,
　　Or aid to help me punish or protect.

Almanzor—
　　Thou want'st them both, or better thou wouldst know,
　　Than to let factions in thy kingdoms grow.

339

Divided interests, while thou think'st to sway,
Draw, like two brooks, thy middle stream away:
For though they band and jar, yet both combine
To make their greatness by the fall of thine.
Thus, like a buckler, thou art held in sight,
While they behind thee with each other fight.

Boabdelin—

Away, and execute him instantly! (*To his Guards.*)

Almanzor—

Stand off; I have not leisure yet to die.

To them, enter Abdalla *hastily.*

Abdalla—

Hold, sir! for heaven's sake hold!
Defer this noble stranger's punishment,
Or your rash orders you will soon repent.

Boabdelin—

Brother, you know not yet his insolence.

Abdalla—

Upon yourself you punish his offense:
If we treat gallant strangers in this sort,
Mankind will shun the inhospitable court;
And who, henceforth, to our defense will come,
If death must be the brave Almanzor's doom?
From Africa I drew him to your aid,
And for his succor have his life betrayed.

Boabdelin—

Is this the Almanzor whom at Fez you knew,
When first their swords the Xeriff brothers drew?

Abdalla—

This, sir, is he, who for the elder fought,
And to the juster cause the conquest brought;
Till the proud Santo, seated on the throne,
Disdained the service he had done to own:
Then to the vanquished part his fate he led;
The vanquished triumphed, and the victor fled.
Vast is his courage, boundless is his mind,
Rough as a storm, and humorous as wind:
Honor's the only idol of his eyes;
The charms of beauty like a pest he flies;
And, raised by valor from a birth unknown,
Acknowledges no power above his own.

340

Boabdelin (coming to Almanzor) —
Impute your danger to our ignorance;
The bravest men are subject most to chance:
Granada much does to your kindness owe;
But towns, expecting sieges, cannot show
More honor than to invite you to a foe.

Almanzor —
I do not doubt but I have been to blame:
But, to pursue the end for which I came,
Unite your subjects first; then let us go,
And pour their common rage upon the foe.

Boabdelin (to the factions) —
Lay down your arms, and let me beg you cease
Your enmities.

Zulema —
We will not hear of peace,
Till we by force have first revenged our slain.

Abdelmelech —
The action we have done we will maintain.

Selin —
Then let the king depart, and we will try
Our cause by arms.

Zulema —
For us and victory.

Boabdelin —A king entreats you.

Almanzor —
What subjects will precarious kings regard?
A beggar speaks too softly to be heard:
Lay down your arms! 'tis I command you now.
Do it—or, by our prophet's soul I vow,
My hands shall right your king on him I seize.
Now let me see whose look but disobeys.

All —
Long live king Mahomet Boabdelin!

Almanzor —
No more; but hushed as midnight silence go:
He will not have your acclamations now.
Hence, you unthinking crowd!—
(*The Common People go off in both parties.*)
Empire, thou poor and despicable thing,
When such as these make or unmake a king!

341

ALEXANDRE DUMAS

ALEXANDRE DUMAS (1802-1870). Prolific romantic novelist. *The Three Musketeers, The Count of Monte Cristo, The Man in the Iron Mask,* still read for their vitality and narrative ingenuity. With team of collaborators, produced 300 such romances. Also wrote melodramas for stage, and was active in political affairs.

MARGUERITE DE VALOIS

1. *Henry of Navarre and Marguerite*

ON Monday, August 18, 1572, a great festival was held in the palace of the Louvre. It was to celebrate the marriage of Henry of Navarre and Marguerite de Valois, a marriage that perplexed a good many people, and alarmed others.

For Henry de Bourbon, King of Navarre, was the leader of the Huguenot party, and Marguerite was the daughter of Catherine de Medici, and the sister of the king, Charles IX., and this alliance between a Protestant and a Catholic, it seemed, was to end the strife that rent the nation. The king, too, had set his heart on this marriage, and the Huguenots were somewhat reassured by the king's declaration that Catholic and Huguenot alike were now his subjects, and were equally beloved by him. Still, there were many on both sides who feared and distrusted the alliance.

At midnight, six days later, on August 24, the tocsin sounded, and the massacre of St. Bartholomew began.

The marriage, indeed, was in no sense a love match; but Henry succeeded at once in making Marguerite his friend, for he was alive to the dangers that surrounded him.

"Madame," he said, presenting himself at Marguerite's rooms on the night of the wedding festival, "whatever many persons may have said, I think our marriage is a good marriage. I stand well with you—you stand well with me. Therefore, we ought to act towards each other like good allies, since to-day we have been allied in the sight of God! Don't you think so?"

"Without question, sir!"

"I know, madame, that the ground at court is full of dangerous abysses; and I know that, though I am young and have never injured any person, I have many enemies. The king hates me, his brothers, the Duke of Anjou and the Duke d' Alençon, hate me. Catherine de Medici hated my mother too much not to hate me.

Well, against these menaces, which must soon become attacks, I
can only defend myself by your aid, for you are beloved by all
those who hate me!"

"I?" said Marguerite.

"Yes, you!" replied Henry. "And if you will—I do not say love
me—but if you will be my ally I can brave anything; while, if
you become my enemy, I am lost."

"Your enemy! Never, sir!" exclaimed Marguerite.

"And my ally?"

"Most decidedly!"

And Marguerite turned round and presented her hand to the king.
"It is agreed," she said.

"Political alliance, frank and loyal?" asked Henry.

"Frank and loyal," was the answer.

At the door Henry turned and said softly, "Thanks, Marguerite;
thanks! You are a true daughter of France. Lacking your love, your
friendship will not fail me. I rely on you, as you, for your part,
may rely on me. Adieu, madame."

He kissed his wife's hand; and then, with a quick step, the king
went down the corridor to his own apartment. "I have more need
of fidelity in politics than in love," he said to himself.

If on both sides there was little attempt at fidelity in love, there
was an honourable alliance, which was maintained unbroken and
saved the life of Henry of Navarre from his enemies on more than
one occasion.

On the day of the St. Bartholomew massacre, while the Huguenots
were being murdered throughout Paris, Charles IX., instigated by
his mother, summoned Henry of Navarre to the royal armoury, and
called upon him to turn Catholic or die.

"Will you kill me, sire—me, your brother-in-law?" exclaimed
Henry.

Charles IX turned away to the open window. "I must kill someone," he cried, and firing his arquebuse, struck a man who was
passing.

Then, animated by a murderous fury, Charles loaded and fired his
arquebuse without stopping, shouting with joy when his aim was
successful.

"It's all over with me!" said Henry to himself. "When he sees
no one else to kill, he will kill me!"

Catherine de Medici entered as the king fired his last shot. "Is
it done?" she said, anxiously.

343

"No," the king exclaimed, throwing his arquebuse on the floor. "No; the obstinate blockhead will not consent!"

Catherine gave a glance at Henry which Charles understood perfectly, and which said, "Why, then, is he alive?"

"He lives," said the king, "because he is my relative."

Henry felt that it was with Catherine he had to contend.

"Madame," he said, addressing her, "I can see quite clearly that all this comes from you and not from brother-in-law Charles. It was you who planned this massacre to ensnare me into a trap which was to destroy us all. It was you who made your daughter the bait. It has been you who have separated me now from my wife, that she might not see me killed before her eyes!"

"Yes; but that shall not be!" cried another voice; and Marguerite, breathless and impassioned, burst into the room.

"Sir," said Marguerite to Henry, "your last words were an accusation, and were both right and wrong. They have made me the means for attempting to destroy you, but I was ignorant that in marrying me you were going to destruction. I myself owe my life to chance, for this very night they all but killed me in seeking you. Directly I knew of your danger I sought you. If you are exiled, sir, I will be exiled too; if they imprison you they shall imprison me also; if they kill you, I will also die!"

She gave her hand to her husband, and he seized it eagerly.

"Brother," cried Marguerite to Charles IX., "remember, you made him my husband!"

"Faith, Margot is right, and Henry is my brother-in-law," said the king.

II

THE BOAR HUNT

As time went on, if Catherine's hatred of Henry of Navarre did not diminish, Charles IX. certainly became more friendly.

Catherine was for ever intriguing and plotting for the fortunes of her sons and the downfall of her son-in-law, but Henry always managed to evade the webs she wove. At a certain boar-hunt Charles was indebted to Henry for his life.

It was at the time when the king's brother, D'Anjou, had accepted the crown of Poland, and the second brother, D'Alençon, a weak-minded, ambitious man, was secretly hoping for a crown somewhere, that Henry paid his debt for the king's mercy to him on the night of St. Bartholomew.

Charles was an intrepid hunter, but the boar had swerved as the king's spear was aimed at him, and, maddened with rage, the animal had rushed at him. Charles tried to draw his hunting-knife, but the sheath was so tight it was impossible.

"The boar! the boar!" shouted the king. "Help, D'Alençon, help!"

D'Alençon was ghastly white as he placed his arquebuse to his shoulder and fired. The ball, instead of hitting the boar, felled the king's horse.

"I think," D'Alençon murmured to himself, "that D'Anjou is King of France, and I King of Poland."

The boar's tusk had indeed grazed the king's thigh when a hand in an iron glove dashed itself against the mouth of the beast, and a knife was plunged into its shoulder.

Charles rose with difficulty, and seemed for a moment as if about to fall by the dead boar. Then he looked at Henry of Navarre, and for the first time in four-and-twenty years his heart was touched.

"Thanks, Harry!" he said. "D'Alençon, for a first-rate marksman you made a most curious shot."

On Marguerite coming up to congratulate the king and thank her husband, Charles added, "Margot, you may well thank him. But for him Henry III. would be King of France."

"Alas, madame," returned Henry, "M. D'Anjou, who is always my enemy, will now hate me more than ever; but everyone has to do what he can."

Had Charles IX. been killed, the Duke d'Anjou would have been King of France, and D'Alençon most probably King of Poland. Henry of Navarre would have gained nothing by this change of affairs.

Instead of Charles IX., who tolerated him, he would have had the Duke d'Anjou on the throne, who, being absolutely at one with his mother, Catherine, had sworn his death, and would have kept his oath.

These ideas were in his brain when the wild boar rushed on Charles, and like lightning he saw that his own existence was bound up with the life of Charles IX. But the king knew nothing of the spring and motive of the devotion which had saved his life, and on the following day he showed his gratitude to Henry by carrying him off from his apartments, and out of the Louvre. Catherine, in her fear lest Henry of Navarre should some day be King of France, had arranged the assassination of her son-in-law; and Charles, getting wind of this, warned him that the air of the

Louvre was not good for him that night, and kept him in his company. Instead of Henry, it was one of his followers who was killed.

III

THE POISONED BOOK

Once more Catherine resolved to destroy Henry. The Huguenots had plotted with D'Alençon that he should be King of Navarre, since Henry not only abjured Protestantism but remained in Paris, being kept there indeed by the will of Charles IX.

Catherine, aware of D'Alençon's scheme, assured her son that Henry was suffering from an incurable disease, and must be taken away from Paris when D'Alencon started for Navarre.

"Are you sure that Henry will die?" asked D'Alencon.

"The physician who gave me a certain book assured me of it."

"And where is this book? What is it?"

Catherine brought the book from her cabinet.

"Here it is. It is a treatise on the art of rearing and training falcons by an Italian. Give it to Henry, who is going hawking with the king to-day, and will not fail to read it."

"I dare not!" said D'Alençon shuddering.

"Nonsense!" replied Catherine. "It is a book like any other, only the leaves have a way of sticking together. Don't attempt to read it yourself, for you will have to wet the finger in turning over each leaf, which takes up so much time."

"Oh," said D'Alençon, "Henry is with the court! Give me the book, and while he is away I will put it in his room."

D'Alençon's hand was trembling as he took the book from the queen-mother, and with some hesitation and fear he entered Henry's apartment and placed the volume, open at the title page.

But it was not Henry, but Charles, seeking his brother-in-law, who found the book and carried it off to his own room. D'Alençon found the king reading.

"By heavens, this is an admirable book!" cried Charles. "Only it seems as if they had stuck the leaves together on purpose to conceal the wonders it contains."

D'Alençon's first thought was to snatch the book from his brother, but he hesitated.

The king again moistened his finger and turned over a page.

346

"Let me finish this chapter," he said, "and then tell me what you please. I have already read fifty pages."

"He must have tasted the poison five-and-twenty times," thought D'Alençon. "He is a dead man!"

The poison did its deadly work. Charles was taken ill while out hunting, and returned to find his dog dead, and in its mouth pieces of paper from the precious book on falconry. The king turned pale. The book was poisoned! Many things flashed across his memory, and he knew his life was doomed.

Charles summoned René, a Florentine, the court perfumer to Catherine de Medici, to his presence, and bade him examine the dog.

"Sire," said René, after a close investigation, "the dog has been poisoned by arsenic."

"He has eaten a leaf of this book," said Charles; "and if you do not tell me whose book it is I will have your flesh torn from your bones by red-hot pincers."

"Sire," stammered the Florentine, "this book belongs to me!"

"And how did it leave your hands?"

"Her majesty the queen-mother took it from my house."

"Why did she do that?"

"I believe she intended sending it to the King of Navarre, who had asked for a book on hawking."

"Ah," said Charles, "I understand it all! The book was in Harry's room. It is destiny; I must yield to it. Tell me," he went on, turning to René, "this poison does not always kill at once?"

"No, sire; but it kills surely. It is a matter of time."

"Is there no remedy?"

"None, sire, unless it be instantly administered."

Charles compelled the wretched man to write in the fatal volume, "This book was given by me to the queen-mother, Catherine de Medici.—René," and then dismissed him.

Henry, at his own prayer and for his personal safety, was confined in the prison of Vincennes by the king's order. Charles grew worse, and the physicians discussed his malady without daring to guess at the truth.

Then Catherine came one day and explained to the king the cause of his disease.

"Listen, my son; you believe in magic?"

"Oh, fully," said Charles, repressing his smile of incredulity.

"Well," continued Catherine, "all your sufferings proceed from

347

magic. An enemy afraid to attack you openly has done so in secret; a terrible conspiracy has been directed against your majesty. You doubt it, perhaps, but I know it for a certainty."

"I never doubt what you tell me," replied the king sarcastically. "I am curious to know how they have sought to kill me."

"By magic. Look here." The queen drew from under her mantle a figure of yellow wax about ten inches high, wearing a robe covered with golden stars, and over this a royal mantle.

"See, it has on its head a crown," said Catherine, "and there is a needle in its heart. Now do you recognise yourself?"

"Myself?"

"Yes, in your royal robes, with the crown on your head."

"And who made this figure?" asked the king, weary of the wretched farce. "The King of Navarre, of course!"

"No, sire; he did not actually make it, but it was found in the rooms of M. de la Mole, who serves the King of Navarre."

"So, then, the person who seeks to kill me is M. de la Mole?" said Charles.

"He is only the instrument, and behind the instrument is the hand that directs it," replied Catherine.

"This, then, is the cause of my illness. And now what must I do —for I know nothing of sorcery?"

"The death of the conspirator destroys the charm. Its power ends with his life. You are convinced now, are you not, of the cause of your illness?"

"Oh, certainly," Charles answered ironically. "And I am to punish M. de la Mole, as you say he is the guilty party?"

"I say he is the instrument, and," muttered Catherine, "we have infallible means for making him confess the name of his principal."

Catherine left hurriedly without understanding the sardonic laughter of the king, and as she went out Marguerite appeared.

"Oh, sire—sire," cried Marguerite, "you know what *she* says is false. It is terrible to accuse one's own mother, but she only lives to persecute the man who is devoted to you, Henry—your Henry— and I swear to you that what she says is false!"

"I think so, too, Margot. But Henry is safe. Safer in disgrace in Vincennes than in favour at the Louvre."

"Oh, thanks, thanks! But there is another person in whose welfare I am interested, whom I hardly dare mention to my brother, much less to my king."

"M. de la Mole, is it not? But do you know that a figure dressed

348

in royal robes and pierced to the heart was found in his rooms?"

"I know it; but it was the figure of a woman, not of a man."

"And the needle?"

"Was a charm not to kill a man, but to make a woman love him."

"What was the name of this woman?"

"Marguerite!" cried the queen, throwing herself down and bathing the king's hand in her tears.

"Margot, what if I know the real author of the crime? For a crime has been committed, and I have not three months to live. I am poisoned, but it must be thought I die by magic."

"You know who is guilty?"

"Yes; but it must be kept from the world, and so it must be believed I die of magic, and by the agency of him they accuse."

"But it is monstrous!" exclaimed Marguerite. "You know he is innocent. Pardon him—pardon him!"

"I know it, but the world must believe him guilty. Let your friend die. His death alone can save the honour of our family. I am dying that the secret may be preserved."

M. de la Mole, after enduring excruciating tortures at the hands of Catherine, without making any admissions, died on the scaffold.

IV

"THE BOURBON SHALL NOT REIGN!"

Before he died Charles showed Catherine the poisoned book, which he had kept under lock and key.

"And now burn it, madame. I read this book too much, so fond was I of the chase. And the world must not know the weaknesses of kings. When it is burnt, please summon my brother Henry. I wish to speak to him about the regency."

Catherine brought Henry of Navarre to the king, and warned him that if he accepted the regency he was a dead man.

Charles, however, though on his deathbed, declared Henry should be regent.

"Madame," he said, addressing his mother, "if I had a son he would be king, and you would be regent. In your stead, did you decline, the King of Poland would be regent; and in his stead, D'Alencon. But I have no son, and therefore the throne belongs to D'Anjou, who is absent. To make D'Alencon regent is to invite civil war. I have therefore chosen the fittest person for regent. Salute him, madame; salute him, D'Alençon. It is the King of Navarre!"

"Never," cried Catherine, "shall my race yield to a foreign one! Never shall a Bourbon reign while a Valois lives!"

She left the room, followed by D'Alençon.

"Henry," said Charles, "after my death you will be great and powerful. D'Anjou will not leave Poland—they will not let him. D'Alençon is a traitor. You alone are capable of governing. It is not the regency only, but the throne I give you."

A stream of blood choked his speech.

"The fatal moment is come," said Henry. "Am I to reign, or to live?"

"Live, sire!" a voice answered, and René appeared. "The queen has sent me to ruin you, but I have faith in your star. It is foretold that you shall be king. Do you know that the King of Poland will be here very soon? He has been summoned by the queen. A messenger has come from Warsaw. You shall be king, but not yet."

"What shall I do, then?"

"Fly instantly to where your friends wait for you."

Henry stooped and kissed his brother's forehead, then disappeared down a secret passage, passed through the postern, and, springing on his horse, galloped off.

"He flies! The King of Navarre flies!" cried the sentinels.

"Fire on him! Fire!" said the queen.

The sentinels levelled their pieces, but the king was out of reach.

"He flies!" muttered D'Alençon. "I am king, then!"

At the same moment the drawbridge was hastily lowered, and Henry D'Anjou galloped into the court, followed by four knights, crying, "France! France!"

"My son!" cried Catherine joyfully.

"Am I too late?" said D'Anjou.

"No. You are just in time. Listen!"

The captain of the king's guards appeared at the balcony of the king's apartment. He broke the wand he held in two pieces, and holding a piece in either hand, called out three times, "King Charles the Ninth is dead! King Charles the Ninth is dead! King Charles the Ninth is dead!"

"Charles the Ninth is dead!" said Catherine, crossing herself. "God save Henry the Third!"

All repeated the cry.

"I have conquered," said Catherine, "and the odious Bourbon shall not reign!"

350

E

JOSEPH VON EICHENDORFF

JOSEPH VON EICHENDORFF (German, 1788-1857). The latter-day poet of German medievalism. Characterized by typical Romantic themes: love of nature, wanderlust, romantic longings. Wrote in many forms, but most characteristic work, a novella, *Aus dem Leben eines Taugenichts (From the Life of a Good-for-Nothing)*, is combination of poetry and prose.

Poems from
"FROM THE LIFE OF A GOOD-FOR-NOTHING"

The favoured ones, the loved of Heaven,
  God sends to roam the world at will;
His wonders to their gaze are given
  By field and forest, stream and hill.

The dullards who at home are staying
  Are not refreshed by morning's ray;
They grovel, earth-born calls obeying,
  And petty cares beset their day.

The little brooks o'er rocks are springing,
  The lark's gay carol fills the air:
Why should not I with them be singing
  A joyous anthem free from care?

I wander on, in God confiding,
  For all are His, wood, field, and fell;
O'er earth and skies He still presiding,
  For me will order all things well.

*   *   *

I gaze around me, going
  By forest, dale, and lea,
O'er heights where streams are flowing,
My every thought bestowing,
  Ah, Lady fair, on thee.

351

And in my garden, finding
  Bright flowers fresh and rare,
While many a wreath I'm binding,
Sweet thoughts therein I'm winding
  Of thee, my Lady fair.

For me 'twould be too daring
  To lay them at her feet.
They'll soon away be wearing,
But love beyond comparing
  Is thine, my Lady sweet.

In early morning waking,
  I toil with ready smile,
And though my heart be breaking,
I'll sing to hide its aching,
  And dig my grave the while.

*　*　*

When the earliest morning ray
Through the valley finds its way,
Hill and forest fair awaking,
All who can their flight are taking.

And the lad who's free from care
Shouts, with cap flung high in air,
'Song its flight can aye be winging;
Let me, then, be ever singing.'

THE BROKEN RING

Adown in yon cool valley
  I hear a mill-wheel go:
Alas! my love has left me,
  Who once dwelt there below.

A ring of gold she gave me,
  And vowed she would be true;
The vow long since was broken,
  The gold ring snapped in two.

I would I were a minstrel,
  To rove the wide world o'er,
And sing afar my measures,
  And rove from door to door;

Or else a soldier, flying
  Deep into furious flight,
By silent camp-fires lying
  A-field in gloomy night.

Hear I the mill-wheel going:
  I know not what I will;
'Twere best if I were dying—
  Then all were calm and still.

MORNING PRAYER

O silence, wondrous and profound!
  O'er earth doth solitude still reign;
The woods alone incline their heads,
  As if the Lord walked o'er the plain.

I feel new life within me glow;
  Where now is my distress and care?
Here in the blush of waking morn,
  I blush at yesterday's despair.

To me, a pilgrim, shall the world,
  With all its joy and sorrows, be
But as a bridge that leads, O Lord,
  Across the stream of time to Thee.

And should my song woo worldly gifts,
  The base rewards of vanity—
Dash down my lyre! I'll hold my peace
  Before thee to eternity.

353

GEORGE ELIOT

GEORGE ELIOT (Mary Ann Evans, English 1819-1880). Leading author of the Victorian novel. Was assistant editor of *Westminster Review*, knew many intellectuals of her day. Novels marked by deep humanity, subtle psychology, concern for philosophical issues. *Middlemarch*, her masterpiece, a detailed study of Victorian Era. Others: *Adam Bede, The Mill on the Floss, Silas Marner, Romola.*

SILAS MARNER

I. *Why Silas Came to Raveloe*

IN the early years of the nineteenth century a linen-weaver named Silas Marner worked at his vocation in a stone cottage that stood among the nutty hedgerows near the village of Raveloe, and not far from the edge of a deserted stone-pit.

It was fifteen years since Silas Marner had first come to Raveloe; he was then simply a pallid young man with prominent, short-sighted brown eyes. To the villagers among whom he had to settle he seemed to have mysterious peculiarities, chiefly owing to his advent from an unknown region called "Northard." He invited no comer to step across his door-sill, and he never strolled into the village to drink a pint at the Rainbow, or to gossip at the wheel-wrights'; he sought no man or woman, save for the purposes of his calling, or in order to supply himself with necessaries.

At the end of fifteen years the Raveloe men said just the same things about Silas Marner as at the beginning. There was only one important addition which the years had brought; it was that Master Marner had laid by a fine sight of money somewhere, and that he could buy up "bigger men than himself."

But while his daily habits presented scarcely any visible change, Marner's inward life had been a history and a metamorphosis as that of every fervid nature must be when it has been condemned to solitude. His life, before he came to Raveloe, had been filled with the close fellowship of a narrow religious sect, where the poorest layman had the chance of distinguishing himself by gifts of speech; and Marner was highly thought of in that little hidden world, known to itself as the church assembling in Lantern Yard. He was believed to be a young man of exemplary life and ardent faith, and a peculiar interest had been centred in him ever since he had fallen at

a prayer-meeting into a trance or cataleptic fit, which lasted for an hour.

Among the members of his church there was one young man, named William Dane, with whom he lived in close friendship; and it seemed to the unsuspecting Silas that the friendship suffered no chill, even after he had formed a closer attachment, and had become engaged to a young servant-woman.

At this time the senior deacon was taken dangerously ill, and Silas and William, with others of the brethren, took turns at night-watching. On the night the old man died, Silas fell into one of his trances, and when he awoke at four o'clock in the morning death had come, and further, a little bag of money had been stolen from the deacon's bureau, and Silas's pocket-knife was found inside the bureau. For some time Silas was mute with astonishment, then he said, "God will clear me; I know nothing about the knife being there, or the money being gone. Search me and my dwelling."

The search was made, and it ended in William Dane finding the deacon's bag, empty, tucked behind the chest of drawers in Silas's chamber.

According to the principles of the church in Lantern Yard prosecution was forbidden to Christians. But the members were bound to take other measures for finding out the truth, and they resolved on praying and drawing lots; there was nothing unusual about such proceedings a hundred years ago. Silas knelt with his brethren, relying on his own innocence being certified by immediate Divine interference. *The lots declared that Silas Marner was guilty.* He was solemnly suspended from church-membership, and called upon to render up the stolen money; only on confession and repentance could he be received once more within the fold of the church. Marner listened in silence. At last, when everyone rose to depart, he went towards William Dane and said, in a voice shaken by agitation, "The last time I remember using my knife was when I took it to cut a strap for you. I don't remember putting it in my pocket again. *You* stole the money, and you have woven a plot to lay the sin at my door. But you may prosper for all that; there is no just God, but a God of lies, that bears witness against the innocent!"

There was a general shudder at this blasphemy. Poor Marner went out with that despair in his soul—that shaken trust in God and man which is little short of madness to a loving nature. In the bitterness of his wounded spirit, he said to himself, "*She* will cast me off, too!" and for a whole day he sat alone, stunned by despair.

The second day he took refuge from benumbing unbelief by getting into his loom and working away as usual, and before many hours were past, the minister and one of the deacons came to him with a message from Sarah, the young woman to whom he had been engaged, that she held her engagement at an end. In little more than a month from that time Sarah was married to William Dane, and not long afterwards it was known to the brethren in Lantern Yard that Silas Marner had departed from the town.

II. *The Second Blow*

When Silas Marner first came to Raveloe he seemed to weave like a spider, from pure impulse, without reflection. Then there were the calls of hunger, and Silas, in his solitude, had to provide his own breakfast, dinner, and supper, to fetch his own water from the well, and put his own kettle on the fire; and all these immediate promptings helped to reduce his life to the unquestioning activity of a spinning insect. He hated the thought of the past; there was nothing that called out his love and fellowship towards the strangers he had come amongst; and the future was all dark, for there was no Unseen Love that cared for him.

It was then, when all purpose of life was gone, that Silas got into the habit of looking towards the money he received for his weaving, and grasping it with a sense of fulfilled effort. Gradually, the guineas, the crowns, and the half-crowns, grew to a heap, and Marner drew less and less for his own wants, trying to solve the problem of keeping himself strong enough to work sixteen hours a day on as small an outlay as possible. He handled his coins, he counted them, till their form and colour were like the satisfaction of a thirst to him; but it was only in the night, when his work was done, that he drew them out, to enjoy their companionship. He had taken up some bricks in his floor underneath his loom, and here he had made a hole in which he set the iron pot that contained his guineas and silver coins, covering the bricks with sand whenever he replaced them.

So, year after year, Silas Marner lived in this solitude, his guineas rising in the iron pot, and his life narrowing and hardening itself more and more as it became reduced to the functions of weaving and hoarding.

This is the history of Silas Marner until the fifteenth year after

he came to Raveloe. Then, about the Christmas of that year, a second great change came over his life.

It was a raw, foggy night, with rain, and Silas was returning from the village, plodding along, with a sack thrown round his shoulders, and with a horn lantern in his hand. His legs were weary, but his mind was at ease with the sense of security that springs from habit. Supper was his favorite meal, because it was his time of revelry, when his heart warmed over his gold.

He reached his door in much satisfaction that his errand was done; he opened it, and to his short-sighted eyes everything remained as he had left it, except that the fire sent out a welcome increase of heat.

As soon as he was warm he began to think it would be a long while to wait till after supper before he drew out his guineas, and it would be pleasant to see them on the table before him as he ate his food.

He rose and placed his candle unsuspectingly on the floor near his loom, swept away the sand, without noticing any change, and removed the bricks. The sight of the empty hole made his heart leap violently, but the belief that his gold was gone could not come at once—only terror, and the eager effort to put an end to the terror. He passed his trembling hand all about the hole, then he held the candle and examined it curiously, trembling more and more. He searched in every corner, he turned his bed over, and shook it, and kneaded it; he looked in the brick oven; and when there was no other place to be searched, he felt once more all round the hole.

He could see every object in his cottage, and his gold was not there. He put his trembling hands to his head, and gave a wild, ringing scream—the cry of desolation. Then the idea of a thief began to present itself, and he entertained it eagerly, because a thief might be caught and made to release the gold. The robber must be laid hold of. Marner's ideas of legal authority were confused, but he felt that he must go and proclaim his loss; and the great people in the village — the clergyman, the constable, and Squire Cass — would make the thief deliver up the stolen money.

It was to the village inn Silas Marner went, where the parish clerk and a select company were assembled, and told the story of his loss—£272 12s. 6d. in all. The machinery of the law was set in motion, but no thief was ever captured, nor could grounds be found for suspicion against any persons.

What had really happened was that Dunsey Cass, Squire Cass's

second son — a mean, boastful rascal — on his way home on foot from hunting, saw the light in the weaver's cottage, and knocked, hoping to borrow a lantern, for the lane was unpleasantly slippery, and the night dark. But all was silence in the cottage, for the weaver at that moment had not yet reached home. For a minute Dunsey thought that old Marner might be dead, fallen over the stone pits. And from that came the decision that he must be dead. If so, the question arose, what would become of the money that everybody said the old miser had put by?

Dunstan Cass was in difficulties for want of money, and he had killed his brother's horse that day on the hunting-field. Who would know, if Marner was dead, that anybody had come to take his hoard of money away?

There were only three hiding-places where he had heard of cottagers' hoards being found: the thatch, the bed, and a hole in the floor. His eyes traveling eagerly over the floor, noted a spot where the sand had been more carefully spread.

Dunstan found the hole and the money, now hidden in two leathern bags. From their weight he judged they must be filled with guineas. Quickly he hastened out into the darkness with the bags, and Dunstan Cass was seen no more alive.

At the very moment when he turned his back on the cottage Silas Marner was not more than a hundred yards away.

III. *Silas Marner's Visitor*

It was New Year's Eve, and Squire Cass was giving a dance to the neighbouring gentry of Raveloe. There had been snow in the afternoon, but at seven o'clock it had ceased, and a freezing wind had sprung up.

A woman, shabbily dressed, with a child in her arms, was making her way towards Raveloe, seeking the Red House, where Squire Cass lived. It was not the squire she wanted, but his eldest son, Godfrey, to whom she was secretly married. The marriage—the result of rash impulse—had been an unhappy one from the first, for Godfrey's wife was the slave of opium. The squire had long desired that his son should marry Miss Nancy Lammeter, and would have turned him out of house and home had he known of the unfortunate marriage already contracted. Cold and weariness drove the woman, even while she walked, to the only comfort she knew. She raised the black

remnant to her lips, and then flung the empty phial away. Now she walked, always more and more drowsily, and clutched more and more automatically the sleeping child at her bosom. Soon she felt nothing but a supreme longing to lie down and sleep; and so sank down against a straggling furze-bush, an easy pillow enough; and the bed of snow, too, was soft. The cold was no longer felt, but her arms did not at once relax their instinctive clutch, and the little one slumbered on.

The complete torpor came at last; the fingers lost their tension, the arms unbent; then the little head fell away from the bosom, and the blue eyes of the child opened wide on the cold starlight. At first there was a little peevish cry of "Mammy," as the child rolled downward; and then, suddenly, its eyes were caught by a bright gleaming light on the white ground, and with the ready transition of infancy it decided the light must be caught.

In an instant the child had slipped on all fours, and, after making out that the cunning gleam came from a very bright place, the little one, rising on its legs, toddled through the snow—toddled on to the open door of Silas Marner's cottage, and right up to the warm hearth where was a bright fire.

The little one, accustomed to be left to itself for long hours without notice, squatted down on the old sack spread out before the fire, in perfect contentment. Presently the little golden head sank down, and the blue eyes were veiled by their delicate half-transparent lids.

But where was Silas Marner while this strange visitor had come to his hearth? He was in the cottage, but he did not see the child. Since he had lost his money he had contracted the habit of opening his door, and looking out from time to time, as if he thought that his money might, somehow, be coming back to him.

That morning he had been told by some of his neighbours that it was New Year's Eve, and that he must sit up and hear the old year rung out, and the new rung in, because that was good luck, and might bring his money back again. Perhaps this friendly Raveloe way of jesting had helped to throw Silas into a more than usually excited state. Certainly he opened his door again and again that night, and the last time, just as he put out his hand to close it, the invisible wand of catalepsy arrested him, and there he stood like a graven image, powerless to resist either the good or evil that might enter.

When Marner's sensibility returned he was unaware of the break

in his consciousness, and only noticed that he was chilled and faint. Turning towards the hearth it seemed to his blurred vision as if there was a heap of gold on the floor; but instead of hard coin his fingers encountered soft, warm curls. In utter amazement, Silas fell on his knees to examine the marvel: it was a sleeping child, a round, fair thing, with soft, yellow rings all over its head. Could this be the little sister come back to him in a dream—his little sister whom he had carried about in his arms for a year before she died? That was the first thought. *Was* it a dream? It was very much like his little sister. How and when had the child come in without his knowledge?

But there was a cry on the hearth; the child had awakened, and Marner stooped to lift it on to his knee. He had plenty to do through the next hour. The porridge, sweetened with some dry brown sugar, stopped the cries of the little one for "mammy." Then it occurred to Silas's dull bachelor mind that the child wanted its wet boots off, and this having been done, the wet boots suggested that the child had been walking on the snow.

He made out the marks of the little feet in the snow, and, holding the child in his arms, followed their track to the furze-bush. Then he became aware that there was a human body, half covered with the shifting snow.

With the child in his arms, Silas at once went for the doctor, who was spending the evening at the Red House. And Godfrey Cass recognised that it was his own child he saw in Marner's arms.

The woman was dead—had been dead for some hours, the doctor said: and Godfrey, who had accompanied him to Marner's cottage, understood that he was free to marry Nancy Lammeter.

"You'll take the child to the parish to-morrow?" Godfrey asked, speaking as indifferently as he could.

"Who says so?" said Marner sharply. "Will they make me take her? I shall keep her till anybody shows they've a right to take her away from me. The mother's dead, and I reckon it's got no father. It's a lone thing, and I'm a lone thing. My money's gone—I don't know where, and this is come from I don't know where."

Godfrey returned to the Red House with a sense of relief and gladness, and Silas kept the child. There had been a softening of feeling to him in the village since the day of his robbery, and now an active sympathy was aroused amongst the women. The child was christened Hephzibah, after Marner's mother, and was called Eppie for short.

IV. *Eppie's Decision*

Eppie had come to link Silas Marner once more with the whole world. The disposition to hoard had utterly gone, and there was no longer any repulsion around to him.

As the child grew up, one person watched with keener, though more hidden interest than any other the prosperous growth of Eppie under the weaver's care. The squire was dead, and Godfrey Cass was married to Nancy Lammeter. He had no child of his own save the one that knew him not. No Dunsey had ever turned up, and people had ceased to think of him.

Sixteen years had passed, and now Aaron Winthrop, a well-behaved young gardener, is wanting to marry Eppie, and Eppie is willing to have him "some time."

" 'Everybody's married some time,' Aaron says," said Eppie. "But I told him that wasn't true, for I said look at father—he's never been married."

"No, child," said Silas, "your father was a lone man till you was sent to him."

"But you'll never be lone again, father," said Eppie tenderly. "That was what Aaron said—'I could never think o' taking you away from Master Marner, Eppie.' And I said, 'It 'ud be no use if you did, Aaron.' And he wants us all to live together, so as you needn't work a bit, father, only what's for your own pleasure, and he'd be as good as a son to you—that was what he said."

The proposal to separate Eppie from her foster-father came from Godfrey Cass.

When the old stone-pit by Marner's cottage went dry, owing to drainage operations, the skeleton of Dunstan Cass was found, wedged between two great stones. The watch and seals were recognised, and all the weaver's money was at the bottom of the pit. The shock of this discovery moved Godfrey to tell Nancy the secret of his earlier marriage.

"Everything comes to light, Nancy, sooner or later," he said. "That woman Marner found dead in the snow—Eppie's mother—was my wife. Eppie is my child. I oughtn't to have left the child unowned. I oughtn't to have kept it from you."

"It's but little wrong to me, Godfrey," Nancy answered sadly. "You've made it up to me—you've been good to me for fifteen years. It'll be a different coming to us, now she's grown up."

They were childless, and it hadn't occurred to them as they ap-

proached Silas Marner's cottage that Godfrey's offer might be declined. At first Godfrey explained that he and his wife wanted to adopt Eppie in place of a daughter.

"Eppie, my child, speak," said old Marner faintly. "I won't stand in your way. Thank Mr. and Mrs. Cass."

"Thank you, ma'am—thank you, sir," said Eppie dropping a curtsy; "but I can't leave my father, nor own anybody nearer than him."

Godfrey Cass was irritated at this obstacle.

"But I've a claim on you, Eppie," he returned. "It's my duty, Marner, to own Eppie as my child, and provide for her. She's my own child. Her mother was my wife. I've a natural claim on her."

"Then, sir, why didn't you say so sixteen years ago, and claim her before I'd come to love her, i'stead o' coming to take her from me now, when you might as well take the heart out o' my body? When a man turns a blessing from his door, it falls to them as take it in. But let it be as you will. Speak to the child. I'll hinder nothing."

"Eppie, my dear," said Godfrey, looking at his daughter not without some embarrassment, "it'll always be our wish that you should show your love and gratitude to one who's been a father to you so many years; but we hope you'll come to love us as well, and though I haven't been what a father should ha' been to you all these years, I wish to do the utmost in my power for you now, and provide for you as my only child. And you'll have the best of mothers in my wife."

Eppie did not come forward and curtsy as she had done before, but she held Silas's hand in hers and grasped it firmly.

"Thank you, ma'am—thank you, sir, for your offers—they're very great and far above my wish. For I should have no delight in life any more if I was forced to go away from my father."

In vain Nancy expostulated mildly.

"I can't feel as I've got any father but one," said Eppie. "I've always thought of a little home where he'd sit i' the corner, and I should fend and do everything for him. I can't think o' no other home. I wasn't brought up to be a lady, and," she ended passionately, "I'm promised to marry a working man, as'll live with father and help me to take care of him."

Godfrey Cass and his wife went out.

A year later Eppie was married, and Mrs. Godfrey Cass provided

362

the wedding dress, and Mr. Cass made some necessary alterations to suit Silas's larger family.

"Oh, father," said Eppie, when the bridal party returned from the church, "what a pretty home ours is! I think nobody could be happier than we are!"

MIHAIL EMINESCU

MIHAIL EMINESCU (Rumanian, 1850-1889). Outstanding Rumanian poet. Highly sensitive and romantic, unable to adjust to everyday life. Killed by another inmate in insane asylum. Wrote 60 poems, a novel, fairy tales, and articles on wide range of subjects. His pessimism reflected in later Rumanian writers.

SONNET

How many stars in lofty heaven ascending;
How many billows seam the ocean's flowing,
With serried lights and scintillations glowing,
And endless movement—is our thought transcending.
Choose as thou wilt, the road of Life's bestowing;
Rising to greatness, or to crime descending;
Dust and the darkness Fate for each is sending;
To mute oblivion, like the rest, art going.
I saw me dying; 'mid the shadowed porches
They did appear in lonely earth would lay me;
I heard the requiem chants, and saw the torches.
O dulcet shadow; pray thee, draw more nigh me,
That I may feel Death's hovering shade approaches,
With weeping lids and dark wings, pausing by me.

O'ER THE TREES

O'er the trees the moon is showing;
    Stir the leaves in forest brake,
And the alder branches shake,
    Whilst the wistful horn is blowing.

Further wending, further wending;
  Heard more faint, and yet more faint;
To my soul with sorrow blent,
  Healing hope of Death thou'rt sending.

Why art silent, when, becalmèd,
  Turns my sad heart to thy strain?
Gentle horn, wilt sound again,
  Sound for me thy notes encharmèd?

WHY COMEST NOT? WHY COMEST NOT?

Behold the swallows quit the eaves,
And fall the yellowed walnut leaves,
The hoar frost doth the vineyard rot;
Why comest not? Why comest not?

Unto mine arms, O love, return;
Mine eager eyes to thee shall yearn;
My weary head find gentle rest
Upon thy breast; upon thy breast.

Dost thou remember? Oft indeed
We twain did hie o'er vale and mead;
And oft I raised thee, sweetheart mine;
Ah, many a time! Ah, many a time!

On earth full many women dwell
Whose eyes the sparkling stars excel;
But how so bright their eyes may be,
They're not like thee! They're not like thee!

Since thy dear bounty sweet affords
My life the joys of love's accords,
For me thou dost the stars outshine;
Beloved mine! Beloved mine!

Now speed the last of Autumn days,
The dead leaves scatter on the ways,
The lonely fields are dank and drear—
Why art not here? Why art not here?

EURIPIDES

EURIPIDES (Greek, 485-406 B.C.). The most influential and popular of the Greek tragedians. The dramatist of great human passions, as opposed to more philosophic conceptions of Aeschylus and Sophocles. Wrote over 80 plays, of which 19 survive—including *Alcestis, Medea, Electra, Orestes.* These seem almost modern in portrayal of strong personalities in grip of warring emotions.

MEDEA'S WRONGS

Nurse of Medea.   All is variance now
And hate: for Jason, to his children false,
False to my mistress, for a royal bride
Hath left her couch, and wedded Creon's daughter,
Lord of this land. Ill doth Medea brook
This base dishonor; on his oath she calls,
Recalls their plighted hands, the firmest pledge
Of mutual faith, and calls the gods to witness
What a requital she from Jason finds.
Of food regardless, and in sorrow sunk
She lies, and melts in tears each tedious hour
Since first she knew her lord had injured her;
Nor lifts her eye, nor lifts her face from the earth
Deaf to her friends' entreaties as a rock,
Or billow of the sea; save when she turns
Her snowy neck, and to herself bewails
Her father, and her country, and her house,
Which she betray'd to follow this base man,
Who treats her now with such indignity.
Affliction now hath taught her what it is
Not to forsake a parent and his house.
She hates her children, nor with pleasure sees them.
I fear her, lest she form some strange design;
For violent her temper, and of wrongs
Impatient: well I know her, and I fear her,
Lest, in the dead of night, when all are laid
In deep repose, she steal into the house,
And plunge into their breast the piercing sword;
Or murder ev'n the monarch of the land,
Or the new-married Jason, on herself
Drawing severer ills: for like a storm
Her passions swell, and he that dares enrage her
Will have small cause to boast his victory.

365

But see, her sons from the gymnastic ring
Returning, heedless of their mother's ills;
For youth holds no society with grief.

Enter Tutor, with the Sons of Medea.

Tut. Thou old domestic servant of my mistress,
Why dost thou take thy station at the gates,
And ruminate in silence on thy griefs?
How hath Medea wish'd to be alone?

Nur. Thou good old man, attendant on the sons
Of Jason, faithful servants with their lords
Suffer in their afflictions, and their hearts
Are touch'd with social sorrow; and my griefs
Swell, for Medea's sufferings, to such height,
That strong desire impell'd me to come forth,
And tell them to the earth and to the skies.

Tut. Admits she yet no respite to her groans?

Nur. I wonder at thee: no, these ills but now
Are rising, to their height not yet advanced.

Tut. I heard one say, not seeming to attend,
But passing on to where they play with dice,
Among the grave old men, who then by chance
Were sitting near Pirene's hallow'd stream,
That Creon, lord of this fair land, will drive
These children and their mother from the state
Of Corinth: whether this report be true
I know not, but I wish it otherwise.

Nur. Will Jason bear to see his sons thus wrong'd,
Though he regards their mother now no more?

Tut. To new alliances the old gives place,
And to this house he is no more a friend.

Nur. Ruin would follow, to the former ill
If this were added ere the first subsides.

Tut. Be cautious then; it were unseasonable
Our queen knew this; in silence close thy lips.

Nur. Go in, my children, go: all will be well;
And take thou heed, keep them aloof, nor let them
Come near their mother while her griefs are fresh:
Cruel her eye, and wild; I mark'd it late,
Expressive of some dark design on these:

366

Nor will she check her fury, well I know,
Till the storm bursts on some one: may its stroke
Fall on some hostile head, not on a friend.
  Medea (within.) Wretch that I am, what anguish rends my
    heart!
Wretched Medea, how art thou undone!
  Nur. Ay, thus it is. Your mother, my dear children,
Swells with resentment, swells with rage. Go in,
Go quickly in; but come not in her eye,
Approach her not, but keep you from the wild
And dreadful fury of her violent temper.
Go now, go quickly in; this rising cloud
Of grief forebodes a storm, which soon will fall
With greater rage: inflamed with injuries,
What will not her tempestuous spirit dare?
  Med. Ah me! ah me! what mighty wrongs I bear,
Wrongs that demand my tears and loud laments!
Ye sons accursed of a detested mother,
Perish, together with your father perish,
And in one general ruin sink your house!
  Nur. Ah me unhappy! in their father's fault
Why make thy sons associates? Why on them
Rises thy hatred? Oh, I fear, I fear,
My children, lest some evil threatens you.
Kings have a fiery quality of soul,
Accustom'd to command; if once they feel
Control, though small, their anger blazes out,
Not easily extinguish'd; hence I deem
An equal mediocrity of life
More to be wish'd; if not in gorgeous state,
Yet without danger glides it on to age.
There's a protection in its very name,
And happiness dwells with it: but the height
Of towering greatness long to mortal man
Remains not fix'd, and, when misfortune comes
Enraged, in deeper ruin sinks the house.
  Chorus. I heard the voice, I heard the loud laments
Of the unhappy Colchian: do her griefs
(Say, reverend matron), find no respite yet?
From the door's opening valve I heard her voice.
No pleasure in the sorrows of your home

367

I take; for deeds are done not grateful to me.

    Nur.   This is no more a home; all here is vanish'd,
Nor leaves a trace behind. The monarch's house
He makes his own; while my unhappy mistress
In her lone chamber melts her life away
In tears, unmoved by all the arguments
Urged by her friends to soothe her sorrowing soul.

    Med.   O that the ethereal lightning on this head
Would fall! Why longer should I wish to live?
Unhappy me! Death would be welcome now,
And kindly free me from this hated life.

    Cho.   Dost thou hear this, O Jove, O Earth, O Light,
The mournful voice of this unhappy dame?
Why thus indulge this unabated force
Of nuptial love, self-rigorous, hastening death?
Let it not be thy wish: if a new bed
Now charms thy husband, be not his offence
Engraved too deep: Jove will avenge thy wrongs;
Let not thy sorrows prey upon thy heart.

    Med.   O powerful Themis, O revered Diana,
See what I suffer, though with sacred oaths
This vile, accursed husband I had bound!
Oh, might I one day see him and his bride
Rent piecemeal in their house, who unprovoked
Have dared to wrong me thus! Alas, my father!
Alas, my country! whom my shameful flight
Abandon'd, having first my brother slain!

    Cho.   I hear her lamentations mixed with groans,
Which in the anguish of her heart she vents;
And on her faithless husband, who betray'd
Her bed, she calls aloud; upon the gods,
Thus basely wrong'd, she calls, attesting Themis,
Daughter of Jove, the arbitress of oaths,
Who led her to the shores of Greece, across
The rolling ocean, when the shades of night
Darken'd its waves, and steer'd her through the straits.

MEDEA'S LAST WORDS TO HER CHILDREN

O children, children! you have still a city,
A home, where, lost to me and all my woe,
You will live out your lives without a mother!

368

But I—lo! I am for another land,
Leaving the joy of you. To see you happy,
To deck your marriage-bed, to greet your bride,
To light your wedding torch shall not be mine!
O me, thrice wretched in my own self-will!
In vain then, dear my children! did I rear you;
In vain I travailed, and with wearing sorrow
Bore bitter anguish in the hour of childbirth!
Yea, of a sooth, I had great hope of you,
That you should cherish my old age, and deck
My corpse with loving hands, and make me blessed
'Mid women in my death. But now, ah me!
Hath perished that sweet dream. For long without you
I shall drag out a dreary, doleful age.
And you shall never see your mother more
With your dear eyes: for all your life is changed.
Woe, woe!
Why gaze you at me with your eyes, my children?
Why smile your last sweet smile? Ah me! ah me!
What shall I do? My heart dissolves within me,
Friends, when I see the glad eyes of my sons!
I cannot. No: my will that was so steady,
Farewell to it. They too shall go with me:
Why should I wound their sire with what wounds them,
Heaping tenfold his woes on my own head?
No, no, I shall not. Perish my proud will.
Yet whence this weakness? Do I wish to reap
The scorn that springs from enemies unpunished?
Dare it I must. What craven fool am I,
To let soft thoughts flow trickling from my soul!
Go, boys, into the house: and he who may not
Be present at my solemn sacrifice—
Let him see to it. My hand shall not falter.
Ah! ah!
Nay, do not, O my heart! do not this thing!
Suffer them, O poor fool; yea, spare thy children!
There in thy exile they will gladden thee.
Not so: by all the plagues of nethermost Hell,
It shall not be that I, that I should suffer
My foes to triumph and insult my sons!
Die must they: this must be, and since it must,

369

I, I myself will slay them, I who bore them.
So it is fixed, and there is no escape.
Even as I speak, the crown is on her head,
The bride is dying in her robes, I know it.
But since this path most piteous I tread,
Sending them forth on paths more piteous far,
I will embrace my children. O my sons,
Give, give your mother your dear hands to kiss!
O dearest hands, and mouths most dear to me,
And forms and noble faces of my sons!
Be happy even there: what here was yours,
Your father robs you of. O loved embrace!
O tender touch and sweet breath of my boys!
Go, go, go, leave me! Lo, I cannot bear
To look on you, my woes have overwhelmed me!
Now know I all the ill I have to do:
But rage is stronger than my better mind;
Rage, cause of greatest crimes and griefs to mortals.

ABRAHAM IBN EZRA

ABRAHAM IBN EZRA (Spanish-Hebrew, 1092-1167). Wandering hymnist and
philosopher. Traveled through many non-Moslem lands, so became first
Hebrew-Spaniard to write entirely in Hebrew. Wrote many liturgical poems,
philosophic works, and an Arabic study of Spanish-Hebrew poetry.

I. SONGS

I

The shadow of the houses leave behind,
In the cool boscage of the grove reclined,
The wine of friendship from love's goblet drink,
And entertain with cheerful speech the mind.

Drink, friend! behold, the dreary winter's gone,
The mantle of old age has time withdrawn.
The sunbeam glitters in the morning dew,
O'er hill and vale youth's bloom is surging on.

Cup-bearer! quench with snow the goblet's fire,
Even as the wise man cools and stills his ire.
Look, when the jar is drained, upon the brim
The light foam melteth with the heart's desire.

Cup-bearer! bring anear the silver bowl,
And with the glowing gold fulfil the whole,
Unto the weak new vigor it imparts,
And without lance subdues the hero's soul.

My love sways, dancing, like the myrtle-tree,
The masses of her curls disheveled, see!
She kills me with her darts, intoxicates
My burning blood, and will not set me free.

Within the aromatic garden come,
And slowly in its shadows let us roam,
The foliage be the turban for our brows,
And the green branches o'er our heads a dome.

All pain thou with the goblet shalt assuage,
The wine-cup heals the sharpest pangs that rage,
Let others crave inheritance of wealth,
Joy be our portion and our heritage.

Drink in the garden, friend, anigh the rose,
Richer than spice's breath the soft air blows.
If it should cease a little traitor then,
A zephyr light its secret would disclose.

II

Thou who art clothed in silk, who drawest on
Proudly thy raiment of fine linen spun,
Bethink thee of the day when thou alone
Shalt dwell at last beneath the marble stone.

Anigh the nests of adders thine abode,
With the earth-crawling serpent and the toad.
Trust in the Lord, He will sustain thee there,
And without fear thy soul shall rest with God.

371

If the world flatter thee with soft-voiced art,
Know 'tis a cunning witch who charms thy heart,
Whose habit is to wed man's soul with grief,
And those who are close-bound in love to part.

He who bestows his wealth upon the poor,
Has only lent it to the Lord, be sure—
Of what avail to clasp it with clenched hand?
It goes not with us to the grave obscure.

The voice of those who dwell within the tomb,
Who in corruption's house have made their home;
"O ye who wander o'er us still today,
When will ye come to share with us the gloom?"

How can'st thou ever of the world complain,
And murmuring, burden it with all thy pain?
Silence! thou art a traveller at an inn,
A guest, who may but over night remain.

Be thou not wroth against the proud, but show
How he who yesterday great joy did know,
Today is begging for his very bread,
And painfully upon a crutch must go.

How foolish they whose faith is fixed upon
The treasures of their worldly wealth alone,
Far wiser were it to obey the Lord,
And only say, "The will of God be done!"

Has Fortune smiled on thee? Oh, do not trust
Her reckless joy, she still deceives and must.
Perpetual snares she spreads about thy feet,
Thou shalt not rest till thou art mixed with dust.

Man is a weaver on the earth, 'tis said,
Who weaves and weaves—his own days are the thread,
And when the length allotted he hath spun,
All life is over, and all hope is dead.

Unto the house of prayer my spirit yearns,
Unto the sources of her being turns,
To where the sacred light of heaven burns,
She struggles thitherward by day and night.

The splendor of God's glory blinds her eyes,
Up without wings she soareth to the skies,
With silent aspiration seeks to rise,
In dusky evening and in darksome night.

To her the wonders of God's works appear,
She longs with fervor Him to draw anear,
The tidings of His glory reach her ear,
From morn to even, and from night to night.

The banner of thy grace did o'er me rest,
Yet was thy worship banished from my breast.
Almighty, thou didst seek me out and test
To try and to instruct me in the night.

Infatuate I trifled youth away,
In nothingness dreamed through my manhood's day.
Therefore my streaming tears I may not stay,
They are my meat and drink by day and night.

In flesh imprisoned is the son of light,
This life is but a bridge when seen aright.
Rise in the silent hour and pray with might,
Awake and call upon the God by night!

Hasten to cleanse thyself of sin, arise!
Follow Truth's path that leads unto the skies,
As swift as yesterday existence flies,
Brief even as a watch within the night.

Man enters life for trouble; all he has,
And all that he beholds, is pain, alas!
Like to a flower does he bloom and pass,
He fadeth like a vision of the night.

The surging floods of life around him roar,
Death feeds upon him, pity is no more,
To others all his riches he gives o'er,
And dieth in the middle hour of night.

Crushed by the burden of my sins I pray,
Oh, wherefore shunned I not the evil way?
Deep are my sighs, I weep the livelong day,
And wet my couch with tears night after night.

My spirit stirs, my streaming tears still run,
Like to the wild birds' notes my sorrows' tone,
In the hushed silence loud resounds my groan,
My soul arises moaning in the night.

Within her narrow soul oppressed with dread,
Bare of adornment and with grief-bowed head
Lamenting, many a tear her sad eyes shed,
She weeps with anguish in the gloomy night.

For tears my burden seem to lighten best,
Could I but weep my heart's blood, I might rest.
My spirit bows with mighty grief oppressed,
I utter forth my prayer within the night.

Youth's charm has like a fleeting shadow gone,
With eagle wings the hours of life have flown.
Alas! the time when pleasure I have known,
I may not now recall by day or night.

The haughty scorn pursues me of my foe,
Evil his thought, yet soft his speech and low.
Forget it not, but bear his purpose so
Forever in thy mind by day and night.

Observe a pious fast, be whole again,
Hasten to purge thy heart of every stain.
No more from prayer and penitence refrain,
But turn unto thy God by day and night.

He speaks: "My son, yea, I will send thee aid,
Bend thou thy steps to me, be not afraid.
No nearer friend than I am, hast thou made,
Possess thy soul in patience one more night."

III. ELEGY

My thoughts impelled me to the resting-place
Where sleep my parents, many a friend and brother.
I asked them (no one heard and none replied) : .
"Do ye forsake me, too, oh father, mother?"
Then from the grave, without a tongue, these cried,
And showed my own place waiting by their side.

F

WILLIAM FAULKNER

WILLIAM FAULKNER (American, 1897-   ). Considered by some the most important American novelist, but until recently more admired abroad than in this country. Nobel Prize winner, 1949. Novels describe decay of a Southern county and its major families. Major works: *The Sound and the Fury, As I Lay Dying, Light in August, Intruder in the Dust, A Fable.*

A ROSE FOR EMILY

WHEN Miss Emily Grierson died, our whole town went to her funeral: the men through a sort of respectful affection for a fallen monument, the women mostly out of curiosity to see the inside of her house, which no one save an old man-servant—a combined gardener and cook—had seen in at least ten years.

It was a big, squarish frame house that had once been white, decorated with cupolas and spires and scrolled balconies in the heavily lightsome style of the Seventies, set on what had once been our most select street. But garages and cotton gins had encroached and obliterated even the august names of that neighborhood; only Miss Emily's house was left, lifting its stubborn and coquettish decay above the cotton wagons and the gasoline pumps—an eyesore among eyesores. And now Miss Emily had gone to join the representatives of those august names where they lay in the cedar-bemused cemetery among the ranked and anonymous graves of Union and Confederate soldiers who fell at the battle of Jefferson.

Alive, Miss Emily had been a tradition, a duty, and a care; a sort of hereditary obligation upon the town, dating from that day in 1894 when Colonel Sartoris, the mayor—he who fathered the edict that no Negro woman should appear on the streets without an apron —remitted her taxes, the dispensation dating from the death of her

father on into perpetuity. Not that Miss Emily would have accepted charity. Colonel Sartoris invented an involved tale to the effect that Miss Emily's father had loaned money to the town, which the town, as a matter of business, preferred this way of repaying. Only a man of Colonel Sartoris' generation and thought could have invented it, and only a woman could have believed it.

When the next generation, with its more modern ideas, became mayors and aldermen, this arrangement created some little dissatisfaction. On the first of the year they mailed her a tax notice. February came, and there was no reply. They wrote her a formal letter, asking her to call at the sheriff's office at her convenience. A week later the mayor wrote her himself, offering to call or send his car for her, and received in reply a note on paper of an archaic shape, in a thin, flowing calligraphy in faded ink, to the effect that she no longer went out at all. The tax notice was also enclosed, without comment.

They called a special meeting of the Board of Aldermen. A deputation waited upon her, knocked at the door through which no visitor had passed since she ceased giving china-painting lessons eight or ten years earlier. They were admitted by the old Negro into a dim hall from which a stairway mounted into still more shadow. It smelled of dust and disuse—a close, dank smell. The Negro led them into the parlor. It was furnished in heavy, leather-covered furniture. When the Negro opened the blinds of one window, they could see that the leather was cracked; and when they sat down, a faint dust rose sluggishly about their thighs, spinning with slow motes in the single sun-ray. On a tarnished gilt easel before the fireplace stood a crayon portrait of Miss Emily's father.

They rose when she entered—a small, fat woman in black, with a thin gold chain descending to her waist and vanishing into her belt, leaning on an ebony cane with a tarnished gold head. Her skeleton was small and spare; perhaps that was why what would have been merely plumpness in another was obesity in her. She looked bloated, like a body long submerged in motionless water, and of that pallid hue. Her eyes, lost in the fatty ridges of her face, looked like two small pieces of coal pressed into a lump of dough as they moved from one face to another while the visitors stated their errand.

She did not ask them to sit. She just stood in the door and listened quietly until the spokesman came to a stumbling halt. Then they could hear the invisible watch ticking at the end of the gold chain. Her voice was dry and cold. "I have no taxes in Jefferson. Colonel

377

Sartoris explained it to me. Perhaps one of you can gain access to the city records and satisfy yourselves."

"But we have. We are the city authorities, Miss Emily. Didn't you get a notice from the sheriff, signed by him?"

"I received a paper, yes," Miss Emily said. "Perhaps he considers himself the sheriff . . . I have no taxes in Jefferson."

"But there is nothing on the books to show that, you see. We must go by the—"

"See Colonel Sartoris. I have no taxes in Jefferson."

"But, Miss Emily—"

"See Colonel Sartoris." (Colonel Sartoris had been dead almost ten years.) "I have no taxes in Jefferson. Tobe!" The Negro appeared. "Show these gentlemen out."

II

So she vanquished them, horse and foot, just as she had vanquished their fathers thirty years before about the smell. That was two years after her father's death and a short time after her sweetheart—the one we believed would marry her—had deserted her. After her father's death she went out very little; after her sweetheart went away, people hardly saw her at all. A few of the ladies had the temerity to call, but were not received, and the only sign of life about the place was the Negro man—a young man then—going in and out with a market basket.

"Just as if a man—any man—could keep a kitchen properly," the ladies said; so they were not surprised when the smell developed. It was another link between the gross, teeming world and the high and mighty Griersons.

A neighbor, a woman, complained to the mayor, Judge Stevens, eighty years old.

"But what will you have me do about it, madam?" he said.

"Why, send her word to stop it," the woman said. "Isn't there a law?"

"I'm sure that won't be necessary," Judge Stevens said. "It's probably a snake or a rat that nigger of hers killed in the yard. I'll speak to him about it."

The next day he received two more complaints, one from a man who came in diffident deprecation. "We really must do something about it, Judge. I'd be the last one in the world to bother Miss

378.

Emily, but we've got to do something." That night the Board of Aldermen met—three gray-beards and one younger man, a member of the rising generation.

"It's simple enough," he said. "Send her word to have her place cleaned up. Give her a certain time to do it in, and if she don't . . ."

"Dammit, sir," Judge Stevens said, "will you accuse a lady to her face of smelling bad?"

So the next night, after midnight, four men crossed Miss Emily's lawn and slunk about the house like burglars, sniffing along the base of the brickwork and at the cellar openings while one of them performed a regular sowing motion with his hand out of a sack slung from his shoulder. They broke open the cellar door and sprinkled lime there, and in all the outbuildings. As they recrossed the lawn, a window that had been dark was lighted and Miss Emily sat in it, the light behind her, and her upright torso motionless as that of an idol. They crept quietly across the lawn and into the shadow of the locusts that lined the street. After a week or two the smell went away.

That was when people had begun to feel really sorry for her. People in our town, remembering how Old Lady Wyatt, her great-aunt, had gone completely crazy at last, believed that the Griersons held themselves a little too high for what they really were. None of the young men was quite good enough to Miss Emily and such. We had long thought of them as a tableau: Miss Emily a slender figure in white in the background, her father a spraddled silhouette in the foreground, his back to her and clutching a horse-whip, the two of them framed by the back-flung front door. So when she got to be thirty and was still single, we were not pleased exactly, but vindicated; even with insanity in the family she wouldn't have turned down all of her chances if they had really materialized.

When her father died, it got about that the house was all that was left to her; and in a way, people were glad. At last they could pity Miss Emily. Being left alone, and a pauper, she had become humanized. Now she too would know the old thrill and the old despair of a penny more or less.

The day after his death all the ladies prepared to call at the house and offer condolence and aid, as is our custom. Miss Emily met them at the door, dressed as usual and with no trace of grief on her face. She told them that her father was not dead. She did that for three days, with the ministers calling on her, and the doctors, try-

ing to persuade her to let them dispose of the body. Just as they were about to resort to law and force, she broke down, and they buried her father quickly.

We did not say she was crazy then. We believed she had to do that. We remembered all the young men her father had driven away, and we knew that with nothing left, she would have to cling to that which had robbed her, as people will.

III

She was sick for a long time. When we saw her again, her hair was cut short, making her look like a girl, with a vague resemblance to those angels in colored church windows—sort of tragic and serene.

The town had just let the contracts for paving the sidewalks, and in the summer after her father's death they began the work. The construction company came with niggers and mules and machinery, singing in time to the rise and fall of picks. Pretty soon he knew everybody in town. Whenever you heard a lot of laughing any-man, with a big voice and eyes lighter than his face. The little boys would follow in groups to hear him cuss the niggers, and the niggers and a foreman named Homer Barron, a Yankee—a big, dark, ready where about the square, Homer Barron would be in the center of the group. Presently we began to see him and Miss Emily on Sunday afternoons driving in the yellow-wheeled buggy and the matched team of bays from the livery stable.

At first we were glad that Miss Emily would have an interest because the ladies all said, "Of course a Grierson would not think seriously of a Northerner, a day laborer." But there were still others, older people, who said that even grief could not cause a real lady to forget *noblesse oblige*—without calling it *noblesse oblige*. They just said, "Poor Emily. Her kinsfolk should come to her." She had some kin in Alabama; but years ago her father had fallen out with them over the estate of Old Lady Wyatt, the crazy woman, and there was no communication between the two families. They had not even been represented at the funeral.

And as soon as the old people said, "Poor Emily," the whispering began. "Do you suppose it's really so?" they said to one another. "Of course it is. What else could . . ." This behind their hands; rustling of craned silk and satin behind jalousies closed upon the sun of Sunday afternoon as the thin, swift clop-clop-clop of the matched team passed: "Poor Emily."

She carried her head high enough—even when we believed that she was fallen. It was as if she demanded more than ever the recognition of her dignity as the last Grierson; as if it had wanted that touch of earthiness to reaffirm her imperviousness. Like when she bought the rat poison, the arsenic. That was over a year after they had begun to say "Poor Emily," and while the two female cousins were visiting her.

"I want some poison," she said to the druggist. She was over thirty then, still a slight woman, though thinner than usual, with cold, haughty black eyes in a face the flesh of which was strained across the temples and about the eye-sockets as you imagine a light-house-keeper's face ought to look. "I want some poison," she said.

"Yes, Miss Emily. What kind? For rats and such? I'd recom—"

"I want the best you have. I don't care what kind."

The druggist named several. "They'll kill anything up to an elephant. But what you want is—"

"Arsenic," Miss Emily said. "Is that a good one?"

"Is . . . arsenic? Yes, ma'am. But what you want—"

"I want arsenic."

The druggist looked down at her. She looked back at him, erect, her face like a strained flag. "Why, of course," the druggist said. "If that's what you want. But the law requires you to tell what you are going to use it for."

Miss Emily just stared at him, her head tilted back in order to look him eye for eye, until he looked away and went and got the arsenic and wrapped it up. The Negro delivery boy brought her the package; the druggist didn't come back. When she opened the package at home there was written on the box, under the skull and bones: "For rats."

IV

So the next day we all said, "She will kill herself"; and we said it would be the best thing. When she had first begun to be seen with Homer Barron, we had said, "She will marry him." Then we said, "She will persuade him yet," because Homer himself had remarked—he liked men, and it was known that he drank with the younger men in the Elk's Club—that he was not a marrying man. Later we said, "Poor Emily" behind the jalousies as they passed on Sunday afternoon in the glittering buggy, Miss Emily with her head high and Homer Barron with his hat cocked and a cigar in his teeth, reins and whip in a yellow glove.

Then some of the ladies began to say that it was a disgrace to the town and a bad example to the young people. The men did not want to interfere, but at last the ladies forced the Baptist minister—Miss Emily's people were Episcopal—to call upon her. He would never divulge what happened during that interview, but he refused to go back again. The next Sunday they again drove about the streets, and the following day the minister's wife wrote to Miss Emily's relations in Alabama.

So she had blood-kin under her roof again and we sat back to watch developments. At first nothing happened. Then we were sure that they were to be married. We learned that Miss Emily had been to the jeweler's and ordered a man's toilet set in silver, with the letter H. B. on each piece. Two days later we learned that she had bought a complete outfit of men's clothing, including a nightshirt, and we said, "They are married." We were really glad. We were glad because the two female cousins were even more Grierson than Miss Emily had ever been.

So we were not surprised when Homer Barron—the streets had been finished some time since—was gone. We were a little disappointed that there was not a public blowing-off, but we believed that he had gone on to prepare for Miss Emily's coming, or to give her a chance to get rid of the cousins. (By that time it was a cabal, and we were all Miss Emily's allies to help circumvent the cousins.) Sure enough, after another week they departed. And, as we had expected all along, within three days Homer Barron was back in town. A neighbor saw the Negro man admit him at the kitchen door at dusk one evening.

And that was the last we saw of Homer Barron. And of Miss Emily for some time. The Negro man went in and out with the market basket, but the front door remained closed. Now and then we would see her at a window for a moment, as the men did that night when they sprinkled the lime, but for almost six months she did not appear on the streets. Then we knew that this was to be expected too; as if that quality of her father which had thwarted her woman's life so many times had been too virulent and too furious to die.

When we next saw Miss Emily, she had grown fat and her hair was turning gray. During the next few years it grew grayer and grayer until it attained an even pepper-and-salt iron-gray, when it ceased turning. Up to the day of her death at seventy-four it was still that vigorous iron-gray, like the hair of an active man.

From that time on her front door remained closed, save for a period of six or seven years, when she was about forty, during which she gave lessons in china-painting. She fitted up a studio in one of the downstairs rooms, where the daughters and granddaughters of Colonel Sartoris' contemporaries were sent to her with the same regularity and in the same spirit that they were sent to church on Sundays with a twenty-five-cent piece for the collection plate. Meanwhile her taxes had been remitted.

Then the newer generation became the backbone and the spirit of the town, and the painting pupils grew up and fell away and did not send their children to her with boxes of color and tedious brushes and pictures cut from the ladies' magazines. The front door closed upon the last one and remained closed for good. When the town got free postal delivery, Miss Emily alone refused to let them fasten the metal numbers above her door and attach a mailbox to it. She would not listen to them.

Daily, monthly, yearly we watched the Negro grow grayer and more stooped, going in and out with the market basket. Each December we sent her a tax notice, which would be returned by the post office a week later, unclaimed. Now and then we would see her in one of the downstairs windows—she had evidently shut up the top floor of the house—like the carven torso of an idol in a niche, looking or not looking at us, we could never tell which. Thus she passed from generation to generation—dear, inescapable, impervious, tranquil, and perverse.

And so she died. Fell ill in the house filled with dust and shadows, with only a doddering Negro man to wait on her. We did not even know she was sick; we had long since given up trying to get any information from the Negro. He talked to no one, probably not even to her, for his voice had grown harsh and rusty, as if from disuse.

She died in one of the downstairs rooms, in a heavy walnut bed with a curtain, her gray head propped on a pillow yellow and moldy with age and lack of sunlight.

V

The Negro met the first of the ladies at the front door and let them in, with their hushed, sibilant voices and their quick, curious glances, and then he disappeared. He walked right through the house and out the back and was not seen again.

The two female cousins came at once. They held the funeral on

383

the second day, with the town coming to look at Miss Emily beneath a mass of bought flowers, with the crayon face of her father musing profoundly above the bier and the ladies sibilant and macabre; and the very old men—some in their brushed Confederate uniforms— on the porch and the lawn, talking of Miss Emily as if she had been a contemporary of theirs, believing that they had danced with her and courted her perhaps, confusing time with its mathematical progression, as the old do, to whom all the past is not a diminishing road but, instead, a huge meadow which no winter ever quite touches, divided from them now by the narrow bottle-neck of the most recent decade of years.

Already we knew that there was one room in that region above stairs which no one had seen in forty years, and which would have to be forced. They waited until Miss Emily was decently in the ground before they opened it.

The violence of breaking down the door seemed to fill this room with pervading dust. A thin, acrid pall as of the tomb seemed to lie everywhere upon this room decked and furnished as for a bridal; upon the valence curtains of faded rose color, upon the rose-shaded lights, upon the dressing table, upon the delicate array of crystal and the man's toilet things backed with tarnished silver, silver so tarnished that the monogram was obscured. Among them lay a collar and tie, as if they had just been removed, which, lifted, left upon the surface a pale crescent in the dust. Upon a chair hung the suit, carefully folded; beneath it the two mute shoes and the discarded socks.

The man himself lay in the bed.

For a long while we just stood there, looking down at the profound and fleshless grin. The body had apparently once lain in the attitude of an embrace, but now the long sleep that outlasts love, that conquers even the grimace of love, had cuckolded him. What was left of him, rotted beneath what was left of the nightshirt, had become inextricable from the bed in which he lay; and upon him and upon the pillow beside him lay that even coating of the patient and biding dust.

Then we noticed that in the second pillow was the indentation of a head. One of us lifted something from it, and leaning forward, that faint and invisible dust dry and acrid in the nostrils, we saw a long strand of iron-gray hair.

384

FIRDAUSI

FIRDAUSI (Abul Kasim Mansur, Persian, *ca.* 941-1025). The Persian Homer.
The *Shah-namah*, commissioned by Persia's ruler, recounts in 60,000 couplets
Iran's legends and history from prehistoric times to Arab conquest. Spent most
of life on this, one of world's great epics. Influenced all later Persian poets.

RUSTAM AND AKWAN DEV

Kai Khosrau sat in a garden bright
  With all the beauties of balmy Spring;
And many a warrior armor-dight
With a stout kamand and an arm of might
    Supported Persia's King.

With trembling mien and a pallid cheek,
  A breathless hind to the presence ran;
And on bended knee, in posture meek,
With faltering tongue that scarce could speak,
    His story thus began:—

"Alackaday! for the news I bear
  Will like to the follies of Fancy sound;
Thy steeds were stabled and stalled with care,
When a Wild Ass sprang from its forest lair
    With a swift resistless bound,—

"A monster fell, of a dusky hue,
  And eyes that flashed with a hellish glow;
Many it maimed and some it slew,
Then back to the forest again it flew,
    As an arrow leaves the bow."

Kai Khosrau's rage was a sight to see:
  "Now curses light on the foul fiend's head!
Full rich and rare shall his guerdon be
Whose stalwart arm shall bring to me
    The monster, alive or dead!"

But the mail-clad warriors kept their ground,
    And their bronzèd cheeks were blanched with fear;
With scorn the Shah on the cowards frowned,—
"One champion bold may yet be found
    While Rustam wields a spear!"

No tarrying made the son of Zal,
    Small reck had he of the fiercest fray;
But promptly came at the monarch's call,
And swore that the monster fiend should fall
    Ere closed the coming day.

The swift Rakush's sides he spurred,
    And speedily gained the darksome wood;
Nor was the trial for long deferred,—
But soon a hideous roar was heard,
    Had chilled a baser blood.

Then darting out like a flashing flame,
    Traverse his path the Wild Ass fled;
And the hero then with unerring aim
Hurled his stout kamand, but as erst it came,
    Unscathed the monster fled.

"Now Khuda in heaven!" bold Rustam cried,—
    "Thy chosen champion deign to save!
Not all in vain shall my steel be tried,
Though he who my powers has thus defied
    Be none but Akwan Dev."

Then steadily chasing his fiendish foe,
    He thrust with hanger, he smote with brand:
But ever avoiding the deadly blow
It vanished away like the scenes that show
    On Balkh's delusive sand.

For full three wearisome nights and days
    Stoutly he battled with warlike skill;
But the Demon such magical shifts essays
That leaving his courser at large to graze,
    He rests him on a hill.

386

But scare can slumber his eyelids close,
   Ere Akwan Dev from afar espies;
And never disturbing his foe's repose
The earth from under the mound he throws,
   And off with the summit flies.

"Now, daring mortal!" the Demon cried,—
   "Whither wouldst have me carry thee?
Shall I cast thee forth on the mountain side,
Where the lions roar and the reptiles glide,
   Or hurl thee into the sea?"

"O bear me off to the mountain side,
   Where the lions roar and the serpents creep!
For I fear not the creatures that spring or glide;
But where is the arm that can stem the tide,
   Or still the raging deep?"

Loud laughed the fiend as his load he threw
   Far plunging into the roaring flood;
And louder laughed Rustam as out he flew,
For he fain had chosen the sea, but knew
   The fiend's malignant mood.

Soon all the monsters that float or swim,
   With ravening jaws down on him bore;
But he hewed and hacked them limb from limb,
And the wave pellucid grew thick and dim
   With streaks of crimson gore.

With thankful bosom he gains the strand,
   And seeketh his courser near and far,
Till he hears him neigh, and he sees him stand
Among the herds of a Tartar band,
   The steeds of Isfendiyar.

But Rustam's name was a sound of dread,
   And the Tartar heart it had caused to quake;
The herd was there, but the hinds had fled,—
So all the horses he captive led
   For good Kai Khosrau's sake.

387

Then loud again through the forest rings
   The fiendish laugh and the taunting cry;
But his kamand quickly the hero flings,
And around the Demon it coils and clings,
   As a cobweb wraps a fly.

Kai Khosrau sat in his garden fair,
   Mourning his Champion lost and dead,
When a shout of victory rent the air,
And Rustam placed before his chair
   A Demon Giant's head.

GUSTAVE FLAUBERT

GUSTAVE FLAUBERT (French, 1821-1880). One of the great French stylists. Recluse because of epilepsy, devoted self to cult of classical art. *Salammbô* and *The Temptation of Saint Anthony*, masterpieces of romanticism; *Madame Bovary*, the great novel of French realism. Other works: *The Sentimental Education, Bouvard and Pécuchet.* Flaubert's struggle for objectivity defeated itself, but he remains one of greatest novelists.

SALAMMBÔ AND HER LOVER

MATHO was bound on the elephant's back, his four limbs crosswise, and all the unwounded escorted him, hurrying with a great commotion back to Carthage.

The water-clock of Khamoûn marked the fifth hour of the night when they reached Malqua. Here Matho reopened his eyes. There were such vast numbers of lights on the houses that the city seemed to be all in flames.

A mighty clamor came confusedly to him, and lying on his back he gazed at the stars. Then a door closed upon him, and darkness enveloped him. . . .

There were rejoicings at Carthage — rejoicings deep, universal, extravagant, frantic; the holes of the ruins had been stopped up, the statues of the Gods had been repainted, the streets were strewn with myrtle branches, incense smoked at the corners of the crossways, and the throng on the terraces looked, in their variegated garments, like heaps of flowers blooming in the air.

The people accosted one another, and embraced one another with tears;—the Tyrian towns were taken, the Nomads dispersed, and all the Barbarians annihilated. The Acropolis was hidden beneath colored velaria; the beaks of the triremes, drawn up in line outside the mole, shone like a dike of diamonds; everywhere there was a sense of the restoration of order, the beginning of a new existence, and the diffusion of vast happiness: it was the day of Salammbô's marriage with the king of the Numidians.

On the terrace of the temple of Khamon there were three long tables laden with gigantic plates, at which the Priests, Ancients and Rich were going to sit, and there was a fourth and higher one for Hamilcar, Narr' Havas, and Salammbô; for as she saved her country by the restoration of the zaïmph, the people turned her wedding into a national rejoicing, and were waiting in the square below till she should appear.

But their impatience was excited by another and more acrid longing: Matho's death had been promised for the ceremony.

It had been proposed at first to flay him alive, to pour lead into his entrails, to kill him with hunger; he should be tied to a tree, and an ape behind him should strike him on the head with a stone; he had offended Tanith, and the cynocephaluses of Tanith should avenge her. Others were of the opinion that he should be led about on a dromedary after linen wicks, dipped in oil, had been inserted in his body in several places—and they took pleasure in the thought of the large animal wandering through the streets with this man writhing beneath the fires like a candelabrum blown about by the wind.

But what citizens should be charged with his torture, and why disappoint the rest? They would have liked a kind of death in which the whole town might take part, in which every hand, every weapon, everything Carthaginian, to the very paving stones in the streets and the waves in the gulf, could rend him, and crush him, and annihilate him. Accordingly the Ancients decided that he should go from his prison to the square of Khamon without any escort, and with his arms fastened to his back; it was forbidden to strike him to the heart, in order that he might live the longer; to put out his eyes, so that he might see his torture through; to hurl anything against his person, or to lay more than three fingers upon him at a time.

Although he was not to appear until the end of the day, the people sometimes fancied that he could be seen, and the crowd would rush

toward the Acropolis, and empty the streets, to return with length-ened murmurings. Some people had remained standing in the same place since the day before, and they would call on one another from a distance and show their nails, which they had allowed to grow, the better to bury them in his flesh. Others walked restlessly up and down; some were as pale as though they were awaiting their own execution.

Suddenly lofty feather fans rose above the heads, behind the Map-palian district. It was Salammbô leaving her palace; a sigh of relief found vent.

But the procession was long in coming; it marched with delib-eration.

First there filed past the priests of the Pataec Gods, then those of Eschmoun, of Melkarth, and all the other colleges in succession, with the same insignia, and in the same order as had been observed at the time of the sacrifice. The pontiffs of Moloch passed with heads bent, and the multitude stood aside from them in a kind of remorse. But the priests of Rabbetna advanced with a proud step, and with lyres in their hands; the priestesses followed them in transparent robes of yellow or black, uttering cries like birds and writhing like vipers, or else whirling round to the sound of flutes to imitate the dance of the stars, while their light garments wafted puffs of deli-cate scents through the streets.

The Kedeschim, with painted eyelids, who symbolized the her-maphroditism of the Divinity, received applause among these wo-men, and, being perfumed and dressed like them, they resembled them in spite of their flat breasts and narrower hips. Moreover, on this day the female principle dominated and confused all things; a mystic lasciviousness moved in the heavy air; the torches were al-ready lighted in the depths of the sacred woods; there was to be a great prostitution there during the night; three vessels had brought courtesans from Sicily, and others had come from the desert.

As the colleges arrived they ranged themselves in the courts of the temples, on the outer galleries, and along double staircases which rose against the walls, and drew together at the top. Files of white robes appeared between the colonnades, and the architecture was peopled with human statues, motionless as statues of stone.

Then came the masters of the exchequer, the governors of the pro-vinces, and all the Rich. A great tumult prevailed below. Adjacent streets were discharging the crowd, hierodules were driving it back with blows of sticks; and then Salammbô appeared in a litter sur-

390

mounted by a purple canopy, and surrounded by the Ancients crowned with their golden tiaras.

Thereupon an immense shout arose; the cymbols and crotala sounded more loudly, the tambourines thundered, and the great purple canopy sank between the two pylons.

It appeared again on the first landing. Salammbô was walking slowly beneath it; then she crossed the terrace to take her seat behind on a kind of throne cut out of the carapace of a tortoise. An ivory stool with three steps was pushed beneath her feet; two negro children knelt on the edge of the first step, and sometimes she would rest both arms, which were laden with rings of excessive weight, upon their heads.

From ankle to hip she was covered with a network of narrow meshes which were in imitation of fish scales, and shone like mother-of-pearl; her waist was clasped by a blue zone, which allowed her breasts to be seen through two crescent-shaped slashings; the nipples were hidden by carbuncle pendants. She had a headdress made of peacock's feathers studded with gems; an ample cloak, as white as snow, fell behind her—and with her elbows at her sides, her knees pressed together, and circles of diamonds on the upper part of her arms, she remained perfectly upright in a hieratic attitude.

Her father and her husband were on two lower seats, Narr' Havas dressed in a light simar and wearing his crown of rock salt, from which there strayed two tresses of hair as twisted as the horns of Ammon; and Hamilcar in a violet tunic figured with gold vine branches, and with a battle sword at his side.

The python of the temple of Eschmoun lay on the ground amid pools of pink oil in the space inclosed by the tables, and, biting its tail, described a large, black circle. In the middle of the circle there was a copper pillar bearing a crystal egg; and, as the sun shone upon it, rays were emitted on every side.

Behind Salammbô, stretched the priests of Tanith in linen robes; on her right the Ancients, in their tiaras, formed a great gold line, and on the other side the Rich, with their emerald scepters, a great green line—while quite in the background, where the priests of Moloch were ranged, the cloaks looked like a wall of purple. The other colleges occupied the lower terraces. The multitude obstructed the streets. It reached to the house tops, and extended in long files to the summit of the Acropolis. Having thus the people at her feet, the firmament above her head, and around her the immensity of the sea, the gulf, the mountains, and the distant provinces, Salammbô in her

splendor was blended with Tanith, and seemed the very Genius of Carthage, and its embodied soul.

The feast was to last all night, and lamps with several branches were planted like trees on the painted woolen cloths which covered the low tables. Large electrum flagons, blue glass amphoras, tortoise-shell spoons, and small round loaves were crowded between the double row of pearl-bordered plates; bunches of grapes with their leaves had been rolled round ivory vine stocks after the fashion of the thyrsus; blocks of snow were melting on ebony trays, and lemons, pomegranates, gourds, and watermelons formed hillocks beneath the lofty silver plate; boars with open jaws were wallowing in the dust of spices; hares, covered with their fur, appeared to be bounding amid the flowers; there were shells filled with forcemeat; the pastry had symbolic shapes; when the covers of the dishes were removed doves flew out.

The slaves, meanwhile, with tunics tucked up, were going about on tiptoe; from time to time a hymn sounded on the lyres, or a choir of voices rose. The clamor of the people, continuous as the noise of the sea, floated vaguely around the feast, and seemed to lull it in a broader harmony; some recalled the banquet of the Mercenaries; they gave themselves up to dreams of happiness; the sun was beginning to go down, and the crescent of the moon was already rising in another part of the sky.

But Salammbô turned her head as though some one had called her; the people, who were watching her, followed the direction of her eyes.

The door of the dungeon, hewn in the rock at the foot of the temple, on the summit of the Acropolis, had just opened; and a man was standing on the threshold of this black hole.

He came forth bent double, with the scared look of fallow deer when suddenly enlarged.

The light dazzled him, he stood motionless awhile. All had recognized him and they held their breath.

In their eyes the body of this victim was something peculiarly theirs, and was adorned with almost religious splendor. They bent forward to see him, especially the women. They burned to gaze upon him who had caused the deaths of their children and husbands; and from the bottom of their souls there sprang up in spite of themselves an infamous curiosity, a desire to know him completely, a wish mingled with remorse which turned to increased execration.

At last he advanced; then the stupefaction of surprise disappeared. Numbers of arms were raised, and he was lost to sight.

The staircase of the Acropolis had sixty steps. He descended them as though he were rolled down in a torrent from the top of a mountan; three times he was seen to leap, and then he alighted below on his feet.

His shoulders were bleeding, his breast was panting with great shocks; and he made such efforts to burst his bonds that his arms, which were crossed on his naked loins, swelled like pieces of a serpent.

Several streets began in front of him, leading from the spot at which he found himself. In each of them a triple row of bronze chains fastened to the navels of the Pataec Gods extended in parallel lines from one end to the other; the crowd was massed against the houses, and servants, belonging to the Ancients, walked in the middle brandishing thongs.

One of them drove him forward with a great blow; Matho began to move.

They thrust their arms over the chains, shouting out that the road had been left too wide for him; and he passed along, felt, pricked, and slashed by all those fingers; when he reached the end of one street another appeared; several times he flung himself to one side to bite them; they speedily dispersed, the chains held him back, and the crowd burst out laughing.

A child rent his ear; a young girl, hiding the point of a spindle in her sleeve, split his cheek; they tore handfuls of hair from him and strips of flesh; others smeared his face with sponges steeped in filth and fastened upon their sticks. A stream of blood started from the right side of his neck; frenzy immediately set in. This last Barbarian was to them a representative of all the Barbarians, and all the army; they were taking vengeance on him for their disasters, their terrors, and their shame. The rage of the mob developed with its gratification; the curving chains were overstrained, and were on the point of breaking; the people did not feel the blows of the slaves who struck at them to drive them back; some clung to the projections of the houses; all the openings in the walls were stopped up with heads; and they howled at him the mischief that they could not inflict upon him.

It was atrocious, filthy abuse, mingled with ironical encouragements and with imprecations; and, his present tortures not being

393

enough for them, they foretold to him others that should be still more terrible in eternity.

This vast baying filled Carthage with stupid continuity. Frequently a single syllable—a hoarse, deep, and frantic intonation—would be repeated for several minutes by the entire people. The walls would vibrate with it from top to bottom, and both sides of the street would seem to Matho to be coming against him, and carrying him off the ground, like two immense arms stifling him in the air.

Nevertheless he remembered that he had experienced something like it before. The same crowd was on the terraces, there were the same looks and the same wrath; but then he had walked free, all had then dispersed, for a God covered him—and the recollection of this, gaining precision by degrees, brought a crushing sadness upon him. Shadows passed before his eyes; the town whirled round his head, his blood streamed from a wound in his hip, he felt that he was dying; his hams bent, and he sank quite gently upon the pavement.

Some one went to the peristyle of the temple of Melkarth, took thence the bar of a tripod, heated red hot in the coals, and, slipping it beneath the first chain, pressed it against his wound. The flesh was seen to smoke; the hootings of the people drowned his voice; he was standing again.

Six paces further on, and he fell a third and again a fourth time; but some new torture always made him rise. They discharged little drops of boiling oil through tubes at him; they strewed pieces of broken glass beneath his feet; still he walked on. At the corner of the street of Satheb he leaned his back against the wall beneath the penthouse of a shop, and advanced no further.

The slaves of the Council struck him with their whips of hippopotamus leather, so furiously and long that the fringes of their tunics were drenched with sweat. Matho appeared insensible; suddenly he started off and began to run at random, making noise with his lips like one shivering with severe cold. He threaded the streets of Boudes, and the street of Sœpo, crossed the Green Market, and reached the square of Khamon.

He now belonged to the priests; the slaves had just dispersed the crowd, and there was more room. Matho gazed round him and his eyes encountered Salammbô.

At the first step that he had taken she had risen; then, as he approached, she had involuntarily advanced by degrees to the edge of the terrace; and soon all external things were blotted out, and she

394

saw only Matho. Silence fell in her soul—one of those abysses wherein the whole world disappears beneath the pressure of a single thought, a memory, a look. This man who was walking toward her attracted her.

Excepting his eyes he had no appearance of humanity left; he was a long, perfectly red shape; his broken bonds hung down his thighs, but they could not be distinguished from the tendons of his wrists, which were laid quite bare; his mouth remained wide open; from his eye sockets there darted flames which seemed to rise up to his hair—and the wretch still walked on!

He reached the foot of the terrace. Salammbô was leaning over the balustrade; those frightful eyeballs were scanning her, and there rose within her a consciousness of all that he had suffered for her. Although he was in his death agony, she could see him once more kneeling in his tent, encircling her waist with his arms, and stammering out gentle words; she thirsted to feel them and hear them again; she did not want him to die! At this moment Matho gave a great start: she was on the point of shrieking aloud. He fell backward and did not stir again.

Salammbô was borne back, nearly swooning, to her throne by the priests who flocked about her. They congratulated her; it was her work. All clapped their hands and stamped their feet, howling her name.

A man darted upon the corpse. Although he had no beard he had the cloak of a priest of Moloch on his shoulder, and in his belt that species of knife which they employed for cutting up the sacred meat, and which terminated, at the end of the handle, in a golden spatula. He cleft Matho's breast with a single blow, then snatched out the heart and laid it upon the spoon; and Schahabarim, uplifting his arm, offered it to the sun.

The sun sank behind the waves; his rays fell like long arrows upon the red heart. As the beatings diminished the planet sank into the sea; and at the last palpitation it disappeared.

Then from the gulf to the lagoon, and from the isthmus to the pharos, in all the streets, on all the houses, and on all the temples, there was a single shout; sometimes it paused, to be again renewed; the building shook with it; Carthage was convulsed, as it were, in the spasm of Titanic joy and boundless hope.

Narr' Havas, drunk with pride, passed his left arm beneath Salammbô's waist in token of possession; and taking a gold patera in his right hand, he drank to the Genius of Carthage.

Salammbô rose like her husband, with a cup in her hand, to drink also. She fell down again with her head lying over the back of the throne,—pale, stiff, with parted lips,—and her loosened hair hung to the ground.

FRIEDRICH DE LA MOTTE-FOUQUE

FRIEDRICH DE LA MOTTE-FOUQUÉ (German, 1777-1843). German novelist, given to romantic fantasies. Very popular in his day for medieval and nordic romances. Now remembered chiefly for fairy tale, "Undine."

UNDINE

I. *The Water Sprite*

ABOUT a century ago an aged fisherman sat mending his nets by his cottage door, in front of a lovely lake. Behind his dwelling stretched a sombre forest, reputed to be haunted by goblin creatures. Through this gloomy solitude the pious old fisherman frequently passed, religiously dispelling all terrors by singing hymns as he went with his fish to a town near the border of the forest.

One evening he heard the sound of a horse's hoofs, and presently appeared a knight riding on a splendid steed, and clad in resplendent armour. The stranger stopped, and besought shelter for the night, and the good old fisherman accorded him a most cheery welcome, taking him into the cottage, where sat his aged wife by a scanty fire. Soon the three were freely conversing. The knight told of his travels and revealed that he was Sir Huldbrand of Ringstetten, where he had a castle by the Rhine.

A splash against the window surprising the guest he was informed by his host, with some little show of vexation, that little tricks were often played by a foster-child of the old couple, named Undine, a girl of eighteen.

The door flew open, and a lovely girl glided, laughing, into the room. Without the slightest token of shyness she gazed at the knight for a few moments, then asked why he had come to the poor cottage. "Have you come through the wild forest?"

He confessed that he had, and she instantly demanded a recital of

his adventures. With a slight shudder at his own recollections of the strange creatures he had encountered, Huldbrand consented, but a reproof from the fisherman at her obtrusiveness angered Undine. The girl sprang up and rushed forth into the night, exclaiming, "Sleep alone in your smoky old hut!"

In great alarm, the fisherman and Huldbrand rose to follow the girl, but she had vanished in the darkness. Remarking that she had acted so before, the old fisherman invited Huldbrand to sit by the fire and talk awhile, and began to relate how Undine had come to live with them.

The couple had lost their only child, a wonderfully beautiful little girl. At the age of three, when sitting in her mother's lap at the edge of the lake, she seemed to be attracted by some lovely apparition in the water, for, suddenly stretching out her hands and laughing, she had in a moment sprung into the lake. No trace of the child could ever be found. But the same evening a lovely little girl, three or four years old, with water streaming from her golden tresses, suddenly entered the cottage, smiling sweetly at the fisherman and his wife. They hastily undressed the little stranger and put her to bed. She uttered not a word, but simply smiled. In the morning she talked a little, confusedly telling how she had been in a boat on the lake with her mother, and had fallen in, and could recollect nothing more. She could say nothing as to who she was or whence she came. But she talked often of golden castles and crystal domes.

While the fisherman was talking thus to the knight, he was suddenly interrupted by the noise of rushing water. Floods seemed to be bursting forth, and he and his guest, going hastily to the door, saw by the moonlight that the brook which issued from the forest was surging in a wild torrent over its margin, while a roaring wind was lashing the lake. In great alarm both shouted, "Undine! Undine!" But there was no response, and the two ran off in different directions in search of the fugitive.

It was Huldbrand who discovered the girl. Clambering down some rocks at the edge of the stream, thinking Undine might have fallen there, he was hailed by the sweet voice of the girl herself.

"Venture not," she cried. "The old man of the stream is full of tricks."

Looking across at a tiny isle in the stream, the knight saw her nestling in the grass, smiling, and in an instant he had crossed.

"The fisherman is distressed at your absence," said he. "Let us go back."

Looking at him with her beautiful blue eyes, the girl replied, "If you think so, well; whatever you think is right to me."

Taking Undine in his arms, Huldbrand bore her over the stream to the cottage, where she was received with joy. Dawn was breaking, and breakfast was prepared under the trees. Undine flung herself on the grass at Huldbrand's feet, and at her renewed request the knight told the story of his forest adventures.

"It is now about eight days since I rode into the city on the other side of the forest to join in a great tournament. In one of the intervals between the jousts I noticed a lovely lady among the spectators. I learned that she was Bertalda, foster-daughter of a great duke, and each evening I became her partner in the dances.

"This Bertalda was a wayward girl, and each day pleased me less and less; but I continued in her company, and asked her jestingly to give me a glove. She said she would do so if I would explore alone the haunted forest. As an honorable knight I could not decline the challenge, and yesterday I set out on the enterprise. Before I had penetrated very far within the glades, I saw what looked like a bear in the branches of an oak; but the creature, in a harsh, human voice, growled that it was getting branches with which to roast me at night. My horse was scared at this, and other grim apparitions, but at last I emerged from the forest, and saw the lake and this cottage."

When he had finished, the fisherman spoke of the best way by which the visitor could return to the city; but, with sly laughter, Undine declared that the knight could not depart, for if he attempted now to cross the deluged wood, he would be overwhelmed.

II. "I Have No Soul!"

HULDBRAND, detained at the cottage by the increasing overflow of the stream, enjoyed the most perfect satisfaction with his sojourn.

The old folks with pleasure regarded the two young people as betrothed, and Huldbrand assumed that he was accepted by the girl, whom he had come to look upon as not being in reality one of this poor household, but one of some illustrious family, and when, one evening, an aged priest appeared at the cottage, driven in by the storm, Huldbrand addressed to him a request that he should on the spot at once unite him and the maiden, as they were pledged to each other. A discussion arose, but matters were at length settled, and

the old wife produced two consecrated tapers. Lighting these, the priest, with brief, solemn ceremony, celebrated the nuptials.

Undine had been quiet and grave during these proceedings, but a singular change took place in her demeanour as soon as the rite had been performed. She began at intervals to indulge in wild freaks, teasing the priest, and indulging in a variety of silly tricks. At length the priest gently expostulated with Undine, exhorting her so to attune her soul that it might always be in concord with that of her husband.

Her reply amazed the listeners, for she said, "If one has no soul, as I have none, what is there to harmonise?" Then she burst into a fit of passionate weeping, to the consternation of all the little company. As she again and again wept, the priest, fearing that she was possessed by some evil spirit, sought to exorcise it. The priest turned to the bridegroom with the assurance that he could discover nothing evil in the bride, mysterious though her behaviour was, and he commended him to be loving and true to her.

The next morning Undine, when she and her husband made their appearance, responded gracefully to the paternal greeting of the priest, beseeching his pardon for her folly of the previous evening, and begging him to pray for the good of her soul. Through the whole day Undine behaved angelically. She was kind, quiet, and gentle. At eventide she led her husband out to the edge of the stream, which, to the wonder of Huldbrand, had subsided into gentle, rippling waves.

She whispered, "Carry me across to that little isle, and we will decide there."

Wondering, he carried her across, and, laying her on the turf, listened as she began.

"My loved one, know that there are strange beings which, though seeming almost like mortals, are rarely visible to human eyes—salamanders in the flames, gnomes down in the earth, spirits in the air. And in the water are myriads of spirits dwelling in crystal domes, in the coral-trees, and in the lovely shells. These are far more beautiful than the fairest of human beings, and sometimes a fisherman has seen a tender mermaid, and has listened to her song. Such wonderful creatures are called Undines, and one of these you see now before you!

"We should be far superior to other beings—for we consider ourselves human—but for one defect. We have no souls, and nothing

remains of us after this mortal life is over. Yet every being aspires to rise higher, and so my father, who is a great water prince in the Mediterranean Sea, desired that his only daughter should become possessed of a soul. But this can only come to pass with loving union with one of your race. Now, O my dearly beloved, I have to thank you that I am gifted with a soul, and it will be due to you should all my life be made wretched. For what will become of me if you forsake me? If you would do so, do it now! Then I will plunge into the stream—which is my uncle—and as he brought me here, so will he take me back to my parents, a loving, suffering woman with a soul."

Undine would have said yet more, but Huldbrand, astonishing though the recital was, with tears and kisses vowed he would never leave his lovely wife; and with her leaning in loving trustfulness on his arm,.they returned to the hut.

The next day, at Undine's strange urgency, farewell was said with bitter tears and lamentations.

Undine was placed on the beautiful horse, and Huldbrand and the priest walked on either side as the three passed through the solemn glades of the wood. A fourth soon joined them. He was dressed in a white robe, like that of the priest, and presently attempted to speak to Undine. But she shrank from him, declaring she wished to have nothing to do with him.

"Oh, oh!" cried the stranger, with a laugh. "What kind of a marriage is this you have made, that you must not speak to your relative? Do you not know I am your uncle Kühleborn, who brought you to this region, and that I am here to protect you from goblins and sprites? So let me quietly accompany you."

"We are near the end of the forest, and shall not need you further," was her rejoinder. But he grinned at her so frightfully that she shrieked for help, and the knight aimed at his head a blow from his sword. Instantly Kühleborn was transformed into a gushing waterfall, foaming over them from a rock near by and drenching all three.

III. *"Woe! Woe!"*

THE sudden disappearance of the young knight had caused a sensation in the city, for the duke and duchess, and the friends and servants of Huldbrand, feared he had perished in the forest during the terrible tempest. When he suddenly reappeared, all rejoiced ex-

cept Bertalda, who was profoundly vexed at seeing with him a beautiful bride. She so far reconciled herself to the conditions that a warm friendship sprang up between Undine and herself.

It was agreed that Bertalda should accompany the wedded pair to Ringstetten, and with the consent of the noble foster-parents of Bertalda the three appointed a day for the departure. One beautiful evening, as they walked about the market-place round the great fountain, suddenly a tall man emerged from among the people and stopped in front of Undine. He quickly whispered something in her ear, and though at first she seemed vexed at the intrusion, presently she clapped her hands and laughed joyously. Then the stranger mysteriously vanished, and seemed to disappear in the fountain.

Huldbrand had suspected that he had seen this man before, and now felt assured that he was Kühleborn. Undine admitted the fact, and said that her uncle had told her a secret, which she was to reveal on the third day afterwards, which would be the anniversary of Bertalda's nameday.

The anniversary came, and strange incidents happened. After the banquet given by the duke and duchess, Undine suddenly gave a signal, and from among the retainers at the door came forth the old fisherman and his wife, and Undine declared that in these Bertalda saw her real parents. The proud maiden instantly flew into a violent rage, weeping passionately, and utterly refused to acknowledge the old couple as her father and mother. She declared that Undine was an enchantress and a witch, sustaining intercourse with evil spirits.

Undine, with great dignity, indignantly denied the accusation, while Bertalda's violent conduct created a feeling of disgust in the minds of all in the assembly. The matter was settled in a simple manner, for the duke commanded Bertalda to withdraw to a private apartment with the duchess and the two old folks from the hut, that an investigation might be made. It was soon over, for the noble lady was able presently to inform the company that Undine's story was absolutely true. The guests silently departed, and Undine sank sobbing into her husband's arms.

Next day Bertalda, humbled by these events, sought pardon of Undine for her evil behaviour, and was instantly welcomed with loving assurances of forgiveness. Moreover, she was cordially invited to go with the pair to Ringstetten.

"We will share all things there as sisters," said Undine.

The three journeyed to the distant castle, and took up their abode together. Soon Kühleborn appeared on the scene, but Undine at once

repulsed him. Next, when her husband was one day hunting, she ordered the great well in the courtyard to be covered with a big stone, on which she cut some curious characters.

Bertalda waywardly complained that this proceeding deprived her of water that was good for her complexion, but Undine privately explained to Huldbrand that she had caused the servants to seal up this spring because only by that way of access could her uncle Kühleborn come to disturb their peace.

As time passed on, Huldbrand gradually cooled towards his wife and turned affectionately towards Bertalda. Undine bore patiently and silently the sorrow thus inflicted on her. But when her husband was impatient and angry she would plead with him never to speak to her in accents of unkindness when they happened to be on the water, for the water spirits had her completely in their power on their element, and would seek to protect her and even seize her and take her down for ever to dwell in the crystal castles of the deep.

After some estrangements, Undine and Bertalda had again become loving friends, and Huldbrand's affection for his wife had revived with its old and welcome warmth, while the attachment between him and Bertalda seemed forgotten.

One day the three were enjoying a delightful excursion on the glorious Danube. Bertalda had taken off a beautiful coral necklace which Huldbrand had given her. She leaned over and drew the coral beads across the surface, enjoying the glitter thus caused, when suddenly a great hand from beneath seized the necklace and snatched it down. The maiden's scream of terror was answered by mocking laughter from the water.

In an outburst of passion, Huldbrand started up and poured forth curses on the river and its denizens, whether spirits or sirens. With tears in her eyes, Undine besought him softly not to scold her there, and she took from her neck a beautiful necklace and offered it to Bertalda as a compensation.

But the angry knight snatched it away, and hurled it into the river, exclaiming, "Are you still connected with them? In the name of all the witches, remain among them with your presents, and leave us mortals in peace, you sorceress!"

Bitterly weeping and crying, "Woe! Woe!" she vanished over the side of the vessel. Her last words were, "Remain true! Woe! Woe!" Huldbrand lay swooning on the deck, and little waves seemed to be sobbing on the surface of the Danube, "Woe! Woe! Remain true!"

For a time deep sorrow fell on the lord of Ringstetten and Bertalda. They lived long in the castle quietly, often weeping for Undine, tenderly cherishing her memory. Undine often visited Huldbrand in his dreams, caressing him and weeping silently so that his cheeks were wet when he awoke. But these visions grew less frequent, and the knight's grief diminished by degrees. At length he and Bertalda were married, but it was in spite of a grave warning from Father Heilmann, who declared that Undine had appeared to him in visions, beseeching him to warn Huldbrand and Bertalda to leave each other. They were too infatuated to heed the admonition, and a priest from a neighbouring monastery promised to perform the ceremony in a few days.

Meantime, when lying between sleeping and waking, the knight seemed fanned by the wings of a swan, and, as he fell asleep, seemed borne along on the wings of swans which sang their sweetest music. All at once he seemed to be hovering over the Mediterranean Sea. Its waters were so crystalline that he could see through them to the bottom, and there, under a crystal arch, sat Undine, weeping bitterly. She seemed not to perceive him. Kühleborn approached her, and told her that Huldbrand was to be wedded again, and that it would be her duty, from which nothing could release her, to end his life.

"That I cannot do," said she. "I have sealed up the fountain against me and my race."

Huldbrand felt as if he were soaring back again over the sea, and at length he seemed to reach his castle. He awoke on his couch, but he could not bring himself to break off the arrangements that had been made.

The marriage feast at Ringstetten was not as bright and happy as such occasions usually are, for a veil of gloom seemed to rest over the company. Even the bride affected a happy and thoughtless demeanour which she did not really feel. The company dispersed early, Bertalda retiring with her maidens, and Huldbrand with his attendants.

In her apartment Bertalda, with a sigh, noticed how freckled was her neck, and a remark she made to her maidens as she gazed in the mirror excited the eager attention of one of them. She heard her fair mistress say, "Oh, that I had a flask of the purifying water from the closed fountain!" Presently the officious waiting-woman

was seen leading men to the fountain. With levers they quickly lifted the stone, for some mysterious force seemed to aid them.

Then from the fountain solemnly rose a white column of water. It was presently perceived that it was a pale female figure, veiled in white. She was weeping bitterly as she walked slowly to the building, while Bertalda and her attendants, pale with terror, watched from the window. The figure passed on, and at the door of Huldbrand's room, where the knight was partly undressed, was heard a gentle tap. The white figure slowly entered. It was Undine, who softly said, "They have opened the spring, and now I am here and you must die." Said the knight, "It must be so! But let me die in your embrace."

"Most gladly, my beloved one," said she, throwing back her veil and disclosing her face divinely smiling. Imprinting on his lips a sacred kiss, Undine clasped the knight in her arms, weeping as if she would weep her very soul away. Huldbrand fell softly back on the pillows of his couch, a corpse.

At the funeral of Huldbrand the veiled figure appeared when the procession formed a circle round the grave. All knelt in mute devotion at a signal from Father Heilmann. When they rose again the white stranger had vanished, and on the spot where she had knelt a silvery little fountain gushed forth, which almost encircled the grave and then ran on till it reached a lake near by. And to this day the inhabitants cherish the tradition that thus the poor rejected Undine still lovingly embraces her husband.

ANATOLE FRANCE

ANATOLE FRANCE (Jacques Anatole François Thibault, French, 1844-1924). The poet of irony and pity, with his heart in the Middle Ages. Novelist, historian, short story writer: *Thaïs, Penguin Island, The Crime of Sylvestre Bonnard, Life of Joan of Arc.* Nobel Prize, 1921. Though his work dates, its survival seems ensured because of its wit and stylistic talent.

A ROMAN SENATOR

Cæsar, on the stones of the deserted hall,
Under the folds of his toga, lay in majesty.
The green-lipped bronze of Pompey, proud and tall,
Smiled at the white corpse bloodily.

The spirit just fled through a road made clear
By the steel of Brutus and of Liberty,
Hovered sadly over the lifeless, dear
Flesh fond death made pale yet fair to see.

On a bare marble bench near by, at rest,
The even movements of his mighty chest
Marking his snores, a Senator took his leisure.

The silence woke him and, disturbed, he cried
Across the silent horror at his side:
"I vote to give the imperial crown to Cæsar!"

EVE'S BLOOD

Love hides many treasures in its deeps.
Nature's primordial hardihoods,
That mingled nude thighs in woodland quest,
Still modestly surge in the bride's breast:
Watchful of our conventions, she keeps
The blood of that Eve of the early woods.

THE BAD WORKMAN

Master Laurent Coster, with poetry in his heart,
Left his companions who, from morn to night,
Born vintners, made the boards of the wine-press start—
And Coster dreaming followed his fancy's flight.

For he loved the demon Aspasia with all his soul.
Sometimes he'd sit upon his bench at church
And see in the fumes above the incense bowl
The Woman of Hell who was his only search.

Or else alone at the brink of a mossy well,
Clasping the hands no labor could impel,
He'd hark forever to her siren song. . . .

And I, as well, can neither work nor pray;
I am like Coster, a laborer astray
Through looking in your dark eyes overlong.

"I have burned my garments of gold, and my violin.
While the brazier of repentance shines on me
I shall seek the Pope to wash away my sin.

"O Holy Father, hear with clemency
By what rare sins and demon joy thereof,
Remote from Jesus, I was blind to his decree.

"In the enchanted city, all other peaks above,
With beauteous Venus I dwelt seven years.
Absolve me now, by Jesus whom we love."

The cross of the Holy Father, as he hears,
Trembles: "Your frightful sins the Lord will pardon
When leaf or flower on his cross appears!"

Tears do the gallant's heavy spirit harden.
"Since, Madame Virgin, I no more may yearn
To tend the flowers of your heavenly garden,

"Nor as a shining taper for you burn,
The tender Lady Venus will comfort me:
Never to leave her more, I now return!"

"In truth I'm glad, yes, glad, to see
Thee, Knight; sit down and drink, I pray.
A long time, Tannhäuser, I have longed for thee."

The cross having blossomed on the third day,
The Holy Father sent a post full speed
To seek Tannhäuser up hill and away.

With Venus, he was drinking mellow mead,—
And there will linger, while marriage songs are played,
Until the Angel's trump to Judgment lead.

Not thus should man's bright soul be overlaid:
If they are damned who love the brave device
Of the clear word and the clear smile of a maid

There'll be no one to sing in Paradise.

FERDINAND FREILIGRATH

FERDINAND FREILIGRATH (German, 1810-1876). German poet whose revolutionary sentiments forced him frequently abroad. Influenced by Byron and Victor Hugo, whom he translated.

THE SPECTER CARAVAN

'Twas midnight in the Desert, where we rested on the ground;
There my Beddaweens were sleeping and their steeds were stretched
  around;
In the farness lay the moonlight of the Mountains of the Nile,
And the camel bones that strewed the sands for many an arid mile.

With my saddle for a pillow did I prop my weary head,
And my kaftan cloth unfolded o'er my limbs was lightly spread,
While beside me, as the Kapitan and watchman of my band,
Lay my Bazra sword and pistols twain a shimmering on the sand.

And the stillness was unbroken, save at moments by a cry
From some stray belated vulture sailing blackly down the sky,
Or the snortings of a sleeping steed at waters fancy-seen,
Or the hurried warlike mutterings of some dreaming Beddaween.

When, behold!—a sudden sandquake,—and between the earth and
  moon
Rose a mighty Host of Shadows, as from out some dim lagoon;
Then our coursers gasped with terror, and a thrill shook every man;
And the cry was—"Allah Akbar! 'tis the Specter Caravan!"

On they came, their hueless faces toward Mecca evermore;
On they came, long files of camels, and of women whom they bore,
Guides, and merchants, youthful maidens bearing pitchers in their
  hands,
And behind them troops of horsemen following, sumless as the
  sands!

More and more! the phantom pageant overshadowed all the plains;
Yea! the ghastly camel bones arose, and grew to camel trains;
And the whirling column clouds of sand to forms in dusky garbs,—
Here afoot as Hadjee pilgrims, there as warriors on their barbs!

407

Whence we knew the Night was come when all whom Death had
    sought and found,
Long ago amid the sands whereon their bones yet bleach around,
Rise by legions from the darkness of their prisons low and lone,
And in dim procession march to kiss the Kaaba's Holy Stone.

And yet more, and more forever!—still they swept in pomp along,
Till I asked me,—Can the Desert hold so vast a muster throng?
Lo! the Dead are here in myriads; the whole World of Hades
    waits,
As with eager wish to press beyond the Babelmandeb Straits!

Then I spake: "Our steeds are frantic: To your saddles, every one!
Never quail before these Shadows! You are children of the Sun!
If their garments rustle past you, if their glances reach you here,
Cry Bismillah! and that mighty Name shall banish every fear.

"Courage, comrades! Even now the moon is waning far a-west,—
Soon the welcome Dawn will mount the skies, in gold and crimson
    vest,—
And in thinnest air will melt away those phantom shapes forlorn,
When again upon your brows you feel the odor winds of Morn!"

THE LION'S RIDE

King of deserts reigns the lion; will he through his realm go
    riding,
Down to the lagoon he paces, in the tall sedge there lies hiding.
Where gazelles and camelopards drink, he crouches by the shore;
Ominous, above the monster, moans the quivering sycamore.

When, at dusk, the ruddy hearth-fires in the Hottentot kraals are
    glowing,
And the motley, changeful signals on the Table Mountain growing
Dim and distant—when the Caffre sweeps along the lone karroo—
When in the bush the antelope slumbers, and beside the stream the
    gnu—

Lo! majestically stalking, yonder comes the tall giraffe,
Hot with thirst, the gloomy waters of the dull lagoon to quaff;
O'er the naked waste behold her, with parched tongue, all panting
hasten—
Now she sucks the cool draught, kneeling, from the stagnant, slimy
basin.

Hark, a rustling in the sedges! with a roar, the lion springs
On her back now. What a race-horse! Say, in proudest stalls of
kings,
Saw one ever richer housings than the courser's motley hide,
On whose back the tawny monarch of the beasts tonight will ride?

Fixed his teeth are in the muscles of the nape, with greedy strain;
Round the giant courser's withers waves the rider's yellow mane.
With a hollow cry of anguish, leaps and flies the tortured steed;
See her, how with skin of leopard she combines the camel's speed!

See, with lightly beating footsteps, how she scours the moonlit
plains!
From their sockets start the eyeballs; from the torn and bleeding
veins,
Fast the thick, black drops come trickling, o'er the brown and
dappled neck,
And the flying beast's heart-beatings audible the stillness make.

Like the cloud, that, guiding Israel through the land of Yemen,
shone,
Like a spirit of the desert, like a phantom, pale and wan,
O'er the desert's sandy ocean, like a waterspout at sea,
Whirls a yellow, cloudy column, tracking them where'er they flee.

On their track the vulture follows, flapping, croaking, through the
air,
And the terrible hyena, plunderer of tombs, is there;
Follows them the stealthy panther—Cape-town's folds have known
him well;
Them their monarch's dreadful pathway, blood and sweat full
plainly tell.

409

On his living throne, they, quaking, see their ruler sitting there,
With sharp claw the painted cushion of his seat they see him tear.
Restless the giraffe must bear him on, till strength and lifeblood
    fail her;
Mastered by such daring rider, rearing, plunging, naught avail her.

To the desert's verge she staggers—sinks—one groan—and all is
    o'er.
Now the steed shall feast the rider, dead, and smeared with dust
    and gore.
Far across, o'er Madagascar, faintly now the morning breaks;
Thus the king of beasts his journey nightly through his empire
    makes.

ROBERT FROST

ROBERT FROST (American, 1875-   ). The poet of the ordinary tongue.
Called the interpreter of New England. Spent much of life as professor at
Amherst College. His supremely simple poems convey universal truths through
homely, country images. Collections: *North of Boston, Mountain Interval,
New Hampshire, West-running Brook, A Further Range, A Masque of Reason.*

The Need of Being Versed in Country Things

The house had gone to bring again
To the midnight sky a sunset glow.
Now the chimney was all of the house that stood,
Like a pistil after the petals go.

The barn opposed across the way,
That would have joined the house in flame
Had it been the will of the wind, was left
To bear forsaken the place's name.

No more it opened with all one end
For teams that came by the stony road
To drum on the floor with scurrying hoofs
And brush the mow with the summer load.

The birds that came to it through the air
At broken windows flew out and in,
Their murmur like the sigh we sigh
From too much dwelling on what has been.

Yet for them the lilac renewed its leaf,
And the aged elm, though touched with fire;
And the dry pump flung up an awkward arm;
And the fence post carried a strand of wire.

For them there was really nothing sad.
But though they rejoiced in the nest they kept,
One had to be versed in country things
Not to believe the phoebes wept.

The Gift Outright

The land was ours before we were the land's.
She was our land more than a hundred years
Before we were her people. She was ours
In Massachusetts, in Virginia,
But we were England's, still colonials,
Possessing what we were still unpossessed by,
Possessed by what we now no more possessed.
Something we were withholding made us weak
Until we found out that it was ourselves
We were withholding from our land of living,
And forthwith found salvation in surrender.
Such as we were we gave ourselves outright
(The deed of gift was many deeds of war)
To the land vaguely realizing westward,
But still unstoried, artless, unenhanced,
Such as she was, such as she would become.

411

FUZULI

FUZULî (Mehmet Suleiman Oglou, Turkish, *ca.* 1494-1572). Leading representative of the classical school of Turkish literature. Wrote also in Arabic and Persian. Led humble, unhappy life, died of plague. Called "the poet of the heart." Chief works: *Divan* (a collection of short odes known as *ghazals* or "gazels") and *Leyla ve Mejnun,* a romance of unhappy lovers.

GAZEL

O breeze, thou'rt kind, of balm to those whom pangs affright, thou
    news hast brought,
To wounded frame of life, to life of life's delight thou news hast
    brought.
Thou'st seen the mourning nightingale's despair in sorrow's autumn
    drear,
Like springtide days, of smiling roseleaf fresh and bright, thou
    news hast brought.
If I should say thy words are heaven-inspired, in truth, blaspheme
    I not;
Of Faith, whilst unbelief doth earth hold fast and tight, thou news
    hast brought.
They say the loved one comes to soothe the hearts of all her lovers
    true;
If that the case, to yon fair maid of lovers' plight thou news hast
    brought.
Of rebel demon thou hast cut the hope Suleyman's throne to gain;
That in the sea secure doth lie his Ring of might, thou news hast
    brought.
Fuzuli, through the parting night, alas, how dark my fortune grew!
Like zephyr of the dawn, of shining sun's fair light thou news hast
    brought.

GAZEL

O thou Perfect Being, Source whence wisdom's mysteries arise;
Things, the issue of thine essence, show wherein thy nature lies.
Manifester of all wisdom, thou art he whose pen of might
Hath with rays of stars illumined yonder gleaming page, the skies.
That a happy star, indeed, the essence clear of whose bright self
Truly knoweth how the blessings from thy word that flow to prize.

412

But a jewel flawed am faulty I: alas, forever stands
Blank the page of my heart's journal from thought of thy writing
   wise.
In the journal of my actions Evil's lines are black indeed;
When I think of Day of Gathering's terrors, blood flows from my
   eyes.
Gathering of my tears will form a torrent on the Reckoning Day,
If the pearls, my tears, rejecting, he but view them to despise:
Pearls my tears are, O Fuzuli, from the ocean deep of love;
But they're pearls these, oh! most surely, that the Love of Allah
   buys!

GAZEL

Is't strange if beauties' hearts turn blood through envy of thy cheek
   most fair?
For that which stone to ruby turns is but the radiant sunlight's glare.
Or strange is't if thine eyelash conquer all the stony-hearted ones?
For meet an ebon shaft like that a barb of adamant should bear!
Thy cheek's sun-love hath on the hard, hard hearts of fairy beauties
   fall'n,
And many a steely-eyed one hath received thy bright reflection fair.
The casket, thy sweet mouth, doth hold spell-bound the *huri*-faced
   ones all;
The virtue of Suleyman's Ring was that fays thereto fealty sware.
Is't strange if, seeing thee, they rub their faces lowly midst the dust?
That down to Adam bowed the angel throng doth the Qur'an
   declare!
On many and many a heart of stone have fall'n the pangs of love
   for thee!
A fire that lies in stone concealed is thy heart-burning love's dread
   glare!
Within her ward, with garments rent, on all sides rosy-cheeked ones
   stray;
Fuzuli, through those radiant hues, that quarter beams a garden
   fair.

GAZEL

From the turning of the Sphere my luck hath seen reverse and woe;
Blood I've drunk, for from my banquet wine arose and forth did go.
With the flame, my burning sighs, I've lit the wand'ring wildered
   heart;

413

I'm a fire, doth not all that which turns about me roasted glow?
With thy rubies wine contended—oh! how it hath lost its wits!
Need 'tis yon ill-mannered wretch's company that we forego.
Yonder Moon saw not my burning's flame upon the parting day—
How can e'er the sun about the taper all night burning know?
Every eye that all around tears scatters, thinking of thy shaft,
Is an oyster-shell that causeth rain-drops into pearls to grow.
Forms my sighing's smoke a cloud that veils the bright cheek of
    the moon;
Ah! that yon fair Moon will ne'er the veil from off her beauty
    throw!
Ne'er hath ceased the rival e'en within her ward to vex me sore;
How say they, Fuzuli, "There's in Paradise nor grief nor woe"?

G

SOLOMON IBN GABIROL

SOLOMON IBN GABIROL (Spanish-Hebrew, 1021-1058). The Hebrew poet of the Golden Period of Moorish Spain. Little is known of his life. One of the greatest of medieval poets, deeply religious and philosophical. Philosophic works, written in Arabic, influenced Duns Scotus, Spinoza, Schopenhauer. Most noted poem: *Kether Meluth (Royal Crown)*.

NIGHT

Night, and the heavens beam serene with peace,
Like a pure heart benignly smiles the moon.
Oh, guard thy blessed beauty from mischance,
This I beseech thee in all tender love.
See where the Storm his cloudy mantle spreads,
An ashy curtain covereth the moon.
As if the tempest thirsted for the rain,
The clouds he presses, till they burst in streams.
Heaven wears a dusky raiment, and the moon
Appeareth dead—her tomb is yonder cloud,
And weeping shades come after, like the people
Who mourn with tearful grief a noble queen.
But look! the thunder pierced night's close-linked mail,
His keen-tipped lance of lightning brandishing;
He hovers like a seraph-conqueror.—
Dazed by the flaming splendor of his wings,
In rapid flight as in a whirling dance,
The black cloud-ravens hurry scared away.
So, though the powers of darkness chain my soul,
My heart, a hero, chafes and breaks its bonds.

NIGHT-THOUGHTS

Will night already spread her wings and weave
Her dusky robe about the day's bright form,
Boldly the sun's fair countenance displacing,
And swathe it with her shadow in broad day?
So a green wreath of mist enrings the moon,
Till envious clouds do quite encompass her.
No wind! and yet the slender stem is stirred,
With faint, slight motion as from inward tremor.
Mine eyes are full of grief—who sees me, asks,
"Oh, wherefore dost thou cling unto the ground?"
My friends discourse with sweet and soothing words;
They all are vain, they glide above my head.
I fain would check my tears; would fain enlarge
Unto infinity, my heart—in vain!
Grief presses hard my breast, therefore my tears
Have scarcely dried, ere they again spring forth.
For these are streams no furnace heat may quench,
Nebuchadnezzar's flames may dry them not.
What is the pleasure of the day for me,
If, in its crucible, I must renew
Incessantly the pangs of purifying?
Up, challenge, wrestle, and o'ercome! Be strong!
The late grapes cover all the vine with fruit.
I am not glad, though even the lion's pride
Content itself upon the field's poor grass.
My spirit sinks beneath the tide, soars not
With fluttering seamews on the moist, soft strand.
I follow Fortune not, where'er she lead.
Lord o'er myself, I banish her, compel.
And though her clouds should rain no blessed dew,
Though she withhold the crown, the heart's desire,
Though all deceive, though honey change to gall,
Still am I lord, and will in freedom strive.

MEDITATIONS

Forget thine anguish,
  Vexed heart, again.
Why shouldst thou languish,
  With earthly pain?

416

The husk shall slumber,
    Bedded in clay
Silent and sombre,
    Oblivion's prey!
But, Spirit immortal,
Thou at Death's portal,
    Tremblest with fear.
    If he caress thee,
    Curse thee or bless thee,
    Thou must draw near,
From him the worth of thy works to hear.

    Why full of terror,
    Compassed with error,
    Trouble thy heart,
    For thy mortal part?
    The soul flies home—
    The corpse is dumb.
    Of all thou didst have,
Follows naught to the grave.
    Thou fliest thy nest,
Swift as a bird to thy place of rest.

    What avail grief and fasting,
    Where nothing is lasting?
    Pomp, domination,
    Become tribulation.
    In a health-giving draught,
    A death-dealing shaft.
    Wealth—an illusion,
    Power—a lie,
    Over all, dissolution
    Creeps silent and sly.
    Unto others remain
    The goods thou didst gain
    With infinite pain.

Life is a vine-branch;
    A vintager, Death.
He threatens and lowers
    More near with each breath.

Then hasten, arise!
   Seek God, O my soul!
For time quickly flies,
   Still far is the goal.
Vain heart praying dumbly,
   Learn to prize humbly,
   The meanest of fare.
Forget all thy sorrow,
   Behold, Death is there!

   Dove-like lamenting,
   Be full of repenting,
Lift vision supernal
To raptures eternal.
   On ev'ry occasion
   Seek lasting salvation.
Pour thy heart out in weeping,
While others are sleeping.
   Pray to Him when all's still,
   Performing his will.
And so shall the angel of peace be thy warden,
And guide thee at last to the heavenly garden.

JOHN GALSWORTHY

JOHN GALSWORTHY (English, 1867-1933). Novelist and playwright. A gentle critic of our social disorder. Trained for the bar, but turned to literature. His major work, *The Forsyte Saga*, paints detailed picture of late Victorian era. Other novels more superficial. Still performed play, *Justice*, displays a concern over social wrongs.

QUALITY

I KNEW him from the days of my extreme youth, because he made my father's boots; inhabiting with his elder brother two little shops let into one, in a small by-street—now no more, but then most fashionably placed in the West End.

That tenement had a certain quiet distinction; there was no sign upon its face that he made for any of the Royal Family—merely his

own German name of Gessler Brothers; and in the window a few pairs of boots. I remember that it always troubled me to account for those unvarying boots in the window, for he made only what was ordered, reaching nothing down, and it seemed so inconceivable that what he made could ever have failed to fit. Had he bought them to put there? That, too, seemed inconceivable. He would never have tolerated in his house leather on which he had not worked himself. Besides, they were too beautiful—the pair of pumps, so inexpressibly slim; the patent leathers with cloth tops, making water come into one's mouth; the tall brown riding boots, with marvellous sooty glow, as if, though new, they had been worn a hundred years. Those pairs could only have been made by one who saw before him the Soul of Boot—so truly were they prototypes incarnating the very spirit of all foot-gear. These thoughts, of course, came to me later, though even when I was promoted to him, at the age of perhaps fourteen, some inkling haunted me of the dignity of himself and brother. For to make boots—such boots as he made—seemed to me then, and still seems to me, mysterious and wonderful.

I remember well my shy remark, one day, while stretching out to to him my youthful foot:

"Isn't it awfully hard to do, Mr. Gessler?"

And his answer, given with a sudden smile from out of the sardonic redness of his beard: "Id is an Ardt!"

Himself, he was as little as if made from leather, with his yellow crinkly reddish hair and beard, and neat folds slanting down his cheeks to the corners of his mouth, and his guttural and one-toned voice; for leather is a sardonic substance, and stiff and slow of purpose. And that was the character of his face, save that his eyes, which were grey-blue, had in them the simple gravity of one secretly possessed by the Ideal. His elder brother was so very like him— though watery, paler in every way, with a great industry—that sometimes in early days I was not quite sure of him until the interview was over. Then I knew that it was he, if the words, "I will ask my brudder," had not been spoken; and that, if they had, it was his elder brother.

When one grew old and wild and ran up bills, one somehow never ran them up with Gessler Brothers. It would not have seemed becoming to go in there and stretch out one's foot to that blue iron-spectacled glance, owing him for more than—say—two pairs, just the comfortable reassurance that one was still his client.

For it was not possible to go to him very often—his boots lasted

419

terribly, having something beyond the temporary—some, as it were, essence of boot stitched into them.

One went in, not as into most shops, in the mood of; "Please serve me, and let me go!" but restfully, as one enters a church; and, sitting on the single wooden chair, waited—for there was never anybody there. Soon, over the top edge of that sort of well—rather dark, as smelling soothingly of leather—which formed the shop, there would be seen his face, or that of his elder brother, peering down. A guttural sound, and the tip-tap of bast slippers beating the narrow wooden stairs, and he would stand before one without coat, a little bent, in leather apron, with sleeves turned back, blinking—as if awakened from some dream of boots, or like an owl surprised in daylight and annoyed at his interruption.

And I would say: "How do you do, Mr. Gessler? Could you make me a pair of Russian leather boots?"

Without a word he would leave me, retiring whence he came, or into the other portion of the shop, and I would continue to rest in the wooden chair, inhaling the incense of his trade. Soon he would come back, holding in his thin, veined hand a piece of gold-brown leather. With eyes fixed on it, he would remark: "What a beautiful biece!" When I, too, had admired it, he would speak again. "When do you wand dem?" And I would answer: "Oh! As soon as you conveniently can." And he would say: "To-morrow fordnight?" Or if he were his elder brother: "I will ask my brudder!"

Then I would murmur: "Thank you! Good morning, Mr. Gessler." "Goot morning!" he would reply, still looking at the leather in his hand. And as I moved to the door, I would hear the tip-tap of his bast slippers restoring him, up the stairs, to his dream of boots. But if it were some new kind of foot-gear that he had not yet made me, then indeed he would observe ceremony—divesting me of my boot and holding it long in his hand, looking at it with eyes at once critical and loving, as if recalling the glow with which he had created it, and rebuking the way in which one had disorganised this master-piece. Then, placing my foot on a thin piece of paper, he would two or three times tickle the outer edges with a pencil and pass his nervous fingers over my toes, feeling himself into the heart of my requirements.

I cannot forget that day on which I had occasion to say to him: "Mr. Gessler, that last pair of town walking-boots creaked, you know."

He looked at me for a time without replying, as if expecting me to withdraw or qualify the statement, then said:

"Id shouldn't 'ave greaked."

"It did, I'm afraid."

"You goddem wed before dey found demselves?"

"I don't think so."

At that he lowered his eyes, as if hunting for memory of those boots, and I felt sorry I had mentioned this grave thing.

"Zend dem back!" he said; "I will look at dem."

A feeling of compassion for my creaking boots surged up in me, so well could I imagine the sorrowful long curiosity of regard which he would bend on them.

"Zome boods," he said slowly, "are bad from birdt. If I can do noding wid dem, I dake dem off your bill."

Once (once only) I went absent-mindedly into his shop in a pair of boots bought in an emergency at some large firm's. He took my order without showing me any leather, and I could feel his eyes penetrating the inferior integument of my foot. At last he said:

"Dose are nod my boods."

The tone was not one of anger, nor of sorrow, not even of contempt, but there was in it something quiet that froze the blood. He put his hand down and pressed a finger on the place where the left boot, endeavoring to be fashionable, was not quite comfortable.

"Id 'urds you dere," he said. "Dose big virms 'ave no self-respect. Drash!" And then as if something had given way within him, he spoke long and bitterly. It was the only time I ever heard him discuss the conditions and hardships of the trade.

"Dey get id all," he said, "dey get id by adverdisement, nod by work. Dey dake it way from us, who lofe our boods. Id gomes to this—bresently I haf no work. Every year id gets less—you will see." And looking at his lined face I saw things I had never noticed before, bitter things and bitter struggle—and what a lot of grey hairs there seemed suddenly in his red beard!

As best I could, I explained the circumstances of the purchase of those ill-omened boots. But his face and voice made so deep impression that during the next few minutes I ordered many pairs. Nemesis fell! They lasted more terribly than ever. And I was not able conscientiously to go to him for nearly two years.

When at last I went I was surprised to find that outside one of the two little windows of his shop another name was painted, also that

of a boot-maker—making, of course, for the Royal Family. The old familiar boots, no longer in dignified isolation, were huddled in the window. Inside, the now contracted well of the one little shop was more scented and darker than ever. And it was longer than usual, too, before a face peered down, and the tip-tap of the bast slippers began. At last he stood before me, and, gazing through those rusty iron spectacles, said:

"Mr. ——, isn'd id?"

"Ah! Mr. Gessler," I stammered, "but your boots are really *too* good, you know! See, these are quite decent still!" And I stretched out to him my foot. He looked at it.

"Yes," he said, "beople do nod wand good boods, id seems."

To get away from his reproachful eyes and voice I hastily remarked: "What have you done to your shop?"

He answered quietly: "Id was too exbensive. Do you wand some boods?"

I ordered three pairs, though I had only wanted two, and quickly left. I had, I do not know quite what feeling of being part, in his mind, of a conspiracy against him; or not perhaps so much against him as against his idea of boot. One does not, I suppose, care to feel like that; for it was again many months before my next visit to his shop, paid I remember, with the feeling: "Oh, well, I can't leave the old boy—so here goes! Perhaps it will be his elder brother!"

For his elder brother, I knew, had not character enough to reproach me, even dumbly.

And, to my relief, in the shop there did appear to be his elder brother, handling apiece of leather.

"Well, Mr. Gessler," I said, "how are you?"

He came close and peered at me.

"I am breddy well," he said slowly: "but my elder brudder is dead."

And I saw that it was indeed himself—but how aged and wan! And never before had I heard him mention his brother. Much shocked, I murmured: "Oh! I am sorry!"

"Yes," he answered, "he was a good man, he made a good bood; but he is dead." And he touched the top of his head, where the hair had suddenly gone as thin as it had been on that of his poor brother, to indicate, I suppose, the cause of death. "He could nod ged over losing de oder shop. Do you wand any boods?" And he held up the leather in his hand: "Id's a beaudiful biece."

I ordered several pairs. It was very long before they came—but

422

they were better than ever. One simply could not wear them out. And soon after that I went abroad.

It was over a year before I was again in London. And the first shop I went to was my old friend's. I had left a man of sixty, I came back to one of seventy-five, pinched and worn and tremulous, who genuinely, this time, did not at first know me.

"Oh! Mr. Gessler," I said, sick at heart; "how splendid your boots are! See, I've been wearing this pair nearly all the time I've been abroad; and they're not half worn out, are they?"

He looked long at my boots—a pair of Russian leather, and his face seemed to regain steadiness. Putting his hand on my instep, he said:

"Do dey vid you here? I 'ad drouble wid dat bair, I remember."

I assured him that they had fitted beautifully.

"Do you wand any boods? he said. "I can make dem quickly; id is a slack dime."

I answered: "Please, please! I want boots all round—every kind!"

"I will make a vresh model. Your foot must be bigger." And with utter slowness, he traced round my foot, and felt my toes, only once looking up to say:

"Did I tell you my brudder was dead?"

To watch him was painful, so feeble had he grown; I was glad to get away.

I had given those boots up, when one evening they came. Opening the parcel, I set the four pairs out in a row. Then one by one I tried them on. There was no doubt about it. In shape and fit, in finish and quality of leather, they were the best he had ever made me. And in the mouth of one of the Town walking-boots I found his bill. The amount was the same as usual, but it gave me quite a shock. He had never before sent it till quarter day. I flew down-stairs, and wrote a cheque, and posted it at once with my own hand.

A week later, passing the little street, I thought I would go in and tell him how splendidly the new boots fitted. But when I came to where his shop had been, his name was gone. Still there, in the window, were the slim pumps, the patent leathers with cloth tops, the sooty riding boots.

I went in, very much disturbed. In the two little shops—again made into one—was a young man with an English face.

"Mr. Gessler in?" I said.

He gave me a strange, ingratiating look.

"No, sir," he said, "no. But we can attend to anything with

pleasure. We've taken the shop over. You've seen our name, no doubt, next door. We make for some very good people."

"Yes, yes," I said; "but Mr. Gessler?"

"Oh!" he answered; "dead.'

"Dead! But I received these boots from him last Wednesday week."

"Ah!" he said, "a shockin' go. Poor old man starved 'imself."

"Good God!"

"Slow starvation, the doctor called it! You see he went to work in such a way! Would keep the shop on; wouldn't have a soul touch his boots except himself. When he got an order, it took him such a time. People won't wait. He lost everybody. And there he'd sit, goin' on and on—I will say that for him—not a man in London made a better boot! But look at the competition! He never advertised! Would 'ave the best leather, too, and do it all 'imself. Well, there it is. What could you expect with his ideas?"

"But starvation——!"

"That may be a bit flowery, as the sayin' is—but I know myself he was sittin' over his boots day and night, to the very last. You see I used to watch him. Never gave himself time to eat; never had a penny in the house. All went in rent and leather. How he lived so long I don't know. He regular let his fire go out. He was a character. But he made good boots."

"Yes," I said, "he made good boots."

And I turned and went out quickly, for I did not want that youth to know that I could hardly see.

VSEVOLOD GARSHIN

VSEVOLOD GARSHIN (Russian, 1855-1888). Russian writer of novellas. Lived his short adult life in melancholy frustration, suffering from experiences in Serbian and Turkish wars. Committed suicide. Stories permeated with urgent sense of justice and compassion.

THE SIGNAL

SEMYON IVANOV was a track-walker. His hut was ten versts away from a railroad station in one direction and twelve versts away in the other. About four versts away there was a cotton mill that had opened the year before, and its tall chimney rose up darkly from

424

behind the forest. The only dwellings around were the distant huts of the other track-walkers.

Semyon Ivanov's health had been completely shattered. Nine years before he had served right through the war as servant to an officer. The sun had roasted him, the cold frozen him, and hunger famished him on the forced marches of forty and fifty versts a day in the heat and the cold and the rain and the shine. The bullets had whizzed about him, but, thank God! none had struck him.

Semyon's regiment had once been on the firing line. For a whole week there had been skirmishing with the Turks, only a deep ravine separating the two hostile armies; and from morn till eve there had been a steady cross-fire. Thrice daily Semyon carried a steaming samovar and his officer's meals from the camp kitchen to the ravine. The bullets hummed about him and rattled viciously against the rocks. Semyon was terrified and cried sometimes, but still he kept right on. The officers were pleased with him, because he always had hot tea ready for them.

He returned from the campaign with limbs unbroken but crippled with rheumatism. He had experienced no little sorrow since then. He arrived home to find that his father, an old man, and his little four-year-old son had died. Semyon remained alone with his wife. They could not do much. It was difficult to plow with rheumatic arms and legs. They could no longer stay in their village, so they started off to seek their fortune in new places. They stayed for a short time on the line, in Kherson and Donshchina, but nowhere found luck. Then the wife went out to service, and Semyon continued to travel about. Once he happened to ride on an engine, and at one of the stations the face of the station-master seemed familiar to him. Semyon looked at the station-master and the station-master looked at Semyon, and they recognized each other. He had been an officer in Semyon's regiment.

"You are Ivanov?" he said.

"Yes, your Excellency."

"How do you come to be here?"

Semyon told him all.

"Where are you off to?"

"I cannot tell you, sir."

"Idiot! What do you mean by 'cannot tell you'?"

"I mean what I say, your Excellency. There is nowhere for me to go to. I must hunt for work, sir."

The station-master looked at him, thought a bit, and said: "See

425

here, friend, stay a while at the station. You are married, I think. Where is your wife?"

"Yes, your Excellency, I am married. My wife is at Kursk, in service with a merchant."

"Well, write to your wife to come here. I will give you a free pass for her. There is a position as track-walker open. I will speak to the Chief on your behalf."

"I shall be very grateful to you, your Excellency," replied Semyon.

He stayed at the station, helped in the kitchen, cut firewood, kept the yard clean, and swept the platform. In a fortnight's time his wife arrived, and Semyon went on a hand-trolley to his hut. The hut was a new one and warm, with as much wood as he wanted. There was a little vegetable garden, the legacy of a former track-walker, and there was about half a dessiatin of plowed land on either side of the railway embankment. Semyon was rejoiced. He began to think of doing some farming, of purchasing a cow and a horse.

He was given all necessary stores—a green flag, a red flag, lanterns, a horn, hammer, screw-wrench for the nuts, a crow-bar, spade, broom, bolts and nails: they gave him two books of regulations and a time-table of the trains. At first Semyon could not sleep at night, and learned the whole time-table by heart. Two hours before a train was due he would go over his section, sit on the bench at his hut, and look and listen whether the rails were trembling or the rumble of the train could be heard. He even learned the regulations by heart, although he could only read by spelling out each word.

It was summer; the work was not heavy; there was no snow to clear away and the trains on that line were infrequent. Semyon used to go over his verst twice a day, examine and screw up nuts here and there, keep the bed level, look at the water-pipes, and then go home to his own affairs. There was only one drawback—he always had to get the inspector's permission for the least little thing he wanted to do. Semyon and his wife were even beginning to be bored.

Two months passed, and Semyon commenced to make the acquaintance of his neighbors, the track-walkers on either side of him. One was a very old man, whom the authorities were always meaning to relieve. He scarcely moved out of his hut. His wife used to do all his work. The other track-walker, nearer the station, was a young man, thin but muscular. He and Semyon met for the first time on the line midway between the huts. Semyon took off his hat and bowed. "Good health to you, neighbor," he said.

The neighbor glanced askance at him. "How do you do?" he replied; then turned around and made off.

Later the wives met. Semyon's wife passed the time of day with her neighbor, but neither did she say much.

On one occasion Semyon said to her: "Young woman, your husband is not very talkative."

The woman said nothing at first, then replied: "But what is there for him to talk about? Every one has his own business. Go your way, and God be with you."

However after another month or so they became acquainted. Semyon would go with Vasily along the line, sit on the edge of a pipe, smoke, and talk of life. Vasily, for the most part, kept silent, but Semyon talked of his village and of the campaign through which he had passed.

"I have had no little sorrow in my day," he would say; "and goodness knows I have not lived long. God has not given me happiness, but what He may give, so will it be. That's so, friend Vasily Stepanych."

Vasily Stepanych knocked the ashes out of his pipe against a rail, stood up and said: "It is not luck which follows us in life, but human beings. There is no crueller beast on this earth than man. Wolf does not eat wolf, but man will readily devour man."

"Come, friend, don't say that; a wolf eats wolf."

"The words came into my mind and I said it. All the same, there is nothing crueller than man. If it were not for his wickedness and greed, it would be possible to live. Everybody tries to sting you to the quick, to bite and eat you up."

Semyon pondered a bit. "I don't know, brother," he said; "perhaps it is as you say, and perhaps it is God's will."

"And perhaps," said Vasily, "it is waste of time for me to talk to you. To put everything unpleasant on God, and sit and suffer, means, brother, being not a man but an animal. That's what I have to say." And he turned and went off without saying good-bye.

Semyon also got up. "Neighbor," he called, "why do you lose your temper?" But his neighbor did not look round, and kept on his way.

Semyon gazed after him until he was lost to sight in the cutting at the turn. He went home and said to his wife: "Arina, our neighbor is a wicked person, not a man."

However, they did not quarrel. They met again and discussed the same topics.

427

"Ah, friend, if it were not for men we should not be poking in these huts," said Vasily on one occasion.

"And what if we are poking in these huts? It's not so bad. You can live in them."

"Live in them, indeed! Bah, you! . . . You have lived long and learned little, looked at much and seen little. What sort of life is there for a poor man in a hut here or there? The cannibals are devouring you. They are sucking up all your life-blood, and when you become old, they will throw you out just as they do husks to feed the pigs on. What pay do you get?"

"Not much, Vasily Stepanych—twelve rubles."

"And I, thirteen and a half rubles. Why? By the regulations the company should give us fifteen rubles a month with firing and lighting. Who decides that you should have twelve rubles, or I thirteen and a half? Ask yourself! And you say a man can live on that? You understand it is not a question of one and a half rubles or three rubles—even if they paid us each the whole fifteen rubles. I was at the station last month. The director passed through. I saw him. I had that honor. He had a separate coach. He came out and stood on the platform. . . . I shall not stay here long; I shall go somewhere, anywhere, follow my nose."

"But where will you go, Stepanych? Leave well enough alone. Here you have a house, warmth, a little piece of land. Your wife is a worker."

"Land! You should look at my piece of land. Not a twig on it— nothing. I planted some cabbages in the spring, just when the inspector came along. He said: 'What is this? Why have you not reported this? Why have you done this without permission? Dig them up, roots and all.' He was drunk. Another time he would not have said a word, but this time it struck him. Three rubles fine! . . ."

Vasily kept silent for a while, pulling at his pipe, then added quietly: "A little more and I should have done for him."

"You are hot-tempered."

"No, I am not hot-tempered, but I tell the truth and think. Yes, he will still get a bloody nose from me. I will complain to the Chief. We will see then!" And Vasily did complain to the Chief.

Once the Chief came to inspect the line. Three days later important personages were coming from St. Petersburg and would pass over the line. They were conducting an inquiry, so that previous to their journey it was necessary to put everything in order. Ballast

was laid down, the bed was leveled, the sleepers carefully examined, spikes driven in a bit, nuts screwed up, posts painted, and orders given for yellow sand to be sprinkled at the level crossings. The woman at the neighboring hut turned her old man out to weed. Semyon worked for a whole week. He put everything in order, mended his kaftan, cleaned and polished his brass plate until it fairly shone. Vasily also worked hard. The Chief arrived on a trolley, four men working the handles and the levers, making the six wheels hum. The trolley traveled at twenty versts an hour, but the wheels squeaked. It reached Semyon's hut, and he ran out and reported in soldierly fashion. All appeared to be in repair.

"Have you been here long?" inquired the Chief.

"Since the second of May, your Excellency."

"All right. Thank you. And who is at hut No. 164?"

The traffic inspector (he was traveling with the Chief on the trolley) replied: "Vasily Spiridov."

"Spiridov, Spiridov. . . . .Ah! is he the man against whom you made a note last year?"

"He is."

"Well, we will see Vasily Spiridov. Go on!" The workmen laid to the handles, and the trolley got under way. Semyon watched it, and thought, "There will be trouble between them and my neighbor."

About two hours later he started on his round. He saw some one coming along the line from the cutting. Something white showed on his head. Semyon began to look more attentively. It was Vasily. He had a stick in his hand, a small bundle on his shoulder, and his cheek was bound up in a handkerchief.

"Where are you off to?" cried Semyon.

Vasily came quite close. He was very pale, white as chalk, and his eyes had a wild look. Almost choking, he muttered: "To town— to Moscow—to the head office."

"Head office? Ah, you are going to complain, I suppose. Give it up! Vasily Stepanych, forget it."

"No, mate, I will not forget. It is too late. See! He struck me in the face, drew blood. So long as I live I will not forget. I will not leave it like this!"

Semyon took his hand. "Give it up, Stepanych. I am giving you good advice. You will not better things. . . ."

"Better things! I know myself I shan't better things. You were right about Fate. It would be better for me not to do it, but one must stand up for the right."

"But tell me, how did it happen?"

"How? He examined everything, got down from the trolley, looked into the hut. I knew beforehand that he would be strict, and so I had put everything into proper order. He was just going when I made my complaint. He immediately cried out: 'Here is a Government inquiry coming, and you make a complaint about a vegetable garden. Here are privy councilors coming, and you annoy me with cabbages!' I lost patience and said something—not very much, but it offended him, and he struck me in the face. I stood still; I did nothing, just as if what he did was perfectly all right. They went off; I came to myself, washed my face, and left."

"And what about the hut?"

"My wife is staying there. She will look after things. Never mind about the roads."

Vasily got up and collected himself. "Good-bye, Ivanov. I do not know whether I shall get any one at the office to listen to me."

"Surely you are not going to walk?"

"At the station I will try to get on a freight train, and to-morrow I shall be in Moscow."

The neighbors bade each other farewell. Vasily was absent for some time. His wife worked for him night and day. She never slept, and wore herself out waiting for her husband. On the third day the commission arrived. An engine, luggage-van, and two first-class saloons; but Vasily was still away. Semyon saw his wife on the fourth day. Her face was swollen from crying and her eyes were red.

"Has your husband returned?" he asked. But the woman only made a gesture with her hands, and without saying a word went her way.

Semyon had learned when still a lad to make flutes out of a kind of reed. He used to burn out the heart of the stalk, make holes where necessary, drill them, fix a mouth-piece at one end, and tune them so well that it was possible to play almost any air on them. He made a number of them in his spare time, and sent them by his friends amongst the freight brakemen to the bazaar in the town. He got two kopeks apiece for them. On the day following the visit of the commission he left his wife at home to meet the six o'clock train, and started off to the forest to cut some sticks. He went to the end of his section—at this point the line made a sharp turn—descended the embankment, and struck into the wood at the foot of the mountain. About half a verst away there was a big marsh, around which

splendid reeds for his flutes grew. He cut a whole bundle of stalks and started back home. The sun was already dropping low, and in the dead stillness only the twittering of the birds was audible, and the crackle of the dead wood under his feet. As he walked along rapidly, he fancied he heard the clang of iron striking iron, and he redoubled his pace. There was no repair going on in his section. What did it mean? He emerged from the woods, the railway embankment stood high before him; on the top a man was squatting on the bed of the line busily engaged in something. Semyon commenced quietly to crawl up towards him. He thought it was some one after the nuts which secure the rails. He watched, and the man got up, holding a crow-bar in his hand. He had loosened a rail, so that it would move to one side. A mist swam before Semyon's eyes; he wanted to cry out, but could not. It was Vasily! Semyon scrambled up the bank, as Vasily with crow-bar and wrench slid headlong down the other side.

"Vasily Stepanych! My dear friend, come back! Give me the crow-bar. We will put the rail back; no one will know. Come back! Save your soul from sin!"

Vasily did not look back, but disappeared into the woods.

Semyon stood before the rail which had been torn up. He threw down his bundle of sticks. A train was due; not a freight, but a passenger-train. And he had nothing with which to stop it, no flag. He could not replace the rail and could not drive in the spikes with his bare hands. It was necessary to run, absolutely necessary to run to the hut for some tools. "God help me!" he murmured.

Semyon started running towards his hut. He was out of breath, but still ran, falling every now and then. He had cleared the forest; he was only a few hundred feet from his hut, not more, when he heard the distant hooter of the factory sound—six o'clock! In two minutes' time No 7 train was due. "Oh, Lord! have pity on innocent souls!" In his mind Semyon saw the engine strike against the loosened rail with its left wheel, shiver, careen, tear up and splinter the sleepers—and just there, there was a curve and the embankment seventy feet high, down which the engine would topple — and the third-class carriages would be packed . . . little children. . . . All sitting in the train now, never dreaming of danger. "Oh, Lord! Tell me what to do! . . . No, it is impossible to run to the hut and get back in time."

Semyon did not run on to the hut, but turned back and ran faster

431

than before. He was running almost mechanically, blindly; he did not know himself what was to happen. He ran as far as the rail which had been pulled up; his sticks were lying in a heap. He bent down, seized one without knowing why, and ran on farther. It seemed to him the train was already coming. He heard the distant whistle; he heard the quiet, even tremor of the rails; but his strength was exhausted, he could run no farther, and came to a halt about six hundred feet from the awful spot. Then an idea came into his head, literally like a ray of light. Puilling off his cap, he took out of it a cotton scarf, drew his knife out of the upper part of his boot, and crossed himself, muttering, "God bless me!"

He buried the knife in his left arm above the elbow; the blood spurted out, flowing in a hot stream. In this he soaked his scarf, smoothed it out, tied it to the stick and hung out his red flag.

He stood waving his flag. The train was already in sight. The driver would not see him—would come close up, and a heavy train cannot be pulled up in six hundred feet.

And the blood kept on flowing. Semyon pressed the sides of the wound together so as to close it, but the blood did not diminish. Evidently he had cut his arm very deep. His head commenced to swim, black spots began to dance before his eyes, and then it became dark. There was a ringing in his ears. He could not see the train or hear the noise. Only one thought possessed him. "I shall not be able to keep standing up. I shall fall and drop the flag; the train will pass over me. Help me, O Lord!"

All turned black before him, his mind became a blank, and he dropped the flag; but the blood-stained banner did not fall to the ground. A hand seized it and held it high to meet the approaching train. The engineer saw it, shut the regulator, and reversed steam. The train came to a standstill.

People jumped out of the carriages and collected in a crowd. They saw a man lying senseless on the footway, drenched in blood, and another man standing beside him with a blood-stained rag on a stick.

Vasily looked around at all. Then, lowering his head, he said: "Bind me, I tore up a rail!"

THEOPHILE GAUTIER

THÉOPHILE GAUTIER (French, 1811-1872). One of the prominent founders of the French Romantic Movement. Painter, newspaperman, extensive traveler. Wrote art, dramatic and literary criticism, ballets and pantomimes. Both poetry and prose are highly polished, exotic, objective. Best-known novel: *Mademoiselle de Maupin.*

THE MUMMY'S FOOT

I HAD entered, in an idle mood, the shop of one of those curiosity-vendors, who are called *marchands de bric-à-brac* in that Parisian *argot*, which is so perfectly unintelligible elsewhere in France.

You have doubtless glanced occasionally through the windows of some of these shops, which have become so numerous now that it is fashionable to buy antiquated furniture, and that every petty stock-broker thinks he must have his *chambre au moyen âge.*

There is one thing there which clings alike to the shop of the dealer in old iron, the wareroom of the tapestry-maker, the laboratory of the chemist, and the studio of the painter:—in all those gloomy dens where a furtive daylight filters in through the window-shutters, the most manifestly ancient thing is dust;—the cobwebs are more authentic than the guimp laces; and the old pear-tree furniture on exhibition is actually younger than the mahogany which arrived but yesterday from America.

The warehouse of my *bric-à-brac* dealer was a veritable Caphar-naum; all ages and all nations seemed to have made their rendezvous there; an Etruscan lamp of red clay stood upon a Boule cabinet, with ebony panels, brightly striped by lines of inlaid brass; a duchess of the court of Louis XV nonchalantly extended her fawn-like feet under a massive table of the time of Louis XIII with heavy spiral supports of oak, and carven designs of chimeras and foliage inter-mingled.

Upon the denticulated shelves of several sideboards glittered immense Japanese dishes with red and blue designs relieved by gilded hatching; side by side with enameled works by Bernard Palissy, representing serpents, frogs, and lizards in relief.

From disemboweled cabinets escaped cascades of silver-lustrous Chinese silks and waves of tinsel, which an oblique sunbeam shot through with luminous beads; while portraits of every era, in

frames more or less tarnished, smiled through their yellow varnish.

The striped breastplate of a damascened suit of Milanese armor glittered in one corner; Loves and Nymphs of porcelain; Chinese Grotesques, vases of *céladon* and crackle-ware; Saxon and old Sèvres cups encumbered the shelves and nooks of the apartment.

The dealer followed me closely through the tortuous way contrived between the piles of furniture; warding off with his hand the hazardous sweep of my coat-skirts; watching my elbows with the uneasy attention of an antiquarian and a usurer.

It was a singular face, that of the merchant:—an immense skull, polished like a knee, and surrounded by a thin aureole of white hair, which brought out the clear salmon tint of his complexion all the more strikingly, lent him a false aspect of patriarchal *bonhomie*, counteracted, however, by the scintillation of two little yellow eyes which trembled in their orbits like two louis-d'or upon quicksilver. The curve of his nose presented an aquiline silhouette, which suggested the Oriental or Jewish type. His hands—thin, slender, full of nerves which projected like strings upon the fingerboard of a violin, and armed with claws like those on the terminations of bats' wings—shook with senile trembling; both those convulsively agitated hands became firmer than steel pincers or lobsters' claws when they lifted any precious article—an onyx cup, a Venitian glass, or a dish of Bohemian crystal. This strange old man had an aspect so thoroughly rabbinical and cabalistic that he would have been burnt on the mere testimony of his face three hundred centuries ago.

"Will you not buy something from me to-day, sir? Here is a Malay kreese with a blade undulating like flame; look at those grooves contrived for the blood to run along, those teeth set backwards so as to tear out the entrails in withdrawing the weapon— it is a fine character of ferocious arm, and will look well in your collection: this two-handed sword is very beautiful—it is the work of Josepe de la Hera; and this *colichemarde,* with its fenestrated guard—what a superb specimen of handicraft!"

"No; I have quite enough weapons and instruments of carnage;— I want a small figure, something which will suit me as a paper-weight; for I cannot endure those trumpery bronzes which the stationers sell, and which may be found on everybody's desk."

The old gnome foraged among his ancient wares, and finally arranged before me some antique bronzes—so-called, at least; fragments of malachite; little Hindoo or Chinese idols—a kind of pussah

toys in jadestone, representing the incarnations of Brahma or Vishnoo, and wonderfully appropriate to the very undivine office of holding papers and letters in place.

I was hesitating between a porcelain dragon, all constellated with warts—its mouth formidable with bristling tusks and ranges of teeth—and an abominable Mexican fetish, representing the god Zitziliputzili *au naturel,* when I caught sight of a charming foot, which I at first took for a fragment of some antique Venus.

It had those beautifully ruddy and tawny tints that lend to Florentine bronze that warm living look so much preferable to the gray-green aspect of common bronzes, which might easily be mistaken for statues in a state of putrefaction: satin gleams played over its rounded forms, doubtless polished by the amorous kiss of twenty centuries; for it seemed a Corinthian bronze, a work of the best era of art—perhaps molded by Lysippus himself.

"That foot will be my choice," I said to the merchant, who regarded me with an ironical and saturnine air, and held out the object desired that I might examine it more fully.

I was surprised at its lightness; it was not a foot of metal, but in sooth a foot of flesh—an embalmed foot—a mumy's foot: on examining it still more closely the very grain of the skin, and the almost imperceptible lines impressed upon it by the texture of the bandages, became perceptible. The toes were slender and delicate, and terminated by perfectly formed nails, pure and transparent as agates; the great toe, slightly separated from the rest, afforded a happy contrast, in the antique style, to the position of the other toes, and lent it an aerial lightness—the grace of a bird's foot,— the sole, scarcely streaked by a few almost imperceptible cross lines, afforded evidence that it had never touched the bare ground, and had only come in contact with the finest matting of Nile rushes, and the softest carpets of panther skin.

"Ha, ha!—you want the foot of the Princess Hermonthis,"— exclaimed the merchant, with a strange giggle, fixing his owlish eyes upon me—"ha, ha ha!—for a paper-weight!—an original idea!—artistic idea! Old Pharaoh would certainly have been surprised had some one told him that the foot of his adored daughter would be used for a paperweight after he had a mountain of granite hollowed out as a receptacle for the triple coffin, painted and gilded—covered with hieroglyphics and beautiful paintings of the Judgment of Souls,"—continued the queer little merchant, half audibly, as though talking to himself!

435

"How much will you charge me for this mummy fragment?"

"Ah, the highest price I can get; for it is a superb piece: if I had the match of it you could not have it for less than five hundred francs;—the daughter of a Pharaoh! nothing is more rare."

"Assuredly that is not a common article; but, still, how much do you want? In the first place I can buy anything that costs five louis, but nothing dearer;—you might search my vest pockets and most secret drawers without even finding one poor five-franc piece more."

"Five louis for the foot of the Princess Hermonthis! that is very little, very little indeed; 'tis an authentic foot," muttered the merchant, shaking his head, and imparting a peculiar rotary motion to his eyes. "Well, take it, And I will give you the bandages into the bargain," he added, wrapping the foot in an ancient damask rag—"very fine! real damask—Indian damask which has never been redyed; it is strong, and yet it is soft," he mumbled, stroking the frayed tissue with his fingers, through the trade-acquired habit which moved him to praise even an object of so little value that he himself deemed it only worth the giving away.

He poured the gold coins into a sort of medieval alms-purse hanging at his belt, repeating:

"The foot of the Princess Hermonthis, to be used for a paper-weight."

Then turning his phosphorescent eyes upon me, he exclaimed in a voice strident as the crying of a cat which has swallowed a fish-bone:

"Old Pharaoh will not be well pleased; he loved his daughter—the dear man!"

"You speak as if you were a contemporary of his: you are old enough, goodness knows! but you do not date back to the Pyramids of Egypt," I answered, laughingly, from the threshold.

I went home, delighted with my acquisition.

With the idea of putting it to profitable use as soon as possible, I placed the foot of the divine Princess Hermonthis upon a heap of papers scribbled over with verses, in themselves an undecipherable mosaic work of erasures; articles freshly begun; letters forgotten, and posted in the table drawer instead of the letter-box—an error of which absent-minded people are peculiarly liable. The effect was charming, *bizarre*, and romantic.

Well satisfied with this embellishment, I went out with the gravity and pride becoming one who feels that he has the ineffable ad-

vantage over all the passers-by whom he elbows, of possessing a piece of the Princess Hermonthis, daughter of Pharaoh.

I looked upon all who did not possess, like myself, a paper-weight so authentically Egyptian, as very ridiculous people; and it seemed to me that the proper occupation of every sensible man should consist in the mere fact of having a mummy's foot upon his desk.

Happily I met some friends, whose presence distracted me in my infatuation with this new acquisition: I went to dinner with them; for I could not very well have dined with myself.

When I came back that evening, with my brain slightly confused by a few glasses of wine, a vague whiff of Oriental perfume delicately titillated my olfatory nerves: the heat of the room had warmed the natron, bitumen, and myrrh in which the *paraschistes, who cut* open the bodies of the dead, had bathed the corpse of the princess;— it was a perfume at once sweet and penetrating—a perfume that four thousand years had not been able to dissipate.

The Dream of Egypt was Eternity: her odors have the solidity of granite, and endure as long.

I soon drank deeply from the black cup of sleep: for a few hours all remained opaque to me; Oblivion and Nothingness inundated me with their somber waves.

Yet light gradually dawned upon the darkness of my mind; dreams commenced to touch me softly in their silent flight.

The eyes of my soul were opened; and I beheld my chamber as it actually was; I might have believed myself awake, but for a vague consciousness which assured me that I slept, and that something fantastic was about to take place.

The odor of the myrrh had augmented in intensity: and I felt a slight headache, which I very naturally attributed to several glasses of champagne that we had drunk to the unknown gods and our future fortunes.

I peered through my room with a feeling of expectation which I saw nothing to justify: every article of furniture was in its proper place; the lamp, softly shaded by its globe of ground crystal, burned upon its bracket; the water-color sketches shone under their Bohemian glass; the curtains hung down languidly; everything wore an aspect of tranquil slumber.

After a few moments, however, all this calm interior appeared to become disturbed; the woodwork cracked stealthily; the ash-covered log suddenl emitted a jet of blue flame; and the disks of the

437

pateras seemed like great metallic eyes, watching, like myself, for the things which were about to happen.

My eyes accidentally fell upon the desk where I had placed the foot of the Princess Hermonthis.

Instead of remaining quiet—as behooved a foot which had been embalmed for four thousand years— it commenced to act in a nervous manner; contracted itself, and leaped over the papers like a startled frog;—one would have imagined that it had suddenly been brought into contact with a galvanic battery: I could distinctly hear the dry sound made by its little heel, hard as the hoof of a gazelle.

I became rather discontented with my acquisition, inasmuch as I wished my paper-weights to be of a sedentary disposition, and thought it very unnatural that feet should walk about without legs; and I commenced to experience a feeling closely akin to fear.

Suddenly I saw the folds of my bed-curtain stir; and heard a bumping sound, like that caused by some person hopping on one foot across the floor. I must confess I became alternately hot and cold; that I felt a strange wind chill my back; and that my suddenly rising hair caused my nightcap to execute a leap of several yards.

The bed-curtains opened and I beheld the strangest figure imaginable before me.

It was a young girl of a very deep coffee-brown complexion, like the bayadere Amani, and possessing the purest Egyptian type of perfect beauty: her eyes were almond-shaped and oblique, with eyebrows so black that they seemed blue; her nose was exquisitely chiseled, almost Greek in its delicacy of outline; and she might indeed have been taken for a Corinthian statue of bronze, but for the prominence of her cheekbones and the slightly African fullness of her lips, which compelled one to recognize her as belonging beyond all doubt to the hieroglyphic race which dwelt upon the banks of the Nile.

Her arms, slender and spindle-shaped, like those of very young girls, were encircled by a peculiar kind of metal bands and bracelets of glass beads; her hair was all twisted into little cords; and she wore upon her bosom a little idol-figure of green paste, bearing a whip with seven lashes, which proved it to be an image of Isis: her brow was adorned with a shining plate of gold; and a few traces of paint relieved the coppery tint of her cheeks.

As for her costume, it was very odd indeed.

Fancy a *pagne* or skirt all formed of little strips of material be-

438

dizened with red and black hieroglyphics, stiffened with bitumen, and apparently belonging to a freshly unbandaged mummy.

In one of those sudden flights of thought so common in dreams I heard the hoarse falsetto of the *bric-à-brac* dealer, repeating like a monotonous refrain the phrase he had uttered in his shop with so enigmatic an intonation:

"Old Pharaoh will not be well pleased: he loved his daughter, the dear man!"

One strange circumstance, which was not at all calculated to restore my equanimity, was that the apparition had but one foot; the other was broken off at the ankle!

She approached the table where the foot was starting and fidgeting about more than ever, and there supported herself upon the edge of the desk. I saw her eyes fill with pearly-gleaming tears.

Although she had not as yet spoken, I fully comprehended the thoughts which agitated her: she looked at her foot—for it was indeed her own—with an exquisitely graceful expression of coquettish sadness; but the foot leaped and ran hither and thither as though impelled on steel springs.

Twice or thrice she extended her hand to seize it, but could not succeed.

Then commenced between Princess Hermonthis and her foot—which appeared to be endowed with a special life of its own—a very fantastic dialogue in a most ancient Coptic tongue, such as might have been spoken thirty centuries ago in the syrinxes of the land of Ser: luckily, I understood Coptic perfectly well that night.

The Princess Hermonthis cried, in a voice sweet and vibrant as the tones of a crystal bell:

"Well, my dear little foot, you always flee from me; yet I always took good care of you. I bathed you with perfumed water in a bowl of alabaster; I smoothed your heel with pumice-stone mixed with palm oil; your nails were cut with golden scissors and polished with a hippopotamus tooth; I was careful to select *tatbebs* for you, painted and embroidered and turned up at the toes, which were the envy of all the young girls in Egypt: you wore on your great toe rings bearing the device of the sacred Scarabæus; and you supported one of the lightest bodies that a lazy foot could sustain."

The foot replied, in a pouting and chagrined tone:

"You know well that I do not belong to myself any longer;—I have been bought and paid for; the old merchant knew what he was about; he bore you a grudge for having refused to espouse him;—

this is an ill turn which he has done you. The Arab who violated your royal coffin in the subterranean pits of the necropolis of Thebes was sent thither by him: he desired to prevent you from being present at the reunion of the shadowy nations in the cities below. Have you five pieces of gold for my ransom?"

"Alas, no!—my jewels, my rings, my purses of gold and silver, they were all stolen from me," answered the Princess Hermonthis, with a sob.

"Princess," I then exclaimed, "I never retained anybody's foot unjustly;—even though you have not got the five louis which it cost me, I present it to you gladly: I should feel unutterably wretched to think that I were the cause of so amiable a person as the Princess Hermonthis being lame."

I delivered this discourse in a royally gallant, troubadour tone, which must have astonished the beautiful Egyptian girl.

She turned a look of deepest gratitude upon me; and her eyes shone with bluish gleams of light.

She took her foot—which surrendered itself willingly this time— like a woman about to put on her little shoe, and adjusted it to her leg with much skill.

This operation over, she took a few steps about the room, as though to assure herself that she was really no longer lame.

"Ah, how pleased my father will be!—he who was so unhappy because of my mutilation, and who from the moment of my birth set a whole nation at work to hollow me out a tomb so deep that he might preserve me intact until that last day, when souls must be weighed in the balance of Amenthi! Come with me to my father;— he will receive you kindly; for you have given me back my foot."

I thought this proposition natural enough. I arrayed myself in a dressing-gown of large-flowered pattern, which lent me a very Pharaonic aspect; hurriedly put on a pair of Turkish slippers, and informed the Princess Hermonthis that I was ready to follow her.

Before starting, Hermonthis took from her neck the little idol of green paste, and laid it on the scattered sheets of paper which covered the table.

"It is only fair," she observed smilingly, "that I should replace your paper-weight."

She gave me her hand, which felt soft and cold, like the skin of a serpent; and we departed.

We passed for some time with the velocity of an arrow through

a fluid and grayish expanse, in which half-formed silhouettes flitted swiftly by us, to right and left.

For an instant we saw only sky and sea.

A few moments later obelisks commenced to tower in the distance: pylons and vast flights of steps guarded by sphinxes became clearly outlined against the horizon.

We had reached our destination.

The princess conducted me to the mountain of rose-colored granite, in the face of which appeared an opening so narrow and low that it would have been difficult to distinguish it from the fissures in the rock, had not its location been marked by two stelæ wrought with sculptures.

Hermonthis kindled a torch, and led the way before me.

We traversed corridors hewn through the living rock: their walls, covered with hieroglyphics and paintings of allegorical processions, might well have occupied thousands of arms for thousands of years in their formation;—these corridors, of interminable length, opened into square chambers, in the midst of which pits had been contrived, through which we descended by cramp-irons or spiral stairways;—these pits again conducted us into other chambers, opening into other corridors, likewise decorated with painted sparrow-hawks, serpents coiled in circles, the symbols of the *tau* and *pedum*—prodigious works of art which no living eye can ever examine—interminable legends of granite which only the dead have time to read through all eternity.

At last we found ourselves in a hall so vast, so enormous, so immeasurable, that the eye could not reach its limits; files of monstrous columns stretched far out of sight on every side, between which twinkled livid stars of yellowish flame;—points of light which revealed further depths incalculable in the darkness beyond.

The Princess Hermonthis still held my hand, and graciously saluted the mummies of her acquaintance.

My eyes became accustomed to the dim twilight, and objects became discernible.

I beheld the kings of the subterranean races seated upon thrones —grand old men, though dry, withered, wrinkled like parchment, and blackened with naphtha and bitumen—all wearing *pshents* of gold, and breastplates with gorgets glittering with precious stones; their eyes immovably fixed like the eyes of sphinxes, and their long beards whitened by the snow of centuries. Behind them stood their

441

peoples, in the stiff and constrained posture enjoined by Egyptian art, all eternally preserving the attitude prescribed by the hieratic code. Behind these nations, the cats, ibises, and crocodiles contemporary with them—rendered monstrous of aspect by their swathing bands—mewed, flapped their wings, or extended their jaws in a saurian giggle.

All the Pharaohs were there—Cheops, Chephrenes, Psammetichus, Sesostris, Amenotaph—all the dark rulers of the pyramids and syrinxes;—on yet higher thrones sat Chronos and Xixouthros—who was contemporary with the deluge; and Tubal Cain, who reigned before it.

The beard of King Xixouthros had grown seven times around the granite table, upon which he leaned, lost in deep reverie—and buried in dreams.

Further back, through a dusty cloud, I beheld dimly the seventy-two pre-Adamite Kings, with their seventy-two peoples — forever passed away.

After permitting me to gaze upon this bewildering spectacle a few moments, the Princess Hermonthis presented me to her father Pharaoh, who favored me with a most gracious nod.

"I have found my foot again!—I have found my foot!" cried the Princess, clapping her little hands together with every sign of frantic joy: "it was this gentleman who restored it to me."

The races of Kemi, the races of Nahasi—all the black, bronzed, and copper-colored nations repeated in chorus:

"The Princess Hermonthis has found her foot again!"

Even Xixouthros himself was visibly affected.

He raised his heavy eyelids, stroked his mustache with his fingers, and turned upon me a glance weighty with centuries.

"By Oms, the dog of Hell, and Tmei, daughter of the Sun and of Truth! this is a brave and worthy lad!" exclaimed Pharaoh, pointing to me with his scepter, which was terminated with a lotus-flower.

"What recompense do you desire?"

Filled with that daring inspired by dreams in which nothing seems impossible, I asked him for the hand of the Princess Hermonthis;—the hand seemed to me a very proper antithetic recompense for the foot.

Pharaoh opened wide his great eyes of glass in astonishment at my witty request.

"What country do you come from? and what is your age?"

442

"I am a Frenchman; and I am twenty-seven years old, venerable Pharaoh."

"——Twenty-seven years old! and he wishes to espouse the Princess Hermonthis, who is thirty centuries old!" cried out at once all the Thrones and all the Circles of Nations.

Only Hermonthis herself did not seem to think my request unreasonable.

"If you were even only two thousand years old," replied the ancient King, "I would willingly give you the Princess; but the disproportion is too great; and, besides, we must give our daughters husbands who will last well: you do not know how to preserve yourselves any longer; even those who died only fifteen centuries ago are already no more than a handful of dust;—behold! my flesh is solid as basalt; my bones are bars of steel!

"I shall be present on the last day of the world, with the same body and the same features which I had during my lifetime: my daughter Hermonthis will last longer than a statue of bronze.

"Then the last particles of your dust will have been scattered abroad by the winds; and even Isis herself, who was able to find the atoms of Osiris, would scarce be able to recompose your being.

"See how vigorous I yet remain, and how mighty is my grasp," he added, shaking my hand in the English fashion with a strength that buried my rings in the flesh of my fingers.

He squeezed me so hard that I awoke, and found my friend Alfred shaking me by the arm to make me get up.

"O you everlasting sleeper!—must I have you carried out into the middle of the street, and fireworks exploded in your ears? It is after noon; don't you recollect your promise to take me with you to see M. Aguado's Spanish pictures?"

"God! I forgot all, all about it," I answered, dressing myself hurriedly; "we will go there at once; I have the permit lying on my desk."

I started to find it;—but fancy my astonishment when I beheld, instead of the mummy's foot I had purchased the evening before, the little green paste idol left in its place by the Princess Hermonthis!

KHALIL GIBRAN

KHALIL GIBRAN (Syro-American, 1883-1931). Syro-American writer of inspirational literature. Born in Lebanon, came to America at 11. Studied in Europe, then formed coterie of Syrian writers in New York. Early works in Arabic: *Al-arwāh al-mutamarridat (Spirits Rebellious)*. Later ones in English: *The Prophet*. Taught a religion of love, beauty and redemption.

BEHIND THE GARMENT

RACHEL woke at midnight and gazed intently at something invisible in the sky of her chamber. She heard a voice more soothing than the whispers of Life, and more dismal than the moaning call of the abyss, and softer than the rustling of white wings, and deeper than the message of the waves. . . . It vibrated with hope and with futility, with joy and with misery, and with affection for life, yet with desire for death. Then Rachel closed her eyes and sighed deeply, and gasped, saying, "Dawn has reached the extreme end of the valley; we should go toward the sun and meet him." Her lips were parted, resembling and echoing a deep wound in the soul.

At that moment the priest approached her bed and felt her hand, but found it as cold as the snow; and when he grimly placed his fingers upon her heart, he determined that it was as immobile as the ages, and as silent as the secret of his heart.

The reverend father bowed his head in deep despair. His lips quivered as if wanting to utter a divine word, repeated by the phantoms of the night in the distant and deserted valleys.

After crossing her arms upon her bosom, the priest looked toward a man sitting in an obscured corner of the room, and with a kind and merciful voice he said, "Your beloved has reached the great circle of light. Come, my brother, let us kneel and pray."

The sorrowful husband lifted his head; his eyes stared, gazing at the unseen, and his expression then changed as if he saw understanding in the ghost of an unknown God. He gathered the remnants of himself and walked reverently toward the bed of his wife, and knelt by the side of the clergyman who was praying and lamenting and making the sign of the cross.

Placing his hand upon the shoulder of the grief-stricken husband, the Father said quietly, "Go to the adjoining room, brother, for you are in great need of rest."

He rose obediently, walked to the room and threw his fatigued

body upon a narrow bed, and in a few moments he was sailing in the world of sleep like a little child taking refuge in the merciful arms of his loving mother.

*　　*　　*　　*　　*

The priest remained standing like a statue in the center of the room, and a strange conflict gripped him. And he looked with tearful eyes at the cold body of the young woman and then through the parted curtain at her husband, who had surrendered himself to the allure of slumber. An hour, longer than an age and more terrible than Death, had already passed, and the priest was still standing between two parted souls. One was dreaming as a field dreams of the coming Spring after the tragedy of Winter, and the other was resting eternally.

Then the priest came close to the body of the young woman and knelt as if worshipping before the altar; he held her cold hand and placed it against his trembling lips, and looked at her face that was adorned with the soft veil of Death. His voice was at the same time calm as the night and deep as the chasm and faltering as with the hopes of man. And in voice he wept, "Oh Rachel, bride of my soul, hear me! At last I am able to talk! Death has opened my lips so that I can now reveal to you a secret deeper than Life itself. Pain has unpinioned my tongue and I can disclose to you my suffering, more painful than pain. Listen to the cry of my soul, Oh Pure Spirit, hovering between the earth and the firmament. Give heed to the youth who waited for you to come from the field, gazing upon you from behind the trees, in fear of your beauty. Hear the priest, who is serving God, calling to you unashamed, after you have reached the City of God. I have proved the strength of my love by concealing it!"

Having thus opened his soul, the Father leaned over and printed three long, warm, and mute kisses upon her forehead, eyes and throat, pouring forth all his heart's secret of love and pain, and the anguish of the years. Then he suddenly withdrew to the dark corner and dropped in agony upon the floor, shaking like an Autumn leaf, as if the touch of her cold face had awakened within him the spirit to repent; whereupon he composed himself and knelt, hiding his face with his cupped hands, and he whispered softly, "God. . . . Forgive my sin; forgive my weakness, Oh Lord. I could no longer resist disclosing that which You knew. Seven years have I kept the deep secrets hidden in my heart from the spoken word, until Death

445

came and tore them from me. Help me, Oh God, to hide this terrible and beautiful memory which brings sweetness from life and bitterness from You. Forgive me, My Lord, and forgive my weakness."

Without looking at the young woman's corpse, he continued suffering and lamenting until Dawn came and dropped a rosy veil upon those two still images, revealing the conflict of Love and Religion to one man; the peace of Life and Death to the other.

ANDRE GIDE

ANDRÉ GIDE (French, 1869-1951). Contemporary French novelist. Sensitive and sensuous protagonist of egotism. Rebelled against Puritan background after meeting Oscar Wilde in Algeria. Insisted on doctrine of individual morality, but became a stylist in classic tradition. Most widely read novel: *The Counterfeiters*. Others: *The Immoralist, The Pastoral Symphony, Strait Is the Gate*. Autobiography: *If It Die . . .*

MY MOTHER

I

WHEN I had finished my first studies, my mother thought it would be a good thing to introduce me to "society". But aside from some not too distant cousins and the wives of a few of my father's colleagues at the Faculty of Law, transplanted from Rouen to Paris, she had never tried to make any acquaintances. Furthermore, the world in which it seemed I was to be interested, that of men of letters or artists, was not "her" world; she would have felt herself out of place in it.

I no longer know to what drawing-room she took me that day. It must have been that of my cousin Saussine, at whose home, on the rue d'Athènes, I took tiresome dancing lessons twice a week. It was the day they received. There were numerous introductions, and the conversation was approximately what all society conversations are, made up of little nothings and affectations. I turned my attention less to the other ladies than to my mother. I scarcely recognized her. She, ordinarily so modest, so reserved, and seemingly fearful of her own opinion, appeared in that social gathering, full of assurance and, without pushing herself forward at all, perfectly at her

446

ease. One would have said that she was playing a role exactly as it should be, without, moreover, attaching any importance to it, but willingly consenting to mingle in the game of the society parade to which one contributes hardly anything but outward appearances. It even seemed to me that, in the twaddle and foolishness all about, a few particularly sensible sentences of hers threw the general conversation into disorder; the ridiculous remarks immediately collapsed and disappeared into thin air, like ghosts at the crowing of the cock. I was amazed, and told her so, as soon as we escaped from that Vanity Fair, and found ourselves alone together.

For my part, I dined that evening with Pierre Louÿs, I believe. At any rate, I remember that I left her as we turned the corner of rue d'Athènes. But I came back to her almost immediately after dinner. I was in a hurry to see her. We were then living on the rue de Commaille. The windows of our apartment opened on a deep garden that no longer exists to-day. My mother was on the balcony. She had taken off her finery, and I rediscovered her in her simple, drab, everyday clothes. It was the season when the first acacias smell sweet. My mother seemed worried; she did not make confidences easily and doubtless the co-operation of springtime was needed to invite her to speak.

"Is what you said to me as we left our cousin's true?" she began with a great effort. "You really think so? I was . . . well, as good as the others?"

And as I began to exclaim, she continued mournfully:

"If your father had told me so even once . . . I never dared ask him, and I needed so terribly to know, when we went out together, if he was . . . "

She was silent for a moment. I looked at her trying to hold back her tears. She finished in a lower tone of voice, hardly audible:

". . . if he was pleased with me."

I think that those were her exact words which suddenly let me understand how many worries, unasked questions and expectations could, under the appearance of happiness, still dwell in even the most united of couples. And such were my parents in the eyes of everyone and of their son. What my mother had vainly awaited was not a compliment from my father, but only the assurance that she had been able to prove herself worthy of him, that he had not been disappointed in her. But what my father thought, I knew no more than she; and I understood, that evening, that every soul carries to the tomb to hide it there, some secret.

447

II

Everything that was natural in my mother, I loved. But it happened that her impulses were checked by covention and the bent that a bourgeois education too often leaves behind it. (Not always; thus I remember that she dared brave the disapproval of all her family when she went to care for the farmers of La Roque attacked during a typhus epidemic.) That education, excellent, doubtless, when it is a question of curbing evil instincts, attacks equally, but then very unfortunately, the generous emotions of the heart; then a sort of calculation restrains or directs them. I should like to give an example of this:

My mother announced to me her intention of making a gift of Littré to Anna Shackleton, our poor friend, whom I loved as a son. I was bursting with joy, when she added:

"The one I gave your father is bound in morocco. I thought that, for Anna, a shagreen binding would be sufficient."

I understood at once, what I had not known before, that shagreen costs much less. The joy suddenly left my heart. And without a doubt my mother noticed it, for she went on quickly:

"She won't see the difference."

No, that shabby cheating was not natural to her. To her giving was natural. But I was irritated also by that sort of complicity to which she had invited me.

I have lost the memory of a thousand more important things. Why did those few sentences of my mother's engrave themselves so deeply on my heart? Perhaps because I felt myself capable of thinking and saying them myself, in spite of the violent reprobation they aroused in me. Perhaps because I became conscious of that bent against which I should have to struggle and that I was sadly amazed to discover in my mother. Everything else melted into the harmonious ensemble of her face; and it is perhaps just because I did not recognize her any more by that trait, truly unworthy of her, that my memory took possession of it. What a warning! What strength that educational bent had, then, to triumph in this way from time to time! But my mother remained too surrounded by beings deformed in the same way, to be able to recognize in herself, among all the acquired characteristics, those spontaneous to her nature; above all, she remained too fearful and unsure of herself to give them the upper hand. She remained worried about others and their opinions; always desirous of the best, but a best answering to

accepted rules; always tending toward this best, and without even suspecting (and too modest to recognize it) that the best in her was exactly what she obtained with the least effort.

JEAN GIRAUDOUX

JEAN GIRAUDOUX (French, 1882-1944). Influential modern playwright and novelist. Profound and searching in thought. Was diplomat after First World War. Achieved first success as novelist *(Siegfried et le Limousin)*, then as dramatist. Chose fantastic themes to treat serious problems of our time. Plays translated: *Amphitryon 38, Intermezzo, The Madwoman of Chaillot, Ondine, Tiger at the Gates.*

MAY ON LAKE ASQUAM

I AM stretched out in the middle of a great ring of mountains. When I get up onto my feet, I become their very pivot. I have put the sun on my left, as they taught me to do at school, and I am writing to you. The lake below me bears fragile islands on its surface, and pine logs, from the drifts broken up during the winter, wash vagrantly in its bays and coves. Humming-birds thrusting voraciously among the apple-blossoms, wound their swift bills on the hard wood and glance off again. To soothe the sore feet of the farm turkeys—a degenerate race—Mrs. Green is greasing the limbs of the tree where they come to roost. A thrush grazes me, a little breeze begins to stir. As when a bird alights by a dreaming poet and he is moved to see the very thought he was seeking within himself drop then, perfect— so a sweet and tender love, instead of stirring in my heart, lifts this page, fans me with its soft breath. In boat-houses hidden in the reeds the farmers are testing the motors of the boats which will be launched for their masters next month. Mrs. Green is beating a rose-colored puff for me, because my bed ends under the window, and when I wake in the morning I see my sunny feet under the spread—and yet feel cold. In the depths of the creeks where the new-cut pines are floating, the lumbermen jump from one log to the next, whistling as they go. I envy them their balance; I feel over-weighted with a lake and a sun on my left, and nothing on my right.

Where am I? I am in a land which I instantly recognize to be

enormous, because these wasps that are this second buzzing about my head are three times bigger than they are in Europe. I am in the middle of New Hampshire, which is having its first sight of the sky-blue uniform, and, supposing that I have chosen this color myself, imagines me to be sensitive and generous. The Harvard Regiment is having a week of examinations, and I am taking a rest.

The motor left Boston early on Monday, reaching the suburbs at the hour when the typewriters, perched on their high-heeled, pointed shoes, in their low-necked foulard dresses, and bent slant-wise to the wind, climb into the tramcars without touching the rail, anxious only for their hands; the stenographers following them rigidly erect, thinking only of their heads. On the door-steps Irish girls with brown braids looped over their ears passed on to us, through soft blue eyes, the holiest thoughts they had been pondering in the night. We were following the highway bordered with Washington elms, very old trees whose trunks had been repaired with the sort of cement of which they make statues in this country; and immortality —as sap was lacking—had already reached the topmost branches. Lakes that grew clearer and clearer the farther we went held the water of the richer and richer parts of Boston, and we came at last to the very round, very blue lake that supplies Beacon Street.

At noon we were at Portsmouth, where I presided at a meeting the children were holding on the beach to sell their pet animals, for the benefit of their French godchildren. There were at least a hundred of them, all grave, eager, or at least acquiescent, save Grace Henderson, who clung to her white calf and wept. They bought it of her quickly, and in pity gave it back to her; but her brother obliged her to sell it again, and so she had to struggle and suffer three times over. There were Cuban birds, that you bought with their cages; native birds that you bought so as to set them free; turtles which sold badly, as they wore the initials of their first master carved on their backs; goats; and there were animals which were also immolated for the cause—sad dogs, who had no resistance left in them, and sold themselves; a little elephant which clasped his mistress by a belt that gave, by a sleeve that tore, and so did not dare to take her by the pigtail. The governesses, to console their children, quickly bought these other animals, and took turns standing on a platform to read out letters from the godsons: *"Venez chez moi, j'irai chez vous,"* wrote Jean Perrot, *"et si je meurs je veux vous voir."* Some professors who were there were amazed to discover that all French children use rhythmic prose.

450

Then came green forests cut by tumbling brooks, where little boys, who were fishing for trout with both hands, hailed us with a wink, as they did not dare to move or call out. Then came the country of the field-mice, where the owls have such fat haunches that they have to perch sideways for fear of tumbling off their twigs head first. Then came Sandwich, where a Lithuanian was waving his national flag, protesting all by himself against conscription. Then came Lake Asquam, and this local hilltop where I have lain stretched out ever since, at the foot of a slim giant birch, which has only one tuft of verdure at its top, and will fall if it puts out a single other leaf.

My hostess is Mrs. Green, the farmer's wife, who wears her gray hair braided down her back, and a big striped shawl, and eyeglasses; but she twists the calves' tails, and fights with the rooster. When a word gets stuck in my fountain pen I shake it out into the lake from my steamer-chair. Sometimes, though, it is inside me that it hesitates, and then I have to get up myself, lean on my elbows, sometimes even stoop all the way over.

Who am I with? With two friends—a forester and an Australian poet. The morning belongs to Carnegie, the forester. By six o'clock he has me up and off on a dash to his district, straight across the islands where every owner keeps a different scheme of hours, according as he likes to see his children get up early or late. Silent beasts are waking in woods that still have their Indian names; the muskrat is taking his bath, the blue heron flies from an isthmus to an island, from an island to an islet, flying ever toward that little round point of noon. We land in haste, to avoid an upset—for a new-cut pine log is already sliding down the toboggan to the lake—and go to the sawmill by a path that was once covered with sawdust, but that my forester has had tarred since he lost his gold chain. He teaches me the secret sign by which one may recognize the red pine, the white pine, and the black pine; he gathers together his group of woodcutters, who are going off to France, and forces me to pronounce our biggest trees in French—the oak, the elm; I saw my favorite beeches with difficulty. In the short cuts we walk through the briars stiffly, as people who do not speak the same tongue always do, and not one of these noble gestures is lost, my dear, for the forest is full of lynxes. In the clearings he shows me the remains of the wood fires he has kindled since his childhood, and twenty years of embers still blacken his fingers. He is moved and sits down, my love, to dream . . . and suddenly four little woodchucks, my sweet, hurry timidly out of the ground; real little woodchucks, my heart.

451

We catch them—they bite us, and try to get away—we pet them, my dear love.

But the night belongs to Rogers, the Australian. The whole world is dark, invisible; only one red point to be seen, Carnegie's cigar—he is noiselessly paddling on the lake. But miles away the chosen tree that announces the moon suddenly twinkles down its whole length. That is because a whole moon is coming. Everything is radiant, everything shines. Rocks begin to show themselves, as white and polished as bleached bones. Far around the lake the reflection of the forest, just now cleft and jutting, becomes an even border. It is the hour when the Indians gave a name to all the things that surround us. The white mountains turn white, the yellow birches yellow, and blue, blue grow the owls. Every separate plane of the lake seems to lie on a different level, and the moon gnaws the water where it falls over the dams. A divine night, this, when the White Mountains are of silver and the birches of gold. At last the hour has come when I can find an epithet for my soul, and a name for my house. The bull-frog groans; the loon, black swan of the lake, utters cries, first piercing, then muffled, for he continuously ducks his head under the water and pulls it out again. The true moon cautiously climbs farther and farther from the false moon. . . .

But Rogers insists on talking. He wants me to talk to him of Seeger, who is dead, of Blakely, who is dead—of all the American poets who were killed before the American war began. He persists in talking French, without allowing me to help him, and circles about the words he no longer knows: about the word "debonair," the word "ladder," the word "serenity." From my refuge in the very heart of the word I wait placidly for him, sometimes in the heart of a proper name, in the heart of Baudelaire—a stuffy place, his statue. Then he reads me his verses, which he wishes to adapt to Europe, because the Australian mouths are so different from our own.

"July has frozen the rivers," he says, "and the useless bridges are collected in the barn."

I shake my head; he understands, and corrects himself:

"Summer has frozen the rivers, and the bridges" . . .

The loon sings on. The lake suddenly bursts into flame, for Carnegie is lighting a second cigar. Rogers grows emotional, takes my hand and circles about a word which expresses both loons and friendships, a word which even we in France, alas, do not know.

When the storm breaks; when, by millions, the owners of the

wooden houses bring their red-striped tents in from the rain: when a flash of lightning allows you to see—through the isinglass of the top of the car in front of you—the shadow of two gray heads; when the black bird with the red wings folds his wings; when the pro-German shuts his window and suddenly feels so lonely and beaten that he bursts into tears; when, in the public parks, the crowds swarm under the tents of the recruiting sergeants, and help them move their posters, and torpedoes, and mortars under shelter; when the mother astride the purple motor-cycle tries in vain to reach out a hand and feel the baby dozing in the side-car; when the golden stags, the dragons and the golden cows whirl madly on the clock-towers of the barns, but always in time; when a Hannan shoe lies on the deserted avenue; when a blast of wind lifts the page of the one-armed accountant, and he holds it down with the point of his pen, calling for help; when one hears nothing on the sidewalks, on on the sea, on the buildings, but the rain . . . then when a sunbeam comes down, and a sharp cloud cuts it, and it falls; when the rain-bow shivers, its left on the solid city cement, its right on the sea; when you gather the sun into a corner of the sky, as if it were your one last match—and it finally burns; when a victorious sunbeam, fall-ing on the terrace beats by the fraction of an inch a rain-drop that has come from thousands of miles less far away; when the baby in the side-car gets the last drop of all, and begins to cry—then when the pond-lilies climb up to the level of the new pond that has formed about them; when the farmer in his rubber boots tramps out to empty his pitch cans and his maple syrup cans of their water; when a child, for no reason at all, wants to burn a joss-stick; when the traveler, at the turn of the Cañon, gets down to pat his mule and all at once remounts quickly for the storm is rumbling again, and he wants to keep his saddle dry; when the rain begins to beat down once more, in a deluge, the very same rain, as you can plainly recognize by its drops: then I think of him, of Seeger, who loved storms, and I shudder.

"How did Seeger die?" asks Rogers.

In a month Rogers will be leaving for the war, and he loses no opportunity of informing himself how the poets, his colleagues, were killed. It would be very odd if two poets were killed in the same way, the same identical way; each one of these deaths is death that fate will deny him. He will not wander, like Rupert Brooke, repeating one Christian name after another, and dying at the first woman's name. He will not have him, as Dollero did, to write me three letters; the

453

first with a splinter and his blood saying good by; the second with his nurse's pencil, hoping to see me; the last with the doctor's fountain pen—confident, happy, unfinished. He will not drop dead like Hesslin, the German poet, on the back of a mystical sergeant who rose slowly with his load, and bore it to the hospital without casting a backward look. He will need a whole grave to himself, since he is not to die like Blakely, whose poor remains fitted into a Palmer's biscuit box. It will not be at dark, as it was with Drouot, or at noon, as it was with Clermont. If Seeger died at dawn, there is no time left for him but night. Bitter night, running under the days like some infernal strawberry vine. Soft night, with its lake, its loons. Night on the Sydney steamers, when the world turns silent, and nothing stands in the way of a poet's thoughts but the mute strain of a vessel. Night near some French spring where you lie, scarcely aware of your wound, and nibble a leaf of water-cress. Somber night, in whose very center, sharp cut against the velvet dark, the sun suddenly appears. Happy he who dies at night!

"How did Seeger die? Did you know him?"

Rogers is astigmatic, wears heavy gold-rimmed spectacles with lenses of different pattern, and always asks you two questions at a time. Yes, I had seen him. Once it was in the Luxembourg, in summer; he was just coming into the unreal garden, with its world of fantastic and tender Parisians—those who felt themselves too heavy could buy little balloons at the gate. Another time it was at the house of a friend whom he had tried to find the two preceding evenings; on the first he left a couplet, on the second a sonnet. My friend allowed himself to be surprised in bed, the third day, and so did not get his poem.

"Did he suffer? Have you seen his last verses?"

For Rogers also collects the last poems of all the poets who have been killed. He even collects their last letters in prose, where sometimes two words clash into each other and rhyme—the same thing happens when a departing warrior is dressing in his apartment, with his friends standing about—and makes them tremble. It may be a last letter written to an aunt between the two last poems, when, in spite of himself, he uses the poetic epithet (as the other does not come)—talks of "steeds," and "blades," and "meads," and feels obliged to be somewhat ironic. Last poems where nearly all of them saw death as it was, in fact, to overtake them, Seeger like a mistress, longing for a rendezvous, Dollero like a storm with three stray birds, Blakely like a headless monster—and when only Brooke foresaw

things all wrong. Poor Brooke who told us *"Si je meurs, dites vous que dans une terre ètrangère il y aura toujours un coin de terre anglaise. Une poussière plus riche que la terre y sera contenue, un corps d'Angleterre lavé par les rivières anglaises, brûle par le soleil anglais," "un corps horizontal tendu sur la ligne de tous les corps anglais,"* and in the end died on a boat, and was thrown into the sea with a cannon ball to keep his shroud upright. So that, for all one's pity one is put on one's guard, and when one turns over his other poems one no longer believes exactly what they say; no longer believes that love is *une rue ouverte où se precipite ce qui jamais ne voient, un traître qui livre au destin la citadelle du coeur, un enfant étendu.* One grows obstinate about it, insists on believing that love is a street, if you like, but a street with no outlet; a traitor perhaps, but in that case a friendly traitor; and sometimes one sees the charming fellow standing quite vertical, floating sadly in the air.

"How did Seeger die?"

It is summer. Everything that prevents one from breathing in the summer—his cap, his gas-mask—he throws off. He holds his cigar behind him, because of the smoke; the company thief steals it away from him—thank heaven, for so his hands will not burn up after his death. Then he stretches himself, but without lifting his arms, crosswise. He has just one minute to live. There is your watch before you, with its second hand: one minute and he will be dead. In his pocket is the bottle of heliotrope perfume that he is to break as he falls. Now you have not even time, before he dies, to write that short sentence which he took for his motto, the one that he wrote at the head of every poem—about the poplars. If it is a shell, the cannon is being loaded. If it is a bullet, the German soldier is tapping his charge and slipping it in. Seeger raises his head. The sky is very blue. A poplar, yes, a poplar is outlined on the horizon. Seeger climbs the firing step—a bird, yes, a . . .

So my three days of rest have gone, and now it is noon. I think of you who wrote me every week from Europe, a letter of variable mood —Even the color of the paper is inconstant, and each one, like the flash of a revolving lighthouse, throws a new region into high relief. Love is a restive horse, a saddled antelope, a faithful traitor. The sun is just above me now. I was writing, to spare my eyes, in the shadow of my head; there is no shadow left; adieu, Madame, I write the last word, I write your name, full in the sun.

455

JOHANN WOLFGANG VON GOETHE

JOHANN WOLFGANG VON GOETHE (German, 1749-1832). Germany's greatest poet and the philosopher of classical poetry. Writer of universal scope—even his recorded conversations are significant. Wielded tremendous influence during life and afterward. Initiated *Sturm und Drang* movement *(Sorrows of Werther)*. Autobiographical novel: *Wilhelm Meister*. Epic: *Hermann and Dorothea*. Drama: *Egmont*. His masterpiece, *Faust*, philosophic-poetic drama, one of Western world's supreme classics.

FAUST

A Tragedy

Faust. All that philosophy can teach,
The craft of lawyer and of leech,
I've mastered, ah! and sweated through
Theology's dreary deserts, too;
Yet here, poor fool! for all my lore,
I stand no wiser than before.
They call me magister, save the mark!
Doctor, withal! and these ten years I
Have been leading my pupils a dance in the dark,
Up hill, down dale, through wet and through dry—
And yet, that nothing can ever be
By mortals known, too well I see!
This is burning the heart clean out of me.
More brains have I than all the tribe
Of doctor, magister, parson, and scribe.
From doubts and scruples my soul is free;
Nor hell nor devil has terrors for me:
But just for this I am dispossessed
Of all that gives pleasure to life and zest.
I can't even juggle myself to own
There is any one thing to be truly known,
Or aught to be taught in science or arts,
To better mankind and to turn their hearts.
Besides, I have neither land nor pence,
Nor worldly honour nor influence.
A dog in my case would scorn to live!

So myself to magic I've vowed to give,
And see, if through spirit's might and tongue
The heart from some mysteries cannot be wrung;
If I cannot escape from the bitter woe
Of babbling of things that I do not know,
And get to the root of those secret powers
Which hold together this world of ours,
The sources and centres of force explore,
And chaffer and dabble in words no more.
Oh, broad bright moon, if this might be
The last of the nights of agony,
The countless midnights, these weary eyes
Have from this desk here watched thee rise!
Then, sad-eyed friend, thy wistful looks
Shone in upon me o'er paper and books;
But oh! might I wander, in thy dear light,
O'er the trackless slopes of some mountain height,
Round mountain caverns with spirits sail,
Or float o'er the meads in thy hazes pale;
And, freed from the fumes of a fruitless lore,
Bathe in thy dews, and be whole once more!

Ah me! am I penned in this dungeon still?
Accursed doghole, clammy and chill!
Where heaven's own blessed light must pass,
Shorn of its rays, through the painted glass,
Narrowed and cumbered by piles of books,
That are gnawed by worms and grimed with dust,
And which, with its smoke-stained paper looks
Swathed to the roof in a dingy rust;
Stuck round with phials, and chests untold,
With instruments littered, and lumbered with old,
Crazy, ancestral household ware—
This is your world! A world most rare!

And yet can you wonder why your soul
Is numbed within your breast, and why
A dead, dull anguish makes your whole
Life's pulses falter, and ebb, and die?

457

How should it be but so? Instead
Of the living nature, whereinto
God has created man, things dead
And drear alone, encompass you—
Smoke, litter, dust, the skeletons
Of birds and beasts, and dead men's bones!

Up, up! Away to the champaign free!
And this mysterious volume, writ
By Nostradamus' self, is it
Not guide and counsel enough for thee?
Then wilt thou learn by what control
The stars within their orbits roll,
And if thou wilt let boon Nature be
The guide and monitress to thee,
Thy soul shall expand with tenfold force,
As spirit with spirit holds discourse.
Dull poring, think not, that can here
Expound these holy signs to thee!
Ye spirits, ye are hovering near,
If ye can hear me, answer me!

Throws open the book, and discovers the sign of the Macrocosm.

Ha! as it meets my gaze, what rapture, gushing
Through all my senses, mounts into my brain!
Youth's ecstasy divine, I feel it rushing,
Like quickening fire, through every nerve and vein!
Was it a god who chronicled these signs,
Which all the war within me still,
The aching heart with sweetness fill,
And to mine eyes, in clearest lines,
Unveil all Nature's powers as with a mystic thrill?
Am I a god? All grows so bright.
In these pure outlines I behold
Nature at work before my soul unrolled.
Now can I read the sage's saw aright:
"Not barred to man the world of spirits is;
Thy sense is shut, thy heart is dead!
Up, student, lave,—nor dread the bliss,—
Thy earthly breast in the morning red!"

Gazes intently at the sign.

458

Into one whole how all the things blend,
One in the other working, living!
What powers celestial, lo! ascend, descend,
Each unto each the golden pitchers giving!
And, wafting blessings from their wings,
From heaven through farthest earth career,
While through the universal sphere
One universal concord rings!

Oh, what a show! yet but a show! Ah me!
Where, boundless Nature, shall I clutch at thee?
Ye breasts, where are ye? Ye perennial springs
Of life, whereon hang heaven and earth,
Whereto the blighted bosom clings,
Ye gush, ye slake all thirst, yet I pine on in dearth!

*Turns the leaves of the book angrily, and sees the sign of the Earth
Spirit.*

How differently I feel before this sign!
Earth Spirit, thou to me art nearer;
My faculties grow loftier, clearer,
Even now I glow as with new wine.
Courage I feel, into the world to roam,
To bid earth's joy and sorrows hail,
'Mid storm and struggle to make my home,
And in the crash of shipwreck not to quail.
Clouds gather o'er my head;
The moon conceals her light,
The lamp's gone out. The air
Grows thick and close! Red flashes play
Around me. From the vaulted roof
A shuddering horror creeps
And on me lays its gripe!
Spirit by me invoked, I feel
Thou'rt hovering near,—thou art, thou art!
Unveil thyself!
Ha! What a tugging at my heart!
Stirred through their depths, my senses reel
With passions new and strange! I feel
My heart is thine, thine wholly! Hear!
Thou must! ay, though it cost my life, thou must appear!

459

Seizes the book, and utters the sign of the Spirit mysteriously. A red light flashes, in which the Spirit appears.

Spirit. Who calls on me?

Faust (turning away). Dread vision gaunt!

Spirit. By potent art thou'st dragged me here;
Thou'st long been sucking at my sphere,
And now—

Faust. I loathe thee. Hence, avaunt!

Spirit. To view me were thy prayer and choice,
To see my face, to hear my voice.
Well! by thy potent prayer won o'er,
I come. And thou, that wouldst be more
Than mortal, having thy behest,
Art with a craven fear possessed!
Where is thy pride of soul? Where now the breast
Which in itself a universe created,
Sustained and fostered,—which dilated
With giant throes of rapture, in the hope
As peer with spirits such as me to cope?
Where art thou, Faust, whose summons rang so wide,
Is this thing thou? This, my mere breath doth make
Through every nerve and fibre quake?
A crawling, cowering, timorous worm?

Faust. Thou film of flame, art thou a thing to fear?
I am, I am that Faust! I am thy peer!

Spirit. In the currents of Life, in Action's storm,
I wander and I wave;
Everywhere I be!
Birth and the grave,
An infinite sea,
A web ever growing,
A life ever glowing;
Thus at Time's whizzing loom I spin,
And weave the living vesture that God is mantled in!

Faust. Thou busy Spirit, who dost sweep
From sphere to sphere, from deep to deep,
Ranging the world from end to end,
How near akin I feel to thee!

Spirit. Thou'rt like the Spirit, thou dost comprehend,
But not like me!

Vanishes.

460

Faust.   O happy he who still can hope
Out of this sea of error to arise!
We long to use what lies beyond our scope,
Yet cannot use even what within it lies.
But let us not, by saddening thoughts like these,
The blessing of this happy hour o'errun.
See, how they gleam, the green-girt cottages,
Fired by the radiance of the evening sun!
It slopes, it sets. Day wanes. On with a bound
It speeds, and lo! a new world is alive!
O God, for wings to lift me from the ground,
Onward, still onward, after it to strive!
Beneath me, I should see, as on I pressed,
The hushed world ever bathed in evening's beams,
Each mountain-top on fire, each vale at rest,
The silver brook flow into golden streams.
Nor peak nor mountain-chasm should then defeat
My onward course, so godlike and so free.
Lo, with its bays all winking in the heat,
Bursts on my wonder-smitten eyes the sea!
But now the god appears about to sink!
Fresh impulse stirs me, not to be confined.
I hurry on, his deathless light to drink,
The day before me, and the night behind.
The heavens above me, and the waves below.
A lovely dream! Meanwhile, the sun his face
Has hid. Ah, with the spirit's wing will no
Corporeal wings so readily keep pace!
Yet is the yearning with us all inborn,
Upwards and onwards to be struggling still,
When over us we hear the lark, at morn,
Lost in the sky, her quivering carol trill;
When o'er the mountains' pine-clad summits drear
The eagle wheels afar on outstretched wing,
When over flat and over mere
The crane is homewards labouring.
    Wagner.   I too have often had my whims and moods,
But never was by such an impulse stirred.
A man soon looks his fill at fields and woods;
The wings I ne'er shall envy of a bird.
How differently the spirit's pure delights

461

Waft us from book to book, from page to page!
They give a beauty to the winter's nights,
A cheerful glow that can its chill assuage.
And some fine manuscript when you unroll,
Ah, then all heaven descends into your soul!

    Faust. One only aspiration thou hast known,
Oh, never seek to know the other, never!
Two souls, alas! within my bosom throne,
That each from other fiercely longs to sever.
One, with a passionate love that never tires,
Cleaves as with cramps of steel to things of earth,
The other upwards through earth's mists aspires
To kindred regions of a loftier worth.
Oh, in the air if spirits be,
That float 'twixt earth and heaven, and lord it there,
Then from your golden haze descend, and me
Far hence to fields of new existence bear!
Yes, if a magic mantle were but mine,
To stranger lands to waft me at my call,
I'd prize it more than robes of costliest shine,
I would not change it for a monarch's pall

* * *

    Mephistopheles. These my tiny spirits be.
Hark, with what sagacity
They advise thee to pursue
Action, pleasure ever new!
Out into the world so fair
They would lure and lead thee hence,
From this lonely chamber, where
Stagnate life and soul and sense.
No longer trifle with the wretchedness,
That, like a vulture, gnaws your life away!
The worst society will teach you this,
You are a man 'mongst men, and feel as they.
Yet 'tis not meant, I pray you, see,
To thrust you 'mong the rabble rout;—
I'm done of your great folks, no doubt,
But if, in fellowship with me,
To range through life you are content,
I will most cheerfully consent

To be your own upon the spot.
I am your chum. You'd rather not?
Well! If your scruples it will save,
I am your servant, yea, your slave!

    Faust.   And in return what must I do for you?

    Mephistopheles.   Oh, time enough to talk of that!

    Faust.   Nay, nay!
The devil's selfish—is and was always—
And is not like for mere God's sake to do
A liberal turn to any child of clay.
Out with the terms, and plainly! Such as thou
Are dangerous servants in a house, I trow.

    Mephistopheles.   I bind myself to serve you here,—**to do**
Your bidding promptly, whatsoe'er it be,
And, when we come together yonder, you
Are then to do the same for me.

    Faust.   I prize that yonder at a rush!
Only this world to atoms crush,
And then that other may arise!
From earth my every pleasure flows,
Yon Sun looks down upon my woes;
Let me but part myself from those.
Then come what may, in any guise!
To idle prate I'll close mine ears,
If we hereafter hate or love,
Or if there be in yonder spheres,
As here, an Under and Above!

    Mephistopheles.   You're in the proper mood to venture! **Bind**
Yourself, and pleasure in my sleights you'll find,
While this life lasts. I'll give you more
Than eye of man hath ever seen before.

    Faust.   What wilt thou give, thou sorry devil? When
Were the aspiring souls of men
Fathomed by such a thing as thee?
Oh, thou hast food that satisfieth never,
Gold, ruddy gold thou hast, that restlessly
Slips, like quicksilver, through the hand for ever;
A game, where we must losers be;
A girl, that, on my very breast,
My neighbour woos with smile and wink;
Fame's rapturous flash of godlike zest,

That, meteor-like, is doomed to sink.
Show me the fruit that, ere 'tis plucked, doth rot,
And trees that every day grow green anew!

Mephistopheles. Such task as this affrights me not.
I have such treasures at command for you.
But, my good friend, the time draws nigh
When we may banquet on the best in peace!

Faust. If e'er at peace on sluggard's couch I lie,
Then may my life upon the instant cease!
Cheat thou me ever by thy glozing wile,
So that I cease to scorn myself, or e'er
My senses with a perfect joy beguile,
Then be that day my last! I offer fair,
How say'st thou?

Mephistopheles. Done!

Faust. My hand upon it! There!
If to the passing moment e'er I say,
"Oh, linger yet, thou art so fair!"
Then cast me into chains you may,
Then will I die without a care!
Then may the death-bell sound its call,
Then art thou from thy service free,
The clock may stand, the index fall,
And time and tide may cease for me!

Mephistopheles. Think well; we sha'n't forget the terms you
name.

Faust. Your perfect right I must allow.
Not rashly to the pact I came.
I am a slave as I am now;
Yours or another's, 'tis to me the same!

Mephistopheles. Then at the Doctors' feast this very day
Will I my post, as your attendant take.
Just one thing more! To guard against mistake,
Oblige me with a line or two, I pray.

Faust. Pedant, must thou have writing, too?
Hast thou no true man, or man's promise, known?
Is not my word of mouth enough for you,
To pledge my days for all eternity?
Does not the universe go raving on,
In all its ever-eddying currents, free

464

To pass from change to change and I alone,
Shall a mere promise curb or fetter me?
Yet doth man's heart so hug the dear deceit,
Who would its hold without a pang undo?
Blest he, whose soul is with pure truth replete,
No sacrifice shall ever make him rue.
But, oh, your stamped and scribbled parchment sheet
A spectre is, which all men shrink to view.
The word dies ere it quits the pen,
And wax and sheepskin lord it then.
What would you have, spirit of ill!
Brass, marble, parchment, paper?—Say,
Am I to write with pen, or style, or graver?
I care not—choose whiche'er you will.

 Mephistopheles. Why, throw your eloquence away,
Or give it such a very pungent savour?
Pshaw! Any scrap will do—'tis quite the same—
With the least drop of blood just sign your name.

 Faust. If that will make you happy, why, a claim
So very whimsical I'll freely favour.

 Mephistopheles. Blood is a juice of quite peculiar kind.

 Faust. Fear not that I the compact will evade!
My life's whole struggle, heart and mind,
Chimes with the promise I have made.
Too high I've soared—too proudly dreamt,
I'm only peer for such as thee;
The Mighty Spirit spurns me with contempt,
And Nature veils her face from me.
Thought's chain is snapt;—for many a day
I've loathed all knowledge every way.
So quench we now our passion's fires
In sense and sensual delights,
Unveil all hidden magic sleights,
To minister to our desires!
Let us plunge in the torrent of time, and range
Through the weltering chaos of chance and change,
Then pleasure and pain, disaster and gain,
May course one another adown my brain.
Change and excitement may work as they can,
Rest there is none for the spirit of man.

Forest and Cavern

Faust (alone).   Majestic spirit, thou hast given me all
For which I prayed. Thou not in vain didst turn
  Thy countenance to me in fire and flame.
Thou glorious Nature for my realm hast given,
With power to feel, and to enjoy her. Thou
No mere cold glance of wonder hast vouchsafed,
But let'st me peer deep down into her breast,
Even as into the bosom of a friend.
Before me thou in long procession lead'st
All things that live, and teachest me to know
My kindred in still grove, in air, and stream.
And, when the storm sweeps roaring through the woods,
Upwrenching by the roots the giant pines,
Whose neighbouring trunks, and intertangled boughs,
In crashing ruin tear each other down,
And shake with roar of thunder all the hills,
Then dost thou guide me to some sheltering cave,
There show'st me to myself, and mine own soul
Teems marvels forth I weened not of before.
And when the pure moon, with her mellowing light,
Mounts as I gaze, then from the rocky walls,
And out from the dank underwood, ascend
Forms silvery-clad of ages long ago,
And soften the austere delight of thought.

  Oh, now I feel no perfect boon is e'er
Achieved by man. With this ecstatic power,
Which brings me hourly nearer to the gods,
A yokemate thou hast given me, whom even now
I can no more dispense with, though his cold
Insulting scorn degrades me to myself,
And turns my gifts to nothing with a breath.
Within my breast he fans unceasingly
A raging fire for that bewitching form.
So to fruition from desire I reel,
And 'midst fruition languish for desire.

466

NIKOLAI GOGOL

NIKOLAI GOGOL (Russian, 1809-1852). One of the founders of Russian literature. Primarily a realist, wrote comedy with pathetic overtones. Personally an eccentric and hypochondriac. Famous satiric play: *The Inspector General*. Important nationalistic novels: *Dead Souls, Taras Bulba*. Exerted tremendous influence on later Russians, especially Dostoyevsky and the Soviets.

ST. JOHN'S EVE

THOMA GRIGOROVITCH had one very strange eccentricity: to the day of his death he never liked to tell the same thing twice. There were times when, if you asked him to relate a thing afresh, he would interpolate new matter, or alter it so that it was impossible to recognize it. Once upon a time, one of those gentlemen who like every sort of frippery, and issue mean little volumes, no thicker than an A B C book, every month, or even every week, wormed this same story out of Thoma Grigorovitch, and the latter completely forgot about it. But that same young gentleman, in the pea-green caftan, came from Poltava, bringing with him a little book, and, opening it in the middle, showed it to us. Thoma Grigorovitch was on the point of setting his spectacles astride of his nose, but recollected that he had forgotten to wind thread about them and stick them together with wax, so he passed it over to me. As I understand something about reading and writing, and do not wear spectacles, I undertook to read it. I had not turned two leaves when all at once he caught me by the hand and stopped me.

"Stop! tell me first what you are reading."

I confess that I was a trifle stunned by such a question.

"What! what am I reading, Thoma Grigorovitch? Why? your own words."

"Who told you that they were my words?"

"Why, what more would you have? Here it is printed: 'Related by such and such a sacristan.'"

"Spit on the head of the man who printed that! he lies, the dog of a Moscow peddler! Did I say that? ''Twas just the same as though one hadn't his wits about him!' Listen, I'll tell the tale to you on the spot." We moved up to the table, and he began.

My grandfather (the kingdom of heaven be his! may he eat only wheaten rolls and poppy-seed cakes with honey, in the other world!)

467

could tell a story wonderfully well. When he used to begin a tale you could not stir from the spot all day, but kept on listening. He was not like the story-teller of the present day, when he begins to lie, with a tongue as though he had had nothing to eat for three days, so that you snatch your cap and flee from the house. I remember my old mother was alive then, and in the long winter evenings when the frost was crackling out of doors, and had sealed up hermetically the narrow panes of our cottage, she used to sit at her wheel, drawing out a long thread in her hand, rocking the cradle with her foot, and humming a song, which I seem to hear even now.

The lamp, quivering and flaring up as though in fear of something, lighted up our cottage; the spindle hummed; and all of us children, collected in a cluster, listened to our grandfather, who had not crawled off the stove for more than five years, owing to his great age. But the wondrous tales of the incursions of the Zaporozhian Cossacks and the Poles, the bold deeds of Polkova, of Poltar-Kozhukh, and Sagaidatchnii, did not interest us so much as the stories about some deed of old, which always sent a shiver through our frames and made our hair rise upright on our heads. Sometimes such terror took possession of us in consequence of them, that, from that evening forward, Heaven knows how wonderful everything seemed to us. If one chanced to go out of the cottage after nightfall for anything, one fancied that a visitor from the other world had lain down to sleep in one's bed; and I have often taken my own smock, at a distance, as it lay at the head of the bed, for the Evil One rolled up in a ball! But the chief thing about grandfather's stories was, that he had never lied in all his life; and whatever he said was so was so.

I will now tell you one of his wonderful tales. I know that there are a great many wise people who copy in the courts, and can even read civil documents, but who, if you were to put into their hand a simple prayer-book, could not make out the first letter in it, and would show all their teeth in derision. These people laugh at everything you tell them. Along comes one of them—and doesn't believe in witches! Yes, glory to God that I have lived so long in the world! I have seen heretics to whom it would be easier to lie in confession than it would be to our brothers and equals to take snuff, and these folk would deny the existence of witches! But let them just dream about something and they won't even tell what it was! There, it is no use talking about them!

No one could have recognized the village of ours a little over a

hundred years ago; it was a hamlet, the poorest kind of a hamlet. Half a score of miserable farmhouses, unplastered and badly thatched, were scattered here and there about the fields. There was not a yard or a decent shed to shelter animals or wagons. That was the way the wealthy lived; and if you had looked for our brothers, the poor—why, a hole in the ground—that was a cabin for you! Only by the smoke could you tell that a God-created man lived there. You ask why they lived so? It was not entirely through poverty; almost everyone led a raiding Cossack life, and gathered not a little plunder in foreign lands; it was rather because it was little use building up a good wooden house. Many folk were engaged in raids all over the country—Crimeans, Poles, Lithuanians! It was quite possible that their own countrymen might make a descent and plunder everything. Anything was possible.

In this hamlet a man, or rather a devil in human form, often made his appearance. Why he came, and whence, no one knew. He prowled about, got drunk, and suddenly disappeared as if into the air, leaving no trace of his existence. Then, behold, he seemed to have dropped from the sky again, and went flying about the street of the village, of which no trace now remains, and which was not more than a hundred paces from Dikanka. He would collect together all the Cossacks he met; then there were songs, laughter, and cash in plenty, and vodka flowed like water. . . . He would address the pretty girls, and give them ribbons, earrings, strings of beads—more than they knew what to do with. It is true that the pretty girls rather hesitated about accepting his presents: God knows, perhaps, what unclean hands they had passed through. My grandfather's aunt, who kept at that time a tavern, in which Basavriuk (as they called this devil-man) often caroused, said that no consideration on the earth would have induced her to accept a gift from him. But then, again, how avoid accepting? Fear seized on every one when he knit his shaggy brows, and gave a sidelong glance which might send your feet God knows whither: whilst if you did accept, then the next night some fiend from the swamp, with horns on his head, came and began to squeeze your neck, if there was a string of beads upon it, or bite your finger, if there was a ring upon it; or drag you by the hair, if ribbons were braided in it. God have mercy, then, on those who held such gifts! But here was the difficulty: it was impossible to get rid of them; if you threw them into the water, the diabolical ring or necklace would skim along the surface and into your hand.

There was a church in the village—St. Pantelei, if I remember

rightly. There lived there a priest, Father Athanasii, of blessed memory. Observing that Basavriuk did not come to church even at Easter, he determined to reprove him and impose penance upon him. Well, he hardly escaped with his life. "Hark ye, sir!" he thundered in reply, "learn to mind your own business instead of meddling in other people's if you don't want that throat of yours stuck together with boiling kutya."

What was to be done with this unrepentant man? Father Athanasii contented himself with announcing that any one who should make the acquaintance of Basavriuk would be counted a Catholic, an enemy of Christ's orthodox church, not a member of the human race.

In this village there was a Cossack named Korzh, who had a laborer whom people called Peter the Orphan—perhaps because no one remembered either his father or mother. The church elder, it is true, said that they had died of the pest in his second year; but my grandfather's aunt would not hear of that, and tried with all her might to furnish him with parents, although poor Peter needed them about as much as we need last year's snow. She said that his father had been in Zaporozhe, and had been taken prisoner by the Turks, amongst whom he underwent God only knows what tortures, until, having by some miracle disguised himself as a eunuch, he made his escape. Little cared the black-browed youths and maidens about Peter's parents. They merely remarked that if he only had a new coat, a red sash, a black lambskin cap with a smart blue crown on his head, a Turkish saber by his side, a whip in one hand and a pipe with handsome mountings in the other, he would surpass all the young men. But the pity was, that the only thing poor Peter had was a gray gaberdine with more holes in it than there are gold pieces in a Jew's pockets. But that was not the worst of it. Korzh had a daughter, such a beauty as I think you can hardly have chanced to see. My grandfather's aunt used to say—and you know that it is easier for a woman to kiss the Evil One than to call any one else a beauty—that this Cossack's maiden's cheeks were as plump and fresh as the pinkest poppy when, bathed in God's dew, it unfolds its petals, and coquets with the rising sun; that her brows were evenly arched over her bright eyes like black cords, such as our maidens buy nowadays, for their crosses and ducats, off the Moscow peddlers who visit the villages with their baskets; that her little mouth, at sight of which the youths smacked their lips, seemed made to warble the songs of nightingales; that her hair, black as the raven's wing, and soft as young flax, fell in curls over her shoulders, for our

maidens did not then plait their hair in pigtails interwoven with pretty, bright-hued ribbons. Eh! may I never intone another alleluia in the choir, if I would not have kissed her, in spite of the gray which is making its way through the old wool which covers my pate, and of the old woman beside me, like a thorn in my side! Well, you know what happens when young men and maidens live side by side. In the twilight the heels of red boots were always visible in the place where Pidorka chatted with her Peter. But Korzh would never have suspected anything out of the way, only one day—it is evident that none but the Evil One could have inspired him—Peter took into his head to kiss the maiden's rosy lips with all his heart, without first looking well about him; and that same Evil One—may the son of a dog dream of the holy cross!—caused the old graybeard, like a fool, to open the cottage door at that moment. Korzh was petrified, dropped his jaw, and clutched at the door for support. Those unlucky kisses completely stunned him.

Recovering himself, he took his grandfather's hunting whip from the wall, and was about to belabor Peter's back with it, when Pidorka's little six-year-old brother Ivas rushed up from somewhere or other, and grasping his father's legs with his little hands, screamed out, "Daddy, Daddy! don't beat Peter!" What was to be done? A father's heart is not made of stone. Hanging the whip again upon the wall, he led Peter quietly from the house. "If you ever show yourself in my cottage again, or even under the windows, look out, Peter, for, by heaven, your black mustache will disappear; and your black locks, though wound twice about your ears will take leave of your pate, or my name is not Terentiy Korzh." So saying, he gave him such a taste of his fist in the nape of his neck, that all grew dark before Peter, and he flew headlong out of the place.

So there was an end of their kissing. Sorrow fell upon our turtle doves; and a rumor grew rife in the village that a certain Pole, all embroidered with gold, with mustaches, saber, spurs, and pockets jingling like bells of the bag with which our sacristan Taras goes through the church every day, had begun to frequent Korzh's house. Now, it is well known why a father has visitors when there is a black-browed daughter about. So, one day, Pidorka burst into tears, and caught the hand of her brother Ivas. "Ivas, my dear! Ivas, my love! fly to Peter, my child of gold, like an arrow from a bow. Tell him all: I would have loved his brown eyes, I would have kissed his fair face, but my fate decrees otherwise. More than one handkerchief have I wet with burning tears. I am sad and heavy at heart. And my

471

own father is my enemy. I will not marry the Pole, whom I do not love. Tell him they are making ready for a wedding, but there will be no music at our wedding: priests will sing instead of pipes and viols. I shall not dance with my bridegroom; they will carry me out. Dark, dark will be my dwelling of maple wood; and instead of chimneys, a cross will stand upon the roof."

Peter stood petrified, without moving from the spot, when the innocent child lisped out Pidorka's words to him. "And I, wretched man, had thought to go to the Crimea and Turkey, to win gold and return to thee, my beauty! But it may not be. We have been overlooked by the evil eye. I too shall have a wedding, dear one; but no ecclesiastics will be present at that wedding. The black crow instead of the pope will caw over me; the bare plain will be my dwelling; the dark blue cloud my roof-tree. The eagle will claw out my brown eyes; the rain will wash my Cossack bones, and the whirlwinds will dry them. But what am I? Of what should I complain? 'Tis clear God willed it so. If I am to be lost, then so be it!" and he went straight to the tavern.

My late grandfather's aunt was somewhat surprised at seeing Peter at the tavern, at an hour when good men go to morning mass; and stared at him as though in a dream when he called for a jug of brandy, about half a pailful. But the poor fellow tried in vain to drown his woe. The vodka stung his tongue like nettles, and tasted more bitter than worm-wood. He flung the jug from him upon the ground.

"You have sorrowed enough, Cossack," growled a bass voice behind him. He looked round—it was Basavriuk! Ugh, what a face! His hair was like a brush, his eyes like those of a bull. "I know what you lack: here it is." As he spoke he jingled a leather purse which hung from his girdle and smiled diabolically. Peter shuddered. "Ha, ha, ha! how it shines!" he roared, shaking out ducats into his hands: "Ha, ha, ha! how it jingles! And I only ask one thing for a whole pile of such shiners."

"It is the Evil One!" exclaimed Peter. "Give me them! I'm ready for anything!"

They struck hands upon it, and Basavriuk said, "You are just in time, Peter: to-morrow is St. John the Baptist's day. Only on this one night in the year does the fern blossom. I will await you at midnight in the Bear's ravine."

I do not believe that chickens await the hour when the housewife brings their corn with as much anxiety as Peter awaited the evening.

472

He kept looking to see whether the shadows of the trees were not lengthening, whether the sun was not turning red towards setting; and, the longer he watched, the more impatient he grew. How long it was! Evidently God's day had lost its end somewhere. But now the sun has set. The sky is red only on one side, and it is already growing dark. It grows colder in the fields. It gets gloomier and gloomier, and at last quite dark. At last! With heart almost bursting from his bosom, he set out and cautiously made his way down through the thick woods into the deep hollow called the Bear's ravine. Basavriuk was already waiting there. It was so dark that you could not see a yard before you. Hand in hand they entered the ravine, pushing through the luxuriant thorn-bushes and stumbling at almost every step. At last they reached an open spot. Peter looked about him; he had never chanced to come there before. Here Basavriuk halted.

"Do you see before you three hillocks? There are a great many kinds of flowers upon them. May some power keep you from plucking even one of them. But as soon as the fern blossoms, seize it, and look not round, no matter what may seem to be going on behind thee."

Peter wanted to ask some questions, but behold, Basavriuk was no longer there. He approached the three hillocks—where were the flowers? He saw none! The wild steppe-grass grew all around, and hid everything in its luxuriance. But the lightning flashed; and before him was a whole bed of flowers, all wonderful, all strange: whilst amongst them there were also the simple fronds of fern. Peter doubted his senses, and stood thoughtfully before them, arms akimbo.

"What manner of prodigy is this? why, one can see these weeds ten times a day. What is there marvelous about them? Devil's-face must be mocking me!"

But behold! the tiny flower-bud of the fern reddened and moved as though alive. It was a marvel, in truth. It grew larger and larger, and glowed like a burning coal. The tiny stars of light flashed up, something burst softly, and the flower opened before his eyes like a flame, lighting the others about it.

"Now is the time," thought Peter and extended his hand. He saw hundreds of hairy hands reach also for the flower from behind him, and there was a sound of scampering in his rear. He half closed his eyes, and plucked sharply at the stalk, and the flower remained in his hand.

Upon a stump sat Basavriuk, quite blue like a corpse. He did not move so much as a finger. His eyes were immovably fixed on some-

473

thing visible to him alone: his mouth was half open and speechless. Nothing stirred around. Ugh! it was horrible!—But then a whistle was heard, which made Peter's heart grow cold within him; and it seemed to him that the grass whispered, and the flowers began to talk among themselves in delicate voices, like little silver bells, whilst the trees rustled in murmuring contention;—Basavriuk's face suddenly became full of life, and his eyes sparkled. "The witch has just returned," he muttered between his teeth. "Hearken, Peter: a charmer will stand before you in a moment; do whatever she commands; if not—you are lost forever."

Then he parted the thorn-bushes with a knotty stick, and before him stood a tiny farmhouse. Basavriuk smote it with his fist, and the wall transformed itself into a cat and flew straight at his eyes.

"Don't be angry, don't be angry, you old Satan!" said Basavriuk, employing such words as would have made a good man stop his ears. Behold, instead of a cat, an old woman all bent into a bow, with a face wrinkled like a baked apple, and a nose and chin like a pair of nut-crackers.

"A fine charmer!" thought Peter; and cold chills ran down his back. The witch tore the flower from his hand, stooped and muttered over it for a long time, sprinkling it with some kind of water. Sparks flew from her mouth, and foam appeared on her lips.

"Throw it away," she said, giving it back to Peter.

Peter threw it, but what wonder was this? The flower did not fall straight to the earth, but for a long while twinkled like a fiery ball through the darkness, and swam through the air like a boat. At last it began to sink lower and lower, and fell so far away that the little star, hardly larger than a poppy-seed, was barely visible. "There!" croaked the old woman, in a dull voice; and Basavriuk, giving him a spade, said, "Dig here Peter: you will find more gold than you or Korzh ever dreamed of."

Peter spat on his hands, seized the spade, pressed his foot on it, and turned up the earth, a second, a third, a fourth time. The spade clinked against something hard, and would go no farther. Then his eyes began to distinguish a small, iron-bound coffer. He tried to seize it, but the chest began to sink into the earth, deeper, farther and deeper still: whilst behind him he heard a laugh like a serpent's hiss.

"No, you shall not have the gold until you shed human blood," said the witch, and she led up to him a child of six, covered with a white sheet, and indicated by a sign that he was to cut off his head.

Peter was stunned. A trifle, indeed, to cut off a man's, or even an innocent child's, head for no reason whatsoever! In wrath he tore off the sheet enveloping the victim's head, and behold! before him stood Ivas. The poor child crossed his little hands, and hung his head. Peter flew at the witch with the knife like a madman, and was on the point of laying hands on her.

"What did you promise for the girl?" thundered Basavriuk; and like a shot he was on his back. The witch stamped her foot; a blue flame flashed from the earth and illuminated all within it. The earth became transparent as if molded of crystal; and all that was within it became visible as if in the palm of the hand. Ducats, precious stones, in chests and pots, were piled in heaps beneath the very spot they stood on. Peter's eyes flashed, his mind grew troubled. . . . He grasped the knife like a madman, and the innocent blood spurted into his eyes. Diabolical laughter resounded on all sides. Misshapen monsters flew past him in flocks. The witch, fastening her hands in the headless trunk like a wolf, drank its blood. His head whirled. Collecting all his strength, he set out to run. Everything grew red before him. The trees seemed steeped in blood, and burned and groaned. The sky glowed and threatened. Burning points, like lightning, flickered before his eyes. Utterly exhausted, he rushed into his miserable hovel and fell to the ground like a log. A deathlike sleep overpowered him.

Two days and two nights did Peter sleep, without once wakening. When he came to himself, on the third day, he looked long at all the corners of his hut; but in vain did he endeavor to recollect what had taken place; his memory was like a miser's pocket from which you cannot entice a quarter of a kopek. Stretching himself, he heard something clash at his feet. He looked; there were two bags of gold. Then only, as if in a dream, he recollected that he had been seeking for treasure, and that something had frightened him in the woods. But at what price he had obtained it, and how, he could by no means tell.

Korzh saw the sacks—and was mollified. "A fine fellow Peter, quite unequalled! yes, and did I not love him? Was he not to me as my own son?" And the old man repeated this fiction until he wept over it himself. Pidorka began to tell Peter how some passing gipsies had stolen Ivas; but he could not even recall him—to such a degree had the Devil's influence darkened his mind. There was no reason for delay. The Pole was dismissed and the wedding-feast prepared; rolls were baked, towels and handkerchiefs embroidered; the young

people were seated at table; the wedding-loaf was cut; guitars, cymbals, pipes, viols sounded, and pleasure was rife.

A wedding in the olden times was not like one of the present day. My grandfather's aunt used to tell how the maidens—in festive head-dresses, of yellow, blue and pink ribbons, above which they bound gold braid; in thin chemisettes embroidered on all the seams with red silk, and strewn with tiny silver flowers; in morocco shoes, with high iron heels—danced the gorlitza as swimmingly as peacocks, and as wildly as the whirlwind; how the youths—with their ship-shaped caps upon their heads, the crowns of gold brocade, and two horns projecting, one in front and another behind, of the very finest black lambskin; in tunics of the finest blue silk with red borders—stepped forward one by one, their arms akimbo in stately form, and executed the hopak; how the lads—in tall Cossack caps, and light cloth gaberdines, girt with silver embroidered belts, their short pipes in their teeth—skipped before them and talked nonsense. Even Korzh as he gazed at the young people could not help getting gay in his old age. Guitar in hand, alternately puffing at his pipe and singing, a brandy-glass upon his head, the graybeard began the national dance amid loud shouts from the merrymakers.

What will not people devise in merry mood? They even began to disguise their faces till they did not look like human beings. On such occasions one would dress himself as a Jew, another as the devil; they would begin by kissing each other, and end by seizing each other by the hair. God be with them! you laughed till you held your sides. They dressed themselves in Turkish and Tatar garments. All upon them glowed like a conflagration, and they began to joke and play pranks. . . .

An amusing thing happened to my grandfather's aunt, who was at this wedding. She was wearing an ample Tatar robe, and, wineglass in hand, was entertaining the company. The Evil One instigated one man to pour vodka over her from behind. Another, at the same moment, evidently not by accident, struck a light, and held it to her. The flame flashed up, and poor aunt, in terror, flung her dress off, before them all. Screams, laughter, jests arose as if at a fair. In a word, the old folks could not recall so merry a wedding.

Pidorka and Peter began to live like a gentleman and lady. There was plenty of everything and everything was fine. . . . But honest folk shook their heads when they marked their way of living. "From the devil no good can come," they unanimously agreed. "Whence, except from the tempter of orthodox people, came this wealth?

Where else could he have got such a lot of gold? Why, on the very day that he got rich, did Basavriuk vanish as if into thin air?"

Say, if you can, that people only imagine things! A month had not passed, and no one would have recognized Peter. He sat in one spot, saying no word to anyone; but continually thinking and seemingly trying to recall something. When Pidorka succeeded in getting him to speak, he appeared to forget himself, and would carry on a conversation, and even grow cheerful; but if he inadvertently glanced at the sacks, "Stop, stop! I have forgotten," he would cry, and again plunge into reverie and strive to recall something. Sometimes when he sat still a long time in one place, it seemed to him as though it were coming, just coming back to mind, but again all would fade away. It seemed as if he was sitting in the tavern: they brought him vodka; vodka stung him; vodka was repulsive to him. Some one came along and struck him on the shoulder; but beyond that everything was veiled in darkness before him. The perspiration would stream down his face, and he would sit exhausted in the same place.

What did not Pidorka do? She consulted the sorceresses; and they poured out fear, and brewed stomachache—but all to no avail. and so the summer passed. Many a Cossack had mowed and reaped; many a Cossack, more enterprising than the rest, had set off upon an expedition. Flocks of ducks were already crowding the marshes, but there was not even a hint of improvement.

It was red upon the steppes. Ricks of grain, like Cossack's caps, dotted the fields here and there. In the highway were to be encountered wagons loaded with brushwood and logs. The ground had become more solid, and in places was touched with frost. Already had the snow begun to fall and the branches of the trees were covered with rime like rabbitskin. Already on frosty days the robin redbreast hopped about on the snow-heaps like a foppish Polish nobleman, and picked out grains of corn; and children, with huge sticks, played hockey upon the ice; while their fathers lay quietly on the stove, issuing forth at intervals with lighted pipes in their lips, to growl in regular fashion, at the orthodox frost or to take the air, and thresh the grain spread out in the barn. At last the snow began to melt, and the ice slipped away: but Peter remained the same; and, the more time went on, the more morose he grew. He sat in the cottage as though nailed to the spot, with the sacks of gold at his feet. He grew averse to look at Pidorka; and still he thought of but one thing, still he tried to recall something, and got angry and ill-tempered because he could not. Often, rising wildly from his seat, he gesticulated

477

violently and fixed his eyes on something as though desirous of catching it: his lips moved as though desirous of uttering some long-forgotten word, but remained speechless. Fury would take possession of him: he would gnaw and bite his hands like a man half crazy, and in his vexation would tear out his hair by the handful, until, calming down, he would relapse into forgetfulness, as it were, and then would again strive to recall the past and be again seized with fury and fresh tortures. What visitation of God was this?

Pidorka was neither dead nor alive. At first it was horrible to her to remain alone with him in the cottage; but, in course of time, the poor woman grew accustomed to her sorrow. But it was impossible to recognize the Pidorka of former days. No blushes, no smiles: she was thin and worn with grief, and had wept her bright eyes away. Once someone who took pity on her advised her to go to the witch who dwelt in the Bear's ravine, and enjoyed the reputation of being able to cure every disease in the world. She determined to try this last remedy: and finally persuaded the old woman to come to her. This was on St. John's Eve, as it chanced. Peter lay insensible on the bench, and did not observe the newcomer. Slowly he rose, and looked about him. Suddenly he trembled in every limb, as though he were on the scaffold: his hair rose upon his head, and he laughed a laugh that thrilled Pidorka's heart with fear.

"I have remembered, remembered!" he cried, in terrible joy; and, swinging a hatchet round his head, he struck at the old woman with all his might. The hatchet penetrated the oaken door nearly four inches. The old woman disappeared; and a child of seven, covered in a white sheet, stood in the middle of the cottage. . . . The sheet flew off. "Ivas!" cried Pidorka, and ran to him; but the apparition became covered from head to foot with blood, and illumined the whole room with red light.

She ran into the passage in her terror, but, on recovering herself a little, wished to help Peter. In vain! The door had slammed to behind her, so that she could not open it. People ran up, and began to knock: they broke in the door, as though there were but one mind among them. The whole cottage was full of smoke; and just in the middle, where Peter had stood, was a heap of ashes from whence smoke was still rising. They flung themselves upon the sacks: only broken potsherds lay there instead of ducats. The Cossacks stood with staring eyes and open mouths, as if rooted to the earth, not daring to move a hair, such terror did this wonder inspire in them.

I do not remember what happened next. Pidorka made a vow to

478

go upon a pilgrimage, collected the property left her by her father, and in a few days it was as if she had never been in the village. Whither she had gone, no one could tell. Officious old women would have despatched her to the same place whither Peter had gone; but a Cossack from Kief reported that he had seen, in a cloister, a nun withered to a mere skeleton who prayed unceasingly. Her fellow-villagers recognized her as Pidorka by the tokens—that no one heard her utter a word; and that she had come on foot, and had brought a frame for the picture of God's mother, set with such brilliant stones that all were dazzled at the sight.

But this was not the end, if you please. On the same day that the Evil One made away with Peter, Basavriuk appeared again; but all fled from him. They knew what sort of a being he was—none else than Satan, who had assumed human form in order to unearth treasures; and, since treasures do not yield to unclean hands, he seduced the young. That same year, all deserted their earthen huts and collected in a village; but even there there was was no peace on account of that accursed Basavriuk.

My late grandfather's aunt said that he was particularly angry with her because she had abandoned her former tavern, and tried with all his might to revenge himself upon her. Once the village elders were assembled in the tavern, and, as the saying goes, were arranging the precedence at the table, in the middle of which was placed a small roasted lamb, shame to say. They chattered about this, that and the other—among the rest about various marvels and strange things. Well, they saw something; it would have been nothing if only one had seen it, but all saw it, and it was this: the sheep raised his head; his goggling eyes became alive and sparkled; and the black, bristling mustache, which appeared for one instant, made a significant gesture at those present. All at once recognized Basavriuk's countenance in the sheep's head; my grandfather's aunt thought it was on the point of asking her for vodka. The worthy elders seized their hats and hastened home.

Another time, the church elder himself, who was fond of an occasional private interview with my grandfather's brandy-glass, had not succeeded in getting to the bottom twice, when he beheld the glass bowing very low to him. "Satan, take you, let us make the sign of the cross over you!" And the same marvel happened to his better half. She had just begun to mix the dough in a huge kneading-trough when suddenly the trough sprang up. "Stop, stop! where are you going?" Putting its arms akimbo, with dignity, it went skipping all

479

about the cottage. You may laugh, but it was no laughing matter to our grandfathers. And in vain did Father Athanasii go through the village with holy water, and chase the devil through all the streets with his brush. My late grandfather's aunt long complained that, as soon as it was dark, some one came knocking at her door and scratching at the wall.

Well! all appears to be quiet now, in the place where our village stands; but it was not so very long ago—my father was still alive—that I remember how a good man could not pass the ruined tavern which a dishonest race had long managed for their own interest. From the smoke-blackened chimneys smoke poured out in a pillar and, rising high in the air, rolled off like a cap, scattering burning coals over the steppe; and Satan (the son of a dog should not be mentioned) sobbed so pitifully in his lair that the startled ravens rose in flocks from the neighboring oak-wood and flew through the air with wild cries.

CARLO GOLDONI

CARLO GOLDONI (Italian, 1707-1793). Reformed native Italian comedy in 18th century by replacing artificial pantomime with realistic character and situations. Author of some 150 plays—many in French, since he spent last 20 years in France. Influenced by Molière and English writers. Works: *The Clever Widow, The Hostess, Pamela, The Beneficent Bear, The Fan.*

THE BENEFICENT BEAR

(Act II, scene 4)

Angelica (aside). What have I to do with Signor Dorval? I can go away.

Dorval. Mademoiselle Angelica!

Ang. Sir?

Dor. Have you seen your uncle? Has he told you nothing?

Ang. I saw him this morning, sir.

Dor. Before he went out of the house?

Ang. Yes, sir.

Dor. Has he returned?

Ang. No, sir.

Dor. (aside). Good. She knows nothing of it.

Ang. Excuse me, sir. Is there anything new in which I am concerned?

480

Dor. Your uncle takes much interest in you.

Ang. (with modesty). He is very kind.

Dor. (seriously). He thinks often of you.

Ang. It is fortunate for me.

Dor. He thinks of marrying you. *(Angelica blushes.)* What say you to it? Would you like to be married?

Ang. I depend on my uncle.

Dor. Shall I say anything more to you on the subject?

Ang. (with a little curiosity). But—as you please, sir.

Dor. The choice of a husband is already made.

Ang. (aside). O heavens! I tremble.

Dor. (aside). She seems to be pleased.

Ang. (trembling). Sir, I am curious to know—

Dor. What, Mademoiselle?

Ang. Do you know who is intended for me?

Dor. Yes, and you know him too.

Ang. (with joy). I know him too?

Dor. Certainly, you know him.

Ang. May I, sir, have the boldness—

Dor. Speak, Mademoiselle.

Ang. To ask you the name of the young man?

Dor. The name of the young man?

Ang. Yes, if you know him.

Dor. Suppose he were not so young?

Ang. (aside, with agitation). Good heavens!

Dor. You are sensible—you depend on your uncle—

Ang. (trembling). Do you think, sir, my uncle would sacrifice me?

Dor. What do you mean by sacrificing you?

Ang. Mean—without the consent of my heart. My uncle is so good—but who could have advised him—who could have proposed this match? *(With temper.)*

Dor. (a little hurt.) But this match—Mademoiselle—suppose it were I.

Ang. (with joy). You, sir? Heaven grant it!

Dor. (pleased). Heaven grant it!

Ang. Yes, I know you; I know you are reasonable. You are sensible; I can trust you. If you have given my uncle this advice, if you have proposed this match, I hope you will now find some means of making him change his plan.

481

Dor. (aside). Eh! this is not so bad. *(To Angelica.)* Mademoiselle—

Ang. (distressed). Signor?

Dor. (with feeling). Is your heart engaged?

Ang. Ah, sir—

Dor. I understand you.

Ang. Have pity on me!

Dor. (aside). I said so, I foresaw right; it is fortunate for me I am not in love—yet I began to perceive some little symptoms of it.

Ang. But you do not tell me, sir.

Dor. But, Mademoiselle—

Ang. You have perhaps some particular interest in the person they wish me to marry?

Dor. A little.

Ang. I tell you I shall hate him.

Dor. (aside). Poor girl! I am pleased with her sincerity.

Ang. Come, have compassion; be generous.

Dor. Yes, I will be so, I promise you; I will speak to your uncle in your favor, and will do all I can to make you happy.

Ang. (with joy and transport). Oh, how dear a man you are! You are my benefactor, my father. *(Takes his hand.)*

Dor. My dear girl!

(Enter Geronte.)

Geronte (with animation). Excellent, excellent! Courage, my children, I am delighted with you. *(Angelica retires, mortified; Dorval smiles.)* How! does my presence alarm you? I do not condemn this proper show of affection. You have done well, Dorval, to inform her. Come, my niece, embrace your future husband.

Ang. (in consternation). What do I hear?

Dor. (aside and smiling). Now I am unmasked.

Ger. (to Angelica, with warmth). What scene is this? Your modesty is misplaced. When I am not present, you are near enough to each other; when I come in, you go far apart. Come here. *(To Dorval with anger.)* And do you too come here.

Dor. (laughing). Softly, my friend.

Ger. Why do you laugh? Do you feel your happiness? I am very willing you should laugh, but do not put me in a passion; do you hear, you laughing gentleman? Come here and listen to me.

Dor. But listen yourself.

482

Ger. (to Angelica, and endeavoring to take her hand). Come near, both of you.

Ang. (weeping). My uncle!

Ger. Weeping! What's the matter, my child? I believe you are making a jest of me. *(Takes her hand, and draws her forward; then turns to Dorval.)* You shall escape me no more.

Dor. At least let me speak.

Ger. No, no!

Ang. My dear uncle—

Ger. (with warmth). No, no. *(He becomes serious.)* I have been to my notary's, and have arranged everything; he has taken a note of it in my presence, and will soon bring the contract here for us to subscribe.

Dor. But will you listen to me?

Ger. No, no. As to her fortune, my brother had the weakness to leave it in the hands of his son; this will no doubt cause some obstacle on his part, but it will not embarrass me. Every one who has transactions with him suffers. The fortune cannot be lost, and in any event I will be responsible for it.

Ang. (aside). I can bear this no longer.

Dor. (embarrassed). All proceeds well, but—

Ger. But what?

Dor. The young lady may have something to say in this matter. *(Looking at Angelica.)*

Ang. (hastily and trembling). I, sir?

Ger. I should like to know if she can say anything against what I do, what I order, and what I wish. My wishes, my orders, and what I do, are all for her good. Do you understand me?

Dor. Then I must speak myself.

Ger. What have you to say?

Dor. That I am very sorry, but this marriage cannot take place.

Ger. Not take place! *(Angelica retreats frightened; Dorval steps back.)* *(To Dorval.)* You have given me your word of honor.

Dor. Yes, on condition—

Ger. (turning to Angelica). It must then be this impertinent. If I could believe it! if I had any reason to suspect it! *(Threatens her.)*

Dor. (seriously). No, sir, you are mistaken.

Ger. (to Dorval. Angelica makes her escape). It is you, then, who refuse? So you abuse my friendship and affection for you!

Dor. (raising his voice). But hear reason—

Ger. What reason? what reason? There is no reason. I am a

man of honor, and if you are so, too, it shall be done at once. *(Turning round, he calls)* Angelica!

Dor. What possesses the man? He will resort to violence on the spot. *(Runs off.)*

Ger. (alone). Where is she gone? Angelica! Hallo! who's there? Piccardo! Martuccia! Pietro! Cortese!—But I'll find her. It is you I want. *(Turns round and, not seeing Dorval, remains motionless.)* What! he treat me so! *(Calls.)* Dorval! my friend! Dorval—Dorval! my friend! Oh, shameful—ungrateful! Hallo! Is no one there? Piccardo!

(Enters Piccardo.)

Piccardo. Here, sir.

Ger. You rascal! Why don't you answer?

Pic. Pardon me, sir, here I am.

Ger. Shameful! I called you ten times.

Pic. I am sorry, but—

Ger. Ten times! It is scandaious.

Pic. (aside and angry). He is in a fury now.

Ger. Have you seen Dorval?

Pic. Yes, sir.

Ger. Where is he?

Pic. He is gone.

Ger. How is he gone?

Pic. (roughly). He is gone as other people go.

Ger. Ah, insolent! do you answer your master in this manner? *(Threatens him.)*

Pic. (very angrily). Give me my discharge, sir.

Ger. Your discharge—worthless fellow! *(Makes him retreat. Piccardo falls between the chair and the table. Geronte runs and helps him up.)*

Pic. Oh! *(He shows much pain.)*

Ger. Are you hurt? Are you hurt?

Pic. Very much hurt; you have crippled me.

Ger. Oh, I am sorry! Can you walk?

Pic. (still angry). I believe so, sir. *(He tries, and walks badly.)*

Ger. (sharply). Go on.

Pic. Do you drive me away, sir?

Ger. (warmly). No. Go to your wife's house, that you may be taken care of. *(Pulls out his purse and offers him money.)* Take this to get cured.

Pic. (aside, with tenderness). What a master!

484

Ger. Take it. *(Giving him money.)*

Pic. (with modesty). No, sir, I hope it will be nothing.

Ger. Take it, I tell you.

Pic. (Still refusing it). Sir—

Ger. (very warmly). What! you refuse my money Do you refuse it from pride, or spite, or hatred? Do you believe I did it on purpose? Take this money. Take it. Come, don't put me in a passion.

Pic. Do not get angry, sir. I thank you for all your kindness. *(Takes the money.)*

Ger. Go quickly.

Pic. Yes, sir. *(Walks badly.)*

Ger. Go slowly.

Pic. Yes, sir.

Ger. Wait, wait; take my cane.

Pic. Sir—

Ger. Take it, I tell you! I wish you to do it.

Pic. (takes the cane). What goodness!

(Exit.)

(Enter Martuccia.)

Ger. It is the first time in my life that—Plague on my temper! *(Taking long strides.)* It is Dorval who put me in a passion.

Martuccia. Do you wish to dine, sir?

Ger. May the devil take you! *(Runs out and shuts himself in his room.)*

Mar. Well, well! He is in a rage: I can do nothing for Angelica to-day; Valerio can go away.

OLIVER GOLDSMITH

OLIVER GOLDSMITH (English, 1728-1774). Forerunner of the English Romantic School. From wealthy family, tried numerous professions before settling on literature. Produced classics in three fields: *The Deserted Village* (romantic poem), *The Vicar of Wakefield* (sentimental-realistic novel), *She Stoops to Conquer* (comedy drama). Also short stories of merit.

THE DISABLED SOLDIER

No OBSERVATION is more common, and at the same time more true, than that one half of the world are ignorant how the other half lives. The misfortunes of the great are held up to engage our atten-

485

tion; are enlarged upon in tones of declamation; and the world is called upon to gaze at the noble sufferers: the great, under the pressure of calamity, are conscious of several others sympathizing with their distress; and have, at once, the comfort of admiration and pity.

There is nothing magnanimous in bearing misfortunes with fortitude, when the whole world is looking on: men in such circumstances will act bravely even from motives of vanity: but he who, in the vale of obscurity, can brave adversity; who without friends to encourage, acquaintances to pity, or even without hope to alleviate his misfortunes, can behave with tranquillity and indifference, is truly great: whether peasant or courtier, he deserves admiration, and should be held up for our imitation and respect.

While the slightest inconveniences of the great are magnified into calamities; while tragedy mouths out their sufferings in all the strains of eloquence, the miseries of the poor are entirely disregarded; and yet some of the lower ranks of people undergo more real hardships in one day, than those of a more exalted station suffer in their whole lives. It is inconceivable what difficulties the meanest of our common sailors and soldiers endure without murmuring or regret; without passionately declaiming against providence, or calling their fellows to be gazers on their intrepidity. Every day is to them a day of misery, and yet they entertain their hard fate without repining.

With what indignation do I hear an Ovid, a Cicero, or a Rabutin complain of their misfortunes and hardships, whose greatest calamity was that of being unable to visit a certain spot of earth, to which they had foolishly attached an idea of happiness. Their distresses were pleasures, compared to what many of the adventuring poor every day endure without murmuring. They ate, drank, and slept; they had slaves to attend them, and were sure of subsistence for life; while many of their fellow creatures are obliged to wander without a friend to comfort or assist them, and even without shelter from the severity of the season.

I have been led into these reflections from accidentally meeting, some days ago, a poor fellow, whom I knew when a boy, dressed in a sailor's jacket, and begging at one of the outlets of the town, with a wooden leg. I knew him to have been honest and industrious when in the country, and was curious to learn what had reduced him to his present situation. Wherefore, after giving him what I thought proper, I desired to know the history of his life and misfortunes, and the manner in which he was reduced to his present distress. The

486

disabled soldier, for such he was, though dressed in a sailor's habit, scratching his head, and leaning on his crutch, put himself into an attitude to comply with my request, and gave me his history as follows:

"As for my misfortunes, master, I can't pretend to have gone through any more than other folks; for, except the loss of my limb, and my being obliged to beg, I don't know any reason, thank Heaven, that I have to complain. There is Bill Tibbs, of our regiment, he has lost both his legs, and an eye to boot; but, thank Heaven, it is not so bad with me yet.

"I was born in Shropshire; my father was a laborer, and died when I was five years old, so I was put upon the parish. As he had been a wandering sort of a man, the parishioners were not able to tell to what parish I belonged, or where I was born, so they sent me to another parish, and that parish sent me to a third. I thought in my heart, they kept sending me about so long, that they would not let me be born in any parish at all; but at last, however, they fixed me. I had some disposition to be a scholar, and was resolved at least to know my letters: but the master of the workhouse put me to business as soon as I was able to handle a mallet; and here I lived an easy kind of life for five years. I only wrought ten hours in the day, and had my meat and drink provided for my labor. It is true, I was not suffered to stir out of the house, for fear, as they said, I should run away; but what of that? I had the liberty of the whole house, and the yard before the door, and that was enough for me. I was then bound out to a farmer, where I was up both early and late; but I ate and drank well; and liked my business well enough, till he died, when I was obliged to provide for myself; so I resolved to go seek my fortune.

"In this manner I went from town to town, worked when I could get employment, and starved when I could get none; when, happening one day to go through a field belonging to a justice of peace, I spied a hare crossing the path just before me; and I believe the devil put it into my head to fling my stick at it. Well, what will you have on't? I killed the hare, and was bringing it away, when the justice himself met me; he called me a poacher and a villain, and collaring me, desired I would give an account of myself. I fell upon my knees, begged his worship's pardon, and began to give a full account of all that I knew of my breed, seed, and generation; but though I gave a very true account, the justice said I could give no account; so I was indicted at the sessions, found guilty of being

poor, and sent up to London to Newgate, in order to be transported as a vagabond.

"People may say this and that of being in jail, for my part, I found Newgate as agreeable a place as ever I was in in all my life. I had my belly full of eat and drink, and did no work at all. This kind of life was too good to last forever; so I was taken out of prison, after five months, put on board of ship, and sent off, with two hundred more, to the plantations. We had but an indifferent passage, for being all confined in the hold, more than a hundred of our people died for want of sweet air; and those that remained were sickly enough, God knows. When we came ashore we were sold to the planters, and I was bound for seven years more. As I was no scholar, for I did not know my letters, I was obliged to work among the negroes; and I served out my time, as in duty bound to do.

"When my time was expired, I worked my passage home, and glad I was to see old England again, because I loved my country. I was afraid, however, that I should be indicted for a vagabond once more, so did not much care to go down into the country, but kept about the town, and did little jobs when I could get them.

"I was very happy in this manner for some time till one evening, coming home from work, two men knocked me down, and then desired me to stand. They belonged to a press-gang. I was carried before the justice, and as I could give no account of myself, I had my choice left, whether to go on board a man-of-war, or list for a soldier. I chose the latter, and in this post of a gentleman, I served two campaigns in Flanders, was at the battles of Val and Fontenoy, and received but one wound through the breast here; but the doctor of our regiment soon made me well again.

"When the peace came on I was discharged; and as I could not work, because my wound was sometimes troublesome, I listed for a landman in the East India Company's service. I have fought the French in six pitched batles; and I verily believe that if I could read or write, our captain would have made me a corporal. But it was not my good fortune to have any promotion, for I soon fell sick, and so got leave to return home again with forty pounds in my pocket. This was at the beginning of the present war, and I hoped to be set on shore, and to have the pleasure of spending my money; but the Government wanted men, and so I was pressed for a sailor, before ever I could set a foot on shore.

"The boatswain found me, as he said, an obstinate fellow: he swore he knew that I understood my business well, but that I

shammed Abraham, to be idle; but God knows, I knew nothing of sea-business, and he beat me without considering what he was about. I had still, however, my forty pounds, and that was some comfort to me under every beating; and the money I might have had to this day, but that our ship was taken by the French, and so I lost all.

"Our crew was carried into Brest, and many of them died, because they were not used to live in a jail; but, for my part, it was nothing to me, for I was seasoned. One night, as I was asleep on the bed of boards, with a warm blanket about me, for I always loved to lie well, I was awakened by the boatswain, who had a dark lantern in his hands. 'Jack,' says he to me 'will you knock out the French sentry's brains?' 'I don't care,' says I, striving to keep myself awake, 'if I lend a hand.' 'Then, follow me,' says he, 'and I hope we shall do business.' So up I got, and tied my blanket, which was all the clothes I had, about my middle; and went with him to fight the Frenchman. I hate the French because they are all slaves, and wear wooden shoes.

"Though we had no arms, one Englishman is able to beat five French at any time; so we went down to the door where both the sentries were posted, and rushing upon them, seized their arms in a moment, and knocked them down. From thence nine of us ran together to the quay, and seizing the first boat we met, got out of the harbor and put to sea. We had not been here three days before we were taken up by the Dorset privateer, who were glad of so many good hands; and we consented to run our chance. However, we had not as much luck as we expected. In three days we fell in with the *Pompadour* privateer of forty guns, while we had but twenty-three, so to it we went, yard-arm and yard-arm. The fight lasted three hours, and I verily believe we should have taken the Frenchman, had we but had some men left behind; but unfortunately we lost all our men just as we were going to get the victory.

"I was once more in the power of the French, and I believe it would have gone hard with me had I been brought back to Brest; but by good fortune we were retaken by the *Viper*. I had almost forgotten to tell you that in that engagement I was wounded in two places: I lost four fingers off the left hand, and my leg was shot off. If I had the good fortune to have lost my leg and use of my hand on board a king's ship, and not aboard a privateer, I should have been entitled to clothing and maintenance during the rest of my life; but that was not my chance: one man is born with a silver spoon in his mouth, and another with a wooden ladle. However, blessed be God, I enjoy

good health, and will forever love liberty and old England. Liberty, property, and old England, forever, huzza!"

Thus saying, he limped off, leaving me in admiration at his intrepidity and content; nor could I avoid acknowledging that an habitual acquaintance with misery serves better than philosophy to teach us to despise it.

IVAN ALEXANDROVICH GONCHAROV

IVAN ALEXANDROVICH GONCHAROV (Russian, 1812-1891). One of foremost of the great roll of Russian novelists of 19th century. Best-known to Western readers for *Oblomof*, a realistic novel about Russia's so-called "superfluous man."

THE EVOLUTION OF OBLOMOF

ILYA ILYICH OBLOMOF, nobleman by birth, college secretary by occupation, was living for the twelfth consecutive year at Petersburg.

At first, during his parents' lifetime, he lived in rather close quarters, occupying two rooms, and contenting himself with the one servant, Zakhar, brought with him from the country. But after the death of his father and mother he became the sole possessor of three hundred and fifty souls, which fell to him as a legacy in one of the remote provinces, almost in Asia. Instead of five thousand he received now from seven to ten thousand paper rubles income, and his living too assumed another and more generous scale. He rented larger apartments, added a cook to his household, and bought a span of horses. At that time he was still young, and if it cannot be said that he was lively, at any rate he was livelier than now. He still had a thousand different aspirations, was always hoping for something, and expecting much of fate as well as of himself. He was preparing himself for a career; above all, of course, for a role in the government service, which was the very object of his coming to Petersburg. Afterwards he thought, too, of a rôle in society. Finally, in a distant perspective, in the turning of youth to mature age, domestic happiness gleamed and smiled in fancy. But day after day passed, and years followed years; the down on his chin turned to a rough beard, the beaming eyes faded to two dull spots, the shape

grew stout, the hair began to fall out pitilessly;—it struck thirty, but he had not advanced a step on any career, and still stood at the threshold of his arena where he was ten years before.

Life, to him, was divided into halves: one of which consisted of work and weariness—which with him were synonymous; the other of rest and quiet enjoyment. That is why his principal career, the government service, jarred on him most unpleasantly from the first.

Brought up in a remote provincial corner, amidst the gentle and hearty native manners and customs, passing in the course of twenty years from embrace to embrace of relatives, friends, and acquaintances, he had become so thoroughly imbued with the family principle that even his future service appeared to him a sort of domestic occupation,—like that, for example, of making entries in a book of receipts and expenditures, as his father used to. He imagined that the officials of a place formed a small, harmonious family among themselves, unceasingly solicitous for their mutual repose and contentment; that invariable attendance at the office was not an obligatory custom, which had to be observed every day; and that wetness, heat, or merely indisposition would always serve as sufficient and legitimate excuses for neglect of his work. But how distressed he was when he saw that nothing short of an earthquake would entitle a well man to remain away from his office, and by ill luck, earthquakes are unknown in Petersburg; a flood, it is true, might serve equally well as a hindrance, but floods seldom occur either. Still more was Oblomof startled when packets gleamed before his eyes with the superscription "important" and "very urgent"; when he was required to make various researches and extracts, to rummage among documents, and to write reports two fingers thick, which are humorously called "memoranda." Besides, everything was wanted in a hurry. Everybody was hurrying some way or other, and no one kept still at anything; a man scarcely got one thing out of his hands when he eagerly seized something else, as if his whole existence were in that; this finished, he forgot it and flew at a third—there was never once an end to it. Once or twice he was wakened in the night and obliged to write "memoranda"; sometimes he would be called away from company by a courier—always on account of these "memoranda": all of which alarmed him and wearied him greatly. "When am I to live? *live?*" he repeated sorrowfully.

He had been told at home that the chief was the father of his subordinates, and so he formed the pleasantest and fondest idea of this person. He pictured him somewhat in the light of a second

491

father, who breathed only to recompense his subordinates one after another, deservedly or undeservedly, and to provide for not only their needs but their pleasures. Ilya Ilyich thought that a chief was so much concerned about the welfare of a subordinate that he would anxiously inquire how he had passed the night, why his eyes looked heavy, and didn't his head ache? But he was cruelly unde-ceived the first day of his service. With the arrival of the chief began scurrying and confusion; all were upset, all hustled each other about; many rearranged their toilet; fearing that as they were they didn't look fine enough to show themselves to the chief. This, as Oblomof noticed later, was because there are some chiefs who read in the faces confronting them, of underlings almost out of their wits, not only respect for them, but zeal as well, and often fitness for the service.

Ilya Ilyich did not need to stand in such fear of his own chief, a kind and chatty man, who never harmed any one; his clerks were as content as could be, and asked no better. No one ever heard him say an unpleasant word, or shout or storm; and he never ordered anything done, but always begged it. Work to do—he begged you; to dine with him—he begged you; to put yourself under arrest —he begged you. He never called any one "thou," but every one "you" whether a single official or all in a body. Yet his subordinates were inexplicably timid in the chief's presence: they answered his friendly questions not with their own voice, but with a strangely different one, which they never used in speaking with others. Ilya Ilyich, too, became suddenly afraid, without himself knowing why, when his superior entered the room, and his voice would fail and give place to an unpleasant falsetto as soon as the chief started to speak with him. Ilya Ilyich suffered from fear and weariness in the service, even under this good, indulgent chief. God knows what would have become of him if he had fallen under a stern, exacting one. Oblomof had to serve two years; possibly he would have held out a third also, till he received a title, but a peculiar accident oc-casioned his quitting the service earlier.

He once sent some important papers to Archangel instead of to Astrakhan. The matter came to light; the culprit was sought for. All the others waited with curiosity for the chief to call Oblomof and coldly and calmly inquire, "Was it you who sent these papers to Astrakhan?" and all were in doubt with what voice Ilya Ilyich would reply. Some thought he would not answer at all—would not have the power. Glancing at the others, Ilya Ilyich was afraid too, though

492

he knew as well as the rest that the chief would confine himself to a reproof. But his own conscience was far more severe than any reproach. Oblomof did not wait for the deserved punishment; he went home and sent a medical certificate. In this certificate it was recited that "I, the subscriber, testify, over my seal, that the college secretary Ilya Oblomof is attacked by hypertrophy of the heart, with dilitation of the left ventricle" (*hypertrophia cordis cum dilatatione ejus ventriculi sinistri*), "and at the same time by a chronic pain in the liver" (*hepatitis*) "which threatens development dangerous to the health and life of the patient, which ailments forbid his daily attendance at the office. Therefore, to prevent a repetition and aggravation of these painful attacks, I deem it necessary for Mr. Oblomof to discontinue for a time his attendance at the office, and I prescribe generally the abstention from mental occupation and every kind of activity."

But this availed for a short time only: he would have to get well—and there again in perspective was the daily round of duty. Oblomof could not endure it, and tendered his resignation. Thus ended—and never to be resumed—his official employment.

His role in society was more successful. In the first years of his residence in Petersburg, in his fresh youthful days, his calm features were oftener animated, his eyes shone for a long period with a vital fire, and beamed forth rays of light, of hope, and of strength. He had emotions like every one else, hoped, found delight in trivialities, and suffered because of bagatelles. But all that was long ago, at that tender time when man fancies every other man a sincere friend, falls in love with almost every woman, and is prepared to offer each his hand and his heart,—which often results in anguish to others for the rest of their lives. In these happy days there likewise fell to Ilya Ilyich's share, from the host of pretty women, not a few tender, velvety, even passionate glances, an ocean of smiles that promised much, two or three unprivileged kisses, and still more of affectionate hand-pressures actually painful even to tears.

Still, he never fell a victim to the fair sex, never was its slave, nor even a very assiduous adorer, for the very reason that association with women brings great disquietude. Oblomof generally confined himself to adoring them afar at a respectful distance. Seldom did chance bring him to that point in his companionship with a woman where he could glow for some days and think himself beloved. So his love affairs never went the length of a romance; they stopped at the beginning, and from innocence, simplicity, and purity he never

yielded to love for some boarding-school girl in her teens. . . .
Immediately after the overseer's first letter, about unpaid rents and
bad harvests, he first replaced his friend the cook by a woman cook,
then sold his horses, and finally discharged his other "friends."
Scarcely anything took him out of doors, and he shut himself up in
his lodgings closer and more immovably every day.

From the first he found it hard to remain dressed all day; then he
became too lazy to dine out, except with intimate friends—preferably
in bachelor households where one could take off his cravat, unbutton
his waistcoat, "lop out," or even sleep an hour or so. Soon even these
evening calls wearied him; for you had to put on a coat and shave
every day. He had read somewhere that only the morning exhalations
were wholesome, while those of the evening were injurious; and he
began to be afraid of dampness. Despite all these whims, his friend
Stoltz succeeded in dragging him out into the world; but Stoltz was
often absent from Petersburg, in Moscow, Nijni, the Crimea, even
foreign lands, and without him Oblomof sank clean to the ears again
in solitude and isolation, out of which only something unusual could
bring him, something out of the course of the every-day incidents of
life. Nothing of the sort happened, however, nor could be forecast in
the future.

Added to all this, there returned to him with age a certain childish
timidity, an apprehension of danger and misfortune in whatever lay
without the sphere of his daily existence—the result of estrangement
from the varieties of external phenomena. He was not frightened,
for example, by a crack in the ceiling of his bedroom: he was used
to that. No more did it occur to him that the air in a room always
closed, and the constant sitting in seclusion, were more injurious to
the health than evening damp, and that overfilling the stomach daily
is a kind of gradual suicide; but he was wonted to these and did not
fear them. He was not accustomed to movement, to life, to throngs
and confusion. In a large crowd he was stifled; he got into a boat
with but uncertain hope of reaching the other shore; he rode in a
carriage expecting a runaway and smash-up. Or else a nervous fear
overcame him: he was afraid of the silence around him—or simply,
without himself knowing why, chills would run over his body. He
often glanced fearfully sidewise at a dark corner, expecting his
imagination to play him a trick and conjure up some supernatural
vision.

So played itself out his rôle in society. Slothfully he let go all
youthful hopes, which disappointed him or which he disappointed;

494

all those tenderly sad, luminous memories with which many a heart throbs even in declining years.

What then did he do at home? Read, write, study? Yes, if a book or a newspaper fell into his hands, he set out to read it. Did he chance to hear of a notable work, he was seized with a desire to become acquainted with it; he hunted about, asked for the book, and if it were brought soon, threw himself on it, and an idea of the subject began to take shape in his mind—another page and he would have grasped it: but look, he is lying down already, gazing apathetically at the ceiling, the book beside him, unread, uncomprehended. His ardor cooled even quicker than it kindled; and he never returned to the forsaken book. His head was a confused magazine of dead facts, persons, epochs, figures, religions, unrelated political economics or mathematics or other sciences, problems, and the like. It was a library composed solely of odd volumes in all branches of learning.

Study affected Ilya Ilyich curiously. For him, between learning and life there was an absolute gulf, which he made no attempt to cross. For him life was life and science was science. He studied all existent and long non-existent laws, he even went through a course in practical law procedure: then when a theft in his house made it necessary to compose a letter to the police, took a sheet of paper and a pen, thought and thought, and finally sent for the public scrivener. The accounts of the estate were kept by the overseer. "What has science to do with that!" he argued, with dubitation.

He returned to his solitude without sufficient weight of knowledge to give direction to the thoughts that wandered at will in his head or slumbered in idleness. What then did he do? He kept on tracing the pattern of his own life. In it he found, not without reason, more philosophy and poetry than could be exhausted, even without books or learning. Having deserted the service and society, he began to solve the problem of his existence by other means. He reflected upon his destiny, and finally discovered that the sphere of his activity and profession reposed in himself. He realized that the welfare of the family and the care of the property fell to his share. Up to this time he had no systematic knowledge of his own affairs, which Stoltz sometimes attended to in his stead; he did not know his exact receipts and expenditures, struck no balance sheet—nothing.

The senior Oblomof had transmitted the estate to his son just as he received it from his father. Though he spent his whole life in the country, he did not elaborate nor break his head over innovations, as men do nowadays; how to discover new sources of productivity

495

for the soil, or increase and reënforce the old, and so on. As and wherewith the fields had been sown by his grandfather, and such as were then the methods of marketing the crops, such they remained under him. The old man was wont to be delighted if a good harvest or advanced prices gave him an income larger than last year's: he called that a blessing of God. But he disliked to scheme and strive for a harvest of money. "God gives, let us be satisfied," he said.

Ilya Ilyich pinned his faith no longer to father or grandfather. He had studied and lived in the world: it all suggested to him a variety of ideas strange till then. He understood that not only i gain no sin, but that it is every citizen's duty to contribute by honest work to the general well-being. Thus it was that the largest part of the life-design he traced in his solitude was devoted to a new and fresh plan, in accordance with the needs of the time, for administering his property and managing his peasants. The fundamental idea of the plan, the arrangement, the principal parts—all have long been ready in his head; there remain now only details, estimates, and figures. He has worked untiringly for several years on this plan; he thinks about it and ponders it, both afoot and in bed, at home as well as in company; now filling out, now changing various portions, now recalling to mind some point conceived yesterday and forgotten during the night; and sometimes, swift as lightning, a new, unexpected idea flashes upon him and begins to seethe in his brain—the work is going on swimmingly. He is not petty executive of others' ready-made notions: himself is the creator and himself the executor of his ideas. As soon as he rises from bed in the morning, after his tea he throws himself at once on the sofa, rests his head in his hands and meditates, without sparing his strength, till his head at length is fatigued by the arduous labor, and his conscience says: "Enough done to-day for the public good."

Free from business cares, Oblomof loved to retire into himself and live in a self-created world. He was accessible to the joy of lofty purpose; he was no stranger to the general interests of humanity. Many a time in the depth of his soul he wept bitterly over the miseries of mankind; he experienced mysterious nameless suffering and sorrow, and vague longing for a distant land, probably for that world where his teacher, Stoltz, had often led him;—and sweet tears trickled down his cheeks. Sometimes, too, he is filled with contempt for human vices, for the falsehood, the calumny, the evil that floods the world, and he is inflamed with a desire to show mankind his hurts: suddenly there glow within him ideas that come and g·

in his mind, like waves on the sea, then grow to purposes, setting all his blood on fire; the purposes are transformed to endeavor; impelled by a moral force, he changes his attitude twice or thrice in a minute; with sparkling eyes he half rises in his bed, stretches forth his hand and casts an inspired look about him. Now, now the endeavor is about to be realized, turn into a fact—and then, great Heaven! what miracles, what beneficial results might not be expected from an effort so sublime!—But see, the morning passes, the day is already inclining to its end, and with it Oblomof's wearied strength inclines to repose; the storms and tempests in his soul abate, his head cools from thought, the blood courses more slowly in his veins. Oblomof, tranquil and pensive, stretches himself on his back, and casting a mournful glance toward the window, with melancholy eyes follows the sun as it sinks majestically behind some four-story house. How many times he has thus followed the setting sun!

In the morning life returns; once more emotions and illusions. He often loves to fancy himself some invincible general, before whom not only Napoleon but Yeruslan Lazarevich are as nothing; he pictures a war and its causes: in his mind, for example, the people of Africa hurl themselves on Europe; or he organizes new crusades, makes war, decides the destinies of nations, destroys cities, spares, puts to death, does deeds of kindness and magnanimity. Or else he chooses the career of the thinker, or the great artist: all do him honor; he reaps laurels; the crowd follows him, crying, "There he is, there he is, there goes Oblomof, our celebrated Ilya Ilyich!"

In bitter moments he is tormented by cares, turns from one side to the other, lies face down, sometimes even completely loses himself; then he rises from bed, falls on his knees, and begins to pray warmly, fervently, beseeching Heaven to avert from him some threatening storm. Then, having shifted the care of his fate on Heaven, he becomes calm and indifferent toward everything in the world, and the storm is wholly forgotten.

Thus he puts his moral strength in play; thus he often agitates himself for entire days, and only awakes with a deep sigh from enchanting visions or painful anxieties when the day is declining, and the great sphere of the sun begins to descend in glory behind the four-story house. Then he follows it again with a dreamy look and a melancholy smile, and rests peacefully from his emotions.

497

MAXIM GORKY

MAXIM GORKY (Alexei Maximovich Peshkov, Russian, 1868-1936). Pioneer
of Russian Revolution in his magnificent, socially-conscious stories. Orphaned
when a child, spent years wandering through Russia. Short stories notable
for compassionate treatment of outcasts. Famous also for uncompromising
realistic drama, *The Lower Depths*. Autobiographical works: *My Childhood*,
My University Days, *My Mother*. Successfully hid bitter disappointment with
Stalinist dictatorship, but died under mysterious circumstances.

ONE AUTUMN NIGHT

ONCE in the autumn I happened to be in a very unpleasant and
inconvenient position. In the town where I had just arrived and
where I knew not a soul, I found myself without a farthing in my
pocket and without a night's lodging.

Having sold during the first few days every part of my costume
without which it was still possible to go about, I passed from the
town into the quarter called "Yste," where were the steamship
wharves—a quarter which during the navigation season fermented
with boisterous, laborous life, but now was silent and deserted, for
we were in the last days of October.

Dragging my feet along the moist sand, and obstinately scrutiniz-
ing it with the desire to discover in it any sort of fragment of food,
I wandered alone among the deserted buildings and warehouses,
and thought how good it would be to get a full meal.

In our present state of culture hunger of the mind is more quickly
satisfied than hunger of the body. You wander about the streets,
you are surrounded by buildings not bad-looking from the outside
and—you may safely say it—not so badly furnished inside, and
the sight of them may excite within you stimulating ideas about
architecture, hygiene, and many other wise and high-flying subjects.
You may meet warmly and neatly dressed folks—all very polite, and
turning away from you tactfully, not wishing offensively to notice the
lamentable fact of your existence. Well, well, the mind of a hungry
man is always better nourished and healthier that the mind of the
well-fed man; and there you have a situation from which you may
draw a very ingenious conclusion in favor of the ill fed.

The evening was approaching, the rain was falling, and the wind blew violently from the north. It whistled in the empty booths and shops, blew into the plastered window-panes of the taverns, and whipped into foam the wavelets of the river which splashed noisily on the sandy shore, casting high their white crests, racing one after another into the dim distance, and leaping impetuously over one another's shoulders. It seemed as if the river felt the proximity of winter, and was running at random away from the fetters of ice which the north wind might well have flung upon her that very night. The sky was heavy and dark; down from it swept incessantly scarcely visible drops of rain, and the melancholy elegy in nature all around me was emphasized by a couple of battered and mis-shapen willow-trees and a boat, bottom upwards, that was fastened to their roots.

The overturned canoe with its battered keel and the miserable old trees rifled by the cold wind—everything around me was bankrupt, barren, and dead, and the sky flowed with undryable tears. . . . Everything around was waste and gloomy . . . it seemed as if everything were dead, leaving me alone among the living, and for me also a cold death waited.

I was then eighteen years old—a good time!

I walked and walked along the cold wet sand, making my chattering teeth warble in honor of cold and hunger, when suddenly, as I was carefully searching for something to eat behind one of the empty crates, I perceived behind it, crouching on the ground, a figure in woman's clothes dank with the rain and clinging fast to her stooping shoulders. Standing above her, I watched to see what she was doing. It appeared that she was digging a trench in the sand with her hands—digging away under one of the crates.

"Why are you doing that?" I asked, crouching down on my heels quite close to her.

She gave a little scream and was quickly on her legs again. Now that she stood there staring at me, with her wide-open gray eyes full of terror, I perceived that it was a girl of my own age, with a very pleasant face embellished unfortunately by three large blue marks. This spoilt her, although these blue marks had been distributed with a remarkable sense of proportion, one at a time, and all were of equal size—two under the eyes, and one a little bigger on the forehead just over the bridge of the nose. This symmetry was evidently the work of an artist well inured to the business of spoiling the human physiognomy.

The girl looked at me, and the terror in her eyes gradually died out. . . . She shook the sand from her hands, adjusted her cotton head-gear, cowered down, and said:

"I suppose you, too, want something to eat? Dig away then! My hands are tired. Over there"—she nodded her head in the direction of a booth—"there is bread for certain . . . and sausages too. . . . That booth is still carrying on business."

I began to dig. She, after waiting a little and looking at me, sat down beside me and began to help me.

We worked in silence. I cannot say now whether I thought at that moment of the criminal code, of morality, of proprietorship, and all the other things about which, in the opinion of many experienced persons, one ought to think every moment of one's life. Wishing to keep as close to the truth as possible, I must confess that apparently I was so deeply engaged in digging under the crate that I completely forgot about everything else except one thing: What could be inside that crate?

The evening drew on. The gray, mouldy, cold fog grew thicker and thicker around us. The waves roared with a hollower sound than before, and the rain pattered down on the boards of that crate more loudly and more frequently. Somewhere or other the night-watchman began springing his rattle.

"Has it got a bottom or not?" softly inquired my assistant. I did not understand what she was talking about, and kept silence.

"I say, has the crate got a bottom? If it has we shall try in vain to break into it. Here we are digging a trench, and we may, after all come upon nothing but solid boards. How shall we take them off? Better smash the lock; it is a wretched lock."

Good ideas rarely visit the heads of women, but as you see, they visit them sometimes. I have always valued good ideas, and have always tried to utilize them as far as possible.

Having found the lock, I tugged at it and wrenched off the whole thing. My accomplice immediately stooped down and wriggled like a serpent into the gaping-open, four-cornered cover of the crate whence she called to me approvingly, in a low tone:

"You're a brick!"

Nowadays a little crumb of praise from a woman is dearer to me than a whole dithyramb from a man, even though he be more eloquent than all the ancient and modern orators put together. Then, however, I was less amiably disposed than I am now, and paying

no attention to the compliment of my comrade, I asked her curtly and anxiously:

"Is there anything?"

In a monotonous tone she set about calculating our discoveries.

"A basketful of bottles—thick furs—a sunshade—an iron pail."

All this was uneatable. I felt that my hopes had vanished. . . . But suddenly she exclaimed vivaciously:

"Aha! here it is!"

"What?"

"Bread . . . a loaf . . . it's only wet . . . take it!"

A loaf flew to my feet and after it herself, my valiant comrade. I had already bitten off a morsel, stuffed it in my mouth, and was chewing it. . . .

"Come, give me some too! . . . And we mustn't stay here. . . . Where shall we go?" She looked inquiringly about on all sides. . . . It was dark, wet, and boisterous.

"Look! there's an upset canoe yonder . . . let us go there."

"Let us go then!" And off we set, demolishing our booty as we went, and filling our mouths with large portions of it. . . . The rain grew more violent, the river roared; from somewhere or other resounded a prolonged mocking whistle—just as if someone great who feared nobody was whistling down all earthly institutions and along with them this horrid autumnal wind and us, its heroes. This whistling made my heart throb painfully, in spite of which I greedily went on eating, and in this respect the girl walking on my left, kept even pace with me.

"What do they call you?" I asked her—why I know not.

"Natasha," she answered shortly, munching loudly.

I stared at her. My heart ached within me; and then I stared into the mist before me, and it seemed to me as if the inimical countenance of my Destiny was smiling at me enigmatically and coldly.

The rain scourged the timbers of the skiff incessantly, and its soft patter induced melancholy thoughts, and the wind whistled as it flew down into the boat's battered bottom through a rift, where some loose splinters of wood were rattling together—a disquieting and depressing sound. The waves of the river were splashing on the shore, and sounded so monotonous and hopeless, just as if they were telling something unbearably dull and heavy, which was boring them into utter disgust, something from which they wanted to run away and yet were obliged to talk about all the same. The

sound of the rain blended with their splashing, and a long-drawn sigh seemed to be floating above the overturned skiff—the endless, laboring sigh of the earth, injured and exhausted by the eternal changes from the bright and warm summer to the cold, misty and damp autumn. The wind blew continually over the desolate shore and the foaming river—blew and sang its melancholy songs. . . .

Our position beneath the shelter of the skiff was utterly devoid of comfort; it was narrow and damp, tiny cold drops of rain dribbled through the damaged bottom; gusts of wind penetrated it. We sat in silence and shivered with cold. I remembered that I wanted to go to sleep. Natasha leaned her back against the hull of the boat and curled herself up into a tiny ball. Embracing her knees with her hands, and resting her chin upon them, she stared doggedly at the river with wide-open eyes; on the pale patch of her face they seemed immense, because of the blue marks below them. She never moved, and this immobility and silence—I felt it—gradually produced within me a terror of my neighbor. I wanted to talk to her, but I knew not how to begin.

It was she herself who spoke.

"What a cursed thing life is!" she exclaimed plainly, abstractedly, and in a tone of deep conviction.

But this was no complaint. In these words there was too much of indifference for a complaint. This simple soul thought according to her understanding—thought and proceeded to form a certain conclusion which she expressed aloud, and which I could not confute for fear of contradicting myself. Therefore I was silent, and she, as if she had not noticed me, continued to sit there immovable.

"Even if we croaked . . . what then . . .?" Natasha began again, this time quietly and reflectively, and still there was not one note of complaint in her words. It was plain that this person, in the course of her reflections on life, was regarding her own case, and had arrived at the conviction that in order to preserve herself from the mockeries of life, she was not in a position to do anything else but simply "croak"—to use her own expression.

The clearness of this line of thought was inexpressibly sad and painful to me, and I felt that if I kept silence any longer I was really bound to weep. . . . And it would have been shameful to have done this before a woman, especially as she was not weeping herself. I resolved to speak to her.

"Who was it that knocked you about?" I asked. For the moment I could not think of anything more sensible or more delicate.

502

"Pashka did it all," she answered in a dull and level tone.

"And who is he?"

"My lover. . . . He was a baker."

"Did he beat you often?"

"Whenever he was drunk he beat me. . . . Often!"

And suddenly, turning towards me, she began to talk about herself, Pashka, and their mutual relations. He was a baker with red mustaches and played very well on the banjo. He came to see her and greatly pleased her, for he was a merry chap and wore nice clean clothes. He had a vest which cost fifteen rubles and boots with dress tops. For these reasons she had fallen in love with him, and he became her "creditor." And when he became her creditor, he made it his business to take away from her the money which her other friends gave to her for bonbons, and, getting drunk on this money, he would fall to beating her; but that would have been nothing if he hadn't also begun to "run after" other girls before her very eyes.

"Now wasn't that an insult? I am not worse than the others. Of course that meant that he was laughing at me, the blackguard. The day before yesterday I asked leave of my mistress to go out for a bit, went to him, and here I found Dimka sitting beside him, drunk. And he, too, was half seas over. I said, 'You scoundrel, you!' And he gave me a thorough hiding. He kicked me and dragged me by the hair. But that was nothing to what came after. He spoiled everything I had on—left me just as I am now! How could I appear before my mistress? He spoiled everything . . . my dress and my jacket too—it was quite a new one; I gave a fiver for it . . . and tore my kerchief from my head. . . . Oh, Lord! What will become of me now?" she suddenly whined in a lamentable, overstrained voice.

The wind howled, and became ever colder and more boisterous. . . . Again my teeth began to dance up and down, and she, huddled up to avoid the cold, pressed as closely to me as she could, so that I could see the gleam of her eyes through the darkness.

"What wretches all you men are! I'd burn you all in an oven; I'd cut you in pieces. If any one of you was dying I'd spit in his mouth, and not pity him a bit. Mean skunks! You wheedle and wheedle, you wag your tails like cringing dogs, and we fools give ourselves up to you, and it's all up with us! Immediately you trample us underfoot. . . . Miserable loafers!"

She cursed us up and down, but there was no vigor, no malice,

no hatred of these "miserable loafers" in her cursing that I could hear. The tone of her language was by no means corresponded with its subject-matter, for it was calm enough, and the gamut of her voice was terribly poor.

Yet all this made a stronger impression on me than the most eloquent and convincing pessimistic books and speeches, of which I had read a good many and which I still read to this day. And this, you see, was because the agony of a dying person is much more natural and violent than the most minute and picturesque descriptions of death.

I felt really wretched—more from cold than from the words of my neighbor. I groaned softly and ground my teeth.

Almost at the same moment I felt two little arms about me—one of them touched my neck and the other lay upon my face—and at the same time an anxious, gentle, friendly voice uttered the question: "What ails you?"

I was really to believe that someone else was asking me this and not Natasha, who had just declared that all men were scoundrels, and expressed a wish for their destruction. But she it was, and now she began speaking quickly, hurriedly.

"What ails you, eh? Are you cold? Are you frozen? Ah, what a one you are, sitting there so silent like a little owl! Why, you should have told me long ago that you were cold. Come . . . Lie on the ground . . . stretch yourself out and I will lie . . . there! How's that? Now put your arms round me? . . . tighter! How's that? You shall be warm very soon now. . . . And then we'll lie back to back. . . . The night will pass so quickly, see if it won't. I say . . . have you too been drinking . . . ? Turned out of your place, eh? . . . It doesn't matter."

And she comforted me. . . . She encouraged me.

May I be thrice accursed! What a world of irony was in this single fact for me! Just imagine! Here was I, seriously occupied at this very time with the destiny of humanity, thinking of the re-organization of the social system, of political revolutions, reading all sorts of devilishly wise books whose abysmal profundity was certainly unfathomable by their very authors—at this very time, I say, I was trying with all my might to make of myself "a potent, active social force." It even seemed to me that I had partially accomplished my object; anyhow, at this time, in my ideas about myself, I had got so far as to recognize that I had an exclusive right to exist, that I had the necessary greatness to deserve to live

my life, and that I was fully competent to play a great historical part therein. And a woman was now warming me with her body, a wretched, battered, hunted creature, who had no place and no value in life, and whom I had never thought of helping till she helped me herself, and whom I really would not have known how to help in any way even if the thought of it had occurred to me.

Ah! I was ready to think that all this was happening to me in a dream—in a disagreable, an oppressive dream.

But, ugh! it was impossible for me to think that, for cold drops of rain were dripping down upon me, the woman was pressing close to me, her warm breath was fanning my face, and—despite a slight odor of vodka—it did me good. The wind howled and raged, the rain smote upon the skiff, the waves splashed, and both of us, embracing each other convulsively, nevertheless shivered with cold. All this was only too real, and I am certain that nobody ever dreamed such an oppressive and horrid dream as that reality.

But Natasha was talking all the time of something or other, talking kindly and sympathetically, as only women can talk. Beneath the influence of her voice and kindly words, a little fire began to burn up within me, and something inside my heart thawed in consequence.

Then tears poured from my eyes like a hailstorm, washing away from my heart much that was evil, much that was stupid, much sorrow and dirt which had fastened upon it before that night. Natasha comforted me.

"Come, come, that will do, little one! Don't take on! That'll do! God will give you another chance . . . you will right yourself and stand in your proper place again . . . and it will be all right. . . ."

And she kept kissing me . . . many kisses did she give me . . . burning kisses . . . and all for nothing. . . .

Those were the first kisses from a woman that had ever been bestowed upon me, and they were the best kisses too, for all the subsequent kisses cost me frightfully dear, and really gave me nothing at all in exchange.

"Come, don't take on so, funny one! I'll manage for you to-morrow if you cannot find a place." Her quiet, persuasive whispering sounded in my ears as if it came through a dream. . . .

There we lay till dawn. . . .

And when the dawn came, we crept from behind the skiff and went into the town. . . .Then we took friendly leave of each other and never met again, although for half a year I searched in every

505

hole and corner for that kind Natasha with whom I spent the
autumn night just described.

If she be already dead—and well for her if it were so—may she
rest in peace! And if she be alive . . . still I say "Peace to her soul!"
And may the consciousness of her fall never enter her soul . . .
for that would be a superfluous and fruitless suffering if life is to
be lived. . . .

THOMAS GRAY

THOMAS GRAY (English, 1716-1771). Precursor of English Romanticism.
Magnificent craftsman, with classical background. Passed most of life as
professor, wrote frequently in Latin. *Elegy Written in a Country Churchyard*
one of favorite and most quoted poems in the language. Excellent *Pindaric
Odes* less well known.

ELEGY IN A COUNTRY CHURCHYARD

The curfew tolls the knell of parting day,
    The lowing herd winds slowly o'er the lea,
The ploughman homeward plods his weary way,
    And leaves the world to darkness and to me.

Now fades the glimmering landscape on the sight,
    And all the air a solemn stillness holds,
Save where the beetle wheels his droning flight,
    And drowsy tinklings lull the distant folds;

Save that from yonder ivy-mantled tower,
    The moping owl does to the moon complain
Of such as, wandering near her secret bower,
    Molest her ancient solitary reign.

Beneath those rugged elms, that yew-tree's shade,
    Where heaves the turf in many a mouldering heap
Each in his narrow cell forever laid,
    The rude forefathers of the hamlet sleep.

The breezy call of incense breathing-morn,
  The swallow twittering from the straw-built shed,
The cock's shrill clarion, or the echoing horn,
  No more shall rouse them from their lowly bed.

For them no more the blazing hearth shall burn,
  Or busy housewife ply her evening care;
No children run to lisp their sire's return,
  Or climb his knees the envied kiss to share.

Oft did the harvest to their sickle yield;
  Their furrow oft the stubborn glebe has broke;
How jocund did they drive their team afield!
  How bowed the woods beneath their sturdy stroke!

Let not ambition mock their useful toil,
  Their homely joys and destiny obscure;
Nor grandeur hear, with a disdainful smile,
  The short and simple annals of the poor.

The boast of heraldry, the pomp of power,
  And all that beauty, all that wealth e'er gave,
Await alike the inevitable hour—
  The paths of glory lead but to the grave.

Nor you, ye proud, impute to these the fault,
  If memory o'er their tomb no trophies raise,
Where, through the long-drawn aisle and fretted vault,
  The pealing anthem swells the note of praise.

Can storied urn or animated bust
  Back to its mansion call the fleeting breath?
Can honor's voice provoke the silent dust,
  Or flattery soothe the dull cold ear of death?

Perhaps in this neglected spot is laid
  Some heart once pregnant with celestial fire,
Hands that the rod of empire might have swayed
  Or waked to ecstasy the living lyre.

But knowledge to their eyes her ample page,
　Rich with the spoils of time, did ne'er unroll;
Chill penury repressed their noble rage,
　And froze the genial current of the soul.

Full many a gem of purest ray serene
　The dark, unfathomed caves of ocean bear;
Full many a flower is born to blush unseen,
　And waste its sweetness in the desert air.

Some village Hampden, that, with dauntless breast,
　The little tyrant of his fields withstood
Some mute inglorious Milton here may rest,
　Some Cromwell, guiltless of his country's blood.

The applause of listening senates to command,
　The threats of pain and ruin to despise,
To scatter plenty o'er a smiling land,
　And read their history in a nation's eyes,—

Their lot forbade; nor circumscribed alone
　Their growing virtues, but their crimes confined;
Forbade to wade through slaughter to a throne,
　And shut the gates of mercy on mankind;

The struggling pangs of conscious truth to hide,
　To quench the blushes of ingenious shame,
Or heap the shrine of luxury and pride
　With incense kindled at the muse's flame.

Far from the madding crowd's ignoble strife,
　Their sober wishes never learned to stray;
Along the cool sequestered vale of life
　They kept the noiseless tenor of their way.

Yet e'en these bones from insult to protect,
　Some frail memorial still erected nigh,
With uncouth rhymes and shapeless sculpture decked,
　Implores the passing tribute of a sigh.

Their names, their years, spelled by the unlettered muse,
 The place of fame and eulogy supply;
And many a holy text around she strews,
 That teach the rustic moralist to die.

For who, to dumb forgetfulness a prey,
 This pleasing, anxious being e'er resigned,
Left the warm precincts of the cheerful day,
 Nor cast one longing, lingering look behind?

On some fond breast the parting soul relies,
 Some pious hand the closing eye requires;
Even from the tomb the voice of nature cries,
 Even in our ashes live their wonted fires.

For thee, who, mindful of the unhonored dead,
 Dost in these lines their artless tale relate,
If chance, by lonely contemplation led,
 Some kindred spirit shall inquire thy fate.

Haply some hoary-headed swain may say,
 "Oft have we seen him at the peep of dawn,
Brushing with hasty steps the dews away,
 To meet the sun upon the upland lawn.

"There at the foot of yonder nodding beech,
 That wreathes its old fantastic roots so high,
His listless length at noontide would he stretch,
 And pore upon the brook that bubbles by.

"Hard by yon wood, now smiling as in scorn,
 Muttering his wayward fancies, he would rove,
Now drooping, woeful wan, like one forlorn,
 Or crazed with care, or crossed in hopeless love.

"One morn I missed him on the 'customed hill,
 Along the heath, and near his favorite tree;
Another came; nor yet beside the rill,
 Nor up the lawn, nor at the wood was he;

"The next, with dirges due, in sad array,
  Slow through the churchyard path we saw him borne—
Approach and read (for thou canst read) the lay
  'Graved on the stone beneath yon aged thorn."

THE EPITAPH

Here rests his head upon the lap of earth,
  A youth to fortune and to fame unknown;
Fair science frowned not on his humble birth,
  And melancholy marked him for her own.

Large was his bounty, and his soul sincere,
  Heaven did a recompense as largely send;
He gave to misery all he had—a tear;
  He gained from Heaven ('twas all he wished) a friend.

No farther seek his merits to disclose,
  Or draw his frailties from their dread abode
(There they alike in trembling hope repose),
  The bosom of his Father and his God.

FRANZ GRILLPARZER

FRANZ GRILLPARZER (Austrian, 1791-1872). Chief Austrian dramatist.
Developed classical and historical themes in contemporary terms, informing
them with 19th century idealism and psychology. Mood of pessimism prevails.
Suffered from political censorship of his time. Major works: *The Golden
Fleece* (treatment of Medea legend), *The Dream of Life, Woe to Him
That Lies!*

SAPPHO

Act V

Rhamnes— Her name upon the stars
She has traced with diamond-pointed letters,
And only with the stars 'twill fade away.
In distant lands, among strange men, 'twill

510

Echo, long after these our mortal frames
Have perished, our graves no more are found.
Then Sappho's soul will speak from out strange lips;
Her songs will live embalmed in unknown tongues,
And thine, thy name will live! Be proud of thy
Undying name! In distant lands, by men
Unknown, when centuries have passed away,
And time has swallowed all, 'twill echo then
From every mouth, "'Twas Sappho sang the song,
And Phaon caused her death."

Melitta— Forbear! forbear!

Phaon— A maniac wouldst thou make me? Who'll save me
from this torment?

Eucharis enters.

Eucharis— Rhamnes, thou art here! come! hasten!
Rhamnes— Whither?
Eucharis— To Sappho. I fear she is ill.
Rhamnes— The gods
Forbid!
Eucharis— I followed her afar, till gained
The largest hall. Concealed, and with sharp eye,
Her motions all I watched. Leaning, and raised
Upon a pedestal, she looked far o'er
The distant sea, that raged and chafed upon
The rock-bound coast. With pallid cheek and eyes,
Veiled with their lids, all motionless she stood,
Among those marble statues, one of them.
Only she seized upon the altar flowers,
The gold and ornaments within her reach,
And cast them, musing, deep in the raging sea.
Their fall with longing eyes she seemed to follow.
I nearer drew; but now a sound I heard
That shook her inmost soul. Suspended from
On high, the sea breeze touched the lyre,
And pensive played within its untuned strings;
Deep sighing, she looked up, and all her being
Thrilled, shaken invisibly by higher
Powers. Her eyes with a strange fire illumed,
A lovely smile played o'er her mouth.
The firm-closed lips were parted now, and words

511

Came forth so solemn and profound they seemed
Not Sappho's words, but edicts of the gods!
"O friend!" she said, "thou dost admonish me
Of passing time; O thanks! I understand
Thee well." How the wall she gained, and how
The lyre high-hanging reached, I know not.
Her arm, a beam of light it seemed; and as
I looked she held the lyre and pressed the strings
Upon her storm-moved breast; while audibly
The breathing sounds came forth and passed away.
Suspended as a votive wreath upon
The domestic altar, hung her crown; she took
And wound it round her head; the purple robe,
A glowing veil, o'er her fair shoulders threw.
Who first had seen her now, with lyre in hand,
And look inspired, upraised, the altar steps
Ascending, with her whole light form enwrapped
In light, in prayer had bent his trembling knees,
And hailed her the immortal. Silent
And motionless she stood, yet through my limbs
Crept shuddering fear; I quailed beneath
Her piercing eye, and fled to thee.
    Rhamnes— Left her?
Return! yet see, herself comes near!
*(Sappho enters richly dressed as in the first act: the purple mantle on
her shoulders, the laurel crown upon her head, and the golden
lyre in her hand. She is surrounded by her women, and descends
the steps of the marble colonnade.)*
    Melitta— Sappho! dearest mistress!
    Sappho (calm and earnest)— What wouldst thou, then?
    Melitta— Rent is the bandage from my opened eyes.
Let me again become thy slave. Receive
Again what's thine, and pardon me.
    Sappho— So ill
Advised believe me not. No gift from thee
Will Sappho take. That was my own, thou canst
Not give nor take.
    Phaon (kneeling)— O listen, Sappho!
    Sappho— Beware! kneel not to me; devoted am I to the gods!
    Phaon— With gentle eye thou look'st at me, O Sappho!
Rememberest thou—

512

Sappho— Thou speakest of things long past,
Thee, Phaon, I sought! and found myself.
Thou understood me not. Farewell! on firmer
Ground my hopes must rest!
    Phaon— Hatest thou me, then?
    Sappho— Hatred! Love! Is there no third? Worthy wert
Thou, and are so still, and ever will to me
Be so; like a dear chance companion
That accident awhile led in my boat. The goal
Once reached, we part, each wandering on
His path alone; yet often from the path,
The widening path, recall the friendly meeting.
                              (Her voice fails.

    Phaon (much moved)— O Sappho!
    Sappho— Forbear! we part in peace!
    (To the others)— You who have Sappho's weakness seen, O
    pardon!
To Sappho's weakness be ye reconciled!
The bow when bent first shows its power.
    (She points to the altar in the background)— The flame
Is lit. To Aphrodite it mounts, clear as
The beam of coming day.
    (To her Servants and Phaon)— And now remove!
Leave me to counsel with mine own—mine own!
    Rhamnes— Obey her will. Let all withdraw   *(They draw back.*
    Sappho (approaches the altar that stands close to the cliff)—
Ye lofty gods! divine! With blessings rich
You've crowned my life. My hand the muses' lyre
Has touched; the poet's cup for me runs o'er.
A heart to feel, a mind to think, and power
   To form my thought to music, you have given.
With rich blessings you have blessed me. I thank you!
With victory you've crowned my feeble brow,
And sowed in distant lands the poet's fame,
Of immortality the seed. Echoes
From strangers' tongues the song I struck upon
My golden lyre, and only with the earth
The fame of Sappho dies.
I thank you!
In life's unmingled cup, crowned high with sweets,
The poet only sips, but does not drink.

Obedient to your highest wish, the sweet,
Unemptied cup I place aside, and drink not.
What you decreed, all-powerful gods,
Has Sappho finished! Deny me not
The last reward within your power to grant—
No weakness, no decay, let Sappho know.
In her full strength, in nature's bloom, O take
Her quickly to yourselves!
Forbid that e'er a priestess of the gods
Should be the theme of god-denying foes!
The sport of fools, in their own folly wise!
You bruised the flower, break now the stem;
Perfect in truth what was begun in love,
And spare the conflict's bleeding struggle. Grant,
O grant the victory! the victor's weakness spare!
The flame is kindling while the sun ascends!
I feel I'm heard! Great gods, I thank you!
Melitta! Phaon! come nearer to me!
    (She kisses Phaon on the forehead)—
A friend from distant worlds salutes thee thus!
    (Embracing Melitta)—
Thy mother, dead, sends thee this kiss! Farewell!
There, on the altar of love's goddess, love
Fulfills, of love, the melancholy fate!
    (She hastens to the altar.)
Rhamnes— What means she? Inspired is all her being.
The splendor of immortals wraps her round.
*(Sappho, who has gradually approached the edge of the cliff, upon
    which the altar stands, stretches both hands over Melitta and
    Phaon.)*
Sappho— To men give love! ambition to the gods!
What for you blooms, enjoy, and think of Sappho!
Of life the last debt I pay! The gods,
To you, grant blessings; and to me—themselves.
    (She springs from the cliff into the sea.)
Phaon— Hold! Sappho! hold!
Melitta— Alas, she falls! she dies.
Phaon *(busied with Melitta)—*
Quick! quick! She dies! Forth from the shore to save!
    Rhamnes (has climbed upon the rock)—
The gods protect! There on that cliff she falls;

514

There is she crushed, destroyed! Bears she off?
Impossible! alas! too late!

   Phaon—   Why weep
You here? a boat! haste! haste to save her.

   Rhamnes (descending)—
Forbear! it is too late! Grant her the grave
The gods decree. That she, disdaining this
False earth, within the sacred waves has
Chosen for her rest.

   Phaon—   Dead!

   Rhamnes—   Dead!

   Phaon—   Dead! alas!
Impossible! She is not dead! not dead!

   Rhamnes—   Withered the laurel! broken are the strings;
Upon the earth there was no home for her;
To heaven has Sappho, to her own, returned!

H

HAFIZ

HĀFIZ (Shams ud-Din Mohammed, Persian, *ca.* 1320-1389). Unequaled master of the *ghazal* (short lyric poem). His *Divan,* containing over 500 *ghazals,* influenced later Persian, Indian and Turkish poets, and Westerners such as Goethe. A subtle mystic and superb satirist.

CHARMS THAT CHARM NOT

Without the loved one's cheek the rose
    Can charm not.
The spring, unless the wine-cup flows,
    Can charm not.
The greenwood's border and the orchard's air,
Unless some tulip cheek be there,
    Can charm not.
The sugar-lipped, the fair of rosy frame,
Whom kisses nor embrace can claim,
    Can charm not.
The dancing cypress, the enrapturing flower,
If no nightingale gladden the bower,
    Can charm not.
The painter's picture, though with genius rife,
Without the picture that has life,
    Can charm not.
Wine, flower, and bower abound in charm, yet they,
Lack we the friend who makes us gay,
    Can charm not.
Thy soul, O Hafiz! is a coin that none prize;
And it, though poured forth largess-wise,
    Can charm not.

My breast is filled with roses,
   My cup is crowned with wine,
And the veil her face discloses—
   The maid I hail as mine.
The monarch, wheresoe'er he be,
Is but a slave compared to me.

Their glare no torches throwing,
   Shall in our bower be found—
Her eyes, like moonbeams glowing,
   Cast light enough around:
And other odors I can spare
Who scent the perfume of her hair.

The honey-dew thy charm might borrow,
   Thy lip alone to me is sweet;
When thou art absent, faint with sorrow
   I hide me in some lone retreat.
Why talk to me of power or fame?
   What are those idle toys to me?
Why ask the praises of my name,
   My joy, my triumph is in thee.

How blest am I! around me swelling
   The notes of melody arise!
I hold the cup with wine excelling,
   And gaze upon thy radiant eyes.

O Hafiz—never waste thy hours
   Without the cup, the lute, and love,
For 'tis the sweetest time of flowers,
   And none these moments shall reprove.
The nightingales around thee sing;
It is the joyous feast of spring.

THE DRUNKARD'S EXCUSE

Know you the true reason and cause why it is that I drink?
   From pride and from folly I strutted and swelled through the
     town:

517

And now those detestable vices, from which the saints shrink,
  I will in the depths of the ocean of drunkenness drown.

MY BIRD

My soul is as a sacred bird, the highest heaven its nest,
Fretting within its body-bars, it finds on earth its nest;
When rising from its dusty heap this bird of mine shall soar
'Twill find upon the lofty gate the nest it had before.
The Sidrah shall receive my bird, when it has winged its way,
And on the Empyrean's top, my falcon's foot shall stay.
Over the ample field of earth is fortune's shadow cast,
Where upon wings and pennons borne this bird of mine has passed.
No spot in the two worlds it owns, above the sphere its goal,
Its body from the quarry is, from "No Place" is its soul.
'Tis only in the glorious world my bird its splendor shows,
The rosy bowers of Paradise its daily food bestows.

JUDAH HALEVI

JUDAH HALEVI (Spanish-Hebrew, *ca.* 1080-1140). One of greatest Hebrew
poets of Spanish Golden Period, called the Sweet Singer of Zion. Physician
by profession, emigrated to Palestine to devote rest of life to writing *Songs of
Zion.* Also famous: *Sefer ha-Kuzari,* a dialogue on Jewish religion and history,
in effect an essay on national revival. Religious and liturgical poems still used
in prayer.

I. A LETTER TO HIS FRIEND ISAAC

But yesterday the earth drank like a child
  With eager thirst the autumn rain.
Or like a wistful bride who waits the hour
  Of love's mysterious bliss and pain.
And now the Spring is here with yearning eyes;
  Midst shimmering golden flower-beds,
On meadows carpeted with varied hues,
  In richest raiment clad, she treads.

518

She weaves a tapestry of bloom o'er all,
    And myriad eyed young plants upspring,
White, green, or red like lips that to the mouth
    Of the beloved one sweetly cling.
Whence come these radiant tints, these blended beams?
    Here's such a dazzle, such a blaze,
As though earth stole the splendor of the stars,
    Fain to eclipse them with her rays.
Come! go we to the garden with our wine,
    Which scatters sparks of hot desire,
Within our hand 't is cold, but in our veins
    It flashes clear, it glows like fire.
It bubbles sunnily in earthen jugs.
We catch it in the crystal glass,
    Then wander through cool, shadowy lanes and breathe
    The spicy freshness of the grass.
Whilst we with happy hearts our circuit keep,
    The gladness of the Earth is shown.
She smileth, though the trickling rain-drops weep
    Silently o'er her, one by one.
She loves to feel the tears upon her cheek,
    Like a rich veil, with pearls inwove.
Joyous she listens when the swallows chirp,
    And warbles to her mate, the dove.
Blithe as a maiden midst the young green leaves,
    A wreath she'll wind, a fragrant treasure;
All living things in graceful motion leap,
    As dancing to some merry measure.
The morning breezes rustle cordially,
    Love's thirst is sated with the balm they send.
Sweet breathes the myrtle in the frolic wind,
    As though remembering a distant friend.
The myrtle branch now proudly lifted high,
    Now whispering to itself drops low again.
The topmost palm-leaves rapturously stir,
    For all at once they hear the birds' soft strain.
So stirs, so yearns all nature, gayly decked,
    To honor *Isaac* with her best array.
Hear'st thou the word? She cries—I beam with joy,
Because with Isaac I am wed today.

519

II. ADMONITION

Long in the lap of childhood didst thou sleep,
Think how thy youth like chaff did disappear;
Shall life's sweet Spring forever last? Look up,
Old age approaches ominously near.
Oh, shake thou off the world, even as the bird
Shakes off the midnight dew that clogged his wings.
Soar upward, seek redemption from thy guilt
And from the earthly dross that round thee clings.
Draw near to God, His holy angels know,
For whom His bounteous streams of mercy flow.

III. LOVE SONGS

"See'st thou o'er my shoulders falling,
    Snake-like ringlets waving free?
Have no fear, for they are twisted
    To allure thee unto me."

Thus she spake, the gentle dove,
    Listen to thy plighted love:—
"Ah, how long I wait, until
    Sweetheart cometh back (she said)
Laying his caressing hand
    Underneath my burning head."

KNUT HAMSUN

KNUT HAMSUN (Norwegian, 1859-1952). One of great literary figures of modern Norway. Novelist, playwright and poet. Nobel Prize, 1920. Famous novel: *Growth of the Soil*. Nature mystic and biting critic of materialist civilization—yet succumbed to one of its lowest forms, Nazism.

THE CALL OF LIFE

Down near the inner harbor in Copenhagen there is a street called Vestervold, a relatively new, yet desolate, boulevard. There are few houses to be seen on it, few gas lamps, and almost no people whatever. Even now, in summer, it is rare that one sees people promenading there.

Well, last evening I had something of a surprise in that street.

I had taken a few turns up and down the sidewalk when a lady came towards me from the opposite direction. There were no other people in sight. The gas lamps were lighted, but it was nevertheless dark—so dark that I could not distinguish the lady's face. One of the usual creatures of the night, I thought to myself, and passed her by.

At the end of the boulevard I turned about and walked back. The lady had also turned about, and I met her again. She is waiting for some one, I thought, and I was curious to see whom she could be waiting for. And again I passed her by.

When I met her the third time I tipped my hat and spoke to her. "Good evening! Are you waiting for some one?"

She was startled. No—that is, yes—she was waiting for some one.

Did she object to my keeping her company till the person she was expecting arrived?

No—she did not object in the least, and she thanked me. For that matter, she explained, she was not expecting any one. She was merely taking the air—it was so still here.

We strolled about side by side. We began talking about various things of no great consequence. I offered my arm.

"Thank you, no," she said, and shook her head.

There was no great fun promenading in this way; I could not see her in the dark. I struck a match to see what time it was. I held the match up and looked at her too.

"Nine-thirty," I said.

She shivered as if she were freezing. I seized the opportunity.

"You are freezing?" I asked. "Shan't we drop in some place and get something to drink? At Tivoli? At the National?"

"But, don't you see, I can't go anywhere now," she answered.

And I noticed then for the first time that she wore a very long black veil.

I begged her pardon, and blamed the darkness for my mistake. And the way in which she took my apology at once convinced me that she was not one of the usual night wanderers.

"Won't you take my arm?" I suggested again. "It may warm you a bit."

She took my arm.

We paced up and down a few turns. She asked me to look at the time again.

"It is ten," I said. "Where do you live?"

521

"On Gamle Kongevei."

I stopped her.

"And may I see you to your door?" I asked.

"Not very well," she answered. "No, I can't let you . . . You live on Bredgade, don't you?"

"How do you know that?" I asked surprised.

"Oh, I know who you are," she answered.

A pause. We walked arm in arm down the lighted streets. She walked rapidly, her long veil streaming behind.

"We had better hurry," she said.

At her door in Gamle Kongevei she turned toward me as if to thank me for my kindness in escorting her. I opened the door for her, and she entered slowly. I thrust my shoulder gently against the door and followed her in. Once inside she seized my hand. Neither of us said anything.

We mounted two flights of stairs and stopped on the third floor. She herself unlocked the door to her apartment, then opened a second door, and took me by the hand and led me in. It was presumably a drawing-room; I could hear a clock ticking on the wall. Once inside the door the lady paused a moment, threw her arms about me suddenly, and kissed me tremblingly, passionately, on the mouth. Right on the mouth.

"Won't you be seated," she suggested. "Here is a sofa. Meanwhile I'll get a light."

And she lit a lamp.

I looked about me, amazed, yet curious. I found myself in a spacious and extremely well furnished drawing-room with other, half open, doors leading into several rooms on the side. I could not for the life of me make out what sort of person it was I had come across.

"What a beautiful room!" I exclaimed. "Do you live here?"

"Yes, this is my home," she answered.

"Is this your home? You live with your parents then?"

"Oh, no," she laughed. "I am an old woman, as you'll see!"

And she removed her veil and her wraps.

"There—see! What did I tell you!" she said, and threw her arms about me once again, abruptly, driven by some uncontrollable urge.

She might have been twenty-two or three, wore a ring on her right hand, and might for that matter really have been a married woman. Beautiful? No, she was freckled, and had scarcely any

522

eyebrows. But there was an effervescent life about her, and her mouth was strangely beautiful.

I wanted to ask her who she was, where her husband was, if she had any, and whose house this was I was in, but she threw herself about me every time I opened my mouth and forbade me to be inquisitive.

"My name is Ellen," she explained. "Would you care for something to drink? It really won't disturb any one if I ring. Perhaps you'd step in here, in the bed-room, meanwhile."

I went into the bed-room. The light from the drawing room illumined it partially. I saw two beds. Ellen rang and ordered wine, and I heard a maid bring in the wine and go out again. A little later Ellen came into the bed-room after me, but she stopped short in the door. I took a step towards her. She uttered a little cry and at the same time came towards me.

This was last evening.

What further happened? Ah, patience! There is much more!

It was beginning to grow light this morning when I awoke. The daylight crept into the room on either side of the curtain. Ellen was also awake and smiled toward me. Her arms were white and velvety, her breast unusually high. I whispered something to her, and she closed my mouth with hers, mute with tenderness. The day grew lighter and lighter.

Two hours later I was on my feet. Ellen was also up, busy dressing herself—she had got her shoes on. Then it was I experienced something which even now strikes me as a gruesome dream. I was at the wash stand. Ellen had some errand or other in the adjoining room, and as she opened the door I turned around and glanced in. A cold draft from the open windows in the room rushed in upon me, and in the center of the room I could just make out a corpse stretched out on a table. A corpse, in a coffin, dressed in white, with a gray beard, the corpse of a man. His bony knees protruded like madly clenched fists underneath the sheet, and his face was sallow and ghastly in the extreme. I could see everything in full daylight. I turned away and said not a word.

When Ellen returned I was dressed and ready to go out. I could scarcely bring myself to respond to her embraces. She put on some additional clothes; she wanted to accompany me down as far as the street door, and I let her come, still saying nothing. At the door she pressed close to the wall so as not to be seen.

523

"Well, good-bye," she whispered.

"Till to-morrow?" I asked, in part to test her.

"No, not to-morrow."

"Why not to-morrow?"

"Not so many questions, dear. I am going to a funeral to-morrow, a relation of mine is dead. Now there—you know it."

"But the day after to-morrow?"

"Yes, the day after to-morrow, at the door here, I'll meet you. Good-bye!"

I went.

Who was she? And the corpse? With its fists clenched and the corners of its mouth drooping—how ghastly comic! The day after to-morrow she would be expecting me. Ought I to see her again?

I went straight down to the Bernina Café and asked for a directory. I looked up number so and so Gamle Kongevei, and—there—there was the name. I waited some little time till the morning papers were out. Then I turned quickly to the announcements of deaths. And—sure enough—there I found hers too, the very first in the list, in bold type: "My husband, fifty-three years old, died to-day after a long illness." The announcement was dated the day before yesterday.

I sat for a long time and pondered.

A man marries. His wife is thirty years younger than he. He contracts a lingering illness. One fair day he dies.

And the young widow breathes a sigh of relief.

THOMAS HARDY

THOMAS HARDY (English, 1840-1928). Novelist and poet. Realistic observer of village and palace, at his best when writing of native Wessex. Began career as architect. His major novels are tragedies: *The Mayor of Casterbridge, The Return of the Native, Tess of the D'Urbervilles, Jude the Obscure.* Pessimistic epic drama, *The Dynasts,* considered by some his masterpiece.

SQUIRE PETRICK'S LADY

FOLK who are at all acquainted with the traditions of Stapleford Park will not need to be told that in the middle of the last century it was owned by that trump of mortgagees, Timothy Petrick, whose

524

skill in gaining possession of fair estates by granting sums of money on their title-deeds has seldom if ever been equaled in our part of England. Timothy was a lawyer by profession, and agent to several noblemen, by which means his special line of business became opened to him by a sort of revelation. It is said that a relative of his, a very deep thinker, who afterwards had the misfortune to be transported for life for mistaken notions on the signing of a will, taught him considerable legal lore, which he creditably resolved never to throw away for the benefit of other people, but to reserve it entirely for his own.

However, I have nothing in particular to say about his early and active days, but rather of the time when, an old man, he had become the owner of vast estates by the means I have signified—among them the great manor of Stapleford, on which he lived, in the splendid old mansion now pulled down; likewise estates at Marlott, estates near Sherton Abbas, nearly all the borough of Millpool, and many properties near Ivell. Indeed, I can't call to mind half his landed possessions, and I don't know that it matters much at this time of day, seeing that he's been dead and gone many years. It is said that when he bought an estate he would not decide to pay the price till he had walked over every single acre with his own two feet, and prodded the soil at every point with his own spud, to test its quality, which, if we regard the extent of his properties, must have been a stiff business for him.

At the time I am speaking of he was a man over eighty, and his son was dead; but he had two grandsons, the eldest of whom, his namesake, was married, and was shortly expecting issue. Just then the grandfather was taken ill, for death, as it seemed, considering his age. By his will the old man had created an entail (as I believe the lawyers call it), devising the whole of the estates to his elder grandson and his issue male, failing which to his younger grandson and his issue male, failing which, to remoter relatives, who need not be mentioned now.

While old Timothy Petrick was lying ill, his elder grandson's wife, Annetta, gave birth to her expected child, who, as fortune would have it, was a son. Timothy, her husband, though sprung of a scheming family, was no great schemer himself; he was the single one of the Petricks then living whose heart had never been greatly moved by sentiments which did not run in the groove of ambitions; and on this account he had not married well, as the saying is, his wife having been the daughter of a family of no better beginnings

525

than his own; that is to say, her father was a country townsman of the professional class. But she was a very pretty woman, by all accounts, and her husband had seen, courted, and married her in a high tide of infatuation, after a very short acquaintance, and with very little knowledge of her heart's history. He had never found reason to regret his choice as yet, and his anxiety for her recovery was great.

She was supposed to be out of danger, and herself and the child progressing well, when there was a change for the worse, and she sank so rapidly that she was soon given over. When she felt she was about to leave him, Annetta sent for her husband, and, on his speedy entry and assurance that they were alone, she made him solemnly vow to give the child every care in any circumstances that might arise, if it should please Heaven to take her. This, of course, he readily promised. Then after some hesitation she told him that she could not die with a falsehood upon her soul, and dire deceit in her life; she must make a terrible confession to him before her lips were sealed forever. She thereupon related an incident concerning the the baby's parentage which was not as he supposed.

Timothy Petrick, though a quick-feeling man, was not of a sort to show nerves outwardly; and he bore himself as heroically as he possibly could do in this trying moment of his life. That same night his wife died; and while she lay dead, and before her funeral, he hastened to the bedside of his sick grandfather, and revealed to him all that had happened—the baby's birth, his wife's confession, and her death, beseeching the aged man, as he loved him, to bestir himself now, at the eleventh hour, and alter his will so as to dish the intruder. Old Timothy, seeing matters in the same light as his grandson, required no urging against allowing anything to stand in the way of legitimate inheritance; he executed another will, limiting the entail to Timothy, his grandson, for life, and his male heirs thereafter to be born, after them to his other grandson, Edward, and Edward's heirs. Thus the newly born infant, who had been the center of so many hopes, was cut off and scorned as none of the elect.

The old mortgagee lived but a short time after this, the excitement of the discovery having told upon him considerably, and he was gathered to his fathers like the most charitable man in his neighborhood. Both his wife and grandparent being buried, Timothy settled down to his usual life as well as he was able, mentally satis-

526

fied that he had, by prompt action, defeated the consequences of such dire domestic treachery as had been shown towards him, and resolving to marry a second time as soon as he could satisfy himself in the choice of a wife.

But men do not always know themselves. The imbittered state of Timothy Petrick's mind bred in him by degrees such a hatred and mistrust of womankind that, though several specimens of high attractiveness came under his eyes, he could not bring himself to the point of proposing marriage. He dreaded to take up the position of husband a second time, discerning a trap in every petticoat, and a Slough of Despond in possible heirs. "What has happened once, when all seemed so fair, may happen again," he said to himself. "I'll risk my name no more." So he abstained from marriage, and overcame his wish for a lineal descendant to follow him in the ownership of Stapleford.

Timothy had scarcely noticed the unfortunate child that his wife had borne, after arranging for a meager fulfillment of his promise to her to take care of the boy, by having him brought up in his house. Occasionally, remembering his promise, he went and glanced at the child, saw that he was doing well, gave a few special directions, and again went his solitary way. Thus he and the child lived on in the Stapleford mansion-house till two or three years had passed by. One day he was walking in the garden, and by some accident left his snuff-box on a bench. When he came back to find it he saw the little boy standing there; he had escaped his nurse, and was making a plaything of the box, in spite of the convulsive sneezings which the game brought in its train. Then the man with the incrusted heart became interested in the little fellow's persistence in his play under such discomforts; he looked in the child's face, saw there his wife's countenance, though he did not see his own, and fell into thought on the piteousness of childhood—particularly of despised and rejected childhood, like this before him.

From that hour, try as he would to counteract the feeling, the human necessity to love something or other got the better of what he had called his wisdom, and shaped itself in a tender anxiety for the youngster Rupert. This name had been given him by his dying mother when, at her request, the child was baptized in her chamber, lest he should not survive for public baptism; and her husband had never thought of it as a name of any significance till, about this time, he learned by accident that it was the name of the young Marquis

527

of Christminster, son of the Duke of Southwesterland, for whom Annetta had cherished warm feelings before her marriage. Recollecting some wandering phrases in his wife's last words, which he had not understood at the time, he perceived at last that this was the person to whom she had alluded when affording him a clew to little Rupert's history.

He would sit in silence for hours with the child, being no great speaker at the best of times; but the boy, on his part, was too ready with his tongue for any break in discourse to arise because Timothy Petrick had nothing to say. After idling away his mornings in this manner, Petrick would go to his own room and swear in long, loud whispers, and walk up and down, calling himself the most ridiculous dolt that ever lived, and declaring that he would never go near the little fellow again; to which resolve he would adhere for the space, perhaps, of a day. Such cases are happily not new to human nature, but there never was a case in which a man more completely befooled his former self than in this.

As the child grew up, Timothy's attachment to him grew deeper, till Rupert became almost the sole object for which he lived. There had been enough of the family ambition latent in him for Timothy Petrick to feel a little envy when, some time before this date, his brother Edward had been accepted by the Honorable Harriet Mountclere, daughter of the second viscount of that name and title; but having discovered, as I have before stated, the paternity of his boy Rupert to lurk in even a higher stratum of society, those envious feelings speedily dispersed. Indeed, the more he reflected thereon, after his brother's aristocratic marriage, the more content did he become. His late wife took softer outline in his memory, as he thought of the lofty taste she had displayed, though only a plain burgher's daughter, and the justification for this weakness in loving the child—the justification that he had longed for—was afforded now in the knowledge that the boy was by nature, if not by name, a representative of one of the noblest houses in England.

"She was a woman of grand instincts, after all," he said to himself, proudly. "To fix her choice upon the immediate successor in that ducal line—it was finely conceived! Had he been of low blood like myself or my relations she would scarce have deserved the harsh measure that I have dealt out to her and her offspring. How much less, then, when such groveling tastes were farthest from her soul! The man Annetta loved was noble, and my boy is noble in spite of me."

528

The after-clap was inevitable, and it soon came. "So far," he reasoned, "from cutting off his child from inheritance of my estates, as I have done, I should have rejoiced in the possession of him! He is of pure stock on one side at least, while in the ordinary run of affairs he would have been a commoner to the bone."

Being a man, whatever his faults, of good old beliefs in the divinity of kings and those about 'em, the more he overhauled the case in this light the more strongly did his poor wife's conduct in improving the blood and breed of the Petrick family win his heart. He considered what ugly, idle, hard-drinking scamps many of his own relations had been; the miserable scriveners, usurers, and pawnbrokers that he had numbered among his forefathers, and the probability that some of their bad qualities would have come out in a merely corporeal child, to give him sorrow in his old age, turn his black hairs gray, his gray hairs white, cut down every stick of timber, and Heaven knows what all, had he not, like a skillful gardener, minded his grafting and changed the sort; till at length this right-minded man fell down on his knees every night and morning and thanked God that he was not as other meanly descended fathers in such matters.

It was in the peculiar disposition of the Petrick family that the satisfaction which ultimately settled in Timothy's breast found nourishment. The Petricks had adored the nobility, and plucked them at the same time. That excellent man Izaak Walton's feelings about fish were much akin to those of old Timothy Petrick, and of his descendants in a lesser degree, concerning the landed aristocracy. To torture and to love simultaneously is a proceeding strange to reason, but possible to practise, as these instances show.

Hence, when Timothy's brother Edward said slightingly one day that Timothy's son was well enough, but that he had nothing but shops and offices in his backward perspective, while his own children, should he have any, would be far different, in possessing such a mother as the Honorable Harriet, Timothy felt a bound of triumph within him at the power he possessed of contradicting that statement if he chose.

So much was he interested in his boy in this new aspect that he now began to read up chronicles of the illustrious house ennobled as the Dukes of Southwesterland, from their very beginning in the glories of the Restoration of the blessed Charles till the year of his own time. He mentally noted their gifts from royalty, grants of lands, purchases, intermarriages, plantings, and buildings; more particular-

ly their political and military achievements, which had been great, and their performances in arts and letters, which had been by no means contemptible. He studied prints of the portraits of that family, and then, like a chemist watching a crystallization, began to examine young Rupert's face for the unfolding of those historic curves and shades that the painters Vandyke and Lely had perpetuated on canvas.

When the boy reached the most fascinating age of childhood, and his shouts of laughter rang through Stapleford House from end to end, the remorse that oppressed Timothy Petrick knew no bounds. Of all people in the world this Rupert was the one on whom he could have wished the estates to devolve; yet Rupert, by Timothy's own desperate strategy at the time of his birth, had been ousted from all inheritance of them; and, since he did not mean to remarry, the manors would pass to his brother and his brother's children, who would be nothing to him, whose boasted pedigree on one side would be nothing to his Rupert's.

Had he only left the first will of his grandfather alone!

His mind ran on the wills continually, both of which were in existence, and the first, the canceled one, in his own possession. Night after night, when the servants were all abed, and the click of safety-locks sounded as loud as a crash, he looked at that first will, and wished it had been the second and not the first.

The crisis came at last. One night, after having enjoyed the boy's company for hours, he could no longer bear that his beloved Rupert should be dispossessed, and he committed the felonious deed of altering the date of the earlier will to a fortnight later, which made its execution appear subsequent to the date of the second will already proved. He then boldly propounded the first will as the second.

His brother Edward submitted to what appeared to be not only incontestible fact, but a far more likely disposition of old Timothy's property; for, like many others, he had been much surprised at the limitations defined in the other will, having no clew to their cause. He joined his brother Timothy in setting aside the hitherto accepted document, and matters went on in their usual course, there being no dispositions in the substituted will differing from those in the other, except such as related to a future which had not yet arrived.

The years moved on. Rupert had not yet revealed the anxiously expected historic lineaments which should foreshadow the political

530

abilities of the ducal family aforesaid, when it happened on a certain day that Timothy Petrick made the acquaintance of a well-known physician of Budmouth, who had been the medical adviser and friend of the late Mrs. Petrick's family for many years, though after Annetta's marriage, and consequent removal to Stapleford, he had seen no more of her, the neighboring practitioner who attended the Petricks having then become her doctor as a matter of course. Timothy was impressed by the insight and knowledge disclosed in the conversation of the Budmouth physician, and the acquaintance ripening to intimacy, the physician alluded to a form of hallucination to which Annetta's mother and grandmother had been subject —that of believing in certain dreams as realities. He delicately inquired if Timothy had ever noticed anything of the sort in his wife during her lifetime; he, the physician, had fancied that he discerned germs of the same peculiarity in Annetta when he attended her in her girlhood. One explanation begat another, till the dumbfounded Timothy Petrick was persuaded in his own mind that Annetta's confession to him had been based on a delusion.

"You look down in the mouth!" said the doctor, pausing.

"A bit unmanned. 'Tis unexpected-like," sighed Timothy.

But he could hardly believe it possible; and, thinking it best to be frank with the doctor, told him the whole story which, till now, he had never related to living man, save his dying grandfather. To his surprise, the physician informed him that such a form of delusion was precisely what he would have expected from Annetta's antecedents at such a physical crisis in her life.

Petrick prosecuted his inquiries elsewhere; and the upshot of his labors was, briefly, that a comparison of dates and places showed irrefutably that his poor wife's assertion could not have foundation in fact. The young Marquis of her tender passion—a highly moral and bright-minded nobleman—had gone abroad the year before Annetta's marriage, and had not returned until after her death. The young girl's love for him had been a delicate ideal dream—no more.

Timothy went home, and the boy ran out to meet him; whereupon a strangely dismal feeling of discontent took possession of his soul. After all, then, there was nothing but plebeian blood in the veins of the heir to his name and estates; he was not to be succeeded by a noble-natured line. To be sure, Rupert was his son; but that glory and halo he believed him to have inherited from the ages, outshining that of his brother's children, had departed from Rupert's brow for-

ever; he could no longer read history in the boy's face and centuries of domination in his eyes.

His manner towards his son grew colder and colder from that day forward; and it was with bitterness of heart that he discerned the characteristic features of the Petricks unfolding themselves by degrees. Instead of the elegant knife-edged nose, so typical of the Dukes of Southwesterland, there began to appear on his face the broad nostril and hollow bridge of his grandfather Timothy. No illustrious line of politicians was promised a continuator in that graying blue eye, for it was acquiring the expression of the orb of a particularly objectionable cousin of his own; and, instead of the mouth-curves which had thrilled Parliamentary audiences in speeches now bound in calf in every well-ordered library, there was the bull-lip of that very uncle of his who had had the misfortune with the signature of a gentleman's will, and had been transported for life in consequence.

To think how he himself, too, had sinned in this same matter of a will for this mere fleshly reproduction of a wretched old uncle whose very name he wished to forget! The boy's Christian name, even, was an imposture and an irony, for it implied hereditary force and brilliancy to which he plainly would never attain. The consolation of real sonship was always left him certainly; but he could not help groaning to himself, "Why cannot a son be one's own and somebody else's likewise?"

The Marquis was shortly afterwards in the neighborhood of Stapleford, and Timothy Petrick met him, and eyed his noble countenance admiringly. The next day, when Petrick was in his study, somebody knocked at the door.

"Who's there?"

"Rupert."

"I'll Rupert thee, you young imposter! Say, only a poor commonplace Petrick!" his father grunted. "Why didn't you have a voice like the Marquis I saw yesterday!" he continued, as the lad came in. "Why haven't you his looks, and a way of commanding as if you'd done it for centuries—hey?"

"Why? How can you expect it, father, when I'm not related to him?"

"Ugh! Then you ought to be!" growled his father.

BRET HARTE

BRET HARTE (American, 1836-1902). The sentimental popularizer of the Western tale in America. Born in Albany, New York, went to California in 1854, and worked as teacher, miner, printer, editor. Best-known stories: "The Outcasts of Poker Flat" and "The Luck of Roaring Camp."

THE OUTCASTS OF POKER FLAT

As Mr. John Oakhurst, gambler, stepped into the main street of Poker Flat on the morning of the 23d of November, 1850, he was conscious of a change in its moral atmosphere since the preceding night. Two or three men, conversing earnestly together, ceased as he approached, and exchanged significant glances. There was a Sabbath lull in the air, which, in a settlement unused to Sabbath influences, looked ominous.

Mr. Oakhurst's calm, handsome face betrayed small concern in these indications. Whether he was conscious of any predisposing cause was another question. "I reckon they're after somebody," he reflected: "likely it's me." He returned to his pocket the handkerchief with which he had been wiping away the red dust of Poker Flat from his neat boots, and quietly discharged his mind of any further conjecture.

In point of fact, Poker Flat was "after somebody." It had lately suffered the loss of several thousand dollars, two valuable horses, and a prominent citizen. It was experiencing a spasm of virtuous reaction, quite as lawless and ungovernable as any of the acts that had provoked it. A secret committee had determined to rid the town of all improper persons. This was done permanently in regard to two men who were then hanging from the boughs of a sycamore in the gulch, and temporarily in the banishment of certain ladies. It is but due to the sex, however, to state that their impropriety was professional, and it was only in such easily established standards of evil that Poker Flat ventured to sit in judgment.

Mr. Oakhurst was right in supposing that he was included in this category. A few of the committee had urged hanging him as a possible example and a sure method of reimbursing themselves from his pockets of the sums he had won from them. "It's agin justice," said Jim Wheeler, "to let this yer young man from Roaring Camp—an entire stranger—carry away our money." But a crude sentiment of equity residing in the breasts of those who had been fortunate

533

enough to win from Mr. Oakhurst overruled this narrower local prejudice.

Mr. Oakhurst received his sentence with philosophic calmness, none the less coolly that he was aware of the hesitation of his judges. He was too much of a gambler not to accept his fate. With him life was at best an uncertain game, and he recognized the usual percentage in favor of the dealer.

A body of armed men accompanied the deported wickedness of Poker Flat to the outskirts of the settlement. Besides Mr. Oakhurst, who was known to be a coolly desperate man, and for whose intimidation the armed escort was intended, the expatriated party consisted of a young woman familiarly known as "The Duchess"; another who had won the title of "Mother Shipton"; and "Uncle Billy," a suspected sluice-robber and confirmed drunkard. The cavalcade provoked no comments from the spectators, nor was any word uttered by the escort. Only when the gulch which marked the uttermost limit of Poker Flat was reached, the leader spoke briefly and to the point. The exiles were forbidden to return at the peril of their lives.

As the escort disappeared, their pent-up feelings found vent in a few hysterical tears from the Duchess, some bad language from Mother Shipton, and a Parthian volley of expletives from Uncle Billy. The philosophic Oakhurst alone remained silent. He listened calmly to Mother Shipton's desire to cut somebody's heart out, to the repeated statements of the Duchess that she would die in the road, and to the alarming oaths that seemed to be bumped out of Uncle Billy as he rode forward. With the easy good humor characteristic of his class, he insisted upon exchanging his own riding-horse, "Five-spot," for the sorry mule which the Duchess rode. But even this act did not draw the party into any closer sympathy. The young woman readjusted her somewhat draggled plumes with a feeble, faded coquetry; Mother Shipton eyed the possessor of "Five-spot" with malevolence, and Uncle Billy included the whole party in one sweeping anathema.

The road to Sandy Bar—a camp that, not having as yet experienced the regenerating influences of Poker Flat, consequently seemed to offer some invitation to the emigrants—lay over a steep mountain range. It was distant a day's severe travel. In that advanced season the party soon passed out of the moist, temperate regions of the foothills into the dry, cold bracing air of the Sierras. The trail was narrow and difficult. At noon the Duchess, rolling out of her saddle

534

upon the ground, declared her intention of going no farther, and the party halted.

The spot was singularly wild and impressive. A wooded amphitheater surrounded on three sides by precipitous cliffs of naked granite, sloped gently toward the crest of another precipice that overlooked the valley. It was, undoubtedly, the most suitable spot for a camp, had camping been advisable. But Mr. Oakhurst knew that scarcely half the journey to Sandy Bar was accomplished, and the party was not equipped or provisioned for delay. This fact he pointed out to his companions curtly, with a philosophic commentary on the folly of "throwing up their hand before the game was played out." But they were furnished with liquor, which in this emergency stood them in place of food, fuel, rest and prescience. In spite of his remonstrances, it was not long before they were more or less under its influence. Uncle Billy passed rapidly from a bellicose state into one of stupor, the Duchess became maudlin, and Mother Shipton snored. Mr. Oakhurst alone remained erect, leaning against a rock, calmly surveying them.

Mr. Oakhurst did not drink. It interfered with a profession which required coolness, impassiveness, and presence of mind, and, in his own language, he "couldn't afford it." As he gazed at his recumbent fellow exiles, the loneliness begotten of his pariah trade, his habits of life, his very vices, for the first time seriously oppressed him. He bestirred himself in dusting his black clothes, washing his hands and face, and other acts characteristic of his studiously neat habits, and for a moment forgot his annoyance. The thought of deserting his weaker and more pitiable companions never perhaps occurred to him. Yet he could not help feeling the want of that excitement which, singularly enough, was most conducive to that calm equanimity for which he was notorious. He looked at the gloomy walls that rose a thousand feet sheer above the circling pines around him, at the sky ominously clouded, at the valley below, already deepening into shadow; and, doing so, suddenly he heard his own name called.

A horseman slowly ascended the trail. In the fresh, open face of the newcomer Mr. Oakhurst recognized Tom Simson, otherwise known as "The Innocent," of Sandy Bar. He had met him some months before over a "little game," and had, with perfect equanimity, won the entire fortune—amounting to some forty dollars—of that guileless youth. After the game was finished, Mr. Oakhurst drew the youthful speculator behind the door and thus addressed him:

"Tommy, you're a good little man, but you can't gamble worth a cent. Don't try it ever again." He then handed him his money back, pushed him gently from the room, and so made a devoted slave of Tom Simson.

There was a remembrance of this in his boyish and enthusiastic greeting of Mr. Oakhurst. He had started, he said, to go to Poker Flat to seek his fortune. "Alone?" No, not exactly alone; in fact (a giggle), he had run away with Piney Woods. Didn't Mr Oakhurst remember Piney? She that used to wait on the table at the Temperance House? They had been engaged a long time, but old Jake Woods had objected, and so they had run away, and were going to Poker Flat to be married, and here they were. And they were tired out, and how lucky it was they had found a place to camp, and company. All this the Innocent delivered rapidly, while Piney, a stout, comely damsel of fifteen, emerged from behind the pine tree, where she had been blushing unseen, and rode to the side of her lover.

Mr. Oakhurst seldom troubled himself with sentiment, still less with propriety; but he had a vague idea that the situation was not fortunate. He retained, however, his presence of mind sufficiently to kick Uncle Billy, who was about to say something, and Uncle Billy, was sober enough to recognize in Mr. Oakhurst's kick a superior power that would not bear trifling. He then endeavored to dissuade Tom Simson from delaying further, but in vain. He even pointed out the fact that there was no provision, nor means of making a camp. But, unluckily, the Innocent met this objection by assuring the party that he was provided with an extra mule loaded with provisions, and by the discovery of a rude attempt at a log house near the trail. "Piney can stay with Mrs. Oakhurst," said the Innocent, pointing to the Duchess, "and I can shift for myself."

Nothing but Mr. Oakhurst's admonishing foot saved Uncle Billy from bursting into a roar of laughter. As it was, he felt compelled to retire up the cañon until he could recover his gravity. There he confided the joke to the tall pine trees, with many slaps of his leg, contortions of his face, and the usual profanity. But when he returned to the party, he found them seated by a fire—for the air had grown strangely chill and the sky overcast—in apparently amicable conversation. Piney was actually talking in an impulsive girlish fashion to the Duchess, who was listening with an interest and animation she had not shown for many days. The Innocent was holding forth, apparently with equal effect, to Mr. Oakhurst and Mother

Shipton, who was actually relaxing into inward amiability. "Is this yer a d—d picnic?" said Uncle Billy, with inward scorn, as he surveyed the sylvan group, the glancing firelight, and the tethered animals in the foreground. Suddenly an idea mingled with the alcoholic fumes that disturbed his brain. It was apparently of a jocular nature, for he felt impelled to slap his leg again and cram his fist into his mouth.

As the shadows crept slowly up the mountain, a slight breeze rocked the tops of the pine trees and moaned through their long and gloomy aisles. The ruined cabin, patched and covered with pine boughs, was set apart for the ladies. As the lovers parted, they unaffectedly exchanged a kiss, so honest and sincere that it might have been heard above the swaying pines. The frail Duchess and the malevolent Mother Shipton were probably too stunned to remark upon this last evidence of simplicity, and so turned without a word to the hut. The fire was replenished, the men lay down before the door, and in a few minutes were asleep.

Mr. Oakhurst was a light sleeper. Toward morning he awoke benumbed and cold. As he stirred the dying fire, the wind, which was now blowing strongly, brought to his cheek that which caused the blood to leave it—snow!

He started to his feet with the intention of awakening the sleepers, for there was no time to lose. But turning to where Uncle Billy had been lying, he found him gone. A suspicion leaped to his brain, and a curse to his lips. He ran to the spot where the mules had been tethered—they were no longer there. The tracks were already rapidly disappearing in the snow.

The momentary excitement brought Mr. Oakhurst back to the fire with his usual calm. He did not waken the sleepers. The Innocent slumbered peacefully, with a smile on his good-humored, freckled face; the virgin Piney slept beside her frailer sisters as sweetly as though attended by celestial guardians; and Mr. Oakhurst, drawing his blanket over his shoulders, stroked his mustaches and waited for the dawn. It came slowly in a whirling mist of snow-flakes that dazzled and confused the eye. What could be seen of the landscape appeared magically changed. He looked over the valley, and summed up the present and future in two words, "Snowed in!"

A careful inventory of the provisions, which, fortunately for the party, had been stored within the hut, and so escaped the felonious fingers of Uncle Billy, disclosed the fact that with care and prudence they might last ten days longer. "That is," said Mr. Oakhurst *sotto*

voce to the Innocent, "if you're willing to board us. If you ain't—
and perhaps you'd better not—you can wait till Uncle Billy gets back
with provisions." For some occult reason, Mr. Oakhurst could not
bring himself to disclose Uncle Billy's rascality, and so offered the
hypothesis that he had wandered from the camp and had accidentally
stampeded the animals. He dropped a warning to the Duchess and
Mother Shipton, who, of course, knew the facts of their associate's
defection. "They'll find out the truth about us *all* when they find out
anything," he added significantly, "and there's no good frightening
them now."

Tom Simson not only put all his worldly store at the disposal of
Mr. Oakhurst, but seemed to enjoy the prospect of their enforced
seclusion. "We'll have a good camp for a week, and then the snow'll
melt, and we'll all go back together." The cheerful gayety of the
young man and Mr. Oakhurst's calm infected the others. The Innocent, with the aid of pine boughs, extemporized a thatch for the roof
less cabin, and the Duchess directed Piney in the rearrangement of
the interior with a taste and a tact that opened the blue eyes of that
provincial maiden to their fullest extent. "I reckon now you're used
to fine things at Poker Flat," said Piney. The Duchess turned away
sharply to conceal something that reddened her cheeks through their
professional tint, and Mother Shipton requested Piney not to "chatter." But when Mr. Oakhurst returned from a weary search for the
trail, he heard the sound of happy laughter echoed from the rocks.
He stopped in some alarm, and his thoughts first naturally reverted
to the whiskey, which he had prudently cached. "And yet it don't
somehow sound like whiskey," said the gambler. It was not until he
caught sight of the blazing fire through the still blinding storm, and
the group around it, that he settled to the conviction that it was
"square fun."

Whether Mr. Oakhurst had cached his cards with the whiskey as
something debarred the free access of the community, I cannot say.
It was certain that, in Mother Shipton's words, he "didn't say 'cards'
once" during that evening. Haply the time was beguiled by an accordian, produced somewhat ostentatiously by Tom Simson from his
pack. Notwithstanding some difficulties attending the manipulation
of this instrument, Piney Woods managed to pluck several reluctant melodies from its keys, to an accompaniment by the Innocent
on a pair of bone castanets. But the crowning festivity of the evening was reached in a rude camp-meeting hymn, which the lovers,
joining hands, sang with great earnestness and vociferation. I fear

538

that a certain defiant tone and Covenanter's swing to its chorus, rather than any devotional quality, caused it speedily to infect the others, who at last joined in the refrain:—

"I'm proud to live in the service of the Lord,
And I'm bound to die in his army."

The pines rocked, the storm eddied and whirled above the miserable group, and the flames of their altar leaped heavenward, as if in token of the vow.

At midnight the storm abated, the rolling clouds parted, and the stars glittered keenly above the sleeping camp. Mr. Oakhurst, whose professional habits had enabled him to live on the smallest possible amount of sleep, in dividing the watch with Tom Simson somehow managed to take upon himself the greater part of that duty. He excused himself to the Innocent by saying that he had "often been a week without sleep." "Doing what?" asked Tom. "Poker!" replied Oakhurst sententiously. "When a man gets a streak of luck—nigger-luck—he don't get tired. The luck gives in first. Luck," continued the gambler reflectively, "is a mighty queer thing. All you know about it for certain is that it's bound to change. And it's finding out when it's going to change that makes you. We've had a streak of bad luck since we left Poker Flat—you come along, and, slap, you get into it, too. If you can hold your cards right along you're all right. For," added the gambler, with cheerful irrelevance—

" 'I'm proud to live in the service of the Lord,
And I'm bound to die in his army.' "

The third day came, and the sun, looking through the white-curtained valley, saw the outcasts divide their slowly decreasing store of provisions for the morning meal. It was one of the peculiarities of that mountain climate that its rays diffused a kindly warmth over the wintry landscape, as if in regretful commiseration of the past. But it revealed drift on drift of snow piled high around the hut—a hopeless, uncharted, trackless sea of white lying below the rocky shores to which the castaways still clung. Through the marvelously clear air the smoke of the pastoral village of Poker Flat rose miles away. Mother Shipton saw it, and from a remote pinnacle of her rocky fastness hurled in that direction a final malediction. It was her last vituperative attempt, and perhaps for that reason was invested with a certain degree of sublimity. It did her good, she privately informed the Duchess. "Just you go out there and cuss, and

539

see." She then set herself to the task of amusing "the child," as she and the Duchess were pleased to call Piney. Piney was no chicken, but it was a soothing and original theory of the pair thus to account for the fact that she didn't swear and wasn't improper.

When night crept up again through the gorges, the reedy notes of the accordian rose and fell in fitful spasms and long-drawn gasps by the flickering camp-fire. But music failed to fill entirely the aching void left by insufficient food, and a new diversion was proposed by Piney,—story-telling. Neither Mr. Oakhurst nor his female companions caring to relate their personal experiences, this plan would have failed too, but for the Innocent. Some months before he had chanced upon a stray copy of Mr. Pope's ingenious translation of the Iliad. He now proposed to narrate the principle incidents of that poem— having thoroughly mastered the argument and fairly forgotten the words—in the current vernacular of Sandy Bar. And so for the rest of that night the Homeric demigods again walked the earth. Trojan bully and wily Greek wrestled in the winds, and the great pines in the cañon seemed to bow to the wrath of the son of Peleus. Mr. Oakhurst listened with quiet satisfaction. Most especially was he interested in the fate of "Ash-heels," as the Innocent persisted in denominating the "swift-footed Achilles."

So, with small food and much of Homer and the accordian, a week passed over the heads of the outcasts. The sun again forsook them, and again from leaden skies the snowflakes were sifted over the land. Day by day closer around them drew the snowy circle, until at last they looked from their prison over drifted walls of dazzling white, that towered twenty feet above their heads. It became more and more difficult to replenish their fires, even from the fallen trees beside them, now half hidden in the drifts. And yet no one complained. The lovers turned from the dreary prospect and looked into each other's eyes, and were happy. Mr. Oakhurst settled himself coolly to the losing game before him. The Duchess, more cheerful than she had been, assumed the care of Piney. Only Mother Shipton—once the strongest of the party—seemed to sicken and fade. At midnight on the tenth day she called Oakhurst to her side. "I'm going," she said, in a voice of querulous weakness, "but don't say anything about it. Don't waken the kids. Take the bundle from under my head, and open it." Mr. Oakhurst did so. It contained Mother Shipton's rations for the last week, untouched. "Give 'em to the child," she said, pointing to the sleeping Piney. "You've starved yourself," said the gambler. "That's what they call it," said the woman querulously,

540

as she lay down again, and, turning her face to the wall, passed quietly away.

The accordian and the bones were put aside that day, and Homer was forgotten. When the body of Mother Shipton had been committed to the snow, Mr. Oakhurst took the Innocent aside, and showed him a pair of snow-shoes, which he had fashioned from the old pack-saddle. "There's one chance in a hundred to save her yet," he said, pointing to Piney; "but it's there," he added, pointing toward Poker Flat. "If you can reach there in two days, she's safe." "And you?" asked Tom Simson. "I'll stay here," was the curt reply.

The lovers parted with a long embrace. "You are not going, too?" said the Duchess, as she saw Mr. Oakhurst apparently waiting to accompany him. "As far as the cañon," he replied. He turned suddenly and kissed the Duchess, leaving her pallid face aflame, and her trembling limbs rigid with amazement.

Night came, but not Mr. Oakhurst. It brought the storm again and the whirling snow. Then the Duchess, feeding the fire, found that some one had quietly piled beside the hut enough fuel to last a few days longer. The tears rose to her eyes, but she hid them from Piney.

The women slept but little. In the morning, looking into each other's faces, they read their fate. Neither spoke, but Piney, accepting the position of the stronger, drew near and placed her arm around the Duchess's waist. They kept this attitude for the rest of the day. That night the storm reached its greatest fury, and, rending asunder the protecting vines, invaded the very hut.

Toward morning they found themselves unable to feed the fire, which gradually died away. As the embers slowly blackened, the Duchess crept closer to Piney, and broke the silence of many hours: "Piney, can you pray?" "No, dear," said Piney simply. The Duchess, without knowing exactly why, felt relieved, and, putting her head upon Piney's shoulder, spoke no more. And so reclining, the younger and purer pillowing the head of her soiled sister upon her virgin breast, they fell asleep.

The wind lulled as if it feared to waken them. Feathery drifts of snow, shaken from the long pine boughs, flew like white winged birds, and settled about them as they slept. The moon through the rifted clouds looked down upon what had been the camp. But all human stain, all trace of earthly travail, was hidden beneath the spotless mantle mercifully flung from above.

They slept all that day and the next, nor did they waken when

541

voices and footsteps broke the silence of the camp. And when pitying fingers brushed the snow from their wan faces, you could scarcely have told from the equal peace that dwelt upon them which was she that had sinned. Even the law of Poker Flat recognized this, and turned away, leaving them still locked in each other's arms.

But at the head of the gulch, on one of the largest pine trees, they found the deuce of clubs pinned to the bark with a bowie-knife. It bore the following, written in pencil in a firm hand:—

†

BENEATH THIS TREE

LIES THE BODY

OF

JOHN OAKHURST

WHO STRUCK A STREAK OF BAD LUCK

ON THE 23D OF NOVEMBER 1850,

AND

HANDED IN HIS CHECKS

ON THE 7TH DECEMBER 1850

And pulseless and cold, with a derringer by his side and a bullet in his heart, though still calm as in life, beneath the snow lay he who was at once the strongest and yet the weakest of the outcasts of Poker Flat.

GERHART HAUPTMANN

GERHART HAUPTMANN (German, 1862-1946). Won early, and most lasting, fame as revolutionary naturalist with *The Weavers*, drama of social protest. In later years leaned to classicism and symbolism: *The Fool in Christ* (novel), *Iphegenia in Aulis* (play). Early social consciousness did not prevent his final association with Nazism.

THE WEAVERS

Enter Ansorge, an earthenware pan with soup in one hand, in the other a half-finished quarter-bushel basket.

Ansorge. Glad to see you again, Moritz!

Jaeger. Thank you, Father Ansorge—same to you!

Ansorge (shoving his pan into the oven). Why, lad, you look like a duke!

542

Old Baumert. Show him your watch, Moritz. An' he's got a new suit of clothes besides them he's on, an' thirty shillings in his purse.

Ansorge (shaking his head). Is that so? Well, well!

Emma (puts the potato-parings into a bag). I must be off; I'll maybe get a drop o' skim milk for these.   *(Goes out.)*

Jaeger (the others hanging on his words). You know how you all used to be down on me. It was always: Wait, Moritz, till your soldiering time comes—you'll catch it then. But you see how well I've got on. At the end of the first half-year I had my good-conduct stripes. You've got to be willing—that's where the secret lies. I brushed the sergeant's boots; I groomed his horse; I fetched his beer. I was as sharp as a needle. Always ready, accouterments clean and shining—first at stables, first at roll-call, first in the saddle. And when the bugle sounded to the assault—why, then, blood and thunder, and ride to the devil with you!! I was as keen as a pointer. Says I to myself: There's no help for it now, my boy, it's got to be done; and I set my mind to it and did it. Till at last the major said before the whole squadron: There's a hussar, now, that shows you what a hussar should be!

(Silence. He lights his pipe.)

Ansorge (shaking his head). Well, well, well! You had luck with you, Moritz. *(Sits down on the floor, with his willow twigs beside him, and continues mending the basket, which he holds between his legs.)*

Old Baumert. Let's hope you've brought some of it to us.—Are we to have a drop to drink your health in?

Jaeger. Of course you are, Father Baumert. And when this bottle's done, we'll send for more. *(He flings a coin on the table.)*

Ansorge (open mouthed with amazement). Oh my! Oh my! What goings on, to be sure! Roast meat frizzlin' in the oven! A bottle o' brandy on the table! *(He drinks out of the bottle.)* Here's to you, Moritz!—Well, well, well!

(The bottle circulates freely after this.)

Old Baumert. If we could any way have a bit o' meat on Sundays and holidays, instead of never seein' the sight of it from year's end to year's end! Now we'll have to wait till another poor little dog finds its way into the house like this one did four weeks gone by—an' that's not likely to happen soon again.

Ansorge. Have you killed the little dog?

Old Baumert. We had to do that or starve.

Ansorge. Well, well!

543

Mother Baumert. A nice, kind little beast he was, too!

Jaeger. Are you as keen as ever on roast dog hereabouts?

Old Baumert. My word, if we could only get enough of it!

Mother Baumert. A nice little bit o' meat like that does you a lot o' good.

Old Baumert. Have you lost the taste for it, Moritz? Stay with us a bit, and it'll soon come back to you.

Ansorge (sniffing). Yes, yes! That will be a tasty bite—what a good smell it has!

Old Baumert (sniffing). Splendid!

Ansorge. Come, then, Moritz, tell us your opinion, you that's been out and seen the world. Are things at all like improving for us weavers, eh?

Jaeger. They would need to.

Ansorge. We're in an awful state here. It's not livin' an' it's not dyin'. A man fights to the bitter end, but he's bound to be beat at last—to be left without a room over his head, you may say without ground under his feet. As long as he can work at the loom he can earn some sort o' poor, miserable livin'. But it's many a day since I've been able to get that sort o' job. Now I tries to put a bite into my mouth with this here basket-makin'. I sits at it late into the night, and by the time I tumbles into bed I've earned three-halfpence. I put it to you if a man can live on that, when everything's so dear? Nine shillin' goes in one lump for house tax, three shillin' for land tax, nine shillin' for mortgage interest—that makes one pound one. I may reckon my year's earnin' at just double that money, and that leaves me twenty-one shillin' for a whole year's food, an' fire, an' clothes, an' shoes; and I've got to keep up some sort of a place to live in. Is it any wonder if I'm behindhand with my interest payments?

Old Baumert. Some one would need to go to Berlin an' tell the King how hard put to it we are.

Jaeger. Little good that would do, Father Baumert. There's been plenty written about it in the newspapers. But the rich people, they can turn and twist things round—as cunning as the devil himself.

Old Baumert (shaking his head). To think they've no more sense than that in Berlin!

Ansorge. And is it really true, Moritz? Is there no law to help us? If a man hasn't been able to scrape together enough to pay his mortgage interest, though he's worked the very skin off his hands, must his house be taken from him? The peasant that's lent the

544

money on it, he wants his rights—what else can you look for from him? But what's to be the end of it all, I don't know. If I'm put out o' the house—*(In a voice choked by tears.)* I was born here, and here my father sat at his loom for more than forty year. Many was the time he said to mother: Mother, when I'm gone, the house'll still be here. I've worked hard for it. Every nail means a night's weaving, every plank a year's dry bread. A man would think that—

Jaeger. They're quite fit to take the last bite out of your mouth—that's what they are.

Ansorge. Well, well, well! I would rather be carried out than have to walk out now in my old days. Who minds dyin'? My father, he was glad to die. At the very end he got frightened, but I crept into bed beside him, an' he quieted down again. I was a lad of thirteen then. I was tired and fell asleep beside him—I knew no better—and when I woke he was quite cold.

Mother Baumert (after a pause). Give Ansorge his soup out o' the oven, Bertha.

Bertha. Here, Father Ansorge, it'll do you good.

Ansorge (eating and shedding tears). Well, well, well!

(Old Baumert has begun to eat meat out of the saucepan.)

Mother Baumert. Father, father, can't you have patience an' let Bertha serve it up properly?

Old Baumert (chewing). It's two years now since I took the sacrament. I went straight after that an' sold my Sunday coat, an' we bought a good bit o' pork, an' since then never a mouthful of meat has passed my lips till to-night.

Jaeger. How should *we* need meat? The manufacturers eat it for us. It's the fat of the land *they* live on. Whoever doesn't believe that has only to go down to Bielau and Peterswaldau. He'll see fine things there—palace upon palace, with towers and iron railings and plate-glass windows. Who do they all belong to? Why, of course, the manufacturers! No signs of bad times there! Baked and boiled and fried—horses and carriages and governesses—they've money to pay for all that and goodness knows how much more. They're swelled out to bursting with pride and good living.

Ansorge. Things was different in my young days. Then the manufacturers let the weaver have his share. Now they keep everything to theirselves. An' would you like to know what's at the bottom of it all? It's that the fine folks nowadays believes neither in God nor devil. What do they care about commandments or punishments? And so they steal our last scrap o' bread, and leave us

545

no chance of earnin' the barest living. For it's their fault. If our manufacturers was good men, there would be no bad times for us.

Jaeger. Listen, then, and I'll read you something that will please you. *(He takes one or two loose papers from his pocket.)* I say, August, run and fetch another quart from the public house. Eh, boy, do you laugh all day long?

Mother Baumert. No one knows why, but our August's always happy—grins an' laughs, come what may. Off with you then, quick! *(Exit August with the empty brandy bottle.)* You've got something good now, eh, father?

Old Baumert (still chewing; spirits rising from the effect of food and drink). Moritz, you're the very man we want. You can read an' write. You understand the weaving trade, and you've a heart to feel for the poor weaver's sufferin's. You should stand up for us here.

Jaeger. I'd do that quick enough! There's nothing I'd like better than to give the manufacturers round here a bit of a fright—dogs that they are! I'm an easy-going fellow, but let me once get worked up into a real rage, and I'll take Dreissiger in the one hand and Dittrich in the other, and knock their heads together till the sparks fly out of their eyes.—If we could only arrange all to join together, we'd soon give the manufacturers a proper lesson—without help from King or Government—all we'd have to do would be to say, We want this and that, and we don't want the other thing. There would be a change of days then. As soon as they see that there's some pluck in us, they'll cave in. I know the rascals; they're a pack of cowardly hounds.

Mother Baumert. There's some truth in what you say. I'm not an ill-natured woman. I've always been the one to say as how there must be rich folks as well as poor. But when things comes to such a pass as this—

Jaeger. The devil may take them all, for what I care. It would be no more than they deserve.

(Old Baumert has quietly gone out.)

Bertha. Where's father?

Mother Baumert. I don't know where he can have gone.

Bertha. Do you think he's not been able to stomach the meat, with not gettin' none for so long?

Mother Baumert (in distress, crying). There now, there! He's not even able to keep it down when he's got it. Up it comes again, the only bite o' good food as he's tasted this many a day.

546

Old Baumert. It's no good! I'm too far gone! Now that I've at last got hold of somethin' with a taste in it, my stomach won't keep it. *(He sits down on the bench by the stove, crying.)*

Jaeger (with a sudden violent ebullition of rage). And yet there are people not far from here, justices they call themselves too, over-fed brutes, that have nothing to do all the year round but invent new ways of wasting their time. And these people say that the weavers would be quite well off if only they weren't so lazy.

Ansorge. The men as say that are no men at all, they're monsters.

Jaeger. Never mind, Father Ansorge; we're making the place hot for 'em. Becker and I have been and given Dreissiger a piece of our mind, and before we came away we sang him "Bloody Justice."

Ansorge. Good Lord! Is that the song?

Jaeger. Yes; I have it here.

Ansorge. They call it Dreissiger's song, don't they?

Jaeger. I'll read it to you.

Mother Baumert. Who wrote it?

Jaeger. That's what nobody knows. Now listen.

(He reads, hesitating like a schoolboy, with incorrect accentuation, but unmistakably strong feeling. Despair, suffering, rage, hatred, thirst for revenge, all find utterance.

The justice to us weavers dealt
 Is bloody, cruel, and hateful;
Our life's one torture, long drawn out:
 For Lynch law we'd be grateful.

Stretched on the rack day after day,
 Hearts sick and bodies aching,
Our heavy sighs their witness bear
 To spirit slowly breaking.

(The words of the song make a strong impression on Old Baumert. Deeply agitated, he struggles against the temptation to interrupt Jaeger. At last he can keep quiet no longer.)

Old Baumert (to his wife, half laughing, half crying, stammering). Stretched on the rack day after day. Whoever wrote that, mother,

547

wrote the truth. You can bear witness—eh, how does it go? "Our heavy sighs their witness bear"—what's the rest?

Jaeger. "To spirit slowly breaking."

Old Baumert. You know the way we sigh, mother, day and night, sleepin' and wakin'.

(Ansorge has stopped working, and cowers on the floor, strongly agitated. Mother Baumert and Bertha wipe their eyes frequently during the course of the reading.

Jaeger (continues to read)—

The Dreissigers true hangmen are,
    Servants no whit behind them;
Masters and men with one accord
    Set on the poor to grind them.

You villains all, you brood of hell!—

Old Baumert (trembling with rage, stamping on the floor)— Yes, brood of hell!!!

Jaeger (reads)—
You fiends in fashion human,
A curse will fall on all like you,
    Who prey on man and woman.

Ansorge. Yes, yes, a curse upon them!

Old Baumert (clenching his fist, threateningly). You prey on man and woman.

Jaeger (reads)—

The suppliant knows he asks in vain,
    Vain every word that's spoken.
"If not content, then go and starve—
    Our rules cannot be broken."

Old Baumert. What is it? "The suppliant knows he asks in vain"? Every word of it's true—every word—as true as the Bible. He knows he asks in vain.

Ansorge. Yes, yes! It's all no good.

Jaeger (reads)—

Then think of all our woe and want,
    O ye who hear this ditty!
Our struggle vain for daily bread
    Hard hearts would move to pity.

548

But pity's what *you've* never known,—
  You'd take both skin and clothing,
You cannibals, whose cruel deeds
  Fill all good men with loathing.

Old Baumert (jumps up, beside himself with excitement). Both skin and clothing. It's true, it's all true! Here I stand, Robert Baumert, master-weaver, of Kaschbach. Who can bring up anything against me?—I've been an honest, hard-working man all my life long, an' look at me now! What have I to show for it? Look at me! See what they've made of me! Stretched on the rack day after day. *(He holds out his arms.)* Feel that! Skin and bone! "You villains all, you brood of hell!!" *(He sinks down on a chair, weeping with rage and despair.)*

Ansorge (flings his basket from him into a corner, rises, his whole body trembling with rage, gasps). And the time's come now for a change, I say. We'll stand it no longer! We'll stand it no longer! Come what may!

NATHANIEL HAWTHORNE

NATHANIEL HAWTHORNE (American, 1804-1864). Classic American novelist of New England. Housebound by boyhood leg injury. Worked as adult for port of Salem, became U.S. Consul abroad. Puritan heritage centers his novels about problems of guilt and moral pride. Most famous: *The Scarlet Letter.* Others: *The House of the Seven Gables, The Marble Faun, The Blithedale Romance, Twice-Told Tales*

THE AMBITIOUS GUEST

One September night a family had gathered round their hearth and piled it high with the driftwood of mountain streams, the dry cones of the pine, and the splintered ruins of great trees, that had come crashing down the precipice. Up the chimney roared the fire, and brightened the room with its broad blaze. The faces of the father and mother had a sober gladness; the children laughed. The eldest daughter was the image of Happiness at seventeen, and the aged grandmother, who sat knitting in the warmest place, was the image of Happiness grown old. They had found the "herb heart's-ease" in the

bleakest spot of all New England. This family were situated in the Notch of the White Hills, where the wind was sharp throughout the year and piteously cold in the winter, giving their cottage all its fresh inclemency before it descended on the valley of the Saco. They dwelt in a cold spot and a dangerous one, for a mountain towered above their heads so steep that the stones would often rumble down its sides and startle them at midnight.

The daughter had just uttered some simple jest that filled them all with mirth, when the wind came through the Notch and seemed to pause before their cottage, rattling the door with a sound of wailing and lamentation before it passed into the valley. For a moment it saddened them, though there was nothing unusual in the tones. But the family were glad again when they perceived that the latch was lifted by some traveler whose footsteps had been unheard amid the dreary blast which heralded his approach and wailed as he was entering, and went moaning away from the door.

Though they dwelt in such a solitude, these people held daily converse with the world. The romantic pass of the Notch is a great artery through which the life-blood of internal commerce is continually throbbing between Maine on one side and the Green Mountains and the shores of the St. Lawrence on the other. The stage coach always drew up before the door of the cottage. The wayfarer with no companion but his staff paused here to exchange a word, that the sense of loneliness might not utterly overcome him ere he could pass through the cleft of the mountain or reach the first house in the valley. And here the teamster on his way to Portland market would put up for the night, and, if a bachelor, might sit an hour beyond the usual bedtime and steal a kiss from the mountain maid at parting. It was one of those primitive taverns where the traveler pays only for food and lodging, but meets with a homely kindness beyond all price. When the footsteps were heard, therefore, between the outer door and the inner one, the whole family rose up, grandmother, children, and all as if about to welcome someone who belonged to them, and whose fate was linked with theirs.

The door was opened by a young man. His face at first wore the melancholy expression, almost despondency, of one who travels a wild and bleak road at nightfall and alone, but soon brightened up when he saw the kindly warmth of his reception. He felt his heart spring forward to meet them all, from the old woman who wiped the chair with her apron to the little child that held out its arms

to him. One glance and smile placed the stranger on a footing of innocent familiarity with the oldest daughter.

"Ah! this fire is the right thing," cried he, "especially when there is such a pleasant circle around it. I am quite benumbed, for the Notch is just like the pipe of a great pair of bellows; it has blown a terrible blast in my face all the way from Bartlett."

"Then you are going toward Vermont?" said the master of the house as he helped to take a light knapsack off the young man's shoulders.

"Yes, to Burlington, and far enough beyond," replied he. "I meant to have been at Ethan Crawford's tonight, but a pedestrian lingers along such a road as this. It is no matter; for when I saw this good fire and all your cheerful faces, I felt as if you had kindled it on purpose for me and were waiting my arrival. So I shall sit down among you and make myself at home."

The frank-hearted stranger had just drawn his chair to the fire when something like a heavy footstep was heard without, rushing down the steep side of the mountain as with long and rapid strides, and taking such a leap in passing the cottage as to strike the opposite precipice. The family held their breath, because they knew the sound, and their guest held his by instinct.

"The old mountain has thrown a stone at us for fear we should forget him," said the landlord, recovering himself. "He sometimes nods his head and threatens to come down, but we are old neighbors, and agree together pretty well upon the whole. Besides, we have a sure place of refuge hard by if he should be coming in good earnest."

Let us now suppose the stranger to have finished his supper of bear's meat, and by his natural felicity of manner to have placed himself on a footing of kindness with the whole family; so that they talked as freely together as if he belonged to their mountain brood. He was of a proud yet gentle spirit, haughty and reserved among the rich and great, but ever ready to stoop his head to the lowly cottage door and be like a brother or a son at the poor man's fireside. In the household of the Notch he found warmth and simplicity of feeling, the pervading intelligence of New England, and a poetry of native growth which they had gathered when they little thought of it from the mountain-peaks and chasms, and at the very threshold of their romantic and dangerous abode. He had traveled far and alone; his whole life, indeed, had been a solitary path, for, with the lofty caution of his nature, he had kept himself apart from

those who might otherwise have been his companions. The family, too, though so kind and hospitable, had that consciousness of unity among themselves and separation from the world at large which in every domestic circle should still keep a holy place where no stranger may intrude. But this evening a prophetic sympathy impelled the refined and educated youth to pour out his heart before the simple mountaineers, and constrained them to answer him with the same free confidence. And thus it should have been. Is not the kindred of a common fate a closer tie than that of birth?

The secret of the young man's character was a high and abstracted ambition. He could have borne to live an undistinguished life, but not to be forgotten in the grave. Yearning desire had been transformed to hope, and hope, long cherished, had become like certainty that, obscurely as he journeyed now, a glory was to beam on all his pathway, though not, perhaps, while he was treading it. But when present, they would trace the brightness of his footsteps, brightening as meaner glories faded, and confess that a gifted one had passed from his cradle to his tomb with none to recognize him.

"As yet," cried the stranger, his cheek glowing and his eye flashing with enthusiasm— "as yet I have done nothing. Were I to vanish from the earth tomorrow, none would know so much of me as you—that a nameless youth came up at nightfall from the valley of the Saco, and opened his heart to you in the evening, and passed through the Notch by sunrise, and was seen no more. Not a soul would ask, 'Who was he? Whither did the wanderer go?' But I cannot die till I have achieved my destiny. Then let Death come; I shall have built my monument."

There was a continual flow of natural emotion gushing forth amid abstracted reverie which enabled the family to understand this young man's sentiments, though so foreign from their own. With quick sensibility of the ludicrous, he blushed at the ardor into which he had been betrayed.

"You laugh at me," said he, taking the eldest daughter's hand and laughing himself. "You think my ambition as nonsensical as if I were to freeze myself to death on the top of Mount Washington only that people might spy at me from the country roundabout. And truly that would be a noble pedestal for a man's statue."

"It is better to sit here by this fire," answered the girl, blushing, "and be comfortable and contented, though nobody thinks about us."

"I suppose," said her father, after a fit of musing, "there is something natural in what the young man says; and if my mind had been turned that way, I might have felt just the same. It is strange, wife, how his talk has set my head running on things that are pretty certain never to come to pass."

"Perhaps they may," observed the wife. "Is the man thinking what he will do when he is a widower?"

"No, no!" cried he, repelling the idea with reproachful kindness. "When I think of your death, Esther, I think of mine, too. But I was wishing we had a good farm in Bartlett or Bethlehem or Littleton, or some other township round the White Mountains, but not where they could tumble on our heads. I should want to stand well with my neighbors and be called squire and sent to General Court for a term or two; for a plain, honest man may do as much good there as a lawyer. And when I should be grown quite an old man, and you an old woman, so as not to be long apart, I might die happy enough in my bed, and leave you all crying around me. A slate gravestone would suit me as well as a marble one, with just my name and age, and a verse of a hymn, and something to let people know that I lived an honest man and died a Christian."

"There, now!" exclaimed the stranger; "it is our nature to desire a monument, be it slate or marble, or a pillar of granite, or a glorious memory in the universal heart of man."

"We're in a strange way tonight," said the wife, with tears in her eyes. "They say it's a sign of something when folks' minds go a-wandering so. Hark to the children!"

They listened accordingly. The younger children had been put to bed in another room, but with an open door between; so that they could be heard talking busily among themselves. One and all seemed to have caught the infection from the fireside circle, and were outvying each other in wild wishes and childish projects of what they would do when they came to be men and women. At length a little boy, instead of addressing his brothers and sisters, called out to his mother:

"I'll tell you what I wish, mother," cried he: "I want you and father and grandma'm, and all of us, and the stranger, too, to start right away and go and take a drink out of the basin of the Flume."

Nobody could help laughing at the child's notion of leaving a warm bed and dragging them from a cheerful fire to visit the basin of the Flume—a brook which tumbles over the precipe deep within the Notch.

553

The boy had hardly spoken, when a wagon rattled along the road and stopped a moment before the door. It appeared to contain two or three men who were cheering their hearts with the rough chorus of a song which resounded in broken notes between the cliffs, while the singers hesitated whether to continue their journey or put up here for the night.

"Father," said the girl, "they are calling you by name."

But the good man doubted whether they had really called him, and was unwilling to show himself too solicitous of gain by inviting people to patronize his house. He therefore did not hurry to the door, and, the lash being soon applied, the travelers plunged into the Notch, still singing and laughing, though their music and mirth came back drearily from the heart of the mountain.

"There, mother!" cried the boy again; "they'd have given us a ride to the Flume."

Again they laughed at the child's pertinacious fancy for a night ramble. But it happened that a light cloud passed over the daughter's spirit; she looked gravely into the fire and drew a breath that was almost a sigh. It forced its way, in spite of a little struggle to repress it. Then, starting and blushing, she looked quickly around the circle, as if they had caught a glimpse into her bosom. The stranger asked what she had been thinking of.

"Nothing," answered she, with a downcast smile; "only I felt lonesome just then."

"Oh, I have always had a gift of feeling what is in other people's hearts," said he, half seriously. "Shall I tell the secrets of yours? For I know what to think when a young girl shivers by a warm hearth and complains of lonesomeness at her mother's side. Shall I put these feelings into words?"

"They would not be a girl's feelings any longer if they could be put into words," replied the mountain nymph, laughing, but avoiding his eye.

All this was said apart. Perhaps a germ of love was springing in their hearts so pure that it might blossom in Paradise, since it could not be matured on earth; for women worship such gentle dignity as his, and the proud, contemplative, yet kindly, soul is oftenest captivated by simplicity like hers. But while they spoke softly, and he was watching the happy sadness, the lightsome shadows, the shy yearnings of a maiden's nature, the wind through the Notch took a deeper and drearier sound. It seemed, as the fanciful stranger said, like the choral strain of the spirits of the blast who

in old Indian times had their dwelling among these mountains, and made their heights and recesses a sacred region. There was a wail along the road as if a funeral were passing. To chase away the gloom, the family threw pine-branches on their fire till the dry leaves crackled and the flame arose, discovering once again a scene of peace and humble happiness. The light hovered about them fondly and caressed them all. There were the little faces of the children peeping from their bed apart, and here the father's frame of strength, the mother's subdued and careful mien, the high-browed youth, the budding girl, and the good old grandam still knitting in the warmest place.

The aged woman looked up from her task, and with fingers ever busy was the next to speak.

"Old folks have their notions," said she, "as well as young ones. You've been wishing and planning and letting your heads run on one thing and another till you've set my mind a-wandering too. Now, what should an old woman wish for when she can go but a step or two before she comes to her grave? Children, it will haunt me night and day till I tell you."

"What is it, mother?" cried the husband and wife, at once.

Then the old woman, with an air of mystery which drew the circle closer round the fire, informed them that she had provided her grave-clothes some years before—a nice linen shroud, a cap with a muslin ruff, and everything of a finer sort than she had worn since her wedding day. But this evening an old superstition had strangely recurred to her. It used to be said in her younger days that if anything were amiss with a corpse, if only the ruff were not smooth or the cap did not set right, the corpse, in the coffin and beneath the clods, would strive to put up its cold hands and arrange it. The bare thought made her nervous.

"Don't talk so, grandmother," said the girl, shuddering.

"Now," continued the old woman with singular earnestness, yet smiling strangely at her own folly, "I want one of you, my children, when your mother is dressed and in the coffin,—I want one of you to hold a looking-glass over my face. Who knows but I may take a glimpse at myself, and see whether all's right."

"Old and young, we dream of graves and monuments," murmured the stranger youth. "I wonder how mariners feel when the ship is sinking and they, unknown and undistinguished, are to be buried together in the ocean, that wide and nameless sepulcher?"

For a moment the old woman's ghastly conception so engrossed

the minds of her hearers that a sound abroad in the night, rising like the roar of a blast, had grown broad, deep and terrible before the fated group were conscious of it. The house and all within it trembled; the foundations of the earth seemed to be shaken, as if this awful sound were the peal of the last trump. Young and old exchanged one wild glance and remained an instant pale, affrighted, without utterance or power to move. Then the same shriek burst simultaneously from all their lips:

"The slide! The slide!"

The simplest words must intimate, but not portray, the unutterable horror of the catastrophe. The victims rushed from their cottage, and sought refuge in what they deemed a safer spot, where, in contemplation of such an emergency, a sort of barrier had been reared. Alas! they had quitted their security and fled right into the pathway of destruction. Down came the whole side of the mountain in a cataract of ruin. Just before it reached the house the stream broke into two branches, shivered not a window there, but overwhelmed the whole vicinity, blocked up the road and and annihilated everything in its dreadful course. Long ere the thunder of that great slide had ceased to roar among the mountains the mortal agony had been endured and the victims were at peace. Their bodies were never found.

The next morning the light smoke was seen stealing from the cottage chimney, up the mountain-side. Within, the fire was yet smoldering on the hearth, and the chairs in a circle round it, as if the inhabitants had but gone forth to view the devastation of the slide, and would shortly return to thank Heaven for their miraculous escape. All had left separate tokens by which those who had known the family were made to shed a tear for each. Who has not heard their name? The story has been told far and wide, and will forever be a legend of these mountains. Poets have sung their fate.

There were circumstances which led some to suppose that a stranger had been received into the cottage on this awful night, and had shared the catastrophe of all its inmates; others denied that there were sufficient grounds for such a conjecture. Woe for the high souled youth with his dream of earthly immortality! His name and person utterly unknown, his history, his way of life, his plans, a mystery never to be solved, his death and his existence equally a doubt,—whose was the agony of that death moment?

556

JOHANN PETER HEBEL

JOHANN PETER HEBEL (German, 1760-1826). German poet and storyteller.
Son of a servant, became teacher and prelate. Goethe considered him among
greatest dialect poets. Published annual almanac of stories and anecdotes
(Schatzkästlein des Rheinischen Hausfreundes), from which he collected the
volume that established his fame.

KANNITVERSTAN

IN EMMENDINGEN and Gundelfingen, as well as in Amsterdam, a
man has the opportunity every day, I dare say, to reflect on the inconstancy of all earthly things—if he wants to—and to learn how
to be satisfied with his lot even though life is no bed of roses. But
it was by the oddest roundabout route that a German journeyman
in Amsterdam came, through error, to the perception of this truth.

After he had come to that great and prosperous city of commerce,
full of splendid houses, heaving ships, and busy people, his eye fell
upon a house larger and more beautiful than any he had ever seen
on all his travels from Tuttlingen to Amsterdam. For a long time he
gazed in wonder at this costly building, at the six chimneys on its
roof, at its beautiful cornices, and at the high windows, each larger
than the front door to his father's house.

Finally, yielding to an impulse, he addressed a passer-by. "My
good friend," he asked, "can you tell me the name of the gentleman
who owns this marvelous house with the windows full of tulips,
asters, and gilliflowers?" But the man, who probably had something
more important to attend to and, unfortunately, understood just as
much German as his questioner did Dutch—to wit, nothing—growled:
"Kannitverstan," and whisked by. This is a Dutch word—or three
of them, if one looks at it properly—and means no more than "I
cannot understand you."

But the good stranger thought it to be the name of the gentleman
he'd asked about. "That must be a mighty rich man, that Mr. Kannitverstan," he said to himself, and walked on.

Making his way through the narrow streets, he came at length to
the estuary that is called Het Ey, meaning "the Y." There stood ship
after ship and mast after mast, and he was beginning to wonder
how he could ever manage to take in all of these marvels with his
own two eyes, when his glance fell upon a large merchantman that

557

recently had put in from the East Indies and was being unloaded. Whole rows of piled crates and bales stood side by side on the wharf, and more were being rolled out: casks full of sugar and coffee, full of rice and pepper, and with them—pardon—mouse droppings too.

After he had watched for a long time, he asked a fellow who was carrying a crate on his shoulders the name of the fortunate man to whom the sea had brought all these wares. *"Kannitverstan,"* was the answer.

Then he thought: "Aha, so that's how it is! If the sea floats him such riches, no wonder he can put up houses with gilt-potted tulips in the windows." So he went away, sorrowfully reflecting how poor a man he was among so many rich people in this world. But just as he was thinking: "I wish I, too, would be as well off some day as this Mr. Kannitverstan," he turned a corner and saw a great funeral procession. Four black-draped horses were pulling a black-covered hearse slowly and lugubriously, as though they were aware they were carrying a dead man to his peace. A long cortege of friends and acquaintances of the departed followed behind, pair after pair, muffled in black cloaks, and mute. A solitary bell sounded in the distance. Our stranger was seized by the melancholy feeling that no good man can suppress at the sight of a funeral, and he remained standing reverently, with his hat in his hands, until all was over. Then he attached himself to the last mourner (who was just figuring how much he would make on his cotton if the bale price should rise ten florins), tugged at his coat, guilelessly begged his pardon, and said: "He must indeed have been a good friend of yours, the gentleman for whom the bell is tolling, that you follow his coffin so grieved and pensive."

"Kannitverstan," was the answer.

A few large tears descended from the eyes of our good journeyman from Tuttlingen, and he felt sad and relieved at once. "Poor Kannitverstan," he exclaimed, "what have you now of all your riches? Exactly what I shall get one day from my poverty: a linen shroud! And of all your beautiful flowers, you have, perhaps, a rosemary on your cold breast, or some rue." With these thoughts he accompanied the funeral procession to the grave as though he belonged with it, and saw the supposed Mr. Kannitverstan sink down to his final resting-place, and was more moved by the Dutch funeral oration, of which he understood not a word, than by many a German one to which he had paid no attention.

He left with the others and went away with a light heart, and at an inn where German was understood, he ate, with relish, a piece of Limburg cheese. And whenever afterward his heart became heavy because so many people in this world were so rich and he was so poor, he only thought of Mr. Kannitverstan of Amsterdam—of his big house, his opulent ship, and his narrow grave.

HEINRICH HEINE

HEINRICH HEINE (German, 1797-1856). Greatest lyricist in the German tongue. Regarded as leader of Young Germany. Settled in Paris, and interpreted French and Germans to each other. A hasty convert who remained a tender admirer of Judaism and acid critic of Christianity all his life. Noted for his irony, wit, mercurial intelligence. Famous poems: *"Die Lorelei,"* *"Du Bist Wie eine Blume."*

SONGS

Thou Who Art So Fair and Pure

Thou, so fair, so pure of guile,
Maiden of the sunny smile
Would to thee it were my fate
All my life to dedicate!

Like the moonbeams' tender shine
Gleam these gentle eyes of thine;
Thy soft cheeks so ruddy bright
Scatter rays of rosy light.

Thy dear little mouth doth show
Pearls within, a shining row;
But the gem of gems the best
Is enshrined within thy breast.

It was love divinely deep,
That into my heart did leap,
When I looked on thee erewhile,
Maiden of the sunny smile!

'Neath the Forest Boughs I Stept

Alone with the anguish that tore me
  'Neath the forest boughs I stept;
Anon came the old dream o'er me,
  And into my heart it crept.

Who taught ye this word, not to fear it,
  Little birds, singing up there so free?
Oh, hush! if my heart should hear it,
  Very sad it again would be.

"This way came a fair girl, she taught **it**;
  As she sang it, it was all we heard;
And up we little birds caught it,
  The dainty-sweet golden word."

Never think with such fables to wile me!
  Little birds, ye are wondrously sly;
You wish of my grief to beguile me,
  But I trust nothing living, not I.

The Two Grenadiers

For France two grenadiers held their way,
  Had prisoners been in Russia;
And sorrowful men they were, when they
  The frontier reached of Prussia.

For there they heard of a dire event,—
  How the world 'gainst France had risen, her
Grande armée had shattered and shent,
  And taken her Emperor prisoner.

They mingled their tears, these two grenadiers,
  To the sad tale ever returning;
"Oh would," said one, "that my days were done!
  My old wounds, how they're burning!"

"All's up!" said the other; "and sooner than not
  I would die like you, never doubt me;
But a wife and child at home I've got,
  And they must be starved without me!"

"Hang wife and child! It is something more,
    And better far, that I pant for;
My Emperor prisoner! My Emperor!
    Let them go beg what they want for!

"If I die just now, as 'tis like I may,
    Then, comrade, this boon grant me,
Take my body with you to France away,
    And in France's dear earth plant me.

"The *Croix d'Honneur*, with its crimson band,
    On my heart see that you place it;
Then give me my rifle in my hand,
    And my sword, around me to brace it.

"So will I lie, and listen all ear,
    Like a sentinel, low in my bed there,
Till the roar of the cannon some day I hear,
    And the chargers' neigh and their tread there.

"Then I'll know 'tis my Emperor riding by;
    The sabres flash high that attend him,
And out from my grave full-armed spring I
    The Emperor! to shield and defend him!"

Whene'er I Look into Thine Eyes

Whene'er I look into thine eyes,
Then every fear that haunts me flies;
But when I kiss thy mouth, oh then
I feel a giant's strength again.

Whene'er I couch me on thy breast,
I know what heaven is to the blest;
But when thou sayest, "I love thee!"
Then must I weep, and bitterly.

Thou Lovest Me Not

My love you cannot, cannot brook!
    I don't let that distress me;
So I but on thy face may look,
    In that's enough to bless me.

561

You hate, you hate, you hate me! is
  Your rosy-red mouth's greeting:
But let me have that mouth to kiss,
  And I'm content, my sweeting!

A Pine-Tree Stands Alone

A pine-tree stands alone on
  A bare bleak northern height;
The ice and snow they swathe it,
  As it sleeps there, all in white.

'Tis dreaming of a palm-tree,
  In a far-off Eastern land,
That mourns, alone and silent,
  On a ledge of burning sand.

My Songs Are Poisoned!

My songs, they are poisoned—poisoned!
  How otherwise could it be?
Over the flowers of my life's fresh hours
  Has poison been poured by thee.

My songs, they are poisoned—poisoned!
  How otherwise could it be?
Many serpents I bear in my heart, and there
  I bear with them, thee, love, thee.

In Dreams, Oh, I Have Wept, Love!

In dreams, oh, I have wept, love!
  I dreamed in the grave you were laid;
I awoke, and my cheek was wet, love,
  And tears still adown it strayed.

In dreams, oh, I have wept, love!
  I dreamt you were false to me;
I awoke, and I went on weeping
  Long, long and bitterly.

562

In dreams, oh, I have wept, love!
  I dreamed you still held me dear;
I awoke, and unto this hour, love,
  Weep many a scalding tear.

The Loreley

I cannot tell what's coming o'er me,
  That makes me so eerie and low:
An old-world legend before me,
  Keeps rising, and will not go.

The air chills, day is declining,
  And smoothly Rhine's waters run,
And the peaks of the mountains are shining
  Aloft in the setting sun.

A maiden of wondrous seeming,
  Most beautiful, sits up there;
Her jewels in gold are gleaming,
  She combs out her golden hair.

With a comb of red gold she parts it,
  And still as she combs it, she sings;
Her song pierces home to our hearts, it
  Has tones of a sweetness that stings.

The boatman, he thrills as he hears it
  Out there in his little skiff:
He sees not the reef as he nears it,
  He only looks up to the cliff.

The waters will sweep, I am thinking,
  O'er skiff, and o'er boatman ere long;
And this is, when daylight is sinking,
  What Loreley did with her song.

Thou Lovely Fisher-Maiden

My bonnie blithe fisher-maiden,
  Row in your boat to the strand;
Come here and sit down beside me,
  And chat with me hand in hand.

563

Rest your dear little head on my bosom,
    And be not so frightened, child;
Every day you trust without thinking
    Yourself to the ocean wild.

My heart is quite like the ocean,
    It has tempests, and ebb, and flow;
And fine pearls lie there a-many,
    Down, down in its depths below.

Thou Art Even as a Flower Is

Thou art even as a flower is,
    So gentle, and pure, and fair;
I gaze on thee, and sadness
    Comes over my heart unaware.

I feel as though I should lay, sweet,
    My hands on thy head, with a prayer
That God may keep thee alway, sweet,
    As gentle, and pure, and fair!

Oh, the Sweet Lies Lurk in Kisses!

Oh, the sweet lies lurk in kisses!
    Oh, the charm of make-believe!
Oh, to be deceived sweet bliss is,
    Bliss still sweeter to deceive!

What thou'lt grant, I know, my fairest,
    Vowing, "Nay, I never must!"
I will trust whate'er thou swearest,
    I will swear what thou wilt trust.

The Shades of the Summer Evening

The shades of the summer evening lie
    On forest and meadows green;
The golden moon shines in the azure sky
    Through balm-breathing air serene.

564

The cricket is chirping, the brooklet near,
  In the water a something stirs,
And the wanderer can in the stillness hear
  A plash and a sigh through the furze.

There all by herself the fairy bright
  Is bathing down in the stream;
Her arms and throat, betwitching and white,
  In the moonshine glance and gleam.

There Was an Aged King

There was an aged king,
  His heart was heavy, his locks were grey;
This poor old king, he wedded
  A maiden young and gay.

There was a pretty foot-page,
  His looks were fair, and his heart was light;
The sammet train he carried
  Of that queen so young and bright.

Dost know the old, old story?
  So sweet in the telling, so sad to tell!
They had both to die, oh the pity!
  They had loved each other too well.

MEMOIRS

Little Veronica

Whether it be because of the rhythmic beat of the oars, or the
swaying of the boat, or the fragrance of the hills of the river bank,
where joy doth grow, it always comes to pass that the most troubled
spirit finds peace in floating lightly in a little boat on the bosom of
the dear, clear river Rhine. In truth, kind old Father Rhine cannot
endure his children weeping; to stay their tears he takes them in
his trusty arms and rocks them and tells them his most lovely tales

and promises them his most golden treasures, perhaps even the hoard of the Niblungs sunk there in the dim distant past. . . .

O! it is a fair country full of loveliness and sunshine. The hills of the river bank are mirrored in the blue stream with their ruined castles and woods and ancient towns. There on their thresholds sit the townsfolk in the summer evenings and drink out of great mugs, and gossip, how the vines flourish, thank God, and how trials must be held in public, and how Marie Antoinette had been guillotined without more ado, and how the tobacco monopoly had raised the price of tobacco, and how all men are equal, and what a capital fellow Gôrres is.

For my part I never bothered about such conversations, but much preferred to sit with the girls in the arched window and laugh as they laughed, and have flowers thrown in my face and pretend to be angry, until they told me their secrets or some other vastly important story. The fair Gertrude could scarcely contain her delight when I sat with her; she was like a flaming rose, and when she fell upon my neck I used to think she would burst into flame and go off in smoke in my arms. The fair Catherine used to melt away in tender melody, when she talked to me, and her eyes were of a blue pure and sweet such as I have never found in human beings or beasts and only very rarely in flowers; it was lovely to look upon them, and so many sweet thoughts would come into my head as I gazed. But the fair Hedwig loved me; for when I came to her she bowed her head so that her black tresses fell over her blushing face, and her bright eyes shone like stars in the dark sky. Never a word came from her modest lips, and I, too, had nothing to say to her. I coughed, and she trembled. Often she would beg me through her sisters not to climb the rocks so fast, and not to bathe in the Rhine when I was hot with running or had been drinking. I used to listen sometimes when she prayed devoutly before the little picture of the Virgin Mary, which, spangled with gold, and lit up by a little flickering lamp, stood in a niche of the hall of the house. I heard clearly how she prayed the Mother of God to forbid Him to climb and drink and bathe. I might have loved her if she had been indifferent to me; and I was indifferent to her because I knew that she loved me.

The fair Johanna was a cousin of the three sisters; I liked much to be with her. She knew the most beautiful stories, and when she reached out of the window with her white hand towards the hills, where all the happenings of the story had been, a spell was cast

566

over me and I could see the old knights coming out of the ruined castles and hacking away at each other's armour, and the Lorelei stood once more on the hill-top and sang her sweet, seductive song, and the Rhine lapped so peacefully, so wisely, and yet with such dreadful mocking—and the fair Johanna looked at me strangely, as warily, and as mysteriously brooding as though she herself belonged to the fairy world of which she told. She was a slim, pale girl; she was consumptive and had long, long thoughts; her eyes were clear as truth; her lips pious and arched; in her features was a great story, but a sacred story—perhaps a legend of love? I know not, and I never had the courage to ask her. When I gazed for long upon her, I became peaceful and glad, and it was as though there were Sunday in my breast, and the angels were holding divine service in it.

At such times I used to tell her stories of my childhood, and she always listened gravely, and, strange, when I could not remember the names, she used to call them to mind for me. When I asked her in my astonishment how she knew the names, she used to smile and tell me by way of answer that the birds had told her who had made their nest in the eaves of her window; and she would have me believe that they were the very same birds which, as a boy, I had once bought from the cruel peasant children with my pocket-money to let them fly away. But I believe that she knew everything, because she was so pale and died so young. She knew also when she was to die, and wished me to leave Andenach the day before. When I left her, she gave me both her hands—they were clear, white hands and pure as the Host—and said: "You are very kind, and when you are angry, think of little Veronica, who is no more."

First Impressions in Paris

I had done and suffered much, and when the sun of the July Revolution rose in France I was very weary and stood in need of some relaxation. The air of my own country was every day more unwholesome for me, and I had seriously to think of a change of climate, and I had visions; the clouds oppressed me and cut all sorts of terrible capers before me. Often I thought the sun was a Prussian cockade; at night I dreamed of an ugly black vulture that ate my liver, and I was very melancholy. I also made the acquaintance of an old judge of Berlin who had passed many years in the

fortress of Spandau, and he told me how unpleasant it is to have to wear irons in winter. It seemed to me very unchristian not to warm the irons a little. If our chains were warmed a little they would not make so unpleasant an impression, and even men of a chilly nature could then bear them well; care should also be taken to scent fetters with roses and laurel as they do here in this country. I asked my old judge if he had often been given oysters to eat at Spandau. He said, "No," and that Spandau was far from the sea. Meat, too, he said, was rare there, and there was no other winged creature than the flies that fell in the soup. At the same time I made the acquaintance of a French *commis voyageur*, who travelled in wine and could not praise enough the jolly life in Paris, saying, how the sky is hung with fiddles, and how they sing from morning to night the Marseillaise and *"En avant, marchons!"* and *"Lafayette aux cheveux blancs,"* and how liberty, equality, and fraternity are written up at all the street corners; incidentally he praised the champagne of his firm, of whose cards he gave me a great number, and he promised me letters of introduction to the best Parisian restaurants, in case I should ever visit the capital in search of pleasure. And now as some sort of recreation is necessary, and Spandau is too far from the sea to eat oysters there, and the fly soup of Spandau did not attract me much, and also the Prussian chains are very cold in winter and would not be good for my health, I made up my mind to go to Paris and in the fatherland of champagne and the Marseillaise to drink the one and to hear the other, together with *"En avant, marchons!"* and *"Lafayette aux cheveux blancs."*

On May 1, 1831, I crossed the Rhine. I did not see the old river god, Father Rhine; I contented myself with throwing my visiting card into the water. I only saw the cathedral of Strassburg from a distance; he wagged his head like good Old Eckart when he sees a youngster going to the Venusberg.

At Saint Denis I awoke from a sweet morning sleep and heard for the first time the cry of the driver—"Paris! Paris!"—and the handbells of the cocoa-sellers. Here already you breathe the air of the capital which is visible on the horizon. An old rascal of a tout tried to persuade me to visit the tombs of the kings, but I had not come to France to see the kings; I contented myself with letting the guide tell me the legends of the place, how, for instance, the wicked Pagan king had Saint Denis' head cut off, and the Saint ran from Paris to Saint Denis with his head in his hand to be buried there, and to have the place called after him. "If you think," said my

guide, "if you think of the distance you cannot but be amazed at the miracle that any one could go so far on foot without a head"—and he added with a strange smile: *"Dans des cas pareils il n'y a que le premier pas qui coûte."* It was worth two francs and I gave them to him *pour l'amour de Voltaire*, whose mocking smile I had already met in him. In twenty minutes I was in Paris, and entered through the triumphal arch of the Boulevard Saint Denis, which was originally erected in honour of Louis XIV, but now served to glorify my entry into Paris. I was really surprised by the crowd of gay people, dressed very tastefully like fashion plates. Then I was impressed by them all speaking French, which is with us the mark of the polite world; but everybody is as polite here as the aristocracy in my country. The men were all so courteous, and the lovely ladies all so smiling. If any one jostled me without at once begging my pardon, then I could wager that he was a fellow countryman; and if ever a pretty woman looked sourly, then she had either been eating Sauerkraut or could read Klopstock in the original. I found everything so amazing, and the sky was so blue, and the air so sweet, so generous, and the beams of the July sun flickered hither and thither; the cheeks of the fair Lutetia were touched with the flaming kisses of that sun, and in her bosom her bridal nosegay was not yet withered. At the street corners *"Liberté, égalité, fraternité"* had in places been erased.

I sought at once the restaurants for which I had my letters of introduction; the proprietors assured me that they would have received me without letters of introduction, that I had such an honest and distinguished appearance as to be a recommendation in itself. Never did a German cookshop-keeper say the like to me, even if he thought it; such a fellow thinks that he must say nothing pleasant, and that his German frankness compels him only to say to one's face disagreeable things. In the manners and speech of the French there is so much of that precious flattery that costs so little and yet is so kindly and refreshing. My poor sensitive soul, that often recoiled in shyness from German coarseness, opened out to the flattering sounds of French urbanity. God gave us our tongues so that we might say pleasant things to our fellow men.

There was a hitch in my French when I arrived; but after half an hour's conversation with a little flower-seller in the Passage de l'Opéra, my French, which had grown rusty since the Battle of Waterloo, became fluent again and I stumbled about in the most gallant conjugations and explained to my little friend the Linnaean

system, by which flowers are classified according to the filaments; she herself followed another method and divided the flowers into those which smelled sweet and those which smelled offensive. I believed that she applied the same method of classification to men. She was astonished that I was so learned, in spite of my youth, and she trumpeted the fame of my learning through all the Passage de l'Opéra. I drank in delightedly the sweet scents of flattery and was much amused. I walked on flowers, and many a roast pigeon flew into my open gaping maw. What amusing things I saw on my arrival! All the notabilities of public pleasure and official absurdity.

Paris delighted me much with the cheeriness which appears in everything, and influences even the most doleful disposition. Strange! Paris is the scene of the greatest tragedies of the history of the world, tragedies at the memory of which hearts in the most distant lands tremble, eyes grow wet; but it is with the spectator of these great tragedies as it was once with me when I saw the *Tour de Nesle* at the Porte St. Martin. I was sitting behind a lady who was wearing a hat of rose-red gauze, and this hat was so wide that it cut off altogether my view of the stage, so that I could see the tragedy enacted through the red gauze of the hat, so that all the horrors of the *Tour de Nesle* appeared in the rosiest light. Yes, there is such a rosy light in Paris, which makes bright every tragedy for the spectator, so that it does not touch his enjoyment of life, and so the terrors which we bring to Paris lose their most bitter sting. Sorrows are strangely softened. In the air of Paris wounds are healed quicker than anywhere else; there is something so noble, so gentle, so sweet in the air, as in the people themselves.

ERNEST HEMINGWAY

ERNEST HEMINGWAY (American, 1898-   ). Influential novelist, brought to modern fiction new techniques of clipped dialogue and excessive scenes of violence. Experience in First World War produced *A Farewell to Arms.* Postwar "lost generation" classic: *The Sun Also Rises.* Covered Spanish Civil War as journalist, and wrote *For Whom the Bell Tolls.* Also addicted to hunting *(The Green Hills of Africa)* and bullfighting *(Death in the Afternoon)*—both nonfiction. Nobel Prize, 1954.

TEN INDIANS

AFTER one Fourth of July, Nick, driving home late from town in the big wagon with Joe Garner and his family, passed nine drunken Indians along the road. He remembered there were

nine because Joe Garner, driving along in the dusk, pulled up the
horses, jumped down into the road and dragged an Indian out of
the wheel rut. The Indian had been asleep, face down in the sand.
Joe dragged him into the bushes and got back up on the wagon-
box.

"That makes nine of them," Joe said, "just between here and the
edge of town."

"Them Indians," said Mrs. Garner.

Nick was on the back seat with the two Garner boys. He was
looking out from the back seat to see the Indian where Joe had
dragged him alongside of the road.

"Was it Billy Tabeshaw?" Carl asked.

"No."

"His pants looked mighty like Billy."

"All Indians wear the same kind of pants."

"I didn't see him at all," Frank said. "Pa was down into the road
and back up again before I seen a thing. I thought he was killing a
snake."

"Plenty of Indians'll kill snakes tonight, I guess," Joe Garner
said.

"Them Indians," said Mrs. Garner.

They drove along. The road turned off from the main highway
and went up into the hills. It was hard pulling for the horses
and the boys got down and walked. The road was sandy. Nick
looked back from the top of the hill by the schoolhouse. He
saw the lights of Petoskey and, off across Little Traverse Bay, the
lights of Harbour Springs. They climbed back in the wagon again.

"They ought to put some gravel on that stretch," Joe Garner
said. The wagon went along the road through the woods. Joe and
Mrs. Garner sat close together on the front seat. Nick sat between
the two boys. The road came out into a clearing.

"Right here was where Pa ran over the skunk."

"It was further on."

"Where?"

"Down by the lake. They were looking for dead fish along the
beach."

"They were coons probably," Carl said.

"They were skunks. I guess I know skunks."

"You ought to," Carl said. "You got an Indian girl."

"Stop talking that way, Carl," said Mrs. Garner.

"Well, they smell about the same."

571

Joe Garner laughed.

"You stop laughing, Joe," Mrs. Garner said. "I won't have Carl talk that way."

"Have you got an Indian girl, Nickie?" Joe asked.

"No."

"He has too, Pa," Frank said. "Prudence Mitchell's his girl."

"She's not."

"He goes to see her every day."

"I don't." Nick, sitting between the two boys in the dark, felt hollow and happy inside himself to be teased about Prudence Mitchell. "'She ain't my girl," he said.

"Listen to him," said Carl. "I see them together every day."

"Carl can't get a girl," his mother said, "not even a squaw." Carl was quiet.

"Carl ain't no good with girls," Frank said.

"You shut up."

"You're all right, Carl," Joe Garner said. "Girls never got a man anywhere. Look at your pa."

"Yes, that's what you would say," Mrs. Garner moved close to Joe as the wagon jolted. "Well, you had plenty of girls in your time."

"I'll bet Pa wouldn't ever have had a squaw for a girl."

"Don't you think it," Joe said. "You better watch out to keep Prudie, Nick."

His wife whispered to him and Joe laughed.

"What you laughing at?" asked Frank

"Don't you say it, Garner," his wife warned. Joe laughed again.

"Nickie can have Prudence," Joe Garner said. "I got a good girl."

"That's the way to talk," Mrs. Garner said.

The horses were pulling heavily in the sand. Joe reached out in the dark with the whip.

"Come on, pull into it. You'll have to pull harder than this tomorrow."

They trotted down the long hill, the wagon jolting. At the farmhouse everybody got down. Mrs. Garner unlocked the door, went inside, and came out with a lamp in her hand. Carl and Nick unloaded the things from the back of the wagon. Frank sat on the front seat to drive to the barn and put up the horses. Nick went up the steps and opened the kitchen door. Mrs. Garner was building a fire in the stove. She turned from pouring kerosene on the wood.

"Good-by, Mrs. Garner," Nick said. "Thanks for taking me."

572

"Oh shucks, Nickie."

"I had a wonderful time."

"We like to have you. Won't you stay and eat some supper?"

"I better go. I think Dad probably waited for me."

"Well, get along then. Send Carl up to the house, will you?"

"All right."

"Good night, Nickie."

"Good night, Mrs. Garner."

Nick went out the farmyard and down to the barn. Joe and Frank were milking.

"Good night," Nick said. "I had a swell time."

"Good night, Nick," Joe Garner called. "Aren't you going to stay and eat?"

"No, I can't. Will you tell Carl his mother wants him?"

"All right. Good night, Nickie."

Nick walked barefoot along the path through the meadow below the barn. The path was smooth and the dew was cool on his bare feet. He climbed a fence at the end of the meadow, went down through a ravine, his feet wet in the swamp mud, and then climbed up through the dry beech woods until he saw the lights of the cottage. He climbed over the fence and walked around to the front porch. Through the window he saw his father sitting by the table, reading in the light from the big lamp. Nick opened the door and went in.

"Well, Nickie," his father said, "was it a good day?"

"I had a swell time, Dad. It was a swell Fourth of July."

"Are you hungry?"

"You bet."

"What did you do with your shoes?"

"I left them in the wagon at Garner's."

"Come on out to the kitchen."

Nick's father went ahead with the lamp. He stopped and lifted the lid of the ice-box. Nick went on into the kitchen. His father brought in a piece of old chicken on a plate and a pitcher of milk and put them on the table before Nick. He put down the lamp.

"There's some pie too," he said. "Will that hold you?"

"It's grand."

His father sat down in a chair beside the oil-cloth-covered table. He made a big shadow on the kitchen wall.

"Who won the ball game?"

"Petoskey. Five to three."

His father sat watching him eat and filled his glass from the milk-

573

pitcher. Nick drank and wiped his mouth on his napkin. His father reached over to the shelf for the pie. He cut Nick a big piece. It was huckleberry pie.

"What did you do, Dad?"

"I went out fishing in the morning."

"What did you get?"

"Only perch."

His father sat watching Nick eat the pie.

"What did you do this afternoon?" Nick asked.

"I went for a walk up by the Indian camp."

"Did you see anybody?"

"The Indians were all in town getting drunk."

"Didn't you see anybody at all?"

"I saw your friend, Prudie."

"Where was she?"

"She was in the woods with Frank Washburn. I ran onto them. They were having quite a time."

His father was not looking at him.

"What were they doing?"

"I didn't stay to find out."

"Tell me what they were doing."

"I don't know," his father said. "I just heard them threshing around."

"How did you know it was them?"

"I saw them."

"I thought you said you didn't see them."

"Oh, yes, I saw them."

"Who was it with her?" Nick asked.

"Frank Washburn."

"Were they—were they—"

"Were they what?"

"Were they happy?"

"I guess so."

His father got up from the table and went out the kitchen screen door. When he came back Nick was looking at his plate. He had been crying.

"Have some more?" His father picked up the knife to cut the pie.

"No," said Nick.

"You better have another piece."

"No, I don't want any."

His father cleared off the table.

574

"Where were they in the woods?" Nick asked.

"Up back of the camp." Nick looked at his plate. His father said, "You better go to bed, Nick."

"All right."

Nick went into his room, undressed, and got into bed. He heard his father moving around in the living room. Nick lay in the bed with his face in the pillow.

"My heart's broken," he thought. "If I feel this way my heart must be broken."

After a while he heard his father blow out the lamp and go into his own room. He heard a wind come up in the trees outside and felt it come in cool through the screen. He lay for a long time with his face in the pillow, and after a while he forgot to think about Prudence and finally he went to sleep. When he awoke in the night he heard the wind in the hemlock trees outside the cottage and the waves of the lake coming in on the shore, and he went back to sleep. In the morning there was a big wind blowing and the waves were running high up on the beach and he was awake a long time before he remembered that his heart was broken.

O. HENRY

O. HENRY (William Sydney Porter, American, 1862-1910). Imaginative, ironic storyteller, famous for surprise endings. At one time America's most widely read story writer. Author of some 600 tales. Characters drawn from everyday life, with sympathy for the underdog. Titles of collections: *Cabbages and Kings, The Four Million, Heart of the West.*

THE WHIRLIGIG OF LIFE

JUSTICE-OF-THE-PEACE BENAJA WIDDUP sat in the door of his office smoking his elder-stem pipe. Halfway to the zenith the Cumberland range rose blue-gray in the afternoon haze. A speckled hen swaggered down the main street of the "settlement," cackling foolishly.

Up the road came a sound of creaking axles, and then a slow cloud of dust, and then a bull-cart bearing Ransie Bilbro and his wife. The cart stopped at the Justice's door, and the two climbed down. Ransie was a narrow six feet of sallow brown skin and yellow hair.

The imperturbability of the mountains hung upon him like a suit of armor. The woman was calicoed, angled, snuff-brushed, and weary with unknown desires. Through it all gleamed a faint protest of cheated youth unconscious of its loss.

The Justice of the Peace slipped his feet into his shoes, for the sake of dignity, and moved to let them enter.

"We-all," said the woman, in a voice like the wind blowing through pine boughs, "wants a divo'ce." She looked at Ransie to see if he noted any flaw or ambiguity or evasion or partiality or self-partisanship in her statement of their business.

"A divo'ce," repeated Ransie, with a solemn nod. "We-all can't git along together nohow. It's lonesome enough fur to live in the mount'ins when a man and a woman keers fur one another. But when she's a-spittin' like a wildcat or a-sullenin' like a hoot-owl in the cabin, a man ain't got no call to live with her."

"When he's a no-'count varmint," said the woman, without any especial warmth, "a-traipsin' along of scalawags and moonshiners and a-layin' on his back pizen 'ith co'n whiskey, and a-pesterin' folks with a pack o' hungry, triflin' houn's to feed!"

"When she keeps a-throwin' skillet lids," came Ransie's antiphony, "slings b'ilin' water on the best coon-dog in the Cumberlands, and sets herself agin' cookin' a man's victuals, and keeps him awake o' nights accusin' him of a sight of doin's!"

"When he's al'ays a-fightin' the revenues, and gits a hard name in the mount'ins fur a mean man, who's gwine to be able fur to sleep o' nights?"

The Justice of the Peace stirred deliberately to his duties. He placed his one chair and a wooden stool for his petitioners. He opened his book of statutes on the table and scanned the index. Presently he wiped his spectacles and shifted his inkstand.

"The law and the statutes," said he, "air silent on the subjeck of divo'ce as fur as the jurisdiction of this co't air concerned. But, accordin' to equity and the Constitution and the golden rule, it's a bad barg'in that can't run both ways. If a justice of the peace can marry a couple, it's plain that he is bound to be able to divo'ce 'em. This here office will issue a decree of divo'ce and abide by the decision of the Supreme Co't to hold it good."

Ransie Bilbro drew a small tobacco-bag from his trousers pocket. Out of this he shook upon the table a five-dollar note. "Sold a b'er-skin and two foxes fur that," he remarked. "It's all the money we got."

576

"The regular price of a divo'ce in this co't," said the Justice, "air five dollars." He stuffed the bill into the pocket of his homespun vest with a deceptive air of indifference. With much bodily toil and mental travail he wrote the decree upon half a sheet of foolscap, and then copied it upon the other. Ransie Bilbro and his wife listened to his reading of the document that was to give them freedom:

"Know all men by these presents that Ransie Bilbro and his wife, Ariela Bilbro, this day personally appeared before me and promised that hereinafter they will neither love, honor, nor obey each other, neither for better nor worse, being of sound mind and body, and accept summons for divorce according to the peace and dignity of the State. Herein fail not, so help you God. Benaja Widdup, justice of the peace in and for the county of Piedmont, State of Tennessee."

The Justice was about to hand one of the documents to Ransie. The voice of Ariela delayed the transfer. Both men looked at her. Their dull masculinity was confronted by something sudden and unexpected in the woman.

"Judge, don't you give him that air paper yit. 'Tain't all settled, nohow. I got to have my rights first. I got to have my ali-money. 'Tain't no kind of a way to do fur a man to divo'ce his wife 'thout her havin' a cent fur to do with. I'm a-layin' off to be a-goin' up to brother Ed's up on Hogback Mount'in. I'm bound fur to hev a pa'r of shoes and some snuff and things besides. Ef Rance kin affo'd a divo'ce, let him pay me ali-money."

Ransie Bilbro was stricken to dumb perplexity. There had been no previous hint of alimony. Women were always bringing up startling and unlooked-for issues.

Justice Benaja Widdup felt that the point demanded judicial decision. The authorities were also silent on the subject of alimony. But the woman's feet were bare. The trail to Hogback Mountain was steep and flinty.

"Ariela Bilbro," he asked, in official tones, "how much did you 'low would be good and sufficient ali-money in the case befo' the co't."

"I 'lowed," she answered, "fur the shoes and all, to say five dollars. That ain't much fur ali-money, but I reckon that'll git me up to brother Ed's."

"The amount," said the Justice, "air not onreasonable. Ransie Bilbro, you air ordered by the co't to pay the plaintiff the sum of five dollars befo' the decree of divo'ce air issued."

"I hain't no mo' money," breathed Ransie, heavily. "I done paid you all I had."

"Otherwise," said the Justice, looking severely over his spectacles, "you air in contempt of co't."

"I reckon if you gimme till to-morrow," pleaded the husband, "I mout be able to rake or scrape it up somewhars. I never looked for to be a-payin' no ali-money."

"The case air adjourned," said Benaja Widdup "till to-morrow, you-all will present yo'selves and obey the order of the co't. Followin' of which the decrees of divo'ce will be delivered." He sat down in the door and began to loosen a shoestring.

"We mout as well go down to Uncle Ziah's," decided Ransie, "and spend the night." He climbed into the cart on one side, and Ariela climbed in on the other. Obeying the flap of his rope the little red bull slowly came around on a tack, and the cart crawled away in the nimbus arising from its wheels.

Justice-of-the-peace Benaja Widdup smoked his elder-stem pipe. Late in the afternoon he got his weekly paper, and read it until the twilight dimmed its lines. Then he lit the tallow candle on his table, and read until the moon rose, marking the time for supper. He lived in the double log cabin on the slope near the girdled poplar. Going home to supper he crossed a little branch darkened by a laurel thicket. The dark figure of a man stepped from the laurels and pointed a rifle at his breast. His hat was pulled down low, and something covered most of his face.

"I want yo' money," said the figure, " 'thout any talk. I'm gettin' nervous, and my finger's a-wabblin on this here trigger."

"I've only got f-f-five dollars," said the Justice, producing it from his vest pocket.

"Roll it up," came the order, "and stick it in the end of this here gun-bar'l."

The bill was crisp and new. Even fingers that were clumsy and trembling found little difficulty in making a spill of it and inserting it (this with less ease) into the muzzle of the rifle.

"Now I reckon you kin be goin' along," said the robber.

The Justice lingered not on his way.

The next day came the little red bull, drawing the cart to the office door. Justice Benaja Widdup had his shoes on, for he was expecting the visit. In his presence Ransie Bilbro handed to his wife a five-dollar bill. The official's eye sharply viewed it. It seemed to curl up as though it had been rolled and inserted into the end of a

gun-barrel. But the Justice refrained from comment. It is true that other bills might be inclined to curl. He handed each one a decree of divorce. Each stood awkwardly silent, slowly folding the guarantee of freedom. The woman cast a shy glance full of constraint at Ransie.

"I reckon you'll be goin' back up to the cabin," she said, "along 'ith the bull-cart. There's bread in the tin box settin' on the shelf. I put the bacon in the b'ilin'-pot to keep the hounds from gittin' it. Don't forget to wind the clock to-night."

"You air a-goin' to your brother Ed's?" asked Ransie, with fine unconcern.

"I was 'lowin' to get along up thar afore night. I ain't sayin' as they'll pester theyselves any to make me welcome, but I hain't no-whar else fur to go. It's a right smart ways, and I reckon I better be goin'. I'll be a-sayin' good-bye, Ranse—that is, if you keer fur to say so."

"I don't know as anybody's a hound dog," said Ransie, in a martyr's voice, "fur to not want to say good-bye—'less you air so anxious to git away that you don't want me to say it."

Ariela was silent. She folded the five-dollar bill and her decree carefully, and placed them in the bosom of her dress. Benaja Wid-dup watched the money disappear with mournful eyes behind his spectacles.

And then with his next words he achieved rank (as his thoughts ran) with either the great crowd of the world's sympathizers or the little crowd of its great financiers.

"Be kind o' lonesome in the old cabin to-night, Ranse," he said.

Ransie Bilbro stared out at the Cumberlands, clear blue now in the sunlight. He did not look at Ariela.

"I 'low it might be lonesome," he said; "but when folks git mad and wants a divo'ce, you can't make folks to stay."

"Nobody never said they didn't."

"Nobody never said they did. I reckon I better start on now to brother Ed's."

"Nobody can't wind that old clock."

"Want me to go back along 'ith you in the cart and wind it fur you, Ranse?"

The mountaineer's countenance was proof against emotion. But he reached out a big hand and enclosed Ariela's thin brown one. Her soul peeped out once through her impassive face, hallowing it.

"Them hounds shan't pester you no more," said Ransie. "I reckon I been mean and low down. You wind that clock, Ariela."

"My heart, hit's in that cabin, Ranse," she whispered, "along 'ith you. I ain't a-goin' to git mad no more. Le's be startin', Ranse, so's we kin git home by sundown.'

Justice-of-the-peace Benaja Widdup interposed as they started for the door, forgetting his presence.

"In the name of the State of Tennessee," he said, "I forbid you-all to be a-defyin' of its laws and statutes. This co't is mo' than willin' and full of joy to see the clouds of discord and misunderstandin' rollin' away from two lovin' hearts, but it air the duty of the co't to p'eserve the morals and integrity of the State. The co't reminds you that you air no longer man and wife, but air divo'ced by regular decree, and as such air not entitled to the benefits and 'purtenances of the mattermonal estate."

Ariela caught Ransie's arm. Did those words mean that she must lose him now when they had just learned the lesson of life?

"But the co't air prepared," went on the Justice, "fur to remove the disabilities set up by the decree of divo'ce. The co't air on hand to perform the solemn ceremony of mari'ge, thus fixin' things up and enablin' the parties in the case to resume the honor'ble and elevatin' state of mattermony which they desires. The fee fur performin' said ceremony will be, in this case, to wit, five dollars."

Ariela caught the gleam of promise in his words. Swiftly her hand went to her bosom. Freely as an alighting dove the bill fluttered to the Justice's table. Her sallow cheek colored as she stood hand in hand with Ransie and listened to the reuniting words.

Ransie helped her into the cart, and climbed in beside her. The little red bull turned once more, and they set out, hand-clasped, for the mountains.

Justice-of-the-peace Benaja Widdup sat in his door and took off his shoes. Once again he fingered the bill tucked down in his vest pocket. Once again he smoked his elder-stem pipe. Once again the speckled hen swaggered down the main street of the "settlement," cackling foolishly.

JOHANN GOTTFRIED VON HERDER

JOHANN GOTTFRIED VON HERDER (German, 1744-1803). A sage among
the poets. Disciple of Kant, friend of Goethe. Wrote many essays on literature
(On German Life and Art), translated folk songs *(Voices of the Nations in
Song)*. A brilliant critic, important in shaping 18th and 19th century literature.

SIR OLAF

Sir Olaf he rideth west and east
To bid the folk to his bridal feast.

On the wold are dancing an elvish band,
And Erl-king's daughter proffers her hand.

"Now welcome, Sir Olaf: what haste's with thee?
Step into our circle and dance with me."

"To dance I neither will nor may,
To-morrow's dawn is my bridal-day."

"Nay, stay, Sir Olaf, and dance with me,
And golden spurs will I give to thee."

"To dance I neither will nor may,
To-morrow's dawn is my bridal-day."

"Nay, stay, Sir Olaf, and dance with me,
A heap of gold will I give to thee."

"For all thy gold I will not stay,
And dance I neither will nor may."

"If thou wilt not dance, Sir Olaf, with me,
Then Pest and Sickness shall follow thee."

She touched Sir Olaf upon the heart—
Ne'er in his life had he felt such smart.

She lifted him up on his steed that tide,
"Ride home! ride fast to thy troth-plight bride!"

And when he came to his castle-door,
His mother stood there, and trembled sore.

"Now say, sweet son, right speedilie
Why art thou wan, and white of blee?"

"Well may my face be wan and white.
I was in Erl-king's realm last night."

"Now tell me, my son so true and tried,
What thing shall I say to thy plighted bride?"

"Say that I hunt in the good greenwood,
With hound and horse as a good knight should."

When scarce the dawn in heaven shone red,
Came the train with the bride Sir Olaf should wed.

They sat at meat, they sat at wine;
"Now where is Sir Olaf, bridegroom of mine?"

"Sir Olaf rode out to the greenwood free,
With horse and hound to the hunt rode he."

The bride she lifted a cloth of red:
Beneath, Sir Olaf was lying dead.

ESTHONIAN BRIDAL SONG

Deck thyself, maiden,
With the hood of thy mother;
Put on the ribands
Which thy mother once wore:
On thy head the band of duty,
On thy forehead the band of care.
Sit in the seat of thy mother,
And walk in thy mother's footsteps.
And weep not, weep not, maiden:
If thou weepest in thy bridal attire,
Thou wilt weep all thy life.

582

HERMANN HESSE

HERMANN HESSE (German, 1877-   ). Swiss glorifier of nature and child-hood. After school, became locksmith and bookseller. Moved from Germany to Switzerland in 1912 to escape German militarism. Nobel Prize, 1946. *Peter Camenzind*, first successful novel. *Steppenwolf*, celebrated psychoanalytic novel. Others: *Demian, Death and the Lover, Magister Ludi.*

TALK IN A GONDOLA

What I dream, you ask? That yesterday
We had died, we two. In fair array—
Clad in white, our hair with flowers wound,
In our gondola we're seaward bound;
Bells from yonder campanile peal,
But the water gurgles round the keel,
Drowns the distant toll that's gently failing.
Onward, onward to the sea we're sailing,
Where the ships with masts that tower high,
Sombre shadows, rest against the sky,
Where on fishing-boats there gleam the moist
Deep-stained red and yellow sails they hoist,
Where the roaring mighty waves are swelling,
Where the sailors lurid tales are telling.
Through a gate of bluest water, deeply
Downward now our boat is gliding steeply.
In the depths we find a wid'ning range
Filled with many trees of coral strange,
Where in lustrous shells that hidden gleam
Pale gigantic pearls with beauty beam.
Silvery fishes pass us, glist'ning, shy,
Leaving tinted trails as they flit by,
In whose furrows other fish instead
Gleam with slender tails of golden red.
At the bottom, fathoms deep, we dream;
As if bells were calling it will seem,
Now and then, as if a wind that fanned
Sang us songs we cannot understand,
Songs of narrow streets we long ago
Left behind, of things we used to know,

583

Songs so far, far off about the ways
That we trod in long forgotten days.
And with wonder we'll remember slowly
Now a street, now some cathedral holy,
Or the shouting of a gondolier,
Many names that once we used to hear.
Smiling then as children smile in sleep,
Moving still our silent lips we keep,
And the word will, ere it spoken seems,
Fall into oblivion, death in dreams.
Over us the mighty vessels float,
Sails are bright on many a sombre boat,
Snow-white birds in gleaming sunshine fly,
Glistening nets upon the water lie,
Spanning all, with arches high and true
Glows the heavens' vault of sunlit blue.

IN THE FOG

In the fog to wander, how queer!
Lonely is every bush and stone,
No tree sees the other near,
Each is alone.

Once my world was full of friends,
When my life still had light;
Now that the fog descends,
Not one is in sight.

Only he is wise who knows
The steady gloom to fall
That slowly round him grows,
Severed from all.

In the fog to wander, how queer!
Solitude is life's own.
No man sees the other near,
Each is alone.

HITOMARO KAKINOMOTO

HITOMARO KAKINOMOTO (Japanese, *ca.* 655-710). Greatest of the Japanese Manyō poets. Nothing known of his life. Surviving work collected in the *Manyōshū*—scores of long poems and several hundred *tanka*, vigorous epics and delicate lyrics.

Poems from
THE MANYOSHU

In the sea of Iwami,
By the cape of Kara,
There amid the stones under sea
Grows the deep-sea *miru* weed;
There along the rocky strand
Grows the sleek sea-tangle.

Like the swaying sea-tangle,
Unresisting would she lie beside me—
My wife whom I love with a love
Deep as the *miru*-growing ocean.
But few are the nights
We two have lain together.

Away I have come, parting from her
Even as the creeping vines do part.
My heart aches within me;
I turn back to gaze—
But because of the yellow leaves
Of Watari Hill,
Flying and fluttering in the air,

I cannot see plainly
My wife waving her sleeve to me.
Now as the moon, sailing through the cloud rift
Above the mountain of Yakami,
Disappears, leaving me full of regret,
So vanishes my love out of sight;
Now sinks at last the sun,
Coursing down the western sky.

I thought myself a strong man,
But the sleeves of my garment
Are wetted through with tears.

585

My black steed
Galloping fast,
Away have I come,
Leaving under distant skies
The dwelling-place of my love.

Oh, yellow leaves
Falling on the autumn hill,
Cease a while
To fly and flutter in the air
That I may see my love's dwelling-place!

AFTER THE DEATH OF HIS WIFE

Since in Karu lived my wife,
I wished to be with her to my heart's content;
But I could not visit her constantly
Because of the many watching eyes—
Men would know of our troth,
Had I sought her too often
So our love remained secret like a rock-pent pool;
I cherished her in my heart,
Looking to after-time when we should be together,
And lived secure in my trust
As one riding a great ship.
Suddenly there came a messenger
Who told me she was dead—
Was gone like a yellow leaf of autumn.
Dead as the day dies with the setting sun,
Lost as the bright moon is lost behind the cloud,
Alas, she is no more, whose soul
Was bent to mine like the bending seaweed!

When the word was brought to me
I knew not what to do nor what to say;
But restless at the mere news,
And hoping to heal my grief
Even a thousandth part,
I journed to Karu and searched the market-place
Where my wife was wont to go!

There I stood and listened,
But no voice of her I heard,
Though the birds sang in the Unebi Mountain;
None passed by, who even looked like my wife.
I could only call her name and wave my sleeve.

ENVOYS

In the autumn mountains
The yellow leaves are so thick.
Alas, how shall I seek my love
Who has wandered away?—
I know not the mountain track.

I see the messenger come
As the yellow leaves are falling.
Oh, well I remember
How on such a day we used to meet—
My wife and I!

In the days when my wife lived,
We went out to the embankment near by—
We two, hand in hand—
To view the elm-trees standing there
With their outspreading branches
Thick with spring leaves. Abundant as their
     greenery
Was my love. On her leaned my soul.
But who evades mortality?—
One morning she was gone, flown like an early bird.
Clad in a heavenly scarf of white,
To the wide fields where the shimmering *kagero* rises
She went and vanished like the setting sun.

The little babe—the keepsake
My wife has left me—
Cries and clamours.
I have nothing to give; I pick up the child
And clasp it in my arms.

587

In her chamber, where our two pillows lie,
Where we two used to sleep together,
Days I spend alone, broken-hearted:
Nights I pass, sighing till dawn.

Though I grieve, there is no help;
Vainly I long to see her.
Men tell me that my wife is
In the mountains of Hagai—
Thither I go,
Toiling along the stony path;
But it avails me not,
For of my wife, as she lived in this world,
I find not the faintest shadow.

ENVOYS

To-night the autumn moon shines—
The moon that shone a year ago,
But my wife and I who watched it then together
Are divided by ever-widening wastes of time.

When leaving my love behind
In the Hikité mountains—
Leaving her there in her grave,
I walk down the mountain path,
I feel not like one living.

THE MOUNTAIN TOP

Because the plum trees on the peak
   Are up so high,
The buzz of bees about their bloom
   Comes from the sky!

MY LOVE WHO LOVES ME NOT
*But who must at least come with the
rest of the village to my funeral*

If I die of love, why, let me die,
   For then, since I have died,
She'll cross the threshold where I lie
   And stand—once—by my side.

FRIEDRICH HOLDERLIN

FRIEDRICH HÖLDERLIN (German, 1770-1843). Classical poet of Germany.
A poor tutor, lost his reason as a man of thirty, spent better part of life as a
ward of a carpenter. Most of works published by friends after his madness.
Reputation slight in own day, grew later.

HYPERION'S SONG OF FATE

Ye wander there in the light
On flower-soft fields, ye blest immortal
    Spirits.
Radiant godlike zephyrs
Touch you as gently
As the hand of a master might
Touch the awed lute-string.
Free of fate as the slumbering
Infant, breathe the divine ones.
Guarded well
In the firm-sheathed bud
Blooms eternal
Each happy soul;
And their rapture-lit eyes
Shine with a tranquil
Unchanging lustre.
But we, 'tis our portion,
We never may be at rest.
They stumble, they vanish,
The suffering mortals,
Hurtling from one hard
Hour to another,
Like waves that are driven
From cliff-side to cliff-side,
Endlessly down the uncertain abyss.

EVENING PHANTASIE

Before his hut reposes in restful shade
The ploughman; wreaths of smoke from his hearth ascend.
    And sweet to wand'rers comes the tone of
        Evening bells from the peaceful village.

The sailor too puts into the haven now,
In distant cities cheerily dies away
  The busy tumult; in the arbor
    Gleams the festal repast of friendship.

But whither I? In labor, for slight reward
We mortals live; in alternate rest and toil
  Contentment dwells; but why then sleeps not
    Hid in my bosom the thorn unsparing?

The ev'ning heaven blooms as with springtime's hue;
Uncounted bloom the roses, the golden world
  Seems wrapt in peace; oh, bear me thither,
    Purple-wrought clouds! And may for me there

Both love and grief dissolve in the joyous light!
But see, as if dispelled by the foolish prayer,
  The wonder fades! 'Tis dark, and lonely
    Under the heaven I stand as erstwhile.

Come then to me, soft Sleep. Overmuch requires
The heart; and yet thou too at the last shalt fade,
  Oh youth, thou restless dream-pursuer!
    Peaceful and happy shall age then follow.

HOMER

HOMER (Greek, 9th century B.C.). According to tradition, the blind author
of the *Iliad* and the *Odyssey*, great epics based on the Greek legends. Exact
identity never established. Homer set standard for epic poetry of Western
literature: swift, brilliant narrative, primitive imagery, celebration of exploits
of a whole people through an epic hero.

PRIAM RECLAIMS HECTOR'S BODY

On did the old man pass; and he entered, and found the Peleides
Seated apart from his train: two only of Myrmidons trustful,
Hero Automedon only, and Alkimus, sapling of Ares,
Near to him minist'ring stood; he reposed him but now from the
  meal-time,

Sated with food and with wine, nor removed from him yet was the
  table.
All unobserved of them entered the old man stately, and forthwith
Grasped with his fingers the knees and was kissing the hands of
  Achilles—
Terrible, murderous hands, by which son upon son had been slaugh-
  tered.
As when a man who has fled from his home with the curse of the
  blood-guilt,
Kneels in a far-off land, at the hearth of some opulent stranger,
Begging to shelter his head, there is stupor on them that behold
  him;
So was Achilles dumb at the sight of majestical Priam—
He and his followers all, each gazing on other bewildered.
But he uplifted his voice in their silence, and made supplication:
"Think of thy father at home" (he began), "O godlike Achilles!
Him, my coeval, like me within age's calamitous threshold.
Haply this day there is trouble upon him, some insolent neighbors
Round him in arms, nor a champion at hand to avert the disaster:
Yet even so there is comfort for him, for he hears of thee living;
Day unto day there is hope for his heart amid worst tribulation,
That yet again he shall see his beloved from Troia returning.
Misery only is mine; for of all in the land of my fathers,
Bravest and best were the sons I begat, and not one is remaining.
Fifty were mine in the hour that the host of Achaia descended:
Nineteen granted to me out of one womb, royally mothered,
Stood by my side; but the rest were of handmaids born in my dwell-
  ing.
Soon were the limbs of the many unstrung in the fury of Ares:
But one peerless was left, sole prop of the realm and the people;
And now at last he too, the protector of Ilion, Hector,
Dies by thy hand. For his sake have I come to the ships of Achaia,
Eager to ransom the body with bountiful gifts of redemption.
Thou have respect for the gods, and on me, O Peleides! have pity,
Calling thy father to mind; but more piteous is my desolation,
Mine, who alone of mankind have been humbled to this of en-
  durance
Pressing my mouth to the hand that is red with the blood of my
  children."
  Hereon Achilles, awaked to a yearning remembrance of Peleus,

Rose up, took by the hand, and removed from him gently the old man.
Sadness possessing the twain—one, mindful of valorous Hector,
Wept with o'erflowing tears, low laid at the feet of Achilles;
He, sometime for his father, anon at the thought of Patroclus,
Wept, and aloft in the dwelling their long lamentation ascended.
But when the bursting of grief had contented the godlike Peleides,
And from his heart and his limbs irresistible yearning departed,
Then from his seat rose he, and with tenderness lifted the old man,
Viewing the hoary head and the hoary beard with compassion;
And he addressed him, and these were the air-winged words that he uttered:—
"Ah unhappy! thy spirit in truth has been burdened with evils.
How could the daring be thine to come forth to the ships of Achaia
Singly, to stand in the eyes of the man by whose weapon thy children,
Many and gallant, have died? full surely thy heart is of iron.
But now seat thee in peace, old man, and let mourning entirely
Pause for a space in our minds, although heavy on both be affliction;
For without profit and vain is the fullness of sad lamentation,
Since it was destined so of the gods for unfortunate mortals
Ever in trouble to live, but they only partake not of sorrow;
For by the threshold of Zeus two urns have their station of old time,
Whereof the one holds dolings of good, but the other of evil;
And to whom mixt are the doles of the thunder-delighting Kronion,
He sometime is of blessing partaker, of misery sometime;
But if he gives him the ill, he has fixed him the mark of disaster,
And over bountiful earth the devouring Necessity drives him,
Wandering ever forlorn, unregarded of gods and of mortals.
Thus of a truth did the gods grant glorious gifts unto Peleus,
Even from the hour of his birth, for above compare was he favored,
Whether in wealth or in power, in the land of the Myrmidons reigning;
And albeit a mortal, his spouse was a goddess appointed.
Yet even to him, of the god there was evil apportioned,—that never
Lineage of sons should be born in his home, to inherit dominion.
One son alone he begat, to untimely calamity foredoomed;
Nor do I cherish his age, since afar from the land of my fathers
Here in the Troas I sit, to the torment of thee and thy children.
And we have heard, old man, of thine ancient prosperity also,

Lord of whatever is held between Lesbos the seat of the Macar,
Up to the Phrygian bound and the measureless Hellespontos;
Ruling and blest above all, nor in wealth nor in progeny equaled:
Yet from the hour that the gods brought this visitation upon thee,
Day unto day is thy city surrounded with battles and bloodshed.
Howso, bear what is sent, nor be grieved in thy soul without ceas-
   ing.
Nothing avails it, O king! to lament for the son that has fallen;
Him thou canst raise up no more, but thyself may have new tribu-
   lation."

  So having said, he was answered by Priam the aged and god-
   like:—
'Seat not me on the chair, O beloved of Olympus! while Hector
Lies in the tent uninterred; but I pray thee deliver him swiftly,
That I may see with mine eyes; and, accepting the gifts of redemp-
   tion,
Therein have joy to thy heart; and return thou homeward in safety,
Since of thy mercy I live and shall look on the light of the morning."
  Darkly regarding the king, thus answered the rapid Achilles:—
"Stir me to anger no more, old man: of myself I am minded
To the release of the dead; for a messenger came from Kronion
Hither, the mother that bore me, the child of the Ancient of Ocean.
Thee, too, I know in my mind, nor has aught of thy passage escaped
   me;
How that some god was the guide of thy steps to the ships of Achaia.
For never mortal had dared to advance, were he blooming in man-
   hood,
Here to the host by himself; nor could sentinels all be avoided;
Nor by an imbecile push might the bar be dislodged at my bulwark.
Therefore excite me no more, old man, when my soul is in sorrow,
Lest to thyself peradventure forebearance continue not alway,
Suppliant all that thou art—but I break the behest of the godhead."
  So did he speak; but the old man feared, and obeyed his com-
   mandment.
Forth of the door of his dwelling then leapt like a lion Peleides;
But not alone: of his household were twain that attended his going,
Hero Automedon first, and young Alkimus, he that was honored
Chief of the comrades around since the death of belovèd Patroclus.
These from the yoke straightway unharnessed the mules and the
   horses,

And they conducted within the coeval attendant of Priam,
Bidding him sit in the tent; then swiftly their hands from the mule-
wain,
Raise the uncountable wealth of the king's Hectorean head-gifts.
But two mantles they leave, and a tunic of beautiful texture,
Seemly for wrapping the dead as the ransomer carries him home-
ward.
Then were the handmaidens called, and commanded to wash and
anoint him,
Privately lifted aside, lest the son should be seen of the father,
Lest in the grief of his soul he restrain not his anger within him,
Seeing the corse of his son, but enkindle the heart of Achilles,
And he smite him to death, and transgress the command of Kronion.
But when the dead had been washed and anointed with oil by the
maidens,
And in the tunic arrayed and enwrapt in the beautiful mantle,
Then by Peleides himself was he raised and composed on the hand-
bier;
Which when the comrades had lifted and borne to its place in the
mule-wain,
Then groaned he; and he called on the name of his friend, the
beloved:—
"Be not wroth with me now, O Patroclus, if haply thou hearest,
Though within Hades obscure, that I yield the illustrious Hector
Back to his father dear. Not unworthy the gifts of redemption;
And unto thee will I render thereof whatsoever is seemly."

HORACE

HORACE (Roman, 65-8 B.C.). Latin poet, subtle, elegant, cheerful, profoundly
influential. One of notable group whose patron was the wealthy Maecenas.
Friend of Virgil. First work: *Satires*. Later: *Epistles*, *Odes*. His *Ars Poetica*,
written toward end of life, had permanent influence on all European criticism.

ODES

BOOK III, ODE 1

I scorn and shun the rabble's noise.
    Abstain from idle talk. A thing
    That ear hath not yet heard, I sing,
The Muses' priest, to maids and boys.

To Jove the flocks which great kings sway,
  To Jove great kings allegiance owe.
  Praise him: he laid the giants low:
All things that are, his nod obey.

This man may plant in broader lines
  His fruit trees: that, the pride of race
  Enlists a candidate for place:
In worth, in fame, a third outshines

His mates; or, thronged with clients, claims
  Precedence. Even-handed Fate
  Hath but one law for small and great:
That ample urn holds all men's names.

He o'er whose doomed neck hangs the sword
  Unsheathed, the dainties of the South
  Shall lack their sweetness in his mouth:
No note of bird or harpsichord

Shall bring him Sleep. Yet Sleep is kind,
  Nor scorns the huts of laboring men;
  The bank where shadows play, the glen
Of Temple dancing in the wind.

He, who but asks "Enough," defies
  Wild waves to rob him of his ease;
  He fears no rude shocks, when he sees
Arcturus set or Hædus rise:

When hailstones lash his vines, or fails
  His farm its promise, now of rains
  And now of stars that parch the plains
Complaining, unkindly gales.

—In straitened seas the fish are pent;
  For dams are sunk into the deep:
  Pile upon pile the builders heap,
And he, whom earth could not content,

The Master. Yet shall Fear and Hate
    Climb where the Master climbs: nor e'er
    From the armed trireme parts black Care;
He sits behind, the horseman's mate.

And if red marble shall not ease
    The heartache; nor the shell that shines
    Star-bright; nor all Falernum's vines,
All scents that charmed Achæmenes:

Why should I rear me halls of rare
    Design, on proud shafts mounting high?
    Why bid my Sabine vale good-by
For doubled wealth and doubled care?

EPODE 2

Alphius

Happy the man, in busy schemes unskilled,
    Who, living simply, like our sires of old,
Tills the few acres which his father tilled,
    Vexed by no thoughts of usury or gold;

The shrilling clarion ne'er his slumber mars,
    Nor quails he at the howl of angry seas;
He shuns the forum, with its wordy jars,
    Nor at a great man's door consents to freeze.

The tender vine-shoots, budding into life,
    He with the stately poplar tree doth wed,
Lopping the fruitless branches with his knife,
    And grafting shoots of promise in their stead;

Or in some valley, up among the hills,
    Watches his wandering herds of lowing kine,
Or fragrant jars with liquid honey fills,
    Or shears his silly sheep in sunny shine;

596

Or when Autumnus o'er the smiling land
 Lifts up his head with rosy apples crowned,
Joyful he plucks the pears, which erst his hand
 Graffed on the stem they're weighing to the ground;

Plucks grapes in noble clusters purple-dyed,
 A gift for thee, Priapus, and for thee,
Father Sylvanus, where thou dost preside,
 Warding his bounds beneath thy sacred tree.

Now he may stretch his careless limbs to rest,
 Where some old ilex spreads its sacred roof;
Now in the sunshine lie, as likes him best,
 On grassy turf of close elastic woof.

And streams the while glide on with murmurs low,
 And birds are singing 'mong the thickets deep,
And fountains babble, sparkling as they flow,
 And with their noise invite to gentle sleep.

But when grim winter comes, and o'er his grounds
 Scatters its biting snows with angry roar,
He takes the field, and with a cry of hounds
 Hunts down into the toils the foaming boar;

Or seeks the thrush, poor starveling, to ensnare,
 In filmy net with bait delusive stored,
Entraps the traveled crane, and timorous hare,
 Rare dainties these to glad his frugal board.

Who amid joys like these would not forget
 The pangs which love to all its victims bears,
The fever of the brain, the ceaseless fret,
 And all the heart's lamentings and despairs?

But if a chaste and blooming wife, beside,
 The cheerful home with sweet young blossoms fills,
Like some stout Sabine, or the sunburnt bride
 Of the lithe peasant of the Apulian hills

597

Who piles the hearth with logs well dried and old
    Against the coming of her wearied lord,
And, when at eve the cattle seek the fold,
    Drains their full udders of the milky hoard;

And bringing forth from her well-tended store
    A jar of wine, the vintage of the year,
Spreads an unpurchased feast,—oh then, not more
    Could choicest Lucrine oysters give me cheer,

Or the rich turbot, or the dainty char,
    If ever to our bays the winter's blast
Should drive them in its fury from afar;
    Nor were to me a welcomer repast

The Afric hen or the Ionic snipe,
    Than olives newly gathered from the tree,
That hangs abroad its clusters rich and ripe,
    Or sorrel, that doth love the pleasant lea,

Or mallows wholesome for the body's need,
    Or lamb foredoomed upon some festal day
In offering to the guardian gods to bleed,
    Or kidling which the wolf hath marked for prey.

What joy, amidst such feasts, to see the sheep,
    Full of the pasture, hurrying homewards come;
To see the wearied oxen, as they creep,
    Dragging the upturned plowshare slowly home!

Or, ranged around the bright and blazing hearth,
    To see the hinds, a house's surest wealth,
Beguile the evening with their simple mirth,
    And all the cheerfulness of rosy health!

Thus spake the miser Alphius; and, bent
    Upon a country life, called in amain
The money he at usury had lent;—
    But ere the month was out, 'twas lent again.

RICARDA HUCH

RICARDA HUCH (German, 1864-1947). Neo-romantic lyricist. Outstanding woman poet in modern German literature. Also wrote novels, including remarkable detective story, *The Deruga Trial.* Verse traditional in form, but rich in imagination and intuition.

MIDNIGHT

To this grave of mine
Come not in the morning,
Come on ways of darkness,
Dearest, by the dim moonshine.

For when through the skies
Bells are tolling midnight,
From my earthly prison
To the lovely air I rise.

In my death-dress white
On my grave I linger,
Watch the stars and measure
Time's placid tread at night.

Come and have no fear!
Can you still give kisses?
I forgot them never
While I slept the winters drear.

Kiss me hard and long.
In the east already
Sings the morning sunlight
—Lack-a-day!—its joyful song.

You were mine again!
Go and taste life's sweetness!—
I in deep, deep darkness
Sleep once more with pain.

VICTOR HUGO

VICTOR HUGO (French, 1802-1885). Chief exponent of the Romantic School of the drama; turned later to the novel. Among his main works: *The Punishments, Contemplation, The Legend of the Centuries, Les Misérables, The Hunchback of Notre Dame.* Also wrote poetry, somewhat stilted. Incurred displeasure of Napoleon III, was banished to the Channel Isles. The most widely known author of 19th century France.

LES MISERABLES

I.

Jean Valjean, Galley Slave

EARLY in October 1815, at the close of the afternoon, a man came into the little town of D——. He was on foot, and the few people about looked at him suspiciously. The traveller was of wretched appearance, though stout and robust, and in the full vigour of life. He was evidently a stranger, and tired, dusty, and wearied with a long day's tramp.

But neither of the two inns in the town would give him food or shelter though he offered good money for payment.

He was an ex-convict—that was enough to exclude him.

In despair he went to the prison, and asked humbly for a night's lodging, but the jailer told him that was impossible unless he got arrested first.

It was a cold night and the wind was blowing from the Alps; it seemed there was no refuge open to him.

Then, as he sat down on a stone bench in the market-place and tried to sleep, a lady coming out of the cathedral noticed him, and, learning his homeless state, bade him knock at the bishop's house, for the good bishop's charity and compassion were known in all the neighborhood.

At the man's knock the bishop, who lived alone with his sister, Madame Magloire, and an old housekeepes, said "Come in"; and the ex-convict entered.

He told them at once that his name was Jean Valjean, that he was a galley-slave, who had spent nineteen years at the hulks, and that he had been walking for four days since his release. "It is the same wherever I go," the man went on. "They all say to me, 'Be off!'

I am very tired and hungry. Will you let me stay here? I will pay."

"Madame Magloire," said the bishop, "please lay another knife and fork. Sit down, monsieur, and warm yourself. We shall have supper directly, and your bed will be got ready while you are supping."

Joy and amazement were on the man's face; he stammered his thanks as though beside himself.

The bishop, in honour of his guest, had silver forks and spoons placed on the table.

The man took his food with frightful voracity, and paid no attention to anyone till the meal was over. Then the bishop showed him his bed in an alcove, and an hour later the whole household was asleep.

Jean Valjean soon woke up again.

For nineteen years he had been at the galleys. Originally a pruner of trees, he had broken a baker's window and stolen a loaf one hard winter when there was no work to be had, and for this the sentence was five years. Time after time he had tried to escape, and had always been recaptured; and for each offence a fresh sentence was imposed.

Nineteen years for breaking a window and stealing a loaf! He had gone into prison sobbing and shuddering. He came out full of hatred and bitterness.

That night, at the bishop's house, for the first time in nineteen years, Jean Valjean had received kindness. He was moved and shaken. It seemed inexplicable.

He got up from his bed. Everyone was asleep, the house was perfectly still.

Jean Valjean seized the silver plate-basket which stood in the bishop's room, put the silver into his knapsack, and fled out of the house.

In the morning, while the bishop was breakfasting, the gendarmes brought in Jean Valjean. The sergeant explained that they had met him running away, and had arrested him, because of the silver they found on him.

"I gave you the candlesticks, too!" said the bishop; "they are silver. Why did not you take them with the rest of the plate?" Then, turning to the gendarmes, "It is a mistake."

"We are to let him go?" said the sergeant.

"Certainly," said the bishop.

The gendarmes retired.

"My friend," said the bishop to Jean Valjean, "here are your candlesticks. Take them with you." He added in a low voice, "Never forget that you have promised me to use this silver to become an honest man. My brother, you belong no longer to evil, but to good."

Jean Valjean never remembered having promised anything. He left the bishop's house and the town dazed and stupefied. It was a new world he had come into.

He walked on for miles, and then sat down by the roadside to think.

Presently a small Savoyard boy passed him, and as he passed dropped a two-franc piece on the ground.

Jean Valjean placed his foot upon it. In vain the boy prayed him for the coin. Jean Valjean sat motionless, deep in thought.

Only when the boy had gone on, in despair, did Jean Valjean wake from his reverie.

He shouted out, "Little Gervais, little Gervais!" for the boy had told him his name. The lad was out of sight and hearing, and no answer came.

The enormity of his crime came home to him, and Jean Valjean fell on the ground, and for the first time in nineteen years he wept.

II

Father Madeleine

On a certain December night in 1815 a stranger entered the town of M——, at the very time when a great fire had just broken out in the town hall.

This man at once rushed into the flames, and at the risk of his own life saved the two children of the captain of gendarmes. In consequence no one thought of asking for his passport.

The stranger settled in the town; by a happy invention he improved the manufacture of the black beads, the chief industry of M——, and in three years, from a very small capital, he became a rich man, and brought prosperity to the place.

In 1820, Father Madeleine, for so the stranger was called, was made Mayor of M—— by unanimous request, an honour he had declined the previous year. Before he came everything was languishing in the town, and now, a few years later, there was healthy life for all.

Father Madeleine employed everybody who came to him. The only

condition he made was—honesty. From the men he expected good-will, from the women, purity.

Prosperity did not make Father Madeleine change his habits. He performed his duties as mayor, but lived a solitary and simple life, avoiding society. His strength, although he was a man of fifty, was enormous. It was noticed that he read more as his leisure increased, and that as the years went by his speech became gentler and more polite.

One person only in all the district looked doubtfully at the mayor, and that was Javert, inspector of police.

Javert, born in prison, was the incarnation of police duty—implacable, resolute, fanatical. He arrived in M—— when Father Madeleine was already a rich man, and he felt sure he had seen him before.

One day in 1823 the mayor interfered to prevent Javert sending a poor woman, named Fantine, to prison. Fantine had been dismissed from the factory without the knowledge of M. Madeleine; and her one hope in life was her little girl, whom she called Cosette. Now, Cosette was boarded out at the village of Montfermeil, some leagues distance from M——, with a family grasping and dishonest, and to raise money for Cosette's keep had brought Fantine to misery and sickness.

The mayor could save Fantine from prison, he could not save her life; but before the unhappy woman died she had delivered a paper to M. Madeleine authorising him to take her child, and M. Madeleine had accepted the trust.

It was when Fantine lay dying in the hospital that Javert, who had quite decided in his own mind who M. Madeleine was, came to the mayor and asked to be dismissed from the service.

"I have denounced you, M. le Maire, to the prefect of police at Paris, as Jean Valjean, an ex-convict, who has been wanted for the robbery of a little Savoyard more than five years ago."

"And what answer did you receive?"

"That I was mad, for the real Jean Valjean has been found."

"Ah!"

Javert explained that an old man had been arrested for breaking into an orchard; that on being taken to the prison he had been recognised by several people as Jean Valjean, and that he, Javert, himself recognised him. To-morrow he was to be tried at Arras, and, as he was an ex-convict, his sentence would be for life.

Terrible was the anguish of M. Madeleine that night. He had

done all that man could do to obliterate the past, and now it seemed another was to be taken in his place. The torture and torment ended. In the morning M. Madeleine set out for Arras.

M. Madeleine arrived before the orchard-breaker was condemned. He proved to the court's astonishment that he, the revered and philanthropic Mayor of M——, was Jean Valjean, and that the prisoner had merely committed a trivial theft. Then he left the court, returned to M——, removed what money he had, buried it, and arranged his affairs.

A few days later Jean Valjean was sent back to the galleys at Toulon, and with his removal the prosperity of M—— speedily collapsed. This was in July 1823. In November of that year the following paragraph appeared in the Toulon paper.

"Yesterday, a convict, on his return from rescuing a sailor, fell into the sea and was drowned. His body has not been found. His name was registered as Jean Valjean."

III

A Hunted Man

At Christmas in the year 1823, an old man came to the village of Montfermeil, called at the inn, paid money to the rascally innkeeper, Thénardier, and carried off little Cosette to Paris.

The old man rented a large garret in an old house, and Cosette became inexpressibly happy with her doll and the good man who loved her so tenderly.

Till then Jean Valjean had never loved anything. He had never been a father, lover, husband, or friend. When he saw Cosette, and had rescued her, he felt his heart strangely moved. All the affection he had was aroused, and went out towards this child. Jean Valjean was fifty-five and Cosette eight, and all the love of his life, hitherto untouched, melted into a benevolent devotion.

Cosette, too, changed. She had been separated from her mother at such an early age that she could not remember her. And the Thénardiers had treated her harshly. In Jean Valjean she found a father, just as he found a daughter in Cosette.

Weeks passed away. These two beings led a wonderfully happy life in the old garret; Cosette would chatter, laugh, and sing all day.

Jean Valjean was careful never to go out in the daytime, but he began to be known in the district as "the mendicant who gives away money." There was one old man who sat by some church steps, and

who generally seemed to be praying, whom Jean Valjean always liked to relieve. One night when Jean Valjean had dropped a piece of money into his hand as usual, the beggar suddenly raised his eyes, stared hard at him, and then quickly dropped his head. The movement was like a flash. Jean Valjean started, and went home greatly troubled. The face which he fancied he had seen was that of Javert.

A few nights later Jean Valjean found that Javert had taken lodgings in the same house where he and Cosette lived. Taking the child by the hand, he at once set out for fresh quarters. They passed through silent and empty streets, and crossed the river, and it seemed to Jean Valjean that no one was in pursuit. But soon he noticed four men plainly shadowing him, and a shudder went over him. He turned from street to street, trying to escape from the city, and at last found himself entrapped in a *cul-de sac*. What was to be done?

There was no time to turn back. Javert had undoubtedly picketed every outlet. Fortunately for Jean Valjean, there was a deep shadow in the street, so that his own movements were unseen.

While he stood hesitating, a patrol of soldiers entered the street, with Javert at their head. They frequently halted. It was evident that they were exploring every hole and corner, and one might judge they would take a quarter of an hour before they reached the spot where Jean Valjean was. It was a frightful moment. Capture meant the galleys, and Cosette lost for ever. There was only one thing possible—to scale the wall which ran along a wide portion of the street. But the difficulty was Cosette; there was no thought of abandoning her.

First, Jean Valjean procured a rope from the lamp-post, for the lamps had not been lit that night owing to the moonlight. This he fastened round the child, taking the other end between his teeth. Half a minute later he was on his knees on top of the wall. Cosette watched him in silence. All at once she heard Jean Valjean saying in a very low voice. "Lean against the wall. Don't speak, and don't be afraid."

She felt herself lifted from the ground, and before she had time to think where she was she found herself on top of the wall.

Jean Valjean grasped her, put the child on his back, and crawled along the wall till he came to a sloping roof. He could hear the thundering voice of Javert giving orders to the patrol to search the *cul-de-sac* to the end.

Jean Valjean slipped down the roof, still carrying Cosette, and leaped on the ground. It was a convent garden he had entered.

On the other side of the wall the clatter of muskets and the imprecations of Javert resounded; from the convent came a hymn. Cosette and Jean Valjean fell on their knees. Presently Jean Valjean discovered that the gardener was an old man whose life he had saved at M——, and who, in his gratitude, was prepared to do anything for M. Madeleine.

It ended in Cosette entering the convent school as a pupil, and Jean Valjean being accepted as the gardener's brother. The good nuns never left the precincts of their convent, and cared nothing for the world beyond their gates.

As for Javert, he had delayed attempting an arrest, even when his suspicions had been aroused, because, after all, the papers said the convict was dead. But once convinced, he hesitated no longer.

His disappointment when Jean Valjean escaped him was midway between despair and fury. All night the search went on; but it never occurred to Javert that a steep wall of fourteen feet could be climbed by an old man with a child.

Several years passed at the convent.

Jean Valjean worked daily in the garden, and shared the hut and the name of the old gardener, M. Fauchelevent. Cosette was allowed to see him for an hour every day.

The peaceful garden, the fragrant flowers, the merry cries of the children, the grave and simple women, gradually brought happiness to Jean Valjean; and his heart melted into gratitude for the security he had found.

IV

Something Higher Than Duty

For six years Cosette and Jean Valjean stayed at the convent; and then, on the death of the old gardener, Jean Valjean, now bearing the name of Fauchelevent, decided that as Cosette was not going to be a nun, and as recognition was no longer to be feared, it would be well to remove into the city.

So a house was taken in the Rue Plumet, and here, with a faithful servant, the old man dwelt with his adopted child. But Jean Valjean took other rooms in Paris, in case of accidents.

Cosette was growing up. She was conscious of her good looks, and she was in love with a well-connected youth named Marius, the son of Baron Pontmercy.

606

Jean Valjean learnt of this secret lovemaking with dismay. The idea of parting from Cosette was intolerable to him.

Then, in June, 1832, came desperate street fighting in Paris, and Marius was in command of one of the revolutionary barricades.

At this barricade Javert had been captured as a spy, and Jean Valjean, who was known to the revolutionaries, found his old, implacable enemy tied to a post, waiting to be shot. Jean Valjean requested to be allowed to blow out Javert's brain himself, and permission was given.

Holding a pistol in his hand, Jean Valjean led Javert, who was still bound, to a lane out of sight of the barricade, and there with his knife cut the ropes from the wrists and feet of his prisoner.

"You are free," he said. "Go; and if by any chance I leave this place alive, I am to be found under the name of Fauchelevent, in the Rue de l'Homme-Armé, No. 7."

Javert walked a few steps, and then turned back, and cried, "You worry me. I would rather you killed me!"

"Go!" was the only answer from Jean Valjean.

Javert moved slowly away; and when he had disappeared Jean Valjean discharged his pistol in the air.

Soon the last stand of the insurgents was at an end, and the barricade destroyed. Jean Valjean, who had taken no part in the struggle, beyond exposing himself to the bullets of the soldiers, was unhurt; but Marius lay wounded and insensible in his arms.

The soldiers were shooting down all who tried to escape. The situation was terrible.

There was only one chance for life—underground. An iron grating, which led to the sewers, was at his feet. Jean Valjean tore it open, and disappeared with Marius on his shoulders.

He emerged, after a horrible passage through a grating by the bank of the river, only to find there the implacable Javert!

Jean Valjean was quite calm.

"Inspector Javert," he said, "help me to carry this man home; then do with me what you please."

A cab was waiting for the inspector. He ordered the man to drive to the address Jean Valjean gave him. Marius, still unconscious, was taken to his grandfather's house.

"Inspector Javert," said Jean Valjean, "grant me one thing more. Let me go home for a minute; then you may take me where you will."

Javert told the driver to go to Rue de l'Homme-Armé, No. 7.

When they reached the house, Javert said, "Go up; I will wait here for you!"

But before Jean Valjean reached his rooms Javert had gone, and the street was empty.

Javert had not been at ease since his life had been spared. He was now in horrible uncertainty. To owe his life to an ex-convict, to accept this debt, and then to repay him by sending him back to the galleys was impossible. To let a malefactor go free while he, Inspector Javert, took his pay from the government was equally impossible. It seemed there was something higher and above his code of duty, something he had not come into collision with before. The uncertainty of the right thing to be done destroyed Javert, to whom life had hitherto been perfectly plain. He could not live recognising Jean Valjean as his saviour, and he could not bring himself to arrest Jean Valjean.

Inspector Javert made his last report at the police-station, and then, unable to face the new conditions of life, walked slowly to the river and plunged into the Seine, where the water rolls round and round in an endless whirlpool.

Marius recovered, and married Cosette; and Jean Valjean lived alone. He had told Marius who he was—Jean Valjean, an escaped convict; and Marius and Cosette gradually saw less and less of the old man.

But before Jean Valjean died Marius learnt the whole truth of the heroic life of the old man who had rescued him from the lost barricade. For the first time he realised that Jean Valjean had come to the barricade only to save him, knowing him to be in love with Cosette.

He hastened with Cosette to Jean Valjean's room; but the old man's last hour had come.

"Come closer, come closer, both of you," he cried. "I love you so much. It is good to die like this! You love me too, my Cosette. I know you've always had a fondness for the poor old man. And you, M. Pontmercy, will always make Cosette happy. There were several things I wanted to say, but they don't matter now. Come nearer, my children, I am happy in dying!"

Cosette and Marius fell on their knees, and covered his hands with kisses.

Jean Valjean was dead!

I

HENRIK IBSEN

HENRIK IBSEN (Norwegian, 1828-1906). From poor family. Was apprenticed
to an apothecary. Decided to devote himself to poetry and playwrighting.
Became theater director. Among major works: *Brand, Peer Gynt, A Doll's
House, Ghosts, The Wild Duck, Hedda Gabler.* One of the great antagonists
of social shams and pretenses.

PEER GYNT

Scene IX

Peer Gynt. (Throwing turban away)
There goes the Turk and Prophet—I'm Peer once more.
Those heathen customs I cannot endure.
I'm lucky that it's only a matter of clothes,
And not bred in the bone, as the old saw goes.
It behooves a man to live like a Christian,
To shun the gaudy peacock dress of a Pagan,
To fear God, walk in His steps, break no laws,
Be yourself and keep out of the devil's claws.
These folks will some day say kind words, revere
Your name, and place a wreath upon your bier.
     (taking a few steps)
Why, that ornery rascal, that little faker!
She surely took me, hook, line and sinker.
She was on the verge of turning my head.
Well, that's over, thank heaven! The less said
The better. But it's some comfort, I was off guard
In a weak moment. Soothsaying's a hazard—
That's not my forte. After all, I'm still a man—

609

In courting the little goose, I was only human.
Ha! There's no fool like an old fool, they say.

(*Bursts out laughing*)

Sir Peter Gynt singing, dancing, so blithe and gay;
Strumming the lute, crowing like a rooster.
Ha! Then plucked by a hen of every feather.
Yes, plucked, plucked clean to the bone—
I have only a trifle I can call my own.

(*feeling in his pockets*)

A little cash in hand, in America some holdings—
Not quite broke, not enough to hobnob with kings.
I feel better foot-loose, with no trappings—
Horses, coachmen, servants and the like.
No! I'm not washed up yet. I'll soon strike
Something good; of course, as a merchantman
And lover, I'm finished. However, I don't plan
To retrace my steps. No, I'll turn over a new leaf.
I must find some noble task. I'll find relief—
Say in my autobiography. No, 'twould be too long,
I'll just write a history of the world—a song
Of humanity, with all its joy and grief.
Like a feather, I'll float down history's stream,
And make it live again, as in a dream.

(*With quiet emotion*)

See brave men battle for truth and right,
Of course, I'll keep safely out of sight;
See saints and sages sacrificed for spite;
See war, the trade of Kings, wax and wane;
See the conquering heroes come and go—
In short, I'll skim off the cream of history,
I'll give them something different and new,
I can always fall back on my lying.
Aye, I'll bury myself in antiquity
And forsake the beaten paths of the living.
The present's not worth a pair of shoe-strings.
Here, I think, I may find myself again.
Proud and vain are the ways of men and kings—
Their souls have no wings, their deeds no salt.

(*Shrugs his shoulders*)

And woman—ah, that's the Maker's fault!

Scene X

A summer day, far up North. A hut in the woods. A door, with a large wooden bar, stands open. Above the door a pair of large antlers. A small herd of goats grazes by the side of the hut. Solveig, now middle-aged but fair and comely, sits and spins outside in the sunlight.

Solveig. (*Looks down the path and sings*)
The seasons slowly come and go;
  I know you will return some day;
  Here I abide, lad, and spin and pray
As I promised, lad, long, long ago.
        (*calls the goats, and spins and sings again*)
God guard you, wherever you are;
  God bless you when you kneel in prayer;
  I'll abide in thee, lad, forever;
If above, lad, I'll meet you there.

Scene XI

In Egypt, Dawn at the foot of the Statue of Memnon.

Peer Gynt. (*Comes on, stops and looks around.*)
Just the right place for Gynt, the Historian
To begin. For the present I'm an Egyptian,
And, of course, with the emphasis on I.
Next, I'll take ancient Assyria on high.
To begin right back at the world's creation
Would lead only to trouble and confusion.
Anyhow, Bible lore's not popular to-day—
I'll just take a bird's-eye view, as they say.
I'll abridge or elaborate here and there,
Pick out the high spots in true Gynt flair—
When you describe a horse you don't enumerate
All the hairs in his tail.

611

MUHAMMAD IQBAL

MUHAMMAD IQBAL (Indian, 1876-1938). Foremost poet of Moslem India in 20th century. Uneventful life, educated at Lahore and in England, earned living as lawyer. Wrote in several languages, most of poetry in Urdu or Persian. Persian works are more philosophical, the Urdu more lyrical and popular. Strong social consciousness.

COMMUNITY

Upon what manner man is bound to man:
That tale's a thread, the end whereof is lost
Beyond unravelling. We can descry
The Individual within the Mass,
And we can pluck him as a flower is plucked
Out of the garden. All his nature is
Entranced with individuality,
Yet only in Society he finds
Security and preservation. On
The road of life, the furnace of life's fire,
That roaring battle-field, sets him aflame.
Men grow habituated each to each,
Like jewels threaded on a single cord;
Succour each other in the war of life
In mutual bond, like workmen bent upon
A common task. Through such polarity
The constellations congregate, each star
In several attraction keeping each
Poised firmly and unshaken. Caravans
May pitch their tents on mountain or on hill,
Broad meadow, fringe of desert, sandy mound.
Yet slack and lifeless hangs the warp and woof
Of the Group's labour, unresolved the bud
Of its deep meditation, still unplayed
The flickering levin of its instrument,
Its music hushed within its muted strings,
Unsmitten by the pounding of the quest,
The plectrum of desire; disordered still
Its new-born concourse, and so thin its wine
As to be blotted up with cotton flock;

New-sprung the verdure of its soil, and cold
The blood in its vine's veins; a habitat
Of demons and of fairy sprites its thoughts,
So that it leaps in terror from the shapes
Conjured by its own surmise; shrunk the scope
Of its crude life, its narrow thoughts confined
Beneath the rim of its constricting roof;
Fear for its life the meagre stock-in-trade
Of its constituent elements; its heart
Trembling before the whistle of the wind;
Its spirit shies away from arduous toil,
Little disposed to pluck at Nature's skirt,
But whatsoever springs of its own self
Or falls from heaven, that it gathers up.
Till God discovers a man pure of heart
In His good time, who in a single word
A volume shall rehearse; a minstrel he
Whose piercing music gives new life to dust.
Through him the unsubstantial atom glows
Radiant with life, the meanest merchandise
Takes on new worth. Out of his single breath
Two hundred bodies quicken; with one glass
He livens an assembly. His bright glance
Slays, but forthwith his single uttered word
Bestows new life, that so Duality
Expiring, Unity may come to birth.
His thread, whose end is knotted to the skies,
Weaves all together life's dissevered parts.
Revealing a new vista to the gaze,
He can convert broad desert and bare vale
Into a garden. At his fiery breath
A people leap like rue upon a fire
In sudden tumult, in their heart one spark
Caught from his kindling, and their sullen clay
Breaks instantly aflame. Where'er he treads
The earth receiving vision, every mote
May wink the eye at Moses' Sinai.
The naked understanding he adorns,
With wealth abundant fills its indigence,
Fans with his skirts its embers, purifies
Its gold of every particle of dross.

He strikes the shackles from the fettered slave,
Redeems him from his masters, and declares:
'No other's slave thou art, nor any less
Than those mute idols.' So unto one goal
Drawing each on, he circumscribes the feet
Of all within the circle of one Law,
Reschools them in God's wondrous Unity,
And teaches them the habit and the use
Of self-surrender to the Will Divine.

WASHINGTON IRVING

WASHINGTON IRVING (American, 1783-1859). First American man of
letters, supporting self by writing. Traveled widely abroad, first American
literary ambassador. Fame established with *The Sketch Book*, containing
"Rip Van Winkle" and "The Legend of Sleepy Hollow." Interest in Spain
created *The Alhambra*. Later became ambassador to Spain. Charm lies in his
urbane style, genial temperament.

THE LEGEND OF THE ENCHANTED SOLDIER

EVERYBODY has heard of the Cave of St. Cyprian at Salamanca,
where in old times judicial astronomy, necromancy, chiromancy,
and other dark and damnable arts were secretly taught by an
ancient sacristan; or, some will have it, by the devil himself in
that disguise. The cave has long been shut up and the very site
of it forgotten; though, according to tradition, the entrance was
somewhere about where the stone cross stands in the small square
of the seminary of Carvajal, and this tradition appears in some
degree corroborated by the circumstances of the following story:—

There was at one time a student of Salamanca, Don Vicente by
name, of that merry but mendicant class who set out on the road
to learning without a penny in pouch for the journey, and who
during college vacations beg from town to town and village to
village to raise funds to enable them to pursue their studies through
the ensuing term. He was now about to set forth on his wanderings,
and, being somewhat musical, slung on his back a guitar with
which to amuse the villagers and pay for a meal or a night's
lodging.

614

As he passed by the stone cross in the seminary square he pulled off his hat and made a short invocation to St. Cyprian for good luck, when casting his eyes upon the earth he perceived something glitter at the foot of the cross. On picking it up, it proved to be a seal ring of mixed metal, in which gold and silver appeared to be blended. The seal bore as a device two triangles crossing each other so as to form a star. This device is said to be a cabalistic sign invented by King Solomon the Wise, and of mighty power in all cases of enchantment; but the honest student, being neither sage or conjurer, knew nothing of the matter. He took the ring as a present from St. Cyprian in reward of his prayer, slipped it on his finger, made a bow to the cross, and strumming his guitar set off merrily on his wandering.

The life of a mendicant student in Spain is not the most miserable in the world, especially if he has any talent at making himself agreeable. He rambles at large from village to village and city to city wherever curiosity or caprice may conduct him. The country curates, who, for the most part, have been mendicant students in their time, give him shelter for the night and a comfortable meal, and often enrich him with several quartos or halfpence in the morning. As he presents himself from door to door in the streets of the cities he meets with no harsh rebuff, no chilling contempt, for there is no disgrace attending his mendicity. Many of the most learned men in Spain have commenced their career in this manner; but if, like the student in question, he is a good-looking varlet and a merry companion, and, above all, if he can play the guitar, he is sure of a hearty welcome among the peasants, and smiles and favors from their wives and daughters.

In this way, then, did our ragged and musical son of learning make his way over half the kingdom, with the fixed determination to visit the famous city of Granada before his return. Sometimes he was gathered for the night into the fold of some village pastor; sometimes he was sheltered under the humble but hospitable roof of the peasant. Seated at the cottage door with his guitar he delighted the simple folk with his ditties; or striking up a fandango or bolero, set the brown country lads and lasses dancing in the mellow twilight. In the morning he departed with kind words from host and hostess.

At length he arrived at the great object of his musical vaga-bondizing, the far-famed city of Granada, and hailed with wonder and delight its Moorish towers, its lovely Vega, and its snowy

615

mountains glistening through a summer atmosphere. It is needless to say with what eager curiosity he entered its gates and wandered through its streets, and gazed upon its Oriental monuments. Every female face peering through a window or beaming from a balcony was to him a Zorayda or a Zelinda, nor could he meet a stately dame on the Alameda, but he was ready to fancy her a Moorish princess and to spread his student's robe beneath her feet.

His musical talent, his happy humor, his youth, and his good looks won him a universal welcome in spite of his ragged robes, and for several days he led a gay life in the old Moorish capital and its environs. One of his occasional haunts was the fountain of Avellanos, in the valley of the Darro. It is one of the popular resorts of Granada, and has been so since the days of the Moors; and here the student had an opportunity of pursuing his studies of female beauty, a branch of study to which he was a little prone.

Here he would take his seat with his guitar, improvise love ditties to admiring groups, or prompt with his music the ever ready dance. He was thus engaged one evening, when he beheld a padre of the Church advancing, at whose approach every one touched the hat. He was evidently a man of consequence; he certainly was a mirror of good, if not of holy, living; robust and rosy-faced, and breathing at every pore, with the warmth of the weather and the exercise of the walk. As he passed along he would every now and then draw a maravedi out of his pocket, and bestow it on a beggar, with an air of signal beneficence. "Ah, the blessed father!" would be the cry. "Long life to him, and may he soon be a bishop!"

To aid his steps in ascending the hill, he leaned gently now and then on the arm of a handmaid.

The good padre looked benignantly on the company about the fountain, and took his seat with some emphasis on a stone bench, while the handmaid hastened to bring him a glass of sparkling water. He sipped it deliberately, and with relish, tempering it with one of those spongy pieces of frosted eggs and sugar so dear to Spanish epicures, and on returning the glass to the hand of the damsel pinched her cheek with infinite loving-kindness.

"Ah, the good pastor!" whispered the student to himself. "What a happiness would it be to be gathered into his fold with such a damsel for a companion!"

But no such good fare was likely to befall him. In vain he essayed

those powers of pleasing which he had found so irresistible with country curates and country lasses. Never had he touched his guitar with such skill; never had he poured forth more soul-moving ditties; but he had no longer a country curate or country lass to deal with. The worthy priest evidently did not relish music, and the modest damsel never raised her eyes from the ground. They remained but a short time at the fountain. The good padre hastened their return to Granada. The damsel gave the student one shy glance in retiring, but it plucked the heart out of his bosom!

He inquired about them after they had gone. Padre Thomas was one of the saints of Granada, a model of regularity—punctual in his hour of rising; his hour of taking a paseo for an appetite; his hour of playing his game of tresillo, of an evening, with some of the dames of the cathedral circle; his hour of supping; and his hour of retiring to rest, to gather fresh strength for another day's round of similar duties. He had an easy, sleek mule for his riding; a matronly housekeeper, skilled in preparing titbits for his table.

Adieu now to the gay, thoughtless life of the student; the side glance of a bright eye had been the undoing of him. Day and night he could not get the image of this most modest damsel out of his mind. He sought the mansion of the padre. Alas! it was above the class of houses accessible to a strolling student like himself. The worthy padre had no sympathy with him; he had never been obliged to sing for his supper. He blockaded the house by day, catching a glance of the damsel now and then as she appeared at a casement; but these glances only fed his flame without encouraging his hope. He serenaded her balcony at night, and at one time was flattered by the appearance of something white at a window. Alas, it was only the nightcap of the padre.

Never was lover more devoted; never damsel more shy; the poor student was reduced to despair. At length arrived the eve of St. John, when the lower classes of Granada swarm into the country, dance away the afternoon, and pass midsummer's night on the banks of the Darro and the Xenil. Happy are they who, on this eventful night, can wash their faces in those waters just as the cathedral bell tells midnight; for at that precise moment they have a beautifying power. The student, having nothing to do, suffered himself to be carried away by the holiday-seeking throng until he found himself in the narrow valley of the Darro, below the lofty hill and ruddy towers of the Alhambra. The dry bed of the river,

the rocks which border it, the terraced gardens which overhang it, were alive with variegated groups, dancing under the vines and fig trees to the sound of the guitar and castanets.

The student remained for some time in doleful dumps, leaning against one of the huge misshapen stone pomegranates which adorn the ends of the little bridge over the Darro. He cast a wistful glance upon the merry scene, where every cavalier had his dame; or, to speak more appropriately, every Jack his Jill; sighed at his own solitary state, a victim to the black eye of the most unapproachable of damsels, and repined at his ragged garb, which seemed to shut the gate of hope against him.

By degrees his attention was attracted to a neighbor equally solitary with himself. This was a tall soldier, of a stern aspect and grizzled beard, who seemed posted as a sentry at the opposite pomegranate. His face was bronzed by time; he was arrayed in ancient Spanish armor, with buckler and lance, and stood immovable as a statue. What surprised the student was, that though thus strangely equipped, he was totally unnoticed by the passing throng, albeit that many almost brushed against him.

"This is a city of old-time peculiarities," thought the student, "and doubtless this is one of them with which the inhabitants are too famliar to be surprised." His own curiosity, however, was awakened; and, being of a social disposition, he accosted the soldier.

"A rare old suit of armor that which you wear, comrade. May I ask what corps you belong to?"

The soldier gasped out a reply from a pair of jaws which seemed to have rusted on their hinges.

"The roval guard of Ferdinand and Isabella."

"Santa Maria! Why, it is three centuries since that corps was in service."

"And for three centuries have I been mounting guard. Now I trust my tour of duty draws to a close. Dost thou desire fortune?"

The student held up his tattered cloak in reply.

"I understand thee. If thou hast faith and courage, follow me, and thy fortune is made."

"Softly, comrade. To follow thee would require small courage in one who has nothing to lose but life and an old guitar, neither of much value; but my faith is of a different matter, and not to be put in temptation. If it be any criminal act by which I am to mend my fortune, think not my ragged cloak will make me undertake it."

618

The soldier turned on him a look of high displeasure. "My sword," said he, "has never been drawn but in the cause of the faith and the throne. I am an old Christian; trust in me and fear no evil."

The student followed him, wondering. He observed that no one heeded their conversation, and that the soldier made his way through the various groups of idlers unnoticed, as if invisible.

Crossing the bridge, the soldier led the way by a narrow and steep path past a Moorish mill and aqueduct, and up the ravine which separates the domains of the Generalife from those of the Alhambra. The last ray of the sun shone upon the red battlements of the latter, which beetled far above; and the convent bells were proclaiming the festival of the ensuing day. The ravine was overshadowed by fig trees, vines, and myrtles, and the outer towers and walls of the fortress. It was dark and lonely, and the twilight-loving bats began to flit about. At length the soldier halted at a remote and ruined tower, apparently intended to guard a Moorish aqueduct. He struck the foundation with the butt end of his spear. A rumbling sound was heard, and the solid stones yawned apart, leaving an opening as wide as a door.

"Enter in the name of the Holy Trinity," said the soldier, "and fear nothing." The student's heart quaked, but he made the sign of the cross, muttered his Ave Maria, and followed his mysterious guide into a deep vault cut out the solid rock under the tower, and covered with Arabic inscriptions. The soldier pointed to a stone seat hewn along one side of the vault. "Behold," said he, "my couch for three hundred years." The bewildered student tried to force a joke. "By the blessed St Anthony," said he, "but you must have slept soundly, considering the hardness of your couch."

"On the contrary, sleep has been a stranger to these eyes; incessant watchfulness has been my doom. Listen to my lot. I was one of the royal guards of Ferdinand and Isabella, but was taken prisoner by the Moors in one of their sorties, and confined a captive in this tower. When preparations were made to surrender the fortress to the Christian sovereigns, I was prevailed upon by an alfaqui, a Moorish priest, to aid him in secreting some of the treasures of Boabdil in this vault. I was justly punished for my fault. The alfaqui was an African necromancer, and by his infernal arts cast a spell upon me to guard his treasures. Something must have happened to him, for he never returned, and here I have remained ever since, buried alive. Years and years have rolled

619

away; earthquakes have shaken this hill; I have heard stone by stone of the tower above tumbling to the ground in the natural operation of time; but the spellbound walls of the vault have set both time and earthquakes at defiance.

"Once every hundred years, on the festival of St. John, the enchantment ceases to have thorough sway. I am permitted to go forth and post myself upon the bridge of the Darro, where you met me, waiting until some one shall arrive who may have power to break this magic spell. I have hitherto mounted guard there in vain. I walk as in a cloud, concealed from mortal sight. You are the first to accost me for now three hundred years. I behold the reason. I see on your finger the seal ring of Solomon the Wise, which is proof against all enchantment. With you it remains to deliver me from this awful dungeon, or to leave me to keep guard here for another hundred years."

The student listened to this tale in mute wonderment. He had heard many tales of treasure shut up under strong enchantment in the vaults of the Alhambra, but had treated them as fables. He now felt the value of the seal ring, which had, in a manner, been given to him by St. Cyprian. Still, though armed by so potent a talisman, it was an awful thing to find himself tête-à-tête in such a place with an enchanted soldier, who, according to the laws of nature, ought to have been quietly in his grave for nearly three centuries.

A personage of this kind, however, was quite out of the ordinary run, and not to be trifled with, and he assured him he might rely upon his friendship and good will to do everything in his power for his deliverance.

"I trust to a motive more powerful than friendship," said the soldier.

He pointed to a ponderous iron coffer, secured by locks inscribed with Arabic characters. "That coffer," said he, "contains countless treasure in gold and jewels and precious stones. Break the magic spell by which I am enthralled, and one-half of this treasure shall be thine."

"But how am I to do it?"

"The aid of a Christian priest and a Christian maid is necessary; the priest to exorcise the powers of darkness, the damsel to touch this chest with the seal of Solomon. This must be done at night. But have a care. This is solemn work, and not to be effected by

620

the carnal-minded. The priest must be an old Christian, a model of sanctity; and must mortify the flesh, before he comes here, by a rigorous fast of four-and-twenty hours; and as to the maiden, she must be above reproach, and proof against temptation. Linger not in finding such aid. In three days my furlough is at an end; if not delivered before midnight of the third, I shall have to mount guard for another century."

"Fear not," said the student, "I have in my eye the very priest and damsel you describe; but how am I to regain admission to this tower?"

"The seal of Solomon will open the way for thee."

The student issued forth from the tower much more gaily than he had entered. The wall closed behind him, and remained solid as before.

The next morning he repaired boldly to the mansion of the priest, no longer a poor, strolling student, thrumming his way with a guitar; but an ambassador from the shadowy world, with enchanted treasures to bestow. No particulars are told of his negotiation, excepting that the zeal of the worthy priest was easily kindled at the idea of rescuing an old soldier of the faith and a strong box of King Chico from the very clutches of Satan; and then what alms might be dispensed, what churches built, and how many poor relatives enriched with the Moorish treasure!

As to the handmaid, she was ready to lend her hand, which was all that was required, to the pious work; and if a shy glance now and then might be believed, the ambassador began to find favor in her modest eyes.

The greatest difficulty, however, was the fast to which the good padre had to subject himself. Twice he attempted it, and twice the flesh was too strong for the spirit. It was only on the third day that he was enabled to withstand the temptations of the cupboard; but it was still a question whether he would hold out until the spell was broken.

At a late hour of the night the party groped their way up the ravine, by the light of a lantern, and bearing a basket with provisions for exorcising the demon of hunger so soon as the other demons should be laid in the Red Sea.

The seal of Solomon opened their way into the tower. They found the soldier, seated on the enchanted strong box, awaiting their arrival. The exorcism was performed in due style. The damsel advanced, and touched the locks of the coffer with the seal of

621

Solomon. The lid flew open, and such treasures of gold and jewels and precious stones as flashed upon the eye!

"Here's cut, and come again!" cried the student, exultingly, as he proceeded to cram his pockets.

"Fairly and softly," exclaimed the soldier. "Let us get the coffer out entire, and then divide."

They accordingly went to work with might and main, but it was a difficult task; the chest was enormously heavy, and had been embedded there for centuries. While they were thus employed, the good dominie drew on one side, and made a vigorous onslaught on the basket, by way of exorcising the demon of hunger which was raging within him. In a little while a fat capon was devoured, and washed down by a deep potation; and, by way of grace after meat, he gave a kind-hearted kiss to the damsel who waited on him. It was quietly done in a corner, but the tell-tale walls babbled it forth as if in triumph. Never was chaste salute more awful in its effects. At the sound the soldier gave a great cry of despair; the coffer, which was half raised, fell back in its place and was locked once more. Priest, student, and damsel found themselves outside of the tower, the wall of which closed with a thundering jar. Alas! the good padre had broken his fast too soon.

When recovered from his surprise, the student would have re-entered the tower, but learnt to his dismay that the damsel, in her fright, had let fall the seal of Solomon; it remained within the vault.

In a word, the cathedral bell tolled midnight; the spell was renewed; the soldier was doomed to mount guard for another hundred years; and there he and the treasure remain to this day, and all because the kind-hearted padre kissed his handmaid.

Thus ends the legend as far as it has been authenticated. There is a tradition, however, that the student had brought off treasure enough in his pocket to set him up in the world; that he prospered in his affairs, that the worthy padre gave him the damsel in marriage, by way of amends for the blunder in the vault; and she proved a pattern for wives.

The story of the enchanted soldier remains one of the popular traditions of Granada, though told in a variety of ways; the common people affirm that he still mounts guard on midsummer eve, beside the gigantic stone pomegranate on the bridge of the Darro, but remains invisible excepting to such lucky mortal as may possess the seal of Solomon.

J

JENS PETER JACOBSEN

JENS PETER JACOBSEN (Danish, 1847-1885). Danish realistic novelist and
poet. Sought to find the laws of nature in the realm of literature. Disciple of
great Danish critic Brandes. Worked with such care that he produced only
two novels *(Fru Marie Grubbe, Niels Lyhne)*, a volume of tales *(Mogens and
Other Stories)*, and a few poems.

THE PLAGUE AT BERGAMO

OLD Bergamo lay up there at the top of a squatty mountain encircled by walls and towers. New Bergamo lay below at the foot of
the mountain, exposed to every wind that blows.

In the new town the plague broke out and wrought havoc indescribable. Many died, and the rest fled across the plains to every
point of the compass. The men of Old Bergamo set fire to the
deserted town, to disinfect the air. In vain. Men began to die on
the mountain, also; at first one a day, then five, then ten, then a
dozen.

There were many who sought to escape, but they could not flee
as those in the new town had done; they lived like hunted beasts,
hiding in tombs, under bridges, behind hedges, and in the tall grass
of the green fields. For the peasants stoned all strangers from their
hearths, or beat them as they would mad dogs, cruelly, pitilessly—
in self-protection, as they thought, for the first fugitives had brought
with them the pestilence into their houses.

So the people of Old Bergamo were as prisoners in their own
town. Day by day the sun blazed hotter, and day by day the terrible
infection carried off more victims.

In the very beginning, when the plague came among them, they
bound themselves together in unity and peace, and had taken care
to decently bury the dead, and had kindled great fires in the mar-

kets and open places, so that the purging fumes might be blown through the streets. Juniper and vinegar had been given to the poor. Above all they had gone to church, early and late, singly and in processions; each day they lifted their voices in prayer. As the sun sank behind the mountains the church bells tolled their dirge from a hundred hanging mouths. Days were set aside for fasting, and the relics were placed upon the altars.

At last, in their extremity, amid the blare of trumpets and tubas, they proclaimed the Holy Virgin forevermore Podesta of the city.

All this was of no help. And when the people saw that nothing could aid them, that Heaven either would not or could not send them relief, they did not fold their hands together and say, "God's will be done." It was as if sin, growing by a secret, stealthy sickness, had flared into an evil, open, raging pestilence, stalking hand in hand with the body's disease, the one to kill their souls, even as the other defiled their flesh—so incredible were their deeds, so monstrous their cruelty.

"Let us eat to-day, for to-morrow we die!" It was as if this theme, set to music, were played in an endless, devilish symphony on instruments without number. The most unnatural vices flourished among them. Even such rare arts as necromancy, sorcery, and devil worship became familiar to them; for there were many who sought from the powers of hell that protection which Providence had not been willing to accord them. Everything that suggested charity and sympathy had vanished; each thought only of himself. If a beggar, faint with the first delirium of the plague, fell in the street, he was driven from door to door with sharp weapons and with stones. From the dead that lay rotting in the houses, and from the bodies hastily buried in the earth, arose a sickening stench that mingled with the heavy air of the streets, and drew ravens and crows hither in swarms and in clouds, so that the walls and housetops were black with them. And about the town walls great strange birds perched here and there—birds that came from afar, with rapacious beaks and talons expectantly curved; and they sat and stared with their quiet, hungry eyes as if awaiting the moment when the doomed town would be reduced to a heap of carrion.

Eleven weeks had passed since the plague had first broken out. Then the tower watchman and others who chanced to be on high ground perceived a singular procession winding from the plains into the narrow streets of the new town, between the smoke-blackened stone walls and the charred frames of houses. A great

throng! Assuredly six hundred and more, men and women, young and old. Some among them bore large, black crosses, and some held above their heads broad banners, red as blood and fire. They sang as they marched, and strange, despairingly plaintive melodies rose in the still, oppressively hot air.

Brown, gray, black, were the colors these people wore. Yet all had a red sign on their breasts. As they came nearer and nearer this was seen to be the sign of the cross. They crowded up the steep, stone-girt space that led to the old town. Their faces were as waves of white sea; they bore scourges in their hands; a rain of fire was painted on their banners. And in the surging mass the black crosses swung from side to side. Face after face plunged into the gloom of the tower gate and emerged into the light on the other side with blinking eyes.

Then the chant was taken up anew—a *miserere*. They grasped their scourges and marched even more sturdily than if their chant had been a battle song. Their aspect was that of a people who had come from a starving town. Their cheeks were sunken; their cheek-bones protruded; their lips were bloodless, and dark rings encircled their eyes. All the scourges were stained with blood.

With astonishment and uneasiness all Bergamo flocked together to gaze upon them. Red, bloated faces stood out against those that were pale; heavy, lust-weary eyes were lowered before the keen, flashing glances of the pilgrims; grinning, blasphemous mouths were struck dumb by these chants. The townspeople were spellbound.

But it was not long before the pall was shaken off. Some recognized among the cross-bearers a half-crazed cobbler of Brescia, and in a moment the procession became a butt of ridicule. Moreover, this was something new, a diversion from the monotony of every-day life, and as the strangers marched on to the cathedral, they were followed as a band of jugglers might be or as a tame bear is followed.

But soon anger seized the jostling crowd. It was clear that these cobblers and tailors had come to convert them, to pray, and to speak words that none wished to hear. Two gaunt, grizzled philosophers who had formulated blasphemy into a system incited the populace out of sheer wickedness of heart, so that the mob grew more threatening as the procession marched to the church, and more fiercely enraged. Bergamo was about to lay hands on these singular, scourge-bearing tailors. Not a hundred paces from the portal of the church a tavern opened its doors and a whole band of

roisterers poured out, one on the shoulders of another. And they took their places at the head of the procession, singing and howling, assuming a mock-religious mien—all save one, who jerked his thumbs contemptuously toward the grass-grown steps of the church. Rough laughter then arose, and pilgrims and blasphemers entered the sanctuary in peace.

It was strange to be in that place again, to roam through the great cool nave, in air heavy with the stale fumes of snuffed wax tapers, over sunken flagstones so familiar to the foot, and over stones with their worn ornaments and polished inscriptions, in contemplation of which the mind had often grown so weary. And while the eye, half curiously, half involuntarily rested in the dim half-light of the vaults or strayed over the mellow gaudiness of dusty gold and grimy colors, or began to lose itself in the grotesque shadows of the apse, a kind of longing arose, not to be suppressed.

Meanwhile the tavern roisterers played their pranks on the main altar itself. A tall, strong young butcher removed his white apron and wound it about his neck so that it hung at his back like a cloak. Thus arrayed, he celebrated mass, with the wildest and most shocking words of sacrilege. A small, elderly, round-bellied fellow, lively and agile in spite of his fat, with the face of a peeled pumpkin, played sexton and responded with ribald songs; he made his genuflexions and turned his back upon the altar, and rang his bell like a clown; and the other tipplers, as they made their genuflexions, threw themselves flat on the ground and roared with laughter, hiccuping drunkenly.

All within the church laughed, hooted, and jeered at the strangers, and bade them notice how God was esteemed in Old Bergamo. Yet they wished not so much to mock God as to rack the souls of these penitents with their impiety.

In the centre of the nave the pilgrims halted and groaned, such was their anguish. Their blood boiled with hate, and they thirsted for vengeance. They prayed to God, with hands and eyes uplifted, that He might smite His blasphemers for the mockery offered Him in His house. Gladly would they perish with the presumptuous infidels, if He would but show His might; blissfully would they be crushed beneath His feet, if He would but triumph, and if these godless throats might be made to shriek in agony and despair.

They lifted up their voices in a *miserere*, each note of which rang like a prayer for that rain of fire that once swept over Sodom, for the strength that was Samson's when he grasped the pillars of the

626

Philistine temple. They prayed with words and with song; they bared their shoulders and prayed with their scourges. Kneeling, row on row, stripped to the waist they whirled stinging, knotted cords over their backs.

Frantically they scourged, until the blood spurted under their hissing lashes. Each stroke was an offering to God. Stroke on stroke came down, until arms sank or were cramped into knots. Thus they lay, row on row, with frenzied look and foaming mouth, blood dripping from their bodies.

And those that saw this of a sudden felt their hearts beat, felt the blood mount to their temples, their breathing grow hard. Their knees shook. To be the slave of a powerful, stern divinity, to fling one's self at the feet of the Lord, to be His own, not in mute devotion, not in the mild inefficacy of prayer, but in a fury of passion, in the intoxication of self-humiliation, in blood and lamentation, and smitten with the moist, glistening tongues of scourges—this they could understand. Even the butcher held his peace; and the toothless philosophers bowed their grizzled heads.

Silence reigned in the church; only a gentle breathing passed through the multitude.

Then one of the strangers, a young friar, rose and spoke. His was the pallor of bloodless flesh; his black eyes glowed; and the sad lines of his mouth were as if cut with a knife in wood, and not mere furrows in a human face.

He lifted up his thin, suffering hands in prayer to Heaven, and the black sleeves of his gown slipped back from his lean arms.

Then he spoke—of hell, of its eternity, of the eternity of Heaven, of the solitary world of pain which each of the damned must suffer and must fill with his cries of agony. In that world were seas of sulphur, meadows of wasps, flames to be wrapped about them like a cloak, and hard flames that would pierce them like a probe twisting in a wound.

Breathlessly all listened to his words; for he spoke as if he had seen these things with his own eyes. And they asked themselves: "Is this man not one of the damned, sent to us from the mouth of hell, to testify?"

Then he preached long of the commandments and their rigor, of the need of obeying them to the very letter, and of the dire punishment that awaited him who sinned against them. " 'But Christ died for our sins,' ye say. 'We are no longer bound by the Word.' But I say that hell will not be cheated of one of you, and not one of the

627

iron teeth of hell's wheel will your flesh escape. Ye build upon Calvary's cross? Come! Come and see it! I will lead you to its foot. It was on a Friday, as ye know, when they cast Him from their gates and laid the heavier end of a cross upon His shoulders and suffered Him to bear it to a barren and naked hill without the city; and they walked beside Him and stirred up the dust with their feet, so that it rested over them like a red cloud. And they tore His garments from Him, even as the lords of justice strip a criminal before all eyes, that all might see His body. And they threw Him down upon His cross, and stretched Him upon it, and drove an iron nail through each of His unresistant hands and a nail through His crossed feet. And they raised the cross in a hole dug in the earth; but it would stand neither firm nor upright. So they shook it and drove wedges and blocks around it. And those that did this turned down the brims of their hats so that the blood of His hands might not drip into their eyes.

"And He from on high looked down upon the soldiers casting dice for His seamless coat, and down upon all the howling mob for whose salvation He suffered. Not one tearful eye was there in all the multitude. And those who were below looked up at Him, hanging from the cross, suffering, and faint. They read the inscription above His head: 'King of the Jews,' and they mocked Him and called up to Him: 'Thou that destroyest the temple, and buildest it in three days, save Thyself. If Thou be the Son of God, come down from the cross.'

"Then God's noble Son waxed wroth and saw that these were unworthy of salvation, this mob that swarmed over the earth; and He wrenched His feet from the nail, and He clenched His fingers and tore His hands away, so that the arms of the cross bent as a bow. And He leaped to the earth and caught up His garment, so that the dice rolled over the precipice of Golgotha, and threw it about His person with the righteous wrath of a king, and ascended into heaven. And the cross stood bare; and the great work of atonement remained unfulfilled. No mediator stands between us and God. No Jesus died for us on the cross! No Jesus died for us on the cross!"

He ceased.

As he uttered the last words he bent toward the multitude and with his lips and hands flung his words, as it were, upon their heads. A groan of fear ran through the church. Sobs could be heard. Then the butcher with uplifted, threatening hands, pallid as a

corpse, stepped forward and commanded:

"Monk, nail Him to the cross again, nail Him—!"

And from all lips, pleadingly, threateningly, a storm of voices rolled to the vault above: "Crucify Him!"

But the monk looked down upon these fluttering, uplifted hands, upon these distorted faces with the dark openings of their screaming mouths, from which the teeth flashed like those of tormented beasts of prey; and in the ecstasy of the moment he extended his arms toward Heaven, and laughed. Then he descended; and his people raised the banners of the fiery rain and their plain, black crosses and pushed out of the church. Once more they marched, singing, across the marketplace, and once more they passed through the mouth of the tower gate.

And the people of Old Bergamo stared after them, as they proceeded down the mountain. The steep, wall-girt road was obscured in the uncertain light of the setting sun, and the procession could be only half seen in the glare. Their huge crosses, swaying in the crowd from side to side, cast sharp, black shadows on the glowing walls of the town.

In the distance a chant could be heard. A banner or two gleamed red from the charred site of the new town, and the pilgrims vanished into the bright plain.

HENRY JAMES

HENRY JAMES (American, 1843-1916). Novelist and critic, noted as precise stylist. Educated in Europe, led cosmopolitan life, eventually became British citizen. Favorite theme: contrast between naïve Americans and sophisticated Europeans. Later writing became more and more subtle, overrefined, idiosyncratic. Some of novels: *The American, The Portrait of a Lady, The Wings of the Dove, Washington Square, The Ambassadors, The Golden Bowl.*

CONFIDENCE

CHAPTER I

IT WAS in the early days of April; Bernard Longueville had been spending the winter in Rome. He had travelled northward with the consciousness of several social duties that appealed to him from the further side of the Alps, but he was under the charm of the Italian

spring, and he made a pretext for lingering. He had spent five days at Siena, where he had intended to spend but two, and still it was impossible to continue his journey. He was a young man of a contemplative and speculative turn, and this was his first visit to Italy, so that if he dallied by the way he should not be harshly judged. He had a fancy for sketching, and it was on his conscience to take a few pictorial notes. There were two old inns at Siena, both of them very shabby and very dirty. The one at which Longueville had taken up his abode was entered by a dark, pestiferous archway, surmounted by a sign which at a distance might have been read by the travellers as the Dantean injunction to renounce all hope. The other was not far off, and the day after his arrival, as he passed it, he saw two ladies going in who evidently belonged to the large fraternity of Anglo-Saxon tourists, and one of whom was young and carried herself very well. Longueville had his share—or more than his share—of gallantry, and this incident awakened a regret. If he had gone to the other inn he might have had charming company: at his own establishment there was no one but an æsthetic German who smoked bad tobacco in the dining-room. He remarked to himself that this was always his luck, and the remark was characteristic of the man; it was charged with the feeling of the moment, but it was not absolutely just; it was the result of an acute impression made by the particular occasion; but it failed in appreciation of a providence which had sprinkled Longueville's career with happy accidents—accidents, especially, in which his characteristic gallantry was not allowed to rust for want of exercise. He lounged, however, contentedly enough through these bright, still days of a Tuscan April, drawing much entertainment from the high picturesqueness of the things about him. Siena, a few years since, was a flawless gift of the Middle Ages to the modern imagination. No other Italian city could have been more interesting to an observer fond of reconstructing obsolete manners. This was a taste of Bernard Longueville's, who had a relish for serious literature, and at one time had made several lively excursions into mediæval history. His friends thought him very clever, and at the same time had an easy feeling about him which was a tribute to his freedom from pedantry. He was clever, indeed, and an excellent companion; but the real measure of his brilliancy was in the success with which he entertained himself. He was much addicted to conversing with his own wit, and he greatly enjoyed his own society. Clever as he often was in talking with his friends, I am not sure that his best things, as the

phrase is, were not for his own ears. And this was not on account of any cynical contempt for the understanding of his fellow-creatures: it was simply because what I have called his own society was more of a stimulus than that of most other people. And yet he was not for this reason fond of solitude; he was, on the contrary, a very sociable animal. It must be admitted at the outset that he had a nature which seemed at several points to contradict itself, as will probably be perceived in the course of this narration.

He entertained himself greatly with his reflections and meditations upon Sienese architecture and early Tuscan art, upon Italian street-life and the geological idiosyncrasies of the Apennines. If he had only gone to the other inn, that nice-looking girl whom he had seen passing under the dusky portal with her face turned away from him might have broken bread with him at this intellectual banquet. There came a day, however, when it seemed for a moment that if she were disposed she might gather up the crumbs of the feast. Longueville, every morning after breakfast, took a turn in the great square of Siena—the vast *piazza*, shaped like a horse-shoe, where the market is held beneath the windows of that crenellated palace from whose overhanging cornice a tall, straight tower springs up with a movement as light as that of a single plume in the bonnet of a captain. Here he strolled about, watching a brown *contadino* dis-embarrass his donkey, noting the progress of half an hour's chaffer over a bundle of carrots, wishing a young girl with eyes like ani-mated agates would let him sketch her, and gazing up at intervals at the beautiful, slim tower, as it played at contrasts with the large blue air. After he had spent the greater part of a week in these grave considerations, he made up his mind to leave Siena. But he was not content with what he had done for his portfolio. Siena was eminently sketchable, but he had not been industrious. On the last morning of his visit, as he stood staring about him in the crowded piazza, and feeling that, in spite of its picturesqueness, this was an awkward place for setting up an easel, he bethought himself, by contrast, of a quiet corner in another part of the town, which he had chanced upon in one of his first walks—an angle of a lonely terrace that abutted upon the city-wall, where three or four super-annuated objects seemed to slumber in the sunshine—the open door of an empty church, with a faded fresco exposed to the air in the arch above it, and an ancient beggar woman sitting beside it on a three-legged stool. The little terrace had an old polished parapet, about as high as a man's breast, above which was a view of strange,

sad-colored hills. Outside, to the left, the wall of the town made an outward bend, and exposed its rugged and rusty complexion. There was a smooth stone bench set into the wall of the church, on which Longueville had rested for an hour, observing the composition of the little picture of which I have indicated the elements, and of which the parapet of the terrace would form the foreground. The thing was what painters call a subject, and he had promised himself to come back with his utensils. This morning he returned to the inn and took possession of them, and then he made his way through a labyrinth of empty streets, lying on the edge of the town, within the wall, like the superfluous folds of a garment whose wearer has shrunken with old age. He reached his little grass-grown terrace, and found it as sunny and as private as before. The old mendicant was mumbling petitions, sacred and profane, at the church door; but save for this the stillness was unbroken. The yellow sunshine warmed the brown surface of the city-wall, and lighted the hollows of the Etruscan hills. Longueville settled himself on the empty bench, and, arranging his little portable apparatus, began to ply his brushes. He worked for some time smoothly and rapidly, with an agreeable sense of the absence of obstacles. It seemed almost an interruption when, in the silent air, he heard a distant bell in the town strike noon. Shortly after this, there was another interruption. The sound of a soft footstep caused him to look up; whereupon he saw a young woman standing there and bending her eyes upon the graceful artist. A second glance assured him that she was that nice girl whom he had seen going into the other inn with her mother, and suggested that she had just emerged from the little church. He suspected, however—I hardly know why—that she had been looking at him for some moments before he perceived her. It would perhaps be impertinent to inquire what she thought of him; but Longueville, in the space of an instant, made two or three reflections upon the young lady. One of them was to the effect that she was a handsome creature, but that she looked rather bold; the burden of the other was that—yes, decidedly—she was a compatriot. She turned away almost as soon as she met his eyes; he had hardly time to raise his hat, as, after a moment's hesitation, he proceeded to do. She herself appeared to feel a certain hesitation; she glanced back at the church door, as if under the impulse to retrace her steps. She stood there a moment longer—long enough to let him see that she was a person of easy attitudes—and then she walked away slowly to the parapet of the terrace. Here she stationed her-

self, leaning her arms upon the high stone ledge, presenting her back to Longueville, and gazing at rural Italy. Longueville went on with his sketch, but less attentively than before. He wondered what this young lady was doing there alone, and then it occurred to him that her companion—her mother, presumably—was in the church. The two ladies had been in the church when he arrived; women liked to sit in churches; they had been there more than half an hour, and the mother had not enough of it even yet. The young lady, however, at present preferred the view that Longueville was painting; he became aware that she had placed herself in the very centre of his foreground. His first feeling was that she would spoil it; his second was that she would improve it. Little by little she turned more into profile, leaning only one arm upon the parapet, while the other hand, holding her folded parasol, hung down at her side. She was motionless; it was almost as if she were standing there on purpose to be drawn. Yes, certainly she improved the picture. Her profile, delicate and thin, defined itself against the sky, in the clear shadow of a coquettish hat; her figure was light; she bent and leaned easily; she wore a gray dress, fastened up as was then the fashion, and displaying the broad edge of a crimson petticoat. She kept her position; she seemed absorbed in the view. "Is she *posing*—is she attitudinizing for my benefit?" Longueville asked of himself. And then it seemed to him that this was a needless assumption, for the prospect was quite beautiful enough to be looked at for itself, and there was nothing impossible in a pretty girl having a love of fine landscape. "But posing or not," he went on, "I will put her into my sketch. She has simply put herself in. It will give it a human interest. There is nothing like having a human interest." So, with the ready skill that he possessed, he introduced the young girl's figure into his foreground, and at the end of ten minutes he had almost made something that had the form of a likeness. "If she will only be quiet for another ten minutes," he said, "the thing will really be a picture." Unfortunately, the young lady was not quiet; she had apparently had enough of her attitude and her view. She turned away, facing Longueville again, and slowly came back, as if to re-enter the church. To do so she had to pass near him, and as she approached he instinctively got up, holding his drawing in one hand. She looked at him again, with that expression that he had mentally characterized as "bold" a few minutes before—with dark, intelligent eyes. Her hair was dark and dense; she was a strikingly handsome girl.

633

"I am so sorry you moved," he said, confidently, in English. "You were so—so beautiful."

She stopped, looking at him more directly than ever; and she looked at his sketch, which he held out toward her. At the sketch, however, she only glanced, whereas there was observation in the eye that she bent upon Longueville. He never knew whether she had blushed; he afterward thought she might have been frightened. Nevertheless, it was not exactly terror that appeared to dictate her answer to Longueville's speech.

"I am much obliged to you. Don't you think you have looked at me enough?"

"By no means. I should like so much to finish my drawing."

"I am not a professional model," said the young lady.

"No. That's my difficulty," Longueville answered, laughing. "I can't propose to remunerate you."

The young lady seemed to think this joke in indifferent taste. She turned away in silence; but something in her expression, in his feeling at the time, in the situation, incited Longueville to higher play. He felt a lively need of carrying his point.

"You see it will be pure kindness," he went on,—"a simple act of charity. Five minutes will be enough. Treat me as an Italian beggar."

He had laid down his sketch and had stepped forward. He stood there, obsequious, clasping his hands and smiling.

His interruptress stopped and looked at him again, as if she thought him a very odd person; but she seemed amused. Now, at any rate, she was not frightened. She seemed even disposed to provoke him a little.

"I wish to go to my mother," she said.

"Where is your mother?" the young man asked.

"In the church, of course. I didn't come here alone!"

"Of course not; but you may be sure that your mother is very contented. I have been in that little church. It is charming. She is just resting there; she is probably tired. If you will kindly give me five minutes more, she will come out to you."

"Five minutes?" the young girl asked.

"Five minutes will do. I shall be eternally grateful." Longueville was amused at himself as he said this. He cared infinitely less for his sketch than the words appeared to imply; but, somehow, he cared greatly that this graceful stranger should do what he had proposed.

The graceful stranger dropped an eye on the sketch again.

"Is your picture so good as that?" she asked.

"I have a great deal of talent," he answered, laughing. "You shall see for yourself, when it is finished."

She turned slowly toward the terrace again.

"You certainly have a great deal of talent, to induce me to do what you ask." And she walked to where she had stood before. Longueville made a movement to go with her, as if to show her the attitude he meant; but, pointing with decision to his easel, she said—

"You have only five minutes." He immediately went back to his work, and she made a vague attempt to take up her position. "You must tell me if this will do," she added, in a moment.

"It will do beautifully," Longueville answered, in a happy tone, looking at her and plying his brush. "It is immensely good of you to take so much trouble."

For a moment she made no rejoinder, but presently she said—

"Of course if I pose at all I wish to pose well."

"You pose admirably," said Longueville.

After this she said nothing, and for several minutes he painted rapidly and in silence. He felt a certain excitement, and the movement of his thoughts kept pace with that of his brush. It was very true that she posed admirably; she was a fine creature to paint. Her prettiness inspired him, and also her audacity, as he was content to regard it for the moment. He wondered about her—who she was, and what she was—perceiving that the so-called audacity was not vulgar boldness, but the play of an original and probably interesting character. It was obvious that she was a perfect lady, but it was equally obvious that she was irregularly clever. Longueville's little figure was a success—a charming success, he thought, as he put on the last touches. While he was doing this, his model's companion came into view. She came out of the church, pausing a moment as she looked from her daughter to the young man in the corner of the terrace; then she walked straight over to the young girl. She was a delicate little gentlewoman, with a light, quick step.

Longueville's five minutes were up; so, leaving his place, he approached the two ladies, sketch in hand. The elder one, who had passed her hand into her daughter's arm, looked up at him with clear, surprised eyes; she was a charming old woman. Her eyes were very pretty, and on either side of them, above a pair of fine dark brows, was a band of silvery hair, rather coquettishly arranged.

635

"It is my portrait," said her daughter, as Longueville drew near. "This gentleman has been sketching me."

"Sketching you, dearest?" murmured her mother. "Wasn't it rather sudden?"

"Very sudden—very abrupt!" exclaimed the young girl with a laugh.

"Considering all that, it's very good," said Longueville, offering his picture to the elder lady, who took it and began to examine it. "I can't tell you how much I thank you," he said to his model.

"It's very well for you to thank me now," she replied. "You really had no right to begin."

"The temptation was so great."

"We should resist temptation. And you should have asked my leave."

"I was afraid you would refuse it; and you stood there, just in my line of vision."

"You should have asked me to get out of it."

"I should have been very sorry. Besides, it would have been extremely rude."

The young girl looked at him a moment.

"Yes, I think it would. But what you have done is ruder."

"It is a hard case!" said Longueville. "What could I have done, then, decently?"

"It's a beautiful drawing," murmured the elder lady, handing the thing back to Longueville. Her daughter, meanwhile, had not even glanced at it.

"You might have waited till I should go away," this argumentative young person continued.

Longueville shook his head.

"I never lose opportunities!"

"You might have sketched me afterwards, from memory."

Longueville looked at her, smiling.

"Judge how much better my memory will be now!"

She also smiled a little, but instantly became serious.

"For myself, it is an episode I shall try to forget. I don't like the part I have played in it."

"May you never play a less becoming one!" cried Longueville. "I hope that your mother, at least, will accept a memento of the occasion." And he turned again with the sketch to her companion, who had been listening to the girl's conversation with this enter-

636

prising stranger, and looking from one to the other with an air of earnest confusion. "Won't you do me the honor of keeping my sketch?" he said. "I think it really looks like your daughter."

"Oh, thank you, thank you; I hardly dare," murmured the lady, with a deprecating gesture.

"It will serve as a kind of amends for the liberty I have taken," Longueville added; and he began to remove the drawing from its paper block.

"It makes it worse for you to give it to us," said the young girl.

"Oh, my dear, I am sure it's lovely!" exclaimed her mother. "It's wonderfully like you."

"I think that also makes it worse!"

Longueville was at last nettled. The young lady's perversity was perhaps not exactly malignant; but it was certainly ungracious. She seemed to desire to present herself as a beautiful tormentress.

"How does it make it worse?" he asked, with a frown.

He believed she was clever, and she was certainly ready. Now, however, she reflected a moment before answering.

"That you should give us your sketch," she said at last.

"It was to your mother I offered it," Longueville observed.

But this observation, the fruit of his irritation, appeared to have no effect upon the young girl.

"Isn't it what painters call a study?" she went on. "A study is of use to the painter himself. Your justification would be that you should keep your sketch, and that it might be of use to you."

"My daughter is a study, sir, you will say," said the elder lady in a little, light, conciliating voice, and graciously accepting the drawing again.

"I will admit," said Longueville, "that I am very inconsistent. Set it down to my esteem, madam," he added, looking at the mother.

"That's for you, mamma," said his model, disengaging her arm from her mother's hand and turning away.

The mamma stood looking at the sketch with a smile which seemed to express a tender desire to reconcile all accidents.

"It's extremely beautiful," she murmured, "and if you insist on my taking it——"

"I shall regard it as a great honor."

"Very well, then; with many thanks, I will keep it." She looked at the young man a moment, while her daughter walked away.

Longueville thought her a delightful little person; she struck him as a sort of transfigured Quakeress—a mystic with a practical side. "I am sure you think she is a strange girl," she said.

"She is extremely pretty."

"She is very clever," said the mother.

"She is wonderfully graceful."

"Ah, but she's good!" cried the old lady.

"I am sure she comes honestly by that," said Longueville, expressively, while his companion, returning his salutation with a certain scrupulous grace of her own, hurried after her daughter.

Longueville remained there staring at the view, but not especially seeing it. He felt as if he had at once enjoyed and lost an opportunity. After a while he tried to make a sketch of the old beggar-woman who sat there in a sort of palsied immobility, like a rickety statue at a church-door. But his attempt to reproduce her features was not gratifying, and he suddenly laid down his brush. She was not pretty enough—she had a bad profile.

JAMI

JAMI (Persian, 1414-1492). The last great classical poet of Persia. Mystic and scholar, devoted to Sufism. Highly honored by the Ottoman sultans. Wrote three *Divans* of lyric poetry, seven long *Masnavīs*, and great variety of prose works.

ZULAIKHA

... There was a King in the West. His name
Taimùs, was spread wide by the drum of Fame.
Of royal power and wealth possessed,
No wish unanswered remained in his breast.
His brow gave luster to Glory's crown,
And his foot gave the thrones of the Mighty renown.
With Orion from heaven his host to aid,
Conquest was his when he bared his blade.
His child Zulaikha was passing fair:
None in his heart might with her compare,—

638

Of his royal house the most brilliant star,
A gem from the chest where the treasures are.
Praise cannot equal her beauty; no!
But its faint, faint shadow my pen may show.
Like her own bright hair falling loosely down,
I will touch each charm to her feet from her crown.
May the soft reflection of that bright cheek
Lend light to my spirit and bid me speak!
And that flashing ruby, her mouth, bestow
The power to tell of the things I know!

    Her stature was like to a palm tree grown
In the Garden of Grace, where no sin is known;
Bedewed by the love of her father the King,
She mocked the cypress that rose by the spring.
Sweet with the odor of musk, a snare
For the heart of the Wise, was the maiden's hair;
Tangled at night, in the morning through
Her long thick tresses a comb she drew,
And cleft the heart of the musk deer in twain
As for that rare odor he sighed in vain.
A dark shade fell from her loose hair sweet
As jasmine over the rose of her feet.
A broad silver tablet her forehead displayed
For the heaven-set lessons of beauty made;
Under its edge two inverted Núns
Showed black as musk their splendid half-moons,
And beneath them lively and bright were placed
Two Sáds by the pen of her Maker traced.
From Nún to the ring of the Mim there rose
Pure as silver, like Alif, her nose.
To the cipher, her mouth, add Alif: then
She had ten strong spells for the conquest of men.
That laughing ruby to view exposed
A Sín when the knot of her lips unclosed
At the touch of her pure white teeth, and between
The lines of crimson their flash was seen.
Her face was the garden of Iram, where
Roses of every hue are fair.
The dusky moles that enhanced the red
Were like Moorish boys playing in each rose bed.

Of silver that paid no tithe, her chin
Had a well with the Water of Life therein.
If a sage in his thirst came near to drink,
He would feel the spray ere he reached the brink;
But lost were his soul if he nearer drew,
For it was a well and a whirlpool too.
Her neck was of ivory. Thither drawn,
Came with her tribute to beauty the fawn;
And the rose hung her head at the gleam of the skin
Of the shoulders fairer than jessamine.
Her breasts were orbs of a light most pure,
Twin bubbles new risen from Fount Kafúr;
Two young pomegranates grown on one spray,
Where bold hope never a finger might lay.
The touchstone itself was proved false when it tried
Her arms' fine silver thrice purified;
But the pearl-pure amulets fastened there
Were the hearts of the holy absorbed in prayer.
The loveliest gave her their souls for rue;
And round the charm their own heartstrings drew.
Her arms filled her sleeves with silver from them
Whose brows are bound with a diadem.
To labor and care her soft hand lent aid,
And to wounded hearts healing unction laid.
Like reeds were those taper fingers of hers
To write on each heart love's characters.
Each nail on those fingers so long and slim
Showed a new moon laid on a full moon's rim;
And her small closed hand made the moon confess
That she never might rival its loveliness.
Two columns fashioned of silver upheld
That beauty which never was paralleled;
And, to make the tale of her charms complete,
They were matched by the shape of her exquisite feet,—
Feet so light and elastic no maid might show,
So perfectly fashioned from heel to toe,—
If on the eye of a lover she stepped,
Her foot would float on the tear he wept.

THE JATAKA

THE JATAKA (Pali-Sanskrit, 1st century B.C.). One of the sacred books of Buddhism. A collection of some 550 *jatakas*, or brief tales combining legends and maxims of the Buddha with animal fables and the theme of reincarnation.

THE STRIDER OVER BATTLE-FIELDS

THIS was related by the Teacher while dwelling at Jetavana monastery; and it was concerning Nanda the elder.

For when the Teacher made his visit home to Kapilapura, he induced his youngest brother, Prince Nanda, to join the Order. Then he departed from Kapilapura and, traveling from place to place, he came and dwelt at Savatthi.

Now when the venerable Nanda had taken the Blessed One's bowl, and was leaving home, Belle-of-the-Country heard the report that Prince Nanda was going away in company with the Teacher, and with hair half-braided she looked out of the window, and called out to him: 'Come back quickly, my love!' And her speech remained in the venerable Nanda's mind, so that he became lovesick, and discontented, and pined away until the network of his veins showed on the surface of his body.

When the Teacher heard of all this, he thought: 'What if now I were to establish Nanda in saintship?' And going to the cell which was Nanda's sleeping-room, and taking his seat on the mat that was offered him, he said:

'Nanda, are you contented under this dispensation?'

'Reverend Sir, I am not contented, for I am exceedingly in love with Belle-of-the-Country.'

'Nanda, have you ever taken a trip through the Himalya mountains?'

'Reverend Sir, I never have.'

'Then let us go now.'

'Reverend Sir, I have no magical power. How can I go?'

'I will take you, Nanda,' said the Teacher, 'by my own magical power.'

Then he took the elder by the hand, and sprang into the air. As they passed along he pointed out to him a field that had been burned over, and on a charred stump was seated a she-monkey with her nose and tail destroyed, her hair singed off, her skin fissured and peeled to the quick, and all smeared with blood.

'Nanda, do you see this she-monkey?'

'Yes, Reverend Sir.'

'Take good note of her.'

Then he took him and showed him Manosila table-land, which is sixty leagues in extent, and Anotatta, and the rest of the seven great lakes, and the five great rivers, and the Himalya range containing many hundred pleasant spots, and graced with Gold Mountain, Silver Mountain, and Jewel Mountain.

Then said he: 'Nanda, have you ever seen the Heaven of the Suite of the Thirty-three?'

'Reverend Sir, I never have.'

'Come then, Nanda, and I will show it to you.'

And he took him thither, and sat down on Sakka's marble throne.

And Sakka, the king of the gods, came up with the gods of two heavens, and did obeisance, and sat down respectfully at one side. And his female attendants, twenty-five million in number, and five hundred pink-footed, celestial nymphs came up also, and did obeisance, and sat down respectfully at one side.

The Teacher suffered the venerable Nanda to look upon these five hundred celestial nymphs again and again with passion.

'Nanda,' said he, 'do you see these pink-footed celestial nymphs?'

'Yes, Reverend Sir.'

'Pray, now, are these or Belle-of-the-Country the prettier?'

'Reverend Sir, as is the burned she-monkey compared to Belle-of-the-Country, so is Belle-of-the-Country compared to these.'

'Well, Nanda, what then?'

'Reverend Sir, what does one do to obtain these celestial nymphs?'

'By performing the duties of a monk does one obtain these nymphs.'

'Reverend Sir, if the Blessed One will be my guarantee that if I perform the duties of a monk I shall obtain these nymphs, I will perform the duties of a monk.'

'Do so, Nanda. I am your guarantee.'

Thus did the elder take the Tathagata as a guarantee in the presence of the assembled gods. Then he said:

'Reverend Sir, do not delay. Come, let us go. I will perform the duties of a monk.'

Then the Teacher returned with him to Jetavana monastery; and the elder began to perform the duties of a monk.

'Sariputta,' said then the Teacher, addressing the Captain of the Doctrine, 'my youngest brother, Nanda, took me as guarantee for some celestial nymphs in the presence of the gods assembled in the Heaven of the Suite of the Thirty-three.'

Thus he told him. And in the same way he told it to Maha-Moggallana the elder, the Maha-Kassapa the elder, to Anuruddha the elder, to Ananda the elder and Treasurer of the Doctrine, and so on to all the eighty great disciples, and also to the greater part of the other priests.

The Captain of the Doctrine, Sariputta the elder, then drew near to Nanda the elder, then said:

'Is it true, as they say, brother Nanda, that in the presence of the gods assembled in the Heaven of the Suite of the Thirty-three you took The One Possessing the Ten Forces as a guarantee for some celestial nymphs, if you performed the duties of a monk? If that be so, is not your chaste religious life all for the sake of women? All for the sake of your passions? What is the difference between your thus doing the duties of a monk for the sake of women, and a laborer who performs his work for hire?'

This speech put the elder to shame, and made him quite dispirited. And in the same way all the eighty great disciples, and the remaining priests also, shamed the venerable Nanda. And realizing that he had behaved in an unworthy manner, in shame and remorse he summoned up his heroism, and attained to insight and to saintship; and coming to the Teacher, he said:

'Reverend Sir, I release the Blessed One from his promise.'

Said the Teacher: 'When you attained to saintship, O Nanda, I became released from my promise.'

When the priests heard of this occurrence, they raised a discussion in the lecture-hall.

'Brethren, how amenable to admonition is Nanda the elder! One admonition was sufficient to arouse in him shame and remorse, so that he performed the duties of a monk, and attained to saintship.'

The Teacher came and inquired: 'Priests, what now is the subject of your discourse?'

And they told him.

'Priests, formerly also, and not now for the first time, was Nanda amenable to admonition.' So saying, he related the bygone occurrence:

Once upon a time, when Brahmadatta was ruling at Benares, the future Buddha was born in the family of an elephant-trainer; and when he had come of age, and become accomplished as an elephant-trainer, he took service under a king who was hostile to the King of Benares. And he trained the State elephant until it was very well trained.

643

Then the King resolved to conquer the kingdom of Benares, and taking the future Buddha with him, and mounting the State elephant, with a mighty army he went to Benares, and surrounded the place. Then he sent a letter to the King saying, 'Give me the kingdom, or give me battle.'

Brahmadatta resolved to give battle; and having manned the walls, the watchtowers, and the gates, he did so.

His enemy had his State elephant armed with a defensive suit of mail, put on armor himself, and mounted on the elephant's shoulders. 'I will break into the city, kill my enemy, and take possession of the kingdom.' With this thought he seized a sharp goad, and urged the elephant in the direction of the city.

But the elephant, when he saw the hot mud, the stones from the catapults, and the various kinds of missiles thrown by the defenders, did not dare to advance, but retreated in mortal terror.

Then his trainer drew near: 'Old fellow,' said he, 'you are a hero, a strider over battle-fields. Retreat at such a time is not worthy of you.' And thus admonishing the elephant, he pronounced the following stanzas:

'A strider over battle-fields,
A hero, strong one, art thou called.
Why, then, behemoth, dost retreat
On coming near the gateway arch?

'Break down in haste the great crossbar!
The city-pillars take away!
And crashing through the gateway arch,
Enter, behemoth, quickly in!'

This one admonition was sufficient. For when the elephant heard it, he turned back, twisted his trunk round the city-pillars, and pulled them up like so many mushrooms. Then, crashing down the gateway arch, and forcing the cross-bar, he broke his way into the city, captured the kingdom, and gave it to his master.

When the Teacher had given this doctrinal instruction, he identified the characters of the birth-story:

'In that existence the elephant was Nanda, the King was Ananda, while the elephant-trainer was I myself.'

644

JAYADEVA

JAYADEVA (Sanskrit, *ca.* 1119-1179). Sanskrit poet at the court of the last king of Bengal. Author of celebrated love poem, the *Gītā Govinda* (*Song of the Cowherd*).

HYMN TO VISHNU

O thou that held'st the blessed Veda dry
   When all things else beneath the floods were hurled;
Strong Fish-God! Ark of Men! *Jai!* Hari, *jai!*
   Hail, Keshav, hail; thou Master of the world!

The round world rested on thy spacious nape;
   Upon thy neck, like a mere mole, it stood:
O thou, that took'st for us the Tortoise-shape,
   Hail, Keshav, Hail! Ruler of wave and wood!

The world upon thy curving tusk sate sure,
   Like the Moon's dark disc in her crescent pale;
O thou who didst for us assume the Boar,
   Immortal Conqueror! hail, Keshav, hail!

When thou thy Giant-Foe didst seize and rend,
   Fierce, fearful, long, and sharp were fang and nail;
Thou who the Lion and the Man didst blend,
   Lord of the Universe, hail, Narsingh, hail!

Wonderful Dwarf!—who with a threefold stride
   Cheated King Bali—where thy footsteps fall
Men's sins, O Wamuna! are set aside:
   O Keshav, hail! thou Help and Hope of all!

The sins of this sad earth thou didst assail,
   The anguish of its creatures thou didst heal;
Freed are we from all terrors by thy toil:
   Hail, Purshuram, hail! Lord of the biting steel!

To thee the fell Ten-Headed yielded life.
   Thou in dread battle laid'st the monster low!
Ah, Rama! dear to Gods and men that strife;
   We praise thee, Master of the matchless bow!

With clouds for garments glorious thou dost fare,
　Veiling thy dazzling majesty and might,
As when Jamuna saw thee with the share,
　A peasant—yet the King of Day and Night.

Merciful-hearted! when thou camest as Boodh—
　Albeit 'twas written in the Scriptures so—
Thou bad'st our altars to be no more imbrued
　With blood of victims: Keshav! bending low—

We praise thee, Wielder of the sweeping sword,
　Brilliant as curving comets in the gloom,
Whose edge shall smite the fierce barbarian horde;
　Hail to thee, Keshav! hail, and hear, and come,

And fill this song of Jayadev with thee,
　And make it wise to teach, strong to redeem,
And sweet to living souls. Thou Mystery!
　Thou Light of Life! Thou Dawn beyond the dream!

Fish! that didst outswim the flood;
Tortoise! whereon earth hath stood;
Boar! who with thy tush held'st high
The world, that mortals might not die;
Lion! who hast giants torn;
Dwarf! who laugh'dst a king to scorn;
Sole Subduer of the Dreaded!
Slayer of the many-headed!
Mighty Ploughman! Teacher tender!
Of thine own the sure Defender!
Under all thy ten disguises
Endless praise to thee arises.

JUAN RAMON JIMENEZ

JUAN RAMON JIMÉNEZ (Spanish, 1881-　　). Influential modern Spanish poet, leader of Darío-French-Symbolist School. A native of Andalusia, went into exile at time of Civil War. Now living in America. Highly polished artist, whose aim is "pure poetry." Important publications: *Baladas de primavera, Diario de un poeta recién casado, Poesías escojidas.*

FORTUNATE BEING

Singing you go, and laughing through the water,
and through the air you go whistling and laughing,

646

a round of blue and gold, of green and silver,
so happy passing and repassing ever
amidst the first red blossoming of April,
the distinct form of instantaneous
equalities of light, of life, of color,
with us, kindled like river banks aflame!

What a happy being you are,
with universal and eternal happiness!
Happy, you break through the waves of the air,
you swim contrary to the waves of water!
Do you not have to eat, neither to sleep?
All the springtime, is it yours to enjoy?
All of the green, all of the blue,
the flowering all, is it yours?
There is no fear in your glory;
your fate is to return, return, return,
in rounds of green and silver, blue and gold,
through an eternity of eternities!

You give your hand to us in a moment
of possible affinity, of sudden love,
of radiant concession;
and with your warm contact,
in wild vibration of flesh and of soul,
we are enkindled with sweet harmony,
and we, made new, forget the usual,
we shine for an instant, happy with gold.
It seems that we too are going to be
perennial as you,
that we shall fly from ocean to the mountain,
that we shall leap from heaven to the sea,
and that we shall return, return, return
for an eternity of eternities.
We sing and we laugh through the air,
through the water we laugh and whistle.

But you must not forget yourself,
you are the casual, perpetual presence,
you are the fortunate creature,
the only magic being without shadow,
the one adored for warmth and grace,

647

the free, enraptured robber
that, in rounds of blue and gold, green and silver,
goes laughing, whistling through the air,
through the water singing and laughing!

THE BEST THAT I HAVE

Green sea and grey sky and blue sky
and loving albatross upon the waves,
and in all, the sun, and thou in the sun,
observing desired and desiring god,
lighting with distinct golden rays my arrival;
the arrival of him that I am today,
of him that even yesterday I doubted
he could be in thee as I am.

What a changed man in me, desiring god,
from the being doubting the legend
of the god of the many glib speakers,
to be the firm believer
in the story I myself have created
all through my life for thee.

Now I come to this termination
of a year of my natural life,
in the depths of the air where I keep thee,
above this sea, these depths of water,
to this beautiful, blinding termination,
where thou art gradually entering me,
content to be thine, to be mine,
through the best that I have, my own expression.

From ELEGIES

The dazzling whiteness of my first love
At the sweet, sad sound of reveille!
What celestial joy was it that opened those oriental gardens
To my youthful soul, that morning?
It was a holiday. All pallid sorrow died out
In the green of false springtime;
Everything was charged with laughter, with flowers.
The ground was rushes, the air was pennons.

648

And that sweet blue night, on that bench,
Under the doubled shadow of the drooping acacia,
While the moon gave its white flax to the world,
She said she had loved me all her life long.

Alas! I would live through all my sorrows again,
Even the darkest, to see such a morning
As that on which the sun purified my brow
At the sweet, sad sound of reveille.

From THE DIARY OF A NEWLY-MARRIED MAN

Remorse
(Between Philadelphia and New York, a rainy night, May 24)

Must you acquiesce, my soul,
In forgetting in the morning?
If four great nails, well nailed,
My soul, right into your entrails,
Were to open four great, pure roses
From those four livid words
That he will hold nailed
In his kind heart
From then on!

Must you acquiesce
Merely in being quite happy,
Soul?

From STONE AND HEAVEN

Dream Nocturne

The earth leads by the earth.
But, sea,
You lead by the heavens.
With what security of gold and silver light
Do the stars mark the road for us!
One would think
That the earth was the road
Of the body,

That the sea was the road
Of the soul.
Yes. It seems
That the soul is the only traveler
Of the sea; that the body, alone,
Remains behind, on the beach,
Without her, saying goodbye,
Heavy, cold, as though dead.
How like
Is a journey by sea
To death,
To eternal life!

MAURUS JOKAI

MAURUS JOKAI (Hungarian, 1825-1904). Most widely read Hungarian novelist. Unusual narrative skill, wrote chiefly to entertain. Author of 100 novels. Most colorful are those celebrating glories of old Hungary; 22 translated into English, including: *Midst the Wild Carpathians, The Baron's Sons, Timar's Two Worlds, The Yellow Rose.*

TIMAR'S TWO WORLDS

I. How Ali Saved His Daughter

A MOUNTAIN-CHAIN, pierced through from base to summit—a gorge four miles in length walled in by lofty precipices; and between these walls flows the Danube in its rocky bed.

At this time there were no steamers on the Danube, but a vessel, called the St. Barbara, approaches, drawn against the stream by thirty-two horses. The fate of the vessel lies in the hands of two men—the pilot and the captain.

The name of the captain is Michael Timar. He is a man of about thirty, with fair hair and dreamy blue eyes.

At the door of the ship's cabin sits a man of fifty, smoking a Turkish chibouque. Euthemio Trikaliss is the name under which he is registered in the way-book, and he is the owner of the cargo. The ship itself belongs to a merchant of Komorn called Athanas Brazovics.

Out of one of the cabin windows looks the face of a young girl,

Timéa, the daughter of Euthemio, and the face is as white as marble. Timéa and her father are the only passengers of the St. Barbara.

When the captain lays aside his speaking-trumpet he has time to chat with Timéa, who understands only modern Greek, which the captain speaks fluently.

It is always a dangerous voyage, for the current is fierce and the rocks are death-traps. To-day, too, the St. Barbara was pursued by a Turkish gunboat. But the vessel makes its way safely, in spite of current and rocks, and the Turkish gunboat gives up the chase.

Three days later the St. Barbara had reached the island of Orsova; the plains of Hungary are to the north of the river, Servia to the south.

Provisions had run short, and Timar decided to go on shore. There were no signs of human habitation at first, but Timar's sharp eyes had discovered a faint smoke rising above the tops of the poplars. He worked his way in a small skiff through the reeds, reached dry land, pushed through hedges and bushes, and then stood transfixed with admiration.

A cultivated orchard of some five or six acres was before him, and beyond that a flower-garden, full of summer bloom.

Timar went up through the orchard and flower garden to a cottage, built partly in the rock, and covered with creepers. A huge, black Newfoundland dog was lying before the door.

A woman's voice answered Timar's "good-morning," and the dog raised no objection to the captain going indoors.

"It never hurts good people," said the woman.

Timar explained his mission. The wind had brought his vessel to a standstill; he was short of provisions, and he had two passengers who would be grateful for shelter on land for the night.

The woman promised him food and a room for his passengers in exchange for grain, and at her word the dog brought him by a better path to the river.

Presently Timar was back again with Euthemio and Timéa, and now a young girl appeared, whom the housewife called Noemi.

Before supper was over, the growling of the dog announced a new arrival, and a man of youthful appearance, who introduced himself as Theodor Krisstyan, an old friend of the lady of the house, whom he called Madame Therese, entered and made himself quickly at home. It was plain that his hostess both feared and disliked Theodor, while Timar, who had met him before, regarded him as a spy in the pay of the Turkish government.

651

In the morning the wind had gone down, Theodor had vanished, and Timar and his passengers prepared to renew their journey.

Therese told Timar her story before he left; how she and her daughter Noemi had lived there for twelve years, and who the objectionable Theodor was. Then she added, in a whisper. "I fancy this man Krisstyan's visit was either on your account, or that of the other gentleman. Be on your guard if either of you dread the discovery of a secret."

Trikaliss looked very gloomy when he heard the stranger had left before sunrise, and the following night he called Timar to his cabin.

"I am dying," he said. "I want to die—I have taken poison. Timéa will not wake till all is over. My true name is not Euthemio Trikaliss, but Ali Tschorbadschi. I was once governor of Candia, and then treasurer in Stamboul. You know there is a revolution proceeding in Turkey; my turn was coming. Not that I was a conspirator, but the treasury wanted my money and the seraglio my daughter. Death is easy for me, but I will not let my daughter go into the harem nor myself be made a beggar. Therefore I hired your vessel, and loaded it with grain. The owner, Athanas Brazovics, is a connection of mine; I have often shown him kindness, he can return it now. By a miracle we got safely through the rocks and whirlpools of the river, and eluded the pursuit of the Turkish brigantine, and now I stumble over a straw into my grave.

"That man who followed us last evening was a spy of the Turkish government. He recognised me, and sealed my fate. The government would not demand me from Austria as a political refugee, but as a thief. This is unjust, for what I took was my own. But I am pursued as a thief, and Austria gives up escaped thieves if Turkish spies can trace them. By dying I can save my daughter and her property. Swear to me by your faith and your honour you will carry out my instructions. Here in this casket is about a thousand ducats. Take Timéa to Athanas Brazovics, and beg him to adopt my daughter. Give him the money, he must spend it on the education of the child, and give him also the cargo, and beg him to be present when the sacks are emptied. You understand!"

The dying man looked in Timar's face, and struggled for breath. "Yes—the Red Crescent!" he stammered. "The Red Crescent!" Then the death-throes closed his lips—one struggle, and he was a corpse.

WHEN the St. Barbara had nearly reached Komorn it struck an uprooted tree, lying in ambush under water, and immediately began to sink. It is absolutely impossible to save a vessel wrecked in this way. The crew all left the sinking craft, and Timar rescued Timéa, and with her the casket with the thousand ducats.

Then the captain drove off with the fatherless girl to the house of Athanas Brazovics in the town of Komorn.

At first Athanas kissed Timéa very heartily, but when he learnt that his vessel was lost, and all Timéa's property, except the thousand ducats, and the wheat sacks—now spoilt by water—he altered his tune.

He and his wife Sophie decided that Timéa should live with them as an adopted child, and at the same time attend on their daughter Athalie as a waiting-maid. Athalie and her mother treated the poor girl with scornful contempt.

As for Timar, Athanas turned on him savagely, as though the captain could have prevented the wreck!

On the advice of his friend, Lieutenant Katschuka, who was betrothed to Athalie, Timar purchased the sunken grain next day when it was put up for auction, buying the whole cargo for 10,000 gulden. "You will do the poor orphan a good turn if you buy it," said the lieutenant. "Otherwise, the value of the cargo will all go in salvage."

Timar at once made arrangements for hauling up the sacks, and for the immediate drying and grinding of the corn, and all day labourers were at work on the wreck.

At nightfall Timar, left alone, noticed one sack differently marked from the rest—marked with a red crescent! Within this sack was a long leathern bag. He broke it open and found it full of diamonds, emeralds, and sapphires richly set in girdles and bracelets and rings. A whole heap of unset diamonds were in an agate box. The whole treasure was worth at least 1,000,000 gulden. The St. Barbara had carried a million on board!

"To whom does this treasure belong?"

So Timar put the question to himself, and answered it.

"Why, whom should it belong to but you? You bought the sunken cargo, just as it is, with the sacks and the grain. If the treasurer stole the jewels from the sultan, the sultan probably stole them in his campaigns."

"And Timéa?"

"Timéa would not know how to use the treasure, and her adopted father would absorb it, and get rid of nine-tenths of it. What would be the result if Timéa gets it? She would be a rich lady, and would not cast a look at you from her height. Now things are the other way—you will be a rich man and she a poor girl. You do not want the treasure for yourself. You will invest it profitably, and when you have earned with the first million a second and a third, you will go to the poor girl and say, 'There, take it—it is all yours; and take me, too.' You only wish to become rich in order to make her happy."

The moon and the waves cried to Timar, "You are rich—you are a made man!"

But when it was dark an inward voice whispered, "You are a thief!"

From that day all Timar's undertakings flourished, and step by step he reached the summit of an ordinary successful business man's ambition—the title of nobility. At the same time Brazovics, who had treated Timar with brutal inconsiderateness because of the wreck of the St. Barbara, went steadily down-hill, borrowing and embezzling trust moneys in his fall.

Lieutenant Katschuka had declared all along that he could not marry Athalie without a dowry, and when the wedding day arrived, Brazovics, unable to face his creditors, and knowing himself bankrupt, penniless, and fraudulent, committed suicide. Katschuka immediately declared the engagement at an end. In his heart he had long wearied of Athalie, and looked with desire on Timéa. The orphan girl from the first had loved the lieutenant with silent, unspoken affection.

When the Brazovics' house was put up for sale Timar bought it outright, furniture and all, and then said to Timéa, "From this day forth you are the mistress of this house. Everything in it belongs to you, all is inscribed in your name. Accept it from me. You are the owner of the house, and if there is a little shelter for me in your heart, and you did not refuse my hand—then I should be only too happy."

Timéa gave her hand to Timar, and said in a low, firm voice, "I accept you as my husband, and will be a faithful and obedient wife."

This man had always been so good to her. He had never made sport of her nor flattered her, and he had saved her life on the

Danube when the St. Barbara was sinking. He had given her all her heart could desire except one thing, and that belonged to another.

III. The Ownerless Island

On his betrothal to Timéa a great burden was lifted from the soul of Timar. Since the day when the treasure of Ali Tschorbadschi had enabled him to achieve power and riches, Timar had been haunted by the voice of self-accusation: "This money does not belong to you—it was the property of an orphan. You are a man of gold! You are a thief!"

But now the defrauded orphan had received back her property. Only Timar forgot that he had demanded in exchange the girl's heart.

Timéa promised to be a faithful and obedient wife, but on the wedding-day when Timar said, "Do you love me?" she only opened her eyes, and asked, "What is love?"

Timar found he had married a marble statue; and that all his riches would not buy his wife's love. He became wretched, conscious that his wife was unhappy, that he was the author of their mutual misery.

Then, in the early summer, Timar went off from Komorn to shoot water-fowl. He meant to go to the ownerless island at Ostrova —it was three years since that former visit.

Therese and Noemi welcomed him cordially at the island, and Timar forgot his troubles when he was with them. Therese told him her story; how her husband, ruined by the father of Theodor Krisstyan and by Athanas Brazovics, had committed suicide, and how, forsaken and friendless, she had brought her child to this island, which neither Austria nor Turkey claimed, and where no tax-collector called. With her own hands she had turned the wilderness into a paradise, and the only fear she had was that Theodor Krisstyan, who had discovered her retreat, might reveal it to the Turkish government.

Therese had no money and no use for it, but she exchanged fruit and honey for grain, salt, clothes, and hardware, and the people with whom she bartered were not inclined to gossip about her affairs.

So no news concerning the island ever went to Vienna, Komorn, or Constantinople, and the fact of Timar's great prosperity had not reached the islanders. He was welcomed as a hard-working man,

and Therese did not know that Timar had been powerful enough to get a ninety years' lease of the island from both Turkish and Austrian governments; perhaps no very difficult matter, as the existence of the island was unknown, and there were fees to be paid over the concession.

When he told her what he had done, Noemi threw her arms round his neck.

Theodor Krisstyan was furious, but Timar procured him a post in Brazil, and for a long time the disreputable spy was too far off to be troublesome.

And now on this island Timar found health and rest. It became his home, and for the summer months every year he would slip away from Komorn, and no one, not even Timéa, guessed his secret. When he returned Timéa's cold, white face was still an unsolved riddle to her husband. She would greet him kindly, but never was there any token that she loved him. Timar's ever-increasing business operations were excuse for his long absences, but all the same the double life he was leading made him ill. He could not tell Timéa of Therese and Noemi, and he could not tell them on the island that he was married.

Timéa, on her side, devoted herself more and more to her husband's business in his absence, and when Major Katschuka once called and asked her if she could not arrange for a divorce, she answered gently, "My husband is the noblest man in the world. Should I separate from him who has no one but me to love him? Am I to tell him that I hate him, I who owe everything to him, and who brought him no dowry but a loveless heart?"

Timar learnt from Athalie, who lived in Timéa's house, of this reply, and felt more in despair than ever. He wanted Timéa to be happy, she had never been his wife except in name, for he had been waiting for her love.

And he wanted to go away, and leave all his riches behind, and settle on the island. Now more than ever was he wanted on the island, for Therese had died of heart failure, and the years had made Noemi a woman.

IV. "My Name is Nobody"

It was winter, and Timar had gone off alone to a house that belonged to him near a frozen lake. He felt the time had come for flight, but whither?

656

Theodor Krisstyan had turned up again. In Brazil he had heard a story of Ali Tschorbadschi's jewels from an old criminal from Turkey, and he had returned to blackmail Timar. But he did not find him till Timar was at the frozen lake.

Krisstyan's story was not true. Timar knew that the accusations were false as he listened to the vagabond's indictment. He had not "killed" Timéa's father, nor "stolen" his treasure. But he had played a false game, and his position was a false one. Krisstyan demanded a change of raiment, and Timar let him take clothes and shirts. But at last the blackmailer's demands became too insolent, and Timar drove him out of the house.

And now it seemed to Timar that his own career was finished. This ruffian Krisstyan could expose the foundation of his wealth, and how could he live discredited before the world?

On the frozen water there were great fissures between the blocks of ice. Within the waves of the lake death would come quickly. Timar walked out on the ice, and there before him the head of Theodor Krisstyan rose in the water and then sank. The spy had not known the treachery of the fissures.

Timar fled to the ownerless island, and when the corpse of Krisstyan was recovered, in an advanced stage of decomposition, Timéa declared she recognised her husband's clothes.

So the body of Theodor Krisstyan was buried with great pomp, and a year later Timéa married Major Katschuka, and then, haunted by the doubt whether her first husband was really dead, pined away.

No blessing rested on the wealth Timar left behind him. The only son Timéa bore to the major was a great spendthrift, and in his hands the fabulous wealth vanished as quickly as it had grown.

And what is passing meanwhile on the ownerless island?

Forty years have passed since Timar's disappearance from Komorn, and the island is now a complete model farm. Recently, a friend of mine, an ardent naturalist, took me to the island. I had heard as a child of Timar and his wealth.

Every inch of ground is utilised or serves to beautify the place. The tobacco grown here has the most exquisite aroma, and the beehives look from a distance like a small town with many-shaped roofs.

It is easy to see that the owner of the island understands luxury, and yet that owner never has a farthing to call his own; no money ever enters the island. Those, however, who need the exports know also the requirements of the islanders, and bring them for barter.

The whole colony consisted of one family, and each was called only by his Christian name. The six sons of the first settler had married women of the district, and the numbers of grandchildren and great-grandchildren already exceeded forty, but the island maintained them all. Poverty was unknown; they lived in luxury; each knew some trade, and if they had been ten times as many, their labour would have supported them.

When we arrived on the island, the nominal head of the family, a well-built man of forty, received us cordially, and in the evening presented us to his parents.

When my name was mentioned to the old man he looked long at me, and a visible colour rose in his cheeks. I began to tell him of what was going on in the world, that Hungary was now united to Austria, and that the taxes were very heavy.

He blew a cloud from his pipe, and the smoke said, "My island has nothing to do with that, we have no taxes here."

I told him of wars, financial panics, the strife of religion and politics, and the smoke seemed to say, "We wage war with no one here. Thank God, we have no money here and no elections or ministers."

Presently the old man asked me where I was born, and what my profession was? And when I told him that I wrote romances, he said, "Guess my story. There was once a man who left a world in which he was admired and respected, and created a second world in which he was loved."

"May I venture to ask your name?" I said.

The old man seemed to grow a head taller; then, raising his trembling hands, he laid them on my head. And it seemed to me as if once, long, long before those same hands had rested on my head when childish curls covered it, and that I had seen that noble face before.

"My name is Nobody," he replied to my question; and after that night I saw him no more during our stay on the island.

The privileges granted by two governments to the owner of the island will last for fifty years more. And who knows what may happen to the world in fifty years?

BEN JONSON

BEN JONSON (English, 1572-1637). Delightful singer of Shakespeare's time and later. Also actor, dramatist and critic. Wrote masques for noble patrons and popular plays: *Every Man in His Humour, Volpone.* Had large coterie in London and was literary dictator for quarter of century. Loved most for his lyrics, such as "Drink to Me Only with Thine Eyes."

EPITAPH ON ELIZABETH, L. H.

Wouldst thou hear what man can say
　　In a little? Reader, stay.
Underneath this stone doth lie
　　As much beauty as could die;
Which in life did harbor give
　　To more virtue than doth live.
If at all she had a fault,
　　Leave it buried in this vault.
One name was Elizabeth,
　　Th' other let it sleep with death;
Fitter, where it died to tell,
　　Than that it lived at all. Farewell.

WHY I WRITE NOT OF LOVE

Some act of Love's bound to rehearse,
I thought to bind him in my verse;
Which when he felt, Away, quoth he,
Can poets hope to fetter me?
It is enough they once did get
Mars and my mother in their net;
I wear not these my wings in vain.
With which he fled me, and again
Into my rhymes could ne'er be got
By any art. Then wonder not
That since my numbers are so cold,
When Love is fled, and I grow old.

SONG, TO CELIA [1]

Come, my Celia, let us prove
While we may the sports of love;
Time will not be ours forever,
He at length our good will sever.
Spend not then his gifts in vain;
Suns that set may rise again,
But if once we lose this light,
'Tis with us perpetual night.
Why should we defer our joys?
Fame and rumor are but toys.
Cannot we delude the eyes
Of a few poor household spies?
Or his easier ears beguile,
So removed by our wile?
'Tis no sin love's fruit to steal;
But the sweet theft to reveal,
To be taken, to be seen,
These have crimes accounted been.

SONG, TO CELIA [2]

Drink to me only with thine eyes,
    And I will pledge with mine;
Or leave a kiss but in the cup,
    And I'll not look for wine.
The thirst that from the soul doth rise
    Doth ask a drink divine;
But might I of Jove's nectar sup,
    I would not change for thine.

I sent thee late a rosy wreath,
    Not so much honoring thee,
As giving it a hope that there
    It could not withered be.
But thou thereon didst only breathe,
    And sent'st it back to me,
Since when it grows and smells, I swear,
    Not of itself, but thee.

Let it not your wonder move,
Less your laughter, that I love.
Though I now write fifty years,
I have had, and have, my peers;
Poets though divine are men,
Some have loved as old again.
And it is not always face,
Clothes, or fortune, gives the grace,
Or the feature, or the youth;
But the language and the truth,
With the ardor and the passion,
Gives the lover weight and fashion.

If you then will read the story,
First prepare you to be sorry
That you never knew till now
Either whom to love, or how;
But be glad, as soon with me,
When you know that this is she
Of whose beauty it was sung:
She shall make the old man young,
Keep the middle age at stay,
And let nothing high decay;
Till she be the reason why
All the world for love may die.

HER TRIUMPH

See the chariot at hand here of love,
    Wherein my lady rideth!
Each that draws is a swan or a dove,
    And well the car love guideth.
As she goes all hearts do duty
        Unto her beauty,
And enamoured do wish so they might
        But enjoy such a sight,
That they still were to run by her side,
Through swords, through seas, whither she would ride.

Do but look on her eyes; they do light
  All that love's world compriseth!
Do but look on her hair; it is bright
  As love's star when it riseth!
Do but mark, her forehead's smoother
  Than words that soothe her;
And from her arched brows, such a grace
  Sheds itself through the face,
As alone there triumphs to the life
All the gain, all the good of the elements' strife.

Have you seen but a bright lily grow
  Before rude hands have touched it?
Ha' you marked but the fall o' the snow
  Before the soil hath smutched it?
Ha' you felt the wool of beaver,
  Or swan's down ever?
Or have smelt o' the bud o' the briar?
  Or the nard in the fire?
Or have tasted the bag of the bee?
O so white! O so soft! O so sweet is she!

THE PLANT AND FLOWER OF LIGHT

It is not growing like a tree
In bulk, doth make man better be;
Or standing long an oak, three hundred year,
To fall a log at last, dry, bald, and sere;
A lily of a day
Is fairer far in May,
Although it fall and die that night,
It was the plant and flower of light.
In small proportions we just beauties see;
And in short measures, life may perfect be.

TO CYNTHIA

Queen and huntress, chaste and fair,
Now the sun is laid to sleep,
Seated in thy silver chair
State in wonted manner keep;

Hesperus entreats thy light,
Goddess excellently bright.

Earth, let not thy envious shade
Dare itself to interpose;
Cynthia's shining orb was made
Heaven to clear, when day did close;
  Bless us then with wishëd sight,
  Goddess excellently bright.

Lay thy bow of pearl apart,
And thy crystal shining quiver;
Give unto the flying hart
Space to breathe, how short soever,
  Thou that mak'st a day of night,
  Goddess excellently bright.

JAMES JOYCE

JAMES JOYCE (Irish, 1882-1941). Most controversial innovator of modern
letters. Experiments with new techniques influenced "stream-of-consciousness"
school. Unhappy youth in Ireland reflected in *A Portrait of the Artist as a
Young Man*. In self-imposed exile to Paris, wrote *Ulysses*, description of a
day's life in Dublin. Published first in Paris, permitted in America by famous
court decision. Last work, *Finnegans Wake*, so difficult only Joyce *aficionados*
understand it.

ARABY

NORTH Richmond Street, being blind, was a quiet street except at
the hour when the Christian Brothers' School set the boys free. An
uninhabited house of two storeys stood at the blind end, detached
from its neighbours in a square ground. The other houses of the
street, conscious of decent lives within them, gazed at one another
with brown imperturbable faces.

The former tenant of our house, a priest, had died in the back
drawing-room. Air, musty from having been long enclosed, hung
in all the rooms, and the waste room behind the kitchen was
littered with old useless papers. Among these I found a few paper-

663

covered books, the pages of which were curled and damp: *The Abbot*, by Walter Scott, *The Devout Communicant* and *The Memoirs of Vidocq*. I liked the last best because its leaves were yellow. The wild garden behind the house contained a central apple-tree and a few straggling bushes under one of which I found the late tenant's rusty bicycle-pump. He had been a very charitable priest; in his will he had left all his money to institutions and the furniture of his house to his sister.

When the short days of winter came, dusk fell before we had well eaten our dinners. When we met in the street the houses had grown somber. The space of sky above us was the color of ever-changing violet and towards it the lamps of the street lifted their feeble lanterns. The cold air stung us and we played till our bodies glowed. Our shouts echoed in the silent street. The career of our play brought us through the dark muddy lanes behind the houses where we ran the gauntlet of the rough tribes from the cottages, to the back doors of the dark dripping gardens where odors arose from the ashpits, to the dark odorous stables where a coachman smoothed and combed the horse or shook music from the buckled harness. When we returned to the street, light from the kitchen windows had filled the areas. If my uncle was seen turning the corner we hid in the shadow until we had seen him safely housed. Or if Mangan's sister came out on the doorstep to call her brother in to his tea we watched her from our shadow peer up and down the street. We waited to see whether she would remain or go in and, if she remained, we left our shadow and walked up to Mangan's steps resignedly. She was waiting for us, her figure defined by the light from the half-opened door. Her brother always teased her before he obeyed and I stood by the railings looking at her. Her dress swung as she moved her body and the soft rope of her hair tossed from side to side.

Every morning I lay on the floor in the front parlor watching her door. The blind was pulled down to within an inch of the sash so that I could not be seen. When she came out on the doorstep my heart leaped. I ran to the hall, seized my books and followed her. I kept her brown figure always in my eye and, when we came near the point at which our ways diverged, I quickened my pace and passed her. This happened morning after morning. I had never spoken to her, except for a few casual words, and yet her name was like a summons to all my foolish blood.

Her image accompanied me even in places the most hostile to

romance. On Saturday evenings when my aunt went marketing I had to go to carry some of the parcels. We walked through the flaring streets, jostled by drunken men and bargaining women, amid the curses of laborers, the shrill litanies of shop-boys who stood on guard by the barrels of pigs' cheeks, the nasal chanting of street-singers, who sang a *come-all-you* about O'Donovan Rossa, or a ballad about the troubles in our native land. These noises converged in a single sensation of life for me: I imagined that I bore my chalice safely through a throng of foes. Her name sprang to my lips at moments in strange prayers and praises which I myself did not understand. My eyes were often full of tears (I could not tell why) and at times a flood from my heart seemed to pour out into my bosom. I thought little of the future. I did not know whether I would ever speak to her or not or, if I spoke to her, how I could tell her of my confused adoration. But my body was like a harp and her words and gestures were like fingers running upon the wires.

One evening I went into the back drawing-room in which the priest had died. It was a dark rainy evening and there was no sound in the house. Through one of the broken panes I heard the rain impinge upon the earth, the fine incessant needles of water playing in the sodden beds. Some distant lamp or lighted window gleamed below me. I was thankful that I could see so little. All my senses seemed to desire to veil themselves and, feeling that I was about to slip from them, I pressed the palms of my hands together until they trembled, murmuring: *"O love! O love!"* many times.

At last she spoke to me. When she addressed the first words to me I was so confused that I did not know what to answer. She asked me was I going to *Araby*. I forgot whether I answered yes or no. It would be a splendid bazaar, she said she would love to go.

"And why can't you?" I asked.

While she spoke she turned a silver bracelet round and round her wrist. She could not go, she said, because there would be a retreat that week in her convent. Her brother and two other boys were fighting for their caps and I was alone at the railings. She held one of the spikes, bowing her head towards me. The light from the lamp opposite our door caught the white curve of her neck, lit up her hair that rested there and, falling, lit up the hand upon the railing. It fell over one side of her dress and caught the white border of a petticoat, just visible as she stood at ease.

"It's well for you," she said.

"If I go," I said, "I will bring you something."

What innumerable follies laid waste my waking and sleeping thoughts after that evening! I wished to annihilate the tedious intervening days. I chafed against the work of school. At night in my bedroom and by day in the classroom her image came between me and the page I strove to read. The syllables of the word *Araby* were called to me through the silence in which my soul luxuriated and cast an Eastern enchantment over me. I asked for leave to go to the bazaar on Saturday night. My aunt was surprised and hoped it was not some Freemason affair. I answered few questions in class. I watched my master's face pass from amiability to sternness; he hoped I was not beginning to idle. I could not call my wandering thoughts together. I had hardly any patience with the serious work of life which, now that it stood between me and my desire, seemed to me child's play, ugly monotonous child's play.

On Saturday morning I reminded my uncle that I wished to go to the bazaar in the evening. He was fussing at the hallstand, looking for the hat-brush, and answered me curtly:

"Yes, boy, I know."

As he was in the hall I could not go into the front parlor and lie at the window. I left the house in bad humor and walked slowly towards the school. The air was pitilessly raw and already my heart misgave me.

When I came home to dinner my uncle had not yet been home. Still it was early. I sat staring at the clock for some time and, when its ticking began to irritate me, I left the room. I mounted the staircase and gained the upper part of the house. The high, cold, empty gloomy rooms liberated me and I went from room to room singing. From the front window I saw my companions playing below in the street. Their cries reached me weakened and indistinct and, leaning my forehead against the cool glass, I looked over at the dark house where she lived. I may have stood there for an hour, seeing nothing but the brown-clad figure cast by my imagination, touched discreetly by the lamplight at the curved neck, at the hand upon the railings and at the border below the dress.

When I came downstairs again I found Mrs. Mercer sitting at the fire. She was an old garrulous woman, a pawnbroker's widow, who collected used stamps for some pious purpose. I had to endure the gossip of the tea-table. The meal was prolonged beyond an hour and still my uncle did not come. Mrs. Mercer stood up to

go: she was sorry she couldn't wait any longer, but it was after eight o'clock and she did not like to be out late, as the night air was bad for her. When she had gone I began to walk up and down the room, clenching my fists. My aunt said:

"I'm afraid you may put off your bazaar for this night of Our Lord."

At nine o'clock I heard my uncle's latchkey in the halldoor. I heard him talking to himself and heard the hallstand rocking when it had received the weight of his overcoat. I could interpret these signs. When he was midway through his dinner I asked him to give me the money to go to the bazaar. He had forgotten.

"The people are in bed and after their first sleep now," he said.

I did not smile. My aunt said to him energetically:

"Can't you give him the money and let him go? You've kept him late enough as it is."

My uncle said he was very sorry he had forgotten. He said he believed in the old saying: "All work and no play makes Jack a dull boy." He asked me where I was going and, when I had told him a second time he asked me did I know *The Arab's Farewell to his Steed*. When I left the kitchen he was about to recite the opening lines of the piece to my aunt.

I held a florin tightly in my hand as I strode down Buckingham Street towards the station. The sight of the streets thronged with buyers and glaring with gas recalled to me the purpose of my journey. I took my seat in a third-class carriage of a deserted train. After an intolerable delay the train moved out of the station slowly. It crept onward among ruinous houses and over the twinkling river. At Westland Row Station a crowd of people pressed to the carriage doors; but the porters moved them back, saying that it was a special train for the bazaar. I remained alone in the bare carriage. In a few minutes the train drew up beside an improvised wooden platform. I passed out on to the road and saw by the lighted dial of a clock that it was ten minutes to ten. In front of me was a large building which displayed the magical name.

I could not find any sixpenny entrance and, fearing that the bazaar would be closed, I passed in quickly through a turnstile, handing a shilling to a weary-looking man. I found myself in a big hall girdled at half its height by a gallery. Nearly all the stalls were closed and the greater part of the hall was in darkness. I recognised a silence like that which pervades a church after a service. I walked into the center of the bazaar timidly. A few people

667

were gathered about the stalls which were still open. Before a curtain, over which the words *Café Chantant* were written in colored lamps, two men were counting money on a salver. I listened to the fall of the coins.

Remembering with difficulty why I had come I went over to one of the stalls and examined porcelain vases and flowered tea-sets. At the door of the stall a young lady was talking and laughing with two young gentlemen. I remarked their English accents and listened vaguely to their conversation.

"O, I never said such a thing!"

"O, but you did!"

"O, but I didn't!"

"Didn't she say that?"

"Yes. I heard her."

"O, there's a . . . fib!"

Observing me the young lady came over and asked me did I wish to buy anything. The tone of her voice was not encouraging; she seemed to have spoken to me out of a sense of duty. I looked humbly at the great jars that stood like eastern guards at either side of the dark entrance to the stall and murmured:

"No, thank you."

The young lady changed the position of one of the vases and went back to the two young men. They began to talk of the same subject. Once or twice the young lady glanced at me over her shoulder.

I lingered before her stall, though I knew my stay was useless, to make my interest in her wares seem the more real. Then I turned away slowly and walked down the middle of the bazaar. I allowed the two pennies to fall against the sixpence in my pocket. I heard a voice call from one end of the gallery that the light was out. The upper part of the hall was now completely dark.

Gazing up into the darkness I saw myself as a creature driven and derided by vanity; and my eyes burned with anguish and anger.

K

FRANZ KAFKA

FRANZ KAFKA (German, 1883-1924). Austrian-born novelist, whose influence became international 20 years after death. A lonely, tormented figure, who suffered from tuberculosis. Published only few stories during lifetime. Three posthumous novels—*The Castle, The Trial, Amerika*—notable for atmosphere of paranoia, the individual struggling against anonymous powers. Fantastic motives combined with detailed realism.

A COUNTRY DOCTOR

I was in great perplexity; I had to start on an urgent journey; a seriously ill patient was waiting for me in a village ten miles off; a thick blizzard of snow filled all the wide spaces between him and me; I had a gig, a light gig with big wheels, exactly right for our country roads; muffled in furs, my bag of instruments in my hand, I was in the courtyard all ready for the journey; but there was no horse to be had, no horse. My own horse had died in the night, worn out by the fatigues of this icy winter; my servant girl was now running round the village trying to borrow a horse; but it was hopeless, I knew it, and I stood there forlornly, with the snow gathering more and more thickly upon me, more and more unable to move. In the gateway the girl appeared, alone, and waved the lantern; of course, who would lend a horse at this time for such a journey? I strode through the courtyard once more; I could see no way out; in my confused distress I kicked at the dilapidated door of the year-long uninhabited pigsty. It flew open and flapped to and fro on its hinges. A steam and smell as of horses came out from it. A dim stable lantern was swinging inside from a rope. A man, crouching on his hams in that low space, showed an open blue-eyed face. "Shall I yoke up?" he asked, crawling out on all fours. I did not know what to say and merely stooped down to see what else was in the sty. The servant girl was standing beside me. "You never know what

669

you're going to find in your own house," she said, and we both laughed. "Hey there, Brother, hey there, Sister!" called the groom, and two horses, enormous creatures with powerful flanks, one after the other, their legs tucked close to their bodies, each well-shaped head lowered like a camel's, by sheer strength of buttocking squeezed out through the door hole which they filled entirely. But at once they were standing up, their legs long and their bodies steaming thickly. "Give him a hand," I said, and the willing girl hurried to help the groom with the harnessing. Yet hardly was she beside him when the groom clipped hold of her and pushed his face against hers. She screamed and fled back to me; on her cheek stood out in red the marks of two rows of teeth. "You brute," I yelled in fury, "do you want a whipping?" but in the same moment reflected that the man was a stranger; that I did not know where he came from, and that of his own free will he was helping me out when everyone else had failed me. As if he knew my thoughts he took no offense at my threat but, still busied with the horse, only turned round once towards me. "Get in," he said then, and indeed: everything was ready. A magnificent pair of horses, I observed, such as I had never sat behind, and I climbed in happily. "But I'll drive, you don't know the way," I said. "Of course," said he, " I'm not coming with you anyway. I am staying with Rose." "No," shrieked Rose, fleeing in the house with a justified presentiment that her fate was inescapable; I heard the key turn in the locks; I could see, moreover, how she put out the lights in the entrance hall and in further flight all through the rooms keep herself from being discovered. "You're coming with me," I said to the groom, "or I won't go, urgent as my journey is. I'm not thinking of paying for it by handing the girl over to you." "Gee up!" he said; clapped his hands; the gig whirled off like a log in a freshet; I could just hear the door of my house splitting and bursting as the groom charged at it and then I was deafened and blinded by a storming rush that steadily buffeted all my senses. But this only for a moment, since, as if my patient's farmyard had opened out just before my courtyard gate, I was already there; the horses had come quietly to a standstill; the blizzard had stopped; moonlight all around; my patient's parents hurried out of the house, his sister behind them; I was almost lifted out of the gig; from their confused ejaculations I gathered not a word; in the sickroom the air was almost unbreathable; the neglected stove was smoking; I wanted to push open a window; but first I had to look at my patient. Gaunt, without any

fever, not cold, not warm, with vacant eyes, without a shirt, the youngster heaved himself up from under the feather bedding, threw his arms around my neck, and whispered in my ear: "Doctor, let me die." I glanced round the room; no one had heard it; the parents were leaning forward in silence waiting for my verdict; the sister had set a chair for my handbag; I opened the bag and hunted among my instruments; the boy kept clutching at me from his bed to remind me of his entreaty; I picked up a pair of tweezers, examined them in the candlelight and laid them down again. "Yes," I thought blasphemously, "in cases like this the gods are helpful, send the missing horse, add to it a second because of the urgency, and to crown everything bestow even a groom—" And only now did I remember Rose again; what was I to do, how could I rescue her, how could I pull her away from under that groom at ten miles' distance, with a team of horses I couldn't control. These horses, now, they had somehow slipped the reins loose, pushed the windows open from outside, I did not know how; each of them had stuck a head in at a window and, quite unmoved by the startled cries of the family, stood eyeing the patient. "Better go back at once," I thought, as if the horses were summoning me to the return journey, yet I permitted the patient's sister, who fancied that I was dazed by the heat, to take my fur coat from me. A glass of rum was poured out for me, the old man clapped me on the shoulder, a familiarity justified by this offer of his treasure. I shook my head; in the narrow confines of the old man's thoughts I felt ill; that was my only reason for refusing the drink. The mother stood by the bedside and cajoled me towards it; I yielded, and, while one of the horses whinnied loudly to the ceiling, laid my head to to the boy's breast, which shivered under my wet beard. I confirmed what I already knew; the boy was quite sound, something a little wrong with his circulation, saturated with coffee by his solicitous mother, but sound and best turned out of bed with one shove. I am no world reformer and so I let him lie. I was the district doctor and did my duty to the uttermost, to the point where it became almost too much. I was badly paid and yet generous and helpful to the poor. I had still to see that Rose was all right, and then the boy might have his way and I wanted to die too. What was I doing there in that endless winter! My horse was dead, and not a single person in the village would lend me another. I had to get my team out of the pigsty; if they hadn't chanced to be horses I should have had to travel with swine. That was how it was. And

671

I nodded to the family. They knew nothing about it, and, had they known, would not have believed it. To write prescriptions is easy, but to come to an understanding with people is hard. Well, this should be the end of my visit, I had once more been called out needlessly. I was used to that, the whole district made my life a torment with my night bell, but that I should have to sacrifice Rose this time as well, the pretty girl who had lived in my house for years almost without noticing her—that sacrifice was too much to ask, and I had somehow to get it reasoned out in my head with the help of what craft I could muster, in order not to let fly at this family, which with the best will in the world could not restore Rose to me. But as I shut my bag and put an arm out for my fur coat, the family meanwhile standing together, the father sniffing at the glass of rum in his hand, the mother, apparently disappointed in me—why, what do people expect?—biting her lips with tears in her eyes, the sister fluttering a blood-soaked towel, I was somehow ready to admit conditionally that the boy might be ill after all. I went towards him, he welcomed me smiling as if I were bringing him the most nourishing invalid broth—ah, now both horses were whinnying together; the noise, I suppose, was ordained by heaven to assist my examination of the patient—and this time, I discovered that the boy was indeed ill. His right side, near the hip, was an open wound as big as the palm of my hand. Rose-red, in many variations of shade, dark in the hollows, lighter at the edges, softly granulated, with irregular clots of blood, open as a surface mine to the daylight. That was how it looked from a distance. But on closer inspection there was another complication. I could not help a low whistle of surprise. Worms, as thick and as long as my little finger, themselves rose-red and blood-spotted as well, were wriggling from their fastness in the interior of the wound towards the light, with small white heads and many little legs. Poor boy, you were past helping. I had discovered your great wound; this blossom in your side was destroying you. The family was pleased; they saw me busying myself; the sister told the mother, the mother the father, the father told several guests who were coming in, through the moonlight at the open door, walking on tiptoe, keeping their balance with outstretched arms. "Will you save me?" whispered the boy with a sob, quite blinded by the life within his wound. That is what people are like in my district. Always expecting the impossible from the doctor. They have lost their ancient beliefs; the parson sits at home and unravels his vestments,

one after another; but the doctor is supposed to be omnipotent with his merciful surgeon's hand. Well, as it pleases them; I have not thrust my services on them; if they misuse me for sacred ends, I let that happen to me too; what better do I want, old country doctor that I am, bereft of my servant girl! And so they came, the family and the village elders, and stripped my clothes off me; a scholar choir with the teacher at the head of it stood before the house and sang these words to an utterly simple tune:

> Strip his clothes off, then he'll heal us,
> If he doesn't, kill him dead!
> Only a doctor, only a doctor.

Then my clothes were off and I looked at the people quietly, my fingers in my beard and my head cocked to one side. I was altogether composed and equal to the situation and remained so, although it was no help to me, since they now took me by the head and feet and carried me to the bed. The laid me down in it next to the wall, on the side of the wound. Then they all left the room; the door was shut; the singing stopped; clouds covered the moon; the bedding was warm around me; the horses' heads in the open windows wavered like shadows. "Do you know," said a voice in my ear, "I have very little confidence in you. Why, you were only blown in here, you didn't come on your own feet. Instead of helping me, you're cramping me on my deathbed. What I'd like best is to scratch your eyes out." "Right," I said, " it is a shame. And yet I am a doctor. What am I to do? Belive me, it is not too easy for me either." "Am I supposed to be content with this apology? Oh, I must be, I can't help it. I always have to put up with things. A fine wound is all I brought into the world; that was my sole endowment." "My young friend," said I, "your mistake is: you have not a wide enough view. I have been in all the sickrooms, far and wide, and I tell you: your wound is not so bad. Done in a tight corner with two strokes of the ax. Many a one proffers his side and can hardly hear the ax in the forest, far less that it is coming nearer to him." "Is that really so, or are you deluding me in my fever?" "It is really so, take the word of honor of an official doctor." And he took it and lay still. But now it was time for me to think of escaping. The horses were still standing faithfully in their places. My clothes, my fur coat, my bag were quickly collected; I didn't want to waste time dressing; if the horses raced home as they had come, I should only be springing, as it were, out of this bed into my own. Obediently a horse backed away from the window; I

threw my bundle into the gig; the fur coat missed its mark and was caught on a hook only by the sleeve. Good enough. I swung myself on to the horse. With the reins loosely trailing, one horse barely fastened to the other, the gig swaying behind, my fur coat last of all in the snow. "Gee up!" I said, but there was no galloping; slowly, like old men, we crawled through the snowy wastes; a long time echoed behind us the new but faulty song of the children:

> O be joyful, all you patients,
> The doctor's laid in bed beside you!

Never shall I reach home at this rate; my flourishing practice is done for; my successor is robbing me, but in vain, for he cannot take my place; in my house the disgusting groom is raging; Rose is his victim; I do not want to think about it any more. Naked, exposed to the frost of this most unhappy of ages, with an earthly vehicle, unearthly horses, old man that I am, I wander astray. My fur coat is hanging from the back of the gig, but I cannot reach it and none of my limber pack of patients lifts a finger. Betrayed! Betrayed! A false alarm on the night bell once answered—it cannot be made good, not ever.

NAGAI KAFU

NAGAI KAFU (Japanese, 1879-   ). Modern Japanese fiction writer, strongly influenced by American and French literature. Spent most of youth in China, America and France.

THE BILL-COLLECTING

I

INSTANTLY after she got up from the bed where she was sleeping with Omatsu, her companion, Oyo put on her narrow-sleeved Hanten as usual, and, wrapping her head with a towel in the manner of the "sister's cap," she began to sweep the parlour.

Oyo is the maidservant in Kinugawa, an assignation house.

As they had guests in the inner room of Yojohan, who had been lodging there since the evening before, Oyo wiped up every place with the dust cloth except that room, including the railings and

stairways of the first floor. Coming down to the fireplace near the counter she found the mistress, with toothbrush in her mouth, already uncovering the charcoal fire of the previous evening. In contrast to the dark, humid interior where the odour of wine seemed to drift from somewhere, the winter sunshine glittering on the opposite side of the street and through the frosted-glass screen of the front lattice gate, looked quite warm and cheerful. As soon as the mistress saw Oyo, who was bidding her "Good-morning," she said all at once:

"Now, Oyo, I wish you would go directly after breakfast, as the place is far."

Being thus ordered, Oyo took up her chopsticks for breakfast, eating before Omatsu and Otetsu the cook. After having finished her toilet and changed her dress, and listening again to the instructions and messages from the mistress, she started. It was almost seven o'clock when she set out in the new wooden clogs that were given her by the regular geisha girls as a present at the end of the last year, and she heard the voice of the cook-supplier at the kitchen, the man who came to get the plates and bowls.

Oyo went out by the familiar short-cut through the lane between the houses of the geisha girls. Coming out into the open street of Ginza, which was filled with sunshine, she looked around her as though surprised at the new appearance of things. Her bosom pulsated to the sounds of trolleys passing by, and she not only felt that she had forgotten all the messages charged by the mistress, but even the route which she thought she had understood well when she left home. She became confused, so that the way seemed further than she had supposed.

It had been five years since Oyo entered service, in the autumn, at the age of fourteen, at Kinugawa, the assignation house. She had been at Hakone and at Enoshima, she knew Haneda and the shrine of Narita, but it was only as an attendant of the guests and geisha girls in the great carousels of many people that she went to these places. Once, though she was a woman, she had walked alone through the night with two or three hundred yen in cash in her sash. But it was not further than a few blocks where she went to an accustomed bank on behalf of the mistress. It was only once or twice in a year that she rode a really long distance by trolley, to visit her home at Minami-Senju for holiday.

To a woman of down-town who knows nothing about the suburbs of Tokyo, except Fukagawa, Shinagawa, and Asakusa, even to

hear the name of Okubo in the uptown district where Oyo was going to-day to collect the bill, caused her to imagine a place where foxes and badgers live. As she also felt fearful that she might not be able to return home that day if she did not catch the trolley as soon as possible, she hurried to the square of Owaricho, not even stopping at the beautiful show windows of Matsuya, and Mikamiya and Tenshodo.

"Good-morning, Maid Oyo!"

Suddenly, being thus addressed from the crowd which was waiting for the trolley, Oyo turned back and saw an unemployed girl of Tamaomiya, who had her hair dressed in Hisashigami and wore the half-coat of Koki silk.

"Kimi chan. Going to temple?"

As is a habit of woman, Oyo looked at the hair and clothing of this geisha girl, which was not particularly unusual.

"No. I have a patient at home," Kimi chan, the employed girl, said apologetically, as though answering the question of the employer. "Where are you going?"

"To the place called Okubo. I was told to take the Shinjuku line. Is this the place to wait for it?"

"Shinjuku. . . . Then it is on the other side. You must take the car from the other side of the street."

"Oh!" Oyo cried, with such a loud voice that she surprised herself. And as if she could not hear the formal salutation of the employed girl, "Please keep me in mind again . . ." she crossed the square to the other side almost in rapture. Though it was a winter morning her forehead perspired. Having heaved a sigh of relief before the glass door of the Café Lion, Oyo turned back with a wonder-stricken look to the other side of the street where was the clock on the roof of the Hattori clock store, thinking that it was a marvellous thing that she was not killed in the midst of the square where so many trolleys are crossing. By that time the employed girl of Tamaomiya, almost crushed among the crowds on the conductor's platform, went away toward the Mihara bridge, and though many almost empty cars followed it, the only thing that passed the tracks where Oyo was waiting was a lumbering horse truck loaded with casks. The sidewalk near to the Café Lion was so filled with persons waiting for transfers that they overflowed on to the street pavement. Unconsciously, Oyo looked at the blue sky of winter, calling to mind the clock on the roof of Hattori's

676

building, which pointed to half-past eleven. She became so impatient that she felt she could not wait any longer. The complaints of the persons who were waiting for transfers, speaking in loud voices, the breaking of the wires or the stoppage of the electric current, disturbed her as though it were the announcement of a fire burning her house. Exhausted by waiting, Oyo, like the others, leaned against the glass door of the Café and hung her head. Suddenly becoming conscious of a commotion, Oyo also ran in order not to be too late for the car, but, being only a helpless woman, she could hardly approach the first car. Even the next one she missed, for a big man of dark complexion, crossing in from the side, had pushed her away when her foot was already on the step. Moreover, her side lock of Ichogaeshi was rubbed up by the sleeve of the double manteau with great force.

"Now I won't mind what becomes of me. I will wait even half a day, or a day, as long as they want me to wait."

Oyo, who had already become desperate, purposely followed behind the crowd, to take the next approaching car.

When they came to Hibiya park, a seat was left, so Oyo could at last rest her tired back. Then the inside of the car was calmer and the streets outside opened out and became more quiet, and in the warmth of the inside of the car, with the sun shining on the back of her neck and shoulders, she nodded involuntarily with the light jolting of the car. The fatigue of the body, which has to work every night until one o'clock at the earliest, pressed on her eyelids all at once. As Oyo is the favourite servant of the mistress, raised by her from childhood, she must help her not only in the parlour of the guests, but also as chambermaid. To be made a companion in the late drinking of the guests in her busy time is bearable, but the most disgusting thing is the troublesome task of washing clean, in a hot-water cup, the whole set of artificial teeth of a guest nearly sixty years of age, every time after his meal.

In a short time there were indications of the stopping of the car and passengers coming and going. Oyo awakened all at once, surprised, and looked out of the window. She saw a leafy tree, a high bank and a low bridge on the waterless moat. The conductors, enough to frighten her, were assembled in front of the new house at the corner. Many empty cars were left as if they were to be given away. With this sight of unfamiliar streets, Oyo felt unutterable helplessness. She became anxious about the thing in her sash, fear-

ing that it had been stolen in her absent-minded moments. Also she doubted whether this was the place to leave the car. Impatiently she moved a bit from the end and said:

"Please, what is this place?"

The high-boned, flat-faced, slant-eyed conductor, who seemed to perceive the embarrassed figure of Oyo by a glance, did not move from the platform. Shrugging his shoulders, as if cold, and turning his head to the other side, he pulled the bell so that Oyo, who had left her seat, was upset by the moving car and thrown with all the weight of her body on the lap of a man looking like a foreman of the labourers, who was sitting near to the entrance. Feeling abashed, Oyo tried to get up quickly; she noticed that a big arm, as heavy as iron, was laid on her back as if to embrace her body; she struggled with all her might.

"Ehe! he! he!"

With the vile, frightful laughter there was a smell of wine.

"How can I stand it when I am held fast by a girl!"

"What good luck to have!" chanted one of the group that was sitting on the other side, and they burst into laughter.

Oyo flushed like fire, and wished even to jump out of the moving car. After that she felt that all the eyes in the car were looking constantly at her. Even then, she had not gained her composure after the fright of the moment when she felt herself closely embraced by a labourer. All at once Oyo became conscious that no one in the car was dressed like her—in Meisen silk, with folds laid somewhat loose, grey Hawori with an embroidered crest on it, and an apron of Itoöri neatly tied. All the other women were in Hisashigami and in close folds, and most of the men passengers were soldiers. Her helplessness riding among these unknown people became more keen. Just at the time when she was about to ask the conductor, who came to inspect the transfer tickets, regarding the station before Shinjuku, her embarrassment and helplessness became all but overwhelming.

"This is the Awoyama line, Miss. If you wish to go to Shinjuku, there is no other way but to transfer at Awoyama Itchome, and again at Shiocho." Throwing the transfer ticket on the lap of Oyo, the conductor hurried to fix the dislocated pole.

As she had understood that she could go all the way without transferring, Oyo, on hearing that she had to transfer not once but twice, felt as if she was thrown at last into the labyrinthine jungle of Yawata.

After going here and there, Oyo was able at last to realise that Tenmacho Nichome was the station before Shinjuku. How far would the trouble of the unknown route continue? Oyo regretted that she had come, and thought that she would never again go on an errand to an unknown place, no matter how she might be scolded. It is far better to stay at home with the sweeping, and to dry the bed-clothes or to wash the Yukata to offer to the guests. In this broad street, more bustling than she could have expected, she could not tell whether she had to turn to the right or to the left. Nevertheless, as she could not stand in the middle of the street, she was thinking about paying her own money secretly to ride in a Kuruma, when she saw a Kurumaya from the stand, and asked him how much she would have to pay to ride to Okubo.

"Give me fifty sen."

"Don't fool me."

Being much provoked, Oyo did not even turn to the Kurumaya, who called out something to her from her back, and walked aimlessly to a side street. Seeing a little girl with tucks at her shoulders in front of a tobacco shop, she asked in an almost weeping tone:

"Please, my girl, will you kindly let me know how to get to Yochomachi of Okubo?"

"Yochomachi?" said the girl cheerfully. "Go straight this way, and going down a slope you will find a policeman's post. . . . You had better ask at the policeman's post."

Oyo felt revived for the first time.

"Thank you ever so much."

Putting an overwhelming sentiment of thanks into these simple words, Oyo walked away, looking curiously at the sights on both sides of the somewhat narrow street. There was a European building for moving pictures on one side. From the lane near to the building a few geisha girls came out, laughing about something in loud voices. Looking at them, Oyo wondered: "Why are there geisha girls in such a place?" Suddenly she heard a tremendous noise. Before she could think what was the matter, she saw many soldiers on horseback riding from the open street to this narrow side street. There was the gate of a temple at one side of the beginning of the slope, and, taking advantage of an open place, Oyo was fortunate enough to get out of the way. She saw six or seven men employed on the telegraph wires, squatting on the earth, eating

679

their luncheon. A bamboo ladder was leaned against a wire pole on the other side of the street.

"Hello! The beauty!"

Their teasing started Oyo running away in embarrassment.

"We are receiving an extraordinary Benten."

"Hey, my girl! May I offer you a glass?"

Some of them were looking intently at the folds of her skirts. They could not contain themselves any longer, when a sudden wind had brushed aside the skirts of her underclothes. All of them burst in at once.

"Luck to see!"

"It is worth two yen at Sinjuku!"

"The red clothes are said to keep long!" And they continued to say things which were unbearable to hear. But is not the procession of the soldiers endless, stirring up the sand on all sides? And how much Oyo wished to escape!

Oyo finally got away from the place and went down the slope, almost running, when she suddenly stumbled on a stone and hardly kept from falling. In front of it she saw something that looked like a squirming heap of rags, which said:

"Ladies and gentlemen, passing by, please, a penny . . ."

Two or three leper beggars, at whom one could not bear to look a second time, were making bows on the sand of the street. The town at the foot of the slope was visible, with the dirty roofs in confusion, at the bottom of the valley-like lowland. Oyo wondered without any reason whether the town over yonder was the outcasts' quarter.

Going down the slope and turning to the left as she was instructed by the girl of the tobacco shop she easily found a policeman's post. As a policeman who looked good-natured was standing in the middle of the street, she asked him her route.

"What number of Yochomachi is it?"

"It is number sixty-two. The house is Mr. Inuyama's."

"Number sixty-two—then you have to go straight along this way, and go up the slope before a big wine-shop."

"I see."

"And let me see, is it the third side street after you go straight up the slope? . . . You turn there to the left, where you will find number sixty-two."

"Much obliged to you."

680

Before she had gone less than half a block, she found a wine-shop that looked like the one she was told about, and also a slope, so she thought the rest of the route was quite short. Feeling somewhat proud that she had come this far alone without the Kuruma or without going much out of the way, she forgot a while even the fatigue of her legs, but when she began to go up the slope, she had to meet another unexpected trouble.

Though the down-town district had had such continuous clear weather that it was annoyed by the dust, the up-town quarter of the city seemed to have had rain the night before and the street, which was not broad, was so deep in mud that Oyo could not even find the sidewalk. By the time she discovered that the mud was melting frost, which had not had time to dry, not only the toes of her new wooden clogs, but also her white socks newly washed, were all splashed with mud. On one side of the road was the bank covered with sepiaria and on the other side was a cryptomeria hedge, where, taking advantage of the fact that there were no passers-by, Oyo took out her pocket-papers and wiped, she knew not how often, the mud from the mat lining of her wooden clogs. As she glanced up she thought the third side street to which she had been directed by the policeman might be the corner she sought.

III

The mud of the melting frost became harder and harder. A big, masterless dog was roaming about with a menacing look. The rasping sounds of a violin were heard. The dreary sigh of the wind came from the trees near by. Far at the end of the side street the ground seemed to slope again, and, though the winter sunshine was falling gently on the roofs of the new houses and on the deep forest that covered the rears of all the houses, either side of the road was dark in shade, and all the houses were surrounded with fences of four-inch boards. Each had a small gate containing a slide-door, the faces of which were smeared with mud that had not been washed off, which seemed to have been placed there in mischief by the boys in the neighbourhood.

The number and name of the house, which Oyo found at last, after examining all the labels on the houses on both sides, was on the support of the small gate, where the mud was splashed thickest and dirtiest.

Inuyama Takemasa. . . .

Oyo looked at it again before she entered the gate. The gentleman called Mr. Inuyama was the most captious, unsympathetic and unreasonable among the numerous guests that came to Kinugawa. No matter how busy they were in attendance in the parlours, he would not be satisfied if he could not call up Oyo and all the other maids into his room. If the mistress did not come to salute him every time he came he would be angry and say: "You insult me," or "You treat me coldly." It was said that he gave up his membership in the parliament as it did not suit his dignity. His profession at present was that of a politician. He was fond of geishas as young as babies, and if the girls did not obey his will, he was so furious that nobody could touch him, and Oyo not only despised him more than any of the other guests, but also was afraid, without any reason, of his forbidding appearance and loud voice. He always wore European clothes and used to come in a Kuruma pulled by two drawers, saying that the lower class of people ride in the trolley. Once in a certain conversation, when the mistress had said to him that "in these days not only the expenses of your pleasure and the tips for geisha become dearer, but even your expense for Kuruma must be very considerable," he laughed:

"Mistress, the money is earned to spend. Ha! ha! ha! ha!"

But these prosperous days were no longer. When it was hardly December of that year, Mr. Inuyama suddenly stopped coming, and in spite of many letters he would not respond to the bill of two hundred yen of that month and the fifty-yen balance of the previous month. Kinugawa was obliged to talk it over with a geisha who first brought Mr. Inuyama after their meeting at a certain Matsumotoro, but, it was almost clear that she could not shake her sleeve when she had none, and so January passed in this way, and now it was February. The mistress sent Oyo to the mansion of Mr. Inuyama to reconnoitre.

Oyo had known numerous cases of this kind, not only of men like Mr. Inuyama, but also of many other guests. She thought this nothing more than the bad ways of people. She thought only that they will be enjoying themselves at some other house, if they do not come to hers, then, it will be good of them if they will be more considerate and pay the bill. The reason Oyo looked again at the label on the gate was the fact that the gate of his mansion was so dirty. But, to enter the gate was better than the annoyance of walking around aimlessly any longer in the frost-melting road, so

682

she looked around from the porch with its dirty and broken paper-screen, wondering which was the servants' entrance.

On the right hand, beyond the bamboo fence, was visible the roof of a one-storied house looking cold under the garden trees. She got a glimpse of an old red blanket and a dirty cotton gown hung on a clothes-pole, through the crevices of the bamboo fence. On the left hand, further on, were one-storied houses with lattice gates, and another that looked like a rented house. Beside the wheel-well, where the plum-blossoms showed their buds, a fishmonger was cutting a salted salmon. Two maidservants in careless Hisashigami, who carried babies under quilted gowns and wore European aprons which had become grey, seemed to be at the height of their silly conversation with the fishmonger. As soon as they caught sight of Oyo, whose appearance was quite different, they sharpened their eyes, and, seeming rather to fear her, looked her over attentively from top to toe. The road from the well to the servants' entrance was spread with straw bags of charcoal, and the muddy water of the melting frost ran into the feet of people walking on them. Being in much perplexity Oyo could not move a step, and bending her waist, said:

"I beg your pardon."

Both of the maidservants stood wonder-stricken with open mouths.

"Is this Mr. Inuyama's house?"

Suddenly one of the maidservants began to grow uneasy, and, perceiving her manner, Oyo said:

"I came with a message from Kyobashi. Is the master at home?"

"He is absent."

Then the baby on her back began to cry.

Oyo, as she was ordered by the mistress, remembered how to proceed when she was told the master was absent, namely, to call madam to the servants' entrance and leave the word that she was the messenger from Mizuta, which was the name of her mistress. However, as Oyo was only eighteen or nineteen, she felt somewhat timid and stood on the walk, forgetting even that the water of the melting frost was overflowing on her polished wooden clogs. The baby on the back of the maidservant cried more and more.

"Chiyo! Chiyo!" Suddenly, a voice of woman, close to her ears, aroused her.

Being astonished, Oyo turned and saw at the broken paper-screens of the servants' entrance not farther than six inches, the big face of a woman, like a horse, with the eyes widely separated from

each other. The careless Hisashigami could not be beaten by the maidservants. She was a big, clumsy madam in a dirty and creased Higu.

Just then, the fishmonger came to offer three slices of the salted salmon to madam. Madam continued talking with the fishmonger, and Oyo, at last somewhat aroused and feeling at the same time a sense of deep disappointment, went out from the gate as if to escape. For she felt that her troubles in coming so far had been all in vain. She was exceedingly sorry for her mistress, as she had been entirely deceived by this humbug.

When Oyo rode again in the trolley she felt, at first, the fatigue of the vain effort and at the same time the fact that she was unbearably hungry, but being unable to do anything about it, she arrived at Ginza. The sun was already declining. Calling to her mind the clockstand of Hattori, which she saw when she was waiting for the car that morning, she looked up, and lo! was it not already near to four o'clock. Oyo felt her heart sinking with melancholy, picturing in her mind the flash of her mistress' eye, who never would say to her: "How early you are!" when she returned from the far-away errand. The electric lights were already lit in the shops. . . .

KAGAWA KAGEKI

KAGAWA KAGEKI (Japanese, 1768-1843). Leading *tanka* poet of his day. A prodigy who composed verse as a child. Earned living as instructor of poetry. Famous collection of verse: *Keien isshi*. Also prepared important editions of early Japanese texts.

SWALLOWS

Although the swallows are not like
  The friends with whom I freely may
Hold converse, what a joy it is
  To meet these birds from far away!

PINE-TREES AND THE MOON

The forms of all the pine-trees
  Have stood forth into sight;
But yet the moon has not left
  The rim of the mountain height.

WILD GEESE

Far in the distance, across the hazy sky,
  I saw the wild geese flock and fly away;
Yesterday I saw them take their flight,
    Also to-day.

A MAIDEN

The girl of whom in olden days
I once caught glimpses through a hedge,
Making my horse tread on young grass—
Alas! she, too, by now must have grown old!

THE CRICKET

O, cricket, chirruping
  Under my bed,
Do not tell other men
  My whispers with my beloved.

KALIDASA

KĀLIDĀSA (Sanskrit, 5th century A.D.). Legendary, greatest of all Sanskrit dramatists and poets. Nothing known of life, though apparently he was a thorough scholar and wide traveler throughout India. Left three dramas, two epics, two shorter poems. His masterpiece, the play *Sakuntalā*, created sensation when translated in 1789, influenced Goethe, Schiller, Herder.

THE CITY OF UJJAIN

Swerve from thy northern path; for westward rise
The palace balconies thou may'st not slight
  In fair Ujjain; and if bewitching eyes,
That flutter at thy gleams, should not delight
  Thine amorous bosom, useless were thy gift of sight.

The neighbouring mountain-stream that gliding grants
A glimpse of charms in whirling eddies pursed,
  While noisy swans accompany her dance
Like a tinkling zone, will slake thy loving thirst—
A woman always tells her love in gestures first.

Thou only, happy lover! canst repair
The desolation that thine absence made:
    Her shrinking current seems the careless hair
That brides deserted wear in single braid,
And dead leaves falling give her face a paler shade.

    Oh, fair Ujjain! Gem to Avanti given,
Where village ancients tell their tales of mirth
    And old romance! Oh, radiant glimpse of heaven,
Home of a blest celestial band whose worth
Sufficed, though fallen from heaven, to bring down heaven on earth.

    Where the river-breeze at dawn, with fragrant gain
From friendly lotus-blossoms, lengthens out
    The clear, sweet passion-warbling of the crane,
To cure the women's languishing, and flout
With a lover's coaxing all their hesitating doubt.

    Enriched with odours through a window drifting
From perfumed hair, and greeted as a friend
    By peacock pets their wings in dances lifting,
On flower-sweet balconies thy labour end,
Where prints of dear pink feet an added glory lend.

    Black as the neck of Siva, very God,
Dear therefore to his hosts, thou mayest go
    To his dread shrine, round which the gardens nod,
When breezes rich with lotus-pollen blow
And ointments that the gaily bathing maidens know.

    Reaching that temple at another time,
Wait till the sun is lost to human eyes;
    For if thou mayest play the part sublime
Of Siva's drum at evening sacrifice,
Then hast thou in thy thunders grave a priceless prize.

    The women there, whose girdles long have tinkled
In answer to the dance, whose hands yet seize
    And wave their fans with lustrous gems besprinkled,
Will feel thine early drops that soothe and please,
And recompense thee from black eyes like clustering bees.

Clothing thyself in twilight's rose-red glory,
Embrace the dancing Siva's tree-like arm;
  He will prefer thee to his mantle hoary,
And spare his grateful goddess-bride's alarm,
Whose eager gaze will manifest no fear of harm.

JOHN KEATS

JOHN KEATS (English, 1795-1821). A major poet of English Romantic Period. Exquisite workmanship made him the "poet of the most poetical type." Short, unhappy life, died in Rome of tuberculosis. Hopeless love for Fanny Brawne inspired many poems and letters. Shakespeare and Milton his models. Wrote some of most perfect poems in the language: "La Belle Dame Sans Merci," "The Eve of St. Agnes," Odes and Sonnets.

ODE TO A NIGHTINGALE

My heart aches, and a drowsy numbness pains
  My sense, as though of hemlock I had drunk,
Or emptied some dull opiate to the drains
  One minute past, and Lethe-wards had sunk:
'Tis not through envy of thy happy lot,
  But being too happy in thy happiness,
    That thou, light-winged Dryad of the trees,
      In some melodious plot
Of beechen green, and shadows numberless,
    Singest of summer in full-throated ease.

O for a draught of vintage! that hath been
  Cooled a long age in the deep-delved earth,
Tasting of Flora and the country green,
  Dance, and Provençal song, and sunburnt mirth!
O for a beaker full of the warm South!
  Full of the true, the blushful Hippocrene,
    With beaded bubbles winking at the brim,
      And purple-stained mouth;
That I might drink, and leave the world unseen,
  And with thee fade away into the forest dim:

Fade far away, dissolve, and quite forget
  What thou among the leaves hast never known,

The weariness, the fever, and the fret
    Here, where men sit and hear each other groan;
Where palsy shakes a few, sad, last grey hairs,
    Where youth grows pale, and spectre-thin, and dies;
        Where but to think is to be full of sorrow
            And leaden-eyed despairs;
        Where beauty cannot keep her lustrous eyes,
            Or new love pine at them beyond tomorrow.

Away! away! for I will fly to thee,
    Not charioted by Bacchus and his pards,
But on the viewless wings of Poesy,
    Though the dull brain perplexes and retards:
Already with thee! tender is the night,
    And haply the Queen-Moon is on her throne,
        Clustered around by all her starry Fays;
            But here there is no light,
    Save what from heaven is with the breezes blown
        Through verdurous glooms and winding mossy ways.

I cannot see what flowers are at my feet,
    Nor what soft incense hangs upon the boughs,
But, in embalmed darkness, guess each sweet
    Wherewith the seasonable month endows
The grass, the thicket, and the fruit-tree wild;
    White hawthorn, and the pastoral eglantine;
        Fast-fading violets covered up in leaves;
            And mid-May's eldest child,
    The coming musk-rose, full of dewy wine,
        The murmurous haunt of flies on summer eves.

Darkling I listen; and for many a time
    I have been half in love with easeful Death,
Called him soft names in many a mused rhyme,
    To take into the air my quiet breath;
Now more than ever seems it rich to die,
    To cease upon the midnight with no pain,
        While thou art pouring forth thy soul abroad
            In such an ecstasy!
    Still wouldst thou sing, and I have ears in vain—
        To thy high requiem become a sod.

Thou wast not born for death, immortal Bird!
  No hungry generations tread thee down;
The voice I hear this passing night was heard
  In ancient days by emperor and clown:
Perhaps the self-same song that found a path
  Through the sad heart of Ruth, when, sick for home,
    She stood in tears amid the alien corn;
      The same that ofttimes hath
Charmed magic casements, opening on the foam
Of perilous seas, in faery lands forlorn.

Forlorn! the very word is like a bell
  To toll me back from thee to my sole self!
Adieu! the fancy cannot cheat so well
  As she is famed to do, deceiving elf.
Adieu! adieu! thy plaintive anthem fades
  Past the near meadows, over the still stream,
    Up the hill-side; and now 'tis buried deep
      In the next valley-glades:
Was it a vision, or a waking dream?
Fled is that music:—do I wake or sleep?

ODE ON A GRECIAN URN

Thou still unravish'd bride of quietness,
  Thou foster-child of silence and slow time,
Sylvian historian, who canst thus express
  A flowery tale more sweetly than our rhyme:
What leaf-fring'd legend haunts about thy shape
  Of deities or mortals, or of both,
    In Tempe or the dales of Arcady?
What men or gods are these? What maidens loth?
  What mad pursuit? What struggle to escape?
    What pipes and timbrels? What wild ecstasy?

Heard melodies are sweet, but those unheard
  Are sweeter; therefore, ye soft pipes, play on;
Not to the sensual ear, but, more endear'd,
  Pipe to the spirit ditties of no tone:

Fair youth, beneath the trees, thou canst not leave
　　Thy song, nor ever can those trees be bare;
　　　　Bold Lover, never, never canst thou kiss,
Though winning near the goal—yet, do not grieve;
　　She cannot fade, though thou hast not thy bliss,
　　　　For ever wilt thou love, and she be fair!

Ah, happy, happy boughs! that cannot shed
　　Your leaves, nor ever bid the Spring adieu;
And, happy melodist, unwearied,
　　For ever piping songs for ever new;
More happy love! more happy, happy love!
　　For ever warm and still to be enjoy'd,
　　　　For ever panting, and for ever young;
All breathing human passion far above,
　　That leaves a heart high-sorrowful and cloy'd,
　　　　A burning forehead, and a parching tongue.

Who are these coming to the sacrifice?
　　To what green altar, O mysterious priest,
Lead'st thou that heifer lowing at the skies,
　　And all her silken flanks with garlands drest?
What little town by river or sea shore,
　　Or mountain-built with peaceful citadel,
　　　　Is emptied of its folk, this pious morn?
And, little town, thy streets for evermore
　　Will silent be: and not a soul to tell
　　　　Why thou art desolate, can e'er return.

O Attic shape! Fair attitude! with brede
　　Of marble men and maidens overwrought,
With forest branches and the trodden weed;
　　Thou, silent form, dost tease us out of thought
As doth eternity: Cold Pastoral!
　　When old age shall this generation waste,
　　　　Thou shalt remain, in midst of other woe
Than ours, a friend to man, to whom thou say'st,
　　'Beauty is truth, truth beauty'—that is all
　　　　Ye know on earth, and all ye need to know.

Season of mists and mellow fruitfulness,
    Close bosom-friend of the maturing sun;
Conspiring with him how to load and bless
    With fruit the vines that round the thatch-eves run;
To bend with apples the moss'd cottage-trees,
    And fill all fruit with ripeness to the core;
        To swell the gourd, and plump the hazel shells
With a sweet kernel; to set budding more,
    And still more, later flowers for the bees,
        Until they think warm days will never cease,
        For Summer has o'er-brimm'd their clammy cells.

Who hath not seen thee oft amid thy store?
    Sometimes whoever seeks abroad may find
Thee sitting careless on a granary floor,
    Thy hair soft-lifted by the winnowing wind;
Or on a half-reap'd furrow sound asleep,
    Drows'd with the fume of poppies, while thy hook
        Spares the next swath and all its twined flowers:
And sometimes like a gleaner thou dost keep
    Steady thy laden head across a brook;
    Or by a cyder-press, with patient look,
        Thou watchest the last oozings hours by hours.

Where are the songs of Spring? Ay, where are they?
    Think not of them, thou hast thy music too,—
While barred clouds bloom the soft-dying day,
    And touch the stubble-plains with rosy hue;
Then in a wailful choir the small gnats mourn
    Among the river sallows, borne aloft
        Or sinking as the light wind lives or dies;
And full-grown lambs loud bleat from hilly bourn;
    Hedge-crickets sing; and now with treble soft
    The red-breast whistles from a garden-croft;
        And gathering swallows twitter in the skies.

GOTTFRIED KELLER

GOTTFRIED KELLER (Swiss, 1819-1890). A Swiss writer who wrote some
of best German literature of 19th century. Largely self-educated, became first
a painter, then a writer. Autobiographical novel, *Der Grüne Heinrich,* one of
most praised "educational novels." Short stories skillful, realistic, sensitive.

A LEGEND OF THE DANCE

ACCORDING to Saint Gregory, Musa was the dancer among the
saints. The child of good people, she was a bright young lady, a
diligent servant of the Mother of God, and subject only to one
weakness, such an uncontrollable passion for the dance that when
the child was not praying she was dancing, and that on all imaginable occasions. Musa danced with her playmates, with children, with
the young men, and even by herself. She danced in her own room
and every other room in the house, in the garden, in the meadows.
Even when she went to the altar it was to a gracious measure rather
than a walk, and even on the smooth marble flags before the church
door, she did not scruple to practice a few hasty steps.

In fact, one day when she found herself alone in the church, she
could not refrain from executing some figures before the altar, and,
so to speak, dancing a pretty prayer to the Virgin Mary. She became
so oblivious of all else that she fancied she was merely dreaming
when she saw an oldish but handsome gentleman dancing opposite
her and supplementing her figures so skilfully that the pair got into
the most elaborate dance imaginable. The gentleman had a royal
purple robe, a golden crown on his head, and a glossy black curled
beard, which age had touched as with streaks of starlight. At the
same time music sounded from the choir where half a dozen small
angels stood, or sat with their chubby little legs hanging over the
screen, and fingered or blew their various instruments. The urchins
were very pleasant and skilful. Each rested his music on one of the
stone angels with which the choir screen was adorned, except the
smallest, a puffy-cheeked piper who sat crosslegged and contrived to
hold his music with his pink toes. He was the most diligent of them
all. The others dangled their feet, kept spreading their pinions, one
or other of them, with a rustle, so that their colors shimmered like
doves' breasts, and they teased each other as they played.

Musa found no time to wonder at all this until the dance, which

lasted a pretty long time, was over; for the merry gentleman seemed to enjoy himself as much as the maid, who felt as if she were danc- ing about in heaven. But when the music ceased and Musa stood there panting, she began to be frightened in good earnest, and looked in astonishment at the ancient, who was neither out of breath nor warm, and who now began to speak. He introduced himself as David, the Virgin Mary's royal ancestor, and her ambassador. He asked if she would like to pass eternal bliss in an unending pleasure dance, compared with which the dance they had just finished could only be called a miserable crawl.

To this she promptly answered that she would like nothing better. Whereupon the blessed King David said again that in that case she had nothing more to do than to renounce all pleasure and all danc- ing for the rest of her days on earth and devote herself wholly to penance and spiritual exercises, and that without hesitation or re- lapse. The maiden was taken aback at these conditions, and asked whether she must really give up dancing altogether. She questioned indeed whether there was any dancing in Heaven; for there was a time for everything. This earth looked very fit and proper for dancing; it stood to reason that Heaven must have very different attractions, else death were a superfluity.

But David explained to her that her notions on the subject were erroneous, and proved from many Bible texts, and from his own example that dancing was assuredly a sanctified occupation for the blessed. But what was wanted just now was an immediate decision, Yes or No, whether she wished to enter into eternal joy by way of temporal self-denial, or not. If she did not, then he would go farther on; for they wanted some dancers in Heaven.

Musa stood, still doubtful and undecided, and fumbled anxiously with her finger-tips in her mouth. It seemed too hard never to dance again from that moment, all for the sake of an unknown reward. At that, David gave a signal, and suddenly the musicians struck up some bars of a dance of such unheard-of bliss and unearthliness that the girl's soul leaped in her body, and her limbs twitched; but she could not get one of them to dance, and she noticed that her body was far too heavy and stiff for the tune. Full of longing, she thrust her hand into the King's and made the promise which he demanded.

Forthwith he was no more to be seen, and the angel-musicians whirred and fluttered and crowded out and away through an open window. But, in mischievous childish fashion, before going they

dealt the patient stone angels a sounding slap on the cheeks with their rolled-up music.

Musa went home with devout step, carrying that celestial melody in her ears; and having laid all her dainty raiment aside, she got a coarse gown made and put it on. At the same time she built herself a cell at the end of her parents' garden, where the deep shade of the trees lingered, made a scant bed of moss and from that day onward separated herself from all her kindred, and took up her abode there as a penitent and saint. She spent all her time in prayer, and often disciplined herself with a scourge. But her severest penance consisted in holding her limbs stiff and immovable, for whenever she heard a sound, the twitter of a bird or the rustling of the leaves in the wind, her feet twitched as much as to tell her they must dance.

As this involuntary twitching would not forsake her, and often seduced her to a little skip before she was aware, she caused her tender feet to be fastened together by a light chain. Her relatives and friends marveled day and night at the transformation, rejoiced to possess such a saint, and guarded the hermitage under the trees as the apple of their eye. Many came for her counsel and intercession. In particular, they used to bring young girls to her who were rather clumsy on their feet, for it was observed that everyone whom she touched at once became light and graceful in gait.

So she spent three years in her cell, but by the end of the third year Musa had become almost as thin and transparent as a summer cloud. She lay continually on her bed of moss, gazed wistfully into Heaven, and was convinced that she could already see the golden sandals of the blessed, dancing and gliding about through the azure.

At last one harsh autumn day the tidings spread that the saint lay on her death-bed. She had taken off her dark penitential robe, and caused herself to be arrayed in bridal garments of dazzling white. So she lay with folded hands and smilingly awaited the hour of death. The garden was all filled with devout persons, the breezes murmured, and the leaves were falling from the trees on all sides. But suddenly the sighing of the wind changed into music, which appeared to be playing in the tree-tops, and as the people looked up, lo, all the branches were clad in fresh green, the myrtles and pomegranates put out blossom and fragrance, the earth decked itself with flowers, and a rosy glow settled upon the white, frail form of the dying saint.

That same instant she yielded up her spirit. The chain about her

694

feet sprang asunder with a sharp twang, Heaven opened wide all around, full of unbounded radiance so that all could see in. Then they saw many thousands of beautiful young men and maidens in the utmost splendor, dancing circle upon circle farther than the eye could reach. A magnificent King enthroned on a cloud, with a special band of small angels seated on its edge, bore down a little way towards earth, and received the form of the sainted Musa from before the eyes of all the beholders who filled the garden. They saw, too, how she sprang into the open Heaven and immediately danced out of sight among the jubilant radiant circle.

That was a high feast-day in Heaven. Now the custom (to be sure, it is denied by Saint Gregory of Nyssa, but stoutly maintained by his namesake of Nazianza) on feast-days was to invite the nine Muses, who sat for the rest of their time in Hell and to admit them to Heaven that they might be of assistance. They were well entertained, but once the feast was over had to go back to the other place.

When, now, the dances and songs and all the ceremonies had come to an end and the heavenly company sat down, Musa was taken taken to a table where the nine Muses were being served. They sat huddled together half scared, glancing about with their fiery black or dark-blue eyes. The busy Martha of the Gospels was caring for them in person. She had on her finest kitchen-apron and a tiny little smudge on her white chin and was pressing all manner of good things on the Muses in the friendliest possible way, but when Musa and Saint Cecilia and some other artistic women arrived and greeted the shy Pierians cheerfully, and joined their company, they began to thaw, grew confidential, and the feminine circle became quite pleasant and happy. Musa sat beside Terpsichore, and Cecilia between Polyhymnia and Euterpe, and all took one another's hands. Next came the little minstrel urchins and made up to the beautiful women with an eye to the bright fruit which shone on the ambrosial table. King David himself came and brought a golden cup, out of which all drank, so that gracious joy warmed them. He went round the table, not omitting as he passed to chuck pretty Erato under the chin. While things were going on so favorably at the Muses' table, Our Gracious Lady herself appeared in all her beauty and goodness, sat down a few minutes beside the Muses, and kissed the august Urania with the starry coronet tenderly upon the lips, when she took her departure, whispering to her that she would not rest until the Muses could remain in Paradise forever.

But that never came about. To declare their gratitude for the

695

kindness and friendliness which had been shown them, and to prove their goodwill, the Muses took counsel together and practised a hymn of praise in a retired corner of the Underworld. They tried to give it the form of the solemn chorals which were the fashion in Heaven. They arranged it in two parts of four voices each, with a sort of principal part, which Urania took, and they thus produced a remarkable piece of vocal music.

The next time a feast-day was celebrated in Heaven, and the Muses again rendered their assistance, they seized what appeared to be a favorable moment for their purpose, took their places, and began their song. It began softly, but soon swelled out mightily, but in those regions it sounded so dismal, almost defiant and harsh, yet so wistful and mournful that first of all a horrified silence prevailed, and next the whole assembly was seized with a sad longing for earth and home, and broke into universal weeping.

A sigh without end throbbed throughout Heaven. All the Elders and Prophets started up in dismay while the Muses, with the best of intentions, sang louder and more mournfully, and all Paradise, with the Patriarchs and Elders and Prophets and all who ever walked or lay in green pastures, lost all command of themselves. Until at last, the High and Mighty Trinity Himself came to put things right, and reduced the too zealous Muses to silence with a long reverberating peal of thunder.

Then quiet and composure were restored to Heaven, but the poor nine Sisters had to depart and never dared enter it again from that day onward.

OMAR KHAYYAM

OMAR KHAYYAM (Persian, 1050-1123). Most widely known of the Persian poets through Edward Fitzgerald's translation of the *Rubaiyat*. Honored in Iran as astronomer, algebraist and philosopher. Compiled astronomical tables and first Arabic algebra. Left 280 quatrains, epigrammatic in style, counseling a temperate hedonism as antidote to the cruelties of fate.

RUBAIYAT OF OMAR KHAYYAM

I

Awake! for Morning in the Bowl of Night
Has flung the Stone that puts the Stars to Flight;
   And Lo! the Hunter of the East has caught
The Sultan's Turret in a Noose of Light.

II

Dreaming when Dawn's Left Hand was in the Sky
I heard a Voice within the Tavern cry,
    "Awake, my Little ones, and fill the Cup
Before Life's Liquor in its Cup be dry."

III

And, as the Cock crew, those who stood before
The Tavern shouted—"Open then the Door!
    You know how little while we have to stay,
And, once departed, may return no more."

IV

Now the New Year reviving old Desires,
The thoughtful Soul to Solitude retires,
    Where the *white hand of Moses* on the Bough
Puts out, and Jesus from the Ground suspires.

V

Iram indeed is gone with all its Rose,
And Jamshyd's Sev'n-ring'd Cup where no one knows;
    But still the Vine her ancient Ruby yields,
And still a Garden by the Water blows.

VI

And David's Lips are lock't; but in divine
High-piping Pehlevi, with "Wine! Wine! Wine!
    Red Wine!"—the Nightingale cries to the Rose
That yellow Cheek of hers to incarnadine.

VII

Come, fill the Cup, and in the Fire of Spring
The Winter Garment of Repentance fling:
    The Bird of Time has but a little way
To fly—and Lo! the Bird is on the Wing.

697

VIII

And look—a thousand Blossoms with the Day
Woke—and a thousand scatter'd into Clay:
    And this first Summer Month that brings the Rose
Shall take Jamshyd and Kaikobad away.

IX

But come with old Khayyam, and leave the Lot
Of Kaikobad and Kaihosru forgot:
    Let Rustum lay about him as he will,
Or Hatim Tai cry Supper—heed them not.

X

With me along some Strip of Herbage strown
That just divides the desert from the town,
    Where name of Slave and Sultan scarce is known,
And pity Sultan Mahmud on his Throne.

XI

Here with a Loaf of Bread beneath the Bough,
A flask of Wine, a Book of Verse—and Thou
    Beside me singing in the Wilderness—
And Wilderness is Paradise enow.

XII

"How sweet is mortal Sovranty"—think some:
Others—"How blest the Paradise to come!"
    Ah, take the Cash in hand and waive the Rest;
Oh, the brave Music of a *distant* Drum!

XIII

Look to the Rose that blows about us—"Lo,
Laughing," she says, "into the World I blow:
    At once the silken Tassel of my Purse
Tear, and its Treasure on the Garden throw."

XIV

The Worldly Hope men set their Hearts upon
Turns Ashes—or it prospers; and anon,
   Like Snow upon the Desert's dusty Face
Lighting a little Hour or two—is gone.

XV

And those who husbanded the Golden Grain,
And those who flung it to the Winds like Rain,
   Alike to no such aureate Earth are turn'd
As, buried once, Men want dug up again.

XVI

Think, in this batter'd Caravanserai
Whose Doorways are alternate Night and Day,
   How Sultan after Sultan with his Pomp
Abode his Hour or two, and went his way.

XVII

They say the Lion and the Lizard keep
The Courts where Jamshyd gloried and drank deep:
   And Bahram, that great Hunter—the Wild Ass
Stamps O'er his Head, and he lies fast asleep.

XVIII

I sometimes think that never blows so red
The Rose as where some buried Cæsar bled;
   That every Hyacinth the Garden wears
Dropt in its Lap from some once lovely Head.

XIX

And this delightful Herb whose tender Green
Fledges the River's Lip on which we lean—
   Ah, lean upon it lightly! for who knows
From what once lovely Lip it springs unseen!

KAN KIKUCHI

KAN KIKUCHI (Japanese, 1888-1948). Contemporary Japanese short story writer, novelist and playwright. Precise, clear-cut stylist. Influenced by West, helped introduce realism into Japanese theater. Plays translated: *The Miracle, Love and Four Other Plays, The Father Returns, The Madman on the Roof, Better Than Revenge.*

THE MADMAN ON THE ROOF

Characters

Yoshitaro Katsushima, *the madman, 24 years of age*
Suejiro Katsushima, *his brother, a 17-year-old high school student*
Gisuke Katsushima, *their father*
Oyoshi Katsushima, *their mother*
Tosaku, *a neighbor*
Kichiji, *a man-servant, 20 years of age*
A Priestess, *about 50 years of age*

Place: *a small island in Sanuki Strait*
Time: *1900*

The stage-setting represents the backyard of the Katsushimas, who are the richest family on the island. A bamboo fence prevents one from seeing more of the house than the high roof, which stands out sharply against the rich greenish sky of the southern island summer. At the left of the stage one can catch a glimpse of the sea shining in the sunlight.

Yoshitaro, the elder son of the family, is sitting astride the ridge of the roof, and is looking out over the sea.

Gisuke (*speaking from within the house*). Yoshi is sitting on the roof again. He will get a sunstroke—the sun is so terribly hot. (*Coming out.*) Kichiji!—Where is Kichiji?

Kichiji (*appearing from the right*). Yes! What do you want?

Gisuke. Bring Yoshitaro down. He has no hat on, up there in the hot sun. He will get a sunstroke. How did he get up there, anyway? (*Coming through the gate to the center of the stage, and looking up to the roof.*) I don't see how he can stand it, sitting on that hot slate roof. (*He calls.*) Yoshitaro! You better come down. If you stay up there you will get a sunstroke, and maybe die. Come

700

on now—hurry! If you don't come down, I'll get after you with a stick.

Yoshitaro (protesting like a spoiled child). No; I don't want to. Something interesting. The priest of the Konpira God is dancing in the clouds. Dancing with an angel in pink robes. They are calling to me to come. *(Crying out ecstatically.)* Wait! I am coming!

Gisuke. If you talk like that you will fall, as you did the other day. You are already crippled and insane. How you worry your parents! Come down, you fool!

Kichiji. Master, don't get so angry. The young master doesn't understand anything. He's under the influence of evil spirits. Why, he climbed the roof of the Honzen Temple without even a ladder; a low roof like this one is the easiest thing in the world for him. I tell you it's the evil spirits that make him climb. Nothing can stop him.

Gisuke. You may be right; but he worries me to death.

Kichiji. Everyone on the island says he is under the influence of the evil fox-spirit, but I don't believe that, for I never heard of a fox climbing trees.

Gisuke (He calls again). Yoshi! Come down! *(Dropping his voice.)* Kichiji, you had better go up and fetch him.

(Kichiji goes out after the ladder. Tosaku, the neighbor, enters.)

Tosaku. Good-day, sir. Your son is on the roof again.

Gisuke. Yes; he is up there as usual. I don't like it, but when I keep him locked in a room he is unhappy as a fish out of water. Then, when I think that is too cruel, and let him out, back he goes up on the roof.

Tosaku. By the way, a Priestess has just come to the island. How would you like to have her pray for your son?—That is really what I came to see you about.

Gisuke. Is that so? Well, we have tried prayers several times before, but it has never done any good.

Tosaku. The Priestess who is here now believes in the Konpira God. She is very miraculous. People say she is inspired by the Konpira God, so that her prayers are quite different from those of a mountain priest. Why don't you try her once?

Gisuke. Suejiro says he doesn't believe in any prayers. . . . But there isn't any harm in letting her try.

(Kichiji enters carrying the ladder, and disappears behind the fence.)

701

Tosaku. Then I will go Kinkichi's house and bring her here. In the meantime you get your son down off the roof.

Gisuke. All right. Thanks for your trouble. *(After seeing that Tosaku has gone, he calls again.)* Yoshi! Be quiet now and come down.

Yoshitaro (drawing away from Kichiji as a Buddhist might from a heathen). If you touch me the fairies will destroy you!

(Kichiji hurriedly catches Yoshitaro by the shoulder and pulls him to the ladder. Yoshitaro suddenly becomes gentle. He comes down to the center of the stage, followed by Kichiji. Yoshitaro is lame in his right leg.)

Gisuke (calling). Oyoshi! Come out here a minute.

Oyoshi (from within). What do you want?

Gisuke. I have sent for the Priestess.

Oyoshi (appearing at the gate). That may be a good idea. You never can tell what may help him.

(Tosaka enters, leading the Priestess. She has a cunning look.)

Tosaku. This is the lady I spoke to you about.

Gisuke. Ah, good-afternoon! You are welcome.—This boy is a great worry, and causes us much shame.

Priestess (casually). Don't worry about him. I will cure him immediately with the help of the God. *(Looking at Yoshitaro.)* This is the one?

Gisuke. Yes. He is twenty-four years old, and can do nothing but climb up to high places.

Priestess. How long has he been this way?

Gisuke. Ever since he was born. Even when he was a baby, he wanted to be climbing. When he was four or five years old he climbed onto the low shrine, then onto the high shrine of Buddha, and finally onto a very high shelf. When he was seven or eight he began climbing trees. At fifteen or sixteen he climbed to the top of mountains, and stayed there all day long, where he says he talked with fairies and with gods, and such things. What do you think is the matter with him?

Priestess. There's no doubt but that it is the evil fox-spirit. All right, I will pray for him. *(Looking at Yoshitaro.)* Listen now! I am the messenger of the Konpira God of this island. And all that I say comes from the God.

702

Yoshitaro (uneasily). You say the Konpira God? Did you ever see him?

Priestess (staring at him). Don't say such sacrilegious things! The God cannot be seen.

Yoshitaro (exultantly). Oh, I have seen him many times! He is an old man with white robes and a golden crown. He is my best friend.

Priestess (taken aback at this assertion, and speaking to Gisuke). This is the evil fox-spirit, all right, but a very extreme case. Now then, I will ask the God.

(She chants a prayer in a ridiculous manner. Yoshitaro, held fast by Kichiji, watches the Priestess blankly. She works herself into a frenzy, and falls to the ground in a faint. Presently she rises to her feet and looks about her strangely.)

Priestess (in a changed voice). I am the Konpira God residing in this island!

(All except Yoshitaro fall to their knees with exclamations of reverence.)

Priestess (with affected dignity). The elder son of this family is under the influence of the evil fox-spirit. Hang him up on the branch of a tree and purify him with the smoke of green pine-needles. If you doubt what I say, you are condemned!

(She faints again. There are more exclamations of astonishment.)

Priestess (rising and looking about her as though unconscious of what has taken place). What has happened? Did the God speak?

Gisuke. It was miraculous. The God answered.

Priestess. Whatever the God told you to do, you must do at once, or be condemned. I warn you for your own sake.

Gisuke (hesitating somewhat). Kichiji, you may go and get the green pine-needles.

Yoshitaro. That was not the voice of the Konpira God. He wouldn't listen to a priestess like you!

Priestess (as though insulted). I will get even with you. Just wait! Don't you talk back to the God like that, you wretched fox!

(Kichiji enters with an armful of green pine-needles. Oyoshi becomes frightened. Gisuke and Kichiji rather reluctantly set fire to

703

the pine-needles, then bring Yoshitaro to the fire. Gisuke and Kichiji attempt to get Yoshitaro's face into the smoke. Suddenly Suejiro appears in the gateway. He wears a high-school uniform, and is a dark-complexioned, active boy. He stands amazed at the scene before him.)

Suejiro. What is the meaning of this smoke?

Yoshitaro (coughing from the smoke, and looking at his brother as at a savior). That you, Sue? Father and Kichiji have been putting me in the smoke.

Suejiro (angrily). Father! What foolish thing are you doing? Haven't I told you time and again about this sort of business?

Gisuke. But the miraculous Priestess, inspired by the God of——

Suejiro (interrupting). Rubbish! You do these foolish things merely because he is so helpless. *(He looks contemptuously at the Priestess and crosses over and stamps the fire out with his feet.)*

Gisuke (more courageously). Suejiro, I have no education, and you have, so I am always willing to listen to you. But this fire was made at the God's command, and you mustn't stamp on it.

Suejiro. Smoke won't cure him. People will laugh at you for talking about the fox-spirit. Why, if all the gods in the country were called upon together, they couldn't cure even a cold. When the doctors can't cure him, no one can. I've told you before that he doesn't suffer. If he did, we would have to do something for him. But as long as he can climb up on the roof, he is happy from morning till night. There is no one in the whole country as happy as he is—perhaps no one in the world. Besides, if you cure him now, what can he do? He is twenty-four years old and knows nothing—not even the alphabet; and he has had no experience. If he were cured, he would be conscious of being crippled, and would be the most miserable man in the country. Is that what you want to see? It's all because you want to make him normal. But isn't it foolish to become normal merely to suffer? *(Looking sidewise at the Priestess.)* Tosaku-san, if you brought her here, you had better take her away.

Tosaku. Well, we'll go home right away. It was my mistake that I brought you here.

Gisuke (giving Tosaku some money). Maybe you will excuse him. He is young and he has such a temper.

(The Priestess and Tosaku go out.)

704

Oyoshi. I suspected her from the very first. If she was inspired by a real god, she wouldn't do such cruel things.

Gisuke (suddenly). But where has Yoshitaro gone, anyway?

Kichiji (pointing at the roof). He is up there.

Gisuke (having to smile). As usual.

(During the preceding excitement, Yoshitaro has slipped away and climbed back up on the roof. The four persons below look at each other and smile.)

Suejiro. A normal person would be angry with you for having put him in the smoke; but you see, he has forgotten everything. *(He calls.)* Brother!

Yoshitaro (as brotherly affection springs from his heart). Suejiro! I asked the Konpira God, and he says he doesn't know her!

Suejiro (smiling). You are right. The God will inspire you instead of a Priestess like her.

(Through a rift in the clouds, the golden light of sunset strikes on the roof.)

Suejiro (exclaiming). What a beautiful sunset!

Yoshitaro (his face lighted by the sun's reflection). Sue, look! Can't you see a golden palace in yonder cloud? There! There! Can't you see? Just look! How beautiful!

Suejiro (as he feels the sorrow of sanity). Yes, I see. I see it, too. Wonderful.

Yoshitaro (filled with joy). There! From within the palace I hear the music of flutes—which I love best of all! Is it not beautiful?

(The parents have gone into the house. The mad brother on the roof, and the sane brother on the ground, remain looking at the golden sunset.)

CURTAIN

705

RUDYARD KIPLING

RUDYARD KIPLING (English, 1865-1936). Poet and novelist of British imperialism. Born in India, he brought to the West the life of English society in the colony. Emphasized patriotism, comradeship, physical courage. Excellent craftsman, phenomenally popular in his day. *Barrack-Room Ballads, Plain Tales from the Hills, Just So Stories, The Light That Failed, The Jungle Books.*

FALSE DAWN

No MAN will ever know the exact truth of this story; though women may sometimes whisper it to one another after a dance, when they are putting up their hair for the night and comparing lists of victims. A man, of course, cannot assist at these functions. So the tale must be told from the outside—in the dark—all wrong.

Never praise a sister to a sister, in the hope of your compliments reaching the proper ears, and so preparing the way for you later on. Sisters are women first, and sisters afterwards; and you will find that you do yourself harm.

Saumarez knew this when he made up his mind to propose to the elder Miss Copleigh. Saumarez was a strange man, with a few merits, so far as men could see, though he was popular with women, and carried enough conceit to stock a Viceroy's Council, and leave a little over for the commander-in-chief's staff. He was a civilian. Very many women took an interest in Saumarez, perhaps because his manner to them was inoffensive. If you hit a pony over the nose at the outset of your acquaintance, he may not love you, but he will take a deep interest in your movements ever afterward. The elder Miss Copleigh was nice, plump, winning and pretty. The younger was not so pretty, and, from men disregarding the hint set forth above, her style was repellent and unattractive. Both girls had, practically, the same figure, and there was a strong likeness between them in look and voice; though no one could doubt for an instant which was the nicer of the two.

Saumarez made up his mind, as soon as they came into the station from Behar, to marry the elder one. At least, we all made sure that he would, which comes to the same thing. She was twenty-two and he was thirty-three, with pay and allowances of nearly fourteen hundred rupees a month. So the match, as we arranged it, was in

every way a good one. Saumarez was his name, and summary was his nature, as a man once said. Having drafted his resolution, he formed a select committee of one to sit upon it, and resolved to take his time. In our unpleasant slang, the Copleigh girls "hunted in couples." That is to say, you could do nothing with one without the other. They were very loving sisters; but their mutual affection was sometimes inconvenient. Saumarez held the balance-hair true between them, and none but himself could have said to which side his heart inclined; though every one guessed. He rode with them a good deal, and danced with them, but he never succeeded in detaching them from each other for any length of time.

Women said that the two girls kept together through deep mistrust, each fearing that the other would steal a march on her. But that has nothing to do with a man. Saumarez was silent for good or bad, and as business-likely attentive as he could be, having due regard to his work and his polo. Beyond doubt both girls were fond of him.

As the hot weather drew nearer and Saumarez made no sign, women said that you could see their trouble in the eyes of the girls —that they were looking strained, anxious, and irritable. Men are quite blind in these matters unless they have more of the woman than the man in their composition, in which case it does not matter what they say or think. I maintain it was the hot April days that took the color out of the Copleigh girls' cheeks. They should have been sent to the Hills early. No one—man or woman—feels an angel when the hot weather is approaching. The younger sister grew more cynical—not to say acid—in her ways; and the winningness of the elder wore thin. There was more effort in it.

Now the Station wherein all these things happened was, though not a little one, off the line of rail, and suffered through want of attention. There were no gardens, or bands or amusements worth speaking of, and it was nearly a day's journey to come into Lahore for a dance. People were grateful for small things to interest them.

About the beginning of May, and just before the final exodus of Hill-goers, when the weather was very hot and there were not more than twenty people in the Station, Saumarez gave a moonlight riding picnic at an old tomb, six miles away, near the bed of the river. It was a "Noah's Ark" picnic; and there was to be the usual arrangement of quarter-mile intervals between each couple, on account of the dust. Six couples came altogether, including chap-

707

erones. Moonlight picnics are useful just at the very end of the season, before all the girls go away to the Hills. They lead to understandings, and should be encouraged by chaperones; especially those whose girls look sweetest in riding habits. I knew a case once. But that is another story. That picnic was called the "Great Pop Picnic," because everyone knew Saumarez would propose then to the eldest Miss Copleigh; and, besides his affair, there was another which might possibly come to happiness. The social atmosphere was heavily charged and wanted clearing.

We met at the parade ground at 10; the night was fearfully hot. The horses sweated even at walking pace, but anything was better than sitting still in our own dark houses. When we moved off under the full moon we were four couples, one triplet, and Mr. Saumarez rode with the Copleigh girls, and I loitered at the tail of the procession wondering with whom Saumarez would ride home. Every one was happy and contented; but we all felt that things were going to happen. We rode slowly; and it was nearly midnight before we reached the old tomb, facing the ruined tank, in the decayed gardens where we were going to eat and drink. I was late in coming up; and, before I went in to the garden I saw that the horizon to the north carried a faint, dun-colored feather. But no one would have thanked me for spoiling so well-managed an entertainment as this picnic—and a dust-storm, more or less, does no great harm.

We gathered by the tank, some one had brought out a banjo—which is a most sentimental instrument—and three or four of us sang. You must not laugh at this. Our amusements in out-of-the-way stations are very few indeed. Then we talked in groups, or together, lying under the trees, with the sun-baked roses dropping their petals on our feet, until supper was ready. It was a beautiful supper, as cold and as iced as you could wish; and we stayed long over it.

I had felt that the air was growing hotter and hotter; but nobody seemed to notice it until the moon went out and a burning hot wind began lashing the orange trees with a sound like the noise of the sea. Before we knew where we were, the dust-storm was on us, and everything was roaring, whirling darkness. The supper table was blown bodily into the tank. We were afraid of staying anywhere near the old tomb for fear it might be blown down. So we felt our way to the orange trees where the horses were picketed and waited for the storm to blow over. Then the little light that was left van-

ished, and you could not see your hand before your face. The air was heavy with dust and sand from the bed of the river, that filled boots and pockets and drifted down necks and coated eyebrows and mustaches. It was one of the worst dust-storms of the year. We were all huddled together close to the trembling horses, with the thunder chattering overhead, and the lightning spurting like water from a sluice, all ways at once.

There was no danger, of course, unless the horses broke loose. I was standing with my head down wind and my hands over my mouth, hearing the trees thrashing each other. I could not see who was next me till the flashes came. Then I found that I was packed near Saumarez and the eldest Miss Copleigh, with my own horse just in front of me. I recognized the eldest Miss Copleigh, because she had a *pagri* round her helmet and the younger had not. All the electricity in the air had gone into my body and I was quivering and tingling from head to foot—exactly as a corn shoots and tingles before rain. It was a grand storm. The wind seemed to be picking up the earth and pitching it to leeward in great heaps; and the heat beat up from the ground like the heat of the Day of Judgment.

The storm lulled slightly after the first half-hour, and I heard a despairing little voice close to my ear, saying to itself, quietly and softly, as if some lost soul were flying about with the wind: "O my God!" Then the younger Miss Copleigh stumbled into my arms, saying: "Where is my horse? Get my horse. I want to go home. I *want* to go home. Take me home."

I thought that the lightning and the black darkness had frightened her; so I said there was no danger, but she must wait till the storm blew over. She answered: "It is not *that!* It is not *that!* I want to go home! Oh, take me away from here!"

I said that she could not go till the light came; but I felt her brush past me and go away. It was too dark to see where. Then the whole sky was split open with one tremendous flash, as if the end of the world were coming, and all the women shrieked.

Almost directly after this I felt a man's hand on my shoulder and heard Saumarez bellowing in my ear. Through the rattling of the trees and howling of the wind, I did not catch his words at once, but at last I heard him say: "I've proposed to the wrong one! What shall I do?" Saumarez had no occasion to make this confidence to me. I was never a friend of his, nor am I now; but I fancy neither of us were ourselves just then. He was shaking as

709

he stood with excitement, and I was feeling queer all over with the electricity. I could not think of anything to say except: "More fool you for proposing in a dust storm." But I did not see how that would improve the mistake.

Then he shouted: "Where's Edith—Edith Copleigh?" Edith was the younger sister. I answered out of my astonishment: "What do you want with *her?*" Would you believe it, for the next two minutes, he and I were shouting at each other like maniacs—he vowing that it was the younger sister he had meant to propose to all along, and I telling him till my throat was hoarse that he must have made a mistake. I can't account for this except, again, by the fact that we were neither of us ourselves. Everything seemed to me like a bad dream—from the stamping of the horses in the darkness to Saumarez telling me the story of his loving Edith Copleigh since the first. He was still clawing my shoulder and begging me to tell him where Edith Copleigh was, when another lull came and brought light with it, and we saw the dust-cloud forming on the plain in front of us. So we knew the worst was over. The moon was low down, and there was just the glimmer of the false dawn that comes about an hour before the real one. But the light was very faint, and the dun cloud roared like a bull. I wondered where Edith Copleigh had gone; and as I was wandering I saw three things together: First, Maud Copleigh's face come smiling out of the darkness and move toward Saumarez, who was standing by me. I heard the girl whisper, "George," and slide her arm through the arm that was not clawing my shoulder, and I saw that look on her face which only comes once or twice in a lifetime—when a woman is perfectly happy, and the air is full of trumpets and gorgeous-colored fire and the Earth turns into cloud because she loves and is loved. At the same time, I saw Saumarez's face as he heard Maud Copleigh's voice, and fifty yards away from the clump of orange trees I saw a brown holland habit getting upon a horse.

It must have been my state of over-excitement that made me so quick to meddle with what did not concern me. Saumarez was moving off to the habit; but I pushed him back and said: "Stop here and explain. I'll fetch her back!" And I ran out to get at my own horse. I had a perfectly unnecessary notion that everything must be done decently and in order, and that Saumarez's first care was to wipe the happy look out of Maud Copleigh's face. All the time I was linking up the curb-chain I wondered how he would do it.

I cantered after Edith Copleigh, thinking to bring her back slowly on some pretense or another. But she galloped away as soon as she saw me, and I was forced to ride after her in earnest. She called back over her shoulder, "Go away! I'm going home. Oh, go *away!*" two or three times; but my business was to catch her first, and argue later. The ride just fitted in with the rest of the evil dream. The ground was very bad, and now and again we rushed through the whirling, choking "dust-devils" in the skirts of the flying storm. There was a burning hot wind blowing that brought up a stench of stale brick-kilns with it; and through the half light and through the dust-devils, across that desolate plain, flickered the brown holland habit on the gray horse. She headed for the Station at first.

Then she wheeled round and set off for the river through beds of burned-down jungle-grass, bad even to ride a pig over. In cold blood I should never have dreamed of going over such a country at night, but it seemed quite right and natural with the lightning crackling over head, and a reek like the smell of the Pit in my nostrils. I rode and shouted, and she bent forward and lashed her horse, and the aftermath of the dust-storm came up and caught us both, and drove us down wind like pieces of paper.

I don't know how far we rode; but the drumming of the horse-hoofs and the roar of the wind and the race of the faint blood-red moon through the yellow mist seemed to have gone on for years and years, and I was literally drenched with sweat from my helmet to my gaiters when the gray stumbled, recovered himself, and pulled up dead lame. My brute was used up altogether. Edith Copleigh was in a sad state, plastered with dust, her helmet off, and crying bitterly. "Why can't you let me alone?" she said. "I only wanted to get away and go home. Oh, *please* let me go!"

"You have got to come back with me, Miss Copleigh. Saumarez has something to say to you."

It was a foolish way of putting it; but I hardly knew Miss Copleigh, and, though I was playing Providence at the cost of my horse, I could not tell her in as many words what Saumarez had told me. I thought he could do that better himself. All her pretense about being tired and wanting to go home broke down, and she rocked herself to and fro in the saddle as she sobbed, and the hot wind blew her black hair to leeward. I am not going to repeat what she said, because she was utterly unstrung.

This, if you please, was the cynical Miss Copleigh. Here was I,

711

almost an utter stranger to her, trying to tell her that Saumaraz loved her, and she was to come back to hear him say so. I believe I made myself understood, for she gathered the gray together and made him hobble somehow, and we set off for the tomb, while the storm went thundering down to Umballa and a few big drops of warm rain fell. I found out that she had been standing close to Saumarez when he proposed to her sister, and had wanted to go home to cry in peace, as an English girl should. She dabbed her eyes with her pocket handkerchief as we went along, and babbled to me out of sheer lightness of heart and hysteria. That was perfectly unnatural; and yet, it seemed all right at the time and in the place. All the world was only the two Copleigh girls, Saumarez and I, ringed in with the lightning and the dark; and the guidance of this misguided world seemed to lie in my hands.

When we returned to the tomb in the deep, dead stillness that followed the storm, the dawn was just breaking and nobody had gone away. They were waiting for our return. Saumarez most of all. His face was white and drawn. As Miss Copleigh and I limped up, he came forward to meet us, and, when he helped her down from her saddle, he kissed her before all the picnic. It was like a scene in a theater, and the likeness was heightened by all the dust-white, ghostly-looking men and women under the orange trees clapping their hands—as if they were watching a play—at Saumarez' choice. I never knew anything so un-English in my life.

Lastly, Saumarez said we must all go home, or the Station would come out to look for us, and *would* I be good enough to ride home with Maud Copleigh? Nothing would give me greater pleasure, I said.

So we formed up, six couples in all, and went back two by two, Saumarez walking at the side of Edith Copleigh, who was riding his horse.

The air was cleared; and little by little, as the sun rose, I felt we were all dropping back again into ordinary men and women, and that the "Great Pop Picnic" was a thing altogether apart and out of the world—never to happen again. It had gone with the dust-storm and the tingle in the hot air.

712

JOSEPH KISS

JOSEPH KISS (Hungarian, 1843-1921). Most genuine Hungarian poet. Taught in Hebrew schools.

JEHOVAH

I

I have seen the great world, I have wandered afar,
I have worshipped the southern clime's beauteous star;
From Tisra's bright shore I have wandered far forth,
By my spirit of roving sent south and sent north.
At the foot of the Alps, where the rose grows knee-deep,
And the blue sky of Italy never doth weep,
But sweet odors and colors bright fade into naught,
And fly, like the cloudlets on zephyr's wings caught;
Tossed hither and thither, like chaff o'er the plain,
As to hold it you long, but the longing is vain,
Even thus from my soul, like a dream of the dawn,
Fades this picture so bright, from mem'ry withdrawn.

The years, in their flight, efface as by stealth,
Every trace of its beauty, its splendour and wealth;
Yet sometimes the sight of some tall, barren rock,
The floodgates of memories sad will unlock.
Its crags seem like features that me terrify,
I watch it with dread, reaching up to the sky,
In bleakness so bare, though majestic withal
It stands, and its frowning my soul doth appall,
And concealed at its base, 'neath foliage green,
A part of itself, that broke from it, is seen,
By the force of the storm and by tempest 'twas wrought,
To which once more these storms new life have brought,
They are parts of himself, sweet children, his own,
Yet a different life from his own they have known.

Where saw I that face which haunts, fills my heart?
From marble was't hewn, a creature of art?
The flashing of the eye, and the majestic pose,
The Titanic genius of Angelo shows.

713

On his forehead he beareth the imprint of woe,
From his visage of iron his soul we may know.
Does it live, or did fancy the image create,
While I, 'neath Saint Peter's dome, mighty and great,
Once did stand? No. There I was dreaming again,
A winter morn's dream, which still I retain.

II

I know it now, from home did hail that face,—
How could I see it and not sooner trace,—
In cassock dark, the figure gaunt, erect,
Whose every slow movement commandeth respect.
And the boys, we who romped in the street,
With awe avoided him, afraid to greet;
We gathered then and put our heads together,
As sparrows seek the trees in stormy weather.
An hundred years, it seems, upon his shoulders weigh,
Yet proud he walks, as in his manliest day;
A living legend, covered with a shroud
He movéd thus among the human crowd,
Full of foreboding, yet 'twas never known,
What in his seeming endless life had grown.
This sage, in fame of greatest learning stood,
To tell though, where acquired, no one could;
And yet 'twas whispered e'en, that learned was he
In holy Cabalah's dark secrecy;
That he himself, at his own wish could bring
About, that he could live as lives a king;
That he had vowed to be forever poor,
A straw-thatched hut he did as home secure.
He read his books, to synagogue he went,
To worldly things he no attention lent.
He spoke the tongue of races that are dead,
And Syrian and Chaldaic filled his head;
Late into night, and in the early dawn,
Queer hieroglyphics had his attention drawn.
Wisdom and wine, he thinks the worthier far
When ripened both by passing age they are;
Wisdom is One; and faith its foremost claim,
Wisdom is One; Jehovah is his name . . .

714

Who sends chastisement to the fourth degree,
That God who saith: "Revenge is my decree!"
That is his God, and like a breath upon a glass,
Or like the burning tears shed by a child, alas!
Thus came and went before his aged eyes
Some generations, and dissolved the ties
That he had known, and all was frail that came,
Steadfast but he and great Jehovah's name.

Unspeaking, melancholy and morose,
Beneath his eyelids, it seems in deep repose
A world of thought doth lie, a boundless world,
Which storm and lightning flash had oft-times hurled
And tossed about. His fellow-men he shunned;
Indeed, it seemed as if he lived beyond
His days; but when one was about to die,—
Unbid or bid, he promptly came to try
With hope divine to fill the dying soul,
And sacred hymns then from his lips would roll.
The dying man would ope his shaded eye,
And gather strength and faith wherewith to die.
Full many a night no sleep nor rest he had,
But needs must struggle for his daily bread.
O'er parchment leaves he would for hours bend,
And trace thereon the writ, with iron hand;
The holy writ, the testament of old,
He copied carefully, and strong and bold
His letters were, and day and night he wrote
The name of Him, who in his anger smote
Him, who revered not Him, with iron rod, . . .
The name of Him he loved, Jehovah, God, . . .
Because all day these letters dead he saw,
The letters dead became for him the law.
Fanatically he, the bygone days
Did wish returned, the awful dark, dread ways
And when on earth Jehovah was—the torch,—
And who profaned Him and died by sword or scorch.
The letters dead to him were living law,
To punish swift, the high priest would but draw
His sword; and burned on stake or stoned to death
He who the wrath of God encountereth.

And at this barren rock's stone feet there grew
A beauteous flower, fair and sweet to view.
The brooklet's murmur and the zephyr's sigh
To nourish her, would with each other vie.
The soil was barren, no moisture from above,
Privation, poverty, no parent's love
Her share, and yet, in spite of all, she grows,—
This child of Job,—as lovely as a rose.
So sweet and pure, a fairy queen she is,
There blend in her in charming harmonies.
Those gifts of heaven which heart and mind most please.
Her form divine, her movement queenly grace,
And radiantly beautiful her face.
Melodious her voice, like silver bell
Which holds the rustic listener in spell
When in the eve he hears the distant knell;
And what she says and what she thinks is bright
As wings of gaudy butterflies, which light
On flowers fair, in dewy morn and night.
Above all these, her eyes, ah, me! those eyes!
It matters nothing how my fish-line tries
To hook the proper word, I'll not succeed
The superb beauty of those eyes to read;
But I will tell a tale, do you give heed:
The midnight's depth, the height of mid-day's sun
Each from the other loving glances won;
They longed to meet, and for each other sighed;
They met, each other loved, and ever bide
Each with the other, and until to-day
They live in bliss; the truth of what I've told,
Do Miriam's flaming, darkling eyes enhold.

The fields and gardens gave her needed food,
Her soul grew in its very solitude,
A kindly nursing which in its due course
Matured her feelings and with hidden force
Her fancy rose. From tattered leaves she found,
She learned to read and write; and held her bound

716

Full many a night, when she would read by stealth
Each word, each line, each tale, each song; and wealth
Of thought did gain. Her hungry soul did yearn
In learning's banquet hall to sit and learn;
Her soul with almost holy fire aglow,
To rise above her sphere, so dull and slow,
Aspired; and she did vow to learn, to know;
Her daily life to cast away, not prone
'Fore fate to lie; but make her life her own;
And this she did, more pure her life, more bold
Half dream of hers and half as story told. . . .

And once a book came in her hands, complete,—
Though coverless and gone the title-sheet,
And pity 'twas, the author was unknown.
She read it oft, an hundred times a year,
As if it were a song which to the ear
Melodiously clings, and we repeat,
Because it fills our hearts and souls complete.

She read each play and felt that every role
Had taken hold, and filled her very soul;
Now Juliet, she roamed in love's estate,
To-morrow moaned o'er Desdemona's fate;
Then Lady Macbeth, with her blood-stained hands,
Then Imogen,—Cordelia now she stands,
And when the foolish, simple country swain
Would seek with awkward praise her love to gain,
She would the role of Queen Titania play, . . .
Thus Miriam, Job's daughter, lived her day.

IV

In autumn eve, the poplar tree tops sigh,
The swallow soon will flit, soon homeward fly:
To-morrow's dawn may find unfilled the nest,
Sweet bird, wilt here, thou seek again thy rest?
The window of the straw-thatched hut now brightly shines,
The poplar's trembling crown it illumines.
The poplar's trembling crown seems golden bright,
Its beauteous hue lends glory to the night.

717

V

His hoary head old Job leans on his hands,
Lost in deep thought, though work his care commands;
Before him lies the yellow parchment leaf,
And quill and ink, and yet, some hidden grief
Keeps him from work; he cannot trace his pen,
The very letters dance when now and then
He tries to work; some cloud bedulls his brain;
But as a lion wakening, his mane
Doth toss, so now old Job doth seem to wake;
Into his hand the quill doth firmly take,
And, dipping deep in ink, begins to write,
And what he writes, brings to his soul delight.
It suits his mood, 'tis Moses' second book
And chapter thirty-two, and he, whose look
At holy writ is frequent, knows how there
'Tis told, the old law-giver was aware,
That while he was with God, on their behalf,
The people made and worshipped the golden calf;
How great his wroth, his sorrow greater still,
And Moses' song men's souls must ever thrill.

Joshua said: "Dost, Master, hear the voice
From yonder camp? O'er victories they rejoice."
The Master said: "It is not so, my son;
'Tis not the joyous voice of victory won
That comes from camp, nor yet defeat's sad wail,
But other voices reach us from the vale." . . .
And marvel: As these things he now indited;
His ravished ears hear song and shout and hail
As once old Moses heard in ancient tale.
And song and shout and shout and song he hears,
Roused are the spirits of those bygone years,
Yet no, no spirit voices these, 'tis plain,
This music earthly is, this noise profane,
A band of strolling players at the inn
Have built a tent, and there their plays begin;
The villagers, or all who could but go,
Are there, enjoying this uncommon show.
They cheer and weep, the play has touched their heart,
The play and players gain the praise of art.

718

This was the voice old Job had heard, and then
He slowly takes again in hand his pen
To write, but lo! he soon again must cease,
It seems his soul to-night can find no peace.
The music dies away, no noise below,
He sees the wraiths of days of long ago
That torture him, the weary, hoary head—
Why are the days gone by not really dead!

He once three manly boys had called his own;
Life took them all, not death; aye, life alone
Robbed him of them; the one who really died,
Alone, lives in his heart with loving pride.
The strife, the times, the change, the very air
Of the to-day, which dawns ere one's aware,
And which we notice only when their wave
Prevails, and yesterdays are in their grave:
The spirit of the times which ever runs,
Had swallowed, Moloch-like, all his three sons.
No faith, no aim, ideals none, no rite,
The father and the son do now unite;
The holy tie, which with its powers divine
Men in their hearts with loving care enshrine,
The ties of heart and blood, old Job, with scorn
And pride, from his parental heart had torn.

He blessed his son, and for his welfare prayed;
Told him to go. A last farewell him bade!
The boy was only thirteen years of age,
Too young, think you, to enter on life's stage?
But custom and the law demand it so,
And out into the world the lad did go.
For years he seemed as lost, but once there came
A letter from a place of strangest name:
"Dear father,"—wrote the son,—"here in this land,
The victories of steam are truly grand."
The father's answer was one single word:
"Jehovah!"—as the son had often heard.
Another letter came: "Here on the banks
Of the Missouri I, in labor's ranks

719

Toil day and night to fell the ancient trees,
And inch by inch new territories seize;
Lay railroad ties, and oft the Indian chase.
At night, to starlit heaven I often gaze,
And think of home when the hyena's howl
And Indians' shrieks around our camp who prowl
Keep me awake; but then the amulet,
Dear father, which you gave, I have it yet."

And then no further news, and years rolled by, . . .
The young grew old, the old perforce must die.
The eldest son of Job was long forgot, . . .
When to the village came with lively trot
On horse and wheel, as might a king in state,
A train of men; what stir it did create,
The horses, carriages, the lively swarm;
The negro servants in their uniform;
It was a lively, captivating scene,
The like of which the village ne'er had seen.
Before the straw-thatched hut they stopped, behold
Upon the threshold stands erect, though old,
Proud Job: and from a carriage steps a man,—
The southern sun had turned his skin to tan,—
A giant figure, he, a worthy son
Of worthy sire, pleasant to look upon.
A lady, too, alights; a woman fair;
He leads her to his father, standing there.
Old Job outspreads his arms, about to kiss
His long-lost son and daughter, his is bliss!
When suddenly he shrieks and starts aback,
A golden cross hangs on the woman's neck.
"Apostate, thou!" he cries; "thou'rt not my son!
Apostate, thou! No nearer come! begone!
Ne'er shalt thou o'er my threshold step, swear I,
Jehovah, witness! I my son deny!"

VII

His memories are sad. Beneath their weight
His soul doth rise, as even then, too late . . .

The old wound opes and freely bleeds again
As it bled once when first he knew life's bane.
He sobs and weeps, his heart may almost break,
Most painful are the ways his thoughts do take.
He had, yea, it is true, another son,
A splendid boy, who admiration won
By his bright thought and brain and mind.
He, too, went forth,—and onward, but to find
Himself on paths his sires had never trod;
In plant and stone he sought to find his God.
The highest goals of learning he did gain,
Found everything, but sought a God in vain.
His name and fame shine brightly as a star
Among the great men who immortal are.
Savant, philosopher, known o'er the globe,
Alas! no longer he a son of Job!

And silently a sentient, burning tear
Rolls down his face, so strong and yet austere.
God only knows, these tears well from his heart,
The thought for his third, youngest son impart.
He suffered not, that he the world should roam,
He loved this boy the best, kept him at home.
A lively youth, of mischief full and fun,
That kind of boy who's loved by every one,
The picture of himself while he a boy,
This youngest son of his, his greatest joy.
He was not yet fifteen, . . . when lo! the world
Did seem to turn and quake; flags were unfurled,
Thrones shook, and shouts did mark the Bastille's fall.
With martial noise "To arms!" goes forth the call!
Blood-red the very grass, blood-red the dawn . . .
The boy enlists, nor waits till he be drawn.
Beneath a heavy gun he would succumb,
And his the burden was to bear the drum.
And with his drum from field to field he went,
Until at last a bullet his rest sent. . . .

VIII

The taper's burning low, and now to bed
He is about to take his weary head;

721

And as he rises, 't seems a deeper gloom
Obtains; his own dark shadow fills the room.
"Miriam, my darling child!" he whispers low,
Thou art still mine; the boys, oh, great my woe,
I've lost them all! May angels guard thy sleep,
Gabriel, Raphael, o'er thee watch and keep
From thee the evil spirit of the night,
That naught thy golden dream and slumber blight;
Jehovah, keep my Miriam sweet, secure!"
And then, to still the pain he must endure,
He goes to look upon his child, his own;
And to her room on tip-toe steals; a throne
To him her couch, on which his child inclines!
But, lo! the pale moon only illumines,—
Has he seen right? he stares,—he sees, to-night
An empty couch,—Miriam has taken flight!

IX

And as the stag, who hears the shot and feels
It whistling, grazing past, and knows it deals
A deadly aim: though once that aim was bad,
And suddenly stands still,—with eyes like mad
Looks right and left, and sniffs the air; then he
With sudden leap will fly, but to be free,
Though danger lurks perhaps behind each tree:
Thus acted Job. First stunned, he gasps for breath,
His glaring eyes are shadowed, as by death;
His mind grows blank; he knows not what to do;
The heart is broken of the poor old Jew.
And then in accents slow: "She, too, she, too;
My last and only child is gone from me,
My Miriam is taken by God's decree."
And then he sobs, and freely flow his tears,
He weeps as those who stand before friends' biers;
Not for himself he feels the awful blow,
'Tis for his child his burning tears do flow.
When past the agony of his great woe,
While still convulsed his sturdy, giant frame:
"All gone, all lost, yet I fore'er exclaim:
Steadfast is One! Jehovah is His Name!"

722

And then his window opes. His eye is dry;
But here and there a star is in the sky;
His eagle eye far into night doth spy.
The heavens, it seems, are overcast with clouds,
As if all nature donned funeral shrouds.
As if to list to him had come in crowds;
As if all heaven and earth had come to know
That he, in spite of awful blow and woe,
His ancient faith in Him did not forego!
Then with a voice, which shakes the very walls
Of his small hut, and by its power appals,
Into the night with trembling voice he calls:
"Lord! God! Thou givest and taketh with thy breath,
Adonai, God, Thine is all life and death!"

HEINRICH VON KLEIST

HEINRICH VON KLEIST (German, 1777-1811). Playwright and journalist.
Impulsive peregrinant. While traveling, once arrested as spy and spent six
months in French jail. His plays slow to gain recognition. When financial
situation became desperate, staged double suicide with a Berlin merchant's
wife. Works: *Penthesilea, The Prince of Homburg, Michael Kolhaas.*

THE BEGGAR-WOMAN OF LOCARNO

At the foot of the Alps, near Locarno in Upper Italy, stood once a
castle, the property of a marquis; of this castle, as one goes southward from the St. Gotthard, one sees now only the ashes and ruins.
In one of its high and spacious rooms there once lay, on a bundle
of straw which had been thrown down for her, an old, sick woman,
who had come begging to the door, and had been taken in and
given shelter out of pity by the mistress of the castle. The Marquis,
returning from the hunt, happened to enter this room, where he
usually kept his guns, while the old woman lay there, and angrily
ordered her to come out of the corner where the bundle of straw had
been placed and to get behind the stove. In rising the old woman
slipped on the polished floor and injured her spine severely; so much
did she hurt herself that only with unspeakable agony could she
manage to cross the room, as she was ordered, to sink moaning
behind the stove and there to die.

Some years later the Marquis, owing to war and bad harvests, having lost most of his fortune, decided to sell his estates. One day a nobleman from Florence arrived at the castle which, on account of its beautiful situation, he wished to buy. The Marquis, who was very anxious to bring the business to a successful conclusion, gave instructions to his wife to prepare for their guest the above-mentioned room, which was now very beautifully furnished. But imagine their horror when, in the middle of the night, the nobleman, pale and distracted, entered their room, solemnly assuring them that his room was haunted by something which was not visible, but which sounded as if somebody lying on straw in one corner of the room got up and slowly and feebly but with distinct steps crossed the room to lie down moaning and groaning behind the stove.

The Marquis, horrified, he did not himself know why, laughed with forced merriment at the nobleman and said he would get up at once and keep him company for the rest of the night in the haunted room, and when the morning came he ordered his horses to be brought round, bade farewell, and departed.

This incident, which created a great sensation, unhappily for the Marquis frightened away several would-be buyers; and when amongst his own servants strangely and mysteriously the rumour arose that queer things happened in the room at midnight, he determined to make a definite stand in the matter and to investigate it himself the same night. For that reason he had his bed moved into the room at twilight, and watched there without sleeping until midnight. To his horror, as the clock began to strike midnight, he became aware of the mysterious noise; it sounded as though somebody rose from straw which rustled beneath him, crossed the room and sank down sighing and groaning behind the stove. The next morning when he came downstairs his wife inquired what he had discovered; he looked round with nervous and troubled glances, and after fastening the door assured her that the rumour was true. The Marquise was more terrified than ever in her life, and begged him, before the rumour grew, to make a cold-blooded trial in her company. Accompanied by a loyal servant, they spent the following night in the room and heard the same ghostly noises; and only the pressing need to get rid of the castle at any cost enabled the Marquise in the presence of the servant to smother the terror which she felt, and to put the noise down to some ordinary and casual event which it would be easy to discover. On the evening of the third day, as both of them, with beating hearts, went up the stairs to the guest-room, anxious to get

at the cause of the disurbance, they found that the watch-dog, who happened to have been let off his chain, was standing at the door of the room; so that, without giving a definite reason, both perhaps unconsciously wishing to have another living thing in the room besides themselves, they took him into the room with them. About eleven o'clock the two of them, two candles on the table, the Marquise fully dressed, the Marquis with dagger and pistol which he had taken from the cupboard beside him, sat down one on each bed; and while they entertained one another as well as they could by talking, the dog lay down, his head on his paws, in the middle of the room and slept. As the clock began to strike midnight the horrible sound began; somebody whom human eyes could not see raised himself on crutches in the corner of the room; the straw could be heard rustling beneath him; and at the first step the dog woke, pricked up his ears, rose from the ground growling and barking, and, just as though somebody were making straight for him, moved backwards towards the stove. At the sight the Marquise, her hair rising, rushed from the room, and while the Marquis, who had snatched up his dagger, called 'Who is there?' and received no answer, she, like a mad woman, had ordered the coach to be got out, determined to drive away to the town immediately. But before she had packed a few things together and got them out of the door she noticed that all around her the castle was in flames. The Marquis, overcome with horror, and tired of life, had taken a candle and set fire to the wooden panelling on all sides. In vain she sent people in to rescue the wretched man; he had already found his end in the most horrible manner possible; and his white bones, gathered together by his people, still lie in that corner of the room from which he once ordered the beggar-woman of Locarno to rise.

FRIEDRICH GOTTLIEB KLOPSTOCK

FRIEDRICH GOTTLIEB KLOPSTOCK (German, 1724-1803). Main architect of 18th century independent German writing. Author of great biblical epic, *The Messiah*, and *Odes*. Both works influential on contemporaries, bringing deeply felt emotion into classical forms. Late "bardic" poems stimulated German nationalism.

THE CONTEMPLATION OF GOD

Trembling I rejoice,
Nor would believe the Voice,

If that the Eternal were
Not the Greater Promiser!
For, oh! I know, I feel
I am a sinner still—
Should know, should feel the same,
The sorrow and the shame;
Albeit Deity my spot
More clearly shown to me had not,
Unveiling to my wiser view
The wounded soul's condition true.
  With bended knee,
Astonished and intensely praying,
  That I my God shall see!

Oh! meditate the thought divine,
Thou thought-capacious soul of mine,
Who near the body's grave art ever,
Yet art eternal, and shalt perish never!
Not that thou venturest into
The Holiest of all to go—
Much unconsidered, never prized,
Ne'er celebrated, ne'er agonized!—
Celestial graces
Have in the Sanctuary their dwelling places;—
From afar only but one softened glimmer,
  So that therewith I die not suddenly—
One beam, which night of earth for me makes dimmer,
  Of Thy bright glory let me see!

The man how great! who thus his prayer preferred—
  "Grace have I found of Thee!
  Then show Thy glory unto me!"—
Thus dared, and by the Infinite was heard!
That Land of Golgotha he never entered;—
Once, only once, he failed in God to trust—
An early death avenged the doubt he ventured!—
  How great proved him a punishment so just!
Him hid the Father on the clouded Hill;
  The Filial Glory passed the finite o'er;—
God of God spake! the trump the while was still,
  Nor did the thunder's voice on Sinai roar!

726

Now, in that cloud of seeming night
He sees already, in the light
Of day, no shade makes visibler,
Long centuries—(so we aver)—
Beyond the bounds of time; and, feeling free
    Of moments passed successively,
Thy glory now beholdeth he—
    Holy! Holy! Holy!

Most nameless rapture of my soul!
    Thought of the Vision blest to come!
My great assurance and my goal!
    The Rock whereon I stand, and gaze up to my heavenly home!

When that the terrors both of Sin and Death
Fearfully threat to prostrate me beneath,
Upon this rock, oh! let me stand,
    Thou whom the Dead of God behold!
When grasped in the almighty hand
    Of death, that may not be controlled!
My soul, above mortality
Exalt thyself! Look up and see—
Behold the Father's glory radiant shine
In the human face of Jesus Christ divine!
Hosanna! let the loud Hosanna tell—
    The plenitude of Deity
Doth in the man Christ Jesus dwell—
Yet scarcely sounds the cherub's harp—it shakes!
Scarce sounds the voice—it trembles—trembles! Now wakes!

    Hosanna! Hosanna!
    The plenitude of Deity
    Doth in the humanity
        Of Christ Jesus dwell!

Even then when on our world shone brighter still
A god-beam, and Redemption did fulfill
That prophecy of blood—when he knew scorn
And woe, whereto none else was ever born—
Unseen by mortals, Cherubim beheld
The Father's glory, unexcelled,

727

Shine in the face, where aye it shone,
Of the co-eternal Son!

I see—I see the Witness! Lo!
Seven midnights, sore perplexed, had he
Doubted, and with severest agony
    Adoring, wrestled so!—
Yes, him I see—
To him appears the Risen! His hands explore
The wounds divine; and now perceiveth he
(About him heaven and earth expire!)
In the Son's face the glory of his Sire!—
I hear him! He exclaims—in doubt no more—
(About him heaven and earth expire!)
"Thou art my Lord and God—the God whom I adore!"

HERMAN AND THUSNELDA

"Ha! there comes he, with sweat, with Roman blood,
With battle dust bedecked! Never so fair
    Was Herman—never flamed
    His eye so brightly yet!

Come! for desire I tremble! Reach to me
The eagle, the blood-dropping sword! Come, breathe
    Here—rest in mine embrace
    From the too fearful fight!

Rest here, that I may wipe away the sweat
Off from thy brow, and from thy cheek the blood—
    How glows thy cheek! Thus ne'er
    Thusnelda Herman loved!

Not even then, when in the oak shade first
With thy brown arm thou wilder compassed me;
    Flying, I stayed, and saw
    The' undying fame in thee

Which now is thine. Relate it all in groves,
That timidly Augustus, with his gods,

728

Drinks nectar now—that more
Immortal Herman is!"

"Why curlest thou my hair? Lies not the dumb
Dead father before us? Oh, had his host
   Augustus led—there he
   Might lie yet bloodier!"

"Herman—nay, let me raise thy sinking hair,
That o'er the garland thread its tresses may;—
   Siegmar is with the gods!—
   Follow—nor weep for him!"

THE TWO MUSES

I saw—oh, tell me, saw I what now is,
Or what shall be?—with Britain's Muse I saw
   The German in the race compete,
   Fly ardent for the crowning goal.

There, where the prospect terminates, two goals
Closed the career. Oaks of the forest one
   Shaded; and near the other waved
   Palms in the glimmering of the eve.

To contest used, the Muse of Albion stept
Into the arena proudly, as when she
   Dared mate the Grecian Muse, and brave
   The heroine of the Capitol.

She saw her young and trembling rival, who
With high emotion trembled; yea, her cheek
   With roses, worthy of victory,
   Glowed, and her golden hair flew wide.

With pain already in her throbbing breast,
She held the breath restrained; hung, forward bent,
   Towards the goal;—the herald raised
   His trump—her eyes swam drunkenly.

729

Proud of thy courage, of herself, thee scanned
The lofty Britoness with noble glance.
 Tuiscone. "Yes, near the bards
 I grew with thee in oaken groves;—

But I was told thou wert no more. O Muse!
Pardon, if that thou art immortal, me
 Pardon, that now I first am taught
 What at the goal I'll better learn!

Yonder it stands;—but mark the further one!
Seest thou its crown? This courage thus suppressed,
 This silence proud, this look of fire
 Fixed on the earth—I knew it well!

Yet, ponder once again, ere sounds to thee
The herald's dangerous signal. Strove not I
 With her of old Thermopylæ,
 And eke with her of the Seven Hills?"

She spake. The solemn, the decisive time
Approaches with the herald. With a look
 Of ardor spake Teutona quick—
 "Thee I, admiring, love, O Muse!

But dearer yet love immortality
And yonder palms! Oh—if thy genius will,—
 Touch them before me;—but, e'en then,
 Will I seize likewise on the crown!

Oh, how I tremble! Ye immortal gods!
I haply may reach first the goal sublime!—
 Then may I feel, O Britoness!
 Thy breath on my loose-flowing locks!"

The herald clanged. With eagle speed they flew,—
Their far career smoked up with dust, like clouds;—
 I looked—beyond the oak the dust,
 Still billowing, hid them from my sight!

730

VLADIMIR KOROLENKO

VLADIMIR KOROLENKO (Russian, 1853-1921). Half-Ukrainian, half-Polish writer. Spent much of life in Siberian exile, but remained genial and optimistic. Courageous defender of freedom. As story writer, forms link between Turgenev and Chekhov. Best-known novels: *Makar's Dream, The Blind Musician*; stories: "The Frost," "The Old Bell-Ringer."

THE OLD BELL-RINGER

IT was growing dark.

The tiny village, nestling by the distant stream, in a pine forest, was merged in that twilight peculiar to starry spring nights, when the fog, rising from the earth, deepens the shadows of the woods and fills the open spaces with a silvery blue mist. . . . Everything was still, pensive and sad. The village quietly slumbered.

The dark outlines of the wretched cabins were barely visible; here and there lights glimmered; now and then you could hear a gate creak; or a dog would suddenly bark and then stop. Occasionally, out of the dark, murmuring forest emerged the figure of a pedestrian, or that of a horseman; or a cart would jolt by. These were the inhabitants of lone forest hamlets going to their church for the great spring holiday.

The church stood on a gentle hill in the center of the village. The ancient belfry, tall and murky, was lost in the blue sky.

The creaking of the staircase could be heard as the old bell-ringer Mikheyich mounted to the belfry, and his little lantern, suspended in mid-air, looked like a star in space.

It was difficult for the old man to climb the staircase. His legs served him badly, and his eyes saw but dimly. . . . An old man like him should have been at rest by now, but God spared him from death. He had buried his sons and his grandsons; he had accompanied old men and young men to their resting place, but he still lived on. 'Twas hard. Many the times he had greeted the spring holiday, and he could not remember how often he had waited in that very belfry the appointed hour. And how God had again willed that . . .

The old man went to the opening in the tower and leaned on the banister. In the darkness below, around the church, he made out the village cemetery in which the old crosses with their outstretched arms seemed to protect the ill-kept graves. Over these bowed here and there a few leafless birch trees. The aromatic odor of young

731

buds, wafted to Mikheyich from below, brought with it a feeling of the melancholy of eternal sleep.

Where would he be a year hence? Would he again climb to this height, beneath the brass bell to awaken the slumbering night with its metallic peal, or would he be lying in a dark corner of the graveyard, under a cross? God knows! . . . He was prepared; in the meantime God granted him the happiness of greeting the holiday once more.

"Glory be to God!" His lips whispered the customary formula as his eyes looked up to the heaven bright with a million twinkling stars and made the sign of the cross.

"Mikheyich, ay, Mikheyich!" called out to him the tremulous voice of an old man. The aged sexton gazed up at the belfry, shading his unsteady, tear-dimmed eyes with his hand, trying to see Mikheyich.

"What do you want? Here I am," replied the bell-ringer, looking down from the belfry. "Can't you see me?"

"No, I can't. It must be time to ring. What do you say?"

Both looked at the stars. Myriads of God's lights twinkled on high. The fiery Wagoner was above them. Mikheyich meditated.

"No, not yet a while. . . . I know when. . . ."

Indeed he knew. He did not need a watch. God's stars would tell him when. . . . Heaven and earth, the white cloud gently floating in the sky, the dark forest with its indistinct murmur and the rippling of the stream enveloped by the darkness—all that was familiar to him, part of him. Not in vain had he spent his life here.

The distant past arose before him. He recalled how for the first time he had mounted to this belfry with his father. Lord! how long ago that was, and yet how recent it seemed! . . . He saw himself a blond lad; his eyes sparkled; the wind—not the wind that raises the dust in the streets, but a strange one, that flaps its noiseless wings, tousled his hair. . . . Way down below, tiny beings walked about, and the village huts looked small; the forest had receded, and the oval clearing on which the village stood seemed enormous, so endless . . .

"And there it is, all of it!" smiled the gray-haired old man, gazing at the little clearing. . . . That was the way of life. As a young man one can not see the end of it. And now, there it was, as if in the palm of one's hand, from the beginning to the grave over there which he had fancied for himself in the corner of the

732

cemetery. . . . Well, glory be to God! it was time to rest. The burden of life he had borne honorably, and the damp earth seemed like his mother. . . . Soon, very soon!

But the hour had come. Mikheyich looked once more at the stars, took off his cap, made the sign of the cross, and grasped the bell-ropes. In a moment, the night air echoed with the resounding stroke. Another, a third, a fourth . . . one after the other, filling the quiescent, holy eve, there poured forth powerful, drawn-out, singing sounds.

The bell stopped. The church service had begun. Mikheyich had formerly been in the habit of going down to stand in the corner by the door in order to pray and hear the singing. This time he remained in the belfry. It was too much to walk the stairs, and, moreover, he felt rather tired. He sat down on the bench and, as he listened to the melting sounds of brass, fell to musing. About what? He would have been unable to say. . . . The tower was dimly lit by the feeble light of his lantern. The still vibrating bells were invisible in the darkness; from time to time a faint murmur of singing in the church below reached him, and the night wind stirred the ropes attached to the iron tongues of the bells.

The old man let his head droop upon his breast, while his mind was confused with fancies. "Now they are singing a hymn," he thought, and imagined himself in church, where he heard the children's voices in the choir, and saw Father Naum, long since dead, leading the congregation in prayer; hundreds of peasants' heads rose and fell, like ripened stalks of grain before the wind. . . . The peasants made the sign of the cross. . . . All of these are familiar, although they are all dead. . . . There he beheld his father's severe face; there was his brother fervently praying. And he also stood there, abloom with health and strength, filled with unconscious hope of happiness. . . . And where was that happiness? . . . For a moment, the old man's thoughts flared up, illuminating various episodes in his past life. . . .

He saw hard work, sorrow, care . . . where was this happiness? A hard lot will trace furrows even in a young face, will bend a powerful back and teach him to sigh as it had taught his older brother.

There on the left, among the village women, with her head humbly bowed, stood his sweetheart. A good woman, may she inherit the kingdom of Heaven! How much she had suffered, poor

733

woman. . . . Constant poverty and work, and the inevitable sorrows of a woman's life will wither her beauty; her eyes will lose their luster, and instead of the customary serenity, dull fear of unexpected calamities will settle perpetually on her face. . . . Well, then, where was her happiness? . . . One son was left to them, their one hope and joy; but he was too weak to withstand temptation.

And there was his rich enemy, kneeling and praying to be forgiven for the many tears he had caused orphans to shed. He crossed himself ardently and struck his forehead against the ground. . . . Mikheyich's heart boiled within him, and the dusky faces of the ikons frowned down upon human sorrow and human wickedness.

All that was past, behind him. For him the whole world was now bounded by this bell-tower, where the wind moaned in the darkness and stirred the ropes. . . . "God be your judge!" muttered the old man, drooping his gray head, while tears rolled gently down his cheeks.

"Mikheyich, ay, Mikheyich! Have you fallen asleep up there?" shouted someone from below.

"What?" the old man answered, rising to his feet. "God! Have I really been sleeping? Such a thing never happened before!"

With quick, experienced hands he grasped the ropes. Below him, the peasant mob moved about like an ant-hill; banners, sparkling with gilt brocade, fluttered in the air. . . . The procession made the circuit of the church, and soon the joyous call reached Mikheyich, "Christ is risen from the dead!"

The old man's heart responded fervently to this call. . . . It seemed to him that the tapers were burning more brightly, and the crowd was more agitated; the banners seemed to be animated, and the wakened wind gathered the billows of sound on its wings, floated them up and blended them with the loud festal pealing of the bells.

Never before had old Mikheyich rung like this!

It seemed as if the old man's heart had passed into the lifeless brass, and the tones of the bells sang and laughed and wept, and, welding in a sublime stream of harmony, rose high and higher into a heaven resplendent with myriad stars, and, trembling, flowed down to earth.

A powerful bass bell proclaimed, "Christ is risen!" And two tenors, trembling with the alternate beats of their iron tongues, repeated joyfully, "Christ is risen!"

And two small sopranos, seemingly hastening so as not to be left

734

behind, crowded in among the more powerful voices and, like little children, sang hurriedly, cheerfully, "Christ is risen!"

The old belfry seemed to tremble and shake, and the wind, flapping its wings in the old bell-ringer's face. repeated, "Christ is risen!"

The old heart forgot its life, full of cares and grief. The old bell-ringer forgot that his life was confined to the narrow limits of the dreary belfry, that he was alone in the world, like an old storm-broken stump. . . . He heard those singing and weeping sounds that rose to heaven and fell again to the sorrowing earth, and it seemed to him that he was surrounded by his sons and grandsons, that he heard their joyful voices; the voices of young and old blend into a chorus and sing to him of happiness and joy which he had never tasted in his life. . . . He pulled the ropes, while tears rolled down his cheeks, and his heart beat violently with the illusion of happiness. . . .

Below, people listened and said to each other that never before had old Mikheyich rung so well.

Suddenly the large bell uttered an uncertain sound, and grew dumb. The smaller ones rang out an unfinished tone, and then stopped, as if abashed, to listen to the lugubrious echo of the prolonged and palpitating note gradually dying away upon the air. . . . The old bell-ringer, utterly exhausted, fell back on the bench, and the last two tears trickled slowly down his pallid cheeks. . . .

"Ho, there! Send up a substitute; the old bell-ringer has rung his final stroke."

ZYGMUNT KRASINSKI

ZYGMUNT KRASINSKI (Polish, 1812-1859). Poet, playwright and novelist. Romanticist with deep philosophical undertone. Embittered by hostile Polish reaction to father's loyalty to Russia, lived most of life abroad. Best-known work: *The Undivine Comedy*, a mystic vision of social revolution. Also ranks high among Polish poets.

A LEGEND

IT seemed to me that precisely during the vigil at the Birth of our Lord I emerged from the gates of Rome and walked along the Campanile. The pagan graves were warming themselves in the rays of the sun—it was early morn—and the sky as clear and the plain as sad as in ages past.

735

I walked all day long borne by the strength of the soul. The ancient aqueducts ran along beside me but I went on beyond. The ivy, as in the pictured models of the manger of Christ, rustled on the walls of the ancient ruins. Above me swept flocks of white birds—before me on the ground wriggled a glistening snake. The roar of the ocean began to call me!

And when I stood on the highest summit of the earth, when I beheld the sea the sun was already setting—and far out over the water stood a black blot like a living thing, constantly growing larger and flying landward towards me—until it increased to a huge size when the sun had faded completely and twilight had begun to descend.

It was a great black ship, without sails or masts—dashing the waves into foam with its timbers. From the centre of the ship a column of smoke belched forth gliding back into the infinite.

Ever more darkly—like an inky spectre it circled in the expanse with thunderous roar—when two night lights gleamed before it on the ocean and a voice sounded from the deck, "Is this the last night of the vigil of the Birth of our Lord?"

Alarmed in spirit I answered from my height, "It is true, to-day is the vigil." And at once the ship stopped at the very edge, the pale stream enveloped her, and slack and sparks were emitted from her sides. In the ruddy glow rapidly declining—for a moment the deck gleamed brightly. Figures stood there in crimson caps and white cloaks—I heard the jangling of chains.—It seemed to me that a heavy long bridge was lowered from the ship to the shore —and upon it in the darkness the figures came rushing out directing their steps toward me.

And when they were very close, they asked us with one voice, "Which way is the road that leads to Rome?" I answered, "There is no road. This is a wilderness." And they answered, "Then lead us." And when I hesitated, they again spoke in low, sad tones, "We are what is left of the Polish nobility, an angel appeared to us, an angel not unlike those whom our forefathers saw, for he had wings without brilliance and a mourning veil over his brow—but we know he was sent from heaven, and he it was who directed us hither. We have been sailing for a long time, the gales have been terrific and many difficulties have we had at sea but the will of the Lord shall be accomplished if to-day at midnight, we arrive at the basilica of St. Peter."

Thereupon I said to them, "Follow me, thou unhappy people."

And I turned to go back from the shore of the ocean toward the city, trembling and praying as if I were crossing a cemetery and as if the dead were rising up and following me.

A wind arose and no more clouds were visible. Everywhere in the deep dark sky the stars were twinkling, while below was a vast black plain! Only now and then we passed dusky mounds or a pile of grey ruins or mayhap the gates of an aqueduct. In the distance one could hear the rustle of tall reeds—above at times sounded the shriek of a night bird, and near by, somewhere among the sunken graves came the murmurings from beneath the earth!

They strode along behind me—I could feel on my back their heavy breathing—I moved on swiftly for they were in haste—I could hear the plumes on their caps flutter in the breeze and the very folds of their capes puff up with the wind!

It seemed to me that I beheld a wandering light in the distance —and immediately a second and a third. When I advanced I beheld a great number of lights on the plain moving rapidly from all sides in one direction. And the sound of many voices began to hum in the wilderness.

When I came nearer I saw a great body of pilgrims passing over the Campanile with torches in their hands. The glow which they cast went with them between two solid walls of blackness but the light glistened on the tall crosses, pictures of saints and on the flags of various nations which fluttered in the breezes.

Into the very centre of the multitudes I led my own group, and at that instant I beheld the melancholy features of those who followed me. A strange ectasy was in their eyes but it was not the lustre of life. They carried swords on which they leaned as did the other pilgrims upon their staffs.

Hardly had I entered with them into the light of the torches when it seemed to me that the masses stood still asking, "Who are you and whence do you come?"

They paused and a strange smile passed over their lips while they answered as one, "Is there no longer anyone on this earth who recognises us?"

A low hum constantly growing in strength filled the air and it seemed to me that all the bands of pilgrims of a sudden cried out, "We know you—you are the last heroes of the earth."

Then they marched forward saying, "We saw an angel with a black band on his brow who commanded us to hasten to Rome. Tell us, did any of you also hear that voice?"

In the multitude a great tumult arose in answer, "Amen,—that same angel bade us leave our homes—his voice increased in the night about our heads and he gave us no peace. In these days, he said, Christ would be born for the last time at the grave of Peter and from that moment nothing shall be born nor nothing shall die on earth."

And the multitude became silent and stood as if startled by its own words.

The Poles were the first to move onward—throwing back their white capes over their shoulders—. From all sides of the Campanile a greater and greater mass of pilgrims crowded forward. Already we saw the battlements of the city—already we heard the harmony of the bells—sounding more clearly the nearer we came.

On the gates, on the towers, festoons of lights appeared and more loudly echoed the bells as one after another awoke to join the rest until soon all the church bells of Rome resounded.

It seemed to me that the night was transformed into white day. I did not in the least recognise the streets from which I had departed in the morning. There where once ruins projected frequented only by owls—baskets of blooming flowers and glowing lamps now swung. The Roman populace came forth in throngs shouting: "Let us rejoice—rejoice ye all, for today Christ is born to us."

And when they beheld the Polish nobles entering the gates and the stream of pilgrims behind them gaily springing forward they cried out: "Why are you so sad, you, our guests? If the long voyage has wearied you, moisten your lips with the juice of the orange. Remove your white caps and your black cloaks—behold, here are clusters of myrtle—here, camelias, we offer them to you to adorn your temples with garlands!"

But in silence and with furrowed brows, the Poles advanced through their midst and marching said to me, "Where is the basilica of Peter? We must hasten and our hearts are downcast. Is the midnight hour close in truth?"

I led them across the Forum. It seemed to me that the Amphitheatre of Flavianus—recently empty, dark and ancient—stood now like a giant of resplendant light from its base to its massive shields gleaming with lamps so that every ivy leaf upon them could be plainly distinguished. Women and children in glistening garments promenaded through various portions of the structure and clapped their hands in welcome to us who approached.

738

Every arch in the Forum and every column glo red and blazed. At the summit a wall of golden flames, the Capitol, shone forth. The very stars in heaven had grown pallid before the great flood of brilliance.

The people continued to shout: "Hosanna, Hosanna!" And the pilgrims sang psalms of penitence. The masses perpetually surged hither and thither, sounding guitars, scattering flaring sparks in the air, and through the centre of all this sea we proceeded in garments of blackness, slowly, in sorrow of soul.

From every balcony, every roof, from the streets, violets and roses descended upon us.

Already the bell of the Capitol boomed far behind us, and before us in the wide space sounded the bell of St. Peter. At last it rang independently, more sonorously than all the rest.

We hastened in the direction of that voice, we crossed the bridge over the Tiber, the houses on its banks standing out like quiet conflagrations, the river like a ribbon of flame. The angel palace bristled with cannon, every instant one of them blazed forth and thundered.

We turned and entered the courtyard of St Peter's. Its dome was hung with thousands of scarlet lamps, the cross at its summit like a diamond, the pillars at either side of the courts as if of twisted fires. In the centre were two fountains like two flowing rainbows, and I beheld a vast mass of people waiting there. The doors of the cathedral stood open and within an infinitude of blazing brightness.

While it was possible the Poles and the other pilgrims advanced but at the steps and at the base of the portico, the throng closed up the way. Pausing therefore, they demanded a passageway, but ever more closely from the front, from the rear and from the sides, the crowds pressed in upon them.

Then the voices of the Romans arose: "Are we not the first, has not this church been our own for ages upon ages?" And among the pilgrims were heard other voices saying: "Up to this time the Polish nobles have led the way for us, shall they be allowed to enter the holy place before us?"

And I looked and saw that the Poles had lifted their swords in token that they would defend themselves. With a pure fire their blades flashed in the clear air!

But at that instant on the battlements of the basilica high above the heads of the people appeared a figure in royal purple which

739

spoke in thunderous tones: "Let pass those who for the Catholic faith ransomed another nation from death and later for that faith perished themselves. Give passageway to the dead, first of all!" And the cardinal extended his hand toward the right and toward the left as if he were dividing the multitude, and down below the masses did indeed separate and make way—which seeing, he turned back into the building.

And together with the Poles I mounted the steps and advanced directly through the portico into the church and on up to the chief altar before the lamps which burn at the tomb of Peter. Here they paused, and removing their crimson caps, they unfastened their white capes and kneeling, worshipped, holding their unsheathed weapons in hand.

The snowy gleam of marble shone in the vast cathedral, the silvery transparent smoke of the incense rose to the arched dome and floated above us. On the mosaic floor lay scattered flowers and palms. From all the chapels echoed choirs of gentle joyful voices and off in the distance around the doors, the space began to fill. The pilgrims marched through that world of song and light just as they did through the city, dark and unrejoicing. A stream of Romans rolled into the basilica, noisily. And when each group had taken its place under its own banner, at its own altar, then the great expanse became silent again, as if it were a vast vacant space. The songs in the chapels were stilled and from the Vatican echoed the sounds of trumpets giving sign that the people were approaching.

Through the centre of the church proceeded all the friars and monks of Rome, the elders one after another, some in white robes, others in grey horse-hair cloth, with crucifixes in their hands. Then came the bishops wearing their mitres and silvery trains and after them the cardinals in splendid crimson, around them priests in dalmatics and troops of children in white garments, carrying wine, incense and wreaths.

And when the procession arrived at the main altar where the crowds separated forming a clear path between walls of living people who now suddenly fell to their knees, an aged grey-haired man walked slowly forward, wearing on his head a triple crown and a white vestment over his golden surplice.

At a great distance behind him remained the soldiers, attendants and the throne borne by priests. He stood alone in the centre of the throng and of the cathedral, alone he ascended the main altar.

740

It semed to me, that each step took an interminable length of time and that he never would come to us.

And as he thus advanced in the centre of those bowing before him touching their foreheads to the ground, he closed his eyes at times as if seeking relief from so many lights. Now and then he essayed to make but tremblingly left unfinished the sign of his blessing, until, pausing, he sighed and lifted up his hands to heaven, but he was unable to hold them upraised—they sank exhaustedly!

At his deep drawn sigh, the people lifted their heads. The sorrow of their father caused all to grow pale and then, I noted, that from the main altar one of the cardinals had turned away, the same one who had ordered that we should be admitted. With grave step, he descended towards the aged eldest of elders and extended his hand, turning shining eyes upon the grave of Peter. The aged man advanced a few steps but with lingering difficulty. The cardinal shook the rings of his long hair with a sidelong motion giving signal to those who had remained in the rear who at once hastened forward carrying the golden throne.

Then the father who is on earth grasped the arm of the throne with his pallid hand and seated himself. Quickly they lifted him up and the trumpets in the church again thundered forth. The cardinal walked along beside the throne. The people lifted themselves from the floor, the bell began to ring and twelve times the arched dome quivered. Around the main altar a cloud of incense arose and from it the pope ascended the steps as the cardinal announced: "Christ is born."

From amid the group of pilgrims at once a voice cried out mournfully: "Will not the words of the angel be borne out in truth that Christ is born for the last time?"

And the Roman people shouted out angrily: "Who dares blaspheme in the church of Peter?"

One of the Polish nobles stepped fortn crying: "They are not blaspheming. We do not fear you—they speak the truth—I myself and my brethren beheld the angel of sorrow."

The cardinal again like a prince of power waved his hand and said, "Peace unto the people of good will, pray ye now for the mass has begun—the time is short and today there must be prayers on earth as in heaven."

We all began to pray awaiting great things. And our holy fath_ᴸ sat before us on the throne.

From the chapels again rose voices like angels' choirs, full of heavenly rapture. A portion of the night passed and white-robed priests came and offered their hands to our father. He descended from the throne and approached the altar taking the chalice in his hands, for the moment had come for the holy sacrifice. The cardinal poured wine into the chalice.

Just at the moment the chalice was being uplifted, when all had fallen to their knees, a voice from the air was heard which uttered, "I live!" And when, aquiver, we raised our heads, we beheld a large figure with head bent upon the central gate, slowly dissolving —ever becoming more misty—the hands bloody, the feet bleeding, but the figure itself of snowy whiteness—and—melting like snow —it vanished.

Then the cardinal, as the pope holding the chalice in his hands, still hesitated, himself uttered the words: "Ite, missa est!" and then he cried in a powerful voice, "The times are fulfilled!" and rending the purple on his breast, he extended his hand toward the grave of Peter saying, "Awake and speak!"

From every lamp above the tomb a fiery tongue burst forth and a wreath of flames swung over the dark sepulcher. From the depths of that darkness, a body arose with hands upstretched to the dome, and standing buried in the tomb to its breast, it shrieked, "Woe!"

After this outcry it seemed to all of us that the vaulted arch of the dome cracked for the first time.

The cardinal then said, "Peter, do you recognise me?"

And the body answered, "Your head rested on the bosom of the Master at the last supper and you have never perished from the earth."

The cardinal responded, "Now it is commanded to me to linger among human beings and to embrace the earth and hold it to my bosom as the Master held mine that last night of His life on earth."

And the body replied, "Do as you have been commanded."

Then the cardinal again waved his hands as with the authority of a prince, and the body repeated: "Woe be unto me!" and fell with a terrible crash as into an abyss, back into its grave. Above, the vaulted arches began anew to shiver and break.

Horror overwhelmed us all. Only the Polish nobles gazed with dauntless eyes, leaning upon their swords.

The pope in his triple crown had knelt down on the steps of the altar and, as immovable as a statue, continued kneeling.

742

The cardinal spoke: "Go forth, all of you—you and you and you,—lest some of you perish beneath the ruins of these walls."

The people answered from all sides, "Lead us—you—under whose protection we have this day entered."

A cry of terror arose for the arches ever more thunderously burst into fissures, the pillars and columns all about shook and lamps were shattered and extinguished by a great wind.

Then spoke the cardinal, "Father—mine—do you wish to remain here?"

And the aged man lifting his hands to his crown, answered in a sorrowful voice: "I wish to die here—leave me, my son."

All the people heard these words, and shrieked, "Run—let us run away!"

And the Romans were the first to recover and began to flee.

And each troop or band moved from its altar with its banner and made haste to fly away.

Then the cardinal, kneeling at last, pressed his lips to the old man's brow and made the sign of a blessing around his crown like a garland of livid light in the air, then he descended and walked toward the gate of the church with a marvellous glow encircling his brow. The entire church was twisted and bent as a dying body in the last throes, but he, with uplifted hand, stayed the cracking, tumbling vault above the people and stood watching until the last one of them had gone.

And departing he said to the Polish nobles, "People, follow after me."

But these did not answer.

He turned his head back again and said, "Follow after me."

They did not move.

When he had reached the gate, driving the people before him like a shepherd, he beckoned them for the last time with his hand.

But they only lifted up their swords as if with their edges they would hold up the falling walls and they cried out altogether, "We shall not desert that aged man—it is bitter, indeed, to die all alone —and who should die with him if not we?—Go you, all—we do not know how to run away."

The cardinal stopped on the very threshold and from a distance made to them the sign of his blessing and of the garland of livid light. In his eyes that moment a tear glistened as he said, "Yet a moment more and you perish."

743

But in that moment they were hastening to the main altar to offer a hand to the kneeling and dying. They advanced in their white caps and in the gleaming of their swords—and the four twisted columns of the altar snapped like a split tree and came crashing down—even the metal canopy dropped in ruins—the entire cupola like a sinking world, fell to the ground.

And all the porticoes, even the palace of the Vatican and the colonnade in the court cracked and burst, falling into dust. Both of the fountains like two white doves, fell to the ground perishing. The populace rushed ever farther on like a sea forced from its shores and, it seemed that it was already morn, though the sun had not yet risen. But I seemed to see only the morning star above a pile of ruins, as high, as immense as had formerly been the basilica of Peter.

Upon this gigantic mountain the cardinal ascended and it seemed that I followed after him carried on by strength of soul.

When he had attained the summit, he seated himself there as on a throne and gazed at the world. His purple robes dropped from his body and he was transformed into a figure of white ensilvered by the mild glow. In his hands was a book and over it he bent his head reading attentively.

His face was entranced with an expression of love and fulness of peace.

I approached him and said just as the sun began to rise: "Sir, is it true that Christ was born for the last time yesterday in that church which to-day is no more?"

With a strange smile and without lifting his eyes from his book, he responded, "From the time of Christ none are born and none die on this earth."

Hearing this I lost my great fear and asked, "Sir, and those whom I led thither yesterday, shall they lie forever under those ruins,—all those dead around the aged dead man?"

And the white saint answered me, "Fear not for them. Because they performed the last service for him, God will reward them—for those who pass out of life are like those who are entering upon it, the dead just as the living are of God. Instead of loss—they gain —it will be better for them and for the sons of their sons."

And when I understood, I rejoiced and my soul awakened.

L

SELMA LAGERLOF

SELMA LAGERLÖF (Swedish, 1858-1940). Most important Swedish woman novelist. Deeply imbued with love of the supernatural and wondersome. Decided to write book based on traditions and stories of her province; *Gösta Berlings Saga* became world classic. Also famous: *Jerusalem*, novel of Swedish farmers who emigrated to Palestine; *The Wonderful Adventures of Nils*, children's story. Nobel Prize, 1909.

THE ECLIPSE

THERE were Stina of Ridgecote and Lina of Birdsong and Kajsa of Littlemarsh and Maja of Skypeak and Beda of Finn-darkness and Elin, the new wife on the old soldier's place, and two or three other peasant women besides—all of them lived at the far end of the parish, below Storhöjden, in a region so wild and rocky none of the big farmowners had bothered to lay hands on it.

One had her cabin set up on a shelf of rock, another had hers put up at the edge of a bog, while a third had one that stood at the crest of a hill so steep it was a toilsome climb getting to it. If by chance any of the others had a cottage built on more favorable ground, you may be sure it lay so close to the mountain as to shut out the sun from autumn fair time clear up to Annunciation Day.

They each cultivated a little potato patch close by the cabin, though under serious difficulties. To be sure, there were many kinds of soil there at the foot of the mountain, but it was hard work to make the patches of land yield anything. In some places they had to clear away so much stone from their fields, it would have built a cow-house on a manorial estate; in some they had dug ditches as deep as graves, and in others they had brought their earth in sacks and spread it on the bare rocks. Where the soil was not so poor, they were forever fighting the tough thistle and pig-

745

weed which sprang up in such profusion you would have thought the whole potato land had been prepared for their benefit.

All the livelong day the women were alone in their cabins; for even where one had a husband and children, the man went off to his work every morning and the children went to school. A few among the older women had grown sons and daughters, but they had gone to America. And some there were with little children, who were always around, of course; but these could hardly be regarded as company.

Being so much alone, it was really necessary that they should meet sometimes over the coffee cups. Not that they got on so very well together, nor had any great love for each other; but some liked to keep posted on what the others were doing, and some grew despondent living like that, in the shadow of the mountain, unless they met people now and then. And there were those, too, who needed to unburden their hearts, and talk about the last letter from America, and those who were naturally talkative and jocular, and who longed for opportunity to make use of these happy God-given talents.

Nor was it any trouble at all to prepare for a little party. Coffee-pot and coffee cups they all had of course, and cream could be got at the manor, if one had no cow of one's own to milk; fancy biscuits and small cakes one could, at a pinch, get the dairyman's driver to fetch from the municipal bakery, and country merchants who sold coffee and sugar were to be found everywhere. So, to get up a coffee party was the easiest thing imaginable. The difficulty lay in finding an occasion.

For Stina of Ridgecote, Lina of Birdsong, Kajsa of Littlemarsh, Maja of Skypeak, Beda of Finn-darkness, and Elin, the new wife at the old soldier's, were all agreed that it would never do for them to celebrate in the midst of the common everyday life. Were they to be that wasteful of the precious hours which never return, they might get a bad name. And to hold coffee parties on Sundays or great Holy Days was out of the question; for then the married women had husband and children at home, which was quite company enough. As for the rest—some liked to attend church, some wished to visit relatives, while a few preferred to spend the day at home, in perfect peace and stillness, that they might really feel it was a Holy Day.

Therefore they were all the more eager to take advantage of every possible opportunity. Most of them gave parties on their name-

746

days, though some celebrated the great event when the wee little one cut its first tooth, or when it took its first steps. For those who received money-letters from America that was always a convenient excuse, and it was also in order to invite all the women of the neighborhood to come and help tack a quilt or stretch a web just off the loom.

All the same, there were not nearly as many occasions to meet as were needed. One year one of the women was at her wit's end. It was her turn to give a party, and she had no objection to carrying out what was expected of her; but she could not seem to hit upon anything to celebrate. Her own name-day she could not celebrate, being named Beda, as Beda has been stricken out of the almanac. Nor could she celebrate that of any member of her family, for all her dear ones were resting in the churchyard. She was very old, and the quilt she slept under would probably outlast her. She had a cat of which she was very fond. Truth to tell, it drank coffee just as well as she did; but she could hardly bring herself to hold a party for a cat!

Pondering, she searched her almanac again and again, for there she felt she must surely find the solution of her problem.

She began at the beginning, with "The Royal House" and "Signs and Forecasts," and read on, right through to "Markets and Postal Transmittances for 1912," without finding anything.

As she was reading the book for the seventh time, her glance rested on "Eclipses." She noted that that year, which was the year of our Lord nineteen-hundred twelve, on April seventeenth there would be a solar eclipse. It would begin at twenty minutes past high noon and end at 2:40 o'clock, and would cover nine-tenths of the sun's disk.

This she had read before, many times, without attaching any significance to it; but now, all at once, it became dazzling clear to her.

"Now I have it!" she exclaimed.

But it was only for a second or two that she felt confident; and then she put the thought away, fearing that the other women would just laugh at her.

The next few days, however, the idea that had come to her when reading her almanac kept recurring to her mind, until at last she began to wonder whether she hadn't better venture. For when she thought about it, what friend had she in all the world she loved better than the Sun? Where her hut lay not a ray of sunlight pene-

747

trated her room the whole winter long. She counted the days until the Sun would come back to her in the spring. The Sun was the only one who was always friendly and gracious to her and of whom she could never see enough.

She looked her years, and felt them, too. Her hands shook as if she were in a perpetual chill and when she saw herself in the looking-glass, she appeared so pale and washed out, as if she had been lying out to bleach. It was only when she stood in a strong, warm, down-pouring sunshine that she felt like a living human being and not a walking corpse.

The more she thought about it, the more she felt there was no day in the whole year she would rather celebrate than the one when her friend the Sun battled against darkness, and after a glorious conquest, came forth with new splendor and majesty.

The seventeenth of April was not far away, but there was ample time to make ready for a party. So, on the day of the eclipse Stina, Lina, Kajsa, Maja, and the other women all sat drinking coffee with Beda at Finn-darkness. They drank their second and their third cups, and chatted about everything imaginable. For one thing, they said they coudn't for the life of them understand why Beda should be giving a party.

Meanwhile, the eclipse was under way. But they took little notice of it. Only for a moment, when the sky turned blackish gray, when all nature seemed under a leaden pall, and there came driving a howling wind with sounds as of the Trumpet of Doom and the lamentations of Judgment Day—only then did they pause and feel a bit awed. But here they each had a fresh cup of coffee, and the feeling soon passed.

When all was over, and the Sun stood out in the heavens so beamingly happy—it seemed to them it had not shone with such brilliancy and power the whole year—they saw old Beda go over to the window, and stand with folded hands. Looking out toward the sunlit slope, she sang in her quavering voice:

"Thy shining sun goes up again,
I thank Thee, O my Lord!
With new-found courage, strength and hope,
I raise a song of joy."

Thin and transparent, old Beda stood there in the light of the window, and as she sang the sunbeams danced about her, as if wanting to give her, also, of their life and strength and color.

When she had finished the old hymn-verse she turned and looked at her guests, as if in apology.

"You see," she said, "I haven't any better friend than the Sun, and I wanted to give her a party on the day of her eclipse. I felt that we should come together to greet her, when she came out of her darkness."

Now they understood what old Beda meant, and their hearts were touched. They began to speak well of the Sun. "She was kind to rich and poor alike, and when she came peeping into the hut on a winter's day, she was as comforting as a glowing fire on the hearth. Just the sight of her smiling face made life worth living, whatever the troubles one had to bear."

The women went back to their homes after the party, happy and content. They somehow felt richer and more secure in the thought that they had a good, faithful friend in the Sun.

LAO SHE

LAO SHÊ (Shu Ch'ing-ch'un, Chinese, 1897-   ). Leading writer of satirical fiction. During war with Japan was president of Writer's League, wrote patriotic plays. *Ssu-shih t'ung-t'ang*, novel of occupied Peking, widely acclaimed.

THE LAST TRAIN

THE train started a long while ago, and now the wheels rumbled mournfully along the rails, the passengers sighed and counted the hours: seven o'clock, eight, nine, ten—by ten o'clock the train would arrive, and they would be home around midnight. It might not be too late, for the children might already be put to bed. It was New Year's Day, and they were all in a hurry to get home. They looked at the cans, the fruit and the toys heaped up on the shelves, and already they could hear the children crying 'Papa, papa!', and thinking of all this, they lost themselves in their thoughts; but there were others who were well aware that they would not be home before daybreak.

There were not many passengers in the second-class carriage. There was fat Mr. Chang and thin Mr. Chiao, and they sat in the

same compartment opposite one another. Whenever they got up, they spread their blankets over their seats to show that intruders would not be welcomed. When the train started they found to their surprise that there were very few passengers indeed, and somehow this led them more than ever to feel grieved at the thought that they were travelling in a train on New Year's Day. There were other similarities between the two passengers: they were both holding free passes, and both of them had been unable to obtain the pass until the previous day. They were both indignant at this treatment, for in the good old days friends were made of sterner stuff, and so they shook their heads and put the blame on these so-called friends who had prevented them from reaching their home before the New Year's Day.

Old Mr. Chang removed his fox-fur coat and tucked his legs under his body, but he discovered that the seat was too narrow for sitting comfortably in this posture. Meanwhile, the temperature of the carriage rose and beads of perspiration began to roll down his brow. 'Boy, towels!' he shouted, and then to Mr. Chiao he said: 'I wonder why they turn so much heat on nowadays'. He gasped. 'It wouldn't be so hot if we were travelling on an aeroplane.'

Old Mr. Chiao had taken off his coat a long while ago, and now he was wearing a robe lined with white sheep's fur, and over that a sleeveless jacket of shining black satin. He showed no sign of feeling faint. He said: 'One can get a free pass on an aeroplane, too. It isn't difficult'. And he drawled off with a faint smile.

'It's better not to risk travelling by air', old Mr. Chang said, trying hard to keep his crossed legs under him, but succeeding only with great difficulty. 'Boy, towels!'

The 'boy' was over forty, and his neck was as thin as a stick, so thin that one imagined that it was quite easy to pluck off his head and plant it back again. You could see him hurrying backwards and forwards along the passageway, his hands full of steaming towels. He was always eager to serve, but really—the way the management made you work on such a sacred day—it was really inconceivable. Taking advantage of the rocking movement of the train, he swung his body towards a certain Mr. K'ou. 'Like a towel, sir? It's trying to travel at this time of the year.'

Mr. K'ou was dressed with considerable éclat. He wore a dark serge overcoat with a beaver collar, with a brand new black satin, melon-shaped hat. He had removed neither his coat nor his hat, and he sat there as rigid as a chairman on a platform waiting

750

solemnly for the moment when he would address a huge audience. He took the towel, stretching out his arm at full length, and taking care not to fold his elbow he described a semi-circle with the towel until it reached his face. Then he rubbed his face fastidiously and ostentatiously. When his face emerged from the whirling cloud of the towel it dazzled and lent to his person a renewed splendour and dignity. He nodded to the 'boy', without explaining why he was travelling on New Year's Day.

And meanwhile the waiter knew perfectly well that the man was a friend of the manager. The carriage began to rock again, and the movement of the carriage hurled him into the passage way. Steadying himself, he untwisted a towel and holding it delicately by two corners he offered it to Mr. Chang. 'Would you like one, sir?', and the man reached out for it, his thick palm touching the central part of it, which was the hottest. He pressed it to his face, rubbing hard as though he were cleaning a mirror. Then he handed another one to Mr. Chiao, who showed no enthusiasm, but took the towel and with it proceeded to clean his nostrils and fingernails delicately. When he returned it to the waiter, it was all greasy and black.

'The inspectors will soon be coming now', he began. 'When they have gone, you will want to have a rest, and if any of you gentlemen would like a cushion, just let me know.' And he went on a little later: 'There are not many passengers on board, and you'll all be able to have a nap. It's a pity you gentlemen are spending a day like this on a train, but as for us waiters—'. He sighed. He realized that he had been talking too much.

'What's wrong with the heating system?' Mr. Chang asked, as he tossed back the towel.

'I wouldn't advise you to open the window', the waiter answered. 'Nine to ten you'll catch cold. The railway is under a rotten management.' The chance lay wide open for him, and he entered quickly. 'They make you work all the year round, and don't even let you rest on New Year's Day. Well, all talking is vain.'

And so it was, for the train had drawn into a small wayside station. Half a dozen soldiers came into the compartment. Their boots thundered on the floor, their leather belts flashed in the light and their luggage consisted of four large cases of fireworks wrapped in scarlet paper and decorated with characters cut out of gold paper. The boxes were so large that for a long time they were undecided what to do with them. Finally, a man who resembled a

751

battalion commander, said that they should be put on the floor. Boots thundered. A cloud of grey caps, grey uniforms and grey leggings. A moment later someone said: 'Hurry!', and they obediently disappeared. A whistle sounded from the train, rather muffled. Lights and shadows flitted about, and the wheels began to rumble and the train to roll out of the station.

The waiter walked from one end of the carriage to the other, looking as though there was something on his mind. He stole a glance at the two soldiers and then at the heap of fireworks which lay so uncompromisingly on the floor, barring his way; but he dared not say anything. The battalion commander was lying down, tired out, his pistol on the little table at the side of the carriage. The platoon commander had not yet dared to imitate him, but he had removed his cap and was now violently scratching his scalp. The waiter took care not to awaken the senior officer, but he smiled voluminously at the junior. 'What was I going to say?' he said in a half-apologetic tone of voice, hesitantly. 'Oh yes, I was going to suggest that it might be a better idea to put the crackers up on the shelf.'

'Why?' the officer answered, mouth awry with head scratching.

'You know, I was afraid people might step on them', the waiter replied, his head shrinking tortoise-fashion into his shoulders.

'If I have any more trouble from you, what about fighting it out?' the officer suddenly shouted. He had been worn thin by the ill-humour of his senior officer, and he was perfectly prepared to fight.

But the waiter was in no need of a fight, and he abruptly disappeared. As he passed Mr. Chang, he said: 'The inspectors will be here soon, sir'.

Mr. Chang and Mr. Chiao were developing a cordial friendship. The ticket inspection began.

Meanwhile the waiter was taking this opportunity to inform Mr. Chang and Mr. Chiao to get their tickets ready. They gave him their tickets. He was awestruck when he realized that the tickets were free passes, and his reverence for the two gentlemen became even greater than before. He returned Mr. Chang's pass at once, but he ventured to detain Mr. Chiao's for a moment because it was clearly indicated on the pass that the holder was a woman, and there was indisputable evidence that Mr. Chiao was a man. The two inspectors drew apart and began to whisper into each other's

ear. A moment later they nodded to one another, and it was clear that they had reached a common understanding that on New Year's Day a man might pass for a woman. The waiter returned Mr. Chiao's ticket with both hands, apologetically.

The battalion commander was now snoring. As soon as he noticed the arrival of the inspectors, the platoon commander put his legs up on the seat and showed every sign of an unwillingness to be disturbed. The inspectors' attention was immediately arrested by the pile of fireworks which littered the passageway. They nodded in admiration, overcome by the length and the solidity of the fire-works. And they passed through the compartment, and it was not until the first inspector reached the door that he turned to the waiter and said: 'You'd better tell them to put the fireworks on the shelves', and in order to save the waiter from further embarrass-ment the second inspector added quickly: 'Better still if you did it for them'. The waiter nodded his thin neck like a pendulum without saying anything, but all the while he was asking himself: 'You haven't the courage to tell them—that's what it is—so what can I do except nod my head?—and besides, there is a great difference between nodding and doing.' The truth dawned on his mind. The fireworks must *not* be moved.

Go-home-go-home-go-home-go-home. The wheels roared in chorus. But they were very slow. The star-strewn sky undulated. Hills, trees, villages, graves, flashed past in clusters. The train dashed on and on in the darkness. Smoke, soot and sparks shot up furiously, and then disappeared. The train ran on, flying breathlessly, one patch of darkness following on another. The lights were ablaze, the tempera-ture steaming, all the passengers were weary to death, and not one was inclined to sleep. Go-home-go-home-go-home. The farewell rites to the Old Year, the libations to the gods, the offerings to the Ancestors, the writing on the spring scrolls, the firecrackers, the dumplings, the sweetmeats, the dinners and the wine—all these became suddenly very real to them, filling their eyes and their ears, their palates and their nostrils. A smile would light upon their lips and instantly disappear, dying away at the recollection that they were still physically in the train. Go-home-go-home-go-home-go-home.

Mr. Chang took down from the shelf two bottles of distilled wine, and said to Mr. Chiao: 'We're just like old friends now. How about a drop of this? We might as well enjoy New Year's Day

753

—no reason why we shouldn't enjoy ourselves'. He handed over a cup of the wine. 'Real Yinkow wine. Twenty years old. You can't get it on the market. Bottoms up.'

Mr. Chiao was too polite to refuse.

'Marvellous!' Mr. Chiao wetted his lips. 'Marvellous! Nothing like it anywhere.'

They filled up one another's cups, and slowly and imperceptibly their faces turned crimson. Their tongues were unloosened. They talked of their families, their jobs, their friends, the difficulty of earning money, free passes. Their cups clinked, their hearts clinked, their eyes moistened, they were permeated with warmth.

Mr. Chang looked at his bottle—there was not very much left now. He untied his collar. Beads of perspiration stood out on his brow; his eyes were bloodshot and his tongue was stiff. Though still talkative, his talk was reduced to mere babbling; he had not yet completely lost his self-control, he could still put a curb on the curious inner urge which nearly led him to curse in front of his new-found friend, and the resultant of these forces took the form, not of a quarrel, or incivility, but rather of exultation and gaiety. Mr. Chiao, on the other hand, had been able to stomach only half of the bottle assigned to him, but his face was already turning deathly pale. He produced a packet of cigarettes and threw one at Mr. Chang. Both lit their cigarettes.

Go-home-go-home-go-home-go-home. In Mr. Chang's ears the wheels sounded as though they were going at breakneck speed. His heart beat fast, and suddenly everything began buzzing. His head turned round and round in the air, buzzing like a fly. All objects were dancing and glowing in red circles. When the buzzing ceased, his heart once more began to beat at its accustomed ritual, and he opened his eyes slightly, partially regaining his strength. He pretended nothing had happened, and groping for the matchbox he relit his extinguished cigarette. Then he threw the match away. Suddenly on the table a greenish flame flared up, smelling of alcohol, spinning among the cups and bottles, fluttering, rising, spreading out. Mr. Chiao was startled out of his dreams as the cigarette which he held in his hand suddenly caught fire. He threw it away. He beat the table with both hands to extinguish the fire, and in doing this he knocked down the cups and bottles. Iridescent tongues licked the unopened parcels. Mr. Chang's face was hidden in flames. Mr. Chiao thought of running away. The flames on the table soared up, and the parcels on the shelf above seemed to reach down to

catch the rising columns of flames. Flame linked with flame. Mr. Chiao himself was ablaze. The fire reached his eyebrows, charring them, snapping at his hair, which sizzled, lighting up the alcohol on his lips and turning him into a fire-breathing monster.

Suddenly: pop, pop, pop . . . It sounded like machine-gun fire. The platoon commander had hardly opened his eyes when a cracker exploded on his nose and sent sparks and blood flying in fine sprays. He rose, and began frantically running. There were explosions everywhere, under his feet, all round his body. The noise was deafening as though they had stepped on a land mine. The battalion commander was swallowed up in the fire before he could open his eyes. He was trying to open his eyes when the right eye received a direct hit from one of the exploding crackers.

Mr. K'ou started up. He cast a quick glance at his luggage on the shelf. Some of the parcels were already burning, and the fire was closing in from all sides—from above, from below, and even from a long way away. Flames licked at him, and an idea flashed through his mind. He picked up one of his shoes from the floor and smote at the windowpane. He wanted to jump out of the window. The glass was broken, a gale rushed in, the fire turned wild. His collar of beaver-skin, the four bedrolls, the five boxes, his clothes—they were all swallowed up in the flames. The train ran on, the wind was roaring, the firecrackers kept going off. Mr. K'ou ran like a wild animal.

Mr. Chang was dead-drunk, and he lay there like a log. Mr. Chiao, Mr. K'ou and the platoon commander were running about in all directions, stark staring mad. The battalion commander knelt on the bench and wailed. The fire had already penetrated every corner of the carriage; the smell of sulphur was suffocating. The crackers were no longer exploding—they had all been burnt. The noise died away, but the smoke grew thicker. And at last those who were running about no longer ran about, and those who were wailing no longer wailed. The fire began to devour the furniture. The train kept darting forward, the wind kept roaring. Red tongues of flame struggled within the dense clouds of smoke, hoping for an outlet. The smoke turned milky, and the flames began to thrash at the windows. The whole carriage was transparent with light, and tongues of fire streamed away like streamers, a thousand torches burning brightly in the wind.

Brilliant rockets shot out in sprays. The night was dark and the train was a chain of lanterns pouring out licking flames. Of the

second-class carriage, only a charred skeleton remained. The flames, having nothing to feed on, moved backwards and forwards, and finally entered the third-class carriage. Smoke came first, sending out a pungent, and slightly sweet smell of charred flesh and furniture. Fire followed. 'Fire! Fire' Fire' Everyone was shouting in fearful panic. They lost their heads. They broke the windows in an attempt to leap out, and then hesitated. Some began to run, and then they would fall against one another and fall down. Some sat transfixed to their seats, unable even to cry. Turbulence. Panic. Every effort proved vain. They howled, folded their arms round their heads, beat off the flames with their clothes, ran, jumped out of the carriage. . . .

The fire had discovered a new colony, with rich resources and a great population. It was mad with joy. Hundreds of flames began dancing in the most fantastic patterns. They rolled themselves up into balls, shot out like meteors, gathered in red-and-green pools of fire. They squeaked and gibbered as they burned human flesh and broiled human hair. The crowd howled, the wind roared, the fire crackled. The whole car was on fire. The smoke was heavy. It was a lovely cremation.

The train arrived at the next station, where it was due to stop. It stopped. Signalmen, ticket-inspectors, guards, the stationmaster and the assistant stationmaster, the clerks and the hangers-on all looked at the burning carriages in amazement, and could do nothing, because there were no fire engines and no implements for putting out fires. The second-class carriage, and the two adjacent third-class carriages in front and behind were silent and still. From them a plume of blue smoke curled up—languidly and leisurely.

It was reported later that fifty-two corpses were found on the train, and the bodies of eleven more, who had jumped off and killed themselves, were found along the line.

After the Lantern Festival—that is, fifteen days after the New Year—an inspector arrived.

The guard knew nothing. The first inspector knew nothing. The second inspector knew nothing.

Finally, the waiter was examined. He declared that he knew nothing about the fire, which must have started when he was in the dining-car. The tribunal decided that he was irrevocably wrong, and should be punished for having left his post of duty. And he was duly discharged from the service.

756

The inspector submitted his report with a detailed account of the tragedy written in the most admirable style.

'I don't care at all', the waiter said to his wife. 'They put you on duty on New Year's Day, and then, when everything goes wrong, they think we will be starved if we leave their wretched railway.'

'What nonsense!' his wife answered. 'I'm not worried about that. What I am worried about is the cabbage that got burnt.'

LAO-TZU

LAO-TZU (Chinese, 6th century B.C.). Legendary sage of China. Author of the celebrated *Tao Te Ching*, 81 chapters of prose and verse. Important in the whole Taoist movement ("Tao," "the Eternal" or "Way of Life" according to reason and virtue).

PARAPHRASE

1

There are ways but the Way is uncharted;
There are names but not nature in words:
Nameless indeed is the source of creation
But things have a mother and she has a name.

The secret waits for the insight
Of eyes unclouded by longing;
Those who are bound by desire
See only the outward container.

These two come paired but distinct
By their names.
Of all things profound,
Say that their pairing is deepest,
The gate to the root of the world.

2

Since the world points up beauty as such,
There is ugliness too.
If goodness is taken as goodness,
Wickedness enters as well.

757

For is and is-not come together;
Hard and easy are complementary;
Long and short are relative;
High and low are comparative;
Pitch and sound make harmony;
Before and after are a sequence.

Indeed the Wise Man's office
Is to work by being still;
He teaches not by speech
But by accomplishment;
He does for everything,
Neglecting none;
Their life he gives to all,
Possessing none;
And what he brings to pass
Depends on no one else.
As he succeeds,
He takes no credit
And just because he does not take it,
Credit never leaves him.

3

A man of highest virtue
Will not display it as his own;
His virtue then is real.
Low virtue makes one miss no chance
To show his virtue off;
His virtue then is nought.
High virtue is at rest;
It knows no need to act.
Low virtue is a busyness
Pretending to accomplishment.

Compassion at its best
Consists in honest deeds;
Morality at best
Is something done, aforethought;
High etiquette, when acted out
Without response from others,
Constrains a man to bare his arms
And make them do their duty!

Truly, once the Way is lost,
There comes then virtue;
Virtue lost, comes then compassion;
After that morality;
And when that's lost, there's etiquette,
The husk of all good faith,
The rising point of anarchy.

Foreknowledge is, they say,
The Doctrine come to flower;
But better yet, it is
The starting point of silliness.
So once full-grown, a man will take
The meat and not the husk,
The fruit and not the flower.
Rejecting one, he takes the other.

4

These things in ancient times received the One:

The sky obtained it and was clarified;
The earth received it and was settled firm;
The spirits got it and were energized;
The valleys had it, filled to overflow;
All things, as they partook it came alive;
The nobles and the king imbibed the One
In order that the realm might upright be;
Such things were then accomplished by the One.

Without its clarity the sky might break;
Except it were set firm, the earth might shake;
Without their energy the gods would pass;
Unless kept full, the valleys might go dry;
Except for life, all things would pass away;
Unless the One did lift and hold them high,
The nobles and the king might trip and fall.

The humble folk support the mighty ones;
They are base on which the highest rest.
The nobles and the king speak of themselves

759

As "orphans," "desolate" and "needy ones."
Does this not indicate that they depend
Upon the lowly people for support?

Truly, a cart is more than the sum of its parts.

Better to rumble like rocks
Than to tinkle like jade.

DAVID HERBERT LAWRENCE

DAVID HERBERT LAWRENCE (English, 1885-1930). Controversial English novelist and poet. An enigmatic battler against social prejudice. Son of a coal miner, rebelled bitterly against industrialism. Also concerned with better relations between sexes. *Sons and Lovers*, partly autobiographical novel. *Lady Chatterly's Lover*, banned in England and America because of frankness. Spent last years of life in Mexico and Italy.

DREAMS OLD AND NASCENT

My world is a painted fresco, where coloured shapes
Of old, ineffectual lives linger blurred and warm;
An endless tapestry the past has woven drapes
The halls of my life, compelling my soul to conform.

The surface of dreams is broken,
The picture of the past is shaken and scattered.
Fluent, active figures of men pass along the railway, and I am woken
From the dreams that the distance flattered.

Along the railway, active figures of men.
They have a secret that stirs in their limbs as they move
Out of the distance, nearer, commanding my dreamy world.

Here in the subtle, rounded flesh
Beats the active ectasy.
In the sudden lifting of my eyes, it is clearer,
The fascination of the quick, restless Creator moving through the
    mesh
Of men, vibrating in ecstasy through the rounded flesh.

Oh my boys, bending over your books,
In you is trembling and fusing
The creation of a new-patterned dream, dream of a generation:
And I watch to see the Creator, the power that patterns the dream.

The old dreams are beautiful, beloved, soft-toned, and sure,
But the dream-stuff is molten and moving mysteriously,
Alluring my eyes; for I, am I not also dream-stuff,
Am I not quickening, diffusing myself in the pattern, shaping and
   shapen?

Here in my class is the answer for the great yearning:
Eyes where I can watch the swim of old dreams reflected on the
   molten metal of dreams,
Watch the stir which is rhythmic and moves them all as a heart-beat
   moves the blood,
Here in the swelling flesh the great activity working,
Visible there in the change of eyes and the mobile features.

Oh the great mystery and fascination of the unseen Shaper,
The power of the melting, fusing Force—heat, light, all in one,
Everything great and mysterious in one, swelling and shaping the
   dream in the flesh,
As it swells and shapes a bud into blossom.

Oh the terrible ecstasy of the consciousness that I am life!
Oh the miracle of the whole, the widespread, labouring concentration
Swelling mankind like one bud to bring forth the fruit of a dream,
Oh the terror of lifting the innermost I out of the sweep of the
   impulse of life,
And watching the Great Thing labouring through the whole round
   flesh of the world;
And striving to catch a glimpse of the shape of the coming dream,
As it quickens within the labouring, white-hot metal,
Catch the scent and the colour of the coming dream,
Then to fall back exhausted into the unconscious, molten life!

761

LEE HOU-CHU

LEE HOU-CHU (Chinese, 937-978). King of the South T'ang Kingdom in the time of the Ten Kingdoms, and greatest poet of his time. His administration, more devoted to arts than wars, fell easily to Sung Emperor. Great lover of music, women and Buddhism. Master of the *tzu*, a song set to a definite tune.

THE FISHERMAN

The vernal breeze an oar;
My skiff a leaf;
A line of fishing string;
A light hook.
An islet full of flowers;
A pitcher full of wine.
Among ten thousand ching of waves
I have my freedom.

The wave-flowers break into a thousand layers of snow.
Peach and plum blossoms from the quiet army of Spring.
A flask of wine;
A fishing rod and line.
Who is as happy as I?

FADING FLOWERS

The morning moon sets;
Last night's smoke is blown away.
Speechless I recline on the pillow.
Returning from my dreams I hanker after the scented grass.

In the far sky, the cry of swans is thin.

The singing orioles scatter;
The fading flowers fall;
Lonely are the painted hall and the deep courtyard.
Do not sweep away the red petals;
Let them await the feet of the returning dancers.

762

SPRING

To find spring one must walk out in the early Spring.
To love a flower do not wait till the flower is old.
She holds the bluish cup in her supple hand;
The brimming wine is clear.

What harm is there in smiling and laughing?
In the Forbidden Garden spring yet lingers.
Ah, to be drunk together and to converse leisurely!
Poems flow to the sound of the goat-drum
Calling on the flowers to blossom forth.

PALE MOON

In the long night,
I loiter round the bower,
Indolent.
The feast of ching-min is just over;
I already feel the Spring wane.
The sound of falling rain is stifled by the wind.
The blurred moon is pale among the shifting clouds.

Breezes pass lightly through the yearning peach and apricot.
Who is chattering there at the swing with laughter?
My heart is one, but its threads of thoughts are ten thousand.
There is no place on earth for me to smooth them out.

NIKOLAUS LENAU

NIKOLAUS LENAU (Nikolaus Niembsch von Strehlenau, Austrian, 1802-
1850). Austrian lyric poet. The bohemian of the Balkans. Lived erratically,
died in delusion. Like Leopardi, a poet of despair. An accomplished violinist,
with deep feeling for nature.

SONGS BY THE LAKE

I

In the sky the sun is failing,
And the weary day would sleep.
Here the willow fronds are trailing
In the water still and deep.

From my darling I must sever:
  Stream, oh tears, stream forth amain!
In the breeze the rushes quiver
  And the willow sighs in pain.

On my soul in silence grieving
  Mild thou gleamest from afar,
As through rushes interweaving
  Gleams the mirrored evening star.

IV

Sunset dull and drear;
  Dark the clouds drive past;
Sultry, full of fear,
  All the winds fly fast.

Through the sky's wild rack
  Shoots the lightning pale;
O'er the waters black
  Burns its flickering trail.

In the vivid glare
  Half I see thy form,
And thy streaming hair
  Flutters in the storm.

V

On the lake as it reposes
  Dwells the moon with glow serene
Interweaving pallid roses
  With the rushes' crown of green.

Stags from out the hillside bushes
  Gaze aloft into the night,
Waterfowl amid the rushes
  Vaguely stir with fluttering light.

Down my tear-dim glance I bend now,
  While through all my soul a rare
Thrill of thought toward thee doth tend now
  Like an ecstasy of prayer.

Passing lovely was the night,
  Silver clouds flew o'er us,
Spring, methought, with splendor dight
  Led the happy chorus.

Sleep-entranced lay wood and dale,
  Empty now each by-way;
No one but the moonlight pale
  Roamed upon the highway.

Breezes wandering in the gloom
  Soft their footsteps numbered
Through Dame Nature's sleeping-room
  Where her children slumbered.

Timidly the brook stole by,
  While the beds of blossom
Breathed their perfume joyously
  On the still night's bosom.

My postilion, heedless all,
  Cracked his whip most gaily,
And his merry trumpet-call
  Rang o'er hill and valley.

Hoofs beat steadily the while,
  As the horses gamboled,
And along the shady aisle
  Spiritedly rambled.

Grove and meadow gliding past
  Vanished at a glimmer:
Peaceful towns were gone as fast,
  Like to dreams that shimmer.

Midway in the Maytide trance
  Tombs were shining whitely;
'Twas the churchyard met our glance—
  None might view it lightly.

Close against the mountain braced
  Ran the long white wall there,
And the cross, in sorrow placed,
  Silent rose o'er all there.

Jehu straight, his humor spent,
  Left his tuneful courses;
On the cross his gaze he bent
  Then pulled up his horses.

"Here's where horse and coach must wait—
  You may think it odd, sir:—
But up yonder, lies my mate
  Underneath the sod, sir.

"Better lad was never born—
  (Sir, 'twas God's own pity!)
No one else could blow the horn
  Half as shrill and pretty.

"So I stop beside the wall
  Every time I pass here,
And I blow his favorite call
  To him under grass here."

Toward the churchyard then he blew
  One call after other,
That they might go ringing through
  To his sleeping brother.

From the cliff each lively note
  Echoing resounded,
As it were the dead man's throat
  Answering strains had sounded.

On we went through field and hedge,
  Loosened bridles jingling;
Long that echo from the ledge
  In my ear kept tingling.

TO THE BELOVED FROM AFAR

His sweet rose here oversea
    I must gather sadly;
Which, beloved, unto thee
    I would bring how gladly!

But alas! if o'er the foam
    I this flower should carry,
It would fade ere I could come;
    Roses may not tarry.

Farther let no mortal fare
    Who would be a wooer,
Than unwithered he may bear
    Blushing roses to her,

Or than nightingale may fly
    For her nesting grasses,
Or than with the west wind's sigh
    Her soft warbling passes.

THE THREE GIPSIES

Three gipsy men I saw one day
    Stretched out on the grass together,
As wearily o'er the sandy way
    My wagon brushed the heather.

The first of the three was fiddling there
    In the glow of evening pallid,
Playing a wild and passionate air,
    The tune of some gipsy ballad.

From the second's pipe the smoke-wreaths curled,
    He watched them melt at his leisure.
So full of content, it seemed the world
    Had naught to add to his pleasure.

767

And what of the third?—He was fast asleep,
   His harp to a bough confided;
The breezes across the strings did sweep,
   A dream o'er his heart-strings glided.

The garb of all was worn and frayed,
   With tatters grotesquely mended;
But flouting the world, and undismayed,
   The three with fate contended.

They showed me how, by three-fold scoff,
   When cares of life perplex us,
To smoke, or sleep, or fiddle them off,
   And scorn the ills that vex us.

GIACOMO LEOPARDI

GIACOMO LEOPARDI (Italian, 1798-1837). Italian poet of pessimism and despair. Unhappy childhood and ill health throughout life. A visionary and mystic naturalist, who rejected civilization and thought Italy corrupt and decadent. Intense personal emotion gave his work strength and validity. Best-known: *To Italy, On the Monument to Dante, The Lone Sparrow, The Broom Plant.*

THE LAST SONG OF SAPPHO

Thou peaceful night, thou chaste and silver ray
Of the declining Moon; and thou, arising
Amid the quiet forest on the rocks,
Herald of day; O cherished and endeared,
Whilst Fate and Doom were to my knowledge closed,
Objects of sight! No lovely land or sky
Doth longer gladden my despairing mood.
By unaccustomed joy we are revived
When o'er the liquid spaces of the Heavens
And o'er the fields alarmed doth wildly whirl
The tempest of the winds, and when the car,
The ponderous car of Jove, above our heads
Thundering, divides the heavy air obscure.
O'er mountain peaks and o'er abysses deep
We love to float amid the swiftest clouds;

768

We love the terror of the herds dispersed,
The streams that flood the plain,
And the victorious, thunderous fury of the main.

Fair is thy sight, O sky divine, and fair
Art thou, O dewy Earth! Alas! of all
This beauty infinite, no slightest part
To wretched Sappho did the Gods or Fate
Inexorable give. Unto thy reign
Superb, O Nature, an unwelcome guest
And a disprized adorer doth my heart
And do mine eyes implore thy lovely forms;
But all in vain. The sunny land around
Smiles not for me, nor from ethereal gates
The blush of early dawn; not me the songs
Of brilliant-feathered birds, not me the trees
Salute with murmuring leaves; and where in shade
Of drooping willows doth a liquid stream
Display its pure and crystal course, from my
Advancing foot the soft and flowing waves
Withdrawing with affright,
Disdainfully it takes through flowery dell its flight.

What fault so great, what guiltiness so dire
Did blight me ere my birth, that adverse grew
To me the brow of fortune and the sky?
How did I sin, a child, when ignorant
Of wickedness is life, that from that time
Despoiled of youth and of its fairest flowers,
The cruel Fates wove with relentless wrath
The web of my existence? Reckless words
Rise on thy lips; the events that are to be
A secret council guides. Secret is all,
Our agony excepted. We were born,
Neglected race, for tears; the reason lies
Amid the Gods on high. O cares and hopes
Of early years! To beauty did the Sire,
To glorious beauty an eternal reign
Give o'er this human kind; for warlike deed,
For learned lyre or song,
In unadornèd shape, no charms to fame belong.

769

Ah! let us die. The unworthy garb divested,
The naked soul will take to Dis its flight
And expiate the cruel fault of blind
Dispensers of our lot. And thou for whom
Long love in vain, long faith, and fruitless rage
Of unappeased desire assailed my heart,
Live happily, if happily on earth
A mortal yet hath lived. Not me did Jove
Sprinkle with the delightful liquor from
The niggard urn, since of my childhood died
The dreams and fond delusions. The glad days
Of our existence are the first to fly;
And then disease and age approach, and last,
The shade of frigid Death. Behold! of all
The palms I hoped for and the errors sweet,
Hades remains; and the transcendent mind
Sinks to the Stygian shore
Where sable Night doth reign, and silence evermore.

THE VILLAGERS' SATURDAY NIGHT

From copse and glade the maiden takes her way
When in the west the setting sun reposes;
She gathered flowers; her slender fingers bear
A fragrant wealth of violets and roses,
And with their beauty she will deck her hair,
Her lovely bosom with their leaves entwine;
Such is her wont on every festive day.
The aged matron sits upon the steps
And with her neighbors turns the spinning wheel,
Facing the heavens where the rays decline;
And she recalls the years,—
The happy years when on the festive day
It was her wont her beauty to array,
And when amidst her lovers and compeers
In youth's effulgent pride
Her rapid feet through mazy dance did glide.

The sky already darkens, and serene
The azure vault its loveliness reveals;

770

From hill and tower a lengthened shadow steals
In silvery whiteness of the crescent moon.
We hear the distant bell
Of festive morrow tell;
To weary hearts how generous a boon!
The happy children in the open space
In dancing numbers throng
With game and jest and song;
And to his quiet home and simple fare
The laborer doth repair
And whistles as he goes,
Glad of the morrow that shall bring repose.

   Then, when no other light around is seen,
No other sound or stir,
We hear the hammer strike,
The grating saw of busy carpenter;
He is about and doing, so unlike
His quiet neighbors; his nocturnal lamp
With helpful light the darkened workshop fills,
And he makes haste his business to complete
Ere break of dawn the heavenly regions greet.

   This of the seven is the happiest day,
With hope and joyance gay;
To-morrow grief and care
The unwelcome hours will in their progress bear;
To-morrow one and all
In thought their wonted labors will recall.

   O merry youth! Thy time of life so gay
Is like a joyous and delightful day,—
A day clear and serene
That doth the approaching festival precede
Of thy fair life. Rejoice! Divine indeed
Is this fair day, I ween.
I'll say no more; but when it comes to thee,
Thy festival, may it not evil be.

MIKHAIL YURYEVICH LERMONTOV

MIKHAIL YURYEVICH LERMONTOV (Russian, 1814-1841). Russian poet,
whose work marked end of era inaugurated by Pushkin. Led wild life, died in
duel after brief, rancorous military career. Gloomy cynicism makes him most
Byronic of Russian poets. Had great sympathy for the common people. Best
work: lyric poems and a novel, *A Hero of Our Time.*

DAGGER

I love you well, my steel-white dagger,
Comrade luminous and cold;
Forged by a Georgian dreaming vengeance,
Whetted by Circassians bold.

A tender hand, in grace of parting,
Gave you to mark a meeting brief;
For blood there glimmered on your metal
A shining tear—the pearl of grief.

And black eyes, clinging to my glances,
Filled deep with liquid sorrow seemed;
Like your clear blade where flame is trembling,
They darkened quickly and they gleamed.

You were to be my long companion.
Give me your counsel to the end!
I will be hard of soul and faithful,
Like you, my iron-hearted friend!

A SAIL

White is the sail and lonely
    On the misty infinite blue;
Flying from what in the homeland?
    Seeking for what in the new?

The waves romp, and the winds whistle,
    And the mast leans and creaks;
Alas! He flies not from fortune,
    And no good fortune he seeks.

Beneath him the stream, luminous, azure,
    Above him the sun's golden breast;
But he, a rebel, invites the storms,
    As though in the storms were rest.

COMPOSED WHILE UNDER ARREST

When waves invade the yellowing wheat,
And the saplings sway with a wind-song brief;
When the raspberry plum in the garden sweet
Hides him under the cool green leaf;

When sprinkled with lights of limpid dew,
At rose of evening or gold of morn,
The lilies-of-the-valley strew
Their silver nodding under the thorn;

When the brook in the valley with cooling breast,
Plunging my soul in a cloudy dream,
Murmurs a legend of lands of rest
At the rise of his happy and rapid stream;

Then humbled is my heart's distress,
And lulled the anguish of my blood;
Then in the earth my happiness,
Then in the heaven my God.

A THOUGHT

I gaze with grief upon our generation.
Its future black or vacant—and to-day,
Bent with a load of doubt and understanding,
In sloth and cold stagnation it grows old.
When scarcely from the cradle we were rich
In follies, in our fathers' tardy wits.
Life wearied us—a road without a goal,
A feast upon a foreign holiday.
Toward good and evil shamefully impassive,
In mid-career we fade without a fight.

Before a danger pusillanimous,
Before a power that scorns us we are slaves.
Precocious fruit, untimely ripe, we hang,
Rejoicing neither sight nor touch nor tongue,
A wrinkled orphan runt among the blossoms,
Their beauty's hour the hour of its decay.

The hues of poetry, the shapes of art,
Wake in our minds no lovely ecstasy.
We hoard the dregs of feelings that are dead,
Misers, we dig and hide a debased coin.
We hate by chance, we love by accident;
We make no sacrifice to hate or love.
Within our minds presides a secret chill
Even while the flame is burning in our blood.
A bore to us our fathers' gorgeous sporting,
Their conscientious childish vast debauch.
We hasten tomb-wards without joy or glory,
With but a glance of ridicule thrown back.
A surly-hearted crowd and soon forgotten,
We pass in silence, trackless from the world,
Tossing no fruit of dreaming to the ages,
No deed of genius even half begun.
Our dust the justice of the citizen
In future time will judge in songs of venom. . . .
Will celebrate the weak and squandering father
In bitter mockery the cheated son.

THE MOUNTAIN

A golden cloud slept for her pleasure
All night on the gaunt hill's breast;
Light-heart to her play-ground of azure,
How early she sped from the nest.
But the soft moist trace of her sleeping
Lay in the folds of the hill.
He pondered; his tears are creeping
Down to the desert still.

GOTTHOLD EPHRAIM LESSING

GOTTHOLD EPHRAIM LESSING (German, 1729-1781). German critic and dramatist. One of the very distinguished Continental liberals. Gave up clerical career to become playwright. With Moses Mendelssohn and Nicolai, produced critical journal. *Laokoon*, famous treatise defining differences between poetry and other arts. *Nathan the Wise*, important drama pleading religious tolerance.

SALADIN AND NATHAN

Saladin. Draw nearer, Jew—yet nearer—close to me!
Lay fear aside.
 Nathan. Fear, Sultan, 's for your foes.
 Saladin. Your name is Nathan?
 Nathan. Yes.
 Saladin. Nathan the Wise.
 Nathan. No.
 Saladin. But, at least the people call you so.
 Nathan. That may be true. The people!
 Saladin. Do you think
I treat the people's voice contemptuously.
I have been wishing long to know the man
Whom it has called the Wise.
 Nathan. What if it named
Him so in scorn? If wise means prudent only—
And prudent, one who knows his interest well?
 Saladin. Who knows his real interest, you mean.
 Nathan. Then, Sultan, selfish men were the most prudent,
And wise, and prudent, then, would mean the same.
 Saladin. You're proving what your speeches contradict.
You know the real interests of man:
The people know them not—have never sought
To know them. That alone can make man wise.
 Nathan. Which every man conceives himself to be.
 Saladin. A truce to modesty! To meet it ever,
When we are seeking truth is wearisome. (*Springs up.*)
So, let us to the point. Be candid, Jew,
Be frank and honest.
 Nathan. I will serve you, prince,
And prove that I am worthy of your favor.
 Saladin. How will you serve me?

775

Nathan. You shall have the best
Of all I have, and at the cheapest rate.
Saladin. What mean you? Not your wares?—My sister, then,
Shall make the bargain with you. (That's for the listener!)
I am not versed in mercantile affairs,
And with a merchant's craft I've naught to do.
Nathan. Doubtless you would inquire if I have marked
Upon my route the movements of the foe?
Whether he's stirring? If I may presume——
Saladin. Neither was that my object. On that point
I know enough. But hear me.
Nathan. I obey.
Saladin. It is another, a far different thing
On which I seek for wisdom; and since you
Are called the Wise, tell me which faith or law
You deem the best.
Nathan. Sultan, I am a Jew.
Saladin.—And I a Mussulman. The Christian stands
Between us. Here are three religions, then,
And of these three one only can be true.
A man like you remains not where his birth
By accident has cast him; or if so,
Conviction, choice, or ground of preference,
Supports him. Let me, Nathan, hear from you,
In confidence, the reasons of your choice,
Which I have lacked the leisure to examine.
It may be, Nathan, that I am the first
Sultan who has indulged this strange caprice,
Which need not, therefore, make a Sultan blush.
Am I first? Nay, speak; or if you seek
A brief delay to shape your scattered thoughts,
I yield it freely. (Has she overheard?
She will inform me if I've acted right.)
Reflect then, Nathan, I shall soon return.
                                        (*Exit.*)

Nathan. (*alone*). Strange! how is this? What can the Sultan want?
I came prepared for cash—he asks for truth!
Truth! as if truth were cash! A coin disused—
Valued by weight! If so, 'twere well, indeed!
But coin quite new, not coin but for the die,

776

To be flung down and on the counter told—
It is not that. Like gold tied up in bags,
Will truth lie hoarded in the wise man's head,
To be produced at need? Now, in this case,
Which of us plays the Jew? He asks for truth.
Is truth what he requires? his aim, his end?
Or does he use it as a subtle snare?
That were too petty for his noble mind.
Yet what is e'er too petty for the great?
Did he not rush at once into the house,
Whilst, as a friend, he would have paused or knocked?
I must beware. Yet to repel him now,
And act the stubborn Jew, is not the thing;
And wholly to fling off the Jew, still less.
For if no Jew, he might with justice ask,
Why not a Mussulman?—That thought may serve.—
Others than children may be quieted
With tales well told. But see, he comes—he comes.

    Saladin. (*aside*). (The coast is clear)—I am not come too soon?
Have you reflected on this matter, Nathan?
Speak! no one hears.

    Nathan.   Would all the world might hear!

    Saladin.   And are you of your cause so confident.
'Tis wise, indeed, of you to hide no truth,
For truth to hazard all, even life and goods.

    Nathan.   Ay, when necessity and profit bid.

    Saladin.   I hope that henceforth I shall rightly bear
One of my names, "Reformer of the world
And of the law!"

    Nathan.   A noble title, truly;
But, Sultan, ere I quite explain myself,
Permit me to relate a tale.

    Saladin.   Why not?
I ever was a friend of tales well told.

    Nathan.   Well told! Ah, Sultan! that's another thing.

    Saladin.   What! still so proudly modest? But begin.

    Nathan.   In days of yore, there dwelt in Eastern lands
A man, who from a valued hand received
A ring of priceless worth. An opal stone
Shot from within an ever-changing hue,
And held this virtue in its form concealed,

777

To render him of God and man beloved,
Who wore it in this fixed unchanging faith.
No wonder that its Eastern owner ne'er
Withdrew it from his finger, and resolved
That to his house the ring should be secured.
Therefore he thus bequeathed it: first to him
Who was the most beloved of his sons,
Ordaining then that he should leave the ring
To the most dear among his children; then,
That without heeding birth, the fav'rite son,
In virtue of the ring alone, should still
Be lord of all the house. You hear me, Sultan?

    Saladin. I understand. Proceed.

    Nathan. From son to son,
The ring at length descended to a sire
Who had three sons, alike obedient to him,
And whom he loved with just and equal love.
The first, the second, and the third, in turn,
According as they each apart received
The overflowings of his heart, appeared
Most worthy, as his heir, to take the ring,
Which, with good-natured weakness, he in turn
Had promised privately to each; and thus
Things lasted for a while. But death approached,
The father now embarrassed, could not bear
To disappoint two sons, who trusted him.
What's to be done? In secret he commands
The jeweler to come, that from the form
Of the true ring, he may bespeak two more.
Nor cost nor pains are to be spared, to make
The rings alike—quite like the true one. This
The artist managed. When the rings were brought
The father's eye could not distinguish which
Had been the model. Overjoyed, he calls
His sons, takes leave of each apart—bestows
His blessing and his ring on each—and dies.
You hear me?

    Saladin. (*who has turned away in perplexity*). Ay! I hear. Con-
clude the tale.

    Nathan. 'Tis ended, Sultan! All that follows next
May well be guessed. Scarce is the father dead,

When with his ring each separate son appears,
And claims to be the lord of all the house.
Question arises, tumult and debate—
But all in vain—the true ring could no more
Be then distinguished than—(*after a pause, in which he awaits the
Sultan's reply*) the true faith now.

    Saladin.   Is that your answer to my question?

    Nathan. No!
But it may serve as my apology.
I cannot venture to decide between
Rings which the father had expressly made,
To baffle those who would distinguish them.

    Saladin.   Rings, Nathan! Come, a truce to this! The creeds
Which I have named have broad, distinctive marks,
Differing in raiment, food, and drink!

    Nathan. 'Tis true!
But then they differ not in their foundation.
Are not all built on history alike,
Traditional or written? History
Must be received on trust. Is it not so?
In whom are we most likely to put trust?
In our own people? in those very men
Whose blood we are? who, from our earliest youth,
Have proved their love for us, have ne'er deceived,
Except in cases where 'twere better so?
Why should I credit my forefathers less
Than you do yours? or can I ask of you
To charge your ancestors with falsehood, that
The praise of truth may be bestowed on mine?
And so of Christians.

    Saladin.   By our Prophet's faith,
The man is right. I have no more to say.

    Nathan. Now let us to our rings once more return.
We said the sons complained; each to the judge
Swore from his father's hand immediately
To have received the ring—as was the case—
In virtue of a promise that he should
One day enjoy the ring's prerogative.
In this they spoke the truth. Then each maintained
It was not possible that to himself
His father had been false. Each could not think

779

His father guilty of an act so base.
Rather than that, reluctant as he was
To judge his brethren, he must yet declare
Some treach'rous act of falsehood had been done.

   Saladin. Well! and the judge? I'm curious now to hear
What you will make him say. Go on, go on!

   Nathan. The judge said: If the father is not brought
Before my seat, I cannot judge the case.
Am I to judge enigmas? Do you think
That the true ring will here unseal its lips?
But, hold! You tell me that the real ring
Enjoys the secret power to make the man
Who wears it, both by God and man beloved.
Let that decide. Who of the three is loved
Best by his brethren? Is there no reply?
What! do these love-exciting rings alone
Act inwardly? Have they no outward charm?
Does each one love himself alone? You're all
Deceived deceivers. All your rings are false.
The real ring, perchance, has disappeared;
And so your father, to supply the loss,
Has caused three rings to fill the place of one.

   Saladin. O, charming, charming!

   Nathan. And, the judge continued,
If you insist on judgment, and refuse
My counsel, be it so. I recommend
That you consider how the matter stands.
Each from his father has received a ring:
Let each then think the real ring his own.
Your father, possibly, desired to free
His power from one ring's tyrannous control.
He loved you all with an impartial love,
And equally, and had no inward wish
To prove the measure of his love for one
By pressing heavily upon the rest.
Therefore, let each one imitate this love;
So, free from prejudice, let each one aim
To emulate his brethren in the strife
To prove the virtues of his several ring,
By offices of kindness and of love,
And trust in God. And if, in years to come,

780

The virtues of the ring shall reappear
Amongst your children, then, once more
Come to this judgment seat. A greater far
Than I shall sit upon it, and decide.
So spake the modest judge.

    Saladin. O God, O God!

    Nathan. And if now, Saladin, you think you're he——

    Saladin (*approaches* Nathan *and takes his hand, which he retains to the end of the scene*). This promised judge— I? Dust! I? —Naught! O God!

    Nathan. What is the matter, Sultan?

    Saladin. Dearest Nathan!
That judge's thousand years are not yet past;
His judgment seat is not for me. But go,
And still remain my friend.

    Nathan. Has Saladin aught else to say?

    Saladin. No.

    Nathan. Nothing?

    Saladin. Truly nothing.

    Nathan. I could have wished
An opportunity to ask a boon.

    Saladin. Wait not for opportunity. Speak now.

    Nathan. I have been trav'ling, and am just returned
From a long journey, from collecting debts.
Hard cash is troublesome these perilous times,
I know not where I may bestow it safely.
These coming wars need money; and, perchance,
You can employ it for me, Saladin?

    Saladin. (*fixing his eyes upon Nathan*). I ask not, Nathan, have you seen Al-Hafi?
Nor if some shrewd suspicion of your own
Moves you to make this offer.

    Nathan. What suspicion?

    Saladin. I do not ask—forgive me,—it is just,
For what avails concealment? I confess
I was about——

    Nathan. To ask this very thing?

    Saladin. Yes!

    Nathan. Then our objects are at once fulfilled.

SINCLAIR LEWIS

SINCLAIR LEWIS (American, 1885-1951). The satirist of American middle-
class life. After six early novels, achieved recognition with *Main Street*, followed by *Babbitt, Arrowsmith, Dodsworth.* Later work less effective, except
for *It Can't Happen Here,* exposing perils of Fascism. First American to win
Nobel Prize in Literature, 1930.

YOUNG MAN AXELBROD

THE cottonwood is a tree of a slovenly and plebeian habit. Its
woolly wisps turn gray the lawns and engender neighborhood
hostilities about our town. Yet it is a mighty tree, a refuge and an
inspiration; the sun flickers in its towering foliage, whence the
tattoo of locusts enlivens our dusty summer afternoons. From the
wheat country out to the sagebrush plains between the buttes and
the Yellowstone it is the cottonwood that keeps a little grateful
shade for sweating homesteaders.

In Joralemon we call Knute Axelbrod "Old Cottonwood." As a
matter of fact, the name was derived not so much from the quality
of the man as from the wide grove about his gaunt white house
and red barn. He made a comely row of trees on each side of
the country road, so that a humble, daily sort of a man, driving
beneath them in his lumber wagon, might fancy himself lord of
a private avenue.

And at sixty-five Knute was like one of his own cottonwoods, his
roots deep in the soil, his trunk weathered by rain and blizzard
and baking August noons, his crown spread to the wide horizon
of day and the enormous sky of a prairie night.

This immigrant was an American even in speech. Save for a
weakness about his j's and w's, he spoke the twangy Yankee English
of the land. He was the more American because in his native
Scandinavia he had dreamed of America as a land of light. Always
through disillusion and weariness he beheld America as the world's
nursery for justice, for broad, fair towns, and eager talk; and always
he kept a young soul that dared to desire beauty.

As a lad Knute Axelbrod had wished to be a famous scholar,
to learn the ease of foreign tongues, the romance of history, to
unfold in the graciousness of wise books. When he first came to
America he worked in a sawmill all day and studied all evening.
He mastered enough book-learning to teach district school for two

terms; then, when he was only eighteen, a great-hearted pity for faded little Lena Wesselius moved him to marry her. Gay enough, doubtless, was their hike by prairie schooner to new farmlands, but Knute was promptly caught in a net of poverty and family. From eighteen to fifty-eight he was always snatching children away from death or the farm away from mortgages.

He had to be content—and generously content he was—with the second-hand glory of his children's success and, for himself, with pilfered hours of reading—that reading of big, thick, dismal volumes of history and economics which the lone mature learner chooses. Without ever losing his desire for strange cities and the dignity of towers he stuck to his farm. He acquired a half-section, free from debt, fertile, well-stocked, adorned with a cement silo, a chicken-run, a new windmill. He became comfortable, secure, and then he was ready, it seemed, to die; for at sixty-three his work was done, and he was unneeded and alone.

His wife was dead. His sons had scattered afar, one a dentist in Fargo, another a farmer in the Golden Valley. He had turned over his farm to his daughter and son-in-law. They had begged him to live with them, but Knute refused.

"No," he said, "you must learn to stand on your own feet. I vill not give you the farm. You pay me four hundred dollars a year rent, and I live on that and vatch you from my hill."

On a rise beside the lone cottonwood which he loved best of all his trees Knute built a tar-paper shack, and here he "bached it"; cooked his meals, made his bed, sometimes sat in the sun, read many books from the Joralemon library, and began to feel that he was free of the yoke of citizenship which he had borne all his life.

For hours at a time he sat on a backless kitchen chair before the shack, a wide-shouldered man, white-bearded, motionless; a seer despite his grotesquely baggy trousers, his collarless shirt. He looked across the miles of stubble to the steeple of the Jackrabbit Forks church and meditated upon the uses of life. At first he could not break the rigidity of habit. He rose at five, found work in cleaning his cabin and cultivating his garden, had dinner exactly at twelve, and went to bed by afterglow. But little by little he discovered that he could be irregular without being arrested. He stayed abed till seven or even eight. He got a large, deliberate, tortoise-shell cat, and played games with it; let it lap milk upon the table,

called it the Princess, and confided to it that he had a "sneaking idee" that men were fools to work so hard. Around this coatless old man, his stained waistcoat flapping about a huge torso, in a shanty of rumpled bed and pine table covered with sheets of food-daubed newspaper, hovered all the passionate aspiration of youth and the dreams of ancient beauty.

He began to take long walks by night. In his necessitous life night had ever been a period of heavy slumber in close rooms. Now he discovered the mystery of the dark; saw the prairies wide-flung and misty beneath the moon, heard the voices of grass and cottonwoods and drowsy birds. He tramped for miles. His boots were dew-soaked, but he did not heed. He stopped upon hillocks, shyly threw wide his arms, and stood worshiping the naked, slumbering land.

These excursions he tried to keep secret, but they were bruited abroad. Neighbors, good, decent fellows with no sense about walking in the dew at night, when they were returning late from town, drunk, lashing their horses and flinging whisky bottles from racing democrat wagons, saw him, and they spread the tidings that Old Cottonwood was "getting nutty since he gave up his farm to that son-in-law of his and retired. Seen the old codger wandering around at midnight. Wish I had his chance to sleep. Wouldn't catch me out in the night air."

Any rural community from Todd Center to Seringapatam is resentful of any person who varies from its standard, and is morbidly fascinated by any hint of madness. The countryside began to spy on Knute Axelbrod, to ask him questions, and to stare from the road at his shack. He was sensitively aware of it, and inclined to be surly to inquisitive acquaintances. Doubtless that was the beginning of his great pilgrimage.

As a part of the general wild license of his new life—really, he once roared at that startled cat, the Princess: "By gollies! I ain't going to brush my teeth tonight. All my life I've brushed 'em, and alvays vanted to skip a time vunce"—Knute took considerable pleasure in degenerating in his taste in scholarship. He wilfully declined to finish *The Conquest of Mexico*, and began to read light novels borrowed from the Joralemon library. So he rediscovered the lands of dancing and light wines, which all his life he had desired. Some economics and history he did read, but every evening he would stretch out in his buffalo-horn chair, his feet on the cot

and the Princess in his lap, and invade Zenda or fall in love with Trilby.

Among the novels he chanced upon a highly optimistic story of Yale in which a worthy young man "earned his way through" college, stroked the crew, won Phi Beta Kappa, and had the most entertaining, yet moral, conversations on or adjacent to "the dear old fence."

As a result of this chronicle, at about three o'clock one morning, when Knute Axelbrod was sixty-four years of age, he decided that he would go to college. All his life he had wanted to. Why not do it?

When he awoke he was not so sure about it as when he had gone to sleep. He saw himself as ridiculous, a ponderous, oldish man among clean-limbed youths, like a dusty cottonwood among silver birches. But for months he wrestled and played with that idea of a great pilgrimage to the Mount of Muses; for he really supposed college to be that sort of place. He believed that all college students, except for the wealthy idlers, burned to acquire learning. He pictured Harvard and Yale and Princeton as ancient groves set with marble temples, before which large groups of Grecian youths talked gently about astronomy and good government. In his picture they never cut classes or ate.

With a longing for music and books and graciousness such as the most ambitious boy could never comprehend, this thick-faced farmer dedicated himself to beauty, and defied the unconquerable power of approaching old age. He sent for college catalogues and school books, and diligently began to prepare himself for college.

He found Latin irregular verbs and the whimsicalities of algebra fiendish. They had nothing to do with actual life as he had lived it. But he mastered them; he studied twelve hours a day, as once he had plodded through eighteen hours a day in the hayfield. With history and English he knew much of them from his recreative reading. From German neighbors he had picked up enough Platt-deutsch to make German easy. The trick of study began to come back to him from his small school teaching of forty-five years before. He began to believe that he could really put it through. He kept assuring himself that in college, with rare and sympathetic instructors to help him, there would not be this baffling search, this nervous strain.

But the unreality of the things he studied did disillusion him, and

785

he tired of his new game. He kept it up chiefly because all his life he had kept up onerous labor without any taste for it. Toward the autumn of the second year of his eccentric life he no longer believed that he would ever go to college.

Then a busy little grocer stopped him on the street in Joralemon and quizzed him about his studies, to the delight of the informal club which always loafs at the corner of the hotel.

Knute was silent, but dangerously angry. He remembered just in time how he had once laid wrathful hands upon a hired man, and somehow the man's collar bone had been broken. He turned away and walked home, seven miles, still boiling. He picked up the Princess, and, with her mewing on his shoulder, tramped out again to enjoy the sunset.

He stopped at a reedy slough. He gazed at a hopping plover without seeing it. Suddenly he cried:

"I am going to college. It opens next veek. I t'ink that I can pass the examinations."

Two days later he had moved the Princess and his sticks of furniture to his son-in-law's house, had bought a new slouch hat, a celluloid collar and a solemn suit of black, had wrestled with God in prayer through all of a star-clad night, and had taken the train for Minneapolis, on the way to New Haven.

While he stared out of the car window Knute was warning himself that the millionaires' sons would make fun of him. Perhaps they would haze him. He bade himself avoid all these sons of Belial and cleave to his own people, those who "earned their way through."

At Chicago he was afraid with a great fear of the lightning flashes that the swift crowds made on his retina, the batteries of ranked motor cars that charged at him. He prayed, and ran for his train to New York. He came at last to New Haven.

Not with gibing rudeness, but with politely quizzical eyebrows, Yale received him, led him through entrance examinations, which after sweaty plowing with the pen, he barely passed, and found for him a roommate. The roommate was a large-browed soft white grub named Ray Gribble, who had been teaching school in New England and seemed chiefly to desire college training so that he might make more money as a teacher. Ray Gribble was a hustler, he instantly got work tutoring the awkward son of a steel man, and for board he waited on table.

He was Knute's chief acquaintance. Knute tried to fool himself into thinking he liked the grub, but Ray couldn't keep his damp

786

hands off the old man's soul. He had the skill of a professional exhorter of young men in finding out Knute's motives, and when he discovered that Knute had a hidden desire to sip at gay, polite literature, Ray said in a shocked way:

"Strikes me a man like you, that's getting old, ought to be thinking more about saving your soul than about all these frills. You leave this poetry and stuff to these foreigners and artists, and you stick to Latin and math. and the Bible. I tell you, I've taught school, and I've learned by experience."

With Ray Gribble, Knute lived grubbily, an existence of torn comforters and smelly lamp, of lexicons and logarithm tables. No leisurely loafing by fireplaces was theirs. They roomed in West Divinity, where gather the theologues, the lesser sort of law students, a whimsical genius or two, and a horde of unplaced freshmen and "scrub seniors."

Knute was shockingly disappointed, but he stuck to his room because outside of it he was afraid. He was a grotesque figure, and he knew it, a white-polled giant squeezed into a small seat in a classroom, listening to instructors younger than his own sons. Once he tried to sit on the fence. No one but "ringers" sat on the fence any more, and at the sight of him trying to look athletic and young, two upper-class men snickered, and he sneaked away.

He came to hate Ray Gribble and his voluble companions of the submerged tenth of the class, the hewers of tutorial wood. It is doubtless safer to mock the flag than to question that best-established tradition of our democracy—that those who "earn their way through" college are necessarily stronger, braver, and more assured of success than the weaklings who talk by the fire. Every college story presents such a moral. But tremblingly the historian submits that Knute discovered that waiting on table did not make lads more heroic than did football or happy loafing. Fine fellows, cheerful and fearless, were many of the boys who "earned their way," and able to talk to richer classmates without fawning; but just as many of them assumed an abject respectability as the most convenient pose. They were pickers up of unconsidered trifles; they toadied to the classmates whom they tutored; they wriggled before the faculty committee on scholarships; they looked pious at Dwight Hall prayer-meetings to make an impression on the serious minded; and they drank one glass of beer at Jake's to show the light minded that they meant nothing offensive by their piety. In revenge for cringing to the insolent athletes whom they tutored, they would,

787

when safe among their own kind, yammer about the "lack of democracy of college today." Not that they were so indiscreet as to do anything about it. They lacked the stuff of really rebellious souls. Knute listened to them and marveled. They sounded like young hired men talking behind his barn at harvest time.

This submerged tenth hated the dilettantes of the class even more than they hated the bloods. Against one Gilbert Washburn, a rich esthete with more manner than any freshman ought to have, they raged righteously. They spoke of seriousness and industry till Knute, who might once have desired to know lads like Washburn, felt ashamed of himself as a wicked, wasteful old man.

Humbly though he sought, he found no inspiration and no comradeship. He was the freak of the class, and aside from the submerged tenth, his classmates were afraid of being "queered" by being seen with him.

As he was still powerful, one who could take up a barrel of pork on his knees, he tried to find friendship among the athletes. He sat at Yale Field, watching the football tryouts, and tried to get acquainted with the candidates. They stared at him and answered his questions grudgingly—beefy youths who in their simple-hearted way showed that they considered him plain crazy.

The place itself began to lose the haze of magic through which he had first seen it. Earth is earth, whether one sees it in Camelot or Joralemon or on the Yale campus—or possibly even in the Harvard yard! The buildings ceased to be temples to Knute; they became structures of brick or stone, filled with young men who lounged at windows and watched him amusedly as he tried to slip by.

The Gargantuan hall of Commons became a tri-daily horror because at the table where he dined were two youths who, having uncommonly penetrating minds, discerned that Knute had a beard, and courageously told the world about it. One of them, named Atchison, was a superior person, very industrious and scholarly, glib in mathematics and manners. He despised Knute's lack of definite purpose in coming to college. The other was a play-boy, a wit and a stealer of street signs, who had a wonderful sense for a subtle jest; and his references to Knute's beard shook the table with jocund mirth three times a day. So these youths of gentle birth drove the shambling, wistful old man away from Commons, and thereafter he ate at the lunch counter at the Black Cat.

Lacking the stimulus of friendship, it was the harder for Knute to keep up the strain of studying the long assignments. What had been a week's pleasant reading in his shack was now thrown at him as a day's task. But he would not have minded the toil if he could have found one as young as himself. They were all so dreadfully old, the money-earners, the serious laborers at athletics, the instructors who worried over their life work of putting marks in class-record books.

Then, on a sore, bruised day, Knute did meet one who was young.

Knute had heard that the professor who was the idol of the college had berated the too-earnest lads in his Browning class, and insisted that they read *Alice in Wonderland*. Knute floundered dustily about in a second-hand bookshop till he found an "Alice," and he brought it home to read over his lunch of a hot-dog sandwich. Something in the grave absurdity of the book appealed to him, and he was chuckling over it when Ray Gribble came into the room and glanced at the reader.

"Huh!" said Mr. Gribble.

"That's a fine, funny book," said Knute.

"Huh! *Alice in Wonderland!* I've heard of it. Silly nonsense. Why don't you read something really fine, like Shakespeare or *Paradise Lost?*"

"Vell——" said Knute, all he could find to say.

With Ray Gribble's glassy eye on him, he could no longer roll and roar with the book. He wondered if indeed he ought not to be reading Milton's pompous anthropological misconceptions. He went unhappily out to an early history class, ably conducted by Blevins, Ph.D.

Knute admired Blevins, Ph.D. He was so tubbed and eyeglassed and terribly right. But most of Blevins' lambs did not like Blevins. They said he was a "crank." They read newspapers in his class and covertly kicked one another.

In the smug, plastered classroom, his arm leaning heavily on the board tablet-arm of his chair, Knute tried not to miss one of Blevins' sardonic proofs that the correct date of the second marriage of Themistocles was two years and seven days later than the date assigned by that illiterate ass, Frutari of Padua. Knute admired young Blevins' performance, and he felt virtuous in application to these hard, unnonsensical facts.

He became aware that certain lewd fellows of the lesser sort were

playing poker just behind him. His prairie-trained ear caught whispers of "Two to dole," and "Raise you two beans." Knute revolved, and frowned upon these mockers of sound learning. As he turned back he was aware that the offenders were chuckling, and continuing their game. He saw that Blevins, Ph.D., perceived that something was wrong; he frowned, but he said nothing. Knute sat in meditation. He saw Blevins as merely a boy. He was sorry for him. He would do the boy a good turn.

When class was over he hung about Blevins' desk till the other students had clattered out. He rumbled:

"Say, Professor, you're a fine fellow. I do something for you. If any of the boys make themselves a nuisance, you yust call on me, and I spank the son of a guns."

Blevins, Ph.D., spake in a manner of culture and nastiness:

"Thanks so much, Axelbrod, but I don't fancy that will ever be necessary. I am supposed to be a reasonably good disciplinarian. Good day. Oh, one moment. There's something I've been wishing to speak to you about. I do wish you wouldn't try quite so hard to show off whenever I call on you during quizzes. You answer at such needless length, and you smile as though there were something highly amusing about me. I'm quite willing to have you regard me as a humorous figure, privately, but there are certain classroom conventions, you know, certain little conventions."

"Why, Professor!" wailed Knute, "I never make fun of you! I didn't know I smile. If I do, I guess it's yust because I am so glad when my stupid old head gets the lesson good."

"Well, well, that's very gratifying, I'm sure. And if you will be a little more careful——"

Blevins, Ph.D., smiled a toothy, frozen smile, and trotted off to the Graduates' Club, to be witty about old Knute and his way of saying "yust," while in the deserted classroom Knute sat chill, an old man and doomed. Through the windows came the light of Indian summer; clean, boyish cries rose from the campus. But the lover of autumn smoothed his baggy sleeve, stared at the blackboard, and there saw only the gray of October stubble about his distant shack. As he pictured the college watching him, secretly making fun of him and his smile, he was now faint and ashamed, now bull-angry. He was lonely for his cat, his fine chair of buffalo horns, the sunny doorstep of his shack, and the understanding land. He had been in college for about one month.

Before he left the classroom he stepped behind the instructor's desk and looked at an imaginary class.

"I might have stood there as a prof if I could have come earlier," he said softly to himself.

Calmed by the liquid autumn gold that flowed through the streets, he walked out Whitney Avenue toward the butte-like hill of East Rock. He observed the caress of the light upon the scarped rock, heard the delicate music of leaves, breathed in air pregnant with tales of old New England. He exulted: " 'Could write poetry now if yust—if I yust could write poetry!"

He climbed to the top of East Rock, whence he could see the Yale buildings like the towers of Oxford, and see Long Island Sound, and the white glare of Long Island beyond the water. He marveled that Axelbrod of the cottonwood country was looking across an arm of the Atlantic to New York state. He noticed a freshman on a bench at the edge of the rock, and he became irritated. The freshman was Gilbert Washburn, the snob, the dilettante, of whom Ray Gribble had once said: "That guy is the disgrace of the class. He doesn't go out for anything, high stand or Dwight Hall or anything else. Thinks he's so doggone much better than the rest of the fellows that he doesn't associate with anybody. Thinks he's literary, they say, and yet he doesn't even heel the 'Lit,' like the regular literary fellows! Got no time for a loafing, mooning snob like that."

As Knute stared at the unaware Gil, whose profile was fine in outline against the sky, he was terrifically public-spirited and disapproving and that sort of moral thing. Though Gil was much too well dressed, he seemed moodily discontented.

"What he needs is to vork in a threshing crew and sleep in the hay," grumbled Knute almost in the virtuous manner of Gribble. "Then he vould know when he vas vell off, and not look like he had the earache. Pff!" Gil Washburn rose, trailed toward Knute, glanced at him, sat down on Knute's bench.

"Great view!" he said. His smile was eager.

That smile symbolized to Knute all the art of life he had come to college to find. He tumbled out of his moral attitude with ludicrous haste, and every wrinkle of his weathered face creased deep as he answered:

"Yes: I t'ink the Acropolis must be like this here."

"Say, look here, Axelbrod; I've been thinking about you."

791

"Yas?"

"We ought to know each other. We two are the class scandal. We came here to dream, and these busy little goats like Atchison and Giblets, or whatever your roommate's name is, think we're fools not to go out for marks. You may not agree with me, but I've decided that you and I are precisely alike."

"What makes you t'ink I come here to dream?" bristled Knute.

"Oh, I used to sit near you at Commons and hear you try to quell old Atchison whenever he got busy discussing the reasons for coming to college. That old, moth-eaten topic! I wonder if Cain and Abel didn't discuss it at the Eden Agricultural College. You know, Abel the markgrabber, very pious and high stand, and Cain wanting to read poetry."

"Yes," said Knute, "and I guess Prof. Adam say, 'Cain, don't you read this poetry; it von't help you in algebry.'"

"Of course. Say, wonder if you'd like to look at this volume of Musset I was sentimental enough to lug up here today. Picked it up when I was abroad last year."

From his pocket Gil drew such a book as Knute had never seen before, a slender volume, in a strange language, bound in hand-tooled crushed levant, an effeminate bibelot over which the prairie farmer gasped with luxurious pleasure. The book almost vanished in his big hands. With a timid forefinger he stroked the levant, ran through the leaves.

"I can't read it, but that's the kind of book I alvays t'ought there must be some like it," he sighed.

"Listen!" cried Gil. "Ysaye is playing up at Hartford tonight. Let's go hear him. We'll trolley up. Tried to get some of the fellows to come, but they thought I was a nut."

What an Ysaye was, Knute Axelbrod had no notion; but "Sure!" he boomed.

When they got to Hartford they found that between them they had just enough money to get dinner, hear Ysaye from gallery seats, and return only as far as Meriden. At Meriden Gil suggested:

"Let's walk back to New Haven, then. Can you make it?"

Knute had no knowledge as to whether it was four miles or forty back to the campus, but "Sure!" he said. For the last few months he had been noticing that, despite his bulk, he had to be careful, but tonight he could have flown.

In the music of Ysaye, the first real musician he had ever heard,

Knute had found all the incredible things of which he had slowly been reading in William Morris and "Idylls of the King." Tall knights he had beheld, and slim princesses in white samite, the misty gates of forlorn towns, and the glory of the chivalry that never was.

They did walk, roaring down the road beneath the October moon, stopping to steal apples and to exclaim over silvered hills, taking a puerile and very natural joy in chasing a profane dog. It was Gil who talked, and Knute who listened, for the most part; but Knute was lured into tales of the pioneer days, of blizzards, of harvesting, and of the first flame of the green wheat. Regarding the Atchisons and Gribbles of the class both of them were youthfully bitter and supercilious. But they were not bitter long, for they were atavisms tonight. They were wandering minstrels, Gilbert the troubadour with his man-at-arms.

They reached the campus at about five in the morning. Fumbling for words that would express hs feeling, Knute stammered:

"Vell, it vas fine. I go to bed now and I dream about——"

"Bed? Rats! Never believe in winding up a party when it's going strong. Too few good parties. Besides, it's only the shank of the evening. Besides, we're hungry. Besides—oh, besides! Wait here a second. I'm going up to my room to get some money, and we'll have some eats. Wait! Please do!"

Knute would have waited all night. He had lived almost seventy years and traveled fifteen hundred miles and endured Ray Gribble to find Gil Washburn.

Policemen wondered to see the celluloid-collared old man and the expensive-looking boy rolling arm in arm down Chapel Street in search of a restaurant suitable to poets. They were all closed.

"The Ghetto will be awake by now," said Gil. "We'll go buy some eats and take 'em up to my room. I've got some tea there."

Knute shouldered through dark streets beside him as naturally as though he had always been a nighthawk, with an aversion to anything as rustic as beds. Down on Oak Street, a place of low shops, smoky lights and alley mouths, they found the slum already astir. Gil contrived to purchase boxed biscuits, cream cheese, chicken-loaf, a bottle of cream. While Gil was chaffering, Knute stared out into the street milkily lighted by wavering gas and the first feebleness of coming day; he gazed upon Kosher signs and advertisements in Russian letters, shawled women and bearded

rabbis; and as he looked he gathered contentment which he could never lose. He had traveled abroad tonight.

The room of Gil Washburn was all the useless, pleasant things Knute wanted it to be. There was more of Gil's Paris days in it than of his freshmanhood: Persian rugs, a silver tea service, etchings, and books. Knute Axelbrod of the tar-paper shack and piggy farmyards gazed in satisfaction. Vast, bearded, sunk in an easy chair, he clucked amiably while Gil lighted a fire.

Over supper they spoke of great men and heroic ideals. It was good talk, and not unspiced with lively references to Gribble and Atchison and Blevins, all asleep now in their correct beds. Gil read snatches of Stevenson and Anatole France; then at last he read his own poetry.

It does not matter whether that poetry was good or bad. To Knute it was a miracle to find one who actually wrote it.

The talk grew slow, and they began to yawn. Knute was sensitive to the lowered key of their Indian-summer madness, and he hastily rose. As he said good-by he felt as though he had but to sleep a little while and return to his unending night of romance.

But he came out of the dormitory upon day. It was six-thirty of the morning, with a still, hard light upon red-brick walls.

"I can go to his room plenty times now; I find my friend," Knute said. He held tight the volume of Musset, which Gil had begged him to take.

As he started to walk the few steps to West Divinity Knute felt very tired. By daylight the adventure seemed more and more incredible.

As he entered the dormitory he sighed heavily:

"Age and youth, I guess they can't team together long." As he mounted the stairs he said: "If I saw the boy again, he vould get tired of me. I tell him all I got to say." And as he opened his door, he added: "This is what I come to college for—this one night. I go avay before I spoil it."

He wrote a note to Gil, and began to pack his telescope. He did not even wake Ray Gribble, sonorously sleeping in the stale air.

At five that afternoon, on the day coach of a westbound train, an old man sat smiling. A lasting content was in his eyes, and in his hands a small book in French.

LIN HO-CHING

LIN HO-CHING (Chinese, 967-1028). A rustic word painter of the Sung Period. Received classical Chinese education. Due to delicate health, retired to home in the country. Also a skillful painter, fond of plum trees. Poetry simple, serene, refined.

MAKING A POEM ON MY DEAR PLUM BLOSSOM

All these years I have been the owner of this pretty garden,
And have never written a poem to my beloved plum blossom.
Patiently I wait for your buds to open and bloom.
The moon has shed her light upon you many times.
The lonely scene is always reflected in the moonlight.
Still prettier looks the evening landscape in the falling snow.
Let me only talk about your pure scent, and I never feel lonely
    and sad,
For I am always singing and drinking to keep you company.

WEST LAKE

How wonderful and skillful is the universal spirit!
Though itself shapeless, it has formed the West Lake
Like a beautiful picture painted on a screen.
In Spring its water is purer than the eyes of a monk.
A greenish-blue sheen is spread like a veil over the evening hills.

My hut's white-washed walls reflect the moving shadow of a fish.
A crane's feather drops upon the dewy orchid.
The boat drifts along to the sounds of a flute.
In gentle breeze and slanting rain these are vague and distant.

THE SHADOWS OF SPRING

It looks like rain. This is the time for meditation.
When drunk I enjoy lying in the shadows in Spring.
It is so cold that I pity myself and the swallow.
I fear the pear blossoms cannot endure this cold night breeze.
My thin curtain cannot keep off the chilly wind.

795

Even a far-playing flute saddens me.
In the garden and fields a bitter wind blows.
And the fragrant flowers seem to sense the danger.

IN RETREAT

Few people pass through my humble door.
My hut lies near by the tree-covered hills.
When I fish at evening a lake breeze refreshes me.
The scent of sun-warmed Spring flowers makes me drowsy.
Little by little the moss becomes like a smooth cloth.
Bolstering the edges of the rock
Why stand so many people by the cave?
Perhaps they wait for an immortal there.

LI PO

LI PO (Chinese, 701-762). Greatest of the Chinese lyricists. A wandering, melancholy troubadour. Occasionally accepted employment—for two years a court poet. Imprisoned briefly for involvement in a rebellion just before death. His lyrics the model for spontaneous romantic verse in China. Poetry gives impression that he lived for the moment, intoxicated by nature, wine or love.

WEEP NOT, YOUNG WOMEN

It is always in sad Autumn that our enemies sweep down from their mountains to invade us.

The trumpets summon the warriors! They will ride on till they reach the Great Wall, and then they will ride beyond it out on the great Kobi desert.

There, only the cold bare moon. Only cold beads of dew on swords and shields. How they shiver!

Weep not, young women . . . this is no time to start your weeping. Who knows how long that you must weep?

796

THE FISHERMAN

The earth has swallowed the snow. Again we see the plum-trees in blossom.

The new willow-leaves are gold, the waters of the lakes are silver.

Now the butterflies powdered with gold lay velvet heads within the hearts of flowers.

In his still boat the fisherman pulls up his dripping net, rippling the still water.

He thinks of a girl at home, like a dark swallow in the nest. He think of a girl at home, waiting like a swallow for her mate.

BIRDS SINGING AT DUSK

The cool wind of evening blows bird-song to the window where a maiden sits. She is embroidering bright flowers on a piece of silk.

Her head is raised; her work falls through her fingers; her thoughts have flown to him who is away.

"A bird can easily find its mate among the leaves, but all a maiden's tears, falling like rain from Heaven, will not bring back her distant lover."

She bends again to her embroidery: "I will weave a little verse among these flowers of his robe . . . perhaps he will read it and come back again."

PICKING THE LOTUS

My boat is rising and falling underneath the harvest moon. Drifting alone on the Southern Lake, I reach to pick the white flowers of the lotus.

Fierce desire pulls me . . . I yearn to tell them of my passion. Alas, my boat floats away at the mercy of the moving current. My heart looks back in sadness.

When you were but a schoolboy
  And I a little lass,
You used to walk on bamboo stilts—
  I peeped to see you pass.
We were such merry children
  In the village of Chang-kan,
But now I am a woman
  And now you are a man.

I'd scarce seen fourteen summers
  When I was made your wife;
I could not raise my eyes to yours,
  Afraid of love and life.
I hid in dusky corners,
  I came not at your call,
But ere the year was ended
  Love overshadowed all.

I thought that you were steadfast
  As the lover by the stream
Who waited in the rising tide
  The lady of his dream;
But now I stand awatching
  On my terrace all alone
Like her who watched and waited
  Until she turned to stone.

You travel to the whirlpools
  And even to Chu-tang
Where chattering monkeys climb the cliff;
  I wait here in Chang-kan.
I watch your fading footprints,
  Now overgrown with green,
And though I sweep and sweep them
  They keep their mossy sheen.

Sere in my western garden
  The autumn leafage lies;
Yellow with August sunshine
  Flit pairing butterflies.

I watch them as they hover
 From bending grass to grass,
And my heart is wrung with weeping
 When I see them pass.

I've sat so long with sorrow
 My red cheeks lose their red.
Send me a letter from afar
 By tireless rider sped:
Let me but know in season
 Your boat is going through
The three grim Gorges of the West,
 And I will come to you.

I'll come as far to meet you
 As ever you may say;
The treacherous sands of the Chang-fang,
 They shall not bar my way.
No danger, toil or trouble
 Shall keep me as I go,
For now I am a woman
 And I love you so.

PASSIONATE GRIEF
A lady weeping in the night

She who rolls up her pearl-hung shade
 Is fair as any,
Yet drawn with grief are her delicate brows,
 Frail moth antennae.

Hot tears course down her cheeks—
 How fast they flow!—
But why, ah, we in the street
 Will never know.

799

LI SHANG-YIN

LI SHANG-YIN (Chinese, 813-858). Imaginative allegorist, who had undistinguished public career but high literary reputation. Poems formal in style, suffused with personal feeling. Many of them love poems, headed "No Title."

Part I. THE MAN

In how many folds of scented gauze patterned with phoenix tails
    is the round jade top of your awning enclosed for the night?
(Though) you have a fan like a full moon, yet your blushes find
    it hard to hide behind it.
The carts rumble by to a sound like thunder and so many words
    cannot reach you.
Otherwise it is quiet and still and the golden lamp has burnt low.
There is no word that can pass from where you are to where I am,
    where the pomegranate flowers are red.
The dappled horse is tethered to the weeping willow on the bank
Whither in the south west could we go trusting to a favorable wind?

Part II. THE WOMAN

Up here behind fold upon fold of curtains is my Mo-ch'ou Hall
After a long night the early dawn creeps slowly along.
It was in a dream that the fairy girl lived on the banks (of a river).
The small maiden who lived by the bridge after all (managed to)
    live without a husband.
The wind and waves do not realize how weak are the stems of the
    water chestnut.

A POEM WITH NO TITLE

It seems only last night that the stars shone and the wind blew;
Your quarters were at the painted tower in the west,
Mine in the pavilion of the cinnamon tree hall in the east.
Alas, to-day, I am no coloured phoenix that can fly to you with
    double wings,
But my mind is quick to apprehend spiritual affinity and can get
    through to you.
(On that evening) we sat opposite to each other and we amused

ourselves with sending across the hook while the spring wine was warm.

Each in our place we played "hitting the cover" to the light of red candles

Until, alas, I had to go, hearing the drum that called for the early morning audience.

Then I rode away home to the orchid tower;

Now I am like the river weed that flows this way and that.

NO TITLE

When we were able to meet it was hard enough and now we are parted for ever it is harder still;

The east wind has died down, and the hundred flowers have faded.

The silkworm of spring spins its silk up to the moment of its death;

The wax candle is burnt down to the end and only then are its tears dry.

In the morning I gaze into my mirror and grieve that my cloudy hair must change;

In the night the bright cold moon calls forth my sad songs,

(Yet after all) it is only a short road from here to paradise.

Will not the blue bird be indulgent and allow me to steal a glance.

THE INLAID ZITHER

The brocade-embroidered zither had fifty strings, no one knows why;

Each string and each support made one think of the years of one's prime.

Chuang Tzu dreamt at morning he was a butterfly.

After death, the soul of the Emperor Wang took up its brief springtime abode in the body of a nightjar,

While in the wide ocean under the bright moon the mermaids drop their tears which become pearls.

Why at Lan-t'ien in the warm sunshine does jade engender mists?

Can we hope for these kinds of portents to come again?

Or are they only things that had form once but have vanished away?

801

LIU CHI

LIU CHI (Chinese, 1311-1375). Most celebrated poet of the Mongol Period. Court adviser of first Ming Emperor. Prolific poet and author of philosophic dialogues. Poems distinguished by charm and feeling for beauty rather than by depth.

THE CONVENT OF SIANG-FU

So I sprang to horse at cockcrow all a fever to depart,
    Galloped, galloped to the convent, ere the calling bells were still,
Over dimpled lawns a zephyr woke the lily's jewelled heart,
    And the moon's faint crescent faltered down the cleft of wooded hill.
Oh the lonely little convent with its secret haunts of prayer!
    With its shadowed cells for dreaming, where eternities abide.
Down the cedar-scented alley not a footfall stirred the air,
    But the monks' low droning echoed in the green gloom far and wide.

NIGHT, SORROW, AND SONG

The rain's in the air
And the winds arouse,
Shaking the cinnamon boughs,
And the begonias' gay parterre;
Raising dust and wreathing mist,
Whirling all things where they list—
Leaves in many-coloured showers,
Bright petals of innumerable flowers.
Knocking at all doors their hustling
Sets the silken curtains rustling,
Till, as shrunken draughts, they creep
Into the shrouded halls of sleep,
Raise the hair and ruck the skin
Of the startled folk therein.

I am grown weary of my lonely state,
Tired of the tongueless hours that wait,
Dreaming of her whom skies of blue
And twilight æons hid from view.

802

Swiftly the waters take their flight
Grandly the mountains rise,
Yon birds that taper to the skies
Why have they lost their plumage bright?
Would they might bear my messages of love!
Alas! the trackless heav'ns unroll above;
From west to east the river flows,
But the waves return not to my calling;
Once more the rare magnolia blows,
But hour by hour her flowers are falling.
My jasper lyre is laid apart,
Hushed for a while the lute of jade;
I hear the beating of my heart,
And watch the moon lean down the glade.

Then, ere the shadows wane,
Out of the night's unrest
Ballad and old refrain
Lure me to seek again
The dream-built Isles of the Blest.

JACK LONDON

JACK LONDON (American, 1876-1916). Novelist, adventurer and utopian. An illegitimate child, worked for his living as a boy in California. Joined Klondike gold rush without making fortune. After *The Call of the Wild,* became one of most popular writers of his day. Wrote over 50 books inspired by faith in socialism. Well-known works: *The Sea Wolf, White Fang, Martin Eden.*

TO BUILD A FIRE

DAY HAD broken cold and grey, exceedingly cold and grey, when the man turned aside from the main Yukon trail and climbed the high earth-bank, where a dim and little-travelled trail led eastward through the fat spruce timberland. It was a steep bank, and he paused for breath at the top, excusing the act to himself by looking at his watch. It was nine o'clock. There was no sun nor a hint of

sun, though there was not a cloud in the sky. It was a clear day, and yet there seemed an intangible pall over the face of things, a subtle gloom that made the day dark, and that was due to the absence of sun. This fact did not worry the man. He was used to the lack of sun. It had been days since he had seen the sun, and he knew that a few more days must pass before that cheerful orb, due south, would just peep above the sky-line and dip immediately from view.

The man flung a look back along the way he had come. The Yukon lay a mile wide and hidden under three feet of ice. On top of this ice were as many feet of snow. It was all pure white, rolling in gentle undulations where the ice-jams of the freeze-up had formed. North and south, as far as his eye could see, it was unbroken white, save for a dark hair-line that curved and twisted from around the spruce-covered island to the south, and that curved and twisted away into the north, where it disappeared behind another spruce-covered island. This dark hair-line was the trail—the main trail—that led south five hundred miles to the Chilkoot Pass, Dyea, and salt water; and that led north seventy miles to Dawson, and still on to the north a thousand miles to Nulato, and finally to St. Michael on Bering Sea, a thousand miles and a half a thousand more.

But all this—the mysterious, far-reaching hair-line trail, the absence of sun from the sky, the tremendous cold, and the strangeness and weirdness of it all—made no impression on the man. It was not because he was long used to it. He was a newcomer in the land, a *chechaquo*, and this was his first winter. The trouble with him was that he was without imagination. He was quick and alert in the things of life, but only in the things, and not in the significances. Fifty degrees below zero meant eighty-odd degrees of frost. Such fact impressed him as being cold and uncomfortable, and that was all. It did not lead him to meditate upon his frailty as a creature of temperature, and upon man's frailty in general, able only to live within certain narrow limits of heat and cold; and from there on it did not lead him to the conjectural field of immortality and man's place in the universe. Fifty degrees below zero stood for a bite of frost that hurt and that must be guarded against by the use of mittens, ear-flaps, warm moccasins, and thick socks. Fifty degrees below zero was to him just precisely fifty degrees below zero. That there should be anything more to it than that was a thought that never entered his head.

As he turned to go on, he spat speculatively. There was a sharp, explosive crackle that startled him. He spat again. And again, in the

air, before it could fall to the snow, the spittle crackled. He knew that at fifty below spittle crackled on the snow, but this spittle had crackled in the air. Undoubtedly it was colder than fifty below—how much colder he did not know. But the temperature did not matter. He was bound for the old claim on the left fork of Henderson Creek, where the boys were already. They had come over across the divide from the Indian Creek country, while he had come the roundabout way to take a look at the possibilities of getting out logs in the spring from the islands in the Yukon. He would be in to camp by six o'clock; a bit after dark, it was true, but the boys would be there, a fire would be going, and a hot supper would be ready. As for lunch, he pressed his hand against the protruding bundle under his jacket. It was also under his shirt, wrapped up in a handkerchief and lying against the naked skin. It was the only way to keep the biscuits from freezing. He smiled agreeably to himself as he thought of those biscuits, each cut open and sopped in bacon grease, and each enclosing a generous slice of fried bacon.

He plunged in among the big spruce trees. The trail was faint. A foot of snow had fallen since the last sled had passed over, and he was glad he was without a sled, travelling light. In fact, he carried nothing but the lunch wrapped in the handkerchief. He was surprised, however, at the cold. It certainly was cold, he concluded, as he rubbed his numb nose and cheek-bones with his mittened hand. He was a warm-whiskered man, but the hair on his face did not protect the high cheek-bones and the eager nose that thrust itself aggressively into the frosty air.

At the man's heels trotted a dog, a big native husky, the proper wolf-dog, grey-coated and without any visible or temperamental difference from its brother, the wild wolf. The animal was depressed by the tremendous cold. It knew that it was no time for travelling. Its instinct told it a truer tale than was told to the man by the man's judgment. In reality, it was not merely colder than fifty below zero; it was colder than sixty below, than seventy below. It was seventy-five below zero. Since the freezing-point is thirty-two above zero, it meant that one hundred and seven degrees of frost obtained. The dog did not know anything about thermometers. Possibly in its brain there was no sharp consciousness of a condition of very cold such as was in the man's brain. But the brute had its instincts. It experienced a vague but menacing apprehension that subdued it and made it slink along at the man's heels, and that made it question eagerly every unwonted movement of the man as if expecting him to go into camp

or to seek shelter somewhere and build a fire. The dog had learned fire, and it wanted fire, or else to burrow under the snow and cuddle its warmth away from the air.

The frozen moisture of its breathing had settled on its fur in a fine powder of frost, and especially were its jowls, muzzle, and eye-lashes whitened by its crystalled breath. The man's red beard and mustache were likewise frosted, but more solidly, the deposit taking the form of ice and increasing with every warm, moist breath he exhaled. Also, the man was chewing tobacco, and the muzzle of ice held his lips so rigidly that he was unable to clear his chin when he expelled the juice. The result was that a crystal beard of the color and solidity of amber was increasing its length on his chin. If he fell down it would shatter itself, like glass, into brittle fragments. But he did not mind the appendage. It was the penalty all tobacco-chewers paid in that country, and he had been out before in two cold snaps. They had not been so cold as this, he knew, but by the spirit thermometer at Sixty Mile he knew they had been registered at fifty below and at fifty-five.

He held on through the level stretch of woods for several miles, crossed a wide flat of nigger-heads, and dropped down a bank to the frozen bed of a small stream. This was Henderson Creek, and he knew he was ten miles from the forks. He looked at his watch. It was ten o'clock. He was making four miles an hour, and he calculated that he would arrive at the forks at half-past twelve. He decided to celebrate that event by eating his lunch there.

The dog dropped in again at his heels, with a tail drooping dis-couragement, as the man swung along the creek-bed. The furrow of the old sled-trail was plainly visible, but a dozen inches of snow covered the marks of the last runners. In a month no man had come up or down that silent creek. The man held steadily on. He was not much given to thinking, and just then particularly he had nothing to think about save that he would eat lunch at the forks and that at six o'clock he would be in camp with the boys. There was nobody to talk to; and, had there been, speech would have been impossible be-cause of the ice-muzzle on his mouth. So he continued monotonously to chew tobacco and to increase the length of his amber beard.

Once in a while the thought reiterated itself that it was very cold and that he had never experienced such cold. As he walked along he rubbed his cheek-bones and nose with the back of his mittened hand. He did this automatically, now and again changing hands. But rub as he would, the instant he stopped his cheek-bones went numb, and

the following instant the end of his nose went numb. He was sure to frost his cheeks; he knew that, and experienced a pang of regret that he had not devised a nose-strap of the sort Bud wore in cold snaps. Such a strap passed across the cheeks, as well, and saved them. But it didn't matter much, after all. What were frosted cheeks? A bit painful, that was all; they were never serious.

Empty as the man's mind was of thoughts, he was keenly observant, and he noticed the changes in the creek, the curves and bends and timber-jams, and always he sharply noted where he placed his feet. Once, coming around a bend, he shied abruptly, like a startled horse, curved away from the place where he had been walking, and retreated several paces back along the trail. The creek he knew was frozen clear to the bottom,—no creek could contain water in that arctic winter,—but he knew also that there were springs that bubbled out from the hillsides and ran along under the snow and on top the ice of the creek. He knew that the coldest snaps never froze these springs, and he knew likewise their danger. They were traps. They hid pools of water under the snow that might be three inches deep, or three feet. Sometimes a skin of ice half an inch thick covered them, and in turn was covered by the snow. Sometimes there were alternate layers of water and ice-skin, so that when one broke through he kept on breaking through for a while, sometimes wetting himself to the waist.

That was why he had shied in such panic. He had felt the give under his feet and heard the crackle of a snow-hidden ice-skin. And to get his feet wet in such a temperature meant trouble and danger. At the very least it meant delay, for he would be forced to stop and build a fire, and under its protection to bare his feet while he dried his socks and moccasins. He stood and studied the creek-bed and its banks, and decided that the flow of water came from the right. He reflected awhile, rubbing his nose and cheeks, then skirted to the left, stepping gingerly and testing the footing for each step. Once clear of the danger, he took a fresh chew of tobacco and swung along at his four-mile gait.

In the course of the next two hours he came upon several similar traps. Usually the snow above the hidden pools had a sunken, candied appearance that advertised the danger. Once again, however, he had a close call; and once, suspecting danger, he compelled the dog to go on in front. The dog did not want to go. It hung back until the man shoved it forward, and then it went quickly across the white, unbroken surface. Suddenly it broke through, floundered to one side,

and got away to firmer footing. It had wet its forefeet and legs, and almost immediately the water that clung to it turned to ice. It made quick efforts to lick the ice off its legs, then dropped down in the snow and began to bite out the ice that had formed between the toes. This was a matter of instinct. To permit the ice to remain would mean sore feet. It did not know this. It merely obeyed the mysterious prompting that arose from the deep crypts of its being. But the man knew, having achieved a judgment on the subject, and he removed the mitten from his right hand and helped tear out the ice-particles. He did not expose his fingers more than a minute, and was astonished at the swift numbness that smote them. It certainly was cold. He pulled on the mitten hastily, and beat the hand savagely across his chest.

At twelve o'clock the day was at its brightest. Yet the sun was too far south on its winter journey to clear the horizon. The bulge of the earth intervened between it and Henderson Creek, where the man walked under a clear sky at noon and cast no shadow. At half-past twelve, to the minute, he arrived at the forks of the creek. He was pleased at the speed he had made. If he kept it up, he would certainly be with the boys by six| He unbuttoned his jacket and shirt and drew forth his lunch. The action consumed no more than a quarter of a minute, yet in that brief moment the numbness laid hold of the exposed fingers. He did not put the mitten on, but, instead, struck the fingers a dozen sharp smashes against his leg. Then he sat down on a snow-covered log to eat. The sting that followed upon the striking of his fingers against his leg ceased so quickly that he was startled. He had had no chance to take a bite of biscuit. He struck the fingers repeatedly and returned them to the mitten, baring the other hand for the purpose of eating. He tried to take a mouthful, but the ice-muzzle prevented. He had forgotten to build a fire and thaw out. He chuckled at his foolishness, and as he chuckled he noted the numbness creeping into the exposed fingers. Also, he noted that the stinging which had first come to his toes when he sat down was already passing away. He wondered whether the toes were warm or numb. He moved them inside the moccasins and decided that they were numb.

He pulled the mitten on hurriedly and stood up. He was a bit frightened. He stamped up and down until the stinging returned into the feet. It certainly was cold, was his thought. That man from Sulphur Creek had spoken the truth when telling how cold it sometimes got in the country. And he had laughed at him at the time!

That showed one must not be too sure of things. There was no mistake about it, it *was* cold. He strode up and down, stamping his feet and threshing his arms, until reassured by the returning warmth. Then he got out matches and proceeded to make a fire. From the undergrowth, where high water of the previous spring had lodged a supply of seasoned twigs, he got his fire-wood. Working carefully from a small beginning, he soon had a roaring fire, over which he thawed the ice from his face and in the protection of which he ate his biscuits. For the moment the cold of space was outwitted. The dog took satisfaction in the fire, stretching out close enough for warmth and far enough away to escape being singed.

When the man had finished, he filled his pipe and took his comfortable time over a smoke. Then he pulled on his mittens, settled the earflaps of his cap firmly about his ears, and took the creek trail up the left fork. The dog was disappointed and yearned back toward the fire. This man did not know cold. Possibly all the generations of his ancestry had been ignorant of cold, of real cold, of cold one hundred and seven degrees below freezing-point. But the dog knew; all its ancestry knew, and it had inherited the knowledge. And it knew that it was not good to walk abroad in such fearful cold. It was the time to lie snug in a hole in the snow and wait for a curtain of cloud to be drawn across the face of outer space whence this cold came. On the other hand, there was no keen intimacy between the dog and the man. The one was the toil-slave of the other, and the only caresses it had ever received were the caresses of the whip-lash and of harsh and menacing throat-sounds that threatened the whiplash. So the dog made no effort to communicate its apprehension to the man. It was not concerned in the welfare of the man; it was for its own sake that it yearned back toward the fire. But the man whistled, and spoke to it with the sound of whip-lashes, and the dog swung in at the man's heels and followed after.

The man took a chew of tobacco and proceeded to start a new amber beard. Also, his moist breath quickly powdered with white his mustache, eyebrows, and lashes. There did not seem to be so many springs on the left fork of the Henderson, and for half an hour the man saw no signs of any. And then it happened. At a place where there were no signs, where the soft, unbroken snow seemed to advertise solidity beneath, the man broke through. It was not deep. He wet himself halfway to the knees before he floundered out to the firm crust.

He was angry, and cursed his luck aloud. He had hoped to get

809

into camp with the boys at six o'clock, and this would delay him an hour, for he would have to build a fire and dry out his foot-gear. This was imperative at that low temperature—he knew that much; and he turned aside to the bank, which he climbed. On top, tangled in the underbrush about the trunks of several small spruce trees, was a high-water deposit of dry fire-wood—sticks and twigs, principally, but also larger portions of seasoned branches and fine, dry, last-year's grasses. He threw down several large pieces on top of the snow. This served for a foundation and prevented the young flame from drowning itself in the snow it otherwise would melt. The flame he got by touching a match to a small shred of birch-bark that he took from his pocket. This burned even more readily than paper. Placing it on the foundation, he fed the young flame with wisps of dry grass and with the tiniest dry twigs.

He worked slowly and carefully, keenly aware of his danger. Gradually, as the flame grew stronger, he increased the size of the twigs with which he fed it. He squatted in the snow, pulling the twigs out from their entanglement in the brush and feeding directly to the flame. He knew there must be no failure. When it is seventy-five below zero, a man must not fail in his first attempt to build a fire—that is, if his feet are wet. If his feet are dry, and he fails, he can run along the trail for half a mile and restore his circulation. But the circulation of wet and freezing feet cannot be restored by running when it is seventy-five below. No matter how fast he runs, the wet feet will freeze the harder.

All this the man knew. The old timer on Sulphur Creek had told him about it the previous fall, and now he was appreciating the advice. Already all sensation had gone out of his feet. To build the fire he had been forced to remove his mittens, and the fingers had quickly gone numb. His pace of four miles an hour had kept his heart pumping blood to the surface of his body and to all the ex-tremities. But the instant he stopped, the action of the pump eased down. The cold of space smote the unprotected tip of the planet, and he, being on that unprotected tip, received the full force of the blow. The blood of his body recoiled before it. The blood was alive, like the dog, and like the dog it wanted to hide away and cover itself up from the fearful cold. So long as he walked four miles an hour, he pumped that blood, willy-nilly, to the surface; but now it ebbed away and sank down into the recesses of his body. The extremities were the first to feel its absence. His wet feet froze the faster, and his exposed fingers numbed the faster, though they had not yet be-

gun to freeze. Nose and cheeks were already freezing, while the skin of all his body chilled as it lost its blood.

But he was safe. Toes and nose and cheeks would be only touched by the frost, for the fire was beginning to burn with strength. He was feeding it with twigs the size of his finger. In another minute he would be able to feed it with branches the size of his wrist, and then he could remove his wet foot-gear, and, while it dried, he could keep his naked feet warm by the fire, rubbing them at first, of course, with snow. The fire was a success. He was safe. He remembered the advice of the old-timer on Sulphur Creek, and smiled. The old-timer had been very serious in laying down the law that no man must travel alone in the Klondike after fifty below. Well, here he was; he had had the accident; he was alone; and he had saved himself. Those old-timers were rather womanish, some of them, he thought. All a man had to do was to keep his head, and he was all right. Any man who was a man could travel alone. But it was surprising, the rapidity with which his cheeks and nose were freezing. And he had not thought his fingers could go lifeless in so short a time. Lifeless they were, for he could scarcely make them move together to grip a twig, and they seemed remote from his body and from him. When he touched a twig, he had to look and see whether or not he had hold of it. The wires were pretty well down between him and his finger-ends.

All of which counted for little. There was the fire, snapping and crackling and promising life with every dancing flame. He started to untie his moccasins. They were coated with ice; the thick German socks were like sheaths of iron halfway to the knees; and the moccasin strings were like rods of steel all twisted and knotted as by some conflagration. For a moment he tugged with his numb fingers, then, realizing the folly of it, he drew his sheath-knife.

But before he could cut the strings, it happened. It was his own fault or, rather, his mistake. He should not have built the fire under the spruce tree. He should have built it in the open. But it had been easier to pull the twigs from the brush and drop them directly on the fire. Now the tree under which he had done this carried a weight of snow on its boughs. No wind had blown for weeks, and each bough was fully freighted. Each time he had pulled a twig he had communicated a slight agitation to the tree—an imperceptible agitation, so far as he was concerned, but an agitation sufficient to bring about the disaster. High up in the tree one bough capsized its load of snow. This fell on the boughs beneath, capsizing them. This process continued, spreading out and involving the whole tree.

It grew like an avalanche, and it descended without warning upon the man and the fire, and the fire was blotted out! Where it had burned was a mantle of fresh and disordered snow.

The man was shocked. It was as though he had just heard his own sentence of death. For a moment he sat and stared at the spot where the fire had been. Then he grew very calm. Perhaps the old-timer on Sulphur Creek was right. If he had only had a trail-mate he would have been in no danger now. The trail-mate could have built the fire. Well, it was up to him to build the fire over again, and this second time there must be no failure. Even if he succeeded, he would most likely lose some toes. His feet must be badly frozen by now, and there would be some time before the second fire was ready.

Such were his thoughts, but he did not sit and think them. He was busy all the time they were passing through his mind. He made a new foundation for a fire, this time in the open, where no treacherous tree could blot it out. Next, he gathered dry grasses and tiny twigs from the high-water flotsam. He could not bring his fingers together to pull them out, but he was able to gather them by the handful. In this way he got many rotten twigs and bits of green moss that were undesirable, but it was the best he could do. He worked methodically, even collecting an armful of the larger branches to be used later when the fire gathered strength. And all the while the dog sat and watched him, a certain yearning wistfulness in its eyes, for it looked upon him as the fire-provider, and the fire was slow in coming.

When all was ready, the man reached in his pocket for a second piece of birch-bark. He knew the bark was there, and, though he could not feel it with his fingers, he could hear its crisp rustling as he fumbled for it. Try as he would, he could not clutch hold of it. And all the time, in his consciousness, was the knowledge that each instant his feet were freezing. This thought tended to put him in a panic, but he fought against it and kept calm. He pulled on his mittens with his teeth, and threshed his arms back and forth, beating his hands with all his might against his sides. He did this sitting down, and he stood up to do it; and all the while the dog sat in the snow, its wolf-brush of a tail curled around warmly over its fore-feet, its sharp wolf-ears pricked forward intently as it watched the man. And the man as he beat and threshed with his arms and hands, felt a great surge of envy as he regarded the creature that was warm and secure in its natural covering.

After a time he was aware of the first far-away signals of sensa-

tion in his beaten fingers. The faint tingling grew stronger till it evolved into a stinging ache that was excruciating, but which the man hailed with satisfaction. He stripped the mitten from his right hand and fetched forth the birch-bark. The exposed fingers were quickly going numb again. Next he brought out his bunch of sulphur matches. But the tremendous cold had already driven the life out of his fingers. In his effort to separate one match from the others, the whole bunch fell in the snow. He tried to pick it out of the snow, but failed. The dead fingers could neither touch nor clutch. He was very careful. He drove the thought of his freezing feet, and nose, and cheeks, out of his mind, devoting his whole soul to the matches. He watched, using the sense of vision in place of that of touch, and when he saw his fingers on each side the bunch, he closed them—that is, he willed to close them, for the wires were down, and the fingers did not obey. He pulled the mitten on the right hand, and beat it fiercely against his knee. Then, with both mittened hands, he scooped the bunch of matches, along with much snow, into his lap. Yet he was no better off.

After some manipulation he managed to get the bunch between the heels of his mittened hands. In this fashion he carried it to his mouth. The ice crackled and snapped when by a violent effort he opened his mouth. He drew the lower jaw in, curled the upper lip out of the way, and scraped the bunch with his upper teeth in order to separate a match. He succeeded in getting one, which he dropped on his lap. He was no better off. He could not pick it up. Then he devised a way. He picked it up in his teeth and scratched it on his leg. Twenty times he scratched before he succeeded in lighting it. As it flamed he held it with his teeth to the birch-bark. But the burning brimstone went up his nostrils and into his lungs, causing him to cough spasmodically. The match fell into the snow and went out.

The old-timer on Sulphur Creek was right, he thought in the moment of controlled despair that ensued; after fifty below, a man should travel with a partner. He beat his hands, but failed in exciting any sensation. Suddenly he bared both his hands, removing the mittens with his teeth. He caught the whole bunch between the heels of his hands. His arm-muscles not being frozen enabled him to press the hand-heels tightly against the matches. Then he scratched the bunch along his leg. It flared into flame, seventy sulphur matches at once! There was no wind to blow them out. He kept his head to one side to escape the strangling fumes, and held the blazing bunch to the birch-bark. As he so held it, he became aware of sensation

813

in his hand. His flesh was burning. He could smell it. Deep down below the surface he could feel it. The sensation developed into pain that grew acute. And still he endured it, holding the flame of the matches clumsily to the bark that would not light readily because his own burning hands were in the way, absorbing most of the flame.

At last, when he could endure no more, he jerked his hands apart. The blazing matches fell sizzling into the snow, but the birch-bark was alight. He began laying dry grasses and the tiniest twigs on the flame. He could not pick and choose, for he had to lift the fuel between the heels of his hands. Small pieces of rotten wood and green moss clung to the twigs, and he bit them off as well as he could with his teeth. He cherished the flame carefully and awkwardly. It meant life, and it must not perish. The withdrawal of blood from the surface of his body now made him begin to shiver, and he grew more awkward. A large piece of green moss fell squarely on the little fire. He tried to poke it out with his fingers, but his shivering frame made him poke too far, and he disrupted the nucleus of the little fire, the burning grasses and tiny twigs separating and scattering.He tried to poke them together again, but in spite of the tenseness of the effort, his shivering got away with him, and the twigs were hopelessly scattered. Each twig gushed a puff of smoke and went out. The fire-provider had failed. As he looked apathetically about him, his eyes chanced on the dog, sitting across the ruins of the fire from him, in the snow, making restless, hunching movement, slightly lifting one forefoot and then the other, shifting its weight back and forth on them with wistful eagerness.

The sight of the dog put a wild idea into his head. He remembered the tale of the man, caught in a blizzard, who killed a steer and crawled inside the carcass, and so was saved. He would kill the dog and bury his hands in the warm body until the numbness went out of them. Then he could build another fire. He spoke to the dog, calling it to him; but in his voice was a strange note of fear that frightened the animal, who had never known the man to speak in such way before. Something was the matter, and its suspicious nature sensed danger—it knew not what danger, but somewhere, somehow, in its brain arose an apprehension of the man. It flattened its ears down at the sound of the man's voice, and its restless, hunching movements and the liftings and shiftings of its forefeet became more pronounced; but it would not come to the man. He got on his hands and knees and crawled toward the dog. This

814

unusual posture again excited suspicion, and the animal sidled mincingly away.

The man sat up in the snow for a moment and struggled for calmness. Then he pulled on his mittens, by means of his teeth, and got upon his feet. He glanced down at first in order to assure himself that he was really standing up, for the absence of sensation in his feet left him unrelated to the earth. His erect position in itself started to drive the webs of suspicion from the dog's mind; and when he spoke peremptorily, with the sound of whip-lashes in his voice, the dog rendered its customary allegiance and came to him. As it came within reaching distance, the man lost his control. His arms flashed out to the dog, and he experienced genuine surprise when he discovered that his hands could not clutch, that there was neither bend nor feeling in the fingers. He had forgotten for the moment that they were frozen and that they were freezing more and more. All this happened quickly, and before the animal could get away, he encircled its body with his arms. He sat down in the snow, and in this fashion held the dog, while it snarled and whined and struggled.

But it was all he could do, hold its body encircled in his arms and sit there. He realized that he could not kill the dog. There was no way to do it. With his helpless hands he could neither draw nor hold his sheathknife nor throttle the animal. He released it, it plunged wildly away, with tail between its legs, and still snarling. It halted forty feet away and surveyed him curiously, with ears sharply pricked forward. The man looked down at his hands in order to locate them, and found them hanging on the ends of his arms. It struck him as curious that one should have to use his eyes in order to find out where his hands were. He began threshing his arms back and forth, beating the mittened hands against his sides. He did this for five minutes, violently, and his heart pumped enough blood up to the surface to put a stop to his shivering. But no sensation was aroused in the hands. He had an impression that they hung like weights on the ends of his arms, but when he tried to run the impression down, he could not find it.

A certain fear of death, dull and oppressive, came to him. This fear quickly became poignant as he realized that it was no longer a mere matter of freezing his fingers and toes, or of losing his hands and feet, but that it was a matter of life and death with the chances against him. This threw him into a panic, and he turned and ran

815

up the creek-bed along the old dim trail. The dog joined in behind and kept up with him. He ran blindly, without intention, in fear such as he had never known in his life. Slowly, as he ploughed and floundered through the snow, he began to see things again,—the banks of the creek, the old timber-jams, the leafless aspens, and the sky. The running made him feel better. He did not shiver. Maybe, if he ran on, his feet would thaw out; and, anyway, if he ran far enough, he would reach camp and the boys. Without doubt he would lose some fingers and toes and some of his face; but the boys would take care of him, and save the rest of him when he got there. And at the same time there was another thought in his mind that said he would never get to the camp and the boys; that it was too many miles away, that the freezing had too great a start on him, and that he would soon be stiff and dead. This thought he kept in the background and refused to consider. Sometimes it pushed itself forward and demanded to be heard, but he thrust it back and strove to think of other things.

It struck him as curious that he could run at all on feet so frozen that he could not feel them when they struck the earth and took the weight of his body. He seemed to himself to skim along above the surface, and to have no connection with the earth. Somewhere he had once seen a winged Mercury, and he wondered if Mercury felt as he felt when skimming over the earth.

His theory of running until he reached camp and the boys had one flaw in it: he lacked the endurance. Several times he stumbled, and finally he tottered, crumpled up, and fell. When he tried to rise, he failed. He must sit and rest, he decided, and next time he would merely walk and keep on going. As he sat and regained his breath, he noted that he was feeling quite warm and comfortable. He was not shivering, and it even seemed that a warm glow had come to his chest and trunk. And yet, when he touched his nose or cheeks, there was no sensation. Running would not thaw them out. Nor would it thaw out his hands and feet. Then the thought came to him that the frozen portions of his body must be extending. He tried to keep this thought down, to forget it, to think of something else; he was aware of the panicky feeling that it caused, and he was afraid of the panic. But the thought asserted itself, and persisted, until it produced a vision of his body totally frozen. This was too much, and he made another wild run along the trail. Once he slowed down to a walk, but the thought of the freezing extending itself made him run again.

And all the time the dog ran with him, at his heels, When he fell down a second time, it curled its tail over its forefeet and sat in front of him, facing him, curiously eager and intent. The warmth and security of the animal angered him, and he cursed it till it flattened down its ears appeasingly. This time the shivering came more quickly upon the man. He was losing in his battle with the frost. It was creeping into his body from all sides. The thought of it drove him on, but he ran no more than a hundred feet, when he staggered and pitched headlong. It was his last panic. When he had recovered his breath and control, he sat up and entertained in his mind the conception of meeting death with dignity. However, the conception did not come to him in such terms. His idea of it was that he had been making a fool of himself, running around like a chicken with its head cut off—such was the simile that occurred to him. Well he was bound to freeze anyway, and he might as well take it decently. With this new-found peace of mind came the first glimmerings of drowsiness. A good idea, he thought, to sleep off to death. It was like taking an anaesthetic. Freezing was not so bad as people thought. There were lots worse ways to die.

He pictured the boys finding his body next day. Suddenly he found himself with them, coming along the trail and looking for himself. And, still with them, he came around a turn in the trail and found himself lying in the snow. He did not belong with himself any more, for even then he was out of himself, standing with the boys and looking at himself in the snow. It certainly was cold, was his thought. When he got back to the States he could tell the folks what real cold was. He drifted on from this to a vision of the old-timer on Sulphur Creek. He could see him quite clearly, warm and comfortable, and smoking a pipe.

"You were right, old hoss; you were right," the man mumbled to the old timer of Sulphur Creek.

Then the man drowsed off into what seemed to him the most comfortable and satisfying sleep he had ever known. The dog sat facing him and waiting. The brief day drew to a close in a long, slow twilight. There were no signs of a fire to be made, and, besides, never in the dog's experience had it known a man to sit like that in the snow and make no fire. As the twilight drew on, its eager yearning for the fire mastered it, and with a great lifting and shifting of forefeet, it whined softly, then flattened its ears down in anticipation of being chided by the man. But the man remained silent. Later, the dog whined loudly. And still later it crept close to

the man and caught the scent of death. This made the animal bristle and back away. A little longer it delayed, howling under the stars that leaped and danced and shone brightly in the cold sky. Then it turned and trotted up the trail in the direction of the camp it knew, where were the other food-providers and fire-providers.

HENRY WADSWORTH LONGFELLOW

HENRY WADSWORTH LONGFELLOW (American, 1807-1882). At one time (possibly still) America's most popular poet. After traveling abroad, took professorship at Harvard. Verses combined the romantic, the sentimental, and the ethical in a proportion that instantly caught popular taste. Famous narrative poems: *Evangeline, The Song of Hiawatha, The Courtship of Miles Standish.* Later critics prefer less-known lyrics, which show true poetic gift.

MY LOST YOUTH

Often I think of the beautiful town
    That is seated by the sea;
Often in thought go up and down
The pleasant streets of that dear old town,
    And my youth comes back to me.
        And a verse of a Lapland song
        Is haunting my memory still:
        "A boy's will is the wind's will,
And the thoughts of youth are long, long thoughts."

I can see the shadowy lines of its trees,
    And catch, in sudden gleams,
The sheen of the far-surrounding seas,
And islands that were the Hesperides
    Of all my boyish dreams.
        And the burden of that old song,
        It murmurs and whispers still:
        "A boy's will is the wind's will,
And the thoughts of youth are long, long thoughts."

I remember the black wharves and the slips,
    And the sea-tides tossing free;

818

And Spanish sailors with bearded lips,
And the beauty and mystery of the ships,
   And the magic of the sea.
     And the voice of that wayward song
     Is singing and saying still:
     "A boy's will is the wind's will,
And the thoughts of youth are long, long thoughts."

I remember the bulwarks by the shore,
   And the fort upon the hill;
The sunrise gun, with its hollow roar,
The drum-beat repeated o'er and o'er,
   And the bugle wild and shrill.
     And the music of that old song
     Throbs in my memory still:
     "A boy's will is the wind's will,
And the thoughts of youth are long, long thoughts."

I remember the sea-fight far away,
   How it thundered o'er the tide!
And the dead captains, as they lay
In their graves, o'erlooking the tranquil bay
   Where they in battle died.
     And the sound of that mournful song
     Goes through me with a thrill:
     "A boy's will is the wind's will,
And the thoughts of youth are long, long thoughts."

I can see the breezy dome of groves,
   The shadows of Deering's Woods;
And the friendships old and the early loves
Come back with a Sabbath sound, as of doves
   In quiet neighborhoods.
     And the verse of that sweet old song,
     It flutters and murmurs still:
     "A boy's will is the wind's will,
And the thoughts of youth are long, long thoughts."

I remember the gleams and glooms that dart
   Across the school-boy's brain;
The song and the silence in the heart,

That in part are prophecies, and in part
  Are longings wild and vain.
    And the voice of that fitful song
    Sings on, and is never still:
    "A boy's will is the wind's will,
And the thoughts of youth are long, long thoughts."

There are things of which I may not speak;
  There are dreams that cannot die;
There are thoughts that make the strong heart weak,
And bring a pallor into the cheek,
  And a mist before the eye.
    And the words of that fatal song
    Come over me like a chill:
    "A boy's will is the wind's will,
And the thoughts of youth are long, long thoughts."

Strange to me now are the forms I meet
  When I visit the dear old town;
But the native air is pure and sweet,
And the trees that o'ershadow each well-known street,
  As they balance up and down,
    Are singing the beautiful song,
    Are sighing and whispering still:
    "A boy's will is the wind's will,
And the thoughts of youth are long, long thoughts."

And Deering's Woods are fresh and fair,
  And with joy that is almost pain
My heart goes back to wander there,
And among the dreams of the days that were,
  I find my lost youth again.
    And the strange and beautiful song,
    The groves are repeating it still:
    "A boy's will is the wind's will,
And the thoughts of youth are long, long thoughts."

THE SKELETON IN ARMOR

Speak! speak! thou fearful guest!
Who, with thy hollow breast

Still in rude armor drest,
    Comest to daunt me!
Wrapt not in Eastern balms,
But with thy fleshless palms
Stretched, as if asking alms,
    Why dost thou haunt me?

Then, from those cavernous eyes
Pale flashes seemed to rise,
As when the Northern skies
    Gleam in December;
And, like the water's flow
Under December's snow,
Came a dull voice of woe
    From the heart's chamber.

'I was a Viking old!
My deeds, though manifold,
No Skald in song has told,
    No Saga taught thee!
Take heed, that in thy verse
Thou dost the tale rehearse,
Else dread a dead man's curse;
    For this I sought thee.

'Far in the Northern Land,
By the wild Baltic's strand,
I, with my childish hand,
    Tamed the gerfalcon;
And, with my skates fast-bound
Skimmed the half-frozen Sound,
That the poor whimpering hound
    Trembled to walk on.

'Oft to his frozen lair
Tracked I the grisly bear,
While from my path the hare
    Fled like a shadow;
Oft through the forest dark
Followed the were-wolf's bark,
Until the soaring lark
    Sang from the meadow.

'But when I older grew,
Joining a corsair's crew,
O'er the dark sea I flew
    With the marauders.
Wild was the life we led;
Many the souls that sped,
Many the hearts that bled,
    By our stern orders.

'Many a wassail-bout
Wore the long Winter out;
Often our midnight shout
    Set the cocks crowing,
As we the Berserk's tale
Measured in cups of ale,
Draining the oaken pail,
    Filled to o'erflowing.

'Once as I told in glee
Tales of the stormy sea,
Soft eyes did gaze on me,
    Burning yet tender:
And as the white stars shine
On the dark Norway pine,
On that dark heart of mine
    Fell their soft splendor.

'I wooed the blue-eyed maid,
Yielding, yet half afraid,
And in the forest's shade
    Our vows were plighted.
Under its loosened vest
Fluttered her little breast,
Like birds within their nest
    By the hawk frighted.

'Bright in her father's hall
Shields gleamed upon the wall.
Loud sang the minstrels all,

822

Chanting his glory;
When of old Hildebrand
I asked his daughter's hand,
Mute did the minstrels stand
  To hear my story.

'While the brown ale he quaffed,
Loud then the champion laughed,
And as the wind-gusts waft
  The sea-foam brightly,
So the loud laugh of scorn,
Out of those lips unshorn,
From the deep drinking-horn
  Blew the foam lightly.

'She was a Prince's child,
I but a Viking wild,
And though she blushed and smiled,
  I was discarded!
Should not the dove so white
Follow the sea-mew's flight,
Why did they leave that night
  Her nest unguarded?

'Scarce had I put to sea,
Bearing the maid with me,
Fairest of all was she
  Among the Norsemen!
When on the white sea-strand,
Waving his armed hand,
Saw we old Hildebrand,
  With twenty horsemen.

'Then launched they to the blast,
Bent like a reed each mast,
Yet we were gaining fast,
  When the wind failed us;
And with a sudden flaw
Came round the gusty Skaw,
So that our foe we saw
  Laugh as he hailed us.

'And as to catch the gale
Round veered the flapping sail,
"Death!" was the helmsman's hail,
   "Death without quarter!"
Mid-ships with iron keel
Struck we her ribs of steel;
Down her black hulk did reel
   Through the black water!

'As with his wings aslant,
Sails the fierce cormorant,
Seeking some rocky haunt,
   With his prey laden,—
So toward the open main,
Beating to sea again,
Through the wild hurricane,
   Bore I the maiden.

'Three weeks we westward bore,
And when the storm was o'er,
Cloud-like we saw the shore
   Stretching to leeward;
There for my lady's bower
Built I the lofty tower,
Which, to this very hour,
   Stands looking seaward.

"There lived we many years;
Time dried the maiden's tears;
She had forgot her fears,
   She was a mother;
Death closed her mild blue eyes,
Under that tower she lies;
Ne'er shall the sun arise
   On such another!

'Still grew my bosom then,
Still as a stagnant fen!
Hateful to me were men,
   The sunlight hateful!

In the vast forest here,
Clad in my warlike gear,
Fell I upon my spear,
    Oh, death was grateful!

'Thus, seamed with many scars,
Bursting these prison bars,
Up to its native stars
    My soul ascended!
There from the flowing bowl
Deep drinks the warrior's soul,
Skoal! to the Northland! *skoal!*'
    Thus the tale ended.

FEDERICO GARCIA LORCA

FEDERICO GARCIA LORCA (Spanish, 1899-1936). Best-known contemporary Spanish poet and dramatist. Fiery anti-Fascist, executed during the Spanish Civil War. Folklorist, musician, lecturer, amateur painter. As a dramatist, dealt with primitive passions: trilogy—*Bodas de Sangre, Yerma, La Casa de Bernarda Alba*. Poetry, in translation: *Lament for the Death of a Bullfighter, The Poet in New York, Poems.*

JOURNEY

A hundred riders in mourning,
where will they go
by the lowering sky
of the orange grove?
Neither in Cordova nor in Seville
will they appear;
nor in Granada that longs
for the sea.
Those sleepy horses
will carry them
to the labyrinth of crosses
where song trembles.
With seven piercing cries,
where will they go,
the hundred Andalusian riders
of the orange grove?

AFTER PASSING

The children gaze
at a distant point.

The candles die.
Some blind girls
question the moon,
and spirals of weeping
climb on the wind.

The mountains gaze
at a distant point.

THE SILENCE

Hear the silence, my child.
It is an undulated silence
where valleys and echoes slip,
a silence
that bows heads
to the ground.

VILLAGE

Upon the barren mountain
a Calvary.
Clear water
and centenary olive trees.
Through the narrow streets
cloaked men,
and on the towers
weathercocks turning.
Eternally
turning.
Oh lost village
in the Andalusia of tears!

SURPRISED

Left dead in the street
with a dagger in his chest.
No one knew him.
How the street lamp trembled!

826

Mother.
How the tiny lamp trembled
in the street!
Early dawn. No one
could face his eyes
open wide in the cruel wind.
Dead he was left in the street
with a dagger in his chest
and no one knew him.

AND THEN

Labyrinths
born of time
vanish.

(Only desert
remains.)

The heart,
fountain of desires,
vanishes.

(Only desert
remains.)

The illusion of dawn
and kisses
vanishes.

Only desert
remains.
Undulating
desert.

AY!

The cry leaves in the wind
a shadow of cypress.

(Leave me in this field,
weeping.)

All has been demolished in the world.
Nothing remains but silence.

(Leave me in this field,
weeping.)

The lightless horizon
is bitten with bonfires.

(I have told you, leave me
in this field,
weeping.)

LUSIN

LUSIN (Chou Shu-jen, Chinese, 1881-1936). Important leader in modern Chinese literary revolution. While a student in Japan, studied Western literature and took European ideals back to China. Forced to leave professorship at Peking National University because of radical ideas. Essays had immediate influence; 26 short stories more likely to endure. *Ah Q and Others* has been translated into many languages.

MEDICINE

IT IS autumn, and late at night, so that the moon has already gone. The sky is a sheet of darkling blue. Everything still sleeps, except those who wander in the night, and Hua Lao-shuan. He sits up suddenly in his bed; leaning over, he rubs a match and touches it to a lamp which is covered with grease. A pale greenish light flickers and reveals the two rooms of a tea house.

"Father of Hsiao-shuan, are you leaving?" queries the voice of a woman. There is a series of tearing coughs in the small room in the rear.

"M-m." Lao-shuan, listening for a moment, fastens his garment and then stretches forth a hand toward the woman. "Give it," he says.

Hua Ta-ma fumbles beneath her pillow and drags forth a small packet of silver dollars, which she hands to him. Nervously he

thrusts it into his pocket, then pats it twice, to reassure himself. He lights a paper lantern and blows out the oil lamp. Carrying the lantern, he goes into the small rear room. There is a rustle and then more coughing. When it is quiet again, Lao-shuan calls out, in an undertone: "Hsiao-shuan—don't bother getting up. The shop—your mother will see to that."

His son does not answer him, and Lao-shuan, thinking he will sleep undisturbed, goes through the low door into the street. In the blackness nothing is at first visible save a gray ribbon of path. The lantern illumines only his two feet, which move rhythmically. Dogs appear here and there, then sidle off again. None even barks. Outside, the air is cold, and it refreshes Lao-shuan, so that it seems to him he is all at once a youth, and possesses the miraculous power of touching men into life. He takes longer strides. Gradually the sky brightens, till the road is more clearly marked.

Absorbed in his walking, Lao-shuan is startled when, almost in front of him, he sees a crossroad. He stops, and then withdraws a few steps, to stand under the eaves of a shop, in front of its closed door. After a long wait, his bones are chilled.

"Unh, an old fellow?"

"High-spirited, up so early . . ."

Opening his eyes, Lao-shuan sees several people passing near him. One of them turns back and looks at him intently. He cannot distinguish the features clearly, but the man's eyes are bright with a cold, lusting gleam, eyes of famishment suddenly coming upon something edible. Looking at his lantern, Lao-shuan sees that it has gone out. He feels quickly at his pocket; the hard substance is still there. Then he peers out, and on either side of him are numerous strange people, loitering and looking oddly like ghosts in the dim light. Then he gazes fixedly at them, and gradually they do not seem unusual at all.

He discerns several soldiers among the crowd. On their coats they wear, both in front and behind, the large white circle of cloth of the government troops, which can be seen for some distance. As one draws nearer, the wine-colored border of their uniform is also evident. There is a trampling of many feet, and a large number of people gathers, little groups here and there merging swiftly into one crush that advances like the ocean's tide. Reaching the crossroad, they halt and form a semicircle, with their backs toward Lao-shuan.

Necks stretch forth from collars and incline toward the same

point, as if, like so many ducks, they are held by some invisible hand. For a moment all is still. Lao-shuan seems to hear a sound from somewhere beyond the necks. A stir sweeps through the on-lookers. With a sudden movement, they abruptly disperse. People jostle one another hurriedly, and some, pushing past Lao-shuan, almost tumble him to the ground in their haste.

"*Hai!* One hand gives the money, another hand gives the goods! " screams a man clad entirely in black, who halts before Lao-shuan. In his eyes is a metallic glitter. They resemble the bright luster of a pair of swords. They stab into Lao-shuan's soul, and his body seems to shrivel to half its normal size. The dark man thrusts one huge, empty paw at him, while in the other he offers a steamed roll, stained with a fresh and still warm red substance, drops of which trickle to the earth.

Hurriedly, Lao-shuan fumbles for his dollars. He attempts to hand them over to the black-garbed man, from whose hand slowly depend the drops of red, but somehow he cannot embolden himself to receive the saturated roll.

"What's he afraid of? Why not take it?" the fellow demands, brusque and impatient. Lao-shuan continues to hesitate until the other roughly snatches his lantern, tears off its paper shade and uses it to wrap up the roll. Then he thrusts this package into Lao-shaun's hand, and at the same time seizes the silver and gives it a cursory feel. As he turns away he murmurs, "That old fool . . ."

"And to cure what person?" Lao shuan seems to hear someone ask him. He does not reply. His attention is centered upon the package, and he embraces it as if it were the only child descended from a house of ten generations. Nothing else in the world matters, now that he is about to transplant into his own home the robust life which he holds in his hands. He hopes, thereby, to reap much happiness.

The sun lifts over the horizon. Before him, the long street leads straight into his tea house. Behind him, the light of day caresses a worn tablet at the crossroad, on which are four characters limned in faint gold: "Ancient—Pavilion—"

Lao-shuan, reaching home, finds the tea house swept clean, with the rows of tables smooth and glistening but as yet serving no customers. Only Hsiao-shuan sits alone at a table by the wall and eats his food. Large drops of sweat drip down his forehead, and his little

lined coat sticks against his sunken spine. His shoulder blades project sharply, from under his coat, so that there appears on his back, as though embossed, the character *pa*. Seeing it causes Lao-shuan to pinch his brow together. He wife emerges hastily from the kitchen, her mouth open, her lips quivering.

"Do you have it?" she asks.

"Yes, I have it."

The pair disappears into the kitchen for a time, where they consult. Then Hua Ta-ma comes hurriedly forth, goes out and in a moment returns with a dried lotus leaf, which she spreads on the table. Lao-shuan unwraps the crimson-stained roll and neatly repacks it in the sheet of lotus. Meanwhile, Hsiao-shuan has finished his meal and his mother warns him: "Sit still, Little Door-latch. Don't come here yet."

When the fire burns briskly in the mud stove, the father thrusts his little green and red parcel into the oven. There is a red and black flame. A strange odor permeates the rooms.

"*Hao.* It smells good, but is it? What are you eating?" demands Camel-Back Fifth, who arrives at this moment and sniffs the air questioningly. He is one of those who pass their days in tea houses, the first to come in the morning, the last to leave at night. Now, tumbling to a table by the lane, he sits down to make idle inquiry.

"Could it be baked rice *congee?*"

Nobody replies. Lao-shuan silently serves him boiled tea.

"Come in, Hsiao-shuan," Hua Ta-ma calls from the inner room, in the center of which she has placed a stool. The Little Door-latch sits, and his mother, saying in a low voice, "Eat it, and your sickness will vanish," hands him a plate on which is a round object, black in color.

Hsiao-shuan picks it up. For a moment he gazes at it curiously, as if he might somehow hold his own life in his hand. His heart is unspeakably moved with wonder. Very carefully, he splits the object. A jet of white vapor gushes forth, and immediately dissolves in the air. Now Hsiao-shuan sees that it is a white flour roll, broken in half. Soon it has entered his stomach, so that even the taste of it cannot be clearly remembered. In front of him there is the empty dish; on one side stands his father and, on the opposite side, his mother. Their eyes are potent with a strange look, as if they desire to pour something into him, yet at the same draw something forth. It is exciting. It is too much for Hsaio-shuan's little heart, which

831

throbs furiously. He presses his hands against his chest and begins to cough.

"Sleep a little; you'll be well."

So Hsiao-shuan coughs himself to sleep, obeying the advice of his mother. Having waited patiently till he is quiet, she drapes over him a lined quilt, which consists mostly of patches.

In the tea house are many customers, and Lao-shaun is kept engaged in his enterprise. He darts from one table to another, pouring hot water and tea, and seemingly intent on his tasks. But under his eyes are dark hollows.

"Lao-shuan," inquires a man with whiskers streaked with white, "are you not a little unwell?"

"No."

"No? But I already see that it's unlikely. Your smile now—" The bearded one contradicts himself.

"Lao-shuan is always busy. Of course if his son were—" begins Camel-Back Fifth. His remarks is interrupted by the arrival of a man whose face is massive, with distorted muscles. He wears a black cotton shirt, unbuttoned and pulled together carelessly around the waist with a broad black cloth girdle [the apparel of an executioner]. As he enters, he shouts to Lao-shuan:

"Eaten, eh? Is he well already? Lao-shuan, luck is with you! Indeed lucky! If it were not that I get news quickly—"

With the kettle in one hand and the other hanging straight beside him in an attitude of respect, Lao-shuan listens and smiles. All the guests listen with deference, and Hua Ta-ma, her eyes dark and sleepless, also comes forth and smiles, serving the new arrival some tea leaves, with the added flourish of a green olive. Lao-shuan himself fills the cup with boiling water.

"It is a guaranteed cure! Different from all others! Think of it, brought back while still warm, eaten while warm!" shouts the gentleman with the coarse face.

"Truly, were it not for Big Uncle Kan's services, how could it be—" Hua Ta-ma thanks him, in deep gratitude.

"Guaranteed cure! Guaranteed cure! Eaten up like that while still warm. A roll with human blood is an absolute cure for any kind of consumption!"

Mention of the word "consumption" seems to disconcert Hua Ta-ma; for her face suddenly turns pallid, though the smile quickly creeps back. She manages to withdraw so inconspicuouly that Big Uncle Kan still shouts with the full vigor of his lungs and does not

832

notice that she is gone till from the inner room, where Hsiao-shuan sleeps, there comes the sound of dry, raucous coughing.

"So, it is true Hsiao-shuan has come upon friendly luck. That sickness will unquestionably be cured utterly. There's no surprise in Lao-shuan's constant smiling." Thus speaks the whiskered old man, who walks toward Big Uncle Kan. "I hear," he says to the latter in a suppressed voice, "that the criminal executed today is a son of the Hsia family. Now, whose son is he? And, in fact, executed for what?"

"Whose?" demands Big Uncle. "Can he be other than the son of the fourth daughter-in-law of the Hsias? That little *tung-hsii!*" Observing that he has an alert audience, Big Uncle expands, his facial muscles become unusually active and he raises his voice to heroic heights, shouting: "The little thing did not want to live! He simply did not want life, that's all."

"And I got what from the execution this time? Not the merest profit! Even the clothes stripped from him were seized by Red Eye Ah Yi, the jailer. Our Uncle Lao-shuan was the luckiest. Second comes the Third Father of the Hsia family. He actually pocketed the reward—twenty-five ounces of silver!—all alone. He gave not so much as a single cash to anyone!"

Hsiao-shuan walks slowly from the little room, his hands pressed to his chest, and coughing without respite. He enters the kitchen, fills a bowl with cold rice and sits down at once to eat. Hua Ta-ma goes to him and inquires softly: "Hsiao-shuan, are you better? Still as hungry as ever?"

"Guaranteed cure, guaranteed!" Big Uncle Kan casts a glance at the lad but quickly turns back to the crowd and declares: "Third Father of Hsia is clever. Had he not been the first to report the matter to the official, his whole house would have been beheaded, and all their property confiscated. But instead? Silver!"

"That little tung-hsi was an altogether rotten egg. He even attempted to induce the head jailer to join the rebellion!"

"*Ai-ya!* If it were actually done, think of it," indignantly comments a youth in his twenties, sitting at a back table.

"You should know that Red Eye Ah Yi was anxious to gather some details; so he entered into conversation. 'The realm of *Ta Ching Dynasty* really belongs to us all,' he told Red Eye. Now, what do you make of that? Is it possible that such talk is actually human?

"Red Eye knew that there was only a mother in his home, but he could not believe that he was so poor that 'not a drop of oil and

833

water' could be squeezed from him. His rage already had burst his abdomen, yet the boy attempted to 'scratch the tiger's head'! Ah Yi gave him several smacks on the face."

"Ah Yi knows his boxing. His blows must have done the wretch good!" exults Camel-Back Fifth, from a corner table.

"No! Would you believe it? His worthless bones were unafraid. The fellow actually said, what is more, that it was a pity!"

Black-and-White Whiskers snorted, "What is it? How could pity be shown in beating a thing like that?"

"You've not listened well," sneers Big Uncle contemptuously. "The little tung-hsi meant to say that Ah Yi hmself was to be pitied!"

The listeners' eyes suddenly dull, and there is a pause in the conversation. Hsiao-shuan perspiring copiously, had finished his rice. His head seems to be steaming.

"So he said Red Eye should be pitied! Now, that is pure insanity!" Black-and-White Whiskers feels proudly that he has logically solved the whole matter. "Obviously, he had gone mad!"

"Gone mad," approvingly echoes the youth who spoke earlier. He too feels like a discoverer.

Equanimity is restored to the other teahouse visitors. They renew their laughing and talking. Hsiao-shuan, under cover of the confusion of sounds, seizes the opportunity to cough hoarsely, with all his emaciated strength.

Big Uncle Kan moves over to pat the child's shoulder, repeating, "Guaranteed cure, Hsiao-shuan. You mustn't cough like that. Guaranteed cure!"

"Gone mad," says Camel-Back Fifth, nodding his head.

Originally, the land adjacent to the city wall beyond the West Gate was public property. The narrow path that now cavorts through it was first made by feet seeking a short cut, which in time came to be a natural boundary line. On the left of it, as one goes out from the gate, are buried those who have been executed or have starved to death in prison. On the right are grouped the graves of the paupers. All of these graves are so numerous and closely arranged that they remind one of the sweet buns laid out in a rich man's home for a birthday celebration.

The Clear and Bright Day, when graves are visited, has dawned unusually cold, and willows have just issued new buds about the size of a half-grain of rice. Hua Ta-ma has laid out four dishes and a bowl of rice in front of a new grave on the right side, has left tears

834

over it and has burned imitation money. Now she sits dazedly on the ground, as if waiting for something, but nothing which she herself could explain. A light breeze sweeps by, and her short hair flutters. It is much grayer than last year.

Down the narrow path comes another woman, gray also, and in torn rags. She carries a worn round basket, lacquered red, with a string of paper ingots hanging from it. Now and then she halts her slow walk. Finally she notices Hua Ta-ma gazing at her, and she hesitates, embarrassed. A look of confused shame crosses her pale, melancholy face. Then, emboldening herself, she walks to a grave on the left of the path and lays down her lacquered basket.

It so happens that the grave is directly opposite Hsiao-shuan's with only the narrow path between them. Hua Ta-ma watches mechanically as the woman lays out four dishes and a bowl of rice; burns paper money and weeps. It occurs to her that in that grave also there is a woman's son. She watches curiously as the woman moves about absently and stares vacantly into space. Suddenly she sees her begin to tremble and stagger backward, as if in stupor.

Hua Ta-ma is touched. "She may be mad with sorrow," she fears. She rises, and, stepping across the path, speaks to her quietly: "Old Mother, don't grieve any more. Let us both go home." The woman nods stupidly, her eyes still staring. Suddenly she utters an exclamation, "Look! What is that?"

Looking along the woman's pointing finger, Hua Ta-ma's eyes take in the grave before them, which is unkempt and has ugly patches of yellow earth on it. Looking more closely she is startled to see, at the top of the little mound, a circlet of scarlet and white flowers.

For many years neither of them has seen clearly, and yet now both see these fresh blossoms. They are not many, but they are neatly arranged; they are not very splendid, but they are comely in an orderly way. Hua Ta-ma looks quickly at her son's grave, and at the others, but only here and there are a few scattered blossoms of blue and white that have braved the cold; there are no others of scarlet. She experiences a nameless emptiness of heart, as if in need, but of what she does not wish to know. The other walks nearer and examines the flowers closely. "What could be the explanation?" she muses.

Tears stream from her face, and she cries out: "Yü, my son! You have been wronged, but you do not forget. Is it that your heart is still full of pain, and you choose this day and this method of telling

me?" She gazes around, but, seeing only a black crow brooding in a leafless tree, she continues: "Yü, my son! It was a trap; you were 'buried alive.' Yet Heaven knows! Rest your eyes in peace, but give me a sign. If you are here in the grave, if you are listening to me, cause the crow to fly here and alight on your grave. Let me know!"

There is no more breeze, and everywhere the dry grass stands erect, like bristles of copper. A faint sound hangs in the air and vibrates, growing less and less audible, till finally it ceases entirely. Then everything becomes as quiet as death. The two old women stood motionless in the midst of the dry grass, intently watching the crow. Among the straight limbs of the tree, its head drawn in, the crow sits immobile and as if cast in iron.

Much time passes. Those who come to visit graves begin to increase in numbers. To Hua Ta-ma it seems that gradually a heavy burden lifts from her, and to the other she says, "Come, let us go."

The old woman sighs dejectedly and gathers up her offertory dishes. She lingers for still another moment, then at length walks slowly, murmuring, "What could it have been?"

When they have walked only some thirty paces they suddenly hear a sharp cry from above. "Yah-h-h." Turning round with a shudder they see the crow brace itself on a limb and then push forth, spreading its broad wings and flying like an arrow toward the far horizon.

M

ANTONIO MACHADO

ANTONIO MACHADO (Spanish, 1875-1939). Poet of the inner life. Andalusian Professor of French, who fled to France after the Spanish Civil War. Poetry of great simplicity, bare of adornment, has been compared with that of Yeats. Books: *Soledades, Campos de Castilla, Nuevas canciones.*

PERCHANCE IN DREAMS

Perchance, in dreams, the hand
of the sower of stars
struck the chords of some forgotten music

as a note of the immense lyre,
and the humble wave reached our lips
as a few simple words of truth.

IBERIAN GOD

As the gambler drew his bow
For vengeance in the song,
So the Iberian recklessly let go
A sharp shaft to the Lord of blighting wrong
Who felled his wheat with hail and killed his fruit;
But he praised the Lord who brought his crops to head
Full eared, gold to the root,
The rye and wheat that tomorrow would be his bread.

"Lord of ruin and loss,
I adore because I fear, because I wait,
But my heart is blasphemous:
Bowing to earth, I pray in pride and hate.

837

"I know Thy power, my chain I recognize,
Lord, for Thee I dig my bread in sweat and sighs;
O master of the flooding clouds that cost
So dear to summer yield,
Of the autumn drought and spring's belated frost,
Of the scorching heat that sears the harvest field.

"Lord of the bow above the tender grass
Where the white ewe grazes,
Lord of the hut undone when tempests pass
And of the fruit where the worm carves its mazes,

"Thy breathing quickens the hearth fire when it
Is low, Thy splendor ripens ruddy grain,
And on Midsummer Eve the olive pit
Forms and hardens where Thy hand has lain.

"O master of fortunes and of poverties,
Good luck and bad, who yet
Giv'st to the rich man favors and soft ease
And to the poor, his hope and bitter sweat,

"Lord, Lord, in the twelve months' whirling round
I have watched my seed with patient labor sown
Run the same risk in the hard and faithless ground
As a gambler's cash on the losing hazard thrown.

"Lord, paternal now, who wert before a God
Cruel, two-faced, Thy love with vengeance dimmed,
To Thee my prayer of blasphemy and laud
Ascends, a gambler's die cast on the wind."

This man who, insulting God, at his altar prayed,
Defiant of all fate's frowning might forbode,
With dreaming tamed the seas and highways laid
Across them, saying, He is the ocean road.

Is it not this man who raised his God to be
Above all war? Beyond
Fate, beyond earth and sea,
Beyond death and dying, free of every bond?

Did not the Iberian tree,
The encina, yield her branch for holy fire
And, burning, find unity
With God in love's pure flame on the sacred pyre?

But now, so quickly day grows into day!
There are new hearths; for these
New roses thrive in field and wooded bay
And fresh green branches on the ancient trees.

The fatherland is still
Waiting to open furrows to the plow;
For the seed of God there is a field to till
Overgrown with burdocks, thorns, and thistles now.

Day merges into day; the past is wide
To the morrow, the morrow to the infinite;
Men of Spain, no yesterday has died,
Future and past have yet no holy writ.

Did ever the Spanish God His face reveal?
My heart awaits the hand
Of an Iberian, vigorous and leal,
To carve in oaken timbers of Castile
The God austere who reigns in this brown land.

AUTUMN DAWN

A highroad's barren scar
Among the grey rock-spires
And humble pastures far
Where strong black bulls are grazing. Brambles, thickets, briars.

The dew has drenched with cold
The landscape in the dark
And the poplars' frieze of gold,
Toward the river's arc.

A hint of dawn half seen
With purple crags for frame.
Beside his greyhounds keen,
His eager gun at rest, a hunter stalking game.

AT THE BURIAL OF A FRIEND

They gave him earth, one horrible afternoon
Of the month of July, under a fiery sun.

At a step from the open sepulchre
There were roses with rotting petals
Amongst geraniums whose scent was keen
And whose flowers were red. The sky

Pure and blue. A breeze
That was strong and dry was blowing.

Suspended from the great cords,
The coffin was let down,
Heavily, to the bottom of the ditch,
By the two gravediggers. . . .

And, as it came to rest, it struck with a loud, solemn noise, in the
   silence.

The thud of a coffin on the earth is a thing
That is, absolutely, serious.

Against the black box broke
The heavy, dusty lumps of earth. . . .

The air drew its whitish breath
From the deep ditch.

—And thou, already shadowless, sleepest and restest.
Long peace to thy bones. . . .

Definitively,
Sleep thou, a quiet, and real, sleep.

POEM

The street in shadow. The high old mansions hide
The dying sun; there are echoes of light in the balconies.

Do you not see, in the charm of that flowered balcony,
The rosy oval of a face you know?

The image, behind the pane, with its equivocal reflection,
Gleams and vanishes, like an old daguerreotype.

In the street only the sound of your step is heard.
Slowly the echoes of its passing die away.

Oh, anguish. The heart grows heavy and hurts. "Is it she?"
It could not be. . . . Go on. . . . The star in the sky.

CHILDISH DREAM

A clear night
Of holiday and moonlight
Night of my dreams
Night of joy

—my soul was brightness
That, to-day, is all fog
My hair
Was not yet black—

The youngest fairy
Took me in her arms
When that joyous holiday
Burned in the square

So, in the crackling
Of the illuminations
Love wove
Its skeins of dances

And in that night
Of holiday and moonlight
Night of my dreams
Night of joy

The youngest fairy
Kissed my forehead. . . .
With her fine hand
Said her goodbyes to me

All the rose trees
Give their perfumes
All the loves
Unfold love

POEM

The loved house
In which she lived
Shows,
On a pile of rubble, ruined
And demolished
A shapeless, wooden skeleton
Black, eaten away.

The moon throws its clear light
In dreams that gleam like silver
On the windows. Ill-dressed, sad,
I walk through the old street.

MAURICE MAETERLINCK

MAURICE MAETERLINCK (Belgian, 1862-1949). Natural scientist and shadowy symbolist. Poet, dramatist and philosopher. Won first recognition as playwright: *Pelléas and Mélisande* (set to music by Debussy), *The Bluebird, Interior.* His theater permeated by sense of doom and death. In *Life of the Bee* and *Life of the Ant,* he wrote artfully on scientific matters. Nobel Prize, 1911.

THE LIFE OF THE DEAD

LAST night, I had a visit from an uncle who died about fifty years ago. During his lifetime, he was what we call a "jolly old fellow," a positive and practical mind. He told me that the cemetery which we had chosen as his quarters was cozy and well managed by one of his friends of the Great Beyond, a remarkable, decent and distinguished gravedigger. My dear uncle was feeling at home and

842

was very happy. A part of himself, in which he never had been seriously interested, had left him to go he knew not where; but all that was human, solid and well balanced had accompanied him in his new and last abode. The dead had organized, underground, small but very lively friendly, or rather brotherly gatherings, where neighbors met to talk over the happenings of the cemetery, for every day brought new arrivals, two or three dead, sometimes even one or two dozens, in the prosperous days of an epidemic. These unexpected tourists had to be received affectionately if they were relatives or friends, and with every courtesy if they were strangers. These gatherings were highly exclusive, and no one was admitted without serious investigations. A class system had spontaneously been established. The deceased were divided in three classes, that is those who, to speak as you speak up here, did not have as yet an evil smell, that is, the new arrivals whose odorless stage was rather transitory; then the ones who emitted strong exhalations, you judge disagreeable, who constituted the middle class, the most numerous, and finally the superior class, the sepulchral aristocracy, whose members were proclaimed immortal because they had ceased emitting any scent, and consisted only of bleached bones, aseptic and carefully polished.

"But, uncle," I interrupted, "why is it that you do not feel certain emanations that we deem unpleasant? Is it because you do not have a nose?"

"It is not a question of nose anymore, but a purely scientific question. There are no evil smells. It is a regrettable error of the inhabitants on the surface. All odors are chemically pure, whether they come from the lily, the rose, the violet or the gardens of the Great Beyond."

"Uncle, another question, if I may? . . ."

"Go ahead, dear, go ahead. I am here to answer you, for we know almost everything. . . ."

"Uncle, how do you receive those who have been incinerated?"

"We despise them! They are renegades, traitors, deserters. They are ashamed of death. They disavow it. They would like to abolish it; and when they come here begging for a place for their little jars of human preserves, we throw those little jars out of the window, into eternity, for we are eternal . . .

"But do not speak to me about those people. . . . When do you expect to join me?"

"I do not know yet. Do you?"

"I could know, if I wanted to, but I would not tell you. Anyhow, as soon as you arrive, let me know. I shall take you under my wing and facilitate your admission in our circles, for it involves a lot of red tape. The dead are even worse bureaucrats than the Americans, and for the most unimportant formality, such as recuperating a lost nail, a tooth, or a radius one has to go through twenty offices, give sixty signatures, disclose the first and last names of one's parents, grand-parents; produce one's birth certificate, marriage certificate, death certificate of sisters, brothers, first and other cousins. It is a deplorable habit of which we have as yet not been able to rid ourselves. It is true that it takes care of our moments of leisure which are long, although very agreeable. . . ."

"Uncle, I also would like to ask you . . ."

"Go on, go on, my child, I am at your disposal."

"What will you do when there is no more place left in your garden in the Great Beyond? It seems to be rather crowded already."

"We will take the one of the living."

"And if they do not want to give it up to you?"

"We will make dead out of them."

"Does that mean that you have the right to kill?"

"We do not have to kill them. We have only to wait. It is time which kills them."

"But uncle, what happens in case of exhumation? What happens to you? What do you feel?"

"We did not have any exhumation yet; but there has been some talk about it. . . . It is supposed to be more unpleasant than moving. You lose everything and do not find your own friendships and little schemes anymore. Happily, exhumation occurs rather seldom. . . ."

"I can see, uncle, that not even death is free of troubles."

"What do you expect, my child, all lives have their little inconveniences."

"Uncle, I would also like to ask you . . . Uncle, where are you? . . . Are not you going to answer me anymore? . . ."

I insisted in vain, I did not get an answer. He had returned into eternal silence. . . .

STEPHANE MALLARME

STÉPHANE MALLARMÉ (French, 1842-1898). Dreamlike symbolist poet. Small output, of wide influence on modern poetry. As youth studied in England, returned to France to teach English. Later celebrated for his literary soirées. His most famous poem, "Afternoon of a Faun," was inspiration for first great piece of impressionist music (by Debussy). His entire work delicate, evasive, often obscure.

THE AFTERNOON OF A FAUN

These nymphs, I would make them eternal.
   So rare,
Their delicate rose, that it drifts on the air,
Drowsy with clustering sleep.
   Did I love a dream?
My doubt, fruit of the ancient night, breaks forth
In many a subtle branch, which, on the swell
Of the true forest,
Proves that I proffer to myself,—alas!
The triumph of an ideal want
Of roses.
   Think:
Perhaps these women of your niceties
Are but the figures of your fabled hope!
Faun, the illusion leaps from the blue, cold eyes
As a spring all of tears, of her most pure:
And she all sighs is a contrast
As a warm day's breath on the fleece!
No! By the weary and motionless swoon
Stifling with summer the fresh lilting morn,
No murmur of water but my flute wafts
To the dew-sprinkled woods of consent.
   The only wind
Hustling its sound through the twin-born pipes
Dispersing its arid rain—
The while the horizon unfrowning—
Is the calm, artificial, evident sigh
Of Inspiration, rising to its source.

845

O Sicilian shores of a quiet fen
Which my vanity sacks to the jealous suns
Submissive under the flowers of sparks,
Reveal:
"Here was I culling hollow reeds,
Tamed by my talent, when, on the glaucous gold
Of distant verdures yielding to the flood
Their richest vines,
A living whiteness surged to its repose:
At the soft prelude to the birth of song
The flock of swans—no!—naiads, fled or plunged."

Inert and scorched in the tawny hour,
Unnoticing by what collective art
Too many hymens scamper off, desired
By him who seeketh Woman:
Then I shall waken, lone, erect,
Under an ancient surge of light,
At the first fervor:
Lilies! and candor in one of you all.

Else that sweet nothing rumored from their lip,
The kiss, that whispers low of perfidy;
My breast, virgin of evidence, testifies a sting
Mysterious, and of a sacred tooth;
But bah! such a secret elects to confide
In the vast twin-born reed that plays to the clouds:
That, sloughing off the cheek's pale pain,
Dreams, in a lengthy solo, I'll delight
The beauty of the roundabout with it
And false confusions with my credulous song;
Of notes so loud that modulated love
Shrinks from the inconsiderable dream
Of back or pure flank in my closed regard,
A resounding, vain, and endless-dreary line.

Strain then, O instrument of flights, malign Syrinx,
To flower anew by bords where you await me!
I, in my noisy pride, shall sing,
Sing long and longingly of goddesses;
And by the paintings of idolaters
Still in their shadows charm the girdle free:

So, when I've sucked the splendor from the grape
To banish regret dispelled by my deceit,
Mocking the summer sky,
I raise the empty cluster, with a puff
Belling the luminous skins, for frenzy flushed,
And watch through them till night fall.
Oh, nymphs, bell them with many memories:
"My gaze, piercing the rushes,
Lances each deathless form, that in the wave
Drowns its mad burning, while its passion-cry
Leaps to the forest-heaven;
And the glorious bath of tresses drops below
In lightnings and shudders—O diadems!
I hasten; when, at my ankles (bruised,
Knowing the languor of the ill of being twain)
Are sleepers conjoined, in danger of themselves.
I embrace them, not disentwining,
And bear to this grove, which futile shadows flee,
Roses yielding their fragrance to the sun;
Here our frolic shall linger with the day it burns."

I adore you, O wrath of virgins,
O untamed delight of the holy nude burden
That glides, to escape my lips of drinking fire,
As the lightning leaps! The silent dread of the flesh:
From the head of the cruel to the heart of the weak
From whom their innocence droppeth, moist
With tears of frenzy, or less mournful dew.
"I sinned, gay at defeating these treacherous terrors,
In having divided the disheveled cluster
Of kisses the gods had so close intermingled;
For, as my lips moved in the passionate smiling
I plunged in the sensuous joy of one only
(Holding by a single finger
So that the frozen candor of her breast
Her sister's crimson ferment might encolor—
Her sister enkindled—
The little one artless, unblushing)
Out of my arms, weak with uncertain dyings,
The ever thankless prey was gone
Without ruth for the sob of my frenzy."

847

Shall I grieve? toward pleasure others will draw me on
By their tresses bound to the horns of my brow:
You know, my passion, how, purple and overripe,
Each pomegranate bursts and hums of bees;
And our blood, smitten with what will capture it,
Flows for the eternal swarming of desire.
When these woods are tinted of ashes and gold
A festival exults in the darkened forest:
Etna! it is to you that Venus comes
Setting on your lava her ingenuous heels,
When in sad thundering sleep the fires die.
I hold the queen!
    O sure chastisement!
    No,
But the soul empty of words and the dull form
Slowly succumb to the proud silence of noon:
Now I must sleep and forget the blasphemy,
Outspread on the parched sand—and, as I love,
Open my mouth to the healing star of wine!

Couple, farewell; I shall see the shadow that you are.

THOMAS MANN

THOMAS MANN (German, 1875-1955). One of the most distinguished modern men of letters. Came to America to escape Nazism, preferred to return to Europe after war. Early fiction depicted life in Germany (*Buddenbrooks*) and prewar Europe *(The Magic Mountain)*. In stories *(Death in Venice)* and essays, he was arbiter between the artist and the average man. In later years, preoccupied with social and moral issues (in the *Joseph* cycle and *Doctor Faustus*).

A WEARY HOUR

HE GOT up from the table, his little, fragile writing-desk; got up as though desperate, and with hanging head crossed the room to the tall, thin, pillar-like stove in the opposite corner. He put his hands to it; but the hour was long past midnight and the tiles were nearly

stone cold. Not getting even his little comfort that he sought, he leaned back against them and, coughing, drew together the folds of his dressing-gown, between which a draggled lace shirt-frill stuck out; he snuffed hard through his nostrils to get a little air, for as usual he had a cold.

It was a particular, a sinister cold, which scarcely ever quite disappeared. It inflamed his eyelids and made the flanges of his nose all raw; in his head and limbs it lay like a heavy, sombre intoxication. Or was this cursed confinement to his room, to which the doctor had weeks ago condemned him, to blame for all his languor and flabbiness? God knew if it was the right thing—perhaps so, on account of his chronic catarrh and the spasms of his chest and belly. And for weeks on end now, yes, weeks, bad weather had reigned in Jena—hateful, horrible weather, which he felt in every nerve of his body—cold, wild, gloomy. The December wind roared in the stove-pipe with a desolate god-forsaken sound—he might have been wandering on a heath, by night and storm, his soul full of unappeasable grief. Yet this close confinement—that was not good either; not good for thought, nor for the rhythm of the blood, where thought was engendered.

The six-sided room was bare and colourless and devoid of cheer: a whitewashed ceiling wreathed in tobacco smoke, walls covered with trellis-patterned paper and hung with silhouettes in oval frames, half a dozen slender-legged pieces of furniture; the whole lighted by two candles burning at the head of the manuscript on the writing-table. Red curtains draped the upper part of the window-frames; mere festooned wisps of cotton they were, but red, a warm, sonorous red, and he loved them and would not have parted from them; they gave a little air of ease and charm to the bald unlovely poverty of his surroundings. He stood by the stove and blinked repeatedly, straining his eyes across at the work from which he had just fled: that load, that weight, that gnawing conscience, that sea which to drink up, that frightful task which to perform, was all his pride and all his misery, at once his heaven and his hell. It dragged, it stuck, it would not budge—and now again . . . ! It must be the weather; or his catarrh, or his fatigue. Or was it the work? Was the thing itself an unfortunate conception, doomed from its beginning to despair?

He had risen in order to put a little space between him and his task, for physical distance would often result in improved perspective, a wider view of his material and a better chance of conspectus.

Yes, the mere feeling of relief on turning away from the battlefield had been known to work like an inspiration. And a more innocent one than that purveyed by alcohol or strong, black coffee.

The little cup stood on the side-table. Perhaps it would help him out of the impasse? No, no, not again! Not the doctor only, but somebody else too, a more important somebody, had cautioned him against that sort of thing—another person, who lived over in Weimar and for whom he felt a love which was a mixture of hostility and yearning. That was a wise man. He knew how to live and create; did not abuse himself, was full of self-regard.

Quiet reigned in the house. There was only the wind, driving down the Schlossgasse and dashing the rain in gusts against the panes. They were all asleep—the landlord and his family. Lotte and the children. And here he stood by the cold stove, awake, alone, tormented; blinking across at the work in which his morbid self-dissatisfaction would not let him believe.

His neck rose long and white out of his stock and his knock-kneed legs showed between the skirts of his dressing-gown. The red hair was smoothed back from a thin, high forehead; it retreated in bays from his veined white temples and hung down in thin locks over the ears. His nose was aquiline, with an abrupt whitish tip; above it the well-marked line of the brows almost met. They were darker than his hair and gave the deep-set, inflamed eyes a tragic, staring look. He could not breathe through his nose; so he opened his thin lips and made the freckled, sickly cheeks look even more sunken thereby.

No, it was a failure, it was all hopelessly wrong. The army ought to have been brought in! The army was the root of the whole thing. But it was impossible to present it before the eyes of the audience —and was art powerful enough thus to enforce the imagination? Besides, his hero was no hero; he was contemptible, he was frigid. The situation was wrong, the language was wrong; it was a dry pedestrian lecture, good for a history class, but as drama absolutely hopeless!

Very good, then, it was over. A defeat. A failure. Bankruptcy. He would write to Körner, the good Körner, who believed in him, who clung with childlike faith to his genius. He would scoff, scold, beseech—this friend of his; would remind him of the *Carlos*, which likewise had issued out of doubts and pains and rewritings and after all the anguish turned out to be something really fine, a genuine masterpiece. But times were changed. Then he had been a man still capable of taking a strong, confident grip on a thing and giving it

850

triumphant shape. Doubts and struggles? Yes. And ill he had been, perhaps more ill than now; a fugitive, oppressed and hungry, at odds with the world; humanly speaking, a beggar. But young, still young! Each time, however low he had sunk, his resilient spirit had leaped up anew; upon the hour of affliction had followed the feeling of triumphant self-confidence. That came no more, or hardly ever, now. There might be one night of glowing exaltation—when the fires of his genius lighted up an impassioned vision of all that he might do if only they burned on; but it had always to be paid for with a week of enervation and gloom. Faith in the future, his guiding star in times of stress, was dead. Here was the despairing truth: the years of need and nothingness, which he had thought of as the painful testing-time, turned out to have been the rich and fruitful ones; and now that a little happiness had fallen to his lot, now that he had ceased to be an intellectual freebooter and occupied a position of civic dignity, with office and honours, wife and children—now he was exhausted, worn out. To give up, to own himself beaten—that was all there was left to do. He groaned; he pressed his hands to his eyes and dashed up and down the room like one possessed. What he had just thought was so frightful that he could not stand still on the spot where he had thought it. He sat down on a chair by the further wall and stared gloomily at the floor, his clasped hands hanging down between his knees.

His conscience . . . how loudly his conscience cried out! He had sinned, sinned against himself all these years, against the delicate instrument that was his body. Those youthful excesses, the nights without sleep, the days spent in close, smoke-laden air, straining his mind and heedless of his body; the narcotics with which he had spurred himself on—all that was now taking its revenge.

And if it did—then he would defy the gods, who decreed the guilt and then imposed the penalties. He had lived as he had to live, he had not had time to be wise, not time to be careful. Here in this place in his chest, when he breathed, coughed, yawned, always in the same spot came this pain, this piercing, stabbing, diabolical little warning; it never left him, since that time in Erfurt five years ago when he had catarrhal fever and inflammation of the lungs. What was it warning him of? Ah, he knew only too well what it meant—no matter how the doctor chose to put him off. He had no time to be wise and spare himself, no time to save his strength by submission to moral laws. What he wanted to do he must do soon, quickly, do today.

And the moral laws? . . . Why was it that precisely sin, surrender to the harmful and the consuming, actually seemed to him more moral than any amount of wisdom and frigid self-discipline? Not that constituted morality: not the contemptible knack of keeping a good conscience—rather the struggle and compulsion, the passion and pain.

Pain . . . how his breast swelled at the word! He drew himself up and folded his arms; his gaze, beneath the close-set auburn brows, was kindled by the nobility of his suffering. No man was utterly wretched so long as he could still speak of his misery in high-sounding and noble words. One thing only was indispensable; the courage to call his life by large and fine names. Not to ascribe his sufferings to bad air and constipation; to be well enough to cherish emotions, to scorn and ignore the material. Just on this one point to be naïve, though in all else sophisticated. To believe, to have strength to believe, in suffering. . . . But he *did* believe in it; so profoundly, so ardently, that nothing which came to pass with suffering could seem to him either useless or evil. His glance sought the manuscript, and his arms tightened across his chest. Talent itself— was that not suffering? And if the manuscript over there, his unhappy effort, made him suffer, was not that quite as it should be—a good sign, so to speak? His talents had never been of the copious, ebullient sort; were they to become so he would feel mistrustful. That only happened with beginners and bunglers, with the ignorant and easily satisfied, whose life was not shaped and disciplined by the possession of a gift. For a gift, my friends down there in the audience, a gift is not anything simple, not anything to play with; it is not mere ability. At bottom it is a compulsion; a critical knowledge of the ideal, a permanent dissatisfaction, which rises only through suffering to the height of its powers. And it is to the greatest, the most unsatisfied, that their gift is the sharpest scourge. Not to complain, not to boast; to think modestly, patiently of one's pain; and if not a day in the week, not even an hour, be free from it— what then? To make light and little of it all, of suffering and achievement alike—that was what made a man great.

He stood up, pulled out his snuff-box and sniffed eagerly, then suddenly clasped his hands behind his back and strode so briskly through the room that the flames of the candles flickered in the draught. Greatness, distinction, world conquest and an imperishable name! To be happy and unknown, what was that by comparison? To be known—known and loved by all the world—ah, they might

call that egotism, those who knew naught of the urge, naught of the sweetness of this dream! Everything out of the ordinary is egotistic, in proportion to its suffering. "Speak for yourselves," it says, "ye without mission on this earth, ye whose life is so much easier than mine!" And Ambition says: "Shall my sufferings be vain? No, they must make me great!"

The nostrils of his great nose dilated, his gaze darted fiercely about the room. His right hand was thrust hard and far into the opening of his dressing-gown, his left arm hung down, the fist clenched. A fugitive red played in the gaunt cheeks—a glow thrown up from the fire of his artistic egoism; that passion for his own ego, which burnt unquenchably in his being's depths. Well he knew it, the secret intoxication of this love! Sometimes he needed only to contemplate his own hand, to be filled with the liveliest tenderness towards himself, in whose service he was bent on spending all the talent, all the art that he owned. And he was right so to do, there was nothing base about it. For deeper still than his egoism lay the knowledge that he was freely consuming and sacrificing himself in the service of a high ideal, not as a virtue, of course, but rather out of sheer necessity. And this was his ambition: that no one should be greater than he who had not also suffered more for the sake of the high ideal. No one. He stood still, his hand over his eyes, his body turned aside in a posture of shrinking and avoidance. For already the inevitable thought had stabbed him: the thought of that other man, that radiant being, so sense-endowed, so divinely unconscious, that man over there in Weimar, whom he loved and hated. And once more, as always, in deep disquiet, in feverish haste, there began working within him the inevitable sequence of his thoughts: he must assert and define his own nature, his own art, against that other's. Was the other greater? Wherein, then, and why? If he won, would he have sweated blood to do so? If he lost, would his downfall be a tragic sight? He was no hero, no; a god, perhaps. But it was easier to be a god than a hero. Yes, things were easier for him. He was wise, he was deft, he knew how to distinguish between knowing and creating; perhaps that was why he was so blithe and carefree, such an effortless and gushing spring! But if creation was divine, knowledge was heroic, and he who created in knowledge was hero as well as god.

The will to face difficulties. . . . Did anyone realize what discipline and self-control it cost him to shape a sentence or follow out a hard train of thought? For after all he was ignorant, undisci-

plined, a slow, dreamy enthusiast. One of Cæsar's letters was harder to write than the most effective scene—and was it not almost for that very reason higher? From the first rhythmical urge of the inward creative force towards matter, towards the material, towards casting in shape and form—from that to the thought, the image, the word, the line—what a struggle, what a Gethsemane! Everything that he wrote was a marvel of yearning after form, shape, line, body; of yearning after the sunlit world of that other man who had only to open his godlike lips and straightway call the bright unshadowed things he saw by name!

And yet—and despite that other man. Where was there an artist, a poet, like himself? Who like him created out of nothing, out of his own breast? A poem was born as music in his soul, as pure, primitive essence, long before it put on a garment of metaphor from the visible world. History, philosophy, passion were no more than pretexts and vehicles for something which had little to do with them, but was at home in orphic depths. Words and conceptions were keys upon which his art played and made vibrate the hidden strings. No one realized. The good souls praised him, indeed, for the power of feeling with which he struck one note or another. And his favourite note, his final emotional appeal, the great bell upon which he sounded his summons to the highest feasts of the soul—many there were who responded to its sound. Freedom! But in all their exaltation, certainly he meant by the word both more and less than they did. Freedom—what was it? A self-respecting middle-class attitude towards thrones and princes? Surely not that. When one thinks of all that the spirit of man has dared to put into the word! Freedom from what? After all, from what? Perhaps, indeed, even from happiness, from human happiness, that silken bond, that tender, sacred tie. . . .

From happiness. His lips quivered. It was as though his glance turned inward upon himself; slowly his face sank into his hands. . . . He stood by the bed in the next room, where the flowered curtains hung in motionless folds across the window, and the lamp shed a bluish light. He bent over the sweet head on the pillow . . . a ringlet of dark hair lay across her cheek, that had the paleness of pearl; the childlike lips were open in slumber. "My wife! Beloved, didst thou yield to my yearning and come to me to be my joy? And that thou art. . . . Lie still and sleep; nay, lift not those sweet shadowy lashes and gaze up at me, as sometimes with thy great, dark, questioning, searching eyes. I love thee so! By God I swear

it. It is only that sometimes I am tired out, struggling at my self-imposed task, and my feelings will not respond. And I must not be too utterly thine, never utterly happy in thee, for the sake of my mission."

He kissed her, drew away from her pleasant, slumbrous warmth, looked about him, turned back to the outer room. The clock struck; it warned him that the night was already far spent; but likewise it seemed to be mildly marking the end of a weary hour. He drew a deep breath, his lips closed firmly; he went back and took up his pen. No, he must not brood, he was too far down for that. He must not descend into chaos; or at least he must not stop there. Rather out of chaos, which is fullness, he must draw up to the light whatever he found there fit and ripe for form. No brooding! Work! Define, eliminate, fashion, complete!

And complete it he did, that effort of a labouring hour. He brought it to an end, perhaps not to a good end, but in any case to an end. And being once finished, lo, it was also good. And from his soul, from music and idea, new works struggled upward to birth and, taking shape, gave out light and sound, ringing and shimmering, and giving hint of their infinite origin—as in a shell we hear the sighing of the sea whence it came.

ALESSANDRO MANZONI

ALESSANDRO MANZONI (Italian, 1785-1873). Profound historical romanticist. Founder of the Romantic School in Italy. His novel, *I Promessi Sposi* (*The Betrothed*), Italians sometimes rank next to the *Divine Comedy*. Influenced by Sir Walter Scott, but probes more deeply into historical issues. Also wrote poems and verse plays.

THE INTERRUPTED WEDDING

DON ABBONDIO (the priest) was sitting in an old armchair, wrapped in a dilapidated dressing-gown, with an ancient cap on his head, which made a frame all round his face. By the faint light of a small lamp the two thick white tufts of hair which projected from under the cap, his bushy white eyebrows, moustache, and pointed beard all seemed, on his brown and wrinkled face, like bushes covered with snow on a rocky hillside seen by moonlight.

"Ah! ah!" was his salutation, as he took off his spectacles and put them into the book he was reading.

"Your Reverence will say we are late in coming," said Tonio, bowing, as did Gervaso, but more awkwardly.

"Certainly it is late—late in every way. Do you know that I am ill?"

"Oh! I am very sorry, sir!"

"You surely must have heard that I am ill, and don't know when I can see anyone. . . . But why have you brought that—that fellow with you?"

"Oh! just for company, like, sir!"

"Very good—now let us see."

"There are twenty-five new *berlinghe*, sir— those with Saint Ambrose on horseback on them," said Tonio, drawing a folded paper from his pocket.

"Let us see," returned Abbondio, and taking the paper, he put on his spectacles, unfolded it, took out the silver pieces, turned them over and over, counted them and found them correct.

"Now, your Reverence, will you kindly give me my Teckla's necklace?"

"Quite right," replied Don Abbondio; and going to a cupboard, he unlocked it, and having first looked round, as if to keep away any spectators, opened one side, stood in front of the open door, so that no one could see in, put in his head to look for the pledge, and his arm to take it out, and, having extracted it, locked the cupboard, unwrapped the paper, said interrogatively, "All right?" wrapped it up again and handed it over to Tonio.

"Now," said the latter, "would you please let me have a little black and white, sir?"

"This, too!" exclaimed Don Abbondio; "they are up to every trick! Eh! how suspicious the world has grown! Can't you trust me?"

"How, your Reverence, not trust you? You do me wrong! But as my name is down on your book, on the debtor side, . . . and you have already had the trouble of writing it once, so . . . in case anything were to happen, you know . . ."

"All right, all right," interrupted Don Abbondio, and, grumbling to himself, he opened the table drawer, took out pen, paper and inkstand, and began to write, repeating the words out loud as he set them down. Meanwhile, Tonio, and, at a sign from him, Gervaso, placed themselves in front of the table, so as to prevent the writer from seeing the door, and, as if in mere idleness, began to move

856

their feet about noisily on the floor, in order to serve as a signal to those outside, and, at the same time, to deaden the sound of their footsteps. Don Abbondio, intent on his work, noticed nothing. Renzo and Lucia, hearing the signal, entered on tiptoe, holding their breath, and stood close behind the two brothers. Meanwhile, Don Abbondio, who had finished writing, read over the document attentively, without raising his eyes from the paper, folded it and saying, "Will you be satisfied now?" took off his spectacles with one hand, and held out the sheet to Tonio with the other. Tonio, while stretching out his hand to take it, stepped back on one side, and Gervaso, at a sign from him, on the other, and between the two appeared Renzo and Lucia. Don Abbondio saw them, started, was dumfounded, became furious, thought it over, and came to a resolution, all in the time that Renzo took in uttering these words: "Your Reverence, in the presence of these witnesses, this is my wife!" His lips had not yet ceased moving when Don Abbondio let fall the receipt, which he was holding in his left hand, raised the lamp and seizing the table-cloth with his right hand, dragged it violently towards him, throwing book, papers and inkstand to the ground, and, springing between the chair and table, approached Lucia. The poor girl, with her sweet voice all trembling, had only just been able to say "This is . . ." when Don Abbondio rudely flung the table-cloth over her head, and immediately dropping the lamp which he held in his other hand, used the latter to wrap it tightly round her face, nearly suffocating her, while he roared at the top of his voice, like a wounded bull, "Perpetua! Perpetua! treason! help!" When the light was out the priest let go his hold of the girl, went groping about for the door leading into an inner room, and, having found it, entered and locked himself in, still shouting, "Perpetua! treason! help! get out of this house! get out of this house!" In the other room all was confusion; Renzo, trying to catch the priest, and waving his hands about as though he had been playing at blindman's buff, had reached the door and kept knocking, crying out, "Open! open! don't make a noise!" Lucia called Renzo in a feeble voice, and said supplicatingly, "Let us go! do let us go!" Tonio was down on his hands and knees, feeling about the floor to find his receipt, while Gervaso jumped about and yelled like one possessed, trying to get out by the door leading to the stairs.

In the midst of this confusion we cannot refrain from a momentary reflection. Renzo, raising a noise by night in another man's

house, which he had surreptitiously entered, and keeping its owner besieged in an inner room, has every appearance of being an oppressor,—yet, after all, when you come to look at it, he was the oppressed. Don Abbondio, surprised, put to flight, frightened out of his wits while quietly attending to his own business, would seem to be the victim; and yet in reality, it was he who did the wrong. So goes the world, as it often happens; at least, so it used to go in the seventeenth century.

CHRISTOPHER MARLOWE

CHRISTOPHER MARLOWE (English, 1564-1593). Precursor of Shakespeare in English drama. After brief diplomatic career, settled in London, to become one of "University Wits." Killed, under questionable circumstances, in a tavern brawl, at 29. Greatest plays: *Tamburlaine the Great, The Tragicall History of Dr. Faustus, The Jew of Malta.*

THE PASSIONATE SHEPHERD
TO HIS LOVE

Come live with me and be my Love,
And we will all the pleasures prove
That hills and valleys, dale and field,
And all the craggy mountains yield.

There will we sit upon the rocks
And see the shepherds feed their flocks,
By shallow rivers, to whose falls
Melodious birds sing madrigals.

There will I make thee beds of roses
And a thousand fragrant posies,
A cap of flowers and a kirtle
Embroider'd all with leaves of myrtle.

A gown made of the finest wool,
Which from our pretty lambs we pull,
Fair linéd slippers for the cold,
With buckles of the purest gold.

A belt of straw and ivy buds
With coral clasps and amber studs:
And if these pleasures may thee move,
Come live with me and be my Love.

Thy silver dishes for thy meat
As precious as the gods do eat,
Shall on an ivory table be
Prepared each day for thee and me.

The shepherd swains shall dance and sing
For thy delights each May morning:
If these delights thy mind may move,
Then live with me and be my Love.

JOHN MASEFIELD

JOHN MASEFIELD (English, 1878-   ). Exultant poet of the ordinary man.
British Poet Laureate from 1930. Ran away to sea at 14. Worked for a time
in New York. In his poetry, influenced by Kipling; in novels, by Conrad. Best-
known volumes of verse: *Salt-Water Ballads, The Everlasting Mercy, Reynard
the Fox.*

THE WESTERN ISLANDS

ONCE there were two sailors; and one of them was Joe, and the
other one was Jerry, and they were fishermen. And they'd a young
apprentice-feller, and his name was Jim. And he was a great one for
his pot, and Jerry was a wonder at his pipe; and Jim did all the
work, and both of them banged him. So one time Joe and Jerry
were in the beer-house, and there was a young parson there, telling
the folks about foreign things, about plants and that. 'A,' he says,
'what wonders there are in the west.'

" 'What sort of wonders, begging your pardon, sir,' says Joe.
'What sort of wonders might them be?'

" 'Why, all sorts of wonders,' says the parson. 'Why in the west,'
he says, 'there's things you wouldn't believe. No, you wouldn't be-

lieve; not till you'd seen them,' he says. 'There's diamonds growing on the trees. And great, golden, glittering pearls as common as pea-straw. And there's islands in the west. Ah, I could tell you of them. Islands? I rather guess there's islands. None of your Isles of Man. None of your Alderney and Sark. Not in them seas.'

" 'What sort of islands might they be, begging your pardon, sir?' says Jerry.

" 'Why,' he says (the parson feller says), 'ISLANDS. Islands as big as Spain. Islands with rivers of rum and streams of sarsaparilla. And none of your roses. Rubies and ame-thynes is all the roses grows in them parts. With golden stalks to them, and big diamond sticks to them, and the taste of pork-crackling if you eat them. They're the sort of roses to have in your area,' he says.

" 'And what else might there be in them parts, begging your pardon, sir?' says Joe.

" 'Why,' he says, this parson says, 'there's wonders. There's not only wonders but miracles. And not only miracles, but sperrits.'

" 'What sort of sperrits might they be, begging your pardon?' says Jerry, 'Are they rum and that?'

" 'When I says sperrits,' says the parson feller, 'I mean ghosts.'

" 'Of course ye do,' says Joe.

" 'Yes, ghosts' says the parson, 'And by ghosts I mean sperrits. And by sperrits I mean white things. And by white things I mean things as turn your hair white. And there's red devils there, and blue devils there, and a great gold queen a-waiting for a man to kiss her. And the first man as dares to kiss that queen, why he becomes king, and all her sacks of gold become his.'

" 'Begging your pardon, sir,' said Jerry, 'but whereabouts might these here islands be?'

" 'Why, in the west,' says the parson. 'In the west, where the sun sets.'

" 'Ah,' said Joe and Jerry. 'What wonders there are in the world.'

"Now, after that, neither one of them could think of anything but these here western islands. So at last they take their smack, and off they go in search of them. And Joe had a barrel of beer in the bows, and Jerry had a box of twist in the waist, and pore little Jim stood and steered abaft all. And in the evenings Jerry and Joe would bang their pannikins together, and sing of the great times they meant to have when they were married to the queen. Then they would clump pore little Jim across the head, and tell him to watch out, and keep her to her course, or they'd ride him down like you would a main

tack. And he'd better mind his eye, they told him, or they'd make him long to be boiled and salted. And he'd better put more sugar in the tea, they said, or they'd cut him up for cod-bait. And who was he, they asked, to be wanting meat for dinner, when there was that much weevilly biscuit in the bread-barge? And boys was going to the dogs, they said, when limbs the like of him had the heaven-born insolence to want to sleep. And a nice pass things was coming to, they said, when a lad as they'd done everything for, and saved, so to speak, from the workhouse, should go for to snivel when they hit him a clip. If they'd said a word, when they was hit, when they was boys, they told him, they'd have had their bloods drawed, and been stood in the wind to cool. But let him take heed, they said, and be a good lad, and do the work of five, and they wouldn't half wonder, they used to say, as he'd be a man before his mother. So the sun shone, and the stars came out golden, and all the sea was a sparkle of gold with them. Blue was the sea, and the wind blew, too, and it blew Joe and Jerry west as fast as a cat can eat sardines.

"And one fine morning the wind fell calm, and a pleasant smell came over the water, like nutmegs on a rum-milk-punch. Presently the dawn broke. And, lo, and behold, a rousing great wonderful island, all scarlet with coral and with rubies. The surf that was beating on her sands went shattering into silver coins, into dimes; and pesetas, and francs, and fourpenny bits. And the flowers on the cliffs was all one gleam and glitter. And the beauty of that island was a beauty beyond the beauty of Sally Brown, the lady as kept the beer-house. And on the beach of that island, on a golden throne, like, sat a women so lovely that to look at her was as good as a church-service for one.

" 'That's the party I got to kiss,' said Jerry. 'Steady, and beach her, Jim, boy,' he says. 'Run her ashore, lad. That's the party is to be my queen.'

" 'You've got a neck on you, all of a sudden,' said Joe. 'You ain't the admiral of this fleet. Not by a wide road you ain't. I'll do all the kissing as there's any call for. You keep clear, my son.'

" 'Keep clear, is it?' said Jerry. 'You tell me to keep clear? You tell me again, and I'll put a head on you—'ll make you sing like a kettle. Who are you to tell me to keep clear?'

" 'I tell you who I am,' said Joe. 'I'm a better man than you are. That's what I am. I'm Joe the Tank, from Limehouse Basin, and there's no tinker's donkey-boy'll make me stand from under. Who are you to go kissing queens? Who are you that talk so proud and

861

so mighty? You've a face on you would make a Dago tired. You look like a sea-sick Kanaka that's boxed seven rounds with a buzz-saw. You've no more manners than a hog, and you've a lip on you would fetch the enamel off a cup.'

" 'If it comes to calling names,' said Jerry, 'you ain't the only pebble on the beach. Whatever you might think, I tell you you ain't. You're the round turn and two-half hitches of a figure of fun as makes the angels weep. That's what you are. And you're the right-hand strand, and the left-hand strand, and the centre strand, and the core, and the serving, and the marling, of a three-stranded, left-handed, poorly worked junk of a half-begun and never finished odds and ends of a Port Mahon soldier. You look like a Portuguese drummer. You've a whelky red nose that shines like a port side-light. You've a face like a muddy field where they've been playing football in the rain. Your hair is an insult and a shame. I blush when I look at you. You give me a turn like the first day out to a first voyager. Kiss, will you? Kiss? Man, I tell you you'd paralyze a shark if you kissed him. Paralyze him, strike him cold. That's what a kiss of yours'd do.'

" 'You ought to 'a' been a parson,' said Joe, 'that's what you'd ought. There's many would 'a' paid you for talk like that. But for all your fine talk, and for all your dandy language, you'll not come the old soldier over me. No, nor ten of you. You talk of kissing, when there's a handsome young man, the likes of me, around. Neither you nor ten of you. To hear you talk one'd think you was a Emperor or a Admiral. One would think you was a Bishop or a King. One might mistake you for a General or a Member of Parliament. You might. Straight, you might. A General or a Bishop or a King. And what are you? What are you? I ask you plain. What are you?—I'll tell you what you are.

" 'You're him as hired himself out as a scarecrow, acos no one'd take you as a fo'c'sle hand. You're him as give the colic to a weather-cock. You're him as turned old Mother Bomby's beer. You're him as drowned the duck and stole the monkey. You're him as got the medal give him for having a face that made the bull tame. You're——'

' 'Now don't you cast no more to me," said Jerry. 'For I won't take no lip from a twelve-a-shilling, cent-a-corner, the likes of you are. You're the clippings of old junk, what the Dagoes smoke in cigarettes. A swab, and a-wash-deck-broom, and the half pint of paint'd make a handsomer figger of a man than what you are. I've

seen a coir whisk, what they grooms a mule with, as had a sweeter face than you got. So stand aside, before you're put aside. I'm the king of this here island. You can go chase yourself for another. Stand clear, I say, or I'll give you a jog'll make your bells ring.'

"Now, while they were argufying, young Jim, the young apprentice feller, he creeps up to the queen upon the throne. She was beautiful, she was, and she shone in the sun, and she looked straight ahead of her like a wax-work in a show. And in her hand she had a sack full of jewels, and at her feet she had a sack full of gold, and by her side was an empty throne ready for the king she married. But round her right hand there was a red snake, and round her left hand there was a blue snake, and the snakes hissed and twisted, and they showed their teeth full of poison. So Jim looked at the snakes, and he hit them a welt, right and left, and he kissed the lady.

"And immediately all the bells and the birds of the world burst out a-ringing and a-singing. The lady awoke from her sleep, and Jim's old clothes were changed to cloth of gold. And there he was, a king, on the throne besides the lady.

"But the red snake turned to a big red devil who took a-hold of Joe, and the blue snake turned to a big blue devil, who took a-hold of Jerry. And 'Come you here, you brawling pugs,' they said, 'come and shovel sand.' And Joe and Jerry took the spades that were given to them. And 'Dig, now,' said the devils. 'Heave round. Let's see you dig. Dig, you scarecrows. And tell us when you've dug to London.' "

WILLIAM SOMERSET MAUGHAM

WILLIAM SOMERSET MAUGHAM (English, 1874-   ). Popular novelist, playwright and story teller. Early life and study of medicine mirrored in semi-autobiographical novel, *Of Human Bondage* (considered his masterpiece). Others: *The Moon and Sixpence, Cakes and Ale.* Effective society plays: *The Circle, Our Betters.* In his stories (*The Trembling of a Leaf*, including the famous "Rain") he is romancer of the Far East par excellence.

THE PATTERN

PHILIP felt a shiver pass through his heart. He had never before lost a friend of his own age, for the death of Cronshaw, a man so much older than himself, had seemed to come in the normal course

of things. The news gave him a peculiar shock. It reminded him of his own mortality, for like everyone else Philip, knowing perfectly that all men must die, had no intimate feeling that the same must apply to himself; and Hayward's death, though he had long ceased to have any warm feeling for him, affected him deeply. He remembered on a sudden all the good talks they had had, and it pained him to think that they would never talk with one another again; he remembered their first meeting and the pleasant months they had spent together in Heidelberg. Philip's heart sank as he thought of the lost years. He walked on mechanically not noticing where he went, and realised suddenly, with a movement of irritation, that instead of turning down the Haymarket he had sauntered along Shaftesbury Avenue. It bored him to retrace his steps; and besides, with that news, he did not want to read, he wanted to sit alone and think. He made up his mind to go to the British Museum. Solitude was now his only luxury. Since he had been at Lynn's he had often gone there and sat in front of the groups from the Parthenon; and, not deliberately thinking, had allowed their divine masses to rest his troubled soul. But this afternoon they had nothing to say to him, and after a few minutes, impatiently, he wandered out of the room. There were too many people, provincials with foolish faces, foreigners poring over guide-books; their hideousness besmirched the everlasting masterpieces, their restlessness troubled the god's immortal repose. He went into another room and here there was hardly anyone. Philip sat down wearily. His nerves were on edge. He could not get the people out of his mind. Sometimes at Lynn's they affected him in the same way, and he looked at them file past him with horror; they were so ugly and there was such meanness in their faces, it was terrifying; their features were distorted with paltry desires, and you felt they were strange to any ideas of beauty. They had furtive eyes and weak chins. There was no wickedness in them, but only pettiness and vulgarity. Their humour was a low facetiousness. Sometimes he found himself looking at them to see what animal they resembled, (he tried not to, for it quickly became an obsession,) and he saw in them all the sheep or the horse or the fox, or the goat. Human beings filled him with disgust.

But presently the influence of the place descended upon him. He felt quieter. He began to look absently at the tombstones with which the room was lined. They were the work of Athenian stone masons

of the fourth and fifth centuries before Christ, and they were very simple, work of no great talent but with the exquisite spirit of Athens upon them; time had mellowed the marble to the colour of honey, so that unconsciously one thought of the bees of Hymettus, and softened their outlines. Some represented a nude figure, seated on a bench, some the departure of the dead from those who loved him, and some the dead clasping hands with one who remained behind. On all was the tragic word farewell; that and nothing more. Their simplicity was infinitely touching. Friend parted from friend, the son from his mother, and the restraint made the survivor's grief more poignant. It was so long, long ago, and century upon century had passed over that unhappiness; for two thousand years those who wept had been dust as those they wept for. Yet the woe was alive still, and it filled Philip's heart so that he felt compassion spring up in it, and he said:

'Poor things, poor things.'

And it came to him that the gaping sight-seers and the fat strangers with their guide-books, and all those mean, common people who thronged the shop, with their trivial desires and vulgar cares, were mortal and must die. They too loved and must part from those they loved, the son from his mother, the wife from her husband; and perhaps it was more tragic because their lives were ugly and sordid, and they knew nothing that gave beauty to the world. There was one stone which was very beautiful, a bas relief of two young men holding each other's hand; and the reticence of line, the simplicity, made one like to think that the sculptor here had been touched with a genuine emotion. It was an exquisite memorial to that than which the world offers but one thing more precious, to a friendship; and as Philip looked at it, he felt the tears come to his eyes. He thought of Hayward and his eager admiration for him when first they met, and how disillusion had come and then indifference, till nothing held them together but habit and old memories. It was one of the queer things of life that you could not imagine existence without him; then separation came, and everything went on in the same way, and the companion who had seemed essential proved unnecessary. Your life proceeded and you did not even miss him. Philip thought of those early days in Heidelberg when Hayward, capable of great things, had been full of enthusiasm for the future, and how, little by little, achieving nothing, he had resigned himself to failure. Now he was dead. His

death had been as futile as his life. He died ingloriously, of a stupid disease, failing once more, even at the end, to accomplish anything. It was just the same now as if he had never lived.

Philip asked himself desperately what was the use of living at all. It all seemed inane. It was the same with Cronshaw: it was quite unimportant that he had lived; he was dead and forgotten, his book of poems sold in remainder by second-hand booksellers; his life seemed to have served nothing except to give a pushing journalist occasion to write an article in a review. And Philip cried out in his soul:

'What is the use of it?'

The effort was so incommensurate with the result. The bright hopes of youth had to be paid for at such a bitter price of disillusionment. Pain and disease and unhappiness weighed down the scale so heavily. What did it all mean? He thought of his own life, the high hopes with which he had entered upon it, the limitations which his body forced upon him, his friendlessness, and the lack of affection which had surrounded his youth. He did not know that he had ever done anything but what seemed best to do, and what a cropper he had come! Other men, with no more advantages than he, succeeded, and others again, with many more, failed. It seemed pure chance. The rain fell alike upon the just and upon the unjust, and for nothing was there a why and a wherefore.

Thinking of Cronshaw, Philip remembered the Persian rug which he had given him, telling him that it offered an answer to his question upon the meaning of life; and suddenly the answer occurred to him: he chuckled: now that he had it, it was like one of the puzzles which you worry over till you are shown the solution and then cannot imagine how it could ever have escaped you. The answer was obvious. Life had no meaning. On the earth, satellite of a star speeding through space, living things had arisen under the influence of conditions which were part of the planet's history; and as there had been a beginning of life upon it so, under the influence of other conditions, there would be an end: man, no more significant than other forms of life, had come not as the climax of creation but as a physical reaction to the environment. Philip remembered the story of the Eastern King who, desiring to know the history of man, was brought by a sage five hundred volumes; busy with affairs of state, he bade him go and condense it; in twenty years the sage returned and his history now was in no more than fifty volumes, but the King, too old then to read so many ponderous

tomes, bade him go and shorten it once more; twenty years passed again and the sage, old and gray, brought a single book in which was the knowledge the King had sought; but the King lay on his deathbed, and he had no time to read even that; and then the sage gave him the history of man in a single line; it was this: he was born, he suffered, and he died. There was no meaning in life, and man by living served no end. It was immaterial whether he was born or not born, whether he lived or ceased to live. Life was insignificant and death without consequence. Philip exulted, as he had exulted in his boyhood when the weight of a belief in God was lifted from his shoulders: it seemed to him that the last burden of responsibility was taken from him; and for the first time he was utterly free. His insignificance was turned to power, and he felt himself suddenly equal with the cruel fate which had seemed to persecute him; for, if life was meaningless, the world was robbed of its cruelty. What he did or left undone did not matter. Failure was unimportant and success amounted to nothing. He was the most inconsiderable creature in that swarming mass of mankind which for a brief space occupied the surface of the earth; and he was almighty because he had wrenched from chaos the secret of its nothingness. Thoughts came tumbling over one another in Philip's eager fancy, and he took long breaths of joyous satisfaction. He felt inclined to leap and sing. He had not been so happy for months.

'Oh, life,' he cried in his heart, 'Oh life, where is thy sting?'

For the same uprush of fancy which had shown him with all the force of mathematical demonstration that life had no meaning, brought with it another idea; and that was why Cronshaw, he imagined, had given him the Persian rug. As the weaver elaborated his pattern for no end but the pleasure of his aesthetic sense, so might a man live his life, or if one was forced to believe that his actions were outside his choosing, so might a man look at his life, that it made a pattern. There was as little need to do this as there was use. It was merely something he did for his own pleasure. Out of the manifold events of his life, his deeds, his feelings, his thoughts, he might make a design, regular, elaborate, complicated, or beautiful; and though it might be no more than an illusion that he had the power of selection, though it might be no more than a fantastic legerdemain in which appearances were interwoven with moonbeams, that did not matter: it seemed, and so to him it was. In the vast warp of life, (a river arising from no spring and flowing

867

endlessly to no sea,) with the background to his fancies that there was no meaning and that nothing was important, a man might get a personal satisfaction in selecting the various strands that worked out the pattern. There was one pattern, the most obvious, perfect, and beautiful, in which a man was born, grew to manhood, married, produced children, toiled for his bread, and died; but there were others intricate and wonderful, in which happiness did not enter and in which success was not attempted; and in them might be discovered a more troubling grace. Some lives, and Hayward's was among them, the blind indifference of chance cut off while the design was still imperfect; and then the solace was comfortable that it did not matter; other lives, such as Cronshaw's, offered a pattern which was difficult to follow: the point of view had to be shifted and old standards had to be altered before one could understand that such a life was its own justification. Philip thought that in throwing over the desire for happiness he was casting aside the last of his illusions. His life had seemed horrible when it was measured by something else. Happiness mattered as little as pain. They came in, both of them, as all the other details of his life came in, to the elaboration of the design. He seemed for an instant to stand above the accidents of his existence, and he felt that they could not affect him again as they had done before. Whatever happened to him now would be one more motive to add to the complexity of the pattern, and when the end approached he would rejoice in its completion. It would be a work of art, and it would be none the less beautiful because he alone knew of its existence, and with his death it would at once cease to be.

Philip was happy.

GUY DE MAUPASSANT

GUY DE MAUPASSANT (French, 1850-1893). The great realist of French literature. Strongly influenced by Flaubert, a personal friend. After success at 30, became one of most popular French writers. Ten years later he was hopelessly insane. Slick craftsmanship makes him father of modern commercial story. Most famous tale: *"Boule de Suif."* Novels: *Une Vie, Bel-Ami.*

THE NECKLACE

SHE was one of those pretty and charming girls who are sometimes, as if by a mistake of destiny, born in a family of clerks. She had

no dowry, no expectations, no means of being known, understood, loved, wedded, by any rich and distinguished man; and she let herself be married to a little clerk at the Ministry of Public Instruction.

She dressed plainly because she could not dress well, but she was as unhappy as though she had really fallen from her proper station; since with women there is neither caste nor rank; and beauty, grace, and charm act instead of family and birth. Natural fineness, instinct for what is elegant, suppleness of wit, are the sole hierarchy, and make from women of the people the equals of the very greatest ladies.

She suffered ceaselessly, feeling herself born for all the delicacies and all the luxuries. She suffered from the poverty of her dwelling, from the wretched look of the walls, from the worn-out chairs, from the ugliness of the curtains. All those things, of which another woman of her rank would never even have been conscious, tortured her and made her angry. The sight of the little Breton peasant who did her humble housework aroused in her regrets which were despairing, and distracted dreams. She thought of the silent ante-chambers hung with Oriental tapestry, lit by tall bronze candelabra, and of the two great footmen in knee-breeches who sleep in the big armchairs, made drowsy by the heavy warmth of the hot-air stove. She thought of the long *salons* fitted up with ancient silk, of the delicate furniture carrying priceless curiosities, and of the coquettish perfumed boudoirs made for talks at five o'clock with intimate friends, with men famous and sought after, whom all women envy and whose attention they all desire.

When she sat down to dinner, before the round table covered with a table-cloth three days old, opposite her husband, who uncovered the soup tureen and declared with an enchanted air, "Ah, the good *pot-au-feu!* I don't know anything better than that," she thought of dainty dinners, of shining silverware, of tapestry which peopled the walls with ancient personages and with strange birds flying in the midst of a fairy forest; and she thought of delicious dishes served on marvelous plates, and of the whispered gallantries which you listen to with a sphinx-like smile, while you are eating the pink flesh of a trout or the wings of a quail.

She had no dresses, no jewels, nothing. And she loved nothing but that; she felt made for that. She would so have liked to please, to be envied, to be charming, to be sought after.

She had a friend, a former schoolmate at the convent, who was

869

rich, and whom she did not like to go and see any more, because she suffered so much when she came back.

But, one evening, her husband returned home with a triumphant air, and holding a large envelope in his hand.

"There," said he, "here is something for you."

She tore the paper sharply, and drew out a printed card which bore these words:

"The Minister of Public Instruction and Mme. Georges Ramponneau request the honor of M. and Mme. Loisel's company at the palace of the Ministry on Monday evening, January 18th."

Instead of being delighted, as her husband hoped, she threw the invitation on the table with disdain, murmuring:

"What do you want me to do with that?"

"But, my dear, I thought you would be glad. You never go out, and this is such a fine opportunity. I had awful trouble to get it. Every one wants to go; it is very select, and they are not giving many invitations to clerks. The whole official world will be there."

She looked at him with an irritated eye, and she said, impatiently:

"And what do you want me to put on my back?"

He had not thought of that; he stammered:

"Why, the dress you go to the theater in. It looks very well, to me."

He stopped, distracted, seeing that his wife was crying. Two great tears descended slowly from the corners of her eyes towards the corners of her mouth. He stuttered:

"What's the matter? What's the matter?"

But, by a violent effort, she had conquered her grief, and she replied, with a calm voice, while she wiped her wet cheeks:

"Nothing. Only I have no dress, and therefore I can't go to this ball. Give your card to some colleague whose wife is better equipped than I."

He was in despair. He resumed:

"Come, let us see, Mathilde. How much would it cost, a suitable dress, which you could use on other occasions, something very simple?"

She reflected several seconds, making her calculations and wondering also what sum she could ask without drawing on herself an immediate refusal and a frightened exclamation from the economical clerk.

Finally, she replied, hesitatingly:

"I don't know exactly, but I think I could manage it with four hundred francs."

He had grown a little pale, because he was laying aside just that amount to buy a gun and treat himself to a little shooting next summer on the plain of Nanterre, with several friends who went to shoot larks down there, of a Sunday.

But he said:

"All right. I will give you four hundred francs. And try to have a pretty dress."

The day of the ball drew near, and Mme. Loisel seemed sad, uneasy, anxious. Her dress was ready, however. Her husband said to her one evening:

"What is the matter? Come, you've been so queer these last three days."

And she answered:

"It annoys me not to have a single jewel, not a single stone, nothing to put on. I shall look like distress. I should almost rather not go at all."

He resumed:

"You might wear natural flowers. It's very stylish at this time of the year. For ten francs you can get two or three magnificent roses."

She was not convinced.

"No; there's nothing more humiliating than to look poor among other women who are rich."

But her husband cried:

"How stupid you are! Go look up your friend Mme. Forestier, and ask her to lend you some jewels. You're quite thick enough with her to do that."

She uttered a cry of joy:

"It's true. I never thought of it."

The next day she went to her friend and told of her distress.

Mme. Forestier went to a wardrobe with a glass door, took out a large jewel-box, brought it back, opened it, and said to Mme. Loisel:

"Choose, my dear."

She saw first of all some bracelets, then a pearl necklace, then a Venetian cross, gold, and precious stones of admirable workmanship. She tried on the ornaments before the glass, hesitated, could

871

not make up her mind to part with them, to give them back. She kept asking:

"Haven't you any more?"

"Why, yes. Look. I don't know what you like."

All of a sudden she discovered, in a black satin box, a superb necklace of diamonds; and her heart began to beat with an immoderate desire. Her hands trembled as she took it. She fastened it around her throat, outside her high-necked dress, and remained lost in ecstasy at the sight of herself.

Then she asked, hesitating, filled with anguish:

"Can you lend me that, only that?"

"Why, yes, certainly."

She sprang upon the neck of her friend, kissed her passionately, then fled with her treasure.

The day of the ball arrived. Mme. Loisel made a great success. She was prettier than them all, elegant, gracious, smiling, and crazy with joy. All the men looked at her, asked her name, endeavored to be introduced. All the attachés of the Cabinet wanted to waltz with her. She was remarked by the minister himself.

She danced with intoxication, with passion, made drunk by pleasure, forgetting all, in the triumph of her beauty, in the glory of her success, in a sort of cloud of happiness composed of all this homage, of all this admiration, of all these awakened desires, and of that sense of complete victory which is so sweet to woman's heart.

She went away about four o'clock in the morning. Her husband had been sleeping since midnight, in a little deserted ante-room, with three other gentlemen whose wives were having a very good time.

He threw over her shoulders the wraps which he had brought, modest wraps of common life, whose poverty contrasted with the elegance of the ball dress. She felt this and wanted to escape so as not to be remarked by the other women, who were enveloping themselves in costly furs.

Loisel held her back.

"Wait a bit. You will catch cold outside. I will go and call a cab."

But she did not listen to him, and rapidly descended the stairs. When they were in the street they did not find a carriage; and they began to look for one, shouting after the cabmen whom they saw passing by at a distance.

They went down towards the Seine, in despair, shivering with cold. At last they found on the quay one of those ancient noctambulant coupés which, exactly as if they were ashamed to show their misery during the day, are never seen round Paris until after nightfall.

It took them to their door in the Rue des Martyrs, and once more, sadly, they climbed up homeward. All was ended for her. And as to him, he reflected that he must be at the Ministry at ten o'clock.

She removed the wraps, which covered her shoulders, before the glass, so as once more to see herself in all her glory. But suddenly she uttered a cry. She had no longer the necklace around her neck!

Her husband, already half-undressed, demanded:

"What is the matter with you?"

She turned madly towards him:

"I have—I have—I've lost Mme. Forestier's necklace."

He stood up, distracted.

"What!—how?—Impossible!"

And they looked in the folds of her dress, in the folds of her cloak, in her pockets, everywhere. They did not find it.

He asked:

"You're sure you had it on when you left the ball?"

"Yes, I felt it in the vestibule of the palace."

"But if you had lost it in the street we should have heard it fall. It must be in the cab."

"Yes. Probably. Did you take his number?"

"No. And you, didn't you notice it?"

"No."

They looked, thunderstruck, at one another. At last Loisel put on his clothes.

"I shall go back on foot," said he, "over the whole route which we have taken, to see if I can't find it."

And he went out. She sat waiting on a chair in her ball dress, without strength to go to bed, overwhelmed, without fire, without a thought.

Her husband came back about seven o'clock. He had found nothing.

He went to Police Headquarters, to the newspaper offices, to offer a reward; he went to the cab companies—everywhere, in fact, whither he was urged by the least suspicion of hope.

She waited all day, in the same condition of mad fear before this terrible calamity.

Loisel returned at night with a hollow, pale face; he had discovered nothing.

"You must write to your friend," said he, "that you have broken the clasp of her necklace and that you are having it mended. That will give us time to turn round."

She wrote at his dictation.

At the end of a week they had lost all hope.

And Loisel, who had aged five years, declared:

"We must consider how to replace that ornament."

The next day they took the box which had contained it, and they went to the jeweler whose name was found within. He consulted his books.

"It was not I, madame, who sold that necklace; I must simply have furnished the case."

Then they went from jeweler to jeweler, searching for a necklace like the other, consulting their memories, sick both of them with chagrin and with anguish.

They found, in a shop at the Palais Royal, a string of diamonds which seemed to them exactly like the one they looked for. It was worth forty thousand francs. They could have it for thirty-six.

So they begged the jeweler not to sell it for three days yet. And they made a bargain that he should buy it back for thirty-four thousand francs, in case they found the other one before the end of February.

Loisel possessed eighteen thousand francs which his father had left him. He would borrow the rest.

He did borrow, asking a thousand francs of one, five hundred of another, five louis here, three louis there. He gave notes, took up ruinous obligations, dealt with usurers, and all the race of lenders. He compromised all the rest of his life, risked his signature without even knowing if he could meet it; and, frightened by the pains yet to come, by the black misery which was about to fall upon him, by the prospect of all the physical privations and of all the moral tortures which he was to suffer, he went to get the new necklace, putting down upon the merchant's counter thirty-six thousand francs.

When Mme. Loisel took back the necklace Mme. Forestier said to her, with a chilly manner:

"You should have returned it sooner, I might have needed it."

She did not open the case, as her friend had so much feared. If she had detected the substitution, what would she have thought, what would she have said? Would she not have taken Mme. Loisel for a thief?

Mme. Loisel now knew the horrible existence of the needy. She took her part, moreover, all on a sudden, with heroism. That dreadful debt must be paid. She would pay it. They dismissed their servant; they changed their lodgings; they rented a garret under the roof.

She came to know what heavy housework meant and the odious cares of the kitchen. She washed the dishes, using her rosy nails on the greasy pots and pans. She washed the dirty linen, the shirts, and the dish-cloths, which she dried upon a line; she carried the slops down to the street every morning, and carried up the water, stopping for breath at every landing. And, dressed like a woman of the people, she went to the fruiterer, the grocer, the butcher, her basket on her arm, bargaining, insulted, defending her miserable money sou by sou.

Each month they had to meet some notes, renew others, obtain more time.

Her husband worked in the evening making a fair copy of some tradesman's accounts, and late at night he often copied manuscript for five sous a page.

And this life lasted ten years.

At the end of ten years they had paid everything, everything, with the rates of usury, and the accumulations of the compound interest.

Mme. Loisel looked old now. She had become the woman of impoverished households—strong and hard and rough. With frowsy hair, skirts askew, and red hands, she talked loud while washing the floor with great swishes of water. But sometimes, when her husband was at the office, she sat down near the window, and she thought of that gay evening of long ago, of that ball where she had been so beautiful and so fêted.

What would have happened if she had not lost that necklace? Who knows? who knows? How life is strange and how changeful! How little a thing is needed for us to be lost or to be saved!

But, one Sunday, having gone to take a walk in the Champs Elysées to refresh herself from the labors of the week, she suddenly

perceived a woman who was leading a child. It was Mme. Forestier, still young, still beautiful, still charming.

Mme. Loisel felt moved. Was she going to speak to her? Yes, certainly. And now that she had paid, she was going to tell her all about it. Why not?

She went up.

"Good-day, Jeanne."

The other, astonished to be familiarly addressed by this plain good-wife, did not recognize her at all, and stammered:

"But—madame!—I—do not know— You must have mistaken."

"No. I am Mathilde Loisel."

Her friend uttered a cry.

"Oh, my poor Mathilde! How you are changed!"

"Yes, I have had days hard enough, since I have seen you, days wretched enough—and that because of you!"

"Of me! How so?"

"Do you remember that diamond necklace which you lent me to wear at the ministerial ball?"

"Yes. Well?"

"Well, I lost it."

"What do you mean? You brought it back."

"I brought you back another just like it. And for this we have been ten years paying. You can understand that it was not easy for us, us who had nothing. At last it is ended, and I am very glad."

Mme. Forestier had stopped.

"You say that you bought a necklace of diamonds to replace mine?"

"Yes. You never noticed it, then! They were very like."

And she smiled with a joy which was proud and naïve at once.

Mme. Forestier, strongly moved, took her two hands.

"Oh, my poor Mathilde! Why, my necklace was paste. It was worth at most five hundred francs!"

FRANCOIS MAURIAC

FRANÇOIS MAURIAC (French, 1885-   ). Devout and highly principled
Catholic essayist and novelist. Member of French Academy, Nobel Prize-
winner, 1952. A soldier in World War I, member of the Resistance in War II.
His novels (including *A Woman of the Pharisees, Knot of Vipers, The Dark
Angels*) deal primarily with violent passions, in which sinners ultimately
receive grace.

THE ETERNAL BOURGEOISE

A WOMAN who belonged to the highest society of Cortona, a very
pious woman, gave proof of so much devotion to Margaret that
the saint prayed for her benefactress incessantly. One day Christ
spoke to her about this soul. "My daughter," he told her, "tell
your confessor about the shortcomings of her for whom you pray
to Me so often. I shall tell you what they are one after the other
so that your confessor may be able to tell her about them to her
great gain." It is Christ Himself Who proposes this terrifyingly
minute examination of conscience to so many perfect people who,
every week, bring trifles to the confessional and glory in finding
no sin in themselves.

"Tell her that she who is so devoted to you out of love for Me
had, before her marriage, a heart of doubtful virtue. Let her confess
having desired too passionately the man who is now her husband
and of having sought him with immoderate desire. Let her confess
this false virtue in her looks, her words, her gestures. . . .

Let her confess that at the time when a misfortune occurred to
one of her parents, she gave false testimony and helped, as much
as was in her power to do so, to render the judge's sentence unjust,
and that she felt less grief for the degrading record which the
accused thereby incurred than for the money which she made him
lose.

Let her reveal her offense against Me when she betook herself
to the Palace of the Podestat to hear herself proclaimed the most
beautiful among her friends (already queens of beauty!).

Let her admit often having accused servants secretly to their
masters, hoping to win their friendship by an indiscreet zeal in
meddling in their affairs, a zeal which was only hypocrisy since
she had no real affection either for them or for anyone except her
husband and children whom she loved excessively.

Let her reveal her inordinate fondness for delicate foods.

Let her bewail her hardness of heart toward the poor.

Let her admit the use she has made of ill-gotten gains. Let her remember everything she has thus spent. How much money has she not spent in this way, money pilfered from her husband, money coming from frauds, money extorted by violence, money won at gambling. . . .

As the mother of a family, she was in charge of household expenses; let her remember how many useless purchases she made, how many superfluous things she bought with money that was wrongly acquired. . . . (What rich and pious woman ever asks herself questions about 'those things which make one shudder,' which Bourdaloue has denounced as being at the source of every great fortune?).

Let her admit the jealousy that she harbored against her parents who did not support her husband's quarrels, the proud domination she exercised in her husband's family, she who would never have allowed her sister-in-law to behave so in her own. Let her admit her greed in regard to her husband's wards whom she had to take care of because they were poor. Let her remember all the injuries she directed against persons of the household in season and out, and with what pride she adorned her body. . . .

Let her confess the bad things she said and the rash judgments she made concerning the neighbor whose qualities she scorned and disparaged, recalling the faults that she knew about and concealing the good and finding the means of accusing him of other faults of which he was not guilty.

Let her confess the harsh disclosures she made about those who were absent and her flatteries before those who were present.

Let her admit her thirst for honor and praise, her desire to seem richer than others, her jealousy at the idea that others might be superior to her in wealth and beauty, her distraction at church in the presence of other women.

In spite of what I have done for her, I have been unable to attach Myself to her, and if at times she has served Me, it has been out of fear, not out of love.

Although she is free of the vice of impurity, yet she has soiled the marriage bed. She has felt no repugnance at finding herself among those who offend Me in their flesh, she who is full of spiritual vices.

Let her admit how careful she has been to blame others, whether for their ill-gotten gains, their lands, the luxuriousness of their

clothes and their perfumes, she who has sought the pleasures of good living and has given alms out of ostentation.

Let her confess her indiscretions concerning her servants, her rash judgments concerning the poor and how she scorned their pleadings, their tears, and their pleasures, their games, and their eating and drinking as well (this last trait is wonderful).

She denies herself nothing in what concerns the number and richness of her garments and does not worry herself at all about covering their nakedness nor appeasing their hunger.

Let her admit having usurped the name which befitted My Mother only when she had herself called Sovereign, she who ridiculed others when they assumed that name.

Although she has moved in the society of the most beautiful and best dressed persons, she has always thought herself superior to them.

Let her admit the frivolity which brings her to exaggerate her sufferings, always regarding them as greater than those of others, she who remains cold and indifferent before their misfortunes.

Let her confess her harshness in regard to her servants to whom she gave no rest after hard work, whether they were ill or not. Instead of the comforting which they needed they received only insults and abuse and were accused of gluttony and negligence. As for herself, their mistress treated herself with high consideration, spoke when she should have kept quiet, and kept quiet when she should have spoken. Let her confess having avoided deformed persons. . . . In spite of all these faults let her have confidence in My mercy. Let her not delay going to her confessor. Yet I say unto you, Margaret, My daughter, that this woman whom you recommend so urgently to My mercy will not fully agree to these favors."

HERMAN MELVILLE

HERMAN MELVILLE (American, 1819-1891). American fiction writer, whose major work, *Moby Dick*, was an utter failure when published—now justly considered one of world's masterpieces. Unable to support family as writer, worked for 20 years as New York Inspector of Customs. His South Sea stories (*Typee, Omoo, Mardi*) enjoyed limited popularity. Navy classic, *Billy Budd*, completed just before death, not published till 1924.

"THE WHALE WATCH" and "THE CHASE"
Chapter CXVII

THE four whales slain that evening had died wide apart; one, far to windward; one, less distant, to leeward; one ahead; one astern.

These last three were brought alongside ere nightfall; but the windward one could not be reached till morning; and the boat that had killed it lay by its side all night; and that boat was Ahab's.

The waif-pole was thrust upright into the dead whale's spout-hole and the lantern hanging from its top, cast a troubled flickering glare upon the black, glossy back, and far out upon the midnight waves, which gently chafed the whale's broad flank, like soft surf upon a beach.

Ahab and all his boat's crew seemed asleep but the Parsee; who crouching in the bow, sat watching the sharks, that spectrally played round the whale, and tapped the light cedar planks with their tails. A sound like the moaning in squadrons over Asphaltites of unforgiven ghosts of Gomorrah, ran shuddering through the air.

Started from his slumbers, Ahab, face to face, saw the Parsee; and hooped round by the gloom of the night they seemed the last men in a flooded world. "I have dreamed it again," said he.

"Of the hearses? Have I not said, old man, that neither hearse nor coffin can be thine?"

"And who are hearsed that die on the sea?"

"But I said, old man, that ere thou couldst die on this voyage, two hearses must verily be seen by thee on the sea; the first not made by mortal hands; and the visible wood of the last one must be grown in America."

"Aye, aye! a strange sight that, Parsee:—a hearse and its plumes floating over the ocean with the waves for the pall-bearers. Ha! Such a sight we shall not soon see."

"Believe it or not, thou canst not die till it be seen, old man."

"And what was that saying about thyself?"

"Though it come to the last, I shall still go before thee thy pilot."

"And when thou art so gone before—if that ever befall—then ere I can follow, thou must still appear to me, to pilot me still?— Was it not so? Well, then, did I believe all ye say, oh my pilot! I have here two pledges that I shall yet slay Moby-Dick and survive it."

"Take another pledge, old man," said the Parsee, as his eyes lighted up like fireflies in the gloom—"Hemp only can kill thee."

"The gallows, ye mean.—I am immortal then, on land and on sea," cried Ahab, with a laugh of derision:—"Immortal on land and on sea!"

Both were silent again, as one man. The gray dawn came on, and the slumbering crew arose from the boat's bottom, and ere noon the dead whale was brought to the ship.

. . . "Great God! but for one single instant show thyself," cried Starbuck; "never, never wilt thou capture him, old man—In Jesus' name no more of this, that's worse than devil's madness. Two days chased; twice stove to splinters; thy very leg once more snatched from under thee; thy evil shadow gone—all good angels mobbing thee with warnings:—what more wouldst thou have?—Shall we keep chasing this murderous fish till he swamps the last man? Shall we be dragged by him to the bottom of the sea? Shall we be towed by him to the infernal world? Oh, oh,—Impiety and blasphemy to hunt him more!"

"Starbuck, of late I've felt strangely moved to thee; ever since that hour we both saw—thou know'st what, in one another's eyes. But in this matter of the whale, be the front of thy face to me as the palm of this hand—a lipless, unfeatured blank. Ahab is for ever Ahab, man. This whole act's immutably decreed. 'Twas rehearsed by thee and me a billion years before this ocean rolled. Fool! I am the Fates' lieutenant; I act under orders. Look thou, underling! that thou obeyest mine.—Stand round me, men. Ye see an old man cut down to the stump; leaning on a shivered lance; propped up on a lonely foot. 'Tis Ahab—his body's part; but Ahab's soul's a centipede, that moves upon a hundred legs. I feel strained, half-stranded, as ropes that tow dismasted frigates in a gale; and I may look so. But ere I break, ye'll hear me crack; and till ye hear *that*, know that Ahab's hawser tows his purpose yet. Believe ye, men, in the things called omens? Then laugh aloud, and cry encore! For ere they drown, drowning things will twice rise to the surface; then rise again, to sink for evermore. So with Moby-Dick —two days he's floated—to-morrow will be the third. Aye, men, he'll rise once more,—but only to spout his last! D'ye feel brave, men, brave?"

"As fearless fire," cried Stubb.

"And as mechanical," muttered Ahab. Then as the men went forward, he muttered on: "The things called omens! And yesterday I talked the same to Starbuck there, concerning my broken boat. Oh! how valiantly I seek to drive out of others' hearts what's clinched so fast in mine!—The Parsee—the Parsee!—gone, gone? and he was to go before:—but still was to be seen again ere I could perish—How's that?—There's a riddle now might baffle all

881

the lawyers backed by the ghosts of the whole line of judges:—like a hawk's beak it pecks my brain. *I'll, I'll* solve it, though!"

When dusk descended, the whale was still in sight to leeward.

So once more the sail was shortened, and everything passed nearly as on the previous night; only, the sound of hammers, and the hum of the grindstone was heard till nearly daylight, as the men toiled by lanterns in the complete and careful rigging of the spare boats and sharpening their fresh weapons for the morrow. Meantime, of the broken keel of Ahab's wrecked craft the carpenter made him another leg; while still as on the night before, slouched Ahab stood fixed within his scuttle; his hid, heliotrope glance anticipatingly gone backward on its dial; sat due eastward for the earliest sun. . . .

Chapter CXXXV

. . . The boats had not gone very far, when by a signal from the mastheads—a downward pointed arm, Ahab knew that the whale had sounded; but intending to be near him at the next rising, he held on his way a little sideways from the vessel; the becharmed crew maintaining the profoundest silence, as the head-beat waves hammered and hammered against the opposing bow.

"Drive, drive in your nails, oh ye waves! to their uttermost heads drive them in! ye but strike a thing without a lid; and no coffin and no hearse can be mine:—and hemp only can kill me! Ha! ha!"

Suddenly the waters around them slowly swelled in broad circles; then quickly upheaved, as if sideways sliding from a submerged berg of ice, swiftly rising to the surface. A low rumbling sound was heard; a subterraneous hum; and then all held their breaths; as bedraggled with trailing ropes, and harpoons, and lances, a vast form shot lengthwise, but obliquely from the sea. Shrouded in a thin drooping veil of mist, it hovered for a moment in the rainbowed air; and then fell swamping back into the deep. Crushed thirty feet upwards, the waters flashed for an instant like heaps of fountains, then brokenly sank in a shower of flakes, leaving the circling surface creamed like new milk round the marble trunk of the whale.

"Give way!" cried Ahab to the oarsmen, and the boats darted forward to the attack; but maddened by yesterday's fresh irons that corroded in him, Moby Dick seemed combinedly possessed by

882

all the angels that fell from heaven. The wide tiers of welded tendons overspreading his broad white forehead, beneath the transparent skin, looked knitted together; as head on, he came churning his tail among the boats; and once more flailed them apart; spilling out the irons and lances from the two mates' boats, and dashing in one side of the upper part of their bows, but leaving Ahab's almost without a scar.

While Daggoo and Queequeg were stopping the strained planks; and as the whale swimming out from them, turned, and showed one entire flank as he shot by them again; at that moment a quick cry went up. Lashed round and round to the fish's back; pinioned in the turns upon turns in which, during the past night, the whale had reeled the involutions of the lines around him, the half torn body of the Parsee was seen; his sable raiment frayed to shreds; his distended eyes turned full upon old Ahab.

The harpoon dropped from his hand.

"Befooled, befooled!"—drawing in a long lean breath—"Aye, Parsee! I see thee again.—Aye, and thou goest before; and this, *this* then is the hearse that thou didst promise. But I hold thee to the last letter of thy word. Where is the second hearse? Away, mates, to the ship! those boats are useless now; repair them if ye can in time, and return to me; if not, Ahab is enough to die—Down, men! the first thing that but offers to jump from this boat I stand in, that thing I harpoon. Ye are not other men, but my arms and my legs; and so obey me.—Where's the whale? gone down again?"

But he looked too nigh the boat; for as if bent upon escaping with the corpse he bore, and as if the particular place of the last encounter had been a stage in his leeward voyage, Moby-Dick was now again steadily swimming forward; and had almost passed the ship,—which thus far had been sailing in the contrary direction to him, though for the present her headway had been stopped. He seemed swimming with his utmost velocity, and now only intent upon pursuing his own straight path in the sea.

"Oh! Ahab," cried Starbuck, "not too late is it, even now, the third day, to desist. See! Moby-Dick seeks thee not. It is thou, thou, that madly seekest him!" ...

From the ship's bows, nearly all the seamen now hung inactive; hammers, bits of plank, lances, and harpoons, mechanically retained in their hands, just as they had darted from their various employments; all their enchanted eyes intent upon the whale, which from side to side strangely vibrating his predestinating head, sent a

broad band of overspreading semicircular foam before him as he rushed. Retribution, swift vengeance, eternal malice were in his whole aspect, and spite of all that mortal man could do, the solid white buttress of his forehead smote the ship's starboard bow, till men and timbers reeled. Some fell flat upon their faces. Like dislodged trucks, the heads of the harpooneers aloft shook on their bull-like necks. Through the breach, they heard the waters pour, as mountain torrents down a flume.

"The ship! The hearse!—the second hearse!" cried Ahab from the boat; "its wood could only be American!"

Diving beneath the settling ship, the whale ran quivering along its keel; but turning under water, swiftly shot to the surface again, far off the other bow, but within a few yards of Ahab's boat, where, for a time, he lay quiescent.

"I turn my body from the sun. What ho, Tashtego! let me hear thy hammer. Oh! ye three unsurrendered spires of mine; thou uncracked keel; the only god-bullied hull; thou firm deck, and haughty helm, and Pole-pointed prow,—death-glorious ship! must ye then perish, and without me? Am I cut off from the last fond pride of meanest shipwrecked captains? Oh, lonely death on lonely life! Oh, now I feel my topmost greatness lies in my topmost grief! Ho, ho! from all your furthest bounds, pour ye now in, ye bold billows of my whole foregone life, and top this one piled comber of my death! Towards thee I roll, thou all-destroying but unconquering whale; to the last I grapple with thee; from hell's heart I stab at thee; for hate's sake I spit my last breath at thee. Sink all coffins and hearses to one common pool! and since neither can be mine, let me then tow to pieces, while still chasing thee, though tied to thee, thou damned whale! *Thus* I give up the spear!"

The harpoon was darted; the stricken whale flew forward; with igniting velocity the line ran through the groove;—ran foul. Ahab stooped to clear it; he did clear it; but the flying turn caught him round the neck, and voicelessly as Turkish mutes bowstring their victim, he was shot out of the boat, ere the crew knew he was gone. Next instant, the heavy eye-splice in the rope's final end flew out of the stark-empty tub, knocked down an oarsman, and smiting the sea, disappeared in its depths.

For an instant, the tranced boat's crew stood still; then turned. "The ship? Great God, where is the ship?" Soon they through dim, bewildering mediums saw her sidelong fading phantom, as in the gaseous Fata Morgana; only the uppermost masts out of water;

while fixed by infatuation, or fidelity, or fate, to their once lofty perches, the pagan harpooneers still maintained their sinking lookouts on the sea. And now, concentric circles seized the lone boat itself, and all its crew, and each floating oar, and every lance-pole, and spinning, animate and inanimate, all round and round in one vortex, carried the smallest chip of the Pequod out of sight.

But as the last whelmings intermixingly poured themselves over the sunken head of the Indian at the mainmast, leaving a few inches of the erect spar yet visible, together with long streaming yards of the flag, which calmly undulated, with ironical coincidings, over the destroying billows they almost touched;—at that instant, a red arm and a hammer hovered backwardly uplifted in the open air, in the act of nailing the flag faster and yet faster to the subsiding spar. A sky-hawk that tauntingly had followed the main-truck downwards from its natural home among the stars, pecking at the flag, and incommoding Tashtego there; this bird now chanced to intercept its broad fluttering wings between the hammer and the wood; and simultaneously feeling that ethereal thrill, the submerged savage beneath, in his death-gasp, kept his hammer frozen there; and so the bird of heaven, with arch-angelic shrieks, and his imperial beak thrust upwards, and his whole captive form folded in the flag of Ahab, went down with his ship, which, like Satan, would not sink to hell till she had dragged a living part of heaven along with her, and helmeted herself with it.

Now small fowls flew screaming over the yet yawning gulf; a sullen white surf beat against its steep sides; then all collapsed, and the great shroud of the sea rolled on as it rolled five thousand years ago.

MENG HAO-JAN

MÉNG HAO-JAN (Chinese, 689-740). Political satirist and lyricist. Spent early days studying in the mountains. When he failed to pass official examination, decided to devote remaining life to literature. Satirical poems incurred Emperor's wrath. Friend and disciple of famous Buddhist poet, Wang Wei.

THE LOST ONE

The red gleam o'er the mountains
   Goes wavering from sight,
And the quiet moon enhances
   The loveliness of night.

I open wide my casement
  To breathe the rain-cooled air,
And mingle with the moonlight
  The dark waves of my hair.

The night wind tells me secrets
  Of lotus lilies blue;
And hour by hour the willows
  Shake down the chiming dew.

I fain would take the zither,
  By some stray fancy led;
But there are none to hear me,
  And who can charm the dead?

So all my day-dreams follow
  The bird that leaves the nest;
And in the night I gather
  The lost one to my breast.

A FRIEND EXPECTED

Over the chain of giant peaks
  The great red sun goes down,
And in the stealthy floods of night
  The distant valleys drown.

Yon moon that cleaves the gloomy pines
  Has freshness in her train;
Low wind, faint stream, and waterfall
  Haunt me with their refrain.

The tired woodman seeks his cot
  That twinkles up the hill;
And sleep has touched the wanderers
  That sang the twilight still.

To-night—ah! beauty of to-night
  I need my friend to praise,
So take the lute to lure him on
  Through the frgrant, dew-lit ways.

GEORGE MEREDITH

GEORGE MEREDITH (English, 1828-1909). Long ignored because of his halting style, later became revered as master of Victorian novel. Striking creator of human portraits in *The Egoist, Diana of the Crossways.* Elaborate analyst of psychological situations, in the light of what he called "the comic spirit." Best poem, *Modern Love,* is based on his own first marriage.

THE PUNISHMENT OF SHAHPESH, THE
PERSIAN, ON KHIPIL, THE BUILDER

THEY relate that Shahpesh, the Persian, commanded the building of a palace, and Khipil was his builder. The work lingered from the first year of the reign of Shahpesh even to his fourth. One day Shahpesh went to the river-side where it stood, to inspect it. Khipil was sitting on a marble slab among the stones and blocks; round him stretched lazily the masons and stonecutters and slaves of burden; and they with the curve of humorous enjoyment on their lips, for he was reciting to them adventures, interspersed with anecdotes and recitations and poetic instances, as was his wont. They were like pleased flocks whom the shepherd hath led to a pasture freshened with brooks, there to feed indolently; he, the shepherd, in the midst.

Now, the King said to him, "O Khipil, show me my palace where it standeth, for I desire to gratify my sight with its fairness."

Khipil abased himself before Shahpesh, and answered, " 'Tis even here, O King of the age, where thou delightest the earth with thy foot and the ear of thy slave with sweetness. Surely a site of vantage, one that dominateth earth, air, and water, which is the builder's first and chief requisition for a noble palace, a palace to fill foreign kings and sultans with the distraction of envy; and it is, O Sovereign of the time, a site, this site I have chosen, to occupy the tongues of travellers and awaken the flights of poets!"

Shahpesh smiled and said, "The site is good! I laud the site! Likewise I laud the wisdom of Ebn Busrac, where he exclaims:

> *"Be sure, where Virtue faileth to appear,*
> *For her a gorgeous mansion men will rear;*
> *And day and night her praises will be heard,*
> *Where never yet she spake a single word."*

Then said he, "O Khipil, my builder, there was once a farm-servant that, having neglected in the seed-time to sow, took to singing the richness of his soil when it was harvest, in proof of which he displayed the abundance of weeds that coloured the land everywhere. Discover to me now the completeness of my halls and apartments, I pray thee, O Khipil, and be the excellence of thy construction made visible to me!"

Quoth Khipil, "To hear is to obey."

He conducted Shahpesh among the unfinished saloons and imperfect courts and roofless rooms, and by half-erected obelisks, and columns pierced and chipped, of the palace of his building. And he was bewildered at the words spoken by Shahpesh; but now the King exalted him, and admired the perfection of his craft, the greatness of his labour, the speediness of his construction, his assiduity; feigning not to behold his negligence.

Presently they went up winding balusters to a marble terrace, and the King said, "Such is thy devotion and constancy in toil, O Khipil, that thou shalt walk before me here."

He then commanded Khipil to precede him, and Khipil was heightened with the honour. When Khipil had paraded a short space he stopped quickly, and said to Shahpesh, "Here is, as it chanceth, a gap, O King! and we can go no further this way."

Shahpesh said, "All is perfect, and it is my will thou delay not to advance."

Khipil cried, "The gap is wide, O mighty King, and manifest, and it is an incomplete part of thy palace."

Then said Shahpesh, "O Khipil, I see no distinction between one part and another; excellent are all parts in beauty and proportion, and there can be no part incomplete in this palace that occupieth the builder four years in its building: so advance, do my bidding."

Khipil yet hesitated, for the gap was of many strides, and at the bottom of the gap was a deep water, and he one that knew not the motion of swimming. But Shahpesh ordered his guard to point their arrows in the direction of Khipil, and Khipil stepped forward hurriedly, and fell in the gap, and was swallowed by the water below. When he rose the second time, succour reached him, and he was drawn to land trembling, his teeth chattering. And Shahpesh praised him, and said, "This is an apt contrivance for a bath, Khipil O my builder! well conceived; one that taketh by surprise; and it shall be thy reward daily when much talking hath fatigued thee."

Then he bade Khipil lead him to the hall of state. And when they were there Shahpesh said, "For a privilege, and as a mark of my approbation, I give thee permission to sit in the marble chair of yonder throne, even in my presence, O Khipil."

Khipil said, "Surely, O King, the chair is not yet executed."

And Shahpesh exclaimed, "If this be so, thou art but the length of thy measure on the ground, O talkative one!"

Khipil said, "Nay, 'tis not so, O King of splendours! blind that I am! yonder 's indeed the chair."

And Khipil feared the King, and went to the place where the chair should be, and bent his body in a sitting posture, eyeing the King, and made pretence to sit in the chair of Shahpesh, as in conspiracy to amuse his master.

Then said Shahpesh, "For a token that I approve thy execution of the chair, thou shalt be honoured by remaining seated in it up to the hour of noon; but move thou to the right or to the left, showing thy soul insensible of the honour done thee, transfixed thou shalt be with twenty arrows and five."

The King then left him with a guard of twenty-five of his bodyguard; and they stood around him with bent bows, so that Khipil dared not move from his sitting posture. And the masons and the people crowded to see Khipil sitting on his master's chair, for it became rumoured about. When they beheld him sitting upon nothing, and he trembling to stir for fear of the loosening of the arrows, they laughed so that they rolled upon the floor of the hall, and the echoes of laughter were a thousand-fold. Surely the arrows of the guards swayed with the laughter that shook them.

Now, when the time had expired for his sitting in the chair, Shahpesh returned to him, and he was cramped, pitiable to see; and Shahpesh said, "Thou hast been exalted above men, O Khipil! for that thou didst execute for thy master has been found fitting for thee."

Then he bade Khipil lead the way to the noble gardens of dalliance and pleasure that he had planted and contrived. And Khipil went in that state described by the poet, when we go draggingly, with remonstrating members,

> Knowing a dreadful strengh behind,
> And a dark fate before.

They came to the gardens, and behold, these were full of weeds and nettles, the fountains dry, no tree to be seen—a desert. And Shahpesh

889

cried, "This is indeed of admirable design, O Khipil! Feelest thou not the coolness of the fountains?—their refreshingness? Truly I am grateful to thee! And these flowers, pluck me now a handful, and tell me of their perfume."

Khipil plucked a handful of the nettles that were there in the place of flowers, and put his nose to them before Shahpesh, till his nose was reddened; and desire to rub it waxed in him, and possessed him, and became a passion, so that he could scarce refrain from rubbing it even in the King's presence. And the King encouraged him to sniff and enjoy their fragrance, repeating the poet's words:

> *Methinks I am a lover and a child,*
> *A little child and happy lover, both!*
> *When by the breath of flowers I am beguiled*
> *From sense of pain, and lulled in odorous sloth.*
> *So I adore them, that no mistress sweet*
> *Seems worthier of the love which they awake:*
> *In innocence and beauty more complete,*
> *Was never maiden cheek in morning lake.*
> *Oh, while I live, surround me with fresh flowers,*
> *Oh, when I die, then bury me in their bowers!*

And the King said, "What sayest thou, O my builder? that is a fair quotation, applicable to thy feelings, one that expresseth them?

Khipil answered, "'Tis eloquent, O great King! comprehensiveness would be its portion, but that it alludeth not to the delight of chafing."

Then Shahpesh laughed, and cried, "Chafe not! it is an ill thing and a hideous! This nosegay, O Khipil, it is for thee to present to thy mistress. Truly she will receive thee well after its presentation! I will have it now sent in thy name, with word that thou followest quickly. And for thy nettled nose, surely if the whim seize thee that thou desirest its chafing, to thy neighbour is permitted what to thy hand is refused."

The King set a guard upon Khipil to see that his orders were executed, and appointed a time for him to return to the gardens.

At the hour indicated Khipil stood before Shahpesh again. He was pale, saddened; his tongue drooped like the tongue of a heavy bell, that when it soundeth giveth forth mournful sounds only: he had also the look of one battered with many beatings. So the King said, "How of the presentation of the flowers of thy culture, O Khipil?"

He answered, "Surely, O King, she received me with wrath, and I am shamed by her."

And the King said, "How of my clemency in the matter of the chafing?"

Khipil answered, "O King of splendours! I made petition to my neighbours whom I met, accosting them civilly and with imploring, for I ached to chafe, and it was the very raging thirst of desire to chafe that was mine, devouring eagerness for solace of chafing. And they chafed me, O King; yet not in those parts which throbbed for the chafing, but in those which abhorred it."

Then Shahpesh smiled and said, " 'Tis certain that the magnanimity of monarchs is as the rain that falleth, the sun that shineth: and in this spot it fertilizeth richness; in that encourageth rankness. So art thou but a weed, O Khipil! and my grace is thy chastisement."

Now, the King ceased not persecuting Khipil, under pretence of doing him honour and heaping favours on him. Three days and three nights was Khipil gasping without water, compelled to drink the drought of the fountain, as an honour at the hands of the King. And he was seven days and seven nights made to stand with stretched arms, as they were the branches of a tree, in each hand a pomegranate. And Shahpesh brough the people of his court to regard the wondrous pomegranate-shoot planted by Khipil, very wondrous, and a new sort, worthy the gardens of a King. So the wisdom of the King was applauded, and men wotted he knew how to punish offences in coin, by the punishment inflicted on Khipil the builder. Before that time his affairs had languished, and the currents of business instead of flowing had become stagnant pools. It was the fashion to do as did Khipil, and fancy the tongue a constructor rather than a commentator; and there is a doom upon that people and that man which runneth to seed in gabble, as the poet says in his wisdom:

> *If thou wouldst be famous, and rich in splendid fruits,*
> *Leave to bloom the flower of things, and dig among the roots.*

Truly after Khipil's punishment there were few in the dominions of Shahpesh who sought to win the honours bestowed by him on gabblers and idlers: as again the poet:

> *When to loquacious fools with patience rare*
> *I listen, I have thoughts of Khipil's chair:*
> *His bath, his nosegay, and his fount I see,—*
> *Himself stretch'd out as a pomegranate-tree.*

And that I am not Shahpesh I regret,
So to inmesh the babbler in his net.
Well is that wisdom worthy to be sung,
Which raised the Palace of the Wagging Tongue!

And whoso is punished after the fashion of Shahpesh, the Persian, on Khipil the Builder, is said to be one "in the Palace of the Wagging Tongue" to this time.

ADAM MICKIEWICZ

ADAM MICKIEWICZ (Polish, 1798-1855). Polish patriot, admired for his deep humanity and sentiment. Arrested for political activities, exiled to Russia. Died in Constantinople trying to raise Polish legion to fight for country's liberation. Playwright and poet. *Pan Tadeusz,* his masterwork, a tribute to the free Poland of his dreams.

ZEVILA

THE HISTORIES of many women of fair virtue and men of courage are recorded in the chronicles of Greece and Rome. So, too, would we find them in our own chronicles of Lithuania if some learned scribe had bent his efforts to the golden stylus and inscribed their stories in our annals; but since none have been moved to do so, I, myself, have resolved to set down here in homely words a short history from our ancient books.

About the year of Our Lord 1400, Prince Koryat, a great and powerful monarch, reigned over Novogrodek and Soinim and Leda. His only daughter, Zevila, (which is in our tongue, Diana), was a comely damsel and fair, but it was rumored that she dreaded the marriage vows, since she shook her head when princes and great barons from distant lands sent their ambassadors requesting her hand, saying she would rest a maid for the days of her life. Howbeit, the Princess Zevila had for a long time loved in her secret heart the Knight Poray, a man of her own country in whose prowess and military cunning her father, Prince Koryat, found good comfort and who, in the absence of the prince, was left in command of the kingdom. Poray was at no small pains to meet his lady in secret, so that they might together unbosom their sweet sentiments the one for the other.

It befell that Prince Koryat when he returned from the wars was sore aggrieved to see a change in his beloved daughter. Her sighs and tears, her ashen cheeks and trembling words when she greeted him, told him at once how matters stood.

"A bawd! My Zevila a bawd!" he cried. "So, thy debauch has led thee to assoil thy father's line. Be gone from my eyes and know that you and the man who brought you to this dishonor shall die a hard death together!"

So it was trumpeted throughout the city that he who would name Zevila's lover and prove the fellow's guilt should receive a rich reward. Yet with all the trumpeting, there was no man who knew about the secret amours of the princess or who would bear a tale to Koryat. Love of Zevila lay deep in the hearts of her subjects and serving folk, and furthermore, no breath of suspicion had fallen upon the Knight Poray who, although he discreetly bewailed his misfortune, showed to the court a jovial face.

When Prince Koryat found that all the trumpeting and inquests stirred no man to speak, he tried with mighty threats to force the secret from his daughter's lips. But no force prevailed upon her.

"My father," she said. "I do confess my own full share of guilt, so punish me, as I am not worthy to cry thee mercy for what I have done; but 'tis not for me to visit like ruin upon another. That would be an even greater offense against the gods."

On hearing this the prince put aside his threatening manner and fell to wheedling. Concealing his ire with silken speech he pledged himself in honeyed words to forgive her of her sin if only he might learn the name of her seducer.

Zevila spoke not, replying only with sobs and tears. Then the prince, waxing angry, commanded that his only daughter be put in chains and cast into a dungeon, from which she was to be led forth anon and put to death.

Now hath any writing man the words to relate the sound of the grief and lamenting that arose from the whole city! The people likened the Princess Zevila in their hearts unto a deity, and looked upon her as a tender mother who helped the poor and softened as much as she could the hard will of the prince. Wherefore, the people surged to the court, weeping bitterly and begging the prince to be merciful toward poor Zevila. But they gained nothing for their tears.

Now in those days, says the history, there was always strife between the men of Lithuania and the Russian *kniazes* or princes. One day the *kniaz* Ivan who wished to take Koryat's city, marched

with great haste to spread his camps around the place. He attacked so swiftly that before the full tidings of his deeds were heard much blood had been spilled.

All this happened on the day before the Great Feast, the morning on which Princess Zevila was to die.

Seeing his plight, Prince Koryat prayed Poray to ride forth with a small company of knights and lay on the foe with guile, while the prince strengthened the walls of his city. Poray, not knowing how strong the foe was but never losing heart, rode forth and fell upon Ivan's men who, he found, were out of sorts and craven. He dealt them such a mighty blow that they ran back to their Cossack camp and would have met their doom had not night fallen to end their sorry plight.

Without tarrying Poray set his men about the enemy, encompassing them, then he, himself, rode back into the city to bring the glad tidings to Koryat. The people made merry and the prince rode forth with his train and was full of praise for his knight. He called Poray the defender of the city and bade him to the castle for a mighty feast.

Now when those two were alone Poray fell down at the feet of his prince, speaking many words.

"Forsooth, my lord, my prince," he said, "I have laid heavy defeat upon your foe and, the gods willing, we shall destroy them to the last one, for which I pray as my reward that you do not put to death your only daughter but, by your grace give her to me as wife. For such a reward I swear to repay you with my blood and all my prowess, in all ways I am able."

The prince was angered and spoke thus his displeasure!

"How now, Poray! Why do you make me rejoice and sadden my heart in the same breath. I rejoice in your noble service, but what you ask is not in my power. Our revered forefathers, the Lithuanian princes, have never given their daughters to wed with their subjects, and woe be unto him who follows not the customs of his ancestors. As for the man who, goaded by success and pride, seeketh beyond his station—I will not dwell on that! Still there is the fact that my wanton child has assoiled the honor of our princely house. I trust it was not you who led her astray and put this shame upon her, and yet, why your sudden heart for this trollop?"

Thus they discoursed, then parted, each seeming still in a friendly mind with the other; each having mastered his wrath at least long enough to conceal it. Poray, hurt by his lord's ingratitude and fore-

894

seeing evil for his fortune, let seeds of vengeance spring up in his soul. The prince, no less, was fearful that Poray, for the love if his mistress and his knightly fortune, might seize the capital for his own. Koryat brooded over his need to take the knight's life but he dared not do it at once, because such a deed would sit ill on the people who were now making a great noise and calling Poray their defender. And, furthermore, he himself was still in need of Poray's right hand to crush his enemy.

This, sayeth the chronicle, was on the eve of the Great Feast. In the morning the Princess Zevila was to die.

Meanwhile Ivan, the Russian *kniaz*, hard beaten and surrounded, sat fretting in his camp, waiting for the dawn of the day of his defeat, hopeless, not knowing what more he could do. Suddenly into his tent ran sentries with word that a man in black armor had ridden into the encampment and would have audience with him. Did Ivan wish to hear the man?

When the knight in black armor was fetched he spoke thus to Ivan, "*Kniaz* Ivan, I am Poray who has twice beaten your Russian men and who holds you surrounded. I come to deliver to you the city, the prince, and all his possessions and men-at-arms on one condition: you must swear with a mighty oath that you will not harm our folk with fire or sword and that you will grant me to wife the princess inprisoned in the city, as well as the full protection of your men-at-arms."

As the *kniaz* agreed, cocks crowed in the early light and it was the day of the Great Feast, the day on which the Princess Zevila was to die.

A great tumult arose throughout the whole city, the like of which no man hath the cunning to describe. Those of the townsfolk who were hot of blood and resisted forfeited their heads; their fellows, being struck by fear, yielded themselves to the foe.

Poray then broke open the prison and found—oh, the horror of it!—his beloved, pale as ashes, alone and forgotten on a bed of rags there in the dungeon hole. When she saw Poray she fell in a swoon.

They bore her forth into the light and did what they could, yet she lay as one dead. A great press of folk about her crowded around, crying and calling unto her, but she did not open her eyes.

For a long time she lay there, then between her lids she marveled to see the people pressing about her and among them the armed foe. Then Poray spoke to her, "Pray, quiet your fears, my sweet.

895

Those are Ivan's men-at-arms who avenge our hurt and will serve as our protectors."

Zevila, hearing this, almost swooned again, but suddenly she drew the sword of Poray and smote him fair in the breast with such might that the blade sank deep.

"Traitor," she cried, "is your homeland such a mean thing in your heart that you would sell it for the smoothness of a woman's flesh? Oh, man of no honor, is this the way you would repay me for my so great a love? And ye, vassals, why do you not spend your wrath and vengeance on Ivan's brigands there?"

So saying, Zevila struck out with the sword at the foemen nigh about; then all the people stirred as though a fire had touched them and each man of them fell upon the unsuspecting Russians with swords and whatever weapons he could find to hand. Many foemen were done to death indoors and in the streets and others were taken alive for captives. Zevila hastened to the place where Prince Koryat, her father, stood fettered to the barricade.

"My father," she cried, then fell down there dead at his feet.

They buried Zevila at the foot of the mountain called Mendoga, and there the people came to make a *kopiec* or memorial mound and planted trees about. And even unto this day the old folk, being thankful to Almighty God that He did not offer them up to disgrace and the scorn of their foe, tell the story of Zevila to their young.

EDNA ST. VINCENT MILLAY

EDNA ST. VINCENT MILLAY (American, 1882-1950). One of the great figures in modern American poetry. Became famous at 19, while still in college, for long poem, "Renascence." In New York, worked with Provincetown Players and Theatre Guild. Among many volumes of verse: *A Few Figs from Thistles, Wine from These Grapes, Fatal Interview*. Her sonnets have been called best since Shakespeare.

WHAT LIPS MY LIPS HAVE KISSED

What lips my lips have kissed, and where, and why,
I have forgotten, and what arms have lain
Under my head till morning; but the rain
Is full of ghosts tonight, that tap and sigh

Upon the glass and listen for reply;
And in my heart there stirs a quiet pain
For unremembered lads that not again
Will turn to me at midnight with a cry.
Thus in the winter stands the lonely tree,
Nor knows what birds have vanished one by one,
Yet knows its boughs more silent than before:
I cannot say what loves have come and gone;
I only know that summer sang in me
A little while, that in me sings no more.

ELEGY BEFORE DEATH

There will be rose and rhododendron
   When you are dead and under ground;
Still will be heard from white syringas
   Heavy with bees, a sunny sound.

Still will the tamaracks be raining
   After the rain has ceased, and still
Will there be robins in the stubble,
   Brown sheep upon the warm green hill.

Spring will not ail nor autumn falter;
   Nothing will know that you are gone,
Saving alone some sullen plough-land
   None but yourself set foot upon;

Saving the may-weed and the pig-weed
   Nothing will know that you are dead,—
These, and perhaps a useless wagon
   Standing beside some tumbled shed.

Oh, there will pass with your great passing
   Little of beauty not your own,—
Only the light from common water,
   Only the grace from simple stone.

JOHN MILTON

JOHN MILTON (English, 1608-1674). The noblest of England's poets. In youth wrote more lyric poems (*Lycidas, L'Allegro, Il Penseroso*). In middle years composed pamphlets on civil and religious liberty (*Areopagitica*) and sonnets. Late in life, blind and in retirement, wrote *Paradise Lost, Paradise Regained, Samson Agonistes*. His command of blank verse unrivaled in English.

IL PENSEROSO

Hence, vain, deluding Joys,
    The brood of Folly without father bred!
How little you bestéd,
    Or fill the fixéd mind with all your toys!
Dwell in some idle brain,
    And fancies fond with gaudy shapes possess,
As thick and numberless
    As the gay motes that people the sunbeams,
Or likest hovering dreams,
    The fickle pensioners of Morpheus' train.
But, hail! thou Goddess, sage and holy!
Hail, divinest Melancholy!
Whose saintly visage is too bright
To hit the sense of human sight,
And therefore to our weaker view,
O'erlaid with black, staid Wisdom's hue;
Black, but such as in esteem
Prince Memnon's sister might beseem,
Or that starred Ethiop queen that strove
To set her beauty's praise above
The Sea-nymphs, and their powers offended.
Yet thou art higher far descended;
Thee bright-haired Vesta long of yore
To solitary Saturn bore;
His daughter she; in Saturn's reign
Such mixture was not held a stain.
Oft in glimmering bowers and glades
He met her, and in secret shades
Of woody Ida's inmost grove,
Whilst yet there was no fear of Jove.

Come, pensive Nun, devout and pure,
Sober, steadfast, and demure,
All in a robe of darkest grain,
Flowing with majestic train,
And sable stole of cypress lawn
Over thy decent shoulders drawn.
Come; but keep thy wonted state
With even step, and musing gait,
And looks commercing with the skies
Thy rapt soul sitting in thine eyes;
There, held in holy passion still,
Forget thyself to marble, till
With a sad, leaden, downward cast
Thou fix them on the earth as fast.
And join with thee calm Peace and Quiet,
Spare Fast, that oft with gods doth diet,
And hears the Muses in a ring
Aye round about Jove's altar sing;
And add to these retiréd Leisure,
That in trim gardens takes his pleasure;
But, first and chiefest, with thee bring
Him that yon soars on golden wing,
Guiding the fiery-wheeléd throne,
The cherub Contemplation;
And the mute Silence hist along,
'Less Philomel will deign a song,
In her sweetest, saddest plight,
Smoothing the rugged brow of Night,
While Cynthia checks her dragon yoke
Gently o'er the accustomed oak.
Sweet bird, that shun'st the noise of folly,
Most musical, most melancholy!
Thee, chauntress, oft the woods among
I woo, to hear thy evensong;
And, missing thee, I walk unseen
On the dry, smooth-shaven green,
To behold the wandering moon
Riding near her highest noon,
Like one that had been led astray
Through the heaven's wide, pathless way,

And oft, as if her head she bowed,
Stooping through a fleecy cloud.
Oft, on a plat of rising ground,
I hear the far-off curfew sound,
Over some wide-watered shore,
Swinging slow with sullen roar;
Or, if the air will not permit,
Some still, removéd place will fit,
Where glowing embers through the room
Teach light to counterfeit a gloom,
Far from all resort of mirth,
Save the cricket on the hearth,
Or the bellman's drowsy charm
To bless the doors from nightly harm.
Or let my lamp, at midnight hour,
Be seen in some high, lonely tower
Where I may oft outwatch the Bear,
With thrice-great Hermes, or unsphere
The spirit of Plato, to unfold
What world or what vast regions hold
The immortal mind that hath forsook
Her mansion in this fleshly nook;
And of those demons that are found
In fire, air, flood, or underground,
Whose power hath a true consent
With planet or with element.
Sometime let gorgeous Tragedy
In sceptered pall come sweeping by,
Presenting Thebes, or Pelops' line,
Or the tale of Troy divine.
Or what—though rare—of later age
Ennobled hath the buskined stage.
But, O sad Virgin! that thy power
Might raise Musæus from his bower;
Or bid the soul of Orpheus sing
Such notes as, warbled to the string,
Drew iron tears down Pluto's cheek,
And made Hell grant what love did seek;
Or call up him that left half told
The story of Cambuscan bold,

Of Camball, and of Algarsife,
And who had Canace to wife,
That owned the virtuous ring and glass,
And of the wondrous horse of brass
On which the Tartar king did ride;
And if aught else great bards beside
In sage and solemn tunes have sung,
Of tourneys, and of trophies hung,
Of forests, and enchantments drear,
Where more is meant than meets the ear.
Thus, Night, oft see me in thy pale career,
Till civil-suited Morn appear,
Not tricked and frounced, as she was wont
With the Attic boy to hunt,
But kerchiefed in a comely cloud,
While rocking winds are piping loud,
Or ushered with a shower still,
When the gust hath blown his fill,
Ending on the rustling leaves,
With minute-drops from off the eaves.
And, when the sun begins to fling
His flaring beams, me, Goddess, bring
To archéd walks of twilight groves,
And shadows brown, that Silvan loves,
Of pine, or monumental oak,
Where the rude ax with heavéd stroke
Was never heard the nymphs to daunt,
Or fright them from their hallowed haunt.
There in close covert, by some brook,
Where no profaner eye may look,
Hide me from day's garish eye,
While the bee with honeyed thigh,
That at her flowery work doth sing,
And the waters murmuring,
With such dewy-feathered Sleep.
And let some strange, mysterious dream
Wave at his wings, in airy stream
Of lively portraiture displayed,
Softly on my eyelids laid;
And, as I wake, sweet music breathe
Above, about, or underneath,

Sent by some Spirit to mortals good,
Or the unseen Genius of the wood.
But let my due feet never fail
To walk the studious cloister's pale,
And love the high embowéd roof,
With antique pillars massy-proof,
And storied windows richly dight,
Casting a dim, religious light,
There let the pealing organ blow,
To the full-voiced choir below,
In service high and anthems clear,
As may with sweetness, through mine ear,
And may at last my weary age
Find out the peaceful hermitage
The hairy gown and mossy cell,
Where I may sit and rightly spell
Of every star that heaven doth shew,
And every herb that sips the dew,
Till old experience do attain
To something like prophetic strain.
These pleasures, Melancholy, give,
And I with thee will choose to live.

MOLIERE

MOLIÈRE (Jean-Baptiste Poquelin, French, 1622-1673). France's greatest
comic poet. A complete man of the theater, passing his life as actor, playwright, manager. Company he founded is ancestor of present Théatre
Française. His greatest works are comedies of character: *Le Tartuffe, Dom
Juan, Le Misanthrope, Le Bourgeois Gentilhomme.* Unremitting satirist of
sham and hypocrisy. Founded the comedy of manners in France.

FIRST LESSON IN PHILOSOPHY

Philosophy-Master. What have you a mind to learn?
Mr. Jourdain. Everything I can, for I have all the desire in the
world to be a scholar, and it vexes me that my father and mother
had not made me study all the sciences when I was young.

902

Master. That's a very reasonable feeling. *Nam sine doctrina vita est quasi mortis imago.* You understand that, and are acquainted with the Latin, of course?

M. Jour. Yes; but act as if I were not acquainted with it. Tell me what it means.

Master. It means that "without learning life is as it were an image of death."

M. Jour. That same Latin's in the right.

Master. Don't you know some principles, some rudiments of science?

M. Jour. Oh, yes! I can read and write. . . . But now I must confide a secret to you. I'm in love with a person of quality, and I should be glad if you would help me to write something to her in a short billet-doux, which I'll drop at her feet.

Master. Very well.

M. Jour. That will be gallant, won't it?

Master. Undoubtedly. Is it verse you wish to write to her?

M. Jour. No, no; none of your verse.

Master. You would only have prose?

M. Jour. No, I would neither have verse nor prose.

Master. It must be one or the other.

M. Jour. Why so?

Master. Because, sir, there's nothing to express oneself by but prose or verse.

M. Jour. Is there nothing, then, but verse or prose?

Master. No, sir; whatever is not prose is verse, and whatever is not verse is prose.

M. Jour. And when one talks what may that be, then?

Master. Prose.

M. Jour. How? When I say, "Nicole, bring me my slippers and give me my nightcap," is that prose?

Master. Yes, sir.

M. Jour. On my conscience, I have spoken prose above these forty years without knowing it; and I am hugely obliged to you for informing me of this.

M. Jour. (*to his wife*). I am ashamed of your ignorance. For example, do you know what it is you now speak?

Mme. Jour. Yes, I know that what I speak is right, and that you ought to think of living in another manner.

M. Jour. I don't talk of that. I ask you what the words are that you now speak?

Mme. Jour. They are words that have a good deal of sense in them, and your conduct is by no means such.

M. Jour. I don't talk of that, I tell you. I ask you what it is that I now speak to you, which I say this very moment?

Mme. Jour. Mere stuff.

M. Jour. Pshaw, no, it is not that. That which we both of us say, the language we speak this instant?

Mme. Jour. Well?

M. Jour. How is it called?

Mme. Jour. It's called just what you please to call it.

M. Jour. It's prose, you ignorant creature.

Mme. Jour. Prose?

M. Jour. Yes, prose. Whatever is prose is not verse, and whatever is not verse, is prose. Now, see what it is to study.

THOMAS MOORE

THOMAS MOORE (Irish, 1779-1852). Famous Irish versifier of most melodious rhythms. Student of law in London, government official in Bermuda, traveler in United States and Canada. Author of *Lalla Rookh* and *Life of Sheridan*, but chiefly remembered for his *Irish Melodies*, based on traditional Irish airs.

GO WHERE GLORY WAITS THEE

Go where glory waits thee;
But while fame elates thee,
　Oh still remember me!
When the praise thou meetest
To thine ear is sweetest,
　Oh then remember me!
Other arms may press thee,
Dearer friends caress thee,
All the joys that bless thee
　Sweeter far may be;
But when friends are nearest,
And when joys are dearest
　Oh then remember me!

When at eve thou rovest
By the star thou lovest,
   Oh then remember me!
Think, when home returning,
Bright we've seen it burning,
   Oh thus remember me!
Oft as summer closes,
When thine eye reposes
On its lingering roses,
      Once so loved by thee,
Think of her who wove them,
Her who made thee love them—
   Oh then remember me!

When around thee dying
Autumn leaves are lying,
   Oh then remember me!
And at night when gazing
On the gay hearth blazing,
   Oh still remember me!
Then should music, stealing
All the soul of feeling,
To thy heart appealing,
      Draw one tear from thee;
Then let memory bring thee
Strains I used to sing thee—
   Oh then remember me!

OFT, IN THE STILLY NIGHT

Oft, in the stilly night,
Ere Slumber's chain has bound me,
Fond Memory brings the light
   Of other days around me;
      The smiles, the tears,
      Of boyhood's years,
The words of love then spoken;
      The eyes that shone,
      Now dimm'd and gone,
   The cheerful hearts now broken!

Thus, in the stilly night,
  Ere Slumber's chain has bound me,
Sad Memory brings the light
  Of other days around me.

When I remember all
  The friends, so link'd together,
I've seen around me fall,
  Like leaves in wintry weather;
    I feel like one,
    Who treads alone
Some banquet-hall deserted,
    Whose lights are fled,
    Whose garlands dead,
And all but he departed!
Thus, in the stilly night,
  Ere Slumber's chain has bound me,
Sad Memory brings the light
  Of other days around me.

SWEET INNISFALLEN

Sweet Innisfallen, fare thee well,
May calm and sunshine long be thine!
How fair thou art let others tell—
  To *feel* how fair shall long be mine.

Sweet Innisfallen, long shall dwell
  In memory's dream that sunny smile,
Which o'er thee on that evening fell
  When first I saw thy fairy isle.

'Twas light, indeed, too blest for one,
  Who had to turn to paths of care—
Through crowded haunts again to run,
  And leave thee bright and silent there;

No more unto thy shores to come,
  But, on the world's rude ocean tost,
Dream of thee sometimes as a home
  Of sunshine he had seen and lost.

Far better in thy weeping hours
　　To part from thee, as I do now,
When mist is o'er thy blooming bowers,
　　Like sorrow's veil on beauty's brow.

For, though unrivall'd still thy grace,
　　Thou dost not look, as then, too blest,
But thus in shadow, seem'd a place
　　Where erring man might hope to rest—

Might hope to rest, and find in thee
　　A gloom like Eden's, on the day
He left its shade, when every tree,
　　Like thine, hung weeping o'er his way.

Weeping or smiling, lovely isle!
　　And all the lovelier for thy tears—
For tho' but rare thy sunny smile,
　　'Tis heaven's own glance when it appears.

Like feeling hearts, whose joys are few,
　　But, when indeed they come, divine—
The brightest life the sun e'er threw
　　Is lifeless to one gleam of thine!

LOVE'S YOUNG DREAM

Oh! the days are gone when Beauty bright
　　My heart's chain wove!
When my dream of life, from morn till night,
　　Was love, still love,
　　　New hope may bloom,
　　　And days may come
　　Of milder, calmer beam,
But there's nothing half so sweet in life
　　As Love's young dream!
Oh! there's nothing half so sweet in life
　　As Love's young dream!

907

Though the bard to purer fame may soar,
    When wild youth's past;
Though he win the wise, who frowned before,
    To smile at last;
        He'll never meet
        A joy so sweet,
    In all his noon of fame,
As when first he sang to woman's ear
    His soul-felt flame,
And, at every close, she blushed to hear
    The one loved name!

Oh! that hallowed form is ne'er forgot
    Which first love traced;
Still it lingering haunts the greenest spot
    On memory's waste!
        'Twas odor fled
        As soon as shed;
    'Twas morning's wingéd dream;
'Twas a light that ne'er can shine again
    On life's dull stream!
Oh! 'twas light that ne'er can shine again
    On life's dull stream.

COME, YE DISCONSOLATE

Come, ye disconsolate, where'er you languish;
    Come, at God's altar fervently kneel;
Here bring your wounded hearts, here tell your anguish—
    "Earth has no sorrow that Heaven cannot heal."

Joy of the desolate, Light of the straying
    Hope, when all others die, fadeless and pure,
Here speaks the Comforter, in God's name saying,
    "Earth has no sorrow that Heaven cannot cure."

Go, ask the infidel what boon he brings us,
    What charm for aching hearts *he* can reveal
Sweet as that heavenly promise Hope sings us,
    "Earth has no sorrow that God cannot heal."

908

BELIEVE ME, IF ALL THOSE ENDEARING
YOUNG CHARMS

Believe me, if all those endearing young charms
    Which I gaze on so fondly to-day
Were to change by to-morrow, and fleet in my arms,
    Like fairy-gifts fading away,
Thou wouldst still be adored, as this moment thou art,
    Let thy loveliness fade as it will;
And around the dear ruin each wish of my heart
    Would entwine itself verdantly still.

It is not while beauty and youth are thine own,
    And thy cheeks unprofaned by a tear,
That the fervor and faith of a soul can be known
    To which time will but make thee more dear;
No, the heart that as truly loved never forgets,
    But as truly loves on to the close,
As the sunflower turns on his god when he sets
    The same look which she turned when he rose.

THE TURF SHALL BE MY FRAGRANT
SHRINE

The turf shall be my fragrant shrine;
My temple, Lord ! that arch of thine;
My censer's breath the mountain airs,
And silent thoughts my only prayers.

My choir shall be the monlight waves,
When murmuring homeward to their caves,
Or when the stillness of the sea,
Even more than music, breathes of Thee!

I'll seek, by day, some glade unknown,
All light and silence, like thy throne!
And the pale stars shall be, at night,
The only eyes that watch my rite.

Thy heaven, on which 'tis bliss to look,
Shall be my pure and shining book,
Where I shall read, in words of flame,
The glories of thy wondrous name.

I'll read thy anger in the rack
That clouds awhile the day-beam's track;
Thy mercy in the azure hue
Of sunny brightness breaking through!

There's nothing bright above, below,
From flowers that bloom to stars that glow,
But in its light my soul can see
Some feature of thy Deity!

There's nothing dark below, above,
But in its gloom I trace thy love,
And meekly wait that moment when
Thy touch shall turn all bright again!

MORI OGAI

MORI OGAI (Japanese, 1860-1922). Classical stylist, noted as both original writer and translator. As an army doctor, went to Germany to study army hygiene. Later translated many German classics into Japanese. Also author of over 60 novels and short stories. Major influence in modern Japanese literature.

THE PIER

THE pier is long—long—
    The rails of four railroads cut straight and obliquely the beams of the iron bridge on which the long and short cross-beams are like the bars of the xylophone on which children play. Through the cracks of the cross-beams, that almost catch the heels of shoes and wooden clogs, here and there the black waves are shown, reflected on the white flashes of sunshine.
    The sky has cleared into a deep blue. On the inside of the train where she was sitting with her husband starting today, she did not think the wind was blowing.

When leaving the jinriksha, in which she rode from the station of Yokohama, and standing on this pier, she found that the wind of the fifth of March was still blowing as if to bite the skin, fluttering the skirts of the Azuma coat.

It is the Azuma coat in silver gray, which she loosely wears on her body, that carries the child of her husband, who is starting to-day, this day which is not far from the month of confinement.

She came with her hair in Sokuhatsu. Her boa is of white ostrich. Holding the light green umbrella with tassels, she walks along, surrounded by four or five maidservants.

The pier is long—long——

The big ships are anchoring on the right and the left of the pier. Some are painted in black, some in white.

The anchored ships are making a fence for the wind. Every time she leaves the place where there are ships, a gust of wind blows and flutters the skirts of her Azuma coat.

Two years ago, immediately after he was graduated from the university of literature, the count, her husband, had married her. It was during the previous year that she gave birth to her first child, a princess like a jewel. At the end of the year her husband became a Master of Ceremonies at the Court. And, now, he is starting to London, charged with his official duty.

In his newly made gray overcoat, flinging the cane with crooked handle, her husband is walking rapidly along the pier. The viscount, who is going with him, and whose height is taller by a head than his, also walks rapidly beside him, clad in a suit of similar color.

The French ship, on which her husband is about to go abroad, is anchoring at the extreme end of the right side of the pier.

A stool, like that which is used to repair the wires of a trolley, is stationed on the pier, and from it a gangplank is laid across to the bulwark.

While walking slowly, she sees her husband and the viscount, his companion, crossing the gangplank and entering the ship.

The group of people looking after them are standing, here and there, on the pier. Almost all of them are those who came to bid adieu to her husband and the viscount. Perhaps there are no other passengers on this ship about to sail who are so important and are looked at by so many people.

Some of them are going to the foot of the stool on which the gangplank is laid, and stop there to wait for their companions.

911

Some of them are standing at the place, a bit before the stool, where the blocks and ropes are laid down.

Among these people there must be some who are intimately known to her husband, and some who know him but slightly. But, standing under this clear sky, they all seem dejected; or is it only her fancy?

The pier is long—long——

Following slowly after them, unconsciously she looks off to her right where there were many round windows on the side of the ship. The faces and chests of women are seen from one of those round windows. Three of them are from thirty to forty years of age; all with white aprons on their chests. They must be the waitresses of the ship. Supposing them to be the waitresses who wait on the passengers of the ship, on which her husband is on board, she feels envious of even those humble women.

There is also a woman at the bulwark, looking down on the pier, who wears a big bonnet with white cloth and carries a small leather bag in her hand. Two big eyes, as if painted with shadows, are shining on her wrinkled face above the large nose, like a hook. She looks like a Jewess. She also must be a traveler who is going on this ship. She is also envious of her.

The pier is long—long——

At last she arrives at the foot of the gangplank. Cautiously she carries her body, which has the second infant of her husband under the Azuma coat, and descends on the deck of the big, black-painted ship. She hands the umbrella to a maidservant.

Led by the people who have come to say farewell and were already on board, she goes back along the bulwark toward the prow. There are rooms for passengers at the end of the way, the numbers of which increase from twenty-seven to twenty-nine.

The viscount is standing at the entrance and addresses her.

"This is the room, madam."

Peeping into the room she finds two beds, under which the familiar packages and trunks are deposited. Her husband is standing before one of the beds.

"Look it through, madam. It is like this."

This is the room; she must look through it carefully. During the long, long voyage of her husband, this is the room where her dreams must come and go.

A man, who looks like the captain, comes, and, addressing her

912

husband in French, guides him to the saloon of the ship. She follows her husband and the viscount and enters the room.

This is a spacious and beautiful saloon. Several tables are arranged, each bearing a flower basket. . . . Gradually the people who came to say farewell gather into the room.

By the order of this man, who looks like the captain, a waiter brings forth many cups in the shape of morning-glories, and, pouring champagne into them, he distributes them among the people. Another waiter brings cakes, like those which are brought with ice cream, piled on a plate in the form of the well crib, and distributes them among the people.

The people who received the cups go after another, and stand before her husband and the viscount, wishing them a happy voyage, and drink from the cups.

Sitting on a small chair beside the table, she is waiting for the time when the congratulations are at an end. During his busy moments, now and then, her husband lifts his eyes to her.

However, there is no more to be said to her before many people. Also, there is no more to be said to him, before many people.

The bell rings. Having bidden farewell to her husband and to the viscount the people are going out, one after another. She also follows them, saluting her husband and the viscount.

Again crossing the dangerous gangplank, she descends to the pier. She receives the light green umbrella from the hand of her maidservant, and raises it.

Her husband and the viscount are standing on the bulwark, looking in her direction. She is looking up at them from under her umbrella. She feels that her eyes, as she looks up, are growing gradually larger and larger.

Again the bell rings. A few French sailors begin to untie the rope from the gangplank. A Japanese laborer in Hanten is standing on the stool like that which is used in repairing the trolley, preparing to draw down the gangplank. Hanging on the rope of the wheel, pulled by the man in Hanten, the gangplank at last leaves the bulwark.

The noon-gun of the city of Yokohama resounds. With this as a signal, the ship, from the hold of which for some time a noise has been issuing, silently begins to move.

The elderly Europeans, who seem to be a married couple, are standing at the bulwark. They are talking about something of a jolly nature with a white-haired old man who is standing on the

913

pier, with one of his feet placed on an apparatus to roll the ropes, which looks like a big bobbin. They do not seem to regret the parting.

It looks as if the ship is moving. It looks as if the pier is moving. There seems to be the distance of a Pallaraxe between the place where her husband and the viscount are standing and the place where she is standing. She feels her eyes growing larger and larger.

Some of the people who are looking after them are running to the end of the pier. She cannot do such an immodest thing. Suddenly something white waves at the bulwark. It was a handkerchief waved by the hand of a woman who wears a big bonnet decorated with a white cloth. A tall man stands at the end of the pier, in red waistcoat and tan shoes. A white handkerchief waves also from the hand of this man. This also must be a parting in human life.

These two persons set the fashion, and the handkerchiefs are waved here and there. White things are waving also from the people who are looking after the group surrounding the count. She also grasps the batiste handkerchief which she has brought in her sleeve, but she cannot do such an immodest thing.

When the ship seemed to have left the pier, it turned its prow a bit to the right. The place where her husband and the viscount were standing has disappeared at last.

Still she can see a boy about fifteen or sixteen, standing at the stern, in a blue, cold-looking garment like a blouse. What mother is waiting for him in France? Or has he no parents? What is he looking at, standing by the rail at the stern?

Slowly she turned her feet and walked among the maidservants surrounding her.

The pier is long—long——

At the place where the black-painted ship was anchored, until a short time ago, the water is glittering like the scales of fish, as the small ripples are reflecting the pale sunshine.

914

EDUARD MORIKE

EDUARD MÖRIKE (German, 1804-1875). German poet and novelist, creative in both the classical and the folk manner. His private life was not happy —career as vicar and marriage were unsuccessful. Famous novella: *Mozart on His Trip to Prague.* Best poems are extremely simple, remarkable imitations of folk songs.

BEAUTY ROHTRAUT

What is the name of King Ringang's daughter?
   Rohtraut, Beauty Rohtraut!
And what does she do the livelong day,
Since she dare not knit and spin alway?
O hunting and fishing is ever her play!
And, heigh! that her huntsman I might be!
I'd hunt and fish right merrily!
     Be silent, heart!

And it chanced that, after this some time,
   Rohtraut, Beauty Rohtraut!
The boy in the Castle has gained access,
And a horse he has got and a huntsman's dress,
To hunt and to fish with the merry Princess;
And, O! that a king's son I might be!
Beauty Rohtraut I love so tenderly.
     Hush! hush! my heart.

Under a gray old oak they sat,
   Beauty, Beauty Rohtraut!
She laughs: "Why look you so slyly at me?
If you have heart enough, come, kiss me."
Cried the breathless boy, "Kiss thee?"
But he thinks kind fortune has favored my youth;
And thrice he has kissed Beauty Rohtraut's mouth.
     Down! down! mad heart.

Then slowly and silently they rode home,—
   Rohtraut, Beauty Rohtraut!
The boy was lost in his delight:

"And, wert thou Empress this very night,
I would not heed or feel the blight;
Ye thousand leaves of the wild wood wist
How Beauty Rohtraut's mouth I kiss'd.
            Hush! hush! wild heart."

AN ERROR CHANCED

An error chanced in the moonlight garden
Of a once inviolate love.
Shuddering I came on an outworn deceit,
And with sorrowing look, yet cruel,
Bade I the slender
Enchanting maiden
Leave me and wander far.
Alas! her lofty forehead
Was bowed, for she loved me well;
Yet did she go in silence
Into the dim gray
World outside.

Sick since then,
Wounded and woeful heart!
Never shall it be whole.

Meseems that, spun of the air, a thread of magic
Binds her yet to me, an unrestful bond;
It draws, it draws me faint with love toward her.
Might it yet be some day that on my threshold
I should find her, as erst, in the morning twilight,
Her traveler's bundle beside her,
And her eye true-heartedly looking up to me,
Saying, "See, I've come back,
Back once more from the lonely world!"

A SONG FOR TWO IN THE NIGHT

She: How soft the night wind strokes the meadow grasses
And, breathing music, through the woodland passes!

916

Now that the upstart day is dumb,
One hears from the still earth a whispering throng
Of forces animate, with murmured song
Joining the zephyrs' well-attunèd hum.

He: I catch the tone from wondrous voices brimming,
Which sensuous on the warm wind drifts to me,
While, streaked with misty light uncertainly,
The very heavens in the glow are swimming.

She: The air like woven fabric seems to wave,
Then more transparent and more lustrous groweth;
Meantime a muted melody outgoeth
From happy fairies in their purple cave.
To sphere-wrought harmony
Sing they, and busily
The thread upon their silver spindles floweth.

He: Oh lovely night! how effortless and free
O'er samite black—though green by day—thou movest!
And to the whirring music that thou lovest
Thy foot advances imperceptibly.
Thus hour by hour thy step doth measure—
In trancèd self-forgetful pleasure
Thou'rt rapt; creation's soul is rapt with thee!

EARLY AWAY

The morning frost shines gray
    Along the misty field
Beneath the pallid way
    Of early dawn revealed.

Amid the glow one sees
    The day-star disappear;
Yet o'er the western trees
    The moon is shining clear.

So, too, I send my glance
    On distant scenes to dwell;
I see in torturing trance
    The night of our farewell.

917

Blue eyes, a lake of bliss,
   Swim dark before my sight,
Thy breath, I feel, thy kiss;
   I hear thy whispering light.

My cheek upon thy breast
   The streaming tears bedew,
Till, purple-black, is cast
   A veil across my view.

The sun comes out; he glows,
   And straight my dreams depart,
While from the cliffs he throws
   A chill across my heart.

THE FORSAKEN MAIDEN

Early when cocks do crow
   Ere the stars dwindle,
Down to the hearth I go,
   Fire must I kindle.

Fair leap the flames on high,
   Sparks they whirl drunken;
I watch them listlessly
   In sorrow sunken.

Sudden it comes to me,
   Youth so fair seeming,
That all the night of thee
   I have been dreaming.

Tears then on tears do run
   For my false lover;
Thus has the day begun—
   Would it were over!

WEYLA'S SONG

Thou art Orplede, my land
Remotely gleaming;
The mist arises from thy sun-bright strand
To where the faces of the gods are beaming.

Primeval rivers spring renewed
Thy silver girdle weaving, child!
Before the godhead bow subdued
Kings, thy worshipers and watchers mild.

SECLUSION

Let, oh world, ah let me be!
Tempt me not with gifts of pleasure.
Leave alone this heart to treasure
All its joy, its misery.

What my grief I can not say,
'Tis a strange, a wistful sorrow;
Yet through tears at every morrow
I behold the light of day.

When my weary soul finds rest
Oft a beam of rapture brightens
All the gloom of cloud, and lightens
This oppression in my breast.

Let, oh world, ah, let me be!
Tempt me not with gifts of pleasure.
Leave alone this heart to treasure
All its joy, its misery.

THE SOLDIER'S BETROTHED

Oh dear, if the king only knew
How brave is my sweetheart, how true!
He would give his heart's blood for the king,
But for me he would do the same thing.

My love has no ribbon or star,
No cross such as gentlemen wear,
A gen'ral he'll never become;
If only they'd leave him at home!

919

For stars there are three shining bright
O'er the Church of St. Mary each night;
We are bound by a rose-woven band,
And a house-cross is always at hand.

THE OLD WEATHERCOCK: AN IDYLL

At Cleversulzbach in the Underland
A hundred and thirteen years did I stand
Up on the tower in wind and rain,
An ornament and a weathervane.
Through night and tempest gazing down,
Like a good old cock I watched the town.

THINK OF IT, MY SOUL!

Somewhere a pine is green,
Just where who knoweth,
And in a garth unseen
A rose-tree bloweth.
These are ordained for thee—
Think, oh, soul, fixedly—
Over thy grave to be;
Swift the time floweth.

Two black steeds on the down
Briskly are faring,
Or on their way to town
Canter uncaring.
These may with heavy tread
Slowly convey the dead
E'en ere the shoes be shed
They now are wearing.

ERINNA TO SAPPHO

"Many the paths to Hades," an ancient proverb
Tells us, "and one of them thou thyself shalt follow,
Doubt not!" My sweetest Sappho, who can doubt it?
Tells not each day the old tale?

Yet the foreboding word in a youthful bosom
Rankles not, as a fisher bred by the seashore,
Deafened by use, perceives the breaker's thunder no more.
—Strangely, however, today my heart misgave me. Attend:
Sunny the glow of morn-tide, pouring
Through the trees of my well-walled garden,
Roused the slugabed (so of late thou calledst Erinna)
Early up from her sultry couch.
Full was my soul of quiet, although my blood beat
Quick with uncertain waves o'er the thin cheek's pallor.
Then, as I loosed the plaits of my shining tresses,
Parting with nard-moist comb above my forehead
The veil of hair—in the glass my own glance met me.
Eyes, strange eyes, I said, what will ye?
Spirit of me, that within there dwelled securely as yet,
Occultly wed to my living senses—
Demon-like, half smiling thy solemn message,
Thou dost nod to me, Death presaging!
—Ha! all at once like lightning a thrill went through me,
Or as a deadly arrow with sable feathers
Whizzing had grazed my temples,
So that, with hands pressed over my face, a long time
Dumb-struck I sat, while my thought reeled at the frightful
    abyss.

Tearless at first I pondered,
Weighing the terror of Death;
Till I bethought me of thee, my Sappho,
And of my comrades all,
And of the muses' lore,
When straightway the tears ran fast.

But there on the table gleamed a beautiful hair-net, thy gift,
Costly handwork of Byssos, spangled with golden bees.
This, when next in the flowery festal season
We shall worship the glorious child of Demeter,
This will I offer to her for thy and my sake,
So may she favor us both (for she much availeth),
That no mourning lock thou untimely sever
From thy beloved head for thy poor Erinna.

MULTATULI

MULTATULI (Eduard Douwes Dekker), (Dutch, 1820-1887). One of the most powerful novelists of Holland. At 18 left for Dutch East Indies, became bitter foe of colonialism. Fame rests on two novels: *Max Havelaar* and *Woutertje Pieterse*. Exerted considerable influence on succeeding generation of Dutch writers.

THE STORY OF SAÏDJAH

SAÏDJAH's father had a buffalo, which he used for plowing his field. When this buffalo was taken away from him by the district chief at Parang-Koodjang he was very dejected, and spoke no word for many a day. For plowing time was come, and he feared that if the rice-field was not worked in time, the opportunity to sow would be lost, and lastly, that there would be no paddy to cut, and none to keep in the store-room of the house. I have here to tell readers who know Java, but not Bantam, that in that Residency there is personal landed property, which is not the case elsewhere. Saïdjah's father, then, was very uneasy. He feared that his wife would have no rice, nor Saïdjah himself, who was still a child, nor his little brothers and sisters. And the district chief, too, would denounce him to the Assistant Resident if he was behindhand in the payment of his taxes, for this is punished by the law. Saïdjah's father then took a poniard, which he had inherited from his father. It was not very handsome, but there were silver bands round the sheath, and at the end a silver plate. He sold it to a Chinaman in the capital, and came home with twenty-four guilders, with which he bought another buffalo.

Saïdjah, who was then about seven, soon made friends with the new buffalo. I purposely say "made friends," for it was indeed touching to see how the buffalo was attached to the little boy who watched over and fed him. Of this attachment I shall soon give an example. The large strong animal bends its heavy head to the right, to the left, or downwards, just as the pressure of the child's finger directs. Such a friendship the little Saïdjah had soon been able to make with the newcomer; and it seemed as if the encouraging voice of the child gave more strength to the heavy shoulders of the animal, when it tore open the stiff clay and traced its way in deep sharp furrows. The buffalo turned willingly, on reaching the end of the field, not losing an inch of ground when plowing backwards the new furrow, which was ever near the old, as if the *sawah* was a garden

922

ground raked by a giant. Quite near were the *sawahs* of the father of Adinda (the child who was to marry Saïdjah), and when the little brothers of Adinda came to the limit of their fields, as the father of Saïdjah was there with his plow, the children called out merrily to each other, and each praised the strength and docility of his buffalo. But I believe that Saïdjah's buffalo was the best of all, perhaps because its master knew better how to speak to the animal, for buffaloes are very responsive to kind words.

Saïdjah was nine and Adinda six, when this buffalo was taken from Saïdjah's father by the chief. Saïdjah's father, who was very poor, thereupon sold to the Chinaman two silver curtain-hooks—inheritances from his wife's parents—for eighteen guilders, and with that money he bought a new buffalo. Saïdjah was very dejected, for he knew from Adinda's little brothers that the other buffalo had been driven to the capital, and he had asked his father if he had not seen the animal when he was there to sell the curtain-hooks. To this question his father refused to give an answer, and therefore the lad feared that his buffalo had been slaughtered, like the others which the chief had taken from the people. And Saïdjah wept much when he thought of the poor buffalo, which he had known for so long, and could eat nothing for days. It must be remembered that he was only a child.

The new buffalo soon got acquainted with the boy and obtained in the heart of Saïdjah the same place as his predecessor—alas, too soon, for the wax impressions of the heart are soon smoothed to make room for other writing. However this may be, the new buffalo was not so strong as the former: true, the old yoke was too large for his neck, but the poor animal was willing, like the other, and though Saïdjah could boast no more of the strength of his buffalo when he met Adinda's brothers at the boundaries, yet maintained that none surpassed his in willingness, and if the furrow was not so straight as before, or if lumps of earth had been turned but not cut, he willingly made this right as well as he could by means of his spade. Moreover, no buffalo had any such star on his forehead as this one had. The village priest himself said that there was good luck in the course of the hair-whorls on its shoulders.

Once when they were in the field, Saïdjah called in vain to his buffalo to make haste. The animal did not move. Saïdjah grew angry at this unusual refractoriness, and could not refrain from scolding. He called him a s——. Anyone who has been in India will understand me, and he who has not is the gainer if I spare him the explanation.

923

Saïdjah did not mean anything bad. He only used the word because he had often heard it used by others when they were dissatisfied with their buffaloes. But it was useless: his buffalo did not move. He shook his head as if to throw off the yoke, he blew and trembled, there was anguish in his blue eye, and the upper lip was curled, baring the gums.

"Fly, fly!" Adinda's brothers cried, "Fly, Saïdjah, there's a tiger!" And they all unyoked their buffaloes, and throwing themselves on their broad backs, galloped away through *sawahs*, irrigation trenches, mud, brushwood, forest and jungle, along fields and roads, but when they tore panting and dripping with perspiration into the village of Badoer, Saïdjah was not with them. For when he had freed his buffalo from the yoke and mounted him as the others had done in order to escape, an unexpected jump made him lose his seat and fall to the ground. The tiger was very close. . . . The buffalo, driven on by his own speed alone, and not of his own will, had gone further than Saïdjah, and scarcely had it conquered the momentum when it returned and, placing its big body, supported by its feet like a roof over the child, turned its horned head toward the tiger, which bounded forward—but for the last time. The buffalo caught him on his horns, and only lost some flesh, which the tiger took out of his neck. The tiger lay there with his belly torn open. Saïdjah was saved. Certainly there had been luck in the star on the buffalo's head.

When this buffalo had been taken away from Saïdjah's father and slaughtered, Saïdjah was just twelve, and Adinda was wearing *sarongs* and making figures on them. She had already learned to express thoughts in melancholy drawings on her tissue, for she had seen Saïdjah's sadness. And Saïdjah's father was also sad, but his mother still more so. For she had cured the wound in the neck of the faithful animal which had brought her child home unhurt. As often as she saw this wound, she thought how far the gashes of the tiger might have gone into the tender body of her child; and every time she put fresh dressings on the wound, she caressed the buffalo and spoke kindly to him, that the faithful animal might know how grateful a mother can be. Afterwards she hoped that the buffalo understood her, for he must have known why she wept when he was taken away, and that it was not Saïdjah's mother who caused him to be slaughtered. Some days afterward, Saïdjah's father fled out of the country, for he was afraid of being punished for not paying his

924

taxes, and he had no other heirlooms to sell with which to buy another buffalo. His parents had left him but few things. However, he went on for some years after the loss of his last buffalo by working with hired animals: but that is a very unremunerative labor, and moreover sad for one who has had buffaloes of his own.

Saïdjah's mother died of grief, and his father, in a moment of dejection, left Bantam to find work in the Buitenzorg district. But he was punished with stripes because he had left Lebak without a passport, and brought back by the police to Badoer. There he was put in prison, because he was supposed to be mad, which I can well believe, and it was feared he would run amok in a moment of frenzy. But he was not long in prison, for he died soon after. What became of Saïdjah's brothers and sisters I do not know. The house they lived in at Badoer was empty for some time, and then fell down, for it was only built of bamboo covered with cane. A little dust and dirt covered the spot where there had been so much suffering. There are many such places in Lebak.

Saïdjah was already fifteen when his father set out for Buitenzorg, and he did not accompany him thither, because he had other plans in mind. He had been told that there were gentlemen in Batavia who drove in carriages, and that it would be easy to get work as a carriage boy, for which young lads are used, so as not to disturb the equilibrium of the two-wheeled carriage by too much motion. He would, they said, earn much that way if he behaved himself—perhaps in three years he would be able to save enough to buy two buffaloes. This was a pleasant prospect. With the proud gait of one who had conceived a grand idea, he entered Adinda's house one day after his father had gone away, and communicated his plans to her.

"Think of it," said he. "When I come back we shall be old enough to marry, and have enough to buy two buffaloes!"

"I will gladly marry you, Saïdjah, when you come back. I will spin and weave *sarongs* and *slendangs*, and be very diligent all the while."

"Oh, I believe you, Adinda, but—if I find you already married?"

"Saïdjah, you know very well I will marry nobody but you. My father promised me to your father."

"And you yourself—?"

"When I come back, I will call from afar off."

"Who will hear it, if we are stamping rice in the village?"

"That is true, but, Adinda—oh, yes, this is better: wait for me

925

in the wood, under the Ketapan, where you gave me the Melatti flowers."

"But, Saïdjah, how am I to know when I am to go to the Ketapan?"

Saïdjah considered a moment and said: "Count the moons. I shall stay away three times twelve moons, not counting this moon. See, Adinda, at every new moon cut a notch in your rice block on the floor. When you have cut three times twelve lines, I will be under the Ketapan the next day. Do you promise to be there?"

"Yes, Saïdjah. I will be there, under the Ketapan, near the djatis, when you come back."

Thereupon Saïdjah tore a piece off his much-worn blue turban and gave it to Adinda to keep as a pledge, and then left her and Badoer. He walked many days, passing through Rankas-Belong, not yet capital of Lebak, through Warong-Goonoong, the home of the Assistant Resident, and the next day he came to Pamarangand, which lies in a garden. The day after, he came to Serang, and was astonished at the magnificence and size of the place, and the number of tiled stone houses. He had never before seen the like. He remained there a day, because he was tired, but in the coolness of the night he went his way, and the following day arrived at Tangerang. There he bathed in the river and rested at the home of an acquaintance of his father's who showed him how to make straw hats like those from Manila. He remained a day in order to learn the art, because he thought he might be able to turn it to use later on, if by chance he should fail to find other work in Batavia. The following day toward evening he thanked his host and departed. As soon as it was dark, and no one could see him, he took out the Melatti leaves Adinda had given him, for he was sad, thinking that he would not see her for so long. Neither on the first nor the second day had he realized how lonely he was, because he was captivated by the grand idea of earning money enough to buy two buffaloes, whereas his father had never had more than one, and was too excited over the prospect of seeing Adinda again to grieve over his departure. He had left her in anxious hope. The prospect of seeing her again so occupied his heart that on leaving Badoer and passing the tree, he felt something akin to joy, as if the thirty-six moons were already past. It had seemed that he had only to turn round to see Adinda waiting for him. But the further he went, the more did he realize the length of the period before him. There was something in his soul that made

him walk more slowly—he felt an affliction in his knees, and though it was not dejection that overcame him it was a mournful sadness. He thought of returning, but what would Adinda think of his want of courage?

Therefore he walked on, though not so fast as on the first day. He had the Melatti in his hand and often pressed them to his breast. He had aged much during the past few days, and could not understand how he had been able to live so calmly before, when Adinda was so near that he could see her as often as he liked. Now he could not recapture that calmness. Nor did he understand why, after having taken his leave, he had not gone back once again to see her. He recalled how recently he had quarreled with her about a cord she had made for her brother's kite, which had broken because there was some defect in her work. This made him lose a bet he had with the Tjipoeroet children. "How was it possible," he thought, "to have been angry over that with Adinda?" If there was a defect in the cord, and if the bet *was* lost, ought he to have been so rude and called her names? What, he wondered, if he died at Batavia without having asked her forgiveness? Would it not make him seem a wicked man? When it was learned that he had died in a distant place, would not everyone at Badoer say, "It is well Saïdjah has died—he spoke insolently to Adinda!"

Thus his thoughts ran, uttered at first involuntarily and softly, soon in a quiet monologue, and finally in a melancholy song.

He arrived at Batavia, and asked a certain gentleman to take him into his service, which the gentleman did, because Saïdjah spoke no Malay—an advantage there, for servants who do not understand that language are not so corrupt as the others, who have been longer in touch with the Europeans. But Saïdjah soon learned Malay, though he behaved well, for he always remembered the two buffaloes he was going to buy. He grew tall and strong, because he ate every day— not always the case at Badoer. In the stable he was liked, and would certainly not have been rejected if he had asked the hand of the coachman's daughter. His master liked him so much that he soon promoted him to be a house servant, increased his wages, and continually made him presents, to show how pleased he was. Saïdjah's mistress had read Sue's novel, so popular for a short while, and always thought of Prince Djalma when she saw Saïdjah, and the young girls, too, understood better than before why the Javanese painter, Radeen Saleh, had been so successful at Paris. But they

927

thought Saïdjah ungrateful when after almost a three years he asked for his dismissal and a certificate of good behavior. This could not be refused, and Saïdjah went on his journey with a joyful heart.

He counted the treasures he was carrying home. In a roll of bamboo he had his passport and certificate. In a case fastened to a leather girdle something heavy swung against his shoulder, but he enjoyed the feel of that, and no wonder! What would Adinda say? It contained thirty piastres—enough to buy three buffaloes! Nor was that all: on his back was a silver-covered sheath with his poniard. The hilt was indeed a fine one, for he had wound it round with a silk wrapper. And he had still more treasures! In the folds of his loin-cloth he kept a belt of silver links with gold clasps. True, the belt was short, but then Adinda was slender! Suspended by a cord round his neck, and under his clothes, he wore a silken bag in which were the withered Melatti leaves.

Is it to be wondered at that he stopped no longer at Sangerang than to visit the acquaintances who made such fine straw hats? That he said so little to the girls on his way who asked him whence he came and where he was going—the usual salutations; that he no longer thought Serang so beautiful (he who had learned to know Batavia); that he no longer hid himself behind the enclosure as he did three years before when he saw the Resident go riding out (he who had seen the much grander Lord at Buitenzorg, grandfather of Solo); that he paid little attention to the tales of those who went part of the way with him and gave news of Bantam-Kidool—is no wonder. No, he had sublime visions in his mind's eye. He looked for the Ketapan tree in the clouds when he was still far from Badoer. He caught at the air as if to embrace the form that was to meet him under the tree. He pictured to himself the face of Adinda, her head, her shoulders, saw the heavy chignon, black and glossy, confined in a net, hanging down her back; her large eyes glistening in dark reflection, the nostrils raised so proudly as a child (was it possible?), when he had vexed her; and the corner of her lips, when she smiled; and finally, her breasts, now doubtless swelling under her shawl. He could imagine her saying to him, "Welcome, Saïdjah! I have thought of you as I was spinning and weaving and stamping the rice on the floor which shows three times twelve lines cut by my hand. And I am under the Ketapan the first day of the new moon. Welcome, Saïdjah! I will be your wife."

928

That was the music that resounded in his ears and prevented him from listening to all the news that was told him on the road.

At last he saw Ketapan, or rather a large, dark spot with many stars above it. That must be the Ljati wood, near the tree where he should again see Adinda next morning, after sunrise. He sought in the dark and felt many trunks, finding at last a rough spot on the south side of a tree, and thrust his finger into a hole which Si-Panteh had cut with his knife to exorcise the Evil Spirit that had caused his mother's toothache, a short time before the birth of Panteh's little brother. That was the Ketapan he sought.

Yes, this was indeed the spot where he had looked upon Adinda for the first time with a different eye. She had become different from his other comrades. There she had given him the leaves. He sat down at the foot of the tree and looked at the stars, and when he saw a shooting-star he took it as a welcome of his return to Badoer, and wondered whether Adinda were now asleep, whether she had correctly cut the number of moons on the wood? How terrible if she had missed a moon, as if thirty-six were not quite enough! Had she, he wondered, made him some nice *sarongs* and *slendangs?* Who would now be living in her father's house? Then he thought of his childhood, and his mother, and how the buffalo had saved him from the tiger, of what would have become of Adinda if the buffalo had not been so faithful. He watched the sinking of the stars, and as each disappeared, he calculated how much nearer he was to Adinda. For she would certainly come at the first beam—at daybreak she would be there. Why had she not come the day before?

He was hurt that she had not anticipated the supreme moment that had lighted his soul for three years with indescribable brightness; unjust as he was in his selfishness, it seemed to him that Adinda ought to have been waiting for him. He complained unjustly, for the sun had not yet risen. But the stars were growing pale, and strange colors floated over the mountain tops, which appeared darker as they contrasted sharply with places elsewhere illuminated. Here and there something glowed in the east—arrows of gold and fire darted along the horizon, but disappeared again and seemed to fall down behind the impenetrable curtain which hid the day. It grew lighter and lighter around him: he now saw the landscape and could already distinguish a part of the wood behind which Badoer lay. There Adinda slept.

No, surely, she did not sleep! How could she? Did she not know

929

that Saïdjah would be waiting for her. She had not slept the whole night certainly; the village night police had knocked at her door to ask why her lamp burned so long, and with a sweet laugh she had replied that she had vowed to weave a *slendang* which must be ready before the first day of the new moon. Or perhaps she had passed the night in darkness, sitting on the rice floor, counting with eager fingers the thirty-six lines. Or possibly amused herself by pretending that she miscalculated, and had counted the lines all over again each time, enjoying the delicious assurance that the thirty-six moons had come and gone since her Saïdjah had left her.

Now that it was becoming light, she would be busying herself with useless little things, glancing from time to time over the wide horizon, looking for the sun, the lazy sluggard!

There was a line of bluish red, touching the clouds and making their edges light. The arrows of fire shot higher and higher, and ran over the dark ground, illuminating wide spaces of the earth, meeting, crossing, unrolling, running, and at last uniting in vast patches of fire, painting the azure earth in pigments of shining gold. There was red, blue, and purple, yellow gold. God in Heaven—it was at last daybreak!—Adinda!

Saïdjah had never learned to pray, and it would have been a pity to teach him: a more devout prayer and a more fervent expression of gratitude than his would have been impossible. He would no go to Badoer: actually to see her again was not so wonderful as to await her coming. He sat down at the foot of the Ketapan, and his eyes wandered over the landscape. Nature smiled at him, and seemed to welcome him like a mother. Saïdjah was overjoyed at seeing so many spots that reminded him of his earlier life. Though his eyes and thoughts wandered, his longings always reverted to the path which leads from Badoer to the Ketapan tree. His senses were wholly alive to Adinda. He saw the abyss to the left, where the earth was yellow, the spot where once a young buffalo had sunk down to the depths: they had all descended there with strong rattan cords, and Adinda's father had been the bravest of the rescue party. How Adinda had clapped her hands! Farther along, over there on the other side by the clump of cocoa-trees, whose leaves waved over the village, Si-Penah had fallen from a tree and been killed. How his mother had wailed—because, she said, Si-Penah was still such a little one—as if her grief had been less if he were larger! True, he *was* small, smaller and more fragile than Adinda.

930

There was no one on the little road leading from Badoer to the tree.

—By and by she would come. It was still very early.

Saïdjah saw a squirrel spring playfully up the trunk of a cocoanut tree and run untiringly to and fro. He forced himself to stand and regard the animal, for this calmed his thoughts, which had been working hard since early morning. His thoughts then ran into song. There was still no one on the little road. . . .

He caught sight of a butterfly disporting joyously in the increasing warmth. . . .

Still, there was no one on the little road. The sun climbed higher into the heavens, and it grew warm. . . .

Still, no one appeared on the little road. . . . No one.

She must have fallen asleep toward morning, weary with watching during the night, during many nights. She had not slept for weeks. That was it! Ought he to get up and go to Badoer? That would look as though he doubted her coming. . . . That man over there was too far away, and Saïdjah did not wish to speak to anyone about Adinda. He would see her alone. Surely, surely, she would come soon!

He would wait. . . .

But what if she were ill—dead?

Like a wounded stag he flew along the pathway toward the village. He saw nothing and heard nothing. Normally he would have heard, for there were men standing in the road at the entrance to the village, who cried out, "Saïdjah! Saïdjah!"

Was it his eagerness, or what, that prevented his finding Adinda's house? He had already run to the end of the village, and as if mad, he turned back, beating his head in despair to think that he had passed her house. But he soon found himself back at the entrance of the village, and—was it a dream? Again he had missed the house. Once more he flew back and suddenly stood still, and took his head in both hands to press out the madness that stunned him.

"Drunk, drunk!" he exclaimed. "I am drunk!"

The women of Badoer came out of their houses and saw with sorrow poor Saïdjah standing there, for they knew that he had been looking for Adinda's house, and that the house was no longer there. . . .

When the chief of Parang-Koodjang had taken away the buffaloes belonging to Adinda's father, Adinda's mother had died of grief,

931

and her baby sister soon after, for there was no one to suckle her. Adinda's father, fearing punishment for failing to pay his land taxes, had fled the district, taking with him Adinda and her brothers. He had heard how Saïdjah's father had been punished at Buitenzorg with stripes, because he had left Badoer without a passport. He had therefore not gone to Buitenzorg, nor to the Preangan, nor to Bantam, but to Tjilangkahan, bordering upon the sea. There he had hidden in the woods, awaiting the arrival of Pa-Ento, Pa-Lontah, Si-Penah, Pa-Ansive, Abdoel Isma, and others who had been robbed of their buffaloes by the chief of Parang-Koodjang, all of whom feared punishment for failure to pay their taxes. There, during the night, they had taken possession of a fishing-boat, and gone to sea. They steered toward the west, as far as Java Head. There they turned northward, until they came in sight of Prince's Island, and sailed round the east coast, going thence to the Lampoons. That at least was what people whispered to one another in Lebak whenever there was any question about buffaloes or land-taxes.

But Saïdjah could scarcely understand what they had told him. There was a buzzing in his ears, as if a gong were sounding in his head. He felt the blood throbbing convulsively in his temples; it seemed as though his head would burst under the pressure. He said nothing, and looked about stupified, not seeing anything. At last he laughed horribly. An old woman led him to her cottage. She would take care of the piteous fool. His laugh gradually became less horrible, but he still spoke no word. During the night the inmates of the hut were frightened by the sound of his voice. He sang out monotonously: "I don't know where I shall die!"

Some of the natives collected a little money in order to offer a sacrifice to the crocodile of the Tji-Udjiung, in order to cure Saïdjah, whom they thought insane. But he was not insane, for on a certain night when the moon was extraordinarily clear, he rose from his couch and quietly left the hut, and sought out the place where Adinda's house had stood. It was not easy to find it, for many houses had fallen down. But he recognized the spot by looking at the rays of moonlight that filtered down through the trees, as sailors measure their positions by lighthouses and mountain-tops.

That was the spot. There had Adinda lived!

Stumbling over half-decayed bamboos and pieces of fallen roof, he made his way to the sanctuary which he sought. He found some few remains of the enclosure still standing erect. There had been

Adinda's room, and there was the bamboo pin on which she had hung her dress when she was retiring at night. The walls of the room were turned to dust. He took up a handful of it, pressed it to his lips, and breathed hard. . . .

The next day he asked the old woman who had taken him in, where the rice-floor was, that stood in Adinda's house. The woman was glad at last to hear him speak, and ran through the village to look for the remains of the floor. She pointed out to Saïdjah the proprietor, and Saidjah followed in silence. He came to the rice-floor. On it he counted thirty-two lines. . . .

He gave the old woman piastres enough to buy a buffalo, and left Badoer. At Tjilangkahan he bought a fishing-boat, and after sailing for two days, reached the Lampoon Islands, where the insurgents had arisen against the Dutch rule. He joined a troop of Badoer men, not so much with the idea of fighting as of finding Adinda, for he was naturally tender-hearted, and more disposed to sorrow than to bitterness.

One day after the insurgents had suffered a defeat, he wandered through a village that had just been taken by the Dutch army, and was therefore in flames. Saïdjah knew that the defeated troop was composed largely of Badoer men. He wandered like a ghost among the houses that had not yet been burned. In one of them he found the dead body of Adinda's father with a bayonet wound in the breast. Near him lay the bodies of Adinda's three brothers, still boys—children, in fact.

Not far off lay the body of Adinda, naked and horribly mutilated. A small piece of blue linen had penetrated into the gaping wound in the breast, which seemed to have made an end to a long struggle.

Saïdjah went off to meet some Dutch soldiers who were driving the surviving insurgents at the point of the bayonet into the fire of the burning houses. He went out to meet the broad bayonets, and pressed forward with all his might, until the steel was buried up to the hilt in his breast.

Not long after there was much rejoicing at Batavia for the new victory, which so added to the laurels of the Dutch-Indian army. And the Government wrote that tranquillity had been restored in the Lampoons. The King of Holland, enlightened by his statesmen, again rewarded so much heroism with many orders of knighthood.

LADY MURASAKI

LADY MURASAKI (Japanese, *ca.* 978-1031). Realistic court diarist, novelist
and poet. Lived most of life connected with Emperor's court at Kyoto, and
last years in the entourage of Empress Akiko. Chief work, *The Tale of Genji,*
is most impressive of Japanese novels—54 sections, translated into 6 English
volumes by Arthur Waley. Her *Diary* also a classic.

THE FESTIVAL OF RED LEAVES

THERE was an elderly lady-of-the-bedchamber who, though she was
an excellent creature in every other way and was very much liked
and respected, was an outrageous flirt. It astonished Genji that
despite her advancing years she showed no sign of reforming her
reckless and fantastic behaviour. Curious to see how she would
take it, he one day came up and began joking with her. She appeared to be quite unconscious of the disparity between their ages
and at once counted him as an admirer. Slightly alarmed, he nevertheless found her company rather agreeable and often talked with
her. But, chiefly because he was frightened of being laughed at
if anyone found out, he refused to become her lover, and this she
very much resented. One day she was dressing the Emperor's hair.
When this was over His Majesty sent for his valets and went with
them into another room. Genji and the elderly lady were left alone
together. She was fuller than ever of languishing airs and poses,
and her costume was to the last degree stylish and elaborate. 'Poor
creature,' he thought, 'how little difference it all makes!' and he
was passing her on his way out of the room when suddenly the
temptation to give a tug at her dress became irresistible. She
glanced swiftly round, eyeing him above the rim of a marvellously
painted summer-fan. The eyelids beneath which she ogled at him
were blackened and sunken; wisps of hair projected untidily around
her forehead. There was something singularly inappropriate about
this gawdy, coquettish fan. Handing her his own instead, he took
it from her and examined it. On paper coated with a red so thick
and lustrous that you could see yourself reflected in it a forest of
tall trees was painted in gold. At the side of this design, in a hand
which though out-of-date was not lacking in distinction was written
the poem about the Forest of Oaraki. He made no doubt that the
owner of the fan had written it in allusion to her own advancing
years and was expecting him to make a gallant reply. Turning over

in his mind how best to divert the extravagant ardour of this strange creature, he could, to his own amusement, think only of another poem about the same forest; but to this it would have been ill-bred to allude He was feeling very uncomfortable lest someone should come in and see them together. She however was quite at her ease and seeing that he remained silent she recited with many arch looks the poem: 'Come to me in the forest and I will cut pasture for your horse, though it be but the under leaf whose season is past.' 'Should I seek your woodland,' he answered, 'my fair name would be gone, for down its glades at all times the pattering of hoofs is heard,' and he tried to get away; but she held him back saying: 'How odious you are! That is not what I mean at all. No one has ever insulted me like this before,' and she burst into tears. 'Let us talk about it some other time,' said Genji; 'I did not mean . . .' and freeing himself from her grasp he rushed out of the room, leaving her in great dudgeon. She felt indeed after this repulse prodigiously old and tottering. All this was seen by His Majesty who, his toilet long ago completed, had watched the ill-assorted pair with great amusement from behind his Imperial screen. 'I am always being told,' he said, 'that the boy takes no interest in the members of my household. But I cannot say that he seems to me unduly shy,' and he laughed. For a moment she was slightly embarrassed; but she felt that any relationship with Genji, even if it consisted of being rebuffed by him in public, was distinctly a feather for her cap, and she made no attempt to defend herself against the Emperor's raillery. The story soon went round of the Court. It astonished no one more than To no Chujo who, though he knew that Genji was given to odd experiments, could not believe that his friend was really launched upon the fantastic courtship which rumour was attributing to him. There seemed no better way of discovering whether it was conceivably possible to regard the lady in such a light than to make love to her himself.

The attentions of so distinguished a suitor went a long way towards consoling her for her late discomfiture. Her new intrigue was of course carried on with absolute secrecy and Genji knew nothing about it. When he next met her she seemed to be very cross with him, and feeling sorry for her because she was so old he made up his mind that he must try to console her. But for a long while he was completely occupied by tiresome business of one kind and another. At last one very dismal evening when he was strolling in the neighborhood of the Ummeiden he heard this lady playing most

agreeably on her lute. She was so good a performer that she was often called upon to play with the professional male musicians in the Imperial orchestra. It happened that at this moment she was somewhat downcast and discontented, and in such a mood she played with even greater feeling and verve. She was singing the 'Melon-grower's Song'; admirably, he thought, despite its inappropriateness to her age. So must the voice of the mysterious lady at O-Chou have sounded in Po Chü-i's ears when he heard her singing on her boat at night; and he stood listening. At the end of her song the player sighed heavily as though quite worn out by the passionate vehemence of her serenade. Genji approached softly humming the 'Azumaya': 'Here in the portico of the eastern house rain splashes on me while I wait. Come, my beloved, open the door and let me in.' Immediately, indeed with an unseemly haste, she answered as does the lady in the song, 'Open the door and come in,' adding the verse: 'In the wide shelter of that portico no man yet was ever splashed with rain,' and again she sighed so portentously that although he did not at all suppose that he alone was the cause of this demonstration, he felt it in any case to be somewhat exaggerated and answered with the poem: 'Your sighs show clearly that, despite the song, you are an-other's bride, and I for my part have no mind to haunt the loggias of your eastern house.' He would gladly have passed on, but he felt that this would be too unkind, and seeing that someone else was coming towards her room, he stepped inside and began talking lightly of indifferent subjects, in a style which though it was in reality some-what forced she found very entertaining.

It was intolerable, thought To no Chujo, that Genji should be praised as a quiet and serious young man and should constantly re-buke him for his frivolity, while all the time he was carrying on a multiplicity of interesting intrigues which out of mere churlishness he kept entirely hidden from all his friends. For a long while Chujo had been waiting for an opportunity to expose this sanctimonious imposture and when he saw Genji enter the gentlewoman's apartment you may be sure he was delighted. To scare him a little at such a moment would be an excellent way to punish him for his unfriend-liness. He slackened his pace and watched. The wind sighed in the trees. It was getting very late. Surely Genji would soon begin to doze? And indeed he did now look as though he had fallen asleep. Chujo stole on tiptoe into the room; but Genji who was only half-dreaming instantly heard him, and not knowing that Chujo had fol-lowed him, got it into his head that it was a certain Commissioner

936

of Works who years ago had been supposed to be an admirer of the lady. The idea of being discovered in such a situation by this important old gentleman filled him with horror. Furious with his companion for having exposed him to the chance of such a predicament: 'This is too bad,' he whispered, 'I am going home. What possessed you to let me in on a night when you knew that someone else was coming?' He had only time to snatch up his cloak and hide behind a long folding-screen before Chujo entered the room and going straight up to the screen began in a businesslike manner to fold it up. Though she was no longer young, the lady did not lose her head in this alarming crisis. Being a woman of fashion, she had on more than one occasion found herself in an equally agitating position, and now despite her astonishment, after considering for a moment what had best be done with the intruder, she seized him by the back of his coat and with a practised though trembling hand pulled him away from the screen. Genji had still no idea that it was Chujo. He had half a mind to show himself, but quickly remembered that he was oddly and inadequately clad, with his headdress all awry. He felt that if he ran for it he would cut much too strange a figure as he left the room, and for a moment he hesitated. Wondering how much longer Genji would take to recognize him, Chujo did not say a word but putting on the most ferocious air imaginable, drew his sword from the scabbard. Whereupon the lady crying 'Gentlemen! Gentlemen!' flung herself between them in an attitude of romantic supplication. They could hardly refrain from bursting into laughter. It was only by day when very carefully painted and bedizened that she still retained a certain superficial air of youth and charm. But now this woman of fifty-seven or eight, disturbed by a sudden brawl in the midst of her amours, created the most astonishing spectacle as she knelt at the feet of two young men in their 'teens beseeching them not to die for her. Chujo however refrained from showing the slightest sign of amusement and continued to look as alarming and ferocious as he could. But he was now in full view and Genji realized in a moment that Chujo had all the while known who he was and had been amusing himself at his expense. Much relieved at this discovery, he grabbed at the scabbard from which Chujo had drawn the sword and held it fast lest his friend should attempt to escape and then, despite his annoyance at having been followed, burst into an uncontrollable fit of laughter. 'Are you in your right mind?' said Genji at last. 'This is really a very poor sort of joke. Do you mind letting me get into my cloak?' Wherupon Chujo snatched the cloak

937

from him and would not give it back. 'Very well then,' said Genji; 'if you are to have my cloak I must have yours,' and so saying he pulled open the clasp of Chujo's belt and began tugging his cloak from his shoulders. Chujo resisted and a long tussle followed in which the cloak was torn to shreds. 'Should you now get it in exchange for yours, this tattered cloak will but reveal the secrets it is meant to hide,' recited To no Chujo; to which Genji replied with an acrostic poem in which he complained that Chujo with whom he shared so many secrets should have found it necessary to spy upon him in this fashion. But neither was really angry with the other and setting their disordered costumes to rights they both took their departure.

SANEATSU MUSHAKOJI

SANEATSU MUSHAKOJI (Japanese, 1885-   ). Modern Japanese dramatist, noted for unconventional ideological plots. Embarked on impressive literary career after leaving school. Influenced by European dramatists: Ibsen, Maeterlinck, Tolstoy. Authored several novels, books of essays, and many plays. Plays known in translation: *A Family Affair, The Sister.*

A FAMILY AFFAIR

ACT III

A living room in the Yamada home, luxuriously furnished in Western style. Shuzo is alone, seated in a rocking-chair. He is smoking a cigar and reading a newspaper. There is a knock at the door.

Shuzo.   Come in.

(*Enter* Hiroko, *his wife.*)

Hiroko.   What is it you wish?

(*She seats herself on a chair near him.*)

Shuzo (*still reading the paper*).   I want to talk over something with you.

Hiroko: Is it something very important?

Shuzo: Not especially so. It is about Jiro, your son.

Hiroko: About Jiro! Oh! that frightens me.

Shuzo: Why should you be frightened? (*Puts down the news-paper.*)

938

Hiroko: He is capable of doing such alarming things.

Shuzo: Oh, he is not so rash as all that.

Hiroko: No; he isn't exactly rash, but if he made up his mind to do a certain thing, he would do it even at the expense of his life.

Shuzo: You are right. But he is a very interesting boy. He will be a great man some day, if he doesn't get switched off on the wrong track.

Hiroko: And he has no regard whatever for his home and family.

Shuzo: That is true. Heaven knows he pays no attention to me. He thinks I am old and stupid, and that I want everything my own way.

Hiroko: Now, I doubt if he thinks that.

Shuzo: Oh, yes, he does. He has a stronger will than I have, and he has more brains, too. He is a deep one. We get on his nerves, and he pities us.

Hiroko: Do you think so?

Shuzo: Certainly. Now I am a self-made man and had to fight my way up in the world, but Jiro has always been taken care of, and has led an easy life. That is why I cannot understand how he comes to be so strong-willed.

Hiroko: Somehow he has changed a great deal since his brother Taro went abroad.

Shuzo: He has seemed to me very gloomy lately, and very obstinate.

Hiroko: Don't you think he will get over that when Taro comes back.

Shuzo: No; I don't think he will. He will dominate Taro. Taro has strong passions, but his will is weaker than Jiro's. I doubt if Taro is capable of anything more dangerous than falling prey to women.

Hiroko: You class women as a danger, do you?

Shuzo: I was only joking. At any rate, Taro will be all right. He isn't foolish.

Hiroko: I don't like that kind of joking.

Shuzo: Well, what I want to tell you about Jiro has to do with Fuji.

Hiroko: With Fuji? Surely not!

Shuzo: You think not? Then listen. To-day the father of Fuji, our former maid, came to see me, and told me that Fuji had refused to marry the man her family had chosen for her. I think Jiro is

939

behind this. I heard, also, that about two weeks ago, Jiro went to Fuji's house to see her.

Hiroko: Did her father tell you that?

Shuzo: No; he didn't tell me that. You know what I think? That he and Jiro are working together—that they have framed up against me. I tried to catch the old fellow by remarking that we appreciated the hospitable way in which he had received Jiro at his house. He said, "Not at all. We were surprised to have him drop in so unexpectedly." So much for that. I am certain, too, that about two weeks ago, when I was discussing Fuji's marriage with you, Jiro was listening on the sly. I thought so at the time, and that is why I asked you the next day where Jiro had gone. But you are so stupid you had no idea where he was.

Hiroko: And you are too clever for anything, of course.

Shuzo: I'm keeping a sharp eye on Jiro because I am more interested in his future than I am in Taro's.

Hiroko: Taro is more dependable.

Shuzo: Maybe so. And I admit that if Jiro should succeed me as head of the family, things might all go to smash. But to finish my story. When I asked Ota, the man I sent to arrange Fuji's marriage, how her family took to the idea, he reported that they showed neither surprise nor interest. That means Jiro had been there first. Later on I remarked in Jiro's presence that Fuji had refused the marriage proposal, and I knew he was laughing up his sleeve at me, but I didn't want to have a scene with him just then, so I ignored it. The disobedient rascal! And I thought he promised you he wouldn't go to see Fuji.

Hiroko: So he did promise.

Shuzo: You are sure?

Hiroko: Certainly. He gave me his promise not to see her, on condition that I keep my promise to him.

Shuzo: That's interesting. I am going to cross-examine him, and I want you here as a witness. But remember that you are to be on the side of the prosecution, not the defence. He's a tough customer. He knows already that we are on his trail.

Hiroko: That doesn't seem very likely.

Shuzo: But he knows that Fuji's father has been here to see me.

(A knock at the door.)

Who is it?

Jiro (outside): Jiro.

Shuzo: Come in.

940

(Jiro *enters calmly and sits on a chair near his mother.*)

Jiro: What is it you want?

Shuzo: Don't you know what I want?

Jiro: Well, I think perhaps I do.

Shuzo: What makes you think so.

Jiro: Something I heard from Fuji's father. Besides, you are so sharp that I have to be sharp, too.

Shuzo: I have a number of things to say to you. But first of all, why did you interfere with Fuji's marriage?

Jiro: I didn't go that far. I merely went to see her father.

Shuzo: To get him to interfere, eh?

Jiro: Perhaps—though I have absolute confidence in Fuji. The point is, I knew that if her father tried to dictate to her, it would only cause trouble, so I went to win him over to her side.

Shuzo: That's a strange line of talk. What do you mean when you say you have absolute confidence in her?

Jiro: Oh, you are not clever enough to understand that. Fuji is deeply in love with someone who is also in love with her. I knew that she would refuse this arranged marriage, and I wanted to make the refusal as easy for her as possible.

Shuzo: Who is it that is in love with her?

Jiro: I can't tell you that.

Shuzo: It is not likely that it is you, is it? (*Smiles.*) If it should be, you would both have to commit suicide.

Jiro: Do you really think it is I? And do you really care as much as that about the family name, and the laws of conventionality?

Hiroko: Jiro! What are you saying? How dare you! Say that again!

Jiro: I can repeat it as often as you like. Would you drive apart two who are so deeply in love? Of course I can't tell whether or not they would actually commit suicide. That is a matter of secondary importance, anyway. But you are really so afraid of conventional laws that you would drive them apart?

Hiroko: Do you mean that you are not afraid of the criticism of society?

Jiro: Not at all. I am afraid of it. But I am much more afraid of ruining human life.

Hiroko: What an unnatural child you are. You were born to disgrace your parents.

Jiro: No, mother. I think I was not born for that purpose,

941

though I admit I do not know why I was born. But certainly not for anything as easy as disgracing my parents. My task is more difficult than that.

Hiroko: Jiro, be still! You are going too far.

Jiro: Mother!

Hiroko: I am shocked at you!

Jiro: Mother!

Hiroko: I am not your mother, and you are not my child. Go ahead—say what you please!

Shuzo (to Hiroko): Be quiet! Jiro didn't say that he wanted to marry Fuji. (*To* Jiro): You don't know how sacred the family name is, nor how important public opinion is, and you don't frighten me by all that wild talk. I haven't the slightest use for the sort of man that kills himself for the sake of a woman. Now see here, Jiro. Isn't it true that when we discharged Fuji, you promised your mother that you would have no correspondence with her?

Jiro: Yes, that is true. That is why I have had no correspondence with her.

Shuzo: You are sure you haven't?

Jiro: Absolutely. Some day, two or three years from now, the man who will then be her husband will prove my innocence.

Shuzo: You had no correspondence. All right. But you also promised your mother that you would not go to see Fuji, either.

Jiro: Yes, I promised that.

Shuzo: But you did see her after all, didn't you?

Jiro: Yes, I saw her.

Shuzo: Ah! And why?

Jiro: Well, I went to her home, and she was there, and I couldn't help meeting her. But I didn't go there with that purpose. I did not break the spirit of my promise to mother. If you still think I did, please forgive me.

Shuzo: I may forgive that. But you don't mind, do you, if Fuji becomes a geisha girl?

Jiro: Father! You are not going to punish Fuji because of my actions! I had to make those promises to mother in order to convince her of my innocence. I ought never to have made them!

Shuzo: You are ready to accept your punishment?

Jiro: If it is what I deserve.

Shuzo: Well then . . . you will never be Fuji's husband!

Jiro: Oh! Why, I wouldn't be if you wanted me to. In the first place, Fuji doesn't want to marry me.

Hiroko: She doesn't? You are not telling us that to clear yourself?

Jiro: Mother, you are so suspicious!

Shuzo: You are sure she doesn't want to marry you?

Jiro: Of course I am.

Shuzo: Absolutely certain?

Jiro: Absolutely.

Shuzo: You have given me your word as a man.

Jiro: And you mistrust me like a woman.

Shuzo: You have been acting very strangely.

Jiro: How?

Shuzo: First, you made a special trip to Fuji's house. Next, you concealed from us the name of the man who is in love with her. Finally, you got angry when I said you would be getting mixed up in a double-suicide.

Jiro: The first charge I think I have already explained to you. The second is made necessary by the fact that I have not the man's permission to reveal his identity. To the last accusation I will say that I got angry thinking how cruel you are, and how differently I should look at things if I were in your position. I pitied you, father and mother, for being so stupid as to worry over such a matter.

Shuzo: Do you still imagine that we will allow you to marry Fuji?

Jiro: No. I never suspected you of being that liberal. But if I were in love with Fuji so desperately that I contemplated suicide, then I think you would allow me to marry her, because it would be better for you to make your son happy than to let him kill himself after a scandal.

Hiroko: You are trying to make fools of us.

Jiro: Yes; I am.

Hiroko: You have no respect for your parents.

Jiro: I have always gone on the assumption that parents love their children.

Hiroko: No child talks back to his parents as you do.

Jiro: Perhaps not. But why worry over that?

Hiroko: Father, why don't you do something to him? He makes me angry!

Jiro: And you make me angry.

Shuzo: Jiro, you are amusing yourself at our expense just because you are clever. You are forgetting the beneficence of your parents.

943

Jiro: The beneficence of parents! That should mean giving the child happiness. When a child grows up he doesn't love his parents any longer—he wants to run away from them. That is true in my case, but you are still trying to impose your beneficence on me, and it won't work.

Hiroko: A queer sort of child you are!

Jiro: Father! Mother! You don't understand what you are talking about. You know nothing of a young man's heart. These times are different from those of your own youth. And besides, a young tree doesn't want to stay in the shade of an old tree. A young tree wants the sunlight. It wants to brave the winds. Old people think life is made for suffering; young people think it is made for enjoyment. To enjoy to the fullest one's own life! to find one's own happiness—are not those words beautiful?

Shuzo: But, Jiro, you must not forget self-sacrifice.

Jiro: I am not forgetting self-sacrifice. I would gladly sacrifice myself by my own will, but not by the will of others. If I were the man you suspected me of being, I am certain I should leave this house and run away with the girl. I would willingly disgrace my parents and become an outcast from society.

Hiroko: How dare you say such a thing?

Shuzo (to Hiroko): Be still. Jiro doesn't know what he is saying. But I believe him when he says he is not the man in question. (*To* Jiro): Now that I am convinced you are not he, you may go. I have nothing more to say to you.

(*Jiro opens the door and goes out.* Shutzo *and* Hiroko *look after him. There is a silence. Then——*)

Hiroko: Such trouble! What are we going to do?

Shuzo: After all, Jiro is our younger son. Maybe we will let him marry her. Anyway, don't worry about it.

Hiroko: Jiro is a very queer boy. I can't understand him.

Shuzo: Say!

Hiroko: Well?

Shuzo: I have thought of something—something terrible!

Hiroko: What is it?

Shuzo: The man may be—Taro!

Hiroko: Surely not!

Shuzo: Perhaps not. But why, otherwise, should Jiro talk so strangely? Taro stopped writing just about the time we sent him word of Fuji's dismissal. Before that he had written two or three times a week. In fact, I couldn't understand why he should write

so often, but I supposed it was merely because the two boys were so fond of each other. Now I realise more than ever how peculiar it was. And Jiro swore he would never correspond with Fuji, and that he would never marry her. I don't think he was lying.

Hiroko: Oh, if it is true, it is terrible!

Shuzo: Quite right. What shall we do?

Hiroko: Do you think they will commit suicide if we separate them?

Shuzo: I don't think Taro is as foolish as that.

Hiroko: Then do you think it will ruin his health?

Shuzo: I don't think so.

Hiroko: But he will hate us.

Shuzo: Yes; I suppose he will. And Jiro will hate us, too.

Hiroko: Still, if we were to let Taro marry her, it would mean the disgrace of our house.

Shuzo: That is just it. We would be ashamed for the rest of our lives. (*He glances at the door and speaks in a lower tone.*) Jiro may be listening to us.

Hiroko: No, surely not!

Shuzo: You can't trust him.

Jiro (*outside the door*): No; you can't trust him. (*He opens the door and appears.*) You were right when you guessed that Taro is the man; but you were wrong about their relationship. You have no idea how deeply they are in love.

Shuzo: Never mind about that. I shall write to Taro and tell him that we know all about his affair with Fuji, and that we are very sorry, but we cannot countenance it.

Jiro: If you write him that, I shall write him this: "Father and mother are very happy over the affair, and everything has been settled much easier than you expected." I swear I will do this. The thing has come to light through my carelessness, and I am responsible for its solution. Both of them trusted me, and I considered myself worthy of their trust. I shall therefore help them get married.

Shuzo: If you do what you threaten, I will drive you out of this house.

Jiro: I am ready to be driven out. I am ready to stand on my own feet. I knew that when I told Taro and Fuji not to worry about me. When I cried a while ago, it was merely because I pitied you both so much.

(*There is an astonished silence on the part of the parents for a few moments, then—*)

Hiroko: What kind of a child is this!

Shuzo: Even I am astonished!

Jiro: Death would be nothing to me. (*Tears start from his eyes.*)

Shuzo: I wish I could turn you out, but I haven't the courage. It is harder for a parent to lose his child than for a child to lose his parent. Jiro, haven't you someone you want to marry?

Jiro: I? Not yet.

Shuzo: Then I shall find someone for you.

Jiro: All right.

Shuzo: You are in love with Fuji, aren't you?

Jiro: I can't answer that.

Shuzo: Jiro, I will consent to anything you wish. You may write whatever you like to Taro. It will make him happy. And even if I lose the whole world, I won't lose you. I love you.

Jiro: Thank you, father. Taro and Fuji will be so happy! And mother, don't you worry. If you do lose the respect of society, you will gain our love. Please forgive me everything I said to you before.

Shuzo: Jiro, you are not thinking about dying?

Jiro: Far from it. I have something else to do.

(*He bows and goes out quietly.*)

Shuzo (*to Hiroko*): Don't worry any more. All your children have come back to you. I feel that I, too, am coming back to you. Year after next we shall see our first grandchild.

(Hiroko *looks up at Shuzo. They smile at each other.*)

CURTAIN.

MU'TAMID

MU'TAMID (Arabic, 1040-1095). A member of the Abbasid Dynasty, who became King of Seville when Moslem Spain was broken into petty states. Later lost his kingdom and was exiled to Morocco. Of some importance as a poet.

THE PHILOSOPHER PENITENT

Then must I lose my all of joy to thee,
    Thou plunderer, Time, and thief of my delight,
And in my cup of sadness shall there be
No lingering lees of my felicity?

True, I have been of late no little while
   A stranger to the lute-string and the cup;
Sweet looks, and tremulous eyes, and subtle smile
Have tempted not, nor crafty fingers' guile.

And now behold, my head is waxen grey,
   Yet not with plentitude of years; and lo,
My limbs are lean, my flesh consumed away,
Yet not with waste and ravage of decay,

But because I have sinned, and mocked the wise,
   And fouled the fountain of my hopes. Alas,
My spring of youth is muddied and there rise
No waters but the salt tears of these eyes.

But I will chide my sorrow, I will speak
   Thus to my weeping, saying: "Hence, my tears!
And, O sad heart, strew not upon my cheek
These symbols of the coward and the weak."

For if the shaft of Destiny hath quit
   The bow of Fate, whose hand shall be so skilled
To pluck the flying arrow back? Whose wit
Shall by a hair's breadth change the course of it?

Not ours, not ours, who spend our little time
   Tracing a broken couplet on the sand,
Till, wearied of the pleasant pantomime,
Death, the great poet, adds the lacking rhyme.

TEARS OF THE WORLD

Weep for me, friend, for now that I am hence,
   Lo, in Time's dust the footprints of my pride!
Lament, strong lions of my great defence,
   Shed tears, my young gazelles and dewy-eyed!
Look ye, the cold stars even in the height
Weep, and the clouds lift not their mournful night.

Weep, Wahîd, weep, and Zahi with the towers,
  Weep ye for him that shall not come again.
All waters of the earth, all dew and showers
  Have tears for Mu'tamid, and the summer rain
That once strewed pearls upon him, is become
A sea-wave full of sand and sound and foam.

N

SAROJINI NAIDU

SAROJINI NAIDU (Indian, 1879-1949). Gifted English language lyricist of Indian themes. One of first Indians to achieve mastery of English verse. A woman who married out of her caste, and later became President of the Indian National Congress. Principal volumes: *The Golden Threshold*, *The Bird of Time*, *The Broken Wing*.

SUMMER WOODS

O I am tired of painted roofs and soft and silken floors,
And long for wind-blown canopies of crimson *gulmohurs!*

O I am tired of strife and song and festivals and fame,
And long to fly where cassia-woods are breaking into flame.

Love, come with me where koels call from flowering glade and glen,
Far from the toil and weariness, the praise and prayers of men.

O let us fling all care away, and lie alone and dream
'Neath tangled boughs of tamarind and *molsari* and *neem!*

And bind our brows with jasmine sprays and play on carven flutes,
To wake the slumbering serpent-kings among the banyan roots,

And roam at fall of eventide along the river's brink,
And bathe in water-lily pools where golden panthers drink!

You and I together, Love, in the deep blossoming woods
Engirt with low-voiced silences and gleaming solitudes,

Companions of the lustrous dawn, gay comrades of the night,
Like Krishna and like Radhika, encompassed with delight.

NATSUME SOSEKI

NATSUME SOSEKI (Japanese, 1867-1916). Writer of bizarre and fantastic tales. Essayist, critic and poet. Studied in England and taught English in Japan. First enormously successful novel: *I Am a Cat*. Later works: *Young Master, Kusamakura*. His style, marked by wit and urbanity, influenced the contemporary Japanese novel.

OUR CAT'S GRAVE

AFTER we removed to Waseda our cat began to grow lean and lank. She did not seem to want to join the children in frisking about at all. When the sun shone, she would go to sleep on the verandah. Stretching her front legs out straight, she would put her square chin down on them, and, fixing her eyes on the plants in the garden, would not move for hours. No matter how noisily the children might play about her, she did not seem to be at all disturbed.

As to the children, they practically refused to associate with their old friend whom they treated like a stranger, as much as to say, "This kitten isn't friendly enough for a playmate."

Not only the children but also our maid-servant cared little for Puss: she took the trouble to put the three meals for the poor animal in a corner of the kitchen but would do nothing else.

The three meals, however, were usually made away with by a big and thievish tabby-cat of the neighbourhood before our cat had touched them. She did not even appear to get angry at this, and never quarreled. She slept quietly all the time.

But her manner of sleeping was without freedom or ease. She did not lie comfortably and enjoy the pleasant sunshine. It seemed she could not afford to move but this is not sufficient to describe her state. In other words she found life exceedingly dull and she knew that she could not shake off this feeling without moving, but to move would make her feel more lonely. She seemed to have decided to lie still and put up with her surroundings.

Her eyes were ever upon the plants in the garden, but she was probably entirely unconscious of the shapes of the leaves and of their stalks. She lay with her vacant bluish-yellow eyes riveted upon some spot.

Just as the children, her former playmates, did not seem to recognize her existence, she herself did not seem to recognize the very existence of the world around her.

950

Sometimes, however, she would go out, like one who had business to attend to. On these occasions she was invariably driven home by the same tom-cat of the neighbourhood, and, terror-stricken, she would spring upon the verandah, break her way through one of the closed paper doors and rush to the hearthside.

It was only at these times that the family were reminded of her existence and that she seemed to feel any satisfaction in realizing that she was still alive.

After several repetitions of this experience, the hair on her tail grew thinner little by little. At first the hair dropped out in several spots leaving small hole-like patches. These patches grew larger till her whole tail was bare. Later on it hung down like a piece of rope.

Utterly tired of all things, she began to lick the affected parts. "My dear, I'm afraid there must be something wrong with the cat," said I to my wife.

"Perhaps so;" said she quite indifferently, "perhaps it's due to her advanced age." So after this I too left the wretched animal in her pitiable plight.

Then after a few days I noticed that the poor cat was throwing up everything she ate. Moving the forepart of her neck with a wavy motion she gave a mournful sound which was something between a sneeze and a hiccup. Pitiable as she looked, I could not help her. So every time I found her in this awkward situation, I thought I would drive her out.

Otherwise she would go on spoiling the mats and cushions without compunction. Most of the *hattan* silk cusions used for visitors had already been spoiled by her.

"This won't do," I said to my wife. "She has some kind of stomach trouble, I suppose. Dissolve some *hotan* in water and give it to the poor beast."

But she did not deign to answer. A few days later, I asked her if she had given the cat any *hotan* and she replied: "Why, my dear, I've tried in vain to make her take the medicine, but she would not open her mouth. As you see, even when we give her fishbones, she vomits." She added explanatorily.

"All right, then you had not better give her any," said I crossly, returning to my book.

No sooner had the cat got rid of her nausea than she slept quietly. Lately she had shrunk into herself in an uncomfortable way and

951

appeared to feel that she had no place to go except the verandah upon which she slept.

Some changes were visible in the expression of her eyes. First they looked as if they were fixed on some distant object brought suddenly into the near field of her vision and there was something calm about her eyes even in the midst of her wretchedness. But then they began to move in a strange way. The fire of her eyes, however, sank lower and lower like sheet lightning after a summer sunset.

However, I left her just as she was. My wife also did not seem to care for the poor creature. The children had long ceased to think of their former pet, of course.

One evening she was lying on her stomach at the foot of one of the children's beds, when, all at once she gave a deep growl such as she used to do when some one tried to seize her fish.

I was the only one who thought it very strange at the time. The children were sound asleep. Their mother was busy sewing.

After a while the cat uttered another growl. At last my wife dropped her work. "What's the matter with the cat?" I cried. "It would be terrible if the cat should bite our children during the night."

"Nonsense!" said she, resuming her sewing on the sleeves of an undershirt. The cat growled again at intervals.

The next day, the poor creature lay down on the edge of the hearth and mewed all day long. That seemed somewhat repulsive to us when we went there for the tea kettle or to make tea. But when it was evening my wife as well as myself forgot all about the cat. That night the cat died. The next morning when the maid-servant went to the backyard shed to fetch some firewood, it was already lying stiff on an old kitchen stove.

My wife took the trouble of going there to see the body of the poor creature. Thereupon, her former indifference was gone and she suddenly began making a great fuss about it. She sent for our rickshaman, and getting him to buy an oblong grave-post, she asked me to write something on it. I wrote: "In Memory of A Cat" on its front and "*Konoshitani, Inazuma okoru yoi aran*," on its back. The rickshaman wanted to know if he might bury the cat as it was, and the maid-servant added that she could not think of cremating it.

The children also began to make much of the cat again suddenly. They planted two glass bottles, one on each side of the grave-post, and filled them with twigs of blossoming *hagi*. They filled a cup with water and placed it before the grave. The flowers and the water were

changed every day. In the evening on the third day, my three-year-old daughter—I was watching her through a window of my study—walked up to the grave all alone, and after gazing at the plainwood grave-post for a while, put out her toy dipper, scooped up water from the cup which was offered to the cat, and drank it. That was not the only time she did so. The water strewn with the fallen petals of *hagi* flowers often served to cure the thirst of little Aiko in the evening quiet.

On each death-anniversary of the cat, my wife has made it a rule to offer a small slice of salted salmon and a bowl of rice with dried bonito shavings on it before the grave. She has never forgotten to do so even until now. Only she seems to have come recently to place them on top of the wardrobe in her sitting room instead of walking out into the garden with them.

NIZAMI

NIZAMI (Persian, 1140-1203). First great romantic poet of Persia. Spent 30 years composing his *Khamsa* (*Five Treasures*), of which best-known is *Khosru and Shireen*. Dedicated poems to various rulers, but avoided court life. Also composed religious and moral poems. Works exhibit extravagant imagination, are highly ornamented.

FERHAD THE SCULPTOR

The first epic of Nizami was "Khosru and Shireen," which relates the love story of the King of Persia and the beautiful Princess Shireen. Ferhad was an eminent sculptor whose passionate love for the same maiden gave the monarch vexation. To remove him from his court the king required him to hew a channel for a river through the lofty mountain of Beysitoun, and to decorate it with sculpture. He promised also that if Ferhad should accomplish this stupendous task, he should receive as his bride the object of his love. The enamored artist accepted the work on this condition. It is related that as he struck the rock, he constantly invoked the name of Shireen.

On lofty Beysitoun the lingering sun
Looks down on ceaseless labors, long begun;

953

The mountain trembles to the echoing sound
Of falling rocks that from her sides rebound.
Each day, all respite, all repose, denied,
Without a pause the thundering strokes are plied;
The mist of night around the summit coils,
But still Ferhad, the lover-artist, toils.
And still, the flashes of his axe between,
He sighs to every wind, "Alas, Shireen!"
A hundred arms are weak one block to move
Of thousands moulded by the hand of love
Into fantastic shapes and forms of grace,
That crowd each nook of that majestic place.
The piles give way, the rocky peaks divide,
The stream comes gushing on, a foaming tide,—
A mighty work for ages to remain,
The token of his passion and his pain.
As flows the milky flood from Allah's throne,
Rushes the torrent from the yielding stone.
And, sculptured there, amazed, stern Khosru stands,
And frowning sees obeyed his harsh commands:
While she, the fair beloved, with being rife,
Awakes from glowing marble into life.
O hapless youth? O toil repaid by woe!
A king thy rival, and the world thy foe.
Will she wealth, splendor, pomp, for thee resign,
And only genius, truth, and passion thine?
Around the pair, lo! chiselled courtiers wait,
And slaves and pages grouped in solemn state;
From columns imaged wreaths their garlands throw,
And fretted roofs with stars appear to glow:
Fresh leaves and blossoms seem around to spring,
And feathered throngs their loves seem murmuring.
The hands of Peris might have wrought those stems
Where dew-drops hang their fragile diadems,
And strings of pearl and sharp-cut diamonds shine,
New from the wave, or recent from the mine.
"Alas, Shireen!" at every stroke he cries,—
At every stroke fresh miracles arise.
"For thee my life one ceaseless toil has been;
Inspire my soul anew,—alas, Shireen!"

One evening Jesus lingered in the market-place,
Teaching the people parables of truth and grace,
When in the square remote a crowd was seen to rise,
And stop with loathing gestures and abhorring cries.

The Master and his meek disciples went to see
What cause for this commotion and disgust could be,
And found a poor dead dog beside the gutter laid;
Revolting sight! at which each face its hate betrayed.

One held his nose, one shut his eyes, one turned away;
And all among themselves began aloud to say,—
"Destested creature! he pollutes the earth and air!"
"His eyes are blear!" "His ears are foul!" "His ribs are bare!"

"In his torn hide there's not a decent shoe-string left!"
"No doubt the execrable cur was hung for theft!"
Then Jesus spake, and dropped on him this saving wreath,—
"Even pearls are dark before the whiteness of his teeth!"

The pelting crowd grew silent and ashamed, like one
Rebuked by sight of wisdom higher than his own;
And one exclaimed, "No creature so accursed can be,
But some good thing in him a loving eye will see."

NOVALIS

NOVALIS (Friedrich von Hardenberg, German 1772-1801). One of most original writers of German Romantic School. Catholic medievalist, imbued with mystical and mythological inspirations. Created the "blue flower," favorite romantic symbol. Died young of tuberculosis. Most significant work: an unfinished novel, *Heinrich von Ofterdingen*. Free-verse poem: *Hymns to the Night*.

THE POET'S DAUGHTER

THE journey was now ended. It was toward evening when our travelers arrived, safe and in good spirits, in the world-renowned city of Augsburg, and rode through the lofty streets to the house of old

Schwaning. . . . They found the house illuminated, and a merry music reached their ears. "What will you wager," said the merchants, "that your grandfather is giving a merry entertainment? We come as if called. How surprised he will be at the uninvited guests! Little does he dream that the true festival is now to begin." . . .

Among the guests, Heinrich had noticed a man who appeared to be the person that he had seen often at his side, in that book. His noble aspect distinguished him before all the rest. A cheerful earnestness was the spirit of his countenance. An open, beautifully arched brow; great, black, piercing and firm eyes; a roguish trait about the merry mouth, and altogether clear and manly proportions made it significant and attractive. He was strongly built, his movements were easy and full of expression, and where he stood, it seemed as if he would stand forever. Heinrich asked his grandfather about him. "I am glad," said the old man, "that you have remarked him at once. It is my excellent friend Klingsohr, the poet. Of his acquaintance and friendship you may be prouder than of the emperor's. But how stands it with your heart? He has a beautiful daughter; perhaps she will supplant the father in your regards. I shall be surprised if you have not observed her." Heinrich blushed. "I was absent, dear grandfather. The company was numerous, and I noticed only your friend." "It is very easy to see," replied Schwaning, "that you are from the North. We will soon find means to thaw you here. You shall soon learn to look out for pretty eyes."

The old Schwaning led Heinrich to Klingsohr, and told him how Heinrich had observed him at once, and felt a very lively desire to be acquainted with him. Heinrich was diffident. Klingsohr spoke to him in a very friendly manner of his country and his journey. There was something so confidential in his voice, that Heinrich soon took heart and conversed with him freely. After some time Schwaning returned, and brought with him the beautiful Mathilde. "Have compassion on my shy grandson, and pardon him for seeing your father before he did you. Your gleaming eyes will awaken his slumbering youth. In his country the spring is late."

Heinrich and Mathilde colored. They looked at each other with wondering eyes. She asked him with gentle, scarce audible words: "Did he like to dance?" Just as he was affirming this question a merry dancing-music struck up. Silently he offered her his hand, she gave hers, and they mingled in the ranks of the waltzing pairs. Schwaning and Klingsohr looked on. The mother and the merchant rejoiced in Heinrich's activity, and in his beautiful partner. . . .

956

Heinrich wished the dance never to end. With intense satisfaction his eye rested on the roses of his partner. Her innocent eye shunned him not. She seemed the spirit of her father in the loveliest disguise. Out of her large, calm eyes, spoke eternal youth. On a light, heaven-blue ground reposed the mild glory of the dusky stars. Around them brow and nose sloped gracefully. A lily inclined toward the rising sun was her face; and from the slender white neck, blue veins meandered in tempting curves around the delicate cheeks. Her voice was like a far-away echo, and the small brown curly head seemed to hover over the light form.

The music banished reserve and roused every inclination to cheerful sport. Baskets of flowers in full splendor breathed forth odors on the table, and the wine crept about among the dishes and the flowers, shook his golden wings, and wove curtains of bright tapestry between the guests and the world. Heinrich now, for the first time, understood what a feast was. A thousand gay spirits seemed to him to dance about the table, and in still sympathy with gay men, to live by their joys and to intoxicate themselves with their delights. The joy of life stood like a sounding tree full of golden fruits before him. Evil did not show itself, and it seemed to him impossible that ever human inclination should have turned from this tree to the dangerous fruit of knowledge, to the tree of conflict. He now understood wine and food. He found their savor surpassingly delicious. They were seasoned for him by a heavenly oil, and sparkled from the cup the glory of earthly life. . . .

It was deep in the night when the company separated. The first and only feast of my life, said Heinrich to himself when he was alone.

He went to the window. The choir of the stars stood in the dark sky, and in the east a white sheen announced the coming day. With full transport Heinrich exclaimed: "You, ye everlasting stars, ye silent pilgrims, you I invoke as witnesses of my sacred oath! For Mathilde I will live, and eternal truth shall bind my heart to hers. For me too the morn of an everlasting day is breaking. The night is past. I kindle myself, a never-dying sacrifice to the rising sun!"

Heinrich was heated, and it was late, toward morning, when he fell asleep. The thoughts of his soul ran together into wondrous dreams. A deep blue river shimmered from the green plain. On the smooth surface swam a boat. Mathilde sat and rowed. She was decked with garlands, sang a simple song, and looked toward him with a sweet sorrow. His bosom was oppressed, he knew not why. The sky was bright, and peaceful the flood. Her heavenly coun-

957

tenance mirrored itself in the waves. Suddenly the boat began to spin round. He called to her, alarmed. She smiled, and laid the oar in the boat, which continued incessantly to whirl. An overwhelming anxiety seized him. He plunged into the stream, but could make no progress, the water bore him. She beckoned, she appeared desirous to say something. Already the boat shipped water, but she smiled with an ineffable inwardness, and looked cheerfully into the whirlpool. All at once it drew her down. A gentle breath streaked across the waves, which flowed as calm and as shining as before. The terrific agony deprived him of consciousness. His heart beat no more. He did not come to himself until he found himself on dry ground. He might have swam far, it was a strange country. He knew not what had befallen him; his mind was gone;—thoughtless he wandered farther into land. He felt himself dreadfully exhausted. A little fountain trickled from a hill, it sounded like clear bells. With his hand he scooped a few drops, and wetted his parched lips. Like an anxious dream the terrible event lay behind him. He walked on and on; flowers and trees spoke to him. He felt himself so well, so at home. Then he heard again that simple song. He pursued the sound. Suddenly some one held him back by his garment. "Dear Heinrich!" called a well-known voice. He looked round, and Mathilda clasped him in her arms. "Why didst thou run from me, dear heart?" said she, drawing a long breath, "I could scarce overtake thee." Heinrich wept. He pressed her to his bosom.—"Where is the river?" he exclaimed with tears. "Seest thou not its blue waves above us?" He looked up, and the blue river was flowing gently above their heads. "Where are we, dear Mathilda?" "With our parents." "Shall we remain together?" "Forever," she replied, while she pressed her lips to his, and so clasped him that she could not be separated from him again. She whispered a strange mysterious word into his mouth, which vibrated through his whole being. He wished to repeat it, when his grandfather called and he awoke. He would have given his life to remember that word.

O

EUGENE O'NEILL

EUGENE O'NEILL (American, 1888-1953). Dramatist of the tragic sense of life, often judged America's most important playwright. Experiences as young seaman recorded in early *Plays of the Sea*. After period in tuberculosis sanatorium, studied in Harvard's "47 Workshop" and joined Provincetown Players. Styles range from naturalism of *Beyond the Horizon*, to expressionism of *The Emperor Jones*, to symbolism of *The Great God Brown*, to special techniques of *Strange Interlude* and *Mourning Becomes Electra*. Nobel Prize, 1936.

THE GREAT GOD BROWN

SCENE. Cybel's parlor. An automatic, nickel-in-the-slot player-piano is at center, rear. On its right is a dirty gilt second-hand sofa. At the left is a bald-spotted crimson plush chair. The backdrop for the rear wall is cheap wall-paper of a dull yellow-brown, resembling a blurred impression of a fallow field in early spring. There is a cheap alarm clock on top of the piano. Beside it her mask is lying.

DION is seated on his back, fast asleep on the sofa, His mask has fallen down on his chest. His pale face is singularly pure, spiritual and sad.

The player-piano is groggily banging out a sentimental medley of "Mother—Mammy" tunes.

CYBEL is seated on the stool in front of the piano. She is a strong, calm, sensual, blonde girl of twenty or so, her complexion fresh and healthy, her figure full-breasted and wide-hipped, her movements slow and solidly languorous like an animal's, her large eyes dreamy with the reflected stirring of profound instincts. She chews gum like a sacred cow forgetting time with an eternal cud. Her eyes are fixed, incuriously, on DION's pale face.

959

Cybel (*as the tune runs out, glances at the clock, which indicates midnight, then goes slowly to to Dion and puts her hand gently on his forehead*). Wake up!

Dion (*stirs, sighs and murmurs dreamily*). "And He laid His hands on them and healed them." (*Then with a start he opens his eyes and, half sitting up, stares at her bewilderedly*) What—where —who are you? (*He reaches for his mask and claps it on defensively*).

Cybel (*placidly*). Only another female. You was camping on my steps, sound asleep. I didn't want to run any risk getting into more trouble with the cops pinching you there and blaming me, so I took you to sleep it off.

Dion (*mockingly*). Blessed are the pitiful, Sister! I'm broke— but you will be rewarded in Heaven!

Cybel (*calmly*). I wasn't wasting my pity. Why should I? You were happy, weren't you?

Dion (*approvingly*). Excellent! You're not a moralist, I see.

Cybel (*going on*). And you look like a good boy, too—when you're asleep. Say you better beat it home to bed or you'll be locked out.

Dion (*mockingly*). Now you're becoming maternal, Miss Earth. Is that the only answer—to pin my soul into every vacant diaper? (*She stares down at his mask, her face growing hard. He laughs*) But please don't stop stroking my aching brow. Your hand is cool mud poultice on the sting of thought!

Cybel (*calmly*). Stop acting. I hate ham fats. (*She looks at him as if waiting for him to remove his mask—then turns her back indifferently and goes to the piano*) Well, if you simply got to be a regular devil like all the other visiting sports, I s'pose I got to play with you. (*She takes her mask and puts it on—then turns. The mask is the rouged and eye-blackened countenance of the hardened prostitute. In a coarse, harsh voice*) Kindly state your dishonorable intentions, if any! I can't sit up all night keeping company! Let's have some music! (*She puts a plug in the machine. The same sentimental medley begins to play. The two masks stare at each other. She laughs*) Shoot! I'm all set! It's your play, Kid Lucifer!

Dion (*slowly removes hs mask She stops the music with a jerk. His face is gentle and sad—humbly*). I'm sorry. It has always been such an agony for me to be touched!

Cybel (*taking off her mask—sympathetically as she comes back and sits down on her stool*). Poor kid! I've never had one, but I

can guess. They hug and kiss you and take you on their laps and pinch you and want to see you getting dressed and undressed—as if they owned you—I bet you I'd never let them treat one of mine that way!

Dion (turning to her). You're lost in blind alleys, too. (*Suddenly holding out his hand to her*) But you're strong. Let's be friends.

Cybel (with a strange sternness, searches his face). And never nothing more?

Dion (with a strange smile). Let's say, never anything less (*She takes his hand. There is a ring at the outside door bell. They stare at each other. There is another ring*).

Cybel (puts on her mask, Dion does likewise. Mockingly). When you got to love to live it's hard to love living. I better join the A.F. of. L. and soap-box for the eight-hour night! Got a nickel, baby? Play a tune. (*She goes out. Dion puts a nickel in. The same sentimental tune starts. Cybel returns, followed by Billy Brown. His face is rigidly composed, but his superior disgust for Dion can be seen. Dion jerks off the music and he and Billy look at each other for a moment, Cybel watching the both—then, bored, she yawns*) He's hunting for you. Put out the lights when you go. I'm going to sleep. (*She starts to go—then, as if reminded of something—to Dion*) Life's all right, if you let it alone. (*Then mechanically flashing a trade smile at Billy*) Now you know the way, Handsome, call again! (*She goes*).

Brown (after an awkward pause). Hello, Dion! I've been looking all over town for you. This place was the very last chance. . . . (*Another pause—embarrassedly*) Let's take a walk.

Dion (mockingly). I've given up exercise. They claim it lengthens your life.

Brown (persuasively). Come on, Dion, be a good fellow. You're certainly not staying here——

Dion. Billy would like to think me taken in *flagrante delicto*, eh?

Brown. Don't be a damn fool! listen to me! I've been looking you up for purely selfish reasons. I need your help.

Dion (astonished). What?

Brown. I've a proposition to make that I hope you'll consider favorably out of old friendship. To be frank, Dion, I need you to lend me a hand down at the office.

Dion (with a harsh laugh). So it's the job, is it? Then my poor wife did a-begging go!

961

Brown (repelled—sharply). On the contrary, I had to beg her to beg you to take it. *(More angrily)* Look here, Dion! I won't listen to you talk that way about Margaret! And you wouldn't if you weren't drunk! *(Suddenly shaking him)* What in hell has come over you, anyway! You didn't use to be like this! What the devil are you going to do with yourself—sink into the gutter and drag Margaret with you? If you'd heard her defend you, lie about you, tell me how hard you were working. what beautiful things you were painting, how you stayed at home and idolized the children! —when everyone knows you've been out every night sousing and gambling away the last of your estate. . . . *(He stops, ashamed, controlling himself).*

Dion (wearily). She was lying about her husband, not me, you fool! But it's no use explaining. *(Then, in a sudden, excitable passion)* What do you want? I agree to anything—except the humiliation of yelling secrets at the deaf!

Brown (trying a bullying tone—roughly). Bunk! Don't try to crawl out! There's no excuse and you know it. *(Then as Dion doesn't reply—penitently)* But I know I shouldn't talk this way old man! It's only because we're such old pals—and I hate to see you wasting yourself—you who had more brains than any of us! But, damn it, I suppose you're too much of a rotten cynic to believe I mean what I've just said!

Dion (touched). I know Billy was always Dion Anthony's friend.

Brown. You're damn right I am—and I'd proved it long ago if you'd given me half a chance. After all, I couldn't keep chasing after you and be snubbed every time. A man has some pride!

Dion (bitterly mocking). Dead wrong! Never more! None whatever! It's immoral! Blessed are the poor in spirit, Brother! When shall I report?

Brown (eagerly). Then you'll take the—you'll help me?

Dion (wearily bitter). I'll take the job. One must do something to pass away the time, while one is waiting—for one's next incarnation.

Brown (jokingly). I'd say it was a bit early to be worrying Humorist had given me weak eyes, so now I'll have to foreswear about that. *(Trying to get Dion started)* Come along, now. It's pretty late.

Dion (shakes his hand off his shoulder and walks away from him —after a pause). Is my father's chair still there?

Brown (*turns away—embarrassed*). I— don't really remember, Dion—I'll look it up.

Dion (*taking off his mask slowly*). I'd like to sit where he spun what I have spent. What aliens we were to each other! When he lay dead, his face looked so familiar that I wondered where I had met that man before. Only at the second of my conception. After that, we grew hostile with concealed shame. And my mother? I remember a sweet strange girl, with affectionate, bewildered eyes as if God had locked her in dark closet without any explanation. I was the sole doll our ogre, her husband, allowed her and she played mother and child with me for many years in that house until at last through two tears I watched her die with the shy pride of one who has lengthened her dress and put up her hair. And I felt like a forsaken toy and cried to be buried with her, because her hands alone had caressed without clawing. She lived long and aged greatly in the two days before they closed her coffin. The last time I looked, her purity had forgotten me, she was stainless and imperishable, and I knew my sobs were ugly and meaningless to her virginity; so I shrank away, back into life, with naked nerves jumping like fleas, and in due course of nature another girl called me her boy in the moon and married me and became three mothers in one person, while I got paint on my paws in an endeavor to see God! (*He laughs wildly—claps on his mask*) But that Ancient Humorist had given me weak eyes, so now I'll have to forswear my quest for Him and go in for the Omnipresent Successful Serious One, the Great God Mr. Brown, instead! (*He makes him a sweeping, mocking bow*).

Brown (*repelled but cajolingly*). Shut up, you nut! You're still drunk. Come on! Let's start! (*He grabs Dion by the arm and switches off the light*).

Dion. (*from the darkness—mockingly*). I am thy shorn, bald, nude sheep! Lead on, Almighty Brown, thou Kindly Light!

Curtain

963

JIRO OSARAGI

OSARAGI JIRO (Japanese, 1897-   ). Eminent Japanese novelist and historical writer. Majored in political science and French law and literature. Taught language and history, then worked in Foreign Office. Author of 6 major novels and innumerable short stories. In his fiction, a concise psychological observant.

From
HOMECOMING

SAEKO said good-night and went up to her apartment on the second floor. She undressed, put on a chemise, and sat down at her dressing-table to take the pins out of her hair.

The door opened suddenly and Nobu's reflection in the mirror startled Saeko.

"I'd like to talk to you a minute," he announced from the door-way. "I didn't want Otane around. I thought it might be embarrassing."

"I'll put something on. Wait in the next room."

"Pardon me for bursting in, but, after all, I'm—"

"Never mind that. Please do as I say."

There was only a thin piece of silk around her body. Saeko felt ashamed suddenly and blushed. Nobu had looked away, but stood there waiting. She walked over to the bed and wrapped a light kimono around her. She spoke as she was picking out an obi. "Can't this wait until tomorrow morning?"

"No. It would be better to talk about it now," he insisted. "It concerns Otane. I want to send her away. . . . I want to throw off this whole slovenly existence I'm leading now. That's what I want to talk over with you."

"I hardly see that it's any of my business. But aren't you being rather hard on Otane? She's served you faithfully all these years."

"But her life never meant anything anyway. What about me? Do I have to go on dragging the sins of my youth with me the rest of my life? They become a pretty heavy load at my age. I realized I was wrong at the time, but my friends all acted that way, and I was young, so I just slipped into it. . . ."

"If you can talk so selfishly about it, it's plain you still haven't repented what you did. Of course, it takes a human being to repent." Saeko finished tying her obi and turned around toward him. "Let's go into the next room. This place is a mess."

964

"Saeko!" He looked into her face, his eyes intense. "That's not nice of you. This is your room, isn't it? I'm your husband. How can you order me out? . . . I'm sorry from the bottom of my heart. You don't understand how I've suffered these six years. I've tried to tell you, but you just wouldn't listen."

"You're breaking your promise now. We made an agreement, and you can't change it when it pleases you. And be kind enough to leave that door open."

"You're cold, Saeko—to stay angry so long about a trifle."

"I'm not in the least angry. I have nothing to be angry about."

"You say that, and torture me like this?"

"Torture you, indeed!"

"Saeko, I didn't want to say it, but a woman is a woman."

"Are you trying to get me really angry? Are you trying to make me say what I'd rather not say?"

"Don't get angry! Don't get angry! That's all I ask."

The color of fear on his elegant face provoked Saeko to speak. "You who crushed the feelings of my youth, you come here now and speak this way? And think of Otane, if you will. She's not like me. That poor creature's been trained to accept this kind of life and think herself lucky to have it. She's given herself to you entirely, with utter faith—and you want to get rid of her now she no longer suits your convenience. It would be an abominable thing to do."

"But—if you gave her a decent sum of money, she'd be glad to go back to her parents."

Saeko burst out laughing. "I shall most certainly do nothing of the kind. I refuse, definitely. I find it a very amusing idea. Who's buying what?"

"All right. I can manage to scrape that much together myself."

"Tell me—when you've sent Otane away, with whom do you intend to go on living in this house?"

Nobu paled. He understood well enough what she meant, but was too choked with humiliation to speak.

"Aren't you being cruel? Otane's a good, simple woman. What a shock it'll be for her! And have you thought what things are like outside now that you're pushing her into the streets?"

"That's why I'm giving her the money."

"Has she agreed to this? Or is it all your own idea? When I first found out about you and her, the only reason I felt I could forgive you was that at least you loved her. But if you slighted my feelings out of pure whim, if you tell me now that everything you've

been saying is a lie—aren't you making it all the harder for me to bear as a woman? I've left it all up to you. I've stayed out of your way."

"But you were all wrong about it. You're completely mistaken about what happened between us."

"I know nothing about it and don't want to! The man is responsible in such cases. Otane and I felt embarrassed toward each other as women, and you and she were shy of discussing the matter because you both knew that what you were doing was wrong. Well, good night now. Think it over. If this is what you intend to do, it's absurd to complain about needing more money."

Nobu's eyes flashed, and he shouted: "Saeko! You're in love with someone!"

"What?"

"You are! You must be!"

"I'll leave it to your imagination. Of course, I don't know what may happen in the future, but surely you can see how improbable it is that I'm in love now. I go in for things the whole way. If I were really in love with someone else, I wouldn't be at all in the mood to go on feeding a purely nominal husband and his Number Two. You can be sure of that, can't you?"

Nobu said nothing, but he put his arms around her shoulders and pulled her toward him. They were strong arms, the arms of an oarsman, but Saeko pressed her two hands against his chest and bent her body back bow-like to ward him off.

"Saeko, it's you I've always loved. Really, from my heart—"

"Take your hands off me. I'll call Otane. The plain truth is you're saying that because you want money."

"Saeko! Don't say things like that!"

"Never mind. I know you and your blood and your background Things have gone badly for you, haven't they? But stop this disgusting, unmanly display. Instead of these attentions, give me Otane's consolation money. Then we can separate for good. I hadn't thought of it until you mentioned it, but there is a man I could fall in love with. I want to go to him."

The strength ebbed out of Nobu's arms. He stood stiff and spiritless. His face sagged, pale and ugly, with his mouth open. Saeko took her chance, walked out the door, and called Otane's name in her ordinary tone.

"Forgive me, Saeko, forgive me. You shouldn't torture me so cruelly." Nobu was whining like a beaten puppy. "If you're satisfied,

966

let's leave things as they are. I'll try to bear it. . . . But don't get angry. Please don't get angry."

Saeko was listening to the stillness of the house. Otane wasn't coming.

"Just try to act like a man," she said irritably. "But I seem to be more manly than you, don't I? Good night!"

Nobu was slow to move. Saeko had reached the point where she could have loosened her sash and lain down on the bed right in front of him. She could have undressed, indifferent to his presence. She had always taken good care of herself, and her body was still young. It always gave her confidence to look at it in a full-length mirror. The man's slowness was irritating her beyond endurance. She felt there was nothing too cruel for her to do. Nobu apologized one last time and finally went out. She didn't even bother to lock the door behind him.

"Aah!" She sighed out all the feeling she'd been holding in, and sprawled her thinly covered body on the bed, throwing out her arms and legs. She could feel the dark stillness of the peony garden outside her window. The waves broke at intervals on the pebbled shore, but the sudden sounds only made the night more quiet.

Her eyes were shut. She could hear her troubled blood. Her mind was calm. It had come out of the incident indifferent. But she was becoming conscious of the weight of her extended body.

Her heartbeat quickened suddenly. She had moved her arms and legs deliberately, and then realized that her new position was the same as the one she had taken automatically that night in Singapore after parting from Kyogo Moriya. She thought about it, comparing the two positions in detail as though reviewing a school lesson. She lay still, her eyes closed, and the sense of fulfillment she had had that night seeped into her body and lured her mind into a trance. She was like a sponge growing heavy as it takes in water. At the height of fullness, she bit her lip and moaned low.

He was so much older than she, and he could make her feel this way! Her inner eyes stared at this fact in growing surprise, while the inhuman loneliness of the way she was living now shadowed her heart. She had nothing in the world to fear now. But what would become of her if she went on as she was? Kyogo Moriya hated her, there could be no doubt. She thought of these things, and something like a tremor of fear ran up and down her almost naked body.

She sighed, sat up, and turned off the lamp beside her bed.

967

OVID

OVID (Latin, 43 B.C.-19 A.D.). Urbane and sophisticated Latin poet. Of equestrian family, traveled widely before devoting self to fashionable life of Rome. Early exiled for wantonness in writings. Remains one of most influential and graceful poets of antiquity. Major works: *Amores, Heroides, Ars Amatoria, Metamorphoses, Epistulae ex Ponto.*

SAPPHO TO PHAON

Say, lovely youth, that doth my heart command,
Can Phaon's eyes forget his Sappho's hand?
Must then her name the wretched writer prove,
To thy remembrance lost, as to thy love?
Ask not the cause that I new members choose,
The lute neglected, and the Lyric Muse.
Love taught my tears in sadder notes to flow,
And tuned my heart to elegies of woe.
I burn, I burn, as when through ripened corn
By driving winds the spreading flames are borne.
Phaon to Etna's scorching fields retires,
While I consume with more than Etna's fires!
No more my soul a charm in music finds,
Music has charms alone for peaceful minds:
Soft scenes of solitude no more can please,
Love enters there, and I'm my own disease.
No more the Lesbian dames my passion move,
Once the dear objects of my guilty love;
All other loves are lost in only thine,
Ah, youth ungrateful to a flame like mine!
Whom would not all those blooming charms surprise,
Those heavenly looks, and dear deluding eyes?
The harp and bow would you like Phœbus bear,
A brighter Phœbus Phaon might appear;
Would you with ivy wreathe your flowing hair,
Not Bacchus' self with Phaon could compare:
Yet Phœbus loved, and Bacchus felt the flame,
One Daphne warmed, and one the Cretan dame;
Nymphs that in verse no more could rival me,
Than e'en those gods contend in charms with thee. . . .

Brown as I am, an Ethiopian dame
Inspired young Perseus with a generous flame;
Turtles and doves of different hues unite,
And glossy jet is paired with shining white.
If to no charms thou wilt thy heart resign,
But such as merit, such as equal thine,
By none, alas! by none thou canst be moved:
Phaon alone by Phaon must be loved!
Yet once thy Sappho could thy cares employ;
Once in her arms you centered all your joy:
No time the dear remembrance can remove,
For, oh! how vast a memory has love!
My music, then you could not ever hear,
And all my words were music to your ear.
You stopped with kisses my enchanting tongue,
And found my kisses sweeter than my song.
In all I pleased, but most in what was best;
And the last joy was dearer than the rest.
Then with each word, each glance, each motion fired,
You still enjoyed, and yet you still desired,
Till all dissolving in the trance we lay,
And in tumultuous raptures died away. . . .

O scarce a youth, yet scarce a tender boy!
O useful time for lovers to employ!
Pride of thy age and glory of thy race,
Come to these arms, and melt in this embrace!
The vows you never will return, receive;
And take at least the love you will not give.
See, while I write, my words are lost in tears!
The less my sense, the more my love appears.
Sure 'twas not much to bid one kind adieu;
(At least to feign was never hard to you!)
"Farewell, my Lesbian love," you might have said;
Or coldly thus, "Farewell, oh Lesbian maid!"
No tear did you, no parting kiss receive,
Nor knew I then how much I was to grieve.
No lover's gift your Sappho could confer,
And wrongs and woes were all you left with her.
No charge I gave you, and no charge could give,
But this, "Be mindful of your loves, and live."

969

Now by the Nine, those powers adored by me,
And Love, the god that ever waits on thee,
When first I heard (from whom I hardly knew)
That you were fled, and all my joys with you,
Like some sad statue, speechless, pale I stood,
Grief chilled my breast, and stopped my freezing blood;
No sigh to rise, no tear had power to flow,
Fixed in a stupid lethargy of woe:
But when its way the impetuous passion found,
I rend my tresses, and my breast I wound;
I rave, then weep; I curse, and then complain;
Now fiercer pangs distract the mournful dame
Whose firstborn infant feeds the funeral flame. . . .
Stung with my love, and furious with despair,
All torn my garments, and my bosom bare,
My woes, thy crimes, I to the world proclaim:
Such inconsistent things are love and shame!
'Tis thou art all my care and my delight,
My daily longing, and my dream by night.
O night, more pleasing than the brightest day,
When fancy gives what absence takes away,
And dressed in all its visionary charms,
Restores my fair deserter to my arms! . . .
But when with day, the sweet delusions fly,
And all things wake to life and joy, but I;
As if once more forsaken, I complain,
And close my eyes to dream of you again.

P

YITSKHOK LEYBUSH PERETZ

YITSKHOK LEYBUSH PERETZ (Polish-Hebrew, 1852-1915). The classic of
modern Yiddish literature. Born in Poland, exposed early to ideological conflict between traditionalism and modernism. After 10 years of law practice,
became leader of new trend in Yiddish literature. Works include poetry,
socially oriented stories, and symbolic dramas (*The Golden Chain, At Night
in the Old Market Place*).

IF NOT HIGHER

EARLY every Friday morning, at the time of the Penitential Prayers,
the Rabbi of Nemirov would vanish.

He was nowhere to be seen—neither in the synagogue nor in the
two Houses of Study nor at a *minyan*. And he was certainly not at
home. His door stood open; whoever wished could go in and out;
no one would steal from the rabbi. But not a living creature was
within.

Where could the rabbi be? Where should he be? In heaven, no
doubt. A rabbi has plenty of business to take care of just before the
Days of Awe. Jews, God bless them, need livelihood, peace, health,
and good matches. They want to be pious and good, but our sins are
so great, and Satan of the thousand eyes watches the whole earth
from one end to the other. What he sees he reports; he denounces,
informs. Who can help us if not the rabbi!

That's what the people thought.

But once a Litvak came, and he laughed. You know the Litvaks.
They think little of the Holy Books but stuff themselves with Talmud
and law. So this Litvak points to a passage in the *Gemarah*—it
sticks in your eyes—where it is written that even Moses, our Teacher, did not ascend to heaven during his lifetime but remained suspended two and a half feet below. Go argue with a Litvak!

971

So where can the rabbi be?

"That's not my business," said the Litvak, shrugging. Yet all the while—what a Litvak can do!—he is scheming to find out.

That same night, right after the evening prayers, the Litvak steals into the rabbi's room, slides under the rabbi's bed, and waits. He'll watch all night and discover where the rabbi vanishes and what he does during the Penitential Prayers.

Someone else might have got drowsy and fallen asleep, but a Litvak is never at a loss; he recites a whole tractate of the Talmud by heart.

At dawn he hears the call to prayers.

The rabbi has already been awake for a long time. The Litvak has heard him groaning for a whole hour.

Whoever has heard the Rabbi of Nemirov groan knows how much sorrow for all Israel, how much suffering, lies in each groan. A man's heart might break, hearing it. But a Litvak is made of iron; he listens and remains where he is. The rabbi, long life to him, lies on the bed, and the Litvak under the bed.

Then the Litvak hears the beds in the house begin to creak; he hears people jumping out of their beds, mumbling a few Jewish words, pouring water on their fingernails, banging doors. Everyone has left. It is again quiet and dark; a bit of light from the moon shines through the shutters.

(Afterward the Litvak admitted that when he found himself alone with the rabbi a great fear took hold of him. Goose pimples spread across his skin, and the roots of his earlocks pricked him like needles. A trifle: to be alone with the rabbi at the time of the Penitential Prayers! But a Litvak is stubborn. So he quivered like a fish in water and remained where he was.)

Finally the rabbi, long life to him, arises. First he does what befits a Jew. Then he goes to the clothes closet and takes out a bundle of peasant clothes: linen trousers, high boots, a coat, a big felt hat, and a long wide leather belt studded with brass nails. The rabbi gets dressed. From his coat pocket dangles the end of a heavy peasant rope.

The rabbi goes out, and the Litvak follows him.

On the way the rabbi stops in the kitchen, bends down, takes an ax from under the bed, puts it in his belt, and leaves the house. The Litvak trembles but continues to follow.

The hushed dread of the Days of Awe hangs over the dark streets.

972

Every once in a while a cry rises from some *minyan* reciting the Penitential Prayers, or from a sickbed. The rabbi hugs the sides of the streets, keeping to the shade of the houses. He glides from house to house, and the Litvak after him. The Litvak hears the sound of his heartbeats mingling with the sound of the rabbi's heavy steps. But he keeps on going and follows the rabbi to the outskirts of the town.

A small wood stands behind the town.

The rabbi, long life to him, enters the wood. He takes thirty or forty steps and stops by a small tree. The Litvak, overcome with amazement, watches the rabbi take the ax out of his belt and strike the tree. He hears the tree creak and fall. The rabbi chops the tree into logs and the logs into sticks. Then he makes a bundle of the wood and ties it with the rope in his pocket. He puts the bundle of wood on his back, shoves the ax back into his belt, and returns to the town.

He stops at a back street beside a small broken-down shack and knocks at the window.

"Who is there?" asks a frightened voice. The Litvak recognizes it as the voice of a sick Jewish woman.

"I," answers the rabbi in the accent of a peasant.

"Who is I?"

Again the rabbi answers in Russian. "Vassil."

"Who is Vassil, and what do you want?"

"I have wood to sell, very cheap." And, not waiting for the woman's reply, he goes into the house.

The Litvak steals in after him. In the gray light of early morning he sees a poor room with broken, miserable furnishings. A sick woman, wrapped in rags, lies on the bed. She complains bitterly, "Buy? How can I buy? Where will a poor widow get money?"

"I'll lend it to you," answers the supposed Vassil. "It's only six cents."

"And how will I ever pay you back?" said the poor woman, groaning.

"Foolish one," says the rabbi reproachfully. "See, you are a poor sick Jew, and I am ready to trust you with a little wood. I am sure you'll pay. While you, you have such a great and mighty God and you don't trust him for six cents."

"And who will kindle the fire?" said the widow. "Have I the strength to get up? My son is at work."

973

"I'll kindle the fire," answers the rabbi.

As the rabbi put the wood into the oven he recited, in a groan, the first portion of the Penitential Prayers.

As he kindled the fire and the wood burned brightly, he recited, a bit more joyously, the second portion of the Penitential Prayers. When the fire was set he recited the third portion, and then he shut the stove.

The Litvak who saw all this became a disciple of the rabbi.

And ever after, when another disciple tells how the Rabbi of Nemirov ascends to heaven at the time of the Penitential Prayers, the Litvak does not laugh. He only adds quietly, "If not higher."

BENITO PEREZ GALDOS

BENITO PÉREZ GALDOS (Spanish, 1843-1920). Prolific Spanish novelist, often compared with Dickens and Tolstoy. An observing narrator of real life with depth and sympathy. Many of his books motivated by liberal ideas—e.g., *Gloria*, an indictment of religious and racial prejudice, and *Misericordia*, a study of the Madrid underworld. Left some 80 novels, 24 plays and 15 volumes of miscellaneous writings.

MADAMA ESTHER

ESTHER Spinoza, the wife of Moses Morton, a very wealthy Jewish merchant of Hamburg, who had afterwards settled in London, was, like her husband, descended from a family of Spanish Jews; but the Morton family had got itself involved with German and Dutch alliances, while that of Spinoza had kept itself unmixed, and its pedigree could be clearly traced as far back as to Daniel Spinoza, a Jew of Cordova, banned by the edict of proscription of 1492. Esther Spinoza was a Spaniard by blood, though not by birth; Spanish too in her serious character, her deeply-seated and strongly-controlled vehemence, her strict sense of duty—while the melancholy light of her black eyes, her tall figure, and her graceful gait were those of a true Spaniard. Spanish too was her mother-tongue that she had spoken like a native, from her cradle. It is a well-known fact that all the Hebrew families descended from the Spanish exiles have clung to that language, though for lack of replanting on its

974

native soil it has often degenerated greatly; and the Spaniard who, even at the present day, visits Constantinople, Belgrade, Jerusalem, Venice, Rome or Cairo—all of them places whither some of the miserable dust was blown that the storm swept from Spain—may hear among the Jews an archaic form of Castilian which rings in his ears as a melancholy and sweet surprise, as if it were an echo from the dead past of his native land—a sigh from the grave after four centuries of oblivion. The Spanish Jews, most of them very abject, have clung to the language of their oppressors and read the rabbinical books in that tongue; their love for the country that has been so ruthless a step-mother is as fervent as their devotion to that ancient eastern home which they have never recovered, and they weep for her as hundreds of years ago they wept by the waters of Babylon. The feeling is less strong, no doubt, among the wealthier Hebrews. The Spinozas loved the memory of the second country they had lost, but Esther hated the land with all her heart, excepting the language which she kept up diligently and took care to teach to her children.

She did not profess her own faith with any fervor of enthusiasm; still, she was loyal to it with a steady and dutiful feeling which was not so much devotion as respect for the creed of her ancestors and attachment to the name and history of an unhappy and persecuted race. This indeed amounted to a passion, a fanaticism, which might have reproduced in her the grand characteristics of Deborah the "Mother in Israel," of Jael who transfixed the foe with a nail of the tragical Judith and gentler heroine Esther. The spirit of her race filled her and inspired her, but she had not the same devotion to its formulas and rites; and though she fulfilled its precepts with her children and servants, she did so because she thought it well to perpetuate this potent bond of union—a sort of ideal father-land— on whose sacred ground a hapless nation, bereft of soil, might meet. Esther was a model of the domestic virtues which are universal among the higher class of Hebrew women, and which need neither cause surprise nor give rise to invidious reflections. There is no need to analyze them, nor to wonder whether, as many have thought, the secret of them lies in superior culture or in intrinsic natural morality. She was a good wife and a tender mother, and those who said she was worthy to have been a Christian did her no more than justice.

Esther and her husband were enormously wealthy; it might be said of them that the Lord had prospered the work of their hands.

They lived in perfect harmony, surrounded by every luxury that art could produce. Their houses almost revived the fabulous glories of the palace of Haroun-al-Raschid. They were respected by all and the guests even of Kings; and having acquired a financial position which almost gave them the importance of a political power, they had extricated Nations from difficulties. They had no native soil, but the proudest rulers had sued to them; titles, honors, respect, consideration, position and adulation—all that potentates enjoy or covet, was theirs. They stood like divinities, before whom every minister of finance was ready to burn incense; and the Pope himself, as secular sovereign, gave them titles and crosses and never called them *Deicides*, but on the contrary, "potent seignors." Esther Spinoza having visited Rome, a Cardinal constituted himself her guide through the collections, and another presented her with mosaics, cameos and carnelians, while a third sold her a marble crucifix for a thousand *livres*, and for five hundred a Spanish manuscript of the Talmud, on vellum, of the XIIIth century.

They had no kingdom but they reigned everywhere, for the dominion of Mammon is a wide one; "the earth is *his*," we may say, "and the fulness thereof," and the home of the north and the south winds. No one had ever thought of asking any member of this illustrious family in the exalted position they occupied, whether they too had said: *"Crucify Him and release unto us Barrabas."*

In spite of her fifty years, Madama Esther was still extremely handsome, as among Spanish women of rank is not uncommon; it may be accounted for by the finely-tempered balance of certain natures, combined with easy circumstances and the inestimable advantage of a life free from anxiety, menial toil and no more suffering or sorrow than is enough to prove that perfect happiness is but a myth. She indulged in few arts of the toilet, and those she used were not to conceal her years, but merely to make them look beautiful, as though she were proud of her bright and fresh maturity, the true homage of age to youth. In looking at her it became easy to understand the lasting spring of the women of whom we are told in the Bible that they lived a hundred and twenty years and more, as though it were nothing.

SAINT-JOHN PERSE

SAINT-JOHN PERSE (Alexis Saint-Léger Léger, French, 1887-   ). Elegant poet and diplomat. Born in Guadeloupe, went to Paris for education. Entered the Foreign Service, working closely with Briand. Came to America when Nazis took France. Painter of rich and unusual images, especially admired by poets and intellectuals. Most famous work, *Anabasis*, has been translated by T. S. Eliot.

SNOWS

AND then came the snows, the first snows of absence, falling upon the great woven cloths of dreams and reality; and with every affliction remitted to men of memory, there came the freshness of clean sheets on our temples. And it was in the morning, under the grey salt of dawn, a little before the sixth hour, as in a haven of fortune, an asylum of grace and mercy where the swarm of the great odes of silence could be scattered.

And all the night, unknown to us, beneath that canopy of feather, bearing its noble imprint and cure of souls, the high towns of pumice-stone perforated by luminous insects had not ceased to grow and excel, in the oblivion of their weight. And they alone knew something about it whose memory is uncertain whose story aberrant. The share that the mind took in these conspicuous things, we do not know.

No one surprised, no one knew the first laying of that silky hour on the loftiest brow of stone, the first touch of that agile and very futile thing, the sweep as it were of eyelashes. On the bronze revetments and the out-thrusts of chromium-plated steel, on the rubble of heavy porcelain, on the coarse-glass tiles, on the black-marble spindle and on the white-metal spur, no one surprised, no one tarnished it,

This mist of a breath at its birth, like the first fright of a blade unsheathed . . . it was snowing and we shall tell the wonder of it: dawn silent in its plumes, like a great fabulous owl a prey to the winds of the spirit, puffed out its white dahlia body. On all sides a miracle and a fête. May grace alight on this terrace-slope where the Architect showed to us one recent summer the eggs of a night-jar.

ALEXANDER PETOFI

ALEXANDER PETÖFI (Hungarian, 1822-1849). Most widely known Hungarian poet. Fighter for Hungarian independence in the 1840's. Majority of his compositions are simple lyrics, modeled on folk poetry. Notable for vivid imagination, fiery patriotism.

LONGING FOR DEATH

Give me a coffin and a grave,
  And let the grave be deep and low;
And bury with me all I feel,
  All passions strong, all thoughts of woe.

O, mind and heart, twice cursed, e'er have
  You been the bane of my whole life!
Why torture me with burning scourge?
  Why should not end now all this strife?

Why should this feverish brain inspire
  To rise above the stars on high?
When angry Fate hath it ordained
  That crawl upon the earth should I.

Why have I not fair heavenly wings,
  If my aims soar to heaven's dome?
To carry me into heights where
  Immortality is at home!

And if to me this world is void
  Of joy, why have I, then, a breast?
Created that of human joys
  It be the home, the shelt'ring nest!

Or if there be a heart which flames
  And burns in passion's deep abyss,
Why, then, this icy look on me,
  Thou God of happiness and bliss?

Give me a coffin and a grave,
    And let the grave be deep and low;
And bury with me all I feel,
    All passions strong, all thoughts of woe.

IF GOD

If God Almighty thus did speak to me:
"My son, I grant permission unto thee
To have thy Death as thou thyself shalt say;"
Thus unto my Creator I would pray:

"Let it be autumn, when the zephyrs sway
The sere leaves wherewith mellow sunbeams play;
And let me hear once more the sad, sweet song
Of errant birds, that will be missed ere long.

"And unperceived, as winter's chilling breath
Waiting o'er autumn bearing subtle Death
Thus let Death come; most welcome will He be
If I observe Him when he's close to me.

"Like to the birds, again I will outpour
A mellower tune than e'er I sang before,
A song which moves the heart, makes dim the eyes
And mounts up swelling to the very skies.

"And, as my swan song draweth to its end,
My sweetheart fair and true may o'er me bend;
Thus would I die, caressing her fair face,
Kissing the one on earth who holds most grace.

"But if the Lord this boon should disallow,
With spring of war let Him the land endow;
When the rose-blooms that color earth again
Are blood-red roses in the breasts of men."

FRANCESCO PETRARCA

FRANCESCO PETRARCA (Italian, 1304-1374). Latin and Italian Poet Laureate. Precursor of the Renaissance, has been called "the first modern man of letters." Now best remembered for his Italian lyrics, *Le Rime*, addressed to his beloved, Laura. These remained models of style for centuries. Also wrote Latin epic, *Africa*, and many letters and philosophic treatises in the classic Latin manner.

SONNETS TO LAURA

All ye who list, in wildly warbled strain,
  Those sighs with which my youthful heart was fed,
  Erewhile fond passion's maze I wont to tread,
Erewhile I lived estrang'd to manlier pain;
For all those vain desires, and griefs as vain,
  Those tears, those plaints, by am'rous fancy bred,
  If ye by love's strong power have e'er been led,
Pity, nay, haply pardon, I may gain.
Oft on my check the conscious crimson glows,
  And sad reflection tells—ungrateful thought!—
How jeering crowds have mock'd my love-lorn woes:
But folly's fruits are penitence and shame,
  With this just maxim, I've too dearly bought,
That man's applause is but a transient dream.

Poor, solitary bird, that pour'st thy lay,
  Or haply mournest the sweet season gone,
  As chilly night and winter hurry on,
And daylight fades, and summer flies away!
If, as the cares that swell thy little throat,
  Thou knew'st alike the woes that wound my rest,
  Oh, thou wouldst house thee in this kindred breast,
And mix with mine thy melancholy note!
Yet little know I ours are kindred ills:
  She still may live the object of thy song:
Not so for me stern Death or Heaven wills!
  But the sad season, and less grateful hour,
And of past joy and sorrow thoughts that throng,
  Prompt my full heart this idle lay to pour.

Alone and pensive, the deserted strand
  I wander o'er with slow and measured pace,

And shun with eager eye the lightest trace
Of human foot imprinted on the sand.
I find, alas! no other resting-place
  From the keen eye of man; for, in the show
  Of joys gone by, it reads upon my face
The traces of the flame that burns below.
And thus, at length, each leafy mount and plain,
  Each wandering stream and shady forest, know,
What others know not, all my life of pain.
  And e'en as through the wildest tracts I go,
Love whispers in my ear his tender strain,
Which I with trembling lip repeat to him again.

Swift current, that from rocky Alpine vein,
  Gathering the tribute to thy waters free,
  Mov'st joyous onward night and day with me,
Where nature leads thee, me love's tyrant chain!
Roll freely on; nor toil nor rest restrain
  Thine arrowy course; but ere thou yieldest in
The tribute of thy waters to the main,
  Seek out heaven's purest sky, earth's deepest green;
There wilt thou find the bright and living beam
  That o'er thy left bank sheds its heavenly rays:
If unto her too slow my footsteps seem,—
  While by her feet thy lingering current strays,
Forming to words the murmurs of its stream,—
  Say that the weary flesh the willing soul delays.

In what ideal world or part of heaven
  Did Nature find the model of that face
  And form, so fraught with loveliness and grace,
In which to our creation she has given
Her prime proof of creative power above?
What fountain nymph or goddess ever let
  Such lovely tresses float of gold refined
  Upon the breeze, or in a single mind
Where have so many virtues ever met,
E'en though those charms have slain my bosom's weal?
  He knows not love, who has not seen her eyes
  Turn when she sweetly speaks, or smiles, or sighs,
Or how the power of love can hurt or heal.

Creatures there be, of sight so keen and high,
  That even on the sun they bend their gaze;
  Others, who, dazzled by too fierce a blaze,
Issue not forth till evening veils the sky;
Others, who, with insane desire, would try
  The bliss which dwells within the fire's bright rays,
  But, in their sport, find that its fervor slays.
Alas! of this last heedless band am I:
  Since strength I boast not, to support the light
Of that fair form, nor in obscure sojourn
  Am skilled to fence me, nor enshrouding night.
Wherefore, with eyes which ever weep and mourn,
  My fate compels me still to court her sight,
Conscious I follow flames which shine to burn.

Waved to the winds were those long locks of gold
  Which in a thousand burnished ringlets flowed,
  And the sweet light beyond all measure glowed
Of those fair eyes which I no more behold,
Nor (so it seemed) that face aught harsh or cold
  To me (if true or false, I know not) showed;
  Me, in whose breast the amorous lure abode,
If flames consumed, what marvel to unfold?
That step of hers was of no mortal guise,
  But of angelic nature; and her tongue
Had other utterance than of human sounds.
A living sun, a spirit of the skies,
  I saw her. Now, perhaps, not so. But wounds
  Heal not, for that the bow is since unstrung.

PILPAY

PILPAY (Sanskrit, dates unknown). Legendary fabulist, known through an
ancient Sanskrit collection called *Panchatantra*. Translated into Pahlavi about
550, thereafter into Arabic. Versions also exist in Mongol, Malay and Afghan
languages.

THE MAN AND THE ADDER

A MAN mounted upon a Camel once rode into a thicket, and went
to rest himself in that part of it from whence a caravan was just

982

departed, and where the people having left a fire, some sparks of it, being driven by the wind, had set a bush, wherein lay an Adder, all in a flame. The fire environed the Adder in such a manner that he knew not how to escape, and was just giving himself over to destruction, when he perceived the Man already mentioned, and with a thousand mournful conjurations begged of him to save his life. The Man, on this, being naturally compassionate, said to himself, "It is true these creatures are enemies to mankind; however, good actions are of great value, even of the very greatest when done to our enemies; and whoever sows the seed of good works, shall reap the fruit of blessings." After he had made this reflection, he took a sack, and tying it to the end of his lance, reached it over the flame to the Adder, who flung himself into it; and when he was safe in, the traveler pulled back the bag, and gave the Adder leave to come forth, telling him he might go about his business; but hoped he would have the gratitude to make him a promise, never to do any more harm to men, since a man had done him so great a piece of service.

To this the ungrateful creature answered, "You much mistake both yourself and me: think not that I intend to be gone so calmly; no, my design is first to leave thee a parting blessing, and throw my venom upon thee and thy Camel."

"Monster of ingratitude!" replied the Traveler, "desist a moment at least, and tell me whether it be lawful to recompense good with evil."

"No," replied the Adder, "it certainly is not; but in acting in that manner I shall do no more than what yourselves do every day; that is to say, retaliate good deeds with wicked actions, and requite benefits with ingratitude."

"You cannot prove this slanderous and wicked aspersion," replied the Traveler: "nay, I will venture to say that if you can show me any one other creature in the world that is of your opinion, I will consent to whatever punishment you think fit to inflict on me for the faults of my fellow-creatures."

"I agree to this willingly," answered the Adder; and at the same time spying a Cow, "Let us propound our question," said he, "to this creature before us, and we shall see what answer she will make." The Man consented; and so both of them accosting the Cow, the Adder put the question to her, how a good turn was to be requited. "By its contrary," replied the Cow, "if you mean according to the custom of men; and this I know by sad experience. I belong," said

983

she, "to a man, to whom I have long been several ways extremely beneficial: I have been used to bring him a calf every year, and to supply his house with milk, butter, and cheese; but now I am grown old, and no longer in a condition to serve him as formerly I did, he has put me in this pasture to fat me, with a design to sell me to a butcher, who is to cut my throat, and he and his friends are to eat my flesh: and is not this requiting good with evil?"

On this, the Adder, taking upon him to speak, said to the Man, "What say you now? are not your own customs a sufficient warrant for me to treat you as I intend to do?"

The Traveler, not a little confounded at this ill-timed story, was cunning enough, however, to answer, "This is a particular case only, and give me leave to say, one witness is not sufficient to convince me; therefore pray let me have another."

"With all my heart," replied the Adder; "let us address ourselves to this Tree that stands here before us." The Tree, having heard the subject of their dispute, gave his opinion in the following words: "Among men, benefits are never requited but with ungrateful actions. I protect travelers from the heat of the sun, and yield them fruit to eat, and a delightful liquor to drink; nevertheless, forgetting the delight and benefit of my shade, they barbarously cut down my branches to make sticks, and handles for hatchets, and saw my body to make planks and rafters. Is not this requiting good with evil?"

The Adder, on this, looking upon the Traveler, asked if he was satisfied. But he was in such a confusion that he knew not what to answer. However, in hopes to free himself from the danger that threatened him, he said to the Adder, "I desire only one favor more; let us be judged by the next beast we meet; give me but that satisfaction, it is all I crave: you know life is sweet; suffer me therefore to beg for the means of continuing it." While they were thus parlaying together, a Fox passing by was stopped by the Adder, who conjured him to put an end to their controversy.

The Fox, upon this, desiring to know the subject of their dispute, said the Traveler, "I have done this Adder a signal piece of service, and he would fain persuade me that, for my reward, he ought to do me a mischief." "If he means to act by you as you men do by others, he speaks nothing but what is true," replied the Fox; "but, that I may be better able to judge between you, let me understand what service it is that you have done him."

The Traveler was very glad of this opportunity of speaking for

984

himself, and recounted the whole affair to him: he told him after what manner he had rescued him out of the flames with that little sack, which he showed him.

"How!" said the Fox, laughing outright, "would you pretend to make me believe that so large an Adder as this could get into such a little sack? It is impossible!" Both the Man and the Adder, on this, assured him of the truth of that part of the story; but the Fox positively refused to believe it. At length said he, "Words will never convince me of this monstrous improbability; but if the Adder will go into it again, to convince me of the truth of what you say, I shall then be able to judge of the rest of this affair."

"That I will do most willingly," replied the Adder; and, at the same time, put himself into the sack.

Then said the Fox to the Traveler, "Now you are the master of your enemy's life: and, I believe, you need not be long in resolving what treatment such a monster of ingratitude deserves of you." With that the Traveler tied up the mouth of the sack, and, with a great stone, never left off beating it till he had pounded the Adder to death; and, by that means, put an end to his fears and the dispute at once.

PINDAR

PINDAR (Greek, 518-438 B.C.). Sublime poetic eulogist, most accomplished writer of Greek choral lyrics. His major surviving works are celebration odes, written for aristocratic families and dedicated to the victors of the Panhellenic Games. Characterized by brilliant imagery and use of myths to point a moral.

JASON

(From the Fourth Pythian Ode. In honor of Arcesilaus, King of Cyrene, victor in chariot race, 466 B.C.

In time a noble stranger came,
A youth of glorious port; his manly frame
The country tunic clasped; two spears he bore.
    Above, to fence the shivering rain,
      A skin of spotted pard he threw.
    Adown his youthful neck amain
      His hair in glittering ringlets flew.

('Twas then in thronging crowds the people pressed,
　　What time the busy forum filled),
　　Then first he proved his manly breast,
And stood amid the throng by timorous fears unchilled.

　　Who might he be? thus each in wonder cried;
　　Is he Apollo? Is he Mars,
　　　So awful from the brazen cars,
　　So fair to win bright Venus for his bride?
　　　In Naxus sure men said
　　　Otus and Ephialte were dead;
　　And earth-born Tityus' giant form
　　　The winged shaft of Dian slew,
　　What time in dread avenging storm
　　　From her unconquered bow it flew,
　　A warning dread that men should fear,
Nor aim audacious love beyond their mortal sphere.

So each to the other babbled;—but in haste
　　High on his mule-drawn chariot Pelias came,
　　Eager, and full of fear: in stealthy shame
A frightened glance upon the ground he cast,
　　That glance the single sandal spied,
　　　The left foot bare! with easy grace
　　As bent his inward dread to hide,
　　"Tell, friend," he cried, "thy dwelling place;
What nameless mother sent her darling here,
　　　The darling of her doting age?
　　Speak nor let glozing falsehood sear
Thy birth, whate'er it be, nor lies thy soul engage."

Then frank and brave the gentle youth replied,
　　" From Chiron's cave I come, his nurseling I,
　　Where Philyra my innocent infancy
And Chariclo, the Centaur's child, did guide.
　　Twice ten the years I count, yet ne'er
　　Hath word of falsehood stained my tongue,
　　　Nor deed of ill, nor ribald jeer.
　　I come to claim mine own from wrong.
Home to mine own I come, my father's heir.
　　That crown usurped by lawless might,

986

Which erst old Æolus did wear,
He and his sons. From Jove, I claim my father's right.

For yielding to vile greed of power, men say,
    The promptings of a felon breast,
    Pelias my sire hath dispossessed,
And torn his long descended crown away.
    So when I first drew breath,
    Lest ruffian hands should do me death,
    My parents in the king's despite,
    Feigning an infant's early doom,
    Drest up with tears a funeral rite,
    And laid a puppet in the tomb.
    But me to Chiron's loving care,
All wrapt in princely robe, at dead of night, they bare.

Such is my tale;—no more the occasion needs;
    Then deign, kind citizens, to show me plain
    The dwelling whence my sires in lawful reign
Issued, all princely drawn by milk-white steeds.
    For Æson's son, no stranger I
    Come welcome to my home and free.
    Ask ye my name? The Centaur high
    Who bred me, bade me Jason be."
He spoke: but him his father's heart had known;
    Down his cheeks rolled the happy tears,
    To see his long-lost stripling grown
A prince of noble youths, the fairest of his peers.

Soon flock his brethren at the wondrous tale.
    Pheres from Hypereia's neighbor spring,
    Admetus eke, and brave Melampus bring,
And Amythaon from Messenia's vale,
    Cousinly greeting. He the while
    Spread bounteous forth the genial feast,
    And with kind word and courteous smile
    Received each new arriving guest.
High was the lordly cheer, and loud and long;
    Flew swiftly by each mirthful hour;
    Echoed five days and nights the song,
Five days and nights they culled joy's holiest, brightest flower.

987

But when the sixth day dawned, his tale of wrong
    To his assembled kinsman bold,
      In manly phrase the Chieftain told;
  Approving murmurs broke from all the throng.
      Forth from the council-tent
      Amid his peers the hero went
    Straightway the robber king to seek.
    They passed within the portal high.
  He heard and with a smiling cheek
    Wore a deceitful courtesy.
     Then, in sage words of peaceful flow
And counsel calm, the hero thus addressed his foe:

  " Son of Poseidon! oft the blinded heart
    Of man in folly seeks for crafty gain,
      Nor heeds the after-reckoning of grim pain,
  To choose the juster and the wiser part.
      Yet were it well that I and you,
        With peaceful words and counsel sage,
      Should weave a web both wise and true,
        And turn to peace our mutual rage.
  I speak of what thou know'st. A single womb
    Cretheus and bold Salmoneus bore.
    From these in third descent we come;
But Fate shrinks back ashamed when kinsmen join in war.

  It must not be that we with sword and steel
    Our great forefather's heritage should share.
      Freely the flocks and herds,—my father's heir,
  Yea, and the fruitful lands to thee I deal.
      Long hast thou these unduly held.
      Keep them, and swell thy robber store.
      It doth not yearn my soul to yield
      All these to thee; do thou restore
    The royal sceptre and the righteous throne,
      Where Cretheus' son, my sire, erewhile
      With princely justice ruled his own.
These, without sterner force or trick of fraudful guile,

Restore, lest thence worse evil should ensue."
        Briefly, as best his grief to hide,
        In accents calm the king replied:
" That which thy words invite me, will I do,
        But now mine age is old;
        Thy blood is young, thy heart is bold;
        Thou may'st the infernal wrath allay:
    For murdered Phrixus bids us come
    Where lives Æetes far away,
    And call his exiled spirit home,
        And fetch the fleece of golden sheen,
On which he soared erewhile to 'scape the vengeful Queen.

    For so a wondrous vision of my sleep
        Enjoined; without delay my way I took,
        Lest aught of vain or false my soul should mock,
    To seek the God of Delphi's holy steep.
        He bade me brook no slow delay,
        But man a bark with instant speed
        The sacred vision to obey.
        Do thou perform the holy deed;
    And by great Jove, our common sire, I swear,
        Sceptre and throne to yield thee free."
        Their mutual faith they promised fair,
That strong and sure to both should their high compact be.

OLYMPIA

(Eighth Olympian Ode. To Alcimedon of Ægina, victor in wrestling,
460 B.C.)

Olympia! mother of the old-crowned games!
        Great spring of Truth divine!
    Where seers around the holy shrine,
    With augury of sacred flames,
Essay the mind of Jove, the Thunder-King,
        If aught of hope he bring
To heroes straining for the glorious wreath,
Which bids the aching heart in triumph breathe.

989

(And oft success attends on pious prayers)
　　　　O holy Pisan grove,
　　Receive our revel-pomp in love!
　For glorious is his praise who shares
The grace which thy victorious garlands shed!
　　　　Yet many a path men tread,
And various are the roads of sweet success,
When the good Gods the toils of mortals bless.

DAVID PINSKI

DAVID PINSKI (Russian-Hebrew, 1872-　　). Foremost dramatist in Yiddish.
Born in Ukraine, studied in Vienna. Under influence of I. L. Peretz in Warsaw,
attached self to Jewish Socialist Movement. Came to U.S.A. in 1899, emigrated
to Israel in 1950. Wrote historical romances, realistic novels of Jewish life,
and plays: *The Treasure, King David and His Wives, The Final Balance.*

AND THEN HE WEPT

BEREL the carrier, poor but cheerful, lived in a cellar. Its two small
windows below the cobbled pavement of the courtyard were gray
and muddy, scarcely admitting the sunbeams that sometimes reached
them. Dampness leaked from the walls, mold glittered and sparkled
in the corners.

A table stood near the wall, between the two windows. Two of
the legs were its own, the others proxies—sticks of wood, which
often disappeared when there was nothing else with which to heat
the stove. At such times the table was shoved against the wall and
remained standing, Berel said, "with God's help."

There were three white chairs as well, all without backs. As soon
as a back toppled, Berel intended to hammer it into place again, but
meanwhile the two sticks supporting the table had been burned up
and no other firewood remained. So Berel would pull a solemn face
and hand down a truly philosophical decision: one can sit on a chair
even though it has no back, but potatoes must be cooked. And he
would intone in a Passover voice, most impressively, while the
chairback entered the oven along with other scraps that Berel and
his children had scavenged.

Two beds completed the furnishings. Rags, which Berel persisted
in calling pillows and blankets, covered them, and under and near

990

them stood boxes filled with more rags. Berel announced proudly that these were shirts, tablecloths—all sorts of household riches.

Did all this worry Berel? He laughed.

"What more do I need? Not a thing. As long as there's life . . ."

He had four children; two slept with him in one bed, two with the mother in the second bed. But he had no fear of more children. "Children," he said, "are a delight, a joy. Of course, they need a lot, but what's the difference? As long as I can come home and there's someone to play with, to make myself foolish with. What a pleasure! What a gang I have!"

Only his wife Bas-Sheve caused Berel dissatisfaction. He couldn't bear her moaning, her wailing and complaining.

"Eh," Berel said, shrugging, "my wife isn't fit for anything—always crying. She wants so much—what is there that she doesn't want? You'd think she had a contract with God, and He had promised to provide for her."

The tears had barely come to her eyes when Berel began to pose in front of her, his right hand against his cheek, his left hand supporting the right, his face twisted into woe and his head rocking back and forth. Bas-Sheve didn't find the imitation amusing. She grew angry. "All you do is laugh!"

"But I'm crying. Can't you see?" mocked Berel in his weepy voice.

"I wish we were crying for you, you great provider!" Her piece recited, she turned her back sharply. Berel wasn't insulted. Curses couldn't bother him. It almost seemed that without her curses life would be dull.

Only when she began to curse herself did Berel really become angry. "Almighty God," she cried out once when there was nothing to eat and a child was ill into the bargain (not at all a rare co-incidence in Berel's house), "Almighty God, rescue me from this dark and bitter life!" Her voice trembled; she meant it in earnest. At that moment she had no fear of death, and Berel felt it. His ribs seemed to crack with anguish. Outraged, furious, he began to scream, "May your tongue wither!"

Bas-Sheve, reduced to silence, wept instead, while Berel cast angry glances at her. "What good does crying do? That's all I want to know. You fool!"

As far as Berel was concerned, a human being should never cry unless, God forbid, someone died. But once . . .

Once of an evening Berel played so hard with the children,

wrestled and cavorted and carried on so lustily, that he plummeted onto his bed—and the bed exploded into bits.

He rose from the ruins, laughing. "Hoorah! Just wait, children. We'll deliver a funeral oration over the bed." Crouching like the humpbacked village orator, Berel made as if to speak. Bas-Sheve, clutching her head, broke into a wail. "It's too much—I can't stand any more. It's the last straw. I'll kill myself."

"Shh, let me say the eulogy." Berel tried to calm her, to draw her into the game. But she kept on moaning, "God in heaven, how can I be rid of this miserable life? At least we owned two beds, and now we don't even have that."

Berel grew angry. "Cow! What shall I do with you? Come on, cry some more. So the bed's smashed! You cow! Come on, moo-oo. Why aren't you bellowing?"

"May I bellow for the loss of your head!" She threw herself at him. "If only I could get rid of you I'd see daylight! Whenever you lift a finger it turns out a misfortune. Murderer, you're my private Angel of Death."

Berel's good humor was restored by the familiar accusations. "Come on, tell the truth—why all this uproar? Why upset the universe? What's a broken bed—a catastrophe? Has the sky collapsed? Listen. Think what might have happened to one of us, and instead it's happened to the bed!"

He remonstrated. She wept.

Blotting the tears with her apron, she thought of the future. No new shoes for the children. The first few pennies that came into the house would have to go for a new bed . . . though perhaps the old one could still be fixed. Meanwhile she and the two girls would sleep on the floor, and he—that foul hunk of disaster—he'd sleep in the remaining bed.

When Berel finished she answered tartly and with tears, "Sure, you have lots of beds, don't you? Go, crawl on the floor in the mud and the damp, and you'll learn how to laugh—may this be your last laugh!" Bas-Sheve glared at him.

Berel laughed. "What a joke! Berel, that great gentleman, has to sleep on the floor. Come on, kids, drag down the mattress," he told the boys.

"Not while I'm alive will I let you sleep on the floor!" She leaped up and shielded the mattress with her body.

Berel was astonished. "What's wrong? Are you crazy?"

"When you're dead, then you can lie on the ground. Not now."

Berel grew stern. "Bas-Sheve, this is no time for foolishness. Let me get some sleep." He reached for the mattress.

She pushed his head away and pointed to the bed. "Lie down, and may you never get up."

"I don't sleep in women's beds," he joked. "Come on, let me get some sleep." He grabbed the mattress.

"I said no and I meant it," screamed Bas-Sheve, clutching the mattress with both hands.

"So I'll lie down without a mattress!" Berel laughed and took off his coat.

Bas-Sheve rushed at him with her nails. Her cheeks flushed, her eyes burned. Berel grew excited. It was his young Bas-Sheve again! Warmth flooded his heart, a smile flowed across his face. "Ah, my pretty wife," he called and wanted to embrace her. But she thrust him off, her hatred absolute. "Get away from me quietly. If you don't I'll break your head."

She turned her back and began to prepare the bed for him. In that instant he grabbed the mattress, spun it onto the floor near the stove, and threw himself on top of it.

"Come on, boys," he ordered, "let's get to sleep."

Bas-Sheve cried out in fury, "Get on that bed!"

"Tomorrow."

"Stop ordering me around—may you wither and rot."

He laughed.

"Get into that bed! Do you hear what I say?"

"Ho-hum."

Frenzied, she began to kick the one remaining bed with her feet. "There—take that! There!"

Berel and the children jumped up in horror while she kept kicking with all her strength.

Berel tried to control her, to soothe her. He caught and held her tightly. "Have you gone mad?"

She tore herself away. Her heart contracted, her head blazed. She wanted to smash, smash, smash . . . But he held her too strongly. She tried to bite him.

"Bas-Sheve! Look, Bas Sheve," he stammered, twisting away from her teeth. He managed to lower her to a chair. Slowly Bas-Sheve calmed herself and began to weep. The children formed a chorus, wailing with fright.

Berel felt lost. He stood before Bas-Sheve and didn't take his sorrowful eyes off her. "Bas-Shevenke, little Bas-Sheve, stop, please stop!"

His voice twitched. "Bas-Shevenke," he pleaded gently, softly. His heart warmed with a marvelous tenderness, his throat seemed to choke and thicken. And that time Berel wept too.

LUIGI PIRANDELLO

LUIGI PIRANDELLO (Italian, 1867-1936). Leading modern dramatist of Italy. Began career as naturalistic novelist and story writer. Turned to theater in middle age. Developed highly individual technique, to explore metaphysical problems—especially the question of personal identity. Most famous plays: *Right You Are If You Think You Are, Six Characters in Search of an Author.* Nobel Prize, 1934.

HORSE IN THE MOON

IN SEPTEMBER, upon that high and arid clayey plain, jutting perilously over the African sea, the melancholy countryside still lay parched from the merciless summer sun; it was still shaggy with blackened stubble, while a sprinkling of almond trees and a few aged olive trunks were to be seen here and there. Nevertheless, it had been decided that the bridal pair should spend at least the first few days of their honeymoon in this place, to oblige the bridegroom.

The wedding feast, which was held in a room of the deserted villa, was far from being a festive occasion for the invited guests. None of those present was able to overcome the embarrassment, or rather the feeling of dismay inspired in him by the aspect and bearing of that fleshy youth, barely twenty years of age, with purplish face and with the little darting black eyes, which were preternaturally bright, like a madman's. The latter no longer heard what was being said around him; he did not eat, and he did not drink, but became, from moment to moment, redder and more purple of countenance.

Everyone knew that he had been madly in love with the one who now sat beside him as his bride, and that he had done perfectly mad things on her account, even to the point of attempting to kill himself. He was very rich, the sole heir to the Bernardi fortune, while she, after all, was only the daughter of an infantry colonel who had come there the year before, with the regiment from Sicily.

But in spite of this, the colonel, who had been warned against the inhabitants of the island, had been reluctant about giving his consent to this match, for the reason that he had not wanted to leave his daughter there among people that were little better than savages. The dismay which the bridegroom's aspect and actions inspired in the guests increased when the latter came to contrast him with his extremely young bride. She was really but a child, fresh, vivacious, and aloof; it seemed that she always shook off every unpleasant thought with a liveliness that was, at once, charming, ingenuous and roguish. Roguish as that of a little tomboy who as yet knows nothing of the world. A half-orphan, she had grown up without a mother's care; and indeed, it was all too evident that she was going into matrimony without any preparation whatsoever. Everyone smiled, but everyone felt a chill, when, at the end of the meal, she turned to the bridegroom and exclaimed:

"For goodness' sake, Nino, why do you make those tiny eyes? Let me—no, they burn! Why do your hands burn like that? Feel, Papa, feel how hot his hands are—Do you suppose he has a fever?"

The colonel, on pins and needles, did what he could to speed up the departure of the countryside guests. He wanted to put an end to a spectacle that impressed him as being indecent. They all piled into a half-dozen carriages. The one in which the colonel rode proceeded slowly down the lane and lagged a little behind, for the reason that the bridal couple, one on one side and one on the other, holding hands with the mother and father, had wanted to follow a short distance on foot, down to where the highway which led to the distant city began. At that point, the colonel leaned down and kissed his daughter on the head; he coughed and muttered: "Goodby, Nino."

"Goodby, Ida," said the bridegroom's mother with a laugh; and the carriage rattled away at a good pace, in order to overtake the others.

The two stood there for a moment gazing after it. But it was really only Ida who gazed; for Nino saw nothing, was conscious of nothing; his eyes were fastened upon his bride as she stood there, alone with him at last—his, all his—But what was this? Was she weeping?

"Daddy—" said Ida, as she waved her handkerchief in farewell. "There, do you see? He, too—"

"No, Ida—Ida dear—" and stammering, almost sobbing, trembling violently, Nino made an effort to embrace her.

995

"No, let me alone, please."

"I just wanted to dry your eyes—"

"Thanks, my dear; I'll dry them myself."

Nino stood there awkwardly. His face, as he looked at her, was pitiful to behold, and his mouth was half-open. Ida finished drying her eyes.

"But what's the matter?" she asked him. "You're trembling all over—No, no, Nino, for heaven's sake, no; don't stand there like that! You make me laugh. And if I once start laughing—you'll see—I'll never stop! Wait a minute; I'll wake you up."

She put her hands on his temples and blew in his eyes. At the touch of those fingers, at the breath from those lips, he felt his legs giving way beneath him; he was about to sink down on one knee, but she held him up and burst into a loud laugh:

"Upon the highway? Are you crazy? Come on, let's go! Look at that little hill over there! We shall be able to see the carriages still. Let's go look!"

And she impetuously dragged him away by one arm.

From all the countryside roundabout, where so many weeds and grasses, so many things dispersed by the hand of time lay withered, there mounted into the heat-ridden air something like a dense and ancient drought, mingling with the warm, heavy odor of the manure that lay fermenting in little piles upon the fallow fields, and with the sharper fragrance of sage and wildmint. Of that dense drought, those warm and heavy odors, that piercing fragrance, he alone was aware. She, as she ran, could hear how gaily the wood-larks sang up to the sun, from behind the thick hedges and from between the rugged yellowish tufts of burnt-over stubble; she could hear, too, in that impressive silence, the prophetic crow of cocks from distant barnyards; and she felt herself wrapped, every now and then, in the cool, keen breath that came up from the neighboring sea, to stir the few tired and yellowed leaves that were left on the almond trees, and the close-clustering, sharp-pointed, ashen-hued olive leaves.

It did not take them long to reach the hilltop; but he was so exhausted from running that he could no longer stand; he wanted to sit down, and tried to make her sit down also, there on the ground beside him, with his arm about her waist. But Ida put him off with "Let me have a look first."

She was beginning to feel restless inside, but she did not care to show it. Irritated by a certain strange and curious stubbornness

996

on his part, she could not, she would not stand still, but longed to keep on fleeing, still farther away; she wanted to shake him up, to distract him, to distract herself as well, so long as the day lasted.

Down there, on the other side of the hill, there stretched away a devastated plain, a sea of stubble, amid which one could make out occasionally the black and meandering traces of wood-ashes that had been sprinkled there; now and again, too, the crude yellow gleam was broken by a few clumps of caper or of licorice. Away over there, as if on the other shore of that vast yellow sea, the roofs of a hamlet rose from the tall dark poplars.

And now Ida suggested to her husband that they go over there, all the way over to that hamlet. How long would it take? An hour or less. It was not more than five o'clock. Back home, in the villa, the servants must still be busy clearing away the things. They would be home before evening.

Nino made a feeble attempt at opposition, but she took him by the hands and dragged him to his feet; in a moment, she was running down the side of the hill and was off through the sea of stubble, as light and quick as a young doe. He was not fast enough to keep up with her, but, redder-faced than ever and seemingly stunned by it all, ran after her, pantingly and perspiringly, and kept calling to her to wait and give him her hand.

"Give me your hand, at least! At least, give me your hand!" he shouted.

All of a sudden, she uttered a cry and stopped short. A flock of cawing ravens had just flown up from in front of her, stretched out upon the earth, was a dead horse. Dead? No, no, it wasn't dead; it had its eyes open. Heavens, what eyes! What eyes! A skeleton, that was what it was. And those ribs! And those flanks!

Nino came up fuming and fretting:

"Come on, let's go—let's go back—at once!"

"It's alive, look!" cried Ida, shivering from compassion. "Lift its head—heavens, what eyes! Look, Nino!'

"Yes, yes," said he, panting still. "They've just put it out here —Leave it alone; let's go! What a sight! Don't you smell?"

"And those ravens!" she exclaimed with a shudder. "Are those ravens going to eat it alive?"

"But Ida, for heaven's sake!" he implored her, clasping his hands.

"Nino, that will do!" she cried. It was more than she could endure to see him so stupid and so contrite. "Answer me: what if they eat it alive?"

"What do I know about whether or not they'll eat it? They'll wait—"

"Until it dies here, of hunger, of thirst?" Her face was all drawn, with horror and pity. "Just because it's old? Because it can't work any more? Ah, poor beast! What a shame! What a shame! Haven't you any heart, standing there like that?"

"Excuse me," he said, losing his temper, "but you feel so much sympathy for an animal—"

"And oughtn't I to?"

"But you don't feel any for me!"

"And are you an animal? Are you dying of hunger and thirst as you sit there in the stubble? You feel—Oh, look at the ravens, Nino, look, up there, circling around—Oh, what a horrible, shameful, monstrous thing!—Look—Oh, the poor beast—try to lift him up! Come, Nino, get up; maybe he can still walk—Nino, get up, help me—shake yourself out of it!"

"But what do you expect me to do?" he burst out, exasperatedly. "Do you expect me to drag him back? Put him on my shoulders? What's a horse more or less? How do you think he is going to walk? Can't you see he's half-dead?"

"And if we brought him something to eat?"

"And to drink, too?"

"Oh, Nino, you're wicked!" And the tears stood in Ida's eyes.

Overcoming her shudders, she bent over very gently to caress the horse's head. The animal, with a great effort had managed to get to its knees; and even in its last degrading agony, it showed the traces of a noble beauty in head and neck.

Nino, owing possibly to the blood that was pounding in his veins, possibly owing to the bitterness and contempt she had manifested, or to the perspiration that was trickling from him, now suddenly felt his breath failing him; he grew giddy, his teeth began chattering, and he was conscious of a weird trembling all over his body. He instinctively turned up his coat collar, and with his hands in his pockets, went over and huddled down in gloomy despair upon a rock some distance away.

The sun had already set, and from the distant highway could be heard the occasional sound of horses' bells.

Why were his teeth chattering like that? For his forehead was burning up, the blood in his veins stung him, and there was a roaring in his ears. It seemed to him that he could hear so many far-away bells. All that anxiety, that spasm of expectation, her

998

coldness and caprice, that last foot-race, and that horse there, that cursed horse—Oh, God! was it a dream? A nightmare within a dream? Did he have a fever? Or perhaps, a worse illness? Ah! How dark it was, God—how dark! And now, his sight was clouding over. And he could not speak, he could not cry out. He tried to call "Ida, Ida!" but he could not get the words out of his parched throat.

Where was Ida? What was she doing?

She had gone off to the distant hamlet, to seek aid for that horse; she did not stop to think that the peasants had brought the animal there to die.

He remained there, alone upon the rock, a prey to those growing tremors; and as he sat there, huddled to himself like a great owl upon a perch, he suddenly beheld a sight that seemed—Ah, yes— he could see it plainly enough now—an atrocious sight, like a vision from another world. The moon. A huge moon, coming slowly up from behind that sea of stubble. And black against that enormous. vapory copper disk, the headstrong head of that horse, waiting still with its neck stretched out—it had, perhaps, been waiting like that always, darkly etched upon that copper disk, while from far up in the sky could be heard the caw of circling ravens.

When Ida, angry and disillusioned, came groping her way back over the plain, calling "Nino, Nino!" the moon had already risen; the horse had dropped down as if dead; and Nino—where was Nino? Oh, there he was over there; he was on the ground, too.

Had he fallen asleep there?

She ran up to him, and found him with a death-rattle in his throat. His face, also, was on the ground; it was almost black, and his eyes, nearly closed, were puffed and bloodshot.

"Oh, God!"

She looked about her, as if in a swoon. She opened her hands which held a few dried beans that she had brought from the hamlet over there to feed to the horse. She looked at the moon, then at the horse, and then at the man lying on the ground as if dead. She felt faint, assailed as she was by the sudden suspicion that everything she saw was unreal. Terrified, she fled back to the villa calling in a loud voice for her father, her father—to come and take her away. Oh, God! away from that man with the rattle in his throat—that rattle, the meaning of which she did not understand! away from under that mad moon, away from under those cawing ravens in the sky—away, away, away—

999

PO CHU-I

PO CHÜ-I (Chinese, 772-846). One of China's greatest statesmen. Many of his poems are occasional, others written to protest social evils. Most famous, *Song of Everlasting Remorse* and *Lute Song*, are long narratives in ballad form. Also composed verse to folk tunes. Had great influence on his contemporaries.

IN YUNG-YANG

I was a child in Yung-yang,
A little child I waved farewell.
After long years again I dwell
In world-forgotten Yung-yang.
Yet I recall my play-time,
And in my dreams I see
The little ghosts of May-time
Waving farewell to me.

My father's house in Yung-yang
Has fallen upon evil days.
No kinsmen o'er the crooked ways
Hail me as once in Yung-yang.

No longer stands the old Moot-hall;
Gone is the market from the town;
The very hills have tumbled down
And stoned the valleys in their fall.

Only the waters of the Ch'in and Wei
Roll green and changeless as in days gone by.

Yet I recall my play-time,
And in my dreams I see
The little ghosts of May-time
Waving farewell to me.

RAIN AT DAWN

At dawn the crickets shrill, then cease their 'plain,
The dying candle flickers through my eaves;
Though windows bar the wild dust and the rain,
I hear the drip, drip, dripping on the broad banana leaves.

1000

SHE WHO MUST PART FROM HER SONS

The First Wife Speaks:

Sons say farewell to their mother, mother farewell to her sons;
The bright day loses its brightness at the sobs of such little ones.
He is the great Commander who conquered the West Frontier;
Last year he won the battle; the Emperor holds him dear.
Two million silver pieces were his in a shining shower—
And he went to Lo-yang and wedded this woman fair as a flower!

When the new life comes to the castle, the old wife goes from the
    door;
But my babies, my lotus blossoms, she hated them even more.
To take a new wife to your bosom and send the old wife away
Is bad enough, but the worst thing is that my babes must stay,
Stay in your house without me: one is learning to walk,
And the other just sits up swaying, a gurgle his only talk.
The boy baby cries, and the toddler weeps and clings to my dress
With a faint foreboding of evil that would vanish at my caress.
Just that you two may make merry, you turn from your former wife.
The mother of little children, and shut her out, in her life.
It isn't even so happy as the crow's or the blackbird's fate;
Their young do not leave the mother; mate does not leave his mate.
Or the plum trees abloom in the garden, haven of bird and bee;
Though their blossoms fall to the greensward, their fruit still clings
    to the tree.

New wife, new wife to my husband, hear but this word from me:
Still in Lo-yang, our native city, there are many as fair as we.
May our General win one more victory, one more great gift
    from the throne!
Then a newer wife yet will enter, and you shall go forth—alone.

CHAO CHUN IN TARTARY

When the Han envoy turns his horses homeward,
    Pray him to bear this message back for me:
"The Lady Chao Chun asks but this one question—
    'When will they send the gold to set me free?'"

And if the Emperor inquire about me,
Whether my face has grown less fair or more,
Say not that I have lost my beauty grieving!
Say not that I'm less lovely than before!

EDGAR ALLAN POE

EDGAR ALLAN POE (American, 1809-1849). Erratic, intemperate genius, whose influence has been world-wide—particularly in France. A journalist in Philadelphia and New York. His life a ceaseless struggle with poverty and alcoholism. Originated the modern detective story ("The Murders in the Rue Morgue"), wrote remarkable tales of terror ("Fall of the House of Usher") and America's most quoted poem ("The Raven").

THE MASQUE OF THE RED DEATH

THE "Red Death" had long devastated the country. No pestilence had ever been so fatal, or so hideous. Blood was its Avatar and its seal—the redness and the horror of blood. There were sharp pains, and sudden dizziness, and then profuse bleeding at the pores, with dissolution. The scarlet stains upon the body and especially upon the face of the victim, were the pest ban which shut him out from the aid and from the sympathy of his fellowmen. And the whole seizure, progress and termination of the disease, were the incidents of half an hour.

But the Prince Prospero was happy and dauntless and sagacious. When his dominions were half depopulated, he summoned to his presence a thousand hale and lighthearted friends from among the knights and dames of his court, and with these retired to the deep seclusion of one of his castellated abbeys. This was an extensive and magnificent structure, the creation of the prince's own eccentric yet august taste. A strong and lofty wall girdled it in. This wall had gates of iron. The courtiers, having entered, brought furnaces and massy hammers and welded the bolts. They resolved to leave means neither of ingress or egress to the sudden impulses of despair or of frenzy from within. The abbey was amply provisioned. With such precautions the courtiers might bid defiance to contagion. The external world could take care of itself. In the meantime it was folly to grieve, or to think. The prince had provided all the appliances of pleasure. There were buffoons, there were improvisatori, there

1002

were ballet-dancers, there were musicians, there was Beauty, there was wine. All these and security were within. Without was the "Red Death."

It was toward the close of the fifth or sixth month of his seclusion, and while the pestilence raged most furiously abroad, that the Prince Prospero entertained his thousand friends at a masked ball of the most unusual magnificence.

It was a voluptuous scene, that masquerade. But first let me tell of the rooms in which it was held. There were seven—an imperial suite. In many palaces, however, such suites form a long and straight vista, while the folding doors slide back nearly to the walls on either hand, so that the view of the whole extent is scarcely impeded. Here the case was very different; as might have been expected from the duke's love of the *bizarre*. The apartments were so irregularly disposed that the vision embraced but little more then one at a time. There was a sharp turn at every twenty or thirty yards, and at each turn a novel effect. To the right and left, in the middle of each wall, a tall and narrow Gothic window looked out upon a closed corridor which pursued the windings of the suite. These windows were of stained glass whose color varied in accordance with the prevailing hue of the decorations of the chamber into which it opened. That at the eastern extremity was hung, for example, in blue—and vividly blue were its windows. The second chamber was purple in its ornaments and tapestries, and here the panes were purple. The third was green throughout, and so were the casements. The fourth was furnished and lighted with orange —the fifth with white—the sixth with violet. The seventh apartment was closely shrouded in black velvet tapestries that hung all over the ceiling and down the walls, falling in heavy folds upon a carpet of the same material and hue. But in this chamber only, the color of the windows failed to correspond with the decorations. The panes here were scarlet—a deep blood color. Now in no one of the seven apartments was there any lamp or candelabrum, amid the profusion of golden ornaments that lay scattered to and fro or depended from the roof. There was no light of any kind emanating from lamp or candle within the suite of chambers. But in the corridors that followed the suite, there stood, opposite to each window, a heavy tripod, bearing a brazier of fire that projected its rays through the tinted glass and so glaringly illumined the room. And thus were produced a multitude of gaudy and fantastic appearances. But in the western or black chamber the effect of the

fire-light that streamed upon the dark hangings through the blood-tinted panes, was ghastly in the extreme, and produced so wild a look upon the countenances of those who entered, that there were few of the company bold enough to set foot within its precincts at all.

It was in this apartment, also, that there stood against the western wall, a gigantic clock of ebony. Its pendulum swung to and fro with a dull, heavy, monotonous clang; and when the minute-hand made the circuit of the face, and the hour was to be stricken, there came from the brazen lungs of the clock a sound which was clear and loud and deep and exceedingly musical, but of so peculiar a note and emphasis that, at each lapse of an hour, the musicians of the orchestra were constrained to pause, momentarily, in their performance, to hearken to the sound; and thus the waltzers per-force ceased their evolutions; and there was a brief disconcert of the whole gay company; and, while the chimes of the clock yet rang, it was observed that the giddiest grew pale, and the more aged and sedate passed their hands over their brows as if in confused revery or meditation. But when the echoes had fully ceased, a light laughter at once pervaded the assembly; the musicians looked at each other and smiled as if at their own nervousness and folly, and made whispering vows, each to the other, that the next chiming of the clock should produce in them no similar emotion; and then, after the lapse of sixty minutes (which embrace three thousand and six hundred seconds of the Time that flies), there came yet another chiming of the clock, and then were the same disconcert and tremulousness and meditation as before.

But, in spite of these things, it was a gay and magnificent revel. The tastes of the duke were peculiar. He had a fine eye for colors and effects. He disregarded the *decora* of mere fashion. His plans were bold and fiery, and his conceptions glowed with barbaric lustre. There are some who would have thought him mad. His followers felt that he was not. It was necessary to hear and see and touch him to be *sure* that he was not.

He had directed, in great part, the movable embellishments of the seven chambers, upon occasion of this great *fête;* and it was his own guiding taste which had given character to the masqueraders. Be sure they were grotesque. There were much glare and glitter and piquancy and phantasm—much of what has been since seen in "Hernani." There were arabesque figures with unsuited limbs and appointments. There were delirious fancies such as the madman

1004

fashions. There was much of the beautiful, much of the wanton, much of the *bizarre*, something of the terrible, and not a little of that which might have excited disgust. To and fro in the seven chambers there stalked, in fact, a multitude of dreams. And these —the dreams—writhed in and about, taking hue from the rooms, and causing the wild music of the orchestra to seem as the echo of their steps. And, anon, there strikes the ebony clock which stands in the hall of the velvet. And then, for a moment, all is still, and all is silent save the voice of the clock. The dreams are stiff-frozen as they stand. But the echoes of the chime die away—they have endured but an instant—and a light, half-subdued laughter floats after them as they depart. And now again the music swells, and the dreams live, and writhe to and fro more merrily than ever, taking hue from the many tinted windows through which stream the rays from the tripods. But to the chamber which lies most west-wardly of the seven, there are now none of the maskers who venture, for the night is waning away; and there flows a ruddier light through the blood-colored panes; and the blackness of the sable drapery appalls; and to him whose foot falls upon the sable carpet, there comes from the near clock of ebony a muffled peal more solemnly emphatic than any which reaches *their* ears who indulge in the more remote gayeties of the other apartments.

But these other apartments were densely crowded, and in them beat feverishly the heart of life. And the revel went whirlingly on, until at length there commenced the sounding of midnight upon the clock. And then the music ceased, as I have told; and the evolu-tions of the waltzers were quieted; and there was an uneasy cessation of all things as before. But now there were twelve strokes to be sounded by the bell of the clock; and thus it happened, perhaps, that before the last echoes of the last chime had utterly sunk into silence, there were many individuals in the crowd who had found leisure to become aware of the presence of a masked figure which had arrested the attention of no single individual before. And the rumor of this new presence having spread itself whispering around, there arose at length from the whole company, a buzz, or murmur, expressive of disapprobation and surprise—then, finally, of terror, of horror, and of disgust.

In an assembly of phantasms such as I have painted, it may well be supposed that no ordinary appearance could have excited such sensation. In truth the masquerade license of the night was nearly unlimited; but the figure in question had out-Heroded Herod,

and gone beyond the bounds of even the prince's indefinite decorum. There are chords in the hearts of the most reckless which cannot be touched without emotion. Even with the utterly lost, to whom life and death are equally jests, there are matters of which no jest can be made. The whole company, indeed, seemed now deeply to feel that in the costume and bearing of the stranger neither wit nor propriety existed. The figure was tall and gaunt, and shrouded from head to foot in the habiliments of the grave. The mask which concealed the visage was made so nearly to resemble the countenance of a stiffened corpse that the closest scrutiny must have had difficulty in detecting the cheat. And yet all this might have been endured, if not approved, by the mad revellers around. But the mummer had gone so far as to assume the type of the Red Death. His vesture was dabbled in *blood*—and his broad brow, with all the features of the face, was besprinkled with the scarlet horror.

When the eyes of Prince Prospero fell upon this spectral image (which with a slow and solemn movement, as if more fully to sustain its *rôle*, stalked to and fro among the waltzers) he was seen to be convulsed, in the first moment, with a strong shudder either of terror or distaste; but, in the next, his brow reddened with rage.

"Who dares?" he demanded hoarsely of the courtiers who stood near him—"who dares insult us with this blasphemous mockery? Seize him and unmask him—that we may know whom we have to hang at sunrise, from the battlements!"

It was in the eastern or blue chamber in which stood the Prince Prospero as he uttered these words. They rang throughout the seven rooms loudly and clearly—for the prince was a bold and robust man, and the music had become hushed at the waving of his hand.

It was in the blue room where stood the prince, with a group of pale courtiers by his side. At first, as he spoke, there was a slight rushing movement of this group in the direction of the intruder, who at the moment was also near at hand, and now, with deliberate and stately step, made closer approach to the speaker. But from a certain nameless awe with which the mad assumptions of the mummer had inspired the whole party, there were found none who put forth hand to seize him; so that, unimpeded, he passed within a yard of the prince's person; and, while the vast assembly, as if with one impulse, shrank from the centres of the room to the walls, he made his way uninterruptedly, but with the same solemn and measured step which had distinguished him from

1006

the first, through the blue chamber to the purple—through the purple to the green—through the green to the orange—through this again to the white—and even thence to the violet, ere a decided movement had been made to arrest him. It was then, however, that the Prince Prospero, maddening with rage and the shame of his own momentary cowardice, rushed hurriedly through the six chambers, while none followed him on account of a deadly terror that had seized upon all. He bore aloft a drawn dagger, and had approached, in rapid impetuosity, to within three or four feet of the retreating figure, when the latter, having attained the extremity of the velvet apartment, turned suddenly and confronted his pursuer. There was a sharp cry—and the dagger dropped gleaming upon the sable carpet, upon which, instantly afterwards, fell prostrate in death the Prince Prospero. Then, summoning the wild courage of despair, a throng of the revellers at once threw themselves into the black apartment, and, seizing the mummer, whose tall figure stood erect and motionless within the shadow of the ebony clock, gasped in unutterable horror at finding the grave-cerements and corpse-like mask which they handled with so violent a rudeness, untenanted by any tangible form.

And now was acknowledged the presence of the Red Death. He had come like a thief in the night. And one by one dropped the revellers in the blood-bedewed halls of their revel, and died each in the despairing posture of his fall. And the life of the ebony clock went out with that of the last of the gay. And the flames of the tripods expired. And Darkness and Decay and the Red Death held illimitable dominion over all.

ALEXANDER POPE

ALEXANDER POPE (English, 1688-1744). Foremost literary figure of the 18th century Classicists. A dwarfed cripple, 4½ feet tall. Famous for his translation of Homer, *An Essay on Criticism* and the poem, "The Rape of the Lock." Gave English verse a technical finish it had never previously possessed. Hence, in an age of formal standards, was acknowledged Europe's greatest poet during his lifetime.

AN ESSAY ON MAN

Hope humbly then; with trembling pinions soar;
Wait the great teacher Death, and God adore.

What future bliss, he gives not thee to know,
But gives that hope to be thy blessing now;
Hope springs eternal in the human breast—
Man never is, but always to be blessed
The soul, uneasy and confined from home,
Rests and expatiates in a life to come.
Lo, the poor Indian! whose untutored mind
Sees God in clouds, or hears him in the wind;
His soul proud science never taught to stray
Far as the solar walk, or milky way,
Yet simple nature to his hope has given,
Behind the cloud-topped hill, an humbler heaven.

Know then thyself, presume not God to scan,
The proper study of mankind is man.
Placed on this isthmus of a middle state,
A being darkly wise, and rudely great:
With too much knowledge for the sceptic side,
With too much weakness for the stoic's pride,
He hangs between; in doubt to act, or rest;
In doubt to deem himself a god, or beast;
In doubt his mind or body to prefer;
Born but to die, and reasoning but to err;
Alike in ignorance, his reason such,
Whether he thinks too little or too much:
Chaos of thought and passion, all confused;
Still by himself abused or disabused;
Created half to rise and half to fall;
Great lord of all things, yet a prey to all;
Sole judge of truth, in endless error hurled:
The glory, jest, and riddle of the world!

Whate'er the passion—knowledge, fame, or pelf,
Not one will change his neighbor with himself.
The learned is happy nature to explore,
The fool is happy that he knows no more;
The rich is happy in the plenty given,
The poor contents him with the care of Heaven.
See the blind beggar dance, the cripple sing,
The sot a hero, lunatic a king;
The starving chemist in his golden views
Supremely blest, the poet in his muse.

See some strange comfort every state attend,
And pride bestowed on all, a common friend;
See some fit of passion every age supply,
Hope travels through nor quits us when we die.
  Behold the child, by nature's kindly law,
Pleased with a rattle, tickled with a straw:
Some livelier plaything gives his youth delight,
A little louder, but as empty quite:
Scarfs, garters, gold, amuse his riper stage,
And beads and prayer-books are the toys of age:
Pleased with this bauble still, as that before;
Till tired he sleeps, and life's poor play is o'er.

Honor and shame from no condition rise:
Act well your part, there all the honor lies.
Fortune in men has some small difference made,
One flaunts in rags, one flutters in brocade;
The cobbler aproned, and the parson gowned,
The friar hooded, and the monarch crowned.
"What differ more (you cry) than crown and cowl!"
I'll tell you, friend! a wise man and a fool.
You'll find, if once the monarch acts the monk,
Or, cobbler-like, the parson will be drunk,
Worth makes the man, and want of it the fellow;
The rest is all but leather or prunella.

MARCEL PROUST

MARCEL PROUST (French, 1871-1922). Creator of the most fabulous single
work in modern literature: *Remembrance of Things Past*. He spent many
years in a dark, cork-lined chamber writing this 7-volume novel; then published it at his own expense. Ostensibly a meticulous recreation of the author's
early life and later social excursions, it is actually a kind of metaphysical
exploration of concepts like Time, Memory, Art and Reality.

THE DEATH OF BERGOTTE

I LEARNED that a death had occurred during the day which distressed
me greatly, that of Bergotte. It was known that he had been ill for
a long time past. Not, of course, with the illness from which he had

1009

suffered originally and which was natural. Nature hardly seems capable of giving us any but quite short illnesses. But medicine has annexed to itself the art of prolonging them. Remedies, the respite that they procure, the relapses that a temporary cessation of them provokes, compose a sham illness to which the patient grows so accustomed that he ends by making it permanent, just as children continue to give way to fits of coughing long after they have been cured of the whooping cough. Then remedies begin to have less effect, the doses are increased, they cease to do any good, but they have begun to do harm thanks to that lasting indisposition. Nature would not have offered them so long a tenure. It is a great miracle that medicine can almost equal nature in forcing a man to remain in bed, to continue on pain of death the use of some drug. From that moment the illness artificially grafted has taken root, has become a secondary but a genuine illness, with this difference only that natural illnesses are cured, but never those which medicine creates, for it knows not the secret of their cure.

For years past Bergotte had ceased to go out of doors. Anyhow, he had never cared for society, or had cared for it for a day only, to despise it as he despised everything else and in the same fashion, which was his own, namely to despise a thing not because it was beyond his reach but as soon as he had reached it. He lived so simply that nobody suspected how rich he was, and anyone who had known would still have been mistaken, for he would have thought him a miser, whereas no one was ever more generous. He was generous above all towards women—girls, one ought rather to say—who were ashamed to receive so much in return for so little. He excused himself in his own eyes because he knew that he could never produce such good work as in an atmosphere of amorous feelings. Love is too strong a word, pleasure that is at all deeply rooted in the flesh is helpful to literary work because it cancels all other pleasures, for instance the pleasures of society, those which are the same for everyone. And even if this love leads to disillusionment, it does at least stir, even by so doing, the surface of the soul which otherwise would be in danger of becoming stagnant. Desire is therefore not without its value to the writer in detaching him first of all from his fellow men and from conforming to their standards, and afterwards in restoring some degree of movement to a spiritual machine which, after, a certain age, tends to become paralysed. We do not succeed in being happy but we make observation of the reasons which prevent us from being happy and which

1010

would have remained invisible to us but for these loopholes opened by disappointment. Dreams are not to be converted into reality, that we know; we would not form any, perhaps, were it not for desire, and it is useful to us to form them in order to see them fail and to be instructed by their failure. And so Bergotte said to himself· 'I am spending more than a multimillionaire would spend upon girls, but the pleasures or disappointments that they give me make me write a book which brings me money." Economically, this argument was absurd, but no doubt he found some charm in thus transmitting gold into caresses and caresses into gold. We saw, at the time of my grandmother's death, how a weary old age loves repose. Now in society, there is nothing but conversation. It may be stupid, but it has the faculty of suppressing women who are nothing more than questions and answers. Removed from society, women become once more what is so reposeful to a weary old man, an object of contemplation. In any case, it was no longer a question of anything of this sort. I have said that Bergotte never went out of doors, and when he got out of bed for an hour in his room, he would be smothered in shawls, plaids, all the things with which a person covers himself before exposing himself to intense cold or getting into a railway train. He would apologise to the few friends whom he allowed to penetrate to his sanctuary, and, pointing to his tartan plaids, his travelling-rugs, would say merrily: "After all, my dear fellow, life, as Anaxagoras has said, is a journey." Thus he went on growing steadily colder, a tiny planet that offered a prophetic image of the greater, when gradually heat will withdraw from the earth, then life itself. Then the resurrection will have to come to an end, for if, among future generations, the works of men are to shine, there must first of all be men. If certain kinds of animals hold out longer against the invading chill, when there are no longer any men, and if we suppose Bergotte's fame to have lasted so long, suddenly it will be extinguished for all time. It will not be the last animals that will read him, for it is scarcely probable that, like the Apostles on the Day of Pentecost, they will be able to understand the speech of the various races of mankind without having learned it.

In the months that preceded his death, Bergotte suffered from insomnia, and what was worse, whenever he did fall asleep, from nightmares which, if he awoke, made him reluctant to go to sleep again. He had long been a lover of dreams, even of bad dreams, because thanks to them and to the contradiction they present to

the reality which we have before us in our waking state, they give us, at the moment of waking if not before, the profound sensation of having slept. But Bergotte's nightmares were not like that. When he spoke of nightmares, he used in the past to mean unpleasant things that passed through his brain. Latterly, it was as though proceeding from somewhere outside himself that he would see a hand armed with a damp cloth which, passed over his face by an evil woman, kept scrubbing him awake, an intolerable itching in his thighs, the rage—because Bergotte had murmured in his sleep that he was driving badly—of a raving lunatic of a cabman who flung himself upon the writer, biting and gnawing his fingers. Finally, as soon as in his sleep it had grown sufficiently dark, nature arranged a sort of undress rehearsal of the apoplectic stroke that was to carry him off: Bergotte arrived in a carriage beneath the porch of Swann's new house, and tried to alight. A stunning giddiness glued him to his seat, the porter came forward to help him out of the carriage, he remained seated, unable to rise, to straighten his legs. He tried to pull himself up with the help of the stone pillar that was by his side, but did not find sufficient support in it to enable him to stand.

He consulted doctors who, flattered at being called in by him, saw in his virtue as an incessant worker (it was twenty years since he had written anything), in his overstrain, the cause of his ailments. They advised him not to read thrilling stories (he never read anything), to benefit more by the sunshine, which was "indispensable to life" (he had owed a few years of comparative health only to his rigorous seclusion indoors), to take nourishment (which made him thinner, and nourished nothing but his nightmares). One of his doctors was blessed with the spirit of contradiction, and whenever Bergotte consulted him in the absence of the others, and, in order not to offend him, suggested to him as his own ideas what the others had advised, this doctor, thinking that Bergotte was seeking to have prescribed for him something that he himself liked, at once forbade it, and often for reasons invented so hurriedly to meet the case that in face of the material objections which Bergotte raised, this argumentative doctor was obliged in the same sentence to contradict himself, but, for fresh reasons, repeated the original prohibition. Bergotte returned to one of the first of these doctors, a man who prided himself on his cleverness, especially in the presence of one of the leading men of letters, and who, if Bergotte insinuated: "I seem to remember, though, that

Dr. X—— told me—long ago, of course—that that might congest my kidneys and brain . . ." would smile sardonically, raise his fingers and enounce: "I said use, I did not say abuse. Naturally every remedy, if one takes it in excess, becomes a two-edged sword." There is in the human body a certain instinct for what is beneficial to us, as there is in the heart for what is our moral duty, an instinct which no authorisation by a Doctor of Medicine or Divinity can replace. We know that cold baths are bad for us, we like them, we can always find a doctor to recommend them, not to prevent them from doing us harm. From each of these doctors Bergotte took something which, in his own wisdom, he had forbidden himself for years past. After a few weeks, his old troubles had reappeared, the new had become worse. Maddened by an unintermittent pain, to which was added insomnia broken only by brief spells of nightmare, Bergotte called in no more doctors and tried with success, but to excess, different narcotics, hopefully reading the prospectus that accompanied each of them, a prospectus which proclaimed the necessity of sleep but hinted that all the preparations which induce it (except that contained in the bottle round which the prospectus was wrapped, which never produced any toxic effect) were toxic, and therefore made the remedy worse than the disease. Bergotte tried them all. Some were of a different family from those to which we are accustomed, preparations for instance of amyl and ethyl. When we absorb a new drug, entirely different in composition, it is always with a delicious expectancy of the unknown. Our heart beats as at a first assignation. To what unknown forms of sleep, of dreams, is the newcomer going to lead us? He is inside us now, he has the control of our thoughts. In what fashion are we going to fall asleep? And, once we are asleep, by what strange paths, up to what peaks, into what unfathomed gulfs is he going to lead us? With what new grouping of sensations are we to become acquainted on this journey? Will it bring us to the end of illness? To blissful happiness? To death? Bergotte's death had come to him overnight, when he had thus entrusted himself to one of these friends (a friend? or an enemy, rather?) who proved too strong for him. The circumstances of his death were as follows. An attack of uraemia, by no means serious, had led to his being ordered to rest. But one of the critics having written somewhere that in *Vermeer's Street in Delft* (lent by the Gallery at The Hague for an exhibition of Dutch painting), a picture which he adored and imagined that he knew by heart, a little patch of yellow wall (which he could not remember)

was so well painted that it was, if one looked at it by itself, like some priceless specimen of Chinese art, of a beauty that was sufficient in itself. Bergotte ate a few potatoes, left the house, and went to the exhibition. At the first few steps that he had to climb he was overcome by giddiness. He passed in front of several pictures and was struck by the stiffness and futility of so artificial a school, nothing of which equalled the fresh air and sunshine of a Venetian palazzo, or of an ordinary house by the sea. At last he came to the Vermeer which he remembered as more striking, more different from anything else that he knew, but in which, thanks to the critic's article, he remarked for the first time some small figures in blue, that the ground was pink, and finally the precious substance of the tiny patch of yellow wall. His giddiness increased; he fixed his eyes, like a child upon a yellow butterfly which it is trying to catch, upon the precious little patch of wall. "That is how I ought to have written," he said. "My last books are too dry, I ought to have gone over them with several coats of paint, made my language exquisite in itself, like this little patch of yellow wall." Meanwhile he was not unconscious of the gravity of his condition. In a celestial balance there appeared to him, upon one of its scales, his own life, while the other contained the little patch of wall so beautifully painted in yellow. He felt that he had rashly surrendered the former for the latter. "All the same," he said to himself, "I have no wish to provide the 'feature' of this exhibition for the evening papers."

He repeated to himself: "Little patch of yellow wall, with a sloping roof, little patch of yellow wall." While doing so he sank down upon a circular divan; and then at once he ceased to think that his life was in jeopardy and, reverting to his natural optimism, told himself: "It is just an ordinary indigestion from those potatoes; they weren't properly cooked; it is nothing." A fresh attack beat him down; he rolled from the divan to the floor, as visitors and attendants came hurrying to his assistance. He was dead. Permanently dead? Who shall say? Certainly our experiments in spiritualism prove no more than the dogmas of religion that the soul survives death. All that we can say is that everything is arranged in this life as though we entered it carrying the burden of obligations contracted in a former life; there is no reason inherent in the conditions of life on this earth that can make us consider ourselves obliged to do good, to be fastidious, to be polite even, nor make the talented artist consider himself obliged to begin over again a score of times a piece of work the admiration aroused by which

will matter little to his body devoured by worms, like the patch of yellow wall painted with so much knowledge and skill by an artist who must for ever remain unknown and is barely identified under the name Vermeer. All these obligations which have not their sanction in our present life seem to belong to a different world, founded upon kindness, scrupulosity, self-sacrifice, a world entirely different from this, which we leave in order to be born into this world, before perhaps returning to the other to live once again beneath the sway of those unknown laws which we have obeyed because we bore their precepts in our hearts, knowing not whose hand had traced them there—those laws to which every profound work of the intellect brings us nearer and which are invisible only—and still!—to fools. So that the idea that Bergotte was not wholly and permanently dead is by no means improbable.

They buried him, but all through the night of mourning, in the lighted windows, his books arranged three by three kept watch like angels with outspread wings and seemed, for him who was no more, the symbol of his resurrection.

ALEXANDER SERGEYEVICH PUSHKIN

ALEXANDER SERGEYEVICH PUSHKIN (Russian, 1799-1837). The first great figure in Russian literature, and fountainhead of much of its later glory. *Evgeny Onegin, Pique Dame* (both turned into operas by Tchaikovsky), *Boris Godunov* (similarly treated by Moussorgsky), *Ruslan and Ludmila,* and *Fairy Tales* are major works. Partly of African ancestry, exiled for a time because of his liberalism. Later joined the Czar's entourage, killed in duel. Great champion of Russian genius.

OUTLIVED DESIRE

Outlived desire now departs,
  My dreams I cannot love again;
I reap the fruit of empty hearts,
  The fruit of pain.

The tempest of a cruel fate
  My fair and flowery garlands rend;
Unhappy and alone I wait:
  When comes the end?

1015

So, stricken by the early cold,
    The whistling, bitter gales of grief,
Still the autumnal branches hold
    One shuddering leaf.

THE PRISONER

In a damp cell behind bars sit I;
Outside an eagle, young and born to fly,
The sad companion of my prisoned day
Flutters his wing and pecks his bleeding prey.

Then pecks no more, but through the window stares
As though we thought the same thing unawares,
As though with look and cry his heart would say:
'Brother, the time is come to fly away.

We are free birds together, free and proud;
Fly where the mountains whiten through the cloud
To that sea country blue beneath the sky
Where only walks the wind, the wind and I'.

THE COACH OF LIFE

The swaying coach, for all its load,
    Runs lightly as it rocks;
Grey Time goes driving down the road,
    Nor ever leaves the box.

We jump into the coach at dawn,
    Alert and fresh and free,
And holding broken bones in scorn,
    'Go on' shout we.

By midday all is changed about,
    Our morning hearts are cool;
We fear the steep descents, and shout:
    'Go slow, you fool!'

By dusk we're used to jolt and din,
    And when the light is gone
We sleep before we reach the inn,
    As Time drives on.

THE PROPHET

I dragged my steps across a desert bare,
    My spirit parched with heat;
And lo, a seraph with six wings was there;
    He stood where two roads meet.

Soft as the coming of a dream at night,
    His fingers touched my head;
He raised the lids of my prophetic sight,
    An eagle's, wide with dread.

He touched my ears. They filled with sound and song:
    I heard the heaven's motion,
The flight of angels, and the reptile throng
    That moves beneath the ocean.

I heard the soundless growth of plant and tree:
    Then, stooping to my face,
With his right hand he tore my tongue from me.
    Vain, sinful tongue and base.

A serpent's fiery fang he thrust instead
    Through my faint lips apart;
He slit my breast, and with a sword stained red
    Hewed out my quaking heart.

A coal of living fire his fingers placed
    Deep in my gaping side.
Dead as I lay upon the desert waste,
    I heard God's Voice that cried:

'Arise, O prophet, having seen and heard;
    Strong in my Spirit, span
The universal earth, and make my word
    Burn in the heart of man'.

1017

THE POET

When the poet by Apollo
For his service is not claimed,
In a life inane and hollow
He is sunken, he is maimed.
Then his soul, as cold as clay,
Sleeps unvisited by Song:
He frequents the wordly throng,
Insignificant as they.
But let once Apollo's word
Fall upon his listening ear,
His awakened soul is stirred
Like an eagle soaring clear.
Wild and sad, he turns away
From the pleasures of the town,
Scorning man and man's renown
And the idols of a day.
Full of voices, in the throes
Of confusion forth he goes,
Lonely, to the forest trees
And the shores of barren seas.

THE UPAS TREE

Across the desert dry as bone,
    Stark sentinel of burning sands,
In the wide universe alone
    The deadly Upas stands.

Born in a day of wrath it rose
    Out of the waste, whose nature sent
Deep through its roots and sombre boughs
    Poison for nourishment.

In noonday heat from out its bark
    The beads of oozing venom come,
And with the cooler breath of dark
    Set in a shining gum.

No bird among its boughs may fly,
   Beneath its shade no tiger stray:
The whirlwind when it ventures nigh
   Infected storms away.

The wandering showers of the plain,
   Caught on its branches interlaced,
In drops of dark unwholesome rain
   Sink in the thirsty waste.

Yet once a man, with cold command,
   Dared send a man to seek the tree.
All night across the dreadful sand
   He went obediently.

He brought the deathly gum at dawn
   With leaves by poison withered brown,
And from his forehead pale and drawn
   Coldly the sweat ran down.

Before his master as he went
   His steps grew weak and faltering,
And the poor slave died in the tent
   Of the remorseless King.

The venom taken from his hand
   The King's obedient arrows fed,
And they through every neighbouring land
   Death and disaster sped.

THE DON

Through open fields, across the plain
   I see him yonder, streaming on!
From all your distant sons, again
   I greet you, shining Don.

O quiet Don, each river knows
   That you their famous brother are;
Araxes greets you as he flows,
   And Oxus from afar.

By cruel foes no longer chased
  The horses of the Don draw nigh,
Already scent there home, and taste
  The streams of Arpachai.

Then watch, O holy Don, for there
  They come, brave Cossacks, born your own!
Once more the sparkling wine prepare
  From vineyards you have grown.

R

FRANCOIS RABELAIS

FRANÇOIS RABELAIS (French, *ca.* 1490-1553). A monk who later became a physician and scholar. *Gargantua and Pantagruel,* his sprawling comic allegory, was written over period of 20 years to entertain patients and patrons. Today the symbol of the burlesque and ribald, it nonetheless carried a message: that man is basically good and only needs new kind of education to call forth that goodness.

THE LOST HATCHET

THERE once lived a poor honest country fellow of Gravot, Tom Wellhung by name, a wood cleaver by trade, who in that low drudgery made shift so to pick up a sorry livelihood. It happened that he lost his hatchet. Now, tell me, who ever had more cause to be vexed than poor Tom? Alas, his whole estate and life depended on his hatchet; by his hatchet he earned many a fair penny of the best woodmongers or log merchants, among whom he went a jobbing; for want of his hatchet he was like to starve; and had Death but met him six days after without a hatchet, the grim fiend would have mowed him down in the twinkling of a bedstaff. In this sad case he began to be in a heavy taking, and called upon Jupiter with most eloquent prayers (for, you know, Necessity was the mother of Eloquence). With the whites of his eyes turned up towards heaven, down on his marrowbones, his arms reared high, his fingers stretched wide, and his head bare, the poor wretch without ceasing was roaring out by way of Litany at every repetition of his supplications, "My hatchet, Lord Jupiter, my hatchet, my hatchet, only my hatchet, O Jupiter, or money to buy another, and nothing else; alas, my poor hatchet!"

Jupiter happened then to be holding a grand council about certain urgent affairs, and old Gammer Cybele was just giving her opinion,

or, if you had rather have it so, it was young Phœbus the Beau; but, in short, Tom's outcry and lamentations were so loud that they were heard with no small amazement at the council board by the whole consistory of the gods. "What a devil have we below," quoth Jupiter, "that howls so horridly? By the mud of Styx, haven't we had all along, and haven't we here still, enough to do to set to rights a world of puzzling business of consequence? . . . Let us, however, dispatch this howling fellow below: you, Mercury, go see who it is, and know what he wants." Mercury looked out at heaven's trapdoor, through which, as I am told, they hear what's said here below; by the way, one might well enough mistake it for the scuttle of a ship; though Icaromenippus said it was like the mouth of a well. The light-heeled deity saw it was honest Tom, who asked for his lost hatchet; and accordingly he made his report to the Synod. "Marry," said Jupiter, "we are finely holped up, as if we had now nothing else to do here but to restore lost hatchets. Well, he must then have it for all this, for so 'tis written in the Book of Fate (do you hear?), as well as if it was worth the whole duchy of Milan. The truth is, the fellow's hatchet is as much to him as a kingdom to a king. Come, come, let no more words be scattered about it; let him have his hatchet again. Run down immediately, and cast at the poor fellow's feet three hatchets,—his own, another of gold, and a third of massy silver, all of one size: then, having left it to his will to take his choice, if he take his own, and be satisfied with it, give him t'other two. If he take another, chop his head off with his own; and henceforth serve me all those losers of hatchets after that manner." Having said this, Jupiter, with an awkward turn of his head, like a jackanapes swallowing of pills, made so dreadful a phiz that all the vast Olympus quaked again. Heaven's foot messenger, thanks to his low-crowned, narrow-brimmed hat, and plume of feathers, heelpieces, and running stick with pigeon wings, flings himself out at heaven's wicket, through the empty deserts of the air, and in a trice nimbly alights on the earth, and throws at friend Tom's feet the three hatchets, saying to him, "Thou hast bawled long enough to be a-dry; thy prayers and requests are granted by Jupiter: see which of these three is thy hatchet, and take it away with thee."

Wellhung lifts up the golden hatchet, peeps upon it, and finds it very heavy, then, staring at Mercury, cries, "Godzouks, this is none of mine; I won't ha' 't!" The same he did with the silver one, and said, " 'Tis not this, either: you may e'en take them again."

1022

At last he takes up his own hatchet, examines the end of the helve, and finds his mark there; then, ravished with joy, like a fox that meets some straggling poultry, and sneering from the top of his nose, he cried, "By the mass, this is my hatchet! Master god, if you will leave it me, I will sacrifice to you a very good and huge pot of milk, brimful, covered with fine strawberries, next Ides (*i.e.* the 15th) of March."

"Honest fellow," said Mercury, "I leave it thee; take it; and because thou hast wished and chosen moderately, in point of hatchet, by Jupiter's command I give thee these two others. Thou hast now wherewith to make thyself rich; be honest." Honest Tom gave Mercury a whole cart load of thanks, and revered the most great Jupiter. His old hatchet he fastens close to his leathern girdle, and girds it about his breech like Martin of Cambray; the two others, being more heavy, he lays on his shoulder. Thus he plods on, trudging over the fields, keeping a good countenance among his neighbors and fellow-parishioners with one merry saying or other after Patelin's way. The next day, having put on a clean white jacket, he takes on his back the two precious hatchets, and comes to Chinon, the famous city, noble city, ancient city, yea, the first city of the world, according to the judgment and assertion of the most learned Massoreths. In Chinon he turned his silver hatchet into fine testons, crown pieces, and other white cash; his golden hatchet into fine angels, curious ducats, substantial ridders, spankers, and rose nobles. Then with them he purchases a good number of farms, barns, houses, outhouses, thatch houses, stables, meadows, orchards, fields, vineyards, woods, arable lands, pastures, ponds, mills, gardens, nurseries, oxen, cows, sheep, goats, swine, hogs, asses, horses, hens, cocks, capons, chickens, geese, ganders, ducks, drakes and a world of other necessaries, and in a short time became the richest man in all the country. His brother bumpkins, and the yeomen and other country-puts thereabouts, perceiving his good fortune were not a little amazed, insomuch that their pity of poor Tom was soon changed into an envy of his so great and unexpected rise; and, as they could not for their souls devise how this came about, they made it their business to pry up and down, and lay their heads together, to inquire, seek, and inform themselves by what means, in what place, on what day, what hour, how, why, and wherefore, he had come by this great treasure.

At last, hearing it was by losing his hatchet, "Ha! ha!" said they, "was there no more to do but lose a hatchet, to make us rich?"

1023

With this they all fairly lost their hatchets out of hand. The devil a one that had a hatchet left; he was not his mother's son that did not lose his hatchet. No more was wood felled or cleared in that country, through want of hatchets. Nay, the Æsopian apologue even saith that certain petty country gents of the lower class, who had sold Wellhung their little mill and little field to have wherewithal to make a figure at the next muster, having been told that this treasure was come to him by that means only, sold the only badge of their gentility, their swords, to purchase hatchets to go to lose them, as the silly clodpates did, in hopes to gain store of chink by that loss.

You would have truly sworn they had been a parcel of your petty spiritual usurers, Rome-bound, selling their all, and borrowing of others to buy store of mandates, a pennyworth of a new-made pope.

Now they cried out and brayed, and prayed and bawled, and lamented and invoked Jupiter: "My hatchet! my hatchet! Jupiter, my hatchet!" on this side, "My hatchet!" on that side, "My hatchet! Ho, ho, ho, ho, Jupiter, my hatchet!" The air round about rang again with the cries and howlings of these rascally losers of hatchets.

Mercury was nimble in bringing them hatchets,—to each offering that which he had lost, as also another of gold and a third of silver.

Everywhere he still was for that of gold, giving thanks in abundance to the great giver, Jupiter; but, in the very nick of time that they bowed and stooped to take it from the ground, whip in a trice Mercury lopped off their heads, as Jupiter had commanded; and of heads thus cut off the number was just equal to that of the lost hatchets.

You see how it is now; you see how it goes with those who in the simplicity of their hearts wish and desire with moderation. Take warning by this, all you greedy, fresh-water shirks, who scorn to wish for anything under ten thousand pounds; and do not, for the future, run on impudently, as I have sometimes heard you wishing, "Would to God I had now one hundred and seventy-eight millions of gold! oh, how I should tickle it off!" The deuce on you, what more might a king, an emperor, or a pope wish for? For that reason, indeed, you see that after you have made such hopeful wishes all the good that comes to you of it is the itch or scab, and not a cross in your breeches to scare the devil that tempts you to make these wishes; no more than those two mumpers, one of whom only wished to have in good old gold as much as hath been spent, bought, and sold in Paris, since its first foundations were laid, to

this hour, all of it valued at the price, sale, and rate of the dearest
year in all that space of time. Do you think the fellow was bashful?
had he eaten sour plums unpeeled? were his teeth on edge, I pray
you? The other wished Our Lady's church brimful of steel needles,
from the floor to the top of the roof, and to have as many ducats
as might be crammed into as many bags as might be sewed with
each and every one of those needles, till they were all either broke
at the point or eye. This is to wish with a vengeance! What think
you of it? What did they get by it, in your opinion? Why, at night
both my gentlemen had kibed heels, a tetter in the chin, a churchyard cough in the lungs, a catarrh in the throat, a swingeing boil
at the rump, and the devil of one musty crust of a brown George
the poor dogs had to scour their grinders with. Wish, therefore, for
mediocrity, and it shall be given unto you, and over and above yet;
that is to say, provided you bestir yourselves manfully and do your
best in the mean time.

JEAN BAPTISTE RACINE

JEAN BAPTISTE RACINE (French, 1639-1699). Classical tragedian who
brought French drama to its highest peak. Adhered to the Greek unities and
concentrated on psychological conflict between characters. Used mainly Latin
and Greek themes in his 11 plays. Best: *Andromaque*, *Bérénice*, *Phèdre*,
Athalie. Emotional range of his poetry unsurpassed in French.

ORESTES AND HERMIONE

Hermione. What have I done? Where am I? Where is Pyrrhus?
Ye gods! what mean these horrors? I'm undone!
My soul is on the rack! I cannot bear it!
Why do I wander like some guilty ghost?
What brought me to this place? What keeps me here?
The court of Pyrrhus has no room for me!
Do I still doubt if I should love or hate him?
Hard-hearted man! how unconcerned he left me!
Did he once sigh? bestow one pitying look?
Once shed a tear? or speak one soft, kind word?
Did he so much as feign one moment's sorrow,
To calm my griefs, and mitigate his falsehood?
Why am I still thus anxious for his life?
Why do I start at his impending fate?

1025

Shall he, then, live? Shall the base traitor live
To laugh at my distress? No, let him perish!
Be quick, Orestes! Execute my orders!
Alas! my orders! O preposterous guilt!
Can I decree the death of him I love?
Was it for this my soul delighted in him?
Was it for this I left my father's court?
Have I, then, crossed so many realms and seas
To murder Pyrrhus?——

       (*Cleone enters.*)
O Cleone, help me!
What have I done? Is Pyrrhus yet alive?
What say'st thou? Answer me: where is the king?
 Cleone. Madam, I saw the cruel prince set forward,
Triumphant in his looks, and full of joy.
Still as he walked, his ravished eyes were fixed
On the fair captive; while through shouting crowds
She passed along with a dejected air,
And seemed to mourn her Hector to the last.
 Herm. Insulting tyrant! I shall burst with rage!
But say, Cleone, didst thou mark him well?
Was his brow smooth? Say did there not appear
Some shade of grief, some little cloud of sorrow?
Did he not stop? Did he not once look back?
Didst thou approach him? Was he not confounded?
Did he not——Oh, be quick, and tell me all!
 Cle. Madam, the tumult of his joy admits
No thought but love. Unguarded he marches on,
'Midst a promiscuous throng of friends and foes.
His cares all turn upon Astyanax,
Whom he has lodged within the citadel,
Defended by the strength of all his guards.
 Herm. Enough! he dies! the traitor! Where's Orestes?
 Cle. Madam, I fear——
 Herm. Is he still resolute? Is he still determined?
 Cle. Madam, I fear——
 Herm. How! Is Orestes false? Does he betray me, too?
 Cle. A thousand doubts
Perplex his soul, and wound him with remorse:
His virtue and his love prevail by turns.
He told me Pyrrhus should not fall ignobly,—

Pyrrhus, the warlike son of great Achilles.
He dreads the censure of the Grecian states,—
Of all mankind, and fears to stain his honor.

   Herm.   Poor timorous wretch! 'Tis false! He basely fears
To cope with dangers, and encounter death;
'Tis that he fears! Am I bright Helen's daughter?
To vindicate her wrongs all Greece conspired;
For her, confederate nations fought, and kings were slain,
Troy was o'erthrown, and a whole empire fell:
My eyes want force to raise a lover's arm
Against a tyrant that has dared to wrong me!

   Cle.   Madam, like Helen, trust your cause to Greece.

   Herm.   No! I'll avenge myself: I'll to the temple;
I'll overturn the altar, stab the priest;
I'll hurl destruction like a whirlwind round me!
They must not wed! they must not live! they shall not!
Let me begone! I have no time to lose!
Stand off! hold me not! I am all distraction!
O Pyrrhus, tyrant! traitor! thou shalt bleed!

               (*Orestes enters.*)

   Orestes.   Madam, 'tis done; your orders are obeyed:
The tyrant lies expiring at the altar.

   Herm.   Is Pyrrhus slain?

   Or.   Even now he gasps in death.
Our Greeks, all undistinguished in the crowd,
Flocked to the temple and dispersed themselves
On every side the altar. I was there:
Pyrrhus observed me with a haughty eye,
And, proud to triumph over Greece in me,
From his own brows he took the diadem,
And bound it on the temples of his captive:
"Receive," said he, "my crown! receive my faith!
Mine and my people's sovereign reign, forever!
From this blessed hour, a father to your son,
I'll scourge his foes: henceforth be he styled
The Trojan king: I swear it at the altar,
And call the gods to ratify my vows!"
His subjects with loud acclamations shook
The spacious dome. Our Greeks, enraged, cried out,
"Revenge! revenge!" broke through the thronging press,
And rushed tumultuous on the unguarded king:

Their eager fury left no work for me.
Pyrrhus awhile opposed their clashing swords,
And dealt his fatal blows on every side
With manly fierceness; till, oppressed by numbers,
Streaming with blood, all over gashed with wounds,
He reeled, he groaned, and at the altar fell.
Haste, Madam, let us fly! Haste to our ships!
They lie unmoored,—our friends attend us there.

Herm. What have they done?

Or. Madam, forgive their rage!
I own your vengeance had been more complete
Had Pyrrhus fallen by me, and had he known
Hermione chastised him by my arm.

Herm. Peace, monster, peace! Go, tell thy horrid **tale**
To savages, and howl it in the deserts!
Wouldst thou impute to me thy barbarous guilt?
Me wouldst thou make the accomplice of thy crimes?
Hence to thy Greeks, and boast thy foul exploits!
My soul abhors them! I disclaim the deed!
Begone! I know thee not, thou fell barbarian!
What had he done? What could provoke thy madness
To assassinate so great, so brave a man?
Who set thee on?

Or. Oh, grant me patience, Heaven!
With your own lips did you not curse the tyrant,
Pronounce his death, and urge me to destroy him?

Herm. What if, transported by my boundless passion,
I could not bear to see him wed another,—
Were you to obey a jealous woman's frenzy?
You should have div'd into my inmost thoughts:
My heart, though full of rage, was free from malice;
And all my anger was excess of love.
Why did you take me at my word? You saw
The struggles of my soul; you heard me rave:
You should have questioned me a thousand times,
Yet still have doubted, and still questioned on,
Before you ventured on a life so precious.

Or. Hear me but speak: Heaven knows, against my will——

Herm. Why did you not return? why not consult me
A second time? and, undetermined still,
Again return, and still find new delays?

What had your rash, officious Greeks—dire bloodhounds!
To do with my revenge? What drew you hither?
To bring on me the vengeful woes that haunt you?
Are these the fruits of your detested love?
Your fatal embassy, your hateful presence,
Drove Pyrrhus to my rival, and destroys
Both him and me. He might have loved me still,
Had you ne'er interposed. Avaunt! Begone!
And leave me in Epirus. I renounce
My friends, my country, Greece, and all mankind:
But, chiefly, I renounce thee, monster! thee!
                                                        (*Exit.*)
    Or. Am I awake? Where am I? Soft, my soul!
Be not too rash.——Was that Hermione?
Why should her anger thunder against me?
Was not this blood shed all by her command?
I am, indeed, a most outrageous monster!
A ruffian, murderer, a base assassin!
And all to please a false, ungrateful woman.
Henceforward let the laws of nations cease;
And let the pale that severs right and wrong,
Things sacred and profane, be broken down:
Gods in their temples, kings upon their thrones,
Are not in safety while Orestes lives.
Oh, never more shall my torn mind be healed,
Nor taste the gentle comforts of repose;
A dreadful band of gloomy cares surround me,
And lay strong siege to my distracted soul!

JEAN PAUL RICHTER

JEAN PAUL RICHTER (German, 1763-1825). Sentimental interpreter of
everyday life. After early poverty, was supported by numerous patronesses.
Settled in Weimar and Bayreuth. Extravagantly popular during his lifetime,
his novels are seldom read today. Most famous: *Titan*, *'Teens*, *The Life of
Quintus Fixlein.*

THE NEW-YEAR'S NIGHT OF AN UNHAPPY MAN

AN old man stood on the new-year's midnight at the window, and
gazed with a look of long despair, upwards to the immovable ever-

blooming heaven, and down upon the still, pure, white earth, on which no one was then so joyless and sleepless as he. For his grave stood near him; it was covered over only with the snow of age, not with the green of youth; and he brought nothing with him out of the whole rich life, nothing with him, but errors, sins and disease, a wasted body, a desolated soul, the breast full of poison, an old age full of remorse. The beautiful days of his youth turned round to-day, as spectres, and drew him back again to that bright morning on which his father first placed him at the cross-road of life, which, on the right hand, leads by the sun-path of Virtue into a wide peaceful land full of light and of harvests, and full of angels, and which, on the left hand, descends into the mole-ways of Vice, into a black cavern full of down-dropping poison, full of aiming serpents, and of gloomy, sultry vapours.

Ah! the serpents hung about his breast, and the drops of poison on his tongue.—And he knew, now, where he was!

Frantic, and with unspeakable grief, he called upwards to Heaven: "Oh! give me back my youth again!—O, Father! place me once more at the cross-path of life, that I may choose otherwise than I did."

But his father and his youth had long since passed away.

He saw fiery exhalations dancing on the marshes, and extinguishing themselves in the churchyard, and he said: "These are the days of my folly!"—He saw a star fly from heaven, and, in falling, glimmer and dissolve upon the earth. "That am I!" said his bleeding heart, and the serpent-teeth of remorse dug therein further in its wounds.

His flaming fancy showed him sleepwalkers slinking away on the house-tops; and a windmill raised up its arms threateningly to destroy him; and a mask that remained behind in the empty charnel-house, assumed by degrees his own features.

In the midst of this paroxysm, suddenly the music for the new-year flowed down from the steeple, like distant church-anthems. He became more gently moved.—He looked round on the horizon and upon the wide world, and thought on the friends of his youth, who, better and more happy than he, were now instructors of the earth, fathers of happy children, and blest men—and he exclaimed: "Oh! I also might have slumbered, like you, this new-year's night with dry eyes, had I chosen it—Ah! I might have been happy, beloved parents! had I fulfilled your new-year's wishes and instructions."

In feverish recollection of the period of his youth, it appeared

to him as if the mask with his features raised itself up in the charnel-house—at length, through the superstition, which, on the new-year's night, beholds spirits and futurity, it grew to a living youth in the position of the beautiful boy of the Capitol, pulling out a thorn; and his former blooming figure was bitterly placed as a phantasma before him.

He could behold it no longer—he covered his eyes.—A thousand, hot, draining tears streamed into the snow.—He, now, only softly sighed, inconsolably and unconsciously: "Only come again, youth! come again!"

And it came again, for he had only dreamed so fearfully on the new-year's night.—He was still a youth.—His errors alone had been no dream; but he thanked God, that, still young, he could turn round in the foul ways of Vice, and fall back on the sun-path which conducts into the ·pure land of harvests.

Turn with him, youthful reader, if thou standest on his path of error: This frightful dream will, in future, become thy judge; but shouldst thou one day call out, full of anguish: "Come again, beautiful youth!"—it would not come again.

RAINER MARIA RILKE

RAINER MARIA RILKE (German, 1875-1926). Highly disciplined and dedicated German poet. Extensive traveler and love correspondent. Painter and translator. Born Catholic, became mystic. Bulk of his work concerned with the ultimate themes of nature, love, death. Most widely known works: *The Journal of My Other Self, Sonnets to Orpheus, Duinese Elegies, Stories of God.*

O SELDOM

O seldom into the breathless
Restless rustle of life,
Reaches one of the crowning, deathless
Hours that consecrate strife;
Hour that accidentally seest,
That imprisons thy hand with fingers gentle:
      Come and be the only
      Guest at my lonely feast.

HOW GLORIOUS THE CHRYSANTHEMUMS

How glorious the chrysanthemums that day!
I almost shuddered at their splendour white . . .
And then you came to take my soul away
Deep in the night . . .

Such fear had I, and you came dear and wary,
Just when a dream had flashed you on my sight.
You came—and like a song from lips of fairy,
Rang out the night . . .

PRAYER OF THE MAIDENS TO MARY

I

O see how narrow are our days,
    How full of fear our bed;
We reach out awkward arms always
    To gather the roses red.

Thou must be mild to us, Mary,
    Out of Thy blood we blow;
And what a pain is yearning
    Thou alone canst know;

For Thou hast known this maiden's woe
    In Thine own soul's desire;
It feels as cold as Christmas snow,
    And yet is all on fire . . .

AFTER THE PRAYER

II

But I feel how my heart is glowing
    Warmer and warmer in my breast,
And every evening poorer growing,
    Nor any night can bring me rest.

I tear at the white silken tissue,
And my shy dreams cry out to Thee:
    Let me be sorrow of Thy sorrow,
    O let us both
By the same wonder wounded be.

THY GREAT TOWNS, LORD

Thy great towns, Lord, are lost to shame,
    Things merged in misery and maddened;
The greatest is like flight from flame,—
    Comfort is none for them to be gladdened,
Their life is shorter than their name.

Therein dwell men from kennelled door to door,
    Starved into meagre shape and timid gesture,
Like herded lambkins shepherded before:
    Thine earth breathes sweet outside in springtide vesture,
But they are not and know of it no more.

And children there grow up on blind staircases,
    And up and down the self-same shadows wind,
And know not of the outside sunny spaces,
    Where flowers bloom fair for happy hands to bind,
And must be children, children of a kind.

And budding girls are to the unknown turning,
    And wishing back the peace of childhood eves;
They find not that for which their hearts are burning,
    And close again their open-trembling leaves.
And have in black back-garrets all untended
    The days of disappointed motherhood,

The listless whimpering of long nights unended,
    And cold years with no courage in the blood.
And all in darkness stand the beds for dying
    To which they like a beggar woman fade,
Till by the slow consumption of their sighing
    They at the last are on the death-bed laid.

Behold how all is opened: we are so;
   For we are but such blessedness in space.
What in a beast was blood and dark, did grow
   To be a soul in us, and cries apace

For thee, as a soul ever. Thou indeed
   Takest it only up into thy face
As it were landscape: gently and with no greed.
   And so we think, for whom its pulses race

It is not thou. And yet, art thou not he
   To whom we lost ourselves till naught remained?
And shall we ever in any other be?

With us infinity fades like a mist.
   But thou, O mouth, so that it be explained,
Be! O thou teller unto us, exist.

ABISHAG

I

She lay, and serving-men her lithe arms took,
And bound them round the withering old man,
And on him through the long sweet hours she lay,
A little fearful of his many years.

And many times she turned amidst his beard
Her face, as often as the night-owl screeched,
And all that was the night around them reached
Its feelers manifold of longing fears.

As they had been the sisters of the child
The stars trembled, and fragrance searched the room,
The curtain stirring sounded with a sign
Which drew her gentle glances after it.

But she clung close upon the dim old man,
And, by the night of nights not overtaken,
Upon the cooling of the King she lay
Maidenly, and lightly as a soul.

1034

The King sate thinking out the empty day
Of deeds accomplished and untasted joys,
And of his favorite bitch that he had bred—
But with the evening Abishag was arched
Above him. His dishevelled life lay bare,
Abandoned as diffamèd coasts, beneath
The quiet constellation of her breasts.

But many times, as one in women skilled,
He through his eye-brows recognized the mouth
Unmoved, unkissed; and saw: the comet green
Of her desires reached not to where he lay.
He shivered. And he listened like a hound,
And sought himself in his remaining blood.

LOVE-SONG

By what device shall I my soul prevent
From touching thine? My soul how shall I lift
To other things above thee? Great
Indeed is my desire to have it pent
In something lost in some still spot, and let it mate
With darkness which thy gladness shall not rift,
And which shall not with thy own deeps vibrate.

But all that touches us,
Takes us together, thee and me, as does
A fiddle-bow one voice prolong
Out of two chords. Upon what instrument
Then are we stretched? What master's face is o'er us bent?
O sweet song.

THE ELOPEMENT

Often as a child she had escaped
Her women to behold beneath the skies,
Because inside they are so otherwise,
The wind weave when the evening first is draped;

And yet no night of tempest ever had
Into such fragments torn the giant park
As it was now torn into by her bad

Conscience, since down the silken ladder's fall
He took and bore her onward through the dark

Until the carriage was all.
And the black vehicle she smelt,
And round it chase in hiding,
And danger.
And he was faced with cold, she felt,
And the blackness and the coldness in her gliding,
She crept into the collar of her cloak,
And felt her hair, as if it were not riding,
And she, strange, heard how a stranger
Spoke:
Iambytheeabiding.

ESTHER

The serving-women combed her seven days through
The ashes of her torment and her sorrow
Out of her hair the sediment and deposit,
And bore it out and dried it in the sun,
Spice that they did not feed it with was none
Another day and this one; but then was it

The time when she, now being all anointed
Even as a corpse is, at no hour appointed
Should enter in the open palace grim
In order at the way's end to behold
The face of him concerning whom we are told
That any one must die who looks on him.

As though the ruby of her crown were dull
Before, she felt it flash ere he was seen
And filled herself already with his mien
Like to a vessel, till she grew so full

1036

That she flowed over with the monarch's might
Or ever on her face the third hall gleamed,
That ran green over her with the malachite
Of its four walls. But she had never dreamed
With all her gems so long a way to wend her,
And they grew heavier with the King's great splendour
And with her terror cold. She, wandering,
Went on till, when she saw him there recline,
Towering upon a throne of tourmaline,
Before her, looking verily like a thing:

The right handmaiden took her fainting, and
Upreared her in the reach of the monarch's hand.
He touched her with his sceptre's point, and she
Conceived it without senses, inwardly.

JEAN ARTHUR RIMBAUD

JEAN ARTHUR RIMBAUD (French, 1854-1891). Brilliant poetic genius,
who at 19 deliberately ceased writing. Ran away from home as adolescent.
After year of literary life in Paris, set off on walking tour with Verlaine. Was
shot by him, but recovered. After much travel, settled in Ethiopa as a slave-
trader. His aesthetic theories had marked influence on modern literature.
Major works: *Les Illuminations, Une Saison en Enfer.*

DRUNKEN BOAT

As I descended the impassable streams
I felt myself no longer held by the drag-poles:
Clamorous Redskins had taken my crew for targets,
First having nailed them naked to the flagpoles.

But I was unconcerned for any crew,
Porters of Flemish grain or English cotton.
And when my haulers had done with their hurly-burly
The streams let me pass on as though forgotten.

Amidst the furious chopping of the tides
Last winter, muffled as a midnight scurvy,
I ran! and peninsulas that slip their bonds
Have never been more gloriously topsy-turvy.

The tempest blessed my maritime alarms.
Lighter than a cork I danced upon the waves,
Ten nights, nor missed the silly eyes of lanterns,
On the eternal rolling of those graves.

Sweeter than the juice of held fruit to a child
The green water would my broken cockle whelm,
And streaks of bluish wines and of disgorgements
Washed me and bore off grappling-irons and helm.

And thenceforth I was deluged in the poem
Of the sea infused with meteors latescent
Devouring the green azure where, wan flotation,
A pensive drowned man is at times quiescent.

Or, of a sudden tinting the bluishness, swirls
And soft rhythms under the rutilant day,
Stronger than alcohol, larger than your lyres,
The bitter red vortices of love stew away!

I know the heavens lightning-rived, the waterspout,
Surfs, and the currents; I know the evening sky,
The dawn exalted as a poplar light with doves;
And I have sometimes seen what man thinks he may descry.

I have seen the low sun stained with mystic terrors,
Lighting long violet coagulations;
Like olden actors in an antique drama
The waves roll off their compass-agitations.

I have dreamed through green nights of dazzling snows,
Of a kiss that, welling in the eyes of the sea, over long stirs,
The circulation of unheard-of saps,
And the yellow and blue alarm of phosphorous songsters.

I have followed, months through, like the noise of hysterical stables,
The shore-battering blows of the billows' barrages,
Without thinking that over the short-winded ocean
Their luminous feet might force forward the snouts of the barges.

I have come, understand! on incredible Floridas
Where flowers blend with panther-eyes, and the skin
Of men with rainbows taut as a bridle,
Under ocean horizons, where sea-green hordes rush in.

I have seen swamps ferment, enormous fish-traps
Where in the rushes Leviathan rotting sleeps;
Downpourings of waters in the midst of calm,
And the distances whirled to the cataract deeps,

Glaciers, suns of silver, pearl floods, skies of embers,
Hideous jetsam in deep gulfs of gloom,
Where giant serpents eaten of grubbing maggots
Fall from the gnarled trees with black perfume.

I'd have liked to show children these ocean doradoes,
The great gold fish, the fish that sings;
Foam-wreaths of flowers have blessed my far-sea driftings
And at times ineffable winds have lent me wings.

At times, weary martyr of the zones and poles,
The ocean, whose sobbing softly cradles me,
Lifts me its flowers of dark with yellow air-holes;
And I have stayed there as a woman on her knee,

Peninsula tossing to my sides the quarrels
And the guano of chattering birds with pallid eyes;
And I floated on, while across my slender lines
Drowned men came drifting down to sleep sidewise.

Then I, lost boat beneath the leafy bays,
Hurled by tornadoes to the birdless ether,
I whose sea-drunk carcass no Monitor
Nor packet of the Guilds would have fished for beneath her,

1039

Free, fumid, risen with violet mists,
I who bored through the ruddy sky's diadem
Like a wall that was decked, to the poet's taste,
With sun-touched lichen and azure phlegm,

I who ran spotted with electric lunes,
Mad plank, with hippocampi at the gunwales,
When July was battering with bludgeon blows
The ultramarine skies with their flaming funnels,

I who trembled, sensing at fifty leagues
The rut of Behemoth, the loud Maelstrom's frets,
Eternal spinner of blue fixities—
I long for Europe's ancient parapets.

I have seen starry archipelagoes, and isles
Whose frenzied skies are clear above the rower;
Is it in those deep nights you in your exile sleep,
Mid millions of golden birds, O future Overthrower?

True, I have wept too long. Dawn breaks the heart.
All moons are hateful, every sun is gall.
Tart love has swollen me with dizzying torpors.
Oh, that my keel were darting! Oh, that I fled the squall!

If I want water of Europe, it is the black
Cold puddle where, as evening gathers nigh,
A squatting plaintive youngster will release
A boat as fragile as a butterfly.

I can no longer, bathed in your languor, waves,
Take the backwash of freighters as they bowse,
Nor breast the pride of colours and salutes,
Nor sail beneath the horrid eyes of scows!

EDWIN ARLINGTON ROBINSON

EDWIN ARLINGTON ROBINSON (American, 1869-1935). Reflective poetic traditionalist, who achieved individual style through precision and simplicity. Worked at odd jobs until President Theodore Roosevelt's recognition got him job in New York Custom House. *The Children of the Night* contains famous character portraits of Richard Cory, Miniver Cheevy, Luke Havergal, *et al.* *The Man Against the Sky* brought national fame. Also: *Merlin, Lancelot, Tristram.*

STAFFORD'S CABIN

Once there was a cabin here, and once there was a man;
And something happened here before my memory began.
Time has made the two of them the fuel of one flame
And all we have of them is now a legend and a name.

All I have to say is what an old man said to me,
And that would seem to be as much as there will ever be.
"Fifty years ago it was we found it where it sat."
And forty years ago it was old Archibald said that.

"An apple tree that's yet alive saw something, I suppose,
Of what it was that happened there, and what no mortal knows
Some one on the mountain heard far off a master shriek,
And then there was a light that showed the way for men to seek.

"We found it in the morning with an iron bar behind,
And there were chains around it; but no search could ever find,
Either in the ashes that were left, or anywhere,
A sign to tell of who or what had been with Stafford there.

"Stafford was a likely man with ideas of his own—
Though I could never like the kind that likes to live alone;
And when you met, you found his eyes were always on your shoes,
As if they did the talking when he asked you for the news.

"That's all, my son. Were I to talk for a half a hundred years
I'd never clear away from there the cloud that never clears.
We buried what was left of it,—the bar, too, and the chains;
And only for the apple tree there's nothing that remains."

1041

Forty years ago it was I heard the old man say,
"That's all, my son." And here again I find the place today,
Deserted and told only by the tree that knows the most,
And overgrown with goldenrod as if there were no ghost.

NEW ENGLAND

Here where the wind is always north-north-east
And children learn to walk on frozen toes,
Wonder begets an envy of all those
Who boil elsewhere with such a lyric yeast
Of love that you will hear them at a feast
Where demons would appeal for some repose,
Still clamoring where the chalice overflows
And crying wildest who have drunk the least.

Passion is here a soilure of the wits,
We're told, and Love a cross for them to bear;
Joy shivers in the corner where she knits
And Conscience always has the rocking-chair,
Cheerful as when she tortured into fits
The first cat that was ever killed by Care.

ROMAIN ROLLAND

ROMAIN ROLLAND (French, 1866-1944). Renowned novelist and playwright.
Leading pacifist at beginning of present century. In later years turned Stalinist
fellow traveler. Author of biographies of Beethoven, Michelangelo, Tolstoy and
others. Winner of Nobel Prize in 1915 for *Jean-Christophe*, heroic novel modeled
roughly on life of Beethoven.

THE TRAP

THE first questions that enter my childish mind:
    "Where did I come from? and where am I confined?——"
I was born into a comfortable middle-class family, surrounded
by loving relatives, in a pleasant part of the country whose joyous
flavor I later tasted and celebrated through the voice of my *Colas*.
    How does it happen that, from the moment of my birth, the first
feeling—the strongest, most persistent of my early childhood—

should be—dim, haunting, sometimes rebellious, sometimes resigned: "I am a prisoner!"

Francis the First, on entering the tottering nave of my old Saint Martin of Clamecy, said (so the legend runs): "There's a fine trap!"—I was in "the Trap."

At the beginning, a visual impression: the first horizon presented to my childish view—a rather large paved court, with a garden in the middle, surrounded on three sides by three walls of the house that to me seemed very high. On the fourth side, the street and the houses opposite, separated by a canal. Although this quadrangle was terraced above the water, it seemed to the child, confined to his room on the ground floor, like a ditch in the zoological gardens at the foot of four walls.

A significant impression: children's diseases and a delicate constitution. Although I come of healthy parents and robust ancestry— (The Rollands and the Courots, tall, bony, without physical defects, and endowed with boundless nervous energy that keeps them up and about until their last day, have all lived to a ripe old age; my maternal grandparents lived merrily on past their eightieth year; at the very moment of this writing my eighty-eight-year-old father is happily watering his garden)—I, made of the same lime and sand that, in spite of everything, have resisted fatigue and the trials of a busy existence, have borne, all my life, the painful consequences of a childhood accident: the carelessness of a young servant who, forgetting me in the winter-cold when I was less than a year old, brought me close to death and bequeathed to me for life a bronchial weakness and shortness of breath. Over and over again one can find in my works, spurting up, involuntarily, like an interrupted flight, the "respiratory" expressions: "stifling," "open windows," "fresh air," "the breath of the heroes . . ."—the bird that flutters its wings, or crouches, feverish, in the cage of the wounded breast.

Finally, moral impressions, powerful and penetrating: the thought of death that enveloped the first ten years of my life. Death had entered the family circle: it had struck down at my side a little sister, younger than I, of whom I shall speak later; and her shadow continued to inhabit the house. An excitable mother, whose grief was never allayed, feverishly nursed the memory of the departed child. And I, who had seen her disappear in a few days, and whom the constant sight of this mother, brooding over her solitary thought, also bound, despite the heedlessness of my age that sought an escape —I was all the more readily exposed to the idea that was going

1043

about, since, until I was ten or twelve years old, my own life was threatened. Frequent colds, bronchitis, sore throats, persistent nose-bleeds took away my zest for life; and in my little bed I would keep repeating:

"I don't want to die!"

while my mother, in tears, would answer, hugging me to her:

"No, my little boy. The good God will not want to take you away from me, too!"

This only half convinced me, for what did I know about God, except that, from my first steps, he had taken advantage of his power. And my most lucid thought in regard to him was, without my realizing it, that of the Gardener for his Lord: '

"The good man said: Those are the moves of a prince . . . .
In appealing to kings, you make great fools of yourselves.
You must never let them enter your lands. . . ."

In the threefold prison of the old house, my weak chest, and the ill-omened circle of death, the earliest consciousness of my child-hood grew up under the anxious surveillance of my mother's affec-tion. Fragile plant, sister to the wistaria and the petunias blooming in the court and along the walls, whose breath from short-lived lips mingled with the dank odor of the stagnant canal; like them, rooted to the ground, yet aspiring to the light, the little prisoner, only half-awakened, kept groping blindly and instinctively in the air for invisible roads of escape.

The closest at hand: the murky canal, flowing along the terrace-wall over which I hung. Muddy and green, without a ripple, it bore up the deep, heavy boats that the bargemen forced along by the sheer forward thrust of their thin bodies. I could hear the grinding of the cables along the railing at the edge. A turn-bridge creaked and began to move slowly. From the cabin of the boat whose sky-light was decorated with a pot of geraniums, mounted a thin blue spiral of smoke. Seated before the door in silence, a woman was knitting; from time to time she glanced indifferently in my direction. The boat passed. . . . And I, leaning over the wall, saw the wall and myself passing. We were leaving the boat behind us; it was ·we who were going away. Now we are far out in the open: without a jar, without a motion. So slowly we slipped along that it seemed as though we should glide, like the night-sky, into eternity, without a change. And then we found each other again, the wall and I,

still dreaming in the same place. The boat had gone. Would it ever reach its destination? Another was coming up after it. It looked just the same. . . .

Then I imagined another route, free and without locks: the air. A child often lifts his face toward the sky, toward the wandering clouds and the twittering swallows, toward the great white clouds, like whimsical monuments formed by the childish eye. (That is his first sculpture; the child uses the air as his clay.) It is needless to speak of the rest: the threatening clouds, the rumbling storms of Central France with their crashing thunder. It is in them that the enemy returns—the Master with his beetling eyebrows closes the shutters of the sky on the frail prisoner. Then come the hands of deliverance, the fingers of the sorceress that open my window on the plains of the air. . . . And now come the bells, the bells of Saint Martin! They sound in the first pages of my *Jean-Christophe*. Their music is engraved on my unawakened heart. They pealed forth from the open tower of the old cathedral above my house. But it was not the church that these ecclesiastical songsters called forth in me. Later I shall tell of my encounters with the God of the church. They were cold, ceremonious and distant. In spite of my honest efforts, I never succeeded in getting in touch with him. God alone knows whether I sought him. But the God who knows it is not the same God. The God who heard me—the God whom I created so that he would listen to me, and in whom I have confided all my life—was in the hovering song-birds; the bells, and in the air. Not the Lord of Saint Martin's hidden in his retreat above the sculptured arches. But the God Liberty—At that time, to be sure, I had no knowledge of the span of his wings, but I heard them flutter in the airy heights. Nor was I even sure that they were more real than the white clouds. They ever remained for me a nostalgic dream that let me glance at space for a moment before taking their flight and letting the trap-door fall again over the cave of my life. . . . Much, much later (I shall tell how), I climbed, I pushed upward, I forced the trap with my forehead and, freed at last, I found traces of the bells once more. But all through childhood I groped about in a sealed cave— the great, beautiful cave of Burgundy, like a crypt full of wine-casks set in rows, and covered with cobwebs. Everyone else was at ease there, except one, and I heard them laugh as one laughs in my country. I did not look down upon the laughter and the drinking— But oh! for a taste of the sun outside! Was there really a sun? (If only I had the answer!) Or even the night?—And since none of

those strong men tried to leave, I conscious of my weakness, crouched in my corner, beaten.

At sixteen or seventeen years of age, when I read *Hamlet,* with what resonance these fraternal words echoed under the vault of my cave:

"*. . . what have you, my good friends, deserved at the hands of Fortune, that she sends you to prison hither?*"

"*Prison, my lord?*"

"*Denmark's a prison.*"

"*Then is the world one.*"

"*A goodly one, in which there are many confines, wards and dungeons, . . .*"

It is true that, a few lines further on, a magic word fills me with infinite hope:

"*O God, I could be bounded in a nut-shell and count myself a king of infinite space, . . .*"

That is the story of my life.

PIERRE DE RONSARD

PIERRE DE RONSARD (French, 1524-1585). Most eminent of Renaissance poets. Plans for diplomatic career frustrated by deafness at 18. Became leader of group of poets called La Pléiade. Received rich honors from French kings during lifetime, was neglected after death. Has since taken place among great French lyricists. Best work: the sonnets in three sets of *Amours.*

THE ROSE

See, Mignonne! hath not the Rose,
That this morning did unclose
  Her purple mantle to the light,
Lost, before the day be dead,
The glory of her raiment red,
  Her color, bright as yours is bright?

Ah, Mignonne! in how few hours
The petals of her purple flowers
  All have faded, fallen, died!
Sad Nature! mother ruinous!
That seest thy fair child perish thus
  'Twixt matin song and eventide.

Hear me, Darling! speaking sooth:
Gather the fleet flower of your youth!
    Take ye your pleasure at the best!
Be merry ere your beauty flit!
For length of days will tarnish it.
    Like roses that were loveliest.

WELCOME TO SPRING

God shield ye, heralds of the spring,
Ye faithful swallows fleet of wing,
    Hoops, cuckoos, nightingales,
Turtles and every wilder bird,
That make your hundred chirpings heard
    Through the green woods and dales.

God shield ye, Easter daisies all,
Fair roses, buds and blossoms small;
    And ye, whom erst the gore
Of Ajax and Narciss did print,
Ye wild thyme, anise, balm, and mint
    I welcome ye once more.

God shield ye, bright embroidered train
Of butterflies, that, on the plain,
    Of each sweet herblet sip;
And ye new swarm of bees that go
Where the pink flowers and yellow grow
    To kiss them with your lip.

A hundred thousand times I call—
A hearty welcome on ye all:

    This season how I love!
This merry din on every shore,
For winds and storms, whose sullen roar
    Forbade my steps to rove.

OF HIS LADY'S OLD AGE

When you are very old, at evening
  You'll sit and spin beside the fire, and say,
    Humming my songs, "Ah well, ah well-a-day!
When I was young, of me did Ronsard sing."
None of your maidens that doth hear the thing,
  Albeit with her weary task foredone,
    But wakens at my name, and calls you one
Blest, to be held in long remembering.

I shall be low beneath the earth, and laid
On sleep, a phantom in the myrtle shade,
  While you beside the fire, a grandame gray,
My love, your pride, remember and regret;
Ah, love me, love! we may be happy yet,
  And gather roses, while 'tis called to-day.

EDMOND ROSTAND

EDMOND ROSTAND (French, 1868-1918). Colorful virtuoso of the drama, whose name is chiefly associated with florid heroic masterpiece, *Cyrano de Bergerac*. Other works: *L'Aiglon, Chantecler, La dernière nuit de Don Juan*.
His work the final flower of the romantic theater of Victor Hugo.

TO SARAH

In these drab days, alone there never cloys
Your pallid grace, descending a wide stair,
Wreathing a frontlet, holding a lily, sword in air:
Queen of Fair Gestures, Princess of Poise.
In these tame times your flames are mutinous!
You speak verse. You die of love. You are ever fresh.
You hold forth arms of dream, then arms of flesh,
And when Phèdre appears, we are all incestuous.

Avid of suffering, you deepen with the years;
We have seen flowing—for they flow!—your tears:

All the dew of our soul on your cheek lingers.
But you know, Sarah, that at times there stray—
And furtively you feel them as you play—
The lips of Shakespeare on your jeweled fingers.

CYRANO TO HIS CHIDING FRIENDS

Do what?
Seek a potent protector, slink under a patron,
And like the low ivy, both early and late run
Round a trunk-prop and, licking the bark,
Climb by a ruse instead of rising stark?
No, thanks! Like everyone, set dearly down
Lines to a financier? Change into a clown
In the base hope of seeing, on the lips of a minister,
A smile spread, at last, that may not be sinister?
No, thanks! Dine daily on a bitter pill?
Have a belly worn with walking? A skin still
Quicker to catch the dirt upon the knees?
Execute daily dorsal suppleties?
No, thanks! With one hand pet a goat until it preens,
And with the other confiscate its greens?
Donor of senna that rhubarb be neared,
Always burn incense in somebody's beard?
No, thanks! From one lap leap to the lap beyond,
To become a big man in a small pond,
To navigate with madrigal-propellers
And the sighs of old maids as my sail-swellers?
No, thanks! At the publishing house of kindly Blanks
Pay to have my verses done? No, thanks!
Be named high-priest by the council of buffoons
That meets before the bars of old saloons?
No, thanks! Work that my name shall go
High with one sonnet, and write no more? No,
Thanks! Discover talent only in loons,
Be terrorized by threats of vague lampoons,
And endlessly to say "Just let me be
Among the personals in the *Mercury!*"
No, thanks! Calculate? Have fears—and show 'em?
And rather make a visit than poem?

Draw up petitions, be presented . . . everything!!!
No, thanks! No, thanks! No, thanks! No, thanks! But—sing,
Dream, laugh, go by, be alone, be free,
With a vibrant voice, and a steady eye to see,
And when I please, to set my hat awry,
At a yea or a nay take arms—or versify!
To work, unheeding wealth or glory's tune,
Toward the journey I'm thinking of making to the moon!
Never to write a line save from the heart,
Modestly to say to myself from the very start:
"Be satisfied with flowers, fruits, even leaves,
If it is your own garden that achieves!"
Then if fame and fortune send a soft appeaser,
Not to be obliged to render aught unto Cæsar,
But clear in your own eyes make your merit shine:
In short, disdaining the parasitic vine,
Even if you haven't to the oak's crest grown,
Not to soar high, perhaps, but rise alone!

JALAL UD-DIN RUMI

JALAL UD-DIN RUMI (Persian, 1207-1273). Most eminent mystic poet and
Dervish of Persia. A devotee of Sufism, regarded by contemporaries as a
spiritual guide. Founded the order of Mowlavies ("Whirling Dervishes").
His greatest work: *Masnavi*, a poem in 6 books, containing stories, fables,
and moral precepts.

THE MERCHANT AND THE PARROT

There was once a merchant, who had a parrot,
A parrot fair to view, confined in a cage;
And when the merchant prepared for a journey,
He resolved to bend his way towards Hindustan.
Every servant and maiden in his generosity
He asked, what present he should bring them home,
And each one named what he severally wished,
And to each one the good master promised his desire.

Then he said to the parrot, "And what gift wishest thou,
That I should bring to thee from Hindustan?"
The parrot replied, "When thou seest the parrots there,
Oh, bid them know of my condition.
Tell them, 'A parrot, who longs for your company,
Through Heaven's decree is confined in my cage.
He sends you his salutation, and demands his right,
And seeks from you help and counsel.
He says, "Is it right that I in my longings
Should pine and die in this prison through separation?
Is it right that I should be here fast in this cage,
While you dance at will on the grass and the trees?
Is this the fidelity of friends,
I here in a prison, and you in a grove?
Oh remember, I pray you, that bower of ours,
And our morning-draughts in the olden time;
Oh remember all our ancient friendships,
And all the festive days of our intercourse!" ' "
The merchant received its message,
The salutation which he was to bear to its fellows;
And when he came to the borders of Hindustan,
He beheld a number of parrots in the desert.
He stayed his horse, and he lifted his voice,
And he repeated his message, and deposited his trust;
And one of those parrots suddenly fluttered,
And fell to the ground, and presently died.
Bitterly did the merchant repent his words;
"I have slain," he cried, "a living creature.
Perchance this parrot and my little bird were close of kin,
Their bodies perchance were two and their souls one.
Why did I this? why gave I the message?
I have consumed a helpless victim by my foolish words!
My tongue is as flint, and my lips as steel;
And the words that burst from them are sparks of fire.
Strike not together in thy folly the flint and steel,
Whether for the sake of kind words or vain boasting;
The world around is as a cotton-field by night;
In the midst of cotton, how shall the spark do no harm?"
  The merchant at length completed his traffic,
And he returned right glad to his home once more.
To every servant he brought a present,

1051

To every maiden he gave a token;
And the parrot said, "Where is my present?
Tell all that thou hast said and seen!"
He answered, "I repeated thy complaints
To that company of parrots, thy old companions,
And one of those birds, when it inhaled the breath of thy sorrow,
Broke its heart, and fluttered, and died."
And when the parrot heard what its fellow had done,
It too fluttered, and fell down, and died.
When the merchant beheld it thus fall,
Up he sprang, and dashed his cap to the ground.
"Oh, alas!" he cried, "my sweet and pleasant parrot,
Companion of my bosom and sharer of my secrets!
Oh alas! alas! and again alas!
That so bright a moon is hidden under a cloud!"
After this, he threw its body out of the cage;
And lo! the little bird flew to a lofty bough.
The merchant stood amazed at what it had done;
Utterly bewildered he pondered its mystery.
It answered, "Yon parrot taught me by its action:
'Escape,' it told me, 'from speech and articulate voice,
Since it was thy voice that brought thee into prison;'
And to prove its own words itself did die."
    It then gave the merchant some words of wise counsel,
And at last bade him a long farewell.
"Farewell, my master, thou hast done me a kindness,
Thou hast freed me from the bond of this tyranny.
Farewell, my master, I fly towards home;
Thou shalt one day be free like me!"

THE DESTINY OF MAN

Seeks thy spirit to be gifted
    With a deathless life?
Let it seek to be uplifted
    O'er earth's storm and strife.

Spurn its joys—its ties dissever;
    Hopes and fears divest;
Thus aspire to live forever—
    Be forever blest!

Faith and doubt leave far behind thee;
   Cease to love or hate;
Let not Time's illusions blind thee;
   Thou shalt Time outdate.

Merge thine individual being
   In the Eternal's love;
All this sensuous nature fleeing
   For pure bliss above.

Earth receives the seed and guards it;
   Trustfully it dies;
Then, what teeming life rewards it
   For self-sacrifice!

With green leaf and clustering blossom
   Clad, and golden fruit,
See it from earth's cheerless bosom
   Ever sunward shoot!

Thus, when self-abased, Man's spirit
   From each earthly tie
Rises disenthralled t' inherit
   Immortality!

S

SA'DI

SA'DI (Persian, 1184-1291). One of the most versatile figures in Persian literature: poet, philosopher, teacher, Sufi. Great traveler and a soldier against the Christians during the Crusades. His *Gulistan* (*Rose Garden*), in prose and verse, is most widely read Persian classic.

THE GULISTAN

Purgatory May Be Paradise

A KING was embarked along with a Persian slave on board a ship. The boy had never been at sea, nor experienced the inconvenience of a ship. He set up a weeping and wailing, and all his limbs were in a state of trepidation; and, however much they soothed him, he was not to be pacified. The king's pleasure-party was disconcerted by him; but they had no help. On board that ship there was a physician. He said to the king: "If you will order it, I can manage to silence him." The king replied: "It will be an act of great favor." The physician so directed that they threw the boy into the sea, and after he had plunged repeatedly, they seized him by the hair of the head and drew him close to the ship, when he clung with both hands by the rudder, and, scrambling upon the deck, slunk into a corner and sat down quiet. The king, pleased with what he saw, said: "What art is there in this?" The physician replied: "Originally he had not experienced the danger of being drowned, and undervalued the safety of being in a ship; in like manner as a person is aware of the preciousness of health when he is overtaken with the the calamity of sickness. *A barley loaf of bread has, O epicure, no relish for thee. That is my mistress who appears so ugly to thy eye. —To the houris, or nymphs of paradise, purgatory would be a hell: ask the inmates of hell whether purgatory is not paradise.—There is a distinction between the man that folds his mistress in his arms and him whose two eyes are fixed on the door expecting her.*"

1054

The Wrestler

A person had become a master in the art of wrestling; he knew three hundred and sixty sleights in this art, and could exhibit a fresh trick for every day throughout the year. Perhaps owing to a liking that a corner of his heart took for the handsome person of one of his scholars, he taught him three hundred and fifty-nine of those feats, but he was putting off the last one, and under some pretence deferring it.

In short, the youth became such a proficient in the art and talent of wrestling that none of his contemporaries had ability to cope with him, till he at length had one day boasted before the reigning sovereign, saying: "To any superiority my master possesses over me, he is beholden to my reverence of his seniority, and in virtue of his tutorage; otherwise I am not inferior in power, and am his equal in skill." This want of respect displeased the king. He ordered a wrestling match to be held, and a spacious field to be fenced in for the occasion. The ministers of state, nobles of the court, and gallant men of the realm were assembled, and the ceremonials of the combat marshalled. Like a huge and lusty elephant, the youth rushed into the ring with such a crash that had a brazen mountain opposed him he would have moved it from its base. The master being aware that the youth was his superior in strength, engaged him in that strange feat of which he had kept him ignorant. The youth was unacquainted with its guard. Advancing, nevertheless, the master seized him with both hands, and, lifting him bodily from the ground, raised him above his head and flung him on the earth. The crowd set up a shout. The king ordered them to give the master an honorary dress and handsome largess, and the youth he addressed with reproach and asperity, saying: "You played the traitor with your own patron, and failed in your presumption of opposing him." He replied: "O sire! my master did not overcome my by strength and ability, but one cunning trick in the art of wrestling was left which he was reserved in teaching me, and by that little feat had today the upper hand of me." The master said: "I reserved myself for such a day as this. As the wise have told us, put not so much into a friend's power that, if hostilely disposed, he can do you an injury. Have you not heard what that man said who was treacherously dealt with by his own pupil: *'Either in fact there was no good faith in this world, or nobody has perhaps practised it in our days. No person learned the art of archery from me who did not in the end make me his butt.'* "

1055

Having taken offence with the society of my friends at Damascus, I retired into the wilderness of the Holy Land, or Jerusalem, and sought the company of brutes till such time as I was made a prisoner by the Franks, and employed by them, along with some Jews, in digging earth in the ditches of Tripoli. At length one of the chiefs of Aleppo, between whom and me an intimacy had of old subsisted, happening to pass that way, recognized me, and said: "How is this? and how came you to be thus occupied?" I replied: "What can I say? *I was flying from mankind into the forests and mountains, for my resource was in God and in none else. Fancy to thyself what my condition must now be, when forced to associate with a tribe scarcely human?—To be linked in a chain with a company of acquaintance were pleasanter than to walk in a garden with strangers.*"

He took pity on my situation; and, having for ten dinars redeemed me from captivity with the Franks, carried me along with him to Aleppo. Here he had a daughter, and her he gave me in marriage, with a dower of a hundred dinars. Soon after this damsel turned out a termagant and vixen, and discovered such a perverse spirit and virulent tongue as quite unhinged all my domestic comfort. *A scolding wife in the dwelling of a peaceable man is his hell even in this world. Protect and guard us against a wicked inmate. Save us, O Lord, and preserve us from the fiery, or hell, torture.*

Having on one occasion given a liberty to the tongue of reproach, she was saying: "Are you not the fellow whom my father redeemed from the captivity of the Franks for ten dinars?" I replied: "Yes, I am that same he delivered from captivity for ten dinars, and enslaved me with you for a hundred!" *I have heard that a reverend and mighty man released a sheep from the paws and jaws of a wolf. That same night he was sticking a knife into its throat, when the spirit of the sheep reproached him, saying: "Thou didst deliver me from the clutches of a wolf, when I at length saw that thou didst prove a wolf to me thyself."*

WEALTH

He that owns wealth, in mountain, wold, or waste,
Plays master—pitches tent at his own taste;
Whilst he who lacks that which the world commends
Must pace a stranger, e'en in his own lands.

1056

PRIEST SAIGYO

PRIEST SAIGYO (Japanese, 1118-1190). *Tanka* nature poet. At 23 gave up the life of a courtier to become an itinerant priest, his wife becoming a nun. His poetry admired for its lucidity and simplicity. Principal collection: *Sankashū.*

FORSAKEN

Why should I bitter be,
   Although he cold has grown?
There was a time when he to me
   And I to him were quite unknown.

THE AUTUMN MOON

I envy much the autumn moon,
   Which, journeying without delay,
Can follow, in the western sky,
   My friend who travels far away.

THE OLD CHERRY-TREE

Particularly will I gaze
   Upon the agéd cherry tree;
It and its flowers are pitiful.
   How many more springs can it see?

FLOWERS AND THE MOON

Suppose no clouds ever covered the moon
   And cherry flowers did not fall,
Why, then, I think in such a world,
   No sorrow should I know at all!

THE MOON

All things are ever changing
   In this transitory world,
But yet the moon is shining
   With the same light as of old.

SPRING AND AUTUMN

In spring when we see flowers,
  Would that there were no night!
In autumn when we see the moon,
  That there were no light!

GEORGE SAND

GEORGE SAND (Amandine Aurore Lucie Dupin, Baroness Dudevant, French, 1804-1876). Scandalous libertine and liberal. A remarkable woman who flouted the conventions of her time to leave husband, become novelist, and have series of notorious amours (including De Musset and Chopin). Her rather facile works favored the sociological theme. An ardent feminist—her best stories depict rebellious women: *Consuelo, Lélia, Elle et Lui.*

THE PLOUGHMAN AND HIS CHILD

I WAS walking on the border of a field which some peasants were carefully preparing for the approaching seed-time. The area was vast; the landscape was vast also, and enclosed with great lines of verdure, somewhat reddened by the approach of autumn, that broad field of vigorous brown, where recent rains had left, in some furrows, lines of water which the sun made glitter like fine threads of silver. The day had been clear and warm, and the earth, freshly opened by the cutting of the ploughshares, exhaled a light vapor. In the upper part of the field, an old man gravely held his plough of antique form, drawn by two oxen, with pale yellow skins—real patriarchs of the meadow—large in stature, rather thin, with long turned-down horns, old laborers whom long habit had made "brothers," as they are called by our country people, and who, when separated from each other, refuse to work with a new companion, and let themselves die of sorrow. The old husbandman worked slowly, in silence, without useless efforts; his docile team did not hurry any more than he; but, owing to the continuity of a labor without distraction, and the appliance of tried and well-sustained strength, his furrow was as soon turned as that of his son, who was ploughing at a short distance from him, with four oxen not so stout, in a vein of stronger and more stony soil.

But that which afterwards attracted my attention was really a beautiful spectacle—a noble subject for a painter. At the other ex-

1058

tremity of the arable field, a good-looking young man was driving a magnificent team: four pairs of young animals of a dark color, a mixture of black and bay with streaks of fire, with those short and frizzly heads which still savor of the wild bull, those large savage eyes, those sudden motions, that nervous and jerking labor which still is irritated by the yoke and the goad, and only obeys with a start of anger the recently imposed authority. They were what are called newly-yoked steers. The man who governed them had to clear a corner formerly devoted to pasturage, and filled with century-old stumps, the task of an athlete, for which his energy, his youth, and eight almost unbroken animals were barely sufficient.

A child six or seven years old, beautiful as an angel, with his shoulders covered, over his blouse, by a lamb-skin, which made him resemble the little Saint John the Baptist of the painters of the Restoration, walked in a furrow parallel to the plough, and touched the flank of the oxen with a long and light stick pointed with a slightly sharpened goad. The proud animals quivered under the small hand of the child, and made their yokes and the thongs bound over their foreheads creak, while they gave violent shocks to the plough handles. When a root stopped the ploughshare, the husbandman shouted with a powerful voice, calling each beast by his name, but rather to calm than excite; for the oxen, irritated by this sudden resistance, leaped, dug up the ground with their broad forked feet, and would have cast themselves out of the track, carrying the plough across the field, if, with his voice and goad, the young man had not restrained the four nearest him, while the child governed the other four. He also, shouted, the poor little fellow, with a voice he wished to make terrible, but which remained as gentle as his angelic face. It was all beautiful in strength or in grace, the landscape, the man, the child, the bulls under the yoke; and in spite of this powerful struggle in which the earth was overcome, there was a feeling of gentleness and deep calm which rested upon all things. When the obstacle was surmounted, and the team had resumed its equal and solemn step, the husbandman, whose feigned violence was only an exercise of vigor, and an expenditure of activity, immediately recovered the serenity of simple souls, and cast a look of paternal satisfaction on his child, who turned to smile on him.

Then the manly voice of this young father of a family struck up the melancholy and solemn strain which the ancient tradition of the country transmits, not to all ploughmen indiscriminately, but to those most consummate in the art of exciting and sustaining the ardor of

1059

the oxen at work. This chant, the origin of which was perhaps considered sacred, and to which mysterious influences must formerly have been attributed, is still reputed, at this day, to possess the virtue of keeping up the courage of the animals, of appeasing their dissatisfaction, and of charming the ennui of their long task. It is not enough to know how to drive them well while tracing a perfectly straight furrow, to lighten their labor by raising or depressing the point of the ploughshare opportunely in the soil: no one is a perfect ploughman if he does not know how to sing to the oxen, and this is a science apart, which requires taste and peculiar adaptation. This chant is, to say the truth, only a kind of recitative, interrupted and resumed at will. Its irregular form and its false intonations, speaking according to the rules of musical art, render it untranslatable. But it is none the less a beautiful chant, and so appropriate to the nature of the labor which it accompanies, to the gait of the oxen, to the calmness of those rural scenes, to the simplicity of the men who sing it, that no genius, a stranger to the labors of the soil, could have invented it, and no singer other than a "finished ploughman" of that country could repeat it. At those epochs of the year when there is no other labor and no other movement in the country than that of ploughing, this chant, so simple and so powerful, rises like the voice of a breeze, to which its peculiar toning gives it a kind of resemblance. The final note of each phrase, continued and trilled with an incredible length and power of breath, ascends a quarter of a note with systematic dissonance. This is wild, but the charm of it is invincible, and when you become accustomed to hear it, you cannot conceive how any song could be sung at those hours and in those places without disturbing their harmony.

It was then that, on seeing this beautiful pair, the man and the child, accomplish under such poetical conditions, and with so much gracefulness united with strength, a labor full of grandeur and solemnity, I felt a deep pity mingled with an involuntary respect. "Happy the husbandman!" Yes, doubtless, I should be happy in his place, if my arm, suddenly become strong, and my chest, become powerful, could thus fertilize and sing nature, without my eyes ceasing to see and my brain to comprehend the harmony of colors and of sounds, the fineness of tones, and the gracefulness of outlines—in one word, the mysterious beauty of things! and especially without my heart ceasing to be in relation with the divine feeling which presided over the immortal and sublime creation!

CARL SANDBURG

CARL SANDBURG (American, 1878-   ). The folk singer of America. Of
Swedish immigrant parentage, became a great rover over the U.S. His poems
of the prairies and early days of industrialism are already classics (*Chicago
Poems, Smoke and Steel*). His militant sympathy for working classes dominates
The People, Yes. Most impressive accomplishment: a monumental biography
of Lincoln.

THE PEOPLE, YES

The people will live on.
The learning and blundering people will live on.
They will be tricked and sold and again sold
And go back to the nourishing earth for rootholds,
The people so peculiar in renewal and comeback,
You can't laugh off their capacity to take it.
The mammoth rests between his cyclonic dramas.

The people so often sleepy, weary, enigmatic.
is a vast huddle with many units saying:
"I earn my living.
I make enough to get by
and it takes all my time.
If I had more time
I could do more for myself
and maybe for others.
I could read and study
and talk things over
and find out about things.
It takes time.
I wish I had the time."

The people is a tragic and comic two-face:
hero and hoodlum: phantom and gorilla twisting to moan with a gargoyle mouth: "They
buy and sell me . . . it's game . . .
sometime I'll break loose . . ."

Once having marched
Over the margins of animal necessity,
Over the grim line of sheer subsistence
   Then man came
To the deeper rituals of his bones,
To the lights lighter than any bones,
To the time for thinking things over,
To the dance, the song, the story,
Or the hours given over to dreaming,
   Once having so marched.
Between the finite limitations of the five senses
and the endless yearnings of man for the beyond
the people hold to the humdrum bidding of work and food
while reaching out when it comes their way
for lights beyond the prison of the five senses,
for keepsakes lasting beyond any hunger or death.
   This reaching is alive.
The panderers and liars have violated and smutted it.
   Yet this reaching is alive yet
   for lights and keepsakes.

   The people know the salt of the sea
   and the strength of the winds
   lashing the corners of the earth.
   The people take the earth
   as a tomb of rest and a cradle of hope.
   Who else speaks for the Family of Man?
   They are in tune and step
   with constellations of universal law.

   The people is a polychrome,
   a spectrum and a prism
   held in a moving monolith,
   a console organ of changing themes,
   a clavilux of color poems
   wherein the sea offers fog
   and the fog moves off in rain
   and the labrador sunset shortens
   to a nocturne of clear stars
   serene over the shot spray
   of northern lights.

1062

The steel mill sky is alive.
The fire breaks white and zigzag
shot on a gun-metal gloaming.
Man is a long time coming.
    Man will yet win.
Brother may yet line up with brother:

This old anvil laughs at many broken hammers.
    There are men who can't be bought.
    The fireborn are at home in fire.
    The stars make no noise.
    You can't hinder the wind from blowing.
    Time is a great teacher.
    Who can live without hope?

In the darkness with a great bundle of grief
    the people march.
In the night, and overhead a shovel of stars for
    keeps, the people march:
            "Where to? what next?"

GEORGE SANTAYANA

GEORGE SANTAYANA (Spanish-American, 1863-1952). America's philosopher-poet. Though born in Spain, he was educated in Boston and taught at
Harvard for 20-odd years. Primarily a philosopher and aesthetician, he began
by writing verse. Later composed a popular novel: *The Last Puritan*. Most
important philosophic works: *The Life of Reason* and *The Realms of Being*.
           Autobiography: *Persons and Places*.

SOLIPSISM

I could believe that I am here alone,
    And all the world my dream;
The passion of the scene is all my own,
    And things that seem but seem.

Perchance an exhalation of my sorrow
    Hath raised this vaporous show,
For whence but from my soul should all things borrow
    So deep a tinge of woe?

I keep the secret doubt within my breast
    To be the gods' defence,
To ease the heart by too much ruth oppressed
    And drive the horror hence.

O sorrow that the patient brute should cower
    And die, not having sinned!
O pity that the wild and fragile flower
    Should shiver in the wind!

Then were I dreaming dreams I know not of,
    For that is part of me
That feels the piercing pang of grief and love
    And doubts eternally.

But whether all to me the vision come
    Or break in many beams,
The pageant ever shifts, and being's sum
    Is but the sum of dreams.

MY HEART REBELS AGAINST MY GENERATION

My heart rebels against my generation,
That talks of freedom and is slave to riches,
And, toiling 'neath each day's ignoble burden,
    Boasts of the morrow.

No space for noonday rest or midnight watches,
No purest joy of breathing under heaven!
Wretched themselves, they heap, to make them happy,
    Many possessions.

But thou, O silent Mother, wise, immortal,
To whom our toil is laughter,—take, divine one,
This vanity away, and to thy lover
    Give what is needful:—

A staunch heart, nobly calm, averse to evil,
The windy sky for breath, the sea, the mountain,
A well-born, gentle friend, his spirit's brother,
    Ever beside him.

What would you gain, ye seekers, with your striving,
Or what vast Babel raise you on your shoulders?
You multiply distress, and your children
    Surely will curse you.

O leave them rather friendlier gods, and fairer
Orchards and temples, and a freer bosom!
What better comfort have we, or what other
    Profit in living,

Than to feed, sobered by the truth of Nature,
Awhile upon her bounty and her beauty,
And hand her torch of gladness to the ages
    Following after?

She hath not made us, like her other children,
Merely for peopling of her spacious kingdoms,
Beasts of the wild, or insects of the summer,
    Breeding and dying,

But also that we might, half knowing, worship
The deathless beauty of her guiding vision,
And learn to love, in all things mortal, only
    What is eternal.

I WOULD I MIGHT FORGET THAT I AM I

I would I might forget that I am I,
And break the heavy chain that binds me fast,
Whose links about myself my deeds have cast.
What in the body's tomb doth buried lie
Is boundless; 'tis the spirit of the sky,
Lord of the future, guardian of the past,
And soon must forth, to know his own at last.
In his large life to live, I fain would die.
Happy the dumb beast, hungering for food,
But calling not his suffering his own;
Blessed the angel, gazing on all good,
But knowing not he sits upon a throne;
Wretched the mortal, pondering his mood,
And doomed to know his aching heart alone.

1065

As in the midst of battle there is room
For thoughts of love, and in foul sin for mirth;
As gossips whisper of a trinket's worth
Spied by the death-bed's flickering candle-gloom;
As in the crevices of Cæsar's tomb
The sweet herbs flourish on a little earth:
So in this great disaster of our birth
We can be happy, and forget our doom.
For morning, with a ray of tendered joy
Gilding the iron heaven, hides the truth,
And evening gently woos us to employ
Our grief in idle catches. Such is youth;
Till from that summer's trance we wake, to find
Despair before us, vanity behind.

SAPPHO

SAPPHO (Greek, *ca.* 650 B.C.). Historiographically maligned gentle poetess of ancient Greece. Born on the island of Lesbos of noble family. Headed band of feminine worshipers of Aphrodite. Her simple emotional style has been imitated for centuries.

HYMN TO APHRODITE
(Translation by Henry T. Wharton)

Immortal Aphrodite of the broidered throne (*Poikilóthron, some-*
times printed *Poikilóphron,* various-minded), daughter of Zeus,
weaver of wiles, I pray thee break not my spirit with anguish and
distress, O Queen. But come hither, if ever before thou didst hear
my voice afar and listen, and, leaving thy father's golden house,
camest with chariot yoked, and fair, fleet sparrows drew thee, flapping fast their wings around the dark earth, from heaven through
mid sky. Quickly arrived they; and thou, blessed one, smiling with
immortal countenance, didst ask, What now is befallen me, and
why now I call, and what I in my weak heart most desire to see?
"What beauty now wouldst thou draw to love thee? Who wrongs

thee, Sappho? For even if she flies, she shall soon follow; and if she rejects gifts, shall yet live; if she loves not, shall soon love, however loth." Come, I pray thee, now too, and release me from cruel cares; and all that my heart desires to accomplish, accomplish thou, and be thyself my ally.

(*Translation of J. H. Merivale*)

Immortal Venus, throned above
In radiant beauty, child of Jove,
O skilled in every art of love
    And artful snare;
Dread power, to whom I bend the knee,
Release my soul and set it free
From bonds of piercing agony
    And gloomy care.
Yet come thyself, if e'er, benign,
Thy listening ears thou didst incline
To my rude lay, the starry shine
    Of Jove's court leaving.
In chariot yoked with coursers fair,
Thine own immortal birds, that bear
Thee swift to earth, the middle air
    With bright wings cleaving.
Soon they were sped—and thou, most blest,
In thine own smiles ambrosial dressed,
Didst ask what griefs my mind oppressed—
    What meant my song—
What end my frenzied thoughts pursue—
For what loved youth I spread anew
My amorous nets—"Who, Sappho, who
    Hath done thee wrong?
What though he fly, he'll soon return;
Still press thy gifts, though now he spurn;
Heed not his coldness—soon he'll burn,
    E'en though thou chide."
And saidst thou this, dread goddess? Oh,
Come then once more to ease my woe;
Grant all, and thy great self bestow,
    My shield and guide!

Glittering-throned, undying Aphrodite,
Wile-weaving daughter of high Zeus, I pray thee,
Tame not my soul with heavy woe, dread mistress,
      Nay, nor with anguish!
But hither come, if ever erst of old time
Thou didst incline, and listenedst to my crying,
And from thy father's palace down descending,
      Camest with golden
Chariot yoked: the fair swift-flying sparrows
Over dark earth with multitudinous fluttering,
Pinion on pinion, through middle ether
      Down from heaven hurried.
Quickly they came like light, and thou, blest lady,
Smiling with clear undying eyes didst ask me
What was the woe that troubled me, and wherefore
      I had cried to thee:
What thing I longed for to appease my frantic
Soul; and whom now must I persuade, thou askedst,
Whom must entangle to thy love, and who now,
      Sappho, hath wronged thee?
Yea, for if now he shun, he soon shall chase thee;
Yea, if he take not gifts he soon shall give them;
Yea, if he love not, soon shall he begin to
      Love thee, unwilling.
Come to me now too, and from tyrannous sorrow
Free me, and all things that my soul desires to
Have done, do for me, queen, and let thyself too
      Be my great ally!

(*Translation of Francis T. Palgrave*)

Golden-throned beyond the sky,
Jove-born immortality:
Hear and heal a suppliant's pain;
Let not love be love in vain!

Come, as once to Love's imploring
Accents of a maid's adoring,

Wafted 'neath the golden dome,
Bore thee from thy father's home;

When far off thy coming glowed,
Whirling down th' ethereal road,
On thy dove-drawn progress glancing,
'Mid the light of wings advancing;

And at once the radiant hue
Of immortal smiles I knew;
Heard the voice of reassurance
Ask the tale of love's endurance:

Why such prayer? And who for thee,
Sappho, should be touched by me;
Passion-charmed in frenzy strong,
Who hath wrought my Sappho wrong?

"Soon for flight pursuit wilt find
Proffered gifts for gifts declined;
Soon, through long resistance earned,
Love refused be love returned."

To thy suppliant so returning,
Consummate a maiden's yearning;
Love, from deep despair set free,
Championing to Victory!

JEAN-PAUL SARTRE

JEAN-PAUL SARTRE (French, 1905-   ). The philosopher of postwar
opportunism. Leader of French School of Existentialism, and author of its
bible: *L'Être et le Néant*. Active during war in the Resistance, afterward
editor of his own journal. Successful plays: *Les Mouches, Huis-Clos, Les
Mains Sales*. Widely known novel: 4-volume *Les Chemins de la Liberté*.

THE WALL

THEY pushed us into a big white room and I began to blink because
the light hurt my eyes. Then I saw a table and four men behind the

table, civilians, looking over the papers. They had bunched another group of prisoners in the back and we had to cross the whole room to join them. There were several I knew and some others who must have been foreigners. The two in front of me were blond with round skulls; they looked alike. I supposed they were French. The smaller one kept hitching up his pants; nerves.

It lasted about three hours; I was dizzy and my head was empty; but the room was well heated and I found that pleasant enough: for the past 24 hours we hadn't stopped shivering. The guards brought the prisoners up to the table, one after the other. The four men asked each one his name and occupation. Most of the time they didn't go any further—or they would simply ask a question here and there: "Did you have anything to do with the sabotage of munitions?" Or "Where were you the morning of the 9th and what were you doing?" They didn't listen to the answers or at least didn't seem to. They were quiet for a moment and then looking straight in front of them began to write.

It was my turn.

"Your name is Pablo Ibbieta?"

"Yes."

The man looked at the papers and asked me, "Where's Ramon Gris?"

"I don't know."

"You hid him in your house from the 6th to the 19th."

"No."

They wrote for a minute and then the guards took me out. In the corridor Tom and Juan were waiting between two guards. We started walking. Tom asked one of the guards, "So?"

"So what?" the guard said.

"Was that the cross-examination or the sentence?"

"Sentence," the guard said.

"What are they going to do with us?"

The guard answered dryly. "Sentence will be read in your cell."

As a matter of fact, our cell was one of the hospital cellars. It was terrifically cold there because of these drafts. We shivered all night and it wasn't much better during the day.

There was a bench in the cellar and four mats. When they took us back we sat and waited in silence. After a long moment, Tom said, "We're screwed."

"I think so too," I said, "but I don't think they'll do anything to the kid."

1070

"They don't have a thing against him," said Tom. "He's the brother of a militiaman and that's all."

Around eight o'clock in the evening a major came in with two *falangistas*. He had a sheet of paper in his hand. He asked the guard, "What are the names of those three?"

"Steinbock, Ibbieta and Mirbal," the guard said.

The major put on his eyeglasses and scanned the list: "Steinbock . . . Steinbock . . . Oh yes . . . You are sentenced to death.You will be shot tomorrow morning." He went on looking. "The other two as well."

"That's not possible," Juan said. "Not me."

The major looked at him amazed. "What's your name?"

"Juan Mirbal," he said.

"Well, your name is there," said the major. "You're sentenced."

"I didn't do anything," Juan said.

The major shrugged his shoulders. "A Belgian doctor is coming shortly. He is authorized to spend the night with you." He made a military salute and left.

"What did I tell you," Tom said. "We get it."

"Yes," I said, "it's a rotten deal for the kid."

I said that to be decent but I didn't like the kid. His face was too thin and fear and suffering had disfigured it, twisting all his features. Three days before he was a smart sort of kid, not too bad; but now he looked like an old fairy and I thought how he'd never be young again, even if they were to let him go. It wouldn't have been too hard to have a little pity for him but pity disgusts me, or rather it horrifies me.

It was almost dark, a dim glow filtered through the airholes and the pile of coal and made a big stain beneath the spot of sky; I could already see a star through the hole in the ceiling: the night would be pure and icy.

The door opened and two guards came in, followed by a blond man in a tan uniform. He saluted us. "I am the doctor," he said. "I have authorization to help you in these trying hours."

He had an agreeable and distinguished voice. I said, "What do you want here?"

"I am at your disposal. I shall do all I can to make your last moments less difficult."

"What did you come here for? You aren't here on an errand of mercy. Besides, I know you. I saw you with the fascists in the barracks yard the day I was arrested."

I was going to continue, but something surprising suddenly happened to me; the presence of this doctor no longer interested me. Generally when I'm on somebody I don't let go. But the desire to talk left me completely; I shrugged and turned my eyes away. A little later I raised my head; he was watching me curiously. The guards were sitting on a mat. Pedro, the tall thin one, was twiddling his thumbs, the other shook his head from time to time to keep from falling asleep.

I looked at my two friends. Tom had hidden his face in his hands. I could only see the fat white nape of his neck. Little Juan was the worst, his mouth was open and his nostrils trembled. The doctor went to him and put his hand on his shoulder to comfort him: but his eyes stayed cold. Then I saw the Belgian's hand drop stealthily along Juan's arm, down to the wrist. Juan paid no attention. The Belgian took his wrist between three fingers, distractedly, the same time drawing back a little and turning his back to me. But I leaned backward and saw him take a watch from his pocket and look at it for a moment, never letting go of the wrist. After a minute he let the hand fall inert and went and leaned his back against the wall, then, as if he suddenly remembered something very important which had to be jotted down on the spot, he took a notebook from his pocket and wrote a few lines. "Bastard," I thought angrily, "let him come and take my pulse. I'll shove my fist in his rotten face."

He didn't come but I felt him watching me. I raised my head and returned his look. Impersonally, he said to me, "Doesn't it seem cold to you here?" He looked cold, he was blue.

"I'm not cold," I told him.

He never took his hard eyes off me. Suddenly I understood and my hands went to my face: I was drenched in sweat. In this cellar, in the midst of winter, in the midst of drafts, I was sweating. I ran my hands through my hair, gummed together with perspiration; at the same time I saw my shirt was damp and sticking to my skin: I had been dripping for an hour and hadn't felt it. But that swine of a Belgian hadn't missed a thing; he had seen the drops rolling down my cheeks and thought: this is the manifestation of an almost pathological state of terror; and he had felt normal and proud of being alive because he was cold. I wanted to stand up and smash his face but no sooner had I made the slightest gesture than my rage and shame were wiped out; I fell back on the bench with indifference.

Suddenly Juan spoke. "You're a doctor?"

"Yes," the Belgian said.

"Does it hurt . . . very long?"

"Huh? When . . . ? Oh, no," the Belgian said paternally. "Not at all. It's over quickly." He acted as though he were calming a cash customer.

"But I . . . they told me . . . sometimes they had to fire twice."

"Sometimes," the Belgian said, nodding. "It may happen that the first volley reaches no vital organs."

"Then they had to reload their rifles and aim all over again?" He thought for a moment and then added hoarsely, "That takes time!"

He had a terrible fear of suffering, it was all he thought about: it was his age. I never thought much about it and it wasn't fear of suffering that made me sweat.

Tom began speaking in a low voice. He had to talk, without that he wouldn't have been able to recognize himself in his own mind.

"Do you understand?" he said. " I don't understand."

I began to speak in a low voice too. I watched the Belgian. "Why? What's the matter?"

"Something is going to happen to us that I can't understand."

There was a strange smell about Tom. It seemed to me I was more sensitive than usual to odors. I grinned. "You'll understand in a while."

"It isn't clear," he said obstinately. "I want to be brave but first I have to know . . . Listen, they're going to take us into the court-yard. Good. They're going to stand up in front of us. How many?"

"I don't know. Five or eight. Not more."

"All right. There'll be eight. Someone'll holler 'aim!' and I'll see eight rifles looking at me. I'll think how I'd like to get inside the wall, I'll push against it with my back . . . with every ounce of strength I have, but the wall will stay, like in a nightmare. I can imagine all that. If you only knew how well I can imagine it."

"All right, all right!" I said, "I can imagine it too."

"It must hurt like hell. You know, they aim at the eyes and the mouth to disfigure you," he added mechanically. "I can feel the wounds already; I've had pains in my head and in my neck for the past hour. Not real pains. Worse. This is what I'm going to feel tomorrow morning. And then what?"

I well understood what he meant but I didn't want to act as if I did. I had pains too, pains in my body like a crowd of tiny scars. I couldn't get used to it. But I was like him, I attached no impor-tance to it. "After," I said, "you'll be pushing up daisies."

He kept on chewing his words, with something like distraction.

1073

He certainly talked to keep himself from thinking. Naturally, I agreed with him, I could have said everything he said: it isn't *natural* to die. And since I was going to die, nothing seemed natural to me. Only it didn't please me to think the same things as Tom. And I knew that, all through the night, every five minutes, we would keep on thinking things at the same time. I looked at him sideways and for the first time he seemed strange to me: he wore death on his face. My pride was wounded: for the past 24 hours I had lived next to Tom, I had listened to him, I had spoken to him and I knew we had nothing in common. And now we looked as much alike as twin brothers, simply because we were going to die together. Tom took my hand without looking at me . . .

I felt relaxed and over-excited at the same time. I didn't want to think any more about what would happen at dawn, at death. It made no sense. I only found words or emptiness. But as soon as I tried to think of anything else I saw rifle barrels pointing at me. Perhaps I lived through my execution twenty times; once I even thought it was for good: I must have slept a minute. They were dragging me to the wall and I was struggling; I was asking for mercy. If I had wanted to, I think I could have slept a while; I had been awake for 48 hours. I was at the end of my rope. But I didn't want to lose two hours of life: they would come to wake me up at dawn, I would follow them, stupefied with sleep and I would have croaked without so much as an "Oof!"; I didn't want that, I didn't want to die like an animal, I wanted to understand. Then I was afraid of having nightmares. I got up, walked back and forth, and, to change my ideas, I began to think about my past life. A crowd of memories came back to me pell-mell. There were good and bad ones—or at least I called them that *before*. There were faces and incidents. I saw the face of a little *novillero* who was gored in Valencia during the *Feria*, the face of one of my uncles, the face of Ramon Gris. I remembered my whole life: how I was out of work for three months in 1926, how I almost starved to death. I remembered a night I spent on a bench in Granada: I hadn't eaten for three days. I was angry, I didn't want to die. That made me smile. How madly I ran after happiness, after women, after liberty. Why? I wanted to free Spain, I admired Pi y Margall, I joined the anarchist movement, I spoke in public meetings: I took everything as seriously as if I were immortal.

At that moment I felt that I had my whole life in front of me and I thought, "It's a damned lie." It was worth nothing because it

was finished. I wondered how I'd been able to walk, to laugh with the girls: I wouldn't have moved so much as my little finger if I had only imagined I would die like this. My life was in front of me, shut, closed, like a bag and yet everything inside of it was unfinished. For an instant I tried to judge it. I wanted to tell myself, this is a beautiful life. But I couldn't pass judgment on it; it was only a sketch; I had spent my time counterfeiting eternity, I had understood nothing. I missed nothing: there were so many things I could have missed, the taste of *manzanilla* or the baths I took in summer in a little creek near Cadiz; but death had disenchanted everything.

In the state I was in, if somebody had come and told me I could go home quietly, that they would leave me my life whole, it would have left me cold: several hours or several years of waiting is all the same when you have lost the illusion of being eternal. I clung to nothing, in a way I was calm. But it was a horrible calm— because of my body; my body, I saw with its eyes, I heard with its ears, but it was no longer me; it sweated and trembled by itself and I didn't recognize it any more. I had to touch it and look at it to find out what was happening, as if it were the body of someone else. At times I could still feel it, I felt sinkings, and fallings, as when you're in a plane taking a nosedive, or I felt my heart beating. But that didn't reassure me. Everything that came from my body was all cockeyed. Most of the time it was quiet and I felt no more than a sort of weight, a filthy presence against me; I had the impression of being tied to an enormous vermin.

The Belgian took out his watch, looked at it. He said, "It is three-thirty."

Bastard! He must have done it on purpose. Tom jumped; we hadn't noticed time was running out; night surrounded us like a shapeless, somber mass, I couldn't even remember that it had begun.

Little Juan began to cry. He wrung his hands, pleaded, "I don't want to die. I don't want to die."

He ran across the whole cellar waving his arms in the air then fell sobbing on one of the mats. He wept: I could clearly see he was pitying himself; he wasn't thinking about death. For one second, one single second, I wanted to weep myself, to weep with pity for myself. But the opposite happened: I glanced at the kid, I saw his thin sobbing shoulders and I felt inhuman: I could pity neither the others nor myself. I said to myself, "I want to die cleanly."

1075

Tom had gotten up, he placed himself just under the round opening and began to watch for daylight. I was determined to die cleanly and I only thought of that. But ever since the doctor told us the time, I felt time flying, flowing away drop by drop.

It was still dark when I heard Tom's voice: "Do you hear them?" Men were marching in the courtyard.

"Yes."

"What the hell are they doing? They can't shoot in the dark."

After a while we heard no more. I said to Tom, "It's day."

Pedro got up, yawning, and came to blow out the lamp. He said to his buddy, "Cold as hell."

The cellar was all grey. We heard shots in the distance.

"It's starting," I told Tom. "They must do it in the court in the rear."

Tom asked the doctor for a cigarette. I didn't want one; I didn't want cigarettes or alcohol. From that moment on they didn't stop firing.

"Do you realize what's happening," Tom said.

He wanted to add something but kept quiet, watching the door. The door opened and a lieutenant came in with four soldiers. Tom dropped his cigarette.

"Steinbock?"

Tom didn't answer. Pedro pointed him out.

"Juan Mirbal?"

"On the mat."

"Get up," the lieutenant said.

Juan did not move. Two soldiers took him under the arms and set him on his feet. But he fell as soon as they released him.

The soldiers hesitated.

"He's not the first sick one," said the lieutenant. "You two carry him; they'll fix it up down there."

He turned to Tom. "Let's go."

Tom went out between two soldiers. Two others followed, carrying the kid by the armpits. He hadn't fainted; his eyes were wide open and tears ran down his cheeks. When I wanted to go out the lieutenant stopped me.

"You Ibbieta?"

"Yes."

"You wait here; they'll come for you later."

They left. The Belgian and the two jailers left too, I was alone. I did not understand what was happening to me but I would have

liked it better if they had gotten it over with right away. I heard shots at almost regular intervals; I shook with each one of them. I wanted to scream and tear out my hair. But I gritted my teeth and pushed my hands in my pockets because I wanted to stay clean.

After an hour they came to get me and led me to the first floor, to a small room that smelt of cigars and where the heat was stifling. There were two officers sitting smoking in the armchairs, papers on their knees.

"You're Ibbieta?"

"Yes."

"Where is Ramon Gris?"

"I don't know."

The one questioning me was short and fat. His eyes were hard behind his glasses. He said to me, "Come here."

I went to him. He got up and took my arms, staring at me with a look that should have pushed me into the earth. At the same time he pinched my biceps with all his might. It wasn't to hurt me, it was only a game: he wanted to dominate me. He also thought he had to blow his stinking breath square in my face. We stayed for a moment like that, and I almost felt like laughing. It takes a lot to intimidate a man who is going to die; it didn't work. He pushed me back violently and sat down again. He said, "It's his life against yours. You can have yours if you tell us where he is."

These men dolled up with their riding crops and boots were still going to die. A little later than I, but not too much. They busied themselves looking for names in their crumpled papers, they ran after other men to imprison or suppress them; they had opinions on the future of Spain and on other subjects. Their little activities seemed shocking and burlesqued to me; I couldn't put myself in their place, I thought they were insane. The little man was still looking at me, whipping his boots with the riding crop. All his gestures were calculated to give him the look of a live and ferocious beast.

"So? You understand?"

"I don't know where Gris is," I answered. "I thought he was in Madrid."

The other officer raised his pale hand indolently. This indolence was also calculated. I saw through all their little schemes and I was stupefied to find there were men who amused themselves that way.

"You have a quarter of an hour to think it over." he said slowly.

"Take him to the laundry, bring him back in fifteen minutes. If he still refuses he will be executed on the spot."

They knew what they were doing: I had passed the night in waiting; then they had made me wait an hour in the cellar while they shot Tom and Juan and now they were locking me up in the laundry; they must have prepared their game the night before. They told themselves that nerves eventually wear out and they hoped to get me that way.

They were badly mistaken. In the laundry I sat on a stool because I felt very weak and I began to think. But not about their proposition. Of course I knew where Gris was; he was hiding with his cousins, four kilometers from the city. I also knew that I would not reveal his hiding place unless they tortured me (but they didn't seem to be thinking about that). All that was perfectly regulated, definite and in no way interested me. Only I would have liked to understand the reasons for my conduct. I would rather die than give up Gris. Why? I didn't like Ramon Gris any more. My friendship for him had died a little while before dawn at the same time as my desire to live. Undoubtedly I thought highly of him: he was tough. But it was not for this reason that I consented to die in his place; his life had no more value than mine; no life had value. They were going to slap a man up against a wall and shoot at him till he died, whether it was I or Gris or somebody else made no difference. I knew he was more useful than I to the cause of Spain but I thought to hell with Spain and anarchy; nothing was important. Yet I was there, I could save my skin and give up Gris and I refused to do it. I found that somehow comic; it was obstinacy. I thought, "I must be stubborn!" And a droll sort of gaiety spread over me.

They came for me and brought me back to the two officers. A rat ran out from under my feet and that amused me. I turned to one of the *falangistas* and said, "Did you see the rat?"

He didn't answer. He was very sober, he took himself seriously. I wanted to laugh but I held myself back because I was afraid that once I got started I wouldn't be able to stop.

"Well," said the fat officer, "have you thought about it?"

I looked at them with curiosity, as insects of a very rare species. I told them, "I know where he is. He is hidden in the cemetery. In a vault or in the gravediggers' shack."

It was a farce. I wanted to see them stand up, buckle their belts and give orders busily.

1078

They jumped to their feet. "Let's go. Molés, go get fifteen men from Lieutenant Lopez. You," the fat man said, "I'll let you off if you're telling the truth, but it'll cost you plenty if you're making monkeys out of us."

They left in a great clatter and I waited peacefully under the guard of *falangistas*. From time to time I smiled, thinking about the spectacle they would make. I felt stunned and malicious. I imagined them lifting up tombstones, opening the doors of the vaults one by one. I represented this situation to myself as if I had been someone else: this prisoner obstinately playing the hero, these grim *falangistas* with their moustaches and their men in uniform running among the graves; it was irresistibly funny. After half an hour the little fat man came back alone. I thought he had come to give the orders to execute me. The others must have stayed in the cemetery.

The officer looked at me. He didn't look at all sheepish. "Take him into the big courtyard with the others," he said. "After the military operations a regular court will decide what happens to him."

"Then they're not ... not going to shoot me? ..."

"Not now, anyway. What happens afterwards is none of my business."

I still didn't understand. I asked, "But why ... ?"

He shrugged his shoulders without answering and the soldiers took me away. In the big courtyard there were about a hundred prisoners, women, children and a few old men. I began walking around the central grass-plot, I was stupefied. At noon they let us eat in the mess hall. Two or three people questioned me. I must have known them, but I didn't answer: I didn't even know where I was.

Around evening they pushed about ten new prisoners into the court. I recognized Garcia, the baker. He said, "What damned luck you have! I didn't think I'd see you alive."

"They sentenced me to death," I said, "and then they changed their minds. I don't know why."

"They arrested me at two o'clock," Garcia said.

"Why?" Garcia had nothing to do with politics.

"I don't know," he said. "They arrest everybody who doesn't think the way they do. He lowered his voice. "They got Gris."

I began to tremble. "When?"

"This morning. He messed it up. He left his cousin's on Tuesday because they had an argument. There were plenty of people to

1079

hide him but he didn't want to owe anything to anybody. He said, 'I'd go and hide in Ibbieta's place, but they got him, so I'll go hide in the cemetery.' "

"In the cemetery?"

"Yes. What a fool. Of course they went by there this morning, that was sure to happen. They found him in the gravediggers' shack. He shot at them and they got him."

"In the cemetery!"

Everything began to spin and I found myself sitting on the ground: I laughed so hard I cried.

FRIEDRICH VON SCHILLER

FRIEDRICH VON SCHILLER (German, 1759-1805). Germany's greatest dramatist. After years of antagonism, a great friend of Goethe's. His life was a triumph of creative will over disease. His 9 great plays, technically of the first order, are deeply imbued with pathos for moral freedom. Prominent among them: *Don Carlos, Wallenstein's Camp, Mary Stuart, William Tell.*

WILLIAM TELL AND THE TYRANT

Scene—*The hollow way at Küssnacht*

Tell (among the rocks overhanging the pass). Here through the
    hollow way he'll pass; there is
No other road to Küssnacht. Here I'll do it! . . .
The opportunity is good: the bushes
Of alder there will hide me; from that point
My arrow hits him; the strait pass prevents
Pursuit. Now, Gessler, balance thy account
With Heaven! Thou must be gone; thy sand is run! . . .
Remote and harmless I have lived; my bow
Ne'er bent save on the wild beast of the forest;
My thoughts were free of murder. Thou hast scared me
From my peace; to fell asp-poison hast thou
Changed the milk of kindly temper in me;
Thou hast accustomed me to horrors. Gessler!
The archer who could aim at his boy's head
Can send an arrow to his enemy's heart. . . .

Poor little boys! My kind, true wife! I will
Protect them from thee. Viceroy! when I drew
That bowstring and my hand was quivering,
And with devilish joy thou mad'st me point it
At the child, and I in fainting anguish
Entreated thee in vain; then, with a grim,
Irrevocable oath, deep in my soul,
I vowed to God in Heaven that the next aim
I took should be thy heart. The vow I made
In that despairing moment's agony,
Became a holy debt—and I will pay it.

(Various characters gradually appear upon the scene, among
them Stüssi, Frau Armgart, and the members of a wedding procession, who come up the pass; at length Gessler [the Austrian
Landvogt or Viceroy], and Rudolph der Harras approach, riding
up the pass, while Tell disappears among the rocks.)

Gessler. Say what you like, I am the Kaiser's servant,
And must think of pleasing him. He sent me,
Not to caress these hinds, to soothe or nurse them.
Obedience is the word! The point at issue is,
Shall Boor or Kaiser here be lord o' th' lands?
Armgart. Now is the moment! Now for my petition.
Gess. This Hat at Altdorf, mark you, I set up,
Not for the joke's sake, or to try the hearts
O' th' people—these I know of old—but that
They might be taught to bend their necks to me,
Which are too straight and stiff; and in the way
Where they are hourly passing I have planted
This offence, so that their eyes may fall on't,
And remind them of their lord, whom they forgot.
Rudolph. But the people have some rights—
Gess. Which now
Is not a time for settling or admitting.
Mighty things are on the anvil. The House
Of Hapsburg must wax powerful; what the Father
Gloriously began, the Son must forward.
This people is a stone of stumbling, which
One way or t' other must be put aside.
Arm. Mercy, gracious Viceroy! Justice! Justice!

1081

Gess. Why do you plague me here and stop my way
I' th' open road? Off! Let me pass!
    Arm. My husband
Is in prison; these orphans cry for bread.
Have pity, good your grace, have pity on us!
    Rud. Who or what are you, then? Who is your husband?
    Arm. A poor wild-hay-man of the Rigiberg,
Whose trade is, on the brow of the abyss,
To mow the common grass from craggy shelves
And nooks to which the cattle dare not climb.
    Rud. By Heaven, a wild and miserable life!
Do now! do let this poor drudge free, I pray you!—
Whatever be his crime, that horrid trade
Is punishment enough. You shall have justice;
In the castle there make your petition;
This is not the place.
    Arm. No, no! I stir not
From this spot till you give up my husband!
'Tis the sixth month he has lain i' th' dungeon,
Waiting for the sentence of some judge in vain.
    Gess. Woman! Would'st lay thy hands on me? Begone!
    Arm. Justice Viceroy! thou art judge o' th' land here,
I' th' Kaiser's stead and God's. Perform thy duty!
As thou expectest justice from above,
Show it to us.
    Gess. Off! take the mutinous rabble from my sight.
    Arm. No, no! I now have nothing
More to lose. Thou shalt not move a step, Lord,
Till thou hast done me right. Ay, knit thy brows,
And roll thy eyes as sternly as thou wilt;
We are so wretched, wretched now we care not
Aught more for thy anger.
    Gess. Woman, make way!
Or else my horse shall crush thee.
    Arm. Let it! there!
Here am I with my children. Let the orphans
Be trodden underneath thy horse's hoofs!
'Tis not the worst that thou hast done.
    Rud. Woman, art mad?
    Arm. 'Tis long that thou has trodden
The Kaiser's people under foot. Too long!

Oh, I am but a woman! Were I a man
I should find something else to do
Than lie here crying in the dust.

Gess. Where are my servants?
Quick! take her hence! I may forget myself,
And do the thing I shall repent.

Rud. My lord,
The servants cannot pass; the place above
Is crowded with a bridal company.

Gess. I've been too mild a ruler to this people;
They are not tamed as they should be; their tongues
Are still at liberty. This shall be altered!
I will break that stubborn humor. Freedom,
With its pert vauntings, shall no more be heard of.
I will enforce a new law in these lands;
There shall not—

(An arrow pierces him; he presses his hand on his heart, and
slides from his horse into the arms of Rudolph, who has dis-
mounted.)

Rud. Lord Viceroy—God! What is it? whence came it?
Gess. 'Tis Tell's arrow.
Tell (from a rock above). Thou hast found the archer;
Seek no other. Free are the cottages,
Secure is innocence from thee; thou wilt
Torment the land no more.

ARTHUR SCHNITZLER

ARTHUR SCHNITZLER (Austrian, 1862-1931). Impressionist playwright and
novelist. Physician and literary interpreter of Vienna's *"belle epoche."* His
sophisticated, pessimistic plays have been accused of immorality and decadence, but they brilliantly preserve the flavor of an era. Among them: *Anatol,
Reigen, Professor Bernhardi.*

FLOWERS

I WANDERED about the streets the whole afternoon, while the snow
fell slowly, in large flakes—and now I am at home, my lamp is
burning, my cigar is lighted and my books lie close by; in fact, I
have everything that affords true comfort. Yet all is in vain; I can
think of but one thing.

But had she not been dead for a long time as far as I was concerned?—yes, dead; or, as I thought with the childish pathos of the deceived, "worse than dead?" And now that I know that she is not "worse than dead," but simply dead, like the many others who lie out there, under the ground, forever—in spring, in the hot summer, and when the snow falls, as today—without any hope of ever returning—since that time I know that she did not die a moment sooner for me than she did for the rest of the world. Sorrow?—no. It is only the general horror that we all feel when something that once belonged to us, and whose entire being is still clear in our minds, sinks into the grave.

It was very sad when I discovered that she was deceiving me; —but there was so much else with it!—the fury and sudden hatred, and the horror of existence, and—ah, yes—the wounded vanity; —the sorrow only came later! But then there was the consolation that she also must be suffering.—I have them all yet, I can reread them at any time, those dozens of letters which sob, pray, and beseech forgiveness!—And I can still see her before me, in her dark dress and small straw hat, standing at the street corner in the twilight as I stepped out of the gate—looking after me.—And I still think of the last meeting when she stood in front of me with her large, beautiful eyes, set in that round, childlike face that now had become pale and wan.—I did not give her my hand when she left me;—when she left me for the last time.—And I watched her go down the street from my window and then she disappeared —forever. Now she can never return. . . .

My knowing it at all is due to an accident. I could have been unaware of it for weeks and months. I happened to meet her uncle one morning. I had not seen him for at least a year, as he does not come to Vienna very often. In fact, I had only met him two or three times before this. Our first meeting was three years ago at a bowling party. She and her mother were there also.—And then the following summer: I was in the Prater with a few friends. Her uncle was sitting at the next table with some gentlemen. They were all gay, and he drank to my health. And before he left he came up to me and told me confidentially that his niece was madly in love with me!—And in my half-giddiness it seemed very foolish and queer that the old gentleman should tell such a thing here, midst the music of the cymbals and violins—to me, who knew it so well, and on whose lips still clung the impression of her last kiss. And now, this morning! I almost walked past him. I asked for his niece,

more out of politeness than interest. I knew nothing more about her; her letters had stopped coming a long time ago; only flowers she sent me, regularly. Recollections of our happiest days! Once a month they came; no card: just silent, humble flowers.—And when I asked the old gentleman he was all astonishment. "You don't know that the poor girl died a week ago?" It was a terrible shock! —Then he told me more. And her illness? "Melancholia—anæmia. —The doctors themselves were not quite sure."

I remained a long while on the spot where the old gentleman had left me;—I was enervated, as if I had just gone through some great trouble.—And now it seems to me as if today marks the termination of a part of my life. Why—why? It was simply something external. I had no more feeling for her; in fact, I seldom thought of her any more. But now that I have written this all down I feel better; I am more composed—I am beginning to appreciate the coziness of my home.—It is foolish and tormenting to think of it any more.—There are certainly others today who have a great deal more to mourn about than I.

I have taken a walk. It is a serene winter's day. The sky looks so grey, so cold, so far away.—And I am very calm. The old gentleman whom I met yesterday—it seems as if it had been weeks ago. And when I think of her I can see her in a peculiarly sharp and finished outline; only one thing is lacking: the anger which always associated itself with my thoughts of her. The real appreciation that she is no more on earth, that she is lying in a coffin, that she has been buried, I have not—I feel no sorrow. The world seemed calmer to me today. I once knew for just one moment that there is neither happiness nor sorrow; no, there are only the grimaces of joy and sadness; we laugh and we weep and we invite our soul to be present. I could sit down now and read deep, serious books, and should soon be able to penetrate into all of their learning. Or, I could stand in front of old pictures, which heretofore have meant nothing to me, and now appreciate their true beauty.—And when I think of certain dear friends who have died, my heart does not feel as sad as it used to—death has become something friendly; it stalks among us but does not want to harm us.

Snow, high, white snow on all the streets. Little Gretel came to me and suggested that we ought to take a sleigh ride. And we drove out into the country, over the smooth road, the sleigh bells ringing and the blue-grey sky above us. Gretel rested against my shoulder and looked out upon the long road with happy eyes. We came to

an inn that we knew well from the summer. The oven was all aglow, and it was so hot that we had to move the table away, as Gretel's left ear and cheek became fire red. I had to kiss the paler cheek. Afterwards, the return home in the twilight! Gretel sat very close to me and held both of my hands in hers.—Then she said: "At last I have you again." She had thus, without racking her brain, struck the right note to make me happy. But perhaps it was the biting, clear air that unchained my thoughts, for I feel freer and more contented than I have in the last few days.

A short while ago again, as I lay dozing on my couch, a strange thought came to my mind. I appeared hard and cold to myself. As one who, without tears, in fact, without any emotion, stands at the grave in which he has buried a dear one. As one who has grown so hard that he cannot reconcile the horror of death.—Yes, irreconcilable, that is it.

Gone, quite gone! Life, happiness, and a little love drives all that foolishness away. I go again among people. I like them; they are harmless, they chatter about all sorts of jolly things. And Gretel is a dear, kind creature; and she is prettiest when she stands at my window and the sunbeams shine on her golden hair.

Something strange happened today.—It is the day on which she always sent me flowers. And the flowers came again as—as if nothing had changed. They came with the first mail, in a long, narrow white box. It was quite early, and I was still sleepy. And only when I was actually opening the box did I gain full consciousness. Then I almost had a shock. And there lay, daintily tied with a golden string, violets and pinks.—They lay as in a coffin. And as I took the flowers in my hand a shudder went through my heart. —But I understand how it is that they came again today. When she felt her illness, perchance even when she felt death approaching, she gave her usual order to the florist so that I would not miss her attention. Certainly, that is the explanation; as something quite natural, as something touching perhaps.—And still as I held them in my hands, these flowers, and they seemed to nod and tremble, then, in spite of reason and will power, I looked upon them as something ghostly, as if they had come from her, as if they were her greeting—as if she wanted always, even now that she was dead, to tell me of her love—of her tardy faithfulness. Ah, we do not understand death, we will never understand it; and a person is dead only after all that have known him have also passed away. To-day I grasped the flowers differently than usual, as if I might injure

them were I to hold them too tight—as if their souls might begin to sob softly. And as they now stand in front of me on my desk, in a narrow, light-green vase, they seem to nod their heads in mournful gratitude. The full pain of a useless yearning spreads over me from them, and I believe that they could tell me something if we could only understand the language of *all* living things—not only of the things that talk.

I do not want to let myself be fooled. They are only flowers. They are a message from the past. They are no call, surely no call from the grave. They are simply flowers, and some florist tied them together mechanically, put a bit of cotton around them, then laid them in the white box, and mailed it.—And now that they are here, why do I think about them?

I spend many hours in the open air and take long, lonely walks. When I am among people I do not feel compatible with them. And I noticed it when the sweet, blonde girl sits in my room, chattering away about all sorts of things—I don't know about what. When she is gone, in a moment it is as if she were miles away from me, as if the flood of people had engulfed her and left no traces behind. I should hardly be surprised if she did not come again.

The flowers are in the tall, green vase; their stems are in the water and their scent fills the room. They still retain their odour —in spite of the fact that I have had them a week and that they are already fading. And I believe all sorts of nonsense that I used to laugh at: I believe in the possibility of conversing with things in nature—I believe that one can communicate with clouds and springs; and I am waiting for these flowers to begin to talk. But no, I feel sure that they are always speaking—even now—they are forever crying out; and I can almost understand them.

How glad I am that the winter is over! Already the breath of spring throbs in the air. I am not living any differently than before, still I sometimes feel as if the boundaries of my existence are expanding. Yesterday seems far off, and the happenings of a few days past are like vague dreams. It is still the same when Gretel leaves me, especially when I have not seen her for several days; then our friendship appears like an affair of the past ages. She always comes, from afar, from so far away!—But when she begins to chatter it is like olden times again, and I then have a clear consciousness of the present. And then her words are almost too loud and the colours seem too harsh. Yet as soon as she leaves me all is gone; there are no after-pictures or gradual, fading recollec-

tions.—And then I am alone with my flowers. They are now quite faded, quite faded. They have no more perfume. Gretel had not noticed them at all; but today she saw them and it seemed as if she wanted to question me, but then she suddenly appeared to have a secret horror for them;—she stopped speaking altogether and soon left me.

The petals are slowly falling off. I never touch them; anyway, if I did they would crumble. It makes me very sad to see them faded. I do not know why I have not the courage to make an end of all this nonsense. The faded flowers make me ill. I cannot stand them and I rush out. Once in the street, I feel that I have to hurry back to them, to care for them. And then I find them in the same green vase where I left them, tired and sad. Last evening I wept before them, as one weeps at a grave. Yet I never gave a thought to the sender of them. Perhaps I am wrong, yet it seems as if Gretel feels that there is something strange in my room. She does not laugh any more. She does not speak so loud, with that clear, lively voice to which I am accustomed. And I do not receive her as I used to. Then there is the fear that she will question me; and I realise what torture those questions would be.

She frequently brings her sewing, and if I am still at my books she sits quietly at the table and sews or crochets; and she waits patiently until I have finished and put my books away and come up to her and take her sewing out of her hands. Then I remove the green shade from the lamp so that a mellow light floods the room. I do not like dark corners.

Spring! My window is wide open. Late last evening Gretel and I looked out on to the street. The air was warm and balmy. And when I looked at the corner, where the street lamp spreads a weak light, I suddenly saw a shadow. I saw it and I did not—I know that I did not see it—I closed my eyes and I could suddenly see through my eyelids. There stood the miserable creature, in the pale lamp light, and I saw her face very clearly, as if the yellow sunshine were on it, and I saw in the pale, emaciated face those wounded eyes. Then I walked slowly away from the window and sat down at my desk; the candle spluttered in the breeze. And I remained motionless, for I knew that the poor creature was standing at the corner, waiting; and if I had dared to touch the faded flowers I would have taken them out of the vase and brought them to her. Thus I thought, and sincerely thought; yet I knew all the while that it was foolish. Now Gretel also left the window and came over to the back of my chair

where she remained a moment to touch my hair with her lips. Then she went and left me alone.

I stared at the flowers. There are hardly any more. Mostly bare stems, dry and pitiful. They make me ill and drive me mad. And it must be evident; otherwise Gretel would have asked me; but she feels it, too. Now she had fled as if there were ghosts in my room. Ghosts!—They are, they are!—Dead things playing with life! And if faded flowers smell mouldy it is only the remembrance of the time when they were in bloom. And the dead return as long as we do not forget them. What difference does it make if they cannot speak now;—I hear them! She does not appear any more, yet I can see her! And the spring outside, and the sunshine on my rug, and the perfume of the lilacs in the park, and the people who pass below and do not interest me, are they life? If I pull down the curtains, the sun is dead. I do not care to know about all these people, and they are dead. I close my window, and the perfume of the lilacs is gone and spring is dead. I am more powerful than the sun, the people, and the spring. But more powerful than I is remembrance, for that comes when it wills and from it there is no escape. And these dry stems are more powerful than the perfume of the lilacs and the spring.

I was pondering over these pages when Gretel entered. She had never come so early. I was surprised, astonished. She remained a moment on the threshold, and I gazed at her without greeting her. Then she smiled and approached me. In her hand she carried a bouquet of fresh flowers. Then, without speaking, she laid them on my desk. In the next moment, she seized the withered stems in the green vase. It seemed as if someone had grasped my heart;—but I could not utter a sound. And when I wanted to rise and take her by the arm, she smiled at me. Holding the faded flowers high above her, she hurried to the window and threw them out into the street. I felt I wanted to throw myself after them; but Gretel stood at the sill, facing me. And on her head was the sunshine, the bright sunshine. And the aroma of lilacs came in through the window. And I looked at the empty, green vase on my desk;—I am not sure, yet I think I felt freer,—yes, freer. Then Gretel approached me, picked up her bouquet, and held in front of my face cool, white lilacs. Such a healthy, fresh perfume—so soft, so cool; I wanted to bury my face in them. Laughing, white, beautiful flowers—and I felt that the spectre was gone. Gretel stood behind me and ran her hands

through my hair. "You silly boy," she said. Did she know what she had done? I grasped her hands and kissed her.

In the evening we went out into the open, into the spring. We have just returned! I have lighted my candle. We took a long walk, and Gretel is so tired that she has fallen asleep in the chair. She is very beautiful when she smiles thus in her sleep.

Before me, in the narrow, green vase are the lilacs. Down on the street—no, no, they are not there any longer. Already the wind has blown them away with the rest of the dust.

SIR WALTER SCOTT

SIR WALTER SCOTT (Scottish, 1771-1832). Prolific as well as imaginative practitioner of the historical romance and sentimental novel. Based adventure stories on sound research, heavily influencing French and other period novelists. Most famous of these: *Ivanhoe, Quentin Durward, The Talisman.* His long narrative poems still effective: *The Lay of the Last Minstrel, Lady of the Lake.*

THE NUBIAN

RICHARD surveyed the Nubian in silence as he stood before him, his looks bent upon the ground, his arms folded on his bosom, with the appearance of a black marble statue of the most exquisite workmanship waiting life from the touch of a Prometheus. The king of England, who, as it was emphatically said of his successor, Henry the Eighth, loved to look upon a man, was well pleased with the thews, sinews, and symmetry of him whom he now surveyed and questioned him in the lingua Franca, "Art thou a pagan?"

The slave shook his head, and raising his finger to his brow crossed himself in token of his Christianity, then resumed his posture of motionless humility.

"A Nubian Christian, doubtless," said Richard, "and mutilated of the organ of speech by these heathen dogs?"

The mute again slowly shook his head, in token of negative, pointed with his forefinger to heaven, and then laid it upon his own lips.

"I understand thee," said Richard; "thou doest suffer under the infliction of God, not by the cruelty of man. Canst thou clean an armor and belt, and buckle it in time of need?"

The mute nodded, and stepping toward the coat of mail, which hung with the shield and helmet of the chivalrous monarch, upon

the pillar of the tent, he handled it with such nicety of address, as sufficiently to show that he fully understood the business of the armor bearer.

"Thou art an apt, and wilt doubtless be a useful, knave. Thou shalt wait in my chamber, and on my person," said the king, "to show how much I value the gift of the royal Soldan. If thou hast no tongue, it follows thou canst carry no tales, neither provoke me to be sudden by an unfit reply."

The Nubian again prostrated himself till his brow touched the earth, then stood erect, at some paces distant, as waiting for his new master's commands.

"Nay, thou shalt commence thy office presently," said Richard, "for I see a speck of rust darkening on that shield; and when I shake it in the face of Saladin, it should be bright and unsullied as the Soldan's honor and mine own."

A horn was winded without, and presently Sir Henry Neville entered with a packet of dispatches. "From England, my lord," he said, as he delivered it. "From England,—our own England" repeated Richard, in a tone of melancholy enthusiasm. "Alas! they little think how hard their sovereign has been beset by sickness and sorrow, faint friends, and forward enemies." Then, opening the dispatches, he said hastily, "Ha! this comes from no peaceful land; they too have their feuds. Neville, begone; I must peruse these tidings alone, and at leisure."

Neville withdrew accordingly, and Richard was soon absorbed in the melancholy details which had been conveyed to him from England, concerning the factions that were tearing to pieces his native dominions,—the disunion of his brothers, John and Geoffrey, and the quarrels of both with the High Justiciary Longchamp, Bishop of Ely; the oppressions practiced by the nobles upon the peasantry, and rebellion of the latter against their masters, which had produced everywhere scenes of discord, and in some instances the effusion of blood. Details of incidents mortifying to his pride, and derogatory from his authority, were intermingled with the earnest advice of his wisest and most attached counselors, that he should presently return to England, as his presence offered the only hope of saving the kingdom from all the horrors of civil discord, of which France and Scotland were likely to avail themselves.

Filled with the most painful anxiety, Richard read, and again read, the ill-omened letters, compared the intelligence with some of them contained with the same facts as differently stated in others,

1091

and soon became totally insensible to whatever was passing around him although seated, for the sake of coolness, close to the entrance of his tent, and having the curtains withdrawn, so that he could see and be seen by the guards and others who were stationed without.

Deeper in the shadow of the pavilion, and busied with the task his new master had imposed, sat the Nubian slave, with his back rather turned toward the king. He had finished adjusting the hauberk and brigandine, and was now busily employed on a broad pavise, or buckler, of unusual size, and covered with steel plating, which Richard often used in reconnoitering, or actually storming, fortified places, as a more effectual protection against missile weapons than the narrow triangular shield used on horseback.

This pavise bore neither the royal lions of England, nor any other device, to attract the observation of the defenders of the walls against which it was advanced. The care, therefore, of the armorer was addressed to causing its surface to shine as bright crystal, in which he seemed to be peculiarly successful. Beyond the Nubian, and scarcely visible from without, lay the large dog, which might be termed his brother slave, and which, as if he felt awed by being transferred to a royal owner, was couched close to the side of the mute, with his head and ears on the ground, and his limbs and tail drawn close around and under him.

While the monarch and his new attendant were thus occupied, another actor crept upon the scene, and mingled among the group of English yeomen, about a score of whom, respecting the unusually pensive posture and close occupation of their sovereign, were, contrary to their wont, keeping a silent guard in front of his tent. It was not, however, more vigilant than usual. Some were playing at games of hazard with small pebbles, other spoke together in whispers of the approaching day of battle, and several lay asleep, their bulky limbs folded in their green mantles.

Amid these careless warders glided the puny form of a little old Turk, poorly dressed like a marabout or santon of the desert,—a sort of enthusiast, who sometimes ventured into the camp of the Crusaders, though treated always with contumely, and often with violence. Indeed, the luxury and profligate indulgence of the Christian leaders had occasioned a motley concourse in their tents, of musicians, Jewish merchants, Copts, Turks, and all the varied refuse of the Eastern nations; so that the caftan and turban—though to drive both from the Holy Land was the professed object of the expedition

—were nevertheless neither an uncommon nor an alarming sight in the camp of the Crusaders. When, however, the little insignificant figure we have described approached so nigh as to receive some interruption from the warders, he dashed his dusky green turban from his head, showed that his beard and eyebrows were shaved like those of a professed buffoon, and that the expression of his fantastic and writhen features, as well as of his little black eyes, which glittered like jet, was that of a crazed imagination.

"Dance, marabout," cried the soldiers, acquainted with the manners of these wandering enthusiasts,—"dance, or we will scourge thee with our bowstrings, till thou spin as never top did under schoolboy's lash." Thus shouted the reckless warders, as much delighted at having a subject to tease as a child when he catches a butterfly, or a schoolboy upon discovering a bird's nest.

The marabout, as if happy to do their behests, bounded from the earth, and spun his giddy round before them with singular agility, which when contrasted with his slight and wasted figure and diminutive appearance, made him resemble a withered leaf twirled round and round at the pleasure of the winter's breeze. His single lock of hair streamed upwards from his bald and shaven head, as if some genie upheld him by it; and indeed it seemed as if supernatural art were necessary to the execution of the wild whirling dance, in which scarce the tiptoe of the performer was seen to touch the ground.

Amid the vagaries of his performance, he flew here and there, from one spot to another, still approaching, however, though almost imperceptibly, to the entrance of the royal tent; so that, when at length he sunk exhausted on the earth, after two or three bounds still higher than those which he had yet executed, he was not above thirty yards from the king's person.

For the space of a quarter of an hour, or longer, after the incident related, all remained perfectly quiet in the front of the royal habitation. The king read and mused in the entrance of his pavilion; behind, and with his back turned to the same entrance, the Nubian slave still burnished the ample pavise; in front of all, at an hundred paces distant, the yeomen of the guard stood, sat, or lay extended on the grass, attentive to their own sports, but pursuing them in silence; while on the esplanade betwixt them and the front of the tent lay, scarcely to be distinguished from a bundle of rags, the senseless form of the marabout.

But the Nubian had the advantage of a mirror, from the brilliant

1093

reflection which the surface of the highly polished shield now afforded, by means of which he beheld, to his alarm and surprise, that the marabout raised his head gently from the ground, so as to survey all around him, moving with a well-adjusted precaution, which seemed entirely inconsistent with a state of inebriety. He couched his head instantly, as if satisfied he was unobserved, and began, with the slightest possible appearance of voluntary effort, to drag himself, as if by chance, ever nearer and nearer to the king, but stopping and remaining fixed at intervals, like the spider, which, moving towards her object, collapses into apparent lifelessness when she thinks she is the subject of observation. This species of movement appeared suspicious to the Ethiopian, who, on his part, prepared himself as quietly as possible to interfere the instant that interference should seem to be necessary.

The merchant meanwhile glided on gradually and imperceptibly, serpent-like, or rather snail-like, till he was about ten yards' distance from Richard's person, when, starting on his feet, he sprang forward with the bound of a tiger, stood at the king's back in less than an instant, and brandished aloft the cangiar, or poniard, which he had hidden in his sleeve.

Not the presence of his whole army could have saved their heroic monarch; but the motions of the Nubian had been as well calculated as those of the enthusiast, and, ere the latter could strike, the former caught his uplifted arm. Turning his fanatical wrath upon what thus unexpectedly interposed betwixt him and his object, the Charegite, for such was the seeming marabout, dealt the Nubian a blow with the dagger, which, however, only grazed his arm, while the far superior strength of the Ethiopian easily dashed him to the ground.

Aware of what had passed, Richard had now arisen, and with little more of surprise, anger, or interest of any kind in his countenance than an ordinary man would show in brushing up the stool on which he had been sitting, and exclaiming only "Ha, dog!" dashed almost to pieces the skull of the assassin, who uttered twice, once in a loud and once in a broken tone, the words "Allah ackbar!" —God is victorious.—and expired at the king's feet.

"Ye are careful warders," said Richard to his archers, in a tone of scornful reproach, as, aroused by the bustle of what had passed, in terror and tumult they now rushed into his tent; "watchful sentinels ye are, to leave me to do such hangman's work with my own hand. Be silent, all of you, and cease your senseless clamor!

1094

Saw ye never a dead Turk before? Here, cast that carrion out of the camp, strike the head from the trunk, and stick it on a lance, taking care to turn the face to Mecca, that he may the easier tell the foul impostor, on whose inspiration he came hither, how he has sped on his errand.—For thee, my swart and silent friend," he added, turning to the Ethiopian. "But how's this? thou art wounded, and with a poisoned weapon, I warrant me; for by force of stab so weak an animal as that could scarce hope to do more than raise the lion's hide. Suck the poison from the wound, one of you; the venom is harmless on the lips, though fatal when it mingles with the blood."

The yeomen looked on each other confusedly and with hesitation, the apprehension of so strange a danger prevailing with those who feared no other.

"How now, sirrah?" continued the king; "are you dainty-lipped, or do you fear death, that you dally thus?"

"Not the death of a man," said Long Allan, to whom the king looked as he spoke; "but methinks I would not die like a poisoned rat for the sake of a black chattel there, that is bought and sold in market like a Martlemas ox."

"His Grace speaks to men of sucking poison," muttered another yeoman, "as if he said, 'Go to, swallow a gooseberry!'"

"Nay," said Richard, "I never bade a man do that which I would do not myself."

And without further ceremony, and in spite of the general expostulations of those around, and the respectful opposition of the Nubian himself, the king of England applied his lips to the wound of the black slave, treating with ridicule all remonstrances, and overpowering all resistance. He had no sooner intermitted his singular occupation, than the Nubian started from him, and casting a scarf over his arm, intimated by gestures, as firm in purpose as they were respectful in manner, his determination not to permit the monarch to renew so degrading an employment. Long Allan also interposed, saying that if it were necessary to prevent the king engaging again in a treatment of this kind, his own lips, tongue, and teeth were at the service of the negro (as he called the Ethiopian), and that he would eat him up bodily, rather than King Richard's mouth again should approach him.

Neville, who entered with other officers, added his remonstrances.

"Nay, nay, make not a needless halloo about a hart that the hounds have lost, or a danger when it is over," said the king. "The

wound will be a trifle, for the blood is scarce drawn,—an angry cat had dealt a deeper scratch,—and, for me, I have but to take a dram of orvietan by way of precaution, though it is needless."

Thus spoke Richard, a little ashamed, perhaps, of his own condescension, though sanctioned both by humanity and gratitude. But when Neville continued to make remonstrances on the peril to his royal person, the king imposed silence on him.

"Peace, I prithee; make no more of it. I did it but to show these ignorant prejudiced knaves how they might help each other when these cowardly caitiffs come against us with sarbacanes and poisoned shafts."

SE'AMI

SE'AMI (Japanese, 1363-1443). Chief representative of the *Nō* play, created by self and father. Author of nearly half the *Nō* plays still performed. Most famous: *Takasago*. Was also praised as an actor and dramatic critic.

SOTOBA KOMACHI

Characters:
First Priest
Second Priest
Chorus
Komachi, as herself
and as her former
lover

Both Priests:
The mountains are not high on which we hide
The mountains are not high on which we hide
The lonely deepness of our hearts.
First Priest:
I am a priest from the Koya Hills
Coming down now to make my way to the city.
Second Priest:
The Buddha that was is gone away.
The Buddha to be has not yet come to the world.
Both Priests:
At birth we woke to dream in this world between
What then shall we say is real?
By chance we took the forms of men

From a thousand possibilities.
We stumbled on the treasure of the holy law
The seed of all salvation
And then with thoughtful hearts we put our bodies
In these thin and ink-black robes,
We knew of lives before this birth
We knew of lives before this birth
And knew we owed no love to those who to this life
Engendered us.
We recognize no parents.
No children cared for us.
We walked a thousand miles and the way seemed short.
In the fields we lay down
And slept the night in the hills
Which now became our proper dwelling place
Our proper home.

Komachi:
'Like a root-cut reed
Should the tide entice
I would come
I would come I know but no wave asks
No stream invites this grief.'

How sad that once I was proud
Long ago
Proud and graceful
Golden birds in my raven hair
When I walked like willows nodding, charming
As the breeze in spring.
The voice of the nightingale
The petals of the wood rose wide stretched
Holding dew
At the hour before their breathless fall:
I was lovlier than these.
Now
I am foul in the eyes of the humblest creatures
To whom my shame is shown.
Unwelcome months and days pile over me
The wreck of a hundred years
In the city to avoid the eyes of men
Lest they should say "Can it be she?"

1097

In the evening
West with the moon I steal past the palace,
Past the towers
Where no guard will question in the mountains
In the shadows of the trees
None challenge so wretched a pilgrim as this
To Love's Tomb
The autumn hills
The River Katsura
Boats in the moonlight rowed by whom?
I cannot see. . . .
But rowed by whom!

Oh, too, too, painful. . . .
Here on this withered stump of tree
Let me sit and collect my senses.

First Priest:
Come on. The sun is down. We must hurry on our way. But look!
that old beggar woman sitting there on a sacred stupa. We should
warn her to come away.

Second Priest:
Yes, of course.

First Priest:
Excuse me, old lady, but don't you know that's a stupa there you're
sitting on? the holy image of the Buddha's incarnation. You'd better
come away and rest some other place.

Komachi:
The holy image of the Buddha you say? But I saw no words or
carvings on it. I took it for a tree stump only.

First Priest:
'Withered stumps
Are known as pine or cherry still
On the loneliest mountain.'

Komachi:
I, too, am a fallen tree.
But still the flowers of my heart
Might make some offering to the Buddha.
But this you call the Buddha's body. Why?

First Priest:
The stupa represents the body of Kongosatta Buddha, the Diamond

Lord, when he assumed the temporary form of each of his manifestations.

Komachi:
In what forms then is he manifested?

First Priest:
In Earth and Water and Wind and Fire and Space.

Komachi:
The same five elements as man. What was the difference then?

First Priest:
The form was the same but not the power.

Komachi:
And what is a stupa's power?

First Priest:
"He that has once looked upon a stupa shall for all eternity avoid the three worst catastrophes."

Komachi:
"One sudden thought can strike illumination."
Is that not just as good?

Second Priest:
If you've had such an illumination, why are you lingering here in this world of illusion?

Komachi:
Though my body lingers, my heart has left it long ago.

First Priest:
Unless you had no heart at all you wouldn't have failed to feel the presence of a stupa.

Komachi:
It was because I felt it that I came perhaps.

Second Priest:
In that case you shouldn't have spread yourself out on it without so much as a word of prayer.

Komachi:
It was on the ground already. . . .

First Priest:
Just the same it was an act of discord.

Komachi:
"Even from discord salvation springs."

Second Priest:
From the evil of Daiba

1099

Komachi:
Or the love of Kannon.
First Priest:
From the folly of Handoku
Komachi:
Or the wisdom of
Monju.
First Priest:
What we call evil
Komachi:
Is also good.
First Priest:
Illusion
Komachi:
Is Salvation.
Second Priest:
"Salvation
Komachi:
Cannot be watered like trees."
First Priest:
"The brightest mirror
Komachi:
Is not on the wall."
Chorus:
Nothing is separate.
Nothing persists.
Of Buddha and man there is no distinction,
At most a seeming difference planned
For the humble, ill-instructed men
He has vowed from the first to save.
"Even from discord salvation springs."
So said Komachi. And the priests:
"Surely this beggar is someone beyond us."
Then bending their heads to the ground
Three times did they do her homage
The difficult priests
The difficult priests
Who thought to correct her.
First Priest:
Who are you then? Give us your name; we will pray for your soul.

Komachi:

For all my shame I will tell you. Pray for the wreck of Komachi, the
daughter of Yoshizane of Ono, Lord of Dewa.

Both Priests:

How sad to think that you were she.

Exquisite Komachi

The brightest flower long ago

Her dark brows arched

Her face bright powdered always

When cedar-scented halls could scarce contain

Her damask robes.

Komachi:

I made verses in our speech

And in the speech of the foreign Court.

Chorus:

When she passed the banquet cup

Reflected moonlight lay on her sleeve.

How was ever such lovliness lost?

When did she change?

Her hair a tangle of frosted grass

Where the black curls lay on her neck

And the color lost from the twin arched peaks

Of her brow.

Komachi:

'Oh shameful in the dawning light

These silted seaweed locks that of a hundred years

Now lack but one.'

Chorus:

What do you have in the bag at your waist?

Komachi:

Death today or hunger tomorrow.

Only some beans I've put in my bag.

Chorus:

And in the bundle on you back?

Komachi:

A soiled and dusty robe.

Chorus:

And in the basket on your arm?

Komachi:

Sagittaries black and white.

1101

Chorus:
Tattered coat
Komachi:
Broken hat
Chorus:
Can scarcely hide her face.
Komachi:
Think of the frost and the snow and the rain.
I've not even sleeves enough to dry my tears.
But I wander begging things from men
That come and go along the road.
When begging fails
An awful madness seizes me
And my voice is no longer the same. . . .
          Hey! Give me something, you priests!
First Priest:
What do you want?
Komachi:
To go to Komachi!
First Priest:
What are you saying? You *are* Komachi!
Komachi:
No. Komachi was beautiful.
Many letters came, many messages
Thick as rain from a summer sky
But she made no answer, even once,
Even an empty word.
Age is her retribution now.
Oh, I love her!
I love her!
First Priest:
You love her! What spirit has possessed you to make you say such
things?
Komachi:
Many loved her
But among them all
It was Shosho who loved her deepest
Shii no Shosho, the Captain.
Chorus:
The wheel turns back.

I live again a cycle of unhappiness
Riding with the wheels
That came and went again each night.
The sun.
What time is it now?
Dusk.
The moon will be my friend on the road
And though the watchmen stand at the pass
They shall not bar my way.

Komachi: (*re-costumed as her lover*)
My wide white skirts hitched up

Chorus:
My wide white skirts hitched up
My tall black hat pulled down
And my sleeves thrown over my head
Hidden from the eyes of men on the road
In the moonlight
In the darkness coming, coming
When the night rains fell
When the night winds blew the leaves like rain
When the snow lay deep

Komachi:
And the melting drops fell
One by one from the rafters

Chorus:
I came and went, came and went
One night, two nights, three,
Ten (and this was the Harvest Night).
And did not see her.
Faithful as a cock that marks each dawn
I came and carved my mark upon the pillar.
I was to come a hundred nights,
I lacked but one. . . .
Oh, dizziness . . . pain. . . .

Chorus:
He was grieved at the pain in his breast
When the last night came and he died
Shii no Shosho, the Captain.

Komachi:
It was his unsatisfied love possessed me so

1103

His anger that turned my wits.
In the face of this I will pray
For life in the worlds to come
The sands of goodness I will pile
Into a towering hill.
Before the golden, gentle Buddha I will lay
Poems as my flowers
Entering in the way
Entering in the way

SEI SHONAGON

SEI SHONAGON (Japanese, *ca.* 966-1013). Early Japanese poetical court diarist. The daughter of a poet. Served as lady-in-waiting to the Empress. Her private sketchbook or diary later became celebrated literary work. It is made up of epigrammatic, anecdotal pictures of court life.

A CUCKOO PICNIC

SINCE the 1st May it had been raining or cloudy every day, and we were bored to death. I suggested that we should go and hear the cuckoo, and everyone was wildly excited at once and agreed, saying: "I too! I too!" Someone said: "Far away near Kamo River is a bridge. It is not called Tanabata's Bridge, but something like it and more difficult. However, near there the cuckoo sings nearly every day."

"No, no! It's only a cicada," said another. Anyway, we decided to go out there, and asked the officer on duty to order the carriage to the veranda.

"It would certainly be allowed, as it is raining," we said, and when the carriage came from the north guard-room it arrived at our veranda and four of us got in and started from the northern gate. The others said enviously: "What a pity we can't order another carriage and go together."

But the Empress said "No," so we paid no attention to this.

On our way past the racecourse we saw crowds of noisy people. "What can be going on?" we asked.

"They are practising archery on horseback. Pray stop and see," the man who runs beside the carriage answered. He stopped the

carriage, but we could see nothing of the General of the Left, who they said had arrived, and only a few sixth-grade people were strolling about.

"It isn't worth watching. Let us get on quickly," we agreed.

And on we went. This road is quite interesting about the time of Kamo festival.

"By and by we shall come to the house of the Empress's uncle," we said, and we got out of the carriage there.

Lord Akinobu Ason's house is built in the simplest way and very rustic—paper screens with pictures of horses, and others woven of strips of bamboo and fine grass-woven blinds, and so on. One could see they kept up the old customs, and the house itself had little spaciousness. Just as we were looking about us with interest the cuckoos burst into song with such zest as to be absolutely noisy. We were dreadfully sorry the Empress could not hear them, and also for those of us who had wanted to come and could not.

"Now you are in the country, you must see our country ways," said Akinobu Ason, and accordingly rice plants were brought and some cleanly dressed young women showed us how the stripping of the grain is done and how it is put into a kind of revolving machine. Two of them kept it turning while they marked time with a song. It was very curious, and we laughed so much that we quite forgot the cuckoo and the poems to be written about her.

Then in came food on the beautiful old tables one sees in Chinese pictures, but that did not interest any of us, and he said: "I know this is very countrified stuff, but the only way is to keep on attacking the host until he provides something you really like. If you have no appetite it is not like our usual City visitors."

So he cheered us on, saying: "These bracken fronds I picked myself."

"But surely you don't expect us to sit round the tables like common people," I remonstrated and at once he had the refreshment taken from the little tables.

"Why, no! one sees all of you are accustomed to the strictest etiquette in the August Presence," he said, and so served us separately.

While we were making merry we heard the driver calling: "It's going to rain," and out we all hurried and into the carriage.

"But I want to get my poem done before we start," I cried.

"No, No! On the way back!" someone said.

We picked any amount of lovely deutzia along the road and stuck

the sprays into the blinds and the sides of the carriage, and thatched the roofs with great boughs of it, until it looked exactly as if the carriage were covered with white damask. Our men, much interested, helped us, sticking the sprays into every crevice of the wickerwork, crying, "More, more. A bit just here!" thoroughly enjoying themselves.

In we all got, hoping to meet someone who would notice our display. But no one turned up. There were only dull priests and a few servants on the road. Such a pity! Presently we arrived at the East Ward and said to each other: "It will never do if we meet no one and not the least notice is taken of our gorgeously decorated carriage!"

So we stopped forthwith in front of the palace in that ward and asked for the Lord Chamberlain sending word by the messenger: "Is the Lord Chamberlain at home? We are just returning from a cuckoo picnic."

Back came the messenger.

"His Lordship says: 'I will come out at once.' Do please wait."

It seems he was putting on his ceremonial trousers in a hurry. So we thought there was no need to wait and whipping up set off for the Eastern Gate. And there he followed us, rushing down the road and tying his trousers as he ran. Behind him rushed his followers and valets. We urged the driver on, faster! faster! and when we arrived at the gate he overtook us, perfectly breathless. It was then he noticed the splendour of our carriage and said: "What in the world—! Are there common mortals in such a carriage? Do get out and let me see!"

And he and his followers laughed with delight over the joke.

"But your poems—your poems! I want to hear them now!" he begged.

"Now? Certainly not! Her Majesty will hear them first!" I said demurely.

The rain began to pelt while we were talking, and he said: "Why in the world has this gate no roof when every other gate is weatherproof? And to-day of all days, when we want shelter. And how am I to get home? I rushed out after you regardless of consequences, and what am I to do?"

We all chorused: "Come into the Palace!"

"And may I ask how I am to go there in a soft-crowned cap?"

"Send home for what you want," we suggested.

Down came the rain, and our men began pulling us with all

1106

speed. Off went the Lord Chamberlain, and under an umbrella. Slowly and reluctantly he trudged along, turning to look back with a spray of deutzia in his hand. It was very amusing.

In the Palace her Majesty asked for the story of our adventures, and we told the tale of the Lord Chamberlain and Ichijo Street. Everyone laughed, even the sulky stay-at-homes. But then came the question: "And where are the poems?"

Of course, it had to come out that we had made none. The Empress said at once; "Oh what a pity! All the officers will have heard of the picnic, and with what face can we say no poems came of such an adventure? You had much better have done it while the cuckoo was singing and you were considering it seriously. But set to work even now, for if not your visit will be wasted!"

Really, we had been idiots. And while we were regretting all this and consulting over poems, in comes a short poem from the Lord Chamberlain written on fine white flower-paper and fastened to the deutzia spray he had taken.

"The cuckoo's cry. Had I known you
were fled to seek it
I should have bid you carry my whole
heart's greeting today."

I thought the messenger might be waiting, so I sent someone hurrying for my writing-box, but the Empress said: "No—be quick. Use mine!"

And she did me the honor to slip in some paper. So I said to Saisho: "Be quick. Your turn, please."

"No, yours, please!" said she. And in the midst of our polite wrangling the sky grew black and the rain came down in sheets and the thunder roared so terrifically that we were frightened into rushing away to shut all the blinds and the outside doors in a perfect panic. And poetry was forgotten.

The thunder lasted so long that as it stopped darkness came on. And still we would have struggled with the poems but that many of the officers and other visitors came up to inquire for the Empress's health after the storm, and of course we had to meet them and do the honors, so again the poems went to the wall as far as I was concerned, and the other ladies did not trouble about it, for they declared the Lord Chamberlain's poem was addressed to me, and it was my business to answer. I was not in the mood for it, much as I regretted it.

1107

"I really wish no one knew anything about the picnic," I said, and the Empress retorted: "You could certainly patch up a poem among you. It is only that you don't care to."

I think she was a little cross. It was strange altogether.

"But we missed our chance, and now the mood has evaporated," I said.

"You mean your interest has evaporated," she said.

And there we left it.

Two days passed and we were discussing the cuckoo picnic. Saishō said: "But how did you like the bracken-shoots which our host said he had picked himself?"

The Empress, listening, said with a laugh: "I think your refreshments were the only things you remembered." And she scribbled the end of a verse on a piece of paper:

"The longing for the bracken haunts her memory still."

"Do be poetical and finish it!" she said.

It was really rather amusing, and I took my brush and wrote:

"And drowns the cuckoo's note we sallied out to hear."

"Candid enough!" said the laughing Empress. "But why didn't you remember the cuckoo as affectionately?"

I felt a little out of countenance.

"I don't know why," I said, "but I have a kind of feeling I shall compose no more short poems. I always am uncomfortable when the subject comes up and your Majesty commands me to set to work. Besides, how am I to do it when I am so stupid as to have no knowledge of metre and evolve a winter poem in spring and a spring one in autumn, and in plum-blossom time descant upon chrysanthemums? You see, my ancestor was a well-known poet, so that mine really ought to be better than others, and, if they were, one might really plume oneself when people said, 'This short poem absolutely fitted the occasion. But then, of course, she had the advantage of a poetical heritage.' But if one has no special aptitude and yet thinks oneself clever, and so composes at large, it really is a little hard on the ancestor!"

The Empress laughed and answered: "Well, well! Do as you please. I shall not insist on your poetising any more!"

So I was feeling easier in my mind.

But while all this was in my head the Empress's brother was eagerly preparing to hold the All Night Waking. As it grew late a

competition for short poems was announced, and all the ladies asked
to compete. Great excitement! I was there and talking to the Empress about something else, when the Prince came up to me and
said: "Why, is it possible you are not going to write us a poem?
Do, I beseech you!"

I answered: "I have been honored by permission to do exactly
as I please, and so I am not going to write. I have not one idea
to rattle on another."

"But how extraordinary! Do you really mean to say you have
permission to be dumb? Did her Majesty give it? I don't so much
mind about other times, but to-night of all times you cannot refuse!"

He was as eager as possible and I as decided! While they were
criticising the other poems the Empress wrote me a tiny note. I
opened it at once and found this:

"Even though a descendant of the famous Motosuke,
Why—why not join in the battle of the poems to-night?"

I was really obliged to laugh. It was so very amusing, and the
Prince called out: "But what is it? What is it?"

[I wrote:]

"If I had not the reputation of my heritage to consider,
Would I not gaily join in the battle of poems to-night?"

And I said to the Empress: "If I had not this incubus of reputation
to keep up, I would turn out thousands of poems on the spot."

MENDELE MOCHER SFORIM

MENDELE MOCHER SFORIM (Shalom Jacob Abramowitsch, Lithuanian-
Hebrew, 1836-1917). Yiddish folklorist, sometimes called the grandfather of
Yiddish literature. Earlier works, written in Hebrew, helped revive that
language as a literary medium. He then transformed Yiddish from a colloquial
tongue to an exact literary form. Introduced the novel of social criticism.
Novels: *Dos Kleine Menshele, Die Takse, Die Klyatsche.*

THE NAG

THIS is Mendele the book peddler speaking. Glory be to the Creator!
For, after His creation of all this enormous universe, He took
counsel with His host of heavenly angels and did create a universe

1109

in-little—by which you may take to mean man, who is justly called *olam katan* (a microcosm), since man, if you look at him closely, combines in himself all species of creatures and creations. You will find in him all possible wild beasts, as well as all the different breeds of cattle. You will find in him the lizard, the leech, the Spanish fly, the Prussian cockroach, and, to top it all off, a devil and a werewolf, a clown, a Jew-baiter, and many another uncanny foe of man and scourge of God. You will see, as well, among these universes-in-little all sorts of amazing sights. Here's a tomcat, for instance, playing with a baby mouse; here's a polecat making its way into a hencoop and sinking its teeth into the necks of the poor little fowl; here's a monkey mimicking and mocking everyone in sight; here's a dog standing up on its hind legs and wagging its tail for anybody who throws it a crust; here's a spider leading a fly astray, enmeshing it, strangling it, and sucking all the juices out of it; here are midges, overtaking a passer-by and humming all sorts of secrets in his ears; here are thousands of things no less amazing.

However, that's not at all what I'm leading up to.

Glory to the Holy Name (I have said), Who contemplates in silence all that is going on in this universe-in-little and still does not give it the quietus, and puts off His wrath, and tolerates transgressions, and evinces not a little mercy toward man the imperfect. In short, I was about to tell you, at this point, of a certain great favor bestowed upon me right after He had, at first, chastised me just a little.

My little nag, kind masters, is no more. My faithful horse, who passed all the days of her life in righteous toil, who served me faithfully and truly, who could have given pointers in topography to the natives of all the tiny hamlets and crossroads settlements, who was a remarkable connoisseur of little wayside inns, who had, in my company, crisscrossed almost all the pales of Israel, who was personally known to almost all of our orthodox communities— my poor nag departed this life one fine day, as a matter of fact it was on Lag Baomer, in the town of Glupsk [Foolstown]. It is painful to give the reason; poverty, however, is no disgrace; the poor little thing simply passed away from starvation. Her daily fodder consisted of chopped straw, and only on rare occasions would there fall to her lot a few dry crusts of bread that I had bought from beggars who wandered about with sacks over their shoulders. Ah, woe to the horse that falls into the hands of a peddler of Jewish books!

A wanderer, she wanders without end and in all probability labors more than her fellow creatures who draw wares more choice than ours and yet she is supposed to exist on practically nothing. A Jewish bookman lives all his life on virtually the same footing, and, one might say, he himself, with his wife and children, dies from hunger ten times a day. . . .

However, that's still not what I'm leading up to.

The Lord (I have said) sent me a visitation. I was left without a horse, had nothing with which to buy another, and yet I had to get to the fairs in time. As you can see, I was up against it.

And there I was, sitting all by myself in the House of Prayer, in low spirits, when suddenly a friend of mine walked in, headed straight for me, and asked:

"Reb Mendele, would you like to buy a nag, maybe?"

"I'd buy it with pleasure," I answered with a sigh, "but where would I get the money?"

"Bah!" said he. "That's no trouble at all. You won't have to pay a copper of spot cash. It's quite possible they'll lend you a little something besides. Never fear, they know you're an honest man."

"In that case," I said, "I am most willing to buy your nag right now, without any further beating around the bush. Well, let's go, if you please—we'll have a look at her."

"Why, there's no need of putting yourself out, actually. I have the nag right here with me. . . ."

"What do you mean, you have it here with you?" I voiced my astonishment.

"Why, right here—inside my coat," my friend smiled.

"Are you laughing at me or what?" I asked in vexation. "Look for someone else to make fun of—I don't find your little jokes at all entertaining right now."

"God forbid! I'm not joking at all," said my friend, and took from under his coat a whole stack of papers. "You see, Reb Mendele, all this belongs to a certain gentleman, a good friend of mine—you'll find his name right here on his stories. And it is one of these tales that bears the title, *The Nag*. The man who wrote it is, at present— and may this never be said of you!— he is . . . well, how am I to put it to you? He has bees in his bonnet, as the saying goes, but just the same, we who are his good friends would very much like to see his stories in print, as is fit and proper. To whom else were we to turn in this matter but to you, Reb Mendele, who enjoys such

1111

well-earned prestige in our region? We are asking you to go through these stories quite thoroughly and put them in shape. We rely upon you in this. You can go right ahead and print *The Nag*. We'll talk over the terms later, and I can assure you that you won't be out anything. If you need some money right now, why, we won't quibble over a small amount. Well, now, do you want to do it, Reb Mendele?"

"Do I? What a question, really! I want to with all my heart," I answered, and almost launched into a dance, so overjoyed was I.

I attended to my affairs and, full of zeal, tackled *The Nag*. I spared no labor and did my work properly.

And now, gentlemen, just a word or two concerning *The Nag*.

The Nag is written in a high-flown manner, after the fashion in which the ancients wrote. Each man will understand it in his own way and in keeping with his common sense. For honest folk who don't go grabbing at the stars in the sky, it will be simply a fairy tale. Those who look deeper may find in it a reflection of all of us who are sinners. Take me, now—I have seen in the nag all our little Jewish souls and have grasped the secret of why they exist in this world. I'm ready to wager that, in turning the pages of this book, many of us—each according to his nature—will exclaim vehemently: "Why, this aimed at our Nusen Reb Heikes"—"—at our Zalman Yukele Reb Moteles"—"—at Hershke Reb Abeles." Still others will declare: "He has discovered the secret of our poor-box collections, of our benevolent city fathers and all our lovely ways," and so on and on.

That's the sort of problem I posed to the Rabbinical judiciary in the town of Glupsk and to all the bigwigs in the vicinity. "As you know," I told them, "at the time I put out *The Tax*, I promised the public a sequel. It was more than a promise. It was a vow. Tell me, my dear sirs, what's the proper, lawful thing to do now? I am publishing *The Nag*. May I consider that I have fulfilled my promise concerning a sequel to *The Tax*?"

Well, they certainly pondered, and then pondered some more. They scratched and scratched behind their ears and, at last, came to a decision. "Yes, Reb Mendele," they answered, "after due deliberation, we do hereby release you from your vow. Let *The Nag* be considered the equivalent of your having kept your word, as if you had turned out the second part of *The Tax* and everything appertaining thereto. The thing isn't so bad, really, and, after all, you've appealed to almost every taste."

1112

How many thanks, then, should I render to the All Highest! Had I acquired *The Nag* just so, without any deposit toward the purchase of a horse, it would have been well. Had I acquired it with a small deposit, but it did not serve as a substitute for the second part of *The Tax*, and had the Rabbinical judiciary not absolved me of my vow without scratching behind their ears, that, too, would have been well. And even if they had scratched, but had given no reason for doing so, even then everything would have been well.

And therefore I should render thanks to the All Highest over and over again, because *The Nag* did have something of *The Tax* about it, and because the Rabbinical judiciary had released me from my vow, and because they did scratch themselves most horrendously as they gave me absolution, and because I know why they scratched themselves and understand that *The Nag* is worth scratching oneself behind the ear about . . . by way of redemption for all our transgressions.

That, gentlemen, is precisely what I wanted to say right out in my brief foreword. Whatever I have in mind is on the tip of my tongue.

Humbly,
Mendele the Book Peddler

Written the first day of the month
of Elul, in a cart laden with books,
on the road between the town of Glupsk
and Teterevka (Grouseville).

WILLIAM SHAKESPEARE

WILLIAM SHAKESPEARE (English, 1564-1616). The Bard of England, against whose works all English poetry and drama are measured. Little known of his life, except that he was an actor and playwright. His understanding of humanity unsurpassed, his dramatic and lyric poetry the finest flower of Elizabethan Age. Used every form of his time: The great tragedies: *Hamlet, Othello, Macbeth, King Lear.* Comedies: *Twelfth Night, A Midsummer Night's Dream.* Historicals: *Henry IV* and *V.* Romantic drama: *The Tempest.*

Speech by John of Gaunt from *King Richard the Second*

This royal throne of kings, this scepter'd isle,
This earth of majesty, this seat of Mars,

This other Eden, demi-paradise,
This fortress built by Nature for herself
Against infection and the hand of war,
This happy breed of men, this little world,
This precious stone set in the silver sea,
Which serves it in the office of a wall,
Or as a moat defensive to a house,
Against the envy of less happier lands,
This blessed plot, this earth, this realm, this England,
This nurse, this teeming womb of royal kings,
Fear'd by their breed and famous by their birth,
Renowned for their deeds as far from home,—
For Christian service and true chivalry,—
As is the sepulchre in stubborn Jewry
Of the world's ransom, blessed Mary's Son:
This land of such dear souls, this dear, dear land,
Dear for her reputation through the world,
Is now leas'd out,—I die pronouncing it,—
Like to a tenement, or pelting farm:
England, bound in with the triumphant sea,
Whose rocky shore beats back the envious siege
Of watery Neptune, is now bound in with shame,
With inky blots, and rotten parchment bonds:
That England, that was wont to conquer others,
Hath made a shameful conquest of itself.

Speech by Prince Henry over the body of Hotspur **from**
King Henry the Fourth, Part I

. . . Fare thee well, great heart!
Ill-weaved ambition, how much art thou shrunk!
When that this body did contain a spirit,
A kingdom for it was too small a bound;
But now two paces of the vilest earth
Is room enough: this earth that bears thee dead
Bears not alive so stout a gentleman.
If thou wert sensible of courtesy,
I should not make so dear a show of zeal:
But let my favours hide thy mangled face;
And, even in thy behalf, I'll thank myself
For doing these fair rites of tenderness.

Adieu, and take thy praise with thee to heaven!
Thy ignomy sleep with thee in the grave,
But not remember'd in thy epitaph!

Speech by Berowne from *Love's Labour's Lost*

Why, all delights are vain; but that most vain,
Which, with pain purchased, doth inherit pain:
As, painfully to pore upon a book
To seek the light of truth; while truth the while
Doth falsely blind the eyesight of his look:
Light, seeking light, doth light of light beguile:
So, ere you find where light in darkness lies,
Your light grows dark by losing of your eyes.
Study me how to please the eye indeed,
By fixing it upon a fairer eye;
Who dazzling so, that eye shall be his heed,
And give him light that it was blinded by.
Study is like the heaven's glorious sun,
That will not be deep-search'd with saucy looks:
Small have continual plodders ever won,
Save base authority from others' books.
These earthly godfathers of heaven's lights,
That give a name to every fixèd star,
Have no more profit of their shining nights
Than those that walk and wot not what they are.
Too much to know, is to know naught but fame;
And every godfather can give a name.

Speech by the Archbishop of Canterbury from *King Henry the Fifth*

Therefore doth heaven divide
The state of man in divers functions,
Setting endeavour in continual motion;
To which is fixèd, as an aim or butt,
Obedience: for so work the honey-bees,
Creatures that by a rule in nature teach
The act of order to a peopled kingdom.
They have a king and officers of sorts;
Where some, like magistrates, correct at home,
Others, like merchants, venture trade abroad,
Others, like soldiers, armed in their stings,

1115

Make boot upon the summer's velvet buds;
Make pillage they with merry march bring home
To the tent-royal of their emperor:
Who, busied in his majesty, surveys
The singing masons building roofs of gold,
The civil citizens kneading up the honey,
The poor mechanic porters crowding in
Their heavy burdens at his narrow gate,
The sad-ey'd justice, with his surly hum,
Delivering o'er to executors pale
The lazy yawning drone. I this infer
That many things, having all reference
To one consent, may work contrariously;
As many arrows, loosèd several ways,
Fly to one mark; as many ways meet in one town;
As many fresh streams meet in one salt sea;
As many lines close in the dial's centre;
So may a thousand actions, once afoot,
End in one purpose, and be all well borne
Without defeat.

Speech by Titania from *A Midsummer Night's Dream*

These are the forgeries of jealousy:
And never, since the middle summer's spring,
Met we on hill, in dale, forest, or mead,
By pavéd fountain or by rushy brook,
Or in the beached margent of the sea,
To dance our ringlets to the whistling wind,
But with thy brawls thou hast disturb'd our sport.
Therefore the winds, piping to us in vain,
As in revenge, have suck'd up from the sea
Contagious fogs; which falling in the land,
Hath every pelting river made so proud,
That they have overborne their continents:
The ox hath therefore stretch'd his yoke in vain,
The ploughman lost his sweat; and the green corn
Hath rotted ere his youth attain'd a beard:
The fold stands empty in the drownéd field,
And crows are fatted with the murrion flock;
The nine-men's-morris is fill'd up with mud;

1116

And the quaint mazes in the wanton green,
For lack of tread, are undistinguishable:
The human mortals want their winter here;
No night is now with hymn or carol blest:—
Therefore the moon, the governess of floods,
Pale in her anger, washes all the air,
That rheumatic diseases do abound:
And thorough this distemperature we see
The seasons alter: hoary-headed frosts
Fall in the fresh lap of the crimson rose;
And on old Hiems' thin and icy crown
An odorous chaplet of sweet summer buds
Is, as in mockery, set: the spring, the summer,
The childing autumn, angry winter, change
Their wonted liveries; and the mazèd world,
By their increase, now knows not which is which:
And this same progeny of evil comes
From our debate, from our dissension;
We are their parents and original.

Speech by Jaques from *As You Like It*

                All the world's a stage,
And all the men and women merely players;
They have their exits and their entrances;
And one man in his time plays many parts,
His acts being seven ages. At first the infant,
Mewling and puking in the nurse's arms.
And then the whining school-boy with his satchel,
And shining morning face, creeping like snail,
Unwillingly to school. And then the lover,
Sighing like furnace, with a woful ballad,
Made to his mistress' eyebrow. Then a soldier,
Full of strange oaths, and bearded like the pard,
Jealous in honour, sudden and quick in quarrel,
Seeking the bubble reputation
Even in the cannon's mouth. And then the justice,
In fair round belly with good capon lin'd,
With eyes severe, and beard of formal cut,
Full of wise saws and modern instances;

And so he plays his part. The sixth age shifts
Into the lean and slipper'd pantaloon,
With spectacles on nose and pouch on side,
His youthful hose well sav'd, a world too wide
For his shrunk shank; and his big manly voice,
Turning again toward childish treble, pipes
And whistles in his sound. Last scene of all,
That ends this strange eventful history,
Is second childishness and mere oblivion,
Sans teeth, sans eyes, sans taste, sans everything.

Clown's Songs from *Twelfth Night*

I

O mistress mine! where are you roaming?
O! stay and hear; your true love's coming,
   That can sing both high and low.
Trip no further, pretty sweeting;
Journeys end in lovers meeting,
   Every wise man's son doth know.

What is love? 'tis not hereafter;
Present mirth hath present laughter;
   What's to come is still unsure.
In delay there lies no plenty;
Then come kiss me, sweet-and-twenty,
   Youth's a stuff will not endure.

IV

Come away, come away, death,
   And in sad cypress let me be laid.
Fly away, fly away, breath;
   I am slain by a fair cruel maid.
My shroud of white, stuck all with yew,
    O! prepare it.
My part of death, no one so true
    Did share it.

Not a flower, not a flower sweet,
  On my black coffin let there be strown;
Not a friend, not a friend greet
  My poor corse, where my bones shall be thrown.
A thousand thousand sighs to save,
    Lay me, O! where
Sad true lover never find my grave,
    To weep there.

Soliloquy by Ophelia from *Hamlet*

O, what a noble mind is here o'erthrown!
The courtier's, soldier's, scholar's eye, tongue, sword;
Th' expectancy and rose of the fair state,
The glass of fashion and the mould of form,
The observ'd of all observers,—quite, quite down!
And I, of ladies most deject and wretched,
That suckt the honey of his music vows,
Now see that noble and most sovereign reason,
Like sweet bells jangled, out of tune and harsh;
That unmatcht form and feature of blown youth
Blasted with ecstasy: O, woe is me
To have seen what I have seen, see what I see!

Speech by King Lear from *King Lear*

You see me here, you gods, a poor old man,
As full of grief as age; wretched in both!
If it be you that stir these daughters' hearts
Against their father, fool me not so much
To bear it tamely; touch me with noble anger,
And let not women's weapons, water-drops,
Stain my man's cheeks! No, you unnatural hags,
I will have such revenges on you both
That all the world shall—I will do such things,—
What they are yet I know not,—but they shall be
The terrors of the earth. You think I'll weep;
No, I'll not weep:
I have full cause of weeping, but this heart
Shall break into a hundred thousand flaws
Or ere I'll weep. O fool! I shall go mad.

1119

Speech by Coriolanus from *Coriolanus*

You common cry of curs! whose breath I hate
As reek o' the rotten fens, whose loves I prize
As the dead carcases of unburied men
That do corrupt my air, I banish you;
And here remain with your uncertainty!
Let every feeble rumour shake your hearts!
Your enemies, with nodding of their plumes,
Fan you into despair! Have the power still
To banish your defenders; till at length
Your ignorance,—which finds not, till it feels,—
Making but reservation of yourselves,—
Still your own foes,—deliver you as most
Abated captives to some nation
That won you without blows! Despising,
For you, the city, thus I turn my back:
There is a world elsewhere.

Speech by Prince Henry from *King John*

O vanity of sickness! fierce extremes
In their continuance will not feel themselves.
Death, having prey'd upon the outward parts,
Leaves them invisible; and his siege is now
Against the mind, the which he pricks and wounds
With many legions of strange fantasies,
Which, in their throng and press to that last hold,
Confound themselves. 'Tis strange that death should sing.
I am the cygnet to this pale faint swan,
Who chants a doleful hymn to his own death,
And from the organ-pipe of frailty sings
His soul and body to their lasting rest.

Speech by King Henry from *King Henry the Sixth, Part III*

This battle fares like to the morning's war,
When dying clouds contend with growing light,
What time the shepherd, blowing of his nails,

1120

Can neither call it perfect day nor night.
Now sways it this way, like a mighty sea
Forc'd by the tide to combat with the wind;
Now sways it that way, like the self-same sea
Forc'd to retire by fury of the wind:
Sometime the flood prevails, and then the wind;
Now one the better, then another best;
Both tugging to be victors, breast to breast,
Yet neither conqueror nor conqueréd:
So is the equal poise of this fell war.
Here on this molehill will I sit me down.
To whom God will, there be the victory!
For Margaret my queen, and Clifford too,
Have chid me from the battle; swearing both
They prosper best of all when I am thence.
Would I were dead! if God's good will were so;
For what is in this world but grief and woe?
O God! methinks it were a happy life,
To be no better than a homely swain;
To sit upon a hill, as I do now,
To carve out dials quaintly, point by point,
Thereby to see the minutes how they run,
How many make the hour full complete;
How many hours bring about the day;
How many days will finish up the year;
How many years a mortal man may live.
When this is known, then to divide the times:
So many hours must I tend my flock;
So many hours must I take my rest;
So many hours must I contemplate;
So many hours must I sport myself;
So many days my ewes have been with young;
So many weeks ere the poor fools will ean;
So many years ere I shall shear the fleece:
So minutes, hours, days, months, and years,
Pass'd over to the end they were created,
Would bring white hairs unto a quiet grave.
Ah! what a life were this! how sweet! how lovely!
Gives not the hawthorn bush a sweeter shade
To shepherds looking on their silly sheep,
Than doth a rich embroider'd canopy

To kings, that fear their subjects' treachery?
O, yes! it doth; a thousand-fold it doth.
And to conclude, the shepherd's homely curds,
His cold thin drink out of his leather bottle,
His wonted sleep under a fresh tree's shade,
All which secure and sweetly he enjoys,
Is far beyond a prince's delicates,
His viands sparkling in a golden cup,
His body couchéd in a curious bed,
When care, mistrust, and treason wait on him.

"Blow, Winds" from *King Lear*

Blow, winds, and crack your cheeks! rage! blow!
You cataracts and hurricanoes, spout
Till you have drenched our steeples, drowned the cocks!
You sulphurous and thought-executing fires,
Vaunt-couriers to oak-cleaving thunderbolts,
Singe my white head! And thou, all-shaking thunder,
Smite flat the thick rotundity o' the world!
Crack nature's molds, all germins spill at once
That make ingrateful man! . . .
Rumble thy bellyful! Spit, fire! spout, rain!
Nor rain, wind, thunder, fire, are my daughters:
I tax not you, you elements, with unkindness;
I never gave you kingdom, called you children,
You owe me no subscription: then let fall
Your horrible pleasure; here I stand, your slave,
A poor, infirm, weak and despised old man:
But yet I call you servile ministers,
That have with two pernicious daughters joined
Your high-engendered battles 'gainst a head
So old and white as this. O! O! 'tis foul!

Portrait of Brutus from *Julius Caesar*

This was the noblest Roman of them all:
All the conspirators, save only he,
Did that they did in envy of great Cæsar;

1122

He only, in a general honest thought
And common good to all, made one of them.
His life was gentle, and the elements
So mixed in him that Nature might stand up
And say to all the world "This was a man!"

Portrait of Caesar from *Julius Caesar*

Why, man, he doth bestride the narrow world
Like a Colossus, and we petty men
Walk under his huge legs and peep about
To find ourselves dishonorable graves.
Men at some time are masters of their fates:
The fault, dear Brutus, is not in our stars,
But in ourselves, that we are underlings.
Brutus, and Cæsar: what should be in that Cæsar?
Why should that name be sounded more than yours?
Write them together, yours is as fair a name;
Sound them, it doth become the mouth as well;
Weigh them, it is as heavy; conjure with 'em,
Brutus will start a spirit as soon as Cæsar.
Now, in the names of all the gods at once,
Upon what meat doth this our Cæsar feed,
That he is grown so great? Age, thou art shamed!
Rome, thou hast lost the breed of noble bloods!
When went there by an age, since the great flood,
But it was famed with more than with one man?
When could they say till now that talked of Rome
That her wide walls encompassed but one man?
Now is it Rome indeed, and room enough,
When there is in it but one only man.

"Fear" from *Julius Caesar*

Cowards die many times before their death;
The valiant never taste of death but once.
Of all the wonders that I yet have heard,
It seems to me most strange that men should fear;
Seeing that death, a necessary end,
Will come when it will come.

Anthony's Oration from *Julius Caesar*

Friends, Romans, countrymen, lend me your ears;
I come to bury Cæsar, not to praise him.
The evil that men do lives after them;
The good is oft interred with their bones;
So let it be with Cæsar. The noble Brutus
Hath told you Cæsar was ambitious:
If it were so, it was a grievous fault,
And grievously hath Cæsar answered it.
Here, under leave of Brutus and the rest—
For Brutus is an honorable man;
So are they all, all honorable men—
Come I to speak in Cæsar's funeral.
He was my friend, faithful and just to me:
But Brutus says he was ambitious;
And Brutus is an honorable man.
He hath brought many captives home to Rome,
Whose ransoms did the general coffers fill:
Did this in Cæsar seem ambitious?
When that the poor have cried, Cæsar hath wept:
Ambition should be made of sterner stuff:
Yet Brutus says he was ambitious;
And Brutus is an honorable man.
You all did see that on the Lupercal
I thrice presented him a kingly crown,
Which he did thrice refuse: was this ambition?
Yet Brutus says he was ambitious;
And, sure, he is an honorable man.
I speak not to disprove what Brutus spoke,
But here I am to speak what I do know.
You all did love him once, not without cause:
What cause withholds you then to mourn for him?
O judgment! thou art fled to brutish beasts,
And men have lost their reason. Bear with me;
My heart is in the coffin there with Cæsar,
And I must pause till it come back to me.

If you have tears, prepare to shed them now.
You all do know this mantle: I remember
The first time ever Cæsar put it on;
'Twas on a summer's evening, in his tent,

That day he overcame the Nervii:
Look, in this place ran Cassius' dagger through:
See what a rent the envious Casca made:
Through this the well-beloved Brutus stabbed;
And as he plucked his cursed steel away,
Mark how the blood of Cæsar followed it,
As rushing out of doors, to be resolved
If Brutus so unkindly knocked, or no:
For Brutus, as you know, was Cæsar's angel:
Judge, O you gods, how dearly Cæsar loved him!
This was the most unkindest cut of all;
For when the noble Cæsar saw him stab,
Ingratitude, more strong than traitors' arms,
Quite vanquished him: then burst his mighty heart;
And, in his mantle muffling up his face,
Even at the base of Pompey's statue,
Which all the while ran blood, great Cæsar fell.
O, what a fall was there, my countrymen!
Then I, and you, and all of us fell down,
Whilst bloody treason flourished over us.

"I Have Lived Long Enough" from *Macbeth*

I have lived long enough: my way of life
Is fallen into the sere, the yellow leaf,
And that which should accompany old age,
As honor, love, obedience, troops of friends,
I must not look to have; but, in their stead,
Curses, not loud but deep, mouth-honor, breath,
Which the poor heart would fain deny, and dare not.

Canst thou not minister to a mind diseased,
Pluck from the memory a rooted sorrow,
Raze out the written troubles of the brain,
And with some sweet oblivious antidote
Cleanse the stuffed bosom of that perilous stuff
Which weighs upon the heart?

"Tomorrow, and Tomorrow, and Tomorrow" from *Macbeth*

Tomorrow, and tomorrow, and tomorrow,
Creeps in this petty pace from day to day,

To the last syllable of recorded time;
And all our yesterdays have lighted fools
The way to dusty death. Out, out, brief candle!
Life's but a walking shadow, a poor player
That struts and frets his hour upon the stage
And then is heard no more: it is a tale
Told by an idiot, full of sound and fury,
Signifying nothing.

"This Above All" from *Hamlet*

And these few precepts in thy memory
See thou character. Give thy thoughts no tongue,
Nor any unproportioned thought his act.
Be thou familiar, but by no means vulgar.
Those friends thou hast, and their adoption tried,
Grapple them to thy soul with hoops of steel,
But do not dull thy palm with entertainment
Of each new-hatched unfledged comrade. Beware
Of entrance to a quarrel; but being in,
Bear't, that the opposed may beware of thee.
Give every man thy ear, but few thy voice:
Take each man's censure, but reserve thy judgment.
Costly thy habit as thy purse can buy,
But not expressed in fancy; rich, not gaudy:
For the apparel oft proclaims the man;
And they in France of the best rank and station
Are most select and generous in that.
Neither a borrower nor a lender be:
For loan oft loses both itself and friend,
And borrowing dulls the edge of husbandry.
This above all: to thine own self be true,
And it must follow, as the night the day,
Thou canst not then be false to any man.

"Frailty, Thy Name Is Woman" from *Hamlet*

O, that this too too solid flesh would melt,
Thaw and resolve itself into a dew!
Or that the Everlasting had not fix'd
His canon 'gainst self-slaughter! O God! O God!

How weary, stale, flat and unprofitable
Seem to me all the uses of this world!
Fie on't! oh fie! 'tis an unweeded garden,
That grows to seed; things rank and gross in nature
Possess it merely. That it should come to this!
But two months dead! nay, not so much, not two:
So excellent a king; that was, to this,
Hyperion to a satyr: so loving to my mother,
That he might not beteem the winds of heaven
Visit her face too roughly. Heaven and earth!
Must I remember? why, she would hang on him,
As if increase of appetite had grown
By what it fed on: and yet, within a month—
Let me not think on't—Frailty, thy name is woman!—
A little month, or ere those shoes were old
With which she follow'd my poor father's body,
Like Niobe, all tears:—why she, even she—
O God! a beast that wants discourse of reason
Would have mourned longer—married with my uncle,
My father's brother, but no more like my father
Than I to Hercules: within a month;
Ere yet the salt of most unrighteous tears
Had left the flushing in her galled eyes,
She married. O, most wicked speed, to post
With such dexterity to incestuous sheets!
It is not, nor it cannot come to good:
But break, my heart, for I must hold my tongue!

"To Be, Or Not To Be" from *Hamlet*

To be, or not to be: that is the question:
Whether 'tis nobler in the mind to suffer
The slings and arrows of outrageous fortune,
Or to take arms against a sea of troubles,
And by opposing end them. To die: to sleep;
No more; and by a sleep to say we end
The heart-ache, and the thousand natural shocks
That flesh is heir to. 'Tis a consummation
Devoutly to be wish'd. To die, to sleep;
To sleep? Perchance to dream! aye, there's the rub;

For in that sleep of death what dreams may come,
When we have shuffled off this mortal coil,
Must give us pause: there's the respect
That makes calamity of so long life;
For who would bear the whips and scorns of time,
The oppressor's wrong, the proud man's contumely,
The pangs of despised love, the law's delay,
The insolence of office, and the spurns
That patient merit of the unworthy takes,
When he himself might his quietus make
With a bare bodkin? who would fardels bear,
To grunt and sweat under a weary life,
But that the dread of something after death,
The undiscovered country from whose bourn
No traveler returns, puzzles the will,
And makes us rather bear those ills we have
Than fly to others that we know not of?
Thus conscience does make cowards of us all,
And thus the native hue of resolution
Is sicklied o'er with the pale cast of thought,
And enterprises of great pitch and moment
With this regard their currents turn awry
And lose the name of action.

GEORGE BERNARD SHAW

GEORGE BERNARD SHAW (Irish, 1856-1950). Leading English dramatist, novelist and critic. Wit and reformer as well. First worked as music critic and founded Socialist Fabian Society. Propagandistic prefaces to his plays are sometimes more brilliant than the plays. Disciple of Ibsen, but created own witty drama of ideas. Most-praised works: *St. Joan, Pygmalion, Major Barbara, Candida, Caesar and Cleopatra, Man and Superman.*

THE MIRACULOUS REVENGE

I ARRIVED in Dublin on the evening of the 5th of August, and drove to the residence of my uncle, the Cardinal Archbishop. He is, like most of my family, deficient in feeling, and consequently cold to me personally. He lives in a dingy house, with a side-long view of

the portico of his cathedral from the front windows, and of a monster national school from the back. My uncle maintains no retinue. The people believe that he is waited upon by angels. When I knocked at the door, an old woman, his only servant, opened it, and informed me that her master was then officiating in the cathedral, and that he had directed her to prepare dinner for me in his absence. An unpleasant smell of salt fish made me ask her what the dinner consisted of. She assured me that she had cooked all that could be permitted in His Holiness's house on a Friday. On my asking her further why on a Friday, she replied that Friday was a fast day. I bade her tell His Holiness that I had hoped to have the pleasure of calling on him shortly, and drove to a hotel in Sackville Street, where I engaged apartments and dined.

After dinner I resumed my eternal search—I know not for what; it drives me to and fro like another Cain. I sought in the streets without success. I went to the theatre. The music was execrable, the scenery poor. I had seen the play a month before in London, with the same beautiful artist in the chief part. Two years had passed since, seeing her for the first time, I had hoped that she, perhaps, might be the long-sought mystery. It had proved otherwise. On this night I looked at her and listened to her for the sake of that bygone hope, and applauded her generously when the curtain fell. But I went out lonely still. When I had supped at a restaurant, I returned to my hotel, and tried to read. In vain. The sound of feet in the corridors as the other occupants of the hotel went to bed distracted my attention from my book. Suddenly it occurred to me that I had never quite understood my uncle's character. He, father to a great flock of poor and ignorant Irish; an austere and saintly man, to whom livers of hopeless lives daily appealed for help heavenward; who was reputed never to have sent away a troubled peasant without relieving him of his burden by sharing it; whose knees were worn less by the altar steps than by the tears and embraces of the guilty and wretched: he had refused to humour my light extravagances, or to find time to talk with me of books, flowers, and music. Had I not been mad to expect it? Now that I needed sympathy myself, I did him justice. I desired to be with a true-hearted man, and to mingle my tears with his.

I looked at my watch. It was nearly an hour past midnight. In the corridor the lights were out, except one jet at the end. I threw a cloak upon my shoulders, put on a Spanish hat, and left my apartment, listening to the echoes of my measured steps retreating

through the deserted passages. A strange sight arrested me on the landing of the grand staircase. Through an open door I saw the moonlight shining through the windows of a saloon in which some entertainment had recently taken place. I looked at my watch again. It was but one o'clock; and yet the guests had departed. I entered the room, my boots ringing loudly on the waxed boards. On a chair lay a child's clock and a broken toy. The entertainment had been a children's party. I stood for a time looking at the shadow of my cloaked figure upon the floor, and at the disordered decorations, ghostly in the white light. Then I saw that there was a grand piano, still open, in the middle of the room. My fingers throbbed as I sat down before it, and expressed all that I felt in a grand hymn which seemed to thrill the cold stillness of the shadows into a deep hum of approbation, and to people the radiance of the moon with angels. Soon there was a stir without too, as if the rapture was spreading abroad. I took up the chant triumphantly with my voice, and the empty saloon resounded as though to the thunder of an orchestra.

"Hallo, sir!" "Confound you, sir—" "Do you suppose that this—" "What the deuce—?"

I turned, and silence followed. Six men, partially dressed, and with dishevelled hair, stood regarding me angrily. They all carried candles. One of them had a bootjack, which he held like a truncheon. Another, the foremost, had a pistol. The night porter was behind trembling.

"Sir," said the man with the revolver, coarsely, "may I ask whether you are mad, that you disturb people at this hour with such an unearthly noise?"

"Is it possible that you dislike it?" I replied, courteously.

"Dislike it!" said he, stamping with rage. "Why—damn everything—do you suppose we were enjoying it?"

"Take care. He's mad," whispered the man with the bootjack.

I began to laugh. Evidently they did think me mad. Unaccustomed to my habits, and ignorant of music as they probably were, the mistake, however absurd, was not unnatural. I rose. They came closer to one another; and the night porter ran away.

"Gentlemen," I said, "I am sorry for you. Had you lain still and listened, we should all have been the better and happier. But what you have done, you cannot undo. Kindly inform the night porter that I am gone to visit my uncle, the Cardinal Archbishop. Adieu!"

I strode past them, and left them whispering among themselves.

1130

Some minutes later I knocked at the door of the Cardinal's house. Presently a window on the first floor was opened; and the moonbeams fell on a grey head, with a black cap that seemed ashy pale against the unfathomable gloom of the shadow beneath the stone sill.

"Who are you?"

"I am Zeno Legge."

"What do you want at this hour?"

The question wounded me. "My dear uncle," I exclaimed, "I know you do not intend it, but you make me feel unwelcome. Come down and let me in, I beg."

"Go to your hotel," he said sternly. "I will see you in the morning. Goodnight" He disappeared and closed the window.

I felt that if I let this rebuff pass, I should not feel kindly towards my uncle in the morning, nor, indeed, at any future time. I therefore plied the knocker with my right hand, and kept the bell ringing with my left until I heard the doorchain rattle within. The Cardinal's expression was grave nearly to moroseness as he confronted me on the threshold.

"Uncle," I cried, grasping his hand, "do not reproach me. Your door is never shut against the wretched. I am wretched. Let us sit up all night and talk"

"You may thank my position and not my charity for your admission, Zeno," he said. "For the sake of the neighbours, I had rather you played the fool in my study than upon my doorstep at this hour. Walk upstairs quietly, if you please. My housekeeper is a hard-working woman: the little sleep she allows herself must not be disturbed."

"You have a noble heart, uncle. I shall creep like a mouse."

"This is my study," he said, as we entered an ill-furnished den on the second floor. "The only refreshment I can offer you, if you desire any, is a bunch of raisins. The doctors have forbidden you to touch stimulants, I believe."

"By heaven—!" He raised his finger. "Pardon me: I was wrong to swear. But I had totally forgotten the doctors. At dinner I had a bottle of *Grave*."

"Humph! You have no business to be travelling alone. Your mother promised me that Bushy should come over here with you."

"Pshaw! Bushy is not a man of feeling. Besides, he is a coward. He refused to come with me because I purchased a revolver."

"He should have taken the revolver from you, and kept to his post."

"Why will you persist in treating me like a child, uncle? I am very impressionable, I grant you; but I have gone round the world alone, and do not need to be dry-nursed through a tour in Ireland."

"What do you intend to do during your stay here?"

I had no plans; and instead of answering I shrugged my shoulders and looked around the apartment. There was a statuette of the Virgin upon my uncle's desk. I looked at its face, as he was wont to look in the midst of his labours, I saw there eternal peace. The air became luminous with an infinite network of the jewelled rings of Paradise descending in roseate clouds upon us.

"Uncle," I said, bursting into the sweetest tears I had ever shed, "my wanderings are over. I will enter the Church, if you will help me. Let us read together the third part of *Faust*; for I understand it at last."

"Hush, man," he said, half rising with an expression of alarm, "Control yourself."

"Do not let my tears mislead you. I am calm and strong. Quick, let us have Goethe:

> *Das Unbeschreibliche,*
> *Hier ist gethan;*
> *Das Ewig-Weibliche,*
> *Zieht uns hinan."*

"Come, come. Dry your eyes and be quiet. I have no library here."

"But I have—in my portmanteau at the hotel," I said, rising. "Let me go for it, I will return in fifteen minutes."

"The devil is in you, I believe. Cannot—"

I interrupted him with a shout of laughter. "Cardinal," I said noisily, "you have become profane; and a profane priest is always the best of good fellows. Let us have some wine; and I will sing you a German beer song."

"Heaven forgive me if I do you wrong," he said; "but I believe God has laid the expiation of some sin on your unhappy head. Will you favor me with your attention for a while? I have something to say to you, and I have also to get some sleep before my hour for rising, which is half-past five."

"My usual hour for retiring—when I retire at all. But proceed. My fault is not inattention, but over-susceptibility."

"Well, then, I want you to go to Wicklow. My reasons—"

1132

"No matter what they may be," said I, rising again. "It is enough that you desire me to go. I shall start forthwith."

"Zeno! will you sit down and listen to me?"

I sank upon my chair reluctantly. "Ardor is a crime in your eyes, even when it is shown in your service," I said. "May I turn down the light?"

"Why?"

"To bring on my sombre mood, in which I am able to listen with tireless patience."

"I will turn it down myself. Will that do?"

I thanked him, and composed myself to listen in the shadow. My eyes, I felt, glittered. I was like Poe's raven.

"Now for my reasons for sending you to Wicklow. First, for your own sake. If you stay in town, or in any place where excitement can be obtained by any means, you will be in Swift's Hospital in a week. You must live in the country, under the eye of one upon whom I can depend. And you must have something to do to keep you out of mischief, and away from your music and painting and poetry, which, Sir John Richards writes to me, are dangerous for you in your present morbid state. Second, because I can entrust you with a task which, in the hands of a sensible man, might bring discredit on the Church. In short, I want you to investigate a miracle."

He looked attentively at me. I sat like a statue.

"You understand me?" he said.

"Nevermore," I replied, hoarsely. "Pardon me," I added, amused at the trick my imagination had played me, "I understand you perfectly. Proceed."

"I hope you do. Well, four miles distant from the town of Wicklow is a village called Four Mile Water. The resident priest is Father Hickey. You have heard of the miracles at Knock?"

I winked.

"I did not ask you what you think of them, but whether you have heard of them. I see you have. I need not tell you that even a miracle may do more harm than good to the Church in the country, unless it can be proved so thoroughly that her powerful and jealous enemies are silenced by the testimony of followers of their heresy. Therefore, when I saw in a Wexford newspaper last week a description of a strange manifestation of the Divine Power which was said to have taken place at Four Mile Water, I was troubled in my mind about it. So I wrote to Father Hickey, bidding him give me an

1133

account of the matter if it were true, and, if not, to denounce from the altar the author of the report, and to contradict it in the paper at once. This is his reply. He says—well, the first part is about Church matters: I need not trouble you with it. He goes on to say—"

"One moment. Is that his own handwriting? It does not look like a man's."

"He suffers from rheumatism in the fingers of his right hand, and his niece, who is an orphan, and lives with him, acts as his amanuensis. Well—"

"Stay. What is her name?"

"Her name? Kate Hickey."

"How old is she?"

"Tush, man, she is only a little girl. If she were old enough to concern you, I should not send you into her way. Have you any more questions to ask about her?"

"None. I can fancy her in a white veil at the rite of confirmation, a type of faith and innocence. Enough of her. What says the Reverend Hickey of the apparitions?"

"They are not apparitions. I will read you what he says. Ahem!

'In reply to your inquiries concerning the late miraculous event in this parish, I have to inform you that I can vouch for its truth, and that I can be confirmed not only by the inhabitants of the place, who are all Catholics, but by every person acquainted with the former situation of the graveyard referred to, including the Protestant Archdeacon of Baltinglas, who spends six weeks annually in the neighbourhood. The newspaper account is incomplete and inaccurate. The following are the facts: About four years ago, a man named Wolfe Tone Fitzgerald settled in this village as a farrier. His antecedents did not transpire, and he had no family. He lived by himself, was very careless of his person; and when in his cups, as he often was, regarded the honor neither of God nor man in his conversation. Indeed if it were not speaking ill of the dead, one might say that he was a dirty, drunken, blasphemous blackguard. Worse again, he was, I fear, an atheist, for he never attended Mass, and gave his Holiness worse language even than he gave the Queen. I should have mentioned that he was a bitter rebel, and boasted that his grandfather had been out in '98, and his father with Smith O'Brien. At last he went by the name of Brimstone Billy, and was held up in the village as the type of all wickedness.

'You are aware that our graveyard, situated on the north side of the water, is famous throughout the country as the burial place of the nuns of St. Ursula, the hermit of Four Mile Water, and many other holy people. No Protestant has ever ventured to enforce his legal right of interment there, though two have died in the parish within my own recollection. Three weeks ago, this Ftzgerald died in a fit brought on by drink, and a great hullabaloo was raised in the village when it became known that he would be buried in the graveyard. The body had to be watched to prevent its being stolen and buried at the cross-roads. My people were greatly disappointed when they were told I could do nothing to stop the burial, particularly as I of course refused to read any service on the occasion. However, I bade them not interfere; and the interment was effected on the 14th of July, late in the evening, and long after the legal hour. There was no disturbance. Next morning, the graveyard was found moved to the south side of the water, with the one newly-filled grave left behind on the north side; and thus they both remain. The departed saints would not lie with the reprobate. I can testify to it on the oath of a Christian priest; and if this will not satisfy those outside the Church, everyone, as I said before, who remembers where the graveyard was two months ago, can confirm me.

'I respectfully suggest that a thorough investigation into the truth of this miracle be proposed to a committee of Protestant gentlemen. They shall not be asked to accept a single fact on hearsay from my people. The ordnance maps show where the graveyard was; and anyone can see for himself where it is. I need not tell your Eminence what a rebuke this would be to those enemies of the holy Church that have sought to put a stain on her by discrediting the late wonderful manifestations at Knock Chapel. If they come to Four Mile Water, they need cross-examine no one. They will be asked to believe nothing but their own senses.

'Awaiting your Eminence's counsel to guide me further in the matter,

'I am, etc.'

"Well, Zeno," said my uncle, "what do you think of Father Hickey now?"

"Uncle, do not ask me. Beneath this roof I desire to believe everything. The Reverend Hickey has appealed strongly to my love

1135

of legend. Let us admire the poetry of his narrative and ignore the balance of probability between a Christian priest telling a lie on his oath and a graveyard swimming across a river in the middle of the night and forgetting to return."

"Tom Hickey is not telling a lie, sir. You may take my word for that. But he may be mistaken."

"Such a mistake amounts to insanity. It is true that I myself, awaking suddenly in the depth of night, have found myself convinced that the position of my bed had been reversed. But on opening my eyes the illusion ceased. I fear Mr. Hickey is mad. Your best course is this. Send down to Four Mile Water a perfectly sane investigator; an acute observer; one whose perceptive faculties, at once healthy and subtle, are absolutely unclouded by religious prejudice. In a word, send me. I will report to you the true state of affairs in a few days, and you can then make arrangements for transferring Hickey from the altar to the asylum."

"Yes, I had intended to send you. You are wonderfully sharp and you would make a capital detective if you could only keep your mind to one point. But your chief qualification for this business is that you are too crazy to excite the suspicions of those whom you may have to watch. For the affair may be a trick. If so, I hope and believe that Hickey has no hand in it. Still, it is my duty to take every precaution."

"Cardinal; may I ask whether traces of insanity have ever appeared in our family?"

"Except in you and in my grandmother, no. She was a Pole; and you resemble her personally. Why do you ask?"

"Because it has often occurred to me that you are, perhaps, a little cracked. Excuse my candour, but a man who has devoted his life to the pursuit of a red hat, who accuses everyone else besides himself of being mad, and who is disposed to listen seriously to a tale of a peripatetic graveyard, can hardly be quite sane. Depend upon it, uncle, you want rest and change. The blood of your Polish grandmother is in your veins."

"I hope I may not be committing a sin in sending a ribald on the Church's affairs," he replied, fervently. "However, we must use the instruments put into our hands. Is it agreed that you go?"

"Had you not delayed me with this story, which I might as well have learned on the spot, I should have been there already."

"There is no occasion for impatience, Zeno. I must first send to Hickey to find a place for you. I shall tell him that you are going

1136

to recover your health, as, in fact, you are. And, Zeno, in Heaven's name be discreet. Try to act like a man of sense. Do not dispute with Hickey on matters of religion. Since you are my nephew, you had better not disgrace me."

"I shall become an ardent Catholic, and do you infinite credit, uncle."

"I wish you would, although you would hardly be an acquisition to the Church. And now I must turn you out. It is nearly three o'clock, and I need some sleep. Do you know your way back to your hotel?"

"I need not stir. I can sleep in this chair. Go to bed, and never mind me."

"I shall not close my eyes until you are safely out of the house. Come, rouse yourself, and say goodnight."

The following is a copy of my first report to the Cardinal:

Four Mile Water, County Wicklow,
10th August

My Dear Uncle,

The miracle is genuine. I have affected perfect credulity in order to throw the Hickeys and the countryfolk off their guard with me. I have listened to their method of convincing sceptical strangers. I have examined the ordnance maps, and cross-examined the neighbouring Protestant gentle folk. I have spent a day upon the ground on each side of the water, and have visited it at midnight. I have considered the upheaval theories, subsidence theories, volcanic theories, and tidal wave theories which the provincial *savants* have suggested. They are all untenable. There is only one scoffer in the district, an Orangeman; and he admits the removal of the cemetery, but says it was dug up and transplanted in the night by a body of men under the command of Father Tom. This also is out of the question. The interment of Brimstone Billy was the first which had taken place for four years; and his is the only grave which bears a trace of recent digging. It is alone on the north bank, and the inhabitants shun it after nightfall. As each passer-by during the day throws a stone upon it, it will soon be marked by a large cairn. The graveyard, with a ruined stone chapel still standing in its midst, is on the south side. You may send down a committee to investigate the matter as soon as you please. There can be no doubt as to the miracle

1137

having actually taken place, as recorded by Hickey. As for me, I have grown so accustomed to it that if the county Wicklow were to waltz off with me to Middlesex, I should be quite impatient of any expressions of surprise from my friends in London.

Is not the above a businesslike statement? Away then, with this stale miracle. If you would see for yourself a miracle which can never pall, a vision of youth and health to be crowned with garlands for ever, come down and see Kate Hickey, whom you suppose to be a little girl. Illusion, my lord Cardinal, illusion! She is seventeen, with a bloom and a brogue that would lay your asceticism in ashes at a flash. To her I am an object of wonder, a strange man bred in wicked cities. She is courted by six feet of farming material, chopped off a spare length of coarse humanity by the Almighty, and flung into Wicklow to plough the fields. His name is Phil Langan; and he hates me. I have to consort with him for the sake of Father Tom, whom I entertain vastly by stories of your wild oats at Salamanca. I exhausted all my authentic anecdotes the first day; and now I invent gallant escapades with Spanish donnas, in which you figure as a youth of unstable morals. This delights Father Tom infinitely. I feel that I have done you a service by thus casting on the cold sacerdotal abstraction which formerly represented you in Kate's imagination a ray of vivifying passion.

What a country this is! A Hesperidean garden: such skies! Adieu, uncle.

Zeno Legge.

Behold me, then, at Four Mile Water, in love. I had been in love frequently; but not oftener than once a year had I encountered a woman who affected me as seriously as Kate Hickey. She was so shrewd, and yet so flippant! When I spoke of art she yawned. When I deplored the sordidness of the world she laughed, and called me "poor fellow!" When I told her what a treasure of beauty and freshness she had she ridiculed me. When I reproached her with brutality she became angry, and sneered at me for being what she called a fine gentleman. One sunny afternoon we were standing at the gate of her uncle's house, she looking down the dusty road for the detestable Langan, I watching the spotless azure sky, when she said:

"How soon are you going back to London?"

"I am not going back to London, Miss Hickey. I am not yet tired of Four Mile Water."

1138

"I'm sure Four Mile Water ought to be proud of your approbation."

"You disapprove of my liking it, then? Or is it that you grudge me the happiness I have found here? I think Irish ladies grudge a man a moment's peace."

"I wonder you have ever prevailed on yourself to associate with Irish ladies, since they are so far beneath you."

"Did I say they were beneath me, Miss Hickey? I feel that I have made a deep impression on you."

"Indeed! Yes, you're quite right. I assure you I can't sleep at night for thinking of you, Mr. Legge. It's the best a Christian can do, seeing you think so mighty little of yourself."

"You are triply wrong, Miss Hickey: wrong to be sarcastic with me, wrong to pretend that there is anything unreasonable in my belief that you think of me sometimes, and wrong to discourage the candour with which I always avow that I think constantly of myself."

"Then you had better not speak to me, since I have no manners."

"Again! Did I say you had no manners? The warmest expressions of regard from my mouth seem to reach your ears transformed into insults. Were I to repeat the Litany of the Blessed Virgin, you would retort as though I had been reproaching you. This is because you hate me. You never misunderstand Langan, whom you love."

"I don't know what London manners are, Mr. Legge; but in Ireland gentlemen are expected to mind their own business. How dare you say I love Mr. Langan?"

"Then you do not love him?"

"It is nothing to you whether I love him or not."

"Nothing to me that you hate me and love another?"

"I did not say that I hated you. You are not so very clever yourself at understanding what people say, though you make such fuss because they don't understand you." Here, as she glanced down the road again, she suddenly looked glad.

"Aha!" I said.

"What do you mean by 'Aha!'?"

"No matter. I will now show you what a man's sympathy is. As yon perceived just then, Langan—who is too tall for his age, by-the-bye—is coming to pay you a visit. Well, instead of staying with you, as a jealous woman would, I will withdraw."

"I don't care whether you go or stay, I'm sure. I wonder what you would give to be as fine a man as Mr. Langan."

1139

"All I possess: I swear it! But solely because you admire tall men more than broad views. Mr. Langan may be defined geometrically as length without breadth; altitude without position; a line on the landscape, not a point in it."

"How very clever you are!"

"You do not understand me, I see. Here comes your lover, stepping over the wall like a camel. And here go I, out through the gate like a Christian. Good afternoon, Mr. Langan. I am going because Miss Hickey has something to say to you about me which she would rather not say in my presence. You will excuse me?"

"Oh, I'll excuse you," said he boorishly. I smiled, and went out. Before I was quite out of hearing, Kate whispered vehemently to him, "I *hate* that fellow."

I smiled again; but I had scarcely done so when my spirits fell. I walked hastily away with a coarse threatening sound in my ears like that of the clarionets whose sustained low notes darken the woodland in "Der Freischütz." I found myself presently at the graveyard. It was a barren place, enclosed by a mud wall with a gate to admit funerals, and numerous gaps to admit the peasantry, who made short cuts across it as they went to and fro between Four Mile Water and the market town The graves were mounds overgrown with grass; there was no keeper; nor were there flowers, railings or any of the conventionalities that make an English graveyard repulsive. A great thornbush, near what was called the grave of the holy sisters, was covered with scraps of cloth and flannel, attached by peasant women who had prayed before it. There were three kneeling there as I entered, for the reputation of the place had been revived of late by the miracle, and a ferry had been established close by, to conduct visitors over the route taken by the graveyard. From where I stood I could see on the opposite bank the heap of stones, perceptibly increased since my last visit, marking the deserted grave of Brimstone Billy. I strained my eyes broodingly at it for some minutes, and then descended the river bank and entered the boat.

"Good evenin' t'your honour," said the ferryman, and set to work to draw the boat hand-over-hand by a rope stretched across the water.

"Good evening. Is your business beginning to fall off yet?"

"Faith, it never was as good as it might ha' been. The people that comes from the south side can see Billy's grave—Lord have mercy on him—across the wather; and they think bad of payin' a

1140

penny to put a stone over him. It's them that lives tow'rst Dublin that makes the journey. Your honour is the third I've brought from south to north this blessed day."

"When do most people come? In the afternoon, I suppose?"

"All hours, sur, except afther dusk. There isn't a sowl in the counthry ud come within sight of that grave wanst the sun goes down."

"And you! Do you stay here all night by yourself?"

"The holy heavens forbid! Is it me stay here all night? No, your honour; I tether the boat at siven o'hlyock, and lave Brimstone Billy—God forgimme!—to take care of it t'll mornin."

"It will be stolen some night, I'm afraid."

"Arra, who'd dar come next or near it, let alone stale it? Faith, I'd think twice before lookin at it meself in the dark. God bless your honour, and gran'che long life."

I had given him sixpence. I went to the reprobate's grave and stood at the foot of it, looking at the sky, gorgeous with the descent of the sun.To my English eyes, accustomed to giant trees, broad lawns, and stately mansions, the landscape was wild and inhospitable. The ferryman was already tugging at the rope on his way back (I had told him I did not intend to return that way), and presently I saw him make the painter fast o the south bank; put on his coat; and trudge homeward. I turned towards the grave at my feet. Those who had interred Brimstone Billy, working hastily at an unlawful hour, and in fear of molestation by the people, had hardly dug a grave. They had scooped out earth enough to hide their burden, and no more. A stray goat had kicked away a corner of the mound and exposed the coffin. It occurred to me, as I took some of the stones from the cairn, and heaped them so as to repair the breach, that had the miracle been the work of a body of men, they would have moved the one grave instead of the many. Even from a supernatural point of view, it seemed strange that the sinner should have banished the elect, when, by their superior numbers, they might so much more easily have banished him.

It was almost dark when I left the spot, After a walk of half a mile, I recrossed the water by a bridge, and returned to the farm-house in which I lodged. Here, finding that I had had enough of solitude, I only stayed to take a cup of tea. Then I went to Father Hickey's cottage.

Kate was alone when I entered. She looked up quickly as I

1141

opened the door, and turned away disappointed when she recognized me.

"Be generous for once," I said. "I have walked about aimlessly for hours in order to avoid spoiling the beautiful afternoon for you by my presence. When the sun was up I withdrew my shadow from your path. Now that darkness has fallen, shed some light on mine. May I stay half an hour?"

"You may stay as long as you like, of course. My uncle will soon be home. He is clever enough to talk to you."

"What! More sarcasms! Come, Miss Hickey, help me to spend a pleasant evening. It will only cost you a smile. I am somewhat cast down. Four Mile Water is a paradise; but without you, it would be a little lonely."

"It must be very lonely for you. I wonder why you came here."

"Because I heard that the women here were all Zerlinas like you, and the men Masettos, like Mr. Phil—where are you going to?"

"Let me pass, Mr. Legge. I had intended never speaking to you again after the way you went on about Mr. Langan today; and I wouldn't either, only my uncle made me promise not to take any notice of you, because you were—no matter; but I won't listen to you any more on the subject."

"Do not go. I swear never to mention his name again. I beg your pardon for what I said: you shall have no further cause for complaint. Will you forgive me?"

She sat down, evidently disappointed by my submission. I took a chair, and placed myself near her. She tapped the floor impatiently with her foot. I saw that there was not a movement I could make, not a look, not a tone of my voice, which did not irritate her.

"You were remarking," I said, "that your uncle desired you to take no notice of me because—"

She closed her lips, and did not answer.

"I fear I have offended you again by my curiosity. But indeed, I had no idea that he had forbidden you to tell me the reason."

"He did not forbid me. Since you are so determined to find out—"

"No, excuse me. I do not wish to know, I am sorry I asked."

"Indeed! Perhaps you would be sorrier still to be told. I only made a secret of it out of consideration for you."

"Then your uncle has spoken ill of me behind my back. If that be so, there is no such thing as a true man in Ireland. I would not have believed it on the word of any woman alive save yourself."

1142

"I never said my uncle was a backbiter. Just to show you what he thinks of you, I will tell you whether you want to know it or not, that he bid me not mind you because you were only a poor mad creature, sent down here by your family to be out of harm's way."

"Oh, Miss Hickey!"

"There now! You have got it out of me; and I wish I had bit my tongue out first. I sometimes think—that I mayn't sin!—that you have a bad angel in you."

"I am glad you told me this," I said gently. "Do not reproach yourself for having done so, I beg. Your uncle has been misled by what he has heard of my family, who are all more or less insane. Far from being mad, I am actually the only rational man named Legge in the three kingdoms. I will prove this to you, and at the the same time keep your indiscretion in countenance, by telling you something I ought not to tell you. It is this. I am not here as an invalid or a chance tourist. I am here to investigate the miracle. The Cardinal, a shrewd if somewhat erratic man, selected mine from all the long heads at his disposal to come down here, and find out the truth of Father Hickey's story. Would he have entrusted such a task to a madman, think you?"

"The truth of—who dared to doubt my uncle's word? And so you are a spy, a dirty informer."

I started. The adjective she had used, though probably the commonest expression of contempt in Ireland, is revolting to an Englishman.

"Miss Hickey," I said, "there is in me, as you have said, a bad angel. Do not shock my good angel—who is a person of taste—quite away from my heart, lest the other be left undisputed monarch of it. Hark! The chapel bell is ringing the angelus. Can you, with that sound softening the darkness of the village night, cherish a feeling of spite against one who admires you?"

"You come between me and my prayers," she said hysterically, and began to sob. She had scarcely done so, when I heard voices without. Then Langan and the priest entered.

"Oh Phil," she cried, running to him, "take me away from him: I can't bear—" I turned towards him, and showed him my dog-tooth in a false smile. He felled me at one stroke, as he might have felled a poplar tree.

"Murdher!" exclaimed the priest. "What are you doin, Phil?"

"He is an informer," sobbed Kate. "He came down here to spy

1143

on you, uncle, and to try and show that the blessed miracle was a make-up. I knew it long before he told me, by his insulting ways. He wanted to make love to me."

I rose with difficulty from beneath the table, where I had lain motionless for a moment.

"Sir," I said, "I am somewhat dazed by the recent action of Mr. Langan, whom I beg, the next time he converts himself into a fulling-mill, to do so at the expense of a man more nearly his equal in strength than I. What your niece has told you is partly true. I am indeed the Cardinal's spy; and I have already reported to him that the miracle is a genuine one. A committee of gentlemen will wait on you tomorrow to verify it, at my suggestion. I have thought that the proof might be regarded by them as more complete if you were taken by surprise. Miss Hickey, that I admire all that is admirable in you is but to say that I have a sense of the beautiful. To say that I love you would be mere profanity. Mr. Langan, I have in my pocket a loaded pistol, which I carry from a silly English prejudice against you countrymen. Had I been the Hercules of the ploughtail, and you in my place, I should have been a dead man now. Do not redden; you are safe as far as I am concerned."

"Let me tell you before you leave my house for good," said Father Hickey, who seemed to have become unreasonably angry, "that you should never have crossed my threshold if I had known you were a spy; no, not if your uncle were his Holiness the Pope himself."

Here a frightful thing happened to me. I felt giddy, and put my hand to my head. Three warm drops trickled over it. Instantly I became murderous. My mouth filled with blood, my eyes were blinded with it; I seemed to drown in it. My hand went involuntarily to the pistol. It is my habit to obey my impulses instantaneously. Fortunately the impulse to kill vanished before a sudden perception of how I might miraculously humble the mad vanity in which these foolish people had turned upon me. The blood receded from my ears; and I again heard and saw distinctly.

"And let *me* tell you," Langan was saying, "that if you think yourself handier with cold lead than you are with your fists, I'll exchange shots with you, and welcome, whenever you please. Father Tom's credit is the same to me as my own, and if you say a word against it, you lie."

"His credit is in my hands," I said. "I am the Cardinal's witness. Do you defy me?"

"There is the door," said the priest, holding it open before me.

1144

"Until you can undo the visible work of God's hand your testimony can do no harm to me."

"Father Hickey," I replied, "before the sun rises again upon Four Mile Water, I will undo the visible work of God's hand, and bring the pointing finger of the scoffer upon your altar."

I bowed to Kate, and walked out. It was so dark that I could not at first see the garden-gate. Before I found it, I heard through the window Father Hickey's voice, saying. "I wouldn't for ten pound that this had happened, Phil. He's as mad as a March hare. The Cardinal told me so."

I returned to my lodging, and took a cold bath to cleanse the blood from my neck and shoulder. The effect of the blow I had received was so severe, that even after the bath and a light meal I felt giddy and languid. There was an alarum-clock on the mantelpiece. I wound it; set the alarum for half-past twelve; muffled it so that it should not disturb the people in the adjoining room; and went to bed, where I slept soundly for an hour and a quarter. Then the alarum woke me, and I sprang up before I was thoroughly awake. Had I hesitated, the desire to relapse into perfect sleep would have overpowered me. Although the muscles of my neck were painfully stiff, and my hands unsteady from my nervous disturbance, produced by the interruption of my first slumber, I dressed myself resolutely, and, after taking a draught of cold water, stole out of the house. It was exceedingly dark and I had some difficulty in finding the cow-house, whence I borrowed a spade, and a truck with wheels, ordinarily used for moving sacks of potatoes. These I carried in my hands until I was beyond earshot of the house, when I put the spade on the truck, and wheeled it along the road to the cemetery. When I approached the water, knowing that no one would dare to come thereabout at such an hour, I made greater haste, no longer concerning myself about the rattling of the wheels. Looking across to the opposite bank, I could see a phosphorescent glow, marking the lonely grave of Brimstone Billy. This helped me to find the ferry station, where, after wandering a little and stumbling often, I found the boat, and embarked with my implements. Guided by the rope, I crossed the water without difficulty; landed; made fast the boat; dragged the truck up the bank; and sat down to rest on the cairn of the grave. For nearly a quarter of an hour I sat watching the patches of jack-o'-lantern fire, and collecting my strength for the work before me. Then the distant bell of the chapel clock tolled one. I rose, took the spade, and in about ten minutes uncovered the coffin, which

smelt horribly. Keeping to windward of it, and using the spade as a lever, I contrived with great labor to place it on the truck. I wheeled it without accident to the landing-place, where, by placing the shafts of the truck upon the stern of the boat and lifting the foot by main strength, I succeeded in embarking my load after twenty minutes' toil, during which I got covered with clay and perspiration, and several times all but upset the boat. At the southern bank I had less difficulty in getting truck and coffin ashore, and dragging them up to the graveyard.

It was now past two o'clock, and the dawn had begun, so that I had no further trouble from want of light. I wheeled the coffin to a patch of loamy soil which I had noticed in the afternoon near the grave of the holy sisters. I had warmed to my work; my neck no longer pained me; and I began to dig vigorously, soon making a shallow trench, deep enough to hide the coffin with the addition of a mound. The chill pearl-coloured morning had by this time quite dissipated the darkness. I could see, and was myself visible, for miles around. This alarmed me, and made me impatient to finish my task. Nevertheless, I was forced to rest for a moment before placing the coffin in the trench. I wiped my brow and wrists, and again looked about me. The tomb of the holy women, a massive slab supported by four stone spheres, was grey and wet with dew. Near it was the thornbush covered with rags, the newest of which were growing gaudy in the radiance which was stretching up from the coast on the east. It was time to finish my work. I seized the truck; laid it alongside the grave; and gradually prized the coffin off with the spade until it rolled over into the trench with a hollow sound like a drunken remonstrance from the sleeper within. I shovelled the earth round and over it, working as fast as possible. In less than a quarter of an hour it was buried. Ten minutes more sufficed to make the mound symmetrical, and to clear the traces of my work from the adjacent sward. Then I flung down the spade; threw up my arms; and vented a sigh of relief and triumph. But I recoiled as I saw that I was standing on a barren common, covered with furze. No product of man's handiwork was near me except my truck and spade and the grave of Brimstone Billy, now as lonely as before. I turned towards the water. On the opposite bank was the cemetery, with the tomb of the holy women, the thornbush with its rags stirring in the morning breeze, and the broken mud wall. The ruined chapel was there too, not a stone shaken from its crumbling walls,

not a sign to show that it and its precinct were less rooted in their place than the eternal hills around.

I looked down at the grave with a pang of compassion for the unfortunate Wolfe Tone Fitzgerald, with whom the blessed would not rest. I was even astonished, though I had worked expressly to this end. But the birds were astir, and the cocks crowing. My land-lord was an early riser. I put the spade on the truck again, and hastened back to the farm, where I replaced them in the cow-house. Then I stole into the house, and took a clean pair of boots, an over-coat, and a silk hat. These, with a change of linen, were sufficient to make my appearance respectable. I went out again, bathed in the Four Mile Water, took a last look at the cemetery, and walked to Wicklow, whence I travelled by the first train to Dublin.

Some months later, at Cairo, I received a packet of Irish news-papers and a leading article, cut from the *Times*, on the subject of the miracle. Father Hickey had suffered the meed of his inhospit-able conduct. The committee, arriving at Four Mile Water the day after I left, had found the graveyard exactly where it had formerly stood. Father Hickey, taken by surprise, had attempted to defend himself by a confused statement, which led the committee to declare finally that the miracle was a gross imposture. The *Times*, com-menting on this after adducing a number of examples of priestly craft, remarked, "We are glad to learn that the Rev. Mr. Hickey has been permanently relieved of his duties as the parish priest of Four Mile Water by his ecclesiastical superior. It is less gratifying to have to record that it has been found possible to obtain two hundred signatures to a memorial embodying the absurd defense offered to the committee, and expressing unabated confidence in the integrity of Mr. Hickey."

1147

PERCY BYSSHE SHELLEY

PERCY BYSSHE SHELLY (English, 1792-1822). One of major Romantic poets. Lived and wrote in the light of Greek classicism. Expelled from Oxford for pamphlet on atheism. Eloped with Mary Wollstonecraft (author of *Frankenstein*). Drowned in Italy. Many of his long works are didactic and philosophical. Better-loved are such shorter lyrics as "Adonais," "Ode to the West Wind," "To Night," etc.

LOVE

When the lamp is shattered,
   The light in the dust lies dead—
When the cloud is scattered,
   The rainbow's glory is shed.
When the lute is broken,
   Sweet tones are remembered not;
When the lips have spoken,
   Loved accents are soon forgot.

As music and splendour
   Survive not the lamp and the lute,
The heart's echoes render
   No song when the spirit is mute—
No song but sad dirges,
   Like the wind through a ruined cell,
Or the mournful surges
   That ring the dead seaman's knell.

When hearts have once mingled,
   Love first leaves the well-built nest;
The weak one is singled
   To endure what it once possest.
O Love! who bewailest
   The frailty of all things here,
Why choose you the frailest
   For your cradle, your home, and your bier?

Its passions will rock thee
   As the storms rock the ravens on high;
Bright reason will mock thee
   Like the sun from a wintry sky.

1148

From thy nest every rafter
    Will rot, and thine eagle home
Leave thee naked to laughter,
    When leaves fall and cold winds come.

INVOCATION

Rarely, rarely, comest thou,
    Spirit of Delight!
Wherefore hast thou left me now
    Many a day and night?
Many a weary night and day
'Tis since thou art fled away.

How shall ever one like me
    Win thee back again?
With the joyous and the free
    Thou wilt scoff at pain.
Spirit false! thou hast forgot
All but those who need thee not.

As a lizard with the shade
    Of a trembling leaf,
Thou with sorrow art dismay'd;
    Even the sighs of grief
Reproach thee, that thou art not near,
And reproach thou wilt not hear.

Let me set my mournful ditty
    To a merry measure;
Thou wilt never come for pity,
    Thou wilt come for pleasure;
Pity then will cut away
Those cruel wings, and thou wilt stay.

I love all that thou lovest,
    Spirit of Delight!
The fresh Earth in new leaves drest
    And the starry night;
Autumn evening, and the morn
When the golden mists are born.

I love snow and all the forms
  Of the radiant frost;
I love waves, and winds, and storms,
  Everything almost
Which is Nature's, and may be
Untainted by man's misery.

I love tranquil solitude,
  And such society
As is quiet, wise, and good;
  Between thee and me
What diff'rence? but thou dost possess
The things I seek, not love them less.
I love Love—though he has wings,
  And like light can flee,
But above all other things,
  Spirit, I love thee—
Thou art love and life! O come!
Make once more my heart thy home!

DEJECTION

The sun is warm, the sky is clear,
  The waves are dancing fast and bright,
Blue isles and snowy mountains wear
  The purple noon's transparent might:
  The breath of the moist earth is light
Around its unexpanded buds;
  Like many a voice of one delight—
The winds, the birds, the ocean-floods—
The City's voice itself is soft like Solitude's.

I see the Deep's untrampled floor
  With green and purple seaweeds strown;
I see the waves upon the shore,
  Like light dissolved in star-showers, thrown:
  I sit upon the sands alone;
The lightning of the noontide ocean
  Is flashing round me, and a tone
Arises from its measured motion—
How sweet! did any heart now share in my emotion.

1150

Alas! I have nor hope nor health,
    Nor peace within nor calm around,
Nor that content, surpassing wealth,
    The sage in meditation found,
    And walked with inward glory crowned—
Nor fame, nor power, nor love, nor leisure;
    Others I see whom these surround—
Smiling they live, and call life pleasure;
To me that cup has been dealt in another measure.

Yet now despair itself is mild
    Even as the winds and waters are;
I could lie down like a tired child,
    And weep away the life of care
    Which I have borne, and yet must bear,
Till death like sleep might steal on me,
    And I might feel in the warm air
My cheek grow cold, and hear the sea
Breathe o'er my dying brain its last monotony.

ODE TO THE WEST WIND

O wild West Wind, thou breath of Autumn's being,
Thou, from whose unseen presence the leaves dead
Are driven, like ghosts from an enchanter fleeing,
Yellow, and black, and pale, and hectic red,
Pestilence-stricken multitudes: O thou
Who chariotest to their dark wintry bed
The wingéd seeds, where they lie cold and low,
Each like a corpse within its grave, until
Thine azure sister of the Spring shall blow
Her clarion o'er the dreaming earth, and fill
(Driving sweet buds like flocks to feed in air)
With living hues and odours plain and hill:
Wild Spirit, which art moving everywhere;
Destroyer and Preserver; hear, oh, hear!

Thou on whose stream, mid the steep sky's commotion,
Loose clouds like earth's decaying leaves are shed,
Shook from the tangled boughs of Heaven and Ocean,
Angels of rain and lightning: there are spread

On the blue surface of thine airy surge,
Like the bright hair uplifted from the head
Of some fierce Maenad, even from the dim verge
Of the horizon to the zenith's height,
The locks of the approaching storm. Thou dirge
Of the dying year, to which this closing night
Will be the dome of a vast sepulchre,
Vaulted with all thy congregated might
Of vapours, from whose solid atmosphere
Black rain, and fire, and hail, will burst: oh, hear!

Thou who didst waken from his summer dreams
The blue Mediterranean, where he lay,
Lull'd by the coil of his crystalline streams,
Beside a pumice isle in Baiae's bay,
And saw in sleep old palaces and towers
Quivering within the wave's intenser day,
All overgrown with azure moss and flowers
So sweet, the sense faints picturing them! Thou
For whose path the Atlantic's level powers
Cleave themselves into chasms, while far below
The sea-blooms and the oozy woods which wear
The sapless foliage of the ocean, know
Thy voice, and suddenly grow grey with fear,
And tremble and despoil themselves: oh, hear!

If I were a dead leaf thou mightest bear;
If I were a swift cloud to fly with thee;
A wave to pant beneath thy power, and share
The impulse of thy strength, only less free
Than thou, O uncontrollable! If even
I were as in my boyhood, and could be
The comrade of thy wanderings over Heaven,
As then, when to outstrip thy skyey speed
Scarce seemed a vision, I would ne'er have striven
As thus with thee in prayer in my sore need.
Oh, lift me as a wave, a leaf, a cloud!
I fall upon the thorns of life! I bleed!
A heavy weight of hours has chained and bowed
One too like thee: tameless, and swift, and proud.

Make me thy lyre, even as the forest is:
What if my leaves are falling like its own!
The tumult of thy mighty harmonies
Will take from both a deep, autumnal tone,
Sweet though in sadness. Be thou, Spirit fierce,
My spirit! Be thou me, impetuous one!

Drive my dead thoughts over the universe
Like withered leaves to quicken a new birth!
And, by the incantation of this verse,
Scatter, as from an unextinguished hearth
Ashes and sparks, my words among mankind!
Be through my lips to unawakened earth
The trumpet of a prophecy! O Wind,
If Winter comes, can Spring be far behind?

TO NIGHT

Swiftly walk o'er the western wave,
    Spirit of Night!
Out of the misty eastern cave,
Where, all the long and lone daylight,
Thou wovest dreams of joy and fear,
Which make thee terrible and dear—
    Swift be thy flight!

Wrap thy form in a mantle gray,
    Star-inwrought!
Blind with thine hair the eyes of day;
Kiss her until she be wearied out,
Then wander o'er city, and sea, and land,
Touching all with thine opiate wand—
    Come, long-sought!

When I arose and saw the dawn,
    I sighed for thee;
When light rode high, and the dew was gone,
And noon lay heavy on flower and tree,
And the weary day turned to his rest,
Lingering like an unloved guest,
    I sighed for thee.

Thy brother Death came, and cried,
  Wouldst thou me?
Thy sweet child Sleep, the filmy-eyed,
Murmured like a noontide bee,
Shall I nestle near thy side?
Wouldst thou me?—And I replied,
  No, not thee!

Death will come when thou art dead,
  Soon, too soon—
Sleep will come when thou art fled;
Of neither would I ask the boon
I ask of thee, beloved Night—
Swift be thine approaching flight,
  Come soon, soon!

SHEN TS'UNG-WEN

SHÉN TS'UNG-WÉN (Chinese, 1902-   ). Prolific Chinese novelist and critic. Had military rather than conventional academic background. Edited *Ta-kung pao* literary supplement. Author of some 60 novels, volumes of stories and other works.

UNDER COVER OF DARKNESS

THE bamboo raft, nimbly manned by the two men, glided quietly downstream. The raftsmen had passed unseen through the river patrols, and were now only two miles from their destination, but suddenly the raft ran aground on a wild bank overgrown with rushes and reeds, and while the raft remained still and unmoving, they heard the murmuring of the water and the rustling of the wind through the reeds.

Lu-Yi, an officer of the signal corps of the guerrilla troops, began to blame the younger man, hoarsely. "What's the matter?" he asked. "Are you possessed by devils? You think it's funny, don't you? But if we are stranded here, they will soon find us out, and we shall be shot to pieces by their guns."

The boy who had been crouching on the raft stood up slowly, but still he made no sound. There was a faint shimmering light on

the dark surface of the river, and in the water there lay the reflection of two men standing on a raft, a reflection which was upside-down. Silently the boy walked to the other end of the raft.

"Well, we have run aground. I guess we have caught in something!" It was the voice of a very young boy.

He went up to the older man, and still leaning against the oar which he held in one hand, he took over the bamboo pole and tried to push it hither and thither in the marshy water. They were at a bend in the river where the water was shallow, but from the murmur of the water it was clear that the river ran swift round the bend; and there was no reason why the rafts should remain still, unless something had caught hold of the bamboo raft from underneath.

Their spirits were tried. Lu-Yi began to grumble again, impatiently. "There's two miles to go," he said. "It's a desperately dangerous area. There might be enemy patrols at any moment. . . ."

The boy seemed to have no feeling for fear or sorrow. He silently listened to the older man, and then untied the automatic pistol and bullet-case from his belt, rolled up his trousers, and gently slid into the water. He found a foothold and stooped down to push the raft with both hands. They heard the long, low squeak of the bamboos, but the raft did not move, and seemed, indeed, to be constrained by unseen hands.

Lu-Yi was still impatient. "Be careful," he murmured. "I know you are strong, but be careful. Better take off your clothes and feel with your hands underneath the bamboos. There seem to be devils and ghosts there. . . ."

"Yes," the boy answered, with a little giggle. "Devils and ghosts. But let me try. . . ."

He began to move slowly in the water, stretching his hands under the bamboos. Touching the ropes and knots which joined the raft together, he stooped down, his arms and shoulders buried under the cold water, and his chin kissing the rippling surface of the river. Meanwhile his feet sank in mud to the knees, and it took an effort to pull them up again. He was still feeling among the knots and ropes when he felt something hard and round striking against his fingers. He realized then that it was a millstone entangled among ropes and clothes. He reached out his hands and felt the coldwetness of a human body. "A body!" he shouted out in mingled alarm and delight, for now at last he knew what was obstructing the raft. "A body!" he exclaimed. "It's the funniest thing. . . ."

"Well, what is it?"

He did not answer. He ran his fingers over the body and touched the hair, the face, and then the arms. It was bound to the millstone with heavy ropes, which had somewhat curled round the bamboos.

"Even with a millstone round its neck, this body prevents us from moving," the boy laughed silently.

"Then take it away," the other commanded, and he was more impatient than ever when he heard the crowing of the first cocks in the distance. "The body of a good-for-nothing," he added contemptuously. "No good when he was alive, and no good when he was dead," he murmured softly.

The boy was still wading round the raft, trying to disentangle the rope. Lu-Yi drew his knife from his belt and tapped it against the side of the raft. "Boy, come here," he said. "Take the knife and cut the rope in two. If the devil doesn't loosen his hold, cut his hand off. Hurry up! We're in terrible danger, and we have to get to the army."

The boy amused by the expression "loosen his hold," wondered at his companion's impatience.

There was a muffled noise of a knife stirring up the water, and the raft began to turn a little. A little while later he went to the stern of the raft and put his shoulder against it. He began to push hard, but he only succeeded in lifting the raft a little above the level of the water. The raft kept turning, but did not move forward. It was difficult to manage the knife under water, and perhaps in the end they would have to take the raft to pieces and then join the bamboos up again. But there was no time. Besides, less than a mile downstream, they knew there was a pontoon bridge held by the enemy. Lu-Yi could no longer restrain his impatience. He began to curse the boy for his lightheartedness and slowness, and promised to write a report on his negligence, inefficiency, and lack of responsibility. The boy remained calm, unmoved.

"Well, then, we had better walk instead of wasting our time on the river," he said, in a perfectly matter-of-fact voice. "Otherwise we won't get there before dawn."

"There are traps laid for us all over the hills and valley," the other answered. "The devils are ready with their ropes and millstones there. If we walk those two miles, it's likely we'll have millstones round our necks before dawn."

"Fears can't stop us," the boy replied. "There's no other way."

At last the older man was convinced. They carried the two bullet-

cases and the rest of their equipment on to the embankment, groping and stumbling in the dark. Then they sat among the tall reeds and whispered about the routes they would take. They had no idea of the ponds and marshes and streams which lay in their way, and the villages and guard stations through which they would have to pass. In the black sky not a single star lay visible. Each one had brought a shirt torch, but in the enveloping darkness they seemed to see eyes glaring at them, and they knew that the slightest light shown by them would call for a bullet from the enemy. And if the enemy knew that they were passing along the river, the lives of all those who followed them on the bamboo rafts would be endangered.

After a while they decided not to take the road over the hills, but to follow the path which lay along the edge of the river. The flood water had receded during the past few days, and now the path was dry. Besides, there was always the chance that they would come across a sampan or canoe left somewhere along the bank.

The small path wound through bushy reeds. The earth was muddy and slippery underfoot, and there was a strange smell, a smell which grew inexplicably stronger as they went forward.

"Mind your steps! There's probably another body somewhere around. Don't fall over it."

"I forgot to feel the pockets of the fellow under the raft. Probably he was one of our comrades."

"Who else could it be?"

"Now I remember. The message of number seventy-four was stitched into the back of his trousers, the message of thirteen was hidden in a cigarette, and. . . ."

"Rubbish! Don't talk. We are still under close watch. Look out, because we don't want to have two more corpses in the place."

Lu-Yi was embarrassed by the strange smell, and thought the corpse could hardly be more than five yeards away from them. He held his torch in his hand, and made as though he was going to flick on the light. but the boy prevented him. They pricked up their ears and listened intently. They heard the approaching splash of rhythmic oars. They were about five feet away from the river, but thick bushes of reeds screened them from sight. They were both aware of the critical situation they were in, for it was evident that the approaching boat was patrolling the river to prevent the guerrillas from using it as a means of communication. If the patrol boat had reached the bend in the river and discovered the raft and their footprints, they would be followed immediately, and God

knows what would happen then. Fortunately, they were already on land. . . .

At that moment, frightened by the steps of the two wanderers or by the splashing of the oars in the river, a waterfowl rose, flapped its wings, and flew up into the dark sky. And then, after describing aimless and purposeless evolutions, it darted towards the opposite bank of the river. They heard whispers among the oarsmen; probably they had already suspected the presence of strangers among the reeds. But the boat, instead of pursuing them, followed in the direction of the waterfowl, and they heard the leisurely pad of oars as the boat went towards the other bank.

The two wanderers lay on the bank with their pistols pointed in the direction of the boat. They were calm and determined, but when they heard the boat moving into the distance, they held out their hands silently at the same moment and clasped one another's hands with excitement and relief. Then they went on.

They could still smell the corpse, which was evidently lying somewhere to their left, away from the path. Suddenly Lu-Yi felt a hand snatching at his sleve.

"Devil take you! What do you want?" he groaned.

"I think it is comrade seventy-four. Let me go and feel his body. A minute, or half a minute. . . ."

Without waiting for an answer from the older man, who was clearly displeased by the suggestion, the boy bent down and ran swiftly towards the place in the bushes where the heavy foetid smell came from. He was back half a minute later.

"It's him all right," the boy said. "And it smells like him. He was a daring and dauntless fellow when alive, and now, even in corruption, his smell is terrific."

"What have you got?"

"A handful of maggots."

"Are you sure it is him?"

"Yes, I tore off his collar. The papers are there. I knew it right away."

"Nice fellows—both of you!"

They strode along the path in silence. They were soon out of the bushes, but new dangers seemed to be lying in wait for them. Soon they came to a hillside, where the path diverged, one road leading down towards the ford, and the other winding strangely among the battlemented rocks. A few lights were shining above the ford: evidently the place was well guarded. They gazed into one another's

1158

faces and neither could decide which pass was more dangerous or easier to get through.

Each minute gained gave them more hope, but they had no time to lose. They knew that the path to the ford was more familiar to them, and, if necessary, they could wade or swim across the river. They made a dash for the river. The boy saw that a fire was going out, and was probably unattended, but the older man held him back.

"Don't go near the fire, boy!"

"Don't worry. The fire must have been left behind by the patrols who boarded the boat. Probably they left it intentionally, to make us think they were there."

Once more the boy won the older man's consent. Crawling on all fours, they made their way towards the dying embers. They passed the fire unharmed, and found themselves before a long smooth road which wound along the edge of the hills and the river. They were light hearted now, and all the danger forgotten, until some minutes later the boy thought he heard the clop-clop of a horse's hooves along the road. Lu-Yi listened. He too, heard the sound and imagined that the enemy was approaching, followed perhaps by a wolfhound trained to smell out strangers at night. They decided to hide in the woods which bordered the hill, and blindly they crawled among the shadows of rocks and trees. Later, they heard the sound of hoof-beats along the road at the place where they had been, and they even imagined they could see the sparks from under the horse's feet and the white, thick vapour coming from the horse's mouth, and the sleek shadow of its back.

On his way down the slope, Lu-Yi twisted his ankle, but he knew that he would have to go as fast as possible if they were to avoid the guard station.

The sound of cocks crowing was wafted down the river. They decided, then, to bury their automatics among the reeds and swim downstream. If they could once pass the pontoon bridge, they would find themselves in safe territory less than a quarter of a mile away. But Lu-Yi knew that with his twisted ankle, it would be impossible for him to swim. They could go over the hills, but the tracks there were unknown to them, and hardly visible even in broad daylight. Moreover, beyond the hills lay precipitous slopes looking down over a ravine, and it would be easy for the enemy patrols to pick them out.

Knowing that the position was hopeless, Lu-Yi broke out into angry remonstrances.

1159

"Boy, it's a trick played by devils. I know I am going to die here, and become a mess of worms. Next time you pass this way, better feel my collar as well. I can't walk. My right leg hurts abominably, and I am sure I can't swim. You go downstream, and I'll go to the hills—and give me your pistol."

"No, if you are hurt, I'll go with you. We'll go up the hill and die together if we have to."

"Why should we die together, my dear little devil," Lu-Yi answered, in a tone of annoyance. "Give me your pistol, and make your own way downstream."

The boy was silent. The older man repeated his command.

"I'll do as you say," the boy answered at last in a low voice. He unslung his belt, and all the time he was wondering how anyone could climb up hills and down valleys with only one game leg. He hesitated before handing the pistol over. They had gone on many dangerous errands together, and they had worked well together, and now Lu-Yi had to take the most dangerous road of all. He hardly dared to leave his companion. Lu-Yi saw this, and tried to console him.

"Boy, don't worry about me. With two pistols I shall kill many before I am killed. I prefer climbing to swimming, and in any case your journey will be hard. There may be barbed wire rising from the bottom of the river near the pontoon bridge. You may have to climb over the bridge—that's dangerous. I think I shall find my way easily enough over the hill, and when I find you I shall give you your pistol back. We'll meet again, my dear little devil."

Both knew that he was lying. Hardly had Lu-Yi finished speaking when he stepped forward and helped the boy untie his pistol belt, and the bandolier of bullets which fell down from his shoulders. Then he patted the boy on the arm and asked him to jump into the water before he himself went uphill. The kindly dogmatism of the older man, the deep friendship which existed between them, and the strict discipline which existed among the guerrilla troops, all these exhorted the boy to slide down the embankment and into the water without another word.

The stream murmured quietly and coldly, and the boy threw himself in the water, imitating the cry of a wildfowl to show that he was already on his way, and meanwhile the older man, as a sign of final greeting, threw a pebble which landed a little way from the boy's foot. Thus, for the last time, they bade each other farewell and went on their ways.

1160

The boy exerted all the strength of his young limbs, and cautiously moved downstream. He saw fires burning at each end of the pontoon bridge, and each fire cast a dazzling shadow on the water. The bridge was formed of a number of sampans and fishing boats fastened together with iron thews; there was a sentry at each end, and there were also three or four soldiers patrolling the bridge. With his face showing only a little above water, the boy attempted to surrender to the force of the water, hoping to slide under the bridge without making the slightest sound. Suddenly he heard a whistling sound from the hilltop, and a moment later there was the sound of shooting. He knew then that the whereabouts of his friend had been discovered, but what puzzled him was that there was no answering fire from his friend. The bridge was only two yards away from him, shining in the light of the flares. He dived swiftly. There were no obstacles rising from the bottom of the river. Three yards past the bridge he came to the surface, and at that very moment he heard the automatic pistol shooting seven times in rapid succession. Soon afterwards he heard four successive pistol shots, and for the moment there were no more sounds.

Later he heard three rifle shots, then there was silence, followed by a solitary pistol shot. Immediately afterwards he heard a shrill scream from someone on the bridge. A torchlight swept over the bridge, and all around. Once more the boy dived, and when he came to the surface again all was silent in the boundless darkness except for the interminable murmur of the water beneath his body. The black night air permeating all the space overhead seemed to press down on the river and penetrate through his skin and into his veins. He knew that the safety zone lay less than a quarter of a mile away.

He saw a camp fire blazing through the darkness, and the recognition of the friendly light and the illusory warmth which came from the fire gave him new strength.

"Password!"

"Nine . . . ty, with both feet wrapped in cloth."

"Why only one? Where's your companion?"

"Ask the ghost of your ancestor."

"Is he lost then?"

There was no reply. Only a splashing sound was heard when the boy climbed up the river bank.

SHIH NAI-AN

SHIH NAI-AN (Chinese, *ca.* 1290-1365). Traditional author of *All Men Are Brothers*, one of four or five masterpieces of Chinese fiction. Written in the fourteenth century, improved and embellished during two succeeding centuries, receiving its final form. The novel is based on a cycle of stories about a band of outlaws.

"DEATH OF THE TIGERS"

LET it here be told only how Li K'uei feared lest Li Ta lead men out to pursue him. Carrying his mother on his back he turned towards the wilds of the mountain into the small lonely paths where no men were. After a while had passed, he saw that the sky was dark with night, and he carried his mother into a valley. Now his old mother's two eyes were dim and she did not know if it were morning or night. But Li K'uei knew this valley, and it was called the I Valley. On the other side only were there any homes. And the mother and son, taking advantage of the light of the new moon, went slowly step by step up the valley, and the mother said as she was on her son's back, "My son, if you could fetch a mouthful of water for me to drink it would be well."

And again Li K'uel said, "I am suffering more than I can bear, too."

Now Li K'uei saw that step by step he had come to the edge of pine trees and to a place where there was a great green stone. There he put his mother down and he thrust his sword into the earth beside her and he commanded her, saying, "Be patient and sit awhile and I will go and seek water for you to drink."

Now Li K'uei had heard the gurgling sound of water and he sought a path thither and when he had climbed over several foothills he came to the side of a brook and he dipped up water in his hands and he drank several mouthfuls. And to himself he thought, "How can I fetch this water to give my mother to drink?"

He stood up and looked east and he looked west. In the far distance upon the point of the mountain he saw a temple. He said, "Ha, it is well!"

And grasping vines and branches he climbed up the mountain side and went to the front of the temple. When he pushed the gate open and looked in he saw it was a temple to The Dragon God of Sze Chou. In front of the god was a stone urn for incense. Li-K'uei

put his hand out to seize this. Now this urn was fastened upon a stone altar beneath and Li K'uei pulled at it awhile, but how could he pull it up? Then his anger rose and he jerked the altar and urn and all and he pulled them up and carried them to the stone terrace in front of the terrace and threw them down and knocked off the urn from the altar. He took the urn then and went again to the brook and he soaked it clean in the brook and he pulled some wild grass and he washed the urn clean. Then he dipped up half the urn full of water and, bearing it in both hands, he went along his old path, and stumbling along he came again to the valley.

But when he had come to the stone by the pine trees he did not see his mother. There was only the sword thrust into the ground. Then Li K'uei called, "Mother, drink some water!"

But there was no sound anywhere. When he had called and there was no answer, Li K'uei's heart was filled with fear and he put down the urn and staring about he looked in all four directions. He did not see his mother, but when he had gone not more than thirty-odd paces he saw a pool of blood upon the grass. When he saw this his flesh began to tremble. Following the flow of the blood he went to seek, and he sought to the mouth of a great cave. There he saw two tiger cubs gnawing upon a human leg. Li K'uei could not check his shivering and he said, "I returned from the mountain lair especially to seek out my old mother, and I carried her on my back through a thousand pains and bitternesses, and I did, but bring her here for you to eat! As for that leg which that cursed tiger has dragged hither, if it is not my mother's then whose is it?"

When the fire of his anger rose in his heart he ceased his shivering and his red and yellow whiskers stood erect. He lifted up the sword in his hand; he stabbed at those two tiger cubs. Now the two cubs were terrified and with their teeth bared and their claws outspread they charged to attack Li K'uei, but Li K'uei lifted his hand and stabbed one to death. Then the other one turned and hastened into the cave, and Li K'uei pursued it into the cave and stabbed it to death also.

Now when Li K'uei had rushed into the tigers' den, as he stood crouching there and staring about him, he saw the mother tiger standing looking into the den, her teeth bared and her claws outspread. And Li K'uei cried, "Truly it was you, you wicked wild beast, who ate my mother!"

And he put down his sword and he took his dagger out from his person. Now that mother tiger reached the mouth of the cave and

1163

she thrust her tail into the den and whirled it about, and was about to sit down upon her haunches in the den. But Li K'uei could see very clearly there in the den and he reached his dagger to the point below the tigress's tail and with all his strength he thrust forward, and he thrust it straight into the beast's anus. Yet he used his strength too heavily and he had thrust the very handle of the dagger through to the tigress's belly and the tigress gave a great growl and with the dagger in her vitals she rushed out of the cave and leaped to a point on the mountain beyond. Then Li K'uei took his sword and he hastened out of the cave. The tigress, suffering the pain, leaped down the mountain. Li K'uei was just about to hasten after her when he saw a great wind come out of the trees beside him, and the leaves fall from the trees like rain, and to himself he thought, "Clouds come with the dragon, wind with the tiger."

Now the place where this wind rose was beneath the light of the new moon. There came forth a deep growl and all of a sudden there leaped out a slant-eyed, white-browed tiger. That great beast charged at Li K'uei with its whole strength. But Li K'uei was not fearful nor agitated. He took advantage of the force of the beast's attack and he lifted his sword in his hand and thrust it straight into the tiger's throat.

As for the tiger, he did not attack with his hind feet nor strike with his tail, for he tried to save himself his pain, and moreover, Li K'uei had pierced his windpipe. The tiger retreated not more than five or seven paces when Li K'uei heard a sound as though the half of a great mountain fell. Straightway then did the tiger die there beside the rock.

In this short time did Li K'uei kill the two tigers and their cubs. Then he went once more into the den with his knife and looked about, lest there be yet another tiger. But there was none. And Li K'uei was weary by now also, and he went to The Temple To The Dragon God, and he slept there until dawn.

On the morning of the next day Li K'uei went to collect his mother's two legs and such of her bones as had not yet been devoured, and he took a cloth and wrapped them up. He went behind The Temple To The Dragon God and he dug a hole and buried them, and there he did weep mightily for a while. Yet he was hungry and thirsty too, and at last he tied up his bundle again and took his sword and seeking a path he slowly crossed the valley.

HENRYK SIENKIEWICZ

HENRYK SIENKIEWICZ (Polish, 1846-1916). Vivid historical novelist of Poland. Traveled in America and Africa. Won Nobel Prize, 1905. Beloved in native country for patriotic trilogy based on Polish history. Known the world over for *Quo Vadis,* novel of the Roman Empire. Other novels translated: *With Fire and Sword, The Deluge.*

THE LIGHTHOUSE KEEPER OF ASPINWALL

ON a time it happened that the lighthouse keeper in Aspinwall, not far from Panama, disappeared without a trace. Since he disappeared during a storm, it was supposed that the ill-fated man went to the very edge of the small, rocky island on which the lighthouse stood, and was swept out by a wave. This supposition seemed the more likely, as his boat was not found next day in its rocky niche. The place of lighthouse keeper had become vacant. It was necessary to fill this place at the earliest moment possible, since the lighthouse had no small significance for the local movement as well as for vessels going from New York to Panama. Mosquito Bay abounds in sandbars and banks. Among these, navigation, even in the daytime, is difficult; but at night, especially with the fogs which are so frequent on those waters warmed by the sun of the tropics, it is nearly impossible. The only guide at that time for the numerous vessels is the lighthouse.

The task of finding a new keeper fell to the United States consul living in Panama, and this task was no small one: first, because it was absolutely necessary to find a man within twelve hours; second, the man must be unusually conscientious—it was not possible, of course, to take the first comer at random; finally, there was an utter lack of candidates. Life on a tower is uncommonly difficult, and by no means enticing to people of the South, who love idleness and the freedom of vagrant life. That lighthouse keeper is almost a prisoner. He cannot leave his rocky island except on Sundays. A boat from Aspinwall brings him provisions and water once a day, and returns immediately; on the whole island, one acre in area, there is no inhabitant. The keeper lives in the lighthouse; he keeps it in order. During the day he gives signals by displaying flags of various colors to indicate changes of the barometer; in the evening he lights the lantern. This would be no great labor were it not that to reach the lantern at the summit of the tower he must pass over more than

1165

four hundred steep and very high steps; sometimes he must make this journey repeatedly during the day. In general, it is the life of a monk, and indeed more than that—the life of a hermit. It was not wonderful, therefore, that Mr. Isaac Falconbridge was in no small anxiety as to where he should find a permanent successor to the recent keeper; and it is easy to understand his joy when a successor announced himself most unexpectedly on that very day. He was a man already old, seventy years or more, but fresh, erect with the movements and bearing of a soldier. His hair was perfectly white, his face as dark as that of a Creole; but, judging from his blue eyes, he did not belong to the people of the South. His face was somewhat downcast and sad, but honest. At the first glance he pleased Falconbridge. It remained only to examine him. Therefore the following conversation began:

"Where are you from?"

"I am a Pole."

"Where have you worked up to this time?"

"In one place and another."

"A lighthouse keeper should like to stay in one place."

"I need rest."

"Have you served? Have you testimonials of honorable government service?"

The old man drew from his bosom a piece of faded silk, resembling a strip of an old flag, unwound it, and said:

"Here are the testimonials. I received this cross in 1830. This second one is Spanish from the Carlist War; the third is the French legion; the fourth I received in Hungary. Afterward I fought in the States against the South; there they do not give crosses."

Falconbridge took the paper and began to read.

"H'm! Skavinski? Is that your name? H'm! Two flags captured in a bayonet attack. You were a gallant soldier."

"I am able to be a conscientious lighthouse keeper."

"It is necessary to ascend the tower a number of times daily. Have you sound legs?"

"I crossed the plains on foot." (The immense steppes between the East and California are called "the plains.")

"Do you know sea service?"

"I served three years on a whaler."

"You have tried various occupations."

"The only one I have not known is quiet."

"Why is that?"

1166

The old man shrugged his shoulders. "Such is my fate."

"Still you seem to me too old for a lighthouse keeper."

"Sir," exclaimed the candidate suddenly in a voice of emotion, "I am greatly wearied, knocked about. I have passed through much, as you see. This place is one of those which I have wished for most ardently. I am old, I need rest. I need to say to myself, 'Here you will remain; this is your port.' Ah, sir, this depends now on you alone. Another time perhaps such a place will not offer itself. What luck that I was in Panama! I entreat you—as God is dear to me, I am like a ship which if it misses the harbor will be lost. If you wish to make an old man happy—I swear to you that I am honest, but—I have enough of wandering."

The blue eyes of the old man expressed such earnest entreaty that Falconbridge, who had a good, simple heart, was touched.

"Well," said he, "I take you. You are lighthouse keeper."

The old man's face gleamed with inexpressible joy.

"I thank you."

"Can you go to the tower to-day?"

"I can."

"Then good-bye. Another word—for any failure in service you will be dismissed."

"All right."

That same evening, when the sun had descended on the other side of the isthmus, and a day of sunshine was followed by a night without twilight, the new keeper was in his place evidently, for the lighthouse was casting its bright rays on the water as usual. The night was perfectly calm, silent, genuinely tropical, filled with a transparent haze, forming around the moon a great colored rainbow with soft, unbroken edges; the sea was moving only because the tide raised it. Skavinski on the balcony seemed from far below like a small black point. He tried to collect his thoughts and take in his new position; but his mind was too much under pressure to move with regularity. He felt somewhat as a hunted beast feels when at last it has found refuge from pursuit on some inaccessible rock or in a cave. There had come to him, finally, an hour of quiet; the feeling of safety filled his soul with a certain unspeakable bliss. Now on that rock he can simply laugh at his previous wanderings, his misfortunes and failures. He was in truth like a ship whose masts, ropes, and sails had been broken and rent by a tempest, and cast from the clouds to the bottom of the sea—a ship on which the tempest had hurled waves and spat foam, but which still wound its

way to the harbor. The pictures of that storm passed quickly through his mind as he compared it with the calm future now beginning. A part of his wonderful adventures he had related to Falconbridge; he had not mentioned, however, thousands of other incidents. It had been his misfortune that as often as he pitched his tent and fixed his fireplace to settle down permanently, some wind tore out the stakes of his tent, whirled away the fire, and bore him on toward destruction. Looking now from the balcony of the tower at the illuminated waves, he remembered everything through which he had passed. He had campaigned in the four parts of the world, and in wandering had tried almost every occupation. Labor-loving and honest, more than once he had earned money, and had always lost it in spite of every provision and the utmost caution. He had been a gold miner in Australia, a diamond-digger in Africa, a rifleman in public service in the East Indies. He established a ranch in California —the drought ruined him; he tried trading with wild tribes in the interior of Brazil—his raft was wrecked on the Amazon; he himself alone, weaponless, and nearly naked, wandered in the forest for many weeks living on wild fruits, exposed every moment to death from the jaws of wild beasts. He established a forge in Helena, Arkansas, and that was burned in a great fire which consumed the whole town. Next he fell into the hands of Indians in the Rocky Mountains, and only through a miracle was he saved by Canadian trappers. Then he served as a sailor on a vessel running between Bahia and Bordeaux, and as harpooner on a whaling-ship; both vessels were wrecked. He had a cigar factory in Havana, and was robbed by his partner while he himself was lying sick with the vomito. At last he came to Aspinwall, and there was to be the end of his failures—for what could reach him on that rocky island? Neither water nor fire nor men. But from men Skavinski had not suffered much; he had met good men oftener than bad ones.

But it seemed to him that all the four elements were persecuting him. Those who knew him said that he had no luck, and with that they explained everything. He himself became something of a mono-maniac. He believed that some mighty and vengeful hand was pursuing him everywhere, on all lands and waters. He did not like, however, to speak of this; only at times, when someone asked him whose hand that could be, he pointed mysteriously to the Polar Star, and said, "It comes from that place." In reality his failures were so continuous that they were wonderful, and might easily drive a nail into the head, especially of the man who had experienced them. But

Skavinski had the patience of an Indian, and that great calm power of resistance which comes from truth of heart. In his time he had received in Hungary a number of bayonet-thrusts because he would not grasp at a stirrup which was shown as means of salvation to him, and cry for quarter. In like manner he did not bend to misfortune. He crept up against the mountain as industriously as an ant. Pushed down a hundred times, he began his journey calmly for the hundred and first time. He was in his way a most peculiar original. This old soldier, tempered, God knows in how many fires, hardened in suffering, hammered and forged, had the heart of a child. In the time of the epidemic in Cuba, the vomito attacked him because he had given to the sick all his quinine, of which he had a considerable supply, and left not a grain for himself.

There had been in him also this wonderful quality—that after so many disappointments he was ever full of confidence, and did not lose hope that all would be well yet. In winter he grew lively, and predicted great events. He waited for these events with impatience, and lived with the thought of them whole summers. But the winters passed one after another, and Skavinski lived only to this—that they whitened his head. At last he grew old, began to lose energy; his endurance was becoming more and more like resignation, his former calmness was tending toward supersensitiveness, and that tempered soldier was degenerating into a man ready to shed tears for any cause. Besides this, from time to time he was weighed down by a terrible homesickness which was roused by any circumstance—the sight of swallows, gray birds like sparrows, snow on the mountains, or melancholy music like that heard on a time. It mastered the old man thoroughly, and swallowed all other desires and hopes. This ceaseless wanderer could not imagine anything more precious, than a quiet corner in which to rest, and wait in silence for the end. Perhaps specially because some whim of fate had so hurried him over all seas and lands that he could hardly catch his breath, did he imagine that the highest human happiness was his due; but he was so accustomed to disappointments that he thought of rest as people in general think of something which is beyond reach. He did not dare to hope for it. Meanwhile, unexpectedly, in the course of twelve hours he had gained a position which was as if chosen for him out of all the world. We are not to wonder, then, that when he lighted his lantern in the evening he became as it were dazed— that he asked himself if that was reality, and he did not dare to answer that it was. But at the same time reality convinced him with

1169

incontrovertible proofs; hence hours one after another passed while he was on the balcony. He gazed, and convinced himself. It might seem that he was looking at the sea for the first time in his life. The lens of the lantern cast into the darkness an enormous triangle of light, beyond which the eye of the old man was lost in the black distance completely, in the distance mysterious and awful. But that distance seemed to run toward the light. The long waves following one another rolled out from the darkness, and went bellowing towards the base of the island; and then their foaming backs were visible, shining rose-coloured in the light of the lantern. The incoming tide swelled more and more, and covered the sandy bars. The mysterious speech of the ocean came with a fullness more powerful and louder, at one time like the thunder of cannon, at another like the distant dull sound of the voices of people. At moments it was quiet; then to the ears of the old man came some great sigh, then a kind of sobbing, and again threatening outbursts. At last the wind bore away the haze, but brought black, broken clouds, which hid the moon. From the west it began to blow more and more; the waves sprang with rage against the rock of the lighthouse, licking with foam the foundation walls. In the distance a storm was beginning to bellow. On the dark, disturbed expanse certain green lanterns gleamed from the masts of ships. These green points rose high and then sank; now they swayed to the right, and now to the left. Skavinski descended to his room. The storm began to howl. Outside, people on those ships were struggling with night, with darkness, with waves but inside the tower it was calm and still. Even the sounds of the storm hardly came through the thick walls, and only the measured tick-tack of the clock lulled the wearied old man to his slumber.

Hours, days, and weeks began to pass. Sailors assert that sometimes when the sea is greatly roused, something from out of the midst of night and darkness calls them by name. If the infinity of the sea may call out thus, perhaps when a man is growing old, calls come to him, too, from another infinity still darker and more deeply mysterious; and the more he is wearied by life the dearer are those calls to him. But to hear them quiet is needed. Besides old age loves to put itself aside, as if with a foreboding of the grave. The lighthouse had become for Skavinski such a half grave. Nothing is more monotonous than life on a beacon-tower. If young people consent to take up this service they leave it after a time. Lighthouse keepers are generally men not young, gloomy, and confined to

themselves. If by chance one of them leaves his lighthouse and goes among men, he walks in the midst of them like a person roused from deep slumber. On the tower there is a lack of minute impressions which in ordinary life teach men to adapt themselves to everything. All that a lighthouse keeper comes in contact with is gigantic and devoid of definitely outlined forms. The sky is one whole, the water another; and between those two infinities the soul of man is in loneliness. That is a life in which thought is continual meditation, and out of that meditation nothing rouses the keeper, not even his work. Day is like day as two beads in a rosary, unless changes of weather form the only variety. But Skavinski felt more happiness than ever in life before. He rose with the dawn, took his breakfast, polished the lens, and then sitting in the balcony gazed into the distance of the water; and his eyes were never sated with the pictures which he saw before him. On the enormous turquoise ground of the ocean were to be seen generally flocks of swollen sails gleaming in the rays of the sun so brightly, that the eyes were blinking before the excess of light. Sometimes the ships, favored by the so-called trade winds, went in an extended line one after another, like a chain of sea-mews or albatrosses. The red casks indicating the channel swayed on the light wave with gentle movement. Among the sails appeared every afternoon grayish feather-like plumes of smoke. That was a steamer from New York which brought passengers and goods to Aspinwall, drawing behind it a frothy path of foam. On the other side of the balcony Skavinski saw, as if on his palm, Aspinwall and its busy harbor, and in it a forest of masts, boats, and craft; a little farther, white houses and the towers of the town. From the height of his tower the small houses were like the nests of sea-mews, the boats were like beetles, and the people moved around like small points on the white stone boulevard. From early morning a light eastern breeze brought a confused hum of human life, above which predominated the whistle of steamers. In the afternoon six o'clock came; the movements in the harbor began to cease; the mews hid themselves in the rents of the cliffs; the waves grew feeble and became in some sort lazy; and then on the land, on the sea, and on the tower came a time of stillness unbroken by anything. The yellow sands from which the waves had fallen back glittered like golden stripes on the width of the waters; the body of the tower was outlined definitely in blue. Floods of sunbeams were poured from the the sky on the water and the sands and the cliff. At that time a certain lassitude full of sweetness seized the old man. He felt that

1171

the rest which he was enjoying was excellent; and when he thought that it would be continuous nothing was lacking to him.

Skavinski was intoxicated with his own happiness; and since a man adapts himself easily to improved conditions, he gained faith and confidence by degrees; for he thought that if men built houses for invalids, why should not God gather up at last His own invalids? Time passed, and confirmed him in this conviction. The old man grew accustomed to his tower, to the lantern, to the rock, to the sand-bars, to solitude. He grew accustomed also to the sea-mews which hatched in the crevices of the rock, and in the evening held meetings on the roof of the lighthouse. Skavinski threw them generally the remnants of his food; and soon they grew tame, and afterward when he fed them, a real storm of white wings encircled him, and the old man went among the birds like a shepherd among sheep. When the tide ebbed he went to the low sandbanks, on which he collected savory periwinkles and beautiful pearl shells of the nautilus, which receding waves had left on the sand. In the night by the moonlight and the tower he went to catch fish, which frequented the windings of the cliff in myriads. At last he was in love with his rocks and his treeless little island, grown over only with small thick plants exuding sticky resin. The distant views repaid him for the poverty of the island, however. During afternoon hours, when the air became very clear he could see the whole isthmus covered with the richest vegetation. It seemed to Skavinski at such times that he saw one gigantic garden—bunches of cocoa, and enormous musa, combined as it were in luxurious tufted bouquets, right there behind the houses of Aspinwall. Farther on, between Aspinwall and Panama, was a great forest over which every morning and evening hung a reddish haze of exhalations—a real tropical forest with its feet in stagnant water, interlaced with lianas and filled with the sound of one sea of gigantic orchids, palms, milk-trees, iron-trees, gum-trees.

Through his field-glass the old man could see not only trees and the broad leaves of bananas, but even legions of monkeys and great marabous and flocks of parrots, rising at times like a rainbow cloud over the forest. Skavinski knew such forests well, for after being wrecked on the Amazon he had wandered whole weeks among similar arches and thickets. He had seen how many dangers and deaths lie concealed under those wonderful and smiling exteriors. During the nights which he had spent in them he heard close at hand the sepulchral voices of howling monkeys and the roaring of

the jaguars; he saw gigantic serpents coiled like lianas on trees; he knew those slumbering forest lakes full of torpedo-fish and swarming with crocodiles; he knew under what a yoke man lives in those unexplored wildernesses in which are single leaves that exceed a man's size ten times—wildernesses swarming with blood-drinking mosquitoes, tree-leeches, and gigantic poisonous spiders. He had experienced that forest life himself, had witnessed it, had passed through it; therefore it gave him the greater enjoyment to look from his height and gaze on those *matos,* admire their beauty, and be guarded from their treacherousness. His tower preserved him from every evil. He left it only for a few hours on Sunday. He put on then his blue keeper's coat with silver buttons, and hung his crosses on his breast. His milk-white head was raised with a certain pride when he heard at the door, while entering the church, the Creoles say among themselves, "We have an honorable lighthouse keeper and not a heretic, though he is a Yankee." But he returned straightway after Mass to his island, and returned happy, for he had still no faith in the mainland. On Sunday also he read the Spanish newspaper which he bought in the town, or the *New York Herald,* which he borrowed from Falconbridge; and he sought in it European news eagerly. The poor old heart on that lighthouse tower, and in another hemisphere, was beating yet for its birthplace. At times too, when the boat brought his daily supplies and water to the island, he went down from the tower to talk with Johnson, the guard. But after a while he seemed to grow shy. He ceased to go to the town, to read the papers and to go down to talk politics with Johnson. Whole weeks passed in this way, so that no one saw him and he saw no one. The only signs that the old man was living were the disappearance of the provisions left on shore, and the light of the lantern kindled every evening with the same regularity with which the sun rose in the morning from the waters of those regions. Evidently, the old man had become indifferent to the world. Homesickness was not the cause, but just this—that even homesickness had passed into resignation. The whole world began now and ended for Skavinski on his island. He had grown accustomed to the thought that he would not leave the tower till his death, and he simply forgot that there was anything else besides it. Moreover, he had become a mystic; his mild blue eyes began to stare like the eyes of a child, and were as if fixed on something at a distance. In presence of a surrounding uncommonly simple and great, the old man was losing the feeling of personality; he was ceasing to exist as an individual,

1173

was becoming merged more and more in that which inclosed him. He did not understand anything beyond his environment; he felt only unconsciously. At last it seems to him that the heavens, the water, his rock, the tower, the golden sand-banks, and the swollen sails, the sea-mews, the ebb and flow of the tide—all form a mighty unity, one enormous mysterious soul; that he is sinking in that mystery, and feels that soul which lives and lulls itself. He sinks and is rocked, forgets himself; and in that narrowing of his own individual existence, in that half-waking, half-sleeping, he has discovered a rest so great that it nearly resembles half-death.

But the awakening came.

On a certain day, when the boat brought water and a supply of provisions, Skavinski came down an hour later from the tower, and saw that besides the usual cargo there was an additional package. On the outside of this package were postage stamps of the United States, and the address: "Skavinski, Esq.," was written on coarse canvas.

The old man, with aroused curiosity, cut the canvas, and saw books; he took one in his hand, looked at it, and put it back; thereupon his hands began to tremble greatly. He covered his eyes as if he did not believe them; it seemed to him as if he were dreaming. The book was Polish—what did that mean? Who could have sent the book? Clearly, it did not occur to him at the first moment that in the beginning of his lighthouse career he had read in the *Herald*, borrowed from the consul, of the formation of a Polish society in New York, and had sent at once to that society half his month's salary, for which he had, moreover, no use on the tower. The society had sent him the books with thanks. The books came in the natural way; but at the first moment the old man could not seize those thoughts. Polish books in Aspinwall, on his tower, amid his solitude—that was for him something uncommon, a certain breath from past times, a kind of miracle. Now it seemed to him, as to those sailors in the night, that something was calling him by name with a voice greatly beloved and nearly forgotten. He sat for a while with closed eyes, and was almost certain that, when he opened them, the dream would be gone.

The package, cut open, lay before him, shone upon clearly by the afternoon sun, and on it was an open book. When the old man stretched his hand toward it again, he heard in the stillness the beating of his own heart. He looked; it was poetry. On the outside stood printed in great letters the title, underneath the name of the

1174

author. The name was not strange to Skavinski; he saw that it belonged to the great poet, whose production he had read in 1830 in Paris. Afterward, when campaigning in Algiers and Spain, he had heard from his countrymen of the growing fame of the great seer; but he was so accustomed to the musket at that time that he took no book in hand. In 1849, he went to America, and in the adventurous life which he led he hardly ever met a Pole, and never a Polish book. With the greater eagerness, therefore, and with a livelier beating of the heart, did he turn to the title-page. It seemed to him then that on his lonely rock some solemnity is about to take place. Indeed it was a moment of great calm and silence. The clocks of Aspinwall were striking five in the afternoon. Not a cloud darkened the clear sky; only a few sea-mews were sailing through the air. The ocean was as if cradled to sleep. The waves on the shore stammered quietly, spreading softly on the sand. In the distance the white houses of Aspinwall, and the wonderful groups of palm, were smiling. In truth, there was something there solemn, calm, and full of dignity. Suddenly, in the midst of that calm of Nature, was heard the trembling voice of the old man, who read aloud as if to understand himself better:

"Thou art like health, O my birth-land Litva!
How much we should prize thee he only can know who has
    lost thee.
Thy beauty in perfect adornment this day
I see and describe, because I am yearning for thee."

His voice failed Skavinski. The letters began to dance before his eyes; something broke in his breast, and went like a wave from his heart higher and higher, choking his voice and pressing his throat. A moment more he controlled himself, and read further:

"O Holy Lady, who guardest bright Chenstohova,
Who shinest in Ostrobrama and preservest
The castle town Novgrodek with its trusty people,
As Thou didst give me back to health in childhood,
When by my weeping mother placed beneath Thy care
I raised my lifeless eyelids upward,
And straightway walked unto Thy holy threshold,
To thank God for the life restored me,—
So by wonder now restore us to the bosom of our birthplace."

1175

The swollen wave broke through the restraint of his will. The old man sobbed, and threw himself on the ground; his milk-white hair was mingled with the sand of the sea. Forty years had passed since he had seen his country, and God knows how many since he heard his native speech; and now that speech had come to him itself—it had sailed to him over the ocean, and found him in solitude on another hemisphere—it so loved, so dear, so beautiful! In the sobbing which shook him there was no pain—only a suddenly aroused immense love, in the presence of which other things are as nothing. With that great weeping he had simply implored forgiveness of that beloved one, set aside because he had grown so old, had become so accustomed to his solitary rock, and had so forgotten it that in him even longing had begun to disappear. But now it returned as if by a miracle; therefore the heart leaped in him.

Moments vanished one after another; he lay there continually. The mews flew over the lighthouse, crying as if alarmed for their old friend. The hour in which he fed them with the remnants of his food had come; therefore, some of them flew down from the lighthouse to him; then more and more came, and began to pick and shake their wings over his head. The sound of the wings roused him. He had wept his fill, and had now a certain calm and brightness; but his eyes were as if inspired. He gave unwittingly all his provisions to the birds, which rushed at him with an uproar, and he himself took the book again. The sun had gone already behind the gardens and the forest of Panama, and was going slowly beyond the isthmus to the other ocean; but the Atlantic was full of light yet; in the open air there was still perfect vision; therefore, he read further:

"Now bear my longing soul to those forest slopes, to those green meadows."

At last the dusk obliterates the letters on the white paper—the dusk short as a twinkle. The old man rested his head on the rock, and closed his eyes. Then "She who defends bright Chenstohova" took his soul and transported it to "those fields colored by various grain." On the sky were burning yet those long stripes, red and golden, and on those brightnesses he was flying to beloved regions. The pine-woods were sounding in his ears; the streams of his native place were murmuring. He saw everything as it was; everything asked him, "Dost remember?" He remembers! He sees broad fields;

1176

between the fields, wood and villages. It is night now. At this hour his lantern usually illuminates the darkness of the sea; but now he is in his native village. His old head has dropped on his breast, and he is dreaming. Pictures are passing before his eyes quickly, and a little disorderly. He does not see the house in which he was born, for war had destroyed it; he does not see his father and mother, for they died when he was a child; but still the village is as if he had left it yesterday—the line of cottages with lights in the windows, the mound, the mill, the two ponds opposite each other, and thundering all night with a chorus of frogs. Once he had been on guard in that village all night; now that past stood before him at once in a series of views. He is an Uhlan again, and he stands there on guard; at a distance is the public-house; he looks with swimming eyes. There is thundering and singing and shouting amid the silence of the night, with voices of fiddles and bass-viols "U-ha! U-ha!" Then the Uhlans knock out fire with their horseshoes, and it is wearisome for him there on his horse. The hours drag on slowly; at last the lights are quenched: now as far as the eye reaches there is mist, and mist impenetrable; now the fog rises, evidently from the fields, and embraces the whole world with a whitish cloud. You would say, a complete ocean. But that is fields; soon the land-rail will be heard in the darkness, and the bitterns will call from the reeds. The night is calm and cool—in truth, a Polish night! In the distance the pine-wood is sounding without wind, like the roll of the sea. Soon dawn will whiten the east. In fact, the cocks are beginning to crow behind the hedges. One answers to another from cottage to cottage; the storks are screaming somewhere on high. The Uhlan feels well and bright. Someone had spoken of a battle tomorrow. Hei! that will go on, like all the others, with shouting, with flutterings of flaglets. The young blood is playing like a trumpet, though the night cools it. But it is dawning. Already night is growing pale; out of the shadows come forests, the thicket, a row of cottages, the mill, the poplars. The well is squeaking like a metal banner on a tower. What a beloved land, beautiful in the rosy gleams of the morning! Oh, the one land, the one land!

Quiet! the watchful picket hears that someone is approaching. Of course, they are coming to relieve the guard.

Suddenly some voice is heard above Skavinski:

"Here, old man! Get up! What's the matter?

The old man opens his eyes, and looks with wonder at the person standing before him. The remnants of the dream-visions struggle in

his head with reality. At last the visions pale and vanish. Before him stands Johnson, the harbor guide.

"What's this?" asked Johnson; "are you sick?"

"No."

"You didn't light the lantern. You must leave your place. A vessel from St. Geromo was wrecked on the bar. It is lucky that no one was drowned, or you would go to trial. Get into the boat with me; you'll hear the rest at the Consulate."

The old man grew pale; in fact he had not lighted the lantern that night.

A few days later, Skavinski was seen on the deck of a steamer, which was going from Aspinwall to New York. The poor man had lost his place. There opened before him new roads of wandering; the wind had torn that leaf away again to whirl it over lands and seas, to sport with it till satisfied. The old man had failed greatly during those few days, and was bent over; only his eyes were gleaming. On his new road of life he held at his breast his book, which from time to time he pressed with his hand as if in fear that that too might go from him.

SOLOMON

SOLOMON (Hebrew, 10th Century, B.C.). Kingly poet and philosopher. Most powerful ruler of the Hebrew monarchy. Organizer, builder and reformer. The exceptionally lyrical, erotic "Song of Songs," attributed to him, has been endlessly disputed and interpreted by scholars—the commonest and most ingenious interpretation being that it is an allegory.

"THE SONG OF SOLOMON"

IV

Behold, thou art fair, my love; behold, thou art fair; thou hast doves' eyes within thy locks: thy hair is as a flock of goats, that appear from mount Gilead.

Thy teeth are like a flock of sheep that are even shorn, which came up from the washing; whereof every one bear twins, and none is barren among them.

Thy lips are like a thread of scarlet, and thy speech is comely; thy temples are like a piece of a pomegranate within thy locks.

Thy neck is like the tower of David builded for an armoury, whereon there hang a thousand bucklers, all shields of mighty men.

Thy two breast are like two young roes that are twins which feed among the lilies.

Until the day break, and the shadows flee away, I will get me to the mountain of myrrh, and to the hill of frankincense.

Thou art all fair, my love; there is no spot in thee.

Come with me from Lebanon, my spouse, with me from Lebanon: look from the top of Amana, from the top of Shenir and Hermon, from the lions' dens. from the mountains of the leopards.

Thou hast ravished my heart, my sister, my spouse; thou hast ravished my heart with one of thine eyes, with one chain of thy neck.

How fair is thy love, my sister, my spouse! How much better is thy love than wine! and the smell of thine ointments than all spices!

Thy lips, O my spouse, drop as the honeycomb: honey and milk are under thy tongue; and the smell of thy garments is like the smell of Lebanon.

A garden inclosed is my sister, my spouse; a spring shut up, a fountain sealed.

Thy plants are an orchard of pomegranates, with pleasant fruits; camphire, with spikenard,

Spikenard and saffron; calamus and cinnamon, with all trees of frankincense; myrrh and aloes, with all the chief spices:

A fountain of gardens, a well of living waters, and streams from Lebanon.

Awake, O north wind; and come, thou south; blow upon my garden, that the spices thereof may flow out. Let my beloved come into his garden, and eat his pleasant fruits.

V

I AM come into my garden, my sister, my spouse: I have gathered my myrrh with my spice; I have eaten my honeycomb with my honey; I have drunk my wine with my milk: eat, O friends; drink, yea, drink abundantly. O beloved.

I sleep, but my heart waketh: it is the voice of my beloved that knocketh, saying, Open to me, my sister, my love, my dove, my undefiled: for my head is filled with dew, and my locks with the drops of the night.

I have put off my coat; how shall I put it on? I have washed my feet; how shall I defile them?

My beloved put in his hand by the hole of the door, and my
bowels were moved for him.

I rose up to open to my beloved; and my hands dropped with
myrrh, and my fingers with sweet smelling myrrh, upon the handles
of the lock.

I opened to my beloved; but my beloved had withdrawn himself,
and was gone: my soul failed when he spake: I sought him, but I
could not find him; I called him, but he gave me no answer.

The watchmen that went about the city found me, they smote me,
they wounded me; the keepers of the walls took away my veil
from me.

I charge you, O daughters of Jerusalem, if ye find my beloved,
that ye tell him, that I am sick of love.

What is thy beloved more than another beloved, O thou fairest
among women? What is thy beloved more than another beloved,
that thou dost so charge us?

My beloved is white and ruddy, the chiefest among ten thousand.

His head is as the most fine gold, his locks are bushy, and black
as a raven.

His eyes are as the eyes of doves by the rivers of waters, washed
with milk, and fitly set.

His cheeks are as a bed of spices, as sweet flowers: his lips like
lilies, dropping sweet smelling myrrh.

His hands are as gold rings set with the beryl: his belly is as
bright ivory overlaid with sapphires.

His legs are as pillars of marble, set upon sockets of fine gold:
his countenance is as Lebanon, excellent as the cedars.

His mouth is most sweet; yea, he is altogether lovely. This is my
beloved, and this is my friend, O daughters of Jerusalem.

SOMADEVA

SOMADEVA (Sanskrit, 11th Century). Legendary Kashmir Brahmin. Little
known of his life. His celebrated collection of stories, *The Ocean of the
Streams of Story*, is based on a still earlier collection.

DEVASMITA

THERE is a city in the world famous under the name of Támraliptá,
and in that city there was a very rich merchant named Dhanadatta.

And he, being childless, assembled many Bráhmans and said to them with due respect, "Take such steps as will procure me a son soon." Then those Bráhmans said to him: "This is not at all difficult, for Bráhmans can accomplish all things in this world by means of ceremonies in accordance with the Scriptures. To give you an instance, there was in old times a king who had no sons, and he had a hundred and five wives in his harem. And by means of a sacrifice to procure a son, there was born to him a son named Jantu, who was like the rising of the new moon to the eyes of his wives. Once on a time an ant bit the boy on the thigh as he was crawling about on his knees, so that he was very unhappy and sobbed loudly. Thereupon the whole harem was full of confused lamentation, and the king himself shrieked out 'My son! my son;' like a common man. The boy was soon comforted, the ant having been removed, and the king blamed the misfortune of his only having one son as the cause of all his grief. And he asked the Bráhmans in his affliction if there was any expedient by which he might obtain a large number of children. They answered, 'O king, there is one expedient open to you; you must slay this son and offer up all his flesh in the fire. By smelling the smell of that sacrifice all thy wives will obtain sons.' When he heard that, the king had the whole ceremony performed as they directed; and he obtained as many sons as he had wives. So we can obtain a son for you also by a burnt-offering." When they had said this to Dhanadatta, the Bráhmans, after a sacrificial fee had been promised them, performed a sacrifice: then a son was born to that merchant. That son was called Guhasena, and he gradually grew up to man's estate. Then his father Dhanadatta began to look out for a wife for him.

Then his father went with that son of his to another country, on the pretence of traffic, but really to get a daughter-in-law. There he asked an excellent merchant of the name of Dharmagupta to give him his daughter named Devasmitá for his son Guhasena. But Dharmagupta, who was tenderly attached to his daughter, did not approve of that connection, reflecting that the city of Támraliptá was very far off. But when Devasmitá beheld that Guhasena, her mind was immediately attracted by his virtues, and she was set on abandoning her relations, and so she made an assignation with him by means of a confidante, and went away from that country at night with her beloved and his father. When they reached Támraliptá they were married, and the minds of the young couple were firmly knit together by the bond of mutual love. Then Guhasena's

father died, and he himself was urged by his relations to go to the country of Katáha for the purpose of trafficking; but his wife Devasmitá was too jealous to approve of that expedition, fearing exceedingly that he would be attracted by some other lady. Then, as his wife did not approve of it, and his relations kept inciting him to it, Guhasena, whose mind was firmly set on doing his duty, was bewildered. Then he went and performed a vow in the temple of the god, observing a rigid fast, trusting that the god would show him some way out of his difficulty. And his wife Devasmitá also performed a vow with him; then Siva was pleased to appear to that couple in a dream; and giving them two red lotuses the god said to them, "Take each of you one of these lotuses in your hand. And if either of you shall be unfaithful during your separation, the lotus in the hand of the other shall fade, but not otherwise." After hearing this, the two woke up, and each beheld in the hand of the other a red lotus, and it seemed as if they had got one another's hearts. Then Guhasena set out, lotus in hand. but Devasmitá remained in the house with her eyes fixed upon her flower. Guhasena for his part quickly reached the country of Katáha, and began to buy and sell jewels there. And four young merchants in that country, seeing that that unfading lotus was ever in his hand, were greatly astonished. Accordingly they got him to their house by an artifice, and made him drink a great deal of wine, and then asked him the history of the lotus, and he being intoxicated told them the whole story. Then those four young merchants, knowing that Guhasena would take a long time to complete his sales and purchases of jewels and other wares, planned together, like rascals as they were, the seduction of his wife out of curiosity, and eager to accomplish it set out quickly for Támraliptá without their departure being noticed. There they cast about for some instrument, and at last had recourse to a female ascetic of the name of Yogakaramdiká, who lived in a sanctuary of Buddha; and they said to her in an affectionate manner, "Reverend madam, if our object is accomplished by your help, we will give you much wealth." She answered them: "No doubt you young men desire some woman in this city, so tell me all about it, I will procure you the object of your desire. What woman do you desire? I will quickly procure her for you." When they heard that they said, "Procure us an interview with the wife of the merchant Guhasena named Devasmitá." When she heard that, the ascetic undertook to manage that business for them. and she gave those young merchants her own house to reside in. Then she gratified the ser-

vants at Guhasena's house with gifts of sweetmeats and other things, and afterwards entered it with her pupil. Then, as she approached the private rooms of Devasmitá, a hound, that was fastened there with a chain, would not let her come near, but opposed her entrance in the most determined way. Then Devasmitá seeing her, of her own accord sent a maid, and had her brought in, thinking to herself, "What can this person be come for?" After she had entered, the wicked ascetic gave Devasmitá her blessing, and treating the virtuous woman with affected respect, said to her, "I have always had a desire to see you, but to-day I saw you in a dream, therefore I have come to visit you with impatient eagerness; and my mind is afflicted at beholding you separated from your husband, for beauty and youth are wasted when one is deprived of the society of one's beloved." With this and many other speches of the same kind she tried to gain the confidence of the virtuous woman in a short interview, and then taking leave of her she returned to her own house. On the second day she took with her a piece of meat full of pepper dust, and went again to the house of Devasmitá, and there she gave that piece of meat to the hound at the door, and the hound gobbled it up, pepper and all. Then owing to the pepper dust, the tears flowed in profusion from the animal's eyes, and her nose began to run. And the cunning ascetic immediately went into the apartment of Devasmitá, who received her hospitably, and began to cry. When Devasmitá asked why she shed tears, she said with affected reluctance: "My friend, look at this hound weeping outside here. This creature recognised me to-day as having been its companion in a former birth, and began to weep; for that reason my tears gushed through pity." When she heard that, and saw that hound outside apparently weeping, Devasmitá thought for a moment to herself, "What can be the meaning of this wonderful sight?" Then the ascetic said to her, "My daughter, in a former birth, I and that hound were the two wives of a certain Bráhman. And our husband frequently went about to other countries on embassies by order of the king. Now while he was away from home, I lived at my good will and pleasure, and so did not cheat the elements, of which I was composed, and my senses, of their lawful enjoyment. For considerate treatment of the elements and senses is held to be the highest duty. Therefore I have been born in this birth with a recollection of my former existence. But she, in her former life, through ignorance, confined all her attention to the preservation of her character, therefore, she has been degraded and born again as one of the canine race, however, she too remem-

1183

bers her former birth." The wise Devasmitá said to herself, "This is a novel conception of duty; no doubt this woman has laid a treacherous snare for me"; and so she said to her, "Reverend lady, for this long time I have been ignorant of this duty, so procure me an interview with some charming man." Then the ascetic said, "There are residing here some young merchants that have come from another country, so I will bring them to you." When she had said this, the ascetic returned home delighted, and Devasmitá of her own accord said to her maids: "No doubt those scoundrelly young merchants, whoever they may be, have seen that unfading lotus in the hand of my husband, and have on some occasion or other, when he was drinking wine, asked him out of curiosity to tell the whole story of it, and have now come here from that island to deceive me, and this wicked ascetic is employed by them. So bring quickly some wine mixed with Datura, and when you have brought it, have a dog's foot of iron made as quickly as possible." When Devasmitá had given these orders, the maids executed them faithfully, and one of the maids, by her orders, dressed herself up to resemble her mistress. The ascetic for her part chose out of the party of four merchants (each of whom in his eagerness said—"Let me go first"—) one individual, and brought him with her. And concealing him in the dress of her pupil, she introduced him in the evening into the house of Devasmitá, and coming out, disappeared. Then that maid, who was disguised as Devasmitá, courteously persuaded the young merchant to drink some of that wine drugged with Datura. That liquor, like his own immodesty, robbed him of his senses, and then the maids took away his clothes and other equipments and left him stark naked; then they branded him on the forehead with the mark of a dog's foot, and during the night took him and pushed him into a ditch full of filth. Then he recovered consciousness in the last watch of the night, and found himself plunged in a ditch, as it were the hell *Avíchi* assigned to him by his sins. Then he got up and washed himself and went to the house of the female ascetic, in a state of misery, feeling with his fingers the mark on his forehead. And when he got there, he told his friends that he had been robbed on the way, in order that he might not be the only person made ridiculous. And the next morning he sat with a cloth wrapped round his branded forehead, giving as an excuse that he had a headache from keeping awake so long, and drinking too much. In the same way the next young merchant was maltreated, when he got to the house of Devasmitá, and when he returned home stripped, he said,

1184

"I put on my ornaments there, and as I was coming out I was plundered by robbers." In the morning he also, on the plea of a headache, put a wrapper on to cover his branded forehead.

In the same way all the four young merchants suffered in turn branding and other humiliating treatment, though they concealed the fact. And they went away from the place, without revealing to the female Buddhist ascetic the ill-treatment they had experienced, hoping that she would suffer in a similar way. On the next day the ascetic went with her disciple to the house of Devasmitá, much delighted at having accomplished what she undertook to do. Then Devasmitá received hr courteously, and made her drink wine drugged with Datura, offered as a sign of gratitude. When she and her disciple were intoxicated with it, that chaste wife cut off their ears and noses, and flung them also into a filthy pool. And being distressed by the thought that perhaps these young merchants might go and slay her husband, she told the whole circumstance to her mother-in-law. Then her mother-in-law said to her, "My daughter, you have acted nobly, but possibly some misfortune may happen to my son in consequence of what you have done."

So the wise Devasmitá forthwith put on the dress of a merchant. Then she embarked on a ship, on the pretence of a mercantile expedition, and came to the country of Katáha where her husband was. And when she arrived there, she saw that husband of hers, Guhasena, in the midst of a circle of merchants, like consolation in external bodily form. He seeing her afar off in the dress of a man, as it were, drank her in with his eyes, and thought to himself, "Who may this merchant be that looks so like my beloved wife?" So Devasmitá went and represented to the king that she had a petition to make, and asked him to assemble all his subjects. Then the king full of curiosity assembled all the citizens, and said to that lady disguised as a merchant, "What is your petition?" Then Devasmitá said, "There are residing here in your midst four slaves of mine who have escaped, let the king make them over to me." Then the king said to her, "All the citizens are present here, so look at everyone in order to recognise him, and take those slaves of yours." Then she seized upon the four young merchants, whom she had before treated in such a humiliating way in her house, and who had wrappers bound round their heads. Then the merchants, who were there, flew in a passion, and said to her, "These are the sons of distinguished merchants, how then can they be your slaves?" Then she answered them, "If you do not believe what I say, examine their

1185

foreheads which I marked with a dog's foot." They consented, and removing the head-wrappers of these four, they all beheld the dog's foot on their foreheads. Then all the merchants were abashed, and the king, being astonished, himself asked Devasmitá what all this meant. She told the whole story, and all the people burst out laughing, and the king said to the lady, "They are your slaves by the best of titles." Then the other merchants paid a large sum of money to the chaste wife, to redeem those four from slavery, and a fine to the king's treasury. Devasmitá received that money, and recovered her husband, and being honoured by all good men, returned then to her own city Támraliptá, and she was never afterwa ds separated from her beloved.

SOPHOCLES

SOPHOCLES (Greek, 496-406 B.C.). Early master of the drama, next to Aeschylus in time and rank. Is said to have introduced third actor into the drama, and made each play a unit instead of part of a trilogy. Of his 123 plays, 7 survive. Among them: *Antigone, Electra, Ajax, Oedipus Tyrannus.* Notable for humanizing his characters and for skillful play construction.

ANTIGONE

Antigone, the daughter of Œdipus, having buried her father, returns to Thebes. Eteocles and Polynices, her brothers, having fallen by each other's hand, the kingdom devolves on Creon, their uncle. The tragedy of Antigone begins with Creon's edict forbidding the rites of burial to Polynices, as a traitor, and threatening with death any one who should dare to bury him. In violation of the decree, Antigone sprinkles dust and pours libations over the body of her brother, but is arrested and condemned to be immured in a cave. Tiresias, the seer, warns Creon that the offended people will rage, that his cities shall be polluted and his palace filled with woe. Creon relents and gives orders for the burial of Polynices, and goes himself to free Antigone. He is too late; she has killed herself, and her lover, Creon's son Hæmon, lies slain by her side. In the meantime, Eurydice, the queen, has stabbed herself before the altar. As the play closes, Creon is in utter mi ry.

ANTIGONE BEFORE KING CREON

Guards bring in Antigone

Guard. I come, although I swore the contrary,
Bringing this maiden, whom in act we found
Decking the grave.
And now, O king, take her, and as thou wilt,
Judge and convict her.
   Creon. How and where was it that ye seized and brought her?
   Guard. She was in act of burying. Thou knowest all.
   Creon. Dost know and rightly speak the tale thou tell'st?
   Guard. I saw her burying that self-same corpse
Thou bad'st us not to bury. Speak I clear?
   Creon. How was she seen, and taken in the act?
   Guard. The matter passed as follows:—When we came,
With all those dreadful threats of thine upon us,
Sweeping away the dust which, lightly spread,
Covered the corpse, and laying stripped and bare
The tainted carcase, on the hill we sat
To windward, shunning the infected air,
Each stirring up his fellow with strong words,
If any shirked his duty. This went on
Some time, until the glowing orb of day
Stood in mid heaven, and the scorching heat
Fell on us. Then a sudden whirlwind rose,
A scourge from heaven, raising squalls on earth,
And filled the plain, the leafage stripping bare
Of all the forest, and the air's vast space
Was thick and troubled, and we closed our eyes,
Until the plague the Gods had sent was past;
And when it ceased, a weary time being gone,
The girl is seen, and with a bitter cry,
Shrill as a bird's, when it beholds its nest
All emptied of its infant brood, she wails;
Thus she, when she beholds the corpse all stripped,
Groaned loud with many moanings, and she called
Fierce curses down on those who did the deed.
And in her hand she brings some fine, dry dust,
And from a vase of bronze, well wrought, upraised,
She pours the three libations o'er the dead.

1187

And we, beholding, give her chase forthwith,
And run her down, naught terrified at us.
And then we charged her with the former deed,
As well as this. And nothing she denied.
But this to me both bitter is and sweet,
For to escape one's-self from ill is sweet,
But to bring friends to trouble, this is hard
And painful. Yet my nature bids me count
Above all these things safety for myself.

 Creon (*to Antigone*). Thou, then — yes, thou, who bend'st thy
 face to earth—
Confessest thou, or dost deny the deed?
 Antig. I own I did it, and will not deny.
 Creon (*to Guard*). Go thou thy way, where'er thy will may
 choose,
Freed from a weighty charge.

(Exit Guard.)

(*To Antigone*). And now for thee.
Say in few words, not lengthening out thy speech,
Knew'st thou the edicts which forbade these things?
 Antig. I knew them. Could I fail? Full clear were they.
 Creon. And thou didst dare to disobey these laws?
 Antig. Yes, for it was not Zeus who gave them forth,
Nor Justice, dwelling with the Gods below,
Who traced these laws for all the sons of men;
Nor did I deem thy edicts strong enough,
That thou, a mortal man, shouldst over-pass
The unwritten laws of God that know not change.
They are not of to-day nor yesterday,
But live for ever, nor can man assign
When first they sprang to being. Not through fear
Of any man's resolve was I prepared
Before the Gods to bear the penalty
Of sinning against these. That I should die
I knew, (how should I not?) though thy decree
Had never spoken. And, before my time
If I shall die, I reckon this a gain;
For whoso lives, as I, in many woes,
How can it be but he shall gain by death?

1188

And so for me to bear this doom of thine
Has nothing painful. But, if I had left
My mother's son unburied on his death,
In that I should have suffered; but in this
I suffer not. And should I seem to thee
To do a foolish deed, 'tis simply this,—
I bear the charge of folly from a fool. . . . .
And yet how could I higher glory gain
Than placing my true brother in his tomb?
There is not one of these but would confess
It pleases them, did fear not seal their lips.
The tyrant's might in much besides excels,
And it may do and say whate'er it will.

    Creon.   Of all the race of Cadmos thou alone
Look'st thus upon the deed.

    Antig.   They see it too
As I do, but their tongue is tied for thee.

    Creon.   Art not ashamed against their thoughts to think?

    Antig.   There is naught base in honoring our own blood.

    Creon.   And was he not thy kin who fought against him?

    Antig.   Yea, brother, of one father and one mother.

    Creon.   Why then give honor which dishonors him?

    Antig.   The dead below will not repeat thy words.

    Creon.   Yes, if thou give like honor to the godless.

    Antig.   It was his brother, not his slave, that died.

    Creon.   Wasting this land, while *he* died fighting for it.

    Antig.   Yet Hades still craves equal rites for all.

    Creon.   The good craves not the portion of the bad.

    Antig.   Who knows if this be holy deemed below?

    Creon.   Not even when he dies can foe be friend.

    Antig.   My nature leads to sharing love, not hate.

    Creon.   Go then below; and if thou must have love,
Love them. While I live, women shall not rule.

ANTIGONE AND ISMENE

Ismene, sister of Antigone, had in fear of the king's decree refused to join her in performing the burial rites for her brother Polynices. But when Antigone is arrested, Ismene is willing and eager to share her fate.

Enter Ismene, led in by Attendants

Chorus. And, lo! Ismene at the gate
Comes shedding tears of sisterly regard,
And o'er her brow a gathering cloud
    Mars the deep roseate blush,
    Bedewing her fair cheek.

Creon (to Ismene). And thou who, creeping as a viper creeps
Didst drain my life in secret, and I knew not
That I was rearing two accursed ones,
Subverters of my throne,—come, tell me, then,
Wilt thou confess thou tookst thy part in this,
Or wilt thou swear thou didst not know of it?

Ism. I did the deed, if she did go; with her
I share the guilt, and bear an equal blame.

Antig. Nay, justice will not suffer this, for thou
Didst not consent, nor did I let thee join.

Ism. Nay, in thy troubles, I am not ashamed
in the same boat with thee to share thy fate.

Antig. Who did it, Hades knows, and those below:
I do not love a friend who loves in words.

Ism. Do not, my sister, put me to such shame,
As not to let me join in death with thee,
And so to pay due reverence to the dead.

Antig. Share not my death, nor make thine own this deed
Thou hadst no hand in. My death shall suffice.

Ism. What life to me is sweet, bereaved of thee?

Antig. Save thou thyself. I grudge not thy escape.

Ism. Ah, woe is me! and must I miss thy fate?

Antig. Thou mad'st thy choice to live, and I to die.

Ism. 'Twas not because I failed to speak my thoughts.

Antig. To these didst thou, to those did I seem wise.

Ism. And yet the offence is equal in us both.

Antig. Take courage. Thou dost live. My soul long since
Hath died to render service to the dead.

Creon. Of these two girls the one goes mad but now,
The other ever since her life began.

Ism. E'en so, O king; no mind that ever lived
Stands firm in evil days, but goes astray.

Creon. Thine did. when. with the vile, vile deeds thou chosest.

Ism. How could I live without her presence here?

Creon. Speak not of presence. She is here no more.

Ism. And wilt thou slay thy son's betrothed bride?

Creon. Full many a field there is which he may plough.

Ism. None like that plighted troth 'twixt him and her.

Creon. Wives that are vile I love not for my sons.

Ism. Ah, dearest Hæmon, how thy father shames thee!

Creon. Thou with that marriage dost but vex my soul.

Chor. And wilt thou rob thy son of her he loved?

Creon. 'Tis Death, not I, shall break the marriage off.

Chor. Her doom is fixed, it seems, then. She must die.

Creon. Fixed, yes, by me and thee. No more delay,
Lead them within, ye slaves. These must be kept
Henceforth as women, suffered not to roam;
For even boldest natures shrink in fear
When they see Hades overshadowing life.

KING ŒDIPUS

The terrible story of Œipus had a strong fascination for the
Greeks, as illustrating the conflict of moral laws and the supremacy
of destiny. Laius, King of Thebes, learned from the oracle of
Apollo, at Delphi, that he was destined to perish by the hand of
his own son. He ordered his wife Jocasta, therefore, to destroy the
infant. She gave it to a herdsman, who left it, tied with thongs, on
Mount Cithæron. But a shepherd of Corinth found the babe and
delivered it to King Polybus, who adopted it as his own child, and
called it Œdipus (Swollen-foot). When grown up, Œdipus is told
by the oracle that he would slay his father and marry his mother.
On his return to Corinth he met Laius in a narrow pass and, in a
dispute about the road, slew him. Passing to Thebes, he destroyed
the Sphinx, a monster which had been inflicting damage on the
city. Œdipus was, therefore, raised to the throne and the widowed
Jocasta receives him as her husband. A pestilence arises, and the
oracle declares that it cannot be abated until the murder of Laius
is avenged. On investigation the appalling secret is discovered,
whereupon Jocasta commits suicide, and Œdipus tears out his own
eyes and goes into exile.

Jocasta. Princes of Thebes, we deemed it meet to seek
The temples of the gods, and in our hands
These votive wreaths, this odorous incense bear.
The soul of Œdipus on a wild sea
Of anxious care is tossed;—nor, as becomes

The prudent, weighs by former oracles
This late response, but lends a willing ear
To all who speak of terrors. Since my voice
Avails no more, Lycæan king, to thee
I fly, for thou art nearest to our need,
And come in prayer a suppliant to thy shrine,
That thou mayst grant us thine auspicious aid;
Since all now tremble, when we thus behold
Our very pilot shuddering and appalled.

Enter Corinthian

Corinthian. Can ye inform me, strangers, where your king,
Great Œdipus, his regal state maintains;
Or, if ye know, where I may find the monarch?
Chorus. These are th' imperial halls—he is within—
This is his wife, the mother of his children.
Cor. Blest may she be, and ever with the blest
Hold glad communion; to her royal lord
A most accomplished consort.
Joc. Equal joy
Attend thee, stranger,—thy kind greeting claims
This due return of courtesy. But say,
Whence cam'st thou to our Thebes, and what thy tidings?
Cor. Joy to thy house, O lady! and thy lord.
Joc. What joy?—and from what region art thou come?
Cor. From Corinth. At my words thou wilt rejoice:
Why shouldst thou not—yet fond regrets will rise.
Joc. What dost thou mean, and whence this two-fold influence?
Cor. The assembled States of Isthmus, rumor tells,
Will choose thy lord to mount the vacant throne.
Joc. How vacant? Reigns not Polybus in Corinth?
Cor. No more!—His only kingdom is the tomb.
Joc. Haste, haste, attendant, and convey with speed
These tidings to your lord. Vain oracles!
Where are your bodings now? My Œdipus,
Fearing to slay this man, forsook his country;
Now Fate, and not his hand, hath laid him low.

Enter Œdipus

Œdipus. Why, my beloved Jocasta, has thou sent
To bid my presence hither?

Joc.   Hear this man—
Attend his tidings, and observe the end
Of these most true and reverend oracles.
   Œd.   Who is this stranger—with what message charged?
   Joc.   He is from Corinth, thence despatched to tell thee
That Polybus, thy father, is no more.
   Œd.   What sayest thou, stranger? Be thyself the speaker.
   Cor.   Then, in plain terms, the king is dead and gone.
   Œd.   Died he by treason, or the chance of sickness?
   Cor.   Slight ills dismiss the aged to their rest.
   Œd.   Then by disease, it seems, the monarch died.
   Cor.   And bowed beneath a withering weight of years.
   Œd.   Ha! is it thus? Then, lady, who would heed
The Pythian shrine oracular, or birds
Clanging in air, by whose vain auspices
I was fore-doomed the murderer of my father?
In the still silence of the tomb he sleeps.
While I am here—the fatal sword untouched,
Unless he languished for his absent child,
And I was thus the author of his doom.
Now in the grave he lies, and with him rest
Those vain predictions, worthy of our scorn.
   Joc.   Did I not tell thee this before?
   Œd.   Thou didst,
But terror urged me onward.
   Joc.   Banish now
This vain solicitude.
   Œd.   Should I not fear
The dark pollution of my mother's bed?
   Joc.   Oh, why should mortals fear, when fortune's sway
Rules all, and wariest foresight naught avails?
Best to live on unheeding, as thou may'st.
   Œd.   Phœbus foretold that I should wed my mother,
And shed with impious hand a father's blood.
For this I fled my own Corinthian towers
To seek a distant home—that home was blest;
Though still I languished to embrace my parents,
   Cor.   This fear then urged thee to renounce thy country?
   Œd.   Old man, I would not be a father's murderer.
   Cor.   Then wherefore, since thy welfare I regard,
Should I forbear to rid thee of this terror?

Œd. Do so, and rich shall be thy recompense.

Cor. This hope impell'd me here, that when our State
Hails thee her monarch, I might win thy favor.

Œd. Ne'er will I seek the authors of my birth.

Cor. 'Tis plain, my son, thou know'st not what thou doest!

Œd. How! how! old man, by heaven, unfold thy meaning.

Cor. If this preclude thee from returning home—

Œd. I fear lest Phœbus saw, alas! too clearly!

Cor. If thou dost dread pollution from thy parents—

Œd. That restless dread for ever haunts my soul.

Cor. Know, then, thy terrors all are causeless here.

Œd. How so? if of these parents I was born?

Cor. But Polybus is not allied to thee.

Œd. How say'st thou? was not Polybus my father?

Cor. No more than I—our claims are equal here.

Œd. Had he who gave me life no nearer claim
Than thou, a stranger?

Cor. Nor to him or me
Ow'st thou thy birth.

Œd. Then wherefore did he grant
A son's beloved name?

Cor. He from my hand
Received thee as a gift.

Œd. With such fond love
How could he cherish thus an alien child?

Cor. His former childless state to this impelled him.

Œd. Gav'st thou a purchased slave, or thy own child?

Cor. I found thee in Cithæron's shadowy glades.

Œd. Why didst thou traverse those remoter vales?

Cor. It was my charge to tend the mountain herds.

Œd. Wert thou a herdsman, and engaged for hire?

Cor. I was, my son, but thy preserver too.

Œd. From what affliction didst thou then preserve me?

Cor. This let thy scarr'd and swollen feet attest.

Œd. Ha! why dost thou revive a woe long passed?

Cor. I loosed thy bound and perforated feet.

Œd. Such foul reproach mine infancy endured.

Cor. From this event arose the name thou bear'st.

Œd. Thou didst receive me then from other hands,
Nor find me as by chance?

Cor.   No; to my hand
Another herdsman gave thee.

Œd.   Who was he?
Canst thou inform me this?

Cor.   He was, I believe,
A slave of Laius.

Œd.   What! of him who erst
Ruled o'er this land?

Cor.   The same;—this man to him
Discharged an herdsman's office.

Œd.   Lives he yet
That I may see him?

Cor.   Ye, his countrymen,
Are best prepared this question to resolve.

Œd.   Is there, of you who now attend our presence,
One who would know the herdsman he describes,
Familiar erst or here, or in the field?
Speak—for the time demands a prompt disclosure.

Ch.   He is, I deem, no other than the man
Whom thou before didst summon from the fields.
This none can know more than the Queen.

Œd.   Think'st thou, O Queen, the man whose presence late
We bade, is he of whom this stranger speaks?

Joc.   Who—spake of whom?—Regard him not, nor dwell,
With vain remembrance, on unmeaning words!

Œd.   Nay, Heaven forfend, when traces of my birth
Are thus unfolding, I should cease to follow.

Joc.   Nay, by the Gods I charge thee! search no more,
If life be precious still. Be it enough
That I am most afflicted.

Œd.   Cheer thee, lady,
Though my descent were proved e'en trebly servile,
No stain of infamy would light on thee.

Joc.   Ah yield, I do conjure thee—seek no more.

Œd.   I will not yield, till all be clearly known.

Joc.   'Tis for thy peace I warn thee—yet be wise.

Œd.   That very wisdom wounds my peace most deeply.

Joc.   Unhappy—never may'st thou know thy birth.

Œd.   Will none conduct this shepherd to our presence?
Leave her to triumph in her lordly race.

1195

Joc.   Woe! woe! unhappy! henceforth by that name
Alone can I address thee, and by that
Alone for ever.

Œd.   I will on
To trace my birth, though it be most obscure.
Pride swells her thus, for in a woman's breast
Pride reigns despotic, and she thinks foul scorn
Of my ignoble birth. I deem myself
The child of Fortune, in whose favoring smile
I shall not be dishonored. She alone
Hath been my fostering parent; from low state
My kindred mouths have raised me into greatness.
Sprung from such lineage, none I heed beside,
Nor blush reluctant to explore my birth.

Enter Herdsman

Œd.   Approach, old man! look on me, and reply
To my demand. Wert thou the slave of Laius?

Herd.   I was his slave—bred in his house—not purchased.
My better part of life was passed in tending
The monarch's flocks.

Œd.   What regions wert thou then
Wont to frequent?

Herd.   Cithæron and the meads
Adjacent.

Cor.   Then answer, dost thou recollect the babe
Thou gav'st me there, as mine own child to cherish?

Herd.   What wouldst thou? Whither do thy questions tend?

Cor.   This is that child, my friend, who stands before thee.

Herd.   A curse light on thee! wilt thou not be silent?

Œd.   Reprove him not, old man, for thine own words,
Far more than his, demand a stern reprover.

Herd.   I did:—Oh, had that moment been my last!

Œd.   This shall be, if thou wilt not speak the truth.

Herd.   And if I speak it, I am trebly lost.

Œd.   This man, it seems, still struggles to elude us.

Herd.   No, I confessed long since I gave the child.

Œd.   And whence received? thine own, or from another?

Herd.   No, not mine own; I from another's hand
Bare him.

Œd.   And from what Theban, from what roof?

1196

Herd.   Oh, by the gods! my lord, inquire no further.
Œd.   If I repeat th' inquiry, thou art lost.
Herd.   The palace of King Laius gave him birth.
Œd.   Sprung from a slave, or of the royal stock?
Herd.   The child was called the son of Laius; here
The royal consort can inform thee better.
Œd.   Didst thou from her receive him?
Herd.   Yea, O king!—
Œd.   And for what purpose?
Herd.   That I might destroy him—
Œd.   What—the unnatural mother!
Herd.   She was awed
By woe-denouncing oracles.
Œd.   What woe?
Herd.   That he should prove the murderer of his parents.
Œd.   Why, then, to this old man thy charge consign?
Herd.   From pity, O my lord, I deemed that he
To his own land would bear the child afar.
He saved him to despair. If thou art he
Of whom he spake, how dark a doom is thine!
Œd.   Woe! woe! 'tis all too fatally unveiled.
Thou Light! Oh, may I now behold thy beams
For the last time! Unhallowed was my birth;
In closest ties united, where such ties
Were most unnatural;—with that blood defiled,
From whose pollution most the heart recoils.

CARL SPITTELER

CARL SPITTELER (Swiss, 1845-1924). Swiss poet and essayist. A rebellious neo-classicist, whose position in German literature is still in dispute. Though he wrote both realistic and romantic works, his major career was spent on a modern Greek epic, *Olympian Spring*. A lonely and unusual figure. Nobel Prize-winner, 1919.

THEME

Bell, my silver tonguéd bell,
Oh, thy secret prithee tell:

Dwellst where bats and night-owls roam,
Lonely in thy moldered home;
Tell me, whence thy solemn ring?
And who taught thee, pray, to sing?

When in gloomy shaft I lay,
Night of hell I saw alway.
In this tower high and free
Through the whirling winds I see
Human sorrow graced by soul.
And thou wonderst why I toll?

"HERACLES PASSING TO EARTH"

But now the king the host of heralds did invite.
"The harpers bring, the singing maids, into my sight,
That Heracles unto the lovely sounds of mirth,
With courage fortified, may tread his way to earth!"
Before the gate there rose the buzz of strings subdued,
And laughter from the throat, as if a bird had cooed,
Betrayed the sportive singing-maidens' coming nigh.
Spake Zeus to Heracles: "It hurts to say good-by!"
And leads him to the court and fountain. At the brink
A little, and the rest he gives his son with cheer:
"Drink heartily!" he says, "this spring is true and clear!"
Then, with his hands upon the youthful shoulders: "Man!
Now let there happen what there will and come what can:
Into a royal font baptismal thou hast dipped,
And from the dripping fountain-flood of truth hast sipped.
That thou hast drunk with Zeus out of one glass today
The might of thousand rascals cannot wrench away.
In some dark hour shouldst thou in want of comfort be,
Look up, remember then: thou hast a bond with me
What I could do for thee is done. The retinue
That is to follow on thy way, come let us view."

With playing of the strings and bursts of song about,
Now from the house the king doth with his son step out.
Hark: cracks of whips and jingling! Plumes and pinions bold!
A chariot train of princely Titans now behold.
"I welcome ye!" spake Zeus. "What do ye bring me now?"
"We came the son of Zeus with talents to endow."
"Then thanks! For thus I know the way of kinsmen dear."
And now round Heracles the princes formed a sphere:
Nobility from Artemis and from Apollo
Comes valor, thought so keen that no mistake can follow
From Pallas—Hermes now his glance with kindness fills,
And Aphrodite mirth into his hearts instils.
Zeus spake and bound about the bosom of his son
The scroll of fate: "Now that thou really must be gone,
Receive my counsel: keep a stubborn head!
And be no simple fool—no rascal dread!"
The escorts then round Heracles with song and play
All turned into the fields to journey far away.
Ahead into the sky rang high the travel-song,
And golden grain looked down the hillsides all along.
No working-man, when Heracles did come in sight,
But sent to him some little words of kindness bright.
"Fare well on earth and prosper in the human land!"
And every lad ran toward him with outstreched hand.
A maiden laughs with eyes and mouth and checks—in zest
A bunch of flowers now she fastens to his breast.
And other human souls that came across his ways
At him with wonder in their dreamy eyes would gaze:
"Who cometh there whose steps sound victory so loud?
This hero's stature is of upright stock and proud!"
A maiden of the human beings one, but fairer
By far than all the other maidens be and rarer,
Drew near to him, her locks as if in slumber swaying,
And made him halt, upon his breast her finger laying.
Then pensively she bowed her forehead, sighing: "Oh,
Where is the street that we on earth do not yet know

1199

—Oh, tell me this, thou great unknown, oh tell thou me—
That over mountains, sombre forests, leads to thee?
If 'twere a thousand miles through many nights and days,
I would with quick'ning pulse o'ertake thee on thy ways.
If sharpest thorns should give me wounds, I would not bind
My bleeding foot at all, until I thee should find.
Forsee: on earth I know not where thou shalt be with me."
So I will go and dwell where thou shalt be with me."
Thus, dreaming, sighed the maid. Her speech was done; at last
She passed along her way with glances backward cast.
And Heracles, with all about him loving, kind,
In ecstasy of soul began within his mind:
"On earth I see a mountain looming to remind me.
A vow I'll make in solemn worship that shall bind me:
Ye joyous fields of high Olympos, beauty-bright,
Thou sky that floatest o'er the clouds in lofty height,
Ye dear ones all, unto my vow oh witness bear:
Now for my work I live, not for myself, I swear,
With heart and hands, nor rest nor pleasure taking more,
To love the great and do what ne'er was done before.
Oh, ye my human brothers, human sisters dear,
Your friend I'll be, your help devoted and sincere.
And no reward, except upon accomplished deed,
A silent, knowing glance but from the best, I need.
Hail, earth! I gladly pay the tax of pain you ask,
With courage spirited I come to do my task."
Thus cried he. Harps resounded, choirs rejoiced in song,
And through the folds of golden fields they passed along.

SSU-K'UNG T'U

SSÜ-K'UNG T'U (Chinese, 837-908). Scholarly pedantic stylist. Like many another Chinese poet, gave up an official career to write in retirement. His work shows great erudition rather than originality. Most famous: a 24-stanza poem, Êrh-shih-ssu shih-p'in.

RETURN OF SPRING

A lovely maiden, roaming
  The wild dark valley through,
Culls from the shining waters
  Lilies and lotus blue.
With leaves the peach-trees are laden,
  The wind sighs through the haze,
And the willows wave their shadows
  Down the oriole-haunted ways.
As, passion-tranced, I follow,
  I hear the old refrain
Of Spring's eternal story,
  That was old and is young again.

THE COLOUR OF LIFE

Would that we might for ever stay
The rainbow glories of the world,
The blue of the unfathomed sea,
The rare azalea late unfurled,
The parrot of a greener spring,
The willows and the terrace line,
The stranger from the night-steeped hills,
The roselit brimming cup of wine.
Oh for a life that stretched afar,
Where no dead dust of books were rife,
Where spring sang clear from star to star;
Alas! what hope for such a life?

SET FREE

I revel in flowers without let,
An atom at random in space;
My soul dwells in regions ethereal,
And the world is my dreaming-place.

As the tops of the ocean I tower,
As the winds of the air spreading wide,
I am 'stablished in might and dominion and power,
With the universe ranged at my side.

Before me the sun, moon, and stars,
Behind me the phœnix doth clang;
In the morning I lash my leviathans,
And I bathe my feet in Fusang.

FASCINATION

Fair is the pine grove and the mountain stream
That gathers to the valley far below,
The black-winged junks on the dim sea reach,
    adream,
The pale blue firmament o'er banks of snow.
And her, more fair, more supple smooth than jade,
Gleaming among the dark red woods I follow:
Now lingering, now as a bird afraid
Of pirate wings she seeks the haven hollow.
Vague, and beyond the daylight of recall,
Into the cloudland past my spirit flies,
As though before the gold of autumn's fall,
Before the glow of the moon-flooded skies.

TRANQUIL REPOSE

It dwells in the quiet silence,
    Unseen upon hill and plain,
'Tis lapped by the tideless harmonies,
    It soars with the lonely crane.

As the springtime breeze whose flutter
    The silken skirts hath blown,
As the wind-drawn note of the bamboo flute
    Whose charm we would make our own,—

Chance-met, it seems to surrender;
    Sought, and it lures us on;
Ever shifting in form and fantasy,
    It eludes us, and is gone.

JOHN ERNST STEINBECK

JOHN ERNST STEINBECK (1902-   ). Contemporary writer of powerful sociological novels. Born in the California country celebrated in *Tortilla Flat* and *Cannery Row*. Labored as newsman and bricklayer in New York. Best works are infused with sympathy for the underprivileged. *Grapes of Wrath*, epic of the dust bowl, has been compared with *Uncle Tom's Cabin*. Other novels: *Of Mice and Men, The Pearl.*

OWNERS AND TENANTS

THE owners of the land had come onto the land, or more often a spokesman for the owners came. They came in closed cars, and they felt the dry earth with their fingers, and sometimes they drove big earth augers into the ground for soil tests. The tenants from their sun-beaten dooryards, watched uneasily when the closed cars drove along the fields. And at last the owner men drove into the dooryards and sat in their cars to talk out of the windows. The tenant men stood beside the cars for a while, and then sqatted on their hams and found sticks with which to mark the dust.

In the open doors the women stood looking out, and behind them the children—corn-headed children, with wide eyes, one bare foot on top of the other bare foot, and the toes working. The women and the children watched their men talking to the owner men. They were silent.

Some of the owner men were kind because they hated what they had to do, and some of them were angry because they hated to be cruel, and some of them were cold because they had long ago found that one could not be an owner unless one were cold. And all of them were caught in something larger than themselves. Some of them hated the mathematics that drove them, and some were afraid, and some worshiped the mathematics because it provided a refuge from thought and from feeling. If a bank or a finance company owned the land, the owner man said, The Bank—or the Company— needs—wants—insists—must have— as though the Bank or the Company were a monster, with thought and feeling, which had ensnared them. These last would take no responsibility for the banks or the companies because they were men and slaves, while the banks were machines and masters all at the same time. Some of the owner men were a little proud to be slaves to such cold and powerful masters. The owner men sat in the cars and explained. You know the land is poor. You've scrabbled at it long enough, God knows.

The squatting tenant men nodded and wondered and drew figures in the dust, and yes, they knew, God knows. If the dust only wouldn't fly. If the top would only stay on the soil, it might not be so bad.

The owner men went on leading to their point: You know the land's getting poorer. You know what cotton does to the land; robs it, sucks all the blood out of it.

The squatters nodded—they knew, God knew. If they could only rotate the crops they might pump blood back into the land.

Well, it's too late. And the owner men explained the workings and thinkings of the monster that was stronger than they were. A man can hold land if he can just eat and pay taxes; he can do that.

Yes, he can do that until his crops fail one day and he has to borrow money from the bank.

But—you see, a bank or a company can't do that, because those creatures don't breathe air, don't eat side-meat. They breathe profits; they eat the interest on money. If they don't get it, they die the way you die without air, without side-meat. It is a sad thing, but it is so. It is just so.

The squatting men raised their eyes to understand. Can't we just hang on? Maybe the next year will be a good year. God knows how much cotton next year. And with all the wars—God knows what price cotton will bring. Don't they make explosives out of cotton? And uniforms? Get enough wars and cotton'll hit the ceiling. Next year, maybe. They looked up questioningly.

We can't depend on it. The bank—the monster has to have profits all the time. It can't wait. It'll die. No, taxes go on. When the monster stops growing, it dies. It can't stay one size.

Soft fingers began to tap the sill of the car window, and hard fingers tightened on the restless drawing sticks. In the doorways of the sun-beaten tenant houses, women sighed and shifted feet so that the one that had been down was now on top, and the toes working. Dogs came sniffing near the owner cars and wetted on all four tires one after another. And the chickens lay in the sunny dust and fluffed their feathers to get the cleansing dust down to the skin. In the little sties the pigs grunted inquiringly over the muddy remnants of the slops.

The squatting men looked down again. What do you want us to do? We can't take less share of the crop—we're half starved now. The kids are hungry all the times. We got no clothes, torn an' ragged. If all the neighbors weren't the same, we'd be ashamed to go to meeting.

1204

And at last the owner men came to the point. The tenant system won't work any more. One man on a tractor can take the place of twelve or fourteen families. Pay him a wage and take all the crop. We have to do it. We don't like to do it. But the monster's sick. Something's happened to the monster.

But you'll kill the land with cotton.

We know. We've got to take cotton quick before the land dies. Then we'll sell the land. Lots of families in the East would like to own a piece of land.

The tenant men looked up alarmed. But what'll happen to us? How'll we eat?

You'll have to get off the land. The plows'll go through the dooryard.

And now the squatting men stood up angrily. Grampa took up the land, and he had to kill the Indians and drive them away. And Pa was born here, and he killed weeds and snakes. Then a bad year came and he had to borrow a little money. An' we was born here. There in the door—our children born here. And Pa had to borrow money. The bank owned the land then, but we stayed and we got a little bit of what we raised.

We know that—all that. It's not us, it's the bank. A bank isn't like a man. Or an owner with fifty thousand acres, he isn't like a man either. That's the monster.

Sure, cried the tenant men, but it's our land. We measured it and broke it up. We were born on it, and we got killed on it, died on it. Even if it's no good, it's still ours. That's what makes it ours—being born on it, working it, dying on it. That makes ownership, not a paper with numbers on it.

We're sorry. It's not us. It's the monster. The bank isn't like a man.

Yes, but the bank is only made of men.

No, you're wrong there—quite wrong there. The bank is something else than men. It happens that every man in a bank hates what the bank does, and yet the bank does it. The bank is something more than men, I tell you. It's the monster. Men made it, but they can't control it.

The tenants cried: Grampa killed Indians, Pa killed snakes for the land. Maybe we can kill banks—they're worse than Indians and snakes. Maybe we got to fiight to keep our land, like Pa and Grampa did.

And now the owner men grew angry. You'll have to go.

But it's ours, the tenant men cried. We—

No. The bank, the monster owns it. You'll have to go.

We'll get our guns, like Grandpa when the Indians came. What then?

Well—first the sheriff, and then the troops. You'll be stealing if you try to stay, you'll be murderers if you kill to stay. The monster isn't men, but it can make men do what it wants.

But if we go, where'll we go? How'll we go? We got no money.

We're sorry, said the owner men. The bank, the fifty-thousand-acre owner can't be responsible. You're on land that isn't yours. Once over the line maybe you can pick cotton in the fall. Maybe you can go on relief. Why don't you go on West to California? There's work there and it never gets cold. Why, you can reach out anywhere and pick an orange. Why, there's always some kind of crop to work in. Why don't you go there? And the owner men started their cars and rolled away.

The tenant men squatted down on their hams again to mark the dust with a stick, to figure, to wonder. Their sun-burned faces were dark, and their sun-whipped eyes were light. The women moved cautiously out of the door-ways towards their men, and the children crept behind the women, cautiously, ready to run. The bigger boys squatted beside their fathers, because that made them men. After a time the women asked, What did he want?

And the men looked up for a second, and the smolder of pain was in their eyes. We got to get off. A tractor and a superintendent. Like factories.

Where'll we go? the women asked.

We don't know. We don't know.

And the women went quickly, quietly back into the houses and herded the children ahead of them. They knew that a man so hurt and so perplexed may turn in anger, even on people he loves. They left the men alone to figure and wonder in the dust.

After a time perhaps the tenant man looked about—at the pump put in ten years ago, with a goose-neck handle and iron flowers on the spout, at the chopping block where a thousand chickens had been killed, at the hand plow lying in the shed, and the patent crib hanging in the rafters over it.

The children crowded about the women in the houses. What are we going to do, Ma? Where are we going to go?

The women said: We don't know, yet. Go out and play. But don't go near your father. He might whale you if you go near him. And

1206

the women went on with the work, but all the time they watched the men squatting in the dust—perplexed and figuring.

The tractors came over the roads and into the fields, great crawlers moving like insects, having the incredible strength of insects. They crawled over the ground, laying the track and rolling on it and picking it up. Diesel tractors, puttering while they stood idle; they thundered when they moved, and then settled down to a droning roar. Snub-nosed monsters, raising the dust and sticking their snouts into it, straight down the country, through fences, through dooryards, in and out of gullies in straight lines. They did not run on the ground, but on their own roadbeds. They ignored hills and gulches, water courses, fences, houses.

The man sitting in the iron seat did not look like a man; gloved, goggled, rubber dust mask over the nose and mouth, he was a part of the monster, a robot in the seat. The thunder of the cylinders sounded through the country, became one with the air and the earth, so that earth and air muttered in sympathetic vibration. The driver could not control it—straight across the country it went, cutting through a dozen farms and straight back. A twitch at the controls could swerve the cat, but the driver's hands could not twitch because the monster that built the tractor, the monster that sent the tractor out, had somehow got into the driver's hands, into his brain and muscle, had goggled him and muzzled him—goggled his mind, muzzled his speech, goggled his perception, muzzled his protest. He could not see the land as it was, he could not smell the land as it smelled; his feet did not stamp the clods or feel the warmth and power of the earth. He sat in an iron seat and stepped on iron pedals. He could not cheer or beat or curse or encourage the extension of his power, and because of this he could not cheer or whip or curse or encourage himself. He did not know or own or trust or beseech the land. If a seed dropped did not germinate, it was nothing. If the young trusting plant withered in drought or drowned in a flood of rain, it was no more to the driver than to the tractor.

He loved the land no more than the bank loved the land. He could admire the tractor—its machined surfaces, its surge of power, the roar of its detonating cylinders; but it was not his tractor. Behind the tractor rolled the shining disks, cutting the earth with blades—not plowing but surgery, pushing the cut earth to the right where

1207

the second row of disks cut it and pushed it to the left; slicing blades shining, polished by the cut earth. And pulled behind the disks, the harrows combing with iron teeth so that the little clods broke up and the earth lay smooth. Behind the harrows, the long seeders—twelve curved iron penes erected in the foundry, orgasms set by gears, raping methodically, raping without passion. The driver sat in his iron seat and he was proud of the straight lines he did not will, proud of the tractor he did not own or love, proud of the power he could not control. And when that crop grew, and was harvested, no man had crumbled a hot clod in his fingers and let the earth sift through his fingertips. No man had touched the seed, or lusted for the growth. Men ate what they had not raised, had no connection with the bread. The land bore under iron, and under iron gradually died; for it was not loved or hated, it had no prayers or curses.

At noon the tractor driver stopped sometimes near a tenant house and opened his lunch; sandwiches wrapped in waxed paper, white bread, pickle, cheese, Spam, a piece of pie branded like an engine part. He ate without relish. And tenants not yet moved away came out to see him, looked curiously while the goggles were taken off, and the rubber dusk mask, leaving white circles around the eyes and a large white circle around nose and mouth. The exhaust of the tractor putted on, for fuel is so cheap it is more efficient to leave the engine running than to heat the Diesel nose for a new start. Curious children crowded close, ragged children who ate their fried dough as they watched. They watch hungrily the unwrapping of the sandwiches, and their hunger-sharpened noses smelled the pickle, cheese, and Spam. They didn't speak to the driver. They watched his hand as it carried food to his mouth. They did not watch him chewing; their eyes followed the hand that held the sandwich. After a while the tenant who could not leave the place came out and squatted in the shade beside the tractor.

"Why, you're Joe Davis's boy!"

"Sure," the driver said.

"Well, what are you doing this kind of work for—against your own people?"

"Three dollars a day. I got damn sick of creeping for my dinner —and not getting it. I got a wife and kids. We got to eat. Three dollars a day, and it comes every day."

"That's right," the tenant said. "But for your three dollars a day fifteen or twenty families can't eat at all. Nearly a hundred people have to go out and wander on the roads for your three dollars a day. Is that right?"

And the driver said, "Can't think of that. Got to think of my own kids. Three dollars a day, and it comes every day. Times are changing, mister, don't you know? Can't make a living on the land unless you've got two, five, ten thousand acres and a tractor. Crop land isn't for little guys like us any more. You don't kick up a howl because you can't make Fords, or because you're not the telephone company. Well, crops are like that now. Nothing to do about it. You try to get three dollars a day someplace. That's the only way."

The tenant pondered. "Funny thing how it is. If a man owns a little property, the property is him, it's part of him, and it's like him. If he owns property only so he can walk on it and handle it and be sad when it isn't doing well, and feel fine when the rain falls on it, the property is him, and someway he's bigger because he owns it. Even if he isn't successful he's big with his property. That is so."

And the tenant pondered more. "But let a man get property he doesn't see, or can't take time to get his fingers in, or can't be there to walk on it—why, then the property is the man. He can't do what he wants, he can't think what he wants. The property is the man, stronger than he is. And he is small, not big. Only his possessions are big—and he's the servant of his property. That is so, too."

The driver munched the branded pie and threw the crust away. "Times are changed, don't you know? Thinking about stuff like that don't feed the kids. Get your three dollars a day, feed your kids. You got no call to worry about anybody's kids but your own. You get a reputation for talking like that, and you'll never get three dollars a day. Big shots won't give you three dollars a day if you worry about anything but your three dollars a day."

"Nearly a hundred people on the road for your three dollars. Where will we go?"

"And that reminds me," the driver said, "you'd better get out soon. I'm going through the dooryard after dinner."

"You filled in the well this morning."

"I know. Had to keep the line straight. But I'm going through the dooryard after dinner. Got to keep the lines straight. And—well, you know Joe Davis, my old man, so I'll tell you this. I got orders wherever there's a family not moved out—if I have an

1209

accident—you know, get too close and cave the house in a little—well, I might get a couple of dollars. And my youngest kid never had no shoes yet."

"I built it with my hands. Straightened old nails to put the sheathing on. Rafters are wired to the stringers with baling wire. It's mine. I built it. You bump it down—I'll be in the window with a rifle. You even come too close and I'll pot you like a rabbit."

"It's not me. There's nothing I can do. I'll lose my job if I don't do it. And look—suppose you kill me? They'll just hang you, but long before you're hung there'll be another guy on the tractor, and he'll bump the house down. You're not killing the right guy."

"That's so," the tenant said. "Who gave you orders? I'll go after him. He's the one to kill."

"You're wrong. He got his orders from the bank. The bank told him, 'Clear those people out or it's your job!'"

"Well, there's a president of the bank. There's a board of directors. I'll fill up the magazine of the rifle and go into the bank."

The driver said, "Fellow was telling me the bank gets orders from the East. The orders were, 'Make the land show profit or we'll close you up.'"

"But where does it stop? Who can we shoot? I don't aim to starve to death before I kill the man that's starving me."

"I don't know. Maybe there's nobody to shoot. Maybe the thing isn't men at all. Maybe, like you said, the property's doing it. Anyway I told you my orders."

"I got to figure," the tenant said. "We all got to figure. There's some way to stop this. It's not like lightning or earthquakes. We've got a bad thing made by men, and by God that's something we can change." The tenant sat in his doorway, and the driver thundered his engine and started off, tracks falling and curving, harrows combing, and the phalli of the seeder slipping into the ground. Across the dooryard the tractor cut, and the hard, foot-beaten ground was seeded field, and the tractor cut through again: the uncut space was ten feet wide. And back he came. The iron guard bit into the house-corner, crumbled the wall, and wrenched the little house from its foundation so that it fell sideways, crushed like a bug. And the driver was goggled and a rubber mask covered his nose and mouth. The tractor cut a straight line on, and the air and the ground vibrated with its thunder. The tenant man stared after it, his rifle in his hand. His wife was beside him, and the quiet children behind. And all of them stared after the tractor.

1210

STENDHAL

STENDHAL (Marie-Henri Beyle, French, 1783-1842). Forerunner of the modern novel. Rejecting provincial life, became soldier under Bonaparte, later a French consul. As a novelist, possessed acute psychological insight, a disenchanted viewpoint. In his two masterpieces, *Le Rouge et le Noir* and *La Chartreuse de Parme*, the "Stendhal hero" is always at odds with his world.

THE CHARTREUSE OF PARMA

I.—Fabrice del Dongo

"THREE members of your family," said Count Mosca to the Duchess of Sanseverina, "have been Archbishops of Parma. Could a better career be open to your nephew Fabrice?"

The Duchess disliked the notion; and indeed Fabrice del Dongo seemed a person but little fitted for an ecclesiastical career. His ambitions were military; his hero was Napoleon. The great escapade of his life had been a secret journey into France to fight at Waterloo. His father, the Marquis del Dongo, was loyal to the Austrian masters of Lombardy; and during Fabrice's absence his elder brother Arcanio had laid an information against him as a conspirator against Austrian rule. Consequently Fabrice, on his return, found himself exposed to the risk of ten years in an Austrian prison. By his own address and by the good offices of his aunt, the Countess Pietravera, Fabrice was able to escape from Milanese territory.

Immediately afterwards the Countess wedded the aged and wealthy Duke of Sanseverina, and transferred her beauty and unbounded social talents from Milan to the court of Prince Ranuce Ernest IV., absolute ruler of Parma. The Duke had his ambitions gratified by an appointment as Ambassador to a distant country; the Duchess, left behind at Parma, was able to devote herself to the interests of Count Mosca, the Prince's chief Minister, and to counteract the intrigues of the celebrated Marchioness Raversi, head of the party that sought to overthrow him.

The welfare of her beloved nephew was the most cherished of all the Duchess's aims, and she succeeded in inspiring Count Mosca with an equal enthusiasm for the prosperity of that errant youth. But she hesitated over the project of making him an Archbishop.

"You must understand," explained the Count, "that I do not intend to make Fabrice an exemplary priest of the conventional kind.

1211

No, he will above all remain a great noble; he may continue to be absolutely ignorant if he so pleases, and will become a Bishop and an Archbishop just the same—provided, of course, that I succeed in retaining the Prince's confidence."

Ultimately the Duchess agreed, and undertook to persuade Fabrice to enter the Church. The persuasion was not easy; but at length Fabrice, having been convinced that the clerical yoke would bear but lightly upon him, consented to the step, and as a preliminary spent three years in a theological college at Naples.

When at the end of three years Fabrice, now a Monsignore, returned to Parma, matters there were at a crisis; the Raversi party were gaining ground, and Count Mosca was in danger. Nor did the Prince's interview with the young cleric improve matters. Ranuce Ernest IV. had two ruling passions—an ambition to become ruler of united Italy, and a fear of revolution. Count Mosca, the diplomatist, was the only man who could further his hopes in one direction; his fears in the other were carefully kept alive by Rassi, the fiscal-general—to such an extent that each night the Prince looked under his bed to see if by chance a liberal were lurking there. Rassi was a man of low origin, who kept his place partly by submitting good-humouredly to the abuse and even the kicks of his master, and partly by rousing that master's alarms and afterwards allaying them by hanging or imprisoning liberals, with the ready assistance of a carefully corrupted judicial bench.

Towards this nervous Prince, Fabrice bore himself with an aristocratic assurance, and a promptness and coolness in conversation that made a bad impression. His political notions were correct enough, according to the Prince's standard; but plainly, he was a man of spirit, and the Prince did not like men of spirit; they were all cousins-germane of Voltaire and Rousseau. He deemed Fabrice, in short, a potential if not an actual liberal, and therefore dangerous.

Nevertheless Count Mosca carried the day against his rivals—a triumph due less to his own efforts than to those of the Duchess, to whose charms as the court's chief ornament the Prince was far from insusceptible. The Count's success was Fabrice's; that youth found himself established as co-adjutor to the Archbishop of Parma, with a reversion to the Archbishopric on the demise of its worthy occupant.

On Fabrice's return from Naples, the Duchess had found him developed from a boy into a young man, and the handsomest young

1212

man in Italy; her affection for him became sisterly; she was nearly
in love with him. She had no cause for jealousy, for Fabrice,
although prone to flirtation, had no affairs of the heart. The word
love, as yet, had no meaning for him.

II.—Giletti

One of our hero's flirtations had consequences with a very pronounced bearing on his after career. During a surreptitious visit to
the theatre he became captivated with the actress, Marietta Valserra.
Stolen visits of two minutes' duration to Marietta's lodging on the
fourth floor of an old house behind the theatre were an agreeable
variation of the monotony of Fabrice's clerical duties, and of his
visits among the most important and least entertaining families in
Parma. But the trifling little intrigue came to the ears of Count
Mosca, with the result that the travelling company to which Marietta
belonged received its passports and was requested to move on.

In the affair, moreover, Fabrice had a rival. Giletti was the low
comedian of the company, and the ugliest member of it; he assumed
proprietorship over Marietta, who, although she did not love him,
was at any rate horribly afraid of him. Giletti several times
threatened to kill Fabrice; whereby Fabrice was not disturbed.

Count Mosca was passionately archæological, and this taste he
shared with Fabrice, who had cultivated the hobby at Naples. It so
happened that the two were engaged in excavations near the bridge
over the Po where the main road passes into Austrian territory at
Castel-Maggiore. Early one morning Fabrice, after surveying the
work that was going on in the trenches, strolled away with a gun,
intent upon lark-shooting. A wounded bird dropped on the road;
and as Fabrice followed it he encountered a battered old carriage
driving towards the frontier. In it were Giletti, Marietta and an old
woman who passed as Marietta's mother.

Giletti leapt to the conclusion that Fabrice had come there, gun
in hand, to insult him, and possibly to carry off Marietta. He leapt
out of the carriage.

"Brigand!" he yelled, "we are only a league from the frontier—
now I can finish you!"

Fabrice saw a pistol levelled at him at a distance of three feet;
he knocked it aside with the butt of his gun, and it went off harmlessly. Giletti then clutched the gun; the two men wrestled for it,
and it exploded close to Giletti's ear. Staggered for an instant, he

1213

quickly recovered himself; drawing from its sheath a "property" sword, he fell once more upon Fabrice.

"Look out! he will kill you," came an agitated whisper from Marietta; "take this!"

A sort of hunting knife was flung out of the carriage door. Fabrice picked it up, and was nearly stunned forthwith by a blow from the handle of the "property" sword. Happily Giletti was too near to use his sword-point. Pulling himself together, Fabrice gave his enemy a gash on the thigh. Giletti, swearing furiously, injured Fabrice on the cheek. Blood poured down our hero's face. The thought, "I am disfigured for life!" flashed through his mind. Enraged at the idea, he thrust the hunting knife at Giletti's breast with all his force. Giletti fell and lay motionless.

"He is dead!" said Fabrice to himself. Then, turning to the coach, he asked, "Have you a looking-glass?"

His eyes and teeth were undamaged; he was not permanently disfigured. Hastily, then, he turned to thoughts of escape. Marietta gave him Giletti's passport; obviously his first business was to get across the frontier. And yet the Austrian frontier was no safe one for him to cross. Were he recognised, he might expect ten years in an Imperial fortress. But this was the less immediate danger, and he determined to risk it.

With considerable trepidation he walked across the bridge, and presented Giletti's passport to the Austrian gendarme.

The gendarme looked at it, and rose, "You must wait, monsieur; there is a difficulty," he said, and left the room. Fabrice was profoundly uncomfortable; he was nearly for bolting, when he heard the gendarme say to another, "I am done up with the heat; just go and put your visa on a passport in there when you have finished your pipe; I'm going for some coffee."

This gendarme, in fact, knew Giletti, and was quite well aware that the man before him was not the actor. But, for all he could tell, Giletti had lent the passport for reasons of his own. The easiest way out of the difficulty was to get another gendarme to see to the visa. This man affixed it as a matter of course, and Fabrice escaped danger number one.

The rest was very easy, thanks to Ludovico, an old servant of the Duchess, whom Fabrice met at an eating-house where he had turned in for some very necessary refreshment. With the aid of this excellent fellow Fabrice had his wounds attended to, and was safely smuggled out of Austrian territory into Bologna.

The party opposed to Count Mosca hastened to take advantage of Fabrice's offence. He was represented as a murderer; the workmen in the trenches who had seen the affray, and knew that Fabrice had acted in self-defence, were either bribed or got out of the way. Rassi accused Fabrice of being a liberal; and since the Prince was ill-disposed towards the young man, not all the endeavours of Count Mosca could save him from a sentence of twenty years' imprisonment, should he be so impudent as to venture upon the territory of Parma.

Just before the sentence was presented to the Prince for final confirmation, the Prince learned that the Dutchess of Sanseverina sought an audience with him. He rubbed his hands; the greatest beauty of his court had come to beg mercy for her nephew; there would be tears and frantic appeals. For a quarter of an hour the Prince gloated over the prospect; then he ordered that the Duchess be admitted.

She entered—in travelling costume; never had she looked more charming, never more cheerful. "I trust your Serene Highness will pardon my unorthodox costume," she said, smiling archly; "but as I am about to leave Parma for a very long time, I have felt it my duty to come and thank you ere I go for all the kindnesses you have deigned to confer upon me."

The Prince was astonished and profoundly chagrined. "Why are you going?" he asked, as calmly as he could.

"I have had the project for some time," she replied, "and a little insult paid to Monsignor del Dongo has hastened it."

The Prince was beside himself. What would his court be without the Duchess? At all costs he much check her flight.

At this moment Count Mosca, pale with anxiety, begged admittance. He had just heard of the Duchess's intention to leave Parma.

"Let me speak as a friend to friends," said the Prince, collecting himself; "what can I do, Madame, to arrest your hasty resolution?"

"If your highness were to write a gracious letter revoking the unjust sentence upon Fabrice del Dongo, I might re-consider my decision; and, let me add, if the Marchioness Raversi were advised by you to retire to the country early to-morrow morning for the benefit of her health—"

"Was there ever such a woman?" cried the Prince, stamping up and down the room.

But he agreed. At his orders Count Mosca sat down and wrote the letter required. The Prince objected to the phrase "unjust sentence," and Count Mosca, courtier-like, abstained from using it. The Prince did not mind the banishment of the Marchioness Raversi; he liked exiling people.

At seven o'clock next morning the Prince summoned Rassi, and dictated to him another letter. The sentence of twenty years, upon the criminal del Dongo was to be reduced by the Prince's clemency, at the supplication of the Duchess Sanseverina, to twelve years; and the police were instructed to do their utmost to arrest the offender.

The only difficulty was that of tempting Fabrice into the territory of Parma. A hint to the Marchioness Raversi and her associates removed the obstacle. A forged letter, purporting to be from the Duchess, reached Fabrice at Bologna, telling him that there would be little danger in his meeting her at Castelnovo, within the frontier. Fabrice repaired joyfully to Castelnovo. That night he lay a prisoner in the citadel of Parma; while the Duchess, alone in her room with locked door, sobbed her heart out and raved helplessly against the treachery of princes.

"So long as her nephew is in the citadel," said the Prince to himself, "the Duchess will be in Parma."

The citadel of Parma is a colossal building with a flat roof 180 feet above the level of the ground. On this roof are erected two structures: one, the governor's residence; the other, the Farnese tower, a prison specially erected for a recalcitrant prince of earlier days. In this tower Fabrice, as a prisoner of importance, was confined; and as he looked from the window on the evening of his arrival and beheld the superb panorama of the distant Alps, he reflected pleasantly that he might have found a worse dungeon.

On the next morning his attention was absorbed by something nearer at hand. His window overlooked one belonging to the governor's palace; in this window were many bird cages, and at eleven o'clock a maiden came to feed the birds. Fabrice recognised her as Clelia Conti, the governor's daughter. He succeeding in attracting her attention; she blushed and withdrew. But next day she came again at the same hour. On the third day, however, a heavy wooden shutter was clapped upon the window. Nothing daunted, Fabrice proceeded patiently to cut a peep-hole in the shutter by aid of the main-spring of his watch. When he had succeeded in removing

a square piece of the wood, he looked with delight upon Clelia gazing at his window with eyes of profound pity, unconscious that she was observed.

Gradually he broke down the maiden's reserve. She discovered the secret of the peep-hole; she consented to communicate with him; finally the two conversed by a system of signals. Fabrice even dared to tell Clelia that he loved her—and truly he was in love, for the first time in his life. The worst of it was that these declarations were apt to bring the conversation to an end; so Fabrice was sparing of them.

Clelia, meanwhile, was in sore perplexity. Her father, General Fabio Conti the governor, was a political opponent of Count Mosca, and had ambitions of office. These ambitions might be forwarded, he deemed, by the successful marriage of his daughter. He did not desire that she should remain a lovely recluse, feeding birds at the top of the citadel. Accordingly he had presented to her an ultimatum; either she must marry the Marquis Crescenzi, the wealthiest nobleman of Parma, who sought her hand, or she must retire to a convent.

The signalled conversation with Fabrice, therefore, could not last long. And yet she had beyond doubt fallen deeply in love with Fabrice. She knew he was her father's prisoner, and belonged to the party hostile to her father; she was ashamed, as a daughter, of her love for him. But she admired him, and pitied him; she was well aware that he was a victim of political intrigue, for why should a nobleman of Fabrice's standing be thus punished for killing a mere actor? The stolen interviews with the captive were as dear to her as to him; and so dear were they to him that, after months of imprisonment he declared that he had never been so happy in his life.

IV.—The Escape

One night, as Fabrice looked through his peep-hole, he became aware of a light flashing from the town. Obviously some attempt was being made at signalling. He observed the flashes, counting them in relation to the order of the letters in the alphabet—one for A, two for B, and so on. He discovered that the message was from the Duchess, and was directed to himself. He replied, on the same system, by passing his lantern in front of the peep-hole. The answer from the distance was important; arrangements were being made for his escape. But he did not want to escape.

1217

Next day he told Clelia of his message, and of his unwillingness to leave the prison. She gave no answer, but burst into tears. How could she tell him that she herself must presently leave—for marriage or a convent?

Next day, Fabrice, by his goaler's connivance, received a long letter from Clelia. She urged him to escape, declaring that at any time the Prince might order his execution, and in addition that he was in danger of death by poison. Straightway he sought an interview with Clelia, with whom he had not hitherto conversed save by signals from their windows. The goaler arranged that they should meet when Fabrice was being conducted from his cell to the roof of the Farnese tower, where he was occasionally allowed to take exercise.

"I can speak but few words to you," she said trembling, with tears in her eyes. "Swear that you will obey the Duchess, and escape when she wishes and as she wishes."

"And condemn myself to live far away from her whom I love?"

"Swear it! for my sake, swear it!" she implored him.

"Well then, I swear it!"

The preparations were quickly advanced. Three knotted ropes were smuggled with Clelia's aid into Fabrice's cell—one for descending the 35 feet between his window and the roof of the citadel; another for descending the tremendous wall of 180 feet between the roof and the ramparts; a third for the 30 feet between the top of the ramparts and the ground.

A feast-day, when the garrison of the citadel would presumably be drunk, was chosen for the attempt. Fabrice spent the time of waiting in cutting a hole in his shutter large enough to enable him to get through. Fortunately, on the night of the feast-day a thick fog arose and enveloped the citadel. The Duchess had seen to it that the garrison was plentifully supplied with wine.

Fabrice attached one of the shorter ropes to his bed, and struggled through the shutter—an ungainly figure, for round his body were wound the immense ropes necessary for the long descent. Once on the roof-platform he made his way along the parapet until he came to a new stove which he had been told marked the best spot for lowering the rope. He could hear the soldiers talking near at hand, but the fog made him invisible. Unrolling his rope, and fastening his rope to the parapet by threading it through a water-duct, he flung it over; then, with a prayer and a thought of Clelia, he began to descend.

1218

At first he went down mechanically, as if doing the feat for a wager. About half-way down his arms seemed to lose their strength; he nearly let go—he might have fallen had he not supported himself by clinging to the vegetation on the wall. From time to time he felt horrible pain between the shoulders. Birds hustled against him now and then; he feared at the first contact with them that pursuers were coming down the rope after him. But he reached the rampart undamaged save for bleeding hands.

He was quite exhausted; for a few minutes he slept. On waking and realising the situation, he attached his third rope to a cannon, and hurried down to the ground. Two men seized him just as he fainted at the foot.

A few hours afterwards a carriage crossed the frontier with Ludovico on the box, and within it the Duchess watching over the sleeping Fabrice. The journey did not end until they had reached Locarno on Lake Maggiore.

V.—Clelia's Vow

To Locarno soon afterwards came the news that Ranuce Ernest IV. was dead. Fabrice could now safely return, for the young Ranuce Ernest V. was believed to be entirely under the influence of Count Mosca, and was an honest youth without the tyrannical instincts of his father. Nevertheless the Duchess returned first, to make certain of Fabrice's security. She employed her whole influence to hasten forward the wedding of Clelia with the Marquis Crescenzi; she was jealous of the ascendancy the girl had gained over her beloved nephew.

Fabrice, on reaching Parma, was well received by the young Prince. Witnesses, he was told, had been found who could prove that he had killed Giletti in self defence. He would spend a few days in a purely nominal confinement in the city goal, and then would be tried by impartial judges and released.

Imagine the consternation of the Duchess when she learnt that Fabrice, having to go to prison, had deliberately given himself up at the citadel!

She saw the danger clearly. Fabrice was in the hands of Count Mosca's political opponents, among whom General Conti was still a leading spirit. They would not suffer him to escape this time. Fabrice would be poisoned.

1219

Clelia, too, knew that this would be his fate. When she saw him once again at the old window, happily signalling to her, she was smitten with panic terror. Her alarm was realised when she learnt of a plot between Rassi and her father to poison the prisoner.

On the second day of his confinement Fabrice was about to eat his dinner when Clelia, in desperate agitation, forced her way into his cell.

"Have you tasted it?" she cried, grasping his arm.

Fabrice guessed the state of affairs with delight. He seized her in his arms and kissed her.

"Help me to die," he said.

"Oh, my beloved," she answered, "let me die with you."

"Let me not spoil our happiness with a lie," said he as he embraced her. "I have not yet tasted."

For an instant Clelia looked at him in anger; then she fell into his arms.

At that instant there came a sound of men hurrying. There entered the Prince's aide-de-camp, with order to remove Fabrice from the citadel and to seize the poisoned food. The Duchess had heard of the plot, and had persuaded the Prince to take instant action.

Clelia, when her father was in danger of death on account of the plot, vowed before the Virgin Mary never again to look upon the face of Fabrice. Her father escaped with a sentence of banishment; and Clelia, to the profound satisfaction of the Duchess, was wedded to the Marquis Crescenzi. The Duchess was now a widow, Count Mosca a widower. Their long friendship, after Fabrice's acquittal, was cemented by marriage.

The loss of Clelia left Fabrice inconsolable. He shunned society; he lived a life of religious retirement, and gained a reputation for piety that even inspired the jealousy of his good friend the Archbishop.

At length Fabrice emerged from his solitude; he came forth as a preacher, and his success was unequalled. All Parma, gentle and simple, flocked to hear the famous devotee—slender, ill-clad, so handsome and yet so profoundly melancholy. And ere he began each sermon, Fabrice looked earnestly round his congregation to see if Clelia was there.

But Clelia, adhering to her vow, stayed away. It was not until she was told that a certain Anetta Marini was in love with the

preacher, and that gossip asserted that the preacher was smitten with Anetta Marini, that she changed her mind.

One evening, as Fabrice stood in the pulpit, he saw Clelia before him. Her eyes were filled with tears; he looked so pale, so thin, so worn. But never had he preached as he preached that night.

After the sermon he received a note asking him to be at a small garden door of the Crescenzi Palace at midnight on the next night. Eagerly he obeyed; when he reached the door, a voice called him to enter. The darkness was intense; he could see nothing.

"I have asked you to come here," said the voice, "to say that I still love you. But I have vowed to the Virgin never to see your face; that is why I receive you in this darkness. And let me beg you—never preach before Anetta Marini."

"My angel," replied the enraptured Fabrice, "I shall never preach again before anyone; it was only in the hope of seeing you that I preached at all."

During the following three years the two often met in darkness. But twice, by accident, Clelia broke her vow by looking on Fabrice's face. Her conscience preyed upon her; she wore away and died.

A few days afterwards Fabrice resigned his reversion to the Archbishopric, and retired to the Chartreuse of Parma. He ended his days in the monastery only a year afterwards.

WALLACE STEVENS

WALLACE STEVENS (American, 1879-1955). Poet of enchanting imagery. Educated for the law, spent most of life with an insurance company. Was slow winning recognition—first from other poets, finally from reading public. Now acknowledged one of important American poets. Books of verse: *Harmonium, Ideas of Order, Parts of a World.*

DOMINATION OF BLACK

At night, by the fire,
The colors of the bushes
And of the fallen leaves,
Repeating themselves,
Turned in the room,

Like the leaves themselves
Turning in the wind.
Yes: but the color of the heavy hemlocks
Came striding.
And I remembered the cry of the peacocks.

The colors of their tails
Were like the leaves themselves
Turning in the wind.
In the twilight wind.
They swept over the room,
Just as they flew from the boughs of the hemlocks
Down to the ground.
I heard them cry—the peacocks.
Was it a cry against the twilight
Or against the leaves themselves
Turning in the wind.
Turning as the flames
Turned in the fire,
Turning as the tails of the peacocks
Turned in the loud fire,
Loud as the hemlocks
Full of the cry of the peacocks,
Or was it a cry against the hemlocks.

Out of the window,
I saw how the planets gathered
Like the leaves themselves
Turning in the wind.
I saw how the night came,
Came striding like the color of the heavy hemlocks.
I felt afraid.
And I remembered the cry of the peacocks.

AN EXTRACT

from Addresses to the Academy of Fine Ideas

On an early Sunday in April, a feeble day,
He felt curious about the winter hills
And wondered about the water in the lake.

It had been cold since December. Snow fell first,
At New Year and, from then until April, lay
On everything. Now it had melted, leaving
The gray grass like a pallet, closely pressed;
And dirt. The wind blew in the empty place.
The winter wind blew in an empty place—
There was that difference between the and an,
The difference between himself and no man,
No man that heard a wind in an empty place.
It was time to be himself again, to see
If the place, in spite of its witheredness, was still
Within the difference. He felt curious
Whether the water was black and lashed about
Or whether the ice still covered the lake. There was still
Snow under the trees and on the northern rocks,
The dead rocks, not the green rocks, the live rocks. If,
When he looked, the water ran up the air or grew white
Against the edge of the ice, the abstraction would
Be broken and winter would be broken and done,
And being would be being himself again,
Being, becoming seeing and feeling and self,
Black water breaking into reality.

ANECDOTE OF THE JAR

I placed a jar in Tennessee,
And round it was, upon a hill.
It made the slovenly wilderness
Surround that hill.

The wilderness rose up to it,
And sprawled around, no longer wild.
The jar was round upon the ground
And tall and of a port in air.

It took dominion everywhere.
The jar was gray and bare.
It did not give of bird or bush,
Like nothing else in Tennessee.

ROBERT LOUIS STEVENSON

ROBERT LOUIS STEVENSON (Scottish, 1850-1894). Writer of essays and novels in the Scott-Dumas manner. A sickly traveler, who died in the South Seas. Affectionately venerated by his generation. Most popular work: adventure novel, *Treasure Island*. First-rate tales of supernatural: *Dr. Jekyll and Mr. Hyde* and *Thrawn Janet*.

THRAWN JANET

THE Reverend Murdoch Soulis was long minister of the moorland parish of Balweary, in the vale of Dule. A severe, bleak-faced old man, dreadful to his hearers, he dwelt in the last years of his life, without relative or servant or any human company, in the small and lonely manse under the Hanging Shaw. In spite of the iron composure of his features, his eye was wild, seared, and uncertain; and when he dwelt, in private admonitions, on the future of the impenitent, it seemed as if his eye pierced through the storms of time to the terrors of eternity. Many young persons, coming to prepare themselves against the season of the Holy Communion, were dreadfully affected by his talk. He had a sermon on 1st Peter, v. and 8th, "The devil as a roaring lion," on the Sunday after every seventeenth of August, and he was accustomed to surpass himself upon that text both by the appalling nature of the matter and the terror of his bearing in the pulpit. The children were frightened into fits, and the old looked more than usually oracular, and were, all that day, full of those hints that Hamlet deprecated. The manse itself, where it stood by the water of Dule among some thick trees, with the Shaw overhanging it on the one side, and on the other many cold, moorish hilltops rising toward the sky, had begun, at a very early period of Mr. Soulis's ministry, to be avoided in the dusk hours by all who valued themselves upon their prudence; and guidmen sitting at the clachan alehouse shook their heads together at the thought of passing late by that uncanny neighborhood. There was one spot, to be more particular, which was regarded with special awe. The manse stood between the high road and the water of Dule, with a gable to each; its back was toward the kirktown of Balweary, nearly half a mile away; in front of it, a bare garden, hedged with thorn, occupied the land between the river and the road. The house was two stories high, with two large rooms on each. It opened not directly on the garden, but on a causewayed path, or passage, giving on the road on the one hand, and closed on the

1224

other by the tall willows and elders that bordered on the stream. And it was this strip of causeway that enjoyed among the young parishioners of Balweary so infamous a reputation. The minister walked there often after dark, sometimes groaning aloud in the instancy of his unspoken prayers; and when he was from home, and the manse door was locked, the more daring schoolboys ventured, with beating hearts, to "follow my leader" across that legendary spot.

This atmosphere of terror, surrounding, as it did, a man of God of spotless character and orthodoxy, was a common cause of wonder and subject of inquiry among the few strangers who were led by chance or business into that unknown, outlying country. But many even of the people of the parish were ignorant of the strange events which had marked the first year of Mr. Soulis's ministrations; and among those who were better informed, some were naturally reticent, and others shy of that particular topic. Now and again, only, one of the older folk would warm into courage over his third tumbler, and recount the cause of the minister's strange looks and solitary life.

Fifty years syne, when Mr. Soulis cam' first into Ba'weary, he was still a young man—a callant, the folk said—fu' o' book learnin' and grand at the exposition, but, as was natural in sae young man, wi' nae leevin' experience in religion. The younger sort were greatly taken wi' his gifts and his gab; but auld, concerned, serious men and women were moved even to prayer for the young man, whom they took to be a self-deceiver, and the parish that was like to be sae ill-supplied. It was before the days o' the moderates—weary fa' them; but ill things are like guid—they baith come bit by bit, a pickle at a time; and there were folk even then that said the Lord had left the college professors to their ain devices, an' the lads that went to study wi' them wad hae done mair and better sittin' in a peat-bog, like their forebears of the persecution, wi' a Bible under their oxter and a speerit o' prayer in their heart. There was nae doubt, onyway, but that Mr. Soulis had been ower lang at the college. He was careful and troubled for mony things besides the ae thing needful. He had a feck o' books wi' him—mair than had ever been seen before in a' that presbytery; and a sair wark the carrier had wi' them, for they were a' like to have smoored in the Deil's Hag between this and Kilmackerlie. They were books o' divinity, to be sure, or so they ca'd them; but the serious were o' opinion

there was little service for sae mony, when the hail o' God's Word would gang in the neuk of a plaid. Then he wad sit half the day and half the nicht forbye, which was scant decent—writin', nae less; and first, they were feared he wad read his sermons; and syne it proved he was writin' a book himsel', which was surely no fittin' for ane of his years an' sma' experience.

Onyway it behooved him to get an auld, decent wife to keep the manse for him an' see to his bit denners; and he was recommended to an auld limmer—Janet M'Clour, they ca'd her—and sae far left to himsel' as to be ower persuaded. There was mony advised him to the contrar, for Janet was mair than suspeckit by the best folk in Ba'weary. Lang or that, she had had a wean to a dragoon; she hadnae come forrit for maybe thretty year; and bairns had seen her mumblin' to hersel' up on Key's Loan in the gloamin', whilk was an unco time an' place for a God-fearin' woman. Howsoever, it was the laird himsel' that had first tauld the minister o' Janet; and in thae days he wad have gane a far gate to pleesure the laird. When folk tauld him that Janet was sib to the deil, it was a' superstition by his way of it; an' when they cast up the Bible to him an' the witch of Endor, he wad threep it doun their thrapples that thir days were a' gane by, and the deil was mercifully restrained.

Weel, when it got about the clachan that Janet M'Clour was to be servant at the manse, the folk were fair mad wi' her an' him thegether; and some o' the guidwives had nae better to dae than get round her door cheeks and chairge her wi' a' that was ken't again her, frae the sodger's bairn to John Tamson's twa kye. She was nae great speaker; folk usually let her gang her ain gate, an' she let them gang theirs, wi' neither Fair-guid-een nor Fair-guid-day; but when she buckled to she had a tongue to deave the miller. Up she got, an' there wasnae an auld story in Ba'weary but she gart somebody lowp for it that day; they couldnae say ae thing but she could say twa to it; till, at the hinder end, the guidwives up and claught haud of her, and clawed the coats aff her back, and pu'd her doun the clachan to the water o' Dule, to see if she were a witch or no, soum or droun. The carline skirled till ye could hear her at the Hangin' Shaw, and she focht like ten; there was mony a guidwife bure the mark of her neist day, an' mony a lang day after; and just in the hettest o' the collieshangie, wha suld come up (for his sins) but the new minister.

"Women," said he (and he had a grand voice), "I charge you in the Lord's name to let her go."

Janet ran to him—she was fair wud wi' terror—an' clang to him an' prayed him, for Christ's sake, save her frae the cummers; an' they, for their pairt, tauld him a' that was ken't, and maybe mair.

"Woman," says he to Janet, "is this true?"

"As the Lord sees me," says she, "as the Lord made me, no a word o't. Forbye the bairn," says she, 'I've been a decent woman a' my days."

"Will you,' says Mr. Soulis, "in the name of God, and before me, His unworthy minister, renounce the devil and his works?"

Well, it wad appear that when he askit that, she gave a girn that fairly frichtit them that saw her, an' they could hear her teeth play dirl thegether in her chafts; but there was naething for it but the ae way or the ither; an' Janet lifted up her hand and renounced the deil before them a'.

"And now," said Mr. Soulis to the guidwives, "home with ye, one and all, and pray to God for His forgiveness."

And he gied Janet his arm, though she had little on her but a sark, and took her up the clachan to her ain door like a leddy of the land; an' her skreighin' and laughin' as was a scandal to be heard.

There were mony grave folk lang ower their prayers that nicht; but when the morn cam' there was sic a fear fell upon a' Ba'weary that the bairns hid theirsels, and even the men-folk stood and keekit frae their doors. For there was Janet comin' doun the clachan—her or her likeness, nane could tell—wi' her neck thrawn, and her heid on ae side, like a body that has been hangit, and a girn on her face like an unstreakit corp. By an' by they got used wi' it, and even speered at her to ken what was wrang; but frae that day forth she couldnae speak like a Christian woman, but slavered and played click wi' her teeth like a pair o' shears; and frae that day forth the name o' God cam' never on her lips. Whiles she wad try to say it, but it michtnae be. Them that kenned best said least; but they never gied that Thing the name o' Janet M'Clour; for the auld Janet, by their way o't, was in muckle hell that day. But the minister was neither to haud nor to bind; he preached about naething but the folks' cruelty that had gi'en her a stroke of the palsy; he skelpt the bairns that meddled her; and he had her up to the manse that same nicht and dwalled there a' his lane wi' her under the Hangin' Shaw.

Weel, time gaed by: and the idler sort commenced to think mair lichtly o' that black business. The minister was weel thocht o'; he

was aye late at the writing, folk wad see his can'le doun by the Dule water after twal' at e'en; and he seemed pleased wi' himsel' and upsitten as at first though a' body could see that he was dwining. As for Janet she cam' an' she gaed; if she didnae speak muckle afore, it was reason she should speak less then; she meddled naebody; but she was an eldritch thing to see, an' nane wad hae mistrysted wi' her for Ba'weary glebe. About the end o' July there cam' a spell o' weather, the like o't never was in that countryside; it was lown an' het an' heartless; the herds couldnae win up the Black Hill, the bairns were ower weariet to play; an' yet it was gousty too, wi' claps o' het wund that rumm'led in the glens, and bits o' shouers that slockened naething. We aye thocht it but to thun'er on the morn; but the morn cam', and the morn's morning, and it was aye the same uncanny weather, sair on folks and bestial. Of a' that were the waur, nane suffered like Mr. Soulis; he could neither sleep nor eat, he tauld his elders; an' when he wasnae writin' at his weary book, he wad be stravaguin' ower a' the countryside like a man possessed, when a' body else was blythe to keep caller ben the house.

Abune Hangin' Shaw, in the bield o' the Black Hill, there's a bit inclosed grund wi' an iron yett; and it seems in the auld days, that was the kirkyaird o' Ba'weary, and consecrated by the Papists before the blessed licht shone upon the kingdom. It was a great howff o' Mr. Soulis's, onyway; there he would sit an' consider his sermons; and indeed it's a bieldy bit. Weel, as he cam' ower the wast end o' the Black Hill, ae day, he saw first twa, an' syne fower, an' syne seven corbie craws fleein' round an' round abune the auld kirkyard. They flew laigh and heavy, an' squawked to ither as they gaed; and it was clear to Mr. Soulis that something had put them frae ordinar. He wasnae easy fleyed, an' gaed straucht up to the wa's; an' what suld he find there but a man, or the appearance of a man, sittin' in the inside upon a grave. He was of a great stature, an' black as hell, and his een were singular to see. Mr. Soulis had heard tell o' black men, mony's the time; but there was something unco about this black man that daunted him. Het as he was, he took a kind o' cauld grue in the marrow o' his banes; but up he spak for a' that; an' says he: "My friend, are you a stranger in this place?" The black man answered never a word; he got upon his feet, an' begude to hirstle to the wa' on the far side; but he aye lookit at the minister; an' the minister stood an' lookit back, till a' in a meenute the black man was over the wa' an' rinnin' for

the bield o' the trees. Mr. Soulis, he hardly kenned why, ran after him; but he was sair forjaskit wi' his walk an' the het, unhalesome weather; and rin as he likit, he got nae mair than a glisk o' the black man amang the birks, till he won doun to the foot o' the hillside, an' there he saw him ance mair, gaun, hap, step, an' lowp, ower Dule water to the manse.

Mr. Soulis wasnae weel pleased that this fearsome gangrel suld mak' sae free wi' Ba'weary manse; an' he ran the harder, an', wet shoon, ower the burn, an' up the walk; but the deil a black man was there to see. He stepped out upon the road, but there was naebody there; he gaed a' ower the gairden, but na, nae black man. At the hinder end, and a bit feared as was but natural, he lifted the hasp and into the manse; and there was Janet M'Clour before his een, wi' her thrawn craig, and nane sae pleased to see him. And he aye minded sinsyne, when first he set his een upon her, he had the same cauld and deidly grue.

"Janet," says he, "have you seen a black man?"

"A black man?" quo' she. "Save us a'! Ye're no wise, minister. There's nae black man in a' Ba'weary."

But she didnae speak plain, ye maun understand; but yam-yammered, like a powney wi' the bit in its moo.

"Weel," says he, "Janet, if there was nae black man, I have spoken with the Accuser of the Brethren."

And he sat down like ane wi' a fever, an' his teeth chittered in his heid.

"Hoots," says she, "think shame to yoursel', minister"; an' gied him a drap brandy that she keept aye by her.

Syne Mr. Soulis gaed into his study amang a' his books. It's a lang, laigh, mirk chalmer, perishin' cauld in winter, an' no very dry even in the tap o' the simmer, for the manse stands near the burn. Sae doun he sat, and thocht of a' that had come an' gane since he was in Ba'weary, an' his hame, an' the days when he was a bairn an' ran daffin' on the braes; and that black man aye ran in his heid like the owercome of a sang. Aye the mair he thocht, the mair he thocht o' the black man. He tried the prayer, an' the words wouldnae come to him; an' he tried, they say, to write at his book, but he couldnae mak' nae mair o' that. There was whiles he thocht the black man was at his oxter, an' the swat stood upon him cauld as well-water; and there was other whiles, when he cam' to himsel' like a christened bairn and minded naething.

The upshot was that he gaed to the window an' stood glowrin' at

Dule water. The trees are unco thick, an' the water lies deep an' black under the manse; an' there was Janet washin' the cla'es wi' her coats kilted. She had her back to the minister, an' he, for his pairt, hardly kenned what he was lookin' at. Syne she turned round an' shawed her face; Mr. Soulis had the same cauld grue as twice that day afore, an' it was borne in upon him what folk said, that Janet was deid lang syne, an' this was a bogle in her clay cauld flesh. He drew back a pickle and he scanned her narrowly. She was tramp-trampin' in the cla'es, croonin' to hersel'; and eh! Gude guide us, but it was a fearsome face. Whiles she sang louder, but there was nae man born o' woman that could tell the words o' her sang; an' whiles she lookit side-lang doun, but there was naething there for her to look at. There gaed a scunner through the flesh upon his banes; and that was Heeven's advertisement. But Mr. Soulis just blamed himsel', he said, to think sae ill of a puir, auld afflicted wife that hadnae a freend forby himsel'; and he put up a bit prayer for him and her, an' drank a little caller water—for his heart rose again the meat—an' gaed up to his naked bed in the gloaming.

That was a nicht that has never been forgotten in Ba'weary, the nicht o' the seeventeenth of August, seeventeen hun'er and twal'. It had been het afore, as I hae said, but that nicht it was hetter than ever. The sun gaed doun amang unco-lookin' clouds; it fell as mirk as the pit; no a star, no a breath o' wund; ye couldnae see your han' before your face, and even the auld folk cuist the covers frae their beds and lay pechin' for their breath. Wi' a' that he had upon his mind, it was gey and unlikely Mr. Soulis wad get muckle sleep. He lay an' he tummled; the gude, caller bed that he got into brunt his very banes; whiles he slept, and whiles he waukened; whiles he heard the time o' nicht, and whiles a tyke yowlin' up the muir, as if somebody was deid; whiles he thocht he heard bogles claverin' in his lug, an' whiles he saw spunkies in the room. He behooved, he judged, to be sick; an' sick he was—little he jaloosed the sickness.

At the hinder end, he got a clearness in his mind, sat up in his sark on the bedside, and fell thinkin' ance mair o' the black man an' Janet. He couldnae well tell how—maybe it was the cauld to his feet—but it cam' in upon him wi' a spat that there was some connection between their twa, an' that either or baith o' them were bogles. And just at that moment, in Janet's room which was neist to his, there cam' a stramp o' feet as if men were wars'lin', an' then a loud bang; an' then a wund gaed reishling round the fower

1230

quarters of the house; an' then a' was aince mair as seelent as the grave.

Mr. Soulis was feared for neither man nor deevil. He got his tinder box, an' lighted a can'le, an' made three steps o't ower to Janet's door. It was on the hasp, an' he pushed it open, an' keeked bauldly in. It was a big room, as big as the minister's ain, an' plenished wi' grand, auld, solid gear, for he had naething else. There was a fower-posted bed wi' auld tapestry; and a braw cabinet of aik, that was fu' o' the minister's divinity books, an' put there to be out o' the gate; an' a wheen duds o' Janet's lying here and there about the floor. But nae Janet could Mr. Soulis see; nor ony sign of a contention. In he gaed (an' there's few that wad ha'e followed him) an' lookit a' round, an' listened. But there was naethin' to be heard, neither inside the manse nor in a' Ba'weary parish, an' naethin' to be seen but the muckle shadows turnin' round the can'le. An' then a' at aince, the minister's heart played dunt an' stood stock-still; an' a cauld wund blew amang the hairs o' his heid. Whaten a weary sicht was that for the puir man's een! For there was Janet hangin' frae a nail beside the auld aik cabinet: her heid aye lay on her shouther, her een were steeked, the tongue projekit frae her mouth, and her heels were twa feet clar abune the floor.

"God forgive us all!" thocht Mr. Soulis; "poor Janet's dead."

He cam' a step nearer to the corp; an' then his heart fair whammled in his inside. For by what cantrip it wad ill-beseem a man to judge, she was hingin' fae a single nail an' by a single wursted thread for darnin' hose.

It's an awfu' thing to be your lane at nicht wi' siccan prodigies o' darkness; but Mr. Soulis was strong in the Lord. He turned an' gaed his ways oot o' that room, and lockit the door ahint him; and step by step, doon the stairs, as heavy as leed; and set doon the can'le on the table at the stairfoot. He couldnae pray, he couldnae think, he was dreepin' wi' caul' swat, an' naething could he hear but the dunt-dunt-duntin' o' his ain heart. He micht maybe have stood there an hour, or maybe twa, he minded sae little; when a' o' a sudden he heard a laigh, uncanny steer upstairs; a foot gaed to an' fro in the cha'mer whaur the corp was hingin'; syne the door was opened, though he minded weel that he had lockit it; an' syne there was a step upon th landin', an' it seemed to him as if the corp was lookin' ower the rail and doun upon him whaur he stood.

He took up the can'le again (for he couldnae want the licht) and,

as saftly as ever he could, gaed straucht out o' the manse an' to the far end o' the causeway. It was aye pitmirk; the flame o' the can'le, when he set it on the grund, brunt steedy and clear as in a room; naething moved, but the Dule water seepin' and sabbin' doon the glen, an' yon unhaly footstep that cam' ploddin' doun the stairs inside the manse. He kenned the foot ower weel, for it was Janet's; and at ilka step that cam' a wee thing nearer, the cauld got deeper in his vitals. He commended his soul to Him that made an' keepit him; "and O Lord," said he, "give me strength this night to war against the powers of evil."

By this time the foot was comin' through the passage for the door; he could hear a hand skirt alang the wa', as if the fearsome thing was feelin' for its way. The saughs tossed an' maned thegether, a lang sigh cam' ower the hills, the flame o' the can'le was blawn aboot; an' there stood the corp of Thrawn Janet, wi' her grogram goun an' her black mutch, wi' the heid aye upon the shouther, an' the girn still upon the face o't—leevin', ye wad hae said—deid, as Mr. Soulis weel kenned—upon the threshold o' the manse.

It's a strange thing that the saul of man should be that thirled into his perishable body; but the minister saw, an' his heart didnae break.

She didnae stand there lang; she began to move again an' cam' slowly toward Mr. Soulis whaur he stood under the saughs. A' the life o' his body, a' the strength o' his speerit, were glowerin' frae his een. It seemed she was gaun to speak, but wanted words, an' made a sign wi' the left hand. There cam' a clap o' wund, like a cat's fuff; oot gaed the can'le, the saughs skrieghed like folk; an' Mr. Soulis kenned that, live or die, this was the end o't.

"Witch, beldam, devil!" he cried, "I charge you, by the power of God, begone—if you be dead, to the grave—if you be damned, to hell."

An' at that moment the Lord's ain hand out o' the Heevens struck the Horror whaur it stood; the auld, deid, desecrated corp o' the witchwife, sae lang keepit frae the grave and hirsled round by deils, lowed up like a brunstane spunk and fell in ashes to the grund; the thunder followed, peal on dirling peal, the rairing rain upon the back o' that; and Mr. Soulis lowped through the garden hedge, and ran, wi' skelloch upon skellock, for the clachan.

That same mornin', John Christie saw the Black Man pass the Muckle Cairn as it was chappin' six; before eicht, he gaed by the change-house at Knockdow; an' no lang after, Sandy M'Lellan saw

1232

him gaun linkin' doun the braes frae Kilmackerlie. There's little doubt it was him that dwalled sae lang in Janet's body; but he was awa' at last; and sinsyne the deil has never fashed us in Ba'weary.

But it was a sair dispensation for the minister; lang, lang he lay ravin' in his bed; and frae that hour to this, he was the man ye ken the day.

THEODOR STORM

THEODOR STORM (German, 1817-1888). Lawyer and judge, who was exiled to Prussia for 10 years for his sympathies in the Schleswig-Holstein dispute with Denmark. Devoted his evenings to creating a literature of romantic mood-pictures. Of his stories, "Immensee" is a universal favorite.

VERONIKA

I. At the Mill

IT WAS at the beginning of April on the day before Palm Sunday. The mild rays of the late afternoon sun shone on the young grass at the side of the path which led down gradually along a mountain slope. At this moment one of the most respected jurists of the city, a man of middle age, with calm but distinctive features, was walking leisurely, exchanging only an occasional word with the clerk at his side. Their destination was a water-mill not far off whose owner, troubled by age and illness, wished to make over his property to his son.

A few paces behind followed another couple; beside a young man with fresh, intelligent features walked a beautiful, still very youthful woman. He spoke to her, but she did not seem to hear. Her dark eyes gazing straight ahead, she walked silently, as though unaware of anyone at her side.

As the mill became visible in the valley below, the counsellor turned his head. "Well cousin," he called, "you write a passable hand; how would you like to learn a little about making contracts?"

But the cousin waved his hand in protest. "Go on!" he said and looked questioningly at his companion. "Meanwhile I'll have a conversation-lesson with your wife!"

"Well, at least don't teach him too much, Veronika!"

The young woman only inclined her head as in assent. Behind them, from the towers of the city, the sound of the evening chimes came spreading over the country-side. Her hand, which had just stroked back the black hair beneath her white satin hat, glided down over her breast and, making the sign of the cross, she began softly to recite the Angelus. The glance of the young man who, like his relative, belonged to a protestant family, followed the uniform movement of her lips with an expression of impatience.

Several months ago he had come to the city as an architect to work on the addition to a church and since then had been an almost daily guest in the house of the counsellor. He had entered immediately into a lively and friendly association with the wife of his cousin. The two were drawn together through the youth which they had in common as well as through his accomplishment in drawing, which she also practiced with enthusiasm and skill. Now she had found him a friend and teacher at the same time. Soon, however, as he sat beside her evenings, it was not so much the drawing lying before her upon which his eyes rested, as it was her small, busy hand; and she who had been wont to cast aside her pencil at any given moment, now drew silently and obediently without looking up, as though caught in his gaze. It may be that they hardly realized themselves, that, every evening when saying "Good night," their hands remained together a little longer and their fingers were clasped a little tighter. The counsellor, whose thoughts were usually with his business, thought still less about it; he was glad that his wife had found stimulation and understanding for her favorite occupation, which he himself was unable to give her. Only once, just after the young architect had left their house, the dreamy expression in her eyes had surprised him. "Vroni," he said, holding her back by the hand as she tried to pass, "It's true then, isn't it, what your sisters say." "What is, Franz?" "Of course," he said, "now I see it myself, you have spiritual eyes." She blushed and submitted without speaking as he drew her closer and kissed her.

Today, in the fine weather, she and Rudolf had been invited by the counsellor to accompany him on his official errand to the near-by mill.

Since yesterday's social gathering, when she had displayed, at the request of her husband, a drawing which had been completed under his eyes, everything had become different between them. Rudolf felt it only too well; he recalled how it had come about that he had

1234

opposed the excessive praise of the others with such sharp and passionate criticism.

Veronika had long ended her prayer, but he waited in vain for her to turn her eyes toward him.

"You are angry with me, Veronika," he said at last. The young woman nodded slightly, but her lips remained firmly closed.

He looked at her. Obstinacy still lay upon her brow.

"I should think," he said, "you might know how it could happen! Or don't you know, Veronika?"

"I know only," she said, "that you have hurt me. And," she added, "that you wanted to hurt me."

He remained silent for a while. "Did you not notice," he asked hesitantly, "the knowing eye of the old man who stood opposite you?"

She turned her head and glanced up at him fleetingly.

"I had to do it myself, Veronika. Forgive me! I can't bear to have you criticized by others."

It seemed as though a veil drew over her eyes, and long black lashes sank upon her cheeks; but she did not answer.

A short time later they had reached the mill. The counsellor was led into the house by the miller's son; Rudolf and Veronika entered the garden lying at the side, and continued to walk silently up the long incline; it was almost as though they were angry with each other, as though they had to stop for want of breath when they tried to speak an occasional word.

When they had wandered through the garden, they passed over a narrow foot-bridge into the lower door of the mill-building, which stood by a swift stream at the edge of the garden. Through the clattering of the works and the roar of the falling water which drowned every sound coming from outside, a strange sense of separation reigned in the almost dusky room. Veronika had walked over to the door which led to the mill-race and gazed down into the thrashing wheels upon which the water glistened in the evening sun. Rudolf did not follow; he stood within, beside the big cogwheel, his gloomy eyes unswervingly upon her. Finally she turned her head. She spoke, he saw how her lips moved, but he did not understand her words.

"I don't understand!" he said and shook his head.

As he was about to go to her, she had already stepped back into the inner room. In passing she came so close to the wheel beside which he stood, that the teeth almost touched her hair. She did not see it, since she was still blinded by the evening sun; but she felt

1235

her hands seized and herself drawn quickly to the side. As she looked up, her eyes met his. They remained silent; a sudden unmindfulness dropped like a shadow over them. At their heads thundered the mill works; from outside came the monotonous rushing of the water, plunging over the wheels into the depths. Gradually, however, the young man's lips began to move, and, protected by the deafening noise, in which his voice was lost, he whispered intoxicated, maddening words. Her ears could not discern them, but she read their meaning from his lips, from the impassioned pallor of his face. She threw her head back and closed her eyes; only her mouth smiled and betrayed life. Thus she stood holding her face toward him helplessly, her hands obliviously in his.

Then suddenly the roaring ceased; the mill stood still. They heard the mill-hands walking above, and outside, the dripping water fell from the wheels, tinkling into the pond. The lips of the young man became dumb, and when Veronika withdrew from him, he did not try to hold her back. Not until she had gone out through the door into the open, did he seem to regain his speech. He called her name and extended his arms to her, pleadingly. But she shook her head, without turning to look at him, and walked slowly through the garden to the dwelling.

As she went in through the door which had been left partly open, she saw opposite her the old miller, with folded hands lying in his bed. Over it a wooden crucifix was attached, from which hung a rosary. A young woman with a child in her arm had just come over to the bedside and was bending over the covers. "He only needs air." she said. "He enjoys his food well enough."

"Who is your doctor?" asked the counsellor, who was standing close by, holding a document in his hand.

"Doctor?" she repeated. " We have no doctor."

"You're doing wrong there!"

The young woman let out an embarrassed laugh. "It's old age," she said, as she wiped her chubby boy's little nose with her apron, "The doctor couldn't help that."

Veronika listened breathlessly to this conversation. The old man began to cough and put his hand to his eyes.

"Is this your will, Martin, as it is written here?" the counsellor now asked. But the sick man seemed not to hear him.

"Father," said the young woman, "Is that right as the counsellor has just read it?"

"Of course," said the sick man, "Everything is all right."

1236

"And you have considered everything well?" asked the counsellor.

The old man nodded. "Yes, yes," he said, "I have worked hard; but the boy shouldn't have it too bad. . . ."

The son, who until now had been sitting in the corner smoking, entered into the conversation. "Of course, the old man's part has to be considered too," he said, and cleared his throat several times, "The old man will live away a neat sum yet."

The counsellor cast his gray eyes down upon the coarse peasant. "Is that your son, Weismann?" he asked, pointing at the child playing at the bed side. "Send him out, if you expect to do any more talking!"

The man was silent; but his eyes met those of the counsellor with an almost threatening expression.

The old man stroked his hard hand over the cover. And said quietly, "It won't be so very long, Jakob!—But," he added, turning to the counsellor, "in keeping with the village customs, he will have to bury me; that will cost something, too."

The young lady disappeared without a sound, just as she had come, from the open door in which she had been standing during these proceedings.

Outside she saw Rudolf on the other side of the garden in conversation with the mill-hand, but she turned away and followed a footpath, which led below the mill down to the stream. Her eyes strayed unconsciously into the distance; she did not notice how dusk was sinking upon the mountains ahead of her, nor how, gradually, even while she was strolling up and down, the moon was rising behind them and pouring its light over the silent valley. Life in its naked poverty confronted her as she had never before seen it; an endless, arid way,—at the end, death. She felt as though she had been living in a dream until now, and as if she were now wandering in a reality without solace, in which she did not know how to find her way.

It was late when the voice of her husband called her back to the mill where he awaited her at the door. On the way home she walked silently at his side, without feeling his understanding eyes upon her. "You have been frightened, Veronika!" he said and laid his hand upon her cheek. "But," he added, "these people live according to different standards; they are harsh, not only towards their kin, but also towards themselves."

She looked up at her husband's calm face for a moment; then she cast her eyes upon the ground and walked humbly at his side.

Just as silently Rudolf walked at the side of the old clerk. His eyes

1237

hung upon the hand of the woman, illuminated by the moonlight, which had only a short time ago rested so weakly in his own. He hoped that he would be able to hold it once more, if only for a moment when saying good night.—But it was to be otherwise; for, as they approached the city, he noticed the small hands, one after the other, slip into a pair of dark gloves which, as he well knew, Veronika usually carried only for the sake of completing her costume.

Finally they had reached the house; but before he was quite aware of it in his dejection, he felt the hasty touch of her covered fingers upon his own. With a distinctly spoken "Good night" Veronika had opened the door and had disappeared into the darkness of the hall ahead of her husband.

II. Palm Sunday

The morning of Palm Sunday had arrived. The streets of the city were thronged with country-folk from the neighboring villages. Here and there in the sunshine in front of the house-doors stood the children of protestant inhabitants, gazing down toward the open door of the Catholic Church. This was the day of the great Easter procession. —Now the bells were ringing, and the procession became visible under the Gothic arch, and surged out into the street. At the head the orphan boys with black crosses in their hands, behind them in white veiled hoods, the Sisters of Mercy, then the various public schools and finally the whole endless train of country and city folk, of men, women, of children, and old people, all singing, praying, dressed in their best clothes, men and boys bare-headed, their caps in their hands. Overhead at measured intervals, carried upon shoulders, the colossal religious pictures: Christ at Calvary, Christ jeered by the soldiers, in the center, high above everything, the tremendous cross, finally the Holy Sepulchre.

The ladies of the city did not customarily participate in the public festivities.

Veronika sat half dressed in her bedroom at a small dressing table. Before her lay open a small, gilt-edge Testament, such as the Catholic Church permits its members. She seemed to have forgotten herself over her reading, for her long black hair hung loose over her white night-gown, while her hand, holding a tortoise-shell comb lay idly in her lap.

As the din of the approaching procession reached her ears she raised her head and listened. Ever more distinctly came the dull

1238

sound of steps, the singing, monotonous murmuring of prayers. "Holy Mary, Mother of Mercy!," it came from outside, and from the rear of the procession resounded a subdued: "Pray for us poor sinners, now, and in the hour of death."

Veronika recited the familiar words softly. She had pushed back her chair; with her arms at her sides, she stood in the back of the room, her eyes steadfastly directed toward the window. New people came and went continuously, new voices spoke, one picture after the other was carried by. Then suddenly a heart-rending tone penetrated the air. The *castrum doloris* approached, accompanied by the sound of trumpets, surrounded by people, followed by the acolytes and the highest priests in festive vestment. The ribbons fluttered, the black crepe of the canopy rippled in the air; underneath it in a garden of flowers lay the image of the Crucified One. The metallic peal of the trumpets was like a summons to the Day of Judgment.

Veronika was still standing motionless; her knees trembled; beneath the accentuated black eyebrows her eyes lay as if extinguished in the pale countenance.

When the procession had passed, she sank to the floor beside the chair upon which she had been sitting, and covering her face with both hands, she cried, with the words in Luke: "Father, I have sinned against Heaven, and I am not worthy of being called your child!"

III. In the Confessional

The counsellor belonged to that ever increasing community of those who saw in the appearance of Christianity not so much a miracle, but rather the natural result of the spiritual development of humanity. He himself, therefore, did not go to any church; nevertheless, he permitted his wife to retain the habits of her youth and parental home, perhaps in the expectation of her gradual, independent liberation from them.

Since their wedding two years before Veronika had gone to confession and communion only at Easter-time, which had now begun again. He was already acquainted with the way in which she went about in the house on the preceding days, quiet and apparently indifferent; therefore, it had not struck him that the enthusiastically undertaken drawing lessons had ceased ever since that evening walk. But the time passed, the May sun began to beam warmly into the room, and Veronika put off her confession again. At last it could escape him no longer that her cheeks became paler from day to day,

1239

that little shadows became visible under her eyes, left there by sleepless nights. Thus he found her one morning upon entering the bedroom unnoticed, standing at the window lost in thought.

"Vroni," he said, putting his arm around her, "Won't you try holding up your little head again?"

She shuddered, as if he had surprised unguarded thoughts in her, but she sought to control herself. "Go, Franz!," she said, taking his hand tenderly and leading him back to the door.

Then, soon after he had left her alone, she dressed and departed from the house, prayer-book in hand.

A short time later she entered St. Lambert's. Meanwhile the morning was advancing. Outside the windows of the vast hall the leaf-covered branches of the Linden trees cast their shadows; in the choir, upon the doors of the reliquary, a broken sunray fell through the stained glass panes. In the confessionals in the nave of the church here and there people sat or kneeled before opened prayer-books, preparing for confessions. There was no sound but the whispering from the confessionals, now and then a deep breath, the rustling of a dress, or a soft footfall upon the flagstones. Soon Veronika, too, was kneeling in one of the confessionals, not far from the picture of the Holy Mother, who looked down upon her, smiling compassionately. Her completely black costume made the transparent pallor of her face still more striking. The priest, a robust middle-aged man, leaned his head against the screen which separated him from his penitent.

Veronika began the introductory formula in a half whisper: "Forgive me, Father, for I have sinned," and with wavering voice she continued: "I confess to Almighty God and to you, Father, . . ." Her words became slower and slower, less and less understandable; then she stopped.

The dark eye of the priest was calm and directed upon her with an expession almost of fatigue, since he had been hearing confessions for hours. "Turn ye to the Lord!" he said mildly. "Sin is death; but repentance is life."

She tried to collect her thoughts. And again, as so often since that hour, her inward ear heard the turbulent roar of the mill; and again she stood before him in the mysterious twilight—her hands caught in his, closing her eyes under the stress of the overwhelming emotion, transfixed in mortification, not daring to escape, and even less, to remain.—Her lips moved, but she could not get it out; she tried in vain.

The Priest remained silent for a moment. "Courage! my daughter!" he then said, raising his head with the rich black hair. "Think of the words of the Lord: 'Receive ye the Holy Spirit; those whom ye free from sin, their sins shall be forgiven!' "

She glanced up. The flushed countenance, the powerful bull-neck of the man in vestments was close before her eyes. She began once more; but an unconquerable resentment came over her, a reluctance, as before something unchaste, worse than that which she had come here to confess. She was frightened. Was not this revolt in her a temptation of the deadly sin from which she wanted to be released? She bowed her head in silent conflict upon the prayer-book lying before her. Meanwhile, the expression of fatigue had vanished from the face of the priest. He began to speak, earnestly and forcibly, and then with all the magic of persuasion; softly, yet sonorously the tone of his voice came to her ears. At any other time she would have sunk to the dust, enraptured; but this time the newly awakened emotion was stronger than all the power of rhetoric and all the habit of her youth. Her hand fumbled at her veil which was thrown back over her hat.

"Forgive me, father," she stammered. Then, silently shaking her head, she drew the veil down without having received the sign of the cross, stood up, and went hastily down the aisle. Her clothes rustled past the church benches; she gathered them in her hand; it seemed to her as though unseen hands were reaching out to keep her there.

Outside, beneath the high doorway she stood still, breathing deeply. She was troubled in spirit; she had rejected the redeeming hand which had led her since childhood; she knew no other which she might grasp now. Then, as she stood undecided on the sunny square, she heard the voice of a child beside her, and a small brown hand offered her a bouquet of primroses for sale. It was indeed spring outside in the world. As though she had not known it, like a messenger it came to her heart.

She bent down to the child and bought his flowers; then, the bouquet in her hand, she walked down the street towards the city gate. The sun glittered on the stones; from the open window of a house a canary sent forth its loud song. She walked slowly on and soon reached the last houses. From there a foot-path led off to the side up toward the hills which bounded the city. Veronika breathed more freely; her eyes rested upon the green of the fields which bordered the path; now and then the air stirred and brought the gentle fragrance of the cowslips growing at the foot of the mountain. Farther

1241

on, where, at the border of the fields the forest began, the path rose steeper, and physical effort became necessary although Veronika had been used to mountain climbing since her early youth. Now and then she stopped and gazed from the shadows of the firs into the sunny valley which sank deeper and deeper below her.

When she had reached the summit she sat on the ground among the wild thyme which had spun itself over the mountain at this spot. As she breathed the spicy air of the forest her eye swept over toward the blue mountan-chain which lay on the horizon like a haze. Behind her, at short intervals, the spring wind was blowing through the tops of the pines. Now and then the call of a blackbird sounded out of the depths of the forest, or above her the cry of a bird of prey which floated invisible in the immeasurable vastness of space.

Veronika removed her hat and supported her head with her hand.

Thus in solitude and quiet a period of time passed. Nothing approached her but the pure breezes which touched her brow and the calls of the birds which reached her ear from the distance. At times a bright glow flushed her cheeks and her eyes became large and shining.

Now the bells sounded up from the city. She raised her head and listened. They rang shrilly and hastily. "Requiescat!," she said softly, for she had recognized the little bell from St. Lambert's tower which informed the community that beneath one of its roofs the grim messenger of the Lord had entered.

At the foot of the mountains lay the cemetery. She could see the stone cross towering over the grave of her father who, but a few years before, had passed away in her arms as a priest intoned his prayers. And farther on, there, where the water glistened, was that ugly barren patch of earth which she had so often entered as a child, full of shy curiosity, where, according to the commandment of the church, those who had not received the sacrament of the altar were buried beside those who had taken their own lives. This would now be her resting place, too, since Easter confessions were at an end for her.

An expression of pain crept about her mouth and then disappeared. She stood up, a decision firm and clear in her soul.

A moment longer she looked down upon the city and let her eyes wander over the sunlit roofs as if in search of something. Then she turned and walked through the pines down the mountain the way she had come. Soon she was in the green of the fields again. She seemed to hurry, walking erect with firm steps.

Thus she reached her house. From the maid she learned that her husband was in his room. As she opened the door and saw him sitting calmly at his desk she remained hesitantly on the threshold.

"Franz," she called softly.

He laid his pen aside.

"Is it you, Vroni?," he said, turning to her. "You're late! Was your list of transgressions so long?"

"Don't joke!" she said pleadingly as she stepped up to him and took his hand. "I did not confess."

He looked up at her, surprised. She, however, knelt before him and pressed her lips upon his hand.

"Franz," she said, "I have hurt you!"

"Me, Veronika?" he asked, and took her face softly between his hands.

"And now you have come to confess to your husband?"

"No, Franz," she replied, "Not to confess, but to confide in you, in you alone,—and you,—help me, and if you can,—forgive me!"

For a moment he gazed at her earnestly, then he raised her with both arms and laid her head upon his breast. "Then speak, Veronika!"

She did not stir, but her mouth began to speak and, as his eyes hung upon her lips, she felt how his arms tightened about her.

TO A DECEASED

But this is more than I can bear,
That still the laughing sun is bright,
As in the days when you were there,
That clocks are striking, unaware,
And mark the change of day and night—

That we, as twilight dims the air,
Assemble when the day is done,
And that the place where stood your chair
Already many others share,
And that you seem thus missed by none;

When meanwhile from the gate below
The narrow strips of moonlight spare
Into your vault down deeply go
And with a ghostly pallid glow
Are stealing o'er your coffin there.

1243

THE CITY

The shore is gray, the sea is gray,
And there the city stands;
The mists upon the houses weigh
And through the calm, the ocean gray
Roars dully on the strands.

There are no rustling woods, there fly
No birds at all in May,
The wild goose with its callous cry
Along on autumn nights soars by,
The wind-blown grasses sway.

And yet my whole heart clings to thee,
Gray city by the sea;
And e'er the spell of youth for me
Doth smiling rest on thee, on thee
Gray city by the sea.

THE HEATH

It is so quiet here. There lies
The heath in noon's warm sunshine gold.
A gleam of light, all rosy, flies
And hovers round the mounds of old.
The herbs are blooming; fragrance fair
Now fills the bluish summer air.

The beetles rush through bush and trees,
In little golden coats of mail;
And on the heather-bells the bees
Alight on all its branches frail.
From out the grass there starts a throng
Of larks and fills the air with song.

A lonely house, half-crumbled, low:
The farmer, in the doorway bent,
Stands watching in the sunlight's glow
The busy bees in sweet content.
And on a stone near by his boy
Is carving pipes from reeds with joy.

1244

Scarce trembling through the peace of noon
The town-clock strikes—from far, it seems.
The old man's eye-lids droop right soon,
And of his honey crops he dreams.—
The sounds that tell our time of stress
Have not yet reached this loneliness.

CONSOLATION

Let come to me whatever may,
While you are with me it is day.

Though in the world I wander far,
My home is ever—where you are.

Your face is all in all to me,
The future's frown I do not see.

HARRIET BEECHER STOWE

HARRIET BEECHER STOWE (American, 1811-1896). Author of a book that changed the face of a country. Daughter and wife of clergymen. Wrote her novels and stories while raising six children. *Uncle Tom's Cabin*, hardly a great work of art, nonetheless had powerful influence in turning the country's attention toward evils of slavery. It has been translated into nearly every written language.

TOPSY

ONE morning, while Miss Ophelia was busy in some of her domestic cares, St. Clare's voice was heard, calling her at the foot of the stairs.

"Come down here, cousin; I've something to show you."

"What is it?" said Miss Ophelia, coming down, with her sewing in her hand.

"I've made a purchase for your department—see here," said St. Clare; and, with the word, he pulled along a little negro girl, about eight or nine years of age.

She was one of the blackest of her race; and her round, shining eyes, glittering as glass beads, moved with quick and restless glances over everything in the room. Her mouth, half open with astonish-

ment at the wonders of the new Mas'r's parlor, displayed a white and brilliant set of teeth. Her woolly hair was braided in sundry little tails, which stuck out in every direction. The expression of her face was an odd mixture of shrewdness and cunning, over which was oddly drawn, like a kind of veil, an expression of the most doleful gravity and solemnity. She was dressed in a single filthy, ragged garment, made of bagging; and stood with her hands demurely folded before her. Altogether, there was something odd and goblin-like about her appearance,—something, as Miss Ophelia afterwards said, "so heathenish," as to inspire that good lady with utter dismay; and, turning to St. Clare, she said:

"Augustine, what in the world have you brought that thing here for?"

"For you to educate, to be sure, and train in the way she should go. I thought she was rather a funny specimen in the Jim Crow line. Here, Topsy," he added, giving a whistle, as a man would call the attention of a dog, "give us a song, now, and show us some of your dancing."

The black, glassy eyes glittered with a kind of wicked drollery, and the thing struck up, in a clear shrill voice, an old negro melody, to which she kept time with her hands and feet, spinning round, clapping her hands, knocking her knees together, in a wild, fantastic sort of time, and producing in her throat all those odd guttural sounds which distinguish the native music of her race; and finally, turning a somerset or two, and giving a prolonged closing note as odd and unearthly as that of a steam-whistle, she came suddenly down on the carpet, and stood with her hands folded, and a most sanctimonious expression of meekness and solemnity over her face, only broken by the cunning glances which she shot askance from the corners of her eyes.

Miss Ophelia stood silent, perfectly paralyzed with amazement.

St. Clare, like a mischievous fellow as he was, appeared to enjoy her astonishment; and, addressing the child again, said:

"Topsy, this is your new mistress. I'm going to give you up to her; see, now, that you behave yourself."

"Yes, Mas'r," said Topsy, with sanctimonious gravity, her wicked eyes twinkling as she spoke.

"You're going to be good, Topsy, you understand," said St. Clare.

"Oh, yes, Mas'r," said Topsy, with another twinkle, her hands still devoutly folded.

"Now, Augustine, what upon earth is this for?" said Miss Ophelia.

"Your house is so full of these little plagues, now, that a body can't set down their foot without treading on 'em. I get up in the morning, and find one asleep behind the door, and see one black head poking out from under the table, one lying on the door-mat,—and they are mopping and mowing and grinning between all the railings, and tumbling over the kitchen floor! What on earth did you want to bring this one for?"

"For you to educate,—didn't I tell you? You're always preaching about educating. I thought I would make you a present of a fresh-caught specimen, and let you try your hand on her, and bring her up in the way she should go."

"*I* don't want her, I am sure;—I have more to do with 'em now than I want to."

"That's you Christians, all over!—you'll get up a society, and get some poor missionary to spend all his days among just such heathen. But let me see one of you that would take one into your house with you, and take the labor of their conversion on yourselves! No; when it comes to that, they are dirty and disagreeable, and it's too much care, and so on."

"Augustine, you know I didn't think of it in that light," said Miss Ophelia, evidently softening. "Well, it might be a real missionary work," said she, looking rather more favorably on the child.

St. Clare had touched the right string. Miss Ophelia's conscientiousness was ever on the alert. "But," she added, "I really didn't see the need of buying this one:—there are enough now, in your house, to take all my time and skill."

"Well, then, cousin," said St. Clare, drawing her aside, "I ought to beg your pardon for my good-for-nothing speeches. You are so good, after all, that there's no sense in them. Why, the fact is, this concern belonged to a couple of drunken creatures that keep a low restaurant that I have to pass by every day, and I was tired of hearing her screaming, and them beating and swearing at her. She looked bright and funny, too, as if something might be made of her,—so I bought her, and I'll give her to you. Try, now, and give her a good orthodox New England bringing up, and see what it'll make of her. You know I haven't any gift that way; but I'd like you to try."

"Well, I'll do what I can," said Miss Ophelia; and she approached her new subject very much as a person might be supposed to approach a black spider, supposing them to have benevolent designs toward it.

1247

"She's dreadfully dirty, and half naked," she said.

"Well, take her down stairs, and make some of them clean and clothe her up."

Miss Ophelia carried her to the kitchen regions.

"Don't see what Mas'r St. Clare wants of 'nother nigger!" said Dinah, surveying the new arrival with no friendly air. "Won't have her round under *my* feet, *I* know!"

"Pah!" said Rosa and Jane, with supreme disgust; "let her keep out of our way! What in the world Mas'r wanted another of these low niggers for, I can't see!"

"You go 'long! No more nigger dan you be, Miss Rosa," said Dinah, who felt this last remark a reflection on herself. "You seem to tink yourself white folks. You an't nerry one, black *nor* white. I'd like to be one or turrer."

Miss Ophelia saw that there was nobody in the camp that would undertake to oversee the cleansing and dressing of the new arrival; and so she was forced to do it herself, with some very ungracious and reluctant assistance from Jane.

When she saw, on the back and shoulders of the child, great welts and calloused spots, ineffaceable marks of the system under which she had grown up thus far, her heart became pitiful within her.

"See there!" said Jane, pointing to the marks, "don't that show she's a limb? We'll have fine works with her, I reckon. I hate these nigger young uns! so disgusting! I wonder that Mas'r would buy her!"

The "young un" alluded to heard all these comments with the subdued and doleful air which seemed habitual to her, only scanning, with a keen and furtive glance of her flickering eyes, the ornaments which Jane wore in her ears. When arrayed at last in a suit of decent and whole clothing, her hair cropped short to her head, Miss Ophelia, with some satisfaction, said she looked more Christianlike than she did, and in her own mind began to mature some plans for her instruction.

Sitting down before her, she began to question her. "How old are you, Topsy?"

"Dunno, Missis," said the image, with a grin that showed all her teeth.

"Don't know how old you are? Didn't anybody ever tell you? Who was your mother?"

"Never had none!" said the child, with another grin.

"Never had any mother? What do you mean? Where were you born?"

"Never was born!" persisted Topsy, with another grin, that looked so goblin-like, that, if Miss Ophelia had been at all nervous, she might have fancied that she had got hold of some sooty gnome from the land of Diablerie; but Miss Ophelia was not nervous, but plain and business-like, and she said, with some sternness:

"You mustn't answer me in that way, child; I'm not playing with you. Tell me where you were born, and who your father and mother were."

"Never was born," reiterated the creature, more emphatically; "never had no father nor mother, nor nothin'. I was raised by a speculator, with lots of others. Old Aunt Sue used to take car on us."

The child was evidently sincere; and Jane, breaking into a short laugh, said:

"Laws, Missis, there's heaps of 'em. Speculators buys 'em up cheap, when they's little, and get's 'em raised for market."

"How long have you lived with your master and mistress?"

"Dunno, Missis."

"Is it a year, or more, or less?"

"Dunno, Missis."

"Laws, Missis, those low negroes,—they can't tell; they don't know anything about time," said Jane; "they don't know what a year is; they don't know their own ages."

"Have you ever heard anything about God, Topsy?"

The child looked bewildered, but grinned as usual.

"Do you know who made you?"

"'Nobody, as I knows on," said the child, with a short laugh. The idea appeared to amuse her considerably; for her eyes twinkled, and she added:

"I spect I grow'd. Don't think nobody never made me."

"Do you know how to sew?" said Miss Ophelia, who thought she would turn her inquiries to something more tangible.

"No, Missis."

"What can you do?—what did you do for your master and mistress?"

"Fetch water, and wash dishes, and rub knives, and wait on folks."

"Were they good to you?"

"Spect they was," said the child, scanning Miss Ophelia cunningly.

1249

Miss Ophelia rose from this encouraging colloquy; St. Clare was leaning over the back of her chair.

"You find virgin soil there, cousin; put in your own ideas,—you won't find many to pull up."

AUGUST STRINDBERG

AUGUST STRINDBERG (Swedish, 1849-1912). One of the leading literary rebels of Europe at turn of the century. Unhappy teacher, actor, newspaperman. Prolific dramatist, novelist, critic. Lifelong conflict with women reflected in his naturalistic plays—*The Father* and *Miss Julia*—and novels like *Confessions of a Fool*. Tendency to emotional instability apparent in all his work, but experiments in dramatic form had lasting influence.

A FUNERAL

THE cooper sat with the barber in the inn at Engsung and played a harmless game of lansquenet for a barrel of beer. It was one o'clock in the afternoon of a snowy November day. The tavern was quite empty, for most people were still at work. The flames burned brightly in the clay fire-place which stood on four wooden feet in a corner, and looked like a coffin; the fir twigs on the ground smelt pleasantly; the well-panelled walls kept out all draughts and looked warm; the bull-finch in his cage twittered now and then, and looked out of the window, but he had to put his head on one side to see if it was fine. But it was snowing outside. The innkeeper sat behind his counter and reckoned up chalk-strokes on a black slate; now and then he interjected a humorous remark or a bright idea which seemed to please the other two.

Then the great bell in the church began to toll with a dull and heavy sound, in keeping with the November day.

"What the devil is that cursed ringing for?" said the cooper, who felt too comfortable in life to enjoy being reminded of death.

"Another funeral," answered the innkeeper. "There is never anything else."

"Why the deuce do people want to have such a fuss made about them after they are dead," said the barber. "Trump that, Master Cooper!"

1250

"So I did," said the cooper, and pocketed the trick in his leather apron.

Down the sloping road which led to the Nicholai Gate, a funeral procession wended its way. There was a simple, roughly planed coffin, thinly coated with black paint so that the knots in the wood showed through. A single wreath of whortleberries lay on the coffin lid. The undertaker's men who carried the bier looked indifferent and almost humiliated because they were carrying a bier without a cover and fringes.

Behind the coffin walked three women—the dead man's mother and her two daughters; they looked crushed with grief. When the funeral reached the gate of the churchyard, the priest met it and shook hands with the mourners; then the service began in the presence of some old women and apprentices who had joined the procession.

"I see now—it is the clerk, Hans Schönschreiber," said the innkeeper, who had gone to the window, from which he could overlook the churchyard.

"And none of his fellow-clerks follow him to the grave," said the cooper. "A bad lot, these clerks."

"I know the poor fellow," said the barber. "He lived like a church mouse and died of hunger."

"And a little of pride," added the innkeeper.

"Not so little though," the cooper corrected him. "I knew his father; he was a clerk too. See now! these fellows who go in for reading and writing die before their time. They go without dinner and beg if necessary in order to look fine gentlemen; and yet a clerk is only a servant and can never be his own master for only the King is his own master in this life."

"And why should it be more gentleman-like to write?" asked the barber. "Isn't it perhaps just as difficult to cut a courtier's hair and to make him look smart, or to let someone's blood when he is in danger of his life?"

"I would like to see the clerk who would take less than ten years to make a big beer barrel," said the cooper. "Why, one knows the fellows require two years to draw up their petitions and such-like."

"And what is the good of it all?" asked the innkeeper. "Can I scribble such letters as they do, but don't I keep my accounts right? See here I draw a crucifix on the slate—that means the sexton; here I scribble the figure of a barrel—that stands for the cooper; then in

1251

a twinkling, however many strokes I have to make, I know exactly how many each has drunk."

"Yes, but no one else except yourself can read it, Mr. Innkeeper," objected a young man who had hitherto sat silent in a corner.

"That is the best of it," answered the innkeeper, "that no one can poke his nose into my accounts, and therefore I am just as good a clerk as anyone."

The cooper and the barber grinned approval.

"I knew the dead man's father," resumed the innkeeper. "He was a clerk too! And when he died I had to rub out many chalk-strokes which made up his account, for he wanted to be a fine gentleman, you see. All the inheritance he left to the son, who now lies with his nose pointing upwards, was a mother and two sisters. The young fellow wanted to be a tradesman in order to get food for four mouths, but his mother would not consent; she said it was a shame to step downward when one was above. And heavens, how the poor young fellow had to write! I know exactly what went on. The three women lived in one room and he in a rat-hole. All he could scrape together he had to give them; and when he came from work to eat his dinner, they deafened him with complaints. There was no butter on the bread, no sugar on the cakes; the elder sister wanted to have a new dress, and the younger a new mantle. Then he had to write through the whole night, and how he wrote! At last when his breast-bone stuck out like a hook and his face was as yellow as a leather strap, one day he felt tired; he came to me and borrowed a bottle of brandy. He was melancholy but also angry, for the elder sister had said she wanted a velvet jacket such as she had seen in the German shop, and his mother said ladies of their class could not do with less. The young fellow worked and slaved, but not with the same zest as formerly. And fancy! when he came here and took a glass to ease his chest, his conscience reproached him so much that he really believed he was stealing. And he had other troubles, the poor young fellow. A wooer came after the younger sister—a pewterer from Peter Apollo Street. But the sister said 'No!' and so did the mother, for he was only a pewterer. Had he been a clerk, she would have said 'Yes' and persuaded him that she loved him, and it is likely that she would really have done so, for such is love!"

All laughed except the young man, who struck in, "Well, innkeeper, but he loved her, although she was so poor and he was well off; that proves that love can be sincere, doesn't it?"

"Pooh!" said the innkeeper, who did not wish to be interrupted.

"But something else happened, and that finished him. He went and fell in love. His mother and sister had not counted on that, but it was the law of nature. And when he came and said that he thought of marrying, do you know what they said?—'Have you the means to?' And the youth, who was a little simple, considered and discovered that he had not means to establish a new family since he had one already, and so he did not marry; but he got engaged. And then there was a lot of trouble! His mother would not receive his fiancée, because her father could not write, and especially because she herself had been a dressmaker. It was still worse when the young man went in the evenings to her, and would not stay at home. A fine to-do there was! But still he went on working for his mother and sisters, and I know that in the evening he sat and wrote by his fiancée's side, while she sewed, only to save time and to be able to be near her. But his mother and sisters believed evil of the pair, and showed it too. It was one Sunday about dinner-time; he told me himself the young fellow, when he came here to get something for his chest, for now he coughed terribly. He had gone out with his fiancée to Brunke-berg, and as they were coming home over the North Bridge, whom did they meet but his mother and sisters? His fiancée wanted to turn back, but he held her arm firmly and drew her forward. But his mother remained standing by the bridge railings and looked into the water; the elder sister spat before her, and did the same, but the younger—she was a beauty! She stood still and stared at the young woman's woollen mantle and laughed, for she had one of English cloth—and just because of that, her brother's fiancée had to wear wool. Fancy the impudent hussy!"

"That was simply want of sense in the child," said the young man.

"Want of sense!" exclaimed the cooper indignantly. "Want of sense!" But he could not say any more.

The innkeeper took no notice of the interruption and continued: "It was a Christmas Eve, the last Christmas Eve on which he was alive. He came to me as usual to get something for his chest, which was very bad. 'A Merry Christmas, Hans!' I said. I sat where I am sitting now, and he sat just where you are sitting, young sir. 'Are you bad?' I asked. 'Yes,' he answered, 'and your slate is full.' 'It doesn't matter,' I answered, 'we can write down the rest in the great book up there. A glass of hot *Schnapps* does one good on Christmas Eve.' He was coughing terribly, and so he took a drink. Then his tongue was loosened. He said how miserable and forlorn he felt this evening. He had just left his home. The Christmas table was laid.

1253

His mother and sisters were soft and mild, as one usually is on such an evening. They said nothing, they did not reproach him, but when he took his coat and was about to go out, his mother wept and said it was the first Christmas Eve that her son was absent. But do you think that she had so much heart as to say 'Go to her, bring her here, and let us be at peace like friends.' No! she only thought of herself, and so he went with an aching heart. Poor fellow! But hear what followed. Then he came to his fiancée. She was glad and happy to have him, and now she saw that he loved her better than anything else on earth. But the young man, whose heart was torn in two, was not so cheerful as she wished him to be, and then she was vexed with him, a little only of course. Then they talked about marriage, but he could not agree with her. No, he had duties towards his father's widow. But she quoted the priest who had said a man should leave father and mother and remain with his wife. He asked whether he had not left his mother and home this evening with a bleeding heart in order to be with her. She replied that she had already noticed, when he came, that he was depressed because he was going to spend the evening with her. He answered it was not that which depressed him, but his having to leave his old mother on Christmas Eve. Then she objected that he could not deny he had been depressed when he came to her—and so they went on arguing, you can imagine how!"

The cooper nodded intelligently.

"Well, it was a pleasant Christmas for him. Enough! The young fellow was torn in two, piece by piece; he never married. But now he lies at rest, if the coffin nails hold; but it was a sad business for him, poor devil, even if he was a fool. And God bless his soul! Hans Schönschreiber, if you have no greater list of debts than you had with me, they are easily settled!"

So saying, the innkeeper took his black slate from the counter, and with his elbow rubbed out a whole row of chalk-strokes which had been made under a hieroglyph which looked like a pen in an inkpot.

"See," said the barber, who had been looking through the window to hide his red eyes, "see, there she is!"

Outside in the churchyard the funeral service was at an end; the priest had pressed the hands of the mourners and was about to go; the sexton plied his spade in order to fill up the grave again, as a woman dressed in black pressed through the crowd, fell on her knees by the edge of the grave, and offered a silent prayer. Then she let fall a wreath of white roses into the grave, and a faint

1254

sobbing and whispering was audible as the rose leaves fell apart on the black coffin lid. Then she stood up to go, erect and proud, but did not at first notice in the crowd that her dead lover's mother was regarding her with wild and angry looks as though she saw her worst enemy, who had robbed her of her dearest. Then they stood for a moment opposite one another, revengeful and ready for battle; but suddenly their features assumed a milder expression, their pale faces twitched, and they fell in each other's arms and wept. They held each other in a long, convulsive embrace, and then departed side by side.

The innkeeper wept like a child without attempting to hide his emotion, the barber pressed his face against the window, and the cooper took the cards out of his pocket as though to arrange them; but the young man, his head propped in his hands, had placed himself against the wall in order to have a support, for he wept so that his whole body shook and his legs trembled.

The innkeeper first broke the silence. "Who will now help the poor family? The pewterer would be accepted now, were he to make another proposal."

"How do you know that, innkeeper?" asked the young man, much moved, as he stepped into the centre of the room.

"Well, I heard it yesterday when I was up there helping at the preparations for the funeral. But the pewterer will not have her now, as she would not have him then."

"Yes he will, innkeeper!" said the young man. "He will have her though she were ever so selfish and bad-tempered, poor, and wretched, for such is love!"

So saying, he left the astonished innkeeper and his friends.

"Deuce take me—that was he himself!" said the barber.

"Things do not always end so happily," remarked the cooper.

"How about the clerk?" objected the barber.

"No, they did not end well with him, but with the others, you know. They had, as it were, more right to live than he, the young one; for they were alive first, and he who first comes to the mill, grinds his corn first."

"The young fellow was stupid, that was the whole trouble," said the barber.

"Yes, yes," concluded the inkeeper. "He certainly was stupid, but it was fine of him anyhow."

In that they were all agreed.

SUDRAKA

SUDRAKA (Sanskrit, 1st or 2nd century B.C.). Legendary Hindu Prince and Sanskrit dramatist, to whom the drama *Mricchakatikā* (*The Clay Cart*) is attributed. Even this is dubious, since play probably dates from fifth century A.D. Nothing known of his life.

THE CLAY CART

The first scene represents a court in front of Caru-datta's house. His friend Maitreya—who, although a Brahman, acts the part of a sort of jovial companion, and displays a disposition of mixed shrewdness and simplicity—laments Caru-datta's fallen fortunes, caused by his too great liberality. Caru-datta replies thus:—

Caru-datta. Think not, my friend, I mourn departed wealth.
One thing alone torments me.—that my guests
Desert my beggared house, like to the bees
That swarm around the elephant, when dews
Exhale from his broad front; but quickly leave
His dried-up temples when they yield no sweets.
Maitreya. The sons of slaves! These guests you speak of are always ready to make a morning meal off a man's property.
Caru-datta. It is most true, but I bestow no thought
On my lost property,—as fate decrees
Wealth comes and goes; but this is torture to me,—
That friendships I thought firm hang all relaxed
And loose, when poverty sticks closest to me.
From poverty 'tis but a step to shame—
From shame to loss of manly self-respect;
Then comes disdainful scorn, then dark despair
O'erwhelms the mind with melancholy thoughts,
Then reason goes, and last of all comes ruin.
Oh! poverty is source of every ill.
Maitreya. Ah well, cheer up! Let's have no more of these woebegone memories. What's lost can't be recovered.
Caru-datta. Good! I will grieve no more. Go you, my friend,
And offer this oblation, just prepared,
Unto the gods, and mothers of us all.
Maitreya. Not I.

Caru-datta. And why not, pray?

Maitreya. Why, what's the use, when the gods you have worshiped have done nothing for you?

Caru-datta. Friend, speak not thus, for worship is the duty
Of every family; the gods are honored
By offerings, and gratified by acts
Of penance and restraint in thought and word.
Therefore, delay not to present the oblation.

Maitreya. I don't intend to go; send some one else.

Caru-datta. Stay quiet then for a little, till I have finished
My religious meditations and prayer.

They are supposed here to retire, and a voice is heard behind the scenes:—

Stop! Vasanta-sena, stop!

The heroine of the play now appears in front of Caru-datta's house, pursued by the king's worthless but wealthy brother-in-law, called Samsthanaka, who is an embodiment of everything vicious and mean, in exact contrast to Caru-datta.

Samsthanaka. Stop! Vasanta-sena, stop! Why do you run away? Don't be alarmed. I am not going to kill you. My poor heart is on fire with love, like a piece of meat placed on a heap of burning coals.

Vasanta-sena. Noble sir, I am only a weak woman.

Samsthanaka. That is just why I don't intend murdering you.

Vasanta-sena. Why then do you pursue me? Do you seek my jewels?

Samsthanaka. No, I only seek to gain your affections.

At this point the frightened Vasanta-sena discovers that she is close to Caru-datta's house. He is not only loved by her, but greatly respected as a man of honor; and under cover of the evening darkness, now supposed to have supervened, she slips into the courtyard of his house by a side door, and hides herself. A companion who is with the king's brother now counsels him to desist from following her, by remarking:—

An elephant is bound by a chain,
A horse is curbed by a bridle and rein;
But a woman is only held by her heart—
If you can't hold that, you had better depart.

Samsthanaka, however, forces his way into Caru-datta's house; and there finding Caru-datta's friend and companion Maitreya, thus addresses him:—

Take this message to Caru-datta.—Vasanta-sena loves you, and has taken refuge in your house. If you will deliver her up, you shall be rewarded by my everlasting friendship; if not, I shall remain your enemy till death. Give this message, so that I may hear you from the neighboring terrace; refuse to say exactly what I have told you, and I will crush your head as I would a wood apple beneath a door.

He then leaves the stage.

Maitreya accordingly delivers the message. Soon afterwards the heroine Vasanta-sena ventures into the presence of Caru-datta, asks pardon for intruding into his house, requests him to take charge of a golden casket containing her ornaments as a deposit left in trust, and solicits his friend's escort back to her own house.

Maitreya is too much alarmed to accompany her, so Caru-datta himself escorts Vasanta-sena home.

So far is an epitome of the first act.

At the commencement of the second act a gambler is introduced running away from the keeper of a gaming house, named Mathura, and another gambler to whom the first gambler has lost money, who are both pursuing him.

First Gambler. The master of the tables and the gamester are at my heels: how can I escape them? Here is an empty temple: I will enter it walking backwards, and pretend to be its idol.

Mathura. Ho there! stop, thief! A gambler has lost ten suvarnas, and is running off without paying. Stop him, stop him!

Second Gambler. He has run as far as this point; but here the track is lost.

Marthura. Ah! I see,—the footsteps are reversed: the rogue has walked backwards into this temple which has no image in it.

They enter and make signs to each other on discovering the object of their search, who pretends to be an idol fixed on a pedestal.

Second Gambler. Is this a wooden image, I wonder?

Mathura. No, no, it must be made of stone, I think. (*So saying,*

1258

they shake and pinch him.) Never mind, sit we down here, and play out our game. (*They commence playing.*)

First Gambler (*still acting the image, but looking on and with difficulty restraining his wish to join in the game. Aside*). The rattling of dice is as tantalizing to a penniless man as the sound of drums to a dethroned monarch; verily it is sweet as the note of a nightingale.

Second Gambler. The throw is mine, the throw is mine!

Mathura. No, it is mine, I say.

First Gambler (*forgetting himself and jumping off his pedestal*). No, I tell you it is mine.

Second Gambler. We've caught him!

Mathura. Yes, rascal, you're caught at last: hand over the suvarnas.

First Gambler. Worthy sir, I'll pay them in good time.

Mathura. Hand them over this very minute, I say. (*They beat him.*)

First Gambler (*aside to Second Gambler*). I'll pay you half if you will forgive me the rest.

Second Gambler. Agreed.

First Gambler (*aside to Mathura*). I'll give you security for half if you will let me off the other half.

Mathura. Agreed.

First Gambler. Then good morning to you, sirs; I'm off.

Mathura. Hullo! stop there, where are you going so fast? Hand over the money.

First Gambler. See here, my good sirs, one has taken security for half, and the other has let me off another half. Isn't it clear I have nothing to pay?

Mathura. No, no, my fine fellow: my name is Mathura, and I'm not such a fool as you take me for. Don't suppose I'm going to be cheated out of my ten suvarnas in this way. Hand them over, you scoundrel.

Upon that they set to work beating the unfortunate gambler, whose cries for help bring to his rescue another gamster who happens to be passing. A general scuffle now takes place, and in the midst of the confusion the first gambler escapes. In his flight he comes to the house of Vasanta-sena, and finding the door open, rushes in. Vasanta-sena inquires who he is and what he wants. He then recites his story, and makes known to her that having been once in the

service of Caru-datta, and having been discharged by him on account of his reduced circumstances, he has been driven to seek a livelihood by gambling. The mention of Caru-datta at once secures Vasanta-sena's aid; and the pursuers having now tracked their fugitive to the door of her house, she sends them out a jeweled bracelet, which satisfies their demands, and they retire. The gambler expresses the deepest gratitude, hopes in return to be of use to Vasanta-sena at some future time, and announces his intention of abandoning his disreputable mode of life and becoming a Buddhist mendicant.

The third act opens with a scene inside Caru-datta's house. The time is supposed to be night. Caru-datta and Maitreya are absent at a concert. A servant is preparing their sleeping couches, and commences talking to himself thus:—

A good master who is kind to his servants, even though he be poor, is their delight; while a harsh fellow, who is always finding fault and has nothing but his money to be proud of, is a perpetual torment from morning to night. Well, well! one can't alter nature; an ox can't be kept out of a field of corn, and a man once addicted to gambling can't be induced to leave off. My good master has gone to a concert. I must await his return; so I may as well take a nap in the hall.

Meanwhile Caru-datta and Maitreya come back, and the servant delivers Vasanta-sena's golden casket, saying that it is his turn to take charge of it by night. They now lie down.

Maitreya. Are you sleepy?
Caru-datta. Yes:
I feel inconstant sleep, with shadowy form
Viewless and wayward, creep across my brow
And weigh my eyelids down; her soft approach
Is like Decay's advance, which stronger grows
Till it has mastered all our faculties,
And life is lost in blank unconsciousness.

The whole household is soon buried in slumber, when a thief named Sarvilaka is seen to approach. His soliloquy, while he proceeds to accomplish his design of breaking into the house, is curious, as showing that an Indian burglar's mode of operation in ancient

1260

times differed very little from that now in fashion. Moreover, it appears that the whole practice of housebreaking was carried on by professional artists according to certain fixed rules and principles, which a master of the science, named Yogacarya, had embodied in a kind of "Thieves' Manual" for the better training of his disciples. It is evident, too, that the fraternity of thieves, burglars, and rogues had a special presiding Deity and Patron in India, much in the same way as in ancient Greece and Rome.

It may be noted also, as still more curious, that the particular burglar here introduced is represented as a Brahman, that he is made to speak the learned language, Sanskrit, and to display acquaintance with Sanskrit literature; while all the subordinate characters in Indian dramas, including women of rank, are represented as speaking one or other of the provincial dialects called Prakrit. Here is part of the burglar's soliloquy:—

I advance creeping stealthily along the ground, like a snake wiggling out of its worn-out skin, making a path for my operations by the sheer force of my scientific craft, and artfully constructing an opening just big enough to admit my body with ease.

This friendly night which covers all the stars
With a thick coat of darkness, acts the part
Of a kind mother, shrouding me, her son,
Whose valor is displayed in night assaults
Upon my neighbors, and whose only dread
Is to be pounced upon by royal watchmen.

Good! I have made a hole in the garden wall, and am now in the midst of the premises. Now for an attack on the four walls of the house itself.

Men call this occupation mean, which thrives
By triumphing o'er sleeping enemies.
This, they say, is not chivalry but burglary:
But better far reproach with independence,
Than cringing service without liberty;
And did not Aswatthaman long ago
O'erpower in night attack his slumbering foe?

Where shall I make my breach? Ah! here's a rat hole—this is the very thing we disciples of the god Skanda hail as the best guide

to our operations, and the best omen of success. Here then I must begin my excavation, that is clear; but how shall I proceed? The golden-speared god has taught four methods of making a breach: namely,—pulling out baked bricks, cutting through unbaked ones; soaking a mud wall with water, and boring through one made of wood. This wall is evidently of baked bricks, so they must be pulled out. Now for the shape of the hole. It must be carved according to some orthodox pattern: shall it be like a lotus blossom, the sun, a crescent, a lake, a triangle, or a jar? I must do it cleverly, so that to-morrow morning people may look at my handiwork with wonder, and say to each other, "None but a skilled artist could have done this!" The jar shape looks best in a wall of baked bricks. Be it so: now, then, to work! Reverence to the golden-speared god Karttikeya, the giver of all boons! Reverence to Yogacarya, whose chief disciple I am, and who was so pleased with his pupil that he gave me a magical pigment, which, when spread over my body, prevents any police officer from catching sight of me and any weapons from harming my limbs. Ah! what a pity! I have forgotten my measuring line. Never mind, I can use my Brahmanical cord,—a most serviceable implement to all Brahmans, especially to men of my profession. It serves to measure a wall, or to throw round ornaments which have to be drawn from their places, or to lift the latch of a door, or to bind up one's finger when bitten by insects or snakes. And now, to commence measuring. Good! the hole is exactly the right size; only one brick remains! Ah! botheration! I am bitten by a snake: I must bind up my finger and apply the antidote that's the only cure. Now I am all right again. Let me first peep in. What! A light gleams somewhere! Never mind! the breach being perfect, I must creep in. Reverence to Karttikeya! How now! two men asleep! Are they really asleep, or only shamming? If they are shamming, they won't bear the glimmer of this lamp when passed over their faces;—they are fast asleep, I believe,—their breathing is regular, their eyes are firmly closed, their joints are all relaxed, and their limbs protrude beyond the bed. What have we here? Here are tabors, a lute, flutes, and books; why, I must have broken into the house of a dancing master; I took it for the mansion of a man of rank.

He helps himself to the casket, and proceeds to make good his escape.

The noise he makes in going out rouses its inmates, and they

discover that the house has been robbed. Caru-datta is greatly shocked at the loss of Vasanta-sena's casket, which had been deposited with him in trust. He has only one valuable thing left, —a necklace or string of jewels, forming part of the private property of his wife. This he sends by Maitreya to Vasanta-sena as a substitute for the casket.

SUN HSI-CHEN

SUN HSI-CHEN (Chinese, 1906-   ). Novelist popular among Chinese youth. Admired for his stories of rural life. Most widely known books: *Beaten Gold, Woman of the Night,* and a war trilogy: *The Field of War, War,* and *After War.*

AH AO

THROUGHOUT the day, from early dawn Ah Ao had remained hidden under a bed in the small dark room, her head bent, her body still, scarcely daring to breathe.

At the foot of the Purple-Red Mountain, down which spilled a dense growth of fragrant pines and other trees, a small stream ran into the open cornfields, and beside it stood a row of seven houses, most of them old and dilapidated. This place was known as Tao Village, although none of the inhabitants was named Tao. In four of the seven houses lived the family Chen, the house on the western end was a family temple reserved for the spirits, while in the center of the row stood a comparatively new and handsome residence (some eighteen years old) which was owned by Chin the Rich.

It was in the seventh house, poorest of all, consisting of five little rooms, where the Wang family dwelt, that Ah Ao lay hidden. Half of this house was in fact mortgaged to Chin the Rich who, two years before, when old Wang died, had lent his widow forty thousand cash to pay for the funeral feast and obsequies. Consequently she now lived with her son, Small One Brother, and her daughter, Ah Ao, in only the nether part of the little hut, which did not belong to Chin the Rich. In the room next to the kitchen—or rather in one corner of the kitchen itself, since the bed was separated from it only by a few thin planks—Ah Ao, in secret dread, trembled and stifled her lungs all day.

Some grindstones and empty bamboo baskets leaned against the wall of the kitchen, which was just now very noisy. There were four

square wooden tables, with long benches ranged on each side, and these, with their occupants, completely choked up the little room. Altogether one could count more than thirty men, including not only the male population of Tao Village but also guests from the neighboring villages of Yu and Red Wall. They sat drinking and feasting in exuberant mood. Most of them wore blue or white cotton shirts and trousers and were in their bare feet. Chin the Rich, Wu the Merchant, who could read and write, and the Hairy-Headed Village Elder, respected for his age, wore long gowns, however, made of linen. Only on rare occasions did these long-gown men visit such a lowly establishment, and it was plain that they were now quite aware of the extraordinary dignity their appearance lent to the feast.

The food seemed simple enough, with but four big bowls of meat, fish, turnips and soup, spread on each table, but they were refilled again and again, and each time emptied almost as soon as replenished. Later on, besides, the women of the village would have to be fed. Everybody gorged, helping himself to great hunks of meat and full bowls of wine without any pretense at etiquette; their presence at the feast was not in the interest of good will, but a punitive measure against the mother of a shameless daughter. Never mind the financial burden to Widow Wang! It was the only way of justice.

The fact was that only by mortgaging the other half of her house had the unhappy woman managed to get together the money to finance this strange banquet. A sentimental person might have observed that what the guests clipped between the blades of chopsticks was actually Widow Wang's flesh and blood; for the feast meant utter ruin to her. By this sacrifice, however, she was saving the life of her daughter, who was, no one could deny it, guilty of that crime. Now, although a crime of such a nature necessarily required two to commit it, the unwritten but powerful law of custom nevertheless made her alone responsible, and gave any villager the right to attack, insult, abuse or kill her, as he saw fit. By what other means, then, could the child's life be saved, than through this, an expensive banquet in honor of the offended villagers, with the especial aim of winning mercy from Chin the Rich, Wu the Merchant and the Hairy-Headed Village Elder? Even though it meant her own death in the end, still the widow would have gone through with it.

Two days before, in the afternoon, she had sent her son to Chin. He had bowed, begged mercy and requested the loan of thirty thousand cash, pledging the rest of the Wang House as security. Then with this money the boy had, again at his mother's instruction, gone

to the market where he bought thirty pounds of meat, more than twenty pounds of fish, fully a bushel of turnips and some other ingredients of the feast. Since early in the morning of the previous day she had busied herself with cleaning and making ready this food, preparing rice wine and attending to other duties, so that she had not once had a moment to rest.

With the arrival of the guests she had become even busier. All alone, she worked ceaselessly, serving everybody, keeping all the bowls filled with food, pouring forth the warm wine that was like emptying the vessels of her own body, but all the same managing to smile and give the appearance of enjoying her duties immensely.

"Brother Lucky Root," shouted one coarse fellow, "don't hesitate! This isn't an occasion for ceremony, but a free feed. See, you don't have to give anything in return: so eat up! Fill yourself to the brim!"

"You are quite right," agreed Lucky Root. "Why be slow about it, eh? Let's eat; for such opportunities as this are rare indeed. As a matter of fact this girl now, Ah Ao; shameless, but still rather good-looking. How many girls around compare with her? Actually—?"

"The more girls like Ah Ao the more free feasts," yelled a third. "Personally I hope we'll have others."

"Ai-ya. Old Fa! Always boasting. You, the hungry devil with women! But don't forget the facts in this case; the girl right under your noses chooses instead a fellow from a neighboring village, not you!"

"Old Fa, ha, ha!"

"Ho, what an—Old Fa!"

The Widow Wang did not appear to understand these remarks, but bent her attention on the tasks of service and of maintaining the smile on her face. She did not once frown. But Ah Ao heard and trembled and crawled still farther toward the wall. She did not know whether the feeling she experienced was humiliation or terror or indignation or merely a heavy sadness, but something like a great stone seemed to be crushing her down, and her heart burned as if pierced by a shaft of red-hot iron. A few days ago she had boldly resigned herself to whatever fate might bring, but now she wanted only to crawl, crawl, crawl.

The Hairy-Headed Elder at last came to the issue. "To be precise," he began slowly, "this is perhaps after all not so serious a matter. It is natural for a grown girl to want marriage, isn't it so? But to make love—to a young man—in secret, you know, and without anybody's knowledge—without the usual formalities—who can excuse it?"

1265

"Exactly!" exclaimed Wu the Merchant. "Widow Wang, this is something that can come to a mother only as punishment for her own sins in the past. Such a daughter, just consider, is not only a disgrace to your own family name but to the whole Tao Village as well. You very well know that according to age-old custom this crime merits nothing less than death. Recall, now, the case of the Chao girl—it happened three or four years ago in Stone Gate Village—who was beaten to death for the very same offense. Do you remember, she was buried without even a coffin? Nobody could call it cruelty, but only justice; for she had violated the laws of right conduct. Moreover, the worst of it is that even after their death such girls continue to dishonor the good name of the community. Ending life does not end their sin—no, indeed, and, as everyone knows, death doesn't begin to make up for it!"

"What you have just said is undeniably true. Death doesn't cover up the crime at all. But, on the other hand, it's not altogether the girl's fault. The mother is to blame also—a certain laxness, a waning of discipline. Again, in this case it may be that the mother was not herself very virtuous in some previous incarnation. Widow Wang, let me advise you to take care—in this life you had better be more strict."

The Village Elder was the donor of this speech, which oddly did not seem to anger the Widow, but on the contrary encouraged her to speak. She moved forward timidly, her hands pulling nervously on the edge of her worn dress. She spoke, in a very low voice, and smiled painfully:

"Yes, Honored Elder—that is correct. If she did wrong it was really my fault. I don't know what unpardonable sin I have back of me in some previous existence, but it must be as you say. And this terrible crime of my daughter, you're quite right, death would only be the punishment deserved. Still—" she broke suddenly into tears. "But I can't speak, I haven't 'face' to say—only I ask—*mercy!* Spare her life at least."

This was a reckless demand, an extraordinary request indeed, and were it not that the villagers were at that moment eating her food she would never have escaped ridicule by them. They believed in enforcing justice and morality to the letter, and ordinarily would stand no nonsense. Yet it seemed generally understood that because they had appeared, and had eaten, and had enjoyed themselves, and had some of them even come on their own invitation, they would not be altogether adamant. But their decision rested upon the opinions voiced

1266

by Chin the Rich, Wu the Merchant and the Hairy-Headed. Everybody remained silent until Chin finally gave the verdict.

"Wu has, I agree, spoken very wisely, and very much to the point. 'Death doesn't begin to cover up the crime.' Precisely! Then, perhaps, or so it seems to me, little is to be gained by taking her life now. The guilt has been admitted, and the Widow Wang, asking mercy, has begged us also to give 'face' to her late husband. She wants us to spare her daughter's life, and everything considered that is perhaps possible, but at the same time we cannot permit such an altogether immoral woman to continue to besmirch the village good name. She must leave at once!"

The Elder shared this view. "What is done is done; though totally without honor, still it's no use, now, to kill her. Better, as you say, expel her—move her out immediately."

These two having rendered a judgment, the rest of the guests, who considered themselves a kind of "jury," reined in their tongues. The decision was unanimously approved. The pale, weary face of the Widow Wang broke out suddenly into a genuine smile; she bowed low to the three wise men and obsequiously thanked the members of the self-appointed jury. But, back in the darkness, the hidden Ah Ao heard and yet curiously did not feel happy at all at this reprieve. She understood well enough that life had been miraculously restored to her, but although the prospect of death had been terrifying she was after all too young to have a deep fear of it, whereas to be banished from the village, to leave and never again to see her mother, to bid farewell to her brother, to plunge into an unknown, uncertain future —that was something which she knew to be worse than death. Grief shook her body, seemed to break, to shatter it, so that it was no longer whole, but a heap of something that mysteriously still trembled with life.

It had happened two months before, in early April, on a day filled with an ineffable softness, an unbearable languor and gladness that made men dreamy-eyed, drowsy and as if drunk with some wonderful wine.

Ah Ao, on her way home in the afternoon from the near-by Yu Village, thought that she had never known such a glorious day. There was a new warmth in her body, a strange vigor in her as if she had just begun to live. The fields bordering the road were touched from a withered yellow into a lush new green, the trees were coming to life, and in their budding limbs birds had appeared and were joyously

1267

chattering. The whole world, as far as she could see, was young, fresh, growing, awakened, expectant. She felt in harmony with all that she saw, and expectant too. Of what? She did not know, but somehow she found herself walking more slowly. Her face burned as from some inner fire, and she became all at once conscious of her body, vibrant and warm against the fabric of her garments.

"Ah Ao—" a voice called from somewhere.

Surprised and a little afraid, she stopped, looked around, peered over the fields into the clustered pines and through the rocky pass, but saw no one. Above her head a pair of eagles circled. She blushed, rubbed her burning face and walked on.

"Ah Ao—" someone cried again, but this time much nearer. She stopped, more puzzled, but saw no one, and started to go on, when once more she heard the same voice, now quite close, speak out, "Ah Ao, it's me!" Turning round quickly, she saw, protruding from the bushes and greenery, a head. Then slowly a young man in a long linen gown gave her a full-length view of himself, including his handsome red-buttoned cap. He was perhaps twenty years old, not a bad-looking fellow, and he wore on his face a pleased look. Ah Ao recognized him. He was the son of Li, a shop-owner in the neighboring village. His name, she knew as Ah Hsian.

"*Ai-ya!* so it's you," said Ah Ao. "You frightened me almost to death. Where did you come from?" Nevertheless, she seemed not altogether dissatisfied that he had appeared.

"I?" he demanded. "I? I just happened to be coming from town, saw you in the distance and hid myself to have some fun with you."

" You impudent rascal!" she shouted gaily, raising her hand as if to slap him. "Frightening a person to death!"

"I apologize, Ah Ao, with all my heart. The truth is I have something very important to tell you."

"For example?"

But the youth suddenly became weak or timid. He kept murmuring "I—I—I—" Then he seized her hand.

"What is this?" Ah Ao started back quickly, but for some reason her legs refused to move. Her body quivered, as from some shock, and again she felt her flesh warm beneath her garments. All the strength seemed to run out of her. He put his arms around her, pulled her toward him, and then led her into the forest. She could not summon up any resistance, her mind did not seem to work as usual, she was hardly conscious that they moved at all, and she did not utter a

1268

sound. She only knew that within she felt intolerably buoyant and enlarged.

They sat down under the leafy arm of a tree, her head resting upon his shoulder. Her eyes closed and she breathed rapidly. She felt his hand close softly over her breast, over her beating heart. She felt his lips upon hers, and suddenly she knew a bodily glow that she had never felt before.

"Caw-w-w," a magpie circling overhead, startled her, and for a moment recalled to her that the world existed. She trembled. "Ah Hsian! No, no! Don't, please! Mother will beat me to death!"

"Don't, you must not worry. Trust me, believe in me; everything will be wonderful, like this always."

His voice shook too, and some strange vibrancy of it, some summons which she had never heard before, and which would not be denied, completely overpowered her. He caressed her arms, her face, her throat. She ceased to resist.

"What is the matter with you, Ah Ao?" Widow Wang asked her daughter when, very much agitated, she returned home late that afternoon. "Fever?" She touched her forehead, which was covered with a short fringe of hair. "Have you caught a cold?"

"Nothing at all. I—I simply don't feel very well—" Ah Ao murmured, half to herself. She went to the bed and lay down and for a long time she did not stir. She knew very well the risks, the danger, the fate opening up ahead of her, but just as well she knew that she would meet Ah Hsian again, whenever he asked, yes, even tomorrow!

She expected something dreadful to happen; she prepared herself for it. In the future, after each interval with him, she waited dully for the exposure of their crime, and each time was rather surprised when no one came to denounce her. Nevertheless, she resigned herslf to ultimate discovery, but found comfort in the thought that her lover would come to her defense, take punishment as pronounced: and she imagined herself, in his moment of disgrace, going proudly to his side, sharing whatever fate imposed upon him. And what she constantly feared did happen at last, but its consequences were nothing like what she had romantically foreseen. It was just three days before the Widow Wang offered the villagers such a splendid banquet.

Behind Purple-Red Mountain there was a small hill, the name of which had long been forgotten. Halfway up its flank, nearly buried in the foliage, was a temple to the mountain god. The surrounding forests were owned by one of the great landlords, and few ventured

1269

to trespass through the leafy lanes. The place was pervaded by a ghostly stillness, but it was gentle shelter for young lovers.

On this day Lao Teh, the Spotted Face, a woodcutter, had stealthily crept into the forest to steal wood. He had gathered a load and was prepared to leave just as the setting sun splashed ruddily against the wall behind the mountain temple. The sight invited him, and he sat down on the threshold of the enclosure, sighed, lighted his pipe and gazed at the sky.

But was that not a sound? Thrusting the pipe into his girdle, he seized his ax and stood ready to combat with any wild animal that might rush forth. He waited for several minutes, tense and excited. He thought of running away but reconsidered, remembering that "an offensive is the best defensive." Picking up a stone as big as a goose egg, he threw it with all his strength into the thickest part of the forest.

To his astonishment it was not a wild beast but a man that burst from the trees. He did not stop or even look in Lao Teh's direction, but vanished like a devil. Lao Teh nevertheless saw enough of him to recognize Ah Hsian. Somewhat perplexed, he advanced toward the spot whence he had emerged.

Then, in a moment he came upon Ah Ao, languidly spread out, with her dress loosened, her dark hair starred with bits of green leaves, and altogether wearing a look of abandon. The spectacle somehow aroused in Lao Teh, the Spotted Face, an intense fury. He stared with wide-open eyes, and then he bent down and severely struck her.

"Ha! Ah Ao! The devil! You've done a fine thing!" She did not speak, but lifted up eyes that implored and eloquently begged pity. "Scandalous and shameless one! To come here in secret and lie with him!"

Later on, this scene and the subsequent abuse flung upon her by the infuriated Lao Teh remained rather obscure in Ah Ao's mind. She could not remember how, under his guidance, she returned home in disgrace, nor how news of her love spread throughout the village in a few minutes. Only afterward all the eyes she looked into were full of wrath, cold-gleaming eyes of hate. Even her mother gazed at her with anger and bitterness, yet deeper, deep down in those eyes, was a look of poignant sadness that troubled her heart. But the blows of bamboo sticks, the beatings that came in rapid succession, the curses hurled at her, not one of these caused her any pain, nor any shame, nor even the least regret.

She had expected all this, and now it had come. It was no accident,

but had all along been in the certainty of fate, and she was prepared for everything that happened. The single unforeseen development that dismayed and depressed her was that her lover suffered none of the consequences and did not appear to be in the least interested in her any longer.

Even before the men guests had finished sipping the last of their wine, the women began to come for their share, and during all this time Ah Ao continued to press closely against the wall, hovering in her hiding place, hungry and shivering, not because it was cold, not because she felt any longer the fear of death, but from some nameless malady that had seized her inmost being. The women ate no more lightly than their menfolk, and like the men they dropped cynical, sardonic remarks meant to stab mother and daughter cruelly.

The air seemed charged with heightened drama when Mrs. Li, the fat mother of Ah Hsian, unexpectedly appeared at the feast. She had come, it was soon apparent, not to apologize for the part her son had taken in the affair, but on the contrary to curse the Widow Wang for permitting her daughter to induce him to commit adultery. At sight of the unhappy mother, she pointed fixedly at her and began loudly to revile her: "Miserable woman! Where there is such a daughter, there is such a mother also! And you have the 'face' to come to meet me? Actually? My son is pure, chaste, good; he has made the genuflections before the image of Confucius; he has understood well the teachings of the great sage. Yet you, shameless mother and immoral daughter, attempt to seduce and ruin him! I am resolved to die with you this instant!"

And, saying this, she did indeed rush toward the Widow Wang and appeared to be determined to dash her brains out against her. Other woman guests grouped round them, forming a little circle, not without experiencing an inner satisfaction at the scene, and comforting and soothing the wrath of the offended Mrs. Li. The fat woman in fact so far forgot her original intention that she partook heartily of the feast and in the end contented herself with muttering now and then, "She abused my son, seduced him—from now on he will be unable to raise his head above others!"

When the last guest had gone, the old woman stepped slowly into the little dark enclosure, carrying an oil lamp in her hand. She called to Ah Ao to come out and eat, and the girl dragged herself forth, but she had scarcely strength enough to stand erect. A moment ago she had thought herself famished; now she could not swallow a morsel.

1271

Midnight. Widow Wang was not yet in bed. She moved about in the little room, picking up articles from here and there, busily arranging them in the baggage which Ah Ao must take with her when she left at tomorrow's dawn. Finally she fastened the bag.

Spring nights are brief; in a very short time the cocks began to crow. The widow awoke her son and daughter, lighted a lantern, gave them their morning food and then accompanied Ah Ao almost at once to the barrow which stood beside the door.

"Understand, daughter, it's not I who wants to desert you—you have spoiled yourself—" But the stooped figure shook with sudden tears. She seemed to brace herself against the air, and continued, managing to smile very gently: "Just be careful, Ah Ao. From now on stand firmly on your own feet, and I shall have no more cause for worry. As for me, daughter, well just think that I am dead, no longer in this world. If we can't meet here again, then perhaps after death; anyway, let's hope!"

She sat beside Ah Ao on the barrow pushed by her son until they reached the great oak, at the main road, half a mile from her home. She alighted there, bade a last farewell to her daughter and stood watching the receding lantern till, like the last flutter of life in a great void of death, its dim spark crept into utter darkness.

SU TUNG-P'O

SU TUNG-P'O (Su Shih, 1036-1101). Statesman and poet, highly revered by Chinese literary public. Also a great calligrapher and painter. Great number of his poems survive, as well as many brilliant prose essays. Collected works: *Tung-p'o ch'uan-chi.*

AUTUMN SUN

A DESCENDANT of Yüeh Wang, a worthy gentleman, dwells in a village without soil and croons verses without words. He once told Tung-p'o, the retired Scholar, that his mind was as pure as the rays of the Autumn Sun, his emotions as peaceful as its tranquillity. 'I love virtue,' he said, 'and am determined to bring it to perfection with the persistence of the Autumn Sun. I dislike all crops, and, in my dislike, desire to chastise them even as the Autumn Sun strikes that group of trees. So I am anxious to write some verses upon it. What does the master think?'

1272

The retired Scholar with a smile answered, 'How can a gentleman like yourself appreciate the Autumn Sun? Born into a luxurious mansion, when older you roamed through the Emperor's Courts.— Out of doors you were sheltered by a large umbrella, at home you were waited upon behind curtain and veil. You could stand the hot weather up to the point of warmth and the winter to the point of coolness—that's all! What then can you know about the Autumn Sun?

'Now, a man like myself really appreciates it. When the summer floods become excessive, when the clouds become vapour and the rains fall, when the thunder rolls and the lightning flashes, rivers and lakes merge together and the god of the soil is in danger of drowning, then do boats sail on the city walls, the fish and the dragon enter the house, mildew covers the utensils, frogs and earth-worms crawl about the tables. At night, one must move five times to avoid the damp; in daytime, one must dry the clothes in the sun for three changes. But still there is nothing in all this to worry about!

'Now, in San-Wu there is a plot of ploughed land. The ripened grain becomes covered with fungi, the matured rice curls up into the mud. Drains and dykes overflow into one other, walls are ruined with holes and collapse into the mud. One's eyes glisten with tears as the smoke from the fuel in boiler and cauldron fills the room. All around, the neighborhood is silent. The crane cries in the doorway; the wife rises in the night and heaves a deep sigh, when she reckons up the number of foodless days, and wonders whether the clothing will last to the end of the year.

'Suddenly the cauldron sends out sparks in myriad confusion, and the lamp-wick hangs down in double blossom. Clear blows the west wind; the drums and bells resound. The slaves joyously tell me that this is the sign of no more rain. So I rise early to divine it, and I find that Hesperus, the evening star, is placid and no longer flashes as it bathes in the Valley of Sunshine and rises over Fu-Sang. Ere one has winked, the whole prospect has changed with wingéd flight to the crossbeams of the house. In that moment I feel as though I am awakening from a drunken slumber, like a dumb man who can speak, a paralytic who can rise and walk, or as though I am returning to my ancestral village and get my first glimpse of the elders! Have you, Sir, also tasted joy like this?' 'That's fine!' he answered, 'Although I cannot say that I have personally experienced this, yet I can well appreciate it.'

'The Sun,' continued the retired Scholar, 'moves through the South-

ern and the Northern Heavens in different ways. Its fierce and fiery heat is not the result of tyranny, nor is its soothing warmth due to tenderness, for the warmth of to-day is the heat of yesterday. Why then consider Summer as Tun and Winter as Ts'ui? We little men are easily vexed or glad, so that the dread of summer or the love of winter is just the same to us as the numbers 3 and 4 to a crowd of monkeys!

'From now onwards, understand this and be not in doubt. Live without plastering the door; go out without putting on a labourer's hat; and do not complain of the summer heat if you would not forget the virtues of the Autumn Sun.'

Whereat my nobleman clapped his hands and laughed as he wrote this down.

JONATHAN SWIFT

JONATHAN SWIFT (Irish, 1667-1745). Creator of one of world's most brutal and morbid satires on mankind, *Gulliver's Travels*, that later generations used as a children's book. Other famous satire, *The Tale of a Tub*, castigates Christianity. A masterful prose stylist, whose life was embittered by political setbacks. His ambiguous relations with two women, "Stella" and "Vanessa," have intrigued scholars, but remain unsolved.

THE EMPEROR OF LILLIPUT

THE Emperor is taller by almost the breadth of my nail than any of his court, which alone is sufficient to strike an awe into the beholders. His features are strong and masculine, with an Austrian lip, and arched nose; his complexion olive, his countenance erect, his body and limbs well-proportioned, all his movements graceful, and his deportment majestic. He was then past his prime, being twenty-eight years and three-quarters old, of which he had reigned seven in great felicity, and generally victorious. For the better convenience of beholding him, I lay on my side, so that my face was parallel to his, and he stood but three yards off. However, I have had him since many times in my hand, and therefore cannot be mistaken in my description. His dress was very plain and simple, and the fashion of it between the Asiatic and the European; but he had on his head a light helmet of gold, adorned with jewels, and a plume on the crest.

He held his sword drawn in his hand, to defend himself if I should happen to break loose. It was almost three inches long; the hilt and scabbard were gold, enriched with diamonds. His voice was shrill, but very clear and articulate; and I could distinctly hear it when I stood up. His Imperial Majesty spoke often to me, and I returned answers; but neither of us could understand a syllable.

THOUGHTS AND APHORISMS

An old miser kept a tame jackdaw, that used to steal pieces of money, and hide them in a hole, which the cat observing, asked, "Why he would hoard up those round shining things that he could make no use of?"

"Why," said the jackdaw, "my master has a whole chestful, and makes no more use of them than I."

If the men of wit and genius would resolve never to complain in their works of critics and detractors, the next age would not know that they ever had any.

I never wonder to see men wicked, but I often wonder to see them not ashamed.

Imaginary evils soon become real ones, by indulging our reflections on them; as he, who in a melancholy fancy sees something like a face on the wall or the wainscot, can, by two or three touches with lead pencil, make it look visible, and agreeing with what he fancied.

Men of great parts are often unfortunate in the management of public business, because they art apt to go out of the common road by the quickness of their imagination. This I once said to my Lord Bolingbroke, and desired he would observe, that the clerks in his office used a sort of ivory knife with a blunt edge to divide a sheet of paper, which never failed to cut it even, only requiring a steady hand; whereas if they should make use of a sharp penknife, the sharpness would make it often go out of the crease, and disfigure the paper.

"He who does not provide for his own house," St. Paul says, "is worse than an infidel!" And I think he who provides only for his own house is just equal with an infidel.

When I am reading a book, whether wise or silly, it seems to me to be alive, and talking to me.

I never yet knew a wag (as the term is) who was not a dunce.

A person reading to me a dull poem of his own making, I prevailed on him to scratch out six lines together; in turning over the

1275

leaf, the ink being wet, it marked as many lines on the other side; whereof the poet complaining, I bid him be easy, for it would be better if those were out too.

We have just enough religion to make us hate, but not enough to make us love one another.

When we desire or solicit anything, our minds run wholly on the good side or circumstances of it; when it is obtained, our minds run wholly on the bad ones.

The latter part of a wise man's life is taken up in curing the follies, prejudices, and false opinions he had contracted in the former.

Would a writer know how to behave himself with relation to posterity, let him consider in old books what he finds that he is glad to know, and what omissions he most laments.

It is grown a word of course for writers to say, "the critical age," as divines say, "this sinful age."

It is pleasant to observe how free the present age is in laying taxes on the next: "Future ages shall talk of this: this shall be famous to all posterity;" whereas their time and thoughts will be taken up about present things, as ours are now.

I never heard a finer piece of satire against lawyers, than that of astrologers, when they pretend by rules of art to tell when a suit will end, and whether to the advantage of the plaintiff or defendant; thus making the matter depend entirely upon the influence of the stars, without the least regard to the merits of the cause.

I have known some men possessed of good qualities, which were very serviceable to others, but useless to themselves; like a sun-dial on the front of a house, to inform the neighbors and passengers, but not the owner within.

If a man would register all his opinions upon love, politics, religion, learning, &c., beginning from his youth, and so go on to old age, what a bundle of inconsistencies and contradictions would appear at last!

The stoical scheme of supplying our wants by lopping off our desires, is like cutting off our feet when we want shoes.

The reason why so few marriages are happy, is because young ladies spend their time in making nets, not in making cages.

The power of fortune is confessed only by the miserable; for the happy impute all their success to prudence or merit.

Ambition often puts men upon doing the meanest offices; so climbing is performed in the same posture with creeping.

Although men are accused for not knowing their own weakness, yet perhaps as few know their own strength. It is in men as in soils, where sometimes there is a vein of gold which the owner knows not of.

An idle reason lessens the weight of the good ones you gave before.

Arbitrary power is the natural object of temptation to a prince; as wine or women to a young fellow, or a bribe to a judge, or avarice to old age, or vanity to a woman.

The humor of exploding many things under the name of trifles, fopperies and only imaginary goods, is a very false proof either of wisdom or magnanimity, and a great check to virtuous actions. For instance, with regard to fame; there is in most people a reluctance and unwillingness to be forgotten. We observe, even among the vulgar, how fond they are to have an inscription over their grave. It requires but little philosophy to discover and observe that there is no intrinsic value in all this; however, if it be founded in our nature, as an incitement to virtue, it ought not to be ridiculed.

Complaint is the largest tribute Heaven receives, and the sincerest part of our devotion.

The common fluency of speech in many men, and most women, is owing to a scarcity of matter, and a scarcity of words; for whoever is a master of language, and hath a mind full of ideas, will be apt in speaking to hesitate upon the choice of both; whereas common speakers have only one set of ideas, and one set of words to clothe them in; and these are always ready at the mouth; so people come faster out of church when it is almost empty, than when a crowd is at the door.

To be vain is rather a mark of humility than pride. Vain men delight in telling what honors have been done them, what great company they have kept, and the like, by which they plainly confess that these honors were more than their due, and such as their friends would not believe if they had not been told: whereas a man truly proud thinks the greatest honors below his merit, and consequently scorns to boast. I therefore deliver it as a maxim, that whoever desires the character of a proud man ought to conceal his vanity.

I have known several persons of great fame for wisdom in public affairs and councils governed by foolish servants.

I have known great ministers, distinguished for wit and learning, who preferred none but dunces.

I have known men of great valor cowards to their wives.

I have known men of the greatest cunning perpetually cheated.

1277

Dignity, high station, or great riches, are in some sort necessary to old men, in order to keep the younger at a distance, who are otherwise too apt to insult them upon the score of their age.

Every man desires to live long, but no man would be old.

Love of flattery, in most men, proceeds from the mean opinion they have of themselves; in women, from the contrary.

Kings are commonly said to have long hands; I wish they had as long ears.

Princes, in their infancy, childhood and youth, are said to discover prodigious parts and wit, to speak things that surprise and astonish: strange, so many hopeful princes, so many shameful kings! If they happen to die young, they would have been prodigies of wisdom and virtue: if they live, they are often prodigies, indeed, but of another sort.

Apollo was held the god of physic and sender of diseases. Both were originally the same trade, and still continue.

"That was excellently observed," said I, when I read a passage in an author where his opinion agrees with mine: when we differ, there I pronounce him to be mistaken.

Very few men, properly speaking, live at present; but are providing to live another time.

As universal a practice as lying is, and as easy a one as it seems, I do not remember to have heard three good lies in all my conversation, even from those who were most celebrated in that faculty.

ALGERNON CHARLES SWINBURNE

ALGERNON CHARLES SWINBURNE (English, 1837-1909). Poet of late Victorian Era, who shocked his contemporaries by personal life (dipsomaniac) and literary output (earlier works, *Poems and Ballads*, seemed sex-obsessed). Other famous works: *Atalanta in Calydon* and *Songs Before Sunrise*. Master of verbal music and the singing line.

WHEN THE HOUNDS OF SPRING

When the hounds of spring are on winter's traces,
  The mother of months in meadow or plain
Fills the shadows and windy places
  With lisp of leaves and ripple of rain;

And the brown bright nightingale amorous
Is half assuaged for Itylus,
For the Thracian ships and the foreign faces,
  The tongueless vigil, and all the pain.

Come with bows bent, and with emptying of quivers,
  Maiden most perfect, lady of light,
With a noise of winds and many rivers,
  With a clamor of waters, and with might;
Bind on thy sandals, O thou most fleet,
Over the splendor and speed of thy feet;
For the faint east quickens, the wan west shivers,
  Round the feet of the day and the feet of the night.

Where shall we find her, how shall we sing to her,
  Fold our hands round her knees, and cling?
O that man's heart were as fire and could spring to her,
  Fire, or the strength of the streams that spring!
For the stars and the winds are unto her
As raiment, as songs of the harp-player;
For the risen stars and the fallen cling to her,
  And the southwest-wind and the west-wind sing.

For winter's rains and ruins are over,
  And all the season of snows and sins;
The days dividing lover and lover,
  The light that loses, the night that wins;
And time remembered is grief forgotten,
And frosts are slain and flowers begotten,
And in green underwood and cover
  Blossom by blossom the spring begins.

The full streams feed on flower of rushes,
  Ripe grasses trammel a traveling foot,
The faint fresh flame of the young year flushes
  From leaf to flower and flower to fruit;
And fruit and leaf are as gold and fire,
And the oat is heard above the lyre,
And the hoofed heel of a satyr crushes
  The chestnut-husk at the chestnut-root.

1279

And Pan by noon and Bacchus by night,
　　Fleeter of foot than the fleet-foot kid,
Follows with dancing and fills with delight
　　The Maenad and the Bassarid;
And soft as lips that laugh and hide
The laughing leaves of the trees divide,
And screen from seeing and leave in sight
　　The god pursuing the maiden hid.

The ivy falls with the Bacchanal's hair
　　Over her eyebrows hiding her eyes;
The wild vine slipping down leaves bare
　　Her bright breast shortening into sighs;
The wild vine slips with the weight of its leaves,
But the berried ivy catches and cleaves
To the limbs that glitter, the feet that scare
　　The wolf that follows, the fawn that flies.

MAN

Before the beginning of years,
　　There came to the making of man
Time, with a gift of tears;
　　Grief, with a glass that ran;
Pleasure, with pain for leaven;
　　Summer, with flowers that fell;
Remembrance fallen from heaven,
　　And madness risen from hell;
Strength without hands to smite;
　　Love that endures for a breath;
Night, the shadow of light,
　　And life, the shadow of death.
And the high gods took in hand
　　Fire, and the falling of tears,
And a measure of sliding sand
　　From under the feet of the years;
And froth and drift of the sea;
　　And dust of the laboring earth;
And bodies of things to be
　　In the houses of death and of birth;

And wrought with weeping and laughter,
  And fashioned with loathing and love,
With life before and after
  And death beneath and above,
For a day and a night and a morrow,
  That his strength might endure for a span
With travail and heavy sorrow,
  The holy spirit of man.

From the winds of the north and the south
  They gathered as unto strife;
They breathed upon his mouth,
  They filled his body with life;
Eyesight and speech they wrought
  For the veils of the soul therein,
A time for labor and thought,
They gave him light in his ways,
  And love, and a space for delight,
And beauty and length of days.
  And night, and sleep in the night.
His speech is a burning fire;
  With his lips he travaileth;
In his heart is a blind desire,
  In his eyes foreknowledge of death;
He weaves, and is clothed with derision;
  Sows, and he shall not reap;
His life is a watch or a vision
  Between a sleep and a sleep.

THE GARDEN OF PROSERPINE

Here, where the world is quiet;
  Here, where all trouble seems
Dead winds' and spent waves' riot
  In doubtful dreams of dreams;
I watch the green field growing
For reaping folk and sowing,
For harvest-time and moving,
  A sleepy world of streams.

I am tired of tears and laughter,
    And men that laugh and weep;
Of what may come hereafter
    For men that sow to reap:
I am weary of days and hours,
Blown buds of barren flowers,
Desires and dreams and powers
    And everything but sleep.

Here life has death for neighbor,
    And far from eye or ear
Wan waves and wet winds labor,
    Weak ships and spirits steer;
They drive adrift, and whither
They wot not who make thither;
But no such winds blow hither,
And no such things grow here.

No growth of moor or coppice,
    No heather-flower or vine,
But bloomless buds of poppies,
    Green grapes of Proserpine,
Pale beds of blowing rushes,
Where no leaf blooms or blushes
Save this whereout she crushes
    For dead men deadly wine.

Pale, without name or number,
    In fruitless fields of corn,
They bow themselves and slumber
    All night till light is born;
And like a soul belated,
In hell and heaven unmated,
By cloud and mist abated
    Comes out of darkness morn.

Though one were strong as seven,
    He too with death shall dwell,
Nor wake with wings in heaven,
    Nor weep for pains in hell;

Though one were fair as roses,
His beauty clouds and closes;
And well though love reposes,
  In the end it is not well.

Pale, beyond porch and portal,
  Crowned with calm leaves, she stands
Who gathers all things mortal
  With cold immortal hands;
Her languid lips are sweeter
Than love's who fears to greet her,
To men that mix and meet her
  From many times and lands.

She waits for each and other,
  She waits for all men born;
Forgets the earth her mother,
  The life of fruits and corn;
And spring and seed and swallow
Take wing for her and follow
Where summer song rings hollow
  And flowers are put to scorn.

There go the loves that wither,
  The old loves with wearier wings;
And all dead years draw thither,
  And all disastrous things;
Dead dreams of days forsaken,
Blind buds that snows have shaken,
Wild leaves that winds have taken,
  Red strays of ruined springs.

We are not sure of sorrow;
  And joy was never sure;
Today will die tomorrow;
  Time stoops to no man's lure;
And love, grown faint and fretful,
With lips but half regretful
Sighs, and with eyes forgetful
  Weeps that no loves endure.

From too much love of living,
    From hope and fear set free,
We thank with brief thanksgiving
    Whatever gods may be
That no life lives for ever;
That dead men rise up never;
That even the weariest river
    Winds somewhere safe at sea.

Then star nor sun shall waken,
    Nor any change of light:
Nor sound of waters shaken,
    Nor any sound or sight:
Nor wintry leaves nor vernal,
Nor days nor things diurnal;
Only the sleep eternal
    In an eternal night.

T

RABINDRANATH TAGORE

RABINDRANATH TAGORE (Indian, 1861-1941). Foremost Bengali **poet**. Member of famous family of artists, musicians and reformers. When translated, won immediate favor in the West. Outstanding works: *Chitrā (Beauty)*, *Gitanjali (Handful of Songs)*, and *Gorā*, a novel after Kipling.

TO NATURE

1

Thou tanglest my heart in a hundred nooses of love,
What is this thy play?
It is but a little feeble life—
Why so many bonds to bind it?
At every turn and every moment
Thou winnest my love with thy wiles,
But hast none to give, thou stealer of hearts!
I wander about in search of thy heart,
   O cruel Nature;
So many flowers, such light, such songs and scents,
   But where is love?
Hidden in the wealth of thy beauty thou laughest
   While we weep.

2

Day and night in the deserted playfield
   Thou playest in jest;
We wot not whom thou lovest or slightest;
He to whom thou art kind and loving in the morning,
The evening finds him lying neglected in the dust.

Still I love thee and cannot forget,
   Thou enchantress!
Thy loveless embrace awakes in the heart
   A thousand songs;
In happiness and grief and misery I live in the sunlight,
Nor crave the frozen stillness of the endless night.

      3

Half open, half-veiled, thy face
   Is the abode of mystery;
To the heart it brings the ache of love
   Mingled with fear;
Thy ever-new phases pass understanding,
And the heart is filled with laughter and tears.
Stretching forth my heart and soul I rush towards thee,
   But thou eludest my grasp;
I see the slight, sweet, mocking smile
   On thy sun-red lips;
If I wish to flee thou spreadest thy nets for my feet,—
What arts, what strength, fleet-footed, quick of tongue!

      4

Thou knowest not thy own limits,
   Thine own mystery;
So in the blind night when the seven worlds
   Are steeped in slumber,
Curious and silent-footed thou standest in the sky
Lighting million torches of star-rays.

      5

In another place thou sittest ever lone
   With a vow of eternal silence,
All around is the hard, treeless, dreary
   Solitude of the desert;
Eon after eon rise overhead the sun and the moon,
They look and they pass without a word.

Again, thou rompest and playest like a girl
  With hair and garments flying in the wind,
With laughter overflowing as a fountain,
  Without a trace of shame;
Thy heart cannot hold its own measure,—
Words and songs without end.

7

Yet again with wrath-lit frenzied eyes,
  Slaying in a moment,
Thou strikest the breast of hapless Earth
  With incessant curses of fire;
Sometimes in the dusk moved by a noble grief
A pale shadow as of pity falls on thy face.

8

It is thus thou hast conquered
  Innumerable hearts;
For ages and ages thy countenance
  Has been fresh and sweet;
Disguised in many forms thou art near all,
Yet hast thou given thyself to none.

9

The more am I baffled the more I remember
  The great opulence of thy beauty;
So grows my love as increases my pain,
  As I laugh and cry;
The farther thou goest the heavier is my soul trammelled,
The less I understand thee the more I love thee.

JUNICHIRO TANIZAKI

JUNICHIRO TANIZAKI (Japanese, 1886-   ). One of Japan's most distinguished modern novelists. Started his career under Western influence of Baudelaire, Wilde and Poe. After earthquake of 1923, turned to classical Japanese literature and wrote most important novels, including *Some Prefer Nettles*. Recently engaged in new translation of *The Tale of Genji*.

From *SOME PREFER NETTLES*

O-HISA, his father-in-law's mistress, drove a moth from the clear-lacquer table, the breeze from her fan cool through Kaname's light kimono. The clean smell of spring mushrooms rose faintly from the soup. It was pitch-dark now in the garden, and the croaking of the rain-frogs had risen to a clamor.

"I'd like to learn the Tokyo style of singing myself."

"You'll be scolded for dangerous thoughts. And I'm afraid I'll have to join the scolding—you've no idea how much better the Osaka style is for you."

"I don't object to it so much. But the teacher is rather a problem."

"Let me see—you go to someone in Osaka, don't you?"

"That's right. But I was thinking more of the teacher here."

Kaname laughed.

"He's unbearable. Lecture, lecture, lecture."

"All old people are that way." Kaname laughed again. "That reminds me. I noticed the bran bag. You still use it?"

"That's right. Your father-in-law uses soap himself, but he won't let me. He says women mustn't ruin their skin with soap."

"And the nightingale dung?"

"I go on with that too. But it hasn't made my skin a bit whiter."

Kaname was finishing off the meal with his second decanter of saké, and O-hisa had brought in a dish of loquats when the telephone rang. She ran to answer it, leaving a half-peeled loquat in an antique glass saucer.

"Yes . . . yes . . . I see. I'll tell him." Kaname could see her in the hall nodding into the telephone. In a minute or two she was back. "Misako will stay here too, he says. They'll be home before long."

"Really? And she said she wouldn't. . . . It seems an awfully long time since I last spent the night here."

"It has been a long time."

More than that, though, it seemed a long time since he and his wife, Misako, had slept alone together. There had of course been those two or three nights—their first alone in he did not know how many years—when little Hiroshi was in Tokyo with Takanatsu; but they had been able then to lie down side by side and go off to sleep as unconcernedly as two strangers at an inn, so deadened had their marital nerves become. He suspected that tonight, however, her father hoped for great changes to come from throwing them together. This benevolent scheming was a little disconcerting, but not enough so that Kaname felt pressed to try for an escape. He was sure that the time had passed when one night could make a difference.

"Hasn't it grown heavy?" said Kaname. "Not a breath of air." He looked out to the veranda. The incense, on the point of going out, sent a column of smoke straight and unwavering into the air. The breeze in the garden had died, and with it the breeze from O-hisa's fan, motionless in her lap and as though forgotten.

"It's clouding over. I wonder if it will rain."

"It might well. I almost hope it will."

Above the motionless leaves a star here and there broke through the clouds. For a moment he thought he could hear, as with a sixth sense, Misako's voice fighting back the old man; and he knew that almost unconsciously he had come to a point where he could support his wife's decision with an even stronger one of his own.

"What time do you suppose it is?"

"Eight thirty, possibly."

"Only eight thirty. Isn't it quiet, though?"

"It's still early, but you may want to go to bed. They should be back before long."

"I suppose it seemed from what he said over the telephone that the conversation was not going very well?" Kaname was secretly more interested in having O-hisa's views than the old man's.

"Shall I bring you something to read?"

"Thank you. What sort of things do you read?"

"He brings home old wood-block books and tells me I should read them. But I can't get interested in the dusty old things."

"You'd rather read a woman's magazine?"

"He says if I have time for that sort of trash I should be practising my calligraphy."

"What copybook does he have you on?"

"There are a couple. O-ie method."

"Well, let me look at one of your dusty books."

"How about a travel guide?"

"That should do, I suppose."

"Let's go out to the cottage, then. I have everything ready."

O-hisa led the way along a covered passage to the garden cottage. As she slid back the paper-paneled door to the rear of the tearoom, Kaname caught the rustling of a mosquito net in the darkness beyond. A cool breath of air came through the open door.

"The wind seems to have come up again."

"And all of a sudden it's a little chilly," Kaname answered.

"We'll have a shower before long."

The mosquito net rustled again, this time not from the wind. O-hisa felt her way inside and, groping for the lamp; at Kaname's pillow, turned the switch.

"Shall I get you a larger bulb?"

"This will do nicely. The print's always big in old books."

"Suppose I leave the shutters open. You won't want it too hot."

"I wish you would. I can close them later."

Kaname crawled under the net himself when O-hisa had gone. The room was not a large one, and the linen mosquito netting cut it off smaller yet, so that the two mattresses were almost touching. It was a novel arrangement for Kaname and Misako. At home these summer nights they hung up as large a mosquito net as possible and slept, one at each end, with Hiroshi between them. Kaname rolled over on his stomach, a little bored, and lighted a cigarette. He tried to make out the picture in the alcove beyond the light-green netting. Something in modest, neutral colors, a landscape it seemed to be, wider than it was high. With the light inside the net, however, the rest of the room lay in deep shadow, and he could make out neither the details nor the artist's signature. Below it in a bowl was what he took to be a blue and white porcelain burner. There was a faint smell of incense through the room—he noticed it for the first time. Plum blossom, he judged. For an instant he thought he saw O-hisa's face, faint and white, in a shadowy corner beside the bed. He started up, but quickly caught himself. It was the puppet the old man had brought back from Awaji, a lady puppet in a modest dotted kimono.

A gust of wind came through the open window and the shower began. Kaname could hear large drops falling against the leaves. He raised himself on an elbow and stared out into the wooden depths of the garden. A small green frog, a refugee from the rain,

1290

clung halfway up the fluttering side of the net, its belly reflecting the light from the bed lamp.

"It's finally begun."

The door slid open, and this time, half a dozen old-style Japanese books in arm, it was no puppet that sat faintly white in the shadows beyond the netting.

T'AO CH'IEN

T'AO CH'IEN (Chinese, 372-427). Profoundly influential rustic poet of China. After brief official career, retired to live rural life. His prose poem, *Kuei-ch'ü-lai tz'u (Returning to Live on the Farm)*, and shorter lyric poems are known to all Chinese school children. Simplicity of his life and work earned him reputation as "the most harmonious product of Chinese culture."

RETURNING TO LIVE ON THE FARM

Six Poems

When I was young, I was not fitted for a worldly rhythm.
By nature I loved the mountains and the hills.
I fell into the net of the world by mistake,
And I have stayed there for thirty years.
A bird in the cage longs for the old forest,
And a fish in the pond thinks of his former pool.
I cultivated rough land in the south,
And, keeping to simple ways, I returned to the field and garden.
I have over ten *mu* of land
And a thatched house of eight or nine rooms.
Birch and willow shade the back eaves;
Peach and plum spread their branches in the front courtyard.
Villages lie in the distance.
Smoke rises like mist from faraway fields.
Dogs bark in hidden lanes,
And roosters crow.
There is no worldly hubbub.
There is space, and I have leisure.
For a long time I was in a cage,
But now I am back with nature.

1291

In the country there is little of human affairs.
The lane has but few wheel tracks,
And white sun shines on the closed door.
In the empty room I have no thoughts of the world.
Often, strolling along the winding roads
And wearing cotton garments, we visit each other.
When we meet, we do not gossip,
But simply talk about how the hemp and mulberry have shot up.
Daily the hemp and mulberry grow taller,
And our fields each day are extended.
Frequently we fear that a frost will come
And kill the plants as if they were weeds.

I plant beans at the foot of the southern hill.
Grass flourishes, but the beans rarely sprout.
In the early morning I go out to weed,
And in the moonlight I return, carrying my hoe.
The path is narrow, and as the shrubs and grasses are tall,
Evening dew moistens my clothes.
These wet clothes are not worth worrying about.
I only hope that my dream will not leave me.

I have been away from the pleasure of the hills and streams,
From the rushing sound of the wild trees.
Wearing a raincoat, I go with my nephews and children
To walk in the meadows
And stroll on the hills and dikes.
This seems to be a spot where once someone lived;
There are the remains of a well and an oven,
And mulberry and bamboo wither among the other trees.
I ask a wood-gatherer
What kind of man lived here.
He replies
That all have died,
And that they saw the shift of power at court.
These words are not empty.
Man's life is like a shifting illusion;
At the end we shall return to emptiness.

Depressed and alone, I take my staff and return,
Passing along the zigzag, rough, and thorny roads.

The stream of the mountain is clear and shallow;
Coming upon it I wash my feet.
I strain my fresh wine
And, having a chicken, invite my close neighbors.
The sunset enters my gate.
The glow of firewood takes the place of a bright candle.
When I am happy I regret that the evening is too short,
And in no time it is dawn!

I plant sprouts on the eastern hill,
And they grow lushly in the field.
Although I am tired of carrying the hoe,
This muddy wine comforts me.
The sun sets, and I return with a cart of firewood.
The road is dim, the light already dusky.
Returning farmers watch the chimney smoke.
A child, waiting behind the crack of the door under the eaves,
Asks what I have been doing.
For a hundred years I have been on the road,
And now I only wish that the mulberry and hemp were ripe.
In the month of the silkworm we can weave,
And my simple heart wants just this!
I clear three paths and watch for my friends.

TORQUATO TASSO

TORQUATO TASSO (Italian, 1544-1595). Classicist of the idyllic pastoral
and ardent religiosity. Most celebrated works: *Rinaldo*, epic poem; *Aminta*,
pastoral play; *Jerusalem Delivered*, Counter-Reformation epic of the Crusades.
In later years his mind was clouded as result of excessive religious scruples.

THE GOLDEN AGE

O lovely age of gold!
Not that the rivers rolled
With milk, or that the woods wept honey-dew;
Not that the ready ground
Produced without a wound,
Or the mild serpent had no tooth that slew:

1293

Not that a cloudless blue
　Forever was in sight,
Or that the heaven, which burns
And now is cold by turns,
Looked out in glad and everlasting light;
No, nor that even the insolent ships from far
Brought war to no new lands, nor riches worse than war.

　　But solely that that vain
　　And breath-invented pain,
That idol of mistake, that worshiped cheat,
　　That Honor—since so called
　　By vulgar minds appalled,—
Played not the tyrant with our nature yet.
　　It had not come to fret
　　The sweet and happy fold
　　Of gentle human kind;
　　Nor did its hard law bind
Souls nursed in freedom; but that law of gold,
That glad and golden law, all free. all fitted.
Which Nature's own hand wrote—what pleases is permitted.

　　Then among streams and flowers.
　　The little winged Powers
Went singing carols without torch or bow;
　　The nymphs and shepherds sat
　　Mingling with innocent chat
Sports and low whispers, and with whispers low,
　　Kisses that would not go.
　　The maid, her childhood o'er,
　　Kept not her bloom uneyed,
　　Which now a veil must hide,
Nor the crisp apples which her bosom bore;
And oftentimes, in river or in lake,
The lover and his love their merry bath would take.

　　'Twas thou, thou, Honor, first
　　That didst deny our thirst
Its drink, and on the fount thy covering set;
　　Thou badst kind eyes withdraw
　　Into constrainèd awe,

1294

And keep the secret for their tears to wet;
　　Thou gatherdst in a net
　　　The tresses from the air,
　　And mad'st the sports and plays
　　Turn all to sullen ways,
And put'st on speech a rein—in steps a care.
Thy work it is—thou shade that wilt not move—
That what was once the gift, is now the theft, of love.

　　　Our sorrows and our pains,
　　　These are thy noble gains.
But oh, thou Love's and Nature's masterer,
　　Thou conqueror of the crowned,
　　What dost thou on this ground,
Too small a circle for thy mighty sphere?
　　　Go, and make slumber dear
　　　　To the renowned and high;
　　　We here, a lowly race,
　　　Can live without thy grace,
After the use of mild antiquity.
　　　Go, let us love—since years
No truce allow, and life soon disappears.
Go let us love: the daylight dies, is born;
　　　But unto us the light
Dies once for all, and sleep brings on eternal night.

ALFRED LORD TENNYSON

ALFRED LORD TENNYSON (English, 1808-1892). Poet of English national
life. Artful, subtle, often morbid. In disciplined sensibility and concern for
traditional morality, represents peak of Victorian literature. Most popular
work: *Idylls of the King*, based on Arthurian legends. Most moving: *In
Memoriam*, elegy on his friend Arthur Hallam. Succeeded Wordsworth as
Poet Laureate.

CHORIC SONG FROM THE LOTOS-EATERS

I

There is sweet music here that softer falls
Than petals from blown roses on the grass,
Or night-dews on still waters between walls
Of shadowy granite, in a gleaming pass;

Music that gentlier on the spirit lies,
Than tired eyelids upon tired eyes;
Music that brings sweet sleep down from the blissful skies.
Here are cool mosses deep,
And through the moss the ivies creep,
And in the stream the long-leaved flowers weep,
And from the craggy ledge the poppy hangs in sleep.

II

Why are we weighed upon with heaviness,
And utterly consumed with sharp distress,
While all things else have rest from weariness?
All things have rest; why should we toil alone,
We only toil, who are the first of things,
And make perpetual moan,
Still from one sorrow to another thrown;
Nor ever fold our wings,
And cease from wanderings,
Nor steep our brows in slumber's holy balm;
Nor harken what the inner spirit sings,
"There is no joy but calm!"—
Why should we only toil, the roof and crown of things?

III

Lo! in the middle of the wood,
The folded leaf is wooed from out the bud
With winds upon the branch, and there
Grows green and broad, and takes no care,
Sun-steeped at noon, and in the moon
Nightly dew-fed; and turning yellow
Falls, and floats adown the air.
Lo! sweetened with the summer light,
The full-juiced apple, waxing over-mellow,
Drops in a silent autumn night.
All its allotted length of days
The flower ripens in its place,
Ripens and fades, and falls, and hath no toil,
Fast-rooted in the fruitful soil.

IV

Hateful is the dark-blue sky,
Vaulted o'er the dark-blue sea.
Death is the end of life; ah, why
Should life all labor be?
Let us alone. Time driveth onward fast,
And in a little while our lips are dumb.
Let us alone. What is it that will last?
All things are taken from us, and become
Portions and parcels of the dreadful past.
Let us alone. What pleasure can we have
To war with evil? Is there any peace
In ever climbing up the climbing wave?
All things have rest, and ripen toward the grave
In silence—ripen, fall, and cease.
Give us long rest or death, dark death, or dreamful ease.

V

How sweet it were, hearing the downward stream,
With half-shut eyes ever to seem
Falling asleep in a half-dream!
To dream and dream, like yonder amber light,
Which will not leave the myrrh-bush on the height;
To hear each other's whispered speech;
Eating the Lotos day by day,
To watch the crisping ripples on the beach,
And tender curving lines of creamy spray;
To lend our hearts and spirits wholly
To the influence of mild-minded melancholy;
To muse and brood and live again in memory,
With those old faces of our infancy
Heaped over with a mound of grass,
Two handfuls of white dust, shut in an urn of brass!

VI

Dear is the memory of our wedded lives,
And dear the last embraces of our wives

And their warm tears; but all hath suffered change;
For surely now our household hearths are cold,
Our sons inherit us, our looks are strange,
And we should come like ghosts to trouble joy.
Or else the island princes over-bold
Have eat our substance, and the minstrel sings
Before them of the ten years' war in Troy,
And our great deeds, as half-forgotten things.
Is there confusion in the little isle?
Let what is broken so remain.
The gods are hard to reconcile;
'Tis hard to settle order once again.
There *is* confusion worse than death,
Trouble on trouble, pain on pain,
Long labor unto aged breath,
Sore task to hearts worn out by many wars
And eyes grown dim with gazing on the pilot stars.

VII

But, propped on beds of amaranth and moly,
How sweet—while warm airs lull us, blowing lowly—
With half-dropped eyelid still,
Beneath a heaven dark and holy,
To watch the long bright river drawing slowly
His waters from the purple hill—
To hear the dewy echoes calling
From cave to cave through the thick-twined vine—
To watch the emerald-colored water falling
Through many a woven acanthus-wreath divine!
Only to hear and see the far-off sparkling brine,
Only to hear were sweet, stretched out beneath the pine.

VIII

The Lotos blooms below the barren peak,
The Lotos blows by every winding creek;
All day the wind breathes low with mellower tone;
Through every hollow cave and alley lone
Round and round the spicy downs the yellow Lotos-dust is blown.

We have had enough of action, and of motion we,
Rolled to starboard, rolled to larboard, when the surge was seething
    free,
Where the wallowing monster spouted his foam-fountains in the sea.
Let us swear an oath, and keep it with an equal mind,
In the hollow Lotos-land to live and lie reclined
On the hills like gods together, careless of mankind.
For they lie beside their nectar, and the bolts are hurled
Far below them in the valleys, and the clouds are lightly curled
Round their golden houses, girdled with the gleaming world;
Where they smile in secret, looking over wasted lands,
Blight and famine, plague and earthquake, roaring deeps and fiery
    sands,
Clanging fights, and flaming towns, and sinking ships, and praying
    hands.
But they smile, they find a music centered in a doleful song
Steaming up, a lamentation and an ancient tale of wrong,
Like a tale of little meaning though the words are strong;
Chanted from an ill-used race of men that cleave the soil,
Sow the seed, and reap the harvest with enduring toil,
Storing yearly little dues of wheat, and wine and oil;
Till they perish and they suffer—some, 'tis whispered—down in
    hell
Suffer endless anguish, others in Elysian valleys dwell,
Resting weary limbs at last on beds of asphodel.
Surely, surely, slumber is more sweet than toil, the shore
Than labor in the deep mid-ocean, wind and wave and oar;
Oh, rest ye, brother mariners, we will not wander more.

WILLIAM MAKEPEACE THACKERAY

WILLIAM MAKEPEACE THACKERAY (English, 1811-1863). Voluminous
novelist of Victorian Period. Well born, wrote unceasingly after losing fortune.
A keen satirist of social snobbery, using unaffected conversational, sometimes
sermonizing, style. *Vanity Fair*, one of the masterpieces of the English novel,
Becky Sharp one of its celebrated heroines. Other novels: *Pendennis, The
Virginians, Henry Esmond, The Newcomes.*

VANITY FAIR

ONE gusty, raw day at the end of April—the rain whipping the
pavement of that ancient street where the old Slaughter's Coffee-

house was once situated—George Osborne came into the coffee-room, looking very haggard and pale, although dressed rather smartly in a blue coat and brass buttons, and a neat buff waistcoat of the fashion of those days. Here was his friend Captain Dobbin, in blue and brass too, having abandoned the military frock and French-gray trousers, which were the usual coverings of his lanky person.

Dobbin had been in the coffee-room for an hour or more. He had tried all the papers, but could not read them. He had looked at the clock many scores of times; and at the street, where the rain was pattering down, and the people, as they clinked by in pattens, left long reflections on the shining stone; he tattooed at the table; he bit his nails most completely, and nearly to the quick (he was accustomed to ornament his great big hands in this way); he balanced the tea-spoon on the milkjug; upset it, etc., etc.; and in fact showed those signs of disquietude, and practised those desperate attempts at amusement, which men are accustomed to employ when very anxious and expectant, and perturbed in mind.

Some of his comrades, gentlemen who used the room, joked him about the splendour of his costume and his agitation of manner. One asked him if he was going to be married. Dobbin laughed and said he would send his acquaintance (Major Wagstaff of the Engineers) a piece of cake when that event took place. At length Captain Osborne made his appearance, very smartly dressed, but very pale and agitated, as we have said. He wiped his pale face with a large yellow bandana pocket-handkerchief that was prodigiously scented. He shook hands with Dobbin, looked at the clock, and told John, the waiter, to bring him some curaçoa. Of this cordial he swallowed off a couple of glasses with nervous eagerness. His friend asked with some interest about his health.

"Couldn't get a wink of sleep till daylight, Dob," said he. "Infernal headache and fever. Got up at nine, and went down to the Hummums for a bath. I say, Dob, I feel just as I did on the morning I went out with Rocket at Quebec."

"So do I," William responded. "I was a deuce deal more nervous than you were, that morning. You made a famous breakfast, I remember. Eat something now."

"You're a good old fellow, Will. I'll drink your health, old boy, and farewell to—"

"No, no; two glasses are enough," Dobbin interrupted him. "Here, take away the *liqueurs*, John. Have some cayenne-pepper with your fowl. Make haste, though, for it is time we were there."

1300

It was about half an hour from twelve when this brief meeting and colloquy took place between the two captains. A coach, into which Captain Osborne's servant put his master's desk and dressing-case, had been in waiting for some time; and into this the two gentlemen hurried under an umbrella, and the valet mounted on the box, cursing the rain and the dampness of the coachman who was steaming beside him. "We shall find a better trap than this at the carriage door," says he; "that's a comfort." And the carriage drove on, taking the road down Piccadilly, where Apsley House and St. George's Hospital wore red jackets still; where there were oil lamps; where Achilles was not yet born; nor the Pimlico arch raised; nor the hideous equestrian monster which pervades it and the neighborhood—and so they drove down by Brompton to a certain chapel near the Fulham road there.

A chariot was in waiting with four horses; likewise a coach of the kind called glass coaches. Only a very few idlers were collected, on account of the dismal rain.

"Hang it!" said George, "I said only a pair."

"My master would have four," said Mr. Joseph Sedley's servant, who was in waiting; and he and Mr. Osborne's man agreed, as they followed George and William into the church, that it was a "reg'lar shabby turnhout; and with scarce so much as a breakfast or a wedding faviour."

"Here you are," said our old friend, Jos Sedley, coming forward. "You're five minutes late, George my boy. What a day, eh? Demmy, it's like the commencement of the rainy season in Bengal. But you'll find my carriage is water-tight. Come along, my mother and Emmy are in the vestry."

Jos Sedley was splendid. He was fatter than ever. His shirt-collars were higher; his face was redder; his shirt-frill flaunted gorgeously out of his variegated waistcoat. Varnished boots were not invented as yet; but the Hessians on his beautiful legs shone so, that they must have been the identical pair in which the gentleman in the old picture used to shave himself; and on his light green coat there bloomed a fine wedding favour, like a great white spreading magnolia.

In a word, George had thrown the great cast. He was going to be married. Hence his pallor and nervousness—his sleepless night and agitation in the morning. I have heard people who have gone through the same thing own to the same emotion. After three or four ceremonies, you get accustomed to it, no doubt; but the first dip, everybody allows, is awful.

The bride was dressed in a brown silk pelisse (as Captain Dobbin

has since informed me), and wore a straw bonnet with a pink ribbon; over the bonnet she had a veil of white Chantilly lace, a gift from Mr. Joseph Sedley, her brother. Captain Dobbin himself had asked leave to present her with a gold chain and watch, which she sported on this occasion; and her mother gave her her diamond brooch— almost the only trinket which was left to the old lady. As the service went on, Mrs. Sedley sat and whimpered a great deal in a pew, consoled by the Irish maid-servant and Mrs. Clapp from the lodgings. Old Sedley would not be present. Jos acted for his father, giving away the bride, whilst Captain Dobbin stepped up as groomsman to his friend George.

There was nobody in the church besides the officiating persons and the small marriage party and their attendants. The two valets sat aloof superciliously. The rain came rattling down on the windows. In the intervals of the service you heard it, and the sobbing of old Mrs. Sedley in the pew. The parson's tones echoed sadly through the empty walls. Osborne's "I will" was sounded in very deep bass. Emmy's response came fluttering up to her lips from her heart, but was scarcely heard by anybody except Captain Dobbin.

When the service was completed, Jos Sedley came forward and kissed his sister, the bride, for the first time for many months— George's look of gloom had gone, and he seemed quite proud and radiant. "It's your turn, William," says he, putting his hand fondly upon Dobbin's shoulder; and Dobbin went up and touched Amelia on the cheek.

Then they went into the vestry and signed the register. "God bless you, old Dobbin," George said, grasping him by the hand, with something very like moisture glistening in his eyes. William replied only by nodding his head. His heart was too full to say much.

"Write directly, and come down as soon as you can, you know," Osborne said. After Mrs. Sedley had taken an hysterical adieu of her daughter, the pair went off to the carriage. "Get out of the way, you little devils," George cried to a small crowd of damp urchins, that were hanging about the chapel door. The rain drove into the bride and bridegroom's faces as they passed to the chariot. The postillion's favours draggled on their dripping jackets. The few children made a dismal cheer as the carriage, splashing mud, drove away.

William Dobbin stood in the church porch, looking at it, a quiet figure. The small crew of spectators jeered him. He was not thinking about them or their laughter.

"Come home and have some tiffin, Dobbin," a voice cried behind

him, as a pudgy hand was laid on his shoulder, and the honest fellow's reverie was interrupted. But the captain had no heart to go a feasting with Jos Sedley. He put the weeping old lady and her attendants into the carriage along with Jos, and left them without further words passing. This carriage, too, drove away, and the urchins gave another sarcastical cheer.

"Here, you little beggars," Dobbin said, giving some sixpences amongst them, and then went off by himself through the rain. It was all over. They were married, and happy, he prayed God. Never since he was a boy, had he felt so miserable and so lonely. He longed with a heart-sick yearning for the first few days to be over, that he might see her again.

JOHANN LUDWIG TIECK

JOHANN LUDWIG TIECK (1773-1853). One of the leaders of the German Romantic School. Experimented in every literary form, was most successful with short stories and *novellen*. Influenced not only German writers, but such men as Gogol, Coleridge, Scott, Longfellow, Hawthorne. Best work: *Puss-in-Boots*, satirical fairy tales.

THE FRIENDS

It was a beautiful spring morning, when Lewis Wandel went out to visit a sick friend, in a village some miles distant from his dwelling. This friend had written to him to say that he was lying dangerously ill, and would gladly see him and speak to him once more.

The cheerful sunshine now sparkled in the bright green bushes; the birds twittered and leapt to and fro on the branches; the larks sang merrily above the thin fleeting clouds; sweet scents rose from the fresh meadows, and the fruit-trees of the garden were white and gay in blossom.

Lewis's eye roamed intoxicate around him; his soul seemed to expand; but he thought of his invalid friend, and he bent forward in silent dejection. Nature had decked herself all in vain, so serenely and so brightly; his fancy could only picture to him the sick bed and his suffering brother.

"How song is sounding from every bough!" cried he; "the notes of the birds mingle in sweet unison with the whisper of the leaves;

and yet in the distance, through all the charm of the concert, come the sighs of the sick one."

Whilst he thus communed, a troop of gaily-clad peasant girls issued from the village; they all gave him a friendly salutation, and told him that they were on their merry way to a wedding; that work was over for that day, and had to give place to festivity. He listened to their tale, and still their merriment rang in the distance on his ear; still he caught the sound of their songs, and became more and more sorrowful. In the wood he took his seat on a dismantled tree, drew the oft-read letter from his pocket, and ran through it once more:—

"My very dear friend,—I cannot tell why you have so utterly forgotten me, that I receive no news from you. I am not surprised that men forsake me; but it heartily pains me to think that you too care nothing about me. I am dangerously ill; a fever that saps my strength: if you delay visiting me any longer, I cannot promise you that you will see me again. All nature revives, and feels fresh and strong; I alone sink lower in languor; the returning warmth cannot animate me; I see not the green fields, nothing but the tree that rustles before my window, and sings death-songs to my thoughts; my bosom is pent, my breathing is hard; and often I think the walls of my room will press closer together and crush me. The rest of you in the world are holding the most beautiful festival of life, whilst I must languish in the dwelling of sickness. Gladly would I dispense with spring, if I could but see your dear face once more: but you that are in health never earnestly think what it really is to be ill, and how dear to us then, in our helplessness, the visit of a friend is: you do not know how to prize those precious minutes of consolation, because the whole world receives you in the warmth and the fervour of its friendship. Ah! if you did but know, as I do, how terrible is death, and how still more terrible it is to be ill,—O Lewis, how would you hasten then to behold once more this frail form, that you have hitherto called your friend, and that by and by will be so ruthlessly dismembered! If I were well, I would haste to meet you, or fancy that you may perhaps be ill at this moment. If I never see you again—farewell."

What a painful impression did the suffering depicted in this letter make upon Lewis's heart, amid the liveliness of Nature, as she lay in brilliancy before him! He melted into tears, and rested his head on his hand.—"Carol now, ye foresters," thought he; "for ye know no

1304

lamentation; ye lead a buoyant poetic existence, and for this are those swift pinions granted you; oh, how happy are ye, that ye need not mourn; warm summer calls you, and ye wish for nothing more; ye dance forth to meet it, and when winter is advancing, ye are gone! O light-winged merry forest-life, how do I envy thee! Why are so many heavy cares burdened upon poor man's heart? Why may he not love without purchasing his love by wailing—his happiness by misery? Life purls on like a fleeting rivulet beneath his feet, and quenches not his thirst, his fervid longing."

He became more and more absorbed in thought, and at last he rose and pursued his way through the thick forest. "If I could but help him," cried he; "if Nature could but supply me with a means of saving him; but as it is, I feel nothing but my own impotency, and the pain of losing my friend. In my childhood I used to believe in enchantment and its supernatural aids; would I now could hope in them as happily as then!"

He quickened his steps; and involuntarily all the remembrances of the earliest years of his childhood crowded back upon him: he followed those forms of loveliness, and was soon entangled in such a labyrinth as not to notice the objects that surrounded him. He had forgotten that it was spring—that his friend was ill: he hearkened to the wondrous melodies, which came borne, as if from distant shores, upon his ear: all that was most strange united itself to what was most ordinary: his whole soul was transmuted. From the far vista of memory, from the abyss of the past, all those forms were summoned forth that ever had enraptured or tormented him: all those dubious phantoms were aroused, that flutter formlessly about us, and gather in dizzy hum around our heads. Puppets, the toys of childhood, and spectres, danced along before him, and so mantled over the green turf, that he could not see a single flower at his feet. First love encircled him with its twilight morning gleam, and let down its sparkling rainbow over the mead: his earliest sorrows glided past him in review, and threatened to greet him in the same guise at the end of his pilgrimage. Lewis sought to arrest all these changeful feelings, and to retain a consciousness of self amid the magic of enjoyment,—but in vain. Like enigmatic books, with figures grotesquely gay, that open for a moment and in a moment are closed, so unstably and fleetingly all floated before his soul.

The wood opened, and in the open country on one side lay some old ruins, encompassed with watch-towers and ramparts. Lewis was astonished at having advanced so quickly amid his dreams. He

emerged from his melancholy, as he did from the shades of the wood; for often the pictures within us are but the reflection of outward objects. Now rose on him, like the morning sun, the memory of his first poetical enjoyments, of his earliest appreciations of that luscious harmony which many a human ear never inhales.

"How incomprehensibly," said he, "did those things commingle then, which seemed to me eternally parted by such vast chasms; my most undefined presentiments assumed a form and outline, and gleamed on me in the shape of a thousand subordinate phantoms, which till then I had never descried! So names were found me for things that I had long wished to speak of: I became recipient of earth's fairest treasures, which my yearning heart had so long sought for in vain: and how much have I to thank thee for since then, divine power of fancy and of poetry! How hast thou smoothed for me the path of life, that erst appeared so rough and perplexed! Ever hast thou revealed to me new sources of enjoyment and happiness, so that no arid desert presents itself to me now: every stream of sweet voluptuous inspiration hath wound its way through my earth-born heart: I have become intoxicate with bliss, and have communed with beings of heaven."

The sun sank below the horizon, and Lewis was astonished that it was already evening. He was insensible of fatigue, and was still far from the point which he had wished to reach before night: he stood still, without being able to understand how the crimson of evening could be so early mantling the clouds; how the shadows of everything were so long, while the nightingale warbled her song of wail in the thicket. He looked around him: the old ruins lay far in the background, clad in blushing splendour; and he doubted whether he had not strayed from the direct and well-known road.

Now he remembered a phantasy of his early childhood, that till that moment had never recurred to him: it was a female form of awe, that glided before him over the lonely fields: she never looked round, yet he was compelled, against his will, to follow her, and to be drawn on into unknown scenes, without in the least being able to extricate himself from her power. A slight thrill of fear came over him, and yet he found it impossible to obtain a more distinct recollection of that figure, or to usher back his mind into the frame, in which this image had first appeared to him. He sought to individualise all these singular sensations, when, looking round by chance, he really found himself on a spot which, often as he had been that way, he had never seen before.

"Am I spell-bound?" cried he; "or have my dreams and fancies crazed me? Is it the wonderful effect of solitude that makes me irrecognisable to myself; or do spirits and genii hover round me and hold my senses in thrall? Sooth, if I cannot enfranchise myself from myself, I will await that woman-phantom that floated before me in every lonely place in my childhood."

He endeavoured to rid himself of every kind of phantasy, in order to get into the right road again; but his recollections became more and more perplexed; the flowers at his feet grew larger, the red glow of evening more brilliant, and wondrously shaped clouds hung drooping on the earth, like the curtains of some mystic scene that was soon to unfold itself. A ringing murmur arose from the high grass, and the blades bowed to one another, as if in friendly converse; while a light warm spring rain dropped pattering amongst them, as if to wake every slumbering harmony in wood, and bush, and flower. Now all was rife with song and sound; a thousand sweet voices held promiscuous parley; song entwined itself in song, and tone in tone; while in the waning crimson of eve lay countless blue butterflies rocking, with its radiance sparkling from their wavy wings. Lewis fancied himself in a dream, when the heavy dark-red clouds suddenly rose again, and a vast prospect opened on him in unfathomable distance. In the sunshine lay a gorgeous plain, sparkling with verdant forests and dewy underwood. In its centre glittered a palace of a myraid hues, as if composed all of undulating rainbows and gold and jewels: a passing stream reflected its various brilliancy, and a soft crimson æther environed this hall of enchantment; strange birds, he had never seen before, flew about, sportively flapping each other with their red and green wings: larger nightingales warbled their clear notes to the echoing landscape: lambent flames shot through the green grass, flickering here and there, and then darting in coils round the mansion. Lewis drew nearer, and heard ravishing voices sing the following words:—

Traveller from earth below,
Wend thee not farther,
In our hall's magic glow
Bide with us rather.
Hast thou with longing scann'd
Joy's distant morrow,
Cast away sorrow,
And enter the wish'd-for land.

1307

Without further scruple, Lewis stepped to the shining threshold, and lingering but a moment ere he set his foot on the polished stone, he entered. The gates closed after him.

"Hitherward! hitherward!" cried invisible lips, as from the inmost recesses of the palace; and with loudly throbbing heart he followed the voices. All his cares, all his olden remembrances were cast away: his inmost bosom rang with the songs that outwardly encompassed him: his every regret was stilled: his every conscious and unconscious wish was satisfied. The summoning voices grew so loud, that the whole building re-echoed them, and still he could not find their origin, though he long seemed to have been standing in the central hall of the palace.

At length a ruddy-cheeked boy stepped up to him, and saluted the stranger guest: he led him through magnificent chambers, full of splendour and melody, and at last entered the garden, where Lewis, as he said, was expected. Entranced he followed his guide, and the most delicious fragrance from a thousand flowers floated forth to meet him. Broad shady walks received them. Lewis's dizzy gaze could scarcely gain the tops of the high immemorial trees: bright-coloured birds sat perched upon the branches: children were playing on guitars in the shade, and they and the birds sang to the music. Fountains shot up, with the clear red of morning, sparkling upon them: the flowers were as high as shrubs, and parted spontaneously as the wanderer pressed through them. He had never before felt the hallowed sensations that then enkindled in him; never had such pure heavenly enjoyment been revealed to him: he was over-happy.

But bells of silver sound rang through the trees, and their tops were bowed: the birds and children with the guitars were hushed: the rose-buds unfolded: and the boy now conducted the stranger into the midst of a brilliant assembly.

Lovely dames of lofty form were seated on beautiful banks of turf, in earnest conference. They were above the usual height of the human race, and their more than earthly beauty had at the same time something of awe in it, from which the heart shrunk back in alarm. Lewis dared not interrupt their conversation: it seemed as if he were among the god-like forms of Homer's song, where every thought must be excluded that formed the converse of mortals. Odd little spirits stood round, as ready ministers, waiting attentively for the wink of the moment that should summon them from their posture of quietude: they fixed their glances on the stranger, and then looked jeeringly and significantly at each other. At last the beautiful women ceased

speaking, and beckoned Lewis to approach; he was still standing with an embarrassed air, and drew near to them with trembling.

"Be not alarmed," said the fairest of them all; "you are welcome to us here, and we have long been expecting you: long have you wished to be in our abode,—are you satisfied now?"

"Oh, how unspeakably happy I am!" exclaimed Lewis; "all my dearest dreams have met with their fulfilment, all my most daring wishes are gratified now: yes, I am, I live among them. How it has happened so, I cannot comprehend: sufficient for me, that it is so. Why should I raise a new wail over this enigma, ere my olden lamentations are scarcely at an end?"

"Is this life," asked the lady, "very different from your former one?"

"My former life," said Lewis, "I can scarcely remember. But has, then, this golden state of existence fallen to my lot? this beautiful state, after which my every sense and prescience so ardently aspired; to which every wish wandered, that I could conceive in fancy, or realise in my inmost thought; though its image, veiled in mist, seemed ever strange in me—and is it, then, mine at last? have I, then, achieved this new existence, and does it hold me in its embrace? Oh, pardon me, I know not what I say in my delirium of ecstasy, and might well weigh my words more carefully in such an assemblage."

The lady sighed; and in a moment every minister was in motion; there was a stirring among the trees, everywhere a running to and fro, and speedily a banquet was placed before Lewis of fair fruits and fragrant wines. He sat down again, and music rose anew on the air. Rows of beautiful boys and girls sped round him, intertwined in the dance, while uncouth little cobolds lent life to the scene, and excited loud laughter by their ludicrous gambols. Lewis noted every sound and every gesture: he seemed newly-born since his initiation into this joyous existence. "Why," thought he, "are those hopes and reveries of ours so often laughed at, that pass into fulfilment sooner than ever had been expected? Where, then, is that border-mark between truth and error which mortals are ever ready with such temerity to set up? Oh, I ought in my former life to have wandered oftener from the way, and then perhaps I should have ripened all the earlier for this happy transmutation."

The dance died away; the sun sank to rest; the august dames arose; Lewis too left his seat, and accompanied them on their walk through the quiet garden. The nightingales were complaining in a softened tone, and a wondrous moon rose above the horizon. The blossoms

opened to its silver radiance, and every leaf kindled in its gleam; the wide avenues became of a glow, casting shadows of a singular green; red clouds slumbered on the green grass of the fields: the fountains turned to gold, and played high in the clear air of heaven.

"Now you will wish to sleep," said the loveliest of the ladies, and shewed the enraptured wanderer a shadowy bower, strewed with soft turf and yielding cushions. Then they left him, and he was alone.

He sat down and watched the magic twilight glimmering through the thickly-woven foliage. "How strange is this!" said he to himself; "perhaps I am now only asleep, and I may dream that I am sleeping a second time, and may have a dream in my dream; and so it may go on for ever, and no human power ever be able to awake me. No! unbeliever that I am! it is beautiful reality that animates me now, and my former state perhaps was but the dream of gloom." He lay down, and light breezes played round him. Perfume was wafted on the air, and little birds sang lulling songs. In his dreams he fancied the garden all around him changed: the tall trees withered away; the golden moon fallen from the sky, leaving a dismal gap behind her; instead of the watery jet from the fountains, little genii gushed out, caracolling over each in the air, and assuming the strangest attitudes. Notes of woe supplanted the sweetness of song, and every trace of that happy abode had vanished. Lewis awoke amid impressions of fear, and chid himself for still feeding his fancy in the perverse manner of the habitants of earth, who mingle all received images in rude disorder, and present them again in this garb in a dream. A lovely morning broke over the scene, and the ladies saluted him again. He spoke to them more intrepidly, and was to-day more inclined to cheerfulness, as the surrounding world had less power to astonish him. He contemplated the garden of the palace, and fed upon the magnificence and the wonders that he met there. Thus he lived many days happily, in the belief that his felicity was incapable of increase.

But sometimes the crowing of a cock seemed to sound in the vicinity; and then the whole edifice would tremble, and his compainions turn pale: this generally happened of an evening, and soon afterwards they retired to rest. Then often there would come a thought of earth into Lewis's soul; then he would often lean out of the windows of the glittering palace to arrest and fix these fleeting remembrances, and to get a glimpse of the high road again, which, as he thought, must pass that way. In this sort of mood, he was one afternoon alone, musing within himself why it was just as impossible for him to recall a distinct remembrance of the world, as formerly it had been to feel

a presage of this poetic place of sojourn,—when all at once a post-horn seemed to sound in the distance, and the rattle of carriage-wheels to make themselves heard. "How strangely," said he to himself, "does a faint gleam, a slight reminiscence of earth, break upon my delight—rendering me melancholy and dejected! Then, do I lack anything here? Is my happiness still incomplete?"

The beautiful women returned. "What do you wish for?" said they, in a tone of concern; "you seem sad."

"You will laugh," replied Lewis; "yet grant me one favour more. In that other life I had a friend, whom I now but faintly remember: he is ill, I think; restore him by your skill."

"Your wish is already gratified," said they.

"But," said Lewis, "vouchsafe me two questions."

"Speak!"

"Does no gleam of love fall on this wondrous world? Does no friendship perambulate these bowers? I thought the morning blush of spring-love would be eternal here, which in that other life is too prone to be extinguished, and which men afterwards speak of as of a fable. To confess to you the truth, I feel an unspeakable yearning after those sensations."

"Then you long for earth again?"

"Oh, never!" cried Lewis; "for in that cold earth I used to sigh for friendship and for love, and they came not near me. The longing for those feelings had to supply the place of those feelings themselves; and for that reason I turned my aspirations hitherward, and hoped here to find every thing in the most beautiful harmony."

"Fool!" said the venerable woman: "so on earth you sighed for earth, and knew not what you did in wishing to be here; you have overshot your desires, and substituted phantasies for the sensations of mortals."

"Then who are ye?" cried Lewis, astounded.

"We are the old fairies," said she, "of whom you surely must have heard long ago. If you ardently long for earth, you will return thither again. Our kingdom flourishes when mortals are shrouded in night; but their day is *our* night. Our sway is of ancient date, and will long endure. It abides invisibly among men—to your eye alone has it been revealed." She turned away, and Lewis remembered that it was the same form which had resistlessly dragged him after it in his youth, and of which he felt a secret dread. He followed now also, crying, "No, I will not go back to earth! I will stay here!" "So then," said he to himself, "I divined this lofty being even in my childhood! And

so the solution of many a riddle, which we are too idle to investigate, may be within ourselves."

He went on much further than usual, till the fairy garden was soon left far behind him. He stood on a romantic mountain-range, where the ivy climbed in wild tresses up the rocks; cliff was piled on cliff, and awe and grandeur seemed to hold universal sway. Then there came a wandering stranger to him, who accosted him kindly, and addressed him thus:—"Glad I am after all, to see you again."

"I know you not," said Lewis.

"That may well be," replied the other; "but once you thought you knew me well. I am your late sick friend."

"Impossible! you are quite a stranger to me!"

"Only," said the stranger, "because to-day you see me for the first time in my true form: till now you only found in me a reflection of yourself. You are right too in remaining here; for there is no love, no friendship—not here, I mean, where all illusion vanishes."

Lewis sat down and wept.

"What ails you?" said the stranger.

"That it is you—you who were the friend of my youth: is not that mournful enough? Oh, come back with me to our dear, dear earth, where we shall know each other once more under illusive forms— where there exists the superstition of friendship! What am I doing here?"

"What will that avail?" answered the stranger. "You will want to be back again; earth is not bright enough for you: the flowers are too small for you, the song too suppressed. Colour there, cannot emerge so brilliantly from the shade; flowers there are of small comfort, and so prone to fade; the little birds think of their death, and sing in modest constraint: but here every thing is on a scale of grandeur."

"Oh, I will be contented!" cried Lewis, as the tears gushed profusely from his eyes. "Do but come back with me, and be my friend once more; let us leave this desert, this glittery misery!"

Thus saying, he opened his eyes, for some one was shaking him roughly. Over him leant the friendly but pale face of his once sick friend. "But are you dead?" cried Lewis.

"Recovered am I, wicked sleeper," he replied. "Is it thus you visit your sick friend? Come along with me; my carriage is waiting there, and a thunder-storm is rising."

Lewis rose: in his sleep he had glided off the trunk of the tree; his friend's letter lay open beside him. "So am I really on the earth

again?" he exclaimed with joy; "really? and is this no new dream?"

"You will not escape from the earth," answered his friend with a smile; and both were locked in heart-felt embraces.

"How happy I am," said Lewis, "that I have you once more, that I feel as I used to do, and that you are well again!"

"Suddenly," replied his friend, "I felt ill; and as suddenly I was well again. So I wished to go to you, and do away with the alarm that my letter must have caused you; and here, half-way, I find you asleep."

"I do not deserve your love at all," said Lewis.

"Why?"

"Because I just now doubted of your friendship."

"But only in sleep."

"It would be strange enough though," said Lewis, "if there really were such things as fairies."

"There are such, of a certainty," replied the other; "but it is all a fable, that their whole pleasure is to make men happy. They plant those wishes in our bosoms which we ourselves do not know of; those over-wrought pretensions—that super-human covetousness of super-human gifts; so that in our desponding delirium we afterwards despise the beautiful earth with all its glorious stores."

Lewis answered with a pressure of the hand.

LEO TOLSTOY

LEO TOLSTOY (Russian, 1828-1910). The sage among the master Russian novelists. An aristocrat who, after a spiritual conversion, altered his life in effort to become a later-day saint. Moral conflict forms basis of all his writing. Two of his novels belong among the greatest: *Anna Karenina* and *War and Peace*, world's most ambitious war story. Also notable are his plays and short stories.

WHERE LOVE IS

In a certain town there lived a shoemaker named Martin Avdeitch. He lived in a basement room which possessed but one window. This window looked onto the street, and through it a glimpse could be caught of the passers-by. It is true that only their legs could be seen, but that did not matter, as Martin could recognize people by their boots alone. He had lived here for a long time, and so had many

acquaintances. There were very few pairs of boots in the neighborhood which had not passed through his hands at least once, if not twice. Some he had resoled, others he had fitted with side-pieces, others, again, he had resewn where they were split, or provided with new toe-caps. Yes, he often saw his handiwork through that window. He was given plenty of custom, for his work lasted well, his materials were good, his prices moderate, and his word to be depended on. If he could do a job by a given time it should be done; but if not, he would warn you beforehand rather than disappoint you. Everyone knew Avdeitch, and no one ever transferred his custom from him. He had always been an upright man, but with the approach of old age he had begun more than ever to think of his soul, and to draw nearer to God.

His wife had died while he was still an apprentice, leaving behind her a little boy of three. This was their only child, indeed, for the two elder ones had died previously. At first Martin thought of placing the little fellow with a sister of his in the country, but changed his mind, thinking: "My Kapitoshka would not like to grow up in a strange family, so I will keep him by me." Then Avdeitch finished his apprenticeship, and went to live in lodgings with his little boy. But God had not seen fit to give Avdeitch happiness in his children. The little boy was just growing up and beginning to help his father and to be a pleasure to him, when he fell ill, was put to bed, and died after a week's fever.

Martin buried the little fellow and was inconsolable. Indeed, he was so inconsolable that he began to murmur against God. His life seemed so empty that more than once he prayed for death and reproached the Almighty for taking away his only beloved son instead of himself, the old man. At last he ceased altogether to go to church.

Then one day there came to see him an ancient peasant-pilgrim—one who was now in the eighth year of his pilgrimage. To him Avdeitch talked, and then went on to complain of his great sorrow.

"I no longer wish to be a God-fearing man," he said. "I only wish to die. That is all I ask of God. I am a lonely, hopeless man."

"You should not speak like that, Martin," replied the old pilgrim. "It is not for us to judge the acts of God. We must rely, not upon our own understanding, but upon the Divine wisdom. God saw fit that your son should die and that you should live. Therefore it must be better so. If you despair, it is because you have wished to live too much for your own pleasure."

"For what, then, should I live?" asked Martin.

"For God alone," replied the old man. "It is He who gave you life, and therefore it is He for whom you should live. When you come to live for Him you will cease to grieve, and your trials will become easy to bear."

Martin was silent. Then he spoke again.

"But how am I to live for God?" he asked.

"Christ has shown us the way," answered the old man. "Can you read? If so, buy a Testament and study it. You will learn there how to live for God. Yes, it is all shown you there."

These words sank into Avdeitch's soul. He went out the same day, bought a large-print copy of the New Testament, and set himself to read it.

At the beginning Avdeitch had meant only to read on festival days, but when he once began his reading he found it so comforting to the soul that he came never to let a day pass without doing so. On the second occasion he became so engrossed that all the kerosene was burnt away in the lamp before he could tear himself away from the book.

Thus he came to read it every evening, and, the more he read, the more clearly did he understand what God required of him, and in what way he could live for God; so that his heart grew ever lighter and lighter. Once upon a time, whenever he had lain down to sleep, he had been used to moan and sigh as he thought of his little Kapitoshka; but now he only said—"Glory to Thee, O Lord! Glory to Thee! Thy will be done!"

From that time onwards Avdeitch's life became completely changed. Once he had been used to go out on festival days and drink tea in a tavern, and had not denied himself even an occasional glass of *vodka*. This he had done in the company of a boon companion, and, although no drunkard, would frequently leave the tavern in an excited state and talk much nonsense as he shouted and disputed with this friend of his. But now he had turned his back on all this, and his life had become quiet and joyous. Early in the morning he would sit down to his work, and labour through his appointed hours. Then he would take the lamp down from a shelf, light it, and sit down to read. And the more he read, the more he understood, and the clearer and happier he grew at heart.

It happened once the Martin had been reading late. He had been reading those verses in the sixth chapter of the Gospel of St. Luke which run:

"And unto him that smiteth thee on the one cheek offer also the other; and him that taketh away thy cloak forbid not to take thy coat also. Give to every man that asketh of thee; and of him that taketh thy goods ask them not again. And as ye would that men should do to you, do ye also to them likewise."

Then, further on, he had read those verses where the Lord says: "And why call ye Me, Lord, Lord, and do not the things which I say? Whosoever cometh to Me and heareth my sayings, and doeth them, I will show you to whom he is like: He is like a man which built an house, and digged deep, and laid the foundation on a rock: and when the flood arose, the storm beat vehemently upon that house, and could not shake it: for it was founded upon a rock. But he that heareth and doeth not, is like a man that without a foundation built an house upon the earth; against which the stream did beat vehemently, and immediately it fell; and the ruin of that house was great."

Avdeitch read these words, and felt greatly cheered in soul. He took off his spectacles, laid them on the book, leaned his elbows upon the table, and gave himself up to meditation. He set himself to measure his own life by those words, and thought to himself:

"Is my house founded upon a rock or upon sand? It is well if it be upon a rock. Yet it seems so easy to me as I sit here alone. I may so easily come to think that I have done all that the Lord has commanded me, and grow careless and—sin again. Yet I will keep on striving, for it is goodly so to do. Help Thou me, O Lord."

Thus he kept on meditating, though conscious that it was time for bed; yet he was loathe to tear himself away from the book. He began to read the seventh chapter of St. Luke, and read on about the centurion, the widow's son, and the answer given to John's disciples; until in time he came to the passage where the rich Pharisee invited Jesus to his house, and the woman washed the Lord's feet with her tears and He justified her. So he came to the forty-fourth verse and read:

"And He turned to the woman, and said unto Simon, Seest thou this woman? I entered into thine house, and thou gavest Me no water for My feet: but she hath washed My feet with tears, and wiped them with the hairs of her head. Thou gavest Me no kiss: but this woman since the time I came in hath not ceased to kiss My feet. My head with oil thou didst anoint: but this woman hath anointed My feet with ointment."

He read these verses and thought:

" 'Thou gavest Me no water for My feet' . . . 'Thou gavest Me no

1316

kiss' . . . 'My head with oil thou didst not anoint' . . . "—and once
again he took off his spectacles, laid them on the book, and became
lost in meditation.

"I am even as that Pharisee," he thought to himself. "I drink tea
and think only of my deeds. Yes, I think only of having plenty
to eat and drink, of being warm and clean—but never of entertaining
a guest. And Simon too was mindful only of himself, although the
guest who had come to visit him was—who? Why, even the Lord
Himself! If, then, He should come to visit *me*, should I receive Him
any better?"—and, leaning forward upon his elbows, he was asleep
almost before he was aware of it.

"Martin!" someone seemed to breathe in his ear.

He started from his sleep.

"Who is there?" he said. He turned and looked toward the door,
but could see no one. Again he bent forward over the table. Then
suddenly he heard the words:

"Martin, Martin! Look thou into the street to-morrow, for I am
coming to visit thee."

Martin roused himself, got up from the chair, and rubbed his
eyes. He did not know whether it was dreaming or awake that he
had heard these words, but he turned out the lamp and went to bed.

The next morning Avdeitch rose before daylight and said his
prayers. Then he made up the stove, got ready some cabbage soup
and porridge, lighted the samovar, slung his leather apron about
him, and sat down to his work in the window. He sat and worked
hard, yet all the time his thoughts were centered upon the night
before. He was of two minds about the vision. At one moment he
would think that it must have been his fancy, while the next moment
he would find himself convinced that he had really heard the voice.
"Yes, it must have been so," he concluded.

As Martin sat thus by the window he kept looking out of it as
much as working. Whenever a pair of boots passed with which he
was acquainted he would bend down to glance upwards through
the window and see their owner's face as well. The doorkeeper passed
in new felt boots, and then a water-carrier. Next, an old soldier,
a veteran of Nicholas' army, in old, patched boots, and carrying
a shovel in his hands, halted close by the window. Avdeitch knew
him by his boots. His name was Stepanitch, and he was kept by a
neighbouring tradesman out of charity, his duties being to help
the doorkeeper. He began to clear away the snow from in front of

Avdeitch's window, while the shoemaker looked at him and then resumed his work.

"I think I must be getting into my dotage," thought Avdeitch with a smile. "Just because Stepanitch begins clearing away the snow I at once jump to the conclusion that Christ is about to visit me. Yes, I am growing foolish now, old greybeard that I am."

Yet he had hardly made a dozen stitches before he was craning his neck again to look out of the window. He could see that Stepanitch had placed his shovel against the wall, and was resting and trying to warm himself a little.

"He is evidently an old man now and broken," thought Avdeitch to himself. "He is not strong enough to clear away snow. Would he like some tea, I wonder? That reminds me that the samovar must be ready now."

He made fast his awl in his work and got up. Placing the samovar on the table, he brewed the tea, and then tapped with his finger on the window-pane. Stepanitch turned round and approached. Avdeitch beckoned to him, and then went to open the door.

"Come in and warm yourself," he said. "You must be frozen."

"Christ requite you!" answered Stepanitch. "Yes, my bones are almost cracking."

He came in, shook the snow off himself, and, though tottering on his feet, took pains to wipe them carefully, that he might not dirty the floor.

"Nay, do not trouble about that," said Avdeitch. "I will wipe your boots myself. It is part of my business in this trade. Come you here and sit down, and we will empty this tea-pot together."

He poured out two tumblerfuls, and offered one to his guest; after which he emptied his own into the saucer, and blew upon it to cool it. Stepanitch drank his tumblerful, turned the glass upside down, placed his crust upon it, and thanked his host kindly. But it was plain that he wanted another one.

"You must drink some more," said Avdeitch, and refilled his guest's tumbler and his own. Yet, in spite of himself, he had no sooner drunk his tea than he found himself looking out into the street again.

"Are you expecting anyone?" asked his guest.

"Am—am I expecting anyone? Well, to tell the truth, yes. That is to say, I am, and I am not. The fact is that some words have got fixed in my memory. Whether it was a vision or not I cannot tell, but at all events, my old friend, I was reading in the Gospels last

1318

night about Our Little Father Christ, and how He walked this earth and suffered. You have heard of Him, have you not?"

"Yes, yes, I have heard of Him," answered Stepanitch; "but we are ignorant folk and do not know our letters."

"Well, I was reading of how He walked this earth, and how He went to visit a Pharisee, and yet received no welcome from him at the door. All this I read last night, my friend, and then fell to thinking about it—to thinking how some day I too might fail to pay Our Little Father Christ due honour. 'Suppose,' I thought to myself, 'He came to me or to anyone like me? Should we, like the great lord Simon, not know how to receive Him and not go out to meet Him?' Thus I thought, and fell asleep where I sat. Then as I sat sleeping there I heard someone call my name; and as I raised myself the voice went on (as though it were the voice of someone whispering in my ear): 'Watch thou for me to-morrow, for I am coming to visit thee.' It said that twice. And so those words have got into my head, and, foolish though I know it to be, I keep expecting *Him*—the Little Father—every moment."

Stepanitch nodded and said nothing, but emptied his glass and laid it aside. Nevertheless Avdeitch took and refilled it.

"Drink it up; it will do you good," he said. "Do you know," he went on, "I often call to mind how, when Our Little Father walked this earth, there was never a man, however humble, whom He despised, and how it was chiefly among the common people that He dwelt. It was always with *them* that He walked; it was from among *them*—from among such men as you and I—from among sinners and working folk—that He chose His disciples. 'Whosoever,' He said, 'shall exalt himself, the same shall be abased; and whosoever shall abase himself, the same shall be exalted.' 'You,' He said again, 'call me Lord; yet will I wash you feet.' 'Whosoever,' He said, 'would be chief among you, let him be the servant of all. Because,' He said, 'blessed are the lowly, the peacemakers, the merciful, and the charitable.' "

Stepanitch had forgotten all his tea. He was an old man, and his tears came easily. He sat and listened, with the tears rolling down his cheeks.

"Oh, but you must drink your tea," said Avdeitch; yet Stepanitch only crossed himself and said the thanksgiving, after which he pushed his glass away and rose.

"I thank you, Martin Avdeitch," he said. "You have taken me in, and fed both soul and body."

"Nay, but I beg of you to come again," replied Avdeitch. "I am only too glad of a guest."

So Stepanitch departed, while Martin poured out the last of the tea and drank it. Then he cleaned the crockery, and sat down again to his work by the window—to the stitching of a back-piece. He stitched away, yet kept on looking through the window—looking for Christ, as it were—and ever thinking of Christ and His works. Indeed, Christ's many sayings were never absent from Avdeitch's mind.

Two soldiers passed the window, the one in military boots, and the other in civilian. Next, there came a neighbouring householder, in polished goloshes; then a baker with a basket. All of them passed on. Presently a woman in woollen stockings and rough country shoes approached the window, and halted near the buttress outside it. Avdeitch peered up at her from under the lintel of his window, and could see that she was a plain-looking, poorly-dressed woman and had a child in her arms. It was in order to muffle the child up more closely—little though she had to do it with!—that she had stopped near the buttress and was now standing there with her back to the wind. Her clothing was ragged and fit only for summer, and even from behind his window-panes Avdeitch could hear the child crying miserably and its mother vainly trying to soothe it. Avdeitch rose, went to the door, climbed the steps, and cried out: "My good woman, my good woman!"

She heard him and turned round.

"Why need you stand there in the cold with your baby?" he went on. "Come into my room, where it is warm, and where you will be able to wrap the baby up more comfortably than you can here. Yes, come in with you."

The woman was surprised to see an old man in a leather apron and with spectacles upon his nose calling out to her, yet she followed him down the steps, and they entered his room. The old man led her to the bedstead.

"Sit you down here, my good woman," he said. "You will be near the stove, and can warm yourself and feed your baby."

"Ah, but I have no milk left in my breast," she replied. "I have had nothing to eat this morning." Nevertheless she put the child to suck.

Avdeitch nodded his head approvingly, went to the table for some bread and a basin, and opened the stove door. From the stove he took and poured some soup into the basin, and drew out also

1320

a bowl of porridge. The latter, however, was not yet boiling, so he set out only the soup, after first laying the table with a cloth.

"Sit down and eat, my good woman," he said, "while I hold your baby. I have had little ones of my own, and know how to nurse them."

The woman crossed herself and sat down, while Avdeitch seated himself upon the bedstead with the baby. He smacked his lips at it once or twice, but made a poor show of it, for he had no teeth left. Consequently the baby went on crying. Then he bethought him of his finger, which he wriggled to and fro towards the baby's mouth and back again—without, however, actually touching the little one's lips, since the finger was blackened with work and sticky with shoemaker's wax. The baby contemplated the finger and grew quiet—then actually smiled. Avdeitch was delighted. Meanwhile the woman had been eating the meal, and now she told him, unasked, who she was and whither she was going.

"I am a soldier's wife," she said, "but my husband was sent to a distant station eight months ago, and I have heard nothing of him since. At first I got a place as cook, but when the baby came they said they could not do with it and dismissed me. That was three months ago, and I have got nothing since, and have spent all my savings. I tried to get taken as a wet nurse but no one would have me, for they said I was too thin. I have just been to see a tradesman's wife where our grandmother is in service. She had promised to take me on, and I quite thought that she would, but when I arrived to-day she told me to come again next week. She lives a long way from here, and I am quite worn out and have tired my baby for nothing. Thank Heaven, however, my landlady is good to me, and gives me shelter for Christ's sake. Otherwise I should not have known how to bear it all."

Avdeitch sighed and said: "But have you nothing warm to wear?"

"Ah, sir," replied the woman, "although it is the time for warm clothes I had to pawn my last shawl yesterday for two *grivenki*."

Then the woman returned to the bedstead to take her baby, while Avdeitch rose and went to a cupboard. There he rummaged about, and presently returned with an old jacket.

"Here," he said. "It is a poor old thing, but it will serve to cover you."

The woman looked at the jacket, and then at the old man. Then she took the jacket and burst into tears. Avdeitch turned away, and went creeping under the bedstead, whence he extracted a box and

1321

pretended to rummage about in it for a few moments; after which he sat down again before the woman.

Then the woman said to him: "I thank you in Christ's name, good grandfather. Surely it was He Himself who sent me to your window. Otherwise I should have seen my baby perish with the cold. When I first came out the day was warm, but now it has begun to freeze. But He, Our Little Father, had placed you in your window, that you might see me in my bitter plight and have compassion upon me."

Avdeitch smiled and said: "He did indeed place me there; yet, my poor woman, it was for a special purpose that I was looking out."

Then he told his guest, the soldier's wife, of his vision, and how he had heard a voice foretelling that to-day the Lord Himself would come to visit him.

"That may very well be," said the woman as she rose, took the jacket, and wrapped her baby in it. Then she saluted him once more and thanked him.

"Also, take this in Christ's name," said Avdeitch, and gave her a two-*grivenka* piece with which to buy herself a shawl. The woman crossed herself, and he likewise. Then he led her to the door and dismissed her.

When she had gone Avdeitch ate a little soup, washed up the crockery again, and resumed his work. All the time, though, he kept his eye upon the window, and as soon as ever a shadow fell across it he would look up to see who was passing. Acquaintances of his came past, and people whom he did not know, yet never anyone very particular.

Then suddenly he saw something. Opposite his window there had stopped an old pedlar-woman, with a basket of apples. Only a few of the apples, however, remained, so that it was clear that she was almost sold out. Over her shoulder was slung a sack of shavings, which she must have gathered near some new building as she was going home. Apparently, her shoulder had begun to ache under their weight, and she therefore wished to shift them to the other one. To do this, she balanced her basket of apples on the top of a post, lowered the sack to the pavement, and began shaking up its contents. As she was doing this, a boy in a ragged cap appeared from somewhere, seized an apple from the basket, and tried to make off. But the old woman, who had been on her guard, managed to turn and seize the boy by the sleeve, and although he struggled and

1322

tried to break away, she clung to him with both hands, snatched his cap off, and finally grasped him by the hair. Thereupon the youngster began to shout and abuse his captor. Avdeitch did not stop to make fast his awl, but threw his work down upon the floor, ran to the door, and went stumbling up the steps—losing his spectacles as he did so. Out into the street he ran, where the old woman was still clutching the boy by the hair and threatening to take him to the police, while the boy, for his part, was struggling in the endeavour to free himself.

"I never took it," he was saying. "What are you beating me for? Let me go."

Avdeitch tried to part them as he took the boy by the hand and said:

"Let him go, my good woman. Pardon him for Christ's sake."

"Yes, I will pardon him," she retorted, "but not until he has tasted a new birch-rod. I mean to take the young rascal to the police."

But Avdeitch still interceded for him.

"Let him go, my good woman," he said. "He will never do it again. Let him go for Christ's sake."

The old woman released the boy, who was for making off at once had not Avdeitch stopped him.

"You must beg the old woman's pardon," he said, "and never do such a thing again. I saw you take the apple."

The boy burst out crying, and begged the old woman's pardon as Avdeitch commanded.

"There, there," said Avdeitch. "Now I will give you one. Here you are,"—and he took an apple from the basket and handed it to the boy. "I will pay you for it, my good woman," he added.

"Yes, but you spoil the young rascal by doing that," she objected. "He ought to have received a reward that would have made him glad to stand for a week."

"Ah, my good dame, my good dame," exclaimed Avdeitch. "That may be *our* way of rewarding, but it is not God's. If this boy ought to have been whipped for taking the apple, ought not we also to receive something for our sins?"

The old woman was silent. Then Avdeitch related to her the parable of the master who absolved his servant from the great debt which he owed him, whereupon the servant departed and took his own debtor by the throat. The old woman listened, and also the boy.

1323

"God has commanded us to pardon one another," went on Avdeitch, "or *He* will not pardon us. We ought to pardon all men, and especially the thoughtless."

The old woman shook her head and sighed.

"Yes, that may be so," she said, "but these young rascals are so spoilt already!"

"Then it is for us, their elders, to teach them better," he replied.

"That is what I say myself at times," rejoined the old woman. "I had seven of them once at home, but have only one daughter now." And she went on to tell Avdeitch where she and her daughter lived, and how they lived, and how many grandchildren she had.

"I have only such strength as you see," she said, "yet I work hard, for my heart goes out to my grandchildren—the bonny little things that they are! No children could run to meet me as they do. Aksintka, for instance, will go to no one else. 'Grandmother,' she cries, 'dear grandmother, you are tired' "—and the old woman became thoroughly softened. "Everyone knows what boys are," she added presently, referring to the culprit. "May God go with him!"

She was raising the sack to her shoulders again when the boy darted forward and said:

"Nay, let me carry it, grandmother. It will be all on my way home."

The old woman nodded assent, gave up the sack to the boy, and went away with him down the street. She had quite forgotten to ask Avdeitch for the money for the apple. He stood looking after them, and observing how they were talking together as they went.

Having seen them go, he returned to his room, finding his spectacles—unbroken—on the steps as he descended them. Once more he took up his awl and fell to work, but had done little before he found it difficult to distinguish the stitches, and the lamplighter had passed on his rounds. "I too must light up," he thought to himself. So he trimmed the lamp, hung it up, and resumed his work. He finished one boot completely, and then turned it over to look at it. It was all good work. Then he laid aside his tools, swept up the cuttings, rounded off the stitches and loose ends, and cleaned his awl. Next he lifted the lamp down, placed it on the table, and took his Testament from the shelf. He had intended opening the book at the place which he had marked last night with a strip of leather, but it opened itself at another instead. The instant it did so, his vision of last night came back to his memory, and, as instantly, he thought he heard a movement behind him as of someone moving

1324

towards him. He looked round and saw in the shadow of a dark corner what appeared to be figures—figures of persons standing there, yet could not distinguish them clearly. Then the voice whispered in his ear:

"Martin, Martin, dost thou not know Me?"

"Who art Thou?" said Avdeitch.

"Even I!" whispered the voice again. "Lo, it is I!"—and there stepped from the dark corner Stepanitch. He smiled, and then, like the fading of a little cloud, was gone.

"It is I!" whispered the voice again—and there stepped from the same corner the woman with her baby. She smiled, and the baby smiled, and they were gone.

"And it is I!" whispered the voice again—and there stepped forth the old woman and the boy with the apple. They smiled, and were gone.

Joy filled the soul of Martin Avdeitch as he crossed himself, put on his spectacles, and set himself to read the Testament at the place where it had opened. At the top of the page he read:

"For I was an hungred, and ye gave Me meat: I was thirsty, and ye gave Me drink: I was a stranger, and ye took Me in."

And further down the page he read:

"Inasmuch as ye have done it unto one of the least of these my brethren ye have done it unto Me."

Then Avdeitch understood that the vision had come true, and that his Saviour had in very truth visited him that day, and that he had received Him.

ANTHONY TROLLOPE

ANTHONY TROLLOPE (English, 1815-1882). Novelist recreator of the average in life and conduct. Spent early years as Irish civil servant. Famous for his methodical way of writing—1,000 words an hour—and frank admission that he did it for money. Author of over 40 novels, most famous being the 6 Barsetshire stories, including *The Warden* and *Barchester Towers*.

HE KNEW HE WAS RIGHT

The Glascock marriage was a great affair in Florence; so much so that there were not a few who regarded it as a strengthening of peaceful relations between the United States and the United King-

dom, and who thought that the Alabama claims and the question of naturalisation might now be settled with comparative ease. An English lord was about to marry the niece of an American Minister to a foreign court. The bridegroom was not, indeed, quite a lord as yet, but it was known to all men that he must be a lord in a very short time, and the bride was treated with more than usual bridal honours because she belonged to a legation. She was not, indeed, an ambassador's daughter, but the niece of a daughterless ambassador, and therefore almost as good as a daughter. The wives and daughters of other ambassadors, and the other ambassadors themselves, of course, came to the wedding; and as the palace in which Mr. Spalding had apartments stood alone, in a garden, with a separate carriage entrance, it seemed for all wedding purposes as though the whole palace were his own.

The English Minister came, and his wife,—although she had never quite given over turning up her nose at the American bride whom Mr. Glascock had chosen for himself. It was such a pity, she said, that such a man as Mr. Glascock should marry a young woman from Providence, Rhode Island. Who in England would know anything of Providence, Rhode Island? And it was so expedient, in her estimation, that a man of family should strengthen himself by marrying a woman of family. It was so necessary, she declared, that a man when marrying should remember that his child would have two grandfathers, and would be called upon to account for four great-grandfathers. Nevertheless Mr. Glascock was —Mr. Glascock; and, let him marry whom he would, his wife would be the future Lady Peterborough. Remembering this, the English Minister's wife gave up the point, when the thing was really settled, and benignly promised to come to the breakfast with all the secretaries and attachés belonging to the legation, and all the wives and daughters thereof. What may a man not do, and do with éclat, if he be heir to a peer and have plenty of money in his pocket?

Mr. and Mrs. Spalding were covered with glory on the occasion; and perhaps they did not bear their glory as meekly as they should have done. Mrs. Spalding laid herself open to some ridicule from the English Minister's wife because of her inability to understand with absolute clearness the condition of her niece's husband in respect to his late and future seat in Parliament, to the fact of his being a commoner and a nobleman at the same time, and to certain information which was conveyed to her, surely in a most unnecessary manner, that if Mr. Glascock were to die before his father her

niece would never become Lady Peterborough, although her niece's son, if she had one, would be the future lord. No doubt she blundered, as was most natural; and then the British Minister's wife made the most of the blunders; and when once Mrs. Spalding ventured to speak of Caroline as her ladyship, not to the British Minister's wife, but to the sister of one of the secretaries, a story was made out of it almost as false as it was ill-natured. Poor Caroline was spoken of as her ladyship backwards and forwards among the ladies of the legation in a manner which might have vexed her had she known anything about it; but, nevertheless, all the ladies prepared their best flounces to go to the wedding. The time soon would come when she would in truth be a "ladyship," and she might be of social use to any one of the ladies in question.

. . . Everybody who was anybody in Florence was to be present. There were only to be four bridesmaids, Caroline herself having strongly objected to a greater number. As Wallach Petrie had fled at the first note of preparation for these trivial and unpalatable festivities, another American young lady was found; and the sister of the English secretary of legation, who had so maliciously spread that report about her "ladyship," gladly agreed to be the fourth.

It was generally admitted among the various legations in Florence that there had not been such a wedding in the City of Flowers since it had become the capital of Italia. Mr. Glascock and Miss Spalding were married in the chapel of the legation,—a legation chapel on the ground floor having been extemporised for the occasion. This greatly enhanced the pleasantness of the thing, and saved the necessity of matrons and bridesmaids packing themselves and their finery into close fusty carriages. A portion of the guests attended in the chapel, and the remainder, when the ceremony was over, were found strolling about the shady garden.

The whole affair of the breakfast was very splendid and lasted some hours. In the midst of the festivities the bride and bridegroom were whisked away with a pair of gray horses to the railway station, and before the last toast of the day had been proposed by the Belgian Councillor of Legation, they were half-way up the Apennines on their road to Bologna.

Mr. Spalding behaved himself like a man on this occasion Nothing was spared in the way of expense, and when he made that celebrated speech, in which he declared that the republican

1327

virtue of the New World had linked itself in a happy alliance with the aristocratic splendour of the Old, and went on with a simile about the lion and the lamb, everybody accepted it with good humour in spite of its being a little too long for the occasion.

"It has gone off very well, mamma, has it not?" said Nora, as she returned home with her mother to her lodgings.

"Yes, my dear; much, I fancy, as these things generally do."

"I thought it was so nice. And she looked very well. And he was so pleasant, and so much like a gentleman,—not noisy, you know, and yet not too serious."

"I dare say, my love."

"It is easy enough, mamma, for a girl to be married, for she has nothing to do but wear her clothes and look as pretty as she can. And if she cries and has a red nose it is forgiven her. But a man has so difficult a part to play. If he tries to carry himself as though it were not a special occasion, he looks like a fool that way; and if he is very special, he looks like a fool the other way. I thought Mr. Glascock did it very well."

TU FU

TU FU (Chinese, 712-770). Once called the God of Verse. Friend of Li Po. Became a courtier; was exiled by Emperor Su Tsung because of his outspoken demeanor. For a time traveled as a homeless wanderer. Did some painting. A certain sadness overshadows his poetry.

TO A LOST LADY

Be still!
Tell me no more of spring,
No more of flowers.
Bring mourning boughs
And black weeds stricken by blight.

Be still!
Let the glad sun
Dip down behind the mountains,
While I put on grief's robe
And lie
Among the leaves she loved—
For it is night.

1328

Fire wrecked the house where I was born
  And stripped the rafters bare:
I put to sea in my gilded barque,
  But I could not shake despair.

I took my flute and played to the moon,
  But she hid behind a cloud,
For my song was sad, the music faint;
  Only my heart beat loud.

I turned me to the mountain,
  But I found no solace there,
For childhood joys seemed vanished,
  With my home into thin blue air.

I longed for death—but then the moon
  Shone mirrored in the sea,
And I caught one glimpse of a maiden's face
  As her boat was passing me.

Were it her wish, I'd rout despair
  And bear a true man's part:
I'd build another dwelling—
  And this one, in her heart!

ON THE RIVER CHOU

Beneath the wide cloud-ridden sky
My boat is gliding swiftly by.

I watch the quiet water; soon
The drifting clouds have hid the moon.

As I lean back within my boat,
Upon the sky I seem to float.

And as I drift, I like to dream
That my heart is the quiet stream,

The River Chou so still and fair—
And my beloved is mirrored there.

Now the sad rains are falling. Let us say now: the sky weeps because its fine weather is all gone. Boredom piles up on us like heavy rain-clouds: where is our gaiety and wit? Let us sit indoors.

Now is the time for poetry that remembers summer. Let it be put down gently on white paper like full-blown petals falling from exquisite trees. And let my lips drink from this cup of summer wine each time my brush is dipped into the ink. Thus will I keep my fancy from floating off like clouds or smoke: for time past escapes from us, my love, quicker than a flight of birds.

IVAN SERGEYEVICH TURGENEV

IVAN SERGEYEVICH TURGENEV (Russian, 1818-1883). The most consciously artistic and "Western" of the great Russian novelists. Admired particularly by stylists like Henry James. Interested in politics of his day. Considerably responsible through his novels for abolition of serfdom in Russia. Major works: (novels) *Fathers and Sons, Virgin Soil,* and (play) *A Month in the Country.*

THE NIHILIST

"WHERE is your new friend?" he asked Arkadi.

"He has gone out already. He generally gets up very early and makes some excursion. But I must tell you, once for all, that you need not take any notice of him; he does not care for conventionalities."

"Yes, so I perceive."

Paul Petrovitch began slowly to spread butter on his bread.

"Will he remain here any length of time?"

"That depends. He will go from here to his father's."

"And where does his father live?"

"In our district; eighty versts from here. He has a little estate there. He used to be the regimental doctor."

"Ta-ta, ta-ta! I have been continually asking myself, where could I have heard that name before? Bazarof, Bazarof! Nicholas, do

you not remember that in our father's division there was a Dr. Bazarof?"

"I seem to remember something of the sort."

"Yes, it is right enough. So this doctor is his father—hm!" Paul Petrovitch twisted his moustache.

"Well, and what is Mr. Bazarof junior?" asked he slowly.

"What is Bazarof?" Arkadi smiled. "Shall I tell you, uncle, what he really is?"

"Do me that favor, my dear nephew."

"He is a Nihilist."

"What?" asked Nicholas Petrovitch.

As for Paul Petrovitch, he suddenly raised the knife, on whose point was a little piece of butter, and remained motionless.

"He is a Nihilist," repeated Arkadi.

"Nihilist!" said Nicholas Petrovitch. "The word comes from the Latin *nihil*, nothing, as far as I can tell, and therefore designates a person who acknowledges nothing."

"Or rather, who respects nothing," said Paul Petrovitch, who recommenced buttering his bread.

"Or rather, who regards everything from a critical point of view," remarked Arkadi.

"Does not that come to the same thing?" asked Paul Petrovitch.

"No, by no means. A Nihilist is a man who bows to no authority, who accepts no principles on faith alone, however high may be the regard in which this principle is held in human opinion."

"And do you consider that right?" asked Paul Petrovitch.

"That depends on the point of view, uncle; some think it right, while others consider it quite wrong."

"Indeed. Well, I see it is not *our* point of view. We of the old school are of opinion that without principles, that are received on faith alone, as you express it, the world could not exist. But *vous avez changé tout cela*. Well, may God give you good health and the rank of general; as for us, we will be content with admiring you, you—what do you call yourselves?"

"Nihilists," said Arkadi, accenting each syllable.

"Yes. We used to have Hegelists, now we have Nihilists. We shall see how you manage to exist in the nothing, the vacuum, as under an air-pump. And now, brother Nicholas, be so good as to ring; I should like to drink my cocoa."

The combat took place the same evening at tea. Paul had come down into the drawing-room in a state of irritation, and ready for

the fight. He only awaited an opportunity to throw himself on the enemy; but he had long to wait. Bazarof never spoke much before the "two old fellows," as he called the two brothers; besides, he did not feel very well this evening, and swallowed one cup of tea after another in silence. Paul was devoured by impatience: at length he found the opportunity he had been seeking.

The conversation turned on one of the neighboring landholders.

"He is a simpleton, a bad aristocrat," said Bazarof, who had known him at St. Petersburg.

"Permit me to ask you," said Paul, with trembling lips, "whether the words 'simpleton' and 'aristocrat' are in your opinion synonymous?"

"I said 'bad aristocrat,' " replied Bazarof carelessly, sipping his tea.

"That is true; But I assume that you rank aristocrats and bad aristocrats in the same category. I think it right to inform you that such is not my opinion. I venture to say that I am generally considered a liberal man and lover of progress; but it is just on that account that I respect the aristocrats, the true aristocrats. Consider, my dear sir"—Bazarof fixed his eyes on Paul—"my dear sir," continued he, with dignity, "consider the English nobility: they do not give up one iota of their rights, and yet they respect the rights of others just as much; they demand what is due to them, and yet they are always careful to render their due to others. It is the nobility that has given England its liberty, and that is its strongest support."

"That is an old song we have often heard," replied Bazarof; "but what do you mean by it?"

"I mean to prove by it, my dear sir, that without the consciousness of one's own dignity, without self-respect—and all these sentiments prevail among the aristocracy—there can be no solid foundation for the commonwealth, for the edifice of the State. The individual, the personality, my dear sir—that is the essential; a man's personality must stand firm as a rock, for everything rests on this basis. I know quite well that you think my manners, my dress, even my habit of cleanliness, absurd; but all this springs from self-respect, from a feeling of duty—yes, yes, sir, from a feeling of duty. I live in an out-of-the-way corner of the province; but I do not neglect my person on that account—in my own person I respect the man."

"Excuse me, Paul Petrovitch," replied Bazarof; "you say that you respect yourself, and you sit there with your arms crossed. What advantage can that be to the commonwealth? If you did not respect yourself you would not act differently."

Paul Petrovitch turned pale.

"That is quite another matter," replied he. "I have no intention of telling you why I stay with my arms crossed, as you are pleased to call it. I merely wished to tell you that aristocracy depends upon principle; and it is only immoral or worthless men who can live nowadays without principles. I said so to Arkadi the day after his arrival; and I am merely repeating it to you today. Is it not the case, Nicholas Petrovitch?"

Nicholas Petrovitch nodded assent.

"Aristocracy, liberalism, principles, progress," repeated Bazarof— "all words quite foreign to our language, and perfectly useless. A true Russian need not use them."

"What does he need, then, in your opinion? According to you, we are outside the limits of humanity, outside its laws. That is going rather too far; the logic of history requires—"

"What do you need that logic for? We can do very well without it."

"How?"

"I will give an example. I fancy that you do not need the aid of logic in carrying a piece of bread to your mouth when you are hungry. What is the use of all these abstractions?"

Paul lifted up his hands.

"I no longer understand you," said he. "You insult the Russian people. I do not understand how it is possible not to acknowledge principles—rules! What have you, then, to guide you through life?"

"I have told you before, uncle," interposed Arkadi, "that we do not acknowledge any authorities."

"We act according as anything seems useful to us," added Bazarof; "to-day it seems to us useful to deny, and we do deny."

"Everything?"

"Absolutely everything."

"What? Not only art, poetry, but even—I hesitate to say it."

"Everything," repeated Bazarof, with most indomitable calm.

Paul looked at him fixedly. He had not expected this answer. Arkadi blushed with pleasure.

"Excuse me," said Nicholas, "you deny everything, or, to speak more correctly, you destroy everything; but you must also rebuild."

"That does not concern us. First of all, we must clear the ground."

"The present state of the people requires it," added Arkadi seriously. "We must fulfill this duty; we have no right to abandon ourselves to the satisfaction of our personal vanity."

This last speech did not please Bazarof. It smacked of philosophy,

1333

that is, of romanticism; for he gave this name even to philosophy. But he did not think this a fitting moment to contradict his young pupil.

"No, no!" exclaimed Paul, with sudden emotion. "I will not believe that you gentlemen have a right idea of the Russian people, and that you express its real wants, its surest wishes. No, the Russian people is not what you represent it. It has a reverent respect for tradition; it is patriarchal; it cannot live without faith."

"I shall not attempt to contradict you," replied Bazarof. "I am even ready to admit that this once you are right."

"But if I am right?"

"That proves nothing whatever."

"Nothing whatever," repeated Arkadi, with the assurance of an experienced chess-player, who, having foreseen a move that his opponent considers dangerous, does not seem in the least disconcerted by it.

"How can you say that proves nothing?" said Paul, stupefied. "Do you then separate yourself from your people?"

"And what if I did? The people believe that when it thunders, the prophet Elijah is riding over the heavens in his chariot. Well, must I share its opinion in this matter? You think you will confound me by telling me that the people is Russian. Well, am I not Russian, too?"

"No; after all that you have just said, you are not. I will no longer acknowledge you to be Russian."

"My grandfather followed the plough," replied Bazarof, with lofty pride. "Ask any one of your peasants which of us two—you or me—he is readiest to acknowledge as his fellow-citizen. You cannot even talk to him."

"And you, who can talk to him, you despise him."

"Why not, if he deserves it? You condemn the tendency of my ideas; but how do you know that it is accidental, that it is not rather determined by the universal spirit of the people whom you defend so well?"

"Come, the Nihilists are very useful."

"Whether they are or not is not for us to decide. Do not you also think that you are good for something?"

"Gentlemen, gentlemen, no personalities," exclaimed Nicholas, rising.

Paul smiled, and placing his hand on his brother's shoulder, forced him to sit down again.

"Set your mind at rest," said he; "I shall not forget myself, if only

1334

because of that feeling of dignity of which this gentleman speaks so scornfully. Excuse me," continued he, once more addressing Bazarof; "you probably think that your mode of looking at things is a new one; that is a mistake on your part. The materialism you profess has been held in honor more than once, and has always proved itself insufficient."

"Another foreign word!" replied Bazarof. He was beginning to become bitter, and the complexion of his face was assuming an unpleasant yellow. "In the first place, let me tell you that we do not preach; that is not one of our habits."

"What do you do, then?"

"I will tell you. We have begun by calling attention to the extortionate officials, the need of roads, the absence of trade, the manner of executing justice."

"Yes, yes; you are informers, *divulgators*, that is the name given to you, if I am not much mistaken. I agree with you in many of your criticisms; but—"

"Then we soon discovered that it was not enough to talk about the wounds to which we are succumbing, that all this only tended to platitudes and dogmatism. We perceived that our advanced men, our *divulgators*, were worth nothing whatever; that we were taking up our time with follies, such as art for art's sake, creative power which does not know itself, the parliamentary system, the need of lawyers, and a thousand other foolish tales; while we were overwhelmed by the grossest superstition; while all our joint-stock companies were becoming bankrupt. All this is only because there is a dearth of honest men; while even the liberation of the serfs, with which Government is much occupied, will produce no good effects, because our peasants are themselves ready to steal, so that they may go and drink poisonous drugs in the taverns."

"Good," replied Paul, "very good. You have discovered all that, and all the same you are determined to undertake nothing serious?"

"Yes, we are determined!" repeated Bazarof, somewhat sharply. Suddenly he began to reproach himself for having said so much before this gentleman.

"And you confine yourself to abuse?"

"We abuse, if necessary."

"And that is what is called Nihilism?"

"That is what is called Nihilism!" repeated Bazarof, this time in a particularly irritating tone.

Paul winced a little.

1335

"Good!" said he, with forced calm and constrained manner. "The mission of Nihilism is to remedy all things, and you are our saviours and our heroes. Excellent! But why do you abuse the others so much, and call them chatterboxes? Do you not chatter as much as the rest?"

"Come, if there is anything we have to reproach ourselves with, it is certainly not this," muttered Bazarof between his teeth.

"What! can you say that you act, or even prepare for action?"

Bazarof remained silent. Paul trembled, but he restrained his anger.

"Then act, destroy," continued he; "but how dare you destroy without ever knowing why you destroy?"

"We destroy because we are a force," said Arkadi, gravely.

Paul looked at his nephew and smiled.

"Yes, force is responsible to no one," continued Arkadi, drawing himself up.

"Wretched man," exclaimed Paul Petrovitch, no longer able to contain himself, "if you would but consider what you assert of Russia alone, with your absurd phrases! No, it would require an angel's patience to endure that force! The Mongol and the savage Kalmuk have force, too. But how can this force help us? What ought to be dear to us is civilization; yes, yes, my dear sirs, the fruits of civilization. And do not tell me that these fruits are worthless; the merest dauber of signboards, the most wretched fiddler, who, for five kopecks an evening, plays polkas and mazurkas, are more useful than you, because they are representatives of civilization, and not of the Mongolian brute force! You consider yourselves advanced, and your proper place would be in a Kalmuk kibitka. Force! Consider one moment, you strong gentlemen, that at most there are only a few dozen of you, while the others may be counted by millions, and that they will not allow you to tread under foot their most sacred traditions; no, they will tear you to pieces."

"If they tear us to pieces, we must put up with it," replied Bazarof. "But you are quite out in your reckoning. We are not so few as you suppose."

"What! You seriously believe that you will be able to bring the whole people into your ranks?"

"Do you not know that a kopeck candle is enough to set the whole city of Moscow on fire?" answered Bazarof.

"Excellent! First, almost Satanic pride, and then irony, which reveals your bad taste. This is how youth is carried away; this is how the inexperienced hearts of these boys are seduced. Look! there is one of them by your side; he almost worships you." Arkadi turned

1336

away, frowning. "And this contagion has already spread. I have been told that at Rome our painters no longer set foot into the Vatican; they call Raphael a bungler, because, as they say, he is considered an authority—and those who say this are themselves incapacity personified; their imagination cannot soar beyond the 'Girl at the Well;' however they may try, they cannot attain anything better! And how ugly is this 'Girl at the Well!' I suppose you have the highest opinion of these fellows, have you not?"

"As far as I am concerned," replied Bazarof, "I would not give twopence for Raphael, and I do not suppose that the others are worth much more."

"Bravo, bravo! Do you hear, Arkadi? That is how young people should express themselves now! O, I can quite understand why they follow in your footsteps! Formerly they used to feel the need of learning something. As they did not wish to be considered ignorant, they were forced to work. But now they need only say, 'There is nothing but folly and rubbish in the world;' and there is an end to everything. The students may well rejoice. Formerly they were only foolish boys —behold them suddenly transformed into Nihilists!"

"It appears to me that you are forgetting the sentiment of personal dignity, on which you laid so much stress just now," remarked Bazarof phlegmatically, while Arkadi's face flushed with indignation, and his eyes flashed. "Our dispute has led us too far. I think we should do well to stop here. Yet," added he, rising, "I should agree with you if you could name to me a single institution of our social, civil, or family life, which does not deserve to be swept away without mercy."

"I could name a million such," exclaimed Paul Petrovitch, "a million! Take, for instance, the commune."

A cold smile passed over Bazarof's lips.

"As for the commune," said he, "you had better talk to your brother about that. I suppose he must know by this time what to think of the commune, the solidarity of the peasants, their temperance, and similar jokes."

"And the family, the family, such as we still find it among our peasants!" exclaimed Paul Petrovitch.

"In my opinion that is another question that you would do well not to examine too closely. Come, take my advice, Paul Petrovitch, and take two days to consider the matter. Nothing else will occur to you just at present; consider all our institutions one after another, and contemplate them carefully. Meantime Arkadi and I will—"

"Turn everything to ridicule," interrupted Paul Petrovitch.

"No; dissect frogs. Come, Arkadi. Good afternoon, gentlemen."
The two friends went out. The brothers remained alone together,
and for some time could only look at each other in silence.

"So that is the youth of to-day," began Paul Petrovitch at length;
"those are our successors!"

MARK TWAIN

MARK TWAIN (Samuel Langhorne Clemens, American, 1835-1910). Humane
and gentle satirist, whose last works reveal strain of disillusioned pessimism.
Adventures of childhood on the Mississippi appear in the beloved boys' stories,
Adventures of Tom Sawyer and *Adventures of Huckleberry Finn* (considered
by some the great American novel). Later satirical novel: *A Connecticut
Yankee at King Arthur's Court.*

THE CELEBRATED JUMPING FROG
OF CALAVERAS COUNTY

IN compliance with the request of a friend of mine, who wrote me
from the East, I called on good-natured, garrulous old Simon Wheeler,
and inquired after my friend's friend, Leonidas W. Smiley, as requested to do, and I hereunto append the result. I have a lurking
suspicion that *Leonidas W.* Smiley is a myth; that my friend never
knew such a personage; and that he only conjectured that if I asked
old Wheeler about him, it would remind him of his infamous *Jim*
Smiley, and he would go to work and bore me to death with some
exasperating reminiscence of him as long as and as tedious as it
should be useless to me. If that was the design, it succeeded.

I found Simon Wheeler dozing comfortably by the barroom stove
of the dilapidated tavern in the decayed mining camp of Angel's, and
I noticed that he was fat and bald-headed, and had an expression of
winning gentleness and simplicity upon his tranquil countenance. He
roused up and gave me good-day. I told him a friend of mine had
commissioned me to make some inquiries about a cherished companion of his boyhood named *Leonidas W.* Smiley—*Reverend Leonidas W.* Smiley, a young minister of the Gospel, who he had heard
was at one time a resident of Angel's Camp. I added that if Mr.
Wheeler could tell me anything about this Reverend Leonidas W.
Smiley I would feel under many obligations to him.

1338

Simon Wheeler backed me into a corner and blockaded me there with his chair, and then sat down and reeled off the monotonous narrative which follows this paragraph. He never smiled, he never frowned, he never changed his voice from the gentle-flowing key to which he tuned his initial sentence, he never betrayed the slightest suspicion of enthusiasm; but all through the interminable narrative there ran a vein of impressive earnestness and sincerity which showed me plainly that, so far from his imagining that there was anything ridiculous or funny about his story, he regarded it as a really important matter, and admired its two heroes as men of transcendent genius in *finesse*. I let him go on his own way, and never interrupted him once.

Reverend Leonidas W. H'm, Reverend Le—well, there was a feller here once by the name of *Jim* Smiley, in the winter of '49—or maybe it was the spring of '50—I don't recollect exactly, somehow, though what makes me think it was one or the other is because I remember the big flume warn't finished when he first came to the camp; but anyway, he was the curiousest man about always betting on anything that turned up you ever see, if he could get anybody to bet on the other side; and if he couldn't he'd change sides. Anyway what suited the other man would suit *him*—anyway just so's he got a bet, *he* was satisfied. But still he was lucky, uncommon lucky; he most always come out winner. He was always ready and laying for a chance; there couldn't be no solit'ry thing mentioned but that feller'd offer to bet on it, and take ary side you please, as I was just telling you. If there was a horse-race, you'd find him flush or you'd find him busted at the end of it; if there was a dog-fight, he'd bet on it; if there was a cat-fight, he'd bet on it; if there was a chicken-fight, he'd bet on it; why if there was two birds setting on a fence, he would bet you which one would fly first; or if there was a camp-meeting he would be there reg'lar to bet on Parson Walker which he judged to be the best exhorter about here, and so he was, too, and a good man. If he even see a straddle-bug start to go anywhere, he would bet how long it would take him to get to—to wherever he was going to, and if you took him up, he would foller that straddle-bug to Mexico but what he would find out where he was bound for and how long he was on the road. Lots of the boys here has seen that Smiley and can tell you about him. Why, it never made no difference to *him* —he'd bet on *anything*—the dangdest feller. Parson Walker's wife laid very sick once, for a good while, and it seemed as if they warn't going to save her; but one morning he come in, and Smiley up and

1339

asked him how she was, and he said she was considerable better—
thank the Lord for His inf'nite mercy—and coming on so smart that
with the blessing of Prov'dence she'd get well yet; and Smiley, before
he thought, says, "Well, I'll resk two-and-a-half she don't anyway."

Thish-yer Smiley had a mare—the boys called her the fifteen-
minute nag, but that was only in fun, you know, because of course,
for all she was slow and always had the asthma, or the distemper, or
the consumption, or something of that kind. They used to give her
two or three hundred yards' start, and then pass her under way; but
always at the fag end of the race she'd get excited and desparate like,
and come cavorting and straddling up, and scattering her legs around
limber, sometimes in the air and sometimes out to one side among
the fences, and kicking up m-o-r-e dust and raising m-o-r-e racket
with her coughing and sneezing and blowing her nose—and *always*
fetch up at the stand just about a neck ahead, as near as you cipher
it down.

And he had a little small bull-pup, that to look at him you'd think
he warn't worth a cent but to set around and look ornery and lay for
a chance to steal something. But as soon as money was up on him he
was a different dog; his under-jaw'd begin to stick out like the fo'-
castle of a steamboat, and his teeth would uncover and shine like the
furnaces. And a dog might tackle him and bully-rag him, and bite
him, and throw him over his shoulder two or three times, and Andrew
Jackson—which was the name of the pup—Andrew Jackson would
never let on but what *he* was satisfied, and hadn't expected nothing
else—and the bets being doubled and doubled on the other side all
the time, till the money was all up; and then all of a sudden he would
grab that other dog just by the j'int of his hind leg and freeze to it—
not chaw, you understand, but only just grip and hang on till they
throwed up the sponge, if it was a year. Smiley always come out winner on that pup, till he harnessed a dog once that didn't have no
hind legs, because they'd been sawed off in a circular saw, and when
the thing had gone along far enough, and the money was all up, and
he came to make a snatch for his pet holt, he see in a minute how
he'd been imposed on, and how the other dog had him in the door,
so to speak, and he 'peared surprised, and then he looked sorter dis-
couraged-like, and didn't try no more to win the fight, and so he got
shucked out bad. He gave Smiley a look, as much as to say his heart
was broke, and it was *his* fault for putting up a dog that hadn't no
hind legs for him to take holt of, which was his main dependence in
a fight, and then he limped off a piece and laid down and died. It

was a good pup, was that Andrew Jackson, and would have made a name for hisself if he'd lived, for the stuff was in him and he had genius—I know it, because he hadn't no opportunities to speak of, and it don't stand to reason that a dog could make such a fight as he could under them circumstances if he hadn't no talent. It always makes me feel sorry when I think of that last fight of his'n, and the way it turned out.

Well, thish-yer Smiley had rat-terriers, and chicken cocks, and tom-cats, and all them kind of things till you couldn't rest, and you couldn't fetch nothing for him to bet on but he'd match you. He ketched a frog one day, and took him home, and said he cal'lated to educate him; and so he never done nothing for three months but set in his back yord and learn that frog to jump. And you bet you he *did* learn him, too. He'd give him a little punch behind, and the next minute you'd see that frog whirling in the air like a doughnut—see him turn one summerset, or maybe a couple, if he got a good start, and come down flat-footed and all right like a cat. He got him up so in the matter of ketching flies, and kep' him in practice so constant, that he'd nail a fly every time as fur as he could see him. Smiley said all a frog wanted was education and he could do 'most anything—and I believe him. Why, I've seen him set Dan'l Webster down here on this floor—Dan'l Webster was the name of the frog—and sing out, "Flies, Dan'l, flies!" and quicker'n you could wink he'd spring straight up and snake a fly off'n the counter there, and flop ag'in as solid as a gob of mud, and fall to scratching the side of his head with his hind foot as indifferent as if he hadn't no idea he'd been doin' any more'n any frog might do. You never see a frog so modest and straightfor'-ard as he was, for all he was so gifted. And when it come to fair and square jumping on a dead level, he could get over more ground at one straddle than any animal of his breed you ever see. Jumping on a dead level was his strong suit, you understand; and when it come to that, Smiley would ante up money on him as long as he had a red. Smiley was monstrous proud of his frog, and well he might be, for fellers that had traveled and been everywhere all said he laid over any frog that ever *they* see.

Well, Smiley kep' the beast in a little lattice box, and he used to fetch him down-town sometimes and lay for a bet. One day a feller—a stranger in the camp, he was—come acrost him with his box, and says:

"What might it be that you've got in the box?"

And Smiley says, sorter indifferent like, "It might be a parrot, or

1341

it might be a canary, maybe, but it ain't—it's only just a frog."

And the feller took it, and looked at it careful, and turned it round this way and that, and says, "H'm—so 'tis. Well, what's *he* good for?"

"Well," Smiley says, easy and careless, "he's good enough for *one* thing, I should judge—he can outjump any frog in Calaveras County."

The feller took the box again, and took another long, particular look, and give it back to Smiley, and says, very deliberate, "Well," he says, "I don't see no p'ints about that frog that's any better'n any other frog."

"Maybe you don't," Smiley says. "Maybe you understand frogs and maybe you don't understand 'em; maybe you've had experience, and maybe you ain't only a amature, as it were. Anyways, I've got *my* opinion, and I'll resk forty dollars that he can outjump any frog in Calaveras County."

And the feller studied a minute, and then says, kinder sad like, "Well, I'm only a stranger here, and I ain't got no frog; but if I had a frog I'd bet you."

And then Smiley says, "That's all right—that's all right—if you'll hold my box a minute I'll go and get you a frog." And so the feller took the box, and put up his forty dollars along with Smiley's, and set down to wait.

So he set there a good while thinking and thinking to himself, and then he got the frog out and pried his mouth open and took a tea-spoon and filled him full of quail shot—filled him pretty near up to his chin—and set him on the floor. Smiley he went to the swamp and slopped around in the mud for a long time, and finally he ketched a frog, and fetched him in, and give him to this feller, and says:

"Now, if you're ready, set him alongside of Dan'l, with his fore-paws just even with Dan'l's, and I'll give the word." Then he says, "One—two—three—*git!*" and him and the feller touched up the frogs from behind, and the new frog hopped off lively, but Dan'l give a heave, and hysted up his shoulders—so—like a Frenchman, but it warn't no use—he couldn't budge; he was planted as solid as a church, and he couldn't no more stir than if he was anchored out. Smiley was a good deal surprised, and he was disgusted, too, but he didn't have no idea what the matter was, of course.

The feller took the money and started away; and when he was going out at the door, he sorter jerked his thumb over his shoulder—so—at Dan'l, and says again, very deliberate, "Well," he says, "*I* don't see no p'ints about that frog that's any better'n any other frog."

Smiley he stood scratching his head and looking down at Dan'l a long time, and at last he says, "I do wonder what in the nation that frog throw'd off for—I wonder if there ain't something the matter with him—he 'pears to look mighty baggy, somehow." And he ketched Dan'l by the nap of the neck and hefted him, and says, "Why, blame my cats, if he don't weigh five pound!" and turned him upside down and he belched out a double handful of shot. And then he see how it was, and he was the maddest man—he set the frog down and took out after that feller, but he never ketched him. And——

[Here Simon Wheeler heard his name called from the front yard, and got up to see what was wanted.] And turning to me as he moved away, he said: "Jest set where you are, stranger, and rest easy—I ain't going to be gone a second."

But by your leave, I did not think that a continuation of the history of the enterprising vagabond *Jim* Smiley would be likely to afford me much information concerning the Reverend *Leonidas W.* Smiley, and so I started away.

At the door I met the sociable Wheeler returning, and he button-holed me and recommenced:

"Well, thish-yer Smiley had a yaller, one-eyed cow that didn't have no tail, only just a short stump like a bannanner, and——"

However, lacking both time and inclination, I did not wait to hear about the afflicted cow, but took my leave.

1343

U

MIGUEL DE UNAMUNO

MIGUEL DE UNAMUNO (Spanish, 1864-1936). Unique philosopher and powerful personality of modern Spain. A professor of Greek, exiled for his lofty spirit and writings. He attempted to synthesize the many aspects of present-day culture. Admired poem: *El Cristo de Vélazquez*. Novels: *Niebla, Tres novelas ejemplares*. Internationally famous philosophic work: *Del sentimiento trágico de la vida*.

THREE GENERATIONS

SCENE: the dining room of a village inn in my native Basque country; actors: grandfather, son, and grandson; audience: myself, profoundly moved. Three generations of the same family had met there to eat together. The old man, an honorable independent workman, was plain and uneducated, speaking Castilian only with difficulty; his son, a mature man, who in his youth had gone to America where he had made a fortune, married and raised a family, was returning to his native soil to visit his aged father and introduce the grandson; and the grandson, still very young, was a good looking boy, very neat, very finical, and very well groomed, whose careful training was apparent in every move of his knife and fork.

Between frequent draughts of wine, the grandfather was evidencing his joy at the sight of such an elegant grandson, repeating dotingly again and again in his meagre Castilian, "I thought I was going to die without ever seeing you." The father, between the grandfather and his son, between his memories and his hopes, was thinking of God knows what, and the youngster was eating politely and coldly, looking impatiently at his grandfather from time to time as if bored.

That scene was full of meaning, not because of what its actors said, but rather what they left unsaid.

That pretty youth did not seem to be interested in anything and was paying no attention to his father's father. They were separated by an abyss. I doubt that he had ever stopped to consider that he owed his good fortune, his education, and everything that was serving as a base for his egoism to the simple, noble, honorable spirit that the old man transmitted to his son, the stalwart toiler who had made a fortune.

Immediately I was reminded that a few years ago I had heard a poor man confess sadly and bitterly that, having amassed a fortune, married and raised a family also in America, he was disdained by his children. "They scorn me," he said tearfully, "they scorn me because I don't speak correctly and because I don't know the things they have learned from the teachers I hired." Later I had the opportunity of meeting one of his sons and I can assure you that he knew less than his father. He could talk about bookish things, jabber a little French and even less English, sigh for Paris, and find fault with his father's people.

You should have heard him constantly comparing our country and the one in which he was born. There was no limit to the superficiality of his comparisons. To him everything revolved around paved streets, water-closets, street cars, restaurants, and theatres. To him civilization meant urbanization and conveniences and, in addition, a certain show of good manners. The real essence of culture was completely unknown to him. He possessed not one grain of poetic feeling or sensibility. He told me that he was not interested in old stones.

Only this lack of sensibility, this want of poetic feeling, or—let us state it clearly—this cold-heartedness can explain certain things. Many an American of Spanish parents comes to Europe without enough piety, or curiosity even, to visit his parents' fatherland; Paris calls him. In his father's town, perhaps a tiny village hidden in the mountains, there are no asphalt boulevards or electric trollies; above all, there is no *Moulin Rouge* or *chez Maxim*. Not all can feel the deep penetrating poetry of one of those little villages.

How beautiful, how deeply pious and poetical is the account by that great poet, Zorrilla de San Martín, of his visit to his father's people in the mountains behind Santander! Zorrilla de San Martín is a poet, a true poet, a noble delicate spirit, guarding the treasure of our secular culture.

I am not known as a flatterer of my country; I could more correctly be called a bitter critic of its defects. I have never hidden our weaknesses, but when I happen to meet one of those pretty youths

who find fault with everything around here, I find myself turning against them and the superiorities of the lands that they have come to boast about. Because they both fail to see our real ills and to comprehend the best features of their own countries.

One of my neighbors in Salamanca, where I now live and write, once went to Bilbao, my native city, and in front of the city hall, a massive, showy, poorly designed building, he stopped and exclaimed, "I wish we had something like this in Salamanca." A native of Salamanca, who has never been near the beautiful old cathedral of this city except to show it to some visitor, said this.

At the end of each year I receive many letters spontaneously from my unknown American readers. The vast majority of them are written in a kindly, amiable tone, urging me to keep on with my work, or, if they do censure me for something, they do it discreetly, honestly, and respectfully. But there are also some, although very few, mostly anonymous, written in a sly, under-handed manner, saying injurious things about me, or more correctly, about my country, its men, and its ways. What nonsense comes from the pens of those artful nitwits. Not long ago I received a letter whose author, after using the term Galician in its derogatory sense—an act which belittles the user more than anyone else—asked me if certain Spanish family names, such as *Iglesias* and *de la Iglesia* originate in foundling asylums, or if they are given to children found in their vicinity.

If I were a spiteful, ill-natured individual, I would have answered that these names and many more had their origin in such asylums, and among them the names of some saints, including the name of San Martín, so justly famous in Argentina.

In my Basque country there has been developing for some time, because of the material prosperity of the region, a most blameworthy feeling of disdain toward those who come there from other parts of Spain to earn a living, working there and increasing the general prosperity of the country. They call them *maquis* and say that they have come there to kill their hunger. That is right, but they also kill the hunger of those that are making sport of them. It is a line of reasoning like that of the factory owner who seriously asserts that he is feeding two or three hundred workers, when it is they who are feeding him and giving him something more in addition.

That poorly disguised hostility toward the immigrant or stranger is a phenomenon that arises when the partner in production becomes a competitor in consumption, when the planting and the reaping are ended and it is time to divide the harvest. It is then that the descend-

ants of the first inhabitants resort to trickery and seek to obtain special privileges as if they had created the fertility of the soil. Is it any merit of mine that my native mountains are filled with rich iron mines?

It is all right for those poor laborers to drag out their lives extracting ore from the depths of the mountains or doing any other work that adds to the wealth of the region; it is all right for them to work. But, as soon as they show any interest in political or social affairs, they are reminded that they came there to work, they are ridiculed for being industrious.

On one occasion an Argentine friend, whose name I had given to an emigrant, wrote me an interesting letter saying, among other things, "Do not encourage ambitious people to come here; we need hands and capital, but not talent. There are too many scholars here in America. In some countries, having nothing else to do, they plan revolutions." I understood immediately what my friend was saying and, by reading between the lines, I understood many things that he did not say. I recalled the bitter tale of a friend and countryman of mine who was a doctor. He suffered a great deal overseas precisely because he was a competent doctor. His learned colleagues outdid themselves to help him . . . suffer.

What have I been led to say by the sight of that family represented by three generations? I can see them yet: the old man striving to use a fork and not his hands as he would have done at home, the youth daintily cutting his meat and peeling his peaches with studied elegance, and between them, the rude man who had made a fortune. I do not know whether he was ashamed to have such a father or such a son or proud of one or the other or of both of them. How well groomed the boy was! How artistic was his head on the outside! I do not know what it was like on the inside but most surely it was furnished with the latest fads from Parisian books.

The mature man, the maker of fortunes, seemed to me to be only the connecting link between his father and his son. And I set about comparing the strong plain old man with the delicate disdainful youth. And, of the two, the old man seemed to be the younger, hardly more than a child. He was probably more than seventy but his was the illusion and the enthusiasm, while the youth seemed to have been born bored and carrying the weight of the greatest disillusionment on his artistic head.

Why was that reunion held in a place as public as the dining room of an inn? Why were those three not before the grandfather's hearth,

in the house where the father was born? Perhaps it was on a mountain top whither one had to climb along a stony path, possibly muddy in spots. The youth's delicate feet were only accustomed to smooth macadam and his shining boots had never been spattered by mud. Surely that house did not have even the inn's primitive conveniences. I imagine that in the opinion of the pretty boy with well combed locks it was not a dwelling of a civilized country. For I am almost certain that I know what concept of civilization that scornful, finical upstart had. It was ridiculous and extremely superficial.

No people can progress far until it has lost that concept of civilization which looks upon it mainly as conveniences and facilities for material well-being. Hygiene is important and comfort is more so; but we must agree that among a people that is hygienically careless, the life of the spirit can be far more carefully guarded than among people that is daily sprinkled with antiseptics. Hygiene itself is indispensable but it should not become a monomania or superstition.

The maxim says: *mens sana in corpore sano,* a sound mind in a sound body, and not *corpus sanum in mente sana;* let us put first things first. Of the two extremes, and they are both abominable, I prefer Job on the dung-heap to a spruce young gentleman whose principle occupation is bathing and perfuming himself.

It is evident that not all the grandsons of our rude, homespun mountain folk feel like the pretty youth I have described; besides, I am glad to believe most of them pride themselves on their ancestry, and if they do not visit their ancestral homes, it is because they cannot and not through laziness. I know all that very well, but I would not like to fail to add my protest against those vain superficial striplings who come here and disdain everything they cannot comprehend, those who judge a people by its manners and who seem to think that the most important agents of civilization are the janitor, the cook, the tailor, and the dancer.

V

PAUL VALERY

PAUL VALÉRY (French, 1871-1945). Poet of philosophical abstractions.
Influenced early by Mallarmé. First works were prose: *Introduction à la
méthode de Léonard de Vinci* and *La Soirée avec Monsieur Teste*. Most
famous poem: *"La Jeune parque." Charmes:* poems on love and death.
Skeptical, disillusioned, he advocated refined discipline of the mind.

NARCISSUS

A Fragment

. . . Perhaps you expected a face that was free from tears,
You calms, you always decked with leaves and flowers,
And haunted depths of the incorruptible,
O nymphs! . . . But yielding to the enchanted slopes
That were my irretrievable roadway to you,
Permit this fair reflection of man's disorder.
Happy your blended forms, you deep and level waters!
I am alone. . . . If the gods, the waves, and the echoes
And so many sighs allow! I am alone!
But still I am he who comes unto himself
When he comes near the banks this growth adorns.

On the peaks the light has halted its pure plunder,
The voice of the fountains turns to talk of dusk,
Calm concord hearkens, wherein I hear hope.
I hear the night grass grow in the holy shadows,
And the perfidious moon now elevates her mirror
Even to the secrets of the dying pool.

1349

And I! My body cast upon these reeds,
I languish, Sapphire, in my mournful beauty!
I must henceforth adore the magic waters
Where I have forgotten the olden smile and the rose.
Let me bewail your pure and fatal glory,
Fountain so softly closed around by me,
Where my eyes draw forth from the lethal azure
Those same dark eyes of their astounded soul!
What loss within oneself so calm a place affords!
The soul, even unto destruction, seeks a god
Demanding of the wave, the lonely wave
That gleams inviting soft advent of swan . . .
Never have thirsty flocks bemired these waters!
Others who have wandered here have found repose,
And in the dark earth a clear, opening tomb;
But it is not calm, alas! that I shall find,
When the opaque delight where the splendor sleeps
Yields to my body the horror of widening leafage
And, driving back the shade and the frightening thickness,
I see! I fall! and come from this tyrant body
Peacefully to share the eternal charms!
There, nude between the arms that spring from the forest,
A tender gleam of daylight doubtfully plays;
And there the glimmer of day becomes a bridegroom,
Pure in the place where the sad water lures me,
Delightful spirit, desirable and cold!
I behold in the water my flesh of moon and the dawn-dew,
Obedient form opposed to my desires!
There are the pure stirrings of my silver arms!
My lingering hands in the adorable gold grow weary
Of seeking the captive whom the leaves entwine,
And I cry to echo the names of the hidden gods!

But how fair his mouth in that mute blasphemy!
O likeness! . . . Yet more perfect than myself,
Immortal ephemeron, clear before my eyes,
Pale limbs of pearl and softly silken hair,
Must the shadow darken us who scarce have loved,
Must the night already part us, O Narcissus,
And press between us the blade that halves a fruit!

1350

What is it?
                    My plaint is baneful? . . .
                                        The mere stir
Of the breath I set upon your lips, my double,
Has coursed a tremor on your limpid wave? . . .
You tremble! But these words I, kneeling, breathe
Are still no more than a hesitant soul between us,
Between that clear brow and my spent memory . . . .
I am so near you I can drink you in,
O countenance? . . . My thirst is a naked slave . . . .

Till this rapt hour I did not know myself,
Nor how to cherish, how attain my soul? . . .
But watching you, dear slave, obey the least
Of the shadows sadly retreating in my heart,
And on my brow a secret fire and storm,
Watching, O marvel! watching my murmurous mouth
Betray . . . snare on the water a flower of fancy,
And mad events that sparkle in the eye! · · · ·
I have found a treasure of impotence and pride!
May no sweet virgin whom the satyr stalks,
None! Swift in flight, deft in unfeeling fall,
No nymph, no maiden, ever lure me on
As you within the waters, my illimitable soul!

THE SYLPH

Seen not nor known
I am the scent shed
Living and dead
In the wind blown

Seen not nor known
Genius or chance?
Hardly seed sown
When the flowers dance!

Nor read nor possessed!
What errors shown
For swift renowns—

Seen not nor known,
The glimpse of a breast
Between two gowns!

LOST WINE

One day I cast into the sea
(But I no longer remember under what skies)
As an offering unto Nonentity
A little wine of a sort I prize.

Who, O liquor, wished you to part?
Perhaps you were an omen I could not divine:
Perhaps concerned with my heart,
Thinking of blood, and pouring wine?
I watched the sea resume,
After a rosy spume,
Its usual transparency. . . .

Lost the wine, drunk the waves!
I saw leaping from sea-caves
Figures of greatest profundity.

VALMIKI

VALMIKI (Indian, *ca.* 4th century B. C.). Legendary author of a poem of
24,000 verses on the exploits of Rama *(Rāmāyana)*. In Hindu literature this
work compares with the Greek *Odyssey*, and exists in several versions.

NÁRAD

Om

To sainted Nárad, prince of those
Whose lore in words of wisdom flows,
Whose constant care and chief delight
Were Scripture and ascetic rite,
The good Válmíki, first and best
Of hermit saints, these words addressed:—

1352

"In all this world, I pray thee, who
Is virtuous, heroic, true?
Firm in his vows, of grateful mind,
To every creature good and kind?
Bounteous, and holy, just, and wise,
Alone most fair to all men's eyes?
Devoid of envy, firm, and sage,
Whose tranquil soul ne'er yields to rage?
Whom, when his warrior wrath is high,
Do Gods embattled fear and fly?
Whose noble might and gentle skill
The triple world can guard from ill?
Who is the best of princes, he
Who loves his people's good to see?
The store of bliss, the living mine
Where brightest joys and virtues shine?
Queen Fortune's best and dearest friend,
Whose steps her choicest gifts attend?
Who may with Sun and Moon compare,
With Indra, Vishnu, Fire, and Air?
Grant, Saint divine, the boon I ask,
For thee, I ween, an easy task,
To whom the power is given to know
If such a man breathe here below."

Then Nárad, clear before whose eye
The present, past, and future lie,
Made ready answer: "Hermit, where
Are graces found so high and rare?
Yet listen, and my tongue shall tell
In whom alone these virtues dwell.
From old Ikshváku's line he came,
Known to the world by Ráma's name:—
With soul subdued, a chief of might,
In Scripture versed, in glory bright.
His steps in virtue's paths are bent,
Obedient, pure, and eloquent.
In each emprise he wins success,
And dying foes his power confess.
Tall and broad-shouldered, strong of limb,
Fortune has set her mark on him.

Graced with a conch-shell's triple line,
His throat displays the auspicious sign.
High destiny is clear impressed
On massive jaw and ample chest.
His mighty shafts he truly aims,
And foemen in the battle tames.
Deep in the muscle, scarcely shown,
Embedded lies his collar-bone.
His lordly steps are firm and free,
His strong arms reach below his knee;
All fairest graces join to deck
His head, his brow, his stately neck,
And limbs in fair proportion set:—
The manliest form e'er fashioned yet.
Graced with each high imperial mark,
His skin is soft and lustrous dark.
Large are his eyes that sweetly shine
With majesty almost divine.
His plighted word he ne'er forgets;
On erring sense a watch he sets.
By nature wise, his teacher's skill
Has trained him to subdue his will.
Good, resolute and pure, and strong,
He guards mankind from scathe and wrong,
And lends his aid, and ne'er in vain,
The cause of justice to maintain.
Well has he studied o'er and o'er
The Vedas and their kindred lore.
Well skilled is he the bow to draw,
Well trained in arts and versed in law;
High-souled and meet for happy fate,
Most tender and compassionate;
The noblest of all lordly givers,
Whom good men follow, as the rivers
Follow the King of Floods, the sea:—
So liberal, so just is he.
The joy of Queen Kausalyá's heart,
In every virtue he has part;
Firm as Himálaya's snowy steep,
Unfathomed like the mighty deep;

The peer of Vishnu's power and might,
And lovely as the Lord of Night;
Patient as Earth, but, roused to ire,
Fierce as the world-destroying fire;
In bounty like the Lord of Gold,
And Justice' self in human mould.
With him, his best and eldest son,
By all his princely virtues won
King Dasaratha willed to share
His kingdom as the Regent Heir.
But when Kaikeyí, youngest queen,
With eyes of envious hate had seen
The solemn pomp and regal state
Prepared the prince to consecrate,
She bade the hapless king bestow
Two gifts he promised long ago,
That Ráma to the woods should flee,
And that her child the heir should be.

By chains of duty firmly tied,
The wretched King perforce complied.
Ráma, to please Kaikeyí went
Obedient forth, to banishment.
Then Lakshman's truth was nobly shown,
Then were his love and courage known,
When for his brother's sake he dared
All perils, and his exile shared.
And Sítá, Ráma's darling wife,
Loved even as he loved his life,
Whom happy marks combined to bless,
A miracle of loveliness,
Of Janak's royal lineage sprung,
Most excellent of women, clung
To her dear lord, like Rohiní
Rejoicing with the Moon to be.
The King and People, sad of mood,
The hero's car awhile pursued.
But when Prince Ráma lighted down
At Sringavera's pleasant town,

Where Gangá's holy waters flow,
He bade his driver turn and go.
Guha, Nishádas' King, he met,
And on the farther bank was set.
Then on from wood to wood they strayed,
O'er many a stream, through constant shade,
As Bharadvája bade them, till
They came to Chitrakúta's hill.
And Ráma there, with Lakshman's aid,
A pleasant little cottage made,
And spent his days with Sítá, dressed
In coat of bark and deerskin vest.
And Chitrakúta grew to be
As bright with those illustrious three
As Meru's sacred peaks that shine
With glory, when the Gods recline
Beneath them: Siva's self between
The Lord of Gold and Beauty's Queen.

The aged King for Ráma pined,
And for the skies the earth resigned.
Bharat, his son, refused to reign,
Though urged by all the twice-born train.
Forth to the woods he fared to meet
His brother, fell before his feet,
And cried "Thy claim all men allow:—
O come, our lord and King be thou."
But Ráma nobly chose to be
Observant of his sire's decree.
He placed his sandals in his hand,
A pledge that he would rule the land:—
And bade his brother turn again.
Then Bharat, finding prayer was vain,
The sandals took and went away;
Nor in Ayodhyá would he stay,
But turned to Nandigráma, where
He ruled the realm with watchful care,
Still longing eagerly to learn
Tidings of Ráma's safe return.

Then lest the people should repeat
Their visit to his calm retreat,
Away from Chitrakúta's hill
Fared Ráma, ever onward till
Beneath the shady trees he stood
Of Dandaká's primeval wood.
Virádha, giant fiend, he slew,
And then Agastya's friendship knew.
Counselled by him he gained the sword
And bow of Indra, heavenly lord:—
A pair of quivers too, that bore
Of arrows an exhaustless store.
While there he dwelt in greenwood shade,
The trembling hermits sought his aid,
And bade him with his sword and bow
Destroy the fiends who worked them woe:—
To come like Indra strong and brave,
A guardian God to help and save.
And Ráma's falchion left its trace
Deep cut on Súrpanakhá's face:—
A hideous giantess who came
Burning for him with lawless flame.
Their sister's cries the giants heard,
And vengeance in each bosom stirred;
The monster of the triple head,
And Dúshan to the contest sped.
But they and myriad fiends beside
Beneath the might of Ráma died.

When Rávan, dreaded warrior, knew
The slaughter of his giant crew—
Rávan, the King, whose name of fear
Earth, hell, and heaven all shook to hear—
He bade the fiend Márícha aid
The vengeful plot his fury laid.
In vain the wise Márícha tried
To turn him from his course aside:—
Not Rávan's self, he said, might hope
With Ráma and his strength to cope.

1357

Impelled by fate and blind with rage
He came to Ráma's hermitage.
There, by Márícha's magic art,
He wiled the princely youths apart,
The vulture slew, and bore away
The wife of Ráma as his prey.
The son of Raghu came and found
Jatáyu slain upon the ground.
He rushed within his leafy cot;
He sought his wife, but found her not.
Then, then the hero's senses failed;
In mad despair he wept and wailed.
Upon the pile that bird he laid,
And still in quest of Sítá strayed.
A hideous giant then he saw,
Kabandha named, a shape of awe.

The monstrous fiend he smote and slew,
And in the flame the body threw;
When straight from out the funeral flame
In lovely form Kabandha came,
And bade him seek in his distress
A wise and holy hermitess.
By counsel of this saintly dame
To Pampá's pleasant flood he came,
And there the steadfast friendship won
Of Hanumán the Wind-God's son.
Counselled by him he told his grief
To great Sugríva, Vánar chief,
Who, knowing all the tale, before
The sacred flame alliance swore.
Sugríva to his new-found friend
Told his own story to the end:—
His hate of Báli for the wrong
And insult he had borne so long.
And Ráma lent a willing ear
And promised to allay his fear.
Sugríva warned him of the might
Of Báli, matchless in the fight,
And, credence for his tale to gain,
Showed the huge fiend by Báli slain.

1358

The prostrate corse of mountain size
Seemed nothing in the hero's eyes;
He lightly kicked it, as it lay,
And cast it twenty leagues away.
To prove his might his arrows through
Seven palms in line, uninjured, flew.
He cleft a mighty hill apart,
And down to hell he hurled his dart.
Then high Sugríva's spirit rose,
Assured of conquest o'er his foes.
With his new champion by his side
To vast Kishkindhá's cave he hied.
Then, summoned by his awful shout,
King Báli came in fury out,
First comforted his trembling wife,
Then sought Sugriva in the strife.
One shaft from Ráma's deadly bow
The monarch in the dust laid low.
Then Ráma bade Sugríva reign
In place of royal Báli slain.
Then speedy envoys hurried forth
Eastward and westward, south and north,
Commanded by the grateful King
Tidings of Ráma's spouse to bring.
Then by Sampáti's counsel led,
Brave Hanumán, who mocked at dread,
Sprang at one wild tremendous leap
Two hundred leagues, across the deep.
To Lanká's town he urged his way,
Where Rávan held his royal sway.
There pensive 'neath Asoka boughs
He found poor Sítá, Ráma's spouse.
He gave the hapless girl a ring,
A token from her lord and King.
A pledge from her fair hand he bore;
Then battered down the garden door.
Five captains of the host he slew,
Seven sons of councillors o'erthrew;
Crushed youthful Aksha on the field,
Then to his captors chose to yield.

Soon from their bonds his limbs were free,
But honoring the high decree
Which Brahmá had pronounced of yore,
He calmly all their insults bore.
The town he burnt with hostile flame,
And spoke again with Ráma's dame,
Then swiftly back to Ráma flew
With tidings of the interview.

Then with Sugríva for his guide,
Came Ráma to the ocean side.
He smote the sea with shafts as bright
As sunbeams in their summer height,
And quick appeared the River's King
Obedient to the summoning.
A bridge was thrown by Nala o'er
The narrow sea from shore to shore.
They crossed to Lanká's golden town,
Where Ráma's hand smote Rávan down.
Vibhíshan there was left to reign
Over his brother's wide domain.
To meet her husband Sítá came;
But Ráma, stung with ire and shame,
With bitter words his wife addressed
Before the crowd that round her pressed.
But Sítá, touched with noble ire,
Gave her fair body to the fire.
Then straight the God of Wind appeared,
And words from heaven her honor cleared.
And Ráma clasped his wife again,
Uninjured, pure from spot and stain,
Obedient to the Lord of Fire
And the high mandate of his sire.
Led by the Lord who rules the sky,
The Gods and heavenly saints drew nigh,
And honored him with worthy meed,
Rejoicing in each glorious deed.
His task achieved, his foe removed,
He triumphed, by the Gods approved.
By grace of Heaven he raised to life
The chieftains slain in mortal strife;

1360

Then in the magic chariot through
The clouds to Nandigráma flew.
Met by his faithful brothers there,
He loosed his votive coil of hair;
Thence fair Ayodhyá's town he gained,
And o'er his father's kingdom reigned.
Disease or famine ne'er oppressed
His happy people, richly blest
With all the joys of ample wealth,
Of sweet content and perfect health.
No widow mourned her well-loved mate,
No sire his son's untimely fate.
They feared not storm or robber's hand,
No fire or flood laid waste the land:
The Golden Age seemed come again
To bless the days of Ráma's reign.
From him the great and glorious King,
Shall many a princely scion spring.
And he shall rule, beloved by men,
Ten thousand years and hundreds ten,
And when his life on earth is past
To Brahmá's world shall go at last.

Whoe'er this noble poem reads
That tells the tale of Ráma's deeds,
Good as the Scriptures, he shall be
From every sin and blemish free.
Whoever reads the saving strain,
With all his kin the heavens shall gain.
Bráhmans who read shall gather hence
The highest praise for eloquence.
The warrior, o'er the land shall reign,
The merchant, luck in trade obtain;
And Súdras, listening, ne'er shall fail
To reap advantage from the tale.

GIOVANNI VERGA

GIOVANNI VERGA (Italian, 1840-1922). One of Italy's leading realistic fiction writers. Immortalized in his novels the peasants of Sicily. Spent a time in the fashionable world of Florence, but returned to Sicily to do best work: *Vita dei Campi* (stories), *Mastro Don Gesualdo* (novel). Author of *Cavalleria Rusticana*, basis of Mascagni's popular opera.

GRAMIGNA'S MISTRESS

THIS is no more than the sketch of a story, but it has the merit of being very short, and of being historical—a human document, as they say nowadays; and as such will perhaps be interesting to those who study the great book of the heart. I will tell it just as I heard it myself among the fields and country lanes; almost with the same simple and picturesque words as are used in the popular narrative.

Some years ago, down in the district of the Simeto, they were hunting a brigand; one Gramigna, if I mistake not,—and that is as ill a name as the weed that bears it,—who had filled the whole countryside with the terror of his renown.

Police, soldiery, and mounted militia had pursued him for two months, and had never succeeded in fastening their claws upon him; he was alone, but he was as good as ten others, and the evil weed threatened to take root.

To make matters worse, it was nearly harvest time, the hay already lay scattered upon the meadows, and the ears of corn bowed their heads, as if nodding consent to the reapers, who were ready with sickle in hand; and yet not a single farmer dared show his nose beyond his garden hedge, for fear of finding Gramigna lying among the furrows, his carbine between his knees, ready to blow out the brains of the first man who should offer to meddle with him.

Hence the complaints were universal. So the prefect summoned before him all these gentlemen of the police, the "*carabinieri*," and the soldiery, and said a few words to them of a kind that made them prick up their ears. The next day there was a general earthquake: patrols, troops, vedettes in every ditch and behind every wall—they drove him before them like a wild beast, through a whole province, by day and by night, on foot, on horseback, and by the telegraph. Still Gramigna slipped through their hands, and answered them with volleys of shot when they trod too closely on his heels. In the fields, in the villages, at the farms, beneath the boughs that overshadow

1362

the tavern doors, in every place of meeting, people talked of nothing but him, Gramigna, and that furious chase, that desperate flight.

The *carabinieri's* horses dropped down from sheer weariness, the worn-out soldiers flung themselves to rest upon the ground in every stable, the patrols fell asleep as they walked. Only he, Gramigna, was never weary, never slept, but still fled on, clambering up precipices, creeping among the corn, crawling on all fours through the thickets of prickly pear, scrambling like a wolf along the dry torrent-beds. The principal topic of conversation among the gossips at the village doors was the consuming thirst that the hunted creature must be enduring, down there on the vast, arid plain, beneath the June sun. The idlers stood agape at the very thought.

Peppa, one of the handsomest girls of Licodia, was at this time about to be married to Master Finu, surnamed the "Tallow-candle," who owned sunny lands and had a bay mule in his stable, and was a fine young fellow, "beautiful as the sun," who could carry the banner of St. Margaret as straight as a pillar, without bending his back. Peppa's mother wept for joy at the good luck that had befallen her daughter, and spent her time in turning over the bride's outfit as it lay in its trunk—"all of white stuff, in fours," like that of a queen, and golden earrings that hung down to the shoulders, and gold rings for all the ten fingers; she had as much gold as St. Margaret herself, and was to be married just about St. Margaret's Day, which fell in June, after the hay was cut. Every evening, "Tallow-candle," as he returned from the fields, would leave his mule at Peppa's door and come in to tell her that the crops were a joy to behold, if only Gramigna did not set fire to them, that the corn-bin behind the bed would not be large enough to hold all the grain that harvest, and that it seemed to him a thousand years till the time should come when he might take his bride home behind him on the bay mule.

But one fine day Peppa said to him, "Let your mule be—for I will not marry you."

Poor "Tallow-candle" stood aghast, and the old woman began tearing her hair when she heard her daughter give up the best match in the village.

"I love Gramigna," the girl said to her, "and I will marry no one else."

"Ah me!" the mother went crying about the house, her gray hair flying in the wind like a witch's—"Ah me! that demon has got even in here and bewitched my daughter!"

1363

"No," Peppa would reply, and her eye was fixed and as hard as steel, "no, he has not been here."

"Where have you seen him, then?"

"I have not seen him, I have heard of him. But listen—I feel him, here, burning me."

The affair made a stir in the village, though they tried to hush it up. The gossips who had envied Peppa the prosperous crops, the bay mule, and the fine young fellow who carried St. Margaret's banner without bending his back, now went about telling all manner of ugly tales—how Gramigna came to visit her by night in the kitchen, and how he had been seen hiding under the bed.

The poor mother had a lamp lighted "for the souls in purgatory," and the priest even came to the house and laid his stole upon Peppa's heart, so as to drive out that devil of a Gramigna, who had taken possession of it. Still she persisted in saying that she did not even know the fellow by sight, but that she saw him at night in her dreams; and she rose every morning with parched lips, almost as though she too had suffered the burning thirst that he must be enduring.

Then the old woman shut her up in the house, that she might no longer hear them talk of Gramigna, and stopped up the very cracks in the door with pictures of the saints. But Peppa listened from behind the sacred images to what the people in the street were saying, and grew red and pale, as though the devil were blowing all the flames of hell across her face. At last she heard them say that Gramigna had been brought to bay, among the prickly-pear thickets of Palagonia.

"He kept up a two hours' fire," they said, "and there is one *carabiniere* killed, and three soldiers and more are wounded. But they sent such a hail of shot upon him, that this time they found a pool of blood where he had stood."

Then Peppa made the sign of the cross at her old woman's bedside, and fled through the window.

Gramigna was among the prickly pears of Palagonia, for they had not been able to dislodge him from such a rabbit-warren. Wounded and blood-stained, pale from a two days' fast, burnt with fever, he stood there, his carbine leveled.

When he saw her coming towards him, fearless and firm, through the thickets of prickly pear, in the dim light of the dawn, he debated for a moment whether he should pull the trigger.

"What do you want?" he asked; "what have you come here for?"

"I have come to be with you," she replied, looking at him fixedly. "Are you Gramigna?"

"Yes, I am Gramigna. If you have come here after those twenty ounces of the reward, you have mistaken your reckoning."

"No, I have come to stay by you," she replied.

"Get you gone," said he; "you cannot stay here, and I will have no one with me. If you have come after money, you have made a mistake, I tell you; I have nothing—see; it is two days since I have even had a bit of bread."

"I cannot go home again now," she said; "the road is full of soldiers."

"Go! What do I care for that? Every one for himself!"

As she was turning away, like a dog driven off by kicks, he called after her:—

"Look here, go and get me a flask of water from the torrent down there; if you want to stay with me, you must risk your skin."

She went without a word; and when Gramigna heard the fusillade, he laughed out, saying to himself, "That was meant for me!"

But when he saw her return in a little while, pale and bleeding, with the flask on her arm, first he tore it from her, and drank so long and deep a draught that his very breath failed him, and then —"Did you escape it?" he asked; "how did you manage?"

"The soldiers were on the opposite bank, and on this side the bushes were thick."

"But they put a bullet into you? Your clothes are stained with blood."

"Yes."

"Where are you wounded?"

"In the shoulder."

"That's no matter—you can still walk."

So he suffered her to stay with him. She followed him, barefooted, all torn and feverish from her wound; she would go hunting after a flask of water or a crust of bread for him, and when she returned empty-handed, amid the volleys of shot, her lover, devoured by hunger and thirst, would beat her. At last, one night when the moon shone brightly through the thickets of prickly pear, Gramigna said, "They are coming," and made her stand with her back against a rock at the bottom of a cleft; then he fled in the opposite direction.

The shots echoed nearer and nearer among the bushes, and the darkness was lighted up by sudden bursts of flame. All at once

1365

Peppa heard a trampling close by, and Gramigna reappeared, dragging himself along, with one leg broken, so that he had to prop himself against the shoots of the prickly pear to reload his carbine.

"It is over," he said; "now they will take me."

And what froze her blood more than all was the glitter in his eye, that made him look like a madman. Then, when he fell like a log upon the dead branches, the soldiers were upon him, all at once.

Next day they dragged him on a cart through the streets of the village, mangled and bleeding. The crowd that pressed round to gaze at him, laughed when they saw how small and pale and ugly he was, like a clown. It was for him that Peppa had left Master Finu, the "Tallow-candle"!

Poor "Tallow-candle" went away and hid himself, as though it were his part to be ashamed.

And Peppa was led along between the soldiers, handcuffed, as if she too had been a thief—she, who had as much gold as St. Margaret.

Her poor mother had to sell all the "white stuff" of the bridal outfit, and the golden earrings, and the rings for the ten fingers, to pay lawyers for her daughter, and get her home again once more, poor, sickly, and shame-faced—ugly, too, now, like Gramigna, and with Gramigna's child upon her bosom. Yet when she was restored to her at the end of the trial, the old woman recited the "Ave Maria" there in the bare and fast-darkening barrack-room, among all the *carabinieri;* it was as though they had given her back a treasure —to her, the poor old woman who had nothing else in the world, and she wept like a fountain for joy.

But Peppa seemed to have no more tears left, and she spoke never a word; nor did the village folk ever see her again, though the two women had to work with their hands for their daily bread. People said that Peppa had learnt her trade, there in the wood, and that she went out thieving by night. In reality, she sat crouching in the corner of the kitchen, like a wild beast, and only left it when her old woman was dead of hard work, and she had to sell the house.

"Do you see now!" the "Tallow-candle" said to her, for he loved her still, "I could crush your head between two stones for all the harm you have done to yourself and others."

"It is true," Peppa answered, "I know it. It was the will of God."

When the house and her few remaining goods and chattels were sold, she left the village by night, as she had come—without turning back to give one look at the roof beneath which she had slept so long—and went away with her boy to do the will of God in the city, near the prison where Gramigna was shut up.

She could only see the dark shutters upon the great, silent face of the building, and when she stood looking at it, trying to make out where he might be, the sentries drove her away. At last they told her that for some time back he had no longer been there—that they had taken him away over the sea, handcuffed, and with his wallet about his neck.

She said nothing. She never left the place, because she did not know where to go, and no one was expecting her anywhere. She made shift to live, doing jobs for the soldiers and the jailers, as if she herself were a part of that great, dark silent building; and for the *carabinieri*, who had taken Gramigna from her, there among the prickly-pear thickets, and had broken his leg with gun-shots, she felt a sort of respectful tenderness—an animal admiration for strength.

On holidays, when she saw them with their plumes and their glittering epaulettes, stiff and straight in their gala uniforms, she devoured them with her eyes; and she was always about the barracks, sweeping out the halls and polishing the boots, so that they nick-named her "the dust-clout of the *carabinieri*."

Only when, at nightfall, she saw them load their guns and go out, two by two, with their trousers turned up, and revolvers slung across their chests, or when they mounted their horses, under the great lantern that gleamed upon the muzzles of the carbines, and she heard the trampling of the horses' hoofs and the clink of the scabbards die away in the darkness, then she would turn pale and shiver as she closed the stable doors. And when her little one played with the rest in the great square before the prison running in and out among the soldiers' legs, and the other children would call after him, "The son of Gramigna!—the son of Gramigna!" then she would fly into a rage and pursue them, pelting them with stones.

EMILE VERHAEREN

ÉMILE VERHAEREN (Belgian, 1855-1916). Poet Laureate of Belgium. Apostle of industrial progress. Frequent visitor in England. Early work realistic and violent—later poetry symbolic free verse. Has been compared with Whitman. Major works: *Les Rythmes Souverains, Les Flamandes, Les Heures Claires.*

THE MILL

Slowly in the depths of the night the windmill turns.
Under a somber, melancholy sky
It turns and turns, and its wind-burnt canvas moans
A sad and worn and heavy lullaby.

Since the dawn its arms, like arms in supplication,
Have stretched out and have fallen, and they will
Fall on and on across the darkened air
And weary nature slumbering now and still.

A cheerless winter night broods over the hamlet,
The weary clouds are restless overhead;
And along the thickets that gather up their shadows,
The pathways point a horizon that is dead.

Under a rim of earth, a few beechen shanties
Wretchedly huddle in a miserable round;
A brass lamp that is hanging from the ceiling
Speckles with light the window and the ground.

And across the wide field, and the slumbering void
They hold—puny hovels—with the blinking eyes
Of their broken panes with the ragged curtain,
The old mill that turns and, weary, turns, and dies.

1368

THE POOR

There are poor souls
Where tears are starred
And pale as stones
In a graveyard.

There are poor backs
Weighed down with ills
Like the roofs of hovels
In the hills.

There are poor hands
Like leaves the wind wore,
Like yellow, dying leaves
By the door.

There are poor eyes
Humble and kind and warm,
Sadder than the eyes of beasts
Beneath the storm.

There are poor folk
With movements forbearing and worn,
On whom misery battens—
Wherever men are born.

PIOUS EVENINGS

To farthest off the sun at setting sheds
The haircloth of its silence and its calm;
On Byzantine backgrounds carefully it spreads
All things as clearly as a quiet psalm.

The downpour slashed the air with blades of hail
And now the heavens shine like a sanctuary;
It is the hour when the western fires fail,
When the day's gold and the twilight's silver vary.

Nothing stirs on the horizon, unless it be
An infinite giant march of oaks in the gloom,
Stretching beyond the farms one just can see,
Along the fallow fields and the corners of broom.

1369

The trees move on—as mortuary friars
Pass by, and twilight weighs upon their bands,
As the long troop of penitents aspires
On pilgrimage to ancient holy lands.

And as the road leads upward to the sky,
Where the setting sun far peony petals strews,
To see those long bare trees, to see those monks pass by,
You'd say they were setting out tonight, by twos,

Toward their God who fills the heavens with sprinkled gold;
And the stars, gleaming high ahead of them,
Are each the light of a candle that they hold
Of which we cannot see the towering stem.

PAUL VERLAINE

PAUL VERLAINE (French, 1844-1896). Chief figure in the French Symbolist Movement. Poetic descendant of Baudelaire. Began career as middle-class clerk. Left wife to go vagabonding with Rimbaud. Died in misery and poverty. Major volumes: *Fêtes galantes, Romances sans paroles, La Bonne chanson.* His life and legend almost as influential as his actual work.

MYSTIC TWILIGHT

Memory with the twilight
Flushes and trembles on the horizon
Of hope that soars with a high light,
Recoils, collects, and flies on
Like a mysterious valley up
Which many a flaunting flower—
Tulip, lily, buttercup—
Thrusts forth in a bower
Where the poison-perfume stilly—
Buttercup, tulip, and lily—
In a ghostly, weird, and wry light
With my reason, soul and senses strewn,
Blends in an unbounded swoon
Memory with the twilight.

STREETS

Let us dance!

Surpassingly I loved her eyes,
Clearer than the starry skies;
I loved their swift surprise.

Let us dance!

She had such wild ways, truly
A sweetheart most unruly;
And she took life so coolly.

Let us dance!

But beyond these memories start
The kisses her flower-lips dart. . . .
Since she is dead to my heart.

Let us dance!

I recall, still I recall
Pensive hours at evenfall:
And they are best of all.
Let us dance!

MY FAMILIAR DREAM

I often have the queer and radiant dream
Of an unknown woman I love, and who loves me,
Who never will be wholly as before, nor seem
Quite other; who loves, and probes my mystery.

She understands me; my translucent heart—
Only for her, alas!—quite plain appears,
Only for her; and the dampness that will start
On my brow, she alone can dry it with her tears.

Is she blonde, brunette, or red-haired? I do not know.
Her name? I remember it is resonant and sweet
As those of lovers life has beaten low.

1371

Her look is as the look in a statue's head,
And for her voice, where calm and sorrow meet,
She has the tone of loved ones who are dead.

WOMAN AND CAT

She was playing with her cat;
They were enraptured who saw
The white hand and the white paw
In their evening frolic-pat.

It hid—O innocent gazer!—
Under black silken veils
Murderous agate nails
Clear and sharp as a razor.

She too was compact of sweets,
Withholding her steely claws;
But the devil's eye has no beam . . .

And in her boudoir, when the dark meets
Her airy laughter, and withdraws,—
Four points of phosphorus gleam.

THE SONG OF THE INGÉNUES

We are the ingénues—
Blue eyes, long hair, sweet looks—
Who live with rainbow dews
In seldom read books.

We set forth intertwined,
And the day no purer seems
Than the depths of our mind
And our azure dreams;

And we romp through the fields,
Where our happy calls rise
Till day to dusk yields—
Chasing butterflies.

And a shepherdess' bonnet
Screens our face from strong light,
And our gown—lace upon it—
Is immaculate white.

Cavaliers of romances
Who capture the skies
Shower their glances,
Greetings, and sighs,

But in vain their romantic
Stir, their fine flirts—
Before the gigantic
Guardian, our skirts.

And our free laughter falls
At the imagination
Of these cling-to-the-walls—
Though at times a sensation

Stirs the frock that covers
Our heart that preens
To know we're the future lovers
Of libertines.

YOUNGLINGS

High heels in a struggle with a long skirt,
As the wind roused or as the land lay,
Twinkled a glimpse above, if we were alert—
Intercepted!—and we loved that gulls' play.

Sometimes the sting of an insect bolder
Than we, sought a fair neck to scrutinize,
And there was the sudden lightning of a shoulder
And that feast overwhelmed our young fools' eyes.

Twilight came, an uncertain autumnal glow:
The fair ones, clinging dreamily to our arms,
Spoke words that were so specious and so low
That our souls forever hold their eager qualms.

1373

CAVITRI

Mahabharatta

To save her husband, Cavitri's deep vow bids
Her stand, while three days and three nights unroll,
Erect, nor move limbs, body, nor eyelids—
Rigid, Vyaca tells us, as a pole.

Neither your cruel rays, Curya, nor the swoon
Chandra spreads over the summits of the moon
Can weaken, as your mighty spheres revolve,
That glorious woman's flesh nor her resolve. . . .

Should forgetfulness with black, bleak treachery
Or lean-faced envy toward me incline,
Impassive as Cavitri may I be,
And in my soul as lofty a design.

WHAT HAVE YOU DONE?

The sky, above the roof,
   Is so blue and so calm!
The tree above the roof
   Cradles its palm.

The bell, in the sky we watch,
   Quietly rings;
A bird on the tree we watch,
   Mournfully sings.

Lord, O Lord, life is here
   Gently fluttering down.
That peaceful stir we hear
   Comes from the town.

—What have you done, you there
   Endlessly weeping; in sooth,
What have you done, you there,
   With your youth?

1374

The heavy thrall
Of the sobbing call
Of the fall
Weighs, nor departs,
Like my heart's
Pall.

Overcome
And dumb,
As the hours creep
I see the haze
Of olden days
And weep.

And I go away
The wind's prey,
In barren, brief
Whirl hither and yon
Like a wan
Dead leaf.

JULES VERNE

JULES VERNE (French, 1828-1905). The father of science fiction. Began career as opera librettist till he discovered gift for imagining adventures of the future. His works are still read with entertainment, especially *Twenty Thousand Leagues Under the Sea* and *Around the World in Eighty Days*.

THE BOTTOM OF THE SEA

AND now, how can I retrace the impression left upon me by that walk under the waters? Words are impotent to relate such wonders! Captain Nemo walked in front, his companions followed some steps behind. Conseil and I remained near each other, as if an exchange of words had been possible through our metallic cases. I no longer felt the weight of my clothing, or my shoes, of my reservoir of air,

or of my thick helmet, in the midst of which my head rattled like an almond in its shell.

The light, which lit the soil thirty feet below the surface of the ocean, astonished me by its power. The solar rays shone through the watery mass easily and dissipated all color, and I clearly distinguished objects at a distance of a hundred and fifty yards. Beyond that the tints darkened into fine gradations of ultra-marine, and faded into vague obscurity. Truly this water which surrounded me was but another air denser than the terrestrial atmosphere, but almost as transparent. Above me was the calm surface of the sea. We were walking on fine, even sand, not wrinkled, as on a flat shore, which retains the impression of the billows. This dazzling carpet, really a reflector, repelled the rays of the sun with wonderful intensity, which accounted for the vibration which penetrated every atom of liquid. Shall I be believed when I say that, at the depth of thirty feet, I could see as if I was in broad daylight?

For a quarter of an hour I trod on this sand sown with the impalpable dust of shells. The hull of the "Nautilus," resembling a long shoal, disappeared by degrees; but its lantern, when darkness should overtake us in the waters, would help to guide us on board by its distinct rays. Soon forms of objects outlined in the distance were discernible. I recognized magnificent rocks, hung with a tapestry of zoophytes of the most beautiful kind, and I was at first struck by the peculiar effect of this medium.

It was then ten in the morning, the rays of the sun struck the surface of the waves at rather an oblique angle, and at the touch of their light, decomposed by refraction as through a prism, flowers, rocks, plants, shells, and polypi were shaded at the edges by the seven solar colors. It was marvelous, a feast for the eyes, this complication of colored tints, a perfect kaleidoscope of green, yellow, orange, violet, indigo, and blue; in one word, the whole palette of an enthusiastic colorist! Why could I not communicate to Conseil the lively sensations which were mounting to my brain, and rival him in expressions of admiration? For aught I knew, Captain Nemo and his companion might be able to exchange thoughts by means of signs previously agreed upon. So for want of better, I talked to myself; I declaimed in the copper box which covered my head, thereby expending more air in vain words than was, perhaps, expedient.

Various kinds of isis, clusters of pure tuft-coral, prickly fungi, and anemones, formed a brilliant garden of flowers, enameled with

porplutæ, decked with their collarettes of blue tentacles, sea-stars studding the sandy bottom, together with asterophytons like fine lace embroidered by the hands of naiads; whose festoons were waved by the gentle undulations caused by our walk. It was a real grief to me to crush under my feet the brilliant specimens of molluscs which strewed the ground by thousands, of hammerheads, donaciæ (veritable bounding shells), of staircases, and red helmet-shells, angel-wings, and many others produced by this inexhaustible ocean. But we were bound to walk, so we went on, whilst above our heads waved shoals of physalides, leaving their tentacles to float in their train, medusæ whose umbrellas of opal or rose-pink, escaloped with a band of blue, sheltered us from the rays of the sun and fiery pelagiæ which, in the darkness, would have strewn our path with phosphorescent light.

All these wonders I saw in the space of a quarter of a mile, scarcely stopping, and following Captain Nemo, who beckoned me on by signs. Soon the nature of the soil changed; to the sandy plain succeeded an extent of slimy mud, which the Americans call "ooze," composed of equal parts of silicious and calcareous shells. We then traveled over a plain of sea-weed of wild and luxuriant vegetation. This sward was of close texture, and soft to the feet, and rivalled the softest carpet woven by the hand of man. But whilst verdure was spread at our feet, it did not abandon our heads. A light network of marine plants, of that inexhaustible family of sea-weeds of which more than two thousand kinds are known, grew on the surface of the water. I saw long ribbons of fucus floating, some globular, others tuberous, laurenciæ and cladostephi of most delicate foliage, and some rhodomeniæ palmatæ, resembling the fan of a cactus. I noticed that the green plants kept nearer the top of the sea whilst the red were at a greater depth, leaving to the black or brown hydrophytes the care of forming gardens and parterres in the remote beds of the ocean.

We had quitted the "Nautilus" about an hour and a half. It was near noon; I knew by the perpendicularity of the sun's rays, which were no longer refracted. The magical colors disappeared by degrees, and the shades of emerald and sapphire were effaced. We walked with a regular step, which rang upon the ground with astonishing intensity; the slightest noise was transmitted with a quickness to which the ear is unaccustomed on the earth; indeed, water is a better conductor of sound than air, in the ratio of four to one. At this period the earth sloped downward; the light took a uniform

tint. We were at a depth of a hundred and five yards and twenty inches, undergoing a pressure of six atmospheres.

At this depth I could still see the rays of the sun, though feebly; to their intense brilliancy had succeeded a reddish twilight, the lowest state between day and night; and we could still see well enough.

FRANCOIS VILLON

FRANÇOIS VILLON (French, *ca.* 1431-1465?). One of the brightest stars of medieval France. Wrecked by debauchery, jail and torture, he was sentenced to death, then banished. His total work: *Le Petit Testament, Le Grand Testament* and some 40 shorter poems. He crystallized vivid perceptions of life's pleasures and ironies.

BALLAD OF OLD-TIME LADIES

Tell me where, in what land of shade,
  Bides fair Flora of Rome, and where
Are Thais and Archipiade,
  Cousins-german of beauty rare,
  And Echo, more than mortal fair,
That, when one calls by river-flow
  Or marish, answers out of the air?
But what is become of last year's snow?

Where did the learn'd Helosa vade,
  For whose sake Abelard might not spare
(Such dole for love on him was laid)
  Manhood to lose and a cowl to wear?
  And where is the queen who willed whilere
That Buridan, tied in a sack, should go
  Floating down Seine from the turret-stair?
But what is become of last year's snow?

Blanche, too, the lily-white queen, that made
  Sweet music as if she a siren were;
Broad-foot Bertha; and Joan the maid,

The good Lorrainer, the English bare
Captive to Rouen and burned her there;
Beatrix, Eremburge, Alys,—lo!
    Where are they, Virgin debonair?
    But what is become of last year's snow?

ENVOI

Prince, you may question how they fare
This week, or liefer this year, I trow:
Still shall the answer this burden bear,
    But what is become of last year's snow?

BALLAD OF OLD-TIME LORDS

Where is Calixtus, third of the name,
    That died in the purple whiles ago,
Four years since he to the tiar came?
    And the King of Aragon, Alfonso?
    The Duke of Bourbon, sweet of show,
And the Duke Arthur of Brittaine?
    And Charles the Seventh, the Good? Heigho!
But where is the doughty Charlemaine?

Likewise the King of Scots, whose shame
    Was the half of his face (or folks say so),
Vermeil as amethyst held to the flame,
    From chin to forehead all of a glow?
    The King of Cyprus, of friend and foe
Renowned; and the gentle King of Spain,
    Whose name, God 'ield me, I do not know?
But where is the doughty Charlemaine?

Of many more might I ask the same,
    Who are but dust that the breezes blow;
But I desist, for none may claim
    To stand against Death, that lays all low,
    Yet one more question before I go:
Where is Lancelot, King of Behaine?
    And where are his valiant ancestors, trow?
But where is the doughty Charlemaine?

1379

ENVOI

Where is Du Guesclin, the Breton prow?
    Where Auvergne's Dauphin, and where again
The late good duke of Alençon? Lo!
    But where is the doughty Charlemaine?

VILLON'S EPITAPH

The following is the epitaph, in ballad form, that Villon made for himself and his companions, expecting no better than to be hanged in their company.

Brothers, that after us on life remain,
    Harden your hearts against us not as stone;
For, if to pity us poor wights you're fain,
    God shall the rather grant you benison.
    You see us six, the gibbet here upon:
As for the flesh that we too well have fed,
'Tis all devoured and rotted, shred by shred.
    Let none make merry of our piteous case,
Whose crumbling bones the life long since hath fled:
    The rather pray, God grant us of His grace!

Yea, we conjure you, look not with disdain,
    Brothers, on us, though we to death were done
By justice. Well, you know the saving grain
    Of sense springs not in every mother's son:
    Commend us, therefore, now we're dead and gone,
To Christ, the Son of Mary's maidenhead,
That He leave not His grace on us to shed
    And save us from the nether torture-place.
Let no one harry us: forsooth we're sped:
    The rather pray, God grant us of His grace!

We are whiles scoured and sodden of the rain
    And whiles burnt up and blackened of the sun:
Corbies and pyets have our eyes outa'en
    And plucked our beard and hair out, one by one.
    Whether by night or day; rest have we none:

1380

Now here, now there, as the wind shifts its stead,
We swing and creak and rattle overhead,
  No thimble dinted like our bird-pecked face.
Brothers, have heed and shun the life we led:
  The rather pray, God grant us of his grace!

ENVOI

Prince Jesus, over all empoweréd,
Let us not fall into the Place of Dread,
  But all our reckoning with the Fiend efface.
Folk, mock us not that are forspent and dead:
  The rather pray, God grant us of His grace!

VIRGIL

VIRGIL (Latin, 70-19 B.C.). Didactic poet, heavily imitative of the Greeks. The *Aeneid*, glorifying the birth of Rome, derives from Homer's epics, but remains most imposing work of Latin literature. His patriotism manifest in the *Georgics*, his love of the rural in the early *Eclogues*.

ECLOGUE IV: "THE MESSIAH"

Sicilian Muse, begin a loftier strain!
Tho' lowly shrubs, and trees that shade the plain,
Delight not all; Sicilian Muse, prepare
To make the vocal woods deserve a consul's care.
The last great age, foretold by sacred rhymes,
Renews its finished course: Saturnian times
Roll round again; and mighty years, begun
From their first orb, in radiant circles run.
The base degenerate iron offspring ends;
A golden progeny from heaven descends.
O chaste Lucina, speed the mother's pains,
And haste the glorious birth! thy own Apollo reigns!
The lovely boy, with his auspicious face,
Shall Pallio's consulship and triumph grace;
Majestic months set out with him to their appointed race.

The father banished virtue shall restore,
And crimes shall threat the guilty world no more.
The son shall lead the life of gods, and be
By gods and heroes seen, and gods and heroes see.
The jarring nations he in peace shall bind,
And with paternal virtues rule mankind.
Unbidden Earth shall wreathing ivy bring,
And fragrant herbs (the promises of spring),
As her first offerings to her infant king.
The goats with strutting dugs shall homeward speed,
And lowing herds secure from lions feed.
His cradle shall with rising flowers be crowned:
The serpent's brood shall die; the sacred ground
Shall weeds and poisonous plants refuse to bear;
Each common bush shall Syrian roses wear.
But when heroic verse his youth shall raise,
And form it to hereditary praise,
Unlabored harvests shall the fields adorn,
And clustered grapes shall blush on every thorn;
The knotted oaks shall showers of honey weep,
And thro' the matted grass the liquid gold shall creep.
Yet of old fraud some footsteps shall remain:
The merchant still shall plow the deep for gain;
Great cities shall with walls be compassed round,
And sharpened shares shall vex the fruitful ground;
Another Tiphys shall new seas explore;
Another Argo land the chiefs upon the Iberian shore;
Another Helen other wars create,
And great Achilles urge the Trojan fate.
But when to ripened manhood he shall grow,
The greedy sailor shall the seas forego;
No keel shall cut the waves for foreign ware,
For every soil shall every product bear.
The laboring hind his oxen shall disjoin;
No plow shall hurt the glebe, no pruning hook the vine;
Nor wool shall in dissembled colors shine.
But the luxurious father of the fold,
With native purple, or unborrowed gold,
Beneath his pompous fleece shall proudly sweat;
And under Tyrian robes the lamb shall bleat.

The Fates, when they this happy web have spun,
Shall bless the sacred clew, and bid it smoothly run.
Mature in years, to ready honors move,
O of celestial seed! O foster son of Jove!
See, laboring Nature calls thee to sustain
The nodding frame of heaven, and earth, and main!
See to their base restored, earth, seas, and air;
And joyful ages, from behind, in crowding ranks appear.
To sing thy praise, would Heaven my breath prolong,
Infusing spirits worthy such a song,
Not Thracian Orpheus should transcend my lays,
Nor Linus crowned with never-fading bays;
Tho' each his heavenly parent should inspire;
The Muse instruct the voice, and Phœbus tune the lyre.
Should Pan contend in verse, and thou my theme,
Arcadian judges should their god condemn.
Begin, auspicious boy, to cast about
Thy infant eyes, and, with a smile, thy mother single out:
Thy mother well deserves that short delight,
The nauseous qualms of ten long months and travel to requite.
Then smile: the frowning infant's doom is read;
No god shall crown the board, nor goddess bless the bed.

WALTHER VON DER VOGELWEIDE

WALTHER VON DER VOGELWEIDE (Austrian, *ca.* 1170-1230). Didactic
wandering court singer of Middle Ages. His accomplishments include political,
religious and love songs. Championed German independence of papal claims,
though his political allegiance shifted with his patrons, as was custom of
the times.

MOURNINGS

To me is barred the door of joy and ease,
There stand I as an orphan, lone, forlorn,
And nothing boots me that I frequent knock.
Strange that on every hand the show'r should fall,

And not one cheering drop should reach to me!
On all around the gen'rous Austrian's gifts,
Gladd'ning the land, like genial rain descend:
A fair and gay adorned mead is he,
Whereon are gathered of the sweetest flowers:
Would that his rich and ever gen'rous hand
Might stoop to pluck one little leaf for me,
So might I fitly praise a scene so fair!

Fain (could it be) would I a home obtain,
And warm me by a hearth-side of my own.
Then, then, I'd sing about the sweet birds' strain,
And fields and flowers, as I have whilome done;
And paint in song the lily and the rose
That dwell upon *her* cheek who smiles on me.
But lone I stray—no home its comfort shows:
Ah, luckless man! still doomed a *guest* to be!

A mournful one am I, above whose head
A day of perfect bliss hath never past;
Whatever joys my soul have ravished,
Soon was the radiance of those joys o'ercast.
And none can show me that substantial pleasure
Which will not pass away like bloom from flowers;
Therefore, no more my heart such joys shall treasure,
Nor pine for fading sweets and fleeting hours.

Ah! where are hours departed fled?
    Is life a dream, or true indeed?
Did all my heart hath fashioned
    From fancy's visitings proceed?
Yes! I have slept; and now unknown
    To me the things best known before:
The land, the people, once mine own,
    Where are they?—they are here no more:
My boyhood's friends, all aged, worn,
    Despoiled the woods, the fields, of home,
Only the stream flows on forlorn;
    (Alas! that e'er such change should come!)

And he who knew me once so well
　　Salutes me now as one estranged:
The very earth to me can tell
　　Of naught but things perverted, changed:
And when I muse on other days,
　　That passed me as the dashing oars
The surface of the ocean raise,
　　Ceaseless my heart its fate deplores.

MAY AND HIS LADY

When from the sod the flow'rets spring,
　　And smile to meet the sun's bright ray,
When birds their sweetest carols sing
　　In all the morning pride of May,
What lovelier than the prospect there?
Can earth boast anything more fair?
To me it seems an almost heaven,
So beauteous to my eyes that vision bright is given.

But when a lady, chaste and fair,
　　Noble, and clad in rich attire,
Walks through the throng with gracious air,
　　As sun that bids the stars retire,—
Then, where are all thy boastings, May?
What hast thou beautiful and gay
Compared with that supreme delight?
We leave thy loveliest flowers, and watch that lady bright.

Wouldst thou believe me,—come and place
　　Before thee all this pride of May;
Then look but on my lady's face,
　　And, which is best and brightest? say:
For me, how soon (if choice were mine)
This would I take, and that resign!
And say, "Though sweet thy beauties, May!
I'd rather forfeit all than lose my lady gay."

1385

"Lady," I said, "this garland wear!
    For thou wilt wear it gracefully:
And on thy brow 'twill sit so fair,
    And thou wilt dance so light and free;
Had I a thousand gems, on thee,
    Fair one! their brilliant light should shine:
Would'st thou such gift accept from me,—
    Oh, doubt me not,—it should be thine.

"Lady, so beautiful thou art,
    That I on thee the wreath bestow,
'Tis the best gift I can impart;
    But whiter, rosier flow'rs, I know,
Upon the distant plain they're springing,
    Where beauteously their heads they rear,
And birds their sweetest songs are singing:
    Come! let us go and pluck them there."

She took the beauteous wreath I chose,
    And like a child at praises glowing,
Her cheeks blushed crimson as the rose,
    When by the snow-white lily growing:
But all from those bright eyes eclipse
    Received; and then, my toil to pay,
Kind, precious words fell from her lips:
    What more than this I shall not say.

W

WANG WEI

WANG WEI (Chinese, *ca.* 700-760). Leading Sung landscape painter. Also devout Buddhist as well as successful politician. Su Shih said of him: "There is painting in his poetry and poetry in his painting." Noted for his four-line *chueh-chu* poems.

BEST HAPPINESS OF ALL

I am old and I am bored. I was never very wise and my mind has not ever walked much further than my feet. Only my forest, my forest . . . I go back and back to wander there.

The blue fingers of the moon play on my old lute there. The wind scatters the clouds there and comes down to flutter my robe.

You ask me what is the best happiness of all? In the forest it is sweet to hear a girl singing on the path, after she has stopped to ask her way, and thanked you with a smile.

THE PEACH GARDEN

The fisherman's boat is carried away along the water hugging
     the spring hills;
By two banks the peach blossom marks the limits of an ancient
     ferry;
The fisherman sits gazing at the pink blossoms regardless of the
     distance,
Drifting to the end of a green mountain stream, careless of where
     he goes.

1387

A narrow passage in the mountains leads by secret detours to the beginning of an open bay,

There the hills open out on a vast expanse of flat land:

He approaches it and it is a village of 1000 homes scattered amid flowers and bamboo.

The stranger begins to distinguish the speech of the Han dynasty.

Those who dwelt there had not changed the fashion of their clothes since the days of Ch'in.

These village dwellers lived together at the source of the Wu Ling River;

They had fled away from the world to live the lives of peasants.

The moon is bright underneath the pines,

Shining on their quiet windows;

The sun rises; dogs bark and chickens crow.

The inhabitants are startled to hear a man has come from the world of men,

And vie with each other in hospitality.

They compete to invite him into their houses and ask him whence he has come.

When morning comes they sweep away the fallen flowers and open the village gates.

When night falls fishermen and woodcutters come home by way of the stream.

Once upon a time these people, seeking a place of refuge, left their fellow men.

They sought to obtain immortality and they did not go back.

In among the ravines and gorges what could they know of the affairs of the world?

All they could see of the world were distant clouds and hills.

Their visitor did not suspect this was a holy place, unknown to mortal men;

His earthly heart had not extinguished earthly desires and he thought of his native home.

Once out of the cave he does not mind that he is separated from it by hills and water.

(When once again) he leaves his family to go on the same long journey,

He says to himself, I have been there before, I cannot miss the way.

How should he know that the mountains and ravines had all changed?

He can only remember that on the former occasion he plunged deep into the green hills

Where mountain rivulets meandered to and fro, leading him to
 misty woods.
(Again) the spring is here and everywhere peach flowers stain
 the water,
But he cannot trace the way to the land of immortality.
Where shall he hunt for it now?

ON A DARK AUTUMN IN A HILL HUT

On the empty hill new rain has fallen;
Out of the dusk comes the autumn.
The bright moon shines forth between the pines,
Above the rocks flows the clear stream,
Babel in the bamboos proclaims the washing girls are returning
 home,
The lotus swing beneath the fisherman's boat,
The fragrance of spring sighs and expires,
How can we detain it before it goes?

JAKOB WASSERMANN

JAKOB WASSERMANN (German, 1873-1934). Problem novelist, whose complex plots and unusual characters gave his stories universal appeal. A wanderer
in his youth, finally settled in Austria. Not identified with any literary school.
His most successful novel: *The World's Illusion*. Others: *The Maurizius Case,
Doctor Kerkhoven*.

THE BEAST

IN one of the former capitals of central Germany great labour riots,
which the citizens still recall with horror, broke out in the wake
of the revolution. Thousands of striking labourers gathered in mobs
and marched, on that misty February morning, towards the busy
streets of the inner city. The jeering rabble, usually idle all the
time, joined them, and the deploying police was soon no longer
able to cope with the threatening throng. The iron shutters rattled
down over the displays in the shop-windows; cafés and restaurants
were locked in panicky haste; house doors were slammed to, and
curious and terrified faces appeared at the windows when the wild
shouting and whistling of the approaching masses became audible.

These broke their way like an unstemmed flood; stones were hurled at the houses and smashed the windows. Here and there a shot was fired. The constabulary force saw itself reduced to take measures of defense and prepared to resist the mob with sabres and clubs. Turmoil and bitterness grew with each passing moment. The shouts and yells sounded more and more horrible. Bare arms and grimly threatening fists were stretched forth; eyes burned with rapacious and vindictive hatred. Women goaded on the men; ragged children filled the air with ear-splitting screams; and the slightest provocation, perhaps an irritating word, and murder and plundering would have been inevitable.

At that moment, there drove across a public square which the most advanced of the throng had just reached, a rather huge wagon resembling a furniture van, but which instead of side-walls had loose brown canvas hangings, and these showed the coat-of-arms of the royal family which had till recently ruled over the country. The sight of the hated emblems whipped the anger of the rioters into fury. In an instant the wagon was surrounded; the efforts of the police to break through the human ring were futile. The driver had pulled up the two horses, which, on being reined in so abruptly, trembled violently. A man jumped from the running-board at the rear of the wagon, unslung a rifle from his shoulder and cocked the trigger. This was the signal for the attack. A well-aimed blow knocked him down; thirty or forty arms reached for the cloth decorated with the escutcheon. The coachman's vehement, threatening gesticulation remained unnoticed; a word which he hurled at them was drowned in the turmoil and the protecting cover fell away in shreds from the frame-work. No sooner had this happened, when all, even the boldest of them, were seized with the utmost horror. The whistling, screaming, howling subsided as if by command, and they who beheld the sight, subdued by their horror-stricken silence those in the rear who, only dimly conscious of something ominous, stared with frightened, reluctant glances at the necks in front of them.

On the wagon was a Nubian lion from the royal zoological gardens. Owing to the high cost of feeding and maintaining him and also because of a certain aversion against such playthings of their erstwhile lords, the new government had decided to sell the beast to a foreign country. And thus, on that very morning the lion had been sent to the railroad station to be forwarded to his new destination.

1390

As the canvas-wall slipped down from the frame, the lion roused himself and then surveyed the thousands of people, so steadily, with an expression of awe-inspiring majesty, until no sound could be heard from them, not a breath was audible. In his flashing eyes was reflected the picture of an alien world. But what was the nature of that world out there? A world as hard and cold as stone, a world with no heaven or horizon, one of mysterious sounds and offensive odours. Did he have an inkling of the wild passions which burst forth from despair and misery, he, who knew neither despair nor misery, and of passions only the elemental, natural ones of his superior kind? Did he actually take in those disturbed, ugly faces before him, or was it only a partial aspect or some impression of a detail that reached him: grinning teeth, distorted forehead, protruding chin; the violent wrath in the glance, the soulless glance of Megæra, the sullen sneer of the emaciated?

But those out there felt, with almost religious awe, something entirely unknown to him. In the dirty holes where they lived and brooded their evil; where their sick ones were lying and their children were born, and where they gave way to gloomy thoughts over the injustice which was their heritage of an evil order. On all their ways and journeys and in all the dreams of their servile imaginations they never had a vision which reminded them so much of what lay beyond their world, of the greatness and might of Nature. An undefinable horror took possession of their gloom-enveloped souls. They trembled, their muscles became limp, and they bowed their heads and cast down their eyes; their closely knitted ranks broke and gaps opened here and there. This enabled the policemen to arrest several dangerous ringleaders, and for the time being the rebellion was nipped in the bud.

FRANZ WERFEL

FRANZ WERFEL (Austrian, 1890-1945). Novelist, playwright and poet, who found success in America where he fled from Nazi Germany. His main theme: humanity and divine providence. His widely popular novels include: *Verdi, The Forty Days of Musa Dagh* and *The Song of Bernadette*. Play: *Jacobowsky and the Colonel*. Admired in Germany for his early lyric poetry.

THEOLOGOUMENA

WHAT argument is there against the notion that man is the center of creation? Are there any more complex and more differentiated orgnisms than he? The stars, for example?

I turned to a modern astronomer for an answer to this question. He informed me that the stars are suns similar to our own sun, many of them thousands of times larger and many of them thousands of times smaller. These tremendous, white-hot, gaseous spheres, he told me, are the only form in which matter occurs in that indescribable void that we call the universe. Though astro-physics determines the weight of the stars and their temperatures, the nature of sidereal matter has nothing to do with what we on earth call matter, least of all with the highly organized matter out of which the bodies of living, terrestrial creatures are constructed. Atoms, I was informed, cannot sustain themselves under the enormous pressure prevailing in sidereal spheres and increasing at a high ratio towards their center; consequently, they disintegrate into their hypothethical components, into protons and electrons that travel as waves and rays out into universal space.

"The stars which compose the comparatively sparse population of the universe," concluded the astronomer, "are, accordingly, nothing but inconceivably rarefied condensations of certain chemical elements (hydrogen, oxygen, nitrogen, carbon, and, to name a few of the less common ones, argon and crypton), spherical in form, a raging whirl of exploded atoms engaged in a mysteriously eruptive vital activity."

"Vital activity?" I repeated questioningly. "Does that mean you believe that the stars might be living bodies, mentally alive bodies, personalities, so to speak, which is, after all, the same thing? The latter-day gnostics held the view that stars are the heavenly hosts in material form and that their glowing, eruptive, vital activity

represents nothing but the great hymn of praise, the 'Holy, Holy, Holy' with which the angels eternally celebrate the Creator."

At these words, the modern scientist gave me a startled look; then his lips tightened, whether with annoyance or irony I do not know. "Intelligence," he corrected me, "is a phenomenon which is developed only by the most highly differentiated matter in animal and human form, and for the one and only purpose of self-defense and self-assertion for survival . . . The stars, on the other hand, consist of inorganic matter in its most primal and simple form."

"Then organic matter," I interrupted, "highly differentiated, organic matter only exists on the planets? What about the planets, professor?"

"They are extremely rare and exceptional cases in the universe," answered the scientist, "if the prevalent hypothesis is correct. According to this hypothesis, planets and families of planets originate when two stars or suns approach too close to each other in their orbits so that the gravitation of the larger star attracts the smaller one so overpoweringly that part of its matter is torn out of its body, assumes shape and begins to rotate about the larger star in the congealing form of one or more planets."

"Could there be masculine and feminine stars?" I interrupted the astronomer. Again I received a look of disapproval as he continued, "As far as inorganic matter is concerned, it can be charged with either positive or negative electricity, nothing more. Sexual differences and characteristics which serve for the propagation of a species exist only in the more differentiated organic matter, beginning with certain plants."

"Thank you, professor. Forget my stupid question . . . But there's one more thing. If I understand you correctly, it's against the traffic regulations of the universe for the orbits of stars to approach each other too closely."

"Quite right," he responded. "This approach of the stars' orbits and the tearing off of planetary systems thus brought about, are, as our research assumes, among the most unusual catastrophes in the universe, far more unusual, for example, than the explosion of stars (which is in itself quite a rare event) and the formation of nova that is associated with it and that we can observe in our telescopes now and then. The planets, my dear fellow, are a catastrophic anomaly in the realm of matter. And of all the planets, a planet with the earth's conditions of life seems to be the most anomalous of anomalies."

"How can that be, my dear professor?" said I abruptly. "Can it be that the highly differentiated organic matter of which we spoke cannot sustain its life upon the other planets that revolve about our sun?"

"In all probability, no," he answered rather glumly. "On one of them, for example, the atmosphere is too dense, on another it is too rarefied, on a third there isn't any at all, on a fourth the temperature is much too high, on a fifth it is much too low."

"Just a moment, professor. Two stars disturb the harmony by coming too close to each other. The result is that sun-like matter is torn off, catapulted outward and finally cools down slowly. That is, it becomes rock and water, sand and mud, this exiled matter that owes its existence to an infraction, a clumsy violation of law. Is that correct, professor?"

"Approximately, my friend," he grumbled, "if we subtract your mythologically moralizing commentary."

"And out of this exiled, out of this banished, out of this deeply humiliated matter," I continued to question, "does the germ of life spring forth until, in a comparatively short time, it has developed into the human soul that is capable of ecstatically comprehending God?"

"Here you are leaving the paths of science," declared the astronomer, disgusted.

"If, as you say, the earth is already an anomaly, my dear professor, what then is humanity?"

"An anomaly raised to the twelfth power," he laughed contemptuously . . .

When I left the learned man, I realized that science had not lessened my faith but had unintentionally strengthened it. If the earth really is the most anomalous of all anomalies, then for that reason alone it revolves in the innermost center of the universe, a center that can only be a *product of the mind;* for indeed, within the universe, all space and time dimensions are meaningless. And if humanity is really the great exceptional case, as modern theory seems disposed to profess, how easy should it be for everyone to believe that this humanity is the crown and the goal of creation, and that God Himself had decided from the very beginning not to become *Sirius, Aldebaran* or *Cassiopeia* in order to incorporate Himself into a created thing and to have experience of it, but to become something far more rare, greater and more precious, a man.

1394

WALT WHITMAN

WALT WHITMAN (American, 1819-1892). Prophetic singer of odes to demo-
cratic Americanism. The U. S.'s most universally praised poet. Served as journalist in New York, became army nurse during Civil War. First edition of
Leaves of Grass was received with hostility, accused of immorality. His own
criticism of America contained in prose work, *Democratic Vistas*. Style, modeled
on Old Testament, extravagantly admired by poets, but has not been successfully
imitated.

From *SONG OF MYSELF*

X

The runaway slave came to my house and stopt outside,
I heard his motions crackling the twigs of the woodpile,
Through the swung half-door of the kitchen I saw him limpsy and
   weak,
And went where he sat on a log and led him in and assured him,
And brought water and fill'd a tub for his sweated body and bruis'd
   feet,

And gave him a room that enter'd from my own, and gave him
   some coarse clean clothes,
And remember perfectly well his revolving eyes and his awkwardness,
And remember putting plasters on the galls of his neck and ankles;
He staid with me a week before he was recuperated and pass'd
   north,
I had him sit next to me at table, my fire-lock lean'd in the corner.

XXIV

Walt Whitman, a kosmos, of Manhattan the son,
Turbulent, fleshy, sensual, eating, drinking and breeding,
No sentimentalist, no stander above men and women or apart from
   them,
No more modest than immodest.

Unscrew the locks from the doors!
Unscrew the doors themselves from their jambs!

1395

Whoever degrades another degrades me,
And whatever is done or said returns at last to me.

Through me the afflatus surging and surging, through me the current
and index.

I speak the pass-word primeval, I give the sign of democracy,
By God! I will accept nothing which all cannot have their counterpart
of on the same terms.

XXXIII

I understand the large hearts of heroes,
The courage of present times and all times,
How the skipper saw the crowded and rudderless wreck of the
steam-ship, and Death chasing it up and down the storm,
How he knuckled tight and gave not an inch, and was faithful of
days and faithful of nights,
And chalk'd in large letters on a board, *Be of good cheer, we will
not desert you;*
How he follow'd with them and tack'd with them three days and
would not give it up,
How he saved the drifting company at last,
How the lank loose-gown'd women look'd when boated from the
side of their prepared graves,
How the silent old-faced infants and the lifted sick, and the sharp-
lipp'd unshaven men;
All this I swallow, it tastes good, I like it well, it becomes mine,
I am the man, I suffer'd, I was there.
The disdain and calmness of martyrs,
The mother of old, condemn'd for a witch, burnt with dry wood,
her children gazing on,
The hounded slave that flags in the race, leans by the fence, blowing,
cover'd with sweat,
The twinges that sting like needles his legs and neck, the murderous
buckshot and the bullets,
All these I feel or am.

I am the hounded slave, I wince at the bite of the dogs,
Hell and despair are upon me, crack and again crack the marksmen,

1396

I clutch the rails of the fence, my gore dribs, thinn'd with the ooze
    of my skin,
I fall on the weeds and stones,
The riders spur their unwilling horses, haul close,
Taunt my dizzy ears and beat me violently over the head with
    whip-stocks.

Agonies are one of my changes of garments,
I do not ask the wounded person how he feels, I myself become
    the wounded person,
My hurts turn livid upon me as I lean on a cane and observe.

O CAPTAIN! MY CAPTAIN!

O Captain! my Captain! our fearful trip is done,
The ship has weathered every rack, the prize we sought is won,
The port is near, the bells I hear, the people all exulting,
While follow eyes the steady keel, the vessel grim and daring;
    But O heart! heart! heart!
      O the bleeding drops of red,
        Where on the deck my Captain lies,
        Fallen cold and dead.

O Captain! my Captain! rise up and hear the bells;
Rise up—for you the flag is flung—for you the bugle trills,
For you bouquets and ribboned wreaths—for you the shores acrowd-
    ing,
For you they call, the swaying mass, their eager faces turning;
    Here Captain! dear father!
      This arm beneath your head!
        It is some dream that on the deck
        You've fallen cold and dead.

My Captain does not answer, his lips are pale and still,
My father does not feel my arm, he has no pulse nor will,
The ship is anchored safe and sound, its voyage closed and done,
From fearful trip the victor ship comes in with object won;
    Exult O shores, and ring O bells!
      But I, with mournful tread,
        Walk the deck my Captain lies,
        Fallen cold and dead.

From TO A FOIL'D EUROPEAN REVOLUTIONAIRE

(No songs of loyalty alone are these,
  But songs of insurrection also;
For I am the sworn poet of every dauntless rebel, the world over,
And he going with me leaves peace and routine behind him,
And stakes his life, to be lost at any moment.)

When liberty goes out of a place, it is not the first to go, nor the
    second or third to go,
It waits for all the rest to go—it is the last.

When there are no more memories of heroes and martyrs,
And when all life, and all the souls of men and women are discharged
    from any part of the earth,
Then only shall liberty, or the idea of liberty, be discharged from
    that part of the earth,
And the infidel come into full possession.

From AS A STRONG BIRD ON PINIONS FREE

Beautiful World of new, superber Birth, that rises to my eyes,
Like a limitless golden cloud, filling the western sky. . . .
Thou Wonder World, yet undefined, unform'd—neither do I define
    thee;
How can I pierce the impenetrable blank of the future?
I feel thy ominous greatness, evil as well as good;
I watch thee, advancing, absorbing the present, transcending the
    past;
I see thy light lighting and thy shadow shadowing, as if the entire
    globe;
But I do not undertake to define thee—hardly to comprehend thee;
I but thee name—thee prophesy—as now!

From SONG OF THE OPEN ROAD

XI

Listen! I will be honest with you,
I do not offer the old smooth prizes, but offer rough new prizes,

These are the days that must happen to you:
You shall not heap up what is call'd riches,
You shall scatter with lavish hand all that you earn or achieve,
You but arrive at the city to which you were destin'd, you hardly
    settle yourself to satisfaction, before you are call'd by an irresist-
    ible call to depart,
You shall be treated to the ironical smiles and mockings of those
    who remain behind you,
What beckonings of love you receive you shall only answer with
    passionate kisses of parting,
You shall not allow the hold of those who spread their reach'd
    hands toward you.

XII

Allons! after the great Companions, and to belong to them!
They too are on the road—they are the swift and majestic men
    —they are the greatest women,
Enjoyers of calms of seas and storms of seas,
Sailors of many a ship, walkers of many a mile of land,
Habitués of many distant countries, habitués of far-distant dwellings,
Trusters of men and women, observers of cities, solitary toilers,
Pausers and contemplators of tufts, blossoms, shells of the shore,
Dancers at wedding-dances, kissers of brides, tender helpers of
    children, bearers of children,
Soldiers of revolts, standers by gaping graves, lowerers-down of
    coffins,
Journeyers over consecutive seasons, over the years, the curious
    years each emerging from that which preceded it,
Journeyers as with companions, namely their own diverse phases,
Forth-steppers from the latent unrealized baby-days,
Journeyers gayly with their own youth, journeyers with their bearded
    and well-grain'd manhood,
Journeyers with their womanhood, ample, unsurpass'd, content,
Journeyers with their own sublime old age of manhood or woman-
    hood,
Old age, calm, expanded, broad with the haughty breadth of the
    universe,
Old age, flowing free with the delicious near-by freedom of death.

I HEAR AMERICA SINGING

I hear America singing, the varied carols I hear,
Those of mechanics, each one singing his as it should be blithe and
strong,
The carpenter singing his as he measures his plank or beam,
The mason singing his as he makes ready for work, or leaves off
work,
The boatman singing what belongs to him in his boat, the deck-hand
singing on the steamboat deck,
The shoemaker singing as he sits on his bench, the hatter singing
as he stands,
The wood-cutter's song, the plowboy's on his way in the morning,
or at noon intermission or at sundown,
The delicious singing of the mother, or of the young wife at work,
or of the girl sewing or washing,
Each singing what belongs to him or her and to none else,
The day what belongs to the day—at night the party of young
fellows, robust, friendly,
Singing with open mouths their strong melodious songs.

FOR YOU, O DEMOCRACY

Come, I will make the continent indissoluble,
I will make the most splendid race the sun ever shone upon,
I will make divine magnetic lands,
    With the love of comrades,
        With the life-long love of comrades.

I will plant companionship thick as trees along all the rivers of
        America, and along the shores of the great lakes, and
        all over the prairies,
I will make inseparable cities with their arms about each other's
        necks,
    By the love of comrades,
        By the manly love of comrades.

For you these from me, O Democracy, to serve you *ma femme*!
For you, for you I am trilling these songs.

JOHN GREENLEAF WHITTIER

JOHN GREENLEAF WHITTIER (American, 1807-1892). Antislavery balladist.
His New England Quaker background painted in narrative poem, *Snowbound*.
Became widely known as pamphleteer and editor of various abolitionist papers.
Now more often remembered as a writer of popular ballads and nature poet.

THE SLAVE-SHIPS

> "That fatal, that perfidious bark,
> Built i' the eclipse, and rigged with curses dark."
> —*Milton's Lycidas*.

"All ready!" cried the captain;
   "Ay, ay!" the seamen said;
"Heave up the worthless lubbers,—
   The dying and the dead."
Up from the slave-ship's prison
   Fierce, bearded heads were thrust:
"Now let the sharks look to it,—
   Toss up the dead ones first!"

Corpse after corpse came up,—
   Death had been busy there;
Where every blow is mercy,
   Why should the spoiler spare?
Corpse after corpse they cast
   Sullenly from the ship,
Yet bloody with the traces
   Of fetter-link and whip.

Gloomily stood the captain,
   With his arms upon his breast,
With his cold brow sternly knotted,
   And his iron lip compressed.
"Are all the dead dogs over?"
   Growled through that matted lip,—
"The blind ones are no better,
   Let's lighten the good ship."

Hark! from the ship's dark bosom,
  The very sounds of hell!
The ringing clank of iron,—
  The maniac's short, sharp yell!—
The hoarse, low curse, throat-stilled,—
  The starving infant's moan,—
The horror of a breaking heart
  Poured through a mother's groan.

Up from that loathsome prison
  The stricken blind ones came:
Below, had all been darkness,—
  Above, was still the same.
Yet the holy breath of heaven
  Was sweetly breathing there,
And the heated brow of fever
  Cooled in the soft sea air.

"Overboard with them, shipmates!"
  Cutlass and dirk were plied;
Fettered and blind, one after one,
  Plunged down the vessel's side.
The saber smote above,—
  Beneath, the lean shark lay,
Waiting with wide and bloody jaw
  His quick and human prey.

God of the earth! what cries
  Rang upward unto thee?
Voices of agony and blood,
  From ship-deck and from sea.
The last dull plunge was heard,—
  The last wave caught its stain,—
And the unsated shark looked up
  For human hearts in vain.

Red glowed the western waters,—
  The setting sun was there,
Scattering alike on wave and cloud
  His fiery mesh of hair.

Amidst a group in blindness,
     A solitary eye
Gazed, from the burdened slaver's deck,
     Into that burning sky.

"A storm," spoke out the gazer,
     "Is gathering and at hand,—
Curse on 't—I'd give my other eye
     For one firm rood of land."
And then he laughed,—but only
     His echoed laugh replied,—
For the blinded and the suffering
     Alone were at his side.

Night settled on the waters,
     And on a stormy heaven,
While fiercely on that lone ship's track
     The thunder-gust was driven.
"A sail!—thank God, a sail!"
     And as the helmsman spoke,
Up through the stormy murmur
     A shout of gladness broke.

Down came the stranger vessel,
     Unheeding on her way,
So near, that on the slaver's deck
     Fell off her driven spray.
"Ho! for the love of mercy,—
     We're perishing and blind!"
A wail of utter agony
     Came back upon the wind:

"Help *us!* for we are stricken
     With blindness every one;
Ten days we've floated fearfully,
     Unnoting star or sun.
Our ship's the slaver Leon,—
     We've but a score on board,—
Our slaves are all gone over,—
     Help,—for the love of God!"

1403

On livid brows of agony
  The broad red lightning shone,—
But the roar of wind and thunder
  Stifled the answering groan
Wailed from the broken waters
  A last despairing cry,
As, kindling in the stormy light,
  The stranger ship went by.

In the sunny Guadaloupe
  A dark-hulled vessel lay,—
With a crew who noted never
  The nightfall or the day
The blossom of the orange,
  Was white by every stream,
And tropic leaf, and flower, and bird
  Were in the warm sunbeam.

And the sky was bright as ever,
  And the moonlight slept as well,
On the palm-trees by the hillside,
  And the streamlet of the dell:
And the glances of the Creole
  Were still as archly deep,
And her smiles as full as ever
  Of passion and of sleep.

But vain were bird and blossom,
  The green earth and the sky,
And the smile of human faces,
  To the slaver's darkened eye;
At the breaking of the morning,
  At the star-lit evening time,
O'er a world of light and beauty
  Fell the blackness of his crime.

CHRISTOPH MARTIN WIELAND

CHRISTOPH MARTIN WIELAND (German, 1733-1813). Translator of Shakespeare. Strongly influenced High German literary style. Edited and published first modern literary review in German. His novel, *Der goldene Spiegel*, brought appointment as tutor to Weimar princes, where he lived most of his life. Most famous work: *Oberon*, a verse romance.

SIR HUON ENTERS THE SULTAN'S PALACE

Now through the outward court swift speeds the knight;
　Within the second from his steed descends;
　Along the third his pace majestic bends:
Where'er he enters, dazzled by his sight,
　The guards make way,—his gait, his dress, his air,
　A nuptial guest of highest rank declare.
Now he advances towards an ebon gate,
Where with drawn swords twelve Moors gigantic wait,
　And piecemeal hack the wretch who steps unbidden there.

But the bold gesture and imperial mien
　Of Huon as he opes the lofty door,
　Drive back the swords that crossed his path before,
And at his entrance flamed with lightning sheen.
　At once, with rushing noise, the valves unfold:
　High throbs the bosom of our hero bold,
When, locked behind him, harsh the portals bray:
Through gardens decked with columns leads the way,
　Where towered a gate incased with plates of massy gold.

There a large fore-court held a various race
　Of slaves, hapless race, sad harem slaves,
　Who die of thirst 'mid joy's o'erflowing waves!
And when a man, whom emir honors grace,
　Swells in his state before their hollow eye,
　Breathless they bend, with looks that seem to die,
Beneath the weight of servitude oppresed;
Bow down, with folded arms across the breast,
　Nor dare look up to mark the pomp that glitters by.

1405

Already cymbals, drums and fifes resound;
  With song and string the festive palace clangs;
  The Sultan's head already heaving hangs,
While vinous vapors float his brain around:
  Already mirth in freer current flows,
  And the gay bridegroom, wild with rapture, glows.
Then, as the bride, in horror turned away,
Casts on the ground her looks that never stray,
  Huon along the hall with noble freedom goes.

Now to the table he advances nigh,
  And with uplifted brow in wild amaze
  The admiring guests upon the stranger gaze:
Fair Rezia, tranced, with fascinated eye
  Still views her dream, and ever downward bends:
  The Sultan, busy with the bowl, suspends
All other thoughts: Prince Bakeban alone,
Warned by no vision, towards the guest unknown,
  All fearless of his fate, his length of neck extends.

Soon as Sir Huon's scornful eyes retrace
  The man of yesterday, that he, the same
  Who lately dared the Christian God defame,
Sits at the left, high-plumed in bridal grace,
  And bows the neck as conscious of his guilt:
  Swift as the light he grasps the sabre's hilt;
Off at the instant flies the heathen's head;
And, o'er the Caliph and the banquet shed,
  Up spirts his boiling blood, by dreadful vengeance spilt!

As the dread visage of Medusa fell,
  Swift flashing on the sight, with instant view
  Deprives of life the wild-revolted crew;
While reeks the tower with blood, while tumults swell,
  And murderous frenzy, fierce and fiercer grown,
  Glares in each eye, and maddens every tone,—
At once, when Perseus shakes the viper hair,
Each dagger stiffens as it hangs in air,
  And every murderer stands transformed to living stone!

1406

Thus, at the view of this audacious feat,
  The jocund blood that warmed each merry guest
  Suspends its frozen course in every breast:
Like ghosts, in heaps, all-shivering from their seat
  They start, and grasp their swords and mark their prey;
  But, shrunk by fear, their vigor dies away:
Each in its sheath their swords remain at rest:
With powerless fury in his look expressed,
  Mute sunk the caliph back, and stared in wild dismay.

The uproar which confounds the nuptial hall
  Forces the dreamer from her golden trance:
  Round her she gazes with astonished glance,
While yells of frantic rage her soul appal:
  But, as she turns her face towards Huon's side,
  How throbs his bosom, when he sees his bride!—
"'Tis she,—'tis she herself!" he wildly calls:
Down drops the bloody steel; the turban falls;
  And Rezia knows her knight, as float his ringlets wide.

"'Tis he!" she wild exclaims: yet virgin shame
  Stops in her rosy mouth the imperfect sound:
  How throbs her heart; what thrillings strange confound,
When, with impatient speed, the stranger came,
  And, love-emboldened, with presumptuous arms
  Clasped, in the sight of all, her angel charms!
And, Oh, how fiery red, how deadly pale
Her cheek, as love and maiden fear assail,
  The while he kissed her lip that glowed with sweet alarms!

Twice had his lip already kissed the maid:—
  "Where shall the bridal ring, Oh, where be found?"
  Lo! by good fortune, as he gazes round,
The elfin ring shines suddenly displayed,
  Won from the giant of the iron tower:
  Now, all-unconscious of its magic power,
This ring, so seeming base, the impatient knight
Slips on her finger, pledge of nuptial rite:—
  "With this, O bride beloved! I wed thee from this hour!"

1407

Then, for the third time, at these words, again
   The bridegroom kissed the soft reluctant fair:
   The Sultan storms and stamps in wild despair:—
"Thou sufferest, then,—inexpiable stain!
   This Christian dog to shame thy nuptial day?—
   Seize, seize him, slaves!—ye die, the least delay!
Haste! drop by drop, from every throbbing vein,
By lengthened agonies his life-blood drain,—
   Thus shall the pangs of hell his monstrous guilt repay."

At once, in flames, before Sir Huon's eyes,
   A thousand weapons glitter at the word;
   And, ere our hero snatches up his sword,
On every side the death-storms fiercely rise:
   On every side he turns his brandished blade:
   By love and anguish wild, at once the maid
Around him wreathes her arm, his shield her breast,
Seizes his sword, by her alone repressed:—
   "Back! daring slaves!" she cries, "I, I the hero aid!

"Back!—to that breast,—here, here the passage lies!—
   No other way than through the midst of mine!"—
   And she, who lately seemed Love's bride divine,
Now flames a Gorgon with Medusa's eyes!
   And ever, as the emirs near inclose,
   She dares with fearless breast their swords oppose:—
"Spare him, my father! spare him! and, O thou,
Destined by fate to claim my nuptial vow,
   Spare him!—in both your lives the blood of Rezia flows!"

The Sultan's frenzy rages uncontrolled:
   Fierce on Sir Huon storm the murderous train;
   Yet still his glittering falchion flames in vain,
While Rezia's gentle hand retains its hold:
   Her agonizing shrieks his bosom rend.
   And what remains the princes to defend?
What but the horn can rescue her from death?—
Soft through the ivory flows his gentle breath,
   And from its spiry folds sweet fairy tones ascend.

1408

Soon as its magic sounds, the powerless steel
  Falls without struggle from the lifted hand:
  In rash vertigo turned, the emir band
Wind arm in arm and spin the giddy reel:
  Throughout the hall tumultuous echoes ring;
  All, old and young, each heel has Hermes' wing:
No choice is left them by the fairy tone:
Pleased and astonished, Rezia stands alone
  By Huon's side unmoved, while all around them spring.

The whole divan, one swimming circle, glides
  Swift without stop: the old bashaws click time:
  As if on polished ice, in trance sublime,
The iman hoar with some spruce courtier slides:
  Nor rank nor age from capering refrain:
  Nor can the king his royal foot restrain;
He, too, must reel amid the frolic row,
Grasp the grand vizier by his beard of snow,
  And teach the aged man once more to bound amain.

The dancing melodies, ne'er heard before,
  From every crowded antechamber round,
  First draw the eunuchs forth with airy bound;
The women next, and slaves that guard the door
  Alike the merry madness seizes all.
  The harem's captives, at the magic call,
Trip gaily to the tune and whirl the dance:
In party-colored shirts the gardeners prance,
  Rush 'mid the youthful nymphs and mingle in the ball.

Entranced, with fearful joy, while doubt alarms,
  Fair Rezia stands almost deprived of breath:—
  "What wonder at the time when instant death
Hangs o'er us, that a dance the god disarms!
  A dance thus rescues from extreme distress!"
  "Some friendly genius deigns our union bless,"
Sir Huon says. Meanwhile amid the throng
With eager step darts Sherasmin along,
  And towards them Fatma hastes unnoticed through the press.

"Haste!" Sherasmin exclaims; "not now the hour
    To pry with curious leisure on the dance,—
    All is prepared,—the steeds impatient prance,—
While raves the castle, while unbarred the tower,
    And every gate wide open, why delay?
    By luck I met Dame Fatma on the way,
Close-packed, like beast of burden, for the flight."
"Peace! 'tis not yet the time," replies the knight;
    "A dreadful task impends,—for that must Huon stay."

Pale Rezia shudders at the dreadful sound,
    And looks with longing eye, that seems to say,
    "Why, on the brink of ruin, why delay?
Oh, hasten! let our footsteps fly the ground,
    Ere bursts the transient charm that binds their brain.
    And rage and vengeance repossess the train!"
Huon, who reads the language of her eyes,
With looks of answering love alone replies,
    Clasps to his heart her hand, nor dares the deed explain.

And now the fairy tones to soft repose
    Melt in the air: each head swims giddy round,
    And every limb o'ertired forgets to bound;
Wet every thread, and every pore o'erflows.
    The breath half-stopped scarce heaves with struggling pain;
    The drowsy blood slow creeps through every vein;
Involuntary joy, like torture, thrills:
The king, as from a bath, in streams distills,
    And pants upon his couch, amid the exhausted train.

Stiff, without motion, scarce with sense endued,
    Down, one by one, the o'erwearied dancers fall,
    Where swelling bolsters heave around the wall:
Emirs and lowly slaves, in contrast rude,
    Mix with the harem goddesses, as chance
    Tangles the mazes of the frantic dance:
At once together by a whirlwind blown,
On the same bed, in ill-paired union thrown,
    The groom and favorite lie confused in breathless trance.

1410

OSCAR WILDE

OSCAR WILDE (English, 1854-1900). Cultivated literary eccentric and social satirist. One of leaders of Aesthetic Movement in 90's. Exotic stylist, particularly in play *Salome*, novel *The Picture of Dorian Gray*, and fairy tales. His drawing room comedies the best since Sheridan: *Lady Windermere's Fan, The Importance of Being Earnest, An Ideal Husband.* His last years darkened by aberrational ignominy.

THE SELFISH GIANT

EVERY afternoon, as they were coming from school, the children used to go and play in the Giant's garden.

It was a large lovely garden, with soft green grass. Here and there over the grass stood beautiful flowers like stars, and there were twelve peach-trees that in the Spring-time broke out into delicate blossoms of pink and pearl, and in the autumn bore rich fruit. The birds sat on the trees and sang so sweetly that the children used to stop their games in order to listen to them. "How happy we are here!" they cried to each other.

One day the Giant came back. He had been to visit his friend the Cornish ogre, and had stayed with him for seven years. After the seven years were over he had said all that he had to say, for his conversation was limited, and he determined to return to his own castle. When he arrived he saw the children playing in the garden.

"What are you doing there?" he cried in a very gruff voice, and the children ran away.

"My own garden is my own garden," said the Giant; "anyone can understand that, and I will allow nobody to play in it but myself." So he built a high wall all round it, and put up a notice-board.

TRESPASSERS
WILL BE
PROSECUTED

He was a very selfish Giant.

The poor children had now nowhere to play. They tried to play on the road, but the road was very dusty and full of hard stones, and they did not like it. They used to wander round the high wall

when their lessons were over, and talk about the beautiful garden inside. "How happy we were there," they said to each other.

Then the Spring came, and all over the country there were little blossoms and little birds. Only in the garden of the Selfish Giant it was still winter. The birds did not care to sing in it, as there were no children, and the trees forgot to blossom. Once a beautiful flower put its head out from the grass, but when it saw the notice-board it was so sorry for the children that it slipped back into the ground again, and went off to sleep. The only people who were pleased were the Snow and the Frost. "Spring has forgotten this garden," they cried, "so we will live here all the year round." The Snow covered up the grass with her great white cloak, and the Frost painted all the trees silver. Then they invited the North Wind to stay with them, and he came. He was wrapped in furs, and he roared all day about the garden, and blew the chimney-pots down. "This is a delightful spot," he said; "we must ask the Hail on a visit." So the Hail came. Every day for three hours he rattled on the roof of the castle till he broke most of the slates, and then he ran round and round the garden as fast as he could go. He was dressed in gray, and his breath was like ice.

"I can not understand why the Spring is so late in coming," said the Selfish Giant, as he sat at the window and looked out at his cold white garden; "I hope there will be a change in the weather."

But the Spring never came, nor the Summer. The Autumn gave golden fruit to every garden, but to the Giant's garden she gave none. "He is too selfish," she said. So it was always Winter there, and the North Wind, and the Hail, and the Frost, and the Snow danced about through the trees.

One morning the Giant was lying awake in bed when he heard some lovely music. It sounded so sweet to his ears that he thought it must be the King's musicians passing by. It was really only a little linnet singing outside his window, but it was so long since he had heard a bird sing in his garden that it seemed to him to be the most beautiful music in the world. Then the Hail stopped dancing over his head, and the North Wind ceased roaring, and a delicious perfume came to him through the open casement. "I believe the Spring has come at last," said the Giant; and he jumped out of bed and looked out.

What did he see?

He saw a most wonderful sight. Through a little hole in the wall the children had crept in, and they were sitting in the branches of

1412

the trees. In every tree that he could see there was a little child. And the trees were so glad to have the children back again that they had covered themselves with blossoms, and were waving their arms gently above the children's heads. The birds were flying about and twittering with delight, and the flowers were looking up through the green grass and laughing. It was a lovely scene, only in one corner it was still winter. It was the farthest corner of the garden, and in it was standing a little boy. He was so small that he could not reach up to the branches of the tree, and he was wandering all round it, crying bitterly. The poor tree was still quite covered with frost and snow, and the North Wind was blowing and roaring above it. "Climb up, little boy," said the Tree, and it bent its branches down as low as it could; but the boy was too tiny.

And the Giant's heart melted as he looked out. "How selfish I have been!" he said; "now I know why the Spring would not come here. I will put that poor little boy on the top of the tree, and then I will knock down the wall, and my garden shall be the children's playground for ever and ever." He was really very sorry for what he had done.

So he crept downstairs and opened the front door quite softly, and went out into the garden. But when the children saw him they were so frightened that they all ran away, and the garden became winter again. Only the little boy did not run, for his eyes were so full of tears that he did not see the Giant coming. And the Giant stole up behind him and took him gently in his hand, and put him up into the tree. And the tree broke at once into blossoms, and the birds came and sang on it, and the little boy stretched out his two arms and flung them round the Giant's neck, and kissed him. And the other children, when they saw that the Giant was not wicked any longer, came running back, and with them came the Spring. "It is your garden now, little children," said the Giant, and he took a great axe and knocked down the wall. And when the people were going to market at twelve o'clock they found the Giant playing with the children in the most beautiful garden they had ever seen.

All day long they played, and in the evening they came to the Giant to bid him good-bye.

"But where is your little companion?" he said: "the boy I put into the tree." The Giant loved him the best because he had kissed him.

"We don't know," answered the children; "he has gone away."

"You must tell him to be sure and come here to-morrow," said

1413

the Giant. But the children said that they did not know where he lived, and had never seen him before; and the Giant felt very sad.

Every afternoon, when school was over, the children came and played with the Giant. But the little boy whom the Giant loved was never seen again. The Giant was very kind to all the children, yet he longed for his first little friend, and often spoke of him. "How I would like to see him!" he used to say.

Years went over, and the Giant grew very old and feeble. He could not play about any more, so he sat in a huge armchair, and watched the children at their games, and admired his garden. "I have many beautiful flowers," he said; "but the children are the most beautiful flowers of all."

One winter morning he looked out of his window as he was dressing. He did not hate the Winter now, for he knew that it was merely the Spring asleep, and that the flowers were resting.

Suddenly he rubbed his eyes in wonder, and looked and looked. It certainly was a marvelous sight. In the farthest corner of the garden was a tree quite covered with lovely white blossoms. Its branches were all golden, and silver fruit hung down from them, and underneath it stood the little boy he had loved.

Downstairs ran the Giant in great joy, and out into the garden. He hastened across the grass, and came near to the child. And when he came quite close his face grew red with anger, and he said, "Who hath dared to wound thee?" For on the palms of the child's hands were the prints of two nails, and the prints of two nails were on the little feet.

"Who hath dared to wound thee?" cried the Giant; "tell me, that I may take my big sword and slay him."

"Nay!" answered the child; "but these are the wounds of Love."

"Who art thou?" said the Giant, and a strange awe fell on him, and he knelt before the little child.

And the child smiled on the Giant, and said to him, "You let me play once in your garden, to-day you shall come with me to my garden, which is Paradise."

And when the children ran in that afternoon, they found the Giant lying dead under the tree, all covered with white blossoms.

WILLIAM WORDSWORTH

WILLIAM WORDSWORTH (English, 1770-1850). Grand poet of the common-place. One of founders (with friend Coleridge) of the English Romantic Movement. Preface to their joint work, *Lyrical Ballads,* became famous manifesto. He glorified the Lake District and its simple inhabitants. More ambitious work: *The Prelude, The Excursion.* Later poetry less inspired. Ended days as Poet Laureate.

INTIMATIONS OF IMMORTALITY

I

There was a time when meadow, grove and stream,
  The earth, and every common sight,
      To me did seem
      Apparelled in celestial light,
The glory and the freshness of a dream.
It is not now as it hath been of yore;—
      Turn wheresoe'er I may,
        By night or day,
The things which I have seen I now can see no more.

II

      The rainbow comes and goes,
      And lovely is the rose;
      The moon doth with delight
Look round her when the heavens are bare;
      Waters on a starry night
      Are beautiful and fair;
    The sunshine is a glorious birth;—
    But yet I know, where'er I go,
That there hath passed away a glory from the earth.

III

Now, while the birds thus sing a joyous song.
  And while the young lambs bound
    As to the tabor's sound,

To me alone there came a thought of grief;
A timely utterance gave that thought relief;
    And I again am strong.
The cataracts blow their trumpets from the steep—
No more shall grief of mine the season wrong:
I hear the echoes through the mountains throng;
The winds come to me from the fields of sleep;
        And all the earth is gay.
            Land and sea
    Give themselves up to jollity;
        And with the heart of May
    Doth every beast keep holiday:—
        Thou child of joy,
Shout round me, let me hear thy shouts, thou happy shepherd-boy!

IV

Ye blessèd creatures, I have heard the call
    Ye to each other make; I see
The heavens laugh with you in your jubilee;
    My heart is at your festival,
        My head hath its coronal,
The fullness of your bliss I feel—I feel it all.
    Oh, evil day! if I were sullen,
        While Earth herself is adorning,
            This sweet May morning;
    And the children are culling,
            On every side,
    In a thousand valleys far and wide,
    Fresh flowers; while the sun shines warm,
And the babe leaps up on his mother's arm:—
    I hear, I hear, with joy I hear!
        —But there's a tree, of many one,
A single field which I have looked upon—
Both of them speak of something that is gone:
            The pansy at my feet
            Doth the same tale repeat:
Whither is fled the visionary gleam?
Where is it now, the glory and the dream?

V

Our birth is but a sleep and a forgetting:
The soul that rises with us, our life's star,
    Hath had elsewhere its setting,
      And cometh from afar:
    Not in entire forgetfulness,
    And not in utter nakedness,
But trailing clouds of glory do we come
      From God, who is our home:
Heaven lies about us in our infancy!
Shades of the prison-house begin to close
      Upon the growing boy;
But he beholds the light, and whence it flows,
      He sees it in his joy;
The youth, who daily farther from the east
   Must travel, still is Nature's priest,
    And by the vision splendid
    Is on his way attended;
At length the man perceives it die away,
And fade into the light of common day.

VI

Earth fills her lap with pleasures of her own;
Yearnings she hath in her own natural kind,
And, even with something of a mother's mind,
    And no unworthy aim,
    The homely nurse doth all she can ·
To make her foster-child, her inmate man,
    Forget the glories he hath known,
And that imperial palace whence he came.

VII

Behold the child among his new-born blisses,
A six-years' darling of a pigmy size!
See, where 'mid work of his own hand he lies,
Fretted by sallies of his mother's kisses,

With light upon him from his father's eyes!
See, at his feet, some little plan or chart,
Some fragment from his dream of human life,
Shaped by himself with newly-learnéd art;
    A wedding or a festival,
    A mourning or a funeral;
      And this hath now his heart,
      And unto this he frames his song:
        Then will he fit his tongue
To dialogues of business, love, or strife;
    But it will not be long
    Ere this be thrown aside,
    And with new joy and pride
The little actor cons another part;
Filling from time to time his "humorous stage"
With all the persons, down to palsied age,
That Life brings with her in her equipage;
    As if his whole vocation
    Were endless imitation.

VIII

Thou, whose exterior semblance dost belie
    Thy soul's immensity;
Thou best philosopher, who yet dost keep
Thy heritage; thou eye among the blind,
That, deaf and silent, readest the eternal deep,
Haunted forever by the eternal mind,—
    Mighty Prophet! Seer blessed!
    On whom those truths do rest,
Which we are toiling all our lives to find;
In darkness lost, the darkness of the grave;
Thou, over whom thy immortality
Broods like the day, a master o'er a slave,
A presence which is not to be put by;
Thou little child, yet glorious in the might
Of heaven-born freedom, on thy being's height,
Why with such earnest pains dost thou provoke
The years to bring the inevitable yoke,

Thus blindly with thy blessedness at strife?
Full soon thy soul shall have her earthly freight,
And custom lie upon thee with a weight,
Heavy as frost, and deep almost as life!

IX

O joy! that in our embers
Is something that does live,
That nature yet remembers
What was so fugitive!
The thought of our past years in me doth breed
Perpetual benedictions: not indeed
For that which is most worthy to be blessed;
Delight and liberty, the simple creed
Of childhood, whether busy or at rest,
With new-fledged hope still fluttering in his breast,—
Not for these I raise
The song of thanks and praise;
But for those obstinate questionings
Of sense and outward things,
Fallings from us, vanishings;
Blank misgivings of a creature
Moving about in worlds not realized,
High instincts, before which our mortal nature
Did tremble, like a guilty thing surprised:
But for those first affections,
Those shadowy recollections,
Which, be they what they may,
Are yet the fountain light of all our day,
Are yet a master light of all our seeing;
Uphold us, cherish, and have power to make
Our noisy years seem moments in the being
Of the eternal silence: truths that wake
To perish never;
Which neither listlessness, nor mad endeavor,
Nor man, nor boy,
Nor all that is at enmity with joy,
Can utterly abolish or destroy!

Hence, in a season of calm weather,
        Though inland far we be,
Our souls have sight of that immortal sea
        Which brought us hither;
        Can in a moment travel thither,
And see the children sport upon the shore,
And hear the mighty waters rolling evermore.

X

Then sing, ye birds—sing, sing a joyous song!
        And let the young lambs bound
        As to the tabor's sound!
    We, in thought, will join your throng,
        Ye that pipe and ye that play,
        Ye that through your hearts to-day
        Feel the gladness of the May!
What though the radiance which was once so bright
Be now forever taken from my sight,—
    Though nothing can bring back the hour
Of splendor in the grass, of glory in the flower;
        We will grieve not, rather find
        Strength in what remains behind;
        In the primal sympathy,
        Which, having been, must ever be
        In the soothing thoughts that spring
        Out of human suffering;
        In the faith that looks through death,
In years that bring the philosophic mind.

XI

And oh, ye fountains, meadows, hills, and groves,
Forbode not any severing of our loves!
Yet in my heart of hearts I feel your might;
I only have relinquished one delight,
To live beneath your more habitual sway.
I love the brooks, which down their channels fret,
Even more than when I tripped lightly as they;
The innocent brightness of a new-born day
        Is lovely yet;

The clouds that gather round the setting sun
Do take a sober coloring from an eye
That hath kept watch o'er man's mortality:
Another race hath been and other palms are won.
Thanks to the human heart by which we live;
Thanks to its tenderness, its joys, and fears,
To me the meanest flower that blows can give
Thoughts that do often lie too deep for tears.

Y

YAMANOE NO OKURA

YAMANOE NO OKURA (Japanese, 659-733). Moralist and philosopher. One
of the best poets from the *Manyōshū* anthology. Notable for his sympathy for
the suffering poor and for children. Pursued a diplomatic career.

AN ELEGY ON THE IMPERMANENCE OF
HUMAN LIFE

We are helpless before time
Which ever speeds away.
And pains of a hundred kinds
Pursue us one after another.
Maidens joy in girlish pleasures,
With ship-borne gems on their wrists,
And hand in hand with their friends;
But the bloom of maidenhood,
As it cannot be stopped,
Too swiftly steals away.
When do their ample tresses
Black as a mud-snail's bowels
Turn white with the frost of age?
Whence come those wrinkles
Which furrow their rosy cheeks?
The lusty young men, warrior-like,
Bearing their sword-blades at their waists,
In their hands the hunting bows,
And mounting their bay horses,
With saddles dressed with twill,
Ride about in triumph;

But can their prime of youth
Favour them for ever?
Few are the nights they keep,
When, sliding back the plank doors,
They reach their beloved ones
And sleep, arms intertwined,
Before, with staffs at their waists,
They totter along the road,
Laughed at here, and hated there.
This is the way of the world;
And, cling as I may to life,
I know no help!

Envoy

Although I wish I were thus,
Like the rocks that stay for ever,
In this world of humanity
I cannot keep old age away.

A DIALOGUE ON POVERTY

On the night when the rain beats,
Driven by the wind,
On the night when the snow-flakes mingle
With the sleety rain,
I feel so helplessly cold.
I nibble at a lump of salt,
Sip the hot, oft-diluted dregs of saké;
And coughing, snuffling,
And stroking my scanty beard,
I say in my pride,
'There's none worthy, save I!'
But I shiver still with cold.
I pull up my hempen bed-clothes,
Wear what few sleeveless clothes I have,
But cold and bitter is the night!
As for those poorer than myself,
Their parents must be cold and hungry,
Their wives and children beg and cry.
Then, how do you struggle through life?

1423

Wide as they call the heaven and earth,
For me they have shrunk quite small;
Bright though they call the sun and moon,
They never shine for me.
Is it the same with all men,
Or for me alone?
By rare chance I was born a man
And no meaner than my fellows,
But, wearing unwadded sleeveless clothes
In tatters, like weeds waving in the sea,
Hanging from my shoulders,
And under the sunken roof,
Within the leaning walls,
Here I lie on straw
Spread on bare earth,
With my parents at my pillow,
My wife and children at my feet,
All huddled in grief and tears.
No fire sends up smoke
At the cooking-place,
And in the cauldron
A spider spins its web.
With not a grain to cook,
We moan like the 'night-thrush.'
Then, 'to cut,' as the saying is,
'The ends of what is already too short,'
The village headman comes,
With rod in hand, to our sleeping-place,
Growling for his dues.
Must it be so hopeless—
The way of this world?

Envoy

Nothing but pain and shame in this world of men,
But I cannot fly away,
Wanting the wings of a bird.

1424

SUFFERING FROM OLD AGE AND PROLONGED ILLNESS, AND THINKING OF HIS CHILDREN

So long as lasts the span of life,
We wish for peace and comfort
With no evil and no mourning,
But life is hard and painful.
As the common saying has it,
Bitter salt is poured into the smarting wound,
Or the burdened horse is packed with an upper load,
Illness shakes my old body with pain.
All day long I breathe in grief
And sigh throughout the night.
For long years my illness lingers,
I grieve and groan month after month,
And though I would rather die,
I cannot, and leave my children
Noisy like the flies of May.
Whenever I watch them
My heart burns within.
And tossed this way and that,
I weep aloud.

Envoys

I find no solace in my heart;
Like the bird flying behind the clouds
I weep aloud.

Helpless and in pain,
I would run out and vanish,
But the thought of my children holds me.

No children to wear them in wealthy homes,
They are thrown away as waste,
Those silks and quilted clothes!

With no sackcloth for my children to wear,
Must I thus grieve,
For ever at a loss!

1425

Though vanishing like a bubble,
I live, praying that my life will be long
Like a rope of a thousand fathoms.

Humble as I am,
Like an arm-band of coarse twill,
How I crave a thousand years of life!

WILLIAM BUTLER YEATS

WILLIAM BUTLER YEATS (Irish, 1865-1939). Greatest Irish poet. Leader of
the Irish Renaissance in literature, co-founder with Lady Gregory of the Abbey
Theatre. Nobel Prize, 1923. Wrote romantic and mythological lyrics, highly
personal poems, plays and critical essays. Among them: *The Wind Among
the Reeds, Responsibilities, The Tower, A Full Moon in March, Stories of
Red Hanrahan.*

AN IRISH AIRMAN FORESEES HIS DEATH

I know that I shall meet my fate
Somewhere among the clouds above;
Those that I fight I do not hate,
Those that I guard I do not love;
My country is Kiltartan Cross,
My countrymen Kiltartan's poor,
No likely end could bring them loss
Or leave them happier than before.
Nor law, nor duty bade me fight,
Nor public men, nor cheering crowds,
A lonely impulse of delight
Drove to this tumult in the clouds;
I balanced all, brought all to mind,
The years to come seemed waste of breath,
A waste of breath the years behind
In balance with this life, this death.

AN APPOINTMENT

Being out of heart with government,
I took a broken root to fling
Where the proud, wayward squirrel went,
Taking delight that he could spring;

And he, with that low whinnying sound
That is like laughter, sprang again
And so to the other tree at a bound.
Nor the tame will, nor timid brain,
Bred that fierce tooth and cleanly limb
And threw him up to laugh on the bough;
No government appointed him.

THE ROSE TREE

'O words are lightly spoken,'
Said Pearse to Connolly,
'Maybe a breath of politic words
Has withered our Rose Tree;
Or maybe but a wind that blows
Across the bitter sea.'

'It needs to be but watered,'
James Connolly replied,
'To make the green come out again
And spread on every side,
And shake the blossom from the bud
To be the garden's pride.'

'But where can we draw water,'
Said Pearse to Connolly,
'When all the wells are parched away?
O plain as plain can be
There's nothing but our own red blood
Can make a right Rose Tree.'

COME GATHER ROUND ME, PARNELLITES

Come gather round me, Parnellites,
And praise our chosen man;
Stand upright on your legs awhile,
Stand upright while you can,
For soon we lie where he is laid,
And he is underground;
Come fill up all those glasses
And pass the bottle round.

1427

And here's a cogent reason,
And I have many more,
He fought the mind of England
And saved the Irish poor,
Whatever good a farmer's got
He brought it all to pass;
And here's another reason,
That Parnell loved a lass.

And here's a final reason,
He was of such a kind
Every man that sings a song
Keeps Parnell in his mind.
For Parnell was a proud man,
No prouder trod the ground,
And a proud man's a lovely man,
So pass the bottle round.

The Bishops and the Party
That tragic story made,
A husband that had sold his wife
And after that betrayed;
But stories that live longest
Are sung above the glass,
And Parnell loved his country,
And Parnell loved his lass.

Z

EMILE ZOLA

ÉMILE ZOLA (French, 1840-1902). Founder of the Naturalistic School of
French literature. Tried to apply new scientific concepts to literature. Remembered, also, for his dedicated defense of Dreyfus, *J'Accuse*. Like Balzac,
he wanted to embrace all French society in his novels. Most nearly successful:
Germinal, L'Assommoir, La Débâcle. Most widely read: *Nana*.

A FIGHT WITH FLAILS

WHEN the relatives, invited to a baptism and supper, had gone to
look over the farm, Buteau, dissatisfied at losing the afternoon, took
off his jacket and began to thresh, in the paved corner of the courtyard; for he needed a sack of wheat. But he soon wearied of
threshing alone, he wanted, to warm him up, the double cadence
of the flails, tapping in measure; and he called Françoise, who often
aided him in this work, her arms as hard as those of a lad:—"Eh,
Françoise, will you come?"

His wife, who was preparing a ragoût of veal with carrots, and
who had alrady put on an old dress, was forced to follow him. She
took a flail, her own. With both hands she made it whirl above her
head, bringing it down upon the wheat, which it struck with a sharp
blow. Buteau, opposite her, did the same, and soon nothing was seen
but the bits of flying wood. The grain leaped, fell like hail, beneath
the panting toc-toc of the two threshers.

At a quarter to seven o'clock, as the night was coming on,
Fouan and the Delhommes presented themselves.

"We must finish," Buteau cried to them, without stopping. "Fire
away, Françoise!"

She did not pause, tapped harder, in the excitement of the work
and the noise. And it was thus that Jean, who arrived in his turn,
with the permission to dine out, found them. Françoise, on seeing

1429

him, stopped short, troubled. Buteau, having wheeled about, stood for an instant motionless with surprise and anger. "What are you doing here?"

But Lise cried out, with her gay air: "Eh! true, I have not told you. I saw him this morning, and asked him to come."

The inflamed face of her husband became so terrible, that she added, wishing to excuse herself: "I have an idea, Père Fouan, that he has a request to make of you."

"What request?" said the old man.

Jean colored, and stammered, greatly vexed that the matter should be broached in this way, so quickly, before everybody. But Buteau interrupted him violently, the smiling glance that his wife had cast upon Françoise had sufficed to enlighten him: "Are you making game of us? She is not for you, you scoundrel!"

This brutal reception restored Jean his courage. He turned his back, and addressed the old man: "This is the story, Père Fouan, it's very simple. As you are Françoise's guardian, it is necessary for me to address myself to you to get her, is it not? If she will take me, I will take her. It is marriage that I ask."

Francoise, who was still holding her flail, dropped it, trembling with fright. She ought, however, to have expected this; but never could she have thought that Jean would dare to demand her thus, immediately. Why had he not talked with her about it first? She was overwhelmed, she could not have said if she trembled with hope or with fear. And, all of a quiver, she stood between the two men.

Buteau did not give Fouan time to answer. He resumed, with a growing fury:—"Eh? you have gall! An old fellow of thirty-three marry a girl of eighteen! Only fifteen years difference! Is it not laughable?"

Jean commenced to get angry. "What difference does it make to you, if I want her and she wants me?" And he turned towards Françoise, that she might give her decision. But she remained frightened, stiffened, and seeming not to understand the case. She could not say No; she did not say Yes, however. Buteau, besides, was looking at her as if he would kill her, to force back the Yes in her throat. If she married, he would lose her land. The sudden thought of this result put the climax to his rage.

"See here, father, see here, Delhomme, it's not right to give this girl to that old villain, who is not even of the district, who comes from nobody knows where, after having dragged his ugly mug in

all directions! A failure of a joiner who has turned farmer, because, very sure, he has some dirty business to hide!"

"And afterwards? If I want her and she wants me!" repeated Jean, who had controlled himself. "Come, Françoise, speak."

"But it's true!" cried Lise, carried away by the desire of marrying off her sister, in order to disembarrass herself of her, "what have you to say, if they come to an understanding? She has no need of your consent; it's very considerate in her not to send you about your business with a flea in your ear. You exhaust our patience!"

Then Buteau saw that the marriage would be decided upon, if the young girl spoke. At that instant La Grande (the old aunt) entered the court-yard, followed by the Charleses, who had returned with Éloide. And he summoned them with a gesture, without knowing yet what he would say. Then his face puffed out, he bawled, shaking his fist at his wife and sister-in-law:

"Name of God! I'll break the heads of both of them, the jades!"

The Charleses caught his words, open-mouthed, with consternation. Madam Charles threw herself forward, as if to cover with her body Éloide, who was listening; then, pushing her towards the kitchen garden, she herself cried out, very loudly: "Go look at the salads; go look at the cabbages! Oh! the fine cabbages!"

Buteau continued, violently abusing the two women, upon whom he heaped all sorts of epithets. Lise, astonished at this sudden fit, shrugging her shoulders, repeating: "He is crazy! he is crazy!"

"Tell him it's none of his business!" cried Jean to Françoise.

"Very sure it's none of his business!" said the young girl, with a tranquil air.

"Ah! it's none of my business, eh?" resumed Buteau. "Well, I'm going to make you both march, jades that you are!"

This mad audacity paralyzed, bewildered Jean. The others, the Delhommes, Fouan, La Grande, held aloof. They did not seem surprised; they thought, evidently, that Buteau had a right to do as he pleased in his own house. Then Buteau felt himself victorious in his undisputed strength of possession. He turned towards Jean. "And now for you, scoundrel, who came here to turn my house upside down! Get out of here on the instant! Eh! you refuse. Wait, wait!"

He picked up his flail, he whirled it about his head, and Jean had only the time to seize the other flail, Françoise's, to defend himself. Cries burst forth, they strove to throw themselves between them; but the two men were so terrible that they drew back. The

1431

long handles of the flails carried the blows for several yards; they swept the court-yard. The two adversaries stood alone, in the centre, at a distance from each other, enlarging the circle of their flails. They uttered not a word, their teeth set. Only the sharp blows of the pieces of wood were heard at each stroke.

Buteau had launched forth the first blow, and Jean, yet stooping, would have had his head broken, if he had not leaped backwards. Instantly, with a sudden stiffening of the muscles, he arose, he raised, he brought down the flail, like a thresher beating the grain. But already the other was striking also, the two flail ends met, bent back upon their leather straps, in the mad flight of wounded birds. Three times the same clash was reproduced. They saw only those bits of wood whirl and hiss in the air at the extremity of the handles, always ready to fall and split the skulls which they menaced.

Delhomme and Fouan, however, had rushed forward, when the women cried out. Jean had just rolled in the straw, treacherously stricken by Buteau, who, with a blow like a whip stroke, along the ground, fortunately deadened, had hit him on the legs. He sprang to his feet, he brandished his flail in a rage that the pain increased. The end described a large circle, fell to the right, when the other expected it to the left. A few lines nearer, and the brains would have been beaten out. Only the ear was grazed. The blow, passing obliquely, fell with all its force upon the arm, which was broken clean. The bone cracked with the sound of breaking glass.

"Ah! the murderer!" howled Buteau, "he has killed me!"

Jean, haggard, his eyes red with blood, dropped his weapon. Then, for a moment, he stared at them all, as if stupefied by what had happened there, so rapidly; and he went away, limping, with a gesture of furious despair.

When he had turned the corner of the house, towards the plain, he saw La Trouille, who had witnessed the fight, over the garden hedge. She was still laughing at it, having come there to skulk around the baptismal repast, to which neither her father nor herself had been invited. Mahomet would split his sides with merriment over the little family fête, over his brother's broken arm! She squirmed as if she had been tickled, almost ready to fall over, so much was she amused at it all.

"Ah! Caporal, what a hit!" cried she. "The bone went crack! It wasn't the least bit funny!"

He did not answer, slackening his step with an over-whelmed

air. And she followed him, whistling to her geese, which she had brought to have a pretext for stationing herself and listening behind the walls. Jean, mechanically, returned towards the threshing machine, which was yet at work amid the fading light. He thought that it was all over, that he could never see the Buteaus again, that they would never give him Françoise. How stupid it was! Ten minutes had sufficed; a quarrel which he had not sought, a blow so unfortunate, just at the moment when matters were progressing favorably! And now there was an end to it all! The roaring of the machine, in the depths of the twilight, prolonged itself like a great cry of distress.

ARNOLD ZWEIG

ARNOLD ZWEIG (German, 1887-   ). Militant pacifist. His most famous novel, *The Case of Sergeant Grischa*, came out of painful World War I experiences. Emigrated to Israel, a refugee from Nazi Germany. There wrote extensively on Zionism. Best stories: in *Playthings of Time*. Essays: *Juden auf der deutschen Bühne.*

THE APPARITION

TELL me a story!—that's easy to say. These mountains bring back almost too vivid memories of blessed, happy days when I was as carefree as a colt and of those others when I was preparing myself for the task (or was it preparing itself for me?) that, for the time being, I hold in abeyance yet dare not interrupt. But as my eyes trouble me and I cannot, just now, enjoy the flights of fancy of others in the delightful pursuit of reading, I must, for better or worse, pass my leisure time in telling stories.

It happened during the coldest part of winter in the eastern Carpathians. This is a country of mountains that rise abruptly from the plains, and of heavy-coated browsing sheep; little hamlets, villages, and farms dot the plain, divided from each other by tongues of woodland slipping down the mountainside, and by fields wrested, ages ago, from the stark Slovak soil. This region lies far away— fully four hundred years! Miracles, saints, and demons still remain familiar phenomena there while fear, superstitious fear, is felt— and perhaps rightly so—only towards government officials, newspapers, machinery, the telephone, and the radio.

1433

The inhabitants are without exception religious. The Jews believe in the Jewish lore, the Slovaks in the Christian, literally and reverently, and they carry on the customs their fathers have handed down to them in writing and by word of mouth. They are also very poor in that region, the Slovakian peasants a little less so, the Jews a little more, and these two are dependent upon each other, inevitably and by turns, as in the good fable of the lion and the mouse.

In this state of poverty and intense cold, Rifke Leah left her cottage early one winter's evening and went into the woods where the snow lay deep and undisturbed. Rifke Leah carried a short spade and, arriving at a familiar spot near the edge of the wood which seemed shielded from prying eyes, she busily began to shovel away the snow and to break up the ice beneath to cleanse herself. She shivered as she cowered and washed herself in the crystal-clear, crystal-cold water which came down from the mountains under a crust of ice and which, suddenly freed of its coverlet, steamed as it came in contact with the warmer air—but she shivered chiefly because she feared someone might pass by and surprise her.

It was early evening, the moon was still low and yellow, but bright wintry stars were shining through the bare branches. . . . Then, as she had divined, she suddenly heard—a short distance away—the voices of some peasants taking a short-cut through the woods from the village tavern to their homes. Merciful God—men! They have been drinking, they are singing—good-natured men but ready for pranks when in liquor. She represses her cry of alarm, throws her skirt over her head so that no one recognizes her, and dashes, or rather glides, silently homeward through the snow under the light of the pale golden moon—a mysterious figure, swathed in white. Rifke Leah succeeds in eluding them; trembling, with beating heart, she makes a detour around the tavern and reaches her cottage a few minutes later.

Meanwhile the three peasants stood mutely beside the dark water, which had miraculously thawed in the midst of the snow and which was still steaming. What had they witnessed? A lovely, white form had floated away amid the trees; it must have been the Holy Mother of God come to assure the village of a better harvest. In their greatest need came heavenly kindness—take off your hats: a miracle has happened here in the midst of the snowy desolation of the forest. Indeed, the vapours were still rising like incense before their eyes! They corroborate each other—they have seen the Holy Mother of God, white and lovely, float away amid the trees.

The next morning and especially on the following Sunday they eagerly told of the miracle whose scene they had hastily marked by sticking branches into the snow around the pool of water. They had not neglected to cross themselves, kneel down, and thank the Mother of God for her visit.

The women and many people in distress made their way to the spot, which was frozen over again and covered with snow. One of the faithful hung a picture of the miraculous visitor and her Divine Child on the nearest tree, paper flowers from the church came next, then a little shed was built to protect the picture from the rain. Devout peasants and townsfolk, in ever-increasing numbers, made pilgrimages thither. The priests, hearing of it and being simple folk like the others, saw no reason to doubt a miracle that had already brought joy, solace, and cure from small ailments to so many of the faithful.

Spring came early that year; warm sunlight flooded the fields which peasants—cheered by the promise of the Queen of Heaven —were confidently tilling with their teams. The Jews had also, in due course, heard of the forest shrine. Oddly enough, Rifke Leah and her husband were the first to know its exact site. "Benjamin always was wide awake," the Jews said, and followed his lead. When the warm weather set in, he and his wife sold bread, wafers, biscuits, lemonade, and candles to the pilgrims.

The following autumn, after an abundant harvest, the foundations of a chapel commemorating the blessed visit of the Mother of God were laid. Before the winter began, the Bishop of Kosice came for the dedication. Not without heavy misgivings had he listened to the remarks of the local clergy, remarks which at first seemed harmless enough but which gradually came to reflect an urgent desire of the people. Many paths led to salvation and none should be disregarded, nor was this the time to ignore spiritual needs because of mental snobbishness. A miracle must have occurred; people believed it and it was working.

He visualized the brown, weatherbeaten faces of the peasants, their eyes opened wide in wonder; if he questioned and cross-questioned them as to what they had actually seen, they would insist it had been the Mother of God floating away through the wintry forest—nothing else. They had found the warm, dewy pool sending vapours into the night—nothing else. Let sceptics jeer, make insinuations, offer explanations of all sorts—he, the bishop, would be unworthy of shepherding these souls, if, through fear of

fostering a delusion, he refused to bestow upon the scene of the apparition the dignity of official as well as spiritual consecration. He came; he stood before them simply and gravely, chanting praises in Latin and asking God's blessing upon the land and the simple faith of these country people.

For Kosice, far off in the east of Europe, is also some hundreds of years behind the times. It isn't so long ago that bloody battles were fought there with gipsies who had made savoury meals of human flesh. The Jews of that region, when they are among themselves, say to each other that it is only fair that their trade, especially that with pilgrims, has so greatly improved.

Benjamin, Rifke Leah's husband, occasionally drinks a glass too much. That is why he happened to be so communicative to an eminent scholar and politician who came there a year later from the capital city of Prague to tell the Jews how and why they should vote. It was he—he clung to the ancient traditions of his land and people with tender mockery—who sometimes told this story, not to sneer at the incident but to characterize these distant people and places, where even today the Middle Ages are alive in human hearts. He possessed a sympathetic understanding of the sincerity and simple piety as well as of the humour and gentle roguishness of this tale. That is why I have retold it—at leisure, beneath green trees, surrounded by green mountains, facing the blue heavens, which we strange creatures so frequently fashion into figments of our own childish desires so that our dreams, fears, and hopes may be as much a part of them as the fleecy clouds and may pass as they do.

1436

ACKNOWLEDGMENTS

Aeschylus: "The Complaint of Prometheus," from *Prometheus Bound*, translated by Elizabeth Barrett Browning; "A Prayer to Artemis," from *The Suppliants*, translated by Miss Swanwick; "The Vision of Cassandra," from *Agamemnon*, translated by Edward Fitzgerald.

Ryunosuke Akutagawa: "Rashomon," from *Rashomon and Other Stories*, translated by Takashi Kojima, reprinted by permission of Liveright Publishing Corp., New York.

Sholem Aleikhem: "The Passover Guest," from *Yiddish Tales*, translated by Helena Frank, reprinted by permission of the Jewish Publication Society of America.

Vittorio Alfieri: "David Soothes Saul's Madness" and "The Death of Saul," from *Saul*.

Hans Christian Andersen: "The Lovers," reprinted from *The Universal Anthology*, edited by Richard Garnett, Merrill & Baker, New York. (Copyright, 1899, by Richard Garnett.)

Leonid Nikolayevic Andreyev: "Valia," translated by Lizzie B. Gorin, reprinted from *Greatest Short Stories*, P. F. Collier & Son, New York.

Guillaume Apollinaire: Poems from *Modern French Poetry*, compiled and translated by Joseph T. Shipley, reprinted by permission of Greenberg, New York.

Ludovico Ariosto: "Alcina the Enchantress," from *Orlando Furioso*, translated by W. S. Rose, reprinted from *The Universal Anthology*, edited by Richard Garnett, Merrill & Baker, New York. (Copyright, 1899, by Richard Garnett.)

Aristophanes: "Grand Chorus of Birds," from *The Birds*, translated by A. C. Swinburne.

Sholem Asch: "A Jewish Child," from *Yiddish Tales*, translated by Helena Frank, reprinted by permission of the Jewish Publication Society of America.

Attar (Farid ud-Din): "The Bird Parliament," translated by Edward Fitzgerald.

Sri Aurobindo: Poems from *Poems, Past and Present*, reprinted by permission of the Sri Aurobindo Ashram Press, Pondicherry, India.

Mary Austin: "Papago Wedding," reprinted from *One Smoke Stories*, by permission of Houghton Mifflin, Boston.

Isaak Babel: "The Birth of a King," from *Benya Krik the Gangster and Other Stories*, translated by Elisaveta Fen, reprinted by permission of Schocken Books, Inc., New York.

1437

James Matthew Barrie: "Courtships," from *Auld Licht Idylls*, reprinted by permission of Charles Scribner's Sons, New York.

Bashō: Poems from *An Anthology of Haiku Ancient and Modern*, translated by Asataro Miyamori, reprinted by permission of Taisei-Do Shobo Co., Kobe, Japan.

Charles Baudelaire: Poems from *Modern French Poetry*, translated by Joseph T. Shipley, reprinted by permission of Greenberg, New York.

Stephen Vincent Benét: "Freedom's a Hard-Bought Thing," from *Selected Works of Stephen Vincent Benét*, published by Rinehart & Co., New York; reprinted by permission of Brandt & Brandt, agents for the estate of Stephen Vincent Benét. (Copyright, 1940, by Stephen Vincent Benét.)

Pierre Jean de Béranger: Poems from *The Universal Anthology*, edited by Richard Garnett, tr. by William Young, Merrill & Baker, New York. Copyright, 1899, by Richard Garnett.)

Bhartrihari: Poems, translated by Arthur W. Ryder, from *1001 Poems of Mankind*, edited by Henry W. Wells, Tupper & Love, Atlanta.

Bhāsa: "True Love" from *Svapnavāsavadatta*, and "Serenity" from *Pratimā Nātakam*, from *Sanskrit Literature*, by K. Chandrasekharan and Brahmasri V. H. Subrahmanya Sastri, reprinted by permission of The P.E.N. All-India Centre, Bombay.

Bhavabhūti: "The Rescue of Malātī," from *Malātī Mādhava*; "The Story of the Ramayana," from *Uttara Rāmacharita*; from *Sanskrit Literature* by K. Chandrasekharan and Brahmasri V. H. Subrahmanya Sastri, reprinted by permission of The P.E.N. All-India Centre, Bombay.

Hayyim Nahman Bialik: Poems translated by Leo Auerbach and Joseph T. Shipley, reprinted from *The Guardian*, Philadelphia, Nov., 1924; courtesy *New Palestine*.

Bilhana: "An Indian Love-Lament," from *Saurīsuratapanchāsikā*, translated by Sir Edwin Arnold.

Björmstjerne Björnson: "The Father," from *The Bridal March*, translated by R. B. Anderson.

Karl Georg Büchner: *Woyzeck*, translated by and reprinted by permission of Theodore Hoffman.

Ivan Bunin: "Sunstroke," translated by Helen Matheson, from *Great Russian Short Stories*, edited by Stephen Graham, reprinted by permission of Ernest Benn Limited, London.

John Bunyan: "The Golden City," from *The Pilgrim's Progress*.

Robert Burns: "The Twa Dogs," from *Burns into English, Renderings of Select Dialect Poems of Robert Burns* by William Kean Seymour, Philosophical Library, New York.

Pedro Calderón de la Barca: "Segismund's Dream," from *La vida es sueño (Life Is a Dream)*, translated by Edward Fitzgerald.

Karel Capek: "The Island," translated by Sarka B. Hrbkova, from *Great Stories of All Nations*, edited by Lieber and Williams, Copyright 1927 by Brentano's, Inc.; reprinted by permission of Coward-McCann, Inc., New York.

Giosué Carducci: Poems from *Italian Lyrists of To-day*, translated by G. A. Greene, Macmillan Co., New York.

Miguel de Cervantes y Saavedra: "Sancho Panza in His Island," from *Don Quixote*, reprinted from *Half Hours with the Best Authors* by Charles Knight, C. Arthur Pearson, Ltd., London.

Adalbert von Chamisso: *Peter Schlemihl, the Shadowless Man,* from *The World's Greatest Books,* edited by Lord Northcliffe, S. S. McClure, McKinlay, Stone, and Mackenzie. (Copyright, 1910, S. S. McClure Co.)

François-René de Chateaubriand: "Chactas Relates the Death of Atala," from *Atala.*

Bankim Chandra Chatteree: "The Bride's Arrival," from *Devi Choudhurani,* Part III, reprinted from *Bengali Literature* by Annadasankar and Lila Ray, by permission of The P.E.N. All-India Centre, Bombay.

Geoffrey Chaucer: "The Pardoner's Tale" from *The Canterbury Tales,* retold in prose by Lieber and Williams, from *Great Stories of All Nations,* edited by Lieber and Williams. (Copyright, 1927, by Brentano's.)

Anton Chekhov: "The Slanderer," translated by Herman Bernstein, reprinted from *Greatest Short Stories,* by permission of P. F. Collier & Son, New York.

Chikamatsu Monzaemon: "Adventures of the Hakata Damsel," translated by Asataro Miyamori, revised by Robert Nichols, from *Masterpieces of Chikamatsu, the Japanese Shakespeare,* reprinted by permission of Routledge & Kegan Paul, Ltd., London.

Ch'u Yuan: Poems from *Li Sao and Other Poems of Ch'u Yuan,* translated by Yang Hsien-yi and Gladys Yang, reprinted by permission of the Foreign Language Press, Peking.

Confucius: Poems from the *Shih Ching,* translated by Williams Jennings, reprinted from *The Universal Anthology,* edited by Richard Garnett, Merrill & Baker, New York. (Copyright, 1899, by Richard Garnett.)

Joseph Conrad: "The Lagoon," from *Tales of Unrest,* reprinted by permission of the trustees of the Joseph Conrad Estate, Messrs. J. M. Dent & Sons, Ltd., London. (Copyright, 1908, 1920, Doubleday, Page and Company.)

James Fenimore Cooper: "The Ariel on the Shoals," from *The Pilot.*

Stephen Crane: "The Bride Comes to Yellow Sky," reprinted from *Stephen Crane: An Omnibus,* edited by R. W. Stallman, by permission of Alfred A. Knopf, Inc., New York. (Copyright, 1925, by William H. Crane and, 1952, by Alfred A. Knopf, Inc.)

Dandin: "The Courtesan's Mother," from *Dasakumāracharita,* reprinted from *Sanskrit Literature* by K. Chandrasekharan and Brahmasri V. H. Subrahmanya Sastri, by permission of The P.E.N. All-India Centre, Bombay.

Gabriele D'Annunzio: "Four Sonnets," translated by G. A. Greene, reprinted by permission of Macmillan Co., New York.

Dante Alighieri: Selection from *The Divine Comedy,* translated by "Mr. Carey," reprinted from *Half Hours with the Best Authors* by Charles Knight, C. Arthur Pearson, Ltd., London, 1899.

Alphonse Daudet: "The Death of the Dauphin," translated by Stuart Merrill. (Copyright, 1890.)

David: "Psalms" from the Book of Psalms, King James Version of The Holy Bible.

Richard Dehmel: Poems from *Contemporary German Poetry,* selected and translated by Jethro Bithell. (Walter Scott Publishing Company, 1909.)

1439

Grazia Deledda: "The Open Door," from *Chiaroscuro* (Fratelli Treves, Milan), translated by E. M. Baker, from *Great Italian Short Stories*, edited by Decio Pettoello, Ernest Benn, Ltd., London, 1930.

Charles Dickens: "The Convict in the Marshes," from *Great Expectations*.

Emily Dickinson: Poems from *The Poems of Emily Dickinson*, edited by Martha Dickinson Bianchi, reprinted by permission of Little, Brown, & Co., Boston.

Feodor Mikhaylovich Dostoyevsky: "The Murderer's Confession to Sonia," from *Crime and Punishment*.

John Dryden: "Zegri and Abencerrage" from *The Conquest of Granada by the Spaniards*.

Joseph von Eichendorff: Poems from *Leaves from the Life of a Good-for-Nothing*, translated by Mrs. A. L. Wister. "The Broken Ring," translated by C. G. Leland, and "Morning Prayer," translated by Alfred Baskerville, reprinted from *Representative German Poems*, Henry Holt & Co., New York.

Mihail Eminescu: Poems from *Poems of Mihail Eminescu*, translated from the Rumanian and rendered into the original metres by E. Sylvia Pankhurst and I. O. Stefanovici, reprinted by permission of Routledge & Kegan Paul, Ltd., London.

Euripides: "Medea's Wrongs" and "Medea's Last Words to Her Children," from *Medea*.

Abraham Ibn Ezra: Poems translated by Emma Lazarus, reprinted from *A Golden Treasury of Jewish Literature*, edited by Leo W. Schwarz, Rinehart & Co., New York, reprinted by permission of Leo W. Schwarz. (Copyright, 1937, by Leo W. Schwarz.)

William Faulkner: "A Rose for Emily," reprinted by permission of Random House, Inc., New York. (Copyright, 1931, by William Faulkner.)

Firdausi: "Rustam and Akwan Dev," from *Shah-namah*, translated by E. H. Palmer, reprinted from *The Universal Anthology*, edited by Richard Garnett, Merrill & Baker, New York. (Copyright, 1899, by Richard Garnett.)

Gustave Flaubert: "Salammbô and Her Lover," from *Salammbô*.

Anatole France: Poems from *Modern French Poetry*, compiled and translated by Joseph T. Shipley, reprinted by permission of Greenberg, New York.

Ferdinand Freiligrath: "The Lion's Ride," translated by C. T. Brooks, and "The Specter Caravan," translated by J. C. Mangan, reprinted from *The German Classics, Masterpieces of German Literature*, edited by Kuno Francke, The German Publication Society, New York.

Robert Frost: Poems from *Complete Poems of Robert Frost*, reprinted by permission of Henry Holt & Co., New York. (Copyright, 1930, 1949, by Henry Holt & Co., Inc., copyright 1936, 1948, by Robert Frost.)

Fuzulî: Poems, reprinted from *Turkish Literature*, P. F. Collier & Son, New York.

Solomon Ibn Gabirol: Poems translated by Emma Lazarus, from *A Golden Treasury of Jewish Literature*, edited by Leo W. Schwarz, Rinehart & Co., New York, reprinted by permission of Leo W. Schwarz. (Copyright, 1937, by Leo W. Schwarz.)

John Galsworthy: "Quality," from *The Inn of Tranquillity*, reprinted by permission of Charles Scribner's Sons, New York.

Vsevolod Garshin: "The Signal," reprinted from *Best Russian Short Stories*, edited by Thomas Seltzer, reprinted by permission of Random House, Inc., New York.

Théophile Gautier: "The Mummy's Foot," from *One of Cleopatra's Nights*, translated by Lafcadio Hearn, Brentano's, New York. (Copyright, 1890.)

Khalil Gibran: "Behind the Garment," from *The Secrets of the Heart*, translated by Anthony Rizcallah Ferris, edited by Martin L. Wolf, Philosophical Library, New York, 1947.

André Gide: "My Mother," from *Autumn Leaves*, translated by Elsie Pell, Philosophical Library, New York, 1950.

Jean Giraudoux: "May on Lake Asquam," from *Campaigns and Intervals*, translated by Elizabeth S. Sargeant, reprinted by permission of Houghton Mifflin Co., Boston.

Johann Wolfgang von Goethe: *Faust*, translated by Sir Theodore Martin.

Nikolai Gogol: "St. John's Eve," from *Evenings on a Farm Near Dikanka*, reprinted from *Taras Bulba, and Other Tales*, Everyman's Library, by permission of E. P. Dutton & Co., New York.

Oliver Goldsmith: "The Disabled Soldier," from *Citizen of the World*, originally titled "Letter CXVIII."

Ivan Alexandrovich Goncharov: Selections from *Oblomof*, reprinted from *The Universal Anthology*, edited by Richard Garnett, Merrill & Baker, New York. (Copyright, 1899, by Richard Garnett.)

Maxim Gorky: "One Autumn Night," reprinted from *Best Russian Short Stories*, edited by Thomas Seltzer, reprinted by permission of Random House, New York.

Judah Halevi: Poems, translated by Emma Lazarus, reprinted from *A Golden Treasury of Jewish Literature*, edited by Leo W. Schwarz, Rinehart & Co., New York, reprinted by permission of Leo W. Schwarz. (Copyright, 1937, by Leo W. Schwarz.)

Knut Hamsun: "The Call of Life," translated by Anders Orbeck, from *Norway's Best Stories*, edited by Hanna Astrup Larsen, W. W. Norton & Co., New York. Reprinted by permission of the American-Scandinavian Foundation.

Thomas Hardy: "Squire Petrick's Lady," from *A Group of Noble Dames*, reprinted by permission of Harper & Brothers, New York. (Copyright, 1891.

Bret Harte: "The Outcasts of Poker Flat," reprinted from *The Luck of Roaring Camp*, by permission of Houghton Mifflin & Co., Boston. (Copyright, 1872.)

Gerhart Hauptmann: Selection from *The Weavers*, translated by Mary Morison, reprinted from *The Universal Anthology*, edited by Richard Garnett, Merrill & Baker, New York. (Copyright, 1899, by Richard Garnett.)

Nathaniel Hawthorne: "The Ambitious Guest," reprinted by permission of Houghton Mifflin Co., New York.

Johann Peter Hebel: "Kannitverstan," translated by Paul Pratt, reprinted by permission of Alfred A. Knopf, Inc., New York.

Heinrich Heine: Poems, translated by Sir Theodore Martin, and selections from *Memoirs*, translated by Gilbert Cannon.

Ernest Hemingway: "Ten Indians," from *Men Without Women*, reprinted by permission of Charles Scribner's Sons, New York. Copyright 1927 by Charles Scribner's Sons, 1955 by Ernest Hemingway.

O. Henry: "The Whirligig of Life," from *Whirligigs*, copyright, 1903, 1931, Doubleday, Doran & Co., New York.

Johann Gottfried von Herder: "Sir Olaf," translated by Elizabeth Craigmyle, "Esthonian Bridal Song," translated by W. Taylor, reprinted from *An Anthology of World Poetry*, edited by Mark Van Doren, Reynal & Hitchcock, New York. (Copyright, 1936.)

Hermann Hesse: Poems, translated by Margarete Münsterberg, reprinted from *The German Classics*, edited by Kuno Francke, The German Publication Society, New York.

Hitomaro Kakinomoto: Poems from *The Manyōshū*. Published for the Nippon Gakujutsu Shinkōkai by the Iwanami Shoten, Tokyo, 1940. "The Mountain Top" and "My Love Who Loves Me Not," translated by Mabel Lorenz Ives, from *Poems for Enjoyment*, ed. Elias Lieberman, Harper & Bros., New York.

Friedrich Hölderlin: Poems, translated by Charles Wharton Stork, reprinted from *The German Classics*, edited by Kuno Francke, The German Publication Society, New York.

Homer: Selection from *The Iliad*, translated by John Gibson Lockhart.

Horace: "Ode 1," translated by Charles Stuart Calverly, "Epode 2," translated by Sir Theodore Martin, reprinted from *The Universal Anthology*, edited by Richard Garnett, Merrill & Baker, New York. (Copyright, 1899, by Richard Garnett.)

Ricarda Huch: "Midnight," translated by Margarete Münsterberg, reprinted from *The German Classics*, edited by Kuno Francke, The German Publication Society, New York.

Victor Hugo: Selections from *Les Misérables*.

Henrik Ibsen: Scenes from *Peer Gynt*, translated by Horace Maynard Finney, published by Philosophical Library, New York.

Muhammad Iqbal: "Community," translated by A. J. Arberry, reprinted from *Mysteries of Selflessness*, by permission of John Murray, Ltd., London.

Jens Peter Jacobsen: "The Plague at Bergamo," reprinted from *Short Story Classics*, P. F. Collier & Son, New York, 1927.

Henry James: Selections from *Confidence*, reprinted by permission of Houghton, Mifflin & Co., Boston.

Jami: "Zulaikha," translated by R. T. H. Griffith, reprinted from *The Universal Anthology*, edited by Richard Garnett, Merrill & Baker, New York. (Copyright, 1899, by Richard Garnett.)

Jataka: "The Strider over Battle-Fields," from *Virtue Is Its Own Reward*, translated by H. C. Warren, reprinted from *Buddhism in Translations* by H. C. Warren, by permission of the Harvard University Press, Cambridge.

Jayadeva: "Hymn to Vishnu," from the *Gītā Govinda*, translated by Sir Edwin Arnold, reprinted from *An Anthology of World Poetry*, edited by Mark Van Doren, Reynal & Hitchcock, New York.

1442

mission of Noel Carrington, Transatlantic Arts Co. Ltd., London and New York. (Copyright, 1946.)

Lao-Tzu: Selections from *The Way of Life*, translated by R. B. Blakney, reprinted by permission of the New American Library, New York. (Copyright, 1955, by Raymond B. Blakney.)

David Herbert Lawrence: "Dreams Old and Nascent," from *Amores*, included in *Collected Poems of D. H. Lawrence*, copyright, 1916, by D. H. Lawrence, 1944 by Frieda Lawrence, reprinted by permission of The Viking Press, New York.

Lee Hou-Chu: Poems from *Poems of Lee Hou-Chu*, translated by Liu Yih-Ling and Shahid Suhrawardy, reprinted by permission of Orient Longmans Ltd., Calcutta.

Nikolaus Lenau: Poems, translated by Charles Wharton Stork, reprinted from *The German Classics, Masterpieces of German Literature*, edited by Kuno Francke, The German Publication Society, New York.

Mikhail Yuryevich Lermontov: Poems, translated by Max Eastman, reprinted by permission of the translator.

Gotthold Ephraim Lessing: "Saladin and Nathan," from *Nathan the Wise*, reprinted by permission of E. P. Dutton & Co., New York.

Sinclair Lewis: "Young Man Axelbrod," reprinted from *Selected Short Stories of Sinclair Lewis*, copyright 1917 by Sinclair Lewis, reprinted by permission of Doubleday & Co., New York.

Lin Ho-Ching: Poems from *Lin Ho-Ching*, translated by Max Perleberg, reprinted by permission of K. Weiss, Hong Kong.

Li Po: "Weep Not, Young Women," "The Fisherman," "Birds Singing at Dusk," "Picking the Lotus," translated by Peter Rudolph, reprinted from *Chinese Love Poems* by permission of the Peter Pauper Press, Mount Vernon. "Song of Chang-kan" and "Passionate Grief," verse renderings by Mabel Lorenz Ives, reprinted from *Chinese Love Songs*, B. L. Hutchinson, Upper Montclair, by permission of the translator.

Li Shang-Yin: Poems from *Three Hundred Poems of the T'ang Dynasty*, reprinted by permission of John Murray Ltd., London.

Liu Chi: Poems, translated by Soames Jenyns, reprinted from *Selections from Three Hundred Poems of the T'ang Dynasty*, John Murray Ltd., London.

Jack London: "To Build a Fire," reprinted by permission of Irving Shepard.

Federico García Lorca: "Seven Lyrics from the *Cante Jondo* Poems," translated by Norman Di Giovanni, reprinted by permission of the *Antioch Review*.

Lusin: *"Medicine,"* translated by Yao Hsin-nang, from *Living China*, reprinted by permission of Edgar Snow.

Antonio Machado: "Perchance in Dreams," translated by Eleanor L. Turnbull, from *Ten Centuries of Spanish Poetry*, edited by Eleanor L. Turnbull. reprinted by permission of the Johns Hopkins Press. "Iberian God," translated by Ruth Matilda Anderson, and "Autumn Dawn," translated by Jean Rogers Longland, reprinted from *Translations from Hispanic Poets*, by permission of the Hispanic Society of America. "At the Burial of a Friend," "Childish Dreams," and "Poem" translated by Thomas McGreevy, reprinted from *The European Caravan*, edited by Samuel Putnam, M. C. Darnton, G. Reavey & J. Bronowski; Brewer, Warren & Putnam, New York, 1931.

Maurice Maeterlinck: "The Life of the Dead," from *The Great Beyond*, translated by Marta K. Neufeld & Renee Spodheim, Philosophical Library, New York, 1947.

Stéphane Mallarmé: "The Afternoon of a Faun," reprinted from *Modern French Poetry*, compiled and translated by Joseph T. Shipley, reprinted by permission of Greenberg Publishers, New York.

Thomas Mann: "A Weary Hour," translated by H. T. Lowe-Porter, from *Stories of Three Decades*, reprinted by permission of Alfred A. Knopf, Inc., New York. Copyright 1936 by Alfred A. Knopf, Inc.

Alessandro Manzoni: "The Interrupted Wedding," from *The Betrothed*.

John Masefield: "The Western Islands," from *A Mainsail Haul*, reprinted by permission of The Macmillan Co., New York. (Copyright, 1913.)

William Somerset Maugham: "The Pattern," from *Of Human Bondage*, reprinted by permission of Doubleday & Co., New York.

Guy de Maupassant: "The Necklace," translated by Jonathan Sturges, reprinted from *The Odd Number* by permission of Harper & Brothers, New York.

François Mauriac: "The Eternal Bourgeoise," from *Saint Margaret of Cortona*, translated by Bernard Frechtman, Philosophical Library, New York.

Mêng Hao-jan: Poems from *A Lute of Jade*, Wisdom of the East Series, edited by J. L. Cranmer-Byng, reprinted by permission of John Murray, Ltd., London.

George Meredith: "The Punishment of Shahpesh, the Persian, on Khipil, the Builder," from *The Shaving of Shagpat*. (Copyright, 1898, by Charles Scribner's Sons.)

Adam Mickiewicz: "Zevila," translated by Lola Gay-Tifft, from *The Blue Flower*, edited by Hermann Kesten, reprinted by permission of Roy Publishers, New York.

Edna St. Vincent Millay: "Elegy Before Death," from *Second April and Other Poems*, published by Harper & Brothers (copyright, 1920, 1948, by Edna St. Vincent Millay); "What Lips My Lips Have Kissed," from *The Harp-Weaver and Other Poems*; published by Harper & Bros. (copyright, 1920, 1948, by Edna St. Vincent Millay), reprinted by permission of Brandt & Brandt, agents for the estate of Edna St. Vincent Millay.

Molière: "First Lesson in Philosophy," from *The Bourgeois Gentleman*.

Mori Ogai: "The Pier," translated by Torao Taketomo, from *Paulownia*, reprinted by permission of Dodd Mead & Co., New York. (Copyright, 1918.)

Eduard Mörike: "Beauty Rohtraut," translated by George Meredith, reprinted by permission of Charles Scribner's Sons. Other poems, translated by Charles Wharton Stork, from *The German Classics, Masterpieces of German Literature*, edited by Kuno Francke, reprinted by permission of the German Publication Society, New York.

Multatuli: "The Story of Saïdjah," from *Max Havelaar*, translated by Alphonse Nahuys, reprinted by permission of Maatschappij der Nederlandse Letterkunde, Leiden, Holland.

Lady Murasaki: "The Festival of Red Leaves," from *The Tale of Genji*, translated by Arthur Waley, reprinted by permission of Houghton Mifflin Co., Boston.

1447

Mendele Mocher Sforim: Selection from *The Nag*, translated by Moshe Spiegel, reprinted by permission of the Beechhurst Press, New York.

George Bernard Shaw: "The Miraculous Revenge," from *Short Stories, Scraps, and Shavings*, reprinted from *44 Irish Short Stories*, edited by Devin A. Garrity by permission of Devin-Adair Co., New York.

Shên Ts'ung-wên: "Under Cover of Darkness," from *Contemporary Chinese Short Stories*, edited and translated by Yuan Chia-Hua and Robert Payne, reprinted by permission of Noel Carrington, Transatlantic Arts Co., Ltd., London.

Shih Nai-an: "Death of the Tigers," from *All Men Are Brothers*, translated by Pearl S. Buck, reprinted by permission of the John Day Company, New York. (Copyright, 1937, by Pearl S. Buck.)

Henryk Sienkiewicz: "The Lighthouse Keeper of Aspinwall," from *Yanko the Musician*, translated by Jeremiah Curtin, Little, Brown & Co., Boston. (Copyright, 1893.)

Solomon: Selection from "The Song of Solomon," from the King James Version of the Bible.

Somadeva: "Devasmita," from the *Katha-sarit-sagara*, reprinted from *Great Stories of All Nations*, edited by Lieber and Williams, Coward-McCann Inc., New York. (Copyright, 1927, by Brentano's.)

Sophocles: Selections from *Antigone* and *Oedipus Tyrannus*. (Copyright, 1900.)

Carl Spitteler: "Theme" and "Heracles' Passing to Earth" from "Olympian Spring," translated by Margarete Münsterberg, from *The German Classics, Masterpieces of German Literature*, edited by Kuno Francke, reprinted by permission of the German Publication Society, New York.

Ssü-k'ung T'u: Poems, from *A Lute of Jade*, translated by L. Cranmer-Byng, reprinted by permission of John Murray, Ltd., London.

John Steinbeck: "Owners and Tenants," from *The Grapes of Wrath*, reprinted by permission of The Viking Press, Inc., New York. (Copyright, 1939, by John Steinbeck.)

Stendhal: Selections from *Chartreuse of Parma*, from *The World's Greatest Books*, edited by Lord Northcliffe, and S. S. McClure, McKinlay, Stone and Mackenzie. (Copyright, 1910, by S. S. McClure Co.)

Wallace Stevens: "Domination of Black" and "Anecdote of the Jar," from *Harmonium*; "An Extract," from *Parts of a World*; reprinted by permission of Alfred A. Knopf, Inc., New York.

Robert Louis Stevenson: "Thrawn Janet," from *The Merry Men*.

Theodor Storm: "Veronika," translated by Charles H. Stubing from Storm's *Sämtliche Schriften* (Braunschweig: G. Westermann, 1868). "To a Deceased," "The City," and "The Heath," translated by Margarete Münsterberg, and "Consolation," translated by Charles Wharton Stork, reprinted from *The German Classics of the Ninteenth and Twentieth Centuries*, edited by Kuno Francke and William Guild Howard, German Publication Society, New York.

Harriet Beecher Stowe: "Topsy," from *Uncle Tom's Cabin*.

August Strindberg: "A Funeral," reprinted from *The German Lieutenant and other Stories*, by permission of T. Werner Laurie, Ltd., London.

Sūdraka: "The Clay Cart," translated by Sir Monier Monier-Williams, reprinted from *The Universal Anthology*, edited by Richard Garnett, Merrill & Baker, New York. (Copyright, 1899, by Richard Garnett.)

Sun Hsi-chen: "Ah Ao," translated by Edgar Snow, from *Living China*, reprinted by permission of the translator.

Su Tung-p'o: "Autumn Sun," from *Selections from the Works of Su Tung-p'o*, translated by Cyril Drummond Le Gros Clark, reprinted by permission of Jonathan Cape Ltd., London.

Jonathan Swift: "The Emperor of Lilliput," from *Gulliver's Travels*.

Algernon Charles Swinburne: "When the Hounds of Spring," and "Man," from *Atalanta in Calydon*.

Rabindranath Tagore: "To Nature," from *Sheaves, Poems and Songs by Rabindranath Tagore*, translated by Nagendranath Gupta, Philosophical Library, New York.

Junichirō Tanizaki: Selection from *Some Prefer Nettles*, translated by Edward G. Seidensticker, reprinted by permission of Alfred A. Knopf, Inc., New York.

T'ao Ch'ien: "Returning to Live on the Farm," from *The Poems of T'ao Ch'ien*, translated by Lily Pao-hu Chang and Marjorie Sinclair, reprinted by permission of the University of Hawaii Press, Honolulu.

Torquato Tasso: "The Golden Age," from *Aminta*, reprinted from *The Universal Anthology*, edited by Richard Garnett, Merrill & Baker, New York. (Copyright, 1899, by Richard Garnett.)

Johann Ludwig Tieck: "The Friends," from *Tales from Phantasus*, James Burns, London, 1845.

Leo Tolstoy: "Where Love Is," from *Master and Man and Other Parables and Tales*, reprinted by permission of E. P. Dutton & Co., New York. (Translated, 1885.)

Tu Fu: "The Poet Dreams" translated by Peter Rudolph from translation of Judith Gautier; from *Chinese Love Poems*, Peter Pauper Press, Mt. Vernon, N. Y. Other poems from *Chinese Love Poems* translated by Mabel Lorenz Ives; published by B. L. Hutchinson, Upper Montclair, N. J.

Ivan Sergeyevich Turgenev: "The Nihilist," from *Fathers and Sons*. (Copyright, 1900.)

Mark Twain: "The Celebrated Jumping Frog of Calaveras County." (Copyright, American Publishing Co.)

Miguel de Unamuno: "Three Generations," from *Perplexities and Paradoxes*, translated by Stuart Gross, Philosophical Library, New York.

Paul Valéry: Poems, from *Modern French Poetry*, compiled and translated by Joseph T. Shipley, reprinted by permission of Greenberg, New York.

Vālmīki: "Nārad," from *Selections from the Rāmāyana*, from *Hindu Literature*, P. F. Collier & Son, New York. (Copyright, 1900, by The Colonial Press.)

Giovanni Verga: "Gramigna's Mistress." (Copyright, 1900.)

Emile Verhaeren: Poems, from *Modern French Poetry*, compiled and translated by Joseph T. Shipley, reprinted by permission of Greenberg, New York.

Paul Verlaine: Poems, from *Modern French Poetry*, compiled and translated by Joseph T. Shipley, reprinted by permission of Greenberg, New York.

They're not so wretched as you'd think,
Though always on privation's brink:
They're so accustomed to the sight,
The view it gives them little fright.

Then chance and fortune are so guided
They're always more or less provided;
And though fatigued with close employment,
A spell of rest's a sweet enjoyment.

The dearest comfort of their lives,
Their thriving brood and faithful wives;
The prattling things are just their pride,
That sweeten board and fireside.

And then, twelvepenny-worth of ale
Will always over care prevail;
They lay aside their private cares
To canvass Church and State affairs:
They'll talk of patronage and priests
With kindling fury in their breasts;
Or tell what new taxation's coming,
And hear the news from London humming.

As bleak-faced Hallowmass returns
They hear the jolly rattling churns,
When rural life of every station
Unite in common recreation;
Love smiles, Wit sparkles, social Mirth
Forgets there's trouble on the earth.

That merry day the year begins
They bar the door on frosty winds;
The strong ale wreathes with mantling cream
And gives a heart-inspiring steam;
The treasured pipe and snuffbox full
Are handed round with right goodwill;
The cheerful elders talk and browse,
The young go romping through the house—
My heart has been so glad to see them
That I for joy ran barking with them.

Still, it's too true what you have said:
That game is far too often played.
There's many a creditable stock
Of decent, honest, kindly folk,

177

Are bundled out both root and branch,
Some rascal's greedy pride to quench,
Who thinks to knit himself the faster
In favour with his absent master,
Who, maybe, is a-parliamenting,
For Britain's good his soul indenting—

CAESAR

Faith, lad, you little know about it;
For Britain's good!—good faith! I doubt it!
Say rather, going as premiers lead him,
With Aye or No just as they bid him!
At operas and plays parading,
Mortgaging, gambling, masquerading.
Or maybe, in a frolic daft,
For Hague or Calais boards a craft.
To make a tour, by pleasure swirled,
To learn *bon ton* and see the world.
　　There, at Vienna or Versailles,
He breaks his father's old entails,
Or to Madrid diverts his route
To strum guitars or fight with nought;
Or down Italian vistas hurtles,
Whore-hunting among groves of myrtles;
Then boozes muddy German water
To make himself look fair and fatter
And clear the consequential sorrows—
Love-gifts of carnival signoras.
For Britain's good!—for her destruction!
With dissipation, feud and faction!

LUATH

Well, well! dear sirs! is that the way
So many great estates decay?
Are we so goaded, cramped and pressed
For wealth to go that way at last?
　　O, if they'd stay away from courts
And please themselves with country sports,
It would for everyone be better,
The laird, the tenant and the cotter!

178

For these wild, noisy, rambling sparks,
They're not ill-natured in their larks:
Except for stripping ancient glades,
Or speaking lightly of their jades,
Or shooting of a hare or moorcock,
They little harm the simple poor folk.
    But will you tell me, Master Caesar,
Sure, great folks live a life of pleasure?
No cold nor hunger's grip can press them,
The very thought need not distress them.

CAESAR

Lord, man, you'd never envy them
If you were sometimes where I am.
    It's true, they needn't starve or sweat
Through winter's cold or summer's heat;
They've no hard work to cramp their bones
And fill old age with aches and groans:
But human beings are such fools,
For all their colleges and schools,
That when no present ills perplex them
They make enough themselves to vex them;
The less they have to disconcert them
In like proportion less will hurt them.
A country fellow at the plough,
His acres tilled, his heart's aglow;
A country lassie at her wheel,
Her dozens done, she's fine and well;
But gentlemen, and ladies worst,
At dusk with idleness are cursed.
They loiter, lounging, lank and lazy;
Though nothing ails them, yet uneasy;
Their days insipid, dull and tasteless;
Their nights unquiet, long and restless.
And even sports, their balls and races,
Their galloping through public places,
Are such parades of pomp and art,
The joy can scarcely reach the heart.
The men fall out in party matches,
Then make it up in wild debauches:

179

One night they're mad with drink and whoring,
Next day their life is past enduring.
The ladies arm-in-arm, in clusters,
Are great and gracious all as sisters;
But hear their thoughts of one another,
They're downright devils all together.
And then, with eggshell cup and platie,
They sip the scandal-brew so pretty,
Or through long nights, with acid looks,
Pore on the devil's picture books;
Stake on a chance a farmer's stackyard,
And cheat like any unhanged blackguard.
    There are exceptions, man and woman;
But this is gentry's life in common.

    By this the sun was out of sight
And twilight darkening brought the night;
A beetle hummed with lazy drone,
The cows stood lowing in the lane;
When up they got with friendly shrugs,
Rejoiced they were not men but dogs;
And each took off his homeward way,
Resolved to meet some other day.

GEORGE GORDON BYRON

GEORGE GORDON BYRON (English, 1788-1824). The most gifted showman
of English Romanticism. Suffered handicap of clubfoot. *Childe Harold's
Pilgrimage* brought early fame and acclaim of English society, despite scandalous private life. Settled in Italy, where he wrote greatest work, the
satirical *Don Juan*. Joined Greek rebels in 1823, died of fever a year later.
    Poetry expresses the essence of romantic melancholy and pessimism.

SHE WALKS IN BEAUTY

SHE walks in beauty, like the night
    Of cloudless climes and starry skies;
And all that's best of dark and bright
    Meet in her aspect and her eyes:
Thus mellowed to that tender light
    Which heaven to gaudy day denies.

One shade the more, one ray the less,
  Had half impaired the nameless grace
Which waves in every raven tress,
  Or softly lightens o'er her face;
Where thoughts serenely sweet express
  How pure, how dear their dwelling-place.

And on that cheek, and o'er that brow,
  So soft, so calm, yet eloquent,
The smiles that win, the tints that glow,
  But tell of days in goodness spent,
A mind at peace with all below,
  A heart whose love is innocent!

SO, WE'LL GO NO MORE A-ROVING

So, we'll go no more a-roving
  So late into the night,
Though the heart be still as loving,
  And the moon be still as bright.

For the sword outwears its sheath,
  And the soul wears out the breast,
And the heart must pause to breathe,
  And Love itself have rest.

Though the night was made for loving,
  And the day returns too soon,
Yet we'll go no more a-roving
  By the light of the moon.

THE ISLES OF GREECE

The isles of Greece! the isles of Greece
  Where burning Sappho loved and sung,
Where grew the arts of war and peace,
  Where Delos rose, and Phœbus sprung!
Eternal summer gilds them yet,
But all, except their sun, is set.

The Scian and the Teian muse,
  The hero's harp, the lover's lute,
Have found the fame your shores refuse;
  Their place of birth alone is mute
To sounds which echo further west
Than your sires' "Islands of the Blest."

The mountains look on Marathon—
  And Marathon looks on the sea;
And musing there an hour alone,
  I dreamed that Greece might still be free;
For standing on the Persians' grave,
I could not deem myself a slave.

A king sate on the rocky brow
  Which looks o'er sea-born Salamis;
And ships, by thousands, lay below,
  And men in nations—all were his!
He counted them at break of day—
And when the sun set, where were they?

And where are they? and where art thou,
  My country? On thy voiceless shore
The heroic lay is tuneless now—
  The heroic bosom beats no more!
And must thy lyre, so long divine,
Degenerate into hands like mine?

'Tis something in the dearth of fame,
  Though linked among a fettered race,
To feel at least a patriot's shame,
  Even as I sing, suffuse my face;
For what is left the poet here?
For Greeks a blush—for Greece a tear.

Must *we* but weep o'er days more blest?
  Must *we* but blush?—Our fathers bled.
Earth! render back from out thy breast
  A remnant of our Spartan dead!
Of the three hundred grant but three,
To make a new Thermopylae!

What, silent still? and silent all?
    Ah! no— the voices of the dead
Sound like a distant torrent's fall,
    And answer, "Let one living head,
But one, arise—we come, we come!"
'Tis but the living who are dumb.

In vain—in vain; strike other chords;
    Fill high the cup with Samian wine!
Leave battles to the Turkish hordes,
    And shed the blood of Scio's vine!
Hark! rising to the ignoble call—
How answers each bold Bacchanal!

You have the Pyrric dance as yet;
    Where is the Pyrric phalanx gone?
Of two such lessons, why forget
    The nobler and the manlier one?
You have the letters Cadmus gave—
Think ye he meant them for a slave?

Fill high the bowl with Samian wine!
    We will not think of themes like these!
It made Anacreon's song divine.
    He served—but served Polycrates—
A tyrant; but our masters then
Were still, at least, our countrymen.

The tyrant of the Chersonese
    Was freedom's best and bravest friend;
That tyrant was Miltiades!
    O that the present hour would lend
Another despot of the kind!
Such chains as his were sure to bind.

Fill high the bowl with Samian wine!
    On Suli's rock, and Parga's shore,
Exists the remnant of a line
    Such as the Doric mothers bore;
And there, perhaps, some seed is sown,
The Heracleidan blood might own.

183

Trust not for freedom to the Franks—
  They have a king who buys and sells;
In native swords and native ranks
  The only hope of courage dwells.
But Turkish force and Latin fraud
Would break your shield, however broad.

Fill high the bowl with Samian wine!
  Our virgins dance beneath the shade—
I see their glorious black eyes shine;
  But gazing on each glowing maid,
My own the burning teardrop laves,
To think such breasts must suckle slaves.

Place me on Sunium's marbled steep,
  Where nothing, save the waves and I,
May hear our mutual murmurs sweep;
  There, swan-like, let me sing and die.
A land of slaves shall ne'er be mine—
Dash down yon cup of Samian wine!

WHEN WE TWO PARTED

When we two parted
  In silence and tears,
Half broken-hearted,
  To sever for years,
Pale grew thy cheek and cold,
  Colder thy kiss;
Truly that hour foretold
  Sorrow to this!

The dew of the morning
  Sunk chill on my brow;
It felt like the waning
  Of what I feel now.
Thy vows are all broken,
  And light is thy fame:
I hear thy name spoken
  And share in its shame.

They name thee before me,
  A knell to mine ear;
A shudder comes o'er me—
  Why wert thou so dear?
They knew not I knew thee
  Who knew thee too well:
Long, long shall I rue thee
  Too deeply to tell.

In secret we met:
  In silence I grieve
That thy heart could forget,
  Thy spirit deceive.
If I should meet thee
  After long years,
How should I greet thee?
  With silence and tears.

ELEGY ON THYRZA

And thou art dead, as young and fair
  As aught of mortal birth;
And form so soft and charms so rare
  Too soon return'd to Earth!
Though Earth received them in her bed,
And o'er the spot the crowd may tread
  In carelessness or mirth,
There is an eye which could not brook
A moment on that grave to look.

I will not ask where thou liest low,
  Nor gaze upon the spot;
There flowers or weeds at will may grow,
  So I behold them not:
It is enough for me to prove
That what I loved and long must love
  Like common earth can rot;
To me there needs no stone to tell
'Tis Nothing that I loved so well.

185

Yet did I love thee to the last,
    As fervently as thou,
Who didst not change through all the past
    And canst not alter now.
The love where Death has set his seal
Nor age can chill, nor rival steal,
    Nor falsehood disavow:
And, what were worse, thou canst not see
Or wrong, or change, or fault in me.

The better days of life were ours;
    The worst can be but mine:
The sun that cheers, the storm that lours,
    Shall never more be thine.
The silence of that dreamless sleep
I envy now too much to weep;
    Nor need I to repine.
That all those charms have pass'd away
I might have watch'd through long decay.

The flower in ripen'd bloom unmatch'd
    Must fall the earliest prey;
Though by no hand untimely snatch'd,
    The leaves must drop away.
And yet it were a greater grief
To watch it withering, leaf by leaf,
    Than see it pluck'd to-day;
Since earthly eye but ill can bear
To trace the change to foul from fair.

I know not if I could have borne
    To see thy beauties fade;
The night that follow'd such a morn
    Had worn a deeper shade:
Thy day without a cloud hath past,
    And thou wert lovely to the last,
    Extinguish'd, not decay'd;
As stars that shoot along the sky
Shine brightest as they fall from high.

As once I wept, if I could weep,
  My tears might well be shed,
To think I was not near, to keep
  One vigil o'er thy bed:
To gaze, how fondly! on thy face,
To fold thee in a faint embrace,
  Uphold thy drooping head;
And show that love, however vain,
Nor thou nor I can feel again.

Yet how much less it were to gain,
  Though thou hast left me free,
The loveliest things that still remain
  Than thus remember thee!
The all of thine that cannot die
Through dark and dread Eternity
  Returns again to me,
And more thy buried love endears
Than aught except its living years.

C

PEDRO CALDERON DE LA BARCA

PEDRO CALDERON DE LA BARCA (Spanish, 1600-1681). Baroque and Catholic playwright and poet. Won early fame as dramatist. After service in Spanish army, became priest at 50. Wrote 120 plays, notable for elaborate construction and philosophic content, and many *autos* (religious mysteries). Among them: *La vida es sueño, El alcalde de Zalamea, El médico de Su Honra.*

SEGISMUND'S DREAM

(The King of Poland, frightened by an omen at his son's birth, which the soothsayers have interpreted to mean that the boy will grow up a mere wild beast, bringing fire and slaughter on the country if he succeeds to power, has imprisoned him in a tower till he shall come of age, with a faithful officer for guard. He then has him released—to see if the oracle has been mistaken!—and told that all this confinement and misery has been a dream—as in the "Induction" to the "Taming of the Shrew.")

   Segismund (within)—
Forbear! I stifle with your perfume! cease
Your crazy salutations! peace, I say—
Begone, or let me go, ere I go mad
With all this babble, mummery, and glare,
For I am growing dangerous—Air! room! air!—
   (*He rushes in. Music ceases.*)
Oh but to save the reeling brain from wreck
With its bewildered senses!—
   (*He covers his eyes for a while.*)
   (*After looking in the mirror.*)
What, this fantastic Segismund the same

188

Who last night, as for all his nights before,
Lay down to sleep in wolfskin on the ground
In a black turret which the wolf howled round.
And woke again upon a golden bed,
Round which as clouds about a rising sun,
In scarce less glittering caparison,
Gathered gay shapes that, underneath a breeze
Of music, handed him upon their knees
The wine of heaven in a cup of gold,
And still in soft melodious undersong
Hailing me Prince of Poland!—"Segismund,"
They said, "Our Prince! The Prince of Poland!" and
Again, "Oh, welcome, welcome, to his own
Our own Prince Segismund—"

If reason, sense, and self-identity
Obliterated from a worn-out brain,
Art thou not maddest striving to be sane,
And catching at that Self of yesterday
That, like a leper's rags, best flung away!
Or if not mad, then dreaming—dreaming?—well—
Dreaming then—Or, if self to self be true,
Not mocked by that, but as poor souls have been
By those who wronged them, to give wrong new relish?
Or have those stars indeed they told me of
As masters of my wretched life of old,
Into some happier constellation rolled,
And brought my better fortune out on earth
Clear as themselves in heav'n!—

(The great officers of state crowd around him with protestations of
fidelity; Clotaldo, his old warder, comes, and after attempts at
explaining and justifying the situation, Segismund in a fury attempts
to strike his head off; the Princess Estrella, betrothed to the Duke
of Muscovy, enters, and Segismund claims her for his own and
attempts to throttle the Duke; the King is called in, and after a
storm of reproaches which the King parries on the ground of good
intentions, Segismund closes as follows:)

Be assured your Savage, once let loose,
Will not be caged again so quickly; not
By threat or adulation to be tamed,

189

Till he have had his quarrel out with those
Who made him what he is.

 King—

Beware! Beware!
Subdue the kindled Tiger in your eye,
Nor dream that it was sheer necessity
Made me thus far relax the bond of fate,
And, with far more of terror than of hope
Threaten myself, my people, and the State.
Know that, if old, I yet have vigor left
To wield the sword as well as wear the crown;
And if my more immediate issue fail,
Not wanting scions of collateral blood,
Whose wholesome growth shall more than compensate
For all the loss of a distorted stem.

 Segismund—

That will I straightway bring to trial—Oh,
After a revelation such as this,
The Last Day shall have little left to show
Of righted wrong and villainy requited!
Nay, Judgment now beginning upon earth,
Myself, methinks, in right of all my wrongs,
Appointed heav'n's avenging minister,
Accuser, judge, and executioner,
Sword in hand, cite the guilty—First, as worst,
The usurper of his son's inheritance;
Him and his old accomplice, time and crime
Inveterate, and unable to repay
The golden years of life they stole away.
What, does he yet maintain his state, and keep
The throne he should be judged from? Down with him,
That I may trample on the false white head
So long has worn my crown! Where are my soldiers?
Of all my subjects and my vassals here
Not one to do my bidding? Hark! A trumpet!
The trumpet—

(*He pauses as the trumpet sounds as in Act I., and masked Soldiers
gradually fill in behind the throne.*)

 King (*rising before his throne*)—

Aye, indeed, the trumpet blows

190

A memorable note, to summon those
Who, if forthwith you fall not at the feet
Of him whose head you threaten with the dust,
Forthwith shall draw the curtain of the Past
About you; and this momentary gleam
Of glory, that you think to hold life-fast,
So coming, so shall vanish, as a dream.

   Segismund—
He prophesies; the old man prophesies;
And, at his trumpet's summons, from the tower
The leash-bound shadows loosened after me
My rising glory reach and overlour—
But, reach not I my height, he shall not hold,
But with me back to his own darkness!
   (*He dashes toward the throne and is inclosed by the soldiers.*)
Traitors!
Hold off! Unhand me! Am not I your king?
And you would strangle him!
But I am breaking with an inward Fire
Shall scorch you off, and wrap me on the wings
Of conflagration from a kindled pyre
Of lying prophecies and prophet kings
Above the extinguished stars—Reach me the sword
He flung me—Fill me such a bowl of wine
As that you woke the day with—
   King—
And shall close,—
But of the vintage that Clotaldo knows.

(He is drugged, returned to the tower, and on waking assured that
the recent taste of freedom and kingship was all a dream, and his
former life in the tower the reality.)

   Segismund—
You know
'Tis nothing but a dream?
   Clotaldo—
Nay, you yourself
Know best how lately you awoke from that
You know you went to sleep on?
Why, have you never dreamt the like before?

Segismund—
Never, to such reality.
   Clotaldo—
Such dreams
Are oftentimes the sleeping exhalations
Of that ambition that lies smoldering
Under the ashes of the lowest fortune;
By which, when reason slumbers, or has lost
The reins of sensible comparison,
We fly at something higher than we are—
Scarce ever dive to lower—to be kings,
Or conquerors, crowned with laurel or with gold,
Nay, mounting heav'n itself on eagle wings.
Which, by the way, now that I think of it,
May furnish us the key to this high flight—
That royal Eagle we were watching, and
Talking of as you went to sleep last night.
   Segismund—
Last night? Last night?
   Clotaldo—
Aye, do you not remember
Envying his immunity of flight,
As, rising from his throne of rock, he sailed
Above the mountains far into the West
That burned about him, while with poising wings
He darkled in it as a burning brand
Is seen to smolder in the fire it feeds?
   Segismund—
Last night—last night—Oh, what a day was that
Between that last night and this sad To-day!
   Clotaldo—
And yet, perhaps,
Only some few dark moments, into which
Imagination, once lit up within
And unconditional of time and space,
Can pour infinities.
   Segismund—
And I remember
How the old man they called the King, who wore
The crown of gold about his silver hair,
And a mysterious girdle round his waist,

192

Just when my rage was roaring at its height,
And after which it was all dark again,
Bid me beware lest all should be a dream.
    Clotaldo—
Aye, there another specialty of dreams,
That once the dreamer 'gins to dream he dreams.
His foot is on the very verge of waking.
    Segismund—
Would it had been upon the verge of death
That knows no waking—
Lifting me up to glory, to fall back,
Stunned, crippled—wretcheder than ev'n before.
    Clotaldo—
Yet not so glorious, Segismund, if you
Your visionary honor wore so ill
As to work murder and revenge on those
Who meant you well.
    Segismund—
Who meant me!—me! their Prince
Chained like a felon—
    Clotaldo—
Stay, stay—Not so fast,
You dreamed the Prince, remember.
    Segismund—
Then in dream
Revenged it only.
True. But as they say
Dreams are rough copies of the waking soul
Yet uncorrected of the higher Will,
So that men sometimes in their dreams confess
An unsuspected, or forgotten, self;
One must beware to check—aye, if one may,
Stifle ere born, such passion in ourselves
As makes, we see, such havoc with our sleep,
And ill reacts upon the waking day.
And, by the bye, for one test, Segismund,
Between such swearable realities—
Since Dreaming, Madness, Passion, are akin
In missing each that salutary rein
Of reason, and the guiding will of man:
One test, I think, of waking sanity

193

Shall be that conscious power of self-control,
To curb all passion, but much most of all
That evil and vindictive, that ill squares
With human, and with holy canon less,
Which bids us pardon ev'n our enemies,
And much more those who, out of no ill will,
Mistakenly have taken up the rod
Which heav'n, they think, has put into their hands.

   Segismund—
I think I soon shall have to try again—
Sleep has not yet done with me.

   Clotaldo—
Such a sleep.
Take my advice—'tis early yet—the sun
Scarce up above the mountain; go within,
And if the night deceived you, try anew
With morning; morning dreams they say come true.

   Segismund—
Oh, rather pray for me a sleep so fast
As shall obliterate dream and waking too.

   (*Exit into the tower.*)

   Clotaldo—
So sleep; sleep fast: and sleep away those two
Night potions, and the waking dream between
Which dream thou must believe; and, if to see
Again, poor Segismund! that dream must be.
And yet, and yet, in these our ghostly lives,
Half night, half day, half sleeping, half awake,
How if our working life, like that of sleep,
Be all a dream in that eternal life
To which we wake not till we sleep in death?
How if, I say, the senses we now trust
For date of sensible comparison,—
Aye, ev'n the Reason's self that dates with them,
Should be in essence or intensity
Hereafter so transcended, and awoke
To a perceptive subtlety so keen
As to confess themselves befooled before,
In all that now they will avouch for most?
One man—like this—but only so much longer
As life is longer than a summer's day,

194

Believed himself a king upon his throne,
And played at hazard with his fellows' lives,
Who cheaply dreamed away their lives to him.
The sailor dreamed of tossing on the flood:
The soldier of his laurels grown in blood:
The lover of the beauty that he knew
Must yet dissolve to dusty residue:
The merchant and the miser of his bags
Of fingered gold; the beggar of his rags:
And all this stage of earth on which we seem
Such busy actors, and the parts we played,
Substantial as the shadow of a shade,
And Dreaming but a dream within a dream.

 Fife—
Was it not said, sir,
By some philosopher as yet unborn
That any chimney sweep who for twelve hours
Dreams himself king is happy as the king
Who dreams himself twelve hours a chimney-sweep?

 Clotaldo—
A theme indeed for wiser heads than yours
To moralize upon.

(An insurrection breaking out to reinstate Segismund, a band of
soldiers bring him, asleep, from the tower.)

 Captain—
O Royal Segismund, our Prince and King,
Look on us—listen to us—answer us,
Your faithful soldiery and subjects, now
About you kneeling, but on fire to rise
And cleave a passage through your enemies,
Until we seat you on your lawful throne.
For though your father, King Basilio,
Now King of Poland, jealous of the stars
That prophesy his setting with your rise,
Here holds you ignominiously eclipsed,
And would Astolfo, Duke of Muscovy,
Mount to the throne of Poland after him;
So will not we, your loyal soldiery

195

And subjects; neither those of us now first
Apprised of your existence and your right:
Nor those that hitherto deluded by
Allegiance false, their vizors now fling down,
And craving pardon on their knees with us
For that unconscious disloyalty,
Offer with us the service of their blood;
Not only we and they; but at our heels
The heart, if not the bulk, of Poland follows
To join their voices and their arms with ours,
In vindicating with our lives our own
Prince Segismund to Poland and her throne.

Soldiers—
Segismund, Segismund, Prince Segismund!
Our own King Segismund, etc.

(*They all arise.*)

Segismund—
Again? So soon?—What, not yet done with me?
The sun is little higher up, I think,
Than when I last lay down,
To bury in the depth of your own sea
You that infest its shallows.

Captain—
Sir!

Segismund—
And now,
Not in a palace, not in the fine clothes
We all were in; but here, in the old place,
And in your old accounterment—
Only your vizors off, and lips unlockt
To mock me with that idle title—

Captain—
Nay,
Indeed no idle title, but your own,
Then, now, and now forever. For, behold,
Ev'n as I speak. the mountain passes fill
And bristle with the advancing soldiery
That glitters in your rising glory, sir;
And, at our signal, echo to our cry,
"Segismund, King of Poland!"

(*Shouts, trumpets, etc.*)

196

Segismund—
Oh, how cheap
The muster of a countless host of shadows,
As impotent to do with as to keep!
All this they said before—to softer music.
   Captain—
Soft music, sir, to what indeed were shadows,
That, following the sunshine of a Court,
Shall back be brought with it—if shadows still,
Yet to substantial reckoning.
   Segismund—
They shall?
The white-haired and white-wandel chamberlain,
So busy with his wand too—the old King
That I was somewhat hard on—he had been
Hard upon me—and the fine feathered Prince
Who crowed so loud—my cousin,—and another,
Another cousin, we will not bear hard on—
And—but Clotaldo?
   Captain—
Fled, my Lord, but close
Pursued; and then—
   Segismund—
Then, as he fled before,
And after he had sworn it on his knees,
Came back to take me—where I am!—No more,
No more of this! Away with you! Begone!
Whether but visions of ambitious night
That morning ought to scatter, or grown out
Of night's proportions you invade the day
To scare me from my little wits yet left,
Begone! I know I must be near awake,
Knowing I dream; or, if not at my voice,
Then vanish at the clapping of my hands,
Or take this foolish fellow for your sport:
Dressing me up in visionary glories,
Which the first air of waking consciousness
Scatters as fast as from the alamander—
That, waking one fine morning in full flower,
One rougher insurrection of the breeze
Of all her sudden honor disadorns

197

To the last blossom, and she stands again
The winter-naked scarecrow that she was!
  (*Shouts, trumpets, etc.*)
  A Soldier—
Challenging King Basilio's now in sight,
And bearing down upon us.
  Captain—
Sir, you hear;
A little hesitation and delay,
And all is lost—your own right, and the lives
Of those who now maintain it at that cost;
With you all saved and won; without, all lost.
That former recognition of your right
Grant but a dream, if you will have it so;
Great things forecast themselves by shadows great:
Or will you have it, this like that dream too,
People, and place, and time itself, all dream—
Yet, being in't, and as the shadows come
Quicker and thicker than you can escape,
Adopt your visionary soldiery,
Who, having struck a solid chain away,
Now put an airy sword into your hand,
And harnessing you piecemeal till you stand
Amidst us all complete in glittering,
If unsubstantial, steel—

(A battle is fought, in which Segismund is victorious; taught by his
former experience, he resolves to be wise and temperate, and closes
with the following moralizing:)

  You stare upon me all, amazed to hear
The word of civil justice from such lips
As never yet seemed tuned to such discourse.
But listen—In that same enchanted tower,
Not long ago, I learned it from a dream
Expounded by this ancient prophet here;
And which he told me, should it come again,
How I should bear myself beneath it; not
As then with angry passion all on fire,
Arguing and making a distempered soul;
But ev'n with justice, mercy, self-control,

198

As if the dream I walked in were no dream,
And conscience one day to account for it.
A dream it was in which I thought myself,
And you that hailed me now then hailed me King,
In a brave palace that was all my own,
Within, and all without it, mine; until,
Drunk with excess of majesty and pride,
Methought I towered so high and swelled so wide,
That of myself I burst the glittering bubble,
That my ambition had about me blown,
And all again was darkness. Such a dream
As this in which I may be walking now;
Dispensing solemn justice to you shadows,
Who make believe to listen; but anon,
With all your glittering arms and equipage,
Kings, princes, captains, warriors, plume and steel,
Aye, ev'n with all your airy theater,
May flit into air you seem to rend
With acclamation, leaving me to wake
In the dark tower; or dreaming that I wake
From this that waking is; or this and that
Both waking or both dreaming; such a doubt
Confounds and clouds our mortal life about.
And, whether wake or dreaming; this I know,
How dream-wise human glories come and go;
Whose momentary tenure not to break,
Walking as one who knows he soon may wake
So fairly carry the full cup, so well
Disordered insolence and passion quell,
That there be nothing after to upbraid
Dreamer or doer in the part he played,
Whether To-morrow's dawn shall break the spell,
Or the Last Trumpet of the eternal Day,
When Dreaming with the Night shall pass away.
    (*Exeunt.*)

KAREL CAPEK

KAREL CAPEK (Czech, 1890-1938). Most widely known Czech writer, through plays, *R.U.R.* and *The Life of the Insects.* Also author of six novels, short story collections, travel books. Ardent humanitarian, fond of utopian themes. Like his friend Masaryk, strongly under influence of American ideas. Said to have died "of the death of his country."

THE ISLAND

AT one time there lived in Lisbon a certain Dom Luiz de Faria who later sailed away in order to see the world, and having visited the greater part of it, died on an island as remote as one's imagination can picture. During his life in Lisbon he was a man full of wisdom and judgment. He lived as such men usually do, in a way to gratify his own desires without doing harm to others, and he occupied a position in affairs commensurate with his innate pride. But even that life eventually bored him and became a burden to him. Therefore he exchanged his property for money and sailed away on the first ship out into the world.

On this ship he sailed first to Cadiz and then to Palermo, Constantinople and Beiruth, to Palestine, Egypt and around Arabia clear up to Ceylon. Then they sailed around lower India and the islands including Java whence they struck for the open sea again heading towards the east and south. Sometimes they met fellow countrymen who were homeward bound and who wept with joy when they asked questions about their native land.

In all the countries they visited Dom Luiz saw so many things that were extraordinary and well-nigh marvellous, that he felt as if he had forgotten all his former life.

While they sailed thus over the wide sea, the stormy season overtook them and their boat tossed on the waves like a cork which has neither a goal nor anchor. For three days the storm increased in violence. The third night the ship struck a coral reef.

Dom Luiz during the terrific crash felt himself lifted to a great height and then plunged down into the water. But the water hurled him back and pitched him unconscious on a broken timber.

When he recovered consciousness, he realised that it was bright noon and that he was drifting on a pile of shattered beams wholly alone on a calm sea. At that instant he felt for the first time a real joy in being alive.

He floated thus until evening and throughout the night and the entire succeeding day, but not a glimpse of land did he have. Besides, the pile of rafters on which he floated was becoming loosened by the action of the water, and piece after piece detached itself, Dom Luiz vainly trying to tie them together with strips of his own clothing. At last only three weak timbers remained to him and he sank back in weariness. With a feeling of being utterly forsaken, Dom Luiz made his adieu to life and resigned himself to the will of God.

The third day at dawn he saw that the waves were bearing him to a beautiful island of charming groves and green thickets which seemed to be floating on the bosom of the ocean.

Finally, covered with salt and foam he stepped out on the land. At that instant several savages emerged from the forest, but Dom Luiz gave utterance to an unfriendly shout for he was afraid of them. Then he knelt down to pray, sank to the earth and fell asleep on the shore of the ocean.

When the sun was setting, he was awakened by a great hunger. The sand all around him was marked by the prints of bare flat feet. Dom Luiz was much rejoiced for he realised that around him had walked and sat many savages who had discussed and wondered about him but had done him no injury. Forthwith he went to seek food but it had already grown dark. When he had passed to the other side of the cliff, he beheld the savages sitting in a circle eating their supper. He saw men, women and children in that circle, but he took a position at some distance, not being bold enough to go closer, as if he were a beggar from some far-off province.

A young female of the savage group arose from her place and brought him a flat basket full of fruit. Luiz flung himself upon the basket and devoured bananas, figs, both dried and fresh, other fruits and fresh clams, meat dried in the sun and sweet bread of a very different sort from ours. The girl also brought him a pitcher of spring water and, seating herself in a squat position, she watched him eat and drink. When Luiz had had his fill, he felt a great relief in his whole body and began to thank the girl aloud for her gifts and for the water, for her kind-heartedness and for the mercifulness of all the others. As he spoke thus, a deep gratitude like the sweet anguish of an overflowing heart grew in him and poured itself out in beautiful words which he had never before been able to utter so well. The savage girl sat in front of him and listened.

The following day he continued his inspection, encircling the

Dom Luiz felt that he must repeat his gratitude in a way to make her understand and so he thanked her as fervently as if he were praying. In the meantime the savages had all gone away into the forest and Luiz was afraid that he would remain alone in the unfamiliar place with this great joy in his heart. So he began to relate things to the girl to detain her—telling her where he came from, how the ship was wrecked and what sufferings he had endured on the sea. All the while the savage maid lay before him flat on her stomach and listened silently. Then Luiz observed that she had fallen asleep with her face on the earth. Seating himself at some distance, he gazed at the heavenly stars and listened to the murmur of the sea until sleep overcame him.

When he awoke in the morning, he looked for the maid but she had vanished. Only the impression of her entire body—straight and long like a green twig—remained in the sand. And when Luiz stepped into the hollow, it was warm and sun-heated. Then he followed the shoreline to inspect the island. Sometimes he had to go through forests or underbrush; often he had to skirt swamps and climb over boulders. At times he met groups of savages but he was not afraid of them. He noted that the ocean was a more beautiful blue than anywhere else in the world and that there were blossoming trees and unusual loveliness of vegetation. Thus he journeyed all day long enjoying the beauty of the island which was the most pleasing of any he had ever seen. Even the natives, he observed, were far more handsome than other savage tribes.

The following day he continued his inspection, encircling the entire island which was of an undulating surface blessed with streams and flowering verdure, just as one would picture paradise. By evening he reached the spot on the shore where he had landed from the sea and there sat the young savage girl all alone braiding her hair. At her feet lay the timbers on which he had floated hither. The waves of the impassable sea splashed up as far as the rafters so that he could advance no farther. Here Dom Luiz seated himself beside her and gazed at the sweep of the water bearing off his thoughts wave on wave. After many hundreds of waves had thus come and gone, his heart overflowed with an immeasurable sorrow and he began to pour out his grief, telling how he had journeyed for two days making a complete circumference of the island but that nowhere had he found a city or a harbour or a human being resembling himself. He told how all his comrades had perished at sea and that he had been cast up on an island from

which there was no return; that he was left alone among low savage beings who spoke another language in which it was impossible to distinguish words or sense. Thus he complained bitterly and the savage maid listened to him lying on the sand until she fell asleep as if rocked to slumber by the grievous lullaby of his tribulations. Then Luiz became silent and breathed softly.

In the morning they sat together on the rock overlooking the sea giving a view of the entire horizon. There Dom Luiz reviewed his whole life, the elegance and splendour of Lisbon, his love affairs, his voyages and all that he had seen in the world and he closed his eyes to vision more clearly the beautiful scenes in his own life. When he again opened his eyes, he saw the savage girl sitting on her heels and looking before her with a somewhat unintelligent gaze. He saw that she was lovely, with a small body and slender limbs, as brown as the earth, and finely erect.

After that he sat often on the rock looking out for a possible passing ship. He saw the sun rise up from the ocean and sink in its depths and he became accustomed to this just as he did to all else. He learned day by day more of the pleasant sweetness of the island and its climate. It was like an isle of love. Sometimes the savages came to him and gazed on him with respect as they squatted in a circle about him like penguins. Among them were tattooed men and venerable ancients and these brought him portions of food that he might live.

When the rainy season came, Dom Luiz took up his abode in the young savage girl's hut. Thus he lived among the wild natives and went naked just as they did but he felt scorn for them and did not learn a single word of their language. He did not know what name they gave to the island on which he lived, to the roof which covered his head or to the woman who in the eyes of God was his only mate. Whenever he returned to the hut, he found there food prepared for him, a couch and the quiet embrace of his brown wife. Although he regarded her as not really or wholly a human being, but rather more nearly like other animals, nevertheless he treated her as if she understood him, telling her everything in his own language and feeling fully satisfied because she listened to him attentively. He narrated to her everything that occupied his mind—events of his former life in Lisbon, things about his home, details of his travels. At first it grieved him that the savage maiden neither understood his words nor the significance of what he was saying but he became accustomed even to that and continued to recount everything in the

same phrases and also with variations and always afterward he took her into his arms.

But in the course of time his narrations grew shorter and more interrupted. The adventures he had had slipped the memory of Dom Luiz just as if they hadn't happened or as if nothing had ever happened. For whole days he would lie on his couch lost in thought and silence. He became accustomed to his new life and continued to sit on his rock but he no longer kept a lookout for passing ships. Thus many years passed and Luiz forgot about returning, forgot the past, even his own native speech, and his mind was as mute as his tongue. Always at night he returned to his hut but he never learned to know the natives any more intimately than he had the day he arrived on the island.

Once in the summer he was deep in the forest when such a strange unrest overwhelmed him suddenly that he ran out of the wood to behold out on the ocean a beautiful ship at anchor. With violently beating heart he rushed to the shore to mount his boulder and when he reached it, he saw on the beach a group of sailors and officers. He concealed himself behind the rock like a savage and listened. Their words touched the margin of his memory and he then realised that the newcomers were speaking his native tongue. He rose then and tried to address them but he only gave utterance to a loud shout. The new arrivals were frightened and he gave a second outcry. They raised their carbines but in that instant his tongue became untangled and he cried out, "Seignors,—have mercy!" All of them cried out in joy and hastened forward to him. But Luiz was seized by a savage instinct to flee before them. They, however, had completely surrounded him and one after another embraced him and overwhelmed him with questions. Thus he stood in the midst of the group—naked and full of anguish, looking in every direction for a loophole of escape.

"Don't be afraid," an elderly officer said to him. "Just recall that you are a human being. Bring him meat and wine for he looks thin and miserable. And you—sit down here among us and rest while you get accustomed again to the speech of human beings instead of to screeches which no doubt apes employ as speech."

They brought Dom Luiz sweet wine, prepared meats and biscuits. He sat among them as if in a dream and ate and gradually began to feel his memory returning. The others also ate and drank and conversed merrily rejoicing that they had found a fellow countryman. When Luiz had partaken of some of the food, a delicious feeling

of gratitude filled him just as that time when the savage maiden had fed him but in addition he now felt a joy in the beautiful speech which he heard and understood and in the companionable people who addressed him as a brother. The words now came to his tongue of themselves and he expressed his thanks to them as best he could.

"Rest a little longer," the old officer said to him, "and then you can tell us who you are and how you got here. Then the precious gift of language will return to you for there is nothing more beautiful than the power of speech which permits a man to talk, to relate his adventures and to pour out his feelings."

While he was speaking a young sailor tuned up and began softly to sing a song about a man who went away beyond the sea while his sweetheart implores the sea and the winds and the sky to restore him to her, the pleading grief of the maiden being expressed in the most touching words one could find anywhere. After him others sang or recited other poems of similar content, each of them a little sadder in strain. All the songs gave voice to the longing for a loved one; they told of ships sailing to far distant lands and of the ever changeful sea. At the last everyone was filled with memories of home and of all whom they had left behind. Dom Luiz wept copious tears, painfully happy in the afflictions he had suffered and in their joyous solution, when after having become unused to civilized speech he now heard the beautiful music of poetry. He wept because it was all like a dream which he feared could not be real.

Finally the old officer arose and said, "Children, now we will inspect the island which we found here in the ocean and before the sun sets we will gather here to row back to the ship. At night we will lift anchor and under God's protection, we will sail back. You, my friend," he turned to Luiz, "if you have anything that is yours and that you want to take with you as a souvenir, bring it here and wait for us till just before sunset."

The sailors scattered over the island shore and Dom Luiz betook himself to the savage woman's hut. The farther he advanced the more he loitered, turning over in his mind just how he should tell the savage that he must go away and forsake her. He sat down on a stone and debated with himself for he could not run away without any show of gratitude when he had lived with her for ten years. He recalled all the things she had done for him, how she had provided his food and shelter and had served him with her body and by her labours. Then he entered her hut, sat down beside her and talked a great deal and very hurriedly as if thus he could the better convince

her. He told her that they had come for him and that he must now sail away to attend to very necessary affairs of which he conjured up a great quantity. Then he took her in his arms and thanked her for everything that she had done for him and he promised her that he would soon return, accompanying his promises with solemn vows and protestations. When he had talked a long time, he noticed that she was listening to him without the faintest understanding or comprehension. This angered him and, losing his patience, he repeated all his arguments as emphatically as possible and he stamped his feet in his irritability. It suddenly occurred to him that the sailors were probably pushing off, not waiting for him, and he rushed out from the hut in the middle of his speech and hastened to the shore.

But as yet no one was there so he sat down to wait. But the thought worried him that in all likelihood the savage woman had not thoroughly understood what he had said to her about being compelled to go away. That seemed such a terrible thing to him that he suddenly started back on a run to explain everything to her once more. However, he did not step into her hut but looked through a crack to see what she was doing. He saw that she had gathered fresh grass to make a soft bed for him for the night; he saw her placing fruit for him to eat and he noted for the first time that she herself ate only the poorer specimens—those that were dwarfed or spotted and for him she selected the most beautiful—all the large and perfect samples of fruit. Then she sat down as immovable as a statue and waited for him. Of a sudden Dom Luis comprehended clearly that he must yet eat the fruit set out for him and lie down on the couch prepared so carefully and complete her expectations before he could depart.

Meanwhile the sun was setting and the sailors gathered on the shore to push off to the ship. Only Dom Luiz was missing and so they called out to him, "Seignor! Seignor!" When he did not come, they scattered in various directions on the edge of the forest to seek him, all the time continuing to call out to him. Two of the seamen ran quite close to him, calling him all the while but he hid among the shrubbery, his heart pounding in his breast for fear they would find him. Then all the voices died down, and the darkness came. Splashing the oars, the seamen rowed to the vessel loudly lamenting the lost survivor of the wreck. Then absolute quiet ensued and Dom Luiz emerged from the underbrush and returned to the hut. The savage woman sat there unmoved and patient. Dom Luiz ate the fruit, lay down on the freshly made couch with her beside him.

When dawn was breaking Dom Luiz lay sleepless and gazed out through the door of the hut where beyond the trees of the forest could be seen the sunlit sea—that sea on which the beautiful ship was just sailing away from the island. The savage woman lay beside him asleep but she was no longer attractive as in former years but ugly and terrible to look upon. Tear after tear rolled down on her bosom while Dom Luiz, in a whisper, lest she might hear, repeated beautiful words, wonderful poems describing the sorrow of longing and of vain eternal yearning.

Then the ship disappeared beyond the horizon and Dom Luiz remained on the island but he never uttered a single word from that day during all the years that preceded his death.

GIOSUE CARDUCCI

GIOSUÈ CARDUCCI (Italian, 1835-1907). Protagonist of the Italian classics in post-Risorgimento literature. Favored return to early literary forms, Roman paganism and imperialism. Opposed to Romanticism and Christianity. Poetry preoccupied with history and landscape of Italy: *Iams and Epodes, Barbarian Odes*. Critical works created great stir in their time.

SONNET

Alone my vessel passes, mid the cry
Of halycons, on the stormy waters borne,
Swept on, by thunder of the billows torn,
Beneath the clamours of the lightening sky.
All Memories turn to that far shore gone by
Their faces wet with tears and sorrow-worn,
And all fair Hopes o'erthrown their glances forlorn
Cast on the splintered oars that broken lie.

Yet at the stern still doth my Genius stand,
While to the creaking masts he hearkeneth,
And cries o'er sea and sky his loud command:
'Row on! row on! O guides of desperate breath,
Toward cloudy ports of the forgetful land.
Toward whitening breakers of the reefs of death.'

PANTHEISM

I told it not, O vigilant stars, to you;
To thee, all-seeing sun, I made no moan;
Her name, the flower of all things fair and true,
Was echoed in my silent heart alone.

Yet now my secret star tells unto star,
Through the brown night, to some vague sphery tune;
The great sun smiles at it, when, sinking far,
He whispers love to the white and rising moon.

On shadowy hills, on shores where life is gay,
Each bush repeats it to each flower that blows;
The flitting birds sing, 'Poet grim and grey,
At last Love's honeyed dreams thy spirit knows.'

I told it not, yet heaven and earth repeat
The name beloved in sounds divine that swell,
And mid the acacia-blossom's perfume sweet
Murmurs the Spirit of All—'She loves thee well.'

SNOWFALL

Slowly flutters the snow from ash-coloured heavens in silence;
Sound or tumult of life rises not up from the town;

Not of herbseller the cry, nor rumorous rattle of wagons,
Not love's passionate song joyous in musical youth.

But, from the belfry swaying, hoarsely the hours thro' the evening
Moan like sighs from a world far from the light of our day.

Wandering song-birds beat at my tarnished window panes; friendly
Spirits returning are they, seeking and calling for me.

Soon, O belovèd ones, soon—be calm, heart ever undaunted—
Soon to the silence I come, soon in the shades to repose.

208

MIGUEL DE CERVANTES Y SAAVEDRA

MIGUEL DE CERVANTES Y SAAVEDRA (Spanish, 1547-1616). Spain's greatest writer and one of foremost in world literature. Wrote poetry and plays, but greatest triumph was novel, *Don Quixote*. Like *Hamlet* and *Faust*, *Quixote* reveals the many contradictions in man's nature. Imbued with deep humanism and gentle humor, Cervantes died same day as his great contemporary, Shakespeare.

SANCHO PANZA IN HIS ISLAND

SANCHO, with all his attendants, came to a town that had about a thousand inhabitants, and was one of the best where the duke had any power. They gave him to understand that the name of the place was the Island of Barataria, either because the town was called Barataria, or because the government cost him so cheap. As soon as he came to the gates (for it was walled) the chief officers and inhabitants, in their formalities, came out to receive him, the bells rung, and all the people gave general demonstrations of their joy. The new governor was then carried in mighty pomp to the great church, to give Heaven thanks: and, after some ridiculous ceremonies, they delivered him the keys of the gates, and received him as perpetual governor of the Island of Barataria. In the meantime, the garb, the port, the huge beard, and the short and thick shape of the new governor, made everyone who knew nothing of the jest wonder: and even those who were privy to the plot, who were many. were not a little surprised.

In short, from the church they carried him to the court of justice; where, when they had placed him in his seat, "My lord governor," said the duke's steward to him, "it is an ancient custom here, that he who takes possession of this famous island must answer to some difficult and intricate question that is propounded to him; and by the return he makes the people feel the pulse of his understanding, and by an estimate of his abilities, judge whether they ought to rejoice or to be sorry for his coming."

All the while the steward was speaking, Sancho was staring on an inscription in large characters on the wall over against his seat; and, as he could not read, he asked what was the meaning of that which he saw painted there upon the wall. "Sir," said they, "it is an account of the day when your lordship took possession of this island; and the inscription runs thus: 'This day, being such a day

of this month, in such a year, the Lord Don Sancho Panza took possession of this island, which may he long enjoy.' " "And who is he?" asked Sancho. "Your lordship," answered the steward; "for we know of no other Panza in the island but yourself, who now sit in this chair." "Well, friend," said Sancho, "pray take notice that Don does not belong to me, nor was it borne by any of my family before me. Plain Sancho Panza is my name; my father was called Sancho, my grandfather Sancho, and all of us have been Panzas, without any Don or Donna added to our name. Now do I already guess your Dons are as thick as stones in this island. But it is enough that Heaven knows my meaning; if my government happens to last but four days to an end, it shall go hard but I will clear the island of these swarms of Dons, that must needs be as troublesome as so many flesh-flies. Come, now for your question, good Mr. Steward, and I will answer it as well as I can, whether the town be sorry or pleased."

At the same instant two men came into the court, the one dressed like a country fellow, the other looked like a tailor, with a pair of shears in his hand. "If it please you, my lord," cried the tailor, "I and this farmer here are come before your worship. This honest man came to my shop yesterday, for, saving your presence, I am a tailor, and, Heaven be praised, free of my company; so, my lord, he showed me a piece of cloth. 'Sir,' quoth he, 'is there enough of this to make a cap?' Whereupon I measured the stuff, and answered him, 'Yes,' if it like your worship. Now, as I imagined, do you see, he could not but imagine (and perhaps he imagined right enough) that I had a mind to cabbage some of his cloth, judging hard of us honest tailors. 'Pr'ythee,' quoth he, 'look there be not enough for two caps?' Now I smelt him out, and told him there was. Whereupon the old knave, (if it like your worship,) going on to the tune, bid me look again, and see whether it would not make three. And at last, if it would not make five. I was resolved to humour my customer, and said it might: so we struck a bargain.

"Just now the man is come for his caps, which I gave him; but when I asked him for my money he will have me give him his cloth again, or pay him for it."—"Is this true, honest man?" said Sancho to the farmer. "Yes, if it please you," answered the fellow; "but pray let him show the five caps he has made me." "With all my heart," cried the tailor; and with that, pulling his hand from under his cloak, he held up five little tiny caps, hanging upon his four fingers and thumb, as upon so many pins. "There," quoth he, "you

see the five caps this good gaffer asks for; and may I never whip a stitch more if I have wronged him of the least snip of his cloth, and let any workman be judge." The sight of the caps, and the oddness of the cause, set the whole court a laughing. Only Sancho sat gravely considering a while, and then, "Methinks," said he, "this suit here needs not be long depending, but may be decided without any more ado, with a great deal of equity; and, therefore, the judgment of the court is, that the tailor shall lose his making, and the countryman his cloth, and that the caps be given to the poor prisoners, and so let there be an end of the business."

If this sentence provoked the laughter of the whole court, the next no less raised their admiration. For, after the governor's order was executed, two old men appeared before him, one of them with a large cane in his hand, which he used as a staff. "My lord," said the other, who had none, "some time ago I lent this man ten gold crowns to do him a kindness, which money he was to repay me on demand. I did not ask him for it again in a good while, lest it should prove a greater inconvenience to him to repay me than he laboured under when he borrowed it. However, perceiving that he took no care to pay me, I have asked him for my due; nay, I have been forced to dun him hard for it. But still he did not only refuse to pay me again, but denied he owed me anything, and said, that if I lent him so much money he certainly returned it. Now, because I have no witnesses of the loan, nor he of the pretended payment, I beseech your lordship to put him to his oath, and if he will swear he has paid me, I will freely forgive him before God and the world." "What say you to this, old gentleman with the staff?" asked Sancho. "Sir," answered the old man, "I own he lent me the gold; and since he requires my oath, I beg you will be pleased to hold down your rod of justice, that I may swear upon it how I have honestly and truly returned him his money." Thereupon the governor held down his rod, and in the meantime the defendant gave his cane to the plaintiff to hold, as if it hindered him, while he was to make a cross and swear over the judge's rod: this done, he declared that it was true the other had lent him ten crowns, but that he had really returned him the same sum into his own hands; and that, because he supposed the plaintiff had forgotten it, he was continually asking him for it. The great governor, hearing this, asked the creditor what he had to reply. He made answer, that since his adversary had sworn it he was satisfied; for he believed him to be a better Christian than to offer to forswear himself, and that perhaps he had forgotten he had

211

been repaid. Then the defendant took his cane again, and, having made a low obeisance to the judge, was immediately leaving the court; which, when Sancho perceived, reflecting on the passage of the cane, and admiring the creditor's patience, after he had studied a while with his head leaning over his stomach, and his forefinger on his nose, on a sudden he ordered the old man with the staff to be called back. When he was returned, "Honest man," said Sancho, "let me see that cane a little, I have a use for it." "With all my heart," answered the other; "sir, here it is," and with that he gave it him. Sancho took it, and giving it to the other old man, "There," said he, "go your ways, and Heaven be with you, for now you are paid." "How so, my lord?" cried the old man; "do you judge this cane to be worth ten gold crowns?" "Certainly," said the governor, "or else I am the greatest dunce in the world. And now you shall see whether I have not a headpiece fit to govern a whole kingdom upon a shift." This said, he ordered the cane to be broken in open court, which was no sooner done, than out dropped the ten crowns. All the spectators were amazed, and began to look on their governor as a second Solomon. They asked him how he could conjecture that the ten crowns were in the cane? He told them that having observed how the defendant gave it to the plaintiff to hold while he took his oath, and then swore that he had truly returned him the money into his own hands, after which he took his cane again from the plaintiff —this considered, it came into his head that the money was lodged within the reed; from whence may be learned, that though sometimes those that govern are destitute of sense, yet it often pleases God to direct them in their judgment. Besides, he had heard the curate of his parish tell of such another business, and he had so special a memory, that were it not that he was so unlucky as to forget all he had a mind to remember, there could not have been a better in the whole island. At last the two old men went away, the one to his satisfaction, the other with eternal shame and disgrace: and the beholders were astonished; insomuch, that the person who was commissioned to register Sancho's words and actions, and observe his behaviour, was not able to determine whether he should not give him the character of a wise man, instead of that of a fool, which he had been thought to deserve.

* * * *

The history informs us that Sancho was conducted from the court of justice to a sumptuous palace, where, in a spacious room,

he found the cloth laid, and a most neat and magnificent entertainment prepared. As soon as he entered, the wind-music played, and four pages waited on him, in order to the washing his hands, which he did with a great deal of gravity. And now, the instruments ceasing, Sancho sat down at the upper end of the table, for there was no seat but there, and the cloth was only laid for one. A certain personage, who afterwards appeared to be a physician, came and stood at his elbow, with a whalebone wand in his hand. Then they took off a curious white cloth that lay over the dishes on the table, and discovered great variety of fruit and other eatables. One that looked like a student said grace: a page put a laced bib under Sancho's chin, and another, who did the office of sewer, set a dish of fruit before him. But he had hardly put one bit into his mouth, before the physician touched the dish with his wand, and then it was taken away by a page in an instant. Immediately another, with meat, was clapped in the place; but Sancho no sooner offered to taste it, than the doctor, with the wand, conjured it away as fast as the fruit. Sancho was annoyed at this sudden removal, and, looking about him on the company, asked them whether they used to tantalise people at that rate, feeding their eyes, and starving their bellies? "My lord governor," answered the physician, "you are to eat here no otherwise than according to the use and custom of other islands where there are governors. I am a doctor of physic, my lord, and have a salary allowed me in this island for taking charge of the governor's health, and I am more careful of it than of my own, studying night and day his constitution, that I may know what to prescribe when he falls sick. Now, the chief thing I do is to attend him always at his meals, to let him eat what I think convenient for him, and to prevent his eating what I imagine to be prejudicial to his health and offensive to his stomach. Therefore, I now ordered the fruit to be taken away because it was too cold and moist: and the other dish, because it is as much too hot, and over seasoned with spices, which are apt to increase thirst, and he that drinks much destroys and consumes the radical moisture, which is the fuel of life." "So, then," quoth Sancho, "this dish of roasted partridges here can do me no manner of harm." "Hold," said the physician, "the lord governor shall not eat of them while I live to prevent it." "Why so?" cried Sancho. "Because," answered the doctor, "our great master, Hippocrates, the north star and luminary of physic, says in one of his aphorisms, *Omnis saturatio mala, perdricis autem pessima*; that is, 'All repletion is bad, but that of

partridges is worst of all!' " "If it be so," said Sancho, "let Mr. Doctor see which of all these dishes on the table will do me the most good, and least harm, and let me eat my bellyful of that, without having it whisked away with his wand. For, by my hopes, and the pleasures of government, as I live, I am ready to die with hunger; and, not to allow me to eat any victuals, (let Mr. Doctor say what he will,) is the way to shorten my life, and not to lengthen it." "Very true, my lord," replied the physician; "however, I am of opinion you ought not to eat of these rabbits, as being a hairy, furry sort of food; nor would I have you taste that veal. Indeed, if it were neither roasted nor par boiled, something might be said; but, as it is, it must not be." "Well, then," said Sancho, "what think you of that huge dish yonder that smokes so? I take it to be an olla podrida, and, that being a hodge-podge of so many sorts of victuals, sure I cannot but light upon something there that will nick me, and be both wholesome and toothsome." "*Absit*," cried the doctor, "far be such an ill thought from us; no diet in the world yields worse nutriment than those wish-washes do. No, leave that luxurious compound to your rich monks and prebendaries, your masters of colleges, and lusty feeders at country weddings; but let them not encumber the tables of governors, where nothing but delicate unmixed viands, in their prime, ought to make their appearance. The reason is, that simple medicines are generally allowed to be better than compounds; for, in a composition, there may happen a mistake by an unequal proportion of the ingredients; but simples are not subject to that accident. Therefore, what I would advise at present, as a fit diet for the governor, for the preservation and support of his health, is a hundred of small wafers, and a few thin slices of marmalade, to strengthen his stomach and help digestion." Sancho, hearing this, leaned back upon his chair, and, looking earnestly in the doctor's face, very seriously asked him what his name was, and where he had studied. "My lord," answered he, "I am called Doctor Pedro Rezio de Augero. The name of the place where I was born is Tirteafuera, and lies between Caraquel and Almodabar del Campo, on the right hand; and I took my degree of Doctor in the University of Ossuna." "Hark you," said Sancho, in a mighty chafe, "Mr. Doctor Pedro Rezio de Augero, born at Tirteafuera, that lies between Caraquel and Almodabar del Campo, on the right hand, and who took your degree of Doctor at the University of Ossuna, and so forth, take yourself away! Avoid the room this moment, or, by the sun's light, I'll get me a good cudgel, and, beginning with

your carcase, will so belabour and rib-roast all the physicmongers in the island, that I will not leave therein one of the tribe, of those, I mean, that are ignorant quacks; for, as for learned and wise physicians, I will make much of them, and honour them like so many angels. Once more, Pedro Rezio, I say, get out of my presence. Avaunt! or I will take the chair I sit upon, and comb your head with it to some purpose, and let me be called to an account about it when I give up my office; I do not care, I will clear myself by saying I did the world good service in ridding it of a bad physician, the plague of the commonwealth. Body of me! let me eat, or let them take their government again; for an office that will not afford a man victuals is not worth two horsebeans."

ADALBERT VON CHAMISSO

ADALBERT VON CHAMISSO (German, 1781-1838). French-born, fled the Revolution with his parents and became page to Queen of Prussia at age of nine. Botanist on round-the-world scientific voyage. Author of romantic poems and the tale of Peter Schlemihl, so widely read it has become an international legend.

PETER SCHLEMIHL, THE SHADOWLESS MAN

I. THE GREY MAN

HAVING safely landed after a fatiguing journey, I took my modest belongings to the nearest cheap inn, engaged a garret room, washed, put on my newly-turned black coat, and proceeded to find Mr. Thomas John's mansion. After a severe cross-examination on the part of the hall-porter, I had the honour of being shown into the park where Mr. John was entertaining a party. He graciously took my letter of introduction, continuing the while to talk to his guests. Then he broke the seal, still joining in the conversation, which turned upon wealth. "Anyone," he remarked, "who has not at least a million is, pardon the word, a rogue." "How true," I exclaimed; which pleased him, for he asked me to stay. Then, offering his arm to a fair lady, he led the party to the rose-clad hill. Everybody was very jolly; and I followed behind, so as not to make myself a nuisance.

215

The beautiful Fanny, who seemed to be the queen of the day, in trying to pick a rose, had scratched her finger, which caused much commotion. She asked for some plaster, and a quiet, lean, tall, elderly man, dressed in grey, who walked by my side, put his hand in his coat pocket, pulled out a pocket-book, and, with a deep bow, handed the lady what she wanted. She took it without thanks, and we all continued to ascend the hill.

Arrived at the top, Mr. John, espying a light spot on the horizon, called for a telescope. Before the servants had time to move, the grey man, bowing modestly, had put his hand in his pocket and pulled out a beautiful telescope, which passed from hand to hand without being returned to its owner. Nobody seemed surprised at the huge instrument issuing from a tiny pocket, and nobody took any more notice of the grey man than of myself.

The ground was damp, and somebody suggested how fine it would be to spread some Turkey carpets. Scarcely had the wish been expressed, when the grey man again put his hand into his pocket, and, with a modest, humble gesture, pulled out a rich Turkey carpet, some twenty yards by ten, which was spread out by the servants without anybody appearing to be surprised. I asked a young gentleman who the obliging man might be. He did not know.

The sun began to get troublesome, and Fanny casually asked the grey man if he might happen to have a tent by him. He bowed deeply, and began to pull out of his pocket canvas, and bars, and ropes, and everything needed for the tent, which was promptly put up. Again nobody seemed surprised. I felt uncanny; especially when, at the next expressed desire, I saw him pull out of his pocket three fine large horses with saddles and trappings! You would not believe it if I did not tell you that I saw it with my own eyes.

It was gruesome. I sneaked away, and had already reached the foot of the hill, when, to my horror, I noticed the grey man approaching. He took off his hat, bowed humbly, and addressed me.

"Forgive my impertinence, sir, but during the short time I have had the happiness to be near you I have been able to look with indescribable admiration upon that beautiful shadow of yours, which you throw from you contemptuously, as it were. Pardon me, but would you feel inclined to sell it?"

I thought he was mad. "Is your own shadow not enough for you? What a strange bargain!"

"No price is too high for this invaluable shadow. I have many a

216

precious thing in my pocket, which you may choose—a mandrake, the dish-cloth of Roland's page, Fortunati's purse——"

"What! Fortunati's purse?"

"Will you condescend to try it?" he said, handing me a money-bag of moderate size, from which I drew ten gold pieces, and another ten, and yet another ten.

I extended my hand, and exclaimed, "A bargain! For this purse you can have my shadow." He seized my hand, knelt down, cleverly detached my shadow from the lawn, rolled it up, folded it, and put it in his pocket. Then he bowed and retired behind the rose-hedge, chuckling gently.

I hurried back to my inn, after having tied the bag around my neck, under my waistcoat. As I went along the sunny street, I heard an old woman's voice, "Heigh, young man, you have lost your shadow!"

"Thank you," I said, threw her a gold piece, and sought the shade of the trees. But I had to cross a broad street again, just as a group of boys were leaving school. They shouted at me, jeered, and threw mud at me. To keep them away I threw a handful of gold among them, and jumped into a carriage. Now I began to feel what I had sacrificed. What was to become of me?

At the inn I sent for my things, and then made the driver take me to the best hotel, where I engaged the state rooms and locked myself up. And what, my dear Chamisso, do you think I did then? I pulled masses of gold out of the bag, covered the floor of the room with ducats, threw myself upon them, made them tinkle, rolled over them, buried my hands in them, until I was exhausted and fell to sleep. Next morning I had to cart all these coins into a cupboard, leaving only just a few handfuls. Then, with the help of the host, I engaged some servants, a certain Bendel, a good, faithful soul, being specially recommended to me as a valet. I spent the whole day with tailors, bootmakers, jewellers, merchants, and bought a heap of precious things, just to get rid of the heaps of gold.

I never ventured out in daytime; and even at night when I happened to step out into the moonlight, I had to suffer untold anguish from the contemptuous sneers of men, the deep pity of women, the shuddering fear of fair maidens. Then I sent Bendel to search for the grey man, giving him every possible indication. He came back late, and told me that none of Mr. John's servants or guests remembered the stranger, and that he could find no trace of him. "By the

way," he concluded, "a gentleman whom I met just as I went out, bid me tell you that he was on the point of leaving the country, and that in a year and a day he would call on you to propose new business. He said you would know who he was."

"How did he look?" Bendel described the man in the grey coat! He was in despair when I told him that this was the very person I wanted. But it was too late; he had gone without leaving a trace.

A famous artist for whom I sent to ask him whether he could paint me a shadow, told me that he might, but I should be bound to lose it again at the slightest movement.

"How did you manage to lose yours?" he asked. I had to lie. "When I was travelling in Russia it froze so firmly to the ground that I could not get it off again."

"The best thing you can do is not to walk in the sun," the artist retorted with a piercing look, and walked out.

I confessed my misfortune to Bendel, and the sympathetic lad, after a terrible struggle with his conscience, decided to remain in my service. From that day he was always with me, ever trying to throw his broad shadow over me to conceal my affliction from the world. Nevertheless, the fair Fanny, whom I often met in the hours of dusk and evening, and who had begun to show me marked favour, discovered my terrible secret one night, as the moon suddenly rose from behind a cloud, and fainted with terror.

There was nothing left for me but to leave the town. I sent for horses, took only Bendel and another servant, a rogue named Gauner, with me, and covered thirty miles during the night. Then we continued our journey across the mountains to a little-frequented watering-place, where I was anxious to seek rest from my troubles.

II. A SOUL FOR A SHADOW

Bendel preceded me to prepare a house for my reception, and spent money so lavishly that the rumour spread the King of Prussia was coming incognito. A grand reception was prepared by the townsfolk, with music and flowers and a chorus of maidens in white, led by a girl of wonderful beauty. And all this in broad sunlight! I did not move in my carriage, and Bendel tried to explain that there must be a mistake, which made the good folk believe that I wanted to remain incognito. Bendel handed a diamond tiara to the beautiful maiden, and we drove on amid cheering and firing of guns.

I became known as Count Peter, and when it was found out that

218

the King of Prussia was elsewhere, they all thought I must be some other king. I gave a grand fête, Bendel taking good care to have such lavish illuminations all round that no one should notice the absence of my shadow. I had masses of gold coins thrown among the people in the street, and gave Mina, the beautiful girl who headed the chorus at my arrival, all the jewels I had brought with me, for distribution among her friends. She was the daughter of the verdurer, and I lost no time in making friends with her parents, and succeeded in gaining Mina's affection.

Continuing to spend money with regal lavishness, I myself led a simple and retired life, never leaving my rooms in daylight. Bendel warned me of Gauner's extensive thefts; but I did not mind. Why should I grudge him the money, of which I had an inexhaustible store? In the evenings I used to meet Mina in her garden, and always found her loving, though awed by my wealth and supposed rank. Yet, conscious of my dreadful secret, I dared not ask for her hand. But the year was nearly up since I had made the fateful bargain, and I look forward to the promised visit of the grey man, whom I hoped to persuade to take back his bag for my shadow. In fact, I told the verdurer that on the first of the next month I should ask him for his daughter's hand.

The anniversary arrived—midday, evening, midnight. I waited through the long hours, heard the clock strike twelve; but the grey man did not come! Towards morning I fell into a fitful slumber. I was awakened by angry voices. Gauner forced his way into my room, which was defended by the faithful Bendel.

"What do you want, you rogue?"

"Only to see your shadow, with your lordship's permission."

"How dare you——"

"I am not going to serve a man without a shadow. Either you show it to me, or I go."

I wanted to offer him money; but he, who had stolen millions, refused to accept money from a man without a shadow. He put on his hat, and left the room whistling.

When at dark I went, with a heavy heart, to Mina's bower, I found her, pale and beautiful, and her father with a letter in his hand. He looked at the letter, then scrutinised me, and said, "Do you happen to know, my lord, a certain Peter Schlemihl, who lost his shadow?"

"Oh, my foreboding!" cried Mina. "I knew it; he has no shadow!"

219

"And you dared," continued the verdurer, "to deceive us? See how she sobs! Confess now how you lost your shadow."

Again I was forced to lie. "Some time ago a man stepped so clumsily into my shadow that he made a big hole. I sent it to be mended, and was promised to have it back yesterday."

"Very well. Either you present yourself within three days with a well-fitting shadow, or, on the next day, my daughter will be another man's wife."

I rushed away, half conscious, groaning and raving. I do not know how long and how far I ran, but I found myself on a sunny heath, when somebody suddenly pulled my sleeve. I turned round. It was the man in the grey coat!

"I announced my visit for to-day. You made a mistake in your impatience. All is well. You buy your shadow back and you will be welcomed by your bride. As for Gauner, who has betrayed you and has asked for Mina's hand—he is ripe for me."

I groped for the bag but the stranger stopped me.

"No, my lord, you keep this; I only want a little souvenir. Be good enough and sign this scrap." On the parchment was written: "I herewith assign to bearer my soul after its natural separation from my body."

I sternly refused. "I am not inclined to stake my soul for my shadow."

He continued to urge, giving the most plausible reasons why I should sign. But I was firm. He even tried to tempt me by unrolling my shadow on the heath. "A line of your pen, and you save your Mina from that rogue's clutches."

At that moment Bendel arrived on the scene, saw me in tears, my shadow on the ground apparently in the stranger's power, and set upon the man with his stick. The grey man walked away, and Bendel followed him, raining blows upon his shoulders, till they disappeared from sight.

I was left with my despair, and spent the day and night on the heath. I was resolved not to return among men, and wandered about for three days, feeding on wild fruit and spring-water. On the morning of the fourth day I suddenly heard a sound, but could see nobody—only a shadow, not unlike my own, but without body. I determined to seize it. and rushed after it. Gradually I gained on it; with a final rush I made for it—and met unexpectedly bodily resistance. We fell on the ground, and a man became visible under me. I understood at once. The man must have had the invisible

bird's nest, which he dropped in the struggle, thus becoming visible himself.

The nest being invisible, I looked for its shadow, found it, seized it quickly, and, of course, disappeared from the man's sight. I left him tearing his hair in despair; and I rejoiced at being able to go again among men. Quickly I proceeded to Mina's garden, which was still empty, although I imagined I heard steps following me. I sat down on a bench, and watched the verdurer leaving the house. Then a fog seemed to pass over my head. I looked around, and—oh, horror!—beheld the grey man sitting by my side. He had pulled his magic cap over my head, at his feet was his shadow and my own, and his hand played with the parchment.

"So we are both under the same cap," he began; "now please give me back my bird's nest. Thanks! You see, sometimes we are forced to do what we refuse when asked kindly. I think you had better buy that shadow back. I'll throw in the magic cap."

Meanwhile, Mina's mother had joined the verdurer, and they began to discuss Mina's approaching marriage and Gauner's wealth, which amounted to ten millions. Then Mina joined them. She was urged to consent, and finally said, sobbingly, "I have no further wish on earth. Do with me as you please." At this moment Gauner approached, and Mina fainted.

"Can you endure this?" asked my companion. "Have you no blood in your veins?" He rapidly scratched a slight wound in my hand, and dipped a pen in the blood. "To be sure, red blood! Then sign." And I took the pen and parchment.

I had scarcely touched food for days, and the excitement of this last hour had completely exhausted my strength. Before I had time to sign I swooned away. When I awoke it was dark. My hateful companion was in a towering rage. The sound of festive music came from the brightly illuminated house; groups of people strolled through the garden, talking of Mina's marriage with the wealthy Mr. Gauner, which had taken place this morning.

Disengaging myself from the magic cap, which act made my companion disappear from my view, I made for the garden gate. But the invisible wretch followed me with his taunts. He only left me at the door of my house, with a mocking *"au revoir."* The place had been wrecked by the mob and was deserted. Only the faithful Bendel was there to receive me with tears of mingled grief and joy. I pressed him to my heart, and bid him leave me to my misery. I told him to keep a few boxes filled with gold, that were still in

the house, made him saddle my horse, and departed, leaving the choice of the road to the animal, for I had neither aim, nor wish, nor hope.

A pedestrian joined me on the sad journey. After tramping along for a while, he asked permission to put his cloak on my horse. I consented; he thanked me, and then, in a kind of soliloquy, began to praise the power of wealth, and to speak cleverly of metaphysics. Meanwhile, day was dawning; the sun was about to rise, the shadows to spread their splendour—and I was not alone! I looked at my companion—it was the man with the grey coat!

He smiled at my surprise, and continued to converse amiably. In fact, he not only offered to replace for the time being my former servant Bendel, but actually lent me my shadow for the journey. The temptation was great. I suddenly gave my horse the spurs and galloped off at full speed; but, alas! my shadow remained behind and I had to turn back shamefacedly.

"You can't escape me," said my compainion, "I hold you by your shadow." And all the time, hour by hour, day by day, he continued his urging. At last we quarrelled seriously, and he decided to leave me. "If ever you want me, you have only to shake your bag. You hold me by my gold. You know I can be useful, especially to the wealthy; and you have seen it."

I thought of the past and asked him quickly, "Did you get Mr. John's signature?" He smiled. "With so good a friend, the formality was not necessary."

"Where is he? I want to know."

He hesitated, then put his hand into his pocket, and pulled out Mr. John's livid body; the blue lips of the corpse moved, and uttered painfully the words: *Justo judico Dei judicatus sum; justo judicio Dei condemnatus sum.*

Seized with horror, I threw the inexhaustible moneybag into the abyss, and then spoke the final words. "You fiend, I exorcise you in the name of God! Be off, and never show yourself before mine eyes again!"

He glared at me furiously and disappeared instantly.

III. THE WANDERER

Left now without shadow and without money, save for the few gold pieces still in my pocket, I could almost have been happy, had it not been for the loss of my love. My horse was down below **at**

the inn; I decided to leave it there and to wander on on foot. In the forest I encountered a peasant, from whom I obtained information about the district and its inhabitants. He was an intelligent man, and I quite enjoyed the talk. When we approached the wide bed of a mountain stream, I made him walk in front, but he turned round to speak to me. Suddenly he broke off—"But how is that? You have no shadow!"

Unfortunately!" I said, with a sigh. "During an illness I lost my hair, nails, and shadow. The hair and nails have grown again, but the shadow won't."

"That must have been a bad illness," said the peasant, and walked on in silence till we reached the nearest side-road, when he turned off without saying another word. I wept bitter tears, and my good spirits had vanished. And so I wandered on sadly, avoiding all villages till nightfall, and often waiting for hours to pass a sunny patch unobserved. I wanted to find work in a mine to save me from my thoughts.

My boots began to be worn out. My slender means made me decide to buy a strong pair that had already been used; new ones were too dear. I put them on at once, and walked out of the village, scarcely noticing the way, since I was thinking deeply of the mine I hoped to reach the same night, and of the manner in which I was to obtain employment. I had scarcely walked two hundred steps, when I noticed that I had lost the road. I was in a wild virginal forest. Another few steps and I was on an endless ice-field. The cold was unbearable, and I had to hasten my steps. I ran for a few minutes, and found myself in rice-fields where Chinese labourers were working. There could be no doubt; I had seven-league boots on my feet!

I fell on my knees, shedding tears of gratitude. Now my future was clear. Excluded from society, study and science were to be my future strength and hope. I wandered through the whole world from east to west, from north to south, comparing the fauna and flora of the different regions. To reduce the speed of my progress, I found I had only to pull a pair of slippers over my boots. When I wanted money, I just took an ivory tusk to sell in London. And finally I made a home in the ancient caves of the desert near Thebes.

Once in the far north I encountered a polar bear. Throwing off my slippers, I wanted to step upon an island facing me. I firmly placed my foot on it, but on the other side I fell into the sea, as the slipper had not come off my boot. I saved my life and hurried to

the Libyan desert to cure my cold in the sun; but the heat made me ill. I lost consciousness, and when I awoke again I was in a comfortable bed among other beds, and on the wall facing me I saw inscribed in golden letters my own name.

To cut things short—the institution which had received me had been founded by Bendel and the widowed Mina with my money, and in my honour had been called the Schlemihlium. As soon as I felt strong enough, I returned to my desert cave, and thus I live to this day.

You, my dear Chamisso, are to be the keeper of my strange history, which may contain useful advice for many. You, if you will live among men, honour first the shadow, then the money. But, if you live only for your better self, you will need no advice.

FRANCOIS-RENE DE CHATEAUBRIAND

FRANÇOIS-RENÉ DE CHATEAUBRIAND (French, 1768-1848). Father of the Romantic Movement in France. Had active, stormy career, both as writer and statesman. Travels in America reflected in *Atala* and *René*, epic romances of "the noble savage." Other major works: *Genius of Christianity* and *The Martyrs*, pleas for Catholicism, and colorful autobiography, *Mémoires d'Outre-Tombe.*

CHACTAS RELATES THE DEATH OF ATALA

The heroine of "Atala" is the daughter of a white man and a Christianized Indian. By her mother's command she took a vow of virginity, but later fell in love with Chactas, a young Indian. When she was tempted by this passion to break her vow she took poison.

As the last rays of light calm the winds and restore serenity to the sky, so the tender words of the hermit appeased the troubles that agitated the breast of my beloved. Her thoughts now rested only upon my grief, which she endeavored to alleviate; and, to fortify my mind to bear the loss, sometimes she told me that she should die happy, if I would dry up my tears; sometimes she talked of my mother, or my native country; seeking to distract my mind from my present sorrow, by awaking other remembrances, she exhorted me to patience and virtue. "Thou wilt not always be unhappy," said she; "if Heaven sends you this severe trial now, it is only to

224

render you more compassionate to the misfortunes of others. The heart, O Chactas, resembles those trees, which yield a balm to heal the wounds of man only when they are wounded by a knife." When she had thus spoken she turned towards the missionary for that comfort which she had administered unto me; and alternately consoling and consoled, she gave and received the word of life upon the couch of death.

The hermit's zeal seemed to increase; his aged limbs were reanimated by the ardor of his charity. He was constantly preparing drugs, re-kindling the fire, attending the couch, and making pious exhortations on God and the happiness of the just. With the torch of religion in his hand, he showed the way to future regions. The humble cell was filled with the splendor of her Christian death; and the celestial spirits, no doubt, attended the edifying scene, where religion struggled with love, youth, and death.

Divine religion triumphed; and the pious melancholy that succeeded in our hearts, to the transports of passion, was the trophy of her victory. Towards the middle of the night, Atala seemed sufficiently revived to repeat the prayers of the holy priest; rising from the side of her couch a short time after, she extended her hand toward me, and in a trembling voice said, "O son of Outalissi, dost thou remember the first night when thou didst take me for the virgin of the last love! Oh! wonderful omen of our future fate." She then stopped, then resumed, "When I think that I am about to leave thee for ever, my heart makes such efforts to revive, that love seems almost to render me immortal; but God, thy will be done." After a short pause, she added, "It now only remains for me to ask your forgiveness for all the uneasiness that I have caused you. I have made you unhappy by my pride and my caprices. Chactas, a little earth will soon separate us, and deliver you from all my misfortunes." "Forgive you," replied I, bathed in tears; "is it not I who have caused your misfortunes?" "Beloved friend," said she, interrupting me, "you have rendered me very happy, and had I to begin life again, I should prefer the happiness of our short love in exile, to a life of tranquillity in my native country."

Here Atala's voice faltered; the films of death covered her glassy eyes and mouth; her wandering hands seemed to seek the shroud, and she whispered to the invisible spirits; then making an effort, she endeavored, but in vain, to untie the golden crucifix that was suspended around her neck; she begged of me to take it off, and in a low voice said, "When I spoke to thee the first time, near the pile,

thou observedst this cross by the light of the fire: it is the only property which Atala possesses. Lopez, thy father and mine, sent it to my mother at my birth. Receive it from me as thine inheritance, preserve it as a memorial of our misfortunes: thou wilt doubtless implore the God of the unfortunate, as thou goest through this life of trouble. O Chactas, I have one last request to make to thee: O my dearest friend, our union on this earth could have been but short, but there is a future state which will be more durable; it is everlasting; and how dreadful to be separated forever. I only precede and wait thy arrival in the celestial regions: if thou lovest me, embrace the Christian religion, which will procure for us an eternal reunion. That divine religion performs a great miracle, since it enables me to quit thee without despair. O Chactas! I only wish to exact one single promise from thee. I know too well the consequence of a rash vow. It might deprive thee of some other woman more happy than myself. O my mother! forgive thy distracted child; O Virgin, take pity on me! I fall again into my former weakness, I avert my thoughts from Thee, O God! when they should all be applied in imploring Thy mercy."

Overwhelmed with grief and sobbing, my heart was ready to burst. I promised Atala that one day I would embrace the Christian religion. At these words, the priest rising as if inspired, extended his arms towards the vault of the cell, and exclaimed, "It is time to call here the presence of the Omnipotent."

As he spoke, methought an invisible hand forced me to prostrate myself at the side of Atala's couch. The priest then opened a secret recess, where a golden urn was concealed, covered by a silk veil; he fell on his knees in devout adoration; the whole cell seemed suddenly illuminated by it. Methought I heard the voices of angels, and the sounds of celestial harps. When the hallowed hermit took the sacred urn from the tabernacle, to me it seemed as if I saw the Great Spirit emerging from the rock.

The priest uncovered the chalice, took a wafer as white as snow between his fingers, and approached Atala, pronouncing mysterious words. She raised her eyes towards Heaven, and was in rapture: all her pains subsided: departing life seemed as if collecting on her faded lips; and her mouth, half opened, received the God concealed under the mystic bread: the holy divine then dipped some cotton in consecrated oil, and anointed her forehead, and after looking a few minutes upon Atala, he suddenly uttered these solemn words: "Depart, Christian soul; go and rejoin thy Creator." Then raising

my drooping head, and steadfastly looking at the vase which contained the consecrated oil, I exclaimed, "Will that remedy restore life to Atala?" "Yes, my son," said the pious anchoret, falling in my arms, "to life eternal." Atala had just expired.——

Here Chactas was again obliged to interrupt his narration; his tears fell; sobs stifled his utterance. The blind sachem uncovered his bosom, and taking out Atala's crucifix, "Here," said he, "this is the pledge of love and misery; René, my son, thou canst behold it—but I,—no more; tell me after so many years is not the gold changed; have not my tears left some traces on it? Couldst thou perceive a place where a saint pressed it to her lips? Why is not old Chactas a Christian? What frivolous reasons of policy could make me still adhere to the idolatry of my forefathers? No! I will delay it no longer: the earth cries to me aloud, When wilt thou descend to the grave? and what do you wait for to embrace this divine religion? O earth, thou wilt not wait long. As soon as a priest shall have renovated by the baptismal flood a head grown white with age and sorrow, I hope to be united to Atala."—But to continue our narration.

I cannot now, O René, describe the despair that seized my soul when Atala had breathed her last; such a description would require more warmth than remains to my grief-worn spirits. Yes, the moon that spreads her silvery rays around our heads, and over the vast plains of Kentucky shall cease to shine, and the rivers to flow, before my tears for Atala shall be dried up. For two days I was insensible to the advice of the hermit. In endeavoring to calm my distress, this holy man did not use vain and worldly arguments; he only said, "My son, the will of God be done;" and clasped me in his arms. Had I not felt, I never should have thought there could have been so much comfort in those few words of a resigned Christian. The tenderness, compassion, and unalterable affection, of the pious servant of the Most High, conquered my obstinate grief. Ashamed of the tears he had shed on my account, "O father," said I, "let not the passions of a miserable youth disturb thy aged breast; let me take the sad remains of my beloved; I will bury them in some remote corner of the desert, and if I am condemned to live, I shall endeavor to render myself worthy of those eternal nuptials promised by Atala."

The hermit was delighted with my returning fortitude, and enthusiastically exclaimed, "May the blood of Jesus Christ, our divine master, which was shed in compassion to our miseries, have

mercy upon this young man; increase his courage, and restore peace to his troubled mind, and only leave in it a useful and humble recollection of his misfortunes."

The holy priest refused to give up the corpse of the daughter of Lopez, but he offered to assemble the inhabitants of the village and to inter her with all Christian pomp, but I refused, saying, "The misfortunes and virtues of Atala are unknown to the rest of mankind; let a solitary grave be dug by our hands to share their obscurity." We agreed to set out the next day by sunrise to inter Atala, at the foot of the natural bridge, and in the entrance to the groves of death.

Towards night we carried the precious remains of this pious saint to the entrance of the cell on the north side. The hermit had enveloped her in a piece of linen cloth of his mother's spinning —the only thing that he had preserved from Europe, and which he intended for his own shroud. Atala lay stretched on a couch of sensitive plants; her feet, head, and shoulders were uncovered, and her hair was adorned with a flower of a magnolia; it was the sensitive flower which I had placed upon the maiden's head. Her lips, that were like a withered rose, seemed endeavoring to smile: dark blue veins appeared upon her marble cheeks, her beauteous eyelids were closed, her feet were joined, and her alabaster hands pressed an ebony crucifix to her heart; the fatal scapulary was suspended on her bosom; she looked as if enchanted by the spirit of melancholy, and resting in the double sleep of innocence and death. Her appearance was quite celestial, and had any one seen her, and been ignorant that she had possessed animation, he would have supposed her the statue of virginity.

The pious anchoret ceased not to pray during the whole night. I sat in silence at the top of Atala's funeral couch: how often had I supported her sleeping head upon my knees, and how often had I bent over her beauteous form listening to her and inhaling her perfumed breath; but now no soft murmur issued from her motionless bosom, and it was in vain that I waited for my beloved to awake. The moon supplied her pale light to the funeral eve: she rose at midnight, as a fair virgin that weeps over the bier of a departed friend: it covered the whole scene with a deep melancholy, displaying the aged oaks and flowing rivers. From time to time the cenobite plunged a bunch of flowers into consecrated water, and bathed the couch of death with the heavenly dew, repeating in a solemn voice some verses from the ancient poet Job.

"Man cometh forth like a flower, and is cut down; he fleeth also as a shadow, and continueth not.

"Wherefore is light given to him that is in misery? and life unto the bitter in soul?"

Thus did the venerable missionary sing; his grave and tremulous voice was re-echoed in the silent woods, and the name of God and the grave was resounded by the neighboring torrents and mountains: the sad warbling of the Virginia dove, the roaring of the waves, and the bell that called travelers, mixed with these funeral chants, and methought I heard in the groves of death the departed spirits join the hermit's voice in mournful chorus. The eastern horizon was now fringed with gold: sparrow-hawks shrieked on the cliffs, and the squirrels hastened into the crevices of old elms: it was the time appointed for Atala's funeral. I carried the corpse upon my shoulders, the hermit preceding me with a spade in his hand. We descended from one mountain to another: old age and death equally retarded our steps. At the sight of the dog which had discovered us in the forest, and who now leaping with joy followed us another road, I could not refrain from tears. Often did the golden tresses of Atala, fanned by the morning gale obscure my eyes, and often was I obliged to deposit my sacred load upon the grass to recover my strength. At last we arrived at the sad spot: we descended under the bridge. O my dear son, what a melancholy sight to see a young savage and an old hermit kneeling opposite each other busily engaged in digging a grave for an innocent virgin, whose corpse lay stretched in a dried ravine.

When we had finished our dismal task we placed the beauteous virgin in her earthly bed: alas! I had hoped to have prepared another couch for her. Then taking a little dust in my hand, and maintaining the most profound silence I scattered it, and for the last time looked at the remains of my beloved; then I spread the earth on a face of eighteen years. I saw the lovely features and graceful form of my sister gradually disappear behind the curtain of eternity. Her snowy bosom appeared rising under the black clay as a lily that lifts its fair head from the dark mold. "Lopez!" I exclaimed, "behold thy son, burying his sister!" and I entirely covered Atala with the earth of sleep. We returned to the cell, when I informed the priest of the project that I had formed of settling near him. The saint, who was thoroughly acquainted with the heart of man, discovered that my thoughts were the effects of

sorrow. He said, "O, Chactas, son of Outalissi, whilst Atala lived, I entreated you to remain here, but now that your destiny is altered, you owe yourself to your native land; believe me, my dear son, grief is not eternal; it will sooner or later forsake the heart of man. Return to Meschacébé [Mississippi], and console your mother, who daily weeps and wants your support.

"Be instructed in the religion of your beloved Atala, and never forget the promise you made her to follow the paths of virtue, and to embrace the Christian religion: I will guard the tomb of your sister. Depart my son; God, the soul of Atala, and the heart of your old friend, will follow you."

Such were the words of the hermit of the rock. His authority was so great, and his wisdom so profound, that it was impossible to disobey him. The next day I quitted my venerable host, who, as he clasped me to his arms, gave me his last counsel and benediction, accompanied with tears. I went to the grave of my Atala, I was surprised to see upon it a little cross, that looked like the top-mast of a wrecked ship seen at a distance. I guessed that the priest had come to pray at the tomb, during the night; this mark of friendship and religion filled my eyes with tears, I felt almost tempted to open the grave, that I might once more behold my beloved Atala; I sat on the earth newly turned, my elbows resting upon my knees, my head supported by my hands; I remained buried in deep and sorrowful meditation. Then for the first time I made the most serious reflections upon the vanity of mankind, and the still greater vanity of human projects.

BANKIM CHANDRA CHATTERJEE

BANKIM CHANDRA CHATTERJEE (Indian, 1838-1894). Leading Bengali novelist and literary pioneer. Historical romances, strongly influenced by Walter Scott: *Ánanda Math, Sitárám, Mrinálinī*. His goal was revival of national pride in protest against foreign rule. Also wrote contemporary social novels and *Krishna Charita*, exposition of religious views.

THE BRIDE'S ARRIVAL

No SOONER had Prafulla's boat put in at Bhutnath landing than the news spread through the village that Brajeswar had again brought

230

home a wife; it was whispered she was full-grown, even old. People came running from all directions to see the bride, the young, the old, the blind, the lame, everybody. The cook left her pots and ran; the cutter of fish turned her basket upside down over her fish and ran; the bather came running in wet clothes. The diner went half-hungry. The disputer suddenly agreed with her opponent. The woman spanking her child spared him for once. Off he went in his mother's arms to see the old bride. When the news came a husband was eating. The curry and dhal had been served but not the fish; he had to do without fish that day. An old woman complained to her granddaughter, "How can I go to the pond unless you take me?" At the news of the bride's coming the girl abandoned the old woman and dashed off. The old woman managed somehow to get there too. A young woman, having just been scolded by her mother, was promising not to leave the house again when she heard the news. Her promise was at once forgotten; away she went towards the bride's house. A mother left her baby and ran; the baby toddled after her, crying. A young wife veiled her face and passed shamelessly in front of her seated husband and his elder brother. Running loosened the young women's clothes but they had no time to set them right. Their hair fell down but they did not stop to twist it up again. In their excitement they did not notice what they pulled where. There was an uproar. The goddess of modesty fled in shame.

The bride and bridegroom were standing on a low stool while his mother went through the formalities of reception. People leaned forward to get a look at the bride. She did not relax proprieties and kept her veil three-fourths of a yard long. No one could see her face. During the ceremony her mother-in-law raised the veil once to look at her. She started a little but said nothing, merely murmuring, "The bride is nice." There were tears in her eyes.

The reception over, her mother-in-law took the bride to her room and then addressed the assembled neighbours: "Mothers! My son's wife has come a long way. She is hungry and thirsty. I am going to give them their food immediately. Our daughter-in-law will stay here in our house. You will see her all the time. Go home now and take your own meals."

Disappointed, the village women went away finding fault. The offence was the mother-in-law's but the bride got most of the blame because no one had seen her face. They all expressed their disgust at an old bride. Again they all opined that such were to be found

231

in Kulin families. Then whoever had seen an old bride in a Kulin home began to tell about it. Govinda Mukerjee had married a woman fifty-five years old. Hari Chatterjee had brought a seventy-year-old maiden wife home. Manu Banerjee married an old woman after she had been brought down to the bank of the Ganges to die. All such tales with embellishments grew familiar on the way. Venting itself in this fashion, the village gradually grew quiet.

GEOFFREY CHAUCER

GEOFFREY CHAUCER (English, *ca.* 1340-1400). The Father of English poetry, whose choice of London dialect determined standard speech. Had full, rich life and sound, practical philosophy. *The Canterbury Tales* shows influence of Boccaccio, Petrarch, and others. Remarkable storyteller, creator of character, humorist. Other works: *Troilus and Criseyde, The Legend of Good Women.*

THE PARDONER'S TALE

THERE dwelt one time in Flanders a company of young folk who followed such folly as riotous living and gaming in stews and taverns, where with harps, lutes and citerns they danced and played at dice both day and night, and ate and drank without restraint. Thus they served the Devil in cursed fashion within those Devil's temples by abominable superfluity.

These rioters, three, of whom I speak, long ere any bell had rung for prime had sat down in a tavern to drink. And as they sat, they heard the tinkle of a bell that was carried before a corpse to his grave. One of them called to his boy. 'Be off with you, and ask straightway what corpse is passing by; and mind you report his name aright.'

'Sir,' quoth the boy, 'that needs not be. It was told me two hours before you came here; he was an old fellow of yours, by God, and he was suddenly slain tonight, as he sat very drunk on his bench. There came a privy thief men call death, that slays all people in this countryside, and with his spear he smote his heart in two, and went his way without a word. A thousand he has slain in this pestilence; and master, ere you come into his presence, methinks

232

it were best to be warned of such an adversary. Be ready to meet him ever; thus my mother taught me, I say no more.'

'By St. Mary,' said the taverner, 'the child speaks truth, for over a mile hence, in a large village, he has slain both woman, child, servant and knave. I trow his habitation be there. It were great wisdom to be advised ere he do injure a man.'

'Yea, God's arms!' quoth this rioter, 'is it such peril to meet with him? I will seek him in the highways and byways, I vow by God's bones. Hearken, fellows, we three be like; let each hold up his hand to the other and become the other's brother, and we will slay this false traitor, Death. He that slays so many shall be slain ere night, by God's Dignity!'

Together these three plighted their troth each to live and die for the rest as though he were their sworn brother, and up they then started in this drunken rage, and forth they went toward that village of which the taverner had spoken; and many a grisly oath they swore, and rent Christ's blessed body. —'Death shall be dead if they can but catch him.'

When they had gone not quite a mile just as they were about to go over a stile, an old man and poor met them and greeted them full meekly, and said, 'Lordings, God be with you!'

The proudest of the three rioters answered, 'What, churl, bad luck to you! Why are you all wrapped up save your face? Why live you so long to so great an age?'

This old man began to peer into his visage, and said, 'Because I cannot find a man, though I walked to India, neither in hamlet nor in city, who will change his youth for mine age. And therefore must I keep mine old age as long as it is God's will. Death, alas will not have me! Thus I walk like a restless caitiff, and early and late I knock with my staff upon the ground which is my mother's gate, and say, "Beloved Mother, let me in. Lo, how I wane away, flesh and blood and skin! Alas when shall my bones be at rest? Mother, with you I would exchange my chest, that has been long time in my chamber, yea for an hair-cloth to wrap me in!" But yet she will not do me that favour; wherefore my face is full pale and withered.—But sirs, it is not courteous to speak churlishly to an old man, unless he trespass in word or deed. You may yourselves read in Holy Writ, "Before an old hoary-head man ye shall arise;" wherefore I counsel you, do no harm now to an old man, no more than you would that men did to you in your old age if it be that

you abide so long. And God be with you, wherever you go or be; I must go whither I have to go.'

'Nay old churl, you shall not go, by God,' said the second gamester straightway. 'You part not so lightly by St. John! You spoke right now of that traitor Death who slays all our friends in this country side. By my troth, you are his spy! Tell where he is, or by God and the Holy Sacrament you shall die. Truly you are of his consent to slay us young folk, false thief!'

'Now, sirs,' quoth he, 'If you be so lief to find Death, turn up this crooked way; for by my faith I left him in that grove under a tree, and there he will abide, nor for all your boasting will he hide him. See you that oak? Right here you shall find him. May God, Who redeemed mankind, save you and amend you!' Thus said this old man.

And each of these rioters ran till he came to the tree, and there they found florins coined of fine round gold well nigh seven bushels, as they thought. No longer sought they then after Death, but each was so glad at the sight that they sat them down by the precious hoard. The worst of them spoke the first word. 'Brethren,' he said, 'heed what I say; my wit is great, though I jest oft and play. This treasure has been given us by Fortune that we may live our lives in mirth and jollity, and lightly as it comes, so we will spend it. Eh! God's precious dignity! Who would have weened today that we should have so fair a grace! But could this gold be carried to my house or else to yours,—for you know well all this gold is ours,—then were we in high felicity! But truly by day it may not be done. Men would say we were sturdy thieves and hang us for our treasure. This treasure must be carried by night, as wisely and as slyly as may be. Wherefore I advise that we draw cuts amongst us all, and he that draws the shortest shall run with a blithe heart to the town and that full swift and privily bring us bread and wine. And two of us shall cunningly guard this treasure, and at night, if he will not tarry, we will carry it where we all agree is safest.'

One of them brought the cuts in his fist and bade them draw and look where the lot should fall. It fell to the youngest of them and he went forth toward the town at once. So soon as he was gone one said to the other, 'You well know you are my sworn brother, and you will profit by what I tell you. Here is gold and plenty of it, to be divided amongst us three. You know well our fellow is gone. If I can shape it so that it be divided betwixt us two, had I not done you a friendly turn?'

234

The other answered, 'I wot not how that may be. He knows well the gold is with us two. What shall we do? What shall we say?'

'Shall it be a secret?' said the first wicked fellow. 'I shall tell you in a few words what we shall do to bring it about.'

'I agree,' quoth the other, 'not to betray you, by my troth.'

'Now,' quoth the first, 'you know well we be two and that two should be stronger than one. Look when he is set down; do you arise as though you would play with him, and I will rive him through the two sides while you struggle with him as in sport; and look that you do the same with your dagger. And then shall all this gold be shared, dear friend, betwixt you and me. Then may we both fulfil all our lusts, and play at dice at our will.' And thus, as you heard me say, were these two villains accorded to slay the third.

The youngest, who went to town, revolved full often in his heart the beauty of those bright new florins. 'Oh Lord,' quoth he, 'if so be I could have all this gold to myself, no man living under God's throne should live so merry as I!' And at last the fiend, our enemy, put it into his thought to buy poison with which he might slay his two fellows; for the fiend found him in such a way of life that he had leave to bring him to sorrow, for this was his full intention namely to slay them both and never to repent. And forth he went without tarrying into the town to an apothecary, and prayed him to sell him some poison that he might kill his rats; and there was also a pole-cat in his yard, which he said, had killed his capons and he would fain wreak him upon the vermin that destroyed him by night. The apothecary answered, 'And you shall have such a thing, that, so may God save my soul, no creature in all this world can eat or drink of this composition the amount of a grain of wheat, but he shall at once forfeit his life. Yea, die he shall, and that in less time than you can walk a mile, this poison is so strong and violent.'

This cursed man clutched the box of poison in his hand and then ran into the next street to a man and borrowed of him three large bottles. Into two of them he poured his poison, but the third he kept clean for his drink, for all night long he planned to labour in carrying away his gold. And when this rioter, the Devil take him! had filled his three great bottles with wine, he repaired again to his fellows.

What need to speak about it more? for just as they had planned his death, even so they slew him, and that anon. And when this was done, one spake thus, 'Now let us sit and drink and make merry,

and then we will bury his body.' And then by chance, he took one of the bottles where the poison was, and he drank and gave his fellow to drink also. Wherefore anon they both died. And certes, Avicenna wrote never in any canon or any chapter more wondrous sufferings of empoisoning than these two wretches showed ere they died. Thus ended these two murderers as well as the poisoner.

ANTON CHEKHOV

ANTON CHEKHOV (Russian, 1860-1904). Great master of Russian short story, whose style heavily influenced modern writing. Meticulously wrought tales, concerned with introspective, inarticulate emotions rather than with outward events. Grandson of a serf, became the artist of twilight Czarist Russia. His great plays, *The Cherry Orchard, The Sea Gull, Three Sisters, Uncle Vanya,* left indelible mark on modern theater, but never successfully imitated.

THE SLANDERER

SERGEY KAPITONICH AKHINEYEV, the teacher of calligraphy, gave his daughter Natalya in marriage to the teacher of history and geography, Ivan Petrovich Loshadinikh. The wedding feast went on swimmingly. They sang, played, and danced in the parlor. Waiters, hired for the occasion from the club, bustled about hither and thither like madmen, in black frock coats and soiled white neckties. A loud noise of voices smote the air. From the outside people looked in at the windows—their social standing gave them no right to enter.

Just at midnight the host, Akhineyev, made his way to the kitchen to see whether everything was ready for the supper. The kitchen was filled with smoke from the floor to the ceiling; the smoke reeked with the odors of geese, ducks, and many other things. Victuals and beverages were scattered about on two tables in artistic disorder. Marfa, the cook, a stout, red-faced woman, was busying herself near the loaded tables.

"Show me the sturgeon, dear," said Akhineyev, rubbing his hands and licking his lips. "What a fine odor! I could just devour the whole kitchen! Well, let me see the sturgeon!"

Marfa walked up to one of the benches and carefully lifted a

236

greasy newspaper. Beneath that paper, in a huge dish, lay a big fat sturgeon, amid capers, olives, and carrots. Akhineyev glanced at the sturgeon and heaved a sigh of relief. His face became radiant, his eyes rolled. He bent down, and, smacking his lips, gave vent to a sound like a creaking wheel. He stood a while, then snapped his fingers for pleasure, and smacked his lips once more.

"Bah! The sound of a hearty kiss. Whom have you been kissing there, Marfusha?" some one's voice was heard from the adjoining room, and soon the closely cropped head of Vankin, the assistant school instructor, appeared in the doorway. "Whom have you been kissing here? A-a-ah! Very good! Sergey Kapitonich! A fine old man indeed! With the female sex tête-à-tête!"

"I wasn't kissing at all," said Akhineyev, confused; "who told you, you fool? I only—smacked my lips on account of—in consideration of my pleasure—at the sight of the fish."

"Tell that to some one else, not to me!" exclaimed Vankin, whose face expanded into a broad smile as he disappeared behind the door. Akhineyev blushed.

"The devil knows what may be the outcome of this!" he thought. "He'll go about tale-bearing now, the rascal. He'll disgrace me before the whole town, the brute!"

Akhineyev entered the parlor timidly and cast furtive glances to see what Vankin was doing. Vankin stood near the piano and, deftly bending down, whispered something to the inspector's sister-in-law, who was laughing.

"That's about me!" thought Akhineyev. "About me, the devil take him! She believes him, she's laughing. My God! No, that mustn't be left like that. No. I'll have to fix it so that no one shall believe him. I'll speak to all of them, and he'll remain a foolish gossip in the end."

Akhineyev scratched his head, and, still confused, walked up to Padekoi.

"I was in the kitchen a little while ago, arranging things there for the supper," he said to the Frenchman. "You like fish, I know, and I have a sturgeon just so big. About two yards. Ha, ha, ha! Yes, by the way, I have almost forgotten. There was a real anecdote about that sturgeon in the kitchen. I entered the kitchen a little while ago and wanted to examine the food. I glanced at the sturgeon and for pleasure, I smacked my lips—it was so piquant! And just at that moment the fool Vankin entered and says—ha, ha, ha—and says: 'A-a! A-a-ah! You have been kissing here?'—with Marfa;

237

just think of it—with the cook! What a piece of invention, that blockhead. The woman is ugly, she looks like a monkey, and he says we were kissing. What a queer fellow!"

"Who's a queer fellow?" asked Tarantulov, as he approached them.

"I refer to Vankin. I went out into the kitchen—"

The story of Marfa and the sturgeon was repeated.

"That makes me laugh. What a queer fellow he is. In my opinion it is more pleasant to kiss the dog than to kiss Marfa," added Akhineyev, and, turning around, he noticed Mzda.

"We have been speaking about Vankin," he said to him. "What a queer fellow. He entered the kitchen and noticed me standing beside Marfa, and immediately he began to invent different stories. 'What?' he says, 'you have been kissing each other!' He was drunk, so he must have been dreaming. 'And I,' I said, 'I would rather kiss a duck than kiss Marfa. And I have a wife,' said I, 'you fool.' He made me appear ridiculous."

"Who made you appear ridiculous?" inquired the teacher of religion, addressing Akhineyev.

"Vankin. I was standing in the kitchen, you know, and looking at the sturgeon—" And so forth. In about half an hour all the guests knew the story about Vankin and the sturgeon.

"Now let him tell," thought Akhineyev, rubbing his hands. "Let him do it. He'll start to tell them, and they'll cut him short: 'Don't talk nonsense, you fool! We know all about it.'"

And Akhineyev felt so much appeased that, for joy, he drank four glasses of brandy over and above his fill. Having escorted his daughter to her room, he went to his own and soon slept the sleep of an innocent child, and on the following day he no longer remembered the story of the sturgeon. But, alas! Man proposes and God disposes. The evil tongue does its wicked work, and even Akhineyev's cunning did not do him any good. One week later, on a Wednesday, after the third lesson, when Akhineyev stood in the teachers' room and discussed the vicious inclinations of the pupil Visyekin, the director approached him, and, beckoning to him, called him aside.

"See here, Sergey Kapitonich," said the director. "Pardon me. It isn't my affair, yet I must make it clear to you, nevertheless. It is my duty— You see, rumors are on foot that you are on intimate terms with that woman—with your cook— It isn't my affair, but— You may be on intimate terms with her, you may kiss

238

her— You may do whatever you like, but, please, don't do it so openly! I beg of you. Don't forget that you are a pedagogue."

Akhineyev stood as though frozen and petrified. Like one stung by a swarm of bees and scalded with boiling water, he went home. On his way it seemed to him as though the whole town stared at him as at one besmeared with tar— At home new troubles awaited him.

"Why don't you eat anything?" asked his wife at their dinner. "What are you thinking about? Are you thinking about Cupid, eh? You are longing for Marfushka. I know everything already, you Mahomet. Kind people have opened my eyes, you barbarian!"

And she slapped him on the cheek.

He rose from the table, and staggering, without cap or coat, directed his footsteps toward Vankin. The latter was at home.

"You rascal!" he said to Vankin. "Why have you covered me with mud before the whole world? Why have you slandered me?"

"How; what slander? What are you inventing?"

"And who told everybody that I was kissing Marfa? Not you, perhaps? Not you, you murderer?"

Vankin began to blink his eyes, and all the fibres of his face began to quiver. He lifted his eyes toward the image and ejaculated:

"May God punish me, may I lose my eyesight and die, if I said even a single word about you to any one! May I have neither house nor home!"

Vankin's sincerity admitted of no doubt. It was evident that it was not he who had gossiped.

"But who was it? Who?" Akhineyev asked himself, going over in his mind all his acquaintances, and striking his chest. "Who was it?"

CHIKAMATSU MONZAEMON

CHIKAMATSU MONZAEMON (Japanese, 1653-1725). The Shakespeare of Japan. Wrote for Kabuki theater, also for puppet theater. Author of numerous plays, mostly historical or domestic dramas. Due to conventions of puppet theater, and allusiveness of writing, plays extremely difficult to translate. Most popular: *Battles of Kokusenya, The Double Suicide of Sonezaki.*

ADVENTURES OF THE HAKATA DAMSEL

FOUR days after leaving the capital Soshichi and Kojoro found themselves at Seki, a post-town in the province of Isé. There the

foot-worn travellers halted before a stone image of Jizo, a guardian god of children. Fervently were they praying to the deity that he might soften Sozaémon toward them when palanquin bearers accosted them.

"Cannot we serve you, sir?"

"That may be. We are going to the province of Owari. How much will you charge to carry us to the next stage?"

"It is five miles to Ishiyakushi, the next stage, so we ask you for *korori*."

Soshichi was startled.

"I don't know how much *korori* is."

"A hundred *mon*, sir."

"Too much. Come down to seventy."

"Very good, sir."

With the care-worn fugitives within their palanquins the bearers presently began a rapid march, keeping in time in their steps to the cries: *"Sokosei!"—"Katasei!"—"Makkasei!"* Mile succeeded mile, until Oiwaki was reached, where it was customary to change palanquins and bearers. The carriers therefore stopped. Kojoro stepped out promptly, but Soshichi would not get down, so great was his fear lest the bearers' sign *"korori"* should prove a bad omen. His mind might be said to be fettered with apprehension ere his body was tied to the detective's cord.

"Well, Kojoro," said Soshichi, "you had better change palanquins and go ahead of me."

"I will."

"And wait for me at a place called Yokkaichi."

"I will, my husband."

Kojoro, all unaware of Soshichi's fears, changed palanquins and let herself be carried ahead. A few minutes later a palanquin arrived from the next stage. The newcomers addressed Soshichi's bearers.

"Isn't your passenger the companion of the young woman who's just gone on? Let us exchange passengers."

"That'll suit us nicely. Now, sir, we're going to do an exchange. Please descend."

The bearers lifted the blind of the palanquin for Soshichi. The passenger of the other palanquin had already stepped out. He was lightly dressed in drawers and leggings, carried a packet in his hand and a *hayanawa* in his belt. Soshochi but glimpsed at him

240

and shuddered. He turned his face away and covered his head with a *tenugui*. Hurriedly he descended and with a brief "Thank you, bearers", stepped into the other palanquin and quickly pulled down the blind.

"I'm in a hurry," he said in a tremulous voice. "I'll give you extra; start quickly."

He had hardly uttered these words when a shrill voice cried, "We arrest Komachiya Soshichi!"

The next moment a strong hempen cord had been wound round his palanquin. The terror-stricken captive struggled in the palanquin but to no purpose; and he could but cry like a caged bird. Armed detectives, lying in ambush, emerged and surrounded him.

"Prisoner, you know what charge we arrest you on. The official information asserts that there are eight in your gang. We have come to arrest you. Do you permit yourself to be arrested, or shall we have to bind you by force?"

To this the prisoner made no reply, but was heard to address a plaintive prayer to Amida Buddha.

"No," said the first detective, "let us take him as he is to the next stage and bind him when we get there. That's more convenient. Now, bearers, move off."

"Certainly, sir, but inasmuch as he can't escape death, why don't you bind him here?"

So murmuring, the bearers approached the palanquin and lifted it, when, to their amazement, blood dribbled down *gaba-gaba* from it, instantaneously forming a scarlet patch upon the ground. The occupant uttered a groan of pain. The affrighted coolies cried, "The prisoner has killed himself in the palanquin! Come and look!"

The palanquin was hastily set to earth. The bearers drew apart. The detectives unwound the cord from the palanquin and raised its blind. Soshichi, with fixed eyes, was gasping after a mortal fashion. The long blade plunged in his right side was buried to the hilt. Its point protruded from his left. The detectives were speechless with terror and dismay.

Kojoro, bound, was brought back. Seeing her husband's plight she was struck with unspeakable grief. She trod the tide of blood. She thrust her face into the palanquin.

"I am here, Soshichi San. Kojoro is here, Soshichi. I was bound a few minutes ago. Till last night we slept together. We had a vow to die in the same hour. And now, despite our vows, you have

241

died alone, leaving me behind to suffer by myself. That is selfish of you. But never mind that now. You must be in pain; I see you are in great pain."

With these words she wept and, sinking down, placed her face in the dying man's lap. Intelligence returned to the eyes of Soshichi.

"Ah, Kojoro," he gasped, "are you bound? I am a wicked man who has broken the national laws and disobeyed my father. I have so narrowed the compass of the wide world that my own home could no longer be a home to me and have wandered to this place till at last I am caught in a heavenly net—quite naturally and justly. Were I brought to my home and there executed I should bring disgrace on all my relatives and prove doubly undutiful to my father. With this thought in my mind I have done the deed you see. This is just retribution I now receive for having joined Kezori Kuémon's gang of smugglers and having lived above my station. And since in the eye of the law a wife cannot escape connection with her husband's crime, you are bound, undergo dishonour and are made to suffer—all of which is caused by my own wicked nature. But for Soshichi you would not have suffered thus. Poor girl? How great must be your grief! You have to sacrifice your life on account of the man with whom you have lived for but a short space of time. Pray forgive me, Kojoro."

Soshichi breathed with difficulty. Death second by second drew nearer. The stern detectives, taking pity upon the sorrowful pair, spoke gently. "When you reach prison you will not be suffered to see each other. Man must help man. Take your fill of speech now."

The more Kojoro listened to Soshichi's kind words the more sorrowful she grew.

"Soshichi San, my dear, you are not to blame. For whose sake is it you have done what you have done? Out of eagerness to prevent Kojoro passing into another's hands you joined Kuémon and forsook even your father. At the risk of your life you became my husband, so dearly have you loved me. So overcome am I at your goodness to me that I cannot find even in Chinese or Hindoo, still less in Japanese, fit words to express my gratitude. Were my hands but unbound I would prostrate myself before you ere I die."

Anguish took her. She wept so bitterly that she seemed almost to lose consciousness.

"Now," gasped Soshichi, "now comes the last moment we behold each other in this life. In the next world, remember, we shall be husband and wife. Namu Amida Buddha."

242

The voice that prayed was faint. Then he drew the sword from his side and almost in the same moment ceased to breathe. Piteous was Kojoro's cry. "Husband, stay for me a moment! I would accompany you! Sooner or later I shall be slain. Officers, have mercy! Slay me here—slay me, I entreat you!"

She wailed and rushed hither and thither in the frenzy of madness. At this moment a police superintendent and his underlings arrived, convoying Kezori Kuémon, his followers and their respective courtesans. All were bound. All had been captured in one place or another. The leader of the party unrolled a scroll and read as follows:

"Prisoners, I read you an Imperial mandate. Listen to it with gratitude. Forasmuch as you have committed the crime of smuggling in connection with great ships in the offing in defiance of the national laws, you richly deserve capital punishment. But in honour of his coronation, His Majesty the Emperor is graciously pleased to pardon you and to release you from such a penalty."

The gratitude of the prisoners knew no bounds. They cried out for joy. The police superintendent addressed the courtesans.

"Forasmuch as your profession compelled you to become the companions of these men you are guilty of no crime. Henceforward you can go whither you choose. Now, men, set these women free."

The constables released the women. The courtesans caressed the abrasions the cords had caused.

"The power of His Majesty the Emperor," they exclaimed, "is great indeed! Our hands are freed from the cords. We feel like birds escaped from their cages."

But Kojoro, albeit set at freedom like her companions, continued to weep. At length she lifted her head.

"Sorrow it is that my husband Soshichi has forsaken me and his soul winged its way to the other world or ever the compassion of this edict could be made known to him. This life is not now worth while the living for this 'Kojoro of Hakata', who is just like a bird which has lost its mate by death. Officers, have mercy! Slay me!"

The bitter tears fell.

"Your grief is natural," said the sympathetic superintendent. "Though your husband was one of a gang of ruffians, he joined them out of youthful folly and infatuation. It follows therefore that his offence was small. We regret that his impetuosity should have led to his suicide. We grieve on your behalf, but nothing is to be done. Your best course will be to serve your father-in-law in

Soshichi's place and busy yourself in prayers for the peace of the departed soul. Now, my men, treat the prisoners as the Imperial edict commands."

Of the smugglers who had escaped death, some were branded or tattooed upon the face, others had their ears or noses cut off that they might not repeat their offences. Then they were set free.

The rumour of the adventures of the hapless Hakata damsel did not take long to spread far and wide. It remained a topic of conversation for generations afterwards.

CH'U YUAN

CH'U YUAN (Chinese, *ca.* 343-277 B.C.). Greatest poet of ancient China. According to legend, a loyal minister who drowned self when he lost emperor's favor. Poems, though personal, are still close to ritual song. The *Li Sao* one of most famous long poems in Chinese.

STRAY THOUGHTS

My Heart with Grief is heavy,
   I sigh with Head down hung.
My Thoughts are like a tangled Skein,
   And yet the Night is young.

In Autumn all Things wither,
   The World is full of Hate,
My Prince is easily enraged,
   And my Affliction great.

The People's Suff'rings move my Heart,
   Our Land I cannot leave.
Here for my Loved One my stray Thoughts
   Into a Song I weave.
Oh, once you gave your Promise,
   At Dusk we two should meet;
But then you went back on your Word,
   For such was your Deceit.

You praise another's Beauty,
  Admire another's Grace,
Forswear your former Pledge to me,
  And turn an angry Face.
I longed for Reconcilement,
  But kept by Fear apart,
I dare no more draw near to you,
  So Grief besets my Heart.

I put my Thought in Verses
  My Prince disdains to hear,
I know true Worth no Favour wins,
  And Enemies will sneer.

All that I said was truthful,
  How could the Prince forget?
By honest Counsel I would make
  Him more illustrious yet.

I take a Sage as Model,
  And in his Steps would tread.
I strive for Excellence so that
  My Prince's Fame may spread.

Virtue is not outside us,
  Fame springs from noble Deeds,
All Reputations must be won,
  As Fruit must grow from Seeds.

Interlude

So I plead before my Love,
But his Heart I cannot move.
He approves another's Grace.
In his Heart I have no Place.

Chorus

A Bird flies from the South once more
To the great Stream's northern Shore.
In fair Splendour see him stand,
All alone in a far-off Land;

245

None to befriend him beneath the Sun,
For Mediators here are none.
Departed Long and in Disgrace,
I have no Way to plead my Case.
Beside the Northern Hill I sigh,
My Tears drop where the Stream flows by,
The short Midsummer Nights are here,
Yet each seems long as one whole Year.
The Capital is far away,
But there each Night in Thought I stray.
By narrow winding Track or wide,
Southward, with Moon and Stars my Guide,
Forward I press, but all in Vain:
My Soul is weary of such Pain!
Yet still my Nature is too Proud
To change or flatter like the Crowd!
For me no one will mediate,
None knows or cares for my sad Fate.

Refrain

Long the Bay and strong the Tide,
    As up the Stream I go.
I make my Journey southward still,
    In Hope to ease my Woe.
The Journey here is hard when Cliffs
    Reach steeply to the Sky,
And hard it is to climb or cross
    The Mountain Paths so high.
Brought to a Halt I hesitate,
    And rest here for the Night.
My Mind is clouded, and there seems
    To be no End in Sight.
My Thoughts have travelled far afield,
    In Grief I heave a Sigh,
This Place is strange and desolate,
    No Go-between have I!
My Thoughts in Verses I have set,
    Some Ease of Mind to seek;
But still my Grief is unassuaged,
    For who will hear me speak?

246

THOUGHTS BEFORE DROWNING

In balmy early Summer Days,
  When Trees and Grasses teem,
With lonely and dejected Heart
  I reach the southern Stream.

Now all around appears forlorn,
  So silent and so still,
While sad and melancholy Thoughts
  Upon me cast a Chill.

Once more I recollect the Past,
  And Wrongs of former Days.
Let Others stoop some Gain to win,
  But I'll not change my Ways.

Such Men as change for selfish Gain
  I always have despised;
But hold the Principles of Old,
  The former Rules have prized.

With Sternness and Benevolence
  An upright Man is filled.
If Craftsmen will not ply the Axe,
  Men doubt that they are skilled.

You see a Picture in the Night,
  And black the Colours find.
If skillful Craftsmen squint to see,
  You need not think them blind.

Now Darkness is construed as Light,
  And Fair to Foul is turned,
Now Hens and Geese can fly on high,
  While Phoenixes are spurned.

Now Good and Bad are thought the same,
  And Jade confused with Stone.
To Men made blind by Prejudice,
  My Virtues are unknown.

247

I feel my Task too hard for me;
    Despairing of Success,
I do not know to whom to show
    The Jewels I possess.

The country Dogs bark savagely
    At One they do not know.
And Fools suspect all Men of Worth,
    And slavish Envy show.

They will not see my Dignity,
    My Learning or my Grace,
And all my subtle Scholarship
    Endeavour to abase.

I double my Benevolence,
    To Honesty I hold;
But who can understand my Worth,
    Since dead the Sage of Old?

How is it that for such long Years
    The Good remain apart?
The ancient Kings are too long gone
    To hold them in our Heart.

I curb my Indignation now,
    My Anger I repress;
I shall not change or hesitate
    In Danger or Distress.

I journey on and take no Rest
    Till darkly sinks the Sun.
But now I ease my heavy Heart—
    My Race will soon be done.

Refrain
On and on the Rivers slow
Down their several Courses flow.
Dark the Way and overgrown,
And the Future all unknown.

248

All my Time in Anguish spent,
No End set to my Lament,
By the World misunderstood,
With no Friend or Kinsman good.

Though my Conscience is quite clear,
I can find no Witness here.
Gone the Charioteer so prized,
The swift Horses are despised.

Sad or happy, each Man's Fate
Overtakes him soon or late.
If I keep a steadfast Heart,
Fear in me can have no Part.

Death, I know, must come to All,
Nor for Mercy would I call.
Saints, I follow in your Wake!
Your Example shall I take!

CONFUCIUS

CONFUCIUS (Chinese, *ca.* 551-479 B.C.). Great poet and philosopher, source
of Chinese wisdom for twenty centuries. His *Shih Ching (Book of Odes)*
laid foundation of Chinese literature. Authorship of other extensive collections
is disputed, probably legendary. His work glorifies the moral virtues: loyalty,
brotherhood, truth, justice, tolerance, etc.

A CHALLENGE

If, boy, thy thoughts of me were kind,
   I'd lift my skirts and wade the Tsin;
But if thou be of other mind,
   Is there none else my love would win?
      O craziest of crazy boys!

Ay, if thy thoughts of me were kind,
   I'd lift my skirts and wade the Wei;
But if thy thoughts are else inclined,
   Is there none other gallant nigh?
      O craziest of crazy boys!

I picked and picked the mouse ears,
    Nor gained one basket load;
My heart was with my husband:
    I flung them on the road.

I climbed yon rugged mountain,
    My ponies all broke down;
I filled my golden goblet
    Long anxious thought to drown.

1 climbed yon lofty ridges,
    With my ponies black and bay;
I filled for me my horn cup
    Long torture to allay.

I climbed yon craggy uplands,
    My steeds grew weak and ill;
My footmen were exhausted;—
    And here I sorrow still!

LAMENT OF A DISCARDED WIFE

When east winds blow unceasingly,
    They bring but gloominess and rain.
Strive, strive to live unitedly,
    And every angry thought restrain.
Some plants we gather for their leaves,
    But leave the roots untouched beneath;
So, while unsullied was my name,
    I should have lived with you till death.

With slow, slow step I took the road,
    My inmost heart rebelling sore,
You came not far with me, indeed,
    You only saw me to the door.
Who calls the lettuce bitter fare,
    The cress is not a whit more sweet.
Ay, feast there with your new-found bride,
    Well pleased, as when fond brothers meet.

250

The Wei, made turbid by the king,
    Grows limpid by the islets there.
There, feasting with your new-found bride
    For me no longer now you care.
Yet leave to me my fishing dam;
    My wicker nets, remove them not.
My person spurned—some vacant hour
    May bring compassion for my lot.

Where ran the river full and deep,
    With raft or boat I paddled o'er;
And where it flowed in shallower stream,
    I dived or swam from shore to shore.
And what we had, or what we lost,
    For that I strained my every nerve;
When other folks had loss, I'd crawl
    Upon my knees, if aught 'twould serve.

And you can show me no kind care,
    Nay, treated like a foe am I!
My virtue stood but in your way,
    Like traders' goods that none will buy.
Once it was feared we could not live;
    In your reverses then I shared:
And now, when fortune smiles on you,
    To very poison I'm compared.

I have laid by a goodly store,—
    For winter's use it was to be;—
Feast on there with your new-found bride,—
    I was for use in poverty!
Rude fits of anger you have shown,
    Now left me to be sorely tried.
Ah, you forget those days gone by,
    When you came nestling to my side!

COMRADES IN WAR TIME

How say we have no clothes?
    One plaid for both will do.
Let but the king, in raising men,
    Our spears and pikes renew,—
    We'll fight as one, we two!

251

How say we have no clothes?
    One skirt our limbs shall hide.
Let but the king, in raising men,
    Halberd and lance provide,—
    We'll do it, side by side!

How say we have no clothes?
    My kirtle thou shalt wear.
Let but the king, in raising men,
    Armor and arms prepare,
    The toils of war we'll share.

TRUST THY LAST FRIEND AGAINST THE WORLD

    A babbling current fails
To float a load of thorns away,—
Of brothers, few are left us now,
Yet we remain, myself and thou:
    Believe not others' tales,
Others will lead thee far astray.

    The babbling current fails
To float the firewood fagots far.—
Of brothers there are left but few,
Yet I and thou remain, we two:
    Believe not others' tales,
For verily untrue they are!

JOSEPH CONRAD

JOSEPH CONRAD (English, 1857-1924). Polish-born novelist, who went early to sea on English ships. Retiring from navy, became British subject, taught self to write English, and became greatest writer of sea stories in the language. Most-praised novel: *Lord Jim*. Others: *Nostromo, Victory, Youth, The Secret Agent, The Nigger of the Narcissus.*

THE LAGOON

THE white man, leaning with both arms over the roof of the little house in the stern of the boat, said to the steersman—
    "We will pass the night in Arsat's clearing. It is late."

The Malay only grunted, and went on looking fixedly at the river. The white man rested his chin on his crossed arms and gazed at the wake of the boat. At the end of the straight avenue of forests cut by the intense glitter of the river, the sun appeared unclouded and dazzling, poised low over the water that shone smoothly like a band of metal. The forests, somber and dull, stood motionless and silent on each side of the broad stream. At the foot of big, towering trees, trunkless nipa palms rose from the mud of the bank, in bunches of leaves enormous and heavy, that hung unstirring over the brown swirl of eddies. In the stillness of the air every tree, every leaf, every bough, every tendril of creeper and every petal of minute blossoms seemed to have been bewitched into an immobility perfect and final. Nothing moved on the river but the eight paddles that rose flashing regularly, dipped together with a single splash; while the steersman swept right and left with a periodic and sudden flourish of his blade describing a glinting semicircle above his head. The churned-up water frothed alongside with a confused murmer. And the white man's canoe, advancing upstream in the short-lived disturbance of its own making, seemed to enter the portals of a land from which the very memory of motion had forever departed.

The white man, turning his back upon the setting sun, looked along the empty and broad expanse of the sea-reach. For the last three miles of its course the wandering, hesitating river, as if enticed irresistibly by the freedom of an open horizon, flows straight into the sea, flows straight to the east—to the east that harbors both light and darkness. Astern of the boat the repeated call of some bird, a cry discordant and feeble, skipped along over the smooth water and lost itself, before it could reach the other shore, in the breathless silence of the world.

The steersman dug his paddle into the stream, and held hard with stiffened arms, his body thrown forward. The water gurgled aloud; and suddenly the long straight reach seemed to pivot on its center, the forests swung in a semicircle, and the slanting beams of sunset touched the broadside of the canoe with a fiery glow, throwing the slender and distorted shadows of its crew upon the streaked glitter of the river. The white man turned to look ahead. The course of the boat had been altered at right angles to the stream, and the carved dragon-head of its prow was pointing now at a gap in the fringing bushes of the bank. It glided through, brushing the overhanging twigs, and disappeared from the river like some slim and amphibious creature leaving the water for its lair in the forests.

The narrow creek was like a ditch: tortuous, fabulously deep; filled with gloom under the thin strip of pure and shining blue of the heaven. Immense trees soared up, invisible behind the festooned draperies of creepers. Here and there, near the glistening blackness of the water, a twisted root of some tall tree showed amongst the tracery of small ferns, black and dull, writhing and motionless, like an arrested snake. The short words of the paddlers reverberated, loudly between the thick and somber walls of vegetation. Darkness oozed out from between the trees, through the tangled maze of the creepers, from behind the great fantastic and unstirring leaves; the darkness, mysterious and invincible; the darkness scented and poisonous of impenetrable forests.

The men poled in the shoaling water. The creek broadened, opening out into a wide sweep of a stagnant lagoon. The forests receded from the marshy bank, leaving a level strip of bright green, reedy grass to frame the reflected blueness of the sky. A fleecy pink cloud drifted high above, trailing the delicate coloring of its image under the floating leaves and the silvery blossoms of the lotus. A little house, perched on high piles, appeared black in the distance. Near it, two tall nibong palms, that seemed to have come out of the forests in the background, leaned slightly over the ragged roof, with a suggestion of sad tenderness and care in the droop of their leafy and soaring heads.

The steersman, pointing with his paddle, said, "Arsat is there. I see his canoe fast between the piles."

The polers ran along the sides of the boat glancing over their shoulders at the end of the day's journey. They would have preferred to spend the night somewhere else than on this lagoon of weird aspect and ghostly reputation. Moreover, they disliked Arsat, first as a stranger, and also because he who repairs a ruined house, and dwells in it, proclaims that he is not afraid to live amongst the spirits that haunt the places abandoned by mankind. Such a man can disturb the course of fate by glances or words; while his familiar ghosts are not easy to propitiate by casual wayfarers upon whom they long to wreak the malice of their human master. White men care not for such things, being unbelievers and in league with the Father of Evil, who leads them unharmed through the invisible dangers of this world. To the warnings of the righteous they oppose an offensive pretense of disbelief. What is there to be done?

So they thought, throwing their weight on the end of their long poles. The big canoe glided on swiftly, noiselessly, and smoothly,

towards Arsat's clearing, till, in a great rattling of poles thrown down, and the loud murmurs of "Allah be praised!" it came with a gentle knock against the crooked piles below the house.

The boatmen with uplifted faces shouted discordantly, "Arsat! O Arsat!" Nobody came. The white man began to climb the rude ladder giving access to the bamboo platform before the house. The juragan of the boat said sulkily, "We will cook in the sampan, and sleep on the water."

"Pass my blankets and the basket," said the white man, curtly.

He knelt on the edge of the platform to receive the bundle. Then the boat shoved off, and the white man, standing up, confronted Arsat, who had come out through the low door of his hut. He was a man young, powerful, with broad chest and muscular arms. He had nothing on but his sarong. His head was bare. His big, soft eyes stared eagerly at the white man, but his voice and demeanor were composed as he asked, without any words of greeting—

"Have you medicine, Tuan?"

"No," said the visitor in a startled tone. "No. Why? Is there sickness in the house?"

"Enter and see," replied Arsat, in the same calm manner, and turning short round, passed again through the small doorway. The white man, dropping his bundles, followed.

In the dim light of the dwelling he made out on a couch of bamboos a woman stretched on her back under a broad sheet of red cotton cloth. She lay still, as if dead; but her big eyes, wide open, glittered in the gloom, staring upwards at the slender rafters, motionless and unseeing. She was in a high fever, and evidently unconscious. Her cheeks were sunk slightly, her lips were partly open, and on the young face there was the ominous and fixed expression—the absorbed, contemplating expression of the unconscious who are going to die. The two men stood looking down at her in silence.

"Has she been long ill?" asked the traveler.

"I have not slept for five nights," answered the Malay, in a deliberate tone. "At first she heard voices calling her from the water and struggled against me who held her. But since the sun of today rose she hears nothing—she hears not me. She sees nothing. She sees not me—me!"

He remained silent for a minute, then asked softly—

"Tuan, will she die?"

"I fear so," said the white man, sorrowfully. He had known Arsat

255

years ago, in a far country in times of trouble and danger, when no friendship is to be despised. And since his Malay friend had come unexpectedly to dwell in the hut on the lagoon with a strange woman, he had slept many times there, in his journeys up and down the river. He liked the man who knew how to keep faith in council and how to fight without fear by the side of his white friend. He liked him—not so much perhaps as a man likes his favorite dog—but still he liked him well enough to help and ask no questions, to think sometimes vaguely and hazily in the midst of his own pursuits, about the lonely man and the long-haired woman with audacious face and triumphant eyes, who lived together hidden by the forests—alone and feared.

The white man came out of the hut in time to see the enormous conflagration of sunset put out by the swift and stealthy shadows that, rising like a black and impalpable vapor above the tree-tops, spread over the heaven, extinguishing the crimson glow of floating clouds and the red brilliance of departing daylight. In a few moments all the stars came out above the intense blackness of the earth and the great lagoon gleaming suddenly with reflected lights resembled an oval patch of night sky flung down into the hopeless and abysmal night of the wilderness. The white man had some supper out of the basket, then collecting a few sticks that lay about the platform, made up a small fire, not for warmth, but for the sake of the smoke, which would keep off the mosquitos. He wrapped himself in the blankets and sat with his back against the reed wall of the house, smoking thoughtfully.

Arsat came through the doorway with noiseless steps and squatted down by the fire. The white man moved his outstretched legs a little.

"She breathes," said Arsat in a low voice, anticipating the expected question. "She breathes and burns as if with a great fire. She speaks not; she hears not—and burns!"

He paused for a moment, then asked in a quiet, incurious tone—

"Tuan . . . will she die?"

The white man moved his shoulders uneasily and muttered in a hesitating manner—

"If such is her fate."

"No, Tuan," said Arsat, calmly. "If such is my fate. I hear, I see, I wait. I remember . . . Tuan, do you remember the old days? Do you remember my brother?"

"Yes," said the white man. The Malay rose suddenly and went in.

256

The other, sitting still outside, could hear the voice in the hut. Arsat said: "Hear me! Speak!" His words were succeeded by a complete silence. "O Diamelen!" he cried, suddenly. After that cry there was a deep sigh. Arsat came out and sank down again in his old place.

They sat in silence before the fire. There was no sound within the house, there was no sound near them; but far away on the lagoon they could hear the voices of the boatmen ringing fitful and distinct on the calm water. The fire in the bows of the sampan shone faintly in the distance with a hazy red glow. Then it died out. The voices ceased. The land and the water slept invisible, unstirring and mute. It was as though there had been nothing left in the world but the glitter of stars streaming, ceaseless and vain, through the black stillness of the night.

The white man gazed straight before him into the darkness with wide-open eyes. The fear and fascination, the inspiration and the wonder of death—of death near, unavoidable, and unseen, soothed the unrest of his race and stirred the most indistinct, the most intimate of his thoughts. The ever-ready suspicion of evil, the gnawing suspicion that lurks in our hearts, flowed out into the stillness round him—into the stillness profound and dumb, and made it appear untrustworthy and infamous, like the placid and impenetrable mask of an unjustifiable violence. In that fleeting and powerful disturbance of his being the earth enfolded in the starlight peace became a shadowy country of inhuman strife, a battle-field of phantoms terrible and charming, august or ignoble, struggling ardently for the possession of our helpless hearts. An unquiet and mysterious country of inextinguishable desires and fears.

A plaintive murmur rose in the night; a murmur saddening and startling, as if the great solitudes of surrounding woods had tried to whisper into his ear the wisdom of their immense and lofty indifference. Sounds hesitating and vague floated in the air round him, shaped themselves slowly into words; and at last flowed on gently in a murmuring stream of soft and monotonous sentences. He stirred like a man waking up and changed his position slightly. Arsat, motionless and shadowy, sitting with bowed head under the stars, was speaking in a low and dreamy tone—

". . . for where can we lay down the heaviness of our trouble but in a friend's heart? A man must speak of war and of love. You, Tuan, know what war is, and you have seen me in time of danger seek death as other men seek life! A writing may be lost; a lie may

be written; but what the eye has seen is truth and remains in the mind!"

"I remember," said the white man, quietly. Arsat went on with mournful composure—

"Therefore I shall speak to you of love. Speak in the night. Speak before both night and love are gone—and the eye of day looks upon my sorrow and my shame; upon my blackened face; upon my burnt-up heart."

A sigh, short and faint, marked an almost imperceptible pause, and then his words flowed on, without a stir, without a gesture.

"After the time of trouble and war was over and you went away from my country in the pursuit of your desires, which we, men of the islands, cannot understand, I and my brother became again, as we had been before, the sword-bearers of the Ruler. You know we were men of family, belonging to a ruling race, and more fit than any to carry on our right shoulder the emblem of power. And in the time of prosperity Si Dendring showed us favor, as we, in time of sorrow, had showed to him the faithfulness of our courage. It was a time of peace. A time of deer-hunts and cock-fights; of idle talks and foolish squabbles between men whose bellies are full and weapons are rusty. But the sower watched the young rice-shoots grow up without fear, and the traders came and went, departed lean and returned fat into the river of peace. They brought news, too. Brought lies and truth mixed together, so that no man knew when to rejoice and when to be sorry. We heard from them about you also. They had seen you here and had seen you there. And I was glad to hear, for I remembered the stirring times, and I always remembered you, Tuan, till the time came when my eyes could see nothing in the past, because they had looked upon the one who is dying there—in the house."

He stopped to exclaim in an intense whisper, "O Mara bahia! O Calamity!" then went on speaking a little louder:

"There's no worse enemy and no better friend than a brother, Tuan, for one brother knows another, and in perfect knowledge is strength for good or evil. I loved my brother. I went to him and told him that I could see nothing but one face, hear nothing but one voice. He told me: 'Open your heart so that she can see what is in it—and wait. Patience is wisdom. Inchi Midah may die or our Ruler may throw off his fear of a woman!' . . . I waited! . . . You remember the lady with the veiled face, Tuan, and the fear of our

258

Ruler before her cunning and temper. And if she wanted her servant, what could I do? But I fed the hunger of my heart on short glances and stealthy words. I loitered on the path to the bath-houses in the daytime, and when the sun had fallen behind the forest I crept along the jasmine hedges of the women's courtyard. Unseeing, we spoke to one another through the scent of flowers, through the veil of leaves, through the blades of long grass that stood still before our lips; so great was our prudence, so faint was the murmur of our great longing. The time passed swiftly . . . and there were whispers amongst women—and our enemies watched—my brother was gloomy, and I began to think of killing and of a fierce death. . . . We are of a people who take what they want—like you whites. There is a time when a man should forget loyalty and respect. Might and authority are given to rulers, but to all men is given love and strength and courage. My brother said, 'You shall take her from their midst. We are two who are like one.' And I answered, 'Let it be soon, for I find no warmth in sunlight that does not shine upon her.' Our time came when the Ruler and all the great people went to the mouth of the river to fish by torchlight. There were hundreds of boats, and on the white sand, between the water and the forests, dwellings of leaves were built for the households of the Rajahs. The smoke of cooking-fires was like a blue mist of the evening, and many voices rang in it joyfully. While they were making the boats ready to beat up the fish, my brother came to me and said, 'Tonight!' I looked to my weapons, and when the time came our canoe took its place in the circle of boats carrying the torches. The lights blazed on the water, but behind the boats there was darkness. When the shouting began and the excitement made them like mad we dropped out. The water swallowed our fire, and we floated back to the shore that was dark with only here and there the glimmer of embers. We could hear the talk of slave-girls amongst the sheds. Then we found a place deserted and silent. We waited there. She came. She came running along the shore, rapid and leaving no trace, like a leaf driven by the wind into the sea. My brother said gloomily, 'Go and take her; carry her into our boat.' I lifted her in my arms. She panted. Her heart was beating against my breast. I said, 'I take you from those people. You came to the cry of my heart, but my arms take you into my boat against the will of the great!' 'It is right,' said my brother. 'We are men who take what we want and can hold it against many. We should have taken her

259

in daylight.' I said, 'Let us be off'; for since she was in my boat I began to think of our Ruler's many men. 'Yes. Let us be off,' said my brother. 'We are cast out and this boat is our country now—and the sea is our refuge.' He lingered with his foot on the shore, and I entreated him to hasten, for I remembered the strokes of her heart against my breast and thought that two men cannot withstand a hundred. We left, paddling downstream close to the bank; and as we passed by the creek where they were fishing, the great shouting had ceased, but the murmur of voices was loud like the humming of insects flying at noonday. The boats floated, clustered together, in the red light of torches, under a black roof of smoke; and men talked of their sport. Men that boasted, and praised, and jeered—men that would have been our friends in the morning, but on that night were already our enemies. We paddled swiftly past. We had no more friends in the country of our birth. She sat in the middle of the canoe with covered face; silent as she is now; unseeing as she is now—and I had no regret at what I was leaving because I could hear her breathing close to me—as I can hear her now."

He paused, listened with his ear turned to the doorway, then shook his head and went on:

"My brother wanted to shout the cry of challenge—one cry only —to let the people know we were freeborn robbers who trusted our arms and the great sea. And again I begged him in the name of our love to be silent. Could I not hear her breathing close to me? I knew the pursuit would come quick enough. My brother loved me. He dipped his paddle without a splash. He only said, 'There is a half a man in you now—the other half is in that woman. I can wait. When you are a whole man again, you will come back with me here to shout defiance. We are sons of the same mother.' I made no answer. All my strength and all my spirit were in my hands that held the paddle—for I longed to be with her in a safe place beyond the reach of men's anger and of women's spite. My love was so great, that I thought it could guide me to a country where death was unknown, if I could only escape from Inchi Midah's fury and from our Ruler's sword. We paddled with haste, breathing through our teeth. The blades bit deep into the smooth water. We passed out of the river; we flew in clear channels amongst the shallows. We skirted the black coast; we skirted the sand beaches where the sea speaks in whispers to the land; and the gleam of white sand flashed back past our boat, so swiftly she ran upon the water. We

spoke not. Only once I said, 'Sleep, Diamelen, for soon you may want all your strength.' I heard the sweetness of her voice, but I never turned my head. The sun rose and still we went on. Water fell from my face like rain from a cloud. We flew in the light and heat. I never looked back, but I knew that my brother's eyes, behind me, were looking steadily ahead, for the boat went as straight as a bushman's dart, when it leaves the end of the sumpitan. There was no better paddler, no better steersman than my brother. Many times, together, we had won races in that canoe. But we never had put out our strength as we did then—then, when for the last time we paddled together! There was no braver or stronger man in our country than my brother. I could not spare the strength to turn my head and look at him, but every moment I heard the hiss of his breath getting louder behind me. Still he did not speak. The sun was high. The heat clung to my back like a flame of fire. My ribs were ready to burst, but I could no longer get enough air into my chest. And then I felt I must cry out with my last breath, 'Let us rest!' . . . 'Good!' he answered; and his voice was firm. He was strong. He was brave. He knew not fear and no fatigue . . . My brother!"

A murmur powerful and gentle, a murmur vast and faint; the murmur of trembling leaves, of stirring boughs, ran through the tangled depths of the forests, ran over the starry smoothness of the lagoon, and the water between the piles lapped the slimy timber once with a sudden splash. A breath of warm air touched the two men's faces and passed on with a mournful sound—a breath loud and short like an uneasy sigh of the dreaming earth.

Arsat went on in an even, low voice.

"We ran our canoe on the white beach of a little bay close to a long tongue of land that seemed to bar our road; a long wooded cape going far into the sea. My brother knew that place. Beyond the cape a river has its entrance, and through the jungle of that land there is a narrow path. We made a fire and cooked rice. Then we lay down to sleep on the soft sand in the shade of our canoe, while she watched. No sooner had I closed my eyes than I heard her cry of alarm. We leaped up. The sun was halfway down the sky already, and coming in sight in the opening of the bay we saw a prau manned by many paddlers. We knew it at once; it was one of our Rajah's praus. They were watching the shore, and saw us. They beat the gong, and turned the head of the prau into the bay.

I felt my heart become weak within my breast. Diamelen sat on the sand and covered her face. There was no escape by sea. My brother laughed. He had the gun you had given him, Tuan, before you went away, but there was only a handful of powder. He spoke to me quickly: 'Run with her along the path. I shall keep them back, for they have no firearms, and landing in the face of a man with a gun is certain death for some. Run with her. On the other side of that wood there is a fisherman's house—and a canoe. When I have fired all the shots I will follow. I am a great runner, and before they can come up we shall be gone. I will hold out as long as I can, for she is but a woman—that can neither run nor fight, but she has your heart in her weak hands.' He dropped behind the canoe. The prau was coming. She and I ran, and as we rushed along the path I heard shots. My brother fired—once—twice—and the booming of the gong ceased. There was silence behind us. That neck of land is narrow. Before I heard my brother fire the third shot I saw the shelving shore, and I saw the water again; the mouth of a broad river. We crossed a grassy glade. We ran down to the water. I saw a low hut above the black mud, and a small canoe hauled up. I heard another shot behind me. I thought, 'That is his last charge.' We rushed down to the canoe; a man came running from the hut, but I leaped on him, and we rolled together in the mud. Then I got up, and he lay still at my feet. I don't know whether I had killed him or not. I and Diamelen pushed the canoe afloat. I heard yells behind me, and I saw my brother run across the glade. Many men were bounding after him. I took her in my arms and threw her into the boat, then leaped in myself. When I looked back I saw that my brother had fallen. He fell and was up again, but the men were closing round him. He shouted, 'I am coming!' The men were close to him. I looked. Many men. Then I looked at her. Tuan, I pushed the canoe! I pushed it into deep water. She was kneeling forward looking at me, and I said, "Take your paddle,' while I struck the water with mine. Tuan, I heard him cry. I heard him cry my name twice; and I heard voices shouting, 'Kill! Strike!' I never turned back. I heard him calling my name again with a great shriek, as when life is going out together with the voice—and I never turned my head. My own name! . . . . My brother; Three times he called—but I was not afraid of life. Was she not there in that canoe? And could I not with her find a country where death is forgotten—where death is unknown!"

262

The white man sat up. Arsat rose and stood, an indistinct and silent figure above the dying embers of the fire. Over the lagoon a mist drifting and low had crept, erasing slowly the glittering images of the stars. And now a great expanse of white vapor covered the land: it flowed cold and gray in the darkness, eddied in noiseless whirls round the tree-trunks and about the platform of the house, which seemed to float upon a restless and impalpable illusion of a sea. Only far away the tops of the trees stood outlined on the twinkle of heaven, like a somber and forbidding shore—a coast deceptive, pitiless and black.

Arsat's voice vibrated loudly in the profound peace.

"I had her there! I had her! To get her I would have faced all mankind. But I had her—and—"

His words went out ringing into the empty distances. He paused, and seemed to listen to them dying away very far—beyond help and beyond recall. Then he said quietly—

"Tuan, I loved my brother."

A breath of wind made him shiver. High above his head, high above the silent sea of mist the drooping leaves of the palms rattled together with a mournful and expiring sound. The white man stretched his legs. His chin rested on his chest, and he murmured sadly without lifting his head—

"We all love our brothers."

Arsat burst out with an intense whispering violence—

"What did I care who died? I wanted peace in my own heart."

He seemed to hear a stir in the house—listened—then stepped in noiselessly. The white man stood up. A breeze was coming in fitful puffs. The stars shone paler as if they had retreated into the frozen depths of immense space. After a chill gust of wind there were a few seconds of perfect calm and absolute silence. Then from behind the black and wavy line of the forest a column of golden light shot up into the heavens and spread over the semicircle of the eastern horizon. The sun had risen. The mist lifted, broke into drifting patches, vanished into thin flying wreaths; and the unveiled lagoon lay, polished and black, in the heavy shadows at the foot of the wall of trees. A white eagle rose over it with a slanting and ponderous flight, reached the clear sunshine and appeared dazzlingly brilliant for a moment, then soaring higher, became a dark and motionless speck before it vanished into the blue as if it had left the earth forever. The white man, standing gazing upwards before

the doorway, heard in the hut a confused and broken murmur of distracted words ending with a loud groan. Suddenly Arsat stumbled out with outstretched hands, shivered, and stood still for some time with fixed eyes. Then he said—

"She burns no more."

Before his face the sun showed its edge above the tree-tops rising steadily. The breeze freshened; a great brilliance burst upon the lagoon, sparkled on the rippling water. The forests came out of the clear shadows of the morning, became distinct, as if they had rushed nearer—to stop short in a great stir of leaves, of nodding boughs, of swaying branches. In the merciless sunshine the whisper of unconscious life grew louder, speaking in an incomprehensible voice round the dumb darkness of that human sorrow. Arsat's eyes wandered slowly, then stared at the rising sun.

"I can see nothing," he said half aloud to himself.

"There is nothing," said the white man, moving to the edge of the platform and waving his hand to his boat. A shout came faintly over the lagoon and the sampan began to glide towards the abode of the friend of ghosts.

"If you want to come with me, I will wait all the morning," said the white man, looking away upon the water.

"No, Tuan," said Arsat, softly. "I shall not eat or sleep in this house, but I must first see my road. Now I can see nothing—see nothing! There is no light and no peace in the world; but there is death—death for many. We are sons of the same mother—and I left him in the midst of enemies; but I am going back now."

He drew a long breath and went on in a dreamy tone:

"In a little while I shall see clear enough to strike—to strike. But she has died, and . . . now . . . darkness."

He flung his arms wide open, let them fall along his body, then stood still with unmoved face and stony eyes, staring at the sun. The white man got down into his canoe. The poles ran smartly along the sides of the boat, looking over their shoulders at the beginning of a weary journey. High in the stern, his head muffled up in white rags, the juragan sat moody, letting his paddle trail in the water. The white man, leaning with both arms over the grass roof of the little cabin, looked back at the shining ripple of the boat's wake. Before the sampan passed out of the lagoon into the creek he lifted his eyes. Arsat had not moved. He stood lonely in the searching sunshine; and he looked beyond the great light of a cloudless day into the darkness of a world of illusions.

JAMES FENIMORE COOPER

JAMES FENIMORE COOPER (American, 1789-1851). The great romancer of the American frontier. Produced more than 50 books: novels, travel sketches, social criticism. Popular reputation rests on sea stories (*The Pilot*), and Leatherstocking tales (*The Last of the Mohicans, The Pathfinder, The Deerslayer*). Labored zealously in 19th century to further international understanding of American democracy.

THE ARIEL ON THE SHOALS

THE SEA was becoming more agitated, and the violence of the wind was gradually increasing. The latter no longer whistled amid the cordage of the vessel, but it seemed to howl surlily as it passed the complicated machinery that the frigate obtruded on its path. An endless succession of white surges rose above the heavy billows, and the very air was glittering with the light that was disengaged from the ocean. The ship yielded each moment more and more before the storm, and, in less than half an hour from the time that she had lifted her anchor, she was driven along with tremendous fury by the full power of a gale of wind. Still, the hardy and experienced mariners who directed her movements, held her to the course that was necessary to their preservation, and still Griffith gave forth, when directed by their unknown pilot, those orders that turned her in the narrow channel where safety was alone to be found.

So far the performance of his duty appeared easy to the stranger, and he gave the required directions in those still, calm tones that formed so remarkable a contrast to the responsibility of his situation. But when the land was becoming dim, in distance as well as darkness, and the agitated sea was only to be discovered as it swept by them in foam, he broke in upon the monotonous roaring of the tempest with the sounds of his voice, seeming to shake off his apathy and rouse himself to the occasion.

"Now is the time to watch her closely, Mr. Griffith," he cried; "here we get the true tide and the real danger. Place the best quarter-master of your ship in those chains, and let an officer stand by him and see that he gives us the right water."

"I will take that office on myself," said the captain; "pass a light into the weather main-chains."

"Stand by your braces!" exclaimed the pilot with startling quickness. "Heave away that lead!"

These preparations taught the crew to expect the crisis, and every officer and man stood in fearful silence at his assigned station awaiting the issue of the trial. Even the quarter-master at the cun gave out his orders to the men at the wheel in deeper and hoarser tones than usual, as if anxious not to disturb the quiet and order of the vessel.

While this deep expectation pervaded the frigate, the piercing cry of the leadsman, as he called, "By the mark seven!" rose above the tempest, crossed over the decks, and appeared to pass away to leeward, borne on the blast like the warnings of some water-spirit.

" 'Tis well," returned the pilot, calmly; "try it again."

The short pause was succeeded by another cry, "and a half-five!"

"She shoals! she shoals!" exclaimed Griffith; "keep her a good full."

"Ay! you must hold the vessel in command, now," said the pilot, with those cool tones that are most appalling in critical moments, because they seem to denote most preparation and care.

The third call of "By the deep four!" was followed by a prompt direction from the stranger to tack.

Griffith seemed to emulate the coolness of the pilot, in issuing the necessary orders to execute this manœuvre.

The vessel rose slowly from the inclined position into which she had been forced by the tempest, and the sails were shaking violently, as if to release themselves from their confinement while the ship stemmed the billows, when the well-known voice of the sailing-master was heard shouting from the forecastle—"Breakers! breakers, dead ahead!"

This appalling sound seemed yet to be lingering about the ship, when a second voice cried—"Breakers on our lee-bow!"

"We are in a bight of the shoals, Mr. Gray," said the commander. "She loses her way; perhaps an anchor might hold her."

"Clear away that best-bower!" shouted Griffith through his trumpet.

"Hold on!" cried the pilot, in a voice that reached the very hearts of all who heard him; "hold on every thing."

The young man turned fiercely to the daring stranger who thus defied the discipline of his vessel, and at once demanded—"Who is it that dares to countermand my orders?—is it not enough that you run the ship into danger, but you must interfere to keep her there? If another word—"

266

"Peace, Mr. Griffith," interrupted the captain, bending from the rigging, his gray locks blowing about in the wind, and adding a look of wildness to the haggard face that he exhibited by the light of his lantern; "yield the trumpet to Mr. Gray; he alone can save us."

Griffith threw his speaking-trumpet on the deck, and as he walked proudly away, muttered in bitterness of feeling—"Then all is lost, indeed, and, among the rest, the foolish hopes with which I visited this coast."

There was, however, no time for reply; the ship had been rapidly running into the wind, and, as the efforts of the crew were paralyzed by the contradictory orders they had heard, she gradually lost her way, and in a few seconds all her sails were taken aback.

Before the crew understood their situation, the pilot had applied the trumpet to his mouth, and, in a voice that rose above the tempest, he thundered forth his orders. Each command was given distinctly, and with a precision that showed him to be master of his profession. The helm was kept fast, the head yards swung up heavily against the wind, and the vessel was soon whirling round on her heel with a retrograde movement.

Griffith was too much of a seaman not to perceive that the pilot had seized, with a perception almost intuitive, the only method that promised to extricate the vessel from her situation. He was young, impetuous and proud, but he was also generous. Forgetting his resentment and his mortification, he rushed forward among the men, and, by his presence and example, added certainty to the experiment. The ship fell off slowly before the gale, and bowed her yards nearly to the water, as she felt the blast pouring its fury on her broadsides while the surly waves beat violently against her stern, as if in reproach at departing from her usual manner of moving.

The voice of the pilot, however, was still heard, steady and calm, and yet so clear and high as to reach every ear; and the obedient seamen whirled the yards at his bidding in despite of the tempest, as if they handled the toys of their childhood. When the ship had fallen off dead before the wind, her head sails were shaken, her aft-yards trimmed, and her helm shifted before she had time to run upon the danger that had threatened, as well to leeward as to windward. The beautiful fabric, obedient to her government, threw her bows up gracefully toward the wind again, and, as her sails were trimmed, moved out from amongst the dangerous shoals in

which she had been embayed, as steadily and swiftly as she had approached them.

A moment of breathless astonishment succeeded the accomplishment of this nice manœuvre, but there was no time for the usual expressions of surprise. The stranger still held the trumpet, and continued to lift his voice amid the howlings of the blast, whenever prudence or skill directed any change in the management of the ship. For an hour longer there was a fearful struggle for their preservation, the channel becoming at each step more complicated, and the shoals thickening around the mariners on every side. The lead was cast rapidly, and the quick eye of the pilot seemed to pierce the darkness with a keenness of vision that exceeded human power. It was apparent to all in the vessel, that they were under the guidance of one who understood the navigation thoroughly, and their exertions kept pace with their reviving confidence. Again and again the frigate appeared to be rushing blindly on shoals, where the sea was covered with foam, and where destruction would have been as sudden as it was certain, when the clear voice of the stranger was heard warning them of the danger and inciting them to their duty. The vessel was implicitly yielding to his government, and during those anxious moments, when she was dashing the waters aside, throwing the spray over her enormous yards, each ear would listen eagerly for those sounds that had obtained a command over the crew that can only be acquired, under such circumstances, by great steadiness and consummate skill. The ship was recovering from the inaction of changing her course in one of those critical tacks that she had made so often when the pilot for the first time addressed the commander of the frigate, who still continued to superintend the all-important duty of the leadsman.

"Now is the pinch," he said; "and if the ship behaves well, we are safe—but if otherwise, all we have yet done will be useless."

The veteran seaman whom he addressed left the chains at this portentous notice, and, calling to his first lieutenant, required of the stranger an explanation of his warning.

"See you yon light on the southern headland?" returned the pilot; "you may know it from the star near it by its sinking, at times, in the ocean. Now observe the hummock a little north of it, looking like a shadow on the horizon—'tis a hill far inland. If we keep that light open from the hill, we shall do well—but if not, we surely go to pieces."

268

"Let us tack again!" exclaimed the lieutenant.

The pilot shook his head, as he replied—"There is no more tacking or box-hauling to be done to-night. We have barely room to pass out of the shoals on this course, and if we can weather the 'Devil's Grip,' we clear their outermost point—but if not, as I said before, there is but an alternative."

"If we had beaten out the way we entered," exclaimed Griffith, "we should have done well."

"Say, also, if the tide would have let us do so," returned the pilot calmly. "Gentlemen, we must be prompt; we have but a mile to go, and the ship appears to fly. That topsail is not enough to keep her up to the wind; we want both jib and mainsail."

" 'Tis a perilous thing to loosen canvas in such a tempest!" observed the doubtful captain.

"It must be done," returned the collected stranger; "we perish without—see! the light already touches the edge of the hummock; the sea casts us to leeward!"

"It shall be done!" cried Griffith, seizing the trumpet from the hand of the pilot.

The orders of the lieutenant were executed almost as soon as issued, and, every thing being ready, the enormous folds of the mainsail were trusted loose to the blast. There was an instant when the result was doubtful; the tremendous threshing of the heavy sails seeming to bid defiance to all restraint, shaking the ship to her centre; but art and strength prevailed, and gradually the canvas was distended, and, bellying as it filled, was drawn down to its usual place by the power of a hundred men. The vessel yielded to this immense addition of force, and bowed before it like a reed bending to a breeze. But the success of the measure was announced by a joyful cry from the stranger that seemed to burst from his inmost soul.

"She feels it! she springs her luff! observe," he said, "the light opens from the hummock already; if she will only bear her canvas, we shall go clear!"

A report like that of a cannon interrupted his exclamation, and something resembling a white cloud was seen drifting before the wind from the head of the ship, till it was driven into the gloom far to leeward.

" 'Tis the jib blown from the bolt-ropes," said the commander of the frigate. "This is no time to spread light duck—but the mainsail may stand it yet."

"The sail would laugh at a tornado," returned the lieutenant; "but that mast springs like a piece of steel."

"Silence all!" cried the pilot. "Now, gentlemen, we shall soon know our fate. Let her luff—luff you can!"

This warning effectually closed all discourse, and the hardy mariners, knowing that they had already done all in the power of man to insure their safety, stood in breathless anxiety awaiting the result. At a short distance ahead of them, the whole ocean was white with foam, and the waves, instead of rolling on in regular succession, appeared to be tossing about in mad gambols. A single streak of dark billows, not half a cable's length in width, could be discerned running into this chaos of water; but it was soon lost to the eye amid the confusion of the disturbed element. Along this narrow path the vessel moved more heavily than before, being brought so near the wind as to keep her sails touching. The pilot silently proceeded to the wheel, and with his own hands he undertook the steerage of the ship. No noise proceeded from the frigate to interrupt the horrid tumult of the ocean, and she entered the channel among the breakers with the silence of a desperate calmness. Twenty times, as the foam rolled away to leeward, the crew were on the eve of uttering their joy, as they supposed the vessel past the danger; but breaker after breaker would still rise before them, following each other into the general mass to check their exultation. Occasionally the fluttering of the sails would be heard; and when the looks of the startled seamen were turned to the wheel, they beheld the stranger grasping its spokes, with his quick eye glancing from the water to the canvas. At length the ship reached a point where she appeared to be rushing directly into the jaws of destruction, when suddenly her course was changed, and her head receded rapidly from the wind. At the same instant the voice of the pilot was heard shouting—"Square away the yards!—in mainsail!"

A general burst from the crew echoed, "Square away the yards!" and quick as thought the frigate was seen gliding along the channel before the wind. The eye had hardly time to dwell on the foam, which seemed like clouds driving in the heavens, and directly the gallant vessel issued from her perils, and rose and fell on the heavy waves of the open sea.

STEPHEN CRANE

STEPHEN CRANE (American, 1871-1900). Great realistic writer, who died
of tuberculosis at 28, after writing greatest Civil War novel—*The Red Badge
of Courage.* Brief life filled with illness and trouble; he was much maligned
as journalist and foreign correspondent. Other masterpieces of realism:
The Open Boat and *Maggie: A Girl of the Streets*, works far in advance of
their time.

THE BRIDE COMES TO YELLOW SKY

I

THE great pullman was whirling onward with such dignity of
motion that a glance from the window seemed simply to prove
that the plains of Texas were pouring eastward. Vast flats of green
grass, dull-hued spaces of mesquit and cactus, little groups of frame
houses, woods of light and tender trees, all were sweeping into
the east, sweeping over the horizon, a precipice.

A newly married pair had boarded this coach at San Antonio.
The man's face was reddened from many days in the wind and
sun, and a direct result of his new black clothes was that his brick-
coloured hands were constantly performing in a most conscious
fashion. From time to time he looked down respectfully at his attire.
He sat with a hand on each knee, like a man waiting in a barber's
shop. The glances he devoted to other passengers were furtive and
shy.

The bride was not pretty, nor was she very young. She wore a
dress of blue cashmere, with small reservations of velvet here and
there, and with steel buttons abounding. She continually twisted
her head to regard her puff sleeves, very stiff, straight, and high.
They embarrassed her. It was quite apparent that she had cooked,
and that she expected to cook, dutifully. The blushes caused by the
careless scrutiny of some passengers as she had entered the car
were strange to see upon this plain, under-class countenance, which
was drawn in placid, almost emotionless lines.

They were evidently very happy. "Ever been in a parlour-car
before?" he asked, smiling with delight.

"No," she answered; "I never was. It's fine, ain't it?"

"Great! And then after a while we'll go forward to the diner,
and get a big lay-out. Finest meal in the world. Charge a dollar."

"Oh, do they?" cried the bride. "Charge a dollar? Why, that's
too much—for us—ain't it, Jack?"

271

"Not this trip, anyhow," he answered bravely. "We're going to go the whole thing."

Later he explained to her about the trains. "You see, it's a thousand miles from one end of Texas to the other; and this train runs right across it, and never stops but four times." He had the pride of an owner. He pointed out to her the dazzling fittings of the coach; and in truth her eyes opened wider as she contemplated the sea-green figured velvet, the shining brass, silver, and glass, the wood that gleamed as darkly brilliant as the surface of a pool of oil. At one end a bronze figure sturdily held a support for a separated chamber, and at convenient places on the ceiling were frescos in olive and silver.

To the minds of the pair, their surroundings reflected the glory of their marriage that morning in San Antonio; this was the environment of their new estate; and the man's face in particular beamed with an elation that made him appear ridiculous to the negro porter. This individual at times surveyed them from afar with an amused and superior grin. On other occasions he bullied them with skill in ways that did not make it exactly plain to them that they were being bullied. He subtly used all the manners of the most unconquerable kind of snobbery. He oppressed them; but of this oppression they had small knowledge, and they speedily forgot that infrequently a number of travellers covered them with stares of derisive enjoyment. Historically there was supposed to be something infinitely humorous in their situation.

"We are due in Yellow Sky at 3:42," he said, looking tenderly into her eyes.

"Oh, are we?" she said, as if she had not been aware of it. To evince surprise at her husband's statement was part of her wifely amiability. She took from a pocket a little silver watch; and as she held it before her, and stared at it with a frown of attention, the new husband's face shone.

"I bought it in San Anton' from a friend of mine," he told her gleefully.

"It's seventeen minutes past twelve," she said, looking up at him with a kind of shy and clumsy coquetry. A passenger, noting this play, grew excessively sardonic, and winked at himself in one of the numerous mirrors.

At last they went to the dining-car. Two rows of negro waiters, in glowing white suits, surveyed their entrance with the interest, and also the equanimity, of men who had been forewarned. The

pair fell to the lot of a waiter who happened to feel pleasure in steering them through their meal. He viewed them with the manner of a fatherly pilot, his countenance radiant with benevolence. The patronage, entwined with the ordinary deference, was not plain to them. And yet, as they returned to their coach, they showed in their faces a sense of escape.

To the left, miles down a long purple slope, was a little ribbon of mist where moved the keening Rio Grande. The train was approaching it at an angle, and the apex was Yellow Sky. Presently it was apparent that, as the distance from Yellow Sky grew shorter, the husband became commensurately restless. His brick-red hands were more insistent in their prominence. Occasionally he was even rather absent-minded and far-away when the bride leaned forward and addressed him.

As a matter of truth, Jack Potter was beginning to find the shadow of a deed weigh upon him like a leaden slab. He, the town marshal of Yellow Sky, a man known, liked, and feared in his corner, a prominent person, had gone to San Antonio to meet a girl he believed he loved, and there, after the usual prayers, had actually induced her to marry him, without consulting Yellow Sky for any part of the transaction. He was now bringing his bride before an innocent and unsuspecting community.

Of course people in Yellow Sky married as it pleased them, in accordance with a general custom; but such was Potter's thought of his duty to his friends, or of their idea of his duty, or of an unspoken form which does not control men in these matters, that he felt he was heinous. He had committed an extraordinary crime. Face to face with this girl in San Antonio, and spurred by his sharp impulse, he had gone headlong over all the social hedges. At San Antonio he was like a man hidden in the dark. A knife to sever any friendly duty, any form, was easy to his hand in that remote city. But the hour of Yellow Sky—the hour of daylight— was approaching.

He knew full well that his marriage was an important thing to his town. It could only be exceeded by the burning of the new hotel. His friends could not forgive him. Frequently he had reflected on the advisability of telling them by telegraph, but a new cowardice had been upon him. He feared to do it. And now the train was hurrying him toward a scene of amazement, glee, and reproach. He glanced out of the window at the line of haze swinging slowly in toward the train.

Yellow Sky had a kind of brass band, which played painfully, to the delight of the populace. He laughed without heart as he thought of it. If the citizens could dream of his prospective arrival with his bride, they would parade the band at the station and escort them, amid cheers and laughing congratulations, to his adobe home.

He resolved that he would use all the devices of speed and plains-craft in making the journey from the station to his house. Once within that safe citadel, he could issue some sort of vocal bulletin, and then not go among the citizens until they had time to wear off a little of their enthusiasm.

The bride looked anxiously at him. "What's worrying you, Jack?"

He laughed again. "I'm not worrying, girl; I'm only thinking of Yellow Sky."

She flushed in comprehension.

A sense of mutual guilt invaded their minds and developed a finer tenderness. They looked at each other with eyes softly aglow. But Potter often laughed the same nervous laugh; the flush upon the bride's face seemed quite permanent.

The traitor to the feelings of Yellow Sky narrowly watched the speeding landscape. "We're nearly there," he said.

Presently the porter came and announced the proximity of Potter's home. He held a brush in his hand, and, with all his airy superiority gone, he brushed Potter's new clothes as the latter slowly turned this way and that way. Potter fumbled out a coin and gave it to the porter, as he had seen others do. It was a heavy and muscle-bound business, as that of a man shoeing his first horse.

The porter took their bag, and as the train began to slow they moved forward to the hooded platform of the car. Presently the two engines and their long string of coaches rushed into the station of Yellow Sky.

"They have to take water here," said Potter, from a constricted throat and in mournful cadence, as one announcing death. Before the train stopped his eye had swept the length of the platform, and he was glad and astonished to see there was none upon it but the station-agent, who, with a slightly hurried and anxious air, was walking toward the water-tanks. When the train had halted, the porter alighted first, and placed in position a little temporary step.

"Come on, girl," said Potter, hoarsely. As he helped her down they each laughed on a false note. He took the bag from the negro,

and bade his wife cling to his arm. As they slunk rapidly away, his hang-dog glance perceived that they were unloading the two trunks, and also that the station-agent, far ahead near the baggage-car, had turned and was running toward him, making gestures. He laughed, and groaned as he laughed, when he noted the first effect of his marital bliss upon Yellow Sky. He gripped his wife's arm firmly to his side, and they fled. Behind them the porter stood, chuckling fatuously.

II

The California express on the Southern Railway was due at Yellow Sky in twenty-one minutes. There were six men at the bar of the Weary Gentleman saloon. One was a drummer who talked a great deal and rapidly; three were Texans who did not care to talk at that time; and two were Mexican sheep-herders, who did not talk as a general practice in the Weary Gentleman saloon. The barkeeper's dog lay on the board walk that crossed in front of the door. His head was on his paws, and he glanced drowsily here and there with the constant vigilance of a dog that is kicked on occasion. Across the sandy street were some vivid green grass-plots, so wonderful in appearance, amid the sands that burned near them in a blazing sun, that they caused a doubt in the mind. They exactly resembled the grass mats used to represent lawns on the stage. At the cooler end of the railway station, a man without a coat sat in a tilted chair and smoked his pipe. The fresh-cut bank of the Rio Grande circled near the town, and there could be seen beyond it a great plum-coloured plain of mesquit.

Save for the busy drummer and his companions in the saloon, Yellow Sky was dozing. The new-comer leaned gracefully upon the bar, and recited many tales with the confidence of a bard who has come upon a new field.

"—and at the moment that the old man fell downstairs with the bureau in his arms, the old woman was coming up with two scuttles of coal, and of course—"

The drummer's tale was interrupted by a young man who suddenly appeared in the open door. He cried: "Scratchy Wilson's drunk, and has turned loose with both hands." The two Mexicans at once set down their glasses and faded out of the rear entrance of the saloon.

The drummer, innocent and jocular, answered: "All right, old man. S'pose he has? Come in and have a drink, anyhow."

But the information had made such an obvious cleft in every skull in the room that the drummer was obliged to see its importance. All had become instantly solemn. "Say," said he, mystified, "what is this?" His three companions made the introductory gesture of eloquent speech; but the young man at the door forestalled them.

"It means, my friend," he answered, as he came into the saloon, "that for the next two hours this town won't be a health resort."

The barkeeper went to the door, and locked and barred it; reaching out of the window, he pulled in heavy wooden shutters, and barred them. Immediately a solemn, chapellike gloom was upon the place. The drummer was looking from one to another.

"But say," he cried, "what is this, anyhow? You don't mean there is going to be a gun-fight?"

"Don't know whether there'll be a fight or not," answered one man, grimly; "but there'll be some shootin'—some good shootin'."

The young man who had warned them waved his hand. "Oh, there'll be a fight fast enough, if any one wants it. Anybody can get a fight out there in the street. There's a fight just waiting."

The drummer seemed to be swayed between the interest of a foreigner and a perception of personal danger.

"What did you say his name was?" he asked.

"Scratchy Wilson," they answered in chorus.

"And will he kill anybody? What are you going to do? Does this happen often? Does he rampage around like this once a week or so? Can he break in that door?"

"No; he can't break down that door," replied the barkeeper. "He's tried it three times. But when he comes you'd better lay down on the floor, stranger. He's dead sure to shoot at it, and a bullet may come through."

Thereafter the drummer kept a strict eye upon the door. The time had not yet been called for him to hug the floor, but, as a minor precaution, he sidled near to the wall. "Will he kill anybody?" he said again.

The men laughed low and scornfully at the question.

"He's out to shoot, and he's out for trouble. Don't see any good in experimentin' with him."

"But what do you do in a case like this? What do you do?"

A man responded: "Why, he and Jack Potter—"

"But," in chorus the other men interrupted, "Jack Potter's in San Anton'."

"Well, who is he? What's he got to do with it?"

"Oh, he's the town marshal. He goes out and fights Scratchy when he gets on one of these tears."

"Wow!" said the drummer, mopping his brow. "Nice job he's got."

The voices had toned away to mere whisperings. The drummer wished to ask further questions, which were born of an increasing anxiety and bewilderment; but when he attempted them, the men merely looked at him in irritation and motioned him to remain silent. A tense waiting hush was upon them. In the deep shadows of the room their eyes shone as they listened for sounds from the street. One man made three gestures at the barkeeper; and the latter, moving like a ghost, handed him a glass and a bottle. The man poured a full glass of whisky in a swallow, and turned again toward the door in immovable silence. The drummer saw that the barkeeper, without a sound, had taken a Winchester from beneath the bar. Later he saw this individual beckoning to him, so he tiptoed across the room.

"You better come with me back of the bar."

"No, thanks," said the drummer, perspiring; "I'd rather be where I can make a break for the back door."

Whereupon the man of bottles made a kindly but peremptory gesture. The drummer obeyed it, and, finding himself seated on a box with his head below the level of the bar, balm was laid upon his soul at sight of various zinc and copper fittings that bore a resemblance to armour-plate. The barkeeper took a seat comfortably upon an adjacent box.

"You see," he whispered, "this here Scratchy Wilson is a wonder with a gun—a perfect wonder; and when he goes on the war-trail, we hunt our holes—naturally. He's about the last one of the old gang that used to hang out along the river here. He's a terror when he's drunk. When he's sober he's all right—kind of simple—wouldn't hurt a fly—nicest fellow in town. But when he's drunk—whoo!"

There were periods of stillness. "I wish Jack Potter was back from San Anton'," said the barkeeper. "He shot Wilson up once —in the leg—and he would sail in and pull out the kinks in this thing."

Presently they heard from a distance the sound of a shot, followed by three wild yowls. It instantly removed a bond from the men in the darkened saloon. There was a shuffling of feet. They looked at each other. "Here he comes," they said.

III

A man in a maroon-coloured flannel shirt, which had been purchased for purposes of decoration, and made principally by some Jewish women on the East Side of New York, rounded a corner and walked into the middle of the main street of Yellow Sky. In either hand the man held a long, heavy, blue-black revolver. Often he yelled, and these cries rang through a semblance of a deserted village, shrilly flying over the roofs in a volume that seemed to have no relation to the ordinary vocal strength of a man. It was as if the surrounding stillness formed the arch of a tomb over him. These cries of ferocious challenge rang against walls of silence. And his boots had red tops with gilded imprints, of the kind beloved in winter by little sledding boys on the hillsides of New England.

The man's face flamed in a rage begot of whisky. His eyes, rolling, and yet keen for ambush, hunted the still doorways and windows. He walked with the creeping movement of the midnight cat. As it occurred to him, he roared menacing information. The long revolvers in his hands were as easy as straws; they were moved with an electric swiftness. The little fingers of each hand played sometimes in a musician's way. Plain from the low collar of the shirt, the cords of his neck straightened and sank, straightened and sank, as passion moved him. The only sounds were his terrible invitations. The calm adobes preserved their demeanour at the passing of this small thing in the middle of the street.

There was no offer of fight—no offer of fight. The man called to the sky. There were no attractions. He bellowed and fumed and swayed his revolvers here and everywhere.

The dog of the barkeeper of the Weary Gentleman saloon had not appreciated the advance of events. He yet lay dozing in front of his master's door. At sight of the dog, the man paused and raised his revolver humorously. At sight of the man, the dog sprang up and walked diagonally away, with a sullen head, and growling. The man yelled, and the dog broke into a gallop. As it was about to enter an alley, there was a loud noise, a whistling, and something spat the ground directly before it. The dog screamed, and, wheeling in terror, galloped headlong in a new direction. Again there was

278

a noise, a whistling, and sand was kicked viciously before it. Fear-stricken, the dog turned and flurried like an animal in a pen. The man stood laughing, his weapons at his hips.

Ultimately the man was attracted by the closed door of the Weary Gentleman saloon. He went to it and, hammering with a revolver, demanded drink.

The door remaining imperturbable, he picked a bit of paper from the walk, and nailed it to the framework with a knife. He then turned his back contemptuously upon this popular resort and, walking to the opposite side of the street and spinning there on his heel quickly and lithely, fired at the bit of paper. He missed it by a half-inch. He swore at himself, and went away. Later he comfortably fusilladed the windows of his most intimate friend. The man was playing with this town; it was a toy for him.

But still there was no offer of fight. The name of Jack Potter, his ancient antagonist, entered his mind, and he concluded that it would be a glad thing if he should go to Potter's house, and by bombardment induce him to come out and fight. He moved in the direction of his desire, chanting Apache scalp-music.

When he arrived at it, Potter's house presented the same still front as had the other adobes. Taking up a strategic position, the man howled a challenge. But this house regarded him as might a great stone god. It gave no sign. After a decent wait, the man howled further challenges, mingling with them wonderful epithets.

Presently there came the spectacle of a man churning himself into deepest rage over the immobility of a house. He fumed at it as the winter wind attacks a prairie cabin in the North. To the distance there should have gone the sound of a tumult like the fighting of two hundred Mexicans. As necessity bade him, he paused for breath or to reload his revolvers.

IV

Potter and his bride walked sheepishly and with speed. Sometimes they laughed together shamefacedly and low.

"Next corner, dear," he said finally.

They put forth the efforts of a pair walking bowed against a strong wind. Potter was about to raise a finger to point the first appearance of the new home when, as they circled the corner, they came face to face with a man in a maroon-coloured shirt, who was feverishly pushing cartridges into a large revolver. Upon the instant the man dropped his revolver to the ground and, like lightning,

whipped another from its holster. The second weapon was aimed at the bridegroom's chest.

There was a silence. Potter's mouth seemed to be merely a grave for his tongue. He exhibited an instinct to at once loosen his arm from the woman's grip, and he dropped the bag to the sand. As for the bride, her face had gone as yellow as old cloth. She was a slave to hideous rites, gazing at the apparitional snake.

The two men faced each other at a distance of three paces. He of the revolver smiled with a new and quiet ferocity.

"Tried to sneak up on me," he said. "Tried to sneak up on me!" His eyes grew more baleful. As Potter made a slight movement, the man thrust his revolver venomously forward. "No; don't you do it, Jack Potter. Don't you move a finger toward a gun just yet. Don't you move an eyelash. The time has come for me to settle with you, and I'm goin' to do it my own way, and loaf along with no interferin'. So if you don't want a gun bent on you, just mind what I tell you."

Potter looked at his enemy, "I ain't got a gun on me, Scratchy," he said. "Honest, I ain't." He was stiffening and steadying, but yet somewhere at the back of his mind a vision of the Pullman floated: the sea-green figured velvet, the shining brass, silver, and glass, the wood that gleamed as darkly brilliant as the surface of a pool of oil—all the glory of the marriage, the environment of the new estate. "You know I fight when it comes to fighting, Scratchy Wilson; but I ain't got a gun on me. You'll have to do all the shootin' yourself."

His enemy's face went livid. He stepped forward, and lashed his weapon to and fro before Potter's chest. "Don't you tell me you ain't got no gun on you, you whelp. Don't tell me no lie like that. There ain't a man in Texas ever seen you without no gun. Don't take me for no kid." His eyes blazed with light, and his throat worked like a pump.

"I ain't takin' you for no kid," answered Potter. His heels had not moved an inch backward. "I'm takin' you for a damn fool. I tell you I ain't got a gun, and I ain't. If you're goin' to shoot me up, you better begin now; you'll never get a chance like this again."

So much enforced reasoning had told on Wilson's rage; he was calmer. "If you ain't got a gun, why ain't you got a gun?" he sneered. "Been to Sunday-school?"

"I ain't got a gun because I've just come from San Anton' with my wife. I'm married," said Potter. "And if I'd thought there was

280

going to be any galoots like you prowling around when I brought my wife home, I'd had a gun, and don't you forget it."

"Married!" said Scratchy, not at all comprehending.

"Yes, married. I'm married," said Potter, distinctly.

"Married?" said Scratchy. Seemingly for the first time, he saw the drooping, drowning woman at the other man's side. "No!" he said. He was like a creature allowed a glimpse of another world. He moved a pace backward, and his arm, with the revolver, dropped to his side. "Is this the lady?" he asked.

"Yes; this is the lady," answered Potter.

There was another period of silence.

"Well," said Wilson at last, slowly, "I s'pose it's all off now."

"It's all off if you say so, Scratchy. You know I didn't make the trouble." Potter lifted his valise.

"Well, I 'low it's off, Jack," said Wilson. He was looking at the ground. "Married!" He was not a student of chivalry; it was merely that in the presence of this foreign condition he was a simple child of the earlier plains. He picked up his starboard revolver, and, placing both weapons in their holsters, he went away. His feet made funnel-shaped tracks in the heavy sand.

D

DANDIN

DANDIN (Sanskrit, *ca.* 7th century A.D.). Colorful and picturesque Sanskrit author of a picaresque novel, *Dasakumāracharita (The Adventures of the Ten Princes)*. The play *Mricchakatika* is attributed to him by some.

THE COURTESAN'S MOTHER

THESE are the aspects on which a courtesan's mother has to concentrate her attention in rearing up her child, namely, to apply perfumed cosmetics to the limbs of the girl even from her childhood; to put her on such nutritious diet as would supply her with enough bodily radiance, strength, complexion and wits as well as her normal appetite and digestion; to keep even the man who gave her life from visiting her frequently after her fifth year of life; to celebrate her birthdays and other events of her life in adequate style; to initiate her into the arts of love-making with all their accessory aids; to familiarise her with the secrets of the arts of dancing, music, instrumental play, histrionics, painting and the culinary art; to teach her how to prepare sandal paste and flower pigments as well as to gain efficiency in calligraphy and conversational graces; to supply her with that amount of acquaintance of the Sastras such as grammar, logic and philosophy so as to enable her to carry on discussions without showing want of information; to guide her in the science of living; to teach her knowledge of games and dice-throwing as well as equip her with the necessary zest for watching cock- and bull-fights; to induce her to learn from adept and experienced gallants the trick of amorous wooing; to decorate her person attractively on occasions of festival and public carnival and to send her out attended upon by a proper retinue; to make her ingratiate herself in the favour of men of influence and rank in order to suc-

282

ceed in her performances before audiences; to propitiate the virtuosos in the various arts in order to gain a favourable atmosphere for her own excursions into them; to make astrologers and palmists spread her prospective fame from a reading of her chart; to gather from that group who visit dancing girls enough of appreciation for her good looks, qualities, wit and figure; to give her away to anyone blindly in love with her in case he is rich and independent also; otherwise, to yield her up to one who has high intellectual attainments though poorly equipped with worldly materials; to persuade her to live with one by Gandharva wedding but later on to extort money from him and finally, if need be, to resort to courts of law for recovering her money claims.

GABRIELE D'ANNUNZIO

GABRIELE D'ANNUNZIO (Italian, 1863-1938). Flamboyant, romantic poet and dramatist. Influential in early 20th century Italy. Pushed anti-religious, anti-democratic ideas of Carducci to grotesque extremes. Attracted by themes of violence, illness, erotic decadence. Most widely read novel: *The Triumph of Death*. Plays include *La Gioconda, Francesca da Rimini*.

FOUR SONNETS

I

He was a love-child. In his gloomy eye
  Burned flames of desperate hatred, prompt to glow,
  Like lurid gleams of sunset from the sky
  Fallen in foul waters of a ditch below;
  Pale, lean he was: his red hair stood up high
  Over his head deformed and marked with woe,
  And his misshapen body made awry
  As if from stone hewn by an axe's blow.

  And yet—! None knew his heart-beats in the night,
  None saw his burning tears, none heard him weep
  Tears breaking his poor heart, in youth's despite,
  When o'er the deck broke from the odorous deep
  Vast waves of perfume 'neath the full moonlight,
  And nought was heard save long-drawn breaths of sleep.

283

II

Ah, none! She passes o'er the sands of gold,
  Singing a song, and with the sunlight crowned;
  Given to the Loves her ample breasts unfold,
  Given to the winds her tresses flow unbound.
Joyous with youth her honest eyes and bold,
  Blue like the tropic skies, seek all around
  Fancies and dreams, while to the heavens out-rolled
  O'er the opal sea her joyous songs resound.

He breathless, quivering with passions vain,
  Crouched in the boat along the swaying keel,
  Holds in his hands his temples filled with pain—
  'See to the nets!' the skipper's orders peal,
As he kicks him where he lies. And o'er the main
  Her jocund songs arise, rebound and wheel.

III

The song said: 'Sea-weeds! flowers o' the ample sea!
  Down in the waters green the mermaids dwell
  In gardens coralline, where mansions be,
  Built for fair maids who love their sweethearts well.'
The song said: 'Flower of may on the hawthorn tree!
  There is a grotto made of many a shell,
  Deep in the waters blue, a home of glee
  Built for fair maids who love's sweet story tell.'

And Rufus thought to himelf: 'I am a cur!
  For me there is no smile for dear love's sake,
  And never a kiss for me! I am a cur!
  Up! draw the bridle tight! I work and ache;
  My blood I sell for bread, while none demur:
  Yet—if one day the worn-out cord should break?'

IV

The murderer climbed the cliff with hurrying feet,
  With pale and anxious face, with aching head,
  Like a wild beast struck mad in the summer heat,
  Grasping the guilty knife still dripping red.

The angry sea-gulls in battalions fleet
Raised o'er the crags their clamorous shout, and fled;
And the death-cry shook far off a lugger's sheet
As he hurled himself to the wave that onward sped.

Far echoed o'er the golden sands the sound
Of human labour: mournful and unblest,
Voices of women surged along the ground;
And tossed upon the sea's sublime unrest,
On emerald deeps with zones of glory crowned,
A corpse turned to the sun its shattered breast.

DANTE ALIGHIERI

DANTE ALIGHIERI (Italian, 1265-1321). One of world's great poets, and Italy's supreme literary figure. Dabbled in politics, banished from Florence, lived in bitter exile. Love for Beatrice de' Portinari glorified in *The Divine Comedy*, philosophical-political allegory of 100 cantos, and in *La Vita Nuovo*, collection of 31 love poems. His writing important in shaping Italian into a literary language.

THE DIVINE COMEDY

"Through me ye enter the abode of woe:
    Through me to endless sorrow are ye brought:
    Through me amid the souls accurst ye go.
Justice did first my lofty Maker move;
    By power Almighty was my fabric wrought,
    By highest Wisdom, and by Primal Love.
Ere I was form'd, no things created were,
    Save those eternal—I eternal last:
    All hope abandon—ye who enter here."
These words, inscribed in colour dark, I saw
    High on the summit of a portal vast;
    Whereat I cried: "O master! with deep awe
Their sense I mark." Like one prepared, he said,
    "Here from thy soul must doubt be cast away;
    Here must each thought of cowardice be dead.—
Now, at that place I told thee of, arrived,
    The melancholy shades shalt thou survey,
    Of God—the mind's supremest good—deprived."

285

Then, as he clasp'd my hand with joyful mien,
   That comfort gave, and bade me cease to fear,
   He led me down into the world unseen.
There sobs, and wailings, and heart-rending cries,
   Resounded through the starless atmosphere,
   Whence tears began to gather in mine eyes.
Harsh tongues discordant—horrible discourse—
   Words of despair—fierce accents of despite—
   Striking of hands—with curses deep and hoarse,
Raised a loud tumult, which unceasing whirl'd
   Throughout that gloom of everlasting night,
   Like to the sand in circling eddies hurl'd.
Then (horror compassing my head around)
   I cried: "O master, what is this I hear?
   And who are these so plunged in grief profound?"
He answered me: "The groans which thou hast heard
   Proceed from those, who, when on earth they were,
   Nor praise deserved, nor infamy incurr'd.
Here with those caitiff angels they abide,
   Who stood aloof in heaven—to God untrue,
   Yet wanting courage with His foes to side.
Heaven drove them forth, its beauty not to stain:
   And Hell refuses to receive them too:—
   From them no glory could the damn'd obtain."
"O master, what infliction do they bear,"
   I said, "which makes them raise such shrieks of woe?
   He answer'd: "That I will in brief declare.
No hope of death have this unhappy crew;
   And their degraded life is sunk so low,
   With envy every other state they view.
No record hath the world of this vile class,
   Alike by Justice and by Pity spurn'd:
   Speak we no more of them—but look—and pass."
And as I look'd, a banner I beheld,
   That seemed incapable of rest, and turn'd,
   In one unvaried round for aye impell'd;
While shades were following in so long a train,
   I ne'er forsooth could have believed it true
   That Death such myriads of mankind had slain

And when I had examined many a shade,
Behold! that abject one appear'd in view,
Who, mean of soul, the grand refusal made.

Straight I perceived, and distant recognised,
In that vast concourse the assembly vile
Of those by God and by His foes despised.

These wretched ones, who never were alive,
All naked stood, for sorely stung the while
By wasps and hornets that around them drive.

The cruel swarm bedew'd their cheeks with blood
Which trickled to their feet with many a tear,
While worms disgusting drank the mingled flood.

Then, onward as I stretch'd mine eye, I saw
A mighty stream, with numbers standing near;
Whereat I said: "O master! by what law

Do these sad souls, whose state I fain would learn,
So eagerly to cross the river haste,
As by the doubtful twilight I discern?"

"These things," he answer'd me, "shall all be told
Soon as our feet upon the bank are placed
Of Acheron, that mournful river old."

Mine eyes cast down, my looks o'erwhelm'd with shame
Fearing my questions had oppress'd the sage,
I spake not till beside the stream we came.

Lo! in a vessel o'er the gloomy tide
An old man comes—his locks all white with age:—
"Woe, woe to you, ye guilty souls!" he cried;

"Hope not that heaven shall ever bless your sight;
I come to bear you to the other shore,—
To ice, and fire, in realms of endless night:

And thou—who breathest still the vital air—
Begone—nor stay with these who live no more."
But when he saw that yet I linger'd there—

"By other port," he said, "by other way,
And not by this, a passage must thou find;
Thee a far lighter vessel shall convey."

"Charon," my guide return'd, "thy wrath restrain,
Thus is it will'd where will and power are join'd;
Therefore submit, nor question us again."

287

The dark lake's pilot heard;—and at the sound
    Fell instant his rough cheeks, while flashing raged
    His angry eyes in flaming circles round.
But they—soon as these threatenings met their ear—
    Poor, naked, weary souls—their colour changed;
    And their teeth chatter'd through excess of fear.
God they blasphemed, their parents, man's whole race,
    The hour, the spot,—and e'en the very seed
    To which their miserable life they trace:
Then, while full bitterly their sorrows flow'd,
    They gather'd to that evil strand, decreed
    To all who live not in the fear of God.
Charon, the fiend, with eyes of living coal,
    Beckoning the mournful troop, collects them there,
    And with his oar strikes each reluctant soul.
As leaves in Autumn, borne before the wind,
    Drop one by one, until the branch, laid bare.
    Sees all its honours to the earth consign'd:
So cast them downward at his summons all
    The guilty race of Adam from that strand,—
    Each, as a falcon, answering to the call,
Thus pass they slowly o'er the water brown;
    And ere on the opposing bank they land,
    Fresh numbers to this shore come crowding down.
"All those, my son," exclaim'd the courteous guide,
    "Who in the wrath of the Almighty die,
    Are gather'd here from every region wide:
Goaded by Heavenly Justice in its ire,
    To pass the stream they rush thus hastily;
    So that their fear is turn'd into desire.
By virtuous soul this wave is never cross'd;
    Wherefore, if Charon warn thee to depart,
    The meaning of his words will not be lost."
This converse closed—the dusky region dread
    Trembled so awfully, that o'er my heart
    Doth terror still a chilly moisture shed.
Sent forth a blast that melancholy realm,
    Which flashing a vermilion light around,
    At once did all my senses overwhelm;
And down I sank like one in slumber bound.

ALPHONSE DAUDET

ALPHONSE DAUDET (French, 1840-1897). Associated with French natural-
ists, but essentially a romanticist. Creator of gentle satires and sentimental
stories. Gave up teaching to write, gained early fame and popularity. Best-
known stories in *Lettres de mon Moulin*. Best-known novel: *Sapho*.

THE DEATH OF THE DAUPHIN

THE little Dauphin is ill; the little Dauphin is dying. In all the
churches of the kingdom the Holy Sacrament remains exposed night
and day, and great tapers burn, for the recovery of the royal child.
The streets of the old capital are sad and silent, the bells ring no
more, the carriages slacken their pace. In the neighborhood of the
palace the curious towns-people gaze through the railings upon the
beadles with gilded paunches, who converse in the courts and put
on important airs.

All the castle is in a flutter. Chamberlains and major-domos run
up and down the marble stair-ways. The galleries are full of pages
and of courtiers in silken apparel, who hurry from one group to
another, begging in low tones for news. Upon the wide perrons the
maids of honor, in tears, exchange low courtesies and wipe their
eyes with daintily embroidered handkerchiefs.

A large assemblage of robed physicians has gathered in the Or-
angery. They can be seen through the panes waving their long black
sleeves and inclining their periwigs with professional gestures. The
governor and the equerry of the little Dauphin walk up and down
before the door awaiting the decision of the Faculty. Scullions pass
by without saluting them. The equerry swears like a pagan; the
governor quotes verses from Horace.

And meanwhile, over there, in the direction of the stables, is
heard a long and plaintive neighing; it is the little Dauphin's sorrel,
forgotten by the hostlers, and calling sadly before his empty manger.

And the King? Where is his Highness the King? The King has
locked himself up in a room at the other end of the castle. Majesties
do not like to be seen weeping. For the Queen it is different. Sitting
by the bedside of the little Dauphin, she bows her fair face, bathed
in tears, and sobs very loudly before everybody, like a mere draper's
wife.

On the bed embroidered with lace the little Dauphin, whiter than
the pillows on which he is extended, lies with closed eyes. They think

that he is asleep; but no, the little Dauphin is not asleep. He turns towards his mother, and seeing her tears, he asks:

"Madame la Reine, why do you weep? Do you really believe that I am going to die?"

The Queen tries to answer. Sobs prevent her from speaking.

"Do not weep, Madame la Reine. You forget that I am the Dauphin, and that Dauphins cannot die thus."

The Queen sobs more violently, and the little Dauphin begins to feel frightened.

"Holloa!" says he, "I do not want Death to come and take me away, and I know how to prevent him from coming here. Order up on the spot forty of the strongest lansquenets to keep guard around our bed! Have a hundred big cannons watch day and night, with lighted fuses, under our windows! And woe to Death if he dares to come near us!"

In order to humor the royal child, the Queen makes a sign. On the spot the great cannons are heard rolling in the courts, and forty tall lansquenets, with halberds in their fists, draw up around the room. They are all veterans, with grizzly mustaches. The little Dauphin claps his hands on seeing them. He recognizes one, and calls,

"Lorrain! Lorrain!"

The veteran makes a step towards the bed.

"I love you well, my old Lorrain. Let me see your big sword. If Death wants to fetch me, you will kill him, won't you?"

Lorrain answers:

"Yes, Monseigneur."

And two great tears roll down his tanned cheeks.

At that moment the chaplain approaches the little Dauphin, and pointing to the crucifix, talks to him in low tones. The little Dauphin listens with astonished air; then, suddenly interrupting him,

"I understand well what you are saying, Monsieur l'Abbé; but still, couldn't my little friend Beppo die in my place, if I gave him plenty of money?"

The chaplain continues to talk to him in low tones, and the little Dauphin looks more and more astonished.

When the chaplain has finished, the little Dauphin resumes, with a heavy sigh:

"What you have said is all very sad, Monsieur l'Abbé; but one thing consoles me, and that is that up there, in the Paradise of the stars, I shall still be the Dauphin. I know that the good God is my cousin, and cannot fail to treat me according to my rank."

Then he adds, turning towards his mother:

"Bring me my fairest clothes, my doublet of white ermine, and my pumps of velvet! I wish to look brave to the angels, and to enter Paradise in the dress of a Dauphin."

A third time the chaplain bends over the little Dauphin, and talks to him in low tones. In the midst of his discourse the royal child interrupts him angrily.

"Why, then," he cries, "to be Dauphin is nothing at all!"

And refusing to listen to anything more, the little Dauphin turns towards the wall and weeps bitterly.

DAVID

DAVID (Hebrew, ca. 1000 B.C.). The kingly harpist. King of Judea and Israel. Famous as a poet and warrior.

PSALM XXXVII

FRET not thyself because of evil doers, neither be thou envious against the workers of iniquity.

For they shall soon be cut down like the grass, and wither as the green herb.

Trust in the Lord, and do good; *so* shall thou dwell in the land, and verily thou shalt be fed.

Delight thyself also in the Lord; and he shall give thee the desires of thy heart.

Commit thy way unto the Lord; trust also in him; and he shall bring *it* to pass.

And he shall bring forth thy righteousness as the light, and thy judgement as the noon-day.

Rest in the Lord, and wait patiently for him: fret not thyself because of him who prospereth in his way, because of the man who bringeth wicked devices to pass.

Cease from anger, and forsake wrath: fret not thyself in any wise to do evil.

For evil doers shall be cut off: but those that wait upon the Lord, they shall inherit the earth.

For yet a little while, and the wicked *shall* not *be*: yea, thou shalt diligently consider his place, and it *shall* not *be*.

291

But the meek shall inherit the earth; and shall delight themselves in the abundance of peace.

The wicked plotteth against the just, and gnasheth upon him with his teeth.

The Lord shall laugh at him: for he seeth that his day is coming.

The wicked have drawn out the sword, and have bent their bow, to cast down the poor and needy, *and* to slay such as be of upright conversation.

Their sword shall enter into their own heart, and their bows shall be broken.

A little that a righteous man hath *is* better than the riches of many wicked.

For the arms of the wicked shall be broken: but the Lord upholdeth the righteous.

The Lord knoweth the days of the upright: and their inheritance shall be forever.

They shall not be ashamed in the evil time: and in the days of famine they shall be satisfied.

But the wicked shall perish, and the enemies of the Lord *shall be* as the fat of lambs: they shall consume; into smoke shall they consume away.

The wicked borroweth, and payeth not again: but the righteous showeth mercy, and giveth.

For *such as be* blessed of him shall inherit the earth; and *they that be* cursed of him shall be cut off.

The steps of a *good* man are ordered by the Lord: and he delighteth in his way.

Though he fall, he shall not be utterly cast down: for the Lord upholdeth *him with* his hand.

I have been young, and *now* am old; yet have I not seen the righteous forsaken, nor his seed begging bread.

He is ever merciful, and lendeth; and his seed *is* blessed.

Depart from evil, and do good; and dwell for evermore.

For the Lord loveth judgement, and forsaketh not his saints; they are preserved for ever: but the seed of the wicked shall be cut off.

The righteous shall inherit the land and dwell therein for ever.

The mouth of the righteous speaketh wisdom, and his tongue talketh of judgement.

The law of his God *is* in his heart; none of his steps shall slide.

The wicked watcheth the righteous, and seeketh to slay him.

The Lord will not leave him in his hand, nor condemn him when he is judged.

Wait on the Lord, and keep his way, and he shall exalt thee to inherit the land: when the wicked are cut off, thou shalt see *it*.

I have seen the wicked in great power, and spreading himself like a green bay-tree.

Yet he passed away, and lo, he *was* not: yea, I sought him, but he could not be found.

Mark the perfect *man*, and behold the upright: for the end of *that* man *is* peace.

But the transgressors shall be destroyed together: the end of the wicked shall be cut off.

But the salvation of the righteous *is* of the Lord: *he is* their strength in the time of trouble.

And the Lord shall help them, and deliver them: he shall deliver them from the wicked, and save them, because they trust in him.

DANIEL DEFOE

DANIEL DEFOE (English, *ca.* 1660-1731). Most celebrated for *The Surprising Adventures of Robinson Crusoe*, now a children's classic, but primarily a journalist and politician. Served two years in jail for political dissent. Forerunners of the early novel and modern realism: *Moll Flanders, Journal of the Plague Year, Roxana.*

IN DEFENCE OF HIS RIGHT

A GENTLEMAN of a very good estate married a lady of also a good fortune, and had one son by her, and one daughter, and no more, and after a few years his lady died. He soon married a second venter; and his second wife, though of an inferior quality and fortune to the former, took upon her to discourage and discountenance his children by his first lady, and made the family very uncomfortable, both to the children and to their father also.

The first thing of consequence which this conduct of the mother-in-law produced in the family, was that the son, who began to be a man, asked the father's leave to go abroad to travel. The mother-in-law, though willing enough to be rid of the young man, yet

because it would require something considerable to support his expenses abroad, violently opposed it, and brought his father also to refuse him after he had freely given him his consent.

This so affected the young gentleman, that after using all the dutiful applications to his father that he could possibly do, as well by himself as by some other relations, but to no purpose; and being a little encouraged by an uncle, who was brother to his mother, his father's first lady, he resolved to go abroad without leave, and accordingly did so.

What part of the world he travelled into I do not remember; it seems his father had constantly intelligence from him for some time, and was prevailed with to make him a reasonable allowance for his subsistence, which the young gentleman always drew bills for, and they were honourably paid; but after some time, the mother-in-law prevailing at home, one of his bills of exchange was refused, and being protested, was sent back without acceptance; upon which he drew no more, nor did he write any more letters, or his father hear anything from him for upwards of four years, or thereabout.

Upon this long silence, the mother-in-law made her advantage several ways; she first intimated to his father that he must needs be dead; and consequently, his estate should be settled upon her eldest son (for she had several children). His father withstood the motion very firmly, but the wife harassed him with her importunities; and she argued upon two points against him, I mean the son.

First, if he was dead, then there was no room to object, her son being heir at law.

Secondly, if he was not dead, his behaviour to his father in not writing for so long a time was inexcusable, and he ought to resent it, and settle the estate as if he were dead; that nothing could be more disobliging, and his father ought to depend upon it that he was dead, and treat him as if he was so; for he that would use a father so, should be taken for one dead, as to his filial relation, and be treated accordingly.

His father, however, stood out a long time, and told her that he could not answer it to his conscience; that there might happen many things in the world, which might render his son unable to write; that he might be taken by the Turks, and carried into slavery; or he might be among the Persians or Arabians (which it seems was the case), and so could not get any letters conveyed; and that he could not be satisfied to disinherit him, till he knew whether he had reason for it or no, or whether his son had offended him or no.

These answers, however just, were far from stopping her importunities, which she carried on so far, that she gave him no rest, and it made an unquiet family; she carried it very ill to him, and in a word, made her children do so too; and the gentleman was so wearied out with it, that once or twice he came to a kind of consent to do it, but his heart failed him, and then he fell back again and refused.

However, her having brought him so near it, was an encouragement to her to go on with her restless solicitations, till at last he came thus far to a provisional agreement, that if he did not hear from his son by such a time, or before it, he would consent to a re-settling the estate.

She was not well satisfied with the conditional agreement, but being able to obtain no other, she was obliged to accept of it as it was; though, as she often told him, she was far from being satisfied with it as to the time, for he had fixed it for four years, as above.

He grew angry at her telling him so, and answered, that she ought to be very well satisfied with it, for that it was time little enough, as his son's circumstances might be.

Well, she teased him however so continually, that at last she brought him down to one year: but before she brought him to that, she told him one day in heat, that she hoped his ghost would one time or other appear to him, and tell him that he was dead, and that he ought to do justice to his other children, for he should never come to claim the estate.

When he came, so much against his will, to consent to shorten the time to one year, he told her that he hoped his son's ghost, though he was not dead, would come to her, and tell her he was alive, before the time expired. "For why," says he, "may not injured souls walk while embodied, as well as afterwards?"

It happened one evening after this, that they had a most violent family quarrel upon this subject, when on a sudden a hand appeared at a casement, endeavouring to open it; but as all the iron casements used in former times opened outward, but hasped and fastened themselves in the inside, so the hand seemed to try to open the casement, but could not. The gentleman did not see it, but his wife did, and she presently started up, as if she was frightened, and, forgetting the quarrel they had upon their hands: "Lord bless me!" says she, "there are thieves in the garden." Her husband ran immediately to the door of the room they sat in, and opening it, looked out.

295

"There's nobody in the garden," says he; so he clapped the door to again, and came back.

"I am sure," says she, "I saw a man there."

"It must be the devil then," says he, "for I'm sure there's nobody in the garden."

"I'll swear," says she, "I saw a man put his hand up to open the casement; but finding it fast, and I suppose," adds she, "seeing us in the room, he walked off."

"It is impossible he could be gone," says he; "did not I run to the door immediately? and you know the garden walls on both sides hinder him going."

"Pry'thee," says she angrily, "I an't drunk nor in a dream, I know a man when I see him, and 'tis not dark, the sun is not quite down."

"You're only frighted with shadows," says he (very full of ill-nature): "folks generally are so that are haunted with an evil conscience: it may be 'twas the devil."

"No, no, I'm not soon frightened," says she; "if 'twas the devil, 'twas the ghost of your son: it may be come to tell you he was gone to the devil, and you might give your estate to your eldest bastard. since you won't settle it on the lawful heir."

"If it was my son," says he, "he's come to tell us he's alive, I warrant you, and to ask how you can be so much a devil to desire me to disinherit him;" and with these words: "Alexander," says he aloud, repeating it twice, starting up out of his chair, "if you are alive, show yourself, and don't let me be insulted thus every day with your being dead."

At those very words, the casement which the hand had been seen at by the mother, opened of itself, and his son Alexander looked in with a full face and staring directly upon the mother with an angry countenance, cried "Here," and then vanished in a moment.

The woman that was so stout before, shrieked out in a most dismal manner, so that the whole house was alarmed; her maid ran into the parlour, to see what was the matter, but her mistress was fainted away in her chair.

She was not fallen upon the ground, because it being a great easy chair, she sunk a little back against the side of the chair, and help coming immediately in, they kept her up; but it was not till a great while after, that she recovered enough to be sensible of anything.

Her husband ran immediately to the parlour door, and opening

296

it, went into the garden, but there was nothing; and after that he ran to another door that opened from the house into the garden, and then to two other doors which opened out of his garden, one into the stable-yard, and another into the field beyond the garden, but found them all fast shut and barred; but on one side was his gardener, and a boy, drawing the rolling-stone: he asked them if anybody else had been in the garden, but they both constantly affirmed nobody had been there; and they were both rolling a gravel-walk near the house.

Upon this he comes back into the room, sits him down again, and said not one word for a good while; the woman and servants being busy all the while, and in a hurry, endeavouring to recover his wife.

After some time she recovered so far as to speak, and the first words she said, were:

"L—d bless me! what was it?"

"Nay," says her husband, "it was Alexander, to be sure."

With that she fell into a fit, and screamed and shrieked out again most terribly.

Her husband not thinking that would have affected her, did what he could to persuade her out of it again; but that would not do, and they were obliged to carry her to bed, and get some help to her; but she continued ill for several days after.

However, this put an end for some considerable time to her solicitations about his disinheriting her son-in-law.

But time, that hardens the mind in cases of a worse nature, wore this off also by degrees, and she began to revive the old cause again, though not at first so eagerly as before.

Nay, he used her a little hardly upon it too, and if ever they had any words about it he would bid her hold her tongue, or that if she talked any more upon that subject, he would call Alexander again to open the casement.

This aggravated things much; and though it terrified her a great while, yet at length she was so exasperated, that she told him she believed he dealt with the devil, and that he had sold himself to the devil only to be able to fright his wife.

He jested with her, and told her any man would be beholden to the devil to hush a noisy woman, and that he was very glad he had found the way to do it, whatever it cost him.

She was so exasperated at this, that she threatened him if he played any more of his hellish arts with her she would have him

indicted for a wizard, and having a familiar; and she could prove it, she said, plain enough, for that he had raised the devil on purpose to fright his wife.

The fray parted that night with ill words and ill nature enough, but he little thought she intended as she said, and the next day he had forgot it all, and was as good-humoured as if nothing had happened.

But he found his wife chagrined and disturbed very much, full of resentment, and threatening him with what she resolved to do.

However, he little thought she intended him the mischief she had in her head, offering to talk friendly to her; but she rejected it with scorn, and told him she would be as good as her word, for she would not live with a man that should bring the devil into the room as often as he thought fit, to murder his wife.

He strove to pacify her by fair words, but she told him she was in earnest with him: and, in a word, she was in earnest; for she goes away to a justce, and making an affidavit that her husband had a familiar spirit, and that she went in danger of her life, she obtained a warrant for him to be apprehended.

In short, she brought home the warrant, showed it to him, and told him she had not given it into the hands of an officer, because he should have the liberty to go voluntarily before the justice of the peace, and if he thought fit to let her know when he would be ready, she would be so too, and would get some of her own friends to go along with her.

He was surprised at this, for he little thought she had been in earnest with him, and endeavoured to pacify her by all the ways possible; but she found she had frightened him heartily, and so indeed she had, for though the thing had nothing in it of guilt, yet he found it might expose him very much, and being loath to have such a thing brought upon the stage against him, he used all the entreaties with her that he was able, and begged her not to do it.

But the more he humbled himself the more she triumphed over him; and carrying things to an unsufferable height of insolence, she told him at last, she would make him do justice, as she called it; that she was sure she could have him punished if he continued obstinate, and she would not be exposed to witchcraft and sorcery; for she did not know to what length he might carry it.

To bring the story to a conclusion; she got the better of him to such a degree, that he offered to refer the thing to indifferent persons, friends on both sides; and they met several times, but could

bring it to no conclusion. His friends said there was nothing in it, and they would not have him comply with anything upon the pretence of it; that he called for his son, and somebody opened the casement and cried, "Here"; that there was not the least evidence of witchcraft in that, and insisted that she could make nothing of it.

Her friends carried it high, instructed by her: she offered to swear that he had threatened her before with his son's ghost; that now he visibly raised a spectre; for that calling upon his son, who was dead to be sure, the ghost immediately appeared; that he could not have called up the devil thus to personate his son, if he had not dealt with the devil himself, and had a familiar spirit, and that this was of dangerous consequence to her.

Upon the whole, the man wanted courage to stand it, and was afraid of being exposed; so that he was grievously perplexed, and knew not what to do.

When she found him humbled as much as she could desire, she told him, if he would do her justice, as she called it (that is to say, settle his estate upon her son), she would put it up, on condition that he should promise to fright her no more with raising the devil.

That part of her proposal exasperated him again, and he upbraided her with the slander of it, and told her he defied her, and she might do her worst.

Thus it broke off all treaty, and she began to threaten him again; however, at length she brought him to comply, and he gives a writing under his hand to her, some of her friends being by, promising that he would comply if his son did not arrive, or send an account of himself, within four months.

She was satisfied with this, and they were all made friends again, and accordingly he gave the writing; but when he delivered it to her in presence of her two arbitrators, he took the liberty to say to her, with a grave and solemn kind of speech:

"Look you," says he, "you have worried me into this agreement by your fiery temper, and I have signed it against justice, conscience, and reason; but depend upon it, I shall never perform it."

One of the arbitrators said, "Why, sir, this is doing nothing; for if you resolve not to perform it, what signifies the writing? why do you promise what you do not intend shall be done? This will but kindle a new flame to begin with, when the time fixed expires."

"Why," says he, "I am satisfied in my mind that my son is alive."

"Come, come," says his wife, speaking to the gentleman that had argued with her husband, "let him sign the agreement, and let me alone to make him perform the conditions."

"Well," says her husband, "you shall have the writing, and you shall be let alone; but I am satisfied you will never ask me to perform it; and yet I am no wizard," adds he, "as you have wickedly suggested."

She replied, that she would prove that he dealt with the devil, for that he raised an evil spirit by only calling his son by name; and so began to tell the story of the hand and the casement.

"Come," says the man to the gentleman that was her friend, "give me the pen; I never dealt with but one devil in my life, and there it sits," turning to his wife; "and now I have made an agreement with her that none but the devil would desire any man to sign, and I will sign it; I say, give me the pen, but she nor all the devils in hell will ever be able to get it executed; remember I say so."

She began to open at him, and so a new flame would have been kindled, but the gentlemen moderated between them, and her husband setting his hand to the writing put an end to the fray at that time.

At the end of four months she challenged the performance, and a day was appointed, and her two friends that had been the arbitrators were invited to dinner upon this occasion, believing that her husband would have executed the deeds; and accordingly the writings were brought all forth, engrossed, and read over; and some old writings, which at her marriage were signed by her trustees, in order to her quitting some part of the estate to her son, were also brought to be cancelled: the husband being brought over, by fair means or foul, I know not whether, to be in a humour, for peace' sake, to execute the deeds, and disinherit his son; alleging that, indeed, if he was dead it was no wrong to him, and if he was alive, he was very unkind and undutiful to his father, in not letting him hear from him in all that time.

Besides, it was urged that if he should at any time afterwards appear to be alive, his father (who had very much increased, it seems, in his wealth) was able to give him another fortune, and to make him a just satisfaction for the loss he should sustain by the paternal estate.

Upon these considerations, I say, they had brought over the poor

low-spirited husband to be almost willing to comply; or, at least, willing or unwilling, it was done, and, as above, they met accordingly.

When they had discoursed upon all the particulars, and, as above, the new deeds were read over, she or her husband took the old writings up to cancel them; I think the story says it was the wife, not her husband, that was just going to tear off the seal, when on a sudden they heard a rushing noise in the parlour where they sat, as if somebody had come in at the door of the room which opened from the hall, and went through the room towards the garden door, which was shut.

They were all surprised at it, for it was very distinct, but they saw nothing. The woman turned pale, and was in a terrible fright; however, as nothing was seen, she recovered a little, but began to ruffle her husband again.

"What," says she, "have you laid your plot to bring up more devils again?"

The man sat composed, though he was under no little surprise too.

One of her gentlemen said to him, "What is the meaning of all this?"

"I protest, sir," says he, "I know no more of it than you do."

"What can it be then?" said the other gentleman.

"I cannot conceive," says he, "for I am utterly unacquainted with such things."

"Have you heard nothing from your son?" says the gentleman.

"Not one word," says the father; "no, not the least word these five years."

"Have you wrote nothing to him," says the gentleman, "about this transaction?"

"Not a word," says he; "for I know not where to direct a letter to him."

"Sir," says the gentleman, "I have heard much of apparitions, but I never saw them in my life, nor did I ever believe there was anything of reality in them; and, indeed, I saw nothing now; but the passing of some body, or spirit, or something, across the room just now is plain; I heard it distinctly. I believe there is some unseen thing in the room, as much as if I saw it."

"Nay," says the other arbitrator, "I felt the wind of it as it

301

passed by me. Pray," adds he, turning to the husband, "do you see nothing yourself?"

"No, upon my word," says he, "not the least appearance in the world."

"I have been told," says the first arbitrator, "and have read, that an apparition may be seen by some people and be invisible to others, though all in the same room together."

However, the husband solemnly protested to them all that he saw nothing.

"Pray, sir," says the first arbitrator, "have you seen anything at any other time, or heard any voices or noises, or had any dreams about this matter?"

"Indeed," says he, "I have several times dreamed my son is alive, and that I had spoken with him; and once that I asked him why he was so undutiful, and slighted me so, as not to let me hear of him in so many years, seeing he knew it was in my power to disinherit him."

"Well, sir, and what answer did he give?"

"I never dreamed so far on as to have him answer; it always waked me."

"And what do you think of it yourself," says the arbitrator; "do you think he's dead?"

"No, indeed," says the father, "I do believe in my conscience he's alive, as much as I believe I am alive myself; and I am going to do as wicked a thing of its kind as ever any man did."

"Truly," says the second arbitrator, "it begins to shock me, I don't know what to say to it; I don't care to meddle any more with it, I don't like driving men to act against their consciences."

With this the wife, who, as I said, having a little recovered her spirits, and especially encouraged because she saw nothing, started up: "What's all this discourse to the purpose," says she; "is it not all agreed already? what do we come here for?"

"Nay," says the first arbitrator, "I think we meet now not to inquire into why it is done, but to execute things according to agreement, and what are we frighted at?"

"I'm not frighted," says the wife, "not I; come," says she to her husband, haughtily, "sign the deed; I'll cancel the old writings if forty devils were in the room;" and with that she takes up one of the deeds, and went to tear off the seal.

That moment the same casement flew open again, though it was

302

fast in the inside, just as it was before; and the shadow of a body was seen, as standing in the garden without, and the head reaching up to the casement, the face looking into the room, and staring directly at the woman with a stern and an angry countenance: "Hold," said the spectre, as if speaking to the woman, and immediately clapped the casement to again, and vanished.

It is impossible to describe here the consternation this second apparition put the whole company into; the wife, who was so bold just before, that she would do it though forty devils were in the room, screamed out like a woman in fits, and let the writing fall out of her hands: the two arbitrators were exceedingly terrified, but not so much as the rest; but one of them took up the award which they had signed, in which they awarded the husband to execute the deed to dispose of the estate from the son.

. "I dare say," said he, "be the spirit a good spirit or a bad, it will not be against cancelling this;" so he tore his name out of the award, and so did the other, by his example, and both of them got up from their seats, and said they would have no more to do in it.

But that which was most unexpected of all was that the man himself was so frighted, that he fainted away; notwithstanding it was, as it might be said, in his favour.

This put an end to the whole affair at that time; and, as I understand by the sequel, it did so for ever.

The story has many particulars more in it, too long to trouble you with: but two particulars, which are to the purpose, I must not omit, viz.:

1. That in about four or five months more after this second apparition, the man's son arrived from the East Indies, whither he had gone four years before in a Portuguese ship from Lisbon.

2. That upon being particularly inquired of about these things, and especially whether he had any knowledge of them, or any apparition to him, or voices, or other intimation as to what was doing in England, relating to him; he affirmed constantly that he had not, except that once he dreamed his father had written him an angry letter, threatening him that if he did not come home he would disinherit him and leave him not one shilling. But he added, that he never did receive any such letter from his father in his life, or from any one else.

303

RICHARD DEHMEL

RICHARD DEHMEL (German, 1863-1920). Ardent anti-traditionalist, who went to extremes opposing prejudice and convention. A virtuoso in poetry (*Zwei Menschen*), theater (*Die Menschenfreunde*), and the essay (*Gott und die Welt*).

THE SILENT TOWN

A town lies in the valley,
A pale day fades and dies;
And it will not be long before
Neither moon nor starlight,
Night only fills the skies.

From all the mountain ridges
Creeps mist, and swathes the town;
No farm, no house, no wet red roof
Can pierce the thickly woven woof,
And scarce even spires and bridges.

But as the wanderer shudders,
Deep down a streak of light rejoices
His heart; and, through the smoke and haze,
Children's voices
Begin a gentle hymn of praise.

HELPLESSNESS

But when thou hadst departed,
I grew so lonely-hearted,
    I longed for thee so sore.
I stood with fingers aching,
As though I should lose thee shaking
    The handle of thy barred and bolted door.

And through the panes between us
I begged with eyes as keen as
    A beggar's in the South;
But up the steps thou wentest,
No backward look thou bentest,
    Thou didst not call me back unto thy mouth.

304

With senses stunned I hearkened,
Heard but in the passage darkened
  The rattling of thy keys;
And then the shadows caught me,
That in the park had sought me,
  When we two saw the moon sink o'er the trees.

ANGRY SEA

Thus once again! Through fog and howling squall:
  The sails shook, and the sailors shouted loudly;
At the bowsprit stood the water like a tall
  Tower: I felt your fear in my knees: and proudly
Your unknown face beside me gloomed.

Yet once again your eye upon me frowned,
  Your hair was like a flame behind you sweeping,
While wrestled in the waves a sound
  As of a little child that will be weeping—
You warded me no more.

You let my arms around your shoulder lie,
  Your wild wet hair my greedy mouth was lashing,
Our kiss was wonderfully sweetened by
  The foam of great salt waves about us crashing—
Then I in joy cried out.

Thus once again! What shadow chills thy brow?
  Or does the open ocean make thee craven?
The sea will whip thee warm! Come soon, come now!
  The ferry is dancing in the foggy haven—
Out! To the heights!

FROM A SAD BREAST

The roses still are like a flame,
  The dark leaves gently shake;
  I in the grass am grown awake,
O that you came,
  For the deep midnight's sake.

305

The moon is hid by the garden door,
 O'er which its light is shed
On the lake with willow-shadowed shore,
 In the moist clover I bury my head;
I never loved you so before!

As now I know I have not known,
 For all that ever I caressed
Your neck, and blind your secretest
Being enjoyed, why you would groan,
 When I o'erflowed, from your sad breast.

Had you but seen yon glowworms glide,
 Two glowworms and their light the same!
Never again will I leave your side!
 O that you came!
 The roses still are like a flame.

KNOW'ST THOU YET?

Know'st thou yet, how pale, how white,
When I lay in eves of Maytime,
After kisses of the daytime,
Poured out at thy feet before thee,
Daffodillies trembled o'er me?

Then in deep June's azure night,
Know'st thou yet, how soft and seething,
When we, tired of wild caresses,
Wove around us thy wild tresses,
Daffodillies scents were breathing?

At thy feet again are gleaming,
When the silvery gloamings shimmer,
When the nights of azure glimmer,
Daffodillies scents are streaming.
Know'st thou yet, how hot? how white?

A GRAVE

These are the evenings prematurely pale.
 The dahlias that in the sunlight shone
Like last frail roses, now are standing stale,
 Rosettes of stone whose colour has grown wan.
The swaths of mist across the churchyard trail.

Come, sister. Yonder hedge of brass you see
  Rails round a lady withered in her spring.
  She loved me well. Come home, I am shivering.
Life gave her nothing but her own heart: she
Did good in silence, suffering silently.

THE LABORER

We have a bed, and a baby too,
My wife!
We have work besides, we have work for two,
And we have the sun, and the wind, and the rain,
And we only need one little thing more,
To be as free as the birds that soar:
Only time.

When we go through the fields on the Sunday morn,
My child,
And far and away o'er the bending corn,
We see the swarming swallows flash,
Then we only need a bit of a dress,
To have the birds' bright loveliness:
Only time.

The storm is gathering black as jet,
Feel the poor.
Only a little eternity yet;
We need nothing else, my wife, my child,
Except all things through us that thrive,
To be bold as the birds through the air that drive:
Only time!

HARVEST SONG

There stands a field of golden sheaves,
To the very edge of the world it heaves.
    Grind, mill, grind!

The wind falls in the wide land,
Many mills at the sky-edge stand.
    Grind, mill, grind!

307

There comes a sunset dark and red,
Many poor people are crying for bread.
> Grind, mill, grind!

The night holds in its lap the storm,
To-morrow the men to work will swarm.
> Grind, mill, grind!

Clean are the fields swept, never again
A man shall cry in hunger-pain.
> Grind, mill, grind!

THREATENING PROSPECT

The sky is whirling, the land flies fast;
> And while, by the express shocked and shaken,
Furrow on furrow whizzes past,
> Thee thy shivering limbs awaken:
>> The sun of morning comes.

Through the hung mist with toiling wings
> Break herded crows that autumn is thinning,
While thick upon the dunged field clings
> The smoke of workshops just beginning;
>> The sun of morning comes.

Under the trailing gray crape lies
> A chain of slag-heaps filling acres,
Chimney on chimney scales the skies,
> Standing by coffins fearsome wakers;
>> The sun of morning comes.

Along the rapid landscape rolls
> A pair of road-dikes from the horizon,
Framed in by gnarled and weathered boles
> Of apple-trees a pale sheen lies on;
>> The sun of morning comes.

Now sweeps thy gaze the opposite verge,
> Where boughs, of fruit despoiled, are showing,
And suddenly tree on tree they surge,
> With crumpled leafage fire-red glowing:
>> The day is there.

GRAZIA DELEDDA

GRAZIA DELEDDA (Italian, 1875-1936). Considered by many Italy's greatest
woman novelist. Nobel Prize winner, 1926. Regionalist of the island of
Sardinia. A woman of great sympathy and understanding for the psychology
of the little people. Has been compared with Thomas Hardy. Novels: *Elias
Portolu, Cenere, Nostalgie.*

THE OPEN DOOR

ON holy Wednesday Simon Barca went to confession. He was
desperate, and a desperate man is glad to remember God, as an
ill man the doctor.

So Simon went to the Basilica, a national monument which still
lends a richness to the once prosperous countryside, and where at
that hour of the morning, only a few monks from the nearby
monastery were celebrating Mass, in chapels where the damp had
spread a green film over the ancient frescoes. The peasant women,
with hoods over their heads and coarse skirts swathed tightly round
them and laced up with thin silver chains, were singing the Rosary
in their Latin dialect: their voices faded away in the airy depths
of the Basilica as amongst the ruins of a temple; through the wide
open doors a wild fragrance of spurge and budding alder trees
wafted in from the valley. Simon went to confess himself to the
prior, who filled the little confessional with his huge body, snoring
and puffing away in there like a bear in a cage.

"Father, I'm a lost man: I want to kill some fellow Christian, I
feel so desperate. I have committed the worst sins. Until a little
time ago I was the dutiful son of a family, the only son, Father.
At twenty I still slept with my mother; but she was hardly dead
when bad companions gathered round me like flies round a raisin
pip; and my uncle, priest though he is, turned me out of the house
instead of helping me, and now when he sees me he looks the
other way. Yes, I have committed the very worst sins: I have gam-
bled, drunk, gone with bad women, consulted witches, blasphemed,
wished my neighbour ill, coveted others' belongings, committed
. . . yes, Father . . . I forged a signature, and the bill of exchange
falls due in a few days . . . and I shall have to go to prison and I
shall be dishonoured. . . . It is all the fault of bad companions, and
they have deserted me now: and every door is closed against me
. . there is not one open door, now, for me! But I'm repentant,

309

Father, and will go to prison and atone, but give me the good Lord's absolution, so that I may fulfil the Easter duties and suffer innocent like Christ our Saviour."

The prior wheezed on and made no answer. Simon, his thin, dark rogue's face in his hands, breathed hard too, and thought:

"Perhaps he's scandalised: perhaps he is pleased to hear that the real cause of my ruin is my uncle Barca the priest. Monks and priests can't bear the sight of each other. Perhaps, to spite my uncle, he'll give me the money to pay the bill."

But the prior snored and said nothing: his warm breath blew on Simon's face. Tired of waiting, the penitent roused himself from his dream of expiation and his malicious thoughts; his big eyes, dark and childish, contracted, and a bitter smile deepened the hallows in his shaven cheeks. The prior was asleep. Ah, even God is deaf to the cries of a despairing sinner.

* * *

Simon stole away very quietly, his heart sad, his mind a ferment of ugly thoughts. The proceedings of the day were starting round the great altar, and the priest Barca's mobile voice could already be heard chanting with trills and shakes. People were coming and going: now men were arriving too; they were tall, with long square beards as in Moses' time, dressed in leather jackets and short serge trousers, full like skirts. Some seemed like prophets, they were so solemn, calm and unaffected; others were small, lean as our Simon, hardened by the wind and by evil thoughts.

The women, too, recalled those in the Bible. Simon met one in the court of the Basilica, a tall dry widow, with an olive face and huge greenish eyes, swathed in her almost priestly clothes as in a black sheath, and she only wanted a bunch of ears of corn to be a second mother-in-law of Boaz. Simon shuddered when he saw her; he shuddered with hatred, for the woman was a kind of housekeeper for Barca, and he shuddered at the sudden thought that at that moment there was no one in his uncle's house: and as if night had suddenly fallen, he began to see things and people in a mist, and he stalked along by the walls, stumbling against the stones which lay about the rough roads. So he found himself before his house, like a surviving bit of a tower, and only then the light seemed to flood back all around him.

He went in, and soon after, at the little window of the first and only storey, his face appeared, pensive as that of a general forming

310

a plan of battle from the height of a fortress. Simon's field of battle was the limited picture spread beneath him: it consisted of the country road crossed by a stream, where rushes and grass grew as in open country; the widow's little house opposite his; the big, dark house of his uncle the priest, and its yard, beside the widow's, shut in by a little chapel with a kitchen garden so overgrown with weeds and shaded by cypress trees that it seemed the corner of a cemetery. Simon thought how he had spent his childhood and his youth jumping the wall between his uncle's yard and the chapel's garden; he wondered if the time had come for repeating the feat, only the other way about, from the church garden into his uncle's yard. No one else was so familiar with the hidden corners, the passages, the twistings and turnings.

He shut his eyes, and saw the jutting out piece of the ground floor wall where the priest Barca used to put the big key of his room before going out; he opened them again, and, agitated, remembered that vast, rather mysterious room, lighted by a tiny lamp, filled with sacred images and bound books. Here, as a child, he had more than once surprised his uncle, in shirt and skull-cap, counting over gold pieces like a wizard, or skilfully piercing his name on bank-notes with a pin. One day, crawling on the floor, crouching down to imitate a wild-boar, Simon had moved one of the floor blocks, and under it had found a box full of money. Now he recalled those times as a prisoner remembers his days of freedom . . . . .

For three days he remained almost continually at the window, only leaving it to eat a mouthful of rye bread and some goat's cheese. Yes, while his uncle stored his money under the floor-blocks, he had to live like a poor shepherd; his house was empty, deserted, without furniture (he had sold it), even without doors (sold as well), and the spiders spun their webs over the rough boar's skin trunk in which he kept his poor mother's wedding dress and widow's weeds.

To console himself he would drink a small glass of brandy and go back to the window.

From below he smelt the fragrance of the cakes the women were getting ready for Easter, and he saw the smoke rise from wood or tiled roofs. Already a nightingale was singing in the valley, and the fluffy April clouds floated by over the chapel garden, white as bits of girls' clothing blown off some hedge by the wind.

On Holy Thursday the widow left his uncle's house and opened

the chapel, usually closed. Helped by the other women of the neighbourhood she pulled down the Christ, laid it on the ground between four lights and four dishes of sprouting corn, and so formed the Sepulchre. But everyone was going to the Basilica, where they were celebrating the Passion and two real thieves (at least they had once been condemned for theft) were tied to the cross beside Christ. From his window Simon saw his uncle himself, short, fat, prancing, and the tall widow, dry and stiff, walk one after the other towards the Basilica. He went down, but once in the street he leant his shoulder against the wall and stood for a long time motionless and pensive, listening to the far-off chanting of the procession. It was dusk; the new moon was sinking behind the violet tinted hills, in a greenish sky, and the evening star was rising, and seemed as if it would come along the streets of the village like Mary and Christ.

"In a few moments the procession will be here," thought Simon, and moved; but he walked close by the wall; he was afraid of going past the dead Christ stretched on the floor between the lights and the corn shoots.

Suddenly, coming to his uncle's door, he shivered. The door was open; someone must be in the house and it was useless to go on. He turned back and once more leant against the wall. But who could be in his uncle's house? The servants, peasants and shepherds, only came back on Saturday evening; the priest and the widow were in the procession. He went forward again to the door, knocked, called: "Basila! Basila!"

His voice lost itself inside the already dark house as in a cave. He went in, closed the door, flung himself up the stairs, traversed the narrow passages, found the jutting-out wall, found the key, opened, and was in his uncle's room. He seemed to be in a dream. The window was shut; a light like those round the dead Christ was burning before the picture of the Holy Martyrs. There was a crowd of them, men, women, old people, children, but all looking up with gentle faces, and Simon was not afraid of them. By the greenish glow of the light he bent and began to feel the floor blocks one by one, like a bricklayer with the job of mending the floor; but not one of the bricks moved, and he stood up and passed his hand across his forehead, wet with cold sweat.

The chanting of the procession reached his ears, and he shivered all over. He leant against his uncle's old bed, and the bed moved aside, creaking and shaking as if seized by the robber's own terror and perturbation. Then Simon looked at the block under the foot

312

of the bed, and it seemed to him that it moved: he bent and pulled it up with his nails, and in the space beneath, buried in the dust, he found an iron box with two thousand lire notes in it.

* * *

On Easter Day Barca the priest discharged the widow Basila, and immediately scandalous tales spread over the whole country. It was common knowledge that Barca had lost many thousand lire, some said two, some three, some twenty; and that Basila had forgotten and left his house door open on Good Friday. The police officer went to the priest's house; but the priest tried to appear unconcerned, clapped his hands and said:

"Trifles! miserable trifles!"

On Tuesday the widow's little house was searched with care, and she was arrested and set free again the next day. There was no evidence against her; but the inhabitants or rather the families in the district split into two parties; the men defended Basila saying that perhaps she had really forgotten the open door, so making it easy for any thief to go in; the women sneered: "And in a few short minutes the robber made himself at home and helped himself?"

Finally people stopped this talk; but the widow was looked down on by everyone. She was given no more work; she stopped going to church and lived in poverty in her wretched house. Simon used to see her, always upright on the threshold, her face pale and sad, but her great greenish eyes turned upwards like those of the Holy Martyrs.

* * *

Simon paid the false bill of exchange and bought back his doors and his cloak. No one was surprised, for like every gambler, he often had these ups and downs of fortune, and only his creditor knew about the bill. What astonished everyone was to see him suddenly change his way of living. He stopped going with bad women and gave up his disreputable companions, he went to church and nodded to his uncle. But his uncle persisted in turning away when he saw him, and one day when Simon went up to him determined to stop him and kiss his hand, he not only ignored his greeting but literally turned his back on him.

Simon stood petrified. He leant against the wall and remained fixed there, overcome by a terrible thought.

"He knows!"

313

Then he went to the widow Basila and said to her:

"Do you think you could bake, and wash, and mend my clothes for me? Fix your own wage."

The widow was standing up before a dead fire combing her hair; it was thick and very long, of a golden chestnut colour, and made a halo of martyrdom round her olive face; but when she saw Simon she covered her cheeks and breast with it like a veil, and shook her head in a threatening way, whilst her greenish eyes flashed beneath her knitted eyebrows, thick and black.

"You have someone already to bake and wash for you! Get out of here!"

He went like a whipped dog and leant against his wall again.

"She knows!"

He spent the days in this way, leaning against the wall, often whittling with a little knife at his walnut stick, or some plug of straw, but more often doing nothing at all. Never before, even at his worst times, had he lived so aimlessly. He was haunted by the widow's threatening eyes, and felt an almost physical ill when he thought that Basila had fallen into poverty and ill-repute through his fault; some nights he had fearsome dreams; the trunk with his mother's clothes in it seemed a live boar, and fixed staring eyes on the doors bought back with that money.

The summer passed, and in the autumn he moved his seat along the wall, seeking the sun. From the new place he saw the widow Basila more clearly, seated too in the sun spinning or sewing, barefooted, and sad as a slave.

The winter was long and severe. The poor people suffered much from hunger, and Barca and a lady who lived in the neighbourhood sent bread and vegetables to all the needy except the widow. For Christmas a lady with whom Simon had often wandered about, sent him a present of a ram's leg. He already had a little pig and a lamb: and thinking that Basila had nothing but potatoes, sent her the ram's leg, and to his astonishment found that she did not refuse the gift. Then all the rest of the winter, seized by a mania for expiation, he went on sending her gifts, often depriving himself of some real necessity.

Spring came again: once more the women put bowls of corn to sprout in cupboards, to adorn the sepulchres. Holy Friday evening Simon went to the procession and afterwards stood for some time in the usual spot, beside the wall, in the warm, whisper-filled evening. A yellowish glow was coming from the crack of Basila's door,

314

and Simon stared with queer eyes at that light which seemed mysterious to him. Suddenly he went and knocked and asked the woman if she would marry him.

*   *   *

People talked, then stopped talking, After all, Basila was only ten years older than Simon, and a good housewife: indeed, before long the young man's house was transformed, clean, with the stove always alight and the little yard swarming with fowls. Simon was seen on a horse again, as in the time when his mother was alive; they all said that he had married Basila to spite his uncle.

He was not in love with his wife, but he followed her advice and was glad at having lifted a weight off his conscience, and married a wise woman. The latter went to church again and talked in a brief manner, and it seemed to Simon that he had gone back to the happy times with his mother when he, still innocent at twenty, went to bed with her and repeated the prayers she suggested to him.

One day, several months after his marriage, the woman who had sent him the ram's leg called him as he was passing by her door, and asked him to lend her a hundred crowns.

He began to laugh: "If I had a hundred crowns I should set out to go round the world."

"I'll pay you the interest, Simon Barca! I can pay; I'll give you twenty per cent, like the others."

"You are going mad, Mallena Porceu!"

"What, mad? Tell me you don't trust me, Simon Barca, but don't insult me. You and your wife have lent money for interest, at twenty per cent., to certain people. Why can't you give me some too? Or is it true what your uncle Barca says? That your wife gives the money without you knowing?"

Simon grew pale, but answered:

"My uncle's in his second childhood, and you're what you are!"

The following days he was seen again leaning against the wall, as in his dark times. He was asking himself ceaselessly: "Why was the door open?" and his brain was toiling and toiling, digging down deep into a black chasm, seeking the truth as the miner seeks gold in the bowels of the earth.

"She must have taken a good part of the money, and left the door open to make people think some robber had gone in. Oh, the sly old cat! . . ." he thought furiously. But before believing his own idea he wanted to make sure with his eyes themselves.

Again it was Good Friday evening, and Basila had gone to

315

church. Simon waited for that time so as to be free to search the whole house; but hunt as he might, in drawers, in lockers, in the mattresses, he found nothing.

He looked round, tired of searching and in the half-light the trunk which still contained his mother's clothes seemed again like a live boar. He tried to open it, but could not. Then he remembered that Basila always kept the key with her. He went down to the kitchen, came back with an axe and began to strike at the trunk as if it were really a fierce boar. The lid came open. Simon knelt down and began to search; he found Basila's widow's clothes, and out of her black hood fluttered, silently, two, three, many bank-notes, red, green, yellowish, like withered walnut leaves. Amongst the others was one of a thousand: he took it up, held it against the candle light and read Barca's name pierced on it with a pin. Then he began to curse and batter his head.

"But why did it happen to me? why me of all people?" he cried aloud.

Suddenly a sad, sweet song like a murmuring wood floated in from the road. Simon grew quiet and stood listening, his head bent and his eyes wide open, and as the procession approached, he shook and sweated as when he had leant against his uncle's old bed.

CHARLES DICKENS

CHARLES DICKENS (English, 1812-1870). Sentimental-realistic novelist, one of the great Victorians. Despised greed and injustice, chose his material from lower classes, usually with some object of reform. Prejudiced but influential. Most prolific, his characters famous in English-speaking world. *David Copperfield, A Tale of Two Cities, Great Expectations, Oliver Twist, Pickwick Papers, A Christmas Carol.*

THE CONVICT IN THE MARSHES

MY FATHER's family name being Pirrip and my Christian name Philip, my infant tongue could make of both names nothing longer or more explicit than Pip. So I called myself Pip, and came to be called Pip.

I give Pirrip as my father's family name, on the authority of his

tombstone and my sister—Mrs. Joe Gargery, who married the black-smith. As I never saw my father or my mother, and never saw any likeness of either of them (for their days were long before the days of photographs), my first fancies regarding what they were like were unreasonably derived from their tombstones. The shape of the letters on my father's gave me an odd idea that he was a square, stout, dark man, with curly black hair. From the character and turn of the inscription, *"Also Georgiana, Wife of the Above,"* I drew a childish conclusion that my mother was freckled and sickly. To five little stone lozenges, each about a foot and a half long, which were arranged in a neat row beside their grave, and were sacred to the memory of five little brothers of mine—who gave up trying to get a living exceedingly early in that universal struggle—I am indebted for a belief I religiously entertained that they had all been born on their backs with their hands in their trousers pockets, and had never taken them out in this state of existence.

Ours was the marsh country, down by the river, within, as the river wound, twenty miles of the sea. My first most vivid and broad impression of the identity of things seems to me to have been gained on a memorable raw afternoon towards evening. At such a time I found out for certain that this bleak place overgrown with nettles was the churchyard; and that Philip Pirrip, late of this parish, and also Georgiana, wife of the above, were dead and buried; and that Alexander, Bartholomew, Abraham, Tobias, and Roger, infant children of the aforesaid, were also dead and buried; and that the dark flat wilderness beyond the churchyard, intersected with dikes and mounds and gates, with scattered cattle feeding on it, was the marshes; and that the low leaden line beyond was the river; and that the distant savage lair from which the wind was rushing was the sea; and that the small bundle of shivers growing afraid of it all and beginning to cry was Pip.

"Hold your noise!" cried a terrible voice, as a man started up from among the graves at the side of the church porch. "Keep still, you little devil, or I'll cut your throat!"

A fearful man, all in coarse gray, with a great iron on his leg. A man with no hat, and with broken shoes, and with an old rag tied round his head. A man who had been soaked in water, and smothered in mud, and lamed by stones, and cut by flints, and stung by nettles and torn by briers; who limped, and shivered, and glared, and growled; and whose teeth chattered in his head as he seized me by the chin.

317

"Oh! Don't cut my throat, sir," I pleaded in terror. "Pray don't do it, sir."

"Tell us your name!" said the man. "Quick!"

"Pip, sir."

"Once more," said the man, staring at me. "Give it mouth!"

"Pip. Pip, sir."

"Show us where you live," said the man. "Pint out the place!"

I pointed to where our village lay, on the flat inshore among the alder trees and pollards, a mile or more from the church.

The man, after looking at me for a moment, turned me upside down and emptied my pockets. There was nothing in them but a piece of bread. When the church came to itself—for he was so sudden and strong that he made it go head over heels before me, and I saw the steeple under my feet—when the church came to itself, I say, I was seated on a high tombstone, trembling, while he ate the bread ravenously.

"You young dog," said the man, licking his lips, "what fat cheeks you ha' got."

I believed they were fat, though I was at that time undersized for my years, and not strong.

"Darn me if I couldn't eat 'em," said the man, with a threatening shake of his head, "and if I han't half a mind to't!"

I earnestly expressed my hope that he wouldn't, and held tighter to the tombstone on which he had put me; partly to keep myself upon it; partly to keep myself from crying.

"Now lookee here!" said the man. "Where's your mother?"

"There, sir!" said I.

He started, made a short run, and stopped and looked over his shoulder.

"There, sir!" I timidly explained. "Also Georgiana. That's my mother."

"Oh!" said he, coming back. "And is that your father alonger your mother?"

"Yes, sir," said I; "him too; late of this parish."

"Ha!" he muttered then, considering. "Who d'ye live with—supposing you're kindly let to live, which I han't made up my mind about?"

"My sister, sir — Mrs. Joe Gargery — wife of Joe Gargery, tne blacksmith, sir."

"Blacksmith, eh?" said he. And looked down at his leg.

After darkly looking at his leg and at me several times, he ⸺ ⸺

closer to my tombstone, took me by both arms, and tilted me back as far as he could hold me; so that his eyes looked most powerfully down into mine, and mine looked most helplessly up into his.

"Now lookee here," he said, "the question being whether you're to be let to live. You know what a file is?"

"Yes, sir."

"And you know what wittles is?"

"Yes, sir."

After each question he tilted me over a little more, so as to give me a greater sense of helplessness and danger.

"You get me a file." He tilted me again. "And you get me wittles." He tilted me again. "You bring 'em both to me." He tilted me again. "Or I'll have your heart and liver out." He tilted me again.

I was dreadfully frightened, and so giddy that I clung to him with both hands, and said, "If you would kindly please to let me keep upright, sir, perhaps I shouldn't be sick, and perhaps I could attend more."

He gave me a most tremendous dip and roll, so that the church jumped over its own weathercock. Then, he held me by the arms in an upright position on the top of the stone, and went on in these fearful terms:—

"You bring me, to-morrow morning early, that file and them wittles. You bring the lot to me, at that old Battery over yonder. You do it, and you never dare to say a word or dare to make a sign concerning your having seen such a person as me, or any person sumever, and you shall be let to live. You fail, or you go from my words in any partickler, no matter how small it is, and your heart and your liver shall be tore out, roasted and ate. Now, I ain't alone, as you may think I am. There's a young man hid with me, in comparison with which young man I am a Angel. That young man hears the words I speak. That young man has a secret way pecooliar to himself of getting at a boy, and at his heart, and at his liver. It is in wain for a boy to attempt to hide himself from that young man. A boy may lock his door, may be warm in bed, may tuck himself up, may draw the clothes over his head, may think himself comfortable and safe, but that young man will softly creep and creep his way to him and tear him open. I am a keeping that young man from harming of you at the present moment, with great difficulty. I find it wery hard to hold that young man off of your inside. Now what do you say?"

319

I said that I would get him the file, and I would get him what broken bits of food I could, and I would come to him at the Battery, early in the morning.

"Say, Lord strike you dead if you don't!" said the man.

I said so, and he took me down.

"Now," he pursued, "you remember what you've undertook, and you remember that young man, and you get home!"

"Goo-good night, sir," I faltered.

"Much of that!" said he, glancing about him over the cold, wet flat. "I wish I was a frog. Or a eel!"

At the same time he hugged his shuddering body in both his arms—clasping himself, as if to hold himself together—and limped towards the low church wall. As I saw him go, picking his way among the nettles, and among the brambles that bound the green mounds, he looked in my young eyes as if he were eluding the hands of the dead people, stretching up cautiously out of their graves, to get a twist upon his ankle and pull him in.

When he came to the low church wall, he got over it, like a man whose legs were numbed and stiff, and then turned round to look for me. When I saw him turning, I set my face towards home, and made the best use of my legs. But presently I looked over my shoulder, and saw him going on again towards the river, still hugging himself in both arms, and picking his way with his sore feet among the great stones dropped into the marshes here and there for stepping places when the rains were heavy, or the tide was in.

The marshes were just a long black horizontal line then, as I stopped to look after him; and the river was just another horizontal line, not nearly so broad nor yet so black; and the sky was just a row of long angry red lines and dense black lines intermixed. On the edge of the river I could faintly make out the only two black things in all the prospect that seemed to be standing upright: one of these was the beacon by which the sailors steered,—like an unhooped cask upon a pole,—an ugly thing when you were near it; the other a gibbet, with some chains hanging to it which had once held a pirate. The man was limping on towards this latter, as if he were the pirate come to life, and come down, and going back to hook himself up again. It gave me a terrible turn when I thought so; and as I saw the cattle lifting their heads to gaze after him, I wondered whether they thought so too. I looked all round for the horrible young man, and could see no signs of him. But now I was frightened again, and ran home without stopping.

EMILY DICKINSON

EMILY DICKINSON (American, 1830-1886). The greatest American woman
poet, whose reputation emerged 40 years after her death. During life, a gentle
recluse intimate with nature and private tragedy. Her poetry remarkable for
its economy of means, whimsey of imagery, intensity of feeling.

THE SOUL SELECTS

The soul selects her own society,
Then shuts the door;
On her divine majority
Obtrude no more.

Unmoved, she notes the chariots pausing
At her low gate;
Unmoved, an emperor is kneeling
Upon her mat.

I've known her from an ample nation
Choose one;
Then close the valves of her attention
Like stone.

MY LIFE CLOSED TWICE

My life closed twice before its close;
It yet remains to see
If Immortality unveil
A third event to me,

So huge, so hopeless to conceive,
As these that twice befell.
Parting is all we know of heaven,
And all we need of hell.

OF ALL THE SOULS THAT STAND CREATE

Of all the souls that stand create
I have elected one.
When sense from spirit files away,
And subterfuge is done;

When that which is and that which was
Apart, intrinsic, stand,
And this brief tragedy of flesh
Is shifted like a sand;

When figures show their royal front
And mists are carved away—
Behold the atom I preferred
To all the lists of clay!

THE MOUNTAINS GROW UNNOTICED

The mountains grow unnoticed,
Their purple figures rise
Without attempt, exhaustion,
Assistance or applause.

In their eternal faces
The sun with broad delight
Looks long—and last—and golden,
For fellowship at night.

I NEVER SAW A MOOR

I never saw a moor,
I never saw the sea;
Yet know I how the heather looks,
And what a wave must be.

I never spoke with God,
Nor visited in Heaven;
Yet certain am I of the spot
As if the chart were given.

APPARENTLY WITH NO SURPRISE

Apparently with no surprise
To any happy flower,
The frost beheads it at its play
In accidental power.

The blond assassin passes on;
The sun proceeds unmoved
To measure off another day
For an approving God.

322

THE HEART ASKS PLEASURE FIRST

The heart asks pleasure first;
And then, excuse from pain;
And then, those little anodynes
That deaden suffering;

And then, to go to sleep;
And then, if it should be
The will of its Inquisitor,
The liberty to die.

THERE IS NO FRIGATE LIKE A BOOK

There is no frigate like a book
    To take us lands away,
Nor any courses like a page
    Of prancing poetry.

This traverse may the poorest take
    Without oppress of toll;
How frugal is the chariot
    That bears a human soul!

THE CHARIOT

Because I could not stop for Death,
He kindly stopped for me;
The carriage held but just ourselves,
And Immortality.

We slowly drove, he knew no haste,
And I had put away
My labor and my leisure, too,
For his civility.

We passed the school where children played,
Their lessons scarcely done;
We passed the fields of gazing grain,
We passed the setting sun.

We paused before a house that seemed
A swelling of the ground:
The roof was scarcely visible,
The cornice but a mound.

Since then, 'tis centuries; but each
Feels shorter than the day
I first surmised the horses' heads
Were toward eternity.

DEATH

Death is a dialogue between
The spirit and the dust.
"Dissolve," says Death; the spirit, "Sir,
I have another trust."
Death doubts it, argues from the ground.
The spirit turns away,
Just laying off, for evidence,
An overcoat of clay.

DEATH

The bustle in the house
The morning after death
Is solemnest of industries
Enacted upon earth;—

The sweeping up the heart
And putting love away
We shall not want to use again
Until eternity.

RESURGAM

At last to be identified!
At last, the lamps upon thy side
The rest of life to see!
Past midnight, past the morning star!
Past sunrise! Ah! what leagues there are
Between our feet and day!

THIRST

We thirst at first,—'tis nature's act;
  And, later, when we die
A little water supplicate
  Of fingers going by.

It intimates the finer wants
  Whose adequate supply
Is that great water in the West,
  Termed Immortality.

JOHN DONNE

JOHN DONNE (English, 1572-1631). Famed as preacher and metaphysical
poet. Left Catholic Church for Church of England, became Dean of St. Paul's.
Turned the English lyric to new subtleties of expression. Early love poems
frankly sensuous. Later religious verse sometimes obscure but always noble.
One of the idols of modern poets.

SONG

Go, and catch a falling star,
  Get with child a mandrake root,
Tell me, where all past years are,
  Or who cleft the Devil's foot,
Teach me to hear Mermaids singing,
  Or to keep off envy's stinging,
      And find
      What wind
Serves to advance an honest mind.

If thou be'st born to strange sights,
  Things invisible to see,
Ride ten thousand days and nights,
  Till age snow white hairs on thee,
Thou, when thou return'st, wilt tell me
All strange wonders that befell thee,
      And swear
      No where
Lives a woman true, and fair.

325

If thou find'st one, let me know,
   Such a Pilgrimage were sweet;
Yet do not, I would not go,
   Though at next door we might meet,
Though she were true, when you met her,
And last, till you write your letter,
      Yet she
      Will be
False, ere I come, to two, or three.

THE SUN RISING

   Busy old fool, unruly sun,
     Why dost thou thus
Through windows and through curtains call on us?
Must to thy motions lovers' seasons run?
    Saucy pedantic wretch, go chide
     Late schoolboys and sour prentices,
  Go tell court-huntsmen that the King will ride,
  Call country ants to harvest offices;
Love, all alike, no season knows, nor clime,
Nor hours, days, months, which are the rags of time.

   Thy beams, so reverend and strong
    Why shouldst thou think?
I could eclipse and cloud them with a wink,
But that I would not lose her sight so long;
    If her eyes have not blinded thine,
     Look, and tomorrow late tell me
  Whether both the Indias of spice and mine
  Be where thou left'st them, or lie here with me.
Ask for those kings whom thou saw'st yesterday,
And thou shalt hear, all here in one bed lay.

   She is all states, and all princes I;
    Nothing else is.
Princes do but play us; compared to this,
All honour's mimic, all wealth alchemy.
    Thou, sun, art half as happy as we,
    In that the world's contracted thus;

Thine age asks ease, and since thy duties be
To warm the world, that's done in warming us.
Shine here to us, and thou art everywhere;
This bed thy center is, these walls thy sphere.

THE ECSTASY

Where, like a pillow on a bed,
    A pregnant bank swelled up to rest
The violet's reclining head,
    Sat we two, one another's best.
Our hands were firmly cemented
    With a fast balm, which thence did spring;
Our eye-beams twisted, and did thread
    Our eyes upon one double string;
So to entergraft our hands, as yet
    Was all the means to make us one,
And pictures in our eyes to get
    Was all our propagation.

SEND BACK MY LONG-STRAY'D EYES
TO ME

Send back my long-stray'd eyes to me,
Which, O! too long have dwelt on thee:
But if from you they've learnt such ill,
    To sweetly smile,
    And then beguile,
Keep the deceivers, keep them still.

Send home my harmless heart again,
Which no unworthy thought could stain;
But if it has been taught by thine
    To forfeit both
    Its word and oath,
Keep it, for then 'tis none of mine.

Yet send me back my heart and eyes,
For I'll know all thy falsities;
That I one day may laugh, when thou
    Shalt grieve and mourn—
    Of one the scorn,
Who proves as false as thou art now.

327

THE GOOD MORROW

I wonder, by my troth, what thou and I
Did, till we loved? were we not weaned till then?
But sucked on country pleasures, childishly?
Or snorted we in the Seven Sleepers' den?
'Twas so; but this, all pleasures fancies be;
If ever any beauty I did see,
Which I desired, and got, 'twas but a dream of thee.

And now good morrow to our waking souls,
Which watch not one another out of fear;
For love all love of other sights controls,
And makes one little room an everywhere.
Let sea-discoverers to new worlds have gone;
Let maps to other, worlds on worlds have shown;
Let us possess one world; each hath one, and is one.

My face in thine eye, thine in mine appears,
And true plain hearts do in the faces rest;
Where can we find two better hemispheres
Without sharp north, without declining west?
Whatever dies, was not mix'd equally;
If our two loves be one, or thou and I
Love so alike that none can slacken, none can die.

THE LEGACY

When last I died, and, dear, I die
    As often as from thee I go,
    Though it be but an hour ago
—And lovers' hours be full eternity—
I can remember yet, that I
    Something did say, and something did bestow;
Though I be dead, which sent me, I might be
Mine own executor, and legacy.

I heard me say, "Tell her anon,
    That myself," that is you, not I,
    "Did kill me," and when I felt me die,
I bid me send my heart, when I was gone;

328

But I alas! could there find none;
    When I had ripp'd, and search'd where hearts should lie,
It kill'd me again, that I who still was true
In life, in my last will should cozen you.

Yet I found something like a heart,
    But colors it and corners had;
    It was not good, it was not bad,
It was entire to none, and few had part;
As good as could be made by art
    It seemed, and therefore for our loss be sad.
I meant to send that heart instead of mine,
But O! no man could hold it, for 'twas thine.

FEODOR MIKHAYLOVICH DOSTOYEVSKY

FEODOR MIKHAYLOVICH DOSTOYEVSKY (Russian, 1821-1881). Master
of the psychological novel. Spokesman for the downtrodden little people of
Czarist Russia. Important factors in life: epilepsy, penal servitude in Siberia,
passion for gambling. Novels concerned with mystery of human personality,
good and evil, God and immortality. Character analysis foreshadows modern
psychology. His four masterpieces: *The Brothers Karamazov, Crime and
Punishment, The Idiot, The Possessed.*

THE MURDERER'S CONFESSION TO SONIA

RASKOLNIKOFF wished to smile, but, do what he would, his countenance retained its sorrow-stricken look. He lowered his head, covering his face with his hands. All at once, he fancied that he was
beginning to hate Sonia. Surprised, frightened even, at so strange
a discovery, he suddenly raised his head and attentively considered
the girl, who, in her turn, fixed on him a look of anxious love.
Hatred fled from Raskolnikoff's heart. It was not that; he had only
mistaken the nature of the sentiment he had experienced. It signified that the fatal moment had come. Once more he hid his face in
his hands and bowed his head. Suddenly he grew pale, rose, and,
after looking at Sonia, he mechanically went and sat on her bed,
without uttering a single word. Raskolnikoff's impression was the
very same he had experienced when standing behind the old wo-

man—he had loosened the hatchet from the loop, and said to himself: "There is not a moment to be lost!"

"What is the matter?" asked Sonia, in bewilderment.

No reply. Raskolnikoff had relied on making explanations under quite different conditions, and did not himself understand what was now at work within him. She gently approached him, sat on the bed by his side, and waited, without taking her eyes from his face. Her heart beat as if it would break. The situation was becoming unbearable; he turned towards the girl his lividly-pale face, his lips twitched with an effort to speak. Fear had seized upon Sonia.

"What is the matter with you?" she repeated, moving slightly away from him.

"Nothing, Sonia; don't be afraid. It is not worth while; it is all nonsense!" he murmured, like a man absent in mind. "Only, why can I have come to torment you?" added he all at once, looking at his interlocutress. "Yes, why? I keep on asking myself this question, Sonia."

Perhaps he had done so a quarter of an hour before, but at this moment his weakness was such that he scarcely retained consciousness; a continued trembling shook his whole frame.

"Oh! how you suffer!" said she, in a voice full of emotion, whilst looking at him.

"It is nothing! But this is the matter in question, Sonia." (For a moment or so, a pale smile hovered on his lips.) "You remember what I wished to tell you yesterday?" Sonia waited anxiously. "I told you, on parting, that I was, perhaps, bidding you farewell for ever, but that if I should come to-day, I would tell you who it was that killed Elizabeth." She began to tremble in every limb. "Well, then, that is why I have come."

"I know you told me that yesterday," she went on in a shaky voice. "How do you know that?" she added vivaciously. Sonia breathed with an effort. Her face grew more and more pale.

"I know it."

"Has *he* been discovered?" she asked, timidly, after a moment's silence.

"No, *he* has not been discovered."

For another moment she remained silent. "Then how do you know it?" she at length asked, in an almost unintelligible voice.

He turned towards the girl, and looked at her with a singular rigidity, whilst a feeble smile fluttered on his lips. "Guess!" he said.

Sonia felt on the point of being seized with convulsions. "But

you—why frighten me like this?" she asked, with a childlike smile. "I know it, because I am very intimate with *him!*" went on Raskolnikoff, whose look remained fixed on her, as if he had not strength to turn his eyes aside. "Elizabeth—he had no wish to murder her—he killed her without premeditation. He only intended to kill the old woman, when he should find her alone. He went to her house—but at the very moment Elizabeth came in—he was there—and he killed her."

A painful silence followed upon these words. For a moment both continued to look at one another. "And so you can't guess?" he asked abruptly, feeling like a man on the point of throwing himself from the top of a steeple.

"No," stammered Sonia, in a scarcely audible voice.

"Try again."

At the moment he pronounced these words, Raskolnikoff experienced afresh, in his heart-of-hearts, that feeling of chilliness he knew so well. He looked at Sonia, and suddenly read on her face the same expression as on that of Elizabeth, when the wretched woman recoiled from the murderer advancing towards he, hatchet in hand. In that supreme moment Elizabeth had raised her arm, as children do when they begin to be afraid, and ready to weep, fix a glaring immovable glance on the object which frightens them. In the same way Sonia's face expressed indescribable fear. She also raised her arm, and gently pushed Raskolnikoff aside, whilst touching his breast with her hand, and then gradually drew back without ceasing to look hard at him. Her fear affected the young man, who, for his part, began to gaze on her with a scared expression.

"Have you guessed?" he murmured at last.

"My God!" exclaimed Sonia.

Then she sank exhausted on the bed, and buried her face in the pillows; a moment after, however, she rose with a rapid movement, approached him, and, seizing him by both hands, which her slender fingers clutched like nippers, she fixed on him a long look. Had he made a mistake? She hoped so, but she had no sooner cast a look on Raskolnikoff's face than the suspicion which had flashed on her mind became certainty.

"Enough, Sonia! enough! Spare me!" he implored in a plaintive voice. The event upset all his calculations, for it certainly was not *thus* that he had intended to confess his crime.

Sonia seemed beside herself; she jumped from her bed, went to the middle of the room wringing her hands, she then quickly re-

turned in the same way, sat once more by the young man's side, almost touching him with her shoulder. Suddenly she shivered, uttered a cry, and, without knowing why, fell on her knees before Raskolnikoff. "You are lost!" she exclaimed, with an accent of despair. And, rising suddenly, she threw herself on his neck, and kissed him, whilst lavishing on him tokens of tenderness.

Raskolnikoff broke away, and, with a sad smile, looked at the girl: "I do not understand you, Sonia. You kiss me after I told you *that*—. You cannot be conscious of what you are doing."

She did not hear the remark. "No, at this moment there cannot be a more wretched man on earth than you are!" she exclaimed with a transport of passion, whilst bursting into sobs.

Raskolnikoff felt his heart grow soft under the influence of a sentiment which for some time past he had not felt. He did not try to fight against the feeling; two tears spurted from his eyes and remained on the lashes. "Then you will not forsake me, Sonia?" said he with an almost suppliant look.

"No, no; never, nowhere!" she cried, "I shall follow you, shall follow you everywhere! Heaven! Wretch that I am! And why have I not known you sooner? Why did you not come before? Heaven!"

"You see I have come."

"Now? What is to be done now? Together, together," she went on, with a kind of exaltation, and once more she kissed the young man. "Yes, I will go with you to the galleys!"

These words caused Raskolnikoff a painful feeling; a bitter and almost haughty smile appeared on his lips. "Perhaps I may not yet wish to go to the galleys, Sonia," said he.

The girl rapidly turned her eyes on him. She had up to the present experienced no more than immense pity for an unhappy man. This statement, and the tone of voice in which it was pronounced, suddenly recalled to the girl that the wretched man was an assassin. She cast on him an astonished look. As yet, she did not know how nor why he had become a criminal. At this moment, these questions suggested themselves to her, and, once more doubting, she asked herself: "He, he a murderer? Is such a thing possible? But no, it cannot be true! Where am I?" she asked herself, as if she could have believed herself the sport of a dream. "How is it possible that you, being what you are, can have thought of such a thing? Oh! why?"

"To steal, if you wish to know. Cease, Sonia!" he replied in wearied and rather vexed accents.

Sonia remained stupefied; suddenly a cry escaped her: "Were you hungry? Did you do so to help your mother? Speak!"

"No, Sonia! no!" he stammered, drooping his head. "I was not so poor as all that. It is true I wanted to help my mother, but that was not the real reason.—Do not torment me, Sonia!"

The girl beat her hands together. "Is it possible that such a thing can be real? Heaven! is it possible? How can I believe such a thing? You say you killed to rob; you, who deprive yourself of all for the sake of others! Ah!" she cried suddenly. "That money you gave to Catherine Ivanovna! — that money! Heavens! can it be that?"

"No, Sonia!" he interrupted somewhat sharply. "This money comes from another source, I assure you. It was my mother who sent it to me during my sickness, through the intervention of a merchant, and I had just received it when I gave it. Razoumikin saw it himself, he even went so far as to receive it for me. The money was really my own property." Sonia listened in perplexity, and strove to understand. "As for the old woman's money, to tell the truth, I really do not know whether there was any money at all," he went on hesitatingly. "I took from her neck a well-filled chamois-leather purse. But I never examined the contents, probably because I had no time to do so. I took different things, sleeve-links, watch-chains. These things I hid, in the same way as the purse, on the following day, under a large stone in a yard which looks out on the V—— Prospect. Everything is still there."

Sonia listened with avidity. "But why did you take nothing, since, as you tell me, you committed murder to steal?" she went on, clinging to a last and very vague hope.

"I don't know—as yet I am undecided whether to take this money or not," replied Raskolnikoff in the same hesitating voice; then he smiled. "What silly tale have I been telling you?"

"Can he be mad?" Sonia asked herself, but she soon dispelled such an idea; no, it was something else, which she most certainly did not understand.

"Do you know what I am going to tell you, Sonia?" he went on in a convinced tone: "If nothing but need had urged me to commit a murder," laying stress on every word, and his look, although frank was more or less puzzling, "I should now be *happy!* Let me tell you that! And what can the motive be to you, since I told you just now that I had acted badly?" he cried despairingly, a moment afterwards. "What was the good of this foolish triumph over my-

333

self? Ah! Sonia, was it for that I came to you?" She once more wished to speak, but remained silent. "Yesterday, I made a proposal to you that we should both of us depart together, because you are all that is left to me."

"Why did you wish me to accompany you?" asked the girl timidly.

"Not to rob or to kill, I assure you," answered Raskolnikoff, with a caustic smile. "We are not of the same way of thinking. And—do you know, Sonia?—it is only of late that I have known why I asked you yesterday to accompany me. When I asked you to do so, I did not as yet know what it would lead to. I see it now. I have but one wish—it is that you should not leave me. You will not do so, will you, Sonia?" She clasped his hand. "And why have I told her this? Why make such a confession?" he exclaimed, a moment afterwards. He looked at her with infinite compassion, whilst his voice expressed the most profound despair. "I see, Sonia, that you are waiting for some kind of explanation, but what am I to say? You understand nothing about the matter, and I should only be causing you additional pain. I see you are once more commencing to weep and embrace me. Why do so at all? Because, failing in courage to bear my own burden, I have imposed it on another—because I seek in the anguish of others some mitigation for my own. And you can love a coward like that?"

"But you are likewise suffering!" exclaimed Sonia.

For a moment he experienced a new feeling of tenderness. "Sonia, my disposition is a bad one, and that can explain much. I have come because I am bad. Some would not have done so. But I am an infamous coward. Why, once more, have I come? I shall never forgive myself for that!"

"No, no!—on the contrary, you have done well to come," cried Sonia; "it is better, much better, I should know all!"

Raskolnikoff looked at her with sorrowful eye. "I was ambitious to become another Napoleon; that was why I committed a murder. Can you understand it now?"

"No," answered Sonia, naïvely and in a timid voice. "But speak! speak! I shall understand it all!"

"You will, say you? God! we shall see!" For some time Raskolnikoff collected his ideas. "That fact is that, one day, I asked myself the following question: 'Supposing Napoleon to have been in my place, supposing that to commence his career he had neither had Toulon, nor Egypt, nor the crossing of Mont Blanc, but, in lieu of

334

all these brilliant exploits, he was on the point of committing a murder with a view to secure his future, would he have recoiled at the idea of killing an old woman, and of robbing her of three thousand roubles? Would he have agreed that such a deed was too much wanting in prestige and much too—criminal a one?' For a long time I have split my head on that question, and could not help experiencing a feeling of shame when I finally came to the conclusion that he not only would not have hesitated, but that he would not have understood the possibility of such a thing. Every other expedient being out of his reach, he would not have flinched, he would have done so without the smallest scruple. Hence, I ought not to hesitate—being justified on the authority of Napoleon!"

JOHN DRYDEN

JOHN DRYDEN (English, 1631-1700). Dominant literary figure of the Restoration. Dramatist, poet, essayist, critic. Influential in establishing heroic couplet, which dominated English poetry for a century. Best-known poem: "Alexander's Feast." Drama: *All for Love.* Prose: *An Essay of Dramatic Poesy.*

ZEGRI AND ABENCERRAGE

Scene: *Granada, and the Christian Camp besieging it.* Present: Boabdelin, Abenamar, Abdelmelech, *and* Guards.

Boabdelin—

The alarm-bell rings from our Alhambra walls,
And from the streets sound drums and atabals.

> *(Within, a bell, drums, and trumpets.)*
Enter *a* Messenger.

How now? from whence proceed these new alarms?
Messenger—

The two fierce factions are again in arms;
And changing into blood the day's delight,
The Zegrys with the the Abencerrages fight;
On each side their allies and friends appear;
The Macas here, the Alabezes there;
The Gazuls with the Bencerrages join,
And, with the Zegrys, all great Gomel's line.

335

Boabdelin—

    Draw up behind the Vivarambla place;

    Double my guards,—these factions I will face;

    And try if all the fury they can bring

    Be proof against the presence of their king.

        (Exit Boabdelin.)

*The Factions appear: At the head of the Abencerrages, Ozmyn; at
the head of the Zegrys, Zulema, Hamet, Gomel, and Selin; Abenamar and Abdelmelech join with the Abencerrages.*

Zulema—

    The faint Abencerrages quit their ground:

    Press them; put home your thrusts to every wound.

Abdelmelech—

    Zegry, on manly force our line relies;

    Thine poorly takes the advantage of surprise:

    Unarmed and much outnumbered we retreat;

    You gain no fame, when basely you defeat.

    If thou art brave, seek nobler victory;

    Save Moorish blood; and, while our bands stand by,

    Let two and two an equal combat try.

Hamet—

    'Tis not for fear the combat we refuse.

    But we our gained advantage will not lose.

Zulema—

    In combating, but two of you will fall;

    And we resolve we will despatch you all.

Ozmyn—

    We'll double yet the exchange before we die,

    And each of ours two lives of yours shall buy.

    Almanzor *enters betwixt them, as they stand ready to engage.*

Almanzor—

    I cannot stay to ask which cause is best:

    But this is so to me, because opprest.

        (Goes to the Abencerrages.)

    To them Boabdelin *and his* Guards, *going betwixt them.*

Boabdelin—

    On your allegiance, I command you stay;

    Who passes here, through me must make his way;

    My life's the Isthmus; through this narrow line

    You first must cut, before those seas can join.

    What fury, Zegrys, has possessed your minds?

What rage the brave Abencerrages blinds?
If of your courage you new proofs would show,
Without much travel you may find a foe.
Those foes are neither so remote nor few
That you should need each other to pursue.
Lean times and foreign wars should minds unite;
When poor men mutter, but they seldom fight.
O holy Allah! that I live to see
Thy Granadines assist their enemy!
You fight the Christians' battles; every life
You lavish thus, in this intestine strife,
Does from our weak foundations take one prop,
Which helped to hold our sinking country up.

Ozmyn—

'Tis fit our private enmity should cease;
Though injured first, yet I will first seek peace.

Zulema—

No, murderer, no; I never will be won
To peace with him, whose hand has slain my son.

Ozmyn—

Our phrophet's curse
On me and all the Abencerrages light,
If unprovoked I with your son did fight.

Abdelmelech—

A band of Zegrys ran within the place,
Matched with a troop of thirty of our race.
Your son and Ozmyn the first squadrons led,
Which, ten by ten, like Parthians, charged and fled,
The ground was strowed with canes where we did meet,
Which crackled underneath our coursers' feet;
When Tarifa (I saw him ride apart)
Changed his blunt cane for a steel-pointed dart,
And, meeting Ozmyn next—
Who wanted time for treason to provide,—
He basely threw it at him, undefied.

Ozmyn (showing his arms)—

Witness this blood—which when by treason sought,
That followed, sir, which to myself I ought.

Zulema—

His hate to thee was grounded on a grudge,
Which all our generous Zegrys just did judge:

337

Thy villain-blood thou openly didst place
Above the purple of our kingly race.
Boabdelin—
From equal stems their blood both houses draw,
They from Morocco, you from Cordova.
Hamet—
Their mongrel race is mixed with Christian breed;
Hence 'tis that they those dogs in prisons feed.
Abdelmelech—
Our holy prophet wills, that charity
Should even to birds and beast extended be:
None knows what fate is for himself designed;
The thought of human chance should make us kind.
Gomel—
We waste that time we to revenge should give:
Fall on; let no Abencerrage live.
Advances before the rest of his party. Almanzor *advances on the
other side, and describes a line with his sword.*
Almanzor—
Upon thy life pass not this middle space;
Sure death stands guarding the forbidden place.
Gomel—
To dare that death, I will approach yet nigher;
Thus,—wert thou compassed in with circling fire.
(*They fight.*)
Boabdelin—
Disarm them both; if they resist you, kill.
Almanzor, *in the midst of the guards, kills* Gomel, *and then is
disarmed.*
Almanzor—
Now you have but the leavings of my will.
Boabdelin—
Kill him! this insolent unknown shall fall,
And be the victim to atone you all.
Ozmyn—
If he must die, not one of us will live:
That life he gave for us, for him we give.
Boabdelin—
It was a traitor's voice that spoke those words;
So are you all, who do not sheathe your swords.

338

Zulema—

    Outrage unpunished, when a prince is by,
    Forfeits to scorn the rights of majesty:
    No subject his protection can expect,
    Who what he owes himself does first neglect.

Abenamar—

    This stranger, sir, is he,
    Who lately in the Vivarambla place
    Did, with so loud applause, your triumphs grace.

Boabdelin—

    The word which I have given, I'll not revoke;
    If he be brave, he's ready for the stroke.

Almanzor—

    No man has more contempt than I of breath,
    But whence hast thou the right to give me death?
    Obeyed as sovereign by thy subjects be,
    But know, that I alone am king of me.
    I am as free as nature first made man,
    Ere the base laws of servitude began,
    When wild in woods the noble savage ran.

Boabdelin—

    Since, then, no power above your own you know,
    Mankind should use you like a common foe;
    You should be hunted like a beast of prey:
    By your own law I take your life away.

Almanzor—

    My laws are made but only for my sake;
    No king against himself a law can make.
    If thou pretend'st to be a prince like me,
    Blame not an act which should thy pattern be.
    I saw the oppressed, and thought it did belong
    To a king's office to redress the wrong:
    I brought that succor which thou ought'st to bring,
    And so, in nature, am thy subjects' king.

Boabdelin—

    I do not want your counsel to direct,
    Or aid to help me punish or protect.

Almanzor—

    Thou want'st them both, or better thou wouldst know,
    Than to let factions in thy kingdoms grow.

Divided interests, while thou think'st to sway,
Draw, like two brooks, thy middle stream away:
For though they band and jar, yet both combine
To make their greatness by the fall of thine.
Thus, like a buckler, thou art held in sight,
While they behind thee with each other fight.

Boabdelin—

Away, and execute him instantly! (*To his Guards.*)

Almanzor—

Stand off; I have not leisure yet to die.

    To them, enter Abdalla *hastily.*

Abdalla—

Hold, sir! for heaven's sake hold!
Defer this noble stranger's punishment,
Or your rash orders you will soon repent.

Boabdelin—

Brother, you know not yet his insolence.

Abdalla—

Upon yourself you punish his offense:
If we treat gallant strangers in this sort,
Mankind will shun the inhospitable court;
And who, henceforth, to our defense will come,
If death must be the brave Almanzor's doom?
From Africa I drew him to your aid,
And for his succor have his life betrayed.

Boabdelin—

Is this the Almanzor whom at Fez you knew,
When first their swords the Xeriff brothers drew?

Abdalla—

This, sir, is he, who for the elder fought,
And to the juster cause the conquest brought;
Till the proud Santo, seated on the throne,
Disdained the service he had done to own:
Then to the vanquished part his fate he led;
The vanquished triumphed, and the victor fled.
Vast is his courage, boundless is his mind,
Rough as a storm, and humorous as wind:
Honor's the only idol of his eyes;
The charms of beauty like a pest he flies;
And, raised by valor from a birth unknown,
Acknowledges no power above his own.

340

Boabdelin (coming to Almanzor)—
Impute your danger to our ignorance;
The bravest men are subject most to chance:
Granada much does to your kindness owe;
But towns, expecting sieges, cannot show
More honor than to invite you to a foe.

Almanzor—
I do not doubt but I have been to blame:
But, to pursue the end for which I came,
Unite your subjects first; then let us go,
And pour their common rage upon the foe.

Boabdelin (to the factions)—
Lay down your arms, and let me beg you cease
Your enmities.

Zulema—
We will not hear of peace,
Till we by force have first revenged our slain.

Abdelmelech—
The action we have done we will maintain.

Selin—
Then let the king depart, and we will try
Our cause by arms.

Zulema—
For us and victory.

*Boabdelin—*A king entreats you.

Almanzor—
What subjects will precarious kings regard?
A beggar speaks too softly to be heard:
Lay down your arms! 'tis I command you now.
Do it—or, by our prophet's soul I vow,
My hands shall right your king on him I seize.
Now let me see whose look but disobeys.

All—
Long live king Mahomet Boabdelin!

Almanzor—
No more; but hushed as midnight silence go:
He will not have your acclamations now.
Hence, you unthinking crowd!—
        (*The Common People go off in both parties.*)
Empire, thou poor and despicable thing,
When such as these make or unmake a king!

341

ALEXANDRE DUMAS

ALEXANDRE DUMAS (1802-1870). Prolific romantic novelist. *The Three Musketeers, The Count of Monte Cristo, The Man in the Iron Mask,* still read for their vitality and narrative ingenuity. With team of collaborators, produced 300 such romances. Also wrote melodramas for stage, and was active in political affairs.

MARGUERITE DE VALOIS

1. *Henry of Navarre and Marguerite*

On Monday, August 18, 1572, a great festival was held in the palace of the Louvre. It was to celebrate the marriage of Henry of Navarre and Marguerite de Valois, a marriage that perplexed a good many people, and alarmed others.

For Henry de Bourbon, King of Navarre, was the leader of the Huguenot party, and Marguerite was the daughter of Catherine de Medici, and the sister of the king, Charles IX., and this alliance between a Protestant and a Catholic, it seemed, was to end the strife that rent the nation. The king, too, had set his heart on this marriage, and the Huguenots were somewhat reassured by the king's declaration that Catholic and Huguenot alike were now his subjects, and were equally beloved by him. Still, there were many on both sides who feared and distrusted the alliance.

At midnight, six days later, on August 24, the tocsin sounded, and the massacre of St. Bartholomew began.

The marriage, indeed, was in no sense a love match; but Henry succeeded at once in making Marguerite his friend, for he was alive to the dangers that surrounded him.

"Madame," he said, presenting himself at Marguerite's rooms on the night of the wedding festival, "whatever many persons may have said, I think our marriage is a good marriage. I stand well with you—you stand well with me. Therefore, we ought to act towards each other like good allies, since to-day we have been allied in the sight of God! Don't you think so?"

"Without question, sir!"

"I know, madame, that the ground at court is full of dangerous abysses; and I know that, though I am young and have never injured any person, I have many enemies. The king hates me, his brothers, the Duke of Anjou and the Duke d' Alençon, hate me. Catherine de Medici hated my mother too much not to hate me.

Well, against these menaces, which must soon become attacks, I can only defend myself by your aid, for you are beloved by all those who hate me!"

"I?" said Marguerite.

"Yes, you!" replied Henry. "And if you will—I do not say love me—but if you will be my ally I can brave anything; while, if you become my enemy, I am lost."

"Your enemy! Never, sir!" exclaimed Marguerite.

"And my ally?"

"Most decidedly!"

And Marguerite turned round and presented her hand to the king. "It is agreed," she said.

"Political alliance, frank and loyal?" asked Henry.

"Frank and loyal," was the answer.

At the door Henry turned and said softly, "Thanks, Marguerite; thanks! You are a true daughter of France. Lacking your love, your friendship will not fail me. I rely on you, as you, for your part, may rely on me. Adieu, madame."

He kissed his wife's hand; and then, with a quick step, the king went down the corridor to his own apartment. "I have more need of fidelity in politics than in love," he said to himself.

If on both sides there was little attempt at fidelity in love, there was an honourable alliance, which was maintained unbroken and saved the life of Henry of Navarre from his enemies on more than one occasion.

On the day of the St. Bartholomew massacre, while the Huguenots were being murdered throughout Paris, Charles IX., instigated by his mother, summoned Henry of Navarre to the royal armoury, and called upon him to turn Catholic or die.

"Will you kill me, sire—me, your brother-in-law?" exclaimed Henry.

Charles IX turned away to the open window. "I must kill some-one," he cried, and firing his arquebuse, struck a man who was passing.

Then, animated by a murderous fury, Charles loaded and fired his arquebuse without stopping, shouting with joy when his aim was successful.

"It's all over with me!" said Henry to himself. "When he sees no one else to kill, he will kill me!"

Catherine de Medici entered as the king fired his last shot. "Is it done?" she said, anxiously.

343

"No," the king exclaimed, throwing his arquebuse on the floor. "No; the obstinate blockhead will not consent!"

Catherine gave a glance at Henry which Charles understood perfectly, and which said, "Why, then, is he alive?"

"He lives," said the king, "because he is my relative."

Henry felt that it was with Catherine he had to contend.

"Madame," he said, addressing her, "I can see quite clearly that all this comes from you and not from brother-in-law Charles. It was you who planned this massacre to ensnare me into a trap which was to destroy us all. It was you who made your daughter the bait. It has been you who have separated me now from my wife, that she might not see me killed before her eyes!"

"Yes; but that shall not be!" cried another voice; and Marguerite, breathless and impassioned, burst into the room.

"Sir," said Marguerite to Henry, "your last words were an accusation, and were both right and wrong. They have made me the means for attempting to destroy you, but I was ignorant that in marrying me you were going to destruction. I myself owe my life to chance, for this very night they all but killed me in seeking you. Directly I knew of your danger I sought you. If you are exiled, sir, I will be exiled too; if they imprison you they shall imprison me also; if they kill you, I will also die!"

She gave her hand to her husband, and he seized it eagerly.

"Brother," cried Marguerite to Charles IX., "remember, you made him my husband!"

"Faith, Margot is right, and Henry is my brother-in-law," said the king.

II

THE BOAR HUNT

As time went on, if Catherine's hatred of Henry of Navarre did not diminish, Charles IX. certainly became more friendly.

Catherine was for ever intriguing and plotting for the fortunes of her sons and the downfall of her son-in-law, but Henry always managed to evade the webs she wove. At a certain boar-hunt Charles was indebted to Henry for his life.

It was at the time when the king's brother, D'Anjou, had accepted the crown of Poland, and the second brother, D'Alençon, a weak-minded, ambitious man, was secretly hoping for a crown somewhere, that Henry paid his debt for the king's mercy to him on the night of St. Bartholomew.

Charles was an intrepid hunter, but the boar had swerved as the king's spear was aimed at him, and, maddened with rage, the animal had rushed at him. Charles tried to draw his hunting-knife, but the sheath was so tight it was impossible.

"The boar! the boar!" shouted the king. "Help, D'Alençon, help!"

D'Alençon was ghastly white as he placed his arquebuse to his shoulder and fired. The ball, instead of hitting the boar, felled the king's horse.

"I think," D'Alençon murmured to himself, "that D'Anjou is King of France, and I King of Poland."

The boar's tusk had indeed grazed the king's thigh when a hand in an iron glove dashed itself against the mouth of the beast, and a knife was plunged into its shoulder.

Charles rose with difficulty, and seemed for a moment as if about to fall by the dead boar. Then he looked at Henry of Navarre, and for the first time in four-and-twenty years his heart was touched.

"Thanks, Harry!" he said. "D'Alençon, for a first-rate marksman you made a most curious shot."

On Marguerite coming up to congratulate the king and thank her husband, Charles added, "Margot, you may well thank him. But for him Henry III. would be King of France."

"Alas, madame," returned Henry, "M. D'Anjou, who is always my enemy, will now hate me more than ever; but everyone has to do what he can."

Had Charles IX. been killed, the Duke d'Anjou would have been King of France, and D'Alençon most probably King of Poland. Henry of Navarre would have gained nothing by this change of affairs.

Instead of Charles IX., who tolerated him, he would have had the Duke d'Anjou on the throne, who, being absolutely at one with his mother, Catherine, had sworn his death, and would have kept his oath.

These ideas were in his brain when the wild boar rushed on Charles, and like lightning he saw that his own existence was bound up with the life of Charles IX. But the king knew nothing of the spring and motive of the devotion which had saved his life, and on the following day he showed his gratitude to Henry by carrying him off from his apartments, and out of the Louvre. Catherine, in her fear lest Henry of Navarre should some day be King of France, had arranged the assassination of her son-in-law; and Charles, getting wind of this, warned him that the air of the

345

Louvre was not good for him that night, and kept him in his company. Instead of Henry, it was one of his followers who was killed.

III

THE POISONED BOOK

Once more Catherine resolved to destroy Henry. The Huguenots had plotted with D'Alençon that he should be King of Navarre, since Henry not only abjured Protestantism but remained in Paris, being kept there indeed by the will of Charles IX.

Catherine, aware of D'Alençon's scheme, assured her son that Henry was suffering from an incurable disease, and must be taken away from Paris when D'Alencon started for Navarre.

"Are you sure that Henry will die?" asked D'Alencon.

"The physician who gave me a certain book assured me of it."

"And where is this book? What is it?"

Catherine brought the book from her cabinet.

"Here it is. It is a treatise on the art of rearing and training falcons by an Italian. Give it to Henry, who is going hawking with the king to-day, and will not fail to read it."

"I dare not!" said D'Alençon shuddering.

"Nonsense!" replied Catherine. "It is a book like any other, only the leaves have a way of sticking together. Don't attempt to read it yourself, for you will have to wet the finger in turning over each leaf, which takes up so much time."

"Oh," said D'Alençon, "Henry is with the court! Give me the book, and while he is away I will put it in his room."

D'Alençon's hand was trembling as he took the book from the queen-mother, and with some hesitation and fear he entered Henry's apartment and placed the volume, open at the title page.

But it was not Henry, but Charles, seeking his brother-in-law, who found the book and carried it off to his own room. D'Alençon found the king reading.

"By heavens, this is an admirable book!" cried Charles. "Only it seems as if they had stuck the leaves together on purpose to conceal the wonders it contains."

D'Alençon's first thought was to snatch the book from his brother, but he hesitated.

The king again moistened his finger and turned over a page.

346

"Let me finish this chapter," he said, "and then tell me what you please. I have already read fifty pages."

"He must have tasted the poison five-and-twenty times," thought D'Alençon. "He is a dead man!"

The poison did its deadly work. Charles was taken ill while out hunting, and returned to find his dog dead, and in its mouth pieces of paper from the precious book on falconry. The king turned pale. The book was poisoned! Many things flashed across his memory, and he knew his life was doomed.

Charles summoned René, a Florentine, the court perfumer to Catherine de Medici, to his presence, and bade him examine the dog.

"Sire," said René, after a close investigation, "the dog has been poisoned by arsenic."

"He has eaten a leaf of this book," said Charles; "and if you do not tell me whose book it is I will have your flesh torn from your bones by red-hot pincers."

"Sire," stammered the Florentine, "this book belongs to me!"

"And how did it leave your hands?"

"Her majesty the queen-mother took it from my house."

"Why did she do that?"

"I believe she intended sending it to the King of Navarre, who had asked for a book on hawking."

"Ah," said Charles, "I understand it all! The book was in Harry's room. It is destiny; I must yield to it. Tell me," he went on, turning to René, "this poison does not always kill at once?"

"No, sire; but it kills surely. It is a matter of time."

"Is there no remedy?"

"None, sire, unless it be instantly administered."

Charles compelled the wretched man to write in the fatal volume, "This book was given by me to the queen-mother, Catherine de Medici.—René," and then dismissed him.

Henry, at his own prayer and for his personal safety, was confined in the prison of Vincennes by the king's order. Charles grew worse, and the physicians discussed his malady without daring to guess at the truth.

Then Catherine came one day and explained to the king the cause of his disease.

"Listen, my son; you believe in magic?"

"Oh, fully," said Charles, repressing his smile of incredulity.

"Well," continued Catherine, "all your sufferings proceed from

347

magic. An enemy afraid to attack you openly has done so in secret; a terrible conspiracy has been directed against your majesty. You doubt it, perhaps, but I know it for a certainty."

"I never doubt what you tell me," replied the king sarcastically. "I am curious to know how they have sought to kill me."

"By magic. Look here." The queen drew from under her mantle a figure of yellow wax about ten inches high, wearing a robe covered with golden stars, and over this a royal mantle.

"See, it has on its head a crown," said Catherine, "and there is a needle in its heart. Now do you recognise yourself?"

"Myself?"

"Yes, in your royal robes, with the crown on your head."

"And who made this figure?" asked the king, weary of the wretched farce. "The King of Navarre, of course!"

"No, sire; he did not actually make it, but it was found in the rooms of M. de la Mole, who serves the King of Navarre."

"So, then, the person who seeks to kill me is M. de la Mole?" said Charles.

"He is only the instrument, and behind the instrument is the hand that directs it," replied Catherine.

"This, then, is the cause of my illness. And now what must I do —for I know nothing of sorcery?"

"The death of the conspirator destroys the charm. Its power ends with his life. You are convinced now, are you not, of the cause of your illness?"

"Oh, certainly," Charles answered ironically. "And I am to punish M. de la Mole, as you say he is the guilty party?"

"I say he is the instrument, and," muttered Catherine, "we have infallible means for making him confess the name of his principal."

Catherine left hurriedly without understanding the sardonic laughter of the king, and as she went out Marguerite appeared.

"Oh, sire—sire," cried Marguerite, "you know what *she* says is false. It is terrible to accuse one's own mother, but she only lives to persecute the man who is devoted to you, Henry—your Henry— and I swear to you that what she says is false!"

"I think so, too, Margot. But Henry is safe. Safer in disgrace in Vincennes than in favour at the Louvre."

"Oh, thanks, thanks! But there is another person in whose welfare I am interested, whom I hardly dare mention to my brother, much less to my king."

"M. de la Mole, is it not? But do you know that a figure dressed

in royal robes and pierced to the heart was found in his rooms?"

"I know it; but it was the figure of a woman, not of a man."

"And the needle?"

"Was a charm not to kill a man, but to make a woman love him."

"What was the name of this woman?"

"Marguerite!" cried the queen, throwing herself down and bathing the king's hand in her tears.

"Margot, what if I know the real author of the crime? For a crime has been committed, and I have not three months to live. I am poisoned, but it must be thought I die by magic."

"You know who is guilty?"

"Yes; but it must be kept from the world, and so it must be believed I die of magic, and by the agency of him they accuse."

"But it is monstrous!" exclaimed Marguerite. "You know he is innocent. Pardon him—pardon him!"

"I know it, but the world must believe him guilty. Let your friend die. His death alone can save the honour of our family. I am dying that the secret may be preserved."

M. de la Mole, after enduring excruciating tortures at the hands of Catherine, without making any admissions, died on the scaffold.

IV

"THE BOURBON SHALL NOT REIGN!"

Before he died Charles showed Catherine the poisoned book, which he had kept under lock and key.

"And now burn it, madame. I read this book too much, so fond was I of the chase. And the world must not know the weaknesses of kings. When it is burnt, please summon my brother Henry. I wish to speak to him about the regency."

Catherine brought Henry of Navarre to the king, and warned him that if he accepted the regency he was a dead man.

Charles, however, though on his deathbed, declared Henry should be regent.

"Madame," he said, addressing his mother, "if I had a son he would be king, and you would be regent. In your stead, did you decline, the King of Poland would be regent; and in his stead, D'Alencon. But I have no son, and therefore the throne belongs to D'Anjou, who is absent. To make D'Alencon regent is to invite civil war. I have therefore chosen the fittest person for regent. Salute him, madame; salute him, D'Alençon. It is the King of Navarre!"

"Never," cried Catherine, "shall my race yield to a foreign one! Never shall a Bourbon reign while a Valois lives!"

She left the room, followed by D'Alençon.

"Henry," said Charles, "after my death you will be great and powerful. D'Anjou will not leave Poland—they will not let him. D'Alençon is a traitor. You alone are capable of governing. It is not the regency only, but the throne I give you."

A stream of blood choked his speech.

"The fatal moment is come," said Henry. "Am I to reign, or to live?"

"Live, sire!" a voice answered, and René appeared. "The queen has sent me to ruin you, but I have faith in your star. It is foretold that you shall be king. Do you know that the King of Poland will be here very soon? He has been summoned by the queen. A messenger has come from Warsaw. You shall be king, but not yet."

"What shall I do, then?"

"Fly instantly to where your friends wait for you."

Henry stooped and kissed his brother's forehead, then disappeared down a secret passage, passed through the postern, and, springing on his horse, galloped off.

"He flies! The King of Navarre flies!" cried the sentinels.

"Fire on him! Fire!" said the queen.

The sentinels levelled their pieces, but the king was out of reach.

"He flies!" muttered D'Alençon. "I am king, then!"

At the same moment the drawbridge was hastily lowered, and Henry D'Anjou galloped into the court, followed by four knights, crying, "France! France!"

"My son!" cried Catherine joyfully.

"Am I too late?" said D'Anjou.

"No. You are just in time. Listen!"

The captain of the king's guards appeared at the balcony of the king's apartment. He broke the wand he held in two pieces, and holding a piece in either hand, called out three times, "King Charles the Ninth is dead! King Charles the Ninth is dead! King Charles the Ninth is dead!"

"Charles the Ninth is dead!" said Catherine, crossing herself. "God save Henry the Third!"

All repeated the cry.

"I have conquered," said Catherine, "and the odious Bourbon shall not reign!"

350

E

JOSEPH VON EICHENDORFF

JOSEPH VON EICHENDORFF (German, 1788-1857). The latter-day poet of German medievalism. Characterized by typical Romantic themes: love of nature, wanderlust, romantic longings. Wrote in many forms, but most characteristic work, a novella, *Aus dem Leben eines Taugenichts (From the Life of a Good-for-Nothing)*, is combination of poetry and prose.

Poems from
"FROM THE LIFE OF A GOOD-FOR-NOTHING"

The favoured ones, the loved of Heaven,
    God sends to roam the world at will;
His wonders to their gaze are given
    By field and forest, stream and hill.

The dullards who at home are staying
    Are not refreshed by morning's ray;
They grovel, earth-born calls obeying,
    And petty cares beset their day.

The little brooks o'er rocks are springing,
    The lark's gay carol fills the air:
Why should not I with them be singing
    A joyous anthem free from care?

I wander on, in God confiding,
    For all are His, wood, field, and fell;
O'er earth and skies He still presiding,
    For me will order all things well.

* * *

I gaze around me, going
    By forest, dale, and lea,
O'er heights where streams are flowing,
My every thought bestowing,
    Ah, Lady fair, on thee.

351

And in my garden, finding
    Bright flowers fresh and rare,
While many a wreath I'm binding,
Sweet thoughts therein I'm winding
    Of thee, my Lady fair.

For me 'twould be too daring
    To lay them at her feet.
They'll soon away be wearing,
But love beyond comparing
    Is thine, my Lady sweet.

In early morning waking,
    I toil with ready smile,
And though my heart be breaking,
I'll sing to hide its aching,
    And dig my grave the while.

*   *   *

When the earliest morning ray
Through the valley finds its way,
Hill and forest fair awaking,
All who can their flight are taking.

And the lad who's free from care
Shouts, with cap flung high in air,
'Song its flight can aye be winging;
Let me, then, be ever singing.'

THE BROKEN RING

Adown in yon cool valley
    I hear a mill-wheel go:
Alas! my love has left me,
    Who once dwelt there below.

A ring of gold she gave me,
    And vowed she would be true;
The vow long since was broken,
    The gold ring snapped in two.

352

I would I were a minstrel,
  To rove the wide world o'er,
And sing afar my measures,
  And rove from door to door;

Or else a soldier, flying
  Deep into furious flight,
By silent camp-fires lying
  A-field in gloomy night.

Hear I the mill-wheel going:
  I know not what I will;
'Twere best if I were dying—
  Then all were calm and still.

MORNING PRAYER

O silence, wondrous and profound!
  O'er earth doth solitude still reign;
The woods alone incline their heads,
  As if the Lord walked o'er the plain.

I feel new life within me glow;
  Where now is my distress and care?
Here in the blush of waking morn,
  I blush at yesterday's despair.

To me, a pilgrim, shall the world,
  With all its joy and sorrows, be
But as a bridge that leads, O Lord,
  Across the stream of time to Thee.

And should my song woo worldly gifts,
  The base rewards of vanity—
Dash down my lyre! I'll hold my peace
  Before thee to eternity.

GEORGE ELIOT

GEORGE ELIOT (Mary Ann Evans, English 1819-1880). Leading author of
the Victorian novel. Was assistant editor of *Westminster Review*, knew many
intellectuals of her day. Novels marked by deep humanity, subtle psychology,
concern for philosophical issues. *Middlemarch*, her masterpiece, a detailed
study of Victorian Era. Others: *Adam Bede, The Mill on the Floss, Silas
Marner, Romola.*

SILAS MARNER

I. *Why Silas Came to Raveloe*

IN the early years of the nineteenth century a linen-weaver named
Silas Marner worked at his vocation in a stone cottage that stood
among the nutty hedgerows near the village of Raveloe, and not far
from the edge of a deserted stone-pit.

It was fifteen years since Silas Marner had first come to Raveloe;
he was then simply a pallid young man with prominent, short-sighted
brown eyes. To the villagers among whom he had to settle he seemed
to have mysterious peculiarities, chiefly owing to his advent from an
unknown region called "Northard." He invited no comer to step
across his door-sill, and he never strolled into the village to drink
a pint at the Rainbow, or to gossip at the wheel-wrights'; he sought
no man or woman, save for the purposes of his calling, or in order
to supply himself with necessaries.

At the end of fifteen years the Raveloe men said just the same
things about Silas Marner as at the beginning. There was only one
important addition which the years had brought; it was that Master
Marner had laid by a fine sight of money somewhere, and that he
could buy up "bigger men than himself."

But while his daily habits presented scarcely any visible change,
Marner's inward life had been a history and a metamorphosis as
that of every fervid nature must be when it has been condemned
to solitude. His life, before he came to Raveloe, had been filled with
the close fellowship of a narrow religious sect, where the poorest
layman had the chance of distinguishing himself by gifts of speech;
and Marner was highly thought of in that little hidden world, known
to itself as the church assembling in Lantern Yard. He was believed
to be a young man of exemplary life and ardent faith, and a peculiar interest had been centred in him ever since he had fallen at

a prayer-meeting into a trance or cataleptic fit, which lasted for an hour.

Among the members of his church there was one young man, named William Dane, with whom he lived in close friendship; and it seemed to the unsuspecting Silas that the friendship suffered no chill, even after he had formed a closer attachment, and had become engaged to a young servant-woman.

At this time the senior deacon was taken dangerously ill, and Silas and William, with others of the brethren, took turns at night-watching. On the night the old man died, Silas fell into one of his trances, and when he awoke at four o'clock in the morning death had come, and further, a little bag of money had been stolen from the deacon's bureau, and Silas's pocket-knife was found inside the bureau. For some time Silas was mute with astonishment, then he said, "God will clear me; I know nothing about the knife being there, or the money being gone. Search me and my dwelling."

The search was made, and it ended in William Dane finding the deacon's bag, empty, tucked behind the chest of drawers in Silas's chamber.

According to the principles of the church in Lantern Yard prosecution was forbidden to Christians. But the members were bound to take other measures for finding out the truth, and they resolved on praying and drawing lots; there was nothing unusual about such proceedings a hundred years ago. Silas knelt with his brethren, relying on his own innocence being certified by immediate Divine interference. *The lots declared that Silas Marner was guilty.* He was solemnly suspended from church-membership, and called upon to render up the stolen money; only on confession and repentance could he be received once more within the fold of the church. Marner listened in silence. At last, when everyone rose to depart, he went towards William Dane and said, in a voice shaken by agitation, "The last time I remember using my knife was when I took it to cut a strap for you. I don't remember putting it in my pocket again. *You* stole the money, and you have woven a plot to lay the sin at my door. But you may prosper for all that; there is no just God, but a God of lies, that bears witness against the innocent!"

There was a general shudder at this blasphemy. Poor Marner went out with that despair in his soul—that shaken trust in God and man which is little short of madness to a loving nature. In the bitterness of his wounded spirit, he said to himself, "*She* will cast me off, too!" and for a whole day he sat alone, stunned by despair.

The second day he took refuge from benumbing unbelief by getting into his loom and working away as usual, and before many hours were past, the minister and one of the deacons came to him with a message from Sarah, the young woman to whom he had been engaged, that she held her engagement at an end. In little more than a month from that time Sarah was married to William Dane, and not long afterwards it was known to the brethren in Lantern Yard that Silas Marner had departed from the town.

II. *The Second Blow*

When Silas Marner first came to Raveloe he seemed to weave like a spider, from pure impulse, without reflection. Then there were the calls of hunger, and Silas, in his solitude, had to provide his own breakfast, dinner, and supper, to fetch his own water from the well, and put his own kettle on the fire; and all these immediate promptings helped to reduce his life to the unquestioning activity of a spinning insect. He hated the thought of the past; there was nothing that called out his love and fellowship towards the strangers he had come amongst; and the future was all dark, for there was no Unseen Love that cared for him.

It was then, when all purpose of life was gone, that Silas got into the habit of looking towards the money he received for his weaving, and grasping it with a sense of fulfilled effort. Gradually, the guineas, the crowns, and the half-crowns, grew to a heap, and Marner drew less and less for his own wants, trying to solve the problem of keeping himself strong enough to work sixteen hours a day on as small an outlay as possible. He handled his coins, he counted them, till their form and colour were like the satisfaction of a thirst to him; but it was only in the night, when his work was done, that he drew them out, to enjoy their companionship. He had taken up some bricks in his floor underneath his loom, and here he had made a hole in which he set the iron pot that contained his guineas and silver coins, covering the bricks with sand whenever he replaced them.

So, year after year, Silas Marner lived in this solitude, his guineas rising in the iron pot, and his life narrowing and hardening itself more and more as it became reduced to the functions of weaving and hoarding.

This is the history of Silas Marner until the fifteenth year after

he came to Raveloe. Then, about the Christmas of that year, a second great change came over his life.

It was a raw, foggy night, with rain, and Silas was returning from the village, plodding along, with a sack thrown round his shoulders, and with a horn lantern in his hand. His legs were weary, but his mind was at ease with the sense of security that springs from habit. Supper was his favorite meal, because it was his time of revelry, when his heart warmed over his gold.

He reached his door in much satisfaction that his errand was done; he opened it, and to his short-sighted eyes everything remained as he had left it, except that the fire sent out a welcome increase of heat.

As soon as he was warm he began to think it would be a long while to wait till after supper before he drew out his guineas, and it would be pleasant to see them on the table before him as he ate his food.

He rose and placed his candle unsuspectingly on the floor near his loom, swept away the sand, without noticing any change, and removed the bricks. The sight of the empty hole made his heart leap violently, but the belief that his gold was gone could not come at once—only terror, and the eager effort to put an end to the terror. He passed his trembling hand all about the hole, then he held the candle and examined it curiously, trembling more and more. He searched in every corner, he turned his bed over, and shook it, and kneaded it; he looked in the brick oven; and when there was no other place to be searched, he felt once more all round the hole.

He could see every object in his cottage, and his gold was not there. He put his trembling hands to his head, and gave a wild, ringing scream—the cry of desolation. Then the idea of a thief began to present itself, and he entertained it eagerly, because a thief might be caught and made to release the gold. The robber must be laid hold of. Marner's ideas of legal authority were confused, but he felt that he must go and proclaim his loss; and the great people in the village — the clergyman, the constable, and Squire Cass — would make the thief deliver up the stolen money.

It was to the village inn Silas Marner went, where the parish clerk and a select company were assembled, and told the story of his loss—£272 12s. 6d. in all. The machinery of the law was set in motion, but no thief was ever captured, nor could grounds be found for suspicion against any persons.

What had really happened was that Dunsey Cass, Squire Cass's

357

second son — a mean, boastful rascal — on his way home on foot from hunting, saw the light in the weaver's cottage, and knocked, hoping to borrow a lantern, for the lane was unpleasantly slippery, and the night dark. But all was silence in the cottage, for the weaver at that moment had not yet reached home. For a minute Dunsey thought that old Marner might be dead, fallen over the stone pits. And from that came the decision that he must be dead. If so, the question arose, what would become of the money that everybody said the old miser had put by?

Dunstan Cass was in difficulties for want of money, and he had killed his brother's horse that day on the hunting-field. Who would know, if Marner was dead, that anybody had come to take his hoard of money away?

There were only three hiding-places where he had heard of cottagers' hoards being found: the thatch, the bed, and a hole in the floor. His eyes traveling eagerly over the floor, noted a spot where the sand had been more carefully spread.

Dunstan found the hole and the money, now hidden in two leathern bags. From their weight he judged they must be filled with guineas. Quickly he hastened out into the darkness with the bags, and Dunstan Cass was seen no more alive.

At the very moment when he turned his back on the cottage Silas Marner was not more than a hundred yards away.

III. *Silas Marner's Visitor*

It was New Year's Eve, and Squire Cass was giving a dance to the neighbouring gentry of Raveloe. There had been snow in the afternoon, but at seven o'clock it had ceased, and a freezing wind had sprung up.

A woman, shabbily dressed, with a child in her arms, was making her way towards Raveloe, seeking the Red House, where Squire Cass lived. It was not the squire she wanted, but his eldest son, Godfrey, to whom she was secretly married. The marriage—the result of rash impulse—had been an unhappy one from the first, for Godfrey's wife was the slave of opium. The squire had long desired that his son should marry Miss Nancy Lammeter, and would have turned him out of house and home had he known of the unfortunate marriage already contracted. Cold and weariness drove the woman, even while she walked, to the only comfort she knew. She raised the black

remnant to her lips, and then flung the empty phial away. Now she walked, always more and more drowsily, and clutched more and more automatically the sleeping child at her bosom. Soon she felt nothing but a supreme longing to lie down and sleep; and so sank down against a straggling furze-bush, an easy pillow enough; and the bed of snow, too, was soft. The cold was no longer felt, but her arms did not at once relax their instinctive clutch, and the little one slumbered on.

The complete torpor came at last; the fingers lost their tension, the arms unbent; then the little head fell away from the bosom, and the blue eyes of the child opened wide on the cold starlight. At first there was a little peevish cry of "Mammy," as the child rolled downward; and then, suddenly, its eyes were caught by a bright gleaming light on the white ground, and with the ready transition of infancy it decided the light must be caught.

In an instant the child had slipped on all fours, and, after making out that the cunning gleam came from a very bright place, the little one, rising on its legs, toddled through the snow—toddled on to the open door of Silas Marner's cottage, and right up to the warm hearth where was a bright fire.

The little one, accustomed to be left to itself for long hours without notice, squatted down on the old sack spread out before the fire, in perfect contentment. Presently the little golden head sank down, and the blue eyes were veiled by their delicate half-transparent lids.

But where was Silas Marner while this strange visitor had come to his hearth? He was in the cottage, but he did not see the child. Since he had lost his money he had contracted the habit of opening his door, and looking out from time to time, as if he thought that his money might, somehow, be coming back to him.

That morning he had been told by some of his neighbours that it was New Year's Eve, and that he must sit up and hear the old year rung out, and the new rung in, because that was good luck, and might bring his money back again. Perhaps this friendly Raveloe way of jesting had helped to throw Silas into a more than usually excited state. Certainly he opened his door again and again that night, and the last time, just as he put out his hand to close it, the invisible wand of catalepsy arrested him, and there he stood like a graven image, powerless to resist either the good or evil that might enter.

When Marner's sensibility returned he was unaware of the break

359

in his consciousness, and only noticed that he was chilled and faint.

Turning towards the hearth it seemed to his blurred vision as if there was a heap of gold on the floor; but instead of hard coin his fingers encountered soft, warm curls. In utter amazement, Silas fell on his knees to examine the marvel: it was a sleeping child, a round, fair thing, with soft, yellow rings all over its head. Could this be the little sister come back to him in a dream—his little sister whom he had carried about in his arms for a year before she died? That was the first thought. *Was* it a dream? It was very much like his little sister. How and when had the child come in without his knowledge?

But there was a cry on the hearth; the child had awakened, and Marner stooped to lift it on to his knee. He had plenty to do through the next hour. The porridge, sweetened with some dry brown sugar, stopped the cries of the little one for "mammy." Then it occurred to Silas's dull bachelor mind that the child wanted its wet boots off, and this having been done, the wet boots suggested that the child had been walking on the snow.

He made out the marks of the little feet in the snow, and, holding the child in his arms, followed their track to the furze-bush. Then he became aware that there was a human body, half covered with the shifting snow.

With the child in his arms, Silas at once went for the doctor, who was spending the evening at the Red House. And Godfrey Cass recognised that it was his own child he saw in Marner's arms.

The woman was dead—had been dead for some hours, the doctor said: and Godfrey, who had accompanied him to Marner's cottage, understood that he was free to marry Nancy Lammeter.

"You'll take the child to the parish to-morrow?" Godfrey asked, speaking as indifferently as he could.

"Who says so?" said Marner sharply. "Will they make me take her? I shall keep her till anybody shows they've a right to take her away from me. The mother's dead, and I reckon it's got no father. It's a lone thing, and I'm a lone thing. My money's gone—I don't know where, and this is come from I don't know where."

Godfrey returned to the Red House with a sense of relief and gladness, and Silas kept the child. There had been a softening of feeling to him in the village since the day of his robbery, and now an active sympathy was aroused amongst the women. The child was christened Hephzibah, after Marner's mother, and was called Eppie for short.

IV. *Eppie's Decision*

Eppie had come to link Silas Marner once more with the whole world. The disposition to hoard had utterly gone, and there was no longer any repulsion around to him.

As the child grew up, one person watched with keener, though more hidden interest than any other the prosperous growth of Eppie under the weaver's care. The squire was dead, and Godfrey Cass was married to Nancy Lammeter. He had no child of his own save the one that knew him not. No Dunsey had ever turned up, and people had ceased to think of him.

Sixteen years had passed, and now Aaron Winthrop, a well-behaved young gardener, is wanting to marry Eppie, and Eppie is willing to have him "some time."

" 'Everybody's married some time,' Aaron says," said Eppie. "But I told him that wasn't true, for I said look at father—he's never been married."

"No, child," said Silas, "your father was a lone man till you was sent to him."

"But you'll never be lone again, father," said Eppie tenderly. "That was what Aaron said—'I could never think o' taking you away from Master Marner, Eppie.' And I said, 'It 'ud be no use if you did, Aaron.' And he wants us all to live together, so as you needn't work a bit, father, only what's for your own pleasure, and he'd be as good as a son to you—that was what he said."

The proposal to separate Eppie from her foster-father came from Godfrey Cass.

When the old stone-pit by Marner's cottage went dry, owing to drainage operations, the skeleton of Dunstan Cass was found, wedged between two great stones. The watch and seals were recognised, and all the weaver's money was at the bottom of the pit. The shock of this discovery moved Godfrey to tell Nancy the secret of his earlier marriage.

"Everything comes to light, Nancy, sooner or later," he said. "That woman Marner found dead in the snow—Eppie's mother—was my wife. Eppie is my child. I oughtn't to have left the child unowned. I oughtn't to have kept it from you."

"It's but little wrong to me, Godfrey," Nancy answered sadly. "You've made it up to me—you've been good to me for fifteen years. It'll be a different coming to us, now she's grown up."

They were childless, and it hadn't occurred to them as they ap-

361

proached Silas Marner's cottage that Godfrey's offer might be de-clined. At first Godfrey explained that he and his wife wanted to adopt Eppie in place of a daughter.

"Eppie, my child, speak," said old Marner faintly. "I won't stand in your way. Thank Mr. and Mrs. Cass."

"Thank you, ma'am—thank you, sir," said Eppie dropping a curt-sy; "but I can't leave my father, nor own anybody nearer than him."

Godfrey Cass was irritated at this obstacle.

"But I've a claim on you, Eppie," he returned. "It's my duty, Marner, to own Eppie as my child, and provide for her. She's my own child. Her mother was my wife. I've a natural claim on her."

"Then, sir, why didn't you say so sixteen years ago, and claim her before I'd come to love her, i'stead o' coming to take her from me now, when you might as well take the heart out o' my body? When a man turns a blessing from his door, it falls to them as take it in. But let it be as you will. Speak to the child. I'll hinder nothing."

"Eppie, my dear," said Godfrey, looking at his daughter not with-out some embarrassment, "it'll always be our wish that you should show your love and gratitude to one who's been a father to you so many years; but we hope you'll come to love us as well, and though I haven't been what a father should ha' been to you all these years, I wish to do the utmost in my power for you now, and provide for you as my only child. And you'll have the best of mothers in my wife."

Eppie did not come forward and curtsy as she had done before, but she held Silas's hand in hers and grasped it firmly.

"Thank you, ma'am—thank you, sir, for your offers—they're very great and far above my wish. For I should have no delight in life any more if I was forced to go away from my father."

In vain Nancy expostulated mildly.

"I can't feel as I've got any father but one," said Eppie. "I've always thought of a little home where he'd sit i' the corner, and I should fend and do everything for him. I can't think o' no other home. I wasn't brought up to be a lady, and," she ended passion-ately, "I'm promised to marry a working man, as'll live with father and help me to take care of him."

Godfrey Cass and his wife went out.

A year later Eppie was married, and Mrs. Godfrey Cass provided

the wedding dress, and Mr. Cass made some necessary alterations to suit Silas's larger family.

"Oh, father," said Eppie, when the bridal party returned from the church, "what a pretty home ours is! I think nobody could be happier than we are!"

MIHAIL EMINESCU

MIHAIL EMINESCU (Rumanian, 1850-1889). Outstanding Rumanian poet. Highly sensitive and romantic, unable to adjust to everyday life. Killed by another inmate in insane asylum. Wrote 60 poems, a novel, fairy tales, and articles on wide range of subjects. His pessimism reflected in later Rumanian writers.

SONNET

How many stars in lofty heaven ascending;
How many billows seam the ocean's flowing,
With serried lights and scintillations glowing,
And endless movement—is our thought transcending.
Choose as thou wilt, the road of Life's bestowing;
Rising to greatness, or to crime descending;
Dust and the darkness Fate for each is sending;
To mute oblivion, like the rest, art going.
I saw me dying; 'mid the shadowed porches
They did appear in lonely earth would lay me;
I heard the requiem chants, and saw the torches.
O dulcet shadow; pray thee, draw more nigh me,
That I may feel Death's hovering shade approaches,
With weeping lids and dark wings, pausing by me.

O'ER THE TREES

O'er the trees the moon is showing;
  Stir the leaves in forest brake,
And the alder branches shake,
  Whilst the wistful horn is blowing.

Further wending, further wending;
  Heard more faint, and yet more faint;
To my soul with sorrow blent,
  Healing hope of Death thou'rt sending.

Why art silent, when, becalmèd,
  Turns my sad heart to thy strain?
Gentle horn, wilt sound again,
  Sound for me thy notes encharmèd?

WHY COMEST NOT? WHY COMEST NOT?

Behold the swallows quit the eaves,
And fall the yellowed walnut leaves,
The hoar frost doth the vineyard rot;
Why comest not? Why comest not?

Unto mine arms, O love, return;
Mine eager eyes to thee shall yearn;
My weary head find gentle rest
Upon thy breast; upon thy breast.

Dost thou remember? Oft indeed
We twain did hie o'er vale and mead;
And oft I raised thee, sweetheart mine;
Ah, many a time! Ah, many a time!

On earth full many women dwell
Whose eyes the sparkling stars excel;
But how so bright their eyes may be,
They're not like thee! They're not like thee!

Since thy dear bounty sweet affords
My life the joys of love's accords,
For me thou dost the stars outshine;
Beloved mine! Beloved mine!

Now speed the last of Autumn days,
The dead leaves scatter on the ways,
The lonely fields are dank and drear—
Why art not here? Why art not here?

364

EURIPIDES

EURIPIDES (Greek, 485-406 B.C.). The most influential and popular of the
Greek tragedians. The dramatist of great human passions, as opposed to more
philosophic conceptions of Aeschylus and Sophocles. Wrote over 80 plays, of
which 19 survive—including *Alcestis, Medea, Electra, Orestes.* These seem
almost modern in portrayal of strong personalities in grip of warring emotions.

MEDEA'S WRONGS

Nurse of Medea.   All is variance now
And hate: for Jason, to his children false,
False to my mistress, for a royal bride
Hath left her couch, and wedded Creon's daughter,
Lord of this land. Ill doth Medea brook
This base dishonor; on his oath she calls,
Recalls their plighted hands, the firmest pledge
Of mutual faith, and calls the gods to witness
What a requital she from Jason finds.
Of food regardless, and in sorrow sunk
She lies, and melts in tears each tedious hour
Since first she knew her lord had injured her;
Nor lifts her eye, nor lifts her face from the earth
Deaf to her friends' entreaties as a rock,
Or billow of the sea; save when she turns
Her snowy neck, and to herself bewails
Her father, and her country, and her house,
Which she betray'd to follow this base man,
Who treats her now with such indignity.
Affliction now hath taught her what it is
Not to forsake a parent and his house.
She hates her children, nor with pleasure sees them.
I fear her, lest she form some strange design;
For violent her temper, and of wrongs
Impatient: well I know her, and I fear her,
Lest, in the dead of night, when all are laid
In deep repose, she steal into the house,
And plunge into their breast the piercing sword;
Or murder ev'n the monarch of the land,
Or the new-married Jason, on herself
Drawing severer ills: for like a storm
Her passions swell, and he that dares enrage her
Will have small cause to boast his victory.

But see, her sons from the gymnastic ring
Returning, heedless of their mother's ills;
For youth holds no society with grief.

Enter Tutor, with the Sons of Medea.

Tut. Thou old domestic servant of my mistress,
Why dost thou take thy station at the gates,
And ruminate in silence on thy griefs?
How hath Medea wish'd to be alone?

Nur. Thou good old man, attendant on the sons
Of Jason, faithful servants with their lords
Suffer in their afflictions, and their hearts
Are touch'd with social sorrow; and my griefs
Swell, for Medea's sufferings, to such height,
That strong desire impell'd me to come forth,
And tell them to the earth and to the skies.

Tut. Admits she yet no respite to her groans?

Nur. I wonder at thee: no, these ills but now
Are rising, to their height not yet advanced.

Tut. I heard one say, not seeming to attend,
But passing on to where they play with dice,
Among the grave old men, who then by chance
Were sitting near Pirene's hallow'd stream,
That Creon, lord of this fair land, will drive
These children and their mother from the state
Of Corinth: whether this report be true
I know not, but I wish it otherwise.

Nur. Will Jason bear to see his sons thus wrong'd,
Though he regards their mother now no more?

Tut. To new alliances the old gives place,
And to this house he is no more a friend.

Nur. Ruin would follow, to the former ill
If this were added ere the first subsides.

Tut. Be cautious then; it were unseasonable
Our queen knew this; in silence close thy lips.

Nur. Go in, my children, go: all will be well;
And take thou heed, keep them aloof, nor let them
Come near their mother while her griefs are fresh:
Cruel her eye, and wild; I mark'd it late,
Expressive of some dark design on these:

366

Nor will she check her fury, well I know,
Till the storm bursts on some one: may its stroke
Fall on some hostile head, not on a friend.

    Medea (within.) Wretch that I am, what anguish rends my
        heart!
Wretched Medea, how art thou undone!

    Nur. Ay, thus it is. Your mother, my dear children,
Swells with resentment, swells with rage. Go in,
Go quickly in; but come not in her eye,
Approach her not, but keep you from the wild
And dreadful fury of her violent temper.
Go now, go quickly in; this rising cloud
Of grief forebodes a storm, which soon will fall
With greater rage: inflamed with injuries,
What will not her tempestuous spirit dare?

    Med. Ah me! ah me! what mighty wrongs I bear,
Wrongs that demand my tears and loud laments!
Ye sons accursed of a detested mother,
Perish, together with your father perish,
And in one general ruin sink your house!

    Nur. Ah me unhappy! in their father's fault
Why make thy sons associates? Why on them
Rises thy hatred? Oh, I fear, I fear,
My children, lest some evil threatens you.
Kings have a fiery quality of soul,
Accustom'd to command; if once they feel
Control, though small, their anger blazes out,
Not easily extinguish'd; hence I deem
An equal mediocrity of life
More to be wish'd; if not in gorgeous state,
Yet without danger glides it on to age.
There's a protection in its very name,
And happiness dwells with it: but the height
Of towering greatness long to mortal man
Remains not fix'd, and, when misfortune comes
Enraged, in deeper ruin sinks the house.

    Chorus. I heard the voice, I heard the loud laments
Of the unhappy Colchian: do her griefs
(Say, reverend matron), find no respite yet?
From the door's opening valve I heard her voice.
No pleasure in the sorrows of your home

I take; for deeds are done not grateful to me.

Nur. This is no more a home; all here is vanish'd,
Nor leaves a trace behind. The monarch's house
He makes his own; while my unhappy mistress
In her lone chamber melts her life away
In tears, unmoved by all the arguments
Urged by her friends to soothe her sorrowing soul.

Med. O that the ethereal lightning on this head
Would fall! Why longer should I wish to live?
Unhappy me! Death would be welcome now,
And kindly free me from this hated life.

Cho. Dost thou hear this, O Jove, O Earth, O Light,
The mournful voice of this unhappy dame?
Why thus indulge this unabated force
Of nuptial love, self-rigorous, hastening death?
Let it not be thy wish: if a new bed
Now charms thy husband, be not his offence
Engraved too deep: Jove will avenge thy wrongs;
Let not thy sorrows prey upon thy heart.

Med. O powerful Themis, O revered Diana,
See what I suffer, though with sacred oaths
This vile, accursed husband I had bound!
Oh, might I one day see him and his bride
Rent piecemeal in their house, who unprovoked
Have dared to wrong me thus! Alas, my father!
Alas, my country! whom my shameful flight
Abandon'd, having first my brother slain!

Cho. I hear her lamentations mixed with groans,
Which in the anguish of her heart she vents;
And on her faithless husband, who betray'd
Her bed, she calls aloud; upon the gods,
Thus basely wrong'd, she calls, attesting Themis,
Daughter of Jove, the arbitress of oaths,
Who led her to the shores of Greece, across
The rolling ocean, when the shades of night
Darken'd its waves, and steer'd her through the straits.

MEDEA'S LAST WORDS TO HER CHILDREN

O children, children! you have still a city,
A home, where, lost to me and all my woe,
You will live out your lives without a mother!

But I—lo! I am for another land,
Leaving the joy of you. To see you happy,
To deck your marriage-bed, to greet your bride,
To light your wedding torch shall not be mine!
O me, thrice wretched in my own self-will!
In vain then, dear my children! did I rear you;
In vain I travailed, and with wearing sorrow
Bore bitter anguish in the hour of childbirth!
Yea, of a sooth, I had great hope of you,
That you should cherish my old age, and deck
My corpse with loving hands, and make me blessed
'Mid women in my death. But now, ah me!
Hath perished that sweet dream. For long without you
I shall drag out a dreary, doleful age.
And you shall never see your mother more
With your dear eyes: for all your life is changed.
Woe, woe!
Why gaze you at me with your eyes, my children?
Why smile your last sweet smile? Ah me! ah me!
What shall I do? My heart dissolves within me,
Friends, when I see the glad eyes of my sons!
I cannot. No: my will that was so steady,
Farewell to it. They too shall go with me:
Why should I wound their sire with what wounds them,
Heaping tenfold his woes on my own head?
No, no, I shall not. Perish my proud will.
Yet whence this weakness? Do I wish to reap
The scorn that springs from enemies unpunished?
Dare it I must. What craven fool am I,
To let soft thoughts flow trickling from my soul!
Go, boys, into the house: and he who may not
Be present at my solemn sacrifice—
Let him see to it. My hand shall not falter.
Ah! ah!
Nay, do not, O my heart! do not this thing!
Suffer them, O poor fool; yea, spare thy children!
There in thy exile they will gladden thee.
Not so: by all the plagues of nethermost Hell,
It shall not be that I, that I should suffer
My foes to triumph and insult my sons!
Die must they: this must be, and since it must,

369

I, I myself will slay them, I who bore them.
So it is fixed, and there is no escape.
Even as I speak, the crown is on her head,
The bride is dying in her robes, I know it.
But since this path most piteous I tread,
Sending them forth on paths more piteous far,
I will embrace my children. O my sons,
Give, give your mother your dear hands to kiss!
O dearest hands, and mouths most dear to me,
And forms and noble faces of my sons!
Be happy even there: what here was yours,
Your father robs you of. O loved embrace!
O tender touch and sweet breath of my boys!
Go, go, go, leave me! Lo, I cannot bear
To look on you, my woes have overwhelmed me!
Now know I all the ill I have to do:
But rage is stronger than my better mind;
Rage, cause of greatest crimes and griefs to mortals.

ABRAHAM IBN EZRA

ABRAHAM IBN EZRA (Spanish-Hebrew, 1092-1167). Wandering hymnist and
philosopher. Traveled through many non-Moslem lands, so became first
Hebrew-Spaniard to write entirely in Hebrew. Wrote many liturgical poems,
philosophic works, and an Arabic study of Spanish-Hebrew poetry.

I. SONGS

I

The shadow of the houses leave behind,
In the cool boscage of the grove reclined,
The wine of friendship from love's goblet drink,
And entertain with cheerful speech the mind.

Drink, friend! behold, the dreary winter's gone,
The mantle of old age has time withdrawn.
The sunbeam glitters in the morning dew,
O'er hill and vale youth's bloom is surging on.

Cup-bearer! quench with snow the goblet's fire,
Even as the wise man cools and stills his ire.
Look, when the jar is drained, upon the brim
The light foam melteth with the heart's desire.

Cup-bearer! bring anear the silver bowl,
And with the glowing gold fulfil the whole,
Unto the weak new vigor it imparts,
And without lance subdues the hero's soul.

My love sways, dancing, like the myrtle-tree,
The masses of her curls disheveled, see!
She kills me with her darts, intoxicates
My burning blood, and will not set me free.

Within the aromatic garden come,
And slowly in its shadows let us roam,
The foliage be the turban for our brows,
And the green branches o'er our heads a dome.

All pain thou with the goblet shalt assuage,
The wine-cup heals the sharpest pangs that rage,
Let others crave inheritance of wealth,
Joy be our portion and our heritage.

Drink in the garden, friend, anigh the rose,
Richer than spice's breath the soft air blows.
If it should cease a little traitor then,
A zephyr light its secret would disclose.

II

Thou who art clothed in silk, who drawest on
Proudly thy raiment of fine linen spun,
Bethink thee of the day when thou alone
Shalt dwell at last beneath the marble stone.

Anigh the nests of adders thine abode,
With the earth-crawling serpent and the toad.
Trust in the Lord, He will sustain thee there,
And without fear thy soul shall rest with God.

If the world flatter thee with soft-voiced art,
Know 'tis a cunning witch who charms thy heart,
Whose habit is to wed man's soul with grief,
And those who are close-bound in love to part.

He who bestows his wealth upon the poor,
Has only lent it to the Lord, be sure—
Of what avail to clasp it with clenched hand?
It goes not with us to the grave obscure.

The voice of those who dwell within the tomb,
Who in corruption's house have made their home;
"O ye who wander o'er us still today,
When will ye come to share with us the gloom?"

How can'st thou ever of the world complain,
And murmuring, burden it with all thy pain?
Silence! thou art a traveller at an inn,
A guest, who may but over night remain.

Be thou not wroth against the proud, but show
How he who yesterday great joy did know,
Today is begging for his very bread,
And painfully upon a crutch must go.

How foolish they whose faith is fixed upon
The treasures of their worldly wealth alone,
Far wiser were it to obey the Lord,
And only say, "The will of God be done!"

Has Fortune smiled on thee? Oh, do not trust
Her reckless joy, she still deceives and must.
Perpetual snares she spreads about thy feet,
Thou shalt not rest till thou art mixed with dust.

Man is a weaver on the earth, 'tis said,
Who weaves and weaves—his own days are the thread,
And when the length allotted he hath spun,
All life is over, and all hope is dead.

II. IN THE NIGHT

Unto the house of prayer my spirit yearns,
Unto the sources of her being turns,
To where the sacred light of heaven burns,
She struggles thitherward by day and night.

The splendor of God's glory blinds her eyes,
Up without wings she soareth to the skies,
With silent aspiration seeks to rise,
In dusky evening and in darksome night.

To her the wonders of God's works appear,
She longs with fervor Him to draw anear,
The tidings of His glory reach her ear,
From morn to even, and from night to night.

The banner of thy grace did o'er me rest,
Yet was thy worship banished from my breast.
Almighty, thou didst seek me out and test
To try and to instruct me in the night.

Infatuate I trifled youth away,
In nothingness dreamed through my manhood's day.
Therefore my streaming tears I may not stay,
They are my meat and drink by day and night.

In flesh imprisoned is the son of light,
This life is but a bridge when seen aright.
Rise in the silent hour and pray with might,
Awake and call upon the God by night!

Hasten to cleanse thyself of sin, arise!
Follow Truth's path that leads unto the skies,
As swift as yesterday existence flies,
Brief even as a watch within the night.

Man enters life for trouble; all he has,
And all that he beholds, is pain, alas!
Like to a flower does he bloom and pass,
He fadeth like a vision of the night.

The surging floods of life around him roar,
Death feeds upon him, pity is no more,
To others all his riches he gives o'er,
And dieth in the middle hour of night.

Crushed by the burden of my sins I pray,
Oh, wherefore shunned I not the evil way?
Deep are my sighs, I weep the livelong day,
And wet my couch with tears night after night.

My spirit stirs, my streaming tears still run,
Like to the wild birds' notes my sorrows' tone,
In the hushed silence loud resounds my groan,
My soul arises moaning in the night.

Within her narrow soul oppressed with dread,
Bare of adornment and with grief-bowed head
Lamenting, many a tear her sad eyes shed,
She weeps with anguish in the gloomy night.

For tears my burden seem to lighten best,
Could I but weep my heart's blood, I might rest.
My spirit bows with mighty grief oppressed,
I utter forth my prayer within the night.

Youth's charm has like a fleeting shadow gone,
With eagle wings the hours of life have flown.
Alas! the time when pleasure I have known,
I may not now recall by day or night.

The haughty scorn pursues me of my foe,
Evil his thought, yet soft his speech and low.
Forget it not, but bear his purpose so
Forever in thy mind by day and night.

Observe a pious fast, be whole again,
Hasten to purge thy heart of every stain.
No more from prayer and penitence refrain,
But turn unto thy God by day and night.

374

He speaks: "My son, yea, I will send thee aid,
Bend thou thy steps to me, be not afraid.
No nearer friend than I am, hast thou made,
Possess thy soul in patience one more night."

III. ELEGY

My thoughts impelled me to the resting-place
Where sleep my parents, many a friend and brother.
I asked them (no one heard and none replied) : .
"Do ye forsake me, too, oh father, mother?"
Then from the grave, without a tongue, these cried,
And showed my own place waiting by their side.

F

WILLIAM FAULKNER

WILLIAM FAULKNER (American, 1897-   ). Considered by some the most important American novelist, but until recently more admired abroad than in this country. Nobel Prize winner, 1949. Novels describe decay of a Southern county and its major families. Major works: *The Sound and the Fury, As I Lay Dying, Light in August, Intruder in the Dust, A Fable.*

A ROSE FOR EMILY

WHEN Miss Emily Grierson died, our whole town went to her funeral: the men through a sort of respectful affection for a fallen monument, the women mostly out of curiosity to see the inside of her house, which no one save an old man-servant—a combined gardener and cook—had seen in at least ten years.

It was a big, squarish frame house that had once been white, decorated with cupolas and spires and scrolled balconies in the heavily lightsome style of the Seventies, set on what had once been our most select street. But garages and cotton gins had encroached and obliterated even the august names of that neighborhood; only Miss Emily's house was left, lifting its stubborn and coquettish decay above the cotton wagons and the gasoline pumps—an eyesore among eyesores. And now Miss Emily had gone to join the representatives of those august names where they lay in the cedar-bemused cemetery among the ranked and anonymous graves of Union and Confederate soldiers who fell at the battle of Jefferson.

Alive, Miss Emily had been a tradition, a duty, and a care; a sort of hereditary obligation upon the town, dating from that day in 1894 when Colonel Sartoris, the mayor—he who fathered the edict that no Negro woman should appear on the streets without an apron —remitted her taxes, the dispensation dating from the death of her

father on into perpetuity. Not that Miss Emily would have accepted charity. Colonel Sartoris invented an involved tale to the effect that Miss Emily's father had loaned money to the town, which the town, as a matter of business, preferred this way of repaying. Only a man of Colonel Sartoris' generation and thought could have invented it, and only a woman could have believed it.

When the next generation, with its more modern ideas, became mayors and aldermen, this arrangement created some little dissatisfaction. On the first of the year they mailed her a tax notice. February came, and there was no reply. They wrote her a formal letter, asking her to call at the sheriff's office at her convenience. A week later the mayor wrote her himself, offering to call or send his car for her, and received in reply a note on paper of an archaic shape, in a thin, flowing calligraphy in faded ink, to the effect that she no longer went out at all. The tax notice was also enclosed, without comment.

They called a special meeting of the Board of Aldermen. A deputation waited upon her, knocked at the door through which no visitor had passed since she ceased giving china-painting lessons eight or ten years earlier. They were admitted by the old Negro into a dim hall from which a stairway mounted into still more shadow. It smelled of dust and disuse—a close, dank smell. The Negro led them into the parlor. It was furnished in heavy, leather-covered furniture. When the Negro opened the blinds of one window, they could see that the leather was cracked; and when they sat down, a faint dust rose sluggishly about their thighs, spinning with slow motes in the single sun-ray. On a tarnished gilt easel before the fireplace stood a crayon portrait of Miss Emily's father.

They rose when she entered—a small, fat woman in black, with a thin gold chain descending to her waist and vanishing into her belt, leaning on an ebony cane with a tarnished gold head. Her skeleton was small and spare; perhaps that was why what would have been merely plumpness in another was obesity in her. She looked bloated, like a body long submerged in motionless water, and of that pallid hue. Her eyes, lost in the fatty ridges of her face, looked like two small pieces of coal pressed into a lump of dough as they moved from one face to another while the visitors stated their errand.

She did not ask them to sit. She just stood in the door and listened quietly until the spokesman came to a stumbling halt. Then they could hear the invisible watch ticking at the end of the gold chain. Her voice was dry and cold. "I have no taxes in Jefferson. Colonel

Sartoris explained it to me. Perhaps one of you can gain access to the city records and satisfy yourselves."

"But we have. We are the city authorities, Miss Emily. Didn't you get a notice from the sheriff, signed by him?"

"I received a paper, yes," Miss Emily said. "Perhaps he considers himself the sheriff . . . I have no taxes in Jefferson."

"But there is nothing on the books to show that, you see. We must go by the—"

"See Colonel Sartoris. I have no taxes in Jefferson."

"But, Miss Emily—"

"See Colonel Sartoris." (Colonel Sartoris had been dead almost ten years.) "I have no taxes in Jefferson. Tobe!" The Negro appeared. "Show these gentlemen out."

II

So she vanquished them, horse and foot, just as she had vanquished their fathers thirty years before about the smell. That was two years after her father's death and a short time after her sweetheart—the one we believed would marry her—had deserted her. After her father's death she went out very little; after her sweetheart went away, people hardly saw her at all. A few of the ladies had the temerity to call, but were not received, and the only sign of life about the place was the Negro man—a young man then—going in and out with a market basket.

"Just as if a man—any man—could keep a kitchen properly," the ladies said; so they were not surprised when the smell developed. It was another link between the gross, teeming world and the high and mighty Griersons.

A neighbor, a woman, complained to the mayor, Judge Stevens, eighty years old.

"But what will you have me do about it, madam?" he said.

"Why, send her word to stop it," the woman said. "Isn't there a law?"

"I'm sure that won't be necessary," Judge Stevens said. "It's probably a snake or a rat that nigger of hers killed in the yard. I'll speak to him about it."

The next day he received two more complaints, one from a man who came in diffident deprecation. "We really must do something about it, Judge. I'd be the last one in the world to bother Miss

378.

Emily, but we've got to do something." That night the Board of Aldermen met—three gray-beards and one younger man, a member of the rising generation.

"It's simple enough," he said. "Send her word to have her place cleaned up. Give her a certain time to do it in, and if she don't . . ."

"Dammit, sir," Judge Stevens said, "will you accuse a lady to her face of smelling bad?"

So the next night, after midnight, four men crossed Miss Emily's lawn and slunk about the house like burglars, sniffing along the base of the brickwork and at the cellar openings while one of them performed a regular sowing motion with his hand out of a sack slung from his shoulder. They broke open the cellar door and sprinkled lime there, and in all the outbuildings. As they recrossed the lawn, a window that had been dark was lighted and Miss Emily sat in it, the light behind her, and her upright torso motionless as that of an idol. They crept quietly across the lawn and into the shadow of the locusts that lined the street. After a week or two the smell went away.

That was when people had begun to feel really sorry for her. People in our town, remembering how Old Lady Wyatt, her great-aunt, had gone completely crazy at last, believed that the Griersons held themselves a little too high for what they really were. None of the young men was quite good enough to Miss Emily and such. We had long thought of them as a tableau: Miss Emily a slender figure in white in the background, her father a spraddled silhouette in the foreground, his back to her and clutching a horse-whip, the two of them framed by the back-flung front door. So when she got to be thirty and was still single, we were not pleased exactly, but vindicated; even with insanity in the family she wouldn't have turned down all of her chances if they had really materialized.

When her father died, it got about that the house was all that was left to her; and in a way, people were glad. At last they could pity Miss Emily. Being left alone, and a pauper, she had become human-ized. Now she too would know the old thrill and the old despair of a penny more or less.

The day after his death all the ladies prepared to call at the house and offer condolence and aid, as is our custom. Miss Emily met them at the door, dressed as usual and with no trace of grief on her face. She told them that her father was not dead. She did that for three days, with the ministers calling on her, and the doctors, try-

ing to persuade her to let them dispose of the body. Just as they were about to resort to law and force, she broke down, and they buried her father quickly.

We did not say she was crazy then. We believed she had to do that. We remembered all the young men her father had driven away, and we knew that with nothing left, she would have to cling to that which had robbed her, as people will.

III

She was sick for a long time. When we saw her again, her hair was cut short, making her look like a girl, with a vague resemblance to those angels in colored church windows—sort of tragic and serene.

The town had just let the contracts for paving the sidewalks, and in the summer after her father's death they began the work. The construction company came with niggers and mules and machinery, singing in time to the rise and fall of picks. Pretty soon he knew everybody in town. Whenever you heard a lot of laughing any-man, with a big voice and eyes lighter than his face. The little boys would follow in groups to hear him cuss the niggers, and the niggers and a foreman named Homer Barron, a Yankee—a big, dark, ready where about the square, Homer Barron would be in the center of the group. Presently we began to see him and Miss Emily on Sunday afternoons driving in the yellow-wheeled buggy and the matched team of bays from the livery stable.

At first we were glad that Miss Emily would have an interest because the ladies all said, "Of course a Grierson would not think seriously of a Northerner, a day laborer." But there were still others, older people, who said that even grief could not cause a real lady to forget *noblesse oblige*—without calling it *noblesse oblige*. They just said, "Poor Emily. Her kinsfolk should come to her." She had some kin in Alabama; but years ago her father had fallen out with them over the estate of Old Lady Wyatt, the crazy woman, and there was no communication between the two families. They had not even been represented at the funeral.

And as soon as the old people said, "Poor Emily," the whispering began. "Do you suppose it's really so?" they said to one another. "Of course it is. What else could . . ." This behind their hands; rustling of craned silk and satin behind jalousies closed upon the sun of Sunday afternoon as the thin, swift clop-clop-clop of the matched team passed: "Poor Emily."

She carried her head high enough—even when we believed that she was fallen. It was as if she demanded more than ever the recognition of her dignity as the last Grierson; as if it had wanted that touch of earthiness to reaffirm her imperviousness. Like when she bought the rat poison, the arsenic. That was over a year after they had begun to say "Poor Emily," and while the two female cousins were visiting her.

"I want some poison," she said to the druggist. She was over thirty then, still a slight woman, though thinner than usual, with cold, haughty black eyes in a face the flesh of which was strained across the temples and about the eye-sockets as you imagine a light-house-keeper's face ought to look. "I want some poison," she said.

"Yes, Miss Emily. What kind? For rats and such? I'd recom—"

"I want the best you have. I don't care what kind."

The druggist named several. "They'll kill anything up to an elephant. But what you want is—"

"Arsenic," Miss Emily said. "Is that a good one?"

"Is . . . arsenic? Yes, ma'am. But what you want—"

"I want arsenic."

The druggist looked down at her. She looked back at him, erect, her face like a strained flag. "Why, of course," the druggist said. "If that's what you want. But the law requires you to tell what you are going to use it for."

Miss Emily just stared at him, her head tilted back in order to look him eye for eye, until he looked away and went and got the arsenic and wrapped it up. The Negro delivery boy brought her the package; the druggist didn't come back. When she opened the package at home there was written on the box, under the skull and bones: "For rats."

IV

So the next day we all said, "She will kill herself"; and we said it would be the best thing. When she had first begun to be seen with Homer Barron, we had said, "She will marry him." Then we said, "She will persuade him yet," because Homer himself had remarked—he liked men, and it was known that he drank with the younger men in the Elk's Club—that he was not a marrying man. Later we said, "Poor Emily" behind the jalousies as they passed on Sunday afternoon in the glittering buggy, Miss Emily with her head high and Homer Barron with his hat cocked and a cigar in his teeth, reins and whip in a yellow glove.

Then some of the ladies began to say that it was a disgrace to the town and a bad example to the young people. The men did not want to interfere, but at last the ladies forced the Baptist minister—Miss Emily's people were Episcopal—to call upon her. He would never divulge what happened during that interview, but he refused to go back again. The next Sunday they again drove about the streets, and the following day the minister's wife wrote to Miss Emily's relations in Alabama.

So she had blood-kin under her roof again and we sat back to watch developments. At first nothing happened. Then we were sure that they were to be married. We learned that Miss Emily had been to the jeweler's and ordered a man's toilet set in silver, with the letter H. B. on each piece. Two days later we learned that she had bought a complete outfit of men's clothing, including a nightshirt, and we said, "They are married." We were really glad. We were glad because the two female cousins were even more Grierson than Miss Emily had ever been.

So we were not surprised when Homer Barron—the streets had been finished some time since—was gone. We were a little disappointed that there was not a public blowing-off, but we believed that he had gone on to prepare for Miss Emily's coming, or to give her a chance to get rid of the cousins. (By that time it was a cabal, and we were all Miss Emily's allies to help circumvent the cousins.) Sure enough, after another week they departed. And, as we had expected all along, within three days Homer Barron was back in town. A neighbor saw the Negro man admit him at the kitchen door at dusk one evening.

And that was the last we saw of Homer Barron. And of Miss Emily for some time. The Negro man went in and out with the market basket, but the front door remained closed. Now and then we would see her at a window for a moment, as the men did that night when they sprinkled the lime, but for almost six months she did not appear on the streets. Then we knew that this was to be expected too; as if that quality of her father which had thwarted her woman's life so many times had been too virulent and too furious to die.

When we next saw Miss Emily, she had grown fat and her hair was turning gray. During the next few years it grew grayer and grayer until it attained an even pepper-and-salt iron-gray, when it ceased turning. Up to the day of her death at seventy-four it was still that vigorous iron-gray, like the hair of an active man.

From that time on her front door remained closed, save for a period of six or seven years, when she was about forty, during which she gave lessons in china-painting. She fitted up a studio in one of the downstairs rooms, where the daughters and granddaughters of Colonel Sartoris' contemporaries were sent to her with the same regularity and in the same spirit that they were sent to church on Sundays with a twenty-five-cent piece for the collection plate. Meanwhile her taxes had been remitted.

Then the newer generation became the backbone and the spirit of the town, and the painting pupils grew up and fell away and did not send their children to her with boxes of color and tedious brushes and pictures cut from the ladies' magazines. The front door closed upon the last one and remained closed for good. When the town got free postal delivery, Miss Emily alone refused to let them fasten the metal numbers above her door and attach a mailbox to it. She would not listen to them.

Daily, monthly, yearly we watched the Negro grow grayer and more stooped, going in and out with the market basket. Each December we sent her a tax notice, which would be returned by the post office a week later, unclaimed. Now and then we would see her in one of the downstairs windows—she had evidently shut up the top floor of the house—like the carven torso of an idol in a niche, looking or not looking at us, we could never tell which. Thus she passed from generation to generation—dear, inescapable, impervious, tranquil, and perverse.

And so she died. Fell ill in the house filled with dust and shadows, with only a doddering Negro man to wait on her. We did not even know she was sick; we had long since given up trying to get any information from the Negro. He talked to no one, probably not even to her, for his voice had grown harsh and rusty, as if from disuse.

She died in one of the downstairs rooms, in a heavy walnut bed with a curtain, her gray head propped on a pillow yellow and moldy with age and lack of sunlight.

V

The Negro met the first of the ladies at the front door and let them in, with their hushed, sibilant voices and their quick, curious glances, and then he disappeared. He walked right through the house and out the back and was not seen again.

The two female cousins came at once. They held the funeral on

the second day, with the town coming to look at Miss Emily beneath a mass of bought flowers, with the crayon face of her father musing profoundly above the bier and the ladies sibilant and macabre; and the very old men—some in their brushed Confederate uniforms—on the porch and the lawn, talking of Miss Emily as if she had been a contemporary of theirs, believing that they had danced with her and courted her perhaps, confusing time with its mathematical progression, as the old do, to whom all the past is not a diminishing road but, instead, a huge meadow which no winter ever quite touches, divided from them now by the narrow bottle-neck of the most recent decade of years.

Already we knew that there was one room in that region above stairs which no one had seen in forty years, and which would have to be forced. They waited until Miss Emily was decently in the ground before they opened it.

The violence of breaking down the door seemed to fill this room with pervading dust. A thin, acrid pall as of the tomb seemed to lie everywhere upon this room decked and furnished as for a bridal; upon the valence curtains of faded rose color, upon the rose-shaded lights, upon the dressing table, upon the delicate array of crystal and the man's toilet things backed with tarnished silver, silver so tarnished that the monogram was obscured. Among them lay a collar and tie, as if they had just been removed, which, lifted, left upon the surface a pale crescent in the dust. Upon a chair hung the suit, carefully folded; beneath it the two mute shoes and the discarded socks.

The man himself lay in the bed.

For a long while we just stood there, looking down at the profound and fleshless grin. The body had apparently once lain in the attitude of an embrace, but now the long sleep that outlasts love, that conquers even the grimace of love, had cuckolded him. What was left of him, rotted beneath what was left of the nightshirt, had become inextricable from the bed in which he lay; and upon him and upon the pillow beside him lay that even coating of the patient and biding dust.

Then we noticed that in the second pillow was the indentation of a head. One of us lifted something from it, and leaning forward, that faint and invisible dust dry and acrid in the nostrils, we saw a long strand of iron-gray hair.

384

FIRDAUSI

FIRDAUSI (Abul Kasim Mansur, Persian, ca. 941-1025). The Persian Homer. The *Shah-namah*, commissioned by Persia's ruler, recounts in 60,000 couplets Iran's legends and history from prehistoric times to Arab conquest. Spent most of life on this, one of world's great epics. Influenced all later Persian poets.

RUSTAM AND AKWAN DEV

Kai Khosrau sat in a garden bright
  With all the beauties of balmy Spring;
And many a warrior armor-dight
With a stout kamand and an arm of might
  Supported Persia's King.

With trembling mien and a pallid cheek,
  A breathless hind to the presence ran;
And on bended knee, in posture meek,
With faltering tongue that scarce could speak,
  His story thus began:—

"Alackaday! for the news I bear
  Will like to the follies of Fancy sound;
Thy steeds were stabled and stalled with care,
When a Wild Ass sprang from its forest lair
  With a swift resistless bound,—

"A monster fell, of a dusky hue,
  And eyes that flashed with a hellish glow;
Many it maimed and some it slew,
Then back to the forest again it flew,
  As an arrow leaves the bow."

Kai Khosrau's rage was a sight to see:
  "Now curses light on the foul fiend's head!
Full rich and rare shall his guerdon be
Whose stalwart arm shall bring to me
  The monster, alive or dead!"

But the mail-clad warriors kept their ground,
   And their bronzèd cheeks were blanched with fear;
With scorn the Shah on the cowards frowned,—
"One champion bold may yet be found
   While Rustam wields a spear!"

No tarrying made the son of Zal,
   Small reck had he of the fiercest fray;
But promptly came at the monarch's call,
And swore that the monster fiend should fall
   Ere closed the coming day.

The swift Rakush's sides he spurred,
   And speedily gained the darksome wood;
Nor was the trial for long deferred,—
But soon a hideous roar was heard,
   Had chilled a baser blood.

Then darting out like a flashing flame,
   Traverse his path the Wild Ass fled;
And the hero then with unerring aim
Hurled his stout kamand, but as erst it came,
   Unscathed the monster fled.

"Now Khuda in heaven!" bold Rustam cried,—
   "Thy chosen champion deign to save!
Not all in vain shall my steel be tried,
Though he who my powers has thus defied
   Be none but Akwan Dev."

Then steadily chasing his fiendish foe,
   He thrust with hanger, he smote with brand:
But ever avoiding the deadly blow
It vanished away like the scenes that show
   On Balkh's delusive sand.

For full three wearisome nights and days
   Stoutly he battled with warlike skill;
But the Demon such magical shifts essays
That leaving his courser at large to graze,
   He rests him on a hill.

But scare can slumber his eyelids close,
    Ere Akwan Dev from afar espies;
And never disturbing his foe's repose
The earth from under the mound he throws,
    And off with the summit flies.

"Now, daring mortal!" the Demon cried,—
    "Whither wouldst have me carry thee?
Shall I cast thee forth on the mountain side,
Where the lions roar and the reptiles glide,
    Or hurl thee into the sea?"

"O bear me off to the mountain side,
    Where the lions roar and the serpents creep!
For I fear not the creatures that spring or glide;
But where is the arm that can stem the tide,
    Or still the raging deep?"

Loud laughed the fiend as his load he threw
    Far plunging into the roaring flood;
And louder laughed Rustam as out he flew,
For he fain had chosen the sea, but knew
    The fiend's malignant mood.

Soon all the monsters that float or swim,
    With ravening jaws down on him bore;
But he hewed and hacked them limb from limb,
And the wave pellucid grew thick and dim
    With streaks of crimson gore.

With thankful bosom he gains the strand,
    And seeketh his courser near and far,
Till he hears him neigh, and he sees him stand
Among the herds of a Tartar band,
    The steeds of Isfendiyar.

But Rustam's name was a sound of dread,
    And the Tartar heart it had caused to quake;
The herd was there, but the hinds had fled,—
So all the horses he captive led
    For good Kai Khosrau's sake.

Then loud again through the forest rings
  The fiendish laugh and the taunting cry;
But his kamand quickly the hero flings,
And around the Demon it coils and clings,
  As a cobweb wraps a fly.

Kai Khosrau sat in his garden fair,
  Mourning his Champion lost and dead,
When a shout of victory rent the air,
And Rustam placed before his chair
  A Demon Giant's head.

GUSTAVE FLAUBERT

GUSTAVE FLAUBERT (French, 1821-1880). One of the great French stylists. Recluse because of epilepsy, devoted self to cult of classical art. *Salammbô* and *The Temptation of Saint Anthony*, masterpieces of romanticism; *Madame Bovary*, the great novel of French realism. Other works: *The Sentimental Education, Bouvard and Pécuchet.* Flaubert's struggle for objectivity defeated itself, but he remains one of greatest novelists.

SALAMMBÔ AND HER LOVER

MATHO was bound on the elephant's back, his four limbs crosswise, and all the unwounded escorted him, hurrying with a great commotion back to Carthage.

The water-clock of Khamoûn marked the fifth hour of the night when they reached Malqua. Here Matho reopened his eyes. There were such vast numbers of lights on the houses that the city seemed to be all in flames.

A mighty clamor came confusedly to him, and lying on his back he gazed at the stars. Then a door closed upon him, and darkness enveloped him. . . .

There were rejoicings at Carthage — rejoicings deep, universal, extravagant, frantic; the holes of the ruins had been stopped up, the statues of the Gods had been repainted, the streets were strewn with myrtle branches, incense smoked at the corners of the crossways, and the throng on the terraces looked, in their variegated garments, like heaps of flowers blooming in the air.

The people accosted one another, and embraced one another with
tears;—the Tyrian towns were taken, the Nomads dispersed, and
all the Barbarians annihilated. The Acropolis was hidden beneath
colored velaria; the beaks of the triremes, drawn up in line outside
the mole, shone like a dike of diamonds; everywhere there was a
sense of the restoration of order, the beginning of a new existence,
and the diffusion of vast happiness: it was the day of Salammbô's
marriage with the king of the Numidians.

On the terrace of the temple of Khamon there were three long
tables laden with gigantic plates, at which the Priests, Ancients and
Rich were going to sit, and there was a fourth and higher one for
Hamilcar, Narr' Havas, and Salammbô; for as she saved her country by the restoration of the zaïmph, the people turned her wedding
into a national rejoicing, and were waiting in the square below till
she should appear.

But their impatience was excited by another and more acrid longing: Matho's death had been promised for the ceremony.

It had been proposed at first to flay him alive, to pour lead into
his entrails, to kill him with hunger; he should be tied to a tree,
and an ape behind him should strike him on the head with a stone;
he had offended Tanith, and the cynocephaluses of Tanith should
avenge her. Others were of the opinion that he should be led about
on a dromedary after linen wicks, dipped in oil, had been inserted
in his body in several places—and they took pleasure in the thought
of the large animal wandering through the streets with this man
writhing beneath the fires like a candelabrum blown about by the
wind.

But what citizens should be charged with his torture, and why
disappoint the rest? They would have liked a kind of death in which
the whole town might take part, in which every hand, every weapon,
everything Carthaginian, to the very paving stones in the streets
and the waves in the gulf, could rend him, and crush him, and annihilate him. Accordingly the Ancients decided that he should go
from his prison to the square of Khamon without any escort, and
with his arms fastened to his back; it was forbidden to strike him
to the heart, in order that he might live the longer; to put out his
eyes, so that he might see his torture through; to hurl anything
against his person, or to lay more than three fingers upon him at
a time.

Although he was not to appear until the end of the day, the people
sometimes fancied that he could be seen, and the crowd would rush

toward the Acropolis, and empty the streets, to return with lengthened murmurings. Some people had remained standing in the same place since the day before, and they would call on one another from a distance and show their nails, which they had allowed to grow, the better to bury them in his flesh. Others walked restlessly up and down; some were as pale as though they were awaiting their own execution.

Suddenly lofty feather fans rose above the heads, behind the Mappalian district. It was Salammbô leaving her palace; a sigh of relief found vent.

But the procession was long in coming; it marched with deliberation.

First there filed past the priests of the Pataec Gods, then those of Eschmoun, of Melkarth, and all the other colleges in succession, with the same insignia, and in the same order as had been observed at the time of the sacrifice. The pontiffs of Moloch passed with heads bent, and the multitude stood aside from them in a kind of remorse. But the priests of Rabbetna advanced with a proud step, and with lyres in their hands; the priestesses followed them in transparent robes of yellow or black, uttering cries like birds and writhing like vipers, or else whirling round to the sound of flutes to imitate the dance of the stars, while their light garments wafted puffs of delicate scents through the streets.

The Kedeschim, with painted eyelids, who symbolized the hermaphroditism of the Divinity, received applause among these women, and, being perfumed and dressed like them, they resembled them in spite of their flat breasts and narrower hips. Moreover, on this day the female principle dominated and confused all things; a mystic lasciviousness moved in the heavy air; the torches were already lighted in the depths of the sacred woods; there was to be a great prostitution there during the night; three vessels had brought courtesans from Sicily, and others had come from the desert.

As the colleges arrived they ranged themselves in the courts of the temples, on the outer galleries, and along double staircases which rose against the walls, and drew together at the top. Files of white robes appeared between the colonnades, and the architecture was peopled with human statues, motionless as statues of stone.

Then came the masters of the exchequer, the governors of the provinces, and all the Rich. A great tumult prevailed below. Adjacent streets were discharging the crowd, hierodules were driving it back with blows of sticks; and then Salammbô appeared in a litter sur-

390

mounted by a purple canopy, and surrounded by the Ancients crowned with their golden tiaras.

Thereupon an immense shout arose; the cymbols and crotala sounded more loudly, the tambourines thundered, and the great purple canopy sank between the two pylons.

It appeared again on the first landing. Salammbô was walking slowly beneath it; then she crossed the terrace to take her seat behind on a kind of throne cut out of the carapace of a tortoise. An ivory stool with three steps was pushed beneath her feet; two negro children knelt on the edge of the first step, and sometimes she would rest both arms, which were laden with rings of excessive weight, upon their heads.

From ankle to hip she was covered with a network of narrow meshes which were in imitation of fish scales, and shone like mother-of-pearl; her waist was clasped by a blue zone, which allowed her breasts to be seen through two crescent-shaped slashings; the nipples were hidden by carbuncle pendants. She had a headdress made of peacock's feathers studded with gems; an ample cloak, as white as snow, fell behind her—and with her elbows at her sides, her knees pressed together, and circles of diamonds on the upper part of her arms, she remained perfectly upright in a hieratic attitude.

Her father and her husband were on two lower seats, Narr' Havas dressed in a light simar and wearing his crown of rock salt, from which there strayed two tresses of hair as twisted as the horns of Ammon; and Hamilcar in a violet tunic figured with gold vine branches, and with a battle sword at his side.

The python of the temple of Eschmoun lay on the ground amid pools of pink oil in the space inclosed by the tables, and, biting its tail, described a large, black circle. In the middle of the circle there was a copper pillar bearing a crystal egg; and, as the sun shone upon it, rays were emitted on every side.

Behind Salammbô, stretched the priests of Tanith in linen robes; on her right the Ancients, in their tiaras, formed a great gold line, and on the other side the Rich, with their emerald scepters, a great green line—while quite in the background, where the priests of Moloch were ranged, the cloaks looked like a wall of purple. The other colleges occupied the lower terraces. The multitude obstructed the streets. It reached to the house tops, and extended in long files to the summit of the Acropolis. Having thus the people at her feet, the firmament above her head, and around her the immensity of the sea, the gulf, the mountains, and the distant provinces, Salammbô in her

splendor was blended with Tanith, and seemed the very Genius of Carthage, and its embodied soul.

The feast was to last all night, and lamps with several branches were planted like trees on the painted woolen cloths which covered the low tables. Large electrum flagons, blue glass amphoras, tortoise-shell spoons, and small round loaves were crowded between the double row of pearl-bordered plates; bunches of grapes with their leaves had been rolled round ivory vine stocks after the fashion of the thyrsus; blocks of snow were melting on ebony trays, and lemons, pomegranates, gourds, and watermelons formed hillocks beneath the lofty silver plate; boars with open jaws were wallowing in the dust of spices; hares, covered with their fur, appeared to be bounding amid the flowers; there were shells filled with forcemeat; the pastry had symbolic shapes; when the covers of the dishes were removed doves flew out.

The slaves, meanwhile, with tunics tucked up, were going about on tiptoe; from time to time a hymn sounded on the lyres, or a choir of voices rose. The clamor of the people, continuous as the noise of the sea, floated vaguely around the feast, and seemed to lull it in a broader harmony; some recalled the banquet of the Mercenaries; they gave themselves up to dreams of happiness; the sun was beginning to go down, and the crescent of the moon was already rising in another part of the sky.

But Salammbô turned her head as though some one had called her; the people, who were watching her, followed the direction of her eyes.

The door of the dungeon, hewn in the rock at the foot of the temple, on the summit of the Acropolis, had just opened; and a man was standing on the threshold of this black hole.

He came forth bent double, with the scared look of fallow deer when suddenly enlarged.

The light dazzled him, he stood motionless awhile. All had recognized him and they held their breath.

In their eyes the body of this victim was something peculiarly theirs, and was adorned with almost religious splendor. They bent forward to see him, especially the women. They burned to gaze upon him who had caused the deaths of their children and husbands; and from the bottom of their souls there sprang up in spite of themselves an infamous curiosity, a desire to know him completely, a wish mingled with remorse which turned to increased execration.

At last he advanced; then the stupefaction of surprise disappeared. Numbers of arms were raised, and he was lost to sight.

The staircase of the Acropolis had sixty steps. He descended them as though he were rolled down in a torrent from the top of a mountan; three times he was seen to leap, and then he alighted below on his feet.

His shoulders were bleeding, his breast was panting with great shocks; and he made such efforts to burst his bonds that his arms, which were crossed on his naked loins, swelled like pieces of a serpent.

Several streets began in front of him, leading from the spot at which he found himself. In each of them a triple row of bronze chains fastened to the navels of the Pataec Gods extended in parallel lines from one end to the other; the crowd was massed against the houses, and servants, belonging to the Ancients, walked in the middle brandishing thongs.

One of them drove him forward with a great blow; Matho began to move.

They thrust their arms over the chains, shouting out that the road had been left too wide for him; and he passed along, felt, pricked, and slashed by all those fingers; when he reached the end of one street another appeared; several times he flung himself to one side to bite them; they speedily dispersed, the chains held him back, and the crowd burst out laughing.

A child rent his ear; a young girl, hiding the point of a spindle in her sleeve, split his cheek; they tore handfuls of hair from him and strips of flesh; others smeared his face with sponges steeped in filth and fastened upon their sticks. A stream of blood started from the right side of his neck; frenzy immediately set in. This last Barbarian was to them a representative of all the Barbarians, and all the army; they were taking vengeance on him for their disasters, their terrors, and their shame. The rage of the mob developed with its gratification; the curving chains were overstrained, and were on the point of breaking; the people did not feel the blows of the slaves who struck at them to drive them back; some clung to the projections of the houses; all the openings in the walls were stopped up with heads; and they howled at him the mischief that they could not inflict upon him.

It was atrocious, filthy abuse, mingled with ironical encouragements and with imprecations; and, his present tortures not being

393

enough for them, they foretold to him others that should be still more terrible in eternity.

This vast baying filled Carthage with stupid continuity. Frequently a single syllable—a hoarse, deep, and frantic intonation—would be repeated for several minutes by the entire people. The walls would vibrate with it from top to bottom, and both sides of the street would seem to Matho to be coming against him, and carrying him off the ground, like two immense arms stifling him in the air.

Nevertheless he remembered that he had experienced something like it before. The same crowd was on the terraces, there were the same looks and the same wrath; but then he had walked free, all had then dispersed, for a God covered him—and the recollection of this, gaining precision by degrees, brought a crushing sadness upon him. Shadows passed before his eyes; the town whirled round his head, his blood streamed from a wound in his hip, he felt that he was dying; his hams bent, and he sank quite gently upon the pavement.

Some one went to the peristyle of the temple of Melkarth, took thence the bar of a tripod, heated red hot in the coals, and, slipping it beneath the first chain, pressed it against his wound. The flesh was seen to smoke; the hootings of the people drowned his voice; he was standing again.

Six paces further on, and he fell a third and again a fourth time; but some new torture always made him rise. They discharged little drops of boiling oil through tubes at him; they strewed pieces of broken glass beneath his feet; still he walked on. At the corner of the street of Satheb he leaned his back against the wall beneath the penthouse of a shop, and advanced no further.

The slaves of the Council struck him with their whips of hippopotamus leather, so furiously and long that the fringes of their tunics were drenched with sweat. Matho appeared insensible; suddenly he started off and began to run at random, making noise with his lips like one shivering with severe cold. He threaded the streets of Boudes, and the street of Sœpo, crossed the Green Market, and reached the square of Khamon.

He now belonged to the priests; the slaves had just dispersed the crowd, and there was more room. Matho gazed round him and his eyes encountered Salammbô.

At the first step that he had taken she had risen; then, as he approached, she had involuntarily advanced by degrees to the edge of the terrace; and soon all external things were blotted out, and she

394

saw only Matho. Silence fell in her soul—one of those abysses wherein the whole world disappears beneath the pressure of a single thought, a memory, a look. This man who was walking toward her attracted her.

Excepting his eyes he had no appearance of humanity left; he was a long, perfectly red shape; his broken bonds hung down his thighs, but they could not be distinguished from the tendons of his wrists, which were laid quite bare; his mouth remained wide open; from his eye sockets there darted flames which seemed to rise up to his hair—and the wretch still walked on!

He reached the foot of the terrace. Salammbô was leaning over the balustrade; those frightful eyeballs were scanning her, and there rose within her a consciousness of all that he had suffered for her. Although he was in his death agony, she could see him once more kneeling in his tent, encircling her waist with his arms, and stammering out gentle words; she thirsted to feel them and hear them again; she did not want him to die! At this moment Matho gave a great start: she was on the point of shrieking aloud. He fell backward and did not stir again.

Salammbô was borne back, nearly swooning, to her throne by the priests who flocked about her. They congratulated her: it was her work. All clapped their hands and stamped their feet, howling her name.

A man darted upon the corpse. Although he had no beard he had the cloak of a priest of Moloch on his shoulder, and in his belt that species of knife which they employed for cutting up the sacred meat, and which terminated, at the end of the handle, in a golden spatula. He cleft Matho's breast with a single blow, then snatched out the heart and laid it upon the spoon; and Schahabarim, uplifting his arm, offered it to the sun.

The sun sank behind the waves; his rays fell like long arrows upon the red heart. As the beatings diminished the planet sank into the sea; and at the last palpitation it disappeared.

Then from the gulf to the lagoon, and from the isthmus to the pharos, in all the streets, on all the houses, and on all the temples, there was a single shout; sometimes it paused, to be again renewed; the building shook with it; Carthage was convulsed, as it were, in the spasm of Titanic joy and boundless hope.

Narr' Havas, drunk with pride, passed his left arm beneath Salammbô's waist in token of possession; and taking a gold patera in his right hand, he drank to the Genius of Carthage.

Salammbô rose like her husband, with a cup in her hand, to drink also. She fell down again with her head lying over the back of the throne,—pale, stiff, with parted lips,—and her loosened hair hung to the ground.

FRIEDRICH DE LA MOTTE-FOUQUE

FRIEDRICH DE LA MOTTE-FOUQUÉ (German, 1777-1843). German novelist, given to romantic fantasies. Very popular in his day for medieval and nordic romances. Now remembered chiefly for fairy tale, "Undine."

UNDINE

I. *The Water Sprite*

ABOUT a century ago an aged fisherman sat mending his nets by his cottage door, in front of a lovely lake. Behind his dwelling stretched a sombre forest, reputed to be haunted by goblin creatures. Through this gloomy solitude the pious old fisherman frequently passed, religiously dispelling all terrors by singing hymns as he went with his fish to a town near the border of the forest.

One evening he heard the sound of a horse's hoofs, and presently appeared a knight riding on a splendid steed, and clad in resplendent armour. The stranger stopped, and besought shelter for the night, and the good old fisherman accorded him a most cheery welcome, taking him into the cottage, where sat his aged wife by a scanty fire. Soon the three were freely conversing. The knight told of his travels and revealed that he was Sir Huldbrand of Ringstetten, where he had a castle by the Rhine.

A splash against the window surprising the guest he was informed by his host, with some little show of vexation, that little tricks were often played by a foster-child of the old couple, named Undine, a girl of eighteen.

The door flew open, and a lovely girl glided, laughing, into the room. Without the slightest token of shyness she gazed at the knight for a few moments, then asked why he had come to the poor cottage. "Have you come through the wild forest?"

He confessed that he had, and she instantly demanded a recital of

his adventures. With a slight shudder at his own recollections of the strange creatures he had encountered, Huldbrand consented, but a reproof from the fisherman at her obtrusiveness angered Undine. The girl sprang up and rushed forth into the night, exclaiming, "Sleep alone in your smoky old hut!"

In great alarm, the fisherman and Huldbrand rose to follow the girl, but she had vanished in the darkness. Remarking that she had acted so before, the old fisherman invited Huldbrand to sit by the fire and talk awhile, and began to relate how Undine had come to live with them.

The couple had lost their only child, a wonderfully beautiful little girl. At the age of three, when sitting in her mother's lap at the edge of the lake, she seemed to be attracted by some lovely apparition in the water, for, suddenly stretching out her hands and laughing, she had in a moment sprung into the lake. No trace of the child could ever be found. But the same evening a lovely little girl, three or four years old, with water streaming from her golden tresses, suddenly entered the cottage, smiling sweetly at the fisherman and his wife. They hastily undressed the little stranger and put her to bed. She uttered not a word, but simply smiled. In the morning she talked a little, confusedly telling how she had been in a boat on the lake with her mother, and had fallen in, and could recollect nothing more. She could say nothing as to who she was or whence she came. But she talked often of golden castles and crystal domes.

While the fisherman was talking thus to the knight, he was suddenly interrupted by the noise of rushing water. Floods seemed to be bursting forth, and he and his guest, going hastily to the door, saw by the moonlight that the brook which issued from the forest was surging in a wild torrent over its margin, while a roaring wind was lashing the lake. In great alarm both shouted, "Undine! Undine!" But there was no response, and the two ran off in different directions in search of the fugitive.

It was Huldbrand who discovered the girl. Clanbering down some rocks at the edge of the stream, thinking Undine might have fallen there, he was hailed by the sweet voice of the girl herself.

"Venture not," she cried. "The old man of the stream is full of tricks."

Looking across at a tiny isle in the stream, the knight saw her nestling in the grass, smiling, and in an instant he had crossed.

"The fisherman is distressed at your absence," said he. "Let us go back."

397

Looking at him with her beautiful blue eyes, the girl replied, "If you think so, well; whatever you think is right to me."

Taking Undine in his arms, Huldbrand bore her over the stream to the cottage, where she was received with joy. Dawn was breaking, and breakfast was prepared under the trees. Undine flung herself on the grass at Huldbrand's feet, and at her renewed request the knight told the story of his forest adventures.

"It is now about eight days since I rode into the city on the other side of the forest to join in a great tournament. In one of the intervals between the jousts I noticed a lovely lady among the spectators. I learned that she was Bertalda, foster-daughter of a great duke, and each evening I became her partner in the dances.

"This Bertalda was a wayward girl, and each day pleased me less and less; but I continued in her company, and asked her jestingly to give me a glove. She said she would do so if I would explore alone the haunted forest. As an honorable knight I could not decline the challenge, and yesterday I set out on the enterprise. Before I had penetrated very far within the glades, I saw what looked like a bear in the branches of an oak; but the creature, in a harsh, human voice, growled that it was getting branches with which to roast me at night. My horse was scared at this, and other grim apparitions, but at last I emerged from the forest, and saw the lake and this cottage."

When he had finished, the fisherman spoke of the best way by which the visitor could return to the city; but, with sly laughter, Undine declared that the knight could not depart, for if he attempted now to cross the deluged wood, he would be overwhelmed.

II. "*I Have No Soul!*"

HULDBRAND, detained at the cottage by the increasing overflow of the stream, enjoyed the most perfect satisfaction with his sojourn.

The old folks with pleasure regarded the two young people as betrothed, and Huldbrand assumed that he was accepted by the girl, whom he had come to look upon as not being in reality one of this poor household, but one of some illustrious family, and when, one evening, an aged priest appeared at the cottage, driven in by the storm, Huldbrand addressed to him a request that he should on the spot at once unite him and the maiden, as they were pledged to each other. A discussion arose, but matters were at length settled, and

the old wife produced two consecrated tapers. Lighting these, the priest, with brief, solemn ceremony, celebrated the nuptials.

Undine had been quiet and grave during these proceedings, but a singular change took place in her demeanour as soon as the rite had been performed. She began at intervals to indulge in wild freaks, teasing the priest, and indulging in a variety of silly tricks. At length the priest gently expostulated with Undine, exhorting her so to attune her soul that it might always be in concord with that of her husband.

Her reply amazed the listeners, for she said, "If one has no soul, as I have none, what is there to harmonise?" Then she burst into a fit of passionate weeping, to the consternation of all the little company. As she again and again wept, the priest, fearing that she was possessed by some evil spirit, sought to exorcise it. The priest turned to the bridegroom with the assurance that he could discover nothing evil in the bride, mysterious though her behaviour was, and he commended him to be loving and true to her.

The next morning Undine, when she and her husband made their appearance, responded gracefully to the paternal greeting of the priest, beseeching his pardon for her folly of the previous evening, and begging him to pray for the good of her soul. Through the whole day Undine behaved angelically. She was kind, quiet, and gentle. At eventide she led her husband out to the edge of the stream, which, to the wonder of Huldbrand, had subsided into gentle, rippling waves.

She whispered, "Carry me across to that little isle, and we will decide there."

Wondering, he carried her across, and, laying her on the turf, listened as she began.

"My loved one, know that there are strange beings which, though seeming almost like mortals, are rarely visible to human eyes—salamanders in the flames, gnomes down in the earth, spirits in the air. And in the water are myriads of spirits dwelling in crystal domes, in the coral-trees, and in the lovely shells. These are far more beautiful than the fairest of human beings, and sometimes a fisherman has seen a tender mermaid, and has listened to her song. Such wonderful creatures are called Undines, and one of these you see now before you!

"We should be far superior to other beings—for we consider ourselves human—but for one defect. We have no souls, and nothing

399

remains of us after this mortal life is over. Yet every being aspires to rise higher, and so my father, who is a great water prince in the Mediterranean Sea, desired that his only daughter should become possessed of a soul. But this can only come to pass with loving union with one of your race. Now, O my dearly beloved, I have to thank you that I am gifted with a soul, and it will be due to you should all my life be made wretched. For what will become of me if you forsake me? If you would do so, do it now! Then I will plunge into the stream—which is my uncle—and as he brought me here, so will he take me back to my parents, a loving, suffering woman with a soul."

Undine would have said yet more, but Huldbrand, astonishing though the recital was, with tears and kisses vowed he would never leave his lovely wife; and with her leaning in loving trustfulness on his arm, they returned to the hut.

The next day, at Undine's strange urgency, farewell was said with bitter tears and lamentations.

Undine was placed on the beautiful horse, and Huldbrand and the priest walked on either side as the three passed through the solemn glades of the wood. A fourth soon joined them. He was dressed in a white robe, like that of the priest, and presently attempted to speak to Undine. But she shrank from him, declaring she wished to have nothing to do with him.

"Oh, oh!" cried the stranger, with a laugh. "What kind of a marriage is this you have made, that you must not speak to your relative? Do you not know I am your uncle Kühleborn, who brought you to this region, and that I am here to protect you from goblins and sprites? So let me quietly accompany you."

"We are near the end of the forest, and shall not need you further," was her rejoinder. But he grinned at her so frightfully that she shrieked for help, and the knight aimed at his head a blow from his sword. Instantly Kühleborn was transformed into a gushing waterfall, foaming over them from a rock near by and drenching all three.

III. *"Woe! Woe!"*

THE sudden disappearance of the young knight had caused a sensation in the city, for the duke and duchess, and the friends and servants of Huldbrand, feared he had perished in the forest during the terrible tempest. When he suddenly reappeared, all rejoiced ex-

400

cept Bertalda, who was profoundly vexed at seeing with him a beautiful bride. She so far reconciled herself to the conditions that a warm friendship sprang up between Undine and herself.

It was agreed that Bertalda should accompany the wedded pair to Ringstetten, and with the consent of the noble foster-parents of Bertalda the three appointed a day for the departure. One beautiful evening, as they walked about the market-place round the great fountain, suddenly a tall man emerged from among the people and stopped in front of Undine. He quickly whispered something in her ear, and though at first she seemed vexed at the intrusion, presently she clapped her hands and laughed joyously. Then the stranger mysteriously vanished, and seemed to disappear in the fountain.

Huldbrand had suspected that he had seen this man before, and now felt assured that he was Kühleborn. Undine admitted the fact, and said that her uncle had told her a secret, which she was to reveal on the third day afterwards, which would be the anniversary of Bertalda's nameday.

The anniversary came, and strange incidents happened. After the banquet given by the duke and duchess, Undine suddenly gave a signal, and from among the retainers at the door came forth the old fisherman and his wife, and Undine declared that in these Bertalda saw her real parents. The proud maiden instantly flew into a violent rage, weeping passionately, and utterly refused to acknowledge the old couple as her father and mother. She declared that Undine was an enchantress and a witch, sustaining intercourse with evil spirits.

Undine, with great dignity, indignantly denied the accusation, while Bertalda's violent conduct created a feeling of disgust in the minds of all in the assembly. The matter was settled in a simple manner, for the duke commanded Bertalda to withdraw to a private apartment with the duchess and the two old folks from the hut, that an investigation might be made. It was soon over, for the noble lady was able presently to inform the company that Undine's story was absolutely true. The guests silently departed, and Undine sank sobbing into her husband's arms.

Next day Bertalda, humbled by these events, sought pardon of Undine for her evil behaviour, and was instantly welcomed with loving assurances of forgiveness. Moreover, she was cordially invited to go with the pair to Ringstetten.

"We will share all things there as sisters," said Undine.

The three journeyed to the distant castle, and took up their abode together. Soon Kühleborn appeared on the scene, but Undine at once

401

repulsed him. Next, when her husband was one day hunting, she ordered the great well in the courtyard to be covered with a big stone, on which she cut some curious characters.

Bertalda waywardly complained that this proceeding deprived her of water that was good for her complexion, but Undine privately explained to Huldbrand that she had caused the servants to seal up this spring because only by that way of access could her uncle Kühleborn come to disturb their peace.

As time passed on, Huldbrand gradually cooled towards his wife and turned affectionately towards Bertalda. Undine bore patiently and silently the sorrow thus inflicted on her. But when her husband was impatient and angry she would plead with him never to speak to her in accents of unkindness when they happened to be on the water, for the water spirits had her completely in their power on their element, and would seek to protect her and even seize her and take her down for ever to dwell in the crystal castles of the deep.

After some estrangements, Undine and Bertalda had again become loving friends, and Huldbrand's affection for his wife had revived with its old and welcome warmth, while the attachment between him and Bertalda seemed forgotten.

One day the three were enjoying a delightful excursion on the glorious Danube. Bertalda had taken off a beautiful coral necklace which Huldbrand had given her. She leaned over and drew the coral beads across the surface, enjoying the glitter thus caused, when suddenly a great hand from beneath seized the necklace and snatched it down. The maiden's scream of terror was answered by mocking laughter from the water.

In an outburst of passion, Huldbrand started up and poured forth curses on the river and its denizens, whether spirits or sirens. With tears in her eyes, Undine besought him softly not to scold her there, and she took from her neck a beautiful necklace and offered it to Bertalda as a compensation.

But the angry knight snatched it away, and hurled it into the river, exclaiming, "Are you still connected with them? In the name of all the witches, remain among them with your presents, and leave us mortals in peace, you sorceress!"

Bitterly weeping and crying, "Woe! Woe!" she vanished over the side of the vessel. Her last words were, "Remain true! Woe! Woe!" Huldbrand lay swooning on the deck, and little waves seemed to be sobbing on the surface of the Danube, "Woe! Woe! Remain true!"

IV. The White Strange

For a time deep sorrow fell on the lord of Ringstetten and Bertalda. They lived long in the castle quietly, often weeping for Undine, tenderly cherishing her memory. Undine often visited Huldbrand in his dreams, caressing him and weeping silently so that his cheeks were wet when he awoke. But these visions grew less frequent, and the knight's grief diminished by degrees. At length he and Bertalda were married, but it was in spite of a grave warning from Father Heilmann, who declared that Undine had appeared to him in visions, beseeching him to warn Huldbrand and Bertalda to leave each other. They were too infatuated to heed the admonition, and a priest from a neighbouring monastery promised to perform the ceremony in a few days.

Meantime, when lying between sleeping and waking, the knight seemed fanned by the wings of a swan, and, as he fell asleep, seemed borne along on the wings of swans which sang their sweetest music. All at once he seemed to be hovering over the Mediterranean Sea. Its waters were so crystalline that he could see through them to the bottom, and there, under a crystal arch, sat Undine, weeping bitterly. She seemed not to perceive him. Kühleborn approached her, and told her that Huldbrand was to be wedded again, and that it would be her duty, from which nothing could release her, to end his life.

"That I cannot do," said she. "I have sealed up the fountain against me and my race."

Huldbrand felt as if he were soaring back again over the sea, and at length he seemed to reach his castle. He awoke on his couch, but he could not bring himself to break off the arrangements that had been made.

The marriage feast at Ringstetten was not as bright and happy as such occasions usually are, for a veil of gloom seemed to rest over the company. Even the bride affected a happy and thoughtless demeanour which she did not really feel. The company dispersed early, Bertalda retiring with her maidens, and Huldbrand with his attendants.

In her apartment Bertalda, with a sigh, noticed how freckled was her neck, and a remark she made to her maidens as she gazed in the mirror excited the eager attention of one of them. She heard her fair mistress say, "Oh, that I had a flask of the purifying water from the closed fountain!" Presently the officious waiting-woman

403

was seen leading men to the fountain. With levers they quickly lifted the stone, for some mysterious force seemed to aid them.

Then from the fountain solemnly rose a white column of water. It was presently perceived that it was a pale female figure, veiled in white. She was weeping bitterly as she walked slowly to the building, while Bertalda and her attendants, pale with terror, watched from the window. The figure passed on, and at the door of Huldbrand's room, where the knight was partly undressed, was heard a gentle tap. The white figure slowly entered. It was Undine, who softly said, "They have opened the spring, and now I am here and you must die." Said the knight, "It must be so! But let me die in your embrace."

"Most gladly, my beloved one," said she, throwing back her veil and disclosing her face divinely smiling. Imprinting on his lips a sacred kiss, Undine clasped the knight in her arms, weeping as if she would weep her very soul away. Huldbrand fell softly back on the pillows of his couch, a corpse.

At the funeral of Huldbrand the veiled figure appeared when the procession formed a circle round the grave. All knelt in mute devotion at a signal from Father Heilmann. When they rose again the white stranger had vanished, and on the spot where she had knelt a silvery little fountain gushed forth, which almost encircled the grave and then ran on till it reached a lake near by. And to this day the inhabitants cherish the tradition that thus the poor rejected Undine still lovingly embraces her husband.

ANATOLE FRANCE

ANATOLE FRANCE (Jacques Anatole François Thibault, French, 1844-1924). The poet of irony and pity, with his heart in the Middle Ages. Novelist, historian, short story writer: *Thaïs, Penguin Island, The Crime of Sylvestre Bonnard, Life of Joan of Arc.* Nobel Prize, 1921. Though his work dates, its survival seems ensured because of its wit and stylistic talent.

A ROMAN SENATOR

Cæsar, on the stones of the deserted hall,
Under the folds of his toga, lay in majesty.
The green-lipped bronze of Pompey, proud and tall,
Smiled at the white corpse bloodily.

The spirit just fled through a road made clear
By the steel of Brutus and of Liberty,
Hovered sadly over the lifeless, dear
Flesh fond death made pale yet fair to see.

On a bare marble bench near by, at rest,
The even movements of his mighty chest
Marking his snores, a Senator took his leisure.

The silence woke him and, disturbed, he cried
Across the silent horror at his side:
"I vote to give the imperial crown to Cæsar!"

EVE'S BLOOD

Love hides many treasures in its deeps.
Nature's primordial hardihoods,
That mingled nude thighs in woodland quest,
Still modestly surge in the bride's breast:
Watchful of our conventions, she keeps
The blood of that Eve of the early woods.

THE BAD WORKMAN

Master Laurent Coster, with poetry in his heart,
Left his companions who, from morn to night,
Born vintners, made the boards of the wine-press start—
And Coster dreaming followed his fancy's flight.

For he loved the demon Aspasia with all his soul.
Sometimes he'd sit upon his bench at church
And see in the fumes above the incense bowl
The Woman of Hell who was his only search.

Or else alone at the brink of a mossy well,
Clasping the hands no labor could impel,
He'd hark forever to her siren song. . . .

And I, as well, can neither work nor pray;
I am like Coster, a laborer astray
Through looking in your dark eyes overlong.

405

"I have burned my garments of gold, and my violin.
While the brazier of repentance shines on me
I shall seek the Pope to wash away my sin.

"O Holy Father, hear with clemency
By what rare sins and demon joy thereof,
Remote from Jesus, I was blind to his decree.

"In the enchanted city, all other peaks above,
With beauteous Venus I dwelt seven years.
Absolve me now, by Jesus whom we love."

The cross of the Holy Father, as he hears,
Trembles: "Your frightful sins the Lord will pardon
When leaf or flower on his cross appears!"

Tears do the gallant's heavy spirit harden.
"Since, Madame Virgin, I no more may yearn
To tend the flowers of your heavenly garden,

"Nor as a shining taper for you burn,
The tender Lady Venus will comfort me:
Never to leave her more, I now return!"

"In truth I'm glad, yes, glad, to see
Thee, Knight; sit down and drink, I pray.
A long time, Tannhäuser, I have longed for thee."

The cross having blossomed on the third day,
The Holy Father sent a post full speed
To seek Tannhäuser up hill and away.

With Venus, he was drinking mellow mead,—
And there will linger, while marriage songs are played,
Until the Angel's trump to Judgment lead.

Not thus should man's bright soul be overlaid:
If they are damned who love the brave device
Of the clear word and the clear smile of a maid

There'll be no one to sing in Paradise.

FERDINAND FREILIGRATH

FERDINAND FREILIGRATH (German, 1810-1876). German poet whose
revolutionary sentiments forced him frequently abroad. Influenced by Byron
and Victor Hugo, whom he translated.

THE SPECTER CARAVAN

'Twas midnight in the Desert, where we rested on the ground;
There my Beddaweens were sleeping and their steeds were stretched
    around;
In the farness lay the moonlight of the Mountains of the Nile,
And the camel bones that strewed the sands for many an arid mile.

With my saddle for a pillow did I prop my weary head,
And my kaftan cloth unfolded o'er my limbs was lightly spread,
While beside me, as the Kapitan and watchman of my band,
Lay my Bazra sword and pistols twain a shimmering on the sand.

And the stillness was unbroken, save at moments by a cry
From some stray belated vulture sailing blackly down the sky,
Or the snortings of a sleeping steed at waters fancy-seen,
Or the hurried warlike mutterings of some dreaming Beddaween.

When, behold!—a sudden sandquake,—and between the earth and
    moon
Rose a mighty Host of Shadows, as from out some dim lagoon;
Then our coursers gasped with terror, and a thrill shook every man;
And the cry was—"Allah Akbar! 'tis the Specter Caravan!"

On they came, their hueless faces toward Mecca evermore;
On they came, long files of camels, and of women whom they bore,
Guides, and merchants, youthful maidens bearing pitchers in their
    hands,
And behind them troops of horsemen following, sumless as the
    sands!

More and more! the phantom pageant overshadowed all the plains;
Yea! the ghastly camel bones arose, and grew to camel trains;
And the whirling column clouds of sand to forms in dusky garbs,—
Here afoot as Hadjee pilgrims, there as warriors on their barbs!

407

Whence we knew the Night was come when all whom Death had
    sought and found,
Long ago amid the sands whereon their bones yet bleach around,
Rise by legions from the darkness of their prisons low and lone,
And in dim procession march to kiss the Kaaba's Holy Stone.

And yet more, and more forever!—still they swept in pomp along,
Till I asked me,—Can the Desert hold so vast a muster throng?
Lo! the Dead are here in myriads; the whole World of Hades
    waits,
As with eager wish to press beyond the Babelmandeb Straits!

Then I spake: "Our steeds are frantic: To your saddles, every one!
Never quail before these Shadows! You are children of the Sun!
If their garments rustle past you, if their glances reach you here,
Cry Bismillah! and that mighty Name shall banish every fear.

"Courage, comrades! Even now the moon is waning far a-west,—
Soon the welcome Dawn will mount the skies, in gold and crimson
    vest,—
And in thinnest air will melt away those phantom shapes forlorn,
When again upon your brows you feel the odor winds of Morn!"

THE LION'S RIDE

King of deserts reigns the lion; will he through his realm go
    riding,
Down to the lagoon he paces, in the tall sedge there lies hiding.
Where gazelles and camelopards drink, he crouches by the shore;
Ominous, above the monster, moans the quivering sycamore.

When, at dusk, the ruddy hearth-fires in the Hottentot kraals are
    glowing,
And the motley, changeful signals on the Table Mountain growing
Dim and distant—when the Caffre sweeps along the lone karroo—
When in the bush the antelope slumbers, and beside the stream the
    gnu—

408

Lo! majestically stalking, yonder comes the tall giraffe,
Hot with thirst, the gloomy waters of the dull lagoon to quaff;
O'er the naked waste behold her, with parched tongue, all panting
  hasten—
Now she sucks the cool draught, kneeling, from the stagnant, slimy
  basin.

Hark, a rustling in the sedges! with a roar, the lion springs
On her back now. What a race-horse! Say, in proudest stalls of
  kings,
Saw one ever richer housings than the courser's motley hide,
On whose back the tawny monarch of the beasts tonight will ride?

Fixed his teeth are in the muscles of the nape, with greedy strain;
Round the giant courser's withers waves the rider's yellow mane.
With a hollow cry of anguish, leaps and flies the tortured steed;
See her, how with skin of leopard she combines the camel's speed!

See, with lightly beating footsteps, how she scours the moonlit
  plains!
From their sockets start the eyeballs; from the torn and bleeding
  veins,
Fast the thick, black drops come trickling, o'er the brown and
  dappled neck,
And the flying beast's heart-beatings audible the stillness make.

Like the cloud, that, guiding Israel through the land of Yemen,
  shone,
Like a spirit of the desert, like a phantom, pale and wan,
O'er the desert's sandy ocean, like a waterspout at sea,
Whirls a yellow, cloudy column, tracking them where'er they flee.

On their track the vulture follows, flapping, croaking, through the
  air,
And the terrible hyena, plunderer of tombs, is there;
Follows them the stealthy panther—Cape-town's folds have known
  him well;
Them their monarch's dreadful pathway, blood and sweat full
  plainly tell.

On his living throne, they, quaking, see their ruler sitting there,
With sharp claw the painted cushion of his seat they see him tear.
Restless the giraffe must bear him on, till strength and lifeblood
    fail her;
Mastered by such daring rider, rearing, plunging, naught avail her.

To the desert's verge she staggers—sinks—one groan—and all is
    o'er.
Now the steed shall feast the rider, dead, and smeared with dust
    and gore.
Far across, o'er Madagascar, faintly now the morning breaks;
Thus the king of beasts his journey nightly through his empire
    makes.

ROBERT FROST

ROBERT FROST (American, 1875-   ). The poet of the ordinary tongue.
Called the interpreter of New England. Spent much of life as professor at
Amherst College. His supremely simple poems convey universal truths through
homely, country images. Collections: *North of Boston, Mountain Interval,
New Hampshire, West-running Brook, A Further Range, A Masque of Reason.*

The Need of Being Versed in Country Things

The house had gone to bring again
To the midnight sky a sunset glow.
Now the chimney was all of the house that stood,
Like a pistil after the petals go.

The barn opposed across the way,
That would have joined the house in flame
Had it been the will of the wind, was left
To bear forsaken the place's name.

No more it opened with all one end
For teams that came by the stony road
To drum on the floor with scurrying hoofs
And brush the mow with the summer load.

The birds that came to it through the air
At broken windows flew out and in,
Their murmur like the sigh we sigh
From too much dwelling on what has been.

Yet for them the lilac renewed its leaf,
And the aged elm, though touched with fire;
And the dry pump flung up an awkward arm;
And the fence post carried a strand of wire.

For them there was really nothing sad.
But though they rejoiced in the nest they kept,
One had to be versed in country things
Not to believe the phoebes wept.

The Gift Outright

The land was ours before we were the land's.
She was our land more than a hundred years
Before we were her people. She was ours
In Massachusetts, in Virginia,
But we were England's, still colonials,
Possessing what we were still unpossessed by,
Possessed by what we now no more possessed.
Something we were withholding made us weak
Until we found out that it was ourselves
We were withholding from our land of living,
And forthwith found salvation in surrender.
Such as we were we gave ourselves outright
(The deed of gift was many deeds of war)
To the land vaguely realizing westward,
But still unstoried, artless, unenhanced,
Such as she was, such as she would become.

411

FUZULI

FUZULÎ (Mehmet Suleiman Oglou, Turkish, *ca.* 1494-1572). Leading representative of the classical school of Turkish literature. Wrote also in Arabic and Persian. Led humble, unhappy life, died of plague. Called "the poet of the heart." Chief works: *Divan* (a collection of short odes known as *ghazals* or "gazels") and *Leyla ve Mejnun*, a romance of unhappy lovers.

GAZEL

O breeze, thou'rt kind, of balm to those whom pangs affright, thou
    news hast brought,
To wounded frame of life, to life of life's delight thou news hast
    brought.
Thou'st seen the mourning nightingale's despair in sorrow's autumn
    drear,
Like springtide days, of smiling roseleaf fresh and bright, thou
    news hast brought.
If I should say thy words are heaven-inspired, in truth, blaspheme
    I not;
Of Faith, whilst unbelief doth earth hold fast and tight, thou news
    hast brought.
They say the loved one comes to soothe the hearts of all her lovers
    true;
If that the case, to yon fair maid of lovers' plight thou news hast
    brought.
Of rebel demon thou hast cut the hope Suleyman's throne to gain;
That in the sea secure doth lie his Ring of might, thou news hast
    brought.
Fuzuli, through the parting night, alas, how dark my fortune grew!
Like zephyr of the dawn, of shining sun's fair light thou news hast
    brought.

GAZEL

O thou Perfect Being, Source whence wisdom's mysteries arise;
Things, the issue of thine essence, show wherein thy nature lies.
Manifester of all wisdom, thou art he whose pen of might
Hath with rays of stars illumined yonder gleaming page, the skies.
That a happy star, indeed, the essence clear of whose bright self
Truly knoweth how the blessings from thy word that flow to prize.

But a jewel flawed am faulty I: alas, forever stands
Blank the page of my heart's journal from thought of thy writing
   wise.
In the journal of my actions Evil's lines are black indeed;
When I think of Day of Gathering's terrors, blood flows from my
   eyes.
Gathering of my tears will form a torrent on the Reckoning Day,
If the pearls, my tears, rejecting, he but view them to despise:
Pearls my tears are, O Fuzuli, from the ocean deep of love;
But they're pearls these, oh! most surely, that the Love of Allah
   buys!

GAZEL

Is't strange if beauties' hearts turn blood through envy of thy cheek
   most fair?
For that which stone to ruby turns is but the radiant sunlight's glare.
Or strange is't if thine eyelash conquer all the stony-hearted ones?
For meet an ebon shaft like that a barb of adamant should bear!
Thy cheek's sun-love hath on the hard, hard hearts of fairy beauties
   fall'n,
And many a steely-eyed one hath received thy bright reflection fair.
The casket, thy sweet mouth, doth hold spell-bound the *huri*-faced
   ones all;
The virtue of Suleyman's Ring was that fays thereto fealty sware.
Is't strange if, seeing thee, they rub their faces lowly midst the dust?
That down to Adam bowed the angel throng doth the Qur'an
   declare!
On many and many a heart of stone have fall'n the pangs of love
   for thee!
A fire that lies in stone concealed is thy heart-burning love's dread
   glare!
Within her ward, with garments rent, on all sides rosy-cheeked ones
   stray;
Fuzuli, through those radiant hues, that quarter beams a garden
   fair.

GAZEL

From the turning of the Sphere my luck hath seen reverse and woe;
Blood I've drunk, for from my banquet wine arose and forth did go.
With the flame, my burning sighs, I've lit the wand'ring wildered
   heart;

413

I'm a fire, doth not all that which turns about me roasted glow?
With thy rubies wine contended—oh! how it hath lost its wits!
Need 'tis yon ill-mannered wretch's company that we forego.
Yonder Moon saw not my burning's flame upon the parting day—
How can e'er the sun about the taper all night burning know?
Every eye that all around tears scatters, thinking of thy shaft,
Is an oyster-shell that causeth rain-drops into pearls to grow.
Forms my sighing's smoke a cloud that veils the bright cheek of
 the moon;
Ah! that yon fair Moon will ne'er the veil from off her beauty
 throw!
Ne'er hath ceased the rival e'en within her ward to vex me sore;
How say they, Fuzuli, "There's in Paradise nor grief nor woe"?

G

SOLOMON IBN GABIROL

SOLOMON IBN GABIROL (Spanish-Hebrew, 1021-1058). The Hebrew poet of the Golden Period of Moorish Spain. Little is known of his life. One of the greatest of medieval poets, deeply religious and philosophical. Philosophic works, written in Arabic, influenced Duns Scotus, Spinoza, Schopenhauer. Most noted poem: *Kether Meluth (Royal Crown)*.

NIGHT

Night, and the heavens beam serene with peace,
Like a pure heart benignly smiles the moon.
Oh, guard thy blessed beauty from mischance,
This I beseech thee in all tender love.
See where the Storm his cloudy mantle spreads,
An ashy curtain covereth the moon.
As if the tempest thirsted for the rain,
The clouds he presses, till they burst in streams.
Heaven wears a dusky raiment, and the moon
Appeareth dead—her tomb is yonder cloud,
And weeping shades come after, like the people
Who mourn with tearful grief a noble queen.
But look! the thunder pierced night's close-linked mail,
His keen-tipped lance of lightning brandishing;
He hovers like a seraph-conqueror.—
Dazed by the flaming splendor of his wings,
In rapid flight as in a whirling dance,
The black cloud-ravens hurry scared away.
So, though the powers of darkness chain my soul,
My heart, a hero, chafes and breaks its bonds.

415

Will night already spread her wings and weave
Her dusky robe about the day's bright form,
Boldly the sun's fair countenance displacing,
And swathe it with her shadow in broad day?
So a green wreath of mist enrings the moon,
Till envious clouds do quite encompass her.
No wind! and yet the slender stem is stirred,
With faint, slight motion as from inward tremor.
Mine eyes are full of grief—who sees me, asks,
"Oh, wherefore dost thou cling unto the ground?"
My friends discourse with sweet and soothing words;
They all are vain, they glide above my head.
I fain would check my tears; would fain enlarge
Unto infinity, my heart—in vain!
Grief presses hard my breast, therefore my tears
Have scarcely dried, ere they again spring forth.
For these are streams no furnace heat may quench,
Nebuchadnezzar's flames may dry them not.
What is the pleasure of the day for me,
If, in its crucible, I must renew
Incessantly the pangs of purifying?
Up, challenge, wrestle, and o'ercome! Be strong!
The late grapes cover all the vine with fruit.
I am not glad, though even the lion's pride
Content itself upon the field's poor grass.
My spirit sinks beneath the tide, soars not
With fluttering seamews on the moist, soft strand.
I follow Fortune not, where'er she lead.
Lord o'er myself, I banish her, compel.
And though her clouds should rain no blessed dew,
Though she withhold the crown, the heart's desire,
Though all deceive, though honey change to gall,
Still am I lord, and will in freedom strive.

MEDITATIONS

Forget thine anguish,
  Vexed heart, again.
Why shouldst thou languish,
  With earthly pain?

416

The husk shall slumber,
　　Bedded in clay
Silent and sombre,
　　Oblivion's prey!
But, Spirit immortal,
Thou at Death's portal,
　　Tremblest with fear.
　　If he caress thee,
　　Curse thee or bless thee,
　　Thou must draw near,
From him the worth of thy works to hear.

　　Why full of terror,
　　Compassed with error,
　　Trouble thy heart,
　　For thy mortal part?
　　The soul flies home—
　　The corpse is dumb.
　　Of all thou didst have,
Follows naught to the grave.
　　Thou fliest thy nest,
Swift as a bird to thy place of rest.

　　What avail grief and fasting,
　　Where nothing is lasting?
　　Pomp, domination,
　　Become tribulation.
　　In a health-giving draught,
　　A death-dealing shaft.
　　Wealth—an illusion,
　　Power—a lie,
　　Over all, dissolution
　　Creeps silent and sly.
　　Unto others remain
　　The goods thou didst gain
　　With infinite pain.

Life is a vine-branch;
　　A vintager, Death.
He threatens and lowers
　　More near with each breath.

417

Then hasten, arise!
   Seek God, O my soul!
For time quickly flies,
   Still far is the goal.
Vain heart praying dumbly,
   Learn to prize humbly,
   The meanest of fare.
Forget all thy sorrow,
   Behold, Death is there!

   Dove-like lamenting,
   Be full of repenting,
Lift vision supernal
To raptures eternal.
   On ev'ry occasion
   Seek lasting salvation.
Pour thy heart out in weeping,
While others are sleeping.
   Pray to Him when all's still,
   Performing his will.
And so shall the angel of peace be thy warden,
And guide thee at last to the heavenly garden.

JOHN GALSWORTHY

JOHN GALSWORTHY (English, 1867-1933). Novelist and playwright. A
gentle critic of our social disorder. Trained for the bar, but turned to literature.
His major work, *The Forsyte Saga*, paints detailed picture of late Victorian
era. Other novels more superficial. Still performed play, *Justice*, displays a
concern over social wrongs.

QUALITY

I KNEW him from the days of my extreme youth, because he made
my father's boots; inhabiting with his elder brother two little shops
let into one, in a small by-street—now no more, but then most
fashionably placed in the West End.

That tenement had a certain quiet distinction; there was no sign
upon its face that he made for any of the Royal Family—merely his

own German name of Gessler Brothers; and in the window a few pairs of boots. I remember that it always troubled me to account for those unvarying boots in the window, for he made only what was ordered, reaching nothing down, and it seemed so inconceivable that what he made could ever have failed to fit. Had he bought them to put there? That, too, seemed inconceivable. He would never have tolerated in his house leather on which he had not worked himself. Besides, they were too beautiful—the pair of pumps, so inexpressibly slim; the patent leathers with cloth tops, making water come into one's mouth; the tall brown riding boots, with marvellous sooty glow, as if, though new, they had been worn a hundred years. Those pairs could only have been made by one who saw before him the Soul of Boot—so truly were they prototypes incarnating the very spirit of all foot-gear. These thoughts, of course, came to me later, though even when I was promoted to him, at the age of perhaps fourteen, some inkling haunted me of the dignity of himself and brother. For to make boots—such boots as he made—seemed to me then, and still seems to me, mysterious and wonderful.

I remember well my shy remark, one day, while stretching out to to him my youthful foot:

"Isn't it awfully hard to do, Mr. Gessler?"

And his answer, given with a sudden smile from out of the sardonic redness of his beard: "Id is an Ardt!"

Himself, he was as little as if made from leather, with his yellow crinkly reddish hair and beard, and neat folds slanting down his cheeks to the corners of his mouth, and his guttural and one-toned voice; for leather is a sardonic substance, and stiff and slow of purpose. And that was the character of his face, save that his eyes, which were grey-blue, had in them the simple gravity of one secretly possessed by the Ideal. His elder brother was so very like him—though watery, paler in every way, with a great industry—that sometimes in early days I was not quite sure of him until the interview was over. Then I knew that it was he, if the words, "I will ask my brudder," had not been spoken; and that, if they had, it was his elder brother.

When one grew old and wild and ran up bills, one somehow never ran them up with Gessler Brothers. It would not have seemed becoming to go in there and stretch out one's foot to that blue iron-spectacled glance, owing him for more than—say—two pairs, just the comfortable reassurance that one was still his client.

For it was not possible to go to him very often—his boots lasted

terribly, having something beyond the temporary—some, as it were, essence of boot stitched into them.

One went in, not as into most shops, in the mood of; "Please serve me, and let me go!" but restfully, as one enters a church; and, sitting on the single wooden chair, waited—for there was never anybody there. Soon, over the top edge of that sort of well—rather dark, as smelling soothingly of leather—which formed the shop, there would be seen his face, or that of his elder brother, peering down. A guttural sound, and the tip-tap of bast slippers beating the narrow wooden stairs, and he would stand before one without coat, a little bent, in leather apron, with sleeves turned back, blinking—as if awakened from some dream of boots, or like an owl surprised in daylight and annoyed at his interruption.

And I would say: "How do you do, Mr. Gessler? Could you make me a pair of Russian leather boots?"

Without a word he would leave me, retiring whence he came, or into the other portion of the shop, and I would continue to rest in the wooden chair, inhaling the incense of his trade. Soon he would come back, holding in his thin, veined hand a piece of gold-brown leather. With eyes fixed on it, he would remark: "What a beautiful biece!" When I, too, had admired it, he would speak again. "When do you wand dem?" And I would answer: "Oh! As soon as you conveniently can." And he would say: "To-morrow fordnight?" Or if he were his elder brother: "I will ask my brudder!"

Then I would murmur: "Thank you! Good morning, Mr. Gessler." "Goot morning!" he would reply, still looking at the leather in his hand. And as I moved to the door, I would hear the tip-tap of his bast slippers restoring him, up the stairs, to his dream of boots. But if it were some new kind of foot-gear that he had not yet made me, then indeed he would observe ceremony—divesting me of my boot and holding it long in his hand, looking at it with eyes at once critical and loving, as if recalling the glow with which he had created it, and rebuking the way in which one had disorganised this masterpiece. Then, placing my foot on a thin piece of paper, he would two or three times tickle the outer edges with a pencil and pass his nervous fingers over my toes, feeling himself into the heart of my requirements.

I cannot forget that day on which I had occasion to say to him: "Mr. Gessler, that last pair of town walking-boots creaked, you know."

He looked at me for a time without replying, as if expecting me to withdraw or qualify the statement, then said:

"Id shouldn't 'ave greaked."

"It did, I'm afraid."

"You goddem wed before dey found demselves?"

"I don't think so."

At that he lowered his eyes, as if hunting for memory of those boots, and I felt sorry I had mentioned this grave thing.

"Zend dem back!" he said; "I will look at dem."

A feeling of compassion for my creaking boots surged up in me, so well could I imagine the sorrowful long curiosity of regard which he would bend on them.

"Zome boods," he said slowly, "are bad from birdt. If I can do noding wid dem, I dake dem off your bill."

Once (once only) I went absent-mindedly into his shop in a pair of boots bought in an emergency at some large firm's. He took my order without showing me any leather, and I could feel his eyes penetrating the inferior integument of my foot. At last he said:

"Dose are nod my boods."

The tone was not one of anger, nor of sorrow, not even of contempt, but there was in it something quiet that froze the blood. He put his hand down and pressed a finger on the place where the left boot, endeavoring to be fashionable, was not quite comfortable.

"Id 'urds you dere," he said. "Dose big virms 'ave no self-respect. Drash!" And then as if something had given way within him, he spoke long and bitterly. It was the only time I ever heard him discuss the conditions and hardships of the trade.

"Dey get id all," he said, "dey get id by adverdisement, nod by work. Dey dake it way from us, who lofe our boods. Id gomes to this—bresently I haf no work. Every year id gets less—you will see." And looking at his lined face I saw things I had never noticed before, bitter things and bitter struggle—and what a lot of grey hairs there seemed suddenly in his red beard!

As best I could, I explained the circumstances of the purchase of those ill-omened boots. But his face and voice made so deep impression that during the next few minutes I ordered many pairs. Nemesis fell! They lasted more terribly than ever. And I was not able conscientiously to go to him for nearly two years.

When at last I went I was surprised to find that outside one of the two little windows of his shop another name was painted, also that

421

of a boot-maker—making, of course, for the Royal Family. The old familiar boots, no longer in dignified isolation, were huddled in the window. Inside, the now contracted well of the one little shop was more scented and darker than ever. And it was longer than usual, too, before a face peered down, and the tip-tap of the bast slippers began. At last he stood before me, and, gazing through those rusty iron spectacles, said:

"Mr. ——, isn'd id?"

"Ah! Mr. Gessler," I stammered, "but your boots are really *too* good, you know! See, these are quite decent still!" And I stretched out to him my foot. He looked at it.

"Yes," he said, "beople do nod wand good boods, id seems."

To get away from his reproachful eyes and voice I hastily remarked: "What have you done to your shop?"

He answered quietly: "Id was too exbensive. Do you wand some boods?"

I ordered three pairs, though I had only wanted two, and quickly left. I had, I do not know quite what feeling of being part, in his mind, of a conspiracy against him; or not perhaps so much against him as against his idea of boot. One does not, I suppose, care to feel like that; for it was again many months before my next visit to his shop, paid I remember, with the feeling: "Oh, well, I can't leave the old boy—so here goes! Perhaps it will be his elder brother!"

For his elder brother, I knew, had not character enough to reproach me, even dumbly.

And, to my relief, in the shop there did appear to be his elder brother, handling a piece of leather.

"Well, Mr. Gessler," I said, "how are you?"

He came close and peered at me.

"I am breddy well," he said slowly: "but my elder brudder is dead."

And I saw that it was indeed himself—but how aged and wan! And never before had I heard him mention his brother. Much shocked, I murmured: "Oh! I am sorry!"

"Yes," he answered, "he was a good man, he made a good bood; but he is dead." And he touched the top of his head, where the hair had suddenly gone as thin as it had been on that of his poor brother, to indicate, I suppose, the cause of death. "He could nod ged over losing de oder shop. Do you wand any boods?" And he held up the leather in his hand: "Id's a beaudiful biece."

I ordered several pairs. It was very long before they came—but

422

they were better than ever. One simply could not wear them out. And soon after that I went abroad.

It was over a year before I was again in London. And the first shop I went to was my old friend's. I had left a man of sixty, I came back to one of seventy-five, pinched and worn and tremulous, who genuinely, this time, did not at first know me.

"Oh! Mr. Gessler," I said, sick at heart; "how splendid your boots are! See, I've been wearing this pair nearly all the time I've been abroad; and they're not half worn out, are they?"

He looked long at my boots—a pair of Russian leather, and his face seemed to regain steadiness. Putting his hand on my instep, he said:

"Do dey vid you here? I 'ad drouble wid dat bair, I remember."

I assured him that they had fitted beautifully.

"Do you wand any boods?" he said. "I can make dem quickly; id is a slack dime."

I answered: "Please, please! I want boots all round—every kind!"

"I will make a vresh model. Your foot must be bigger." And with utter slowness, he traced round my foot, and felt my toes, only once looking up to say:

"Did I tell you my brudder was dead?"

To watch him was painful, so feeble had he grown; I was glad to get away.

I had given those boots up, when one evening they came. Opening the parcel, I set the four pairs out in a row. Then one by one I tried them on. There was no doubt about it. In shape and fit, in finish and quality of leather, they were the best he had ever made me. And in the mouth of one of the Town walking-boots I found his bill. The amount was the same as usual, but it gave me quite a shock. He had never before sent it till quarter day. I flew down-stairs, and wrote a cheque, and posted it at once with my own hand.

A week later, passing the little street, I thought I would go in and tell him how splendidly the new boots fitted. But when I came to where his shop had been, his name was gone. Still there, in the window, were the slim pumps, the patent leathers with cloth tops, the sooty riding boots.

I went in, very much disturbed. In the two little shops—again made into one—was a young man with an English face.

"Mr. Gessler in?" I said.

He gave me a strange, ingratiating look.

"No, sir," he said, "no. But we can attend to anything with

pleasure. We've taken the shop over. You've seen our name, no doubt, next door. We make for some very good people."

"Yes, yes," I said; "but Mr. Gessler?"

"Oh!" he answered; "dead.'

"Dead! But I received these boots from him last Wednesday week."

"Ah!" he said, "a shockin' go. Poor old man starved 'imself."

"Good God!"

"Slow starvation, the doctor called it! You see he went to work in such a way! Would keep the shop on; wouldn't have a soul touch his boots except himself. When he got an order, it took him such a time. People won't wait. He lost everybody. And there he'd sit, goin' on and on—I will say that for him—not a man in London made a better boot! But look at the competition! He never advertised! Would 'ave the best leather, too, and do it all 'imself. Well, there it is. What could you expect with his ideas?"

"But starvation——!"

"That may be a bit flowery, as the sayin' is—but I know myself he was sittin' over his boots day and night, to the very last. You see I used to watch him. Never gave himself time to eat; never had a penny in the house. All went in rent and leather. How he lived so long I don't know. He regular let his fire go out. He was a character. But he made good boots."

"Yes," I said, "he made good boots."

And I turned and went out quickly, for I did not want that youth to know that I could hardly see.

VSEVOLOD GARSHIN

VSEVOLOD GARSHIN (Russian, 1855-1888). Russian writer of novellas. Lived his short adult life in melancholy frustration, suffering from experiences in Serbian and Turkish wars. Committed suicide. Stories permeated with urgent sense of justice and compassion.

THE SIGNAL

SEMYON IVANOV was a track-walker. His hut was ten versts away from a railroad station in one direction and twelve versts away in the other. About four versts away there was a cotton mill that had opened the year before, and its tall chimney rose up darkly from

behind the forest. The only dwellings around were the distant huts of the other track-walkers.

Semyon Ivanov's health had been completely shattered. Nine years before he had served right through the war as servant to an officer. The sun had roasted him, the cold frozen him, and hunger famished him on the forced marches of forty and fifty versts a day in the heat and the cold and the rain and the shine. The bullets had whizzed about him, but, thank God! none had struck him.

Semyon's regiment had once been on the firing line. For a whole week there had been skirmishing with the Turks, only a deep ravine separating the two hostile armies; and from morn till eve there had been a steady cross-fire. Thrice daily Semyon carried a steaming samovar and his officer's meals from the camp kitchen to the ravine. The bullets hummed about him and rattled viciously against the rocks. Semyon was terrified and cried sometimes, but still he kept right on. The officers were pleased with him, because he always had hot tea ready for them.

He returned from the campaign with limbs unbroken but crippled with rheumatism. He had experienced no little sorrow since then. He arrived home to find that his father, an old man, and his little four-year-old son had died. Semyon remained alone with his wife. They could not do much. It was difficult to plow with rheumatic arms and legs. They could no longer stay in their village, so they started off to seek their fortune in new places. They stayed for a short time on the line, in Kherson and Donshchina, but nowhere found luck. Then the wife went out to service, and Semyon continued to travel about. Once he happened to ride on an engine, and at one of the stations the face of the station-master seemed familiar to him. Semyon looked at the station-master and the station-master looked at Semyon, and they recognized each other. He had been an officer in Semyon's regiment.

"You are Ivanov?" he said.

"Yes, your Excellency."

"How do you come to be here?"

Semyon told him all.

"Where are you off to?"

"I cannot tell you, sir."

"Idiot! What do you mean by 'cannot tell you'?"

"I mean what I say, your Excellency. There is nowhere for me to go to. I must hunt for work, sir."

The station-master looked at him, thought a bit, and said: "See

425

here, friend, stay a while at the station. You are married, I think. Where is your wife?"

"Yes, your Excellency, I am married. My wife is at Kursk, in service with a merchant."

"Well, write to your wife to come here. I will give you a free pass for her. There is a position as track-walker open. I will speak to the Chief on your behalf."

"I shall be very grateful to you, your Excellency," replied Semyon.

He stayed at the station, helped in the kitchen, cut firewood, kept the yard clean, and swept the platform. In a fortnight's time his wife arrived, and Semyon went on a hand-trolley to his hut. The hut was a new one and warm, with as much wood as he wanted. There was a little vegetable garden, the legacy of a former track-walker, and there was about half a dessiatin of plowed land on either side of the railway embankment. Semyon was rejoiced. He began to think of doing some farming, of purchasing a cow and a horse.

He was given all necessary stores—a green flag, a red flag, lanterns, a horn, hammer, screw-wrench for the nuts, a crow-bar, spade, broom, bolts and nails: they gave him two books of regulations and a time-table of the trains. At first Semyon could not sleep at night, and learned the whole time-table by heart. Two hours before a train was due he would go over his section, sit on the bench at his hut, and look and listen whether the rails were trembling or the rumble of the train could be heard. He even learned the regulations by heart, although he could only read by spelling out each word.

It was summer; the work was not heavy; there was no snow to clear away and the trains on that line were infrequent. Semyon used to go over his verst twice a day, examine and screw up nuts here and there, keep the bed level, look at the water-pipes, and then go home to his own affairs. There was only one drawback—he always had to get the inspector's permission for the least little thing he wanted to do. Semyon and his wife were even beginning to be bored.

Two months passed, and Semyon commenced to make the acquaintance of his neighbors, the track-walkers on either side of him. One was a very old man, whom the authorities were always meaning to relieve. He scarcely moved out of his hut. His wife used to do all his work. The other track-walker, nearer the station, was a young man, thin but muscular. He and Semyon met for the first time on the line midway between the huts. Semyon took off his hat and bowed. "Good health to you, neighbor," he said.

426

The neighbor glanced askance at him. "How do you do?" he replied; then turned around and made off.

Later the wives met. Semyon's wife passed the time of day with her neighbor, but neither did she say much.

On one occasion Semyon said to her: "Young woman, your husband is not very talkative."

The woman said nothing at first, then replied: "But what is there for him to talk about? Every one has his own business. Go your way, and God be with you."

However after another month or so they became acquainted. Semyon would go with Vasily along the line, sit on the edge of a pipe, smoke, and talk of life. Vasily, for the most part, kept silent, but Semyon talked of his village and of the campaign through which he had passed.

"I have had no little sorrow in my day," he would say; "and goodness knows I have not lived long. God has not given me happiness, but what He may give, so will it be. That's so, friend Vasily Stepanych."

Vasily Stepanych knocked the ashes out of his pipe against a rail, stood up and said: "It is not luck which follows us in life, but human beings. There is no crueller beast on this earth than man. Wolf does not eat wolf, but man will readily devour man."

"Come, friend, don't say that; a wolf eats wolf."

"The words came into my mind and I said it. All the same, there is nothing crueller than man. If it were not for his wickedness and greed, it would be possible to live. Everybody tries to sting you to the quick, to bite and eat you up."

Semyon pondered a bit. "I don't know, brother," he said; "perhaps it is as you say, and perhaps it is God's will."

"And perhaps," said Vasily, "it is waste of time for me to talk to you. To put everything unpleasant on God, and sit and suffer, means, brother, being not a man but an animal. That's what I have to say." And he turned and went off without saying good-bye.

Semyon also got up. "Neighbor," he called, "why do you lose your temper?" But his neighbor did not look round, and kept on his way.

Semyon gazed after him until he was lost to sight in the cutting at the turn. He went home and said to his wife: "Arina, our neighbor is a wicked person, not a man."

However, they did not quarrel. They met again and discussed the same topics.

427

"Ah, friend, if it were not for men we should not be poking in these huts," said Vasily on one occasion.

"And what if we are poking in these huts? It's not so bad. You can live in them."

"Live in them, indeed! Bah, you! . . . You have lived long and learned little, looked at much and seen little. What sort of life is there for a poor man in a hut here or there? The cannibals are devouring you. They are sucking up all your life-blood, and when you become old, they will throw you out just as they do husks to feed the pigs on. What pay do you get?"

"Not much, Vasily Stepanych—twelve rubles."

"And I, thirteen and a half rubles. Why? By the regulations the company should give us fifteen rubles a month with firing and lighting. Who decides that you should have twelve rubles, or I thirteen and a half? Ask yourself! And you say a man can live on that? You understand it is not a question of one and a half rubles or three rubles—even if they paid us each the whole fifteen rubles. I was at the station last month. The director passed through. I saw him. I had that honor. He had a separate coach. He came out and stood on the platform. . . . I shall not stay here long; I shall go somewhere, anywhere, follow my nose."

"But where will you go, Stepanych? Leave well enough alone. Here you have a house, warmth, a little piece of land. Your wife is a worker."

"Land! You should look at my piece of land. Not a twig on it—nothing. I planted some cabbages in the spring, just when the inspector came along. He said: 'What is this? Why have you not reported this? Why have you done this without permission? Dig them up, roots and all.' He was drunk. Another time he would not have said a word, but this time it struck him. Three rubles fine! . . ."

Vasily kept silent for a while, pulling at his pipe, then added quietly: "A little more and I should have done for him."

"You are hot-tempered."

"No, I am not hot-tempered, but I tell the truth and think. Yes, he will still get a bloody nose from me. I will complain to the Chief. We will see then!" And Vasily did complain to the Chief.

Once the Chief came to inspect the line. Three days later important personages were coming from St. Petersburg and would pass over the line. They were conducting an inquiry, so that previous to their journey it was necessary to put everything in order. Ballast

was laid down, the bed was leveled, the sleepers carefully examined, spikes driven in a bit, nuts screwed up, posts painted, and orders given for yellow sand to be sprinkled at the level crossings. The woman at the neighboring hut turned her old man out to weed. Semyon worked for a whole week. He put everything in order, mended his kaftan, cleaned and polished his brass plate until it fairly shone. Vasily also worked hard. The Chief arrived on a trolley, four men working the handles and the levers, making the six wheels hum. The trolley traveled at twenty versts an hour, but the wheels squeaked. It reached Semyon's hut, and he ran out and reported in soldierly fashion. All appeared to be in repair.

"Have you been here long?" inquired the Chief.

"Since the second of May, your Excellency."

"All right. Thank you. And who is at hut No. 164?"

The traffic inspector (he was traveling with the Chief on the trolley) replied: "Vasily Spiridov."

"Spiridov, Spiridov. . . . .Ah! is he the man against whom you made a note last year?"

"He is."

"Well, we will see Vasily Spiridov. Go on!" The workmen laid to the handles, and the trolley got under way. Semyon watched it, and thought, "There will be trouble between them and my neighbor."

About two hours later he started on his round. He saw some one coming along the line from the cutting. Something white showed on his head. Semyon began to look more attentively. It was Vasily. He had a stick in his hand, a small bundle on his shoulder, and his cheek was bound up in a handkerchief.

"Where are you off to?" cried Semyon.

Vasily came quite close. He was very pale, white as chalk, and his eyes had a wild look. Almost choking, he muttered: "To town— to Moscow—to the head office."

"Head office? Ah, you are going to complain, I suppose. Give it up! Vasily Stepanych, forget it."

"No, mate, I will not forget. It is too late. See! He struck me in the face, drew blood. So long as I live I will not forget. I will not leave it like this!"

Semyon took his hand. "Give it up, Stepanych. I am giving you good advice. You will not better things. . . ."

"Better things! I know myself I shan't better things. You were right about Fate. It would be better for me not to do it, but one must stand up for the right."

"But tell me, how did it happen?"

"How? He examined everything, got down from the trolley, looked into the hut. I knew beforehand that he would be strict, and so I had put everything into proper order. He was just going when I made my complaint. He immediately cried out: 'Here is a Government inquiry coming, and you make a complaint about a vegetable garden. Here are privy councilors coming, and you annoy me with cabbages!' I lost patience and said something—not very much, but it offended him, and he struck me in the face. I stood still; I did nothing, just as if what he did was perfectly all right. They went off; I came to myself, washed my face, and left."

"And what about the hut?"

"My wife is staying there. She will look after things. Never mind about the roads."

Vasily got up and collected himself. "Good-bye, Ivanov. I do not know whether I shall get any one at the office to listen to me."

"Surely you are not going to walk?"

"At the station I will try to get on a freight train, and to-morrow I shall be in Moscow."

The neighbors bade each other farewell. Vasily was absent for some time. His wife worked for him night and day. She never slept, and wore herself out waiting for her husband. On the third day the commission arrived. An engine, luggage-van, and two first-class saloons; but Vasily was still away. Semyon saw his wife on the fourth day. Her face was swollen from crying and her eyes were red.

"Has your husband returned?" he asked. But the woman only made a gesture with her hands, and without saying a word went her way.

Semyon had learned when still a lad to make flutes out of a kind of reed. He used to burn out the heart of the stalk, make holes where necessary, drill them, fix a mouth-piece at one end, and tune them so well that it was possible to play almost any air on them. He made a number of them in his spare time, and sent them by his friends amongst the freight brakemen to the bazaar in the town. He got two kopeks apiece for them. On the day following the visit of the commission he left his wife at home to meet the six o'clock train, and started off to the forest to cut some sticks. He went to the end of his section—at this point the line made a sharp turn—descended the embankment, and struck into the wood at the foot of the mountain. About half a verst away there was a big marsh, around which

430

splendid reeds for his flutes grew. He cut a whole bundle of stalks and started back home. The sun was already dropping low, and in the dead stillness only the twittering of the birds was audible, and the crackle of the dead wood under his feet. As he walked along rapidly, he fancied he heard the clang of iron striking iron, and he redoubled his pace. There was no repair going on in his section. What did it mean? He emerged from the woods, the railway embankment stood high before him; on the top a man was squatting on the bed of the line busily engaged in something. Semyon commenced quietly to crawl up towards him. He thought it was some one after the nuts which secure the rails. He watched, and the man got up, holding a crow-bar in his hand. He had loosened a rail, so that it would move to one side. A mist swam before Semyon's eyes; he wanted to cry out, but could not. It was Vasily! Semyon scrambled up the bank, as Vasily with crow-bar and wrench slid headlong down the other side.

"Vasily Stepanych! My dear friend, come back! Give me the crow-bar. We will put the rail back; no one will know. Come back! Save your soul from sin!"

Vasily did not look back, but disappeared into the woods.

Semyon stood before the rail which had been torn up. He threw down his bundle of sticks. A train was due; not a freight, but a passenger-train. And he had nothing with which to stop it, no flag. He could not replace the rail and could not drive in the spikes with his bare hands. It was necessary to run, absolutely necessary to run to the hut for some tools. "God help me!" he murmured.

Semyon started running towards his hut. He was out of breath, but still ran, falling every now and then. He had cleared the forest; he was only a few hundred feet from his hut, not more, when he heard the distant hooter of the factory sound—six o'clock! In two minutes' time No 7 train was due. "Oh, Lord! have pity on innocent souls!" In his mind Semyon saw the engine strike against the loosened rail with its left wheel, shiver, careen, tear up and splinter the sleepers—and just there, there was a curve and the embankment seventy feet high, down which the engine would topple — and the third-class carriages would be packed . . . little children. . . . All sitting in the train now, never dreaming of danger. "Oh, Lord! Tell me what to do! . . . No, it is impossible to run to the hut and get back in time."

Semyon did not run on to the hut, but turned back and ran faster

431

than before. He was running almost mechanically, blindly; he did not know himself what was to happen. He ran as far as the rail which had been pulled up; his sticks were lying in a heap. He bent down, seized one without knowing why, and ran on farther. It seemed to him the train was already coming. He heard the distant whistle; he heard the quiet, even tremor of the rails; but his strength was exhausted, he could run no farther, and came to a halt about six hundred feet from the awful spot. Then an idea came into his head, literally like a ray of light. Puilling off his cap, he took out of it a cotton scarf, drew his knife out of the upper part of his boot, and crossed himself, muttering, "God bless me!"

He buried the knife in his left arm above the elbow; the blood spurted out, flowing in a hot stream. In this he soaked his scarf, smoothed it out, tied it to the stick and hung out his red flag.

He stood waving his flag. The train was already in sight. The driver would not see him—would come close up, and a heavy train cannot be pulled up in six hundred feet.

And the blood kept on flowing. Semyon pressed the sides of the wound together so as to close it, but the blood did not diminish. Evidently he had cut his arm very deep. His head commenced to swim, black spots began to dance before his eyes, and then it became dark. There was a ringing in his ears. He could not see the train or hear the noise. Only one thought possessed him. "I shall not be able to keep standing up. I shall fall and drop the flag; the train will pass over me. Help me, O Lord!"

All turned black before him, his mind became a blank, and he dropped the flag; but the blood-stained banner did not fall to the ground. A hand seized it and held it high to meet the approaching train. The engineer saw it, shut the regulator, and reversed steam. The train came to a standstill.

People jumped out of the carriages and collected in a crowd. They saw a man lying senseless on the footway, drenched in blood, and another man standing beside him with a blood-stained rag on a stick.

Vasily looked around at all. Then, lowering his head, he said: "Bind me, I tore up a rail!"

THEOPHILE GAUTIER

THÉOPHILE GAUTIER (French, 1811-1872). One of the prominent founders of the French Romantic Movement. Painter, newspaperman, extensive traveler. Wrote art, dramatic and literary criticism, ballets and pantomimes. Both poetry and prose are highly polished, exotic, objective. Best-known novel: *Mademoiselle de Maupin.*

THE MUMMY'S FOOT

I HAD entered, in an idle mood, the shop of one of those curiosity-vendors, who are called *marchands de bric-à-brac* in that Parisian *argot*, which is so perfectly unintelligible elsewhere in France.

You have doubtless glanced occasionally through the windows of some of these shops, which have become so numerous now that it is fashionable to buy antiquated furniture, and that every petty stock-broker thinks he must have his *chambre au moyen âge.*

There is one thing there which clings alike to the shop of the dealer in old iron, the wareroom of the tapestry-maker, the laboratory of the chemist, and the studio of the painter:—in all those gloomy dens where a furtive daylight filters in through the window-shutters, the most manifestly ancient thing is dust;—the cobwebs are more authentic than the guimp laces; and the old pear-tree furniture on exhibition is actually younger than the mahogany which arrived but yesterday from America.

The warehouse of my *bric-à-brac* dealer was a veritable Capharnaum; all ages and all nations seemed to have made their rendezvous there; an Etruscan lamp of red clay stood upon a Boule cabinet, with ebony panels, brightly striped by lines of inlaid brass; a duchess of the court of Louis XV nonchalantly extended her fawn-like feet under a massive table of the time of Louis XIII with heavy spiral supports of oak, and carven designs of chimeras and foliage intermingled.

Upon the denticulated shelves of several sideboards glittered immense Japanese dishes with red and blue designs relieved by gilded hatching; side by side with enameled works by Bernard Palissy, representing serpents, frogs, and lizards in relief.

From disemboweled cabinets escaped cascades of silver-lustrous Chinese silks and waves of tinsel, which an oblique sunbeam shot through with luminous beads; while portraits of every era, in

433

frames more or less tarnished, smiled through their yellow varnish.

The striped breastplate of a damascened suit of Milanese armor glittered in one corner; Loves and Nymphs of porcelain; Chinese Grotesques, vases of *céladon* and crackle-ware; Saxon and old Sèvres cups encumbered the shelves and nooks of the apartment.

The dealer followed me closely through the tortuous way contrived between the piles of furniture; warding off with his hand the hazardous sweep of my coat-skirts; watching my elbows with the uneasy attention of an antiquarian and a usurer.

It was a singular face, that of the merchant:—an immense skull, polished like a knee, and surrounded by a thin aureole of white hair, which brought out the clear salmon tint of his complexion all the more strikingly, lent him a false aspect of patriarchal *bon-homie*, counteracted, however, by the scintillation of two little yellow eyes which trembled in their orbits like two louis-d'or upon quicksilver. The curve of his nose presented an aquiline silhouette, which suggested the Oriental or Jewish type. His hands—thin, slender, full of nerves which projected like strings upon the finger-board of a violin, and armed with claws like those on the terminations of bats' wings—shook with senile trembling; both those convulsively agitated hands became firmer than steel pincers or lobsters' claws when they lifted any precious article—an onyx cup, a Venitian glass, or a dish of Bohemian crystal. This strange old man had an aspect so thoroughly rabbinical and cabalistic that he would have been burnt on the mere testimony of his face three hundred centuries ago.

"Will you not buy something from me to-day, sir? Here is a Malay kreese with a blade undulating like flame; look at those grooves contrived for the blood to run along, those teeth set backwards so as to tear out the entrails in withdrawing the weapon—it is a fine character of ferocious arm, and will look well in your collection: this two-handed sword is very beautiful—it is the work of Josepe de la Hera; and this *colichemarde,* with its fenestrated guard—what a superb specimen of handicraft!"

"No; I have quite enough weapons and instruments of carnage;—I want a small figure, something which will suit me as a paper-weight; for I cannot endure those trumpery bronzes which the stationers sell, and which may be found on everybody's desk."

The old gnome foraged among his ancient wares, and finally arranged before me some antique bronzes—so-called, at least; fragments of malachite; little Hindoo or Chinese idols—a kind of pussah

toys in jadestone, representing the incarnations of Brahma or Vishnoo, and wonderfully appropriate to the very undivine office of holding papers and letters in place.

I was hesitating between a porcelain dragon, all constellated with warts—its mouth formidable with bristling tusks and ranges of teeth—and an abominable Mexican fetish, representing the god Zitziliputzili *au naturel*, when I caught sight of a charming foot, which I at first took for a fragment of some antique Venus.

It had those beautifully ruddy and tawny tints that lend to Florentine bronze that warm living look so much preferable to the gray-green aspect of common bronzes, which might easily be mistaken for statues in a state of putrefaction: satin gleams played over its rounded forms, doubtless polished by the amorous kiss of twenty centuries; for it seemed a Corinthian bronze, a work of the best era of art—perhaps molded by Lysippus himself.

"That foot will be my choice," I said to the merchant, who regarded me with an ironical and saturnine air, and held out the object desired that I might examine it more fully.

I was surprised at its lightness; it was not a foot of metal, but in sooth a foot of flesh—an embalmed foot—a mumy's foot: on examining it still more closely the very grain of the skin, and the almost imperceptible lines impressed upon it by the texture of the bandages, became perceptible. The toes were slender and delicate, and terminated by perfectly formed nails, pure and transparent as agates; the great toe, slightly separated from the rest, afforded a happy contrast, in the antique style, to the position of the other toes, and lent it an aerial lightness—the grace of a bird's foot,—the sole, scarcely streaked by a few almost imperceptible cross lines, afforded evidence that it had never touched the bare ground, and had only come in contact with the finest matting of Nile rushes, and the softest carpets of panther skin.

"Ha, ha!—you want the foot of the Princess Hermonthis,"—exclaimed the merchant, with a strange giggle, fixing his owlish eyes upon me—"ha, ha ha!—for a paper-weight!—an original idea!—artistic idea! Old Pharaoh would certainly have been surprised had some one told him that the foot of his adored daughter would be used for a paperweight after he had a mountain of granite hollowed out as a receptacle for the triple coffin, painted and gilded—covered with hieroglyphics and beautiful paintings of the Judgment of Souls,"—continued the queer little merchant, half audibly, as though talking to himself!

435

"How much will you charge me for this mummy fragment?"

"Ah, the highest price I can get; for it is a superb piece: if I had the match of it you could not have it for less than five hundred francs;—the daughter of a Pharaoh! nothing is more rare."

"Assuredly that is not a common article; but, still, how much do you want? In the first place I can buy anything that costs five louis, but nothing dearer;—you might search my vest pockets and most secret drawers without even finding one poor five-franc piece more."

"Five louis for the foot of the Princess Hermonthis! that is very little, very little indeed; 'tis an authentic foot," muttered the merchant, shaking his head, and imparting a peculiar rotary motion to his eyes. "Well, take it, And I will give you the bandages into the bargain," he added, wrapping the foot in an ancient damask rag—"very fine! real damask—Indian damask which has never been redyed; it is strong, and yet it is soft," he mumbled, stroking the frayed tissue with his fingers, through the trade-acquired habit which moved him to praise even an object of so little value that he himself deemed it only worth the giving away.

He poured the gold coins into a sort of medieval alms-purse hanging at his belt, repeating:

"The foot of the Princess Hermonthis, to be used for a paper-weight."

Then turning his phosphorescent eyes upon me, he exclaimed in a voice strident as the crying of a cat which has swallowed a fish-bone:

"Old Pharaoh will not be well pleased; he loved his daughter—the dear man!"

"You speak as if you were a contemporary of his: you are old enough, goodness knows! but you do not date back to the Pyramids of Egypt," I answered, laughingly, from the threshold.

I went home, delighted with my acquisition.

With the idea of putting it to profitable use as soon as possible, I placed the foot of the divine Princess Hermonthis upon a heap of papers scribbled over with verses, in themselves an undecipherable mosaic work of erasures; articles freshly begun; letters forgotten, and posted in the table drawer instead of the letter-box—an error of which absent-minded people are peculiarly liable. The effect was charming, *bizarre*, and romantic.

Well satisfied with this embellishment, I went out with the gravity and pride becoming one who feels that he has the ineffable ad-

vantage over all the passers-by whom he elbows, of possessing a piece of the Princess Hermonthis, daughter of Pharaoh.

I looked upon all who did not possess, like myself, a paper-weight so authentically Egyptian, as very ridiculous people; and it seemed to me that the proper occupation of every sensible man should consist in the mere fact of having a mummy's foot upon his desk.

Happily I met some friends, whose presence distracted me in my infatuation with this new acquisition: I went to dinner with them; for I could not very well have dined with myself.

When I came back that evening, with my brain slightly confused by a few glasses of wine, a vague whiff of Oriental perfume deli-cately titillated my olfatory nerves: the heat of the room had warmed the natron, bitumen, and myrrh in which the *paraschistes, who cut* open the bodies of the dead, had bathed the corpse of the princess;— it was a perfume at once sweet and penetrating—a perfume that four thousand years had not been able to dissipate.

The Dream of Egypt was Eternity: her odors have the solidity of granite, and endure as long.

I soon drank deeply from the black cup of sleep: for a few hours all remained opaque to me; Oblivion and Nothingness in-undated me with their somber waves.

Yet light gradually dawned upon the darkness of my mind; dreams commenced to touch me softly in their silent flight.

The eyes of my soul were opened; and I beheld my chamber as it actually was; I might have believed myself awake, but for a vague consciousness which assured me that I slept, and that some-thing fantastic was about to take place.

The odor of the myrrh had augmented in intensity: and I felt a slight headache, which I very naturally attributed to several glasses of champagne that we had drunk to the unknown gods and our future fortunes.

I peered through my room with a feeling of expectation which I saw nothing to justify: every article of furniture was in its proper place; the lamp, softly shaded by its globe of ground crystal, burned upon its bracket; the water-color sketches shone under their Bo-hemian glass; the curtains hung down languidly; everything wore an aspect of tranquil slumber.

After a few moments, however, all this calm interior appeared to become disturbed; the woodwork cracked stealthily; the ash-covered log suddenl emitted a jet of blue flame; and the disks of the

pateras seemed like great metallic eyes, watching, like myself, for the things which were about to happen.

My eyes accidentally fell upon the desk where I had placed the foot of the Princess Hermonthis.

Instead of remaining quiet—as behooved a foot which had been embalmed for four thousand years— it commenced to act in a nervous manner; contracted itself, and leaped over the papers like a startled frog;—one would have imagined that it had suddenly been brought into contact with a galvanic battery: I could distinctly hear the dry sound made by its little heel, hard as the hoof of a gazelle.

I became rather discontented with my acquisition, inasmuch as I wished my paper-weights to be of a sedentary disposition, and thought it very unnatural that feet should walk about without legs; and I commenced to experience a feeling closely akin to fear.

Suddenly I saw the folds of my bed-curtain stir; and heard a bumping sound, like that caused by some person hopping on one foot across the floor. I must confess I became alternately hot and cold; that I felt a strange wind chill my back; and that my suddenly rising hair caused my nightcap to execute a leap of several yards.

The bed-curtains opened and I beheld the strangest figure imaginable before me.

It was a young girl of a very deep coffee-brown complexion, like the bayadere Amani, and possessing the purest Egyptian type of perfect beauty: her eyes were almond-shaped and oblique, with eyebrows so black that they seemed blue; her nose was exquisitely chiseled, almost Greek in its delicacy of outline; and she might indeed have been taken for a Corinthian statue of bronze, but for the prominence of her cheekbones and the slightly African fullness of her lips, which compelled one to recognize her as belonging beyond all doubt to the hieroglyphic race which dwelt upon the banks of the Nile.

Her arms, slender and spindle-shaped, like those of very young girls, were encircled by a peculiar kind of metal bands and bracelets of glass beads; her hair was all twisted into little cords; and she wore upon her bosom a little idol-figure of green paste, bearing a whip with seven lashes, which proved it to be an image of Isis: her brow was adorned with a shining plate of gold; and a few traces of paint relieved the coppery tint of her cheeks.

As for her costume, it was very odd indeed.

Fancy a *pagne* or skirt all formed of little strips of material be-

dizened with red and black hieroglyphics, stiffened with bitumen, and apparently belonging to a freshly unbandaged mummy.

In one of those sudden flights of thought so common in dreams I heard the hoarse falsetto of the *bric-à-brac* dealer, repeating like a monotonous refrain the phrase he had uttered in his shop with so enigmatic an intonation:

"Old Pharaoh will not be well pleased: he loved his daughter, the dear man!"

One strange circumstance, which was not at all calculated to restore my equanimity, was that the apparition had but one foot; the other was broken off at the ankle!

She approached the table where the foot was starting and fidgeting about more than ever, and there supported herself upon the edge of the desk. I saw her eyes fill with pearly-gleaming tears.

Although she had not as yet spoken, I fully comprehended the thoughts which agitated her: she looked at her foot—for it was indeed her own—with an exquisitely graceful expression of coquettish sadness; but the foot leaped and ran hither and thither as though impelled on steel springs.

Twice or thrice she extended her hand to seize it, but could not succeed.

Then commenced between Princess Hermonthis and her foot—which appeared to be endowed with a special life of its own—a very fantastic dialogue in a most ancient Coptic tongue, such as might have been spoken thirty centuries ago in the syrinxes of the land of Ser: luckily, I understood Coptic perfectly well that night.

The Princess Hermonthis cried, in a voice sweet and vibrant as the tones of a crystal bell:

"Well, my dear little foot, you always flee from me; yet I always took good care of you. I bathed you with perfumed water in a bowl of alabaster; I smoothed your heel with pumice-stone mixed with palm oil; your nails were cut with golden scissors and polished with a hippopotamus tooth; I was careful to select *tatbebs* for you, painted and embroidered and turned up at the toes, which were the envy of all the young girls in Egypt: you wore on your great toe rings bearing the device of the sacred Scarabæus; and you supported one of the lightest bodies that a lazy foot could sustain."

The foot replied, in a pouting and chagrined tone:

"You know well that I do not belong to myself any longer;—I have been bought and paid for; the old merchant knew what he was about; he bore you a grudge for having refused to espouse him;—

439

this is an ill turn which he has done you. The Arab who violated your royal coffin in the subterranean pits of the necropolis of Thebes was sent thither by him: he desired to prevent you from being present at the reunion of the shadowy nations in the cities below. Have you five pieces of gold for my ransom?"

"Alas, no!—my jewels, my rings, my purses of gold and silver, they were all stolen from me," answered the Princess Hermonthis, with a sob.

"Princess," I then exclaimed, "I never retained anybody's foot unjustly;—even though you have not got the five louis which it cost me, I present it to you gladly: I should feel unutterably wretched to think that I were the cause of so amiable a person as the Princess Hermonthis being lame."

I delivered this discourse in a royally gallant, troubadour tone, which must have astonished the beautiful Egyptian girl.

She turned a look of deepest gratitude upon me; and her eyes shone with bluish gleams of light.

She took her foot—which surrendered itself willingly this time—like a woman about to put on her little shoe, and adjusted it to her leg with much skill.

This operation over, she took a few steps about the room, as though to assure herself that she was really no longer lame.

"Ah, how pleased my father will be!—he who was so unhappy because of my mutilation, and who from the moment of my birth set a whole nation at work to hollow me out a tomb so deep that he might preserve me intact until that last day, when souls must be weighed in the balance of Amenthi! Come with me to my father;—he will receive you kindly; for you have given me back my foot."

I thought this proposition natural enough. I arrayed myself in a dressing-gown of large-flowered pattern, which lent me a very Pharaonic aspect; hurriedly put on a pair of Turkish slippers, and informed the Princess Hermonthis that I was ready to follow her.

Before starting, Hermonthis took from her neck the little idol of green paste, and laid it on the scattered sheets of paper which covered the table.

"It is only fair," she observed smilingly, "that I should replace your paper-weight."

She gave me her hand, which felt soft and cold, like the skin of a serpent; and we departed.

We passed for some time with the velocity of an arrow through

440

a fluid and grayish expanse, in which half-formed silhouettes flitted swiftly by us, to right and left.

For an instant we saw only sky and sea.

A few moments later obelisks commenced to tower in the distance: pylons and vast flights of steps guarded by sphinxes became clearly outlined against the horizon.

We had reached our destination.

The princess conducted me to the mountain of rose-colored granite, in the face of which appeared an opening so narrow and low that it would have been difficult to distinguish it from the fissures in the rock, had not its location been marked by two stelæ wrought with sculptures.

Hermonthis kindled a torch, and led the way before me.

We traversed corridors hewn through the living rock: their walls, covered with hieroglyphics and paintings of allegorical processions, might well have occupied thousands of arms for thousands of years in their formation;—these corridors, of interminable length, opened into square chambers, in the midst of which pits had been contrived, through which we descended by cramp-irons or spiral stairways;—these pits again conducted us into other chambers, opening into other corridors, likewise decorated with painted sparrow-hawks, serpents coiled in circles, the symbols of the *tau* and *pedum*—prodigious works of art which no living eye can ever examine—interminable legends of granite which only the dead have time to read through all eternity.

At last we found ourselves in a hall so vast, so enormous, so immeasurable, that the eye could not reach its limits; files of monstrous columns stretched far out of sight on every side, between which twinkled livid stars of yellowish flame;—points of light which revealed further depths incalculable in the darkness beyond.

The Princess Hermonthis still held my hand, and graciously saluted the mummies of her acquaintance.

My eyes became accustomed to the dim twilight, and objects became discernible.

I beheld the kings of the subterranean races seated upon thrones—grand old men, though dry, withered, wrinkled like parchment, and blackened with naphtha and bitumen—all wearing *pshents* of gold, and breastplates with gorgets glittering with precious stones; their eyes immovably fixed like the eyes of sphinxes, and their long beards whitened by the snow of centuries. Behind them stood their

441

peoples, in the stiff and constrained posture enjoined by Egyptian art, all eternally preserving the attitude prescribed by the hieratic code. Behind these nations, the cats, ibises, and crocodiles contemporary with them—rendered monstrous of aspect by their swathing bands—mewed, flapped their wings, or extended their jaws in a saurian giggle.

All the Pharaohs were there—Cheops, Chephrenes, Psammetichus, Sesostris, Amenotaph—all the dark rulers of the pyramids and syrinxes;—on yet higher thrones sat Chronos and Xixouthros—who was contemporary with the deluge; and Tubal Cain, who reigned before it.

The beard of King Xixouthros had grown seven times around the granite table, upon which he leaned, lost in deep reverie—and buried in dreams.

Further back, through a dusty cloud, I beheld dimly the seventy-two pre-Adamite Kings, with their seventy-two peoples — forever passed away.

After permitting me to gaze upon this bewildering spectacle a few moments, the Princess Hermonthis presented me to her father Pharaoh, who favored me with a most gracious nod.

"I have found my foot again!—I have found my foot!" cried the Princess, clapping her little hands together with every sign of frantic joy: "it was this gentleman who restored it to me."

The races of Kemi, the races of Nahasi—all the black, bronzed, and copper-colored nations repeated in chorus:

"The Princess Hermonthis has found her foot again!"

Even Xixouthros himself was visibly affected.

He raised his heavy eyelids, stroked his mustache with his fingers, and turned upon me a glance weighty with centuries.

"By Oms, the dog of Hell, and Tmei, daughter of the Sun and of Truth! this is a brave and worthy lad!" exclaimed Pharaoh, pointing to me with his scepter, which was terminated with a lotus-flower.

"What recompense do you desire?"

Filled with that daring inspired by dreams in which nothing seems impossible, I asked him for the hand of the Princess Hermonthis;—the hand seemed to me a very proper antithetic recompense for the foot.

Pharaoh opened wide his great eyes of glass in astonishment at my witty request.

"What country do you come from? and what is your age?"

"I am a Frenchman; and I am twenty-seven years old, venerable Pharaoh."

"——Twenty-seven years old! and he wishes to espouse the Princess Hermonthis, who is thirty centuries old!" cried out at once all the Thrones and all the Circles of Nations.

Only Hermonthis herself did not seem to think my request unreasonable.

"If you were even only two thousand years old," replied the ancient King, "I would willingly give you the Princess; but the disproportion is too great; and, besides, we must give our daughters husbands who will last well: you do not know how to preserve yourselves any longer; even those who died only fifteen centuries ago are already no more than a handful of dust;—behold! my flesh is solid as basalt; my bones are bars of steel!

"I shall be present on the last day of the world, with the same body and the same features which I had during my lifetime: my daughter Hermonthis will last longer than a statue of bronze.

"Then the last particles of your dust will have been scattered abroad by the winds; and even Isis herself, who was able to find the atoms of Osiris, would scarce be able to recompose your being.

"See how vigorous I yet remain, and how mighty is my grasp," he added, shaking my hand in the English fashion with a strength that buried my rings in the flesh of my fingers.

He squeezed me so hard that I awoke, and found my friend Alfred shaking me by the arm to make me get up.

"O you everlasting sleeper!—must I have you carried out into the middle of the street, and fireworks exploded in your ears? It is after noon; don't you recollect your promise to take me with you to see M. Aguado's Spanish pictures?"

"God! I forgot all, all about it," I answered, dressing myself hurriedly; "we will go there at once; I have the permit lying on my desk."

I started to find it;—but fancy my astonishment when I beheld, instead of the mummy's foot I had purchased the evening before, the little green paste idol left in its place by the Princess Hermonthis!

KHALIL GIBRAN

KHALIL GIBRAN (Syro-American, 1883-1931). Syro-American writer of inspirational literature. Born in Lebanon, came to America at 11. Studied in Europe, then formed coterie of Syrian writers in New York. Early works in Arabic: *Al-arwāh al-mutamarridat (Spirits Rebellious)*. Later ones in English: *The Prophet*. Taught a religion of love, beauty and redemption.

BEHIND THE GARMENT

RACHEL woke at midnight and gazed intently at something invisible in the sky of her chamber. She heard a voice more soothing than the whispers of Life, and more dismal than the moaning call of the abyss, and softer than the rustling of white wings, and deeper than the message of the waves. . . . It vibrated with hope and with futility, with joy and with misery, and with affection for life, yet with desire for death. Then Rachel closed her eyes and sighed deeply, and gasped, saying, "Dawn has reached the extreme end of the valley; we should go toward the sun and meet him." Her lips were parted, resembling and echoing a deep wound in the soul.

At that moment the priest approached her bed and felt her hand, but found it as cold as the snow; and when he grimly placed his fingers upon her heart, he determined that it was as immobile as the ages, and as silent as the secret of his heart.

The reverend father bowed his head in deep despair. His lips quivered as if wanting to utter a divine word, repeated by the phantoms of the night in the distant and deserted valleys.

After crossing her arms upon her bosom, the priest looked toward a man sitting in an obscured corner of the room, and with a kind and merciful voice he said, "Your beloved has reached the great circle of light. Come, my brother, let us kneel and pray."

The sorrowful husband lifted his head; his eyes stared, gazing at the unseen, and his expression then changed as if he saw understanding in the ghost of an unknown God. He gathered the remnants of himself and walked reverently toward the bed of his wife, and knelt by the side of the clergyman who was praying and lamenting and making the sign of the cross.

Placing his hand upon the shoulder of the grief-stricken husband, the Father said quietly, "Go to the adjoining room, brother, for you are in great need of rest."

He rose obediently, walked to the room and threw his fatigued

body upon a narrow bed, and in a few moments he was sailing in the world of sleep like a little child taking refuge in the merciful arms of his loving mother.

*　　*　　*　　*　　*

The priest remained standing like a statue in the center of the room, and a strange conflict gripped him. And he looked with tearful eyes at the cold body of the young woman and then through the parted curtain at her husband, who had surrendered himself to the allure of slumber. An hour, longer than an age and more terrible than Death, had already passed, and the priest was still standing between two parted souls. One was dreaming as a field dreams of the coming Spring after the tragedy of Winter, and the other was resting eternally.

Then the priest came close to the body of the young woman and knelt as if worshipping before the altar; he held her cold hand and placed it against his trembling lips, and looked at her face that was adorned with the soft veil of Death. His voice was at the same time calm as the night and deep as the chasm and faltering as with the hopes of man. And in voice he wept, "Oh Rachel, bride of my soul, hear me! At last I am able to talk! Death has opened my lips so that I can now reveal to you a secret deeper than Life itself. Pain has unpinioned my tongue and I can disclose to you my suffering, more painful than pain. Listen to the cry of my soul, Oh Pure Spirit, hovering between the earth and the firmament. Give heed to the youth who waited for you to come from the field, gazing upon you from behind the trees, in fear of your beauty. Hear the priest, who is serving God, calling to you unashamed, after you have reached the City of God. I have proved the strength of my love by concealing it!"

Having thus opened his soul, the Father leaned over and printed three long, warm, and mute kisses upon her forehead, eyes and throat, pouring forth all his heart's secret of love and pain, and the anguish of the years. Then he suddenly withdrew to the dark corner and dropped in agony upon the floor, shaking like an Autumn leaf, as if the touch of her cold face had awakened within him the spirit to repent; whereupon he composed himself and knelt, hiding his face with his cupped hands, and he whispered softly, "God. . . . Forgive my sin; forgive my weakness, Oh Lord. I could no longer resist disclosing that which You knew. Seven years have I kept the deep secrets hidden in my heart from the spoken word, until Death

445

came and tore them from me. Help me, Oh God, to hide this terrible and beautiful memory which brings sweetness from life and bitterness from You. Forgive me, My Lord, and forgive my weakness."

Without looking at the young woman's corpse, he continued suffering and lamenting until Dawn came and dropped a rosy veil upon those two still images, revealing the conflict of Love and Religion to one man; the peace of Life and Death to the other.

ANDRE GIDE

ANDRÉ GIDE (French, 1869-1951). Contemporary French novelist. Sensitive and sensuous protagonist of egotism. Rebelled against Puritan background after meeting Oscar Wilde in Algeria. Insisted on doctrine of individual morality, but became a stylist in classic tradition. Most widely read novel: *The Counterfeiters*. Others: *The Immoralist, The Pastoral Symphony, Strait Is the Gate*. Autobiography: *If It Die . . .*

MY MOTHER

I

WHEN I had finished my first studies, my mother thought it would be a good thing to introduce me to "society". But aside from some not too distant cousins and the wives of a few of my father's colleagues at the Faculty of Law, transplanted from Rouen to Paris, she had never tried to make any acquaintances. Furthermore, the world in which it seemed I was to be interested, that of men of letters or artists, was not "her" world; she would have felt herself out of place in it.

I no longer know to what drawing-room she took me that day. It must have been that of my cousin Saussine, at whose home, on the rue d'Athènes, I took tiresome dancing lessons twice a week. It was the day they received. There were numerous introductions, and the conversation was approximately what all society conversations are, made up of little nothings and affectations. I turned my attention less to the other ladies than to my mother. I scarcely recognized her. She, ordinarily so modest, so reserved, and seemingly fearful of her own opinion, appeared in that social gathering, full of assurance and, without pushing herself forward at all, perfectly at her

446

ease. One would have said that she was playing a role exactly as it should be, without, moreover, attaching any importance to it, but willingly consenting to mingle in the game of the society parade to which one contributes hardly anything but outward appearances. It even seemed to me that, in the twaddle and foolishness all about, a few particularly sensible sentences of hers threw the general conversation into disorder; the ridiculous remarks immediately collapsed and disappeared into thin air, like ghosts at the crowing of the cock. I was amazed, and told her so, as soon as we escaped from that Vanity Fair, and found ourselves alone together.

For my part, I dined that evening with Pierre Louys, I believe. At any rate, I remember that I left her as we turned the corner of rue d'Athènes. But I came back to her almost immediately after dinner. I was in a hurry to see her. We were then living on the rue de Commaille. The windows of our apartment opened on a deep garden that no longer exists to-day. My mother was on the balcony. She had taken off her finery, and I rediscovered her in her simple, drab, everyday clothes. It was the season when the first acacias smell sweet. My mother seemed worried; she did not make confidences easily and doubtless the co-operation of springtime was needed to invite her to speak.

"Is what you said to me as we left our cousin's true?" she began with a great effort. "You really think so? I was . . . well, as good as the others?"

And as I began to exclaim, she continued mournfully:

"If your father had told me so even once . . . I never dared ask him, and I needed so terribly to know, when we went out together, if he was . . . "

She was silent for a moment. I looked at her trying to hold back her tears. She finished in a lower tone of voice, hardly audible:

". . . if he was pleased with me."

I think that those were her exact words which suddenly let me understand how many worries, unasked questions and expectations could, under the appearance of happiness, still dwell in even the most united of couples. And such were my parents in the eyes of everyone and of their son. What my mother had vainly awaited was not a compliment from my father, but only the assurance that she had been able to prove herself worthy of him, that he had not been disappointed in her. But what my father thought, I knew no more than she; and I understood, that evening, that every soul carries to the tomb to hide it there, some secret.

II

Everything that was natural in my mother, I loved. But it happened that her impulses were checked by covention and the bent that a bourgeois education too often leaves behind it. (Not always; thus I remember that she dared brave the disapproval of all her family when she went to care for the farmers of La Roque attacked during a typhus epidemic.) That education, excellent, doubtless, when it is a question of curbing evil instincts, attacks equally, but then very unfortunately, the generous emotions of the heart; then a sort of calculation restrains or directs them. I should like to give an example of this:

My mother announced to me her intention of making a gift of Littré to Anna Shackleton, our poor friend, whom I loved as a son. I was bursting with joy, when she added:

"The one I gave your father is bound in morocco. I thought that, for Anna, a shagreen binding would be sufficient."

I understood at once, what I had not known before, that shagreen costs much less. The joy suddenly left my heart. And without a doubt my mother noticed it, for she went on quickly:

"She won't see the difference."

No, that shabby cheating was not natural to her. To her giving was natural. But I was irritated also by that sort of complicity to which she had invited me.

I have lost the memory of a thousand more important things. Why did those few sentences of my mother's engrave themselves so deeply on my heart? Perhaps because I felt myself capable of thinking and saying them myself, in spite of the violent reprobation they aroused in me. Perhaps because I became conscious of that bent against which I should have to struggle and that I was sadly amazed to discover in my mother. Everything else melted into the harmonious ensemble of her face; and it is perhaps just because I did not recognize her any more by that trait, truly unworthy of her, that my memory took possession of it. What a warning! What strength that educational bent had, then, to triumph in this way from time to time! But my mother remained too surrounded by beings deformed in the same way, to be able to recognize in herself, among all the acquired characteristics, those spontaneous to her nature; above all, she remained too fearful and unsure of herself to give them the upper hand. She remained worried about others and their opinions; always desirous of the best, but a best answering to

448

accepted rules; always tending toward this best, and without even suspecting (and too modest to recognize it) that the best in her was exactly what she obtained with the least effort.

JEAN GIRAUDOUX

JEAN GIRAUDOUX (French, 1882-1944). Influential modern playwright and novelist. Profound and searching in thought. Was diplomat after First World War. Achieved first success as novelist *(Siegfried et le Limousin)*, then as dramatist. Chose fantastic themes to treat serious problems of our time. Plays translated: *Amphitryon 38, Intermezzo, The Madwoman of Chaillot, Ondine, Tiger at the Gates.*

MAY ON LAKE ASQUAM

I AM stretched out in the middle of a great ring of mountains. When I get up onto my feet, I become their very pivot. I have put the sun on my left, as they taught me to do at school, and I am writing to you. The lake below me bears fragile islands on its surface, and pine logs, from the drifts broken up during the winter, wash vagrantly in its bays and coves. Humming-birds thrusting voraciously among the apple-blossoms, wound their swift bills on the hard wood and glance off again. To soothe the sore feet of the farm turkeys—a degenerate race—Mrs. Green is greasing the limbs of the tree where they come to roost. A thrush grazes me, a little breeze begins to stir. As when a bird alights by a dreaming poet and he is moved to see the very thought he was seeking within himself drop then, perfect— so a sweet and tender love, instead of stirring in my heart, lifts this page, fans me with its soft breath. In boat-houses hidden in the reeds the farmers are testing the motors of the boats which will be launched for their masters next month. Mrs. Green is beating a rose-colored puff for me, because my bed ends under the window, and when I wake in the morning I see my sunny feet under the spread—and yet feel cold. In the depths of the creeks where the new-cut pines are floating, the lumbermen jump from one log to the next, whistling as they go. I envy them their balance; I feel over-weighted with a lake and a sun on my left, and nothing on my right. Where am I? I am in a land which I instantly recognize to be

enormous, because these wasps that are this second buzzing about my head are three times bigger than they are in Europe. I am in the middle of New Hampshire, which is having its first sight of the sky-blue uniform, and, supposing that I have chosen this color myself, imagines me to be sensitive and generous. The Harvard Regiment is having a week of examinations, and I am taking a rest.

The motor left Boston early on Monday, reaching the suburbs at the hour when the typewriters, perched on their high-heeled, pointed shoes, in their low-necked foulard dresses, and bent slant-wise to the wind, climb into the tramcars without touching the rail, anxious only for their hands; the stenographers following them rigidly erect, thinking only of their heads. On the door-steps Irish girls with brown braids looped over their ears passed on to us, through soft blue eyes, the holiest thoughts they had been pondering in the night. We were following the highway bordered with Washington elms, very old trees whose trunks had been repaired with the sort of cement of which they make statues in this country; and immortality —as sap was lacking—had already reached the topmost branches. Lakes that grew clearer and clearer the farther we went held the water of the richer and richer parts of Boston, and we came at last to the very round, very blue lake that supplies Beacon Street.

At noon we were at Portsmouth, where I presided at a meeting the children were holding on the beach to sell their pet animals, for the benefit of their French godchildren. There were at least a hundred of them, all grave, eager, or at least acquiescent, save Grace Henderson, who clung to her white calf and wept. They bought it of her quickly, and in pity gave it back to her; but her brother obliged her to sell it again, and so she had to struggle and suffer three times over. There were Cuban birds, that you bought with their cages; native birds that you bought so as to set them free; turtles which sold badly, as they wore the initials of their first master carved on their backs; goats; and there were animals which were also immolated for the cause—sad dogs, who had no resistance left in them, and sold themselves; a little elephant which clasped his mistress by a belt that gave, by a sleeve that tore, and so did not dare to take her by the pigtail. The governesses, to console their children, quickly bought these other animals, and took turns standing on a platform to read out letters from the godsons: *"Venez chez moi, j'irai chez vous,"* wrote Jean Perrot, *"et si je meurs je veux vous voir."* Some professors who were there were amazed to discover that all French children use rhythmic prose.

450

Then came green forests cut by tumbling brooks, where little boys, who were fishing for trout with both hands, hailed us with a wink, as they did not dare to move or call out. Then came the country of the field-mice, where the owls have such fat haunches that they have to perch sideways for fear of tumbling off their twigs head first. Then came Sandwich, where a Lithuanian was waving his national flag, protesting all by himself against conscription. Then came Lake Asquam, and this local hilltop where I have lain stretched out ever since, at the foot of a slim giant birch, which has only one tuft of verdure at its top, and will fall if it puts out a single other leaf.

My hostess is Mrs. Green, the farmer's wife, who wears her gray hair braided down her back, and a big striped shawl, and eyeglasses; but she twists the calves' tails, and fights with the rooster. When a word gets stuck in my fountain pen I shake it out into the lake from my steamer-chair. Sometimes, though, it is inside me that it hesitates, and then I have to get up myself, lean on my elbows, sometimes even stoop all the way over.

Who am I with? With two friends—a forester and an Australian poet. The morning belongs to Carnegie, the forester. By six o'clock he has me up and off on a dash to his district, straight across the islands where every owner keeps a different scheme of hours, according as he likes to see his children get up early or late. Silent beasts are waking in woods that still have their Indian names; the muskrat is taking his bath, the blue heron flies from an isthmus to an island, from an island to an islet, flying ever toward that little round point of noon. We land in haste, to avoid an upset—for a new-cut pine log is already sliding down the toboggan to the lake— and go to the sawmill by a path that was once covered with sawdust, but that my forester has had tarred since he lost his gold chain. He teaches me the secret sign by which one may recognize the red pine, the white pine, and the black pine; he gathers together his group of woodcutters, who are going off to France, and forces me to pronounce our biggest trees in French—the oak, the elm; I saw my favorite beeches with difficulty. In the short cuts we walk through the briars stiffly, as people who do not speak the same tongue always do, and not one of these noble gestures is lost, my dear, for the forest is full of lynxes. In the clearings he shows me the remains of the wood fires he has kindled since his childhood, and twenty years of embers still blacken his fingers. He is moved and sits down, my love, to dream . . . and suddenly four little woodchucks, my sweet, hurry timidly out of the ground; real little woodchucks, my heart.

451

We catch them—they bite us, and try to get away—we pet them, my dear love.

But the night belongs to Rogers, the Australian. The whole world is dark, invisible; only one red point to be seen, Carnegie's cigar— he is noiselessly paddling on the lake. But miles away the chosen tree that announces the moon suddenly twinkles down its whole length. That is because a whole moon is coming. Everything is radiant, everything shines. Rocks begin to show themselves, as white and polished as bleached bones. Far around the lake the reflection of the forest, just now cleft and jutting, becomes an even border. It is the hour when the Indians gave a name to all the things that surround us. The white mountains turn white, the yellow birches yellow, and blue, blue grow the owls. Every separate plane of the lake seems to lie on a different level, and the moon gnaws the water where it falls over the dams. A divine night, this, when the White Mountains are of silver and the birches of gold. At last the hour has come when I can find an epithet for my soul, and a name for my house. The bullfrog groans; the loon, black swan of the lake, utters cries, first piercing, then muffled, for he continuously ducks his head under the water and pulls it out again. The true moon cautiously climbs farther and farther from the false moon. . . .

But Rogers insists on talking. He wants me to talk to him of Seeger, who is dead, of Blakely, who is dead—of all the American poets who were killed before the American war began. He persists in talking French, without allowing me to help him, and circles about the words he no longer knows: about the word "debonair," the word "ladder," the word "serenity." From my refuge in the very heart of the word I wait placidly for him, sometimes in the heart of a proper name, in the heart of Baudelaire—a stuffy place, his statue. Then he reads me his verses, which he wishes to adapt to Europe, because the Australian mouths are so different from our own.

"July has frozen the rivers," he says, "and the useless bridges are collected in the barn."

I shake my head; he understands, and corrects himself:

"Summer has frozen the rivers, and the bridges" . . .

The loon sings on. The lake suddenly bursts into flame, for Carnegie is lighting a second cigar. Rogers grows emotional, takes my hand and circles about a word which expresses both loons and friendships, a word which even we in France, alas, do not know.

When the storm breaks; when, by millions, the owners of the

wooden houses bring their red-striped tents in from the rain: when a flash of lightning allows you to see—through the isinglass of the top of the car in front of you—the shadow of two gray heads; when the black bird with the red wings folds his wings; when the pro-German shuts his window and suddenly feels so lonely and beaten that he bursts into tears; when, in the public parks, the crowds swarm under the tents of the recruiting sergeants, and help them move their posters, and torpedoes, and mortars under shelter; when the mother astride the purple motor-cycle tries in vain to reach out a hand and feel the baby dozing in the side-car; when the golden stags, the dragons and the golden cows whirl madly on the clock-towers of the barns, but always in time; when a Hannan shoe lies on the deserted avenue; when a blast of wind lifts the page of the one-armed accountant, and he holds it down with the point of his pen, calling for help; when one hears nothing on the sidewalks, on on the sea, on the buildings, but the rain . . . then when a sunbeam comes down, and a sharp cloud cuts it, and it falls; when the rain-bow shivers, its left on the solid city cement, its right on the sea; when you gather the sun into a corner of the sky, as if it were your one last match—and it finally burns; when a victorious sunbeam, fall-ing on the terrace beats by the fraction of an inch a rain-drop that has come from thousands of miles less far away; when the baby in the side-car gets the last drop of all, and begins to cry—then when the pond-lilies climb up to the level of the new pond that has formed about them; when the farmer in his rubber boots tramps out to empty his pitch cans and his maple syrup cans of their water; when a child, for no reason at all, wants to burn a joss-stick; when the traveler, at the turn of the Cañon, gets down to pat his mule and all at once remounts quickly for the storm is rumbling again, and he wants to keep his saddle dry; when the rain begins to beat down once more, in a deluge, the very same rain, as you can plainly recognize by its drops: then I think of him, of Seeger, who loved storms, and I shudder.

"How did Seeger die?" asks Rogers.

In a month Rogers will be leaving for the war, and he loses no opportunity of informing himself how the poets, his colleagues, were killed. It would be very odd if two poets were killed in the same way, the same identical way; each one of these deaths is death that fate will deny him. He will not wander, like Rupert Brooke, repeating one Christian name after another, and dying at the first woman's name. He will not have him, as Dollero did, to write me three letters; the

first with a splinter and his blood saying good by; the second with his nurse's pencil, hoping to see me; the last with the doctor's fountain pen—confident, happy, unfinished. He will not drop dead like Hesslin, the German poet, on the back of a mystical sergeant who rose slowly with his load, and bore it to the hospital without casting a backward look. He will need a whole grave to himself, since he is not to die like Blakely, whose poor remains fitted into a Palmer's biscuit box. It will not be at dark, as it was with Drouot, or at noon, as it was with Clermont. If Seeger died at dawn, there is no time left for him but night. Bitter night, running under the days like some infernal strawberry vine. Soft night, with its lake, its loons. Night on the Sydney steamers, when the world turns silent, and nothing stands in the way of a poet's thoughts but the mute strain of a vessel. Night near some French spring where you lie, scarcely aware of your wound, and nibble a leaf of water-cress. Somber night, in whose very center, sharp cut against the velvet dark, the sun suddenly appears. Happy he who dies at night!

"How did Seeger die? Did you know him?"

Rogers is astigmatic, wears heavy gold-rimmed spectacles with lenses of different pattern, and always asks you two questions at a time. Yes, I had seen him. Once it was in the Luxembourg, in summer; he was just coming into the unreal garden, with its world of fantastic and tender Parisians—those who felt themselves too heavy could buy little balloons at the gate. Another time it was at the house of a friend whom he had tried to find the two preceding evenings; on the first he left a couplet, on the second a sonnet. My friend allowed himself to be surprised in bed, the third day, and so did not get his poem.

"Did he suffer? Have you seen his last verses?"

For Rogers also collects the last poems of all the poets who have been killed. He even collects their last letters in prose, where sometimes two words clash into each other and rhyme—the same thing happens when a departing warrior is dressing in his apartment, with his friends standing about—and makes them tremble. It may be a last letter written to an aunt between the two last poems, when, in spite of himself, he uses the poetic epithet (as the other does not come)—talks of "steeds," and "blades," and "meads," and feels obliged to be somewhat ironic. Last poems where nearly all of them saw death as it was, in fact, to overtake them, Seeger like a mistress, longing for a rendezvous, Dollero like a storm with three stray birds, Blakely like a headless monster—and when only Brooke foresaw

things all wrong. Poor Brooke who told us *"Si je meurs, dites vous que dans une terre ètrangère il y aura toujours un coin de terre anglaise. Une poussière plus riche que la terre y sera contenue, un corps d'Angleterre lavé par les rivières anglaises, brûle par le soleil anglais," "un corps horizontal tendu sur la ligne de tous les corps anglais,"* and in the end died on a boat, and was thrown into the sea with a cannon ball to keep his shroud upright. So that, for all one's pity one is put on one's guard, and when one turns over his other poems one no longer believes exactly what they say; no longer believes that love is *une rue ouverte où se precipite ce qui jamais ne voient, un traître qui livre au destin la citadelle du coeur, un enfant étendu.* One grows obstinate about it, insists on believing that love is a street, if you like, but a street with no outlet; a traitor perhaps, but in that case a friendly traitor; and sometimes one sees the charming fellow standing quite vertical, floating sadly in the air.

"How did Seeger die?"

It is summer. Everything that prevents one from breathing in the summer—his cap, his gas-mask—he throws off. He holds his cigar behind him, because of the smoke; the company thief steals it away from him—thank heaven, for so his hands will not burn up after his death. Then he stretches himself, but without lifting his arms, crosswise. He has just one minute to live. There is your watch before you, with its second hand: one minute and he will be dead. In his pocket is the bottle of heliotrope perfume that he is to break as he falls. Now you have not even time, before he dies, to write that short sentence which he took for his motto, the one that he wrote at the head of every poem—about the poplars. If it is a shell, the cannon is being loaded. If it is a bullet, the German soldier is tapping his charge and slipping it in. Seeger raises his head. The sky is very blue. A poplar, yes, a poplar is outlined on the horizon. Seeger climbs the firing step—a bird, yes, a . . .

So my three days of rest have gone, and now it is noon. I think of you who wrote me every week from Europe, a letter of variable mood —Even the color of the paper is inconstant, and each one, like the flash of a revolving lighthouse, throws a new region into high relief. Love is a restive horse, a saddled antelope, a faithful traitor. The sun is just above me now. I was writing, to spare my eyes, in the shadow of my head; there is no shadow left; adieu, Madame, I write the last word, I write your name, full in the sun.

JOHANN WOLFGANG VON GOETHE

JOHANN WOLFGANG VON GOETHE (German, 1749-1832). Germany's greatest poet and the philosopher of classical poetry. Writer of universal scope—even his recorded conversations are significant. Wielded tremendous influence during life and afterward. Initiated *Sturm und Drang* movement *(Sorrows of Werther)*. Autobiographical novel: *Wilhelm Meister*. Epic: *Hermann and Dorothea*. Drama: *Egmont*. His masterpiece, *Faust*, philosophic-poetic drama, one of Western world's supreme classics.

FAUST
A Tragedy

Faust. All that philosophy can teach,
The craft of lawyer and of leech,
I've mastered, ah! and sweated through
Theology's dreary deserts, too;
Yet here, poor fool! for all my lore,
I stand no wiser than before.
They call me magister, save the mark!
Doctor, withal! and these ten years I
Have been leading my pupils a dance in the dark,
Up hill, down dale, through wet and through dry—
And yet, that nothing can ever be
By mortals known, too well I see!
This is burning the heart clean out of me.
More brains have I than all the tribe
Of doctor, magister, parson, and scribe.
From doubts and scruples my soul is free;
Nor hell nor devil has terrors for me:
But just for this I am dispossessed
Of all that gives pleasure to life and zest.
I can't even juggle myself to own
There is any one thing to be truly known,
Or aught to be taught in science or arts,
To better mankind and to turn their hearts.
Besides, I have neither land nor pence,
Nor worldly honour nor influence.
A dog in my case would scorn to live!

456

So myself to magic I've vowed to give,
And see, if through spirit's might and tongue
The heart from some mysteries cannot be wrung;
If I cannot escape from the bitter woe
Of babbling of things that I do not know,
And get to the root of those secret powers
Which hold together this world of ours,
The sources and centres of force explore,
And chaffer and dabble in words no more.
Oh, broad bright moon, if this might be
The last of the nights of agony,
The countless midnights, these weary eyes
Have from this desk here watched thee rise!
Then, sad-eyed friend, thy wistful looks
Shone in upon me o'er paper and books;
But oh! might I wander, in thy dear light,
O'er the trackless slopes of some mountain height,
Round mountain caverns with spirits sail,
Or float o'er the meads in thy hazes pale;
And, freed from the fumes of a fruitless lore,
Bathe in thy dews, and be whole once more!

Ah me! am I penned in this dungeon still?
Accursed doghole, clammy and chill!
Where heaven's own blessed light must pass,
Shorn of its rays, through the painted glass,
Narrowed and cumbered by piles of books,
That are gnawed by worms and grimed with dust,
And which, with its smoke-stained paper looks
Swathed to the roof in a dingy rust;
Stuck round with phials, and chests untold,
With instruments littered, and lumbered with old,
Crazy, ancestral household ware—
This is your world! A world most rare!

And yet can you wonder why your soul
Is numbed within your breast, and why
A dead, dull anguish makes your whole
Life's pulses falter, and ebb, and die?

How should it be but so? Instead
Of the living nature, whereinto
God has created man, things dead
And drear alone, encompass you—
Smoke, litter, dust, the skeletons
Of birds and beasts, and dead men's bones!

Up, up! Away to the champaign free!
And this mysterious volume, writ
By Nostradamus' self, is it
Not guide and counsel enough for thee?
Then wilt thou learn by what control
The stars within their orbits roll,
And if thou wilt let boon Nature be
The guide and monitress to thee,
Thy soul shall expand with tenfold force,
As spirit with spirit holds discourse.
Dull poring, think not, that can here
Expound these holy signs to thee!
Ye spirits, ye are hovering near,
If ye can hear me, answer me!

    Throws open the book, and discovers the sign of the Macrocosm.

Ha! as it meets my gaze, what rapture, gushing
Through all my senses, mounts into my brain!
Youth's ecstasy divine, I feel it rushing,
Like quickening fire, through every nerve and vein!
Was it a god who chronicled these signs,
Which all the war within me still,
The aching heart with sweetness fill,
And to mine eyes, in clearest lines,
Unveil all Nature's powers as with a mystic thrill?
Am I a god? All grows so bright.
In these pure outlines I behold
Nature at work before my soul unrolled.
Now can I read the sage's saw aright:
"Not barred to man the world of spirits is;
Thy sense is shut, thy heart is dead!
Up, student, lave,—nor dread the bliss,—
Thy earthly breast in the morning red!"

    Gazes intently at the sign.

Into one whole how all the things blend,
One in the other working, living!
What powers celestial, lo! ascend, descend,
Each unto each the golden pitchers giving!
And, wafting blessings from their wings,
From heaven through farthest earth career,
While through the universal sphere
One universal concord rings!

Oh, what a show! yet but a show! Ah me!
Where, boundless Nature, shall I clutch at thee?
Ye breasts, where are ye? Ye perennial springs
Of life, whereon hang heaven and earth,
Whereto the blighted bosom clings,
Ye gush, ye slake all thirst, yet I pine on in dearth!

Turns the leaves of the book angrily, and sees the sign of the **Earth**
Spirit.

How differently I feel before this sign!
Earth Spirit, thou to me art nearer;
My faculties grow loftier, clearer,
Even now I glow as with new wine.
Courage I feel, into the world to roam,
To bid earth's joy and sorrows hail,
'Mid storm and struggle to make my home,
And in the crash of shipwreck not to quail.
Clouds gather o'er my head;
The moon conceals her light,
The lamp's gone out. The air
Grows thick and close! Red flashes play
Around me. From the vaulted roof
A shuddering horror creeps
And on me lays its gripe!
Spirit by me invoked, I feel
Thou'rt hovering near,—thou art, thou art!
Unveil thyself!
Ha! What a tugging at my heart!
Stirred through their depths, my senses reel
With passions new and strange! I feel
My heart is thine, thine wholly! Hear!
Thou must! ay, though it cost my life, thou must **appear!**

459

Seizes the book, and utters the sign of the Spirit mysteriously. A red light flashes, in which the Spirit appears.

Spirit.   Who calls on me?

Faust (turning away).   Dread vision gaunt!

Spirit. By potent art thou'st dragged me here;
Thou'st long been sucking at my sphere,
And now—

Faust.   I loathe thee. Hence, avaunt!

Spirit.   To view me were thy prayer and choice,
To see my face, to hear my voice.
Well! by thy potent prayer won o'er,
I come. And thou, that wouldst be more
Than mortal, having thy behest,
Art with a craven fear possessed!
Where is thy pride of soul? Where now the breast
Which in itself a universe created,
Sustained and fostered,—which dilated
With giant throes of rapture, in the hope
As peer with spirits such as me to cope?
Where art thou, Faust, whose summons rang so wide,
Is this thing thou? This, my mere breath doth make
Through every nerve and fibre quake?
A crawling, cowering, timorous worm?

Faust.   Thou film of flame, art thou a thing to fear?
I am, I am that Faust! I am thy peer!

Spirit.   In the currents of Life, in Action's storm,
I wander and I wave;
Everywhere I be!
Birth and the grave,
An infinite sea,
A web ever growing,
A life ever glowing;
Thus at Time's whizzing loom I spin,
And weave the living vesture that God is mantled in!

Faust.   Thou busy Spirit, who dost sweep
From sphere to sphere, from deep to deep,
Ranging the world from end to end,
How near akin I feel to thee!

Spirit.   Thou'rt like the Spirit, thou dost comprehend,
But not like me!

        Vanishes.

460

Faust.   O happy he who still can hope
Out of this sea of error to arise!
We long to use what lies beyond our scope,
Yet cannot use even what within it lies.
But let us not, by saddening thoughts like these,
The blessing of this happy hour o'errun.
See, how they gleam, the green-girt cottages,
Fired by the radiance of the evening sun!
It slopes, it sets. Day wanes. On with a bound
It speeds, and lo! a new world is alive!
O God, for wings to lift me from the ground,
Onward, still onward, after it to strive!
Beneath me, I should see, as on I pressed,
The hushed world ever bathed in evening's beams,
Each mountain-top on fire, each vale at rest,
The silver brook flow into golden streams.
Nor peak nor mountain-chasm should then defeat
My onward course, so godlike and so free.
Lo, with its bays all winking in the heat,
Bursts on my wonder-smitten eyes the sea!
But now the god appears about to sink!
Fresh impulse stirs me, not to be confined.
I hurry on, his deathless light to drink,
The day before me, and the night behind.
The heavens above me, and the waves below.
A lovely dream! Meanwhile, the sun his face
Has hid. Ah, with the spirit's wing will no
Corporeal wings so readily keep pace!
Yet is the yearning with us all inborn,
Upwards and onwards to be struggling still,
When over us we hear the lark, at morn,
Lost in the sky, her quivering carol trill;
When o'er the mountains' pine-clad summits drear
The eagle wheels afar on outstretched wing,
When over flat and over mere
The crane is homewards labouring.
Wagner.   I too have often had my whims and moods,
But never was by such an impulse stirred.
A man soon looks his fill at fields and woods;
The wings I ne'er shall envy of a bird.
How differently the spirit's pure delights

461

Waft us from book to book, from page to page!
They give a beauty to the winter's nights,
A cheerful glow that can its chill assuage.
And some fine manuscript when you unroll,
Ah, then all heaven descends into your soul!

    Faust.   One only aspiration thou hast known,
Oh, never seek to know the other, never!
Two souls, alas! within my bosom throne,
That each from other fiercely longs to sever.
One, with a passionate love that never tires,
Cleaves as with cramps of steel to things of earth,
The other upwards through earth's mists aspires
To kindred regions of a loftier worth.
Oh, in the air if spirits be,
That float 'twixt earth and heaven, and lord it there,
Then from your golden haze descend, and me
Far hence to fields of new existence bear!
Yes, if a magic mantle were but mine,
To stranger lands to waft me at my call,
I'd prize it more than robes of costliest shine,
I would not change it for a monarch's pall

* * *

    Mephistopheles.   These my tiny spirits be.
Hark, with what sagacity
They advise thee to pursue
Action, pleasure ever new!
Out into the world so fair
They would lure and lead thee hence,
From this lonely chamber, where
Stagnate life and soul and sense.
No longer trifle with the wretchedness,
That, like a vulture, gnaws your life away!
The worst society will teach you this,
You are a man 'mongst men, and feel as they.
Yet 'tis not meant, I pray you, see,
To thrust you 'mong the rabble rout;—
I'm done of your great folks. no doubt,
But if, in fellowship with me,
To range through life you are content,
I will most cheerfully consent

462

To be your own upon the spot.
I am your chum. You'd rather not?
Well! If your scruples it will save,
I am your servant, yea, your slave!

    Faust. And in return what must I do for you?
    Mephistopheles. Oh, time enough to talk of that!
    Faust. Nay, nay!
The devil's selfish—is and was always—
And is not like for mere God's sake to do
A liberal turn to any child of clay.
Out with the terms, and plainly! Such as thou
Are dangerous servants in a house, I trow.

    Mephistopheles. I bind myself to serve you here,—to **do**
Your bidding promptly, whatsoe'er it be,
And, when we come together yonder, you
Are then to do the same for me.

    Faust. I prize that yonder at a rush!
Only this world to atoms crush,
And then that other may arise!
From earth my every pleasure flows,
Yon Sun looks down upon my woes;
Let me but part myself from those.
Then come what may, in any guise!
To idle prate I'll close mine ears,
If we hereafter hate or love,
Or if there be in yonder spheres,
As here, an Under and Above!

    Mephistopheles. You're in the proper mood to venture! **Bind**
Yourself, and pleasure in my sleights you'll find,
While this life lasts. I'll give you more
Than eye of man hath ever seen before.

    Faust. What wilt thou give, thou sorry devil? When
Were the aspiring souls of men
Fathomed by such a thing as thee?
Oh, thou hast food that satisfieth never,
Gold, ruddy gold thou hast, that restlessly
Slips, like quicksilver, through the hand for ever;
A game, where we must losers be;
A girl, that, on my very breast,
My neighbour woos with smile and wink;
Fame's rapturous flash of godlike zest,

463

That, meteor-like, is doomed to sink.
Show me the fruit that, ere 'tis plucked, doth rot,
And trees that every day grow green anew!

Mephistopheles.   Such task as this affrights me not.
I have such treasures at command for you.
But, my good friend, the time draws nigh
When we may banquet on the best in peace!

Faust.   If e'er at peace on sluggard's couch I lie,
Then may my life upon the instant cease!
Cheat thou me ever by thy glozing wile,
So that I cease to scorn myself, or e'er
My senses with a perfect joy beguile,
Then be that day my last! I offer fair,
How say'st thou?

Mephistopheles.   Done!

Faust.   My hand upon it! There!
If to the passing moment e'er I say,
"Oh, linger yet, thou art so fair!"
Then cast me into chains you may,
Then will I die without a care!
Then may the death-bell sound its call,
Then art thou from thy service free,
The clock may stand, the index fall,
And time and tide may cease for me!

Mephistopheles.   Think well; we sha'n't forget the terms you
    name.

Faust.   Your perfect right I must allow.
Not rashly to the pact I came.
I am a slave as I am now;
Yours or another's, 'tis to me the same!

Mephistopheles.   Then at the Doctors' feast this very day
Will I my post, as your attendant take.
Just one thing more! To guard against mistake,
Oblige me with a line or two, I pray.

Faust.   Pedant, must thou have writing, too?
Hast thou no true man, or man's promise, known?
Is not my word of mouth enough for you,
To pledge my days for all eternity?
Does not the universe go raving on,
In all its ever-eddying currents, free

464

To pass from change to change and I alone,
Shall a mere promise curb or fetter me?
Yet doth man's heart so hug the dear deceit,
Who would its hold without a pang undo?
Blest he, whose soul is with pure truth replete.
No sacrifice shall ever make him rue.
But, oh, your stamped and scribbled parchment sheet
A spectre is, which all men shrink to view.
The word dies ere it quits the pen,
And wax and sheepskin lord it then.
What would you have, spirit of ill!
Brass, marble, parchment, paper?—Say,
Am I to write with pen, or style, or graver?
I care not—choose whiche'er you will.
 Mephistopheles. Why, throw your eloquence away,
Or give it such a very pungent savour?
Pshaw! Any scrap will do—'tis quite the same—
With the least drop of blood just sign your name.
 Faust. If that will make you happy, why, a claim
So very whimsical I'll freely favour.
 Mephistopheles. Blood is a juice of quite peculiar kind.
 Faust. Fear not that I the compact will evade!
My life's whole struggle, heart and mind,
Chimes with the promise I have made.
Too high I've soared—too proudly dreamt,
I'm only peer for such as thee;
The Mighty Spirit spurns me with contempt,
And Nature veils her face from me.
Thought's chain is snapt;—for many a day
I've loathed all knowledge every way.
So quench we now our passion's fires
In sense and sensual delights,
Unveil all hidden magic sleights,
To minister to our desires!
Let us plunge in the torrent of time, and range
Through the weltering chaos of chance and change,
Then pleasure and pain, disaster and gain,
May course one another adown my brain.
Change and excitement may work as they can,
Rest there is none for the spirit of man.

Forest and Cavern

Faust (alone). Majestic spirit, thou hast given me all
For which I prayed. Thou not in vain didst turn
   Thy countenance to me in fire and flame.
Thou glorious Nature for my realm hast given,
With power to feel, and to enjoy her. Thou
No mere cold glance of wonder hast vouchsafed,
But let'st me peer deep down into her breast,
Even as into the bosom of a friend.
Before me thou in long procession lead'st
All things that live, and teachest me to know
My kindred in still grove, in air, and stream.
And, when the storm sweeps roaring through the woods,
Upwrenching by the roots the giant pines,
Whose neighbouring trunks, and intertangled boughs,
In crashing ruin tear each other down,
And shake with roar of thunder all the hills,
Then dost thou guide me to some sheltering cave,
There show'st me to myself, and mine own soul
Teems marvels forth I weened not of before.
And when the pure moon, with her mellowing light,
Mounts as I gaze, then from the rocky walls,
And out from the dank underwood, ascend
Forms silvery-clad of ages long ago,
And soften the austere delight of thought.

   Oh, now I feel no perfect boon is e'er
Achieved by man. With this ecstatic power,
Which brings me hourly nearer to the gods,
A yokemate thou hast given me, whom even now
I can no more dispense with, though his cold
Insulting scorn degrades me to myself,
And turns my gifts to nothing with a breath.
Within my breast he fans unceasingly
A raging fire for that bewitching form.
So to fruition from desire I reel,
And 'midst fruition languish for desire.

466

NIKOLAI GOGOL

NIKOLAI GOGOL (Russian, 1809-1852). One of the founders of Russian literature. Primarily a realist, wrote comedy with pathetic overtones. Personally an eccentric and hypochondriac. Famous satiric play: *The Inspector General.* Important nationalistic novels: *Dead Souls, Taras Bulba.* Exerted tremendous influence on later Russians, especially Dostoyevsky and the Soviets.

ST. JOHN'S EVE

THOMA GRIGOROVITCH had one very strange eccentricity: to the day of his death he never liked to tell the same thing twice. There were times when, if you asked him to relate a thing afresh, he would interpolate new matter, or alter it so that it was impossible to recognize it. Once upon a time, one of those gentlemen who like every sort of frippery, and issue mean little volumes, no thicker than an A B C book, every month, or even every week, wormed this same story out of Thoma Grigorovitch, and the latter completely forgot about it. But that same young gentleman, in the pea-green caftan, came from Poltava, bringing with him a little book, and, opening it in the middle, showed it to us. Thoma Grigorovitch was on the point of setting his spectacles astride of his nose, but recollected that he had forgotten to wind thread about them and stick them together with wax, so he passed it over to me. As I understand something about reading and writing, and do not wear spectacles, I undertook to read it. I had not turned two leaves when all at once he caught me by the hand and stopped me.

"Stop! tell me first what you are reading."

I confess that I was a trifle stunned by such a question.

"What! what am I reading, Thoma Grigorovitch? Why? your own words."

"Who told you that they were my words?"

"Why, what more would you have? Here it is printed: 'Related by such and such a sacristan.' "

"Spit on the head of the man who printed that! he lies, the dog of a Moscow peddler! Did I say that? ' 'Twas just the same as though one hadn't his wits about him!' Listen, I'll tell the tale to you on the spot." We moved up to the table, and he began.

My grandfather (the kingdom of heaven be his! may he eat only wheaten rolls and poppy-seed cakes with honey, in the other world!)

could tell a story wonderfully well. When he used to begin a tale you could not stir from the spot all day, but kept on listening. He was not like the story-teller of the present day, when he begins to lie, with a tongue as though he had had nothing to eat for three days, so that you snatch your cap and flee from the house. I remember my old mother was alive then, and in the long winter evenings when the frost was crackling out of doors, and had sealed up hermetically the narrow panes of our cottage, she used to sit at her wheel, drawing out a long thread in her hand, rocking the cradle with her foot, and humming a song, which I seem to hear even now.

The lamp, quivering and flaring up as though in fear of something, lighted up our cottage; the spindle hummed; and all of us children, collected in a cluster, listened to our grandfather, who had not crawled off the stove for more than five years, owing to his great age. But the wondrous tales of the incursions of the Zaporozhian Cossacks and the Poles, the bold deeds of Polkova, of Poltar-Kozhukh, and Sagaidatchnii, did not interest us so much as the stories about some deed of old, which always sent a shiver through our frames and made our hair rise upright on our heads. Sometimes such terror took possession of us in consequence of them, that, from that evening forward, Heaven knows how wonderful everything seemed to us. If one chanced to go out of the cottage after nightfall for anything, one fancied that a visitor from the other world had lain down to sleep in one's bed; and I have often taken my own smock, at a distance, as it lay at the head of the bed, for the Evil One rolled up in a ball! But the chief thing about grandfather's stories was, that he had never lied in all his life; and whatever he said was so was so.

I will now tell you one of his wonderful tales. I know that there are a great many wise people who copy in the courts, and can even read civil documents, but who, if you were to put into their hand a simple prayer-book, could not make out the first letter in it, and would show all their teeth in derision. These people laugh at everything you tell them. Along comes one of them—and doesn't believe in witches! Yes, glory to God that I have lived so long in the world! I have seen heretics to whom it would be easier to lie in confession than it would be to our brothers and equals to take snuff, and these folk would deny the existence of witches! But let them just dream about something and they won't even tell what it was! There, it is no use talking about them!

No one could have recognized the village of ours a little over a

hundred years ago; it was a hamlet, the poorest kind of a hamlet. Half a score of miserable farmhouses, unplastered and badly thatched, were scattered here and there about the fields. There was not a yard or a decent shed to shelter animals or wagons. That was the way the wealthy lived; and if you had looked for our brothers, the poor—why, a hole in the ground—that was a cabin for you! Only by the smoke could you tell that a God-created man lived there. You ask why they lived so? It was not entirely through poverty; almost everyone led a raiding Cossack life, and gathered not a little plunder in foreign lands; it was rather because it was little use building up a good wooden house. Many folk were engaged in raids all over the country—Crimeans, Poles, Lithuanians! It was quite possible that their own countrymen might make a descent and plunder everything. Anything was possible.

In this hamlet a man, or rather a devil in human form, often made his appearance. Why he came, and whence, no one knew. He prowled about, got drunk, and suddenly disappeared as if into the air, leaving no trace of his existence. Then, behold, he seemed to have dropped from the sky again, and went flying about the street of the village, of which no trace now remains, and which was not more than a hundred paces from Dikanka. He would collect together all the Cossacks he met; then there were songs, laughter, and cash in plenty, and vodka flowed like water. . . . He would address the pretty girls, and give them ribbons, earrings, strings of beads—more than they knew what to do with. It is true that the pretty girls rather hesitated about accepting his presents: God knows, perhaps, what unclean hands they had passed through. My grandfather's aunt, who kept at that time a tavern, in which Basavriuk (as they called this devil-man) often caroused, said that no consideration on the earth would have induced her to accept a gift from him. But then, again, how avoid accepting? Fear seized on every one when he knit his shaggy brows, and gave a sidelong glance which might send your feet God knows whither: whilst if you did accept, then the next night some fiend from the swamp, with horns on his head, came and began to squeeze your neck, if there was a string of beads upon it, or bite your finger, if there was a ring upon it; or drag you by the hair, if ribbons were braided in it. God have mercy, then, on those who held such gifts! But here was the difficulty: it was impossible to get rid of them; if you threw them into the water, the diabolical ring or necklace would skim along the surface and into your hand.

There was a church in the village—St. Pantelei, if I remember

rightly. There lived there a priest, Father Athanasii, of blessed memory. Observing that Basavriuk did not come to church even at Easter, he determined to reprove him and impose penance upon him. Well, he hardly escaped with his life. "Hark ye, sir!" he thundered in reply, "learn to mind your own business instead of meddling in other people's if you don't want that throat of yours stuck together with boiling kutya."

What was to be done with this unrepentant man? Father Athanasii contented himself with announcing that any one who should make the acquaintance of Basavriuk would be counted a Catholic, an enemy of Christ's orthodox church, not a member of the human race.

In this village there was a Cossack named Korzh, who had a laborer whom people called Peter the Orphan—perhaps because no one remembered either his father or mother. The church elder, it is true, said that they had died of the pest in his second year; but my grandfather's aunt would not hear of that, and tried with all her might to furnish him with parents, although poor Peter needed them about as much as we need last year's snow. She said that his father had been in Zaporozhe, and had been taken prisoner by the Turks, amongst whom he underwent God only knows what tortures, until, having by some miracle disguised himself as a eunuch, he made his escape. Little cared the black-browed youths and maidens about Peter's parents. They merely remarked that if he only had a new coat, a red sash, a black lambskin cap with a smart blue crown on his head, a Turkish saber by his side, a whip in one hand and a pipe with handsome mountings in the other, he would surpass all the young men. But the pity was, that the only thing poor Peter had was a gray gaberdine with more holes in it than there are gold pieces in a Jew's pockets. But that was not the worst of it. Korzh had a daughter, such a beauty as I think you can hardly have chanced to see. My grandfather's aunt used to say—and you know that it is easier for a woman to kiss the Evil One than to call any one else a beauty—that this Cossack's maiden's cheeks were as plump and fresh as the pinkest poppy when, bathed in God's dew, it unfolds its petals, and coquets with the rising sun; that her brows were evenly arched over her bright eyes like black cords, such as our maidens buy nowadays, for their crosses and ducats, off the Moscow peddlers who visit the villages with their baskets; that her little mouth, at sight of which the youths smacked their lips, seemed made to warble the songs of nightingales; that her hair, black as the raven's wing, and soft as young flax, fell in curls over her shoulders, for our

470

maidens did not then plait their hair in pigtails interwoven with pretty, bright-hued ribbons. Eh! may I never intone another alleluia in the choir, if I would not have kissed her, in spite of the gray which is making its way through the old wool which covers my pate, and of the old woman beside me, like a thorn in my side! Well, you know what happens when young men and maidens live side by side. In the twilight the heels of red boots were always visible in the place where Pidorka chatted with her Peter. But Korzh would never have suspected anything out of the way, only one day—it is evident that none but the Evil One could have inspired him—Peter took into his head to kiss the maiden's rosy lips with all his heart, without first looking well about him; and that same Evil One—may the son of a dog dream of the holy cross!—caused the old graybeard, like a fool, to open the cottage door at that moment. Korzh was petrified, dropped his jaw, and clutched at the door for support. Those unlucky kisses completely stunned him.

Recovering himself, he took his grandfather's hunting whip from the wall, and was about to belabor Peter's back with it, when Pidorka's little six-year-old brother Ivas rushed up from somewhere or other, and grasping his father's legs with his little hands, screamed out, "Daddy, Daddy! don't beat Peter!" What was to be done? A father's heart is not made of stone. Hanging the whip again upon the wall, he led Peter quietly from the house. "If you ever show yourself in my cottage again, or even under the windows, look out, Peter, for, by heaven, your black mustache will disappear; and your black locks, though wound twice about your ears will take leave of your pate, or my name is not Terentiy Korzh." So saying, he gave him such a taste of his fist in the nape of his neck, that all grew dark before Peter, and he flew headlong out of the place.

So there was an end of their kissing. Sorrow fell upon our turtle doves; and a rumor grew rife in the village that a certain Pole, all embroidered with gold, with mustaches, saber, spurs, and pockets jingling like bells of the bag with which our sacristan Taras goes through the church every day, had begun to frequent Korzh's house. Now, it is well known why a father has visitors when there is a black-browed daughter about. So, one day, Pidorka burst into tears, and caught the hand of her brother Ivas. "Ivas, my dear! Ivas, my love! fly to Peter, my child of gold, like an arrow from a bow. Tell him all: I would have loved his brown eyes, I would have kissed his fair face, but my fate decrees otherwise. More than one handkerchief have I wet with burning tears. I am sad and heavy at heart. And my

471

own father is my enemy. I will not marry the Pole, whom I do not love. Tell him they are making ready for a wedding, but there will be no music at our wedding: priests will sing instead of pipes and viols. I shall not dance with my bridegroom; they will carry me out. Dark, dark will be my dwelling of maple wood; and instead of chimneys, a cross will stand upon the roof."

Peter stood petrified, without moving from the spot, when the innocent child lisped out Pidorka's words to him. "And I, wretched man, had thought to go to the Crimea and Turkey, to win gold and return to thee, my beauty! But it may not be. We have been overlooked by the evil eye. I too shall have a wedding, dear one; but no ecclesiastics will be present at that wedding. The black crow instead of the pope will caw over me; the bare plain will be my dwelling; the dark blue cloud my roof-tree. The eagle will claw out my brown eyes; the rain will wash my Cossack bones, and the whirlwinds will dry them. But what am I? Of what should I complain? 'Tis clear God willed it so. If I am to be lost, then so be it!" and he went straight to the tavern.

My late grandfather's aunt was somewhat surprised at seeing Peter at the tavern, at an hour when good men go to morning mass; and stared at him as though in a dream when he called for a jug of brandy, about half a pailful. But the poor fellow tried in vain to drown his woe. The vodka stung his tongue like nettles, and tasted more bitter than worm-wood. He flung the jug from him upon the ground.

"You have sorrowed enough, Cossack," growled a bass voice behind him. He looked round—it was Basavriuk! Ugh, what a face! His hair was like a brush, his eyes like those of a bull. "I know what you lack: here it is." As he spoke he jingled a leather purse which hung from his girdle and smiled diabolically. Peter shuddered. "Ha, ha, ha! how it shines!" he roared, shaking out ducats into his hands: "Ha, ha, ha! how it jingles! And I only ask one thing for a whole pile of such shiners."

"It is the Evil One!" exclaimed Peter. "Give me them! I'm ready for anything!"

They struck hands upon it, and Basavriuk said, "You are just in time, Peter: to-morrow is St. John the Baptist's day. Only on this one night in the year does the fern blossom. I will await you at midnight in the Bear's ravine."

I do not believe that chickens await the hour when the housewife brings their corn with as much anxiety as Peter awaited the evening.

He kept looking to see whether the shadows of the trees were not lengthening, whether the sun was not turning red towards setting; and, the longer he watched, the more impatient he grew. How long it was! Evidently God's day had lost its end somewhere. But now the sun has set. The sky is red only on one side, and it is already growing dark. It grows colder in the fields. It gets gloomier and gloomier, and at last quite dark. At last! With heart almost bursting from his bosom, he set out and cautiously made his way down through the thick woods into the deep hollow called the Bear's ravine. Basavriuk was already waiting there. It was so dark that you could not see a yard before you. Hand in hand they entered the ravine, pushing through the luxuriant thorn-bushes and stumbling at almost every step. At last they reached an open spot. Peter looked about him; he had never chanced to come there before. Here Basavriuk halted.

"Do you see before you three hillocks? There are a great many kinds of flowers upon them. May some power keep you from plucking even one of them. But as soon as the fern blossoms, seize it, and look not round, no matter what may seem to be going on behind thee."

Peter wanted to ask some questions, but behold, Basavriuk was no longer there. He approached the three hillocks—where were the flowers? He saw none! The wild steppe-grass grew all around, and hid everything in its luxuriance. But the lightning flashed; and before him was a whole bed of flowers, all wonderful, all strange: whilst amongst them there were also the simple fronds of fern. Peter doubted his senses, and stood thoughtfully before them, arms akimbo.

"What manner of prodigy is this? why, one can see these weeds ten times a day. What is there marvelous about them? Devil's-face must be mocking me!"

But behold! the tiny flower-bud of the fern reddened and moved as though alive. It was a marvel, in truth. It grew larger and larger, and glowed like a burning coal. The tiny stars of light flashed up, something burst softly, and the flower opened before his eyes like a flame, lighting the others about it.

"Now is the time," thought Peter and extended his hand. He saw hundreds of hairy hands reach also for the flower from behind him, and there was a sound of scampering in his rear. He half closed his eyes, and plucked sharply at the stalk, and the flower remained in his hand.

Upon a stump sat Basavriuk, quite blue like a corpse. He did not move so much as a finger. His eyes were immovably fixed on some-

473

thing visible to him alone: his mouth was half open and speechless. Nothing stirred around. Ugh! it was horrible!—But then a whistle was heard, which made Peter's heart grow cold within him; and it seemed to him that the grass whispered, and the flowers began to talk among themselves in delicate voices, like little silver bells, whilst the trees rustled in murmuring contention;—Basavriuk's face suddenly became full of life, and his eyes sparkled. "The witch has just returned," he muttered between his teeth. "Hearken, Peter: a charmer will stand before you in a moment; do whatever she commands; if not—you are lost forever."

Then he parted the thorn-bushes with a knotty stick, and before him stood a tiny farmhouse. Basavriuk smote it with his fist, and the wall transformed itself into a cat and flew straight at his eyes.

"Don't be angry, don't be angry, you old Satan!" said Basavriuk, employing such words as would have made a good man stop his ears. Behold, instead of a cat, an old woman all bent into a bow, with a face wrinkled like a baked apple, and a nose and chin like a pair of nut-crackers.

"A fine charmer!" thought Peter; and cold chills ran down his back. The witch tore the flower from his hand, stooped and muttered over it for a long time, sprinkling it with some kind of water. Sparks flew from her mouth, and foam appeared on her lips.

"Throw it away," she said, giving it back to Peter.

Peter threw it, but what wonder was this? The flower did not fall straight to the earth, but for a long while twinkled like a fiery ball through the darkness, and swam through the air like a boat. At last it began to sink lower and lower, and fell so far away that the little star, hardly larger than a poppy-seed, was barely visible. "There!" croaked the old woman, in a dull voice; and Basavriuk, giving him a spade, said, "Dig here Peter: you will find more gold than you or Korzh ever dreamed of."

Peter spat on his hands, seized the spade, pressed his foot on it, and turned up the earth, a second, a third, a fourth time. The spade clinked against something hard, and would go no farther. Then his eyes began to distinguish a small, iron-bound coffer. He tried to seize it, but the chest began to sink into the earth, deeper, farther and deeper still: whilst behind him he heard a laugh like a serpent's hiss.

"No, you shall not have the gold until you shed human blood," said the witch, and she led up to him a child of six, covered with a white sheet, and indicated by a sign that he was to cut off his head.

Peter was stunned. A trifle, indeed, to cut off a man's, or even an innocent child's, head for no reason whatsoever! In wrath he tore off the sheet enveloping the victim's head, and behold! before him stood Ivas. The poor child crossed his little hands, and hung his head. Peter flew at the witch with the knife like a madman, and was on the point of laying hands on her.

"What did you promise for the girl?" thundered Basavriuk; and like a shot he was on his back. The witch stamped her foot; a blue flame flashed from the earth and illuminated all within it. The earth became transparent as if molded of crystal; and all that was within it became visible as if in the palm of the hand. Ducats, precious stones, in chests and pots, were piled in heaps beneath the very spot they stood on. Peter's eyes flashed, his mind grew troubled. . . . He grasped the knife like a madman, and the innocent blood spurted into his eyes. Diabolical laughter resounded on all sides. Misshapen monsters flew past him in flocks. The witch, fastening her hands in the headless trunk like a wolf, drank its blood. His head whirled. Collecting all his strength, he set out to run. Everything grew red before him. The trees seemed steeped in blood, and burned and groaned. The sky glowed and threatened. Burning points, like lightning, flickered before his eyes. Utterly exhausted, he rushed into his miserable hovel and fell to the ground like a log. A deathlike sleep overpowered him.

Two days and two nights did Peter sleep, without once wakening. When he came to himself, on the third day, he looked long at all the corners of his hut; but in vain did he endeavor to recollect what had taken place; his memory was like a miser's pocket from which you cannot entice a quarter of a kopek. Stretching himself, he heard something clash at his feet. He looked; there were two bags of gold. Then only, as if in a dream, he recollected that he had been seeking for treasure, and that something had frightened him in the woods. But at what price he had obtained it, and how, he could by no means tell.

Korzh saw the sacks—and was mollified. "A fine fellow Peter, quite unequalled! yes, and did I not love him? Was he not to me as my own son?" And the old man repeated this fiction until he wept over it himself. Pidorka began to tell Peter how some passing gipsies had stolen Ivas; but he could not even recall him—to such a degree had the Devil's influence darkened his mind. There was no reason for delay. The Pole was dismissed and the wedding-feast prepared; rolls were baked, towels and handkerchiefs embroidered; the young

people were seated at table; the wedding-loaf was cut; guitars, cymbals, pipes, viols sounded, and pleasure was rife.

A wedding in the olden times was not like one of the present day. My grandfather's aunt used to tell how the maidens—in festive head-dresses, of yellow, blue and pink ribbons, above which they bound gold braid; in thin chemisettes embroidered on all the seams with red silk, and strewn with tiny silver flowers; in morocco shoes, with high iron heels—danced the gorlitza as swimmingly as peacocks, and as wildly as the whirlwind; how the youths—with their ship-shaped caps upon their heads, the crowns of gold brocade, and two horns projecting, one in front and another behind, of the very finest black lambskin; in tunics of the finest blue silk with red borders—stepped forward one by one, their arms akimbo in stately form, and executed the hopak; how the lads—in tall Cossack caps, and light cloth gaberdines, girt with silver embroidered belts, their short pipes in their teeth—skipped before them and talked nonsense. Even Korzh as he gazed at the young people could not help getting gay in his old age. Guitar in hand, alternately puffing at his pipe and singing, a brandy-glass upon his head, the graybeard began the national dance amid loud shouts from the merrymakers.

What will not people devise in merry mood? They even began to disguise their faces till they did not look like human beings. On such occasions one would dress himself as a Jew, another as the devil; they would begin by kissing each other, and end by seizing each other by the hair. God be with them! you laughed till you held your sides. They dressed themselves in Turkish and Tatar garments. All upon them glowed like a conflagration, and they began to joke and play pranks. . . .

An amusing thing happened to my grandfather's aunt, who was at this wedding. She was wearing an ample Tatar robe, and, wineglass in hand, was entertaining the company. The Evil One instigated one man to pour vodka over her from behind. Another, at the same moment, evidently not by accident, struck a light, and held it to her. The flame flashed up, and poor aunt, in terror, flung her dress off, before them all. Screams, laughter, jests arose as if at a fair. In a word, the old folks could not recall so merry a wedding.

Pidorka and Peter began to live like a gentleman and lady. There was plenty of everything and everything was fine. . . . But honest folk shook their heads when they marked their way of living. "From the devil no good can come," they unanimously agreed. "Whence, except from the tempter of orthodox people, came this wealth?

476

Where else could he have got such a lot of gold? Why, on the very day that he got rich, did Basavriuk vanish as if into thin air?"

Say, if you can, that people only imagine things! A month had not passed, and no one would have recognized Peter. He sat in one spot, saying no word to anyone; but continually thinking and seemingly trying to recall something. When Pidorka succeeded in getting him to speak, he appeared to forget himself, and would carry on a conversation, and even grow cheerful; but if he inadvertantly glanced at the sacks, "Stop, stop! I have forgotten," he would cry, and again plunge into reverie and strive to recall something. Sometimes when he sat still a long time in one place, it seemed to him as though it were coming, just coming back to mind, but again all would fade away. It seemed as if he was sitting in the tavern: they brought him vodka; vodka stung him; vodka was repulsive to him. Some one came along and struck him on the shoulder; but beyond that everything was veiled in darkness before him. The perspiration would stream down his face, and he would sit exhausted in the same place.

What did not Pidorka do? She consulted the sorceresses; and they poured out fear, and brewed stomachache—but all to no avail. and so the summer passed. Many a Cossack had mowed and reaped; many a Cossack, more enterprising than the rest, had set off upon an expedition. Flocks of ducks were already crowding the marshes, but there was not even a hint of improvement.

It was red upon the steppes. Ricks of grain, like Cossack's caps, dotted the fields here and there. In the highway were to be encountered wagons loaded with brushwood and logs. The ground had become more solid, and in places was touched with frost. Already had the snow begun to fall and the branches of the trees were covered with rime like rabbitskin. Already on frosty days the robin redbreast hopped about on the snow-heaps like a foppish Polish nobleman, and picked out grains of corn; and children, with huge sticks, played hockey upon the ice; while their fathers lay quietly on the stove, issuing forth at intervals with lighted pipes in their lips, to growl in regular fashion, at the orthodox frost or to take the air, and thresh the grain spread out in the barn. At last the snow began to melt, and the ice slipped away: but Peter remained the same; and, the more time went on, the more morose he grew. He sat in the cottage as though nailed to the spot, with the sacks of gold at his feet. He grew averse to look at Pidorka; and still he thought of but one thing, still he tried to recall something, and got angry and ill-tempered because he could not. Often, rising wildly from his seat, he gesticulated

violently and fixed his eyes on something as though desirous of catching it: his lips moved as though desirous of uttering some long-forgotten word, but remained speechless. Fury would take possession of him: he would gnaw and bite his hands like a man half crazy, and in his vexation would tear out his hair by the handful, until, calming down, he would relapse into forgetfulness, as it were, and then would again strive to recall the past and be again seized with fury and fresh tortures. What visitation of God was this?

Pidorka was neither dead nor alive. At first it was horrible to her to remain alone with him in the cottage; but, in course of time, the poor woman grew accustomed to her sorrow. But it was impossible to recognize the Pidorka of former days. No blushes, no smiles: she was thin and worn with grief, and had wept her bright eyes away. Once someone who took pity on her advised her to go to the witch who dwelt in the Bear's ravine, and enjoyed the reputation of being able to cure every disease in the world. She determined to try this last remedy: and finally persuaded the old woman to come to her. This was on St. John's Eve, as it chanced. Peter lay insensible on the bench, and did not observe the newcomer. Slowly he rose, and looked about him. Suddenly he trembled in every limb, as though he were on the scaffold: his hair rose upon his head, and he laughed a laugh that thrilled Pidorka's heart with fear.

"I have remembered, remembered!" he cried, in terrible joy; and, swinging a hatchet round his head, he struck at the old woman with all his might. The hatchet penetrated the oaken door nearly four inches. The old woman disappeared; and a child of seven, covered in a white sheet, stood in the middle of the cottage. . . . The sheet flew off. "Ivas!" cried Pidorka, and ran to him; but the apparition became covered from head to foot with blood, and illumined the whole room with red light.

She ran into the passage in her terror, but, on recovering herself a little, wished to help Peter. In vain! The door had slammed to behind her, so that she could not open it. People ran up, and began to knock: they broke in the door, as though there were but one mind among them. The whole cottage was full of smoke; and just in the middle, where Peter had stood, was a heap of ashes from whence smoke was still rising. They flung themselves upon the sacks: only broken potsherds lay there instead of ducats. The Cossacks stood with staring eyes and open mouths, as if rooted to the earth, not daring to move a hair, such terror did this wonder inspire in them.

I do not remember what happened next. Pidorka made a vow to

478

go upon a pilgrimage, collected the property left her by her father, and in a few days it was as if she had never been in the village. Whither she had gone, no one could tell. Officious old women would have despatched her to the same place whither Peter had gone; but a Cossack from Kief reported that he had seen, in a cloister, a nun withered to a mere skeleton who prayed unceasingly. Her fellow-villagers recognized her as Pidorka by the tokens—that no one heard her utter a word; and that she had come on foot, and had brought a frame for the picture of God's mother, set with such brilliant stones that all were dazzled at the sight.

But this was not the end, if you please. On the same day that the Evil One made away with Peter, Basavriuk appeared again; but all fled from him. They knew what sort of a being he was—none else than Satan, who had assumed human form in order to unearth treasures; and, since treasures do not yield to unclean hands, he seduced the young. That same year, all deserted their earthen huts and collected in a village; but even there there was was no peace on account of that accursed Basavriuk.

My late grandfather's aunt said that he was particularly angry with her because she had abandoned her former tavern, and tried with all his might to revenge himself upon her. Once the village elders were assembled in the tavern, and, as the saying goes, were arranging the precedence at the table, in the middle of which was placed a small roasted lamb, shame to say. They chattered about this, that and the other—among the rest about various marvels and strange things. Well, they saw something; it would have been nothing if only one had seen it, but all saw it, and it was this: the sheep raised his head; his goggling eyes became alive and sparkled; and the black, bristling mustache, which appeared for one instant, made a significant gesture at those present. All at once recognized Basavriuk's countenance in the sheep's head; my grandfather's aunt thought it was on the point of asking her for vodka. The worthy elders seized their hats and hastened home.

Another time, the church elder himself, who was fond of an occasional private interview with my grandfather's brandy-glass, had not succeeded in getting to the bottom twice, when he beheld the glass bowing very low to him. "Satan, take you, let us make the sign of the cross over you!" And the same marvel happened to his better half. She had just begun to mix the dough in a huge kneading-trough when suddenly the trough sprang up. "Stop, stop! where are you going?" Putting its arms akimbo, with dignity, it went skipping all

about the cottage. You may laugh, but it was no laughing matter to our grandfathers. And in vain did Father Athanasii go through the village with holy water, and chase the devil through all the streets with his brush. My late grandfather's aunt long complained that, as soon as it was dark, some one came knocking at her door and scratching at the wall.

Well! all appears to be quiet now, in the place where our village stands; but it was not so very long ago—my father was still alive— that I remember how a good man could not pass the ruined tavern which a dishonest race had long managed for their own interest. From the smoke-blackened chimneys smoke poured out in a pillar and, rising high in the air, rolled off like a cap, scattering burning coals over the steppe; and Satan (the son of a dog should not be mentioned) sobbed so pitifully in his lair that the startled ravens rose in flocks from the neighboring oak-wood and flew through the air with wild cries.

CARLO GOLDONI

CARLO GOLDONI (Italian, 1707-1793). Reformed native Italian comedy in 18th century by replacing artificial pantomime with realistic character and situations. Author of some 150 plays—many in French, since he spent last 20 years in France. Influenced by Molière and English writers. Works: *The Clever Widow, The Hostess, Pamela, The Beneficent Bear, The Fan.*

THE BENEFICENT BEAR

(Act II, scene 4)

Angelica (aside). What have I to do with Signor Dorval? I can go away.

Dorval. Mademoiselle Angelica!

Ang. Sir?

Dor. Have you seen your uncle? Has he told you nothing?

Ang. I saw him this morning, sir.

Dor. Before he went out of the house?

Ang. Yes, sir.

Dor. Has he returned?

Ang. No, sir.

Dor. (aside). Good. She knows nothing of it.

Ang. Excuse me, sir. Is there anything new in which I am concerned?

480

Dor. Your uncle takes much interest in you.

Ang. (with modesty). He is very kind.

Dor. (seriously). He thinks often of you.

Ang. It is fortunate for me.

Dor. He thinks of marrying you. *(Angelica blushes.)* What say you to it? Would you like to be married?

Ang. I depend on my uncle.

Dor. Shall I say anything more to you on the subject?

Ang. (with a little curiosity). But—as you please, sir.

Dor. The choice of a husband is already made.

Ang. (aside). O heavens! I tremble.

Dor. (aside). She seems to be pleased.

Ang. (trembling). Sir, I am curious to know—

Dor. What, Mademoiselle?

Ang. Do you know who is intended for me?

Dor. Yes, and you know him too.

Ang. (with joy). I know him too?

Dor. Certainly, you know him.

Ang. May I, sir, have the boldness—

Dor. Speak, Mademoiselle.

Ang. To ask you the name of the young man?

Dor. The name of the young man?

Ang. Yes, if you know him.

Dor. Suppose he were not so young?

Ang. (aside, with agitation). Good heavens!

Dor. You are sensible—you depend on your uncle—

Ang. (trembling). Do you think, sir, my uncle would sacrifice me?

Dor. What do you mean by sacrificing you?

Ang. Mean—without the consent of my heart. My uncle is so good—but who could have advised him—who could have proposed this match? *(With temper.)*

Dor. (a little hurt.) But this match—Mademoiselle—suppose it were I.

Ang. (with joy). You, sir? Heaven grant it!

Dor. (pleased). Heaven grant it!

Ang. Yes, I know you; I know you are reasonable. You are sensible; I can trust you. If you have given my uncle this advice, if you have proposed this match, I hope you will now find some means of making him change his plan.

Dor. (aside). Eh! this is not so bad. *(To Angelica.)* Mademoiselle—

Ang. (distressed). Signor?

Dor. (with feeling). Is your heart engaged?

Ang. Ah, sir—

Dor. I understand you.

Ang. Have pity on me!

Dor. (aside). I said so, I foresaw right; it is fortunate for me I am not in love—yet I began to perceive some little symptoms of it.

Ang. But you do not tell me, sir.

Dor. But, Mademoiselle—

Ang. You have perhaps some particular interest in the person they wish me to marry?

Dor. A little.

Ang. I tell you I shall hate him.

Dor. (aside). Poor girl! I am pleased with her sincerity.

Ang. Come, have compassion; be generous.

Dor. Yes, I will be so, I promise you; I will speak to your uncle in your favor, and will do all I can to make you happy.

Ang. (with joy and transport). Oh, how dear a man you are! You are my benefactor, my father. *(Takes his hand.)*

Dor. My dear girl!

(Enter Geronte.)

Geronte (with animation). Excellent, excellent! Courage, my children, I am delighted with you. *(Angelica retires, mortified; Dorval smiles.)* How! does my presence alarm you? I do not condemn this proper show of affection. You have done well, Dorval, to inform her. Come, my niece, embrace your future husband.

Ang. (in consternation). What do I hear?

Dor. (aside and smiling). Now I am unmasked.

Ger. (to Angelica, with warmth). What scene is this? Your modesty is misplaced. When I am not present, you are near enough to each other; when I come in, you go far apart. Come here. *(To Dorval with anger.)* And do you too come here.

Dor. (laughing). Softly, my friend.

Ger. Why do you laugh? Do you feel your happiness? I am very willing you should laugh, but do not put me in a passion; do you hear, you laughing gentleman? Come here and listen to me.

Dor. But listen yourself.

Ger. (to Angelica, and endeavoring to take her hand). Come near, both of you.

Ang. (weeping). My uncle!

Ger. Weeping! What's the matter, my child? I believe you are making a jest of me. *(Takes her hand, and draws her forward; then turns to Dorval.)* You shall escape me no more.

Dor. At least let me speak.

Ger. No, no!

Ang. My dear uncle—

Ger. (with warmth). No, no. *(He becomes serious.)* I have been to my notary's, and have arranged everything; he has taken a note of it in my presence, and will soon bring the contract here for us to subscribe.

Dor. But will you listen to me?

Ger. No, no. As to her fortune, my brother had the weakness to leave it in the hands of his son; this will no doubt cause some obstacle on his part, but it will not embarrass me. Every one who has transactions with him suffers. The fortune cannot be lost, and in any event I will be responsible for it.

Ang. (aside). I can bear this no longer.

Dor. (embarrassed). All proceeds well, but—

Ger. But what?

Dor. The young lady may have something to say in this matter. *(Looking at Angelica.)*

Ang. (hastily and trembling). I, sir?

Ger. I should like to know if she can say anything against what I do, what I order, and what I wish. My wishes, my orders, and what I do, are all for her good. Do you understand me?

Dor. Then I must speak myself.

Ger. What have you to say?

Dor. That I am very sorry, but this marriage cannot take place.

Ger. Not take place! *(Angelica retreats frightened; Dorval steps back.)* *(To Dorval.)* You have given me your word of honor.

Dor. Yes, on condition—

Ger. (turning to Angelica). It must then be this impertinent. If I could believe it! if I had any reason to suspect it! *(Threatens her.)*

Dor. (seriously). No, sir, you are mistaken.

Ger. (to Dorval. Angelica makes her escape). It is you, then, who refuse? So you abuse my friendship and affection for you!

Dor. (raising his voice). But hear reason—

Ger. What reason? what reason? There is no reason. I am a

man of honor, and if you are so, too, it shall be done at once. *(Turning round, he calls)* Angelica!

Dor. What possesses the man? He will resort to violence on the spot. *(Runs off.)*

Ger. (alone). Where is she gone? Angelica! Hallo! who's there? Piccardo! Martuccia! Pietro! Cortese!—But I'll find her. It is you I want. *(Turns round and, not seeing Dorval, remains motionless.)* What! he treat me so! *(Calls.)* Dorval! my friend! Dorval—Dorval! my friend! Oh, shameful—ungrateful! Hallo! Is no one there? Piccardo!

(Enters Piccardo.)

Piccardo. Here, sir.

Ger. You rascal! Why don't you answer?

Pic. Pardon me, sir, here I am.

Ger. Shameful! I called you ten times.

Pic. I am sorry, but—

Ger. Ten times! It is scandalous.

Pic. (aside and angry). He is in a fury now.

Ger. Have you seen Dorval?

Pic. Yes, sir.

Ger. Where is he?

Pic. He is gone.

Ger. How is he gone?

Pic. (roughly). He is gone as other people go.

Ger. Ah, insolent! do you answer your master in this manner? *(Threatens him.)*

Pic. (very angrily). Give me my discharge, sir.

Ger. Your discharge—worthless fellow! *(Makes him retreat. Piccardo falls between the chair and the table. Geronte runs and helps him up.)*

Pic. Oh! *(He shows much pain.)*

Ger. Are you hurt? Are you hurt?

Pic. Very much hurt; you have crippled me.

Ger. Oh, I am sorry! Can you walk?

Pic. (still angry). I believe so, sir. *(He tries, and walks badly.)*

Ger. (sharply). Go on.

Pic. Do you drive me away, sir?

Ger. (warmly). No. Go to your wife's house, that you may be taken care of. *(Pulls out his purse and offers him money.)* Take this to get cured.

Pic. (aside, with tenderness). What a master!

484

Ger. Take it. *(Giving him money.)*

Pic. (with modesty). No, sir, I hope it will be nothing.

Ger. Take it, I tell you.

Pic. (Still refusing it). Sir—

Ger. (very warmly). What! you refuse my money Do you refuse it from pride, or spite, or hatred? Do you believe I did it on purpose? Take this money. Take it. Come, don't put me in a passion.

Pic. Do not get angry, sir. I thank you for all your kindness. *(Takes the money.)*

Ger. Go quickly.

Pic. Yes, sir. *(Walks badly.)*

Ger. Go slowly.

Pic. Yes, sir.

Ger. Wait, wait; take my cane.

Pic. Sir—

Ger. Take it, I tell you! I wish you to do it.

Pic. (takes the cane). What goodness!

(Exit.)

(Enter Martuccia.)

Ger. It is the first time in my life that—Plague on my temper! *(Taking long strides.)* It is Dorval who put me in a passion.

Martuccia. Do you wish to dine, sir?

Ger. May the devil take you! *(Runs out and shuts himself in his room.)*

Mar. Well, well! He is in a rage: I can do nothing for Angelica to-day; Valerio can go away.

OLIVER GOLDSMITH

OLIVER GOLDSMITH (English, 1728-1774). Forerunner of the English Romantic School. From wealthy family, tried numerous professions before settling on literature. Produced classics in three fields: *The Deserted Village* (romantic poem), *The Vicar of Wakefield* (sentimental-realistic novel), *She Stoops to Conquer* (comedy drama). Also short stories of merit.

THE DISABLED SOLDIER

No OBSERVATION is more common, and at the same time more true, than that one half of the world are ignorant how the other half lives. The misfortunes of the great are held up to engage our atten-

485

tion; are enlarged upon in tones of declamation; and the world is called upon to gaze at the noble sufferers: the great, under the pressure of calamity, are conscious of several others sympathizing with their distress; and have, at once, the comfort of admiration and pity.

There is nothing magnanimous in bearing misfortunes with fortitude, when the whole world is looking on: men in such circumstances will act bravely even from motives of vanity: but he who, in the vale of obscurity, can brave adversity; who without friends to encourage, acquaintances to pity, or even without hope to alleviate his misfortunes, can behave with tranquillity and indifference, is truly great: whether peasant or courtier, he deserves admiration, and should be held up for our imitation and respect.

While the slightest inconveniences of the great are magnified into calamities; while tragedy mouths out their sufferings in all the strains of eloquence, the miseries of the poor are entirely disregarded; and yet some of the lower ranks of people undergo more real hardships in one day, than those of a more exalted station suffer in their whole lives. It is inconceivable what difficulties the meanest of our common sailors and soldiers endure without murmuring or regret; without passionately declaiming against providence, or calling their fellows to be gazers on their intrepidity. Every day is to them a day of misery, and yet they entertain their hard fate without repining.

With what indignation do I hear an Ovid, a Cicero, or a Rabutin complain of their misfortunes and hardships, whose greatest calamity was that of being unable to visit a certain spot of earth, to which they had foolishly attached an idea of happiness. Their distresses were pleasures, compared to what many of the adventuring poor every day endure without murmuring. They ate, drank, and slept; they had slaves to attend them, and were sure of subsistence for life; while many of their fellow creatures are obliged to wander without a friend to comfort or assist them, and even without shelter from the severity of the season.

I have been led into these reflections from accidentally meeting, some days ago, a poor fellow, whom I knew when a boy, dressed in a sailor's jacket, and begging at one of the outlets of the town, with a wooden leg. I knew him to have been honest and industrious when in the country, and was curious to learn what had reduced him to his present situation. Wherefore, after giving him what I thought proper, I desired to know the history of his life and misfortunes, and the manner in which he was reduced to his present distress. The

486

disabled soldier, for such he was, though dressed in a sailor's habit, scratching his head, and leaning on his crutch, put himself into an attitude to comply with my request, and gave me his history as follows:

"As for my misfortunes, master, I can't pretend to have gone through any more than other folks; for, except the loss of my limb, and my being obliged to beg, I don't know any reason, thank Heaven, that I have to complain. There is Bill Tibbs, of our regiment, he has lost both his legs, and an eye to boot; but, thank Heaven, it is not so bad with me yet.

"I was born in Shropshire; my father was a laborer, and died when I was five years old, so I was put upon the parish. As he had been a wandering sort of a man, the parishioners were not able to tell to what parish I belonged, or where I was born, so they sent me to another parish, and that parish sent me to a third. I thought in my heart, they kept sending me about so long, that they would not let me be born in any parish at all; but at last, however, they fixed me. I had some disposition to be a scholar, and was resolved at least to know my letters: but the master of the workhouse put me to business as soon as I was able to handle a mallet; and here I lived an easy kind of life for five years. I only wrought ten hours in the day, and had my meat and drink provided for my labor. It is true, I was not suffered to stir out of the house, for fear, as they said, I should run away; but what of that? I had the liberty of the whole house, and the yard before the door, and that was enough for me. I was then bound out to a farmer, where I was up both early and late; but I ate and drank well; and liked my business well enough, till he died, when I was obliged to provide for myself; so I resolved to go seek my fortune.

"In this manner I went from town to town, worked when I could get employment, and starved when I could get none; when, happening one day to go through a field belonging to a justice of peace, I spied a hare crossing the path just before me; and I believe the devil put it into my head to fling my stick at it. Well, what will you have on't? I killed the hare, and was bringing it away, when the justice himself met me; he called me a poacher and a villain, and collaring me, desired I would give an account of myself. I fell upon my knees, begged his worship's pardon, and began to give a full account of all that I knew of my breed, seed, and generation; but though I gave a very true account, the justice said I could give no account; so I was indicted at the sessions, found guilty of being

487

poor, and sent up to London to Newgate, in order to be transported as a vagabond.

"People may say this and that of being in jail, for my part, I found Newgate as agreeable a place as ever I was in in all my life. I had my belly full of eat and drink, and did no work at all. This kind of life was too good to last forever; so I was taken out of prison, after five months, put on board of ship, and sent off, with two hundred more, to the plantations. We had but an indifferent passage, for being all confined in the hold, more than a hundred of our people died for want of sweet air; and those that remained were sickly enough, God knows. When we came ashore we were sold to the planters, and I was bound for seven years more. As I was no scholar, for I did not know my letters, I was obliged to work among the negroes; and I served out my time, as in duty bound to do.

"When my time was expired, I worked my passage home, and glad I was to see old England again, because I loved my country. I was afraid, however, that I should be indicted for a vagabond once more, so did not much care to go down into the country, but kept about the town, and did little jobs when I could get them.

"I was very happy in this manner for some time till one evening, coming home from work, two men knocked me down, and then desired me to stand. They belonged to a press-gang. I was carried before the justice, and as I could give no account of myself, I had my choice left, whether to go on board a man-of-war, or list for a soldier. I chose the latter, and in this post of a gentleman, I served two campaigns in Flanders, was at the battles of Val and Fontenoy, and received but one wound through the breast here; but the doctor of our regiment soon made me well again.

"When the peace came on I was discharged; and as I could not work, because my wound was sometimes troublesome, I listed for a landman in the East India Company's service. I have fought the French in six pitched batles; and I verily believe that if I could read or write, our captain would have made me a corporal. But it was not my good fortune to have any promotion, for I soon fell sick, and so got leave to return home again with forty pounds in my pocket. This was at the beginning of the present war, and I hoped to be set on shore, and to have the pleasure of spending my money; but the Government wanted men, and so I was pressed for a sailor, before ever I could set a foot on shore.

"The boatswain found me, as he said, an obstinate fellow: he swore he knew that I understood my business well, but that I

shammed Abraham, to be idle; but God knows, I knew nothing of sea-business, and he beat me without considering what he was about. I had still, however, my forty pounds, and that was some comfort to me under every beating; and the money I might have had to this day, but that our ship was taken by the French, and so I lost all.

"Our crew was carried into Brest, and many of them died, because they were not used to live in a jail; but, for my part, it was nothing to me, for I was seasoned. One night, as I was asleep on the bed of boards, with a warm blanket about me, for I always loved to lie well, I was awakened by the boatswain, who had a dark lantern in his hands. 'Jack,' says he to me 'will you knock out the French sentry's brains?' 'I don't care,' says I, striving to keep myself awake, 'if I lend a hand.' 'Then, follow me,' says he, 'and I hope we shall do business.' So up I got, and tied my blanket, which was all the clothes I had, about my middle; and went with him to fight the Frenchman. I hate the French because they are all slaves, and wear wooden shoes.

"Though we had no arms, one Englishman is able to beat five French at any time; so we went down to the door where both the sentries were posted, and rushing upon them, seized their arms in a moment, and knocked them down. From thence nine of us ran together to the quay, and seizing the first boat we met, got out of the harbor and put to sea. We had not been here three days before we were taken up by the Dorset privateer, who were glad of so many good hands; and we consented to run our chance. However, we had not as much luck as we expected. In three days we fell in with the *Pompadour* privateer of forty guns, while we had but twenty-three, so to it we went, yard-arm and yard-arm. The fight lasted three hours, and I verily believe we should have taken the Frenchman, had we but had some men left behind; but unfortunately we lost all our men just as we were going to get the victory.

"I was once more in the power of the French, and I believe it would have gone hard with me had I been brought back to Brest; but by good fortune we were retaken by the *Viper*. I had almost forgotten to tell you that in that engagement I was wounded in two places: I lost four fingers off the left hand, and my leg was shot off. If I had the good fortune to have lost my leg and use of my hand on board a king's ship, and not aboard a privateer, I should have been entitled to clothing and maintenance during the rest of my life; but that was not my chance: one man is born with a silver spoon in his mouth, and another with a wooden ladle. However, blessed be God, I enjoy

good health, and will forever love liberty and old England. Liberty, property, and old England, forever, huzza!"

Thus saying, he limped off, leaving me in admiration at his intrepidity and content; nor could I avoid acknowledging that an habitual acquaintance with misery serves better than philosophy to teach us to despise it.

IVAN ALEXANDROVICH GONCHAROV

IVAN ALEXANDROVICH GONCHAROV (Russian, 1812-1891). One of foremost of the great roll of Russian novelists of 19th century. Best-known to Western readers for *Oblomof*, a realistic novel about Russia's so-called "superfluous man."

THE EVOLUTION OF OBLOMOF

ILYA ILYICH OBLOMOF, nobleman by birth, college secretary by occupation, was living for the twelfth consecutive year at Petersburg.

At first, during his parents' lifetime, he lived in rather close quarters, occupying two rooms, and contenting himself with the one servant, Zakhar, brought with him from the country. But after the death of his father and mother he became the sole possessor of three hundred and fifty souls, which fell to him as a legacy in one of the remote provinces, almost in Asia. Instead of five thousand he received now from seven to ten thousand paper rubles income, and his living too assumed another and more generous scale. He rented larger apartments, added a cook to his household, and bought a span of horses. At that time he was still young, and if it cannot be said that he was lively, at any rate he was livelier than now. He still had a thousand different aspirations, was always hoping for something, and expecting much of fate as well as of himself. He was preparing himself for a career; above all, of course, for a role in the government service, which was the very object of his coming to Petersburg. Afterwards he thought, too, of a rôle in society. Finally, in a distant perspective, in the turning of youth to mature age, domestic happiness gleamed and smiled in fancy. But day after day passed, and years followed years; the down on his chin turned to a rough beard, the beaming eyes faded to two dull spots, the shape

grew stout, the hair began to fall out pitilessly;—it struck thirty, but he had not advanced a step on any career, and still stood at the threshold of his arena where he was ten years before.

Life, to him, was divided into halves: one of which consisted of work and weariness—which with him were synonymous; the other of rest and quiet enjoyment. That is why his principal career, the government service, jarred on him most unpleasantly from the first.

Brought up in a remote provincial corner, amidst the gentle and hearty native manners and customs, passing in the course of twenty years from embrace to embrace of relatives, friends, and acquaintances, he had become so thoroughly imbued with the family principle that even his future service appeared to him a sort of domestic occupation,—like that, for example, of making entries in a book of receipts and expenditures, as his father used to. He imagined that the officials of a place formed a small, harmonious family among themselves, unceasingly solicitous for their mutual repose and contentment; that invariable attendance at the office was not an obligatory custom, which had to be observed every day; and that wetness, heat, or merely indisposition would always serve as sufficient and legitimate excuses for neglect of his work. But how distressed he was when he saw that nothing short of an earthquake would entitle a well man to remain away from his office, and by ill luck, earthquakes are unknown in Petersburg; a flood, it is true, might serve equally well as a hindrance, but floods seldom occur either. Still more was Oblomof startled when packets gleamed before his eyes with the superscription "important" and "very urgent"; when he was required to make various researches and extracts. to rummage among documents, and to write reports two fingers thick, which are humorously called "memoranda." Besides, everything was wanted in a hurry. Everybody was hurrying some way or other, and no one kept still at anything; a man scarcely got one thing out of his hands when he eagerly seized something else, as if his whole existence were in that; this finished, he forgot it and flew at a third—there was never once an end to it. Once or twice he was wakened in the night and obliged to write "memoranda"; sometimes he would be called away from company by a courier—always on account of these "memoranda": all of which alarmed him and wearied him greatly. "When am I to live? *live?*" he repeated sorrowfully.

He had been told at home that the chief was the father of his subordinates, and so he formed the pleasantest and fondest idea of this person. He pictured him somewhat in the light of a second

491

father, who breathed only to recompense his subordinates one after another, deservedly or undeservedly, and to provide for not only their needs but their pleasures. Ilya Ilyich thought that a chief was so much concerned about the welfare of a subordinate that he would anxiously inquire how he had passed the night, why his eyes looked heavy, and didn't his head ache? But he was cruelly undeceived the first day of his service. With the arrival of the chief began scurrying and confusion; all were upset, all hustled each other about; many rearranged their toilet; fearing that as they were they didn't look fine enough to show themselves to the chief. This, as Oblomof noticed later, was because there are some chiefs who read in the faces confronting them, of underlings almost out of their wits, not only respect for them, but zeal as well, and often fitness for the service.

Ilya Ilyich did not need to stand in such fear of his own chief, a kind and chatty man, who never harmed any one; his clerks were as content as could be, and asked no better. No one ever heard him say an unpleasant word, or shout or storm; and he never ordered anything done, but always begged it. Work to do—he begged you; to dine with him—he begged you; to put yourself under arrest —he begged you. He never called any one "thou," but every one "you" whether a single official or all in a body. Yet his subordinates were inexplicably timid in the chief's presence: they answered his friendly questions not with their own voice, but with a strangely different one, which they never used in speaking with others. Ilya Ilyich, too, became suddenly afraid, without himself knowing why, when his superior entered the room, and his voice would fail and give place to an unpleasant falsetto as soon as the chief started to speak with him. Ilya Ilyich suffered from fear and weariness in the service, even under this good, indulgent chief. God knows what would have become of him if he had fallen under a stern, exacting one. Oblomof had to serve two years; possibly he would have held out a third also, till he received a title, but a peculiar accident occasioned his quitting the service earlier.

He once sent some important papers to Archangel instead of to Astrakhan. The matter came to light; the culprit was sought for. All the others waited with curiosity for the chief to call Oblomof and coldly and calmly inquire, "Was it you who sent these papers to Astrakhan?" and all were in doubt with what voice Ilya Ilyich would reply. Some thought he would not answer at all—would not have the power. Glancing at the others, Ilya Ilyich was afraid too, though

he knew as well as the rest that the chief would confine himself to a reproof. But his own conscience was far more severe than any reproach. Oblomof did not wait for the deserved punishment; he went home and sent a medical certificate. In this certificate it was recited that "I, the subscriber, testify, over my seal, that the college secretary Ilya Oblomof is attacked by hypertrophy of the heart, with dilitation of the left ventricle" (*hypertrophia cordis cum dilatatione ejus ventriculi sinistri*), "and at the same time by a chronic pain in the liver" (*hepatitis*) "which threatens development dangerous to the health and life of the patient, which ailments forbid his daily attendance at the office. Therefore, to prevent a repetition and aggravation of these painful attacks, I deem it necessary for Mr. Oblomof to discontinue for a time his attendance at the office, and I prescribe generally the abstention from mental occupation and every kind of activity."

But this availed for a short time only: he would have to get well—and there again in perspective was the daily round of duty. Oblomof could not endure it, and tendered his resignation. Thus ended—and never to be resumed—his official employment.

His role in society was more successful. In the first years of his residence in Petersburg, in his fresh youthful days, his calm features were oftener animated, his eyes shone for a long period with a vital fire, and beamed forth rays of light, of hope, and of strength. He had emotions like every one else, hoped, found delight in trivialities, and suffered because of bagatelles. But all that was long ago, at that tender time when man fancies every other man a sincere friend, falls in love with almost every woman, and is prepared to offer each his hand and his heart,—which often results in anguish to others for the rest of their lives. In these happy days there likewise fell to Ilya Ilyich's share, from the host of pretty women, not a few tender, velvety, even passionate glances, an ocean of smiles that promised much, two or three unprivileged kisses, and still more of affectionate hand-pressures actually painful even to tears.

Still, he never fell a victim to the fair sex, never was its slave, nor even a very assiduous adorer, for the very reason that association with women brings great disquietude. Oblomof generally confined himself to adoring them afar at a respectful distance. Seldom did chance bring him to that point in his companionship with a woman where he could glow for some days and think himself beloved. So his love affairs never went the length of a romance; they stopped at the beginning, and from innocence, simplicity, and purity he never

yielded to love for some boarding-school girl in her teens. . . .

Immediately after the overseer's first letter, about unpaid rents and bad harvests, he first replaced his friend the cook by a woman cook, then sold his horses, and finally discharged his other "friends." Scarcely anything took him out of doors, and he shut himself up in his lodgings closer and more immovably every day.

From the first he found it hard to remain dressed all day; then he became too lazy to dine out, except with intimate friends—preferably in bachelor households where one could take off his cravat, unbutton his waistcoat, "lop out," or even sleep an hour or so. Soon even these evening calls wearied him; for you had to put on a coat and shave every day. He had read somewhere that only the morning exhalations were wholesome, while those of the evening were injurious; and he began to be afraid of dampness. Despite all these whims, his friend Stoltz succeeded in dragging him out into the world; but Stoltz was often absent from Petersburg, in Moscow, Nijni, the Crimea, even foreign lands, and without him Oblomof sank clean to the ears again in solitude and isolation, out of which only something unusual could bring him, something out of the course of the every-day incidents of life. Nothing of the sort happened, however, nor could be forecast in the future.

Added to all this, there returned to him with age a certain childish timidity, an apprehension of danger and misfortune in whatever lay without the sphere of his daily existence—the result of estrangement from the varieties of external phenomena. He was not frightened, for example, by a crack in the ceiling of his bedroom: he was used to that. No more did it occur to him that the air in a room always closed, and the constant sitting in seclusion, were more injurious to the health than evening damp, and that overfilling the stomach daily is a kind of gradual suicide; but he was wonted to these and did not fear them. He was not accustomed to movement, to life, to throngs and confusion. In a large crowd he was stifled; he got into a boat with but uncertain hope of reaching the other shore; he rode in a carriage expecting a runaway and smash-up. Or else a nervous fear overcame him: he was afraid of the silence around him—or simply, without himself knowing why, chills would run over his body. He often glanced fearfully sidewise at a dark corner, expecting his imagination to play him a trick and conjure up some supernatural vision.

So played itself out his rôle in society. Slothfully he let go all youthful hopes, which disappointed him or which he disappointed;

all those tenderly sad, luminous memories with which many a heart throbs even in declining years.

What then did he do at home? Read, write, study? Yes, if a book or a newspaper fell into his hands, he set out to read it. Did he chance to hear of a notable work, he was seized with a desire to become acquainted with it; he hunted about, asked for the book, and if it were brought soon, threw himself on it, and an idea of the subject began to take shape in his mind—another page and he would have grasped it: but look, he is lying down already, gazing apathetically at the ceiling, the book beside him, unread, uncomprehended. His ardor cooled even quicker than it kindled; and he never returned to the forsaken book. His head was a confused magazine of dead facts, persons, epochs, figures, religions, unrelated political economics or mathematics or other sciences, problems, and the like. It was a library composed solely of odd volumes in all branches of learning.

Study affected Ilya Ilyich curiously. For him, between learning and life there was an absolute gulf, which he made no attempt to cross. For him life was life and science was science. He studied all existent and long non-existent laws, he even went through a course in practical law procedure: then when a theft in his house made it necessary to compose a letter to the police, took a sheet of paper and a pen, thought and thought, and finally sent for the public scrivener. The accounts of the estate were kept by the overseer. "What has science to do with that!" he argued, with dubitation.

He returned to his solitude without sufficient weight of knowledge to give direction to the thoughts that wandered at will in his head or slumbered in idleness. What then did he do? He kept on tracing the pattern of his own life. In it he found, not without reason, more philosophy and poetry than could be exhausted, even without books or learning. Having deserted the service and society, he began to solve the problem of his existence by other means. He reflected upon his destiny, and finally discovered that the sphere of his activity and profession reposed in himself. He realized that the welfare of the family and the care of the property fell to his share. Up to this time he had no systematic knowledge of his own affairs, which Stoltz sometimes attended to in his stead; he did not know his exact receipts and expenditures, struck no balance sheet—nothing.

The senior Oblomof had transmitted the estate to his son just as he received it from his father. Though he spent his whole life in the country, he did not elaborate nor break his head over innovations, as men do nowadays; how to discover new sources of productivity

495

for the soil, or increase and reënforce the old, and so on. As and wherewith the fields had been sown by his grandfather, and such as were then the methods of marketing the crops, such they remained under him. The old man was wont to be delighted if a good harvest or advanced prices gave him an income larger than last year's: he called that a blessing of God. But he disliked to scheme and strive for a harvest of money. "God gives, let us be satisfied," he said.

Ilya Ilyich pinned his faith no longer to father or grandfather. He had studied and lived in the world: it all suggested to him a variety of ideas strange till then. He understood that not only i gain no sin, but that it is every citizen's duty to contribute by honest work to the general well-being. Thus it was that the largest part of the life-design he traced in his solitude was devoted to a new and fresh plan, in accordance with the needs of the time, for administering his property and managing his peasants. The fundamental idea of the plan, the arrangement, the principal parts—all have long been ready in his head; there remain now only details, estimates, and figures. He has worked untiringly for several years on this plan; he thinks about it and ponders it, both afoot and in bed, at home as well as in company; now filling out, now changing various portions, now recalling to mind some point conceived yesterday and forgotten during the night; and sometimes, swift as lightning, a new, unexpected idea flashes upon him and begins to seethe in his brain—the work is going on swimmingly. He is not petty executive of others' ready-made notions: himself is the creator and himself the executor of his ideas. As soon as he rises from bed in the morning, after his tea he throws himself at once on the sofa, rests his head in his hands and meditates, without sparing his strength, till his head at length is fatigued by the arduous labor, and his conscience says: "Enough done to-day for the public good."

Free from business cares, Oblomof loved to retire into himself and live in a self-created world. He was accessible to the joy of lofty purpose; he was no stranger to the general interests of humanity. Many a time in the depth of his soul he wept bitterly over the miseries of mankind; he experienced mysterious nameless suffering and sorrow, and vague longing for a distant land, probably for that world where his teacher, Stoltz, had often led him;—and sweet tears trickled down his cheeks. Sometimes, too, he is filled with contempt for human vices, for the falsehood, the calumny, the evil that floods the world, and he is inflamed with a desire to show mankind his hurts: suddenly there glow within him ideas that come and g·

in his mind, like waves on the sea, then grow to purposes, setting all his blood on fire; the purposes are transformed to endeavor; impelled by a moral force, he changes his attitude twice or thrice in a minute; with sparkling eyes he half rises in his bed, stretches forth his hand and casts an inspired look about him. Now, now the endeavor is about to be realized, turn into a fact—and then, great Heaven! what miracles, what beneficial results might not be expected from an effort so sublime!—But see, the morning passes, the day is already inclining to its end, and with it Oblomof's wearied strength inclines to repose; the storms and tempests in his soul abate, his head cools from thought, the blood courses more slowly in his veins. Oblomof, tranquil and pensive, stretches himself on his back, and casting a mournful glance toward the window, with melancholy eyes follows the sun as it sinks majestically behind some four-story house. How many times he has thus followed the setting sun!

In the morning life returns; once more emotions and illusions. He often loves to fancy himself some invincible general, before whom not only Napoleon but Yeruslan Lazarevich are as nothing; he pictures a war and its causes: in his mind, for example, the people of Africa hurl themselves on Europe; or he organizes new crusades, makes war, decides the destinies of nations, destroys cities, spares, puts to death, does deeds of kindness and magnanimity. Or else he chooses the career of the thinker, or the great artist: all do him honor; he reaps laurels; the crowd follows him, crying, "There he is, there he is, there goes Oblomof, our celebrated Ilya Ilyich!"

In bitter moments he is tormented by cares, turns from one side to the other, lies face down, sometimes even completely loses himself; then he rises from bed, falls on his knees, and begins to pray warmly, fervently, beseeching Heaven to avert from him some threatening storm. Then, having shifted the care of his fate on Heaven, he becomes calm and indifferent toward everything in the world, and the storm is wholly forgotten.

Thus he puts his moral strength in play; thus he often agitates himself for entire days, and only awakes with a deep sigh from enchanting visions or painful anxieties when the day is declining, and the great sphere of the sun begins to descend in glory behind the four-story house. Then he follows it again with a dreamy look and a melancholy smile, and rests peacefully from his emotions.

497

MAXIM GORKY

MAXIM GORKY (Alexei Maximovich Peshkov, Russian, 1868-1936). Pioneer
of Russian Revolution in his magnificent, socially-conscious stories. Orphaned
when a child, spent years wandering through Russia. Short stories notable
for compassionate treatment of outcasts. Famous also for uncompromising
realistic drama, *The Lower Depths*. Autobiographical works: *My Childhood,
My University Days, My Mother*. Successfully hid bitter disappointment with
Stalinist dictatorship, but died under mysterious circumstances.

ONE AUTUMN NIGHT

ONCE in the autumn I happened to be in a very unpleasant and
inconvenient position. In the town where I had just arrived and
where I knew not a soul, I found myself without a farthing in my
pocket and without a night's lodging.

Having sold during the first few days every part of my costume
without which it was still possible to go about, I passed from the
town into the quarter called "Yste," where were the steamship
wharves—a quarter which during the navigation season fermented
with boisterous, laborous life, but now was silent and deserted, for
we were in the last days of October.

Dragging my feet along the moist sand, and obstinately scrutiniz-
ing it with the desire to discover in it any sort of fragment of food,
I wandered alone among the deserted buildings and warehouses,
and thought how good it would be to get a full meal.

In our present state of culture hunger of the mind is more quickly
satisfied than hunger of the body. You wander about the streets,
you are surrounded by buildings not bad-looking from the outside
and—you may safely say it—not so badly furnished inside, and
the sight of them may excite within you stimulating ideas about
architecture, hygiene, and many other wise and high-flying subjects.
You may meet warmly and neatly dressed folks—all very polite, and
turning away from you tactfully, not wishing offensively to notice the
lamentable fact of your existence. Well, well, the mind of a hungry
man is always bettei nourished and healthier that the mind of the
well-fed man; and there you have a situation from which you may
draw a very ingenious conclusion in favor of the ill fed.

The evening was approaching, the rain was falling, and the wind blew violently from the north. It whistled in the empty booths and shops, blew into the plastered window-panes of the taverns, and whipped into foam the wavelets of the river which splashed noisily on the sandy shore, casting high their white crests, racing one after another into the dim distance, and leaping impetuously over one another's shoulders. It seemed as if the river felt the proximity of winter, and was running at random away from the fetters of ice which the north wind might well have flung upon her that very night. The sky was heavy and dark; down from it swept incessantly scarcely visible drops of rain, and the melancholy elegy in nature all around me was emphasized by a couple of battered and mis-shapen willow-trees and a boat, bottom upwards, that was fastened to their roots.

The overturned canoe with its battered keel and the miserable old trees rifled by the cold wind—everything around me was bankrupt, barren, and dead, and the sky flowed with undryable tears. . . . Everything around was waste and gloomy . . . it seemed as if every-thing were dead, leaving me alone among the living, and for me also a cold death waited.

I was then eighteen years old—a good time!

I walked and walked along the cold wet sand, making my chat-tering teeth warble in honor of cold and hunger, when suddenly, as I was carefully searching for something to eat behind one of the empty crates, I perceived behind it, crouching on the ground, a figure in woman's clothes dank with the rain and clinging fast to her stooping shoulders. Standing above her, I watched to see what she was doing. It appeared that she was digging a trench in the sand with her hands—digging away under one of the crates.

"Why are you doing that?" I asked, crouching down on my heels quite close to her.

She gave a little scream and was quickly on her legs again. Now that she stood there staring at me, with her wide-open gray eyes full of terror, I perceived that it was a girl of my own age, with a very pleasant face embellished unfortunately by three large blue marks. This spoilt her, although these blue marks had been dis-tributed with a remarkable sense of proportion, one at a time, and all were of equal size—two under the eyes, and one a little bigger on the forehead just over the bridge of the nose. This symmetry was evidently the work of an artist well inured to the business of spoiling the human physiognomy.

The girl looked at me, and the terror in her eyes gradually died out. . . . She shook the sand from her hands, adjusted her cotton head-gear, cowered down, and said:

"I suppose you, too, want something to eat? Dig away then! My hands are tired. Over there"—she nodded her head in the direction of a booth—"there is bread for certain . . . and sausages too. . . . That booth is still carrying on business."

I began to dig. She, after waiting a little and looking at me, sat down beside me and began to help me.

We worked in silence. I cannot say now whether I thought at that moment of the criminal code, of morality, of proprietorship, and all the other things about which, in the opinion of many experienced persons, one ought to think every moment of one's life. Wishing to keep as close to the truth as possible, I must confess that apparently I was so deeply engaged in digging under the crate that I completely forgot about everything else except one thing: What could be inside that crate?

The evening drew on. The gray, mouldy, cold fog grew thicker and thicker around us. The waves roared with a hollower sound than before, and the rain pattered down on the boards of that crate more loudly and more frequently. Somewhere or other the night-watchman began springing his rattle.

"Has it got a bottom or not?" softly inquired my assistant. I did not understand what she was talking about, and kept silence.

"I say, has the crate got a bottom? If it has we shall try in vain to break into it. Here we are digging a trench, and we may, after all come upon nothing but solid boards. How shall we take them off? Better smash the lock; it is a wretched lock."

Good ideas rarely visit the heads of women, but as you see, they visit them sometimes. I have always valued good ideas, and have always tried to utilize them as far as possible.

Having found the lock, I tugged at it and wrenched off the whole thing. My accomplice immediately stooped down and wriggled like a serpent into the gaping-open, four-cornered cover of the crate whence she called to me approvingly, in a low tone:

"You're a brick!"

Nowadays a little crumb of praise from a woman is dearer to me than a whole dithyramb from a man, even though he be more eloquent than all the ancient and modern orators put together. Then, however, I was less amiably disposed than I am now, and paying

500

no attention to the compliment of my comrade, I asked her curtly and anxiously:

"Is there anything?"

In a monotonous tone she set about calculating our discoveries. "A basketful of bottles—thick furs—a sunshade—an iron pail."

All this was uneatable. I felt that my hopes had vanished. . . . But suddenly she exclaimed vivaciously:

"Aha! here it is!"

"What?"

"Bread . . . a loaf . . . it's only wet . . . take it!"

A loaf flew to my feet and after it herself, my valiant comrade. I had already bitten off a morsel, stuffed it in my mouth, and was chewing it. . . .

"Come, give me some too! . . . And we mustn't stay here. . . . Where shall we go?" She looked inquiringly about on all sides. . . . It was dark, wet, and boisterous.

"Look! there's an upset canoe yonder . . . let us go there."

"Let us go then!" And off we set, demolishing our booty as we went, and filling our mouths with large portions of it. . . . The rain grew more violent, the river roared; from somewhere or other resounded a prolonged mocking whistle—just as if someone great who feared nobody was whistling down all earthly institutions and along with them this horrid autumnal wind and us, its heroes. This whistling made my heart throb painfully, in spite of which I greedily went on eating, and in this respect the girl walking on my left, kept even pace with me.

"What do they call you?" I asked her—why I know not.

"Natasha," she answered shortly, munching loudly.

I stared at her. My heart ached within me; and then I stared into the mist before me, and it seemed to me as if the inimical countenance of my Destiny was smiling at me enigmatically and coldly.

The rain scourged the timbers of the skiff incessantly, and its soft patter induced melancholy thoughts, and the wind whistled as it flew down into the boat's battered bottom through a rift, where some loose splinters of wood were rattling together—a disquieting and depressing sound. The waves of the river were splashing on the shore, and sounded so monotonous and hopeless, just as if they were telling something unbearably dull and heavy, which was boring them into utter disgust, something from which they wanted to run away and yet were obliged to talk about all the same. The

501

sound of the rain blended with their splashing, and a long-drawn sigh seemed to be floating above the overturned skiff—the endless, laboring sigh of the earth, injured and exhausted by the eternal changes from the bright and warm summer to the cold, misty and damp autumn. The wind blew continually over the desolate shore and the foaming river—blew and sang its melancholy songs. . . .

Our position beneath the shelter of the skiff was utterly devoid of comfort; it was narrow and damp, tiny cold drops of rain dribbled through the damaged bottom; gusts of wind penetrated it. We sat in silence and shivered with cold. I remembered that I wanted to go to sleep. Natasha leaned her back against the hull of the boat and curled herself up into a tiny ball. Embracing her knees with her hands, and resting her chin upon them, she stared doggedly at the river with wide-open eyes; on the pale patch of her face they seemed immense, because of the blue marks below them. She never moved, and this immobility and silence—I felt it—gradually produced within me a terror of my neighbor. I wanted to talk to her, but I knew not how to begin.

It was she herself who spoke.

"What a cursed thing life is!" she exclaimed plainly, abstractedly, and in a tone of deep conviction.

But this was no complaint. In these words there was too much of indifference for a complaint. This simple soul thought according to her understanding—thought and proceeded to form a certain conclusion which she expressed aloud, and which I could not confute for fear of contradicting myself. Therefore I was silent, and she, as if she had not noticed me, continued to sit there immovable.

"Even if we croaked . . . what then . . .?" Natasha began again, this time quietly and reflectively, and still there was not one note of complaint in her words. It was plain that this person, in the course of her reflections on life, was regarding her own case, and had arrived at the conviction that in order to preserve herself from the mockeries of life, she was not in a position to do anything else but simply "croak"—to use her own expression.

The clearness of this line of thought was inexpressibly sad and painful to me, and I felt that if I kept silence any longer I was really bound to weep. . . . And it would have been shameful to have done this before a woman, especially as she was not weeping herself. I resolved to speak to her.

"Who was it that knocked you about?" I asked. For the moment I could not think of anything more sensible or more delicate.

502

"Pashka did it all," she answered in a dull and level tone.

"And who is he?"

"My lover. . . . He was a baker."

"Did he beat you often?"

"Whenever he was drunk he beat me. . . . Often!"

And suddenly, turning towards me, she began to talk about herself, Pashka, and their mutual relations. He was a baker with red mustaches and played very well on the banjo. He came to see her and greatly pleased her, for he was a merry chap and wore nice clean clothes. He had a vest which cost fifteen rubles and boots with dress tops. For these reasons she had fallen in love with him, and he became her "creditor." And when he became her creditor, he made it his business to take away from her the money which her other friends gave to her for bonbons, and, getting drunk on this money, he would fall to beating her; but that would have been nothing if he hadn't also begun to "run after" other girls before her very eyes.

"Now wasn't that an insult? I am not worse than the others. Of course that meant that he was laughing at me, the blackguard. The day before yesterday I asked leave of my mistress to go out for a bit, went to him, and here I found Dimka sitting beside him, drunk. And he, too, was half seas over. I said, 'You scoundrel, you!' And he gave me a thorough hiding. He kicked me and dragged me by the hair. But that was nothing to what came after. He spoiled everything I had on—left me just as I am now! How could I appear before my mistress? He spoiled everything . . . my dress and my jacket too—it was quite a new one; I gave a fiver for it . . . and tore my kerchief from my head. . . . Oh, Lord! What will become of me now?" she suddenly whined in a lamentable, overstrained voice.

The wind howled, and became ever colder and more boisterous. . . . Again my teeth began to dance up and down, and she, huddled up to avoid the cold, pressed as closely to me as she could, so that I could see the gleam of her eyes through the darkness.

"What wretches all you men are! I'd burn you all in an oven; I'd cut you in pieces. If any one of you was dying I'd spit in his mouth, and not pity him a bit. Mean skunks! You wheedle and wheedle, you wag your tails like cringing dogs, and we fools give ourselves up to you, and it's all up with us! Immediately you trample us underfoot. . . . Miserable loafers!"

She cursed us up and down, but there was no vigor, no malice,

503

no hatred of these "miserable loafers" in her cursing that I could hear. The tone of her language was by no means corresponded with its subject-matter, for it was calm enough, and the gamut of her voice was terribly poor.

Yet all this made a stronger impression on me than the most eloquent and convincing pessimistic books and speeches, of which I had read a good many and which I still read to this day. And this, you see, was because the agony of a dying person is much more natural and violent than the most minute and picturesque descriptions of death.

I felt really wretched—more from cold than from the words of my neighbor. I groaned softly and ground my teeth.

Almost at the same moment I felt two little arms about me—one of them touched my neck and the other lay upon my face—and at the same time an anxious, gentle, friendly voice uttered the question: "What ails you?"

I was really to believe that someone else was asking me this and not Natasha, who had just declared that all men were scoundrels, and expressed a wish for their destruction. But she it was, and now she began speaking quickly, hurriedly.

"What ails you, eh? Are you cold? Are you frozen? Ah, what a one you are, sitting there so silent like a little owl! Why, you should have told me long ago that you were cold. Come . . . Lie on the ground . . . stretch yourself out and I will lie . . . there! How's that? Now put your arms round me? . . . tighter! How's that? You shall be warm very soon now. . . . And then we'll lie back to back. . . . The night will pass so quickly, see if it won't. I say . . . have you too been drinking . . . ? Turned out of your place, eh? . . . It doesn't matter."

And she comforted me. . . . She encouraged me.

May I be thrice accursed! What a world of irony was in this single fact for me! Just imagine! Here was I, seriously occupied at this very time with the destiny of humanity, thinking of the re-organization of the social system, of political revolutions, reading all sorts of devilishly wise books whose abysmal profundity was certainly unfathomable by their very authors—at this very time, I say, I was trying with all my might to make of myself "a potent, active social force." It even seemed to me that I had partially accomplished my object; anyhow, at this time, in my ideas about myself, I had got so far as to recognize that I had an exclusive right to exist, that I had the necessary greatness to deserve to live

504

my life, and that I was fully competent to play a great historical part therein. And a woman was now warming me with her body, a wretched, battered, hunted creature, who had no place and no value in life, and whom I had never thought of helping till she helped me herself, and whom I really would not have known how to help in any way even if the thought of it had occurred to me.

Ah! I was ready to think that all this was happening to me in a dream—in a disagreable, an oppressive dream.

But, ugh! it was impossible for me to think that, for cold drops of rain were dripping down upon me, the woman was pressing close to me, her warm breath was fanning my face, and—despite a slight odor of vodka—it did me good. The wind howled and raged, the rain smote upon the skiff, the waves splashed, and both of us, embracing each other convulsively, nevertheless shivered with cold. All this was only too real, and I am certain that nobody ever dreamed such an oppressive and horrid dream as that reality.

But Natasha was talking all the time of something or other, talking kindly and sympathetically, as only women can talk. Beneath the influence of her voice and kindly words, a little fire began to burn up within me, and something inside my heart thawed in consequence.

Then tears poured from my eyes like a hailstorm, washing away from my heart much that was evil, much that was stupid, much sorrow and dirt which had fastened upon it before that night. Natasha comforted me.

"Come, come, that will do, little one! Don't take on! That'll do! God will give you another chance . . . you will right yourself and stand in your proper place again . . . and it will be all right. . . ."

And she kept kissing me . . . many kisses did she give me . . . burning kisses . . . and all for nothing. . . .

Those were the first kisses from a woman that had ever been bestowed upon me, and they were the best kisses too, for all the subsequent kisses cost me frightfully dear, and really gave me nothing at all in exchange.

"Come, don't take on so, funny one! I'll manage for you to-morrow if you cannot find a place." Her quiet, persuasive whispering sounded in my ears as if it came through a dream. . . .

There we lay till dawn. . . .

And when the dawn came, we crept from behind the skiff and went into the town. . . .Then we took friendly leave of each other and never met again, although for half a year I searched in every

505

hole and corner for that kind Natasha with whom I spent the
autumn night just described.

If she be already dead—and well for her if it were so—may she
rest in peace! And if she be alive . . . still I say "Peace to her soul!"
And may the consciousness of her fall never enter her soul . . .
for that would be a superfluous and fruitless suffering if life is to
be lived. . . .

THOMAS GRAY

THOMAS GRAY (English, 1716-1771). Precursor of English Romanticism.
Magnificent craftsman, with classical background. Passed most of life as
professor, wrote frequently in Latin. *Elegy Written in a Country Churchyard*
one of favorite and most quoted poems in the language. Excellent *Pindaric
Odes* less well known.

ELEGY IN A COUNTRY CHURCHYARD

The curfew tolls the knell of parting day,
  The lowing herd winds slowly o'er the lea,
The ploughman homeward plods his weary way,
  And leaves the world to darkness and to me.

Now fades the glimmering landscape on the sight,
  And all the air a solemn stillness holds,
Save where the beetle wheels his droning flight,
  And drowsy tinklings lull the distant folds;

Save that from yonder ivy-mantled tower,
  The moping owl does to the moon complain
Of such as, wandering near her secret bower,
  Molest her ancient solitary reign.

Beneath those rugged elms, that yew-tree's shade,
  Where heaves the turf in many a mouldering heap
Each in his narrow cell forever laid,
  The rude forefathers of the hamlet sleep.

506

The breezy call of incense breathing-morn,
  The swallow twittering from the straw-built shed,
The cock's shrill clarion, or the echoing horn,
  No more shall rouse them from their lowly bed.

For them no more the blazing hearth shall burn,
  Or busy housewife ply her evening care;
No children run to lisp their sire's return,
  Or climb his knees the envied kiss to share.

Oft did the harvest to their sickle yield;
  Their furrow oft the stubborn glebe has broke;
How jocund did they drive their team afield!
  How bowed the woods beneath their sturdy stroke!

Let not ambition mock their useful toil,
  Their homely joys and destiny obscure;
Nor grandeur hear, with a disdainful smile,
  The short and simple annals of the poor.

The boast of heraldry, the pomp of power,
  And all that beauty, all that wealth e'er gave,
Await alike the inevitable hour—
  The paths of glory lead but to the grave.

Nor you, ye proud, impute to these the fault,
  If memory o'er their tomb no trophies raise,
Where, through the long-drawn aisle and fretted vault,
  The pealing anthem swells the note of praise.

Can storied urn or animated bust
  Back to its mansion call the fleeting breath?
Can honor's voice provoke the silent dust,
  Or flattery soothe the dull cold ear of death?

Perhaps in this neglected spot is laid
  Some heart once pregnant with celestial fire,
Hands that the rod of empire might have swayed
  Or waked to ecstasy the living lyre.

But knowledge to their eyes her ample page,
　Rich with the spoils of time, did ne'er unroll;
Chill penury repressed their noble rage,
　And froze the genial current of the soul.

Full many a gem of purest ray serene
　The dark, unfathomed caves of ocean bear;
Full many a flower is born to blush unseen,
　And waste its sweetness in the desert air.

Some village Hampden, that, with dauntless breast,
　The little tyrant of his fields withstood
Some mute inglorious Milton here may rest,
　Some Cromwell, guiltless of his country's blood.

The applause of listening senates to command,
　The threats of pain and ruin to despise,
To scatter plenty o'er a smiling land,
　And read their history in a nation's eyes,—

Their lot forbade; nor circumscribed alone
　Their growing virtues, but their crimes confined;
Forbade to wade through slaughter to a throne,
　And shut the gates of mercy on mankind;

The struggling pangs of conscious truth to hide,
　To quench the blushes of ingenious shame,
Or heap the shrine of luxury and pride
　With incense kindled at the muse's flame.

Far from the madding crowd's ignoble strife,
　Their sober wishes never learned to stray;
Along the cool sequestered vale of life
　They kept the noiseless tenor of their way.

Yet e'en these bones from insult to protect,
　Some frail memorial still erected nigh,
With uncouth rhymes and shapeless sculpture decked,
　Implores the passing tribute of a sigh.

508

Their names, their years, spelled by the unlettered muse,
   The place of fame and eulogy supply;
And many a holy text around she strews,
   That teach the rustic moralist to die.

For who, to dumb forgetfulness a prey,
   This pleasing, anxious being e'er resigned,
Left the warm precincts of the cheerful day,
   Nor cast one longing, lingering look behind?

On some fond breast the parting soul relies,
   Some pious hand the closing eye requires;
Even from the tomb the voice of nature cries,
   Even in our ashes live their wonted fires.

For thee, who, mindful of the unhonored dead,
   Dost in these lines their artless tale relate,
If chance, by lonely contemplation led,
   Some kindred spirit shall inquire thy fate.

Haply some hoary-headed swain may say,
   "Oft have we seen him at the peep of dawn,
Brushing with hasty steps the dews away,
   To meet the sun upon the upland lawn.

"There at the foot of yonder nodding beech,
   That wreathes its old fantastic roots so high,
His listless length at noontide would he stretch,
   And pore upon the brook that bubbles by.

"Hard by yon wood, now smiling as in scorn,
   Muttering his wayward fancies, he would rove,
Now drooping, woeful wan, like one forlorn,
   Or crazed with care, or crossed in hopeless love.

"One morn I missed him on the 'customed hill,
   Along the heath, and near his favorite tree;
Another came; nor yet beside the rill,
   Nor up the lawn, nor at the wood was he;

509

"The next, with dirges due, in sad array,
  Slow through the churchyard path we saw him borne—
Approach and read (for thou canst read) the lay
  'Graved on the stone beneath yon aged thorn."

THE EPITAPH

Here rests his head upon the lap of earth,
  A youth to fortune and to fame unknown;
Fair science frowned not on his humble birth,
  And melancholy marked him for her own.

Large was his bounty, and his soul sincere,
  Heaven did a recompense as largely send;
He gave to misery all he had—a tear;
  He gained from Heaven ('twas all he wished) a friend.

No farther seek his merits to disclose,
  Or draw his frailties from their dread abode
(There they alike in trembling hope repose),
  The bosom of his Father and his God.

FRANZ GRILLPARZER

FRANZ GRILLPARZER (Austrian, 1791-1872). Chief Austrian dramatist.
Developed classical and historical themes in contemporary terms, informing
them with 19th century idealism and psychology. Mood of pessimism prevails.
Suffered from political censorship of his time. Major works: *The Golden
Fleece* (treatment of Medea legend), *The Dream of Life, Woe to Him
That Lies!*

SAPPHO

Act V

Rhamnes— Her name upon the stars
She has traced with diamond-pointed letters,
And only with the stars 'twill fade away.
In distant lands, among strange men, 'twill

Echo, long after these our mortal frames
Have perished, our graves no more are found.
Then Sappho's soul will speak from out strange lips;
Her songs will live embalmed in unknown tongues,
And thine, thy name will live! Be proud of thy
Undying name! In distant lands, by men
Unknown, when centuries have passed away,
And time has swallowed all, 'twill echo then
From every mouth, "'Twas Sappho sang the song,
And Phaon caused her death."

Melitta— Forbear! forbear!

Phaon— A maniac wouldst thou make me? Who'll save me
from this torment?

Eucharis enters.

Eucharis— Rhamnes, thou art here! come! hasten!
Rhamnes— Whither?
Eucharis— To Sappho. I fear she is ill.
Rhamnes— The gods
Forbid!
Eucharis— I followed her afar, till gained
The largest hall. Concealed, and with sharp eye,
Her motions all I watched. Leaning, and raised
Upon a pedestal, she looked far o'er
The distant sea, that raged and chafed upon
The rock-bound coast. With pallid cheek and eyes,
Veiled with their lids, all motionless she stood,
Among those marble statues, one of them.
Only she seized upon the altar flowers,
The gold and ornaments within her reach,
And cast them, musing, deep in the raging sea.
Their fall with longing eyes she seemed to follow.
I nearer drew; but now a sound I heard
That shook her inmost soul. Suspended from
On high, the sea breeze touched the lyre,
And pensive played within its untuned strings;
Deep sighing, she looked up, and all her being
Thrilled, shaken invisibly by higher
Powers. Her eyes with a strange fire illumed,
A lovely smile played o'er her mouth.
The firm-closed lips were parted now, and words

511

Came forth so solemn and profound they seemed
Not Sappho's words, but edicts of the gods!
"O friend!" she said, "thou dost admonish me
Of passing time; O thanks! I understand
Thee well." How the wall she gained, and how
The lyre high-hanging reached, I know not.
Her arm, a beam of light it seemed; and as
I looked she held the lyre and pressed the strings
Upon her storm-moved breast; while audibly
The breathing sounds came forth and passed away.
Suspended as a votive wreath upon
The domestic altar, hung her crown; she took
And wound it round her head; the purple robe,
A glowing veil, o'er her fair shoulders threw.
Who first had seen her now, with lyre in hand,
And look inspired, upraised, the altar steps
Ascending, with her whole light form enwrapped
In light, in prayer had bent his trembling knees,
And hailed her the immortal. Silent
And motionless she stood, yet through my limbs
Crept shuddering fear; I quailed beneath
Her piercing eye, and fled to thee.
    Rhamnes— Left her?
Return! yet see, herself comes near!
*(Sappho enters richly dressed as in the first act: the purple mantle on
    her shoulders, the laurel crown upon her head, and the golden
    lyre in her hand. She is surrounded by her women, and descends
    the steps of the marble colonnade.)*
    Melitta— Sappho! dearest mistress!
    Sappho (calm and earnest)— What wouldst thou, then?
    Melitta— Rent is the bandage from my opened eyes.
Let me again become thy slave. Receive
Again what's thine, and pardon me.
    Sappho— So ill
Advised believe me not. No gift from thee
Will Sappho take. That was my own, thou canst
Not give nor take.
    Phaon (kneeling)— O listen, Sappho!
    Sappho— Beware! kneel not to me; devoted am I to the gods!
    Phaon— With gentle eye thou look'st at me, O Sappho!
Rememberest thou—

Sappho— Thou speakest of things long past,
Thee, Phaon, I sought! and found myself.
Thou understood me not. Farewell! on firmer
Ground my hopes must rest!
    Phaon— Hatest thou me, then?
    Sappho— Hatred! Love! Is there no third? Worthy wert
Thou, and are so still, and ever will to me
Be so; like a dear chance companion
That accident awhile led in my boat. The goal
Once reached, we part, each wandering on
His path alone; yet often from the path,
The widening path, recall the friendly meeting.
                          (Her voice fails.

    Phaon (much moved)— O Sappho!
    Sappho— Forbear! we part in peace!
    (To the others)— You who have Sappho's weakness seen, O
    pardon!
To Sappho's weakness be ye reconciled!
The bow when bent first shows its power.
    (She points to the altar in the background)— The flame
Is lit. To Aphrodite it mounts, clear as
The beam of coming day.
    (To her Servants and Phaon)— And now remove!
Leave me to counsel with mine own—mine own!
    Rhamnes— Obey her will. Let all withdraw *(They draw back.*
    Sappho (approaches the altar that stands close to the cliff)—
Ye lofty gods! divine! With blessings rich
You've crowned my life. My hand the muses' lyre
Has touched; the poet's cup for me runs o'er.
A heart to feel, a mind to think, and power
    To form my thought to music, you have given.
With rich blessings you have blessed me. I thank you!
With victory you've crowned my feeble brow,
And sowed in distant lands the poet's fame,
Of immortality the seed. Echoes
From strangers' tongues the song I struck upon
My golden lyre, and only with the earth
The fame of Sappho dies.
I thank you!
In life's unmingled cup, crowned high with sweets,
The poet only sips, but does not drink.

Obedient to your highest wish, the sweet,
Unemptied cup I place aside, and drink not.
What you decreed, all-powerful gods,
Has Sappho finished! Deny me not
The last reward within your power to grant—
No weakness, no decay, let Sappho know.
In her full strength, in nature's bloom, O take
Her quickly to yourselves!
Forbid that e'er a priestess of the gods
Should be the theme of god-denying foes!
The sport of fools, in their own folly wise!
You bruised the flower, break now the stem;
Perfect in truth what was begun in love,
And spare the conflict's bleeding struggle. Grant,
O grant the victory! the victor's weakness spare!
The flame is kindling while the sun ascends!
I feel I'm heard! Great gods, I thank you!
Melitta! Phaon! come nearer to me!
    (She kisses Phaon on the forehead)—
A friend from distant worlds salutes thee thus!
    (Embracing Melitta)—
Thy mother, dead, sends thee this kiss! Farewell!
There, on the altar of love's goddess, love
Fulfills, of love, the melancholy fate!
    (She hastens to the altar.)
    Rhamnes— What means she? Inspired is all her being.
The splendor of immortals wraps her round.
*(Sappho, who has gradually approached the edge of the cliff, upon
    which the altar stands, stretches both hands over Melitta and
    Phaon.)*
    Sappho— To men give love! ambition to the gods!
What for you blooms, enjoy, and think of Sappho!
Of life the last debt I pay! The gods,
To you, grant blessings; and to me—themselves.
    (She springs from the cliff into the sea.)
    Phaon— Hold! Sappho! hold!
    Melitta— Alas, she falls! she dies.
    Phaon (busied with Melitta)—
Quick! quick! She dies! Forth from the shore to save!
    Rhamnes (has climbed upon the rock)—
    The gods protect! There on that cliff she falls;

514

There is she crushed, destroyed! Bears she off?
Impossible! alas! too late!
 Phaon— Why weep
You here? a boat! haste! haste to save her.
 Rhamnes (descending)—
Forbear! it is too late! Grant her the grave
The gods decree. That she, disdaining this
False earth, within the sacred waves has
Chosen for her rest.
 Phaon— Dead!
 Rhamnes— Dead!
 Phaon— Dead! alas!
Impossible! She is not dead! not dead!
 Rhamnes— Withered the laurel! broken are the strings;
Upon the earth there was no home for her;
To heaven has Sappho, to her own, returned!

515

H

HAFIZ

HĀFIZ (Shams ud-Din Mohammed, Persian, *ca.* 1320-1389). Unequaled master of the *ghazal* (short lyric poem). His *Divan*, containing over 500 *ghazals*, influenced later Persian, Indian and Turkish poets, and Westerners such as Goethe. A subtle mystic and superb satirist.

CHARMS THAT CHARM NOT

Without the loved one's cheek the rose
    Can charm not.
The spring, unless the wine-cup flows,
    Can charm not.
The greenwood's border and the orchard's air,
Unless some tulip cheek be there,
    Can charm not.
The sugar-lipped, the fair of rosy frame,
Whom kisses nor embrace can claim,
    Can charm not.
The dancing cypress, the enrapturing flower,
If no nightingale gladden the bower,
    Can charm not.
The painter's picture, though with genius rife,
Without the picture that has life,
    Can charm not.
Wine, flower, and bower abound in charm, yet they,
Lack we the friend who makes us gay,
    Can charm not.
Thy soul, O Hafiz! is a coin that none prize;
And it, though poured forth largess-wise,
    Can charm not.

My breast is filled with roses,
  My cup is crowned with wine,
And the veil her face discloses—
  The maid I hail as mine.
The monarch, wheresoe'er he be,
Is but a slave compared to me.

Their glare no torches throwing,
  Shall in our bower be found—
Her eyes, like moonbeams glowing,
  Cast light enough around;
And other odors I can spare
Who scent the perfume of her hair.

The honey-dew thy charm might borrow,
  Thy lip alone to me is sweet;
When thou art absent, faint with sorrow
  I hide me in some lone retreat.
Why talk to me of power or fame?
  What are those idle toys to me?
Why ask the praises of my name,
  My joy, my triumph is in thee.

How blest am I! around me swelling
  The notes of melody arise!
I hold the cup with wine excelling,
  And gaze upon thy radiant eyes.

O Hafiz—never waste thy hours
  Without the cup, the lute, and love,
For 'tis the sweetest time of flowers,
  And none these moments shall reprove.
The nightingales around thee sing;
It is the joyous feast of spring.

THE DRUNKARD'S EXCUSE

Know you the true reason and cause why it is that I drink?
  From pride and from folly I strutted and swelled through the
    town:

And now those detestable vices, from which the saints shrink,
    I will in the depths of the ocean of drunkenness drown.

MY BIRD

My soul is as a sacred bird, the highest heaven its nest,
Fretting within its body-bars, it finds on earth its nest;
When rising from its dusty heap this bird of mine shall soar
'Twill find upon the lofty gate the nest it had before.
The Sidrah shall receive my bird, when it has winged its way,
And on the Empyrean's top, my falcon's foot shall stay.
Over the ample field of earth is fortune's shadow cast,
Where upon wings and pennons borne this bird of mine has passed.
No spot in the two worlds it owns, above the sphere its goal,
Its body from the quarry is, from "No Place" is its soul.
'Tis only in the glorious world my bird its splendor shows,
The rosy bowers of Paradise its daily food bestows.

JUDAH HALEVI

JUDAH HALEVI (Spanish-Hebrew, *ca.* 1080-1140). One of greatest Hebrew
poets of Spanish Golden Period, called the Sweet Singer of Zion. Physician
by profession, emigrated to Palestine to devote rest of life to writing *Songs of
Zion.* Also famous: *Sefer ha-Kuzari*, a dialogue on Jewish religion and history,
in effect an essay on national revival. Religious and liturgical poems still used
in prayer.

I. A LETTER TO HIS FRIEND ISAAC

But yesterday the earth drank like a child
    With eager thirst the autumn rain.
Or like a wistful bride who waits the hour
    Of love's mysterious bliss and pain.
And now the Spring is here with yearning eyes;
    Midst shimmering golden flower-beds,
On meadows carpeted with varied hues,
    In richest raiment clad, she treads.

518

She weaves a tapestry of bloom o'er all,
 And myriad eyed young plants upspring,
White, green, or red like lips that to the mouth
 Of the beloved one sweetly cling.
Whence come these radiant tints, these blended beams?
 Here's such a dazzle, such a blaze,
As though earth stole the splendor of the stars,
 Fain to eclipse them with her rays.
Come! go we to the garden with our wine,
 Which scatters sparks of hot desire,
Within our hand 't is cold, but in our veins
 It flashes clear, it glows like fire.
It bubbles sunnily in earthen jugs.
We catch it in the crystal glass,
 Then wander through cool, shadowy lanes and breathe
 The spicy freshness of the grass.
Whilst we with happy hearts our circuit keep,
 The gladness of the Earth is shown.
She smileth, though the trickling rain-drops weep
 Silently o'er her, one by one.
She loves to feel the tears upon her cheek,
 Like a rich veil, with pearls inwove.
Joyous she listens when the swallows chirp,
 And warbles to her mate, the dove.
Blithe as a maiden midst the young green leaves,
 A wreath she'll wind, a fragrant treasure;
All living things in graceful motion leap,
 As dancing to some merry measure.
The morning breezes rustle cordially,
 Love's thirst is sated with the balm they send.
Sweet breathes the myrtle in the frolic wind,
 As though remembering a distant friend.
The myrtle branch now proudly lifted high,
 Now whispering to itself drops low again.
The topmost palm-leaves rapturously stir,
 For all at once they hear the birds' soft strain.
So stirs, so yearns all nature, gayly decked,
 To honor *Isaac* with her best array.
Hear'st thou the word? She cries—I beam with joy,
Because with Isaac I am wed today.

II. ADMONITION

Long in the lap of childhood didst thou sleep,
Think how thy youth like chaff did disappear;
Shall life's sweet Spring forever last? Look up,
Old age approaches ominously near.
Oh, shake thou off the world, even as the bird
Shakes off the midnight dew that clogged his wings.
Soar upward, seek redemption from thy guilt
And from the earthly dross that round thee clings.
Draw near to God, His holy angels know,
For whom His bounteous streams of mercy flow.

III. LOVE SONGS

"See'st thou o'er my shoulders falling,
   Snake-like ringlets waving free?
Have no fear, for they are twisted
   To allure thee unto me."

Thus she spake, the gentle dove,
   Listen to thy plighted love:—
"Ah, how long I wait, until
   Sweetheart cometh back (she said)
Laying his caressing hand
   Underneath my burning head."

KNUT HAMSUN

KNUT HAMSUN (Norwegian, 1859-1952). One of great literary figures of
modern Norway. Novelist, playwright and poet. Nobel Prize, 1920. Famous
novel: *Growth of the Soil*. Nature mystic and biting critic of materialist
civilization—yet succumbed to one of its lowest forms, Nazism.

THE CALL OF LIFE

DOWN near the inner harbor in Copenhagen there is a street called
Vestervold, a relatively new, yet desolate, boulevard. There are few
houses to be seen on it, few gas lamps, and almost no people whatever. Even now, in summer, it is rare that one sees people promenading there.

Well, last evening I had something of a surprise in that street.

I had taken a few turns up and down the sidewalk when a lady came towards me from the opposite direction. There were no other people in sight. The gas lamps were lighted, but it was nevertheless dark—so dark that I could not distinguish the lady's face. One of the usual creatures of the night, I thought to myself, and passed her by.

At the end of the boulevard I turned about and walked back. The lady had also turned about, and I met her again. She is waiting for some one, I thought, and I was curious to see whom she could be waiting for. And again I passed her by.

When I met her the third time I tipped my hat and spoke to her. "Good evening! Are you waiting for some one?"

She was startled. No—that is, yes—she was waiting for some one.

Did she object to my keeping her company till the person she was expecting arrived?

No—she did not object in the least, and she thanked me. For that matter, she explained, she was not expecting any one. She was merely taking the air—it was so still here.

We strolled about side by side. We began talking about various things of no great consequence. I offered my arm.

"Thank you, no," she said, and shook her head.

There was no great fun promenading in this way; I could not see her in the dark. I struck a match to see what time it was. I held the match up and looked at her too.

"Nine-thirty," I said.

She shivered as if she were freezing. I seized the opportunity.

"You are freezing?" I asked. "Shan't we drop in some place and get something to drink? At Tivoli? At the National?"

"But, don't you see, I can't go anywhere now," she answered.

And I noticed then for the first time that she wore a very long black veil.

I begged her pardon, and blamed the darkness for my mistake. And the way in which she took my apology at once convinced me that she was not one of the usual night wanderers.

"Won't you take my arm?" I suggested again. "It may warm you a bit."

She took my arm.

We paced up and down a few turns. She asked me to look at the time again.

"It is ten," I said. "Where do you live?"

"On Gamle Kongevei."

I stopped her.

"And may I see you to your door?" I asked.

"Not very well," she answered. "No, I can't let you . . . You live on Bredgade, don't you?"

"How do you know that?" I asked surprised.

"Oh, I know who you are," she answered.

A pause. We walked arm in arm down the lighted streets. She walked rapidly, her long veil streaming behind.

"We had better hurry," she said.

At her door in Gamle Kongevei she turned toward me as if to thank me for my kindness in escorting her. I opened the door for her, and she entered slowly. I thrust my shoulder gently against the door and followed her in. Once inside she seized my hand. Neither of us said anything.

We mounted two flights of stairs and stopped on the third floor. She herself unlocked the door to her apartment, then opened a second door, and took me by the hand and led me in. It was presumably a drawing-room; I could hear a clock ticking on the wall. Once inside the door the lady paused a moment, threw her arms about me suddenly, and kissed me tremblingly, passionately, on the mouth. Right on the mouth.

"Won't you be seated," she suggested. "Here is a sofa. Meanwhile I'll get a light."

And she lit a lamp.

I looked about me, amazed, yet curious. I found myself in a spacious and extremely well furnished drawing-room with other, half open, doors leading into several rooms on the side. I could not for the life of me make out what sort of person it was I had come across.

"What a beautiful room!" I exclaimed. "Do you live here?"

"Yes, this is my home," she answered.

"Is this your home? You live with your parents then?"

"Oh, no," she laughed. "I am an old woman, as you'll see!"

And she removed her veil and her wraps.

"There—see! What did I tell you!" she said, and threw her arms about me once again, abruptly, driven by some uncontrollable urge.

She might have been twenty-two or three, wore a ring on her right hand, and might for that matter really have been a married woman. Beautiful? No, she was freckled, and had scarcely any

522

eyebrows. But there was an effervescent life about her, and her mouth was strangely beautiful.

I wanted to ask her who she was, where her husband was, if she had any, and whose house this was I was in, but she threw herself about me every time I opened my mouth and forbade me to be inquisitive.

"My name is Ellen," she explained. "Would you care for something to drink? It really won't disturb any one if I ring. Perhaps you'd step in here, in the bed-room, meanwhile."

I went into the bed-room. The light from the drawing room illumined it partially. I saw two beds. Ellen rang and ordered wine, and I heard a maid bring in the wine and go out again. A little later Ellen came into the bed-room after me, but she stopped short in the door. I took a step towards her. She uttered a little cry and at the same time came towards me.

This was last evening.

What further happened? Ah, patience! There is much more!

It was beginning to grow light this morning when I awoke. The daylight crept into the room on either side of the curtain. Ellen was also awake and smiled toward me. Her arms were white and velvety, her breast unusually high. I whispered something to her, and she closed my mouth with hers, mute with tenderness. The day grew lighter and lighter.

Two hours later I was on my feet. Ellen was also up, busy dressing herself—she had got her shoes on. Then it was I experienced something which even now strikes me as a gruesome dream. I was at the wash stand. Ellen had some errand or other in the adjoining room, and as she opened the door I turned around and glanced in. A cold draft from the open windows in the room rushed in upon me, and in the center of the room I could just make out a corpse stretched out on a table. A corpse, in a coffin, dressed in white, with a gray beard, the corpse of a man. His bony knees protruded like madly clenched fists underneath the sheet, and his face was sallow and ghastly in the extreme. I could see everything in full daylight. I turned away and said not a word.

When Ellen returned I was dressed and ready to go out. I could scarcely bring myself to respond to her embraces. She put on some additional clothes; she wanted to accompany me down as far as the street door, and I let her come, still saying nothing. At the door she pressed close to the wall so as not to be seen.

523

"Well, good-bye," she whispered.

"Till to-morrow?" I asked, in part to test her.

"No, not to-morrow."

"Why not to-morrow?"

"Not so many questions, dear. I am going to a funeral to-morrow, a relation of mine is dead. Now there—you know it."

"But the day after to-morrow?"

"Yes, the day after to-morrow, at the door here, I'll meet you. Good-bye!"

I went.

Who was she? And the corpse? With its fists clenched and the corners of its mouth drooping—how ghastly comic! The day after to-morrow she would be expecting me. Ought I to see her again?

I went straight down to the Bernina Café and asked for a directory. I looked up number so and so Gamle Kongevei, and—there—there was the name. I waited some little time till the morning papers were out. Then I turned quickly to the announcements of deaths. And—sure enough—there I found hers too, the very first in the list, in bold type: "My husband, fifty-three years old, died to-day after a long illness." The announcement was dated the day before yesterday.

I sat for a long time and pondered.

A man marries. His wife is thirty years younger than he. He contracts a lingering illness. One fair day he dies.

And the young widow breathes a sigh of relief.

THOMAS HARDY

THOMAS HARDY (English, 1840-1928). Novelist and poet. Realistic observer of village and palace, at his best when writing of native Wessex. Began career as architect. His major novels are tragedies: *The Mayor of Casterbridge, The Return of the Native, Tess of the D'Urbervilles, Jude the Obscure.* Pessimistic epic drama, *The Dynasts,* considered by some his masterpiece.

SQUIRE PETRICK'S LADY

FOLK who are at all acquainted with the traditions of Stapleford Park will not need to be told that in the middle of the last century it was owned by that trump of mortgagees, Timothy Petrick, whose

skill in gaining possession of fair estates by granting sums of money on their title-deeds has seldom if ever been equaled in our part of England. Timothy was a lawyer by profession, and agent to several noblemen, by which means his special line of business became opened to him by a sort of revelation. It is said that a relative of his, a very deep thinker, who afterwards had the misfortune to be transported for life for mistaken notions on the signing of a will, taught him considerable legal lore, which he creditably resolved never to throw away for the benefit of other people, but to reserve it entirely for his own.

However, I have nothing in particular to say about his early and active days, but rather of the time when, an old man, he had become the owner of vast estates by the means I have signified—among them the great manor of Stapleford, on which he lived, in the splendid old mansion now pulled down; likewise estates at Marlott, estates near Sherton Abbas, nearly all the borough of Millpool, and many properties near Ivell. Indeed, I can't call to mind half his landed possessions, and I don't know that it matters much at this time of day, seeing that he's been dead and gone many years. It is said that when he bought an estate he would not decide to pay the price till he had walked over every single acre with his own two feet, and prodded the soil at every point with his own spud, to test its quality, which, if we regard the extent of his properties, must have been a stiff business for him.

At the time I am speaking of he was a man over eighty, and his son was dead; but he had two grandsons, the eldest of whom, his namesake, was married, and was shortly expecting issue. Just then the grandfather was taken ill, for death, as it seemed, considering his age. By his will the old man had created an entail (as I believe the lawyers call it), devising the whole of the estates to his elder grandson and his issue male, failing which to his younger grandson and his issue male, failing which, to remoter relatives, who need not be mentioned now.

While old Timothy Petrick was lying ill, his elder grandson's wife, Annetta, gave birth to her expected child, who, as fortune would have it, was a son. Timothy, her husband, though sprung of a scheming family, was no great schemer himself; he was the single one of the Petricks then living whose heart had never been greatly moved by sentiments which did not run in the groove of ambitions; and on this account he had not married well, as the saying is, his wife having been the daughter of a family of no better beginnings

525

than his own; that is to say, her father was a country townsman of the professional class. But she was a very pretty woman, by all accounts, and her husband had seen, courted, and married her in a high tide of infatuation, after a very short acquaintance, and with very little knowledge of her heart's history. He had never found reason to regret his choice as yet, and his anxiety for her recovery was great.

She was supposed to be out of danger, and herself and the child progressing well, when there was a change for the worse, and she sank so rapidly that she was soon given over. When she felt she was about to leave him, Annetta sent for her husband, and, on his speedy entry and assurance that they were alone, she made him solemnly vow to give the child every care in any circumstances that might arise, if it should please Heaven to take her. This, of course, he readily promised. Then after some hesitation she told him that she could not die with a falsehood upon her soul, and dire deceit in her life; she must make a terrible confession to him before her lips were sealed forever. She thereupon related an incident concerning the the baby's parentage which was not as he supposed.

Timothy Petrick, though a quick-feeling man, was not of a sort to show nerves outwardly; and he bore himself as heroically as he possibly could do in this trying moment of his life. That same night his wife died; and while she lay dead, and before her funeral, he hastened to the bedside of his sick grandfather, and revealed to him all that had happened—the baby's birth, his wife's confession, and her death, beseeching the aged man, as he loved him, to bestir himself now, at the eleventh hour, and alter his will so as to dish the intruder. Old Timothy, seeing matters in the same light as his grandson, required no urging against allowing anything to stand in the way of legitimate inheritance; he executed another will, limiting the entail to Timothy, his grandson, for life, and his male heirs thereafter to be born, after them to his other grandson, Edward, and Edward's heirs. Thus the newly born infant, who had been the center of so many hopes, was cut off and scorned as none of the elect.

The old mortgagee lived but a short time after this, the excitement of the discovery having told upon him considerably, and he was gathered to his fathers like the most charitable man in his neighborhood. Both his wife and grandparent being buried, Timothy settled down to his usual life as well as he was able, mentally satis-

526

fied that he had, by prompt action, defeated the consequences of such dire domestic treachery as had been shown towards him, and resolving to marry a second time as soon as he could satisfy himself in the choice of a wife.

But men do not always know themselves. The imbittered state of Timothy Petrick's mind bred in him by degrees such a hatred and mistrust of womankind that, though several specimens of high attractiveness came under his eyes, he could not bring himself to the point of proposing marriage. He dreaded to take up the position of husband a second time, discerning a trap in every petticoat, and a Slough of Despond in possible heirs. "What has happened once, when all seemed so fair, may happen again," he said to himself. "I'll risk my name no more." So he abstained from marriage, and overcame his wish for a lineal descendant to follow him in the ownership of Stapleford.

Timothy had scarcely noticed the unfortunate child that his wife had borne, after arranging for a meager fulfillment of his promise to her to take care of the boy, by having him brought up in his house. Occasionally, remembering his promise, he went and glanced at the child, saw that he was doing well, gave a few special directions, and again went his solitary way. Thus he and the child lived on in the Stapleford mansion-house till two or three years had passed by. One day he was walking in the garden, and by some accident left his snuff-box on a bench. When he came back to find it he saw the little boy standing there; he had escaped his nurse, and was making a plaything of the box, in spite of the convulsive sneezings which the game brought in its train. Then the man with the incrusted heart became interested in the little fellow's persistence in his play under such discomforts; he looked in the child's face, saw there his wife's countenance, though he did not see his own, and fell into thought on the piteousness of childhood—particularly of despised and rejected childhood, like this before him.

From that hour, try as he would to counteract the feeling, the human necessity to love something or other got the better of what he had called his wisdom, and shaped itself in a tender anxiety for the youngster Rupert. This name had been given him by his dying mother when, at her request, the child was baptized in her chamber, lest he should not survive for public baptism; and her husband had never thought of it as a name of any significance till, about this time, he learned by accident that it was the name of the young Marquis

527

of Christminster, son of the Duke of Southwesterland, for whom Annetta had cherished warm feelings before her marriage. Recollecting some wandering phrases in his wife's last words, which he had not understood at the time, he perceived at last that this was the person to whom she had alluded when affording him a clew to little Rupert's history.

He would sit in silence for hours with the child, being no great speaker at the best of times; but the boy, on his part, was too ready with his tongue for any break in discourse to arise because Timothy Petrick had nothing to say. After idling away his mornings in this manner, Petrick would go to his own room and swear in long, loud whispers, and walk up and down, calling himself the most ridiculous dolt that ever lived, and declaring that he would never go near the little fellow again; to which resolve he would adhere for the space, perhaps, of a day. Such cases are happily not new to human nature, but there never was a case in which a man more completely befooled his former self than in this.

As the child grew up, Timothy's attachment to him grew deeper, till Rupert became almost the sole object for which he lived. There had been enough of the family ambition latent in him for Timothy Petrick to feel a little envy when, some time before this date, his brother Edward had been accepted by the Honorable Harriet Mountclere, daughter of the second viscount of that name and title; but having discovered, as I have before stated, the paternity of his boy Rupert to lurk in even a higher stratum of society, those envious feelings speedily dispersed. Indeed, the more he reflected thereon, after his brother's aristocratic marriage, the more content did he become. His late wife took softer outline in his memory, as he thought of the lofty taste she had displayed, though only a plain burgher's daughter, and the justification for this weakness in loving the child—the justification that he had longed for—was afforded now in the knowledge that the boy was by nature, if not by name, a representative of one of the noblest houses in England.

"She was a woman of grand instincts, after all," he said to himself, proudly. "To fix her choice upon the immediate successor in that ducal line—it was finely conceived! Had he been of low blood like myself or my relations she would scarce have deserved the harsh measure that I have dealt out to her and her offspring. How much less, then, when such groveling tastes were farthest from her soul! The man Annetta loved was noble, and my boy is noble in spite of me."

The after-clap was inevitable, and it soon came. "So far," he reasoned, "from cutting off his child from inheritance of my estates, as I have done, I should have rejoiced in the possession of him! He is of pure stock on one side at least, while in the ordinary run of affairs he would have been a commoner to the bone."

Being a man, whatever his faults, of good old beliefs in the divinity of kings and those about 'em, the more he overhauled the case in this light the more strongly did his poor wife's conduct in improving the blood and breed of the Petrick family win his heart. He considered what ugly, idle, hard-drinking scamps many of his own relations had been; the miserable scriveners, usurers, and pawnbrokers that he had numbered among his forefathers, and the probability that some of their bad qualities would have come out in a merely corporeal child, to give him sorrow in his old age, turn his black hairs gray, his gray hairs white, cut down every stick of timber, and Heaven knows what all, had he not, like a skillful gardener, minded his grafting and changed the sort; till at length this right-minded man fell down on his knees every night and morning and thanked God that he was not as other meanly descended fathers in such matters.

It was in the peculiar disposition of the Petrick family that the satisfaction which ultimately settled in Timothy's breast found nourishment. The Petricks had adored the nobility, and plucked them at the same time. That excellent man Izaak Walton's feelings about fish were much akin to those of old Timothy Petrick, and of his descendants in a lesser degree, concerning the landed aristocracy. To torture and to love simultaneously is a proceeding strange to reason, but possible to practise, as these instances show.

Hence, when Timothy's brother Edward said slightingly one day that Timothy's son was well enough, but that he had nothing but shops and offices in his backward perspective, while his own children, should he have any, would be far different, in possessing such a mother as the Honorable Harriet, Timothy felt a bound of triumph within him at the power he possessed of contradicting that statement if he chose.

So much was he interested in his boy in this new aspect that he now began to read up chronicles of the illustrious house ennobled as the Dukes of Southwesterland, from their very beginning in the glories of the Restoration of the blessed Charles till the year of his own time. He mentally noted their gifts from royalty, grants of lands, purchases, intermarriages, plantings, and buildings; more particular-

ly their political and military achievements, which had been great, and their performances in arts and letters, which had been by no means contemptible. He studied prints of the portraits of that family, and then, like a chemist watching a crystallization, began to examine young Rupert's face for the unfolding of those historic curves and shades that the painters Vandyke and Lely had perpetuated on canvas.

When the boy reached the most fascinating age of childhood, and his shouts of laughter rang through Stapleford House from end to end, the remorse that oppressed Timothy Petrick knew no bounds. Of all people in the world this Rupert was the one on whom he could have wished the estates to devolve; yet Rupert, by Timothy's own desperate strategy at the time of his birth, had been ousted from all inheritance of them; and, since he did not mean to remarry, the manors would pass to his brother and his brother's children, who would be nothing to him, whose boasted pedigree on one side would be nothing to his Rupert's.

Had he only left the first will of his grandfather alone!

His mind ran on the wills continually, both of which were in existence, and the first, the canceled one, in his own possession. Night after night, when the servants were all abed, and the click of safety-locks sounded as loud as a crash, he looked at that first will, and wished it had been the second and not the first.

The crisis came at last. One night, after having enjoyed the boy's company for hours, he could no longer bear that his beloved Rupert should be dispossessed, and he committed the felonious deed of altering the date of the earlier will to a fortnight later, which made its execution appear subsequent to the date of the second will already proved. He then boldly propounded the first will as the second.

His brother Edward submitted to what appeared to be not only incontestible fact, but a far more likely disposition of old Timothy's property; for, like many others, he had been much surprised at the limitations defined in the other will, having no clew to their cause. He joined his brother Timothy in setting aside the hitherto accepted document, and matters went on in their usual course, there being no dispositions in the substituted will differing from those in the other, except such as related to a future which had not yet arrived.

The years moved on. Rupert had not yet revealed the anxiously expected historic lineaments which should foreshadow the political

530

abilities of the ducal family aforesaid, when it happened on a certain day that Timothy Petrick made the acquaintance of a well-known physician of Budmouth, who had been the medical adviser and friend of the late Mrs. Petrick's family for many years, though after Annetta's marriage, and consequent removal to Stapleford, he had seen no more of her, the neighboring practitioner who attended the Petricks having then become her doctor as a matter of course. Timothy was impressed by the insight and knowledge disclosed in the conversation of the Budmouth physician, and the acquaintance ripening to intimacy, the physician alluded to a form of hallucination to which Annetta's mother and grandmother had been subject —that of believing in certain dreams as realities. He delicately inquired if Timothy had ever noticed anything of the sort in his wife during her lifetime; he, the physician, had fancied that he discerned germs of the same peculiarity in Annetta when he attended her in her girlhood. One explanation begat another, till the dumbfounded Timothy Petrick was persuaded in his own mind that Annetta's confession to him had been based on a delusion.

"You look down in the mouth!" said the doctor, pausing.

"A bit unmanned. 'Tis unexpected-like," sighed Timothy.

But he could hardly believe it possible; and, thinking it best to be frank with the doctor, told him the whole story which, till now, he had never related to living man, save his dying grandfather. To his surprise, the physician informed him that such a form of delusion was precisely what he would have expected from Annetta's antecedents at such a physical crisis in her life.

Petrick prosecuted his inquiries elsewhere; and the upshot of his labors was, briefly, that a comparison of dates and places showed irrefutably that his poor wife's assertion could not have foundation in fact. The young Marquis of her tender passion—a highly moral and bright-minded nobleman—had gone abroad the year before Annetta's marriage, and had not returned until after her death. The young girl's love for him had been a delicate ideal dream—no more.

Timothy went home, and the boy ran out to meet him; whereupon a strangely dismal feeling of discontent took possession of his soul. After all, then, there was nothing but plebeian blood in the veins of the heir to his name and estates; he was not to be succeeded by a noble-natured line. To be sure, Rupert was his son; but that glory and halo he believed him to have inherited from the ages, outshining that of his brother's children, had departed from Rupert's brow for-

ever; he could no longer read history in the boy's face and centuries of domination in his eyes.

His manner towards his son grew colder and colder from that day forward; and it was with bitterness of heart that he discerned the characteristic features of the Petricks unfolding themselves by degrees. Instead of the elegant knife-edged nose, so typical of the Dukes of Southwesterland, there began to appear on his face the broad nostril and hollow bridge of his grandfather Timothy. No illustrious line of politicians was promised a continuator in that graying blue eye, for it was acquiring the expression of the orb of a particularly objectionable cousin of his own; and, instead of the mouth-curves which had thrilled Parliamentary audiences in speeches now bound in calf in every well-ordered library, there was the bull-lip of that very uncle of his who had had the misfortune with the signature of a gentleman's will, and had been transported for life in consequence.

To think how he himself, too, had sinned in this same matter of a will for this mere fleshly reproduction of a wretched old uncle whose very name he wished to forget! The boy's Christian name, even, was an imposture and an irony, for it implied hereditary force and brilliancy to which he plainly would never attain. The consolation of real sonship was always left him certainly; but he could not help groaning to himself, "Why cannot a son be one's own and somebody else's likewise?"

The Marquis was shortly afterwards in the neighborhood of Stapleford, and Timothy Petrick met him, and eyed his noble countenance admiringly. The next day, when Petrick was in his study, somebody knocked at the door.

"Who's there?"

"Rupert."

"I'll Rupert thee, you young imposter! Say, only a poor commonplace Petrick!" his father grunted. "Why didn't you have a voice like the Marquis I saw yesterday!" he continued, as the lad came in. "Why haven't you his looks, and a way of commanding as if you'd done it for centuries—hey?"

"Why? How can you expect it, father, when I'm not related to him?"

"Ugh! Then you ought to be!" growled his father.

BRET HARTE

BRET HARTE (American, 1836-1902). The sentimental popularizer of the Western tale in America. Born in Albany, New York, went to California in 1854, and worked as teacher, miner, printer, editor. Best-known stories: "The Outcasts of Poker Flat" and "The Luck of Roaring Camp."

THE OUTCASTS OF POKER FLAT

As Mr. John Oakhurst, gambler, stepped into the main street of Poker Flat on the morning of the 23d of November, 1850, he was conscious of a change in its moral atmosphere since the preceding night. Two or three men, conversing earnestly together, ceased as he approached, and exchanged significant glances. There was a Sabbath lull in the air, which, in a settlement unused to Sabbath influences, looked ominous.

Mr. Oakhurst's calm, handsome face betrayed small concern in these indications. Whether he was conscious of any predisposing cause was another question. "I reckon they're after somebody," he reflected: "likely it's me." He returned to his pocket the handkerchief with which he had been wiping away the red dust of Poker Flat from his neat boots, and quietly discharged his mind of any further conjecture.

In point of fact, Poker Flat was "after somebody." It had lately suffered the loss of several thousand dollars, two valuable horses, and a prominent citizen. It was experiencing a spasm of virtuous reaction, quite as lawless and ungovernable as any of the acts that had provoked it. A secret committee had determined to rid the town of all improper persons. This was done permanently in regard to two men who were then hanging from the boughs of a sycamore in the gulch, and temporarily in the banishment of certain ladies. It is but due to the sex, however, to state that their impropriety was professional, and it was only in such easily established standards of evil that Poker Flat ventured to sit in judgment.

Mr. Oakhurst was right in supposing that he was included in this category. A few of the committee had urged hanging him as a possible example and a sure method of reimbursing themselves from his pockets of the sums he had won from them. "It's agin justice," said Jim Wheeler, "to let this yer young man from Roaring Camp— an entire stranger—carry away our money." But a crude sentiment of equity residing in the breasts of those who had been fortunate

533

enough to win from Mr. Oakhurst overruled this narrower local prejudice.

Mr. Oakhurst received his sentence with philosophic calmness, none the less coolly that he was aware of the hesitation of his judges. He was too much of a gambler not to accept his fate. With him life was at best an uncertain game, and he recognized the usual percentage in favor of the dealer.

A body of armed men accompanied the deported wickedness of Poker Flat to the outskirts of the settlement. Besides Mr. Oakhurst, who was known to be a coolly desperate man, and for whose intimidation the armed escort was intended, the expatriated party consisted of a young woman familiarly known as "The Duchess"; another who had won the title of "Mother Shipton"; and "Uncle Billy," a suspected sluice-robber and confirmed drunkard. The cavalcade provoked no comments from the spectators, nor was any word uttered by the escort. Only when the gulch which marked the uttermost limit of Poker Flat was reached, the leader spoke briefly and to the point. The exiles were forbidden to return at the peril of their lives.

As the escort disappeared, their pent-up feelings found vent in a few hysterical tears from the Duchess, some bad language from Mother Shipton, and a Parthian volley of expletives from Uncle Billy. The philosophic Oakhurst alone remained silent. He listened calmly to Mother Shipton's desire to cut somebody's heart out, to the repeated statements of the Duchess that she would die in the road, and to the alarming oaths that seemed to be bumped out of Uncle Billy as he rode forward. With the easy good humor characteristic of his class, he insisted upon exchanging his own riding-horse, "Five-spot," for the sorry mule which the Duchess rode. But even this act did not draw the party into any closer sympathy. The young woman readjusted her somewhat draggled plumes with a feeble, faded coquetry; Mother Shipton eyed the possessor of "Five-spot" with malevolence, and Uncle Billy included the whole party in one sweeping anathema.

The road to Sandy Bar—a camp that, not having as yet experienced the regenerating influences of Poker Flat, consequently seemed to offer some invitation to the emigrants—lay over a steep mountain range. It was distant a day's severe travel. In that advanced season the party soon passed out of the moist, temperate regions of the foothills into the dry, cold bracing air of the Sierras. The trail was narrow and difficult. At noon the Duchess, rolling out of her saddle

534

upon the ground, declared her intention of going no farther, and the party halted.

The spot was singularly wild and impressive. A wooded amphitheater surrounded on three sides by precipitous cliffs of naked granite, sloped gently toward the crest of another precipice that overlooked the valley. It was, undoubtedly, the most suitable spot for a camp, had camping been advisable. But Mr. Oakhurst knew that scarcely half the journey to Sandy Bar was accomplished, and the party was not equipped or provisioned for delay. This fact he pointed out to his companions curtly, with a philosophic commentary on the folly of "throwing up their hand before the game was played out." But they were furnished with liquor, which in this emergency stood them in place of food, fuel, rest and prescience. In spite of his remonstrances, it was not long before they were more or less under its influence. Uncle Billy passed rapidly from a bellicose state into one of stupor, the Duchess became maudlin, and Mother Shipton snored. Mr. Oakhurst alone remained erect, leaning against a rock, calmly surveying them.

Mr. Oakhurst did not drink. It interfered with a profession which required coolness, impassiveness, and presence of mind, and, in his own language, he "couldn't afford it." As he gazed at his recumbent fellow exiles, the loneliness begotten of his pariah trade, his habits of life, his very vices, for the first time seriously oppressed him. He bestirred himself in dusting his black clothes, washing his hands and face, and other acts characteristic of his studiously neat habits, and for a moment forgot his annoyance. The thought of deserting his weaker and more pitiable companions never perhaps occurred to him. Yet he could not help feeling the want of that excitement which, singularly enough, was most conducive to that calm equanimity for which he was notorious. He looked at the gloomy walls that rose a thousand feet sheer above the circling pines around him, at the sky ominously clouded, at the valley below, already deepening into shadow; and, doing so, suddenly he heard his own name called.

A horseman slowly ascended the trail. In the fresh, open face of the newcomer Mr. Oakhurst recognized Tom Simson, otherwise known as "The Innocent," of Sandy Bar. He had met him some months before over a "little game," and had, with perfect equanimity, won the entire fortune—amounting to some forty dollars—of that guileless youth. After the game was finished, Mr. Oakhurst drew the youthful speculator behind the door and thus addressed him:

"Tommy, you're a good little man, but you can't gamble worth a cent. Don't try it ever again." He then handed him his money back, pushed him gently from the room, and so made a devoted slave of Tom Simson.

There was a remembrance of this in his boyish and enthusiastic greeting of Mr. Oakhurst. He had started, he said, to go to Poker Flat to seek his fortune. "Alone?" No, not exactly alone; in fact (a giggle), he had run away with Piney Woods. Didn't Mr Oakhurst remember Piney? She that used to wait on the table at the Temperance House? They had been engaged a long time, but old Jake Woods had objected, and so they had run away, and were going to Poker Flat to be married, and here they were. And they were tired out, and how lucky it was they had found a place to camp, and company. All this the Innocent delivered rapidly, while Piney, a stout, comely damsel of fifteen, emerged from behind the pine tree, where she had been blushing unseen, and rode to the side of her lover.

Mr. Oakhurst seldom troubled himself with sentiment, still less with propriety; but he had a vague idea that the situation was not fortunate. He retained, however, his presence of mind sufficiently to kick Uncle Billy, who was about to say something, and Uncle Billy, was sober enough to recognize in Mr. Oakhurst's kick a superior power that would not bear trifling. He then endeavored to dissuade Tom Simson from delaying further, but in vain. He even pointed out the fact that there was no provision, nor means of making a camp. But, unluckily, the Innocent met this objection by assuring the party that he was provided with an extra mule loaded with provisions, and by the discovery of a rude attempt at a log house near the trail. "Piney can stay with Mrs. Oakhurst," said the Innocent, pointing to the Duchess, "and I can shift for myself."

Nothing but Mr. Oakhurst's admonishing foot saved Uncle Billy from bursting into a roar of laughter. As it was, he felt compelled to retire up the cañon until he could recover his gravity. There he confided the joke to the tall pine trees, with many slaps of his leg, contortions of his face, and the usual profanity. But when he returned to the party, he found them seated by a fire—for the air had grown strangely chill and the sky overcast—in apparently amicable conversation. Piney was actually talking in an impulsive girlish fashion to the Duchess, who was listening with an interest and animation she had not shown for many days. The Innocent was holding forth, apparently with equal effect, to Mr. Oakhurst and Mother

536

Shipton, who was actually relaxing into inward amiability. "Is this yer a d—d picnic?" said Uncle Billy, with inward scorn, as he surveyed the sylvan group, the glancing firelight, and the tethered animals in the foreground. Suddenly an idea mingled with the alcoholic fumes that disturbed his brain. It was apparently of a jocular nature, for he felt impelled to slap his leg again and cram his fist into his mouth.

As the shadows crept slowly up the mountain, a slight breeze rocked the tops of the pine trees and moaned through their long and gloomy aisles. The ruined cabin, patched and covered with pine boughs, was set apart for the ladies. As the lovers parted, they unaffectedly exchanged a kiss, so honest and sincere that it might have been heard above the swaying pines. The frail Duchess and the malevolent Mother Shipton were probably too stunned to remark upon this last evidence of simplicity, and so turned without a word to the hut. The fire was replenished, the men lay down before the door, and in a few minutes were asleep.

Mr. Oakhurst was a light sleeper. Toward morning he awoke benumbed and cold. As he stirred the dying fire, the wind, which was now blowing strongly, brought to his cheek that which caused the blood to leave it—snow!

He started to his feet with the intention of awakening the sleepers, for there was no time to lose. But turning to where Uncle Billy had been lying, he found him gone. A suspicion leaped to his brain, and a curse to his lips. He ran to the spot where the mules had been tethered—they were no longer there. The tracks were already rapidly disappearing in the snow.

The momentary excitement brought Mr. Oakhurst back to the fire with his usual calm. He did not waken the sleepers. The Innocent slumbered peacefully, with a smile on his good-humored, freckled face; the virgin Piney slept beside her frailer sisters as sweetly as though attended by celestial guardians; and Mr. Oakhurst, drawing his blanket over his shoulders, stroked his mustaches and waited for the dawn. It came slowly in a whirling mist of snowflakes that dazzled and confused the eye. What could be seen of the landscape appeared magically changed. He looked over the valley, and summed up the present and future in two words, "Snowed in!"

A careful inventory of the provisions, which, fortunately for the party, had been stored within the hut, and so escaped the felonious fingers of Uncle Billy, disclosed the fact that with care and prudence they might last ten days longer. "That is," said Mr. Oakhurst *sotto*

voce to the Innocent, "if you're willing to board us. If you ain't—and perhaps you'd better not—you can wait till Uncle Billy gets back with provisions." For some occult reason, Mr. Oakhurst could not bring himself to disclose Uncle Billy's rascality, and so offered the hypothesis that he had wandered from the camp and had accidentally stampeded the animals. He dropped a warning to the Duchess and Mother Shipton, who, of course, knew the facts of their associate's defection. "They'll find out the truth about us *all* when they find out anything," he added significantly, "and there's no good frightening them now."

Tom Simson not only put all his worldly store at the disposal of Mr. Oakhurst, but seemed to enjoy the prospect of their enforced seclusion. "We'll have a good camp for a week, and then the snow'll melt, and we'll all go back together." The cheerful gayety of the young man and Mr. Oakhurst's calm infected the others. The Innocent, with the aid of pine boughs, extemporized a thatch for the roof less cabin, and the Duchess directed Piney in the rearrangement of the interior with a taste and a tact that opened the blue eyes of that provincial maiden to their fullest extent. "I reckon now you're used to fine things at Poker Flat," said Piney. The Duchess turned away sharply to conceal something that reddened her cheeks through their professional tint, and Mother Shipton requested Piney not to "chatter." But when Mr. Oakhurst returned from a weary search for the trail, he heard the sound of happy laughter echoed from the rocks. He stopped in some alarm, and his thoughts first naturally reverted to the whiskey, which he had prudently cached. "And yet it don't somehow sound like whiskey," said the gambler. It was not until he caught sight of the blazing fire through the still blinding storm, and the group around it, that he settled to the conviction that it was "square fun."

Whether Mr. Oakhurst had cached his cards with the whiskey as something debarred the free access of the community, I cannot say. It was certain that, in Mother Shipton's words, he "didn't say 'cards' once" during that evening. Haply the time was beguiled by an accordian, produced somewhat ostentatiously by Tom Simson from his pack. Notwithstanding some difficulties attending the manipulation of this instrument, Piney Woods managed to pluck several reluctant melodies from its keys, to an accompaniment by the Innocent on a pair of bone castanets. But the crowning festivity of the evening was reached in a rude camp-meeting hymn, which the lovers, joining hands, sang with great earnestness and vociferation. I fear

that a certain defiant tone and Covenanter's swing to its chorus, rather than any devotional quality, caused it speedily to infect the others, who at last joined in the refrain:—

> "I'm proud to live in the service of the Lord,
> And I'm bound to die in his army."

The pines rocked, the storm eddied and whirled above the miserable group, and the flames of their altar leaped heavenward, as if in token of the vow.

At midnight the storm abated, the rolling clouds parted, and the stars glittered keenly above the sleeping camp. Mr. Oakhurst, whose professional habits had enabled him to live on the smallest possible amount of sleep, in dividing the watch with Tom Simson somehow managed to take upon himself the greater part of that duty. He excused himself to the Innocent by saying that he had "often been a week without sleep." "Doing what?" asked Tom. "Poker!" replied Oakhurst sententiously. "When a man gets a streak of luck—nigger-luck—he don't get tired. The luck gives in first. Luck," continued the gambler reflectively, "is a mighty queer thing. All you know about it for certain is that it's bound to change. And it's finding out when it's going to change that makes you. We've had a streak of bad luck since we left Poker Flat—you come along, and, slap, you get into it, too. If you can hold your cards right along you're all right. For," added the gambler, with cheerful irrelevance—

> "'I'm proud to live in the service of the Lord,
> And I'm bound to die in his army.'"

The third day came, and the sun, looking through the white-curtained valley, saw the outcasts divide their slowly decreasing store of provisions for the morning meal. It was one of the peculiarities of that mountain climate that its rays diffused a kindly warmth over the wintry landscape, as if in regretful commiseration of the past. But it revealed drift on drift of snow piled high around the hut—a hopeless, uncharted, trackless sea of white lying below the rocky shores to which the castaways still clung. Through the marvelously clear air the smoke of the pastoral village of Poker Flat rose miles away. Mother Shipton saw it, and from a remote pinnacle of her rocky fastness hurled in that direction a final malediction. It was her last vituperative attempt, and perhaps for that reason was invested with a certain degree of sublimity. It did her good, she privately informed the Duchess. "Just you go out there and cuss, and

539

see." She then set herself to the task of amusing "the child," as she and the Duchess were pleased to call Piney. Piney was no chicken, but it was a soothing and original theory of the pair thus to account for the fact that she didn't swear and wasn't improper.

When night crept up again through the gorges, the reedy notes of the accordian rose and fell in fitful spasms and long-drawn gasps by the flickering camp-fire. But music failed to fill entirely the aching void left by insufficient food, and a new diversion was proposed by Piney,—story-telling. Neither Mr. Oakhurst nor his female companions caring to relate their personal experiences, this plan would have failed too, but for the Innocent. Some months before he had chanced upon a stray copy of Mr. Pope's ingenious translation of the Iliad. He now proposed to narrate the principle incidents of that poem— having thoroughly mastered the argument and fairly forgotten the words—in the current vernacular of Sandy Bar. And so for the rest of that night the Homeric demigods again walked the earth. Trojan bully and wily Greek wrestled in the winds, and the great pines in the cañon seemed to bow to the wrath of the son of Peleus. Mr. Oakhurst listened with quiet satisfaction. Most especially was he interested in the fate of "Ash-heels," as the Innocent persisted in denominating the "swift-footed Achilles."

So, with small food and much of Homer and the accordian, a week passed over the heads of the outcasts. The sun again forsook them, and again from leaden skies the snowflakes were sifted over the land. Day by day closer around them drew the snowy circle, until at last they looked from their prison over drifted walls of dazzling white, that towered twenty feet above their heads. It became more and more difficult to replenish their fires, even from the fallen trees beside them, now half hidden in the drifts. And yet no one complained. The lovers turned from the dreary prospect and looked into each other's eyes, and were happy. Mr. Oakhurst settled himself coolly to the losing game before him. The Duchess, more cheerful than she had been, assumed the care of Piney. Only Mother Shipton—once the strongest of the party—seemed to sicken and fade. At midnight on the tenth day she called Oakhurst to her side. "I'm going," she said, in a voice of querulous weakness, "but don't say anything about it. Don't waken the kids. Take the bundle from under my head, and open it." Mr. Oakhurst did so. It contained Mother Shipton's rations for the last week, untouched. "Give 'em to the child," she said, pointing to the sleeping Piney. "You've starved yourself," said the gambler. "That's what they call it," said the woman querulously,

as she lay down again, and, turning her face to the wall, passed quietly away.

The accordian and the bones were put aside that day, and Homer was forgotten. When the body of Mother Shipton had been committed to the snow, Mr. Oakhurst took the Innocent aside, and showed him a pair of snow-shoes, which he had fashioned from the old pack-saddle. "There's one chance in a hundred to save her yet," he said, pointing to Piney; "but it's there," he added, pointing toward Poker Flat. "If you can reach there in two days, she's safe." "And you?" asked Tom Simson. "I'll stay here," was the curt reply.

The lovers parted with a long embrace. "You are not going, too?" said the Duchess, as she saw Mr. Oakhurst apparently waiting to accompany him. "As far as the cañon," he replied. He turned suddenly and kissed the Duchess, leaving her pallid face aflame, and her trembling limbs rigid with amazement.

Night came, but not Mr. Oakhurst. It brought the storm again and the whirling snow. Then the Duchess, feeding the fire, found that some one had quietly piled beside the hut enough fuel to last a few days longer. The tears rose to her eyes, but she hid them from Piney.

The women slept but little. In the morning, looking into each other's faces, they read their fate. Neither spoke, but Piney, accepting the position of the stronger, drew near and placed her arm around the Duchess's waist. They kept this attitude for the rest of the day. That night the storm reached its greatest fury, and, rending asunder the protecting vines, invaded the very hut.

Toward morning they found themselves unable to feed the fire, which gradually died away. As the embers slowly blackened, the Duchess crept closer to Piney, and broke the silence of many hours: "Piney, can you pray?" "No, dear," said Piney simply. The Duchess, without knowing exactly why, felt relieved, and, putting her head upon Piney's shoulder, spoke no more. And so reclining, the younger and purer pillowing the head of her soiled sister upon her virgin breast, they fell asleep.

The wind lulled as if it feared to waken them. Feathery drifts of snow, shaken from the long pine boughs, flew like white winged birds, and settled about them as they slept. The moon through the rifted clouds looked down upon what had been the camp. But all human stain, all trace of earthly travail, was hidden beneath the spotless mantle mercifully flung from above.

They slept all that day and the next, nor did they waken when

541

voices and footsteps broke the silence of the camp. And when pitying fingers brushed the snow from their wan faces, you could scarcely have told from the equal peace that dwelt upon them which was she that had sinned. Even the law of Poker Flat recognized this, and turned away, leaving them still locked in each other's arms.

But at the head of the gulch, on one of the largest pine trees, they found the deuce of clubs pinned to the bark with a bowie-knife. It bore the following, written in pencil in a firm hand:—

†

BENEATH THIS TREE
LIES THE BODY
OF
JOHN OAKHURST
WHO STRUCK A STREAK OF BAD LUCK
ON THE 23D OF NOVEMBER 1850,
AND
HANDED IN HIS CHECKS
ON THE 7TH DECEMBER 1850

╪

And pulseless and cold, with a derringer by his side and a bullet in his heart, though still calm as in life, beneath the snow lay he who was at once the strongest and yet the weakest of the outcasts of Poker Flat.

GERHART HAUPTMANN

GERHART HAUPTMANN (German, 1862-1946). Won early, and most lasting, fame as revolutionary naturalist with *The Weavers*, drama of social protest. In later years leaned to classicism and symbolism: *The Fool in Christ* (novel), *Iphegenia in Aulis* (play). Early social consciousness did not prevent his final association with Nazism.

THE WEAVERS

Enter Ansorge, an earthenware pan with soup in one hand, in the other a half-finished quarter-bushel basket.

Ansorge. Glad to see you again, Moritz!

Jaeger. Thank you, Father Ansorge—same to you!

Ansorge (shoving his pan into the oven). Why, lad, you look like a duke!

Old Baumert. Show him your watch, Moritz. An' he's got a new suit of clothes besides them he's on, an' thirty shillings in his purse.

Ansorge (shaking his head). Is that so? Well, well!

Emma (puts the potato-parings into a bag). I must be off; I'll maybe get a drop o' skim milk for these. *(Goes out.)*

Jaeger (the others hanging on his words). You know how you all used to be down on me. It was always: Wait, Moritz, till your soldiering time comes—you'll catch it then. But you see how well I've got on. At the end of the first half-year I had my good-conduct stripes. You've got to be willing—that's where the secret lies. I brushed the sergeant's boots; I groomed his horse; I fetched his beer. I was as sharp as a needle. Always ready, accouterments clean and shining—first at stables, first at roll-call, first in the saddle. And when the bugle sounded to the assault—why, then, blood and thunder, and ride to the devil with you!! I was as keen as a pointer. Says I to myself: There's no help for it now, my boy, it's got to be done; and I set my mind to it and did it. Till at last the major said before the whole squadron: There's a hussar, now, that shows you what a hussar should be!

(Silence. He lights his pipe.)

Ansorge (shaking his head). Well, well, well! You had luck with you, Moritz. *(Sits down on the floor, with his willow twigs beside him, and continues mending the basket, which he holds between his legs.)*

Old Baumert. Let's hope you've brought some of it to us.—Are we to have a drop to drink your health in?

Jaeger. Of course you are, Father Baumert. And when this bottle's done, we'll send for more. *(He flings a coin on the table.)*

Ansorge (open mouthed with amazement). Oh my! Oh my! What goings on, to be sure! Roast meat frizzlin' in the oven! A bottle o' brandy on the table! *(He drinks out of the bottle.)* Here's to you, Moritz!—Well, well, well!

(The bottle circulates freely after this.)

Old Baumert. If we could any way have a bit o' meat on Sundays and holidays, instead of never seein' the sight of it from year's end to year's end! Now we'll have to wait till another poor little dog finds its way into the house like this one did four weeks gone by—an' that's not likely to happen soon again.

Ansorge. Have you killed the little dog?

Old Baumert. We had to do that or starve.

Ansorge. Well, well!

Mother Baumert. A nice, kind little beast he was, too!

Jaeger. Are you as keen as ever on roast dog hereabouts?

Old Baumert. My word, if we could only get enough of it!

Mother Baumert. A nice little bit o' meat like that does you a lot o' good.

Old Baumert. Have you lost the taste for it, Moritz? Stay with us a bit, and it'll soon come back to you.

Ansorge (sniffing). Yes, yes! That will be a tasty bite—what a good smell it has!

Old Baumert (sniffing). Splendid!

Ansorge. Come, then, Moritz, tell us your opinion, you that's been out and seen the world. Are things at all like improving for us weavers, eh?

Jaeger. They would need to.

Ansorge. We're in an awful state here. It's not livin' an' it's not dyin'. A man fights to the bitter end, but he's bound to be beat at last—to be left without a room over his head, you may say without ground under his feet. As long as he can work at the loom he can earn some sort o' poor, miserable livin'. But it's many a day since I've been able to get that sort o' job. Now I tries to put a bite into my mouth with this here basket-makin'. I sits at it late into the night, and by the time I tumbles into bed I've earned three-halfpence. I put it to you if a man can live on that, when everything's so dear? Nine shillin' goes in one lump for house tax, three shillin' for land tax, nine shillin' for mortgage interest—that makes one pound one. I may reckon my year's earnin' at just double that money, and that leaves me twenty-one shillin' for a whole year's food, an' fire, an' clothes, an' shoes; and I've got to keep up some sort of a place to live in. Is it any wonder if I'm behindhand with my interest payments?

Old Baumert. Some one would need to go to Berlin an' tell the King how hard put to it we are.

Jaeger. Little good that would do, Father Baumert. There's been plenty written about it in the newspapers. But the rich people, they can turn and twist things round—as cunning as the devil himself.

Old Baumert (shaking his head). To think they've no more sense than that in Berlin!

Ansorge. And is it really true, Moritz? Is there no law to help us? If a man hasn't been able to scrape together enough to pay his mortgage interest, though he's worked the very skin off his hands, must his house be taken from him? The peasant that's lent the

544

money on it, he wants his rights—what else can you look for from him? But what's to be the end of it all, I don't know. If I'm put out o' the house—*(In a voice choked by tears.)* I was born here, and here my father sat at his loom for more than forty year. Many was the time he said to mother: Mother, when I'm gone, the house'll still be here. I've worked hard for it. Every nail means a night's weaving, every plank a year's dry bread. A man would think that—

Jaeger. They're quite fit to take the last bite out of your mouth— that's what they are.

Ansorge. Well, well, well! I would rather be carried out than have to walk out now in my old days. Who minds dyin'? My father, he was glad to die. At the very end he got frightened, but I crept into bed beside him, an' he quieted down again. I was a lad of thirteen then. I was tired and fell asleep beside him—I knew no better—and when I woke he was quite cold.

Mother Baumert (after a pause). Give Ansorge his soup out o' the oven, Bertha.

Bertha. Here, Father Ansorge, it'll do you good.

Ansorge (eating and shedding tears). Well, well, well!

(Old Baumert has begun to eat meat out of the saucepan.)

Mother Baumert. Father, father, can't you have patience an' let Bertha serve it up properly?

Old Baumert (chewing). It's two years now since I took the sacrament. I went straight after that an' sold my Sunday coat, an' we bought a good bit o' pork, an' since then never a mouthful of meat has passed my lips till to-night.

Jaeger. How should *we* need meat? The manufacturers eat it for us. It's the fat of the land *they* live on. Whoever doesn't believe that has only to go down to Bielau and Peterswaldau. He'll see fine things there—palace upon palace, with towers and iron railings and plate-glass windows. Who do they all belong to? Why, of course, the manufacturers! No signs of bad times there! Baked and boiled and fried—horses and carriages and governesses—they've money to pay for all that and goodness knows how much more. They're swelled out to bursting with pride and good living.

Ansorge. Things was different in my young days. Then the manufacturers let the weaver have his share. Now they keep everything to theirselves. An' would you like to know what's at the bottom of it all? It's that the fine folks nowadays believes neither in God nor devil. What do they care about commandments or punishments? And so they steal our last scrap o' bread, and leave us

545

no chance of earnin' the barest living. For it's their fault. If our manufacturers was good men, there would be no bad times for us.

Jaeger. Listen, then, and I'll read you something that will please you. *(He takes one or two loose papers from his pocket.)* I say, August, run and fetch another quart from the public house. Eh, boy, do you laugh all day long?

Mother Baumert. No one knows why, but our August's always happy—grins an' laughs, come what may. Off with you then, quick! *(Exit August with the empty brandy bottle.)* You've got something good now, eh, father?

Old Baumert (still chewing; spirits rising from the effect of food and drink). Moritz, you're the very man we want. You can read an' write. You understand the weaving trade, and you've a heart to feel for the poor weaver's sufferin's. You should stand up for us here.

Jaeger. I'd do that quick enough! There's nothing I'd like better than to give the manufacturers round here a bit of a fright—dogs that they are! I'm an easy-going fellow, but let me once get worked up into a real rage, and I'll take Dreissiger in the one hand and Dittrich in the other, and knock their heads together till the sparks fly out of their eyes.—If we could only arrange all to join together, we'd soon give the manufacturers a proper lesson—without help from King or Government—all we'd have to do would be to say, We want this and that, and we don't want the other thing. There would be a change of days then. As soon as they see that there's some pluck in us, they'll cave in. I know the rascals; they're a pack of cowardly hounds.

Mother Baumert. There's some truth in what you say. I'm not an ill-natured woman. I've always been the one to say as how there must be rich folks as well as poor. But when things comes to such a pass as this—

Jaeger. The devil may take them all, for what I care. It would be no more than they deserve.

(Old Baumert has quietly gone out.)

Bertha. Where's father?

Mother Baumert. I don't know where he can have gone.

Bertha. Do you think he's not been able to stomach the meat, with not gettin' none for so long?

Mother Baumert (in distress, crying). There now, there! He's not even able to keep it down when he's got it. Up it comes again, the only bite o' good food as he's tasted this many a day.

Reënter Old Baumert, crying with rage.

Old Baumert. It's no good! I'm too far gone! Now that I've at last got hold of somethin' with a taste in it, my stomach won't keep it. *(He sits down on the bench by the stove, crying.)*

Jaeger (with a sudden violent ebullition of rage). And yet there are people not far from here, justices they call themselves too, over-fed brutes, that have nothing to do all the year round but invent new ways of wasting their time. And these people say that the weavers would be quite well off if only they weren't so lazy.

Ansorge. The men as say that are no men at all, they're monsters.

Jaeger. Never mind, Father Ansorge; we're making the place hot for 'em. Becker and I have been and given Dreissiger a piece of our mind, and before we came away we sang him "Bloody Justice."

Ansorge. Good Lord! Is that the song?

Jaeger. Yes; I have it here.

Ansorge. They call it Dreissiger's song, don't they?

Jaeger. I'll read it to you.

Mother Baumert. Who wrote it?

Jaeger. That's what nobody knows. Now listen.

(He reads, hesitating like a schoolboy, with incorrect accentuation, but unmistakably strong feeling. Despair, suffering, rage, hatred, thirst for revenge, all find utterance.

The justice to us weavers dealt
  Is bloody, cruel, and hateful;
Our life's one torture, long drawn out:
  For Lynch law we'd be grateful.

Stretched on the rack day after day,
  Hearts sick and bodies aching,
Our heavy sighs their witness bear
  To spirit slowly breaking.

(The words of the song make a strong impression on Old Baumert. Deeply agitated, he struggles against the temptation to interrupt Jaeger. At last he can keep quiet no longer.)

Old Baumert (to his wife, half laughing, half crying, stammering). Stretched on the rack day after day. Whoever wrote that, mother,

547

wrote the truth. You can bear witness—eh, how does it go? "Our heavy sighs their witness bear"—what's the rest?

Jaeger. "To spirit slowly breaking."

Old Baumert. You know the way we sigh, mother, day and night, sleepin' and wakin'.

(Ansorge has stopped working, and cowers on the floor, strongly agitated. Mother Baumert and Bertha wipe their eyes frequently during the course of the reading.

Jaeger (continues to read)—

The Dreissigers true hangmen are,
    Servants no whit behind them;
Masters and men with one accord
    Set on the poor to grind them.

You villains all, you brood of hell!—

Old Baumert (trembling with rage, stamping on the floor)—
Yes, brood of hell!!!

Jaeger (reads)—

You fiends in fashion human,
A curse will fall on all like you,
    Who prey on man and woman.

Ansorge. Yes, yes, a curse upon them!

Old Baumert (clenching his fist, threateningly). You prey on man and woman.

Jaeger (reads)—

The suppliant knows he asks in vain,
    Vain every word that's spoken.
"If not content, then go and starve—
    Our rules cannot be broken."

Old Baumert. What is it? "The suppliant knows he asks in vain"? Every word of it's true—every word—as true as the Bible. He knows he asks in vain.

Ansorge. Yes, yes! It's all no good.

Jaeger (reads)—

Then think of all our woe and want,
    O ye who hear this ditty!
Our struggle vain for daily bread
    Hard hearts would move to pity.

548

But pity's what *you've* never known,—
    You'd take both skin and clothing,
You cannibals, whose cruel deeds
    Fill all good men with loathing.

Old Baumert (jumps up, beside himself with excitement). Both skin and clothing. It's true, it's all true! Here I stand, Robert Baumert, master-weaver, of Kaschbach. Who can bring up anything against me?—I've been an honest, hard-working man all my life long, an' look at me now! What have I to show for it? Look at me! See what they've made of me! Stretched on the rack day after day. *(He holds out his arms.)* Feel that! Skin and bone! "You villains all, you brood of hell!!" *(He sinks down on a chair, weeping with rage and despair.)*

Ansorge (flings his basket from him into a corner, rises, his whole body trembling with rage, gasps). And the time's come now for a change, I say. We'll stand it no longer! We'll stand it no longer! Come what may!

NATHANIEL HAWTHORNE

NATHANIEL HAWTHORNE (American, 1804-1864). Classic American novelist of New England. Housebound by boyhood leg injury. Worked as adult for port of Salem, became U.S. Consul abroad. Puritan heritage centers his novels about problems of guilt and moral pride. Most famous: *The Scarlet Letter.* Others: *The House of the Seven Gables, The Marble Faun, The Blithedale Romance, Twice-Told Tales*

THE AMBITIOUS GUEST

One September night a family had gathered round their hearth and piled it high with the driftwood of mountain streams, the dry cones of the pine, and the splintered ruins of great trees, that had come crashing down the precipice. Up the chimney roared the fire, and brightened the room with its broad blaze. The faces of the father and mother had a sober gladness; the children laughed. The eldest daughter was the image of Happiness at seventeen, and the aged grandmother, who sat knitting in the warmest place, was the image of Happiness grown old. They had found the "herb heart's-ease" in the

bleakest spot of all New England. This family were situated in the Notch of the White Hills, where the wind was sharp throughout the year and piteously cold in the winter, giving their cottage all its fresh inclemency before it descended on the valley of the Saco. They dwelt in a cold spot and a dangerous one, for a mountain towered above their heads so steep that the stones would often rumble down its sides and startle them at midnight.

The daughter had just uttered some simple jest that filled them all with mirth, when the wind came through the Notch and seemed to pause before their cottage, rattling the door with a sound of wailing and lamentation before it passed into the valley. For a moment it saddened them, though there was nothing unusual in the tones. But the family were glad again when they perceived that the latch was lifted by some traveler whose footsteps had been unheard amid the dreary blast which heralded his approach and wailed as he was entering, and went moaning away from the door.

Though they dwelt in such a solitude, these people held daily converse with the world. The romantic pass of the Notch is a great artery through which the life-blood of internal commerce is continually throbbing between Maine on one side and the Green Mountains and the shores of the St. Lawrence on the other. The stage coach always drew up before the door of the cottage. The wayfarer with no companion but his staff paused here to exchange a word, that the sense of loneliness might not utterly overcome him ere he could pass through the cleft of the mountain or reach the first house in the valley. And here the teamster on his way to Portland market would put up for the night, and, if a bachelor, might sit an hour beyond the usual bedtime and steal a kiss from the mountain maid at parting. It was one of those primitive taverns where the traveler pays only for food and lodging, but meets with a homely kindness beyond all price. When the footsteps were heard, therefore, between the outer door and the inner one, the whole family rose up, grandmother, children, and all as if about to welcome someone who belonged to them, and whose fate was linked with theirs.

The door was opened by a young man. His face at first wore the melancholy expression, almost despondency, of one who travels a wild and bleak road at nightfall and alone, but soon brightened up when he saw the kindly warmth of his reception. He felt his heart spring forward to meet them all, from the old woman who wiped the chair with her apron to the little child that held out its arms

550

to him. One glance and smile placed the stranger on a footing of innocent familiarity with the oldest daughter.

"Ah! this fire is the right thing," cried he, "especially when there is such a pleasant circle around it. I am quite benumbed, for the Notch is just like the pipe of a great pair of bellows; it has blown a terrible blast in my face all the way from Bartlett."

"Then you are going toward Vermont?" said the master of the house as he helped to take a light knapsack off the young man's shoulders.

"Yes, to Burlington, and far enough beyond," replied he. "I meant to have been at Ethan Crawford's tonight, but a pedestrian lingers along such a road as this. It is no matter; for when I saw this good fire and all your cheerful faces, I felt as if you had kindled it on purpose for me and were waiting my arrival. So I shall sit down among you and make myself at home."

The frank-hearted stranger had just drawn his chair to the fire when something like a heavy footstep was heard without, rushing down the steep side of the mountain as with long and rapid strides, and taking such a leap in passing the cottage as to strike the opposite precipice. The family held their breath, because they knew the sound, and their guest held his by instinct.

"The old mountain has thrown a stone at us for fear we should forget him," said the landlord, recovering himself. "He sometimes nods his head and threatens to come down, but we are old neighbors, and agree together pretty well upon the whole. Besides, we have a sure place of refuge hard by if he should be coming in good earnest."

Let us now suppose the stranger to have finished his supper of bear's meat, and by his natural felicity of manner to have placed himself on a footing of kindness with the whole family; so that they talked as freely together as if he belonged to their mountain brood. He was of a proud yet gentle spirit, haughty and reserved among the rich and great, but ever ready to stoop his head to the lowly cottage door and be like a brother or a son at the poor man's fireside. In the household of the Notch he found warmth and simplicity of feeling, the pervading intelligence of New England, and a poetry of native growth which they had gathered when they little thought of it from the mountain-peaks and chasms, and at the very threshold of their romantic and dangerous abode. He had traveled far and alone; his whole life, indeed, had been a solitary path, for, with the lofty caution of his nature, he had kept himself apart from

those who might otherwise have been his companions. The family, too, though so kind and hospitable, had that consciousness of unity among themselves and separation from the world at large which in every domestic circle should still keep a holy place where no stranger may intrude. But this evening a prophetic sympathy impelled the refined and educated youth to pour out his heart before the simple mountaineers, and constrained them to answer him with the same free confidence. And thus it should have been. Is not the kindred of a common fate a closer tie than that of birth?

The secret of the young man's character was a high and abstracted ambition. He could have borne to live an undistinguished life, but not to be forgotten in the grave. Yearning desire had been transformed to hope, and hope, long cherished, had become like certainty that, obscurely as he journeyed now, a glory was to beam on all his pathway, though not, perhaps, while he was treading it. But when present, they would trace the brightness of his footsteps, brightening as meaner glories faded, and confess that a gifted one had passed from his cradle to his tomb with none to recognize him.

"As yet," cried the stranger, his cheek glowing and his eye flashing with enthusiasm— "as yet I have done nothing. Were I to vanish from the earth tomorrow, none would know so much of me as you—that a nameless youth came up at nightfall from the valley of the Saco, and opened his heart to you in the evening, and passed through the Notch by sunrise, and was seen no more. Not a soul would ask, 'Who was he? Whither did the wanderer go?' But I cannot die till I have achieved my destiny. Then let Death come; I shall have built my monument."

There was a continual flow of natural emotion gushing forth amid abstracted reverie which enabled the family to understand this young man's sentiments, though so foreign from their own. With quick sensibility of the ludicrous, he blushed at the ardor into which he had been betrayed.

"You laugh at me," said he, taking the eldest daughter's hand and laughing himself. "You think my ambition as nonsensical as if I were to freeze myself to death on the top of Mount Washington only that people might spy at me from the country roundabout. And truly that would be a noble pedestal for a man's statue."

"It is better to sit here by this fire," answered the girl, blushing, "and be comfortable and contented, though nobody thinks about us."

552

"I suppose," said her father, after a fit of musing, "there is something natural in what the young man says; and if my mind had been turned that way, I might have felt just the same. It is strange, wife, how his talk has set my head running on things that are pretty certain never to come to pass."

"Perhaps they may," observed the wife. "Is the man thinking what he will do when he is a widower?"

"No, no!" cried he, repelling the idea with reproachful kindness. "When I think of your death, Esther, I think of mine, too. But I was wishing we had a good farm in Bartlett or Bethlehem or Littleton, or some other township round the White Mountains, but not where they could tumble on our heads. I should want to stand well with my neighbors and be called squire and sent to General Court for a term or two; for a plain, honest man may do as much good there as a lawyer. And when I should be grown quite an old man, and you an old woman, so as not to be long apart, I might die happy enough in my bed, and leave you all crying around me. A slate gravestone would suit me as well as a marble one, with just my name and age, and a verse of a hymn, and something to let people know that I lived an honest man and died a Christian."

"There, now!" exclaimed the stranger; "it is our nature to desire a monument, be it slate or marble, or a pillar of granite, or a glorious memory in the universal heart of man."

"We're in a strange way tonight," said the wife, with tears in her eyes. "They say it's a sign of something when folks' minds go a-wandering so. Hark to the children!"

They listened accordingly. The younger children had been put to bed in another room, but with an open door between; so that they could be heard talking busily among themselves. One and all seemed to have caught the infection from the fireside circle, and were outvying each other in wild wishes and childish projects of what they would do when they came to be men and women. At length a little boy, instead of addressing his brothers and sisters, called out to his mother:

"I'll tell you what I wish, mother," cried he: "I want you and father and grandma'm, and all of us, and the stranger, too, to start right away and go and take a drink out of the basin of the Flume."

Nobody could help laughing at the child's notion of leaving a warm bed and dragging them from a cheerful fire to visit the basin of the Flume—a brook which tumbles over the precipe deep within the Notch.

553

The boy had hardly spoken, when a wagon rattled along the road and stopped a moment before the door. It appeared to contain two or three men who were cheering their hearts with the rough chorus of a song which resounded in broken notes between the cliffs, while the singers hesitated whether to continue their journey or put up here for the night.

"Father," said the girl, "they are calling you by name."

But the good man doubted whether they had really called him, and was unwilling to show himself too solicitous of gain by inviting people to patronize his house. He therefore did not hurry to the door, and, the lash being soon applied, the travelers plunged into the Notch, still singing and laughing, though their music and mirth came back drearily from the heart of the mountain.

"There, mother!" cried the boy again; "they'd have given us a ride to the Flume."

Again they laughed at the child's pertinacious fancy for a night ramble. But it happened that a light cloud passed over the daughter's spirit; she looked gravely into the fire and drew a breath that was almost a sigh. It forced its way, in spite of a little struggle to repress it. Then, starting and blushing, she looked quickly around the circle, as if they had caught a glimpse into her bosom. The stranger asked what she had been thinking of.

"Nothing," answered she, with a downcast smile; "only I felt lonesome just then."

"Oh, I have always had a gift of feeling what is in other people's hearts," said he, half seriously. "Shall I tell the secrets of yours? For I know what to think when a young girl shivers by a warm hearth and complains of lonesomeness at her mother's side. Shall I put these feelings into words?"

"They would not be a girl's feelings any longer if they could be put into words," replied the mountain nymph, laughing, but avoiding his eye.

All this was said apart. Perhaps a germ of love was springing in their hearts so pure that it might blossom in Paradise, since it could not be matured on earth; for women worship such gentle dignity as his, and the proud, contemplative, yet kindly, soul is oftenest captivated by simplicity like hers. But while they spoke softly, and he was watching the happy sadness, the lightsome shadows, the shy yearnings of a maiden's nature, the wind through the Notch took a deeper and drearier sound. It seemed, as the fanciful stranger said, like the choral strain of the spirits of the blast who

554

in old Indian times had their dwelling among these mountains, and made their heights and recesses a sacred region. There was a wail along the road as if a funeral were passing. To chase away the gloom, the family threw pine-branches on their fire till the dry leaves crackled and the flame arose, discovering once again a scene of peace and humble happiness. The light hovered about them fondly and caressed them all. There were the little faces of the children peeping from their bed apart, and here the father's frame of strength, the mother's subdued and careful mien, the high-browed youth, the budding girl, and the good old grandam still knitting in the warmest place.

The aged woman looked up from her task, and with fingers ever busy was the next to speak.

"Old folks have their notions," said she, "as well as young ones. You've been wishing and planning and letting your heads run on one thing and another till you've set my mind a-wandering too. Now, what should an old woman wish for when she can go but a step or two before she comes to her grave? Children, it will haunt me night and day till I tell you."

"What is it, mother?" cried the husband and wife, at once.

Then the old woman, with an air of mystery which drew the circle closer round the fire, informed them that she had provided her grave-clothes some years before—a nice linen shroud, a cap with a muslin ruff, and everything of a finer sort than she had worn since her wedding day. But this evening an old superstition had strangely recurred to her. It used to be said in her younger days that if anything were amiss with a corpse, if only the ruff were not smooth or the cap did not set right, the corpse, in the coffin and beneath the clods, would strive to put up its cold hands and arrange it. The bare thought made her nervous.

"Don't talk so, grandmother," said the girl, shuddering.

"Now," continued the old woman with singular earnestness, yet smiling strangely at her own folly, "I want one of you, my children, when your mother is dressed and in the coffin,—I want one of you to hold a looking-glass over my face. Who knows but I may take a glimpse at myself, and see whether all's right."

"Old and young, we dream of graves and monuments," murmured the stranger youth. "I wonder how mariners feel when the ship is sinking and they, unknown and undistinguished, are to be buried together in the ocean, that wide and nameless sepulcher?"

For a moment the old woman's ghastly conception so engrossed

555

the minds of her hearers that a sound abroad in the night, rising like the roar of a blast, had grown broad, deep and terrible before the fated group were conscious of it. The house and all within it trembled; the foundations of the earth seemed to be shaken, as if this awful sound were the peal of the last trump. Young and old exchanged one wild glance and remained an instant pale, affrighted, without utterance or power to move. Then the same shriek burst simultaneously from all their lips:

"The slide! The slide!"

The simplest words must intimate, but not portray, the unutterable horror of the catastrophe. The victims rushed from their cottage, and sought refuge in what they deemed a safer spot, where, in contemplation of such an emergency, a sort of barrier had been reared. Alas! they had quitted their security and fled right into the pathway of destruction. Down came the whole side of the mountain in a cataract of ruin. Just before it reached the house the stream broke into two branches, shivered not a window there, but overwhelmed the whole vicinity, blocked up the road and and annihilated everything in its dreadful course. Long ere the thunder of that great slide had ceased to roar among the mountains the mortal agony had been endured and the victims were at peace. Their bodies were never found.

The next morning the light smoke was seen stealing from the cottage chimney, up the mountain-side. Within, the fire was yet smoldering on the hearth, and the chairs in a circle round it, as if the inhabitants had but gone forth to view the devastation of the slide, and would shortly return to thank Heaven for their miraculous escape. All had left separate tokens by which those who had known the family were made to shed a tear for each. Who has not heard their name? The story has been told far and wide, and will forever be a legend of these mountains. Poets have sung their fate.

There were circumstances which led some to suppose that a stranger had been received into the cottage on this awful night, and had shared the catastrophe of all its inmates; others denied that there were sufficient grounds for such a conjecture. Woe for the high souled youth with his dream of earthly immortality! His name and person utterly unknown, his history, his way of life, his plans, a mystery never to be solved, his death and his existence equally a doubt,—whose was the agony of that death moment?

JOHANN PETER HEBEL

JOHANN PETER HEBEL (German, 1760-1826). German poet and storyteller. Son of a servant, became teacher and prelate. Goethe considered him among greatest dialect poets. Published annual almanac of stories and anecdotes *(Schatzkästlein des Rheinischen Hausfreundes)*, from which he collected the volume that established his fame.

KANNITVERSTAN

IN EMMENDINGEN and Gundelfingen, as well as in Amsterdam, a man has the opportunity every day, I dare say, to reflect on the inconstancy of all earthly things—if he wants to—and to learn how to be satisfied with his lot even though life is no bed of roses. But it was by the oddest roundabout route that a German journeyman in Amsterdam came, through error, to the perception of this truth.

After he had come to that great and prosperous city of commerce, full of splendid houses, heaving ships, and busy people, his eye fell upon a house larger and more beautiful than any he had ever seen on all his travels from Tuttlingen to Amsterdam. For a long time he gazed in wonder at this costly building, at the six chimneys on its roof, at its beautiful cornices, and at the high windows, each larger than the front door to his father's house.

Finally, yielding to an impulse, he addressed a passer-by. "My good friend," he asked, "can you tell me the name of the gentleman who owns this marvelous house with the windows full of tulips, asters, and gilliflowers?" But the man, who probably had something more important to attend to and, unfortunately, understood just as much German as his questioner did Dutch—to wit, nothing—growled: *"Kannitverstan,"* and whisked by. This is a Dutch word—or three of them, if one looks at it properly—and means no more than "I cannot understand you."

But the good stranger thought it to be the name of the gentleman he'd asked about. "That must be a mighty rich man, that Mr. Kannitverstan," he said to himself, and walked on.

Making his way through the narrow streets, he came at length to the estuary that is called Het Ey, meaning "the Y." There stood ship after ship and mast after mast, and he was beginning to wonder how he could ever manage to take in all of these marvels with his own two eyes, when his glance fell upon a large merchantman that

557

recently had put in from the East Indies and was being unloaded. Whole rows of piled crates and bales stood side by side on the wharf, and more were being rolled out: casks full of sugar and coffee, full of rice and pepper, and with them—pardon—mouse droppings too.

After he had watched for a long time, he asked a fellow who was carrying a crate on his shoulders the name of the fortunate man to whom the sea had brought all these wares. *"Kannitverstan,"* was the answer.

Then he thought: "Aha, so that's how it is! If the sea floats him such riches, no wonder he can put up houses with gilt-potted tulips in the windows." So he went away, sorrowfully reflecting how poor a man he was among so many rich people in this world. But just as he was thinking: "I wish I, too, would be as well off some day as this Mr. Kannitverstan," he turned a corner and saw a great funeral procession. Four black-draped horses were pulling a black-covered hearse slowly and lugubriously, as though they were aware they were carrying a dead man to his peace. A long cortege of friends and acquaintances of the departed followed behind, pair after pair, muffled in black cloaks, and mute. A solitary bell sounded in the distance. Our stranger was seized by the melancholy feeling that no good man can suppress at the sight of a funeral, and he remained standing reverently, with his hat in his hands, until all was over. Then he attached himself to the last mourner (who was just figuring how much he would make on his cotton if the bale price should rise ten florins), tugged at his coat, guilelessly begged his pardon, and said: "He must indeed have been a good friend of yours, the gentleman for whom the bell is tolling, that you follow his coffin so grieved and pensive."

"Kannitverstan," was the answer.

A few large tears descended from the eyes of our good journeyman from Tuttlingen, and he felt sad and relieved at once. "Poor Kannitverstan," he exclaimed, "what have you now of all your riches? Exactly what I shall get one day from my poverty: a linen shroud! And of all your beautiful flowers, you have, perhaps, a rosemary on your cold breast, or some rue." With these thoughts he accompanied the funeral procession to the grave as though he belonged with it, and saw the supposed Mr. Kannitverstan sink down to his final resting-place, and was more moved by the Dutch funeral oration, of which he understood not a word, than by many a German one to which he had paid no attention.

He left with the others and went away with a light heart, and at an inn where German was understood, he ate, with relish, a piece of Limburg cheese. And whenever afterward his heart became heavy because so many people in this world were so rich and he was so poor, he only thought of Mr. Kannitverstan of Amsterdam—of his big house, his opulent ship, and his narrow grave.

HEINRICH HEINE

HEINRICH HEINE (German, 1797-1856). Greatest lyricist in the German tongue. Regarded as leader of Young Germany. Settled in Paris, and interpreted French and Germans to each other. A hasty convert who remained a tender admirer of Judaism and acid critic of Christianity all his life. Noted for his irony, wit, mercurial intelligence. Famous poems: *"Die Lorelei,"* *"Du Bist Wie eine Blume."*

SONGS

Thou Who Art So Fair and Pure

Thou, so fair, so pure of guile,
Maiden of the sunny smile
Would to thee it were my fate
All my life to dedicate!

Like the moonbeams' tender shine
Gleam these gentle eyes of thine;
Thy soft cheeks so ruddy bright
Scatter rays of rosy light.

Thy dear little mouth doth show
Pearls within, a shining row;
But the gem of gems the best
Is enshrined within thy breast.

It was love divinely deep,
That into my heart did leap,
When I looked on thee erewhile,
Maiden of the sunny smile!

Alone with the anguish that tore me
  'Neath the forest boughs I stept;
Anon came the old dream o'er me,
  And into my heart it crept.

Who taught ye this word, not to fear it,
  Little birds, singing up there so free?
Oh, hush! if my heart should hear it,
  Very sad it again would be.

"This way came a fair girl, she taught it;
  As she sang it, it was all we heard;
And up we little birds caught it,
  The dainty-sweet golden word."

Never think with such fables to wile me!
  Little birds, ye are wondrously sly;
You wish of my grief to beguile me,
  But I trust nothing living, not I.

The Two Grenadiers

For France two grenadiers held their way,
  Had prisoners been in Russia;
And sorrowful men they were, when they
  The frontier reached of Prussia.

For there they heard of a dire event,—
  How the world 'gainst France had risen, her
Grande armée had shattered and shent,
  And taken her Emperor prisoner.

They mingled their tears, these two grenadiers,
  To the sad tale ever returning;
"Oh would," said one, "that my days were done!
My old wounds, how they're burning!"

"All's up!" said the other; "and sooner than not
  I would die like you, never doubt me;
But a wife and child at home I've got,
  And they must be starved without me!"

"Hang wife and child! It is something more,
  And better far, that I pant for;
My Emperor prisoner! My Emperor!
  Let them go beg what they want for!

"If I die just now, as 'tis like I may,
  Then, comrade, this boon grant me,
Take my body with you to France away,
  And in France's dear earth plant me.

"The *Croix d'Honneur*, with its crimson band,
  On my heart see that you place it;
Then give me my rifle in my hand,
  And my sword, around me to brace it.

"So will I lie, and listen all ear,
  Like a sentinel, low in my bed there,
Till the roar of the cannon some day I hear,
  And the chargers' neigh and their tread there.

"Then I'll know 'tis my Emperor riding by;
  The sabres flash high that attend him,
And out from my grave full-armed spring I
  The Emperor! to shield and defend him!"

Whene'er I Look into Thine Eyes

Whene'er I look into thine eyes,
Then every fear that haunts me flies;
But when I kiss thy mouth, oh then
I feel a giant's strength again.

Whene'er I couch me on thy breast,
I know what heaven is to the blest;
But when thou sayest, "I love thee!"
Then must I weep, and bitterly.

Thou Lovest Me Not

My love you cannot, cannot brook!
  I don't let that distress me;
So I but on thy face may look,
  In that's enough to bless me.

561

You hate, you hate, you hate me! is
  Your rosy-red mouth's greeting:
But let me have that mouth to kiss,
  And I'm content, my sweeting!

A Pine-Tree Stands Alone

A pine-tree stands alone on
  A bare bleak northern height;
The ice and snow they swathe it,
  As it sleeps there, all in white.

'Tis dreaming of a palm-tree,
  In a far-off Eastern land,
That mourns, alone and silent,
  On a ledge of burning sand.

My Songs Are Poisoned!

My songs, they are poisoned—poisoned!
  How otherwise could it be?
Over the flowers of my life's fresh hours
  Has poison been poured by thee.

My songs, they are poisoned—poisoned!
  How otherwise could it be?
Many serpents I bear in my heart, and there
  I bear with them, thee, love, thee.

In Dreams, Oh, I Have Wept, Love!

In dreams, oh, I have wept, love!
  I dreamed in the grave you were laid;
I awoke, and my cheek was wet, love,
  And tears still adown it strayed.

In dreams, oh, I have wept, love!
  I dreamt you were false to me;
I awoke, and I went on weeping
  Long, long and bitterly.

In dreams, oh, I have wept, love!
   I dreamed you still held me dear;
I awoke, and unto this hour, love,
   Weep many a scalding tear.

The Loreley

I cannot tell what's coming o'er me,
   That makes me so eerie and low:
An old-world legend before me,
   Keeps rising, and will not go.

The air chills, day is declining,
   And smoothly Rhine's waters run,
And the peaks of the mountains are shining
   Aloft in the setting sun.

A maiden of wondrous seeming,
   Most beautiful, sits up there;
Her jewels in gold are gleaming,
   She combs out her golden hair.

With a comb of red gold she parts it,
   And still as she combs it, she sings;
Her song pierces home to our hearts, it
   Has tones of a sweetness that stings.

The boatman, he thrills as he hears it
   Out there in his little skiff:
He sees not the reef as he nears it,
   He only looks up to the cliff.

The waters will sweep, I am thinking,
   O'er skiff, and o'er boatman ere long;
And this is, when daylight is sinking,
   What Loreley did with her song.

Thou Lovely Fisher-Maiden

My bonnie blithe fisher-maiden,
   Row in your boat to the strand;
Come here and sit down beside me,
   And chat with me hand in hand.

563

Rest your dear little head on my bosom,
    And be not so frightened, child;
Every day you trust without thinking
    Yourself to the ocean wild.

My heart is quite like the ocean,
    It has tempests, and ebb, and flow;
And fine pearls lie there a-many,
    Down, down in its depths below.

Thou Art Even as a Flower Is

Thou art even as a flower is,
    So gentle, and pure, and fair;
I gaze on thee, and sadness
    Comes over my heart unaware.

I feel as though I should lay, sweet,
    My hands on thy head, with a prayer
That God may keep thee alway, sweet,
    As gentle, and pure, and fair!

Oh, the Sweet Lies Lurk in Kisses!

Oh, the sweet lies lurk in kisses!
    Oh, the charm of make-believe!
Oh, to be deceived sweet bliss is,
    Bliss still sweeter to deceive!

What thou'lt grant, I know, my fairest,
    Vowing, "Nay, I never must!"
I will trust whate'er thou swearest,
    I will swear what thou wilt trust.

The Shades of the Summer Evening

The shades of the summer evening lie
    On forest and meadows green;
The golden moon shines in the azure sky
    Through balm-breathing air serene.

564

The cricket is chirping, the brooklet near,
  In the water a something stirs,
And the wanderer can in the stillness hear
  A plash and a sigh through the furze.

There all by herself the fairy bright
  Is bathing down in the stream;
Her arms and throat, betwitching and white,
  In the moonshine glance and gleam.

There Was an Aged King

There was an aged king,
  His heart was heavy, his locks were grey;
This poor old king, he wedded
  A maiden young and gay.

There was a pretty foot-page,
  His looks were fair, and his heart was light;
The sammet train he carried
  Of that queen so young and bright.

Dost know the old, old story?
  So sweet in the telling, so sad to tell!
They had both to die, oh the pity!
  They had loved each other too well.

MEMOIRS

Little Veronica

Whether it be because of the rhythmic beat of the oars, or the swaying of the boat, or the fragrance of the hills of the river bank, where joy doth grow, it always comes to pass that the most troubled spirit finds peace in floating lightly in a little boat on the bosom of the dear, clear river Rhine. In truth, kind old Father Rhine cannot endure his children weeping; to stay their tears he takes them in his trusty arms and rocks them and tells them his most lovely tales

565

and promises them his most golden treasures, perhaps even the hoard of the Niblungs sunk there in the dim distant past. . . .

O! it is a fair country full of loveliness and sunshine. The hills of the river bank are mirrored in the blue stream with their ruined castles and woods and ancient towns. There on their thresholds sit the townsfolk in the summer evenings and drink out of great mugs, and gossip, how the vines flourish, thank God, and how trials must be held in public, and how Marie Antoinette had been guillotined without more ado, and how the tobacco monopoly had raised the price of tobacco, and how all men are equal, and what a capital fellow Gôrres is.

For my part I never bothered about such conversations, but much preferred to sit with the girls in the arched window and laugh as they laughed, and have flowers thrown in my face and pretend to be angry, until they told me their secrets or some other vastly important story. The fair Gertrude could scarcely contain her delight when I sat with her; she was like a flaming rose, and when she fell upon my neck I used to think she would burst into flame and go off in smoke in my arms. The fair Catherine used to melt away in tender melody, when she talked to me, and her eyes were of a blue pure and sweet such as I have never found in human beings or beasts and only very rarely in flowers; it was lovely to look upon them, and so many sweet thoughts would come into my head as I gazed. But the fair Hedwig loved me; for when I came to her she bowed her head so that her black tresses fell over hei blushing face, and her bright eyes shone like stars in the dark sky. Never a word came from her modest lips, and I, too, had nothing to say to her. I coughed, and she trembled. Often she would beg me through her sisters not to climb the rocks so fast, and not to bathe in the Rhine when I was hot with running or had been drinking. I used to listen sometimes when she prayed devoutly before the little picture of the Virgin Mary, which, spangled with gold, and lit up by a little flickering lamp, stood in a niche of the hall of the house. I heard clearly how she prayed the Mother of God to forbid Him to climb and drink and bathe. I might have loved her if she had been indifferent to me; and I was indifferent to her because I knew that she loved me.

The fair Johanna was a cousin of the three sisters; I liked much to be with her. She knew the most beautiful stories, and when she reached out of the window with her white hand towards the hills, where all the happenings of the story had been, a spell was cast

over me and I could see the old knights coming out of the ruined castles and hacking away at each other's armour, and the Lorelei stood once more on the hill-top and sang her sweet, seductive song, and the Rhine lapped so peacefully, so wisely, and yet with such dreadful mocking—and the fair Johanna looked at me strangely, as warily, and as mysteriously brooding as though she herself belonged to the fairy world of which she told. She was a slim, pale girl; she was consumptive and had long, long thoughts; her eyes were clear as truth; her lips pious and arched; in her features was a great story, but a sacred story—perhaps a legend of love? I know not, and I never had the courage to ask her. When I gazed for long upon her, I became peaceful and glad, and it was as though there were Sunday in my breast, and the angels were holding divine service in it.

At such times I used to tell her stories of my childhood, and she always listened gravely, and, strange, when I could not remember the names, she used to call them to mind for me. When I asked her in my astonishment how she knew the names, she used to smile and tell me by way of answer that the birds had told her who had made their nest in the eaves of her window; and she would have me believe that they were the very same birds which, as a boy, I had once bought from the cruel peasant children with my pocket-money to let them fly away. But I believe that she knew everything, because she was so pale and died so young. She knew also when she was to die, and wished me to leave Andenach the day before. When I left her, she gave me both her hands—they were clear, white hands and pure as the Host—and said: "You are very kind, and when you are angry, think of little Veronica, who is no more."

First Impressions in Paris

I had done and suffered much, and when the sun of the July Revolution rose in France I was very weary and stood in need of some relaxation. The air of my own country was every day more unwholesome for me, and I had seriously to think of a change of climate, and I had visions; the clouds oppressed me and cut all sorts of terrible capers before me. Often I thought the sun was a Prussian cockade; at night I dreamed of an ugly black vulture that ate my liver, and I was very melancholy. I also made the acquaintance of an old judge of Berlin who had passed many years in the

fortress of Spandau, and he told me how unpleasant it is to have to wear irons in winter. It seemed to me very unchristian not to warm the irons a little. If our chains were warmed a little they would not make so unpleasant an impression, and even men of a chilly nature could then bear them well; care should also be taken to scent fetters with roses and laurel as they do here in this country. I asked my old judge if he had often been given oysters to eat at Spandau. He said, "No," and that Spandau was far from the sea. Meat, too, he said, was rare there, and there was no other winged creature than the flies that fell in the soup. At the same time I made the acquaintance of a French *commis voyageur*, who travelled in wine and could not praise enough the jolly life in Paris, saying, how the sky is hung with fiddles, and how they sing from morning to night the Marseillaise and *"En avant, marchons!"* and *"Lafayette aux cheveux blancs,"* and how liberty, equality, and fraternity are written up at all the street corners; incidentally he praised the champagne of his firm, of whose cards he gave me a great number, and he promised me letters of introduction to the best Parisian restaurants, in case I should ever visit the capital in search of pleasure. And now as some sort of recreation is necessary, and Spandau is too far from the sea to eat oysters there, and the fly soup of Spandau did not attract me much, and also the Prussian chains are very cold in winter and would not be good for my health, I made up my mind to go to Paris and in the fatherland of champagne and the Marseillaise to drink the one and to hear the other, together with *"En avant, marchons!"* and *"Lafayette aux cheveux blancs."*

On May 1, 1831, I crossed the Rhine. I did not see the old river god, Father Rhine; I contented myself with throwing my visiting card into the water. I only saw the cathedral of Strassburg from a distance; he wagged his head like good Old Eckart when he sees a youngster going to the Venusberg.

At Saint Denis I awoke from a sweet morning sleep and heard for the first time the cry of the driver—"Paris! Paris!"—and the handbells of the cocoa-sellers. Here already you breathe the air of the capital which is visible on the horizon. An old rascal of a tout tried to persuade me to visit the tombs of the kings, but I had not come to France to see the kings; I contented myself with letting the guide tell me the legends of the place, how, for instance, the wicked Pagan king had Saint Denis' head cut off, and the Saint ran from Paris to Saint Denis with his head in his hand to be buried there, and to have the place called after him. "If you think," said my

568

guide, "if you think of the distance you cannot but be amazed at the miracle that any one could go so far on foot without a head"—and he added with a strange smile: *"Dans des cas pareils il n'y a que le premier pas ̀qui coûte."* It was worth two francs and I gave them to him *pour l'amour de Voltaire,* whose mocking smile I had already met in him. In twenty minutes I was in Paris, and entered through the triumphal arch of the Boulevard Saint Denis, which was originally erected in honour of Louis XIV, but now served to glorify my entry into Paris. I was really surprised by the crowd of gay people, dressed very tastefully like fashion plates. Then I was impressed by them all speaking French, which is with us the mark of the polite world; but everybody is as polite here as the aristocracy in my country. The men were all so courteous, and the lovely ladies all so smiling. If any one jostled me without at once begging my pardon, then I could wager that he was a fellow countryman; and if ever a pretty woman looked sourly, then she had either been eating Sauerkraut or could read Klopstock in the original. I found everything so amazing, and the sky was so blue, and the air so sweet, so generous, and the beams of the July sun flickered hither and thither; the cheeks of the fair Lutetia were touched with the flaming kisses of that sun, and in her bosom her bridal nosegay was not yet withered. At the street corners *"Liberté, égalité, fraternité"* had in places been erased.

I sought at once the restaurants for which I had my letters of introduction; the proprietors assured me that they would have received me without letters of introduction, that I had such an honest and distinguished appearance as to be a recommendation in itself. Never did a German cookshop-keeper say the like to me, even if he thought it; such a fellow thinks that he must say nothing pleasant, and that his German frankness compels him only to say to one's face disagreeable things. In the manners and speech of the French there is so much of that precious flattery that costs so little and yet is so kindly and refreshing. My poor sensitive soul, that often recoiled in shyness from German coarseness, opened out to the flattering sounds of French urbanity. God gave us our tongues so that we might say pleasant things to our fellow men.

There was a hitch in my French when I arrived; but after half an hour's conversation with a little flower-seller in the Passage de l'Opéra, my French, which had grown rusty since the Battle of Waterloo, became fluent again and I stumbled about in the most gallant conjugations and explained to my little friend the Linnaean

system, by which flowers are classified according to the filaments; she herself followed another method and divided the flowers into those which smelled sweet and those which smelled offensive. I believed that she applied the same method of classification to men. She was astonished that I was so learned, in spite of my youth, and she trumpeted the fame of my learning through all the Passage de l'Opéra. I drank in delightedly the sweet scents of flattery and was much amused. I walked on flowers, and many a roast pigeon flew into my open gaping maw. What amusing things I saw on my arrival! All the notabilities of public pleasure and official absurdity.

Paris delighted me much with the cheeriness which appears in everything, and influences even the most doleful disposition. Strange! Paris is the scene of the greatest tragedies of the history of the world, tragedies at the memory of which hearts in the most distant lands tremble, eyes grow wet; but it is with the spectator of these great tragedies as it was once with me when I saw the *Tour de Nesle* at the Porte St. Martin. I was sitting behind a lady who was wearing a hat of rose-red gauze, and this hat was so wide that it cut off altogether my view of the stage, so that I could see the tragedy enacted through the red gauze of the hat, so that all the horrors of the *Tour de Nesle* appeared in the rosiest light. Yes, there is such a rosy light in Paris, which makes bright every tragedy for the spectator, so that it does not touch his enjoyment of life, and so the terrors which we bring to Paris lose their most bitter sting. Sorrows are strangely softened. In the air of Paris wounds are healed quicker than anywhere else; there is something so noble, so gentle, so sweet in the air, as in the people themselves.

ERNEST HEMINGWAY

ERNEST HEMINGWAY (American, 1898-   ). Influential novelist, brought to modern fiction new techniques of clipped dialogue and excessive scenes of violence. Experience in First World War produced *A Farewell to Arms*. Postwar "lost generation" classic: *The Sun Also Rises*. Covered Spanish Civil War as journalist, and wrote *For Whom the Bell Tolls*. Also addicted to hunting *(The Green Hills of Africa)* and bullfighting *(Death in the Afternoon)*—both nonfiction. Nobel Prize, 1954.

TEN INDIANS

AFTER one Fourth of July, Nick, driving home late from town in the big wagon with Joe Garner and his family, passed nine drunken Indians along the road. He remembered there were

nine because Joe Garner, driving along in the dusk, pulled up the horses, jumped down into the road and dragged an Indian out of the wheel rut. The Indian had been asleep, face down in the sand. Joe dragged him into the bushes and got back up on the wagon-box.

"That makes nine of them," Joe said, "just between here and the edge of town."

"Them Indians," said Mrs. Garner.

Nick was on the back seat with the two Garner boys. He was looking out from the back seat to see the Indian where Joe had dragged him alongside of the road.

"Was it Billy Tabeshaw?" Carl asked.

"No."

"His pants looked mighty like Billy."

"All Indians wear the same kind of pants."

"I didn't see him at all," Frank said. "Pa was down into the road and back up again before I seen a thing. I thought he was killing a snake."

"Plenty of Indians'll kill snakes tonight, I guess," Joe Garner said.

"Them Indians," said Mrs. Garner.

They drove along. The road turned off from the main highway and went up into the hills. It was hard pulling for the horses and the boys got down and walked. The road was sandy. Nick looked back from the top of the hill by the schoolhouse. He saw the lights of Petoskey and, off across Little Traverse Bay, the lights of Harbour Springs. They climbed back in the wagon again.

"They ought to put some gravel on that stretch," Joe Garner said. The wagon went along the road through the woods. Joe and Mrs. Garner sat close together on the front seat. Nick sat between the two boys. The road came out into a clearing.

"Right here was where Pa ran over the skunk."

"It was further on."

"Where?"

"Down by the lake. They were looking for dead fish along the beach."

"They were coons probably," Carl said.

"They were skunks. I guess I know skunks."

"You ought to," Carl said. "You got an Indian girl."

"Stop talking that way, Carl," said Mrs. Garner.

"Well, they smell about the same."

Joe Garner laughed.

"You stop laughing, Joe," Mrs. Garner said. "I won't have Carl talk that way."

"Have you got an Indian girl, Nickie?" Joe asked.

"No."

"He has too, Pa," Frank said. "Prudence Mitchell's his girl."

"She's not."

"He goes to see her every day."

"I don't." Nick, sitting between the two boys in the dark, felt hollow and happy inside himself to be teased about Prudence Mitchell. "'She ain't my girl,'" he said.

"Listen to him," said Carl. "I see them together every day."

"Carl can't get a girl," his mother said, "not even a squaw."

Carl was quiet.

"Carl ain't no good with girls," Frank said.

"You shut up."

"You're all right, Carl," Joe Garner said. "Girls never got a man anywhere. Look at your pa."

"Yes, that's what you would say," Mrs. Garner moved close to Joe as the wagon jolted. "Well, you had plenty of girls in your time."

"I'll bet Pa wouldn't ever have had a squaw for a girl."

"Don't you think it," Joe said. "You better watch out to keep Prudie, Nick."

His wife whispered to him and Joe laughed.

"What you laughing at?" asked Frank

"Don't you say it, Garner," his wife warned. Joe laughed again.

"Nickie can have Prudence," Joe Garner said. "I got a good girl."

"That's the way to talk," Mrs. Garner said.

The horses were pulling heavily in the sand. Joe reached out in the dark with the whip.

"Come on, pull into it. You'll have to pull harder than this tomorrow."

They trotted down the long hill, the wagon jolting. At the farmhouse everybody got down. Mrs. Garner unlocked the door, went inside, and came out with a lamp in her hand. Carl and Nick unloaded the things from the back of the wagon. Frank sat on the front seat to drive to the barn and put up the horses. Nick went up the steps and opened the kitchen door. Mrs. Garner was building a fire in the stove. She turned from pouring kerosene on the wood.

"Good-by, Mrs. Garner," Nick said. "Thanks for taking me."

572

"Oh shucks, Nickie."

"I had a wonderful time."

"We like to have you. Won't you stay and eat some supper?"

"I better go. I think Dad probably waited for me."

"Well, get along then. Send Carl up to the house, will you?"

"All right."

"Good night, Nickie."

"Good night, Mrs. Garner."

Nick went out the farmyard and down to the barn. Joe and Frank were milking.

"Good night," Nick said. "I had a swell time."

"Good night, Nick," Joe Garner called. "Aren't you going to stay and eat?"

"No, I can't. Will you tell Carl his mother wants him?"

"All right. Good night, Nickie."

Nick walked barefoot along the path through the meadow below the barn. The path was smooth and the dew was cool on his bare feet. He climbed a fence at the end of the meadow, went down through a ravine, his feet wet in the swamp mud, and then climbed up through the dry beech woods until he saw the lights of the cottage. He climbed over the fence and walked around to the front porch. Through the window he saw his father sitting by the table, reading in the light from the big lamp. Nick opened the door and went in.

"Well, Nickie," his father said, "was it a good day?"

"I had a swell time, Dad. It was a swell Fourth of July."

"Are you hungry?"

"You bet."

"What did you do with your shoes?"

"I left them in the wagon at Garner's."

"Come on out to the kitchen."

Nick's father went ahead with the lamp. He stopped and lifted the lid of the ice-box. Nick went on into the kitchen. His father brought in a piece of old chicken on a plate and a pitcher of milk and put them on the table before Nick. He put down the lamp.

"There's some pie too," he said. "Will that hold you?"

"It's grand."

His father sat down in a chair beside the oil-cloth-covered table. He made a big shadow on the kitchen wall.

"Who won the ball game?"

"Petoskey. Five to three."

His father sat watching him eat and filled his glass from the milk-

pitcher. Nick drank and wiped his mouth on his napkin. His father reached over to the shelf for the pie. He cut Nick a big piece. It was huckleberry pie.

"What did you do, Dad?"

"I went out fishing in the morning."

"What did you get?"

"Only perch."

His father sat watching Nick eat the pie.

"What did you do this afternoon?" Nick asked.

"I went for a walk up by the Indian camp."

"Did you see anybody?"

"The Indians were all in town getting drunk."

"Didn't you see anybody at all?"

"I saw your friend, Prudie."

"Where was she?"

"She was in the woods with Frank Washburn. I ran onto them. They were having quite a time."

His father was not looking at him.

"What were they doing?"

"I didn't stay to find out."

"Tell me what they were doing."

"I don't know," his father said. "I just heard them threshing around."

"How did you know it was them?"

"I saw them."

"I thought you said you didn't see them."

"Oh, yes, I saw them."

"Who was it with her?" Nick asked.

"Frank Washburn."

"Were they—were they——"

"Were they what?"

"Were they happy?"

"I guess so."

His father got up from the table and went out the kitchen screen door. When he came back Nick was looking at his plate. He had been crying.

"Have some more?" His father picked up the knife to cut the pie.

"No," said Nick.

"You better have another piece."

"No, I don't want any."

His father cleared off the table.

"Where were they in the woods?" Nick asked.

"Up back of the camp." Nick looked at his plate. His father said, "You better go to bed, Nick."

"All right."

Nick went into his room, undressed, and got into bed. He heard his father moving around in the living room. Nick lay in the bed with his face in the pillow.

"My heart's broken," he thought. "If I feel this way my heart must be broken."

After a while he heard his father blow out the lamp and go into his own room. He heard a wind come up in the trees outside and felt it come in cool through the screen. He lay for a long time with his face in the pillow, and after a while he forgot to think about Prudence and finally he went to sleep. When he awoke in the night he heard the wind in the hemlock trees outside the cottage and the waves of the lake coming in on the shore, and he went back to sleep. In the morning there was a big wind blowing and the waves were running high up on the beach and he was awake a long time before he remembered that his heart was broken.

O. HENRY

O. HENRY (William Sydney Porter, American, 1862-1910). Imaginative, ironic storyteller, famous for surprise endings. At one time America's most widely read story writer. Author of some 600 tales. Characters drawn from everyday life, with sympathy for the underdog. Titles of collections: *Cabbages and Kings, The Four Million, Heart of the West.*

THE WHIRLIGIG OF LIFE

JUSTICE-OF-THE-PEACE BENAJA WIDDUP sat in the door of his office smoking his elder-stem pipe. Halfway to the zenith the Cumberland range rose blue-gray in the afternoon haze. A speckled hen swaggered down the main street of the "settlement," cackling foolishly.

Up the road came a sound of creaking axles, and then a slow cloud of dust, and then a bull-cart bearing Ransie Bilbro and his wife. The cart stopped at the Justice's door, and the two climbed down. Ransie was a narrow six feet of sallow brown skin and yellow hair.

The imperturbability of the mountains hung upon him like a suit of armor. The woman was calicoed, angled, snuff-brushed, and weary with unknown desires. Through it all gleamed a faint protest of cheated youth unconscious of its loss.

The Justice of the Peace slipped his feet into his shoes, for the sake of dignity, and moved to let them enter.

"We-all," said the woman, in a voice like the wind blowing through pine boughs, "wants a divo'ce." She looked at Ransie to see if he noted any flaw or ambiguity or evasion or partiality or self-partisanship in her statement of their business.

"A divo'ce," repeated Ransie, with a solemn nod. "We-all can't git along together nohow. It's lonesome enough fur to live in the mount'ins when a man and a woman keers fur one another. But when she's a-spittin' like a wildcat or a-sullenin' like a hoot-owl in the cabin, a man ain't got no call to live with her."

"When he's a no-'count varmint," said the woman, without any especial warmth, "a-traipsin' along of scalawags and moonshiners and a-layin' on his back pizen 'ith co'n whiskey, and a-pesterin' folks with a pack o' hungry, triflin' houn's to feed!"

"When she keeps a-throwin' skillet lids," came Ransie's antiphony, "slings b'ilin' water on the best coon-dog in the Cumberlands, and sets herself agin' cookin' a man's victuals, and keeps him awake o' nights accusin' him of a sight of doin's!"

"When he's al'ays a-fightin' the revenues, and gits a hard name in the mount'ins fur a mean man, who's gwine to be able fur to sleep o' nights?"

The Justice of the Peace stirred deliberately to his duties. He placed his one chair and a wooden stool for his petitioners. He opened his book of statutes on the table and scanned the index. Presently he wiped his spectacles and shifted his inkstand.

"The law and the statutes," said he, "air silent on the subjeck of divo'ce as fur as the jurisdiction of this co't air concerned. But, accordin' to equity and the Constitution and the golden rule, it's a bad barg'in that can't run both ways. If a justice of the peace can marry a couple, it's plain that he is bound to be able to divo'ce 'em. This here office will issue a decree of divo'ce and abide by the decision of the Supreme Co't to hold it good."

Ransie Bilbro drew a small tobacco-bag from his trousers pocket. Out of this he shook upon the table a five-dollar note. "Sold a b'er-skin and two foxes fur that," he remarked. "It's all the money we got."

576

"The regular price of a divo'ce in this co't," said the Justice, "air five dollars." He stuffed the bill into the pocket of his homespun vest with a deceptive air of indifference. With much bodily toil and mental travail he wrote the decree upon half a sheet of foolscap, and then copied it upon the other. Ransie Bilbro and his wife listened to his reading of the document that was to give them freedom:

"Know all men by these presents that Ransie Bilbro and his wife, Ariela Bilbro, this day personally appeared before me and promised that hereinafter they will neither love, honor, nor obey each other, neither for better nor worse, being of sound mind and body, and accept summons for divorce according to the peace and dignity of the State. Herein fail not, so help you God. Benaja Widdup, justice of the peace in and for the county of Piedmont, State of Tennessee."

The Justice was about to hand one of the documents to Ransie. The voice of Ariela delayed the transfer. Both men looked at her. Their dull masculinity was confronted by something sudden and unexpected in the woman.

"Judge, don't you give him that air paper yit. 'Tain't all settled, nohow. I got to have my rights first. I got to have my ali-money. 'Tain't no kind of a way to do fur a man to divo'ce his wife 'thout her havin' a cent fur to do with. I'm a-layin' off to be a-goin' up to brother Ed's up on Hogback Mount'in. I'm bound fur to hev a pa'r of shoes and some snuff and things besides. Ef Rance kin affo'd a divo'ce, let him pay me ali-money."

Ransie Bilbro was stricken to dumb perplexity. There had been no previous hint of alimony. Women were always bringing up startling and unlooked-for issues.

Justice Benaja Widdup felt that the point demanded judicial decision. The authorities were also silent on the subject of alimony. But the woman's feet were bare. The trail to Hogback Mountain was steep and flinty.

"Ariela Bilbro," he asked, in official tones, "how much did you 'low would be good and sufficient ali-money in the case befo' the co't."

"I 'lowed," she answered, "fur the shoes and all, to say five dollars. That ain't much fur ali-money, but I reckon that'll git me up to brother Ed's."

"The amount," said the Justice, "air not onreasonable. Ransie Bilbro, you air ordered by the co't to pay the plaintiff the sum of five dollars befo' the decree of divo'ce air issued."

"I hain't no mo' money," breathed Ransie, heavily. "I done paid you all I had."

"Otherwise," said the Justice, looking severely over his spectacles, "you air in contempt of co't."

"I reckon if you gimme till to-morrow," pleaded the husband, "I mout be able to rake or scrape it up somewhars. I never looked for to be a-payin' no ali-money."

"The case air adjourned," said Benaja Widdup "till to-morrow, you-all will present yo'selves and obey the order of the co't. Followin' of which the decrees of divo'ce will be delivered." He sat down in the door and began to loosen a shoestring.

"We mout as well go down to Uncle Ziah's," decided Ransie, "and spend the night." He climbed into the cart on one side, and Ariela climbed in on the other. Obeying the flap of his rope the little red bull slowly came around on a tack, and the cart crawled away in the nimbus arising from its wheels.

Justice-of-the-peace Benaja Widdup smoked his elder-stem pipe. Late in the afternoon he got his weekly paper, and read it until the twilight dimmed its lines. Then he lit the tallow candle on his table, and read until the moon rose, marking the time for supper. He lived in the double log cabin on the slope near the girdled poplar. Going home to supper he crossed a little branch darkened by a laurel thicket. The dark figure of a man stepped from the laurels and pointed a rifle at his breast. His hat was pulled down low, and something covered most of his face.

"I want yo' money," said the figure, "'thout any talk. I'm gettin' nervous, and my finger's a-wabblin on this here trigger."

"I've only got f-f-five dollars," said the Justice, producing it from his vest pocket.

"Roll it up," came the order, "and stick it in the end of this here gun-bar'l."

The bill was crisp and new. Even fingers that were clumsy and trembling found little difficulty in making a spill of it and inserting it (this with less ease) into the muzzle of the rifle.

"Now I reckon you kin be goin' along," said the robber.

The Justice lingered not on his way.

The next day came the little red bull, drawing the cart to the office door. Justice Benaja Widdup had his shoes on, for he was expecting the visit. In his presence Ransie Bilbro handed to his wife a five-dollar bill. The official's eye sharply viewed it. It seemed to curl up as though it had been rolled and inserted into the end of a

578

gun-barrel. But the Justice refrained from comment. It is true that other bills might be inclined to curl. He handed each one a decree of divorce. Each stood awkwardly silent, slowly folding the guarantee of freedom. The woman cast a shy glance full of constraint at Ransie.

"I reckon you'll be goin' back up to the cabin," she said, "along 'ith the bull-cart. There's bread in the tin box settin' on the shelf. I put the bacon in the b'ilin'-pot to keep the hounds from gittin' it. Don't forget to wind the clock to-night."

"You air a-goin' to your brother Ed's?" asked Ransie, with fine unconcern.

"I was 'lowin' to get along up thar afore night. I ain't sayin' as they'll pester theyselves any to make me welcome, but I hain't no-whar else fur to go. It's a right smart ways, and I reckon I better be goin'. I'll be a-sayin' good-bye, Ranse—that is, if you keer fur to say so."

"I don't know as anybody's a hound dog," said Ransie, in a martyr's voice, "fur to not want to say good-bye—'less you air so anxious to git away that you don't want me to say it."

Ariela was silent. She folded the five-dollar bill and her decree carefully, and placed them in the bosom of her dress. Benaja Widdup watched the money disappear with mournful eyes behind his spectacles.

And then with his next words he achieved rank (as his thoughts ran) with either the great crowd of the world's sympathizers or the little crowd of its great financiers.

"Be kind o' lonesome in the old cabin to-night, Ranse," he said.

Ransie Bilbro stared out at the Cumberlands, clear blue now in the sunlight. He did not look at Ariela.

"I 'low it might be lonesome," he said; "but when folks git mad and wants a divo'ce, you can't make folks to stay."

"Nobody never said they didn't."

"Nobody never said they did. I reckon I better start on now to brother Ed's."

"Nobody can't wind that old clock."

"Want me to go back along 'ith you in the cart and wind it fur you, Ranse?"

The mountaineer's countenance was proof against emotion. But he reached out a big hand and enclosed Ariela's thin brown one. Her soul peeped out once through her impassive face, hallowing it.

"Them hounds shan't pester you no more," said Ransie. "I reckon I been mean and low down. You wind that clock, Ariela."

"My heart, hit's in that cabin, Ranse," she whispered, "along 'ith you. I ain't a-goin' to git mad no more. Le's be startin', Ranse, so's we kin git home by sundown.'

Justice-of-the-peace Benaja Widdup interposed as they started for the door, forgetting his presence.

"In the name of the State of Tennessee," he said, "I forbid you-all to be a-defyin' of its laws and statutes. This co't is mo' than willin' and full of joy to see the clouds of discord and misunderstandin' rollin' away from two lovin' hearts, but it air the duty of the co't to p'eserve the morals and integrity of the State. The co't reminds you that you air no longer man and wife, but air divo'ced by regular decree, and as such air not entitled to the benefits and 'purtenances of the mattermonal estate."

Ariela caught Ransie's arm. Did those words mean that she must lose him now when they had just learned the lesson of life?

"But the co't air prepared," went on the Justice, "fur to remove the disabilities set up by the decree of divo'ce. The co't air on hand to perform the solemn ceremony of mari'ge, thus fixin' things up and enablin' the parties in the case to resume the honor'ble and elevatin' state of mattermony which they desires. The fee fur performin' said ceremony will be, in this case, to wit, five dollars."

Ariela caught the gleam of promise in his words. Swiftly her hand went to her bosom. Freely as an alighting dove the bill fluttered to the Justice's table. Her sallow cheek colored as she stood hand in hand with Ransie and listened to the reuniting words.

Ransie helped her into the cart, and climbed in beside her. The little red bull turned once more, and they set out, hand-clasped, for the mountains.

Justice-of-the-peace Benaja Widdup sat in his door and took off his shoes. Once again he fingered the bill tucked down in his vest pocket. Once again he smoked his elder-stem pipe. Once again the speckled hen swaggered down the main street of the "settlement," cackling foolishly.

JOHANN GOTTFRIED VON HERDER

JOHANN GOTTFRIED VON HERDER (German, 1744-1803). A sage among the poets. Disciple of Kant, friend of Goethe. Wrote many essays on literature *(On German Life and Art)*, translated folk songs *(Voices of the Nations in Song)*. A brilliant critic, important in shaping 18th and 19th century literature.

SIR OLAF

Sir Olaf he rideth west and east
To bid the folk to his bridal feast.

On the wold are dancing an elvish band,
And Erl-king's daughter proffers her hand.

"Now welcome, Sir Olaf: what haste's with thee?
Step into our circle and dance with me."

"To dance I neither will nor may,
To-morrow's dawn is my bridal-day."

"Nay, stay, Sir Olaf, and dance with me,
And golden spurs will I give to thee."

"To dance I neither will nor may,
To-morrow's dawn is my bridal-day."

"Nay, stay, Sir Olaf, and dance with me,
A heap of gold will I give to thee."

"For all thy gold I will not stay,
And dance I neither will nor may."

"If thou wilt not dance, Sir Olaf, with me,
Then Pest and Sickness shall follow thee."

She touched Sir Olaf upon the heart—
Ne'er in his life had he felt such smart.

She lifted him up on his steed that tide,
"Ride home! ride fast to thy troth-plight bride!"

And when he came to his castle-door,
His mother stood there, and trembled sore.

"Now say, sweet son, right speedilie
Why art thou wan, and white of blee?"

"Well may my face be wan and white.
I was in Erl-king's realm last night."

"Now tell me, my son so true and tried,
What thing shall I say to thy plighted bride?"

"Say that I hunt in the good greenwood,
With hound and horse as a good knight should."

When scarce the dawn in heaven shone red,
Came the train with the bride Sir Olaf should wed.

They sat at meat, they sat at wine;
"Now where is Sir Olaf, bridegroom of mine?"

"Sir Olaf rode out to the greenwood free,
With horse and hound to the hunt rode he."

The bride she lifted a cloth of red:
Beneath, Sir Olaf was lying dead.

ESTHONIAN BRIDAL SONG

Deck thyself, maiden,
With the hood of thy mother;
Put on the ribands
Which thy mother once wore:
On thy head the band of duty,
On thy forehead the band of care.
Sit in the seat of thy mother,
And walk in thy mother's footsteps.
And weep not, weep not, maiden:
If thou weepest in thy bridal attire,
Thou wilt weep all thy life.

582

HERMANN HESSE

HERMANN HESSE (German, 1877-   ). Swiss glorifier of nature and child-hood. After school, became locksmith and bookseller. Moved from Germany to Switzerland in 1912 to escape German militarism. Nobel Prize, 1946. *Peter Camenzind*, first successful novel. *Steppenwolf*, celebrated psychoanalytic novel. Others: *Demian, Death and the Lover, Magister Ludi*.

TALK IN A GONDOLA

What I dream, you ask? That yesterday
We had died, we two. In fair array—
Clad in white, our hair with flowers wound,
In our gondola we're seaward bound;
Bells from yonder campanile peal,
But the water gurgles round the keel,
Drowns the distant toll that's gently failing.
Onward, onward to the sea we're sailing,
Where the ships with masts that tower high,
Sombre shadows, rest against the sky,
Where on fishing-boats there gleam the moist
Deep-stained red and yellow sails they hoist,
Where the roaring mighty waves are swelling,
Where the sailors lurid tales are telling.
Through a gate of bluest water, deeply
Downward now our boat is gliding steeply.
In the depths we find a wid'ning range
Filled with many trees of coral strange,
Where in lustrous shells that hidden gleam
Pale gigantic pearls with beauty beam.
Silvery fishes pass us, glist'ning, shy,
Leaving tinted trails as they flit by,
In whose furrows other fish instead
Gleam with slender tails of golden red.
At the bottom, fathoms deep, we dream;
As if bells were calling it will seem,
Now and then, as if a wind that fanned
Sang us songs we cannot understand,
Songs of narrow streets we long ago
Left behind, of things we used to know,

Songs so far, far off about the ways
That we trod in long forgotten days.
And with wonder we'll remember slowly
Now a street, now some cathedral holy,
Or the shouting of a gondolier,
Many names that once we used to hear.
Smiling then as children smile in sleep,
Moving still our silent lips we keep,
And the word will, ere it spoken seems,
Fall into oblivion, death in dreams.
Over us the mighty vessels float,
Sails are bright on many a sombre boat,
Snow-white birds in gleaming sunshine fly,
Glistening nets upon the water lie,
Spanning all, with arches high and true
Glows the heavens' vault of sunlit blue.

IN THE FOG

In the fog to wander, how queer!
Lonely is every bush and stone,
No tree sees the other near,
Each is alone.

Once my world was full of friends,
When my life still had light;
Now that the fog descends,
Not one is in sight.

Only he is wise who knows
The steady gloom to fall
That slowly round him grows,
Severed from all.

In the fog to wander, how queer!
Solitude is life's own.
No man sees the other near,
Each is alone.

HITOMARO KAKINOMOTO

HITOMARO KAKINOMOTO (Japanese, *ca.* 655-710). Greatest of the Japanese Manyō poets. Nothing known of his life. Surviving work collected in the *Manyōshū*—scores of long poems and several hundred *tanka*, vigorous epics and delicate lyrics.

Poems from
THE MANYOSHU

In the sea of Iwami,
By the cape of Kara,
There amid the stones under sea
Grows the deep-sea *miru* weed;
There along the rocky strand
Grows the sleek sea-tangle.

Like the swaying sea-tangle,
Unresisting would she lie beside me—
My wife whom I love with a love
Deep as the *miru*-growing ocean.
But few are the nights
We two have lain together.

Away I have come, parting from her
Even as the creeping vines do part.
My heart aches within me;
I turn back to gaze—
But because of the yellow leaves
Of Watari Hill,
Flying and fluttering in the air,

I cannot see plainly
My wife waving her sleeve to me.
Now as the moon, sailing through the cloud rift
Above the mountain of Yakami,
Disappears, leaving me full of regret,
So vanishes my love out of sight;
Now sinks at last the sun,
Coursing down the western sky.

I thought myself a strong man,
But the sleeves of my garment
Are wetted through with tears.

585

My black steed
Galloping fast,
Away have I come,
Leaving under distant skies
The dwelling-place of my love.

Oh, yellow leaves
Falling on the autumn hill,
Cease a while
To fly and flutter in the air
That I may see my love's dwelling-place!

AFTER THE DEATH OF HIS WIFE

Since in Karu lived my wife,
I wished to be with her to my heart's content;
But I could not visit her constantly
Because of the many watching eyes—
Men would know of our troth,
Had I sought her too often
So our love remained secret like a rock-pent pool;
I cherished her in my heart,
Looking to after-time when we should be together,
And lived secure in my trust
As one riding a great ship.
Suddenly there came a messenger
Who told me she was dead—
Was gone like a yellow leaf of autumn.
Dead as the day dies with the setting sun,
Lost as the bright moon is lost behind the cloud,
Alas, she is no more, whose soul
Was bent to mine like the bending seaweed!

When the word was brought to me
I knew not what to do nor what to say;
But restless at the mere news,
And hoping to heal my grief
Even a thousandth part,
I journed to Karu and searched the market-place
Where my wife was wont to go!

There I stood and listened,
But no voice of her I heard,
Though the birds sang in the Unebi Mountain;
None passed by, who even looked like my wife.
I could only call her name and wave my sleeve.

ENVOYS

In the autumn mountains
The yellow leaves are so thick.
Alas, how shall I seek my love
Who has wandered away?—
I know not the mountain track.

I see the messenger come
As the yellow leaves are falling.
Oh, well I remember
How on such a day we used to meet—
My wife and I!

In the days when my wife lived,
We went out to the embankment near by—
We two, hand in hand—
To view the elm-trees standing there
With their outspreading branches
Thick with spring leaves. Abundant as their
    greenery
Was my love. On her leaned my soul.
But who evades mortality?—
One morning she was gone, flown like an early bird.
Clad in a heavenly scarf of white,
To the wide fields where the shimmering *kagero* rises
She went and vanished like the setting sun.

The little babe—the keepsake
My wife has left me—
Cries and clamours.
I have nothing to give; I pick up the child
And clasp it in my arms.

587

In her chamber, where our two pillows lie,
Where we two used to sleep together,
Days I spend alone, broken-hearted:
Nights I pass, sighing till dawn.

Though I grieve, there is no help;
Vainly I long to see her.
Men tell me that my wife is
In the mountains of Hagai—
Thither I go,
Toiling along the stony path;
But it avails me not,
For of my wife, as she lived in this world,
I find not the faintest shadow.

ENVOYS

To-night the autumn moon shines—
The moon that shone a year ago,
But my wife and I who watched it then together
Are divided by ever-widening wastes of time.

When leaving my love behind
In the Hikité mountains—
Leaving her there in her grave,
I walk down the mountain path,
I feel not like one living.

THE MOUNTAIN TOP

Because the plum trees on the peak
   Are up so high,
The buzz of bees about their bloom
   Comes from the sky!

MY LOVE WHO LOVES ME NOT

But who must at least come with the rest of the village to my funeral

If I die of love, why, let me die,
   For then, since I have died,
She'll cross the threshold where I lie
   And stand—once—by my side.

FRIEDRICH HOLDERLIN

FRIEDRICH HÖLDERLIN (German, 1770-1843). Classical poet of Germany.
A poor tutor, lost his reason as a man of thirty, spent better part of life as a
ward of a carpenter. Most of works published by friends after his madness.
Reputation slight in own day, grew later.

HYPERION'S SONG OF FATE

Ye wander there in the light
On flower-soft fields, ye blest immortal
   Spirits.
Radiant godlike zephyrs
Touch you as gently
As the hand of a master might
Touch the awed lute-string.
Free of fate as the slumbering
Infant, breathe the divine ones.
Guarded well
In the firm-sheathed bud
Blooms eternal
Each happy soul;
And their rapture-lit eyes
Shine with a tranquil
Unchanging lustre.
But we, 'tis our portion,
We never may be at rest.
They stumble, they vanish,
The suffering mortals,
Hurtling from one hard
Hour to another,
Like waves that are driven
From cliff-side to cliff-side,
Endlessly down the uncertain abyss.

EVENING PHANTASIE

Before his hut reposes in restful shade
The ploughman; wreaths of smoke from his hearth ascend.
   And sweet to wand'rers comes the tone of
     Evening bells from the peaceful village.

589

The sailor too puts into the haven now,
In distant cities cheerily dies away
   The busy tumult; in the arbor
     Gleams the festal repast of friendship.

But whither I? In labor, for slight reward
We mortals live; in alternate rest and toil
   Contentment dwells; but why then sleeps not
     Hid in my bosom the thorn unsparing?

The ev'ning heaven blooms as with springtime's hue;
Uncounted bloom the roses, the golden world
   Seems wrapt in peace; oh, bear me thither,
     Purple-wrought clouds! And may for me there

Both love and grief dissolve in the joyous light!
But see, as if dispelled by the foolish prayer,
   The wonder fades! 'Tis dark, and lonely
     Under the heaven I stand as erstwhile.

Come then to me, soft Sleep. Overmuch requires
The heart; and yet thou too at the last shalt fade,
   Oh youth, thou restless dream-pursuer!
     Peaceful and happy shall age then follow.

HOMER

HOMER (Greek, 9th century B.C.). According to tradition, the blind author
of the *Iliad* and the *Odyssey*, great epics based on the Greek legends. Exact
identity never established. Homer set standard for epic poetry of Western
literature: swift, brilliant narrative, primitive imagery, celebration of exploits
of a whole people through an epic hero.

PRIAM RECLAIMS HECTOR'S BODY

On did the old man pass; and he entered, and found the Peleides
Seated apart from his train: two only of Myrmidons trustful,
Hero Automedon only, and Alkimus, sapling of Ares,
Near to him minist'ring stood; he reposed him but now from the
    meal-time,

Sated with food and with wine, nor removed from him yet was the
table.
All unobserved of them entered the old man stately, and forthwith
Grasped with his fingers the knees and was kissing the hands of
Achilles—
Terrible, murderous hands, by which son upon son had been slaugh-
tered.
As when a man who has fled from his home with the curse of the
blood-guilt,
Kneels in a far-off land, at the hearth of some opulent stranger,
Begging to shelter his head, there is stupor on them that behold
him;
So was Achilles dumb at the sight of majestical Priam—
He and his followers all, each gazing on other bewildered.
But he uplifted his voice in their silence, and made supplication:
"Think of thy father at home" (he began), "O godlike Achilles!
Him, my coeval, like me within age's calamitous threshold.
Haply this day there is trouble upon him, some insolent neighbors
Round him in arms, nor a champion at hand to avert the disaster:
Yet even so there is comfort for him, for he hears of thee living;
Day unto day there is hope for his heart amid worst tribulation,
That yet again he shall see his beloved from Troia returning.
Misery only is mine; for of all in the land of my fathers,
Bravest and best were the sons I begat, and not one is remaining.
Fifty were mine in the hour that the host of Achaia descended:
Nineteen granted to me out of one womb, royally mothered,
Stood by my side; but the rest were of handmaids born in my dwell-
ing.
Soon were the limbs of the many unstrung in the fury of Ares:
But one peerless was left, sole prop of the realm and the people;
And now at last he too, the protector of Ilion, Hector,
Dies by thy hand. For his sake have I come to the ships of Achaia,
Eager to ransom the body with bountiful gifts of redemption.
Thou have respect for the gods, and on me, O Peleides! have pity,
Calling thy father to mind; but more piteous is my desolation,
Mine, who alone of mankind have been humbled to this of en-
durance
Pressing my mouth to the hand that is red with the blood of my
children."
  Hereon Achilles, awaked to a yearning remembrance of Peleus,

591

Rose up, took by the hand, and removed from him gently the old
    man.
Sadness possessing the twain—one, mindful of valorous Hector,
Wept with o'erflowing tears, low laid at the feet of Achilles;
He, sometime for his father, anon at the thought of Patroclus,
Wept, and aloft in the dwelling their long lamentation ascended.
But when the bursting of grief had contented the godlike Peleides,
And from his heart and his limbs irresistible yearning departed,
Then from his seat rose he, and with tenderness lifted the old man,
Viewing the hoary head and the hoary beard with compassion;
And he addressed him, and these were the air-winged words that
    he uttered:—
"Ah unhappy! thy spirit in truth has been burdened with evils.
How could the daring be thine to come forth to the ships of Achaia
Singly, to stand in the eyes of the man by whose weapon thy chil-
    dren,
Many and gallant, have died? full surely thy heart is of iron.
But now seat thee in peace, old man, and let mourning entirely
Pause for a space in our minds, although heavy on both be affliction;
For without profit and vain is the fullness of sad lamentation,
Since it was destined so of the gods for unfortunate mortals
Ever in trouble to live, but they only partake not of sorrow;
For by the threshold of Zeus two urns have their station of old time,
Whereof the one holds dolings of good, but the other of evil;
And to whom mixt are the doles of the thunder-delighting Kronion,
He sometime is of blessing partaker, of misery sometime;
But if he gives him the ill, he has fixed him the mark of disaster,
And over bountiful earth the devouring Necessity drives him,
Wandering ever forlorn, unregarded of gods and of mortals.
Thus of a truth did the gods grant glorious gifts unto Peleus,
Even from the hour of his birth, for above compare was he favored,
Whether in wealth or in power, in the land of the Myrmidons reign-
    ing;
And albeit a mortal, his spouse was a goddess appointed.
Yet even to him, of the god there was evil apportioned,—that never
Lineage of sons should be born in his home, to inherit dominion.
One son alone he begat, to untimely calamity foredoomed;
Nor do I cherish his age, since afar from the land of my fathers
Here in the Troas I sit, to the torment of thee and thy children.
And we have heard, old man, of thine ancient prosperity also,

Lord of whatever is held between Lesbos the seat of the Macar,
Up to the Phrygian bound and the measureless Hellespontos;
Ruling and blest above all, nor in wealth nor in progeny equaled:
Yet from the hour that the gods brought this visitation upon thee,
Day unto day is thy city surrounded with battles and bloodshed.
Howso, bear what is sent, nor be grieved in thy soul without ceas-
ing.
Nothing avails it, O king! to lament for the son that has fallen;
Him thou canst raise up no more, but thyself may have new tribu-
lation."
  So having said, he was answered by Priam the aged and god-
like:—
'Seat not me on the chair, O beloved of Olympus! while Hector
Lies in the tent uninterred; but I pray thee deliver him swiftly,
That I may see with mine eyes; and, accepting the gifts of redemp-
tion,
Therein have joy to thy heart; and return thou homeward in safety,
Since of thy mercy I live and shall look on the light of the morning."
  Darkly regarding the king, thus answered the rapid Achilles:—
"Stir me to anger no more, old man: of myself I am minded
To the release of the dead; for a messenger came from Kronion
Hither, the mother that bore me, the child of the Ancient of Ocean.
Thee, too, I know in my mind, nor has aught of thy passage escaped
me;
How that some god was the guide of thy steps to the ships of Achaia.
For never mortal had dared to advance, were he blooming in man-
hood,
Here to the host by himself; nor could sentinels all be avoided;
Nor by an imbecile push might the bar be dislodged at my bulwark.
Therefore excite me no more, old man, when my soul is in sorrow,
Lest to thyself peradventure forebearance continue not alway,
Suppliant all that thou art—but I break the behest of the godhead."
  So did he speak; but the old man feared, and obeyed his com-
mandment.
Forth of the door of his dwelling then leapt like a lion Peleides;
But not alone: of his household were twain that attended his going,
Hero Automedon first, and young Alkimus, he that was honored
Chief of the comrades around since the death of belovèd Patroclus.
These from the yoke straightway unharnessed the mules and the
horses,

And they conducted within the coeval attendant of Priam,
Bidding him sit in the tent; then swiftly their hands from the mule-
    wain,
Raise the uncountable wealth of the king's Hectorean head-gifts.
But two mantles they leave, and a tunic of beautiful texture,
Seemly for wrapping the dead as the ransomer carries him home-
    ward.
Then were the handmaidens called, and commanded to wash and
    anoint him,
Privately lifted aside, lest the son should be seen of the father,
Lest in the grief of his soul he restrain not his anger within him,
Seeing the corse of his son, but enkindle the heart of Achilles,
And he smite him to death, and transgress the command of Kronion.
But when the dead had been washed and anointed with oil by the
    maidens,
And in the tunic arrayed and enwrapt in the beautiful mantle,
Then by Peleides himself was he raised and composed on the hand-
    bier;
Which when the comrades had lifted and borne to its place in the
    mule-wain,
Then groaned he; and he called on the name of his friend, the
    beloved:—
"Be not wroth with me now, O Patroclus, if haply thou hearest,
Though within Hades obscure, that I yield the illustrious Hector
Back to his father dear. Not unworthy the gifts of redemption;
And unto thee will I render thereof whatsoever is seemly."

HORACE

HORACE (Roman, 65-8 B.C.). Latin poet, subtle, elegant, cheerful, profoundly
influential. One of notable group whose patron was the wealthy Maecenas.
Friend of Virgil. First work: *Satires*. Later: *Epistles, Odes*. His *Ars Poetica*,
written toward end of life, had permanent influence on all European criticism.

ODES

BOOK III, ODE 1

I scorn and shun the rabble's noise.
    Abstain from idle talk. A thing
    That ear hath not yet heard, I sing,
The Muses' priest, to maids and boys.

594

To Jove the flocks which great kings sway,
　　To Jove great kings allegiance owe.
　　Praise him: he laid the giants low:
All things that are, his nod obey.

This man may plant in broader lines
　　His fruit trees: that, the pride of race
　　Enlists a candidate for place:
In worth, in fame, a third outshines

His mates; or, thronged with clients, claims
　　Precedence. Even-handed Fate
　　Hath but one law for small and great:
That ample urn holds all men's names.

He o'er whose doomed neck hangs the sword
　　Unsheathed, the dainties of the South
　　Shall lack their sweetness in his mouth:
No note of bird or harpsichord

Shall bring him Sleep. Yet Sleep is kind,
　　Nor scorns the huts of laboring men;
　　The bank where shadows play, the glen
Of Temple dancing in the wind.

He, who but asks "Enough," defies
　　Wild waves to rob him of his ease;
　　He fears no rude shocks, when he sees
Arcturus set or Hædus rise:

When hailstones lash his vines, or fails
　　His farm its promise, now of rains
　　And now of stars that parch the plains
Complaining, unkindly gales.

—In straitened seas the fish are pent;
　　For dams are sunk into the deep:
　　Pile upon pile the builders heap,
And he, whom earth could not content,

The Master. Yet shall Fear and Hate
    Climb where the Master climbs: nor e'er
    From the armed trireme parts black Care;
He sits behind, the horseman's mate.

And if red marble shall not ease
    The heartache; nor the shell that shines
    Star-bright; nor all Falernum's vines,
All scents that charmed Achæmenes:

Why should I rear me halls of rare
    Design, on proud shafts mounting high?
    Why bid my Sabine vale good-by
For doubled wealth and doubled care?

EPODE 2

Alphius

Happy the man, in busy schemes unskilled,
    Who, living simply, like our sires of old,
Tills the few acres which his father tilled,
    Vexed by no thoughts of usury or gold;

The shrilling clarion ne'er his slumber mars,
    Nor quails he at the howl of angry seas;
He shuns the forum, with its wordy jars,
    Nor at a great man's door consents to freeze.

The tender vine-shoots, budding into life,
    He with the stately poplar tree doth wed,
Lopping the fruitless branches with his knife,
    And grafting shoots of promise in their stead;

Or in some valley, up among the hills,
    Watches his wandering herds of lowing kine,
Or fragrant jars with liquid honey fills,
    Or shears his silly sheep in sunny shine;

Or when Autumnus o'er the smiling land
　　Lifts up his head with rosy apples crowned,
Joyful he plucks the pears, which erst his hand
　　Graffed on the stem they're weighing to the ground;

Plucks grapes in noble clusters purple-dyed,
　　A gift for thee, Priapus, and for thee,
Father Sylvanus, where thou dost preside,
　　Warding his bounds beneath thy sacred tree.

Now he may stretch his careless limbs to rest,
　　Where some old ilex spreads its sacred roof;
Now in the sunshine lie, as likes him best,
　　On grassy turf of close elastic woof.

And streams the while glide on with murmurs low,
　　And birds are singing 'mong the thickets deep,
And fountains babble, sparkling as they flow,
　　And with their noise invite to gentle sleep.

But when grim winter comes, and o'er his grounds
　　Scatters its biting snows with angry roar,
He takes the field, and with a cry of hounds
　　Hunts down into the toils the foaming boar;

Or seeks the thrush, poor starveling, to ensnare,
　　In filmy net with bait delusive stored,
Entraps the traveled crane, and timorous hare,
　　Rare dainties these to glad his frugal board.

Who amid joys like these would not forget
　　The pangs which love to all its victims bears,
The fever of the brain, the ceaseless fret,
　　And all the heart's lamentings and despairs?

But if a chaste and blooming wife, beside,
　　The cheerful home with sweet young blossoms fills,
Like some stout Sabine, or the sunburnt bride
　　Of the lithe peasant of the Apulian hills

597

Who piles the hearth with logs well dried and old
    Against the coming of her wearied lord,
And, when at eve the cattle seek the fold,
    Drains their full udders of the milky hoard;

And bringing forth from her well-tended store
    A jar of wine, the vintage of the year,
Spreads an unpurchased feast,—oh then, not more
    Could choicest Lucrine oysters give me cheer,

Or the rich turbot, or the dainty char,
    If ever to our bays the winter's blast
Should drive them in its fury from afar;
    Nor were to me a welcomer repast

The Afric hen or the Ionic snipe,
    Than olives newly gathered from the tree,
That hangs abroad its clusters rich and ripe,
    Or sorrel, that doth love the pleasant lea,

Or mallows wholesome for the body's need,
    Or lamb foredoomed upon some festal day
In offering to the guardian gods to bleed,
    Or kidling which the wolf hath marked for prey.

What joy, amidst such feasts, to see the sheep,
    Full of the pasture, hurrying homewards come;
To see the wearied oxen, as they creep,
    Dragging the upturned plowshare slowly home!

Or, ranged around the bright and blazing hearth,
    To see the hinds, a house's surest wealth,
Beguile the evening with their simple mirth,
    And all the cheerfulness of rosy health!

Thus spake the miser Alphius; and, bent
    Upon a country life, called in amain
The money he at usury had lent;—
    But ere the month was out, 'twas lent again.

RICARDA HUCH

RICARDA HUCH (German, 1864-1947). Neo-romantic lyricist. Outstanding woman poet in modern German literature. Also wrote novels, including remarkable detective story, *The Deruga Trial*. Verse traditional in form, but rich in imagination and intuition.

MIDNIGHT

To this grave of mine
Come not in the morning,
Come on ways of darkness,
Dearest, by the dim moonshine.

For when through the skies
Bells are tolling midnight,
From my earthly prison
To the lovely air I rise.

In my death-dress white
On my grave I linger,
Watch the stars and measure
Time's placid tread at night.

Come and have no fear!
Can you still give kisses?
I forgot them never
While I slept the winters drear.

Kiss me hard and long.
In the east already
Sings the morning sunlight
—Lack-a-day!—its joyful song.

You were mine again!
Go and taste life's sweetness!—
I in deep, deep darkness
Sleep once more with pain.

VICTOR HUGO

VICTOR HUGO (French, 1802-1885). Chief exponent of the Romantic School of the drama; turned later to the novel. Among his main works: *The Punishments, Contemplation, The Legend of the Centuries, Les Misérables, The Hunchback of Notre Dame.* Also wrote poetry, somewhat stilted. Incurred displeasure of Napoleon III, was banished to the Channel Isles. The most widely known author of 19th century France.

LES MISERABLES

I.

Jean Valjean, Galley Slave

EARLY in October 1815, at the close of the afternoon, a man came into the little town of D——. He was on foot, and the few people about looked at him suspiciously. The traveller was of wretched appearance, though stout and robust, and in the full vigour of life. He was evidently a stranger, and tired, dusty, and wearied with a long day's tramp.

But neither of the two inns in the town would give him food or shelter though he offered good money for payment.

He was an ex-convict—that was enough to exclude him.

In despair he went to the prison, and asked humbly for a night's lodging, but the jailer told him that was impossible unless he got arrested first.

It was a cold night and the wind was blowing from the Alps; it seemed there was no refuge open to him.

Then, as he sat down on a stone bench in the market-place and tried to sleep, a lady coming out of the cathedral noticed him, and, learning his homeless state, bade him knock at the bishop's house, for the good bishop's charity and compassion were known in all the neighborhood.

At the man's knock the bishop, who lived alone with his sister, Madame Magloire, and an old housekeepes, said "Come in"; and the ex-convict entered.

He told them at once that his name was Jean Valjean, that he was a galley-slave, who had spent nineteen years at the hulks, and that he had been walking for four days since his release. "It is the same wherever I go," the man went on. "They all say to me, 'Be off!'

I am very tired and hungry. Will you let me stay here? I will pay."

"Madame Magloire," said the bishop, "please lay another knife and fork. Sit down, monsieur, and warm yourself. We shall have supper directly, and your bed will be got ready while you are supping."

Joy and amazement were on the man's face; he stammered his thanks as though beside himself.

The bishop, in honour of his guest, had silver forks and spoons placed on the table.

The man took his food with frightful voracity, and paid no attention to anyone till the meal was over. Then the bishop showed him his bed in an alcove, and an hour later the whole household was asleep.

Jean Valjean soon woke up again.

For nineteen years he had been at the galleys. Originally a pruner of trees, he had broken a baker's window and stolen a loaf one hard winter when there was no work to be had, and for this the sentence was five years. Time after time he had tried to escape, and had always been recaptured; and for each offence a fresh sentence was imposed.

Nineteen years for breaking a window and stealing a loaf! He had gone into prison sobbing and shuddering. He came out full of hatred and bitterness.

That night, at the bishop's house, for the first time in nineteen years, Jean Valjean had received kindness. He was moved and shaken. It seemed inexplicable.

He got up from his bed. Everyone was asleep, the house was perfectly still.

Jean Valjean seized the silver plate-basket which stood in the bishop's room, put the silver into his knapsack, and fled out of the house.

In the morning, while the bishop was breakfasting, the gendarmes brought in Jean Valjean. The sergeant explained that they had met him running away, and had arrested him, because of the silver they found on him.

"I gave you the candlesticks, too!" said the bishop; "they are silver. Why did not you take them with the rest of the plate?" Then, turning to the gendarmes, "It is a mistake."

"We are to let him go?" said the sergeant.

"Certainly," said the bishop.

The gendarmes retired.

"My friend," said the bishop to Jean Valjean, "here are your candlesticks. Take them with you." He added in a low voice, "Never forget that you have promised me to use this silver to become an honest man. My brother, you belong no longer to evil, but to good."

Jean Valjean never remembered having promised anything. He left the bishop's house and the town dazed and stupefied. It was a new world he had come into.

He walked on for miles, and then sat down by the roadside to think.

Presently a small Savoyard boy passed him, and as he passed dropped a two-franc piece on the ground.

Jean Valjean placed his foot upon it. In vain the boy prayed him for the coin. Jean Valjean sat motionless, deep in thought.

Only when the boy had gone on, in despair, did Jean Valjean wake from his reverie.

He shouted out, "Little Gervais, little Gervais!" for the boy had told him his name. The lad was out of sight and hearing, and no answer came.

The enormity of his crime came home to him, and Jean Valjean fell on the ground, and for the first time in nineteen years he wept.

II

Father Madeleine

On a certain December night in 1815 a stranger entered the town of M——, at the very time when a great fire had just broken out in the town hall.

This man at once rushed into the flames, and at the risk of his own life saved the two children of the captain of gendarmes. In consequence no one thought of asking for his passport.

The stranger settled in the town; by a happy invention he improved the manufacture of the black beads, the chief industry of M——, and in three years, from a very small capital, he became a rich man, and brought prosperity to the place.

In 1820, Father Madeleine, for so the stranger was called, was made Mayor of M—— by unanimous request, an honour he had declined the previous year. Before he came everything was languishing in the town, and now, a few years later, there was healthy life for all.

Father Madeleine employed everybody who came to him. The only

condition he made was—honesty. From the men he expected good-will, from the women, purity.

Prosperity did not make Father Madeleine change his habits. He performed his duties as mayor, but lived a solitary and simple life, avoiding society. His strength, although he was a man of fifty, was enormous. It was noticed that he read more as his leisure increased, and that as the years went by his speech became gentler and more polite.

One person only in all the district looked doubtfully at the mayor, and that was Javert, inspector of police.

Javert, born in prison, was the incarnation of police duty—implacable, resolute, fanatical. He arrived in M—— when Father Madeleine was already a rich man, and he felt sure he had seen him before.

One day in 1823 the mayor interfered to prevent Javert sending a poor woman, named Fantine, to prison. Fantine had been dismissed from the factory without the knowledge of M. Madeleine; and her one hope in life was her little girl, whom she called Cosette. Now, Cosette was boarded out at the village of Montfermeil, some leagues distance from M——, with a family grasping and dishonest, and to raise money for Cosette's keep had brought Fantine to misery and sickness.

The mayor could save Fantine from prison, he could not save her life; but before the unhappy woman died she had delivered a paper to M. Madeleine authorising him to take her child, and M. Madeleine had accepted the trust.

It was when Fantine lay dying in the hospital that Javert, who had quite decided in his own mind who M. Madeleine was, came to the mayor and asked to be dismissed from the service.

"I have denounced you, M. le Maire, to the prefect of police at Paris, as Jean Valjean, an ex-convict, who has been wanted for the robbery of a little Savoyard more than five years ago."

"And what answer did you receive?"

"That I was mad, for the real Jean Valjean has been found."

"Ah!"

Javert explained that an old man had been arrested for breaking into an orchard; that on being taken to the prison he had been recognised by several people as Jean Valjean, and that he, Javert, himself recognised him. To-morrow he was to be tried at Arras, and, as he was an ex-convict, his sentence would be for life.

Terrible was the anguish of M. Madeleine that night. He had

603

done all that man could do to obliterate the past, and now it seemed another was to be taken in his place. The torture and torment ended. In the morning M. Madeleine set out for Arras.

M. Madeleine arrived before the orchard-breaker was condemned. He proved to the court's astonishment that he, the revered and philanthropic Mayor of M——, was Jean Valjean, and that the prisoner had merely committed a trivial theft. Then he left the court, returned to M——, removed what money he had, buried it, and arranged his affairs.

A few days later Jean Valjean was sent back to the galleys at Toulon, and with his removal the prosperity of M—— speedily collapsed. This was in July 1823. In November of that year the following paragraph appeared in the Toulon paper.

"Yesterday, a convict, on his return from rescuing a sailor, fell into the sea and was drowned. His body has not been found. His name was registered as Jean Valjean."

III

A Hunted Man

At Christmas in the year 1823, an old man came to the village of Montfermeil, called at the inn, paid money to the rascally innkeeper, Thénardier, and carried off little Cosette to Paris.

The old man rented a large garret in an old house, and Cosette became inexpressibly happy with her doll and the good man who loved her so tenderly.

Till then Jean Valjean had never loved anything. He had never been a father, lover, husband, or friend. When he saw Cosette, and had rescued her, he felt his heart strangely moved. All the affection he had was aroused, and went out towards this child. Jean Valjean was fifty-five and Cosette eight, and all the love of his life, hitherto untouched, melted into a benevolent devotion.

Cosette, too, changed. She had been separated from her mother at such an early age that she could not remember her. And the Thénardiers had treated her harshly. In Jean Valjean she found a father, just as he found a daughter in Cosette.

Weeks passed away. These two beings led a wonderfully happy life in the old garret; Cosette would chatter, laugh, and sing all day.

Jean Valjean was careful never to go out in the daytime, but he began to be known in the district as "the mendicant who gives away money." There was one old man who sat by some church steps, and

who generally seemed to be praying, whom Jean Valjean always liked to relieve. One night when Jean Valjean had dropped a piece of money into his hand as usual, the beggar suddenly raised his eyes, stared hard at him, and then quickly dropped his head. The movement was like a flash. Jean Valjean started, and went home greatly troubled. The face which he fancied he had seen was that of Javert.

A few nights later Jean Valjean found that Javert had taken lodgings in the same house where he and Cosette lived. Taking the child by the hand, he at once set out for fresh quarters. They passed through silent and empty streets, and crossed the river, and it seemed to Jean Valjean that no one was in pursuit. But soon he noticed four men plainly shadowing him, and a shudder went over him. He turned from street to street, trying to escape from the city, and at last found himself entrapped in a *cul-de sac*. What was to be done?

There was no time to turn back. Javert had undoubtedly picketed every outlet. Fortunately for Jean Valjean, there was a deep shadow in the street, so that his own movements were unseen.

While he stood hesitating, a patrol of soldiers entered the street, with Javert at their head. They frequently halted. It was evident that they were exploring every hole and corner, and one might judge they would take a quarter of an hour before they reached the spot where Jean Valjean was. It was a frightful moment. Capture meant the galleys, and Cosette lost for ever. There was only one thing possible—to scale the wall which ran along a wide portion of the street. But the difficulty was Cosette; there was no thought of abandoning her.

First, Jean Valjean procured a rope from the lamp-post, for the lamps had not been lit that night owing to the moonlight. This he fastened round the child, taking the other end between his teeth. Half a minute later he was on his knees on top of the wall. Cosette watched him in silence. All at once she heard Jean Valjean saying in a very low voice. "Lean against the wall. Don't speak, and don't be afraid."

She felt herself lifted from the ground, and before she had time to think where she was she found herself on top of the wall.

Jean Valjean grasped her, put the child on his back, and crawled along the wall till he came to a sloping roof. He could hear the thundering voice of Javert giving orders to the patrol to search the *cul-de-sac* to the end.

Jean Valjean slipped down the roof, still carrying Cosette, and leaped on the ground. It was a convent garden he had entered.

On the other side of the wall the clatter of muskets and the imprecations of Javert resounded; from the convent came a hymn.

Cosette and Jean Valjean fell on their knees. Presently Jean Valjean discovered that the gardener was an old man whose life he had saved at M——, and who, in his gratitude, was prepared to do anything for M. Madeleine.

It ended in Cosette entering the convent school as a pupil, and Jean Valjean being accepted as the gardener's brother. The good nuns never left the precincts of their convent, and cared nothing for the world beyond their gates.

As for Javert, he had delayed attempting an arrest, even when his suspicions had been aroused, because, after all, the papers said the convict was dead. But once convinced, he hesitated no longer.

His disappointment when Jean Valjean escaped him was midway between despair and fury. All night the search went on; but it never occurred to Javert that a steep wall of fourteen feet could be climbed by an old man with a child.

Several years passed at the convent.

Jean Valjean worked daily in the garden, and shared the hut and the name of the old gardener, M. Fauchelevent. Cosette was allowed to see him for an hour every day.

The peaceful garden, the fragrant flowers, the merry cries of the children, the grave and simple women, gradually brought happiness to Jean Valjean; and his heart melted into gratitude for the security he had found.

IV

Something Higher Than Duty

For six years Cosette and Jean Valjean stayed at the convent; and then, on the death of the old gardener, Jean Valjean, now bearing the name of Fauchelevent, decided that as Cosette was not going to be a nun, and as recognition was no longer to be feared, it would be well to remove into the city.

So a house was taken in the Rue Plumet, and here, with a faithful servant, the old man dwelt with his adopted child. But Jean Valjean took other rooms in Paris, in case of accidents.

Cosette was growing up. She was conscious of her good looks, and she was in love with a well-connected youth named Marius, the son of Baron Pontmercy.

Jean Valjean learnt of this secret lovemaking with dismay. The idea of parting from Cosette was intolerable to him.

Then, in June, 1832, came desperate street fighting in Paris, and Marius was in command of one of the revolutionary barricades.

At this barricade Javert had been captured as a spy, and Jean Valjean, who was known to the revolutionaries, found his old, implacable enemy tied to a post, waiting to be shot. Jean Valjean requested to be allowed to blow out Javert's brain himself, and permission was given.

Holding a pistol in his hand, Jean Valjean led Javert, who was still bound, to a lane out of sight of the barricade, and there with his knife cut the ropes from the wrists and feet of his prisoner.

"You are free," he said. "Go; and if by any chance I leave this place alive, I am to be found under the name of Fauchelevent, in the Rue de l'Homme-Armé, No. 7."

Javert walked a few steps, and then turned back, and cried, "You worry me. I would rather you killed me!"

"Go!" was the only answer from Jean Valjean.

Javert moved slowly away; and when he had disappeared Jean Valjean discharged his pistol in the air.

Soon the last stand of the insurgents was at an end, and the barricade destroyed. Jean Valjean, who had taken no part in the struggle, beyond exposing himself to the bullets of the soldiers, was unhurt; but Marius lay wounded and insensible in his arms.

The soldiers were shooting down all who tried to escape. The situation was terrible.

There was only one chance for life—underground. An iron grating, which led to the sewers, was at his feet. Jean Valjean tore it open, and disappeared with Marius on his shoulders.

He emerged, after a horrible passage through a grating by the bank of the river, only to find there the implacable Javert!

Jean Valjean was quite calm.

"Inspector Javert," he said, "help me to carry this man home; then do with me what you please."

A cab was waiting for the inspector. He ordered the man to drive to the address Jean Valjean gave him. Marius, still unconscious, was taken to his grandfather's house.

"Inspector Javert," said Jean Valjean, "grant me one thing more. Let me go home for a minute; then you may take me where you will."

Javert told the driver to go to Rue de l'Homme-Armé, No. 7.

When they reached the house, Javert said, "Go up; I will wait here for you!"

But before Jean Valjean reached his rooms Javert had gone, and the street was empty.

Javert had not been at ease since his life had been spared. He was now in horrible uncertainty. To owe his life to an ex-convict, to accept this debt, and then to repay him by sending him back to the galleys was impossible. To let a malefactor go free while he, Inspector Javert, took his pay from the government was equally impossible. It seemed there was something higher and above his code of duty, something he had not come into collision with before. The uncertainty of the right thing to be done destroyed Javert, to whom life had hitherto been perfectly plain. He could not live recognising Jean Valjean as his saviour, and he could not bring himself to arrest Jean Valjean.

Inspector Javert made his last report at the police-station, and then, unable to face the new conditions of life, walked slowly to the river and plunged into the Seine, where the water rolls round and round in an endless whirlpool.

Marius recovered, and married Cosette; and Jean Valjean lived alone. He had told Marius who he was—Jean Valjean, an escaped convict; and Marius and Cosette gradually saw less and less of the old man.

But before Jean Valjean died Marius learnt the whole truth of the heroic life of the old man who had rescued him from the lost barricade. For the first time he realised that Jean Valjean had come to the barricade only to save him, knowing him to be in love with Cosette.

He hastened with Cosette to Jean Valjean's room; but the old man's last hour had come.

"Come closer, come closer, both of you," he cried. "I love you so much. It is good to die like this! You love me too, my Cosette. I know you've always had a fondness for the poor old man. And you, M. Pontmercy, will always make Cosette happy. There were several things I wanted to say, but they don't matter now. Come nearer, my children, I am happy in dying!"

Cosette and Marius fell on their knees, and covered his hands with kisses.

Jean Valjean was dead!

I

HENRIK IBSEN

HENRIK IBSEN (Norwegian, 1828-1906). From poor family. Was apprenticed to an apothecary. Decided to devote himself to poetry and playwrighting. Became theater director. Among major works: *Brand, Peer Gynt, A Doll's House, Ghosts, The Wild Duck, Hedda Gabler.* One of the great antagonists of social shams and pretenses.

PEER GYNT

Scene IX

Peer Gynt. (Throwing turban away)
There goes the Turk and Prophet—I'm Peer once more.
Those heathen customs I cannot endure.
I'm lucky that it's only a matter of clothes,
And not bred in the bone, as the old saw goes.
It behooves a man to live like a Christian,
To shun the gaudy peacock dress of a Pagan,
To fear God, walk in His steps, break no laws,
Be yourself and keep out of the devil's claws.
These folks will some day say kind words, revere
Your name, and place a wreath upon your bier.
                    (taking a few steps)
Why, that ornery rascal, that little faker!
She surely took me, hook, line and sinker.
She was on the verge of turning my head.
Well, that's over, thank heaven! The less said
The better. But it's some comfort, I was off guard
In a weak moment. Soothsaying's a hazard—
That's not my forte. After all, I'm still a man—

In courting the little goose, I was only human.
Ha! There's no fool like an old fool, they say.
(Bursts out laughing)
Sir Peter Gynt singing, dancing, so blithe and gay;
Strumming the lute, crowing like a rooster.
Ha! Then plucked by a hen of every feather.
Yes, plucked, plucked clean to the bone—
I have only a trifle I can call my own.
(feeling in his pockets)
A little cash in hand, in America some holdings—
Not quite broke, not enough to hobnob with kings.
I feel better foot-loose, with no trappings—
Horses, coachmen, servants and the like.
No! I'm not washed up yet. I'll soon strike
Something good; of course, as a merchantman
And lover, I'm finished. However, I don't plan
To retrace my steps. No, I'll turn over a new leaf.
I must find some noble task. I'll find relief—
Say in my autobiography. No, 'twould be too long,
I'll just write a history of the world—a song
Of humanity, with all its joy and grief.
Like a feather, I'll float down history's stream,
And make it live again, as in a dream.
(With quiet emotion)
See brave men battle for truth and right,
Of course, I'll keep safely out of sight;
See saints and sages sacrificed for spite;
See war, the trade of Kings, wax and wane;
See the conquering heroes come and go—
In short, I'll skim off the cream of history,
I'll give them something different and new,
I can always fall back on my lying.
Aye, I'll bury myself in antiquity
And forsake the beaten paths of the living.
The present's not worth a pair of shoe-strings.
Here, I think, I may find myself again.
Proud and vain are the ways of men and kings—
Their souls have no wings, their deeds no salt.
(Shrugs his shoulders)
And woman—ah, that's the Maker's fault!

610

Scene X

*A summer day, far up North. A hut in the woods. A door, with
a large wooden bar, stands open. Above the door a pair of large
antlers. A small herd of goats grazes by the side of the hut. Solveig,
now middle-aged but fair and comely, sits and spins outside in
the sunlight.*

Solveig.   (*Looks down the path and sings*)
The seasons slowly come and go;
   I know you will return some day;
   Here I abide, lad, and spin and pray
As I promised, lad, long, long ago.
            (*calls the goats, and spins and sings again*)
God guard you, wherever you are;
   God bless you when you kneel in prayer;
   I'll abide in thee, lad, forever;
If above, lad, I'll meet you there.

Scene XI

In Egypt, Dawn at the foot of the Statue of Memnon.

Peer Gynt.   (*Comes on, stops and looks around.*)
Just the right place for Gynt, the Historian
To begin. For the present I'm an Egyptian,
And, of course, with the emphasis on I.
Next, I'll take ancient Assyria on high.
To begin right back at the world's creation
Would lead only to trouble and confusion.
Anyhow, Bible lore's not popular to-day—
I'll just take a bird's-eye view, as they say.
I'll abridge or elaborate here and there,
Pick out the high spots in true Gynt flair—
When you describe a horse you don't enumerate
All the hairs in his tail.

611

MUHAMMAD IQBAL

MUHAMMAD IQBAL (Indian, 1876-1938). Foremost poet of Moslem India in 20th century. Uneventful life, educated at Lahore and in England, earned living as lawyer. Wrote in several languages, most of poetry in Urdu or Persian. Persian works are more philosophical, the Urdu more lyrical and popular. Strong social consciousness.

COMMUNITY

Upon what manner man is bound to man:
That tale's a thread, the end whereof is lost
Beyond unravelling. We can descry
The Individual within the Mass,
And we can pluck him as a flower is plucked
Out of the garden. All his nature is
Entranced with individuality,
Yet only in Society he finds
Security and preservation. On
The road of life, the furnace of life's fire,
That roaring battle-field, sets him aflame.
Men grow habituated each to each,
Like jewels threaded on a single cord;
Succour each other in the war of life
In mutual bond, like workmen bent upon
A common task. Through such polarity
The constellations congregate, each star
In several attraction keeping each
Poised firmly and unshaken. Caravans
May pitch their tents on mountain or on hill,
Broad meadow, fringe of desert, sandy mound.
Yet slack and lifeless hangs the warp and woof
Of the Group's labour, unresolved the bud
Of its deep meditation, still unplayed
The flickering levin of its instrument,
Its music hushed within its muted strings,
Unsmitten by the pounding of the quest,
The plectrum of desire; disordered still
Its new-born concourse, and so thin its wine
As to be blotted up with cotton flock;

New-sprung the verdure of its soil, and cold
The blood in its vine's veins; a habitat
Of demons and of fairy sprites its thoughts,
So that it leaps in terror from the shapes
Conjured by its own surmise; shrunk the scope
Of its crude life, its narrow thoughts confined
Beneath the rim of its constricting roof;
Fear for its life the meagre stock-in-trade
Of its constituent elements; its heart
Trembling before the whistle of the wind;
Its spirit shies away from arduous toil,
Little disposed to pluck at Nature's skirt,
But whatsoever springs of its own self
Or falls from heaven, that it gathers up.
Till God discovers a man pure of heart
In His good time, who in a single word
A volume shall rehearse; a minstrel he
Whose piercing music gives new life to dust.
Through him the unsubstantial atom glows
Radiant with life, the meanest merchandise
Takes on new worth. Out of his single breath
Two hundred bodies quicken; with one glass
He livens an assembly. His bright glance
Slays, but forthwith his single uttered word
Bestows new life, that so Duality
Expiring, Unity may come to birth.
His thread, whose end is knotted to the skies,
Weaves all together life's dissevered parts.
Revealing a new vista to the gaze,
He can convert broad desert and bare vale
Into a garden. At his fiery breath
A people leap like rue upon a fire
In sudden tumult, in their heart one spark
Caught from his kindling, and their sullen clay
Breaks instantly aflame. Where'er he treads
The earth receiving vision, every mote
May wink the eye at Moses' Sinai.
The naked understanding he adorns,
With wealth abundant fills its indigence,
Fans with his skirts its embers, purifies
Its gold of every particle of dross.

He strikes the shackles from the fettered slave,
Redeems him from his masters, and declares:
'No other's slave thou art, nor any less
Than those mute idols.' So unto one goal
Drawing each on, he circumscribes the feet
Of all within the circle of one Law,
Reschools them in God's wondrous Unity,
And teaches them the habit and the use
Of self-surrender to the Will Divine.

WASHINGTON IRVING

WASHINGTON IRVING (American, 1783-1859). First American man of letters, supporting self by writing. Traveled widely abroad, first American literary ambassador. Fame established with *The Sketch Book*, containing "Rip Van Winkle" and "The Legend of Sleepy Hollow." Interest in Spain created *The Alhambra*. Later became ambassador to Spain. Charm lies in his urbane style, genial temperament.

THE LEGEND OF THE ENCHANTED SOLDIER

EVERYBODY has heard of the Cave of St. Cyprian at Salamanca, where in old times judicial astronomy, necromancy, chiromancy, and other dark and damnable arts were secretly taught by an ancient sacristan; or, some will have it, by the devil himself in that disguise. The cave has long been shut up and the very site of it forgotten; though, according to tradition, the entrance was somewhere about where the stone cross stands in the small square of the seminary of Carvajal, and this tradition appears in some degree corroborated by the circumstances of the following story:—

There was at one time a student of Salamanca, Don Vicente by name, of that merry but mendicant class who set out on the road to learning without a penny in pouch for the journey, and who during college vacations beg from town to town and village to village to raise funds to enable them to pursue their studies through the ensuing term. He was now about to set forth on his wanderings, and, being somewhat musical, slung on his back a guitar with which to amuse the villagers and pay for a meal or a night's lodging.

614

As he passed by the stone cross in the seminary square he pulled off his hat and made a short invocation to St. Cyprian for good luck, when casting his eyes upon the earth he perceived something glitter at the foot of the cross. On picking it up, it proved to be a seal ring of mixed metal, in which gold and silver appeared to be blended. The seal bore as a device two triangles crossing each other so as to form a star. This device is said to be a cabalistic sign invented by King Solomon the Wise, and of mighty power in all cases of enchantment; but the honest student, being neither sage or conjurer, knew nothing of the matter. He took the ring as a present from St. Cyprian in reward of his prayer, slipped it on his finger, made a bow to the cross, and strumming his guitar set off merrily on his wandering.

The life of a mendicant student in Spain is not the most miserable in the world, especially if he has any talent at making himself agreeable. He rambles at large from village to village and city to city wherever curiosity or caprice may conduct him. The country curates, who, for the most part, have been mendicant students in their time, give him shelter for the night and a comfortable meal, and often enrich him with several quartos or halfpence in the morning. As he presents himself from door to door in the streets of the cities he meets with no harsh rebuff, no chilling contempt, for there is no disgrace attending his mendicity. Many of the most learned men in Spain have commenced their career in this manner; but if, like the student in question, he is a good-looking varlet and a merry companion, and, above all, if he can play the guitar, he is sure of a hearty welcome among the peasants, and smiles and favors from their wives and daughters.

In this way, then, did our ragged and musical son of learning make his way over half the kingdom, with the fixed determination to visit the famous city of Granada before his return. Sometimes he was gathered for the night into the fold of some village pastor; sometimes he was sheltered under the humble but hospitable roof of the peasant. Seated at the cottage door with his guitar he delighted the simple folk with his ditties; or striking up a fandango or bolero, set the brown country lads and lasses dancing in the mellow twilight. In the morning he departed with kind words from host and hostess.

At length he arrived at the great object of his musical vaga-bondizing, the far-famed city of Granada, and hailed with wonder and delight its Moorish towers, its lovely Vega, and its snowy

mountains glistening through a summer atmosphere. It is needless to say with what eager curiosity he entered its gates and wandered through its streets, and gazed upon its Oriental monuments. Every female face peering through a window or beaming from a balcony was to him a Zorayda or a Zelinda, nor could he meet a stately dame on the Alameda, but he was ready to fancy her a Moorish princess and to spread his student's robe beneath her feet.

His musical talent, his happy humor, his youth, and his good looks won him a universal welcome in spite of his ragged robes, and for several days he led a gay life in the old Moorish capital and its environs. One of his occasional haunts was the fountain of Avellanos, in the valley of the Darro. It is one of the popular resorts of Granada, and has been so since the days of the Moors; and here the student had an opportunity of pursuing his studies of female beauty, a branch of study to which he was a little prone.

Here he would take his seat with his guitar, improvise love ditties to admiring groups, or prompt with his music the ever ready dance. He was thus engaged one evening, when he beheld a padre of the Church advancing, at whose approach every one touched the hat. He was evidently a man of consequence; he certainly was a mirror of good, if not of holy, living; robust and rosy-faced, and breathing at every pore, with the warmth of the weather and the exercise of the walk. As he passed along he would every now and then draw a maravedi out of his pocket, and bestow it on a beggar, with an air of signal beneficence. "Ah, the blessed father!" would be the cry. "Long life to him, and may he soon be a bishop!"

To aid his steps in ascending the hill, he leaned gently now and then on the arm of a handmaid.

The good padre looked benignantly on the company about the fountain, and took his seat with some emphasis on a stone bench, while the handmaid hastened to bring him a glass of sparkling water. He sipped it deliberately, and with relish, tempering it with one of those spongy pieces of frosted eggs and sugar so dear to Spanish epicures, and on returning the glass to the hand of the damsel pinched her cheek with infinite loving-kindness.

"Ah, the good pastor!" whispered the student to himself. "What a happiness would it be to be gathered into his fold with such a damsel for a companion!"

But no such good fare was likely to befall him. In vain he essayed

616

those powers of pleasing which he had found so irresistible with country curates and country lasses. Never had he touched his guitar with such skill; never had he poured forth more soul-moving ditties; but he had no longer a country curate or country lass to deal with. The worthy priest evidently did not relish music, and the modest damsel never raised her eyes from the ground. They remained but a short time at the fountain. The good padre hastened their return to Granada. The damsel gave the student one shy glance in retiring, but it plucked the heart out of his bosom!

He inquired about them after they had gone. Padre Thomas was one of the saints of Granada, a model of regularity—punctual in his hour of rising; his hour of taking a paseo for an appetite; his hour of playing his game of tresillo, of an evening, with some of the dames of the cathedral circle; his hour of supping; and his hour of retiring to rest, to gather fresh strength for another day's round of similar duties. He had an easy, sleek mule for his riding; a matronly housekeeper, skilled in preparing titbits for his table.

Adieu now to the gay, thoughtless life of the student; the side glance of a bright eye had been the undoing of him. Day and night he could not get the image of this most modest damsel out of his mind. He sought the mansion of the padre. Alas! it was above the class of houses accessible to a strolling student like himself. The worthy padre had no sympathy with him; he had never been obliged to sing for his supper. He blockaded the house by day, catching a glance of the damsel now and then as she appeared at a casement; but these glances only fed his flame without encouraging his hope. He serenaded her balcony at night, and at one time was flattered by the appearance of something white at a window. Alas, it was only the nightcap of the padre.

Never was lover more devoted; never damsel more shy; the poor student was reduced to despair. At length arrived the eve of St. John, when the lower classes of Granada swarm into the country, dance away the afternoon, and pass midsummer's night on the banks of the Darro and the Xenil. Happy are they who, on this eventful night, can wash their faces in those waters just as the cathedral bell tells midnight; for at that precise moment they have a beautifying power. The student, having nothing to do, suffered himself to be carried away by the holiday-seeking throng until he found himself in the narrow valley of the Darro, below the lofty hill and ruddy towers of the Alhambra. The dry bed of the river,

the rocks which border it, the terraced gardens which overhang it, were alive with variegated groups, dancing under the vines and fig trees to the sound of the guitar and castanets.

The student remained for some time in doleful dumps, leaning against one of the huge misshapen stone pomegranates which adorn the ends of the little bridge over the Darro. He cast a wistful glance upon the merry scene, where every cavalier had his dame; or, to speak more appropriately, every Jack his Jill; sighed at his own solitary state, a victim to the black eye of the most unapproachable of damsels, and repined at his ragged garb, which seemed to shut the gate of hope against him.

By degrees his attention was attracted to a neighbor equally solitary with himself. This was a tall soldier, of a stern aspect and grizzled beard, who seemed posted as a sentry at the opposite pomegranate. His face was bronzed by time; he was arrayed in ancient Spanish armor, with buckler and lance, and stood immovable as a statue. What surprised the student was, that though thus strangely equipped, he was totally unnoticed by the passing throng, albeit that many almost brushed against him.

"This is a city of old-time peculiarities," thought the student, "and doubtless this is one of them with which the inhabitants are too famliar to be surprised." His own curiosity, however, was awakened; and, being of a social disposition, he accosted the soldier.

"A rare old suit of armor that which you wear, comrade. May I ask what corps you belong to?"

The soldier gasped out a reply from a pair of jaws which seemed to have rusted on their hinges.

"The royal guard of Ferdinand and Isabella."

"Santa Maria! Why, it is three centuries since that corps was in service."

"And for three centuries have I been mounting guard. Now I trust my tour of duty draws to a close. Dost thou desire fortune?"

The student held up his tattered cloak in reply.

"I understand thee. If thou hast faith and courage, follow me, and thy fortune is made."

"Softly, comrade. To follow thee would require small courage in one who has nothing to lose but life and an old guitar, neither of much value; but my faith is of a different matter, and not to be put in temptation. If it be any criminal act by which I am to mend my fortune, think not my ragged cloak will make me undertake it."

The soldier turned on him a look of high displeasure. "My sword," said he, "has never been drawn but in the cause of the faith and the throne. I am an old Christian; trust in me and fear no evil."

The student followed him, wondering. He observed that no one heeded their conversation, and that the soldier made his way through the various groups of idlers unnoticed, as if invisible.

Crossing the bridge, the soldier led the way by a narrow and steep path past a Moorish mill and aqueduct, and up the ravine which separates the domains of the Generalife from those of the Alhambra. The last ray of the sun shone upon the red battlements of the latter, which beetled far above; and the convent bells were proclaiming the festival of the ensuing day. The ravine was over-shadowed by fig trees, vines, and myrtles, and the outer towers and walls of the fortress. It was dark and lonely, and the twilight-loving bats began to flit about. At length the soldier halted at a remote and ruined tower, apparently intended to guard a Moorish aqueduct. He struck the foundation with the butt end of his spear. A rumbling sound was heard, and the solid stones yawned apart, leaving an opening as wide as a door.

"Enter in the name of the Holy Trinity," said the soldier, "and fear nothing." The student's heart quaked, but he made the sign of the cross, muttered his Ave Maria, and followed his mysterious guide into a deep vault cut out the solid rock under the tower, and covered with Arabic inscriptions. The soldier pointed to a stone seat hewn along one side of the vault. "Behold," said he, "my couch for three hundred years." The bewildered student tried to force a joke. "By the blessed St Anthony," said he, "but you must have slept soundly, considering the hardness of your couch."

"On the contrary, sleep has been a stranger to these eyes; incessant watchfulness has been my doom. Listen to my lot. I was one of the royal guards of Ferdinand and Isabella, but was taken prisoner by the Moors in one of their sorties, and confined a captive in this tower. When preparations were made to surrender the fortress to the Christian sovereigns, I was prevailed upon by an alfaqui, a Moorish priest, to aid him in secreting some of the treasures of Boabdil in this vault. I was justly punished for my fault. The alfaqui was an African necromancer, and by his infernal arts cast a spell upon me to guard his treasures. Something must have happened to him, for he never returned, and here I have remained ever since, buried alive. Years and years have rolled

619

away; earthquakes have shaken this hill; I have heard stone by stone of the tower above tumbling to the ground in the natural operation of time; but the spellbound walls of the vault have set both time and earthquakes at defiance.

"Once every hundred years, on the festival of St. John, the enchantment ceases to have thorough sway. I am permitted to go forth and post myself upon the bridge of the Darro, where you met me, waiting until some one shall arrive who may have power to break this magic spell. I have hitherto mounted guard there in vain. I walk as in a cloud, concealed from mortal sight. You are the first to accost me for now three hundred years. I behold the reason. I see on your finger the seal ring of Solomon the Wise, which is proof against all enchantment. With you it remains to deliver me from this awful dungeon, or to leave me to keep guard here for another hundred years."

The student listened to this tale in mute wonderment. He had heard many tales of treasure shut up under strong enchantment in the vaults of the Alhambra, but had treated them as fables. He now felt the value of the seal ring, which had, in a manner, been given to him by St. Cyprian. Still, though armed by so potent a talisman, it was an awful thing to find himself tête-à-tête in such a place with an enchanted soldier, who, according to the laws of nature, ought to have been quietly in his grave for nearly three centuries.

A personage of this kind, however, was quite out of the ordinary run, and not to be trifled with, and he assured him he might rely upon his friendship and good will to do everything in his power for his deliverance.

"I trust to a motive more powerful than friendship," said the soldier.

He pointed to a ponderous iron coffer, secured by locks inscribed with Arabic characters. "That coffer," said he, "contains countless treasure in gold and jewels and precious stones. Break the magic spell by which I am enthralled, and one-half of this treasure shall be thine."

"But how am I to do it?"

"The aid of a Christian priest and a Christian maid is necessary; the priest to exorcise the powers of darkness, the damsel to touch this chest with the seal of Solomon. This must be done at night. But have a care. This is solemn work, and not to be effected by

620

the carnal-minded. The priest must be an old Christian, a model of sanctity; and must mortify the flesh, before he comes here, by a rigorous fast of four-and-twenty hours; and as to the maiden, she must be above reproach, and proof against temptation. Linger not in finding such aid. In three days my furlough is at an end; if not delivered before midnight of the third, I shall have to mount guard for another century."

"Fear not," said the student, "I have in my eye the very priest and damsel you describe; but how am I to regain admission to this tower?"

"The seal of Solomon will open the way for thee."

The student issued forth from the tower much more gaily than he had entered. The wall closed behind him, and remained solid as before.

The next morning he repaired boldly to the mansion of the priest, no longer a poor, strolling student, thrumming his way with a guitar; but an ambassador from the shadowy world, with enchanted treasures to bestow. No particulars are told of his negotiation, excepting that the zeal of the worthy priest was easily kindled at the idea of rescuing an old soldier of the faith and a strong box of King Chico from the very clutches of Satan; and then what alms might be dispensed, what churches built, and how many poor relatives enriched with the Moorish treasure!

As to the handmaid, she was ready to lend her hand, which was all that was required, to the pious work; and if a shy glance now and then might be believed, the ambassador began to find favor in her modest eyes.

The greatest difficulty, however, was the fast to which the good padre had to subject himself. Twice he attempted it, and twice the flesh was too strong for the spirit. It was only on the third day that he was enabled to withstand the temptations of the cupboard; but it was still a question whether he would hold out until the spell was broken.

At a late hour of the night the party groped their way up the ravine, by the light of a lantern, and bearing a basket with provisions for exorcising the demon of hunger so soon as the other demons should be laid in the Red Sea.

The seal of Solomon opened their way into the tower. They found the soldier, seated on the enchanted strong box, awaiting their arrival. The exorcism was performed in due style. The damsel advanced, and touched the locks of the coffer with the seal of

621

Solomon. The lid flew open, and such treasures of gold and jewels and precious stones as flashed upon the eye!

"Here's cut, and come again!" cried the student, exultingly, as he proceeded to cram his pockets.

"Fairly and softly," exclaimed the soldier. "Let us get the coffer out entire, and then divide."

They accordingly went to work with might and main, but it was a difficult task; the chest was enormously heavy, and had been embedded there for centuries. While they were thus employed, the good dominie drew on one side, and made a vigorous onslaught on the basket, by way of exorcising the demon of hunger which was raging within him. In a little while a fat capon was devoured, and washed down by a deep potation; and, by way of grace after meat, he gave a kind-hearted kiss to the damsel who waited on him. It was quietly done in a corner, but the tell-tale walls babbled it forth as if in triumph. Never was chaste salute more awful in its effects. At the sound the soldier gave a great cry of despair; the coffer, which was half raised, fell back in its place and was locked once more. Priest, student, and damsel found themselves outside of the tower, the wall of which closed with a thundering jar. Alas! the good padre had broken his fast too soon.

When recovered from his surprise, the student would have re-entered the tower, but learnt to his dismay that the damsel, in her fright, had let fall the seal of Solomon; it remained within the vault.

In a word, the cathedral bell tolled midnight; the spell was renewed; the soldier was doomed to mount guard for another hundred years; and there he and the treasure remain to this day, and all because the kind-hearted padre kissed his handmaid.

Thus ends the legend as far as it has been authenticated. There is a tradition, however, that the student had brought off treasure enough in his pocket to set him up in the world; that he prospered in his affairs, that the worthy padre gave him the damsel in marriage, by way of amends for the blunder in the vault; and she proved a pattern for wives.

The story of the enchanted soldier remains one of the popular traditions of Granada, though told in a variety of ways; the common people affirm that he still mounts guard on midsummer eve, beside the gigantic stone pomegranate on the bridge of the Darro, but remains invisible excepting to such lucky mortal as may possess the seal of Solomon.

J

JENS PETER JACOBSEN

JENS PETER JACOBSEN (Danish, 1847-1885). Danish realistic novelist and poet. Sought to find the laws of nature in the realm of literature. Disciple of great Danish critic Brandes. Worked with such care that he produced only two novels *(Fru Marie Grubbe, Niels Lyhne)*, a volume of tales *(Mogens and Other Stories)*, and a few poems.

THE PLAGUE AT BERGAMO

OLD Bergamo lay up there at the top of a squatty mountain encircled by walls and towers. New Bergamo lay below at the foot of the mountain, exposed to every wind that blows.

In the new town the plague broke out and wrought havoc indescribable. Many died, and the rest fled across the plains to every point of the compass. The men of Old Bergamo set fire to the deserted town, to disinfect the air. In vain. Men began to die on the mountain, also; at first one a day, then five, then ten, then a dozen.

There were many who sought to escape, but they could not flee as those in the new town had done; they lived like hunted beasts, hiding in tombs, under bridges, behind hedges, and in the tall grass of the green fields. For the peasants stoned all strangers from their hearths, or beat them as they would mad dogs, cruelly, pitilessly— in self-protection, as they thought, for the first fugitives had brought with them the pestilence into their houses.

So the people of Old Bergamo were as prisoners in their own town. Day by day the sun blazed hotter, and day by day the terrible infection carried off more victims.

In the very beginning, when the plague came among them, they bound themselves together in unity and peace, and had taken care to decently bury the dead, and had kindled great fires in the mar-

kets and open places, so that the purging fumes might be blown through the streets. Juniper and vinegar had been given to the poor. Above all they had gone to church, early and late, singly and in processions; each day they lifted their voices in prayer. As the sun sank behind the mountains the church bells tolled their dirge from a hundred hanging mouths. Days were set aside for fasting, and the relics were placed upon the altars.

At last, in their extremity, amid the blare of trumpets and tubas, they proclaimed the Holy Virgin forevermore Podesta of the city.

All this was of no help. And when the people saw that nothing could aid them, that Heaven either would not or could not send them relief, they did not fold their hands together and say, "God's will be done." It was as if sin, growing by a secret, stealthy sickness, had flared into an evil, open, raging pestilence, stalking hand in hand with the body's disease, the one to kill their souls, even as the other defiled their flesh—so incredible were their deeds, so monstrous their cruelty.

"Let us eat to-day, for to-morrow we die!" It was as if this theme, set to music, were played in an endless, devilish symphony on instruments without number. The most unnatural vices flourished among them. Even such rare arts as necromancy, sorcery, and devil worship became familiar to them; for there were many who sought from the powers of hell that protection which Providence had not been willing to accord them. Everything that suggested charity and sympathy had vanished; each thought only of himself. If a beggar, faint with the first delirium of the plague, fell in the street, he was driven from door to door with sharp weapons and with stones. From the dead that lay rotting in the houses, and from the bodies hastily buried in the earth, arose a sickening stench that mingled with the heavy air of the streets, and drew ravens and crows hither in swarms and in clouds, so that the walls and housetops were black with them. And about the town walls great strange birds perched here and there—birds that came from afar, with rapacious beaks and talons expectantly curved; and they sat and stared with their quiet, hungry eyes as if awaiting the moment when the doomed town would be reduced to a heap of carrion.

Eleven weeks had passed since the plague had first broken out. Then the tower watchman and others who chanced to be on high ground perceived a singular procession winding from the plains into the narrow streets of the new town, between the smoke-blackened stone walls and the charred frames of houses. A great

624

throng! Assuredly six hundred and more, men and women, young and old. Some among them bore large, black crosses, and some held above their heads broad banners, red as blood and fire. They sang as they marched, and strange, despairingly plaintive melodies rose in the still, oppressively hot air.

Brown, gray, black, were the colors these people wore. Yet all had a red sign on their breasts. As they came nearer and nearer this was seen to be the sign of the cross. They crowded up the steep, stone-girt space that led to the old town. Their faces were as waves of white sea; they bore scourges in their hands; a rain of fire was painted on their banners. And in the surging mass the black crosses swung from side to side. Face after face plunged into the gloom of the tower gate and emerged into the light on the other side with blinking eyes.

Then the chant was taken up anew—a *miserere*. They grasped their scourges and marched even more sturdily than if their chant had been a battle song. Their aspect was that of a people who had come from a starving town. Their cheeks were sunken; their cheekbones protruded; their lips were bloodless, and dark rings encircled their eyes. All the scourges were stained with blood.

With astonishment and uneasiness all Bergamo flocked together to gaze upon them. Red, bloated faces stood out against those that were pale; heavy, lust-weary eyes were lowered before the keen, flashing glances of the pilgrims; grinning, blasphemous mouths were struck dumb by these chants. The townspeople were spellbound.

But it was not long before the pall was shaken off. Some recognized among the cross-bearers a half-crazed cobbler of Brescia, and in a moment the procession became a butt of ridicule. Moreover, this was something new, a diversion from the monotony of everyday life, and as the strangers marched on to the cathedral, they were followed as a band of jugglers might be or as a tame bear is followed.

But soon anger seized the jostling crowd. It was clear that these cobblers and tailors had come to convert them, to pray, and to speak words that none wished to hear. Two gaunt, grizzled philosophers who had formulated blasphemy into a system incited the populace out of sheer wickedness of heart, so that the mob grew more threatening as the procession marched to the church, and more fiercely enraged. Bergamo was about to lay hands on these singular, scourge-bearing tailors. Not a hundred paces from the portal of the church a tavern opened its doors and a whole band of

625

roisterers poured out, one on the shoulders of another. And they took their places at the head of the procession, singing and howling, assuming a mock-religious mien—all save one, who jerked his thumbs contemptuously toward the grass-grown steps of the church. Rough laughter then arose, and pilgrims and blasphemers entered the sanctuary in peace.

It was strange to be in that place again, to roam through the great cool nave, in air heavy with the stale fumes of snuffed wax tapers, over sunken flagstones so familiar to the foot, and over stones with their worn ornaments and polished inscriptions, in contemplation of which the mind had often grown so weary. And while the eye, half curiously, half involuntarily rested in the dim half-light of the vaults or strayed over the mellow gaudiness of dusty gold and grimy colors, or began to lose itself in the grotesque shadows of the apse, a kind of longing arose, not to be suppressed.

Meanwhile the tavern roisterers played their pranks on the main altar itself. A tall, strong young butcher removed his white apron and wound it about his neck so that it hung at his back like a cloak. Thus arrayed, he celebrated mass, with the wildest and most shocking words of sacrilege. A small, elderly, round-bellied fellow, lively and agile in spite of his fat, with the face of a peeled pumpkin, played sexton and responded with ribald songs; he made his genuflexions and turned his back upon the altar, and rang his bell like a clown; and the other tipplers, as they made their genuflexions, threw themselves flat on the ground and roared with laughter, hiccuping drunkenly.

All within the church laughed, hooted, and jeered at the strangers, and bade them notice how God was esteemed in Old Bergamo. Yet they wished not so much to mock God as to rack the souls of these penitents with their impiety.

In the centre of the nave the pilgrims halted and groaned, such was their anguish. Their blood boiled with hate, and they thirsted for vengeance. They prayed to God, with hands and eyes uplifted, that He might smite His blasphemers for the mockery offered Him in His house. Gladly would they perish with the presumptuous infidels, if He would but show His might; blissfully would they be crushed beneath His feet, if He would but triumph, and if these godless throats might be made to shriek in agony and despair.

They lifted up their voices in a *miserere*, each note of which rang like a prayer for that rain of fire that once swept over Sodom, for the strength that was Samson's when he grasped the pillars of the

626

Philistine temple. They prayed with words and with song; they bared their shoulders and prayed with their scourges. Kneeling, row on row, stripped to the waist they whirled stinging, knotted cords over their backs.

Frantically they scourged, until the blood spurted under their hissing lashes. Each stroke was an offering to God. Stroke on stroke came down, until arms sank or were cramped into knots. Thus they lay, row on row, with frenzied look and foaming mouth, blood dripping from their bodies.

And those that saw this of a sudden felt their hearts beat, felt the blood mount to their temples, their breathing grow hard. Their knees shook. To be the slave of a powerful, stern divinity, to fling one's self at the feet of the Lord, to be His own, not in mute devotion, not in the mild inefficacy of prayer, but in a fury of passion, in the intoxication of self-humiliation, in blood and lamentation, and smitten with the moist, glistening tongues of scourges—this they could understand. Even the butcher held his peace; and the toothless philosophers bowed their grizzled heads.

Silence reigned in the church; only a gentle breathing passed through the multitude.

Then one of the strangers, a young friar, rose and spoke. His was the pallor of bloodless flesh; his black eyes glowed; and the sad lines of his mouth were as if cut with a knife in wood, and not mere furrows in a human face.

He lifted up his thin, suffering hands in prayer to Heaven, and the black sleeves of his gown slipped back from his lean arms.

Then he spoke—of hell, of its eternity, of the eternity of Heaven, of the solitary world of pain which each of the damned must suffer and must fill with his cries of agony. In that world were seas of sulphur, meadows of wasps, flames to be wrapped about them like a cloak, and hard flames that would pierce them like a probe twisting in a wound.

Breathlessly all listened to his words; for he spoke as if he had seen these things with his own eyes. And they asked themselves: "Is this man not one of the damned, sent to us from the mouth of hell, to testify?"

Then he preached long of the commandments and their rigor, of the need of obeying them to the very letter, and of the dire punishment that awaited him who sinned against them. "'But Christ died for our sins,' ye say. 'We are no longer bound by the Word.' But I say that hell will not be cheated of one of you, and not one of the

iron teeth of hell's wheel will your flesh escape. Ye build upon Calvary's cross? Come! Come and see it! I will lead you to its foot. It was on a Friday, as ye know, when they cast Him from their gates and laid the heavier end of a cross upon His shoulders and suffered Him to bear it to a barren and naked hill without the city; and they walked beside Him and stirred up the dust with their feet, so that it rested over them like a red cloud. And they tore His garments from Him, even as the lords of justice strip a criminal before all eyes, that all might see His body. And they threw Him down upon His cross, and stretched Him upon it, and drove an iron nail through each of His unresistant hands and a nail through His crossed feet. And they raised the cross in a hole dug in the earth; but it would stand neither firm nor upright. So they shook it and drove wedges and blocks around it. And those that did this turned down the brims of their hats so that the blood of His hands might not drip into their eyes.

"And He from on high looked down upon the soldiers casting dice for His seamless coat, and down upon all the howling mob for whose salvation He suffered. Not one tearful eye was there in all the multitude. And those who were below looked up at Him, hanging from the cross, suffering, and faint. They read the inscription above His head: 'King of the Jews,' and they mocked Him and called up to Him: 'Thou that destroyest the temple, and buildest it in three days, save Thyself. If Thou be the Son of God, come down from the cross.'

"Then God's noble Son waxed wroth and saw that these were unworthy of salvation, this mob that swarmed over the earth; and He wrenched His feet from the nail, and He clenched His fingers and tore His hands away, so that the arms of the cross bent as a bow. And He leaped to the earth and caught up His garment, so that the dice rolled over the precipice of Golgotha, and threw it about His person with the righteous wrath of a king, and ascended into heaven. And the cross stood bare; and the great work of atonement remained unfulfilled. No mediator stands between us and God. No Jesus died for us on the cross! No Jesus died for us on the cross!"

He ceased.

As he uttered the last words he bent toward the multitude and with his lips and hands flung his words, as it were, upon their heads. A groan of fear ran through the church. Sobs could be heard.

Then the butcher with uplifted, threatening hands, pallid as a

corpse, stepped forward and commanded:

"Monk, nail Him to the cross again, nail Him—!"

And from all lips, pleadingly, threateningly, a storm of voices rolled to the vault above: "Crucify Him!"

But the monk looked down upon these fluttering, uplifted hands, upon these distorted faces with the dark openings of their screaming mouths, from which the teeth flashed like those of tormented beasts of prey; and in the ecstasy of the moment he extended his arms toward Heaven, and laughed. Then he descended; and his people raised the banners of the fiery rain and their plain, black crosses and pushed out of the church. Once more they marched, singing, across the marketplace, and once more they passed through the mouth of the tower gate.

And the people of Old Bergamo stared after them, as they proceeded down the mountain. The steep, wall-girt road was obscured in the uncertain light of the setting sun, and the procession could be only half seen in the glare. Their huge crosses, swaying in the crowd from side to side, cast sharp, black shadows on the glowing walls of the town.

In the distance a chant could be heard. A banner or two gleamed red from the charred site of the new town, and the pilgrims vanished into the bright plain.

HENRY JAMES

HENRY JAMES (American, 1843-1916). Novelist and critic, noted as precise stylist. Educated in Europe, led cosmopolitan life, eventually became British citizen. Favorite theme: contrast between naïve Americans and sophisticated Europeans. Later writing became more and more subtle, overrefined, idiosyncratic. Some of novels: *The American, The Portrait of a Lady, The Wings of the Dove, Washington Square, The Ambassadors, The Golden Bowl.*

CONFIDENCE

CHAPTER I

IT WAS in the early days of April; Bernard Longueville had been spending the winter in Rome. He had travelled northward with the consciousness of several social duties that appealed to him from the further side of the Alps, but he was under the charm of the Italian

629

spring, and he made a pretext for lingering. He had spent five days at Siena, where he had intended to spend but two, and still it was impossible to continue his journey. He was a young man of a contemplative and speculative turn, and this was his first visit to Italy, so that if he dallied by the way he should not be harshly judged. He had a fancy for sketching, and it was on his conscience to take a few pictorial notes. There were two old inns at Siena, both of them very shabby and very dirty. The one at which Longueville had taken up his abode was entered by a dark, pestiferous archway, surmounted by a sign which at a distance might have been read by the travellers as the Dantean injunction to renounce all hope. The other was not far off, and the day after his arrival, as he passed it, he saw two ladies going in who evidently belonged to the large fraternity of Anglo-Saxon tourists, and one of whom was young and carried herself very well. Longueville had his share—or more than his share—of gallantry, and this incident awakened a regret. If he had gone to the other inn he might have had charming company: at his own establishment there was no one but an æsthetic German who smoked bad tobacco in the dining-room. He remarked to himself that this was always his luck, and the remark was characteristic of the man; it was charged with the feeling of the moment, but it was not absolutely just; it was the result of an acute impression made by the particular occasion; but it failed in appreciation of a providence which had sprinkled Longueville's career with happy accidents—accidents, especially, in which his characteristic gallantry was not allowed to rust for want of exercise. He lounged, however, contentedly enough through these bright, still days of a Tuscan April, drawing much entertainment from the high picturesqueness of the things about him. Siena, a few years since, was a flawless gift of the Middle Ages to the modern imagination. No other Italian city could have been more interesting to an observer fond of reconstructing obsolete manners. This was a taste of Bernard Longueville's, who had a relish for serious literature, and at one time had made several lively excursions into mediæval history. His friends thought him very clever, and at the same time had an easy feeling about him which was a tribute to his freedom from pedantry. He was clever, indeed, and an excellent companion; but the real measure of his brilliancy was in the success with which he entertained himself. He was much addicted to conversing with his own wit, and he greatly enjoyed his own society. Clever as he often was in talking with his friends, I am not sure that his best things, as the

phrase is, were not for his own ears. And this was not on account
of any cynical contempt for the understanding of his fellow-
creatures: it was simply because what I have called his own society
was more of a stimulus than that of most other people. And yet he
was not for this reason fond of solitude; he was, on the contrary,
a very sociable animal. It must be admitted at the outset that he
had a nature which seemed at several points to contradict itself, as
will probably be perceived in the course of this narration.

He entertained himself greatly with his reflections and meditations
upon Sienese architecture and early Tuscan art, upon Italian street-
life and the geological idiosyncrasies of the Apennines. If he had
only gone to the other inn, that nice-looking girl whom he had seen
passing under the dusky portal with her face turned away from him
might have broken bread with him at this intellectual banquet.
There came a day, however, when it seemed for a moment that if
she were disposed she might gather up the crumbs of the feast.
Longueville, every morning after breakfast, took a turn in the great
square of Siena—the vast *piazza*, shaped like a horse-shoe, where
the market is held beneath the windows of that crenellated palace
from whose overhanging cornice a tall, straight tower springs up
with a movement as light as that of a single plume in the bonnet of
a captain. Here he strolled about, watching a brown *contadino* dis-
embarrass his donkey, noting the progress of half an hour's chaffer
over a bundle of carrots, wishing a young girl with eyes like animated agates would let him sketch her, and gazing up at intervals
at the beautiful, slim tower, as it played at contrasts with the large
blue air. After he had spent the greater part of a week in these
grave considerations, he made up his mind to leave Siena. But he
was not content with what he had done for his portfolio. Siena was
eminently sketchable, but he had not been industrious. On the last
morning of his visit, as he stood staring about him in the crowded
piazza, and feeling that, in spite of its picturesqueness, this was an
awkward place for setting up an easel, he bethought himself, by
contrast, of a quiet corner in another part of the town, which he
had chanced upon in one of his first walks—an angle of a lonely
terrace that abutted upon the city-wall, where three or four super-
annuated objects seemed to slumber in the sunshine—the open door
of an empty church, with a faded fresco exposed to the air in the
arch above it, and an ancient beggar woman sitting beside it on a
three-legged stool. The little terrace had an old polished parapet,
about as high as a man's breast, above which was a view of strange,

631

sad-colored hills. Outside, to the left, the wall of the town made an outward bend, and exposed its rugged and rusty complexion. There was a smooth stone bench set into the wall of the church, on which Longueville had rested for an hour, observing the composition of the little picture of which I have indicated the elements, and of which the parapet of the terrace would form the foreground. The thing was what painters call a subject, and he had promised himself to come back with his utensils. This morning he returned to the inn and took possession of them, and then he made his way through a labyrinth of empty streets, lying on the edge of the town, within the wall, like the superfluous folds of a garment whose wearer has shrunken with old age. He reached his little grass-grown terrace, and found it as sunny and as private as before. The old mendicant was mumbling petitions, sacred and profane, at the church door; but save for this the stillness was unbroken. The yellow sunshine warmed the brown surface of the city-wall, and lighted the hollows of the Etruscan hills. Longueville settled himself on the empty bench, and, arranging his little portable apparatus, began to ply his brushes. He worked for some time smoothly and rapidly, with an agreeable sense of the absence of obstacles. It seemed almost an interruption when, in the silent air, he heard a distant bell in the town strike noon. Shortly after this, there was another interruption. The sound of a soft footstep caused him to look up; whereupon he saw a young woman standing there and bending her eyes upon the graceful artist. A second glance assured him that she was that nice girl whom he had seen going into the other inn with her mother, and suggested that she had just emerged from the little church. He suspected, however—I hardly know why—that she had been looking at him for some moments before he perceived her. It would perhaps be impertinent to inquire what she thought of him; but Longueville, in the space of an instant, made two or three reflections upon the young lady. One of them was to the effect that she was a handsome creature, but that she looked rather bold; the burden of the other was that—yes, decidedly—she was a compatriot. She turned away almost as soon as she met his eyes; he had hardly time to raise his hat, as, after a moment's hesitation, he proceeded to do. She herself appeared to feel a certain hesitation; she glanced back at the church door, as if under the impulse to retrace her steps. She stood there a moment longer—long enough to let him see that she was a person of easy attitudes—and then she walked away slowly to the parapet of the terrace. Here she stationed her-

self, leaning her arms upon the high stone ledge, presenting her back to Longueville, and gazing at rural Italy. Longueville went on with his sketch, but less attentively than before. He wondered what this young lady was doing there alone, and then it occurred to him that her companion—her mother, presumably—was in the church. The two ladies had been in the church when he arrived; women liked to sit in churches; they had been there more than half an hour, and the mother had not enough of it even yet. The young lady, however, at present preferred the view that Longueville was painting; he became aware that she had placed herself in the very centre of his foreground. His first feeling was that she would spoil it; his second was that she would improve it. Little by little she turned more into profile, leaning only one arm upon the parapet, while the other hand, holding her folded parasol, hung down at her side. She was motionless; it was almost as if she were standing there on purpose to be drawn. Yes, certainly she improved the picture. Her profile, delicate and thin, defined itself against the sky, in the clear shadow of a coquettish hat; her figure was light; she bent and leaned easily; she wore a gray dress, fastened up as was then the fashion, and displaying the broad edge of a crimson petticoat. She kept her position; she seemed absorbed in the view. "Is she *posing*—is she attitudinizing for my benefit?" Longueville asked of himself. And then it seemed to him that this was a needless assumption, for the prospect was quite beautiful enough to be looked at for itself, and there was nothing impossible in a pretty girl having a love of fine landscape. "But posing or not," he went on, "I will put her into my sketch. She has simply put herself in. It will give it a human interest. There is nothing like having a human interest." So, with the ready skill that he possessed, he introduced the young girl's figure into his foreground, and at the end of ten minutes he had almost made something that had the form of a likeness. "If she will only be quiet for another ten minutes," he said, "the thing will really be a picture." Unfortunately, the young lady was not quiet; she had apparently had enough of her attitude and her view. She turned away, facing Longueville again, and slowly came back, as if to re-enter the church. To do so she had to pass near him, and as she approached he instinctively got up, holding his drawing in one hand. She looked at him again, with that expression that he had mentally characterized as "bold" a few minutes before—with dark, intelligent eyes. Her hair was dark and dense; she was a strikingly handsome girl.

633

"I am so sorry you moved," he said, confidently, in English. "You were so—so beautiful."

She stopped, looking at him more directly than ever; and she looked at his sketch, which he held out toward her. At the sketch, however, she only glanced, whereas there was observation in the eye that she bent upon Longueville. He never knew whether she had blushed; he afterward thought she might have been frightened. Nevertheless, it was not exactly terror that appeared to dictate her answer to Longueville's speech.

"I am much obliged to you. Don't you think you have looked at me enough?"

"By no means. I should like so much to finish my drawing."

"I am not a professional model," said the young lady.

"No. That's my difficulty," Longueville answered, laughing. "I can't propose to remunerate you."

The young lady seemed to think this joke in indifferent taste. She turned away in silence; but something in her expression, in his feeling at the time, in the situation, incited Longueville to higher play. He felt a lively need of carrying his point.

"You see it will be pure kindness," he went on,—"a simple act of charity. Five minutes will be enough. Treat me as an Italian beggar."

He had laid down his sketch and had stepped forward. He stood there, obsequious, clasping his hands and smiling.

His interruptress stopped and looked at him again, as if she thought him a very odd person; but she seemed amused. Now, at any rate, she was not frightened. She seemed even disposed to provoke him a little.

"I wish to go to my mother," she said.

"Where is your mother?" the young man asked.

"In the church, of course. I didn't come here alone!"

"Of course not; but you may be sure that your mother is very contented. I have been in that little church. It is charming. She is just resting there; she is probably tired. If you will kindly give me five minutes more, she will come out to you."

"Five minutes?" the young girl asked.

"Five minutes will do. I shall be eternally grateful." Longueville was amused at himself as he said this. He cared infinitely less for his sketch than the words appeared to imply; but, somehow, he cared greatly that this graceful stranger should do what he had proposed.

The graceful stranger dropped an eye on the sketch again.

"Is your picture so good as that?" she asked.

"I have a great deal of talent," he answered, laughing. "You shall see for yourself, when it is finished."

She turned slowly toward the terrace again.

"You certainly have a great deal of talent, to induce me to do what you ask." And she walked to where she had stood before. Longueville made a movement to go with her, as if to show her the attitude he meant; but, pointing with decision to his easel, she said—

"You have only five minutes." He immediately went back to his work, and she made a vague attempt to take up her position. "You must tell me if this will do," she added, in a moment.

"It will do beautifully," Longueville answered, in a happy tone, looking at her and plying his brush. "It is immensely good of you to take so much trouble."

For a moment she made no rejoinder, but presently she said—

"Of course if I pose at all I wish to pose well."

"You pose admirably," said Longueville.

After this she said nothing, and for several minutes he painted rapidly and in silence. He felt a certain excitement, and the movement of his thoughts kept pace with that of his brush. It was very true that she posed admirably; she was a fine creature to paint. Her prettiness inspired him, and also her audacity, as he was content to regard it for the moment. He wondered about her—who she was, and what she was—perceiving that the so-called audacity was not vulgar boldness, but the play of an original and probably interesting character. It was obvious that she was a perfect lady, but it was equally obvious that she was irregularly clever. Longueville's little figure was a success—a charming success, he thought, as he put on the last touches. While he was doing this, his model's companion came into view. She came out of the church, pausing a moment as she looked from her daughter to the young man in the corner of the terrace; then she walked straight over to the young girl. She was a delicate little gentlewoman, with a light, quick step.

Longueville's five minutes were up; so, leaving his place, he approached the two ladies, sketch in hand. The elder one, who had passed her hand into her daughter's arm, looked up at him with clear, surprised eyes; she was a charming old woman. Her eyes were very pretty, and on either side of them, above a pair of fine dark brows, was a band of silvery hair, rather coquettishly arranged.

"It is my portrait," said her daughter, as Longueville drew near. "This gentleman has been sketching me."

"Sketching you, dearest?" murmured her mother. "Wasn't it rather sudden?"

"Very sudden—very abrupt!" exclaimed the young girl with a laugh.

"Considering all that, it's very good," said Longueville, offering his picture to the elder lady, who took it and began to examine it. "I can't tell you how much I thank you," he said to his model.

"It's very well for you to thank me now," she replied. "You really had no right to begin."

"The temptation was so great."

"We should resist temptation. And you should have asked my leave."

"I was afraid you would refuse it; and you stood there, just in my line of vision."

"You should have asked me to get out of it."

"I should have been very sorry. Besides, it would have been extremely rude."

The young girl looked at him a moment.

"Yes, I think it would. But what you have done is ruder."

"It is a hard case!" said Longueville. "What could I have done, then, decently?"

"It's a beautiful drawing," murmured the elder lady, handing the thing back to Longueville. Her daughter, meanwhile, had not even glanced at it.

"You might have waited till I should go away," this argumentative young person continued.

Longueville shook his head.

"I never lose opportunities!"

"You might have sketched me afterwards, from memory."

Longueville looked at her, smiling.

"Judge how much better my memory will be now!"

She also smiled a little, but instantly became serious.

"For myself, it is an episode I shall try to forget. I don't like the part I have played in it."

"May you never play a less becoming one!" cried Longueville. "I hope that your mother, at least, will accept a memento of the occasion." And he turned again with the sketch to her companion, who had been listening to the girl's conversation with this enter-

636

prising stranger, and looking from one to the other with an air of earnest confusion. "Won't you do me the honor of keeping my sketch?" he said. "I think it really looks like your daughter."

"Oh, thank you, thank you; I hardly dare," murmured the lady, with a deprecating gesture.

"It will serve as a kind of amends for the liberty I have taken," Longueville added; and he began to remove the drawing from its paper block.

"It makes it worse for you to give it to us," said the young girl.

"Oh, my dear, I am sure it's lovely!" exclaimed her mother. "It's wonderfully like you."

"I think that also makes it worse!"

Longueville was at last nettled. The young lady's perversity was perhaps not exactly malignant; but it was certainly ungracious. She seemed to desire to present herself as a beautiful tormentress.

"How does it make it worse?" he asked, with a frown.

He believed she was clever, and she was certainly ready. Now, however, she reflected a moment before answering.

"That you should give us your sketch," she said at last.

"It was to your mother I offered it," Longueville observed.

But this observation, the fruit of his irritation, appeared to have no effect upon the young girl.

"Isn't it what painters call a study?" she went on. "A study is of use to the painter himself. Your justification would be that you should keep your sketch, and that it might be of use to you."

"My daughter is a study, sir, you will say," said the elder lady in a little, light, conciliating voice, and graciously accepting the drawing again.

"I will admit," said Longueville, "that I am very inconsistent. Set it down to my esteem, madam," he added, looking at the mother.

"That's for you, mamma," said his model, disengaging her arm from her mother's hand and turning away.

The mamma stood looking at the sketch with a smile which seemed to express a tender desire to reconcile all accidents.

"It's extremely beautiful," she murmured, "and if you insist on my taking it——"

"I shall regard it as a great honor."

"Very well, then; with many thanks, I will keep it." She looked at the young man a moment, while her daughter walked away.

Longueville thought her a delightful little person; she struck him as a sort of transfigured Quakeress—a mystic with a practical side. "I am sure you think she is a strange girl," she said.

"She is extremely pretty."

"She is very clever," said the mother.

"She is wonderfully graceful."

"Ah, but she's good!" cried the old lady.

"I am sure she comes honestly by that," said Longueville, expressively, while his companion, returning his salutation with a certain scrupulous grace of her own, hurried after her daughter.

Longueville remained there staring at the view, but not especially seeing it. He felt as if he had at once enjoyed and lost an opportunity. After a while he tried to make a sketch of the old beggar-woman who sat there in a sort of palsied immobility, like a rickety statue at a church-door. But his attempt to reproduce her features was not gratifying, and he suddenly laid down his brush. She was not pretty enough—she had a bad profile.

JAMI

JAMI (Persian, 1414-1492). The last great classical poet of Persia. Mystic and scholar, devoted to Sufism. Highly honored by the Ottoman sultans. Wrote three *Divans* of lyric poetry, seven long *Masnavīs*, and great variety of prose works.

ZULAIKHA

... There was a King in the West. His name
Taimùs, was spread wide by the drum of Fame.
Of royal power and wealth possessed,
No wish unanswered remained in his breast.
His brow gave luster to Glory's crown,
And his foot gave the thrones of the Mighty renown.
With Orion from heaven his host to aid,
Conquest was his when he bared his blade.
His child Zulaikha was passing fair:
None in his heart might with her compare,—

638

Of his royal house the most brilliant star,
A gem from the chest where the treasures are.
Praise cannot equal her beauty; no!
But its faint, faint shadow my pen may show.
Like her own bright hair falling loosely down,
I will touch each charm to her feet from her crown.
May the soft reflection of that bright cheek
Lend light to my spirit and bid me speak!
And that flashing ruby, her mouth, bestow
The power to tell of the things I know!
    Her stature was like to a palm tree grown
In the Garden of Grace, where no sin is known;
Bedewed by the love of her father the King,
She mocked the cypress that rose by the spring.
Sweet with the odor of musk, a snare
For the heart of the Wise, was the maiden's hair;
Tangled at night, in the morning through
Her long thick tresses a comb she drew,
And cleft the heart of the musk deer in twain
As for that rare odor he sighed in vain.
A dark shade fell from her loose hair sweet
As jasmine over the rose of her feet.
A broad silver tablet her forehead displayed
For the heaven-set lessons of beauty made;
Under its edge two inverted Núns
Showed black as musk their splendid half-moons,
And beneath them lively and bright were placed
Two Sáds by the pen of her Maker traced.
From Nún to the ring of the Mim there rose
Pure as silver, like Alif, her nose.
To the cipher, her mouth, add Alif: then
She had ten strong spells for the conquest of men.
That laughing ruby to view exposed
A Sín when the knot of her lips unclosed
At the touch of her pure white teeth, and between
The lines of crimson their flash was seen.
Her face was the garden of Iram, where
Roses of every hue are fair.
The dusky moles that enhanced the red
Were like Moorish boys playing in each rose bed.

639

Of silver that paid no tithe, her chin
Had a well with the Water of Life therein.
If a sage in his thirst came near to drink,
He would feel the spray ere he reached the brink;
But lost were his soul if he nearer drew,
For it was a well and a whirlpool too.
Her neck was of ivory. Thither drawn,
Came with her tribute to beauty the fawn;
And the rose hung her head at the gleam of the skin
Of the shoulders fairer than jessamine.
Her breasts were orbs of a light most pure,
Twin bubbles new risen from Fount Kafúr;
Two young pomegranates grown on one spray,
Where bold hope never a finger might lay.
The touchstone itself was proved false when it tried
Her arms' fine silver thrice purified;
But the pearl-pure amulets fastened there
Were the hearts of the holy absorbed in prayer.
The loveliest gave her their souls for rue;
And round the charm their own heartstrings drew.
Her arms filled her sleeves with silver from them
Whose brows are bound with a diadem.
To labor and care her soft hand lent aid,
And to wounded hearts healing unction laid.
Like reeds were those taper fingers of hers
To write on each heart love's characters.
Each nail on those fingers so long and slim
Showed a new moon laid on a full moon's rim;
And her small closed hand made the moon confess
That she never might rival its loveliness.
Two columns fashioned of silver upheld
That beauty which never was paralleled;
And, to make the tale of her charms complete,
They were matched by the shape of her exquisite feet,—
Feet so light and elastic no maid might show,
So perfectly fashioned from heel to toe,—
If on the eye of a lover she stepped,
Her foot would float on the tear he wept.

640

THE JATAKA

THE JATAKA (Pali-Sanskrit, 1st century B.C.). One of the sacred books of
Buddhism. A collection of some 550 *jatakas*, or brief tales combining legends
and maxims of the Buddha with animal fables and the theme of reincarnation.

THE STRIDER OVER BATTLE-FIELDS

THIS was related by the Teacher while dwelling at Jetavana monastery; and it was concerning Nanda the elder.

For when the Teacher made his visit home to Kapilapura, he
induced his youngest brother, Prince Nanda, to join the Order.
Then he departed from Kapilapura and, traveling from place to
place, he came and dwelt at Savatthi.

Now when the venerable Nanda had taken the Blessed One's bowl,
and was leaving home, Belle-of-the-Country heard the report that
Prince Nanda was going away in company with the Teacher, and
with hair half-braided she looked out of the window, and called out
to him: 'Come back quickly, my love!' And her speech remained
in the venerable Nanda's mind, so that he became lovesick, and
discontented, and pined away until the network of his veins showed
on the surface of his body.

When the Teacher heard of all this, he thought: 'What if now I
were to establish Nanda in saintship?' And going to the cell which
was Nanda's sleeping-room, and taking his seat on the mat that
was offered him, he said:

'Nanda, are you contented under this dispensation?'

'Reverend Sir, I am not contented, for I am exceedingly in love
with Belle-of-the-Country.'

'Nanda, have you ever taken a trip through the Himalya
mountains?'

'Reverend Sir, I never have.'

'Then let us go now.'

'Reverend Sir, I have no magical power. How can I go?'

'I will take you, Nanda,' said the Teacher, 'by my own magical
power.'

Then he took the elder by the hand, and sprang into the air. As
they passed along he pointed out to him a field that had been
burned over, and on a charred stump was seated a she-monkey with
her nose and tail destroyed, her hair singed off, her skin fissured
and peeled to the quick, and all smeared with blood.

'Nanda, do you see this she-monkey?'

'Yes, Reverend Sir.'

641

'Take good note of her.'

Then he took him and showed him Manosila table-land, which is sixty leagues in extent, and Anotatta, and the rest of the seven great lakes, and the five great rivers, and the Himalya range containing many hundred pleasant spots, and graced with Gold Mountain, Silver Mountain, and Jewel Mountain.

Then said he: 'Nanda, have you ever seen the Heaven of the Suite of the Thirty-three?'

'Reverend Sir, I never have.'

'Come then, Nanda, and I will show it to you.'

And he took him thither, and sat down on Sakka's marble throne.

And Sakka, the king of the gods, came up with the gods of two heavens, and did obeisance, and sat down respectfully at one side. And his female attendants, twenty-five million in number, and five hundred pink-footed, celestial nymphs came up also, and did obeisance, and sat down respectfully at one side.

The Teacher suffered the venerable Nanda to look upon these five hundred celestial nymphs again and again with passion.

'Nanda,' said he, 'do you see these pink-footed celestial nymphs?'

'Yes, Reverend Sir.'

'Pray, now, are these or Belle-of-the-Country the prettier?'

'Reverend Sir, as is the burned she-monkey compared to Belle-of-the-Country, so is Belle-of-the-Country compared to these.'

'Well, Nanda, what then?'

'Reverend Sir, what does one do to obtain these celestial nymphs?'

'By performing the duties of a monk does one obtain these nymphs.'

'Reverend Sir, if the Blessed One will be my guarantee that if I perform the duties of a monk I shall obtain these nymphs, I will perform the duties of a monk.'

'Do so, Nanda. I am your guarantee.'

Thus did the elder take the Tathagata as a guarantee in the presence of the assembled gods. Then he said:

'Reverend Sir, do not delay. Come, let us go. I will perform the duties of a monk.'

Then the Teacher returned with him to Jetavana monastery; and the elder began to perform the duties of a monk.

'Sariputta,' said then the Teacher, addressing the Captain of the Doctrine, 'my youngest brother, Nanda, took me as guarantee for some celestial nymphs in the presence of the gods assembled in the Heaven of the Suite of the Thirty-three.'

Thus he told him. And in the same way he told it to Maha-Moggallana the elder, the Maha-Kassapa the elder, to Anuruddha the elder, to Ananda the elder and Treasurer of the Doctrine, and so on to all the eighty great disciples, and also to the greater part of the other priests.

The Captain of the Doctrine, Sariputta the elder, then drew near to Nanda the elder, then said:

'Is it true, as they say, brother Nanda, that in the presence of the gods assembled in the Heaven of the Suite of the Thirty-three you took The One Possessing the Ten Forces as a guarantee for some celestial nymphs, if you performed the duties of a monk? If that be so, is not your chaste religious life all for the sake of women? All for the sake of your passions? What is the difference between your thus doing the duties of a monk for the sake of women, and a laborer who performs his work for hire?'

This speech put the elder to shame, and made him quite dispirited. And in the same way all the eighty great disciples, and the remaining priests also, shamed the venerable Nanda. And realizing that he had behaved in an unworthy manner, in shame and remorse he summoned up his heroism, and attained to insight and to saintship; and coming to the Teacher, he said:

'Reverend Sir, I release the Blessed One from his promise.'

Said the Teacher: 'When you attained to saintship, O Nanda, I became released from my promise.'

When the priests heard of this occurrence, they raised a discussion in the lecture-hall.

'Brethren, how amenable to admonition is Nanda the elder! One admonition was sufficient to arouse in him shame and remorse, so that he performed the duties of a monk, and attained to saintship.'

The Teacher came and inquired: 'Priests, what now is the subject of your discourse?'

And they told him.

'Priests, formerly also, and not now for the first time, was Nanda amenable to admonition.' So saying, he related the bygone occurrence:

Once upon a time, when Brahmadatta was ruling at Benares, the future Buddha was born in the family of an elephant-trainer; and when he had come of age, and become accomplished as an elephant-trainer, he took service under a king who was hostile to the King of Benares. And he trained the State elephant until it was very well trained.

643

Then the King resolved to conquer the kingdom of Benares, and taking the future Buddha with him, and mounting the State elephant, with a mighty army he went to Benares, and surrounded the place. Then he sent a letter to the King saying, 'Give me the kingdom, or give me battle.'

Brahmadatta resolved to give battle; and having manned the walls, the watchtowers, and the gates, he did so.

His enemy had his State elephant armed with a defensive suit of mail, put on armor himself, and mounted on the elephant's shoulders. 'I will break into the city, kill my enemy, and take possession of the kingdom.' With this thought he seized a sharp goad, and urged the elephant in the direction of the city.

But the elephant, when he saw the hot mud, the stones from the catapults, and the various kinds of missiles thrown by the defenders, did not dare to advance, but retreated in mortal terror.

Then his trainer drew near: 'Old fellow,' said he, 'you are a hero, a strider over battle-fields. Retreat at such a time is not worthy of you.' And thus admonishing the elephant, he pronounced the following stanzas:

'A strider over battle-fields,
A hero, strong one, art thou called.
Why, then, behemoth, dost retreat
On coming near the gateway arch?

'Break down in haste the great crossbar!
The city-pillars take away!
And crashing through the gateway arch,
Enter, behemoth, quickly in!'

This one admonition was sufficient. For when the elephant heard it, he turned back, twisted his trunk round the city-pillars, and pulled them up like so many mushrooms. Then, crashing down the gateway arch, and forcing the cross-bar, he broke his way into the city, captured the kingdom, and gave it to his master.

When the Teacher had given this doctrinal instruction, he identified the characters of the birth-story:

'In that existence the elephant was Nanda, the King was Ananda, while the elephant-trainer was I myself.'

644

JAYADEVA

JAYADEVA (Sanskrit, *ca.* 1119-1179). Sanskrit poet at the court of the last king of Bengal. Author of celebrated love poem, the *Gītā Govinda (Song of the Cowherd).*

HYMN TO VISHNU

O thou that held'st the blessed Veda dry
   When all things else beneath the floods were hurled;
Strong Fish-God! Ark of Men! *Jai!* Hari, *jai!*
   Hail, Keshav, hail; thou Master of the world!

The round world rested on thy spacious nape;
   Upon thy neck, like a mere mole, it stood:
O thou, that took'st for us the Tortoise-shape,
   Hail, Keshav, Hail! Ruler of wave and wood!

The world upon thy curving tusk sate sure,
   Like the Moon's dark disc in her crescent pale;
O thou who didst for us assume the Boar,
   Immortal Conqueror! hail, Keshav, hail!

When thou thy Giant-Foe didst seize and rend,
   Fierce, fearful, long, and sharp were fang and nail;
Thou who the Lion and the Man didst blend,
   Lord of the Universe, hail, Narsingh, hail!

Wonderful Dwarf!—who with a threefold stride
   Cheated King Bali—where thy footsteps fall
Men's sins, O Wamuna! are set aside:
   O Keshav, hail! thou Help and Hope of all!

The sins of this sad earth thou didst assail,
   The anguish of its creatures thou didst heal;
Freed are we from all terrors by thy toil:
   Hail, Purshuram, hail! Lord of the biting steel!

To thee the fell Ten-Headed yielded life.
   Thou in dread battle laid'st the monster low!
Ah, Rama! dear to Gods and men that strife;
   We praise thee, Master of the matchless bow!

645

With clouds for garments glorious thou dost fare,
  Veiling thy dazzling majesty and might,
As when Jamuna saw thee with the share,
  A peasant—yet the King of Day and Night.

Merciful-hearted! when thou camest as Boodh—
  Albeit 'twas written in the Scriptures so—
Thou bad'st our altars to be no more imbrued
  With blood of victims: Keshav! bending low—

We praise thee, Wielder of the sweeping sword,
  Brilliant as curving comets in the gloom,
Whose edge shall smite the fierce barbarian horde;
  Hail to thee, Keshav! hail, and hear, and come,

And fill this song of Jayadev with thee,
  And make it wise to teach, strong to redeem,
And sweet to living souls. Thou Mystery!
  Thou Light of Life! Thou Dawn beyond the dream!

Fish! that didst outswim the flood;
Tortoise! whereon earth hath stood;
Boar! who with thy tush held'st high
The world, that mortals might not die;
Lion! who hast giants torn;
Dwarf! who laugh'dst a king to scorn;
Sole Subduer of the Dreaded!
Slayer of the many-headed!
Mighty Ploughman! Teacher tender!
Of thine own the sure Defender!
Under all thy ten disguises
Endless praise to thee arises.

JUAN RAMON JIMENEZ

JUAN RAMON JIMÉNEZ (Spanish, 1881-   ). Influential modern Spanish poet, leader of Darío-French-Symbolist School. A native of Andalusia, went into exile at time of Civil War. Now living in America. Highly polished artist, whose aim is "pure poetry." Important publications: *Baladas de primavera, Diario de un poeta recién casado, Poesías escojidas.*

FORTUNATE BEING

Singing you go, and laughing through the water,
and through the air you go whistling and laughing,

646

a round of blue and gold, of green and silver,
so happy passing and repassing ever
amidst the first red blossoming of April,
the distinct form of instantaneous
equalities of light, of life, of color,
with us, kindled like river banks aflame!

What a happy being you are,
with universal and eternal happiness!
Happy, you break through the waves of the air,
you swim contrary to the waves of water!
Do you not have to eat, neither to sleep?
All the springtime, is it yours to enjoy?
All of the green, all of the blue,
the flowering all, is it yours?
There is no fear in your glory;
your fate is to return, return, return,
in rounds of green and silver, blue and gold,
through an eternity of eternities!

You give your hand to us in a moment
of possible affinity, of sudden love,
of radiant concession;
and with your warm contact,
in wild vibration of flesh and of soul,
we are enkindled with sweet harmony,
and we, made new, forget the usual,
we shine for an instant, happy with gold.
It seems that we too are going to be
perennial as you,
that we shall fly from ocean to the mountain,
that we shall leap from heaven to the sea,
and that we shall return, return, return
for an eternity of eternities.
We sing and we laugh through the air,
through the water we laugh and whistle.

But you must not forget yourself,
you are the casual, perpetual presence,
you are the fortunate creature,
the only magic being without shadow,
the one adored for warmth and grace,

647

the free, enraptured robber
that, in rounds of blue and gold, green and silver,
goes laughing, whistling through the air,
through the water singing and laughing!

THE BEST THAT I HAVE

Green sea and grey sky and blue sky
and loving albatross upon the waves,
and in all, the sun, and thou in the sun,
observing desired and desiring god,
lighting with distinct golden rays my arrival;
the arrival of him that I am today,
of him that even yesterday I doubted
he could be in thee as I am.

What a changed man in me, desiring god,
from the being doubting the legend
of the god of the many glib speakers,
to be the firm believer
in the story I myself have created
all through my life for thee.

Now I come to this termination
of a year of my natural life,
in the depths of the air where I keep thee,
above this sea, these depths of water,
to this beautiful, blinding termination,
where thou art gradually entering me,
content to be thine, to be mine,
through the best that I have, my own expression.

From ELEGIES

The dazzling whiteness of my first love
At the sweet, sad sound of reveille!
What celestial joy was it that opened those oriental gardens
To my youthful soul, that morning?
It was a holiday. All pallid sorrow died out
In the green of false springtime;
Everything was charged with laughter, with flowers.
The ground was rushes, the air was pennons.

And that sweet blue night, on that bench,
Under the doubled shadow of the drooping acacia,
While the moon gave its white flax to the world,
She said she had loved me all her life long.

Alas! I would live through all my sorrows again,
Even the darkest, to see such a morning
As that on which the sun purified my brow
At the sweet, sad sound of reveille.

From THE DIARY OF A NEWLY-MARRIED MAN

Remorse
(Between Philadelphia and New York, a rainy night, May 24)

Must you acquiesce, my soul,
In forgetting in the morning?
If four great nails, well nailed,
My soul, right into your entrails,
Were to open four great, pure roses
From those four livid words
That he will hold nailed
In his kind heart
From then on!

Must you acquiesce
Merely in being quite happy,
Soul?

From STONE AND HEAVEN

Dream Nocturne

The earth leads by the earth.
But, sea,
You lead by the heavens.
With what security of gold and silver light
Do the stars mark the road for us!
One would think
That the earth was the road
Of the body,

That the sea was the road
Of the soul.
Yes. It seems
That the soul is the only traveler
Of the sea; that the body, alone,
Remains behind, on the beach,
Without her, saying goodbye,
Heavy, cold, as though dead.
How like
Is a journey by sea
To death,
To eternal life!

MAURUS JOKAI

MAURUS JOKAI (Hungarian, 1825-1904). Most widely read Hungarian
novelist. Unusual narrative skill, wrote chiefly to entertain. Author of 100
novels. Most colorful are those celebrating glories of old Hungary; 22 translated into English, including: *Midst the Wild Carpathians, The Baron's Sons,
Timar's Two Worlds, The Yellow Rose.*

TIMAR'S TWO WORLDS

I. How Ali Saved His Daughter

A MOUNTAIN-CHAIN, pierced through from base to summit—a gorge
four miles in length walled in by lofty precipices; and between
these walls flows the Danube in its rocky bed.

At this time there were no steamers on the Danube, but a vessel,
called the St. Barbara, approaches, drawn against the stream by
thirty-two horses. The fate of the vessel lies in the hands of two
men—the pilot and the captain.

The name of the captain is Michael Timar. He is a man of about
thirty, with fair hair and dreamy blue eyes.

At the door of the ship's cabin sits a man of fifty, smoking a
Turkish chibouque. Euthemio Trikaliss is the name under which he
is registered in the way-book, and he is the owner of the cargo. The
ship itself belongs to a merchant of Komorn called Athanas
Brazovics.

Out of one of the cabin windows looks the face of a young girl,

Timéa, the daughter of Euthemio, and the face is as white as marble. Timéa and her father are the only passengers of the St. Barbara.

When the captain lays aside his speaking-trumpet he has time to chat with Timéa, who understands only modern Greek, which the captain speaks fluently.

It is always a dangerous voyage, for the current is fierce and the rocks are death-traps. To-day, too, the St. Barbara was pursued by a Turkish gunboat. But the vessel makes its way safely, in spite of current and rocks, and the Turkish gunboat gives up the chase.

Three days later the St. Barbara had reached the island of Orsova; the plains of Hungary are to the north of the river, Servia to the south.

Provisions had run short, and Timar decided to go on shore. There were no signs of human habitation at first, but Timar's sharp eyes had discovered a faint smoke rising above the tops of the poplars. He worked his way in a small skiff through the reeds, reached dry land, pushed through hedges and bushes, and then stood transfixed with admiration.

A cultivated orchard of some five or six acres was before him, and beyond that a flower-garden, full of summer bloom.

Timar went up through the orchard and flower garden to a cottage, built partly in the rock, and covered with creepers. A huge, black Newfoundland dog was lying before the door.

A woman's voice answered Timar's "good-morning," and the dog raised no objection to the captain going indoors.

"It never hurts good people," said the woman.

Timar explained his mission. The wind had brought his vessel to a standstill; he was short of provisions, and he had two passengers who would be grateful for shelter on land for the night.

The woman promised him food and a room for his passengers in exchange for grain, and at her word the dog brought him by a better path to the river.

Presently Timar was back again with Euthemio and Timéa, and now a young girl appeared, whom the housewife called Noemi.

Before supper was over, the growling of the dog announced a new arrival, and a man of youthful appearance, who introduced himself as Theodor Krisstyan, an old friend of the lady of the house, whom he called Madame Therese, entered and made himself quickly at home. It was plain that his hostess both feared and disliked Theodor, while Timar, who had met him before, regarded him as a spy in the pay of the Turkish government.

651

In the morning the wind had gone down, Theodor had vanished, and Timar and his passengers prepared to renew their journey.

Therese told Timar her story before he left; how she and her daughter Noemi had lived there for twelve years, and who the objectionable Theodor was. Then she added, in a whisper. "I fancy this man Krisstyan's visit was either on your account, or that of the other gentleman. Be on your guard if either of you dread the discovery of a secret."

Trikaliss looked very gloomy when he heard the stranger had left before sunrise, and the following night he called Timar to his cabin.

"I am dying," he said. "I want to die—I have taken poison. Timéa will not wake till all is over. My true name is not Euthemio Trikaliss, but Ali Tschorbadschi. I was once governor of Candia, and then treasurer in Stamboul. You know there is a revolution proceeding in Turkey; my turn was coming. Not that I was a conspirator, but the treasury wanted my money and the seraglio my daughter. Death is easy for me, but I will not let my daughter go into the harem nor myself be made a beggar. Therefore I hired your vessel, and loaded it with grain. The owner, Athanas Brazovics, is a connection of mine; I have often shown him kindness, he can return it now. By a miracle we got safely through the rocks and whirlpools of the river, and eluded the pursuit of the Turkish brigantine, and now I stumble over a straw into my grave.

"That man who followed us last evening was a spy of the Turkish government. He recognised me, and sealed my fate. The government would not demand me from Austria as a political refugee, but as a thief. This is unjust, for what I took was my own. But I am pursued as a thief, and Austria gives up escaped thieves if Turkish spies can trace them. By dying I can save my daughter and her property. Swear to me by your faith and your honour you will carry out my instructions. Here in this casket is about a thousand ducats. Take Timéa to Athanas Brazovics, and beg him to adopt my daughter. Give him the money, he must spend it on the education of the child, and give him also the cargo, and beg him to be present when the sacks are emptied. You understand!"

The dying man looked in Timar's face, and struggled for breath. "Yes—the Red Crescent!" he stammered. "The Red Crescent!" Then the death-throes closed his lips—one struggle, and he was a corpse.

WHEN the St. Barbara had nearly reached Komorn it struck an uprooted tree, lying in ambush under water, and immediately began to sink. It is absolutely impossible to save a vessel wrecked in this way. The crew all left the sinking craft, and Timar rescued Timéa, and with her the casket with the thousand ducats.

Then the captain drove off with the fatherless girl to the house of Athanas Brazovics in the town of Komorn.

At first Athanas kissed Timéa very heartily, but when he learnt that his vessel was lost, and all Timéa's property, except the thousand ducats, and the wheat sacks—now spoilt by water—he altered his tune.

He and his wife Sophie decided that Timéa should live with them as an adopted child, and at the same time attend on their daughter Athalie as a waiting-maid. Athalie and her mother treated the poor girl with scornful contempt.

As for Timar, Athanas turned on him savagely, as though the captain could have prevented the wreck!

On the advice of his friend, Lieutenant Katschuka, who was betrothed to Athalie, Timar purchased the sunken grain next day when it was put up for auction, buying the whole cargo for 10,000 gulden. "You will do the poor orphan a good turn if you buy it," said the lieutenant. "Otherwise, the value of the cargo will all go in salvage."

Timar at once made arrangements for hauling up the sacks, and for the immediate drying and grinding of the corn, and all day labourers were at work on the wreck.

At nightfall Timar, left alone, noticed one sack differently marked from the rest—marked with a red crescent! Within this sack was a long leathern bag. He broke it open and found it full of diamonds, emeralds, and sapphires richly set in girdles and bracelets and rings. A whole heap of unset diamonds were in an agate box. The whole treasure was worth at least 1,000,000 gulden. The St. Barbara had carried a million on board!

"To whom does this treasure belong?"

So Timar put the question to himself, and answered it.

"Why, whom should it belong to but you? You bought the sunken cargo, just as it is, with the sacks and the grain. If the treasurer stole the jewels from the sultan, the sultan probably stole them in his campaigns."

"And Timéa?"

"Timéa would not know how to use the treasure, and her adopted father would absorb it, and get rid of nine-tenths of it. What would be the result if Timéa gets it? She would be a rich lady, and would not cast a look at you from her height. Now things are the other way—you will be a rich man and she a poor girl. You do not want the treasure for yourself. You will invest it profitably, and when you have earned with the first million a second and a third, you will go to the poor girl and say, 'There, take it—it is all yours; and take me, too.' You only wish to become rich in order to make her happy."

The moon and the waves cried to Timar, "You are rich—you are a made man!"

But when it was dark an inward voice whispered, "You are a thief!"

From that day all Timar's undertakings flourished, and step by step he reached the summit of an ordinary successful business man's ambition—the title of nobility. At the same time Brazovics, who had treated Timar with brutal inconsiderateness because of the wreck of the St. Barbara, went steadily down-hill, borrowing and embezzling trust moneys in his fall.

Lieutenant Katschuka had declared all along that he could not marry Athalie without a dowry, and when the wedding day arrived, Brazovics, unable to face his creditors, and knowing himself bankrupt, penniless, and fraudulent, committed suicide. Katschuka immediately declared the engagement at an end. In his heart he had long wearied of Athalie, and looked with desire on Timéa. The orphan girl from the first had loved the lieutenant with silent, unspoken affection.

When the Brazovics' house was put up for sale Timar bought it outright, furniture and all, and then said to Timéa, "From this day forth you are the mistress of this house. Everything in it belongs to you, all is inscribed in your name. Accept it from me. You are the owner of the house, and if there is a little shelter for me in your heart, and you did not refuse my hand—then I should be only too happy."

Timéa gave her hand to Timar, and said in a low, firm voice, "I accept you as my husband, and will be a faithful and obedient wife."

This man had always been so good to her. He had never made sport of her nor flattered her, and he had saved her life on the

Danube when the St. Barbara was sinking. He had given her all her heart could desire except one thing, and that belonged to another.

III. *The Ownerless Island*

On his betrothal to Timéa a great burden was lifted from the soul of Timar. Since the day when the treasure of Ali Tschorbadschi had enabled him to achieve power and riches, Timar had been haunted by the voice of self-accusation: "This money does not belong to you—it was the property of an orphan. You are a man of gold! You are a thief!"

But now the defrauded orphan had received back her property. Only Timar forgot that he had demanded in exchange the girl's heart.

Timéa promised to be a faithful and obedient wife, but on the wedding-day when Timar said, "Do you love me?" she only opened her eyes, and asked, "What is love?"

Timar found he had married a marble statue; and that all his riches would not buy his wife's love. He became wretched, conscious that his wife was unhappy, that he was the author of their mutual misery.

Then, in the early summer, Timar went off from Komorn to shoot water-fowl. He meant to go to the ownerless island at Ostrova —it was three years since that former visit.

Therese and Noemi welcomed him cordially at the island, and Timar forgot his troubles when he was with them. Therese told him her story; how her husband, ruined by the father of Theodor Krisstyan and by Athanas Brazovics, had committed suicide, and how, forsaken and friendless, she had brought her child to this island, which neither Austria nor Turkey claimed, and where no tax-collector called. With her own hands she had turned the wilderness into a paradise, and the only fear she had was that Theodor Krisstyan, who had discovered her retreat, might reveal it to the Turkish government.

Therese had no money and no use for it, but she exchanged fruit and honey for grain, salt, clothes, and hardware, and the people with whom she bartered were not inclined to gossip about her affairs.

So no news concerning the island ever went to Vienna, Komorn, or Constantinople, and the fact of Timar's great prosperity had not reached the islanders. He was welcomed as a hard-working man,

and Therese did not know that Timar had been powerful enough to get a ninety years' lease of the island from both Turkish and Austrian governments; perhaps no very difficult matter, as the existence of the island was unknown, and there were fees to be paid over the concession.

When he told her what he had done, Noemi threw her arms round his neck.

Theodor Krisstyan was furious, but Timar procured him a post in Brazil, and for a long time the disreputable spy was too far off to be troublesome.

And now on this island Timar found health and rest. It became his home, and for the summer months every year he would slip away from Komorn, and no one, not even Timéa, guessed his secret. When he returned Timéa's cold, white face was still an unsolved riddle to her husband. She would greet him kindly, but never was there any token that she loved him. Timar's ever-increasing business operations were excuse for his long absences, but all the same the double life he was leading made him ill. He could not tell Timéa of Therese and Noemi, and he could not tell them on the island that he was married.

Timéa, on her side, devoted herself more and more to her husband's business in his absence, and when Major Katschuka once called and asked her if she could not arrange for a divorce, she answered gently, "My husband is the noblest man in the world. Should I separate from him who has no one but me to love him? Am I to tell him that I hate him, I who owe everything to him, and who brought him no dowry but a loveless heart?"

Timar learnt from Athalie, who lived in Timéa's house, of this reply, and felt more in despair than ever. He wanted Timéa to be happy, she had never been his wife except in name, for he had been waiting for her love.

And he wanted to go away, and leave all his riches behind, and settle on the island. Now more than ever was he wanted on the island, for Therese had died of heart failure, and the years had made Noemi a woman.

IV. "My Name is Nobody"

It was winter, and Timar had gone off alone to a house that belonged to him near a frozen lake. He felt the time had come for flight, but whither?

Theodor Krisstyan had turned up again. In Brazil he had heard a story of Ali Tschorbadschi's jewels from an old criminal from Turkey, and he had returned to blackmail Timar. But he did not find him till Timar was at the frozen lake.

Krisstyan's story was not true. Timar knew that the accusations were false as he listened to the vagabond's indictment. He had not "killed" Timéa's father, nor "stolen" his treasure. But he had played a false game, and his position was a false one. Krisstyan demanded a change of raiment, and Timar let him take clothes and shirts. But at last the blackmailer's demands became too insolent, and Timar drove him out of the house.

And now it seemed to Timar that his own career was finished. This ruffian Krisstyan could expose the foundation of his wealth, and how could he live discredited before the world?

On the frozen water there were great fissures between the blocks of ice. Within the waves of the lake death would come quickly. Timar walked out on the ice, and there before him the head of Theodor Krisstyan rose in the water and then sank. The spy had not known the treachery of the fissures.

Timar fled to the ownerless island, and when the corpse of Krisstyan was recovered, in an advanced stage of decomposition, Timéa declared she recognised her husband's clothes.

So the body of Theodor Krisstyan was buried with great pomp, and a year later Timéa married Major Katschuka, and then, haunted by the doubt whether her first husband was really dead, pined away.

No blessing rested on the wealth Timar left behind him. The only son Timéa bore to the major was a great spendthrift, and in his hands the fabulous wealth vanished as quickly as it had grown.

And what is passing meanwhile on the ownerless island?

Forty years have passed since Timar's disappearance from Komorn, and the island is now a complete model farm. Recently, a friend of mine, an ardent naturalist, took me to the island. I had heard as a child of Timar and his wealth.

Every inch of ground is utilised or serves to beautify the place. The tobacco grown here has the most exquisite aroma, and the beehives look from a distance like a small town with many-shaped roofs.

It is easy to see that the owner of the island understands luxury, and yet that owner never has a farthing to call his own; no money ever enters the island. Those, however, who need the exports know also the requirements of the islanders, and bring them for barter.

The whole colony consisted of one family, and each was called only by his Christian name. The six sons of the first settler had married women of the district, and the numbers of grandchildren and great-grandchildren already exceeded forty, but the island maintained them all. Poverty was unknown; they lived in luxury; each knew some trade, and if they had been ten times as many, their labour would have supported them.

When we arrived on the island, the nominal head of the family, a well-built man of forty, received us cordially, and in the evening presented us to his parents.

When my name was mentioned to the old man he looked long at me, and a visible colour rose in his cheeks. I began to tell him of what was going on in the world, that Hungary was now united to Austria, and that the taxes were very heavy.

He blew a cloud from his pipe, and the smoke said, "My island has nothing to do with that, we have no taxes here."

I told him of wars, financial panics, the strife of religion and politics, and the smoke seemed to say, "We wage war with no one here. Thank God, we have no money here and no elections or ministers."

Presently the old man asked me where I was born, and what my profession was? And when I told him that I wrote romances, he said, "Guess my story. There was once a man who left a world in which he was admired and respected, and created a second world in which he was loved."

"May I venture to ask your name?" I said.

The old man seemed to grow a head taller; then, raising his trembling hands, he laid them on my head. And it seemed to me as if once, long, long before those same hands had rested on my head when childish curls covered it, and that I had seen that noble face before.

"My name is Nobody," he replied to my question; and after that night I saw him no more during our stay on the island.

The privileges granted by two governments to the owner of the island will last for fifty years more. And who knows what may happen to the world in fifty years?

BEN JONSON

BEN JONSON (English, 1572-1637). Delightful singer of Shakespeare's time
and later. Also actor, dramatist and critic. Wrote masques for noble patrons
and popular plays: *Every Man in His Humour, Volpone.* Had large coterie in
London and was literary dictator for quarter of century. Loved most for his
lyrics, such as "Drink to Me Only with Thine Eyes."

EPITAPH ON ELIZABETH, L. H.

Wouldst thou hear what man can say
  In a little? Reader, stay.
Underneath this stone doth lie
  As much beauty as could die;
Which in life did harbor give
  To more virtue than doth live.
If at all she had a fault,
  Leave it buried in this vault.
One name was Elizabeth,
  Th' other let it sleep with death;
Fitter, where it died to tell,
  Than that it lived at all. Farewell.

WHY I WRITE NOT OF LOVE

Some act of Love's bound to rehearse,
I thought to bind him in my verse;
Which when he felt, Away, quoth he,
Can poets hope to fetter me?
It is enough they once did get
Mars and my mother in their net;
I wear not these my wings in vain.
With which he fled me, and again
Into my rhymes could ne'er be got
By any art. Then wonder not
That since my numbers are so cold,
When Love is fled, and I grow old.

Come, my Celia, let us prove
While we may the sports of love;
Time will not be ours forever,
He at length our good will sever.
Spend not then his gifts in vain;
Suns that set may rise again,
But if once we lose this light,
'Tis with us perpetual night.
Why should we defer our joys?
Fame and rumor are but toys.
Cannot we delude the eyes
Of a few poor household spies?
Or his easier ears beguile,
So removed by our wile?
'Tis no sin love's fruit to steal;
But the sweet theft to reveal,
To be taken, to be seen,
These have crimes accounted been.

SONG, TO CELIA [2]

Drink to me only with thine eyes,
    And I will pledge with mine;
Or leave a kiss but in the cup,
    And I'll not look for wine.
The thirst that from the soul doth rise
    Doth ask a drink divine;
But might I of Jove's nectar sup,
    I would not change for thine.

I sent thee late a rosy wreath,
    Not so much honoring thee,
As giving it a hope that there
    It could not withered be.
But thou thereon didst only breathe,
    And sent'st it back to me,
Since when it grows and smells, I swear,
    Not of itself, but thee.

HIS EXCUSE FOR LOVING

Let it not your wonder move,
Less your laughter, that I love.
Though I now write fifty years,
I have had, and have, my peers;
Poets though divine are men,
Some have loved as old again.
And it is not always face,
Clothes, or fortune, gives the grace,
Or the feature, or the youth;
But the language and the truth,
With the ardor and the passion,
Gives the lover weight and fashion.

If you then will read the story,
First prepare you to be sorry
That you never knew till now
Either whom to love, or how;
But be glad, as soon with me,
When you know that this is she
Of whose beauty it was sung:
She shall make the old man young,
Keep the middle age at stay,
And let nothing high decay;
Till she be the reason why
All the world for love may die.

HER TRIUMPH

See the chariot at hand here of love,
    Wherein my lady rideth!
Each that draws is a swan or a dove,
    And well the car love guideth.
As she goes all hearts do duty
    Unto her beauty,
And enamoured do wish so they might
    But enjoy such a sight,
That they still were to run by her side,
Through swords, through seas, whither she would ride.

661

Do but look on her eyes; they do light
   All that love's world compriseth!
Do but look on her hair; it is bright
   As love's star when it riseth!
Do but mark, her forehead's smoother
      Than words that soothe her;
And from her arched brows, such a grace
      Sheds itself through the face,
As alone there triumphs to the life
All the gain, all the good of the elements' strife.

Have you seen but a bright lily grow
   Before rude hands have touched it?
Ha' you marked but the fall o' the snow
   Before the soil hath smutched it?
Ha' you felt the wool of beaver,
      Or swan's down ever?
Or have smelt o' the bud o' the briar?
      Or the nard in the fire?
Or have tasted the bag of the bee?
O so white! O so soft! O so sweet is she!

THE PLANT AND FLOWER OF LIGHT

It is not growing like a tree
In bulk, doth make man better be;
Or standing long an oak, three hundred year,
To fall a log at last, dry, bald, and sere;
A lily of a day
Is fairer far in May,
Although it fall and die that night,
It was the plant and flower of light.
In small proportions we just beauties see;
And in short measures, life may perfect be.

TO CYNTHIA

Queen and huntress, chaste and fair,
Now the sun is laid to sleep,
Seated in thy silver chair
State in wonted manner keep;

Hesperus entreats thy light,
Goddess excellently bright.

Earth, let not thy envious shade
Dare itself to interpose;
Cynthia's shining orb was made
Heaven to clear, when day did close;
　　Bless us then with wishëd sight,
　　Goddess excellently bright.

Lay thy bow of pearl apart,
And thy crystal shining quiver;
Give unto the flying hart
Space to breathe, how short soever,
　　Thou that mak'st a day of night,
　　Goddess excellently bright.

JAMES JOYCE

JAMES JOYCE (Irish, 1882-1941). Most controversial innovator of modern letters. Experiments with new techniques influenced "stream-of-consciousness" school. Unhappy youth in Ireland reflected in *A Portrait of the Artist as a Young Man*. In self-imposed exile to Paris, wrote *Ulysses*, description of a day's life in Dublin. Published first in Paris, permitted in America by famous court decision. Last work, *Finnegans Wake*, so difficult only Joyce *aficionados* understand it.

ARABY

NORTH Richmond Street, being blind, was a quiet street except at the hour when the Christian Brothers' School set the boys free. An uninhabited house of two storeys stood at the blind end, detached from its neighbours in a square ground. The other houses of the street, conscious of decent lives within them, gazed at one another with brown imperturbable faces.

The former tenant of our house, a priest, had died in the back drawing-room. Air, musty from having been long enclosed, hung in all the rooms, and the waste room behind the kitchen was littered with old useless papers. Among these I found a few paper-

covered books, the pages of which were curled and damp: *The Abbot*, by Walter Scott, *The Devout Communicant* and *The Memoirs of Vidocq*. I liked the last best because its leaves were yellow. The wild garden behind the house contained a central apple-tree and a few straggling bushes under one of which I found the late tenant's rusty bicycle-pump. He had been a very charitable priest; in his will he had left all his money to institutions and the furniture of his house to his sister.

When the short days of winter came, dusk fell before we had well eaten our dinners. When we met in the street the houses had grown somber. The space of sky above us was the color of ever-changing violet and towards it the lamps of the street lifted their feeble lanterns. The cold air stung us and we played till our bodies glowed. Our shouts echoed in the silent street. The career of our play brought us through the dark muddy lanes behind the houses where we ran the gauntlet of the rough tribes from the cottages, to the back doors of the dark dripping gardens where odors arose from the ashpits, to the dark odorous stables where a coachman smoothed and combed the horse or shook music from the buckled harness. When we returned to the street, light from the kitchen windows had filled the areas. If my uncle was seen turning the corner we hid in the shadow until we had seen him safely housed. Or if Mangan's sister came out on the doorstep to call her brother in to his tea we watched her from our shadow peer up and down the street. We waited to see whether she would remain or go in and, if she remained, we left our shadow and walked up to Mangan's steps resignedly. She was waiting for us, her figure defined by the light from the half-opened door. Her brother always teased her before he obeyed and I stood by the railings looking at her. Her dress swung as she moved her body and the soft rope of her hair tossed from side to side.

Every morning I lay on the floor in the front parlor watching her door. The blind was pulled down to within an inch of the sash so that I could not be seen. When she came out on the doorstep my heart leaped. I ran to the hall, seized my books and followed her. I kept her brown figure always in my eye and, when we came near the point at which our ways diverged, I quickened my pace and passed her. This happened morning after morning. I had never spoken to her, except for a few casual words, and yet her name was like a summons to all my foolish blood.

Her image accompanied me even in places the most hostile to

romance. On Saturday evenings when my aunt went marketing I had to go to carry some of the parcels. We walked through the flaring streets, jostled by drunken men and bargaining women, amid the curses of laborers, the shrill litanies of shop-boys who stood on guard by the barrels of pigs' cheeks, the nasal chanting of street-singers, who sang a *come-all-you* about O'Donovan Rossa, or a ballad about the troubles in our native land. These noises converged in a single sensation of life for me: I imagined that I bore my chalice safely through a throng of foes. Her name sprang to my lips at moments in strange prayers and praises which I myself did not understand. My eyes were often full of tears (I could not tell why) and at times a flood from my heart seemed to pour out into my bosom. I thought little of the future. I did not know whether I would ever speak to her or not or, if I spoke to her, how I could tell her of my confused adoration. But my body was like a harp and her words and gestures were like fingers running upon the wires.

One evening I went into the back drawing-room in which the priest had died. It was a dark rainy evening and there was no sound in the house. Through one of the broken panes I heard the rain impinge upon the earth, the fine incessant needles of water playing in the sodden beds. Some distant lamp or lighted window gleamed below me. I was thankful that I could see so little. All my senses seemed to desire to veil themselves and, feeling that I was about to slip from them, I pressed the palms of my hands together until they trembled, murmuring: *"O love! O love!"* many times.

At last she spoke to me. When she addressed the first words to me I was so confused that I did not know what to answer. She asked me was I going to *Araby*. I forgot whether I answered yes or no. It would be a splendid bazaar, she said she would love to go.

"And why can't you?" I asked.

While she spoke she turned a silver bracelet round and round her wrist. She could not go, she said, because there would be a retreat that week in her convent. Her brother and two other boys were fighting for their caps and I was alone at the railings. She held one of the spikes, bowing her head towards me. The light from the lamp opposite our door caught the white curve of her neck, lit up her hair that rested there and, falling, lit up the hand upon the railing. It fell over one side of her dress and caught the white border of a petticoat, just visible as she stood at ease.

"It's well for you," she said.

"If I go," I said, "I will bring you something."

What innumerable follies laid waste my waking and sleeping thoughts after that evening! I wished to annihilate the tedious intervening days. I chafed against the work of school. At night in my bedroom and by day in the classroom her image came between me and the page I strove to read. The syllables of the word *Araby* were called to me through the silence in which my soul luxuriated and cast an Eastern enchantment over me. I asked for leave to go to the bazaar on Saturday night. My aunt was surprised and hoped it was not some Freemason affair. I answered few questions in class. I watched my master's face pass from amiability to sternness; he hoped I was not beginning to idle. I could not call my wandering thoughts together. I had hardly any patience with the serious work of life which, now that it stood between me and my desire, seemed to me child's play, ugly monotonous child's play.

On Saturday morning I reminded my uncle that I wished to go to the bazaar in the evening. He was fussing at the hallstand, looking for the hat-brush, and answered me curtly:

"Yes, boy, I know."

As he was in the hall I could not go into the front parlor and lie at the window. I left the house in bad humor and walked slowly towards the school. The air was pitilessly raw and already my heart misgave me.

When I came home to dinner my uncle had not yet been home. Still it was early. I sat staring at the clock for some time and, when its ticking began to irritate me, I left the room. I mounted the staircase and gained the upper part of the house. The high, cold, empty gloomy rooms liberated me and I went from room to room singing. From the front window I saw my companions playing below in the street. Their cries reached me weakened and indistinct and, leaning my forehead against the cool glass, I looked over at the dark house where she lived. I may have stood there for an hour, seeing nothing but the brown-clad figure cast by my imagination, touched discreetly by the lamplight at the curved neck, at the hand upon the railings and at the border below the dress.

When I came downstairs again I found Mrs. Mercer sitting at the fire. She was an old garrulous woman, a pawnbroker's widow, who collected used stamps for some pious purpose. I had to endure the gossip of the tea-table. The meal was prolonged beyond an hour and still my uncle did not come. Mrs. Mercer stood up to

go: she was sorry she couldn't wait any longer, but it was after eight o'clock and she did not like to be out late, as the night air was bad for her. When she had gone I began to walk up and down the room, clenching my fists. My aunt said:

"I'm afraid you may put off your bazaar for this night of Our Lord."

At nine o'clock I heard my uncle's latchkey in the halldoor. I heard him talking to himself and heard the hallstand rocking when it had received the weight of his overcoat. I could interpret these signs. When he was midway through his dinner I asked him to give me the money to go to the bazaar. He had forgotten.

"The people are in bed and after their first sleep now," he said.

I did not smile. My aunt said to him energetically:

"Can't you give him the money and let him go? You've kept him late enough as it is."

My uncle said he was very sorry he had forgotten. He said he believed in the old saying: "All work and no play makes Jack a dull boy." He asked me where I was going and, when I had told him a second time he asked me did I know *The Arab's Farewell to his Steed*. When I left the kitchen he was about to recite the opening lines of the piece to my aunt.

I held a florin tightly in my hand as I strode down Buckingham Street towards the station. The sight of the streets thronged with buyers and glaring with gas recalled to me the purpose of my journey. I took my seat in a third-class carriage of a deserted train. After an intolerable delay the train moved out of the station slowly. It crept onward among ruinous houses and over the twinkling river. At Westland Row Station a crowd of people pressed to the carriage doors; but the porters moved them back, saying that it was a special train for the bazaar. I remained alone in the bare carriage. In a few minutes the train drew up beside an improvised wooden platform. I passed out on to the road and saw by the lighted dial of a clock that it was ten minutes to ten. In front of me was a large building which displayed the magical name.

I could not find any sixpenny entrance and, fearing that the bazaar would be closed, I passed in quickly through a turnstile, handing a shilling to a weary-looking man. I found myself in a big hall girdled at half its height by a gallery. Nearly all the stalls were closed and the greater part of the hall was in darkness. I recognised a silence like that which pervades a church after a service. I walked into the center of the bazaar timidly. A few people

were gathered about the stalls which were still open. Before a curtain, over which the words *Café Chantant* were written in colored lamps, two men were counting money on a salver. I listened to the fall of the coins.

Remembering with difficulty why I had come I went over to one of the stalls and examined porcelain vases and flowered tea-sets. At the door of the stall a young lady was talking and laughing with two young gentlemen. I remarked their English accents and listened vaguely to their conversation.

"O, I never said such a thing!"

"O, but you did!"

"O, but I didn't!"

"Didn't she say that?"

"Yes. I heard her."

"O, there's a . . . fib!"

Observing me the young lady came over and asked me did I wish to buy anything. The tone of her voice was not encouraging; she seemed to have spoken to me out of a sense of duty. I looked humbly at the great jars that stood like eastern guards at either side of the dark entrance to the stall and murmured:

"No, thank you."

The young lady changed the position of one of the vases and went back to the two young men. They began to talk of the same subject. Once or twice the young lady glanced at me over her shoulder.

I lingered before her stall, though I knew my stay was useless, to make my interest in her wares seem the more real. Then I turned away slowly and walked down the middle of the bazaar. I allowed the two pennies to fall against the sixpence in my pocket. I heard a voice call from one end of the gallery that the light was out. The upper part of the hall was now completely dark.

Gazing up into the darkness I saw myself as a creature driven and derided by vanity; and my eyes burned with anguish and anger.

K

FRANZ KAFKA

FRANZ KAFKA (German, 1883-1924). Austrian-born novelist, whose influence
became international 20 years after death. A lonely, tormented figure, who
suffered from tuberculosis. Published only few stories during lifetime. Three
posthumous novels—*The Castle, The Trial, Amerika*—notable for atmosphere
of paranoia, the individual struggling against anonymous powers. Fantastic
motives combined with detailed realism.

A COUNTRY DOCTOR

I was in great perplexity; I had to start on an urgent journey; a
seriously ill patient was waiting for me in a village ten miles off; a
thick blizzard of snow filled all the wide spaces between him and
me; I had a gig, a light gig with big wheels, exactly right for our
country roads; muffled in furs, my bag of instruments in my hand,
I was in the courtyard all ready for the journey; but there was no
horse to be had, no horse. My own horse had died in the night,
worn out by the fatigues of this icy winter; my servant girl was now
running round the village trying to borrow a horse; but it was hopeless, I knew it, and I stood there forlornly, with the snow gathering
more and more thickly upon me, more and more unable to move.
In the gateway the girl appeared, alone, and waved the lantern;
of course, who would lend a horse at this time for such a journey?
I strode through the courtyard once more; I could see no way out;
in my confused distress I kicked at the dilapidated door of the year-
long uninhabited pigsty. It flew open and flapped to and fro on its
hinges. A steam and smell as of horses came out from it. A dim
stable lantern was swinging inside from a rope. A man, crouching
on his hams in that low space, showed an open blue-eyed face. "Shall
I yoke up?" he asked, crawling out on all fours. I did not know
what to say and merely stooped down to see what else was in the
sty. The servant girl was standing beside me. "You never know what

669

you're going to find in your own house," she said, and we both laughed. "Hey there, Brother, hey there, Sister!" called the groom, and two horses, enormous creatures with powerful flanks, one after the other, their legs tucked close to their bodies, each well-shaped head lowered like a camel's, by sheer strength of buttocking squeezed out through the door hole which they filled entirely. But at once they were standing up, their legs long and their bodies steaming thickly. "Give him a hand," I said, and the willing girl hurried to help the groom with the harnessing. Yet hardly was she beside him when the groom clipped hold of her and pushed his face against hers. She screamed and fled back to me; on her cheek stood out in red the marks of two rows of teeth. "You brute," I yelled in fury, "do you want a whipping?" but in the same moment reflected that the man was a stranger; that I did not know where he came from, and that of his own free will he was helping me out when everyone else had failed me. As if he knew my thoughts he took no offense at my threat but, still busied with the horse, only turned round once towards me. "Get in," he said then, and indeed: everything was ready. A magnificent pair of horses, I observed, such as I had never sat behind, and I climbed in happily. "But I'll drive, you don't know the way," I said. "Of course," said he, " I'm not coming with you anyway. I am staying with Rose." "No," shrieked Rose, fleeing in the house with a justified presentiment that her fate was inescapable; I heard the key turn in the locks; I could see, moreover, how she put out the lights in the entrance hall and in further flight all through the rooms keep herself from being discovered. "You're coming with me," I said to the groom, "or I won't go, urgent as my journey is. I'm not thinking of paying for it by handing the girl over to you." "Gee up!" he said; clapped his hands; the gig whirled off like a log in a freshet; I could just hear the door of my house splitting and bursting as the groom charged at it and then I was deafened and blinded by a storming rush that steadily buffeted all my senses. But this only for a moment, since, as if my patient's farmyard had opened out just before my courtyard gate, I was already there; the horses had come quietly to a standstill; the blizzard had stopped; moonlight all around; my patient's parents hurried out of the house, his sister behind them; I was almost lifted out of the gig; from their confused ejaculations I gathered not a word; in the sickroom the air was almost unbreathable; the neglected stove was smoking; I wanted to push open a window; but first I had to look at my patient. Gaunt, without any

fever, not cold, not warm, with vacant eyes, without a shirt, the youngster heaved himself up from under the feather bedding, threw his arms around my neck, and whispered in my ear: "Doctor, let me die." I glanced round the room; no one had heard it; the parents were leaning forward in silence waiting for my verdict; the sister had set a chair for my handbag; I opened the bag and hunted among my instruments; the boy kept clutching at me from his bed to remind me of his entreaty; I picked up a pair of tweezers, examined them in the candlelight and laid them down again. "Yes," I thought blasphemously, "in cases like this the gods are helpful, send the missing horse, add to it a second because of the urgency, and to crown everything bestow even a groom—" And only now did I remember Rose again; what was I to do, how could I rescue her, how could I pull her away from under that groom at ten miles' distance, with a team of horses I couldn't control. These horses, now, they had somehow slipped the reins loose, pushed the windows open from outside, I did not know how; each of them had stuck a head in at a window and, quite unmoved by the startled cries of the family, stood eyeing the patient. "Better go back at once," I thought, as if the horses were summoning me to the return journey, yet I permitted the patient's sister, who fancied that I was dazed by the heat, to take my fur coat from me. A glass of rum was poured out for me, the old man clapped me on the shoulder, a familiarity justified by this offer of his treasure. I shook my head; in the narrow confines of the old man's thoughts I felt ill; that was my only reason for refusing the drink. The mother stood by the bedside and cajoled me towards it; I yielded, and, while one of the horses whinnied loudly to the ceiling, laid my head to to the boy's breast, which shivered under my wet beard. I confirmed what I already knew; the boy was quite sound, something a little wrong with his circulation, saturated with coffee by his solicitous mother, but sound and best turned out of bed with one shove. I am no world reformer and so I let him lie. I was the district doctor and did my duty to the uttermost, to the point where it became almost too much. I was badly paid and yet generous and helpful to the poor. I had still to see that Rose was all right, and then the boy might have his way and I wanted to die too. What was I doing there in that endless winter! My horse was dead, and not a single person in the village would lend me another. I had to get my team out of the pigsty; if they hadn't chanced to be horses I should have had to travel with swine. That was how it was. And

671

I nodded to the family. They knew nothing about it, and, had they known, would not have believed it. To write prescriptions is easy, but to come to an understanding with people is hard. Well, this should be the end of my visit, I had once more been called out needlessly. I was used to that, the whole district made my life a torment with my night bell, but that I should have to sacrifice Rose this time as well, the pretty girl who had lived in my house for years almost without noticing her—that sacrifice was too much to ask, and I had somehow to get it reasoned out in my head with the help of what craft I could muster, in order not to let fly at this family, which with the best will in the world could not restore Rose to me. But as I shut my bag and put an arm out for my fur coat, the family meanwhile standing together, the father sniffing at the glass of rum in his hand, the mother, apparently disappointed in me—why, what do people expect?—biting her lips with tears in her eyes, the sister fluttering a blood-soaked towel, I was somehow ready to admit conditionally that the boy might be ill after all. I went towards him, he welcomed me smiling as if I were bringing him the most nourishing invalid broth—ah, now both horses were whinnying together; the noise, I suppose, was ordained by heaven to assist my examination of the patient—and this time, I discovered that the boy was indeed ill. His right side, near the hip, was an open wound as big as the palm of my hand. Rose-red, in many variations of shade, dark in the hollows, lighter at the edges, softly granulated, with irregular clots of blood, open as a surface mine to the daylight. That was how it looked from a distance. But on closer inspection there was another complication. I could not help a low whistle of surprise. Worms, as thick and as long as my little finger, themselves rose-red and blood-spotted as well, were wriggling from their fastness in the interior of the wound towards the light, with small white heads and many little legs. Poor boy, you were past helping. I had discovered your great wound; this blossom in your side was destroying you. The family was pleased; they saw me busying myself; the sister told the mother, the mother the father, the father told several guests who were coming in, through the moonlight at the open door, walking on tiptoe, keeping their balance with outstretched arms. "Will you save me?" whispered the boy with a sob, quite blinded by the life within his wound. That is what people are like in my district. Always expecting the impossible from the doctor. They have lost their ancient beliefs; the parson sits at home and unravels his vestments,

one after another; but the doctor is supposed to be omnipotent with his merciful surgeon's hand. Well, as it pleases them; I have not thrust my services on them; if they misuse me for sacred ends, I let that happen to me too; what better do I want, old country doctor that I am, bereft of my servant girl! And so they came, the family and the village elders, and stripped my clothes off me; a scholar choir with the teacher at the head of it stood before the house and sang these words to an utterly simple tune:

Strip his clothes off, then he'll heal us,
If he doesn't, kill him dead!
Only a doctor, only a doctor.

Then my clothes were off and I looked at the people quietly, my fingers in my beard and my head cocked to one side. I was altogether composed and equal to the situation and remained so, although it was no help to me, since they now took me by the head and feet and carried me to the bed. The laid me down in it next to the wall, on the side of the wound. Then they all left the room; the door was shut; the singing stopped; clouds covered the moon; the bedding was warm around me; the horses' heads in the open windows wavered like shadows. "Do you know," said a voice in my ear, "I have very little confidence in you. Why, you were only blown in here, you didn't come on your own feet. Instead of helping me, you're cramping me on my deathbed. What I'd like best is to scratch your eyes out." "Right," I said, " it is a shame. And yet I am a doctor. What am I to do? Belive me, it is not too easy for me either." "Am I supposed to be content with this apology? Oh, I must be, I can't help it. I always have to put up with things. A fine wound is all I brought into the world; that was my sole endowment." "My young friend," said I, "your mistake is: you have not a wide enough view. I have been in all the sickrooms, far and wide, and I tell you: your wound is not so bad. Done in a tight corner with two strokes of the ax. Many a one proffers his side and can hardly hear the ax in the forest, far less that it is coming nearer to him." "Is that really so, or are you deluding me in my fever?" "It is really so, take the word of honor of an official doctor." And he took it and lay still. But now it was time for me to think of escaping. The horses were still standing faithfully in their places. My clothes, my fur coat, my bag were quickly collected; I didn't want to waste time dressing; if the horses raced home as they had come, I should only be springing, as it were, out of this bed into my own. Obediently a horse backed away from the window; I

threw my bundle into the gig; the fur coat missed its mark and was caught on a hook only by the sleeve. Good enough. I swung myself on to the horse. With the reins loosely trailing, one horse barely fastened to the other, the gig swaying behind, my fur coat last of all in the snow. "Gee up!" I said, but there was no galloping; slowly, like old men, we crawled through the snowy wastes; a long time echoed behind us the new but faulty song of the children:

O be joyful, all you patients,
The doctor's laid in bed beside you!

Never shall I reach home at this rate; my flourishing practice is done for; my successor is robbing me, but in vain, for he cannot take my place; in my house the disgusting groom is raging; Rose is his victim; I do not want to think about it any more. Naked, exposed to the frost of this most unhappy of ages, with an earthly vehicle, unearthly horses, old man that I am, I wander astray. My fur coat is hanging from the back of the gig, but I cannot reach it and none of my limber pack of patients lifts a finger. Betrayed! Betrayed! A false alarm on the night bell once answered—it cannot be made good, not ever.

NAGAI KAFU

NAGAI KAFU (Japanese, 1879-   ). Modern Japanese fiction writer, strongly influenced by American and French literature. Spent most of youth in China, America and France.

THE BILL-COLLECTING

I

INSTANTLY after she got up from the bed where she was sleeping with Omatsu, her companion, Oyo put on her narrow-sleeved Hanten as usual, and, wrapping her head with a towel in the manner of the "sister's cap," she began to sweep the parlour.

Oyo is the maidservant in Kinugawa, an assignation house.

As they had guests in the inner room of Yojohan, who had been lodging there since the evening before, Oyo wiped up every place with the dust cloth except that room, including the railings and

stairways of the first floor. Coming down to the fireplace near the counter she found the mistress, with toothbrush in her mouth, already uncovering the charcoal fire of the previous evening. In contrast to the dark, humid interior where the odour of wine seemed to drift from somewhere, the winter sunshine glittering on the opposite side of the street and through the frosted-glass screen of the front lattice gate, looked quite warm and cheerful. As soon as the mistress saw Oyo, who was bidding her "Good-morning," she said all at once:

"Now, Oyo, I wish you would go directly after breakfast, as the place is far."

Being thus ordered, Oyo took up her chopsticks for breakfast, eating before Omatsu and Otetsu the cook. After having finished her toilet and changed her dress, and listening again to the instructions and messages from the mistress, she started. It was almost seven o'clock when she set out in the new wooden clogs that were given her by the regular geisha girls as a present at the end of the last year, and she heard the voice of the cook-supplier at the kitchen, the man who came to get the plates and bowls.

Oyo went out by the familiar short-cut through the lane between the houses of the geisha girls. Coming out into the open street of Ginza, which was filled with sunshine, she looked around her as though surprised at the new appearance of things. Her bosom pulsated to the sounds of trolleys passing by, and she not only felt that she had forgotten all the messages charged by the mistress, but even the route which she thought she had understood well when she left home. She became confused, so that the way seemed further than she had supposed.

It had been five years since Oyo entered service, in the autumn, at the age of fourteen, at Kinugawa, the assignation house. She had been at Hakone and at Enoshima, she knew Haneda and the shrine of Narita, but it was only as an attendant of the guests and geisha girls in the great carousels of many people that she went to these places. Once, though she was a woman, she had walked alone through the night with two or three hundred yen in cash in her sash. But it was not further than a few blocks where she went to an accustomed bank on behalf of the mistress. It was only once or twice in a year that she rode a really long distance by trolley, to visit her home at Minami-Senju for holiday.

To a woman of down-town who knows nothing about the suburbs of Tokyo, except Fukagawa, Shinagawa, and Asakusa, even to

675

hear the name of Okubo in the uptown district where Oyo was going to-day to collect the bill, caused her to imagine a place where foxes and badgers live. As she also felt fearful that she might not be able to return home that day if she did not catch the trolley as soon as possible, she hurried to the square of Owaricho, not even stopping at the beautiful show windows of Matsuya, and Mikamiya and Tenshodo.

"Good-morning, Maid Oyo!"

Suddenly, being thus addressed from the crowd which was waiting for the trolley, Oyo turned back and saw an unemployed girl of Tamaomiya, who had her hair dressed in Hisashigami and wore the half-coat of Koki silk.

"Kimi chan. Going to temple?"

As is a habit of woman, Oyo looked at the hair and clothing of this geisha girl, which was not particularly unusual.

"No. I have a patient at home," Kimi chan, the employed girl, said apologetically, as though answering the question of the employer. "Where are you going?"

"To the place called Okubo. I was told to take the Shinjuku line. Is this the place to wait for it?"

"Shinjuku. . . . Then it is on the other side. You must take the car from the other side of the street."

"Oh!" Oyo cried, with such a loud voice that she surprised herself. And as if she could not hear the formal salutation of the employed girl, "Please keep me in mind again . . ." she crossed the square to the other side almost in rapture. Though it was a winter morning her forehead perspired. Having heaved a sigh of relief before the glass door of the Café Lion, Oyo turned back with a wonder-stricken look to the other side of the street where was the clock on the roof of the Hattori clock store, thinking that it was a marvellous thing that she was not killed in the midst of the square where so many trolleys are crossing. By that time the employed girl of Tamaomiya, almost crushed among the crowds on the conductor's platform, went away toward the Mihara bridge, and though many almost empty cars followed it, the only thing that passed the tracks where Oyo was waiting was a lumbering horse truck loaded with casks. The sidewalk near to the Café Lion was so filled with persons waiting for transfers that they overflowed on to the street pavement. Unconsciously, Oyo looked at the blue sky of winter, calling to mind the clock on the roof of Hattori's

676

building, which pointed to half-past eleven. She became so impatient that she felt she could not wait any longer. The complaints of the persons who were waiting for transfers, speaking in loud voices, the breaking of the wires or the stoppage of the electric current, disturbed her as though it were the announcement of a fire burning her house. Exhausted by waiting, Oyo, like the others, leaned against the glass door of the Café and hung her head. Suddenly becoming conscious of a commotion, Oyo also ran in order not to be too late for the car, but, being only a helpless woman, she could hardly approach the first car. Even the next one she missed, for a big man of dark complexion, crossing in from the side, had pushed her away when her foot was already on the step. Moreover, her side lock of Ichogaeshi was rubbed up by the sleeve of the double manteau with great force.

"Now I won't mind what becomes of me. I will wait even half a day, or a day, as long as they want me to wait."

Oyo, who had already become desperate, purposely followed behind the crowd, to take the next approaching car.

When they came to Hibiya park, a seat was left, so Oyo could at last rest her tired back. Then the inside of the car was calmer and the streets outside opened out and became more quiet, and in the warmth of the inside of the car, with the sun shining on the back of her neck and shoulders, she nodded involuntarily with the light jolting of the car. The fatigue of the body, which has to work every night until one o'clock at the earliest, pressed on her eyelids all at once. As Oyo is the favourite servant of the mistress, raised by her from childhood, she must help her not only in the parlour of the guests, but also as chambermaid. To be made a companion in the late drinking of the guests in her busy time is bearable, but the most disgusting thing is the troublesome task of washing clean, in a hot-water cup, the whole set of artificial teeth of a guest nearly sixty years of age, every time after his meal.

In a short time there were indications of the stopping of the car and passengers coming and going. Oyo awakened all at once, surprised, and looked out of the window. She saw a leafy tree, a high bank and a low bridge on the waterless moat. The conductors, enough to frighten her, were assembled in front of the new house at the corner. Many empty cars were left as if they were to be given away. With this sight of unfamiliar streets, Oyo felt unutterable helplessness. She became anxious about the thing in her sash, fear-

677

ing that it had been stolen in her absent-minded moments. Also she doubted whether this was the place to leave the car. Impatiently she moved a bit from the end and said:

"Please, what is this place?"

The high-boned, flat-faced, slant-eyed conductor, who seemed to perceive the embarrassed figure of Oyo by a glance, did not move from the platform. Shrugging his shoulders, as if cold, and turning his head to the other side, he pulled the bell so that Oyo, who had left her seat, was upset by the moving car and thrown with all the weight of her body on the lap of a man looking like a foreman of the labourers, who was sitting near to the entrance. Feeling abashed, Oyo tried to get up quickly; she noticed that a big arm, as heavy as iron, was laid on her back as if to embrace her body; she struggled with all her might.

"Ehe! he! he!"

With the vile, frightful laughter there was a smell of wine.

"How can I stand it when I am held fast by a girl!"

"What good luck to have!" chanted one of the group that was sitting on the other side, and they burst into laughter.

Oyo flushed like fire, and wished even to jump out of the moving car. After that she felt that all the eyes in the car were looking constantly at her. Even then, she had not gained her composure after the fright of the moment when she felt herself closely embraced by a labourer. All at once Oyo became conscious that no one in the car was dressed like her—in Meisen silk, with folds laid somewhat loose, grey Hawori with an embroidered crest on it, and an apron of Itoöri neatly tied. All the other women were in Hisashigami and in close folds, and most of the men passengers were soldiers. Her helplessness riding among these unknown people became more keen. Just at the time when she was about to ask the conductor, who came to inspect the transfer tickets, regarding the station before Shinjuku, her embarrassment and helplessness became all but overwhelming.

"This is the Awoyama line, Miss. If you wish to go to Shinjuku, there is no other way but to transfer at Awoyama Itchome, and again at Shiocho." Throwing the transfer ticket on the lap of Oyo, the conductor hurried to fix the dislocated pole.

As she had understood that she could go all the way without transferring, Oyo, on hearing that she had to transfer not once but twice, felt as if she was thrown at last into the labyrinthine jungle of Yawata.

678

After going here and there, Oyo was able at last to realise that
Tenmacho Nichome was the station before Shinjuku. How far
would the trouble of the unknown route continue? Oyo regretted
that she had come, and thought that she would never again go on
an errand to an unknown place, no matter how she might be scolded.
It is far better to stay at home with the sweeping, and to dry the
bed-clothes or to wash the Yukata to offer to the guests. In this
broad street, more bustling than she could have expected, she
could not tell whether she had to turn to the right or to the left.
Nevertheless, as she could not stand in the middle of the street, she
was thinking about paying her own money secretly to ride in a
Kuruma, when she saw a Kurumaya from the stand, and asked
him how much she would have to pay to ride to Okubo.

"Give me fifty sen."

"Don't fool me."

Being much provoked, Oyo did not even turn to the Kurumaya,
who called out something to her from her back, and walked aimlessly to a side street. Seeing a little girl with tucks at her shoulders
in front of a tobacco shop, she asked in an almost weeping tone:

"Please, my girl, will you kindly let me know how to get to
Yochomachi of Okubo?"

"Yochomachi?" said the girl cheerfully. "Go straight this way,
and going down a slope you will find a policeman's post. . . .
You had better ask at the policeman's post."

Oyo felt revived for the first time.

"Thank you ever so much."

Putting an overwhelming sentiment of thanks into these simple
words, Oyo walked away, looking curiously at the sights on both
sides of the somewhat narrow street. There was a European building for moving pictures on one side. From the lane near to the
building a few geisha girls came out, laughing about something
in loud voices. Looking at them, Oyo wondered: "Why are there
geisha girls in such a place?" Suddenly she heard a tremendous
noise. Before she could think what was the matter, she saw many
soldiers on horseback riding from the open street to this narrow
side street. There was the gate of a temple at one side of the beginning of the slope, and, taking advantage of an open place, Oyo was
fortunate enough to get out of the way. She saw six or seven men
employed on the telegraph wires, squatting on the earth, eating

their luncheon. A bamboo ladder was leaned against a wire pole on the other side of the street.

"Hello! The beauty!"

Their teasing started Oyo running away in embarrassment.

"We are receiving an extraordinary Benten."

"Hey, my girl! May I offer you a glass?"

Some of them were looking intently at the folds of her skirts. They could not contain themselves any longer, when a sudden wind had brushed aside the skirts of her underclothes. All of them burst in at once.

"Luck to see!"

"It is worth two yen at Sinjuku!"

"The red clothes are said to keep long!" And they continued to say things which were unbearable to hear. But is not the procession of the soldiers endless, stirring up the sand on all sides? And how much Oyo wished to escape!

Oyo finally got away from the place and went down the slope, almost running, when she suddenly stumbled on a stone and hardly kept from falling. In front of it she saw something that looked like a squirming heap of rags, which said:

"Ladies and gentlemen, passing by, please, a penny . . ."

Two or three leper beggars, at whom one could not bear to look a second time, were making bows on the sand of the street. The town at the foot of the slope was visible, with the dirty roofs in confusion, at the bottom of the valley-like lowland. Oyo wondered without any reason whether the town over yonder was the outcasts' quarter.

Going down the slope and turning to the left as she was instructed by the girl of the tobacco shop she easily found a policeman's post. As a policeman who looked good-natured was standing in the middle of the street, she asked him her route.

"What number of Yochomachi is it?"

"It is number sixty-two. The house is Mr. Inuyama's."

"Number sixty-two—then you have to go straight along this way, and go up the slope before a big wine-shop."

"I see."

"And let me see, is it the third side street after you go straight up the slope? . . . You turn there to the left, where you will find number sixty-two."

"Much obliged to you."

Before she had gone less than half a block, she found a wine-shop that looked like the one she was told about, and also a slope, so she thought the rest of the route was quite short. Feeling somewhat proud that she had come this far alone without the Kuruma or without going much out of the way, she forgot a while even the fatigue of her legs, but when she began to go up the slope, she had to meet another unexpected trouble.

Though the down-town district had had such continuous clear weather that it was annoyed by the dust, the up-town quarter of the city seemed to have had rain the night before and the street, which was not broad, was so deep in mud that Oyo could not even find the sidewalk. By the time she discovered that the mud was melting frost, which had not had time to dry, not only the toes of her new wooden clogs, but also her white socks newly washed, were all splashed with mud. On one side of the road was the bank covered with sepiaria and on the other side was a cryptomeria hedge, where, taking advantage of the fact that there were no passers-by, Oyo took out her pocket-papers and wiped, she knew not how often, the mud from the mat lining of her wooden clogs. As she glanced up she thought the third side street to which she had been directed by the policeman might be the corner she sought.

III

The mud of the melting frost became harder and harder. A big, masterless dog was roaming about with a menacing look. The rasping sounds of a violin were heard. The dreary sigh of the wind came from the trees near by. Far at the end of the side street the ground seemed to slope again, and, though the winter sunshine was falling gently on the roofs of the new houses and on the deep forest that covered the rears of all the houses, either side of the road was dark in shade, and all the houses were surrounded with fences of four-inch boards. Each had a small gate containing a slide-door, the faces of which were smeared with mud that had not been washed off, which seemed to have been placed there in mischief by the boys in the neighbourhood.

The number and name of the house, which Oyo found at last, after examining all the labels on the houses on both sides, was on the support of the small gate, where the mud was splashed thickest and dirtiest.

681

Inuyama Takemasa. . . .

Oyo looked at it again before she entered the gate. The gentleman called Mr. Inuyama was the most captious, unsympathetic and unreasonable among the numerous guests that came to Kinugawa. No matter how busy they were in attendance in the parlours, he would not be satisfied if he could not call up Oyo and all the other maids into his room. If the mistress did not come to salute him every time he came he would be angry and say: "You insult me," or "You treat me coldly." It was said that he gave up his membership in the parliament as it did not suit his dignity. His profession at present was that of a politician. He was fond of geishas as young as babies, and if the girls did not obey his will, he was so furious that nobody could touch him, and Oyo not only despised him more than any of the other guests, but also was afraid, without any reason, of his forbidding appearance and loud voice. He always wore European clothes and used to come in a Kuruma pulled by two drawers, saying that the lower class of people ride in the trolley. Once in a certain conversation, when the mistress had said to him that "in these days not only the expenses of your pleasure and the tips for geisha become dearer, but even your expense for Kuruma must be very considerable," he laughed:

"Mistress, the money is earned to spend. Ha! ha! ha! ha!"

But these prosperous days were no longer. When it was hardly December of that year, Mr. Inuyama suddenly stopped coming, and in spite of many letters he would not respond to the bill of two hundred yen of that month and the fifty-yen balance of the previous month. Kinugawa was obliged to talk it over with a geisha who first brought Mr. Inuyama after their meeting at a certain Matsumotoro, but, it was almost clear that she could not shake her sleeve when she had none, and so January passed in this way, and now it was February. The mistress sent Oyo to the mansion of Mr. Inuyama to reconnoitre.

Oyo had known numerous cases of this kind, not only of men like Mr. Inuyama, but also of many other guests. She thought this nothing more than the bad ways of people. She thought only that they will be enjoying themselves at some other house, if they do not come to hers, then, it will be good of them if they will be more considerate and pay the bill. The reason Oyo looked again at the label on the gate was the fact that the gate of his mansion was so dirty. But, to enter the gate was better than the annoyance of walking around aimlessly any longer in the frost-melting road, so

she looked around from the porch with its dirty and broken paper-screen, wondering which was the servants' entrance.

On the right hand, beyond the bamboo fence, was visible the roof of a one-storied house looking cold under the garden trees. She got a glimpse of an old red blanket and a dirty cotton gown hung on a clothes-pole, through the crevices of the bamboo fence. On the left hand, further on, were one-storied houses with lattice gates, and another that looked like a rented house. Beside the wheel-well, where the plum-blossoms showed their buds, a fish-monger was cutting a salted salmon. Two maidservants in careless Hisashigami, who carried babies under quilted gowns and wore European aprons which had become grey, seemed to be at the height of their silly conversation with the fishmonger. As soon as they caught sight of Oyo, whose appearance was quite different, they sharpened their eyes, and, seeming rather to fear her, looked her over attentively from top to toe. The road from the well to the servants' entrance was spread with straw bags of charcoal, and the muddy water of the melting frost ran into the feet of people walking on them. Being in much perplexity Oyo could not move a step, and bending her waist, said:

"I beg your pardon."

Both of the maidservants stood wonder-stricken with open mouths.

"Is this Mr. Inuyama's house?"

Suddenly one of the maidservants began to grow uneasy, and, perceiving her manner, Oyo said:

"I came with a message from Kyobashi. Is the master at home?"

"He is absent."

Then the baby on her back began to cry.

Oyo, as she was ordered by the mistress, remembered how to proceed when she was told the master was absent, namely, to call madam to the servants' entrance and leave the word that she was the messenger from Mizuta, which was the name of her mistress. However, as Oyo was only eighteen or nineteen, she felt somewhat timid and stood on the walk, forgetting even that the water of the melting frost was overflowing on her polished wooden clogs. The baby on the back of the maidservant cried more and more.

"Chiyo! Chiyo!" Suddenly, a voice of woman, close to her ears, aroused her.

Being astonished, Oyo turned and saw at the broken paper-screens of the servants' entrance not farther than six inches, the big face of a woman, like a horse, with the eyes widely separated from

each other. The careless Hisashigami could not be beaten by the maidservants. She was a big, clumsy madam in a dirty and creased Higu.

Just then, the fishmonger came to offer three slices of the salted salmon to madam. Madam continued talking with the fishmonger, and Oyo, at last somewhat aroused and feeling at the same time a sense of deep disappointment, went out from the gate as if to escape. For she felt that her troubles in coming so far had been all in vain. She was exceedingly sorry for her mistress, as she had been entirely deceived by this humbug.

When Oyo rode again in the trolley she felt, at first, the fatigue of the vain effort and at the same time the fact that she was unbearably hungry, but being unable to do anything about it, she arrived at Ginza. The sun was already declining. Calling to her mind the clockstand of Hattori, which she saw when she was waiting for the car that morning, she looked up, and lo! was it not already near to four o'clock. Oyo felt her heart sinking with melancholy, picturing in her mind the flash of her mistress' eye, who never would say to her: "How early you are!" when she returned from the far-away errand. The electric lights were already lit in the shops. . . .

KAGAWA KAGEKI

KAGAWA KAGEKI (Japanese, 1768-1843). Leading *tanka* poet of his day. A prodigy who composed verse as a child. Earned living as instructor of poetry. Famous collection of verse: *Keien isshi*. Also prepared important editions of early Japanese texts.

SWALLOWS

Although the swallows are not like
    The friends with whom I freely may
Hold converse, what a joy it is
    To meet these birds from far away!

PINE-TREES AND THE MOON

The forms of all the pine-trees
    Have stood forth into sight;
But yet the moon has not left
    The rim of the mountain height.

WILD GEESE

Far in the distance, across the hazy sky,
  I saw the wild geese flock and fly away;
Yesterday I saw them take their flight,
  Also to-day.

A MAIDEN

The girl of whom in olden days
I once caught glimpses through a hedge,
Making my horse tread on young grass—
Alas! she, too, by now must have grown old!

THE CRICKET

O, cricket, chirruping
  Under my bed,
Do not tell other men
  My whispers with my beloved.

KALIDASA

KĀLIDĀSA (Sanskrit, 5th century A.D.). Legendary, greatest of all Sanskrit dramatists and poets. Nothing known of life, though apparently he was a thorough scholar and wide traveler throughout India. Left three dramas, two epics, two shorter poems. His masterpiece, the play *Sakuntalā,* created sensation when translated in 1789, influenced Goethe, Schiller, Herder.

THE.CITY OF UJJAIN

Swerve from thy northern path; for westward rise
The palace balconies thou may'st not slight
  In fair Ujjain; and if bewitching eyes,
That flutter at thy gleams, should not delight
  Thine amorous bosom, useless were thy gift of sight.

The neighbouring mountain-stream that gliding grants
A glimpse of charms in whirling eddies pursed,
  While noisy swans accompany her dance
Like a tinkling zone, will slake thy loving thirst—
A woman always tells her love in gestures first.

685

Thou only, happy lover! canst repair
The desolation that thine absence made:
    Her shrinking current seems the careless hair
That brides deserted wear in single braid,
And dead leaves falling give her face a paler shade.

    Oh, fair Ujjain! Gem to Avanti given,
Where village ancients tell their tales of mirth
    And old romance! Oh, radiant glimpse of heaven,
Home of a blest celestial band whose worth
Sufficed, though fallen from heaven, to bring down heaven on earth.

    Where the river-breeze at dawn, with fragrant gain
From friendly lotus-blossoms, lengthens out
    The clear, sweet passion-warbling of the crane,
To cure the women's languishing, and flout
With a lover's coaxing all their hesitating doubt.

    Enriched with odours through a window drifting
From perfumed hair, and greeted as a friend
    By peacock pets their wings in dances lifting,
On flower-sweet balconies thy labour end,
Where prints of dear pink feet an added glory lend.

    Black as the neck of Siva, very God,
Dear therefore to his hosts, thou mayest go
    To his dread shrine, round which the gardens nod,
When breezes rich with lotus-pollen blow
And ointments that the gaily bathing maidens know.

    Reaching that temple at another time,
Wait till the sun is lost to human eyes;
    For if thou mayest play the part sublime
Of Siva's drum at evening sacrifice,
Then hast thou in thy thunders grave a priceless prize.

    The women there, whose girdles long have tinkled
In answer to the dance, whose hands yet seize
    And wave their fans with lustrous gems besprinkled,
Will feel thine early drops that soothe and please,
And recompense thee from black eyes like clustering bees.

Clothing thyself in twilight's rose-red glory,
Embrace the dancing Siva's tree-like arm;
He will prefer thee to his mantle hoary,
And spare his grateful goddess-bride's alarm,
Whose eager gaze will manifest no fear of harm.

JOHN KEATS

JOHN KEATS (English, 1795-1821). A major poet of English Romantic
Period. Exquisite workmanship made him the "poet of the most poetical type."
Short, unhappy life, died in Rome of tuberculosis. Hopeless love for Fanny
Brawne inspired many poems and letters. Shakespeare and Milton his models.
Wrote some of most perfect poems in the language: "La Belle Dame Sans
Merci," "The Eve of St. Agnes," Odes and Sonnets.

ODE TO A NIGHTINGALE

My heart aches, and a drowsy numbness pains
  My sense, as though of hemlock I had drunk,
Or emptied some dull opiate to the drains
  One minute past, and Lethe-wards had sunk:
'Tis not through envy of thy happy lot,
  But being too happy in thy happiness,
    That thou, light-winged Dryad of the trees,
      In some melodious plot
  Of beechen green, and shadows numberless,
    Singest of summer in full-throated ease.

O for a draught of vintage! that hath been
  Cooled a long age in the deep-delved earth,
Tasting of Flora and the country green,
  Dance, and Provençal song, and sunburnt mirth!
O for a beaker full of the warm South!
  Full of the true, the blushful Hippocrene,
    With beaded bubbles winking at the brim,
      And purple-stained mouth;
  That I might drink, and leave the world unseen,
    And with thee fade away into the forest dim:

Fade far away, dissolve, and quite forget
  What thou among the leaves hast never known,

687

The weariness, the fever, and the fret
   Here, where men sit and hear each other groan;
Where palsy shakes a few, sad, last grey hairs,
   Where youth grows pale, and spectre-thin, and dies;
     Where but to think is to be full of sorrow
       And leaden-eyed despairs;
   Where beauty cannot keep her lustrous eyes,
     Or new love pine at them beyond tomorrow.

Away! away! for I will fly to thee,
   Not charioted by Bacchus and his pards,
But on the viewless wings of Poesy,
   Though the dull brain perplexes and retards:
Already with thee! tender is the night,
   And haply the Queen-Moon is on her throne,
     Clustered around by all her starry Fays;
       But here there is no light,
   Save what from heaven is with the breezes blown
     Through verdurous glooms and winding mossy ways.

I cannot see what flowers are at my feet,
   Nor what soft incense hangs upon the boughs,
But, in embalmed darkness, guess each sweet
   Wherewith the seasonable month endows
The grass, the thicket, and the fruit-tree wild;
   White hawthorn, and the pastoral eglantine;
     Fast-fading violets covered up in leaves;
       And mid-May's eldest child,
The coming musk-rose, full of dewy wine,
     The murmurous haunt of flies on summer eves.

Darkling I listen; and for many a time
   I have been half in love with easeful Death,
Called him soft names in many a mused rhyme,
   To take into the air my quiet breath;
Now more than ever seems it rich to die,
   To cease upon the midnight with no pain,
     While thou art pouring forth thy soul abroad
       In such an ecstasy!
   Still wouldst thou sing, and I have ears in vain—
     To thy high requiem become a sod.

Thou wast not born for death, immortal Bird!
  No hungry generations tread thee down;
The voice I hear this passing night was heard
  In ancient days by emperor and clown:
Perhaps the self-same song that found a path
  Through the sad heart of Ruth, when, sick for home,
    She stood in tears amid the alien corn;
        The same that ofttimes hath
  Charmed magic casements, opening on the foam
    Of perilous seas, in faery lands forlorn.

Forlorn! the very word is like a bell
  To toll me back from thee to my sole self!
Adieu! the fancy cannot cheat so well
  As she is famed to do, deceiving elf.
Adieu! adieu! thy plaintive anthem fades
  Past the near meadows, over the still stream,
    Up the hill-side; and now 'tis buried deep
        In the next valley-glades:
  Was it a vision, or a waking dream?
    Fled is that music:—do I wake or sleep?

ODE ON A GRECIAN URN

Thou still unravish'd bride of quietness,
  Thou foster-child of silence and slow time,
Sylvian historian, who canst thus express
  A flowery tale more sweetly than our rhyme:
What leaf-fring'd legend haunts about thy shape
  Of deities or mortals, or of both,
    In Tempe or the dales of Arcady?
What men or gods are these? What maidens loth?
  What mad pursuit? What struggle to escape?
    What pipes and timbrels? What wild ecstasy?

Heard melodies are sweet, but those unheard
  Are sweeter; therefore, ye soft pipes, play on;
Not to the sensual ear, but, more endear'd,
  Pipe to the spirit ditties of no tone:

689

Fair youth, beneath the trees, thou canst not leave
　　Thy song, nor ever can those trees be bare;
　　　Bold Lover, never, never canst thou kiss,
Though winning near the goal—yet, do not grieve;
　　She cannot fade, though thou hast not thy bliss,
　　　For ever wilt thou love, and she be fair!

Ah, happy, happy boughs! that cannot shed
　　Your leaves, nor ever bid the Spring adieu;
And, happy melodist, unwearied,
　　For ever piping songs for ever new;
More happy love! more happy, happy love!
　　For ever warm and still to be enjoy'd,
　　　For ever panting, and for ever young;
All breathing human passion far above,
　　That leaves a heart high-sorrowful and cloy'd,
　　　A burning forehead, and a parching tongue.

Who are these coming to the sacrifice?
　　To what green altar, O mysterious priest,
Lead'st thou that heifer lowing at the skies,
　　And all her silken flanks with garlands drest?
What little town by river or sea shore,
　　Or mountain-built with peaceful citadel,
　　　Is emptied of its folk, this pious morn?
And, little town, thy streets for evermore
　　Will silent be: and not a soul to tell
　　　Why thou art desolate, can e'er return.

O Attic shape! Fair attitude! with brede
　　Of marble men and maidens overwrought,
With forest branches and the trodden weed;
　　Thou, silent form, dost tease us out of thought
As doth eternity: Cold Pastoral!
　　When old age shall this generation waste,
　　　Thou shalt remain, in midst of other woe
Than ours, a friend to man, to whom thou say'st,
　　'Beauty is truth, truth beauty'—that is all
　　　Ye know on earth, and all ye need to know.

TO AUTUMN

Season of mists and mellow fruitfulness,
  Close bosom-friend of the maturing sun;
Conspiring with him how to load and bless
  With fruit the vines that round the thatch-eves run;
To bend with apples the moss'd cottage-trees,
  And fill all fruit with ripeness to the core;
    To swell the gourd, and plump the hazel shells
With a sweet kernel; to set budding more,
  And still more, later flowers for the bees,
  Until they think warm days will never cease,
    For Summer has o'er-brimm'd their clammy cells.

Who hath not seen thee oft amid thy store?
  Sometimes whoever seeks abroad may find
Thee sitting careless on a granary floor,
  Thy hair soft-lifted by the winnowing wind;
Or on a half-reap'd furrow sound asleep,
  Drows'd with the fume of poppies, while thy hook
    Spares the next swath and all its twined flowers:
And sometimes like a gleaner thou dost keep
  Steady thy laden head across a brook;
  Or by a cyder-press, with patient look,
    Thou watchest the last oozings hours by hours.

Where are the songs of Spring? Ay, where are they?
  Think not of them, thou hast thy music too,—
While barred clouds bloom the soft-dying day,
  And touch the stubble-plains with rosy hue;
Then in a wailful choir the small gnats mourn
  Among the river sallows, borne aloft
    Or sinking as the light wind lives or dies;
And full-grown lambs loud bleat from hilly bourn;
  Hedge-crickets sing; and now with treble soft
  The red-breast whistles from a garden-croft;
    And gathering swallows twitter in the skies.

GOTTFRIED KELLER

GOTTFRIED KELLER (Swiss, 1819-1890). A Swiss writer who wrote some of best German literature of 19th century. Largely self-educated, became first a painter, then a writer. Autobiographical novel, *Der Grüne Heinrich*, one of most praised "educational novels." Short stories skillful, realistic, sensitive.

A LEGEND OF THE DANCE

ACCORDING to Saint Gregory, Musa was the dancer among the saints. The child of good people, she was a bright young lady, a diligent servant of the Mother of God, and subject only to one weakness, such an uncontrollable passion for the dance that when the child was not praying she was dancing, and that on all imaginable occasions. Musa danced with her playmates, with children, with the young men, and even by herself. She danced in her own room and every other room in the house, in the garden, in the meadows. Even when she went to the altar it was to a gracious measure rather than a walk, and even on the smooth marble flags before the church door, she did not scruple to practice a few hasty steps.

In fact, one day when she found herself alone in the church, she could not refrain from executing some figures before the altar, and, so to speak, dancing a pretty prayer to the Virgin Mary. She became so oblivious of all else that she fancied she was merely dreaming when she saw an oldish but handsome gentleman dancing opposite her and supplementing her figures so skilfully that the pair got into the most elaborate dance imaginable. The gentleman had a royal purple robe, a golden crown on his head, and a glossy black curled beard, which age had touched as with streaks of starlight. At the same time music sounded from the choir where half a dozen small angels stood, or sat with their chubby little legs hanging over the screen, and fingered or blew their various instruments. The urchins were very pleasant and skilful. Each rested his music on one of the stone angels with which the choir screen was adorned, except the smallest, a puffy-cheeked piper who sat crosslegged and contrived to hold his music with his pink toes. He was the most diligent of them all. The others dangled their feet, kept spreading their pinions, one or other of them, with a rustle, so that their colors shimmered like doves' breasts, and they teased each other as they played.

Musa found no time to wonder at all this until the dance, which

692

lasted a pretty long time, was over; for the merry gentleman seemed to enjoy himself as much as the maid, who felt as if she were dancing about in heaven. But when the music ceased and Musa stood there panting, she began to be frightened in good earnest, and looked in astonishment at the ancient, who was neither out of breath nor warm, and who now began to speak. He introduced himself as David, the Virgin Mary's royal ancestor, and her ambassador. He asked if she would like to pass eternal bliss in an unending pleasure dance, compared with which the dance they had just finished could only be called a miserable crawl.

To this she promptly answered that she would like nothing better. Whereupon the blessed King David said again that in that case she had nothing more to do than to renounce all pleasure and all dancing for the rest of her days on earth and devote herself wholly to penance and spiritual exercises, and that without hesitation or relapse. The maiden was taken aback at these conditions, and asked whether she must really give up dancing altogether. She questioned indeed whether there was any dancing in Heaven; for there was a time for everything. This earth looked very fit and proper for dancing; it stood to reason that Heaven must have very different attractions, else death were a superfluity.

But David explained to her that her notions on the subject were erroneous, and proved from many Bible texts, and from his own example that dancing was assuredly a sanctified occupation for the blessed. But what was wanted just now was an immediate decision, Yes or No, whether she wished to enter into eternal joy by way of temporal self-denial, or not. If she did not, then he would go farther on; for they wanted some dancers in Heaven.

Musa stood, still doubtful and undecided, and fumbled anxiously with her finger-tips in her mouth. It seemed too hard never to dance again from that moment, all for the sake of an unknown reward. At that, David gave a signal, and suddenly the musicians struck up some bars of a dance of such unheard-of bliss and unearthliness that the girl's soul leaped in her body, and her limbs twitched; but she could not get one of them to dance, and she noticed that her body was far too heavy and stiff for the tune. Full of longing, she thrust her hand into the King's and made the promise which he demanded.

Forthwith he was no more to be seen, and the angel-musicians whirred and fluttered and crowded out and away through an open window. But, in mischievous childish fashion, before going they

693

dealt the patient stone angels a sounding slap on the cheeks with their rolled-up music.

Musa went home with devout step, carrying that celestial melody in her ears; and having laid all her dainty raiment aside, she got a coarse gown made and put it on. At the same time she built herself a cell at the end of her parents' garden, where the deep shade of the trees lingered, made a scant bed of moss and from that day onward separated herself from all her kindred, and took up her abode there as a penitent and saint. She spent all her time in prayer, and often disciplined herself with a scourge. But her severest penance consisted in holding her limbs stiff and immovable, for whenever she heard a sound, the twitter of a bird or the rustling of the leaves in the wind, her feet twitched as much as to tell her they must dance.

As this involuntary twitching would not forsake her, and often seduced her to a little skip before she was aware, she caused her tender feet to be fastened together by a light chain. Her relatives and friends marveled day and night at the transformation, rejoiced to possess such a saint, and guarded the hermitage under the trees as the apple of their eye. Many came for her counsel and intercession. In particular, they used to bring young girls to her who were rather clumsy on their feet, for it was observed that everyone whom she touched at once became light and graceful in gait.

So she spent three years in her cell, but by the end of the third year Musa had become almost as thin and transparent as a summer cloud. She lay continually on her bed of moss, gazed wistfully into Heaven, and was convinced that she could already see the golden sandals of the blessed, dancing and gliding about through the azure.

At last one harsh autumn day the tidings spread that the saint lay on her death-bed. She had taken off her dark penitential robe, and caused herself to be arrayed in bridal garments of dazzling white. So she lay with folded hands and smilingly awaited the hour of death. The garden was all filled with devout persons, the breezes murmured, and the leaves were falling from the trees on all sides. But suddenly the sighing of the wind changed into music, which appeared to be playing in the tree-tops, and as the people looked up, lo, all the branches were clad in fresh green, the myrtles and pomegranates put out blossom and fragrance, the earth decked itself with flowers, and a rosy glow settled upon the white, frail form of the dying saint.

That same instant she yielded up her spirit. The chain about her

694

feet sprang asunder with a sharp twang, Heaven opened wide all around, full of unbounded radiance so that all could see in. Then they saw many thousands of beautiful young men and maidens in the utmost splendor, dancing circle upon circle farther than the eye could reach. A magnificent King enthroned on a cloud, with a special band of small angels seated on its edge, bore down a little way towards earth, and received the form of the sainted Musa from before the eyes of all the beholders who filled the garden. They saw, too, how she sprang into the open Heaven and immediately danced out of sight among the jubilant radiant circle.

That was a high feast-day in Heaven. Now the custom (to be sure, it is denied by Saint Gregory of Nyssa, but stoutly maintained by his namesake of Nazianza) on feast-days was to invite the nine Muses, who sat for the rest of their time in Hell and to admit them to Heaven that they might be of assistance. They were well entertained, but once the feast was over had to go back to the other place.

When, now, the dances and songs and all the ceremonies had come to an end and the heavenly company sat down, Musa was taken taken to a table where the nine Muses were being served. They sat huddled together half scared, glancing about with their fiery black or dark-blue eyes. The busy Martha of the Gospels was caring for them in person. She had on her finest kitchen-apron and a tiny little smudge on her white chin and was pressing all manner of good things on the Muses in the friendliest possible way, but when Musa and Saint Cecilia and some other artistic women arrived and greeted the shy Pierians cheerfully, and joined their company, they began to thaw, grew confidential, and the feminine circle became quite pleasant and happy. Musa sat beside Terpsichore, and Cecilia between Polyhymnia and Euterpe, and all took one another's hands. Next came the little minstrel urchins and made up to the beautiful women with an eye to the bright fruit which shone on the ambrosial table. King David himself came and brought a golden cup, out of which all drank, so that gracious joy warmed them. He went round the table, not omitting as he passed to chuck pretty Erato under the chin. While things were going on so favorably at the Muses' table, Our Gracious Lady herself appeared in all her beauty and goodness, sat down a few minutes beside the Muses, and kissed the august Urania with the starry coronet tenderly upon the lips, when she took her departure, whispering to her that she would not rest until the Muses could remain in Paradise forever.

But that never came about. To declare their gratitude for the

kindness and friendliness which had been shown them, and to prove their goodwill, the Muses took counsel together and practised a hymn of praise in a retired corner of the Underworld. They tried to give it the form of the solemn chorals which were the fashion in Heaven. They arranged it in two parts of four voices each, with a sort of principal part, which Urania took, and they thus produced a remarkable piece of vocal music.

The next time a feast-day was celebrated in Heaven, and the Muses again rendered their assistance, they seized what appeared to be a favorable moment for their purpose, took their places, and began their song. It began softly, but soon swelled out mightily, but in those regions it sounded so dismal, almost defiant and harsh, yet so wistful and mournful that first of all a horrified silence prevailed, and next the whole assembly was seized with a sad longing for earth and home, and broke into universal weeping.

A sigh without end throbbed throughout Heaven. All the Elders and Prophets started up in dismay while the Muses, with the best of intentions, sang louder and more mournfully, and all Paradise, with the Patriarchs and Elders and Prophets and all who ever walked or lay in green pastures, lost all command of themselves. Until at last, the High and Mighty Trinity Himself came to put things right, and reduced the too zealous Muses to silence with a long reverberating peal of thunder.

Then quiet and composure were restored to Heaven, but the poor nine Sisters had to depart and never dared enter it again from that day onward.

OMAR KHAYYAM

OMAR KHAYYAM (Persian, 1050-1123). Most widely known of the Persian poets through Edward Fitzgerald's translation of the *Rubaiyat*. Honored in Iran as astronomer, algebraist and philosopher. Compiled astronomical tables and first Arabic algebra. Left 280 quatrains, epigrammatic in style, counseling a temperate hedonism as antidote to the cruelties of fate.

RUBAIYAT OF OMAR KHAYYAM

I

Awake! for Morning in the Bowl of Night
Has flung the Stone that puts the Stars to Flight;
   And Lo! the Hunter of the East has caught
The Sultan's Turret in a Noose of Light.

II

Dreaming when Dawn's Left Hand was in the Sky
I heard a Voice within the Tavern cry,
  "Awake, my Little ones, and fill the Cup
Before Life's Liquor in its Cup be dry."

III

And, as the Cock crew, those who stood before
The Tavern shouted—"Open then the Door!
  You know how little while we have to stay,
And, once departed, may return no more."

IV

Now the New Year reviving old Desires,
The thoughtful Soul to Solitude retires,
  Where the *white hand of Moses* on the Bough
Puts out, and Jesus from the Ground suspires.

V

Iram indeed is gone with all its Rose,
And Jamshyd's Sev'n-ring'd Cup where no one knows;
  But still the Vine her ancient Ruby yields,
And still a Garden by the Water blows.

VI

And David's Lips are lock't; but in divine
High-piping Pehlevi, with "Wine! Wine! Wine!
  Red Wine!"—the Nightingale cries to the Rose
That yellow Cheek of hers to incarnadine.

VII

Come, fill the Cup, and in the Fire of Spring
The Winter Garment of Repentance fling:
  The Bird of Time has but a little way
To fly—and Lo! the Bird is on the Wing.

697

And look—a thousand Blossoms with the Day
Woke—and a thousand scatter'd into Clay:
   And this first Summer Month that brings the Rose
Shall take Jamshyd and Kaikobad away.

IX

But come with old Khayyam, and leave the Lot
Of Kaikobad and Kaihosru forgot:
   Let Rustum lay about him as he will,
Or Hatim Tai cry Supper—heed them not.

X

With me along some Strip of Herbage strown
That just divides the desert from the town,
   Where name of Slave and Sultan scarce is known,
And pity Sultan Mahmud on his Throne.

XI

Here with a Loaf of Bread beneath the Bough,
A flask of Wine, a Book of Verse—and Thou
   Beside me singing in the Wilderness—
And Wilderness is Paradise enow.

XII

"How sweet is mortal Sovranty"—think some:
Others—"How blest the Paradise to come!"
   Ah, take the Cash in hand and waive the Rest;
Oh, the brave Music of a *distant* Drum!

XIII

Look to the Rose that blows about us—"Lo,
Laughing," she says, "into the World I blow:
   At once the silken Tassel of my Purse
Tear, and its Treasure on the Garden throw."

XIV

The Worldly Hope men set their Hearts upon
Turns Ashes—or it prospers; and anon,
  Like Snow upon the Desert's dusty Face
Lighting a little Hour or two—is gone.

XV

And those who husbanded the Golden Grain,
And those who flung it to the Winds like Rain,
  Alike to no such aureate Earth are turn'd
As, buried once, Men want dug up again.

XVI

Think, in this batter'd Caravanserai
Whose Doorways are alternate Night and Day,
  How Sultan after Sultan with his Pomp
Abode his Hour or two, and went his way.

XVII

They say the Lion and the Lizard keep
The Courts where Jamshyd gloried and drank deep:
  And Bahram, that great Hunter—the Wild Ass
Stamps O'er his Head, and he lies fast asleep.

XVIII

I sometimes think that never blows so red
The Rose as where some buried Cæsar bled;
  That every Hyacinth the Garden wears
Dropt in its Lap from some once lovely Head.

XIX

And this delightful Herb whose tender Green
Fledges the River's Lip on which we lean—
  Ah, lean upon it lightly! for who knows
From what once lovely Lip it springs unseen!

KAN KIKUCHI

KAN KIKUCHI (Japanese, 1888-1948). Contemporary Japanese short story writer, novelist and playwright. Precise, clear-cut stylist. Influenced by West, helped introduce realism into Japanese theater. Plays translated: *The Miracle, Love and Four Other Plays, The Father Returns, The Madman on the Roof, Better Than Revenge.*

THE MADMAN ON THE ROOF

Characters

Yoshitaro Katsushima, *the madman, 24 years of age*
Suejiro Katsushima, *his brother, a 17-year-old high school student*
Gisuke Katsushima, *their father*
Oyoshi Katsushima, *their mother*
Tosaku, *a neighbor*
Kichiji, *a man-servant, 20 years of age*
A Priestess, *about 50 years of age*

Place: *a small island in Sanuki Strait*
Time: *1900*

The stage-setting represents the backyard of the Katsushimas, who are the richest family on the island. A bamboo fence prevents one from seeing more of the house than the high roof, which stands out sharply against the rich greenish sky of the southern island summer. At the left of the stage one can catch a glimpse of the sea shining in the sunlight.

Yoshitaro, the elder son of the family, is sitting astride the ridge of the roof, and is looking out over the sea.

Gisuke (speaking from within the house). Yoshi is sitting on the roof again. He will get a sunstroke—the sun is so terribly hot. *(Coming out.)* Kichiji!—Where is Kichiji?

Kichiji (appearing from the right). Yes! What do you want?

Gisuke. Bring Yoshitaro down. He has no hat on, up there in the hot sun. He will get a sunstroke. How did he get up there, anyway? *(Coming through the gate to the center of the stage, and looking up to the roof.)* I don't see how he can stand it, sitting on that hot slate roof. *(He calls.)* Yoshitaro! You better come down. If you stay up there you will get a sunstroke, and maybe die. Come

700

on now—hurry! If you don't come down, I'll get after you with a stick.

Yoshitaro (protesting like a spoiled child). No; I don't want to. Something interesting. The priest of the Konpira God is dancing in the clouds. Dancing with an angel in pink robes. They are calling to me to come. *(Crying out ecstatically.)* Wait! I am coming!

Gisuke. If you talk like that you will fall, as you did the other day. You are already crippled and insane. How you worry your parents! Come down, you fool!

Kichiji. Master, don't get so angry. The young master doesn't understand anything. He's under the influence of evil spirits. Why, he climbed the roof of the Honzen Temple without even a ladder; a low roof like this one is the easiest thing in the world for him. I tell you it's the evil spirits that make him climb. Nothing can stop him.

Gisuke. You may be right; but he worries me to death.

Kichiji. Everyone on the island says he is under the influence of the evil fox-spirit, but I don't believe that, for I never heard of a fox climbing trees.

Gisuke (He calls again). Yoshi! Come down! *(Dropping his voice.)* Kichiji, you had better go up and fetch him.

(Kichiji goes out after the ladder. Tosaku, the neighbor, enters.)

Tosaku. Good-day, sir. Your son is on the roof again.

Gisuke. Yes; he is up there as usual. I don't like it, but when I keep him locked in a room he is unhappy as a fish out of water. Then, when I think that is too cruel, and let him out, back he goes up on the roof.

Tosaku. By the way, a Priestess has just come to the island. How would you like to have her pray for your son?—That is really what I came to see you about.

Gisuke. Is that so? Well, we have tried prayers several times before, but it has never done any good.

Tosaku. The Priestess who is here now believes in the Konpira God. She is very miraculous. People say she is inspired by the Konpira God, so that her prayers are quite different from those of a mountain priest. Why don't you try her once?

Gisuke. Suejiro says he doesn't believe in any prayers. . . . But there isn't any harm in letting her try.

(Kichiji enters carrying the ladder, and disappears behind the fence.)

Tosaku. Then I will go Kinkichi's house and bring her here. In the meantime you get your son down off the roof.

Gisuke. All right. Thanks for your trouble. *(After seeing that Tosaku has gone, he calls again.)* Yoshi! Be quiet now and come down.

Yoshitaro (drawing away from Kichiji as a Buddhist might from a heathen). If you touch me the fairies will destroy you!

(Kichiji hurriedly catches Yoshitaro by the shoulder and pulls him to the ladder. Yoshitaro suddenly becomes gentle. He comes down to the center of the stage, followed by Kichiji. Yoshitaro is lame in his right leg.)

Gisuke (calling). Oyoshi! Come out here a minute.

Oyoshi (from within). What do you want?

Gisuke. I have sent for the Priestess.

Oyoshi (appearing at the gate). That may be a good idea. You never can tell what may help him.

(Tosaka enters, leading the Priestess. She has a cunning look.)

Tosaku. This is the lady I spoke to you about.

Gisuke. Ah, good-afternoon! You are welcome.—This boy is a great worry, and causes us much shame.

Priestess (casually). Don't worry about him. I will cure him immediately with the help of the God. *(Looking at Yoshitaro.)* This is the one?

Gisuke. Yes. He is twenty-four years old, and can do nothing but climb up to high places.

Priestess. How long has he been this way?

Gisuke. Ever since he was born. Even when he was a baby, he wanted to be climbing. When he was four or five years old he climbed onto the low shrine, then onto the high shrine of Buddha, and finally onto a very high shelf. When he was seven or eight he began climbing trees. At fifteen or sixteen he climbed to the top of mountains, and stayed there all day long, where he says he talked with fairies and with gods, and such things. What do you think is the matter with him?

Priestess. There's no doubt but that it is the evil fox-spirit. All right, I will pray for him. *(Looking at Yoshitaro.)* Listen now! I am the messenger of the Konpira God of this island. And all that I say comes from the God.

702

Yoshitaro (uneasily). You say the Konpira God? Did you ever see him?

Priestess (staring at him). Don't say such sacrilegious things! The God cannot be seen.

Yoshitaro (exultantly). Oh, I have seen him many times! He is an old man with white robes and a golden crown. He is my best friend.

Priestess (taken aback at this assertion, and speaking to Gisuke). This is the evil fox-spirit, all right, but a very extreme case. Now then, I will ask the God.

(She chants a prayer in a ridiculous manner. Yoshitaro, held fast by Kichiji, watches the Priestess blankly. She works herself into a frenzy, and falls to the ground in a faint. Presently she rises to her feet and looks about her strangely.)

Priestess (in a changed voice). I am the Konpira God residing in this island!

(All except Yoshitaro fall to their knees with exclamations of reverence.)

Priestess (with affected dignity). The elder son of this family is under the influence of the evil fox-spirit. Hang him up on the branch of a tree and purify him with the smoke of green pine-needles. If you doubt what I say, you are condemned!

(She faints again. There are more exclamations of astonishment.)

Priestess (rising and looking about her as though unconscious of what has taken place). What has happened? Did the God speak?
Gisuke. It was miraculous. The God answered.
Priestess. Whatever the God told you to do, you must do at once, or be condemned. I warn you for your own sake.
Gisuke (hesitating somewhat). Kichiji, you may go and get the green pine-needles.
Yoshitaro. That was not the voice of the Konpira God. He wouldn't listen to a priestess like you!
Priestess (as though insulted). I will get even with you. Just wait! Don't you talk back to the God like that, you wretched fox!

(Kichiji enters with an armful of green pine-needles. Oyoshi becomes frightened. Gisuke and Kichiji rather reluctantly set fire to

703

the pine-needles, then bring Yoshitaro to the fire. Gisuke and Kichiji attempt to get Yoshitaro's face into the smoke. Suddenly Suejiro appears in the gateway. He wears a high-school uniform, and is a dark-complexioned, active boy. He stands amazed at the scene before him.)

Suejiro. What is the meaning of this smoke?

Yoshitaro (coughing from the smoke, and looking at his brother as at a savior). That you, Sue? Father and Kichiji have been putting me in the smoke.

Suejiro (angrily). Father! What foolish thing are you doing? Haven't I told you time and again about this sort of business?

Gisuke. But the miraculous Priestess, inspired by the God of——

Suejiro (interrupting). Rubbish! You do these foolish things merely because he is so helpless. *(He looks contemptuously at the Priestess and crosses over and stamps the fire out with his feet.)*

Gisuke (more courageously). Suejiro, I have no education, and you have, so I am always willing to listen to you. But this fire was made at the God's command, and you mustn't stamp on it.

Suejiro. Smoke won't cure him. People will laugh at you for talking about the fox-spirit. Why, if all the gods in the country were called upon together, they couldn't cure even a cold. When the doctors can't cure him, no one can. I've told you before that he doesn't suffer. If he did, we would have to do something for him. But as long as he can climb up on the roof, he is happy from morning till night. There is no one in the whole country as happy as he is— perhaps no one in the world. Besides, if you cure him now, what can he do? He is twenty-four years old and knows nothing—not even the alphabet; and he has had no experience. If he were cured, he would be conscious of being crippled, and would be the most miserable man in the country. Is that what you want to see? It's all because you want to make him normal. But isn't it foolish to become normal merely to suffer? *(Looking sidewise at the Priestess.)* Tosaku-san, if you brought her here, you had better take her away.

Tosaku. Well, we'll go home right away. It was my mistake that I brought you here.

Gisuke (giving Tosaku some money). Maybe you will excuse him. He is young and he has such a temper.

(The Priestess and Tosaku go out.)

Oyoshi. I suspected her from the very first. If she was inspired by a real god, she wouldn't do such cruel things.

Gisuke (suddenly). But where has Yoshitaro gone, anyway?

Kichiji (pointing at the roof). He is up there.

Gisuke (having to smile). As usual.

(During the preceding excitement, Yoshitaro has slipped away and climbed back up on the roof. The four persons below look at each other and smile.)

Suejiro. A normal person would be angry with you for having put him in the smoke; but you see, he has forgotten everything. *(He calls.)* Brother!

Yoshitaro (as brotherly affection springs from his heart). Suejiro! I asked the Konpira God, and he says he doesn't know her!

Suejiro (smiling). You are right. The God will inspire you instead of a Priestess like her.

(Through a rift in the clouds, the golden light of sunset strikes on the roof.)

Suejiro (exclaiming). What a beautiful sunset!

Yoshitaro (his face lighted by the sun's reflection). Sue, look! Can't you see a golden palace in yonder cloud? There! There! Can't you see? Just look! How beautiful!

Suejiro (as he feels the sorrow of sanity). Yes, I see. I see it, too. Wonderful.

Yoshitaro (filled with joy). There! From within the palace I hear the music of flutes—which I love best of all! Is it not beautiful?

(The parents have gone into the house. The mad brother on the roof, and the sane brother on the ground, remain looking at the golden sunset.)

CURTAIN

RUDYARD KIPLING

RUDYARD KIPLING (English, 1865-1936). Poet and novelist of British imperialism. Born in India, he brought to the West the life of English society in the colony. Emphasized patriotism, comradeship, physical courage. Excellent craftsman, phenomenally popular in his day. *Barrack-Room Ballads, Plain Tales from the Hills, Just So Stories, The Light That Failed, The Jungle Books.*

FALSE DAWN

No MAN will ever know the exact truth of this story; though women may sometimes whisper it to one another after a dance, when they are putting up their hair for the night and comparing lists of victims. A man, of course, cannot assist at these functions. So the tale must be told from the outside—in the dark—all wrong.

Never praise a sister to a sister, in the hope of your compliments reaching the proper ears, and so preparing the way for you later on. Sisters are women first, and sisters afterwards; and you will find that you do yourself harm.

Saumarez knew this when he made up his mind to propose to the elder Miss Copleigh. Saumarez was a strange man, with a few merits, so far as men could see, though he was popular with women, and carried enough conceit to stock a Viceroy's Council, and leave a little over for the commander-in-chief's staff. He was a civilian. Very many women took an interest in Saumarez, perhaps because his manner to them was inoffensive. If you hit a pony over the nose at the outset of your acquaintance, he may not love you, but he will take a deep interest in your movements ever afterward. The elder Miss Copleigh was nice, plump, winning and pretty. The younger was not so pretty, and, from men disregarding the hint set forth above, her style was repellent and unattractive. Both girls had, practically, the same figure, and there was a strong likeness between them in look and voice; though no one could doubt for an instant which was the nicer of the two.

Saumarez made up his mind, as soon as they came into the station from Behar, to marry the elder one. At least, we all made sure that he would, which comes to the same thing. She was twenty-two and he was thirty-three, with pay and allowances of nearly fourteen hundred rupees a month. So the match, as we arranged it, was in

every way a good one. Saumarez was his name, and summary was his nature, as a man once said. Having drafted his resolution, he formed a select committee of one to sit upon it, and resolved to take his time. In our unpleasant slang, the Copleigh girls "hunted in couples." That is to say, you could do nothing with one without the other. They were very loving sisters; but their mutual affection was sometimes inconvenient. Saumarez held the balance-hair true between them, and none but himself could have said to which side his heart inclined; though every one guessed. He rode with them a good deal, and danced with them, but he never succeeded in detaching them from each other for any length of time.

Women said that the two girls kept together through deep mistrust, each fearing that the other would steal a march on her. But that has nothing to do with a man. Saumarez was silent for good or bad, and as business-likely attentive as he could be, having due regard to his work and his polo. Beyond doubt both girls were fond of him.

As the hot weather drew nearer and Saumarez made no sign, women said that you could see their trouble in the eyes of the girls —that they were looking strained, anxious, and irritable. Men are quite blind in these matters unless they have more of the woman than the man in their composition, in which case it does not matter what they say or think. I maintain it was the hot April days that took the color out of the Copleigh girls' cheeks. They should have been sent to the Hills early. No one—man or woman—feels an angel when the hot weather is approaching. The younger sister grew more cynical—not to say acid—in her ways; and the winningness of the elder wore thin. There was more effort in it.

Now the Station wherein all these things happened was, though not a little one, off the line of rail, and suffered through want of attention. There were no gardens, or bands or amusements worth speaking of, and it was nearly a day's journey to come into Lahore for a dance. People were grateful for small things to interest them.

About the beginning of May, and just before the final exodus of Hill-goers, when the weather was very hot and there were not more than twenty people in the Station, Saumarez gave a moonlight riding picnic at an old tomb, six miles away, near the bed of the river. It was a "Noah's Ark" picnic; and there was to be the usual arrangement of quarter-mile intervals between each couple, on account of the dust. Six couples came altogether, including chap-

707

erones. Moonlight picnics are useful just at the very end of the season, before all the girls go away to the Hills. They lead to understandings, and should be encouraged by chaperones; especially those whose girls look sweetest in riding habits. I knew a case once. But that is another story. That picnic was called the "Great Pop Picnic," because everyone knew Saumarez would propose then to the eldest Miss Copleigh; and, besides his affair, there was another which might possibly come to happiness. The social atmosphere was heavily charged and wanted clearing.

We met at the parade ground at 10; the night was fearfully hot. The horses sweated even at walking pace, but anything was better than sitting still in our own dark houses. When we moved off under the full moon we were four couples, one triplet, and Mr. Saumarez rode with the Copleigh girls, and I loitered at the tail of the procession wondering with whom Saumarez would ride home. Every one was happy and contented; but we all felt that things were going to happen. We rode slowly; and it was nearly midnight before we reached the old tomb, facing the ruined tank, in the decayed gardens where we were going to eat and drink. I was late in coming up; and, before I went in to the garden I saw that the horizon to the north carried a faint, dun-colored feather. But no one would have thanked me for spoiling so well-managed an entertainment as this picnic—and a dust-storm, more or less, does no great harm.

We gathered by the tank, some one had brought out a banjo—which is a most sentimental instrument—and three or four of us sang. You must not laugh at this. Our amusements in out-of-the-way stations are very few indeed. Then we talked in groups, or together, lying under the trees, with the sun-baked roses dropping their petals on our feet, until supper was ready. It was a beautiful supper, as cold and as iced as you could wish; and we stayed long over it.

I had felt that the air was growing hotter and hotter; but nobody seemed to notice it until the moon went out and a burning hot wind began lashing the orange trees with a sound like the noise of the sea. Before we knew where we were, the dust-storm was on us, and everything was roaring, whirling darkness. The supper table was blown bodily into the tank. We were afraid of staying anywhere near the old tomb for fear it might be blown down. So we felt our way to the orange trees where the horses were picketed and waited for the storm to blow over. Then the little light that was left van-

ished, and you could not see your hand before your face. The air was heavy with dust and sand from the bed of the river, that filled boots and pockets and drifted down necks and coated eyebrows and mustaches. It was one of the worst dust-storms of the year. We were all huddled together close to the trembling horses, with the thunder chattering overhead, and the lightning spurting like water from a sluice, all ways at once.

There was no danger, of course, unless the horses broke loose. I was standing with my head down wind and my hands over my mouth, hearing the trees thrashing each other. I could not see who was next me till the flashes came. Then I found that I was packed near Saumarez and the eldest Miss Copleigh, with my own horse just in front of me. I recognized the eldest Miss Copleigh, because she had a *pagri* round her helmet and the younger had not. All the electricity in the air had gone into my body and I was quivering and tingling from head to foot—exactly as a corn shoots and tingles before rain. It was a grand storm. The wind seemed to be picking up the earth and pitching it to leeward in great heaps; and the heat beat up from the ground like the heat of the Day of Judgment.

The storm lulled slightly after the first half-hour, and I heard a despairing little voice close to my ear, saying to itself, quietly and softly, as if some lost soul were flying about with the wind: "O my God!" Then the younger Miss Copleigh stumbled into my arms, saying: "Where is my horse? Get my horse. I want to go home. I *want* to go home. Take me home."

I thought that the lightning and the black darkness had frightened her; so I said there was no danger, but she must wait till the storm blew over. She answered: "It is not *that!* It is not *that!* I want to go home! Oh, take me away from here!"

I said that she could not go till the light came; but I felt her brush past me and go away. It was too dark to see where. Then the whole sky was split open with one tremendous flash, as if the end of the world were coming, and all the women shrieked.

Almost directly after this I felt a man's hand on my shoulder and heard Saumarez bellowing in my ear. Through the rattling of the trees and howling of the wind, I did not catch his words at once, but at last I heard him say: "I've proposed to the wrong one! What shall I do?" Saumarez had no occasion to make this confidence to me. I was never a friend of his, nor am I now; but I fancy neither of us were ourselves just then. He was shaking as

709

he stood with excitement, and I was feeling queer all over with the electricity. I could not think of anything to say except: "More fool you for proposing in a dust storm." But I did not see how that would improve the mistake.

Then he shouted: "Where's Edith—Edith Copleigh?" Edith was the younger sister. I answered out of my astonishment: "What do you want with *her?*" Would you believe it, for the next two minutes, he and I were shouting at each other like maniacs—he vowing that it was the younger sister he had meant to propose to all along, and I telling him till my throat was hoarse that he must have made a mistake. I can't account for this except, again, by the fact that we were neither of us ourselves. Everything seemed to me like a bad dream—from the stamping of the horses in the darkness to Saumarez telling me the story of his loving Edith Copleigh since the first. He was still clawing my shoulder and begging me to tell him where Edith Copleigh was, when another lull came and brought light with it, and we saw the dust-cloud forming on the plain in front of us. So we knew the worst was over. The moon was low down, and there was just the glimmer of the false dawn that comes about an hour before the real one. But the light was very faint, and the dun cloud roared like a bull. I wondered where Edith Copleigh had gone; and as I was wandering I saw three things together: First, Maud Copleigh's face come smiling out of the darkness and move toward Saumarez, who was standing by me. I heard the girl whisper, "George," and slide her arm through the arm that was not clawing my shoulder, and I saw that look on her face which only comes once or twice in a lifetime—when a woman is perfectly happy, and the air is full of trumpets and gorgeous-colored fire and the Earth turns into cloud because she loves and is loved. At the same time, I saw Saumarez's face as he heard Maud Copleigh's voice, and fifty yards away from the clump of orange trees I saw a brown holland habit getting upon a horse.

It must have been my state of over-excitement that made me so quick to meddle with what did not concern me. Saumarez was moving off to the habit; but I pushed him back and said: "Stop here and explain. I'll fetch her back!" And I ran out to get at my own horse. I had a perfectly unnecessary notion that everything must be done decently and in order, and that Saumarez's first care was to wipe the happy look out of Maud Copleigh's face. All the time I was linking up the curb-chain I wondered how he would do it.

I cantered after Edith Copleigh, thinking to bring her back slowly on some pretense or another. But she galloped away as soon as she saw me, and I was forced to ride after her in earnest. She called back over her shoulder, "Go away! I'm going home. Oh, go *away!*" two or three times; but my business was to catch her first, and argue later. The ride just fitted in with the rest of the evil dream. The ground was very bad, and now and again we rushed through the whirling, choking "dust-devils" in the skirts of the flying storm. There was a burning hot wind blowing that brought up a stench of stale brick-kilns with it; and through the half light and through the dust-devils, across that desolate plain, flickered the brown holland habit on the gray horse. She headed for the Station at first.

Then she wheeled round and set off for the river through beds of burned-down jungle-grass, bad even to ride a pig over. In cold blood I should never have dreamed of going over such a country at night, but it seemed quite right and natural with the lightning crackling over head, and a reek like the smell of the Pit in my nostrils. I rode and shouted, and she bent forward and lashed her horse, and the aftermath of the dust-storm came up and caught us both, and drove us down wind like pieces of paper.

I don't know how far we rode; but the drumming of the horse-hoofs and the roar of the wind and the race of the faint blood-red moon through the yellow mist seemed to have gone on for years and years, and I was literally drenched with sweat from my helmet to my gaiters when the gray stumbled, recovered himself, and pulled up dead lame. My brute was used up altogether. Edith Copleigh was in a sad state, plastered with dust, her helmet off, and crying bitterly. "Why can't you let me alone?" she said. "I only wanted to get away and go home. Oh, *please* let me go!"

"You have got to come back with me, Miss Copleigh. Saumarez has something to say to you."

It was a foolish way of putting it; but I hardly knew Miss Copleigh, and, though I was playing Providence at the cost of my horse, I could not tell her in as many words what Saumarez had told me. I thought he could do that better himself. All her pretense about being tired and wanting to go home broke down, and she rocked herself to and fro in the saddle as she sobbed, and the hot wind blew her black hair to leeward. I am not going to repeat what she said, because she was utterly unstrung.

This, if you please, was the cynical Miss Copleigh. Here was I,

almost an utter stranger to her, trying to tell her that Saumaraz loved her, and she was to come back to hear him say so. I believe I made myself understood, for she gathered the gray together and made him hobble somehow, and we set off for the tomb, while the storm went thundering down to Umballa and a few big drops of warm rain fell. I found out that she had been standing close to Saumarez when he proposed to her sister, and had wanted to go home to cry in peace, as an English girl should. She dabbed her eyes with her pocket handkerchief as we went along, and babbled to me out of sheer lightness of heart and hysteria. That was perfectly unnatural; and yet, it seemed all right at the time and in the place. All the world was only the two Copleigh girls, Saumarez and I, ringed in with the lightning and the dark; and the guidance of this misguided world seemed to lie in my hands.

When we returned to the tomb in the deep, dead stillness that followed the storm, the dawn was just breaking and nobody had gone away. They were waiting for our return. Saumarez most of all. His face was white and drawn. As Miss Copleigh and I limped up, he came forward to meet us, and, when he helped her down from her saddle, he kissed her before all the picnic. It was like a scene in a theater, and the likeness was heightened by all the dust-white, ghostly-looking men and women under the orange trees clapping their hands—as if they were watching a play—at Saumarez' choice. I never knew anything so un-English in my life.

Lastly, Saumarez said we must all go home, or the Station would come out to look for us, and *would* I be good enough to ride home with Maud Copleigh? Nothing would give me greater pleasure, I said.

So we formed up, six couples in all, and went back two by two, Saumarez walking at the side of Edith Copleigh, who was riding his horse.

The air was cleared; and little by little, as the sun rose, I felt we were all dropping back again into ordinary men and women, and that the "Great Pop Picnic" was a thing altogether apart and out of the world—never to happen again. It had gone with the dust-storm and the tingle in the hot air.

JOSEPH KISS

JOSEPH KISS (Hungarian, 1843-1921). Most genuine Hungarian poet. Taught in Hebrew schools.

JEHOVAH

I

I have seen the great world, I have wandered afar,
I have worshipped the southern clime's beauteous star;
From Tisra's bright shore I have wandered far forth,
By my spirit of roving sent south and sent north.
At the foot of the Alps, where the rose grows knee-deep,
And the blue sky of Italy never doth weep,
But sweet odors and colors bright fade into naught,
And fly, like the cloudlets on zephyr's wings caught;
Tossed hither and thither, like chaff o'er the plain,
As to hold it you long, but the longing is vain,
Even thus from my soul, like a dream of the dawn,
Fades this picture so bright, from mem'ry withdrawn.

The years, in their flight, efface as by stealth,
Every trace of its beauty, its splendour and wealth;
Yet sometimes the sight of some tall, barren rock,
The floodgates of memories sad will unlock.
Its crags seem like features that me terrify,
I watch it with dread, reaching up to the sky,
In bleakness so bare, though majestic withal
It stands, and its frowning my soul doth appall,
And concealed at its base, 'neath foliage green,
A part of itself, that broke from it, is seen,
By the force of the storm and by tempest 'twas wrought,
To which once more these storms new life have brought,
They are parts of himself, sweet children, his own,
Yet a different life from his own they have known.

Where saw I that face which haunts, fills my heart?
From marble was't hewn, a creature of art?
The flashing of the eye, and the majestic pose,
The Titanic genius of Angelo shows.

713

On his forehead he beareth the imprint of woe,
From his visage of iron his soul we may know.
Does it live, or did fancy the image create,
While I, 'neath Saint Peter's dome, mighty and great,
Once did stand? No. There I was dreaming again,
A winter morn's dream, which still I retain.

II

I know it now, from home did hail that face,—
How could I see it and not sooner trace,—
In cassock dark, the figure gaunt, erect,
Whose every slow movement commandeth respect.
And the boys, we who romped in the street,
With awe avoided him, afraid to greet;
We gathered then and put our heads together,
As sparrows seek the trees in stormy weather.
An hundred years, it seems, upon his shoulders weigh,
Yet proud he walks, as in his manliest day;
A living legend, covered with a shroud
He movéd thus among the human crowd,
Full of foreboding, yet 'twas never known,
What in his seeming endless life had grown.
This sage, in fame of greatest learning stood,
To tell though, where acquired, no one could;
And yet 'twas whispered e'en, that learned was he
In holy Cabalah's dark secrecy;
That he himself, at his own wish could bring
About, that he could live as lives a king;
That he had vowed to be forever poor,
A straw-thatched hut he did as home secure.
He read his books, to synagogue he went,
To worldly things he no attention lent.
He spoke the tongue of races that are dead,
And Syrian and Chaldaic filled his head;
Late into night, and in the early dawn,
Queer hieroglyphics had his attention drawn.
Wisdom and wine, he thinks the worthier far
When ripened both by passing age they are;
Wisdom is One; and faith its foremost claim,
Wisdom is One; Jehovah is his name . . .

714

Who sends chastisement to the fourth degree,
That God who saith: "Revenge is my decree!"
That is his God, and like a breath upon a glass,
Or like the burning tears shed by a child, alas!
Thus came and went before his aged eyes
Some generations, and dissolved the ties
That he had known, and all was frail that came,
Steadfast but he and great Jehovah's name.

Unspeaking, melancholy and morose,
Beneath his eyelids, it seems in deep repose
A world of thought doth lie, a boundless world,
Which storm and lightning flash had oft-times hurled
And tossed about. His fellow-men he shunned;
Indeed, it seemed as if he lived beyond
His days; but when one was about to die,—
Unbid or bid, he promptly came to try
With hope divine to fill the dying soul,
And sacred hymns then from his lips would roll.
The dying man would ope his shaded eye,
And gather strength and faith wherewith to die.
Full many a night no sleep nor rest he had,
But needs must struggle for his daily bread.
O'er parchment leaves he would for hours bend,
And trace thereon the writ, with iron hand;
The holy writ, the testament of old,
He copied carefully, and strong and bold
His letters were, and day and night he wrote
The name of Him, who in his anger smote
Him, who revered not Him, with iron rod, . . .
The name of Him he loved, Jehovah, God, . . .
Because all day these letters dead he saw,
The letters dead became for him the law.
Fanatically he, the bygone days
Did wish returned, the awful dark, dread ways
And when on earth Jehovah was—the torch,—
And who profaned Him and died by sword or scorch.
The letters dead to him were living law,
To punish swift, the high priest would but draw
His sword; and burned on stake or stoned to death
He who the wrath of God encountereth.

715

And at this barren rock's stone feet there grew
A beauteous flower, fair and sweet to view.
The brooklet's murmur and the zephyr's sigh
To nourish her, would with each other vie.
The soil was barren, no moisture from above,
Privation, poverty, no parent's love
Her share, and yet, in spite of all, she grows,—
This child of Job,—as lovely as a rose.
So sweet and pure, a fairy queen she is,
There blend in her in charming harmonies.
Those gifts of heaven which heart and mind most please.
Her form divine, her movement queenly grace,
And radiantly beautiful her face.
Melodious her voice, like silver bell
Which holds the rustic listener in spell
When in the eve he hears the distant knell;
And what she says and what she thinks is bright
As wings of gaudy butterflies, which light
On flowers fair, in dewy morn and night.
Above all these, her eyes, ah, me! those eyes!
It matters nothing how my fish-line tries
To hook the proper word, I'll not succeed
The superb beauty of those eyes to read;
But I will tell a tale, do you give heed:
The midnight's depth, the height of mid-day's sun
Each from the other loving glances won;
They longed to meet, and for each other sighed;
They met, each other loved, and ever bide
Each with the other, and until to-day
They live in bliss; the truth of what I've told,
Do Miriam's flaming, darkling eyes enhold.

The fields and gardens gave her needed food,
Her soul grew in its very solitude,
A kindly nursing which in its due course
Matured her feelings and with hidden force
Her fancy rose. From tattered leaves she found,
She learned to read and write; and held her bound

Full many a night, when she would read by stealth
Each word, each line, each tale, each song; and wealth
Of thought did gain. Her hungry soul did yearn
In learning's banquet hall to sit and learn;
Her soul with almost holy fire aglow,
To rise above her sphere, so dull and slow,
Aspired; and she did vow to learn, to know;
Her daily life to cast away, not prone
'Fore fate to lie; but make her life her own;
And this she did, more pure her life, more bold
Half dream of hers and half as story told. . . .

And once a book came in her hands, complete,—
Though coverless and gone the title-sheet,
And pity 'twas, the author was unknown.
She read it oft, an hundred times a year,
As if it were a song which to the ear
Melodiously clings, and we repeat,
Because it fills our hearts and souls complete.

She read each play and felt that every role
Had taken hold, and filled her very soul;
Now Juliet, she roamed in love's estate,
To-morrow moaned o'er Desdemona's fate;
Then Lady Macbeth, with her blood-stained hands,
Then Imogen,—Cordelia now she stands,
And when the foolish, simple country swain
Would seek with awkward praise her love to gain,
She would the role of Queen Titania play, . . .
Thus Miriam, Job's daughter, lived her day.

IV

In autumn eve, the poplar tree tops sigh,
The swallow soon will flit, soon homeward fly:
To-morrow's dawn may find unfilled the nest,
Sweet bird, wilt here, thou seek again thy rest?
The window of the straw-thatched hut now brightly shines,
The poplar's trembling crown it illumines.
The poplar's trembling crown seems golden bright,
Its beauteous hue lends glory to the night.

V

His hoary head old Job leans on his hands,
Lost in deep thought, though work his care commands;
Before him lies the yellow parchment leaf,
And quill and ink, and yet, some hidden grief
Keeps him from work; he cannot trace his pen,
The very letters dance when now and then
He tries to work; some cloud bedulls his brain;
But as a lion wakening, his mane
Doth toss, so now old Job doth seem to wake;
Into his hand the quill doth firmly take,
And, dipping deep in ink, begins to write,
And what he writes, brings to his soul delight.
It suits his mood, 'tis Moses' second book
And chapter thirty-two, and he, whose look
At holy writ is frequent, knows how there
'Tis told, the old law-giver was aware,
That while he was with God, on their behalf,
The people made and worshipped the golden calf;
How great his wroth, his sorrow greater still,
And Moses' song men's souls must ever thrill.

Joshua said: "Dost, Master, hear the voice
From yonder camp? O'er victories they rejoice."
The Master said: "It is not so, my son;
'Tis not the joyous voice of victory won
That comes from camp, nor yet defeat's sad wail,
But other voices reach us from the vale." . . .
And marvel: As these things he now indited;
His ravished ears hear song and shout and hail
As once old Moses heard in ancient tale.
And song and shout and shout and song he hears,
Roused are the spirits of those bygone years,
Yet no, no spirit voices these, 'tis plain,
This music earthly is, this noise profane,
A band of strolling players at the inn
Have built a tent, and there their plays begin;
The villagers, or all who could but go,
Are there, enjoying this uncommon show.
They cheer and weep, the play has touched their heart,
The play and players gain the praise of art.

718

This was the voice old Job had heard, and then
He slowly takes again in hand his pen
To write, but lo! he soon again must cease,
It seems his soul to-night can find no peace.
The music dies away, no noise below,
He sees the wraiths of days of long ago
That torture him, the weary, hoary head—
Why are the days gone by not really dead!

He once three manly boys had called his own;
Life took them all, not death; aye, life alone
Robbed him of them; the one who really died,
Alone, lives in his heart with loving pride.
The strife, the times, the change, the very air
Of the to-day, which dawns ere one's aware,
And which we notice only when their wave
Prevails, and yesterdays are in their grave:
The spirit of the times which ever runs,
Had swallowed, Moloch-like, all his three sons.
No faith, no aim, ideals none, no rite,
The father and the son do now unite;
The holy tie, which with its powers divine
Men in their hearts with loving care enshrine,
The ties of heart and blood, old Job, with scorn
And pride, from his parental heart had torn.

He blessed his son, and for his welfare prayed;
Told him to go. A last farewell him bade!
The boy was only thirteen years of age,
Too young, think you, to enter on life's stage?
But custom and the law demand it so,
And out into the world the lad did go.
For years he seemed as lost, but once there came
A letter from a place of strangest name:
"Dear father,"—wrote the son,—"here in this land,
The victories of steam are truly grand."
The father's answer was one single word:
"Jehovah!"—as the son had often heard.
Another letter came: "Here on the banks
Of the Missouri I, in labor's ranks

719

Toil day and night to fell the ancient trees,
And inch by inch new territories seize;
Lay railroad ties, and oft the Indian chase.
At night, to starlit heaven I often gaze,
And think of home when the hyena's howl
And Indians' shrieks around our camp who prowl
Keep me awake; but then the amulet,
Dear father, which you gave, I have it yet."

And then no further news, and years rolled by, . . .
The young grew old, the old perforce must die.
The eldest son of Job was long forgot, . . .
When to the village came with lively trot
On horse and wheel, as might a king in state,
A train of men; what stir it did create,
The horses, carriages, the lively swarm;
The negro servants in their uniform;
It was a lively, captivating scene,
The like of which the village ne'er had seen.
Before the straw-thatched hut they stopped, behold
Upon the threshold stands erect, though old,
Proud Job: and from a carriage steps a man,—
The southern sun had turned his skin to tan,—
A giant figure, he, a worthy son
Of worthy sire, pleasant to look upon.
A lady, too, alights; a woman fair;
He leads her to his father, standing there.
Old Job outspreads his arms, about to kiss
His long-lost son and daughter, his is bliss!
When suddenly he shrieks and starts aback,
A golden cross hangs on the woman's neck.
"Apostate, thou!" he cries; "thou'rt not my son!
Apostate, thou! No nearer come! begone!
Ne'er shalt thou o'er my threshold step, swear I,
Jehovah, witness! I my son deny!"

VII

His memories are sad. Beneath their weight
His soul doth rise, as even then, too late . . .

720

The old wound opes and freely bleeds again
As it bled once when first he knew life's bane.
He sobs and weeps, his heart may almost break,
Most painful are the ways his thoughts do take.
He had, yea, it is true, another son,
A splendid boy, who admiration won
By his bright thought and brain and mind.
He, too, went forth,—and onward, but to find
Himself on paths his sires had never trod;
In plant and stone he sought to find his God.
The highest goals of learning he did gain,
Found everything, but sought a God in vain.
His name and fame shine brightly as a star
Among the great men who immortal are.
Savant, philosopher, known o'er the globe,
Alas! no longer he a son of Job!

And silently a sentient, burning tear
Rolls down his face, so strong and yet austere.
God only knows, these tears well from his heart,
The thought for his third, youngest son impart.
He suffered not, that he the world should roam,
He loved this boy the best, kept him at home.
A lively youth, of mischief full and fun,
That kind of boy who's loved by every one,
The picture of himself while he a boy,
This youngest son of his, his greatest joy.
He was not yet fifteen, . . . when lo! the world
Did seem to turn and quake; flags were unfurled,
Thrones shook, and shouts did mark the Bastille's fall.
With martial noise "To arms!" goes forth the call!
Blood-red the very grass, blood-red the dawn . . .
The boy enlists, nor waits till he be drawn.
Beneath a heavy gun he would succumb,
And his the burden was to bear the drum.
And with his drum from field to field he went,
Until at last a bullet his rest sent. . . .

VIII

The taper's burning low, and now to bed
He is about to take his weary head;

721

And as he rises, 't seems a deeper gloom
Obtains; his own dark shadow fills the room.
"Miriam, my darling child!" he whispers low,
Thou art still mine; the boys, oh, great my woe,
I've lost them all! May angels guard thy sleep,
Gabriel, Raphael, o'er thee watch and keep
From thee the evil spirit of the night,
That naught thy golden dream and slumber blight;
Jehovah, keep my Miriam sweet, secure!"
And then, to still the pain he must endure,
He goes to look upon his child, his own;
And to her room on tip-toe steals; a throne
To him her couch, on which his child inclines!
But, lo! the pale moon only illumines,—
Has he seen right? he stares,—he sees, to-night
An empty couch,—Miriam has taken flight!

IX

And as the stag, who hears the shot and feels
It whistling, grazing past, and knows it deals
A deadly aim: though once that aim was bad,
And suddenly stands still,—with eyes like mad
Looks right and left, and sniffs the air; then he
With sudden leap will fly, but to be free,
Though danger lurks perhaps behind each tree:
Thus acted Job. First stunned, he gasps for breath,
His glaring eyes are shadowed, as by death;
His mind grows blank; he knows not what to do;
The heart is broken of the poor old Jew.
And then in accents slow: "She, too, she, too;
My last and only child is gone from me,
My Miriam is taken by God's decree."
And then he sobs, and freely flow his tears,
He weeps as those who stand before friends' biers;
Not for himself he feels the awful blow,
'Tis for his child his burning tears do flow.
When past the agony of his great woe,
While still convulsed his sturdy, giant frame:
"All gone, all lost, yet I fore'er exclaim:
Steadfast is One! Jehovah is His Name!"

And then his window opes. His eye is dry;
But here and there a star is in the sky;
His eagle eye far into night doth spy.
The heavens, it seems, are overcast with clouds,
As if all nature donned funeral shrouds.
As if to list to him had come in crowds;
As if all heaven and earth had come to know
That he, in spite of awful blow and woe,
His ancient faith in Him did not forego!
Then with a voice, which shakes the very walls
Of his small hut, and by its power appals,
Into the night with trembling voice he calls:
"Lord! God! Thou givest and taketh with thy breath,
Adonai, God, Thine is all life and death!"

HEINRICH VON KLEIST

HEINRICH VON KLEIST (German, 1777-1811). Playwright and journalist.
Impulsive peregrinant. While traveling, once arrested as spy and spent six
months in French jail. His plays slow to gain recognition. When financial
situation became desperate, staged double suicide with a Berlin merchant's
wife. Works: *Penthesilea, The Prince of Homburg, Michael Kolhaas.*

THE BEGGAR-WOMAN OF LOCARNO

At the foot of the Alps, near Locarno in Upper Italy, stood once a
castle, the property of a marquis; of this castle, as one goes southward from the St. Gotthard, one sees now only the ashes and ruins.
In one of its high and spacious rooms there once lay, on a bundle
of straw which had been thrown down for her, an old, sick woman,
who had come begging to the door, and had been taken in and
given shelter out of pity by the mistress of the castle. The Marquis,
returning from the hunt, happened to enter this room, where he
usually kept his guns, while the old woman lay there, and angrily
ordered her to come out of the corner where the bundle of straw had
been placed and to get behind the stove. In rising the old woman
slipped on the polished floor and injured her spine severely; so much
did she hurt herself that only with unspeakable agony could she
manage to cross the room, as she was ordered, to sink moaning
behind the stove and there to die.

Some years later the Marquis, owing to war and bad harvests, having lost most of his fortune, decided to sell his estates. One day a nobleman from Florence arrived at the castle which, on account of its beautiful situation, he wished to buy. The Marquis, who was very anxious to bring the business to a successful conclusion, gave instructions to his wife to prepare for their guest the above-mentioned room, which was now very beautifully furnished. But imagine their horror when, in the middle of the night, the nobleman, pale and distracted, entered their room, solemnly assuring them that his room was haunted by something which was not visible, but which sounded as if somebody lying on straw in one corner of the room got up and slowly and feebly but with distinct steps crossed the room to lie down moaning and groaning behind the stove.

The Marquis, horrified, he did not himself know why, laughed with forced merriment at the nobleman and said he would get up at once and keep him company for the rest of the night in the haunted room, and when the morning came he ordered his horses to be brought round, bade farewell, and departed.

This incident, which created a great sensation, unhappily for the Marquis frightened away several would-be buyers; and when amongst his own servants strangely and mysteriously the rumour arose that queer things happened in the room at midnight, he determined to make a definite stand in the matter and to investigate it himself the same night. For that reason he had his bed moved into the room at twilight, and watched there without sleeping until midnight. To his horror, as the clock began to strike midnight, he became aware of the mysterious noise; it sounded as though somebody rose from straw which rustled beneath him, crossed the room and sank down sighing and groaning behind the stove. The next morning when he came downstairs his wife inquired what he had discovered; he looked round with nervous and troubled glances, and after fastening the door assured her that the rumour was true. The Marquise was more terrified than ever in her life, and begged him, before the rumour grew, to make a cold-blooded trial in her company. Accompanied by a loyal servant, they spent the following night in the room and heard the same ghostly noises; and only the pressing need to get rid of the castle at any cost enabled the Marquise in the presence of the servant to smother the terror which she felt, and to put the noise down to some ordinary and casual event which it would be easy to discover. On the evening of the third day, as both of them, with beating hearts, went up the stairs to the guest-room, anxious to get

at the cause of the disturbance, they found that the watch-dog, who happened to have been let off his chain, was standing at the door of the room; so that, without giving a definite reason, both perhaps unconsciously wishing to have another living thing in the room besides themselves, they took him into the room with them. About eleven o'clock the two of them, two candles on the table, the Marquise fully dressed, the Marquis with dagger and pistol which he had taken from the cupboard beside him, sat down one on each bed; and while they entertained one another as well as they could by talking, the dog lay down, his head on his paws, in the middle of the room and slept. As the clock began to strike midnight the horrible sound began; somebody whom human eyes could not see raised himself on crutches in the corner of the room; the straw could be heard rustling beneath him; and at the first step the dog woke, pricked up his ears, rose from the ground growling and barking, and, just as though somebody were making straight for him, moved backwards towards the stove. At the sight the Marquise, her hair rising, rushed from the room, and while the Marquis, who had snatched up his dagger, called 'Who is there?' and received no answer, she, like a mad woman, had ordered the coach to be got out, determined to drive away to the town immediately. But before she had packed a few things together and got them out of the door she noticed that all around her the castle was in flames. The Marquis, overcome with horror, and tired of life, had taken a candle and set fire to the wooden panelling on all sides. In vain she sent people in to rescue the wretched man; he had already found his end in the most horrible manner possible; and his white bones, gathered together by his people, still lie in that corner of the room from which he once ordered the beggar-woman of Locarno to rise.

FRIEDRICH GOTTLIEB KLOPSTOCK

FRIEDRICH GOTTLIEB KLOPSTOCK (German, 1724-1803). Main architect of 18th century independent German writing. Author of great biblical epic, *The Messiah*, and *Odes*. Both works influential on contemporaries, bringing deeply felt emotion into classical forms. Late "bardic" poems stimulated German nationalism.

THE CONTEMPLATION OF GOD

Trembling I rejoice,
Nor would believe the Voice,

If that the Eternal were
Not the Greater Promiser!
For, oh! I know, I feel
I am a sinner still—
Should know, should feel the same,
The sorrow and the shame;
Albeit Deity my spot
More clearly shown to me had not,
Unveiling to my wiser view
The wounded soul's condition true.
    With bended knee,
Astonished and intensely praying,
    That I my God shall see!

Oh! meditate the thought divine,
Thou thought-capacious soul of mine,
Who near the body's grave art ever,
Yet art eternal, and shalt perish never!
Not that thou venturest into
The Holiest of all to go—
Much unconsidered, never prized,
Ne'er celebrated, ne'er agonized!—
Celestial graces
Have in the Sanctuary their dwelling places;—
From afar only but one softened glimmer,
    So that therewith I die not suddenly—
One beam, which night of earth for me makes dimmer,
    Of Thy bright glory let me see!

The man how great! who thus his prayer preferred—
    "Grace have I found of Thee!
    Then show Thy glory unto me!"—
Thus dared, and by the Infinite was heard!
That Land of Golgotha he never entered;—
Once, only once, he failed in God to trust—
An early death avenged the doubt he ventured!—
    How great proved him a punishment so just!
Him hid the Father on the clouded Hill;
    The Filial Glory passed the finite o'er;—
God of God spake! the trump the while was still,
    Nor did the thunder's voice on Sinai roar!

726

Now, in that cloud of seeming night
He sees already, in the light
Of day, no shade makes visibler,
Long centuries—(so we aver)—
Beyond the bounds of time; and, feeling free
   Of moments passed successively,
Thy glory now beholdeth he—
   Holy! Holy! Holy!

Most nameless rapture of my soul!
   Thought of the Vision blest to come!
My great assurance and my goal!
   The Rock whereon I stand, and gaze up to my heavenly home!

When that the terrors both of Sin and Death
Fearfully threat to prostrate me beneath,
Upon this rock, oh! let me stand,
   Thou whom the Dead of God behold!
When grasped in the almighty hand
   Of death, that may not be controlled!
My soul, above mortality
Exalt thyself! Look up and see—
Behold the Father's glory radiant shine
In the human face of Jesus Christ divine!
Hosanna! let the loud Hosanna tell—
   The plenitude of Deity
Doth in the man Christ Jesus dwell—
Yet scarcely sounds the cherub's harp—it shakes!
Scarce sounds the voice—it trembles—trembles! Now wakes!

   Hosanna! Hosanna!
   The plenitude of Deity
   Doth in the humanity
      Of Christ Jesus dwell!

Even then when on our world shone brighter still
A god-beam, and Redemption did fulfill
That prophecy of blood—when he knew scorn
And woe, whereto none else was ever born—
Unseen by mortals, Cherubim beheld
The Father's glory, unexcelled,

Shine in the face, where aye it shone,
Of the co-eternal Son!

I see—I see the Witness! Lo!
Seven midnights, sore perplexed, had he
Doubted, and with severest agony
    Adoring, wrestled so!—
Yes, him I see—
To him appears the Risen! His hands explore
The wounds divine; and now perceiveth he
(About him heaven and earth expire!)
In the Son's face the glory of his Sire!—
I hear him! He exclaims—in doubt no more—
(About him heaven and earth expire!)
"Thou art my Lord and God—the God whom I adore!"

HERMAN AND THUSNELDA

"Ha! there comes he, with sweat, with Roman blood,
With battle dust bedecked! Never so fair
    Was Herman—never flamed
    His eye so brightly yet!

Come! for desire I tremble! Reach to me
The eagle, the blood-dropping sword! Come, breathe
    Here—rest in mine embrace
    From the too fearful fight!

Rest here, that I may wipe away the sweat
Off from thy brow, and from thy cheek the blood—
    How glows thy cheek! Thus ne'er
    Thusnelda Herman loved!

Not even then, when in the oak shade first
With thy brown arm thou wilder compassed me;
    Flying, I stayed, and saw
    The' undying fame in thee

Which now is thine. Relate it all in groves,
That timidly Augustus, with his gods,

728

Drinks nectar now—that more
Immortal Herman is!"

"Why curlest thou my hair? Lies not the dumb
Dead father before us? Oh, had his host
  Augustus led—there he
  Might lie yet bloodier!"

"Herman—nay, let me raise thy sinking hair,
That o'er the garland thread its tresses may;—
  Siegmar is with the gods!—
  Follow—nor weep for him!"

THE TWO MUSES

I saw—oh, tell me, saw I what now is,
Or what shall be?—with Britain's Muse I saw
  The German in the race compete,
  Fly ardent for the crowning goal.

There, where the prospect terminates, two goals
Closed the career. Oaks of the forest one
  Shaded; and near the other waved
  Palms in the glimmering of the eve.

To contest used, the Muse of Albion stept
Into the arena proudly, as when she
  Dared mate the Grecian Muse, and brave
  The heroine of the Capitol.

She saw her young and trembling rival, who
With high emotion trembled; yea, her cheek
  With roses, worthy of victory,
  Glowed, and her golden hair flew wide.

With pain already in her throbbing breast,
She held the breath restrained; hung, forward bent,
  Towards the goal;—the herald raised
  His trump—her eyes swam drunkenly.

Proud of thy courage, of herself, thee scanned
The lofty Britoness with noble glance.
  Tuiscone. "Yes, near the bards
  I grew with thee in oaken groves;—

But I was told thou wert no more. O Muse!
Pardon, if that thou art immortal, me
  Pardon, that now I first am taught
  What at the goal I'll better learn!

Yonder it stands;—but mark the further one!
Seest thou its crown? This courage thus suppressed,
  This silence proud, this look of fire
  Fixed on the earth—I knew it well!

Yet, ponder once again, ere sounds to thee
The herald's dangerous signal. Strove not I
  With her of old Thermopylæ,
  And eke with her of the Seven Hills?"

She spake. The solemn, the decisive time
Approaches with the herald. With a look
  Of ardor spake Teutona quick—
  "Thee I, admiring, love, O Muse!

But dearer yet love immortality
And yonder palms! Oh—if thy genius will,—
  Touch them before me;—but, e'en then,
  Will I seize likewise on the crown!

Oh, how I tremble! Ye immortal gods!
I haply may reach first the goal sublime!—
  Then may I feel, O Britoness!
  Thy breath on my loose-flowing locks!"

The herald clanged. With eagle speed they flew,—
Their far career smoked up with dust, like clouds;—
  I looked—beyond the oak the dust,
  Still billowing, hid them from my sight!

730

VLADIMIR KOROLENKO

VLADIMIR KOROLENKO (Russian, 1853-1921). Half-Ukrainian, half-Polish
writer. Spent much of life in Siberian exile, but remained genial and optimistic. Courageous defender of freedom. As story writer, forms link between
Turgenev and Chekhov. Best-known novels: *Makar's Dream*, *The Blind Musician*; stories: "The Frost," "The Old Bell-Ringer."

THE OLD BELL-RINGER

IT was growing dark.

The tiny village, nestling by the distant stream, in a pine forest,
was merged in that twilight peculiar to starry spring nights, when
the fog, rising from the earth, deepens the shadows of the woods
and fills the open spaces with a silvery blue mist. . . . Everything
was still, pensive and sad. The village quietly slumbered.

The dark outlines of the wretched cabins were barely visible;
here and there lights glimmered; now and then you could hear a
gate creak; or a dog would suddenly bark and then stop.
Occasionally, out of the dark, murmuring forest emerged the figure
of a pedestrian, or that of a horseman; or a cart would jolt by.
These were the inhabitants of lone forest hamlets going to their
church for the great spring holiday.

The church stood on a gentle hill in the center of the village.
The ancient belfry, tall and murky, was lost in the blue sky.

The creaking of the staircase could be heard as the old bell-ringer
Mikheyich mounted to the belfry, and his little lantern, suspended
in mid-air, looked like a star in space.

It was difficult for the old man to climb the staircase. His legs
served him badly, and his eyes saw but dimly. . . . An old man
like him should have been at rest by now, but God spared him
from death. He had buried his sons and his grandsons; he had
accompanied old men and young men to their resting place, but
he still lived on. 'Twas hard. Many the times he had greeted the
spring holiday, and he could not remember how often he had waited
in that very belfry the appointed hour. And how God had again
willed that . . .

The old man went to the opening in the tower and leaned on the
banister. In the darkness below, around the church, he made out
the village cemetery in which the old crosses with their outstretched
arms seemed to protect the ill-kept graves. Over these bowed here
and there a few leafless birch trees. The aromatic odor of young

buds, wafted to Mikheyich from below, brought with it a feeling of the melancholy of eternal sleep.

Where would he be a year hence? Would he again climb to this height, beneath the brass bell to awaken the slumbering night with its metallic peal, or would he be lying in a dark corner of the graveyard, under a cross? God knows! . . . He was prepared; in the meantime God granted him the happiness of greeting the holiday once more.

"Glory be to God!" His lips whispered the customary formula as his eyes looked up to the heaven bright with a million twinkling stars and made the sign of the cross.

"Mikheyich, ay, Mikheyich!" called out to him the tremulous voice of an old man. The aged sexton gazed up at the belfry, shading his unsteady, tear-dimmed eyes with his hand, trying to see Mikheyich.

"What do you want? Here I am," replied the bell-ringer, looking down from the belfry. "Can't you see me?"

"No, I can't. It must be time to ring. What do you say?"

Both looked at the stars. Myriads of God's lights twinkled on high. The fiery Wagoner was above them. Mikheyich meditated.

"No, not yet a while. . . . I know when. . . ."

Indeed he knew. He did not need a watch. God's stars would tell him when. . . . Heaven and earth, the white cloud gently floating in the sky, the dark forest with its indistinct murmur and the rippling of the stream enveloped by the darkness—all that was familiar to him, part of him. Not in vain had he spent his life here.

The distant past arose before him. He recalled how for the first time he had mounted to this belfry with his father. Lord! how long ago that was, and yet how recent it seemed! . . . He saw himself a blond lad; his eyes sparkled; the wind—not the wind that raises the dust in the streets, but a strange one, that flaps its noiseless wings, tousled his hair. . . . Way down below, tiny beings walked about, and the village huts looked small; the forest had receded, and the oval clearing on which the village stood seemed enormous, so endless . . .

"And there it is, all of it!" smiled the gray-haired old man, gazing at the little clearing. . . . That was the way of life. As a young man one can not see the end of it. And now, there it was, as if in the palm of one's hand, from the beginning to the grave over there which he had fancied for himself in the corner of the

732

cemetery. . . . Well, glory be to God! it was time to rest. The burden of life he had borne honorably, and the damp earth seemed like his mother. . . . Soon, very soon!

But the hour had come. Mikheyich looked once more at the stars, took off his cap, made the sign of the cross, and grasped the bell-ropes. In a moment, the night air echoed with the resounding stroke. Another, a third, a fourth . . . one after the other, filling the quiescent, holy eve, there poured forth powerful, drawn-out, singing sounds.

The bell stopped. The church service had begun. Mikheyich had formerly been in the habit of going down to stand in the corner by the door in order to pray and hear the singing. This time he remained in the belfry. It was too much to walk the stairs, and, moreover, he felt rather tired. He sat down on the bench and, as he listened to the melting sounds of brass, fell to musing. About what? He would have been unable to say. . . . The tower was dimly lit by the feeble light of his lantern. The still vibrating bells were invisible in the darkness; from time to time a faint murmur of singing in the church below reached him, and the night wind stirred the ropes attached to the iron tongues of the bells.

The old man let his head droop upon his breast, while his mind was confused with fancies. "Now they are singing a hymn," he thought, and imagined himself in church, where he heard the children's voices in the choir, and saw Father Naum, long since dead, leading the congregation in prayer; hundreds of peasants' heads rose and fell, like ripened stalks of grain before the wind. . . . The peasants made the sign of the cross. . . . All of these are familiar, although they are all dead. . . . There he beheld his father's severe face; there was his brother fervently praying. And he also stood there, abloom with health and strength, filled with unconscious hope of happiness. . . . And where was that happiness? . . . For a moment, the old man's thoughts flared up, illuminating various episodes in his past life. . . .

He saw hard work, sorrow, care . . . where was this happiness? A hard lot will trace furrows even in a young face, will bend a powerful back and teach him to sigh as it had taught his older brother.

There on the left, among the village women, with her head humbly bowed, stood his sweetheart. A good woman, may she inherit the kingdom of Heaven! How much she had suffered, poor

733

woman. . . . Constant poverty and work, and the inevitable sorrows of a woman's life will wither her beauty; her eyes will lose their luster, and instead of the customary serenity, dull fear of unexpected calamities will settle perpetually on her face. . . . Well, then, where was her happiness? . . . One son was left to them, their one hope and joy; but he was too weak to withstand temptation.

And there was his rich enemy, kneeling and praying to be forgiven for the many tears he had caused orphans to shed. He crossed himself ardently and struck his forehead against the ground. . . . Mikheyich's heart boiled within him, and the dusky faces of the ikons frowned down upon human sorrow and human wickedness.

All that was past, behind him. For him the whole world was now bounded by this bell-tower, where the wind moaned in the darkness and stirred the ropes. . . . "God be your judge!" muttered the old man, drooping his gray head, while tears rolled gently down his cheeks.

"Mikheyich, ay, Mikheyich! Have you fallen asleep up there?" shouted someone from below.

"What?" the old man answered, rising to his feet. "God! Have I really been sleeping? Such a thing never happened before!"

With quick, experienced hands he grasped the ropes. Below him, the peasant mob moved about like an ant-hill; banners, sparkling with gilt brocade, fluttered in the air. . . . The procession made the circuit of the church, and soon the joyous call reached Mikheyich, "Christ is risen from the dead!"

The old man's heart responded fervently to this call. . . . It seemed to him that the tapers were burning more brightly, and the crowd was more agitated; the banners seemed to be animated, and the wakened wind gathered the billows of sound on its wings, floated them up and blended them with the loud festal pealing of the bells.

Never before had old Mikheyich rung like this!

It seemed as if the old man's heart had passed into the lifeless brass, and the tones of the bells sang and laughed and wept, and, welding in a sublime stream of harmony, rose high and higher into a heaven resplendent with myriad stars, and, trembling, flowed down to earth.

A powerful bass bell proclaimed, "Christ is risen!" And two tenors, trembling with the alternate beats of their iron tongues, repeated joyfully, "Christ is risen!"

And two small sopranos, seemingly hastening so as not to be left

734

behind, crowded in among the more powerful voices and, like little children, sang hurriedly, cheerfully, "Christ is risen!"

The old belfry seemed to tremble and shake, and the wind, flapping its wings in the old bell-ringer's face, repeated, "Christ is risen!"

The old heart forgot its life, full of cares and grief. The old bell-ringer forgot that his life was confined to the narrow limits of the dreary belfry, that he was alone in the world, like an old storm-broken stump. . . . He heard those singing and weeping sounds that rose to heaven and fell again to the sorrowing earth, and it seemed to him that he was surrounded by his sons and grandsons, that he heard their joyful voices; the voices of young and old blend into a chorus and sing to him of happiness and joy which he had never tasted in his life. . . . He pulled the ropes, while tears rolled down his cheeks, and his heart beat violently with the illusion of happiness. . . .

Below, people listened and said to each other that never before had old Mikheyich rung so well.

Suddenly the large bell uttered an uncertain sound, and grew dumb. The smaller ones rang out an unfinished tone, and then stopped, as if abashed, to listen to the lugubrious echo of the prolonged and palpitating note gradually dying away upon the air. . . . The old bell-ringer, utterly exhausted, fell back on the bench, and the last two tears trickled slowly down his pallid cheeks. . . .

"Ho, there! Send up a substitute; the old bell-ringer has rung his final stroke."

ZYGMUNT KRASINSKI

ZYGMUNT KRASINSKI (Polish, 1812-1859). Poet, playwright and novelist. Romanticist with deep philosophical undertone. Embittered by hostile Polish reaction to father's loyalty to Russia, lived most of life abroad. Best-known work: *The Undivine Comedy*, a mystic vision of social revolution. Also ranks high among Polish poets.

A LEGEND

IT seemed to me that precisely during the vigil at the Birth of our Lord I emerged from the gates of Rome and walked along the Campanile. The pagan graves were warming themselves in the rays of the sun—it was early morn—and the sky as clear and the plain as sad as in ages past.

I walked all day long borne by the strength of the soul. The ancient aqueducts ran along beside me but I went on beyond. The ivy, as in the pictured models of the manger of Christ, rustled on the walls of the ancient ruins. Above me swept flocks of white birds—before me on the ground wriggled a glistening snake. The roar of the ocean began to call me!

And when I stood on the highest summit of the earth, when I beheld the sea the sun was already setting—and far out over the water stood a black blot like a living thing, constantly growing larger and flying landward towards me—until it increased to a huge size when the sun had faded completely and twilight had begun to descend.

It was a great black ship, without sails or masts—dashing the waves into foam with its timbers. From the centre of the ship a column of smoke belched forth gliding back into the infinite.

Ever more darkly—like an inky spectre it circled in the expanse with thunderous roar—when two night lights gleamed before it on the ocean and a voice sounded from the deck, "Is this the last night of the vigil of the Birth of our Lord?"

Alarmed in spirit I answered from my height, "It is true, to-day is the vigil." And at once the ship stopped at the very edge, the pale stream enveloped her, and slack and sparks were emitted from her sides. In the ruddy glow rapidly declining—for a moment the deck gleamed brightly. Figures stood there in crimson caps and white cloaks—I heard the jangling of chains.—It seemed to me that a heavy long bridge was lowered from the ship to the shore —and upon it in the darkness the figures came rushing out directing their steps toward me.

And when they were very close, they asked us with one voice, "Which way is the road that leads to Rome?" I answered, "There is no road. This is a wilderness." And they answered, "Then lead us." And when I hesitated, they again spoke in low, sad tones, "We are what is left of the Polish nobility, an angel appeared to us, an angel not unlike those whom our forefathers saw, for he had wings without brilliance and a mourning veil over his brow—but we know he was sent from heaven, and he it was who directed us hither. We have been sailing for a long time, the gales have been terrific and many difficulties have we had at sea but the will of the Lord shall be accomplished if to-day at midnight, we arrive at the basilica of St. Peter."

Thereupon I said to them, "Follow me, thou unhappy people."

And I turned to go back from the shore of the ocean toward the city, trembling and praying as if I were crossing a cemetery and as if the dead were rising up and following me.

A wind arose and no more clouds were visible. Everywhere in the deep dark sky the stars were twinkling, while below was a vast black plain! Only now and then we passed dusky mounds or a pile of grey ruins or mayhap the gates of an aqueduct. In the distance one could hear the rustle of tall reeds—above at times sounded the shriek of a night bird, and near by, somewhere among the sunken graves came the murmurings from beneath the earth!

They strode along behind me—I could feel on my back their heavy breathing—I moved on swiftly for they were in haste—I could hear the plumes on their caps flutter in the breeze and the very folds of their capes puff up with the wind!

It seemed to me that I beheld a wandering light in the distance —and immediately a second and a third. When I advanced I beheld a great number of lights on the plain moving rapidly from all sides in one direction. And the sound of many voices began to hum in the wilderness.

When I came nearer I saw a great body of pilgrims passing over the Campanile with torches in their hands. The glow which they cast went with them between two solid walls of blackness but the light glistened on the tall crosses, pictures of saints and on the flags of various nations which fluttered in the breezes.

Into the very centre of the multitudes I led my own group, and at that instant I beheld the melancholy features of those who followed me. A strange ectasy was in their eyes but it was not the lustre of life. They carried swords on which they leaned as did the other pilgrims upon their staffs.

Hardly had I entered with them into the light of the torches when it seemed to me that the masses stood still asking, "Who are you and whence do you come?"

They paused and a strange smile passed over their lips while they answered as one, "Is there no longer anyone on this earth who recognises us?"

A low hum constantly growing in strength filled the air and it seemed to me that all the bands of pilgrims of a sudden cried out, "We know you—you are the last heroes of the earth."

Then they marched forward saying, "We saw an angel with a black band on his brow who commanded us to hasten to Rome. Tell us, did any of you also hear that voice?"

In the multitude a great tumult arose in answer, "Amen,—that same angel bade us leave our homes—his voice increased in the night about our heads and he gave us no peace. In these days, he said, Christ would be born for the last time at the grave of Peter and from that moment nothing shall be born nor nothing shall die on earth."

And the multitude became silent and stood as if startled by its own words.

The Poles were the first to move onward—throwing back their white capes over their shoulders—. From all sides of the Campanile a greater and greater mass of pilgrims crowded forward. Already we saw the battlements of the city—already we heard the harmony of the bells—sounding more clearly the nearer we came.

On the gates, on the towers, festoons of lights appeared and more loudly echoed the bells as one after another awoke to join the rest until soon all the church bells of Rome resounded.

It seemed to me that the night was transformed into white day. I did not in the least recognise the streets from which I had departed in the morning. There where once ruins projected frequented only by owls—baskets of blooming flowers and glowing lamps now swung. The Roman populace came forth in throngs shouting: "Let us rejoice—rejoice ye all, for today Christ is born to us."

And when they beheld the Polish nobles entering the gates and the stream of pilgrims behind them gaily springing forward they cried out: "Why are you so sad, you, our guests? If the long voyage has wearied you, moisten your lips with the juice of the orange. Remove your white caps and your black cloaks—behold, here are clusters of myrtle—here, camelias, we offer them to you to adorn your temples with garlands!"

But in silence and with furrowed brows, the Poles advanced through their midst and marching said to me, "Where is the basilica of Peter? We must hasten and our hearts are downcast. Is the midnight hour close in truth?"

I led them across the Forum. It seemed to me that the Amphitheatre of Flavianus—recently empty, dark and ancient—stood now like a giant of resplendant light from its base to its massive shields gleaming with lamps so that every ivy leaf upon them could be plainly distinguished. Women and children in glistening garments promenaded through various portions of the structure and clapped their hands in welcome to us who approached.

738

Every arch in the Forum and every column glowed and blazed. At the summit a wall of golden flames, the Capitol, shone forth. The very stars in heaven had grown pallid before the great flood of brilliance.

The people continued to shout: "Hosanna, Hosanna!" And the pilgrims sang psalms of penitence. The masses perpetually surged hither and thither, sounding guitars, scattering flaring sparks in the air, and through the centre of all this sea we proceeded in garments of blackness, slowly, in sorrow of soul.

From every balcony, every roof, from the streets, violets and roses descended upon us.

Already the bell of the Capitol boomed far behind us, and before us in the wide space sounded the bell of St. Peter. At last it rang independently, more sonorously than all the rest.

We hastened in the direction of that voice, we crossed the bridge over the Tiber, the houses on its banks standing out like quiet conflagrations, the river like a ribbon of flame. The angel palace bristled with cannon, every instant one of them blazed forth and thundered.

We turned and entered the courtyard of St Peter's. Its dome was hung with thousands of scarlet lamps, the cross at its summit like a diamond, the pillars at either side of the courts as if of twisted fires. In the centre were two fountains like two flowing rainbows, and I beheld a vast mass of people waiting there. The doors of the cathedral stood open and within an infinitude of blazing brightness.

While it was possible the Poles and the other pilgrims advanced but at the steps and at the base of the portico, the throng closed up the way. Pausing therefore, they demanded a passageway, but ever more closely from the front, from the rear and from the sides, the crowds pressed in upon them.

Then the voices of the Romans arose: "Are we not the first, has not this church been our own for ages upon ages?" And among the pilgrims were heard other voices saying: "Up to this time the Polish nobles have led the way for us, shall they be allowed to enter the holy place before us?"

And I looked and saw that the Poles had lifted their swords in token that they would defend themselves. With a pure fire their blades flashed in the clear air!

But at that instant on the battlements of the basilica high above the heads of the people appeared a figure in royal purple which

739

spoke in thunderous tones: "Let pass those who for the Catholic faith ransomed another nation from death and later for that faith perished themselves. Give passageway to the dead, first of all!" And the cardinal extended his hand toward the right and toward the left as if he were dividing the multitude, and down below the masses did indeed separate and make way—which seeing, he turned back into the building.

And together with the Poles I mounted the steps and advanced directly through the portico into the church and on up to the chief altar before the lamps which burn at the tomb of Peter. Here they paused, and removing their crimson caps, they unfastened their white capes and kneeling, worshipped, holding their unsheathed weapons in hand.

The snowy gleam of marble shone in the vast cathedral, the silvery transparent smoke of the incense rose to the arched dome and floated above us. On the mosaic floor lay scattered flowers and palms. From all the chapels echoed choirs of gentle joyful voices and off in the distance around the doors, the space began to fill. The pilgrims marched through that world of song and light just as they did through the city, dark and unrejoicing. A stream of Romans rolled into the basilica, noisily. And when each group had taken its place under its own banner, at its own altar, then the great expanse became silent again, as if it were a vast vacant space. The songs in the chapels were stilled and from the Vatican echoed the sounds of trumpets giving sign that the people were approaching.

Through the centre of the church proceeded all the friars and monks of Rome, the elders one after another, some in white robes, others in grey horse-hair cloth, with crucifixes in their hands. Then came the bishops wearing their mitres and silvery trains and after them the cardinals in splendid crimson, around them priests in dalmatics and troops of children in white garments, carrying wine, incense and wreaths.

And when the procession arrived at the main altar where the crowds separated forming a clear path between walls of living people who now suddenly fell to their knees, an aged grey-haired man walked slowly forward, wearing on his head a triple crown and a white vestment over his golden surplice.

At a great distance behind him remained the soldiers, attendants and the throne borne by priests. He stood alone in the centre of the throng and of the cathedral, alone he ascended the main altar.

740

It semed to me, that each step took an interminable length of time and that he never would come to us.

And as he thus advanced in the centre of those bowing before him touching their foreheads to the ground, he closed his eyes at times as if seeking relief from so many lights. Now and then he essayed to make but tremblingly left unfinished the sign of his blessing, until, pausing, he sighed and lifted up his hands to heaven, but he was unable to hold them upraised—they sank exhaustedly!

At his deep drawn sigh, the people lifted their heads. The sorrow of their father caused all to grow pale and then, I noted, that from the main altar one of the cardinals had turned away, the same one who had ordered that we should be admitted. With grave step, he descended towards the aged eldest of elders and extended his hand, turning shining eyes upon the grave of Peter. The aged man advanced a few steps but with lingering difficulty. The cardinal shook the rings of his long hair with a sidelong motion giving signal to those who had remained in the rear who at once hastened forward carrying the golden throne.

Then the father who is on earth grasped the arm of the throne with his pallid hand and seated himself. Quickly they lifted him up and the trumpets in the church again thundered forth. The cardinal walked along beside the throne. The people lifted themselves from the floor, the bell began to ring and twelve times the arched dome quivered. Around the main altar a cloud of incense arose and from it the pope ascended the steps as the cardinal announced: "Christ is born."

From amid the group of pilgrims at once a voice cried out mournfully: "Will not the words of the angel be borne out in truth that Christ is born for the last time?"

And the Roman people shouted out angrily: "Who dares blaspheme in the church of Peter?"

One of the Polish nobles stepped fortn crying: "They are not blaspheming. We do not fear you—they speak the truth—I myself and my brethren beheld the angel of sorrow."

The cardinal again like a prince of power waved his hand and said, "Peace unto the people of good will, pray ye now for the mass has begun—the time is short and today there must be prayers on earth as in heaven."

We all began to pray awaiting great things. And our holy fath.. sat before us on the throne.

741

From the chapels again rose voices like angels' choirs, full of heavenly rapture. A portion of the night passed and white-robed priests came and offered their hands to our father. He descended from the throne and approached the altar taking the chalice in his hands, for the moment had come for the holy sacrifice. The cardinal poured wine into the chalice.

Just at the moment the chalice was being uplifted, when all had fallen to their knees, a voice from the air was heard which uttered, "I live!" And when, aquiver, we raised our heads, we beheld a large figure with head bent upon the central gate, slowly dissolving —ever becoming more misty—the hands bloody, the feet bleeding, but the figure itself of snowy whiteness—and—melting like snow —it vanished.

Then the cardinal, as the pope holding the chalice in his hands, still hesitated, himself uttered the words: "Ite, missa est!" and then he cried in a powerful voice, "The times are fulfilled!" and rending the purple on his breast, he extended his hand toward the grave of Peter saying, "Awake and speak!"

From every lamp above the tomb a fiery tongue burst forth and a wreath of flames swung over the dark sepulcher. From the depths of that darkness, a body arose with hands upstretched to the dome, and standing buried in the tomb to its breast, it shrieked, "Woe!"

After this outcry it seemed to all of us that the vaulted arch of the dome cracked for the first time.

The cardinal then said, "Peter, do you recognise me?"

And the body answered, "Your head rested on the bosom of the Master at the last supper and you have never perished from the earth."

The cardinal responded, "Now it is commanded to me to linger among human beings and to embrace the earth and hold it to my bosom as the Master held mine that last night of His life on earth."

And the body replied, "Do as you have been commanded."

Then the cardinal again waved his hands as with the authority of a prince, and the body repeated: "Woe be unto me!" and fell with a terrible crash as into an abyss, back into its grave. Above, the vaulted arches began anew to shiver and break.

Horror overwhelmed us all. Only the Polish nobles gazed with dauntless eyes, leaning upon their swords.

The pope in his triple crown had knelt down on the steps of the altar and, as immovable as a statue, continued kneeling.

The cardinal spoke: "Go forth, all of you—you and you and you,—lest some of you perish beneath the ruins of these walls."

The people answered from all sides, "Lead us—you—under whose protection we have this day entered."

A cry of terror arose for the arches ever more thunderously burst into fissures, the pillars and columns all about shook and lamps were shattered and extinguished by a great wind.

Then spoke the cardinal, "Father—mine—do you wish to remain here?"

And the aged man lifting his hands to his crown, answered in a sorrowful voice: "I wish to die here—leave me, my son."

All the people heard these words, and shrieked, "Run—let us run away!"

And the Romans were the first to recover and began to flee.

And each troop or band moved from its altar with its banner and made haste to fly away.

Then the cardinal, kneeling at last, pressed his lips to the old man's brow and made the sign of a blessing around his crown like a garland of livid light in the air, then he descended and walked toward the gate of the church with a marvellous glow encircling his brow. The entire church was twisted and bent as a dying body in the last throes, but he, with uplifted hand, stayed the cracking, tumbling vault above the people and stood watching until the last one of them had gone.

And departing he said to the Polish nobles, "People, follow after me."

But these did not answer.

He turned his head back again and said, "Follow after me."

They did not move.

When he had reached the gate, driving the people before him like a shepherd, he beckoned them for the last time with his hand.

But they only lifted up their swords as if with their edges they would hold up the falling walls and they cried out altogether, "We shall not desert that aged man—it is bitter, indeed, to die all alone —and who should die with him if not we?—Go you, all—we do not know how to run away."

The cardinal stopped on the very threshold and from a distance made to them the sign of his blessing and of the garland of livid light. In his eyes that moment a tear glistened as he said, "Yet a moment more and you perish."

But in that moment they were hastening to the main altar to offer a hand to the kneeling and dying. They advanced in their white caps and in the gleaming of their swords—and the four twisted columns of the altar snapped like a split tree and came crashing down—even the metal canopy dropped in ruins—the entire cupola like a sinking world, fell to the ground.

And all the porticoes, even the palace of the Vatican and the colonnade in the court cracked and burst, falling into dust. Both of the fountains like two white doves, fell to the ground perishing. The populace rushed ever farther on like a sea forced from its shores and, it seemed that it was already morn, though the sun had not yet risen. But I seemed to see only the morning star above a pile of ruins, as high, as immense as had formerly been the basilica of Peter.

Upon this gigantic mountain the cardinal ascended and it seemed that I followed after him carried on by strength of soul.

When he had attained the summit, he seated himself there as on a throne and gazed at the world. His purple robes dropped from his body and he was transformed into a figure of white ensilvered by the mild glow. In his hands was a book and over it he bent his head reading attentively.

His face was entranced with an expression of love and fulness of peace.

I approached him and said just as the sun began to rise: "Sir, is it true that Christ was born for the last time yesterday in that church which to-day is no more?"

With a strange smile and without lifting his eyes from his book, he responded, "From the time of Christ none are born and none die on this earth."

Hearing this I lost my great fear and asked, "Sir, and those whom I led thither yesterday, shall they lie forever under those ruins,—all those dead around the aged dead man?"

And the white saint answered me, "Fear not for them. Because they performed the last service for him, God will reward them—for those who pass out of life are like those who are entering upon it, the dead just as the living are of God. Instead of loss—they gain —it will be better for them and for the sons of their sons."

And when I understood, I rejoiced and my soul awakened.

L

SELMA LAGERLOF

SELMA LAGERLÖF (Swedish, 1858-1940). Most important Swedish woman novelist. Deeply imbued with love of the supernatural and wondersome. Decided to write book based on traditions and stories of her province; *Gösta Berlings Saga* became world classic. Also famous: *Jerusalem,* novel of Swedish farmers who emigrated to Palestine; *The Wonderful Adventures of Nils,* children's story. Nobel Prize, 1909.

THE ECLIPSE

THERE were Stina of Ridgecote and Lina of Birdsong and Kajsa of Littlemarsh and Maja of Skypeak and Beda of Finn-darkness and Elin, the new wife on the old soldier's place, and two or three other peasant women besides—all of them lived at the far end of the parish, below Storhöjden, in a region so wild and rocky none of the big farmowners had bothered to lay hands on it.

One had her cabin set up on a shelf of rock, another had hers put up at the edge of a bog, while a third had one that stood at the crest of a hill so steep it was a toilsome climb getting to it. If by chance any of the others had a cottage built on more favorable ground, you may be sure it lay so close to the mountain as to shut out the sun from autumn fair time clear up to Annunciation Day.

They each cultivated a little potato patch close by the cabin, though under serious difficulties. To be sure, there were many kinds of soil there at the foot of the mountain, but it was hard work to make the patches of land yield anything. In some places they had to clear away so much stone from their fields, it would have built a cow-house on a manorial estate; in some they had dug ditches as deep as graves, and in others they had brought their earth in sacks and spread it on the bare rocks. Where the soil was not so poor, they were forever fighting the tough thistle and pig-

weed which sprang up in such profusion you would have thought the whole potato land had been prepared for their benefit.

All the livelong day the women were alone in their cabins; for even where one had a husband and children, the man went off to his work every morning and the children went to school. A few among the older women had grown sons and daughters, but they had gone to America. And some there were with little children, who were always around, of course; but these could hardly be regarded as company.

Being so much alone, it was really necessary that they should meet sometimes over the coffee cups. Not that they got on so very well together, nor had any great love for each other; but some liked to keep posted on what the others were doing, and some grew despondent living like that, in the shadow of the mountain, unless they met people now and then. And there were those, too, who needed to unburden their hearts, and talk about the last letter from America, and those who were naturally talkative and jocular, and who longed for opportunity to make use of these happy God-given talents.

Nor was it any trouble at all to prepare for a little party. Coffee-pot and coffee cups they all had of course, and cream could be got at the manor, if one had no cow of one's own to milk; fancy biscuits and small cakes one could, at a pinch, get the dairyman's driver to fetch from the municipal bakery, and country merchants who sold coffee and sugar were to be found everywhere. So, to get up a coffee party was the easiest thing imaginable. The difficulty lay in finding an occasion.

For Stina of Ridgecote, Lina of Birdsong, Kajsa of Littlemarsh, Maja of Skypeak, Beda of Finn-darkness, and Elin, the new wife at the old soldier's, were all agreed that it would never do for them to celebrate in the midst of the common everyday life. Were they to be that wasteful of the precious hours which never return, they might get a bad name. And to hold coffee parties on Sundays or great Holy Days was out of the question; for then the married women had husband and children at home, which was quite company enough. As for the rest—some liked to attend church, some wished to visit relatives, while a few preferred to spend the day at home, in perfect peace and stillness, that they might really feel it was a Holy Day.

Therefore they were all the more eager to take advantage of every possible opportunity. Most of them gave parties on their name-

days, though some celebrated the great event when the wee little one cut its first tooth, or when it took its first steps. For those who received money-letters from America that was always a convenient excuse, and it was also in order to invite all the women of the neighborhood to come and help tack a quilt or stretch a web just off the loom.

All the same, there were not nearly as many occasions to meet as were needed. One year one of the women was at her wit's end. It was her turn to give a party, and she had no objection to carrying out what was expected of her; but she could not seem to hit upon anything to celebrate. Her own name-day she could not celebrate, being named Beda, as Beda has been stricken out of the almanac. Nor could she celebrate that of any member of her family, for all her dear ones were resting in the churchyard. She was very old, and the quilt she slept under would probably outlast her. She had a cat of which she was very fond. Truth to tell, it drank coffee just as well as she did; but she could hardly bring herself to hold a party for a cat!

Pondering, she searched her almanac again and again, for there she felt she must surely find the solution of her problem.

She began at the beginning, with "The Royal House" and "Signs and Forecasts," and read on, right through to "Markets and Postal Transmittances for 1912," without finding anything.

As she was reading the book for the seventh time, her glance rested on "Eclipses." She noted that that year, which was the year of our Lord nineteen-hundred twelve, on April seventeenth there would be a solar eclipse. It would begin at twenty minutes past high noon and end at 2:40 o'clock, and would cover nine-tenths of the sun's disk.

This she had read before, many times, without attaching any significance to it; but now, all at once, it became dazzling clear to her.

"Now I have it!" she exclaimed.

But it was only for a second or two that she felt confident; and then she put the thought away, fearing that the other women would just laugh at her.

The next few days, however, the idea that had come to her when reading her almanac kept recurring to her mind, until at last she began to wonder whether she hadn't better venture. For when she thought about it, what friend had she in all the world she loved better than the Sun? Where her hut lay not a ray of sunlight pene-

747

trated her room the whole winter long. She counted the days until the Sun would come back to her in the spring. The Sun was the only one who was always friendly and gracious to her and of whom she could never see enough.

She looked her years, and felt them, too. Her hands shook as if she were in a perpetual chill and when she saw herself in the looking-glass, she appeared so pale and washed out, as if she had been lying out to bleach. It was only when she stood in a strong, warm, down-pouring sunshine that she felt like a living human being and not a walking corpse.

The more she thought about it, the more she felt there was no day in the whole year she would rather celebrate than the one when her friend the Sun battled against darkness, and after a glorious conquest, came forth with new splendor and majesty.

The seventeenth of April was not far away, but there was ample time to make ready for a party. So, on the day of the eclipse Stina, Lina, Kajsa, Maja, and the other women all sat drinking coffee with Beda at Finn-darkness. They drank their second and their third cups, and chatted about everything imaginable. For one thing, they said they coudn't for the life of them understand why Beda should be giving a party.

Meanwhile, the eclipse was under way. But they took little notice of it. Only for a moment, when the sky turned blackish gray, when all nature seemed under a leaden pall, and there came driving a howling wind with sounds as of the Trumpet of Doom and the lamentations of Judgment Day—only then did they pause and feel a bit awed. But here they each had a fresh cup of coffee, and the feeling soon passed.

When all was over, and the Sun stood out in the heavens so beamingly happy——it seemed to them it had not shone with such brilliancy and power the whole year—they saw old Beda go over to the window, and stand with folded hands. Looking out toward the sunlit slope, she sang in her quavering voice:

"Thy shining sun goes up again,
I thank Thee, O my Lord!
With new-found courage, strength and hope,
I raise a song of joy."

Thin and transparent, old Beda stood there in the light of the window, and as she sang the sunbeams danced about her, as if wanting to give her, also, of their life and strength and color.

When she had finished the old hymn-verse she turned and looked at her guests, as if in apology.

"You see," she said, "I haven't any better friend than the Sun, and I wanted to give her a party on the day of her eclipse. I felt that we should come together to greet her, when she came out of her darkness."

Now they understood what old Beda meant, and their hearts were touched. They began to speak well of the Sun. "She was kind to rich and poor alike, and when she came peeping into the hut on a winter's day, she was as comforting as a glowing fire on the hearth. Just the sight of her smiling face made life worth living, whatever the troubles one had to bear."

The women went back to their homes after the party, happy and content. They somehow felt richer and more secure in the thought that they had a good, faithful friend in the Sun.

LAO SHE

LAO SHÊ (Shu Ch'ing-ch'un, Chinese, 1897-   ). Leading writer of satirical fiction. During war with Japan was president of Writer's League, wrote patriotic plays. *Ssu-shih t'ung-t'ang*, novel of occupied Peking, widely acclaimed.

THE LAST TRAIN

THE train started a long while ago, and now the wheels rumbled mournfully along the rails, the passengers sighed and counted the hours: seven o'clock, eight, nine, ten—by ten o'clock the train would arrive, and they would be home around midnight. It might not be too late, for the children might already be put to bed. It was New Year's Day, and they were all in a hurry to get home. They looked at the cans, the fruit and the toys heaped up on the shelves, and already they could hear the children crying 'Papa, papa!', and thinking of all this, they lost themselves in their thoughts; but there were others who were well aware that they would not be home before daybreak.

There were not many passengers in the second-class carriage. There was fat Mr. Chang and thin Mr. Chiao, and they sat in the

same compartment opposite one another. Whenever they got up, they spread their blankets over their seats to show that intruders would not be welcomed. When the train started they found to their surprise that there were very few passengers indeed, and somehow this led them more than ever to feel grieved at the thought that they were travelling in a train on New Year's Day. There were other similarities between the two passengers: they were both holding free passes, and both of them had been unable to obtain the pass until the previous day. They were both indignant at this treatment, for in the good old days friends were made of sterner stuff, and so they shook their heads and put the blame on these so-called friends who had prevented them from reaching their home before the New Year's Day.

Old Mr. Chang removed his fox-fur coat and tucked his legs under his body, but he discovered that the seat was too narrow for sitting comfortably in this posture. Meanwhile, the temperature of the carriage rose and beads of perspiration began to roll down his brow. 'Boy, towels!' he shouted, and then to Mr. Chiao he said: 'I wonder why they turn so much heat on nowadays'. He gasped. 'It wouldn't be so hot if we were travelling on an aeroplane.'

Old Mr. Chiao had taken off his coat a long while ago, and now he was wearing a robe lined with white sheep's fur, and over that a sleeveless jacket of shining black satin. He showed no sign of feeling faint. He said: 'One can get a free pass on an aeroplane, too. It isn't difficult'. And he drawled off with a faint smile.

'It's better not to risk travelling by air', old Mr. Chang said, trying hard to keep his crossed legs under him, but succeeding only with great difficulty. 'Boy, towels!'

The 'boy' was over forty, and his neck was as thin as a stick, so thin that one imagined that it was quite easy to pluck off his head and plant it back again. You could see him hurrying backwards and forwards along the passageway, his hands full of steaming towels. He was always eager to serve, but really—the way the management made you work on such a sacred day—it was really inconceivable. Taking advantage of the rocking movement of the train, he swung his body towards a certain Mr. K'ou. 'Like a towel, sir? It's trying to travel at this time of the year.'

Mr. K'ou was dressed with considerable éclat. He wore a dark serge overcoat with a beaver collar, with a brand new black satin, melon-shaped hat. He had removed neither his coat nor his hat, and he sat there as rigid as a chairman on a platform waiting

750

solemnly for the moment when he would address a huge audience. He took the towel, stretching out his arm at full length, and taking care not to fold his elbow he described a semi-circle with the towel until it reached his face. Then he rubbed his face fastidiously and ostentatiously. When his face emerged from the whirling cloud of the towel it dazzled and lent to his person a renewed splendour and dignity. He nodded to the 'boy', without explaining why he was travelling on New Year's Day.

And meanwhile the waiter knew perfectly well that the man was a friend of the manager. The carriage began to rock again, and the movement of the carriage hurled him into the passage way. Steadying himself, he untwisted a towel and holding it delicately by two corners he offered it to Mr. Chang. 'Would you like one, sir?', and the man reached out for it, his thick palm touching the central part of it, which was the hottest. He pressed it to his face, rubbing hard as though he were cleaning a mirror. Then he handed another one to Mr. Chiao, who showed no enthusiasm, but took the towel and with it proceeded to clean his nostrils and fingernails delicately. When he returned it to the waiter, it was all greasy and black.

'The inspectors will soon be coming now', he began. 'When they have gone, you will want to have a rest, and if any of you gentlemen would like a cushion, just let me know.' And he went on a little later: 'There are not many passengers on board, and you'll all be able to have a nap. It's a pity you gentlemen are spending a day like this on a train, but as for us waiters—'. He sighed. He realized that he had been talking too much.

'What's wrong with the heating system?' Mr. Chang asked, as he tossed back the towel.

'I wouldn't advise you to open the window', the waiter answered. 'Nine to ten you'll catch cold. The railway is under a rotten management.' The chance lay wide open for him, and he entered quickly. 'They make you work all the year round, and don't even let you rest on New Year's Day. Well, all talking is vain.'

And so it was, for the train had drawn into a small wayside station. Half a dozen soldiers came into the compartment. Their boots thundered on the floor, their leather belts flashed in the light and their luggage consisted of four large cases of fireworks wrapped in scarlet paper and decorated with characters cut out of gold paper. The boxes were so large that for a long time they were undecided what to do with them. Finally, a man who resembled a

battalion commander, said that they should be put on the floor. Boots thundered. A cloud of grey caps, grey uniforms and grey leggings. A moment later someone said: 'Hurry!', and they obediently disappeared. A whistle sounded from the train, rather muffled. Lights and shadows flitted about, and the wheels began to rumble and the train to roll out of the station.

The waiter walked from one end of the carriage to the other, looking as though there was something on his mind. He stole a glance at the two soldiers and then at the heap of fireworks which lay so uncompromisingly on the floor, barring his way; but he dared not say anything. The battalion commander was lying down, tired out, his pistol on the little table at the side of the carriage. The platoon commander had not yet dared to imitate him, but he had removed his cap and was now violently scratching his scalp. The waiter took care not to awaken the senior officer, but he smiled voluminously at the junior. 'What was I going to say?' he said in a half-apologetic tone of voice, hesitantly. 'Oh yes, I was going to suggest that it might be a better idea to put the crackers up on the shelf.'

'Why?' the officer answered, mouth awry with head scratching.

'You know, I was afraid people might step on them', the waiter replied, his head shrinking tortoise-fashion into his shoulders.

'If I have any more trouble from you, what about fighting it out?' the officer suddenly shouted. He had been worn thin by the ill-humour of his senior officer, and he was perfectly prepared to fight.

But the waiter was in no need of a fight, and he abruptly disappeared. As he passed Mr. Chang, he said: 'The inspectors will be here soon, sir'.

Mr. Chang and Mr. Chiao were developing a cordial friendship. The ticket inspection began.

Meanwhile the waiter was taking this opportunity to inform Mr. Chang and Mr. Chiao to get their tickets ready. They gave him their tickets. He was awestruck when he realized that the tickets were free passes, and his reverence for the two gentlemen became even greater than before. He returned Mr. Chang's pass at once, but he ventured to detain Mr. Chiao's for a moment because it was clearly indicated on the pass that the holder was a woman, and there was indisputable evidence that Mr. Chiao was a man. The two inspectors drew apart and began to whisper into each other's

ear. A moment later they nodded to one another, and it was clear that they had reached a common understanding that on New Year's Day a man might pass for a woman. The waiter returned Mr. Chiao's ticket with both hands, apologetically.

The battalion commander was now snoring. As soon as he noticed the arrival of the inspectors, the platoon commander put his legs up on the seat and showed every sign of an unwillingness to be disturbed. The inspectors' attention was immediately arrested by the pile of fireworks which littered the passageway. They nodded in admiration, overcome by the length and the solidity of the fire-works. And they passed through the compartment, and it was not until the first inspector reached the door that he turned to the waiter and said: 'You'd better tell them to put the fireworks on the shelves', and in order to save the waiter from further embarrass-ment the second inspector added quickly: 'Better still if you did it for them'. The waiter nodded his thin neck like a pendulum without saying anything, but all the while he was asking himself: 'You haven't the courage to tell them—that's what it is—so what can I do except nod my head?—and besides, there is a great difference between nodding and doing.' The truth dawned on his mind. The fireworks must *not* be moved.

Go-home-go-home-go-home-go-home. The wheels roared in chorus. But they were very slow. The star-strewn sky undulated. Hills, trees, villages, graves, flashed past in clusters. The train dashed on and on in the darkness. Smoke, soot and sparks shot up furiously, and then disappeared. The train ran on, flying breathlessly, one patch of darkness following on another. The lights were ablaze, the tempera-ture steaming, all the passengers were weary to death, and not one was inclined to sleep. Go-home-go-home-go-home. The farewell rites to the Old Year, the libations to the gods, the offerings to the Ancestors, the writing on the spring scrolls, the firecrackers, the dumplings, the sweetmeats, the dinners and the wine—all these became suddenly very real to them, filling their eyes and their ears, their palates and their nostrils. A smile would light upon their lips and instantly disappear, dying away at the recollection that they were still physically in the train. Go-home-go-home-go-home-go-home.

Mr. Chang took down from the shelf two bottles of distilled wine, and said to Mr. Chiao: 'We're just like old friends now. How about a drop of this? We might as well enjoy New Year's Day

753

—no reason why we shouldn't enjoy ourselves'. He handed over a cup of the wine. 'Real Yinkow wine. Twenty years old. You can't get it on the market. Bottoms up.'

Mr. Chiao was too polite to refuse.

'Marvellous!' Mr. Chiao wetted his lips. 'Marvellous! Nothing like it anywhere.'

They filled up one another's cups, and slowly and imperceptibly their faces turned crimson. Their tongues were unloosened. They talked of their families, their jobs, their friends, the difficulty of earning money, free passes. Their cups clinked, their hearts clinked, their eyes moistened, they were permeated with warmth.

Mr. Chang looked at his bottle—there was not very much left now. He untied his collar. Beads of perspiration stood out on his brow; his eyes were bloodshot and his tongue was stiff. Though still talkative, his talk was reduced to mere babbling; he had not yet completely lost his self-control, he could still put a curb on the curious inner urge which nearly led him to curse in front of his new-found friend, and the resultant of these forces took the form, not of a quarrel, or incivility, but rather of exultation and gaiety. Mr. Chiao, on the other hand, had been able to stomach only half of the bottle assigned to him, but his face was already turning deathly pale. He produced a packet of cigarettes and threw one at Mr. Chang. Both lit their cigarettes.

Go-home-go-home-go-home-go-home. In Mr. Chang's ears the wheels sounded as though they were going at breakneck speed. His heart beat fast, and suddenly everything began buzzing. His head turned round and round in the air, buzzing like a fly. All objects were dancing and glowing in red circles. When the buzzing ceased, his heart once more began to beat at its accustomed ritual, and he opened his eyes slightly, partially regaining his strength. He pretended nothing had happened, and groping for the matchbox he relit his extinguished cigarette. Then he threw the match away. Suddenly on the table a greenish flame flared up, smelling of alcohol, spinning among the cups and bottles, fluttering, rising, spreading out. Mr. Chiao was startled out of his dreams as the cigarette which he held in his hand suddenly caught fire. He threw it away. He beat the table with both hands to extinguish the fire, and in doing this he knocked down the cups and bottles. Iridescent tongues licked the unopened parcels. Mr. Chang's face was hidden in flames. Mr. Chiao thought of running away. The flames on the table soared up, and the parcels on the shelf above seemed to reach down to

catch the rising columns of flames. Flame linked with flame. Mr. Chiao himself was ablaze. The fire reached his eyebrows, charring them, snapping at his hair, which sizzled, lighting up the alcohol on his lips and turning him into a fire-breathing monster.

Suddenly: pop, pop, pop . . . It sounded like machine-gun fire. The platoon commander had hardly opened his eyes when a cracker exploded on his nose and sent sparks and blood flying in fine sprays. He rose, and began frantically running. There were explosions everywhere, under his feet, all round his body. The noise was deafening as though they had stepped on a land mine. The battalion commander was swallowed up in the fire before he could open his eyes. He was trying to open his eyes when the right eye received a direct hit from one of the exploding crackers.

Mr. K'ou started up. He cast a quick glance at his luggage on the shelf. Some of the parcels were already burning, and the fire was closing in from all sides—from above, from below, and even from a long way away. Flames licked at him, and an idea flashed through his mind. He picked up one of his shoes from the floor and smote at the windowpane. He wanted to jump out of the window. The glass was broken, a gale rushed in, the fire turned wild. His collar of beaver-skin, the four bedrolls, the five boxes, his clothes—they were all swallowed up in the flames. The train ran on, the wind was roaring, the firecrackers kept going off. Mr. K'ou ran like a wild animal.

Mr. Chang was dead-drunk, and he lay there like a log. Mr. Chiao, Mr. K'ou and the platoon commander were running about in all directions, stark staring mad. The battalion commander knelt on the bench and wailed. The fire had already penetrated every corner of the carriage; the smell of sulphur was suffocating. The crackers were no longer exploding—they had all been burnt. The noise died away, but the smoke grew thicker. And at last those who were running about no longer ran about, and those who were wailing no longer wailed. The fire began to devour the furniture. The train kept darting forward, the wind kept roaring. Red tongues of flame struggled within the dense clouds of smoke, hoping for an outlet. The smoke turned milky, and the flames began to thrash at the windows. The whole carriage was transparent with light, and tongues of fire streamed away like streamers, a thousand torches burning brightly in the wind.

Brilliant rockets shot out in sprays. The night was dark and the train was a chain of lanterns pouring out licking flames. Of the

second-class carriage, only a charred skeleton remained. The flames, having nothing to feed on, moved backwards and forwards, and finally entered the third-class carriage. Smoke came first, sending out a pungent, and slightly sweet smell of charred flesh and furniture. Fire followed. 'Fire! Fire' Fire' Everyone was shouting in fearful panic. They lost their heads. They broke the windows in an attempt to leap out, and then hesitated. Some began to run, and then they would fall against one another and fall down. Some sat transfixed to their seats, unable even to cry. Turbulence. Panic. Every effort proved vain. They howled, folded their arms round their heads, beat off the flames with their clothes, ran, jumped out of the carriage. . . .

The fire had discovered a new colony, with rich resources and a great population. It was mad with joy. Hundreds of flames began dancing in the most fantastic patterns. They rolled themselves up into balls, shot out like meteors, gathered in red-and-green pools of fire. They squeaked and gibbered as they burned human flesh and broiled human hair. The crowd howled, the wind roared, the fire crackled. The whole car was on fire. The smoke was heavy. It was a lovely cremation.

The train arrived at the next station, where it was due to stop. It stopped. Signalmen, ticket-inspectors, guards, the stationmaster and the assistant stationmaster, the clerks and the hangers-on all looked at the burning carriages in amazement, and could do nothing, because there were no fire engines and no implements for putting out fires. The second-class carriage, and the two adjacent third-class carriages in front and behind were silent and still. From them a plume of blue smoke curled up—languidly and leisurely.

It was reported later that fifty-two corpses were found on the train, and the bodies of eleven more, who had jumped off and killed themselves, were found along the line.

After the Lantern Festival—that is, fifteen days after the New Year—an inspector arrived.

The guard knew nothing. The first inspector knew nothing. The second inspector knew nothing.

Finally, the waiter was examined. He declared that he knew nothing about the fire, which must have started when he was in the dining-car. The tribunal decided that he was irrevocably wrong, and should be punished for having left his post of duty. And he was duly discharged from the service.

The inspector submitted his report with a detailed account of the tragedy written in the most admirable style.

'I don't care at all', the waiter said to his wife. 'They put you on duty on New Year's Day, and then, when everything goes wrong, they think we will be starved if we leave their wretched railway.'

'What nonsense!' his wife answered. 'I'm not worried about that. What I am worried about is the cabbage that got burnt.'

LAO-TZU

LAO-TZU (Chinese, 6th century B.C.). Legendary sage of China. Author of the celebrated *Tao Te Ching*, 81 chapters of prose and verse. Important in the whole Taoist movement ("Tao," "the Eternal" or "Way of Life" according to reason and virtue).

PARAPHRASE

1

There are ways but the Way is uncharted;
There are names but not nature in words:
Nameless indeed is the source of creation
But things have a mother and she has a name.

The secret waits for the insight
Of eyes unclouded by longing;
Those who are bound by desire
See only the outward container.

These two come paired but distinct
By their names.
Of all things profound,
Say that their pairing is deepest,
The gate to the root of the world.

2

Since the world points up beauty as such,
There is ugliness too.
If goodness is taken as goodness,
Wickedness enters as well.

757

For is and is-not come together;
Hard and easy are complementary;
Long and short are relative;
High and low are comparative;
Pitch and sound make harmony;
Before and after are a sequence.

Indeed the Wise Man's office
Is to work by being still;
He teaches not by speech
But by accomplishment;
He does for everything,
Neglecting none;
Their life he gives to all,
Possessing none;
And what he brings to pass
Depends on no one else.
As he succeeds,
He takes no credit
And just because he does not take it,
Credit never leaves him.

3

A man of highest virtue
Will not display it as his own;
His virtue then is real.
Low virtue makes one miss no chance
To show his virtue off;
His virtue then is nought.
High virtue is at rest;
It knows no need to act.
Low virtue is a busyness
Pretending to accomplishment.

Compassion at its best
Consists in honest deeds;
Morality at best
Is something done, aforethought;
High etiquette, when acted out
Without response from others,
Constrains a man to bare his arms
And make them do their duty!

Truly, once the Way is lost,
There comes then virtue;
Virtue lost, comes then compassion;
After that morality;
And when that's lost, there's etiquette,
The husk of all good faith,
The rising point of anarchy.

Foreknowledge is, they say,
The Doctrine come to flower;
But better yet, it is
The starting point of silliness.
So once full-grown, a man will take
The meat and not the husk,
The fruit and not the flower.
Rejecting one, he takes the other.

4

These things in ancient times received the One:

The sky obtained it and was clarified;
The earth received it and was settled firm;
The spirits got it and were energized;
The valleys had it, filled to overflow;
All things, as they partook it came alive;
The nobles and the king imbibed the One
In order that the realm might upright be;
Such things were then accomplished by the One.

Without its clarity the sky might break;
Except it were set firm, the earth might shake;
Without their energy the gods would pass;
Unless kept full, the valleys might go dry;
Except for life, all things would pass away;
Unless the One did lift and hold them high,
The nobles and the king might trip and fall.

The humble folk support the mighty ones;
They are base on which the highest rest.
The nobles and the king speak of themselves

759

As "orphans," "desolate" and "needy ones."
Does this not indicate that they depend
Upon the lowly people for support?

Truly, a cart is more than the sum of its parts.

Better to rumble like rocks
Than to tinkle like jade.

DAVID HERBERT LAWRENCE

DAVID HERBERT LAWRENCE (English, 1885-1930). Controversial English
novelist and poet. An enigmatic battler against social prejudice. Son of a coal
miner, rebelled bitterly against industrialism. Also concerned with better
relations between sexes. *Sons and Lovers*, partly autobiographical novel. *Lady
Chatterly's Lover*, banned in England and America because of frankness.
Spent last years of life in Mexico and Italy.

DREAMS OLD AND NASCENT

My world is a painted fresco, where coloured shapes
Of old, ineffectual lives linger blurred and warm;
An endless tapestry the past has woven drapes
The halls of my life, compelling my soul to conform.

The surface of dreams is broken,
The picture of the past is shaken and scattered.
Fluent, active figures of men pass along the railway, and I am woken
From the dreams that the distance flattered.

Along the railway, active figures of men.
They have a secret that stirs in their limbs as they move
Out of the distance, nearer, commanding my dreamy world.

Here in the subtle, rounded flesh
Beats the active ectasy.
In the sudden lifting of my eyes, it is clearer,
The fascination of the quick, restless Creator moving through the
    mesh
Of men, vibrating in ecstasy through the rounded flesh.

Oh my boys, bending over your books,
In you is trembling and fusing
The creation of a new-patterned dream, dream of a generation:
And I watch to see the Creator, the power that patterns the dream.

The old dreams are beautiful, beloved, soft-toned, and sure,
But the dream-stuff is molten and moving mysteriously,
Alluring my eyes; for I, am I not also dream-stuff,
Am I not quickening, diffusing myself in the pattern, shaping and
    shapen?

Here in my class is the answer for the great yearning:
Eyes where I can watch the swim of old dreams reflected on the
    molten metal of dreams,
Watch the stir which is rhythmic and moves them all as a heart-beat
    moves the blood,
Here in the swelling flesh the great activity working,
Visible there in the change of eyes and the mobile features.

Oh the great mystery and fascination of the unseen Shaper,
The power of the melting, fusing Force—heat, light, all in one,
Everything great and mysterious in one, swelling and shaping the
    dream in the flesh,
As it swells and shapes a bud into blossom.

Oh the terrible ecstasy of the consciousness that I am life!
Oh the miracle of the whole, the widespread, labouring concentration
Swelling mankind like one bud to bring forth the fruit of a dream,
Oh the terror of lifting the innermost I out of the sweep of the
    impulse of life,
And watching the Great Thing labouring through the whole round
    flesh of the world;
And striving to catch a glimpse of the shape of the coming dream,
As it quickens within the labouring, white-hot metal,
Catch the scent and the colour of the coming dream,
Then to fall back exhausted into the unconscious, molten life!

761

LEE HOU-CHU

LEE HOU-CHU (Chinese, 937-978). King of the South T'ang Kingdom in the time of the Ten Kingdoms, and greatest poet of his time. His administration, more devoted to arts than wars, fell easily to Sung Emperor. Great lover of music, women and Buddhism. Master of the *tzu*, a song set to a definite tune.

THE FISHERMAN

The vernal breeze an oar;
My skiff a leaf;
A line of fishing string;
A light hook.
An islet full of flowers;
A pitcher full of wine.
Among ten thousand ching of waves
I have my freedom.

The wave-flowers break into a thousand layers of snow.
Peach and plum blossoms from the quiet army of Spring.
A flask of wine;
A fishing rod and line.
Who is as happy as I?

FADING FLOWERS

The morning moon sets;
Last night's smoke is blown away.
Speechless I recline on the pillow.
Returning from my dreams I hanker after the scented grass.

In the far sky, the cry of swans is thin.

The singing orioles scatter;
The fading flowers fall;
Lonely are the painted hall and the deep courtyard.
Do not sweep away the red petals;
Let them await the feet of the returning dancers.

SPRING

To find spring one must walk out in the early Spring.
To love a flower do not wait till the flower is old.
She holds the bluish cup in her supple hand;
The brimming wine is clear.

What harm is there in smiling and laughing?
In the Forbidden Garden spring yet lingers.
Ah, to be drunk together and to converse leisurely!
Poems flow to the sound of the goat-drum
Calling on the flowers to blossom forth.

PALE MOON

In the long night,
I loiter round the bower,
Indolent.
The feast of ching-min is just over;
I already feel the Spring wane.
The sound of falling rain is stifled by the wind.
The blurred moon is pale among the shifting clouds.

Breezes pass lightly through the yearning peach and apricot.
Who is chattering there at the swing with laughter?
My heart is one, but its threads of thoughts are ten thousand.
There is no place on earth for me to smooth them out.

NIKOLAUS LENAU

NIKOLAUS LENAU (Nikolaus Niembsch von Strehlenau, Austrian, 1802-
1850). Austrian lyric poet. The bohemian of the Balkans. Lived erratically,
died in delusion. Like Leopardi, a poet of despair. An accomplished violinist,
with deep feeling for nature.

SONGS BY THE LAKE

I

In the sky the sun is failing,
   And the weary day would sleep.
Here the willow fronds are trailing
   In the water still and deep.

763

From my darling I must sever:
  Stream, oh tears, stream forth amain!
In the breeze the rushes quiver
  And the willow sighs in pain.

On my soul in silence grieving
  Mild thou gleamest from afar,
As through rushes interweaving
  Gleams the mirrored evening star.

IV

Sunset dull and drear;
  Dark the clouds drive past;
Sultry, full of fear,
  All the winds fly fast.

Through the sky's wild rack
  Shoots the lightning pale;
O'er the waters black
  Burns its flickering trail.

In the vivid glare
  Half I see thy form,
And thy streaming hair
  Flutters in the storm.

V

On the lake as it reposes
  Dwells the moon with glow serene
Interweaving pallid roses
  With the rushes' crown of green.

Stags from out the hillside bushes
  Gaze aloft into the night,
Waterfowl amid the rushes
  Vaguely stir with fluttering light.

Down my tear-dim glance I bend now,
  While through all my soul a rare
Thrill of thought toward thee doth tend now
  Like an ecstasy of prayer.

764

Passing lovely was the night,
   Silver clouds flew o'er us,
Spring, methought, with splendor dight
   Led the happy chorus.

Sleep-entranced lay wood and dale,
   Empty now each by-way;
No one but the moonlight pale
   Roamed upon the highway.

Breezes wandering in the gloom
   Soft their footsteps numbered
Through Dame Nature's sleeping-room
   Where her children slumbered.

Timidly the brook stole by,
   While the beds of blossom
Breathed their perfume joyously
   On the still night's bosom.

My postilion, heedless all,
   Cracked his whip most gaily,
And his merry trumpet-call
   Rang o'er hill and valley.

Hoofs beat steadily the while,
   As the horses gamboled,
And along the shady aisle
   Spiritedly rambled.

Grove and meadow gliding past
   Vanished at a glimmer:
Peaceful towns were gone as fast,
   Like to dreams that shimmer.

Midway in the Maytide trance
   Tombs were shining whitely;
'Twas the churchyard met our glance—
   None might view it lightly.

Close against the mountain braced
   Ran the long white wall there,
And the cross, in sorrow placed,
   Silent rose o'er all there.

Jehu straight, his humor spent,
   Left his tuneful courses;
On the cross his gaze he bent
   Then pulled up his horses.

"Here's where horse and coach must wait—
   You may think it odd, sir:—
But up yonder, lies my mate
   Underneath the sod, sir.

"Better lad was never born—
   (Sir, 'twas God's own pity!)
No one else could blow the horn
   Half as shrill and pretty.

"So I stop beside the wall
   Every time I pass here,
And I blow his favorite call
   To him under grass here."

Toward the churchyard then he blew
   One call after other,
That they might go ringing through
   To his sleeping brother.

From the cliff each lively note
   Echoing resounded,
As it were the dead man's throat
   Answering strains had sounded.

On we went through field and hedge,
   Loosened bridles jingling;
Long that echo from the ledge
   In my ear kept tingling.

TO THE BELOVED FROM AFAR

His sweet rose here oversea
    I must gather sadly;
Which, beloved, unto thee
    I would bring how gladly!

But alas! if o'er the foam
    I this flower should carry,
It would fade ere I could come;
    Roses may not tarry.

Farther let no mortal fare
    Who would be a wooer,
Than unwithered he may bear
    Blushing roses to her,

Or than nightingale may fly
    For her nesting grasses,
Or than with the west wind's sigh
    Her soft warbling passes.

THE THREE GIPSIES

Three gipsy men I saw one day
    Stretched out on the grass together,
As wearily o'er the sandy way
    My wagon brushed the heather.

The first of the three was fiddling there
    In the glow of evening pallid,
Playing a wild and passionate air,
    The tune of some gipsy ballad.

From the second's pipe the smoke-wreaths curled,
    He watched them melt at his leisure.
So full of content, it seemed the world
    Had naught to add to his pleasure.

And what of the third?—He was fast asleep,
  His harp to a bough confided;
The breezes across the strings did sweep,
  A dream o'er his heart-strings glided.

The garb of all was worn and frayed,
  With tatters grotesquely mended;
But flouting the world, and undismayed,
  The three with fate contended.

They showed me how, by three-fold scoff,
  When cares of life perplex us,
To smoke, or sleep, or fiddle them off,
  And scorn the ills that vex us.

GIACOMO LEOPARDI

GIACOMO LEOPARDI (Italian, 1798-1837). Italian poet of pessimism and despair. Unhappy childhood and ill health throughout life. A visionary and mystic naturalist, who rejected civilization and thought Italy corrupt and decadent. Intense personal emotion gave his work strength and validity. Best-known: *To Italy, On the Monument to Dante, The Lone Sparrow, The Broom Plant.*

THE LAST SONG OF SAPPHO

Thou peaceful night, thou chaste and silver ray
Of the declining Moon; and thou, arising
Amid the quiet forest on the rocks,
Herald of day; O cherished and endeared,
Whilst Fate and Doom were to my knowledge closed,
Objects of sight! No lovely land or sky
Doth longer gladden my despairing mood.
By unaccustomed joy we are revived
When o'er the liquid spaces of the Heavens
And o'er the fields alarmed doth wildly whirl
The tempest of the winds, and when the car,
The ponderous car of Jove, above our heads
Thundering, divides the heavy air obscure.
O'er mountain peaks and o'er abysses deep
We love to float amid the swiftest clouds;

We love the terror of the herds dispersed,
The streams that flood the plain,
And the victorious, thunderous fury of the main.

Fair is thy sight, O sky divine, and fair
Art thou, O dewy Earth! Alas! of all
This beauty infinite, no slightest part
To wretched Sappho did the Gods or Fate
Inexorable give. Unto thy reign
Superb, O Nature, an unwelcome guest
And a disprized adorer doth my heart
And do mine eyes implore thy lovely forms;
But all in vain. The sunny land around
Smiles not for me, nor from ethereal gates
The blush of early dawn; not me the songs
Of brilliant-feathered birds, not me the trees
Salute with murmuring leaves; and where in shade
Of drooping willows doth a liquid stream
Display its pure and crystal course, from my
Advancing foot the soft and flowing waves
Withdrawing with affright,
Disdainfully it takes through flowery dell its flight.

What fault so great, what guiltiness so dire
Did blight me ere my birth, that adverse grew
To me the brow of fortune and the sky?
How did I sin, a child, when ignorant
Of wickedness is life, that from that time
Despoiled of youth and of its fairest flowers,
The cruel Fates wove with relentless wrath
The web of my existence? Reckless words
Rise on thy lips; the events that are to be
A secret council guides. Secret is all,
Our agony excepted. We were born,
Neglected race, for tears; the reason lies
Amid the Gods on high. O cares and hopes
Of early years! To beauty did the Sire,
To glorious beauty an eternal reign
Give o'er this human kind; for warlike deed,
For learned lyre or song,
In unadornèd shape, no charms to fame belong.

769

Ah! let us die. The unworthy garb divested,
The naked soul will take to Dis its flight
And expiate the cruel fault of blind
Dispensers of our lot. And thou for whom
Long love in vain, long faith, and fruitless rage
Of unappeased desire assailed my heart,
Live happily, if happily on earth
A mortal yet hath lived. Not me did Jove
Sprinkle with the delightful liquor from
The niggard urn, since of my childhood died
The dreams and fond delusions. The glad days
Of our existence are the first to fly;
And then disease and age approach, and last,
The shade of frigid Death. Behold! of all
The palms I hoped for and the errors sweet,
Hades remains; and the transcendent mind
Sinks to the Stygian shore
Where sable Night doth reign, and silence evermore.

THE VILLAGERS' SATURDAY NIGHT

From copse and glade the maiden takes her way
When in the west the setting sun reposes;
She gathered flowers; her slender fingers bear
A fragrant wealth of violets and roses,
And with their beauty she will deck her hair,
Her lovely bosom with their leaves entwine;
Such is her wont on every festive day.
The aged matron sits upon the steps
And with her neighbors turns the spinning wheel,
Facing the heavens where the rays decline;
And she recalls the years,—
The happy years when on the festive day
It was her wont her beauty to array,
And when amidst her lovers and compeers
In youth's effulgent pride
Her rapid feet through mazy dance did glide.

The sky already darkens, and serene
The azure vault its loveliness reveals;

770

From hill and tower a lengthened shadow steals
In silvery whiteness of the crescent moon.
We hear the distant bell
Of festive morrow tell;
To weary hearts how generous a boon!
The happy children in the open space
In dancing numbers throng
With game and jest and song;
And to his quiet home and simple fare
The laborer doth repair
And whistles as he goes,
Glad of the morrow that shall bring repose.

Then, when no other light around is seen,
No other sound or stir,
We hear the hammer strike,
The grating saw of busy carpenter;
He is about and doing, so unlike
His quiet neighbors; his nocturnal lamp
With helpful light the darkened workshop fills,
And he makes haste his business to complete
Ere break of dawn the heavenly regions greet.

This of the seven is the happiest day,
With hope and joyance gay;
To-morrow grief and care
The unwelcome hours will in their progress bear;
To-morrow one and all
In thought their wonted labors will recall.

O merry youth! Thy time of life so gay
Is like a joyous and delightful day,—
A day clear and serene
That doth the approaching festival precede
Of thy fair life. Rejoice! Divine indeed
Is this fair day, I ween.
I'll say no more; but when it comes to thee,
Thy festival, may it not evil be.

771

MIKHAIL YURYEVICH LERMONTOV

MIKHAIL YURYEVICH LERMONTOV (Russian, 1814-1841). Russian poet, whose work marked end of era inaugurated by Pushkin. Led wild life, died in duel after brief, rancorous military career. Gloomy cynicism makes him most Byronic of Russian poets. Had great sympathy for the common people. Best work: lyric poems and a novel, *A Hero of Our Time*.

DAGGER

I love you well, my steel-white dagger,
Comrade luminous and cold;
Forged by a Georgian dreaming vengeance,
Whetted by Circassians bold.

A tender hand, in grace of parting,
Gave you to mark a meeting brief;
For blood there glimmered on your metal
A shining tear—the pearl of grief.

And black eyes, clinging to my glances,
Filled deep with liquid sorrow seemed;
Like your clear blade where flame is trembling,
They darkened quickly and they gleamed.

You were to be my long companion.
Give me your counsel to the end!
I will be hard of soul and faithful,
Like you, my iron-hearted friend!

A SAIL

White is the sail and lonely
 On the misty infinite blue;
Flying from what in the homeland?
 Seeking for what in the new?

The waves romp, and the winds whistle,
 And the mast leans and creaks;
Alas! He flies not from fortune,
 And no good fortune he seeks.

772

Beneath him the stream, luminous, azure,
    Above him the sun's golden breast;
But he, a rebel, invites the storms,
    As though in the storms were rest.

COMPOSED WHILE UNDER ARREST

When waves invade the yellowing wheat,
And the saplings sway with a wind-song brief;
When the raspberry plum in the garden sweet
Hides him under the cool green leaf;

When sprinkled with lights of limpid dew,
At rose of evening or gold of morn,
The lilies-of-the-valley strew
Their silver nodding under the thorn;

When the brook in the valley with cooling breast,
Plunging my soul in a cloudy dream,
Murmurs a legend of lands of rest
At the rise of his happy and rapid stream;

Then humbled is my heart's distress,
And lulled the anguish of my blood;
Then in the earth my happiness,
Then in the heaven my God.

A THOUGHT

I gaze with grief upon our generation.
Its future black or vacant—and to-day,
Bent with a load of doubt and understanding,
In sloth and cold stagnation it grows old.
When scarcely from the cradle we were rich
In follies, in our fathers' tardy wits.
Life wearied us—a road without a goal,
A feast upon a foreign holiday.
Toward good and evil shamefully impassive,
In mid-career we fade without a fight.

Before a danger pusillanimous,
Before a power that scorns us we are slaves.
Precocious fruit, untimely ripe, we hang,
Rejoicing neither sight nor touch nor tongue,
A wrinkled orphan runt among the blossoms,
Their beauty's hour the hour of its decay.

The hues of poetry, the shapes of art,
Wake in our minds no lovely ecstasy.
We hoard the dregs of feelings that are dead,
Misers, we dig and hide a debased coin.
We hate by chance, we love by accident;
We make no sacrifice to hate or love.
Within our minds presides a secret chill
Even while the flame is burning in our blood.
A bore to us our fathers' gorgeous sporting,
Their conscientious childish vast debauch.
We hasten tomb-wards without joy or glory,
With but a glance of ridicule thrown back.
A surly-hearted crowd and soon forgotten,
We pass in silence, trackless from the world,
Tossing no fruit of dreaming to the ages,
No deed of genius even half begun.
Our dust the justice of the citizen
In future time will judge in songs of venom. . . .
Will celebrate the weak and squandering father
In bitter mockery the cheated son.

THE MOUNTAIN

A golden cloud slept for her pleasure
All night on the gaunt hill's breast;
Light-heart to her play-ground of azure,
How early she sped from the nest.
But the soft moist trace of her sleeping
Lay in the folds of the hill.
He pondered; his tears are creeping
Down to the desert still.

GOTTHOLD EPHRAIM LESSING

GOTTHOLD EPHRAIM LESSING (German, 1729-1781). German critic and dramatist. One of the very distinguished Continental liberals. Gave up clerical career to become playwright. With Moses Mendelssohn and Nicolai, produced critical journal. *Laokoon*, famous treatise defining differences between poetry and other arts. *Nathan the Wise*, important drama pleading religious tolerance.

SALADIN AND NATHAN

Saladin.   Draw nearer, Jew—yet nearer—close to me!
Lay fear aside.
    Nathan.   Fear, Sultan, 's for your foes.
    Saladin.   Your name is Nathan?
    Nathan.   Yes.
    Saladin.   Nathan the Wise.
    Nathan.   No.
    Saladin.   But, at least the people call you so.
    Nathan.   That may be true. The people!
    Saladin.   Do you think
I treat the people's voice contemptuously.
I have been wishing long to know the man
Whom it has called the Wise.
    Nathan.   What if it named
Him so in scorn? If wise means prudent only—
And prudent, one who knows his interest well?
    Saladin.   Who knows his real interest, you mean.
    Nathan.   Then, Sultan, selfish men were the most prudent,
And wise, and prudent, then, would mean the same.
    Saladin.   You're proving what your speeches contradict.
You know the real interests of man:
The people know them not—have never sought
To know them. That alone can make man wise.
    Nathan.   Which every man conceives himself to be.
    Saladin.   A truce to modesty! To meet it ever,
When we are seeking truth is wearisome. (*Springs up.*)
So, let us to the point. Be candid, Jew,
Be frank and honest.
    Nathan.   I will serve you, prince,
And prove that I am worthy of your favor.
    Saladin.   How will you serve me?

Nathan.   You shall have the best
Of all I have, and at the cheapest rate.
   Saladin.   What mean you? Not your wares?—My sister, then,
Shall make the bargain with you. (That's for the listener!)
I am not versed in mercantile affairs,
And with a merchant's craft I've naught to do.
   Nathan.   Doubtless you would inquire if I have marked
Upon my route the movements of the foe?
Whether he's stirring? If I may presume——
   Saladin.   Neither was that my object. On that point
I know enough. But hear me.
   Nathan.   I obey.
   Saladin.   It is another, a far different thing
On which I seek for wisdom; and since you
Are called the Wise, tell me which faith or law
You deem the best.
   Nathan.   Sultan, I am a Jew.
   Saladin.—And I a Mussulman. The Christian stands
Between us. Here are three religions, then,
And of these three one only can be true.
A man like you remains not where his birth
By accident has cast him; or if so,
Conviction, choice, or ground of preference,
Supports him. Let me, Nathan, hear from you,
In confidence, the reasons of your choice,
Which I have lacked the leisure to examine.
It may be, Nathan, that I am the first
Sultan who has indulged this strange caprice,
Which need not, therefore, make a Sultan blush.
Am I first? Nay, speak; or if you seek
A brief delay to shape your scattered thoughts,
I yield it freely. (Has she overheard?
She will inform me if I've acted right.)
Reflect then, Nathan, I shall soon return.
                                                     (*Exit.*)
   Nathan. (*alone*).   Strange! how is this? What can the Sultan
want?
I came prepared for cash—he asks for truth!
Truth! as if truth were cash! A coin disused—
Valued by weight! If so, 'twere well, indeed!
But coin quite new, not coin but for the die,

776

To be flung down and on the counter told—
It is not that. Like gold tied up in bags,
Will truth lie hoarded in the wise man's head,
To be produced at need? Now, in this case,
Which of us plays the Jew? He asks for truth.
Is truth what he requires? his aim, his end?
Or does he use it as a subtle snare?
That were too petty for his noble mind.
Yet what is e'er too petty for the great?
Did he not rush at once into the house,
Whilst, as a friend, he would have paused or knocked?
I must beware. Yet to repel him now,
And act the stubborn Jew, is not the thing;
And wholly to fling off the Jew, still less.
For if no Jew, he might with justice ask,
Why not a Mussulman?—That thought may serve.—
Others than children may be quieted
With tales well told. But see, he comes—he comes.

  Saladin. (aside). (The coast is clear)—I am not come too soon?
Have you reflected on this matter, Nathan?
Speak! no one hears.

  Nathan. Would all the world might hear!

  Saladin. And are you of your cause so confident.
'Tis wise, indeed, of you to hide no truth,
For truth to hazard all, even life and goods.

  Nathan. Ay, when necessity and profit bid.

  Saladin. I hope that henceforth I shall rightly bear
One of my names, "Reformer of the world
And of the law!"

  Nathan. A noble title, truly;
But, Sultan, ere I quite explain myself,
Permit me to relate a tale.

  Saladin. Why not?
I ever was a friend of tales well told.

  Nathan. Well told! Ah, Sultan! that's another thing.

  Saladin. What! still so proudly modest? But begin.

  Nathan. In days of yore, there dwelt in Eastern lands
A man, who from a valued hand received
A ring of priceless worth. An opal stone
Shot from within an ever-changing hue,
And held this virtue in its form concealed,

To render him of God and man beloved,
Who wore it in this fixed unchanging faith.
No wonder that its Eastern owner ne'er
Withdrew it from his finger, and resolved
That to his house the ring should be secured.
Therefore he thus bequeathed it: first to him
Who was the most beloved of his sons,
Ordaining then that he should leave the ring
To the most dear among his children; then,
That without heeding birth, the fav'rite son,
In virtue of the ring alone, should still
Be lord of all the house. You hear me, Sultan?

  Saladin. I understand. Proceed.

  Nathan. From son to son,
The ring at length descended to a sire
Who had three sons, alike obedient to him,
And whom he loved with just and equal love.
The first, the second, and the third, in turn,
According as they each apart received
The overflowings of his heart, appeared
Most worthy, as his heir, to take the ring,
Which, with good-natured weakness, he in turn
Had promised privately to each; and thus
Things lasted for a while. But death approached,
The father now embarrassed, could not bear
To disappoint two sons, who trusted him.
What's to be done? In secret he commands
The jeweler to come, that from the form
Of the true ring, he may bespeak two more.
Nor cost nor pains are to be spared, to make
The rings alike—quite like the true one. This
The artist managed. When the rings were brought
The father's eye could not distinguish which
Had been the model. Overjoyed, he calls
His sons, takes leave of each apart—bestows
His blessing and his ring on each—and dies.
You hear me?

  Saladin. (*who has turned away in perplexity*). Ay! I hear. Conclude the tale.

  Nathan. 'Tis ended, Sultan! All that follows next
May well be guessed. Scarce is the father dead,

When with his ring each separate son appears,
And claims to be the lord of all the house.
Question arises, tumult and debate—
But all in vain—the true ring could no more
Be then distinguished than—(*after a pause, in which he awaits the
Sultan's reply*) the true faith now.
    Saladin.   Is that your answer to my question?
    Nathan.   No!
But it may serve as my apology.
I cannot venture to decide between
Rings which the father had expressly made,
To baffle those who would distinguish them.
    Saladin.   Rings, Nathan! Come, a truce to this! The creeds
Which I have named have broad, distinctive marks,
Differing in raiment, food, and drink!
    Nathan.   'Tis true!
But then they differ not in their foundation.
Are not all built on history alike,
Traditional or written? History
Must be received on trust. Is it not so?
In whom are we most likely to put trust?
In our own people? in those very men
Whose blood we are? who, from our earliest youth,
Have proved their love for us, have ne'er deceived,
Except in cases where 'twere better so?
Why should I credit my forefathers less
Than you do yours? or can I ask of you
To charge your ancestors with falsehood, that
The praise of truth may be bestowed on mine?
And so of Christians.
    Saladin.   By our Prophet's faith,
The man is right. I have no more to say.
    Nathan.   Now let us to our rings once more return.
We said the sons complained; each to the judge
Swore from his father's hand immediately
To have received the ring—as was the case—
In virtue of a promise that he should
One day enjoy the ring's prerogative.
In this they spoke the truth. Then each maintained
It was not possible that to himself
His father had been false. Each could not think

779

His father guilty of an act so base.
Rather than that, reluctant as he was
To judge his brethren, he must yet declare
Some treach'rous act of falsehood had been done.

    Saladin.   Well! and the judge? I'm curious now to hear
What you will make him say. Go on, go on!

    Nathan.   The judge said: If the father is not brought
Before my seat, I cannot judge the case.
Am I to judge enigmas? Do you think
That the true ring will here unseal its lips?
But, hold! You tell me that the real ring
Enjoys the secret power to make the man
Who wears it, both by God and man beloved.
Let that decide. Who of the three is loved
Best by his brethren? Is there no reply?
What! do these love-exciting rings alone
Act inwardly? Have they no outward charm?
Does each one love himself alone? You're all
Deceived deceivers. All your rings are false.
The real ring, perchance, has disappeared;
And so your father, to supply the loss,
Has caused three rings to fill the place of one.

    Saladin.   O, charming, charming!

    Nathan.   And, the judge continued,
If you insist on judgment, and refuse
My counsel, be it so. I recommend
That you consider how the matter stands.
Each from his father has received a ring:
Let each then think the real ring his own.
Your father, possibly, desired to free
His power from one ring's tyrannous control.
He loved you all with an impartial love,
And equally, and had no inward wish
To prove the measure of his love for one
By pressing heavily upon the rest.
Therefore, let each one imitate this love;
So, free from prejudice, let each one aim
To emulate his brethren in the strife
To prove the virtues of his several ring,
By offices of kindness and of love,
And trust in God. And if, in years to come,

The virtues of the ring shall reappear
Amongst your children, then, once more
Come to this judgment seat. A greater far
Than I shall sit upon it, and decide.
So spake the modest judge.

Saladin. O God, O God!

Nathan. And if now, Saladin, you think you're he——

Saladin (approaches Nathan *and takes his hand, which he retains
to the end of the scene).* This promised judge— I? Dust! I?
—Naught! O God!

Nathan. What is the matter, Sultan?

Saladin. Dearest Nathan!
That judge's thousand years are not yet past;
His judgment seat is not for me. But go,
And still remain my friend.

Nathan. Has Saladin aught else to say?

Saladin. No.

Nathan. Nothing?

Saladin. Truly nothing.

Nathan. I could have wished
An opportunity to ask a boon.

Saladin. Wait not for opportunity. Speak now.

Nathan. I have been trav'ling, and am just returned
From a long journey, from collecting debts.
Hard cash is troublesome these perilous times,
I know not where I may bestow it safely.
These coming wars need money; and, perchance,
You can employ it for me, Saladin?

Saladin. (fixing his eyes upon Nathan*).* I ask not, Nathan, have
you seen Al-Hafi?
Nor if some shrewd suspicion of your own
Moves you to make this offer.

Nathan. What suspicion?

Saladin. I do not ask—forgive me,—it is just,
For what avails concealment? I confess
I was about——

Nathan. To ask this very thing?

Saladin. Yes!

Nathan. Then our objects are at once fulfilled.

781

SINCLAIR LEWIS

SINCLAIR LEWIS (American, 1885-1951). The satirist of American middle-class life. After six early novels, achieved recognition with *Main Street*, followed by *Babbitt, Arrowsmith, Dodsworth*. Later work less effective, except for *It Can't Happen Here*, exposing perils of Fascism. First American to win Nobel Prize in Literature, 1930.

YOUNG MAN AXELBROD

THE cottonwood is a tree of a slovenly and plebeian habit. Its woolly wisps turn gray the lawns and engender neighborhood hostilities about our town. Yet it is a mighty tree, a refuge and an inspiration; the sun flickers in its towering foliage, whence the tattoo of locusts enlivens our dusty summer afternoons. From the wheat country out to the sagebrush plains between the buttes and the Yellowstone it is the cottonwood that keeps a little grateful shade for sweating homesteaders.

In Joralemon we call Knute Axelbrod "Old Cottonwood." As a matter of fact, the name was derived not so much from the quality of the man as from the wide grove about his gaunt white house and red barn. He made a comely row of trees on each side of the country road, so that a humble, daily sort of a man, driving beneath them in his lumber wagon, might fancy himself lord of a private avenue.

And at sixty-five Knute was like one of his own cottonwoods, his roots deep in the soil, his trunk weathered by rain and blizzard and baking August noons, his crown spread to the wide horizon of day and the enormous sky of a prairie night.

This immigrant was an American even in speech. Save for a weakness about his j's and w's, he spoke the twangy Yankee English of the land. He was the more American because in his native Scandinavia he had dreamed of America as a land of light. Always through disillusion and weariness he beheld America as the world's nursery for justice, for broad, fair towns, and eager talk; and always he kept a young soul that dared to desire beauty.

As a lad Knute Axelbrod had wished to be a famous scholar, to learn the ease of foreign tongues, the romance of history, to unfold in the graciousness of wise books. When he first came to America he worked in a sawmill all day and studied all evening. He mastered enough book-learning to teach district school for two

782

terms; then, when he was only eighteen, a great-hearted pity for faded little Lena Wesselius moved him to marry her. Gay enough, doubtless, was their hike by prairie schooner to new farmlands, but Knute was promptly caught in a net of poverty and family. From eighteen to fifty-eight he was always snatching children away from death or the farm away from mortgages.

He had to be content—and generously content he was—with the second-hand glory of his children's success and, for himself, with pilfered hours of reading—that reading of big, thick, dismal volumes of history and economics which the lone mature learner chooses. Without ever losing his desire for strange cities and the dignity of towers he stuck to his farm. He acquired a half-section, free from debt, fertile, well-stocked, adorned with a cement silo, a chicken-run, a new windmill. He became comfortable, secure, and then he was ready, it seemed, to die; for at sixty-three his work was done, and he was unneeded and alone.

His wife was dead. His sons had scattered afar, one a dentist in Fargo, another a farmer in the Golden Valley. He had turned over his farm to his daughter and son-in-law. They had begged him to live with them, but Knute refused.

"No," he said, "you must learn to stand on your own feet. I vill not give you the farm. You pay me four hundred dollars a year rent, and I live on that and vatch you from my hill."

On a rise beside the lone cottonwood which he loved best of all his trees Knute built a tar-paper shack, and here he "bached it"; cooked his meals, made his bed, sometimes sat in the sun, read many books from the Joralemon library, and began to feel that he was free of the yoke of citizenship which he had borne all his life.

For hours at a time he sat on a backless kitchen chair before the shack, a wide-shouldered man, white-bearded, motionless; a seer despite his grotesquely baggy trousers, his collarless shirt. He looked across the miles of stubble to the steeple of the Jackrabbit Forks church and meditated upon the uses of life. At first he could not break the rigidity of habit. He rose at five, found work ı.ı cleaning his cabin and cultivating his garden, had dinner exactly at twelve, and went to bed by afterglow. But little by little he discovered that he could be irregular without being arrested. He stayed abed till seven or even eight. He got a large, deliberate, tortoise-shell cat, and played games with it; let it lap milk upon the table,

called it the Princess, and confided to it that he had a "sneaking idee" that men were fools to work so hard. Around this coatless old man, his stained waistcoat flapping about a huge torso, in a shanty of rumpled bed and pine table covered with sheets of food-daubed newspaper, hovered all the passionate aspiration of youth and the dreams of ancient beauty.

He began to take long walks by night. In his necessitous life night had ever been a period of heavy slumber in close rooms. Now he discovered the mystery of the dark; saw the prairies wide-flung and misty beneath the moon, heard the voices of grass and cottonwoods and drowsy birds. He tramped for miles. His boots were dew-soaked, but he did not heed. He stopped upon hillocks, shyly threw wide his arms, and stood worshiping the naked, slumbering land.

These excursions he tried to keep secret, but they were bruited abroad. Neighbors, good, decent fellows with no sense about walking in the dew at night, when they were returning late from town, drunk, lashing their horses and flinging whisky bottles from racing democrat wagons, saw him, and they spread the tidings that Old Cottonwood was "getting nutty since he gave up his farm to that son-in-law of his and retired. Seen the old codger wandering around at midnight. Wish I had his chance to sleep. Wouldn't catch me out in the night air."

Any rural community from Todd Center to Seringapatam is resentful of any person who varies from its standard, and is morbidly fascinated by any hint of madness. The countryside began to spy on Knute Axelbrod, to ask him questions, and to stare from the road at his shack. He was sensitively aware of it, and inclined to be surly to inquisitive acquaintances. Doubtless that was the beginning of his great pilgrimage.

As a part of the general wild license of his new life—really, he once roared at that startled cat, the Princess: "By gollies! I ain't going to brush my teeth tonight. All my life I've brushed 'em, and alvays vanted to skip a time vunce"—Knute took considerable pleasure in degenerating in his taste in scholarship. He wilfully declined to finish *The Conquest of Mexico*, and began to read light novels borrowed from the Joralemon library. So he rediscovered the lands of dancing and light wines, which all his life he had desired. Some economics and history he did read, but every evening he would stretch out in his buffalo-horn chair, his feet on the cot

and the Princess in his lap, and invade Zenda or fall in love with Trilby.

Among the novels he chanced upon a highly optimistic story of Yale in which a worthy young man "earned his way through" college, stroked the crew, won Phi Beta Kappa, and had the most entertaining, yet moral, conversations on or adjacent to "the dear old fence."

As a result of this chronicle, at about three o'clock one morning, when Knute Axelbrod was sixty-four years of age, he decided that he would go to college. All his life he had wanted to. Why not do it?

When he awoke he was not so sure about it as when he had gone to sleep. He saw himself as ridiculous, a ponderous, oldish man among clean-limbed youths, like a dusty cottonwood among silver birches. But for months he wrestled and played with that idea of a great pilgrimage to the Mount of Muses; for he really supposed college to be that sort of place. He believed that all college students, except for the wealthy idlers, burned to acquire learning. He pictured Harvard and Yale and Princeton as ancient groves set with marble temples, before which large groups of Grecian youths talked gently about astronomy and good government. In his picture they never cut classes or ate.

With a longing for music and books and graciousness such as the most ambitious boy could never comprehend, this thick-faced farmer dedicated himself to beauty, and defied the unconquerable power of approaching old age. He sent for college catalogues and school books, and diligently began to prepare himself for college.

He found Latin irregular verbs and the whimsicalities of algebra fiendish. They had nothing to do with actual life as he had lived it. But he mastered them; he studied twelve hours a day, as once he had plodded through eighteen hours a day in the hayfield. With history and English he knew much of them from his recreative reading. From German neighbors he had picked up enough Plattdeutsch to make German easy. The trick of study began to come back to him from his small school teaching of forty-five years before. He began to believe that he could really put it through. He kept assuring himself that in college, with rare and sympathetic instructors to help him, there would not be this baffling search, this nervous strain.

But the unreality of the things he studied did disillusion him, and

785

he tired of his new game. He kept it up chiefly because all his life he had kept up onerous labor without any taste for it. Toward the autumn of the second year of his eccentric life he no longer believed that he would ever go to college.

Then a busy little grocer stopped him on the street in Joralemon and quizzed him about his studies, to the delight of the informal club which always loafs at the corner of the hotel.

Knute was silent, but dangerously angry. He remembered just in time how he had once laid wrathful hands upon a hired man, and somehow the man's collar bone had been broken. He turned away and walked home, seven miles, still boiling. He picked up the Princess, and, with her mewing on his shoulder, tramped out again to enjoy the sunset.

He stopped at a reedy slough. He gazed at a hopping plover without seeing it. Suddenly he cried:

"I am going to college. It opens next veek. I t'ink that I can pass the examinations."

Two days later he had moved the Princess and his sticks of furniture to his son-in-law's house, had bought a new slouch hat, a celluloid collar and a solemn suit of black, had wrestled with God in prayer through all of a star-clad night, and had taken the train for Minneapolis, on the way to New Haven.

While he stared out of the car window Knute was warning himself that the millionaires' sons would make fun of him. Perhaps they would haze him. He bade himself avoid all these sons of Belial and cleave to his own people, those who "earned their way through."

At Chicago he was afraid with a great fear of the lightning flashes that the swift crowds made on his retina, the batteries of ranked motor cars that charged at him. He prayed, and ran for his train to New York. He came at last to New Haven.

Not with gibing rudeness, but with politely quizzical eyebrows, Yale received him, led him through entrance examinations, which after sweaty plowing with the pen, he barely passed, and found for him a roommate. The roommate was a large-browed soft white grub named Ray Gribble, who had been teaching school in New England and seemed chiefly to desire college training so that he might make more money as a teacher. Ray Gribble was a hustler, he instantly got work tutoring the awkward son of a steel man, and for board he waited on table.

He was Knute's chief acquaintance. Knute tried to fool himself into thinking he liked the grub, but Ray couldn't keep his damp

786

hands off the old man's soul. He had the skill of a professional exhorter of young men in finding out Knute's motives, and when he discovered that Knute had a hidden desire to sip at gay, polite literature, Ray said in a shocked way:

"Strikes me a man like you, that's getting old, ought to be thinking more about saving your soul than about all these frills. You leave this poetry and stuff to these foreigners and artists, and you stick to Latin and math. and the Bible. I tell you, I've taught school, and I've learned by experience."

With Ray Gribble, Knute lived grubbily, an existence of torn comforters and smelly lamp, of lexicons and logarithm tables. No leisurely loafing by fireplaces was theirs. They roomed in West Divinity, where gather the theologues, the lesser sort of law students, a whimsical genius or two, and a horde of unplaced freshmen and "scrub seniors."

Knute was shockingly disappointed, but he stuck to his room because outside of it he was afraid. He was a grotesque figure, and he knew it, a white-polled giant squeezed into a small seat in a classroom, listening to instructors younger than his own sons. Once he tried to sit on the fence. No one but "ringers" sat on the fence any more, and at the sight of him trying to look athletic and young, two upper-class men snickered, and he sneaked away.

He came to hate Ray Gribble and his voluble companions of the submerged tenth of the class, the hewers of tutorial wood. It is doubtless safer to mock the flag than to question that best-established tradition of our democracy—that those who "earn their way through" college are necessarily stronger, braver, and more assured of success than the weaklings who talk by the fire. Every college story presents such a moral. But tremblingly the historian submits that Knute discovered that waiting on table did not make lads more heroic than did football or happy loafing. Fine fellows, cheerful and fearless, were many of the boys who "earned their way," and able to talk to richer classmates without fawning; but just as many of them assumed an abject respectability as the most convenient pose. They were pickers up of unconsidered trifles; they toadied to the classmates whom they tutored; they wriggled before the faculty committee on scholarships; they looked pious at Dwight Hall prayer-meetings to make an impression on the serious minded; and they drank one glass of beer at Jake's to show the light minded that they meant nothing offensive by their piety. In revenge for cringing to the insolent athletes whom they tutored, they would,

787

when safe among their own kind, yammer about the "lack of democracy of college today." Not that they were so indiscreet as to do anything about it. They lacked the stuff of really rebellious souls. Knute listened to them and marveled. They sounded like young hired men talking behind his barn at harvest time.

This submerged tenth hated the dilettantes of the class even more than they hated the bloods. Against one Gilbert Washburn, a rich esthete with more manner than any freshman ought to have, they raged righteously. They spoke of seriousness and industry till Knute, who might once have desired to know lads like Washburn, felt ashamed of himself as a wicked, wasteful old man.

Humbly though he sought, he found no inspiration and no comradeship. He was the freak of the class, and aside from the submerged tenth, his classmates were afraid of being "queered" by being seen with him.

As he was still powerful, one who could take up a barrel of pork on his knees, he tried to find friendship among the athletes. He sat at Yale Field, watching the football tryouts, and tried to get acquainted with the candidates. They stared at him and answered his questions grudgingly—beefy youths who in their simple-hearted way showed that they considered him plain crazy.

The place itself began to lose the haze of magic through which he had first seen it. Earth is earth, whether one sees it in Camelot or Joralemon or on the Yale campus—or possibly even in the Harvard yard! The buildings ceased to be temples to Knute; they became structures of brick or stone, filled with young men who lounged at windows and watched him amusedly as he tried to slip by.

The Gargantuan hall of Commons became a tri-daily horror because at the table where he dined were two youths who, having uncommonly penetrating minds, discerned that Knute had a beard, and courageously told the world about it. One of them, named Atchison, was a superior person, very industrious and scholarly, glib in mathematics and manners. He despised Knute's lack of definite purpose in coming to college. The other was a play-boy, a wit and a stealer of street signs, who had a wonderful sense for a subtle jest; and his references to Knute's beard shook the table with jocund mirth three times a day. So these youths of gentle birth drove the shambling, wistful old man away from Commons, and thereafter he ate at the lunch counter at the Black Cat.

788

Lacking the stimulus of friendship, it was the harder for Knute to keep up the strain of studying the long assignments. What had been a week's pleasant reading in his shack was now thrown at him as a day's task. But he would not have minded the toil if he could have found one as young as himself. They were all so dreadfully old, the money-earners, the serious laborers at athletics, the instructors who worried over their life work of putting marks in class-record books.

Then, on a sore, bruised day, Knute did meet one who was young.

Knute had heard that the professor who was the idol of the college had berated the too-earnest lads in his Browning class, and insisted that they read *Alice in Wonderland*. Knute floundered dustily about in a second-hand bookshop till he found an "Alice," and he brought it home to read over his lunch of a hot-dog sandwich. Something in the grave absurdity of the book appealed to him, and he was chuckling over it when Ray Gribble came into the room and glanced at the reader.

"Huh!" said Mr. Gribble.

"That's a fine, funny book," said Knute.

"Huh! *Alice in Wonderland!* I've heard of it. Silly nonsense. Why don't you read something really fine, like Shakespeare or *Paradise Lost?*"

"Vell——" said Knute, all he could find to say.

With Ray Gribble's glassy eye on him, he could no longer roll and roar with the book. He wondered if indeed he ought not to be reading Milton's pompous anthropological misconceptions. He went unhappily out to an early history class, ably conducted by Blevins, Ph.D.

Knute admired Blevins, Ph.D. He was so tubbed and eyeglassed and terribly right. But most of Blevins' lambs did not like Blevins. They said he was a "crank." They read newspapers in his class and covertly kicked one another.

In the smug, plastered classroom, his arm leaning heavily on the board tablet-arm of his chair, Knute tried not to miss one of Blevins' sardonic proofs that the correct date of the second marriage of Themistocles was two years and seven days later than the date assigned by that illiterate ass, Frutari of Padua. Knute admired young Blevins' performance, and he felt virtuous in application to these hard, unnonsensical facts.

He became aware that certain lewd fellows of the lesser sort were

789

playing poker just behind him. His prairie-trained ear caught whispers of "Two to dole," and "Raise you two beans." Knute revolved, and frowned upon these mockers of sound learning. As he turned back he was aware that the offenders were chuckling, and continuing their game. He saw that Blevins, Ph.D., perceived that something was wrong; he frowned, but he said nothing. Knute sat in meditation. He saw Blevins as merely a boy. He was sorry for him. He would do the boy a good turn.

When class was over he hung about Blevins' desk till the other students had clattered out. He rumbled:

"Say, Professor, you're a fine fellow. I do something for you. If any of the boys make themselves a nuisance, you yust call on me, and I spank the son of a guns."

Blevins, Ph.D., spake in a manner of culture and nastiness:

"Thanks so much, Axelbrod, but I don't fancy that will ever be necessary. I am supposed to be a reasonably good disciplinarian. Good day. Oh, one moment. There's something I've been wishing to speak to you about. I do wish you wouldn't try quite so hard to show off whenever I call on you during quizzes. You answer at such needless length, and you smile as though there were something highly amusing about me. I'm quite willing to have you regard me as a humorous figure, privately, but there are certain classroom conventions, you know, certain little conventions."

"Why, Professor!" wailed Knute, "I never make fun of you! I didn't know I smile. If I do, I guess it's yust because I am so glad when my stupid old head gets the lesson good."

"Well, well, that's very gratifying, I'm sure. And if you will be a little more careful——"

Blevins, Ph.D., smiled a toothy, frozen smile, and trotted off to the Graduates' Club, to be witty about old Knute and his way of saying "yust," while in the deserted classroom Knute sat chill, an old man and doomed. Through the windows came the light of Indian summer; clean, boyish cries rose from the campus. But the lover of autumn smoothed his baggy sleeve, stared at the blackboard, and there saw only the gray of October stubble about his distant shack. As he pictured the college watching him, secretly making fun of him and his smile, he was now faint and ashamed, now bull-angry. He was lonely for his cat, his fine chair of buffalo horns, the sunny doorstep of his shack, and the understanding land. He had been in college for about one month.

Before he left the classroom he stepped behind the instructor's desk and looked at an imaginary class.

"I might have stood there as a prof if I could have come earlier," he said softly to himself.

Calmed by the liquid autumn gold that flowed through the streets, he walked out Whitney Avenue toward the butte-like hill of East Rock. He observed the caress of the light upon the scarped rock, heard the delicate music of leaves, breathed in air pregnant with tales of old New England. He exulted: "'Could write poetry now if yust—if I yust could write poetry!"

He climbed to the top of East Rock, whence he could see the Yale buildings like the towers of Oxford, and see Long Island Sound, and the white glare of Long Island beyond the water. He marveled that Axelbrod of the cottonwood country was looking across an arm of the Atlantic to New York state. He noticed a freshman on a bench at the edge of the rock, and he became irritated. The freshman was Gilbert Washburn, the snob, the dilettante, of whom Ray Gribble had once said: "That guy is the disgrace of the class. He doesn't go out for anything, high stand or Dwight Hall or anything else. Thinks he's so doggone much better than the rest of the fellows that he doesn't associate with anybody. Thinks he's literary, they say, and yet he doesn't even heel the 'Lit,' like the regular literary fellows! Got no time for a loafing, mooning snob like that."

As Knute stared at the unaware Gil, whose profile was fine in outline against the sky, he was terrifically public-spirited and disapproving and that sort of moral thing. Though Gil was much too well dressed, he seemed moodily discontented.

"What he needs is to vork in a threshing crew and sleep in the hay," grumbled Knute almost in the virtuous manner of Gribble. "Then he vould know when he vas vell off, and not look like he had the earache. Pff!" Gil Washburn rose, trailed toward Knute, glanced at him, sat down on Knute's bench.

"Great view!" he said. His smile was eager.

That smile symbolized to Knute all the art of life he had come to college to find. He tumbled out of his moral attitude with ludicrous haste, and every wrinkle of his weathered face creased deep as he answered:

"Yes: I t'ink the Acropolis must be like this here."

"Say, look here, Axelbrod; I've been thinking about you."

"Yas?"

"We ought to know each other. We two are the class scandal. We came here to dream, and these busy little goats like Atchison and Giblets, or whatever your roommate's name is, think we're fools not to go out for marks. You may not agree with me, but I've decided that you and I are precisely alike."

"What makes you t'ink I come here to dream?" bristled Knute.

"Oh, I used to sit near you at Commons and hear you try to quell old Atchison whenever he got busy discussing the reasons for coming to college. That old, moth-eaten topic! I wonder if Cain and Abel didn't discuss it at the Eden Agricultural College. You know, Abel the markgrabber, very pious and high stand, and Cain wanting to read poetry."

"Yes," said Knute, "and I guess Prof. Adam say, 'Cain, don't you read this poetry; it von't help you in algebry.'"

"Of course. Say, wonder if you'd like to look at this volume of Musset I was sentimental enough to lug up here today. Picked it up when I was abroad last year."

From his pocket Gil drew such a book as Knute had never seen before, a slender volume, in a strange language, bound in hand-tooled crushed levant, an effeminate bibelot over which the prairie farmer gasped with luxurious pleasure. The book almost vanished in his big hands. With a timid forefinger he stroked the levant, ran through the leaves.

"I can't read it, but that's the kind of book I alvays t'ought there must be some like it," he sighed.

"Listen!" cried Gil. "Ysaye is playing up at Hartford tonight. Let's go hear him. We'll trolley up. Tried to get some of the fellows to come, but they thought I was a nut."

What an Ysaye was, Knute Axelbrod had no notion; but "Sure!" he boomed.

When they got to Hartford they found that between them they had just enough money to get dinner, hear Ysaye from gallery seats, and return only as far as Meriden. At Meriden Gil suggested:

"Let's walk back to New Haven, then. Can you make it?"

Knute had no knowledge as to whether it was four miles or forty back to the campus, but "Sure!" he said. For the last few months he had been noticing that, despite his bulk, he had to be careful, but tonight he could have flown.

In the music of Ysaye, the first real musician he had ever heard,

792

Knute had found all the incredible things of which he had slowly been reading in William Morris and "Idylls of the King." Tall knights he had beheld, and slim princesses in white samite, the misty gates of forlorn towns, and the glory of the chivalry that never was.

They did walk, roaring down the road beneath the October moon, stopping to steal apples and to exclaim over silvered hills, taking a puerile and very natural joy in chasing a profane dog. It was Gil who talked, and Knute who listened, for the most part; but Knute was lured into tales of the pioneer days, of blizzards, of harvesting, and of the first flame of the green wheat. Regarding the Atchisons and Gribbles of the class both of them were youthfully bitter and supercilious. But they were not bitter long, for they were atavisms tonight. They were wandering minstrels, Gilbert the troubadour with his man-at-arms.

They reached the campus at about five in the morning. Fumbling for words that would express hs feeling, Knute stammered:

"Vell, it vas fine. I go to bed now and I dream about——"

"Bed? Rats! Never believe in winding up a party when it's going strong. Too few good parties. Besides, it's only the shank of the evening. Besides, we're hungry. Besides—oh, besides! Wait here a second. I'm going up to my room to get some money, and we'll have some eats. Wait! Please do!"

Knute would have waited all night. He had lived almost seventy years and traveled fifteen hundred miles and endured Ray Gribble to find Gil Washburn.

Policemen wondered to see the celluloid-collared old man and the expensive-looking boy rolling arm in arm down Chapel Street in search of a restaurant suitable to poets. They were all closed.

"The Ghetto will be awake by now," said Gil. "We'll go buy some eats and take 'em up to my room. I've got some tea there."

Knute shouldered through dark streets beside him as naturally as though he had always been a nighthawk, with an aversion to anything as rustic as beds. Down on Oak Street, a place of low shops, smoky lights and alley mouths, they found the slum already astir. Gil contrived to purchase boxed biscuits, cream cheese, chicken-loaf, a bottle of cream. While Gil was chaffering, Knute stared out into the street milkily lighted by wavering gas and the first feebleness of coming day; he gazed upon Kosher signs and advertisements in Russian letters, shawled women and bearded

793

rabbis; and as he looked he gathered contentment which he could never lose. He had traveled abroad tonight.

The room of Gil Washburn was all the useless, pleasant things Knute wanted it to be. There was more of Gil's Paris days in it than of his freshmanhood: Persian rugs, a silver tea service, etchings, and books. Knute Axelbrod of the tar-paper shack and piggy farmyards gazed in satisfaction. Vast, bearded, sunk in an easy chair, he clucked amiably while Gil lighted a fire.

Over supper they spoke of great men and heroic ideals. It was good talk, and not unspiced with lively references to Gribble and Atchison and Blevins, all asleep now in their correct beds. Gil read snatches of Stevenson and Anatole France; then at last he read his own poetry.

It does not matter whether that poetry was good or bad. To Knute it was a miracle to find one who actually wrote it.

The talk grew slow, and they began to yawn. Knute was sensitive to the lowered key of their Indian-summer madness, and he hastily rose. As he said good-by he felt as though he had but to sleep a little while and return to his unending night of romance.

But he came out of the dormitory upon day. It was six-thirty of the morning, with a still, hard light upon red-brick walls.

"I can go to his room plenty times now; I find my friend," Knute said. He held tight the volume of Musset, which Gil had begged him to take.

As he started to walk the few steps to West Divinity Knute felt very tired. By daylight the adventure seemed more and more incredible.

As he entered the dormitory he sighed heavily:

"Age and youth, I guess they can't team together long." As he mounted the stairs he said: "If I saw the boy again, he vould get tired of me. I tell him all I got to say." And as he opened his door, he added: "This is what I come to college for—this one night. I go avay before I spoil it."

He wrote a note to Gil, and began to pack his telescope. He did not even wake Ray Gribble, sonorously sleeping in the stale air.

At five that afternoon, on the day coach of a westbound train, an old man sat smiling. A lasting content was in his eyes, and in his hands a small book in French.

LIN HO-CHING

LIN HO-CHING (Chinese, 967-1028). A rustic word painter of the Sung Period. Received classical Chinese education. Due to delicate health, retired to home in the country. Also a skillful painter, fond of plum trees. Poetry simple, serene, refined.

MAKING A POEM ON MY DEAR PLUM BLOSSOM

All these years I have been the owner of this pretty garden,
And have never written a poem to my beloved plum blossom.
Patiently I wait for your buds to open and bloom.
The moon has shed her light upon you many times.
The lonely scene is always reflected in the moonlight.
Still prettier looks the evening landscape in the falling snow.
Let me only talk about your pure scent, and I never feel lonely
    and sad,
For I am always singing and drinking to keep you company.

WEST LAKE

How wonderful and skillful is the universal spirit!
Though itself shapeless, it has formed the West Lake
Like a beautiful picture painted on a screen.
In Spring its water is purer than the eyes of a monk.
A greenish-blue sheen is spread like a veil over the evening hills.

My hut's white-washed walls reflect the moving shadow of a fish.
A crane's feather drops upon the dewy orchid.
The boat drifts along to the sounds of a flute.
In gentle breeze and slanting rain these are vague and distant.

THE SHADOWS OF SPRING

It looks like rain. This is the time for meditation.
When drunk I enjoy lying in the shadows in Spring.
It is so cold that I pity myself and the swallow.
I fear the pear blossoms cannot endure this cold night breeze.
My thin curtain cannot keep off the chilly wind.

Even a far-playing flute saddens me.
In the garden and fields a bitter wind blows.
And the fragrant flowers seem to sense the danger.

IN RETREAT

Few people pass through my humble door.
My hut lies near by the tree-covered hills.
When I fish at evening a lake breeze refreshes me.
The scent of sun-warmed Spring flowers makes me drowsy.
Little by little the moss becomes like a smooth cloth.
Bolstering the edges of the rock
Why stand so many people by the cave?
Perhaps they wait for an immortal there.

LI PO

LI PO (Chinese, 701-762). Greatest of the Chinese lyricists. A wandering, melancholy troubadour. Occasionally accepted employment—for two years a court poet. Imprisoned briefly for involvement in a rebellion just before death. His lyrics the model for spontaneous romantic verse in China. Poetry gives impression that he lived for the moment, intoxicated by nature, wine or love.

WEEP NOT, YOUNG WOMEN

It is always in sad Autumn that our enemies sweep down from their mountains to invade us.

The trumpets summon the warriors! They will ride on till they reach the Great Wall, and then they will ride beyond it out on the great Kobi desert.

There, only the cold bare moon. Only cold beads of dew on swords and shields. How they shiver!

Weep not, young women . . . this is no time to start your weeping. Who knows how long that you must weep?

THE FISHERMAN

The earth has swallowed the snow. Again we see the plum-trees in blossom.

The new willow-leaves are gold, the waters of the lakes are silver.

Now the butterflies powdered with gold lay velvet heads within the hearts of flowers.

In his still boat the fisherman pulls up his dripping net, rippling the still water.

He thinks of a girl at home, like a dark swallow in the nest. He think of a girl at home, waiting like a swallow for her mate.

BIRDS SINGING AT DUSK

The cool wind of evening blows bird-song to the window where a maiden sits. She is embroidering bright flowers on a piece of silk.

Her head is raised; her work falls through her fingers; her thoughts have flown to him who is away.

"A bird can easily find its mate among the leaves, but all a maiden's tears, falling like rain from Heaven, will not bring back her distant lover."

She bends again to her embroidery: "I will weave a little verse among these flowers of his robe . . . perhaps he will read it and come back again."

PICKING THE LOTUS

My boat is rising and falling underneath the harvest moon. Drifting alone on the Southern Lake, I reach to pick the white flowers of the lotus.

Fierce desire pulls me . . . I yearn to tell them of my passion. Alas, my boat floats away at the mercy of the moving current. My heart looks back in sadness.

When you were but a schoolboy
  And I a little lass,
You used to walk on bamboo stilts—
  I peeped to see you pass.
We were such merry children
  In the village of Chang-kan,
But now I am a woman
  And now you are a man.

I'd scarce seen fourteen summers
  When I was made your wife;
I could not raise my eyes to yours,
  Afraid of love and life.
I hid in dusky corners,
  I came not at your call,
But ere the year was ended
  Love overshadowed all.

I thought that you were steadfast
  As the lover by the stream
Who waited in the rising tide
  The lady of his dream;
But now I stand awatching
  On my terrace all alone
Like her who watched and waited
  Until she turned to stone.

You travel to the whirlpools
  And even to Chu-tang
Where chattering monkeys climb the cliff;
  I wait here in Chang-kan.
I watch your fading footprints,
  Now overgrown with green,
And though I sweep and sweep them
  They keep their mossy sheen.

Sere in my western garden
  The autumn leafage lies;
Yellow with August sunshine
  Flit pairing butterflies.

I watch them as they hover
  From bending grass to grass,
And my heart is wrung with weeping
  When I see them pass.

I've sat so long with sorrow
  My red cheeks lose their red.
Send me a letter from afar
  By tireless rider sped:
Let me but know in season
  Your boat is going through
The three grim Gorges of the West,
  And I will come to you.

I'll come as far to meet you
  As ever you may say;
The treacherous sands of the Chang-fang,
  They shall not bar my way.
No danger, toil or trouble
  Shall keep me as I go,
For now I am a woman
  And I love you so.

PASSIONATE GRIEF
A lady weeping in the night

She who rolls up her pearl-hung shade
    Is fair as any,
Yet drawn with grief are her delicate brows,
    Frail moth antennae.

Hot tears course down her cheeks—
    How fast they flow!—
But why, ah, we in the street
    Will never know.

LI SHANG-YIN

LI SHANG-YIN (Chinese, 813-858). Imaginative allegorist, who had undistinguished public career but high literary reputation. Poems formal in style, suffused with personal feeling. Many of them love poems, headed "No Title."

Part I. THE MAN

In how many folds of scented gauze patterned with phoenix tails
    is the round jade top of your awning enclosed for the night?
(Though) you have a 'fan like a full moon, yet your blushes find
    it hard to hide behind it.
The carts rumble by to a sound like thunder and so many words
    cannot reach you.
Otherwise it is quiet and still and the golden lamp has burnt low.
There is no word that can pass from where you are to where I am,
    where the pomegranate flowers are red.
The dappled horse is tethered to the weeping willow on the bank
Whither in the south west could we go trusting to a favorable wind?

Part II. THE WOMAN

Up here behind fold upon fold of curtains is my Mo-ch'ou Hall
After a long night the early dawn creeps slowly along.
It was in a dream that the fairy girl lived on the banks (of a river).
The small maiden who lived by the bridge after all (managed to)
    live without a husband.
The wind and waves do not realize how weak are the stems of the
    water chestnut.

A POEM WITH NO TITLE

It seems only last night that the stars shone and the wind blew;
Your quarters were at the painted tower in the west,
Mine in the pavilion of the cinnamon tree hall in the east.
Alas, to-day, I am no coloured phoenix that can fly to you with
    double wings,
But my mind is quick to apprehend spiritual affinity and can get
    through to you.
(On that evening) we sat opposite to each other and we amused

ourselves with sending across the hook while the spring wine was warm.

Each in our place we played "hitting the cover" to the light of red candles

Until, alas, I had to go, hearing the drum that called for the early morning audience.

Then I rode away home to the orchid tower;

Now I am like the river weed that flows this way and that.

NO TITLE

When we were able to meet it was hard enough and now we are parted for ever it is harder still;

The east wind has died down, and the hundred flowers have faded.

The silkworm of spring spins its silk up to the moment of its death;

The wax candle is burnt down to the end and only then are its tears dry.

In the morning I gaze into my mirror and grieve that my cloudy hair must change;

In the night the bright cold moon calls forth my sad songs,

(Yet after all) it is only a short road from here to paradise.

Will not the blue bird be indulgent and allow me to steal a glance.

THE INLAID ZITHER

The brocade-embroidered zither had fifty strings, no one knows why;

Each string and each support made one think of the years of one's prime.

Chuang Tzu dreamt at morning he was a butterfly.

After death, the soul of the Emperor Wang took up its brief springtime abode in the body of a nightjar,

While in the wide ocean under the bright moon the mermaids drop their tears which become pearls.

Why at Lan-t'ien in the warm sunshine does jade engender mists?

Can we hope for these kinds of portents to come again?

Or are they only things that had form once but have vanished away?

801

LIU CHI

LIU CHI (Chinese, 1311-1375). Most celebrated poet of the Mongol Period. Court adviser of first Ming Emperor. Prolific poet and author of philosophic dialogues. Poems distinguished by charm and feeling for beauty rather than by depth.

THE CONVENT OF SIANG-FU

So I sprang to horse at cockcrow all a fever to depart,
    Galloped, galloped to the convent, ere the calling bells were still,
Over dimpled lawns a zephyr woke the lily's jewelled heart,
    And the moon's faint crescent faltered down the cleft of wooded hill.
Oh the lonely little convent with its secret haunts of prayer!
    With its shadowed cells for dreaming, where eternities abide.
Down the cedar-scented alley not a footfall stirred the air,
    But the monks' low droning echoed in the green gloom far and wide.

NIGHT, SORROW, AND SONG

The rain's in the air
And the winds arouse,
Shaking the cinnamon boughs,
And the begonias' gay parterre;
Raising dust and wreathing mist,
Whirling all things where they list—
Leaves in many-coloured showers,
Bright petals of innumerable flowers.
Knocking at all doors their hustling
Sets the silken curtains rustling,
Till, as shrunken draughts, they creep
Into the shrouded halls of sleep,
Raise the hair and ruck the skin
Of the startled folk therein.

I am grown weary of my lonely state,
Tired of the tongueless hours that wait,
Dreaming of her whom skies of blue
And twilight æons hid from view.

802

Swiftly the waters take their flight
Grandly the mountains rise,
Yon birds that taper to the skies
Why have they lost their plumage bright?
Would they might bear my messages of love!
Alas! the trackless heav'ns unroll above;
From west to east the river flows,
But the waves return not to my calling;
Once more the rare magnolia blows,
But hour by hour her flowers are falling.
My jasper lyre is laid apart,
Hushed for a while the lute of jade;
I hear the beating of my heart,
And watch the moon lean down the glade.

Then, ere the shadows wane,
Out of the night's unrest
Ballad and old refrain
Lure me to seek again
The dream-built Isles of the Blest.

JACK LONDON

JACK LONDON (American, 1876-1916). Novelist, adventurer and utopian. An illegitimate child, worked for his living as a boy in California. Joined Klondike gold rush without making fortune. After *The Call of the Wild*, became one of most popular writers of his day. Wrote over 50 books inspired by faith in socialism. Well-known works: *The Sea Wolf, White Fang, Martin Eden.*

TO BUILD A FIRE

DAY HAD broken cold and grey, exceedingly cold and grey, when the man turned aside from the main Yukon trail and climbed the high earth-bank, where a dim and little-travelled trail led eastward through the fat spruce timberland. It was a steep bank, and he paused for breath at the top, excusing the act to himself by looking at his watch. It was nine o'clock. There was no sun nor a hint of

sun, though there was not a cloud in the sky. It was a clear day, and yet there seemed an intangible pall over the face of things, a subtle gloom that made the day dark, and that was due to the absence of sun. This fact did not worry the man. He was used to the lack of sun. It had been days since he had seen the sun, and he knew that a few more days must pass before that cheerful orb, due south, would just peep above the sky-line and dip immediately from view.

The man flung a look back along the way he had come. The Yukon lay a mile wide and hidden under three feet of ice. On top of this ice were as many feet of snow. It was all pure white, rolling in gentle undulations where the ice-jams of the freeze-up had formed. North and south, as far as his eye could see, it was unbroken white, save for a dark hair-line that curved and twisted from around the spruce-covered island to the south, and that curved and twisted away into the north, where it disappeared behind another spruce-covered island. This dark hair-line was the trail—the main trail—that led south five hundred miles to the Chilkoot Pass, Dyea, and salt water; and that led north seventy miles to Dawson, and still on to the north a thousand miles to Nulato, and finally to St. Michael on Bering Sea, a thousand miles and a half a thousand more.

But all this—the mysterious, far-reaching hair-line trail, the absence of sun from the sky, the tremendous cold, and the strangeness and weirdness of it all—made no impression on the man. It was not because he was long used to it. He was a newcomer in the land, a *chechaquo,* and this was his first winter. The trouble with him was that he was without imagination. He was quick and alert in the things of life, but only in the things, and not in the significances. Fifty degrees below zero meant eighty-odd degrees of frost. Such fact impressed him as being cold and uncomfortable, and that was all. It did not lead him to meditate upon his frailty as a creature of temperature, and upon man's frailty in general, able only to live within certain narrow limits of heat and cold; and from there on it did not lead him to the conjectural field of immortality and man's place in the universe. Fifty degrees below zero stood for a bite of frost that hurt and that must be guarded against by the use of mittens, ear-flaps, warm moccasins, and thick socks. Fifty degrees below zero was to him just precisely fifty degrees below zero. That there should be anything more to it than that was a thought that never entered his head.

As he turned to go on, he spat speculatively. There was a sharp, explosive crackle that startled him. He spat again. And again, in the

air, before it could fall to the snow, the spittle crackled. He knew that at fifty below spittle crackled on the snow, but this spittle had crackled in the air. Undoubtedly it was colder than fifty below—how much colder he did not know. But the temperature did not matter. He was bound for the old claim on the left fork of Henderson Creek, where the boys were already. They had come over across the divide from the Indian Creek country, while he had come the roundabout way to take a look at the possibilities of getting out logs in the spring from the islands in the Yukon. He would be in to camp by six o'clock; a bit after dark, it was true, but the boys would be there, a fire would be going, and a hot supper would be ready. As for lunch, he pressed his hand against the protruding bundle under his jacket. It was also under his shirt, wrapped up in a handkerchief and lying against the naked skin. It was the only way to keep the biscuits from freezing. He smiled agreeably to himself as he thought of those biscuits, each cut open and sopped in bacon grease, and each enclosing a generous slice of fried bacon.

He plunged in among the big spruce trees. The trail was faint. A foot of snow had fallen since the last sled had passed over, and he was glad he was without a sled, travelling light. In fact, he carried nothing but the lunch wrapped in the handkerchief. He was surprised, however, at the cold. It certainly was cold, he concluded, as he rubbed his numb nose and cheek-bones with his mittened hand. He was a warm-whiskered man, but the hair on his face did not protect the high cheek-bones and the eager nose that thrust itself aggressively into the frosty air.

At the man's heels trotted a dog, a big native husky, the proper wolf-dog, grey-coated and without any visible or tempermental difference from its brother, the wild wolf. The animal was depressed by the tremendous cold. It knew that it was no time for travelling. Its instinct told it a truer tale than was told to the man by the man's judgment. In reality, it was not merely colder than fifty below zero; it was colder than sixty below, than seventy below. It was seventy-five below zero. Since the freezing-point is thirty-two above zero, it meant that one hundred and seven degrees of frost obtained. The dog did not know anything about thermometers. Possibly in its brain there was no sharp consciousness of a condition of very cold such as was in the man's brain. But the brute had its instincts. It experienced a vague but menacing apprehension that subdued it and made it slink along at the man's heels, and that made it question eagerly every unwonted movement of the man as if expecting him to go into camp

or to seek shelter somewhere and build a fire. The dog had learned fire, and it wanted fire, or else to burrow under the snow and cuddle its warmth away from the air.

The frozen moisture of its breathing had settled on its fur in a fine powder of frost, and especially were its jowls, muzzle, and eyelashes whitened by its crystalled breath. The man's red beard and mustache were likewise frosted, but more solidly, the deposit taking the form of ice and increasing with every warm, moist breath he exhaled. Also, the man was chewing tobacco, and the muzzle of ice held his lips so rigidly that he was unable to clear his chin when he expelled the juice. The result was that a crystal beard of the color and solidity of amber was increasing its length on his chin. If he fell down it would shatter itself, like glass, into brittle fragments. But he did not mind the appendage. It was the penalty all tobacco-chewers paid in that country, and he had been out before in two cold snaps. They had not been so cold as this, he knew, but by the spirit thermometer at Sixty Mile he knew they had been registered at fifty below and at fifty-five.

He held on through the level stretch of woods for several miles, crossed a wide flat of nigger-heads, and dropped down a bank to the frozen bed of a small stream. This was Henderson Creek, and he knew he was ten miles from the forks. He looked at his watch. It was ten o'clock. He was making four miles an hour, and he calculated that he would arrive at the forks at half-past twelve. He decided to celebrate that event by eating his lunch there.

The dog dropped in again at his heels, with a tail drooping discouragement, as the man swung along the creek-bed. The furrow of the old sled-trail was plainly visible, but a dozen inches of snow covered the marks of the last runners. In a month no man had come up or down that silent creek. The man held steadily on. He was not much given to thinking, and just then particularly he had nothing to think about save that he would eat lunch at the forks and that at six o'clock he would be in camp with the boys. There was nobody to talk to; and, had there been, speech would have been impossible because of the ice-muzzle on his mouth. So he continued monotonously to chew tobacco and to increase the length of his amber beard.

Once in a while the thought reiterated itself that it was very cold and that he had never experienced such cold. As he walked along he rubbed his cheek-bones and nose with the back of his mittened hand. He did this automatically, now and again changing hands. But rub as he would, the instant he stopped his cheek-bones went numb, and

the following instant the end of his nose went numb. He was sure to frost his cheeks; he knew that, and experienced a pang of regret that he had not devised a nose-strap of the sort Bud wore in cold snaps. Such a strap passed across the cheeks, as well, and saved them. But it didn't matter much, after all. What were frosted cheeks? A bit painful, that was all; they were never serious.

Empty as the man's mind was of thoughts, he was keenly observant, and he noticed the changes in the creek, the curves and bends and timber-jams, and always he sharply noted where he placed his feet. Once, coming around a bend, he shied abruptly, like a startled horse, curved away from the place where he had been walking, and retreated several paces back along the trail. The creek he knew was frozen clear to the bottom,—no creek could contain water in that arctic winter,—but he knew also that there were springs that bubbled out from the hillsides and ran along under the snow and on top the ice of the creek. He knew that the coldest snaps never froze these springs, and he knew likewise their danger. They were traps. They hid pools of water under the snow that might be three inches deep, or three feet. Sometimes a skin of ice half an inch thick covered them, and in turn was covered by the snow. Sometimes there were alternate layers of water and ice-skin, so that when one broke through he kept on breaking through for a while, sometimes wetting himself to the waist.

That was why he had shied in such panic. He had felt the give under his feet and heard the crackle of a snow-hidden ice-skin. And to get his feet wet in such a temperature meant trouble and danger. At the very least it meant delay, for he would be forced to stop and build a fire, and under its protection to bare his feet while he dried his socks and moccasins. He stood and studied the creek-bed and its banks, and decided that the flow of water came from the right. He reflected awhile, rubbing his nose and cheeks, then skirted to the left, stepping gingerly and testing the footing for each step. Once clear of the danger, he took a fresh chew of tobacco and swung along at his four-mile gait.

In the course of the next two hours he came upon several similar traps. Usually the snow above the hidden pools had a sunken, candied appearance that advertised the danger. Once again, however, he had a close call; and once, suspecting danger, he compelled the dog to go on in front. The dog did not want to go. It hung back until the man shoved it forward, and then it went quickly across the white, unbroken surface. Suddenly it broke through, floundered to one side,

807

and got away to firmer footing. It had wet its forefeet and legs, and almost immediately the water that clung to it turned to ice. It made quick efforts to lick the ice off its legs, then dropped down in the snow and began to bite out the ice that had formed between the toes. This was a matter of instinct. To permit the ice to remain would mean sore feet. It did not know this. It merely obeyed the mysterious prompting that arose from the deep crypts of its being. But the man knew, having achieved a judgment on the subject, and he removed the mitten from his right hand and helped tear out the ice-particles. He did not expose his fingers more than a minute, and was astonished at the swift numbness that smote them. It certainly was cold. He pulled on the mitten hastily, and beat the hand savagely across his chest.

At twelve o'clock the day was at its brightest. Yet the sun was too far south on its winter journey to clear the horizon. The bulge of the earth intervened between it and Henderson Creek, where the man walked under a clear sky at noon and cast no shadow. At half-past twelve, to the minute, he arrived at the forks of the creek. He was pleased at the speed he had made. If he kept it up, he would certainly be with the boys by six| He unbuttoned his jacket and shirt and drew forth his lunch. The action consumed no more than a quarter of a minute, yet in that brief moment the numbness laid hold of the exposed fingers. He did not put the mitten on, but, instead, struck the fingers a dozen sharp smashes against his leg. Then he sat down on a snow-covered log to eat. The sting that followed upon the striking of his fingers against his leg ceased so quickly that he was startled. He had had no chance to take a bite of biscuit. He struck the fingers repeatedly and returned them to the mitten, baring the other hand for the purpose of eating. He tried to take a mouthful, but the ice-muzzle prevented. He had forgotten to build a fire and thaw out. He chuckled at his foolishness, and as he chuckled he noted the numbness creeping into the exposed fingers. Also, he noted that the stinging which had first come to his toes when he sat down was already passing away. He wondered whether the toes were warm or numb. He moved them inside the moocasins and decided that they were numb.

He pulled the mitten on hurriedly and stood up. He was a bit frightened. He stamped up and down until the stinging returned into the feet. It certainly was cold, was his thought. That man from Sulphur Creek had spoken the truth when telling how cold it sometimes got in the country. And he had laughed at him at the time!

That showed one must not be too sure of things. There was no mistake about it, it *was* cold. He strode up and down, stamping his feet and threshing his arms, until reassured by the returning warmth. Then he got out matches and proceeded to make a fire. From the undergrowth, where high water of the previous spring had lodged a supply of seasoned twigs, he got his fire-wood. Working carefully from a small beginning, he soon had a roaring fire, over which he thawed the ice from his face and in the protection of which he ate his biscuits. For the moment the cold of space was outwitted. The dog took satisfaction in the fire, stretching out close enough for warmth and far enough away to escape being singed.

When the man had finished, he filled his pipe and took his comfortable time over a smoke. Then he pulled on his mittens, settled the earflaps of his cap firmly about his ears, and took the creek trail up the left fork. The dog was disappointed and yearned back toward the fire. This man did not know cold. Possibly all the generations of his ancestry had been ignorant of cold, of real cold, of cold one hundred and seven degrees below freezing-point. But the dog knew; all its ancestry knew, and it had inherited the knowledge. And it knew that it was not good to walk abroad in such fearful cold. It was the time to lie snug in a hole in the snow and wait for a curtain of cloud to be drawn across the face of outer space whence this cold came. On the other hand, there was no keen intimacy between the dog and the man. The one was the toil-slave of the other, and the only caresses it had ever received were the caresses of the whip-lash and of harsh and menacing throat-sounds that threatened the whiplash. So the dog made no effort to communicate its apprehension to the man. It was not concerned in the welfare of the man; it was for its own sake that it yearned back toward the fire. But the man whistled, and spoke to it with the sound of whip-lashes, and the dog swung in at the man's heels and followed after.

The man took a chew of tobacco and proceeded to start a new amber beard. Also, his moist breath quickly powdered with white his mustache, eyebrows, and lashes. There did not seem to be so many springs on the left fork of the Henderson, and for half an hour the man saw no signs of any. And then it happened. At a place where there were no signs, where the soft, unbroken snow seemed to advertise solidity beneath, the man broke through. It was not deep. He wet himself halfway to the knees before he floundered out to the firm crust.

He was angry, and cursed his luck aloud. He had hoped to get

into camp with the boys at six o'clock, and this would delay him an hour, for he would have to build a fire and dry out his foot-gear. This was imperative at that low temperature—he knew that much; and he turned aside to the bank, which he climbed. On top, tangled in the underbrush about the trunks of several small spruce trees, was a high-water deposit of dry fire-wood—sticks and twigs, principally, but also larger portions of seasoned branches and fine, dry, last-year's grasses. He threw down several large pieces on top of the snow. This served for a foundation and prevented the young flame from drowning itself in the snow it otherwise would melt. The flame he got by touching a match to a small shred of birch-bark that he took from his pocket. This burned even more readily than paper. Placing it on the foundation, he fed the young flame with wisps of dry grass and with the tiniest dry twigs.

He worked slowly and carefully, keenly aware of his danger. Gradually, as the flame grew stronger, he increased the size of the twigs with which he fed it. He squatted in the snow, pulling the twigs out from their entanglement in the brush and feeding directly to the flame. He knew there must be no failure. When it is seventy-five below zero, a man must not fail in his first attempt to build a fire—that is, if his feet are wet. If his feet are dry, and he fails, he can run along the trail for half a mile and restore his circulation. But the circulation of wet and freezing feet cannot be restored by running when it is seventy-five below. No matter how fast he runs, the wet feet will freeze the harder.

All this the man knew. The old timer on Sulphur Creek had told him about it the previous fall, and now he was appreciating the advice. Already all sensation had gone out of his feet. To build the fire he had been forced to remove his mittens, and the fingers had quickly gone numb. His pace of four miles an hour had kept his heart pumping blood to the surface of his body and to all the extremities. But the instant he stopped, the action of the pump eased down. The cold of space smote the unprotected tip of the planet, and he, being on that unprotected tip, received the full force of the blow. The blood of his body recoiled before it. The blood was alive, like the dog, and like the dog it wanted to hide away and cover itself up from the fearful cold. So long as he walked four miles an hour, he pumped that blood, willy-nilly, to the surface; but now it ebbed away and sank down into the recesses of his body. The extremities were the first to feel its absence. His wet feet froze the faster, and his exposed fingers numbed the faster, though they had not yet be-

gun to freeze. Nose and cheeks were already freezing, while the skin of all his body chilled as it lost its blood.

But he was safe. Toes and nose and cheeks would be only touched by the frost, for the fire was beginning to burn with strength. He was feeding it with twigs the size of his finger. In another minute he would be able to feed it with branches the size of his wrist, and then he could remove his wet foot-gear, and, while it dried, he could keep his naked feet warm by the fire, rubbing them at first, of course, with snow. The fire was a success. He was safe. He remembered the advice of the old-timer on Sulphur Creek, and smiled. The old-timer had been very serious in laying down the law that no man must travel alone in the Klondike after fifty below. Well, here he was; he had had the accident; he was alone; and he had saved himself. Those old-timers were rather womanish, some of them, he thought. All a man had to do was to keep his head, and he was all right. Any man who was a man could travel alone. But it was surprising, the rapidity with which his cheeks and nose were freezing. And he had not thought his fingers could go lifeless in so short a time. Lifeless they were, for he could scarcely make them move together to grip a twig, and they seemed remote from his body and from him. When he touched a twig, he had to look and see whether or not he had hold of it. The wires were pretty well down between him and his finger-ends.

All of which counted for little. There was the fire, snapping and crackling and promising life with every dancing flame. He started to untie his moccasins. They were coated with ice; the thick German socks were like sheaths of iron halfway to the knees; and the moccasin strings were like rods of steel all twisted and knotted as by some conflagration. For a moment he tugged with his numb fingers, then, realizing the folly of it, he drew his sheath-knife.

But before he could cut the strings, it happened. It was his own fault or, rather, his mistake. He should not have built the fire under the spruce tree. He should have built it in the open. But it had been easier to pull the twigs from the brush and drop them directly on the fire. Now the tree under which he had done this carried a weight of snow on its boughs. No wind had blown for weeks, and each bough was fully freighted. Each time he had pulled a twig he had communicated a slight agitation to the tree—an imperceptible agitation, so far as he was concerned, but an agitation sufficient to bring about the disaster. High up in the tree one bough capsized its load of snow. This fell on the boughs beneath, capsizing them. This process continued, spreading out and involving the whole tree.

It grew like an avalanche, and it descended without warning upon the man and the fire, and the fire was blotted out! Where it had burned was a mantle of fresh and disordered snow.

The man was shocked. It was as though he had just heard his own sentence of death. For a moment he sat and stared at the spot where the fire had been. Then he grew very calm. Perhaps the old-timer on Sulphur Creek was right. If he had only had a trail-mate he would have been in no danger now. The trail-mate could have built the fire. Well, it was up to him to build the fire over again, and this second time there must be no failure. Even if he succeeded, he would most likely lose some toes. His feet must be badly frozen by now, and there would be some time before the second fire was ready.

Such were his thoughts, but he did not sit and think them. He was busy all the time they were passing through his mind. He made a new foundation for a fire, this time in the open, where no treacherous tree could blot it out. Next, he gathered dry grasses and tiny twigs from the high-water flotsam. He could not bring his fingers together to pull them out, but he was able to gather them by the handful. In this way he got many rotten twigs and bits of green moss that were undesirable, but it was the best he could do. He worked methodically, even collecting an armful of the larger branches to be used later when the fire gathered strength. And all the while the dog sat and watched him, a certain yearning wistfulness in its eyes, for it looked upon him as the fire-provider, and the fire was slow in coming.

When all was ready, the man reached in his pocket for a second piece of birch-bark. He knew the bark was there, and, though he could not feel it with his fingers, he could hear its crisp rustling as he fumbled for it. Try as he would, he could not clutch hold of it. And all the time, in his consciousness, was the knowledge that each instant his feet were freezing. This thought tended to put him in a panic, but he fought against it and kept calm. He pulled on his mittens with his teeth, and threshed his arms back and forth, beating his hands with all his might against his sides. He did this sitting down, and he stood up to do it; and all the while the dog sat in the snow, its wolf-brush of a tail curled around warmly over its fore-feet, its sharp wolf-ears pricked forward intently as it watched the man. And the man as he beat and threshed with his arms and hands, felt a great surge of envy as he regarded the creature that was warm and secure in its natural covering.

After a time he was aware of the first far-away signals of sensa-

tion in his beaten fingers. The faint tingling grew stronger till it evolved into a stinging ache that was excruciating, but which the man hailed with satisfaction. He stripped the mitten from his right hand and fetched forth the birch-bark. The exposed fingers were quickly going numb again. Next he brought out his bunch of sulphur matches. But the tremendous cold had already driven the life out of his fingers. In his effort to separate one match from the others, the whole bunch fell in the snow. He tried to pick it out of the snow, but failed. The dead fingers could neither touch nor clutch. He was very careful. He drove the thought of his freezing feet, and nose, and cheeks, out of his mind, devoting his whole soul to the matches. He watched, using the sense of vision in place of that of touch, and when he saw his fingers on each side the bunch, he closed them—that is, he willed to close them, for the wires were down, and the fingers did not obey. He pulled the mitten on the right hand, and beat it fiercely against his knee. Then, with both mittened hands, he scooped the bunch of matches, along with much snow, into his lap. Yet he was no better off.

After some manipulation he managed to get the bunch between the heels of his mittened hands. In this fashion he carried it to his mouth. The ice crackled and snapped when by a violent effort he opened his mouth. He drew the lower jaw in, curled the upper lip out of the way, and scraped the bunch with his upper teeth in order to separate a match. He succeeded in getting one, which he dropped on his lap. He was no better off. He could not pick it up. Then he devised a way. He picked it up in his teeth and scratched it on his leg. Twenty times he scratched before he succeeded in lighting it. As it flamed he held it with his teeth to the birch-bark. But the burning brimstone went up his nostrils and into his lungs, causing him to cough spasmodically. The match fell into the snow and went out.

The old-timer on Sulphur Creek was right, he thought in the moment of controlled despair that ensued; after fifty below, a man should travel with a partner. He beat his hands, but failed in exciting any sensation. Suddenly he bared both his hands, removing the mittens with his teeth. He caught the whole bunch between the heels of his hands. His arm-muscles not being frozen enabled him to press the hand-heels tightly against the matches. Then he scratched the bunch along his leg. It flared into flame, seventy sulphur matches at once! There was no wind to blow them out. He kept his head to one side to escape the strangling fumes, and held the blazing bunch to the birch-bark. As he so held it, he became aware of sensation

in his hand. His flesh was burning. He could smell it. Deep down below the surface he could feel it. The sensation developed into pain that grew acute. And still he endured it, holding the flame of the matches clumsily to the bark that would not light readily because his own burning hands were in the way, absorbing most of the flame.

At last, when he could endure no more, he jerked his hands apart. The blazing matches fell sizzling into the snow, but the birch-bark was alight. He began laying dry grasses and the tiniest twigs on the flame. He could not pick and choose, for he had to lift the fuel between the heels of his hands. Small pieces of rotten wood and green moss clung to the twigs, and he bit them off as well as he could with his teeth. He cherished the flame carefully and awkwardly. It meant life, and it must not perish. The withdrawal of blood from the surface of his body now made him begin to shiver, and he grew more awkward. A large piece of green moss fell squarely on the little fire. He tried to poke it out with his fingers, but his shivering frame made him poke too far, and he disrupted the nucleus of the little fire, the burning grasses and tiny twigs separating and scattering.He tried to poke them together again, but in spite of the tenseness of the effort, his shivering got away with him, and the twigs were hopelessly scattered. Each twig gushed a puff of smoke and went out. The fire-provider had failed. As he looked apathetically about him, his eyes chanced on the dog, sitting across the ruins of the fire from him, in the snow, making restless, hunching movement, slightly lifting one forefoot and then the other, shifting its weight back and forth on them with wistful eagerness.

The sight of the dog put a wild idea into his head. He remembered the tale of the man, caught in a blizzard, who killed a steer and crawled inside the carcass, and so was saved. He would kill the dog and bury his hands in the warm body until the numbness went out of them. Then he could build another fire. He spoke to the dog, calling it to him; but in his voice was a strange note of fear that frightened the animal, who had never known the man to speak in such way before. Something was the matter, and its suspicious nature sensed danger—it knew not what danger, but somewhere, somehow, in its brain arose an apprehension of the man. It flattened its ears down at the sound of the man's voice, and its restless, hunching movements and the liftings and shiftings of its forefeet became more pronounced; but it would not come to the man. He got on his hands and knees and crawled toward the dog. This

unusual posture again excited suspicion, and the animal sidled mincingly away.

The man sat up in the snow for a moment and struggled for calmness. Then he pulled on his mittens, by means of his teeth, and got upon his feet. He glanced down at first in order to assure himself that he was really standing up, for the absence of sensation in his feet left him unrelated to the earth. His erect position in itself started to drive the webs of suspicion from the dog's mind; and when he spoke peremptorily, with the sound of whip-lashes in his voice, the dog rendered its customary allegiance and came to him. As it came within reaching distance, the man lost his control. His arms flashed out to the dog, and he experienced genuine surprise when he discovered that his hands could not clutch, that there was neither bend nor feeling in the fingers. He had forgotten for the moment that they were frozen and that they were freezing more and more. All this happened quickly, and before the animal could get away, he encircled its body with his arms. He sat down in the snow, and in this fashion held the dog, while it snarled and whined and struggled.

But it was all he could do, hold its body encircled in his arms and sit there. He realized that he could not kill the dog. There was no way to do it. With his helpless hands he could neither draw nor hold his sheathknife nor throttle the animal. He released it, it plunged wildly away, with tail between its legs, and still snarling. It halted forty feet away and surveyed him curiously, with ears sharply pricked forward. The man looked down at his hands in order to locate them, and found them hanging on the ends of his arms. It struck him as curious that one should have to use his eyes in order to find out where his hands were. He began threshing his arms back and forth, beating the mittened hands against his sides. He did this for five minutes, violently, and his heart pumped enough blood up to the surface to put a stop to his shivering. But no sensation was aroused in the hands. He had an impression that they hung like weights on the ends of his arms, but when he tried to run the impression down, he could not find it.

A certain fear of death, dull and oppressive, came to him. This fear quickly became poignant as he realized that it was no longer a mere matter of freezing his fingers and toes, or of losing his hands and feet, but that it was a matter of life and death with the chances against him. This threw him into a panic, and he turned and ran

up the creek-bed along the old dim trail. The dog joined in behind and kept up with him. He ran blindly, without intention, in fear such as he had never known in his life. Slowly, as he ploughed and floundered through the snow, he began to see things again,—the banks of the creek, the old timber-jams, the leafless aspens, and the sky. The running made him feel better. He did not shiver. Maybe, if he ran on, his feet would thaw out; and, anyway, if he ran far enough, he would reach camp and the boys. Without doubt he would lose some fingers and toes and some of his face; but the boys would take care of him, and save the rest of him when he got there. And at the same time there was another thought in his mind that said he would never get to the camp and the boys; that it was too many miles away, that the freezing had too great a start on him, and that he would soon be stiff and dead. This thought he kept in the background and refused to consider. Sometimes it pushed itself forward and demanded to be heard, but he thrust it back and strove to think of other things.

It struck him as curious that he could run at all on feet so frozen that he could not feel them when they struck the earth and took the weight of his body. He seemed to himself to skim along above the surface, and to have no connection with the earth. Somewhere he had once seen a winged Mercury, and he wondered if Mercury felt as he felt when skimming over the earth.

His theory of running until he reached camp and the boys had one flaw in it: he lacked the endurance. Several times he stumbled, and finally he tottered, crumpled up, and fell. When he tried to rise, he failed. He must sit and rest, he decided, and next time he would merely walk and keep on going. As he sat and regained his breath, he noted that he was feeling quite warm and comfortable. He was not shivering, and it even seemed that a warm glow had come to his chest and trunk. And yet, when he touched his nose or cheeks, there was no sensation. Running would not thaw them out. Nor would it thaw out his hands and feet. Then the thought came to him that the frozen portions of his body must be extending. He tried to keep this thought down, to forget it, to think of something else; he was aware of the panicky feeling that it caused, and he was afraid of the panic. But the thought asserted itself, and persisted, until it produced a vision of his body totally frozen. This was too much, and he made another wild run along the trail. Once he slowed down to a walk, but the thought of the freezing extending itself made him run again.

And all the time the dog ran with him, at his heels, When he fell down a second time, it curled its tail over its forefeet and sat in front of him, facing him, curiously eager and intent. The warmth and security of the animal angered him, and he cursed it till it flattened down its ears appeasingly. This time the shivering came more quickly upon the man. He was losing in his battle with the frost. It was creeping into his body from all sides. The thought of it drove him on, but he ran no more than a hundred feet, when he staggered and pitched headlong. It was his last panic. When he had recovered his breath and control, he sat up and entertained in his mind the conception of meeting death with dignity. However, the conception did not come to him in such terms. His idea of it was that he had been making a fool of himself, running around like a chicken with its head cut off—such was the simile that occurred to him. Well he was bound to freeze anyway, and he might as well take it decently. With this new-found peace of mind came the first glimmerings of drowsiness. A good idea, he thought, to sleep off to death. It was like taking an anaesthetic. Freezing was not so bad as people thought. There were lots worse ways to die.

He pictured the boys finding his body next day. Suddenly he found himself with them, coming along the trail and looking for himself. And, still with them, he came around a turn in the trail and found himself lying in the snow. He did not belong with himself any more, for even then he was out of himself, standing with the boys and looking at himself in the snow. It certainly was cold, was his thought. When he got back to the States he could tell the folks what real cold was. He drifted on from this to a vision of the old-timer on Sulphur Creek. He could see him quite clearly, warm and comfortable, and smoking a pipe.

"You were right, old hoss; you were right," the man mumbled to the old timer of Sulphur Creek.

Then the man drowsed off into what seemed to him the most comfortable and satisfying sleep he had ever known. The dog sat facing him and waiting. The brief day drew to a close in a long, slow twilight. There were no signs of a fire to be made, and, besides, never in the dog's experience had it known a man to sit like that in the snow and make no fire. As the twilight drew on, its eager yearning for the fire mastered it, and with a great lifting and shifting of forefeet, it whined softly, then flattened its ears down in anticipation of being chided by the man. But the man remained silent. Later, the dog whined loudly. And still later it crept close to

817

the man and caught the scent of death. This made the animal bristle and back away. A little longer it delayed, howling under the stars that leaped and danced and shone brightly in the cold sky. Then it turned and trotted up the trail in the direction of the camp it knew, where were the other food-providers and fire-providers.

HENRY WADSWORTH LONGFELLOW

HENRY WADSWORTH LONGFELLOW (American, 1807-1882). At one time (possibly still) America's most popular poet. After traveling abroad, took professorship at Harvard. Verses combined the romantic, the sentimental, and the ethical in a proportion that instantly caught popular taste. Famous narrative poems: *Evangeline, The Song of Hiawatha, The Courtship of Miles Standish*. Later critics prefer less-known lyrics, which show true poetic gift.

MY LOST YOUTH

Often I think of the beautiful town
   That is seated by the sea;
Often in thought go up and down
The pleasant streets of that dear old town,
   And my youth comes back to me.
     And a verse of a Lapland song
     Is haunting my memory still:
     "A boy's will is the wind's will,
And the thoughts of youth are long, long thoughts."

I can see the shadowy lines of its trees,
   And catch, in sudden gleams,
The sheen of the far-surrounding seas,
And islands that were the Hesperides
   Of all my boyish dreams.
     And the burden of that old song,
     It murmurs and whispers still:
     "A boy's will is the wind's will,
And the thoughts of youth are long, long thoughts."

I remember the black wharves and the slips,
   And the sea-tides tossing free;

And Spanish sailors with bearded lips,
And the beauty and mystery of the ships,
  And the magic of the sea.
    And the voice of that wayward song
    Is singing and saying still:
    "A boy's will is the wind's will,
And the thoughts of youth are long, long thoughts."

I remember the bulwarks by the shore,
  And the fort upon the hill;
The sunrise gun, with its hollow roar,
The drum-beat repeated o'er and o'er,
  And the bugle wild and shrill.
    And the music of that old song
    Throbs in my memory still:
    "A boy's will is the wind's will,
And the thoughts of youth are long, long thoughts."

I remember the sea-fight far away,
  How it thundered o'er the tide!
And the dead captains, as they lay
In their graves, o'erlooking the tranquil bay
  Where they in battle died.
    And the sound of that mournful song
    Goes through me with a thrill:
    "A boy's will is the wind's will,
And the thoughts of youth are long, long thoughts."

I can see the breezy dome of groves,
  The shadows of Deering's Woods;
And the friendships old and the early loves
Come back with a Sabbath sound, as of doves
  In quiet neighborhoods.
    And the verse of that sweet old song,
    It flutters and murmurs still:
    "A boy's will is the wind's will,
And the thoughts of youth are long, long thoughts."

I remember the gleams and glooms that dart
  Across the school-boy's brain;
The song and the silence in the heart,

That in part are prophecies, and in part
    Are longings wild and vain.
       And the voice of that fitful song
       Sings on, and is never still:
       "A boy's will is the wind's will,
And the thoughts of youth are long, long thoughts."

There are things of which I may not speak;
    There are dreams that cannot die;
There are thoughts that make the strong heart weak,
And bring a pallor into the cheek,
    And a mist before the eye.
       And the words of that fatal song
       Come over me like a chill:
       "A boy's will is the wind's will,
And the thoughts of youth are long, long thoughts."

Strange to me now are the forms I meet
    When I visit the dear old town;
But the native air is pure and sweet,
And the trees that o'ershadow each well-known street,
    As they balance up and down,
       Are singing the beautiful song,
       Are sighing and whispering still:
       "A boy's will is the wind's will,
And the thoughts of youth are long, long thoughts."

And Deering's Woods are fresh and fair,
    And with joy that is almost pain
My heart goes back to wander there,
And among the dreams of the days that were,
    I find my lost youth again.
       And the strange and beautiful song,
       The groves are repeating it still:
       "A boy's will is the wind's will,
And the thoughts of youth are long, long thoughts."

THE SKELETON IN ARMOR

Speak! speak! thou fearful guest!
Who, with thy hollow breast

820

Still in rude armor drest,
    Comest to daunt me!
Wrapt not in Eastern balms,
But with thy fleshless palms
Stretched, as if asking alms,
    Why dost thou haunt me?

Then, from those cavernous eyes
Pale flashes seemed to rise,
As when the Northern skies
    Gleam in December;
And, like the water's flow
Under December's snow,
Came a dull voice of woe
    From the heart's chamber.

'I was a Viking old!
My deeds, though manifold,
No Skald in song has told,
    No Saga taught thee!
Take heed, that in thy verse
Thou dost the tale rehearse,
Else dread a dead man's curse;
    For this I sought thee.

'Far in the Northern Land,
By the wild Baltic's strand,
I, with my childish hand,
    Tamed the gerfalcon;
And, with my skates fast-bound
Skimmed the half-frozen Sound,
That the poor whimpering hound
    Trembled to walk on.

'Oft to his frozen lair
Tracked I the grisly bear,
While from my path the hare
    Fled like a shadow;
Oft through the forest dark
Followed the were-wolf's bark,
Until the soaring lark
    Sang from the meadow.

'But when I older grew,
Joining a corsair's crew,
O'er the dark sea I flew
   With the marauders.
Wild was the life we led;
Many the souls that sped,
Many the hearts that bled,
   By our stern orders.

'Many a wassail-bout
Wore the long Winter out;
Often our midnight shout
   Set the cocks crowing,
As we the Berserk's tale
Measured in cups of ale,
Draining the oaken pail,
   Filled to o'erflowing.

'Once as I told in glee
Tales of the stormy sea,
Soft eyes did gaze on me,
   Burning yet tender:
And as the white stars shine
On the dark Norway pine,
On that dark heart of mine
   Fell their soft splendor.

'I wooed the blue-eyed maid,
Yielding, yet half afraid,
And in the forest's shade
   Our vows were plighted.
Under its loosened vest
Fluttered her little breast,
Like birds within their nest
   By the hawk frighted.

'Bright in her father's hall
Shields gleamed upon the wall.
Loud sang the minstrels all,

Chanting his glory;
When of old Hildebrand
I asked his daughter's hand,
Mute did the minstrels stand
  To hear my story.

'While the brown ale he quaffed,
Loud then the champion laughed,
And as the wind-gusts waft
  The sea-foam brightly,
So the loud laugh of scorn,
Out of those lips unshorn,
From the deep drinking-horn
  Blew the foam lightly.

'She was a Prince's child,
I but a Viking wild,
And though she blushed and smiled,
  I was discarded!
Should not the dove so white
Follow the sea-mew's flight,
Why did they leave that night
  Her nest unguarded?

'Scarce had I put to sea,
Bearing the maid with me,
Fairest of all was she
  Among the Norsemen!
When on the white sea-strand,
Waving his armed hand,
Saw we old Hildebrand,
  With twenty horsemen.

'Then launched they to the blast,
Bent like a reed each mast,
Yet we were gaining fast,
  When the wind failed us;
And with a sudden flaw
Came round the gusty Skaw,
So that our foe we saw
  Laugh as he hailed us.

823

'And as to catch the gale
Round veered the flapping sail,
"Death!" was the helmsman's hail,
    "Death without quarter!"
Mid-ships with iron keel
Struck we her ribs of steel;
Down her black hulk did reel
    Through the black water!

'As with his wings aslant,
Sails the fierce cormorant,
Seeking some rocky haunt,
    With his prey laden,—
So toward the open main,
Beating to sea again,
Through the wild hurricane,
    Bore I the maiden.

'Three weeks we westward bore,
And when the storm was o'er,
Cloud-like we saw the shore
    Stretching to leeward;
There for my lady's bower
Built I the lofty tower,
Which, to this very hour,
    Stands looking seaward.

"There lived we many years;
Time dried the maiden's tears;
She had forgot her fears,
    She was a mother;
Death closed her mild blue eyes,
Under that tower she lies;
Ne'er shall the sun arise
    On such another!

'Still grew my bosom then,
Still as a stagnant fen!
Hateful to me were men,
    The sunlight hateful!

824

In the vast forest here,
Clad in my warlike gear,
Fell I upon my spear,
  Oh, death was grateful!

'Thus, seamed with many scars,
Bursting these prison bars,
Up to its native stars
  My soul ascended!
There from the flowing bowl
Deep drinks the warrior's soul,
Skoal! to the Northland! *skoal!*'
  Thus the tale ended.

FEDERICO GARCIA LORCA

FEDERICO GARCIA LORCA (Spanish, 1899-1936). Best-known contemporary Spanish poet and dramatist. Fiery anti-Fascist, executed during the Spanish Civil War. Folklorist, musician, lecturer, amateur painter. As a dramatist, dealt with primitive passions: trilogy—*Bodas de Sangre, Yerma, La Casa de Bernarda Alba*. Poetry, in translation: *Lament for the Death of a Bullfighter, The Poet in New York, Poems*.

JOURNEY

A hundred riders in mourning,
where will they go
by the lowering sky
of the orange grove?
Neither in Cordova nor in Seville
will they appear;
nor in Granada that longs
for the sea.
Those sleepy horses
will carry them
to the labyrinth of crosses
where song trembles.
With seven piercing cries,
where will they go,
the hundred Andalusian riders
of the orange grove?

AFTER PASSING

The children gaze
at a distant point.

The candles die.
Some blind girls
question the moon,
and spirals of weeping
climb on the wind.

The mountains gaze
at a distant point.

THE SILENCE

Hear the silence, my child.
It is an undulated silence
where valleys and echoes slip,
a silence
that bows heads
to the ground.

VILLAGE

Upon the barren mountain
a Calvary.
Clear water
and centenary olive trees.
Through the narrow streets
cloaked men,
and on the towers
weathercocks turning.
Eternally
turning.
Oh lost village
in the Andalusia of tears!

SURPRISED

Left dead in the street
with a dagger in his chest.
No one knew him.
How the street lamp trembled!

Mother.
How the tiny lamp trembled
in the street!
Early dawn. No one
could face his eyes
open wide in the cruel wind.
Dead he was left in the street
with a dagger in his chest
and no one knew him.

AND THEN

Labyrinths
born of time
vanish.

(Only desert
remains.)

The heart,
fountain of desires,
vanishes.

(Only desert
remains.)

The illusion of dawn
and kisses
vanishes.

Only desert
remains.
Undulating
desert.

AY!

The cry leaves in the wind
a shadow of cypress.

(Leave me in this field,
weeping.)

827

All has been demolished in the world.
Nothing remains but silence.

(Leave me in this field,
weeping.)

The lightless horizon
is bitten with bonfires.

(I have told you, leave me
in this field,
weeping.)

LUSIN

LUSIN (Chou Shu-jen, Chinese, 1881-1936). Important leader in modern
Chinese literary revolution. While a student in Japan, studied Western literature and took European ideals back to China. Forced to leave professorship at
Peking National University because of radical ideas. Essays had immediate
influence; 26 short stories more likely to endure. *Ah Q and Others* has been
translated into many languages.

MEDICINE

IT IS autumn, and late at night, so that the moon has already gone.
The sky is a sheet of darkling blue. Everything still sleeps, except
those who wander in the night, and Hua Lao-shuan. He sits up
suddenly in his bed; leaning over, he rubs a match and touches it
to a lamp which is covered with grease. A pale greenish light
flickers and reveals the two rooms of a tea house.

"Father of Hsiao-shuan, are you leaving?" queries the voice of a
woman. There is a series of tearing coughs in the small room in
the rear.

"M-m." Lao-shuan, listening for a moment, fastens his garment
and then stretches forth a hand toward the woman. "Give it,"
he says.

Hua Ta-ma fumbles beneath her pillow and drags forth a small
packet of silver dollars, which she hands to him. Nervously he

thrusts it into his pocket, then pats it twice, to reassure himself. He lights a paper lantern and blows out the oil lamp. Carrying the lantern, he goes into the small rear room. There is a rustle and then more coughing. When it is quiet again, Lao-shuan calls out, in an undertone: "Hsiao-shuan—don't bother getting up. The shop—your mother will see to that."

His son does not answer him, and Lao-shuan, thinking he will sleep undisturbed, goes through the low door into the street. In the blackness nothing is at first visible save a gray ribbon of path. The lantern illumines only his two feet, which move rhythmically. Dogs appear here and there, then sidle off again. None even barks. Outside, the air is cold, and it refreshes Lao-shuan, so that it seems to him he is all at once a youth, and possesses the miraculous power of touching men into life. He takes longer strides. Gradually the sky brightens, till the road is more clearly marked.

Absorbed in his walking, Lao-shuan is startled when, almost in front of him, he sees a crossroad. He stops, and then withdraws a few steps, to stand under the eaves of a shop, in front of its closed door. After a long wait, his bones are chilled.

"Unh, an old fellow?"

"High-spirited, up so early . . ."

Opening his eyes, Lao-shuan sees several people passing near him. One of them turns back and looks at him intently. He cannot distinguish the features clearly, but the man's eyes are bright with a cold, lusting gleam, eyes of famishment suddenly coming upon something edible. Looking at his lantern, Lao-shuan sees that it has gone out. He feels quickly at his pocket; the hard substance is still there. Then he peers out, and on either side of him are numerous strange people, loitering and looking oddly like ghosts in the dim light. Then he gazes fixedly at them, and gradually they do not seem unusual at all.

He discerns several soldiers among the crowd. On their coats they wear, both in front and behind, the large white circle of cloth of the government troops, which can be seen for some distance. As one draws nearer, the wine-colored border of their uniform is also evident. There is a trampling of many feet, and a large number of people gathers, little groups here and there merging swiftly into one crush that advances like the ocean's tide. Reaching the crossroad, they halt and form a semicircle, with their backs toward Lao-shuan.

Necks stretch forth from collars and incline toward the same

829

point, as if, like so many ducks, they are held by some invisible hand. For a moment all is still. Lao-shuan seems to hear a sound from somewhere beyond the necks. A stir sweeps through the onlookers. With a sudden movement, they abruptly disperse. People jostle one another hurriedly, and some, pushing past Lao-shuan, almost tumble him to the ground in their haste.

"*Hai!* One hand gives the money, another hand gives the goods!" screams a man clad entirely in black, who halts before Lao-shuan. In his eyes is a metallic glitter. They resemble the bright luster of a pair of swords. They stab into Lao-shuan's soul, and his body seems to shrivel to half its normal size. The dark man thrusts one huge, empty paw at him, while in the other he offers a steamed roll, stained with a fresh and still warm red substance, drops of which trickle to the earth.

Hurriedly, Lao-shuan fumbles for his dollars. He attempts to hand them over to the black-garbed man, from whose hand slowly depend the drops of red, but somehow he cannot embolden himself to receive the saturated roll.

"What's he afraid of? Why not take it?" the fellow demands, brusque and impatient. Lao-shuan continues to hesitate until the other roughly snatches his lantern, tears off its paper shade and uses it to wrap up the roll. Then he thrusts this package into Lao-shaun's hand, and at the same time seizes the silver and gives it a cursory feel. As he turns away he murmurs, "That old fool . . ."

"And to cure what person?" Lao shuan seems to hear someone ask him. He does not reply. His attention is centered upon the package, and he embraces it as if it were the only child descended from a house of ten generations. Nothing else in the world matters, now that he is about to transplant into his own home the robust life which he holds in his hands. He hopes, thereby, to reap much happiness.

The sun lifts over the horizon. Before him, the long street leads straight into his tea house. Behind him, the light of day caresses a worn tablet at the crossroad, on which are four characters limned in faint gold: "Ancient—Pavilion—"

Lao-shuan, reaching home, finds the tea house swept clean, with the rows of tables smooth and glistening but as yet serving no customers. Only Hsiao-shuan sits alone at a table by the wall and eats his food. Large drops of sweat drip down his forehead, and his little

830

lined coat sticks against his sunken spine. His shoulder blades project sharply, from under his coat, so that there appears on his back, as though embossed, the character *pa*. Seeing it causes Lao-shuan to pinch his brow together. He wife emerges hastily from the kitchen, her mouth open, her lips quivering.

"Do you have it?" she asks.

"Yes, I have it."

The pair disappears into the kitchen for a time, where they consult. Then Hua Ta-ma comes hurriedly forth, goes out and in a moment returns with a dried lotus leaf, which she spreads on the table. Lao-shuan unwraps the crimson-stained roll and neatly repacks it in the sheet of lotus. Meanwhile, Hsiao-shuan has finished his meal and his mother warns him: "Sit still, Little Door-latch. Don't come here yet."

When the fire burns briskly in the mud stove, the father thrusts his little green and red parcel into the oven. There is a red and black flame. A strange odor permeates the rooms.

"*Hao*. It smells good, but is it? What are you eating?" demands Camel-Back Fifth, who arrives at this moment and sniffs the air questioningly. He is one of those who pass their days in tea houses, the first to come in the morning, the last to leave at night. Now, tumbling to a table by the lane, he sits down to make idle inquiry.

"Could it be baked rice *congee*?"

Nobody replies. Lao-shuan silently serves him boiled tea.

"Come in, Hsiao-shuan," Hua Ta-ma calls from the inner room, in the center of which she has placed a stool. The Little Door-latch sits, and his mother, saying in a low voice, "Eat it, and your sickness will vanish," hands him a plate on which is a round object, black in color.

Hsiao-shuan picks it up. For a moment he gazes at it curiously, as if he might somehow hold his own life in his hand. His heart is unspeakably moved with wonder. Very carefully, he splits the object. A jet of white vapor gushes forth, and immediately dissolves in the air. Now Hsiao-shuan sees that it is a white flour roll, broken in half. Soon it has entered his stomach, so that even the taste of it cannot be clearly remembered. In front of him there is the empty dish; on one side stands his father and, on the opposite side, his mother. Their eyes are potent with a strange look, as if they desire to pour something into him, yet at the same draw something forth. It is exciting. It is too much for Hsaio-shuan's little heart, which

throbs furiously. He presses his hands against his chest and begins to cough.

"Sleep a little; you'll be well."

So Hsiao-shuan coughs himself to sleep, obeying the advice of his mother. Having waited patiently till he is quiet, she drapes over him a lined quilt, which consists mostly of patches.

In the tea house are many customers, and Lao-shaun is kept engaged in his enterprise. He darts from one table to another, pouring hot water and tea, and seemingly intent on his tasks. But under his eyes are dark hollows.

"Lao-shuan," inquires a man with whiskers streaked with white, "are you not a little unwell?"

"No."

"No? But I already see that it's unlikely. Your smile now—" The bearded one contradicts himself.

"Lao-shuan is always busy. Of course if his son were—" begins Camel-Back Fifth. His remarks is interrupted by the arrival of a man whose face is massive, with distorted muscles. He wears a black cotton shirt, unbuttoned and pulled together carelessly around the waist with a broad black cloth girdle [the apparel of an executioner]. As he enters, he shouts to Lao-shuan:

"Eaten, eh? Is he well already? Lao-shuan, luck is with you! Indeed lucky! If it were not that I get news quickly—"

With the kettle in one hand and the other hanging straight beside him in an attitude of respect, Lao-shuan listens and smiles. All the guests listen with deference, and Hua Ta-ma, her eyes dark and sleepless, also comes forth and smiles, serving the new arrival some tea leaves, with the added flourish of a green olive. Lao-shuan himself fills the cup with boiling water.

"It is a guaranteed cure! Different from all others! Think of it, brought back while still warm, eaten while warm!" shouts the gentleman with the coarse face.

"Truly, were it not for Big Uncle Kan's services, how could it be—" Hua Ta-ma thanks him, in deep gratitude.

"Guaranteed cure! Guaranteed cure! Eaten up like that while still warm. A roll with human blood is an absolute cure for any kind of consumption!"

Mention of the word "consumption" seems to disconcert Hua Ta-ma; for her face suddenly turns pallid, though the smile quickly creeps back. She manages to withdraw so inconspicuouly that Big Uncle Kan still shouts with the full vigor of his lungs and does not

832

notice that she is gone till from the inner room, where Hsiao-shuan sleeps, there comes the sound of dry, raucous coughing.

"So, it is true Hsiao-shuan has come upon friendly luck. That sickness will unquestionably be cured utterly. There's no surprise in Lao-shuan's constant smiling." Thus speaks the whiskered old man, who walks toward Big Uncle Kan. "I hear," he says to the latter in a suppressed voice, "that the criminal executed today is a son of the Hsia family. Now, whose son is he? And, in fact, executed for what?"

"Whose?" demands Big Uncle. "Can he be other than the son of the fourth daughter-in-law of the Hsias? That little *tung-hsii!*" Observing that he has an alert audience, Big Uncle expands, his facial muscles become unusually active and he raises his voice to heroic heights, shouting: "The little thing did not want to live! He simply did not want life, that's all."

"And I got what from the execution this time? Not the merest profit! Even the clothes stripped from him were seized by Red Eye Ah Yi, the jailer. Our Uncle Lao-shuan was the luckiest. Second comes the Third Father of the Hsia family. He actually pocketed the reward—twenty-five ounces of silver!—all alone. He gave not so much as a single cash to anyone!"

Hsiao-shuan walks slowly from the little room, his hands pressed to his chest, and coughing without respite. He enters the kitchen, fills a bowl with cold rice and sits down at once to eat. Hua Ta-ma goes to him and inquires softly: "Hsiao-shuan, are you better? Still as hungry as ever?"

"Guaranteed cure, guaranteed!" Big Uncle Kan casts a glance at the lad but quickly turns back to the crowd and declares: "Third Father of Hsia is clever. Had he not been the first to report the matter to the official, his whole house would have been beheaded, and all their property confiscated. But instead? Silver!"

"That little tung-hsi was an altogether rotten egg. He even attempted to induce the head jailer to join the rebellion!"

"*Ai-ya!* If it were actually done, think of it," indignantly comments a youth in his twenties, sitting at a back table.

"You should know that Red Eye Ah Yi was anxious to gather some details; so he entered into conversation. 'The realm of *Ta Ching Dynasty* really belongs to us all,' he told Red Eye. Now, what do you make of that? Is it possible that such talk is actually human?

"Red Eye knew that there was only a mother in his home, but he could not believe that he was so poor that 'not a drop of oil and

water' could be squeezed from him. His rage already had burst his abdomen, yet the boy attempted to 'scratch the tiger's head'! Ah Yi gave him several smacks on the face."

"Ah Yi knows his boxing. His blows must have done the wretch good!" exults Camel-Back Fifth, from a corner table.

"No! Would you believe it? His worthless bones were unafraid. The fellow actually said, what is more, that it was a pity!"

Black-and-White Whiskers snorted, "What is it? How could pity be shown in beating a thing like that?"

"You've not listened well," sneers Big Uncle contemptuously. "The little tung-hsi meant to say that Ah Yi hmself was to be pitied!"

The listeners' eyes suddenly dull, and there is a pause in the conversation. Hsiao-shuan perspiring copiously, had finished his rice. His head seems to be steaming.

"So he said Red Eye should be pitied! Now, that is pure insanity!" Black-and-White Whiskers feels proudly that he has logically solved the whole matter. "Obviously, he had gone mad!"

"Gone mad," approvingly echoes the youth who spoke earlier. He too feels like a discoverer.

Equanimity is restored to the other teahouse visitors. They renew their laughing and talking. Hsiao-shuan, under cover of the confusion of sounds, seizes the opportunity to cough hoarsely, with all his emaciated strength.

Big Uncle Kan moves over to pat the child's shoulder, repeating, "Guaranteed cure, Hsiao-shuan. You mustn't cough like that. Guaranteed cure!"

"Gone mad," says Camel-Back Fifth, nodding his head.

Originally, the land adjacent to the city wall beyond the West Gate was public property. The narrow path that now cavorts through it was first made by feet seeking a short cut, which in time came to be a natural boundary line. On the left of it, as one goes out from the gate, are buried those who have been executed or have starved to death in prison. On the right are grouped the graves of the paupers. All of these graves are so numerous and closely arranged that they remind one of the sweet buns laid out in a rich man's home for a birthday celebration.

The Clear and Bright Day, when graves are visited, has dawned unusually cold, and willows have just issued new buds about the size of a half-grain of rice. Hua Ta-ma has laid out four dishes and a bowl of rice in front of a new grave on the right side, has left tears

834

over it and has burned imitation money. Now she sits dazedly on the ground, as if waiting for something, but nothing which she herself could explain. A light breeze sweeps by, and her short hair flutters. It is much grayer than last year.

Down the narrow path comes another woman, gray also, and in torn rags. She carries a worn round basket, lacquered red, with a string of paper ingots hanging from it. Now and then she halts her slow walk. Finally she notices Hua Ta-ma gazing at her, and she hesitates, embarrassed. A look of confused shame crosses her pale, melancholy face. Then, emboldening herself, she walks to a grave on the left of the path and lays down her lacquered basket.

It so happens that the grave is directly opposite Hsiao-shuan's with only the narrow path between them. Hua Ta-ma watches mechanically as the woman lays out four dishes and a bowl of rice; burns paper money and weeps. It occurs to her that in that grave also there is a woman's son. She watches curiously as the woman moves about absently and stares vacantly into space. Suddenly she sees her begin to tremble and stagger backward, as if in stupor.

Hua Ta-ma is touched. "She may be mad with sorrow," she fears. She rises, and, stepping across the path, speaks to her quietly: "Old Mother, don't grieve any more. Let us both go home." The woman nods stupidly, her eyes still staring. Suddenly she utters an exclamation, "Look! What is that?"

Looking along the woman's pointing finger, Hua Ta-ma's eyes take in the grave before them, which is unkempt and has ugly patches of yellow earth on it. Looking more closely she is startled to see, at the top of the little mound, a circlet of scarlet and white flowers.

For many years neither of them has seen clearly, and yet now both see these fresh blossoms. They are not many, but they are neatly arranged; they are not very splendid, but they are comely in an orderly way. Hua Ta-ma looks quickly at her son's grave, and at the others, but only here and there are a few scattered blossoms of blue and white that have braved the cold; there are no others of scarlet. She experiences a nameless emptiness of heart, as if in need, but of what she does not wish to know. The other walks nearer and examines the flowers closely. "What could be the explanation?" she muses.

Tears stream from her face, and she cries out: "Yü, my son! You have been wronged, but you do not forget. Is it that your heart is still full of pain, and you choose this day and this method of telling

me?" She gazes around, but, seeing only a black crow brooding in a leafless tree, she continues: "Yü, my son! It was a trap; you were 'buried alive.' Yet Heaven knows! Rest your eyes in peace, but give me a sign. If you are here in the grave, if you are listening to me, cause the crow to fly here and alight on your grave. Let me know!"

There is no more breeze, and everywhere the dry grass stands erect, like bristles of copper. A faint sound hangs in the air and vibrates, growing less and less audible, till finally it ceases entirely. Then everything becomes as quiet as death. The two old women stood motionless in the midst of the dry grass, intently watching the crow. Among the straight limbs of the tree, its head drawn in, the crow sits immobile and as if cast in iron.

Much time passes. Those who come to visit graves begin to increase in numbers. To Hua Ta-ma it seems that gradually a heavy burden lifts from her, and to the other she says, "Come, let us go."

The old woman sighs dejectedly and gathers up her offertory dishes. She lingers for still another moment, then at length walks slowly, murmuring, "What could it have been?"

When they have walked only some thirty paces they suddenly hear a sharp cry from above. "Yah-h-h." Turning round with a shudder they see the crow brace itself on a limb and then push forth, spreading its broad wings and flying like an arrow toward the far horizon.

M

ANTONIO MACHADO

ANTONIO MACHADO (Spanish, 1875-1939). Poet of the inner life. Anda-lusian Professor of French, who fled to France after the Spanish Civil War. Poetry of great simplicity, bare of adornment, has been compared with that of Yeats. Books: *Soledades, Campos de Castilla, Nuevas canciones.*

PERCHANCE IN DREAMS

Perchance, in dreams, the hand
of the sower of stars
struck the chords of some forgotten music

as a note of the immense lyre,
and the humble wave reached our lips
as a few simple words of truth.

IBERIAN GOD

As the gambler drew his bow
For vengeance in the song,
So the Iberian recklessly let go
A sharp shaft to the Lord of blighting wrong
Who felled his wheat with hail and killed his fruit;
But he praised the Lord who brought his crops to head
Full eared, gold to the root,
The rye and wheat that tomorrow would be his bread.

"Lord of ruin and loss,
I adore because I fear, because I wait,
But my heart is blasphemous:
Bowing to earth, I pray in pride and hate.

837

"I know Thy power, my chain I recognize,
Lord, for Thee I dig my bread in sweat and sighs;
O master of the flooding clouds that cost
So dear to summer yield,
Of the autumn drought and spring's belated frost,
Of the scorching heat that sears the harvest field.

"Lord of the bow above the tender grass
Where the white ewe grazes,
Lord of the hut undone when tempests pass
And of the fruit where the worm carves its mazes,

"Thy breathing quickens the hearth fire when it
Is low, Thy splendor ripens ruddy grain,
And on Midsummer Eve the olive pit
Forms and hardens where Thy hand has lain.

"O master of fortunes and of poverties,
Good luck and bad, who yet
Giv'st to the rich man favors and soft ease
And to the poor, his hope and bitter sweat,

"Lord, Lord, in the twelve months' whirling round
I have watched my seed with patient labor sown
Run the same risk in the hard and faithless ground
As a gambler's cash on the losing hazard thrown.

"Lord, paternal now, who wert before a God
Cruel, two-faced, Thy love with vengeance dimmed,
To Thee my prayer of blasphemy and laud
Ascends, a gambler's die cast on the wind."

This man who, insulting God, at his altar prayed,
Defiant of all fate's frowning might forbode,
With dreaming tamed the seas and highways laid
Across them, saying, He is the ocean road.

Is it not this man who raised his God to be
Above all war? Beyond
Fate, beyond earth and sea,
Beyond death and dying, free of every bond?

838

Did not the Iberian tree,
The encina, yield her branch for holy fire
And, burning, find unity
With God in love's pure flame on the sacred pyre?

But now, so quickly day grows into day!
There are new hearths; for these
New roses thrive in field and wooded bay
And fresh green branches on the ancient trees.

The fatherland is still
Waiting to open furrows to the plow;
For the seed of God there is a field to till
Overgrown with burdocks, thorns, and thistles now.

Day merges into day; the past is wide
To the morrow, the morrow to the infinite;
Men of Spain, no yesterday has died,
Future and past have yet no holy writ.

Did ever the Spanish God His face reveal?
My heart awaits the hand
Of an Iberian, vigorous and leal,
To carve in oaken timbers of Castile
The God austere who reigns in this brown land.

AUTUMN DAWN

A highroad's barren scar
Among the grey rock-spires
And humble pastures far
Where strong black bulls are grazing. Brambles, thickets, briars.

The dew has drenched with cold
The landscape in the dark
And the poplars' frieze of gold,
Toward the river's arc.

A hint of dawn half seen
With purple crags for frame.
Beside his greyhounds keen,
His eager gun at rest, a hunter stalking game.

AT THE BURIAL OF A FRIEND

They gave him earth, one horrible afternoon
Of the month of July, under a fiery sun.

At a step from the open sepulchre
There were roses with rotting petals
Amongst geraniums whose scent was keen
And whose flowers were red. The sky

Pure and blue. A breeze
That was strong and dry was blowing.

Suspended from the great cords,
The coffin was let down,
Heavily, to the bottom of the ditch,
By the two gravediggers. . . .

And, as it came to rest, it struck with a loud, solemn noise, in the
    silence.

The thud of a coffin on the earth is a thing
That is, absolutely, serious.

Against the black box broke
The heavy, dusty lumps of earth. . . .

The air drew its whitish breath
From the deep ditch.

—And thou, already shadowless, sleepest and restest.
Long peace to thy bones. . . .

Definitively,
Sleep thou, a quiet, and real, sleep.

POEM

The street in shadow. The high old mansions hide
The dying sun; there are echoes of light in the balconies.

Do you not see, in the charm of that flowered balcony,
The rosy oval of a face you know?

The image, behind the pane, with its equivocal reflection,
Gleams and vanishes, like an old daguerreotype.

In the street only the sound of your step is heard.
Slowly the echoes of its passing die away.

Oh, anguish. The heart grows heavy and hurts. "Is it she?"
It could not be. . . . Go on. . . . The star in the sky.

CHILDISH DREAM

A clear night
Of holiday and moonlight
Night of my dreams
Night of joy

—my soul was brightness
That, to-day, is all fog
My hair
Was not yet black—

The youngest fairy
Took me in her arms
When that joyous holiday
Burned in the square

So, in the crackling
Of the illuminations
Love wove
Its skeins of dances

And in that night
Of holiday and moonlight
Night of my dreams
Night of joy

The youngest fairy
Kissed my forehead. . . .
With her fine hand
Said her goodbyes to me

841

All the rose trees
Give their perfumes
All the loves
Unfold love

POEM

The loved house
In which she lived
Shows,
On a pile of rubble, ruined
And demolished
A shapeless, wooden skeleton
Black, eaten away.

The moon throws its clear light
In dreams that gleam like silver
On the windows. Ill-dressed, sad,
I walk through the old street.

MAURICE MAETERLINCK

MAURICE MAETERLINCK (Belgian, 1862-1949). Natural scientist and
shadowy symbolist. Poet, dramatist and philosopher. Won first recognition as
playwright: *Pelléas and Mélisande* (set to music by Debussy), *The Bluebird*,
Interior. His theater permeated by sense of doom and death. In *Life of the
Bee* and *Life of the Ant*, he wrote artfully on scientific matters. Nobel Prize,
1911.

THE LIFE OF THE DEAD

LAST night, I had a visit from an uncle who died about fifty years
ago. During his lifetime, he was what we call a "jolly old fellow,"
a positive and practical mind. He told me that the cemetery which
we had chosen as his quarters was cozy and well managed by one
of his friends of the Great Beyond, a remarkable, decent and distinguished gravedigger. My dear uncle was feeling at home and

was very happy. A part of himself, in which he never had been seriously interested, had left him to go he knew not where; but all that was human, solid and well balanced had accompanied him in his new and last abode. The dead had organized, underground, small but very lively friendly, or rather brotherly gatherings, where neighbors met to talk over the happenings of the cemetery, for every day brought new arrivals, two or three dead, sometimes even one or two dozens, in the prosperous days of an epidemic. These unexpected tourists had to be received affectionately if they were relatives or friends, and with every courtesy if they were strangers. These gatherings were highly exclusive, and no one was admitted without serious investigations. A class system had spontaneously been established. The deceased were divided in three classes, that is those who, to speak as you speak up here, did not have as yet an evil smell, that is, the new arrivals whose odorless stage was rather transitory; then the ones who emitted strong exhalations, you judge disagreeable, who constituted the middle class, the most numerous, and finally the superior class, the sepulchral aristocracy, whose members were proclaimed immortal because they had ceased emitting any scent, and consisted only of bleached bones, aseptic and carefully polished.

"But, uncle," I interrupted, "why is it that you do not feel certain emanations that we deem unpleasant? Is it because you do not have a nose?"

"It is not a question of nose anymore, but a purely scientific question. There are no evil smells. It is a regrettable error of the inhabitants on the surface. All odors are chemically pure, whether they come from the lily, the rose, the violet or the gardens of the Great Beyond."

"Uncle, another question, if I may? . . ."

"Go ahead, dear, go ahead. I am here to answer you, for we know almost everything. . . ."

"Uncle, how do you receive those who have been incinerated?"

"We despise them! They are renegades, traitors, deserters. They are ashamed of death. They disavow it. They would like to abolish it; and when they come here begging for a place for their little jars of human preserves, we throw those little jars out of the window, into eternity, for we are eternal . . .

"But do not speak to me about those people. . . . When do you expect to join me?"

"I do not know yet. Do you?"

843

"I could know, if I wanted to, but I would not tell you. Anyhow, as soon as you arrive, let me know. I shall take you under my wing and facilitate your admission in our circles, for it involves a lot of red tape. The dead are even worse bureaucrats than the Americans, and for the most unimportant formality, such as recuperating a lost nail, a tooth, or a radius one has to go through twenty offices, give sixty signatures, disclose the first and last names of one's parents, grand-parents; produce one's birth certificate, marriage certificate, death certificate of sisters, brothers, first and other cousins. It is a deplorable habit of which we have as yet not been able to rid ourselves. It is true that it takes care of our moments of leisure which are long, although very agreeable. . . ."

"Uncle, I also would like to ask you . . ."

"Go on, go on, my child, I am at your disposal."

"What will you do when there is no more place left in your garden in the Great Beyond? It seems to be rather crowded already."

"We will take the one of the living."

"And if they do not want to give it up to you?"

"We will make dead out of them."

"Does that mean that you have the right to kill?"

"We do not have to kill them. We have only to wait. It is time which kills them."

"But uncle, what happens in case of exhumation? What happens to you? What do you feel?"

"We did not have any exhumation yet; but there has been some talk about it. . . . It is supposed to be more unpleasant than moving. You lose everything and do not find your own friendships and little schemes anymore. Happily, exhumation occurs rather seldom. . . ."

"I can see, uncle, that not even death is free of troubles."

"What do you expect, my child, all lives have their little inconveniences."

"Uncle, I would also like to ask you . . . Uncle, where are you? . . . Are not you going to answer me anymore? . . ."

I insisted in vain, I did not get an answer. He had returned into eternal silence. . . .

844

STEPHANE MALLARME

STÉPHANE MALLARMÉ (French, 1842-1898). Dreamlike symbolist poet. Small output, of wide influence on modern poetry. As youth studied in England, returned to France to teach English. Later celebrated for his literary soirées. His most famous poem, "Afternoon of a Faun," was inspiration for first great piece of impressionist music (by Debussy). His entire work delicate, evasive, often obscure.

THE AFTERNOON OF A FAUN

These nymphs, I would make them eternal.
   So rare,
Their delicate rose, that it drifts on the air,
Drowsy with clustering sleep.
   Did I love a dream?
My doubt, fruit of the ancient night, breaks forth
In many a subtle branch, which, on the swell
Of the true forest,
Proves that I proffer to myself,—alas!
The triumph of an ideal want
Of roses.
   Think:
Perhaps these women of your niceties
Are but the figures of your fabled hope!
Faun, the illusion leaps from the blue, cold eyes
As a spring all of tears, of her most pure:
And she all sighs is a contrast
As a warm day's breath on the fleece!
No! By the weary and motionless swoon
Stifling with summer the fresh lilting morn,
No murmur of water but my flute wafts
To the dew-sprinkled woods of consent.
   The only wind
Hustling its sound through the twin-born pipes
Dispersing its arid rain—
The while the horizon unfrowning—
Is the calm, artificial, evident sigh
Of Inspiration, rising to its source.

845

O Sicilian shores of a quiet fen
Which my vanity sacks to the jealous suns
Submissive under the flowers of sparks,
Reveal:
"*Here was I culling hollow reeds,*
Tamed by my talent, when, on the glaucous gold
Of distant verdures yielding to the flood
Their richest vines,
A living whiteness surged to its repose:
At the soft prelude to the birth of song
The flock of swans—no!—naiads, fled or plunged."

Inert and scorched in the tawny hour,
Unnoticing by what collective art
Too many hymens scamper off, desired
By him who seeketh Woman:
Then I shall waken, lone, erect,
Under an ancient surge of light,
At the first fervor:
Lilies! and candor in one of you all.

Else that sweet nothing rumored from their lip,
The kiss, that whispers low of perfidy;
My breast, virgin of evidence, testifies a sting
Mysterious, and of a sacred tooth;
But bah! such a secret elects to confide
In the vast twin-born reed that plays to the clouds:
That, sloughing off the cheek's pale pain,
Dreams, in a lengthy solo, I'll delight
The beauty of the roundabout with it
And false confusions with my credulous song;
Of notes so loud that modulated love
Shrinks from the inconsiderable dream
Of back or pure flank in my closed regard,
A resounding, vain, and endless-dreary line.

Strain then, O instrument of flights, malign Syrinx,
To flower anew by bords where you await me!
I, in my noisy pride, shall sing,
Sing long and longingly of goddesses;
And by the paintings of idolaters
Still in their shadows charm the girdle free:

846

So, when I've sucked the splendor from the grape
To banish regret dispelled by my deceit,
Mocking the summer sky,
I raise the empty cluster, with a puff
Belling the luminous skins, for frenzy flushed,
And watch through them till night fall.
Oh, nymphs, bell them with many memories:
"My gaze, piercing the rushes,
Lances each deathless form, that in the wave
Drowns its mad burning, while its passion-cry
Leaps to the forest-heaven;
And the glorious bath of tresses drops below
In lightnings and shudders—O diadems!
I hasten; when, at my ankles (bruised,
Knowing the languor of the ill of being twain)
Are sleepers conjoined, in danger of themselves.
I embrace them, not disentwining,
And bear to this grove, which futile shadows flee,
Roses yielding their fragrance to the sun;
Here our frolic shall linger with the day it burns."

I adore you, O wrath of virgins,
O untamed delight of the holy nude burden
That glides, to escape my lips of drinking fire,
As the lightning leaps! The silent dread of the flesh:
From the head of the cruel to the heart of the weak
From whom their innocence droppeth, moist
With tears of frenzy, or less mournful dew.
"I sinned, gay at defeating these treacherous terrors,
In having divided the disheveled cluster
Of kisses the gods had so close intermingled;
For, as my lips moved in the passionate smiling
I plunged in the sensuous joy of one only
(Holding by a single finger
So that the frozen candor of her breast
Her sister's crimson ferment might encolor—
Her sister enkindled—
The little one artless, unblushing)
Out of my arms, weak with uncertain dyings,
The ever thankless prey was gone
Without ruth for the sob of my frenzy."

Shall I grieve? toward pleasure others will draw me on
By their tresses bound to the horns of my brow:
You know, my passion, how, purple and overripe,
Each pomegranate bursts and hums of bees;
And our blood, smitten with what will capture it,
Flows for the eternal swarming of desire.
When these woods are tinted of ashes and gold
A festival exults in the darkened forest:
Etna! it is to you that Venus comes
Setting on your lava her ingenuous heels,
When in sad thundering sleep the fires die.
I hold the queen!
   O sure chastisement!
    No,
But the soul empty of words and the dull form
Slowly succumb to the proud silence of noon:
Now I must sleep and forget the blasphemy,
Outspread on the parched sand—and, as I love,
Open my mouth to the healing star of wine!

Couple, farewell; I shall see the shadow that you are.

THOMAS MANN

THOMAS MANN (German, 1875-1955). One of the most distinguished modern men of letters. Came to America to escape Nazism, preferred to return to Europe after war. Early fiction depicted life in Germany (*Buddenbrooks*) and prewar Europe (*The Magic Mountain*). In stories (*Death in Venice*) and essays, he was arbiter between the artist and the average man. In later years, preoccupied with social and moral issues (in the *Joseph* cycle and *Doctor Faustus*).

A WEARY HOUR

HE GOT up from the table, his little, fragile writing-desk; got up as though desperate, and with hanging head crossed the room to the tall, thin, pillar-like stove in the opposite corner. He put his hands to it; but the hour was long past midnight and the tiles were nearly

stone cold. Not getting even his little comfort that he sought, he leaned back against them and, coughing, drew together the folds of his dressing-gown, between which a draggled lace shirt-frill stuck out; he snuffed hard through his nostrils to get a little air, for as usual he had a cold.

It was a particular, a sinister cold, which scarcely ever quite disappeared. It inflamed his eyelids and made the flanges of his nose all raw; in his head and limbs it lay like a heavy, sombre intoxication. Or was this cursed confinement to his room, to which the doctor had weeks ago condemned him, to blame for all his languor and flabbiness? God knew if it was the right thing—perhaps so, on account of his chronic catarrh and the spasms of his chest and belly. And for weeks on end now, yes, weeks, bad weather had reigned in Jena—hateful, horrible weather, which he felt in every nerve of his body—cold, wild, gloomy. The December wind roared in the stove-pipe with a desolate god-forsaken sound—he might have been wandering on a heath, by night and storm, his soul full of unappeasable grief. Yet this close confinement—that was not good either; not good for thought, nor for the rhythm of the blood, where thought was engendered.

The six-sided room was bare and colourless and devoid of cheer: a whitewashed ceiling wreathed in tobacco smoke, walls covered with trellis-patterned paper and hung with silhouettes in oval frames, half a dozen slender-legged pieces of furniture; the whole lighted by two candles burning at the head of the manuscript on the writing-table. Red curtains draped the upper part of the window-frames; mere festooned wisps of cotton they were, but red, a warm, sonorous red, and he loved them and would not have parted from them; they gave a little air of ease and charm to the bald unlovely poverty of his surroundings. He stood by the stove and blinked repeatedly, straining his eyes across at the work from which he had just fled: that load, that weight, that gnawing conscience, that sea which to drink up, that frightful task which to perform, was all his pride and all his misery, at once his heaven and his hell. It dragged, it stuck, it would not budge—and now again . . . ! It must be the weather; or his catarrh, or his fatigue. Or was it the work? Was the thing itself an unfortunate conception, doomed from its beginning to despair?

He had risen in order to put a little space between him and his task, for physical distance would often result in improved perspective, a wider view of his material and a better chance of conspectus.

Yes, the mere feeling of relief on turning away from the battlefield had been known to work like an inspiration. And a more innocent one than that purveyed by alcohol or strong, black coffee.

The little cup stood on the side-table. Perhaps it would help him out of the impasse? No, no, not again! Not the doctor only, but somebody else too, a more important somebody, had cautioned him against that sort of thing—another person, who lived over in Weimar and for whom he felt a love which was a mixture of hostility and yearning. That was a wise man. He knew how to live and create; did not abuse himself, was full of self-regard.

Quiet reigned in the house. There was only the wind, driving down the Schlossgasse and dashing the rain in gusts against the panes. They were all asleep—the landlord and his family. Lotte and the children. And here he stood by the cold stove, awake, alone, tormented; blinking across at the work in which his morbid self-dissatisfaction would not let him believe.

His neck rose long and white out of his stock and his knock-kneed legs showed between the skirts of his dressing-gown. The red hair was smoothed back from a thin, high forehead; it retreated in bays from his veined white temples and hung down in thin locks over the ears. His nose was aquiline, with an abrupt whitish tip; above it the well-marked line of the brows almost met. They were darker than his hair and gave the deep-set, inflamed eyes a tragic, staring look. He could not breathe through his nose; so he opened his thin lips and made the freckled, sickly cheeks look even more sunken thereby.

No, it was a failure, it was all hopelessly wrong. The army ought to have been brought in! The army was the root of the whole thing. But it was impossible to present it before the eyes of the audience —and was art powerful enough thus to enforce the imagination? Besides, his hero was no hero; he was contemptible, he was frigid. The situation was wrong, the language was wrong; it was a dry pedestrian lecture, good for a history class, but as drama absolutely hopeless!

Very good, then, it was over. A defeat. A failure. Bankruptcy. He would write to Körner, the good Körner, who believed in him, who clung with childlike faith to his genius. He would scoff, scold, beseech—this friend of his; would remind him of the *Carlos*, which likewise had issued out of doubts and pains and rewritings and after all the anguish turned out to be something really fine, a genuine masterpiece. But times were changed. Then he had been a man still capable of taking a strong, confident grip on a thing and giving it

850

triumphant shape. Doubts and struggles? Yes. And ill he had been, perhaps more ill than now; a fugitive, oppressed and hungry, at odds with the world; humanly speaking, a beggar. But young, still young! Each time, however low he had sunk, his resilient spirit had leaped up anew; upon the hour of affliction had followed the feeling of triumphant self-confidence. That came no more, or hardly ever, now. There might be one night of glowing exaltation—when the fires of his genius lighted up an impassioned vision of all that he might do if only they burned on; but it had always to be paid for with a week of enervation and gloom. Faith in the future, his guiding star in times of stress, was dead. Here was the despairing truth: the years of need and nothingness, which he had thought of as the painful testing-time, turned out to have been the rich and fruitful ones; and now that a little happiness had fallen to his lot, now that he had ceased to be an intellectual freebooter and occupied a position of civic dignity, with office and honours, wife and children— now he was exhausted, worn out. To give up, to own himself beaten —that was all there was left to do. He groaned; he pressed his hands to his eyes and dashed up and down the room like one possessed. What he had just thought was so frightful that he could not stand still on the spot where he had thought it. He sat down on a chair by the further wall and stared gloomily at the floor, his clasped hands hanging down between his knees.

His conscience . . . how loudly his conscience cried out! He had sinned, sinned against himself all these years, against the delicate instrument that was his body. Those youthful excesses, the nights without sleep, the days spent in close, smoke-laden air, straining his mind and heedless of his body; the narcotics with which he had spurred himself on—all that was now taking its revenge.

And if it did—then he would defy the gods, who decreed the guilt and then imposed the penalties. He had lived as he had to live, he had not had time to be wise, not time to be careful. Here in this place in his chest, when he breathed, coughed, yawned, always in the same spot came this pain, this piercing, stabbing, diabolical little warning; it never left him, since that time in Erfurt five years ago when he had catarrhal fever and inflammation of the lungs. What was it warning him of? Ah, he knew only too well what it meant—no matter how the doctor chose to put him off. He had no time to be wise and spare himself, no time to save his strength by submission to moral laws. What he wanted to do he must do soon, quickly, do today.

851

And the moral laws? . . . Why was it that precisely sin, surrender to the harmful and the consuming, actually seemed to him more moral than any amount of wisdom and frigid self-discipline? Not that constituted morality: not the contemptible knack of keeping a good conscience—rather the struggle and compulsion, the passion and pain.

Pain . . . how his breast swelled at the word! He drew himself up and folded his arms; his gaze, beneath the close-set auburn brows, was kindled by the nobility of his suffering. No man was utterly wretched so long as he could still speak of his misery in high-sounding and noble words. One thing only was indispensable; the courage to call his life by large and fine names. Not to ascribe his sufferings to bad air and constipation; to be well enough to cherish emotions, to scorn and ignore the material. Just on this one point to be naïve, though in all else sophisticated. To believe, to have strength to believe, in suffering. . . . But he *did* believe in it; so profoundly, so ardently, that nothing which came to pass with suffering could seem to him either useless or evil. His glance sought the manuscript, and his arms tightened across his chest. Talent itself— was that not suffering? And if the manuscript over there, his unhappy effort, made him suffer, was not that quite as it should be—a good sign, so to speak? His talents had never been of the copious, ebullient sort; were they to become so he would feel mistrustful. That only happened with beginners and bunglers, with the ignorant and easily satisfied, whose life was not shaped and disciplined by the possession of a gift. For a gift, my friends down there in the audience, a gift is not anything simple, not anything to play with; it is not mere ability. At bottom it is a compulsion; a critical knowledge of the ideal, a permanent dissatisfaction, which rises only through suffering to the height of its powers. And it is to the greatest, the most unsatisfied, that their gift is the sharpest scourge. Not to complain, not to boast; to think modestly, patiently of one's pain; and if not a day in the week, not even an hour, be free from it— what then? To make light and little of it all, of suffering and achievement alike—that was what made a man great.

He stood up, pulled out his snuff-box and sniffed eagerly, then suddenly clasped his hands behind his back and strode so briskly through the room that the flames of the candles flickered in the draught. Greatness, distinction, world conquest and an imperishable name! To be happy and unknown, what was that by comparison? To be known—known and loved by all the world—ah, they might

call that egotism, those who knew naught of the urge, naught of the sweetness of this dream! Everything out of the ordinary is egotistic, in proportion to its suffering. "Speak for yourselves," it says, "ye without mission on this earth, ye whose life is so much easier than mine!" And Ambition says: "Shall my sufferings be vain? No, they must make me great!"

The nostrils of his great nose dilated, his gaze darted fiercely about the room. His right hand was thrust hard and far into the opening of his dressing-gown, his left arm hung down, the fist clenched. A fugitive red played in the gaunt cheeks—a glow thrown up from the fire of his artistic egoism; that passion for his own ego, which burnt unquenchably in his being's depths. Well he knew it, the secret intoxication of this love! Sometimes he needed only to contemplate his own hand, to be filled with the liveliest tenderness towards himself, in whose service he was bent on spending all the talent, all the art that he owned. And he was right so to do, there was nothing base about it. For deeper still than his egoism lay the knowledge that he was freely consuming and sacrificing himself in the service of a high ideal, not as a virtue, of course, but rather out of sheer necessity. And this was his ambition: that no one should be greater than he who had not also suffered more for the sake of the high ideal. No one. He stood still, his hand over his eyes, his body turned aside in a posture of shrinking and avoidance. For already the inevitable thought had stabbed him: the thought of that other man, that radiant being, so sense-endowed, so divinely unconscious, that man over there in Weimar, whom he loved and hated. And once more, as always, in deep disquiet, in feverish haste, there began working within him the inevitable sequence of his thoughts: he must assert and define his own nature, his own art, against that other's. Was the other greater? Wherein, then, and why? If he won, would he have sweated blood to do so? If he lost, would his downfall be a tragic sight? He was no hero, no; a god, perhaps. But it was easier to be a god than a hero. Yes, things were easier for him. He was wise, he was deft, he knew how to distinguish between knowing and creating; perhaps that was why he was so blithe and carefree, such an effortless and gushing spring! But if creation was divine, knowledge was heroic, and he who created in knowledge was hero as well as god.

The will to face difficulties. . . . Did anyone realize what discipline and self-control it cost him to shape a sentence or follow out a hard train of thought? For after all he was ignorant, undisci-

plined, a slow, dreamy enthusiast. One of Cæsar's letters was harder to write than the most effective scene—and was it not almost for that very reason higher? From the first rhythmical urge of the inward creative force towards matter, towards the material, towards casting in shape and form—from that to the thought, the image, the word, the line—what a struggle, what a Gethsemane! Everything that he wrote was a marvel of yearning after form, shape, line, body; of yearning after the sunlit world of that other man who had only to open his godlike lips and straightway call the bright unshadowed things he saw by name!

And yet—and despite that other man. Where was there an artist, a poet, like himself? Who like him created out of nothing, out of his own breast? A poem was born as music in his soul, as pure, primitive essence, long before it put on a garment of metaphor from the visible world. History, philosophy, passion were no more than pretexts and vehicles for something which had little to do with them, but was at home in orphic depths. Words and conceptions were keys upon which his art played and made vibrate the hidden strings. No one realized. The good souls praised him, indeed, for the power of feeling with which he struck one note or another. And his favourite note, his final emotional appeal, the great bell upon which he sounded his summons to the highest feasts of the soul—many there were who responded to its sound. Freedom! But in all their exaltation, certainly he meant by the word both more and less than they did. Freedom—what was it? A self-respecting middle-class attitude towards thrones and princes? Surely not that. When one thinks of all that the spirit of man has dared to put into the word! Freedom from what? After all, from what? Perhaps, indeed, even from happiness, from human happiness, that silken bond, that tender, sacred tie. . . .

From happiness. His lips quivered. It was as though his glance turned inward upon himself; slowly his face sank into his hands. . . . He stood by the bed in the next room, where the flowered curtains hung in motionless folds across the window, and the lamp shed a bluish light. He bent over the sweet head on the pillow . . . a ringlet of dark hair lay across her cheek, that had the paleness of pearl; the childlike lips were open in slumber. "My wife! Beloved, didst thou yield to my yearning and come to me to be my joy? And that thou art. . . . Lie still and sleep; nay, lift not those sweet shadowy lashes and gaze up at me, as sometimes with thy great, dark, questioning, searching eyes. I love thee so! By God I swear

854

it. It is only that sometimes I am tired out, struggling at my self-imposed task, and my feelings will not respond. And I must not be too utterly thine, never utterly happy in thee, for the sake of my mission."

He kissed her, drew away from her pleasant, slumbrous warmth, looked about him, turned back to the outer room. The clock struck; it warned him that the night was already far spent; but likewise it seemed to be mildly marking the end of a weary hour. He drew a deep breath, his lips closed firmly; he went back and took up his pen. No, he must not brood, he was too far down for that. He must not descend into chaos; or at least he must not stop there. Rather out of chaos, which is fullness, he must draw up to the light whatever he found there fit and ripe for form. No brooding! Work! Define, eliminate, fashion, complete!

And complete it he did, that effort of a labouring hour. He brought it to an end, perhaps not to a good end, but in any case to an end. And being once finished, lo, it was also good. And from his soul, from music and idea, new works struggled upward to birth and, taking shape, gave out light and sound, ringing and shimmering, and giving hint of their infinite origin—as in a shell we hear the sighing of the sea whence it came.

ALESSANDRO MANZONI

ALESSANDRO MANZONI (Italian, 1785-1873). Profound historical romanticist. Founder of the Romantic School in Italy. His novel, *I Promessi Sposi* (*The Betrothed*), Italians sometimes rank next to the *Divine Comedy*. Influenced by Sir Walter Scott, but probes more deeply into historical issues. Also wrote poems and verse plays.

THE INTERRUPTED WEDDING

DON ABBONDIO (the priest) was sitting in an old armchair, wrapped in a dilapidated dressing-gown, with an ancient cap on his head, which made a frame all round his face. By the faint light of a small lamp the two thick white tufts of hair which projected from under the cap, his bushy white eyebrows, moustache, and pointed beard all seemed, on his brown and wrinkled face, like bushes covered with snow on a rocky hillside seen by moonlight.

"Ah! ah!" was his salutation, as he took off his spectacles and put them into the book he was reading.

"Your Reverence will say we are late in coming," said Tonio, bowing, as did Gervaso, but more awkwardly.

"Certainly it is late—late in every way. Do you know that I am ill?"

"Oh! I am very sorry, sir!"

"You surely must have heard that I am ill, and don't know when I can see anyone. . . . But why have you brought that—that fellow with you?"

"Oh! just for company, like, sir!"

"Very good—now let us see."

"There are twenty-five new *berlinghe*, sir— those with Saint Ambrose on horseback on them," said Tonio, drawing a folded paper from his pocket.

"Let us see," returned Abbondio, and taking the paper, he put on his spectacles, unfolded it, took out the silver pieces, turned them over and over, counted them and found them correct.

"Now, your Reverence, will you kindly give me my Teckla's necklace?"

"Quite right," replied Don Abbondio; and going to a cupboard, he unlocked it, and having first looked round, as if to keep away any spectators, opened one side, stood in front of the open door, so that no one could see in, put in his head to look for the pledge, and his arm to take it out, and, having extracted it, locked the cupboard, unwrapped the paper, said interrogatively, "All right?" wrapped it up again and handed it over to Tonio.

"Now," said the latter, "would you please let me have a little black and white, sir?"

"This, too!" exclaimed Don Abbondio; "they are up to every trick! Eh! how suspicious the world has grown! Can't you trust me?"

"How, your Reverence, not trust you? You do me wrong! But as my name is down on your book, on the debtor side, . . . and you have already had the trouble of writing it once, so . . . in case anything were to happen, you know . . ."

"All right, all right," interrupted Don Abbondio, and, grumbling to himself, he opened the table drawer, took out pen, paper and inkstand, and began to write, repeating the words out loud as he set them down. Meanwhile, Tonio, and, at a sign from him, Gervaso, placed themselves in front of the table, so as to prevent the writer from seeing the door, and, as if in mere idleness, began to move

their feet about noisily on the floor, in order to serve as a signal to those outside, and, at the same time, to deaden the sound of their footsteps. Don Abbondio, intent on his work, noticed nothing. Renzo and Lucia, hearing the signal, entered on tiptoe, holding their breath, and stood close behind the two brothers. Meanwhile, Don Abbondio, who had finished writing, read over the document attentively, without raising his eyes from the paper, folded it and saying, "Will you be satisfied now?" took off his spectacles with one hand, and held out the sheet to Tonio with the other. Tonio, while stretching out his hand to take it, stepped back on one side, and Gervaso, at a sign from him, on the other, and between the two appeared Renzo and Lucia. Don Abbondio saw them, started, was dumfounded, became furious, thought it over, and came to a resolution, all in the time that Renzo took in uttering these words: "Your Reverence, in the presence of these witnesses, this is my wife!" His lips had not yet ceased moving when Don Abbondio let fall the receipt, which he was holding in his left hand, raised the lamp and seizing the table-cloth with his right hand, dragged it violently towards him, throwing book, papers and inkstand to the ground, and, springing between the chair and table, approached Lucia. The poor girl, with her sweet voice all trembling, had only just been able to say "This is . . ." when Don Abbondio rudely flung the table-cloth over her head, and immediately dropping the lamp which he held in his other hand, used the latter to wrap it tightly round her face, nearly suffocating her, while he roared at the top of his voice, like a wounded bull, "Perpetua! Perpetua! treason! help!" When the light was out the priest let go his hold of the girl, went groping about for the door leading into an inner room, and, having found it, entered and locked himself in, still shouting, "Perpetua! treason! help! get out of this house! get out of this house!" In the other room all was confusion; Renzo, trying to catch the priest, and waving his hands about as though he had been playing at blindman's buff, had reached the door and kept knocking, crying out, "Open! open! don't make a noise!" Lucia called Renzo in a feeble voice, and said supplicatingly, "Let us go! do let us go!" Tonio was down on his hands and knees, feeling about the floor to find his receipt, while Gervaso jumped about and yelled like one possessed, trying to get out by the door leading to the stairs.

In the midst of this confusion we cannot refrain from a momentary reflection. Renzo, raising a noise by night in another man's

857

house, which he had surreptitiously entered, and keeping its owner besieged in an inner room, has every appearance of being an oppressor,—yet, after all, when you come to look at it, he was the oppressed. Don Abbondio, surprised, put to flight, frightened out of his wits while quietly attending to his own business, would seem to be the victim; and yet in reality, it was he who did the wrong. So goes the world, as it often happens; at least, so it used to go in the seventeenth century.

CHRISTOPHER MARLOWE

CHRISTOPHER MARLOWE (English, 1564-1593). Precursor of Shakespeare in English drama. After brief diplomatic career, settled in London, to become one of "University Wits." Killed, under questionable circumstances, in a tavern brawl, at 29. Greatest plays: *Tamburlaine the Great, The Tragicall History of Dr. Faustus, The Jew of Malta.*

THE PASSIONATE SHEPHERD
TO HIS LOVE

Come live with me and be my Love,
And we will all the pleasures prove
That hills and valleys, dale and field,
And all the craggy mountains yield.

There will we sit upon the rocks
And see the shepherds feed their flocks,
By shallow rivers, to whose falls
Melodious birds sing madrigals.

There will I make thee beds of roses
And a thousand fragrant posies,
A cap of flowers and a kirtle
Embroider'd all with leaves of myrtle.

A gown made of the finest wool,
Which from our pretty lambs we pull,
Fair linéd slippers for the cold,
With buckles of the purest gold.

A belt of straw and ivy buds
With coral clasps and amber studs:
And if these pleasures may thee move,
Come live with me and be my Love.

Thy silver dishes for thy meat
As precious as the gods do eat,
Shall on an ivory table be
Prepared each day for thee and me.

The shepherd swains shall dance and sing
For thy delights each May morning:
If these delights thy mind may move,
Then live with me and be my Love.

JOHN MASEFIELD

JOHN MASEFIELD (English, 1878-   ). Exultant poet of the ordinary man.
British Poet Laureate from 1930. Ran away to sea at 14. Worked for a time
in New York. In his poetry, influenced by Kipling; in novels, by Conrad. Best-
known volumes of verse: *Salt-Water Ballads, The Everlasting Mercy, Reynard
the Fox.*

THE WESTERN ISLANDS

ONCE there were two sailors; and one of them was Joe, and the
other one was Jerry, and they were fishermen. And they'd a young
apprentice-feller, and his name was Jim. And he was a great one for
his pot, and Jerry was a wonder at his pipe; and Jim did all the
work, and both of them banged him. So one time Joe and Jerry
were in the beer-house, and there was a young parson there, telling
the folks about foreign things, about plants and that. 'A,' he says,
'what wonders there are in the west.'

" 'What sort of wonders, begging your pardon, sir,' says Joe.
'What sort of wonders might them them be?'

" 'Why, all sorts of wonders,' says the parson. 'Why in the west,'
he says, 'there's things you wouldn't believe. No, you wouldn't be-

lieve; not till you'd seen them,' he says. 'There's diamonds growing on the trees. And great, golden, glittering pearls as common as peastraw. And there's islands in the west. Ah, I could tell you of them. Islands? I rather guess there's islands. None of your Isles of Man. None of your Alderney and Sark. Not in them seas.'

" 'What sort of islands might they be, begging your pardon, sir?' says Jerry.

" 'Why,' he says (the parson feller says), 'ISLANDS. Islands as big as Spain. Islands with rivers of rum and streams of sarsaparilla. And none of your roses. Rubies and ame-thynes is all the roses grows in them parts. With golden stalks to them, and big diamond sticks to them, and the taste of pork-crackling if you eat them. They're the sort of roses to have in your area,' he says.

" 'And what else might there be in them parts, begging your pardon, sir?' says Joe.

" 'Why,' he says, this parson says, 'there's wonders. There's not only wonders but miracles. And not only miracles, but sperrits.'

" 'What sort of sperrits might they be, begging your pardon?' says Jerry, 'Are they rum and that?'

" 'When I says sperrits,' says the parson feller, 'I mean ghosts.'

" 'Of course ye do,' says Joe.

" 'Yes, ghosts' says the parson, 'And by ghosts I mean sperrits. And by sperrits I mean white things. And by white things I mean things as turn your hair white. And there's red devils there, and blue devils there, and a great gold queen a-waiting for a man to kiss her. And the first man as dares to kiss that queen, why he becomes king, and all her sacks of gold become his.'

" 'Begging your pardon, sir,' said Jerry, 'but whereabouts might these here islands be?'

" 'Why, in the west,' says the parson. 'In the west, where the sun sets.'

" 'Ah,' said Joe and Jerry. 'What wonders there are in the world.'

"Now, after that, neither one of them could think of anything but these here western islands. So at last they take their smack, and off they go in search of them. And Joe had a barrel of beer in the bows, and Jerry had a box of twist in the waist, and pore little Jim stood and steered abaft all. And in the evenings Jerry and Joe would bang their pannikins together, and sing of the great times they meant to have when they were married to the queen. Then they would clump pore little Jim across the head, and tell him to watch out, and keep her to her course, or they'd ride him down like you would a main

tack. And he'd better mind his eye, they told him, or they'd make him long to be boiled and salted. And he'd better put more sugar in the tea, they said, or they'd cut him up for cod-bait. And who was he, they asked, to be wanting meat for dinner, when there was that much weevilly biscuit in the bread-barge? And boys was going to the dogs, they said, when limbs the like of him had the heaven-born insolence to want to sleep. And a nice pass things was coming to, they said, when a lad as they'd done everything for, and saved, so to speak, from the workhouse, should go for to snivel when they hit him a clip. If they'd said a word, when they was hit, when they was boys, they told him, they'd have had their bloods drawed, and been stood in the wind to cool. But let him take heed, they said, and be a good lad, and do the work of five, and they wouldn't half wonder, they used to say, as he'd be a man before his mother. So the sun shone, and the stars came out golden, and all the sea was a sparkle of gold with them. Blue was the sea, and the wind blew, too, and it blew Joe and Jerry west as fast as a cat can eat sardines.

"And one fine morning the wind fell calm, and a pleasant smell came over the water, like nutmegs on a rum-milk-punch. Presently the dawn broke. And, lo, and behold, a rousing great wonderful island, all scarlet with coral and with rubies. The surf that was beating on her sands went shattering into silver coins, into dimes; and pesetas, and francs, and fourpenny bits. And the flowers on the cliffs was all one gleam and glitter. And the beauty of that island was a beauty beyond the beauty of Sally Brown, the lady as kept the beer-house. And on the beach of that island, on a golden throne, like, sat a women so lovely that to look at her was as good as a church-service for one.

" 'That's the party I got to kiss,' said Jerry. 'Steady, and beach her, Jim, boy,' he says. 'Run her ashore, lad. That's the party is to be my queen.'

" 'You've got a neck on you, all of a sudden,' said Joe. 'You ain't the admiral of this fleet. Not by a wide road you ain't. I'll do all the kissing as there's any call for. You keep clear, my son.'

" 'Keep clear, is it?' said Jerry. 'You tell me to keep clear? You tell me again, and I'll put a head on you—'ll make you sing like a kettle. Who are you to tell me to keep clear?'

" 'I tell you who I am,' said Joe. 'I'm a better man than you are. That's what I am. I'm Joe the Tank, from Limehouse Basin, and there's no tinker's donkey-boy'll make me stand from under. Who are you to go kissing queens? Who are you that talk so proud and

so mighty? You've a face on you would make a Dago tired. You look like a sea-sick Kanaka that's boxed seven rounds with a buzz-saw. You've no more manners than a hog, and you've a lip on you would fetch the enamel off a cup.'

" 'If it comes to calling names,' said Jerry, 'you ain't the only pebble on the beach. Whatever you might think, I tell you you ain't. You're the round turn and two-half hitches of a figure of fun as makes the angels weep. That's what you are. And you're the right-hand strand, and the left-hand strand, and the centre strand, and the core, and the serving, and the marling, of a three-stranded, left-handed, poorly worked junk of a half-begun and never finished odds and ends of a Port Mahon soldier. You look like a Portuguese drummer. You've a whelky red nose that shines like a port side-light. You've a face like a muddy field where they've been playing football in the rain. Your hair is an insult and a shame. I blush when I look at you. You give me a turn like the first day out to a first voyager. Kiss, will you? Kiss? Man, I tell you you'd paralyze a shark if you kissed him. Paralyze him, strike him cold. That's what a kiss of yours'd do.'

" 'You ought to 'a' been a parson,' said Joe, 'that's what you'd ought. There's many would 'a' paid you for talk like that. But for all your fine talk, and for all your dandy language, you'll not come the old soldier over me. No, nor ten of you. You talk of kissing, when there's a handsome young man, the likes of me, around. Neither you nor ten of you. To hear you talk one'd think you was a Emperor or a Admiral. One would think you was a Bishop or a King. One might mistake you for a General or a Member of Parliament. You might. Straight, you might. A General or a Bishop or a King. And what are you? What are you? I ask you plain. What are you?—I'll tell you what you are.

" 'You're him as hired himself out as a scarecrow, acos no one'd take you as a fo'c'sle hand. You're him as give the colic to a weather-cock. You're him as turned old Mother Bomby's beer. You're him as drowned the duck and stole the monkey. You're him as got the medal give him for having a face that made the bull tame. You're——'

' 'Now don't you cast no more to me," said Jerry. 'For I won't take no lip from a twelve-a-shilling, cent-a-corner, the likes of you are. You're the clippings of old junk, what the Dagoes smoke in cigarettes. A swab, and a-wash-deck-broom, and the half pint of paint'd make a handsomer figger of a man than what you are. I've

862

seen a coir whisk, what they grooms a mule with, as had a sweeter face than you got. So stand aside, before you're put aside. I'm the king of this here island. You can go chase yourself for another. Stand clear, I say, or I'll give you a jog'll make your bells ring.'

"Now, while they were argufying, young Jim, the young apprentice feller, he creeps up to the queen upon the throne. She was beautiful, she was, and she shone in the sun, and she looked straight ahead of her like a wax-work in a show. And in her hand she had a sack full of jewels, and at her feet she had a sack full of gold, and by her side was an empty throne ready for the king she married. But round her right hand there was a red snake, and round her left hand there was a blue snake, and the snakes hissed and twisted, and they showed their teeth full of poison. So Jim looked at the snakes, and he hit them a welt, right and left, and he kissed the lady.

"And immediately all the bells and the birds of the world burst out a-ringing and a-singing. The lady awoke from her sleep, and Jim's old clothes were changed to cloth of gold. And there he was, a king, on the throne besides the lady.

"But the red snake turned to a big red devil who took a-hold of Joe, and the blue snake turned to a big blue devil, who took a-hold of Jerry. And 'Come you here, you brawling pugs,' they said, 'come and shovel sand.' And Joe and Jerry took the spades that were given to them. And 'Dig, now,' said the devils. 'Heave round. Let's see you dig. Dig, you scarecrows. And tell us when you've dug to London.' "

WILLIAM SOMERSET MAUGHAM

WILLIAM SOMERSET MAUGHAM (English, 1874-   ). Popular novelist, playwright and story teller. Early life and study of medicine mirrored in semi-autobiographical novel, *Of Human Bondage* (considered his masterpiece). Others: *The Moon and Sixpence, Cakes and Ale*. Effective society plays: *The Circle, Our Betters*. In his stories (*The Trembling of a Leaf*, including the famous "Rain") he is romancer of the Far East par excellence.

THE PATTERN

PHILIP felt a shiver pass through his heart. He had never before lost a friend of his own age, for the death of Cronshaw, a man so much older than himself, had seemed to come in the normal course

of things. The news gave him a peculiar shock. It reminded him of his own mortality, for like everyone else Philip, knowing perfectly that all men must die, had no intimate feeling that the same must apply to himself; and Hayward's death, though he had long ceased to have any warm feeling for him, affected him deeply. He remembered on a sudden all the good talks they had had, and it pained him to think that they would never talk with one another again; he remembered their first meeting and the pleasant months they had spent together in Heidelberg. Philip's heart sank as he thought of the lost years. He walked on mechanically not noticing where he went, and realised suddenly, with a movement of irritation, that instead of turning down the Haymarket he had sauntered along Shaftesbury Avenue. It bored him to retrace his steps; and besides, with that news, he did not want to read, he wanted to sit alone and think. He made up his mind to go to the British Museum. Solitude was now his only luxury. Since he had been at Lynn's he had often gone there and sat in front of the groups from the Parthenon; and, not deliberately thinking, had allowed their divine masses to rest his troubled soul. But this afternoon they had nothing to say to him, and after a few minutes, impatiently, he wandered out of the room. There were too many people, provincials with foolish faces, foreigners poring over guide-books; their hideousness besmirched the everlasting masterpieces, their restlessness troubled the god's immortal repose. He went into another room and here there was hardly anyone. Philip sat down wearily. His nerves were on edge. He could not get the people out of his mind. Sometimes at Lynn's they affected him in the same way, and he looked at them file past him with horror; they were so ugly and there was such meanness in their faces, it was terrifying; their features were distorted with paltry desires, and you felt they were strange to any ideas of beauty. They had furtive eyes and weak chins. There was no wickedness in them, but only pettiness and vulgarity. Their humour was a low facetiousness. Sometimes he found himself looking at them to see what animal they resembled, (he tried not to, for it quickly became an obsession,) and he saw in them all the sheep or the horse or the fox, or the goat. Human beings filled him with disgust.

But presently the influence of the place descended upon him. He felt quieter. He began to look absently at the tombstones with which the room was lined. They were the work of Athenian stone masons

864

of the fourth and fifth centuries before Christ, and they were very simple, work of no great talent but with the exquisite spirit of Athens upon them; time had mellowed the marble to the colour of honey, so that unconsciously one thought of the bees of Hymettus, and softened their outlines. Some represented a nude figure, seated on a bench, some the departure of the dead from those who loved him, and some the dead clasping hands with one who remained behind. On all was the tragic word farewell; that and nothing more. Their simplicity was infinitely touching. Friend parted from friend, the son from his mother, and the restraint made the survivor's grief more poignant. It was so long, long ago, and century upon century had passed over that unhappiness; for two thousand years those who wept had been dust as those they wept for. Yet the woe was alive still, and it filled Philip's heart so that he felt compassion spring up in it, and he said:

'Poor things, poor things.'

And it came to him that the gaping sight-seers and the fat strangers with their guide-books, and all those mean, common people who thronged the shop, with their trivial desires and vulgar cares, were mortal and must die. They too loved and must part from those they loved, the son from his mother, the wife from her husband; and perhaps it was more tragic because their lives were ugly and sordid, and they knew nothing that gave beauty to the world. There was one stone which was very beautiful, a bas relief of two young men holding each other's hand; and the reticence of line, the simplicity, made one like to think that the sculptor here had been touched with a genuine emotion. It was an exquisite memorial to that than which the world offers but one thing more precious, to a friendship; and as Philip looked at it, he felt the tears come to his eyes. He thought of Hayward and his eager admiration for him when first they met, and how disillusion had come and then indifference, till nothing held them together but habit and old memories. It was one of the queer things of life that you could not imagine existence without him; then separation came, and everything went on in the same way, and the companion who had seemed essential proved unnecessary. Your life proceeded and you did not even miss him. Philip thought of those early days in Heidelberg when Hayward, capable of great things, had been full of enthusiasm for the future, and how, little by little, achieving nothing, he had resigned himself to failure. Now he was dead. His

death had been as futile as his life. He died ingloriously, of a stupid disease, failing once more, even at the end, to accomplish anything. It was just the same now as if he had never lived.

Philip asked himself desperately what was the use of living at all. It all seemed inane. It was the same with Cronshaw: it was quite unimportant that he had lived; he was dead and forgotten, his book of poems sold in remainder by second-hand booksellers; his life seemed to have served nothing except to give a pushing journalist occasion to write an article in a review. And Philip cried out in his soul:

'What is the use of it?'

The effort was so incommensurate with the result. The bright hopes of youth had to be paid for at such a bitter price of disillusionment. Pain and disease and unhappiness weighed down the scale so heavily. What did it all mean? He thought of his own life, the high hopes with which he had entered upon it, the limitations which his body forced upon him, his friendlessness, and the lack of affection which had surrounded his youth. He did not know that he had ever done anything but what seemed best to do, and what a cropper he had come! Other men, with no more advantages than he, succeeded, and others again, with many more, failed. It seemed pure chance. The rain fell alike upon the just and upon the unjust, and for nothing was there a why and a wherefore.

Thinking of Cronshaw, Philip remembered the Persian rug which he had given him, telling him that it offered an answer to his question upon the meaning of life; and suddenly the answer occurred to him: he chuckled: now that he had it, it was like one of the puzzles which you worry over till you are shown the solution and then cannot imagine how it could ever have escaped you. The answer was obvious. Life had no meaning. On the earth, satellite of a star speeding through space, living things had arisen under the influence of conditions which were part of the planet's history; and as there had been a beginning of life upon it so, under the influence of other conditions, there would be an end: man, no more significant than other forms of life, had come not as the climax of creation but as a physical reaction to the environment. Philip remembered the story of the Eastern King who, desiring to know the history of man, was brought by a sage five hundred volumes; busy with affairs of state, he bade him go and condense it; in twenty years the sage returned and his history now was in no more than fifty volumes, but the King, too old then to read so many ponderous

tomes, bade him go and shorten it once more; twenty years passed
again and the sage, old and gray, brought a single book in which
was the knowledge the King had sought; but the King lay on his
deathbed, and he had no time to read even that; and then the sage
gave him the history of man in a single line; it was this: he was
born, he suffered, and he died. There was no meaning in life, and
man by living served no end. It was immaterial whether he was
born or not born, whether he lived or ceased to live. Life was
insignificant and death without consequence. Philip exulted, as he
had exulted in his boyhood when the weight of a belief in God
was lifted from his shoulders: it seemed to him that the last
burden of responsibility was taken from him; and for the first
time he was utterly free. His insignificance was turned to power,
and he felt himself suddenly equal with the cruel fate which had
seemed to persecute him; for, if life was meaningless, the world
was robbed of its cruelty. What he did or left undone did not
matter. Failure was unimportant and success amounted to nothing.
He was the most inconsiderable creature in that swarming mass of
mankind which for a brief space occupied the surface of the earth;
and he was almighty because he had wrenched from chaos the
secret of its nothingness. Thoughts came tumbling over one another
in Philip's eager fancy, and he took long breaths of joyous satisfaction. He felt inclined to leap and sing. He had not been so
happy for months.

'Oh, life,' he cried in his heart, 'Oh life, where is thy sting?'

For the same uprush of fancy which had shown him with all
the force of mathematical demonstration that life had no meaning,
brought with it another idea; and that was why Cronshaw, he
imagined, had given him the Persian rug. As the weaver elaborated
his pattern for no end but the pleasure of his aesthetic sense, so
might a man live his life, or if one was forced to believe that his
actions were outside his choosing, so might a man look at his life,
that it made a pattern. There was as little need to do this as there
was use. It was merely something he did for his own pleasure. Out
of the manifold events of his life, his deeds, his feelings, his thoughts,
he might make a design, regular, elaborate, complicated, or beautiful; and though it might be no more than an illusion that he had
the power of selection, though it might be no more than a fantastic
legerdemain in which appearances were interwoven with moonbeams, that did not matter: it seemed, and so to him it was. In
the vast warp of life, (a river arising from no spring and flowing

867

endlessly to no sea,) with the background to his fancies that there was no meaning and that nothing was important, a man might get a personal satisfaction in selecting the various strands that worked out the pattern. There was one pattern, the most obvious, perfect, and beautiful, in which a man was born, grew to manhood, married, produced children, toiled for his bread, and died; but there were others intricate and wonderful, in which happiness did not enter and in which success was not attempted; and in them might be discovered a more troubling grace. Some lives, and Hayward's was among them, the blind indifference of chance cut off while the design was still imperfect; and then the solace was comfortable that it did not matter; other lives, such as Cronshaw's, offered a pattern which was difficult to follow: the point of view had to be shifted and old standards had to be altered before one could understand that such a life was its own justification. Philip thought that in throwing over the desire for happiness he was casting aside the last of his illusions. His life had seemed horrible when it was measured by something else. Happiness mattered as little as pain. They came in, both of them, as all the other details of his life came in, to the elaboration of the design. He seemed for an instant to stand above the accidents of his existence, and he felt that they could not affect him again as they had done before. Whatever happened to him now would be one more motive to add to the complexity of the pattern, and when the end approached he would rejoice in its completion. It would be a work of art, and it would be none the less beautiful because he alone knew of its existence, and with his death it would at once cease to be.

Philip was happy.

GUY DE MAUPASSANT

GUY DE MAUPASSANT (French, 1850-1893). The great realist of French literature. Strongly influenced by Flaubert, a personal friend. After success at 30, became one of most popular French writers. Ten years later he was hopelessly insane. Slick craftsmanship makes him father of modern commercial story. Most famous tale: *"Boule de Suif."* Novels: *Une Vie, Bel-Ami.*

THE NECKLACE

SHE was one of those pretty and charming girls who are sometimes, as if by a mistake of destiny, born in a family of clerks. She had

no dowry, no expectations, no means of being known, understood, loved, wedded, by any rich and distinguished man; and she let herself be married to a little clerk at the Ministry of Public Instruction.

She dressed plainly because she could not dress well, but she was as unhappy as though she had really fallen from her proper station; since with women there is neither caste nor rank; and beauty, grace, and charm act instead of family and birth. Natural fineness, instinct for what is elegant, suppleness of wit, are the sole hierarchy, and make from women of the people the equals of the very greatest ladies.

She suffered ceaselessly, feeling herself born for all the delicacies and all the luxuries. She suffered from the poverty of her dwelling, from the wretched look of the walls, from the worn-out chairs, from the ugliness of the curtains. All those things, of which another woman of her rank would never even have been conscious, tortured her and made her angry. The sight of the little Breton peasant who did her humble housework aroused in her regrets which were despairing, and distracted dreams. She thought of the silent ante-chambers hung with Oriental tapestry, lit by tall bronze candelabra, and of the two great footmen in knee-breeches who sleep in the big armchairs, made drowsy by the heavy warmth of the hot-air stove. She thought of the long *salons* fitted up with ancient silk, of the delicate furniture carrying priceless curiosities, and of the coquettish perfumed boudoirs made for talks at five o'clock with intimate friends, with men famous and sought after, whom all women envy and whose attention they all desire.

When she sat down to dinner, before the round table covered with a table-cloth three days old, opposite her husband, who uncovered the soup tureen and declared with an enchanted air, "Ah, the good *pot-au-feu!* I don't know anything better than that," she thought of dainty dinners, of shining silverware, of tapestry which peopled the walls with ancient personages and with strange birds flying in the midst of a fairy forest; and she thought of delicious dishes served on marvelous plates, and of the whispered gallantries which you listen to with a sphinx-like smile, while you are eating the pink flesh of a trout or the wings of a quail.

She had no dresses, no jewels, nothing. And she loved nothing but that; she felt made for that. She would so have liked to please, to be envied, to be charming, to be sought after.

She had a friend, a former schoolmate at the convent, who was

869

rich, and whom she did not like to go and see any more, because she suffered so much when she came back.

But, one evening, her husband returned home with a triumphant air, and holding a large envelope in his hand.

"There," said he, "here is something for you."

She tore the paper sharply, and drew out a printed card which bore these words:

"The Minister of Public Instruction and Mme. Georges Ramponneau request the honor of M. and Mme. Loisel's company at the palace of the Ministry on Monday evening, January 18th."

Instead of being delighted, as her husband hoped, she threw the invitation on the table with disdain, murmuring:

"What do you want me to do with that?"

"But, my dear, I thought you would be glad. You never go out, and this is such a fine opportunity. I had awful trouble to get it. Every one wants to go; it is very select, and they are not giving many invitations to clerks. The whole official world will be there."

She looked at him with an irritated eye, and she said, impatiently:

"And what do you want me to put on my back?"

He had not thought of that; he stammered:

"Why, the dress you go to the theater in. It looks very well, to me."

He stopped, distracted, seeing that his wife was crying. Two great tears descended slowly from the corners of her eyes towards the corners of her mouth. He stuttered:

"What's the matter? What's the matter?"

But, by a violent effort, she had conquered her grief, and she replied, with a calm voice, while she wiped her wet cheeks:

"Nothing. Only I have no dress, and therefore I can't go to this ball. Give your card to some colleague whose wife is better equipped than I."

He was in despair. He resumed:

"Come, let us see, Mathilde. How much would it cost, a suitable dress, which you could use on other occasions, something very simple?"

She reflected several seconds, making her calculations and wondering also what sum she could ask without drawing on herself an immediate refusal and a frightened exclamation from the economical clerk.

Finally, she replied, hesitatingly:

"I don't know exactly, but I think I could manage it with four hundred francs."

He had grown a little pale, because he was laying aside just that amount to buy a gun and treat himself to a little shooting next summer on the plain of Nanterre, with several friends who went to shoot larks down there, of a Sunday.

But he said:

"All right. I will give you four hundred francs. And try to have a pretty dress."

The day of the ball drew near, and Mme. Loisel seemed sad, uneasy, anxious. Her dress was ready, however. Her husband said to her one evening:

"What is the matter? Come, you've been so queer these last three days."

And she answered:

"It annoys me not to have a single jewel, not a single stone, nothing to put on. I shall look like distress. I should almost rather not go at all."

He resumed:

"You might wear natural flowers. It's very stylish at this time of the year. For ten francs you can get two or three magnificent roses."

She was not convinced.

"No; there's nothing more humiliating than to look poor among other women who are rich."

But her husband cried:

"How stupid you are! Go look up your friend Mme. Forestier, and ask her to lend you some jewels. You're quite thick enough with her to do that."

She uttered a cry of joy:

"It's true. I never thought of it."

The next day she went to her friend and told of her distress.

Mme. Forestier went to a wardrobe with a glass door, took out a large jewel-box, brought it back, opened it, and said to Mme. Loisel:

"Choose, my dear."

She saw first of all some bracelets, then a pearl necklace, then a Venetian cross, gold, and precious stones of admirable workmanship. She tried on the ornaments before the glass, hesitated, could

not make up her mind to part with them, to give them back. She kept asking:

"Haven't you any more?"

"Why, yes. Look. I don't know what you like."

All of a sudden she discovered, in a black satin box, a superb necklace of diamonds; and her heart began to beat with an immoderate desire. Her hands trembled as she took it. She fastened it around her throat, outside her high-necked dress, and remained lost in ecstasy at the sight of herself.

Then she asked, hesitating, filled with anguish:

"Can you lend me that, only that?"

"Why, yes, certainly."

She sprang upon the neck of her friend, kissed her passionately, then fled with her treasure.

The day of the ball arrived. Mme. Loisel made a great success. She was prettier than them all, elegant, gracious, smiling, and crazy with joy. All the men looked at her, asked her name, endeavored to be introduced. All the attachés of the Cabinet wanted to waltz with her. She was remarked by the minister himself.

She danced with intoxication, with passion, made drunk by pleasure, forgetting all, in the triumph of her beauty, in the glory of her success, in a sort of cloud of happiness composed of all this homage, of all this admiration, of all these awakened desires, and of that sense of complete victory which is so sweet to woman's heart.

She went away about four o'clock in the morning. Her husband had been sleeping since midnight, in a little deserted ante-room, with three other gentlemen whose wives were having a very good time.

He threw over her shoulders the wraps which he had brought, modest wraps of common life, whose poverty contrasted with the elegance of the ball dress. She felt this and wanted to escape so as not to be remarked by the other women, who were enveloping themselves in costly furs.

Loisel held her back.

"Wait a bit. You will catch cold outside. I will go and call a cab."

But she did not listen to him, and rapidly descended the stairs. When they were in the street they did not find a carriage; and they began to look for one, shouting after the cabmen whom they saw passing by at a distance.

They went down towards the Seine, in despair, shivering with cold. At last they found on the quay one of those ancient noctambulant coupés which, exactly as if they were ashamed to show their misery during the day, are never seen round Paris until after nightfall.

It took them to their door in the Rue des Martyrs, and once more, sadly, they climbed up homeward. All was ended for her. And as to him, he reflected that he must be at the Ministry at ten o'clock.

She removed the wraps, which covered her shoulders, before the glass, so as once more to see herself in all her glory. But suddenly she uttered a cry. She had no longer the necklace around her neck!

Her husband, already half-undressed, demanded:

"What is the matter with you?"

She turned madly towards him:

"I have—I have—I've lost Mme. Forestier's necklace."

He stood up, distracted.

"What!—how?—Impossible!"

And they looked in the folds of her dress, in the folds of her cloak, in her pockets, everywhere. They did not find it.

He asked:

"You're sure you had it on when you left the ball?"

"Yes, I felt it in the vestibule of the palace."

"But if you had lost it in the street we should have heard it fall. It must be in the cab."

"Yes. Probably. Did you take his number?"

"No. And you, didn't you notice it?"

"No."

They looked, thunderstruck, at one another. At last Loisel put on his clothes.

"I shall go back on foot," said he, "over the whole route which we have taken, to see if I can't find it."

And he went out. She sat waiting on a chair in her ball dress, without strength to go to bed, overwhelmed, without fire, without a thought.

Her husband came back about seven o'clock. He had found nothing.

He went to Police Headquarters, to the newspaper offices, to offer a reward; he went to the cab companies—everywhere, in fact, whither he was urged by the least suspicion of hope.

She waited all day, in the same condition of mad fear before this terrible calamity.

Loisel returned at night with a hollow, pale face; he had discovered nothing.

"You must write to your friend," said he, "that you have broken the clasp of her necklace and that you are having it mended. That will give us time to turn round."

She wrote at his dictation.

At the end of a week they had lost all hope.

And Loisel, who had aged five years, declared:

"We must consider how to replace that ornament."

The next day they took the box which had contained it, and they went to the jeweler whose name was found within. He consulted his books.

"It was not I, madame, who sold that necklace; I must simply have furnished the case."

Then they went from jeweler to jeweler, searching for a necklace like the other, consulting their memories, sick both of them with chagrin and with anguish.

They found, in a shop at the Palais Royal, a string of diamonds which seemed to them exactly like the one they looked for. It was worth forty thousand francs. They could have it for thirty-six.

So they begged the jeweler not to sell it for three days yet. And they made a bargain that he should buy it back for thirty-four thousand francs, in case they found the other one before the end of February.

Loisel possessed eighteen thousand francs which his father had left him. He would borrow the rest.

He did borrow, asking a thousand francs of one, five hundred of another, five louis here, three louis there. He gave notes, took up ruinous obligations, dealt with usurers, and all the race of lenders. He compromised all the rest of his life, risked his signature without even knowing if he could meet it; and, frightened by the pains yet to come, by the black misery which was about to fall upon him, by the prospect of all the physical privations and of all the moral tortures which he was to suffer, he went to get the new necklace, putting down upon the merchant's counter thirty-six thousand francs.

When Mme. Loisel took back the necklace Mme. Forestier said to her, with a chilly manner:

"You should have returned it sooner, I might have needed it."

She did not open the case, as her friend had so much feared. If she had detected the substitution, what would she have thought, what would she have said? Would she not have taken Mme. Loisel for a thief?

Mme. Loisel now knew the horrible existence of the needy. She took her part, moreover, all on a sudden, with heroism. That dreadful debt must be paid. She would pay it. They dismissed their servant; they changed their lodgings; they rented a garret under the roof.

She came to know what heavy housework meant and the odious cares of the kitchen. She washed the dishes, using her rosy nails on the greasy pots and pans. She washed the dirty linen, the shirts, and the dish-cloths, which she dried upon a line; she carried the slops down to the street every morning, and carried up the water, stopping for breath at every landing. And, dressed like a woman of the people, she went to the fruiterer, the grocer, the butcher, her basket on her arm, bargaining, insulted, defending her miserable money sou by sou.

Each month they had to meet some notes, renew others, obtain more time.

Her husband worked in the evening making a fair copy of some tradesman's accounts, and late at night he often copied manuscript for five sous a page.

And this life lasted ten years.

At the end of ten years they had paid everything, everything, with the rates of usury, and the accumulations of the compound interest.

Mme. Loisel looked old now. She had become the woman of impoverished households—strong and hard and rough. With frowsy hair, skirts askew, and red hands, she talked loud while washing the floor with great swishes of water. But sometimes, when her husband was at the office, she sat down near the window, and she thought of that gay evening of long ago, of that ball where she had been so beautiful and so fêted.

What would have happened if she had not lost that necklace? Who knows? who knows? How life is strange and how changeful! How little a thing is needed for us to be lost or to be saved!

But, one Sunday, having gone to take a walk in the Champs Elysées to refresh herself from the labors of the week, she suddenly

875

perceived a woman who was leading a child. It was Mme. Forestier, still young, still beautiful, still charming.

Mme. Loisel felt moved. Was she going to speak to her? Yes, certainly. And now that she had paid, she was going to tell her all about it. Why not?

She went up.

"Good-day, Jeanne."

The other, astonished to be familiarly addressed by this plain good-wife, did not recognize her at all, and stammered:

"But—madame!—I—do not know— You must have mistaken."

"No. I am Mathilde Loisel."

Her friend uttered a cry.

"Oh, my poor Mathilde! How you are changed!"

"Yes, I have had days hard enough, since I have seen you, days wretched enough—and that because of you!"

"Of me! How so?"

"Do you remember that diamond necklace which you lent me to wear at the ministerial ball?"

"Yes. Well?"

"Well, I lost it."

"What do you mean? You brought it back."

"I brought you back another just like it. And for this we have been ten years paying. You can understand that it was not easy for us, us who had nothing. At last it is ended, and I am very glad."

Mme. Forestier had stopped.

"You say that you bought a necklace of diamonds to replace mine?"

"Yes. You never noticed it, then! They were very like."

And she smiled with a joy which was proud and naïve at once.

Mme. Forestier, strongly moved, took her two hands.

"Oh, my poor Mathilde! Why, my necklace was paste. It was worth at most five hundred francs!"

FRANCOIS MAURIAC

FRANÇOIS MAURIAC (French, 1885-   ). Devout and highly principled
Catholic essayist and novelist. Member of French Academy, Nobel Prize-
winner, 1952. A soldier in World War I, member of the Resistance in War II.
His novels (including *A Woman of the Pharisees, Knot of Vipers, The Dark
Angels*) deal primarily with violent passions, in which sinners ultimately
receive grace.

THE ETERNAL BOURGEOISE

A WOMAN who belonged to the highest society of Cortona, a very
pious woman, gave proof of so much devotion to Margaret that
the saint prayed for her benefactress incessantly. One day Christ
spoke to her about this soul. "My daughter," he told her, "tell
your confessor about the shortcomings of her for whom you pray
to Me so often. I shall tell you what they are one after the other
so that your confessor may be able to tell her about them to her
great gain." It is Christ Himself Who proposes this terrifyingly
minute examination of conscience to so many perfect people who,
every week, bring trifles to the confessional and glory in finding
no sin in themselves.

"Tell her that she who is so devoted to you out of love for Me
had, before her marriage, a heart of doubtful virtue. Let her confess
having desired too passionately the man who is now her husband
and of having sought him with immoderate desire. Let her confess
this false virtue in her looks, her words, her gestures. . . .

Let her confess that at the time when a misfortune occurred to
one of her parents, she gave false testimony and helped, as much
as was in her power to do so, to render the judge's sentence unjust,
and that she felt less grief for the degrading record which the
accused thereby incurred than for the money which she made him
lose.

Let her reveal her offense against Me when she betook herself
to the Palace of the Podestat to hear herself proclaimed the most
beautiful among her friends (already queens of beauty!).

Let her admit often having accused servants secretly to their
masters, hoping to win their friendship by an indiscreet zeal in
meddling in their affairs, a zeal which was only hypocrisy since
she had no real affection either for them or for anyone except her
husband and children whom she loved excessively.

Let her reveal her inordinate fondness for delicate foods.

Let her bewail her hardness of heart toward the poor.

Let her admit the use she has made of ill-gotten gains. Let her remember everything she has thus spent. How much money has she not spent in this way, money pilfered from her husband, money coming from frauds, money extorted by violence, money won at gambling. . . .

As the mother of a family, she was in charge of household expenses; let her remember how many useless purchases she made, how many superfluous things she bought with money that was wrongly acquired. . . . (What rich and pious woman ever asks herself questions about 'those things which make one shudder,' which Bourdaloue has denounced as being at the source of every great fortune?).

Let her admit the jealousy that she harbored against her parents who did not support her husband's quarrels, the proud domination she exercised in her husband's family, she who would never have allowed her sister-in-law to behave so in her own. Let her admit her greed in regard to her husband's wards whom she had to take care of because they were poor. Let her remember all the injuries she directed against persons of the household in season and out, and with what pride she adorned her body. . . .

Let her confess the bad things she said and the rash judgments she made concerning the neighbor whose qualities she scorned and disparaged, recalling the faults that she knew about and concealing the good and finding the means of accusing him of other faults of which he was not guilty.

Let her confess the harsh disclosures she made about those who were absent and her flatteries before those who were present.

Let her admit her thirst for honor and praise, her desire to seem richer than others, her jealousy at the idea that others might be superior to her in wealth and beauty, her distraction at church in the presence of other women.

In spite of what I have done for her, I have been unable to attach Myself to her, and if at times she has served Me, it has been out of fear, not out of love.

Although she is free of the vice of impurity, yet she has soiled the marriage bed. She has felt no repugnance at finding herself among those who offend Me in their flesh, she who is full of spiritual vices.

Let her admit how careful she has been to blame others, whether for their ill-gotten gains, their lands, the luxuriousness of their

878

clothes and their perfumes, she who has sought the pleasures of good living and has given alms out of ostentation.

Let her confess her indiscretions concerning her servants, her rash judgments concerning the poor and how she scorned their pleadings, their tears, and their pleasures, their games, and their eating and drinking as well (this last trait is wonderful).

She denies herself nothing in what concerns the number and richness of her garments and does not worry herself at all about covering their nakedness nor appeasing their hunger.

Let her admit having usurped the name which befitted My Mother only when she had herself called Sovereign, she who ridiculed others when they assumed that name.

Although she has moved in the society of the most beautiful and best dressed persons, she has always thought herself superior to them.

Let her admit the frivolity which brings her to exaggerate her sufferings, always regarding them as greater than those of others, she who remains cold and indifferent before their misfortunes.

Let her confess her harshness in regard to her servants to whom she gave no rest after hard work, whether they were ill or not. Instead of the comforting which they needed they received only insults and abuse and were accused of gluttony and negligence. As for herself, their mistress treated herself with high consideration, spoke when she should have kept quiet, and kept quiet when she should have spoken. Let her confess having avoided deformed persons. . . . In spite of all these faults let her have confidence in My mercy. Let her not delay going to her confessor. Yet I say unto you, Margaret, My daughter, that this woman whom you recommend so urgently to My mercy will not fully agree to these favors."

HERMAN MELVILLE

HERMAN MELVILLE (American, 1819-1891). American fiction writer, whose major work, *Moby Dick*, was an utter failure when published—now justly considered one of world's masterpieces. Unable to support family as writer, worked for 20 years as New York Inspector of Customs. His South Sea stories (*Typee, Omoo, Mardi*) enjoyed limited popularity. Navy classic, *Billy Budd*, completed just before death, not published till 1924.

"THE WHALE WATCH" and *"THE CHASE"*
Chapter CXVII

THE four whales slain that evening had died wide apart; one, far to windward; one, less distant, to leeward; one ahead; one astern.

These last three were brought alongside ere nightfall; but the windward one could not be reached till morning; and the boat that had killed it lay by its side all night; and that boat was Ahab's.

The waif-pole was thrust upright into the dead whale's spout-hole and the lantern hanging from its top, cast a troubled flickering glare upon the black, glossy back, and far out upon the midnight waves, which gently chafed the whale's broad flank, like soft surf upon a beach.

Ahab and all his boat's crew seemed asleep but the Parsee; who crouching in the bow, sat watching the sharks, that spectrally played round the whale, and tapped the light cedar planks with their tails. A sound like the moaning in squadrons over Asphaltites of unforgiven ghosts of Gomorrah, ran shuddering through the air.

Started from his slumbers, Ahab, face to face, saw the Parsee; and hooped round by the gloom of the night they seemed the last men in a flooded world. "I have dreamed it again," said he.

"Of the hearses? Have I not said, old man, that neither hearse nor coffin can be thine?"

"And who are hearsed that die on the sea?"

"But I said, old man, that ere thou couldst die on this voyage, two hearses must verily be seen by thee on the sea; the first not made by mortal hands; and the visible wood of the last one must be grown in America."

"Aye, aye! a strange sight that, Parsee:—a hearse and its plumes floating over the ocean with the waves for the pall-bearers. Ha! Such a sight we shall not soon see."

"Believe it or not, thou canst not die till it be seen, old man."

"And what was that saying about thyself?"

"Though it come to the last, I shall still go before thee thy pilot."

"And when thou art so gone before—if that ever befall—then ere I can follow, thou must still appear to me, to pilot me still?— Was it not so? Well, then, did I believe all ye say, oh my pilot! I have here two pledges that I shall yet slay Moby-Dick and survive it."

"Take another pledge, old man," said the Parsee, as his eyes lighted up like fireflies in the gloom—"Hemp only can kill thee."

"The gallows, ye mean.—I am immortal then, on land and on sea," cried Ahab, with a laugh of derision:—"Immortal on land and on sea!"

Both were silent again, as one man. The gray dawn came on, and the slumbering crew arose from the boat's bottom, and ere noon the dead whale was brought to the ship.

. . . "Great God! but for one single instant show thyself," cried Starbuck; "never, never wilt thou capture him, old man—In Jesus' name no more of this, that's worse than devil's madness. Two days chased; twice stove to splinters; thy very leg once more snatched from under thee; thy evil shadow gone—all good angels mobbing thee with warnings:—what more wouldst thou have?—Shall we keep chasing this murderous fish till he swamps the last man? Shall we be dragged by him to the bottom of the sea? Shall we be towed by him to the infernal world? Oh, oh,—Impiety and blasphemy to hunt him more!"

"Starbuck, of late I've felt strangely moved to thee; ever since that hour we both saw—thou know'st what, in one another's eyes. But in this matter of the whale, be the front of thy face to me as the palm of this hand—a lipless, unfeatured blank. Ahab is for ever Ahab, man. This whole act's immutably decreed. 'Twas re-hearsed by thee and me a billion years before this ocean rolled. Fool! I am the Fates' lieutenant; I act under orders. Look thou, underling! that thou obeyest mine.—Stand round me, men. Ye see an old man cut down to the stump; leaning on a shivered lance; propped up on a lonely foot. 'Tis Ahab—his body's part; but Ahab's soul's a centipede, that moves upon a hundred legs. I feel strained, half-stranded, as ropes that tow dismasted frigates in a gale; and I may look so. But ere I break, ye'll hear me crack; and till ye hear *that*, know that Ahab's hawser tows his purpose yet. Believe ye, men, in the things called omens? Then laugh aloud, and cry encore! For ere they drown, drowning things will twice rise to the surface; then rise again, to sink for evermore. So with Moby-Dick —two days he's floated—to-morrow will be the third. Aye, men, he'll rise once more,—but only to spout his last! D'ye feel brave, men, brave?"

"As fearless fire," cried Stubb.

"And as mechanical," muttered Ahab. Then as the men went forward, he muttered on: "The things called omens! And yesterday I talked the same to Starbuck there, concerning my broken boat. Oh! how valiantly I seek to drive out of others' hearts what's clinched so fast in mine!—The Parsee—the Parsee!—gone, gone? and he was to go before:—but still was to be seen again ere I could perish—How's that?—There's a riddle now might baffle all

the lawyers backed by the ghosts of the whole line of judges:—like a hawk's beak it pecks my brain. *I'll, I'll* solve it, though!"

When dusk descended, the whale was still in sight to leeward.

So once more the sail was shortened, and everything passed nearly as on the previous night; only, the sound of hammers, and the hum of the grindstone was heard till nearly daylight, as the men toiled by lanterns in the complete and careful rigging of the spare boats and sharpening their fresh weapons for the morrow. Meantime, of the broken keel of Ahab's wrecked craft the carpenter made him another leg; while still as on the night before, slouched Ahab stood fixed within his scuttle; his hid, heliotrope glance anticipatingly gone backward on its dial; sat due eastward for the earliest sun. . . .

Chapter CXXXV

. . . The boats had not gone very far, when by a signal from the mastheads—a downward pointed arm, Ahab knew that the whale had sounded; but intending to be near him at the next rising, he held on his way a little sideways from the vessel; the becharmed crew maintaining the profoundest silence, as the head-beat waves hammered and hammered against the opposing bow.

"Drive, drive in your nails, oh ye waves! to their uttermost heads drive them in! ye but strike a thing without a lid; and no coffin and no hearse can be mine:—and hemp only can kill me! Ha! ha!"

Suddenly the waters around them slowly swelled in broad circles; then quickly upheaved, as if sideways sliding from a submerged berg of ice, swiftly rising to the surface. A low rumbling sound was heard; a subterraneous hum; and then all held their breaths; as bedraggled with trailing ropes, and harpoons, and lances, a vast form shot lengthwise, but obliquely from the sea. Shrouded in a thin drooping veil of mist, it hovered for a moment in the rainbowed air; and then fell swamping back into the deep. Crushed thirty feet upwards, the waters flashed for an instant like heaps of fountains, then brokenly sank in a shower of flakes, leaving the circling surface creamed like new milk round the marble trunk of the whale.

"Give way!" cried Ahab to the oarsmen, and the boats darted forward to the attack; but maddened by yesterday's fresh irons that corroded in him, Moby Dick seemed combinedly possessed by

all the angels that fell from heaven. The wide tiers of welded tendons overspreading his broad white forehead, beneath the transparent skin, looked knitted together; as head on, he came churning his tail among the boats; and once more flailed them apart; spilling out the irons and lances from the two mates' boats, and dashing in one side of the upper part of their bows, but leaving Ahab's almost without a scar.

While Daggoo and Queequeg were stopping the strained planks; and as the whale swimming out from them, turned, and showed one entire flank as he shot by them again; at that moment a quick cry went up. Lashed round and round to the fish's back; pinioned in the turns upon turns in which, during the past night, the whale had reeled the involutions of the lines around him, the half torn body of the Parsee was seen; his sable raiment frayed to shreds; his distended eyes turned full upon old Ahab.

The harpoon dropped from his hand.

"Befooled, befooled!"—drawing in a long lean breath—"Aye, Parsee! I see thee again.—Aye, and thou goest before; and this, *this* then is the hearse that thou didst promise. But I hold thee to the last letter of thy word. Where is the second hearse? Away, mates, to the ship! those boats are useless now; repair them if ye can in time, and return to me; if not, Ahab is enough to die—Down, men! the first thing that but offers to jump from this boat I stand in, that thing I harpoon. Ye are not other men, but my arms and my legs; and so obey me.—Where's the whale? gone down again?"

But he looked too nigh the boat; for as if bent upon escaping with the corpse he bore, and as if the particular place of the last encounter had been a stage in his leeward voyage, Moby-Dick was now again steadily swimming forward; and had almost passed the ship,—which thus far had been sailing in the contrary direction to him, though for the present her headway had been stopped. He seemed swimming with his utmost velocity, and now only intent upon pursuing his own straight path in the sea.

"Oh! Ahab," cried Starbuck, "not too late is it, even now, the third day, to desist. See! Moby-Dick seeks thee not. It is thou, thou, that madly seekest him!" ...

From the ship's bows, nearly all the seamen now hung inactive; hammers, bits of plank, lances, and harpoons, mechanically retained in their hands, just as they had darted from their various employments; all their enchanted eyes intent upon the whale, which from side to side strangely vibrating his predestinating head, sent a

broad band of overspreading semicircular foam before him as he rushed. Retribution, swift vengeance, eternal malice were in his whole aspect, and spite of all that mortal man could do, the solid white buttress of his forehead smote the ship's starboard bow, till men and timbers reeled. Some fell flat upon their faces. Like dislodged trucks, the heads of the harpooneers aloft shook on their bull-like necks. Through the breach, they heard the waters pour, as mountain torrents down a flume.

"The ship! The hearse!—the second hearse!" cried Ahab from the boat; "its wood could only be American!"

Diving beneath the settling ship, the whale ran quivering along its keel; but turning under water, swiftly shot to the surface again, far off the other bow, but within a few yards of Ahab's boat, where, for a time, he lay quiescent.

"I turn my body from the sun. What ho, Tashtego! let me hear thy hammer. Oh! ye three unsurrendered spires of mine; thou uncracked keel; the only god-bullied hull; thou firm deck, and haughty helm, and Pole-pointed prow,—death-glorious ship! must ye then perish, and without me? Am I cut off from the last fond pride of meanest shipwrecked captains? Oh, lonely death on lonely life! Oh, now I feel my topmost greatness lies in my topmost grief! Ho, ho! from all your furthest bounds, pour ye now in, ye bold billows of my whole foregone life, and top this one piled comber of my death! Towards thee I roll, thou all-destroying but unconquering whale; to the last I grapple with thee; from hell's heart I stab at thee; for hate's sake I spit my last breath at thee. Sink all coffins and hearses to one common pool! and since neither can be mine, let me then tow to pieces, while still chasing thee, though tied to thee, thou damned whale! *Thus* I give up the spear!"

The harpoon was darted; the stricken whale flew forward; with igniting velocity the line ran through the groove;—ran foul. Ahab stooped to clear it; he did clear it; but the flying turn caught him round the neck, and voicelessly as Turkish mutes bowstring their victim, he was shot out of the boat, ere the crew knew he was gone. Next instant, the heavy eye-splice in the rope's final end flew out of the stark-empty tub, knocked down an oarsman, and smiting the sea, disappeared in its depths.

For an instant, the tranced boat's crew stood still; then turned. "The ship? Great God, where is the ship?" Soon they through dim, bewildering mediums saw her sidelong fading phantom, as in the gaseous Fata Morgana; only the uppermost masts out of water;

while fixed by infatuation, or fidelity, or fate, to their once lofty perches, the pagan harpooneers still maintained their sinking lookouts on the sea. And now, concentric circles seized the lone boat itself, and all its crew, and each floating oar, and every lance-pole, and spinning, animate and inanimate, all round and round in one vortex, carried the smallest chip of the Pequod out of sight.

But as the last whelmings intermixingly poured themselves over the sunken head of the Indian at the mainmast, leaving a few inches of the erect spar yet visible, together with long streaming yards of the flag, which calmly undulated, with ironical coincidings, over the destroying billows they almost touched;—at that instant, a red arm and a hammer hovered backwardly uplifted in the open air, in the act of nailing the flag faster and yet faster to the subsiding spar. A sky-hawk that tauntingly had followed the main-truck downwards from its natural home among the stars, pecking at the flag, and incommoding Tashtego there; this bird now chanced to intercept its broad fluttering wings between the hammer and the wood; and simultaneously feeling that ethereal thrill, the submerged savage beneath, in his death-gasp, kept his hammer frozen there; and so the bird of heaven, with arch-angelic shrieks, and his imperial beak thrust upwards, and his whole captive form folded in the flag of Ahab, went down with his ship, which, like Satan, would not sink to hell till she had dragged a living part of heaven along with her, and helmeted herself with it.

Now small fowls flew screaming over the yet yawning gulf; a sullen white surf beat against its steep sides; then all collapsed, and the great shroud of the sea rolled on as it rolled five thousand years ago.

MENG HAO-JAN

MÊNG HAO-JAN (Chinese, 689-740). Political satirist and lyricist. Spent early days studying in the mountains. When he failed to pass official examination, decided to devote remaining life to literature. Satirical poems incurred Emperor's wrath. Friend and disciple of famous Buddhist poet, Wang Wei.

THE LOST ONE

The red gleam o'er the mountains
  Goes wavering from sight,
And the quiet moon enhances
  The loveliness of night.

I open wide my casement
  To breathe the rain-cooled air,
And mingle with the moonlight
  The dark waves of my hair.

The night wind tells me secrets
  Of lotus lilies blue;
And hour by hour the willows
  Shake down the chiming dew.

I fain would take the zither,
  By some stray fancy led;
But there are none to hear me,
  And who can charm the dead?

So all my day-dreams follow
  The bird that leaves the nest;
And in the night I gather
  The lost one to my breast.

A FRIEND EXPECTED

Over the chain of giant peaks
  The great red sun goes down,
And in the stealthy floods of night
  The distant valleys drown.

Yon moon that cleaves the gloomy pines
  Has freshness in her train;
Low wind, faint stream, and waterfall
  Haunt me with their refrain.

The tired woodman seeks his cot
  That twinkles up the hill;
And sleep has touched the wanderers
  That sang the twilight still.

To-night—ah! beauty of to-night
  I need my friend to praise,
So take the lute to lure him on
  Through the frgrant, dew-lit ways.

GEORGE MEREDITH

GEORGE MEREDITH (English, 1828-1909). Long ignored because of his
halting style, later became revered as master of Victorian novel. Striking
creator of human portraits in *The Egoist, Diana of the Crossways*. Elaborate
analyst of psychological situations, in the light of what he called "the comic
spirit." Best poem, *Modern Love*, is based on his own first marriage.

THE PUNISHMENT OF SHAHPESH, THE
PERSIAN, ON KHIPIL, THE BUILDER

THEY relate that Shahpesh, the Persian, commanded the building
of a palace, and Khipil was his builder. The work lingered from
the first year of the reign of Shahpesh even to his fourth. One day
Shahpesh went to the river-side where it stood, to inspect it. Khipil
was sitting on a marble slab among the stones and blocks; round
him stretched lazily the masons and stonecutters and slaves of
burden; and they with the curve of humorous enjoyment on their
lips, for he was reciting to them adventures, interspersed with
anecdotes and recitations and poetic instances, as was his wont.
They were like pleased flocks whom the shepherd hath led to a
pasture freshened with brooks, there to feed indolently; he, the
shepherd, in the midst.

Now, the King said to him, "O Khipil, show me my palace where
it standeth, for I desire to gratify my sight with its fairness."

Khipil abased himself before Shahpesh, and answered, " 'Tis
even here, O King of the age, where thou delightest the earth with
thy foot and the ear of thy slave with sweetness. Surely a site of
vantage, one that dominateth earth, air, and water, which is the
builder's first and chief requisition for a noble palace, a palace to
fill foreign kings and sultans with the distraction of envy; and it
is, O Sovereign of the time, a site, this site I have chosen, to occupy
the tongues of travellers and awaken the flights of poets!"

Shahpesh smiled and said, "The site is good! I laud the site!
Likewise I laud the wisdom of Ebn Busrac, where he exclaims:

> *"Be sure, where Virtue faileth to appear,*
> *For her a gorgeous mansion men will rear;*
> *And day and night her praises will be heard,*
> *Where never yet she spake a single word."*

Then said he, "O Khipil, my builder, there was once a farm-servant that, having neglected in the seed-time to sow, took to singing the richness of his soil when it was harvest, in proof of which he displayed the abundance of weeds that coloured the land everywhere. Discover to me now the completeness of my halls and apartments, I pray thee, O Khipil, and be the excellence of thy construction made visible to me!"

Quoth Khipil, "To hear is to obey."

He conducted Shahpesh among the unfinished saloons and imperfect courts and roofless rooms, and by half-erected obelisks, and columns pierced and chipped, of the palace of his building. And he was bewildered at the words spoken by Shahpesh; but now the King exalted him, and admired the perfection of his craft, the greatness of his labour, the speediness of his construction, his assiduity; feigning not to behold his negligence.

Presently they went up winding balusters to a marble terrace, and the King said, "Such is thy devotion and constancy in toil, O Khipil, that thou shalt walk before me here."

He then commanded Khipil to precede him, and Khipil was heightened with the honour. When Khipil had paraded a short space he stopped quickly, and said to Shahpesh, "Here is, as it chanceth, a gap, O King! and we can go no further this way."

Shahpesh said, "All is perfect, and it is my will thou delay not to advance."

Khipil cried, "The gap is wide, O mighty King, and manifest, and it is an incomplete part of thy palace."

Then said Shahpesh, "O Khipil, I see no distinction between one part and another; excellent are all parts in beauty and proportion, and there can be no part incomplete in this palace that occupieth the builder four years in its building: so advance, do my bidding."

Khipil yet hesitated, for the gap was of many strides, and at the bottom of the gap was a deep water, and he one that knew not the motion of swimming. But Shahpesh ordered his guard to point their arrows in the direction of Khipil, and Khipil stepped forward hurriedly, and fell in the gap, and was swallowed by the water below. When he rose the second time, succour reached him, and he was drawn to land trembling, his teeth chattering. And Shahpesh praised him, and said, "This is an apt contrivance for a bath, Khipil O my builder! well conceived; one that taketh by surprise; and it shall be thy reward daily when much talking hath fatigued thee."

Then he bade Khipil lead him to the hall of state. And when they were there Shahpesh said, "For a privilege, and as a mark of my approbation, I give thee permission to sit in the marble chair of yonder throne, even in my presence, O Khipil."

Khipil said, "Surely, O King, the chair is not yet executed."

And Shahpesh exclaimed, "If this be so, thou art but the length of thy measure on the ground, O talkative one!"

Khipil said, "Nay, 'tis not so, O King of splendours! blind that I am! yonder 's indeed the chair."

And Khipil feared the King, and went to the place where the chair should be, and bent his body in a sitting posture, eyeing the King, and made pretence to sit in the chair of Shahpesh, as in conspiracy to amuse his master.

Then said Shahpesh, "For a token that I approve thy execution of the chair, thou shalt be honoured by remaining seated in it up to the hour of noon; but move thou to the right or to the left, showing thy soul insensible of the honour done thee, transfixed thou shalt be with twenty arrows and five."

The King then left him with a guard of twenty-five of his bodyguard; and they stood around him with bent bows, so that Khipil dared not move from his sitting posture. And the masons and the people crowded to see Khipil sitting on his master's chair, for it became rumoured about. When they beheld him sitting upon nothing, and he trembling to stir for fear of the loosening of the arrows, they laughed so that they rolled upon the floor of the hall, and the echoes of laughter were a thousand-fold. Surely the arrows of the guards swayed with the laughter that shook them.

Now, when the time had expired for his sitting in the chair, Shahpesh returned to him, and he was cramped, pitiable to see; and Shahpesh said, "Thou hast been exalted above men, O Khipil! for that thou didst execute for thy master has been found fitting for thee."

Then he bade Khipil lead the way to the noble gardens of dalliance and pleasure that he had planted and contrived. And Khipil went in that state described by the poet, when we go draggingly, with remonstrating members,

> Knowing a dreadful strengh behind,
> And a dark fate before.

They came to the gardens, and behold, these were full of weeds and nettles, the fountains dry, no tree to be seen—a desert. And Shahpesh

cried, "This is indeed of admirable design, O Khipil! Feelest thou
not the coolness of the fountains?—their refreshingness? Truly I
am grateful to thee! And these flowers, pluck me now a handful,
and tell me of their perfume."

Khipil plucked a handful of the nettles that were there in the place
of flowers, and put his nose to them before Shahpesh, till his nose
was reddened; and desire to rub it waxed in him, and possessed him,
and became a passion, so that he could scarce refrain from rubbing
it even in the King's presence. And the King encouraged him to
sniff and enjoy their fragrance, repeating the poet's words:

> *Methinks I am a lover and a child,*
> *A little child and happy lover, both!*
> *When by the breath of flowers I am beguiled*
> *From sense of pain, and lulled in odorous sloth.*
> *So I adore them, that no mistress sweet*
> *Seems worthier of the love which they awake:*
> *In innocence and beauty more complete,*
> *Was never maiden cheek in morning lake.*
> *Oh, while I live, surround me with fresh flowers,*
> *Oh, when I die, then bury me in their bowers!*

And the King said, "What sayest thou, O my builder? that is a
fair quotation, applicable to thy feelings, one that expresseth them?

Khipil answered, " 'Tis eloquent, O great King! comprehensiveness would be its portion, but that it alludeth not to the delight of
chafing."

Then Shahpesh laughed, and cried, "Chafe not! it is an ill thing
and a hideous! This nosegay, O Khipil, it is for thee to present to
thy mistress. Truly she will receive thee well after its presentation!
I will have it now sent in thy name, with word that thou followest
quickly. And for thy nettled nose, surely if the whim seize thee that
thou desirest its chafing, to thy neighbour is permitted what to thy
hand is refused."

The King set a guard upon Khipil to see that his orders were
executed, and appointed a time for him to return to the gardens.

At the hour indicated Khipil stood before Shahpesh again. He was
pale, saddened; his tongue drooped like the tongue of a heavy bell,
that when it soundeth giveth forth mournful sounds only: he had
also the look of one battered with many beatings. So the King said,
"How of the presentation of the flowers of thy culture, O Khipil?"

890

He answered, "Surely, O King, she received me with wrath, and I am shamed by her."

And the King said, "How of my clemency in the matter of the chafing?"

Khipil answered, "O King of splendours! I made petition to my neighbours whom I met, accosting them civilly and with imploring, for I ached to chafe, and it was the very raging thirst of desire to chafe that was mine, devouring eagerness for solace of chafing. And they chafed me, O King; yet not in those parts which throbbed for the chafing, but in those which abhorred it."

Then Shahpesh smiled and said, " 'Tis certain that the magnanimity of monarchs is as the rain that falleth, the sun that shineth: and in this spot it fertilizeth richness; in that encourageth rankness. So art thou but a weed, O Khipil! and my grace is thy chastisement."

Now, the King ceased not persecuting Khipil, under pretence of doing him honour and heaping favours on him. Three days and three nights was Khipil gasping without water, compelled to drink the drought of the fountain, as an honour at the hands of the King. And he was seven days and seven nights made to stand with stretched arms, as they were the branches of a tree, in each hand a pomegranate. And Shahpesh brough the people of his court to regard the wondrous pomegranate-shoot planted by Khipil, very wondrous, and a new sort, worthy the gardens of a King. So the wisdom of the King was applauded, and men wotted he knew how to punish offences in coin, by the punishment inflicted on Khipil the builder. Before that time his affairs had languished, and the currents of business instead of flowing had become stagnant pools. It was the fashion to do as did Khipil, and fancy the tongue a constructor rather than a commentator; and there is a doom upon that people and that man which runneth to seed in gabble, as the poet says in his wisdom:

If thou wouldst be famous, and rich in splendid fruits,
Leave to bloom the flower of things, and dig among the roots.

Truly after Khipil's punishment there were few in the dominions of Shahpesh who sought to win the honours bestowed by him on gabblers and idlers: as again the poet:

When to loquacious fools with patience rare
I listen, I have thoughts of Khipil's chair:
His bath, his nosegay, and his fount I see,—
Himself stretch'd out as a pomegranate-tree.

And that I am not Shahpesh I regret,
So to inmesh the babbler in his net.
Well is that wisdom worthy to be sung,
Which raised the Palace of the Wagging Tongue!

And whoso is punished after the fashion of Shahpesh, the Persian, on Khipil the Builder, is said to be one "in the Palace of the Wagging Tongue" to this time.

ADAM MICKIEWICZ

ADAM MICKIEWICZ (Polish, 1798-1855). Polish patriot, admired for his deep humanity and sentiment. Arrested for political activities, exiled to Russia. Died in Constantinople trying to raise Polish legion to fight for country's liberation. Playwright and poet. *Pan Tadeusz*, his masterwork, a tribute to the free Poland of his dreams.

ZEVILA

THE HISTORIES of many women of fair virtue and men of courage are recorded in the chronicles of Greece and Rome. So, too, would we find them in our own chronicles of Lithuania if some learned scribe had bent his efforts to the golden stylus and inscribed their stories in our annals; but since none have been moved to do so, I, myself, have resolved to set down here in homely words a short history from our ancient books.

About the year of Our Lord 1400, Prince Koryat, a great and powerful monarch, reigned over Novogrodek and Soinim and Leda. His only daughter, Zevila, (which is in our tongue, Diana), was a comely damsel and fair, but it was rumored that she dreaded the marriage vows, since she shook her head when princes and great barons from distant lands sent their ambassadors requesting her hand, saying she would rest a maid for the days of her life. Howbeit, the Princess Zevila had for a long time loved in her secret heart the Knight Poray, a man of her own country in whose prowess and military cunning her father, Prince Koryat, found good comfort and who, in the absence of the prince, was left in command of the kingdom. Poray was at no small pains to meet his lady in secret, so that they might together unbosom their sweet sentiments the one for the other.

It befell that Prince Koryat when he returned from the wars was sore aggrieved to see a change in his beloved daughter. Her sighs and tears, her ashen cheeks and trembling words when she greeted him, told him at once how matters stood.

"A bawd! My Zevila a bawd!" he cried. "So, thy debauch has led thee to assoil thy father's line. Be gone from my eyes and know that you and the man who brought you to this dishonor shall die a hard death together!"

So it was trumpeted throughout the city that he who would name Zevila's lover and prove the fellow's guilt should receive a rich reward. Yet with all the trumpeting, there was no man who knew about the secret amours of the princess or who would bear a tale to Koryat. Love of Zevila lay deep in the hearts of her subjects and serving folk, and furthermore, no breath of suspicion had fallen upon the Knight Poray who, although he discreetly bewailed his misfortune, showed to the court a jovial face.

When Prince Koryat found that all the trumpeting and inquests stirred no man to speak, he tried with mighty threats to force the secret from his daughter's lips. But no force prevailed upon her.

"My father," she said. "I do confess my own full share of guilt, so punish me, as I am not worthy to cry thee mercy for what I have done; but 'tis not for me to visit like ruin upon another. That would be an even greater offense against the gods."

On hearing this the prince put aside his threatening manner and fell to wheedling. Concealing his ire with silken speech he pledged himself in honeyed words to forgive her of her sin if only he might learn the name of her seducer.

Zevila spoke not, replying only with sobs and tears. Then the prince, waxing angry, commanded that his only daughter be put in chains and cast into a dungeon, from which she was to be led forth anon and put to death.

Now hath any writing man the words to relate the sound of the grief and lamenting that arose from the whole city! The people likened the Princess Zevila in their hearts unto a deity, and looked upon her as a tender mother who helped the poor and softened as much as she could the hard will of the prince. Wherefore, the people surged to the court, weeping bitterly and begging the prince to be merciful toward poor Zevila. But they gained nothing for their tears.

Now in those days, says the history, there was always strife between the men of Lithuania and the Russian *kniazes* or princes. One day the *kniaz* Ivan who wished to take Koryat's city, marched

893

with great haste to spread his camps around the place. He attacked so swiftly that before the full tidings of his deeds were heard much blood had been spilled.

All this happened on the day before the Great Feast, the morning on which Princess Zevila was to die.

Seeing his plight, Prince Koryat prayed Poray to ride forth with a small company of knights and lay on the foe with guile, while the prince strengthened the walls of his city. Poray, not knowing how strong the foe was but never losing heart, rode forth and fell upon Ivan's men who, he found, were out of sorts and craven. He dealt them such a mighty blow that they ran back to their Cossack camp and would have met their doom had not night fallen to end their sorry plight.

Without tarrying Poray set his men about the enemy, encompassing them, then he, himself, rode back into the city to bring the glad tidings to Koryat. The people made merry and the prince rode forth with his train and was full of praise for his knight. He called Poray the defender of the city and bade him to the castle for a mighty feast.

Now when those two were alone Poray fell down at the feet of his prince, speaking many words.

"Forsooth, my lord, my prince," he said, "I have laid heavy defeat upon your foe and, the gods willing, we shall destroy them to the last one, for which I pray as my reward that you do not put to death your only daughter but, by your grace give her to me as wife. For such a reward I swear to repay you with my blood and all my prowess, in all ways I am able."

The prince was angered and spoke thus his displeasure!

"How now, Poray! Why do you make me rejoice and sadden my heart in the same breath. I rejoice in your noble service, but what you ask is not in my power. Our revered forefathers, the Lithuanian princes, have never given their daughters to wed with their subjects, and woe be unto him who follows not the customs of his ancestors. As for the man who, goaded by success and pride, seeketh beyond his station—I will not dwell on that! Still there is the fact that my wanton child has assoiled the honor of our princely house. I trust it was not you who led her astray and put this shame upon her, and yet, why your sudden heart for this trollop?"

Thus they discoursed, then parted, each seeming still in a friendly mind with the other; each having mastered his wrath at least long enough to conceal it. Poray, hurt by his lord's ingratitude and fore-

894

seeing evil for his fortune, let seeds of vengeance spring up in his soul. The prince, no less, was fearful that Poray, for the love if his mistress and his knightly fortune, might seize the capital for his own. Koryat brooded over his need to take the knight's life but he dared not do it at once, because such a deed would sit ill on the people who were now making a great noise and calling Poray their defender. And, furthermore, he himself was still in need of Poray's right hand to crush his enemy.

This, sayeth the chronicle, was on the eve of the Great Feast. In the morning the Princess Zevila was to die.

Meanwhile Ivan, the Russian *kniaz*, hard beaten and surrounded, sat fretting in his camp, waiting for the dawn of the day of his defeat, hopeless, not knowing what more he could do. Suddenly into his tent ran sentries with word that a man in black armor had ridden into the encampment and would have audience with him. Did Ivan wish to hear the man?

When the knight in black armor was fetched he spoke thus to Ivan, "*Kniaz* Ivan, I am Poray who has twice beaten your Russian men and who holds you surrounded. I come to deliver to you the city, the prince, and all his possessions and men-at-arms on one condition: you must swear with a mighty oath that you will not harm our folk with fire or sword and that you will grant me to wife the princess inprisoned in the city, as well as the full protection of your men-at-arms."

As the *kniaz* agreed, cocks crowed in the early light and it was the day of the Great Feast, the day on which the Princess Zevila was to die.

A great tumult arose throughout the whole city, the like of which no man hath the cunning to describe. Those of the townsfolk who were hot of blood and resisted forfeited their heads; their fellows, being struck by fear, yielded themselves to the foe.

Poray then broke open the prison and found—oh, the horror of it!—his beloved, pale as ashes, alone and forgotten on a bed of rags there in the dungeon hole. When she saw Poray she fell in a swoon.

They bore her forth into the light and did what they could, yet she lay as one dead. A great press of folk about her crowded around, crying and calling unto her, but she did not open her eyes.

For a long time she lay there, then between her lids she marveled to see the people pressing about her and among them the armed foe. Then Poray spoke to her, "Pray, quiet your fears, my sweet.

Those are Ivan's men-at-arms who avenge our hurt and will serve as our protectors."

Zevila, hearing this, almost swooned again, but suddenly she drew the sword of Poray and smote him fair in the breast with such might that the blade sank deep.

"Traitor," she cried, "is your homeland such a mean thing in your heart that you would sell it for the smoothness of a woman's flesh? Oh, man of no honor, is this the way you would repay me for my so great a love? And ye, vassals, why do you not spend your wrath and vengeance on Ivan's brigands there?"

So saying, Zevila struck out with the sword at the foemen nigh about; then all the people stirred as though a fire had touched them and each man of them fell upon the unsuspecting Russians with swords and whatever weapons he could find to hand. Many foemen were done to death indoors and in the streets and others were taken alive for captives. Zevila hastened to the place where Prince Koryat, her father, stood fettered to the barricade.

"My father," she cried, then fell down there dead at his feet.

They buried Zevila at the foot of the mountain called Mendoga, and there the people came to make a *kopiec* or memorial mound and planted trees about. And even unto this day the old folk, being thankful to Almighty God that He did not offer them up to disgrace and the scorn of their foe, tell the story of Zevila to their young.

EDNA ST. VINCENT MILLAY

EDNA ST. VINCENT MILLAY (American, 1882-1950). One of the great figures in modern American poetry. Became famous at 19, while still in college, for long poem, "Renascence." In New York, worked with Provincetown Players and Theatre Guild. Among many volumes of verse: *A Few Figs from Thistles, Wine from These Grapes, Fatal Interview.* Her sonnets have been called best since Shakespeare.

WHAT LIPS MY LIPS HAVE KISSED

What lips my lips have kissed, and where, and why,
I have forgotten, and what arms have lain
Under my head till morning; but the rain
Is full of ghosts tonight, that tap and sigh

Upon the glass and listen for reply;
And in my heart there stirs a quiet pain
For unremembered lads that not again
Will turn to me at midnight with a cry.
Thus in the winter stands the lonely tree,
Nor knows what birds have vanished one by one,
Yet knows its boughs more silent than before:
I cannot say what loves have come and gone;
I only know that summer sang in me
A little while, that in me sings no more.

ELEGY BEFORE DEATH

There will be rose and rhododendron
   When you are dead and under ground;
Still will be heard from white syringas
   Heavy with bees, a sunny sound.

Still will the tamaracks be raining
   After the rain has ceased, and still
Will there be robins in the stubble,
   Brown sheep upon the warm green hill.

Spring will not ail nor autumn falter;
   Nothing will know that you are gone,
Saving alone some sullen plough-land
   None but yourself set foot upon;

Saving the may-weed and the pig-weed
   Nothing will know that you are dead,—
These, and perhaps a useless wagon
   Standing beside some tumbled shed.

Oh, there will pass with your great passing
   Little of beauty not your own,—
Only the light from common water,
   Only the grace from simple stone.

JOHN MILTON

JOHN MILTON (English, 1608-1674). The noblest of England's poets. In youth wrote more lyric poems (*Lycidas, L'Allegro, Il Penseroso*). In middle years composed pamphlets on civil and religious liberty (*Areopagitica*) and sonnets. Late in life, blind and in retirement, wrote *Paradise Lost, Paradise Regained, Samson Agonistes*. His command of blank verse unrivaled in English.

IL PENSEROSO

Hence, vain, deluding Joys,
  The brood of Folly without father bred!
How little you bestéd,
  Or fill the fixéd mind with all your toys!
Dwell in some idle brain,
  And fancies fond with gaudy shapes possess,
As thick and numberless
  As the gay motes that people the sunbeams,
Or likest hovering dreams,
  The fickle pensioners of Morpheus' train.
But, hail! thou Goddess, sage and holy!
Hail, divinest Melancholy!
Whose saintly visage is too bright
To hit the sense of human sight,
And therefore to our weaker view,
O'erlaid with black, staid Wisdom's hue;
Black, but such as in esteem
Prince Memnon's sister might beseem,
Or that starred Ethiop queen that strove
To set her beauty's praise above
The Sea-nymphs, and their powers offended.
Yet thou art higher far descended;
Thee bright-haired Vesta long of yore
To solitary Saturn bore;
His daughter she; in Saturn's reign
Such mixture was not held a stain.
Oft in glimmering bowers and glades
He met her, and in secret shades
Of woody Ida's inmost grove,
Whilst yet there was no fear of Jove.

898

Come, pensive Nun, devout and pure,
Sober, steadfast, and demure,
All in a robe of darkest grain,
Flowing with majestic train,
And sable stole of cypress lawn
Over thy decent shoulders drawn.
Come; but keep thy wonted state
With even step, and musing gait,
And looks commercing with the skies
Thy rapt soul sitting in thine eyes;
There, held in holy passion still,
Forget thyself to marble, till
With a sad, leaden, downward cast
Thou fix them on the earth as fast.
And join with thee calm Peace and Quiet,
Spare Fast, that oft with gods doth diet,
And hears the Muses in a ring
Aye round about Jove's altar sing;
And add to these retiréd Leisure,
That in trim gardens takes his pleasure;
But, first and chiefest, with thee bring
Him that yon soars on golden wing,
Guiding the fiery-wheeléd throne,
The cherub Contemplation;
And the mute Silence hist along,
'Less Philomel will deign a song,
In her sweetest, saddest plight,
Smoothing the rugged brow of Night,
While Cynthia checks her dragon yoke
Gently o'er the accustomed oak.
Sweet bird, that shun'st the noise of folly,
Most musical, most melancholy!
Thee, chauntress, oft the woods among
I woo, to hear thy evensong;
And, missing thee, I walk unseen
On the dry, smooth-shaven green,
To behold the wandering moon
Riding near her highest noon,
Like one that had been led astray
Through the heaven's wide, pathless way,

And oft, as if her head she bowed,
Stooping through a fleecy cloud.
Oft, on a plat of rising ground,
I hear the far-off curfew sound,
Over some wide-watered shore,
Swinging slow with sullen roar;
Or, if the air will not permit,
Some still, removéd place will fit,
Where glowing embers through the room
Teach light to counterfeit a gloom,
Far from all resort of mirth,
Save the cricket on the hearth,
Or the bellman's drowsy charm
To bless the doors from nightly harm.
Or let my lamp, at midnight hour,
Be seen in some high, lonely tower
Where I may oft outwatch the Bear,
With thrice-great Hermes, or unsphere
The spirit of Plato, to unfold
What world or what vast regions hold
The immortal mind that hath forsook
Her mansion in this fleshly nook;
And of those demons that are found
In fire, air, flood, or underground,
Whose power hath a true consent
With planet or with element.
Sometime let gorgeous Tragedy
In sceptered pall come sweeping by,
Presenting Thebes, or Pelops' line,
Or the tale of Troy divine.
Or what—though rare—of later age
Ennobled hath the buskined stage.
But, O sad Virgin! that thy power
Might raise Musæus from his bower;
Or bid the soul of Orpheus sing
Such notes as, warbled to the string,
Drew iron tears down Pluto's cheek,
And made Hell grant what love did seek;
Or call up him that left half told
The story of Cambuscan bold,

Of Camball, and of Algarsife,
And who had Canace to wife,
That owned the virtuous ring and glass,
And of the wondrous horse of brass
On which the Tartar king did ride;
And if aught else great bards beside
In sage and solemn tunes have sung,
Of tourneys, and of trophies hung,
Of forests, and enchantments drear,
Where more is meant than meets the ear.
Thus, Night, oft see me in thy pale career,
Till civil-suited Morn appear,
Not tricked and frounced, as she was wont
With the Attic boy to hunt,
But kerchiefed in a comely cloud,
While rocking winds are piping loud,
Or ushered with a shower still,
When the gust hath blown his fill,
Ending on the rustling leaves,
With minute-drops from off the eaves.
And, when the sun begins to fling
His flaring beams, me, Goddess, bring
To archéd walks of twilight groves,
And shadows brown, that Silvan loves,
Of pine, or monumental oak,
Where the rude ax with heavéd stroke
Was never heard the nymphs to daunt,
Or fright them from their hallowed haunt.
There in close covert, by some brook,
Where no profaner eye may look,
Hide me from day's garish eye,
While the bee with honeyed thigh,
That at her flowery work doth sing,
And the waters murmuring,
With such dewy-feathered Sleep.
And let some strange, mysterious dream
Wave at his wings, in airy stream
Of lively portraiture displayed,
Softly on my eyelids laid;
And, as I wake, sweet music breathe
Above, about, or underneath,

Sent by some Spirit to mortals good,
Or the unseen Genius of the wood.
But let my due feet never fail
To walk the studious cloister's pale,
And love the high embowéd roof,
With antique pillars massy-proof,
And storied windows richly dight,
Casting a dim, religious light,
There let the pealing organ blow,
To the full-voiced choir below,
In service high and anthems clear,
As may with sweetness, through mine ear,
And may at last my weary age
Find out the peaceful hermitage
The hairy gown and mossy cell,
Where I may sit and rightly spell
Of every star that heaven doth shew,
And every herb that sips the dew,
Till old experience do attain
To something like prophetic strain.
These pleasures, Melancholy, give,
And I with thee will choose to live.

MOLIERE

MOLIÈRE (Jean-Baptiste Poquelin, French, 1622-1673). France's greatest comic poet. A complete man of the theater, passing his life as actor, playwright, manager. Company he founded is ancestor of present Théatre Française. His greatest works are comedies of character: *Le Tartuffe*, *Dom Juan*, *Le Misanthrope*, *Le Bourgeois Gentilhomme*. Unremitting satirist of sham and hypocrisy. Founded the comedy of manners in France.

FIRST LESSON IN PHILOSOPHY

Philosophy-Master.   What have you a mind to learn?
Mr. Jourdain.   Everything I can, for I have all the desire in the world to be a scholar, and it vexes me that my father and mother had not made me study all the sciences when I was young.

Master. That's a very reasonable feeling. *Nam sine doctrina vita est quasi mortis imago.* You understand that, and are acquainted with the Latin, of course?

M. Jour. Yes; but act as if I were not acquainted with it. Tell me what it means.

Master. It means that "without learning life is as it were an image of death."

M. Jour. That same Latin's in the right.

Master. Don't you know some principles, some rudiments of science?

M. Jour. Oh, yes! I can read and write. . . . But now I must confide a secret to you. I'm in love with a person of quality, and I should be glad if you would help me to write something to her in a short billet-doux, which I'll drop at her feet.

Master. Very well.

M. Jour. That will be gallant, won't it?

Master. Undoubtedly. Is it verse you wish to write to her?

M. Jour. No, no; none of your verse.

Master. You would only have prose?

M. Jour. No, I would neither have verse nor prose.

Master. It must be one or the other.

M. Jour. Why so?

Master. Because, sir, there's nothing to express oneself by but prose or verse.

M. Jour. Is there nothing, then, but verse or prose?

Master. No, sir; whatever is not prose is verse, and whatever is not verse is prose.

M. Jour. And when one talks what may that be, then?

Master. Prose.

M. Jour. How? When I say, "Nicole, bring me my slippers and give me my nightcap," is that prose?

Master. Yes, sir.

M. Jour. On my conscience, I have spoken prose above these forty years without knowing it; and I am hugely obliged to you for informing me of this.

M. Jour. (to his wife). I am ashamed of your ignorance. For example, do you know what it is you now speak?

Mme. Jour. Yes, I know that what I speak is right, and that you ought to think of living in another manner.

903

M. Jour. I don't talk of that. I ask you what the words are that you now speak?

Mme. Jour. They are words that have a good deal of sense in them, and your conduct is by no means such.

M. Jour. I don't talk of that, I tell you. I ask you what it is that I now speak to you, which I say this very moment?

Mme. Jour. Mere stuff.

M. Jour. Pshaw, no, it is not that. That which we both of us say, the language we speak this instant?

Mme. Jour. Well?

M. Jour. How is it called?

Mme. Jour. It's called just what you please to call it.

M. Jour. It's prose, you ignorant creature.

Mme. Jour. Prose?

M. Jour. Yes, prose. Whatever is prose is not verse, and whatever is not verse, is prose. Now, see what it is to study.

THOMAS MOORE

THOMAS MOORE (Irish, 1779-1852). Famous Irish versifier of most melodious rhythms. Student of law in London, government official in Bermuda, traveler in United States and Canada. Author of *Lalla Rookh* and *Life of Sheridan*, but chiefly remembered for his *Irish Melodies*, based on traditional Irish airs.

GO WHERE GLORY WAITS THEE

Go where glory waits thee;
But while fame elates thee,
  Oh still remember me!
When the praise thou meetest
To thine ear is sweetest,
  Oh then remember me!
Other arms may press thee,
Dearer friends caress thee,
All the joys that bless thee
  Sweeter far may be;
But when friends are nearest,
And when joys are dearest
  Oh then remember me!

When at eve thou rovest
By the star thou lovest,
    Oh then remember me!
Think, when home returning,
Bright we've seen it burning,
    Oh thus remember me!
Oft as summer closes,
When thine eye reposes
On its lingering roses,
    Once so loved by thee,
Think of her who wove them,
Her who made thee love them—
    Oh then remember me!

When around thee dying
Autumn leaves are lying,
    Oh then remember me!
And at night when gazing
On the gay hearth blazing,
    Oh still remember me!
Then should music, stealing
All the soul of feeling,
To thy heart appealing,
    Draw one tear from thee;
Then let memory bring thee
Strains I used to sing thee—
    Oh then remember me!

OFT, IN THE STILLY NIGHT

Oft, in the stilly night,
Ere Slumber's chain has bound me,
Fond Memory brings the light
    Of other days around me;
        The smiles, the tears,
        Of boyhood's years,
The words of love then spoken;
        The eyes that shone,
        Now dimm'd and gone,
    The cheerful hearts now broken!

905

Thus, in the stilly night,
 Ere Slumber's chain has bound me,
Sad Memory brings the light
 Of other days around me.

When I remember all
 The friends, so link'd together,
I've seen around me fall,
 Like leaves in wintry weather;
  I feel like one,
  Who treads alone
Some banquet-hall deserted,
  Whose lights are fled,
  Whose garlands dead,
And all but he departed!
Thus, in the stilly night,
 Ere Slumber's chain has bound me,
Sad Memory brings the light
 Of other days around me.

SWEET INNISFALLEN

Sweet Innisfallen, fare thee well,
May calm and sunshine long be thine!
How fair thou art let others tell—
 To *feel* how fair shall long be mine.

Sweet Innisfallen, long shall dwell
 In memory's dream that sunny smile,
Which o'er thee on that evening fell
 When first I saw thy fairy isle.

'Twas light, indeed, too blest for one,
 Who had to turn to paths of care—
Through crowded haunts again to run,
 And leave thee bright and silent there;

No more unto thy shores to come,
 But, on the world's rude ocean tost,
Dream of thee sometimes as a home
 Of sunshine he had seen and lost.

906

Far better in thy weeping hours
    To part from thee, as I do now,
When mist is o'er thy blooming bowers,
    Like sorrow's veil on beauty's brow.

For, though unrivall'd still thy grace,
    Thou dost not look, as then, too blest,
But thus in shadow, seem'd a place
    Where erring man might hope to rest—

Might hope to rest, and find in thee
    A gloom like Eden's, on the day
He left its shade, when every tree,
    Like thine, hung weeping o'er his way.

Weeping or smiling, lovely isle!
    And all the lovelier for thy tears—
For tho' but rare thy sunny smile,
    'Tis heaven's own glance when it appears.

Like feeling hearts, whose joys are few,
    But, when indeed they come, divine—
The brightest life the sun e'er threw
    Is lifeless to one gleam of thine!

LOVE'S YOUNG DREAM

Oh! the days are gone when Beauty bright
    My heart's chain wove!
When my dream of life, from morn till night,
    Was love, still love,
        New hope may bloom,
        And days may come
    Of milder, calmer beam,
But there's nothing half so sweet in life
    As Love's young dream!
Oh! there's nothing half so sweet in life
    As Love's young dream!

Though the bard to purer fame may soar,
    When wild youth's past;
Though he win the wise, who frowned before,
    To smile at last;
      He'll never meet
      A joy so sweet,
    In all his noon of fame,
As when first he sang to woman's ear
    His soul-felt flame,
And, at every close, she blushed to hear
    The one loved name!

Oh! that hallowed form is ne'er forgot
    Which first love traced;
Still it lingering haunts the greenest spot
    On memory's waste!
      'Twas odor fled
      As soon as shed;
    'Twas morning's wingéd dream;
'Twas a light that ne'er can shine again
    On life's dull stream!
Oh! 'twas light that ne'er can shine again
    On life's dull stream.

COME, YE DISCONSOLATE

Come, ye disconsolate, where'er you languish;
    Come, at God's altar fervently kneel;
Here bring your wounded hearts, here tell your anguish—
    "Earth has no sorrow that Heaven cannot heal."

Joy of the desolate, Light of the straying
    Hope, when all others die, fadeless and pure,
Here speaks the Comforter, in God's name saying,
    "Earth has no sorrow that Heaven cannot cure."

Go, ask the infidel what boon he brings us,
    What charm for aching hearts *he* can reveal
Sweet as that heavenly promise Hope sings us,
    "Earth has no sorrow that God cannot heal."

BELIEVE ME, IF ALL THOSE ENDEARING
YOUNG CHARMS

Believe me, if all those endearing young charms
  Which I gaze on so fondly to-day
Were to change by to-morrow, and fleet in my arms,
  Like fairy-gifts fading away,
Thou wouldst still be adored, as this moment thou art,
  Let thy loveliness fade as it will;
And around the dear ruin each wish of my heart
  Would entwine itself verdantly still.

It is not while beauty and youth are thine own,
  And thy cheeks unprofaned by a tear,
That the fervor and faith of a soul can be known
  To which time will but make thee more dear;
No, the heart that as truly loved never forgets,
  But as truly loves on to the close,
As the sunflower turns on his god when he sets
  The same look which she turned when he rose.

THE TURF SHALL BE MY FRAGRANT
SHRINE

The turf shall be my fragrant shrine;
My temple, Lord ! that arch of thine;
My censer's breath the mountain airs,
And silent thoughts my only prayers.

My choir shall be the monlight waves,
When murmuring homeward to their caves,
Or when the stillness of the sea,
Even more than music, breathes of Thee!

I'll seek, by day, some glade unknown,
All light and silence, like thy throne!
And the pale stars shall be, at night,
The only eyes that watch my rite.

909

Thy heaven, on which 'tis bliss to look,
Shall be my pure and shining book,
Where I shall read, in words of flame,
The glories of thy wondrous name.

I'll read thy anger in the rack
That clouds awhile the day-beam's track;
Thy mercy in the azure hue
Of sunny brightness breaking through!

There's nothing bright above, below,
From flowers that bloom to stars that glow,
But in its light my soul can see
Some feature of thy Deity!

There's nothing dark below, above,
But in its gloom I trace thy love,
And meekly wait that moment when
Thy touch shall turn all bright again!

MORI OGAI

MORI OGAI (Japanese, 1860-1922). Classical stylist, noted as both original
writer and translator. As an army doctor, went to Germany to study army
hygiene. Later translated many German classics into Japanese. Also author of
over 60 novels and short stories. Major influence in modern Japanese literature.

THE PIER

THE pier is long—long—
    The rails of four railroads cut straight and obliquely the beams
of the iron bridge on which the long and short cross-beams are like
the bars of the xylophone on which children play. Through the
cracks of the cross-beams, that almost catch the heels of shoes
and wooden clogs, here and there the black waves are shown,
reflected on the white flashes of sunshine.
    The sky has cleared into a deep blue. On the inside of the train
where she was sitting with her husband starting today, she did not
think the wind was blowing.

When leaving the jinriksha, in which she rode from the station of Yokohama, and standing on this pier, she found that the wind of the fifth of March was still blowing as if to bite the skin, fluttering the skirts of the Azuma coat.

It is the Azuma coat in silver gray, which she loosely wears on her body, that carries the child of her husband, who is starting to-day, this day which is not far from the month of confinement.

She came with her hair in Sokuhatsu. Her boa is of white ostrich. Holding the light green umbrella with tassels, she walks along, surrounded by four or five maidservants.

The pier is long—long——

The big ships are anchoring on the right and the left of the pier. Some are painted in black, some in white.

The anchored ships are making a fence for the wind. Every time she leaves the place where there are ships, a gust of wind blows and flutters the skirts of her Azuma coat.

Two years ago, immediately after he was graduated from the university of literature, the count, her husband, had married her. It was during the previous year that she gave birth to her first child, a princess like a jewel. At the end of the year her husband became a Master of Ceremonies at the Court. And, now, he is starting to London, charged with his official duty.

In his newly made gray overcoat, flinging the cane with crooked handle, her husband is walking rapidly along the pier. The viscount, who is going with him, and whose height is taller by a head than his, also walks rapidly beside him, clad in a suit of similar color.

The French ship, on which her husband is about to go abroad, is anchoring at the extreme end of the right side of the pier.

A stool, like that which is used to repair the wires of a trolley, is stationed on the pier, and from it a gangplank is laid across to the bulwark.

While walking slowly, she sees her husband and the viscount, his companion, crossing the gangplank and entering the ship.

The group of people looking after them are standing, here and there, on the pier. Almost all of them are those who came to bid adieu to her husband and the viscount. Perhaps there are no other passengers on this ship about to sail who are so important and are looked at by so many people.

Some of them are going to the foot of the stool on which the gangplank is laid, and stop there to wait for their companions.

911

Some of them are standing at the place, a bit before the stool, where the blocks and ropes are laid down.

Among these people there must be some who are intimately known to her husband, and some who know him but slightly. But, standing under this clear sky, they all seem dejected; or is it only her fancy?

The pier is long—long——

Following slowly after them, unconsciously she looks off to her right where there were many round windows on the side of the ship. The faces and chests of women are seen from one of those round windows. Three of them are from thirty to forty years of age; all with white aprons on their chests. They must be the waitresses of the ship. Supposing them to be the waitresses who wait on the passengers of the ship, on which her husband is on board, she feels envious of even those humble women.

There is also a woman at the bulwark, looking down on the pier, who wears a big bonnet with white cloth and carries a small leather bag in her hand. Two big eyes, as if painted with shadows, are shining on her wrinkled face above the large nose, like a hook. She looks like a Jewess. She also must be a traveler who is going on this ship. She is also envious of her.

The pier is long—long——

At last she arrives at the foot of the gangplank. Cautiously she carries her body, which has the second infant of her husband under the Azuma coat, and descends on the deck of the big, black-painted ship. She hands the umbrella to a maidservant.

Led by the people who have come to say farewell and were already on board, she goes back along the bulwark toward the prow. There are rooms for passengers at the end of the way, the numbers of which increase from twenty-seven to twenty-nine.

The viscount is standing at the entrance and addresses her.

"This is the room, madam."

Peeping into the room she finds two beds, under which the familiar packages and trunks are deposited. Her husband is standing before one of the beds.

"Look it through, madam. It is like this."

This is the room; she must look through it carefully. During the long, long voyage of her husband, this is the room where her dreams must come and go.

A man, who looks like the captain, comes, and, addressing her

912

husband in French, guides him to the saloon of the ship. She follows her husband and the viscount and enters the room.

This is a spacious and beautiful saloon. Several tables are arranged, each bearing a flower basket. . . . Gradually the people who came to say farewell gather into the room.

By the order of this man, who looks like the captain, a waiter brings forth many cups in the shape of morning-glories, and, pouring champagne into them, he distributes them among the people. Another waiter brings cakes, like those which are brought with ice cream, piled on a plate in the form of the well crib, and distributes them among the people.

The people who received the cups go after another, and stand before her husband and the viscount, wishing them a happy voyage, and drink from the cups.

Sitting on a small chair beside the table, she is waiting for the time when the congratulations are at an end. During his busy moments, now and then, her husband lifts his eyes to her.

However, there is no more to be said to her before many people. Also, there is no more to be said to him, before many people.

The bell rings. Having bidden farewell to her husband and to the viscount the people are going out, one after another. She also follows them, saluting her husband and the viscount.

Again crossing the dangerous gangplank, she descends to the pier. She receives the light green umbrella from the hand of her maid-servant, and raises it.

Her husband and the viscount are standing on the bulwark, looking in her direction. She is looking up at them from under her umbrella. She feels that her eyes, as she looks up, are growing gradually larger and larger.

Again the bell rings. A few French sailors begin to untie the rope from the gangplank. A Japanese laborer in Hanten is standing on the stool like that which is used in repairing the trolley, preparing to draw down the gangplank. Hanging on the rope of the wheel, pulled by the man in Hanten, the gangplank at last leaves the bulwark.

The noon-gun of the city of Yokohama resounds. With this as a signal, the ship, from the hold of which for some time a noise has been issuing, silently begins to move.

The elderly Europeans, who seem to be a married couple, are standing at the bulwark. They are talking about something of a jolly nature with a white-haired old man who is standing on the

pier, with one of his feet placed on an apparatus to roll the ropes, which looks like a big bobbin. They do not seem to regret the parting.

It looks as if the ship is moving. It looks as if the pier is moving. There seems to be the distance of a Pallaraxe between the place where her husband and the viscount are standing and the place where she is standing. She feels her eyes growing larger and larger.

Some of the people who are looking after them are running to the end of the pier. She cannot do such an immodest thing. Suddenly something white waves at the bulwark. It was a handkerchief waved by the hand of a woman who wears a big bonnet decorated with a white cloth. A tall man stands at the end of the pier, in red waistcoat and tan shoes. A white handkerchief waves also from the hand of this man. This also must be a parting in human life.

These two persons set the fashion, and the handkerchiefs are waved here and there. White things are waving also from the people who are looking after the group surrounding the count. She also grasps the batiste handkerchief which she has brought in her sleeve, but she cannot do such an immodest thing.

When the ship seemed to have left the pier, it turned its prow a bit to the right. The place where her husband and the viscount were standing has disappeared at last.

Still she can see a boy about fifteen or sixteen, standing at the stern, in a blue, cold-looking garment like a blouse. What mother is waiting for him in France? Or has he no parents? What is he looking at, standing by the rail at the stern?

Slowly she turned her feet and walked among the maidservants surrounding her.

The pier is long—long——

At the place where the black-painted ship was anchored, until a short time ago, the water is glittering like the scales of fish, as the small ripples are reflecting the pale sunshine.

EDUARD MORIKE

EDUARD MÖRIKE (German, 1804-1875). German poet and novelist, creative in both the classical and the folk manner. His private life was not happy —career as vicar and marriage were unsuccessful. Famous novella: *Mozart on His Trip to Prague*. Best poems are extremely simple, remarkable imitations of folk songs.

BEAUTY ROHTRAUT

What is the name of King Ringang's daughter?
    Rohtraut, Beauty Rohtraut!
And what does she do the livelong day,
Since she dare not knit and spin alway?
O hunting and fishing is ever her play!
And, heigh! that her huntsman I might be!
I'd hunt and fish right merrily!
    Be silent, heart!

And it chanced that, after this some time,
    Rohtraut, Beauty Rohtraut!
The boy in the Castle has gained access,
And a horse he has got and a huntsman's dress,
To hunt and to fish with the merry Princess;
And, O! that a king's son I might be!
Beauty Rohtraut I love so tenderly.
    Hush! hush! my heart.

Under a gray old oak they sat,
    Beauty, Beauty Rohtraut!
She laughs: "Why look you so slyly at me?
If you have heart enough, come, kiss me."
Cried the breathless boy, "Kiss thee?"
But he thinks kind fortune has favored my youth;
And thrice he has kissed Beauty Rohtraut's mouth.
    Down! down! mad heart.

Then slowly and silently they rode home,—
    Rohtraut, Beauty Rohtraut!
The boy was lost in his delight:

"And, wert thou Empress this very night,
I would not heed or feel the blight;
Ye thousand leaves of the wild wood wist
How Beauty Rohtraut's mouth I kiss'd.
        Hush! hush! wild heart."

AN ERROR CHANCED

An error chanced in the moonlight garden
Of a once inviolate love.
Shuddering I came on an outworn deceit,
And with sorrowing look, yet cruel,
Bade I the slender
Enchanting maiden
Leave me and wander far.
Alas! her lofty forehead
Was bowed, for she loved me well;
Yet did she go in silence
Into the dim gray
World outside.

Sick since then,
Wounded and woeful heart!
Never shall it be whole.

Meseems that, spun of the air, a thread of magic
Binds her yet to me, an unrestful bond;
It draws, it draws me faint with love toward her.
Might it yet be some day that on my threshold
I should find her, as erst, in the morning twilight,
Her traveler's bundle beside her,
And her eye true-heartedly looking up to me,
Saying, "See, I've come back,
Back once more from the lonely world!"

A SONG FOR TWO IN THE NIGHT

She: How soft the night wind strokes the meadow grasses
And, breathing music, through the woodland passes!

916

Now that the upstart day is dumb,
One hears from the still earth a whispering throng
Of forces animate, with murmured song
Joining the zephyrs' well-attunèd hum.

He: I catch the tone from wondrous voices brimming,
Which sensuous on the warm wind drifts to me,
While, streaked with misty light uncertainly,
The very heavens in the glow are swimming.

She: The air like woven fabric seems to wave,
Then more transparent and more lustrous groweth;
Meantime a muted melody outgoeth
From happy fairies in their purple cave.
To sphere-wrought harmony
Sing they, and busily
The thread upon their silver spindles floweth.

He: Oh lovely night! how effortless and free
O'er samite black—though green by day—thou movest!
And to the whirring music that thou lovest
Thy foot advances imperceptibly.
Thus hour by hour thy step doth measure—
In trancèd self-forgetful pleasure
Thou'rt rapt; creation's soul is rapt with thee!

EARLY AWAY

The morning frost shines gray
    Along the misty field
Beneath the pallid way
    Of early dawn revealed.

Amid the glow one sees
    The day-star disappear;
Yet o'er the western trees
    The moon is shining clear.

So, too, I send my glance
    On distant scenes to dwell;
I see in torturing trance
    The night of our farewell.

917

Blue eyes, a lake of bliss,
   Swim dark before my sight,
Thy breath, I feel, thy kiss;
   I hear thy whispering light.

My cheek upon thy breast
   The streaming tears bedew,
Till, purple-black, is cast
   A veil across my view.

The sun comes out; he glows,
   And straight my dreams depart,
While from the cliffs he throws
   A chill across my heart.

THE FORSAKEN MAIDEN

Early when cocks do crow
   Ere the stars dwindle,
Down to the hearth I go,
   Fire must I kindle.

Fair leap the flames on high,
   Sparks they whirl drunken;
I watch them listlessly
   In sorrow sunken.

Sudden it comes to me,
   Youth so fair seeming,
That all the night of thee
   I have been dreaming.

Tears then on tears do run
   For my false lover;
Thus has the day begun—
   Would it were over!

WEYLA'S SONG

Thou art Orplede, my land
   Remotely gleaming;
The mist arises from thy sun-bright strand
To where the faces of the gods are beaming.

Primeval rivers spring renewed
Thy silver girdle weaving, child!
Before the godhead bow subdued
Kings, thy worshipers and watchers mild.

SECLUSION

Let, oh world, ah let me be!
Tempt me not with gifts of pleasure.
Leave alone this heart to treasure
All its joy, its misery.

What my grief I can not say,
'Tis a strange, a wistful sorrow;
Yet through tears at every morrow
I behold the light of day.

When my weary soul finds rest
Oft a beam of rapture brightens
All the gloom of cloud, and lightens
This oppression in my breast.

Let, oh world, ah, let me be!
Tempt me not with gifts of pleasure.
Leave alone this heart to treasure
All its joy, its misery.

THE SOLDIER'S BETROTHED

Oh dear, if the king only knew
How brave is my sweetheart, how true!
He would give his heart's blood for the king,
But for me he would do the same thing.

My love has no ribbon or star,
No cross such as gentlemen wear,
A gen'ral he'll never become;
If only they'd leave him at home!

919

For stars there are three shining bright
O'er the Church of St. Mary each night;
We are bound by a rose-woven band,
And a house-cross is always at hand.

THE OLD WEATHERCOCK: AN IDYLL

At Cleversulzbach in the Underland
A hundred and thirteen years did I stand
Up on the tower in wind and rain,
An ornament and a weathervane.
Through night and tempest gazing down,
Like a good old cock I watched the town.

THINK OF IT, MY SOUL!

Somewhere a pine is green,
Just where who knoweth,
And in a garth unseen
A rose-tree bloweth.
These are ordained for thee—
Think, oh, soul, fixedly—
Over thy grave to be;
Swift the time floweth.

Two black steeds on the down
Briskly are faring,
Or on their way to town
Canter uncaring.
These may with heavy tread
Slowly convey the dead
E'en ere the shoes be shed
They now are wearing.

ERINNA TO SAPPHO

"Many the paths to Hades," an ancient proverb
Tells us, "and one of them thou thyself shalt follow,
Doubt not!" My sweetest Sappho, who can doubt it?
Tells not each day the old tale?

Yet the foreboding word in a youthful bosom
Rankles not, as a fisher bred by the seashore,
Deafened by use, perceives the breaker's thunder no more.
—Strangely, however, today my heart misgave me. Attend:
Sunny the glow of morn-tide, pouring
Through the trees of my well-walled garden,
Roused the slugabed (so of late thou calledst Erinna)
Early up from her sultry couch.
Full was my soul of quiet, although my blood beat
Quick with uncertain waves o'er the thin cheek's pallor.
Then, as I loosed the plaits of my shining tresses,
Parting with nard-moist comb above my forehead
The veil of hair—in the glass my own glance met me.
Eyes, strange eyes, I said, what will ye?
Spirit of me, that within there dwelled securely as yet,
Occultly wed to my living senses—
Demon-like, half smiling thy solemn message,
Thou dost nod to me, Death presaging!
—Ha! all at once like lightning a thrill went through me,
Or as a deadly arrow with sable feathers
Whizzing had grazed my temples,
So that, with hands pressed over my face, a long time
Dumb-struck I sat, while my thought reeled at the frightful
    abyss.

Tearless at first I pondered,
Weighing the terror of Death;
Till I bethought me of thee, my Sappho,
And of my comrades all,
And of the muses' lore,
When straightway the tears ran fast.

But there on the table gleamed a beautiful hair-net, thy gift,
Costly handwork of Byssos, spangled with golden bees.
This, when next in the flowery festal season
We shall worship the glorious child of Demeter,
This will I offer to her for thy and my sake,
So may she favor us both (for she much availeth),
That no mourning lock thou untimely sever
From thy beloved head for thy poor Erinna.

921

MULTATULI

MULTATULI (Eduard Douwes Dekker), (Dutch, 1820-1887). One of the most powerful novelists of Holland. At 18 left for Dutch East Indies, became bitter foe of colonialism. Fame rests on two novels: *Max Havelaar* and *Woutertje Pieterse*. Exerted considerable influence on succeeding generation of Dutch writers.

THE STORY OF SAÏDJAH

SAÏDJAH's father had a buffalo, which he used for plowing his field. When this buffalo was taken away from him by the district chief at Parang-Koodjang he was very dejected, and spoke no word for many a day. For plowing time was come, and he feared that if the rice-field was not worked in time, the opportunity to sow would be lost, and lastly, that there would be no paddy to cut, and none to keep in the store-room of the house. I have here to tell readers who know Java, but not Bantam, that in that Residency there is personal landed property, which is not the case elsewhere. Saïdjah's father, then, was very uneasy. He feared that his wife would have no rice, nor Saïdjah himself, who was still a child, nor his little brothers and sisters. And the district chief, too, would denounce him to the Assistant Resident if he was behindhand in the payment of his taxes, for this is punished by the law. Saïdjah's father then took a poniard, which he had inherited from his father. It was not very handsome, but there were silver bands round the sheath, and at the end a silver plate. He sold it to a Chinaman in the capital, and came home with twenty-four guilders, with which he bought another buffalo.

Saïdjah, who was then about seven, soon made friends with the new buffalo. I purposely say "made friends," for it was indeed touching to see how the buffalo was attached to the little boy who watched over and fed him. Of this attachment I shall soon give an example. The large strong animal bends its heavy head to the right, to the left, or downwards, just as the pressure of the child's finger directs. Such a friendship the little Saïdjah had soon been able to make with the newcomer; and it seemed as if the encouraging voice of the child gave more strength to the heavy shoulders of the animal, when it tore open the stiff clay and traced its way in deep sharp furrows. The buffalo turned willingly, on reaching the end of the field, not losing an inch of ground when plowing backwards the new furrow, which was ever near the old, as if the *sawah* was a garden

ground raked by a giant. Quite near were the *sawahs* of the father of Adinda (the child who was to marry Saïdjah), and when the little brothers of Adinda came to the limit of their fields, as the father of Saïdjah was there with his plow, the children called out merrily to each other, and each praised the strength and docility of his buffalo. But I believe that Saïdjah's buffalo was the best of all, perhaps because its master knew better how to speak to the animal, for buffaloes are very responsive to kind words.

Saïdjah was nine and Adinda six, when this buffalo was taken from Saïdjah's father by the chief. Saïdjah's father, who was very poor, thereupon sold to the Chinaman two silver curtain-hooks—inheritances from his wife's parents—for eighteen guilders, and with that money he bought a new buffalo. Saïdjah was very dejected, for he knew from Adinda's little brothers that the other buffalo had been driven to the capital, and he had asked his father if he had not seen the animal when he was there to sell the curtain-hooks. To this question his father refused to give an answer, and therefore the lad feared that his buffalo had been slaughtered, like the others which the chief had taken from the people. And Saïdjah wept much when he thought of the poor buffalo, which he had known for so long, and could eat nothing for days. It must be remembered that he was only a child.

The new buffalo soon got acquainted with the boy and obtained in the heart of Saïdjah the same place as his predecessor—alas, too soon, for the wax impressions of the heart are soon smoothed to make room for other writing. However this may be, the new buffalo was not so strong as the former: true, the old yoke was too large for his neck, but the poor animal was willing, like the other, and though Saïdjah could boast no more of the strength of his buffalo when he met Adinda's brothers at the boundaries, yet maintained that none surpassed his in willingness, and if the furrow was not so straight as before, or if lumps of earth had been turned but not cut, he willingly made this right as well as he could by means of his spade. Moreover, no buffalo had any such star on his forehead as this one had. The village priest himself said that there was good luck in the course of the hair-whorls on its shoulders.

Once when they were in the field, Saïdjah called in vain to his buffalo to make haste. The animal did not move. Saïdjah grew angry at this unusual refractoriness, and could not refrain from scolding. He called him a s——. Anyone who has been in India will understand me, and he who has not is the gainer if I spare him the explanation.

923

Saïdjah did not mean anything bad. He only used the word because he had often heard it used by others when they were dissatisfied with their buffaloes. But it was useless: his buffalo did not move. He shook his head as if to throw off the yoke, he blew and trembled, there was anguish in his blue eye, and the upper lip was curled, baring the gums.

"Fly, fly!" Adinda's brothers cried, "Fly, Saïdjah, there's a tiger!" And they all unyoked their buffaloes, and throwing themselves on their broad backs, galloped away through *sawahs*, irrigation trenches, mud, brushwood, forest and jungle, along fields and roads, but when they tore panting and dripping with perspiration into the village of Badoer, Saïdjah was not with them. For when he had freed his buffalo from the yoke and mounted him as the others had done in order to escape, an unexpected jump made him lose his seat and fall to the ground. The tiger was very close. . . . The buffalo, driven on by his own speed alone, and not of his own will, had gone further than Saïdjah, and scarcely had it conquered the momentum when it returned and, placing its big body, supported by its feet like a roof over the child, turned its horned head toward the tiger, which bounded forward—but for the last time. The buffalo caught him on his horns, and only lost some flesh, which the tiger took out of his neck. The tiger lay there with his belly torn open. Saïdjah was saved. Certainly there had been luck in the star on the buffalo's head.

When this buffalo had been taken away from Saïdjah's father and slaughtered, Saïdjah was just twelve, and Adinda was wearing *sarongs* and making figures on them. She had already learned to express thoughts in melancholy drawings on her tissue, for she had seen Saïdjah's sadness. And Saïdjah's father was also sad, but his mother still more so. For she had cured the wound in the neck of the faithful animal which had brought her child home unhurt. As often as she saw this wound, she thought how far the gashes of the tiger might have gone into the tender body of her child; and every time she put fresh dressings on the wound, she caressed the buffalo and spoke kindly to him, that the faithful animal might know how grateful a mother can be. Afterwards she hoped that the buffalo understood her, for he must have known why she wept when he was taken away, and that it was not Saïdjah's mother who caused him to be slaughtered. Some days afterward, Saïdjah's father fled out of the country, for he was afraid of being punished for not paying his

924

taxes, and he had no other heirlooms to sell with which to buy another buffalo. His parents had left him but few things. However, he went on for some years after the loss of his last buffalo by working with hired animals: but that is a very unremunerative labor, and moreover sad for one who has had buffaloes of his own.

Saïdjah's mother died of grief, and his father, in a moment of dejection, left Bantam to find work in the Buitenzorg district. But he was punished with stripes because he had left Lebak without a passport, and brought back by the police to Badoer. There he was put in prison, because he was supposed to be mad, which I can well believe, and it was feared he would run amok in a moment of frenzy. But he was not long in prison, for he died soon after. What became of Saïdjah's brothers and sisters I do not know. The house they lived in at Badoer was empty for some time, and then fell down, for it was only built of bamboo covered with cane. A little dust and dirt covered the spot where there had been so much suffering. There are many such places in Lebak.

Saïdjah was already fifteen when his father set out for Buitenzorg, and he did not accompany him thither, because he had other plans in mind. He had been told that there were gentlemen in Batavia who drove in carriages, and that it would be easy to get work as a carriage boy, for which young lads are used, so as not to disturb the equilibrium of the two-wheeled carriage by too much motion. He would, they said, earn much that way if he behaved himself—perhaps in three years he would be able to save enough to buy two buffaloes. This was a pleasant prospect. With the proud gait of one who had conceived a grand idea, he entered Adinda's house one day after his father had gone away, and communicated his plans to her.

"Think of it," said he. "When I come back we shall be old enough to marry, and have enough to buy two buffaloes!"

"I will gladly marry you, Saïdjah, when you come back. I will spin and weave *sarongs* and *slendangs,* and be very diligent all the while."

"Oh, I believe you, Adinda, but—if I find you already married?"

"Saïdjah, you know very well I will marry nobody but you. My father promised me to your father."

"And you yourself—? "

"When I come back, I will call from afar off."

"Who will hear it, if we are stamping rice in the village?"

"That is true, but, Adinda—oh, yes, this is better: wait for me

925

in the wood, under the Ketapan, where you gave me the Melatti flowers."

"But, Saïdjah, how am I to know when I am to go to the Keta-pan?"

Saïdjah considered a moment and said: "Count the moons. I shall stay away three times twelve moons, not counting this moon. See, Adinda, at every new moon cut a notch in your rice block on the floor. When you have cut three times twelve lines, I will be under the Ketapan the next day. Do you promise to be there?"

"Yes, Saïdjah. I will be there, under the Ketapan, near the djatis, when you come back."

Thereupon Saïdjah tore a piece off his much-worn blue turban and gave it to Adinda to keep as a pledge, and then left her and Badoer. He walked many days, passing through Rankas-Belong, not yet capital of Lebak, through Warong-Goonoong, the home of the Assistant Resident, and the next day he came to Pamarangand, which lies in a garden. The day after, he came to Serang, and was astonished at the magnificence and size of the place, and the number of tiled stone houses. He had never before seen the like. He remained there a day, because he was tired, but in the coolness of the night he went his way, and the following day arrived at Tangerang. There he bathed in the river and rested at the home of an acquaintance of his father's who showed him how to make straw hats like those from Manila. He remained a day in order to learn the art, because he thought he might be able to turn it to use later on, if by chance he should fail to find other work in Batavia. The following day toward evening he thanked his host and departed. As soon as it was dark, and no one could see him, he took out the Melatti leaves Adinda had given him, for he was sad, thinking that he would not see her for so long. Neither on the first nor the second day had he realized how lonely he was, because he was captivated by the grand idea of earning money enough to buy two buffaloes, whereas his father had never had more than one, and was too excited over the prospect of seeing Adinda again to grieve over his departure. He had left her in anxious hope. The prospect of seeing her again so occupied his heart that on leaving Badoer and passing the tree, he felt something akin to joy, as if the thirty-six moons were already past. It had seemed that he had only to turn round to see Adinda waiting for him. But the further he went, the more did he realize the length of the period before him. There was something in his soul that made

926

him walk more slowly—he felt an affliction in his knees, and though it was not dejection that overcame him, it was a mournful sadness. He thought of returning, but what would Adinda think of his want of courage?

Therefore he walked on, though not so fast as on the first day. He had the Melatti in his hand and often pressed them to his breast. He had aged much during the past few days, and could not understand how he had been able to live so calmly before, when Adinda was so near that he could see her as often as he liked. Now he could not recapture that calmness. Nor did he understand why, after having taken his leave, he had not gone back once again to see her. He recalled how recently he had quarreled with her about a cord she had made for her brother's kite, which had broken because there was some defect in her work. This made him lose a bet he had with the Tjipoeroet children. "How was it possible," he thought, "to have been angry over that with Adinda?" If there was a defect in the cord, and if the bet *was* lost, ought he to have been so rude and called her names? What, he wondered, if he died at Batavia without having asked her forgiveness? Would it not make him seem a wicked man? When it was learned that he had died in a distant place, would not everyone at Badoer say, "It is well Saïdjah has died—he spoke insolently to Adinda!"

Thus his thoughts ran, uttered at first involuntarily and softly, soon in a quiet monologue, and finally in a melancholy song.

He arrived at Batavia, and asked a certain gentleman to take him into his service, which the gentleman did, because Saïdjah spoke no Malay—an advantage there, for servants who do not understand that language are not so corrupt as the others, who have been longer in touch with the Europeans. But Saïdjah soon learned Malay, though he behaved well, for he always remembered the two buffaloes he was going to buy. He grew tall and strong, because he ate every day—not always the case at Badoer. In the stable he was liked, and would certainly not have been rejected if he had asked the hand of the coachman's daughter. His master liked him so much that he soon promoted him to be a house servant, increased his wages, and continually made him presents, to show how pleased he was. Saïdjah's mistress had read Sue's novel, so popular for a short while, and always thought of Prince Djalma when she saw Saïdjah, and the young girls, too, understood better than before why the Javanese painter, Radeen Saleh, had been so successful at Paris. But they

927

thought Saïdjah ungrateful when after almost a three years he asked for his dismissal and a certificate of good behavior. This could not be refused, and Saïdjah went on his journey with a joyful heart.

He counted the treasures he was carrying home. In a roll of bamboo he had his passport and certificate. In a case fastened to a leather girdle something heavy swung against his shoulder, but he enjoyed the feel of that, and no wonder! What would Adinda say? It contained thirty piastres—enough to buy three buffaloes! Nor was that all: on his back was a silver-covered sheath with his poniard. The hilt was indeed a fine one, for he had wound it round with a silk wrapper. And he had still more treasures! In the folds of his loin-cloth he kept a belt of silver links with gold clasps. True, the belt was short, but then Adinda was slender! Suspended by a cord round his neck, and under his clothes, he wore a silken bag in which were the withered Melatti leaves.

Is it to be wondered at that he stopped no longer at Sangerang than to visit the acquaintances who made such fine straw hats? That he said so little to the girls on his way who asked him whence he came and where he was going—the usual salutations; that he no longer thought Serang so beautiful (he who had learned to know Batavia); that he no longer hid himself behind the enclosure as he did three years before when he saw the Resident go riding out (he who had seen the much grander Lord at Buitenzorg, grandfather of Solo); that he paid little attention to the tales of those who went part of the way with him and gave news of Bantam-Kidool—is no wonder. No, he had sublime visions in his mind's eye. He looked for the Ketapan tree in the clouds when he was still far from Badoer. He caught at the air as if to embrace the form that was to meet him under the tree. He pictured to himself the face of Adinda, her head, her shoulders, saw the heavy chignon, black and glossy, confined in a net, hanging down her back; her large eyes glistening in dark reflection, the nostrils raised so proudly as a child (was it possible?), when he had vexed her; and the corner of her lips, when she smiled; and finally, her breasts, now doubtless swelling under her shawl. He could imagine her saying to him, "Welcome, Saïdjah! I have thought of you as I was spinning and weaving and stamping the rice on the floor which shows three times twelve lines cut by my hand. And I am under the Ketapan the first day of the new moon. Welcome, Saïdjah! I will be your wife."

928

That was the music that resounded in his ears and prevented him from listening to all the news that was told him on the road.

At last he saw Ketapan, or rather a large, dark spot with many stars above it. That must be the Ljati wood, near the tree where he should again see Adinda next morning, after sunrise. He sought in the dark and felt many trunks, finding at last a rough spot on the south side of a tree, and thrust his finger into a hole which Si-Panteh had cut with his knife to exorcise the Evil Spirit that had caused his mother's toothache, a short time before the birth of Panteh's little brother. That was the Ketapan he sought.

Yes, this was indeed the spot where he had looked upon Adinda for the first time with a different eye. She had become different from his other comrades. There she had given him the leaves. He sat down at the foot of the tree and looked at the stars, and when he saw a shooting-star he took it as a welcome of his return to Badoer, and wondered whether Adinda were now asleep, whether she had correctly cut the number of moons on the wood? How terrible if she had missed a moon, as if thirty-six were not quite enough! Had she, he wondered, made him some nice *sarongs* and *slendangs?* Who would now be living in her father's house? Then he thought of his childhood, and his mother, and how the buffalo had saved him from the tiger, of what would have become of Adinda if the buffalo had not been so faithful. He watched the sinking of the stars, and as each disappeared, he calculated how much nearer he was to Adinda. For she would certainly come at the first beam—at daybreak she would be there. Why had she not come the day before?

He was hurt that she had not anticipated the supreme moment that had lighted his soul for three years with indescribable brightness; unjust as he was in his selfishness, it seemed to him that Adinda ought to have been waiting for him. He complained unjustly, for the sun had not yet risen. But the stars were growing pale, and strange colors floated over the mountain tops, which appeared darker as they contrasted sharply with places elsewhere illuminated. Here and there something glowed in the east—arrows of gold and fire darted along the horizon, but disappeared again and seemed to fall down behind the impenetrable curtain which hid the day. It grew lighter and lighter around him: he now saw the landscape and could already distinguish a part of the wood behind which Badoer lay. There Adinda slept.

No, surely, she did not sleep! How could she? Did she not know

929

that Saïdjah would be waiting for her. She had not slept the whole night certainly; the village night police had knocked at her door to ask why her lamp burned so long, and with a sweet laugh she had replied that she had vowed to weave a *slendang* which must be ready before the first day of the new moon. Or perhaps she had passed the night in darkness, sitting on the rice floor, counting with eager fingers the thirty-six lines. Or possibly amused herself by pretending that she miscalculated, and had counted the lines all over again each time, enjoying the delicious assurance that the thirty-six moons had come and gone since her Saïdjah had left her.

Now that it was becoming light, she would be busying herself with useless little things, glancing from time to time over the wide horizon, looking for the sun, the lazy sluggard!

There was a line of bluish red, touching the clouds and making their edges light. The arrows of fire shot higher and higher, and ran over the dark ground, illuminating wide spaces of the earth, meeting, crossing, unrolling, running, and at last uniting in vast patches of fire, painting the azure earth in pigments of shining gold. There was red, blue, and purple, yellow gold. God in Heaven—it was at last daybreak!—Adinda!

Saïdjah had never learned to pray, and it would have been a pity to teach him: a more devout prayer and a more fervent expression of gratitude than his would have been impossible. He would no go to Badoer: actually to see her again was not so wonderful as to await her coming. He sat down at the foot of the Ketapan, and his eyes wandered over the landscape. Nature smiled at him, and seemed to welcome him like a mother. Saïdjah was overjoyed at seeing so many spots that reminded him of his earlier life. Though his eyes and thoughts wandered, his longings always reverted to the path which leads from Badoer to the Ketapan tree. His senses were wholly alive to Adinda. He saw the abyss to the left, where the earth was yellow, the spot where once a young buffalo had sunk down to the depths: they had all descended there with strong rattan cords, and Adinda's father had been the bravest of the rescue party. How Adinda had clapped her hands! Farther along, over there on the other side by the clump of cocoa-trees, whose leaves waved over the village, Si-Penah had fallen from a tree and been killed. How his mother had wailed—because, she said, Si-Penah was still such a little one—as if her grief had been less if he were larger! True, he *was* small, smaller and more fragile than Adinda.

There was no one on the little road leading from Badoer to the tree.

—By and by she would come. It was still very early.

Saïdjah saw a squirrel spring playfully up the trunk of a cocoanut tree and run untiringly to and fro. He forced himself to stand and regard the animal, for this calmed his thoughts, which had been working hard since early morning. His thoughts then ran into song.

There was still no one on the little road. . . .

He caught sight of a butterfly disporting joyously in the increasing warmth. . . .

Still, there was no one on the little road. The sun climbed higher into the heavens, and it grew warm. . . .

Still, no one appeared on the little road. . . . No one.

She must have fallen asleep toward morning, weary with watching during the night, during many nights. She had not slept for weeks. That was it! Ought he to get up and go to Badoer? That would look as though he doubted her coming. . . . That man over there was too far away, and Saïdjah did not wish to speak to anyone about Adinda. He would see her alone. Surely, surely, she would come soon!

He would wait. . . .

But what if she were ill—dead?

Like a wounded stag he flew along the pathway toward the village. He saw nothing and heard nothing. Normally he would have heard, for there were men standing in the road at the entrance to the village, who cried out, "Saïdjah! Saïdjah!"

Was it his eagerness, or what, that prevented his finding Adinda's house? He had already run to the end of the village, and as if mad, he turned back, beating his head in despair to think that he had passed her house. But he soon found himself back at the entrance of the village, and—was it a dream? Again he had missed the house. Once more he flew back and suddenly stood still, and took his head in both hands to press out the madness that stunned him.

"Drunk, drunk!" he exclaimed. "I am drunk!"

The women of Badoer came out of their houses and saw with sorrow poor Saïdjah standing there, for they knew that he had been looking for Adinda's house, and that the house was no longer there. . . .

When the chief of Parang-Koodjang had taken away the buffaloes belonging to Adinda's father, Adinda's mother had died of grief,

931

and her baby sister soon after, for there was no one to suckle her. Adinda's father, fearing punishment for failing to pay his land taxes, had fled the district, taking with him Adinda and her brothers. He had heard how Saïdjah's father had been punished at Buitenzorg with stripes, because he had left Badoer without a passport. He had therefore not gone to Buitenzorg, nor to the Preangan, nor to Bantam, but to Tjilangkahan, bordering upon the sea. There he had hidden in the woods, awaiting the arrival of Pa-Ento, Pa-Lontah, Si-Penah, Pa-Ansive, Abdoel Isma, and others who had been robbed of their buffaloes by the chief of Parang-Koodjang, all of whom feared punishment for failure to pay their taxes. There, during the night, they had taken possession of a fishing-boat, and gone to sea. They steered toward the west, as far as Java Head. There they turned northward, until they came in sight of Prince's Island, and sailed round the east coast, going thence to the Lampoons. That at least was what people whispered to one another in Lebak whenever there was any question about buffaloes or land-taxes.

But Saïdjah could scarcely understand what they had told him. There was a buzzing in his ears, as if a gong were sounding in his head. He felt the blood throbbing convulsively in his temples; it seemed as though his head would burst under the pressure. He said nothing, and looked about stupified, not seeing anything. At last he laughed horribly. An old woman led him to her cottage. She would take care of the piteous fool. His laugh gradually became less horrible, but he still spoke no word. During the night the inmates of the hut were frightened by the sound of his voice. He sang out monotonously: "I don't know where I shall die!"

Some of the natives collected a little money in order to offer a sacrifice to the crocodile of the Tji-Udjiung, in order to cure Saïdjah, whom they thought insane. But he was not insane, for on a certain night when the moon was extraordinarily clear, he rose from his couch and quietly left the hut, and sought out the place where Adinda's house had stood. It was not easy to find it, for many houses had fallen down. But he recognized the spot by looking at the rays of moonlight that filtered down through the trees, as sailors measure their positions by lighthouses and mountain-tops.

That was the spot. There had Adinda lived!

Stumbling over half-decayed bamboos and pieces of fallen roof, he made his way to the sanctuary which he sought. He found some few remains of the enclosure still standing erect. There had been

932

Adinda's room, and there was the bamboo pin on which she had hung her dress when she was retiring at night. The walls of the room were turned to dust. He took up a handful of it, pressed it to his lips, and breathed hard. . . .

The next day he asked the old woman who had taken him in, where the rice-floor was, that stood in Adinda's house. The woman was glad at last to hear him speak, and ran through the village to look for the remains of the floor. She pointed out to Saïdjah the proprietor, and Saidjah followed in silence. He came to the rice-floor. On it he counted thirty-two lines. . . .

He gave the old woman piastres enough to buy a buffalo, and left Badoer. At Tjilangkahan he bought a fishing-boat, and after sailing for two days, reached the Lampoon Islands, where the insurgents had arisen against the Dutch rule. He joined a troop of Badoer men, not so much with the idea of fighting as of finding Adinda, for he was naturally tender-hearted, and more disposed to sorrow than to bitterness.

One day after the insurgents had suffered a defeat, he wandered through a village that had just been taken by the Dutch army, and was therefore in flames. Saïdjah knew that the defeated troop was composed largely of Badoer men. He wandered like a ghost among the houses that had not yet been burned. In one of them he found the dead body of Adinda's father with a bayonet wound in the breast. Near him lay the bodies of Adinda's three brothers, still boys—children, in fact.

Not far off lay the body of Adinda, naked and horribly mutilated.

A small piece of blue linen had penetrated into the gaping wound in the breast, which seemed to have made an end to a long struggle.

Saïdjah went off to meet some Dutch soldiers who were driving the surviving insurgents at the point of the bayonet into the fire of the burning houses. He went out to meet the broad bayonets, and pressed forward with all his might, until the steel was buried up to the hilt in his breast.

Not long after there was much rejoicing at Batavia for the new victory, which so added to the laurels of the Dutch-Indian army. And the Government wrote that tranquillity had been restored in the Lampoons. The King of Holland, enlightened by his statesmen, again rewarded so much heroism with many orders of knighthood.

933

LADY MURASAKI

LADY MURASAKI (Japanese, *ca.* 978-1031). Realistic court diarist, novelist
and poet. Lived most of life connected with Emperor's court at Kyoto, and
last years in the entourage of Empress Akiko. Chief work, *The Tale of Genji*,
is most impressive of Japanese novels—54 sections, translated into 6 English
volumes by Arthur Waley. Her *Diary* also a classic.

THE FESTIVAL OF RED LEAVES

THERE was an elderly lady-of-the-bedchamber who, though she was
an excellent creature in every other way and was very much liked
and respected, was an outrageous flirt. It astonished Genji that
despite her advancing years she showed no sign of reforming her
reckless and fantastic behaviour. Curious to see how she would
take it, he one day came up and began joking with her. She appeared to be quite unconscious of the disparity between their ages
and at once counted him as an admirer. Slightly alarmed, he nevertheless found her company rather agreeable and often talked with
her. But, chiefly because he was frightened of being laughed at
if anyone found out, he refused to become her lover, and this she
very much resented. One day she was dressing the Emperor's hair.
When this was over His Majesty sent for his valets and went with
them into another room. Genji and the elderly lady were left alone
together. She was fuller than ever of languishing airs and poses,
and her costume was to the last degree stylish and elaborate. 'Poor
creature,' he thought, 'how little difference it all makes!' and he
was passing her on his way out of the room when suddenly the
temptation to give a tug at her dress became irresistible. She
glanced swiftly round, eyeing him above the rim of a marvellously
painted summer-fan. The eyelids beneath which she ogled at him
were blackened and sunken; wisps of hair projected untidily around
her forehead. There was something singularly inappropriate about
this gawdy, coquettish fan. Handing her his own instead, he took
it from her and examined it. On paper coated with a red so thick
and lustrous that you could see yourself reflected in it a forest of
tall trees was painted in gold. At the side of this design, in a hand
which though out-of-date was not lacking in distinction was written
the poem about the Forest of Oaraki. He made no doubt that the
owner of the fan had written it in allusion to her own advancing
years and was expecting him to make a gallant reply. Turning over

in his mind how best to divert the extravagant ardour of this strange creature, he could, to his own amusement, think only of another poem about the same forest; but to this it would have been ill-bred to allude He was feeling very uncomfortable lest someone should come in and see them together. She however was quite at her ease and seeing that he remained silent she recited with many arch looks the poem: 'Come to me in the forest and I will cut pasture for your horse, though it be but the under leaf whose season is past.' 'Should I seek your woodland,' he answered, 'my fair name would be gone, for down its glades at all times the pattering of hoofs is heard,' and he tried to get away; but she held him back saying: 'How odious you are! That is not what I mean at all. No one has ever insulted me like this before,' and she burst into tears. 'Let us talk about it some other time,' said Genji; 'I did not mean . . .' and freeing himself from her grasp he rushed out of the room, leaving her in great dudgeon. She felt indeed after this repulse prodigiously old and tottering. All this was seen by His Majesty who, his toilet long ago completed, had watched the ill-assorted pair with great amusement from behind his Imperial screen. 'I am always being told,' he said, 'that the boy takes no interest in the members of my household. But I cannot say that he seems to me unduly shy,' and he laughed. For a moment she was slightly embarrassed; but she felt that any relationship with Genji, even if it consisted of being rebuffed by him in public, was distinctly a feather for her cap, and she made no attempt to defend herself against the Emperor's raillery. The story soon went round of the Court. It astonished no one more than To no Chujo who, though he knew that Genji was given to odd experiments, could not believe that his friend was really launched upon the fantastic courtship which rumour was attributing to him. There seemed no better way of discovering whether it was conceivably possible to regard the lady in such a light than to make love to her himself.

The attentions of so distinguished a suitor went a long way towards consoling her for her late discomfiture. Her new intrigue was of course carried on with absolute secrecy and Genji knew nothing about it. When he next met her she seemed to be very cross with him, and feeling sorry for her because she was so old he made up his mind that he must try to console her. But for a long while he was completely occupied by tiresome business of one kind and another. At last one very dismal evening when he was strolling in the neighborhood of the Ummeiden he heard this lady playing most

agreeably on her lute. She was so good a performer that she was often called upon to play with the professional male musicians in the Imperial orchestra. It happened that at this moment she was somewhat downcast and discontented, and in such a mood she played with even greater feeling and verve. She was singing the 'Melon-grower's Song'; admirably, he thought, despite its inappropriateness to her age. So must the voice of the mysterious lady at O-Chou have sounded in Po Chü-i's ears when he heard her singing on her boat at night; and he stood listening. At the end of her song the player sighed heavily as though quite worn out by the passionate vehemence of her serenade. Genji approached softly humming the 'Azumaya': 'Here in the portico of the eastern house rain splashes on me while I wait. Come, my beloved, open the door and let me in.' Immediately, indeed with an unseemly haste, she answered as does the lady in the song, 'Open the door and come in,' adding the verse: 'In the wide shelter of that portico no man yet was ever splashed with rain,' and again she sighed so portentously that although he did not at all suppose that he alone was the cause of this demonstration, he felt it in any case to be somewhat exaggerated and answered with the poem: 'Your sighs show clearly that, despite the song, you are an-other's bride, and I for my part have no mind to haunt the loggias of your eastern house.' He would gladly have passed on, but he felt that this would be too unkind, and seeing that someone else was coming towards her room, he stepped inside and began talking lightly of indifferent subjects, in a style which though it was in reality some-what forced she found very entertaining.

It was intolerable, thought To no Chujo, that Genji should be praised as a quiet and serious young man and should constantly re-buke him for his frivolity, while all the time he was carrying on a multiplicity of interesting intrigues which out of mere churlishness he kept entirely hidden from all his friends. For a long while Chujo had been waiting for an opportunity to expose this sanctimonious imposture and when he saw Genji enter the gentlewoman's apartment you may be sure he was delighted. To scare him a little at such a moment would be an excellent way to punish him for his unfriend-liness. He slackened his pace and watched. The wind sighed in the trees. It was getting very late. Surely Genji would soon begin to doze? And indeed he did now look as though he had fallen asleep. Chujo stole on tiptoe into the room; but Genji who was only half-dreaming instantly heard him, and not knowing that Chujo had fol-lowed him, got it into his head that it was a certain Commissioner

of Works who years ago had been supposed to be an admirer of the lady. The idea of being discovered in such a situation by this important old gentleman filled him with horror. Furious with his companion for having exposed him to the chance of such a predicament: 'This is too bad,' he whispered, 'I am going home. What possessed you to let me in on a night when you knew that someone else was coming?' He had only time to snatch up his cloak and hide behind a long folding-screen before Chujo entered the room and going straight up to the screen began in a businesslike manner to fold it up. Though she was no longer young, the lady did not lose her head in this alarming crisis. Being a woman of fashion, she had on more than one occasion found herself in an equally agitating position, and now despite her astonishment, after considering for a moment what had best be done with the intruder, she seized him by the back of his coat and with a practised though trembling hand pulled him away from the screen. Genji had still no idea that it was Chujo. He had half a mind to show himself, but quickly remembered that he was oddly and inadequately clad, with his headdress all awry. He felt that if he ran for it he would cut much too strange a figure as he left the room, and for a moment he hesitated. Wondering how much longer Genji would take to recognize him, Chujo did not say a word but putting on the most ferocious air imaginable, drew his sword from the scabbard. Whereupon the lady crying 'Gentlemen! Gentlemen!' flung herself between them in an attitude of romantic supplication. They could hardly refrain from bursting into laughter. It was only by day when very carefully painted and bedizened that she still retained a certain superficial air of youth and charm. But now this woman of fifty-seven or eight, disturbed by a sudden brawl in the midst of her amours, created the most astonishing spectacle as she knelt at the feet of two young men in their 'teens beseeching them not to die for her. Chujo however refrained from showing the slightest sign of amusement and continued to look as alarming and ferocious as he could. But he was now in full view and Genji realized in a moment that Chujo had all the while known who he was and had been amusing himself at his expense. Much relieved at this discovery, he grabbed at the scabbard from which Chujo had drawn the sword and held it fast lest his friend should attempt to escape and then, despite his annoyance at having been followed, burst into an uncontrollable fit of laughter. 'Are you in your right mind?' said Genji at last. 'This is really a very poor sort of joke. Do you mind letting me get into my cloak?' Wherupon Chujo snatched the cloak

937

from him and would not give it back. 'Very well then,' said Genji;
'if you are to have my cloak I must have yours,' and so saying he
pulled open the clasp of Chujo's belt and began tugging his cloak
from his shoulders. Chujo resisted and a long tussle followed in
which the cloak was torn to shreds. 'Should you now get it in exchange for yours, this tattered cloak will but reveal the secrets it is
meant to hide,' recited To no Chujo; to which Genji replied with an
acrostic poem in which he complained that Chujo with whom he
shared so many secrets should have found it necessary to spy upon
him in this fashion. But neither was really angry with the other and
setting their disordered costumes to rights they both took their departure.

SANEATSU MUSHAKOJI

SANEATSU MUSHAKOJI (Japanese, 1885-   ). Modern Japanese dramatist, noted for unconventional ideological plots. Embarked on impressive
literary career after leaving school. Influenced by European dramatists: Ibsen,
Maeterlinck, Tolstoy. Authored several novels, books of essays, and many
plays. Plays known in translation: *A Family Affair, The Sister.*

A FAMILY AFFAIR
ACT III

*A living room in the Yamada home, luxuriously furnished in West-
ern style. Shuzo is alone, seated in a rocking-chair. He is smoking
a cigar and reading a newspaper. There is a knock at the door.*

Shuzo.   Come in.

(*Enter* Hiroko, *his wife.*)

Hiroko.   What is it you wish?

(*She seats herself on a chair near him.*)

Shuzo (*still reading the paper*).   I want to talk over something
with you.

Hiroko: Is it something very important?

Shuzo: Not especially so. It is about Jiro, your son.

Hiroko: About Jiro! Oh! that frightens me.

Shuzo: Why should you be frightened? (*Puts down the newspaper.*)

938

Hiroko: He is capable of doing such alarming things.

Shuzo: Oh, he is not so rash as all that.

Hiroko: No; he isn't exactly rash, but if he made up his mind to do a certain thing, he would do it even at the expense of his life.

Shuzo: You are right. But he is a very interesting boy. He will be a great man some day, if he doesn't get switched off on the wrong track.

Hiroko: And he has no regard whatever for his home and family.

Shuzo: That is true. Heaven knows he pays no attention to me. He thinks I am old and stupid, and that I want everything my own way.

Hiroko: Now, I doubt if he thinks that.

Shuzo: Oh, yes, he does. He has a stronger will than I have, and he has more brains, too. He is a deep one. We get on his nerves, and he pities us.

Hiroko: Do you think so?

Shuzo: Certainly. Now I am a self-made man and had to fight my way up in the world, but Jiro has always been taken care of, and has led an easy life. That is why I cannot understand how he comes to be so strong-willed.

Hiroko: Somehow he has changed a great deal since his brother Taro went abroad.

Shuzo: He has seemed to me very gloomy lately, and very obstinate.

Hiroko: Don't you think he will get over that when Taro comes back.

Shuzo: No; I don't think he will. He will dominate Taro. Taro has strong passions, but his will is weaker than Jiro's. I doubt if Taro is capable of anything more dangerous than falling prey to women.

Hiroko: You class women as a danger, do you?

Shuzo: I was only joking. At any rate, Taro will be all right. He isn't foolish.

Hiroko: I don't like that kind of joking.

Shuzo: Well, what I want to tell you about Jiro has to do with Fuji.

Hiroko: With Fuji? Surely not!

Shuzo: You think not? Then listen. To-day the father of Fuji, our former maid, came to see me, and told me that Fuji had refused to marry the man her family had chosen for her. I think Jiro is

939

behind this. I heard, also, that about two weeks ago, Jiro went to Fuji's house to see her.

Hiroko: Did her father tell you that?

Shuzo: No; he didn't tell me that. You know what I think? That he and Jiro are working together—that they have framed up against me. I tried to catch the old fellow by remarking that we appreciated the hospitable way in which he had received Jiro at his house. He said, "Not at all. We were surprised to have him drop in so unexpectedly." So much for that. I am certain, too, that about two weeks ago, when I was discussing Fuji's marriage with you, Jiro was listening on the sly. I thought so at the time, and that is why I asked you the next day where Jiro had gone. But you are so stupid you had no idea where he was.

Hiroko: And you are too clever for anything, of course.

Shuzo: I'm keeping a sharp eye on Jiro because I am more interested in his future than I am in Taro's.

Hiroko: Taro is more dependable.

Shuzo: Maybe so. And I admit that if Jiro should succeed me as head of the family, things might all go to smash. But to finish my story. When I asked Ota, the man I sent to arrange Fuji's marriage, how her family took to the idea, he reported that they showed neither surprise nor interest. That means Jiro had been there first. Later on I remarked in Jiro's presence that Fuji had refused the marriage proposal, and I knew he was laughing up his sleeve at me, but I didn't want to have a scene with him just then, so I ignored it. The disobedient rascal! And I thought he promised you he wouldn't go to see Fuji.

Hiroko: So he did promise.

Shuzo: You are sure?

Hiroko: Certainly. He gave me his promise not to see her, on condition that I keep my promise to him.

Shuzo: That's interesting. I am going to cross-examine him, and I want you here as a witness. But remember that you are to be on the side of the prosecution, not the defence. He's a tough customer. He knows already that we are on his trail.

Hiroko: That doesn't seem very likely.

Shuzo: But he knows that Fuji's father has been here to see me.

(*A knock at the door.*)

Who is it?

Jiro (outside): Jiro.

Shuzo: Come in.

940

(Jiro *enters calmly and sits on a chair near his mother.*)

Jiro What is it you want?

Shuzo: Don't you know what I want?

Jiro: Well, I think perhaps I do.

Shuzo: What makes you think so.

Jiro: Something I heard from Fuji's father. Besides, you are so sharp that I have to be sharp, too.

Shuzo: I have a number of things to say to you. But first of all, why did you interfere with Fuji's marriage?

Jiro: I didn't go that far. I merely went to see her father.

Shuzo: To get him to interfere, eh?

Jiro: Perhaps—though I have absolute confidence in Fuji. The point is, I knew that if her father tried to dictate to her, it would only cause trouble, so I went to win him over to her side.

Shuzo: That's a strange line of talk. What do you mean when you say you have absolute confidence in her?

Jiro: Oh, you are not clever enough to understand that. Fuji is deeply in love with someone who is also in love with her. I knew that she would refuse this arranged marriage, and I wanted to make the refusal as easy for her as possible.

Shuzo: Who is it that is in love with her?

Jiro: I can't tell you that.

Shuzo: It is not likely that it is you, is it? (*Smiles.*) If it should be, you would both have to commit suicide.

Jiro: Do you really think it is I? And do you really care as much as that about the family name, and the laws of conventionality?

Hiroko: Jiro! What are you saying? How dare you! Say that again!

Jiro: I can repeat it as often as you like. Would you drive apart two who are so deeply in love? Of course I can't tell whether or not they would actually commit suicide. That is a matter of secondary importance, anyway. But you are really so afraid of conventional laws that you would drive them apart?

Hiroko: Do you mean that you are not afraid of the criticism of society?

Jiro: Not at all. I am afraid of it. But I am much more afraid of ruining human life.

Hiroko: What an unnatural child you are. You were born to disgrace your parents.

Jiro: No, mother. I think I was not born for that purpose,

though I admit I do not know why I was born. But certainly not for anything as easy as disgracing my parents. My task is more difficult than that.

Hiroko: Jiro, be still! You are going too far.

Jiro: Mother!

Hiroko: I am shocked at you!

Jiro: Mother!

Hiroko: I am not your mother, and you are not my child. Go ahead—say what you please!

Shuzo (to Hiroko): Be quiet! Jiro didn't say that he wanted to marry Fuji. *(To* Jiro): You don't know how sacred the family name is, nor how important public opinion is, and you don't frighten me by all that wild talk. I haven't the slightest use for the sort of man that kills himself for the sake of a woman. Now see here, Jiro. Isn't it true that when we discharged Fuji, you promised your mother that you would have no correspondence with her?

Jiro: Yes, that is true. That is why I have had no correspondence with her.

Shuzo: You are sure you haven't?

Jiro: Absolutely. Some day, two or three years from now, the man who will then be her husband will prove my innocence.

Shuzo: You had no correspondence. All right. But you also promised your mother that you would not go to see Fuji, either.

Jiro: Yes, I promised that.

Shuzo: But you did see her after all, didn't you?

Jiro: Yes, I saw her.

Shuzo: Ah! And why?

Jiro: Well, I went to her home, and she was there, and I couldn't help meeting her. But I didn't go there with that purpose. I did not break the spirit of my promise to mother. If you still think I did, please forgive me.

Shuzo: I may forgive that. But you don't mind, do you, if Fuji becomes a geisha girl?

Jiro: Father! You are not going to punish Fuji because of my actions! I had to make those promises to mother in order to convince her of my innocence. I ought never to have made them!

Shuzo: You are ready to accept your punishment?

Jiro: If it is what I deserve.

Shuzo: Well then . . . you will never be Fuji's husband!

Jiro: Oh! Why, I wouldn't be if you wanted me to. In the first place, Fuji doesn't want to marry me.

Hiroko: She doesn't? You are not telling us that to clear yourself?

Jiro: Mother, you are so suspicious!

Shuzo: You are sure she doesn't want to marry you?

Jiro: Of course I am.

Shuzo: Absolutely certain?

Jiro: Absolutely.

Shuzo: You have given me your word as a man.

Jiro: And you mistrust me like a woman.

Shuzo: You have been acting very strangely.

Jiro: How?

Shuzo: First, you made a special trip to Fuji's house. Next, you concealed from us the name of the man who is in love with her. Finally, you got angry when I said you would be getting mixed up in a double-suicide.

Jiro: The first charge I think I have already explained to you. The second is made necessary by the fact that I have not the man's permission to reveal his identity. To the last accusation I will say that I got angry thinking how cruel you are, and how differently I should look at things if I were in your position. I pitied you, father and mother, for being so stupid as to worry over such a matter.

Shuzo: Do you still imagine that we will allow you to marry Fuji?

Jiro: No. I never suspected you of being that liberal. But if I were in love with Fuji so desperately that I contemplated suicide, then I think you would allow me to marry her, because it would be better for you to make your son happy than to let him kill himself after a scandal.

Hiroko: You are trying to make fools of us.

Jiro: Yes; I am.

Hiroko: You have no respect for your parents.

Jiro: I have always gone on the assumption that parents love their children.

Hiroko: No child talks back to his parents as you do.

Jiro: Perhaps not. But why worry over that?

Hiroko: Father, why don't you do something to him? He makes me angry!

Jiro: And you make me angry.

Shuzo: Jiro, you are amusing yourself at our expense just because you are clever. You are forgetting the beneficence of your parents.

943

Jiro: The beneficence of parents! That should mean giving the child happiness. When a child grows up he doesn't love his parents any longer—he wants to run away from them. That is true in my case, but you are still trying to impose your beneficence on me, and it won't work.

Hiroko: A queer sort of child you are!

Jiro: Father! Mother! You don't understand what you are talking about. You know nothing of a young man's heart. These times are different from those of your own youth. And besides, a young tree doesn't want to stay in the shade of an old tree. A young tree wants the sunlight. It wants to brave the winds. Old people think life is made for suffering; young people think it is made for enjoyment. To enjoy to the fullest one's own life! to find one's own happiness—are not those words beautiful?

Shuzo: But, Jiro, you must not forget self-sacrifice.

Jiro: I am not forgetting self-sacrifice. I would gladly sacrifice myself by my own will, but not by the will of others. If I were the man you suspected me of being, I am certain I should leave this house and run away with the girl. I would willingly disgrace my parents and become an outcast from society.

Hiroko: How dare you say such a thing?

Shuzo (to Hiroko): Be still. Jiro doesn't know what he is saying. But I believe him when he says he is not the man in question. (*To* Jiro): Now that I am convinced you are not he, you may go. I have nothing more to say to you.

(*Jiro opens the door and goes out.* Shutzo *and* Hiroko *look after him. There is a silence. Then*———)

Hiroko: Such trouble! What are we going to do?

Shuzo: After all, Jiro is our younger son. Maybe we will let him marry her. Anyway, don't worry about it.

Hiroko: Jiro is a very queer boy. I can't understand him.

Shuzo: Say!

Hiroko: Well?

Shuzo: I have thought of something—something terrible!

Hiroko: What is it?

Shuzo: The man may be—Taro!

Hiroko: Surely not!

Shuzo: Perhaps not. But why, otherwise, should Jiro talk so strangely? Taro stopped writing just about the time we sent him word of Fuji's dismissal. Before that he had written two or three times a week. In fact, I couldn't understand why he should write

so often, but I supposed it was merely because the two boys were so fond of each other. Now I realise more than ever how peculiar it was. And Jiro swore he would never correspond with Fuji, and that he would never marry her. I don't think he was lying.

Hiroko: Oh, if it is true, it is terrible!

Shuzo: Quite right. What shall we do?

Hiroko: Do you think they will commit suicide if we separate them?

Shuzo: I don't think Taro is as foolish as that.

Hiroko: Then do you think it will ruin his health?

Shuzo: I don't think so.

Hiroko: But he will hate us.

Shuzo: Yes; I suppose he will. And Jiro will hate us, too.

Hiroko: Still, if we were to let Taro marry her, it would mean the disgrace of our house.

Shuzo: That is just it. We would be ashamed for the rest of our lives. (*He glances at the door and speaks in a lower tone.*) Jiro may be listening to us.

Hiroko: No, surely not!

Shuzo: You can't trust him.

Jiro (*outside the door*): No; you can't trust him. (*He opens the door and appears.*) You were right when you guessed that Taro is the man; but you were wrong about their relationship. You have no idea how deeply they are in love.

Shuzo: Never mind about that. I shall write to Taro and tell him that we know all about his affair with Fuji, and that we are very sorry, but we cannot countenance it.

Jiro: If you write him that, I shall write him this: "Father and mother are very happy over the affair, and everything has been settled much easier than you expected." I swear I will do this. The thing has come to light through my carelessness, and I am responsible for its solution. Both of them trusted me, and I considered myself worthy of their trust. I shall therefore help them get married.

Shuzo: If you do what you threaten, I will drive you out of this house.

Jiro: I am ready to be driven out. I am ready to stand on my own feet. I knew that when I told Taro and Fuji not to worry about me. When I cried a while ago, it was merely because I pitied you both so much.

(*There is an astonished silence on the part of the parents for a few moments, then—*)

945

Hiroko: What kind of a child is this!

Shuzo: Even I am astonished!

Jiro: Death would be nothing to me. (*Tears start from his eyes.*)

Shuzo: I wish I could turn you out, but I haven't the courage. It is harder for a parent to lose his child than for a child to lose his parent. Jiro, haven't you someone you want to marry?

Jiro: I? Not yet.

Shuzo: Then I shall find someone for you.

Jiro: All right.

Shuzo: You are in love with Fuji, aren't you?

Jiro: I can't answer that.

Shuzo: Jiro, I will consent to anything you wish. You may write whatever you like to Taro. It will make him happy. And even if I lose the whole world, I won't lose you. I love you.

Jiro: Thank you, father. Taro and Fuji will be so happy! And mother, don't you worry. If you do lose the respect of society, you will gain our love. Please forgive me everything I said to you before.

Shuzo: Jiro, you are not thinking about dying?

Jiro: Far from it. I have something else to do.

(*He bows and goes out quietly.*)

Shuzo (to Hiroko): Don't worry any more. All your children have come back to you. I feel that I, too, am coming back to you. Year after next we shall see our first grandchild.

(Hiroko *looks up at Shuzo. They smile at each other.*)

CURTAIN.

MU'TAMID

MU'TAMID (Arabic, 1040-1095). A member of the Abbasid Dynasty, who became King of Seville when Moslem Spain was broken into petty states. Later lost his kingdom and was exiled to Morocco. Of some importance as a poet.

THE PHILOSOPHER PENITENT

Then must I lose my all of joy to thee,
  Thou plunderer, Time, and thief of my delight,
And in my cup of sadness shall there be
No lingering lees of my felicity?

946

True, I have been of late no little while
   A stranger to the lute-string and the cup;
Sweet looks, and tremulous eyes, and subtle smile
Have tempted not, nor crafty fingers' guile.

And now behold, my head is waxen grey,
   Yet not with plentitude of years; and lo,
My limbs are lean, my flesh consumed away,
Yet not with waste and ravage of decay,

But because I have sinned, and mocked the wise,
   And fouled the fountain of my hopes. Alas,
My spring of youth is muddied and there rise
No waters but the salt tears of these eyes.

But I will chide my sorrow, I will speak
   Thus to my weeping, saying: "Hence, my tears!
And, O sad heart, strew not upon my cheek
These symbols of the coward and the weak."

For if the shaft of Destiny hath quit
   The bow of Fate, whose hand shall be so skilled
To pluck the flying arrow back? Whose wit
Shall by a hair's breadth change the course of it?

Not ours, not ours, who spend our little time
   Tracing a broken couplet on the sand,
Till, wearied of the pleasant pantomime,
Death, the great poet, adds the lacking rhyme.

TEARS OF THE WORLD

Weep for me, friend, for now that I am hence,
   Lo, in Time's dust the footprints of my pride!
Lament, strong lions of my great defence,
   Shed tears, my young gazelles and dewy-eyed!
Look ye, the cold stars even in the height
Weep, and the clouds lift not their mournful night.

947

Weep, Wahîd, weep, and Zahi with the towers,
  Weep ye for him that shall not come again.
All waters of the earth, all dew and showers
  Have tears for Mu'tamid, and the summer rain
That once strewed pearls upon him, is become
A sea-wave full of sand and sound and foam.

N

SAROJINI NAIDU

SAROJINI NAIDU (Indian, 1879-1949). Gifted English language lyricist of Indian themes. One of first Indians to achieve mastery of English verse. A woman who married out of her caste, and later became President of the Indian National Congress. Principal volumes: *The Golden Threshold, The Bird of Time, The Broken Wing.*

SUMMER WOODS

O I am tired of painted roofs and soft and silken floors,
And long for wind-blown canopies of crimson *gulmohurs!*

O I am tired of strife and song and festivals and fame,
And long to fly where cassia-woods are breaking into flame.

Love, come with me where koels call from flowering glade and glen,
Far from the toil and weariness, the praise and prayers of men.

O let us fling all care away, and lie alone and dream
'Neath tangled boughs of tamarind and *molsari* and *neem!*

And bind our brows with jasmine sprays and play on carven flutes,
To wake the slumbering serpent-kings among the banyan roots,

And roam at fall of eventide along the river's brink,
And bathe in water-lily pools where golden panthers drink!

You and I together, Love, in the deep blossoming woods
Engirt with low-voiced silences and gleaming solitudes,

Companions of the lustrous dawn, gay comrades of the night,
Like Krishna and like Radhika, encompassed with delight.

NATSUME SOSEKI

NATSUME SOSEKI (Japanese, 1867-1916). Writer of bizarre and fantastic tales. Essayist, critic and poet. Studied in England and taught English in Japan. First enormously successful novel: *I Am a Cat.* Later works: *Young Master, Kusamakura.* His style, marked by wit and urbanity, influenced the contemporary Japanese novel.

OUR CAT'S GRAVE

AFTER we removed to Waseda our cat began to grow lean and lank. She did not seem to want to join the children in frisking about at all. When the sun shone, she would go to sleep on the verandah. Stretching her front legs out straight, she would put her square chin down on them, and, fixing her eyes on the plants in the garden, would not move for hours. No matter how noisily the children might play about her, she did not seem to be at all disturbed.

As to the children, they practically refused to associate with their old friend whom they treated like a stranger, as much as to say, "This kitten isn't friendly enough for a playmate."

Not only the children but also our maid-servant cared little for Puss: she took the trouble to put the three meals for the poor animal in a corner of the kitchen but would do nothing else.

The three meals, however, were usually made away with by a big and thievish tabby-cat of the neighbourhood before our cat had touched them. She did not even appear to get angry at this, and never quarreled. She slept quietly all the time.

But her manner of sleeping was without freedom or ease. She did not lie comfortably and enjoy the pleasant sunshine. It seemed she could not afford to move but this is not sufficient to describe her state. In other words she found life exceedingly dull and she knew that she could not shake off this feeling without moving, but to move would make her feel more lonely. She seemed to have decided to lie still and put up with her surroundings.

Her eyes were ever upon the plants in the garden, but she was probably entirely unconscious of the shapes of the leaves and of their stalks. She lay with her vacant bluish-yellow eyes riveted upon some spot.

Just as the children, her former playmates, did not seem to recognize her existence, she herself did not seem to recognize the very existence of the world around her.

Sometimes, however, she would go out, like one who had business to attend to. On these occasions she was invariably driven home by the same tom-cat of the neighbourhood, and, terror-stricken, she would spring upon the verandah, break her way through one of the closed paper doors and rush to the hearthside.

It was only at these times that the family were reminded of her existence and that she seemed to feel any satisfaction in realizing that she was still alive.

After several repetitions of this experience, the hair on her tail grew thinner little by little. At first the hair dropped out in several spots leaving small hole-like patches. These patches grew larger till her whole tail was bare. Later on it hung down like a piece of rope.

Utterly tired of all things, she began to lick the affected parts. "My dear, I'm afraid there must be something wrong with the cat," said I to my wife.

"Perhaps so;" said she quite indifferently, "perhaps it's due to her advanced age." So after this I too left the wretched animal in her pitiable plight.

Then after a few days I noticed that the poor cat was throwing up everything she ate. Moving the forepart of her neck with a wavy motion she gave a mournful sound which was something between a sneeze and a hiccup. Pitiable as she looked, I could not help her. So every time I found her in this awkward situation, I thought I would drive her out.

Otherwise she would go on spoiling the mats and cushions without compunction. Most of the *hattan* silk cusions used for visitors had already been spoiled by her.

"This won't do," I said to my wife. "She has some kind of stomach trouble, I suppose. Dissolve some *hotan* in water and give it to the poor beast."

But she did not deign to answer. A few days later, I asked her if she had given the cat any *hotan* and she replied: "Why, my dear, I've tried in vain to make her take the medicine, but she would not open her mouth. As you see, even when we give her fishbones, she vomits." She added explanatorily.

"All right, then you had not better give her any," said I crossly, returning to my book.

No sooner had the cat got rid of her nausea than she slept quietly. Lately she had shrunk into herself in an uncomfortable way and

951

appeared to feel that she had no place to go except the verandah upon which she slept.

Some changes were visible in the expression of her eyes. First they looked as if they were fixed on some distant object brought suddenly into the near field of her vision and there was something calm about her eyes even in the midst of her wretchedness. But then they began to move in a strange way. The fire of her eyes, however, sank lower and lower like sheet lightning after a summer sunset.

However, I left her just as she was. My wife also did not seem to care for the poor creature. The children had long ceased to think of their former pet, of course.

One evening she was lying on her stomach at the foot of one of the children's beds, when, all at once she gave a deep growl such as she used to do when some one tried to seize her fish.

I was the only one who thought it very strange at the time. The children were sound asleep. Their mother was busy sewing.

After a while the cat uttered another growl. At last my wife dropped her work. "What's the matter with the cat?" I cried. "It would be terrible if the cat should bite our children during the night."

"Nonsense!" said she, resuming her sewing on the sleeves of an undershirt. The cat growled again at intervals.

The next day, the poor creature lay down on the edge of the hearth and mewed all day long. That seemed somewhat repulsive to us when we went there for the tea kettle or to make tea. But when it was evening my wife as well as myself forgot all about the cat. That night the cat died. The next morning when the maid-servant went to the backyard shed to fetch some firewood, it was already lying stiff on an old kitchen stove.

My wife took the trouble of going there to see the body of the poor creature. Thereupon, her former indifference was gone and she suddenly began making a great fuss about it. She sent for our rickshaman, and getting him to buy an oblong grave-post, she asked me to write something on it. I wrote: "In Memory of A Cat" on its front and *"Konoshitani, Inazuma okoru yoi aran,"* on its back. The rickshaman wanted to know if he might bury the cat as it was, and the maid-servant added that she could not think of cremating it.

The children also began to make much of the cat again suddenly. They planted two glass bottles, one on each side of the grave-post, and filled them with twigs of blossoming *hagi.* They filled a cup with water and placed it before the grave. The flowers and the water were

changed every day. In the evening on the third day, my three-year-old daughter—I was watching her through a window of my study—walked up to the grave all alone, and after gazing at the plain-wood grave-post for a while, put out her toy dipper, scooped up water from the cup which was offered to the cat, and drank it. That was not the only time she did so. The water strewn with the fallen petals of *hagi* flowers often served to cure the thirst of little Aiko in the evening quiet.

On each death-anniversary of the cat, my wife has made it a rule to offer a small slice of salted salmon and a bowl of rice with dried bonito shavings on it before the grave. She has never forgotten to do so even until now. Only she seems to have come recently to place them on top of the wardrobe in her sitting room instead of walking out into the garden with them.

NIZAMI

NIZAMI (Persian, 1140-1203). First great romantic poet of Persia. Spent 30 years composing his *Khamsa* (*Five Treasures*), of which best-known is *Khosru and Shireen*. Dedicated poems to various rulers, but avoided court life. Also composed religious and moral poems. Works exhibit extravagant imagination, are highly ornamented.

FERHAD THE SCULPTOR

The first epic of Nizami was "Khosru and Shireen," which relates the love story of the King of Persia and the beautiful Princess Shireen. Ferhad was an eminent sculptor whose passionate love for the same maiden gave the monarch vexation. To remove him from his court the king required him to hew a channel for a river through the lofty mountain of Beysitoun, and to decorate it with sculpture. He promised also that if Ferhad should accomplish this stupendous task, he should receive as his bride the object of his love. The enamored artist accepted the work on this condition. It is related that as he struck the rock, he constantly invoked the name of Shireen.

On lofty Beysitoun the lingering sun
Looks down on ceaseless labors, long begun;

The mountain trembles to the echoing sound
Of falling rocks that from her sides rebound.
Each day, all respite, all repose, denied,
Without a pause the thundering strokes are plied;
The mist of night around the summit coils,
But still Ferhad, the lover-artist, toils.
And still, the flashes of his axe between,
He sighs to every wind, "Alas, Shireen!"
A hundred arms are weak one block to move
Of thousands moulded by the hand of love
Into fantastic shapes and forms of grace,
That crowd each nook of that majestic place.
The piles give way, the rocky peaks divide,
The stream comes gushing on, a foaming tide,—
A mighty work for ages to remain,
The token of his passion and his pain.
As flows the milky flood from Allah's throne,
Rushes the torrent from the yielding stone.
And, sculptured there, amazed, stern Khosru stands,
And frowning sees obeyed his harsh commands:
While she, the fair beloved, with being rife,
Awakes from glowing marble into life.
O hapless youth? O toil repaid by woe!
A king thy rival, and the world thy foe.
Will she wealth, splendor, pomp, for thee resign,
And only genius, truth, and passion thine?
Around the pair, lo! chiselled courtiers wait,
And slaves and pages grouped in solemn state;
From columns imaged wreaths their garlands throw,
And fretted roofs with stars appear to glow:
Fresh leaves and blossoms seem around to spring,
And feathered throngs their loves seem murmuring.
The hands of Peris might have wrought those stems
Where dew-drops hang their fragile diadems,
And strings of pearl and sharp-cut diamonds shine,
New from the wave, or recent from the mine.
"Alas, Shireen!" at every stroke he cries,—
At every stroke fresh miracles arise.
"For thee my life one ceaseless toil has been;
Inspire my soul anew,—alas, Shireen!"

954

One evening Jesus lingered in the market-place,
Teaching the people parables of truth and grace,
When in the square remote a crowd was seen to rise,
And stop with loathing gestures and abhorring cries.

The Master and his meek disciples went to see
What cause for this commotion and disgust could be,
And found a poor dead dog beside the gutter laid;
Revolting sight! at which each face its hate betrayed.

One held his nose, one shut his eyes, one turned away;
And all among themselves began aloud to say,—
"Destested creature! he pollutes the earth and air!"
"His eyes are blear!" "His ears are foul!" "His ribs are bare!"

"In his torn hide there's not a decent shoe-string left!"
"No doubt the execrable cur was hung for theft!"
Then Jesus spake, and dropped on him this saving wreath,—
"Even pearls are dark before the whiteness of his teeth!"

The pelting crowd grew silent and ashamed, like one
Rebuked by sight of wisdom higher than his own;
And one exclaimed, "No creature so accursed can be,
But some good thing in him a loving eye will see."

NOVALIS

NOVALIS (Friedrich von Hardenberg, German 1772-1801). One of most original writers of German Romantic School. Catholic medievalist, imbued with mystical and mythological inspirations. Created the "blue flower," favorite romantic symbol. Died young of tuberculosis. Most significant work: an unfinished novel, *Heinrich von Ofterdingen*. Free-verse poem: *Hymns to the Night*.

THE POET'S DAUGHTER

THE journey was now ended. It was toward evening when our travelers arrived, safe and in good spirits, in the world-renowned city of Augsburg, and rode through the lofty streets to the house of old

955

Schwaning. . . . They found the house illuminated, and a merry music reached their ears. "What will you wager," said the merchants, "that your grandfather is giving a merry entertainment? We come as if called. How surprised he will be at the uninvited guests! Little does he dream that the true festival is now to begin." . . .

Among the guests, Heinrich had noticed a man who appeared to be the person that he had seen often at his side, in that book. His noble aspect distinguished him before all the rest. A cheerful earnestness was the spirit of his countenance. An open, beautifully arched brow; great, black, piercing and firm eyes; a roguish trait about the merry mouth, and altogether clear and manly proportions made it significant and attractive. He was strongly built, his movements were easy and full of expression, and where he stood, it seemed as if he would stand forever. Heinrich asked his grandfather about him. "I am glad," said the old man, "that you have remarked him at once. It is my excellent friend Klingsohr, the poet. Of his acquaintance and friendship you may be prouder than of the emperor's. But how stands it with your heart? He has a beautiful daughter; perhaps she will supplant the father in your regards. I shall be surprised if you have not observed her." Heinrich blushed. "I was absent, dear grandfather. The company was numerous, and I noticed only your friend." "It is very easy to see," replied Schwaning, "that you are from the North. We will soon find means to thaw you here. You shall soon learn to look out for pretty eyes."

The old Schwaning led Heinrich to Klingsohr, and told him how Heinrich had observed him at once, and felt a very lively desire to be acquainted with him. Heinrich was diffident. Klingsohr spoke to him in a very friendly manner of his country and his journey. There was something so confidential in his voice, that Heinrich soon took heart and conversed with him freely. After some time Schwaning returned, and brought with him the beautiful Mathilde. "Have compassion on my shy grandson, and pardon him for seeing your father before he did you. Your gleaming eyes will awaken his slumbering youth. In his country the spring is late."

Heinrich and Mathilde colored. They looked at each other with wondering eyes. She asked him with gentle, scarce audible words: "Did he like to dance?" Just as he was affirming this question a merry dancing-music struck up. Silently he offered her his hand, she gave hers, and they mingled in the ranks of the waltzing pairs. Schwaning and Klingsohr looked on. The mother and the merchant rejoiced in Heinrich's activity, and in his beautiful partner. . . .

956

Heinrich wished the dance never to end. With intense satisfaction his eye rested on the roses of his partner. Her innocent eye shunned him not. She seemed the spirit of her father in the loveliest disguise. Out of her large, calm eyes, spoke eternal youth. On a light, heaven-blue ground reposed the mild glory of the dusky stars. Around them brow and nose sloped gracefully. A lily inclined toward the rising sun was her face; and from the slender white neck, blue veins meandered in tempting curves around the delicate cheeks. Her voice was like a far-away echo, and the small brown curly head seemed to hover over the light form.

The music banished reserve and roused every inclination to cheerful sport. Baskets of flowers in full splendor breathed forth odors on the table, and the wine crept about among the dishes and the flowers, shook his golden wings, and wove curtains of bright tapestry between the guests and the world. Heinrich now, for the first time, understood what a feast was. A thousand gay spirits seemed to him to dance about the table, and in still sympathy with gay men, to live by their joys and to intoxicate themselves with their delights. The joy of life stood like a sounding tree full of golden fruits before him. Evil did not show itself, and it seemed to him impossible that ever human inclination should have turned from this tree to the dangerous fruit of knowledge, to the tree of conflict. He now understood wine and food. He found their savor surpassingly delicious. They were seasoned for him by a heavenly oil, and sparkled from the cup the glory of earthly life. . . .

It was deep in the night when the company separated. The first and only feast of my life, said Heinrich to himself when he was alone.

He went to the window. The choir of the stars stood in the dark sky, and in the east a white sheen announced the coming day. With full transport Heinrich exclaimed: "You, ye everlasting stars, ye silent pilgrims, you I invoke as witnesses of my sacred oath! For Mathilde I will live, and eternal truth shall bind my heart to hers. For me too the morn of an everlasting day is breaking. The night is past. I kindle myself, a never-dying sacrifice to the rising sun!"

Heinrich was heated, and it was late, toward morning, when he fell asleep. The thoughts of his soul ran together into wondrous dreams. A deep blue river shimmered from the green plain. On the smooth surface swam a boat. Mathilde sat and rowed. She was decked with garlands, sang a simple song, and looked toward him with a sweet sorrow. His bosom was oppressed, he knew not why. The sky was bright, and peaceful the flood. Her heavenly coun-

tenance mirrored itself in the waves. Suddenly the boat began to spin round. He called to her, alarmed. She smiled, and laid the oar in the boat, which continued incessantly to whirl. An overwhelming anxiety seized him. He plunged into the stream, but could make no progress, the water bore him. She beckoned, she appeared desirous to say something. Already the boat shipped water, but she smiled with an ineffable inwardness, and looked cheerfully into the whirlpool. All at once it drew her down. A gentle breath streaked across the waves, which flowed as calm and as shining as before. The terrific agony deprived him of consciousness. His heart beat no more. He did not come to himself until he found himself on dry ground. He might have swam far, it was a strange country. He knew not what had befallen him; his mind was gone;— thoughtless he wandered farther into land. He felt himself dreadfully exhausted. A little fountain trickled from a hill, it sounded like clear bells. With his hand he scooped a few drops, and wetted his parched lips. Like an anxious dream the terrible event lay behind him. He walked on and on; flowers and trees spoke to him. He felt himself so well, so at home. Then he heard again that simple song. He pursued the sound. Suddenly some one held him back by his garment. "Dear Heinrich!" called a well-known voice. He looked round, and Mathilda clasped him in her arms. "Why didst thou run from me, dear heart?" said she, drawing a long breath, "I could scarce overtake thee." Heinrich wept. He pressed her to his bosom.—"Where is the river?" he exclaimed with tears. "Seest thou not its blue waves above us?" He looked up, and the blue river was flowing gently above their heads. "Where are we, dear Mathilda?" "With our parents." "Shall we remain together?" "Forever," she replied, while she pressed her lips to his, and so clasped him that she could not be separated from him again. She whispered a strange mysterious word into his mouth, which vibrated through his whole being. He wished to repeat it, when his grandfather called and he awoke. He would have given his life to remember that word.

O

EUGENE O'NEILL

EUGENE O'NEILL (American, 1888-1953). Dramatist of the tragic sense of life, often judged America's most important playwright. Experiences as young seaman recorded in early *Plays of the Sea*. After period in tuberculosis sanatorium, studied in Harvard's "47 Workshop" and joined Provincetown Players. Styles range from naturalism of *Beyond the Horizon*, to expressionism of *The Emperor Jones*, to symbolism of *The Great God Brown*, to special techniques of *Strange Interlude* and *Mourning Becomes Electra*. Nobel Prize, 1936.

THE GREAT GOD BROWN

SCENE. Cybel's parlor. An automatic, nickel-in-the-slot player-piano is at center, rear. On its right is a dirty gilt second-hand sofa. At the left is a bald-spotted crimson plush chair. The backdrop for the rear wall is cheap wall-paper of a dull yellow-brown, resembling a blurred impression of a fallow field in early spring. There is a cheap alarm clock on top of the piano. Beside it her mask is lying.

DION is seated on his back, fast asleep on the sofa, His mask has fallen down on his chest. His pale face is singularly pure, spiritual and sad.

The player-piano is groggily banging out a sentimental medley of "Mother—Mammy" tunes.

CYBEL is seated on the stool in front of the piano. She is a strong, calm, sensual, blonde girl of twenty or so, her complexion fresh and healthy, her figure full-breasted and wide-hipped, her movements slow and solidly languorous like an animal's, her large eyes dreamy with the reflected stirring of profound instincts. She chews gum like a sacred cow forgetting time with an eternal cud. Her eyes are fixed, incuriously, on DION's pale face.

959

Cybel (*as the tune runs out, glances at the clock, which indicates midnight, then goes slowly to to Dion and puts her hand gently on his forehead*). Wake up!

Dion (*stirs, sighs and murmurs dreamily*). "And He laid His hands on them and healed them." (*Then with a start he opens his eyes and, half sitting up, stares at her bewilderedly*) What—where —who are you? (*He reaches for his mask and claps it on defensively*).

Cybel (*placidly*). Only another female. You was camping on my steps, sound asleep. I didn't want to run any risk getting into more trouble with the cops pinching you there and blaming me, so I took you to sleep it off.

Dion (*mockingly*). Blessed are the pitiful, Sister! I'm broke— but you will be rewarded in Heaven!

Cybel (*calmly*). I wasn't wasting my pity. Why should I? You were happy, weren't you?

Dion (*approvingly*). Excellent! You're not a moralist, I see.

Cybel (*going on*). And you look like a good boy, too—when you're asleep. Say you better beat it home to bed or you'll be locked out.

Dion (*mockingly*). Now you're becoming maternal, Miss Earth. Is that the only answer—to pin my soul into every vacant diaper? (*She stares down at his mask, her face growing hard. He laughs*) But please don't stop stroking my aching brow. Your hand is cool mud poultice on the sting of thought!

Cybel (*calmly*). Stop acting. I hate ham fats. (*She looks at him as if waiting for him to remove his mask—then turns her back indifferently and goes to the piano*) Well, if you simply got to be a regular devil like all the other visiting sports, I s'pose I got to play with you. (*She takes her mask and puts it on—then turns. The mask is the rouged and eye-blackened countenance of the hardened prostitute. In a coarse, harsh voice*) Kindly state your dishonorable intentions, if any! I can't sit up all night keeping company! Let's have some music! (*She puts a plug in the machine. The same sentimental medley begins to play. The two masks stare at each other. She laughs*) Shoot! I'm all set! It's your play, Kid Lucifer!

Dion (*slowly removes hs mask She stops the music with a jerk. His face is gentle and sad—humbly*). I'm sorry. It has always been such an agony for me to be touched!

Cybel (*taking off her mask—sympathetically as she comes back and sits down on her stool*). Poor kid! I've never had one, but I

can guess. They hug and kiss you and take you on their laps and pinch you and want to see you getting dressed and undressed—as if they owned you—I bet you I'd never let them treat one of mine that way!

Dion (turning to her). You're lost in blind alleys, too. (*Suddenly holding out his hand to her*) But you're strong. Let's be friends.

Cybel (with a strange sternness, searches his face). And never nothing more?

Dion (with a strange smile). Let's say, never anything less (*She takes his hand. There is a ring at the outside door bell. They stare at each other. There is another ring*).

Cybel (puts on her mask, Dion does likewise. Mockingly). When you got to love to live it's hard to love living. I better join the A.F. of. L. and soap-box for the eight-hour night! Got a nickel, baby? Play a tune. (*She goes out. Dion puts a nickel in. The same sentimental tune starts. Cybel returns, followed by Billy Brown. His face is rigidly composed, but his superior disgust for Dion can be seen. Dion jerks off the music and he and Billy look at each other for a moment, Cybel watching the both—then, bored, she yawns*) He's hunting for you. Put out the lights when you go. I'm going to sleep. (*She starts to go—then, as if reminded of something—to Dion*) Life's all right, if you let it alone. (*Then mechanically flashing a trade smile at Billy*) Now you know the way, Handsome, call again! (*She goes*).

Brown (after an awkward pause). Hello, Dion! I've been looking all over town for you. This place was the very last chance. . . . (*Another pause—embarrassedly*) Let's take a walk.

Dion (mockingly). I've given up exercise. They claim it lengthens your life.

Brown (persuasively). Come on, Dion, be a good fellow. You're certainly not staying here——

Dion. Billy would like to think me taken in *flagrante delicto,* eh?

Brown. Don't be a damn fool! listen to me! I've been looking you up for purely selfish reasons. I need your help.

Dion (astonished). What?

Brown. I've a proposition to make that I hope you'll consider favorably out of old friendship. To be frank, Dion, I need you to lend me a hand down at the office.

Dion (with a harsh laugh). So it's the job, is it? Then my poor wife did a-begging go!

961

Brown (repelled—sharply). On the contrary, I had to beg her to beg you to take it. *(More angrily)* Look here, Dion! I won't listen to you talk that way about Margaret! And you wouldn't if you weren't drunk! *(Suddenly shaking him)* What in hell has come over you, anyway! You didn't use to be like this! What the devil are you going to do with yourself—sink into the gutter and drag Margaret with you? If you'd heard her defend you, lie about you, tell me how hard you were working. what beautiful things you were painting, how you stayed at home and idolized the children! —when everyone knows you've been out every night sousing and gambling away the last of your estate. . . . *(He stops, ashamed, controlling himself).*

Dion (wearily). She was lying about her husband, not me, you fool! But it's no use explaining. *(Then, in a sudden, excitable passion)* What do you want? I agree to anything—except the humiliation of yelling secrets at the deaf!

Brown (trying a bullying tone—roughly). Bunk! Don't try to crawl out! There's no excuse and you know it. *(Then as Dion doesn't reply—penitently)* But I know I shouldn't talk this way old man! It's only because we're such old pals—and I hate to see you wasting yourself—you who had more brains than any of us! But, damn it, I suppose you're too much of a rotten cynic to believe I mean what I've just said!

Dion (touched). I know Billy was always Dion Anthony's friend.

Brown. You're damn right I am—and I'd proved it long ago if you'd given me half a chance. After all, I couldn't keep chasing after you and be snubbed every time. A man has some pride!

Dion (bitterly mocking). Dead wrong! Never more! None whatever! It's immoral! Blessed are the poor in spirit, Brother! When shall I report?

Brown (eagerly). Then you'll take the—you'll help me?

Dion (wearily bitter). I'll take the job. One must do something to pass away the time, while one is waiting—for one's next incarnation.

Brown (jokingly). I'd say it was a bit early to be worrying Humorist had given me weak eyes, so now I'll have to foreswear about that. *(Trying to get Dion started)* Come along, now. It's pretty late.

Dion (shakes his hand off his shoulder and walks away from him —after a pause). Is my father's chair still there?

Brown (turns away—embarrassed). I— don't really remember, Dion—I'll look it up.

Dion (taking off his mask slowly). I'd like to sit where he spun what I have spent. What aliens we were to each other! When he lay dead, his face looked so familiar that I wondered where I had met that man before. Only at the second of my conception. After that, we grew hostile with concealed shame. And my mother? I remember a sweet strange girl, with affectionate, bewildered eyes as if God had locked her in dark closet without any explanation. I was the sole doll our ogre, her husband, allowed her and she played mother and child with me for many years in that house until at last through two tears I watched her die with the shy pride of one who has lengthened her dress and put up her hair. And I felt like a forsaken toy and cried to be buried with her, because her hands alone had caressed without clawing. She lived long and aged greatly in the two days before they closed her coffin. The last time I looked, her purity had forgotten me, she was stainless and imperishable, and I knew my sobs were ugly and meaningless to her virginity; so I shrank away, back into life, with naked nerves jumping like fleas, and in due course of nature another girl called me her boy in the moon and married me and became three mothers in one person, while I got paint on my paws in an endeavor to see God! (*He laughs wildly—claps on his mask*) But that Ancient Humorist had given me weak eyes, so now I'll have to forswear my quest for Him and go in for the Omnipresent Successful Serious One, the Great God Mr. Brown, instead! (*He makes him a sweeping, mocking bow*).

Brown (repelled but cajolingly). Shut up, you nut! You're still drunk. Come on! Let's start! (*He grabs Dion by the arm and switches off the light*).

Dion. (from the darkness—mockingly). I am thy shorn, bald, nude sheep! Lead on, Almighty Brown, thou Kindly Light!

Curtain

963

JIRO OSARAGI

OSARAGI JIRO (Japanese, 1897-   ). Eminent Japanese novelist and historical writer. Majored in political science and French law and literature. Taught language and history, then worked in Foreign Office. Author of 6 major novels and innumerable short stories. In his fiction, a concise psychological observant.

From
HOMECOMING

SAEKO said good-night and went up to her apartment on the second floor. She undressed, put on a chemise, and sat down at her dressing-table to take the pins out of her hair.

The door opened suddenly and Nobu's reflection in the mirror startled Saeko.

"I'd like to talk to you a minute," he announced from the doorway. "I didn't want Otane around. I thought it might be embarrassing."

"I'll put something on. Wait in the next room."

"Pardon me for bursting in, but, after all, I'm—"

"Never mind that. Please do as I say."

There was only a thin piece of silk around her body. Saeko felt ashamed suddenly and blushed. Nobu had looked away, but stood there waiting. She walked over to the bed and wrapped a light kimono around her. She spoke as she was picking out an obi. "Can't this wait until tomorrow morning?"

"No. It would be better to talk about it now," he insisted. "It concerns Otane. I want to send her away. . . . I want to throw off this whole slovenly existence I'm leading now. That's what I want to talk over with you."

"I hardly see that it's any of my business. But aren't you being rather hard on Otane? She's served you faithfully all these years."

"But her life never meant anything anyway. What about me? Do I have to go on dragging the sins of my youth with me the rest of my life? They become a pretty heavy load at my age. I realized I was wrong at the time, but my friends all acted that way, and I was young, so I just slipped into it. . . ."

"If you can talk so selfishly about it, it's plain you still haven't repented what you did. Of course, it takes a human being to repent." Saeko finished tying her obi and turned around toward him. "Let's go into the next room. This place is a mess."

964

"Saeko!" He looked into her face, his eyes intense. "That's not nice of you. This is your room, isn't it? I'm your husband. How can you order me out? . . . I'm sorry from the bottom of my heart. You don't understand how I've suffered these six years. I've tried to tell you, but you just wouldn't listen."

"You're breaking your promise now. We made an agreement, and you can't change it when it pleases you. And be kind enough to leave that door open."

"You're cold, Saeko—to stay angry so long about a trifle."

"I'm not in the least angry. I have nothing to be angry about."

"You say that, and torture me like this?"

"Torture you, indeed!"

"Saeko, I didn't want to say it, but a woman is a woman."

"Are you trying to get me really angry? Are you trying to make me say what I'd rather not say?"

"Don't get angry! Don't get angry! That's all I ask."

The color of fear on his elegant face provoked Saeko to speak. "You who crushed the feelings of my youth, you come here now and speak this way? And think of Otane, if you will. She's not like me. That poor creature's been trained to accept this kind of life and think herself lucky to have it. She's given herself to you entirely, with utter faith—and you want to get rid of her now she no longer suits your convenience. It would be an abominable thing to do."

"But—if you gave her a decent sum of money, she'd be glad to go back to her parents."

Saeko burst out laughing. "I shall most certainly do nothing of the kind. I refuse, definitely. I find it a very amusing idea. Who's buying what?"

"All right. I can manage to scrape that much together myself."

"Tell me—when you've sent Otane away, with whom do you intend to go on living in this house?"

Nobu paled. He understood well enough what she meant, but was too choked with humiliation to speak.

"Aren't you being cruel? Otane's a good, simple woman. What a shock it'll be for her! And have you thought what things are like outside now that you're pushing her into the streets?"

"That's why I'm giving her the money."

"Has she agreed to this? Or is it all your own idea? When I first found out about you and her, the only reason I felt I could forgive you was that at least you loved her. But if you slighted my feelings out of pure whim, if you tell me now that everything you've

been saying is a lie—aren't you making it all the harder for me to bear as a woman? I've left it all up to you. I've stayed out of your way."

"But you were all wrong about it. You're completely mistaken about what happened between us."

"I know nothing about it and don't want to! The man is responsible in such cases. Otane and I felt embarrassed toward each other as women, and you and she were shy of discussing the matter because you both knew that what you were doing was wrong. Well, good night now. Think it over. If this is what you intend to do, it's absurd to complain about needing more money."

Nobu's eyes flashed, and he shouted: "Saeko! You're in love with someone!"

"What?"

"You are! You must be!"

"I'll leave it to your imagination. Of course, I don't know what may happen in the future, but surely you can see how improbable it is that I'm in love now. I go in for things the whole way. If I were really in love with someone else, I wouldn't be at all in the mood to go on feeding a purely nominal husband and his Number Two. You can be sure of that, can't you?"

Nobu said nothing, but he put his arms around her shoulders and pulled her toward him. They were strong arms, the arms of an oarsman, but Saeko pressed her two hands against his chest and bent her body back bow-like to ward him off.

"Saeko, it's you I've always loved. Really, from my heart—"

"Take your hands off me. I'll call Otane. The plain truth is you're saying that because you want money."

"Saeko! Don't say things like that!"

"Never mind. I know you and your blood and your background Things have gone badly for you, haven't they? But stop this disgusting, unmanly display. Instead of these attentions, give me Otane's consolation money. Then we can separate for good. I hadn't thought of it until you mentioned it, but there is a man I could fall in love with. I want to go to him."

The strength ebbed out of Nobu's arms. He stood stiff and spiritless. His face sagged, pale and ugly, with his mouth open. Saeko took her chance, walked out the door, and called Otane's name in her ordinary tone.

"Forgive me, Saeko, forgive me. You shouldn't torture me so cruelly." Nobu was whining like a beaten puppy. "If you're satisfied,

966

let's leave things as they are. I'll try to bear it. . . . But don't get angry. Please don't get angry."

Saeko was listening to the stillness of the house. Otane wasn't coming.

"Just try to act like a man," she said irritably. "But I seem to be more manly than you, don't I? Good night!"

Nobu was slow to move. Saeko had reached the point where she could have loosened her sash and lain down on the bed right in front of him. She could have undressed, indifferent to his presence. She had always taken good care of herself, and her body was still young. It always gave her confidence to look at it in a full-length mirror. The man's slowness was irritating her beyond endurance. She felt there was nothing too cruel for her to do. Nobu apologized one last time and finally went out. She didn't even bother to lock the door behind him.

"Aah!" She sighed out all the feeling she'd been holding in, and sprawled her thinly covered body on the bed, throwing out her arms and legs. She could feel the dark stillness of the peony garden outside her window. The waves broke at intervals on the pebbled shore, but the sudden sounds only made the night more quiet.

Her eyes were shut. She could hear her troubled blood. Her mind was calm. It had come out of the incident indifferent. But she was becoming conscious of the weight of her extended body.

Her heartbeat quickened suddenly. She had moved her arms and legs deliberately, and then realized that her new position was the same as the one she had taken automatically that night in Singapore after parting from Kyogo Moriya. She thought about it, comparing the two positions in detail as though reviewing a school lesson. She lay still, her eyes closed, and the sense of fulfillment she had had that night seeped into her body and lured her mind into a trance. She was like a sponge growing heavy as it takes in water. At the height of fullness, she bit her lip and moaned low.

He was so much older than she, and he could make her feel this way! Her inner eyes stared at this fact in growing surprise, while the inhuman loneliness of the way she was living now shadowed her heart. She had nothing in the world to fear now. But what would become of her if she went on as she was? Kyogo Moriya hated her, there could be no doubt. She thought of these things, and something like a tremor of fear ran up and down her almost naked body.

She sighed, sat up, and turned off the lamp beside her bed.

967

OVID

OVID (Latin, 43 B.C.-19 A.D.). Urbane and sophisticated Latin poet. Of equestrian family, traveled widely before devoting self to fashionable life of Rome. Early exiled for wantonness in writings. Remains one of most influential and graceful poets of antiquity. Major works: *Amores, Heroides, Ars Amatoria, Metamorphoses, Epistulae ex Ponto.*

SAPPHO TO PHAON

Say, lovely youth, that doth my heart command,
Can Phaon's eyes forget his Sappho's hand?
Must then her name the wretched writer prove,
To thy remembrance lost, as to thy love?
Ask not the cause that I new members choose,
The lute neglected, and the Lyric Muse.
Love taught my tears in sadder notes to flow,
And tuned my heart to elegies of woe.
I burn, I burn, as when through ripened corn
By driving winds the spreading flames are borne.
Phaon to Etna's scorching fields retires,
While I consume with more than Etna's fires!
No more my soul a charm in music finds,
Music has charms alone for peaceful minds:
Soft scenes of solitude no more can please,
Love enters there, and I'm my own disease.
No more the Lesbian dames my passion move,
Once the dear objects of my guilty love;
All other loves are lost in only thine,
Ah, youth ungrateful to a flame like mine!
Whom would not all those blooming charms surprise,
Those heavenly looks, and dear deluding eyes?
The harp and bow would you like Phœbus bear,
A brighter Phœbus Phaon might appear;
Would you with ivy wreathe your flowing hair,
Not Bacchus' self with Phaon could compare:
Yet Phœbus loved, and Bacchus felt the flame,
One Daphne warmed, and one the Cretan dame;
Nymphs that in verse no more could rival me,
Than e'en those gods contend in charms with thee....

Brown as I am, an Ethiopian dame
Inspired young Perseus with a generous flame;
Turtles and doves of different hues unite,
And glossy jet is paired with shining white.
If to no charms thou wilt thy heart resign,
But such as merit, such as equal thine,
By none, alas! by none thou canst be moved:
Phaon alone by Phaon must be loved!
Yet once thy Sappho could thy cares employ;
Once in her arms you centered all your joy:
No time the dear remembrance can remove,
For, oh! how vast a memory has love!
My music, then you could not ever hear,
And all my words were music to your ear.
You stopped with kisses my enchanting tongue,
And found my kisses sweeter than my song.
In all I pleased, but most in what was best;
And the last joy was dearer than the rest.
Then with each word, each glance, each motion fired,
You still enjoyed, and yet you still desired,
Till all dissolving in the trance we lay,
And in tumultuous raptures died away. . . .

O scarce a youth, yet scarce a tender boy!
O useful time for lovers to employ!
Pride of thy age and glory of thy race,
Come to these arms, and melt in this embrace!
The vows you never will return, receive;
And take at least the love you will not give.
See, while I write, my words are lost in tears!
The less my sense, the more my love appears.
Sure 'twas not much to bid one kind adieu;
(At least to feign was never hard to you!)
"Farewell, my Lesbian love," you might have said;
Or coldly thus, "Farewell, oh Lesbian maid!"
No tear did you, no parting kiss receive,
Nor knew I then how much I was to grieve.
No lover's gift your Sappho could confer,
And wrongs and woes were all you left with her.
No charge I gave you, and no charge could give,
But this, "Be mindful of your loves, and live."

969

Now by the Nine, those powers adored by me,
And Love, the god that ever waits on thee,
When first I heard (from whom I hardly knew)
That you were fled, and all my joys with you,
Like some sad statue, speechless, pale I stood,
Grief chilled my breast, and stopped my freezing blood;
No sigh to rise, no tear had power to flow,
Fixed in a stupid lethargy of woe:
But when its way the impetuous passion found,
I rend my tresses, and my breast I wound;
I rave, then weep; I curse, and then complain;
Now fiercer pangs distract the mournful dame
Whose firstborn infant feeds the funeral flame. . . .
Stung with my love, and furious with despair,
All torn my garments, and my bosom bare,
My woes, thy crimes, I to the world proclaim:
Such inconsistent things are love and shame!
'Tis thou art all my care and my delight,
My daily longing, and my dream by night.
O night, more pleasing than the brightest day,
When fancy gives what absence takes away,
And dressed in all its visionary charms,
Restores my fair deserter to my arms! . . .
But when with day, the sweet delusions fly,
And all things wake to life and joy, but I;
As if once more forsaken, I complain,
And close my eyes to dream of you again.

P

YITSKHOK LEYBUSH PERETZ

YITSKHOK LEYBUSH PERETZ (Polish-Hebrew, 1852-1915). The classic of
modern Yiddish literature. Born in Poland, exposed early to ideological conflict between traditionalism and modernism. After 10 years of law practice,
became leader of new trend in Yiddish literature. Works include poetry,
socially oriented stories, and symbolic dramas (*The Golden Chain, At Night
in the Old Market Place*).

IF NOT HIGHER

EARLY every Friday morning, at the time of the Penitential Prayers,
the Rabbi of Nemirov would vanish.

He was nowhere to be seen—neither in the synagogue nor in the
two Houses of Study nor at a *minyan*. And he was certainly not at
home. His door stood open; whoever wished could go in and out;
no one would steal from the rabbi. But not a living creature was
within.

Where could the rabbi be? Where should he be? In heaven, no
doubt. A rabbi has plenty of business to take care of just before the
Days of Awe. Jews, God bless them, need livelihood, peace, health,
and good matches. They want to be pious and good, but our sins are
so great, and Satan of the thousand eyes watches the whole earth
from one end to the other. What he sees he reports; he denounces,
informs. Who can help us if not the rabbi!

That's what the people thought.

But once a Litvak came, and he laughed. You know the Litvaks.
They think little of the Holy Books but stuff themselves with Talmud
and law. So this Litvak points to a passage in the *Gemarah*—it
sticks in your eyes—where it is written that even Moses, our Teacher, did not ascend to heaven during his lifetime but remained suspended two and a half feet below. Go argue with a Litvak!

So where can the rabbi be?

"That's not my business," said the Litvak, shrugging. Yet all the while—what a Litvak can do!—he is scheming to find out.

That same night, right after the evening prayers, the Litvak steals into the rabbi's room, slides under the rabbi's bed, and waits. He'll watch all night and discover where the rabbi vanishes and what he does during the Penitential Prayers.

Someone else might have got drowsy and fallen asleep, but a Litvak is never at a loss; he recites a whole tractate of the Talmud by heart.

At dawn he hears the call to prayers.

The rabbi has already been awake for a long time. The Litvak has heard him groaning for a whole hour.

Whoever has heard the Rabbi of Nemirov groan knows how much sorrow for all Israel, how much suffering, lies in each groan. A man's heart might break, hearing it. But a Litvak is made of iron; he listens and remains where he is. The rabbi, long life to him, lies on the bed, and the Litvak under the bed.

Then the Litvak hears the beds in the house begin to creak; he hears people jumping out of their beds, mumbling a few Jewish words, pouring water on their fingernails, banging doors. Everyone has left. It is again quiet and dark; a bit of light from the moon shines through the shutters.

(Afterward the Litvak admitted that when he found himself alone with the rabbi a great fear took hold of him. Goose pimples spread across his skin, and the roots of his earlocks pricked him like needles. A trifle: to be alone with the rabbi at the time of the Penitential Prayers! But a Litvak is stubborn. So he quivered like a fish in water and remained where he was.)

Finally the rabbi, long life to him, arises. First he does what befits a Jew. Then he goes to the clothes closet and takes out a bundle of peasant clothes: linen trousers, high boots, a coat, a big felt hat, and a long wide leather belt studded with brass nails. The rabbi gets dressed. From his coat pocket dangles the end of a heavy peasant rope.

The rabbi goes out, and the Litvak follows him.

On the way the rabbi stops in the kitchen, bends down, takes an ax from under the bed, puts it in his belt, and leaves the house. The Litvak trembles but continues to follow.

The hushed dread of the Days of Awe hangs over the dark streets.

972

Every once in a while a cry rises from some *minyan* reciting the Penitential Prayers, or from a sickbed. The rabbi hugs the sides of the streets, keeping to the shade of the houses. He glides from house to house, and the Litvak after him. The Litvak hears the sound of his heartbeats mingling with the sound of the rabbi's heavy steps. But he keeps on going and follows the rabbi to the outskirts of the town.

A small wood stands behind the town.

The rabbi, long life to him, enters the wood. He takes thirty or forty steps and stops by a small tree. The Litvak, overcome with amazement, watches the rabbi take the ax out of his belt and strike the tree. He hears the tree creak and fall. The rabbi chops the tree into logs and the logs into sticks. Then he makes a bundle of the wood and ties it with the rope in his pocket. He puts the bundle of wood on his back, shoves the ax back into his belt, and returns to the town.

He stops at a back street beside a small broken-down shack and knocks at the window.

"Who is there?" asks a frightened voice. The Litvak recognizes it as the voice of a sick Jewish woman.

"I," answers the rabbi in the accent of a peasant.

"Who is I?"

Again the rabbi answers in Russian. "Vassil."

"Who is Vassil, and what do you want?"

"I have wood to sell, very cheap." And, not waiting for the woman's reply, he goes into the house.

The Litvak steals in after him. In the gray light of early morning he sees a poor room with broken, miserable furnishings. A sick woman, wrapped in rags, lies on the bed. She complains bitterly, "Buy? How can I buy? Where will a poor widow get money?"

"I'll lend it to you," answers the supposed Vassil. "It's only six cents."

"And how will I ever pay you back?" said the poor woman, groaning.

"Foolish one," says the rabbi reproachfully. "See, you are a poor sick Jew, and I am ready to trust you with a little wood. I am sure you'll pay. While you, you have such a great and mighty God and you don't trust him for six cents."

"And who will kindle the fire?" said the widow. "Have I the strength to get up? My son is at work."

973

"I'll kindle the fire," answers the rabbi.

As the rabbi put the wood into the oven he recited, in a groan, the first portion of the Penitential Prayers.

As he kindled the fire and the wood burned brightly, he recited, a bit more joyously, the second portion of the Penitential Prayers. When the fire was set he recited the third portion, and then he shut the stove.

The Litvak who saw all this became a disciple of the rabbi.

And ever after, when another disciple tells how the Rabbi of Nemirov ascends to heaven at the time of the Penitential Prayers, the Litvak does not laugh. He only adds quietly, "If not higher."

BENITO PEREZ GALDOS

BENITO PÉREZ GALDOS (Spanish, 1843-1920). Prolific Spanish novelist, often compared with Dickens and Tolstoy. An observing narrator of real life with depth and sympathy. Many of his books motivated by liberal ideas—e.g., *Gloria*, an indictment of religious and racial prejudice, and *Misericordia*, a study of the Madrid underworld. Left some 80 novels, 24 plays and 15 volumes of miscellaneous writings.

MADAMA ESTHER

ESTHER Spinoza, the wife of Moses Morton, a very wealthy Jewish merchant of Hamburg, who had afterwards settled in London, was, like her husband, descended from a family of Spanish Jews; but the Morton family had got itself involved with German and Dutch alliances, while that of Spinoza had kept itself unmixed, and its pedigree could be clearly traced as far back as to Daniel Spinoza, a Jew of Cordova, banned by the edict of proscription of 1492. Esther Spinoza was a Spaniard by blood, though not by birth; Spanish too in her serious character, her deeply-seated and strongly-controlled vehemence, her strict sense of duty—while the melancholy light of her black eyes, her tall figure, and her graceful gait were those of a true Spaniard. Spanish too was her mother-tongue that she had spoken like a native, from her cradle. It is a well-known fact that all the Hebrew families descended from the Spanish exiles have clung to that language, though for lack of replanting on its

native soil it has often degenerated greatly; and the Spaniard who, even at the present day, visits Constantinople, Belgrade, Jerusalem, Venice, Rome or Cairo—all of them places whither some of the miserable dust was blown that the storm swept from Spain—may hear among the Jews an archaic form of Castilian which rings in his ears as a melancholy and sweet surprise, as if it were an echo from the dead past of his native land—a sigh from the grave after four centuries of oblivion. The Spanish Jews, most of them very abject, have clung to the language of their oppressors and read the rabbinical books in that tongue; their love for the country that has been so ruthless a step-mother is as fervent as their devotion to that ancient eastern home which they have never recovered, and they weep for her as hundreds of years ago they wept by the waters of Babylon. The feeling is less strong, no doubt, among the wealthier Hebrews. The Spinozas loved the memory of the second country they had lost, but Esther hated the land with all her heart, excepting the language which she kept up diligently and took care to teach to her children.

She did not profess her own faith with any fervor of enthusiasm; still, she was loyal to it with a steady and dutiful feeling which was not so much devotion as respect for the creed of her ancestors and attachment to the name and history of an unhappy and persecuted race. This indeed amounted to a passion, a fanaticism, which might have reproduced in her the grand characteristics of Deborah the "Mother in Israel," of Jael who transfixed the foe with a nail of the tragical Judith and gentler heroine Esther. The spirit of her race filled her and inspired her, but she had not the same devotion to its formulas and rites; and though she fulfilled its precepts with her children and servants, she did so because she thought it well to perpetuate this potent bond of union—a sort of ideal father-land—on whose sacred ground a hapless nation, bereft of soil, might meet. Esther was a model of the domestic virtues which are universal among the higher class of Hebrew women, and which need neither cause surprise nor give rise to invidious reflections. There is no need to analyze them, nor to wonder whether, as many have thought, the secret of them lies in superior culture or in intrinsic natural morality. She was a good wife and a tender mother, and those who said she was worthy to have been a Christian did her no more than justice.

Esther and her husband were enormously wealthy; it might be said of them that the Lord had prospered the work of their hands.

They lived in perfect harmony, surrounded by every luxury that art could produce. Their houses almost revived the fabulous glories of the palace of Haroun-al-Raschid. They were respected by all and the guests even of Kings; and having acquired a financial position which almost gave them the importance of a political power, they had extricated Nations from difficulties. They had no native soil, but the proudest rulers had sued to them; titles, honors, respect, consideration, position and adulation—all that potentates enjoy or covet, was theirs. They stood like divinities, before whom every minister of finance was ready to burn incense; and the Pope himself, as secular sovereign, gave them titles and crosses and never called them *Deicides*, but on the contrary, "potent seignors." Esther Spinoza having visited Rome, a Cardinal constituted himself her guide through the collections, and another presented her with mosaics, cameos and carnelians, while a third sold her a marble crucifix for a thousand *livres*, and for five hundred a Spanish manuscript of the Talmud, on vellum, of the XIIIth century.

They had no kingdom but they reigned everywhere, for the dominion of Mammon is a wide one; "the earth is *his*," we may say, "and the fulness thereof," and the home of the north and the south winds. No one had ever thought of asking any member of this illustrious family in the exalted position they occupied, whether they too had said: *"Crucify Him and release unto us Barrabas."*

In spite of her fifty years, Madama Esther was still extremely handsome, as among Spanish women of rank is not uncommon; it may be accounted for by the finely-tempered balance of certain natures, combined with easy circumstances and the inestimable advantage of a life free from anxiety, menial toil and no more suffering or sorrow than is enough to prove that perfect happiness is but a myth. She indulged in few arts of the toilet, and those she used were not to conceal her years, but merely to make them look beautiful, as though she were proud of her bright and fresh maturity, the true homage of age to youth. In looking at her it became easy to understand the lasting spring of the women of whom we are told in the Bible that they lived a hundred and twenty years and more, as though it were nothing.

SAINT-JOHN PERSE

SAINT-JOHN PERSE (Alexis Saint-Léger Léger, French, 1887-   ). Elegant
poet and diplomat. Born in Guadeloupe, went to Paris for education. Entered
the Foreign Service, working closely with Briand. Came to America when
Nazis took France. Painter of rich and unusual images, especially admired
by poets and intellectuals. Most famous work, *Anabasis*, has been translated
by T. S. Eliot.

SNOWS

AND then came the snows, the first snows of absence, falling upon
the great woven cloths of dreams and reality; and with every
affliction remitted to men of memory, there came the freshness of
clean sheets on our temples. And it was in the morning, under the
grey salt of dawn, a little before the sixth hour, as in a haven of
fortune, an asylum of grace and mercy where the swarm of the
great odes of silence could be scattered.

And all the night, unknown to us, beneath that canopy of feather,
bearing its noble imprint and cure of souls, the high towns of
pumice-stone perforated by luminous insects had not ceased to grow
and excel, in the oblivion of their weight. And they alone knew
something about it whose memory is uncertain whose story aberrant.
The share that the mind took in these conspicuous things, we do
not know.

No one surprised, no one knew the first laying of that silky hour
on the loftiest brow of stone, the first touch of that agile and very
futile thing, the sweep as it were of eyelashes. On the bronze revetments and the out-thrusts of chromium-plated steel, on the rubble
of heavy porcelain, on the coarse-glass tiles, on the black-marble
spindle and on the white-metal spur, no one surprised, no one
tarnished it,

This mist of a breath at its birth, like the first fright of a blade
unsheathed . . . it was snowing and we shall tell the wonder of it:
dawn silent in its plumes, like a great fabulous owl a prey to the
winds of the spirit, puffed out its white dahlia body. On all sides
a miracle and a fête. May grace alight on this terrace-slope where
the Architect showed to us one recent summer the eggs of a night-jar.

977

ALEXANDER PETOFI

ALEXANDER PETÖFI (Hungarian, 1822-1849). Most widely known Hungarian poet. Fighter for Hungarian independence in the 1840's. Majority of his compositions are simple lyrics, modeled on folk poetry. Notable for vivid imagination, fiery patriotism.

LONGING FOR DEATH

Give me a coffin and a grave,
    And let the grave be deep and low;
And bury with me all I feel,
    All passions strong, all thoughts of woe.

O, mind and heart, twice cursed, e'er have
    You been the bane of my whole life!
Why torture me with burning scourge?
    Why should not end now all this strife?

Why should this feverish brain inspire
    To rise above the stars on high?
When angry Fate hath it ordained
    That crawl upon the earth should I.

Why have I not fair heavenly wings,
    If my aims soar to heaven's dome?
To carry me into heights where
    Immortality is at home!

And if to me this world is void
    Of joy, why have I, then, a breast?
Created that of human joys
    It be the home, the shelt'ring nest!

Or if there be a heart which flames
    And burns in passion's deep abyss,
Why, then, this icy look on me,
    Thou God of happiness and bliss?

Give me a coffin and a grave,
    And let the grave be deep and low;
And bury with me all I feel,
    All passions strong, all thoughts of woe.

IF GOD

If God Almighty thus did speak to me:
"My son, I grant permission unto thee
To have thy Death as thou thyself shalt say;"
Thus unto my Creator I would pray:

"Let it be autumn, when the zephyrs sway
The sere leaves wherewith mellow sunbeams play;
And let me hear once more the sad, sweet song
Of errant birds, that will be missed ere long.

"And unperceived, as winter's chilling breath
Waiting o'er autumn bearing subtle Death
Thus let Death come; most welcome will He be
If I observe Him when he's close to me.

"Like to the birds, again I will outpour
A mellower tune than e'er I sang before,
A song which moves the heart, makes dim the eyes
And mounts up swelling to the very skies.

"And, as my swan song draweth to its end,
My sweetheart fair and true may o'er me bend;
Thus would I die, caressing her fair face,
Kissing the one on earth who holds most grace.

"But if the Lord this boon should disallow,
With spring of war let Him the land endow;
When the rose-blooms that color earth again
Are blood-red roses in the breasts of men."

FRANCESCO PETRARCA

FRANCESCO PETRARCA (Italian, 1304-1374). Latin and Italian Poet Laureate. Precursor of the Renaissance, has been called "the first modern man of letters." Now best remembered for his Italian lyrics, *Le Rime*, addressed to his beloved, Laura. These remained models of style for centuries. Also wrote Latin epic, *Africa*, and many letters and philosophic treatises in the classic Latin manner.

SONNETS TO LAURA

All ye who list, in wildly warbled strain,
 Those sighs with which my youthful heart was fed,
 Erewhile fond passion's maze I wont to tread,
Erewhile I lived estrang'd to manlier pain;
For all those vain desires, and griefs as vain,
 Those tears, those plaints, by am'rous fancy bred,
 If ye by love's strong power have e'er been led,
Pity, nay, haply pardon, I may gain.
Oft on my check the conscious crimson glows,
 And sad reflection tells—ungrateful thought!—
How jeering crowds have mock'd my love-lorn woes:
But folly's fruits are penitence and shame,
 With this just maxim, I've too dearly bought,
That man's applause is but a transient dream.

Poor, solitary bird, that pour'st thy lay,
 Or haply mournest the sweet season gone,
 As chilly night and winter hurry on,
And daylight fades, and summer flies away!
If, as the cares that swell thy little throat,
 Thou knew'st alike the woes that wound my rest,
 Oh, thou wouldst house thee in this kindred breast,
And mix with mine thy melancholy note!
Yet little know I ours are kindred ills:
 She still may live the object of thy song:
Not so for me stern Death or Heaven wills!
 But the sad season, and less grateful hour,
And of past joy and sorrow thoughts that throng,
 Prompt my full heart this idle lay to pour.

Alone and pensive, the deserted strand
 I wander o'er with slow and measured pace,

And shun with eager eye the lightest trace
Of human foot imprinted on the sand.
I find, alas! no other resting-place
    From the keen eye of man; for, in the show
    Of joys gone by, it reads upon my face
The traces of the flame that burns below.
And thus, at length, each leafy mount and plain,
    Each wandering stream and shady forest, know,
What others know not, all my life of pain.
    And e'en as through the wildest tracts I go,
Love whispers in my ear his tender strain,
Which I with trembling lip repeat to him again.

Swift current, that from rocky Alpine vein,
    Gathering the tribute to thy waters free,
    Mov'st joyous onward night and day with me,
Where nature leads thee, me love's tyrant chain!
Roll freely on; nor toil nor rest restrain
    Thine arrowy course; but ere thou yieldest in
The tribute of thy waters to the main,
    Seek out heaven's purest sky, earth's deepest green;
There wilt thou find the bright and living beam
    That o'er thy left bank sheds its heavenly rays:
If unto her too slow my footsteps seem,—
    While by her feet thy lingering current strays,
Forming to words the murmurs of its stream,—
    Say that the weary flesh the willing soul delays.

In what ideal world or part of heaven
    Did Nature find the model of that face
    And form, so fraught with loveliness and grace,
In which to our creation she has given
Her prime proof of creative power above?
    What fountain nymph or goddess ever let
    Such lovely tresses float of gold refined
    Upon the breeze, or in a single mind
Where have so many virtues ever met,
E'en though those charms have slain my bosom's weal?
    He knows not love, who has not seen her eyes
    Turn when she sweetly speaks, or smiles, or sighs,
Or how the power of love can hurt or heal.

Creatures there be, of sight so keen and high,
    That even on the sun they bend their gaze;
    Others, who, dazzled by too fierce a blaze,
Issue not forth till evening veils the sky;
Others, who, with insane desire, would try
    The bliss which dwells within the fire's bright rays,
    But, in their sport, find that its fervor slays.
Alas! of this last heedless band am I:
    Since strength I boast not, to support the light
Of that fair form, nor in obscure sojourn
    Am skilled to fence me, nor enshrouding night.
Wherefore, with eyes which ever weep and mourn,
    My fate compels me still to court her sight,
Conscious I follow flames which shine to burn.

Waved to the winds were those long locks of gold
    Which in a thousand burnished ringlets flowed,
    And the sweet light beyond all measure glowed
Of those fair eyes which I no more behold,
Nor (so it seemed) that face aught harsh or cold
    To me (if true or false, I know not) showed;
    Me, in whose breast the amorous lure abode,
If flames consumed, what marvel to unfold?
That step of hers was of no mortal guise,
    But of angelic nature; and her tongue
Had other utterance than of human sounds.
A living sun, a spirit of the skies,
    I saw her. Now, perhaps, not so. But wounds
    Heal not, for that the bow is since unstrung.

PILPAY

PILPAY (Sanskrit, dates unknown). Legendary fabulist, known through an
ancient Sanskrit collection called *Panchatantra*. Translated into Pahlavi about
550, thereafter into Arabic. Versions also exist in Mongol, Malay and Afghan
languages.

THE MAN AND THE ADDER

A MAN mounted upon a Camel once rode into a thicket, and went
to rest himself in that part of it from whence a caravan was just

departed, and where the people having left a fire, some sparks of it, being driven by the wind, had set a bush, wherein lay an Adder, all in a flame. The fire environed the Adder in such a manner that he knew not how to escape, and was just giving himself over to destruction, when he perceived the Man already mentioned, and with a thousand mournful conjurations begged of him to save his life. The Man, on this, being naturally compassionate, said to himself, "It is true these creatures are enemies to mankind; however, good actions are of great value, even of the very greatest when done to our enemies; and whoever sows the seed of good works, shall reap the fruit of blessings." After he had made this reflection, he took a sack, and tying it to the end of his lance, reached it over the flame to the Adder, who flung himself into it; and when he was safe in, the traveler pulled back the bag, and gave the Adder leave to come forth, telling him he might go about his business; but hoped he would have the gratitude to make him a promise, never to do any more harm to men, since a man had done him so great a piece of service.

To this the ungrateful creature answered, "You much mistake both yourself and me: think not that I intend to be gone so calmly; no, my design is first to leave thee a parting blessing, and throw my venom upon thee and thy Camel."

"Monster of ingratitude!" replied the Traveler, "desist a moment at least, and tell me whether it be lawful to recompense good with evil."

"No," replied the Adder, "it certainly is not; but in acting in that manner I shall do no more than what yourselves do every day; that is to say, retaliate good deeds with wicked actions, and requite benefits with ingratitude."

"You cannot prove this slanderous and wicked aspersion," replied the Traveler: "nay, I will venture to say that if you can show me any one other creature in the world that is of your opinion, I will consent to whatever punishment you think fit to inflict on me for the faults of my fellow-creatures."

"I agree to this willingly," answered the Adder; and at the same time spying a Cow, "Let us propound our question," said he, "to this creature before us, and we shall see what answer she will make." The Man consented; and so both of them accosting the Cow, the Adder put the question to her, how a good turn was to be requited. "By its contrary," replied the Cow, "if you mean according to the custom of men; and this I know by sad experience. I belong," said

she, "to a man, to whom I have long been several ways extremely beneficial: I have been used to bring him a calf every year, and to supply his house with milk, butter, and cheese; but now I am grown old, and no longer in a condition to serve him as formerly I did, he has put me in this pasture to fat me, with a design to sell me to a butcher, who is to cut my throat, and he and his friends are to eat my flesh: and is not this requiting good with evil?"

On this, the Adder, taking upon him to speak, said to the Man, "What say you now? are not your own customs a sufficient warrant for me to treat you as I intend to do?"

The Traveler, not a little confounded at this ill-timed story, was cunning enough, however, to answer, "This is a particular case only, and give me leave to say, one witness is not sufficient to convince me; therefore pray let me have another."

"With all my heart," replied the Adder; "let us address ourselves to this Tree that stands here before us." The Tree, having heard the subject of their dispute, gave his opinion in the following words: "Among men, benefits are never requited but with ungrateful actions. I protect travelers from the heat of the sun, and yield them fruit to eat, and a delightful liquor to drink; nevertheless, forgetting the delight and benefit of my shade, they barbarously cut down my branches to make sticks, and handles for hatchets, and saw my body to make planks and rafters. Is not this requiting good with evil?"

The Adder, on this, looking upon the Traveler, asked if he was satisfied. But he was in such a confusion that he knew not what to answer. However, in hopes to free himself from the danger that threatened him, he said to the Adder, "I desire only one favor more; let us be judged by the next beast we meet; give me but that satisfaction, it is all I crave: you know life is sweet; suffer me therefore to beg for the means of continuing it." While they were thus parlaying together, a Fox passing by was stopped by the Adder, who conjured him to put an end to their controversy.

The Fox, upon this, desiring to know the subject of their dispute, said the Traveler, "I have done this Adder a signal piece of service, and he would fain persuade me that, for my reward, he ought to do me a mischief." "If he means to act by you as you men do by others, he speaks nothing but what is true," replied the Fox; "but, that I may be better able to judge between you, let me understand what service it is that you have done him."

The Traveler was very glad of this opportunity of speaking for

himself, and recounted the whole affair to him: he told him after what manner he had rescued him out of the flames with that little sack, which he showed him.

"How!" said the Fox, laughing outright, "would you pretend to make me believe that so large an Adder as this could get into such a little sack? It is impossible!" Both the Man and the Adder, on this, assured him of the truth of that part of the story; but the Fox positively refused to believe it. At length said he, "Words will never convince me of this monstrous improbability; but if the Adder will go into it again, to convince me of the truth of what you say, I shall then be able to judge of the rest of this affair."

"That I will do most willingly," replied the Adder; and, at the same time, put himself into the sack.

Then said the Fox to the Traveler, "Now you are the master of your enemy's life: and, I believe, you need not be long in resolving what treatment such a monster of ingratitude deserves of you." With that the Traveler tied up the mouth of the sack, and, with a great stone, never left off beating it till he had pounded the Adder to death; and, by that means, put an end to his fears and the dispute at once.

PINDAR

PINDAR (Greek, 518-438 B.C.). Sublime poetic eulogist, most accomplished writer of Greek choral lyrics. His major surviving works are celebration odes, written for aristocratic families and dedicated to the victors of the Panhellenic Games. Characterized by brilliant imagery and use of myths to point a moral.

JASON

(*From the Fourth Pythian Ode. In honor of Arcesilaus, King of Cyrene, victor in chariot race, 466 B.C.*

In time a noble stranger came,
A youth of glorious port; his manly frame
The country tunic clasped; two spears he bore.
Above, to fence the shivering rain,
A skin of spotted pard he threw.
Adown his youthful neck amain
His hair in glittering ringlets flew.

985

('Twas then in thronging crowds the people pressed,
  What time the busy forum filled),
  Then first he proved his manly breast,
And stood amid the throng by timorous fears unchilled.

  Who might he be? thus each in wonder cried;
    Is he Apollo? Is he Mars,
    So awful from the brazen cars,
  So fair to win bright Venus for his bride?
    In Naxus sure men said
    Otus and Ephialte were dead;
  And earth-born Tityus' giant form
    The winged shaft of Dian slew,
  What time in dread avenging storm
    From her unconquered bow it flew,
  A warning dread that men should fear,
Nor aim audacious love beyond their mortal sphere.

  So each to the other babbled;—but in haste
  High on his mule-drawn chariot Pelias came,
  Eager, and full of fear: in stealthy shame
A frightened glance upon the ground he cast,
    That glance the single sandal spied,
    The left foot bare! with easy grace
    As bent his inward dread to hide,
  "Tell, friend," he cried, "thy dwelling place;
  What nameless mother sent her darling here,
    The darling of her doting age?
    Speak nor let glozing falsehood sear
Thy birth, whate'er it be, nor lies thy soul engage."

  Then frank and brave the gentle youth replied,
  " From Chiron's cave I come, his nurseling I,
  Where Philyra my innocent infancy
And Chariclo, the Centaur's child, did guide.
    Twice ten the years I count, yet ne'er
    Hath word of falsehood stained my tongue,
    Nor deed of ill, nor ribald jeer.
  I come to claim mine own from wrong.
  Home to mine own I come, my father's heir.
    That crown usurped by lawless might,

986

Which erst old Æolus did wear,
He and his sons. From Jove, I claim my father's right.

For yielding to vile greed of power, men say,
    The promptings of a felon breast,
    Pelias my sire hath dispossessed,
And torn his long descended crown away.
      So when I first drew breath,
      Lest ruffian hands should do me death,
      My parents in the king's despite,
      Feigning an infant's early doom,
      Drest up with tears a funeral rite,
      And laid a puppet in the tomb.
      But me to Chiron's loving care,
All wrapt in princely robe, at dead of night, they bare.

Such is my tale;—no more the occasion needs;
    Then deign, kind citizens, to show me plain
    The dwelling whence my sires in lawful reign
Issued, all princely drawn by milk-white steeds.
      For Æson's son, no stranger I
      Come welcome to my home and free.
      Ask ye my name? The Centaur high
      Who bred me, bade me Jason be."
He spoke: but him his father's heart had known;
    Down his cheeks rolled the happy tears,
    To see his long-lost stripling grown
A prince of noble youths, the fairest of his peers.

Soon flock his brethren at the wondrous tale.
    Pheres from Hypereia's neighbor spring,
    Admetus eke, and brave Melampus bring,
And Amythaon from Messenia's vale,
      Cousinly greeting. He the while
      Spread bounteous forth the genial feast,
      And with kind word and courteous smile
      Received each new arriving guest.
High was the lordly cheer, and loud and long;
    Flew swiftly by each mirthful hour;
    Echoed five days and nights the song,
Five days and nights they culled joy's holiest, brightest flower.

987

But when the sixth day dawned, his tale of wrong
    To his assembled kinsman bold,
     In manly phrase the Chieftain told;
Approving murmurs broke from all the throng.
      Forth from the council-tent
      Amid his peers the hero went
    Straightway the robber king to seek.
      They passed within the portal high.
     He heard and with a smiling cheek
      Wore a deceitful courtesy.
    Then, in sage words of peaceful flow
And counsel calm, the hero thus addressed his foe:

" Son of Poseidon! oft the blinded heart
    Of man in folly seeks for crafty gain,
    Nor heeds the after-reckoning of grim pain,
To choose the juster and the wiser part.
      Yet were it well that I and you,
      With peaceful words and counsel sage,
     Should weave a web both wise and true,
      And turn to peace our mutual rage.
I speak of what thou know'st. A single womb
     Cretheus and bold Salmoneus bore.
     From these in third descent we come;
But Fate shrinks back ashamed when kinsmen join in war.

It must not be that we with sword and steel
    Our great forefather's heritage should share.
    Freely the flocks and herds,—my father's heir,
Yea, and the fruitful lands to thee I deal.
     Long hast thou these unduly held.
      Keep them, and swell thy robber store.
     It doth not yearn my soul to yield
      All these to thee; do thou restore
The royal sceptre and the righteous throne,
     Where Cretheus' son, my sire, erewhile
     With princely justice ruled his own.
These, without sterner force or trick of fraudful guile,

Restore, lest thence worse evil should ensue."
    Briefly, as best his grief to hide,
    In accents calm the king replied:
" That which thy words invite me, will I do,
    But now mine age is old;
    Thy blood is young, thy heart is bold;
    Thou may'st the infernal wrath allay:
For murdered Phrixus bids us come
    Where lives Æetes far away,
And call his exiled spirit home,
    And fetch the fleece of golden sheen,
On which he soared erewhile to 'scape the vengeful Queen.

For so a wondrous vision of my sleep
    Enjoined; without delay my way I took,
    Lest aught of vain or false my soul should mock,
To seek the God of Delphi's holy steep.
    He bade me brook no slow delay,
    But man a bark with instant speed
    The sacred vision to obey.
    Do thou perform the holy deed;
And by great Jove, our common sire, I swear,
    Sceptre and throne to yield thee free."
    Their mutual faith they promised fair,
That strong and sure to both should their high compact be.

OLYMPIA

(Eighth Olympian Ode. To Alcimedon of Ægina, victor in wrestling,
460 B.C.)

Olympia! mother of the old-crowned games!
    Great spring of Truth divine!
    Where seers around the holy shrine,
    With augury of sacred flames,
Essay the mind of Jove, the Thunder-King,
    If aught of hope he bring
To heroes straining for the glorious wreath,
Which bids the aching heart in triumph breathe.

(And oft success attends on pious prayers)
    O holy Pisan grove,
Receive our revel-pomp in love!
For glorious is his praise who shares
The grace which thy victorious garlands shed!
    Yet many a path men tread,
And various are the roads of sweet success,
When the good Gods the toils of mortals bless.

DAVID PINSKI

DAVID PINSKI (Russian-Hebrew, 1872-   ). Foremost dramatist in Yiddish. Born in Ukraine, studied in Vienna. Under influence of I. L. Peretz in Warsaw, attached self to Jewish Socialist Movement. Came to U.S.A. in 1899, emigrated to Israel in 1950. Wrote historical romances, realistic novels of Jewish life, and plays: *The Treasure, King David and His Wives, The Final Balance.*

AND THEN HE WEPT

BEREL the carrier, poor but cheerful, lived in a cellar. Its two small windows below the cobbled pavement of the courtyard were gray and muddy, scarcely admitting the sunbeams that sometimes reached them. Dampness leaked from the walls, mold glittered and sparkled in the corners.

A table stood near the wall, between the two windows. Two of the legs were its own, the others proxies—sticks of wood, which often disappeared when there was nothing else with which to heat the stove. At such times the table was shoved against the wall and remained standing, Berel said, "with God's help."

There were three white chairs as well, all without backs. As soon as a back toppled, Berel intended to hammer it into place again, but meanwhile the two sticks supporting the table had been burned up and no other firewood remained. So Berel would pull a solemn face and hand down a truly philosophical decision: one can sit on a chair even though it has no back, but potatoes must be cooked. And he would intone in a Passover voice, most impressively, while the chairback entered the oven along with other scraps that Berel and his children had scavenged.

Two beds completed the furnishings. Rags, which Berel persisted in calling pillows and blankets, covered them, and under and near

990

them stood boxes filled with more rags. Berel announced proudly that these were shirts, tablecloths—all sorts of household riches.

Did all this worry Berel? He laughed.

"What more do I need? Not a thing. As long as there's life . . ."

He had four children; two slept with him in one bed, two with the mother in the second bed. But he had no fear of more children. "Children," he said, "are a delight, a joy. Of course, they need a lot, but what's the difference? As long as I can come home and there's someone to play with, to make myself foolish with. What a pleasure! What a gang I have!"

Only his wife Bas-Sheve caused Berel dissatisfaction. He couldn't bear her moaning, her wailing and complaining.

"Eh," Berel said, shrugging, "my wife isn't fit for anything—always crying. She wants so much—what is there that she doesn't want? You'd think she had a contract with God, and He had promised to provide for her."

The tears had barely come to her eyes when Berel began to pose in front of her, his right hand against his cheek, his left hand supporting the right, his face twisted into woe and his head rocking back and forth. Bas-Sheve didn't find the imitation amusing. She grew angry. "All you do is laugh!"

"But I'm crying. Can't you see?" mocked Berel in his weepy voice.

"I wish we were crying for you, you great provider!" Her piece recited, she turned her back sharply. Berel wasn't insulted. Curses couldn't bother him. It almost seemed that without her curses life would be dull.

Only when she began to curse herself did Berel really become angry. "Almighty God," she cried out once when there was nothing to eat and a child was ill into the bargain (not at all a rare coincidence in Berel's house), "Almighty God, rescue me from this dark and bitter life!" Her voice trembled; she meant it in earnest. At that moment she had no fear of death, and Berel felt it. His ribs seemed to crack with anguish. Outraged, furious, he began to scream, "May your tongue wither!"

Bas-Sheve, reduced to silence, wept instead, while Berel cast angry glances at her. "What good does crying do? That's all I want to know. You fool!"

As far as Berel was concerned, a human being should never cry unless, God forbid, someone died. But once . . .

Once of an evening Berel played so hard with the children,

991

wrestled and cavorted and carried on so lustily, that he plummeted onto his bed—and the bed exploded into bits.

He rose from the ruins, laughing. "Hoorah! Just wait, children. We'll deliver a funeral oration over the bed." Crouching like the humpbacked village orator, Berel made as if to speak. Bas-Sheve, clutching her head, broke into a wail. "It's too much—I can't stand any more. It's the last straw. I'll kill myself."

"Shh, let me say the eulogy." Berel tried to calm her, to draw her into the game. But she kept on moaning, "God in heaven, how can I be rid of this miserable life? At least we owned two beds, and now we don't even have that."

Berel grew angry. "Cow! What shall I do with you? Come on, cry some more. So the bed's smashed! You cow! Come on, moo-oo. Why aren't you bellowing?"

"May I bellow for the loss of your head!" She threw herself at him. "If only I could get rid of you I'd see daylight! Whenever you lift a finger it turns out a misfortune. Murderer, you're my private Angel of Death."

Berel's good humor was restored by the familiar accusations. "Come on, tell the truth—why all this uproar? Why upset the universe? What's a broken bed—a catastrophe? Has the sky collapsed? Listen. Think what might have happened to one of us, and instead it's happened to the bed!"

He remonstrated. She wept.

Blotting the tears with her apron, she thought of the future. No new shoes for the children. The first few pennies that came into the house would have to go for a new bed . . . though perhaps the old one could still be fixed. Meanwhile she and the two girls would sleep on the floor, and he—that foul hunk of disaster—he'd sleep in the remaining bed.

When Berel finished she answered tartly and with tears, "Sure, you have lots of beds, don't you? Go, crawl on the floor in the mud and the damp, and you'll learn how to laugh—may this be your last laugh!" Bas-Sheve glared at him.

Berel laughed. "What a joke! Berel, that great gentleman, has to sleep on the floor. Come on, kids, drag down the mattress," he told the boys.

"Not while I'm alive will I let you sleep on the floor!" She leaped up and shielded the mattress with her body.

Berel was astonished. "What's wrong? Are you crazy?"

"When you're dead, then you can lie on the ground. Not now."
Berel grew stern. "Bas-Sheve, this is no time for foolishness. Let me get some sleep." He reached for the mattress.

She pushed his head away and pointed to the bed. "Lie down, and may you never get up."

"I don't sleep in women's beds," he joked. "Come on, let me get some sleep." He grabbed the mattress.

"I said no and I meant it," screamed Bas-Sheve, clutching the mattress with both hands.

"So I'll lie down without a mattress!" Berel laughed and took off his coat.

Bas-Sheve rushed at him with her nails. Her cheeks flushed, her eyes burned. Berel grew excited. It was his young Bas-Sheve again! Warmth flooded his heart, a smile flowed across his face. "Ah, my pretty wife," he called and wanted to embrace her. But she thrust him off, her hatred absolute. "Get away from me quietly. If you don't I'll break your head."

She turned her back and began to prepare the bed for him. In that instant he grabbed the mattress, spun it onto the floor near the stove, and threw himself on top of it.

"Come on, boys," he ordered, "let's get to sleep."

Bas-Sheve cried out in fury, "Get on that bed!"

"Tomorrow."

"Stop ordering me around—may you wither and rot."

He laughed.

"Get into that bed! Do you hear what I say?"

"Ho-hum."

Frenzied, she began to kick the one remaining bed with her feet. "There—take that! There!"

Berel and the children jumped up in horror while she kept kicking with all her strength.

Berel tried to control her, to soothe her. He caught and held her tightly. "Have you gone mad?"

She tore herself away. Her heart contracted, her head blazed. She wanted to smash, smash, smash . . . But he held her too strongly. She tried to bite him.

"Bas-Sheve! Look, Bas Sheve," he stammered, twisting away from her teeth. He managed to lower her to a chair. Slowly Bas-Sheve calmed herself and began to weep. The children formed a chorus, wailing with fright.

Berel felt lost. He stood before Bas-Sheve and didn't take his sorrowful eyes off her. "Bas-Shevenke, little Bas-Sheve, stop, please stop!"

His voice twitched. "Bas-Shevenke," he pleaded gently, softly. His heart warmed with a marvelous tenderness, his throat seemed to choke and thicken. And that time Berel wept too.

LUIGI PIRANDELLO

LUIGI PIRANDELLO (Italian, 1867-1936). Leading modern dramatist of Italy. Began career as naturalistic novelist and story writer. Turned to theater in middle age. Developed highly individual technique, to explore metaphysical problems—especially the question of personal identity. Most famous plays: *Right You Are If You Think You Are, Six Characters in Search of an Author,* Nobel Prize, 1934.

HORSE IN THE MOON

IN SEPTEMBER, upon that high and arid clayey plain, jutting perilously over the African sea, the melancholy countryside still lay parched from the merciless summer sun; it was still shaggy with blackened stubble, while a sprinkling of almond trees and a few aged olive trunks were to be seen here and there. Nevertheless, it had been decided that the bridal pair should spend at least the first few days of their honeymoon in this place, to oblige the bridegroom.

The wedding feast, which was held in a room of the deserted villa, was far from being a festive occasion for the invited guests. None of those present was able to overcome the embarrassment, or rather the feeling of dismay inspired in him by the aspect and bearing of that fleshy youth, barely twenty years of age, with purplish face and with the little darting black eyes, which were preternaturally bright, like a madman's. The latter no longer heard what was being said around him; he did not eat, and he did not drink, but became, from moment to moment, redder and more purple of countenance.

Everyone knew that he had been madly in love with the one who now sat beside him as his bride, and that he had done perfectly mad things on her account, even to the point of attempting to kill himself. He was very rich, the sole heir to the Bernardi fortune, while she, after all, was only the daughter of an infantry colonel who had come there the year before, with the regiment from Sicily.

But in spite of this, the colonel, who had been warned against the inhabitants of the island, had been reluctant about giving his consent to this match, for the reason that he had not wanted to leave his daughter there among people that were little better than savages.

The dismay which the bridegroom's aspect and actions inspired in the guests increased when the latter came to contrast him with his extremely young bride. She was really but a child, fresh, vivacious, and aloof; it seemed that she always shook off every unpleasant thought with a liveliness that was, at once, charming, ingenuous and roguish. Roguish as that of a little tomboy who as yet knows nothing of the world. A half-orphan, she had grown up without a mother's care; and indeed, it was all too evident that she was going into matrimony without any preparation whatsoever. Everyone smiled, but everyone felt a chill, when, at the end of the meal, she turned to the bridegroom and exclaimed:

"For goodness' sake, Nino, why do you make those tiny eyes? Let me—no, they burn! Why do your hands burn like that? Feel, Papa, feel how hot his hands are—Do you suppose he has a fever?"

The colonel, on pins and needles, did what he could to speed up the departure of the countryside guests. He wanted to put an end to a spectacle that impressed him as being indecent. They all piled into a half-dozen carriages. The one in which the colonel rode proceeded slowly down the lane and lagged a little behind, for the reason that the bridal couple, one on one side and one on the other, holding hands with the mother and father, had wanted to follow a short distance on foot, down to where the highway which led to the distant city began. At that point, the colonel leaned down and kissed his daughter on the head; he coughed and muttered: "Goodby, Nino."

"Goodby, Ida," said the bridegroom's mother with a laugh; and the carriage rattled away at a good pace, in order to overtake the others.

The two stood there for a moment gazing after it. But it was really only Ida who gazed; for Nino saw nothing, was conscious of nothing; his eyes were fastened upon his bride as she stood there, alone with him at last—his, all his—But what was this? Was she weeping?

"Daddy—" said Ida, as she waved her handkerchief in farewell. "There, do you see? He, too—"

"No, Ida—Ida dear—" and stammering, almost sobbing, trembling violently, Nino made an effort to embrace her.

995

"No, let me alone, please."

"I just wanted to dry your eyes—"

"Thanks, my dear; I'll dry them myself."

Nino stood there awkwardly. His face, as he looked at her, was pitiful to behold, and his mouth was half-open. Ida finished drying her eyes.

"But what's the matter?" she asked him. "You're trembling all over—No, no, Nino, for heaven's sake, no; don't stand there like that! You make me laugh. And if I once start laughing—you'll see—I'll never stop! Wait a minute; I'll wake you up."

She put her hands on his temples and blew in his eyes. At the touch of those fingers, at the breath from those lips, he felt his legs giving way beneath him; he was about to sink down on one knee, but she held him up and burst into a loud laugh:

"Upon the highway? Are you crazy? Come on, let's go! Look at that little hill over there! We shall be able to see the carriages still. Let's go look!"

And she impetuously dragged him away by one arm.

From all the countryside roundabout, where so many weeds and grasses, so many things dispersed by the hand of time lay withered, there mounted into the heat-ridden air something like a dense and ancient drought, mingling with the warm, heavy odor of the manure that lay fermenting in little piles upon the fallow fields, and with the sharper fragrance of sage and wildmint. Of that dense drought, those warm and heavy odors, that piercing fragrance, he alone was aware. She, as she ran, could hear how gaily the wood-larks sang up to the sun, from behind the thick hedges and from between the rugged yellowish tufts of burnt-over stubble; she could hear, too, in that impressive silence, the prophetic crow of cocks from distant barnyards; and she felt herself wrapped, every now and then, in the cool, keen breath that came up from the neighboring sea, to stir the few tired and yellowed leaves that were left on the almond trees, and the close-clustering, sharp-pointed, ashen-hued olive leaves.

It did not take them long to reach the hilltop; but he was so exhausted from running that he could no longer stand; he wanted to sit down, and tried to make her sit down also, there on the ground beside him, with his arm about her waist. But Ida put him off with "Let me have a look first."

She was beginning to feel restless inside, but she did not care to show it. Irritated by a certain strange and curious stubbornness

on his part, she could not, she would not stand still, but longed to keep on fleeing, still farther away; she wanted to shake him up, to distract him, to distract herself as well, so long as the day lasted.

Down there, on the other side of the hill, there stretched away a devastated plain, a sea of stubble, amid which one could make out occasionally the black and meandering traces of wood-ashes that had been sprinkled there; now and again, too, the crude yellow gleam was broken by a few clumps of caper or of licorice. Away over there, as if on the other shore of that vast yellow sea, the roofs of a hamlet rose from the tall dark poplars.

And now Ida suggested to her husband that they go over there, all the way over to that hamlet. How long would it take? An hour or less. It was not more than five o'clock. Back home, in the villa, the servants must still be busy clearing away the things. They would be home before evening.

Nino made a feeble attempt at opposition, but she took him by the hands and dragged him to his feet; in a moment, she was running down the side of the hill and was off through the sea of stubble, as light and quick as a young doe. He was not fast enough to keep up with her, but, redder-faced than ever and seemingly stunned by it all, ran after her, pantingly and perspiringly, and kept calling to her to wait and give him her hand.

"Give me your hand, at least! At least, give me your hand!" he shouted.

All of a sudden, she uttered a cry and stopped short. A flock of cawing ravens had just flown up from in front of her, stretched out upon the earth, was a dead horse. Dead? No, no, it wasn't dead; it had its eyes open. Heavens, what eyes! What eyes! A skeleton, that was what it was. And those ribs! And those flanks!

Nino came up fuming and fretting:

"Come on, let's go—let's go back—at once!"

"It's alive, look!" cried Ida, shivering from compassion. "Lift its head—heavens, what eyes! Look, Nino!'

"Yes, yes," said he, panting still. "They've just put it out here —Leave it alone; let's go! What a sight! Don't you smell?"

"And those ravens!" she exclaimed with a shudder. "Are those ravens going to eat it alive?"

"But Ida, for heaven's sake!" he implored her, clasping his hands.

"Nino, that will do!" she cried. It was more than she could endure to see him so stupid and so contrite. "Answer me: what if they eat it alive?"

"What do I know about whether or not they'll eat it? They'll wait—"

"Until it dies here, of hunger, of thirst?" Her face was all drawn with horror and pity. "Just because it's old? Because it can't work any more? Ah, poor beast! What a shame! What a shame! Haven't you any heart, standing there like that?"

"Excuse me," he said, losing his temper, "but you feel so much sympathy for an animal—"

"And oughtn't I to?"

"But you don't feel any for me!"

"And are you an animal? Are you dying of hunger and thirst as you sit there in the stubble? You feel—Oh, look at the ravens, Nino, look, up there, circling around—Oh, what a horrible, shameful, monstrous thing!—Look—Oh, the poor beast—try to lift him up! Come, Nino, get up; maybe he can still walk—Nino, get up, help me—shake yourself out of it!"

"But what do you expect me to do?" he burst out, exasperatedly. "Do you expect me to drag him back? Put him on my shoulders? What's a horse more or less? How do you think he is going to walk? Can't you see he's half-dead?"

"And if we brought him something to eat?"

"And to drink, too?"

"Oh, Nino, you're wicked!" And the tears stood in Ida's eyes.

Overcoming her shudders, she bent over very gently to caress the horse's head. The animal, with a great effort had managed to get to its knees; and even in its last degrading agony, it showed the traces of a noble beauty in head and neck.

Nino, owing possibly to the blood that was pounding in his veins, possibly owing to the bitterness and contempt she had manifested, or to the perspiration that was trickling from him, now suddenly felt his breath failing him; he grew giddy, his teeth began chattering, and he was conscious of a weird trembling all over his body. He instinctively turned up his coat collar, and with his hands in his pockets, went over and huddled down in gloomy despair upon a rock some distance away.

The sun had already set, and from the distant highway could be heard the occasional sound of horses' bells.

Why were his teeth chattering like that? For his forehead was burning up, the blood in his veins stung him, and there was a roaring in his ears. It seemed to him that he could hear so many far-away bells. All that anxiety, that spasm of expectation, her

coldness and caprice, that last foot-race, and that horse there, that cursed horse—Oh, God! was it a dream? A nightmare within a dream? Did he have a fever? Or perhaps, a worse illness? Ah! How dark it was, God—how dark! And now, his sight was clouding over. And he could not speak, he could not cry out. He tried to call "Ida, Ida!" but he could not get the words out of his parched throat.

Where was Ida? What was she doing?

She had gone off to the distant hamlet, to seek aid for that horse; she did not stop to think that the peasants had brought the animal there to die.

He remained there, alone upon the rock, a prey to those growing tremors; and as he sat there, huddled to himself like a great owl upon a perch, he suddenly beheld a sight that seemed—Ah, yes— he could see it plainly enough now—an atrocious sight, like a vision from another world. The moon. A huge moon, coming slowly up from behind that sea of stubble. And black against that enormous vapory copper disk, the headstrong head of that horse, waiting still with its neck stretched out—it had, perhaps, been waiting like that always, darkly etched upon that copper disk, while from far up in the sky could be heard the caw of circling ravens.

When Ida, angry and disillusioned, came groping her way back over the plain, calling "Nino, Nino!" the moon had already risen; the horse had dropped down as if dead; and Nino—where was Nino? Oh, there he was over there; he was on the ground, too.

Had he fallen asleep there?

She ran up to him, and found him with a death-rattle in his throat. His face, also, was on the ground; it was almost black, and his eyes, nearly closed, were puffed and bloodshot.

"Oh, God!"

She looked about her, as if in a swoon. She opened her hands which held a few dried beans that she had brought from the hamlet over there to feed to the horse. She looked at the moon, then at the horse, and then at the man lying on the ground as if dead. She felt faint, assailed as she was by the sudden suspicion that everything she saw was unreal. Terrified, she fled back to the villa calling in a loud voice for her father, her father—to come and take her away. Oh, God! away from that man with the rattle in his throat—that rattle, the meaning of which she did not understand! away from under that mad moon, away from under those cawing ravens in the sky—away, away, away—

999

PO CHU-I

PO CHÜ-I (Chinese, 772-846). One of China's greatest statesmen. Many of his poems are occasional, others written to protest social evils. Most famous, *Song of Everlasting Remorse* and *Lute Song*, are long narratives in ballad form. Also composed verse to folk tunes. Had great influence on his contemporaries.

IN YUNG-YANG

I was a child in Yung-yang,
A little child I waved farewell.
After long years again I dwell
In world-forgotten Yung-yang.
Yet I recall my play-time,
And in my dreams I see
The little ghosts of May-time
Waving farewell to me.

My father's house in Yung-yang
Has fallen upon evil days.
No kinsmen o'er the crooked ways
Hail me as once in Yung-yang.

No longer stands the old Moot-hall;
Gone is the market from the town;
The very hills have tumbled down
And stoned the valleys in their fall.

Only the waters of the Ch'in and Wei
Roll green and changeless as in days gone by.

Yet I recall my play-time,
And in my dreams I see
The little ghosts of May-time
Waving farewell to me.

RAIN AT DAWN

At dawn the crickets shrill, then cease their 'plain,
The dying candle flickers through my eaves;
Though windows bar the wild dust and the rain,
I hear the drip, drip, dripping on the broad banana leaves.

1000

SHE WHO MUST PART FROM HER SONS

The First Wife Speaks:

Sons say farewell to their mother, mother farewell to her sons;
The bright day loses its brightness at the sobs of such little ones.
He is the great Commander who conquered the West Frontier;
Last year he won the battle; the Emperor holds him dear.
Two million silver pieces were his in a shining shower—
And he went to Lo-yang and wedded this woman fair as a flower!

When the new life comes to the castle, the old wife goes from the
  door;
But my babies, my lotus blossoms, she hated them even more.
To take a new wife to your bosom and send the old wife away
Is bad enough, but the worst thing is that my babes must stay,
Stay in your house without me: one is learning to walk,
And the other just sits up swaying, a gurgle his only talk.
The boy baby cries, and the toddler weeps and clings to my dress
With a faint foreboding of evil that would vanish at my caress.
Just that you two may make merry, you turn from your former wife.
The mother of little children, and shut her out, in her life.
It isn't even so happy as the crow's or the blackbird's fate;
Their young do not leave the mother; mate does not leave his mate.
Or the plum trees abloom in the garden, haven of bird and bee;
Though their blossoms fall to the greensward, their fruit still clings
  to the tree.

New wife, new wife to my husband, hear but this word from me:
Still in Lo-yang, our native city, there are many as fair as we.
May our General win one more victory, one more great gift
  from the throne!
Then a newer wife yet will enter, and you shall go forth—alone.

CHAO CHUN IN TARTARY

When the Han envoy turns his horses homeward,
  Pray him to bear this message back for me:
"The Lady Chao Chun asks but this one question—
  'When will they send the gold to set me free?'

1001

And if the Emperor inquire about me,
  Whether my face has grown less fair or more,
Say not that I have lost my beauty grieving!
  Say not that I'm less lovely than before!

EDGAR ALLAN POE

EDGAR ALLAN POE (American, 1809-1849). Erratic, intemperate genius, whose influence has been world-wide—particularly in France. A journalist in Philadelphia and New York. His life a ceaseless struggle with poverty and alcoholism. Originated the modern detective story ("The Murders in the Rue Morgue"), wrote remarkable tales of terror ("Fall of the House of Usher") and America's most quoted poem ("The Raven").

THE MASQUE OF THE RED DEATH

THE "Red Death" had long devastated the country. No pestilence had ever been so fatal, or so hideous. Blood was its Avatar and its seal—the redness and the horror of blood. There were sharp pains, and sudden dizziness, and then profuse bleeding at the pores, with dissolution. The scarlet stains upon the body and especially upon the face of the victim, were the pest ban which shut him out from the aid and from the sympathy of his fellowmen. And the whole seizure, progress and termination of the disease, were the incidents of half an hour.

But the Prince Prospero was happy and dauntless and sagacious. When his dominions were half depopulated, he summoned to his presence a thousand hale and lighthearted friends from among the knights and dames of his court, and with these retired to the deep seclusion of one of his castellated abbeys. This was an extensive and magnificent structure, the creation of the prince's own eccentric yet august taste. A strong and lofty wall girdled it in. This wall had gates of iron. The courtiers, having entered, brought furnaces and massy hammers and welded the bolts. They resolved to leave means neither of ingress or egress to the sudden impulses of despair or of frenzy from within. The abbey was amply provisioned. With such precautions the courtiers might bid defiance to contagion. The external world could take care of itself. In the meantime it was folly to grieve, or to think. The prince had provided all the appliances of pleasure. There were buffoons, there were improvisatori, there

were ballet-dancers, there were musicians, there was Beauty, there was wine. All these and security were within. Without was the "Red Death."

It was toward the close of the fifth or sixth month of his seclusion, and while the pestilence raged most furiously abroad, that the Prince Prospero entertained his thousand friends at a masked ball of the most unusual magnificence.

It was a voluptuous scene, that masquerade. But first let me tell of the rooms in which it was held. There were seven—an imperial suite. In many palaces, however, such suites form a long and straight vista, while the folding doors slide back nearly to the walls on either hand, so that the view of the whole extent is scarcely impeded. Here the case was very different; as might have been expected from the duke's love of the *bizarre*. The apartments were so irregularly disposed that the vision embraced but little more then one at a time. There was a sharp turn at every twenty or thirty yards, and at each turn a novel effect. To the right and left, in the middle of each wall, a tall and narrow Gothic window looked out upon a closed corridor which pursued the windings of the suite. These windows were of stained glass whose color varied in accordance with the prevailing hue of the decorations of the chamber into which it opened. That at the eastern extremity was hung, for example, in blue—and vividly blue were its windows. The second chamber was purple in its ornaments and tapestries, and here the panes were purple. The third was green throughout, and so were the casements. The fourth was furnished and lighted with orange —the fifth with white—the sixth with violet. The seventh apartment was closely shrouded in black velvet tapestries that hung all over the ceiling and down the walls, falling in heavy folds upon a carpet of the same material and hue. But in this chamber only, the color of the windows failed to correspond with the decorations. The panes here were scarlet—a deep blood color. Now in no one of the seven apartments was there any lamp or candelabrum, amid the profusion of golden ornaments that lay scattered to and fro or depended from the roof. There was no light of any kind emanating from lamp or candle within the suite of chambers. But in the corridors that followed the suite, there stood, opposite to each window, a heavy tripod, bearing a brazier of fire that projected its rays through the tinted glass and so glaringly illumined the room. And thus were produced a multitude of gaudy and fantastic appearances. But in the western or black chamber the effect of the

fire-light that streamed upon the dark hangings through the blood-tinted panes, was ghastly in the extreme, and produced so wild a look upon the countenances of those who entered, that there were few of the company bold enough to set foot within its precincts at all.

It was in this apartment, also, that there stood against the western wall, a gigantic clock of ebony. Its pendulum swung to and fro with a dull, heavy, monotonous clang; and when the minute-hand made the circuit of the face, and the hour was to be stricken, there came from the brazen lungs of the clock a sound which was clear and loud and deep and exceedingly musical, but of so peculiar a note and emphasis that, at each lapse of an hour, the musicians of the orchestra were constrained to pause, momentarily, in their performance, to hearken to the sound; and thus the waltzers perforce ceased their evolutions; and there was a brief disconcert of the whole gay company; and, while the chimes of the clock yet rang, it was observed that the giddiest grew pale, and the more aged and sedate passed their hands over their brows as if in confused revery or meditation. But when the echoes had fully ceased, a light laughter at once pervaded the assembly; the musicians looked at each other and smiled as if at their own nervousness and folly, and made whispering vows, each to the other, that the next chiming of the clock should produce in them no similar emotion; and then, after the lapse of sixty minutes (which embrace three thousand and six hundred seconds of the Time that flies), there came yet another chiming of the clock, and then were the same disconcert and tremulousness and meditation as before.

But, in spite of these things, it was a gay and magnificent revel. The tastes of the duke were peculiar. He had a fine eye for colors and effects. He disregarded the *decora* of mere fashion. His plans were bold and fiery, and his conceptions glowed with barbaric lustre. There are some who would have thought him mad. His followers felt that he was not. It was necessary to hear and see and touch him to be *sure* that he was not.

He had directed, in great part, the movable embellishments of the seven chambers, upon occasion of this great *fête;* and it was his own guiding taste which had given character to the masqueraders. Be sure they were grotesque. There were much glare and glitter and piquancy and phantasm—much of what has been since seen in "Hernani." There were arabesque figures with unsuited limbs and appointments. There were delirious fancies such as the madman

fashions. There was much of the beautiful, much of the wanton, much of the *bizarre*, something of the terrible, and not a little of that which might have excited disgust. To and fro in the seven chambers there stalked, in fact, a multitude of dreams. And these —the dreams—writhed in and about, taking hue from the rooms, and causing the wild music of the orchestra to seem as the echo of their steps. And, anon, there strikes the ebony clock which stands in the hall of the velvet. And then, for a moment, all is still, and all is silent save the voice of the clock. The dreams are stiff-frozen as they stand. But the echoes of the chime die away—they have endured but an instant—and a light, half-subdued laughter floats after them as they depart. And now again the music swells, and the dreams live, and writhe to and fro more merrily than ever, taking hue from the many tinted windows through which stream the rays from the tripods. But to the chamber which lies most west-wardly of the seven, there are now none of the maskers who venture, for the night is waning away; and there flows a ruddier light through the blood-colored panes; and the blackness of the sable drapery appalls; and to him whose foot falls upon the sable carpet, there comes from the near clock of ebony a muffled peal more solemnly emphatic than any which reaches *their* ears who indulge in the more remote gayeties of the other apartments.

But these other apartments were densely crowded, and in them beat feverishly the heart of life. And the revel went whirlingly on, until at length there commenced the sounding of midnight upon the clock. And then the music ceased, as I have told; and the evolu-tions of the waltzers were quieted; and there was an uneasy cessation of all things as before. But now there were twelve strokes to be sounded by the bell of the clock; and thus it happened, perhaps, that before the last echoes of the last chime had utterly sunk into silence, there were many individuals in the crowd who had found leisure to become aware of the presence of a masked figure which had arrested the attention of no single individual before. And the rumor of this new presence having spread itself whispering around, there arose at length from the whole company, a buzz, or murmur, expressive of disapprobation and surprise—then, finally, of terror, of horror, and of disgust.

In an assembly of phantasms such as I have painted, it may well be supposed that no ordinary appearance could have excited such sensation. In truth the masquerade license of the night was nearly unlimited; but the figure in question had out-Heroded Herod,

1005

and gone beyond the bounds of even the prince's indefinite decorum. There are chords in the hearts of the most reckless which cannot be touched without emotion. Even with the utterly lost, to whom life and death are equally jests, there are matters of which no jest can be made. The whole company, indeed, seemed now deeply to feel that in the costume and bearing of the stranger neither wit nor propriety existed. The figure was tall and gaunt, and shrouded from head to foot in the habiliments of the grave. The mask which concealed the visage was made so nearly to resemble the countenance of a stiffened corpse that the closest scrutiny must have had difficulty in detecting the cheat. And yet all this might have been endured, if not approved, by the mad revellers around. But the mummer had gone so far as to assume the type of the Red Death. His vesture was dabbled in *blood*—and his broad brow, with all the features of the face, was besprinkled with the scarlet horror.

When the eyes of Prince Prospero fell upon this spectral image (which with a slow and solemn movement, as if more fully to sustain its *rôle*, stalked to and fro among the waltzers) he was seen to be convulsed, in the first moment, with a strong shudder either of terror or distaste; but, in the next, his brow reddened with rage.

"Who dares?" he demanded hoarsely of the courtiers who stood near him—"who dares insult us with this blasphemous mockery? Seize him and unmask him—that we may know whom we have to hang at sunrise, from the battlements!"

It was in the eastern or blue chamber in which stood the Prince Prospero as he uttered these words. They rang throughout the seven rooms loudly and clearly—for the prince was a bold and robust man, and the music had become hushed at the waving of his hand.

It was in the blue room where stood the prince, with a group of pale courtiers by his side. At first, as he spoke, there was a slight rushing movement of this group in the direction of the intruder, who at the moment was also near at hand, and now, with deliberate and stately step, made closer approach to the speaker. But from a certain nameless awe with which the mad assumptions of the mummer had inspired the whole party, there were found none who put forth hand to seize him; so that, unimpeded, he passed within a yard of the prince's person; and, while the vast assembly, as if with one impulse, shrank from the centres of the room to the walls, he made his way uninterruptedly, but with the same solemn and measured step which had distinguished him from

the first, through the blue chamber to the purple—through the purple to the green—through the green to the orange—through this again to the white—and even thence to the violet, ere a decided movement had been made to arrest him. It was then, however, that the Prince Prospero, maddening with rage and the shame of his own momentary cowardice, rushed hurriedly through the six chambers, while none followed him on account of a deadly terror that had seized upon all. He bore aloft a drawn dagger, and had approached, in rapid impetuosity, to within three or four feet of the retreating figure, when the latter, having attained the extremity of the velvet apartment, turned suddenly and confronted his pursuer. There was a sharp cry—and the dagger dropped gleaming upon the sable carpet, upon which, instantly afterwards, fell prostrate in death the Prince Prospero. Then, summoning the wild courage of despair, a throng of the revellers at once threw themselves into the black apartment, and, seizing the mummer, whose tall figure stood erect and motionless within the shadow of the ebony clock, gasped in unutterable horror at finding the grave-cerements and corpse-like mask which they handled with so violent a rudeness, untenanted by any tangible form.

And now was acknowledged the presence of the Red Death. He had come like a thief in the night. And one by one dropped the revellers in the blood-bedewed halls of their revel, and died each in the despairing posture of his fall. And the life of the ebony clock went out with that of the last of the gay. And the flames of the tripods expired. And Darkness and Decay and the Red Death held illimitable dominion over all.

ALEXANDER POPE

ALEXANDER POPE (English, 1688-1744). Foremost literary figure of the 18th century Classicists. A dwarfed cripple, 4½ feet tall. Famous for his translation of Homer, *An Essay on Criticism* and the poem, "The Rape of the Lock." Gave English verse a technical finish it had never previously possessed. Hence, in an age of formal standards, was acknowledged Europe's greatest poet during his lifetime.

AN ESSAY ON MAN

Hope humbly then; with trembling pinions soar;
Wait the great teacher Death, and God adore.

What future bliss, he gives not thee to know,
But gives that hope to be thy blessing now;
Hope springs eternal in the human breast—
Man never is, but always to be blessed
The soul, uneasy and confined from home,
Rests and expatiates in a life to come.
Lo, the poor Indian! whose untutored mind
Sees God in clouds, or hears him in the wind;
His soul proud science never taught to stray
Far as the solar walk, or milky way,
Yet simple nature to his hope has given,
Behind the cloud-topped hill, an humbler heaven.

Know then thyself, presume not God to scan,
The proper study of mankind is man.
Placed on this isthmus of a middle state,
A being darkly wise, and rudely great:
With too much knowledge for the sceptic side,
With too much weakness for the stoic's pride,
He hangs between; in doubt to act, or rest;
In doubt to deem himself a god, or beast;
In doubt his mind or body to prefer;
Born but to die, and reasoning but to err;
Alike in ignorance, his reason such,
Whether he thinks too little or too much:
Chaos of thought and passion, all confused;
Still by himself abused or disabused;
Created half to rise and half to fall;
Great lord of all things, yet a prey to all;
Sole judge of truth, in endless error hurled:
The glory, jest, and riddle of the world!

Whate'er the passion—knowledge, fame, or pelf,
Not one will change his neighbor with himself.
The learned is happy nature to explore,
The fool is happy that he knows no more;
The rich is happy in the plenty given,
The poor contents him with the care of Heaven.
See the blind beggar dance, the cripple sing,
The sot a hero, lunatic a king;
The starving chemist in his golden views
Supremely blest, the poet in his muse.

See some strange comfort every state attend,
And pride bestowed on all, a common **friend;**
See some fit of passion every age supply,
Hope travels through nor quits us when we die.
  Behold the child, by nature's kindly law,
Pleased with a rattle, tickled with a straw:
Some livelier plaything gives his youth delight,
A little louder, but as empty quite:
Scarfs, garters, gold, amuse his riper stage,
And beads and prayer-books are the toys of age:
Pleased with this bauble still, as that before;
Till tired he sleeps, and life's poor play is o'er.

Honor and shame from no condition rise:
Act well your part, there all the honor lies.
Fortune in men has some small difference made,
One flaunts in rags, one flutters in brocade;
The cobbler aproned, and the parson gowned,
The friar hooded, and the monarch crowned.
"What differ more (you cry) than crown and cowl!"
I'll tell you, friend! a wise man and a fool.
You'll find, if once the monarch acts the monk,
Or, cobbler-like, the parson will be drunk,
Worth makes the man, and want of it the fellow;
The rest is all but leather or prunella.

MARCEL PROUST

MARCEL PROUST (French, 1871-1922). Creator of the most fabulous single
work in modern literature: *Remembrance of Things Past.* He spent many
years in a dark, cork-lined chamber writing this 7-volume novel; then published it at his own expense. Ostensibly a meticulous recreation of the author's
early life and later social excursions, it is actually a kind of metaphysical
exploration of concepts like Time, Memory, Art and Reality.

THE DEATH OF BERGOTTE

I LEARNED that a death had occurred during the day which distressed
me greatly, that of Bergotte. It was known that he had been ill for
a long time past. Not, of course, with the illness from which he had

suffered originally and which was natural. Nature hardly seems capable of giving us any but quite short illnesses. But medicine has annexed to itself the art of prolonging them. Remedies, the respite that they procure, the relapses that a temporary cessation of them provokes, compose a sham illness to which the patient grows so accustomed that he ends by making it permanent, just as children continue to give way to fits of coughing long after they have been cured of the whooping cough. Then remedies begin to have less effect, the doses are increased, they cease to do any good, but they have begun to do harm thanks to that lasting indisposition. Nature would not have offered them so long a tenure. It is a great miracle that medicine can almost equal nature in forcing a man to remain in bed, to continue on pain of death the use of some drug. From that moment the illness artificially grafted has taken root, has become a secondary but a genuine illness, with this difference only that natural illnesses are cured, but never those which medicine creates, for it knows not the secret of their cure.

For years past Bergotte had ceased to go out of doors. Anyhow, he had never cared for society, or had cared for it for a day only, to despise it as he despised everything else and in the same fashion, which was his own, namely to despise a thing not because it was beyond his reach but as soon as he had reached it. He lived so simply that nobody suspected how rich he was, and anyone who had known would still have been mistaken, for he would have thought him a miser, whereas no one was ever more generous. He was generous above all towards women—girls, one ought rather to say—who were ashamed to receive so much in return for so little. He excused himself in his own eyes because he knew that he could never produce such good work as in an atmosphere of amorous feelings. Love is too strong a word, pleasure that is at all deeply rooted in the flesh is helpful to literary work because it cancels all other pleasures, for instance the pleasures of society, those which are the same for everyone. And even if this love leads to disillusion ment, it does at least stir, even by so doing, the surface of the soul which otherwise would be in danger of becoming stagnant. Desire is therefore not without its value to the writer in detaching him first of all from his fellow men and from conforming to their standards, and afterwards in restoring some degree of movement to a spiritual machine which, after, a certain age, tends to become paralysed. We do not succeed in being happy but we make observation of the reasons which prevent us from being happy and which

would have remained invisible to us but for these loopholes opened by disappointment. Dreams are not to be converted into reality, that we know; we would not form any, perhaps, were it not for desire, and it is useful to us to form them in order to see them fail and to be instructed by their failure. And so Bergotte said to himself· 'I am spending more than a multimillionaire would spend upon girls, but the pleasures or disappointments that they give me make me write a book which brings me money." Economically, this argument was absurd, but no doubt he found some charm in thus transmitting gold into caresses and caresses into gold. We saw, at the time of my grandmother's death, how a weary old age loves repose. Now in society, there is nothing but conversation. It may be stupid, but it has the faculty of suppressing women who are nothing more than questions and answers. Removed from society, women become once more what is so reposeful to a weary old man, an object of contemplation. In any case, it was no longer a question of anything of this sort. I have said that Bergotte never went out of doors, and when he got out of bed for an hour in his room, he would be smothered in shawls, plaids, all the things with which a person covers himself before exposing himself to intense cold or getting into a railway train. He would apologise to the few friends whom he allowed to penetrate to his sanctuary, and, pointing to his tartan plaids, his travelling-rugs, would say merrily: "After all, my dear fellow, life, as Anaxagoras has said, is a journey." Thus he went on growing steadily colder, a tiny planet that offered a prophetic image of the greater, when gradually heat will withdraw from the earth, then life itself. Then the resurrection will have to come to an end, for if, among future generations, the works of men are to shine, there must first of all be men. If certain kinds of animals hold out longer against the invading chill, when there are no longer any men, and if we suppose Bergotte's fame to have lasted so long, suddenly it will be extinguished for all time. It will not be the last animals that will read him, for it is scarcely probable that, like the Apostles on the Day of Pentecost, they will be able to understand the speech of the various races of mankind without having learned it.

In the months that preceded his death, Bergotte suffered from insomnia, and what was worse, whenever he did fall asleep, from nightmares which, if he awoke, made him reluctant to go to sleep again. He had long been a lover of dreams, even of bad dreams, because thanks to them and to the contradiction they present to

1011

the reality which we have before us in our waking state, they give us, at the moment of waking if not before, the profound sensation of having slept. But Bergotte's nightmares were not like that. When he spoke of nightmares, he used in the past to mean unpleasant things that passed through his brain. Latterly, it was as though proceeding from somewhere outside himself that he would see a hand armed with a damp cloth which, passed over his face by an evil woman, kept scrubbing him awake, an intolerable itching in his thighs, the rage—because Bergotte had murmured in his sleep that he was driving badly—of a raving lunatic of a cabman who flung himself upon the writer, biting and gnawing his fingers. Finally, as soon as in his sleep it had grown sufficiently dark, nature arranged a sort of undress rehearsal of the apoplectic stroke that was to carry him off: Bergotte arrived in a carriage beneath the porch of Swann's new house, and tried to alight. A stunning giddiness glued him to his seat, the porter came forward to help him out of the carriage, he remained seated, unable to rise, to straighten his legs. He tried to pull himself up with the help of the stone pillar that was by his side, but did not find sufficient support in it to enable him to stand.

He consulted doctors who, flattered at being called in by him, saw in his virtue as an incessant worker (it was twenty years since he had written anything), in his overstrain, the cause of his ailments. They advised him not to read thrilling stories (he never read anything), to benefit more by the sunshine, which was "indispensable to life" (he had owed a few years of comparative health only to his rigorous seclusion indoors), to take nourishment (which made him thinner, and nourished nothing but his nightmares). One of his doctors was blessed with the spirit of contradiction, and whenever Bergotte consulted him in the absence of the others, and, in order not to offend him, suggested to him as his own ideas what the others had advised, this doctor, thinking that Bergotte was seeking to have prescribed for him something that he himself liked, at once forbade it, and often for reasons invented so hurriedly to meet the case that in face of the material objections which Bergotte raised, this argumentative doctor was obliged in the same sentence to contradict himself, but, for fresh reasons, repeated the original prohibition. Bergotte returned to one of the first of these doctors, a man who prided himself on his cleverness, especially in the presence of one of the leading men of letters, and who, if Bergotte insinuated: "I seem to remember, though, that

1012

Dr. X—— told me—long ago, of course—that that might congest my kidneys and brain . . ." would smile sardonically, raise his fingers and enounce: "I said use, I did not say abuse. Naturally every remedy, if one takes it in excess, becomes a two-edged sword." There is in the human body a certain instinct for what is beneficial to us, as there is in the heart for what is our moral duty, an instinct which no authorisation by a Doctor of Medicine or Divinity can replace. We know that cold baths are bad for us, we like them, we can always find a doctor to recommend them, not to prevent them from doing us harm. From each of these doctors Bergotte took something which, in his own wisdom, he had forbidden himself for years past. After a few weeks, his old troubles had reappeared, the new had become worse. Maddened by an unintermittent pain, to which was added insomnia broken only by brief spells of nightmare, Bergotte called in no more doctors and tried with success, but to excess, different narcotics, hopefully reading the prospectus that accompanied each of them, a prospectus which proclaimed the necessity of sleep but hinted that all the preparations which induce it (except that contained in the bottle round which the prospectus was wrapped, which never produced any toxic effect) were toxic, and therefore made the remedy worse than the disease. Bergotte tried them all. Some were of a different family from those to which we are accustomed, preparations for instance of amyl and ethyl. When we absorb a new drug, entirely different in composition, it is always with a delicious expectancy of the unknown. Our heart beats as at a first assignation. To what unknown forms of sleep, of dreams, is the newcomer going to lead us? He is inside us now, he has the control of our thoughts. In what fashion are we going to fall asleep? And, once we are asleep, by what strange paths, up to what peaks, into what unfathomed gulfs is he going to lead us? With what new grouping of sensations are we to become acquainted on this journey? Will it bring us to the end of illness? To blissful happiness? To death? Bergotte's death had come to him overnight, when he had thus entrusted himself to one of these friends (a friend? or an enemy, rather?) who proved too strong for him. The circumstances of his death were as follows. An attack of uraemia, by no means serious, had led to his being ordered to rest. But one of the critics having written somewhere that in *Vermeer's Street in Delft* (lent by the Gallery at The Hague for an exhibition of Dutch painting), a picture which he adored and imagined that he knew by heart, a little patch of yellow wall (which he could not remember)

was so well painted that it was, if one looked at it by itself, like some priceless specimen of Chinese art, of a beauty that was sufficient in itself, Bergotte ate a few potatoes, left the house, and went to the exhibition. At the first few steps that he had to climb he was overcome by giddiness. He passed in front of several pictures and was struck by the stiffness and futility of so artificial a school, nothing of which equalled the fresh air and sunshine of a Venetian palazzo, or of an ordinary house by the sea. At last he came to the Vermeer which he remembered as more striking, more different from anything else that he knew, but in which, thanks to the critic's article, he remarked for the first time some small figures in blue, that the ground was pink, and finally the precious substance of the tiny patch of yellow wall. His giddiness increased; he fixed his eyes, like a child upon a yellow butterfly which it is trying to catch, upon the precious little patch of wall. "That is how I ought to have written," he said. "My last books are too dry, I ought to have gone over them with several coats of paint, made my language exquisite in itself, like this little patch of yellow wall." Meanwhile he was not unconscious of the gravity of his condition. In a celestial balance there appeared to him, upon one of its scales, his own life, while the other contained the little patch of wall so beautifully painted in yellow. He felt that he had rashly surrendered the former for the latter. "All the same," he said to himself, "I have no wish to provide the 'feature' of this exhibition for the evening papers."

He repeated to himself: "Little patch of yellow wall, with a sloping roof, little patch of yellow wall." While doing so he sank down upon a circular divan; and then at once he ceased to think that his life was in jeopardy and, reverting to his natural optimism, told himself: "It is just an ordinary indigestion from those potatoes; they weren't properly cooked; it is nothing." A fresh attack beat him down; he rolled from the divan to the floor, as visitors and attendants came hurrying to his assistance. He was dead. Permanently dead? Who shall say? Certainly our experiments in spiritualism prove no more than the dogmas of religion that the soul survives death. All that we can say is that everything is arranged in this life as though we entered it carrying the burden of obligations contracted in a former life; there is no reason inherent in the conditions of life on this earth that can make us consider ourselves obliged to do good, to be fastidious, to be polite even, nor make the talented artist consider himself obliged to begin over again a score of times a piece of work the admiration aroused by which

will matter little to his body devoured by worms, like the patch of
yellow wall painted with so much knowledge and skill by an artist
who must for ever remain unknown and is barely identified under
the name Vermeer. All these obligations which have not their sanction in our present life seem to belong to a different world, founded
upon kindness, scrupulosity, self-sacrifice, a world entirely different
from this, which we leave in order to be born into this world, before
perhaps returning to the other to live once again beneath the sway
of those unknown laws which we have obeyed because we bore
their precepts in our hearts, knowing not whose hand had traced
them there—those laws to which every profound work of the intellect
brings us nearer and which are invisible only—and still!—to fools.
So that the idea that Bergotte was not wholly and permanently
dead is by no means improbable.

They buried him, but all through the night of mourning, in the
lighted windows, his books arranged three by three kept watch
like angels with outspread wings and seemed, for him who was no
more, the symbol of his resurrection.

ALEXANDER SERGEYEVICH PUSHKIN

ALEXANDER SERGEYEVICH PUSHKIN (Russian, 1799-1837). The first
great figure in Russian literature, and fountainhead of much of its later glory.
Evgeny Onegin, Pique Dame (both turned into operas by Tchaikovsky),
Boris Godunov (similarly treated by Moussorgsky), *Ruslan and Ludmila,* and
Fairy Tales are major works. Partly of African ancestry, exiled for a time
because of his liberalism. Later joined the Czar's entourage, killed in duel.
Great champion of Russian genius.

OUTLIVED DESIRE

Outlived desire now departs,
  My dreams I cannot love again;
I reap the fruit of empty hearts,
  The fruit of pain.

The tempest of a cruel fate
  My fair and flowery garlands rend;
Unhappy and alone I wait:
  When comes the end?

So, stricken by the early cold,
   The whistling, bitter gales of grief,
Still the autumnal branches hold
   One shuddering leaf.

THE PRISONER

In a damp cell behind bars sit I;
Outside an eagle, young and born to fly,
The sad companion of my prisoned day
Flutters his wing and pecks his bleeding prey.

Then pecks no more, but through the window stares
As though we thought the same thing unawares,
As though with look and cry his heart would say:
'Brother, the time is come to fly away.

We are free birds together, free and proud;
Fly where the mountains whiten through the cloud
To that sea country blue beneath the sky
Where only walks the wind, the wind and I'.

THE COACH OF LIFE

The swaying coach, for all its load,
   Runs lightly as it rocks;
Grey Time goes driving down the road,
   Nor ever leaves the box.

We jump into the coach at dawn,
   Alert and fresh and free,
And holding broken bones in scorn,
   'Go on' shout we.

By midday all is changed about,
   Our morning hearts are cool;
We fear the steep descents, and shout:
   'Go slow, you fool!'

1016

By dusk we're used to jolt and din,
  And when the light is gone
We sleep before we reach the inn,
  As Time drives on.

THE PROPHET

I dragged my steps across a desert bare,
  My spirit parched with heat;
And lo, a seraph with six wings was there;
  He stood where two roads meet.

Soft as the coming of a dream at night,
  His fingers touched my head;
He raised the lids of my prophetic sight,
  An eagle's, wide with dread.

He touched my ears. They filled with sound and song:
  I heard the heaven's motion,
The flight of angels, and the reptile throng
  That moves beneath the ocean.

I heard the soundless growth of plant and tree:
  Then, stooping to my face,
With his right hand he tore my tongue from me.
  Vain, sinful tongue and base.

A serpent's fiery fang he thrust instead
  Through my faint lips apart;
He slit my breast, and with a sword stained red
  Hewed out my quaking heart.

A coal of living fire his fingers placed
  Deep in my gaping side.
Dead as I lay upon the desert waste,
  I heard God's Voice that cried:

'Arise, O prophet, having seen and heard;
  Strong in my Spirit, span
The universal earth, and make my word
  Burn in the heart of man'.

THE POET

When the poet by Apollo
For his service is not claimed,
In a life inane and hollow
He is sunken, he is maimed.
Then his soul, as cold as clay,
Sleeps unvisited by Song:
He frequents the wordly throng,
Insignificant as they.
But let once Apollo's word
Fall upon his listening ear,
His awakened soul is stirred
Like an eagle soaring clear.
Wild and sad, he turns away
From the pleasures of the town,
Scorning man and man's renown
And the idols of a day.
Full of voices, in the throes
Of confusion forth he goes,
Lonely, to the forest trees
And the shores of barren seas.

THE UPAS TREE

Across the desert dry as bone,
    Stark sentinel of burning sands,
In the wide universe alone
    The deadly Upas stands.

Born in a day of wrath it rose
    Out of the waste, whose nature sent
Deep through its roots and sombre boughs
    Poison for nourishment.

In noonday heat from out its bark
    The beads of oozing venom come,
And with the cooler breath of dark
    Set in a shining gum.

1018

No bird among its boughs may fly,
   Beneath its shade no tiger stray:
The whirlwind when it ventures nigh
   Infected storms away.

The wandering showers of the plain,
   Caught on its branches interlaced,
In drops of dark unwholesome rain
   Sink in the thirsty waste.

Yet once a man, with cold command,
   Dared send a man to seek the tree.
All night across the dreadful sand
   He went obediently.

He brought the deathly gum at dawn
   With leaves by poison withered brown,
And from his forehead pale and drawn
   Coldly the sweat ran down.

Before his master as he went
   His steps grew weak and faltering,
And the poor slave died in the tent
   Of the remorseless King.

The venom taken from his hand
   The King's obedient arrows fed,
And they through every neighbouring land
   Death and disaster sped.

THE DON

Through open fields, across the plain
   I see him yonder, streaming on!
From all your distant sons, again
   I greet you, shining Don.

O quiet Don, each river knows
   That you their famous brother are;
Araxes greets you as he flows,
   And Oxus from afar.

By cruel foes no longer chased
   The horses of the Don draw nigh,
Already scent there home, and taste
   The streams of Arpachai.

Then watch, O holy Don, for there
   They come, brave Cossacks, born your own!
Once more the sparkling wine prepare
   From vineyards you have grown.

R

FRANCOIS RABELAIS

FRANÇOIS RABELAIS (French, *ca.* 1490-1553). A monk who later became a physician and scholar. *Gargantua and Pantagruel,* his sprawling comic allegory, was written over period of 20 years to entertain patients and patrons. Today the symbol of the burlesque and ribald, it nonetheless carried a message: that man is basically good and only needs new kind of education to call forth that goodness.

THE LOST HATCHET

THERE   once lived a poor honest country fellow of Gravot, Tom Wellhung by name, a wood cleaver by trade, who in that low drudgery made shift so to pick up a sorry livelihood. It happened that he lost his hatchet. Now, tell me, who ever had more cause to be vexed than poor Tom? Alas, his whole estate and life depended on his hatchet; by his hatchet he earned many a fair penny of the best woodmongers or log merchants, among whom he went a jobbing; for want of his hatchet he was like to starve; and had Death but met him six days after without a hatchet, the grim fiend would have mowed him down in the twinkling of a bedstaff. In this sad case he began to be in a heavy taking, and called upon Jupiter with most eloquent prayers (for, you know, Necessity was the mother of Eloquence). With the whites of his eyes turned up towards heaven, down on his marrowbones, his arms reared high, his fingers stretched wide, and his head bare, the poor wretch without ceasing was roaring out by way of Litany at every repetition of his supplications, "My hatchet, Lord Jupiter, my hatchet, my hatchet, only my hatchet, O Jupiter, or money to buy another, and nothing else; alas, my poor hatchet!"

Jupiter happened then to be holding a grand council about certain urgent affairs, and old Gammer Cybele was just giving her opinion,

1021

or, if you had rather have it so, it was young Phœbus the Beau; but, in short, Tom's outcry and lamentations were so loud that they were heard with no small amazement at the council board by the whole consistory of the gods. "What a devil have we below," quoth Jupiter, "that howls so horridly? By the mud of Styx, haven't we had all along, and haven't we here still, enough to do to set to rights a world of puzzling business of consequence? . . . Let us, however, dispatch this howling fellow below: you, Mercury, go see who it is, and know what he wants." Mercury looked out at heaven's trapdoor, through which, as I am told, they hear what's said here below; by the way, one might well enough mistake it for the scuttle of a ship; though Icaromenippus said it was like the mouth of a well. The light-heeled deity saw it was honest Tom, who asked for his lost hatchet; and accordingly he made his report to the Synod. "Marry," said Jupiter, "we are finely holped up, as if we had now nothing else to do here but to restore lost hatchets. Well, he must then have it for all this, for so 'tis written in the Book of Fate (do you hear?), as well as if it was worth the whole duchy of Milan. The truth is, the fellow's hatchet is as much to him as a kingdom to a king. Come, come, let no more words be scattered about it; let him have his hatchet again. Run down immediately, and cast at the poor fellow's feet three hatchets,—his own, another of gold, and a third of massy silver, all of one size: then, having left it to his will to take his choice, if he take his own, and be satisfied with it, give him t'other two. If he take another, chop his head off with his own; and henceforth serve me all those losers of hatchets after that manner." Having said this, Jupiter, with an awkward turn of his head, like a jackanapes swallowing of pills, made so dreadful a phiz that all the vast Olympus quaked again. Heaven's foot messenger, thanks to his low-crowned, narrow-brimmed hat, and plume of feathers, heelpieces, and running stick with pigeon wings, flings himself out at heaven's wicket, through the empty deserts of the air, and in a trice nimbly alights on the earth, and throws at friend Tom's feet the three hatchets, saying to him, "Thou hast bawled long enough to be a-dry; thy prayers and requests are granted by Jupiter: see which of these three is thy hatchet, and take it away with thee."

Wellhung lifts up the golden hatchet, peeps upon it, and finds it very heavy, then, staring at Mercury, cries, "Godszouks, this is none of mine; I won't ha' 't!" The same he did with the silver one, and said, " 'Tis not this, either: you may e'en take them again."

At last he takes up his own hatchet, examines the end of the helve, and finds his mark there; then, ravished with joy, like a fox that meets some straggling poultry, and sneering from the top of his nose, he cried, "By the mass, this is my hatchet! Master god, if you will leave it me, I will sacrifice to you a very good and huge pot of milk, brimful, covered with fine strawberries, next Ides (*i.e.* the 15th) of March."

"Honest fellow," said Mercury, "I leave it thee; take it; and because thou hast wished and chosen moderately, in point of hatchet, by Jupiter's command I give thee these two others. Thou hast now wherewith to make thyself rich; be honest." Honest Tom gave Mercury a whole cart load of thanks, and revered the most great Jupiter. His old hatchet he fastens close to his leathern girdle, and girds it about his breech like Martin of Cambray; the two others, being more heavy, he lays on his shoulder. Thus he plods on, trudging over the fields, keeping a good countenance among his neighbors and fellow-parishioners with one merry saying or other after Patelin's way. The next day, having put on a clean white jacket, he takes on his back the two precious hatchets, and comes to Chinon, the famous city, noble city, ancient city, yea, the first city of the world, according to the judgment and assertion of the most learned Massoreths. In Chinon he turned his silver hatchet into fine testons, crown pieces, and other white cash; his golden hatchet into fine angels, curious ducats, substantial ridders, spankers, and rose nobles. Then with them he purchases a good number of farms, barns, houses, outhouses, thatch houses, stables, meadows, orchards, fields, vineyards, woods, arable lands, pastures, ponds, mills, gardens, nurseries, oxen, cows, sheep, goats, swine, hogs, asses, horses, hens, cocks, capons, chickens, geese, ganders, ducks, drakes and a world of other necessaries, and in a short time became the richest man in all the country. His brother bumpkins, and the yeomen and other country-puts thereabouts, perceiving his good fortune were not a little amazed, insomuch that their pity of poor Tom was soon changed into an envy of his so great and unexpected rise; and, as they could not for their souls devise how this came about, they made it their business to pry up and down, and lay their heads together, to inquire, seek, and inform themselves by what means, in what place, on what day, what hour, how, why, and wherefore, he had come by this great treasure.

At last, hearing it was by losing his hatchet, "Ha! ha!" said they, "was there no more to do but lose a hatchet, to make us rich?"

With this they all fairly lost their hatchets out of hand. The devil a one that had a hatchet left; he was not his mother's son that did not lose his hatchet. No more was wood felled or cleared in that country, through want of hatchets. Nay, the Æsopian apologue even saith that certain petty country gents of the lower class, who had sold Wellhung their little mill and little field to have wherewithal to make a figure at the next muster, having been told that this treasure was come to him by that means only, sold the only badge of their gentility, their swords, to purchase hatchets to go to lose them, as the silly clodpates did, in hopes to gain store of chink by that loss.

You would have truly sworn they had been a parcel of your petty spiritual usurers, Rome-bound, selling their all, and borrowing of others to buy store of mandates, a pennyworth of a new-made pope.

Now they cried out and brayed, and prayed and bawled, and lamented and invoked Jupiter: "My hatchet! my hatchet! Jupiter, my hatchet!" on this side, "My hatchet!" on that side, "My hatchet! Ho, ho, ho, ho, Jupiter, my hatchet!" The air round about rang again with the cries and howlings of these rascally losers of hatchets.

Mercury was nimble in bringing them hatchets,—to each offering that which he had lost, as also another of gold and a third of silver.

Everywhere he still was for that of gold, giving thanks in abundance to the great giver, Jupiter; but, in the very nick of time that they bowed and stooped to take it from the ground, whip in a trice Mercury lopped off their heads, as Jupiter had commanded; and of heads thus cut off the number was just equal to that of the lost hatchets.

You see how it is now; you see how it goes with those who in the simplicity of their hearts wish and desire with moderation. Take warning by this, all you greedy, fresh-water shirks, who scorn to wish for anything under ten thousand pounds; and do not, for the future, run on impudently, as I have sometimes heard you wishing, "Would to God I had now one hundred and seventy-eight millions of gold! oh, how I should tickle it off!" The deuce on you, what more might a king, an emperor, or a pope wish for? For that reason, indeed, you see that after you have made such hopeful wishes all the good that comes to you of it is the itch or scab, and not a cross in your breeches to scare the devil that tempts you to make these wishes; no more than those two mumpers, one of whom only wished to have in good old gold as much as hath been spent, bought, and sold in Paris, since its first foundations were laid, to

this hour, all of it valued at the price, sale, and rate of the dearest year in all that space of time. Do you think the fellow was bashful? had he eaten sour plums unpeeled? were his teeth on edge, I pray you? The other wished Our Lady's church brimful of steel needles, from the floor to the top of the roof, and to have as many ducats as might be crammed into as many bags as might be sewed with each and every one of those needles, till they were all either broke at the point or eye. This is to wish with a vengeance! What think you of it? What did they get by it, in your opinion? Why, at night both my gentlemen had kibed heels, a tetter in the chin, a churchyard cough in the lungs, a catarrh in the throat, a swingeing boil at the rump, and the devil of one musty crust of a brown George the poor dogs had to scour their grinders with. Wish, therefore, for mediocrity, and it shall be given unto you, and over and above yet; that is to say, provided you bestir yourselves manfully and do your best in the mean time.

JEAN BAPTISTE RACINE

JEAN BAPTISTE RACINE (French, 1639-1699). Classical tragedian who brought French drama to its highest peak. Adhered to the Greek unities and concentrated on psychological conflict between characters. Used mainly Latin and Greek themes in his 11 plays. Best: *Andromaque, Bérénice, Phèdre, Athalie.* Emotional range of his poetry unsurpassed in French.

ORESTES AND HERMIONE

Hermione.   What have I done? Where am I? Where is Pyrrhus?
Ye gods! what mean these horrors? I'm undone!
My soul is on the rack! I cannot bear it!
Why do I wander like some guilty ghost?
What brought me to this place? What keeps me here?
The court of Pyrrhus has no room for me!
Do I still doubt if I should love or hate him?
Hard-hearted man! how unconcerned he left me!
Did he once sigh? bestow one pitying look?
Once shed a tear? or speak one soft, kind word?
Did he so much as feign one moment's sorrow,
To calm my griefs, and mitigate his falsehood?
Why am I still thus anxious for his life?
Why do I start at his impending fate?

Shall he, then, live? Shall the base traitor live
To laugh at my distress? No, let him perish!
Be quick, Orestes! Execute my orders!
Alas! my orders! O preposterous guilt!
Can I decree the death of him I love?
Was it for this my soul delighted in him?
Was it for this I left my father's court?
Have I, then, crossed so many realms and seas
To murder Pyrrhus?—

(*Cleone enters.*)

O Cleone, help me!
What have I done? Is Pyrrhus yet alive?
What say'st thou? Answer me: where is the king?
   Cleone. Madam, I saw the cruel prince set forward,
Triumphant in his looks, and full of joy.
Still as he walked, his ravished eyes were fixed
On the fair captive; while through shouting crowds
She passed along with a dejected air,
And seemed to mourn her Hector to the last.
   Herm. Insulting tyrant! I shall burst with rage!
But say, Cleone, didst thou mark him well?
Was his brow smooth? Say did there not appear
Some shade of grief, some little cloud of sorrow?
Did he not stop? Did he not once look back?
Didst thou approach him? Was he not confounded?
Did he not——Oh, be quick, and tell me all!
   Cle. Madam, the tumult of his joy admits
No thought but love. Unguarded he marches on,
'Midst a promiscuous throng of friends and foes.
His cares all turn upon Astyanax,
Whom he has lodged within the citadel,
Defended by the strength of all his guards.
   Herm. Enough! he dies! the traitor! Where's Orestes?
   Cle. Madam, I fear——
   Herm. Is he still resolute? Is he still determined?
   Cle. Madam, I fear——
   Herm. How! Is Orestes false? Does he betray me, too?
   Cle. A thousand doubts
Perplex his soul, and wound him with remorse:
His virtue and his love prevail by turns.
He told me Pyrrhus should not fall ignobly,—

1026

Pyrrhus, the warlike son of great Achilles.
He dreads the censure of the Grecian states,—
Of all mankind, and fears to stain his honor.

Herm. Poor timorous wretch! 'Tis false! He basely fears
To cope with dangers, and encounter death;
'Tis that he fears! Am I bright Helen's daughter?
To vindicate her wrongs all Greece conspired;
For her, confederate nations fought, and kings were slain,
Troy was o'erthrown, and a whole empire fell:
My eyes want force to raise a lover's arm
Against a tyrant that has dared to wrong me!

   Cle. Madam, like Helen, trust your cause to Greece.

   Herm. No! I'll avenge myself: I'll to the temple;
I'll overturn the altar, stab the priest;
I'll hurl destruction like a whirlwind round me!
They must not wed! they must not live! they shall not!
Let me begone! I have no time to lose!
Stand off! hold me not! I am all distraction!
O Pyrrhus, tyrant! traitor! thou shalt bleed!

(Orestes enters.)

   Orestes. Madam, 'tis done; your orders are obeyed:
The tyrant lies expiring at the altar.

   Herm. Is Pyrrhus slain?

   Or. Even now he gasps in death.
Our Greeks, all undistinguished in the crowd,
Flocked to the temple and dispersed themselves
On every side the altar. I was there:
Pyrrhus observed me with a haughty eye,
And, proud to triumph over Greece in me,
From his own brows he took the diadem,
And bound it on the temples of his captive:
"Receive," said he, "my crown! receive my faith!
Mine and my people's sovereign reign, forever!
From this blessed hour, a father to your son,
I'll scourge his foes: henceforth be he styled
The Trojan king: I swear it at the altar,
And call the gods to ratify my vows!"
His subjects with loud acclamations shook
The spacious dome. Our Greeks, enraged, cried out,
"Revenge! revenge!" broke through the thronging press,
And rushed tumultuous on the unguarded king:

1027

Their eager fury left no work for me.
Pyrrhus awhile opposed their clashing swords,
And dealt his fatal blows on every side
With manly fierceness; till, oppressed by numbers,
Streaming with blood, all over gashed with wounds,
He reeled, he groaned, and at the altar fell.
Haste, Madam, let us fly! Haste to our ships!
They lie unmoored,—our friends attend us there.

    Herm. What have they done?

    Or. Madam, forgive their rage!
I own your vengeance had been more complete
Had Pyrrhus fallen by me, and had he known
Hermione chastised him by my arm.

    Herm. Peace, monster, peace! Go, tell thy horrid tale
To savages, and howl it in the deserts!
Wouldst thou impute to me thy barbarous guilt?
Me wouldst thou make the accomplice of thy crimes?
Hence to thy Greeks, and boast thy foul exploits!
My soul abhors them! I disclaim the deed!
Begone! I know thee not, thou fell barbarian!
What had he done? What could provoke thy madness
To assassinate so great, so brave a man?
Who set thee on?

    Or. Oh, grant me patience, Heaven!
With your own lips did you not curse the tyrant,
Pronounce his death, and urge me to destroy him?

    Herm. What if, transported by my boundless passion,
I could not bear to see him wed another,—
Were you to obey a jealous woman's frenzy?
You should have div'd into my inmost thoughts:
My heart, though full of rage, was free from malice;
And all my anger was excess of love.
Why did you take me at my word? You saw
The struggles of my soul; you heard me rave:
You should have questioned me a thousand times,
Yet still have doubted, and still questioned on,
Before you ventured on a life so precious.

    Or. Hear me but speak: Heaven knows, against my will——

    Herm. Why did you not return? why not consult me
A second time? and. undetermined still,
Again return, and still find new delays?

What had your rash, officious Greeks—dire bloodhounds!
To do with my revenge? What drew you hither?
To bring on me the vengeful woes that haunt you?
Are these the fruits of your detested love?
Your fatal embassy, your hateful presence,
Drove Pyrrhus to my rival, and destroys
Both him and me. He might have loved me still,
Had you ne'er interposed. Avaunt! Begone!
And leave me in Epirus. I renounce
My friends, my country, Greece, and all mankind:
But, chiefly, I renounce thee, monster! thee!
                    (*Exit.*)
    Or. Am I awake? Where am I? Soft, my soul!
Be not too rash.——Was that Hermione?
Why should her anger thunder against me?
Was not this blood shed all by her command?
I am, indeed, a most outrageous monster!
A ruffian, murderer, a base assassin!
And all to please a false, ungrateful woman.
Henceforward let the laws of nations cease;
And let the pale that severs right and wrong,
Things sacred and profane, be broken down:
Gods in their temples, kings upon their thrones,
Are not in safety while Orestes lives.
Oh, never more shall my torn mind be healed,
Nor taste the gentle comforts of repose;
A dreadful band of gloomy cares surround me,
And lay strong siege to my distracted soul!

JEAN PAUL RICHTER

JEAN PAUL RICHTER (German, 1763-1825). Sentimental interpreter of everyday life. After early poverty, was supported by numerous patronesses. Settled in Weimar and Bayreuth. Extravagantly popular during his lifetime, his novels are seldom read today. Most famous: *Titan, 'Teens, The Life of Quintus Fixlein*.

THE NEW-YEAR'S NIGHT OF AN UNHAPPY MAN

An old man stood on the new-year's midnight at the window, and gazed with a look of long despair, upwards to the immovable ever-

blooming heaven, and down upon the still, pure, white earth, on which no one was then so joyless and sleepless as he. For his grave stood near him; it was covered over only with the snow of age, not with the green of youth; and he brought nothing with him out of the whole rich life, nothing with him, but errors, sins and disease, a wasted body, a desolated soul, the breast full of poison, an old age full of remorse. The beautiful days of his youth turned round to-day, as spectres, and drew him back again to that bright morning on which his father first placed him at the cross-road of life, which, on the right hand, leads by the sun-path of Virtue into a wide peaceful land full of light and of harvests, and full of angels, and which, on the left hand, descends into the mole-ways of Vice, into a black cavern full of down-dropping poison, full of aiming serpents, and of gloomy, sultry vapours.

Ah! the serpents hung about his breast, and the drops of poison on his tongue.—And he knew, now, where he was!

Frantic, and with unspeakable grief, he called upwards to Heaven: "Oh! give me back my youth again!—O, Father! place me once more at the cross-path of life, that I may choose otherwise than I did."

But his father and his youth had long since passed away.

He saw fiery exhalations dancing on the marshes, and extinguishing themselves in the churchyard, and he said: "These are the days of my folly!"—He saw a star fly from heaven, and, in falling, glimmer and dissolve upon the earth. "That am I!" said his bleeding heart, and the serpent-teeth of remorse dug therein further in its wounds.

His flaming fancy showed him sleepwalkers slinking away on the house-tops; and a windmill raised up its arms threateningly to destroy him; and a mask that remained behind in the empty charnel-house, assumed by degrees his own features.

In the midst of this paroxysm, suddenly the music for the new-year flowed down from the steeple, like distant church-anthems. He became more gently moved.—He looked round on the horizon and upon the wide world, and thought on the friends of his youth, who, better and more happy than he, were now instructors of the earth, fathers of happy children, and blest men—and he exclaimed: "Oh! I also might have slumbered, like you, this new-year's night with dry eyes, had I chosen it—Ah! I might have been happy, beloved parents! had I fulfilled your new-year's wishes and instructions."

In feverish recollection of the period of his youth, it appeared

to him as if the mask with his features raised itself up in the charnel-house—at length, through the superstition, which, on the new-year's night, beholds spirits and futurity, it grew to a living youth in the position of the beautiful boy of the Capitol, pulling out a thorn; and his former blooming figure was bitterly placed as a phantasma before him.

He could behold it no longer—he covered his eyes.—A thousand, hot, draining tears streamed into the snow.—He, now, only softly sighed, inconsolably and unconsciously: "Only come again, youth! come again!"

And it came again, for he had only dreamed so fearfully on the new-year's night.—He was still a youth.—His errors alone had been no dream; but he thanked God, that, still young, he could turn round in the foul ways of Vice, and fall back on the sun-path which conducts into the pure land of harvests.

Turn with him, youthful reader, if thou standest on his path of error: This frightful dream will, in future, become thy judge; but shouldst thou one day call out, full of anguish: "Come again, beautiful youth!"—it would not come again.

RAINER MARIA RILKE

RAINER MARIA RILKE (German, 1875-1926). Highly disciplined and dedicated German poet. Extensive traveler and love correspondent. Painter and translator. Born Catholic, became mystic. Bulk of his work concerned with the ultimate themes of nature, love, death. Most widely known works: *The Journal of My Other Self, Sonnets to Orpheus, Duinese Elegies, Stories of God.*

O SELDOM

O seldom into the breathless
Restless rustle of life,
Reaches one of the crowning, deathless
Hours that consecrate strife;
Hour that accidentally seest,
That imprisons thy hand with fingers gentle:
    Come and be the only
    Guest at my lonely feast.

How glorious the chrysanthemums that day!
I almost shuddered at their splendour white . . .
And then you came to take my soul away
Deep in the night . . .

Such fear had I, and you came dear and wary,
Just when a dream had flashed you on my sight.
You came—and like a song from lips of fairy,
Rang out the night . . .

PRAYER OF THE MAIDENS TO MARY

I

O see how narrow are our days,
 How full of fear our bed;
We reach out awkward arms always
 To gather the roses red.

Thou must be mild to us, Mary,
 Out of Thy blood we blow;
And what a pain is yearning
 Thou alone canst know;

For Thou hast known this maiden's woe
 In Thine own soul's desire;
It feels as cold as Christmas snow,
 And yet is all on fire . . .

AFTER THE PRAYER

II

But I feel how my heart is glowing
 Warmer and warmer in my breast,
And every evening poorer growing,
 Nor any night can bring me rest.

I tear at the white silken tissue,
And my shy dreams cry out to Thee:
    Let me be sorrow of Thy sorrow,
      O let us both
By the same wonder wounded be.

THY GREAT TOWNS, LORD

Thy great towns, Lord, are lost to shame,
    Things merged in misery and maddened;
The greatest is like flight from flame,—
    Comfort is none for them to be gladdened,
Their life is shorter than their name.

Therein dwell men from kennelled door to door,
    Starved into meagre shape and timid gesture,
Like herded lambkins shepherded before:
    Thine earth breathes sweet outside in springtide vesture,
But they are not and know of it no more.

And children there grow up on blind staircases,
    And up and down the self-same shadows wind,
And know not of the outside sunny spaces,
    Where flowers bloom fair for happy hands to bind,
And must be children, children of a kind.

And budding girls are to the unknown turning,
    And wishing back the peace of childhood eves;
They find not that for which their hearts are burning,
    And close again their open-trembling leaves.
And have in black back-garrets all untended
    The days of disappointed motherhood,

The listless whimpering of long nights unended,
    And cold years with no courage in the blood.
And all in darkness stand the beds for dying
    To which they like a beggar woman fade,
Till by the slow consumption of their sighing
    They at the last are on the death-bed laid.

Behold how all is opened: we are so;
    For we are but such blessedness in space.
What in a beast was blood and dark, did grow
    To be a soul in us, and cries apace

For thee, as a soul ever. Thou indeed
    Takest it only up into thy face
As it were landscape: gently and with no greed.
    And so we think, for whom its pulses race

It is not thou. And yet, art thou not he
    To whom we lost ourselves till naught remained?
And shall we ever in any other be?

With us infinity fades like a mist.
    But thou, O mouth, so that it be explained,
Be! O thou teller unto us, exist.

ABISHAG

I

She lay, and serving-men her lithe arms took,
And bound them round the withering old man,
And on him through the long sweet hours she lay,
A little fearful of his many years.

And many times she turned amidst his beard
Her face, as often as the night-owl screeched,
And all that was the night around them reached
Its feelers manifold of longing fears.

As they had been the sisters of the child
The stars trembled, and fragrance searched the room,
The curtain stirring sounded with a sign
Which drew her gentle glances after it.

But she clung close upon the dim old man,
And, by the night of nights not overtaken,
Upon the cooling of the King she lay
Maidenly, and lightly as a soul.

II

The King sate thinking out the empty day
Of deeds accomplished and untasted joys,
And of his favorite bitch that he had bred—
But with the evening Abishag was arched
Above him. His dishevelled life lay bare,
Abandoned as diffamèd coasts, beneath
The quiet constellation of her breasts.

But many times, as one in women skilled,
He through his eye-brows recognized the mouth
Unmoved, unkissed; and saw: the comet green
Of her desires reached not to where he lay.
He shivered. And he listened like a hound,
And sought himself in his remaining blood.

LOVE-SONG

By what device shall I my soul prevent
From touching thine? My soul how shall I lift
To other things above thee? Great
Indeed is my desire to have it pent
In something lost in some still spot, and let it mate
With darkness which thy gladness shall not rift,
And which shall not with thy own deeps vibrate.

But all that touches us,
Takes us together, thee and me, as does
A fiddle-bow one voice prolong
Out of two chords. Upon what instrument
Then are we stretched? What master's face is o'er us bent?
O sweet song.

THE ELOPEMENT

Often as a child she had escaped
Her women to behold beneath the skies,
Because inside they are so otherwise,
The wind weave when the evening first is draped;

And yet no night of tempest ever had
Into such fragments torn the giant park
As it was now torn into by her bad

Conscience, since down the silken ladder's fall
He took and bore her onward through the dark

Until the carriage was all.
And the black vehicle she smelt,
And round it chase in hiding,
And danger.
And he was faced with cold, she felt,
And the blackness and the coldness in her gliding,
She crept into the collar of her cloak,
And felt her hair, as if it were not riding,
And she, strange, heard how a stranger
Spoke:
Iambytheeabiding.

ESTHER

The serving-women combed her seven days through
The ashes of her torment and her sorrow
Out of her hair the sediment and deposit,
And bore it out and dried it in the sun,
Spice that they did not feed it with was none
Another day and this one; but then was it

The time when she, now being all anointed
Even as a corpse is, at no hour appointed
Should enter in the open palace grim
In order at the way's end to behold
The face of him concerning whom we are told
That any one must die who looks on him.

As though the ruby of her crown were dull
Before, she felt it flash ere he was seen
And filled herself already with his mien
Like to a vessel, till she grew so full

That she flowed over with the monarch's might
Or ever on her face the third hall gleamed,
That ran green over her with the malachite
Of its four walls. But she had never dreamed
With all her gems so long a way to wend her,
And they grew heavier with the King's great splendour
And with her terror cold. She, wandering,
Went on till, when she saw him there recline,
Towering upon a throne of tourmaline,
Before her, looking verily like a thing:

The right handmaiden took her fainting, and
Upreared her in the reach of the monarch's hand.
He touched her with his sceptre's point, and she
Conceived it without senses, inwardly.

JEAN ARTHUR RIMBAUD

JEAN ARTHUR RIMBAUD (French, 1854-1891). Brilliant poetic genius,
who at 19 deliberately ceased writing. Ran away from home as adolescent.
After year of literary life in Paris, set off on walking tour with Verlaine. Was
shot by him, but recovered. After much travel, settled in Ethiopa as a slave-
trader. His aesthetic theories had marked influence on modern literature.
Major works: *Les Illuminations, Une Saison en Enfer.*

DRUNKEN BOAT

As I descended the impassable streams
I felt myself no longer held by the drag-poles:
Clamorous Redskins had taken my crew for targets,
First having nailed them naked to the flagpoles.

But I was unconcerned for any crew,
Porters of Flemish grain or English cotton.
And when my haulers had done with their hurly-burly
The streams let me pass on as though forgotten.

Amidst the furious chopping of the tides
Last winter, muffled as a midnight scurvy,
I ran! and peninsulas that slip their bonds
Have never been more gloriously topsy-turvy.

The tempest blessed my maritime alarms.
Lighter than a cork I danced upon the waves,
Ten nights, nor missed the silly eyes of lanterns,
On the eternal rolling of those graves.

Sweeter than the juice of held fruit to a child
The green water would my broken cockle whelm,
And streaks of bluish wines and of disgorgements
Washed me and bore off grappling-irons and helm.

And thenceforth I was deluged in the poem
Of the sea infused with meteors latescent
Devouring the green azure where, wan flotation,
A pensive drowned man is at times quiescent.

Or, of a sudden tinting the bluishness, swirls
And soft rhythms under the rutilant day,
Stronger than alcohol, larger than your lyres,
The bitter red vortices of love stew away!

I know the heavens lightning-rived, the waterspout,
Surfs, and the currents; I know the evening sky,
The dawn exalted as a poplar light with doves;
And I have sometimes seen what man thinks he may descry.

I have seen the low sun stained with mystic terrors,
Lighting long violet coagulations;
Like olden actors in an antique drama
The waves roll off their compass-agitations.

I have dreamed through green nights of dazzling snows,
Of a kiss that, welling in the eyes of the sea, over long stirs,
The circulation of unheard-of saps,
And the yellow and blue alarm of phosphorous songsters.

I have followed, months through, like the noise of hysterical stables,
The shore-battering blows of the billows' barrages,
Without thinking that over the short-winded ocean
Their luminous feet might force forward the snouts of the barges.

I have come, understand! on incredible Floridas
Where flowers blend with panther-eyes, and the skin
Of men with rainbows taut as a bridle,
Under ocean horizons, where sea-green hordes rush in.

I have seen swamps ferment, enormous fish-traps
Where in the rushes Leviathan rotting sleeps;
Downpourings of waters in the midst of calm,
And the distances whirled to the cataract deeps,

Glaciers, suns of silver, pearl floods, skies of embers,
Hideous jetsam in deep gulfs of gloom,
Where giant serpents eaten of grubbing maggots
Fall from the gnarled trees with black perfume.

I'd have liked to show children these ocean doradoes,
The great gold fish, the fish that sings;
Foam-wreaths of flowers have blessed my far-sea driftings
And at times ineffable winds have lent me wings.

At times, weary martyr of the zones and poles,
The ocean, whose sobbing softly cradles me,
Lifts me its flowers of dark with yellow air-holes;
And I have stayed there as a woman on her knee,

Peninsula tossing to my sides the quarrels
And the guano of chattering birds with pallid eyes;
And I floated on, while across my slender lines
Drowned men came drifting down to sleep sidewise.

Then I, lost boat beneath the leafy bays,
Hurled by tornadoes to the birdless ether,
I whose sea-drunk carcass no Monitor
Nor packet of the Guilds would have fished for beneath her,

1039

Free, fumid, risen with violet mists,
I who bored through the ruddy sky's diadem
Like a wall that was decked, to the poet's taste,
With sun-touched lichen and azure phlegm,

I who ran spotted with electric lunes,
Mad plank, with hippocampi at the gunwales,
When July was battering with bludgeon blows
The ultramarine skies with their flaming funnels,

I who trembled, sensing at fifty leagues
The rut of Behemoth, the loud Maelstrom's frets,
Eternal spinner of blue fixities—
I long for Europe's ancient parapets.

I have seen starry archipelagoes, and isles
Whose frenzied skies are clear above the rower;
Is it in those deep nights you in your exile sleep,
Mid millions of golden birds, O future Overthrower?

True, I have wept too long. Dawn breaks the heart.
All moons are hateful, every sun is gall.
Tart love has swollen me with dizzying torpors.
Oh, that my keel were darting! Oh, that I fled the squall!

If I want water of Europe, it is the black
Cold puddle where, as evening gathers nigh,
A squatting plaintive youngster will release
A boat as fragile as a butterfly.

I can no longer, bathed in your languor, waves,
Take the backwash of freighters as they bowse,
Nor breast the pride of colours and salutes,
Nor sail beneath the horrid eyes of scows!

EDWIN ARLINGTON ROBINSON

EDWIN ARLINGTON ROBINSON (American, 1869-1935). Reflective poetic traditionalist, who achieved individual style through precision and simplicity. Worked at odd jobs until President Theodore Roosevelt's recognition got him job in New York Custom House. *The Children of the Night* contains famous character portraits of Richard Cory, Miniver Cheevy, Luke Havergal, *et al.* *The Man Against the Sky* brought national fame. Also: *Merlin, Lancelot, Tristram.*

STAFFORD'S CABIN

Once there was a cabin here, and once there was a man;
And something happened here before my memory began.
Time has made the two of them the fuel of one flame
And all we have of them is now a legend and a name.

All I have to say is what an old man said to me,
And that would seem to be as much as there will ever be.
"Fifty years ago it was we found it where it sat."
And forty years ago it was old Archibald said that.

"An apple tree that's yet alive saw something, I suppose,
Of what it was that happened there, and what no mortal knows
Some one on the mountain heard far off a master shriek,
And then there was a light that showed the way for men to seek.

"We found it in the morning with an iron bar behind,
And there were chains around it; but no search could ever find,
Either in the ashes that were left, or anywhere,
A sign to tell of who or what had been with Stafford there.

"Stafford was a likely man with ideas of his own—
Though I could never like the kind that likes to live alone;
And when you met, you found his eyes were always on your shoes,
As if they did the talking when he asked you for the news.

"That's all, my son. Were I to talk for a half a hundred years
I'd never clear away from there the cloud that never clears.
We buried what was left of it,—the bar, too, and the chains;
And only for the apple tree there's nothing that remains."

Forty years ago it was I heard the old man say,
"That's all, my son." And here again I find the place today,
Deserted and told only by the tree that knows the most,
And overgrown with goldenrod as if there were no ghost.

NEW ENGLAND

Here where the wind is always north-north-east
And children learn to walk on frozen toes,
Wonder begets an envy of all those
Who boil elsewhere with such a lyric yeast
Of love that you will hear them at a feast
Where demons would appeal for some repose,
Still clamoring where the chalice overflows
And crying wildest who have drunk the least.

Passion is here a soilure of the wits,
We're told, and Love a cross for them to bear;
Joy shivers in the corner where she knits
And Conscience always has the rocking-chair,
Cheerful as when she tortured into fits
The first cat that was ever killed by Care.

ROMAIN ROLLAND

ROMAIN ROLLAND (French, 1866-1944). Renowned novelist and playwright.
Leading pacifist at beginning of present century. In later years turned Stalinist
fellow traveler. Author of biographies of Beethoven, Michelangelo, Tolstoy and
others. Winner of Nobel Prize in 1915 for *Jean-Christophe*, heroic novel modeled
roughly on life of Beethoven.

THE TRAP

THE first questions that enter my childish mind:
    "Where did I come from? and where am I confined?——"
    I was born into a comfortable middle-class family, surrounded
by loving relatives, in a pleasant part of the country whose joyous
flavor I later tasted and celebrated through the voice of my *Colas*.
    How does it happen that, from the moment of my birth, the first
feeling—the strongest, most persistent of my early childhood—

should be—dim, haunting, sometimes rebellious, sometimes resigned: "I am a prisoner!"

Francis the First, on entering the tottering nave of my old Saint Martin of Clamecy, said (so the legend runs): "There's a fine trap!"—I was in "the Trap."

At the beginning, a visual impression: the first horizon presented to my childish view—a rather large paved court, with a garden in the middle, surrounded on three sides by three walls of the house that to me seemed very high. On the fourth side, the street and the houses opposite, separated by a canal. Although this quadrangle was terraced above the water, it seemed to the child, confined to his room on the ground floor, like a ditch in the zoological gardens at the foot of four walls.

A significant impression: children's diseases and a delicate constitution. Although I come of healthy parents and robust ancestry— (The Rollands and the Courots, tall, bony, without physical defects, and endowed with boundless nervous energy that keeps them up and about until their last day, have all lived to a ripe old age; my maternal grandparents lived merrily on past their eightieth year; at the very moment of this writing my eighty-eight-year-old father is happily watering his garden)—I, made of the same lime and sand that, in spite of everything, have resisted fatigue and the trials of a busy existence, have borne, all my life, the painful consequences of a childhood accident: the carelessness of a young servant who, forgetting me in the winter-cold when I was less than a year old, brought me close to death and bequeathed to me for life a bronchial weakness and shortness of breath. Over and over again one can find in my works, spurting up, involuntarily, like an interrupted flight, the "respiratory" expressions: "stifling," "open windows," "fresh air," "the breath of the heroes . . ."—the bird that flutters its wings, or crouches, feverish, in the cage of the wounded breast.

Finally, moral impressions, powerful and penetrating: the thought of death that enveloped the first ten years of my life. Death had entered the family circle: it had struck down at my side a little sister, younger than I, of whom I shall speak later; and her shadow continued to inhabit the house. An excitable mother, whose grief was never allayed, feverishly nursed the memory of the departed child. And I, who had seen her disappear in a few days, and whom the constant sight of this mother, brooding over her solitary thought, also bound, despite the heedlessness of my age that sought an escape —I was all the more readily exposed to the idea that was going

about, since, until I was ten or twelve years old, my own life was threatened. Frequent colds, bronchitis, sore throats, persistent nose-bleeds took away my zest for life; and in my little bed I would keep repeating:

"I don't want to die!"

while my mother, in tears, would answer, hugging me to her:

"No, my little boy. The good God will not want to take you away from me, too!"

This only half convinced me, for what did I know about God, except that, from my first steps, he had taken advantage of his power. And my most lucid thought in regard to him was, without my realizing it, that of the Gardener for his Lord: '

"The good man said: Those are the moves of a prince . . . .
In appealing to kings, you make great fools of yourselves.
You must never let them enter your lands. . . ."

In the threefold prison of the old house, my weak chest, and the ill-omened circle of death, the earliest consciousness of my child-hood grew up under the anxious surveillance of my mother's affec-tion. Fragile plant, sister to the wistaria and the petunias blooming in the court and along the walls, whose breath from short-lived lips mingled with the dank odor of the stagnant canal; like them, rooted to the ground, yet aspiring to the light, the little prisoner, only half-awakened, kept groping blindly and instinctively in the air for invisible roads of escape.

The closest at hand: the murky canal, flowing along the terrace-wall over which I hung. Muddy and green, without a ripple, it bore up the deep, heavy boats that the bargemen forced along by the sheer forward thrust of their thin bodies. I could hear the grinding of the cables along the railing at the edge. A turn-bridge creaked and began to move slowly. From the cabin of the boat whose sky-light was decorated with a pot of geraniums, mounted a thin blue spiral of smoke. Seated before the door in silence, a woman was knitting; from time to time she glanced indifferently in my direction. The boat passed. . . . And I, leaning over the wall, saw the wall and myself passing. We were leaving the boat behind us; it was we who were going away. Now we are far out in the open: without a jar, without a motion. So slowly we slipped along that it seemed as though we should glide, like the night-sky, into eternity, without a change. And then we found each other again, the wall and I,

1044

still dreaming in the same place. The boat had gone. Would it ever reach its destination? Another was coming up after it. It looked just the same. . . .

Then I imagined another route, free and without locks: the air. A child often lifts his face toward the sky, toward the wandering clouds and the twittering swallows, toward the great white clouds, like whimsical monuments formed by the childish eye. (That is his first sculpture; the child uses the air as his clay.) It is needless to speak of the rest: the threatening clouds, the rumbling storms of Central France with their crashing thunder. It is in them that the enemy returns—the Master with his beetling eyebrows closes the shutters of the sky on the frail prisoner. Then come the hands of deliverance, the fingers of the sorceress that open my window on the plains of the air. . . . And now come the bells, the bells of Saint Martin! They sound in the first pages of my *Jean-Christophe*. Their music is engraved on my unawakened heart. They pealed forth from the open tower of the old cathedral above my house. But it was not the church that these ecclesiastical songsters called forth in me. Later I shall tell of my encounters with the God of the church. They were cold, ceremonious and distant. In spite of my honest efforts, I never succeeded in getting in touch with him. God alone knows whether I sought him. But the God who knows it is not the same God. The God who heard me—the God whom I created so that he would listen to me, and in whom I have confided all my life—was in the hovering song-birds, the bells, and in the air. Not the Lord of Saint Martin's hidden in his retreat above the sculptured arches. But the God Liberty—At that time, to be sure, I had no knowledge of the span of his wings, but I heard them flutter in the airy heights. Nor was I even sure that they were more real than the white clouds. They ever remained for me a nostalgic dream that let me glance at space for a moment before taking their flight and letting the trap-door fall again over the cave of my life. . . . Much, much later (I shall tell how), I climbed, I pushed upward, I forced the trap with my forehead and, freed at last, I found traces of the bells once more. But all through childhood I groped about in a sealed cave— the great, beautiful cave of Burgundy, like a crypt full of wine-casks set in rows, and covered with cobwebs. Everyone else was at ease there, except one, and I heard them laugh as one laughs in my country. I did not look down upon the laughter and the drinking— But oh! for a taste of the sun outside! Was there really a sun? (If only I had the answer!) Or even the night?—And since none of

those strong men tried to leave, I conscious of my weakness, crouched in my corner, beaten.

At sixteen or seventeen years of age, when I read *Hamlet*, with what resonance these fraternal words echoed under the vault of my cave:

"... *what have you, my good friends, deserved at the hands of Fortune, that she sends you to prison hither?*"

"*Prison, my lord?*"

"*Denmark's a prison.*"

"*Then is the world one.*"

"*A goodly one, in which there are many confines, wards and dungeons, ...*"

It is true that, a few lines further on, a magic word fills me with infinite hope:

"*O God, I could be bounded in a nut-shell and count myself a king of infinite space, ...*"

That is the story of my life.

PIERRE DE RONSARD

PIERRE DE RONSARD (French, 1524-1585). Most eminent of Renaissance poets. Plans for diplomatic career frustrated by deafness at 18. Became leader of group of poets called La Pléiade. Received rich honors from French kings during lifetime, was neglected after death. Has since taken place among great French lyricists. Best work: the sonnets in three sets of *Amours*.

THE ROSE

See, Mignonne! hath not the Rose,
That this morning did unclose
   Her purple mantle to the light,
Lost, before the day be dead,
The glory of her raiment red,
   Her color, bright as yours is bright?

Ah, Mignonne! in how few hours
The petals of her purple flowers
   All have faded, fallen, died!
Sad Nature! mother ruinous!
That seest thy fair child perish thus
   'Twixt matin song and eventide.

Hear me, Darling! speaking sooth:
Gather the fleet flower of your youth!
Take ye your pleasure at the best!
Be merry ere your beauty flit!
For length of days will tarnish it.
Like roses that were loveliest.

WELCOME TO SPRING

God shield ye, heralds of the spring,
Ye faithful swallows fleet of wing,
    Hoops, cuckoos, nightingales,
Turtles and every wilder bird,
That make your hundred chirpings heard
    Through the green woods and dales.

God shield ye, Easter daisies all,
Fair roses, buds and blossoms small;
    And ye, whom erst the gore
Of Ajax and Narciss did print,
Ye wild thyme, anise, balm, and mint
    I welcome ye once more.

God shield ye, bright embroidered train
Of butterflies, that, on the plain,
    Of each sweet herblet sip;
And ye new swarm of bees that go
Where the pink flowers and yellow grow
    To kiss them with your lip.

A hundred thousand times I call—
A hearty welcome on ye all:

    This season how I love!
This merry din on every shore,
For winds and storms, whose sullen roar
    Forbade my steps to rove.

When you are very old, at evening
 You'll sit and spin beside the fire, and say,
 Humming my songs, "Ah well, ah well-a-day!
When I was young, of me did Ronsard sing."
None of your maidens that doth hear the thing,
 Albeit with her weary task foredone,
 But wakens at my name, and calls you one
Blest, to be held in long remembering.

I shall be low beneath the earth, and laid
On sleep, a phantom in the myrtle shade,
 While you beside the fire, a grandame gray,
My love, your pride, remember and regret;
Ah, love me, love! we may be happy yet,
 And gather roses, while 'tis called to-day.

EDMOND ROSTAND

EDMOND ROSTAND (French, 1868-1918). Colorful virtuoso of the drama, whose name is chiefly associated with florid heroic masterpiece, *Cyrano de Bergerac.* Other works: *L'Aiglon, Chantecler, La dernière nuit de Don Juan.* His work the final flower of the romantic theater of Victor Hugo.

TO SARAH

In these drab days, alone there never cloys
Your pallid grace, descending a wide stair,
Wreathing a frontlet, holding a lily, sword in air:
Queen of Fair Gestures, Princess of Poise.
In these tame times your flames are mutinous!
You speak verse. You die of love. You are ever fresh.
You hold forth arms of dream, then arms of flesh,
And when Phèdre appears, we are all incestuous.

Avid of suffering, you deepen with the years;
We have seen flowing—for they flow!—your tears:

All the dew of our soul on your cheek lingers.
But you know, Sarah, that at times there stray—
And furtively you feel them as you play—
The lips of Shakespeare on your jeweled fingers.

CYRANO TO HIS CHIDING FRIENDS

Do what?
Seek a potent protector, slink under a patron,
And like the low ivy, both early and late run
Round a trunk-prop and, licking the bark,
Climb by a ruse instead of rising stark?
No, thanks! Like everyone, set dearly down
Lines to a financier? Change into a clown
In the base hope of seeing, on the lips of a minister,
A smile spread, at last, that may not be sinister?
No, thanks! Dine daily on a bitter pill?
Have a belly worn with walking? A skin still
Quicker to catch the dirt upon the knees?
Execute daily dorsal suppleties?
No, thanks! With one hand pet a goat until it preens,
And with the other confiscate its greens?
Donor of senna that rhubarb be neared,
Always burn incense in somebody's beard?
No, thanks! From one lap leap to the lap beyond,
To become a big man in a small pond,
To navigate with madrigal-propellers
And the sighs of old maids as my sail-swellers?
No, thanks! At the publishing house of kindly Blanks
Pay to have my verses done? No, thanks!
Be named high-priest by the council of buffoons
That meets before the bars of old saloons?
No, thanks! Work that my name shall go
High with one sonnet, and write no more? No,
Thanks! Discover talent only in loons,
Be terrorized by threats of vague lampoons,
And endlessly to say "Just let me be
Among the personals in the *Mercury!*"
No, thanks! Calculate? Have fears—and show 'em?
And rather make a visit than poem?

Draw up petitions, be presented . . . everything!!!
No, thanks! No, thanks! No, thanks! No, thanks! But—sing,
Dream, laugh, go by, be alone, be free,
With a vibrant voice, and a steady eye to see,
And when I please, to set my hat awry,
At a yea or a nay take arms—or versify!
To work, unheeding wealth or glory's tune,
Toward the journey I'm thinking of making to the moon!
Never to write a line save from the heart,
Modestly to say to myself from the very start:
"Be satisfied with flowers, fruits, even leaves,
If it is your own garden that achieves!"
Then if fame and fortune send a soft appeaser,
Not to be obliged to render aught unto Cæsar,
But clear in your own eyes make your merit shine:
In short, disdaining the parasitic vine,
Even if you haven't to the oak's crest grown,
Not to soar high, perhaps, but rise alone!

JALAL UD-DIN RUMI

JALAL UD-DIN RUMI (Persian, 1207-1273). Most eminent mystic poet and
Dervish of Persia. A devotee of Sufism, regarded by contemporaries as a
spiritual guide. Founded the order of Mowlavies ("Whirling Dervishes").
His greatest work: *Masnavi*, a poem in 6 books, containing stories, fables,
and moral precepts.

THE MERCHANT AND THE PARROT

There was once a merchant, who had a parrot,
A parrot fair to view, confined in a cage;
And when the merchant prepared for a journey,
He resolved to bend his way towards Hindustan.
Every servant and maiden in his generosity
He asked, what present he should bring them home,
And each one named what he severally wished,
And to each one the good master promised his desire.

Then he said to the parrot, "And what gift wishest thou,
That I should bring to thee from Hindustan?"
The parrot replied, "When thou seest the parrots there,
Oh, bid them know of my condition.
Tell them, 'A parrot, who longs for your company,
Through Heaven's decree is confined in my cage.
He sends you his salutation, and demands his right,
And seeks from you help and counsel.
He says, "Is it right that I in my longings
Should pine and die in this prison through separation?
Is it right that I should be here fast in this cage,
While you dance at will on the grass and the trees?
Is this the fidelity of friends,
I here in a prison, and you in a grove?
Oh remember, I pray you, that bower of ours,
And our morning-draughts in the olden time;
Oh remember all our ancient friendships,
And all the festive days of our intercourse!" ' "
The merchant received its message,
The salutation which he was to bear to its fellows;
And when he came to the borders of Hindustan,
He beheld a number of parrots in the desert.
He stayed his horse, and he lifted his voice,
And he repeated his message, and deposited his trust;
And one of those parrots suddenly fluttered,
And fell to the ground, and presently died.
Bitterly did the merchant repent his words;
"I have slain," he cried, "a living creature.
Perchance this parrot and my little bird were close of kin,
Their bodies perchance were two and their souls one.
Why did I this? why gave I the message?
I have consumed a helpless victim by my foolish words!
My tongue is as flint, and my lips as steel;
And the words that burst from them are sparks of fire.
Strike not together in thy folly the flint and steel,
Whether for the sake of kind words or vain boasting;
The world around is as a cotton-field by night;
In the midst of cotton, how shall the spark do no harm?"
    The merchant at length completed his traffic,
And he returned right glad to his home once more.
To every servant he brought a present,

To every maiden he gave a token;
And the parrot said, "Where is my present?
Tell all that thou hast said and seen!"
He answered, "I repeated thy complaints
To that company of parrots, thy old companions,
And one of those birds, when it inhaled the breath of thy sorrow,
Broke its heart, and fluttered, and died."
And when the parrot heard what its fellow had done,
It too fluttered, and fell down, and died.
When the merchant beheld it thus fall,
Up he sprang, and dashed his cap to the ground.
"Oh, alas!" he cried, "my sweet and pleasant parrot,
Companion of my bosom and sharer of my secrets!
Oh alas! alas! and again alas!
That so bright a moon is hidden under a cloud!"
After this, he threw its body out of the cage;
And lo! the little bird flew to a lofty bough.
The merchant stood amazed at what it had done;
Utterly bewildered he pondered its mystery.
It answered, "Yon parrot taught me by its action:
'Escape,' it told me, 'from speech and articulate voice,
Since it was thy voice that brought thee into prison;'
And to prove its own words itself did die."
    It then gave the merchant some words of wise counsel,
And at last bade him a long farewell.
"Farewell, my master, thou hast done me a kindness,
Thou hast freed me from the bond of this tyranny.
Farewell, my master, I fly towards home;
Thou shalt one day be free like me!"

THE DESTINY OF MAN

Seeks thy spirit to be gifted
    With a deathless life?
Let it seek to be uplifted
    O'er earth's storm and strife.

Spurn its joys—its ties dissever;
    Hopes and fears divest;
Thus aspire to live forever—
    Be forever blest!

Faith and doubt leave far behind thee;
   Cease to love or hate;
Let not Time's illusions blind thee;
   Thou shalt Time outdate.

Merge thine individual being
   In the Eternal's love;
All this sensuous nature fleeing
   For pure bliss above.

Earth receives the seed and guards it;
   Trustfully it dies;
Then, what teeming life rewards it
   For self-sacrifice!

With green leaf and clustering blossom
   Clad, and golden fruit,
See it from earth's cheerless bosom
   Ever sunward shoot!

Thus, when self-abased, Man's spirit
   From each earthly tie
Rises disenthralled t' inherit
   Immortality!

S

SA'DI

SA'DI (Persian, 1184-1291). One of the most versatile figures in Persian literature: poet, philosopher, teacher, Sufi. Great traveler and a soldier against the Christians during the Crusades. His *Gulistan* (*Rose Garden*), in prose and verse, is most widely read Persian classic.

THE GULISTAN

Purgatory May Be Paradise

A KING was embarked along with a Persian slave on board a ship. The boy had never been at sea, nor experienced the inconvenience of a ship. He set up a weeping and wailing, and all his limbs were in a state of trepidation; and, however much they soothed him, he was not to be pacified. The king's pleasure-party was disconcerted by him; but they had no help. On board that ship there was a physician. He said to the king: "If you will order it, I can manage to silence him." The king replied: "It will be an act of great favor." The physician so directed that they threw the boy into the sea, and after he had plunged repeatedly, they seized him by the hair of the head and drew him close to the ship, when he clung with both hands by the rudder, and, scrambling upon the deck, slunk into a corner and sat down quiet. The king, pleased with what he saw, said: "What art is there in this?" The physician replied: "Originally he had not experienced the danger of being drowned, and undervalued the safety of being in a ship; in like manner as a person is aware of the preciousness of health when he is overtaken with the the calamity of sickness. *A barley loaf of bread has, O epicure, no relish for thee. That is my mistress who appears so ugly to thy eye. —To the houris, or nymphs of paradise, purgatory would be a hell: ask the inmates of hell whether purgatory is not paradise.—There is a distinction between the man that folds his mistress in his arms and him whose two eyes are fixed on the door expecting her.*"

1054

The Wrestler

A person had become a master in the art of wrestling; he knew three hundred and sixty sleights in this art, and could exhibit a fresh trick for every day throughout the year. Perhaps owing to a liking that a corner of his heart took for the handsome person of one of his scholars, he taught him three hundred and fifty-nine of those feats, but he was putting off the last one, and under some pretence deferring it.

In short, the youth became such a proficient in the art and talent of wrestling that none of his contemporaries had ability to cope with him, till he at length had one day boasted before the reigning sovereign, saying: "To any superiority my master possesses over me, he is beholden to my reverence of his seniority, and in virtue of his tutorage; otherwise I am not inferior in power, and am his equal in skill." This want of respect displeased the king. He ordered a wrestling match to be held, and a spacious field to be fenced in for the occasion. The ministers of state, nobles of the court, and gallant men of the realm were assembled, and the ceremonials of the combat marshalled. Like a huge and lusty elephant, the youth rushed into the ring with such a crash that had a brazen mountain opposed him he would have moved it from its base. The master being aware that the youth was his superior in strength, engaged him in that strange feat of which he had kept him ignorant. The youth was unacquainted with its guard. Advancing, nevertheless, the master seized him with both hands, and, lifting him bodily from the ground, raised him above his head and flung him on the earth. The crowd set up a shout. The king ordered them to give the master an honorary dress and handsome largess, and the youth he addressed with reproach and asperity, saying: "You played the traitor with your own patron, and failed in your presumption of opposing him." He replied: "O sire! my master did not overcome my by strength and ability, but one cunning trick in the art of wrestling was left which he was reserved in teaching me, and by that little feat had today the upper hand of me." The master said: "I reserved myself for such a day as this. As the wise have told us, put not so much into a friend's power that, if hostilely disposed, he can do you an injury. Have you not heard what that man said who was treacherously dealt with by his own pupil: *'Either in fact there was no good faith in this world, or nobody has perhaps practised it in our days. No person learned the art of archery from me who did not in the end make me his butt.'* "

1055

Having taken offence with the society of my friends at Damascus, I retired into the wilderness of the Holy Land, or Jerusalem, and sought the company of brutes till such time as I was made a prisoner by the Franks, and employed by them, along with some Jews, in digging earth in the ditches of Tripoli. At length one of the chiefs of Aleppo, between whom and me an intimacy had of old subsisted, happening to pass that way, recognized me, and said: "How is this? and how came you to be thus occupied?" I replied: "What can I say? *I was flying from mankind into the forests and mountains, for my resource was in God and in none else. Fancy to thyself what my condition must now be, when forced to associate with a tribe scarcely human?—To be linked in a chain with a company of acquaintance were pleasanter than to walk in a garden with strangers.*"

He took pity on my situation; and, having for ten dinars redeemed me from captivity with the Franks, carried me along with him to Aleppo. Here he had a daughter, and her he gave me in marriage, with a dower of a hundred dinars. Soon after this damsel turned out a termagant and vixen, and discovered such a perverse spirit and virulent tongue as quite unhinged all my domestic comfort. *A scolding wife in the dwelling of a peaceable man is his hell even in this world. Protect and guard us against a wicked inmate. Save us, O Lord, and preserve us from the fiery, or hell, torture.*

Having on one occasion given a liberty to the tongue of reproach, she was saying: "Are you not the fellow whom my father redeemed from the captivity of the Franks for ten dinars?" I replied: "Yes, I am that same he delivered from captivity for ten dinars, and enslaved me with you for a hundred!" *I have heard that a reverend and mighty man released a sheep from the paws and jaws of a wolf. That same night he was sticking a knife into its throat, when the spirit of the sheep reproached him, saying: "Thou didst deliver me from the clutches of a wolf, when I at length saw that thou didst prove a wolf to me thyself.*"

WEALTH

He that owns wealth, in mountain, wold, or waste,
Plays master—pitches tent at his own taste;
Whilst he who lacks that which the world commends
Must pace a stranger, e'en in his own lands.

PRIEST SAIGYO

PRIEST SAIGYO (Japanese, 1118-1190). *Tanka* nature poet. At 23 gave up the life of a courtier to become an itinerant priest, his wife becoming a nun. His poetry admired for its lucidity and simplicity. Principal collection: *Sankashū.*

FORSAKEN

Why should I bitter be,
  Although he cold has grown?
There was a time when he to me
  And I to him were quite unknown.

THE AUTUMN MOON

I envy much the autumn moon,
  Which, journeying without delay,
Can follow, in the western sky,
  My friend who travels far away.

THE OLD CHERRY-TREE

Particularly will I gaze
  Upon the agéd cherry tree;
It and its flowers are pitiful.
  How many more springs can it see?

FLOWERS AND THE MOON

Suppose no clouds ever covered the moon
  And cherry flowers did not fall,
Why, then, I think in such a world,
  No sorrow should I know at all!

THE MOON

All things are ever changing
  In this transitory world,
But yet the moon is shining
  With the same light as of old.

1057

In spring when we see flowers,
    Would that there were no night!
In autumn when we see the moon,
    That there were no light!

GEORGE SAND

GEORGE SAND (Amandine Aurore Lucie Dupin, Baroness Dudevant, French, 1804-1876). Scandalous libertine and liberal. A remarkable woman who flouted the conventions of her time to leave husband, become novelist, and have series of notorious amours (including De Musset and Chopin). Her rather facile works favored the sociological theme. An ardent feminist—her best stories depict rebellious women: *Consuelo, Lélia, Elle et Lui.*

THE PLOUGHMAN AND HIS CHILD

I WAS walking on the border of a field which some peasants were carefully preparing for the approaching seed-time. The area was vast; the landscape was vast also, and enclosed with great lines of verdure, somewhat reddened by the approach of autumn, that broad field of vigorous brown, where recent rains had left, in some furrows, lines of water which the sun made glitter like fine threads of silver. The day had been clear and warm, and the earth, freshly opened by the cutting of the ploughshares, exhaled a light vapor. In the upper part of the field, an old man gravely held his plough of antique form, drawn by two oxen, with pale yellow skins—real patriarchs of the meadow—large in stature, rather thin, with long turned-down horns, old laborers whom long habit had made "brothers," as they are called by our country people, and who, when separated from each other, refuse to work with a new companion, and let themselves die of sorrow. The old husbandman worked slowly, in silence, without useless efforts; his docile team did not hurry any more than he; but, owing to the continuity of a labor without distraction, and the appliance of tried and well-sustained strength, his furrow was as soon turned as that of his son, who was ploughing at a short distance from him, with four oxen not so stout, in a vein of stronger and more stony soil.

But that which afterwards attracted my attention was really a beautiful spectacle—a noble subject for a painter. At the other ex-

tremity of the arable field, a good-looking young man was driving a magnificent team: four pairs of young animals of a dark color, a mixture of black and bay with streaks of fire, with those short and frizzly heads which still savor of the wild bull, those large savage eyes, those sudden motions, that nervous and jerking labor which still is irritated by the yoke and the goad, and only obeys with a start of anger the recently imposed authority. They were what are called newly-yoked steers. The man who governed them had to clear a corner formerly devoted to pasturage, and filled with century-old stumps, the task of an athlete, for which his energy, his youth, and eight almost unbroken animals were barely sufficient.

A child six or seven years old, beautiful as an angel, with his shoulders covered, over his blouse, by a lamb-skin, which made him resemble the little Saint John the Baptist of the painters of the Restoration, walked in a furrow parallel to the plough, and touched the flank of the oxen with a long and light stick pointed with a slightly sharpened goad. The proud animals quivered under the small hand of the child, and made their yokes and the thongs bound over their foreheads creak, while they gave violent shocks to the plough handles. When a root stopped the ploughshare, the husbandman shouted with a powerful voice, calling each beast by his name, but rather to calm than excite; for the oxen, irritated by this sudden resistance, leaped, dug up the ground with their broad forked feet, and would have cast themselves out of the track, carrying the plough across the field, if, with his voice and goad, the young man had not restrained the four nearest him, while the child governed the other four. He also, shouted, the poor little fellow, with a voice he wished to make terrible, but which remained as gentle as his angelic face. It was all beautiful in strength or in grace, the landscape, the man, the child, the bulls under the yoke; and in spite of this powerful struggle in which the earth was overcome, there was a feeling of gentleness and deep calm which rested upon all things. When the obstacle was surmounted, and the team had resumed its equal and solemn step, the husbandman, whose feigned violence was only an exercise of vigor, and an expenditure of activity, immediately recovered the serenity of simple souls, and cast a look of paternal satisfaction on his child, who turned to smile on him.

Then the manly voice of this young father of a family struck up the melancholy and solemn strain which the ancient tradition of the country transmits, not to all ploughmen indiscriminately, but to those most consummate in the art of exciting and sustaining the ardor of

the oxen at work. This chant, the origin of which was perhaps considered sacred, and to which mysterious influences must formerly have been attributed, is still reputed, at this day, to possess the virtue of keeping up the courage of the animals, of appeasing their dissatisfaction, and of charming the ennui of their long task. It is not enough to know how to drive them well while tracing a perfectly straight furrow, to lighten their labor by raising or depressing the point of the ploughshare opportunely in the soil: no one is a perfect ploughman if he does not know how to sing to the oxen, and this is a science apart, which requires taste and peculiar adaptation. This chant is, to say the truth, only a kind of recitative, interrupted and resumed at will. Its irregular form and its false intonations, speaking according to the rules of musical art, render it untranslatable. But it is none the less a beautiful chant, and so appropriate to the nature of the labor which it accompanies, to the gait of the oxen, to the calmness of those rural scenes, to the simplicity of the men who sing it, that no genius, a stranger to the labors of the soil, could have invented it, and no singer other than a "finished ploughman" of that country could repeat it. At those epochs of the year when there is no other labor and no other movement in the country than that of ploughing, this chant, so simple and so powerful, rises like the voice of a breeze, to which its peculiar toning gives it a kind of resemblance. The final note of each phrase, continued and trilled with an incredible length and power of breath, ascends a quarter of a note with systematic dissonance. This is wild, but the charm of it is invincible, and when you become accustomed to hear it, you cannot conceive how any song could be sung at those hours and in those places without disturbing their harmony.

It was then that, on seeing this beautiful pair, the man and the child, accomplish under such poetical conditions, and with so much gracefulness united with strength, a labor full of grandeur and solemnity, I felt a deep pity mingled with an involuntary respect. "Happy the husbandman!" Yes, doubtless, I should be happy in his place, if my arm, suddenly become strong, and my chest, become powerful, could thus fertilize and sing nature, without my eyes ceasing to see and my brain to comprehend the harmony of colors and of sounds, the fineness of tones, and the gracefulness of outlines—in one word, the mysterious beauty of things! and especially without my heart ceasing to be in relation with the divine feeling which presided over the immortal and sublime creation!

CARL SANDBURG

CARL SANDBURG (American, 1878-   ). The folk singer of America. Of Swedish immigrant parentage, became a great rover over the U.S. His poems of the prairies and early days of industrialism are already classics (*Chicago Poems, Smoke and Steel*). His militant sympathy for working classes dominates *The People, Yes*. Most impressive accomplishment: a monumental biography of Lincoln.

THE PEOPLE, YES

    The people will live on.
The learning and blundering people will live on.
    They will be tricked and sold and again sold
And go back to the nourishing earth for rootholds,
    The people so peculiar in renewal and comeback,
    You can't laugh off their capacity to take it.
The mammoth rests between his cyclonic dramas.

The people so often sleepy, weary, enigmatic.
is a vast huddle with many units saying:
  "I earn my living.
  I make enough to get by
  and it takes all my time.
  If I had more time
  I could do more for myself
  and maybe for others.
  I could read and study
  and talk things over
  and find out about things.
  It takes time.
   I wish I had the time."

The people is a tragic and comic two-face:
hero and hoodlum: phantom and gorilla twisting to moan with a gargoyle mouth: "They
buy and sell me . . . it's game . . .
sometime I'll break loose . . ."

Once having marched
Over the margins of animal necessity,
Over the grim line of sheer subsistence
Then man came
To the deeper rituals of his bones,
To the lights lighter than any bones,
To the time for thinking things over,
To the dance, the song, the story,
Or the hours given over to dreaming,
    Once having so marched.
Between the finite limitations of the five senses
and the endless yearnings of man for the beyond
the people hold to the humdrum bidding of work and food
while reaching out when it comes their way
for lights beyond the prison of the five senses,
for keepsakes lasting beyond any hunger or death.
    This reaching is alive.
The panderers and liars have violated and smutted it.
    Yet this reaching is alive yet
    for lights and keepsakes.

      The people know the salt of the sea
      and the strength of the winds
      lashing the corners of the earth.
      The people take the earth
      as a tomb of rest and a cradle of hope.
      Who else speaks for the Family of Man?
      They are in tune and step
      with constellations of universal law.

      The people is a polychrome,
      a spectrum and a prism
      held in a moving monolith,
      a console organ of changing themes,
      a clavilux of color poems
      wherein the sea offers fog
      and the fog moves off in rain
      and the labrador sunset shortens
      to a nocturne of clear stars
      serene over the shot spray
      of northern lights.

The steel mill sky is alive.
The fire breaks white and zigzag
shot on a gun-metal gloaming.
Man is a long time coming.
   Man will yet win.
Brother may yet line up with brother:

This old anvil laughs at many broken hammers.
  There are men who can't be bought.
  The fireborn are at home in fire.
  The stars make no noise.
  You can't hinder the wind from blowing.
  Time is a great teacher.
  Who can live without hope?

In the darkness with a great bundle of grief
  the people march.
In the night, and overhead a shovel of stars for
  keeps, the people march:
                "Where to? what next?"

GEORGE SANTAYANA

GEORGE SANTAYANA (Spanish-American, 1863-1952). America's philosopher-poet. Though born in Spain, he was educated in Boston and taught at Harvard for 20-odd years. Primarily a philosopher and aesthetician, he began by writing verse. Later composed a popular novel: *The Last Puritan.* Most important philosophic works: *The Life of Reason* and *The Realms of Being.* Autobiography: *Persons and Places.*

SOLIPSISM

I could believe that I am here alone,
   And all the world my dream;
The passion of the scene is all my own,
   And things that seem but seem.

Perchance an exhalation of my sorrow
   Hath raised this vaporous show,
For whence but from my soul should all things borrow
   So deep a tinge of woe?

I keep the secret doubt within my breast
    To be the gods' defence,
To ease the heart by too much ruth oppressed
    And drive the horror hence.

O sorrow that the patient brute should cower
    And die, not having sinned!
O pity that the wild and fragile flower
    Should shiver in the wind!

Then were I dreaming dreams I know not of,
    For that is part of me
That feels the piercing pang of grief and love
    And doubts eternally.

But whether all to me the vision come
    Or break in many beams,
The pageant ever shifts, and being's sum
    Is but the sum of dreams.

MY HEART REBELS AGAINST MY GENERATION

My heart rebels against my generation,
That talks of freedom and is slave to riches,
And, toiling 'neath each day's ignoble burden,
    Boasts of the morrow.

No space for noonday rest or midnight watches,
No purest joy of breathing under heaven!
Wretched themselves, they heap, to make them happy,
    Many possessions.

But thou, O silent Mother, wise, immortal,
To whom our toil is laughter,—take, divine one,
This vanity away, and to thy lover
    Give what is needful:—

A staunch heart, nobly calm, averse to evil,
The windy sky for breath, the sea, the mountain,
A well-born, gentle friend, his spirit's brother,
    Ever beside him.

What would you gain, ye seekers, with your striving,
Or what vast Babel raise you on your shoulders?
You multiply distress, and your children
    Surely will curse you.

O leave them rather friendlier gods, and fairer
Orchards and temples, and a freer bosom!
What better comfort have we, or what other
    Profit in living,

Than to feed, sobered by the truth of Nature,
Awhile upon her bounty and her beauty,
And hand her torch of gladness to the ages
    Following after?

She hath not made us, like her other children,
Merely for peopling of her spacious kingdoms,
Beasts of the wild, or insects of the summer,
    Breeding and dying,

But also that we might, half knowing, worship
The deathless beauty of her guiding vision,
And learn to love, in all things mortal, only
    What is eternal.

I WOULD I MIGHT FORGET THAT I AM I

I would I might forget that I am I,
And break the heavy chain that binds me fast,
Whose links about myself my deeds have cast.
What in the body's tomb doth buried lie
Is boundless; 'tis the spirit of the sky,
Lord of the future, guardian of the past,
And soon must forth, to know his own at last.
In his large life to live, I fain would die.
Happy the dumb beast, hungering for food,
But calling not his suffering his own;
Blessed the angel, gazing on all good,
But knowing not he sits upon a throne;
Wretched the mortal, pondering his mood,
And doomed to know his aching heart alone.

1065

AS IN THE MIDST OF BATTLE THERE IS ROOM

As in the midst of battle there is room
For thoughts of love, and in foul sin for mirth;
As gossips whisper of a trinket's worth
Spied by the death-bed's flickering candle-gloom;
As in the crevices of Cæsar's tomb
The sweet herbs flourish on a little earth:
So in this great disaster of our birth
We can be happy, and forget our doom.
For morning, with a ray of tendered joy
Gilding the iron heaven, hides the truth,
And evening gently woos us to employ
Our grief in idle catches. Such is youth;
Till from that summer's trance we wake, to find
Despair before us, vanity behind.

SAPPHO

SAPPHO (Greek, *ca.* 650 B.C.). Historiographically maligned gentle poetess of ancient Greece. Born on the island of Lesbos of noble family. Headed band of feminine worshipers of Aphrodite. Her simple emotional style has been imitated for centuries.

HYMN TO APHRODITE
(*Translation by Henry T. Wharton*)

Immortal Aphrodite of the broidered throne (*Poikilóthron*, sometimes printed *Poikilóphron*, various-minded), daughter of Zeus, weaver of wiles, I pray thee break not my spirit with anguish and distress, O Queen. But come hither, if ever before thou didst hear my voice afar and listen, and, leaving thy father's golden house, camest with chariot yoked, and fair, fleet sparrows drew thee, flapping fast their wings around the dark earth, from heaven through mid sky. Quickly arrived they; and thou, blessed one, smiling with immortal countenance, didst ask, What now is befallen me, and why now I call, and what I in my weak heart most desire to see? "What beauty now wouldst thou draw to love thee? Who wrongs

thee, Sappho? For even if she flies, she shall soon follow; and if she rejects gifts, shall yet live; if she loves not, shall soon love, however loth." Come, I pray thee, now too, and release me from cruel cares; and all that my heart desires to accomplish, accomplish thou, and be thyself my ally.

(Translation of J. H. Merivale)

Immortal Venus, throned above
In radiant beauty, child of Jove,
O skilled in every art of love
    And artful snare;
Dread power, to whom I bend the knee,
Release my soul and set it free
From bonds of piercing agony
    And gloomy care.
Yet come thyself, if e'er, benign,
Thy listening ears thou didst incline
To my rude lay, the starry shine
    Of Jove's court leaving.
In chariot yoked with coursers fair,
Thine own immortal birds, that bear
Thee swift to earth, the middle air
    With bright wings cleaving.
Soon they were sped—and thou, most blest,
In thine own smiles ambrosial dressed,
Didst ask what griefs my mind oppressed—
    What meant my song—
What end my frenzied thoughts pursue—
For what loved youth I spread anew
My amorous nets—"Who, Sappho, who
    Hath done thee wrong?
What though he fly, he'll soon return;
Still press thy gifts, though now he spurn;
Heed not his coldness—soon he'll burn,
    E'en though thou chide."
And saidst thou this, dread goddess? Oh,
Come then once more to ease my woe;
Grant all, and thy great self bestow,
    My shield and guide!

1067

Glittering-throned, undying Aphrodite,
Wile-weaving daughter of high Zeus, I pray thee,
Tame not my soul with heavy woe, dread mistress,
    Nay, nor with anguish!
But hither come, if ever erst of old time
Thou didst incline, and listenedst to my crying,
And from thy father's palace down descending,
    Camest with golden
Chariot yoked: the fair swift-flying sparrows
Over dark earth with multitudinous fluttering,
Pinion on pinion, through middle ether
    Down from heaven hurried.
Quickly they came like light, and thou, blest lady,
Smiling with clear undying eyes didst ask me
What was the woe that troubled me, and wherefore
    I had cried to thee:
What thing I longed for to appease my frantic
Soul; and whom now must I persuade, thou askedst,
Whom must entangle to thy love, and who now,
    Sappho, hath wronged thee?
Yea, for if now he shun, he soon shall chase thee;
Yea, if he take not gifts he soon shall give them;
Yea, if he love not, soon shall he begin to
    Love thee, unwilling.
Come to me now too, and from tyrannous sorrow
Free me, and all things that my soul desires to
Have done, do for me, queen, and let thyself too
    Be my great ally!

(*Translation of Francis T. Palgrave*)

Golden-throned beyond the sky,
Jove-born immortality:
Hear and heal a suppliant's pain;
Let not love be love in vain!

Come, as once to Love's imploring
Accents of a maid's adoring,

Wafted 'neath the golden dome,
Bore thee from thy father's home;

When far off thy coming glowed,
Whirling down th' ethereal road,
On thy dove-drawn progress glancing,
'Mid the light of wings advancing;

And at once the radiant hue
Of immortal smiles I knew;
Heard the voice of reassurance
Ask the tale of love's endurance:

Why such prayer? And who for thee,
Sappho, should be touched by me;
Passion-charmed in frenzy strong,
Who hath wrought my Sappho wrong?

"Soon for flight pursuit wilt find
Proffered gifts for gifts declined;
Soon, through long resistance earned,
Love refused be love returned."

To thy suppliant so returning,
Consummate a maiden's yearning;
Love, from deep despair set free,
Championing to Victory!

JEAN-PAUL SARTRE

JEAN-PAUL SARTRE (French, 1905-   ). The philosopher of postwar
opportunism. Leader of French School of Existentialism, and author of its
bible: *L'Être et le Néant*. Active during war in the Resistance, afterward
editor of his own journal. Successful plays: *Les Mouches, Huis-Clos, Les
Mains Sales*. Widely known novel: 4-volume *Les Chemins de la Liberté*.

THE WALL

THEY pushed us into a big white room and I began to blink because
the light hurt my eyes. Then I saw a table and four men behind the

1069

table, civilians, looking over the papers. They had bunched another group of prisoners in the back and we had to cross the whole room to join them. There were several I knew and some others who must have been foreigners. The two in front of me were blond with round skulls; they looked alike. I supposed they were French. The smaller one kept hitching up his pants; nerves.

It lasted about three hours; I was dizzy and my head was empty; but the room was well heated and I found that pleasant enough: for the past 24 hours we hadn't stopped shivering. The guards brought the prisoners up to the table, one after the other. The four men asked each one his name and occupation. Most of the time they didn't go any further—or they would simply ask a question here and there: "Did you have anything to do with the sabotage of munitions?" Or "Where were you the morning of the 9th and what were you doing?" They didn't listen to the answers or at least didn't seem to. They were quiet for a moment and then looking straight in front of them began to write.

It was my turn.

"Your name is Pablo Ibbieta?"

"Yes."

The man looked at the papers and asked me, "Where's Ramon Gris?"

"I don't know."

"You hid him in your house from the 6th to the 19th."

"No."

They wrote for a minute and then the guards took me out. In the corridor Tom and Juan were waiting between two guards. We started walking. Tom asked one of the guards, "So?"

"So what?" the guard said.

"Was that the cross-examination or the sentence?"

"Sentence," the guard said.

"What are they going to do with us?"

The guard answered dryly. "Sentence will be read in your cell."

As a matter of fact, our cell was one of the hospital cellars. It was terrifically cold there because of these drafts. We shivered all night and it wasn't much better during the day.

There was a bench in the cellar and four mats. When they took us back we sat and waited in silence. After a long moment, Tom said, "We're screwed."

"I think so too," I said, "but I don't think they'll do anything to the kid."

"They don't have a thing against him," said Tom. "He's the brother of a militiaman and that's all."

Around eight o'clock in the evening a major came in with two *falangistas*. He had a sheet of paper in his hand. He asked the guard, "What are the names of those three?"

"Steinbock, Ibbieta and Mirbal," the guard said.

The major put on his eyeglasses and scanned the list: "Steinbock ... Steinbock ... Oh yes ... You are sentenced to death.You will be shot tomorrow morning." He went on looking. "The other two as well."

"That's not possible," Juan said. "Not me."

The major looked at him amazed. "What's your name?"

"Juan Mirbal," he said.

"Well, your name is there," said the major. "You're sentenced."

"I didn't do anything," Juan said.

The major shrugged his shoulders. "A Belgian doctor is coming shortly. He is authorized to spend the night with you." He made a military salute and left.

"What did I tell you," Tom said. "We get it."

"Yes," I said, "it's a rotten deal for the kid."

I said that to be decent but I didn't like the kid. His face was too thin and fear and suffering had disfigured it, twisting all his features. Three days before he was a smart sort of kid, not too bad; but now he looked like an old fairy and I thought how he'd never be young again, even if they were to let him go. It wouldn't have been too hard to have a little pity for him but pity disgusts me, or rather it horrifies me.

It was almost dark, a dim glow filtered through the airholes and the pile of coal and made a big stain beneath the spot of sky; I could already see a star through the hole in the ceiling: the night would be pure and icy.

The door opened and two guards came in, followed by a blond man in a tan uniform. He saluted us. "I am the doctor," he said. "I have authorization to help you in these trying hours."

He had an agreeable and distinguished voice. I said, "What do you want here?"

"I am at your disposal. I shall do all I can to make your last moments less difficult."

"What did you come here for? You aren't here on an errand of mercy. Besides, I know you. I saw you with the fascists in the barracks yard the day I was arrested."

I was going to continue, but something surprising suddenly happened to me; the presence of this doctor no longer interested me. Generally when I'm on somebody I don't let go. But the desire to talk left me completely; I shrugged and turned my eyes away. A little later I raised my head; he was watching me curiously. The guards were sitting on a mat. Pedro, the tall thin one, was twiddling his thumbs, the other shook his head from time to time to keep from falling asleep.

I looked at my two friends. Tom had hidden his face in his hands. I could only see the fat white nape of his neck. Little Juan was the worst, his mouth was open and his nostrils trembled. The doctor went to him and put his hand on his shoulder to comfort him: but his eyes stayed cold. Then I saw the Belgian's hand drop stealthily along Juan's arm, down to the wrist. Juan paid no attention. The Belgian took his wrist between three fingers, distractedly, the same time drawing back a little and turning his back to me. But I leaned backward and saw him take a watch from his pocket and look at it for a moment, never letting go of the wrist. After a minute he let the hand fall inert and went and leaned his back against the wall, then, as if he suddenly remembered something very important which had to be jotted down on the spot, he took a notebook from his pocket and wrote a few lines. "Bastard," I thought angrily, "let him come and take my pulse. I'll shove my fist in his rotten face."

He didn't come but I felt him watching me. I raised my head and returned his look. Impersonally, he said to me, "Doesn't it seem cold to you here?" He looked cold, he was blue.

"I'm not cold," I told him.

He never took his hard eyes off me. Suddenly I understood and my hands went to my face: I was drenched in sweat. In this cellar, in the midst of winter, in the midst of drafts, I was sweating. I ran my hands through my hair, gummed together with perspiration; at the same time I saw my shirt was damp and sticking to my skin: I had been dripping for an hour and hadn't felt it. But that swine of a Belgian hadn't missed a thing; he had seen the drops rolling down my cheeks and thought: this is the manifestation of an almost pathological state of terror; and he had felt normal and proud of being alive because he was cold. I wanted to stand up and smash his face but no sooner had I made the slightest gesture than my rage and shame were wiped out; I fell back on the bench with indifference.

Suddenly Juan spoke. "You're a doctor?"

"Yes," the Belgian said.

1072

"Does it hurt . . . very long?"

"Huh? When . . . ? Oh, no," the Belgian said paternally. "Not at all. It's over quickly." He acted as though he were calming a cash customer.

"But I . . . they told me . . . sometimes they had to fire twice."

"Sometimes," the Belgian said, nodding. "It may happen that the first volley reaches no vital organs."

"Then they had to reload their rifles and aim all over again?" He thought for a moment and then added hoarsely, "That takes time!"

He had a terrible fear of suffering, it was all he thought about: it was his age. I never thought much about it and it wasn't fear of suffering that made me sweat.

Tom began speaking in a low voice. He had to talk, without that he wouldn't have been able to recognize himself in his own mind.

"Do you understand?" he said. " I don't understand."

I began to speak in a low voice too. I watched the Belgian. "Why? What's the matter?"

"Something is going to happen to us that I can't understand."

There was a strange smell about Tom. It seemed to me I was more sensitive than usual to odors. I grinned. "You'll understand in a while."

"It isn't clear," he said obstinately. "I want to be brave but first I have to know . . . Listen, they're going to take us into the court-yard. Good. They're going to stand up in front of us. How many?"

"I don't know. Five or eight. Not more."

"All right. There'll be eight. Someone'll holler 'aim!' and I'll see eight rifles looking at me. I'll think how I'd like to get inside the wall, I'll push against it with my back . . . with every ounce of strength I have, but the wall will stay, like in a nightmare. I can imagine all that. If you only knew how well I can imagine it."

"All right, all right!" I said, "I can imagine it too."

"It must hurt like hell. You know, they aim at the eyes and the mouth to disfigure you," he added mechanically. "I can feel the wounds already; I've had pains in my head and in my neck for the past hour. Not real pains. Worse. This is what I'm going to feel tomorrow morning. And then what?"

I well understood what he meant but I didn't want to act as if I did. I had pains too, pains in my body like a crowd of tiny scars. I couldn't get used to it. But I was like him, I attached no impor-tance to it. "After," I said, "you'll be pushing up daisies."

He kept on chewing his words, with something like distraction.

1073

He certainly talked to keep himself from thinking. Naturally, I agreed with him, I could have said everything he said: it isn't *natural* to die. And since I was going to die, nothing seemed natural to me. Only it didn't please me to think the same things as Tom. And I knew that, all through the night, every five minutes, we would keep on thinking things at the same time. I looked at him sideways and for the first time he seemed strange to me: he wore death on his face. My pride was wounded: for the past 24 hours I had lived next to Tom, I had listened to him, I had spoken to him and I knew we had nothing in common. And now we looked as much alike as twin brothers, simply because we were going to die together. Tom took my hand without looking at me . . .

I felt relaxed and over-excited at the same time. I didn't want to think any more about what would happen at dawn, at death. It made no sense. I only found words or emptiness. But as soon as I tried to think of anything else I saw rifle barrels pointing at me. Perhaps I lived through my execution twenty times; once I even thought it was for good: I must have slept a minute. They were dragging me to the wall and I was struggling; I was asking for mercy. If I had wanted to, I think I could have slept a while; I had been awake for 48 hours. I was at the end of my rope. But I didn't want to lose two hours of life: they would come to wake me up at dawn, I would follow them, stupefied with sleep and I would have croaked without so much as an "Oof!"; I didn't want that, I didn't want to die like an animal, I wanted to understand. Then I was afraid of having nightmares. I got up, walked back and forth, and, to change my ideas, I began to think about my past life. A crowd of memories came back to me pell-mell. There were good and bad ones—or at least I called them that *before*. There were faces and incidents. I saw the face of a little *novillero* who was gored in Valencia during the *Feria*, the face of one of my uncles, the face of Ramon Gris. I remembered my whole life: how I was out of work for three months in 1926, how I almost starved to death. I remembered a night I spent on a bench in Granada: I hadn't eaten for three days. I was angry, I didn't want to die. That made me smile. How madly I ran after happiness, after women, after liberty. Why? I wanted to free Spain, I admired Pi y Margall, I joined the anarchist movement, I spoke in public meetings: I took everything as seriously as if I were immortal.

At that moment I felt that I had my whole life in front of me and I thought, "It's a damned lie." It was worth nothing because it

was finished. I wondered how I'd been able to walk, to laugh with the girls: I wouldn't have moved so much as my little finger if I had only imagined I would die like this. My life was in front of me, shut, closed, like a bag and yet everything inside of it was unfinished. For an instant I tried to judge it. I wanted to tell myself, this is a beautiful life. But I couldn't pass judgment on it; it was only a sketch; I had spent my time counterfeiting eternity, I had understood nothing. I missed nothing: there were so many things I could have missed, the taste of *manzanilla* or the baths I took in summer in a little creek near Cadiz; but death had disenchanted everything.

In the state I was in, if somebody had come and told me I could go home quietly, that they would leave me my life whole, it would have left me cold: several hours or several years of waiting is all the same when you have lost the illusion of being eternal. I clung to nothing, in a way I was calm. But it was a horrible calm— because of my body; my body, I saw with its eyes, I heard with its ears, but it was no longer me; it sweated and trembled by itself and I didn't recognize it any more. I had to touch it and look at it to find out what was happening, as if it were the body of someone else. At times I could still feel it, I felt sinkings, and fallings, as when you're in a plane taking a nosedive, or I felt my heart beating. But that didn't reassure me. Everything that came from my body was all cockeyed. Most of the time it was quiet and I felt no more than a sort of weight, a filthy presence against me; I had the impression of being tied to an enormous vermin.

The Belgian took out his watch, looked at it. He said, "It is three-thirty."

Bastard! He must have done it on purpose. Tom jumped; we hadn't noticed time was running out; night surrounded us like a shapeless, somber mass, I couldn't even remember that it had begun.

Little Juan began to cry. He wrung his hands, pleaded, "I don't want to die. I don't want to die."

He ran across the whole cellar waving his arms in the air then fell sobbing on one of the mats. He wept: I could clearly see he was pitying himself; he wasn't thinking about death. For one second, one single second, I wanted to weep myself, to weep with pity for myself. But the opposite happened: I glanced at the kid, I saw his thin sobbing shoulders and I felt inhuman: I could pity neither the others nor myself. I said to myself, "I want to die cleanly."

1075

Tom had gotten up, he placed himself just under the round opening and began to watch for daylight. I was determined to die cleanly and I only thought of that. But ever since the doctor told us the time, I felt time flying, flowing away drop by drop.

It was still dark when I heard Tom's voice: "Do you hear them?"

Men were marching in the courtyard.

"Yes."

"What the hell are they doing? They can't shoot in the dark."

After a while we heard no more. I said to Tom, "It's day."

Pedro got up, yawning, and came to blow out the lamp. He said to his buddy, "Cold as hell."

The cellar was all grey. We heard shots in the distance.

"It's starting," I told Tom. "They must do it in the court in the rear."

Tom asked the doctor for a cigarette. I didn't want one; I didn't want cigarettes or alcohol. From that moment on they didn't stop firing.

"Do you realize what's happening," Tom said.

He wanted to add something but kept quiet, watching the door. The door opened and a lieutenant came in with four soldiers. Tom dropped his cigarette.

"Steinbock?"

Tom didn't answer. Pedro pointed him out.

"Juan Mirbal?"

"On the mat."

"Get up," the lieutenant said.

Juan did not move. Two soldiers took him under the arms and set him on his feet. But he fell as soon as they released him.

The soldiers hesitated.

"He's not the first sick one," said the lieutenant. "You two carry him; they'll fix it up down there."

He turned to Tom. "Let's go."

Tom went out between two soldiers. Two others followed, carrying the kid by the armpits. He hadn't fainted; his eyes were wide open and tears ran down his cheeks. When I wanted to go out the lieutenant stopped me.

"You Ibbieta?"

"Yes."

"You wait here; they'll come for you later."

They left. The Belgian and the two jailers left too, I was alone. I did not understand what was happening to me but I would have

liked it better if they had gotten it over with right away. I heard shots at almost regular intervals; I shook with each one of them. I wanted to scream and tear out my hair. But I gritted my teeth and pushed my hands in my pockets because I wanted to stay clean.

After an hour they came to get me and led me to the first floor, to a small room that smelt of cigars and where the heat was stifling. There were two officers sitting smoking in the armchairs, papers on their knees.

"You're Ibbieta?"

"Yes."

"Where is Ramon Gris?"

"I don't know."

The one questioning me was short and fat. His eyes were hard behind his glasses. He said to me, "Come here."

I went to him. He got up and took my arms, staring at me with a look that should have pushed me into the earth. At the same time he pinched my biceps with all his might. It wasn't to hurt me, it was only a game: he wanted to dominate me. He also thought he had to blow his stinking breath square in my face. We stayed for a moment like that, and I almost felt like laughing. It takes a lot to intimidate a man who is going to die; it didn't work. He pushed me back violently and sat down again. He said, "It's his life against yours. You can have yours if you tell us where he is."

These men dolled up with their riding crops and boots were still going to die. A little later than I, but not too much. They busied themselves looking for names in their crumpled papers, they ran after other men to imprison or suppress them; they had opinions on the future of Spain and on other subjects. Their little activities seemed shocking and burlesqued to me; I couldn't put myself in their place, I thought they were insane. The little man was still looking at me, whipping his boots with the riding crop. All his gestures were calculated to give him the look of a live and ferocious beast.

"So? You understand?"

"I don't know where Gris is," I answered. "I thought he was in Madrid."

The other officer raised his pale hand indolently. This indolence was also calculated. I saw through all their little schemes and I was stupefied to find there were men who amused themselves that way.

"You have a quarter of an hour to think it over," he said slowly.

"Take him to the laundry, bring him back in fifteen minutes. If he still refuses he will be executed on the spot."

They knew what they were doing: I had passed the night in waiting; then they had made me wait an hour in the cellar while they shot Tom and Juan and now they were locking me up in the laundry; they must have prepared their game the night before. They told themselves that nerves eventually wear out and they hoped to get me that way.

They were badly mistaken. In the laundry I sat on a stool because I felt very weak and I began to think. But not about their proposition. Of course I knew where Gris was; he was hiding with his cousins, four kilometers from the city. I also knew that I would not reveal his hiding place unless they tortured me (but they didn't seem to be thinking about that). All that was perfectly regulated, definite and in no way interested me. Only I would have liked to understand the reasons for my conduct. I would rather die than give up Gris. Why? I didn't like Ramon Gris any more. My friendship for him had died a little while before dawn at the same time as my desire to live. Undoubtedly I thought highly of him: he was tough. But it was not for this reason that I consented to die in his place; his life had no more value than mine; no life had value. They were going to slap a man up against a wall and shoot at him till he died, whether it was I or Gris or somebody else made no difference. I knew he was more useful than I to the cause of Spain but I thought to hell with Spain and anarchy; nothing was important. Yet I was there, I could save my skin and give up Gris and I refused to do it. I found that somehow comic; it was obstinacy. I thought, "I must be stubborn!" And a droll sort of gaiety spread over me.

They came for me and brought me back to the two officers. A rat ran out from under my feet and that amused me. I turned to one of the *falangistas* and said, "Did you see the rat?"

He didn't answer. He was very sober, he took himself seriously. I wanted to laugh but I held myself back because I was afraid that once I got started I wouldn't be able to stop.

"Well," said the fat officer, "have you thought about it?"

I looked at them with curiosity, as insects of a very rare species. I told them, "I know where he is. He is hidden in the cemetery. In a vault or in the gravediggers' shack."

It was a farce. I wanted to see them stand up, buckle their belts and give orders busily.

1078

They jumped to their feet. "Let's go. Molés, go get fifteen men from Lieutenant Lopez. You," the fat man said, "I'll let you off if you're telling the truth, but it'll cost you plenty if you're making monkeys out of us."

They left in a great clatter and I waited peacefully under the guard of *falangistas*. From time to time I smiled, thinking about the spectacle they would make. I felt stunned and malicious. I imagined them lifting up tombstones, opening the doors of the vaults one by one. I represented this situation to myself as if I had been someone else: this prisoner obstinately playing the hero, these grim *falangistas* with their moustaches and their men in uniform running among the graves; it was irresistibly funny. After half an hour the little fat man came back alone. I thought he had come to give the orders to execute me. The others must have stayed in the cemetery.

The officer looked at me. He didn't look at all sheepish. "Take him into the big courtyard with the others," he said. "After the military operations a regular court will decide what happens to him."

"Then they're not . . . not going to shoot me? . . ."

"Not now, anyway. What happens afterwards is none of my business."

I still didn't understand. I asked, "But why . . . ?"

He shrugged his shoulders without answering and the soldiers took me away. In the big courtyard there were about a hundred prisoners, women, children and a few old men. I began walking around the central grass-plot, I was stupefied. At noon they let us eat in the mess hall. Two or three people questioned me. I must have known them, but I didn't answer: I didn't even know where I was.

Around evening they pushed about ten new prisoners into the court. I recognized Garcia, the baker. He said, "What damned luck you have! I didn't think I'd see you alive."

"They sentenced me to death," I said, "and then they changed their minds. I don't know why."

"They arrested me at two o'clock," Garcia said.

"Why?" Garcia had nothing to do with politics.

"I don't know," he said. "They arrest everybody who doesn't think the way they do. He lowered his voice. "They got Gris."

I began to tremble. "When?"

"This morning. He messed it up. He left his cousin's on Tuesday because they had an argument. There were plenty of people to

1079

hide him but he didn't want to owe anything to anybody. He said, 'I'd go and hide in Ibbieta's place, but they got him, so I'll go hide in the cemetery.'"

"In the cemetery?"

"Yes. What a fool. Of course they went by there this morning, that was sure to happen. They found him in the gravediggers' shack. He shot at them and they got him."

"In the cemetery!"

Everything began to spin and I found myself sitting on the ground: I laughed so hard I cried.

FRIEDRICH VON SCHILLER

FRIEDRICH VON SCHILLER (German, 1759-1805). Germany's greatest dramatist. After years of antagonism, a great friend of Goethe's. His life was a triumph of creative will over disease. His 9 great plays, technically of the first order, are deeply imbued with pathos for moral freedom. Prominent among them: *Don Carlos, Wallenstein's Camp, Mary Stuart, William Tell.*

WILLIAM TELL AND THE TYRANT

Scene—*The hollow way at Küssnacht*

Tell (among the rocks overhanging the pass). Here through the
    hollow way he'll pass; there is
No other road to Küssnacht. Here I'll do it! . . .
The opportunity is good: the bushes
Of alder there will hide me; from that point
My arrow hits him; the strait pass prevents
Pursuit. Now, Gessler, balance thy account
With Heaven! Thou must be gone; thy sand is run! . . .
Remote and harmless I have lived; my bow
Ne'er bent save on the wild beast of the forest;
My thoughts were free of murder. Thou hast scared me
From my peace; to fell asp-poison hast thou
Changed the milk of kindly temper in me;
Thou hast accustomed me to horrors. Gessler!
The archer who could aim at his boy's head
Can send an arrow to his enemy's heart. . . .

1080

Poor little boys! My kind, **true** wife! I will
Protect them from thee. Viceroy! when I drew
That bowstring and my hand was quivering,
And with devilish joy thou mad'st me point it
At the child, and I in fainting anguish
Entreated thee in vain; then, with a grim,
Irrevocable oath, deep in my soul,
I vowed to God in Heaven that the next aim
I took should be thy heart. The vow I made
In that despairing moment's agony,
Became a holy debt—and I will pay it.

(Various characters gradually appear upon the scene, among
them Stüssi, Frau Armgart, and the members of a wedding procession, who come up the pass; at length Gessler [the Austrian
Landvogt or Viceroy], and Rudolph der Harras approach, riding
up the pass, while Tell disappears among the rocks.)

Gessler. Say what you like, I am the Kaiser's servant,
And must think of pleasing him. He sent me,
Not to caress these hinds, to soothe or nurse them.
Obedience is the word! The point at issue is,
Shall Boor or Kaiser here be lord o' th' lands?
  Armgart. Now is the moment! Now for my petition.
  Gess. This Hat at Altdorf, mark you, I set up,
Not for the joke's sake, or to try the hearts
O' th' people—these I know of old—but that
They might be taught to bend their necks to me,
Which are too straight and stiff; and in the way
Where they are hourly passing I have planted
This offence, so that their eyes may fall on't,
And remind them of their lord, whom they forgot.
  Rudolph. But the people have some rights—
  Gess. Which now
Is not a time for settling or admitting.
Mighty things are on the anvil. The House
Of Hapsburg must wax powerful; what the Father
Gloriously began, the Son must forward.
This people is a stone of stumbling, which
One way or t' other must be put aside.
  Arm. Mercy, gracious Viceroy! Justice! Justice!

1081

Gess. Why do you plague me here and stop my way
I' th' open road? Off! Let me pass!

Arm. My husband
Is in prison; these orphans cry for bread.
Have pity, good your grace, have pity on us!

Rud. Who or what are you, then? Who is your husband?

Arm. A poor wild-hay-man of the Rigiberg,
Whose trade is, on the brow of the abyss,
To mow the common grass from craggy shelves
And nooks to which the cattle dare not climb.

Rud. By Heaven, a wild and miserable life!
Do now! do let this poor drudge free, I pray you!—
Whatever be his crime, that horrid trade
Is punishment enough. You shall have justice;
In the castle there make your petition;
This is not the place.

Arm. No, no! I stir not
From this spot till you give up my husband!
'Tis the sixth month he has lain i' th' dungeon,
Waiting for the sentence of some judge in vain.

Gess. Woman! Would'st lay thy hands on me? Begone!

Arm. Justice Viceroy! thou art judge o' th' land here,
I' th' Kaiser's stead and God's. Perform thy duty!
As thou expectest justice from above,
Show it to us.

Gess. Off! take the mutinous rabble from my sight.

Arm. No, no! I now have nothing
More to lose. Thou shalt not move a step, Lord,
Till thou hast done me right. Ay, knit thy brows,
And roll thy eyes as sternly as thou wilt;
We are so wretched, wretched now we care not
Aught more for thy anger.

Gess. Woman, make way!
Or else my horse shall crush thee.

Arm. Let it! there!
Here am I with my children. Let the orphans
Be trodden underneath thy horse's hoofs!
'Tis not the worst that thou hast done.

Rud. Woman, art mad?

Arm. 'Tis long that thou has trodden
The Kaiser's people under foot. Too long!

1082

Oh, I am but a woman! Were I a man
I should find something else to do
Than lie here crying in the dust.

  Gess.   Where are my servants?
Quick! take her hence! I may forget myself,
And do the thing I shall repent.

  Rud.   My lord,
The servants cannot pass; the place above
Is crowded with a bridal company.

  Gess.   I've been too mild a ruler to this people;
They are not tamed as they should be; their tongues
Are still at liberty. This shall be altered!
I will break that stubborn humor. Freedom,
With its pert vauntings, shall no more be heard of.
I will enforce a new law in these lands;
There shall not—

  (An arrow pierces him; he presses his hand on his heart, and
slides from his horse into the arms of Rudolph, who has dis-
mounted.)

  Rud.   Lord Viceroy—God! What is it? whence came it?
  Gess.   'Tis Tell's arrow.
  Tell (*from a rock above*).   Thou hast found the archer;
Seek no other. Free are the cottages,
Secure is innocence from thee; thou wilt
Torment the land no more.

ARTHUR SCHNITZLER

ARTHUR SCHNITZLER (Austrian, 1862-1931). Impressionist playwright and
novelist. Physician and literary interpreter of Vienna's *"belle epoche."* His
sophisticated, pessimistic plays have been accused of immorality and decadence, but they brilliantly preserve the flavor of an era. Among them: *Anatol,
Reigen, Professor Bernhardi.*

FLOWERS

I WANDERED about the streets the whole afternoon, while the snow
fell slowly, in large flakes—and now I am at home, my lamp is
burning, my cigar is lighted and my books lie close by; in fact, I
have everything that affords true comfort. Yet all is in vain; I can
think of but one thing.

But had she not been dead for a long time as far as I was concerned?—yes, dead; or, as I thought with the childish pathos of the deceived, "worse than dead?" And now that I know that she is not "worse than dead," but simply dead, like the many others who lie out there, under the ground, forever—in spring, in the hot summer, and when the snow falls, as today—without any hope of ever returning—since that time I know that she did not die a moment sooner for me than she did for the rest of the world. Sorrow?—no. It is only the general horror that we all feel when something that once belonged to us, and whose entire being is still clear in our minds, sinks into the grave.

It was very sad when I discovered that she was deceiving me; —but there was so much else with it!—the fury and sudden hatred, and the horror of existence, and—ah, yes—the wounded vanity; —the sorrow only came later! But then there was the consolation that she also must be suffering.—I have them all yet, I can reread them at any time, those dozens of letters which sob, pray, and beseech forgiveness!—And I can still see her before me, in her dark dress and small straw hat, standing at the street corner in the twilight as I stepped out of the gate—looking after me.—And I still think of the last meeting when she stood in front of me with her large, beautiful eyes, set in that round, childlike face that now had become pale and wan.—I did not give her my hand when she left me;—when she left me for the last time.—And I watched her go down the street from my window and then she disappeared —forever. Now she can never return. . . .

My knowing it at all is due to an accident. I could have been unaware of it for weeks and months. I happened to meet her uncle one morning. I had not seen him for at least a year, as he does not come to Vienna very often. In fact, I had only met him two or three times before this. Our first meeting was three years ago at a bowling party. She and her mother were there also.—And then the following summer: I was in the Prater with a few friends. Her uncle was sitting at the next table with some gentlemen. They were all gay, and he drank to my health. And before he left he came up to me and told me confidentially that his niece was madly in love with me!—And in my half-giddiness it seemed very foolish and queer that the old gentleman should tell such a thing here, midst the music of the cymbals and violins—to me, who knew it so well, and on whose lips still clung the impression of her last kiss. And now, this morning! I almost walked past him. I asked for his niece,

more out of politeness than interest. I knew nothing more about her; her letters had stopped coming a long time ago; only flowers she sent me, regularly. Recollections of our happiest days! Once a month they came; no card: just silent, humble flowers.—And when I asked the old gentleman he was all astonishment. "You don't know that the poor girl died a week ago?" It was a terrible shock! —Then he told me more. And her illness? "Melancholia—anæmia. —The doctors themselves were not quite sure."

I remained a long while on the spot where the old gentleman had left me;—I was enervated, as if I had just gone through some great trouble.—And now it seems to me as if today marks the termination of a part of my life. Why—why? It was simply something external. I had no more feeling for her; in fact, I seldom thought of her any more. But now that I have written this all down I feel better; I am more composed—I am beginning to appreciate the coziness of my home.—It is foolish and tormenting to think of it any more.—There are certainly others today who have a great deal more to mourn about than I.

I have taken a walk. It is a serene winter's day. The sky looks so grey, so cold, so far away.—And I am very calm. The old gentleman whom I met yesterday—it seems as if it had been weeks ago. And when I think of her I can see her in a peculiarly sharp and finished outline; only one thing is lacking: the anger which always associated itself with my thoughts of her. The real appreciation that she is no more on earth, that she is lying in a coffin, that she has been buried, I have not—I feel no sorrow. The world seemed calmer to me today. I once knew for just one moment that there is neither happiness nor sorrow; no, there are only the grimaces of joy and sadness; we laugh and we weep and we invite our soul to be present. I could sit down now and read deep, serious books, and should soon be able to penetrate into all of their learning. Or, I could stand in front of old pictures, which heretofore have meant nothing to me, and now appreciate their true beauty.—And when I think of certain dear friends who have died, my heart does not feel as sad as it used to—death has become something friendly; it stalks among us but does not want to harm us.

Snow, high, white snow on all the streets. Little Gretel came to me and suggested that we ought to take a sleigh ride. And we drove out into the country, over the smooth road, the sleigh bells ringing and the blue-grey sky above us. Gretel rested against my shoulder and looked out upon the long road with happy eyes. We came to

an inn that we knew well from the summer. The oven was all aglow, and it was so hot that we had to move the table away, as Gretel's left ear and cheek became fire red. I had to kiss the paler cheek. Afterwards, the return home in the twilight! Gretel sat very close to me and held both of my hands in hers.—Then she said: "At last I have you again." She had thus, without racking her brain, struck the right note to make me happy. But perhaps it was the biting, clear air that unchained my thoughts, for I feel freer and more contented than I have in the last few days.

A short while ago again, as I lay dozing on my couch, a strange thought came to my mind. I appeared hard and cold to myself. As one who, without tears, in fact, without any emotion, stands at the grave in which he has buried a dear one. As one who has grown so hard that he cannot reconcile the horror of death.—Yes, irreconcilable, that is it.

Gone, quite gone! Life, happiness, and a little love drives all that foolishness away. I go again among people. I like them; they are harmless, they chatter about all sorts of jolly things. And Gretel is a dear, kind creature; and she is prettiest when she stands at my window and the sunbeams shine on her golden hair.

Something strange happened today.—It is the day on which she always sent me flowers. And the flowers came again as—as if nothing had changed. They came with the first mail, in a long, narrow white box. It was quite early, and I was still sleepy. And only when I was actually opening the box did I gain full consciousness. Then I almost had a shock. And there lay, daintily tied with a golden string, violets and pinks.—They lay as in a coffin. And as I took the flowers in my hand a shudder went through my heart. —But I understand how it is that they came again today. When she felt her illness, perchance even when she felt death approaching, she gave her usual order to the florist so that I would not miss her attention. Certainly, that is the explanation; as something quite natural, as something touching perhaps.—And still as I held them in my hands, these flowers, and they seemed to nod and tremble, then, in spite of reason and will power, I looked upon them as something ghostly, as if they had come from her, as if they were her greeting—as if she wanted always, even now that she was dead, to tell me of her love—of her tardy faithfulness. Ah, we do not understand death, we will never understand it; and a person is dead only after all that have known him have also passed away. To-day I grasped the flowers differently than usual, as if I might injure

them were I to hold them too tight—as if their souls might begin to sob softly. And as they now stand in front of me on my desk, in a narrow, light-green vase, they seem to nod their heads in mournful gratitude. The full pain of a useless yearning spreads over me from them, and I believe that they could tell me something if we could only understand the language of *all* living things—not only of the things that talk.

I do not want to let myself be fooled. They are only flowers. They are a message from the past. They are no call, surely no call from the grave. They are simply flowers, and some florist tied them together mechanically, put a bit of cotton around them, then laid them in the white box, and mailed it.—And now that they are here, why do I think about them?

I spend many hours in the open air and take long, lonely walks. When I am among people I do not feel compatible with them. And I noticed it when the sweet, blonde girl sits in my room, chattering away about all sorts of things—I don't know about what. When she is gone, in a moment it is as if she were miles away from me, as if the flood of people had engulfed her and left no traces behind. I should hardly be surprised if she did not come again.

The flowers are in the tall, green vase; their stems are in the water and their scent fills the room. They still retain their odour —in spite of the fact that I have had them a week and that they are already fading. And I believe all sorts of nonsense that I used to laugh at: I believe in the possibility of conversing with things in nature—I believe that one can communicate with clouds and springs; and I am waiting for these flowers to begin to talk. But no, I feel sure that they are always speaking—even now—they are forever crying out; and I can almost understand them.

How glad I am that the winter is over! Already the breath of spring throbs in the air. I am not living any differently than before, still I sometimes feel as if the boundaries of my existence are expanding. Yesterday seems far off, and the happenings of a few days past are like vague dreams. It is still the same when Gretel leaves me, especially when I have not seen her for several days; then our friendship appears like an affair of the past ages. She always comes, from afar, from so far away!—But when she begins to chatter it is like olden times again, and I then have a clear consciousness of the present. And then her words are almost too loud and the colours seem too harsh. Yet as soon as she leaves me all is gone; there are no after-pictures or gradual, fading recollec-

1087

tions.—And then I am alone with my flowers. They are now quite faded, quite faded. They have no more perfume. Gretel had not noticed them at all; but today she saw them and it seemed as if she wanted to question me, but then she suddenly appeared to have a secret horror for them;—she stopped speaking altogether and soon left me.

The petals are slowly falling off. I never touch them; anyway, if I did they would crumble. It makes me very sad to see them faded. I do not know why I have not the courage to make an end of all this nonsense. The faded flowers make me ill. I cannot stand them and I rush out. Once in the street, I feel that I have to hurry back to them, to care for them. And then I find them in the same green vase where I left them, tired and sad. Last evening I wept before them, as one weeps at a grave. Yet I never gave a thought to the sender of them. Perhaps I am wrong, yet it seems as if Gretel feels that there is something strange in my room. She does not laugh any more. She does not speak so loud, with that clear, lively voice to which I am accustomed. And I do not receive her as I used to. Then there is the fear that she will question me; and I realise what torture those questions would be.

She frequently brings her sewing, and if I am still at my books she sits quietly at the table and sews or crochets; and she waits patiently until I have finished and put my books away and come up to her and take her sewing out of her hands. Then I remove the green shade from the lamp so that a mellow light floods the room. I do not like dark corners.

Spring! My window is wide open. Late last evening Gretel and I looked out on to the street. The air was warm and balmy. And when I looked at the corner, where the street lamp spreads a weak light, I suddenly saw a shadow. I saw it and I did not—I know that I did not see it—I closed my eyes and I could suddenly see through my eyelids. There stood the miserable creature, in the pale lamp light, and I saw her face very clearly, as if the yellow sunshine were on it, and I saw in the pale, emaciated face those wounded eyes. Then I walked slowly away from the window and sat down at my desk; the candle spluttered in the breeze. And I remained motionless, for I knew that the poor creature was standing at the corner, waiting; and if I had dared to touch the faded flowers I would have taken them out of the vase and brought them to her. Thus I thought, and sincerely thought; yet I knew all the while that it was foolish. Now Gretel also left the window and came over to the back of my chair

where she remained a moment to touch my hair with her lips. Then she went and left me alone.

I stared at the flowers. There are hardly any more. Mostly bare stems, dry and pitiful. They make me ill and drive me mad. And it must be evident; otherwise Gretel would have asked me; but she feels it, too. Now she had fled as if there were ghosts in my room. Ghosts!—They are, they are!—Dead things playing with life! And if faded flowers smell mouldy it is only the remembrance of the time when they were in bloom. And the dead return as long as we do not forget them. What difference does it make if they cannot speak now;—I hear them! She does not appear any more, yet I can see her! And the spring outside, and the sunshine on my rug, and the perfume of the lilacs in the park, and the people who pass below and do not interest me, are they life? If I pull down the curtains, the sun is dead. I do not care to know about all these people, and they are dead. I close my window, and the perfume of the lilacs is gone and spring is dead. I am more powerful than the sun, the people, and the spring. But more powerful than I is remembrance, for that comes when it wills and from it there is no escape. And these dry stems are more powerful than the perfume of the lilacs and the spring.

I was pondering over these pages when Gretel entered. She had never come so early. I was surprised, astonished. She remained a moment on the threshold, and I gazed at her without greeting her. Then she smiled and approached me. In her hand she carried a bouquet of fresh flowers. Then, without speaking, she laid them on my desk. In the next moment, she seized the withered stems in the green vase. It seemed as if someone had grasped my heart;—but I could not utter a sound. And when I wanted to rise and take her by the arm, she smiled at me. Holding the faded flowers high above her, she hurried to the window and threw them out into the street. I felt I wanted to throw myself after them; but Gretel stood at the sill, facing me. And on her head was the sunshine, the bright sunshine. And the aroma of lilacs came in through the window. And I looked at the empty, green vase on my desk;—I am not sure, yet I think I felt freer,—yes, freer. Then Gretel approached me, picked up her bouquet, and held in front of my face cool, white lilacs. Such a healthy, fresh perfume—so soft, so cool; I wanted to bury my face in them. Laughing, white, beautiful flowers—and I felt that the spectre was gone. Gretel stood behind me and ran her hands

through my hair. "You silly boy," she said. Did she know what she had done? I grasped her hands and kissed her.

In the evening we went out into the open, into the spring. We have just returned! I have lighted my candle. We took a long walk, and Gretel is so tired that she has fallen asleep in the chair. She is very beautiful when she smiles thus in her sleep.

Before me, in the narrow, green vase are the lilacs. Down on the street—no, no, they are not there any longer. Already the wind has blown them away with the rest of the dust.

SIR WALTER SCOTT

SIR WALTER SCOTT (Scottish, 1771-1832). Prolific as well as imaginative practitioner of the historical romance and sentimental novel. Based adventure stories on sound research, heavily influencing French and other period novelists. Most famous of these: *Ivanhoe, Quentin Durward, The Talisman.* His long narrative poems still effective: *The Lay of the Last Minstrel, Lady of the Lake.*

THE NUBIAN

RICHARD surveyed the Nubian in silence as he stood before him, his looks bent upon the ground, his arms folded on his bosom, with the appearance of a black marble statue of the most exquisite workmanship waiting life from the touch of a Prometheus. The king of England, who, as it was emphatically said of his successor, Henry the Eighth, loved to look upon a man, was well pleased with the thews, sinews, and symmetry of him whom he now surveyed and questioned him in the lingua Franca, "Art thou a pagan?"

The slave shook his head, and raising his finger to his brow crossed himself in token of his Christianity, then resumed his posture of motionless humility.

"A Nubian Christian, doubtless," said Richard, "and mutilated of the organ of speech by these heathen dogs?"

The mute again slowly shook his head, in token of negative, pointed with his forefinger to heaven, and then laid it upon his own lips.

"I understand thee," said Richard; "thou doest suffer under the infliction of God, not by the cruelty of man. Canst thou clean an armor and belt, and buckle it in time of need?"

The mute nodded, and stepping toward the coat of mail, which hung with the shield and helmet of the chivalrous monarch, upon

1090

the pillar of the tent, he handled it with such nicety of address, as sufficiently to show that he fully understood the business of the armor bearer.

"Thou art an apt, and wilt doubtless be a useful, knave. Thou shalt wait in my chamber, and on my person," said the king, "to show how much I value the gift of the royal Soldan. If thou hast no tongue, it follows thou canst carry no tales, neither provoke me to be sudden by an unfit reply."

The Nubian again prostrated himself till his brow touched the earth, then stood erect, at some paces distant, as waiting for his new master's commands.

"Nay, thou shalt commence thy office presently," said Richard, "for I see a speck of rust darkening on that shield; and when I shake it in the face of Saladin, it should be bright and unsullied as the Soldan's honor and mine own."

A horn was winded without, and presently Sir Henry Neville entered with a packet of dispatches. "From England, my lord," he said, as he delivered it. "From England,—our own England" repeated Richard, in a tone of melancholy enthusiasm. "Alas! they little think how hard their sovereign has been beset by sickness and sorrow, faint friends, and forward enemies." Then, opening the dispatches, he said hastily, "Ha! this comes from no peaceful land; they too have their feuds. Neville, begone; I must peruse these tidings alone, and at leisure."

Neville withdrew accordingly, and Richard was soon absorbed in the melancholy details which had been conveyed to him from England, concerning the factions that were tearing to pieces his native dominions,—the disunion of his brothers, John and Geoffrey, and the quarrels of both with the High Justiciary Longchamp, Bishop of Ely; the oppressions practiced by the nobles upon the peasantry, and rebellion of the latter against their masters, which had produced everywhere scenes of discord, and in some instances the effusion of blood. Details of incidents mortifying to his pride, and derogatory from his authority, were intermingled with the earnest advice of his wisest and most attached counselors, that he should presently return to England, as his presence offered the only hope of saving the kingdom from all the horrors of civil discord, of which France and Scotland were likely to avail themselves.

Filled with the most painful anxiety, Richard read, and again read, the ill-omened letters, compared the intelligence with some of them contained with the same facts as differently stated in others,

and soon became totally insensible to whatever was passing around him although seated, for the sake of coolness, close to the entrance of his tent, and having the curtains withdrawn, so that he could see and be seen by the guards and others who were stationed without.

Deeper in the shadow of the pavilion, and busied with the task his new master had imposed, sat the Nubian slave, with his back rather turned toward the king. He had finished adjusting the hauberk and brigandine, and was now busily employed on a broad pavise, or buckler, of unusual size, and covered with steel plating, which Richard often used in reconnoitering, or actually storming, fortified places, as a more effectual protection against missile weapons than the narrow triangular shield used on horseback.

This pavise bore neither the royal lions of England, nor any other device, to attract the observation of the defenders of the walls against which it was advanced. The care, therefore, of the armorer was addressed to causing its surface to shine as bright crystal, in which he seemed to be peculiarly successful. Beyond the Nubian, and scarcely visible from without, lay the large dog, which might be termed his brother slave, and which, as if he felt awed by being transferred to a royal owner, was couched close to the side of the mute, with his head and ears on the ground, and his limbs and tail drawn close around and under him.

While the monarch and his new attendant were thus occupied, another actor crept upon the scene, and mingled among the group of English yeomen, about a score of whom, respecting the unusually pensive posture and close occupation of their sovereign, were, contrary to their wont, keeping a silent guard in front of his tent. It was not, however, more vigilant than usual. Some were playing at games of hazard with small pebbles, other spoke together in whispers of the approaching day of battle, and several lay asleep, their bulky limbs folded in their green mantles.

Amid these careless warders glided the puny form of a little old Turk, poorly dressed like a marabout or santon of the desert,—a sort of enthusiast, who sometimes ventured into the camp of the Crusaders, though treated always with contumely, and often with violence. Indeed, the luxury and profligate indulgence of the Christian leaders had occasioned a motley concourse in their tents, of musicians, Jewish merchants, Copts, Turks, and all the varied refuse of the Eastern nations; so that the caftan and turban—though to drive both from the Holy Land was the professed object of the expedition

—were nevertheless neither an uncommon nor an alarming sight in the camp of the Crusaders. When, however, the little insignificant figure we have described approached so nigh as to receive some interruption from the warders, he dashed his dusky green turban from his head, showed that his beard and eyebrows were shaved like those of a professed buffoon, and that the expression of his fantastic and writhen features, as well as of his little black eyes, which glittered like jet, was that of a crazed imagination.

"Dance, marabout," cried the soldiers, acquainted with the manners of these wandering enthusiasts,—"dance, or we will scourge thee with our bowstrings, till thou spin as never top did under schoolboy's lash." Thus shouted the reckless warders, as much delighted at having a subject to tease as a child when he catches a butterfly, or a schoolboy upon discovering a bird's nest.

The marabout, as if happy to do their behests, bounded from the earth, and spun his giddy round before them with singular agility, which when contrasted with his slight and wasted figure and diminutive appearance, made him resemble a withered leaf twirled round and round at the pleasure of the winter's breeze. His single lock of hair streamed upwards from his bald and shaven head, as if some genie upheld him by it; and indeed it seemed as if supernatural art were necessary to the execution of the wild whirling dance, in which scarce the tiptoe of the performer was seen to touch the ground.

Amid the vagaries of his performance, he flew here and there, from one spot to another, still approaching, however, though almost imperceptibly, to the entrance of the royal tent; so that, when at length he sunk exhausted on the earth, after two or three bounds still higher than those which he had yet executed, he was not above thirty yards from the king's person.

For the space of a quarter of an hour, or longer, after the incident related, all remained perfectly quiet in the front of the royal habitation. The king read and mused in the entrance of his pavilion; behind, and with his back turned to the same entrance, the Nubian slave still burnished the ample pavise; in front of all, at an hundred paces distant, the yeomen of the guard stood, sat, or lay extended on the grass, attentive to their own sports, but pursuing them in silence; while on the esplanade betwixt them and the front of the tent lay, scarcely to be distinguished from a bundle of rags, the senseless form of the marabout.

But the Nubian had the advantage of a mirror, from the brilliant

1093

reflection which the surface of the highly polished shield now afforded, by means of which he beheld, to his alarm and surprise, that the marabout raised his head gently from the ground, so as to survey all around him, moving with a well-adjusted precaution, which seemed entirely inconsistent with a state of inebriety. He couched his head instantly, as if satisfied he was unobserved, and began, with the slightest possible appearance of voluntary effort, to drag himself, as if by chance, ever nearer and nearer to the king, but stopping and remaining fixed at intervals, like the spider, which, moving towards her object, collapses into apparent lifelessness when she thinks she is the subject of observation. This species of movement appeared suspicious to the Ethiopian, who, on his part, prepared himself as quietly as possible to interfere the instant that interference should seem to be necessary.

The merchant meanwhile glided on gradually and imperceptibly, serpent-like, or rather snail-like, till he was about ten yards' distance from Richard's person, when, starting on his feet, he sprang forward with the bound of a tiger, stood at the king's back in less than an instant, and brandished aloft the cangiar, or poniard, which he had hidden in his sleeve.

Not the presence of his whole army could have saved their heroic monarch; but the motions of the Nubian had been as well calculated as those of the enthusiast, and, ere the latter could strike, the former caught his uplifted arm. Turning his fanatical wrath upon what thus unexpectedly interposed betwixt him and his object, the Charegite, for such was the seeming marabout, dealt the Nubian a blow with the dagger, which, however, only grazed his arm, while the far superior strength of the Ethiopian easily dashed him to the ground.

Aware of what had passed, Richard had now arisen, and with little more of surprise, anger, or interest of any kind in his countenance than an ordinary man would show in brushing up the stool on which he had been sitting, and exclaiming only "Ha, dog!" dashed almost to pieces the skull of the assassin, who uttered twice, once in a loud and once in a broken tone, the words "Allah ackbar!" —God is victorious.—and expired at the king's feet.

"Ye are careful warders," said Richard to his archers, in a tone of scornful reproach, as, aroused by the bustle of what had passed, in terror and tumult they now rushed into his tent; "watchful sentinels ye are, to leave me to do such hangman's work with my own hand. Be silent, all of you, and cease your senseless clamor!

Saw ye never a dead Turk before? Here, cast that carrion out of the camp, strike the head from the trunk, and stick it on a lance, taking care to turn the face to Mecca, that he may the easier tell the foul impostor, on whose inspiration he came hither, how he has sped on his errand.—For thee, my swart and silent friend," he added, turning to the Ethiopian. "But how's this? thou art wounded, and with a poisoned weapon, I warrant me; for by force of stab so weak an animal as that could scarce hope to do more than raise the lion's hide. Suck the poison from the wound, one of you; the venom is harmless on the lips, though fatal when it mingles with the blood."

The yeomen looked on each other confusedly and with hesitation, the apprehension of so strange a danger prevailing with those who feared no other.

"How now, sirrah?" continued the king; "are you dainty-lipped, or do you fear death, that you dally thus?"

"Not the death of a man," said Long Allan, to whom the king looked as he spoke; "but methinks I would not die like a poisoned rat for the sake of a black chattel there, that is bought and sold in market like a Martlemas ox."

"His Grace speaks to men of sucking poison," muttered another yeoman, "as if he said, 'Go to, swallow a gooseberry!'"

"Nay," said Richard, "I never bade a man do that which I would do not myself."

And without further ceremony, and in spite of the general expostulations of those around, and the respectful opposition of the Nubian himself, the king of England applied his lips to the wound of the black slave, treating with ridicule all remonstrances, and overpowering all resistance. He had no sooner intermitted his singular occupation, than the Nubian started from him, and casting a scarf over his arm, intimated by gestures, as firm in purpose as they were respectful in manner, his determination not to permit the monarch to renew so degrading an employment. Long Allan also interposed, saying that if it were necessary to prevent the king engaging again in a treatment of this kind, his own lips, tongue, and teeth were at the service of the negro (as he called the Ethiopian), and that he would eat him up bodily, rather than King Richard's mouth again should approach him.

Neville, who entered with other officers, added his remonstrances.

"Nay, nay, make not a needless halloo about a hart that the hounds have lost, or a danger when it is over," said the king. "The

1095

wound will be a trifle, for the blood is scarce drawn,—an angry
cat had dealt a deeper scratch,—and, for me, I have but to take a
dram of orvietan by way of precaution, though it is needless."

Thus spoke Richard, a little ashamed, perhaps, of his own condescension, though sanctioned both by humanity and gratitude.
But when Neville continued to make remonstrances on the peril to
his royal person, the king imposed silence on him.

"Peace, I prithee; make no more of it. I did it but to show these
ignorant prejudiced knaves how they might help each other when
these cowardly caitiffs come against us with sarbacanes and poisoned shafts."

SE'AMI

SE'AMI (Japanese, 1363-1443). Chief representative of the *Nō* play, created
by self and father. Author of nearly half the *Nō* plays still performed. Most
famous: *Takasago*. Was also praised as an actor and dramatic critic.

SOTOBA KOMACHI

Characters:
First Priest
Second Priest
Chorus

Komachi, as herself
and as her former
lover

Both Priests:
The mountains are not high on which we hide
The mountains are not high on which we hide
The lonely deepness of our hearts.

First Priest:
I am a priest from the Koya Hills
Coming down now to make my way to the city.

Second Priest:
The Buddha that was is gone away.
The Buddha to be has not yet come to the world.

Both Priests:
At birth we woke to dream in this world between
What then shall we say is real?
By chance we took the forms of men

1096

From a thousand possibilities.
We stumbled on the treasure of the holy law
The seed of all salvation
And then with thoughtful hearts we put our bodies
In these thin and ink-black robes,
We knew of lives before this birth
We knew of lives before this birth
And knew we owed no love to those who to this life
Engendered us.
We recognize no parents.
No children cared for us.
We walked a thousand miles and the way seemed short.
In the fields we lay down
And slept the night in the hills
Which now became our proper dwelling place
Our proper home.

Komachi:
'Like a root-cut reed
Should the tide entice
I would come
I would come I know but no wave asks
No stream invites this grief.'

How sad that once I was proud
Long ago
Proud and graceful
Golden birds in my raven hair
When I walked like willows nodding, charming
As the breeze in spring.
The voice of the nightingale
The petals of the wood rose wide stretched
Holding dew
At the hour before their breathless fall:
I was lovlier than these.
Now
I am foul in the eyes of the humblest creatures
To whom my shame is shown.
Unwelcome months and days pile over me
The wreck of a hundred years
In the city to avoid the eyes of men
Lest they should say "Can it be she?"

1097

In the evening
West with the moon I steal past the palace,
Past the towers
Where no guard will question in the mountains
In the shadows of the trees
None challenge so wretched a pilgrim as this
To Love's Tomb
The autumn hills
The River Katsura
Boats in the moonlight rowed by whom?
I cannot see. . . .
But rowed by whom!

Oh, too, too, painful. . . .
Here on this withered stump of tree
Let me sit and collect my senses.

First Priest:
Come on. The sun is down. We must hurry on our way. But look!
that old beggar woman sitting there on a sacred stupa. We should
warn her to come away.

Second Priest:
Yes, of course.

First Priest:
Excuse me, old lady, but don't you know that's a stupa there you're
sitting on? the holy image of the Buddha's incarnation. You'd better
come away and rest some other place.

Komachi:
The holy image of the Buddha you say? But I saw no words or
carvings on it. I took it for a tree stump only.

First Priest:
'Withered stumps
Are known as pine or cherry still
On the loneliest mountain.'

Komachi:
I, too, am a fallen tree.
But still the flowers of my heart
Might make some offering to the Buddha.
But this you call the Buddha's body. Why?

First Priest:
The stupa represents the body of Kongosatta Buddha, the Diamond

1098

Lord, when he assumed the temporary form of each of his manifestations.

Komachi:
In what forms then is he manifested?

First Priest:
In Earth and Water and Wind and Fire and Space.

Komachi:
The same five elements as man. What was the difference then?

First Priest:
The form was the same but not the power.

Komachi:
And what is a stupa's power?

First Priest:
"He that has once looked upon a stupa shall for all eternity avoid
the three worst catastrophes."

Komachi:
"One sudden thought can strike illumination."
Is that not just as good?

Second Priest:
If you've had such an illumination, why are you lingering here in
this world of illusion?

Komachi:
Though my body lingers, my heart has left it long ago.

First Priest:
Unless you had no heart at all you wouldn't have failed to feel the
presence of a stupa.

Komachi:
It was because I felt it that I came perhaps.

Second Priest:
In that case you shouldn't have spread yourself out on it without so
much as a word of prayer.

Komachi:
It was on the ground already. . . .

First Priest:
Just the same it was an act of discord.

Komachi:
"Even from discord salvation springs."

Second Priest:
From the evil of Daiba

Komachi:
Or the love of Kannon.
First Priest:
From the folly of Handoku
Komachi:
Or the wisdom of
Monju.
First Priest:
What we call evil
Komachi:
Is also good.
First Priest:
Illusion
Komachi:
Is Salvation.
Second Priest:
"Salvation
Komachi:
Cannot be watered like trees."
First Priest:
"The brightest mirror
Komachi:
Is not on the wall."
Chorus:
Nothing is separate.
Nothing persists.
Of Buddha and man there is no distinction,
At most a seeming difference planned
For the humble, ill-instructed men
He has vowed from the first to save.
"Even from discord salvation springs."
So said Komachi. And the priests:
"Surely this beggar is someone beyond us."
Then bending their heads to the ground
Three times did they do her homage
The difficult priests
The difficult priests
Who thought to correct her.
First Priest:
Who are you then? Give us your name; we will pray for your soul.

1100

Komachi:
For all my shame I will tell you. Pray for the wreck of Komachi, the
daughter of Yoshizane of Ono, Lord of Dewa.
Both Priests:
How sad to think that you were she.
Exquisite Komachi
The brightest flower long ago
Her dark brows arched
Her face bright powdered always
When cedar-scented halls could scarce contain
Her damask robes.
Komachi:
I made verses in our speech
And in the speech of the foreign Court.
Chorus:
When she passed the banquet cup
Reflected moonlight lay on her sleeve.
How was ever such lovliness lost?
When did she change?
Her hair a tangle of frosted grass
Where the black curls lay on her neck
And the color lost from the twin arched peaks
Of her brow.
Komachi:
'Oh shameful in the dawning light
These silted seaweed locks that of a hundred years
Now lack but one.'
Chorus:
What do you have in the bag at your waist?
Komachi:
Death today or hunger tomorrow.
Only some beans I've put in my bag.
Chorus:
And in the bundle on you back?
Komachi:
A soiled and dusty robe.
Chorus:
And in the basket on your arm?
Komachi:
Sagittaries black and white.

Chorus:
Tattered coat

Komachi:
Broken hat

Chorus:
Can scarcely hide her face.

Komachi:
Think of the frost and the snow and the rain.
I've not even sleeves enough to dry my tears.
But I wander begging things from men
That come and go along the road.
When begging fails
An awful madness seizes me
And my voice is no longer the same. . . .
    Hey! Give me something, you priests!

First Priest:
What do you want?

Komachi:
To go to Komachi!

First Priest:
What are you saying? You *are* Komachi!

Komachi:
No. Komachi was beautiful.
Many letters came, many messages
Thick as rain from a summer sky
But she made no answer, even once,
Even an empty word.
Age is her retribution now.
Oh, I love her!
I love her!

First Priest:
You love her! What spirit has possessed you to make you say such things?

Komachi:
Many loved her
But among them all
It was Shosho who loved her deepest
Shii no Shosho, the Captain.

Chorus:
The wheel turns back.

I live again a cycle of unhappiness
Riding with the wheels
That came and went again each night.
The sun.
What time is it now?
Dusk.
The moon will be my friend on the road
And though the watchmen stand at the pass
They shall not bar my way.

Komachi: (re-costumed as her lover)
My wide white skirts hitched up

Chorus:
My wide white skirts hitched up
My tall black hat pulled down
And my sleeves thrown over my head
Hidden from the eyes of men on the road
In the moonlight
In the darkness coming, coming
When the night rains fell
When the night winds blew the leaves like rain
When the snow lay deep

Komachi:
And the melting drops fell
One by one from the rafters

Chorus:
I came and went, came and went
One night, two nights, three,
Ten (and this was the Harvest Night).
And did not see her.
Faithful as a cock that marks each dawn
I came and carved my mark upon the pillar.
I was to come a hundred nights,
I lacked but one. . . .
Oh, dizziness . . . pain. . . .

Chorus:
He was grieved at the pain in his breast
When the last night came and he died
Shii no Shosho, the Captain.

Komachi:
It was his unsatisfied love possessed me so

1103

His anger that turned my wits.
In the face of this I will pray
For life in the worlds to come
The sands of goodness I will pile
Into a towering hill.
Before the golden, gentle Buddha I will lay
Poems as my flowers
Entering in the way
Entering in the way

SEI SHONAGON

SEI SHONAGON (Japanese, *ca.* 966-1013). Early Japanese poetical court diarist. The daughter of a poet. Served as lady-in-waiting to the Empress. Her private sketchbook or diary later became celebrated literary work. It is made up of epigrammatic, anecdotal pictures of court life.

A CUCKOO PICNIC

SINCE the 1st May it had been raining or cloudy every day, and we were bored to death. I suggested that we should go and hear the cuckoo, and everyone was wildly excited at once and agreed, saying: "I too! I too!" Someone said: "Far away near Kamo River is a bridge. It is not called Tanabata's Bridge, but something like it and more difficult. However, near there the cuckoo sings nearly every day."

"No, no! It's only a cicada," said another. Anyway, we decided to go out there, and asked the officer on duty to order the carriage to the veranda.

"It would certainly be allowed, as it is raining," we said, and when the carriage came from the north guard-room it arrived at our veranda and four of us got in and started from the northern gate. The others said enviously: "What a pity we can't order another carriage and go together."

But the Empress said "No," so we paid no attention to this.

On our way past the racecourse we saw crowds of noisy people. "What can be going on?" we asked.

"They are practising archery on horseback. Pray stop and see," the man who runs beside the carriage answered. He stopped the

carriage, but we could see nothing of the General of the Left, who they said had arrived, and only a few sixth-grade people were strolling about.

"It isn't worth watching. Let us get on quickly," we agreed.

And on we went. This road is quite interesting about the time of Kamo festival.

"By and by we shall come to the house of the Empress's uncle," we said, and we got out of the carriage there.

Lord Akinobu Ason's house is built in the simplest way and very rustic—paper screens with pictures of horses, and others woven of strips of bamboo and fine grass-woven blinds, and so on. One could see they kept up the old customs, and the house itself had little spaciousness. Just as we were looking about us with interest the cuckoos burst into song with such zest as to be absolutely noisy. We were dreadfully sorry the Empress could not hear them, and also for those of us who had wanted to come and could not.

"Now you are in the country, you must see our country ways," said Akinobu Ason, and accordingly rice plants were brought and some cleanly dressed young women showed us how the stripping of the grain is done and how it is put into a kind of revolving machine. Two of them kept it turning while they marked time with a song. It was very curious, and we laughed so much that we quite forgot the cuckoo and the poems to be written about her.

Then in came food on the beautiful old tables one sees in Chinese pictures, but that did not interest any of us, and he said: "I know this is very countrified stuff, but the only way is to keep on attacking the host until he provides something you really like. If you have no appetite it is not like our usual City visitors."

So he cheered us on, saying: "These bracken fronds I picked myself."

"But surely you don't expect us to sit round the tables like common people," I remonstrated and at once he had the refreshment taken from the little tables.

"Why, no! one sees all of you are accustomed to the strictest etiquette in the August Presence," he said, and so served us separately.

While we were making merry we heard the driver calling: "It's going to rain," and out we all hurried and into the carriage.

"But I want to get my poem done before we start," I cried.

"No, No! On the way back!" someone said.

We picked any amount of lovely deutzia along the road and stuck

the sprays into the blinds and the sides of the carriage, and thatched the roofs with great boughs of it, until it looked exactly as if the carriage were covered with white damask. Our men, much interested, helped us, sticking the sprays into every crevice of the wickerwork, crying, "More, more. A bit just here!" thoroughly enjoying themselves.

In we all got, hoping to meet someone who would notice our display. But no one turned up. There were only dull priests and a few servants on the road. Such a pity! Presently we arrived at the East Ward and said to each other: "It will never do if we meet no one and not the least notice is taken of our gorgeously decorated carriage!"

So we stopped forthwith in front of the palace in that ward and asked for the Lord Chamberlain sending word by the messenger: "Is the Lord Chamberlain at home? We are just returning from a cuckoo picnic."

Back came the messenger.

"His Lordship says: 'I will come out at once.' Do please wait."

It seems he was putting on his ceremonial trousers in a hurry. So we thought there was no need to wait and whipping up set off for the Eastern Gate. And there he followed us, rushing down the road and tying his trousers as he ran. Behind him rushed his followers and valets. We urged the driver on, faster! faster! and when we arrived at the gate he overtook us, perfectly breathless. It was then he noticed the splendour of our carriage and said: "What in the world—! Are there common mortals in such a carriage? Do get out and let me see!"

And he and his followers laughed with delight over the joke.

"But your poems—your poems! I want to hear them now!" he begged.

"Now? Certainly not! Her Majesty will hear them first!" I said demurely.

The rain began to pelt while we were talking, and he said: "Why in the world has this gate no roof when every other gate is weatherproof? And to-day of all days, when we want shelter. And how am I to get home? I rushed out after you regardless of consequences, and what am I to do?"

We all chorused: "Come into the Palace!"

"And may I ask how I am to go there in a soft-crowned cap?"

"Send home for what you want," we suggested.

Down came the rain, and our men began pulling us with all

speed. Off went the Lord Chamberlain, and under an umbrella. Slowly and reluctantly he trudged along, turning to look back with a spray of deutzia in his hand. It was very amusing.

In the Palace her Majesty asked for the story of our adventures, and we told the tale of the Lord Chamberlain and Ichijo Street. Everyone laughed, even the sulky stay-at-homes. But then came the question: "And where are the poems?"

Of course, it had to come out that we had made none. The Empress said at once; "Oh what a pity! All the officers will have heard of the picnic, and with what face can we say no poems came of such an adventure? You had much better have done it while the cuckoo was singing and you were considering it seriously. But set to work even now, for if not your visit will be wasted!"

Really, we had been idiots. And while we were regretting all this and consulting over poems, in comes a short poem from the Lord Chamberlain written on fine white flower-paper and fastened to the deutzia spray he had taken.

"The cuckoo's cry. Had I known you
were fled to seek it
I should have bid you carry my whole
heart's greeting today."

I thought the messenger might be waiting, so I sent someone hurrying for my writing-box, but the Empress said: "No—be quick. Use mine!"

And she did me the honor to slip in some paper. So I said to Saisho: "Be quick. Your turn, please."

"No, yours, please!" said she. And in the midst of our polite wrangling the sky grew black and the rain came down in sheets and the thunder roared so terrifically that we were frightened into rushing away to shut all the blinds and the outside doors in a perfect panic. And poetry was forgotten.

The thunder lasted so long that as it stopped darkness came on. And still we would have struggled with the poems but that many of the officers and other visitors came up to inquire for the Empress's health after the storm, and of course we had to meet them and do the honors, so again the poems went to the wall as far as I was concerned, and the other ladies did not trouble about it, for they declared the Lord Chamberlain's poem was addressed to me, and it was my business to answer. I was not in the mood for it, much as I regretted it.

"I really wish no one knew anything about the picnic," I said, and the Empress retorted: "You could certainly patch up a poem among you. It is only that you don't care to."

I think she was a little cross. It was strange altogether.

"But we missed our chance, and now the mood has evaporated," I said.

"You mean your interest has evaporated," she said.

And there we left it.

Two days passed and we were discussing the cuckoo picnic. Saisho said: "But how did you like the bracken-shoots which our host said he had picked himself?"

The Empress, listening, said with a laugh: "I think your refreshments were the only things you remembered." And she scribbled the end of a verse on a piece of paper:

"The longing for the bracken haunts her memory still."

"Do be poetical and finish it!" she said.

It was really rather amusing, and I took my brush and wrote:

"And drowns the cuckoo's note we sallied out to hear."

"Candid enough!" said the laughing Empress. "But why didn't you remember the cuckoo as affectionately?"

I felt a little out of countenance.

"I don't know why," I said, "but I have a kind of feeling I shall compose no more short poems. I always am uncomfortable when the subject comes up and your Majesty commands me to set to work. Besides, how am I to do it when I am so stupid as to have no knowledge of metre and evolve a winter poem in spring and a spring one in autumn, and in plum-blossom time descant upon chrysanthemums? You see, my ancestor was a well-known poet, so that mine really ought to be better than others, and, if they were, one might really plume oneself when people said, 'This short poem absolutely fitted the occasion. But then, of course, she had the advantage of a poetical heritage.' But if one has no special aptitude and yet thinks oneself clever, and so composes at large, it really is a little hard on the ancestor!"

The Empress laughed and answered: "Well, well! Do as you please. I shall not insist on your poetising any more!"

So I was feeling easier in my mind.

But while all this was in my head the Empress's brother was eagerly preparing to hold the All Night Waking. As it grew late a

competition for short poems was announced, and all the ladies asked
to compete. Great excitement! I was there and talking to the Empress about something else, when the Prince came up to me and
said: "Why, is it possible you are not going to write us a poem?
Do, I beseech you!"

I answered: "I have been honored by permission to do exactly
as I please, and so I am not going to write. I have not one idea
to rattle on another."

"But how extraordinary! Do you really mean to say you have
permission to be dumb? Did her Majesty give it? I don't so much
mind about other times, but to-night of all times you cannot refuse!"

He was as eager as possible and I as decided! While they were
criticising the other poems the Empress wrote me a tiny note. I
opened it at once and found this:

"Even though a descendant of the famous Motosuke,
Why—why not join in the battle of the poems to-night?"

I was really obliged to laugh. It was so very amusing, and the
Prince called out: "But what is it? What is it?"
[I wrote:]

"If I had not the reputation of my heritage to consider,
Would I not gaily join in the battle of poems to-night?"

And I said to the Empress: "If I had not this incubus of reputation
to keep up, I would turn out thousands of poems on the spot."

MENDELE MOCHER SFORIM

MENDELE MOCHER SFORIM (Shalom Jacob Abramowitsch, Lithuanian-
Hebrew, 1836-1917). Yiddish folklorist, sometimes called the grandfather of
Yiddish literature. Earlier works, written in Hebrew, helped revive that
language as a literary medium. He then transformed Yiddish from a colloquial
tongue to an exact literary form. Introduced the novel of social criticism.
Novels: *Dos Kleine Menshele, Die Takse, Die Klyatsche.*

THE NAG

THIS is Mendele the book peddler speaking. Glory be to the Creator!
For, after His creation of all this enormous universe, He took
counsel with His host of heavenly angels and did create a universe

1109

in-little—by which you may take to mean man, who is justly called *olam katan* (a microcosm), since man, if you look at him closely, combines in himself all species of creatures and creations. You will find in him all possible wild beasts, as well as all the different breeds of cattle. You will find in him the lizard, the leech, the Spanish fly, the Prussian cockroach, and, to top it all off, a devil and a werewolf, a clown, a Jew-baiter, and many another uncanny foe of man and scourge of God. You will see, as well, among these universes-in-little all sorts of amazing sights. Here's a tomcat, for instance, playing with a baby mouse; here's a polecat making its way into a hencoop and sinking its teeth into the necks of the poor little fowl; here's a monkey mimicking and mocking everyone in sight; here's a dog standing up on its hind legs and wagging its tail for anybody who throws it a crust; here's a spider leading a fly astray, enmeshing it, strangling it, and sucking all the juices out of it; here are midges, overtaking a passer-by and humming all sorts of secrets in his ears; here are thousands of things no less amazing.

However, that's not at all what I'm leading up to.

Glory to the Holy Name (I have said), Who contemplates in silence all that is going on in this universe-in-little and still does not give it the quietus, and puts off His wrath, and tolerates transgressions, and evinces not a little mercy toward man the imperfect. In short, I was about to tell you, at this point, of a certain great favor bestowed upon me right after He had, at first, chastised me just a little.

My little nag, kind masters, is no more. My faithful horse, who passed all the days of her life in righteous toil, who served me faithfully and truly, who could have given pointers in topography to the natives of all the tiny hamlets and crossroads settlements, who was a remarkable connoisseur of little wayside inns, who had, in my company, crisscrossed almost all the pales of Israel, who was personally known to almost all of our orthodox communities— my poor nag departed this life one fine day, as a matter of fact it was on Lag Baomer, in the town of Glupsk [Foolstown]. It is painful to give the reason; poverty, however, is no disgrace; the poor little thing simply passed away from starvation. Her daily fodder consisted of chopped straw, and only on rare occasions would there fall to her lot a few dry crusts of bread that I had bought from beggars who wandered about with sacks over their shoulders. Ah, woe to the horse that falls into the hands of a peddler of Jewish books!

A wanderer, she wanders without end and in all probability labors more than her fellow creatures who draw wares more choice than ours and yet she is supposed to exist on practically nothing. A Jewish bookman lives all his life on virtually the same footing, and, one might say, he himself, with his wife and children, dies from hunger ten times a day. . . .

However, that's still not what I'm leading up to.

The Lord (I have said) sent me a visitation. I was left without a horse, had nothing with which to buy another, and yet I had to get to the fairs in time. As you can see, I was up against it.

And there I was, sitting all by myself in the House of Prayer, in low spirits, when suddenly a friend of mine walked in, headed straight for me, and asked:

"Reb Mendele, would you like to buy a nag, maybe?"

"I'd buy it with pleasure," I answered with a sigh, "but where would I get the money?"

"Bah!" said he. "That's no trouble at all. You won't have to pay a copper of spot cash. It's quite possible they'll lend you a little something besides. Never fear, they know you're an honest man."

"In that case," I said, "I am most willing to buy your nag right now, without any further beating around the bush. Well, let's go, if you please—we'll have a look at her."

"Why, there's no need of putting yourself out, actually. I have the nag right here with me. . . ."

"What do you mean, you have it here with you?" I voiced my astonishment.

"Why, right here—inside my coat," my friend smiled.

"Are you laughing at me or what?" I asked in vexation. "Look for someone else to make fun of—I don't find your little jokes at all entertaining right now."

"God forbid! I'm not joking at all," said my friend, and took from under his coat a whole stack of papers. "You see, Reb Mendele, all this belongs to a certain gentleman, a good friend of mine—you'll find his name right here on his stories. And it is one of these tales that bears the title, *The Nag*. The man who wrote it is, at present— and may this never be said of you!— he is . . . well, how am I to put it to you? He has bees in his bonnet, as the saying goes, but just the same, we who are his good friends would very much like to see his stories in print, as is fit and proper. To whom else were we to turn in this matter but to you, Reb Mendele, who enjoys such

1111

well-earned prestige in our region? We are asking you to go through these stories quite thoroughly and put them in shape. We rely upon you in this. You can go right ahead and print *The Nag*. We'll talk over the terms later, and I can assure you that you won't be out anything. If you need some money right now, why, we won't quibble over a small amount. Well, now, do you want to do it, Reb Mendele?"

"Do I? What a question, really! I want to with all my heart," I answered, and almost launched into a dance, so overjoyed was I.

I attended to my affairs and, full of zeal, tackled *The Nag*. I spared no labor and did my work properly.

And now, gentlemen, just a word or two concerning *The Nag*.

The Nag is written in a high-flown manner, after the fashion in which the ancients wrote. Each man will understand it in his own way and in keeping with his common sense. For honest folk who don't go grabbing at the stars in the sky, it will be simply a fairy tale. Those who look deeper may find in it a reflection of all of us who are sinners. Take me, now—I have seen in the nag all our little Jewish souls and have grasped the secret of why they exist in this world. I'm ready to wager that, in turning the pages of this book, many of us—each according to his nature—will exclaim vehemently: "Why, this aimed at our Nusen Reb Heikes"—"—at our Zalman Yukele Reb Moteles"—"—at Hershke Reb Abeles." Still others will declare: "He has discovered the secret of our poorbox collections, of our benevolent city fathers and all our lovely ways," and so on and on.

That's the sort of problem I posed to the Rabbinical judiciary in the town of Glupsk and to all the bigwigs in the vicinity. "As you know," I told them, "at the time I put out *The Tax*, I promised the public a sequel. It was more than a promise. It was a vow. Tell me, my dear sirs, what's the proper, lawful thing to do now? I am publishing *The Nag*. May I consider that I have fulfilled my promise concerning a sequel to *The Tax*?"

Well, they certainly pondered, and then pondered some more. They scratched and scratched behind their ears and, at last, came to a decision. "Yes, Reb Mendele," they answered, "after due deliberation, we do hereby release you from your vow. Let *The Nag* be considered the equivalent of your having kept your word, as if you had turned out the second part of *The Tax* and everything appertaining thereto. The thing isn't so bad, really, and, after all, you've appealed to almost every taste."

1112

How many thanks, then, should I render to the All Highest! Had I acquired *The Nag* just so, without any deposit toward the purchase of a horse, it would have been well. Had I acquired it with a small deposit, but it did not serve as a substitute for the second part of *The Tax*, and had the Rabbinical judiciary not absolved me of my vow without scratching behind their ears, that, too, would have been well. And even if they had scratched, but had given no reason for doing so, even then everything would have been well.

And therefore I should render thanks to the All Highest over and over again, because *The Nag* did have something of *The Tax* about it, and because the Rabbinical judiciary had released me from my vow, and because they did scratch themselves most horrendously as they gave me absolution. and because I know why they scratched themselves and understand that *The Nag* is worth scratching oneself behind the ear about . . . by way of redemption for all our transgressions.

That, gentlemen, is precisely what I wanted to say right out in my brief foreword. Whatever I have in mind is on the tip of my tongue.

Humbly,
Mendele the Book Peddler

Written the first day of the month
of Elul, in a cart laden with books,
on the road between the town of Glupsk
and Teterevka (Grouseville).

WILLIAM SHAKESPEARE

WILLIAM SHAKESPEARE (English, 1564-1616). The Bard of England, against whose works all English poetry and drama are measured. Little known of his life, except that he was an actor and playwright. His understanding of humanity unsurpassed, his dramatic and lyric poetry the finest flower of Elizabethan Age. Used every form of his time: The great tragedies: *Hamlet, Othello, Macbeth, King Lear.* Comedies: *Twelfth Night, A Midsummer Night's Dream.* Historicals: *Henry IV* and *V.* Romantic drama: *The Tempest.*

Speech by John of Gaunt from *King Richard the Second*

This royal throne of kings, this scepter'd isle,
This earth of majesty, this seat of Mars,

This other Eden, demi-paradise,
This fortress built by Nature for herself
Against infection and the hand of war,
This happy breed of men, this little world,
This precious stone set in the silver sea,
Which serves it in the office of a wall,
Or as a moat defensive to a house,
Against the envy of less happier lands,
This blessed plot, this earth, this realm, this England,
This nurse, this teeming womb of royal kings,
Fear'd by their breed and famous by their birth,
Renowned for their deeds as far from home,—
For Christian service and true chivalry,—
As is the sepulchre in stubborn Jewry
Of the world's ransom, blessed Mary's Son:
This land of such dear souls, this dear, dear land,
Dear for her reputation through the world,
Is now leas'd out,—I die pronouncing it,—
Like to a tenement, or pelting farm:
England, bound in with the triumphant sea,
Whose rocky shore beats back the envious siege
Of watery Neptune, is now bound in with shame,
With inky blots, and rotten parchment bonds:
That England, that was wont to conquer others,
Hath made a shameful conquest of itself.

Speech by Prince Henry over the body of Hotspur from
King Henry the Fourth, Part I

. . . Fare thee well, great heart!
Ill-weaved ambition, how much art thou shrunk!
When that this body did contain a spirit,
A kingdom for it was too small a bound;
But now two paces of the vilest earth
Is room enough: this earth that bears thee dead
Bears not alive so stout a gentleman.
If thou wert sensible of courtesy,
I should not make so dear a show of zeal:
But let my favours hide thy mangled face;
And, even in thy behalf, I'll thank myself
For doing these fair rites of tenderness.

Adieu, and take thy praise with thee to heaven!
Thy ignomy sleep with thee in the grave,
But not remember'd in thy epitaph!

Speech by Berowne from *Love's Labour's Lost*

Why, all delights are vain; but that most vain,
Which, with pain purchased, doth inherit pain:
As, painfully to pore upon a book
To seek the light of truth; while truth the while
Doth falsely blind the eyesight of his look:
Light, seeking light, doth light of light beguile:
So, ere you find where light in darkness lies,
Your light grows dark by losing of your eyes.
Study me how to please the eye indeed,
By fixing it upon a fairer eye;
Who dazzling so, that eye shall be his heed,
And give him light that it was blinded by.
Study is like the heaven's glorious sun,
That will not be deep-search'd with saucy looks:
Small have continual plodders ever won,
Save base authority from others' books.
These earthly godfathers of heaven's lights,
That give a name to every fixèd star,
Have no more profit of their shining nights
Than those that walk and wot not what they are.
Too much to know, is to know naught but fame;
And every godfather can give a name.

Speech by the Archbishop of Canterbury from *King Henry the Fifth*

Therefore doth heaven divide
The state of man in divers functions,
Setting endeavour in continual motion;
To which is fixèd, as an aim or butt,
Obedience: for so work the honey-bees,
Creatures that by a rule in nature teach
The act of order to a peopled kingdom.
They have a king and officers of sorts;
Where some, like magistrates, correct at home,
Others, like merchants, venture trade abroad,
Others, like soldiers, armed in their stings,

1115

Make boot upon the summer's velvet buds;
Make pillage they with merry march bring home
To the tent-royal of their emperor:
Who, busied in his majesty, surveys
The singing masons building roofs of gold,
The civil citizens kneading up the honey,
The poor mechanic porters crowding in
Their heavy burdens at his narrow gate,
The sad-ey'd justice, with his surly hum,
Delivering o'er to executors pale
The lazy yawning drone. I this infer
That many things, having all reference
To one consent, may work contrariously;
As many arrows, looséd several ways,
Fly to one mark; as many ways meet in one town;
As many fresh streams meet in one salt sea;
As many lines close in the dial's centre;
So may a thousand actions, once afoot,
End in one purpose, and be all well borne
Without defeat.

Speech by Titania from *A Midsummer Night's Dream*

These are the forgeries of jealousy:
And never, since the middle summer's spring,
Met we on hill, in dale, forest, or mead,
By pavéd fountain or by rushy brook,
Or in the beached margent of the sea,
To dance our ringlets to the whistling wind,
But with thy brawls thou hast disturb'd our sport.
Therefore the winds, piping to us in vain,
As in revenge, have suck'd up from the sea
Contagious fogs; which falling in the land,
Hath every pelting river made so proud,
That they have overborne their continents:
The ox hath therefore stretch'd his yoke in vain,
The ploughman lost his sweat; and the green corn
Hath rotted ere his youth attain'd a beard:
The fold stands empty in the drownéd field,
And crows are fatted with the murrion flock;
The nine-men's-morris is fill'd up with mud;

And the quaint mazes in the wanton green,
For lack of tread, are undistinguishable:
The human mortals want their winter here;
No night is now with hymn or carol blest:—
Therefore the moon, the governess of floods,
Pale in her anger, washes all the air,
That rheumatic diseases do abound:
And thorough this distemperature we see
The seasons alter: hoary-headed frosts
Fall in the fresh lap of the crimson rose;
And on old Hiems' thin and icy crown
An odorous chaplet of sweet summer buds
Is, as in mockery, set: the spring, the summer,
The childing autumn, angry winter, change
Their wonted liveries; and the mazèd world,
By their increase, now knows not which is which:
And this same progeny of evil comes
From our debate, from our dissension;
We are their parents and original.

Speech by Jaques from *As You Like It*

       All the world's a stage,
And all the men and women merely players;
They have their exits and their entrances;
And one man in his time plays many parts,
His acts being seven ages. At first the infant,
Mewling and puking in the nurse's arms.
And then the whining school-boy with his satchel,
And shining morning face, creeping like snail,
Unwillingly to school. And then the lover,
Sighing like furnace, with a woful ballad,
Made to his mistress' eyebrow. Then a soldier,
Full of strange oaths, and bearded like the pard,
Jealous in honour, sudden and quick in quarrel,
Seeking the bubble reputation
Even in the cannon's mouth. And then the justice,
In fair round belly with good capon lin'd,
With eyes severe, and beard of formal cut,
Full of wise saws and modern instances;

And so he plays his part. The sixth age shifts
Into the lean and slipper'd pantaloon,
With spectacles on nose and pouch on side,
His youthful hose well sav'd, a world too wide
For his shrunk shank; and his big manly voice,
Turning again toward childish treble, pipes
And whistles in his sound. Last scene of all,
That ends this strange eventful history,
Is second childishness and mere oblivion,
Sans teeth, sans eyes, sans taste, sans everything.

Clown's Songs from *Twelfth Night*

I

O mistress mine! where are you roaming?
O! stay and hear; your true love's coming,
    That can sing both high and low.
Trip no further, pretty sweeting;
Journeys end in lovers meeting,
    Every wise man's son doth know.

What is love? 'tis not hereafter;
Present mirth hath present laughter;
    What's to come is still unsure.
In delay there lies no plenty;
Then come kiss me, sweet-and-twenty,
    Youth's a stuff will not endure.

IV

Come away, come away, death,
    And in sad cypress let me be laid.
Fly away, fly away, breath;
    I am slain by a fair cruel maid.
My shroud of white, stuck all with yew,
        O! prepare it.
My part of death, no one so true
        Did share it.

Not a flower, not a flower sweet,
  On my black coffin let there be strown;
Not a friend, not a friend greet
  My poor corse, where my bones shall be thrown.
A thousand thousand sighs to save,
    Lay me, O! where
Sad true lover never find my grave,
    To weep there.

Soliloquy by Ophelia from *Hamlet*

O, what a noble mind is here o'erthrown!
The courtier's, soldier's, scholar's eye, tongue, sword;
Th' expectancy and rose of the fair state,
The glass of fashion and the mould of form,
The observ'd of all observers,—quite, quite down!
And I, of ladies most deject and wretched,
That suckt the honey of his music vows,
Now see that noble and most sovereign reason,
Like sweet bells jangled, out of tune and harsh;
That unmatcht form and feature of blown youth
Blasted with ecstasy: O, woe is me
To have seen what I have seen, see what I see!

Speech by King Lear from *King Lear*

You see me here, you gods, a poor old man,
As full of grief as age; wretched in both!
If it be you that stir these daughters' hearts
Against their father, fool me not so much
To bear it tamely; touch me with noble anger,
And let not women's weapons, water-drops,
Stain my man's cheeks! No, you unnatural hags,
I will have such revenges on you both
That all the world shall—I will do such things,—
What they are yet I know not,—but they shall be
The terrors of the earth. You think I'll weep;
No, I'll not weep:
I have full cause of weeping, but this heart
Shall break into a hundred thousand flaws
Or ere I'll weep. O fool! I shall go mad.

Speech by Coriolanus from *Coriolanus*

You common cry of curs! whose breath I hate
As reek o' the rotten fens, whose loves I prize
As the dead carcases of unburied men
That do corrupt my air, I banish you;
And here remain with your uncertainty!
Let every feeble rumour shake your hearts!
Your enemies, with nodding of their plumes,
Fan you into despair! Have the power still
To banish your defenders; till at length
Your ignorance,—which finds not, till it feels,—
Making but reservation of yourselves,—
Still your own foes,—deliver you as most
Abated captives to some nation
That won you without blows! Despising,
For you, the city, thus I turn my back:
There is a world elsewhere.

Speech by Prince Henry from *King John*

O vanity of sickness! fierce extremes
In their continuance will not feel themselves.
Death, having prey'd upon the outward parts,
Leaves them invisible; and his siege is now
Against the mind, the which he pricks and wounds
With many legions of strange fantasies,
Which, in their throng and press to that last hold,
Confound themselves. 'Tis strange that death should sing.
I am the cygnet to this pale faint swan,
Who chants a doleful hymn to his own death,
And from the organ-pipe of frailty sings
His soul and body to their lasting rest.

Speech by King Henry from *King Henry the Sixth, Part III*

This battle fares like to the morning's war,
When dying clouds contend with growing light,
What time the shepherd, blowing of his nails,

1120

Can neither call it perfect day nor night.
Now sways it this way, like a mighty sea
Forc'd by the tide to combat with the wind;
Now sways it that way, like the self-same sea
Forc'd to retire by fury of the wind:
Sometime the flood prevails, and then the wind;
Now one the better, then another best;
Both tugging to be victors, breast to breast,
Yet neither conqueror nor conqueréd:
So is the equal poise of this fell war.
Here on this molehill will I sit me down.
To whom God will, there be the victory!
For Margaret my queen, and Clifford too,
Have chid me from the battle; swearing both
They prosper best of all when I am thence.
Would I were dead! if God's good will were so;
For what is in this world but grief and woe?
O God! methinks it were a happy life,
To be no better than a homely swain;
To sit upon a hill, as I do now,
To carve out dials quaintly, point by point,
Thereby to see the minutes how they run,
How many make the hour full complete;
How many hours bring about the day;
How many days will finish up the year;
How many years a mortal man may live.
When this is known, then to divide the times:
So many hours must I tend my flock;
So many hours must I take my rest;
So many hours must I contemplate;
So many hours must I sport myself;
So many days my ewes have been with young;
So many weeks ere the poor fools will ean;
So many years ere I shall shear the fleece:
So minutes, hours, days, months, and years,
Pass'd over to the end they were created,
Would bring white hairs unto a quiet grave.
Ah! what a life were this! how sweet! how lovely!
Gives not the hawthorn bush a sweeter shade
To shepherds looking on their silly sheep,
Than doth a rich embroider'd canopy

1121

To kings, that fear their subjects' treachery?
O, yes! it doth; a thousand-fold it doth.
And to conclude, the shepherd's homely curds,
His cold thin drink out of his leather bottle,
His wonted sleep under a fresh tree's shade,
All which secure and sweetly he enjoys,
Is far beyond a prince's delicates,
His viands sparkling in a golden cup,
His body couchéd in a curious bed,
When care, mistrust, and treason wait on him.

"Blow, Winds" from *King Lear*

Blow, winds, and crack your cheeks! rage! blow!
You cataracts and hurricanoes, spout
Till you have drenched our steeples, drowned the cocks!
You sulphurous and thought-executing fires,
Vaunt-couriers to oak-cleaving thunderbolts,
Singe my white head! And thou, all-shaking thunder,
Smite flat the thick rotundity o' the world!
Crack nature's molds, all germins spill at once
That make ingrateful man! . . .
Rumble thy bellyful! Spit, fire! spout, rain!
Nor rain, wind, thunder, fire, are my daughters:
I tax not you, you elements, with unkindness;
I never gave you kingdom, called you children,
You owe me no subscription: then let fall
Your horrible pleasure; here I stand, your slave,
A poor, infirm, weak and despised old man:
But yet I call you servile ministers,
That have with two pernicious daughters joined
Your high-engendered battles 'gainst a head
So old and white as this. O! O! 'tis foul!

Portrait of Brutus from *Julius Caesar*

This was the noblest Roman of them all:
All the conspirators, save only he,
Did that they did in envy of great Cæsar;

He only, in a general honest thought
And common good to all, made one of them.
His life was gentle, and the elements
So mixed in him that Nature might stand up
And say to all the world "This was a man!"

Portrait of Caesar from *Julius Caesar*

Why, man, he doth bestride the narrow world
Like a Colossus, and we petty men
Walk under his huge legs and peep about
To find ourselves dishonorable graves.
Men at some time are masters of their fates:
The fault, dear Brutus, is not in our stars,
But in ourselves, that we are underlings.
Brutus, and Caesar: what should be in that Caesar?
Why should that name be sounded more than yours?
Write them together, yours is as fair a name;
Sound them, it doth become the mouth as well;
Weigh them, it is as heavy; conjure with 'em,
Brutus will start a spirit as soon as Caesar.
Now, in the names of all the gods at once,
Upon what meat doth this our Caesar feed,
That he is grown so great? Age, thou art shamed!
Rome, thou hast lost the breed of noble bloods!
When went there by an age, since the great flood,
But it was famed with more than with one man?
When could they say till now that talked of Rome
That her wide walls encompassed but one man?
Now is it Rome indeed, and room enough,
When there is in it but one only man.

"Fear" from *Julius Caesar*

Cowards die many times before their death;
The valiant never taste of death but once.
Of all the wonders that I yet have heard,
It seems to me most strange that men should fear;
Seeing that death, a necessary end,
Will come when it will come.

Friends, Romans, countrymen, lend me your ears;
I come to bury Cæsar, not to praise him.
The evil that men do lives after them;
The good is oft interred with their bones;
So let it be with Cæsar. The noble Brutus
Hath told you Cæsar was ambitious:
If it were so, it was a grievous fault,
And grievously hath Cæsar answered it.
Here, under leave of Brutus and the rest—
For Brutus is an honorable man;
So are they all, all honorable men—
Come I to speak in Cæsar's funeral.
He was my friend, faithful and just to me:
But Brutus says he was ambitious;
And Brutus is an honorable man.
He hath brought many captives home to Rome,
Whose ransoms did the general coffers fill:
Did this in Cæsar seem ambitious?
When that the poor have cried, Cæsar hath wept:
Ambition should be made of sterner stuff:
Yet Brutus says he was ambitious;
And Brutus is an honorable man.
You all did see that on the Lupercal
I thrice presented him a kingly crown,
Which he did thrice refuse: was this ambition?
Yet Brutus says he was ambitious;
And, sure, he is an honorable man.
I speak not to disprove what Brutus spoke,
But here I am to speak what I do know.
You all did love him once, not without cause:
What cause withholds you then to mourn for him?
O judgment! thou art fled to brutish beasts,
And men have lost their reason. Bear with me;
My heart is in the coffin there with Cæsar,
And I must pause till it come back to me.

If you have tears, prepare to shed them now.
You all do know this mantle: I remember
The first time ever Cæsar put it on;
'Twas on a summer's evening, in his tent,

That day he overcame the Nervii:
Look, in this place ran Cassius' dagger through:
See what a rent the envious Casca made:
Through this the well-beloved Brutus stabbed;
And as he plucked his cursed steel away,
Mark how the blood of Cæsar followed it,
As rushing out of doors, to be resolved
If Brutus so unkindly knocked, or no:
For Brutus, as you know, was Cæsar's angel:
Judge, O you gods, how dearly Cæsar loved him!
This was the most unkindest cut of all;
For when the noble Cæsar saw him stab,
Ingratitude, more strong than traitors' arms,
Quite vanquished him: then burst his mighty heart;
And, in his mantle muffling up his face,
Even at the base of Pompey's statue,
Which all the while ran blood, great Cæsar fell.
O, what a fall was there, my countrymen!
Then I, and you, and all of us fell down,
Whilst bloody treason flourished over us.

"I Have Lived Long Enough" from *Macbeth*

I have lived long enough: my way of life
Is fallen into the sere, the yellow leaf,
And that which should accompany old age,
As honor, love, obedience, troops of friends,
I must not look to have; but, in their stead,
Curses, not loud but deep, mouth-honor, breath,
Which the poor heart would fain deny, and dare not.

Canst thou not minister to a mind diseased,
Pluck from the memory a rooted sorrow,
Raze out the written troubles of the brain,
And with some sweet oblivious antidote
Cleanse the stuffed bosom of that perilous stuff
Which weighs upon the heart?

"Tomorrow, and Tomorrow, and Tomorrow" from *Macbeth*

Tomorrow, and tomorrow, and tomorrow,
Creeps in this petty pace from day to day,

To the last syllable of recorded time;
And all our yesterdays have lighted fools
The way to dusty death. Out, out, brief candle!
Life's but a walking shadow, a poor player
That struts and frets his hour upon the stage
And then is heard no more: it is a tale
Told by an idiot, full of sound and fury,
Signifying nothing.

"This Above All" from *Hamlet*

And these few precepts in thy memory
See thou character. Give thy thoughts no tongue,
Nor any unproportioned thought his act.
Be thou familiar, but by no means vulgar.
Those friends thou hast, and their adoption tried,
Grapple them to thy soul with hoops of steel,
But do not dull thy palm with entertainment
Of each new-hatched unfledged comrade. Beware
Of entrance to a quarrel; but being in,
Bear't, that the opposed may beware of thee.
Give every man thy ear, but few thy voice:
Take each man's censure, but reserve thy judgment.
Costly thy habit as thy purse can buy,
But not expressed in fancy; rich, not gaudy:
For the apparel oft proclaims the man;
And they in France of the best rank and station
Are most select and generous in that.
Neither a borrower nor a lender be:
For loan oft loses both itself and friend,
And borrowing dulls the edge of husbandry.
This above all: to thine own self be true,
And it must follow, as the night the day,
Thou canst not then be false to any man.

"Frailty, Thy Name Is Woman" from *Hamlet*

O, that this too too solid flesh would melt,
Thaw and resolve itself into a dew!
Or that the Everlasting had not fix'd
His canon 'gainst self-slaughter! O God! O God!

How weary, stale, flat and unprofitable
Seem to me all the uses of this world!
Fie on't! oh fie! 'tis an unweeded garden,
That grows to seed; things rank and gross in nature
Possess it merely. That it should come to this!
But two months dead! nay, not so much, not two:
So excellent a king; that was, to this,
Hyperion to a satyr: so loving to my mother,
That he might not beteem the winds of heaven
Visit her face too roughly. Heaven and earth!
Must I remember? why, she would hang on him,
As if increase of appetite had grown
By what it fed on: and yet, within a month—
Let me not think on't—Frailty, thy name is woman!—
A little month, or ere those shoes were old
With which she follow'd my poor father's body,
Like Niobe, all tears:—why she, even she—
O God! a beast that wants discourse of reason
Would have mourned longer—married with my uncle,
My father's brother, but no more like my father
Than I to Hercules: within a month;
Ere yet the salt of most unrighteous tears
Had left the flushing in her galled eyes,
She married. O, most wicked speed, to post
With such dexterity to incestuous sheets!
It is not, nor it cannot come to good:
But break, my heart, for I must hold my tongue!

"To Be, Or Not To Be" from *Hamlet*

To be, or not to be: that is the question:
Whether 'tis nobler in the mind to suffer
The slings and arrows of outrageous fortune,
Or to take arms against a sea of troubles,
And by opposing end them. To die: to sleep;
No more; and by a sleep to say we end
The heart-ache, and the thousand natural shocks
That flesh is heir to. 'Tis a consummation
Devoutly to be wish'd. To die, to sleep;
To sleep? Perchance to dream! aye, there's the rub;

For in that sleep of death what dreams may come,
When we have shuffled off this mortal coil,
Must give us pause: there's the respect
That makes calamity of so long life;
For who would bear the whips and scorns of time,
The oppressor's wrong, the proud man's contumely,
The pangs of despised love, the law's delay,
The insolence of office, and the spurns
That patient merit of the unworthy takes,
When he himself might his quietus make
With a bare bodkin? who would fardels bear,
To grunt and sweat under a weary life,
But that the dread of something after death,
The undiscovered country from whose bourn
No traveler returns, puzzles the will,
And makes us rather bear those ills we have
Than fly to others that we know not of?
Thus conscience does make cowards of us all,
And thus the native hue of resolution
Is sicklied o'er with the pale cast of thought,
And enterprises of great pitch and moment
With this regard their currents turn awry
And lose the name of action.

GEORGE BERNARD SHAW

GEORGE BERNARD SHAW (Irish, 1856-1950). Leading English dramatist, novelist and critic. Wit and reformer as well. First worked as music critic and founded Socialist Fabian Society. Propagandistic prefaces to his plays are sometimes more brilliant than the plays. Disciple of Ibsen, but created own witty drama of ideas. Most-praised works: *St. Joan, Pygmalion, Major Barbara, Candida, Caesar and Cleopatra, Man and Superman.*

THE MIRACULOUS REVENGE

I ARRIVED in Dublin on the evening of the 5th of August, and drove to the residence of my uncle, the Cardinal Archbishop. He is, like most of my family, deficient in feeling, and consequently cold to me personally. He lives in a dingy house, with a side-long view of

the portico of his cathedral from the front windows, and of a monster national school from the back. My uncle maintains no retinue. The people believe that he is waited upon by angels. When I knocked at the door, an old woman, his only servant, opened it, and informed me that her master was then officiating in the cathedral, and that he had directed her to prepare dinner for me in his absence. An unpleasant smell of salt fish made me ask her what the dinner consisted of. She assured me that she had cooked all that could be permitted in His Holiness's house on a Friday. On my asking her further why on a Friday, she replied that Friday was a fast day. I bade her tell His Holiness that I had hoped to have the pleasure of calling on him shortly, and drove to a hotel in Sackville Street, where I engaged apartments and dined.

After dinner I resumed my eternal search—I know not for what; it drives me to and fro like another Cain. I sought in the streets without success. I went to the theatre. The music was execrable, the scenery poor. I had seen the play a month before in London, with the same beautiful artist in the chief part. Two years had passed since, seeing her for the first time, I had hoped that she, perhaps, might be the long-sought mystery. It had proved otherwise. On this night I looked at her and listened to her for the sake of that bygone hope, and applauded her generously when the curtain fell. But I went out lonely still. When I had supped at a restaurant, I returned to my hotel, and tried to read. In vain. The sound of feet in the corridors as the other occupants of the hotel went to bed distracted my attention from my book. Suddenly it occurred to me that I had never quite understood my uncle's character. He, father to a great flock of poor and ignorant Irish; an austere and saintly man, to whom livers of hopeless lives daily appealed for help heavenward; who was reputed never to have sent away a troubled peasant without relieving him of his burden by sharing it; whose knees were worn less by the altar steps than by the tears and embraces of the guilty and wretched: he had refused to humour my light extravagances, or to find time to talk with me of books, flowers, and music. Had I not been mad to expect it? Now that I needed sympathy myself, I did him justice. I desired to be with a true-hearted man, and to mingle my tears with his.

I looked at my watch. It was nearly an hour past midnight. In the corridor the lights were out, except one jet at the end. I threw a cloak upon my shoulders, put on a Spanish hat, and left my apartment, listening to the echoes of my measured steps retreating

1129

through the deserted passages. A strange sight arrested me on the landing of the grand staircase. Through an open door I saw the moonlight shining through the windows of a saloon in which some entertainment had recently taken place. I looked at my watch again. It was but one o'clock; and yet the guests had departed. I entered the room, my boots ringing loudly on the waxed boards. On a chair lay a child's clock and a broken toy. The entertainment had been a children's party. I stood for a time looking at the shadow of my cloaked figure upon the floor, and at the disordered decorations, ghostly in the white light. Then I saw that there was a grand piano, still open, in the middle of the room. My fingers throbbed as I sat down before it, and expressed all that I felt in a grand hymn which seemed to thrill the cold stillness of the shadows into a deep hum of approbation, and to people the radiance of the moon with angels. Soon there was a stir without too, as if the rapture was spreading abroad. I took up the chant triumphantly with my voice, and the empty saloon resounded as though to the thunder of an orchestra.

"Hallo, sir!" "Confound you, sir—" "Do you suppose that this—" "What the deuce—?"

I turned, and silence followed. Six men, partially dressed, and with dishevelled hair, stood regarding me angrily. They all carried candles. One of them had a bootjack, which he held like a truncheon. Another, the foremost, had a pistol. The night porter was behind trembling.

"Sir," said the man with the revolver, coarsely, "may I ask whether you are mad, that you disturb people at this hour with such an unearthly noise?"

"Is it possible that you dislike it?" I replied, courteously.

"Dislike it!" said he, stamping with rage. "Why—damn everything—do you suppose we were enjoying it?"

"Take care. He's mad," whispered the man with the bootjack.

I began to laugh. Evidently they did think me mad. Unaccustomed to my habits, and ignorant of music as they probably were, the mistake, however absurd, was not unnatural. I rose. They came closer to one another; and the night porter ran away.

"Gentlemen," I said, "I am sorry for you. Had you lain still and listened, we should all have been the better and happier. But what you have done, you cannot undo. Kindly inform the night porter that I am gone to visit my uncle, the Cardinal Archbishop. Adieu!"

I strode past them, and left them whispering among themselves.

Some minutes later I knocked at the door of the Cardinal's house. Presently a window on the first floor was opened; and the moonbeams fell on a grey head, with a black cap that seemed ashy pale against the unfathomable gloom of the shadow beneath the stone sill.

"Who are you?"

"I am Zeno Legge."

"What do you want at this hour?"

The question wounded me. "My dear uncle," I exclaimed, "I know you do not intend it, but you make me feel unwelcome. Come down and let me in, I beg."

"Go to your hotel," he said sternly. "I will see you in the morning. Goodnight" He disappeared and closed the window.

I felt that if I let this rebuff pass, I should not feel kindly towards my uncle in the morning, nor, indeed, at any future time. I therefore plied the knocker with my right hand, and kept the bell ringing with my left until I heard the doorchain rattle within. The Cardinal's expression was grave nearly to moroseness as he confronted me on the threshold.

"Uncle," I cried, grasping his hand, "do not reproach me. Your door is never shut against the wretched. I am wretched. Let us sit up all night and talk"

"You may thank my position and not my charity for your admission, Zeno," he said. "For the sake of the neighbours, I had rather you played the fool in my study than upon my doorstep at this hour. Walk upstairs quietly, if you please. My housekeeper is a hard-working woman: the little sleep she allows herself must not be disturbed."

"You have a noble heart, uncle. I shall creep like a mouse."

"This is my study," he said, as we entered an ill-furnished den on the second floor. "The only refreshment I can offer you, if you desire any, is a bunch of raisins. The doctors have forbidden you to touch stimulants, I believe."

"By heaven—!" He raised his finger. "Pardon me: I was wrong to swear. But I had totally forgotten the doctors. At dinner I had a bottle of *Grave*."

"Humph! You have no business to be travelling alone. Your mother promised me that Bushy should come over here with you."

"Pshaw! Bushy is not a man of feeling. Besides, he is a coward. He refused to come with me because I purchased a revolver."

"He should have taken the revolver from you, and kept to his post."

1131

"Why will you persist in treating me like a child, uncle? I am very impressionable, I grant you; but I have gone round the world alone, and do not need to be dry-nursed through a tour in Ireland."

"What do you intend to do during your stay here?"

I had no plans; and instead of answering I shrugged my shoulders and looked around the apartment. There was a statuette of the Virgin upon my uncle's desk. I looked at its face, as he was wont to look in the midst of his labours, I saw there eternal peace. The air became luminous with an infinite network of the jewelled rings of Paradise descending in roseate clouds upon us.

"Uncle," I said, bursting into the sweetest tears I had ever shed, "my wanderings are over. I will enter the Church, if you will help me. Let us read together the third part of *Faust;* for I understand it at last."

"Hush, man," he said, half rising with an expression of alarm, "Control yourself."

"Do not let my tears mislead you. I am calm and strong. Quick, let us have Goethe:

> *Das Unbeschreibliche,*
> *Hier ist gethan;*
> *Das Ewig-Weibliche,*
> *Zieht uns hinan.*"

"Come, come. Dry your eyes and be quiet. I have no library here."

"But I have—in my portmanteau at the hotel," I said, rising. "Let me go for it, I will return in fifteen minutes."

"The devil is in you, I believe. Cannot—"

I interrupted him with a shout of laughter. "Cardinal," I said noisily, "you have become profane; and a profane priest is always the best of good fellows. Let us have some wine; and I will sing you a German beer song."

"Heaven forgive me if I do you wrong," he said; "but I believe God has laid the expiation of some sin on your unhappy head. Will you favor me with your attention for a while? I have something to say to you, and I have also to get some sleep before my hour for rising, which is half-past five."

"My usual hour for retiring—when I retire at all. But proceed. My fault is not inattention, but over-susceptibility."

"Well, then, I want you to go to Wicklow. My reasons—"

1132

"No matter what they may be," said I, rising again. "It is enough that you desire me to go. I shall start forthwith."

"Zeno! will you sit down and listen to me?"

I sank upon my chair reluctantly. "Ardor is a crime in your eyes, even when it is shown in your service," I said. "May I turn down the light?"

"Why?"

"To bring on my sombre mood, in which I am able to listen with tireless patience."

"I will turn it down myself. Will that do?"

I thanked him, and composed myself to listen in the shadow. My eyes, I felt, glittered. I was like Poe's raven.

"Now for my reasons for sending you to Wicklow. First, for your own sake. If you stay in town, or in any place where excitement can be obtained by any means, you will be in Swift's Hospital in a week. You must live in the country, under the eye of one upon whom I can depend. And you must have something to do to keep you out of mischief, and away from your music and painting and poetry, which, Sir John Richards writes to me, are dangerous for you in your present morbid state. Second, because I can entrust you with a task which, in the hands of a sensible man, might bring discredit on the Church. In short, I want you to investigate a miracle."

He looked attentively at me. I sat like a statue.

"You understand me?" he said.

"Nevermore," I replied, hoarsely. "Pardon me," I added, amused at the trick my imagination had played me, "I understand you perfectly. Proceed."

"I hope you do. Well, four miles distant from the town of Wicklow is a village called Four Mile Water. The resident priest is Father Hickey. You have heard of the miracles at Knock?"

I winked.

"I did not ask you what you think of them, but whether you have heard of them. I see you have. I need not tell you that even a miracle may do more harm than good to the Church in the country, unless it can be proved so thoroughly that her powerful and jealous enemies are silenced by the testimony of followers of their heresy. Therefore, when I saw in a Wexford newspaper last week a description of a strange manifestation of the Divine Power which was said to have taken place at Four Mile Water, I was troubled in my mind about it. So I wrote to Father Hickey, bidding him give me an

1133

account of the matter if it were true, and, if not, to denounce from the altar the author of the report, and to contradict it in the paper at once. This is his reply. He says—well, the first part is about Church matters: I need not trouble you with it. He goes on to say—"

"One moment. Is that his own handwriting? It does not look like a man's."

"He suffers from rheumatism in the fingers of his right hand, and his niece, who is an orphan, and lives with him, acts as his amanuensis. Well—"

"Stay. What is her name?"

"Her name? Kate Hickey."

"How old is she?"

"Tush, man, she is only a little girl. If she were old enough to concern you, I should not send you into her way. Have you any more questions to ask about her?"

"None. I can fancy her in a white veil at the rite of confirmation, a type of faith and innocence. Enough of her. What says the Reverend Hickey of the apparitions?"

"They are not apparitions. I will read you what he says. Ahem!

'In reply to your inquiries concerning the late miraculous event in this parish, I have to inform you that I can vouch for its truth, and that I can be confirmed not only by the inhabitants of the place, who are all Catholics, but by every person acquainted with the former situation of the graveyard referred to, including the Protestant Archdeacon of Baltinglas, who spends six weeks annually in the neighbourhood. The newspaper account is incomplete and inaccurate. The following are the facts: About four years ago, a man named Wolfe Tone Fitzgerald settled in this village as a farrier. His antecedents did not transpire, and he had no family. He lived by himself, was very careless of his person; and when in his cups, as he often was, regarded the honor neither of God nor man in his conversation. Indeed if it were not speaking ill of the dead, one might say that he was a dirty, drunken, blasphemous blackguard. Worse again, he was, I fear, an atheist, for he never attended Mass, and gave his Holiness worse language even than he gave the Queen. I should have mentioned that he was a bitter rebel, and boasted that his grandfather had been out in '98, and his father with Smith O'Brien. At last he went by the name of Brimstone Billy, and was held up in the village as the type of all wickedness.

'You are aware that our graveyard, situated on the north side of the water, is famous throughout the country as the burial place of the nuns of St. Ursula, the hermit of Four Mile Water, and many other holy people. No Protestant has ever ventured to enforce his legal right of interment there, though two have died in the parish within my own recollection. Three weeks ago, this Ftzgerald died in a fit brought on by drink, and a great hullabaloo was raised in the village when it became known that he would be buried in the graveyard. The body had to be watched to prevent its being stolen and buried at the cross-roads. My people were greatly disappointed when they were told I could do nothing to stop the burial, particularly as I of course refused to read any service on the occasion. However, I bade them not interfere; and the interment was effected on the 14th of July, late in the evening, and long after the legal hour. There was no disturbance. Next morning, the graveyard was found moved to the south side of the water, with the one newly-filled grave left behind on the north side; and thus they both remain. The departed saints would not lie with the reprobate. I can testify to it on the oath of a Christian priest; and if this will not satisfy those outside the Church, everyone, as I said before, who remembers where the graveyard was two months ago, can confirm me.

'I respectfully suggest that a thorough investigation into the truth of this miracle be proposed to a committee of Protestant gentlemen. They shall not be asked to accept a single fact on hearsay from my people. The ordnance maps show where the graveyard was; and anyone can see for himself where it is. I need not tell your Eminence what a rebuke this would be to those enemies of the holy Church that have sought to put a stain on her by discrediting the late wonderful manifestations at Knock Chapel. If they come to Four Mile Water, they need cross-examine no one. They will be asked to believe nothing but their own senses.

'Awaiting your Eminence's counsel to guide me further in the matter,

                                                    'I am, etc.'

"Well, Zeno," said my uncle, "what do you think of Father Hickey now?"

"Uncle, do not ask me. Beneath this roof I desire to believe everything. The Reverend Hickey has appealed strongly to my love

1135

of legend. Let us admire the poetry of his narrative and ignore the balance of probability between a Christian priest telling a lie on his oath and a graveyard swimming across a river in the middle of the night and forgetting to return."

"Tom Hickey is not telling a lie, sir. You may take my word for that. But he may be mistaken."

"Such a mistake amounts to insanity. It is true that I myself, awaking suddenly in the depth of night, have found myself convinced that the position of my bed had been reversed. But on opening my eyes the illusion ceased. I fear Mr. Hickey is mad. Your best course is this. Send down to Four Mile Water a perfectly sane investigator; an acute observer; one whose perceptive faculties, at once healthy and subtle, are absolutely unclouded by religious prejudice. In a word, send me. I will report to you the true state of affairs in a few days, and you can then make arrangements for transferring Hickey from the altar to the asylum."

"Yes, I had intended to send you. You are wonderfully sharp and you would make a capital detective if you could only keep your mind to one point. But your chief qualification for this business is that you are too crazy to excite the suspicions of those whom you may have to watch. For the affair may be a trick. If so, I hope and believe that Hickey has no hand in it. Still, it is my duty to take every precaution."

"Cardinal; may I ask whether traces of insanity have ever appeared in our family?"

"Except in you and in my grandmother, no. She was a Pole; and you resemble her personally. Why do you ask?"

"Because it has often occurred to me that you are, perhaps, a little cracked. Excuse my candour, but a man who has devoted his life to the pursuit of a red hat, who accuses everyone else besides himself of being mad, and who is disposed to listen seriously to a tale of a peripatetic graveyard, can hardly be quite sane. Depend upon it, uncle, you want rest and change. The blood of your Polish grandmother is in your veins."

"I hope I may not be committing a sin in sending a ribald on the Church's affairs," he replied, fervently. "However, we must use the instruments put into our hands. Is it agreed that you go?"

"Had you not delayed me with this story, which I might as well have learned on the spot, I should have been there already."

"There is no occasion for impatience, Zeno. I must first send to Hickey to find a place for you. I shall tell him that you are going

1136

to recover your health, as, in fact, you are. And, Zeno, in Heaven's name be discreet. Try to act like a man of sense. Do not dispute with Hickey on matters of religion. Since you are my nephew, you had better not disgrace me."

"I shall become an ardent Catholic, and do you infinite credit, uncle."

"I wish you would, although you would hardly be an acquisition to the Church. And now I must turn you out. It is nearly three o'clock, and I need some sleep. Do you know your way back to your hotel?"

"I need not stir. I can sleep in this chair. Go to bed, and never mind me."

"I shall not close my eyes until you are safely out of the house. Come, rouse yourself, and say goodnight."

The following is a copy of my first report to the Cardinal:

Four Mile Water, County Wicklow,
10th August

My Dear Uncle,

The miracle is genuine. I have affected perfect credulity in order to throw the Hickeys and the countryfolk off their guard with me. I have listened to their method of convincing sceptical strangers. I have examined the ordnance maps, and cross-examined the neighbouring Protestant gentle folk. I have spent a day upon the ground on each side of the water, and have visited it at midnight. I have considered the upheaval theories, subsidence theories, volcanic theories, and tidal wave theories which the provincial *savants* have suggested. They are all untenable. There is only one scoffer in the district, an Orangeman; and he admits the removal of the cemetery, but says it was dug up and transplanted in the night by a body of men under the command of Father Tom. This also is out of the question. The interment of Brimstone Billy was the first which had taken place for four years; and his is the only grave which bears a trace of recent digging. It is alone on the north bank, and the inhabitants shun it after nightfall. As each passer-by during the day throws a stone upon it, it will soon be marked by a large cairn. The graveyard, with a ruined stone chapel still standing in its midst, is on the south side. You may send down a committee to investigate the matter as soon as you please. There can be no doubt as to the miracle

1137

having actually taken place, as recorded by Hickey. As for me, I have grown so accustomed to it that if the county Wicklow were to waltz off with me to Middlesex, I should be quite impatient of any expressions of surprise from my friends in London.

Is not the above a businesslike statement? Away then, with this stale miracle. If you would see for yourself a miracle which can never pall, a vision of youth and health to be crowned with garlands for ever, come down and see Kate Hickey, whom you suppose to be a little girl. Illusion, my lord Cardinal, illusion! She is seventeen, with a bloom and a brogue that would lay your asceticism in ashes at a flash. To her I am an object of wonder, a strange man bred in wicked cities. She is courted by six feet of farming material, chopped off a spare length of coarse humanity by the Almighty, and flung into Wicklow to plough the fields. His name is Phil Langan; and he hates me. I have to consort with him for the sake of Father Tom, whom I entertain vastly by stories of your wild oats at Salamanca. I exhausted all my authentic anecdotes the first day; and now I invent gallant escapades with Spanish donnas, in which you figure as a youth of unstable morals. This delights Father Tom infinitely. I feel that I have done you a service by thus casting on the cold sacerdotal abstraction which formerly represented you in Kate's imagination a ray of vivifying passion.

What a country this is! A Hesperidean garden: such skies! Adieu, uncle.

Zeno Legge.

Behold me, then, at Four Mile Water, in love. I had been in love frequently; but not oftener than once a year had I encountered a woman who affected me as seriously as Kate Hickey. She was so shrewd, and yet so flippant! When I spoke of art she yawned. When I deplored the sordidness of the world she laughed, and called me "poor fellow!" When I told her what a treasure of beauty and freshness she had she ridiculed me. When I reproached her with brutality she became angry, and sneered at me for being what she called a fine gentleman. One sunny afternoon we were standing at the gate of her uncle's house, she looking down the dusty road for the detestable Langan, I watching the spotless azure sky, when she said:

"How soon are you going back to London?"

"I am not going back to London, Miss Hickey. I am not yet tired of Four Mile Water."

"I'm sure Four Mile Water ought to be proud of your approbation."

"You disapprove of my liking it, then? Or is it that you grudge me the happiness I have found here? I think Irish ladies grudge a man a moment's peace."

"I wonder you have ever prevailed on yourself to associate with Irish ladies, since they are so far beneath you."

"Did I say they were beneath me, Miss Hickey? I feel that I have made a deep impression on you."

"Indeed! Yes, you're quite right. I assure you I can't sleep at night for thinking of you, Mr. Legge. It's the best a Christian can do, seeing you think so mighty little of yourself."

"You are triply wrong, Miss Hickey: wrong to be sarcastic with me, wrong to pretend that there is anything unreasonable in my belief that you think of me sometimes, and wrong to discourage the candour with which I always avow that I think constantly of myself."

"Then you had better not speak to me, since I have no manners."

"Again! Did I say you had no manners? The warmest expressions of regard from my mouth seem to reach your ears transformed into insults. Were I to repeat the Litany of the Blessed Virgin, you would retort as though I had been reproaching you. This is because you hate me. You never misunderstand Langan, whom you love."

"I don't know what London manners are, Mr. Legge; but in Ireland gentlemen are expected to mind their own business. How dare you say I love Mr. Langan?"

"Then you do not love him?"

"It is nothing to you whether I love him or not."

"Nothing to me that you hate me and love another?"

"I did not say that I hated you. You are not so very clever yourself at understanding what people say, though you make such fuss because they don't understand you." Here, as she glanced down the road again, she suddenly looked glad.

"Aha!" I said.

"What do you mean by 'Aha!'?"

"No matter. I will now show you what a man's sympathy is. As yon perceived just then, Langan—who is too tall for his age, by-the-bye—is coming to pay you a visit. Well, instead of staying with you, as a jealous woman would, I will withdraw."

"I don't care whether you go or stay, I'm sure. I wonder what you would give to be as fine a man as Mr. Langan."

"All I possess: I swear it! But solely because you admire tall men more than broad views. Mr. Langan may be defined geometrically as length without breadth; altitude without position; a line on the landscape, not a point in it."

"How very clever you are!"

"You do not understand me, I see. Here comes your lover, stepping over the wall like a camel. And here go I, out through the gate like a Christian. Good afternoon, Mr. Langan. I am going because Miss Hickey has something to say to you about me which she would rather not say in my presence. You will excuse me?"

"Oh, I'll excuse you," said he boorishly. I smiled, and went out. Before I was quite out of hearing, Kate whispered vehemently to him, "I *hate* that fellow."

I smiled again; but I had scarcely done so when my spirits fell. I walked hastily away with a coarse threatening sound in my ears like that of the clarionets whose sustained low notes darken the woodland in "Der Freischütz." I found myself presently at the graveyard. It was a barren place, enclosed by a mud wall with a gate to admit funerals, and numerous gaps to admit the peasantry, who made short cuts across it as they went to and fro between Four Mile Water and the market town The graves were mounds overgrown with grass; there was no keeper; nor were there flowers, railings or any of the conventionalities that make an English graveyard repulsive. A great thornbush, near what was called the grave of the holy sisters, was covered with scraps of cloth and flannel, attached by peasant women who had prayed before it. There were three kneeling there as I entered, for the reputation of the place had been revived of late by the miracle, and a ferry had been established close by, to conduct visitors over the route taken by the graveyard. From where I stood I could see on the opposite bank the heap of stones, perceptibly increased since my last visit, marking the deserted grave of Brimstone Billy. I strained my eyes broodingly at it for some minutes, and then descended the river bank and entered the boat.

"Good evenin' t'your honour," said the ferryman, and set to work to draw the boat hand-over-hand by a rope stretched across the water.

"Good evening. Is your business beginning to fall off yet?"

"Faith, it never was as good as it might ha' been. The people that comes from the south side can see Billy's grave—Lord have mercy on him—across the wather; and they think bad of payin' a

penny to put a stone over him. It's them that lives tow'rst Dublin that makes the journey. Your honour is the third I've brought from south to north this blessed day."

"When do most people come? In the afternoon, I suppose?"

"All hours, sur, except afther dusk. There isn't a sowl in the counthry ud come within sight of that grave wanst the sun goes down."

"And you! Do you stay here all night by yourself?"

"The holy heavens forbid! Is it me stay here all night? No, your honour; I tether the boat at siven o'hlyock, and lave Brimstone Billy—God forgimme!—to take care of it t'll mornin."

"It will be stolen some night, I'm afraid."

"Arra, who'd dar come next or near it, let alone stale it? Faith, I'd think twice before lookin at it meself in the dark. God bless your honour, and gran'che long life."

I had given him sixpence. I went to the reprobate's grave and stood at the foot of it, looking at the sky, gorgeous with the descent of the sun.To my English eyes, accustomed to giant trees, broad lawns, and stately mansions, the landscape was wild and inhospitable. The ferryman was already tugging at the rope on his way back (I had told him I did not intend to return that way), and presently I saw him make the painter fast o the south bank; put on his coat; and trudge homeward. I turned towards the grave at my feet. Those who had interred Brimstone Billy, working hastily at an unlawful hour, and in fear of molestation by the people, had hardly dug a grave. They had scooped out earth enough to hide their burden, and no more. A stray goat had kicked away a corner of the mound and exposed the coffin. It occurred to me, as I took some of the stones from the cairn, and heaped them so as to repair the breach, that had the miracle been the work of a body of men, they would have moved the one grave instead of the many. Even from a supernatural point of view, it seemed strange that the sinner should have banished the elect, when, by their superior numbers, they might so much more easily have banished him.

It was almost dark when I left the spot, After a walk of half a mile, I recrossed the water by a bridge, and returned to the farmhouse in which I lodged. Here, finding that I had had enough of solitude, I only stayed to take a cup of tea. Then I went to Father Hickey's cottage.

Kate was alone when I entered. She looked up quickly as I

1141

opened the door, and turned away disappointed when she recognized me.

"Be generous for once," I said. "I have walked about aimlessly for hours in order to avoid spoiling the beautiful afternoon for you by my presence. When the sun was up I withdrew my shadow from your path. Now that darkness has fallen, shed some light on mine. May I stay half an hour?"

"You may stay as long as you like, of course. My uncle will soon be home. He is clever enough to talk to you."

"What! More sarcasms! Come, Miss Hickey, help me to spend a pleasant evening. It will only cost you a smile. I am somewhat cast down. Four Mile Water is a paradise; but without you, it would be a little lonely."

"It must be very lonely for you. I wonder why you came here."

"Because I heard that the women here were all Zerlinas like you, and the men Masettos, like Mr. Phil—where are you going to?"

"Let me pass, Mr. Legge. I had intended never speaking to you again after the way you went on about Mr. Langan today; and I wouldn't either, only my uncle made me promise not to take any notice of you, because you were—no matter; but I won't listen to you any more on the subject."

"Do not go. I swear never to mention his name again. I beg your pardon for what I said: you shall have no further cause for complaint. Will you forgive me?"

She sat down, evidently disappointed by my submission. I took a chair, and placed myself near her. She tapped the floor impatiently with her foot. I saw that there was not a movement I could make, not a look, not a tone of my voice, which did not irritate her.

"You were remarking," I said, "that your uncle desired you to take no notice of me because—"

She closed her lips, and did not answer.

"I fear I have offended you again by my curiosity. But indeed, I had no idea that he had forbidden you to tell me the reason."

"He did not forbid me. Since you are so determined to find out—"

"No, excuse me. I do not wish to know, I am sorry I asked."

"Indeed! Perhaps you would be sorrier still to be told. I only made a secret of it out of consideration for you."

"Then your uncle has spoken ill of me behind my back. If that be so, there is no such thing as a true man in Ireland. I would not have believed it on the word of any woman alive save yourself."

1142

"I never said my uncle was a backbiter. Just to show you what he thinks of you, I will tell you whether you want to know it or not, that he bid me not mind you because you were only a poor mad creature, sent down here by your family to be out of harm's way."

"Oh, Miss Hickey!"

"There now! You have got it out of me; and I wish I had bit my tongue out first. I sometimes think—that I mayn't sin!—that you have a bad angel in you."

"I am glad you told me this," I said gently. "Do not reproach yourself for having done so, I beg. Your uncle has been misled by what he has heard of my family, who are all more or less insane. Far from being mad, I am actually the only rational man named Legge in the three kingdoms. I will prove this to you, and at the the same time keep your indiscretion in countenance, by telling you something I ought not to tell you. It is this. I am not here as an invalid or a chance tourist. I am here to investigate the miracle. The Cardinal, a shrewd if somewhat erratic man, selected mine from all the long heads at his disposal to come down here, and find out the truth of Father Hickey's story. Would he have entrusted such a task to a madman, think you?"

"The truth of—who dared to doubt my uncle's word? And so you are a spy, a dirty informer."

I started. The adjective she had used, though probably the commonest expression of contempt in Ireland, is revolting to an Englishman.

"Miss Hickey," I said, "there is in me, as you have said, a bad angel. Do not shock my good angel—who is a person of taste—quite away from my heart, lest the other be left undisputed monarch of it. Hark! The chapel bell is ringing the angelus. Can you, with that sound softening the darkness of the village night, cherish a feeling of spite against one who admires you?"

"You come between me and my prayers," she said hysterically, and began to sob. She had scarcely done so, when I heard voices without. Then Langan and the priest entered.

"Oh Phil," she cried, running to him, "take me away from him: I can't bear—" I turned towards him, and showed him my dog-tooth in a false smile. He felled me at one stroke, as he might have felled a poplar tree.

"Murdher!" exclaimed the priest. "What are you doin, Phil?"

"He is an informer," sobbed Kate. "He came down here to spy

1143

on you, uncle, and to try and show that the blessed miracle was a make-up. I knew it long before he told me, by his insulting ways. He wanted to make love to me."

I rose with difficulty from beneath the table, where I had lain motionless for a moment.

"Sir," I said, "I am somewhat dazed by the recent action of Mr. Langan, whom I beg, the next time he converts himself into a fulling-mill, to do so at the expense of a man more nearly his equal in strength than I. What your niece has told you is partly true. I am indeed the Cardinal's spy; and I have already reported to him that the miracle is a genuine one. A committee of gentlemen will wait on you tomorrow to verify it, at my suggestion. I have thought that the proof might be regarded by them as more complete if you were taken by surprise. Miss Hickey, that I admire all that is admirable in you is but to say that I have a sense of the beautiful. To say that I love you would be mere profanity. Mr. Langan, I have in my pocket a loaded pistol, which I carry from a silly English prejudice against you countrymen. Had I been the Hercules of the ploughtail, and you in my place, I should have been a dead man now. Do not redden; you are safe as far as I am concerned."

"Let me tell you before you leave my house for good," said Father Hickey, who seemed to have become unreasonably angry, "that you should never have crossed my threshold if I had known you were a spy; no, not if your uncle were his Holiness the Pope himself."

Here a frightful thing happened to me. I felt giddy, and put my hand to my head. Three warm drops trickled over it. Instantly I became murderous. My mouth filled with blood, my eyes were blinded with it; I seemed to drown in it. My hand went involuntarily to the pistol. It is my habit to obey my impulses instantaneously. Fortunately the impulse to kill vanished before a sudden perception of how I might miraculously humble the mad vanity in which these foolish people had turned upon me. The blood receded from my ears; and I again heard and saw distinctly.

"And let *me* tell you," Langan was saying, "that if you think yourself handier with cold lead than you are with your fists, I'll exchange shots with you, and welcome, whenever you please. Father Tom's credit is the same to me as my own, and if you say a word against it, you lie."

"His credit is in my hands," I said. "I am the Cardinal's witness. Do you defy me?"

"There is the door," said the priest, holding it open before me.

1144

"Until you can undo the visible work of God's hand your testimony can do no harm to me."

"Father Hickey," I replied, "before the sun rises again upon Four Mile Water, I will undo the visible work of God's hand, and bring the pointing finger of the scoffer upon your altar."

I bowed to Kate, and walked out. It was so dark that I could not at first see the garden-gate. Before I found it, I heard through the window Father Hickey's voice, saying. "I wouldn't for ten pound that this had happened, Phil. He's as mad as a March hare. The Cardinal told me so."

I returned to my lodging, and took a cold bath to cleanse the blood from my neck and shoulder. The effect of the blow I had received was so severe, that even after the bath and a light meal I felt giddy and languid. There was an alarum-clock on the mantelpiece. I wound it; set the alarum for half-past twelve; muffled it so that it should not disturb the people in the adjoining room; and went to bed, where I slept soundly for an hour and a quarter. Then the alarum woke me, and I sprang up before I was thoroughly awake. Had I hesitated, the desire to relapse into perfect sleep would have overpowered me. Although the muscles of my neck were painfully stiff, and my hands unsteady from my nervous disturbance, produced by the interruption of my first slumber, I dressed myself resolutely, and, after taking a draught of cold water, stole out of the house. It was exceedingly dark and I had some difficulty in finding the cow-house, whence I borrowed a spade, and a truck with wheels, ordinarily used for moving sacks of potatoes. These I carried in my hands until I was beyond earshot of the house, when I put the spade on the truck, and wheeled it along the road to the cemetery. When I approached the water, knowing that no one would dare to come thereabout at such an hour, I made greater haste, no longer concerning myself about the rattling of the wheels. Looking across to the opposite bank, I could see a phosphorescent glow, marking the lonely grave of Brimstone Billy. This helped me to find the ferry station, where, after wandering a little and stumbling often, I found the boat, and embarked with my implements. Guided by the rope, I crossed the water without difficulty; landed; made fast the boat; dragged the truck up the bank; and sat down to rest on the cairn of the grave. For nearly a quarter of an hour I sat watching the patches of jack-o'-lantern fire, and collecting my strength for the work before me. Then the distant bell of the chapel clock tolled one. I rose, took the spade, and in about ten minutes uncovered the coffin, which

1145

smelt horribly. Keeping to windward of it, and using the spade as a lever, I contrived with great labor to place it on the truck. I wheeled it without accident to the landing-place, where, by placing the shafts of the truck upon the stern of the boat and lifting the foot by main strength, I succeeded in embarking my load after twenty minutes' toil, during which I got covered with clay and perspiration, and several times all but upset the boat. At the southern bank I had less difficulty in getting truck and coffin ashore, and dragging them up to the graveyard.

It was now past two o'clock, and the dawn had begun, so that I had no further trouble from want of light. I wheeled the coffin to a patch of loamy soil which I had noticed in the afternoon near the grave of the holy sisters. I had warmed to my work; my neck no longer pained me; and I began to dig vigorously, soon making a shallow trench, deep enough to hide the coffin with the addition of a mound. The chill pearl-coloured morning had by this time quite dissipated the darkness. I could see, and was myself visible, for miles around. This alarmed me, and made me impatient to finish my task. Nevertheless, I was forced to rest for a moment before placing the coffin in the trench. I wiped my brow and wrists, and again looked about me. The tomb of the holy women, a massive slab supported by four stone spheres, was grey and wet with dew. Near it was the thornbush covered with rags, the newest of which were growing gaudy in the radiance which was stretching up from the coast on the east. It was time to finish my work. I seized the truck; laid it alongside the grave; and gradually prized the coffin off with the spade until it rolled over into the trench with a hollow sound like a drunken remonstrance from the sleeper within. I shovelled the earth round and over it, working as fast as possible. In less than a quarter of an hour it was buried. Ten minutes more sufficed to make the mound symmetrical, and to clear the traces of my work from the adjacent sward. Then I flung down the spade; threw up my arms; and vented a sigh of relief and triumph. But I recoiled as I saw that I was standing on a barren common, covered with furze. No product of man's handiwork was near me except my truck and spade and the grave of Brimstone Billy, now as lonely as before. I turned towards the water. On the opposite bank was the cemetery, with the tomb of the holy women, the thornbush with its rags stirring in the morning breeze, and the broken mud wall. The ruined chapel was there too, not a stone shaken from its crumbling walls,

not a sign to show that it and its precinct were less rooted in their place than the eternal hills around.

I looked down at the grave with a pang of compassion for the unfortunate Wolfe Tone Fitzgerald, with whom the blessed would not rest. I was even astonished, though I had worked expressly to this end. But the birds were astir, and the cocks crowing. My landlord was an early riser. I put the spade on the truck again, and hastened back to the farm, where I replaced them in the cow-house. Then I stole into the house, and took a clean pair of boots, an overcoat, and a silk hat. These, with a change of linen, were sufficient to make my appearance respectable. I went out again, bathed in the Four Mile Water, took a last look at the cemetery, and walked to Wicklow, whence I travelled by the first train to Dublin.

Some months later, at Cairo, I received a packet of Irish newspapers and a leading article, cut from the *Times*, on the subject of the miracle. Father Hickey had suffered the meed of his inhospitable conduct. The committee, arriving at Four Mile Water the day after I left, had found the graveyard exactly where it had formerly stood. Father Hickey, taken by surprise, had attempted to defend himself by a confused statement, which led the committee to declare finally that the miracle was a gross imposture. The *Times*, commenting on this after adducing a number of examples of priestly craft, remarked, "We are glad to learn that the Rev. Mr. Hickey has been permanently relieved of his duties as the parish priest of Four Mile Water by his ecclesiastical superior. It is less gratifying to have to record that it has been found possible to obtain two hundred signatures to a memorial embodying the absurd defense offered to the committee, and expressing unabated confidence in the integrity of Mr. Hickey."

PERCY BYSSHE SHELLEY

PERCY BYSSHE SHELLY (English, 1792-1822). One of major Romantic poets. Lived and wrote in the light of Greek classicism. Expelled from Oxford for pamphlet on atheism. Eloped with Mary Wollstonecraft (author of *Frankenstein*). Drowned in Italy. Many of his long works are didactic and philosophical. Better-loved are such shorter lyrics as "Adonais," "Ode to the West Wind," "To Night," etc.

LOVE

When the lamp is shattered,
   The light in the dust lies dead—
When the cloud is scattered,
   The rainbow's glory is shed.
When the lute is broken,
   Sweet tones are remembered not;
When the lips have spoken,
   Loved accents are soon forgot.

As music and splendour
   Survive not the lamp and the lute,
The heart's echoes render
   No song when the spirit is mute—
No song but sad dirges,
   Like the wind through a ruined cell,
Or the mournful surges
   That ring the dead seaman's knell.

When hearts have once mingled,
   Love first leaves the well-built nest;
The weak one is singled
   To endure what it once possest.
O Love! who bewailest
   The frailty of all things here,
Why choose you the frailest
   For your cradle, your home, and your bier?

Its passions will rock thee
   As the storms rock the ravens on high;
Bright reason will mock thee
   Like the sun from a wintry sky.

From thy nest every rafter
   Will rot, and thine eagle home
Leave thee naked to laughter,
   When leaves fall and cold winds come.

INVOCATION

Rarely, rarely, comest thou,
   Spirit of Delight!
Wherefore hast thou left me now
   Many a day and night?
Many a weary night and day
'Tis since thou art fled away.

How shall ever one like me
   Win thee back again?
With the joyous and the free
   Thou wilt scoff at pain.
Spirit false! thou hast forgot
All but those who need thee not.

As a lizard with the shade
   Of a trembling leaf,
Thou with sorrow art dismay'd;
   Even the sighs of grief
Reproach thee, that thou art not near,
And reproach thou wilt not hear.

Let me set my mournful ditty
   To a merry measure;
Thou wilt never come for pity,
   Thou wilt come for pleasure;
Pity then will cut away
Those cruel wings, and thou wilt stay.

I love all that thou lovest,
   Spirit of Delight!
The fresh Earth in new leaves drest
   And the starry night;
Autumn evening, and the morn
When the golden mists are born.

I love snow and all the forms
　　Of the radiant frost;
I love waves, and winds, and storms,
　　Everything almost
Which is Nature's, and may be
Untainted by man's misery.

I love tranquil solitude,
　　And such society
As is quiet, wise, and good;
　　Between thee and me
What diff'rence? but thou dost possess
The things I seek, not love them less.
I love Love—though he has wings,
　　And like light can flee,
But above all other things,
　　Spirit, I love thee—
Thou art love and life! O come!
Make once more my heart thy home!

DEJECTION

The sun is warm, the sky is clear,
　　The waves are dancing fast and bright,
Blue isles and snowy mountains wear
　　The purple noon's transparent might:
　　The breath of the moist earth is light
Around its unexpanded buds;
　　Like many a voice of one delight—
The winds, the birds, the ocean-floods—
The City's voice itself is soft like Solitude's.

I see the Deep's untrampled floor
　　With green and purple seaweeds strown;
I see the waves upon the shore,
　　Like light dissolved in star-showers, thrown:
　　I sit upon the sands alone;
The lightning of the noontide ocean
　　Is flashing round me, and a tone
Arises from its measured motion—
How sweet! did any heart now share in my emotion.

1150

Alas! I have nor hope nor health,
 Nor peace within nor calm around,
Nor that content, surpassing wealth,
 The sage in meditation found,
 And walked with inward glory crowned—
Nor fame, nor power, nor love, nor leisure;
 Others I see whom these surround—
Smiling they live, and call life pleasure;
To me that cup has been dealt in another measure.

Yet now despair itself is mild
 Even as the winds and waters are;
I could lie down like a tired child,
 And weep away the life of care
 Which I have borne, and yet must bear,
Till death like sleep might steal on me,
 And I might feel in the warm air
My cheek grow cold, and hear the sea
Breathe o'er my dying brain its last monotony.

ODE TO THE WEST WIND

O wild West Wind, thou breath of Autumn's being,
Thou, from whose unseen presence the leaves dead
Are driven, like ghosts from an enchanter fleeing,
Yellow, and black, and pale, and hectic red,
Pestilence-stricken multitudes: O thou
Who chariotest to their dark wintry bed
The wingéd seeds, where they lie cold and low,
Each like a corpse within its grave, until
Thine azure sister of the Spring shall blow
Her clarion o'er the dreaming earth, and fill
(Driving sweet buds like flocks to feed in air)
With living hues and odours plain and hill:
Wild Spirit, which art moving everywhere;
Destroyer and Preserver; hear, oh, hear!

Thou on whose stream, mid the steep sky's commotion,
Loose clouds like earth's decaying leaves are shed,
Shook from the tangled boughs of Heaven and Ocean,
Angels of rain and lightning: there are spread

On the blue surface of thine airy surge,
Like the bright hair uplifted from the head
Of some fierce Maenad, even from the dim verge
Of the horizon to the zenith's height,
The locks of the approaching storm. Thou dirge
Of the dying year, to which this closing night
Will be the dome of a vast sepulchre,
Vaulted with all thy congregated might
Of vapours, from whose solid atmosphere
Black rain, and fire, and hail, will burst: oh, hear!

Thou who didst waken from his summer dreams
The blue Mediterranean, where he lay,
Lull'd by the coil of his crystalline streams,
Beside a pumice isle in Baiae's bay,
And saw in sleep old palaces and towers
Quivering within the wave's intenser day,
All overgrown with azure moss and flowers
So sweet, the sense faints picturing them! Thou
For whose path the Atlantic's level powers
Cleave themselves into chasms, while far below
The sea-blooms and the oozy woods which wear
The sapless foliage of the ocean, know
Thy voice, and suddenly grow grey with fear,
And tremble and despoil themselves: oh, hear!

If I were a dead leaf thou mightest bear;
If I were a swift cloud to fly with thee;
A wave to pant beneath thy power, and share
The impulse of thy strength, only less free
Than thou, O uncontrollable! If even
I were as in my boyhood, and could be
The comrade of thy wanderings over Heaven,
As then, when to outstrip thy skyey speed
Scarce seemed a vision, I would ne'er have striven
As thus with thee in prayer in my sore need.
Oh, lift me as a wave, a leaf, a cloud!
I fall upon the thorns of life! I bleed!
A heavy weight of hours has chained and bowed
One too like thee: tameless, and swift, and proud.

Make me thy lyre, even as the forest is:
What if my leaves are falling like its own!
The tumult of thy mighty harmonies
Will take from both a deep, autumnal tone,
Sweet though in sadness. Be thou, Spirit fierce,
My spirit! Be thou me, impetuous one!
Drive my dead thoughts over the universe
Like withered leaves to quicken a new birth!
And, by the incantation of this verse,
Scatter, as from an unextinguished hearth
Ashes and sparks, my words among mankind!
Be through my lips to unawakened earth
The trumpet of a prophecy! O Wind,
If Winter comes, can Spring be far behind?

TO NIGHT

Swiftly walk o'er the western wave,
    Spirit of Night!
Out of the misty eastern cave,
Where, all the long and lone daylight,
Thou wovest dreams of joy and fear,
Which make thee terrible and dear—
    Swift be thy flight!

Wrap thy form in a mantle gray,
    Star-inwrought!
Blind with thine hair the eyes of day;
Kiss her until she be wearied out,
Then wander o'er city, and sea, and land,
Touching all with thine opiate wand—
    Come, long-sought!

When I arose and saw the dawn,
    I sighed for thee;
When light rode high, and the dew was gone,
And noon lay heavy on flower and tree,
And the weary day turned to his rest,
Lingering like an unloved guest,
    I sighed for thee.

Thy brother Death came, and cried,
  Wouldst thou me?
Thy sweet child Sleep, the filmy-eyed,
Murmured like a noontide bee,
Shall I nestle near thy side?
Wouldst thou me?—And I replied,
  No, not thee!

Death will come when thou art dead,
  Soon, too soon—
Sleep will come when thou art fled;
Of neither would I ask the boon
I ask of thee, beloved Night—
Swift be thine approaching flight,
  Come soon, soon!

SHEN TS'UNG-WEN

SHÉN TS'UNG-WÉN (Chinese, 1902-   ). Prolific Chinese novelist and
critic. Had military rather than conventional academic background. Edited
Ta-kung pao literary supplement. Author of some 60 novels, volumes of stories
and other works.

UNDER COVER OF DARKNESS

THE bamboo raft, nimbly manned by the two men, glided quietly
downstream. The raftsmen had passed unseen through the river
patrols, and were now only two miles from their destination, but
suddenly the raft ran aground on a wild bank overgrown with rushes
and reeds, and while the raft remained still and unmoving, they
heard the murmuring of the water and the rustling of the wind
through the reeds.

Lu-Yi, an officer of the signal corps of the guerrilla troops, began
to blame the younger man, hoarsely. "What's the matter?" he asked.
"Are you possessed by devils? You think it's funny, don't you?
But if we are stranded here, they will soon find us out, and we shall
be shot to pieces by their guns."

The boy who had been crouching on the raft stood up slowly,
but still he made no sound. There was a faint shimmering light on

the dark surface of the river, and in the water there lay the reflection of two men standing on a raft, a reflection which was upside-down. Silently the boy walked to the other end of the raft.

"Well, we have run aground. I guess we have caught in something!" It was the voice of a very young boy.

He went up to the older man, and still leaning against the oar which he held in one hand, he took over the bamboo pole and tried to push it hither and thither in the marshy water. They were at a bend in the river where the water was shallow, but from the murmur of the water it was clear that the river ran swift round the bend; and there was no reason why the rafts should remain still, unless something had caught hold of the bamboo raft from underneath.

Their spirits were tried. Lu-Yi began to grumble again, impatiently. "There's two miles to go," he said. "It's a desperately dangerous area. There might be enemy patrols at any moment. . . ."

The boy seemed to have no feeling for fear or sorrow. He silently listened to the older man, and then untied the automatic pistol and bullet-case from his belt, rolled up his trousers, and gently slid into the water. He found a foothold and stooped down to push the raft with both hands. They heard the long, low squeak of the bamboos, but the raft did not move, and seemed, indeed, to be constrained by unseen hands.

Lu-Yi was still impatient. "Be careful," he murmured. "I know you are strong, but be careful. Better take off your clothes and feel with your hands underneath the bamboos. There seem to be devils and ghosts there. . . ."

"Yes," the boy answered, with a little giggle. "Devils and ghosts. But let me try. . . ."

He began to move slowly in the water, stretching his hands under the bamboos. Touching the ropes and knots which joined the raft together, he stooped down, his arms and shoulders buried under the cold water, and his chin kissing the rippling surface of the river. Meanwhile his feet sank in mud to the knees, and it took an effort to pull them up again. He was still feeling among the knots and ropes when he felt something hard and round striking against his fingers. He realized then that it was a millstone entangled among ropes and clothes. He reached out his hands and felt the coldwetness of a human body. "A body!" he shouted out in mingled alarm and delight, for now at last he knew what was obstructing the raft. "A body!" he exclaimed. "It's the funniest thing. . . ."

"Well, what is it?"

He did not answer. He ran his fingers over the body and touched the hair, the face, and then the arms. It was bound to the millstone with heavy ropes, which had somewhat curled round the bamboos.

"Even with a millstone round its neck, this body prevents us from moving," the boy laughed silently.

"Then take it away," the other commanded, and he was more impatient than ever when he heard the crowing of the first cocks in the distance. "The body of a good-for-nothing," he added contemptuously. "No good when he was alive, and no good when he was dead," he murmured softly.

The boy was still wading round the raft, trying to disentangle the rope. Lu-Yi drew his knife from his belt and tapped it against the side of the raft. "Boy, come here," he said. "Take the knife and cut the rope in two. If the devil doesn't loosen his hold, cut his hand off. Hurry up! We're in terrible danger, and we have to get to the army."

The boy amused by the expression "loosen his hold," wondered at his companion's impatience.

There was a muffled noise of a knife stirring up the water, and the raft began to turn a little. A little while later he went to the stern of the raft and put his shoulder against it. He began to push hard, but he only succeeded in lifting the raft a little above the level of the water. The raft kept turning, but did not move forward. It was difficult to manage the knife under water, and perhaps in the end they would have to take the raft to pieces and then join the bamboos up again. But there was no time. Besides, less than a mile downstream, they knew there was a pontoon bridge held by the enemy. Lu-Yi could no longer restrain his impatience. He began to curse the boy for his lightheartedness and slowness, and promised to write a report on his negligence, inefficiency, and lack of responsibility. The boy remained calm, unmoved.

"Well, then, we had better walk instead of wasting our time on the river," he said, in a perfectly matter-of-fact voice. "Otherwise we won't get there before dawn."

"There are traps laid for us all over the hills and valley," the other answered. "The devils are ready with their ropes and millstones there. If we walk those two miles, it's likely we'll have millstones round our necks before dawn."

"Fears can't stop us," the boy replied. "There's no other way."

At last the older man was convinced. They carried the two bullet-

1156

cases and the rest of their equipment on to the embankment, groping and stumbling in the dark. Then they sat among the tall reeds and whispered about the routes they would take. They had no idea of the ponds and marshes and streams which lay in their way, and the villages and guard stations through which they would have to pass. In the black sky not a single star lay visible. Each one had brought a shirt torch, but in the enveloping darkness they seemed to see eyes glaring at them, and they knew that the slightest light shown by them would call for a bullet from the enemy. And if the enemy knew that they were passing along the river, the lives of all those who followed them on the bamboo rafts would be endangered.

After a while they decided not to take the road over the hills, but to follow the path which lay along the edge of the river. The flood water had receded during the past few days, and now the path was dry. Besides, there was always the chance that they would come across a sampan or canoe left somewhere along the bank.

The small path wound through bushy reeds. The earth was muddy and slippery underfoot, and there was a strange smell, a smell which grew inexplicably stronger as they went forward.

"Mind your steps! There's probably another body somewhere around. Don't fall over it."

"I forgot to feel the pockets of the fellow under the raft. Probably he was one of our comrades."

"Who else could it be?"

"Now I remember. The message of number seventy-four was stitched into the back of his trousers, the message of thirteen was hidden in a cigarette, and. . . ."

"Rubbish! Don't talk. We are still under close watch. Look out, because we don't want to have two more corpses in the place."

Lu-Yi was embarrassed by the strange smell, and thought the corpse could hardly be more than five yeards away from them. He held his torch in his hand, and made as though he was going to flick on the light. but the boy prevented him. They pricked up their ears and listened intently. They heard the approaching splash of rhythmic oars. They were about five feet away from the river, but thick bushes of reeds screened them from sight. They were both aware of the critical situation they were in, for it was evident that the approaching boat was patrolling the river to prevent the guerrillas from using it as a means of communication. If the patrol boat had reached the bend in the river and discovered the raft and their footprints, they would be followed immediately, and God

1157

knows what would happen then. Fortunately, they were already on land. . . .

At that moment, frightened by the steps of the two wanderers or by the splashing of the oars in the river, a waterfowl rose, flapped its wings, and flew up into the dark sky. And then, after describing aimless and purposeless evolutions, it darted towards the opposite bank of the river. They heard whispers among the oarsmen; probably they had already suspected the presence of strangers among the reeds. But the boat, instead of pursuing them, followed in the direction of the waterfowl, and they heard the leisurely pad of oars as the boat went towards the other bank.

The two wanderers lay on the bank with their pistols pointed in the direction of the boat. They were calm and determined, but when they heard the boat moving into the distance, they held out their hands silently at the same moment and clasped one another's hands with excitement and relief. Then they went on.

They could still smell the corpse, which was evidently lying somewhere to their left, away from the path. Suddenly Lu-Yi felt a hand snatching at his sleve.

"Devil take you! What do you want?" he groaned.

"I think it is comrade seventy-four. Let me go and feel his body. A minute, or half a minute. . . ."

Without waiting for an answer from the older man, who was clearly displeased by the suggestion, the boy bent down and ran swiftly towards the place in the bushes where the heavy foetid smell came from. He was back half a minute later.

"It's him all right," the boy said. "And it smells like him. He was a daring and dauntless fellow when alive, and now, even in corruption, his smell is terrific."

"What have you got?"

"A handful of maggots."

"Are you sure it is him?"

"Yes, I tore off his collar. The papers are there. I knew it right away."

"Nice fellows—both of you!"

They strode along the path in silence. They were soon out of the bushes, but new dangers seemed to be lying in wait for them. Soon they came to a hillside, where the path diverged, one road leading down towards the ford, and the other winding strangely among the battlemented rocks. A few lights were shining above the ford: evidently the place was well guarded. They gazed into one another's

1158

faces and neither could decide which pass was more dangerous or easier to get through.

Each minute gained gave them more hope, but they had no time to lose. They knew that the path to the ford was more familiar to them, and, if necessary, they could wade or swim across the river. They made a dash for the river. The boy saw that a fire was going out, and was probably unattended, but the older man held him back.

"Don't go near the fire, boy!"

"Don't worry. The fire must have been left behind by the patrols who boarded the boat. Probably they left it intentionally, to make us think they were there."

Once more the boy won the older man's consent. Crawling on all fours, they made their way towards the dying embers. They passed the fire unharmed, and found themselves before a long smooth road which wound along the edge of the hills and the river. They were light hearted now, and all the danger forgotten, until some minutes later the boy thought he heard the clop-clop of a horse's hooves along the road. Lu-Yi listened. He too, heard the sound and imagined that the enemy was approaching, followed perhaps by a wolfhound trained to smell out strangers at night. They decided to hide in the woods which bordered the hill, and blindly they crawled among the shadows of rocks and trees. Later, they heard the sound of hoof-beats along the road at the place where they had been, and they even imagined they could see the sparks from under the horse's feet and the white, thick vapour coming from the horse's mouth, and the sleek shadow of its back.

On his way down the slope, Lu-Yi twisted his ankle, but he knew that he would have to go as fast as possible if they were to avoid the guard station.

The sound of cocks crowing was wafted down the river. They decided, then, to bury their automatics among the reeds and swim downstream. If they could once pass the pontoon bridge, they would find themselves in safe territory less than a quarter of a mile away. But Lu-Yi knew that with his twisted ankle, it would be impossible for him to swim. They could go over the hills, but the tracks there were unknown to them, and hardly visible even in broad daylight. Moreover, beyond the hills lay precipitous slopes looking down over a ravine, and it would be easy for the enemy patrols to pick them out.

Knowing that the position was hopeless, Lu-Yi broke out into angry remonstrances.

"Boy, it's a trick played by devils. I know I am going to die here, and become a mess of worms. Next time you pass this way, better feel my collar as well. I can't walk. My right leg hurts abominably, and I am sure I can't swim. You go downstream, and I'll go to the hills—and give me your pistol."

"No, if you are hurt, I'll go with you. We'll go up the hill and die together if we have to."

"Why should we die together, my dear little devil," Lu-Yi answered, in a tone of annoyance. "Give me your pistol, and make your own way downstream."

The boy was silent. The older man repeated his command.

"I'll do as you say," the boy answered at last in a low voice. He unslung his belt, and all the time he was wondering how anyone could climb up hills and down valleys with only one game leg. He hesitated before handing the pistol over. They had gone on many dangerous errands together, and they had worked well together, and now Lu-Yi had to take the most dangerous road of all. He hardly dared to leave his companion. Lu-Yi saw this, and tried to console him.

"Boy, don't worry about me. With two pistols I shall kill many before I am killed. I prefer climbing to swimming, and in any case your journey will be hard. There may be barbed wire rising from the bottom of the river near the pontoon bridge. You may have to climb over the bridge—that's dangerous. I think I shall find my way easily enough over the hill, and when I find you I shall give you your pistol back. We'll meet again, my dear little devil."

Both knew that he was lying. Hardly had Lu-Yi finished speaking when he stepped forward and helped the boy untie his pistol belt, and the bandolier of bullets which fell down from his shoulders. Then he patted the boy on the arm and asked him to jump into the water before he himself went uphill. The kindly dogmatism of the older man, the deep friendship which existed between them, and the strict discipline which existed among the guerrilla troops, all these exhorted the boy to slide down the embankment and into the water without another word.

The stream murmured quietly and coldly, and the boy threw himself in the water, imitating the cry of a wildfowl to show that he was already on his way, and meanwhile the older man, as a sign of final greeting, threw a pebble which landed a little way from the boy's foot. Thus, for the last time, they bade each other farewell and went on their ways.

The boy exerted all the strength of his young limbs, and cautiously moved downstream. He saw fires burning at each end of the pontoon bridge, and each fire cast a dazzling shadow on the water. The bridge was formed of a number of sampans and fishing boats fastened together with iron thews; there was a sentry at each end, and there were also three or four soldiers patrolling the bridge. With his face showing only a little above water, the boy attempted to surrender to the force of the water, hoping to slide under the bridge without making the slightest sound. Suddenly he heard a whistling sound from the hilltop, and a moment later there was the sound of shooting. He knew then that the whereabouts of his friend had been discovered, but what puzzled him was that there was no answering fire from his friend. The bridge was only two yards away from him, shining in the light of the flares. He dived swiftly. There were no obstacles rising from the bottom of the river. Three yards past the bridge he came to the surface, and at that very moment he heard the automatic pistol shooting seven times in rapid succession. Soon afterwards he heard four successive pistol shots, and for the moment there were no more sounds.

Later he heard three rifle shots, then there was silence, followed by a solitary pistol shot. Immediately afterwards he heard a shrill scream from someone on the bridge. A torchlight swept over the bridge, and all around. Once more the boy dived, and when he came to the surface again all was silent in the boundless darkness except for the interminable murmur of the water beneath his body. The black night air permeating all the space overhead seemed to press down on the river and penetrate through his skin and into his veins. He knew that the safety zone lay less than a quarter of a mile away.

He saw a camp fire blazing through the darkness, and the recognition of the friendly light and the illusory warmth which came from the fire gave him new strength.

"Password!"

"Nine . . . ty, with both feet wrapped in cloth."

"Why only one? Where's your companion?"

"Ask the ghost of your ancestor."

"Is he lost then?"

There was no reply. Only a splashing sound was heard when the boy climbed up the river bank.

SHIH NAI-AN

SHIH NAI-AN (Chinese, *ca.* 1290-1365). Traditional author of *All Men Are Brothers*, one of four or five masterpieces of Chinese fiction. Written in the fourteenth century, improved and embellished during two succeeding centuries, receiving its final form. The novel is based on a cycle of stories about a band of outlaws.

"DEATH OF THE TIGERS"

LET it here be told only how Li K'uei feared lest Li Ta lead men out to pursue him. Carrying his mother on his back he turned towards the wilds of the mountain into the small lonely paths where no men were. After a while had passed, he saw that the sky was dark with night, and he carried his mother into a valley. Now his old mother's two eyes were dim and she did not know if it were morning or night. But Li K'uei knew this valley, and it was called the I Valley. On the other side only were there any homes. And the mother and son, taking advantage of the light of the new moon, went slowly step by step up the valley, and the mother said as she was on her son's back, "My son, if you could fetch a mouthful of water for me to drink it would be well."

And again Li K'uel said, "I am suffering more than I can bear, too."

Now Li K'uei saw that step by step he had come to the edge of pine trees and to a place where there was a great green stone. There he put his mother down and he thrust his sword into the earth beside her and he commanded her, saying, "Be patient and sit awhile and I will go and seek water for you to drink."

Now Li K'uei had heard the gurgling sound of water and he sought a path thither and when he had climbed over several foothills he came to the side of a brook and he dipped up water in his hands and he drank several mouthfuls. And to himself he thought, "How can I fetch this water to give my mother to drink?"

He stood up and looked east and he looked west. In the far distance upon the point of the mountain he saw a temple. He said, "Ha, it is well!"

And grasping vines and branches he climbed up the mountain side and went to the front of the temple. When he pushed the gate open and looked in he saw it was a temple to The Dragon God of Sze Chou. In front of the god was a stone urn for incense. Li-K'uei

1162

put his hand out to seize this. Now this urn was fastened upon a stone altar beneath and Li K'uei pulled at it awhile, but how could he pull it up? Then his anger rose and he jerked the altar and urn and all and he pulled them up and carried them to the stone terrace in front of the terrace and threw them down and knocked off the urn from the altar. He took the urn then and went again to the brook and he soaked it clean in the brook and he pulled some wild grass and he washed the urn clean. Then he dipped up half the urn full of water and, bearing it in both hands, he went along his old path, and stumbling along he came again to the valley.

But when he had come to the stone by the pine trees he did not see his mother. There was only the sword thrust into the ground. Then Li K'uei called, "Mother, drink some water!"

But there was no sound anywhere. When he had called and there was no answer, Li K'uei's heart was filled with fear and he put down the urn and staring about he looked in all four directions. He did not see his mother, but when he had gone not more than thirty-odd paces he saw a pool of blood upon the grass. When he saw this his flesh began to tremble. Following the flow of the blood he went to seek, and he sought to the mouth of a great cave. There he saw two tiger cubs gnawing upon a human leg. Li K'uei could not check his shivering and he said, "I returned from the mountain lair especially to seek out my old mother, and I carried her on my back through a thousand pains and bitternesses, and I did but bring her here for you to eat! As for that leg which that cursed tiger has dragged hither, if it is not my mother's then whose is it?"

When the fire of his anger rose in his heart he ceased his shivering and his red and yellow whiskers stood erect. He lifted up the sword in his hand; he stabbed at those two tiger cubs. Now the two cubs were terrified and with their teeth bared and their claws outspread they charged to attack Li K'uei, but Li K'uei lifted his hand and stabbed one to death. Then the other one turned and hastened into the cave, and Li K'uei pursued it into the cave and stabbed it to death also.

Now when Li K'uei had rushed into the tigers' den, as he stood crouching there and staring about him, he saw the mother tiger standing looking into the den, her teeth bared and her claws outspread. And Li K'uei cried, "Truly it was you, you wicked wild beast, who ate my mother!"

And he put down his sword and he took his dagger out from his person. Now that mother tiger reached the mouth of the cave and

she thrust her tail into the den and whirled it about, and was about to sit down upon her haunches in the den. But Li K'uei could see very clearly there in the den and he reached his dagger to the point below the tigress's tail and with all his strength he thrust forward, and he thrust it straight into the beast's anus. Yet he used his strength too heavily and he had thrust the very handle of the dagger through to the tigress's belly and the tigress gave a great growl and with the dagger in her vitals she rushed out of the cave and leaped to a point on the mountain beyond. Then Li K'uei took his sword and he hastened out of the cave. The tigress, suffering the pain, leaped down the mountain. Li K'uei was just about to hasten after her when he saw a great wind come out of the trees beside him, and the leaves fall from the trees like rain, and to himself he thought, "Clouds come with the dragon, wind with the tiger."

Now the place where this wind rose was beneath the light of the new moon. There came forth a deep growl and all of a sudden there leaped out a slant-eyed, white-browed tiger. That great beast charged at Li K'uei with its whole strength. But Li K'uei was not fearful nor agitated. He took advantage of the force of the beast's attack and he lifted his sword in his hand and thrust it straight into the tiger's throat.

As for the tiger, he did not attack with his hind feet nor strike with his tail, for he tried to save himself his pain, and moreover, Li K'uei had pierced his windpipe. The tiger retreated not more than five or seven paces when Li K'uei heard a sound as though the half of a great mountain fell. Straightway then did the tiger die there beside the rock.

In this short time did Li K'uei kill the two tigers and their cubs. Then he went once more into the den with his knife and looked about, lest there be yet another tiger. But there was none. And Li K'uei was weary by now also, and he went to The Temple To The Dragon God, and he slept there until dawn.

On the morning of the next day Li K'uei went to collect his mother's two legs and such of her bones as had not yet been devoured, and he took a cloth and wrapped them up. He went behind The Temple To The Dragon God and he dug a hole and buried them, and there he did weep mightily for a while. Yet he was hungry and thirsty too, and at last he tied up his bundle again and took his sword and seeking a path he slowly crossed the valley.

HENRYK SIENKIEWICZ

HENRYK SIENKIEWICZ (Polish, 1846-1916). Vivid historical novelist of Poland. Traveled in America and Africa. Won Nobel Prize, 1905. Beloved in native country for patriotic trilogy based on Polish history. Known the world over for *Quo Vadis,* novel of the Roman Empire. Other novels translated: *With Fire and Sword, The Deluge.*

THE LIGHTHOUSE KEEPER OF ASPINWALL

ON a time it happened that the lighthouse keeper in Aspinwall, not far from Panama, disappeared without a trace. Since he disappeared during a storm, it was supposed that the ill-fated man went to the very edge of the small, rocky island on which the lighthouse stood, and was swept out by a wave. This supposition seemed the more likely, as his boat was not found next day in its rocky niche. The place of lighthouse keeper had become vacant. It was necessary to fill this place at the earliest moment possible, since the lighthouse had no small significance for the local movement as well as for vessels going from New York to Panama. Mosquito Bay abounds in sandbars and banks. Among these, navigation, even in the day-time, is difficult; but at night, especially with the fogs which are so frequent on those waters warmed by the sun of the tropics, it is nearly impossible. The only guide at that time for the numerous vessels is the lighthouse.

The task of finding a new keeper fell to the United States consul living in Panama, and this task was no small one: first, because it was absolutely necessary to find a man within twelve hours; second, the man must be unusually conscientious—it was not possible, of course, to take the first comer at random; finally, there was an utter lack of candidates. Life on a tower is uncommonly difficult, and by no means enticing to people of the South, who love idleness and the freedom of vagrant life. That lighthouse keeper is almost a prisoner. He cannot leave his rocky island except on Sundays. A boat from Aspinwall brings him provisions and water once a day, and returns immediately; on the whole island, one acre in area, there is no inhabitant. The keeper lives in the lighthouse; he keeps it in order. During the day he gives signals by displaying flags of various colors to indicate changes of the barometer; in the evening he lights the lantern. This would be no great labor were it not that to reach the lantern at the summit of the tower he must pass over more than

four hundred steep and very high steps; sometimes he must make this journey repeatedly during the day. In general, it is the life of a monk, and indeed more than that—the life of a hermit. It was not wonderful, therefore, that Mr. Isaac Falconbridge was in no small anxiety as to where he should find a permanent successor to the recent keeper; and it is easy to understand his joy when a successor announced himself most unexpectedly on that very day. He was a man already old, seventy years or more, but fresh, erect with the movements and bearing of a soldier. His hair was perfectly white, his face as dark as that of a Creole; but, judging from his blue eyes, he did not belong to the people of the South. His face was somewhat downcast and sad, but honest. At the first glance he pleased Falconbridge. It remained only to examine him. Therefore the following conversation began:

"Where are you from?"

"I am a Pole."

"Where have you worked up to this time?"

"In one place and another."

"A lighthouse keeper should like to stay in one place."

"I need rest."

"Have you served? Have you testimonials of honorable government service?"

The old man drew from his bosom a piece of faded silk, resembling a strip of an old flag, unwound it, and said:

"Here are the testimonials. I received this cross in 1830. This second one is Spanish from the Carlist War; the third is the French legion; the fourth I received in Hungary. Afterward I fought in the States against the South; there they do not give crosses."

Falconbridge took the paper and began to read.

"H'm! Skavinski? Is that your name? H'm! Two flags captured in a bayonet attack. You were a gallant soldier."

"I am able to be a conscientious lighthouse keeper."

"It is necessary to ascend the tower a number of times daily. Have you sound legs?"

"I crossed the plains on foot." (The immense steppes between the East and California are called "the plains.")

"Do you know sea service?"

"I served three years on a whaler."

"You have tried various occupations."

"The only one I have not known is quiet."

"Why is that?"

1166

The old man shrugged his shoulders. "Such is my fate."

"Still you seem to me too old for a lighthouse keeper."

"Sir," exclaimed the candidate suddenly in a voice of emotion, "I am greatly wearied, knocked about. I have passed through much, as you see. This place is one of those which I have wished for most ardently. I am old, I need rest. I need to say to myself, 'Here you will remain; this is your port.' Ah, sir, this depends now on you alone. Another time perhaps such a place will not offer itself. What luck that I was in Panama! I entreat you—as God is dear to me, I am like a ship which if it misses the harbor will be lost. If you wish to make an old man happy—I swear to you that I am honest, but—I have enough of wandering."

The blue eyes of the old man expressed such earnest entreaty that Falconbridge, who had a good, simple heart, was touched.

"Well," said he, "I take you. You are lighthouse keeper."

The old man's face gleamed with inexpressible joy.

"I thank you."

"Can you go to the tower to-day?"

"I can."

"Then good-bye. Another word—for any failure in service you will be dismissed."

"All right."

That same evening, when the sun had descended on the other side of the isthmus, and a day of sunshine was followed by a night without twilight, the new keeper was in his place evidently, for the lighthouse was casting its bright rays on the water as usual. The night was perfectly calm, silent, genuinely tropical, filled with a transparent haze, forming around the moon a great colored rainbow with soft, unbroken edges; the sea was moving only because the tide raised it. Skavinski on the balcony seemed from far below like a small black point. He tried to collect his thoughts and take in his new position; but his mind was too much under pressure to move with regularity. He felt somewhat as a hunted beast feels when at last it has found refuge from pursuit on some inaccessible rock or in a cave. There had come to him, finally, an hour of quiet; the feeling of safety filled his soul with a certain unspeakable bliss. Now on that rock he can simply laugh at his previous wanderings, his misfortunes and failures. He was in truth like a ship whose masts, ropes, and sails had been broken and rent by a tempest, and cast from the clouds to the bottom of the sea—a ship on which the tempest had hurled waves and spat foam, but which still wound its

1167

way to the harbor. The pictures of that storm passed quickly through his mind as he compared it with the calm future now beginning. A part of his wonderful adventures he had related to Falconbridge; he had not mentioned, however, thousands of other incidents. It had been his misfortune that as often as he pitched his tent and fixed his fireplace to settle down permanently, some wind tore out the stakes of his tent, whirled away the fire, and bore him on toward destruction. Looking now from the balcony of the tower at the illuminated waves, he remembered everything through which he had passed. He had campaigned in the four parts of the world, and in wandering had tried almost every occupation. Labor-loving and honest, more than once he had earned money, and had always lost it in spite of every provision and the utmost caution. He had been a gold miner in Australia, a diamond-digger in Africa, a rifleman in public service in the East Indies. He established a ranch in California —the drought ruined him; he tried trading with wild tribes in the interior of Brazil—his raft was wrecked on the Amazon; he himself alone, weaponless, and nearly naked, wandered in the forest for many weeks living on wild fruits, exposed every moment to death from the jaws of wild beasts. He established a forge in Helena, Arkansas, and that was burned in a great fire which consumed the whole town. Next he fell into the hands of Indians in the Rocky Mountains, and only through a miracle was he saved by Canadian trappers. Then he served as a sailor on a vessel running between Bahia and Bordeaux, and as harpooner on a whaling-ship; both vessels were wrecked. He had a cigar factory in Havana, and was robbed by his partner while he himself was lying sick with the vomito. At last he came to Aspinwall, and there was to be the end of his failures—for what could reach him on that rocky island? Neither water nor fire nor men. But from men Skavinski had not suffered much; he had met good men oftener than bad ones.

But it seemed to him that all the four elements were persecuting him. Those who knew him said that he had no luck, and with that they explained everything. He himself became something of a mono-maniac. He believed that some mighty and vengeful hand was pursuing him everywhere, on all lands and waters. He did not like, however, to speak of this; only at times, when someone asked him whose hand that could be, he pointed mysteriously to the Polar Star, and said, "It comes from that place." In reality his failures were so continuous that they were wonderful, and might easily drive a nail into the head, especially of the man who had experienced them. But

Skavinski had the patience of an Indian, and that great calm power of resistance which comes from truth of heart. In his time he had received in Hungary a number of bayonet-thrusts because he would not grasp at a stirrup which was shown as means of salvation to him, and cry for quarter. In like manner he did not bend to misfortune. He crept up against the mountain as industriously as an ant. Pushed down a hundred times, he began his journey calmly for the hundred and first time. He was in his way a most peculiar original. This old soldier, tempered, God knows in how many fires, hardened in suffering, hammered and forged, had the heart of a child. In the time of the epidemic in Cuba, the vomito attacked him because he had given to the sick all his quinine, of which he had a considerable supply, and left not a grain for himself.

There had been in him also this wonderful quality—that after so many disappointments he was ever full of confidence, and did not lose hope that all would be well yet. In winter he grew lively, and predicted great events. He waited for these events with impatience, and lived with the thought of them whole summers. But the winters passed one after another, and Skavinski lived only to this—that they whitened his head. At last he grew old, began to lose energy; his endurance was becoming more and more like resignation, his former calmness was tending toward supersensitiveness, and that tempered soldier was degenerating into a man ready to shed tears for any cause. Besides this, from time to time he was weighed down by a terrible homesickness which was roused by any circumstance—the sight of swallows, gray birds like sparrows, snow on the mountains, or melancholy music like that heard on a time. It mastered the old man thoroughly, and swallowed all other desires and hopes. This ceaseless wanderer could not imagine anything more precious, than a quiet corner in which to rest, and wait in silence for the end. Perhaps specially because some whim of fate had so hurried him over all seas and lands that he could hardly catch his breath, did he imagine that the highest human happiness was his due; but he was so accustomed to disappointments that he thought of rest as people in general think of something which is beyond reach. He did not dare to hope for it. Meanwhile, unexpectedly, in the course of twelve hours he had gained a position which was as if chosen for him out of all the world. We are not to wonder, then, that when he lighted his lantern in the evening he became as it were dazed— that he asked himself if that was reality, and he did not dare to answer that it was. But at the same time reality convinced him with

incontrovertible proofs; hence hours one after another passed while he was on the balcony. He gazed, and convinced himself. It might seem that he was looking at the sea for the first time in his life. The lens of the lantern cast into the darkness an enormous triangle of light, beyond which the eye of the old man was lost in the black distance completely, in the distance mysterious and awful. But that distance seemed to run toward the light. The long waves following one another rolled out from the darkness, and went bellowing towards the base of the island; and then their foaming backs were visible, shining rose-coloured in the light of the lantern. The incoming tide swelled more and more, and covered the sandy bars. The mysterious speech of the ocean came with a fullness more powerful and louder, at one time like the thunder of cannon, at another like the distant dull sound of the voices of people. At moments it was quiet; then to the ears of the old man came some great sigh, then a kind of sobbing, and again threatening outbursts. At last the wind bore away the haze, but brought black, broken clouds, which hid the moon. From the west it began to blow more and more; the waves sprang with rage against the rock of the lighthouse, licking with foam the foundation walls. In the distance a storm was beginning to bellow. On the dark, disturbed expanse certain green lanterns gleamed from the masts of ships. These green points rose high and then sank; now they swayed to the right, and now to the left. Skavinski descended to his room. The storm began to howl. Outside, people on those ships were struggling with night, with darkness, with waves but inside the tower it was calm and still. Even the sounds of the storm hardly came through the thick walls, and only the measured tick-tack of the clock lulled the wearied old man to his slumber.

Hours, days, and weeks began to pass. Sailors assert that sometimes when the sea is greatly roused, something from out of the midst of night and darkness calls them by name. If the infinity of the sea may call out thus, perhaps when a man is growing old, calls come to him, too, from another infinity still darker and more deeply mysterious; and the more he is wearied by life the dearer are those calls to him. But to hear them quiet is needed. Besides old age loves to put itself aside, as if with a foreboding of the grave. The lighthouse had become for Skavinski such a half grave. Nothing is more monotonous than life on a beacon-tower. If young people consent to take up this service they leave it after a time. Lighthouse keepers are generally men not young, gloomy, and confined to

1170

themselves. If by chance one of them leaves his lighthouse and goes among men, he walks in the midst of them like a person roused from deep slumber. On the tower there is a lack of minute impressions which in ordinary life teach men to adapt themselves to everything. All that a lighthouse keeper comes in contact with is gigantic and devoid of definitely outlined forms. The sky is one whole, the water another; and between those two infinities the soul of man is in loneliness. That is a life in which thought is continual meditation, and out of that meditation nothing rouses the keeper, not even his work. Day is like day as two beads in a rosary, unless changes of weather form the only variety. But Skavinski felt more happiness than ever in life before. He rose with the dawn, took his breakfast, polished the lens, and then sitting in the balcony gazed into the distance of the water; and his eyes were never sated with the pictures which he saw before him. On the enormous turquoise ground of the ocean were to be seen generally flocks of swollen sails gleaming in the rays of the sun so brightly, that the eyes were blinking before the excess of light. Sometimes the ships, favored by the so-called trade winds, went in an extended line one after another, like a chain of sea-mews or albatrosses. The red casks indicating the channel swayed on the light wave with gentle movement. Among the sails appeared every afternoon grayish feather-like plumes of smoke. That was a steamer from New York which brought passengers and goods to Aspinwall, drawing behind it a frothy path of foam. On the other side of the balcony Skavinski saw, as if on his palm, Aspinwall and its busy harbor, and in it a forest of masts, boats, and craft; a little farther, white houses and the towers of the town. From the height of his tower the small houses were like the nests of sea-mews, the boats were like beetles, and the people moved around like small points on the white stone boulevard. From early morning a light eastern breeze brought a confused hum of human life, above which predominated the whistle of steamers. In the afternoon six o'clock came; the movements in the harbor began to cease; the mews hid themselves in the rents of the cliffs; the waves grew feeble and became in some sort lazy; and then on the land, on the sea, and on the tower came a time of stillness unbroken by anything. The yellow sands from which the waves had fallen back glittered like golden stripes on the width of the waters; the body of the tower was outlined definitely in blue. Floods of sunbeams were poured from the the sky on the water and the sands and the cliff. At that time a certain lassitude full of sweetness seized the old man. He felt that

1171

the rest which he was enjoying was excellent; and when he thought that it would be continuous nothing was lacking to him.

Skavinski was intoxicated with his own happiness; and since a man adapts himself easily to improved conditions, he gained faith and confidence by degrees; for he thought that if men built houses for invalids, why should not God gather up at last His own invalids? Time passed, and confirmed him in this conviction. The old man grew accustomed to his tower, to the lantern, to the rock, to the sand-bars, to solitude. He grew accustomed also to the sea-mews which hatched in the crevices of the rock, and in the evening held meetings on the roof of the lighthouse. Skavinski threw them generally the remnants of his food; and soon they grew tame, and afterward when he fed them, a real storm of white wings encircled him, and the old man went among the birds like a shepherd among sheep. When the tide ebbed he went to the low sandbanks, on which he collected savory periwinkles and beautiful pearl shells of the nautilus, which receding waves had left on the sand. In the night by the moonlight and the tower he went to catch fish, which frequented the windings of the cliff in myriads. At last he was in love with his rocks and his treeless little island, grown over only with small thick plants exuding sticky resin. The distant views repaid him for the poverty of the island, however. During afternoon hours, when the air became very clear he could see the whole isthmus covered with the richest vegetation. It seemed to Skavinski at such times that he saw one gigantic garden—bunches of cocoa, and enormous musa, combined as it were in luxurious tufted bouquets, right there behind the houses of Aspinwall. Farther on, between Aspinwall and Panama, was a great forest over which every morning and evening hung a reddish haze of exhalations—a real tropical forest with its feet in stagnant water, interlaced with lianas and filled with the sound of one sea of gigantic orchids, palms, milk-trees, iron-trees, gum-trees.

Through his field-glass the old man could see not only trees and the broad leaves of bananas, but even legions of monkeys and great marabous and flocks of parrots, rising at times like a rainbow cloud over the forest. Skavinski knew such forests well, for after being wrecked on the Amazon he had wandered whole weeks among similar arches and thickets. He had seen how many dangers and deaths lie concealed under those wonderful and smiling exteriors. During the nights which he had spent in them he heard close at hand the sepulchral voices of howling monkeys and the roaring of

1172

the jaguars; he saw gigantic serpents coiled like lianas on trees; he knew those slumbering forest lakes full of torpedo-fish and swarming with crocodiles; he knew under what a yoke man lives in those unexplored wildernesses in which are single leaves that exceed a man's size ten times—wildernesses swarming with blood-drinking mosquitoes, tree-leeches, and gigantic poisonous spiders. He had experienced that forest life himself, had witnessed it, had passed through it; therefore it gave him the greater enjoyment to look from his height and gaze on those *matos*, admire their beauty, and be guarded from their treacherousness. His tower preserved him from every evil. He left it only for a few hours on Sunday. He put on then his blue keeper's coat with silver buttons, and hung his crosses on his breast. His milk-white head was raised with a certain pride when he heard at the door, while entering the church, the Creoles say among themselves, "We have an honorable lighthouse keeper and not a heretic, though he is a Yankee." But he returned straightway after Mass to his island, and returned happy, for he had still no faith in the mainland. On Sunday also he read the Spanish newspaper which he bought in the town, or the *New York Herald*, which he borrowed from Falconbridge; and he sought in it European news eagerly. The poor old heart on that lighthouse tower, and in another hemisphere, was beating yet for its birthplace. At times too, when the boat brought his daily supplies and water to the island, he went down from the tower to talk with Johnson, the guard. But after a while he seemed to grow shy. He ceased to go to the town, to read the papers and to go down to talk politics with Johnson. Whole weeks passed in this way, so that no one saw him and he saw no one. The only signs that the old man was living were the disappearance of the provisions left on shore, and the light of the lantern kindled every evening with the same regularity with which the sun rose in the morning from the waters of those regions. Evidently, the old man had become indifferent to the world. Homesickness was not the cause, but just this—that even homesickness had passed into resignation. The whole world began now and ended for Skavinski on his island. He had grown accustomed to the thought that he would not leave the tower till his death, and he simply forgot that there was anything else besides it. Moreover, he had become a mystic; his mild blue eyes began to stare like the eyes of a child, and were as if fixed on something at a distance. In presence of a surrounding uncommonly simple and great, the old man was losing the feeling of personality; he was ceasing to exist as an individual,

was becoming merged more and more in that which inclosed him. He did not understand anything beyond his environment; he felt only unconsciously. At last it seems to him that the heavens, the water, his rock, the tower, the golden sand-banks, and the swollen sails, the sea-mews, the ebb and flow of the tide—all form a mighty unity, one enormous mysterious soul; that he is sinking in that mystery, and feels that soul which lives and lulls itself. He sinks and is rocked, forgets himself; and in that narrowing of his own individual existence, in that half-waking, half-sleeping, he has discovered a rest so great that it nearly resembles half-death.

But the awakening came.

On a certain day, when the boat brought water and a supply of provisions, Skavinski came down an hour later from the tower, and saw that besides the usual cargo there was an additional package. On the outside of this package were postage stamps of the United States, and the address: "Skavinski, Esq.," was written on coarse canvas.

The old man, with aroused curiosity, cut the canvas, and saw books; he took one in his hand, looked at it, and put it back; thereupon his hands began to tremble greatly. He covered his eyes as if he did not believe them; it seemed to him as if he were dreaming. The book was Polish—what did that mean? Who could have sent the book? Clearly, it did not occur to him at the first moment that in the beginning of his lighthouse career he had read in the *Herald*, borrowed from the consul, of the formation of a Polish society in New York, and had sent at once to that society half his month's salary, for which he had, moreover, no use on the tower. The society had sent him the books with thanks. The books came in the natural way; but at the first moment the old man could not seize those thoughts. Polish books in Aspinwall, on his tower, amid his solitude—that was for him something uncommon, a certain breath from past times, a kind of miracle. Now it seemed to him, as to those sailors in the night, that something was calling him by name with a voice greatly beloved and nearly forgotten. He sat for a while with closed eyes, and was almost certain that, when he opened them, the dream would be gone.

The package, cut open, lay before him, shone upon clearly by the afternoon sun, and on it was an open book. When the old man stretched his hand toward it again, he heard in the stillness the beating of his own heart. He looked; it was poetry. On the outside stood printed in great letters the title, underneath the name of the

author. The name was not strange to Skavinski; he saw that it belonged to the great poet, whose production he had read in 1830 in Paris. Afterward, when campaigning in Algiers and Spain, he had heard from his countrymen of the growing fame of the great seer; but he was so accustomed to the musket at that time that he took no book in hand. In 1849, he went to America, and in the adventurous life which he led he hardly ever met a Pole, and never a Polish book. With the greater eagerness, therefore, and with a livelier beating of the heart, did he turn to the title-page. It seemed to him then that on his lonely rock some solemnity is about to take place. Indeed it was a moment of great calm and silence. The clocks of Aspinwall were striking five in the afternoon. Not a cloud darkened the clear sky; only a few sea-mews were sailing through the air. The ocean was as if cradled to sleep. The waves on the shore stammered quietly, spreading softly on the sand. In the distance the white houses of Aspinwall, and the wonderful groups of palm, were smiling. In truth, there was something there solemn, calm, and full of dignity. Suddenly, in the midst of that calm of Nature, was heard the trembling voice of the old man, who read aloud as if to understand himself better:

"Thou art like health, O my birth-land Litva!
How much we should prize thee he only can know who has
    lost thee.
Thy beauty in perfect adornment this day
I see and describe, because I am yearning for thee."

His voice failed Skavinski. The letters began to dance before his eyes; something broke in his breast, and went like a wave from his heart higher and higher, choking his voice and pressing his throat. A moment more he controlled himself, and read further:

"O Holy Lady, who guardest bright Chenstohova,
Who shinest in Ostrobrama and preservest
The castle town Novgrodek with its trusty people,
As Thou didst give me back to health in childhood,
When by my weeping mother placed beneath Thy care
I raised my lifeless eyelids upward,
And straightway walked unto Thy holy threshold,
To thank God for the life restored me,—
So by wonder now restore us to the bosom of our birthplace."

The swollen wave broke through the restraint of his will. The old man sobbed, and threw himself on the ground; his milk-white hair was mingled with the sand of the sea. Forty years had passed since he had seen his country, and God knows how many since he heard his native speech; and now that speech had come to him itself—it had sailed to him over the ocean, and found him in solitude on another hemisphere—it so loved, so dear, so beautiful! In the sobbing which shook him there was no pain—only a suddenly aroused immense love, in the presence of which other things are as nothing. With that great weeping he had simply implored forgiveness of that beloved one, set aside because he had grown so old, had become so accustomed to his solitary rock, and had so forgotten it that in him even longing had begun to disappear. But now it returned as if by a miracle; therefore the heart leaped in him.

Moments vanished one after another; he lay there continually. The mews flew over the lighthouse, crying as if alarmed for their old friend. The hour in which he fed them with the remnants of his food had come; therefore, some of them flew down from the lighthouse to him; then more and more came, and began to pick and shake their wings over his head. The sound of the wings roused him. He had wept his fill, and had now a certain calm and brightness; but his eyes were as if inspired. He gave unwittingly all his provisions to the birds, which rushed at him with an uproar, and he himself took the book again. The sun had gone already behind the gardens and the forest of Panama, and was going slowly beyond the isthmus to the other ocean; but the Atlantic was full of light yet; in the open air there was still perfect vision; therefore, he read further:

"Now bear my longing soul to those forest slopes, to those green meadows."

At last the dusk obliterates the letters on the white paper—the dusk short as a twinkle. The old man rested his head on the rock, and closed his eyes. Then "She who defends bright Chenstohova" took his soul and transported it to "those fields colored by various grain." On the sky were burning yet those long stripes, red and golden, and on those brightnesses he was flying to beloved regions. The pine-woods were sounding in his ears; the streams of his native place were murmuring. He saw everything as it was; everything asked him, "Dost remember?" He remembers! He sees broad fields;

1176

between the fields, wood and villages. It is night now. At this hour his lantern usually illuminates the darkness of the sea; but now he is in his native village. His old head has dropped on his breast, and he is dreaming. Pictures are passing before his eyes quickly, and a little disorderly. He does not see the house in which he was born, for war had destroyed it; he does not see his father and mother, for they died when he was a child; but still the village is as if he had left it yesterday—the line of cottages with lights in the windows, the mound, the mill, the two ponds opposite each other, and thundering all night with a chorus of frogs. Once he had been on guard in that village all night; now that past stood before him at once in a series of views. He is an Uhlan again, and he stands there on guard; at a distance is the public-house; he looks with swimming eyes. There is thundering and singing and shouting amid the silence of the night, with voices of fiddles and bass-viols "U-ha! U-ha!" Then the Uhlans knock out fire with their horseshoes, and it is wearisome for him there on his horse. The hours drag on slowly; at last the lights are quenched: now as far as the eye reaches there is mist, and mist impenetrable; now the fog rises, evidently from the fields, and embraces the whole world with a whitish cloud. You would say, a complete ocean. But that is fields; soon the land-rail will be heard in the darkness, and the bitterns will call from the reeds. The night is calm and cool—in truth, a Polish night! In the distance the pinewood is sounding without wind, like the roll of the sea. Soon dawn will whiten the east. In fact, the cocks are beginning to crow behind the hedges. One answers to another from cottage to cottage; the storks are screaming somewhere on high. The Uhlan feels well and bright. Someone had spoken of a battle tomorrow. Hei! that will go on, like all the others, with shouting, with flutterings of flaglets. The young blood is playing like a trumpet, though the night cools it. But it is dawning. Already night is growing pale; out of the shadows come forests, the thicket, a row of cottages, the mill, the poplars. The well is squeaking like a metal banner on a tower. What a beloved land, beautiful in the rosy gleams of the morning! Oh, the one land, the one land!

Quiet! the watchful picket hears that someone is approaching. Of course, they are coming to relieve the guard.

Suddenly some voice is heard above Skavinski:

"Here, old man! Get up! What's the matter?

The old man opens his eyes, and looks with wonder at the person standing before him. The remnants of the dream-visions struggle in

1177

his head with reality. At last the visions pale and vanish. Before him stands Johnson, the harbor guide.

"What's this?" asked Johnson; "are you sick?"

"No."

"You didn't light the lantern. You must leave your place. A vessel from St. Geromo was wrecked on the bar. It is lucky that no one was drowned, or you would go to trial. Get into the boat with me; you'll hear the rest at the Consulate."

The old man grew pale; in fact he had not lighted the lantern that night.

A few days later, Skavinski was seen on the deck of a steamer, which was going from Aspinwall to New York. The poor man had lost his place. There opened before him new roads of wandering; the wind had torn that leaf away again to whirl it over lands and seas, to sport with it till satisfied. The old man had failed greatly during those few days, and was bent over; only his eyes were gleaming. On his new road of life he held at his breast his book, which from time to time he pressed with his hand as if in fear that that too might go from him.

SOLOMON

SOLOMON (Hebrew, 10th Century, B.C.). Kingly poet and philosopher. Most powerful ruler of the Hebrew monarchy. Organizer, builder and reformer. The exceptionally lyrical, erotic "Song of Songs," attributed to him, has been endlessly disputed and interpreted by scholars—the commonest and most ingenious interpretation being that it is an allegory.

"THE SONG OF SOLOMON"

IV

BEHOLD, thou art fair, my love; behold, thou art fair; thou hast doves' eyes within thy locks: thy hair is as a flock of goats, that appear from mount Gilead.

Thy teeth are like a flock of sheep that are even shorn, which came up from the washing; whereof every one bear twins, and none is barren among them.

Thy lips are like a thread of scarlet, and thy speech is comely; thy temples are like a piece of a pomegranate within thy locks.

1178

Thy neck is like the tower of David builded for an armoury, whereon there hang a thousand bucklers, all shields of mighty men.

Thy two breast are like two young roes that are twins which feed among the lilies.

Until the day break, and the shadows flee away, I will get me to the mountain of myrrh, and to the hill of frankincense.

Thou art all fair, my love; there is no spot in thee.

Come with me from Lebanon, my spouse, with me from Lebanon: look from the top of Amana, from the top of Shenir and Hermon, from the lions' dens, from the mountains of the leopards.

Thou hast ravished my heart, my sister, my spouse; thou hast ravished my heart with one of thine eyes, with one chain of thy neck.

How fair is thy love, my sister, my spouse! How much better is thy love than wine! and the smell of thine ointments than all spices!

Thy lips, O my spouse, drop as the honeycomb: honey and milk are under thy tongue; and the smell of thy garments is like the smell of Lebanon.

A garden inclosed is my sister, my spouse; a spring shut up, a fountain sealed.

Thy plants are an orchard of pomegranates, with pleasant fruits; camphire, with spikenard,

Spikenard and saffron; calamus and cinnamon, with all trees of frankincense; myrrh and aloes, with all the chief spices:

A fountain of gardens, a well of living waters, and streams from Lebanon.

Awake, O north wind; and come, thou south; blow upon my garden, that the spices thereof may flow out. Let my beloved come into his garden, and eat his pleasant fruits.

V

I AM come into my garden, my sister, my spouse: I have gathered my myrrh with my spice; I have eaten my honeycomb with my honey; I have drunk my wine with my milk: eat, O friends; drink, yea, drink abundantly. O beloved.

I sleep, but my heart waketh: it is the voice of my beloved that knocketh, saying, Open to me, my sister, my love, my dove, my undefiled: for my head is filled with dew, and my locks with the drops of the night.

I have put off my coat; how shall I put it on? I have washed my feet; how shall I defile them?

1179

My beloved put in his hand by the hole of the door, and my bowels were moved for him.

I rose up to open to my beloved; and my hands dropped with myrrh, and my fingers with sweet smelling myrrh, upon the handles of the lock.

I opened to my beloved; but my beloved had withdrawn himself, and was gone: my soul failed when he spake: I sought him, but I could not find him; I called him, but he gave me no answer.

The watchmen that went about the city found me, they smote me, they wounded me; the keepers of the walls took away my veil from me.

I charge you, O daughters of Jerusalem, if ye find my beloved, that ye tell him, that I am sick of love.

What is thy beloved more than another beloved, O thou fairest among women? What is thy beloved more than another beloved, that thou dost so charge us?

My beloved is white and ruddy, the chiefest among ten thousand.

His head is as the most fine gold, his locks are bushy, and black as a raven.

His eyes are as the eyes of doves by the rivers of waters, washed with milk, and fitly set.

His cheeks are as a bed of spices, as sweet flowers: his lips like lilies, dropping sweet smelling myrrh.

His hands are as gold rings set with the beryl: his belly is as bright ivory overlaid with sapphires.

His legs are as pillars of marble, set upon sockets of fine gold: his countenance is as Lebanon, excellent as the cedars.

His mouth is most sweet; yea, he is altogether lovely. This is my beloved, and this is my friend, O daughters of Jerusalem.

SOMADEVA

SOMADEVA (Sanskrit, 11th Century). Legendary Kashmir Brahmin. Little known of his life. His celebrated collection of stories, *The Ocean of the Streams of Story,* is based on a still earlier collection.

DEVASMITA

THERE is a city in the world famous under the name of Támraliptá, and in that city there was a very rich merchant named Dhanadatta.

And he, being childless, assembled many Bráhmans and said to them with due respect, "Take such steps as will procure me a son soon." Then those Bráhmans said to him: "This is not at all difficult, for Bráhmans can accomplish all things in this world by means of ceremonies in accordance with the Scriptures. To give you an instance, there was in old times a king who had no sons, and he had a hundred and five wives in his harem. And by means of a sacrifice to procure a son, there was born to him a son named Jantu, who was like the rising of the new moon to the eyes of his wives. Once on a time an ant bit the boy on the thigh as he was crawling about on his knees, so that he was very unhappy and sobbed loudly. Thereupon the whole harem was full of confused lamentation, and the king himself shrieked out 'My son! my son;' like a common man. The boy was soon comforted, the ant having been removed, and the king blamed the misfortune of his only having one son as the cause of all his grief. And he asked the Bráhmans in his affliction if there was any expedient by which he might obtain a large number of children. They answered, 'O king, there is one expedient open to you; you must slay this son and offer up all his flesh in the fire. By smelling the smell of that sacrifice all thy wives will obtain sons.' When he heard that, the king had the whole ceremony performed as they directed; and he obtained as many sons as he had wives. So we can obtain a son for you also by a burnt-offering." When they had said this to Dhanadatta, the Bráhmans, after a sacrificial fee had been promised them, performed a sacrifice: then a son was born to that merchant. That son was called Guhasena, and he gradually grew up to man's estate. Then his father Dhanadatta began to look out for a wife for him.

Then his father went with that son of his to another country, on the pretence of traffic, but really to get a daughter-in-law. There he asked an excellent merchant of the name of Dharmagupta to give him his daughter named Devasmitá for his son Guhasena. But Dharmagupta, who was tenderly attached to his daughter, did not approve of that connection, reflecting that the city of Támraliptá was very far off. But when Devasmitá beheld that Guhasena, her mind was immediately attracted by his virtues, and she was set on abandoning her relations, and so she made an assignation with him by means of a confidante, and went away from that country at night with her beloved and his father. When they reached Támraliptá they were married, and the minds of the young couple were firmly knit together by the bond of mutual love. Then Guhasena's

father died, and he himself was urged by his relations to go to the
country of Katáha for the purpose of trafficking; but his wife Devasmitá was too jealous to approve of that expedition, fearing
exceedingly that he would be attracted by some other lady. Then,
as his wife did not approve of it, and his relations kept inciting him
to it, Guhasena, whose mind was firmly set on doing his duty, was
bewildered. Then he went and performed a vow in the temple of
the god, observing a rigid fast, trusting that the god would show him
some way out of his difficulty. And his wife Devasmitá also performed a vow with him; then Siva was pleased to appear to that
couple in a dream; and giving them two red lotuses the god said
to them, "Take each of you one of these lotuses in your hand.
And if either of you shall be unfaithful during your separation, the
lotus in the hand of the other shall fade, but not otherwise." After
hearing this, the two woke up, and each beheld in the hand of the
other a red lotus, and it seemed as if they had got one another's
hearts. Then Guhasena set out, lotus in hand. but Devasmitá remained in the house with her eyes fixed upon her flower. Guhasena
for his part quickly reached the country of Katáha, and began to
buy and sell jewels there. And four young merchants in that country,
seeing that that unfading lotus was ever in his hand, were greatly
astonished. Accordingly they got him to their house by an artifice,
and made him drink a great deal of wine, and then asked him the
history of the lotus, and he being intoxicated told them the whole
story. Then those four young merchants, knowing that Guhasena
would take a long time to complete his sales and purchases of jewels
and other wares, planned together, like rascals as they were, the
seduction of his wife out of curiosity, and eager to accomplish it
set out quickly for Támraliptá without their departure being noticed.
There they cast about for some instrument, and at last had recourse
to a female ascetic of the name of Yogakaramdiká, who lived in a
sanctuary of Buddha; and they said to her in an affectionate manner,
"Reverend madam, if our object is accomplished by your help, we
will give you much wealth." She answered them: "No doubt you
young men desire some woman in this city, so tell me all about it,
I will procure you the object of your desire. What woman do you
desire? I will quickly procure her for you." When they heard that
they said, "Procure us an interview with the wife of the merchant
Guhasena named Devasmitá." When she heard that, the ascetic undertook to manage that business for them, and she gave those young
merchants her own house to reside in. Then she gratified the ser-

1182

vants at Guhasena's house with gifts of sweetmeats and other things, and afterwards entered it with her pupil. Then, as she approached the private rooms of Devasmitá, a hound, that was fastened there with a chain, would not let her come near, but opposed her entrance in the most determined way. Then Devasmitá seeing her, of her own accord sent a maid, and had her brought in, thinking to herself, "What can this person be come for?" After she had entered, the wicked ascetic gave Devasmitá her blessing, and treating the virtuous woman with affected respect, said to her, "I have always had a desire to see you, but to-day I saw you in a dream, therefore I have come to visit you with impatient eagerness; and my mind is afflicted at beholding you separated from your husband, for beauty and youth are wasted when one is deprived of the society of one's beloved." With this and many other speches of the same kind she tried to gain the confidence of the virtuous woman in a short interview, and then taking leave of her she returned to her own house. On the second day she took with her a piece of meat full of pepper dust, and went again to the house of Devasmitá, and there she gave that piece of meat to the hound at the door, and the hound gobbled it up, pepper and all. Then owing to the pepper dust, the tears flowed in profusion from the animal's eyes, and her nose began to run. And the cunning ascetic immediately went into the apartment of Devasmitá, who received her hospitably, and began to cry. When Devasmitá asked why she shed tears, she said with affected reluctance: "My friend, look at this hound weeping outside here. This creature recognised me to-day as having been its companion in a former birth, and began to weep; for that reason my tears gushed through pity." When she heard that, and saw that hound outside apparently weeping, Devasmitá thought for a moment to herself, "What can be the meaning of this wonderful sight?" Then the ascetic said to her, "My daughter, in a former birth, I and that hound were the two wives of a certain Bráhman. And our husband frequently went about to other countries on embassies by order of the king. Now while he was away from home, I lived at my good will and pleasure, and so did not cheat the elements, of which I was composed, and my senses, of their lawful enjoyment. For considerate treatment of the elements and senses is held to be the highest duty. Therefore I have been born in this birth with a recollection of my former existence. But she, in her former life, through ignorance, confined all her attention to the preservation of her character, therefore, she has been degraded and born again as one of the canine race, however, she too remem-

1183

bers her former birth." The wise Devasmitá said to herself, "This is a novel conception of duty; no doubt this woman has laid a treacherous snare for me"; and so she said to her, "Reverend lady, for this long time I have been ignorant of this duty, so procure me an interview with some charming man." Then the ascetic said, "There are residing here some young merchants that have come from another country, so I will bring them to you." When she had said this, the ascetic returned home delighted, and Devasmitá of her own accord said to her maids: "No doubt those scoundrelly young merchants, whoever they may be, have seen that unfading lotus in the hand of my husband, and have on some occasion or other, when he was drinking wine, asked him out of curiosity to tell the whole story of it, and have now come here from that island to deceive me, and this wicked ascetic is employed by them. So bring quickly some wine mixed with Datura, and when you have brought it, have a dog's foot of iron made as quickly as possible." When Devasmitá had given these orders, the maids executed them faithfully, and one of the maids, by her orders, dressed herself up to resemble her mistress. The ascetic for her part chose out of the party of four merchants (each of whom in his eagerness said—"Let me go first"—) one individual, and brought him with her. And concealing him in the dress of her pupil, she introduced him in the evening into the house of Devasmitá, and coming out, disappeared. Then that maid, who was disguised as Devasmitá, courteously persuaded the young merchant to drink some of that wine drugged with Datura. That liquor, like his own immodesty, robbed him of his senses, and then the maids took away his clothes and other equipments and left him stark naked; then they branded him on the forehead with the mark of a dog's foot, and during the night took him and pushed him into a ditch full of filth. Then he recovered consciousness in the last watch of the night, and found himself plunged in a ditch, as it were the hell *Avíchi* assigned to him by his sins. Then he got up and washed himself and went to the house of the female ascetic, in a state of misery, feeling with his fingers the mark on his forehead. And when he got there, he told his friends that he had been robbed on the way, in order that he might not be the only person made ridiculous. And the next morning he sat with a cloth wrapped round his branded forehead, giving as an excuse that he had a headache from keeping awake so long, and drinking too much. In the same way the next young merchant was maltreated, when he got to the house of Devasmitá, and when he returned home stripped, he said,

1184

"I put on my ornaments there, and as I was coming out I was plundered by robbers." In the morning he also, on the plea of a headache, put a wrapper on to cover his branded forehead.

In the same way all the four young merchants suffered in turn branding and other humiliating treatment, though they concealed the fact. And they went away from the place, without revealing to the female Buddhist ascetic the ill-treatment they had experienced, hoping that she would suffer in a similar way. On the next day the ascetic went with her disciple to the house of Devasmitá, much delighted at having accomplished what she undertook to do. Then Devasmitá received hr courteously, and made her drink wine drugged with Datura, offered as a sign of gratitude. When she and her disciple were intoxicated with it, that chaste wife cut off their ears and noses, and flung them also into a filthy pool. And being distressed by the thought that perhaps these young merchants might go and slay her husband, she told the whole circumstance to her mother-in-law. Then her mother-in-law said to her, "My daughter, you have acted nobly, but possibly some misfortune may happen to my son in consequence of what you have done."

So the wise Devasmitá forthwith put on the dress of a merchant. Then she embarked on a ship, on the pretence of a mercantile expedition, and came to the country of Katáha where her husband was. And when she arrived there, she saw that husband of hers, Guhasena, in the midst of a circle of merchants, like consolation in external bodily form. He seeing her afar off in the dress of a man, as it were, drank her in with his eyes, and thought to himself, "Who may this merchant be that looks so like my beloved wife?" So Devasmitá went and represented to the king that she had a petition to make, and asked him to assemble all his subjects. Then the king full of curiosity assembled all the citizens, and said to that lady disguised as a merchant, "What is your petition?" Then Devasmitá said, "There are residing here in your midst four slaves of mine who have escaped, let the king make them over to me." Then the king said to her, "All the citizens are present here, so look at everyone in order to recognise him, and take those slaves of yours." Then she seized upon the four young merchants, whom she had before treated in such a humiliating way in her house, and who had wrappers bound round their heads. Then the merchants, who were there, flew in a passion, and said to her, "These are the sons of distinguished merchants, how then can they be your slaves?" Then she answered them, "If you do not believe what I say, examine their

1185

foreheads which I marked with a dog's foot." They consented, and removing the head-wrappers of these four, they all beheld the dog's foot on their foreheads. Then all the merchants were abashed, and the king, being astonished, himself asked Devasmitá what all this meant. She told the whole story, and all the people burst out laughing, and the king said to the lady, "They are your slaves by the best of titles." Then the other merchants paid a large sum of money to the chaste wife, to redeem those four from slavery, and a fine to the king's treasury. Devasmitá received that money, and recovered her husband, and being honoured by all good men, returned then to her own city Támraliptá, and she was never afterwards separated from her beloved.

SOPHOCLES

SOPHOCLES (Greek, 496-406 B.C.). Early master of the drama, next to Aeschylus in time and rank. Is said to have introduced third actor into the drama, and made each play a unit instead of part of a trilogy. Of his 123 plays, 7 survive. Among them: *Antigone, Electra, Ajax, Oedipus Tyrannus*. Notable for humanizing his characters and for skillful play construction.

ANTIGONE

Antigone, the daughter of Œdipus, having buried her father, returns to Thebes. Eteocles and Polynices, her brothers, having fallen by each other's hand, the kingdom devolves on Creon, their uncle. The tragedy of Antigone begins with Creon's edict forbidding the rites of burial to Polynices, as a traitor, and threatening with death any one who should dare to bury him. In violation of the decree, Antigone sprinkles dust and pours libations over the body of her brother, but is arrested and condemned to be immured in a cave. Tiresias, the seer, warns Creon that the offended people will rage, that his cities shall be polluted and his palace filled with woe. Creon relents and gives orders for the burial of Polynices, and goes himself to free Antigone. He is too late; she has killed herself, and her lover, Creon's son Hæmon, lies slain by her side. In the meantime, Eurydice, the queen, has stabbed herself before the altar. As the play closes, Creon is in utter misery.

ANTIGONE BEFORE KING CREON

Guards bring in Antigone

Guard. I come, although I swore the contrary,
Bringing this maiden, whom in act we found
Decking the grave.
And now, O king, take her, and as thou wilt,
Judge and convict her.
    Creon. How and where was it that ye seized and brought her?
    Guard. She was in act of burying. Thou knowest all.
    Creon. Dost know and rightly speak the tale thou tell'st?
    Guard. I saw her burying that self-same corpse
Thou bad'st us not to bury. Speak I clear?
    Creon. How was she seen, and taken in the act?
    Guard. The matter passed as follows:—When we came,
With all those dreadful threats of thine upon us,
Sweeping away the dust which, lightly spread,
Covered the corpse, and laying stripped and bare
The tainted carcase, on the hill we sat
To windward, shunning the infected air,
Each stirring up his fellow with strong words,
If any shirked his duty. This went on
Some time, until the glowing orb of day
Stood in mid heaven, and the scorching heat
Fell on us. Then a sudden whirlwind rose,
A scourge from heaven, raising squalls on earth,
And filled the plain, the leafage stripping bare
Of all the forest, and the air's vast space
Was thick and troubled, and we closed our eyes,
Until the plague the Gods had sent was past;
And when it ceased, a weary time being gone,
The girl is seen, and with a bitter cry,
Shrill as a bird's, when it beholds its nest
All emptied of its infant brood, she wails;
Thus she, when she beholds the corpse all stripped,
Groaned loud with many moanings, and she called
Fierce curses down on those who did the deed.
And in her hand she brings some fine, dry dust,
And from a vase of bronze, well wrought, upraised,
She pours the three libations o'er the dead.

1187

And we, beholding, give her chase forthwith,
And run her down, naught terrified at us.
And then we charged her with the former deed,
As well as this. And nothing she denied.
But this to me both bitter is and sweet,
For to escape one's-self from ill is sweet,
But to bring friends to trouble, this is hard
And painful. Yet my nature bids me count
Above all these things safety for myself.

 Creon (*to Antigone*). Thou, then — yes, thou, who bend'st thy
 face to earth—
Confessest thou, or dost deny the deed?
 Antig. I own I did it, and will not deny.
 Creon (*to Guard*). Go thou thy way, where'er thy will may
 choose,
Freed from a weighty charge.

(Exit Guard.)

(To Antigone). And now for thee.
Say in few words, not lengthening out thy speech,
Knew'st thou the edicts which forbade these things?
 Antig. I knew them. Could I fail? Full clear were they.
 Creon. And thou didst dare to disobey these laws?
 Antig. Yes, for it was not Zeus who gave them forth,
Nor Justice, dwelling with the Gods below,
Who traced these laws for all the sons of men;
Nor did I deem thy edicts strong enough,
That thou, a mortal man, shouldst over-pass
The unwritten laws of God that know not change.
They are not of to-day nor yesterday,
But live for ever, nor can man assign
When first they sprang to being. Not through fear
Of any man's resolve was I prepared
Before the Gods to bear the penalty
Of sinning against these. That I should die
I knew, (how should I not?) though thy decree
Had never spoken. And, before my time
If I shall die, I reckon this a gain;
For whoso lives, as I, in many woes,
How can it be but he shall gain by death?

And so for me to bear this doom of thine
Has nothing painful. But, if I had left
My mother's son unburied on his death,
In that I should have suffered; but in this
I suffer not. And should I seem to thee
To do a foolish deed, 'tis simply this,—
I bear the charge of folly from a fool. . . . .
And yet how could I higher glory gain
Than placing my true brother in his tomb?
There is not one of these but would confess
It pleases them, did fear not seal their lips.
The tyrant's might in much besides excels,
And it may do and say whate'er it will.

 Creon. Of all the race of Cadmos thou alone
Look'st thus upon the deed.

 Antig. They see it too
As I do, but their tongue is tied for thee.

 Creon. Art not ashamed against their thoughts to think?

 Antig. There is naught base in honoring our own blood.

 Creon. And was he not thy kin who fought against him?

 Antig. Yea, brother, of one father and one mother.

 Creon. Why then give honor which dishonors him?

 Antig. The dead below will not repeat thy words.

 Creon. Yes, if thou give like honor to the godless.

 Antig. It was his brother, not his slave, that died.

 Creon. Wasting this land, while *he* died fighting for it.

 Antig. Yet Hades still craves equal rites for all.

 Creon. The good craves not the portion of the bad.

 Antig. Who knows if this be holy deemed below?

 Creon. Not even when he dies can foe be friend.

 Antig. My nature leads to sharing love, not hate.

 Creon. Go then below; and if thou must have love,
Love them. While I live, women shall not rule.

ANTIGONE AND ISMENE

Ismene, sister of Antigone, had in fear of the king's decree
refused to join her in performing the burial rites for her brother
Polynices. But when Antigone is arrested, Ismene is willing and
eager to share her fate.

Enter Ismene, led in by Attendants

Chorus. And, lo! Ismene at the gate
Comes shedding tears of sisterly regard,
And o'er her brow a gathering cloud
    Mars the deep roseate blush,
    Bedewing her fair cheek.
    Creon (to Ismene). And thou who, creeping as a viper creeps
Didst drain my life in secret, and I knew not
That I was rearing two accursed ones,
Subverters of my throne,—come, tell me, then,
Wilt thou confess thou tookst thy part in this,
Or wilt thou swear thou didst not know of it?
    Ism. I did the deed, if she did go; with her
I share the guilt, and bear an equal blame.
    Antig. Nay, justice will not suffer this, for thou
Didst not consent, nor did I let thee join.
    Ism. Nay, in thy troubles, I am not ashamed
in the same boat with thee to share thy fate.
    Antig. Who did it, Hades knows, and those below:
I do not love a friend who loves in words.
    Ism. Do not, my sister, put me to such shame,
As not to let me join in death with thee,
And so to pay due reverence to the dead.
    Antig. Share not my death, nor make thine own this deed
Thou hadst no hand in. My death shall suffice.
    Ism. What life to me is sweet, bereaved of thee?
    Antig. Save thou thyself. I grudge not thy escape.
    Ism. Ah, woe is me! and must I miss thy fate?
    Antig. Thou mad'st thy choice to live, and I to die.
    Ism. 'Twas not because I failed to speak my thoughts.
    Antig. To these didst thou, to those did I seem wise.
    Ism. And yet the offence is equal in us both.
    Antig. Take courage. Thou dost live. My soul long since
Hath died to render service to the dead.
    Creon. Of these two girls the one goes mad but now,
The other ever since her life began.
    Ism. E'en so, O king; no mind that ever lived
Stands firm in evil days, but goes astray.
    Creon. Thine did, when, with the vile, vile deeds thou chosest.
    Ism. How could I live without her presence here?
    Creon. Speak not of presence. She is here no more.
    Ism. And wilt thou slay thy son's betrothed bride?

Creon. Full many a field there is which he may plough.

Ism. None like that plighted troth 'twixt him and her.

Creon. Wives that are vile I love not for my sons.

Ism. Ah, dearest Hæmon, how thy father shames thee!

Creon. Thou with that marriage dost but vex my soul.

Chor. And wilt thou rob thy son of her he loved?

Creon. 'Tis Death, not I, shall break the marriage off.

Chor. Her doom is fixed, it seems, then. She must die.

Creon. Fixed, yes, by me and thee. No more delay,
Lead them within, ye slaves. These must be kept
Henceforth as women, suffered not to roam;
For even boldest natures shrink in fear
When they see Hades overshadowing life.

KING ŒDIPUS

The terrible story of Œipus had a strong fascination for the
Greeks, as illustrating the conflict of moral laws and the supremacy
of destiny. Laius, King of Thebes, learned from the oracle of
Apollo, at Delphi, that he was destined to perish by the hand of
his own son. He ordered his wife Jocasta, therefore, to destroy the
infant. She gave it to a herdsman, who left it, tied with thongs, on
Mount Cithæron. But a shepherd of Corinth found the babe and
delivered it to King Polybus, who adopted it as his own child, and
called it Œdipus (Swollen-foot). When grown up, Œdipus is told
by the oracle that he would slay his father and marry his mother.
On his return to Corinth he met Laius in a narrow pass and, in a
dispute about the road, slew him. Passing to Thebes, he destroyed
the Sphinx, a monster which had been inflicting damage on the
city. Œdipus was, therefore, raised to the throne and the widowed
Jocasta receives him as her husband. A pestilence arises, and the
oracle declares that it cannot be abated until the murder of Laius
is avenged. On investigation the appalling secret is discovered,
whereupon Jocasta commits suicide, and Œdipus tears out his own
eyes and goes into exile.

Jocasta. Princes of Thebes, we deemed it meet to seek
The temples of the gods, and in our hands
These votive wreaths, this odorous incense bear.
The soul of Œdipus on a wild sea
Of anxious care is tossed;—nor, as becomes

1191

The prudent, weighs by former oracles
This late response, but lends a willing ear
To all who speak of terrors. Since my voice
Avails no more, Lycæan king, to thee
I fly, for thou art nearest to our need,
And come in prayer a suppliant to thy shrine,
That thou mayst grant us thine auspicious aid;
Since all now tremble, when we thus behold
Our very pilot shuddering and appalled.

Enter Corinthian

Corinthian. Can ye inform me, strangers, where your king,
Great Œdipus, his regal state maintains;
Or, if ye know, where I may find the monarch?
Chorus. These are th' imperial halls—he is within—
This is his wife, the mother of his children.
Cor. Blest may she be, and ever with the blest
Hold glad communion; to her royal lord
A most accomplished consort.
Joc. Equal joy
Attend thee, stranger,—thy kind greeting claims
This due return of courtesy. But say,
Whence cam'st thou to our Thebes, and what thy tidings?
Cor. Joy to thy house, O lady! and thy lord.
Joc. What joy?—and from what region art thou come?
Cor. From Corinth. At my words thou wilt rejoice:
Why shouldst thou not—yet fond regrets will rise.
Joc. What dost thou mean, and whence this two-fold influence?
Cor. The assembled States of Isthmus, rumor tells,
Will choose thy lord to mount the vacant throne.
Joc. How vacant? Reigns not Polybus in Corinth?
Cor. No more!—His only kingdom is the tomb.
Joc. Haste, haste, attendant, and convey with speed
These tidings to your lord. Vain oracles!
Where are your bodings now? My Œdipus,
Fearing to slay this man, forsook his country;
Now Fate, and not his hand, hath laid him low.

Enter Œdipus

Œdipus. Why, my beloved Jocasta, has thou sent
To bid my presence hither?

Joc.   Hear this man—
Attend his tidings, and observe the end
Of these most true and reverend oracles.
   Œd.   Who is this stranger—with what message charged?
   Joc.   He is from Corinth, thence despatched to tell thee
That Polybus, thy father, is no more.
   Œd.   What sayest thou, stranger? Be thyself the speaker.
   Cor.   Then, in plain terms, the king is dead and gone.
   Œd.   Died he by treason, or the chance of sickness?
   Cor.   Slight ills dismiss the aged to their rest.
   Œd.   Then by disease, it seems, the monarch died.
   Cor.   And bowed beneath a withering weight of years.
   Œd.   Ha! is it thus? Then, lady, who would heed
The Pythian shrine oracular, or birds
Clanging in air, by whose vain auspices
I was fore-doomed the murderer of my father?
In the still silence of the tomb he sleeps.
While I am here—the fatal sword untouched,
Unless he languished for his absent child,
And I was thus the author of his doom.
Now in the grave he lies, and with him rest
Those vain predictions, worthy of our scorn.
   Joc.   Did I not tell thee this before?
   Œd.   Thou didst,
But terror urged me onward.
   Joc.   Banish now
This vain solicitude.
   Œd.   Should I not fear
The dark pollution of my mother's bed?
   Joc.   Oh, why should mortals fear, when fortune's sway
Rules all, and wariest foresight naught avails?
Best to live on unheeding, as thou may'st.
   Œd.   Phœbus foretold that I should wed my mother,
And shed with impious hand a father's blood.
For this I fled my own Corinthian towers
To seek a distant home—that home was blest;
Though still I languished to embrace my parents,
   Cor.   This fear then urged thee to renounce thy country?
   Œd.   Old man, I would not be a father's murderer.
   Cor.   Then wherefore, since thy welfare I regard,
Should I forbear to rid thee of this terror?

Œd. Do so, and rich shall be thy recompense.

Cor. This hope impell'd me here, that when our State
Hails thee her monarch, I might win thy favor.

Œd. Ne'er will I seek the authors of my birth.

Cor. 'Tis plain, my son, thou know'st not what thou doest!

Œd. How! how! old man, by heaven, unfold thy meaning.

Cor. If this preclude thee from returning home—

Œd. I fear lest Phœbus saw, alas! too clearly!

Cor. If thou dost dread pollution from thy parents—

Œd. That restless dread for ever haunts my soul.

Cor. Know, then, thy terrors all are causeless here.

Œd. How so? if of these parents I was born?

Cor. But Polybus is not allied to thee.

Œd. How say'st thou? was not Polybus my father?

Cor. No more than I—our claims are equal here.

Œd. Had he who gave me life no nearer claim
Than thou, a stranger?

Cor. Nor to him or me
Ow'st thou thy birth.

Œd. Then wherefore did he grant
A son's beloved name?

Cor. He from my hand
Received thee as a gift.

Œd. With such fond love
How could he cherish thus an alien child?

Cor. His former childless state to this impelled him.

Œd. Gav'st thou a purchased slave, or thy own child?

Cor. I found thee in Cithæron's shadowy glades.

Œd. Why didst thou traverse those remoter vales?

Cor. It was my charge to tend the mountain herds.

Œd. Wert thou a herdsman, and engaged for hire?

Cor. I was, my son, but thy preserver too.

Œd. From what affliction didst thou then preserve me?

Cor. This let thy scarr'd and swollen feet attest.

Œd. Ha! why dost thou revive a woe long passed?

Cor. I loosed thy bound and perforated feet.

Œd. Such foul reproach mine infancy endured.

Cor. From this event arose the name thou bear'st.

Œd. Thou didst receive me then from other hands,
Nor find me as by chance?

Cor. No; to my hand
Another herdsman gave thee.

Œd. Who was he?
Canst thou inform me this?

Cor. He was, I believe,
A slave of Laius.

Œd. What! of him who erst
Ruled o'er this land?

Cor. The same;—this man to him
Discharged an herdsman's office.

Œd. Lives he yet
That I may see him?

Cor. Ye, his countrymen,
Are best prepared this question to resolve.

Œd. Is there, of you who now attend our presence,
One who would know the herdsman he describes,
Familiar erst or here, or in the field?
Speak—for the time demands a prompt disclosure.

Ch. He is, I deem, no other than the man
Whom thou before didst summon from the fields.
This none can know more than the Queen.

Œd. Think'st thou, O Queen, the man whose presence late
We bade, is he of whom this stranger speaks?

Joc. Who—spake of whom?—Regard him not, nor dwell,
With vain remembrance, on unmeaning words!

Œd. Nay, Heaven forfend, when traces of my birth
Are thus unfolding, I should cease to follow.

Joc. Nay, by the Gods I charge thee! search no more,
If life be precious still. Be it enough
That I am most afflicted.

Œd. Cheer thee, lady,
Though my descent were proved e'en trebly servile,
No stain of infamy would light on thee.

Joc. Ah yield, I do conjure thee—seek no more.

Œd. I will not yield, till all be clearly known.

Joc. 'Tis for thy peace I warn thee—yet be wise.

Œd. That very wisdom wounds my peace most deeply.

Joc. Unhappy—never may'st thou know thy birth.

Œd. Will none conduct this shepherd to our presence?
Leave her to triumph in her lordly race.

1195

Joc.   Woe! woe! unhappy! henceforth by that name
Alone can I address thee, and by that
Alone for ever.

Œd.   I will on
To trace my birth, though it be most obscure.
Pride swells her thus, for in a woman's breast
Pride reigns despotic, and she thinks foul scorn
Of my ignoble birth. I deem myself
The child of Fortune, in whose favoring smile
I shall not be dishonored. She alone
Hath been my fostering parent; from low state
My kindred mouths have raised me into greatness.
Sprung from such lineage, none I heed beside,
Nor blush reluctant to explore my birth.

Enter Herdsman

Œd.   Approach, old man! look on me, and reply
To my demand. Wert thou the slave of Laius?

Herd.   I was his slave—bred in his house—not purchased.
My better part of life was passed in tending
The monarch's flocks.

Œd.   What regions wert thou then
Wont to frequent?

Herd.   Cithæron and the meads
Adjacent.

Cor.   Then answer, dost thou recollect the babe
Thou gav'st me there, as mine own child to cherish?

Herd.   What wouldst thou? Whither do thy questions tend?

Cor.   This is that child, my friend, who stands before thee.

Herd.   A curse light on thee! wilt thou not be silent?

Œd.   Reprove him not, old man, for thine own words,
Far more than his, demand a stern reprover.

Herd.   I did:—Oh, had that moment been my last!

Œd.   This shall be, if thou wilt not speak the truth.

Herd.   And if I speak it, I am trebly lost.

Œd.   This man, it seems, still struggles to elude us.

Herd.   No, I confessed long since I gave the child.

Œd.   And whence received? thine own, or from another?

Herd.   No, not mine own; I from another's hand
Bare him.

Œd.   And from what Theban, from what roof?

Herd.   Oh, by the gods! my lord, inquire no further.

Œd.   If I repeat th' inquiry, thou art lost.

Herd.   The palace of King Laius gave him birth.

Œd.   Sprung from a slave, or of the royal stock?

Herd.   The child was called the son of Laius; here
The royal consort can inform thee better.

Œd.   Didst thou from her receive him?

Herd.   Yea, O king!—

Œd.   And for what purpose?

Herd.   That I might destroy him—

Œd.   What—the unnatural mother!

Herd.   She was awed
By woe-denouncing oracles.

Œd.   What woe?

Herd.   That he should prove the murderer of his parents.

Œd.   Why, then, to this old man thy charge consign?

Herd.   From pity, O my lord, I deemed that he
To his own land would bear the child afar.
He saved him to despair. If thou art he
Of whom he spake, how dark a doom is thine!

Œd.   Woe! woe! 'tis all too fatally unveiled.
Thou Light! Oh, may I now behold thy beams
For the last time! Unhallowed was my birth;
In closest ties united, where such ties
Were most unnatural;—with that blood defiled,
From whose pollution most the heart recoils.

CARL SPITTELER

CARL SPITTELER (Swiss, 1845-1924). Swiss poet and essayist. A rebellious neo-classicist, whose position in German literature is still in dispute. Though he wrote both realistic and romantic works, his major career was spent on a modern Greek epic, *Olympian Spring.* A lonely and unusual figure. Nobel Prize-winner, 1919.

THEME

Bell, my silver tonguéd bell,
Oh, thy secret prithee tell:

Dwellst where bats and night-owls roam,
Lonely in thy moldered home;
Tell me, whence thy solemn ring?
And who taught thee, pray, to sing?

When in gloomy shaft I lay,
Night of hell I saw alway.
In this tower high and free
Through the whirling winds I see
Human sorrow graced by soul.
And thou wonderst why I toll?

"HERACLES PASSING TO EARTH"

But now the king the host of heralds did invite.
"The harpers bring, the singing maids, into my sight,
That Heracles unto the lovely sounds of mirth,
With courage fortified, may tread his way to earth!"
Before the gate there rose the buzz of strings subdued,
And laughter from the throat, as if a bird had cooed,
Betrayed the sportive singing-maidens' coming nigh.
Spake Zeus to Heracles: "It hurts to say good-by!"
And leads him to the court and fountain. At the brink
A little, and the rest he gives his son with cheer:
"Drink heartily!" he says, "this spring is true and clear!"
Then, with his hands upon the youthful shoulders: "Man!
Now let there happen what there will and come what can:
Into a royal font baptismal thou hast dipped,
And from the dripping fountain-flood of truth hast sipped.
That thou hast drunk with Zeus out of one glass today
The might of thousand rascals cannot wrench away.
In some dark hour shouldst thou in want of comfort be,
Look up, remember then: thou hast a bond with me
What I could do for thee is done. The retinue
That is to follow on thy way, come let us view."

With playing of the strings and bursts of song about,
Now from the house the king doth with his son step out.
Hark: cracks of whips and jingling! Plumes and pinions bold!
A chariot train of princely Titans now behold.
"I welcome ye!" spake Zeus. "What do ye bring me now?"
"We came the son of Zeus with talents to endow."
"Then thanks! For thus I know the way of kinsmen dear."
And now round Heracles the princes formed a sphere:
Nobility from Artemis and from Apollo
Comes valor, thought so keen that no mistake can follow
From Pallas—Hermes now his glance with kindness fills,
And Aphrodite mirth into his hearts instils.
Zeus spake and bound about the bosom of his son
The scroll of fate: "Now that thou really must be gone,
Receive my counsel: keep a stubborn head!
And be no simple fool—no rascal dread!"
The escorts then round Heracles with song and play
All turned into the fields to journey far away.
Ahead into the sky rang high the travel-song,
And golden grain looked down the hillsides all along.
No working-man, when Heracles did come in sight,
But sent to him some little words of kindness bright.
"Fare well on earth and prosper in the human land!"
And every lad ran toward him with outstreched hand.
A maiden laughs with eyes and mouth and checks—in zest
A bunch of flowers now she fastens to his breast.
And other human souls that came across his ways
At him with wonder in their dreamy eyes would gaze:
"Who cometh there whose steps sound victory so loud?
This hero's stature is of upright stock and proud!"
A maiden of the human beings one, but fairer
By far than all the other maidens be and rarer,
Drew near to him, her locks as if in slumber swaying,
And made him halt, upon his breast her finger laying.
Then pensively she bowed her forehead, sighing: "Oh,
Where is the street that we on earth do not yet know

1199

—Oh, tell me this, thou great unknown, oh tell thou me—
That over mountains, sombre forests, leads to thee?
If 'twere a thousand miles through many nights and days,
I would with quick'ning pulse o'ertake thee on thy ways.
If sharpest thorns should give me wounds, I would not bind
My bleeding foot at all, until I thee should find.
Forsee: on earth I know not where thou shalt be with me."
So I will go and dwell where thou shalt be with me."
Thus, dreaming, sighed the maid. Her speech was done; at last
She passed along her way with glances backward cast.
And Heracles, with all about him loving, kind,
In ecstasy of soul began within his mind:
"On earth I see a mountain looming to remind me.
A vow I'll make in solemn worship that shall bind me:
Ye joyous fields of high Olympos, beauty-bright,
Thou sky that floatest o'er the clouds in lofty height,
Ye dear ones all, unto my vow oh witness bear:
Now for my work I live, not for myself, I swear,
With heart and hands, nor rest nor pleasure taking more,
To love the great and do what ne'er was done before.
Oh, ye my human brothers, human sisters dear,
Your friend I'll be, your help devoted and sincere.
And no reward, except upon accomplished deed,
A silent, knowing glance but from the best, I need.
Hail, earth! I gladly pay the tax of pain you ask,
With courage spirited I come to do my task."
Thus cried he. Harps resounded, choirs rejoiced in song,
And through the folds of golden fields they passed along.

SSU-K'UNG T'U

SSÜ-K'UNG T'U (Chinese, 837-908). Scholarly pedantic stylist. Like many another Chinese poet, gave up an official career to write in retirement. His work shows great erudition rather than originality. Most famous: a 24-stanza poem, *Êrh-shih-ssu shih-p'in*.

RETURN OF SPRING

A lovely maiden, roaming
    The wild dark valley through,
Culls from the shining waters
    Lilies and lotus blue.
With leaves the peach-trees are laden,
    The wind sighs through the haze,
And the willows wave their shadows
    Down the oriole-haunted ways.
As, passion-tranced, I follow,
    I hear the old refrain
Of Spring's eternal story,
    That was old and is young again.

THE COLOUR OF LIFE

Would that we might for ever stay
The rainbow glories of the world,
The blue of the unfathomed sea,
The rare azalea late unfurled,
The parrot of a greener spring,
The willows and the terrace line,
The stranger from the night-steeped hills,
The roselit brimming cup of wine.
Oh for a life that stretched afar,
Where no dead dust of books were rife,
Where spring sang clear from star to star;
Alas! what hope for such a life?

SET FREE

I revel in flowers without let,
An atom at random in space;
My soul dwells in regions ethereal,
And the world is my dreaming-place.

As the tops of the ocean I tower,
As the winds of the air spreading wide,
I am 'stablished in might and dominion and power,
With the universe ranged at my side.

Before me the sun, moon, and stars,
Behind me the phœnix doth clang;
In the morning I lash my leviathans,
And I bathe my feet in Fusang.

FASCINATION

Fair is the pine grove and the mountain stream
That gathers to the valley far below,
The black-winged junks on the dim sea reach,
    adream,
The pale blue firmament o'er banks of snow.
And her, more fair, more supple smooth than jade,
Gleaming among the dark red woods I follow:
Now lingering, now as a bird afraid
Of pirate wings she seeks the haven hollow.
Vague, and beyond the daylight of recall,
Into the cloudland past my spirit flies,
As though before the gold of autumn's fall,
Before the glow of the moon-flooded skies.

TRANQUIL REPOSE

It dwells in the quiet silence,
    Unseen upon hill and plain,
'Tis lapped by the tideless harmonies,
    It soars with the lonely crane.

As the springtime breeze whose flutter
    The silken skirts hath blown,
As the wind-drawn note of the bamboo flute
    Whose charm we would make our own,—

Chance-met, it seems to surrender;
    Sought, and it lures us on;
Ever shifting in form and fantasy,
    It eludes us, and is gone.

JOHN ERNST STEINBECK

JOHN ERNST STEINBECK (1902-   ). Contemporary writer of powerful
sociological novels. Born in the California country celebrated in *Tortilla Flat*
and *Cannery Row*. Labored as newsman and bricklayer in New York. Best
works are infused with sympathy for the underprivileged. *Grapes of Wrath*,
epic of the dust bowl, has been compared with *Uncle Tom's Cabin*. Other
novels: *Of Mice and Men, The Pearl.*

OWNERS AND TENANTS

THE owners of the land had come onto the land, or more often a
spokesman for the owners came. They came in closed cars, and they
felt the dry earth with their fingers, and sometimes they drove big
earth augers into the ground for soil tests. The tenants from their
sun-beaten dooryards, watched uneasily when the closed cars drove
along the fields. And at last the owner men drove into the dooryards
and sat in their cars to talk out of the windows. The tenant men
stood beside the cars for a while, and then sqatted on their hams
and found sticks with which to mark the dust.

In the open doors the women stood looking out, and behind them
the children—corn-headed children, with wide eyes, one bare foot
on top of the other bare foot, and the toes working. The women
and the children watched their men talking to the owner men. They
were silent.

Some of the owner men were kind because they hated what they
had to do, and some of them were angry because they hated to be
cruel, and some of them were cold because they had long ago found
that one could not be an owner unless one were cold. And all of
them were caught in something larger than themselves. Some of
them hated the mathematics that drove them, and some were afraid,
and some worshiped the mathematics because it provided a refuge
from thought and from feeling. If a bank or a finance company
owned the land, the owner man said, The Bank—or the Company—
needs—wants—insists—must have— as though the Bank or the
Company were a monster, with thought and feeling, which had
ensnared them. These last would take no responsibility for the banks
or the companies because they were men and slaves, while the banks
were machines and masters all at the same time. Some of the owner
men were a little proud to be slaves to such cold and powerful masters. The owner men sat in the cars and explained. You know the
land is poor. You've scrabbled at it long enough, God knows.

The squatting tenant men nodded and wondered and drew figures in the dust, and yes, they knew, God knows. If the dust only wouldn't fly. If the top would only stay on the soil, it might not be so bad.

The owner men went on leading to their point: You know the land's getting poorer. You know what cotton does to the land; robs it, sucks all the blood out of it.

The squatters nodded—they knew, God knew. If they could only rotate the crops they might pump blood back into the land.

Well, it's too late. And the owner men explained the workings and thinkings of the monster that was stronger than they were. A man can hold land if he can just eat and pay taxes; he can do that.

Yes, he can do that until his crops fail one day and he has to borrow money from the bank.

But—you see, a bank or a company can't do that, because those creatures don't breathe air, don't eat side-meat. They breathe profits; they eat the interest on money. If they don't get it, they die the way you die without air, without side-meat. It is a sad thing, but it is so. It is just so.

The squatting men raised their eyes to understand. Can't we just hang on? Maybe the next year will be a good year. God knows how much cotton next year. And with all the wars—God knows what price cotton will bring. Don't they make explosives out of cotton? And uniforms? Get enough wars and cotton'll hit the ceiling. Next year, maybe. They looked up questioningly.

We can't depend on it. The bank—the monster has to have profits all the time. It can't wait. It'll die. No, taxes go on. When the monster stops growing, it dies. It can't stay one size.

Soft fingers began to tap the sill of the car window, and hard fingers tightened on the restless drawing sticks. In the doorways of the sun-beaten tenant houses, women sighed and shifted feet so that the one that had been down was now on top, and the toes working. Dogs came sniffing near the owner cars and wetted on all four tires one after another. And the chickens lay in the sunny dust and fluffed their feathers to get the cleansing dust down to the skin. In the little sties the pigs grunted inquiringly over the muddy remnants of the slops.

The squatting men looked down again. What do you want us to do? We can't take less share of the crop—we're half starved now. The kids are hungry all the times. We got no clothes, torn an' ragged. If all the neighbors weren't the same, we'd be ashamed to go to meeting.

1204

And at last the owner men came to the point. The tenant system won't work any more. One man on a tractor can take the place of twelve or fourteen families. Pay him a wage and take all the crop. We have to do it. We don't like to do it. But the monster's sick. Something's happened to the monster.

But you'll kill the land with cotton.

We know. We've got to take cotton quick before the land dies. Then we'll sell the land. Lots of families in the East would like to own a piece of land.

The tenant men looked up alarmed. But what'll happen to us? How'll we eat?

You'll have to get off the land. The plows'll go through the dooryard.

And now the squatting men stood up angrily. Grampa took up the land, and he had to kill the Indians and drive them away. And Pa was born here, and he killed weeds and snakes. Then a bad year came and he had to borrow a little money. An' we was born here. There in the door—our children born here. And Pa had to borrow money. The bank owned the land then, but we stayed and we got a little bit of what we raised.

We know that—all that. It's not us, it's the bank. A bank isn't like a man. Or an owner with fifty thousand acres, he isn't like a man either. That's the monster.

Sure, cried the tenant men, but it's our land. We measured it and broke it up. We were born on it, and we got killed on it, died on it. Even if it's no good, it's still ours. That's what makes it ours—being born on it, working it, dying on it. That makes ownership, not a paper with numbers on it.

We're sorry. It's not us. It's the monster. The bank isn't like a man.

Yes, but the bank is only made of men.

No, you're wrong there—quite wrong there. The bank is something else than men. It happens that every man in a bank hates what the bank does, and yet the bank does it. The bank is something more than men, I tell you. It's the monster. Men made it, but they can't control it.

The tenants cried: Grampa killed Indians, Pa killed snakes for the land. Maybe we can kill banks—they're worse than Indians and snakes. Maybe we got to fight to keep our land, like Pa and Grampa did.

And now the owner men grew angry. You'll have to go.

But it's ours, the tenant men cried. We—

No. The bank, the monster owns it. You'll have to go.

We'll get our guns, like Grandpa when the Indians came. What then?

Well—first the sheriff, and then the troops. You'll be stealing if you try to stay, you'll be murderers if you kill to stay. The monster isn't men, but it can make men do what it wants.

But if we go, where'll we go? How'll we go? We got no money.

We're sorry, said the owner men. The bank, the fifty-thousand-acre owner can't be responsible. You're on land that isn't yours. Once over the line maybe you can pick cotton in the fall. Maybe you can go on relief. Why don't you go on West to California? There's work there and it never gets cold. Why, you can reach out anywhere and pick an orange. Why, there's always some kind of crop to work in. Why don't you go there? And the owner men started their cars and rolled away.

The tenant men squatted down on their hams again to mark the dust with a stick, to figure, to wonder. Their sun-burned faces were dark, and their sun-whipped eyes were light. The women moved cautiously out of the door-ways towards their men, and the children crept behind the women, cautiously, ready to run. The bigger boys squatted beside their fathers, because that made them men. After a time the women asked, What did he want?

And the men looked up for a second, and the smolder of pain was in their eyes. We got to get off. A tractor and a superintendent. Like factories.

Where'll we go? the women asked.

We don't know. We don't know.

And the women went quickly, quietly back into the houses and herded the children ahead of them. They knew that a man so hurt and so perplexed may turn in anger, even on people he loves. They left the men alone to figure and wonder in the dust.

After a time perhaps the tenant man looked about—at the pump put in ten years ago, with a goose-neck handle and iron flowers on the spout, at the chopping block where a thousand chickens had been killed, at the hand plow lying in the shed, and the patent crib hanging in the rafters over it.

The children crowded about the women in the houses. What are we going to do, Ma? Where are we going to go?

The women said: We don't know, yet. Go out and play. But don't go near your father. He might whale you if you go near him. And

1206

the women went on with the work, but all the time they watched the men squatting in the dust—perplexed and figuring.

The tractors came over the roads and into the fields, great crawlers moving like insects, having the incredible strength of insects. They crawled over the ground, laying the track and rolling on it and picking it up. Diesel tractors, puttering while they stood idle; they thundered when they moved, and then settled down to a droning roar. Snub-nosed monsters, raising the dust and sticking their snouts into it, straight down the country, through fences, through dooryards, in and out of gullies in straight lines. They did not run on the ground, but on their own roadbeds. They ignored hills and gulches, water courses, fences, houses.

The man sitting in the iron seat did not look like a man; gloved, goggled, rubber dust mask over the nose and mouth, he was a part of the monster, a robot in the seat. The thunder of the cylinders sounded through the country, became one with the air and the earth, so that earth and air muttered in sympathetic vibration. The driver could not control it—straight across the country it went, cutting through a dozen farms and straight back. A twitch at the controls could swerve the cat, but the driver's hands could not twitch because the monster that built the tractor, the monster that sent the tractor out, had somehow got into the driver's hands, into his brain and muscle, had goggled him and muzzled him—goggled his mind, muzzled his speech, goggled his perception, muzzled his protest. He could not see the land as it was, he could not smell the land as it smelled; his feet did not stamp the clods or feel the warmth and power of the earth. He sat in an iron seat and stepped on iron pedals. He could not cheer or beat or curse or encourage the extension of his power, and because of this he could not cheer or whip or curse or encourage himself. He did not know or own or trust or beseech the land. If a seed dropped did not germinate, it was nothing. If the young trusting plant withered in drought or drowned in a flood of rain, it was no more to the driver than to the tractor.

He loved the land no more than the bank loved the land. He could admire the tractor—its machined surfaces, its surge of power, the roar of its detonating cylinders; but it was not his tractor. Behind the tractor rolled the shining disks, cutting the earth with blades—not plowing but surgery, pushing the cut earth to the right where

1207

the second row of disks cut it and pushed it to the left; slicing blades shining, polished by the cut earth. And pulled behind the disks, the harrows combing with iron teeth so that the little clods broke up and the earth lay smooth. Behind the harrows, the long seeders—twelve curved iron penes erected in the foundry, orgasms set by gears, raping methodically, raping without passion. The driver sat in his iron seat and he was proud of the straight lines he did not will, proud of the tractor he did not own or love, proud of the power he could not control. And when that crop grew, and was harvested, no man had crumbled a hot clod in his fingers and let the earth sift through his fingertips. No man had touched the seed, or lusted for the growth. Men ate what they had not raised, had no connection with the bread. The land bore under iron, and under iron gradually died; for it was not loved or hated, it had no prayers or curses.

At noon the tractor driver stopped sometimes near a tenant house and opened his lunch; sandwiches wrapped in waxed paper, white bread, pickle, cheese, Spam, a piece of pie branded like an engine part. He ate without relish. And tenants not yet moved away came out to see him, looked curiously while the goggles were taken off, and the rubber dusk mask, leaving white circles around the eyes and a large white circle around nose and mouth. The exhaust of the tractor putted on, for fuel is so cheap it is more efficient to leave the engine running than to heat the Diesel nose for a new start. Curious children crowded close, ragged children who ate their fried dough as they watched. They watch hungrily the unwrapping of the sandwiches, and their hunger-sharpened noses smelled the pickle, cheese, and Spam. They didn't speak to the driver. They watched his hand as it carried food to his mouth. They did not watch him chewing; their eyes followed the hand that held the sandwich. After a while the tenant who could not leave the place came out and squatted in the shade beside the tractor.

"Why, you're Joe Davis's boy!"

"Sure," the driver said.

"Well, what are you doing this kind of work for—against your own people?"

"Three dollars a day. I got damn sick of creeping for my dinner —and not getting it. I got a wife and kids. We got to eat. Three dollars a day, and it comes every day."

"That's right," the tenant said. "But for your three dollars a day fifteen or twenty families can't eat at all. Nearly a hundred people have to go out and wander on the roads for your three dollars a day. Is that right?"

And the driver said, "Can't think of that. Got to think of my own kids. Three dollars a day, and it comes every day. Times are changing, mister, don't you know? Can't make a living on the land unless you've got two, five, ten thousand acres and a tractor. Crop land isn't for little guys like us any more. You don't kick up a howl because you can't make Fords, or because you're not the telephone company. Well, crops are like that now. Nothing to do about it. You try to get three dollars a day someplace. That's the only way."

The tenant pondered. "Funny thing how it is. If a man owns a little property, the property is him, it's part of him, and it's like him. If he owns property only so he can walk on it and handle it and be sad when it isn't doing well, and feel fine when the rain falls on it, the property is him, and someway he's bigger because he owns it. Even if he isn't successful he's big with his property. That is so."

And the tenant pondered more. "But let a man get property he doesn't see, or can't take time to get his fingers in, or can't be there to walk on it—why, then the property is the man. He can't do what he wants, he can't think what he wants. The property is the man, stronger than he is. And he is small, not big. Only his possessions are big—and he's the servant of his property. That is so, too."

The driver munched the branded pie and threw the crust away. "Times are changed, don't you know? Thinking about stuff like that don't feed the kids. Get your three dollars a day, feed your kids. You got no call to worry about anybody's kids but your own. You get a reputation for talking like that, and you'll never get three dollars a day. Big shots won't give you three dollars a day if you worry about anything but your three dollars a day."

"Nearly a hundred people on the road for your three dollars. Where will we go?"

"And that reminds me," the driver said, "you'd better get out soon. I'm going through the dooryard after dinner."

"You filled in the well this morning."

"I know. Had to keep the line straight. But I'm going through the dooryard after dinner. Got to keep the lines straight. And— well, you know Joe Davis, my old man, so I'll tell you this. I got orders wherever there's a family not moved out—if I have an

accident—you know, get too close and cave the house in a little—well, I might get a couple of dollars. And my youngest kid never had no shoes yet."

"I built it with my hands. Straightened old nails to put the sheathing on. Rafters are wired to the stringers with baling wire. It's mine. I built it. You bump it down—I'll be in the window with a rifle. You even come too close and I'll pot you like a rabbit."

"It's not me. There's nothing I can do. I'll lose my job if I don't do it. And look—suppose you kill me? They'll just hang you, but long before you're hung there'll be another guy on the tractor, and he'll bump the house down. You're not killing the right guy."

"That's so," the tenant said. "Who gave you orders? I'll go after him. He's the one to kill."

"You're wrong. He got his orders from the bank. The bank told him, 'Clear those people out or it's your job!'"

"Well, there's a president of the bank. There's a board of directors. I'll fill up the magazine of the rifle and go into the bank."

The driver said, "Fellow was telling me the bank gets orders from the East. The orders were, 'Make the land show profit or we'll close you up.'"

"But where does it stop? Who can we shoot? I don't aim to starve to death before I kill the man that's starving me."

"I don't know. Maybe there's nobody to shoot. Maybe the thing isn't men at all. Maybe, like you said, the property's doing it. Anyway I told you my orders."

"I got to figure," the tenant said. "We all got to figure. There's some way to stop this. It's not like lightning or earthquakes. We've got a bad thing made by men, and by God that's something we can change." The tenant sat in his doorway, and the driver thundered his engine and started off, tracks falling and curving, harrows combing, and the phalli of the seeder slipping into the ground. Across the dooryard the tractor cut, and the hard, foot-beaten ground was seeded field, and the tractor cut through again: the uncut space was ten feet wide. And back he came. The iron guard bit into the house-corner, crumbled the wall, and wrenched the little house from its foundation so that it fell sideways, crushed like a bug. And the driver was goggled and a rubber mask covered his nose and mouth. The tractor cut a straight line on, and the air and the ground vibrated with its thunder. The tenant man stared after it, his rifle in his hand. His wife was beside him, and the quiet children behind. And all of them stared after the tractor.

STENDHAL

STENDHAL (Marie-Henri Beyle, French, 1783-1842). Forerunner of the modern novel. Rejecting provincial life, became soldier under Bonaparte, later a French consul. As a novelist, possessed acute psychological insight, a disenchanted viewpoint. In his two masterpieces, *Le Rouge et le Noir* and *La Chartreuse de Parme*, the "Stendhal hero" is always at odds with his world.

THE CHARTREUSE OF PARMA

I.—Fabrice del Dongo

"THREE members of your family," said Count Mosca to the Duchess of Sanseverina, "have been Archbishops of Parma. Could a better career be open to your nephew Fabrice?"

The Duchess disliked the notion; and indeed Fabrice del Dongo seemed a person but little fitted for an ecclesiastical career. His ambitions were military; his hero was Napoleon. The great escapade of his life had been a secret journey into France to fight at Waterloo. His father, the Marquis del Dongo, was loyal to the Austrian masters of Lombardy; and during Fabrice's absence his elder brother Arcanio had laid an information against him as a conspirator against Austrian rule. Consequently Fabrice, on his return, found himself exposed to the risk of ten years in an Austrian prison. By his own address and by the good offices of his aunt, the Countess Pietravera, Fabrice was able to escape from Milanese territory.

Immediately afterwards the Countess wedded the aged and wealthy Duke of Sanseverina, and transferred her beauty and unbounded social talents from Milan to the court of Prince Ranuce Ernest IV., absolute ruler of Parma. The Duke had his ambitions gratified by an appointment as Ambassador to a distant country; the Duchess, left behind at Parma, was able to devote herself to the interests of Count Mosca, the Prince's chief Minister, and to counteract the intrigues of the celebrated Marchioness Raversi, head of the party that sought to overthrow him.

The welfare of her beloved nephew was the most cherished of all the Duchess's aims, and she succeeded in inspiring Count Mosca with an equal enthusiasm for the prosperity of that errant youth. But she hesitated over the project of making him an Archbishop.

"You must understand," explained the Count, "that I do not intend to make Fabrice an exemplary priest of the conventional kind.

No, he will above all remain a great noble; he may continue to be absolutely ignorant if he so pleases, and will become a Bishop and an Archbishop just the same—provided, of course, that I succeed in retaining the Prince's confidence."

Ultimately the Duchess agreed, and undertook to persuade Fabrice to enter the Church. The persuasion was not easy; but at length Fabrice, having been convinced that the clerical yoke would bear but lightly upon him, consented to the step, and as a preliminary spent three years in a theological college at Naples.

When at the end of three years Fabrice, now a Monsignore, returned to Parma, matters there were at a crisis; the Raversi party were gaining ground, and Count Mosca was in danger. Nor did the Prince's interview with the young cleric improve matters. Ranuce Ernest IV. had two ruling passions—an ambition to become ruler of united Italy, and a fear of revolution. Count Mosca, the diplomatist, was the only man who could further his hopes in one direction; his fears in the other were carefully kept alive by Rassi, the fiscal-general—to such an extent that each night the Prince looked under his bed to see if by chance a liberal were lurking there. Rassi was a man of low origin, who kept his place partly by submitting good-humouredly to the abuse and even the kicks of his master, and partly by rousing that master's alarms and afterwards allaying them by hanging or imprisoning liberals, with the ready assistance of a carefully corrupted judicial bench.

Towards this nervous Prince, Fabrice bore himself with an aristocratic assurance, and a promptness and coolness in conversation that made a bad impression. His political notions were correct enough, according to the Prince's standard; but plainly, he was a man of spirit, and the Prince did not like men of spirit; they were all cousins-germane of Voltaire and Rousseau. He deemed Fabrice, in short, a potential if not an actual liberal, and therefore dangerous.

Nevertheless Count Mosca carried the day against his rivals— a triumph due less to his own efforts than to those of the Duchess, to whose charms as the court's chief ornament the Prince was far from insusceptible. The Count's success was Fabrice's; that youth found himself established as co-adjutor to the Archbishop of Parma, with a reversion to the Archbishopric on the demise of its worthy occupant.

On Fabrice's return from Naples, the Duchess had found him developed from a boy into a young man, and the handsomest young

man in Italy; her affection for him became sisterly; she was nearly in love with him. She had no cause for jealousy, for Fabrice, although prone to flirtation, had no affairs of the heart. The word love, as yet, had no meaning for him.

II.—Giletti

One of our hero's flirtations had consequences with a very pronounced bearing on his after career. During a surreptitious visit to the theatre he became captivated with the actress, Marietta Valserra. Stolen visits of two minutes' duration to Marietta's lodging on the fourth floor of an old house behind the theatre were an agreeable variation of the monotony of Fabrice's clerical duties, and of his visits among the most important and least entertaining families in Parma. But the trifling little intrigue came to the ears of Count Mosca, with the result that the travelling company to which Marietta belonged received its passports and was requested to move on.

In the affair, moreover, Fabrice had a rival. Giletti was the low comedian of the company, and the ugliest member of it; he assumed proprietorship over Marietta, who, although she did not love him, was at any rate horribly afraid of him. Giletti several times threatened to kill Fabrice; whereby Fabrice was not disturbed.

Count Mosca was passionately archæological, and this taste he shared with Fabrice, who had cultivated the hobby at Naples. It so happened that the two were engaged in excavations near the bridge over the Po where the main road passes into Austrian territory at Castel-Maggiore. Early one morning Fabrice, after surveying the work that was going on in the trenches, strolled away with a gun, intent upon lark-shooting. A wounded bird dropped on the road; and as Fabrice followed it he encountered a battered old carriage driving towards the frontier. In it were Giletti, Marietta and an old woman who passed as Marietta's mother.

Giletti leapt to the conclusion that Fabrice had come there, gun in hand, to insult him, and possibly to carry off Marietta. He leapt out of the carriage.

"Brigand!" he yelled, "we are only a league from the frontier—now I can finish you!"

Fabrice saw a pistol levelled at him at a distance of three feet; he knocked it aside with the butt of his gun, and it went off harmlessly. Giletti then clutched the gun; the two men wrestled for it, and it exploded close to Giletti's ear. Staggered for an instant, he

1213

quickly recovered himself; drawing from its sheath a "property" sword, he fell once more upon Fabrice.

"Look out! he will kill you," came an agitated whisper from Marietta; "take this!"

A sort of hunting knife was flung out of the carriage door. Fabrice picked it up, and was nearly stunned forthwith by a blow from the handle of the "property" sword. Happily Giletti was too near to use his sword-point. Pulling himself together, Fabrice gave his enemy a gash on the thigh. Giletti, swearing furiously, injured Fabrice on the cheek. Blood poured down our hero's face. The thought, "I am disfigured for life!" flashed through his mind. Enraged at the idea, he thrust the hunting knife at Giletti's breast with all his force. Giletti fell and lay motionless.

"He is dead!" said Fabrice to himself. Then, turning to the coach, he asked, "Have you a looking-glass?"

His eyes and teeth were undamaged; he was not permanently disfigured. Hastily, then, he turned to thoughts of escape. Marietta gave him Giletti's passport; obviously his first business was to get across the frontier. And yet the Austrian frontier was no safe one for him to cross. Were he recognised, he might expect ten years in an Imperial fortress. But this was the less immediate danger, and he determined to risk it.

With considerable trepidation he walked across the bridge, and presented Giletti's passport to the Austrian gendarme.

The gendarme looked at it, and rose, "You must wait, monsieur; there is a difficulty," he said, and left the room. Fabrice was profoundly uncomfortable; he was nearly for bolting, when he heard the gendarme say to another, "I am done up with the heat; just go and put your visa on a passport in there when you have finished your pipe; I'm going for some coffee."

This gendarme, in fact, knew Giletti, and was quite well aware that the man before him was not the actor. But, for all he could tell, Giletti had lent the passport for reasons of his own. The easiest way out of the difficulty was to get another gendarme to see to the visa. This man affixed it as a matter of course, and Fabrice escaped danger number one.

The rest was very easy, thanks to Ludovico, an old servant of the Duchess, whom Fabrice met at an eating-house where he had turned in for some very necessary refreshment. With the aid of this excellent fellow Fabrice had his wounds attended to, and was safely smuggled out of Austrian territory into Bologna.

The party opposed to Count Mosca hastened to take advantage of Fabrice's offence. He was represented as a murderer; the workmen in the trenches who had seen the affray, and knew that Fabrice had acted in self-defence, were either bribed or got out of the way. Rassi accused Fabrice of being a liberal; and since the Prince was ill-disposed towards the young man, not all the endeavours of Count Mosca could save him from a sentence of twenty years' imprisonment, should he be so impudent as to venture upon the territory of Parma.

Just before the sentence was presented to the Prince for final confirmation, the Prince learned that the Dutchess of Sanseverina sought an audience with him. He rubbed his hands; the greatest beauty of his court had come to beg mercy for her nephew; there would be tears and frantic appeals. For a quarter of an hour the Prince gloated over the prospect; then he ordered that the Duchess be admitted.

She entered—in travelling costume; never had she looked more charming, never more cheerful. "I trust your Serene Highness will pardon my unorthodox costume," she said, smiling archly; "but as I am about to leave Parma for a very long time, I have felt it my duty to come and thank you ere I go for all the kindnesses you have deigned to confer upon me."

The Prince was astonished and profoundly chagrined. "Why are you going?" he asked, as calmly as he could.

"I have had the project for some time," she replied, "and a little insult paid to Monsignor del Dongo has hastened it."

The Prince was beside himself. What would his court be without the Duchess? At all costs he much check her flight.

At this moment Count Mosca, pale with anxiety, begged admittance. He had just heard of the Duchess's intention to leave Parma.

"Let me speak as a friend to friends," said the Prince, collecting himself; "what can I do, Madame, to arrest your hasty resolution?"

"If your highness were to write a gracious letter revoking the unjust sentence upon Fabrice del Dongo, I might re-consider my decision; and, let me add, if the Marchioness Raversi were advised by you to retire to the country early to-morrow morning for the benefit of her health—"

"Was there ever such a woman?" cried the Prince, stamping up and down the room.

But he agreed. At his orders Count Mosca sat down and wrote the letter required. The Prince objected to the phrase "unjust sentence," and Count Mosca, courtier-like, abstained from using it. The Prince did not mind the banishment of the Marchioness Raversi; he liked exiling people.

At seven o'clock next morning the Prince summoned Rassi, and dictated to him another letter. The sentence of twenty years, upon the criminal del Dongo was to be reduced by the Prince's clemency, at the supplication of the Duchess Sanseverina, to twelve years; and the police were instructed to do their utmost to arrest the offender.

The only difficulty was that of tempting Fabrice into the territory of Parma. A hint to the Marchioness Raversi and her associates removed the obstacle. A forged letter, purporting to be from the Duchess, reached Fabrice at Bologna, telling him that there would be little danger in his meeting her at Castelnovo, within the frontier. Fabrice repaired joyfully to Castelnovo. That night he lay a prisoner in the citadel of Parma; while the Duchess, alone in her room with locked door, sobbed her heart out and raved helplessly against the treachery of princes.

"So long as her nephew is in the citadel," said the Prince to himself, "the Duchess will be in Parma."

The citadel of Parma is a colossal building with a flat roof 180 feet above the level of the ground. On this roof are erected two structures: one, the governor's residence; the other, the Farnese tower, a prison specially erected for a recalcitrant prince of earlier days. In this tower Fabrice, as a prisoner of importance, was confined; and as he looked from the window on the evening of his arrival and beheld the superb panorama of the distant Alps, he reflected pleasantly that he might have found a worse dungeon.

On the next morning his attention was absorbed by something nearer at hand. His window overlooked one belonging to the governor's palace; in this window were many bird cages, and at eleven o'clock a maiden came to feed the birds. Fabrice recognised her as Clelia Conti, the governor's daughter. He succeeding in attracting her attention; she blushed and withdrew. But next day she came again at the same hour. On the third day, however, a heavy wooden shutter was clapped upon the window. Nothing daunted, Fabrice proceeded patiently to cut a peep-hole in the shutter by aid of the main-spring of his watch. When he had succeeded in removing

a square piece of the wood, he looked with delight upon Clelia gazing at his window with eyes of profound pity, unconscious that she was observed.

Gradually he broke down the maiden's reserve. She discovered the secret of the peep-hole; she consented to communicate with him; finally the two conversed by a system of signals. Fabrice even dared to tell Clelia that he loved her—and truly he was in love, for the first time in his life. The worst of it was that these declarations were apt to bring the conversation to an end; so Fabrice was sparing of them.

Clelia, meanwhile, was in sore perplexity. Her father, General Fabio Conti the governor, was a political opponent of Count Mosca, and had ambitions of office. These ambitions might be forwarded, he deemed, by the successful marriage of his daughter. He did not desire that she should remain a lovely recluse, feeding birds at the top of the citadel. Accordingly he had presented to her an ultimatum; either she must marry the Marquis Crescenzi, the wealthiest nobleman of Parma, who sought her hand, or she must retire to a convent.

The signalled conversation with Fabrice, therefore, could not last long. And yet she had beyond doubt fallen deeply in love with Fabrice. She knew he was her father's prisoner, and belonged to the party hostile to her father; she was ashamed, as a daughter, of her love for him. But she admired him, and pitied him; she was well aware that he was a victim of political intrigue, for why should a nobleman of Fabrice's standing be thus punished for killing a mere actor? The stolen interviews with the captive were as dear to her as to him; and so dear were they to him that, after months of imprisonment he declared that he had never been so happy in his life.

IV.—The Escape

One night, as Fabrice looked through his peep-hole, he became aware of a light flashing from the town. Obviously some attempt was being made at signalling. He observed the flashes, counting them in relation to the order of the letters in the alphabet—one for A, two for B, and so on. He discovered that the message was from the Duchess, and was directed to himself. He replied, on the same system, by passing his lantern in front of the peep-hole. The answer from the distance was important; arrangements were being made for his escape. But he did not want to escape.

Next day he told Clelia of his message, and of his unwillingness to leave the prison. She gave no answer, but burst into tears. How could she tell him that she herself must presently leave—for marriage or a convent?

Next day, Fabrice, by his goaler's connivance, received a long letter from Clelia. She urged him to escape, declaring that at any time the Prince might order his execution, and in addition that he was in danger of death by poison. Straightway he sought an interview with Clelia, with whom he had not hitherto conversed save by signals from their windows. The goaler arranged that they should meet when Fabrice was being conducted from his cell to the roof of the Farnese tower, where he was occasionally allowed to take exercise.

"I can speak but few words to you," she said trembling, with tears in her eyes. "Swear that you will obey the Duchess, and escape when she wishes and as she wishes."

"And condemn myself to live far away from her whom I love?"

"Swear it! for my sake, swear it!" she implored him.

"Well then, I swear it!"

The preparations were quickly advanced. Three knotted ropes were smuggled with Clelia's aid into Fabrice's cell—one for descending the 35 feet between his window and the roof of the citadel; another for descending the tremendous wall of 180 feet between the roof and the ramparts; a third for the 30 feet between the top of the ramparts and the ground.

A feast-day, when the garrison of the citadel would presumably be drunk, was chosen for the attempt. Fabrice spent the time of waiting in cutting a hole in his shutter large enough to enable him to get through. Fortunately, on the night of the feast-day a thick fog arose and enveloped the citadel. The Duchess had seen to it that the garrison was plentifully supplied with wine.

Fabrice attached one of the shorter ropes to his bed, and struggled through the shutter—an ungainly figure, for round his body were wound the immense ropes necessary for the long descent. Once on the roof-platform he made his way along the parapet until he came to a new stove which he had been told marked the best spot for lowering the rope. He could hear the soldiers talking near at hand, but the fog made him invisible. Unrolling his rope, and fastening his rope to the parapet by threading it through a water-duct, he flung it over; then, with a prayer and a thought of Clelia, he began to descend.

At first he went down mechanically, as if doing the feat for a wager. About half-way down his arms seemed to lose their strength; he nearly let go—he might have fallen had he not supported himself by clinging to the vegetation on the wall. From time to time he felt horrible pain between the shoulders. Birds hustled against him now and then; he feared at the first contact with them that pursuers were coming down the rope after him. But he reached the rampart undamaged save for bleeding hands.

He was quite exhausted; for a few minutes he slept. On waking and realising the situation, he attached his third rope to a cannon, and hurried down to the ground. Two men seized him just as he fainted at the foot.

A few hours afterwards a carriage crossed the frontier with Ludovico on the box, and within it the Duchess watching over the sleeping Fabrice. The journey did not end until they had reached Locarno on Lake Maggiore.

V.—Clelia's Vow

To Locarno soon afterwards came the news that Ranuce Ernest IV. was dead. Fabrice could now safely return, for the young Ranuce Ernest V. was believed to be entirely under the influence of Count Mosca, and was an honest youth without the tyrannical instincts of his father. Nevertheless the Duchess returned first, to make certain of Fabrice's security. She employed her whole influence to hasten forward the wedding of Clelia with the Marquis Crescenzi; she was jealous of the ascendancy the girl had gained over her beloved nephew.

Fabrice, on reaching Parma, was well received by the young Prince. Witnesses, he was told, had been found who could prove that he had killed Giletti in self defence. He would spend a few days in a purely nominal confinement in the city goal, and then would be tried by impartial judges and released.

Imagine the consternation of the Duchess when she learnt that Fabrice, having to go to prison, had deliberately given himself up at the citadel!

She saw the danger clearly. Fabrice was in the hands of Count Mosca's political opponents, among whom General Conti was still a leading spirit. They would not suffer him to escape this time. Fabrice would be poisoned.

Clelia, too, knew that this would be his fate. When she saw him once again at the old window, happily signalling to her, she was smitten with panic terror. Her alarm was realised when she learnt of a plot between Rassi and her father to poison the prisoner.

On the second day of his confinement Fabrice was about to eat his dinner when Clelia, in desperate agitation, forced her way into his cell.

"Have you tasted it?" she cried, grasping his arm.

Fabrice guessed the state of affairs with delight. He seized her in his arms and kissed her.

"Help me to die," he said.

"Oh, my beloved," she answered, "let me die with you."

"Let me not spoil our happiness with a lie," said he as he embraced her. "I have not yet tasted."

For an instant Clelia looked at him in anger; then she fell into his arms.

At that instant there came a sound of men hurrying. There entered the Prince's aide-de-camp, with order to remove Fabrice from the citadel and to seize the poisoned food. The Duchess had heard of the plot, and had persuaded the Prince to take instant action.

Clelia, when her father was in danger of death on account of the plot, vowed before the Virgin Mary never again to look upon the face of Fabrice. Her father escaped with a sentence of banishment; and Clelia, to the profound satisfaction of the Duchess, was wedded to the Marquis Crescenzi. The Duchess was now a widow, Count Mosca a widower. Their long friendship, after Fabrice's acquittal, was cemented by marriage.

The loss of Clelia left Fabrice inconsolable. He shunned society; he lived a life of religious retirement, and gained a reputation for piety that even inspired the jealousy of his good friend the Archbishop.

At length Fabrice emerged from his solitude; he came forth as a preacher, and his success was unequalled. All Parma, gentle and simple, flocked to hear the famous devotee—slender, ill-clad, so handsome and yet so profoundly melancholy. And ere he began each sermon, Fabrice looked earnestly round his congregation to see if Clelia was there.

But Clelia, adhering to her vow, stayed away. It was not until she was told that a certain Anetta Marini was in love with the

preacher, and that gossip asserted that the preacher was smitten with Anetta Marini, that she changed her mind.

One evening, as Fabrice stood in the pulpit, he saw Clelia before him. Her eyes were filled with tears; he looked so pale, so thin, so worn. But never had he preached as he preached that night.

After the sermon he received a note asking him to be at a small garden door of the Crescenzi Palace at midnight on the next night. Eagerly he obeyed; when he reached the door, a voice called him to enter. The darkness was intense; he could see nothing.

"I have asked you to come here," said the voice, "to say that I still love you. But I have vowed to the Virgin never to see your face; that is why I receive you in this darkness. And let me beg you—never preach before Anetta Marini."

"My angel," replied the enraptured Fabrice, "I shall never preach again before anyone; it was only in the hope of seeing you that I preached at all."

During the following three years the two often met in darkness. But twice, by accident, Clelia broke her vow by looking on Fabrice's face. Her conscience preyed upon her; she wore away and died.

A few days afterwards Fabrice resigned his reversion to the Archbishopric, and retired to the Chartreuse of Parma. He ended his days in the monastery only a year afterwards.

WALLACE STEVENS

WALLACE STEVENS (American, 1879-1955). Poet of enchanting imagery. Educated for the law, spent most of life with an insurance company. Was slow winning recognition—first from other poets, finally from reading public. Now acknowledged one of important American poets. Books of verse: *Harmonium, Ideas of Order, Parts of a World.*

DOMINATION OF BLACK

At night, by the fire,
The colors of the bushes
And of the fallen leaves,
Repeating themselves,
Turned in the room,

Like the leaves themselves
Turning in the wind.
Yes: but the color of the heavy hemlocks
Came striding.
And I remembered the cry of the peacocks.

The colors of their tails
Were like the leaves themselves
Turning in the wind.
In the twilight wind.
They swept over the room,
Just as they flew from the boughs of the hemlocks
Down to the ground.
I heard them cry—the peacocks.
Was it a cry against the twilight
Or against the leaves themselves
Turning in the wind.
Turning as the flames
Turned in the fire,
Turning as the tails of the peacocks
Turned in the loud fire,
Loud as the hemlocks
Full of the cry of the peacocks,
Or was it a cry against the hemlocks.

Out of the window,
I saw how the planets gathered
Like the leaves themselves
Turning in the wind.
I saw how the night came,
Came striding like the color of the heavy hemlocks.
I felt afraid.
And I remembered the cry of the peacocks.

AN EXTRACT

from Addresses to the Academy of Fine Ideas

On an early Sunday in April, a feeble day,
He felt curious about the winter hills
And wondered about the water in the lake.

It had been cold since December. Snow fell first,
At New Year and, from then until April, lay
On everything. Now it had melted, leaving
The gray grass like a pallet, closely pressed;
And dirt. The wind blew in the empty place.
The winter wind blew in an empty place—
There was that difference between the and an,
The difference between himself and no man,
No man that heard a wind in an empty place.
It was time to be himself again, to see
If the place, in spite of its witheredness, was still
Within the difference. He felt curious
Whether the water was black and lashed about
Or whether the ice still covered the lake. There was still
Snow under the trees and on the northern rocks,
The dead rocks, not the green rocks, the live rocks. If,
When he looked, the water ran up the air or grew white
Against the edge of the ice, the abstraction would
Be broken and winter would be broken and done,
And being would be being himself again,
Being, becoming seeing and feeling and self,
Black water breaking into reality.

ANECDOTE OF THE JAR

I placed a jar in Tennessee,
And round it was, upon a hill.
It made the slovenly wilderness
Surround that hill.

The wilderness rose up to it,
And sprawled around, no longer wild.
The jar was round upon the ground
And tall and of a port in air.

It took dominion everywhere.
The jar was gray and bare.
It did not give of bird or bush,
Like nothing else in Tennessee.

ROBERT LOUIS STEVENSON

ROBERT LOUIS STEVENSON (Scottish, 1850-1894). Writer of essays and
novels in the Scott-Dumas manner. A sickly traveler, who died in the South
Seas. Affectionately venerated by his generation. Most popular work: adventure
novel, *Treasure Island*. First-rate tales of supernatural: *Dr. Jekyll and Mr.
Hyde* and *Thrawn Janet*.

THRAWN JANET

THE Reverend Murdoch Soulis was long minister of the moorland
parish of Balweary, in the vale of Dule. A severe, bleak-faced old
man, dreadful to his hearers, he dwelt in the last years of his life,
without relative or servant or any human company, in the small and
lonely manse under the Hanging Shaw. In spite of the iron
composure of his features, his eye was wild, seared, and uncertain;
and when he dwelt, in private admonitions, on the future of the
impenitent, it seemed as if his eye pierced through the storms of
time to the terrors of eternity. Many young persons, coming to
prepare themselves against the season of the Holy Communion,
were dreadfully affected by his talk. He had a sermon on 1st Peter, v.
and 8th, "The devil as a roaring lion," on the Sunday after every
seventeenth of August, and he was accustomed to surpass himself
upon that text both by the appalling nature of the matter and the
terror of his bearing in the pulpit. The children were frightened
into fits, and the old looked more than usually oracular, and were,
all that day, full of those hints that Hamlet deprecated. The manse
itself, where it stood by the water of Dule among some thick trees,
with the Shaw overhanging it on the one side, and on the other
many cold, moorish hilltops rising toward the sky, had begun, at
a very early period of Mr. Soulis's ministry, to be avoided in the
dusk hours by all who valued themselves upon their prudence; and
guidmen sitting at the clachan alehouse shook their heads together
at the thought of passing late by that uncanny neighborhood. There
was one spot, to be more particular, which was regarded with
special awe. The manse stood between the high road and the water
of Dule, with a gable to each; its back was toward the kirktown
of Balweary, nearly half a mile away; in front of it, a bare garden,
hedged with thorn, occupied the land between the river and the road.
The house was two stories high, with two large rooms on each. It
opened not directly on the garden, but on a causewayed path, or
passage, giving on the road on the one hand, and closed on the

other by the tall willows and elders that bordered on the stream. And it was this strip of causeway that enjoyed among the young parishioners of Balweary so infamous a reputation. The minister walked there often after dark, sometimes groaning aloud in the instancy of his unspoken prayers; and when he was from home, and the manse door was locked, the more daring schoolboys ventured, with beating hearts, to "follow my leader" across that legendary spot.

This atmosphere of terror, surrounding, as it did, a man of God of spotless character and orthodoxy, was a common cause of wonder and subject of inquiry among the few strangers who were led by chance or business into that unknown, outlying country. But many even of the people of the parish were ignorant of the strange events which had marked the first year of Mr. Soulis's ministrations; and among those who were better informed, some were naturally reticent, and others shy of that particular topic. Now and again, only, one of the older folk would warm into courage over his third tumbler, and recount the cause of the minister's strange looks and solitary life.

Fifty years syne, when Mr. Soulis cam' first into Ba'weary, he was still a young man—a callant, the folk said—fu' o' book learnin' and grand at the exposition, but, as was natural in sae young man, wi' nae leevin' experience in religion. The younger sort were greatly taken wi' his gifts and his gab; but auld, concerned, serious men and women were moved even to prayer for the young man, whom they took to be a self-deceiver, and the parish that was like to be sae ill-supplied. It was before the days o' the moderates—weary fa' them; but ill things are like guid—they baith come bit by bit, a pickle at a time; and there were folk even then that said the Lord had left the college professors to their ain devices, an' the lads that went to study wi' them wad hae done mair and better sittin' in a peat-bog, like their forebears of the persecution, wi' a Bible under their oxter and a speerit o' prayer in their heart. There was nae doubt, onyway, but that Mr. Soulis had been ower lang at the college. He was careful and troubled for mony things besides the ae thing needful. He had a feck o' books wi' him—mair than had ever been seen before in a' that presbytery; and a sair wark the carrier had wi' them, for they were a' like to have smoored in the Deil's Hag between this and Kilmackerlie. They were books o' divinity, to be sure, or so they ca'd them; but the serious were o' opinion

1225

there was little service for sae mony, when the hail o' God's Word would gang in the neuk of a plaid. Then he wad sit half the day and half the nicht forbye, which was scant decent—writin', nae less; and first, they were feared he wad read his sermons; and syne it proved he was writin' a book himsel', which was surely no fittin' for ane of his years an' sma' experience.

Onyway it behooved him to get an auld, decent wife to keep the manse for him an' see to his bit denners; and he was recommended to an auld limmer—Janet M'Clour, they ca'd her—and sae far left to himsel' as to be ower persuaded. There was mony advised him to the contrar, for Janet was mair than suspeckit by the best folk in Ba'weary. Lang or that, she had had a wean to a dragoon; she hadnae come forrit for maybe thretty year; and bairns had seen her mumblin' to hersel' up on Key's Loan in the gloamin', whilk was an unco time an' place for a God-fearin' woman. Howsoever, it was the laird himsel' that had first tauld the minister o' Janet; and in thae days he wad have gane a far gate to pleesure the laird. When folk tauld him that Janet was sib to the deil, it was a' superstition by his way of it; an' when they cast up the Bible to him an' the witch of Endor, he wad threep it doun their thrapples that thir days were a' gane by, and the deil was mercifully restrained.

Weel, when it got about the clachan that Janet M'Clour was to be servant at the manse, the folk were fair mad wi' her an' him thegether; and some o' the guidwives had nae better to dae than get round her door cheeks and chairge her wi' a' that was ken't again her, frae the sodger's bairn to John Tamson's twa kye. She was nae great speaker; folk usually let her gang her ain gate, an' she let them gang theirs, wi' neither Fair-guid-een nor Fair-guid-day; but when she buckled to she had a tongue to deave the miller. Up she got, an' there wasnae an auld story in Ba'weary but she gart somebody lowp for it that day; they couldnae say ae thing but she could say twa to it; till, at the hinder end, the guidwives up and claught haud of her, and clawed the coats aff her back, and pu'd her doun the clachan to the water o' Dule, to see if she were a witch or no, soum or droun. The carline skirled till ye could hear her at the Hangin' Shaw, and she focht like ten; there was mony a guidwife bure the mark of her neist day, an' mony a lang day after; and just in the hettest o' the collieshangie, wha suld come up (for his sins) but the new minister.

"Women," said he (and he had a grand voice), "I charge you in the Lord's name to let her go."

1226

Janet ran to him—she was fair wud wi' terror—an' clang to him an' prayed him, for Christ's sake, save her frae the cummers; an' they, for their pairt, tauld him a' that was ken't, and maybe mair.

"Woman," says he to Janet, "is this true?"

"As the Lord sees me," says she, "as the Lord made me, no a word o't. Forbye the bairn," says she, 'I've been a decent woman a' my days."

"Will you,' says Mr. Soulis, "in the name of God, and before me, His unworthy minister, renounce the devil and his works?"

Well, it wad appear that when he askit that, she gave a girn that fairly frichtit them that saw her, an' they could hear her teeth play dirl thegether in her chafts; but there was naething for it but the ae way or the ither; an' Janet lifted up her hand and renounced the deil before them a'.

"And now," said Mr. Soulis to the guidwives, "home with ye, one and all, and pray to God for His forgiveness."

And he gied Janet his arm, though she had little on her but a sark, and took her up the clachan to her ain door like a leddy of the land; an' her skreighin' and laughin' as was a scandal to be heard.

There were mony grave folk lang ower their prayers that nicht; but when the morn cam' there was sic a fear fell upon a' Ba'weary that the bairns hid theirsels, and even the men-folk stood and keekit frae their doors. For there was Janet comin' doun the clachan—her or her likeness, nane could tell—wi' her neck thrawn, and her heid on ae side, like a body that has been hangit, and a girn on her face like an unstreakit corp. By an' by they got used wi' it, and even speered at her to ken what was wrang; but frae that day forth she couldnae speak like a Christian woman, but slavered and played click wi' her teeth like a pair o' shears; and frae that day forth the name o' God cam' never on her lips. Whiles she wad try to say it, but it michtnae be. Them that kenned best said least; but they never gied that Thing the name o' Janet M'Clour; for the auld Janet, by their way o't, was in muckle hell that day. But the minister was neither to haud nor to bind; he preached about naething but the folks' cruelty that had gi'en her a stroke of the palsy; he skelpt the bairns that meddled her; and he had her up to the manse that same nicht and dwalled there a' his lane wi' her under the Hangin' Shaw.

Weel, time gaed by: and the idler sort commenced to think mair lichtly o' that black business. The minister was weel thocht o'; he

1227

was aye late at the writing, folk wad see his can'le doun by the Dule water after twal' at e'en; and he seemed pleased wi' himsel' and upsitten as at first though a' body could see that he was dwining. As for Janet she cam' an' she gaed; if she didnae speak muckle afore, it was reason she should speak less then; she meddled naebody; but she was an eldritch thing to see, an' nane wad hae mistrysted wi' her for Ba'weary glebe. About the end o' July there cam' a spell o' weather, the like o't never was in that countryside; it was lown an' het an' heartless; the herds couldnae win up the Black Hill, the bairns were ower weariet to play; an' yet it was gousty too, wi' claps o' het wund that rumm'led in the glens, and bits o' shouers that slockened naething. We aye thocht it but to thun'er on the morn; but the morn cam', and the morn's morning, and it was aye the same uncanny weather, sair on folks and bestial. Of a' that were the waur, nane suffered like Mr. Soulis; he could neither sleep nor eat, he tauld his elders; an' when he wasnae writin' at his weary book, he wad be stravaguin' ower a' the countryside like a man possessed, when a' body else was blythe to keep caller ben the house.

Abune Hangin' Shaw, in the bield o' the Black Hill, there's a bit inclosed grund wi' an iron yett; and it seems in the auld days, that was the kirkyaird o' Ba'weary, and consecrated by the Papists before the blessed licht shone upon the kingdom. It was a great howff o' Mr. Soulis's, onyway; there he would sit an' consider his sermons; and indeed it's a bieldy bit. Weel, as he cam' ower the wast end o' the Black Hill, ae day, he saw first twa, an' syne fower, an' syne seeven corbie craws fleein' round an' round abune the auld kirkyard. They flew laigh and heavy, an' squawked to ither as they gaed; and it was clear to Mr. Soulis that something had put them frae ordinar. He wasnae easy fleyed, an' gaed straucht up to the wa's; an' what suld he find there but a man, or the appearance of a man, sittin' in the inside upon a grave. He was of a great stature, an' black as hell, and his een were singular to see. Mr. Soulis had heard tell o' black men, mony's the time; but there was something unco about this black man that daunted him. Het as he was, he took a kind o' cauld grue in the marrow o' his banes; but up he spak for a' that; an' says he: "My friend, are you a stranger in this place?" The black man answered never a word; he got upon his feet, an' begude to hirstle to the wa' on the far side; but he aye lookit at the minister; an' the minister stood an' lookit back, till a' in a meenute the black man was over the wa' an' rinnin' for

1228

the bield o' the trees. Mr. Soulis, he hardly kenned why, ran after him; but he was sair forjaskit wi' his walk an' the het, unhalesome weather; and rin as he likit, he got nae mair than a glisk o' the black man amang the birks, till he won doun to the foot o' the hillside, an' there he saw him ance mair, gaun, hap, step, an' lowp, ower Dule water to the manse.

Mr. Soulis wasnae weel pleased that this fearsome gangrel suld mak' sae free wi' Ba'weary manse; an' he ran the harder, an', wet shoon, ower the burn, an' up the walk; but the deil a black man was there to see. He stepped out upon the road, but there was naebody there; he gaed a' ower the gairden, but na, nae black man. At the hinder end, and a bit feared as was but natural, he lifted the hasp and into the manse; and there was Janet M'Clour before his een, wi' her thrawn craig, and nane sae pleased to see him. And he aye minded sinsyne, when first he set his een upon her, he had the same cauld and deidly grue.

"Janet," says he, "have you seen a black man?"

"A black man?" quo' she. "Save us a'! Ye're no wise, minister. There's nae black man in a' Ba'weary."

But she didnae speak plain, ye maun understand; but yam-yammered, like a powney wi' the bit in its moo.

"Weel," says he, "Janet, if there was nae black man, I have spoken with the Accuser of the Brethren."

And he sat down like ane wi' a fever, an' his teeth chittered in his heid.

"Hoots," says she, "think shame to yoursel', minister"; an' gied him a drap brandy that she keept aye by her.

Syne Mr. Soulis gaed into his study amang a' his books. It's a lang, laigh, mirk chalmer, perishin' cauld in winter, an' no very dry even in the tap o' the simmer, for the manse stands near the burn. Sae doun he sat, and thocht of a' that had come an' gane since he was in Ba'weary, an' his hame, an' the days when he was a bairn an' ran daffin' on the braes; and that black man aye ran in his heid like the owercome of a sang. Aye the mair he thocht, the mair he thocht o' the black man. He tried the prayer, an' the words wouldnae come to him; an' he tried, they say, to write at his book, but he couldnae mak' nae mair o' that. There was whiles he thocht the black man was at his oxter, an' the swat stood upon him cauld as well-water; and there was other whiles, when he cam' to himsel' like a christened bairn and minded naething.

The upshot was that he gaed to the window an' stood glowrin' at

1229

Dule water. The trees are unco thick, an' the water lies deep an' black under the manse; an' there was Janet washin' the cla'es wi' her coats kilted. She had her back to the minister, an' he, for his pairt, hardly kenned what he was lookin' at. Syne she turned round an' shawed her face; Mr. Soulis had the same cauld grue as twice that day afore, an' it was borne in upon him what folk said, that Janet was deid lang syne, an' this was a bogle in her clay cauld flesh. He drew back a pickle and he scanned her narrowly. She was tramp-trampin' in the cla'es, croonin' to hersel'; and eh! Gude guide us, but it was a fearsome face. Whiles she sang louder, but there was nae man born o' woman that could tell the words o' her sang; an' whiles she lookit side-lang doun, but there was naething there for her to look at. There gaed a scunner through the flesh upon his banes; and that was Heeven's advertisement. But Mr. Soulis just blamed himsel', he said, to think sae ill of a puir, auld afflicted wife that hadnae a freend forby himsel'; and he put up a bit prayer for him and her, an' drank a little caller water— for his heart rose again the meat—an' gaed up to his naked bed in the gloaming.

That was a nicht that has never been forgotten in Ba'weary, the nicht o' the seeventeenth of August, seeventeen hun'er and twal'. It had been het afore, as I hae said, but that nicht it was hetter than ever. The sun gaed doun amang unco-lookin' clouds; it fell as mirk as the pit; no a star, no a breath o' wund; ye couldnae see your han' before your face, and even the auld folk cuist the covers frae their beds and lay pechin' for their breath. Wi' a' that he had upon his mind, it was gey and unlikely Mr. Soulis wad get muckle sleep. He lay an' he tummled; the gude, caller bed that he got into brunt his very banes; whiles he slept, and whiles he waukened; whiles he heard the time o' nicht, and whiles a tyke yowlin' up the muir, as if somebody was deid; whiles he thocht he heard bogles claverin' in his lug, an' whiles he saw spunkies in the room. He behooved, he judged, to be sick; an' sick he was—little he jaloosed the sickness.

At the hinder end, he got a clearness in his mind, sat up in his sark on the bedside, and fell thinkin' ance mair o' the black man an' Janet. He couldnae well tell how—maybe it was the cauld to his feet—but it cam' in upon him wi' a spat that there was some connection between their twa, an' that either or baith o' them were bogles. And just at that moment, in Janet's room which was neist to his, there cam' a stramp o' feet as if men were wars'lin', an' then a loud bang; an' then a wund gaed reishling round the fower

quarters of the house; an' then a' was aince mair as seelent as the grave.

Mr. Soulis was feared for neither man nor deevil. He got his tinder box, an' lighted a can'le, an' made three steps o't ower to Janet's door. It was on the hasp, an' he pushed it open, an' keeked bauldly in. It was a big room, as big as the minister's ain, an' plenished wi' grand, auld, solid gear, for he had naething else. There was a fower-posted bed wi' auld tapestry; and a braw cabinet of aik, that was fu' o' the minister's divinity books, an' put there to be out o' the gate; an' a wheen duds o' Janet's lying here and there about the floor. But nae Janet could Mr. Soulis see; nor ony sign of a contention. In he gaed (an' there's few that wad ha'e followed him) an' lookit a' round, an' listened. But there was naethin' to be heard, neither inside the manse nor in a' Ba'weary parish, an' naethin' to be seen but the muckle shadows turnin' round the can'le. An' then a' at aince, the minister's heart played dunt an' stood stock-still; an' a cauld wund blew amang the hairs o' his heid. Whaten a weary sicht was that for the puir man's een! For there was Janet hangin' frae a nail beside the auld aik cabinet: her heid aye lay on her shouther, her een were steeked, the tongue projekit frae her mouth, and her heels were twa feet clar abune the floor.

"God forgive us all!" thocht Mr. Soulis; "poor Janet's dead."

He cam' a step nearer to the corp; an' then his heart fair whammled in his inside. For by what cantrip it wad ill-beseem a man to judge, she was hingin' fae a single nail an' by a single wursted thread for darnin' hose.

It's an awfu' thing to be your lane at nicht wi' siccan prodigies o' darkness; but Mr. Soulis was strong in the Lord. He turned an' gaed his ways oot o' that room, and lockit the door ahint him; and step by step, doon the stairs, as heavy as leed; and set doon the can'le on the table at the stairfoot. He couldnae pray, he couldnae think, he was dreepin' wi' caul' swat, an' naething could he hear but the dunt-dunt-duntin' o' his ain heart. He micht maybe have stood there an hour, or maybe twa, he minded sae little; when a' o' a sudden he heard a laigh, uncanny steer upstairs; a foot gaed to an' fro in the cha'mer whaur the corp was hingin'; syne the door was opened, though he minded weel that he had lockit it; an' syne there was a step upon th landin', an' it seemed to him as if the corp was lookin' ower the rail and doun upon him whaur he stood.

He took up the can'le again (for he couldnae want the licht) and,

as saftly as ever he could, gaed straucht out o' the manse an' to the far end o' the causeway. It was aye pitmirk; the flame o' the can'le, when he set it on the grund, brunt steedy and clear as in a room; naething moved, but the Dule water seepin' and sabbin' doon the glen, an' yon unhaly footstep that cam' ploddin' doun the stairs inside the manse. He kenned the foot ower weel, for it was Janet's; and at ilka step that cam' a wee thing nearer, the cauld got deeper in his vitals. He commended his soul to Him that made an' keepit him; "and O Lord," said he, "give me strength this night to war against the powers of evil."

By this time the foot was comin' through the passage for the door; he could hear a hand skirt alang the wa', as if the fearsome thing was feelin' for its way. The saughs tossed an' maned thegether, a lang sigh cam' ower the hills, the flame o' the can'le was blawn aboot; an' there stood the corp of Thrawn Janet, wi' her grogram goun an' her black mutch, wi' the heid aye upon the shouther, an' the girn still upon the face o't—leevin', ye wad hae said—deid, as Mr. Soulis weel kenned—upon the threshold o' the manse.

It's a strange thing that the saul of man should be that thirled into his perishable body; but the minister saw, an' his heart didnae break.

She didnae stand there lang; she began to move again an' cam' slowly toward Mr. Soulis whaur he stood under the saughs. A' the life o' his body, a' the strength o' his speerit, were glowerin' frae his een. It seemed she was gaun to speak, but wanted words, an' made a sign wi' the left hand. There cam' a clap o' wund, like a cat's fuff; oot gaed the can'le, the saughs skrieghed like folk; an' Mr. Soulis kenned that, live or die, this was the end o't.

"Witch, beldam, devil!" he cried, "I charge you, by the power of God, begone—if you be dead, to the grave—if you be damned, to hell."

An' at that moment the Lord's ain hand out o' the Heevens struck the Horror whaur it stood; the auld, deid, desecrated corp o' the witchwife, sae lang keepit frae the grave and hirsled round by deils, lowed up like a brunstane spunk and fell in ashes to the grund; the thunder followed, peal on dirling peal, the rairing rain upon the back o' that; and Mr. Soulis lowped through the garden hedge, and ran, wi' skelloch upon skellock, for the clachan.

That same mornin', John Christie saw the Black Man pass the Muckle Cairn as it was chappin' six; before eicht, he gaed by the change-house at Knockdow; an' no lang after, Sandy M'Lellan saw

him gaun linkin' doun the braes frae Kilmackerlie. There's little
doubt it was him that dwalled sae lang in Janet's body; but he
was awa' at last; and sinsyne the deil has never fashed us in
Ba'weary.

But it was a sair dispensation for the minister; lang, lang he
lay ravin' in his bed; and frae that hour to this, he was the man
ye ken the day.

THEODOR STORM

THEODOR STORM (German, 1817-1888). Lawyer and judge, who was exiled
to Prussia for 10 years for his sympathies in the Schleswig-Holstein dispute
with Denmark. Devoted his evenings to creating a literature of romantic mood-
pictures. Of his stories, "Immensee" is a universal favorite.

VERONIKA

I. At the Mill

IT WAS at the beginning of April on the day before Palm Sunday.
The mild rays of the late afternoon sun shone on the young grass at
the side of the path which led down gradually along a mountain
slope. At this moment one of the most respected jurists of the city,
a man of middle age, with calm but distinctive features, was walking
leisurely, exchanging only an occasional word with the clerk at his
side. Their destination was a water-mill not far off whose owner,
troubled by age and illness, wished to make over his property to
his son.

A few paces behind followed another couple; beside a young man
with fresh, intelligent features walked a beautiful, still very youthful
woman. He spoke to her, but she did not seem to hear. Her dark eyes
gazing straight ahead, she walked silently, as though unaware of anyone at her side.

As the mill became visible in the valley below, the counsellor
turned his head. "Well cousin," he called, "you write a passable
hand; how would you like to learn a little about making contracts?"

But the cousin waved his hand in protest. "Go on!" he said and
looked questioningly at his companion. "Meanwhile I'll have a conversation-lesson with your wife!"

"Well, at least don't teach him too much, Veronika!"

The young woman only inclined her head as in assent. Behind them, from the towers of the city, the sound of the evening chimes came spreading over the country-side. Her hand, which had just stroked back the black hair beneath her white satin hat, glided down over her breast and, making the sign of the cross, she began softly to recite the Angelus. The glance of the young man who, like his relative, belonged to a protestant family, followed the uniform movement of her lips with an expression of impatience.

Several months ago he had come to the city as an architect to work on the addition to a church and since then had been an almost daily guest in the house of the counsellor. He had entered immediately into a lively and friendly association with the wife of his cousin. The two were drawn together through the youth which they had in common as well as through his accomplishment in drawing, which she also practiced with enthusiasm and skill. Now she had found him a friend and teacher at the same time. Soon, however, as he sat beside her evenings, it was not so much the drawing lying before her upon which his eyes rested, as it was her small, busy hand; and she who had been wont to cast aside her pencil at any given moment, now drew silently and obediently without looking up, as though caught in his gaze. It may be that they hardly realized themselves, that, every evening when saying "Good night," their hands remained together a little longer and their fingers were clasped a little tighter. The counsellor, whose thoughts were usually with his business, thought still less about it; he was glad that his wife had found stimulation and understanding for her favorite occupation, which he himself was unable to give her. Only once, just after the young architect had left their house, the dreamy expression in her eyes had surprised him. "Vroni," he said, holding her back by the hand as she tried to pass. "It's true then, isn't it, what your sisters say." "What is, Franz?" "Of course," he said, "now I see it myself, you have spiritual eyes." She blushed and submitted without speaking as he drew her closer and kissed her.

Today, in the fine weather, she and Rudolf had been invited by the counsellor to accompany him on his official errand to the near-by mill.

Since yesterday's social gathering, when she had displayed, at the request of her husband, a drawing which had been completed under his eyes, everything had become different between them. Rudolf felt it only too well; he recalled how it had come about that he had

1234

opposed the excessive praise of the others with such sharp and passionate criticism.

Veronika had long ended her prayer, but he waited in vain for her to turn her eyes toward him.

"You are angry with me, Veronika," he said at last. The young woman nodded slightly, but her lips remained firmly closed.

He looked at her. Obstinacy still lay upon her brow.

"I should think," he said, "you might know how it could happen! Or don't you know, Veronika?"

"I know only," she said, "that you have hurt me. And," she added, "that you wanted to hurt me."

He remained silent for a while. "Did you not notice," he asked hesitantly, "the knowing eye of the old man who stood opposite you?"

She turned her head and glanced up at him fleetingly.

"I had to do it myself, Veronika. Forgive me! I can't bear to have you criticized by others."

It seemed as though a veil drew over her eyes, and long black lashes sank upon her cheeks; but she did not answer.

A short time later they had reached the mill. The counsellor was led into the house by the miller's son; Rudolf and Veronika entered the garden lying at the side, and continued to walk silently up the long incline; it was almost as though they were angry with each other, as though they had to stop for want of breath when they tried to speak an occasional word.

When they had wandered through the garden, they passed over a narrow foot-bridge into the lower door of the mill-building, which stood by a swift stream at the edge of the garden. Through the clattering of the works and the roar of the falling water which drowned every sound coming from outside, a strange sense of separation reigned in the almost dusky room. Veronika had walked over to the door which led to the mill-race and gazed down into the thrashing wheels upon which the water glistened in the evening sun. Rudolf did not follow; he stood within, beside the big cogwheel, his gloomy eyes unswervingly upon her. Finally she turned her head. She spoke, he saw how her lips moved, but he did not understand her words.

"I don't understand!" he said and shook his head.

As he was about to go to her, she had already stepped back into the inner room. In passing she came so close to the wheel beside which he stood, that the teeth almost touched her hair. She did not see it, since she was still blinded by the evening sun; but she felt

1235

her hands seized and herself drawn quickly to the side. As she looked up, her eyes met his. They remained silent; a sudden unmindfulness dropped like a shadow over them. At their heads thundered the mill works; from outside came the monotonous rushing of the water, plunging over the wheels into the depths. Gradually, however, the young man's lips began to move, and, protected by the deafening noise, in which his voice was lost, he whispered intoxicated, maddening words. Her ears could not discern them, but she read their meaning from his lips, from the impassioned pallor of his face. She threw her head back and closed her eyes; only her mouth smiled and betrayed life. Thus she stood holding her face toward him helplessly, her hands obliviously in his.

Then suddenly the roaring ceased; the mill stood still. They heard the mill-hands walking above, and outside, the dripping water fell from the wheels, tinkling into the pond. The lips of the young man became dumb, and when Veronika withdrew from him, he did not try to hold her back. Not until she had gone out through the door into the open, did he seem to regain his speech. He called her name and extended his arms to her, pleadingly. But she shook her head, without turning to look at him, and walked slowly through the garden to the dwelling.

As she went in through the door which had been left partly open, she saw opposite her the old miller, with folded hands lying in his bed. Over it a wooden crucifix was attached, from which hung a rosary. A young woman with a child in her arm had just come over to the bedside and was bending over the covers. "He only needs air." she said. "He enjoys his food well enough."

"Who is your doctor?" asked the counsellor, who was standing close by, holding a document in his hand.

"Doctor?" she repeated. " We have no doctor."

"You're doing wrong there!"

The young woman let out an embarrassed laugh. "It's old age," she said, as she wiped her chubby boy's little nose with her apron, "The doctor couldn't help that."

Veronika listened breathlessly to this conversation. The old man began to cough and put his hand to his eyes.

"Is this your will, Martin, as it is written here?" the counsellor now asked. But the sick man seemed not to hear him.

"Father," said the young woman, "Is that right as the counsellor has just read it?"

"Of course," said the sick man, "Everything is all right."

1236

"And you have considered everything well?" asked the counsellor.

The old man nodded. "Yes, yes," he said, "I have worked hard; but the boy shouldn't have it too bad. . . ."

The son, who until now had been sitting in the corner smoking, entered into the conversation. "Of course, the old man's part has to be considered too," he said, and cleared his throat several times, "The old man will live away a neat sum yet."

The counsellor cast his gray eyes down upon the coarse peasant. "Is that your son, Weismann?" he asked, pointing at the child playing at the bed side. "Send him out, if you expect to do any more talking!"

The man was silent; but his eyes met those of the counsellor with an almost threatening expression.

The old man stroked his hard hand over the cover. And said quietly, "It won't be so very long, Jakob!—But," he added, turning to the counsellor, "in keeping with the village customs, he will have to bury me; that will cost something, too."

The young lady disappeared without a sound, just as she had come, from the open door in which she had been standing during these proceedings.

Outside she saw Rudolf on the other side of the garden in conversation with the mill-hand, but she turned away and followed a footpath, which led below the mill down to the stream. Her eyes strayed unconsciously into the distance; she did not notice how dusk was sinking upon the mountains ahead of her, nor how, gradually, even while she was strolling up and down, the moon was rising behind them and pouring its light over the silent valley. Life in its naked poverty confronted her as she had never before seen it; an endless, arid way,—at the end, death. She felt as though she had been living in a dream until now, and as if she were now wandering in a reality without solace, in which she did not know how to find her way.

It was late when the voice of her husband called her back to the mill where he awaited her at the door. On the way home she walked silently at his side, without feeling his understanding eyes upon her. "You have been frightened, Veronika!" he said and laid his hand upon her cheek. "But," he added, "these people live according to different standards; they are harsh, not only towards their kin, but also towards themselves."

She looked up at her husband's calm face for a moment; then she cast her eyes upon the ground and walked humbly at his side.

Just as silently Rudolf walked at the side of the old clerk. His eyes

hung upon the hand of the woman, illuminated by the moonlight, which had only a short time ago rested so weakly in his own. He hoped that he would be able to hold it once more, if only for a moment when saying good night.—But it was to be otherwise; for, as they approached the city, he noticed the small hands, one after the other, slip into a pair of dark gloves which, as he well knew, Veronika usually carried only for the sake of completing her costume.

Finally they had reached the house; but before he was quite aware of it in his dejection, he felt the hasty touch of her covered fingers upon his own. With a distinctly spoken "Good night" Veronika had opened the door and had disappeared into the darkness of the hall ahead of her husband.

II. Palm Sunday

The morning of Palm Sunday had arrived. The streets of the city were thronged with country-folk from the neighboring villages. Here and there in the sunshine in front of the house-doors stood the children of protestant inhabitants, gazing down toward the open door of the Catholic Church. This was the day of the great Easter procession. —Now the bells were ringing, and the procession became visible under the Gothic arch, and surged out into the street. At the head the orphan boys with black crosses in their hands, behind them in white veiled hoods, the Sisters of Mercy, then the various public schools and finally the whole endless train of country and city folk, of men, women, of children, and old people, all singing, praying, dressed in their best clothes, men and boys bare-headed, their caps in their hands. Overhead at measured intervals, carried upon shoulders, the colossal religious pictures: Christ at Calvary, Christ jeered by the soldiers, in the center, high above everything, the tremendous cross, finally the Holy Sepulchre.

The ladies of the city did not customarily participate in the public festivities.

Veronika sat half dressed in her bedroom at a small dressing table. Before her lay open a small, gilt-edge Testament, such as the Catholic Church permits its members. She seemed to have forgotten herself over her reading, for her long black hair hung loose over her white night-gown, while her hand, holding a tortoise-shell comb lay idly in her lap.

As the din of the approaching procession reached her ears she raised her head and listened. Ever more distinctly came the dull

1238

sound of steps, the singing, monotonous murmuring of prayers. "Holy Mary, Mother of Mercy!," it came from outside, and from the rear of the procession resounded a subdued: "Pray for us poor sinners, now, and in the hour of death."

Veronika recited the familiar words softly. She had pushed back her chair; with her arms at her sides, she stood in the back of the room, her eyes steadfastly directed toward the window. New people came and went continuously, new voices spoke, one picture after the other was carried by. Then suddenly a heart-rending tone penetrated the air. The *castrum doloris* approached, accompanied by the sound of trumpets, surrounded by people, followed by the acolytes and the highest priests in festive vestment. The ribbons fluttered, the black crepe of the canopy rippled in the air; underneath it in a garden of flowers lay the image of the Crucified One. The metallic peal of the trumpets was like a summons to the Day of Judgment.

Veronika was still standing motionless; her knees trembled; beneath the accentuated black eyebrows her eyes lay as if extinguished in the pale countenance.

When the procession had passed, she sank to the floor beside the chair upon which she had been sitting, and covering her face with both hands, she cried, with the words in Luke: "Father, I have sinned against Heaven, and I am not worthy of being called your child!"

III. In the Confessional

The counsellor belonged to that ever increasing community of those who saw in the appearance of Christianity not so much a miracle, but rather the natural result of the spiritual development of humanity. He himself, therefore, did not go to any church; nevertheless, he permitted his wife to retain the habits of her youth and parental home, perhaps in the expectation of her gradual, independent liberation from them.

Since their wedding two years before Veronika had gone to confession and communion only at Easter-time, which had now begun again. He was already acquainted with the way in which she went about in the house on the preceding days, quiet and apparently indifferent; therefore, it had not struck him that the enthusiastically undertaken drawing lessons had ceased ever since that evening walk. But the time passed, the May sun began to beam warmly into the room, and Veronika put off her confession again. At last it could escape him no longer that her cheeks became paler from day to day,

that little shadows became visible under her eyes, left there by sleepless nights. Thus he found her one morning upon entering the bedroom unnoticed, standing at the window lost in thought.

"Vroni," he said, putting his arm around her, "Won't you try holding up your little head again?"

She shuddered, as if he had surprised unguarded thoughts in her, but she sought to control herself. "Go, Franz!," she said, taking his hand tenderly and leading him back to the door.

Then, soon after he had left her alone, she dressed and departed from the house, prayer-book in hand.

A short time later she entered St. Lambert's. Meanwhile the morning was advancing. Outside the windows of the vast hall the leaf-covered branches of the Linden trees cast their shadows; in the choir, upon the doors of the reliquary, a broken sunray fell through the stained glass panes. In the confessionals in the nave of the church here and there people sat or kneeled before opened prayer-books, preparing for confessions. There was no sound but the whispering from the confessionals, now and then a deep breath, the rustling of a dress, or a soft footfall upon the flagstones. Soon Veronika, too, was kneeling in one of the confessionals, not far from the picture of the Holy Mother, who looked down upon her, smiling compassionately. Her completely black costume made the transparent pallor of her face still more striking. The priest, a robust middle-aged man, leaned his head against the screen which separated him from his penitent.

Veronika began the introductory formula in a half whisper: "Forgive me, Father, for I have sinned," and with wavering voice she continued: "I confess to Almighty God and to you, Father, . . ." Her words became slower and slower, less and less understandable; then she stopped.

The dark eye of the priest was calm and directed upon her with an expession almost of fatigue, since he had been hearing confessions for hours. "Turn ye to the Lord!" he said mildly. "Sin is death; but repentance is life."

She tried to collect her thoughts. And again, as so often since that hour, her inward ear heard the turbulent roar of the mill; and again she stood before him in the mysterious twilight—her hands caught in his, closing her eyes under the stress of the overwhelming emotion, transfixed in mortification, not daring to escape, and even less, to remain.—Her lips moved, but she could not get it out; she tried in vain.

1240

The Priest remained silent for a moment. "Courage! my daughter!" he then said, raising his head with the rich black hair. "Think of the words of the Lord: 'Receive ye the Holy Spirit; those whom ye free from sin, their sins shall be forgiven!' "

She glanced up. The flushed countenance, the powerful bull-neck of the man in vestments was close before her eyes. She began once more; but an unconquerable resentment came over her, a reluctance, as before something unchaste, worse than that which she had come here to confess. She was frightened. Was not this revolt in her a temptation of the deadly sin from which she wanted to be released? She bowed her head in silent conflict upon the prayer-book lying before her. Meanwhile, the expression of fatigue had vanished from the face of the priest. He began to speak, earnestly and forcibly, and then with all the magic of persuasion; softly, yet sonorously the tone of his voice came to her ears. At any other time she would have sunk to the dust, enraptured; but this time the newly awakened emotion was stronger than all the power of rhetoric and all the habit of her youth. Her hand fumbled at her veil which was thrown back over her hat.

"Forgive me, father," she stammered. Then, silently shaking her head, she drew the veil down without having received the sign of the cross, stood up, and went hastily down the aisle. Her clothes rustled past the church benches; she gathered them in her hand; it seemed to her as though unseen hands were reaching out to keep her there.

Outside, beneath the high doorway she stood still, breathing deeply. She was troubled in spirit; she had rejected the redeeming hand which had led her since childhood; she knew no other which she might grasp now. Then, as she stood undecided on the sunny square, she heard the voice of a child beside her, and a small brown hand offered her a bouquet of primroses for sale. It was indeed spring outside in the world. As though she had not known it, like a messenger it came to her heart.

She bent down to the child and bought his flowers; then, the bouquet in her hand, she walked down the street towards the city gate. The sun glittered on the stones; from the open window of a house a canary sent forth its loud song. She walked slowly on and soon reached the last houses. From there a foot-path led off to the side up toward the hills which bounded the city. Veronika breathed more freely; her eyes rested upon the green of the fields which bordered the path; now and then the air stirred and brought the gentle fragrance of the cowslips growing at the foot of the mountain. Farther

on, where, at the border of the fields the forest began, the path rose steeper, and physical effort became necessary although Veronika had been used to mountain climbing since her early youth. Now and then she stopped and gazed from the shadows of the firs into the sunny valley which sank deeper and deeper below her.

When she had reached the summit she sat on the ground among the wild thyme which had spun itself over the mountain at this spot. As she breathed the spicy air of the forest her eye swept over toward the blue mountan-chain which lay on the horizon like a haze. Behind her, at short intervals, the spring wind was blowing through the tops of the pines. Now and then the call of a blackbird sounded out of the depths of the forest, or above her the cry of a bird of prey which floated invisible in the immeasurable vastness of space.

Veronika removed her hat and supported her head with her hand.

Thus in solitude and quiet a period of time passed. Nothing approached her but the pure breezes which touched her brow and the calls of the birds which reached her ear from the distance. At times a bright glow flushed her cheeks and her eyes became large and shining.

Now the bells sounded up from the city. She raised her head and listened. They rang shrilly and hastily. "Requiescat!," she said softly, for she had recognized the little bell from St. Lambert's tower which informed the community that beneath one of its roofs the grim messenger of the Lord had entered.

At the foot of the mountains lay the cemetery. She could see the stone cross towering over the grave of her father who, but a few years before, had passed away in her arms as a priest intoned his prayers. And farther on, there, where the water glistened, was that ugly barren patch of earth which she had so often entered as a child, full of shy curiosity, where, according to the commandment of the church, those who had not received the sacrament of the altar were buried beside those who had taken their own lives. This would now be her resting place, too, since Easter confessions were at an end for her.

An expression of pain crept about her mouth and then disappeared. She stood up, a decision firm and clear in her soul.

A moment longer she looked down upon the city and let her eyes wander over the sunlit roofs as if in search of something. Then she turned and walked through the pines down the mountain the way she had come. Soon she was in the green of the fields again. She seemed to hurry, walking erect with firm steps.

Thus she reached her house. From the maid she learned that her husband was in his room. As she opened the door and saw him sitting calmly at his desk she remained hesitantly on the threshold.

"Franz," she called softly.

He laid his pen aside.

"Is it you, Vroni?," he said, turning to her. "You're late! Was your list of transgressions so long?"

"Don't joke!" she said pleadingly as she stepped up to him and took his hand. "I did not confess."

He looked up at her, surprised. She, however, knelt before him and pressed her lips upon his hand.

"Franz," she said, "I have hurt you!"

"Me, Veronika?" he asked, and took her face softly between his hands.

"And now you have come to confess to your husband?"

"No, Franz," she replied, "Not to confess, but to confide in you, in you alone,—and you,—help me, and if you can,—forgive me!"

For a moment he gazed at her earnestly, then he raised her with both arms and laid her head upon his breast. "Then speak, Veronika!"

She did not stir, but her mouth began to speak and, as his eyes hung upon her lips, she felt how his arms tightened about her.

TO A DECEASED

But this is more than I can bear,
That still the laughing sun is bright,
As in the days when you were there,
That clocks are striking, unaware,
And mark the change of day and night—

That we, as twilight dims the air,
Assemble when the day is done,
And that the place where stood your chair
Already many others share,
And that you seem thus missed by none;

When meanwhile from the gate below
The narrow strips of moonlight spare
Into your vault down deeply go
And with a ghostly pallid glow
Are stealing o'er your coffin there.

1243

THE CITY

The shore is gray, the sea is gray,
And there the city stands;
The mists upon the houses weigh
And through the calm, the ocean gray
Roars dully on the strands.

There are no rustling woods, there fly
No birds at all in May,
The wild goose with its callous cry
Along on autumn nights soars by,
The wind-blown grasses sway.

And yet my whole heart clings to thee,
Gray city by the sea;
And e'er the spell of youth for me
Doth smiling rest on thee, on thee
Gray city by the sea.

THE HEATH

It is so quiet here. There lies
The heath in noon's warm sunshine gold.
A gleam of light, all rosy, flies
And hovers round the mounds of old.
The herbs are blooming; fragrance fair
Now fills the bluish summer air.

The beetles rush through bush and trees,
In little golden coats of mail;
And on the heather-bells the bees
Alight on all its branches frail.
From out the grass there starts a throng
Of larks and fills the air with song.

A lonely house, half-crumbled, low:
The farmer, in the doorway bent,
Stands watching in the sunlight's glow
The busy bees in sweet content.
And on a stone near by his boy
Is carving pipes from reeds with joy.

1244

Scarce trembling through the peace of noon
The town-clock strikes—from far, it seems.
The old man's eye-lids droop right soon,
And of his honey crops he dreams.—
The sounds that tell our time of stress
Have not yet reached this loneliness.

CONSOLATION

Let come to me whatever may,
While you are with me it is day.

Though in the world I wander far,
My home is ever—where you are.

Your face is all in all to me,
The future's frown I do not see.

HARRIET BEECHER STOWE

HARRIET BEECHER STOWE (American, 1811-1896). Author of a book that changed the face of a country. Daughter and wife of clergymen. Wrote her novels and stories while raising six children. *Uncle Tom's Cabin*, hardly a great work of art, nonetheless had powerful influence in turning the country's attention toward evils of slavery. It has been translated into nearly every written language.

TOPSY

ONE morning, while Miss Ophelia was busy in some of her domestic cares, St. Clare's voice was heard, calling her at the foot of the stairs.

"Come down here, cousin; I've something to show you."

"What is it?" said Miss Ophelia, coming down, with her sewing in her hand.

"I've made a purchase for your department—see here," said St. Clare; and, with the word, he pulled along a little negro girl, about eight or nine years of age.

She was one of the blackest of her race; and her round, shining eyes, glittering as glass beads, moved with quick and restless glances over everything in the room. Her mouth, half open with astonish-

1245

ment at the wonders of the new Mas'r's parlor, displayed a white and brilliant set of teeth. Her woolly hair was braided in sundry little tails, which stuck out in every direction. The expression of her face was an odd mixture of shrewdness and cunning, over which was oddly drawn, like a kind of veil, an expression of the most doleful gravity and solemnity. She was dressed in a single filthy, ragged garment, made of bagging; and stood with her hands demurely folded before her. Altogether, there was something odd and goblin-like about her appearance,—something, as Miss Ophelia afterwards said, "so heathenish," as to inspire that good lady with utter dismay; and, turning to St. Clare, she said:

"Augustine, what in the world have you brought that thing here for?"

"For you to educate, to be sure, and train in the way she should go. I thought she was rather a funny specimen in the Jim Crow line. Here, Topsy," he added, giving a whistle, as a man would call the attention of a dog, "give us a song, now, and show us some of your dancing."

The black, glassy eyes glittered with a kind of wicked drollery, and the thing struck up, in a clear shrill voice, an old negro melody, to which she kept time with her hands and feet, spinning round, clapping her hands, knocking her knees together, in a wild, fantastic sort of time, and producing in her throat all those odd guttural sounds which distinguish the native music of her race; and finally, turning a somerset or two, and giving a prolonged closing note as odd and unearthly as that of a steam-whistle, she came suddenly down on the carpet, and stood with her hands folded, and a most sanctimonious expression of meekness and solemnity over her face, only broken by the cunning glances which she shot askance from the corners of her eyes.

Miss Ophelia stood silent, perfectly paralyzed with amazement.

St. Clare, like a mischievous fellow as he was, appeared to enjoy her astonishment; and, addressing the child again, said:

"Topsy, this is your new mistress. I'm going to give you up to her; see, now, that you behave yourself."

"Yes, Mas'r," said Topsy, with sanctimonious gravity, her wicked eyes twinkling as she spoke.

"You're going to be good, Topsy, you understand," said St. Clare.

"Oh, yes, Mas'r." said Topsy, with another twinkle, her hands still devoutly folded.

"Now, Augustine, what upon earth is this for?" said Miss Ophelia.

1246

"Your house is so full of these little plagues, now, that a body can't set down their foot without treading on 'em. I get up in the morning, and find one asleep behind the door, and see one black head poking out from under the table, one lying on the door-mat,—and they are mopping and mowing and grinning between all the railings, and tumbling over the kitchen floor! What on earth did you want to bring this one for?"

"For you to educate,—didn't I tell you? You're always preaching about educating. I thought I would make you a present of a fresh-caught specimen, and let you try your hand on her, and bring her up in the way she should go."

"*I* don't want her, I am sure;—I have more to do with 'em now than I want to."

"That's you Christians, all over!—you'll get up a society, and get some poor missionary to spend all his days among just such heathen. But let me see one of you that would take one into your house with you, and take the labor of their conversion on yourselves! No; when it comes to that, they are dirty and disagreeable, and it's too much care, and so on."

"Augustine, you know I didn't think of it in that light," said Miss Ophelia, evidently softening. "Well, it might be a real missionary work," said she, looking rather more favorably on the child.

St. Clare had touched the right string. Miss Ophelia's conscientiousness was ever on the alert. "But," she added, "I really didn't see the need of buying this one;—there are enough now, in your house, to take all my time and skill."

"Well, then, cousin," said St. Clare, drawing her aside, "I ought to beg your pardon for my good-for-nothing speeches. You are so good, after all, that there's no sense in them. Why, the fact is, this concern belonged to a couple of drunken creatures that keep a low restaurant that I have to pass by every day, and I was tired of hearing her screaming, and them beating and swearing at her. She looked bright and funny, too, as if something might be made of her,—so I bought her, and I'll give her to you. Try, now, and give her a good orthodox New England bringing up, and see what it'll make of her. You know I haven't any gift that way; but I'd like you to try."

"Well, I'll do what I can," said Miss Ophelia; and she approached her new subject very much as a person might be supposed to approach a black spider, supposing them to have benevolent designs toward it.

1247

"She's dreadfully dirty, and half naked," she said.

"Well, take her down stairs, and make some of them clean and clothe her up."

Miss Ophelia carried her to the kitchen regions.

"Don't see what Mas'r St. Clare wants of 'nother nigger!" said Dinah, surveying the new arrival with no friendly air. "Won't have her round under *my* feet, *I* know!"

"Pah!" said Rosa and Jane, with supreme disgust; "let her keep out of our way! What in the world Mas'r wanted another of these low niggers for, I can't see!"

"You go 'long! No more nigger dan you be, Miss Rosa," said Dinah, who felt this last remark a reflection on herself. "You seem to tink yourself white folks. You an't nerry one, black *nor* white. I'd like to be one or turrer."

Miss Ophelia saw that there was nobody in the camp that would undertake to oversee the cleansing and dressing of the new arrival; and so she was forced to do it herself, with some very ungracious and reluctant assistance from Jane.

When she saw, on the back and shoulders of the child, great welts and calloused spots, ineffaceable marks of the system under which she had grown up thus far, her heart became pitiful within her.

"See there!" said Jane, pointing to the marks, "don't that show she's a limb? We'll have fine works with her, I reckon. I hate these nigger young uns! so disgusting! I wonder that Mas'r would buy her!"

The "young un" alluded to heard all these comments with the subdued and doleful air which seemed habitual to her, only scanning, with a keen and furtive glance of her flickering eyes, the ornaments which Jane wore in her ears. When arrayed at last in a suit of decent and whole clothing, her hair cropped short to her head, Miss Ophelia, with some satisfaction, said she looked more Christian-like than she did, and in her own mind began to mature some plans for her instruction.

Sitting down before her, she began to question her. "How old are you, Topsy?"

"Dunno, Missis," said the image, with a grin that showed all her teeth.

"Don't know how old you are? Didn't anybody ever tell you? Who was your mother?"

"Never had none!" said the child, with another grin.

"Never had any mother? What do you mean? Where were you born?"

"Never was born!" persisted Topsy, with another grin, that looked so goblin-like, that, if Miss Ophelia had been at all nervous, she might have fancied that she had got hold of some sooty gnome from the land of Diablerie; but Miss Ophelia was not nervous, but plain and business-like, and she said, with some sternness:

"You mustn't answer me in that way, child; I'm not playing with you. Tell me where you were born, and who your father and mother were."

"Never was born," reiterated the creature, more emphatically; "never had no father nor mother, nor nothin'. I was raised by a speculator, with lots of others. Old Aunt Sue used to take car on us."

The child was evidently sincere; and Jane, breaking into a short laugh, said:

"Laws, Missis, there's heaps of 'em. Speculators buys 'em up cheap, when they's little, and get's 'em raised for market."

"How long have you lived with your master and mistress?"

"Dunno, Missis."

"Is it a year, or more, or less?"

"Dunno, Missis."

"Laws, Missis, those low negroes,—they can't tell; they don't know anything about time," said Jane; "they don't know what a year is; they don't know their own ages."

"Have you ever heard anything about God, Topsy?"

The child looked bewildered, but grinned as usual.

"Do you know who made you?"

"'Nobody, as I knows on," said the child, with a short laugh.

The idea appeared to amuse her considerably; for her eyes twinkled, and she added:

"I spect I grow'd. Don't think nobody never made me."

"Do you know how to sew?" said Miss Ophelia, who thought she would turn her inquiries to something more tangible.

"No, Missis."

"What can you do?—what did you do for your master and mistress?"

"Fetch water, and wash dishes, and rub knives, and wait on folks."

"Were they good to you?"

"Spect they was," said the child, scanning Miss Ophelia cunningly.

1249

Miss Ophelia rose from this encouraging colloquy; St. Clare was leaning over the back of her chair.

"You find virgin soil there, cousin; put in your own ideas,—you won't find many to pull up."

AUGUST STRINDBERG

AUGUST STRINDBERG (Swedish, 1849-1912). One of the leading literary rebels of Europe at turn of the century. Unhappy teacher, actor, newspaperman. Prolific dramatist, novelist, critic. Lifelong conflict with women reflected in his naturalistic plays—*The Father* and *Miss Julia*—and novels like *Confessions of a Fool*. Tendency to emotional instability apparent in all his work, but experiments in dramatic form had lasting influence.

A FUNERAL

THE cooper sat with the barber in the inn at Engsung and played a harmless game of lansquenet for a barrel of beer. It was one o'clock in the afternoon of a snowy November day. The tavern was quite empty, for most people were still at work. The flames burned brightly in the clay fire-place which stood on four wooden feet in a corner, and looked like a coffin; the fir twigs on the ground smelt pleasantly; the well-panelled walls kept out all draughts and looked warm; the bull-finch in his cage twittered now and then, and looked out of the window, but he had to put his head on one side to see if it was fine. But it was snowing outside. The innkeeper sat behind his counter and reckoned up chalk-strokes on a black slate; now and then he interjected a humorous remark or a bright idea which seemed to please the other two.

Then the great bell in the church began to toll with a dull and heavy sound, in keeping with the November day.

"What the devil is that cursed ringing for?" said the cooper, who felt too comfortable in life to enjoy being reminded of death.

"Another funeral," answered the innkeeper. "There is never anything else."

"Why the deuce do people want to have such a fuss made about them after they are dead," said the barber. "Trump that, Master Cooper!"

1250

"So I did," said the cooper, and pocketed the trick in his leather apron.

Down the sloping road which led to the Nicholai Gate, a funeral procession wended its way. There was a simple, roughly planed coffin, thinly coated with black paint so that the knots in the wood showed through. A single wreath of whortleberries lay on the coffin lid. The undertaker's men who carried the bier looked indifferent and almost humiliated because they were carrying a bier without a cover and fringes.

Behind the coffin walked three women—the dead man's mother and her two daughters; they looked crushed with grief. When the funeral reached the gate of the churchyard, the priest met it and shook hands with the mourners; then the service began in the presence of some old women and apprentices who had joined the procession.

"I see now—it is the clerk, Hans Schönschreiber," said the innkeeper, who had gone to the window, from which he could overlook the churchyard.

"And none of his fellow-clerks follow him to the grave," said the cooper. "A bad lot, these clerks."

"I know the poor fellow," said the barber. "He lived like a church mouse and died of hunger."

"And a little of pride," added the innkeeper.

"Not so little though," the cooper corrected him. "I knew his father; he was a clerk too. See now! these fellows who go in for reading and writing die before their time. They go without dinner and beg if necessary in order to look fine gentlemen; and yet a clerk is only a servant and can never be his own master for only the King is his own master in this life."

"And why should it be more gentleman-like to write?" asked the barber. "Isn't it perhaps just as difficult to cut a courtier's hair and to make him look smart, or to let someone's blood when he is in danger of his life?"

"I would like to see the clerk who would take less than ten years to make a big beer barrel," said the cooper. "Why, one knows the fellows require two years to draw up their petitions and such-like."

"And what is the good of it all?" asked the innkeeper. "Can I scribble such letters as they do, but don't I keep my accounts right? See here I draw a crucifix on the slate—that means the sexton; here I scribble the figure of a barrel—that stands for the cooper; then in

1251

a twinkling, however many strokes I have to make, I know exactly how many each has drunk."

"Yes, but no one else except yourself can read it, Mr. Innkeeper," objected a young man who had hitherto sat silent in a corner.

"That is the best of it," answered the innkeeper, "that no one can poke his nose into my accounts, and therefore I am just as good a clerk as anyone."

The cooper and the barber grinned approval.

"I knew the dead man's father," resumed the innkeeper. "He was a clerk too! And when he died I had to rub out many chalk-strokes which made up his account, for he wanted to be a fine gentleman, you see. All the inheritance he left to the son, who now lies with his nose pointing upwards, was a mother and two sisters. The young fellow wanted to be a tradesman in order to get food for four mouths, but his mother would not consent; she said it was a shame to step downward when one was above. And heavens, how the poor young fellow had to write! I know exactly what went on. The three women lived in one room and he in a rat-hole. All he could scrape together he had to give them; and when he came from work to eat his dinner, they deafened him with complaints. There was no butter on the bread, no sugar on the cakes; the elder sister wanted to have a new dress, and the younger a new mantle. Then he had to write through the whole night, and how he wrote! At last when his breast-bone stuck out like a hook and his face was as yellow as a leather strap, one day he felt tired; he came to me and borrowed a bottle of brandy. He was melancholy but also angry, for the elder sister had said she wanted a velvet jacket such as she had seen in the German shop, and his mother said ladies of their class could not do with less. The young fellow worked and slaved, but not with the same zest as formerly. And fancy! when he came here and took a glass to ease his chest, his conscience reproached him so much that he really believed he was stealing. And he had other troubles, the poor young fellow. A wooer came after the younger sister—a pewterer from Peter Apollo Street. But the sister said 'No!' and so did the mother, for he was only a pewterer. Had he been a clerk, she would have said 'Yes' and persuaded him that she loved him, and it is likely that she would really have done so, for such is love!"

All laughed except the young man, who struck in, "Well, innkeeper, but he loved her, although she was so poor and he was well off; that proves that love can be sincere, doesn't it?"

"Pooh!" said the innkeeper, who did not wish to be interrupted.

"But something else happened, and that finished him. He went and fell in love. His mother and sister had not counted on that, but it was the law of nature. And when he came and said that he thought of marrying, do you know what they said?—'Have you the means to?' And the youth, who was a little simple, considered and discovered that he had not means to establish a new family since he had one already, and so he did not marry; but he got engaged. And then there was a lot of trouble! His mother would not receive his fiancée, because her father could not write, and especially because she herself had been a dressmaker. It was still worse when the young man went in the evenings to her, and would not stay at home. A fine to-do there was! But still he went on working for his mother and sisters, and I know that in the evening he sat and wrote by his fiancée's side, while she sewed, only to save time and to be able to be near her. But his mother and sisters believed evil of the pair, and showed it too. It was one Sunday about dinner-time; he told me himself the young fellow, when he came here to get something for his chest, for now he coughed terribly. He had gone out with his fiancée to Brunke-berg, and as they were coming home over the North Bridge, whom did they meet but his mother and sisters? His fiancée wanted to turn back, but he held her arm firmly and drew her forward. But his mother remained standing by the bridge railings and looked into the water; the elder sister spat before her, and did the same, but the younger—she was a beauty! She stood still and stared at the young woman's woollen mantle and laughed, for she had one of English cloth—and just because of that, her brother's fiancée had to wear wool. Fancy the impudent hussy!"

"That was simply want of sense in the child," said the young man.

"Want of sense!" exclaimed the cooper indignantly. "Want of sense!" But he could not say any more.

The innkeeper took no notice of the interruption and continued: "It was a Christmas Eve, the last Christmas Eve on which he was alive. He came to me as usual to get something for his chest, which was very bad. 'A Merry Christmas, Hans!' I said. I sat where I am sitting now, and he sat just where you are sitting, young sir. 'Are you bad?' I asked. 'Yes,' he answered, 'and your slate is full.' 'It doesn't matter,' I answered, 'we can write down the rest in the great book up there. A glass of hot *Schnapps* does one good on Christmas Eve.' He was coughing terribly, and so he took a drink. Then his tongue was loosened. He said how miserable and forlorn he felt this evening. He had just left his home. The Christmas table was laid.

His mother and sisters were soft and mild, as one usually is on such an evening. They said nothing, they did not reproach him, but when he took his coat and was about to go out, his mother wept and said it was the first Christmas Eve that her son was absent. But do you think that she had so much heart as to say 'Go to her, bring her here, and let us be at peace like friends.' No! she only thought of herself, and so he went with an aching heart. Poor fellow! But hear what followed. Then he came to his fiancée. She was glad and happy to have him, and now she saw that he loved her better than anything else on earth. But the young man, whose heart was torn in two, was not so cheerful as she wished him to be, and then she was vexed with him, a little only of course. Then they talked about marriage, but he could not agree with her. No, he had duties towards his father's widow. But she quoted the priest who had said a man should leave father and mother and remain with his wife. He asked whether he had not left his mother and home this evening with a bleeding heart in order to be with her. She replied that she had already noticed, when he came, that he was depressed because he was going to spend the evening with her. He answered it was not that which depressed him, but his having to leave his old mother on Christmas Eve. Then she objected that he could not deny he had been depressed when he came to her—and so they went on arguing, you can imagine how!"

The cooper nodded intelligently.

"Well, it was a pleasant Christmas for him. Enough! The young fellow was torn in two, piece by piece; he never married. But now he lies at rest, if the coffin nails hold; but it was a sad business for him, poor devil, even if he was a fool. And God bless his soul! Hans Schönschreiber, if you have no greater list of debts than you had with me, they are easily settled!"

So saying, the innkeeper took his black slate from the counter, and with his elbow rubbed out a whole row of chalk-strokes which had been made under a hieroglyph which looked like a pen in an inkpot.

"See," said the barber, who had been looking through the window to hide his red eyes, "see, there she is!"

Outside in the churchyard the funeral service was at an end; the priest had pressed the hands of the mourners and was about to go; the sexton plied his spade in order to fill up the grave again, as a woman dressed in black pressed through the crowd, fell on her knees by the edge of the grave, and offered a silent prayer. Then she let fall a wreath of white roses into the grave, and a faint

sobbing and whispering was audible as the rose leaves fell apart on the black coffin lid. Then she stood up to go, erect and proud, but did not at first notice in the crowd that her dead lover's mother was regarding her with wild and angry looks as though she saw her worst enemy, who had robbed her of her dearest. Then they stood for a moment opposite one another, revengeful and ready for battle; but suddenly their features assumed a milder expression, their pale faces twitched, and they fell in each other's arms and wept. They held each other in a long, convulsive embrace, and then departed side by side.

The innkeeper wept like a child without attempting to hide his emotion, the barber pressed his face against the window, and the cooper took the cards out of his pocket as though to arrange them; but the young man, his head propped in his hands, had placed himself against the wall in order to have a support, for he wept so that his whole body shook and his legs trembled.

The innkeeper first broke the silence. "Who will now help the poor family? The pewterer would be accepted now, were he to make another proposal."

"How do you know that, innkeeper?" asked the young man, much moved, as he stepped into the centre of the room.

"Well, I heard it yesterday when I was up there helping at the preparations for the funeral. But the pewterer will not have her now, as she would not have him then."

"Yes he will, innkeeper!" said the young man. "He will have her though she were ever so selfish and bad-tempered, poor, and wretched, for such is love!"

So saying, he left the astonished innkeeper and his friends.

"Deuce take me—that was he himself!" said the barber.

"Things do not always end so happily," remarked the cooper.

"How about the clerk?" objected the barber.

"No, they did not end well with him, but with the others, you know. They had, as it were, more right to live than he, the young one; for they were alive first, and he who first comes to the mill, grinds his corn first."

"The young fellow was stupid, that was the whole trouble," said the barber.

"Yes, yes," concluded the inkeeper. "He certainly was stupid, but it was fine of him anyhow."

In that they were all agreed.

SUDRAKA

SUDRAKA (Sanskrit, 1st or 2nd century B.C.). Legendary Hindu Prince and
Sanskrit dramatist, to whom the drama *Mricchakatikā* (*The Clay Cart*) is at-
tributed. Even this is dubious, since play probably dates from fifth century
A.D. Nothing known of his life.

THE CLAY CART

The first scene represents a court in front of Caru-datta's house.
His friend Maitreya—who, although a Brahman, acts the part of
a sort of jovial companion, and displays a disposition of mixed
shrewdness and simplicity—laments Caru-datta's fallen fortunes,
caused by his too great liberality. Caru-datta replies thus:—

Caru-datta. Think not, my friend, I mourn departed wealth.
One thing alone torments me.—that my guests
Desert my beggared house, like to the bees
That swarm around the elephant, when dews
Exhale from his broad front; but quickly leave
His dried-up temples when they yield no sweets.
Maitreya. The sons of slaves! These guests you speak of are
always ready to make a morning meal off a man's property.
Caru-datta. It is most true, but I bestow no thought
On my lost property,—as fate decrees
Wealth comes and goes; but this is torture to me,—
That friendships I thought firm hang all relaxed
And loose, when poverty sticks closest to me.
From poverty 'tis but a step to shame—
From shame to loss of manly self-respect;
Then comes disdainful scorn, then dark despair
O'erwhelms the mind with melancholy thoughts,
Then reason goes, and last of all comes ruin.
Oh! poverty is source of every ill.
Maitreya. Ah well, cheer up! Let's have no more of these woe-
begone memories. What's lost can't be recovered.
Caru-datta. Good! I will grieve no more. Go you, my friend,
And offer this oblation, just prepared,
Unto the gods, and mothers of us all.
Maitreya. Not I.

Caru-datta. And why not, pray?

Maitreya. Why, what's the use, when the gods you have worshiped have done nothing for you?

Caru-datta. Friend, speak not thus, for worship is the duty
Of every family; the gods are honored
By offerings, and gratified by acts
Of penance and restraint in thought and word.
Therefore, delay not to present the oblation.

Maitreya. I don't intend to go; send some one else.

Caru-datta. Stay quiet then for a little, till I have finished
My religious meditations and prayer.

They are supposed here to retire, and a voice is heard behind
the scenes:—

Stop! Vasanta-sena, stop!

The heroine of the play now appears in front of Caru-datta's
house, pursued by the king's worthless but wealthy brother-in-law,
called Samsthanaka, who is an embodiment of everything vicious
and mean, in exact contrast to Caru-datta.

Samsthanaka. Stop! Vasanta-sena, stop! Why do you run away?
Don't be alarmed. I am not going to kill you. My poor heart is on
fire with love, like a piece of meat placed on a heap of burning coals.

Vasanta-sena. Noble sir, I am only a weak woman.

Samsthanaka. That is just why I don't intend murdering you.

Vasanta-sena. Why then do you pursue me? Do you seek my
jewels?

Samsthanaka. No, I only seek to gain your affections.

At this point the frightened Vasanta-sena discovers that she is
close to Caru-datta's house. He is not only loved by her, but greatly
respected as a man of honor; and under cover of the evening darkness, now supposed to have supervened, she slips into the courtyard
of his house by a side door, and hides herself. A companion who is
with the king's brother now counsels him to desist from following
her, by remarking:—

An elephant is bound by a chain,
A horse is curbed by a bridle and rein;
But a woman is only held by her heart—
If you can't hold that, you had better depart.

1257

Samsthanaka, however, forces his way into Caru-datta's house; and there finding Caru-datta's friend and companion Maitreya, thus addresses him:—

Take this message to Caru-datta.—Vasanta-sena loves you, and has taken refuge in your house. If you will deliver her up, you shall be rewarded by my everlasting friendship; if not, I shall remain your enemy till death. Give this message, so that I may hear you from the neighboring terrace; refuse to say exactly what I have told you, and I will crush your head as I would a wood apple beneath a door.

He then leaves the stage.

Maitreya accordingly delivers the message. Soon afterwards the heroine Vasanta-sena ventures into the presence of Caru-datta, asks pardon for intruding into his house, requests him to take charge of a golden casket containing her ornaments as a deposit left in trust, and solicits his friend's escort back to her own house.

Maitreya is too much alarmed to accompany her, so Caru-datta himself escorts Vasanta-sena home.

So far is an epitome of the first act.

At the commencement of the second act a gambler is introduced running away from the keeper of a gaming house, named Mathura, and another gambler to whom the first gambler has lost money, who are both pursuing him.

First Gambler. The master of the tables and the gamester are at my heels: how can I escape them? Here is an empty temple: I will enter it walking backwards, and pretend to be its idol.

Mathura. Ho there! stop, thief! A gambler has lost ten suvarnas, and is running off without paying. Stop him, stop him!

Second Gambler. He has run as far as this point; but here the track is lost.

Marthura. Ah! I see,—the footsteps are reversed: the rogue has walked backwards into this temple which has no image in it.

They enter and make signs to each other on discovering the object of their search, who pretends to be an idol fixed on a pedestal.

Second Gambler. Is this a wooden image, I wonder?

Mathura. No, no, it must be made of stone, I think. (*So saying,*

1258

they shake and pinch him.) Never mind, sit we down here, and play out our game. (*They commence playing.*)

First Gambler (*still acting the image, but looking on and with difficulty restraining his wish to join in the game. Aside*). The rattling of dice is as tantalizing to a penniless man as the sound of drums to a dethroned monarch; verily it is sweet as the note of a nightingale.

Second Gambler. The throw is mine, the throw is mine!

Mathura. No, it is mine, I say.

First Gambler (*forgetting himself and jumping off his pedestal*). No, I tell you it is mine.

Second Gambler. We've caught him!

Mathura. Yes, rascal, you're caught at last: hand over the suvarnas.

First Gambler. Worthy sir, I'll pay them in good time.

Mathura. Hand them over this very minute, I say. (*They beat him.*)

First Gambler (*aside to Second Gambler*). I'll pay you half if you will forgive me the rest.

Second Gambler. Agreed.

First Gambler (*aside to Mathura*). I'll give you security for half if you will let me off the other half.

Mathura. Agreed.

First Gambler. Then good morning to you, sirs; I'm off.

Mathura. Hullo! stop there, where are you going so fast? Hand over the money.

First Gambler. See here, my good sirs, one has taken security for half, and the other has let me off another half. Isn't it clear I have nothing to pay?

Mathura. No, no, my fine fellow: my name is Mathura, and I'm not such a fool as you take me for. Don't suppose I'm going to be cheated out of my ten suvarnas in this way. Hand them over, you scoundrel.

Upon that they set to work beating the unfortunate gambler, whose cries for help bring to his rescue another gamster who happens to be passing. A general scuffle now takes place, and in the midst of the confusion the first gambler escapes. In his flight he comes to the house of Vasanta-sena, and finding the door open, rushes in. Vasanta-sena inquires who he is and what he wants. He then recites his story, and makes known to her that having been once in the

service of Caru-datta, and having been discharged by him on account of his reduced circumstances, he has been driven to seek a livelihood by gambling. The mention of Caru-datta at once secures Vasanta-sena's aid; and the pursuers having now tracked their fugitive to the door of her house, she sends them out a jeweled bracelet, which satisfies their demands, and they retire. The gambler expresses the deepest gratitude, hopes in return to be of use to Vasanta-sena at some future time, and announces his intention of abandoning his disreputable mode of life and becoming a Buddhist mendicant.

The third act opens with a scene inside Caru-datta's house. The time is supposed to be night. Caru-datta and Maitreya are absent at a concert. A servant is preparing their sleeping couches, and commences talking to himself thus:—

A good master who is kind to his servants, even though he be poor, is their delight; while a harsh fellow, who is always finding fault and has nothing but his money to be proud of, is a perpetual torment from morning to night. Well, well! one can't alter nature: an ox can't be kept out of a field of corn, and a man once addicted to gambling can't be induced to leave off. My good master has gone to a concert. I must await his return; so I may as well take a nap in the hall.

Meanwhile Caru-datta and Maitreya come back, and the servant delivers Vasanta-sena's golden casket, saying that it is his turn to take charge of it by night. They now lie down.

Maitreya. Are you sleepy?
Caru-datta. Yes:
I feel inconstant sleep, with shadowy form
Viewless and wayward, creep across my brow
And weigh my eyelids down; her soft approach
Is like Decay's advance, which stronger grows
Till it has mastered all our faculties,
And life is lost in blank unconsciousness.

The whole household is soon buried in slumber, when a thief named Sarvilaka is seen to approach. His soliloquy, while he proceeds to accomplish his design of breaking into the house, is curious, as showing that an Indian burglar's mode of operation in ancient

times differed very little from that now in fashion. Moreover, it appears that the whole practice of housebreaking was carried on by professional artists according to certain fixed rules and principles, which a master of the science, named Yogacarya, had embodied in a kind of "Thieves' Manual" for the better training of his disciples. It is evident, too, that the fraternity of thieves, burglars, and rogues had a special presiding Deity and Patron in India, much in the same way as in ancient Greece and Rome.

It may be noted also, as still more curious, that the particular burglar here introduced is represented as a Brahman, that he is made to speak the learned language, Sanskrit, and to display acquaintance with Sanskrit literature; while all the subordinate characters in Indian dramas, including women of rank, are represented as speaking one or other of the provincial dialects called Prakrit. Here is part of the burglar's soliloquy:—

I advance creeping stealthily along the ground, like a snake wiggling out of its worn-out skin, making a path for my operations by the sheer force of my scientific craft, and artfully constructing an opening just big enough to admit my body with ease.

This friendly night which covers all the stars
With a thick coat of darkness, acts the part
Of a kind mother, shrouding me, her son,
Whose valor is displayed in night assaults
Upon my neighbors, and whose only dread
Is to be pounced upon by royal watchmen.

Good! I have made a hole in the garden wall, and am now in the midst of the premises. Now for an attack on the four walls of the house itself.

Men call this occupation mean, which thrives
By triumphing o'er sleeping enemies.
This, they say, is not chivalry but burglary:
But better far reproach with independence,
Than cringing service without liberty;
And did not Aswatthaman long ago
O'erpower in night attack his slumbering foe?

Where shall I make my breach? Ah! here's a rat hole—this is the very thing we disciples of the god Skanda hail as the best guide

1261

to our operations, and the best omen of success. Here then I must begin my excavation, that is clear; but how shall I proceed? The golden-speared god has taught four methods of making a breach: namely,—pulling out baked bricks, cutting through unbaked ones; soaking a mud wall with water, and boring through one made of wood. This wall is evidently of baked bricks, so they must be pulled out. Now for the shape of the hole. It must be carved according to some orthodox pattern: shall it be like a lotus blossom, the sun, a crescent, a lake, a triangle, or a jar? I must do it cleverly, so that to-morrow morning people may look at my handiwork with wonder, and say to each other, "None but a skilled artist could have done this!" The jar shape looks best in a wall of baked bricks. Be it so: now, then, to work! Reverence to the golden-speared god Karttikeya, the giver of all boons! Reverence to Yogacarya, whose chief disciple I am, and who was so pleased with his pupil that he gave me a magical pigment, which, when spread over my body, prevents any police officer from catching sight of me and any weapons from harming my limbs. Ah! what a pity! I have forgotten my measuring line. Never mind, I can use my Brahmanical cord,—a most serviceable implement to all Brahmans, especially to men of my profession. It serves to measure a wall, or to throw round ornaments which have to be drawn from their places, or to lift the latch of a door, or to bind up one's finger when bitten by insects or snakes. And now, to commence measuring. Good! the hole is exactly the right size; only one brick remains! Ah! botheration! I am bitten by a snake: I must bind up my finger and apply the antidote that's the only cure. Now I am all right again. Let me first peep in. What! A light gleams somewhere! Never mind! the breach being perfect, I must creep in. Reverence to Karttikeya! How now! two men asleep! Are they really asleep, or only shamming? If they are shamming, they won't bear the glimmer of this lamp when passed over their faces;—they are fast asleep, I believe,—their breathing is regular, their eyes are firmly closed, their joints are all relaxed, and their limbs protrude beyond the bed. What have we here? Here are tabors, a lute, flutes, and books; why, I must have broken into the house of a dancing master; I took it for the mansion of a man of rank.

He helps himself to the casket, and proceeds to make good his escape.
The noise he makes in going out rouses its inmates, and they

discover that the house has been robbed. Caru-datta is greatly
shocked at the loss of Vasanta-sena's casket, which had been
deposited with him in trust. He has only one valuable thing left,
—a necklace or string of jewels, forming part of the private property
of his wife. This he sends by Maitreya to Vasanta-sena as a substitute for the casket.

SUN HSI-CHEN

SUN HSI-CHEN (Chinese, 1906-   ). Novelist popular among Chinese youth.
Admired for his stories of rural life. Most widely known books: *Beaten Gold,
Woman of the Night,* and a war trilogy: *The Field of War, War,* and
After War.

AH AO

THROUGHOUT the day, from early dawn Ah Ao had remained hidden
under a bed in the small dark room, her head bent, her body still,
scarcely daring to breathe.

At the foot of the Purple-Red Mountain, down which spilled a
dense growth of fragrant pines and other trees, a small stream ran
into the open cornfields, and beside it stood a row of seven houses,
most of them old and dilapidated. This place was known as Tao
Village, although none of the inhabitants was named Tao. In four of
the seven houses lived the family Chen, the house on the western end
was a family temple reserved for the spirits, while in the center of
the row stood a comparatively new and handsome residence (some
eighteen years old) which was owned by Chin the Rich.

It was in the seventh house, poorest of all, consisting of five little
rooms, where the Wang family dwelt, that Ah Ao lay hidden. Half
of this house was in fact mortgaged to Chin the Rich who, two years
before, when old Wang died, had lent his widow forty thousand cash
to pay for the funeral feast and obsequies. Consequently she now
lived with her son, Small One Brother, and her daughter, Ah Ao, in
only the nether part of the little hut, which did not belong to Chin
the Rich. In the room next to the kitchen—or rather in one corner of
the kitchen itself, since the bed was separated from it only by a few
thin planks—Ah Ao, in secret dread, trembled and stifled her lungs
all day.

Some grindstones and empty bamboo baskets leaned against the
wall of the kitchen, which was just now very noisy. There were **four**

1263

square wooden tables, with long benches ranged on each side, and these, with their occupants, completely choked up the little room. Altogether one could count more than thirty men, including not only the male population of Tao Village but also guests from the neighboring villages of Yu and Red Wall. They sat drinking and feasting in exuberant mood. Most of them wore blue or white cotton shirts and trousers and were in their bare feet. Chin the Rich, Wu the Merchant, who could read and write, and the Hairy-Headed Village Elder, respected for his age, wore long gowns, however, made of linen. Only on rare occasions did these long-gown men visit such a lowly establishment, and it was plain that they were now quite aware of the extraordinary dignity their appearance lent to the feast.

The food seemed simple enough, with but four big bowls of meat, fish, turnips and soup, spread on each table, but they were refilled again and again, and each time emptied almost as soon as replenished. Later on, besides, the women of the village would have to be fed. Everybody gorged, helping himself to great hunks of meat and full bowls of wine without any pretense at etiquette; their presence at the feast was not in the interest of good will, but a punitive measure against the mother of a shameless daughter. Never mind the financial burden to Widow Wang! It was the only way of justice.

The fact was that only by mortgaging the other half of her house had the unhappy woman managed to get together the money to finance this strange banquet. A sentimental person might have observed that what the guests clipped between the blades of chopsticks was actually Widow Wang's flesh and blood; for the feast meant utter ruin to her. By this sacrifice, however, she was saving the life of her daughter, who was, no one could deny it, guilty of that crime. Now, although a crime of such a nature necessarily required two to commit it, the unwritten but powerful law of custom nevertheless made her alone responsible, and gave any villager the right to attack, insult, abuse or kill her, as he saw fit. By what other means, then, could the child's life be saved, than through this, an expensive banquet in honor of the offended villagers, with the especial aim of winning mercy from Chin the Rich, Wu the Merchant and the Hairy-Headed Village Elder? Even though it meant her own death in the end, still the widow would have gone through with it.

Two days before, in the afternoon, she had sent her son to Chin. He had bowed, begged mercy and requested the loan of thirty thousand cash, pledging the rest of the Wang House as security. Then with this money the boy had, again at his mother's instruction, gone

to the market where he bought thirty pounds of meat, more than twenty pounds of fish, fully a bushel of turnips and some other ingredients of the feast. Since early in the morning of the previous day she had busied herself with cleaning and making ready this food, preparing rice wine and attending to other duties, so that she had not once had a moment to rest.

With the arrival of the guests she had become even busier. All alone, she worked ceaselessly, serving everybody, keeping all the bowls filled with food, pouring forth the warm wine that was like emptying the vessels of her own body, but all the same managing to smile and give the appearance of enjoying her duties immensely.

"Brother Lucky Root," shouted one coarse fellow, "don't hesitate! This isn't an occasion for ceremony, but a free feed. See, you don't have to give anything in return: so eat up! Fill yourself to the brim!"

"You are quite right," agreed Lucky Root. "Why be slow about it, eh? Let's eat; for such opportunities as this are rare indeed. As a matter of fact this girl now, Ah Ao; shameless, but still rather good-looking. How many girls around compare with her? Actually—?"

"The more girls like Ah Ao the more free feasts," yelled a third. "Personally I hope we'll have others."

"Ai-ya. Old Fa! Always boasting. You, the hungry devil with women! But don't forget the facts in this case; the girl right under your noses chooses instead a fellow from a neighboring village, not you!"

"Old Fa, ha, ha!"

"Ho, what an—Old Fa!"

The Widow Wang did not appear to understand these remarks, but bent her attention on the tasks of service and of maintaining the smile on her face. She did not once frown. But Ah Ao heard and trembled and crawled still farther toward the wall. She did not know whether the feeling she experienced was humiliation or terror or indignation or merely a heavy sadness, but something like a great stone seemed to be crushing her down, and her heart burned as if pierced by a shaft of red-hot iron. A few days ago she had boldly resigned herself to whatever fate might bring, but now she wanted only to crawl, crawl, crawl.

The Hairy-Headed Elder at last came to the issue. "To be precise," he began slowly, "this is perhaps after all not so serious a matter. It is natural for a grown girl to want marriage, isn't it so? But to make love—to a young man—in secret, you know, and without anybody's knowledge—without the usual formalities—who can excuse it?"

"Exactly!" exclaimed Wu the Merchant. "Widow Wang, this is something that can come to a mother only as punishment for her own sins in the past. Such a daughter, just consider, is not only a disgrace to your own family name but to the whole Tao Village as well. You very well know that according to age-old custom this crime merits nothing less than death. Recall, now, the case of the Chao girl—it happened three or four years ago in Stone Gate Village—who was beaten to death for the very same offense. Do you remember, she was buried without even a coffin? Nobody could call it cruelty, but only justice; for she had violated the laws of right conduct. Moreover, the worst of it is that even after their death such girls continue to dishonor the good name of the community. Ending life does not end their sin—no, indeed, and, as everyone knows, death doesn't begin to make up for it!"

"What you have just said is undeniably true. Death doesn't cover up the crime at all. But, on the other hand, it's not altogether the girl's fault. The mother is to blame also—a certain laxness, a waning of discipline. Again, in this case it may be that the mother was not herself very virtuous in some previous incarnation. Widow Wang, let me advise you to take care—in this life you had better be more strict."

The Village Elder was the donor of this speech, which oddly did not seem to anger the Widow, but on the contrary encouraged her to speak. She moved forward timidly, her hands pulling nervously on the edge of her worn dress. She spoke, in a very low voice, and smiled painfully:

"Yes, Honored Elder—that is correct. If she did wrong it was really my fault. I don't know what unpardonable sin I have back of me in some previous existence, but it must be as you say. And this terrible crime of my daughter, you're quite right, death would only be the punishment deserved. Still—" she broke suddenly into tears. "But I can't speak, I haven't 'face' to say—only I ask—*mercy!* Spare her life at least."

This was a reckless demand, an extraordinary request indeed, and were it not that the villagers were at that moment eating her food she would never have escaped ridicule by them. They believed in enforcing justice and morality to the letter, and ordinarily would stand no nonsense. Yet it seemed generally understood that because they had appeared, and had eaten, and had enjoyed themselves, and had some of them even come on their own invitation, they would not be altogether adamant. But their decision rested upon the opinions voiced

1266

by Chin the Rich, Wu the Merchant and the Hairy-Headed. Everybody remained silent until Chin finally gave the verdict.

"Wu has, I agree, spoken very wisely, and very much to the point. 'Death doesn't begin to cover up the crime.' Precisely! Then, perhaps, or so it seems to me, little is to be gained by taking her life now. The guilt has been admitted, and the Widow Wang, asking mercy, has begged us also to give 'face' to her late husband. She wants us to spare her daughter's life, and everything considered that is perhaps possible, but at the same time we cannot permit such an altogether immoral woman to continue to besmirch the village good name. She must leave at once!"

The Elder shared this view. "What is done is done; though totally without honor, still it's no use, now, to kill her. Better, as you say, expel her—move her out immediately."

These two having rendered a judgment, the rest of the guests, who considered themselves a kind of "jury," reined in their tongues. The decision was unanimously approved. The pale, weary face of the Widow Wang broke out suddenly into a genuine smile; she bowed low to the three wise men and obsequiously thanked the members of the self-appointed jury. But, back in the darkness, the hidden Ah Ao heard and yet curiously did not feel happy at all at this reprieve. She understood well enough that life had been miraculously restored to her, but although the prospect of death had been terrifying she was after all too young to have a deep fear of it, whereas to be banished from the village, to leave and never again to see her mother, to bid farewell to her brother, to plunge into an unknown, uncertain future —that was something which she knew to be worse than death. Grief shook her body, seemed to break, to shatter it, so that it was no longer whole, but a heap of something that mysteriously still trembled with life.

It had happened two months before, in early April, on a day filled with an ineffable softness, an unbearable languor and gladness that made men dreamy-eyed, drowsy and as if drunk with some wonderful wine.

Ah Ao, on her way home in the afternoon from the near-by Yu Village, thought that she had never known such a glorious day. There was a new warmth in her body, a strange vigor in her as if she had just begun to live. The fields bordering the road were touched from a withered yellow into a lush new green, the trees were coming to life, and in their budding limbs birds had appeared and were joyously

chattering. The whole world, as far as she could see, was young, fresh, growing, awakened, expectant. She felt in harmony with all that she saw, and expectant too. Of what? She did not know, but somehow she found herself walking more slowly. Her face burned as from some inner fire, and she became all at once conscious of her body, vibrant and warm against the fabric of her garments.

"Ah Ao—" a voice called from somewhere.

Surprised and a little afraid, she stopped, looked around, peered over the fields into the clustered pines and through the rocky pass, but saw no one. Above her head a pair of eagles circled. She blushed, rubbed her burning face and walked on.

"Ah Ao—" someone cried again, but this time much nearer. She stopped, more puzzled, but saw no one, and started to go on, when once more she heard the same voice, now quite close, speak out, "Ah Ao, it's me!" Turning round quickly, she saw, protruding from the bushes and greenery, a head. Then slowly a young man in a long linen gown gave her a full-length view of himself, including his handsome red-buttoned cap. He was perhaps twenty years old, not a bad-looking fellow, and he wore on his face a pleased look. Ah Ao recognized him. He was the son of Li, a shop-owner in the neighboring village. His name, she knew as Ah Hsian.

"*Ai-ya!* so it's you," said Ah Ao. "You frightened me almost to death. Where did you come from?" Nevertheless, she seemed not altogether dissatisfied that he had appeared.

"I?" he demanded. "I? I just happened to be coming from town, saw you in the distance and hid myself to have some fun with you."

"You impudent rascal!" she shouted gaily, raising her hand as if to slap him. "Frightening a person to death!"

"I apologize, Ah Ao, with all my heart. The truth is I have something very important to tell you."

"For example?"

But the youth suddenly became weak or timid. He kept murmuring "I—I—I—" Then he seized her hand.

"What is this?" Ah Ao started back quickly, but for some reason her legs refused to move. Her body quivered, as from some shock, and again she felt her flesh warm beneath her garments. All the strength seemed to run out of her. He put his arms around her, pulled her toward him, and then led her into the forest. She could not summon up any resistance, her mind did not seem to work as usual, she was hardly conscious that they moved at all, and she did not utter a

1268

sound. She only knew that within she felt intolerably buoyant and enlarged.

They sat down under the leafy arm of a tree, her head resting upon his shoulder. Her eyes closed and she breathed rapidly. She felt his hand close softly over her breast, over her beating heart. She felt his lips upon hers, and suddenly she knew a bodily glow that she had never felt before.

"Caw-w-w," a magpie circling overhead, startled her, and for a moment recalled to her that the world existed. She trembled. "Ah Hsian! No, no! Don't, please! Mother will beat me to death!"

"Don't, you must not worry. Trust me, believe in me; everything will be wonderful, like this always."

His voice shook too, and some strange vibrancy of it, some summons which she had never heard before, and which would not be denied, completely overpowered her. He caressed her arms, her face, her throat. She ceased to resist.

"What is the matter with you, Ah Ao?" Widow Wang asked her daughter when, very much agitated, she returned home late that afternoon. "Fever?" She touched her forehead, which was covered with a short fringe of hair. "Have you caught a cold?"

"Nothing at all. I—I simply don't feel very well—" Ah Ao murmured, half to herself. She went to the bed and lay down and for a long time she did not stir. She knew very well the risks, the danger, the fate opening up ahead of her, but just as well she knew that she would meet Ah Hsian again, whenever he asked, yes, even tomorrow!

She expected something dreadful to happen; she prepared herself for it. In the future, after each interval with him, she waited dully for the exposure of their crime, and each time was rather surprised when no one came to denounce her. Nevertheless, she resigned herslf to ultimate discovery, but found comfort in the thought that her lover would come to her defense, take punishment as pronounced: and she imagined herself, in his moment of disgrace, going proudly to his side, sharing whatever fate imposed upon him. And what she constantly feared did happen at last, but its consequences were nothing like what she had romantically foreseen. It was just three days before the Widow Wang offered the villagers such a splendid banquet.

Behind Purple-Red Mountain there was a small hill, the name of which had long been forgotten. Halfway up its flank, nearly buried in the foliage, was a temple to the mountain god. The surrounding forests were owned by one of the great landlords, and few ventured

1269

to trespass through the leafy lanes. The place was pervaded by a ghostly stillness, but it was gentle shelter for young lovers.

On this day Lao Teh, the Spotted Face, a woodcutter, had stealthily crept into the forest to steal wood. He had gathered a load and was prepared to leave just as the setting sun splashed ruddily against the wall behind the mountain temple. The sight invited him, and he sat down on the threshold of the enclosure, sighed, lighted his pipe and gazed at the sky.

But was that not a sound? Thrusting the pipe into his girdle. he seized his ax and stood ready to combat with any wild animal that might rush forth. He waited for several minutes, tense and excited. He thought of running away but reconsidered, remembering that "an offensive is the best defensive." Picking up a stone as big as a goose egg, he threw it with all his strength into the thickest part of the forest.

To his astonishment it was not a wild beast but a man that burst from the trees. He did not stop or even look in Lao Teh's direction, but vanished like a devil. Lao Teh nevertheless saw enough of him to recognize Ah Hsian. Somewhat perplexed, he advanced toward the spot whence he had emerged.

Then, in a moment he came upon Ah Ao, languidly spread out, with her dress loosened, her dark hair starred with bits of green leaves, and altogether wearing a look of abandon. The spectacle somehow aroused in Lao Teh, the Spotted Face, an intense fury. He stared with wide-open eyes, and then he bent down and severely struck her.

"Ha! Ah Ao! The devil! You've done a fine thing!" She did not speak, but lifted up eyes that implored and eloquently begged pity. "Scandalous and shameless one! To come here in secret and lie with him!"

Later on, this scene and the subsequent abuse flung upon her by the infuriated Lao Teh remained rather obscure in Ah Ao's mind. She could not remember how, under his guidance, she returned home in disgrace, nor how news of her love spread throughout the village in a few minutes. Only afterward all the eyes she looked into were full of wrath, cold-gleaming eyes of hate. Even her mother gazed at her with anger and bitterness, yet deeper. deep down in those eyes, was a look of poignant sadness that troubled her heart. But the blows of bamboo sticks, the beatings that came in rapid succession, the curses hurled at her, not one of these caused her any pain, nor any shame, nor even the least regret.

She had expected all this, and now it had come. It was no accident,

but had all along been in the certainty of fate, and she was prepared for everything that happened. The single unforeseen development that dismayed and depressed her was that her lover suffered none of the consequences and did not appear to be in the least interested in her any longer.

Even before the men guests had finished sipping the last of their wine, the women began to come for their share, and during all this time Ah Ao continued to press closely against the wall, hovering in her hiding place, hungry and shivering, not because it was cold, not because she felt any longer the fear of death, but from some nameless malady that had seized her inmost being. The women ate no more lightly than their menfolk, and like the men they dropped cynical, sardonic remarks meant to stab mother and daughter cruelly.

The air seemed charged with heightened drama when Mrs. Li, the fat mother of Ah Hsian, unexpectedly appeared at the feast. She had come, it was soon apparent, not to apologize for the part her son had taken in the affair, but on the contrary to curse the Widow Wang for permitting her daughter to induce him to commit adultery. At sight of the unhappy mother, she pointed fixedly at her and began loudly to revile her: "Miserable woman! Where there is such a daughter, there is such a mother also! And you have the 'face' to come to meet me? Actually? My son is pure, chaste, good; he has made the genuflections before the image of Confucius; he has understood well the teachings of the great sage. Yet you, shameless mother and immoral daughter, attempt to seduce and ruin him! I am resolved to die with you this instant!"

And, saying this, she did indeed rush toward the Widow Wang and appeared to be determined to dash her brains out against her. Other woman guests grouped round them, forming a little circle, not without experiencing an inner satisfaction at the scene, and comforting and soothing the wrath of the offended Mrs. Li. The fat woman in fact so far forgot her original intention that she partook heartily of the feast and in the end contented herself with muttering now and then, "She abused my son, seduced him—from now on he will be unable to raise his head above others!"

When the last guest had gone, the old woman stepped slowly into the little dark enclosure, carrying an oil lamp in her hand. She called to Ah Ao to come out and eat, and the girl dragged herself forth, but she had scarcely strength enough to stand erect. A moment ago she had thought herself famished; now she could not swallow a morsel.

Midnight. Widow Wang was not yet in bed. She moved about in the little room, picking up articles from here and there, busily arranging them in the baggage which Ah Ao must take with her when she left at tomorrow's dawn. Finally she fastened the bag.

Spring nights are brief; in a very short time the cocks began to crow. The widow awoke her son and daughter, lighted a lantern, gave them their morning food and then accompanied Ah Ao almost at once to the barrow which stood beside the door.

"Understand, daughter, it's not I who wants to desert you—you have spoiled yourself—" But the stooped figure shook with sudden tears. She seemed to brace herself against the air, and continued, managing to smile very gently: "Just be careful, Ah Ao. From now on stand firmly on your own feet, and I shall have no more cause for worry. As for me, daughter, well just think that I am dead, no longer in this world. If we can't meet here again, then perhaps after death; anyway, let's hope!"

She sat beside Ah Ao on the barrow pushed by her son until they reached the great oak, at the main road, half a mile from her home. She alighted there, bade a last farewell to her daughter and stood watching the receding lantern till, like the last flutter of life in a great void of death, its dim spark crept into utter darkness.

SU TUNG-P'O

SU TUNG-P'O (Su Shih, 1036-1101). Statesman and poet, highly revered by Chinese literary public. Also a great calligrapher and painter. Great number of his poems survive, as well as many brilliant prose essays. Collected works: *Tung-p'o ch'uan-chi.*

AUTUMN SUN

A DESCENDANT of Yüeh Wang, a worthy gentleman, dwells in a village without soil and croons verses without words. He once told Tung-p'o, the retired Scholar, that his mind was as pure as the rays of the Autumn Sun, his emotions as peaceful as its tranquillity. 'I love virtue,' he said, 'and am determined to bring it to perfection with the persistence of the Autumn Sun. I dislike all crops, and, in my dislike, desire to chastise them even as the Autumn Sun strikes that group of trees. So I am anxious to write some verses upon it. What does the master think?'

The retired Scholar with a smile answered, 'How can a gentleman like yourself appreciate the Autumn Sun? Born into a luxurious mansion, when older you roamed through the Emperor's Courts.— Out of doors you were sheltered by a large umbrella, at home you were waited upon behind curtain and veil. You could stand the hot weather up to the point of warmth and the winter to the point of coolness—that's all! What then can you know about the Autumn Sun?

'Now, a man like myself really appreciates it. When the summer floods become excessive, when the clouds become vapour and the rains fall, when the thunder rolls and the lightning flashes, rivers and lakes merge together and the god of the soil is in danger of drowning, then do boats sail on the city walls, the fish and the dragon enter the house, mildew covers the utensils, frogs and earth-worms crawl about the tables. At night, one must move five times to avoid the damp; in daytime, one must dry the clothes in the sun for three changes. But still there is nothing in all this to worry about!

'Now, in San-Wu there is a plot of ploughed land. The ripened grain becomes covered with fungi, the matured rice curls up into the mud. Drains and dykes overflow into one other, walls are ruined with holes and collapse into the mud. One's eyes glisten with tears as the smoke from the fuel in boiler and cauldron fills the room. All around, the neighborhood is silent. The crane cries in the doorway; the wife rises in the night and heaves a deep sigh, when she reckons up the number of foodless days, and wonders whether the clothing will last to the end of the year.

'Suddenly the cauldron sends out sparks in myriad confusion, and the lamp-wick hangs down in double blossom. Clear blows the west wind; the drums and bells resound. The slaves joyously tell me that this is the sign of no more rain. So I rise early to divine it, and I find that Hesperus, the evening star, is placid and no longer flashes as it bathes in the Valley of Sunshine and rises over Fu-Sang. Ere one has winked, the whole prospect has changed with wingéd flight to the crossbeams of the house. In that moment I feel as though I am awakening from a drunken slumber, like a dumb man who can speak, a paralytic who can rise and walk, or as though I am returning to my ancestral village and get my first glimpse of the elders! Have you, Sir, also tasted joy like this?' 'That's fine!' he answered, 'Although I cannot say that I have personally experienced this, yet I can well appreciate it.'

'The Sun,' continued the retired Scholar, 'moves through the South-

ern and the Northern Heavens in different ways. Its fierce and fiery heat is not the result of tyranny, nor is its soothing warmth due to tenderness, for the warmth of to-day is the heat of yesterday. Why then consider Summer as Tun and Winter as Ts'ui? We little men are easily vexed or glad, so that the dread of summer or the love of winter is just the same to us as the numbers 3 and 4 to a crowd of monkeys!

'From now onwards, understand this and be not in doubt. Live without plastering the door; go out without putting on a labourer's hat; and do not complain of the summer heat if you would not forget the virtues of the Autumn Sun.'

Whereat my nobleman clapped his hands and laughed as he wrote this down.

JONATHAN SWIFT

JONATHAN SWIFT (Irish, 1667-1745). Creator of one of world's most brutal and morbid satires on mankind, *Gulliver's Travels*, that later generations used as a children's book. Other famous satire, *The Tale of a Tub*, castigates Christianity. A masterful prose stylist, whose life was embittered by political setbacks. His ambiguous relations with two women, "Stella" and "Vanessa," have intrigued scholars, but remain unsolved.

THE EMPEROR OF LILLIPUT

THE Emperor is taller by almost the breadth of my nail than any of his court, which alone is sufficient to strike an awe into the beholders. His features are strong and masculine, with an Austrian lip, and arched nose; his complexion olive, his countenance erect, his body and limbs well-proportioned, all his movements graceful, and his deportment majestic. He was then past his prime, being twenty-eight years and three-quarters old, of which he had reigned seven in great felicity, and generally victorious. For the better convenience of beholding him, I lay on my side, so that my face was parallel to his, and he stood but three yards off. However, I have had him since many times in my hand, and therefore cannot be mistaken in my description. His dress was very plain and simple, and the fashion of it between the Asiatic and the European; but he had on his head a light helmet of gold, adorned with jewels, and a plume on the crest.

He held his sword drawn in his hand, to defend himself if I should happen to break loose. It was almost three inches long; the hilt and scabbard were gold, enriched with diamonds. His voice was shrill, but very clear and articulate; and I could distinctly hear it when I stood up. His Imperial Majesty spoke often to me, and I returned answers; but neither of us could understand a syllable.

THOUGHTS AND APHORISMS

AN old miser kept a tame jackdaw, that used to steal pieces of money, and hide them in a hole, which the cat observing, asked, "Why he would hoard up those round shining things that he could make no use of?"

"Why," said the jackdaw, "my master has a whole chestful, and makes no more use of them than I."

If the men of wit and genius would resolve never to complain in their works of critics and detractors, the next age would not know that they ever had any.

I never wonder to see men wicked, but I often wonder to see them not ashamed.

Imaginary evils soon become real ones, by indulging our reflections on them; as he, who in a melancholy fancy sees something like a face on the wall or the wainscot, can, by two or three touches with lead pencil, make it look visible, and agreeing with what he fancied.

Men of great parts are often unfortunate in the management of public business, because they art apt to go out of the common road by the quickness of their imagination. This I once said to my Lord Bolingbroke, and desired he would observe, that the clerks in his office used a sort of ivory knife with a blunt edge to divide a sheet of paper, which never failed to cut it even, only requiring a steady hand; whereas if they should make use of a sharp penknife, the sharpness would make it often go out of the crease, and disfigure the paper.

"He who does not provide for his own house," St. Paul says, "is worse than an infidel!" And I think he who provides only for his own house is just equal with an infidel.

When I am reading a book, whether wise or silly, it seems to me to be alive, and talking to me.

I never yet knew a wag (as the term is) who was not a dunce.

A person reading to me a dull poem of his own making, I prevailed on him to scratch out six lines together; in turning over the

1275

leaf, the ink being wet, it marked as many lines on the other side; whereof the poet complaining, I bid him be easy, for it would be better if those were out too.

We have just enough religion to make us hate, but not enough to make us love one another.

When we desire or solicit anything, our minds run wholly on the good side or circumstances of it; when it is obtained, our minds run wholly on the bad ones.

The latter part of a wise man's life is taken up in curing the follies, prejudices, and false opinions he had contracted in the former.

Would a writer know how to behave himself with relation to posterity, let him consider in old books what he finds that he is glad to know, and what omissions he most laments.

It is grown a word of course for writers to say, "the critical age," as divines say, "this sinful age."

It is pleasant to observe how free the present age is in laying taxes on the next: "Future ages shall talk of this: this shall be famous to all posterity;" whereas their time and thoughts will be taken up about present things, as ours are now.

I never heard a finer piece of satire against lawyers, than that of astrologers, when they pretend by rules of art to tell when a suit will end, and whether to the advantage of the plaintiff or defendant; thus making the matter depend entirely upon the influence of the stars, without the least regard to the merits of the cause.

I have known some men possessed of good qualities, which were very serviceable to others, but useless to themselves; like a sun-dial on the front of a house, to inform the neighbors and passengers, but not the owner within.

If a man would register all his opinions upon love, politics, religion, learning, &c., beginning from his youth, and so go on to old age, what a bundle of inconsistencies and contradictions would appear at last!

The stoical scheme of supplying our wants by lopping off our desires, is like cutting off our feet when we want shoes.

The reason why so few marriages are happy, is because young ladies spend their time in making nets, not in making cages.

The power of fortune is confessed only by the miserable; for the happy impute all their success to prudence or merit.

Ambition often puts men upon doing the meanest offices; so climbing is performed in the same posture with creeping.

Although men are accused for not knowing their own weakness, yet perhaps as few know their own strength. It is in men as in soils, where sometimes there is a vein of gold which the owner knows not of.

An idle reason lessens the weight of the good ones you gave before.

Arbitrary power is the natural object of temptation to a prince; as wine or women to a young fellow, or a bribe to a judge, or avarice to old age, or vanity to a woman.

The humor of exploding many things under the name of trifles, fopperies and only imaginary goods, is a very false proof either of wisdom or magnanimity, and a great check to virtuous actions. For instance, with regard to fame; there is in most people a reluctance and unwillingness to be forgotten. We observe, even among the vulgar, how fond they are to have an inscription over their grave. It requires but little philosophy to discover and observe that there is no intrinsic value in all this; however, if it be founded in our nature, as an incitement to virtue, it ought not to be ridiculed.

Complaint is the largest tribute Heaven receives, and the sincerest part of our devotion.

The common fluency of speech in many men, and most women, is owing to a scarcity of matter, and a scarcity of words; for whoever is a master of language, and hath a mind full of ideas, will be apt in speaking to hesitate upon the choice of both; whereas common speakers have only one set of ideas, and one set of words to clothe them in; and these are always ready at the mouth; so people come faster out of church when it is almost empty, than when a crowd is at the door.

To be vain is rather a mark of humility than pride. Vain men delight in telling what honors have been done them, what great company they have kept, and the like, by which they plainly confess that these honors were more than their due, and such as their friends would not believe if they had not been told: whereas a man truly proud thinks the greatest honors below his merit, and consequently scorns to boast. I therefore deliver it as a maxim, that whoever desires the character of a proud man ought to conceal his vanity.

I have known several persons of great fame for wisdom in public affairs and councils governed by foolish servants.

I have known great ministers, distinguished for wit and learning, who preferred none but dunces.

I have known men of great valor cowards to their wives.

I have known men of the greatest cunning perpetually cheated.

1277

Dignity, high station, or great riches, are in some sort necessary to old men, in order to keep the younger at a distance, who are otherwise too apt to insult them upon the score of their age.

Every man desires to live long, but no man would be old.

Love of flattery, in most men, proceeds from the mean opinion they have of themselves; in women, from the contrary.

Kings are commonly said to have long hands; I wish they had as long ears.

Princes, in their infancy, childhood and youth, are said to discover prodigious parts and wit, to speak things that surprise and astonish: strange, so many hopeful princes, so many shameful kings! If they happen to die young, they would have been prodigies of wisdom and virtue: if they live, they are often prodigies, indeed, but of another sort.

Apollo was held the god of physic and sender of diseases. Both were originally the same trade, and still continue.

"That was excellently observed," said I, when I read a passage in an author where his opinion agrees with mine: when we differ, there I pronounce him to be mistaken.

Very few men, properly speaking, live at present; but are providing to live another time.

As universal a practice as lying is, and as easy a one as it seems, I do not remember to have heard three good lies in all my conversation, even from those who were most celebrated in that faculty.

ALGERNON CHARLES SWINBURNE

ALGERNON CHARLES SWINBURNE (English, 1837-1909). Poet of late Victorian Era, who shocked his contemporaries by personal life (dipsomaniac) and literary output (earlier works, *Poems and Ballads*, seemed sex-obsessed). Other famous works: *Atalanta in Calydon* and *Songs Before Sunrise*. Master of verbal music and the singing line.

WHEN THE HOUNDS OF SPRING

When the hounds of spring are on winter's traces,
  The mother of months in meadow or plain
Fills the shadows and windy places
  With lisp of leaves and ripple of rain;

And the brown bright nightingale amorous
Is half assuaged for Itylus,
For the Thracian ships and the foreign faces,
    The tongueless vigil, and all the pain.

Come with bows bent, and with emptying of quivers,
    Maiden most perfect, lady of light,
With a noise of winds and many rivers,
    With a clamor of waters, and with might;
Bind on thy sandals, O thou most fleet,
Over the splendor and speed of thy feet;
For the faint east quickens, the wan west shivers,
    Round the feet of the day and the feet of the night.

Where shall we find her, how shall we sing to her,
    Fold our hands round her knees, and cling?
O that man's heart were as fire and could spring to her,
    Fire, or the strength of the streams that spring!
For the stars and the winds are unto her
As raiment, as songs of the harp-player;
For the risen stars and the fallen cling to her,
    And the southwest-wind and the west-wind sing.

For winter's rains and ruins are over,
    And all the season of snows and sins;
The days dividing lover and lover,
    The light that loses, the night that wins;
And time remembered is grief forgotten,
And frosts are slain and flowers begotten,
And in green underwood and cover
    Blossom by blossom the spring begins.

The full streams feed on flower of rushes,
    Ripe grasses trammel a traveling foot,
The faint fresh flame of the young year flushes
    From leaf to flower and flower to fruit;
And fruit and leaf are as gold and fire,
And the oat is heard above the lyre,
And the hoofed heel of a satyr crushes
    The chestnut-husk at the chestnut-root.

1279

And Pan by noon and Bacchus by night,
    Fleeter of foot than the fleet-foot kid,
Follows with dancing and fills with delight
    The Maenad and the Bassarid;
And soft as lips that laugh and hide
The laughing leaves of the trees divide,
And screen from seeing and leave in sight
    The god pursuing the maiden hid.

The ivy falls with the Bacchanal's hair
    Over her eyebrows hiding her eyes;
The wild vine slipping down leaves bare
    Her bright breast shortening into sighs;
The wild vine slips with the weight of its leaves,
But the berried ivy catches and cleaves
To the limbs that glitter, the feet that scare
    The wolf that follows, the fawn that flies.

MAN

Before the beginning of years,
    There came to the making of man
Time, with a gift of tears;
    Grief, with a glass that ran;
Pleasure, with pain for leaven;
    Summer, with flowers that fell;
Remembrance fallen from heaven,
    And madness risen from hell;
Strength without hands to smite;
    Love that endures for a breath;
Night, the shadow of light,
    And life, the shadow of death.
And the high gods took in hand
    Fire, and the falling of tears,
And a measure of sliding sand
    From under the feet of the years;
And froth and drift of the sea;
    And dust of the laboring earth;
And bodies of things to be
    In the houses of death and of birth;

And wrought with weeping and laughter,
     And fashioned with loathing and love,
With life before and after
     And death beneath and above,
For a day and a night and a morrow,
     That his strength might endure for a span
With travail and heavy sorrow,
     The holy spirit of man.

From the winds of the north and the south
     They gathered as unto strife;
They breathed upon his mouth,
     They filled his body with life;
Eyesight and speech they wrought
     For the veils of the soul therein,
A time for labor and thought,
They gave him light in his ways,
     And love, and a space for delight,
And beauty and length of days.
     And night, and sleep in the night.
His speech is a burning fire;
     With his lips he travaileth;
In his heart is a blind desire,
     In his eyes foreknowledge of death;
He weaves, and is clothed with derision;
     Sows, and he shall not reap;
His life is a watch or a vision
     Between a sleep and a sleep.

THE GARDEN OF PROSERPINE

Here, where the world is quiet;
     Here, where all trouble seems
Dead winds' and spent waves' riot
     In doubtful dreams of dreams;
I watch the green field growing
For reaping folk and sowing,
For harvest-time and moving,
     A sleepy world of streams.

1281

I am tired of tears and laughter,
   And men that laugh and weep;
Of what may come hereafter
   For men that sow to reap:
I am weary of days and hours,
Blown buds of barren flowers,
Desires and dreams and powers
   And everything but sleep.

Here life has death for neighbor,
   And far from eye or ear
Wan waves and wet winds labor,
   Weak ships and spirits steer;
They drive adrift, and whither
They wot not who make thither;
But no such winds blow hither,
And no such things grow here.

No growth of moor or coppice,
   No heather-flower or vine,
But bloomless buds of poppies,
   Green grapes of Proserpine,
Pale beds of blowing rushes,
Where no leaf blooms or blushes
Save this whereout she crushes
   For dead men deadly wine.

Pale, without name or number,
   In fruitless fields of corn,
They bow themselves and slumber
   All night till light is born;
And like a soul belated,
In hell and heaven unmated,
By cloud and mist abated
   Comes out of darkness morn.

Though one were strong as seven,
   He too with death shall dwell,
Nor wake with wings in heaven,
   Nor weep for pains in hell;

Though one were fair as roses,
His beauty clouds and closes;
And well though love reposes,
  In the end it is not well.

Pale, beyond porch and portal,
  Crowned with calm leaves, she stands
Who gathers all things mortal
  With cold immortal hands;
Her languid lips are sweeter
Than love's who fears to greet her,
To men that mix and meet her
  From many times and lands.

She waits for each and other,
  She waits for all men born;
Forgets the earth her mother,
  The life of fruits and corn;
And spring and seed and swallow
Take wing for her and follow
Where summer song rings hollow
  And flowers are put to scorn.

There go the loves that wither,
  The old loves with wearier wings;
And all dead years draw thither,
  And all disastrous things;
Dead dreams of days forsaken,
Blind buds that snows have shaken,
Wild leaves that winds have taken,
  Red strays of ruined springs.

We are not sure of sorrow;
  And joy was never sure;
Today will die tomorrow;
  Time stoops to no man's lure;
And love, grown faint and fretful,
With lips but half regretful
Sighs, and with eyes forgetful
  Weeps that no loves endure.

From too much love of living,
  From hope and fear set free,
We thank with brief thanksgiving
  Whatever gods may be
That no life lives for ever;
That dead men rise up never;
That even the weariest river
  Winds somewhere safe at sea.

Then star nor sun shall waken,
  Nor any change of light:
Nor sound of waters shaken,
  Nor any sound or sight:
Nor wintry leaves nor vernal,
Nor days nor things diurnal;
Only the sleep eternal
  In an eternal night.

T

RABINDRANATH TAGORE

RABINDRANATH TAGORE (Indian, 1861-1941). Foremost Bengali **poet**. Member of famous family of artists, musicians and reformers. When translated, won immediate favor in the West. Outstanding works: *Chitrā* (*Beauty*), *Gitanjali* (*Handful of Songs*), and *Gorā*, a novel after Kipling.

TO NATURE

1

Thou tanglest my heart in a hundred nooses of love,
What is this thy play?
It is but a little feeble life—
Why so many bonds to bind it?
At every turn and every moment
Thou winnest my love with thy wiles,
But hast none to give, thou stealer of hearts!
I wander about in search of thy heart,
   O cruel Nature;
So many flowers, such light, such songs and scents,
   But where is love?
Hidden in the wealth of thy beauty thou laughest
  While we weep.

2

Day and night in the deserted playfield
   Thou playest in jest;
We wot not whom thou lovest or slightest;
He to whom thou art kind and loving in the morning,
The evening finds him lying neglected in the dust.

Still I love thee and cannot forget,
      Thou enchantress!
Thy loveless embrace awakes in the heart
      A thousand songs;
In happiness and grief and misery I live in the sunlight,
Nor crave the frozen stillness of the endless night.

3

Half open, half-veiled, thy face
      Is the abode of mystery;
To the heart it brings the ache of love
      Mingled with fear;
Thy ever-new phases pass understanding,
And the heart is filled with laughter and tears.
Stretching forth my heart and soul I rush towards thee,
      But thou eludest my grasp;
I see the slight, sweet, mocking smile
      On thy sun-red lips;
If I wish to flee thou spreadest thy nets for my feet,—
What arts, what strength. fleet-footed, quick of tongue!

4

Thou knowest not thy own limits,
      Thine own mystery;
So in the blind night when the seven worlds
      Are steeped in slumber,
Curious and silent-footed thou standest in the sky
Lighting million torches of star-rays.

5

In another place thou sittest ever lone
      With a vow of eternal silence,
All around is the hard, treeless, dreary
      Solitude of the desert;
Eon after eon rise overhead the sun and the moon,
They look and they pass without a word.

Again, thou rompest and playest like a girl
    With hair and garments flying in the wind,
With laughter overflowing as a fountain,
    Without a trace of shame;
Thy heart cannot hold its own measure,—
Words and songs without end.

7

Yet again with wrath-lit frenzied eyes,
    Slaying in a moment,
Thou strikest the breast of hapless Earth
    With incessant curses of fire;
Sometimes in the dusk moved by a noble grief
A pale shadow as of pity falls on thy face.

8

It is thus thou hast conquered
    Innumerable hearts;
For ages and ages thy countenance
    Has been fresh and sweet;
Disguised in many forms thou art near all,
Yet hast thou given thyself to none.

9

The more am I baffled the more I remember
    The great opulence of thy beauty;
So grows my love as increases my pain,
    As I laugh and cry;
The farther thou goest the heavier is my soul trammelled,
The less I understand thee the more I love thee.

JUNICHIRO TANIZAKI

JUNICHIRO TANIZAKI (Japanese, 1886-   ). One of Japan's most distinguished modern novelists. Started his career under Western influence of Baudelaire, Wilde and Poe. After earthquake of 1923, turned to classical Japanese literature and wrote most important novels, including *Some Prefer Nettles*. Recently engaged in new translation of *The Tale of Genji*.

From *SOME PREFER NETTLES*

O-HISA, his father-in-law's mistress, drove a moth from the clear-lacquer table, the breeze from her fan cool through Kaname's light kimono. The clean smell of spring mushrooms rose faintly from the soup. It was pitch-dark now in the garden, and the croaking of the rain-frogs had risen to a clamor.

"I'd like to learn the Tokyo style of singing myself."

"You'll be scolded for dangerous thoughts. And I'm afraid I'll have to join the scolding—you've no idea how much better the Osaka style is for you."

"I don't object to it so much. But the teacher is rather a problem."

"Let me see—you go to someone in Osaka, don't you?"

"That's right. But I was thinking more of the teacher here."

Kaname laughed.

"He's unbearable. Lecture, lecture, lecture."

"All old people are that way." Kaname laughed again. "That reminds me. I noticed the bran bag. You still use it?"

"That's right. Your father-in-law uses soap himself, but he won't let me. He says women mustn't ruin their skin with soap."

"And the nightingale dung?"

"I go on with that too. But it hasn't made my skin a bit whiter."

Kaname was finishing off the meal with his second decanter of saké, and O-hisa had brought in a dish of loquats when the telephone rang. She ran to answer it, leaving a half-peeled loquat in an antique glass saucer.

"Yes . . . yes . . . I see. I'll tell him." Kaname could see her in the hall nodding into the telephone. In a minute or two she was back. "Misako will stay here too, he says. They'll be home before long."

"Really? And she said she wouldn't. . . . It seems an awfully long time since I last spent the night here."

"It has been a long time."

More than that, though, it seemed a long time since he and his wife, Misako, had slept alone together. There had of course been those two or three nights—their first alone in he did not know how many years—when little Hiroshi was in Tokyo with Takanatsu; but they had been able then to lie down side by side and go off to sleep as unconcernedly as two strangers at an inn, so deadened had their marital nerves become. He suspected that tonight, however, her father hoped for great changes to come from throwing them together. This benevolent scheming was a little disconcerting, but not enough so that Kaname felt pressed to try for an escape. He was sure that the time had passed when one night could make a difference.

"Hasn't it grown heavy?" said Kaname. "Not a breath of air." He looked out to the veranda. The incense, on the point of going out, sent a column of smoke straight and unwavering into the air. The breeze in the garden had died, and with it the breeze from O-hisa's fan, motionless in her lap and as though forgotten.

"It's clouding over. I wonder if it will rain."

"It might well. I almost hope it will."

Above the motionless leaves a star here and there broke through the clouds. For a moment he thought he could hear, as with a sixth sense, Misako's voice fighting back the old man; and he knew that almost unconsciously he had come to a point where he could support his wife's decision with an even stronger one of his own.

"What time do you suppose it is?"

"Eight thirty, possibly."

"Only eight thirty. Isn't it quiet, though?"

"It's still early, but you may want to go to bed. They should be back before long."

"I suppose it seemed from what he said over the telephone that the conversation was not going very well?" Kaname was secretly more interested in having O-hisa's views than the old man's.

"Shall I bring you something to read?"

"Thank you. What sort of things do you read?"

"He brings home old wood-block books and tells me I should read them. But I can't get interested in the dusty old things."

"You'd rather read a woman's magazine?"

"He says if I have time for that sort of trash I should be practising my calligraphy."

"What copybook does he have you on?"

"There are a couple. *O-ie* method."

"Well, let me look at one of your dusty books."

"How about a travel guide?"

"That should do, I suppose."

"Let's go out to the cottage, then. I have everything ready."

O-hisa led the way along a covered passage to the garden cottage. As she slid back the paper-paneled door to the rear of the tearoom, Kaname caught the rustling of a mosquito net in the darkness beyond. A cool breath of air came through the open door.

"The wind seems to have come up again."

"And all of a sudden it's a little chilly," Kaname answered. "We'll have a shower before long."

The mosquito net rustled again, this time not from the wind. O-hisa felt her way inside and, groping for the lamp; at Kaname's pillow, turned the switch.

"Shall I get you a larger bulb?"

"This will do nicely. The print's always big in old books."

"Suppose I leave the shutters open. You won't want it too hot."

"I wish you would. I can close them later."

Kaname crawled under the net himself when O-hisa had gone. The room was not a large one, and the linen mosquito netting cut it off smaller yet, so that the two mattresses were almost touching. It was a novel arrangement for Kaname and Misako. At home these summer nights they hung up as large a mosquito net as possible and slept, one at each end, with Hiroshi between them. Kaname rolled over on his stomach, a little bored, and lighted a cigarette. He tried to make out the picture in the alcove beyond the light-green netting. Something in modest, neutral colors, a landscape it seemed to be, wider than it was high. With the light inside the net, however, the rest of the room lay in deep shadow, and he could make out neither the details nor the artist's signature. Below it in a bowl was what he took to be a blue and white porcelain burner. There was a faint smell of incense through the room—he noticed it for the first time. Plum blossom, he judged. For an instant he thought he saw O-hisa's face, faint and white, in a shadowy corner beside the bed. He started up, but quickly caught himself. It was the puppet the old man had brought back from Awaji, a lady puppet in a modest dotted kimono.

A gust of wind came through the open window and the shower began. Kaname could hear large drops falling against the leaves. He raised himself on an elbow and stared out into the wooden depths of the garden. A small green frog, a refugee from the rain,

1290

clung halfway up the fluttering side of the net, its belly reflecting the light from the bed lamp.

"It's finally begun."

The door slid open, and this time, half a dozen old-style Japanese books in arm, it was no puppet that sat faintly white in the shadows beyond the netting.

T'AO CH'IEN

T'AO CH'IEN (Chinese, 372-427). Profoundly influential rustic poet of China. After brief official career, retired to live rural life. His prose poem, *Kuei-ch'ü-lai tz'u (Returning to Live on the Farm)*, and shorter lyric poems are known to all Chinese school children. Simplicity of his life and work earned him reputation as "the most harmonious product of Chinese culture."

RETURNING TO LIVE ON THE FARM

Six Poems

When I was young, I was not fitted for a worldly rhythm.
By nature I loved the mountains and the hills.
I fell into the net of the world by mistake,
And I have stayed there for thirty years.
A bird in the cage longs for the old forest,
And a fish in the pond thinks of his former pool.
I cultivated rough land in the south,
And, keeping to simple ways, I returned to the field and garden.
I have over ten *mu* of land
And a thatched house of eight or nine rooms.
Birch and willow shade the back eaves;
Peach and plum spread their branches in the front courtyard.
Villages lie in the distance.
Smoke rises like mist from faraway fields.
Dogs bark in hidden lanes,
And roosters crow.
There is no worldly hubbub.
There is space, and I have leisure.
For a long time I was in a cage,
But now I am back with nature.

1291

In the country there is little of human affairs.
The lane has but few wheel tracks,
And white sun shines on the closed door.
In the empty room I have no thoughts of the world.
Often, strolling along the winding roads
And wearing cotton garments, we visit each other.
When we meet, we do not gossip,
But simply talk about how the hemp and mulberry have shot up.
Daily the hemp and mulberry grow taller,
And our fields each day are extended.
Frequently we fear that a frost will come
And kill the plants as if they were weeds.

I plant beans at the foot of the southern hill.
Grass flourishes, but the beans rarely sprout.
In the early morning I go out to weed,
And in the moonlight I return, carrying my hoe.
The path is narrow, and as the shrubs and grasses are tall,
Evening dew moistens my clothes.
These wet clothes are not worth worrying about.
I only hope that my dream will not leave me.

I have been away from the pleasure of the hills and streams,
From the rushing sound of the wild trees.
Wearing a raincoat, I go with my nephews and children
To walk in the meadows
And stroll on the hills and dikes.
This seems to be a spot where once someone lived;
There are the remains of a well and an oven,
And mulberry and bamboo wither among the other trees.
I ask a wood-gatherer
What kind of man lived here.
He replies
That all have died,
And that they saw the shift of power at court.
These words are not empty.
Man's life is like a shifting illusion;
At the end we shall return to emptiness.

Depressed and alone, I take my staff and return,
Passing along the zigzag, rough, and thorny roads.

The stream of the mountain is clear and shallow;
Coming upon it I wash my feet.
I strain my fresh wine
And, having a chicken, invite my close neighbors.
The sunset enters my gate.
The glow of firewood takes the place of a bright candle.
When I am happy I regret that the evening is too short,
And in no time it is dawn!

I plant sprouts on the eastern hill,
And they grow lushly in the field.
Although I am tired of carrying the hoe,
This muddy wine comforts me.
The sun sets, and I return with a cart of firewood.
The road is dim, the light already dusky.
Returning farmers watch the chimney smoke.
A child, waiting behind the crack of the door under the eaves,
Asks what I have been doing.
For a hundred years I have been on the road,
And now I only wish that the mulberry and hemp were ripe.
In the month of the silkworm we can weave,
And my simple heart wants just this!
I clear three paths and watch for my friends.

TORQUATO TASSO

TORQUATO TASSO (Italian, 1544-1595). Classicist of the idyllic pastoral
and ardent religiosity. Most celebrated works: *Rinaldo*, epic poem; *Aminta*,
pastoral play; *Jerusalem Delivered*, Counter-Reformation epic of the Crusades.
In later years his mind was clouded as result of excessive religious scruples.

THE GOLDEN AGE

O lovely age of gold!
Not that the rivers rolled
With milk, or that the woods wept honey-dew;
Not that the ready ground
Produced without a wound,
Or the mild serpent had no tooth that slew:

1293

Not that a cloudless blue
    Forever was in sight,
Or that the heaven, which burns
And now is cold by turns,
Looked out in glad and everlasting light;
No, nor that even the insolent ships from far
Brought war to no new lands, nor riches worse than war.

    But solely that that vain
    And breath-invented pain,
That idol of mistake, that worshiped cheat,
    That Honor—since so called
    By vulgar minds appalled,—
Played not the tyrant with our nature yet.
    It had not come to fret
      The sweet and happy fold
    Of gentle human kind;
    Nor did its hard law bind
Souls nursed in freedom; but that law of gold,
That glad and golden law, all free. all fitted.
Which Nature's own hand wrote—what pleases is permitted.

    Then among streams and flowers,
    The little winged Powers
Went singing carols without torch or bow;
    The nymphs and shepherds sat
    Mingling with innocent chat
Sports and low whispers, and with whispers low,
    Kisses that would not go.
      The maid, her childhood o'er,
    Kept not her bloom uneyed,
    Which now a veil must hide,
Nor the crisp apples which her bosom bore;
And oftentimes, in river or in lake,
The lover and his love their merry bath would take.

    'Twas thou, thou, Honor, first
    That didst deny our thirst
Its drink, and on the fount thy covering set;
    Thou badst kind eyes withdraw
    Into constrainèd awe,

And keep the secret for their tears to wet;
　　Thou gatherdst in a net
　　　The tresses from the air,
　　And mad'st the sports and plays
　　　Turn all to sullen ways,
And put'st on speech a rein—in steps a care.
Thy work it is—thou shade that wilt not move—
That what was once the gift, is now the theft, of love.

　　Our sorrows and our pains,
　　These are thy noble gains.
But oh, thou Love's and Nature's masterer,
　　Thou conqueror of the crowned,
　　What dost thou on this ground,
Too small a circle for thy mighty sphere?
　　Go, and make slumber dear
　　　To the renowned and high;
　　We here, a lowly race,
　　Can live without thy grace,
After the use of mild antiquity.
　　Go, let us love—since years
No truce allow, and life soon disappears.
Go let us love: the daylight dies, is born;
　　But unto us the light
Dies once for all, and sleep brings on eternal night.

ALFRED LORD TENNYSON

ALFRED LORD TENNYSON (English, 1808-1892). Poet of English national
life. Artful, subtle, often morbid. In disciplined sensibility and concern for
traditional morality, represents peak of Victorian literature. Most popular
work: *Idylls of the King*, based on Arthurian legends. Most moving: *In
Memoriam*, elegy on his friend Arthur Hallam. Succeeded Wordsworth as
Poet Laureate.

CHORIC SONG FROM THE LOTOS-EATERS

I

There is sweet music here that softer falls
Than petals from blown roses on the grass,
Or night-dews on still waters between walls
Of shadowy granite, in a gleaming pass;

Music that gentlier on the spirit lies,
Than tired eyelids upon tired eyes;
Music that brings sweet sleep down from the blissful skies.
Here are cool mosses deep,
And through the moss the ivies creep,
And in the stream the long-leaved flowers weep,
And from the craggy ledge the poppy hangs in sleep.

II

Why are we weighed upon with heaviness,
And utterly consumed with sharp distress,
While all things else have rest from weariness?
All things have rest; why should we toil alone,
We only toil, who are the first of things,
And make perpetual moan,
Still from one sorrow to another thrown;
Nor ever fold our wings,
And cease from wanderings,
Nor steep our brows in slumber's holy balm;
Nor harken what the inner spirit sings,
"There is no joy but calm!"—
Why should we only toil, the roof and crown of things?

III

Lo! in the middle of the wood,
The folded leaf is wooed from out the bud
With winds upon the branch, and there
Grows green and broad, and takes no care,
Sun-steeped at noon, and in the moon
Nightly dew-fed; and turning yellow
Falls, and floats adown the air.
Lo! sweetened with the summer light,
The full-juiced apple, waxing over-mellow,
Drops in a silent autumn night.
All its allotted length of days
The flower ripens in its place,
Ripens and fades, and falls, and hath no toil,
Fast-rooted in the fruitful soil.

IV

Hateful is the dark-blue sky,
Vaulted o'er the dark-blue sea.
Death is the end of life; ah, why
Should life all labor be?
Let us alone. Time driveth onward fast,
And in a little while our lips are dumb.
Let us alone. What is it that will last?
All things are taken from us, and become
Portions and parcels of the dreadful past.
Let us alone. What pleasure can we have
To war with evil? Is there any peace
In ever climbing up the climbing wave?
All things have rest, and ripen toward the grave
In silence—ripen, fall, and cease.
Give us long rest or death, dark death, or dreamful ease.

V

How sweet it were, hearing the downward stream,
With half-shut eyes ever to seem
Falling asleep in a half-dream!
To dream and dream, like yonder amber light,
Which will not leave the myrrh-bush on the height;
To hear each other's whispered speech;
Eating the Lotos day by day,
To watch the crisping ripples on the beach,
And tender curving lines of creamy spray;
To lend our hearts and spirits wholly
To the influence of mild-minded melancholy;
To muse and brood and live again in memory,
With those old faces of our infancy
Heaped over with a mound of grass,
Two handfuls of white dust, shut in an urn of brass!

VI

Dear is the memory of our wedded lives,
And dear the last embraces of our wives

And their warm tears; but all hath suffered change;
For surely now our household hearths are cold,
Our sons inherit us, our looks are strange,
And we should come like ghosts to trouble joy.
Or else the island princes over-bold
Have eat our substance, and the minstrel sings
Before them of the ten years' war in Troy,
And our great deeds, as half-forgotten things.
Is there confusion in the little isle?
Let what is broken so remain.
The gods are hard to reconcile;
'Tis hard to settle order once again.
There *is* confusion worse than death,
Trouble on trouble, pain on pain,
Long labor unto aged breath,
Sore task to hearts worn out by many wars
And eyes grown dim with gazing on the pilot stars.

VII

But, propped on beds of amaranth and moly,
How sweet—while warm airs lull us, blowing lowly—
With half-dropped eyelid still,
Beneath a heaven dark and holy,
To watch the long bright river drawing slowly
His waters from the purple hill—
To hear the dewy echoes calling
From cave to cave through the thick-twined vine—
To watch the emerald-colored water falling
Through many a woven acanthus-wreath divine!
Only to hear and see the far-off sparkling brine,
Only to hear were sweet, stretched out beneath the pine.

VIII

The Lotos blooms below the barren peak,
The Lotos blows by every winding creek;
All day the wind breathes low with mellower tone;
Through every hollow cave and alley lone
Round and round the spicy downs the yellow Lotos-dust is blown.

We have had enough of action, and of motion we,
Rolled to starboard, rolled to larboard, when the surge was seething
   free,
Where the wallowing monster spouted his foam-fountains in the sea.
Let us swear an oath, and keep it with an equal mind,
In the hollow Lotos-land to live and lie reclined
On the hills like gods together, careless of mankind.
For they lie beside their nectar, and the bolts are hurled
Far below them in the valleys, and the clouds are lightly curled
Round their golden houses, girdled with the gleaming world;
Where they smile in secret, looking over wasted lands,
Blight and famine, plague and earthquake, roaring deeps and fiery
   sands,
Clanging fights, and flaming towns, and sinking ships, and praying
   hands.
But they smile, they find a music centered in a doleful song
Steaming up, a lamentation and an ancient tale of wrong,
Like a tale of little meaning though the words are strong;
Chanted from an ill-used race of men that cleave the soil,
Sow the seed, and reap the harvest with enduring toil,
Storing yearly little dues of wheat, and wine and oil;
Till they perish and they suffer—some, 'tis whispered—down in
   hell
Suffer endless anguish, others in Elysian valleys dwell,
Resting weary limbs at last on beds of asphodel.
Surely, surely, slumber is more sweet than toil, the shore
Than labor in the deep mid-ocean, wind and wave and oar;
Oh, rest ye, brother mariners, we will not wander more.

WILLIAM MAKEPEACE THACKERAY

WILLIAM MAKEPEACE THACKERAY (English, 1811-1863). Voluminous
novelist of Victorian Period. Well born, wrote unceasingly after losing fortune.
A keen satirist of social snobbery, using unaffected conversational, sometimes
sermonizing, style. *Vanity Fair*, one of the masterpieces of the English novel,
Becky Sharp one of its celebrated heroines. Other novels: *Pendennis, The
Virginians, Henry Esmond, The Newcomes.*

VANITY FAIR

ONE gusty, raw day at the end of April—the rain whipping the
pavement of that ancient street where the old Slaughter's Coffee-

house was once situated—George Osborne came into the coffee-room, looking very haggard and pale, although dressed rather smartly in a blue coat and brass buttons, and a neat buff waistcoat of the fashion of those days. Here was his friend Captain Dobbin, in blue and brass too, having abandoned the military frock and French-gray trousers, which were the usual coverings of his lanky person.

Dobbin had been in the coffee-room for an hour or more. He had tried all the papers, but could not read them. He had looked at the clock many scores of times; and at the street, where the rain was pattering down, and the people, as they clinked by in pattens, left long reflections on the shining stone; he tattooed at the table; he bit his nails most completely, and nearly to the quick (he was accustomed to ornament his great big hands in this way); he balanced the tea-spoon on the milkjug; upset it, etc., etc.; and in fact showed those signs of disquietude, and practised those desperate attempts at amuse-ment, which men are accustomed to employ when very anxious and expectant, and perturbed in mind.

Some of his comrades, gentlemen who used the room, joked him about the splendour of his costume and his agitation of manner. One asked him if he was going to be married. Dobbin laughed and said he would send his acquaintance (Major Wagstaff of the Engineers) a piece of cake when that event took place. At length Captain Osborne made his appearance, very smartly dressed, but very pale and agi-tated, as we have said. He wiped his pale face with a large yellow bandana pocket-handkerchief that was prodigiously scented. He shook hands with Dobbin, looked at the clock, and told John, the waiter, to bring him some curaçoa. Of this cordial he swallowed off a couple of glasses with nervous eagerness. His friend asked with some inter-est about his health.

"Couldn't get a wink of sleep till daylight, Dob," said he. "Infernal headache and fever. Got up at nine, and went down to the Hummums for a bath. I say, Dob, I feel just as I did on the morning I went out with Rocket at Quebec."

"So do I," William responded. "I was a deuce deal more nervous than you were, that morning. You made a famous breakfast, I re-member. Eat something now."

"You're a good old fellow, Will. I'll drink your health, old boy, and farewell to—"

"No, no; two glasses are enough," Dobbin interrupted him. "Here, take away the *liqueurs*, John. Have some cayenne-pepper with your fowl. Make haste, though, for it is time we were there."

It was about half an hour from twelve when this brief meeting and colloquy took place between the two captains. A coach, into which Captain Osborne's servant put his master's desk and dressing-case, had been in waiting for some time; and into this the two gentlemen hurried under an umbrella, and the valet mounted on the box, cursing the rain and the dampness of the coachman who was steaming beside him. "We shall find a better trap than this at the carriage door," says he; "that's a comfort." And the carriage drove on, taking the road down Piccadilly, where Apsley House and St. George's Hospital wore red jackets still; where there were oil lamps; where Achilles was not yet born; nor the Pimlico arch raised; nor the hideous equestrian monster which pervades it and the neighborhood—and so they drove down by Brompton to a certain chapel near the Fulham road there.

A chariot was in waiting with four horses; likewise a coach of the kind called glass coaches. Only a very few idlers were collected, on account of the dismal rain.

"Hang it!" said George, "I said only a pair."

"My master would have four," said Mr. Joseph Sedley's servant, who was in waiting; and he and Mr. Osborne's man agreed, as they followed George and William into the church, that it was a "reg'lar shabby turnhout; and with scarce so much as a breakfast or a wedding faviour."

"Here you are," said our old friend, Jos Sedley, coming forward. "You're five minutes late, George my boy. What a day, eh? Demmy, it's like the commencement of the rainy season in Bengal. But you'll find my carriage is water-tight. Come along, my mother and Emmy are in the vestry."

Jos Sedley was splendid. He was fatter than ever. His shirt-collars were higher; his face was redder; his shirt-frill flaunted gorgeously out of his variegated waistcoat. Varnished boots were not invented as yet; but the Hessians on his beautiful legs shone so, that they must have been the identical pair in which the gentleman in the old picture used to shave himself; and on his light green coat there bloomed a fine wedding favour, like a great white spreading magnolia.

In a word, George had thrown the great cast. He was going to be married. Hence his pallor and nervousness—his sleepless night and agitation in the morning. I have heard people who have gone through the same thing own to the same emotion. After three or four ceremonies, you get accustomed to it, no doubt; but the first dip, everybody allows, is awful.

The bride was dressed in a brown silk pelisse (as Captain Dobbin

1301

has since informed me), and wore a straw bonnet with a pink ribbon; over the bonnet she had a veil of white Chantilly lace, a gift from Mr. Joseph Sedley, her brother. Captain Dobbin himself had asked leave to present her with a gold chain and watch, which she sported on this occasion; and her mother gave her her diamond brooch— almost the only trinket which was left to the old lady. As the service went on, Mrs. Sedley sat and whimpered a great deal in a pew, consoled by the Irish maid-servant and Mrs. Clapp from the lodgings. Old Sedley would not be present. Jos acted for his father, giving away the bride, whilst Captain Dobbin stepped up as groomsman to his friend George.

There was nobody in the church besides the officiating persons and the small marriage party and their attendants. The two valets sat aloof superciliously. The rain came rattling down on the windows. In the intervals of the service you heard it, and the sobbing of old Mrs. Sedley in the pew. The parson's tones echoed sadly through the empty walls. Osborne's "I will" was sounded in very deep bass. Emmy's response came fluttering up to her lips from her heart, but was scarcely heard by anybody except Captain Dobbin.

When the service was completed, Jos Sedley came forward and kissed his sister, the bride, for the first time for many months— George's look of gloom had gone, and he seemed quite proud and radiant. "It's your turn, William," says he, putting his hand fondly upon Dobbin's shoulder; and Dobbin went up and touched Amelia on the cheek.

Then they went into the vestry and signed the register. "God bless you, old Dobbin," George said, grasping him by the hand, with something very like moisture glistening in his eyes. William replied only by nodding his head. His heart was too full to say much.

"Write directly, and come down as soon as you can, you know," Osborne said. After Mrs. Sedley had taken an hysterical adieu of her daughter, the pair went off to the carriage. "Get out of the way, you little devils," George cried to a small crowd of damp urchins, that were hanging about the chapel door. The rain drove into the bride and bridegroom's faces as they passed to the chariot. The postillion's favours draggled on their dripping jackets. The few children made a dismal cheer as the carriage, splashing mud, drove away.

William Dobbin stood in the church porch, looking at it, a quiet figure. The small crew of spectators jeered him. He was not thinking about them or their laughter.

"Come home and have some tiffin, Dobbin," a voice cried behind

him, as a pudgy hand was laid on his shoulder, and the honest fellow's reverie was interrupted. But the captain had no heart to go a feasting with Jos Sedley. He put the weeping old lady and her attendants into the carriage along with Jos, and left them without further words passing. This carriage, too, drove away, and the urchins gave another sarcastical cheer.

"Here, you little beggars," Dobbin said, giving some sixpences amongst them, and then went off by himself through the rain. It was all over. They were married, and happy, he prayed God. Never since he was a boy, had he felt so miserable and so lonely. He longed with a heart-sick yearning for the first few days to be over, that he might see her again.

JOHANN LUDWIG TIECK

JOHANN LUDWIG TIECK (1773-1853). One of the leaders of the German Romantic School. Experimented in every literary form, was most successful with short stories and *novellen*. Influenced not only German writers, but such men as Gogol, Coleridge, Scott, Longfellow, Hawthorne. Best work: *Puss-in-Boots*, satirical fairy tales.

THE FRIENDS

It was a beautiful spring morning, when Lewis Wandel went out to visit a sick friend, in a village some miles distant from his dwelling. This friend had written to him to say that he was lying dangerously ill, and would gladly see him and speak to him once more.

The cheerful sunshine now sparkled in the bright green bushes; the birds twittered and leapt to and fro on the branches; the larks sang merrily above the thin fleeting clouds; sweet scents rose from the fresh meadows, and the fruit-trees of the garden were white and gay in blossom.

Lewis's eye roamed intoxicate around him; his soul seemed to expand; but he thought of his invalid friend, and he bent forward in silent dejection. Nature had decked herself all in vain, so serenely and so brightly; his fancy could only picture to him the sick bed and his suffering brother.

"How song is sounding from every bough!" cried he; "the notes of the birds mingle in sweet unison with the whisper of the leaves;

1303

and yet in the distance, through all the charm of the concert, come the sighs of the sick one."

Whilst he thus communed, a troop of gaily-clad peasant girls issued from the village; they all gave him a friendly salutation, and told him that they were on their merry way to a wedding; that work was over for that day, and had to give place to festivity. He listened to their tale, and still their merriment rang in the distance on his ear; still he caught the sound of their songs, and became more and more sorrowful. In the wood he took his seat on a dismantled tree, drew the oft-read letter from his pocket, and ran through it once more:—

"My very dear friend,—I cannot tell why you have so utterly forgotten me, that I receive no news from you. I am not surprised that men forsake me; but it heartily pains me to think that you too care nothing about me. I am dangerously ill; a fever that saps my strength: if you delay visiting me any longer, I cannot promise you that you will see me again. All nature revives, and feels fresh and strong; I alone sink lower in languor; the returning warmth cannot animate me; I see not the green fields, nothing but the tree that rustles before my window, and sings death-songs to my thoughts; my bosom is pent, my breathing is hard; and often I think the walls of my room will press closer together and crush me. The rest of you in the world are holding the most beautiful festival of life, whilst I must languish in the dwelling of sickness. Gladly would I dispense with spring, if I could but see your dear face once more: but you that are in health never earnestly think what it really is to be ill, and how dear to us then, in our helplessness, the visit of a friend is: you do not know how to prize those precious minutes of consolation, because the whole world receives you in the warmth and the fervour of its friendship. Ah! if you did but know, as I do, how terrible is death, and how still more terrible it is to be ill,—O Lewis, how would you hasten then to behold once more this frail form, that you have hitherto called your friend, and that by and by will be so ruthlessly dismembered! If I were well, I would haste to meet you, or fancy that you may perhaps be ill at this moment. If I never see you again—farewell."

What a painful impression did the suffering depicted in this letter make upon Lewis's heart, amid the liveliness of Nature, as she lay in brilliancy before him! He melted into tears, and rested his head on his hand.—"Carol now, ye foresters," thought he; "for ye know no

lamentation; ye lead a buoyant poetic existence, and for this are those swift pinions granted you; oh, how happy are ye, that ye need not mourn; warm summer calls you, and ye wish for nothing more; ye dance forth to meet it, and when winter is advancing, ye are gone! O light-winged merry forest-life, how do I envy thee! Why are so many heavy cares burdened upon poor man's heart? Why may he not love without purchasing his love by wailing—his happiness by misery? Life purls on like a fleeting rivulet beneath his feet, and quenches not his thirst, his fervid longing."

He became more and more absorbed in thought, and at last he rose and pursued his way through the thick forest. "If I could but help him," cried he; "if Nature could but supply me with a means of saving him; but as it is, I feel nothing but my own impotency, and the pain of losing my friend. In my childhood I used to believe in enchantment and its supernatural aids; would I now could hope in them as happily as then!"

He quickened his steps; and involuntarily all the remembrances of the earliest years of his childhood crowded back upon him: he followed those forms of loveliness, and was soon entangled in such a labyrinth as not to notice the objects that surrounded him. He had forgotten that it was spring—that his friend was ill: he hearkened to the wondrous melodies, which came borne, as if from distant shores, upon his ear: all that was most strange united itself to what was most ordinary: his whole soul was transmuted. From the far vista of memory, from the abyss of the past, all those forms were summoned forth that ever had enraptured or tormented him; all those dubious phantoms were aroused, that flutter formlessly about us, and gather in dizzy hum around our heads. Puppets, the toys of childhood, and spectres, danced along before him, and so mantled over the green turf, that he could not see a single flower at his feet. First love encircled him with its twilight morning gleam, and let down its sparkling rainbow over the mead: his earliest sorrows glided past him in review, and threatened to greet him in the same guise at the end of his pilgrimage. Lewis sought to arrest all these changeful feelings, and to retain a consciousness of self amid the magic of enjoyment,—but in vain. Like enigmatic books, with figures grotesquely gay, that open for a moment and in a moment are closed, so unstably and fleetingly all floated before his soul.

The wood opened, and in the open country on one side lay some old ruins, encompassed with watch-towers and ramparts. Lewis was astonished at having advanced so quickly amid his dreams. He

emerged from his melancholy, as he did from the shades of the wood; for often the pictures within us are but the reflection of outward objects. Now rose on him, like the morning sun, the memory of his first poetical enjoyments, of his earliest appreciations of that luscious harmony which many a human ear never inhales.

"How incomprehensibly," said he, "did those things commingle then, which seemed to me eternally parted by such vast chasms; my most undefined presentiments assumed a form and outline, and gleamed on me in the shape of a thousand subordinate phantoms, which till then I had never descried! So names were found me for things that I had long wished to speak of: I became recipient of earth's fairest treasures, which my yearning heart had so long sought for in vain: and how much have I to thank thee for since then, divine power of fancy and of poetry! How hast thou smoothed for me the path of life, that erst appeared so rough and perplexed! Ever hast thou revealed to me new sources of enjoyment and happiness, so that no arid desert presents itself to me now: every stream of sweet voluptuous inspiration hath wound its way through my earth-born heart: I have become intoxicate with bliss, and have communed with beings of heaven."

The sun sank below the horizon, and Lewis was astonished that it was already evening. He was insensible of fatigue, and was still far from the point which he had wished to reach before night: he stood still, without being able to understand how the crimson of evening could be so early mantling the clouds; how the shadows of everything were so long, while the nightingale warbled her song of wail in the thicket. He looked around him: the old ruins lay far in the background, clad in blushing splendour; and he doubted whether he had not strayed from the direct and well-known road.

Now he remembered a phantasy of his early childhood, that till that moment had never recurred to him: it was a female form of awe, that glided before him over the lonely fields: she never looked round, yet he was compelled, against his will, to follow her, and to be drawn on into unknown scenes, without in the least being able to extricate himself from her power. A slight thrill of fear came over him, and yet he found it impossible to obtain a more distinct recollection of that figure, or to usher back his mind into the frame, in which this image had first appeared to him. He sought to individualise all these singular sensations, when, looking round by chance, he really found himself on a spot which, often as he had been that way, he had never seen before.

"Am I spell-bound?" cried he; "or have my dreams and fancies crazed me? Is it the wonderful effect of solitude that makes me irrecognisable to myself; or do spirits and genii hover round me and hold my senses in thrall? Sooth, if I cannot enfranchise myself from myself, I will await that woman-phantom that floated before me in every lonely place in my childhood."

He endeavoured to rid himself of every kind of phantasy, in order to get into the right road again; but his recollections became more and more perplexed; the flowers at his feet grew larger, the red glow of evening more brilliant, and wondrously shaped clouds hung drooping on the earth, like the curtains of some mystic scene that was soon to unfold itself. A ringing murmur arose from the high grass, and the blades bowed to one another, as if in friendly converse; while a light warm spring rain dropped pattering amongst them, as if to wake every slumbering harmony in wood, and bush, and flower. Now all was rife with song and sound; a thousand sweet voices held promiscuous parley; song entwined itself in song, and tone in tone; while in the waning crimson of eve lay countless blue butterflies rocking, with its radiance sparkling from their wavy wings. Lewis fancied himself in a dream, when the heavy dark-red clouds suddenly rose again, and a vast prospect opened on him in unfathomable distance. In the sunshine lay a gorgeous plain, sparkling with verdant forests and dewy underwood. In its centre glittered a palace of a myraid hues, as if composed all of undulating rainbows and gold and jewels: a passing stream reflected its various brilliancy, and a soft crimson æther environed this hall of enchantment; strange birds, he had never seen before, flew about, sportively flapping each other with their red and green wings: larger nightingales warbled their clear notes to the echoing landscape: lambent flames shot through the green grass, flickering here and there, and then darting in coils round the mansion. Lewis drew nearer, and heard ravishing voices sing the following words:—

> Traveller from earth below,
> Wend thee not farther,
> In our hall's magic glow
> Bide with us rather.
> Hast thou with longing scann'd
> Joy's distant morrow,
> Cast away sorrow,
> And enter the wish'd-for land.

Without further scruple, Lewis stepped to the shining threshold, and lingering but a moment ere he set his foot on the polished stone, he entered. The gates closed after him.

"Hitherward! hitherward!" cried invisible lips, as from the inmost recesses of the palace; and with loudly throbbing heart he followed the voices. All his cares, all his olden remembrances were cast away: his inmost bosom rang with the songs that outwardly encompassed him: his every regret was stilled: his every conscious and unconscious wish was satisfied. The summoning voices grew so loud, that the whole building re-echoed them, and still he could not find their origin, though he long seemed to have been standing in the central hall of the palace.

At length a ruddy-cheeked boy stepped up to him, and saluted the stranger guest: he led him through magnificent chambers, full of splendour and melody, and at last entered the garden, where Lewis, as he said, was expected. Entranced he followed his guide, and the most delicious fragrance from a thousand flowers floated forth to meet him. Broad shady walks received them. Lewis's dizzy gaze could scarcely gain the tops of the high immemorial trees: bright-coloured birds sat perched upon the branches: children were playing on guitars in the shade, and they and the birds sang to the music. Fountains shot up, with the clear red of morning, sparkling upon them: the flowers were as high as shrubs, and parted spontaneously as the wanderer pressed through them. He had never before felt the hallowed sensations that then enkindled in him; never had such pure heavenly enjoyment been revealed to him: he was over-happy.

But bells of silver sound rang through the trees, and their tops were bowed: the birds and children with the guitars were hushed: the rose-buds unfolded: and the boy now conducted the stranger into the midst of a brilliant assembly.

Lovely dames of lofty form were seated on beautiful banks of turf, in earnest conference. They were above the usual height of the human race, and their more than earthly beauty had at the same time something of awe in it, from which the heart shrunk back in alarm. Lewis dared not interrupt their conversation: it seemed as if he were among the god-like forms of Homer's song, where every thought must be excluded that formed the converse of mortals. Odd little spirits stood round, as ready ministers, waiting attentively for the wink of the moment that should summon them from their posture of quietude: they fixed their glances on the stranger, and then looked jeeringly and significantly at each other. At last the beautiful women ceased

speaking, and beckoned Lewis to approach; he was still standing with an embarrassed air, and drew near to them with trembling.

"Be not alarmed," said the fairest of them all; "you are welcome to us here, and we have long been expecting you: long have you wished to be in our abode,—are you satisfied now?"

"Oh, how unspeakably happy I am!" exclaimed Lewis; "all my dearest dreams have met with their fulfilment, all my most daring wishes are gratified now: yes, I am, I live among them. How it has happened so, I cannot comprehend: sufficient for me, that it is so. Why should I raise a new wail over this enigma, ere my olden lamentations are scarcely at an end?"

"Is this life," asked the lady, "very different from your former one?"

"My former life," said Lewis, "I can scarcely remember. But has, then, this golden state of existence fallen to my lot? this beautiful state, after which my every sense and prescience so ardently aspired; to which every wish wandered, that I could conceive in fancy, or realise in my inmost thought; though its image, veiled in mist, seemed ever strange in me—and is it, then, mine at last? have I, then, achieved this new existence, and does it hold me in its embrace? Oh, pardon me, I know not what I say in my delirium of ecstasy, and might well weigh my words more carefully in such an assemblage."

The lady sighed; and in a moment every minister was in motion; there was a stirring among the trees, everywhere a running to and fro, and speedily a banquet was placed before Lewis of fair fruits and fragrant wines. He sat down again, and music rose anew on the air. Rows of beautiful boys and girls sped round him, intertwined in the dance, while uncouth little cobolds lent life to the scene, and excited loud laughter by their ludicrous gambols. Lewis noted every sound and every gesture: he seemed newly-born since his initiation into this joyous existence. "Why," thought he, "are those hopes and reveries of ours so often laughed at, that pass into fulfilment sooner than ever had been expected? Where, then, is that border-mark between truth and error which mortals are ever ready with such temerity to set up? Oh, I ought in my former life to have wandered oftener from the way, and then perhaps I should have ripened all the earlier for this happy transmutation."

The dance died away; the sun sank to rest; the august dames arose; Lewis too left his seat, and accompanied them on their walk through the quiet garden. The nightingales were complaining in a softened tone, and a wondrous moon rose above the horizon. The blossoms

opened to its silver radiance, and every leaf kindled in its gleam; the wide avenues became of a glow, casting shadows of a singular green; red clouds slumbered on the green grass of the fields: the fountains turned to gold, and played high in the clear air of heaven.

"Now you will wish to sleep," said the loveliest of the ladies, and shewed the enraptured wanderer a shadowy bower, strewed with soft turf and yielding cushions. Then they left him, and he was alone.

He sat down and watched the magic twilight glimmering through the thickly-woven foliage. "How strange is this!" said he to himself; "perhaps I am now only asleep, and I may dream that I am sleeping a second time, and may have a dream in my dream; and so it may go on for ever, and no human power ever be able to awake me. No! unbeliever that I am! it is beautiful reality that animates me now, and my former state perhaps was but the dream of gloom." He lay down, and light breezes played round him. Perfume was wafted on the air, and little birds sang lulling songs. In his dreams he fancied the garden all around him changed: the tall trees withered away; the golden moon fallen from the sky, leaving a dismal gap behind her; instead of the watery jet from the fountains, little genii gushed out, caracolling over each in the air, and assuming the strangest attitudes. Notes of woe supplanted the sweetness of song, and every trace of that happy abode had vanished. Lewis awoke amid impressions of fear, and chid himself for still feeding his fancy in the perverse manner of the habitants of earth, who mingle all received images in rude disorder, and present them again in this garb in a dream. A lovely morning broke over the scene, and the ladies saluted him again. He spoke to them more intrepidly, and was to-day more inclined to cheerfulness, as the surrounding world had less power to astonish him. He contemplated the garden of the palace, and fed upon the magnificence and the wonders that he met there. Thus he lived many days happily, in the belief that his felicity was incapable of increase.

But sometimes the crowing of a cock seemed to sound in the vicinity; and then the whole edifice would tremble, and his compainions turn pale: this generally happened of an evening, and soon afterwards they retired to rest. Then often there would come a thought of earth into Lewis's soul; then he would often lean out of the windows of the glittering palace to arrest and fix these fleeting remembrances, and to get a glimpse of the high road again, which, as he thought, must pass that way. In this sort of mood, he was one afternoon alone, musing within himself why it was just as impossible for him to recall a distinct remembrance of the world, as formerly it had been to feel

a presage of this poetic place of sojourn,—when all at once a post-horn seemed to sound in the distance, and the rattle of carriage-wheels to make themselves heard. "How strangely," said he to himself, "does a faint gleam, a slight reminiscence of earth, break upon my delight—rendering me melancholy and dejected! Then, do I lack anything here? Is my happiness still incomplete?"

The beautiful women returned. "What do you wish for?" said they, in a tone of concern; "you seem sad."

"You will laugh," replied Lewis; "yet grant me one favour more. In that other life I had a friend, whom I now but faintly remember: he is ill, I think; restore him by your skill."

"Your wish is already gratified," said they.

"But," said Lewis, "vouchsafe me two questions."

"Speak!"

"Does no gleam of love fall on this wondrous world? Does no friendship perambulate these bowers? I thought the morning blush of spring-love would be eternal here, which in that other life is too prone to be extinguished, and which men afterwards speak of as of a fable. To confess to you the truth, I feel an unspeakable yearning after those sensations."

"Then you long for earth again?"

"Oh, never!" cried Lewis; "for in that cold earth I used to sigh for friendship and for love, and they came not near me. The longing for those feelings had to supply the place of those feelings themselves; and for that reason I turned my aspirations hitherward, and hoped here to find every thing in the most beautiful harmony."

"Fool!" said the venerable woman: "so on earth you sighed for earth, and knew not what you did in wishing to be here; you have overshot your desires, and substituted phantasies for the sensations of mortals."

"Then who are ye?" cried Lewis, astounded.

"We are the old fairies," said she, "of whom you surely must have heard long ago. If you ardently long for earth, you will return thither again. Our kingdom flourishes when mortals are shrouded in night; but their day is *our* night. Our sway is of ancient date, and will long endure. It abides invisibly among men—to your eye alone has it been revealed." She turned away, and Lewis remembered that it was the same form which had resistlessly dragged him after it in his youth, and of which he felt a secret dread. He followed now also, crying, "No, I will not go back to earth! I will stay here!" "So then," said he to himself, "I divined this lofty being even in my childhood! And

1311

so the solution of many a riddle, which we are too idle to investigate, may be within ourselves."

He went on much further than usual, till the fairy garden was soon left far behind him. He stood on a romantic mountain-range, where the ivy climbed in wild tresses up the rocks; cliff was piled on cliff, and awe and grandeur seemed to hold universal sway. Then there came a wandering stranger to him, who accosted him kindly, and addressed him thus:—"Glad I am after all, to see you again."

"I know you not," said Lewis.

"That may well be," replied the other; "but once you thought you knew me well. I am your late sick friend."

"Impossible! you are quite a stranger to me!"

"Only," said the stranger, "because to-day you see me for the first time in my true form: till now you only found in me a reflection of yourself. You are right too in remaining here; for there is no love, no friendship—not here, I mean, where all illusion vanishes."

Lewis sat down and wept.

"What ails you?" said the stranger.

"That it is you—you who were the friend of my youth: is not that mournful enough? Oh, come back with me to our dear, dear earth, where we shall know each other once more under illusive forms— where there exists the superstition of friendship! What am I doing here?"

"What will that avail?" answered the stranger. "You will want to be back again; earth is not bright enough for you: the flowers are too small for you, the song too suppressed. Colour there, cannot emerge so brilliantly from the shade; flowers there are of small comfort, and so prone to fade; the little birds think of their death, and sing in modest constraint: but here every thing is on a scale of grandeur."

"Oh, I will be contented!" cried Lewis, as the tears gushed profusely from his eyes. "Do but come back with me, and be my friend once more; let us leave this desert, this glittery misery!"

Thus saying, he opened his eyes, for some one was shaking him roughly. Over him leant the friendly but pale face of his once sick friend. "But are you dead?" cried Lewis.

"Recovered am I, wicked sleeper," he replied. "Is it thus you visit your sick friend? Come along with me; my carriage is waiting there, and a thunder-storm is rising."

Lewis rose: in his sleep he had glided off the trunk of the tree; his friend's letter lay open beside him. "So am I really on the earth

again?" he exclaimed with joy; "really? and is this no new dream?"

"You will not escape from the earth," answered his friend with a smile; and both were locked in heart-felt embraces.

"How happy I am," said Lewis, "that I have you once more, that I feel as I used to do, and that you are well again!"

"Suddenly," replied his friend, "I felt ill; and as suddenly I was well again. So I wished to go to you, and do away with the alarm that my letter must have caused you; and here, half-way, I find you asleep."

"I do not deserve your love at all," said Lewis.

"Why?"

"Because I just now doubted of your friendship."

"But only in sleep."

"It would be strange enough though," said Lewis, "if there really were such things as fairies."

"There are such, of a certainty," replied the other; "but it is all a fable, that their whole pleasure is to make men happy. They plant those wishes in our bosoms which we ourselves do not know of; those over-wrought pretensions—that super-human covetousness of super-human gifts; so that in our desponding delirium we afterwards despise the beautiful earth with all its glorious stores."

Lewis answered with a pressure of the hand.

LEO TOLSTOY

LEO TOLSTOY (Russian, 1828-1910). The sage among the master Russian novelists. An aristocrat who, after a spiritual conversion, altered his life in effort to become a later-day saint. Moral conflict forms basis of all his writing. Two of his novels belong among the greatest: *Anna Karenina* and *War and Peace*, world's most ambitious war story. Also notable are his plays and short stories.

WHERE LOVE IS

IN A certain town there lived a shoemaker named Martin Avdeitch. He lived in a basement room which possessed but one window. This window looked onto the street, and through it a glimpse could be caught of the passers-by. It is true that only their legs could be seen, but that did not matter, as Martin could recognize people by their boots alone. He had lived here for a long time, and so had many

acquaintances. There were very few pairs of boots in the neighborhood which had not passed through his hands at least once, if not twice. Some he had resoled, others he had fitted with side-pieces, others, again, he had resewn where they were split, or provided with new toe-caps. Yes, he often saw his handiwork through that window. He was given plenty of custom, for his work lasted well, his materials were good, his prices moderate, and his word to be depended on. If he could do a job by a given time it should be done; but if not, he would warn you beforehand rather than disappoint you. Everyone knew Avdeitch, and no one ever transferred his custom from him. He had always been an upright man, but with the approach of old age he had begun more than ever to think of his soul, and to draw nearer to God.

His wife had died while he was still an apprentice, leaving behind her a little boy of three. This was their only child, indeed, for the two elder ones had died previously. At first Martin thought of placing the little fellow with a sister of his in the country, but changed his mind, thinking: "My Kapitoshka would not like to grow up in a strange family, so I will keep him by me." Then Avdeitch finished his apprenticeship, and went to live in lodgings with his little boy. But God had not seen fit to give Avdeitch happiness in his children. The little boy was just growing up and beginning to help his father and to be a pleasure to him, when he fell ill, was put to bed, and died after a week's fever.

Martin buried the little fellow and was inconsolable. Indeed, he was so inconsolable that he began to murmur against God. His life seemed so empty that more than once he prayed for death and reproached the Almighty for taking away his only beloved son instead of himself, the old man. At last he ceased altogether to go to church.

Then one day there came to see him an ancient peasant-pilgrim—one who was now in the eighth year of his pilgrimage. To him Avdeitch talked, and then went on to complain of his great sorrow.

"I no longer wish to be a God-fearing man," he said. "I only wish to die. That is all I ask of God. I am a lonely, hopeless man."

"You should not speak like that, Martin," replied the old pilgrim. "It is not for us to judge the acts of God. We must rely, not upon our own understanding, but upon the Divine wisdom. God saw fit that your son should die and that you should live. Therefore it must be better so. If you despair, it is because you have wished to live too much for your own pleasure."

"For what, then, should I live?" asked Martin.

1314

"For God alone," replied the old man. "It is He who gave you life, and therefore it is He for whom you should live. When you come to live for Him you will cease to grieve, and your trials will become easy to bear."

Martin was silent. Then he spoke again.

"But how am I to live for God?" he asked.

"Christ has shown us the way," answered the old man. "Can you read? If so, buy a Testament and study it. You will learn there how to live for God. Yes, it is all shown you there."

These words sank into Avdeitch's soul. He went out the same day, bought a large-print copy of the New Testament, and set himself to read it.

At the beginning Avdeitch had meant only to read on festival days, but when he once began his reading he found it so comforting to the soul that he came never to let a day pass without doing so. On the second occasion he became so engrossed that all the kerosene was burnt away in the lamp before he could tear himself away from the book.

Thus he came to read it every evening, and, the more he read, the more clearly did he understand what God required of him, and in what way he could live for God; so that his heart grew ever lighter and lighter. Once upon a time, whenever he had lain down to sleep, he had been used to moan and sigh as he thought of his little Kapitoshka; but now he only said—"Glory to Thee, O Lord! Glory to Thee! Thy will be done!"

From that time onwards Avdeitch's life became completely changed. Once he had been used to go out on festival days and drink tea in a tavern, and had not denied himself even an occasional glass of *vodka*. This he had done in the company of a boon companion, and, although no drunkard, would frequently leave the tavern in an excited state and talk much nonsense as he shouted and disputed with this friend of his. But now he had turned his back on all this, and his life had become quiet and joyous. Early in the morning he would sit down to his work, and labour through his appointed hours. Then he would take the lamp down from a shelf, light it, and sit down to read. And the more he read, the more he understood, and the clearer and happier he grew at heart.

It happened once the Martin had been reading late. He had been reading those verses in the sixth chapter of the Gospel of St. Luke which run:

1315

"And unto him that smiteth thee on the one cheek offer also the other; and him that taketh away thy cloak forbid not to take thy coat also. Give to every man that asketh of thee; and of him that taketh thy goods ask them not again. And as ye would that men should do to you, do ye also to them likewise."

Then, further on, he had read those verses where the Lord says: "And why call ye Me, Lord, Lord, and do not the things which I say? Whosoever cometh to Me and heareth my sayings, and doeth them, I will show you to whom he is like: He is like a man which built an house, and digged deep, and laid the foundation on a rock: and when the flood arose, the storm beat vehemently upon that house, and could not shake it: for it was founded upon a rock. But he that heareth and doeth not, is like a man that without a foundation built an house upon the earth; against which the stream did beat vehemently, and immediately it fell; and the ruin of that house was great."

Avdeitch read these words, and felt greatly cheered in soul. He took off his spectacles, laid them on the book, leaned his elbows upon the table, and gave himself up to meditation. He set himself to measure his own life by those words, and thought to himself:

"Is my house founded upon a rock or upon sand? It is well if it be upon a rock. Yet it seems so easy to me as I sit here alone. I may so easily come to think that I have done all that the Lord has commanded me, and grow careless and—sin again. Yet I will keep on striving, for it is goodly so to do. Help Thou me, O Lord."

Thus he kept on meditating, though conscious that it was time for bed; yet he was loathe to tear himself away from the book. He began to read the seventh chapter of St. Luke, and read on about the centurion, the widow's son, and the answer given to John's disciples; until in time he came to the passage where the rich Pharisee invited Jesus to his house, and the woman washed the Lord's feet with her tears and He justified her. So he came to the forty-fourth verse and read:

"And He turned to the woman, and said unto Simon, Seest thou this woman? I entered into thine house, and thou gavest Me no water for My feet: but she hath washed My feet with tears, and wiped them with the hairs of her head. Thou gavest Me no kiss: but this woman since the time I came in hath not ceased to kiss My feet. My head with oil thou didst anoint: but this woman hath anointed My feet with ointment."

He read these verses and thought:

"'Thou gavest Me no water for My feet' . . . 'Thou gavest Me no

kiss' . . . 'My head with oil thou didst not anoint' . . . "—and once again he took off his spectacles, laid them on the book, and became lost in meditation.

"I am even as that Pharisee," he thought to himself. "I drink tea and think only of my deeds. Yes, I think only of having plenty to eat and drink, of being warm and clean—but never of entertaining a guest. And Simon too was mindful only of himself, although the guest who had come to visit him was—who? Why, even the Lord Himself! If, then, He should come to visit *me*, should I receive Him any better?"—and, leaning forward upon his elbows, he was asleep almost before he was aware of it.

"Martin!" someone seemed to breathe in his ear.

He started from his sleep.

"Who is there?" he said. He turned and looked toward the door, but could see no one. Again he bent forward over the table. Then suddenly he heard the words:

"Martin, Martin! Look thou into the street to-morrow, for I am coming to visit thee."

Martin roused himself, got up from the chair, and rubbed his eyes. He did not know whether it was dreaming or awake that he had heard these words, but he turned out the lamp and went to bed.

The next morning Avdeitch rose before daylight and said his prayers. Then he made up the stove, got ready some cabbage soup and porridge, lighted the samovar, slung his leather apron about him and sat down to his work in the window. He sat and worked hard, yet all the time his thoughts were centered upon the night before. He was of two minds about the vision. At one moment he would think that it must have been his fancy, while the next moment he would find himself convinced that he had really heard the voice. "Yes, it must have been so," he concluded.

As Martin sat thus by the window he kept looking out of it as much as working. Whenever a pair of boots passed with which he was acquainted he would bend down to glance upwards through the window and see their owner's face as well. The doorkeeper passed in new felt boots, and then a water-carrier. Next, an old soldier, a veteran of Nicholas' army, in old, patched boots, and carrying a shovel in his hands, halted close by the window. Avdeitch knew him by his boots. His name was Stepanitch, and he was kept by a neighbouring tradesman out of charity, his duties being to help the doorkeeper. He began to clear away the snow from in front of

Avdeitch's window, while the shoemaker looked at him and then resumed his work.

"I think I must be getting into my dotage," thought Avdeitch with a smile. "Just because Stepanitch begins clearing away the snow I at once jump to the conclusion that Christ is about to visit me. Yes, I am growing foolish now, old greybeard that I am."

Yet he had hardly made a dozen stitches before he was craning his neck again to look out of the window. He could see that Stepanitch had placed his shovel against the wall, and was resting and trying to warm himself a little.

"He is evidently an old man now and broken," thought Avdeitch to himself. "He is not strong enough to clear away snow. Would he like some tea, I wonder? That reminds me that the samovar must be ready now."

He made fast his awl in his work and got up. Placing the samovar on the table, he brewed the tea, and then tapped with his finger on the window-pane. Stepanitch turned round and approached. Avdeitch beckoned to him, and then went to open the door.

"Come in and warm yourself," he said. "You must be frozen."

"Christ requite you!" answered Stepanitch. "Yes, my bones are almost cracking."

He came in, shook the snow off himself, and, though tottering on his feet, took pains to wipe them carefully, that he might not dirty the floor.

"Nay, do not trouble about that," said Avdeitch. "I will wipe your boots myself. It is part of my business in this trade. Come you here and sit down, and we will empty this tea-pot together."

He poured out two tumblerfuls, and offered one to his guest; after which he emptied his own into the saucer, and blew upon it to cool it. Stepanitch drank his tumblerful, turned the glass upside down, placed his crust upon it, and thanked his host kindly. But it was plain that he wanted another one.

"You must drink some more," said Avdeitch, and refilled his guest's tumbler and his own. Yet, in spite of himself, he had no sooner drunk his tea than he found himself looking out into the street again.

"Are you expecting anyone?" asked his guest.

"Am—am I expecting anyone? Well, to tell the truth, yes. That is to say, I am, and I am not. The fact is that some words have got fixed in my memory. Whether it was a vision or not I cannot tell, but at all events, my old friend, I was reading in the Gospels last

1318

night about Our Little Father Christ, and how He walked this earth and suffered. You have heard of Him, have you not?"

"Yes, yes, I have heard of Him," answered Stepanitch; "but we are ignorant folk and do not know our letters."

"Well, I was reading of how He walked this earth, and how He went to visit a Pharisee, and yet received no welcome from him at the door. All this I read last night, my friend, and then fell to thinking about it—to thinking how some day I too might fail to pay Our Little Father Christ due honour. 'Suppose,' I thought to myself, 'He came to me or to anyone like me? Should we, like the great lord Simon, not know how to receive Him and not go out to meet Him?' Thus I thought, and fell asleep where I sat. Then as I sat sleeping there I heard someone call my name; and as I raised myself the voice went on (as though it were the voice of someone whispering in my ear): 'Watch thou for me to-morrow, for I am coming to visit thee.' It said that twice. And so those words have got into my head, and, foolish though I know it to be, I keep expecting *Him*—the Little Father—every moment."

Stepanitch nodded and said nothing, but emptied his glass and laid it aside. Nevertheless Avdeitch took and refilled it.

"Drink it up; it will do you good," he said. "Do you know," he went on, "I often call to mind how, when Our Little Father walked this earth, there was never a man, however humble, whom He despised, and how it was chiefly among the common people that He dwelt. It was always with *them* that He walked; it was from among *them*—from among such men as you and I—from among sinners and working folk—that He chose His disciples. 'Whosoever,' He said, 'shall exalt himself, the same shall be abased; and whosoever shall abase himself, the same shall be exalted.' 'You,' He said again, 'call me Lord; yet will I wash you feet.' 'Whosoever,' He said, 'would be chief among you, let him be the servant of all. Because,' He said, 'blessed are the lowly, the peacemakers, the merciful, and the charitable.' "

Stepanitch had forgotten all his tea. He was an old man, and his tears came easily. He sat and listened, with the tears rolling down his cheeks.

"Oh, but you must drink your tea," said Avdeitch; yet Stepanitch only crossed himself and said the thanksgiving, after which he pushed his glass away and rose.

"I thank you, Martin Avdeitch," he said. "You have taken me in, and fed both soul and body."

"Nay, but I beg of you to come again," replied Avdeitch. "I am only too glad of a guest."

So Stepanitch departed, while Martin poured out the last of the tea and drank it. Then he cleaned the crockery, and sat down again to his work by the window—to the stitching of a back-piece. He stitched away, yet kept on looking through the window—looking for Christ, as it were—and ever thinking of Christ and His works. Indeed, Christ's many sayings were never absent from Avdeitch's mind.

Two soldiers passed the window, the one in military boots, and the other in civilian. Next, there came a neighbouring householder, in polished goloshes; then a baker with a basket. All of them passed on. Presently a woman in woollen stockings and rough country shoes approached the window, and halted near the buttress outside it. Avdeitch peered up at her from under the lintel of his window, and could see that she was a plain-looking, poorly-dressed woman and had a child in her arms. It was in order to muffle the child up more closely—little though she had to do it with!—that she had stopped near the buttress and was now standing there with her back to the wind. Her clothing was ragged and fit only for summer, and even from behind his window-panes Avdeitch could hear the child crying miserably and its mother vainly trying to soothe it. Avdeitch rose, went to the door, climbed the steps, and cried out: "My good woman, my good woman!"

She heard him and turned round.

"Why need you stand there in the cold with your baby?" he went on. "Come into my room, where it is warm, and where you will be able to wrap the baby up more comfortably than you can here. Yes, come in with you."

The woman was surprised to see an old man in a leather apron and with spectacles upon his nose calling out to her, yet she followed him down the steps, and they entered his room. The old man led her to the bedstead.

"Sit you down here, my good woman," he said. "You will be near the stove, and can warm yourself and feed your baby."

"Ah, but I have no milk left in my breast," she replied. "I have had nothing to eat this morning." Nevertheless she put the child to suck.

Avdeitch nodded his head approvingly, went to the table for some bread and a basin, and opened the stove door. From the stove he took and poured some soup into the basin, and drew out also

1320

a bowl of porridge. The latter, however, was not yet boiling, so he set out only the soup, after first laying the table with a cloth.

"Sit down and eat, my good woman," he said, "while I hold your baby. I have had little ones of my own, and know how to nurse them."

The woman crossed herself and sat down, while Avdeitch seated himself upon the bedstead with the baby. He smacked his lips at it once or twice, but made a poor show of it, for he had no teeth left. Consequently the baby went on crying. Then he bethought him of his finger, which he wriggled to and fro towards the baby's mouth and back again—without, however, actually touching the little one's lips, since the finger was blackened with work and sticky with shoemaker's wax. The baby contemplated the finger and grew quiet—then actually smiled. Avdeitch was delighted. Meanwhile the woman had been eating the meal, and now she told him, unasked, who she was and whither she was going.

"I am a soldier's wife," she said, "but my husband was sent to a distant station eight months ago, and I have heard nothing of him since. At first I got a place as cook, but when the baby came they said they could not do with it and dismissed me. That was three months ago, and I have got nothing since, and have spent all my savings. I tried to get taken as a wet nurse but no one would have me, for they said I was too thin. I have just been to see a tradesman's wife where our grandmother is in service. She had promised to take me on, and I quite thought that she would, but when I arrived to-day she told me to come again next week. She lives a long way from here, and I am quite worn out and have tired my baby for nothing. Thank Heaven, however, my landlady is good to me, and gives me shelter for Christ's sake. Otherwise I should not have known how to bear it all."

Avdeitch sighed and said: "But have you nothing warm to wear?"

"Ah, sir," replied the woman, "although it is the time for warm clothes I had to pawn my last shawl yesterday for two *grivenki*."

Then the woman returned to the bedstead to take her baby, while Avdeitch rose and went to a cupboard. There he rummaged about, and presently returned with an old jacket.

"Here," he said. "It is a poor old thing, but it will serve to cover you."

The woman looked at the jacket, and then at the old man. Then she took the jacket and burst into tears. Avdeitch turned away, and went creeping under the bedstead, whence he extracted a box and

1321

pretended to rummage about in it for a few moments; after which he sat down again before the woman.

Then the woman said to him: "I thank you in Christ's name, good grandfather. Surely it was He Himself who sent me to your window. Otherwise I should have seen my baby perish with the cold. When I first came out the day was warm, but now it has begun to freeze. But He, Our Little Father, had placed you in your window, that you might see me in my bitter plight and have compassion upon me."

Avdeitch smiled and said: "He did indeed place me there: yet, my poor woman, it was for a special purpose that I was looking out."

Then he told his guest, the soldier's wife, of his vision, and how he had heard a voice foretelling that to-day the Lord Himself would come to visit him.

"That may very well be," said the woman as she rose, took the jacket, and wrapped her baby in it. Then she saluted him once more and thanked him.

"Also, take this in Christ's name," said Avdeitch, and gave her a two-*grivenka* piece with which to buy herself a shawl. The woman crossed herself, and he likewise. Then he led her to the door and dismissed her.

When she had gone Avdeitch ate a little soup, washed up the crockery again, and resumed his work. All the time, though, he kept his eye upon the window, and as soon as ever a shadow fell across it he would look up to see who was passing. Acquaintances of his came past, and people whom he did not know, yet never anyone very particular.

Then suddenly he saw something. Opposite his window there had stopped an old pedlar-woman, with a basket of apples. Only a few of the apples, however, remained, so that it was clear that she was almost sold out. Over her shoulder was slung a sack of shavings, which she must have gathered near some new building as she was going home. Apparently, her shoulder had begun to ache under their weight, and she therefore wished to shift them to the other one. To do this, she balanced her basket of apples on the top of a post, lowered the sack to the pavement, and began shaking up its contents. As she was doing this, a boy in a ragged cap appeared from somewhere, seized an apple from the basket, and tried to make off. But the old woman, who had been on her guard, managed to turn and seize the boy by the sleeve, and although he struggled and

1322

tried to break away, she clung to him with both hands, snatched his cap off, and finally grasped him by the hair. Thereupon the youngster began to shout and abuse his captor. Avdeitch did not stop to make fast his awl, but threw his work down upon the floor, ran to the door, and went stumbling up the steps—losing his spectacles as he did so. Out into the street he ran, where the old woman was still clutching the boy by the hair and threatening to take him to the police, while the boy, for his part, was struggling in the endeavour to free himself.

"I never took it," he was saying. "What are you beating me for? Let me go."

Avdeitch tried to part them as he took the boy by the hand and said:

"Let him go, my good woman. Pardon him for Christ's sake."

"Yes, I will pardon him," she retorted, "but not until he has tasted a new birch-rod. I mean to take the young rascal to the police."

But Avdeitch still interceded for him.

"Let him go, my good woman," he said. "He will never do it again. Let him go for Christ's sake."

The old woman released the boy, who was for making off at once had not Avdeitch stopped him.

"You must beg the old woman's pardon," he said, "and never do such a thing again. I saw you take the apple."

The boy burst out crying, and begged the old woman's pardon as Avdeitch commanded.

"There, there," said Avdeitch. "Now I will give you one. Here you are,"—and he took an apple from the basket and handed it to the boy. "I will pay you for it, my good woman," he added.

"Yes, but you spoil the young rascal by doing that," she objected. "He ought to have received a reward that would have made him glad to stand for a week."

"Ah, my good dame, my good dame," exclaimed Avdeitch. "That may be *our* way of rewarding, but it is not God's. If this boy ought to have been whipped for taking the apple, ought not we also to receive something for our sins?"

The old woman was silent. Then Avdeitch related to her the parable of the master who absolved his servant from the great debt which he owed him, whereupon the servant departed and took his own debtor by the throat. The old woman listened, and also the boy.

"God has commanded us to pardon one another," went on Avdeitch, "or *He* will not pardon us. We ought to pardon all men, and especially the thoughtless."

The old woman shook her head and sighed.

"Yes, that may be so," she said, "but these young rascals are so spoilt already!"

"Then it is for us, their elders, to teach them better," he replied.

"That is what I say myself at times," rejoined the old woman. "I had seven of them once at home, but have only one daughter now." And she went on to tell Avdeitch where she and her daughter lived, and how they lived, and how many grandchildren she had.

"I have only such strength as you see," she said, "yet I work hard, for my heart goes out to my grandchildren—the bonny little things that they are! No children could run to meet me as they do. Aksintka, for instance, will go to no one else. 'Grandmother,' she cries, 'dear grandmother, you are tired' "—and the old woman became thoroughly softened. "Everyone knows what boys are," she added presently, referring to the culprit. "May God go with him!"

She was raising the sack to her shoulders again when the boy darted forward and said:

"Nay, let me carry it, grandmother. It will be all on my way home."

The old woman nodded assent, gave up the sack to the boy, and went away with him down the street. She had quite forgotten to ask Avdeitch for the money for the apple. He stood looking after them, and observing how they were talking together as they went.

Having seen them go, he returned to his room, finding his spectacles—unbroken—on the steps as he descended them. Once more he took up his awl and fell to work, but had done little before he found it difficult to distinguish the stitches, and the lamplighter had passed on his rounds. "I too must light up," he thought to himself. So he trimmed the lamp, hung it up, and resumed his work. He finished one boot completely, and then turned it over to look at it. It was all good work. Then he laid aside his tools, swept up the cuttings, rounded off the stitches and loose ends, and cleaned his awl. Next he lifted the lamp down, placed it on the table, and took his Testament from the shelf. He had intended opening the book at the place which he had marked last night with a strip of leather, but it opened itself at another instead. The instant it did so, his vision of last night came back to his memory, and, as instantly, he thought he heard a movement behind him as of someone moving

towards him. He looked round and saw in the shadow of a dark corner what appeared to be figures—figures of persons standing there, yet could not distinguish them clearly. Then the voice whispered in his ear:

"Martin, Martin, dost thou not know Me?"

"Who art Thou?" said Avdeitch.

"Even I!" whispered the voice again. "Lo, it is I!"—and there stepped from the dark corner Stepanitch. He smiled, and then, like the fading of a little cloud, was gone.

"It is I!" whispered the voice again—and there stepped from the same corner the woman with her baby. She smiled, and the baby smiled, and they were gone.

"And it is I!" whispered the voice again—and there stepped forth the old woman and the boy with the apple. They smiled, and were gone.

Joy filled the soul of Martin Avdeitch as he crossed himself, put on his spectacles, and set himself to read the Testament at the place where it had opened. At the top of the page he read:

"For I was an hungred, and ye gave Me meat: I was thirsty, and ye gave Me drink: I was a stranger, and ye took Me in."

And further down the page he read:

"Inasmuch as ye have done it unto one of the least of these my brethren ye have done it unto Me."

Then Avdeitch understood that the vision had come true, and that his Saviour had in very truth visited him that day, and that he had received Him.

ANTHONY TROLLOPE

ANTHONY TROLLOPE (English, 1815-1882). Novelist recreator of the average in life and conduct. Spent early years as Irish civil servant. Famous for his methodical way of writing—1,000 words an hour—and frank admission that he did it for money. Author of over 40 novels, most famous being the 6 Barsetshire stories, including *The Warden* and *Barchester Towers.*

HE KNEW HE WAS RIGHT

THE Glascock marriage was a great affair in Florence; so much so that there were not a few who regarded it as a strengthening of peaceful relations between the United States and the United King-

dom, and who thought that the Alabama claims and the question of naturalisation might now be settled with comparative ease. An English lord was about to marry the niece of an American Minister to a foreign court. The bridegroom was not, indeed, quite a lord as yet, but it was known to all men that he must be a lord in a very short time, and the bride was treated with more than usual bridal honours because she belonged to a legation. She was not, indeed, an ambassador's daughter, but the niece of a daughterless ambassador, and therefore almost as good as a daughter. The wives and daughters of other ambassadors, and the other ambassadors themselves, of course, came to the wedding; and as the palace in which Mr. Spalding had apartments stood alone, in a garden, with a separate carriage entrance, it seemed for all wedding purposes as though the whole palace were his own.

The English Minister came, and his wife,—although she had never quite given over turning up her nose at the American bride whom Mr. Glascock had chosen for himself. It was such a pity, she said, that such a man as Mr. Glascock should marry a young woman from Providence, Rhode Island. Who in England would know anything of Providence, Rhode Island? And it was so expedient, in her estimation, that a man of family should strengthen himself by marrying a woman of family. It was so necessary, she declared, that a man when marrying should remember that his child would have two grandfathers, and would be called upon to account for four great-grandfathers. Nevertheless Mr. Glascock was —Mr. Glascock; and, let him marry whom he would, his wife would be the future Lady Peterborough. Remembering this, the English Minister's wife gave up the point, when the thing was really settled, and benignly promised to come to the breakfast with all the secretaries and attachés belonging to the legation, and all the wives and daughters thereof. What may a man not do, and do with éclat, if he be heir to a peer and have plenty of money in his pocket?

Mr. and Mrs. Spalding were covered with glory on the occasion; and perhaps they did not bear their glory as meekly as they should have done. Mrs. Spalding laid herself open to some ridicule from the English Minister's wife because of her inability to understand with absolute clearness the condition of her niece's husband in respect to his late and future seat in Parliament, to the fact of his being a commoner and a nobleman at the same time, and to certain information which was conveyed to her, surely in a most unnecessary manner, that if Mr. Glascock were to die before his father her

1326

niece would never become Lady Peterborough, although her niece's son, if she had one, would be the future lord. No doubt she blundered, as was most natural; and then the British Minister's wife made the most of the blunders; and when once Mrs. Spalding ventured to speak of Caroline as her ladyship, not to the British Minister's wife, but to the sister of one of the secretaries, a story was made out of it almost as false as it was ill-natured. Poor Caroline was spoken of as her ladyship backwards and forwards among the ladies of the legation in a manner which might have vexed her had she known anything about it; but, nevertheless, all the ladies prepared their best flounces to go to the wedding. The time soon would come when she would in truth be a "ladyship," and she might be of social use to any one of the ladies in question.

. . . Everybody who was anybody in Florence was to be present. There were only to be four bridesmaids, Caroline herself having strongly objected to a greater number. As Wallach Petrie had fled at the first note of preparation for these trivial and unpalatable festivities, another American young lady was found; and the sister of the English secretary of legation, who had so maliciously spread that report about her "ladyship," gladly agreed to be the fourth.

It was generally admitted among the various legations in Florence that there had not been such a wedding in the City of Flowers since it had become the capital of Italia. Mr. Glascock and Miss Spalding were married in the chapel of the legation,—a legation chapel on the ground floor having been extemporised for the occasion. This greatly enhanced the pleasantness of the thing, and saved the necessity of matrons and bridesmaids packing themselves and their finery into close fusty carriages. A portion of the guests attended in the chapel, and the remainder, when the ceremony was over, were found strolling about the shady garden.

The whole affair of the breakfast was very splendid and lasted some hours. In the midst of the festivities the bride and bridegroom were whisked away with a pair of gray horses to the railway station, and before the last toast of the day had been proposed by the Belgian Councillor of Legation, they were half-way up the Apennines on their road to Bologna.

Mr. Spalding behaved himself like a man on this occasion Nothing was spared in the way of expense, and when he made that celebrated speech, in which he declared that the republican

1327

virtue of the New World had linked itself in a happy alliance with the aristocratic splendour of the Old, and went on with a simile about the lion and the lamb, everybody accepted it with good humour in spite of its being a little too long for the occasion.

"It has gone off very well, mamma, has it not?" said Nora, as she returned home with her mother to her lodgings.

"Yes, my dear; much, I fancy, as these things generally do."

"I thought it was so nice. And she looked very well. And he was so pleasant, and so much like a gentleman,—not noisy, you know, and yet not too serious."

"I dare say, my love."

"It is easy enough, mamma, for a girl to be married, for she has nothing to do but wear her clothes and look as pretty as she can. And if she cries and has a red nose it is forgiven her. But a man has so difficult a part to play. If he tries to carry himself as though it were not a special occasion, he looks like a fool that way; and if he is very special, he looks like a fool the other way. I thought Mr. Glascock did it very well."

TU FU

TU FU (Chinese, 712-770). Once called the God of Verse. Friend of Li Po. Became a courtier; was exiled by Emperor Su Tsung because of his outspoken demeanor. For a time traveled as a homeless wanderer. Did some painting. A certain sadness overshadows his poetry.

TO A LOST LADY

Be still!
Tell me no more of spring,
No more of flowers.
Bring mourning boughs
And black weeds stricken by blight.

Be still!
Let the glad sun
Dip down behind the mountains,
While I put on grief's robe
And lie
Among the leaves she loved—
For it is night.

THE HOME IN THE HEART

Fire wrecked the house where I was born
   And stripped the rafters bare:
I put to sea in my gilded barque,
   But I could not shake despair.

I took my flute and played to the moon,
   But she hid behind a cloud,
For my song was sad, the music faint;
   Only my heart beat loud.

I turned me to the mountain,
   But I found no solace there,
For childhood joys seemed vanished,
   With my home into thin blue air.

I longed for death—but then the moon
   Shone mirrored in the sea,
And I caught one glimpse of a maiden's face
   As her boat was passing me.

Were it her wish, I'd rout despair
   And bear a true man's part:
I'd build another dwelling—
   And this one, in her heart!

ON THE RIVER CHOU

Beneath the wide cloud-ridden sky
My boat is gliding swiftly by.

I watch the quiet water; soon
The drifting clouds have hid the moon.

As I lean back within my boat,
Upon the sky I seem to float.

And as I drift, I like to dream
That my heart is the quiet stream,

The River Chou so still and fair—
And my beloved is mirrored there.

1329

Now the sad rains are falling. Let us say now: the sky weeps because its fine weather is all gone. Boredom piles up on us like heavy rain-clouds: where is our gaiety and wit? Let us sit indoors.

Now is the time for poetry that remembers summer. Let it be put down gently on white paper like full-blown petals falling from exquisite trees. And let my lips drink from this cup of summer wine each time my brush is dipped into the ink. Thus will I keep my fancy from floating off like clouds or smoke: for time past escapes from us, my love, quicker than a flight of birds.

IVAN SERGEYEVICH TURGENEV

IVAN SERGEYEVICH TURGENEV (Russian, 1818-1883). The most consciously artistic and "Western" of the great Russian novelists. Admired particularly by stylists like Henry James. Interested in politics of his day. Considerably responsible through his novels for abolition of serfdom in Russia. Major works: (novels) *Fathers and Sons, Virgin Soil*, and (play) *A Month in the Country*.

THE NIHILIST

"WHERE is your new friend?" he asked Arkadi.

"He has gone out already. He generally gets up very early and makes some excursion. But I must tell you, once for all, that you need not take any notice of him; he does not care for conventionalities."

"Yes, so I perceive."

Paul Petrovitch began slowly to spread butter on his bread.

"Will he remain here any length of time?"

"That depends. He will go from here to his father's."

"And where does his father live?"

"In our district; eighty versts from here. He has a little estate there. He used to be the regimental doctor."

"Ta-ta, ta-ta! I have been continually asking myself, where could I have heard that name before? Bazarof, Bazarof! Nicholas, do

you not remember that in our father's division there was a Dr. Bazarof?"

"I seem to remember something of the sort."

"Yes, it is right enough. So this doctor is his father—hm!" Paul Petrovitch twisted his moustache.

"Well, and what is Mr. Bazarof junior?" asked he slowly.

"What is Bazarof?" Arkadi smiled. "Shall I tell you, uncle, what he really is?"

"Do me that favor, my dear nephew."

"He is a Nihilist."

"What?" asked Nicholas Petrovitch.

As for Paul Petrovitch, he suddenly raised the knife, on whose point was a little piece of butter, and remained motionless.

"He is a Nihilist," repeated Arkadi.

"Nihilist!" said Nicholas Petrovitch. "The word comes from the Latin *nihil*, nothing, as far as I can tell, and therefore designates a person who acknowledges nothing."

"Or rather, who respects nothing," said Paul Petrovitch, who recommenced buttering his bread.

"Or rather, who regards everything from a critical point of view," remarked Arkadi.

"Does not that come to the same thing?" asked Paul Petrovitch.

"No, by no means. A Nihilist is a man who bows to no authority, who accepts no principles on faith alone, however high may be the regard in which this principle is held in human opinion."

"And do you consider that right?" asked Paul Petrovitch.

"That depends on the point of view, uncle; some think it right, while others consider it quite wrong."

"Indeed. Well, I see it is not *our* point of view. We of the old school are of opinion that without principles, that are received on faith alone, as you express it, the world could not exist. But *vous avez changé tout cela*. Well, may God give you good health and the rank of general; as for us, we will be content with admiring you, you—what do you call yourselves?"

"Nihilists," said Arkadi, accenting each syllable.

"Yes. We used to have Hegelists, now we have Nihilists. We shall see how you manage to exist in the nothing, the vacuum, as under an air-pump. And now, brother Nicholas, be so good as to ring; I should like to drink my cocoa."

The combat took place the same evening at tea. Paul had come down into the drawing-room in a state of irritation, and ready for

the fight. He only awaited an opportunity to throw himself on the enemy; but he had long to wait. Bazarof never spoke much before the "two old fellows," as he called the two brothers; besides, he did not feel very well this evening, and swallowed one cup of tea after another in silence. Paul was devoured by impatience: at length he found the opportunity he had been seeking.

The conversation turned on one of the neighboring landholders.

"He is a simpleton, a bad aristocrat," said Bazarof, who had known him at St. Petersburg.

"Permit me to ask you," said Paul, with trembling lips, "whether the words 'simpleton' and 'aristocrat' are in your opinion synonymous?"

"I said 'bad aristocrat,'" replied Bazarof carelessly, sipping his tea.

"That is true; But I assume that you rank aristocrats and bad aristocrats in the same category. I think it right to inform you that such is not my opinion. I venture to say that I am generally considered a liberal man and lover of progress; but it is just on that account that I respect the aristocrats, the true aristocrats. Consider, my dear sir"—Bazarof fixed his eyes on Paul—"my dear sir," continued he, with dignity, "consider the English nobility: they do not give up one iota of their rights, and yet they respect the rights of others just as much; they demand what is due to them, and yet they are always careful to render their due to others. It is the nobility that has given England its liberty, and that is its strongest support."

"That is an old song we have often heard," replied Bazarof; "but what do you mean by it?"

"I mean to prove by it, my dear sir, that without the consciousness of one's own dignity, without self-respect—and all these sentiments prevail among the aristocracy—there can be no solid foundation for the commonwealth, for the edifice of the State. The individual, the personality, my dear sir—that is the essential; a man's personality must stand firm as a rock, for everything rests on this basis. I know quite well that you think my manners, my dress, even my habit of cleanliness, absurd; but all this springs from self-respect, from a feeling of duty—yes, yes, sir, from a feeling of duty. I live in an out-of-the-way corner of the province; but I do not neglect my person on that account—in my own person I respect the man."

"Excuse me, Paul Petrovitch," replied Bazarof; "you say that you respect yourself, and you sit there with your arms crossed. What advantage can that be to the commonwealth? If you did not respect yourself you would not act differently."

Paul Petrovitch turned pale.

"That is quite another matter," replied he. "I have no intention of telling you why I stay with my arms crossed, as you are pleased to call it. I merely wished to tell you that aristocracy depends upon principle; and it is only immoral or worthless men who can live nowadays without principles. I said so to Arkadi the day after his arrival; and I am merely repeating it to you today. Is it not the case, Nicholas Petrovitch?"

Nicholas Petrovitch nodded assent.

"Aristocracy, liberalism, principles, progress," repeated Bazarof—"all words quite foreign to our language, and perfectly useless. A true Russian need not use them."

"What does he need, then, in your opinion? According to you, we are outside the limits of humanity, outside its laws. That is going rather too far; the logic of history requires—"

"What do you need that logic for? We can do very well without it."

"How?"

"I will give an example. I fancy that you do not need the aid of logic in carrying a piece of bread to your mouth when you are hungry. What is the use of all these abstractions?"

Paul lifted up his hands.

"I no longer understand you," said he. "You insult the Russian people. I do not understand how it is possible not to acknowledge principles—rules! What have you, then, to guide you through life?"

"I have told you before, uncle," interposed Arkadi, "that we do not acknowledge any authorities."

"We act according as anything seems useful to us," added Bazarof; "to-day it seems to us useful to deny, and we do deny."

"Everything?"

"Absolutely everything."

"What? Not only art, poetry, but even—I hesitate to say it."

"Everything," repeated Bazarof, with most indomitable calm.

Paul looked at him fixedly. He had not expected this answer. Arkadi blushed with pleasure.

"Excuse me," said Nicholas, "you deny everything, or, to speak more correctly, you destroy everything; but you must also rebuild."

"That does not concern us. First of all, we must clear the ground."

"The present state of the people requires it," added Arkadi seriously. "We must fulfill this duty; we have no right to abandon ourselves to the satisfaction of our personal vanity."

This last speech did not please Bazarof. It smacked of philosophy,

that is, of romanticism; for he gave this name even to philosophy. But he did not think this a fitting moment to contradict his young pupil.

"No, no!" exclaimed Paul, with sudden emotion. "I will not believe that you gentlemen have a right idea of the Russian people, and that you express its real wants, its surest wishes. No, the Russian people is not what you represent it. It has a reverent respect for tradition; it is patriarchal; it cannot live without faith."

"I shall not attempt to contradict you," replied Bazarof. "I am even ready to admit that this once you are right."

"But if I am right?"

"That proves nothing whatever."

"Nothing whatever," repeated Arkadi, with the assurance of an experienced chess-player, who, having foreseen a move that his opponent considers dangerous, does not seem in the least disconcerted by it.

"How can you say that proves nothing?" said Paul, stupefied. "Do you then separate yourself from your people?"

"And what if I did? The people believe that when it thunders, the prophet Elijah is riding over the heavens in his chariot. Well, must I share its opinion in this matter? You think you will confound me by telling me that the people is Russian. Well, am I not Russian, too?"

"No; after all that you have just said, you are not. I will no longer acknowledge you to be Russian."

"My grandfather followed the plough," replied Bazarof, with lofty pride. "Ask any one of your peasants which of us two—you or me—he is readiest to acknowledge as his fellow-citizen. You cannot even talk to him."

"And you, who can talk to him, you despise him."

"Why not, if he deserves it? You condemn the tendency of my ideas; but how do you know that it is accidental, that it is not rather determined by the universal spirit of the people whom you defend so well?"

"Come, the Nihilists are very useful."

"Whether they are or not is not for us to decide. Do not you also think that you are good for something?"

"Gentlemen, gentlemen, no personalities," exclaimed Nicholas, rising.

Paul smiled, and placing his hand on his brother's shoulder, forced him to sit down again.

"Set your mind at rest," said he; "I shall not forget myself, if only

because of that feeling of dignity of which this gentleman speaks so scornfully. Excuse me," continued he, once more addressing Bazarof; "you probably think that your mode of looking at things is a new one; that is a mistake on your part. The materialism you profess has been held in honor more than once, and has always proved itself insufficient."

"Another foreign word!" replied Bazarof. He was beginning to become bitter, and the complexion of his face was assuming an unpleasant yellow. "In the first place, let me tell you that we do not preach; that is not one of our habits."

"What do you do, then?"

"I will tell you. We have begun by calling attention to the extortionate officials, the need of roads, the absence of trade, the manner of executing justice."

"Yes, yes; you are informers, *divulgators*, that is the name given to you, if I am not much mistaken. I agree with you in many of your criticisms; but—"

"Then we soon discovered that it was not enough to talk about the wounds to which we are succumbing, that all this only tended to platitudes and dogmatism. We perceived that our advanced men, our *divulgators*, were worth nothing whatever; that we were taking up our time with follies, such as art for art's sake, creative power which does not know itself, the parliamentary system, the need of lawyers, and a thousand other foolish tales; while we were overwhelmed by the grossest superstitution; while all our joint-stock companies were becoming bankrupt. All this is only because there is a dearth of honest men; while even the liberation of the serfs, with which Government is much occupied, will produce no good effects, because our peasants are themselves ready to steal, so that they may go and drink poisonous drugs in the taverns."

"Good," replied Paul, "very good. You have discovered all that, and all the same you are determined to undertake nothing serious?"

"Yes, we are determined!" repeated Bazarof, somewhat sharply. Suddenly he began to reproach himself for having said so much before this gentleman.

"And you confine yourself to abuse?"

"We abuse, if necessary."

"And that is what is called Nihilism?"

"That is what is called Nihilism!" repeated Bazarof, this time in a particularly irritating tone.

Paul winced a little.

"Good!" said he, with forced calm and constrained manner. "The mission of Nihilism is to remedy all things, and you are our saviours and our heroes. Excellent! But why do you abuse the others so much, and call them chatterboxes? Do you not chatter as much as the rest?"

"Come, if there is anything we have to reproach ourselves with, it is certainly not this," muttered Bazarof between his teeth.

"What! can you say that you act, or even prepare for action?" Bazarof remained silent. Paul trembled, but he restrained his anger.

"Then act, destroy," continued he; "but how dare you destroy without ever knowing why you destroy?"

"We destroy because we are a force," said Arkadi, gravely.

Paul looked at his nephew and smiled.

"Yes, force is responsible to no one," continued Arkadi, drawing himself up.

"Wretched man," exclaimed Paul Petrovitch, no longer able to contain himself, "if you would but consider what you assert of Russia alone, with your absurd phrases! No, it would require an angel's patience to endure that force! The Mongol and the savage Kalmuk have force, too. But how can this force help us? What ought to be dear to us is civilization; yes, yes, my dear sirs, the fruits of civilization. And do not tell me that these fruits are worthless; the merest dauber of signboards, the most wretched fiddler, who, for five kopecks an evening, plays polkas and mazurkas, are more useful than you, because they are representatives of civilization, and not of the Mongolian brute force! You consider yourselves advanced, and your proper place would be in a Kalmuk kibitka. Force! Consider one moment, you strong gentlemen, that at most there are only a few dozen of you, while the others may be counted by millions, and that they will not allow you to tread under foot their most sacred traditions; no, they will tear you to pieces."

"If they tear us to pieces, we must put up with it," replied Bazarof. "But you are quite out in your reckoning. We are not so few as you suppose."

"What! You seriously believe that you will be able to bring the whole people into your ranks?"

"Do you not know that a kopeck candle is enough to set the whole city of Moscow on fire?" answered Bazarof.

"Excellent! First, almost Satanic pride, and then irony, which reveals your bad taste. This is how youth is carried away; this is how the inexperienced hearts of these boys are seduced. Look! there is one of them by your side; he almost worships you." Arkadi turned

away, frowning. "And this contagion has already spread. I have been told that at Rome our painters no longer set foot into the Vatican; they call Raphael a bungler, because, as they say, he is considered an authority—and those who say this are themselves incapacity personified; their imagination cannot soar beyond the 'Girl at the Well;' however they may try, they cannot attain anything better! And how ugly is this 'Girl at the Well!' I suppose you have the highest opinion of these fellows, have you not?"

"As far as I am concerned," replied Bazarof, "I would not give twopence for Raphael, and I do not suppose that the others are worth much more."

"Bravo, bravo! Do you hear, Arkadi? That is how young people should express themselves now! O, I can quite understand why they follow in your footsteps! Formerly they used to feel the need of learning something. As they did not wish to be considered ignorant, they were forced to work. But now they need only say, 'There is nothing but folly and rubbish in the world;' and there is an end to everything. The students may well rejoice. Formerly they were only foolish boys —behold them suddenly transformed into Nihilists!"

"It appears to me that you are forgetting the sentiment of personal dignity, on which you laid so much stress just now," remarked Bazarof phlegmatically, while Arkadi's face flushed with indignation, and his eyes flashed. "Our dispute has led us too far. I think we should do well to stop here. Yet," added he, rising, "I should agree with you if you could name to me a single institution of our social, civil, or family life, which does not deserve to be swept away without mercy."

"I could name a million such," exclaimed Paul Petrovitch, "a million! Take, for instance, the commune."

A cold smile passed over Bazarof's lips.

"As for the commune," said he, "you had better talk to your brother about that. I suppose he must know by this time what to think of the commune, the solidarity of the peasants, their temperance, and similar jokes."

"And the family, the family, such as we still find it among our peasants!" exclaimed Paul Petrovitch.

"In my opinion that is another question that you would do well not to examine too closely. Come, take my advice, Paul Petrovitch, and take two days to consider the matter. Nothing else will occur to you just at present; consider all our institutions one after another, and contemplate them carefully. Meantime Arkadi and I will—"

"Turn everything to ridicule," interrupted Paul Petrovitch.

"No; dissect frogs. Come, Arkadi. Good afternoon, gentlemen." The two friends went out. The brothers remained alone together, and for some time could only look at each other in silence.

"So that is the youth of to-day," began Paul Petrovitch at length; "those are our successors!"

MARK TWAIN

MARK TWAIN (Samuel Langhorne Clemens, American, 1835-1910). Humane and gentle satirist, whose last works reveal strain of disillusioned pessimism. Adventures of childhood on the Mississippi appear in the beloved boys' stories, *Adventures of Tom Sawyer* and *Adventures of Huckleberry Finn* (considered by some the great American novel). Later satirical novel: *A Connecticut Yankee at King Arthur's Court.*

THE CELEBRATED JUMPING FROG
OF CALAVERAS COUNTY

IN compliance with the request of a friend of mine, who wrote me from the East, I called on good-natured, garrulous old Simon Wheeler, and inquired after my friend's friend, Leonidas W. Smiley, as requested to do, and I hereunto append the result. I have a lurking suspicion that *Leonidas W.* Smiley is a myth; that my friend never knew such a personage; and that he only conjectured that if I asked old Wheeler about him, it would remind him of his infamous *Jim* Smiley, and he would go to work and bore me to death with some exasperating reminiscence of him as long as and as tedious as it should be useless to me. If that was the design, it succeeded.

I found Simon Wheeler dozing comfortably by the barroom stove of the dilapidated tavern in the decayed mining camp of Angel's, and I noticed that he was fat and bald-headed, and had an expression of winning gentleness and simplicity upon his tranquil countenance. He roused up and gave me good-day. I told him a friend of mine had commissioned me to make some inquiries about a cherished companion of his boyhood named *Leonidas W.* Smiley—*Reverend Leonidas W.* Smiley, a young minister of the Gospel, who he had heard was at one time a resident of Angel's Camp. I added that if Mr. Wheeler could tell me anything about this Reverend Leonidas W. Smiley I would feel under many obligations to him.

1338

Simon Wheeler backed me into a corner and blockaded me there with his chair, and then sat down and reeled off the monotonous narrative which follows this paragraph. He never smiled, he never frowned, he never changed his voice from the gentle-flowing key to which he tuned his initial sentence, he never betrayed the slightest suspicion of enthusiasm; but all through the interminable narrative there ran a vein of impressive earnestness and sincerity which showed me plainly that, so far from his imagining that there was anything ridiculous or funny about his story, he regarded it as a really important matter, and admired its two heroes as men of transcendent genius in *finesse*. I let him go on his own way, and never interrupted him once.

Reverend Leonidas W. H'm, Reverend Le—well, there was a feller here once by the name of *Jim* Smiley, in the winter of '49—or maybe it was the spring of '50—I don't recollect exactly, somehow, though what makes me think it was one or the other is because I remember the big flume warn't finished when he first came to the camp; but anyway, he was the curiousest man about always betting on anything that turned up you ever see, if he could get anybody to bet on the other side; and if he couldn't he'd change sides. Anyway what suited the other man would suit *him*—anyway just so's he got a bet, *he* was satisfied. But still he was lucky, uncommon lucky; he most always come out winner. He was always ready and laying for a chance; there couldn't be no solit'ry thing mentioned but that feller'd offer to bet on it, and take ary side you please, as I was just telling you. If there was a horse-race, you'd find him flush or you'd find him busted at the end of it; if there was a dog-fight, he'd bet on it; if there was a cat-fight, he'd bet on it; if there was a chicken-fight, he'd bet on it; why if there was two birds setting on a fence, he would bet you which one would fly first; or if there was a camp-meeting he would be there reg'lar to bet on Parson Walker which he judged to be the best exhorter about here, and so he was, too, and a good man. If he even see a straddle-bug start to go anywhere, he would bet how long it would take him to get to—to wherever he was going to, and if you took him up, he would foller that straddle-bug to Mexico but what he would find out where he was bound for and how long he was on the road. Lots of the boys here has seen that Smiley and can tell you about him. Why, it never made no difference to *him* —he'd bet on *anything*—the dangdest feller. Parson Walker's wife laid very sick once, for a good while, and it seemed as if they warn't going to save her; but one morning he come in, and Smiley up and

1339

asked him how she was, and he said she was considerable better—
thank the Lord for His inf'nite mercy—and coming on so smart that
with the blessing of Prov'dence she'd get well yet; and Smiley, before
he thought, says, "Well, I'll resk two-and-a-half she don't anyway."

Thish-yer Smiley had a mare—the boys called her the fifteen-
minute nag, but that was only in fun, you know, because of course,
for all she was slow and always had the asthma, or the distemper, or
the consumption, or something of that kind. They used to give her
two or three hundred yards' start, and then pass her under way; but
always at the fag end of the race she'd get excited and desparate like,
and come cavorting and straddling up, and scattering her legs around
limber, sometimes in the air and sometimes out to one side among
the fences, and kicking up m-o-r-e dust and raising m-o-r-e racket
with her coughing and sneezing and blowing her nose—and *always*
fetch up at the stand just about a neck ahead, as near as you cipher
it down.

And he had a little small bull-pup, that to look at him you'd think
he warn't worth a cent but to set around and look ornery and lay for
a chance to steal something. But as soon as money was up on him he
was a different dog; his under-jaw'd begin to stick out like the fo'-
castle of a steamboat, and his teeth would uncover and shine like the
furnaces. And a dog might tackle him and bully-rag him, and bite
him, and throw him over his shoulder two or three times, and Andrew
Jackson—which was the name of the pup—Andrew Jackson would
never let on but what *he* was satisfied, and hadn't expected nothing
else—and the bets being doubled and doubled on the other side all
the time, till the money was all up; and then all of a sudden he would
grab that other dog just by the j'int of his hind leg and freeze to it—
not chaw, you understand, but only just grip and hang on till they
throwed up the sponge, if it was a year. Smiley always come out winner on that pup, till he harnessed a dog once that didn't have no
hind legs, because they'd been sawed off in a circular saw, and when
the thing had gone along far enough, and the money was all up, and
he came to make a snatch for his pet holt, he see in a minute how
he'd been imposed on, and how the other dog had him in the door,
so to speak, and he 'peared surprised, and then he looked sorter dis-
couraged-like, and didn't try no more to win the fight, and so he got
shucked out bad. He gave Smiley a look, as much as to say his heart
was broke, and it was *his* fault for putting up a dog that hadn't no
hind legs for him to take holt of, which was his main dependence in
a fight, and then he limped off a piece and laid down and died. It

was a good pup, was that Andrew Jackson, and would have made a name for hisself if he'd lived, for the stuff was in him and he had genius—I know it, because he hadn't no opportunities to speak of, and it don't stand to reason that a dog could make such a fight as he could under them circumstances if he hadn't no talent. It always makes me feel sorry when I think of that last fight of his'n, and the way it turned out.

Well, thish-yer Smiley had rat-terriers, and chicken cocks, and tom-cats, and all them kind of things till you couldn't rest, and you couldn't fetch nothing for him to bet on but he'd match you. He ketched a frog one day, and took him home, and said he cal'lated to educate him; and so he never done nothing for three months but set in his back yord and learn that frog to jump. And you bet you he *did* learn him, too. He'd give him a little punch behind, and the next minute you'd see that frog whirling in the air like a doughnut—see him turn one summerset, or maybe a couple, if he got a good start, and come down flat-footed and all right like a cat. He got him up so in the matter of ketching flies, and kep' him in practice so constant, that he'd nail a fly every time as fur as he could see him. Smiley said all a frog wanted was education and he could do 'most anything—and I believe him. Why, I've seen him set Dan'l Webster down here on this floor—Dan'l Webster was the name of the frog—and sing out, "Flies, Dan'l, flies!" and quicker'n you could wink he'd spring straight up and snake a fly off'n the counter there, and flop ag'in as solid as a gob of mud, and fall to scratching the side of his head with his hind foot as indifferent as if he hadn't no idea he'd been doin' any more'n any frog might do. You never see a frog so modest and straightfor'-ard as he was, for all he was so gifted. And when it come to fair and square jumping on a dead level, he could get over more ground at one straddle than any animal of his breed you ever see. Jumping on a dead level was his strong suit, you understand; and when it come to that, Smiley would ante up money on him as long as he had a red. Smiley was monstrous proud of his frog, and well he might be, for fellers that had traveled and been everywhere all said he laid over any frog that ever *they* see.

Well, Smiley kep' the beast in a little lattice box, and he used to fetch him down-town sometimes and lay for a bet. One day a feller—a stranger in the camp, he was—come acrost him with his box, and says:

"What might it be that you've got in the box?"

And Smiley says, sorter indifferent like, "It might be a parrot, or

it might be a canary, maybe, but it ain't—it's only just a frog."

And the feller took it, and looked at it careful, and turned it round this way and that, and says, "H'm—so 'tis. Well, what's *he* good for?"

"Well," Smiley says, easy and careless, "he's good enough for *one* thing, I should judge—he can outjump any frog in Calaveras County."

The feller took the box again, and took another long, particular look, and give it back to Smiley, and says, very deliberate, "Well," he says, "I don't see no p'ints about that frog that's any better'n any other frog."

"Maybe you don't," Smiley says. "Maybe you understand frogs and maybe you don't understand 'em; maybe you've had experience, and maybe you ain't only a amature, as it were. Anyways, I've got *my* opinion, and I'll resk forty dollars that he can outjump any frog in Calaveras County."

And the feller studied a minute, and then says, kinder sad like, "Well, I'm only a stranger here, and I ain't got no frog; but if I had a frog I'd bet you."

And then Smiley says, "That's all right—that's all right—if you'll hold my box a minute I'll go and get you a frog." And so the feller took the box, and put up his forty dollars along with Smiley's, and set down to wait.

So he set there a good while thinking and thinking to himself, and then he got the frog out and pried his mouth open and took a teaspoon and filled him full of quail shot—filled him pretty near up to his chin—and set him on the floor. Smiley he went to the swamp and slopped around in the mud for a long time, and finally he ketched a frog, and fetched him in, and give him to this feller, and says:

"Now, if you're ready, set him alongside of Dan'l, with his forepaws just even with Dan'l's, and I'll give the word." Then he says, "One—two—three—*git!*" and him and the feller touched up the frogs from behind, and the new frog hopped off lively, but Dan'l give a heave, and hysted up his shoulders—so—like a Frenchman, but it warn't no use—he couldn't budge; he was planted as solid as a church, and he couldn't no more stir than if he was anchored out. Smiley was a good deal surprised, and he was disgusted, too, but he didn't have no idea what the matter was, of course.

The feller took the money and started away; and when he was going out at the door, he sorter jerked his thumb over his shoulder—so—at Dan'l, and says again, very deliberate, "Well," he says, "*I* don't see no p'ints about that frog that's any better'n any other frog."

Smiley he stood scratching his head and looking down at Dan'l a long time, and at last he says, "I do wonder what in the nation that frog throw'd off for—I wonder if there ain't something the matter with him—he 'pears to look mighty baggy, somehow." And he ketched Dan'l by the nap of the neck and hefted him, and says, "Why, blame my cats, if he don't weigh five pound!" and turned him upside down and he belched out a double handful of shot. And then he see how it was, and he was the maddest man—he set the frog down and took out after that feller, but he never ketched him. And——

[Here Simon Wheeler heard his name called from the front yard, and got up to see what was wanted.] And turning to me as he moved away, he said: "Jest set where you are, stranger, and rest easy—I ain't going to be gone a second."

But by your leave, I did not think that a continuation of the history of the enterprising vagabond *Jim* Smiley would be likely to afford me much information concerning the Reverend *Leonidas W.* Smiley, and so I started away.

At the door I met the sociable Wheeler returning, and he button-holed me and recommenced:

"Well, thish-yer Smiley had a yaller, one-eyed cow that didn't have no tail, only just a short stump like a bannanner, and——"

However, lacking both time and inclination, I did not wait to hear about the afflicted cow, but took my leave.

1343

U

MIGUEL DE UNAMUNO

MIGUEL DE UNAMUNO (Spanish, 1864-1936). Unique philosopher and powerful personality of modern Spain. A professor of Greek, exiled for his lofty spirit and writings. He attempted to synthesize the many aspects of present-day culture. Admired poem: *El Cristo de Vélazquez*. Novels: *Niebla, Tres novelas ejemplares*. Internationally famous philosophic work: *Del sentimiento trágico de la vida*.

THREE GENERATIONS

SCENE: the dining room of a village inn in my native Basque country; actors: grandfather, son, and grandson; audience: myself, profoundly moved. Three generations of the same family had met there to eat together. The old man, an honorable independent workman, was plain and uneducated, speaking Castilian only with difficulty; his son, a mature man, who in his youth had gone to America where he had made a fortune, married and raised a family, was returning to his native soil to visit his aged father and introduce the grandson; and the grandson, still very young, was a good looking boy, very neat, very finical, and very well groomed, whose careful training was apparent in every move of his knife and fork.

Between frequent draughts of wine, the grandfather was evidencing his joy at the sight of such an elegant grandson, repeating dotingly again and again in his meagre Castilian, "I thought I was going to die without ever seeing you." The father, between the grandfather and his son, between his memories and his hopes, was thinking of God knows what, and the youngster was eating politely and coldly, looking impatiently at his grandfather from time to time as if bored.

That scene was full of meaning, not because of what its actors said, but rather what they left unsaid.

That pretty youth did not seem to be interested in anything and was paying no attention to his father's father. They were separated by an abyss. I doubt that he had ever stopped to consider that he owed his good fortune, his education, and everything that was serving as a base for his egoism to the simple, noble, honorable spirit that the old man transmitted to his son, the stalwart toiler who had made a fortune.

Immediately I was reminded that a few years ago I had heard a poor man confess sadly and bitterly that, having amassed a fortune, married and raised a family also in America, he was disdained by his children. "They scorn me," he said tearfully, "they scorn me because I don't speak correctly and because I don't know the things they have learned from the teachers I hired." Later I had the opportunity of meeting one of his sons and I can assure you that he knew less than his father. He could talk about bookish things, jabber a little French and even less English, sigh for Paris, and find fault with his father's people.

You should have heard him constantly comparing our country and the one in which he was born. There was no limit to the superficiality of his comparisons. To him everything revolved around paved streets, water-closets, street cars, restaurants, and theatres. To him civilization meant urbanization and conveniences and, in addition, a certain show of good manners. The real essence of culture was completely unknown to him. He possessed not one grain of poetic feeling or sensibility. He told me that he was not interested in old stones.

Only this lack of sensibility, this want of poetic feeling, or—let us state it clearly—this cold-heartedness can explain certain things. Many an American of Spanish parents comes to Europe without enough piety, or curiosity even, to visit his parents' fatherland; Paris calls him. In his father's town, perhaps a tiny village hidden in the mountains, there are no asphalt boulevards or electric trollies; above all, there is no *Moulin Rouge* or *chez Maxim*. Not all can feel the deep penetrating poetry of one of those little villages.

How beautiful, how deeply pious and poetical is the account by that great poet, Zorrilla de San Martín, of his visit to his father's people in the mountains behind Santander! Zorrilla de San Martín is a poet, a true poet, a noble delicate spirit, guarding the treasure of our secular culture.

I am not known as a flatterer of my country; I could more correctly be called a bitter critic of its defects. I have never hidden our weaknesses, but when I happen to meet one of those pretty youths

who find fault with everything around here, I find myself turning against them and the superiorities of the lands that they have come to boast about. Because they both fail to see our real ills and to comprehend the best features of their own countries.

One of my neighbors in Salamanca, where I now live and write, once went to Bilbao, my native city, and in front of the city hall, a massive, showy, poorly designed building, he stopped and exclaimed, "I wish we had something like this in Salamanca." A native of Salamanca, who has never been near the beautiful old cathedral of this city except to show it to some visitor, said this.

At the end of each year I receive many letters spontaneously from my unknown American readers. The vast majority of them are written in a kindly, amiable tone, urging me to keep on with my work, or, if they do censure me for something, they do it discreetly, honestly, and respectfully. But there are also some, although very few, mostly anonymous, written in a sly, under-handed manner, saying injurious things about me, or more correctly, about my country, its men, and its ways. What nonsense comes from the pens of those artful nitwits. Not long ago I received a letter whose author, after using the term Galician in its derogatory sense—an act which belittles the user more than anyone else—asked me if certain Spanish family names, such as *Iglesias* and *de la Iglesia* originate in foundling asylums, or if they are given to children found in their vicinity.

If I were a spiteful, ill-natured individual, I would have answered that these names and many more had their origin in such asylums, and among them the names of some saints, including the name of San Martín, so justly famous in Argentina.

In my Basque country there has been developing for some time, because of the material prosperity of the region, a most blameworthy feeling of disdain toward those who come there from other parts of Spain to earn a living, working there and increasing the general prosperity of the country. They call them *maquis* and say that they have come there to kill their hunger. That is right, but they also kill the hunger of those that are making sport of them. It is a line of reasoning like that of the factory owner who seriously asserts that he is feeding two or three hundred workers, when it is they who are feeding him and giving him something more in addition.

That poorly disguised hostility toward the immigrant or stranger is a phenomenon that arises when the partner in production becomes a competitor in consumption, when the planting and the reaping are ended and it is time to divide the harvest. It is then that the descend-

ants of the first inhabitants resort to trickery and seek to obtain special privileges as if they had created the fertility of the soil. Is it any merit of mine that my native mountains are filled with rich iron mines?

It is all right for those poor laborers to drag out their lives extracting ore from the depths of the mountains or doing any other work that adds to the wealth of the region; it is all right for them to work. But, as soon as they show any interest in political or social affairs, they are reminded that they came there to work, they are ridiculed for being industrious.

On one occasion an Argentine friend, whose name I had given to an emigrant, wrote me an interesting letter saying, among other things, "Do not encourage ambitious people to come here; we need hands and capital, but not talent. There are too many scholars here in America. In some countries, having nothing else to do, they plan revolutions." I understood immediately what my friend was saying and, by reading between the lines, I understood many things that he did not say. I recalled the bitter tale of a friend and countryman of mine who was a doctor. He suffered a great deal overseas precisely because he was a competent doctor. His learned colleagues outdid themselves to help him . . . suffer.

What have I been led to say by the sight of that family represented by three generations? I can see them yet: the old man striving to use a fork and not his hands as he would have done at home, the youth daintily cutting his meat and peeling his peaches with studied elegance, and between them, the rude man who had made a fortune. I do not know whether he was ashamed to have such a father or such a son or proud of one or the other or of both of them. How well groomed the boy was! How artistic was his head on the outside! I do not know what it was like on the inside but most surely it was furnished with the latest fads from Parisian books.

The mature man, the maker of fortunes, seemed to me to be only the connecting link between his father and his son. And I set about comparing the strong plain old man with the delicate disdainful youth. And, of the two, the old man seemed to be the younger, hardly more than a child. He was probably more than seventy but his was the illusion and the enthusiasm, while the youth seemed to have been born bored and carrying the weight of the greatest disillusionment on his artistic head.

Why was that reunion held in a place as public as the dining room of an inn? Why were those three not before the grandfather's hearth,

in the house where the father was born? Perhaps it was on a mountain top whither one had to climb along a stony path, possibly muddy in spots. The youth's delicate feet were only accustomed to smooth macadam and his shining boots had never been spattered by mud. Surely that house did not have even the inn's primitive conveniences. I imagine that in the opinion of the pretty boy with well combed locks it was not a dwelling of a civilized country. For I am almost certain that I know what concept of civilization that scornful, finical upstart had. It was ridiculous and extremely superficial.

No people can progress far until it has lost that concept of civilization which looks upon it mainly as conveniences and facilities for material well-being. Hygiene is important and comfort is more so; but we must agree that among a people that is hygienically careless, the life of the spirit can be far more carefully guarded than among people that is daily sprinkled with antiseptics. Hygiene itself is indispensable but it should not become a monomania or superstition.

The maxim says: *mens sana in corpore sano,* a sound mind in a sound body, and not *corpus sanum in mente sana;* let us put first things first. Of the two extremes, and they are both abominable, I prefer Job on the dung-heap to a spruce young gentleman whose principle occupation is bathing and perfuming himself.

It is evident that not all the grandsons of our rude, homespun mountain folk feel like the pretty youth I have described; besides, I am glad to believe most of them pride themselves on their ancestry, and if they do not visit their ancestral homes, it is because they cannot and not through laziness. I know all that very well, but I would not like to fail to add my protest against those vain superficial striplings who come here and disdain everything they cannot comprehend, those who judge a people by its manners and who seem to think that the most important agents of civilization are the janitor, the cook, the tailor, and the dancer.

V

PAUL VALERY

PAUL VALÉRY (French, 1871-1945). Poet of philosophical abstractions.
Influenced early by Mallarmé. First works were prose: *Introduction à la
méthode de Léonard de Vinci* and *La Soirée avec Monsieur Teste.* Most
famous poem: *"La Jeune parque." Charmes:* poems on love and death.
Skeptical, disillusioned, he advocated refined discipline of the mind.

NARCISSUS

A Fragment

. . . Perhaps you expected a face that was free from tears,
You calms, you always decked with leaves and flowers,
And haunted depths of the incorruptible,
O nymphs! . . . But yielding to the enchanted slopes
That were my irretrievable roadway to you,
Permit this fair reflection of man's disorder.
Happy your blended forms, you deep and level waters!
I am alone. . . . If the gods, the waves, and the echoes
And so many sighs allow! I am alone!
But still I am he who comes unto himself
When he comes near the banks this growth adorns.

On the peaks the light has halted its pure plunder,
The voice of the fountains turns to talk of dusk,
Calm concord hearkens, wherein I hear hope.
I hear the night grass grow in the holy shadows,
And the perfidious moon now elevates her mirror
Even to the secrets of the dying pool.

1349

And I! My body cast upon these reeds,
I languish, Sapphire, in my mournful beauty!
I must henceforth adore the magic waters
Where I have forgotten the olden smile and the rose.
Let me bewail your pure and fatal glory,
Fountain so softly closed around by me,
Where my eyes draw forth from the lethal azure
Those same dark eyes of their astounded soul!
What loss within oneself so calm a place affords!
The soul, even unto destruction, seeks a god
Demanding of the wave, the lonely wave
That gleams inviting soft advent of swan . . .
Never have thirsty flocks bemired these waters!
Others who have wandered here have found repose,
And in the dark earth a clear, opening tomb;
But it is not calm, alas! that I shall find,
When the opaque delight where the splendor sleeps
Yields to my body the horror of widening leafage
And, driving back the shade and the frightening thickness,
I see! I fall! and come from this tyrant body
Peacefully to share the eternal charms!
There, nude between the arms that spring from the forest,
A tender gleam of daylight doubtfully plays;
And there the glimmer of day becomes a bridegroom,
Pure in the place where the sad water lures me,
Delightful spirit, desirable and cold!
I behold in the water my flesh of moon and the dawn-dew,
Obedient form opposed to my desires!
There are the pure stirrings of my silver arms!
My lingering hands in the adorable gold grow weary
Of seeking the captive whom the leaves entwine,
And I cry to echo the names of the hidden gods!

But how fair his mouth in that mute blasphemy!
O likeness! . . . Yet more perfect than myself,
Immortal ephemeron, clear before my eyes,
Pale limbs of pearl and softly silken hair,
Must the shadow darken us who scarce have loved,
Must the night already part us, O Narcissus,
And press between us the blade that halves a fruit!

1350

What is it?
My plaint is baneful? . . .
The mere stir
Of the breath I set upon your lips, my double,
Has coursed a tremor on your limpid wave? . . .
You tremble! But these words I, kneeling, breathe
Are still no more than a hesitant soul between us,
Between that clear brow and my spent memory . . . .
I am so near you I can drink you in,
O countenance? . . . My thirst is a naked slave . . . .

Till this rapt hour I did not know myself,
Nor how to cherish, how attain my soul? . . .
But watching you, dear slave, obey the least
Of the shadows sadly retreating in my heart,
And on my brow a secret fire and storm,
Watching, O marvel! watching my murmurous mouth
Betray . . . snare on the water a flower of fancy,
And mad events that sparkle in the eye!
I have found a treasure of impotence and pride!
May no sweet virgin whom the satyr stalks,
None! Swift in flight, deft in unfeeling fall,
No nymph, no maiden, ever lure me on
As you within the waters, my illimitable soul!

THE SYLPH

Seen not nor known
I am the scent shed
Living and dead
In the wind blown

Seen not nor known
Genius or chance?
Hardly seed sown
When the flowers dance!

Nor read nor possessed!
What errors shown
For swift renowns—

Seen not nor known,
The glimpse of a breast
Between two gowns!

LOST WINE

One day I cast into the sea
(But I no longer remember under what skies)
As an offering unto Nonentity
A little wine of a sort I prize.

Who, O liquor, wished you to part?
Perhaps you were an omen I could not divine:
Perhaps concerned with my heart,
Thinking of blood, and pouring wine?
I watched the sea resume,
After a rosy spume,
Its usual transparency. . . .

Lost the wine, drunk the waves!
I saw leaping from sea-caves
Figures of greatest profundity.

VALMIKI

VALMIKI (Indian, *ca.* 4th century B. C.). Legendary author of a poem of 24,000 verses on the exploits of Rama *(Rāmāyana)*. In Hindu literature this work compares with the Greek *Odyssey*, and exists in several versions.

NÁRAD

Om

To sainted Nárad, prince of those
Whose lore in words of wisdom flows,
Whose constant care and chief delight
Were Scripture and ascetic rite,
The good Válmíki, first and best
Of hermit saints, these words addressed:—

"In all this world, I pray thee, who
Is virtuous, heroic, true?
Firm in his vows, of grateful mind,
To every creature good and kind?
Bounteous, and holy, just, and wise,
Alone most fair to all men's eyes?
Devoid of envy, firm, and sage,
Whose tranquil soul ne'er yields to rage?
Whom, when his warrior wrath is high,
Do Gods embattled fear and fly?
Whose noble might and gentle skill
The triple world can guard from ill?
Who is the best of princes, he
Who loves his people's good to see?
The store of bliss, the living mine
Where brightest joys and virtues shine?
Queen Fortune's best and dearest friend,
Whose steps her choicest gifts attend?
Who may with Sun and Moon compare,
With Indra, Vishnu, Fire, and Air?
Grant, Saint divine, the boon I ask,
For thee, I ween, an easy task,
To whom the power is given to know
If such a man breathe here below."

Then Nárad, clear before whose eye
The present, past, and future lie,
Made ready answer: "Hermit, where
Are graces found so high and rare?
Yet listen, and my tongue shall tell
In whom alone these virtues dwell.
From old Ikshváku's line he came,
Known to the world by Ráma's name:—
With soul subdued, a chief of might,
In Scripture versed, in glory bright.
His steps in virtue's paths are bent,
Obedient, pure, and eloquent.
In each emprise he wins success,
And dying foes his power confess.
Tall and broad-shouldered, strong of limb,
Fortune has set her mark on him.

1353

Graced with a conch-shell's triple line,
His throat displays the auspicious sign.
High destiny is clear impressed
On massive jaw and ample chest.
His mighty shafts he truly aims,
And foemen in the battle tames.
Deep in the muscle, scarcely shown,
Embedded lies his collar-bone.
His lordly steps are firm and free,
His strong arms reach below his knee;
All fairest graces join to deck
His head, his brow, his stately neck,
And limbs in fair proportion set:—
The manliest form e'er fashioned yet.
Graced with each high imperial mark,
His skin is soft and lustrous dark.
Large are his eyes that sweetly shine
With majesty almost divine.
His plighted word he ne'er forgets;
On erring sense a watch he sets.
By nature wise, his teacher's skill
Has trained him to subdue his will.
Good, resolute and pure, and strong,
He guards mankind from scathe and wrong,
And lends his aid, and ne'er in vain,
The cause of justice to maintain.
Well has he studied o'er and o'er
The Vedas and their kindred lore.
Well skilled is he the bow to draw,
Well trained in arts and versed in law;
High-souled and meet for happy fate,
Most tender and compassionate;
The noblest of all lordly givers,
Whom good men follow, as the rivers
Follow the King of Floods, the sea:—
So liberal, so just is he.
The joy of Queen Kausalyá's heart,
In every virtue he has part;
Firm as Himálaya's snowy steep,
Unfathomed like the mighty deep;

1354

The peer of Vishnu's power and might,
And lovely as the Lord of Night;
Patient as Earth, but, roused to ire,
Fierce as the world-destroying fire;
In bounty like the Lord of Gold,
And Justice' self in human mould.
With him, his best and eldest son,
By all his princely virtues won
King Dasaratha willed to share
His kingdom as the Regent Heir.
But when Kaikeyí, youngest queen,
With eyes of envious hate had seen
The solemn pomp and regal state
Prepared the prince to consecrate,
She bade the hapless king bestow
Two gifts he promised long ago,
That Ráma to the woods should flee,
And that her child the heir should be.

By chains of duty firmly tied,
The wretched King perforce complied.
Ráma, to please Kaikeyí went
Obedient forth, to banishment.
Then Lakshman's truth was nobly shown,
Then were his love and courage known,
When for his brother's sake he dared
All perils, and his exile shared.
And Sítá, Ráma's darling wife,
Loved even as he loved his life,
Whom happy marks combined to bless,
A miracle of loveliness,
Of Janak's royal lineage sprung,
Most excellent of women, clung
To her dear lord, like Rohiní
Rejoicing with the Moon to be.
The King and People, sad of mood,
The hero's car awhile pursued.
But when Prince Ráma lighted down
At Sringavera's pleasant town,

Where Gangá's holy waters flow,
He bade his driver turn and go.
Guha, Nishádas' King, he met,
And on the farther bank was set.
Then on from wood to wood they strayed,
O'er many a stream, through constant shade,
As Bharadvája bade them, till
They came to Chitrakúta's hill.
And Ráma there, with Lakshman's aid,
A pleasant little cottage made,
And spent his days with Sítá, dressed
In coat of bark and deerskin vest.
And Chitrakúta grew to be
As bright with those illustrious three
As Meru's sacred peaks that shine
With glory, when the Gods recline
Beneath them: Siva's self between
The Lord of Gold and Beauty's Queen.

The aged King for Ráma pined,
And for the skies the earth resigned.
Bharat, his son, refused to reign,
Though urged by all the twice-born train.
Forth to the woods he fared to meet
His brother, fell before his feet,
And cried "Thy claim all men allow:—
O come, our lord and King be thou."
But Ráma nobly chose to be
Observant of his sire's decree.
He placed his sandals in his hand,
A pledge that he would rule the land:—
And bade his brother turn again.
Then Bharat, finding prayer was vain,
The sandals took and went away;
Nor in Ayodhyá would he stay,
But turned to Nandigráma, where
He ruled the realm with watchful care,
Still longing eagerly to learn
Tidings of Ráma's safe return.

Then lest the people should repeat
Their visit to his calm retreat,
Away from Chitrakúta's hill
Fared Ráma, ever onward till
Beneath the shady trees he stood
Of Dandaká's primeval wood.
Virádha, giant fiend, he slew,
And then Agastya's friendship knew.
Counselled by him he gained the sword
And bow of Indra, heavenly lord:—
A pair of quivers too, that bore
Of arrows an exhaustless store.
While there he dwelt in greenwood shade,
The trembling hermits sought his aid,
And bade him with his sword and bow
Destroy the fiends who worked them woe:—
To come like Indra strong and brave,
A guardian God to help and save.
And Ráma's falchion left its trace
Deep cut on Súrpanakhá's face:—
A hideous giantess who came
Burning for him with lawless flame.
Their sister's cries the giants heard,
And vengeance in each bosom stirred;
The monster of the triple head,
And Dúshan to the contest sped.
But they and myriad fiends beside
Beneath the might of Ráma died.

When Rávan, dreaded warrior, knew
The slaughter of his giant crew—
Rávan, the King, whose name of fear
Earth, hell, and heaven all shook to hear—
He bade the fiend Márícha aid
The vengeful plot his fury laid.
In vain the wise Márícha tried
To turn him from his course aside:—
Not Rávan's self, he said, might hope
With Ráma and his strength to cope.

1357

Impelled by fate and blind with rage
He came to Ráma's hermitage.
There, by Marícha's magic art,
He wiled the princely youths apart,
The vulture slew, and bore away
The wife of Ráma as his prey.
The son of Raghu came and found
Jatáyu slain upon the ground.
He rushed within his leafy cot;
He sought his wife, but found her not.
Then, then the hero's senses failed;
In mad despair he wept and wailed.
Upon the pile that bird he laid,
And still in quest of Sítá strayed.
A hideous giant then he saw,
Kabandha named, a shape of awe.

The monstrous fiend he smote and slew,
And in the flame the body threw;
When straight from out the funeral flame
In lovely form Kabandha came,
And bade him seek in his distress
A wise and holy hermitess.
By counsel of this saintly dame
To Pampá's pleasant flood he came,
And there the steadfast friendship won
Of Hanumán the Wind-God's son.
Counselled by him he told his grief
To great Sugríva, Vánar chief,
Who, knowing all the tale, before
The sacred flame alliance swore.
Sugríva to his new-found friend
Told his own story to the end:—
His hate of Báli for the wrong
And insult he had borne so long.
And Ráma lent a willing ear
And promised to allay his fear.
Sugríva warned him of the might
Of Báli, matchless in the fight,
And, credence for his tale to gain,
Showed the huge fiend by Báli slain.

The prostrate corse of mountain size
Seemed nothing in the hero's eyes;
He lightly kicked it, as it lay,
And cast it twenty leagues away.
To prove his might his arrows through
Seven palms in line, uninjured, flew.
He cleft a mighty hill apart,
And down to hell he hurled his dart.
Then high Sugríva's spirit rose,
Assured of conquest o'er his foes.
With his new champion by his side
To vast Kishkindhá's cave he hied.
Then, summoned by his awful shout,
King Báli came in fury out,
First comforted his trembling wife,
Then sought Sugriva in the strife.
One shaft from Ráma's deadly bow
The monarch in the dust laid low.
Then Ráma bade Sugríva reign
In place of royal Báli slain.
Then speedy envoys hurried forth
Eastward and westward, south and north,
Commanded by the grateful King
Tidings of Ráma's spouse to bring.
Then by Sampáti's counsel led,
Brave Hanumán, who mocked at dread,
Sprang at one wild tremendous leap
Two hundred leagues, across the deep.
To Lanká's town he urged his way,
Where Rávan held his royal sway.
There pensive 'neath Asoka boughs
He found poor Sítá, Ráma's spouse.
He gave the hapless girl a ring,
A token from her lord and King.
A pledge from her fair hand he bore;
Then battered down the garden door.
Five captains of the host he slew,
Seven sons of councillors o'erthrew;
Crushed youthful Aksha on the field,
Then to his captors chose to yield.

1359

Soon from their bonds his limbs were free,
But honoring the high decree
Which Brahmá had pronounced of yore,
He calmly all their insults bore.
The town he burnt with hostile flame,
And spoke again with Ráma's dame,
Then swiftly back to Ráma flew
With tidings of the interview.

Then with Sugríva for his guide,
Came Ráma to the ocean side.
He smote the sea with shafts as bright
As sunbeams in their summer height,
And quick appeared the River's King
Obedient to the summoning.
A bridge was thrown by Nala o'er
The narrow sea from shore to shore.
They crossed to Lanká's golden town,
Where Ráma's hand smote Rávan down.
Vibhíshan there was left to reign
Over his brother's wide domain.
To meet her husband Sítá came;
But Ráma, stung with ire and shame,
With bitter words his wife addressed
Before the crowd that round her pressed.
But Sítá, touched with noble ire,
Gave her fair body to the fire.
Then straight the God of Wind appeared,
And words from heaven her honor cleared.
And Ráma clasped his wife again,
Uninjured, pure from spot and stain,
Obedient to the Lord of Fire
And the high mandate of his sire.
Led by the Lord who rules the sky,
The Gods and heavenly saints drew nigh,
And honored him with worthy meed,
Rejoicing in each glorious deed.
His task achieved, his foe removed,
He triumphed, by the Gods approved.
By grace of Heaven he raised to life
The chieftains slain in mortal strife;

Then in the magic chariot through
The clouds to Nandigráma flew.
Met by his faithful brothers there,
He loosed his votive coil of hair;
Thence fair Ayodhyá's town he gained,
And o'er his father's kingdom reigned.
Disease or famine ne'er oppressed
His happy people, richly blest
With all the joys of ample wealth,
Of sweet content and perfect health.
No widow mourned her well-loved mate,
No sire his son's untimely fate.
They feared not storm or robber's hand,
No fire or flood laid waste the land:
The Golden Age seemed come again
To bless the days of Ráma's reign.
From him the great and glorious King,
Shall many a princely scion spring.
And he shall rule, beloved by men,
Ten thousand years and hundreds ten,
And when his life on earth is past
To Brahmá's world shall go at last.

Whoe'er this noble poem reads
That tells the tale of Ráma's deeds,
Good as the Scriptures, he shall be
From every sin and blemish free.
Whoever reads the saving strain,
With all his kin the heavens shall gain.
Bráhmans who read shall gather hence
The highest praise for eloquence.
The warrior, o'er the land shall reign,
The merchant, luck in trade obtain;
And Súdras, listening, ne'er shall fail
To reap advantage from the tale.

GIOVANNI VERGA

GIOVANNI VERGA (Italian, 1840-1922). One of Italy's leading realistic fiction writers. Immortalized in his novels the peasants of Sicily. Spent a time in the fashionable world of Florence, but returned to Sicily to do best work: *Vita dei Campi* (stories), *Mastro Don Gesualdo* (novel). Author of *Cavalleria Rusticana*, basis of Mascagni's popular opera.

GRAMIGNA'S MISTRESS

THIS is no more than the sketch of a story, but it has the merit of being very short, and of being historical—a human document, as they say nowadays; and as such will perhaps be interesting to those who study the great book of the heart. I will tell it just as I heard it myself among the fields and country lanes; almost with the same simple and picturesque words as are used in the popular narrative.

Some years ago, down in the district of the Simeto, they were hunting a brigand; one Gramigna, if I mistake not,—and that is as ill a name as the weed that bears it,—who had filled the whole countryside with the terror of his renown.

Police, soldiery, and mounted militia had pursued him for two months, and had never succeeded in fastening their claws upon him; he was alone, but he was as good as ten others, and the evil weed threatened to take root.

To make matters worse, it was nearly harvest time, the hay already lay scattered upon the meadows, and the ears of corn bowed their heads, as if nodding consent to the reapers, who were ready with sickle in hand; and yet not a single farmer dared show his nose beyond his garden hedge, for fear of finding Gramigna lying among the furrows, his carbine between his knees, ready to blow out the brains of the first man who should offer to meddle with him.

Hence the complaints were universal. So the prefect summoned before him all these gentlemen of the police, the "*carabinieri*," and the soldiery, and said a few words to them of a kind that made them prick up their ears. The next day there was a general earthquake: patrols, troops, vedettes in every ditch and behind every wall—they drove him before them like a wild beast, through a whole province, by day and by night, on foot, on horseback, and by the telegraph. Still Gramigna slipped through their hands, and answered them with volleys of shot when they trod too closely on his heels. In the fields, in the villages, at the farms, beneath the boughs that overshadow

1362

the tavern doors, in every place of meeting, people talked of nothing but him, Gramigna, and that furious chase, that desperate flight.

The *carabinieri's* horses dropped down from sheer weariness, the worn-out soldiers flung themselves to rest upon the ground in every stable, the patrols fell asleep as they walked. Only he, Gramigna, was never weary, never slept, but still fled on, clambering up precipices, creeping among the corn, crawling on all fours through the thickets of prickly pear, scrambling like a wolf along the dry torrent-beds. The principal topic of conversation among the gossips at the village doors was the consuming thirst that the hunted creature must be enduring, down there on the vast, arid plain, beneath the June sun. The idlers stood agape at the very thought.

Peppa, one of the handsomest girls of Licodia, was at this time about to be married to Master Finu, surnamed the "Tallow-candle," who owned sunny lands and had a bay mule in his stable, and was a fine young fellow, "beautiful as the sun," who could carry the banner of St. Margaret as straight as a pillar, without bending his back. Peppa's mother wept for joy at the good luck that had befallen her daughter, and spent her time in turning over the bride's outfit as it lay in its trunk—"all of white stuff, in fours," like that of a queen, and golden earrings that hung down to the shoulders, and gold rings for all the ten fingers; she had as much gold as St. Margaret herself, and was to be married just about St. Margaret's Day, which fell in June, after the hay was cut. Every evening, "Tallow-candle," as he returned from the fields, would leave his mule at Peppa's door and come in to tell her that the crops were a joy to behold, if only Gramigna did not set fire to them, that the corn-bin behind the bed would not be large enough to hold all the grain that harvest, and that it seemed to him a thousand years till the time should come when he might take his bride home behind him on the bay mule.

But one fine day Peppa said to him, "Let your mule be—for I will not marry you."

Poor "Tallow-candle" stood aghast, and the old woman began tearing her hair when she heard her daughter give up the best match in the village.

"I love Gramigna," the girl said to her, "and I will marry no one else."

"Ah me!" the mother went crying about the house, her gray hair flying in the wind like a witch's—"Ah me! that demon has got even in here and bewitched my daughter!"

1363

"No," Peppa would reply, and her eye was fixed and as hard as steel, "no, he has not been here."

"Where have you seen him, then?"

"I have not seen him, I have heard of him. But listen—I feel him, here, burning me."

The affair made a stir in the village, though they tried to hush it up. The gossips who had envied Peppa the prosperous crops, the bay mule, and the fine young fellow who carried St. Margaret's banner without bending his back, now went about telling all manner of ugly tales—how Gramigna came to visit her by night in the kitchen, and how he had been seen hiding under the bed.

The poor mother had a lamp lighted "for the souls in purgatory," and the priest even came to the house and laid his stole upon Peppa's heart, so as to drive out that devil of a Gramigna, who had taken possession of it. Still she persisted in saying that she did not even know the fellow by sight, but that she saw him at night in her dreams; and she rose every morning with parched lips, almost as though she too had suffered the burning thirst that he must be enduring.

Then the old woman shut her up in the house, that she might no longer hear them talk of Gramigna, and stopped up the very cracks in the door with pictures of the saints. But Peppa listened from behind the sacred images to what the people in the street were saying, and grew red and pale, as though the devil were blowing all the flames of hell across her face. At last she heard them say that Gramigna had been brought to bay, among the prickly-pear thickets of Palagonia.

"He kept up a two hours' fire," they said, "and there is one *carabiniere* killed, and three soldiers and more are wounded. But they sent such a hail of shot upon him, that this time they found a pool of blood where he had stood."

Then Peppa made the sign of the cross at her old woman's bedside, and fled through the window.

Gramigna was among the prickly pears of Palagonia, for they had not been able to dislodge him from such a rabbit-warren. Wounded and blood-stained, pale from a two days' fast, burnt with fever, he stood there, his carbine leveled.

When he saw her coming towards him, fearless and firm, through the thickets of prickly pear, in the dim light of the dawn, he debated for a moment whether he should pull the trigger.

"What do you want?" he asked; "what have you come here for?"

"I have come to be with you," she replied, looking at him fixedly. "Are you Gramigna?"

"Yes, I am Gramigna. If you have come here after those twenty ounces of the reward, you have mistaken your reckoning."

"No, I have come to stay by you," she replied.

"Get you gone," said he; "you cannot stay here, and I will have no one with me. If you have come after money, you have made a mistake, I tell you; I have nothing—see; it is two days since I have even had a bit of bread."

"I cannot go home again now," she said; "the road is full of soldiers."

"Go! What do I care for that? Every one for himself!"

As she was turning away, like a dog driven off by kicks, he called after her:—

"Look here, go and get me a flask of water from the torrent down there; if you want to stay with me, you must risk your skin."

She went without a word; and when Gramigna heard the fusillade, he laughed out, saying to himself, "That was meant for me!"

But when he saw her return in a little while, pale and bleeding, with the flask on her arm, first he tore it from her, and drank so long and deep a draught that his very breath failed him, and then —"Did you escape it?" he asked; "how did you manage?"

"The soldiers were on the opposite bank, and on this side the bushes were thick."

"But they put a bullet into you? Your clothes are stained with blood."

"Yes."

"Where are you wounded?"

"In the shoulder."

"That's no matter—you can still walk."

So he suffered her to stay with him. She followed him, barefooted, all torn and feverish from her wound; she would go hunting after a flask of water or a crust of bread for him, and when she returned empty-handed, amid the volleys of shot, her lover, devoured by hunger and thirst, would beat her. At last, one night when the moon shone brightly through the thickets of prickly pear, Gramigna said, "They are coming," and made her stand with her back against a rock at the bottom of a cleft; then he fled in the opposite direction.

The shots echoed nearer and nearer among the bushes, and the darkness was lighted up by sudden bursts of flame. All at once

Peppa heard a trampling close by, and Gramigna reappeared, dragging himself along, with one leg broken, so that he had to prop himself against the shoots of the prickly pear to reload his carbine.

"It is over," he said; "now they will take me."

And what froze her blood more than all was the glitter in his eye, that made him look like a madman. Then, when he fell like a log upon the dead branches, the soldiers were upon him, all at once.

Next day they dragged him on a cart through the streets of the village, mangled and bleeding. The crowd that pressed round to gaze at him, laughed when they saw how small and pale and ugly he was, like a clown. It was for him that Peppa had left Master Finu, the "Tallow-candle"!

Poor "Tallow-candle" went away and hid himself, as though it were his part to be ashamed.

And Peppa was led along between the soldiers, handcuffed, as if she too had been a thief—she, who had as much gold as St. Margaret.

Her poor mother had to sell all the "white stuff" of the bridal outfit, and the golden earrings, and the rings for the ten fingers, to pay lawyers for her daughter, and get her home again once more, poor, sickly, and shame-faced—ugly, too, now, like Gramigna, and with Gramigna's child upon her bosom. Yet when she was restored to her at the end of the trial, the old woman recited the "Ave Maria" there in the bare and fast-darkening barrack-room, among all the *carabinieri;* it was as though they had given her back a treasure —to her, the poor old woman who had nothing else in the world, and she wept like a fountain for joy.

But Peppa seemed to have no more tears left, and she spoke never a word; nor did the village folk ever see her again, though the two women had to work with their hands for their daily bread. People said that Peppa had learnt her trade, there in the wood, and that she went out thieving by night. In reality, she sat crouching in the corner of the kitchen, like a wild beast, and only left it when her old woman was dead of hard work, and she had to sell the house.

"Do you see now!" the "Tallow-candle" said to her, for he loved her still, "I could crush your head between two stones for all the harm you have done to yourself and others."

"It is true," Peppa answered, "I know it. It was the will of God."

When the house and her few remaining goods and chattels were sold, she left the village by night, as she had come—without turning back to give one look at the roof beneath which she had slept so long—and went away with her boy to do the will of God in the city, near the prison where Gramigna was shut up.

She could only see the dark shutters upon the great, silent face of the building, and when she stood looking at it, trying to make out where he might be, the sentries drove her away. At last they told her that for some time back he had no longer been there—that they had taken him away over the sea, handcuffed, and with his wallet about his neck.

She said nothing. She never left the place, because she did not know where to go, and no one was expecting her anywhere. She made shift to live, doing jobs for the soldiers and the jailers, as if she herself were a part of that great, dark silent building; and for the *carabinieri*, who had taken Gramigna from her, there among the prickly-pear thickets, and had broken his leg with gun-shots, she felt a sort of respectful tenderness—an animal admiration for strength.

On holidays, when she saw them with their plumes and their glittering epaulettes, stiff and straight in their gala uniforms, she devoured them with her eyes; and she was always about the barracks, sweeping out the halls and polishing the boots, so that they nicknamed her "the dust-clout of the *carabinieri*."

Only when, at nightfall, she saw them load their guns and go out, two by two, with their trousers turned up, and revolvers slung across their chests, or when they mounted their horses, under the great lantern that gleamed upon the muzzles of the carbines, and she heard the trampling of the horses' hoofs and the clink of the scabbards die away in the darkness, then she would turn pale and shiver as she closed the stable doors. And when her little one played with the rest in the great square before the prison running in and out among the soldiers' legs, and the other children would call after him, "The son of Gramigna!—the son of Gramigna!" then she would fly into a rage and pursue them, pelting them with stones.

EMILE VERHAEREN

ÉMILE VERHAEREN (Belgian, 1855-1916). Poet Laureate of Belgium. Apostle of industrial progress. Frequent visitor in England. Early work realistic and violent—later poetry symbolic free verse. Has been compared with Whitman. Major works: *Les Rythmes Souverains, Les Flamandes, Les Heures Claires*.

THE MILL

Slowly in the depths of the night the windmill turns.
Under a somber, melancholy sky
It turns and turns, and its wind-burnt canvas moans
A sad and worn and heavy lullaby.

Since the dawn its arms, like arms in supplication,
Have stretched out and have fallen, and they will
Fall on and on across the darkened air
And weary nature slumbering now and still.

A cheerless winter night broods over the hamlet,
The weary clouds are restless overhead;
And along the thickets that gather up their shadows,
The pathways point a horizon that is dead.

Under a rim of earth, a few beechen shanties
Wretchedly huddle in a miserable round;
A brass lamp that is hanging from the ceiling
Speckles with light the window and the ground.

And across the wide field, and the slumbering void
They hold—puny hovels—with the blinking eyes
Of their broken panes with the ragged curtain,
The old mill that turns and, weary, turns, and dies.

THE POOR

There are poor souls
Where tears are starred
And pale as stones
In a graveyard.

There are poor backs
Weighed down with ills
Like the roofs of hovels
In the hills.

There are poor hands
Like leaves the wind wore,
Like yellow, dying leaves
By the door.

There are poor eyes
Humble and kind and warm,
Sadder than the eyes of beasts
Beneath the storm.

There are poor folk
With movements forbearing and worn,
On whom misery battens—
Wherever men are born.

PIOUS EVENINGS

To farthest off the sun at setting sheds
The haircloth of its silence and its calm;
On Byzantine backgrounds carefully it spreads
All things as clearly as a quiet psalm.

The downpour slashed the air with blades of hail
And now the heavens shine like a sanctuary;
It is the hour when the western fires fail,
When the day's gold and the twilight's silver vary.

Nothing stirs on the horizon, unless it be
An infinite giant march of oaks in the gloom,
Stretching beyond the farms one just can see,
Along the fallow fields and the corners of broom.

The trees move on—as mortuary friars
Pass by, and twilight weighs upon their bands,
As the long troop of penitents aspires
On pilgrimage to ancient holy lands.

And as the road leads upward to the sky,
Where the setting sun far peony petals strews,
To see those long bare trees, to see those monks pass by,
You'd say they were setting out tonight, by twos,

Toward their God who fills the heavens with sprinkled gold;
And the stars, gleaming high ahead of them,
Are each the light of a candle that they hold
Of which we cannot see the towering stem.

PAUL VERLAINE

PAUL VERLAINE (French, 1844-1896). Chief figure in the French Symbolist
Movement. Poetic descendant of Baudelaire. Began career as middle-class
clerk. Left wife to go vagabonding with Rimbaud. Died in misery and poverty.
Major volumes: *Fêtes galantes, Romances sans paroles, La Bonne chanson.*
His life and legend almost as influential as his actual work.

MYSTIC TWILIGHT

Memory with the twilight
Flushes and trembles on the horizon
Of hope that soars with a high light,
Recoils, collects, and flies on
Like a mysterious valley up
Which many a flaunting flower—
Tulip, lily, buttercup—
Thrusts forth in a bower
Where the poison-perfume stilly—
Buttercup, tulip, and lily—
In a ghostly, weird, and wry light
With my reason, soul and senses strewn,
Blends in an unbounded swoon
Memory with the twilight.

STREETS

Let us dance!

Surpassingly I loved her eyes,
Clearer than the starry skies;
I loved their swift surprise.

Let us dance!

She had such wild ways, truly
A sweetheart most unruly;
And she took life so coolly.

Let us dance!

But beyond these memories start
The kisses her flower-lips dart. . . .
Since she is dead to my heart.

Let us dance!

I recall, still I recall
Pensive hours at evenfall:
And they are best of all.
Let us dance!

MY FAMILIAR DREAM

I often have the queer and radiant dream
Of an unknown woman I love, and who loves me,
Who never will be wholly as before, nor seem
Quite other; who loves, and probes my mystery.

She understands me; my translucent heart—
Only for her, alas!—quite plain appears,
Only for her; and the dampness that will start
On my brow, she alone can dry it with her tears.

Is she blonde, brunette, or red-haired? I do not know.
Her name? I remember it is resonant and sweet
As those of lovers life has beaten low.

Her look is as the look in a statue's head,
And for her voice, where calm and sorrow meet,
She has the tone of loved ones who are dead.

WOMAN AND CAT

She was playing with her cat;
They were enraptured who saw
The white hand and the white paw
In their evening frolic-pat.

It hid—O innocent gazer!—
Under black silken veils
Murderous agate nails
Clear and sharp as a razor.

She too was compact of sweets,
Withholding her steely claws;
But the devil's eye has no beam . . .

And in her boudoir, when the dark meets
Her airy laughter, and withdraws,—
Four points of phosphorus gleam.

THE SONG OF THE INGÉNUES

We are the ingénues—
Blue eyes, long hair, sweet looks—
Who live with rainbow dews
In seldom read books.

We set forth intertwined,
And the day no purer seems
Than the depths of our mind
And our azure dreams;

And we romp through the fields,
Where our happy calls rise
Till day to dusk yields—
Chasing butterflies.

And a shepherdess' bonnet
Screens our face from strong light,
And our gown—lace upon it—
Is immaculate white.

Cavaliers of romances
Who capture the skies
Shower their glances,
Greetings, and sighs,

But in vain their romantic
Stir, their fine flirts—
Before the gigantic
Guardian, our skirts.

And our free laughter falls
At the imagination
Of these cling-to-the-walls—
Though at times a sensation

Stirs the frock that covers
Our heart that preens
To know we're the future lovers
Of libertines.

YOUNGLINGS

High heels in a struggle with a long skirt,
As the wind roused or as the land lay,
Twinkled a glimpse above, if we were alert—
Intercepted!—and we loved that gulls' play.

Sometimes the sting of an insect bolder
Than we, sought a fair neck to scrutinize,
And there was the sudden lightning of a shoulder
And that feast overwhelmed our young fools' eyes.

Twilight came, an uncertain autumnal glow:
The fair ones, clinging dreamily to our arms,
Spoke words that were so specious and so low
That our souls forever hold their eager qualms.

1373

CAVITRI

Mahabharatta

To save her husband, Cavitri's deep vow bids
Her stand, while three days and three nights unroll,
Erect, nor move limbs, body, nor eyelids—
Rigid, Vyaca tells us, as a pole.

Neither your cruel rays, Curya, nor the swoon
Chandra spreads over the summits of the moon
Can weaken, as your mighty spheres revolve,
That glorious woman's flesh nor her resolve. . . .

Should forgetfulness with black, bleak treachery
Or lean-faced envy toward me incline,
Impassive as Cavitri may I be,
And in my soul as lofty a design.

WHAT HAVE YOU DONE?

The sky, above the roof,
    Is so blue and so calm!
The tree above the roof
    Cradles its palm.

The bell, in the sky we watch,
    Quietly rings;
A bird on the tree we watch,
    Mournfully sings.

Lord, O Lord, life is here
    Gently fluttering down.
That peaceful stir we hear
    Comes from the town.

—What have you done, you there
    Endlessly weeping; in sooth,
What have you done, you there,
    With your youth?

1374

AUTUMN SONG

The heavy thrall
Of the sobbing call
Of the fall
Weighs, nor departs,
Like my heart's
Pall.

Overcome
And dumb,
As the hours creep
I see the haze
Of olden days
And weep.

And I go away
The wind's prey,
In barren, brief
Whirl hither and yon
Like a wan
Dead leaf.

JULES VERNE

JULES VERNE (French, 1828-1905). The father of science fiction. Began
career as opera librettist till he discovered gift for imagining adventures of the
future. His works are still read with entertainment, especially *Twenty Thousand Leagues Under the Sea* and *Around the World in Eighty Days.*

THE BOTTOM OF THE SEA

AND now, how can I retrace the impression left upon me by that
walk under the waters? Words are impotent to relate such wonders!
Captain Nemo walked in front, his companions followed some steps
behind. Conseil and I remained near each other, as if an exchange
of words had been possible through our metallic cases. I no longer
felt the weight of my clothing, or my shoes, of my reservoir of air,

or of my thick helmet, in the midst of which my head rattled like an almond in its shell.

The light, which lit the soil thirty feet below the surface of the ocean, astonished me by its power. The solar rays shone through the watery mass easily and dissipated all color, and I clearly distinguished objects at a distance of a hundred and fifty yards. Beyond that the tints darkened into fine gradations of ultra-marine, and faded into vague obscurity. Truly this water which surrounded me was but another air denser than the terrestrial atmosphere, but almost as transparent. Above me was the calm surface of the sea. We were walking on fine, even sand, not wrinkled, as on a flat shore, which retains the impression of the billows. This dazzling carpet, really a reflector, repelled the rays of the sun with wonderful intensity, which accounted for the vibration which penetrated every atom of liquid. Shall I be believed when I say that, at the depth of thirty feet, I could see as if I was in broad daylight?

For a quarter of an hour I trod on this sand sown with the impalpable dust of shells. The hull of the "Nautilus," resembling a long shoal, disappeared by degrees; but its lantern, when darkness should overtake us in the waters, would help to guide us on board by its distinct rays. Soon forms of objects outlined in the distance were discernible. I recognized magnificent rocks, hung with a tapestry of zoophytes of the most beautiful kind, and I was at first struck by the peculiar effect of this medium.

It was then ten in the morning, the rays of the sun struck the surface of the waves at rather an oblique angle, and at the touch of their light, decomposed by refraction as through a prism, flowers, rocks, plants, shells, and polypi were shaded at the edges by the seven solar colors. It was marvelous, a feast for the eyes, this complication of colored tints, a perfect kaleidoscope of green, yellow, orange, violet, indigo, and blue; in one word, the whole palette of an enthusiastic colorist! Why could I not communicate to Conseil the lively sensations which were mounting to my brain, and rival him in expressions of admiration? For aught I knew, Captain Nemo and his companion might be able to exchange thoughts by means of signs previously agreed upon. So for want of better, I talked to myself; I declaimed in the copper box which covered my head, thereby expending more air in vain words than was, perhaps, expedient.

Various kinds of isis, clusters of pure tuft-coral, prickly fungi, and anemones, formed a brilliant garden of flowers, enameled with

porplutæ, decked with their collarettes of blue tentacles, sea-stars studding the sandy bottom, together with asterophytons like fine lace embroidered by the hands of naiads; whose festoons were waved by the gentle undulations caused by our walk. It was a real grief to me to crush under my feet the brilliant specimens of molluscs which strewed the ground by thousands, of hammerheads, donaciæ (veritable bounding shells), of staircases, and red helmet-shells, angel-wings, and many others produced by this inexhaustible ocean. But we were bound to walk, so we went on, whilst above our heads waved shoals of physalides, leaving their tentacles to float in their train, medusæ whose umbrellas of opal or rose-pink, escaloped with a band of blue, sheltered us from the rays of the sun and fiery pelagiæ which, in the darkness, would have strewn our path with phosphorescent light.

All these wonders I saw in the space of a quarter of a mile, scarcely stopping, and following Captain Nemo, who beckoned me on by signs. Soon the nature of the soil changed; to the sandy plain succeeded an extent of slimy mud, which the Americans call "ooze," composed of equal parts of silicious and calcareous shells. We then traveled over a plain of sea-weed of wild and luxuriant vegetation. This sward was of close texture, and soft to the feet, and rivalled the softest carpet woven by the hand of man. But whilst verdure was spread at our feet, it did not abandon our heads. A light network of marine plants, of that inexhaustible family of sea-weeds of which more than two thousand kinds are known, grew on the surface of the water. I saw long ribbons of fucus floating, some globular, others tuberous, laurenciæ and cladostephi of most delicate foliage, and some rhodomeniæ palmatæ, resembling the fan of a cactus. I noticed that the green plants kept nearer the top of the sea whilst the red were at a greater depth, leaving to the black or brown hydrophytes the care of forming gardens and parterres in the remote beds of the ocean.

We had quitted the "Nautilus" about an hour and a half. It was near noon; I knew by the perpendicularity of the sun's rays, which were no longer refracted. The magical colors disappeared by degrees, and the shades of emerald and sapphire were effaced. We walked with a regular step, which rang upon the ground with astonishing intensity; the slightest noise was transmitted with a quickness to which the ear is unaccustomed on the earth; indeed, water is a better conductor of sound than air, in the ratio of four to one. At this period the earth sloped downward; the light took a uniform

tint. We were at a depth of a hundred and five yards and twenty inches, undergoing a pressure of six atmospheres.

At this depth I could still see the rays of the sun, though feebly; to their intense brilliancy had succeeded a reddish twilight, the lowest state between day and night; and we could still see well enough.

FRANCOIS VILLON

FRANÇOIS VILLON (French, *ca.* 1431-1465?). One of the brightest stars of medieval France. Wrecked by debauchery, jail and torture, he was sentenced to death, then banished. His total work: *Le Petit Testament, Le Grand Testament* and some 40 shorter poems. He crystallized vivid perceptions of life's pleasures and ironies.

BALLAD OF OLD-TIME LADIES

Tell me where, in what land of shade,
  Bides fair Flora of Rome, and where
Are Thais and Archipiade,
  Cousins-german of beauty rare,
  And Echo, more than mortal fair,
That, when one calls by river-flow
  Or marish, answers out of the air?
But what is become of last year's snow?

Where did the learn'd Helosa vade,
  For whose sake Abelard might not spare
(Such dole for love on him was laid)
  Manhood to lose and a cowl to wear?
  And where is the queen who willed whilere
That Buridan, tied in a sack, should go
  Floating down Seine from the turret-stair?
But what is become of last year's snow?

Blanche, too, the lily-white queen, that made
  Sweet music as if she a siren were;
Broad-foot Bertha; and Joan the maid,

1378

The good Lorrainer, the English bare
Captive to Rouen and burned her there;
Beatrix, Eremburge, Alys,—lo!
    Where are they, Virgin debonair?
    But what is become of last year's snow?

ENVOI

Prince, you may question how they fare
    This week, or liefer this year, I trow:
Still shall the answer this burden bear,
    But what is become of last year's snow?

BALLAD OF OLD-TIME LORDS

Where is Calixtus, third of the name,
    That died in the purple whiles ago,
Four years since he to the tiar came?
    And the King of Aragon, Alfonso?
    The Duke of Bourbon, sweet of show,
And the Duke Arthur of Brittaine?
    And Charles the Seventh, the Good? Heigho!
But where is the doughty Charlemaine?

Likewise the King of Scots, whose shame
    Was the half of his face (or folks say so),
Vermeil as amethyst held to the flame,
    From chin to forehead all of a glow?
    The King of Cyprus, of friend and foe
Renowned; and the gentle King of Spain,
    Whose name, God 'ield me, I do not know?
But where is the doughty Charlemaine?

Of many more might I ask the same,
    Who are but dust that the breezes blow;
But I desist, for none may claim
    To stand against Death, that lays all low,
    Yet one more question before I go:
Where is Lancelot, King of Behaine?
    And where are his valiant ancestors, trow?
But where is the doughty Charlemaine?

1379

ENVOI

Where is Du Guesclin, the Breton prow?
    Where Auvergne's Dauphin, and where again
The late good duke of Alençon? Lo!
    But where is the doughty Charlemaine?

VILLON'S EPITAPH

The following is the epitaph, in ballad form, that Villon made for himself and his companions, expecting no better than to be hanged in their company.

Brothers, that after us on life remain,
    Harden your hearts against us not as stone;
For, if to pity us poor wights you're fain,
    God shall the rather grant you benison.
    You see us six, the gibbet here upon:
As for the flesh that we too well have fed,
'Tis all devoured and rotted, shred by shred.
    Let none make merry of our piteous case,
Whose crumbling bones the life long since hath fled:
    The rather pray, God grant us of His grace!

Yea, we conjure you, look not with disdain,
    Brothers, on us, though we to death were done
By justice. Well, you know the saving grain
    Of sense springs not in every mother's son:
    Commend us, therefore, now we're dead and gone,
To Christ, the Son of Mary's maidenhead,
That He leave not His grace on us to shed
    And save us from the nether torture-place.
Let no one harry us: forsooth we're sped:
    The rather pray, God grant us of His grace!

We are whiles scoured and sodden of the rain
    And whiles burnt up and blackened of the sun:
Corbies and pyets have our eyes outa'en
    And plucked our beard and hair out, one by one.
    Whether by night or day; rest have we none:

Now here, now there, as the wind shifts its stead,
We swing and creak and rattle overhead,
  No thimble dinted like our bird-pecked face.
Brothers, have heed and shun the life we led:
  The rather pray, God grant us of his grace!

ENVOI

Prince Jesus, over all empoweréd,
Let us not fall into the Place of Dread,
  But all our reckoning with the Fiend efface.
Folk, mock us not that are forspent and dead:
  The rather pray, God grant us of His grace!

VIRGIL

VIRGIL (Latin, 70-19 B.C.). Didactic poet, heavily imitative of the Greeks. The *Aeneid*, glorifying the birth of Rome, derives from Homer's epics, but remains most imposing work of Latin literature. His patriotism manifest in the *Georgics*, his love of the rural in the early *Eclogues*.

ECLOGUE IV: "THE MESSIAH"

Sicilian Muse, begin a loftier strain!
Tho' lowly shrubs, and trees that shade the plain,
Delight not all; Sicilian Muse, prepare
To make the vocal woods deserve a consul's care.
The last great age, foretold by sacred rhymes,
Renews its finished course: Saturnian times
Roll round again; and mighty years, begun
From their first orb, in radiant circles run.
The base degenerate iron offspring ends;
A golden progeny from heaven descends.
O chaste Lucina, speed the mother's pains,
And haste the glorious birth! thy own Apollo reigns!
The lovely boy, with his auspicious face,
Shall Pallio's consulship and triumph grace;
Majestic months set out with him to their appointed race.

1381

The father banished virtue shall restore,
And crimes shall threat the guilty world no more.
The son shall lead the life of gods, and be
By gods and heroes seen, and gods and heroes see.
The jarring nations he in peace shall bind,
And with paternal virtues rule mankind.
Unbidden Earth shall wreathing ivy bring,
And fragrant herbs (the promises of spring),
As her first offerings to her infant king.
The goats with strutting dugs shall homeward speed,
And lowing herds secure from lions feed.
His cradle shall with rising flowers be crowned:
The serpent's brood shall die; the sacred ground
Shall weeds and poisonous plants refuse to bear;
Each common bush shall Syrian roses wear.
But when heroic verse his youth shall raise,
And form it to hereditary praise,
Unlabored harvests shall the fields adorn,
And clustered grapes shall blush on every thorn;
The knotted oaks shall showers of honey weep,
And thro' the matted grass the liquid gold shall creep.
Yet of old fraud some footsteps shall remain:
The merchant still shall plow the deep for gain;
Great cities shall with walls be compassed round,
And sharpened shares shall vex the fruitful ground;
Another Tiphys shall new seas explore;
Another Argo land the chiefs upon the Iberian shore;
Another Helen other wars create,
And great Achilles urge the Trojan fate.
But when to ripened manhood he shall grow,
The greedy sailor shall the seas forego;
No keel shall cut the waves for foreign ware,
For every soil shall every product bear.
The laboring hind his oxen shall disjoin;
No plow shall hurt the glebe, no pruning hook the vine;
Nor wool shall in dissembled colors shine.
But the luxurious father of the fold,
With native purple, or unborrowed gold,
Beneath his pompous fleece shall proudly sweat;
And under Tyrian robes the lamb shall bleat.

The Fates, when they this happy web have spun,
Shall bless the sacred clew, and bid it smoothly run.
Mature in years, to ready honors move,
O of celestial seed! O foster son of Jove!
See, laboring Nature calls thee to sustain
The nodding frame of heaven, and earth, and main!
See to their base restored, earth, seas, and air;
And joyful ages, from behind, in crowding ranks appear.
To sing thy praise, would Heaven my breath prolong,
Infusing spirits worthy such a song,
Not Thracian Orpheus should transcend my lays,
Nor Linus crowned with never-fading bays;
Tho' each his heavenly parent should inspire;
The Muse instruct the voice, and Phœbus tune the lyre.
Should Pan contend in verse, and thou my theme,
Arcadian judges should their god condemn.
Begin, auspicious boy, to cast about
Thy infant eyes, and, with a smile, thy mother single out:
Thy mother well deserves that short delight,
The nauseous qualms of ten long months and travel to requite.
Then smile: the frowning infant's doom is read;
No god shall crown the board, nor goddess bless the bed.

WALTHER VON DER VOGELWEIDE

WALTHER VON DER VOGELWEIDE (Austrian, ca. 1170-1230). Didactic
wandering court singer of Middle Ages. His accomplishments include political,
religious and love songs. Championed German independence of papal claims,
though his political allegiance shifted with his patrons, as was custom of
the times.

MOURNINGS

To me is barred the door of joy and ease,
There stand I as an orphan, lone, forlorn,
And nothing boots me that I frequent knock.
Strange that on every hand the show'r should fall,

And not one cheering drop should reach to me!
On all around the gen'rous Austrian's gifts,
Gladd'ning the land, like genial rain descend:
A fair and gay adorned mead is he,
Whereon are gathered of the sweetest flowers:
Would that his rich and ever gen'rous hand
Might stoop to pluck one little leaf for me,
So might I fitly praise a scene so fair!

Fain (could it be) would I a home obtain,
And warm me by a hearth-side of my own.
Then, then, I'd sing about the sweet birds' strain,
And fields and flowers, as I have whilome done;
And paint in song the lily and the rose
That dwell upon *her* cheek who smiles on me.
But lone I stray—no home its comfort shows:
Ah, luckless man! still doomed a *guest* to be!

A mournful one am I, above whose head
A day of perfect bliss hath never past;
Whatever joys my soul have ravished,
Soon was the radiance of those joys o'ercast.
And none can show me that substantial pleasure
Which will not pass away like bloom from flowers;
Therefore, no more my heart such joys shall treasure,
Nor pine for fading sweets and fleeting hours.

Ah! where are hours departed fled?
    Is life a dream, or true indeed?
Did all my heart hath fashioned
    From fancy's visitings proceed?
Yes! I have slept; and now unknown
    To me the things best known before:
The land, the people, once mine own,
    Where are they?—they are here no more:
My boyhood's friends, all aged, worn,
    Despoiled the woods, the fields, of home,
Only the stream flows on forlorn;
    (Alas! that e'er such change should come!)

And he who knew me once so well
    Salutes me now as one estranged:
The very earth to me can tell
    Of naught but things perverted, changed:
And when I muse on other days,
    That passed me as the dashing oars
The surface of the ocean raise,
    Ceaseless my heart its fate deplores.

MAY AND HIS LADY

When from the sod the flow'rets spring,
    And smile to meet the sun's bright ray,
When birds their sweetest carols sing
    In all the morning pride of May,
What lovelier than the prospect there?
Can earth boast anything more fair?
To me it seems an almost heaven,
So beauteous to my eyes that vision bright is given.

But when a lady, chaste and fair,
    Noble, and clad in rich attire,
Walks through the throng with gracious air,
    As sun that bids the stars retire,—
Then, where are all thy boastings, May?
What hast thou beautiful and gay
Compared with that supreme delight?
We leave thy loveliest flowers, and watch that lady bright.

Wouldst thou believe me,—come and place
    Before thee all this pride of May;
Then look but on my lady's face,
    And, which is best and brightest? say:
For me, how soon (if choice were mine)
This would I take, and that resign!
And say, "Though sweet thy beauties, May!
I'd rather forfeit all than lose my lady gay."

"Lady," I said, "this garland wear!
  For thou wilt wear it gracefully:
And on thy brow 'twill sit so fair,
  And thou wilt dance so light and free;
Had I a thousand gems, on thee,
  Fair one! their brilliant light should shine:
Would'st thou such gift accept from me,—
  Oh, doubt me not,—it should be thine.

"Lady, so beautiful thou art,
  That I on thee the wreath bestow,
'Tis the best gift I can impart;
  But whiter, rosier flow'rs, I know,
Upon the distant plain they're springing,
  Where beauteously their heads they rear,
And birds their sweetest songs are singing:
  Come! let us go and pluck them there."

She took the beauteous wreath I chose,
  And like a child at praises glowing,
Her cheeks blushed crimson as the rose,
  When by the snow-white lily growing:
But all from those bright eyes eclipse
  Received; and then, my toil to pay,
Kind, precious words fell from her lips:
  What more than this I shall not say.

W

WANG WEI

WANG WEI (Chinese, *ca.* 700-760). Leading Sung landscape painter. Also devout Buddhist as well as successful politician. Su Shih said of him: "There is painting in his poetry and poetry in his painting." Noted for his four-line *chueh-chu* poems.

BEST HAPPINESS OF ALL

I am old and I am bored. I was never very wise and my mind has not ever walked much further than my feet. Only my forest, my forest . . . I go back and back to wander there.

The blue fingers of the moon play on my old lute there. The wind scatters the clouds there and comes down to flutter my robe.

You ask me what is the best happiness of all? In the forest it is sweet to hear a girl singing on the path, after she has stopped to ask her way, and thanked you with a smile.

THE PEACH GARDEN

The fisherman's boat is carried away along the water hugging
    the spring hills;
By two banks the peach blossom marks the limits of an ancient
    ferry;
The fisherman sits gazing at the pink blossoms regardless of the
    distance,
Drifting to the end of a green mountain stream, careless of where
    he goes.

1387

A narrow passage in the mountains leads by secret detours to the beginning of an open bay,

There the hills open out on a vast expanse of flat land:

He approaches it and it is a village of 1000 homes scattered amid flowers and bamboo.

The stranger begins to distinguish the speech of the Han dynasty.

Those who dwelt there had not changed the fashion of their clothes since the days of Ch'in.

These village dwellers lived together at the source of the Wu Ling River;

They had fled away from the world to live the lives of peasants.

The moon is bright underneath the pines,

Shining on their quiet windows;

The sun rises; dogs bark and chickens crow.

The inhabitants are startled to hear a man has come from the world of men,

And vie with each other in hospitality.

They compete to invite him into their houses and ask him whence he has come.

When morning comes they sweep away the fallen flowers and open the village gates.

When night falls fishermen and woodcutters come home by way of the stream.

Once upon a time these people, seeking a place of refuge, left their fellow men.

They sought to obtain immortality and they did not go back.

In among the ravines and gorges what could they know of the affairs of the world?

All they could see of the world were distant clouds and hills.

Their visitor did not suspect this was a holy place, unknown to mortal men;

His earthly heart had not extinguished earthly desires and he thought of his native home.

Once out of the cave he does not mind that he is separated from it by hills and water.

(When once again) he leaves his family to go on the same long journey,

He says to himself, I have been there before, I cannot miss the way.

How should he know that the mountains and ravines had all changed?

He can only remember that on the former occasion he plunged deep into the green hills

1388

Where mountain rivulets meandered to and fro, leading him to
    misty woods.
(Again) the spring is here and everywhere peach flowers stain
    the water,
But he cannot trace the way to the land of immortality.
Where shall he hunt for it now?

ON A DARK AUTUMN IN A HILL HUT

On the empty hill new rain has fallen;
Out of the dusk comes the autumn.
The bright moon shines forth between the pines,
Above the rocks flows the clear stream,
Babel in the bamboos proclaims the washing girls are returning
    home,
The lotus swing beneath the fisherman's boat,
The fragrance of spring sighs and expires,
How can we detain it before it goes?

JAKOB WASSERMANN

JAKOB WASSERMANN (German, 1873-1934). Problem novelist, whose complex plots and unusual characters gave his stories universal appeal. A wanderer
in his youth, finally settled in Austria. Not identified with any literary school.
His most successful novel: *The World's Illusion*. Others: *The Maurizius Case,
Doctor Kerkhoven*.

THE BEAST

IN one of the former capitals of central Germany great labour riots,
which the citizens still recall with horror, broke out in the wake
of the revolution. Thousands of striking labourers gathered in mobs
and marched, on that misty February morning, towards the busy
streets of the inner city. The jeering rabble, usually idle all the
time, joined them, and the deploying police was soon no longer
able to cope with the threatening throng. The iron shutters rattled
down over the displays in the shop-windows; cafés and restaurants
were locked in panicky haste; house doors were slammed to, and
curious and terrified faces appeared at the windows when the wild
shouting and whistling of the approaching masses became audible.

These broke their way like an unstemmed flood; stones were hurled at the houses and smashed the windows. Here and there a shot was fired. The constabulary force saw itself reduced to take measures of defense and prepared to resist the mob with sabres and clubs. Turmoil and bitterness grew with each passing moment. The shouts and yells sounded more and more horrible. Bare arms and grimly threatening fists were stretched forth; eyes burned with rapacious and vindictive hatred. Women goaded on the men; ragged children filled the air with ear-splitting screams; and the slightest provocation, perhaps an irritating word, and murder and plundering would have been inevitable.

At that moment, there drove across a public square which the most advanced of the throng had just reached, a rather huge wagon resembling a furniture van, but which instead of side-walls had loose brown canvas hangings, and these showed the coat-of-arms of the royal family which had till recently ruled over the country. The sight of the hated emblems whipped the anger of the rioters into fury. In an instant the wagon was surrounded; the efforts of the police to break through the human ring were futile. The driver had pulled up the two horses, which, on being reined in so abruptly, trembled violently. A man jumped from the running-board at the rear of the wagon, unslung a rifle from his shoulder and cocked the trigger. This was the signal for the attack. A well-aimed blow knocked him down; thirty or forty arms reached for the cloth decorated with the escutcheon. The coachman's vehement, threatening gesticulation remained unnoticed; a word which he hurled at them was drowned in the turmoil and the protecting cover fell away in shreds from the frame-work. No sooner had this happened, when all, even the boldest of them, were seized with the utmost horror. The whistling, screaming, howling subsided as if by command, and they who beheld the sight, subdued by their horror-stricken silence those in the rear who, only dimly conscious of something ominous, stared with frightened, reluctant glances at the necks in front of them.

On the wagon was a Nubian lion from the royal zoological gardens. Owing to the high cost of feeding and maintaining him and also because of a certain aversion against such playthings of their erstwhile lords, the new government had decided to sell the beast to a foreign country. And thus, on that very morning the lion had been sent to the railroad station to be forwarded to his new destination.

1390

As the canvas-wall slipped down from the frame, the lion roused himself and then surveyed the thousands of people, so steadily, with an expression of awe-inspiring majesty, until no sound could be heard from them, not a breath was audible. In his flashing eyes was reflected the picture of an alien world. But what was the nature of that world out there? A world as hard and cold as stone, a world with no heaven or horizon, one of mysterious sounds and offensive odours. Did he have an inkling of the wild passions which burst forth from despair and misery, he, who knew neither despair nor misery, and of passions only the elemental, natural ones of his superior kind? Did he actually take in those disturbed, ugly faces before him, or was it only a partial aspect or some impression of a detail that reached him: grinning teeth, distorted forehead, protruding chin; the violent wrath in the glance, the soulless glance of Megæra, the sullen sneer of the emaciated?

But those out there felt, with almost religious awe, something entirely unknown to him. In the dirty holes where they lived and brooded their evil; where their sick ones were lying and their children were born, and where they gave way to gloomy thoughts over the injustice which was their heritage of an evil order. On all their ways and journeys and in all the dreams of their servile imaginations they never had a vision which reminded them so much of what lay beyond their world, of the greatness and might of Nature. An undefinable horror took possession of their gloom-enveloped souls. They trembled, their muscles became limp, and they bowed their heads and cast down their eyes; their closely knitted ranks broke and gaps opened here and there. This enabled the policemen to arrest several dangerous ringleaders, and for the time being the rebellion was nipped in the bud.

FRANZ WERFEL

FRANZ WERFEL (Austrian, 1890-1945). Novelist, playwright and poet, who found success in America where he fled from Nazi Germany. His main theme: humanity and divine providence. His widely popular novels include: *Verdi, The Forty Days of Musa Dagh* and *The Song of Bernadette*. Play: *Jacobowsky and the Colonel*. Admired in Germany for his early lyric poetry.

THEOLOGOUMENA

WHAT argument is there against the notion that man is the center of creation? Are there any more complex and more differentiated orgnisms than he? The stars, for example?

I turned to a modern astronomer for an answer to this question. He informed me that the stars are suns similar to our own sun, many of them thousands of times larger and many of them thousands of times smaller. These tremendous, white-hot, gaseous spheres, he told me, are the only form in which matter occurs in that indescribable void that we call the universe. Though astro-physics determines the weight of the stars and their temperatures, the nature of sidereal matter has nothing to do with what we on earth call matter, least of all with the highly organized matter out of which the bodies of living, terrestrial creatures are constructed. Atoms, I was informed, cannot sustain themselves under the enormous pressure prevailing in sidereal spheres and increasing at a high ratio towards their center; consequently, they disintegrate into their hypothethical components, into protons and electrons that travel as waves and rays out into universal space.

"The stars which compose the comparatively sparse population of the universe," concluded the astronomer, "are, accordingly, nothing but inconceivably rarefied condensations of certain chemical elements (hydrogen, oxygen, nitrogen, carbon, and, to name a few of the less common ones, argon and crypton), spherical in form, a raging whirl of exploded atoms engaged in a mysteriously eruptive vital activity."

"Vital activity?" I repeated questioningly. "Does that mean you believe that the stars might be living bodies, mentally alive bodies, personalities, so to speak, which is, after all, the same thing? The latter-day gnostics held the view that stars are the heavenly hosts in material form and that their glowing, eruptive, vital activity

represents nothing but the great hymn of praise, the 'Holy, Holy, Holy' with which the angels eternally celebrate the Creator."

At these words, the modern scientist gave me a startled look; then his lips tightened, whether with annoyance or irony I do not know. "Intelligence," he corrected me, "is a phenomenon which is developed only by the most highly differentiated matter in animal and human form, and for the one and only purpose of self-defense and self-assertion for survival . . . The stars, on the other hand, consist of inorganic matter in its most primal and simple form."

"Then organic matter," I interrupted, "highly differentiated, organic matter only exists on the planets? What about the planets, professor?"

"They are extremely rare and exceptional cases in the universe," answered the scientist, "if the prevalent hypothesis is correct. According to this hypothesis, planets and families of planets originate when two stars or suns approach too close to each other in their orbits so that the gravitation of the larger star attracts the smaller one so overpoweringly that part of its matter is torn out of its body, assumes shape and begins to rotate about the larger star in the congealing form of one or more planets."

"Could there be masculine and feminine stars?" I interrupted the astronomer. Again I received a look of disapproval as he continued, "As far as inorganic matter is concerned, it can be charged with either positive or negative electricity, nothing more. Sexual differences and characteristics which serve for the propagation of a species exist only in the more differentiated organic matter, beginning with certain plants."

"Thank you, professor. Forget my stupid question . . . But there's one more thing. If I understand you correctly, it's against the traffic regulations of the universe for the orbits of stars to approach each other too closely."

"Quite right," he responded. "This approach of the stars' orbits and the tearing off of planetary systems thus brought about, are, as our research assumes, among the most unusual catastrophes in the universe, far more unusual, for example, than the explosion of stars (which is in itself quite a rare event) and the formation of nova that is associated with it and that we can observe in our telescopes now and then. The planets, my dear fellow, are a catastrophic anomaly in the realm of matter. And of all the planets, a planet with the earth's conditions of life seems to be the most anomalous of anomalies."

"How can that be, my dear professor?" said I abruptly. "Can it be that the highly differentiated organic matter of which we spoke cannot sustain its life upon the other planets that revolve about our sun?"

"In all probability, no," he answered rather glumly. "On one of them, for example, the atmosphere is too dense, on another it is too rarefied, on a third there isn't any at all, on a fourth the temperature is much too high, on a fifth it is much too low."

"Just a moment, professor. Two stars disturb the harmony by coming too close to each other. The result is that sun-like matter is torn off, catapulted outward and finally cools down slowly. That is, it becomes rock and water, sand and mud, this exiled matter that owes its existence to an infraction, a clumsy violation of law. Is that correct, professor?"

"Approximately, my friend," he grumbled, "if we subtract your mythologically moralizing commentary."

"And out of this exiled, out of this banished, out of this deeply humiliated matter," I continued to question, "does the germ of life spring forth until, in a comparatively short time, it has developed into the human soul that is capable of ecstatically comprehending God?"

"Here you are leaving the paths of science," declared the astronomer, disgusted.

"If, as you say, the earth is already an anomaly, my dear professor, what then is humanity?"

"An anomaly raised to the twelfth power," he laughed contemptuously . . .

When I left the learned man, I realized that science had not lessened my faith but had unintentionally strengthened it. If the earth really is the most anomalous of all anomalies, then for that reason alone it revolves in the innermost center of the universe, a center that can only be a *product of the mind;* for indeed, within the universe, all space and time dimensions are meaningless. And if humanity is really the great exceptional case, as modern theory seems disposed to profess, how easy should it be for everyone to believe that this humanity is the crown and the goal of creation, and that God Himself had decided from the very beginning not to become *Sirius*, *Aldebaran* or *Cassiopeia* in order to incorporate Himself into a created thing and to have experience of it, but to become something far more rare, greater and more precious, a man.

1394

WALT WHITMAN

WALT WHITMAN (American, 1819-1892). Prophetic singer of odes to demo-cratic Americanism. The U. S.'s most universally praised poet. Served as jour-nalist in New York, became army nurse during Civil War. First edition of *Leaves of Grass* was received with hostility, accused of immorality. His own criticism of America contained in prose work, *Democratic Vistas*. Style, modeled on Old Testament, extravagantly admired by poets, but has not been successfully imitated.

From *SONG OF MYSELF*

X

The runaway slave came to my house and stopt outside,
I heard his motions crackling the twigs of the woodpile,
Through the swung half-door of the kitchen I saw him limpsy and
    weak,
And went where he sat on a log and led him in and assured him,
And brought water and fill'd a tub for his sweated body and bruis'd
    feet,

And gave him a room that enter'd from my own, and gave him
    some coarse clean clothes,
And remember perfectly well his revolving eyes and his awkwardness,
And remember putting plasters on the galls of his neck and ankles;
He staid with me a week before he was recuperated and pass'd
    north,
I had him sit next to me at table, my fire-lock lean'd in the corner.

XXIV

Walt Whitman, a kosmos, of Manhattan the son,
Turbulent, fleshy, sensual, eating, drinking and breeding,
No sentimentalist, no stander above men and women or apart from
    them,
No more modest than immodest.

Unscrew the locks from the doors!
Unscrew the doors themselves from their jambs!

Whoever degrades another degrades me,
And whatever is done or said returns at last to me.

Through me the afflatus surging and surging, through me the current
and index.

I speak the pass-word primeval, I give the sign of democracy,
By God! I will accept nothing which all cannot have their counterpart
of on the same terms.

XXXIII

I understand the large hearts of heroes,
The courage of present times and all times,
How the skipper saw the crowded and rudderless wreck of the
steam-ship, and Death chasing it up and down the storm,
How he knuckled tight and gave not an inch, and was faithful of
days and faithful of nights,
And chalk'd in large letters on a board, *Be of good cheer, we will
not desert you;*
How he follow'd with them and tack'd with them three days and
would not give it up,
How he saved the drifting company at last,
How the lank loose-gown'd women look'd when boated from the
side of their prepared graves,
How the silent old-faced infants and the lifted sick, and the sharp-
lipp'd unshaven men;
All this I swallow, it tastes good, I like it well, it becomes mine,
I am the man, I suffer'd, I was there.
The disdain and calmness of martyrs,
The mother of old, condemn'd for a witch, burnt with dry wood,
her children gazing on,
The hounded slave that flags in the race, leans by the fence, blowing,
cover'd with sweat.
The twinges that sting like needles his legs and neck, the murderous
buckshot and the bullets,
All these I feel or am.

I am the hounded slave, I wince at the bite of the dogs,
Hell and despair are upon me, crack and again crack the marksmen,

I clutch the rails of the fence, my gore dribs, thinn'd with the ooze of my skin,
I fall on the weeds and stones,
The riders spur their unwilling horses, haul close,
Taunt my dizzy ears and beat me violently over the head with whip-stocks.

Agonies are one of my changes of garments,
I do not ask the wounded person how he feels, I myself become the wounded person,
My hurts turn livid upon me as I lean on a cane and observe.

O CAPTAIN! MY CAPTAIN!

O Captain! my Captain! our fearful trip is done,
The ship has weathered every rack, the prize we sought is won,
The port is near, the bells I hear, the people all exulting,
While follow eyes the steady keel, the vessel grim and daring;
    But O heart! heart! heart!
      O the bleeding drops of red,
        Where on the deck my Captain lies,
          Fallen cold and dead.

O Captain! my Captain! rise up and hear the bells;
Rise up—for you the flag is flung—for you the bugle trills,
For you bouquets and ribboned wreaths—for you the shores acrowding,
For you they call, the swaying mass, their eager faces turning;
    Here Captain! dear father!
      This arm beneath your head!
        It is some dream that on the deck
          You've fallen cold and dead.

My Captain does not answer, his lips are pale and still,
My father does not feel my arm, he has no pulse nor will,
The ship is anchored safe and sound, its voyage closed and done,
From fearful trip the victor ship comes in with object won;
    Exult O shores, and ring O bells!
      But I, with mournful tread,
        Walk the deck my Captain lies,
          Fallen cold and dead.

From *TO A FOIL'D EUROPEAN REVOLUTIONAIRE*

(No songs of loyalty alone are these,
    But songs of insurrection also;
For I am the sworn poet of every dauntless rebel, the world over,
And he going with me leaves peace and routine behind him,
And stakes his life, to be lost at any moment.)

When liberty goes out of a place, it is not the first to go, nor the
    second or third to go,
It waits for all the rest to go—it is the last.

When there are no more memories of heroes and martyrs,
And when all life, and all the souls of men and women are discharged
    from any part of the earth,
Then only shall liberty, or the idea of liberty, be discharged from
    that part of the earth,
And the infidel come into full possession.

From *AS A STRONG BIRD ON PINIONS FREE*

Beautiful World of new, superber Birth, that rises to my eyes,
Like a limitless golden cloud, filling the western sky. . . .
Thou Wonder World, yet undefined, unform'd—neither do I define
    thee;
How can I pierce the impenetrable blank of the future?
I feel thy ominous greatness, evil as well as good;
I watch thee, advancing, absorbing the present, transcending the
    past;
I see thy light lighting and thy shadow shadowing, as if the entire
    globe;
But I do not undertake to define thee—hardly to comprehend thee;
I but thee name—thee prophesy—as now!

From *SONG OF THE OPEN ROAD*

XI

Listen! I will be honest with you,
I do not offer the old smooth prizes, but offer rough new prizes,

These are the days that must happen to you:
You shall not heap up what is call'd riches,
You shall scatter with lavish hand all that you earn or achieve,
You but arrive at the city to which you were destin'd, you hardly
    settle yourself to satisfaction, before you are call'd by an irresist-
    ible call to depart,
You shall be treated to the ironical smiles and mockings of those
    who remain behind you,
What beckonings of love you receive you shall only answer with
    passionate kisses of parting,
You shall not allow the hold of those who spread their reach'd
    hands toward you.

XII

Allons! after the great Companions, and to belong to them!
They too are on the road—they are the swift and majestic men
    —they are the greatest women,
Enjoyers of calms of seas and storms of seas,
Sailors of many a ship, walkers of many a mile of land,
Habitués of many distant countries, habitués of far-distant dwellings,
Trusters of men and women, observers of cities, solitary toilers,
Pausers and contemplators of tufts, blossoms, shells of the shore,
Dancers at wedding-dances, kissers of brides, tender helpers of
    children, bearers of children,
Soldiers of revolts, standers by gaping graves, lowerers-down of
    coffins,
Journeyers over consecutive seasons, over the years, the curious
    years each emerging from that which preceded it,
Journeyers as with companions, namely their own diverse phases,
Forth-steppers from the latent unrealized baby-days,
Journeyers gayly with their own youth, journeyers with their bearded
    and well-grain'd manhood,
Journeyers with their womanhood, ample, unsurpass'd, content,
Journeyers with their own sublime old age of manhood or woman-
    hood,
Old age, calm, expanded, broad with the haughty breadth of the
    universe,
Old age, flowing free with the delicious near-by freedom of death.

1399

I HEAR AMERICA SINGING

I hear America singing, the varied carols I hear,
Those of mechanics, each one singing his as it should be blithe and
strong,
The carpenter singing his as he measures his plank or beam,
The mason singing his as he makes ready for work, or leaves off
work,
The boatman singing what belongs to him in his boat, the deck-hand
singing on the steamboat deck,
The shoemaker singing as he sits on his bench, the hatter singing
as he stands,
The wood-cutter's song, the plowboy's on his way in the morning,
or at noon intermission or at sundown,
The delicious singing of the mother, or of the young wife at work,
or of the girl sewing or washing,
Each singing what belongs to him or her and to none else,
The day what belongs to the day—at night the party of young
fellows, robust, friendly,
Singing with open mouths their strong melodious songs.

FOR YOU, O DEMOCRACY

Come, I will make the continent indissoluble,
I will make the most splendid race the sun ever shone upon,
I will make divine magnetic lands,
　With the love of comrades,
　　With the life-long love of comrades.

I will plant companionship thick as trees along all the rivers of
America, and along the shores of the great lakes, and
all over the prairies,
I will make inseparable cities with their arms about each other's
necks,
　By the love of comrades,
　　By the manly love of comrades.

For you these from me, O Democracy, to serve you *ma femme*!
For you, for you I am trilling these songs.

1400

JOHN GREENLEAF WHITTIER

JOHN GREENLEAF WHITTIER (American, 1807-1892). Antislavery balladist.
His New England Quaker background painted in narrative poem, *Snowbound*.
Became widely known as pamphleteer and editor of various abolitionist papers.
Now more often remembered as a writer of popular ballads and nature poet.

THE SLAVE-SHIPS

"That fatal, that perfidious bark,
Built i' the eclipse, and rigged with curses dark."
—*Milton's Lycidas.*

"All ready!" cried the captain;
  "Ay, ay!" the seamen said;
"Heave up the worthless lubbers,—
  The dying and the dead."
Up from the slave-ship's prison
  Fierce, bearded heads were thrust:
"Now let the sharks look to it,—
  Toss up the dead ones first!"

Corpse after corpse came up,—
  Death had been busy there;
Where every blow is mercy,
  Why should the spoiler spare?
Corpse after corpse they cast
  Sullenly from the ship,
Yet bloody with the traces
  Of fetter-link and whip.

Gloomily stood the captain,
  With his arms upon his breast,
With his cold brow sternly knotted,
  And his iron lip compressed.
"Are all the dead dogs over?"
  Growled through that matted lip,—
"The blind ones are no better,
  Let's lighten the good ship."

1401

Hark! from the ship's dark bosom,
   The very sounds of hell!
The ringing clank of iron,—
   The maniac's short, sharp yell!—
The hoarse, low curse, throat-stilled,—
   The starving infant's moan,—
The horror of a breaking heart
   Poured through a mother's groan.

Up from that loathsome prison
   The stricken blind ones came:
Below, had all been darkness,—
   Above, was still the same.
Yet the holy breath of heaven
   Was sweetly breathing there,
And the heated brow of fever
   Cooled in the soft sea air.

"Overboard with them, shipmates!"
   Cutlass and dirk were plied;
Fettered and blind, one after one,
   Plunged down the vessel's side.
The saber smote above,—
   Beneath, the lean shark lay,
Waiting with wide and bloody jaw
   His quick and human prey.

God of the earth! what cries
   Rang upward unto thee?
Voices of agony and blood,
   From ship-deck and from sea.
The last dull plunge was heard,—
   The last wave caught its stain,—
And the unsated shark looked up
   For human hearts in vain.

Red glowed the western waters,—
   The setting sun was there,
Scattering alike on wave and cloud
   His fiery mesh of hair.

Amidst a group in blindness,
    A solitary eye
Gazed, from the burdened slaver's deck,
    Into that burning sky.

"A storm," spoke out the gazer,
    "Is gathering and at hand,—
Curse on 't—I'd give my other eye
    For one firm rood of land."
And then he laughed,—but only
    His echoed laugh replied,—
For the blinded and the suffering
    Alone were at his side.

Night settled on the waters,
    And on a stormy heaven,
While fiercely on that lone ship's track
    The thunder-gust was driven.
"A sail!—thank God, a sail!"
    And as the helmsman spoke,
Up through the stormy murmur
    A shout of gladness broke.

Down came the stranger vessel,
    Unheeding on her way,
So near, that on the slaver's deck
    Fell off her driven spray.
"Ho! for the love of mercy,—
    We're perishing and blind!"
A wail of utter agony
    Came back upon the wind:

"Help *us!* for we are stricken
    With blindness every one;
Ten days we've floated fearfully,
    Unnoting star or sun.
Our ship's the slaver Leon,—
    We've but a score on board,—
Our slaves are all gone over,—
    Help,—for the love of God!"

On livid brows of agony
  The broad red lightning shone,—
But the roar of wind and thunder
  Stifled the answering groan
Wailed from the broken waters
  A last despairing cry,
As, kindling in the stormy light,
  The stranger ship went by.

In the sunny Guadaloupe
  A dark-hulled vessel lay,—
With a crew who noted never
  The nightfall or the day
The blossom of the orange,
  Was white by every stream,
And tropic leaf, and flower, and bird
  Were in the warm sunbeam.

And the sky was bright as ever,
  And the moonlight slept as well,
On the palm-trees by the hillside,
  And the streamlet of the dell:
And the glances of the Creole
  Were still as archly deep,
And her smiles as full as ever
  Of passion and of sleep.

But vain were bird and blossom,
  The green earth and the sky,
And the smile of human faces,
  To the slaver's darkened eye;
At the breaking of the morning,
  At the star-lit evening time,
O'er a world of light and beauty
  Fell the blackness of his crime.

CHRISTOPH MARTIN WIELAND

CHRISTOPH MARTIN WIELAND (German, 1733-1813). Translator of Shakespeare. Strongly influenced High German literary style. Edited and published first modern literary review in German. His novel, *Der goldene Spiegel*, brought appointment as tutor to Weimar princes, where he lived most of his life. Most famous work: *Oberon*, a verse romance.

SIR HUON ENTERS THE SULTAN'S PALACE

Now through the outward court swift speeds the knight;
   Within the second from his steed descends;
   Along the third his pace majestic bends:
Where'er he enters, dazzled by his sight,
   The guards make way,—his gait, his dress, his air,
   A nuptial guest of highest rank declare.
Now he advances towards an ebon gate,
Where with drawn swords twelve Moors gigantic wait,
   And piecemeal hack the wretch who steps unbidden there.

But the bold gesture and imperial mien
   Of Huon as he opes the lofty door,
   Drive back the swords that crossed his path before,
And at his entrance flamed with lightning sheen.
   At once, with rushing noise, the valves unfold:
   High throbs the bosom of our hero bold,
When, locked behind him, harsh the portals bray:
Through gardens decked with columns leads the way,
   Where towered a gate incased with plates of massy gold.

There a large fore-court held a various race
   Of slaves, hapless race, sad harem slaves,
   Who die of thirst 'mid joy's o'erflowing waves!
And when a man, whom emir honors grace,
   Swells in his state before their hollow eye,
   Breathless they bend, with looks that seem to die,
Beneath the weight of servitude oppresed;
Bow down, with folded arms across the breast,
   Nor dare look up to mark the pomp that glitters by.

1405

Already cymbals, drums and fifes resound;
  With song and string the festive palace clangs;
  The Sultan's head already heaving hangs,
While vinous vapors float his brain around:
  Already mirth in freer current flows,
  And the gay bridegroom, wild with rapture, glows.
Then, as the bride, in horror turned away,
Casts on the ground her looks that never stray,
  Huon along the hall with noble freedom goes.

Now to the table he advances nigh,
  And with uplifted brow in wild amaze
  The admiring guests upon the stranger gaze:
Fair Rezia, tranced, with fascinated eye
  Still views her dream, and ever downward bends:
  The Sultan, busy with the bowl, suspends
All other thoughts: Prince Bakeban alone,
Warned by no vision, towards the guest unknown,
  All fearless of his fate, his length of neck extends.

Soon as Sir Huon's scornful eyes retrace
  The man of yesterday, that he, the same
  Who lately dared the Christian God defame,
Sits at the left, high-plumed in bridal grace,
  And bows the neck as conscious of his guilt:
  Swift as the light he grasps the sabre's hilt;
Off at the instant flies the heathen's head;
And, o'er the Caliph and the banquet shed,
  Up spirts his boiling blood, by dreadful vengeance spilt!

As the dread visage of Medusa fell,
  Swift flashing on the sight, with instant view
  Deprives of life the wild-revolted crew;
While reeks the tower with blood, while tumults swell,
  And murderous frenzy, fierce and fiercer grown,
  Glares in each eye, and maddens every tone,—
At once, when Perseus shakes the viper hair,
Each dagger stiffens as it hangs in air,
  And every murderer stands transformed to living stone!

1406

Thus, at the view of this audacious feat,
  The jocund blood that warmed each merry guest
  Suspends its frozen course in every breast:
Like ghosts, in heaps, all-shivering from their seat
  They start, and grasp their swords and mark their prey;
  But, shrunk by fear, their vigor dies away:
Each in its sheath their swords remain at rest:
  With powerless fury in his look expressed,
  Mute sunk the caliph back, and stared in wild dismay.

The uproar which confounds the nuptial hall
  Forces the dreamer from her golden trance:
  Round her she gazes with astonished glance,
While yells of frantic rage her soul appal:
  But, as she turns her face towards Huon's side,
  How throbs his bosom, when he sees his bride!—
"'Tis she,—'tis she herself!" he wildly calls:
Down drops the bloody steel; the turban falls;
  And Rezia knows her knight, as float his ringlets wide.

"'Tis he!" she wild exclaims: yet virgin shame
  Stops in her rosy mouth the imperfect sound:
  How throbs her heart; what thrillings strange confound,
When, with impatient speed, the stranger came,
  And, love-emboldened, with presumptuous arms
  Clasped, in the sight of all, her angel charms!
And, Oh, how fiery red, how deadly pale
Her cheek, as love and maiden fear assail,
  The while he kissed her lip that glowed with sweet alarms!

Twice had his lip already kissed the maid:—
  "Where shall the bridal ring, Oh, where be found?"
  Lo! by good fortune, as he gazes round,
The elfin ring shines suddenly displayed,
  Won from the giant of the iron tower:
  Now, all-unconscious of its magic power,
This ring, so seeming base, the impatient knight
Slips on her finger, pledge of nuptial rite:—
  "With this, O bride beloved! I wed thee from this hour!"

Then, for the third time, at these words, again
    The bridegroom kissed the soft reluctant fair:
    The Sultan storms and stamps in wild despair:—
"Thou sufferest, then,—inexpiable stain!
    This Christian dog to shame thy nuptial day?—
    Seize, seize him, slaves!—ye die, the least delay!
Haste! drop by drop, from every throbbing vein,
By lengthened agonies his life-blood drain,—
    Thus shall the pangs of hell his monstrous guilt repay."

At once, in flames, before Sir Huon's eyes,
    A thousand weapons glitter at the word;
    And, ere our hero snatches up his sword,
On every side the death-storms fiercely rise:
    On every side he turns his brandished blade:
    By love and anguish wild, at once the maid
Around him wreathes her arm, his shield her breast,
Seizes his sword, by her alone repressed:—
    "Back! daring slaves!" she cries, "I, I the hero aid!

"Back!—to that breast,—here, here the passage lies!—
    No other way than through the midst of mine!"—
    And she, who lately seemed Love's bride divine,
Now flames a Gorgon with Medusa's eyes!
    And ever, as the emirs near inclose,
    She dares with fearless breast their swords oppose:—
"Spare him, my father! spare him! and, O thou,
Destined by fate to claim my nuptial vow,
    Spare him!—in both your lives the blood of Rezia flows!"

The Sultan's frenzy rages uncontrolled:
    Fierce on Sir Huon storm the murderous train;
    Yet still his glittering falchion flames in vain,
While Rezia's gentle hand retains its hold:
    Her agonizing shrieks his bosom rend.
    And what remains the princes to defend?
What but the horn can rescue her from death?—
Soft through the ivory flows his gentle breath,
    And from its spiry folds sweet fairy tones ascend.

1408

Soon as its magic sounds, the powerless steel
    Falls without struggle from the lifted hand:
    In rash vertigo turned, the emir band
Wind arm in arm and spin the giddy reel:
    Throughout the hall tumultuous echoes ring;
    All, old and young, each heel has Hermes' wing:
No choice is left them by the fairy tone:
Pleased and astonished, Rezia stands alone
    By Huon's side unmoved, while all around them spring.

The whole divan, one swimming circle, glides
    Swift without stop: the old bashaws click time:
    As if on polished ice, in trance sublime,
The iman hoar with some spruce courtier slides:
    Nor rank nor age from capering refrain:
    Nor can the king his royal foot restrain;
He, too, must reel amid the frolic row,
Grasp the grand vizier by his beard of snow,
    And teach the aged man once more to bound amain.

The dancing melodies, ne'er heard before,
    From every crowded antechamber round,
    First draw the eunuchs forth with airy bound;
The women next, and slaves that guard the door
    Alike the merry madness seizes all.
    The harem's captives, at the magic call,
Trip gaily to the tune and whirl the dance:
In party-colored shirts the gardeners prance,
    Rush 'mid the youthful nymphs and mingle in the ball.

Entranced, with fearful joy, while doubt alarms,
    Fair Rezia stands almost deprived of breath:—
    "What wonder at the time when instant death
Hangs o'er us, that a dance the god disarms!
    A dance thus rescues from extreme distress!"
    "Some friendly genius deigns our union bless,"
Sir Huon says. Meanwhile amid the throng
With eager step darts Sherasmin along,
    And towards them Fatma hastes unnoticed through the press.

"Haste!" Sherasmin exclaims; "not now the hour
    To pry with curious leisure on the dance,—
    All is prepared,—the steeds impatient prance,—
While raves the castle, while unbarred the tower,
    And every gate wide open, why delay?
    By luck I met Dame Fatma on the way,
Close-packed, like beast of burden, for the flight."
"Peace! 'tis not yet the time," replies the knight;
    "A dreadful task impends,—for that must Huon stay."

Pale Rezia shudders at the dreadful sound,
    And looks with longing eye, that seems to say,
    "Why, on the brink of ruin, why delay?
Oh, hasten! let our footsteps fly the ground,
    Ere bursts the transient charm that binds their brain.
    And rage and vengeance repossess the train!"
Huon, who reads the language of her eyes,
With looks of answering love alone replies,
    Clasps to his heart her hand, nor dares the deed explain.

And now the fairy tones to soft repose
    Melt in the air: each head swims giddy round,
    And every limb o'ertired forgets to bound;
Wet every thread, and every pore o'erflows.
    The breath half-stopped scarce heaves with struggling pain;
    The drowsy blood slow creeps through every vein;
Involuntary joy, like torture, thrills:
The king, as from a bath, in streams distills,
    And pants upon his couch, amid the exhausted train.

Stiff, without motion, scarce with sense endued,
    Down, one by one, the o'erwearied dancers fall,
    Where swelling bolsters heave around the wall:
Emirs and lowly slaves, in contrast rude,
    Mix with the harem goddesses, as chance
    Tangles the mazes of the frantic dance:
At once together by a whirlwind blown,
On the same bed, in ill-paired union thrown,
    The groom and favorite lie confused in breathless trance.

OSCAR WILDE

OSCAR WILDE (English, 1854-1900). Cultivated literary eccentric and social satirist. One of leaders of Aesthetic Movement in 90's. Exotic stylist, particularly in play *Salome*, novel *The Picture of Dorian Gray*, and fairy tales. His drawing room comedies the best since Sheridan: *Lady Windermere's Fan*, *The Importance of Being Earnest*, *An Ideal Husband*. His last years darkened by aberrational ignominy.

THE SELFISH GIANT

EVERY afternoon, as they were coming from school, the children used to go and play in the Giant's garden.

It was a large lovely garden, with soft green grass. Here and there over the grass stood beautiful flowers like stars, and there were twelve peach-trees that in the Spring-time broke out into delicate blossoms of pink and pearl, and in the autumn bore rich fruit. The birds sat on the trees and sang so sweetly that the children used to stop their games in order to listen to them. "How happy we are here!" they cried to each other.

One day the Giant came back. He had been to visit his friend the Cornish ogre, and had stayed with him for seven years. After the seven years were over he had said all that he had to say, for his conversation was limited, and he determined to return to his own castle. When he arrived he saw the children playing in the garden.

"What are you doing there?" he cried in a very gruff voice, and the children ran away.

"My own garden is my own garden," said the Giant; "anyone can understand that, and I will allow nobody to play in it but myself." So he built a high wall all round it, and put up a notice-board.

TRESPASSERS
WILL BE
PROSECUTED

He was a very selfish Giant.

The poor children had now nowhere to play. They tried to play on the road, but the road was very dusty and full of hard stones, and they did not like it. They used to wander round the high wall

1411

when their lessons were over, and talk about the beautiful garden inside. "How happy we were there," they said to each other.

Then the Spring came, and all over the country there were little blossoms and little birds. Only in the garden of the Selfish Giant it was still winter. The birds did not care to sing in it, as there were no children, and the trees forgot to blossom. Once a beautiful flower put its head out from the grass, but when it saw the notice-board it was so sorry for the children that it slipped back into the ground again, and went off to sleep. The only people who were pleased were the Snow and the Frost. "Spring has forgotten this garden," they cried, "so we will live here all the year round." The Snow covered up the grass with her great white cloak, and the Frost painted all the trees silver. Then they invited the North Wind to stay with them, and he came. He was wrapped in furs, and he roared all day about the garden, and blew the chimney-pots down. "This is a delightful spot," he said; "we must ask the Hail on a visit." So the Hail came. Every day for three hours he rattled on the roof of the castle till he broke most of the slates, and then he ran round and round the garden as fast as he could go. He was dressed in gray, and his breath was like ice.

"I can not understand why the Spring is so late in coming," said the Selfish Giant, as he sat at the window and looked out at his cold white garden; "I hope there will be a change in the weather."

But the Spring never came, nor the Summer. The Autumn gave golden fruit to every garden, but to the Giant's garden she gave none. "He is too selfish," she said. So it was always Winter there, and the North Wind, and the Hail, and the Frost, and the Snow danced about through the trees.

One morning the Giant was lying awake in bed when he heard some lovely music. It sounded so sweet to his ears that he thought it must be the King's musicians passing by. It was really only a little linnet singing outside his window, but it was so long since he had heard a bird sing in his garden that it seemed to him to be the most beautiful music in the world. Then the Hail stopped dancing over his head, and the North Wind ceased roaring, and a delicious perfume came to him through the open casement. "I believe the Spring has come at last," said the Giant; and he jumped out of bed and looked out.

What did he see?

He saw a most wonderful sight. Through a little hole in the wall the children had crept in, and they were sitting in the branches of

the trees. In every tree that he could see there was a little child. And the trees were so glad to have the children back again that they had covered themselves with blossoms, and were waving their arms gently above the children's heads. The birds were flying about and twittering with delight, and the flowers were looking up through the green grass and laughing. It was a lovely scene, only in one corner it was still winter. It was the farthest corner of the garden, and in it was standing a little boy. He was so small that he could not reach up to the branches of the tree, and he was wandering all round it, crying bitterly. The poor tree was still quite covered with frost and snow, and the North Wind was blowing and roaring above it. "Climb up, little boy," said the Tree, and it bent its branches down as low as it could; but the boy was too tiny.

And the Giant's heart melted as he looked out. "How selfish I have been!" he said; "now I know why the Spring would not come here. I will put that poor little boy on the top of the tree, and then I will knock down the wall, and my garden shall be the children's playground for ever and ever." He was really very sorry for what he had done.

So he crept downstairs and opened the front door quite softly, and went out into the garden. But when the children saw him they were so frightened that they all ran away, and the garden became winter again. Only the little boy did not run, for his eyes were so full of tears that he did not see the Giant coming. And the Giant stole up behind him and took him gently in his hand, and put him up into the tree. And the tree broke at once into blossoms, and the birds came and sang on it, and the little boy stretched out his two arms and flung them round the Giant's neck, and kissed him. And the other children, when they saw that the Giant was not wicked any longer, came running back, and with them came the Spring. "It is your garden now, little children," said the Giant, and he took a great axe and knocked down the wall. And when the people were going to market at twelve o'clock they found the Giant playing with the children in the most beautiful garden they had ever seen.

All day long they played, and in the evening they came to the Giant to bid him good-bye.

"But where is your little companion?" he said: "the boy I put into the tree." The Giant loved him the best because he had kissed him.

"We don't know," answered the children; "he has gone away."

"You must tell him to be sure and come here to-morrow," said

1413

the Giant. But the children said that they did not know where he lived, and had never seen him before; and the Giant felt very sad.

Every afternoon, when school was over, the children came and played with the Giant. But the little boy whom the Giant loved was never seen again. The Giant was very kind to all the children, yet he longed for his first little friend, and often spoke of him. "How I would like to see him!" he used to say.

Years went over, and the Giant grew very old and feeble. He could not play about any more, so he sat in a huge armchair, and watched the children at their games, and admired his garden. "I have many beautiful flowers," he said; "but the children are the most beautiful flowers of all."

One winter morning he looked out of his window as he was dressing. He did not hate the Winter now, for he knew that it was merely the Spring asleep, and that the flowers were resting.

Suddenly he rubbed his eyes in wonder, and looked and looked. It certainly was a marvelous sight. In the farthest corner of the garden was a tree quite covered with lovely white blossoms. Its branches were all golden, and silver fruit hung down from them, and underneath it stood the little boy he had loved.

Downstairs ran the Giant in great joy, and out into the garden. He hastened across the grass, and came near to the child. And when he came quite close his face grew red with anger, and he said, "Who hath dared to wound thee?" For on the palms of the child's hands were the prints of two nails, and the prints of two nails were on the little feet.

"Who hath dared to wound thee?" cried the Giant; "tell me, that I may take my big sword and slay him."

"Nay!" answered the child; "but these are the wounds of Love."

"Who art thou?" said the Giant, and a strange awe fell on him, and he knelt before the little child.

And the child smiled on the Giant, and said to him, "You let me play once in your garden, to-day you shall come with me to my garden, which is Paradise."

And when the children ran in that afternoon, they found the Giant lying dead under the tree, all covered with white blossoms.

WILLIAM WORDSWORTH

WILLIAM WORDSWORTH (English, 1770-1850). Grand poet of the common-place. One of founders (with friend Coleridge) of the English Romantic Movement. Preface to their joint work, *Lyrical Ballads*, became famous manifesto. He glorified the Lake District and its simple inhabitants. More ambitious work: *The Prelude, The Excursion*. Later poetry less inspired. Ended days as Poet Laureate.

INTIMATIONS OF IMMORTALITY

I

There was a time when meadow, grove and stream,
　The earth, and every common sight,
　　　To me did seem
　　　Apparelled in celestial light,
The glory and the freshness of a dream.
It is not now as it hath been of yore;—
　　　Turn wheresoe'er I may,
　　　　By night or day,
The things which I have seen I now can see no more.

II

　　The rainbow comes and goes,
　　And lovely is the rose;
　　The moon doth with delight
Look round her when the heavens are bare;
　　Waters on a starry night
　　Are beautiful and fair;
　The sunshine is a glorious birth;—
　But yet I know, where'er I go,
That there hath passed away a glory from the earth.

III

Now, while the birds thus sing a joyous song,
　And while the young lambs bound
　　As to the tabor's sound,

1415

To me alone there came a thought of grief;
A timely utterance gave that thought relief;
          And I again am strong.
The cataracts blow their trumpets from the steep—
No more shall grief of mine the season wrong:
I hear the echoes through the mountains throng;
The winds come to me from the fields of sleep;
          And all the earth is gay.
              Land and sea
        Give themselves up to jollity;
          And with the heart of May
        Doth every beast keep holiday:—
            Thou child of joy,
Shout round me, let me hear thy shouts, thou happy shepherd-boy!

IV

Ye blessèd creatures, I have heard the call
    Ye to each other make; I see
The heavens laugh with you in your jubilee;
    My heart is at your festival,
        My head hath its coronal,
The fullness of your bliss I feel—I feel it all.
    Oh, evil day! if I were sullen,
    While Earth herself is adorning,
        This sweet May morning;
    And the children are culling,
        On every side,
    In a thousand valleys far and wide,
    Fresh flowers; while the sun shines warm,
And the babe leaps up on his mother's arm:—
    I hear, I hear, with joy I hear!
    —But there's a tree, of many one,
A single field which I have looked upon—
Both of them speak of something that is gone:
        The pansy at my feet
        Doth the same tale repeat:
Whither is fled the visionary gleam?
Where is it now, the glory and the dream?

V

Our birth is but a sleep and a forgetting:
The soul that rises with us, our life's star,
   Hath had elsewhere its setting,
     And cometh from afar;
   Not in entire forgetfulness,
   And not in utter nakedness,
But trailing clouds of glory do we come
     From God, who is our home:
Heaven lies about us in our infancy!
Shades of the prison-house begin to close
     Upon the growing boy;
But he beholds the light, and whence it flows,
     He sees it in his joy;
The youth, who daily farther from the east
   Must travel, still is Nature's priest,
    And by the vision splendid
    Is on his way attended;
At length the man perceives it die away,
And fade into the light of common day.

VI

Earth fills her lap with pleasures of her own;
Yearnings she hath in her own natural kind,
And, even with something of a mother's mind,
    And no unworthy aim,
    The homely nurse doth all she can ·
To make her foster-child, her inmate man,
   Forget the glories he hath known,
And that imperial palace whence he came.

VII

Behold the child among his new-born blisses,
A six-years' darling of a pigmy size!
See, where 'mid work of his own hand he lies,
Fretted by sallies of his mother's kisses,

With light upon him from his father's eyes!
See, at his feet, some little plan or chart,
Some fragment from his dream of human life,
Shaped by himself with newly-learnéd art;
    A wedding or a festival,
    A mourning or a funeral;
      And this hath now his heart,
      And unto this he frames his song:
        Then will he fit his tongue
To dialogues of business, love, or strife;
    But it will not be long
    Ere this be thrown aside,
    And with new joy and pride
The little actor cons another part;
Filling from time to time his "humorous stage"
With all the persons, down to palsied age,
That Life brings with her in her equipage;
    As if his whole vocation
    Were endless imitation.

VIII

Thou, whose exterior semblance dost belie
    Thy soul's immensity;
Thou best philosopher, who yet dost keep
Thy heritage; thou eye among the blind,
That, deaf and silent, readest the eternal deep,
Haunted forever by the eternal mind,—
    Mighty Prophet! Seer blessed!
    On whom those truths do rest,
Which we are toiling all our lives to find;
In darkness lost, the darkness of the grave;
Thou, over whom thy immortality
Broods like the day, a master o'er a slave,
A presence which is not to be put by;
Thou little child, yet glorious in the might
Of heaven-born freedom, on thy being's height,
Why with such earnest pains dost thou provoke
The years to bring the inevitable yoke,

Thus blindly with thy blessedness at strife?
Full soon thy soul shall have her earthly freight,
And custom lie upon thee with a weight,
Heavy as frost, and deep almost as life!

IX

O joy! that in our embers
    Is something that does live,
That nature yet remembers
    What was so fugitive!
The thought of our past years in me doth breed
Perpetual benedictions: not indeed
For that which is most worthy to be blessed;
Delight and liberty, the simple creed
Of childhood, whether busy or at rest,
With new-fledged hope still fluttering in his breast,—
        Not for these I raise
    The song of thanks and praise;
    But for those obstinate questionings
    Of sense and outward things,
    Fallings from us, vanishings;
    Blank misgivings of a creature
Moving about in worlds not realized,
High instincts, before which our mortal nature
Did tremble, like a guilty thing surprised:
    But for those first affections,
    Those shadowy recollections,
        Which, be they what they may,
Are yet the fountain light of all our day,
Are yet a master light of all our seeing;
    Uphold us, cherish, and have power to make
Our noisy years seem moments in the being
Of the eternal silence: truths that wake
            To perish never;
Which neither listlessness, nor mad endeavor,
        Nor man, nor boy,
Nor all that is at enmity with joy,
Can utterly abolish or destroy!

1419

Hence, in a season of calm weather,
        Though inland far we be,
Our souls have sight of that immortal sea
        Which brought us hither;
        Can in a moment travel thither,
And see the children sport upon the shore,
And hear the mighty waters rolling evermore.

X

Then sing, ye birds—sing, sing a joyous song!
        And let the young lambs bound
        As to the tabor's sound!
We, in thought, will join your throng,
        Ye that pipe and ye that play,
        Ye that through your hearts to-day
        Feel the gladness of the May!
What though the radiance which was once so bright
Be now forever taken from my sight,—
        Though nothing can bring back the hour
Of splendor in the grass, of glory in the flower;
        We will grieve not, rather find
        Strength in what remains behind;
        In the primal sympathy,
        Which, having been, must ever be
        In the soothing thoughts that spring
        Out of human suffering;
        In the faith that looks through death,
In years that bring the philosophic mind.

XI

And oh, ye fountains, meadows, hills, and groves,
Forbode not any severing of our loves!
Yet in my heart of hearts I feel your might;
I only have relinquished one delight,
To live beneath your more habitual sway.
I love the brooks, which down their channels fret,
Even more than when I tripped lightly as they;
The innocent brightness of a new-born day
        Is lovely yet;

1420

The clouds that gather round the setting sun
Do take a sober coloring from an eye
That hath kept watch o'er man's mortality:
Another race hath been and other palms are won.
Thanks to the human heart by which we live;
Thanks to its tenderness, its joys, and fears,
To me the meanest flower that blows can give
Thoughts that do often lie too deep for tears.

Y

YAMANOE NO OKURA

YAMANOE NO OKURA (Japanese, 659-733). Moralist and philosopher. One of the best poets from the *Manyōshū* anthology. Notable for his sympathy for the suffering poor and for children. Pursued a diplomatic career.

AN ELEGY ON THE IMPERMANENCE OF HUMAN LIFE

We are helpless before time
Which ever speeds away.
And pains of a hundred kinds
Pursue us one after another.
Maidens joy in girlish pleasures,
With ship-borne gems on their wrists,
And hand in hand with their friends;
But the bloom of maidenhood,
As it cannot be stopped,
Too swiftly steals away.
When do their ample tresses
Black as a mud-snail's bowels
Turn white with the frost of age?
Whence come those wrinkles
Which furrow their rosy cheeks?
The lusty young men, warrior-like,
Bearing their sword-blades at their waists,
In their hands the hunting bows,
And mounting their bay horses,
With saddles dressed with twill,
Ride about in triumph;

But can their prime of youth
Favour them for ever?
Few are the nights they keep,
When, sliding back the plank doors,
They reach their beloved ones
And sleep, arms intertwined,
Before, with staffs at their waists,
They totter along the road,
Laughed at here, and hated there.
This is the way of the world;
And, cling as I may to life,
I know no help!

Envoy

Although I wish I were thus,
Like the rocks that stay for ever,
In this world of humanity
I cannot keep old age away.

A DIALOGUE ON POVERTY

On the night when the rain beats,
Driven by the wind,
On the night when the snow-flakes mingle
With the sleety rain,
I feel so helplessly cold.
I nibble at a lump of salt,
Sip the hot, oft-diluted dregs of saké;
And coughing, snuffling,
And stroking my scanty beard,
I say in my pride,
'There's none worthy, save I!'
But I shiver still with cold.
I pull up my hempen bed-clothes,
Wear what few sleeveless clothes I have,
But cold and bitter is the night!
As for those poorer than myself,
Their parents must be cold and hungry,
Their wives and children beg and cry.
Then, how do you struggle through life?

Wide as they call the heaven and earth,
For me they have shrunk quite small;
Bright though they call the sun and moon,
They never shine for me.
Is it the same with all men,
Or for me alone?
By rare chance I was born a man
And no meaner than my fellows,
But, wearing unwadded sleeveless clothes
In tatters, like weeds waving in the sea,
Hanging from my shoulders,
And under the sunken roof,
Within the leaning walls,
Here I lie on straw
Spread on bare earth,
With my parents at my pillow,
My wife and children at my feet,
All huddled in grief and tears.
No fire sends up smoke
At the cooking-place,
And in the cauldron
A spider spins its web.
With not a grain to cook,
We moan like the 'night-thrush.'
Then, 'to cut,' as the saying is,
'The ends of what is already too short,'
The village headman comes,
With rod in hand, to our sleeping-place,
Growling for his dues.
Must it be so hopeless—
The way of this world?

Envoy

Nothing but pain and shame in this world of men,
But I cannot fly away,
Wanting the wings of a bird.

1424

SUFFERING FROM OLD AGE AND PROLONGED
ILLNESS, AND THINKING OF HIS CHILDREN

So long as lasts the span of life,
We wish for peace and comfort
With no evil and no mourning,
But life is hard and painful.
As the common saying has it,
Bitter salt is poured into the smarting wound,
Or the burdened horse is packed with an upper load,
Illness shakes my old body with pain.
All day long I breathe in grief
And sigh throughout the night.
For long years my illness lingers,
I grieve and groan month after month,
And though I would rather die,
I cannot, and leave my children
Noisy like the flies of May.
Whenever I watch them
My heart burns within.
And tossed this way and that,
I weep aloud.

Envoys

I find no solace in my heart;
Like the bird flying behind the clouds
I weep aloud.

Helpless and in pain,
I would run out and vanish,
But the thought of my children holds me.

No children to wear them in wealthy homes,
They are thrown away as waste,
Those silks and quilted clothes!

With no sackcloth for my children to wear,
Must I thus grieve,
For ever at a loss!

Though vanishing like a bubble,
I live, praying that my life will be long
Like a rope of a thousand fathoms.

Humble as I am,
Like an arm-band of coarse twill,
How I crave a thousand years of life!

WILLIAM BUTLER YEATS

WILLIAM BUTLER YEATS (Irish, 1865-1939). Greatest Irish poet. Leader of
the Irish Renaissance in literature, co-founder with Lady Gregory of the Abbey
Theatre. Nobel Prize, 1923. Wrote romantic and mythological lyrics, highly
personal poems, plays and critical essays. Among them: *The Wind Among
the Reeds, Responsibilities, The Tower, A Full Moon in March, Stories of
Red Hanrahan.*

AN IRISH AIRMAN FORESEES HIS DEATH

I know that I shall meet my fate
Somewhere among the clouds above;
Those that I fight I do not hate,
Those that I guard I do not love;
My country is Kiltartan Cross,
My countrymen Kiltartan's poor,
No likely end could bring them loss
Or leave them happier than before.
Nor law, nor duty bade me fight,
Nor public men, nor cheering crowds,
A lonely impulse of delight
Drove to this tumult in the clouds;
I balanced all, brought all to mind,
The years to come seemed waste of breath,
A waste of breath the years behind
In balance with this life, this death.

AN APPOINTMENT

Being out of heart with government,
I took a broken root to fling
Where the proud, wayward squirrel went,
Taking delight that he could spring;

And he, with that low whinnying sound
That is like laughter, sprang again
And so to the other tree at a bound.
Nor the tame will, nor timid brain,
Bred that fierce tooth and cleanly limb
And threw him up to laugh on the bough;
No government appointed him.

THE ROSE TREE

'O words are lightly spoken,'
Said Pearse to Connolly,
'Maybe a breath of politic words
Has withered our Rose Tree;
Or maybe but a wind that blows
Across the bitter sea.'

'It needs to be but watered,'
James Connolly replied,
'To make the green come out again
And spread on every side,
And shake the blossom from the bud
To be the garden's pride.'

'But where can we draw water,'
Said Pearse to Connolly,
'When all the wells are parched away?
O plain as plain can be
There's nothing but our own red blood
Can make a right Rose Tree.'

COME GATHER ROUND ME, PARNELLITES

Come gather round me, Parnellites,
And praise our chosen man;
Stand upright on your legs awhile,
Stand upright while you can,
For soon we lie where he is laid,
And he is underground;
Come fill up all those glasses
And pass the bottle round.

1427

And here's a cogent reason,
And I have many more,
He fought the mind of England
And saved the Irish poor,
Whatever good a farmer's got
He brought it all to pass;
And here's another reason,
That Parnell loved a lass.

And here's a final reason,
He was of such a kind
Every man that sings a song
Keeps Parnell in his mind.
For Parnell was a proud man,
No prouder trod the ground,
And a proud man's a lovely man,
So pass the bottle round.

The Bishops and the Party
That tragic story made,
A husband that had sold his wife
And after that betrayed;
But stories that live longest
Are sung above the glass,
And Parnell loved his country,
And Parnell loved his lass.

Z

EMILE ZOLA

ÉMILE ZOLA (French, 1840-1902). Founder of the Naturalistic School of
French literature. Tried to apply new scientific concepts to literature. Remembered, also, for his dedicated defense of Dreyfus, *J'Accuse*. Like Balzac,
he wanted to embrace all French society in his novels. Most nearly successful:
Germinal, L'Assommoir, La Débâcle. Most widely read: *Nana*.

A FIGHT WITH FLAILS

WHEN the relatives, invited to a baptism and supper, had gone to
look over the farm, Buteau, dissatisfied at losing the afternoon, took
off his jacket and began to thresh, in the paved corner of the courtyard; for he needed a sack of wheat. But he soon wearied of
threshing alone, he wanted, to warm him up, the double cadence
of the flails, tapping in measure; and he called Françoise, who often
aided him in this work, her arms as hard as those of a lad:—"Eh,
Françoise, will you come?"

His wife, who was preparing a ragoût of veal with carrots, and
who had alrady put on an old dress, was forced to follow him. She
took a flail, her own. With both hands she made it whirl above her
head, bringing it down upon the wheat, which it struck with a sharp
blow. Buteau, opposite her, did the same, and soon nothing was seen
but the bits of flying wood. The grain leaped, fell like hail, beneath
the panting toc-toc of the two threshers.

At a quarter to seven o'clock, as the night was coming on,
Fouan and the Delhommes presented themselves.

"We must finish," Buteau cried to them, without stopping. "Fire
away, Françoise!"

She did not pause, tapped harder, in the excitement of the work
and the noise. And it was thus that Jean, who arrived in his turn,
with the permission to dine out, found them. Françoise, on seeing

1429

him, stopped short, troubled. Buteau, having wheeled about, stood for an instant motionless with surprise and anger. "What are you doing here?"

But Lise cried out, with her gay air: "Eh! true, I have not told you. I saw him this morning, and asked him to come."

The inflamed face of her husband became so terrible, that she added, wishing to excuse herself: "I have an idea, Père Fouan, that he has a request to make of you."

"What request?" said the old man.

Jean colored, and stammered, greatly vexed that the matter should be broached in this way, so quickly, before everybody. But Buteau interrupted him violently, the smiling glance that his wife had cast upon Françoise had sufficed to enlighten him: "Are you making game of us? She is not for you, you scoundrel!"

This brutal reception restored Jean his courage. He turned his back, and addressed the old man: "This is the story, Père Fouan, it's very simple. As you are Françoise's guardian, it is necessary for me to address myself to you to get her, is it not? If she will take me, I will take her. It is marriage that I ask."

Francoise, who was still holding her flail, dropped it, trembling with fright. She ought, however, to have expected this; but never could she have thought that Jean would dare to demand her thus, immediately. Why had he not talked with her about it first? She was overwhelmed, she could not have said if she trembled with hope or with fear. And, all of a quiver, she stood between the two men.

Buteau did not give Fouan time to answer. He resumed, with a growing fury:—"Eh? you have gall! An old fellow of thirty-three marry a girl of eighteen! Only fifteen years difference! Is it not laughable?"

Jean commenced to get angry. "What difference does it make to you, if I want her and she wants me?" And he turned towards Françoise, that she might give her decision. But she remained frightened, stiffened, and seeming not to understand the case. She could not say No; she did not say Yes, however. Buteau, besides, was looking at her as if he would kill her, to force back the Yes in her throat. If she married, he would lose her land. The sudden thought of this result put the climax to his rage.

"See here, father, see here, Delhomme, it's not right to give this girl to that old villain, who is not even of the district, who comes from nobody knows where, after having dragged his ugly mug in

1430

all directions! A failure of a joiner who has turned farmer, because, very sure, he has some dirty business to hide!"

"And afterwards? If I want her and she wants me!" repeated Jean, who had controlled himself. "Come, Françoise, speak."

"But it's true!" cried Lise, carried away by the desire of marrying off her sister, in order to disembarrass herself of her, "what have you to say, if they come to an understanding? She has no need of your consent; it's very considerate in her not to send you about your business with a flea in your ear. You exhaust our patience!"

Then Buteau saw that the marriage would be decided upon, if the young girl spoke. At that instant La Grande (the old aunt) entered the court-yard, followed by the Charleses, who had returned with Éloide. And he summoned them with a gesture, without knowing yet what he would say. Then his face puffed out, he bawled, shaking his fist at his wife and sister-in-law:

"Name of God! I'll break the heads of both of them, the jades!"

The Charleses caught his words, open-mouthed, with consternation. Madam Charles threw herself forward, as if to cover with her body Éloide, who was listening; then, pushing her towards the kitchen garden, she herself cried out, very loudly: "Go look at the salads; go look at the cabbages! Oh! the fine cabbages!"

Buteau continued, violently abusing the two women, upon whom he heaped all sorts of epithets. Lise, astonished at this sudden fit, shrugging her shoulders, repeating: "He is crazy! he is crazy!"

"Tell him it's none of his business!" cried Jean to Françoise.

"Very sure it's none of his business!" said the young girl, with a tranquil air.

"Ah! it's none of my business, eh?" resumed Buteau. "Well, I'm going to make you both march, jades that you are!"

This mad audacity paralyzed, bewildered Jean. The others, the Delhommes, Fouan, La Grande, held aloof. They did not seem surprised; they thought, evidently, that Buteau had a right to do as he pleased in his own house. Then Buteau felt himself victorious in his undisputed strength of possession. He turned towards Jean. "And now for you, scoundrel, who came here to turn my house upside down! Get out of here on the instant! Eh! you refuse. Wait, wait!"

He picked up his flail, he whirled it about his head, and Jean had only the time to seize the other flail, Françoise's, to defend himself. Cries burst forth, they strove to throw themselves between them; but the two men were so terrible that they drew back. The

1431

long handles of the flails carried the blows for several yards; they swept the court-yard. The two adversaries stood alone, in the centre, at a distance from each other, enlarging the circle of their flails. They uttered not a word, their teeth set. Only the sharp blows of the pieces of wood were heard at each stroke.

Buteau had launched forth the first blow, and Jean, yet stooping, would have had his head broken, if he had not leaped backwards. Instantly, with a sudden stiffening of the muscles, he arose, he raised, he brought down the flail, like a thresher beating the grain. But already the other was striking also, the two flail ends met, bent back upon their leather straps, in the mad flight of wounded birds. Three times the same clash was reproduced. They saw only those bits of wood whirl and hiss in the air at the extremity of the handles, always ready to fall and split the skulls which they menaced.

Delhomme and Fouan, however, had rushed forward, when the women cried out. Jean had just rolled in the straw, treacherously stricken by Buteau, who, with a blow like a whip stroke, along the ground, fortunately deadened, had hit him on the legs. He sprang to his feet, he brandished his flail in a rage that the pain increased. The end described a large circle, fell to the right, when the other expected it to the left. A few lines nearer, and the brains would have been beaten out. Only the ear was grazed. The blow, passing obliquely, fell with all its force upon the arm, which was broken clean. The bone cracked with the sound of breaking glass.

"Ah! the murderer!" howled Buteau, "he has killed me!"

Jean, haggard, his eyes red with blood, dropped his weapon. Then, for a moment, he stared at them all, as if stupefied by what had happened there, so rapidly; and he went away, limping, with a gesture of furious despair.

When he had turned the corner of the house, towards the plain, he saw La Trouille, who had witnessed the fight, over the garden hedge. She was still laughing at it, having come there to skulk around the baptismal repast, to which neither her father nor herself had been invited. Mahomet would split his sides with merriment over the little family fête, over his brother's broken arm! She squirmed as if she had been tickled, almost ready to fall over, so much was she amused at it all.

"Ah! Caporal, what a hit!" cried she. "The bone went crack! It wasn't the least bit funny!"

He did not answer, slackening his step with an over-whelmed

air. And she followed him, whistling to her geese, which she had
brought to have a pretext for stationing herself and listening
behind the walls. Jean, mechanically, returned towards the threshing
machine, which was yet at work amid the fading light. He thought
that it was all over, that he could never see the Buteaus again,
that they would never give him Françoise. How stupid it was! Ten
minutes had sufficed; a quarrel which he had not sought, a blow
so unfortunate, just at the moment when matters were progressing
favorably! And now there was an end to it all! The roaring of the
machine, in the depths of the twilight, prolonged itself like a great
cry of distress.

ARNOLD ZWEIG

ARNOLD ZWEIG (German, 1887-   ). Militant pacifist. His most famous
novel, *The Case of Sergeant Grischa*, came out of painful World War I experiences. Emigrated to Israel, a refugee from Nazi Germany. There wrote
extensively on Zionism. Best stories: in *Playthings of Time*. Essays: *Juden
auf der deutschen Bühne*.

THE APPARITION

TELL me a story!—that's easy to say. These mountains bring back
almost too vivid memories of blessed, happy days when I was as
carefree as a colt and of those others when I was preparing myself
for the task (or was it preparing itself for me?) that, for the time
being, I hold in abeyance yet dare not interrupt. But as my eyes
trouble me and I cannot, just now, enjoy the flights of fancy of
others in the delightful pursuit of reading, I must, for better or
worse, pass my leisure time in telling stories.

It happened during the coldest part of winter in the eastern Carpathians. This is a country of mountains that rise abruptly from
the plains, and of heavy-coated browsing sheep; little hamlets,
villages, and farms dot the plain, divided from each other by tongues
of woodland slipping down the mountainside, and by fields wrested,
ages ago, from the stark Slovak soil. This region lies far away—
fully four hundred years! Miracles, saints, and demons still remain
familiar phenomena there while fear, superstitious fear, is felt—
and perhaps rightly so—only towards government officials, newspapers, machinery, the telephone, and the radio.

1433

The inhabitants are without exception religious. The Jews believe in the Jewish lore, the Slovaks in the Christian, literally and reverently, and they carry on the customs their fathers have handed down to them in writing and by word of mouth. They are also very poor in that region, the Slovakian peasants a little less so, the Jews a little more, and these two are dependent upon each other, inevitably and by turns, as in the good fable of the lion and the mouse.

In this state of poverty and intense cold, Rifke Leah left her cottage early one winter's evening and went into the woods where the snow lay deep and undisturbed. Rifke Leah carried a short spade and, arriving at a familiar spot near the edge of the wood which seemed shielded from prying eyes, she busily began to shovel away the snow and to break up the ice beneath to cleanse herself. She shivered as she cowered and washed herself in the crystal-clear, crystal-cold water which came down from the mountains under a crust of ice and which, suddenly freed of its coverlet, steamed as it came in contact with the warmer air—but she shivered chiefly because she feared someone might pass by and surprise her.

It was early evening, the moon was still low and yellow, but bright wintry stars were shining through the bare branches. . . . Then, as she had divined, she suddenly heard—a short distance away—the voices of some peasants taking a short-cut through the woods from the village tavern to their homes. Merciful God—men! They have been drinking, they are singing—good-natured men but ready for pranks when in liquor. She represses her cry of alarm, throws her skirt over her head so that no one recognizes her, and dashes, or rather glides, silently homeward through the snow under the light of the pale golden moon—a mysterious figure, swathed in white. Rifke Leah succeeds in eluding them; trembling, with beating heart, she makes a detour around the tavern and reaches her cottage a few minutes later.

Meanwhile the three peasants stood mutely beside the dark water, which had miraculously thawed in the midst of the snow and which was still steaming. What had they witnessed? A lovely, white form had floated away amid the trees; it must have been the Holy Mother of God come to assure the village of a better harvest. In their greatest need came heavenly kindness—take off your hats: a miracle has happened here in the midst of the snowy desolation of the forest. Indeed, the vapours were still rising like incense before their eyes! They corroborate each other—they have seen the Holy Mother of God, white and lovely, float away amid the trees.

The next morning and especially on the following Sunday they eagerly told of the miracle whose scene they had hastily marked by sticking branches into the snow around the pool of water. They had not neglected to cross themselves, kneel down, and thank the Mother of God for her visit.

The women and many people in distress made their way to the spot, which was frozen over again and covered with snow. One of the faithful hung a picture of the miraculous visitor and her Divine Child on the nearest tree, paper flowers from the church came next, then a little shed was built to protect the picture from the rain. Devout peasants and townsfolk, in ever-increasing numbers, made pilgrimages thither. The priests, hearing of it and being simple folk like the others, saw no reason to doubt a miracle that had already brought joy, solace, and cure from small ailments to so many of the faithful.

Spring came early that year; warm sunlight flooded the fields which peasants—cheered by the promise of the Queen of Heaven —were confidently tilling with their teams. The Jews had also, in due course, heard of the forest shrine. Oddly enough, Rifke Leah and her husband were the first to know its exact site. "Benjamin always was wide awake," the Jews said, and followed his lead. When the warm weather set in, he and his wife sold bread, wafers, biscuits, lemonade, and candles to the pilgrims.

The following autumn, after an abundant harvest, the foundations of a chapel commemorating the blessed visit of the Mother of God were laid. Before the winter began, the Bishop of Kosice came for the dedication. Not without heavy misgivings had he listened to the remarks of the local clergy, remarks which at first seemed harmless enough but which gradually came to reflect an urgent desire of the people. Many paths led to salvation and none should be disregarded, nor was this the time to ignore spiritual needs because of mental snobbishness. A miracle must have occurred; people believed it and it was working.

He visualized the brown, weatherbeaten faces of the peasants, their eyes opened wide in wonder; if he questioned and cross-questioned them as to what they had actually seen, they would insist it had been the Mother of God floating away through the wintry forest—nothing else. They had found the warm, dewy pool sending vapours into the night—nothing else. Let sceptics jeer, make insinuations, offer explanations of all sorts—he, the bishop, would be unworthy of shepherding these souls, if, through fear of

1435

fostering a delusion, he refused to bestow upon the scene of the apparition the dignity of official as well as spiritual consecration. He came; he stood before them simply and gravely, chanting praises in Latin and asking God's blessing upon the land and the simple faith of these country people.

For Kosice, far off in the east of Europe, is also some hundreds of years behind the times. It isn't so long ago that bloody battles were fought there with gipsies who had made savoury meals of human flesh. The Jews of that region, when they are among themselves, say to each other that it is only fair that their trade, especially that with pilgrims, has so greatly improved.

Benjamin, Rifke Leah's husband, occasionally drinks a glass too much. That is why he happened to be so communicative to an eminent scholar and politician who came there a year later from the capital city of Prague to tell the Jews how and why they should vote. It was he—he clung to the ancient traditions of his land and people with tender mockery—who sometimes told this story, not to sneer at the incident but to characterize these distant people and places, where even today the Middle Ages are alive in human hearts. He possessed a sympathetic understanding of the sincerity and simple piety as well as of the humour and gentle roguishness of this tale. That is why I have retold it—at leisure, beneath green trees, surrounded by green mountains, facing the blue heavens, which we strange creatures so frequently fashion into figments of our own childish desires so that our dreams, fears, and hopes may be as much a part of them as the fleecy clouds and may pass as they do.

ACKNOWLEDGMENTS

Aeschylus: "The Complaint of Prometheus," from *Prometheus Bound,* translated by Elizabeth Barrett Browning; "A Prayer to Artemis," from *The Suppliants,* translated by Miss Swanwick; "The Vision of Cassandra," from *Agamemnon,* translated by Edward Fitzgerald.

Ryunosuke Akutagawa: "Rashomon," from *Rashomon and Other Stories,* translated by Takashi Kojima, reprinted by permission of Liveright Publishing Corp., New York.

Sholem Aleikhem: "The Passover Guest," from *Yiddish Tales,* translated by Helena Frank, reprinted by permission of the Jewish Publication Society of America.

Vittorio Alfieri: "David Soothes Saul's Madness" and "The Death of Saul," from *Saul.*

Hans Christian Andersen: "The Lovers," reprinted from *The Universal Anthology,* edited by Richard Garnett, Merrill & Baker, New York. (Copyright, 1899, by Richard Garnett.)

Leonid Nikolayevic Andreyev: "Valia," translated by Lizzie B. Gorin, reprinted from *Greatest Short Stories,* P. F. Collier & Son, New York.

Guillaume Apollinaire: Poems from *Modern French Poetry,* compiled and translated by Joseph T. Shipley, reprinted by permission of Greenberg, New York.

Ludovico Ariosto: "Alcina the Enchantress," from *Orlando Furioso,* translated by W. S. Rose, reprinted from *The Universal Anthology,* edited by Richard Garnett, Merrill & Baker, New York. (Copyright, 1899, by Richard Garnett.)

Aristophanes: "Grand Chorus of Birds," from *The Birds,* translated by A. C. Swinburne.

Sholem Asch: "A Jewish Child," from *Yiddish Tales,* translated by Helena Frank, reprinted by permission of the Jewish Publication Society of America.

Attar (Farid ud-Din): "The Bird Parliament," translated by Edward Fitzgerald.

Sri Aurobindo: Poems from *Poems, Past and Present,* reprinted by permission of the Sri Aurobindo Ashram Press, Pondicherry, India.

Mary Austin: "Papago Wedding," reprinted from *One Smoke Stories,* by permission of Houghton Mifflin, Boston.

Isaak Babel: "The Birth of a King," from *Benya Krik the Gangster and Other Stories,* translated by Elisaveta Fen, reprinted by permission of Schocken Books, Inc., New York.

1437

James Matthew Barrie: "Courtships," from *Auld Licht Idylls*, reprinted by permission of Charles Scribner's Sons, New York.

Bashō: Poems from *An Anthology of Haiku Ancient and Modern*, translated by Asataro Miyamori, reprinted by permission of Taisei-Do Shobo Co., Kobe, Japan.

Charles Baudelaire: Poems from *Modern French Poetry*, translated by Joseph T. Shipley, reprinted by permission of Greenberg, New York.

Stephen Vincent Benét: "Freedom's a Hard-Bought Thing," from *Selected Works of Stephen Vincent Benét*, published by Rinehart & Co., New York; reprinted by permission of Brandt & Brandt, agents for the estate of Stephen Vincent Benét. (Copyright, 1940, by Stephen Vincent Benét.)

Pierre Jean de Béranger: Poems from *The Universal Anthology*, edited by Richard Garnett, tr. by William Young, Merrill & Baker, New York. Copyright, 1899, by Richard Garnett.)

Bhartrihari: Poems, translated by Arthur W. Ryder, from *1001 Poems of Mankind*, edited by Henry W. Wells, Tupper & Love, Atlanta.

Bhāsa: "True Love" from *Svapnavāsavadatta*, and "Serenity" from *Pratimā Nātakam*, from *Sanskrit Literature*, by K. Chandrasekharan and Brahmasri V. H. Subrahmanya Sastri, reprinted by permission of The P.E.N. All-India Centre, Bombay.

Bhavabhūti: "The Rescue of Malātī," from *Malātī Mādhava;* "The Story of the Ramayana," from *Uttara Rāmacharita;* from *Sanskrit Literature* by K. Chandrasekharan and Brahmasri V. H. Subrahmanya Sastri, reprinted by permission of The P.E.N. All-India Centre, Bombay.

Hayyim Nahman Bialik: Poems translated by Leo Auerbach and Joseph T. Shipley, reprinted from *The Guardian*, Philadelphia, Nov., 1924; courtesy *New Palestine*.

Bilhana: "An Indian Love-Lament," from *Saurīsuratapanchāsikā*, translated by Sir Edwin Arnold.

Björnstjerne Björnson: "The Father," from *The Bridal March*, translated by R. B. Anderson.

Karl Georg Büchner: *Woyzeck*, translated by and reprinted by permission of Theodore Hoffman.

Ivan Bunin: "Sunstroke," translated by Helen Matheson, from *Great Russian Short Stories*, edited by Stephen Graham, reprinted by permission of Ernest Benn Limited, London.

John Bunyan: "The Golden City," from *The Pilgrim's Progress*.

Robert Burns: "The Twa Dogs," from *Burns into English, Renderings of Select Dialect Poems of Robert Burns* by William Kean Seymour, Philosophical Library, New York.

Pedro Calderón de la Barca: "Segismund's Dream," from *La vida es sueño (Life Is a Dream)*, translated by Edward Fitzgerald.

Karel Capek: "The Island," translated by Sarka B. Hrbkova, from *Great Stories of All Nations*, edited by Lieber and Williams, Copyright 1927 by Brentano's, Inc.; reprinted by permission of Coward-McCann, Inc., New York.

Giosué Carducci: Poems from *Italian Lyrists of To-day*, translated by G. A. Greene, Macmillan Co., New York.

Miguel de Cervantes y Saavedra: "Sancho Panza in His Island," from *Don Quixote*, reprinted from *Half Hours with the Best Authors* by Charles Knight, C. Arthur Pearson, Ltd., London.

Adalbert von Chamisso: *Peter Schlemihl, the Shadowless Man*, from *The World's Greatest Books*, edited by Lord Northcliffe, S. S. McClure, McKinlay, Stone, and Mackenzie. (Copyright, 1910, S. S. McClure Co.)

François-René de Chateaubriand: "Chactas Relates the Death of Atala," from *Atala*.

Bankim Chandra Chatteree: "The Bride's Arrival," from *Devi Choudhurani*, Part III, reprinted from *Bengali Literature* by Annadasankar and Lila Ray, by permission of The P.E.N. All-India Centre, Bombay.

Geoffrey Chaucer: "The Pardoner's Tale" from *The Canterbury Tales*, retold in prose by Lieber and Williams, from *Great Stories of All Nations*, edited by Lieber and Williams. (Copyright, 1927, by Brentano's.)

Anton Chekhov: "The Slanderer," translated by Herman Bernstein, reprinted from *Greatest Short Stories*, by permission of P. F. Collier & Son, New York.

Chikamatsu Monzaemon: "Adventures of the Hakata Damsel," translated by Asataro Miyamori, revised by Robert Nichols, from *Masterpieces of Chikamatsu, the Japanese Shakespeare*, reprinted by permission of Routledge & Kegan Paul, Ltd., London.

Ch'u Yuan: Poems from *Li Sao and Other Poems of Ch'u Yuan*, translated by Yang Hsien-yi and Gladys Yang, reprinted by permission of the Foreign Language Press, Peking.

Confucius: Poems from the *Shih Ching*, translated by Williams Jennings, reprinted from *The Universal Anthology*, edited by Richard Garnett, Merrill & Baker, New York. (Copyright, 1899, by Richard Garnett.)

Joseph Conrad: "The Lagoon," from *Tales of Unrest*, reprinted by permission of the trustees of the Joseph Conrad Estate, Messrs. J. M. Dent & Sons, Ltd., London. (Copyright, 1908, 1920, Doubleday, Page and Company.)

James Fenimore Cooper: "The Ariel on the Shoals," from *The Pilot*.

Stephen Crane: "The Bride Comes to Yellow Sky," reprinted from *Stephen Crane: An Omnibus*, edited by R. W. Stallman, by permission of Alfred A. Knopf, Inc., New York. (Copyright, 1925, by William H. Crane and, 1952, by Alfred A. Knopf, Inc.)

Dandin: "The Courtesan's Mother," from *Dasakumāracharita*, reprinted from *Sanskrit Literature* by K. Chandrasekharan and Brahmasri V. H. Subrahmanya Sastri, by permission of The P.E.N. All-India Centre, Bombay.

Gabriele D'Annunzio: "Four Sonnets," translated by G. A. Greene, reprinted by permission of Macmillan Co., New York.

Dante Alighieri: Selection from *The Divine Comedy*, translated by "Mr. Carey," reprinted from *Half Hours with the Best Authors* by Charles Knight, C. Arthur Pearson, Ltd., London, 1899.

Alphonse Daudet: "The Death of the Dauphin," translated by Stuart Merrill. (Copyright, 1890.)

David: "Psalms" from the Book of Psalms, King James Version of The Holy Bible.

Richard Dehmel: Poems from *Contemporary German Poetry*, selected and translated by Jethro Bithell. (Walter Scott Publishing Company, 1909.)

1439

Grazia Deledda: "The Open Door," from *Chiaroscuro* (Fratelli Treves, Milan), translated by E. M. Baker, from *Great Italian Short Stories*, edited by Decio Pettoello, Ernest Benn, Ltd., London, 1930.

Charles Dickens: "The Convict in the Marshes," from *Great Expectations*.

Emily Dickinson: Poems from *The Poems of Emily Dickinson*, edited by Martha Dickinson Bianchi, reprinted by permission of Little, Brown, & Co., Boston.

Feodor Mikhaylovich Dostoyevsky: "The Murderer's Confession to Sonia," from *Crime and Punishment*.

John Dryden: "Zegri and Abencerrage" from *The Conquest of Granada by the Spaniards*.

Joseph von Eichendorff: Poems from *Leaves from the Life of a Good-for-Nothing*, translated by Mrs. A. L. Wister. "The Broken Ring," translated by C. G. Leland, and "Morning Prayer," translated by Alfred Baskerville, reprinted from *Representative German Poems*, Henry Holt & Co., New York.

Mihail Eminescu: Poems from *Poems of Mihail Eminescu*, translated from the Rumanian and rendered into the original metres by E. Sylvia Pankhurst and I. O. Stefanovici, reprinted by permission of Routledge & Kegan Paul, Ltd., London.

Euripides: "Medea's Wrongs" and "Medea's Last Words to Her Children," from *Medea*.

Abraham Ibn Ezra: Poems translated by Emma Lazarus, reprinted from *A Golden Treasury of Jewish Literature*, edited by Leo W. Schwarz, Rinehart & Co., New York, reprinted by permission of Leo W. Schwarz. (Copyright, 1937, by Leo W. Schwarz.)

William Faulkner: "A Rose for Emily," reprinted by permission of Random House, Inc., New York. (Copyright, 1931, by William Faulkner.)

Firdausi: "Rustam and Akwan Dev," from *Shah-namah*, translated by E. H. Palmer, reprinted from *The Universal Anthology*, edited by Richard Garnett, Merrill & Baker, New York. (Copyright, 1899, by Richard Garnett.)

Gustave Flaubert: "Salammbô and Her Lover," from *Salammbô*.

Anatole France: Poems from *Modern French Poetry*, compiled and translated by Joseph T. Shipley, reprinted by permission of Greenberg, New York.

Ferdinand Freiligrath: "The Lion's Ride," translated by C. T. Brooks, and "The Specter Caravan," translated by J. C. Mangan, reprinted from *The German Classics, Masterpieces of German Literature*, edited by Kuno Francke, The German Publication Society, New York.

Robert Frost: Poems from *Complete Poems of Robert Frost*, reprinted by permission of Henry Holt & Co., New York. (Copyright, 1930, 1949, by Henry Holt & Co., Inc., copyright 1936, 1948, by Robert Frost.)

Fuzulî: Poems, reprinted from *Turkish Literature*, P. F. Collier & Son, New York.

Solomon Ibn Gabirol: Poems translated by Emma Lazarus, from *A Golden Treasury of Jewish Literature*, edited by Leo W. Schwarz, Rinehart & Co., New York, reprinted by permission of Leo W. Schwarz. (Copyright, 1937, by Leo W. Schwarz.)

John Galsworthy: "Quality," from *The Inn of Tranquillity*, reprinted by permission of Charles Scribner's Sons, New York.

Vsevolod Garshin: "The Signal," reprinted from *Best Russian Short Stories*, edited by Thomas Seltzer, reprinted by permission of Random House, Inc., New York.

Théophile Gautier: "The Mummy's Foot," from *One of Cleopatra's Nights*, translated by Lafcadio Hearn, Brentano's, New York. (Copyright, 1890.)

Khalil Gibran: "Behind the Garment," from *The Secrets of the Heart*, translated by Anthony Rizcallah Ferris, edited by Martin L. Wolf, Philosophical Library, New York, 1947.

André Gide: "My Mother," from *Autumn Leaves*, translated by Elsie Pell, Philosophical Library, New York, 1950.

Jean Giraudoux: "May on Lake Asquam," from *Campaigns and Intervals*, translated by Elizabeth S. Sargeant, reprinted by permission of Houghton Mifflin Co., Boston.

Johann Wolfgang von Goethe: *Faust*, translated by Sir Theodore Martin.

Nikolai Gogol: "St. John's Eve," from *Evenings on a Farm Near Dikanka*, reprinted from *Taras Bulba, and Other Tales*, Everyman's Library, by permission of E. P. Dutton & Co., New York.

Oliver Goldsmith: "The Disabled Soldier," from *Citizen of the World*, originally titled "Letter CXVIII."

Ivan Alexandrovich Goncharov: Selections from *Oblomof*, reprinted from *The Universal Anthology*, edited by Richard Garnett, Merrill & Baker, New York. (Copyright, 1899, by Richard Garnett.)

Maxim Gorky: "One Autumn Night," reprinted from *Best Russian Short Stories*, edited by Thomas Seltzer, reprinted by permission of Random House, New York.

Judah Halevi: Poems, translated by Emma Lazarus, reprinted from *A Golden Treasury of Jewish Literature*, edited by Leo W. Schwarz, Rinehart & Co., New York, reprinted by permission of Leo W. Schwarz. (Copyright, 1937, by Leo W. Schwarz.)

Knut Hamsun: "The Call of Life," translated by Anders Orbeck, from *Norway's Best Stories*, edited by Hanna Astrup Larsen, W. W. Norton & Co., New York. Reprinted by permission of the American-Scandinavian Foundation.

Thomas Hardy: "Squire Petrick's Lady," from *A Group of Noble Dames*, reprinted by permission of Harper & Brothers, New York. (Copyright, 1891.

Bret Harte: "The Outcasts of Poker Flat," reprinted from *The Luck of Roaring Camp*, by permission of Houghton Mifflin & Co., Boston. (Copyright, 1872.)

Gerhart Hauptmann: Selection from *The Weavers*, translated by Mary Morison, reprinted from *The Universal Anthology*, edited by Richard Garnett, Merrill & Baker, New York. (Copyright, 1899, by Richard Garnett.)

Nathaniel Hawthorne: "The Ambitious Guest," reprinted by permission of Houghton Mifflin Co., New York.

Johann Peter Hebel: "Kannitverstan," translated by Paul Pratt, reprinted by permission of Alfred A. Knopf, Inc., New York.

Heinrich Heine: Poems, translated by Sir Theodore Martin, and selections from *Memoirs*, translated by Gilbert Cannon.

Ernest Hemingway: "Ten Indians," from *Men Without Women*, reprinted by permission of Charles Scribner's Sons, New York. Copyright 1927 by Charles Scribner's Sons, 1955 by Ernest Hemingway.

O. Henry: "The Whirligig of Life," from *Whirligigs*, copyright, 1903, 1931, Doubleday, Doran & Co., New York.

Johann Gottfried von Herder: "Sir Olaf," translated by Elizabeth Craigmyle, "Esthonian Bridal Song," translated by W. Taylor, reprinted from *An Anthology of World Poetry*, edited by Mark Van Doren, Reynal & Hitchcock, New York. (Copyright, 1936.)

Hermann Hesse: Poems, translated by Margarete Münsterberg, reprinted from *The German Classics*, edited by Kuno Francke, The German Publication Society, New York.

Hitomaro Kakinomoto: Poems from *The Manyōshū*. Published for the Nippon Gakujutsu Shinkōkai by the Iwanami Shoten, Tokyo, 1940. "The Mountain Top" and "My Love Who Loves Me Not," translated by Mabel Lorenz Ives, from *Poems for Enjoyment*, ed. Elias Lieberman, Harper & Bros., New York.

Friedrich Hölderlin: Poems, translated by Charles Wharton Stork, reprinted from *The German Classics*, edited by Kuno Francke, The German Publication Society, New York.

Homer: Selection from *The Iliad*, translated by John Gibson Lockhart.

Horace: "Ode 1," translated by Charles Stuart Calverly, "Epode 2," translated by Sir Theodore Martin, reprinted from *The Universal Anthology*, edited by Richard Garnett, Merrill & Baker, New York. (Copyright, 1899, by Richard Garnett.)

Ricarda Huch: "Midnight," translated by Margarete Münsterberg, reprinted from *The German Classics*, edited by Kuno Francke, The German Publication Society, New York.

Victor Hugo: Selections from *Les Misérables*.

Henrik Ibsen: Scenes from *Peer Gynt*, translated by Horace Maynard Finney, published by Philosophical Library, New York.

Muhammad Iqbal: "Community," translated by A. J. Arberry, reprinted from *Mysteries of Selflessness*, by permission of John Murray, Ltd., London.

Jens Peter Jacobsen: "The Plague at Bergamo," reprinted from *Short Story Classics*, P. F. Collier & Son, New York, 1927.

Henry James: Selections from *Confidence*, reprinted by permission of Houghton, Mifflin & Co., Boston.

Jami: "Zulaikha," translated by R. T. H. Griffith, reprinted from *The Universal Anthology*, edited by Richard Garnett, Merrill & Baker, New York. (Copyright, 1899, by Richard Garnett.)

Jataka: "The Strider over Battle-Fields," from *Virtue Is Its Own Reward*, translated by H. C. Warren, reprinted from *Buddhism in Translations* by H. C. Warren, by permission of the Harvard University Press, Cambridge.

Jayadeva: "Hymn to Vishnu," from the *Gītā Govinda*, translated by Sir Edwin Arnold, reprinted from *An Anthology of World Poetry*, edited by Mark Van Doren, Reynal & Hitchcock, New York.

1442

Juan Ramon Jiménez: "Fortunate Being" and "The Best That I Have," from *Ten Centuries of Spanish Poetry*, edited by Eleanor L. Turnbull, Johns Hopkins Press, Baltimore, reprinted by permission of the author. "Elegies," "The Diary of a Newly-Married Man," and "Stone and Heaven," translated by Thomas McGreevy, from *The European Caravan*, edited by Putnam, Darnton, Reavey & Bronowsky; Brewer, Warren & Putnam, New York; reprinted by permission of the author.

Maurus Jókai: Selections from *Timar's Two Worlds*, translated by Mrs. Hegan Kennard, published by Messrs. Blackwood, London.

James Joyce: "Araby," from *Dubliners*, included in *The Portable James Joyce*, copyright 1946, 1947, by The Viking Press, Inc., reprinted by permission of The Viking Press, New York.

Franz Kafka: "A Country Doctor," from *The Penal Colony*, translated by Willa and Edwin Muir, reprinted by permission of Schocken Books, Inc., New York.

Nagai Kafu: "The Bill-Collecting," translated by Torao Taketomo, reprinted from *Paulownia*, by permission of Dodd, Mead & Co., New York.

Kagawa Kageki: Poems from *Masterpieces of Japanese Poetry Ancient and Modern*, translated by Miyamori Asatarō, reprinted by permission of the Maruzen Co., Tokyo.

Kālidāsa: "The City of Ujjain," from *The Cloud Messenger*, translated by A. W. Ryder, reprinted from *A Garland of Indian Poetry*, edited by H. G. Rawlinson, by permission of the Royal Indian Society, London.

Gottfried Keller: "A Legend of the Dance," translated by Martin Wyness. reprinted from *Seven Legends*, Gowans & Gray, Glasgow. (Copyright, 1911.)

Omar Khayyam: Poems from the *Rubaiyat*, translated by Edward Fitzgerald.

Kan Kikuchi: "The Madman on the Roof," translated by Yozan T. Iwasaki and Glenn Hughes, reprinted from *Three Modern Japanese Plays* by permission of Appleton-Century-Crofts, Inc., New York. (Copyright, 1923, Stewart Kidd Co.)

Rudyard Kipling: "False Dawn," from *Plain Tales from the Hills*, reprinted by permission of Doubleday & Co., New York.

Joseph Kiss: "Jehovah," translated by William N. Lowe, reprinted from *Magyar Poetry*, Amerikai Magyar Nepszava, New York. (Copyright, 1908.)

Heinrich von Kleist: "The Beggar-Woman of Locarno," translated by E. N. Bennett, reprinted from *Selected German Short Stories* (*World's Classics*), by permission of Oxford University Press, London.

Vladimir Korolenko: "The Old Bell-Ringer," translated by Maxim Lieber, reprinted from "Great Short Stories of the World" edited by Clark and Lieber, Robert M. McBride Co., 1925. Reprinted by permission of the translator.

Zygmunt Krasinski: "A Legend," translated by Sarka Hrbkova, reprinted from *Great Stories of All Nations*, edited by Lieber and Williams. (Copyright. 1927, by Brentano's.)

Selma Lagerlöf: "The Eclipse," translated by Velma Swanston Howard, reprinted from the *American-Scandinavian Review* (December, 1922).

Lao Shê: "The Last Train," from *Contemporary Chinese Short Stories*, edited and translated by Yuan Chia-Hua and Robert Payne, reprinted by per-

1443

1447

Mendele Mocher Sforim: Selection from *The Nag*, translated by Moshe Spiegel, reprinted by permission of the Beechhurst Press, New York.

George Bernard Shaw: "The Miraculous Revenge," from *Short Stories, Scraps, and Shavings*, reprinted from *44 Irish Short Stories*, edited by Devin A. Garrity by permission of Devin-Adair Co., New York.

Shên Ts'ung-wên: "Under Cover of Darkness," from *Contemporary Chinese Short Stories*, edited and translated by Yuan Chia-Hua and Robert Payne, reprinted by permission of Noel Carrington, Transatlantic Arts Co., Ltd., London.

Shih Nai-an: "Death of the Tigers," from *All Men Are Brothers*, translated by Pearl S. Buck, reprinted by permission of the John Day Company, New York. (Copyright, 1937, by Pearl S. Buck.)

Henryk Sienkiewicz: "The Lighthouse Keeper of Aspinwall," from *Yanko the Musician*, translated by Jeremiah Curtin, Little, Brown & Co., Boston. (Copyright, 1893.)

Solomon: Selection from "The Song of Solomon," from the King James Version of the Bible.

Somadeva: "Devasmita," from the *Katha-sarit-sagara*, reprinted from *Great Stories of All Nations*, edited by Lieber and Williams, Coward-McCann Inc., New York. (Copyright, 1927, by Brentano's.)

Sophocles: Selections from *Antigone* and *Oedipus Tyrannus*. (Copyright, 1900.)

Carl Spitteler: "Theme" and "Heracles' Passing to Earth" from "Olympian Spring," translated by Margarete Münsterberg, from *The German Classics, Masterpieces of German Literature*, edited by Kuno Francke, reprinted by permission of the German Publication Society, New York.

Ssü-k'ung T'u: Poems, from *A Lute of Jade*, translated by L. Cranmer-Byng, reprinted by permission of John Murray, Ltd., London.

John Steinbeck: "Owners and Tenants," from *The Grapes of Wrath*, reprinted by permission of The Viking Press, Inc., New York. (Copyright, 1939, by John Steinbeck.)

Stendhal: Selections from *Chartreuse of Parma*, from *The World's Greatest Books*, edited by Lord Northcliffe, and S. S. McClure, McKinlay, Stone and Mackenzie. (Copyright, 1910, by S. S. McClure Co.)

Wallace Stevens: "Domination of Black" and "Anecdote of the Jar," from *Harmonium*; "An Extract," from *Parts of a World*; reprinted by permission of Alfred A. Knopf, Inc., New York.

Robert Louis Stevenson: "Thrawn Janet," from *The Merry Men*.

Theodor Storm: "Veronika," translated by Charles H. Stubing from Storm's *Sämtliche Schriften* (Braunschweig: G. Westermann, 1868). "To a Deceased," "The City," and "The Heath," translated by Margarete Münsterberg, and "Consolation," translated by Charles Wharton Stork, reprinted from *The German Classics of the Ninteenth and Twentieth Centuries*, edited by Kuno Francke and William Guild Howard, German Publication Society, New York.

Harriet Beecher Stowe: "Topsy," from *Uncle Tom's Cabin*.

August Strindberg: "A Funeral," reprinted from *The German Lieutenant and other Stories*, by permission of T. Werner Laurie, Ltd., London.

1448

Sūdraka: "The Clay Cart," translated by Sir Monier Monier-Williams, reprinted from *The Universal Anthology*, edited by Richard Garnett, Merrill & Baker, New York. (Copyright, 1899, by Richard Garnett.)

Sun Hsi-chen: "Ah Ao," translated by Edgar Snow, from *Living China*, reprinted by permission of the translator.

Su Tung-p'o: "Autumn Sun," from *Selections from the Works of Su Tung-p'o*, translated by Cyril Drummond Le Gros Clark, reprinted by permission of Jonathan Cape Ltd., London.

Jonathan Swift: "The Emperor of Lilliput," from *Gulliver's Travels*.

Algernon Charles Swinburne: "When the Hounds of Spring," and "Man," from *Atalanta in Calydon*.

Rabindranath Tagore: "To Nature," from *Sheaves, Poems and Songs by Rabindranath Tagore*, translated by Nagendranath Gupta, Philosophical Library, New York.

Junichirō Tanizaki: Selection from *Some Prefer Nettles*, translated by Edward G. Seidensticker, reprinted by permission of Alfred A. Knopf, Inc., New York.

T'ao Ch'ien: "Returning to Live on the Farm," from *The Poems of T'ao Ch'ien*, translated by Lily Pao-hu Chang and Marjorie Sinclair, reprinted by permission of the University of Hawaii Press, Honolulu.

Torquato Tasso: "The Golden Age," from *Aminta*, reprinted from *The Universal Anthology*, edited by Richard Garnett, Merrill & Baker, New York. (Copyright, 1899, by Richard Garnett.)

Johann Ludwig Tieck: "The Friends," from *Tales from Phantasus*, James Burns, London, 1845.

Leo Tolstoy: "Where Love Is," from *Master and Man and Other Parables and Tales*, reprinted by permission of E. P. Dutton & Co., New York. (Translated, 1885.)

Tu Fu: "The Poet Dreams" translated by Peter Rudolph from translation of Judith Gautier; from *Chinese Love Poems*, Peter Pauper Press, Mt. Vernon, N. Y. Other poems from *Chinese Love Poems* translated by Mabel Lorenz Ives; published by B. L. Hutchinson, Upper Montclair, N. J.

Ivan Sergeyevich Turgenev: "The Nihilist," from *Fathers and Sons*. (Copyright, 1900.)

Mark Twain: "The Celebrated Jumping Frog of Calaveras County." (Copyright, American Publishing Co.)

Miguel de Unamuno: "Three Generations," from *Perplexities and Paradoxes*, translated by Stuart Gross, Philosophical Library, New York.

Paul Valéry: Poems, from *Modern French Poetry*, compiled and translated by Joseph T. Shipley, reprinted by permission of Greenberg, New York.

Vālmīki: "Nārad," from *Selections from the Rāmāyana*, from *Hindu Literature*, P. F. Collier & Son, New York. (Copyright, 1900, by The Colonial Press.)

Giovanni Verga: "Gramigna's Mistress." (Copyright, 1900.)

Emile Verhaeren: Poems, from *Modern French Poetry*, compiled and translated by Joseph T. Shipley, reprinted by permission of Greenberg, New York.

Paul Verlaine: Poems, from *Modern French Poetry*, compiled and translated by Joseph T. Shipley, reprinted by permission of Greenberg, New York.